A

DICTIONARY

OF

Books relating to America,

FROM ITS DISCOVERY TO THE PRESENT TIME.

By JOSEPH SABIN.

Volume I.

"A painfull work it is I'll assure you, and more than difficult, wherein what toyle hath been taken, as no man thinketh so no man believeth, but he hath made the triall."

Ant. à Wood, Preface to the History of Oxford.

Mini-Print Corp. New York

Bibliotheca Americana.

Vol. I. — A to Bedford.

A

DICTIONARY

OF

Books relating to America,

FROM ITS DISCOVERY TO THE PRESENT TIME.

By JOSEPH SABIN.

Volume I.

"A painfull work it is I'll assure you, and more than difficult, wherein what toyle hath been taken, as no man thinketh so no man believeth, but he hath made the triall."
Ant. à Wood, Preface to the History of Oxford.

Mini-Print Corp. New York

TO

J. CARSON BREVOORT, Esq.,

OF BROOKLYN, N. Y.,

TO WHOM I AM GREATLY INDEBTED FOR HIS EARLY ENCOURAGEMENT, CORDIAL COÖPERATION, AND SCHOLARLY SUPERVISION OF MANY OF THESE PAGES,

THIS VOLUME IS RESPECTFULLY DEDICATED BY

JOSEPH SABIN.

New York, *September* 1, 1868.

NOTICE

As it is my intention to issue a preface to the whole work with the last volume, I now, at the conclusion of Vol. I., content myself with reproducing, with some alterations, the Prospectus issued December 5, 1866, and remarking that the list of authorities, therein referred to, will be enlarged and reprinted with the last volume.

Hereafter the work will proceed with more rapidity and greater regularity.

Joseph Sabin.

New York, *September* 1, 1868.

PROSPECTUS.

After nearly four years' labor, in arranging and classifying the material which had accumulated on my hands in the course of some fifteen years of research, I am at last able to publish the following specimen of my projected "Dictionary of Books relating to America."

Had the magnitude and extreme difficulty of the undertaking been presented to my mind in full proportions at the outset, I should never have attempted it; and, indeed, I may remark, that I have more than once almost determined upon its abandonment; but a deep sense of its importance, however imperfectly it may be executed, and a strong partiality for bibliographical pursuits, have stimulated me to continue my labor, until the work has attained such a degree of completeness as to justify its publication, and render its conclusion a task of comparative ease; and I now present this volume as a fair specimen of what the work is intended to be, and respectfully invite for it a candid examination.

The plan I have adopted is briefly this: An alphabetical arrangement, under the names of authors, and, in the case of anonymous writers, under the most obvious subject.

In the arrangement of the Spanish, Portuguese,

French, and Dutch proper names, I have followed the best authorities; but, as these differ, I have made free use of Cross References, and remark, with Plutarch,* "On the subject of names, however, the irregularity of custom, would we insist upon it, might furnish us with discourse enough."

Anonymous works are arranged with more difficulty. The subject most obvious to one mind is obscure to another. Books having reference to a State or City have sometimes been placed under the name of that State or City. *Collections*, *Proceedings*, and *Transactions* of Societies will be found under the *name* of the Society; as for the rest, they will usually be found under the first word of the title-page, particles excepted. The last volume will consist of an Index of Subjects, which will obviate some of these difficulties.

Review "Notices" of the more important books will be referred to, and, in the case of a rare book, a capital letter following the title will indicate some Public Library in which it may be found.

The words "Relating to America" are used with a wide meaning, and it is probable that serious and proper objection may be taken to some titles of books introduced; as, for example, the various works by the early New-England Divines. It must not be forgotten, however, that, in many respects, the New-England Government was a Theocracy, and the works of these Divines had much to do with shaping its institutions; at all

* Life of "Caius Marius."

events, they are books sought for with avidity, and bought at high prices by the collectors of "Americana," and, if only for that reason, have a right to appear here.

I shall not attempt to anticipate the many criticisms which may be made. I shall be glad to have errors pointed out and improvements suggested, and respectfully solicit the coöperation and assistance of gentlemen who have given their attention to any or many particular authors.

I conclude this preliminary notice with the remark, that, whenever possible, I have examined the books for myself, and have described them with all necessary minuteness. Of those not within my reach, I have been compelled to content myself with such descriptions as have come under my notice in the list of authorities quoted on the cover of Part I. of this work,* or sometimes from a less trustworthy source — a Bookseller's Catalogue. Should I wait to make this bibliography as full and exact on all points as I trust it will generally be found, I should never complete it.

It will, perhaps, save inquiry, if I here state that the number of parts of which the work will consist is a question I cannot answer; yet, while I design to make it as complete as possible, my own remarks on the books will be distinguished by their brevity.

The Parts will be issued with all convenient speed, and subscriptions will not be received for anything less than the entire work. Joseph Sabin.

* This Dictionary is published first in parts, of which No. I. appeared in January, 1867.

EXPLANATORY.

The Initials which precede the Numbers, at the end of the Description, indicate certain public Libraries in which the books may be consulted.

A. signifies Astor Library, New York.
B. " Public Library of Boston.
BD. " Bodleian Library.
BM. " British Museum, London.
C. " Library of Congress.
CP. " Library of Parliament, Canada.
H. " Harvard College Library.
M. " Massachusetts Historical Society, Boston.
N. " New York Historical Society.
P. " Library Company of Philadelphia.
Pa. " Pennsylvania State Library.
S. " New York State Library.
W. " Antiquarian Society, Worcester, Mass.

Occasional references are made to private collections, when the books are not to be found in public Libraries. Thus:

J. C. B. stands for the Library of John Carter Brown.
J. C. Bt. " " " J. Carson Brevoort.
G. " " " A. W. Griswold.
J. L. " " " James Lenox.
W. M. " " " William Menzies.
R. " " " John A. Rice.

ll. means leaves.
pp. " pages.
n. p. " no place.
n. d. " no date.
... indicates the omission of words of a title regarded as unimportant.
.... " that the omission began in a sentence and extends to the end, or farther.
. ... " that the omission began a sentence.
|| is used when there is a difference between the titles of different volumes of the same work, to mark the passage from one title-page to another.
[ ] include words which are not on the title-page. When brackets [ ] occur in a title they are represented in this Dictionary by parentheses ( ).
( ) are used to indicate leaves or pages not numbered by the printer. Thus: "(3) l., pp. (3), viii. (13), 464," means 3 unnumbered leaves, followed by three pages unnumbered, 8 numbered with Roman numerals, 13 unnumbered, and 464 numbered with Arabic numerals. It should be noticed that "pp. (4)" implies that all four pages are printed upon; (2) l. that one side of one or both the leaves is blank. Leaves blank on both sides are not counted, unless the contrary is stated.
+ is used when another edition of a work is described without repeating the title-page. It indicates that, so far as is known, the titles of the two editions are essentially alike.

Other references will occur in the course of publication, all of which will be explained in the last volume.

Works which have only a slight relation to America are enumerated briefly in the notes in smaller type—generally in alphabetical succession.

A DICTIONARY OF BOOKS

RELATING TO AMERICA.

A. (B.) *See* A[ntrobus] (B[enjamin]).

A. (G.) The Young Traveller in South America. A popular Introduction to the History and Resources of the Country. *London*, 1835. 12mo. 1

A. (G. A.) Tecumseh; or the Death of the Shawnee Chief. With other Original Poems. By G. A. A. [ynge]. *Weymouth*, 1830. 12mo, pp. 78. 2

"The poem which furnishes the title to this little work occupies ten pages."—Rich.

A. (P.) *See* Sharp (Bartholomew).

A. (T.) *See* A[sh] (T.) and Allen Thomas.

[Aa (P. van der)]. Naaukeurige versameling der gedenkwaardigste Reysen naar Oost en West-Indien, Mitsgaders andere Gewesten gedaan; Sedert De Jaaren 1246. tot op desen tijd. Alles breeder te fien, in, en agter het Voorberigt. [This is the half title preceding Engraved Frontispiece, and a very long descriptive Title, finishing thus]: *In het ligt gegeven Te Leyden, Door Peter Vander Aa.* 1707. 8vo, 30 vols. 3

This collection of the most memorable Voyages to the East and West Indies, from 1246 to 1696, contains translations of all the early voyages to this continent, and is illustrated by a profusion of copper plates. As each voyage has a separate pagination, the work is sometimes found bound up in 28, 29 or 30 volumes, and is worth about $20. There is also an edition in folio, 8 vols. Leyde. This indefatigable publisher, who united within himself the functions of author, editor and publisher, also issued the plates to the above work separately, under the following title: "Atlas nouveau et curieaux des plus celebres itineraires; ou recueil de nouvelles cartes geograph. des voiages modernes de long cours, de depuis l'an 1246 jusqu'a l'an 1696." 2 vols., folio. Leyde. He also published "Grand Theatre Historique, ou Nouvelle

Histoire Universelle tant sacrée que profane." 5 vols., folio. Leyde, 1703; and "La Galerie Agréable du Monde." 66 parts bound in 33 or 22 vols. folio., of which Vol. xvii. relates to America.

Abbeville (Claude d') Histoire | de la Mission | des Peres Capvcins | en l'Isle de Maragnan et | terres circonuoisines | ov est traicte des sin | gularitez admirables & des | Meurs merueilleuses des Indiens | habitans de ce pais Auec les misiues et aduis qui ont este enuoyez de nouue[m] | Par | le R. P. Claude d'Abbeuille | Predicateur Capucin. | *A Paris* | *De l'Imprimerie de François* | *Hvby* 1614. | 8vo. Engraved Title. 7 p. l., 413 leaves, with Table. 4

Puttick, 1859, £3. 10. 0. The Island of Maranham is on the coast of Brazil, and this is the earliest account of it.

Abbeville. L'arrivee des Peres Capucins et la conversion des sauvages à nostre saincte foy. Declaree par le R. P. Claude d'Abbeville, Predicateur Capucin. *Paris, Jean Nigaut*, 1613. 12mo, 16 pp. 5

Abad. Historia geográfica, civil y natural de la isla de Puerto Rico, por Fr. Inigo Abad y Lasserra. Nueva edicion anotada en la parte histórica, y continuada en la estadística y económica por J. J. de Acosta. *Puerto Rico*, n. d. 8vo. 6

Abbring (H. J.) Weemoedstoonen uit de Geschiedenis van mijn Leven, of mijne reis naar Curaçao, en vlugtige beschouwingen van dat eiland gedurende mijn tienjarig verblijf of hetzelve. *Groningen*, 1834. 8vo. 7

Relates the experiences, &c., of the author during a ten years' residence at Curaçoa.

Abbot (Abiel). Artillery Election Sermon, Boston, June 7th, 1812. By Abiel Abbot. *Boston*, 1812. 8vo. 8

Abbot. Discourse at North Coventry, July 4, 1799. By Abiel Abbot. *Hartford*, 1799. 8vo, pp. 16. 9

Abbot. Discourse at Plymouth, Dec. 22, 1809, with Appendix. By Abiel Abbot. *Boston*, 1810. 8vo, pp. 28. 10

Abbot. Ecclesiastical Peace recommended. A Discourse delivered before the Annual Convention of the Congregational Ministers of Massachusetts, in Boston, May 31, 1827. By Abiel Abbot. *Boston*, 1827. 12mo, pp. 20. 11

Abbot. An Eulogy on the Illustrious Life and Character of George Washington, delivered before the inhabitants of the

town of Haverhill, on his Birth-Day, 1800, at the request of their committee. By Abiel Abbot. And the invaluable last Address of President Washington to the Citizens of the United States, the Legacy of the Father of his Country. *Haverhill, Printed by Seth H. Moore.* [1800]. 8vo, pp. 27 and 21. 12

Abbot. History of Andover, from its Settlement to 1829. By Abiel Abbot. *Andover, Flagg & Gould.* 12mo, pp. 204. 13

Abbot. Letters written in the Interior of Cuba, between the Mountains of Arcana, to the East, and of Cusco, to the West, in the Months of February, March, April and May, 1828. By the late Rev. Abiel Abbot, D.D. *Boston*, 1829. 8vo, pp. 272. 14

Reviewed in the N. A. R., xxix., p. 199. Sou. R., iv., p. 123. Christ. E., vi., p. 259.

Abbot. Self-Preservation. Artillery Election Sermon, 1802. By Abiel Abbot. *Boston*, 1802. 8vo. 15

Abbot. Proceedings of the General Association of Connecticut Relative to Rev. Abiel Abbot. *Hartford*, 1812. 8vo. 16

Abbot. Statement of Proceedings in the First Society in Coventry, Conn., which terminated in the Removal of the Pastor; with an Address. *Boston*, 1811. 8vo, pp. 68. 17

Abbot. Reply to Mr. Abbot's Statement of Proceedings in the First Society in Coventry, Conn. By the Association in Tolland County. * * * *Hartford*, 1812. 8vo, pp. 48. 18

Mr. Abbot published other Addresses on Temperance, Missions, &c.

Abbot (A. and E.) Genealogical Register of the Descendants of George Abbot, of Andover; Arthur Abbot, of Ipswich; George Abbot, of Rowley; Thomas Abbot, of Andover; Robert Abbot, of Brentford; and George Abbot, of Brentford. By Abiel and Ephraim Abbot. *Boston*, 1847. 8vo, pp. 197. 19

Abbot (D.) Oration July 4, 1803. By Daniel Abbot. *Nashua, N. H.*, 1803. 8vo. 20

Abbot (G.) A briefe Description of the Whole World, wherein is particularly described all the Monarchies, Empires and Kingdomes of the same, with their *Academies*. As also their several

Titles and Situations thereunto adjoining. Written by the Right Reverend Father in God, *George*, late Archbishop of Canterburie. *London, Printed for William Sheares*, 1634. Sm. 8vo, pp. 329. Engraved Title and Portrait by W. Marshall. 21

In this, the sixth edition, the account of America commences on page 240. This work, which, according to Anthony à Wood, was known as "Abbot's Geography," contains a curious account of the "Discovery of America by the Welsh." It has been frequently reprinted. Copies exist with the dates 1599, 1600, 1603, 1608, 1613. Fourth Edition, 1617. *5th edition* newly augmented and enlarged: with their severall titles and scituations thereunto adjoyning. 4to. *Lond.*, 1620. Other editions, 1622, 1635, 1636, 1642, 1656 and 1664.

Abbot (Hull). The Duty of God's People to pray for the Peace of Jerusalem, and especially for the Preservation and Continuance of their own Privileges, both Civil and Religious, when in Danger at Home or from Abroad. A Sermon on Ocasion of the Rebellion in Scotland Rais'd in Favour of a Popish Pretender, With Design to overthrow our present Happy Establishment, And to Introduce Popery and Arbitrary Power into Our Nations, From which, by a Series of Wonders, in the good Providence of God, they have been often delivered, Preached at Charlestown in New England, Jan. 12, 1745-6. By Hull Abbot, A.M. A Pastor of the Church there. *Boston, Rogers and Fowle*, 1746. 8vo, pp. 26. M. 22

Abbot. Jehovah's Character as a Man of War, illustrated and applied. Artillery-Election Sermon, 1735. By Hull Abbot. *Boston*, 1735. 8vo, pp. 35. 23

Also a Disswasive against Swearing, 1747. + Convention Sermon, 1756. + A Dudleian Lecture, 1764.

Abbot. Trial of Joel Abbot by the General Court Martial, Holden on Board the U. S. Ship Independence, at the Navy Yard, Charlestown, Massachusetts, on Allegations made against Him by Captain David Porter, Navy Commissioner. Printed from the Official Record on File in the Navy Department. *Washington: Davis and Force*, 1822. 8vo, pp. 152. + *Another Edition.* With an Appendix of Documents in relation to the management of Affairs on the Boston Station. *Boston*, 1822. 8vo, pp. 236. 24

Abbot (John). Natural History of the rarer Lepidopterous Insects of Georgia. Including their Systematic Characters, the particulars of their several Metamorphoses, and the Plants on which they Feed. Collected from the Observations of Mr. John Abbot, many years resident in that Country. By James Edward

Smith, M.D., F.R.S., P.L.S. *London, White*, 1796–1798. 2 vols., folio, pp. 208, and 104 Coloured Plates. 25

"Abbot was a most assiduous collector, and an admirable draftsman of insects. His work is one of the most beautiful that this or any other country can boast of. The original coloured impressions are seldom met with."—Swainson. "It is a valuable acquisition to the botanist as well as the entomologist."—Rich. Sold at Edwards' sale for £18 10s. od.; at Saunders' for £14. Some copies are badly coloured and are of much less value.

Abbott (Abbott A.) The Assassination and Death of Abraham Lincoln, April 14, 1865. Full Particulars, with a Short Account of his Life. By Abbott A. Abbott. *New York: American News Co.*, 1865. 16mo, pp. 24. 26

Abbott. Prison Life in the South: at Richmond, Macon, Savannah, Charleston, Columbia, Charlotte, Raleigh, Goldsborough, and Andersonville, during the Years 1864 and 1865. By A. O. Abbott, late Lieutenant First New York Dragoons. With Illustrations. *New York, Harpers*, 1865. 12mo, pp. 374. 27

Abbott (Austin). Popular Government successful in a Great Emergency. An Address delivered at Farmington, Maine, July 4, 1862. By Austin Abbott. 1862. 8vo, pp. 8. 28

[Abbott (J.)] Memoranda of a Settler in Lower Canada, with hints to Emigrants; by an Emigrant Farmer [Rev. J. Abbott]. *Montreal*, 1842. 12mo. 29

Abbott. Philip Musgrave; or, Memoirs of a Church of England Missionary in the North American Colonies. Edited by the Rev. J. Abbott, A.M. *London, John Murray*, 1846. Post 8vo, pp. 164. 30

Abbott (Jacob). American History. Illustrated. Vol. 1. Aboriginal America. Vol. 2. Discovery of America. Vol. 3. Southern Colonies. Vol. 4. Northern Colonies. Vol. 5. The Wars of the Colonies. Vol. 6. Revolt. Vol. 7. War of the Revolution. Vol. 8. Life of Washington. *New York*, 1860–5. 16mo. 31

These Histories were written for young people.

Abbott. Franklin, the apprentice boy. By Jacob Abbott. *New York*, 1855. 16mo, pp. 160. 32

[Abbott.] New England and her Institutions. By One of

her Sons. [Jacob Abbott.] 12mo, pp. 271. *Boston*, 1835. + *Reprinted, London, Seeley*, 1835. Post 8vo, pp. vi, 393. 33

Abbott. Voyages and Travels of Marco Paul. By Jacob Abbott. *New York, Harper*, v. d. Six volumes, 16mo, pp. 192, 203, 191, 208, 192, 192. 34

Accounts of the adventures of a youthful traveller, in New York; on the Erie Canal; in Maine; in Vermont; in Boston; and at the Springfield Armory. Each volume contains from fourteen to twenty-two woodcuts.

Abbott (John Stevens Cabot). An Address upon our National Affairs, delivered in Cheshire, Conn., on the National Fast, January 4th, 1861. By John S. C. Abbott. *New York: Abbey & Abbott*, 1861. 8vo, pp. 16. 35

Abbott. The History of the Civil War in America: comprising a full and Impartial Account of the Origin and Progress of the Rebellion, of the various Naval and Military Engagements, of the Heroic Deeds performed by Armies and Individuals, and of touching Scenes in the Field, the Camp, the Hospital, and the Cabin. By John S. C. Abbott. Illustrated with Maps, Diagrams, and numerous Steel Engravings of Battle Scenes, from original designs, by Darley and other eminent Artists, and Portraits of distinguished men. *New York, H. Bill*, 1863–1865. 2 vols., 8vo, pp. 507, 630. 36

The same in German. Geschichte des Bürger Kreiges in Amerika. *Norwich N. Y.*, 1863–5.

Abbott. History of Hernando Cortes. By John S. C. Abbott. Plates. *New York*, 1855. 18mo. 37

Abbott. Life of Christopher Columbus. By John S. C. Abbott. Plates. *New York*, 1856. 18mo. 38

Abbott. History of King Philip, Sovereign Chief of the Wampanoags; including the early history of the Settlers of New-England. By John S. C. Abbott. With engravings. *New-York, Harper & Brothers*, 1857. 12mo, pp. 410. 39

Abbott. South and North; or, Impressions received during a trip to Cuba and the South. By John S. C. Abbott. *New York, Abbey & Abbott.* 12mo, pp. 352. 40

Abbott. Words of Patriotism and Wisdom now presented to the Freemen of Connecticut for their consideration. By John S. C. Abbott. 8vo, pp. 8. 41

ABBOTT (Nehemiah). Fishing Bounties. Speech delivered in the House of Representatives, Feb. 10, 1859. By Nehemiah Abbott. *Washington*, 1859. 8vo, pp. 8. 42

ABBOTT (Nehemiah). Government Expenditures. Speech delivered in the House of Representatives, Feb. 21, 1859. By Nehemiah Abbott. *Washington*, 1859. 8vo, pp. 8. 43

ABBOTT (Simon C.) A Record of the Births Marriages and Deaths in Worcester, Vermont, from 1813 to 1858, Alphabetically Arranged. By Simon C. Abbott. *Montpelier*, 1858. 8vo, pp. 31. 44

ABDY. Journal of a Residence and Tour in the United States of North America, from April 1833 to October 1835. By E. S. Abdy. *London*, *John Murray*, 1835. Post 8vo, 3 vols., pp. XII., 395; VIII., 415; VIII., 408. 45

See Q. R. LIV., p. 392; W. R. XXIV., p. 244. The republication of this work was commenced in New York, but suspended on account of its remarks on Slavery. The author accompanied Mr. Crawford, who was sent by the English Government to inspect the prisons of the U. S. He gives much information on Public Institutions.

ABDY. American Whites and Blacks in reply to a German Orthodermist. By E. S. Abdy. *London*, 1842. 8vo. 46

ABEILLE. Essai sur nos colonies, et sur le retablissement de Saint Domingue, ou considérations sur leur législation, administration, commerce et agriculture. Par Mr. J. Abeille, administrateur des hospices de Marseille, député du commerce de ladite ville près l'Assemblée constituante, propriétaire et ancien négociant à Saint Domingue. *Paris*, *Chomel*, 1805. 8vo, *half-title and title*, 2 *l.*, xiij., pp. 154. H. 47

L'Abeille Americaine, Journal Historique. *Philadelphia*, 1818. 20 Parts. 48

ABEL. Traveller's and Emigrant's Guide to Wisconsin and Iowa. By Henry J. Abel. Accompanied with a new and improved Map of those Territories, with the addition of parts of Illinois, Indiana, and Michigan. *Philadelphia*, *Printed for the Author*, 1839. 12mo. 49

ABELIN. Newe Welt | Vnd Americanische Historien. | Inhaltende | Warhafftige vnd vollkommene Be- | schreibungen Aller West-Indianischen Landschafften, Insulen, | Königreichen vnd Provintzien, Seecusten, fliessenden vnd stehen- | den Wassern, Port vnd Anländungen, Gebürgen, Thälern, Stätt, Flecken vnd |

Wohnplätzen, zusampt der Natur vnd Eygenschafft dess Erdrichs, der Lufft, der | Mineren vnd Metallen, der Brennenden Vulcanen oder Schwefelbergen, der | Siedenden vnd anderer Heilsamen Quellen, wie auch der Thier, Vögel, Fisch | vnd Gewürm in denselben, sampt andern Wunderbaren Creaturen | vnd Miraculn der Natur, in diesem halben Theil | dess Erdkreyses. | Dessgleichen | Gründlicher Bericht von der Innwohner Beschaffenheit, Sit- | ten, Qualitäten, Policey vnd Götzendienst, Leben vnd Wesen, Barbarischer Vn- | wissenheit vnd vnerhörter Grausamkeit dess meisten theils dieser Wilden Leute, sampt Vn- | terscheyd der Nationen, Sprachen vnd Gebräuchen. | Item, Historische vnd Aussführliche Relation 38. Fürnembster Schiffarten vnter- | schiedlicher Völcker in West-Indien, von der Ersten Entdeckung durch Christopho- | rum Columbum, in 150. Jahren, vollbracht. | Alles auss verscheidenen West-Indianischen Historien-Schreibern, vnnd man- | cherley Sprachen mit sonderm fleiss zusamen getragen, extrahirt, in ein richtige Ordnung | der Materien vnd Zeit, vnd in diese Käuffliche Form gebracht | Durch | Johann Ludwig Gottfriedt. | Mit zugehörigen Landtafeln, Contrafacturen vnd Geschichtmässigen Kupfferstücken, | zum Lust vnd Nachrichtung reichlich gezieret vnd verlegt, | Durch Mattheum Merian, Buchhändlern vnnd | Kunststechern zu Franckfurt am Mäyn. ¶ *Franckfurt, Bey denen Merianischen Erben.* | M.DC.LV. | Fol. 4 p. l. Engraved and Printed Title. pp. 661, 2 p. 4 Maps and many Plates. 50

Jean-Philippe Abelin published this work under the assumed name of Jean-Louis Gottfriedt. It contains a resumé of the Histories of Acosta, Oviedo, Peter Martyr, Herrera, Laet, &c. An account of 33 Voyages to America, from Columbus to Spilbergen and Schouten; notices of the expeditions of Lemaire and Peter Heyn, the Conquests of Brazil by the Dutch, and descriptions of Greenland and Spitzbergen. The first edition was published in 1631. Ternaux (No. 713) quotes an edition 1651, which does not exist.

ABENAQUI Springs, near Bellows Falls, Vermont [Statement concerning]. *New York*, 1858. 16mo, pp. 16. 51

ABERCROMBIE. A Sermon Occasioned by the Death of Major Gen. Alexander Hamilton, who was killed by Aaron Burr, Esq., Vice-President of the United States, in a Duel, July 11, 1804. Preached in Christ Church and St. Peter's, Philadelphia, on Sunday, July 22, 1804. By James Abercrombie, D.D. *Philadelphia*, *H. Max*[illegible] 8vo, pp. vii. 53. Postscript, 1 l. 52

ABERCROMBIE. A serm[illegible] in Christ Church and St.

Peter's, Philadelphia, on Wednesday, May 9th, 1798, being the Day appointed by the President as a day of Fasting, Humiliation, and Prayer, throughout the United States of North America. By James Abercrombie, A.M. *Philadelphia*, *John Ormrod* [1798]. 8vo, pp. 38. 53

ABERCROMBIE (Robert). An Account of the Proceedings of the Presbytery, whereof the Reverend Mr. John Moorhead, &c., are members, against the Rev. Mr. Robert Abercrombie. In a Letter to a Friend. *Boston*, 1754. 12mo, pp. 42. 54

ABERCROMBIE (Robert). Remarks on a late Piece, entitled "A Fair Narrative of the Proceedings of the Presbytery of Boston," &c. *Boston*, 1757. 8vo, pp. 64. 55

ABERCROMBIE (Robert). *See* Moorhead, John. Parsons, Jonathan.

ABERT. Reply of Col. Abert and Mr. Markoe to the Hon. Mr. Tappan, of the U. S. Senate. *Washington*, 1849. 8vo, pp. 18. 56

ABERT. Report of the Secretary of War, communicating a report and map of the examination of New Mexico, made by Lieut. J. W. Abert, of the topographical corps, in the years 1846–47. *Washington*, 1848. 8vo, pp. 195. Plates. 57

Forms Document, No. 23, 30th Congress, 1st Session.

ABERT. Another Edition, with Col. Cook's Report of his March from Santa Fe to San Domingo, and Journal of Capt. Johnson. *Washington*, 1848. 8vo. 58

ABERT. Journal from Bent's Fort to St. Louis, in 1845. *Washington*, 1846. 8vo. 59

Abhandlungen der Philosophisch-Historischen Klasse der Königlichen Akademie der Wissenschaften zu Berlin. *Berlin*, 1855, etc. 4to. 60

Contains several Articles on the North American Indian Languages, etc.

ABINGDON. Thoughts on the Letter of Edmund Burke, Esq., to the Sheriffs of Bristol, on the Affairs of America. By the Earl of Abingdon. *Oxford*, *W. Jackson* [1777]. 8vo, pp. 68. 61

ABINGDON. The Same. Second, Third, Fourth and Fifth Editions. *Oxford*, *W. Jackson* [1777]. Each in 8vo, pp. 68. 62

ABINGDON. Another Edition. *Dublin*, 1777. 8vo, pp. 48. +Reprinted *Lancaster* [*Pa.*], 1778. 8vo, pp. 30. 63

ABINGDON. The Same. Sixth Edition. *Oxford* [1777]. 8vo, XCI. pp. 60. 64

This Edition contains The Dedication to the Collective Body of the People of England, and replies to the several answers to the previous editions.

ABINGDON. Second Thoughts: or, Observations upon Lord Abingdon's Thoughts on the Letter of Edmund Burke, Esq., to the Sheriffs of Bristol. By the Author of the Answer to Mr. Burke's Letter. *London*, *T. Cadell*, 1777. 8vo, pp. 74. 65

ABINGDON. The Same. Second Edition. *London*, *T. Cadell*, 1777. 8vo, pp. 74. 66

"This writer attacks some eminent characters, particularly Dr. Franklin, with an illiberal severity, for which he deserves the reprehension of every considerate and candid reader."—*Monthly Review.*

ABINGDON. Speech of the Earl of Abingdon on the Abolition of the Slave Trade. *London*, 1793. 8vo. 67

ABINGDON. Letter to the Earl of Abingdon. *See* [Linde, Dr.]

ABINGTON. Annual Reports of the Selectmen, Overseers of the Poor, and School Committee; with the Taxable Valuation of the Town of Abington, Mass., 1856. *Boston*, 1856, and continued. 8vo. 68

ABINGTON. Abington, Mass.: Rev. H. D. Walker's Address. Mount-Vernon Cemetery Reports, Oct. 1853. *Boston*, 1853. 69

ABINGTON Baptist Association: Minutes, 1811, &c. *Bethany*, &c. 70

Continued Annually, See Am. Q. Reg. VIII, 149.

ABLON (Claude d'). *See* Dablon.

Abolitionism. *See* Slavery.

Aborigines. *See* Indians.

ABRAHALL (C. H.) Arctic Enterprise, a Poem. In Seven Parts. By Chandos Hoskyns Abrahall. *London*, *Hope*, 1856. Post 8vo. 71

ABRAHALL (J. H.) Western Woods and Waters. Poems and Illustrative Notes. By John Hoskyns Abrahall, Junr., M.A. *London*, *Longman*, 1864. Fcap. 8vo. 72

ABRANTES (M. de). Memoria Sobre meios de promover a Colonisaçao. *Berlin*, 1846. 8vo. 73

Abrégé de la Revolution. *See* [Buisson].

Abrégé des Fruits aquis par l'ordre des freres mineurs es quatres Parties de l'univers nommement la conversion du Nouveau Monde. Recueilles par un Pere Cordelier en Bruxelles. *Bruxelles*, *François Vivien*, 1652. 18mo. Engrv. Title. 8 p. l., pp. 171. 74

ABREU (A. A.) Carta Pastoral del Illustrisimo Señor D. Miguel Anselmo Alvarez de Abreu y Valdes, Obispo de Antequera en el Valle de Oaxaca. *Madrid*, 1768. 4to. 75

ABREU. Victima real legal, discurso unico juridico-historio-politico, sobre que las vacantes Mayores y Menores de las Indias Occidentales pertenecen à la Corona de Castilla, y Leon con pleno y absoluto dominio. Por D. Antonio Joseph Alvarez de Abreu. *Madrid*, 1726. Folio. 76

"In consequence of this vindication of the Royal right to the revenues accruing from vacancies in the churches in America, the author had a pension of a thousand ducats, and the title of Marquis de la Regalia bestowed upon him by Philip V."—RICH. J. R. Smith, No. 39 Catalogue, 1865, quotes an Edition, Madrid, 1769.

ABREU (J. A.) Coleccion de los Tratados de Paz, Alianza, Neutralidad, Garantia, Proteccion, Tregua, Mediacion, Accesion, Reglamento de Limites, Comercio-Navegacion, &c. hechos por los Pueblos, Reyes, y Principes de España, con los Pueblos, Reyes, Principes, &c. de Europa, y otras Partes del Mundo, (A.D. 1598–1700) fielmente sacados de los Originales por D. Joseph Antonio de Abreu y Bértodano. *Madrid*, 1740–52. C. 77

An important collection of all the early Spanish Treaties, many relating to America and the West Indies. 21 vols. folio. Some Copies on Large Paper. The "Prontuario de los Tratados de Paz," *Madrid*, 1749–52, 4 vols., 12mo, is a desirable adjunct. Ebert quotes the 12 vols. at 360 rix dollars; Quaritch at £5.

ABREU (J. J.) Compendio da Historia do Brasil. Por J. J. de Abreu e Lima. *Rio de Janeiro*, 1843. 8vo, 2 vols. Portraits. 78

[ABREU DE GALINEO]. The History of the Discovery and Conquest of the Canary Islands. Translated from a Spanish Manuscript lately found in the Island of Palma. With an Enquiry into the Origin of the Ancient Inhabitants. To which is added A Description of the Canary Islands, Including the Modern History of the Inhabitants, And an Account of their Manners,

Customs, Trade, &c. By George Glas. *London*, *R. and J. Dodsley*, MDCCLXIV. 4to. 79

Reprinted in Pinkerton's Collection of Voyages, Vol. XVI. Referred to by Cook.

An Abridgement of several Acts and Clauses of Acts of Parliament, relating to the Trade and Navigation of Great Britain to, from and in the British Plantations in America, and to the Duty of the Governors and others, His Majesty's Officers in the said Plantations. *London*, 1739. Folio, pp. 44. N. 80

An Abridgement of the Laws in Force and Use in Her Majesty's Plantations, (viz.) of Virginia, Jamaica, Barbadoes, Maryland, New-England, New-York, Carolina, &c. Digested under proper Heads in the Method of Mr. Wingate, and Mr. Washington's Abridgments. *London*, *John Nicholson*, 1704. Sm. 8vo, 2 l., pp. 284; 'Maryland,' pp. 71; 'New-England,' pp. 100; 'Appendix,' pp. 285 to 304. N. 81

An Abridgement of the Laws of the United States. *See* United States.

Abstract of Royal Edicts. 1772. *London*, *Eyre and Strahan*, 1772. Fol. pp. 14. 82

Relates principally to Quebec.

ABRISS. 1779. *See* [Buisson].

Abstract of the Cases of Capture made by France. *Philadelphia*, 1800. 8vo. P. 83

An Abstract of the Charter granted to the Society for the Propagation of the Gospel in Foreign Parts; with a short Account of what hath been, and what is designed to be done by it. *London* [1702]. Folio, pp. 3. 84

An Abstract of the Evidence lately taken in the House of Commons against the Orders in Council, being a Summary of the Facts there proved, respecting the Present State of the Commerce and Manufactures of the Country. *London: Printed by J. M'Creery*, 1812. 8vo, VI. Erratum, 1 l., slip "It was intended, &c." pp. 64. Index 2 l.+Same reprinted. *New York*, 1812. 8vo. 85

An Abstract of the Proceedings of the Corporation, for the Relief of the Widows and Children of Clergymen, in the Communion of the Church of England in America. *Philadelphia*, *J. Humphreys, jun.*, M,DCC,LXXIII. 8vo, pp. 52. 86

Abstracts of the Principal Regulations contained in the Acts of Parliament relative to the Trade of the British Plantations. *Charlestown*, 1774. Sm. 8vo, pp. 28. 87

Acadia and Acadie. *See* Nova Scotia.

ACARETTE. Relation des Voyages dans la Riviere de la Plata et de-là aux terres de Pérou. Par Acarette de Biscaie. *Paris*, 1632. Folio. 88

See Boucher VI., 324. Translated, London, 1698. *See* Acuna & Thevenot.

ACCIOLI. Memorias Historicas e Politicas da Provincia da Bahia. Por Ignacio Accioli de Cerquiera e Silva. *Bahia*, 1835–37. 4to, 4 vols. 89

Account of a Late Conference on the Occurrences in America. In a Letter to a Friend. *London*, 1761. 8vo, pp. 40. 90

"An imaginary conference, managed with decency and good sense, but the strength of the argument lies altogether on the Side of America. The Author is supposed to be Joshua Steele, Esq."—RICH.

Account of a Voyage. *See Voyages.*

Account of Atlantic Steam Ships. *New York*, 1838. 12mo. 91

Account of Discoveries in the South Pacific Ocean. *London*, 1799. 8vo. 92

Quoted by Boucher VI., 351. *See also* Dalrymple (A.)

Account of the Agreement which took place amongst the Burgher and Antiburgher Seceders, and Reformed Presbytery in North America, in Summer 1782. *Glasgow*, 1783. 8vo. 93

An Account of the Conduct of the War in the Middle Colonies. *See* [Galloway, Joseph].

An Account of the Customs and Manners of the Mickmakis and Maricheets Savage Nations, now dependent on the Government of Cape-Breton, from an Original French Manuscript-Letter, never published, Written by a French Abbot, who resided many years, in quality of Missionary, amongst them, To which are annexed, Several Pieces, relative to the Savages, to Nova-Scotia, and to North-America in general. *London*, *S. Hooper and A. Morley*, M,DCC,LVIII. 8vo. Half Title and Title, 2 l., VIII, 138. 94

Account of the European Settlements. *See* [Burke, Ed.]

Account of the French Settlements in North America. By a Gentleman. With an Appendix, giving an Account of Quebec, by P. Charlevoix. *Boston*, 1746. 8vo, pp. 26. N. 95

Account of the part taken, &c. *See* Chatham (Earl).

Account of the proceedings of the *Illinois* and *Ouabache* Land Companies, In pursuance of their purchases made of the Independent Indians, July 5th, 1773, and 18th October, 1775. *Philadelphia*, *W. Young*, 1796. 8vo, 8 p. l., pp. 55. 96

Account of the Progress of the Reformation of Manners in England, Scotland, Ireland, America and other parts. 1702. 8vo. 97

Account of the Propagation of the Gospel in the English Dominions of North America, some West India Islands, &c. A broad sheet. Folio, pp. 4. 98

An Account of the Propagation of the Gospel in Foreign Parts. What the Society established in England by Royal Charter hath done since their Incorporation, June 16, 1701, in Her Majesty's Plantations, Colonies, and Factories. As also what they design to do upon further Encouragement from their own Members and other well disposed Christians, either by Annual subscriptions, present benefactions, or future legacies. *London*, *J. Downing*, 1704. Folio, pp. 4. 99

Drawn up by Rev. Mr. Stubs, *with engraving of the Seal of the Society.*

Account of the Society for the Encouragement of the British Troops in Germany and North America, with the motives of making a Present to those Troops and the Widows and Orphans of such as have died in Defence of their Country, particularly at the Battles of Thonhausen, Quebec, etc. *Quebec and London*, 1760. 8vo. 100

An Account of the Society for Propagating the Gospel in Foreign Parts, Established by the Royal Charter of King William III. With their Proceedings and Success, and Hopes of continual Progress under the Happy Reign of Her Most Excellent Majesty Queen Anne. *London*, *Joseph Downing*, 1706. 4to. *Frontispiece*; *Title*; and pp. 97. P. 101

An Account of the Spanish Settlements in America. In Four Parts. I. An Account of the Discovery of America by the celebrated Christopher Columbus, with a description of the Spanish insular Colonies in the West Indies. II. Their Settlements on the Continent of North America. III. Their Settlements in Peru, Chili, Paraguay and Rio de la Plata. IV. Their Settlements in Terra Firma, Of the different Countries in South America still possessed by the Indians, &c. With a description of the Canary Islands. Each part contains an accurate description of the settlements in it, their situation, extent, climate, soil, produce, former and present condition, trading commodities, manufactures, the genius, disposition, and number of their inhabitants, their government, both civil and ecclesiastic, together with a concise account of their chief cities, ports, bays, rivers, lakes, mountains, minerals, fortifications, &c.; with a very particular account of the trade carried on betwixt them and Old Spain, to which is annexed, A succinct account of the climate, produce, trade, manufactures, &c., of Old Spain, Illustrated with a Map of America. *Edinburgh, A. Donaldson and J. Reid*, MDCCLXII. 8vo, xvi., pp. 512. Map. 102

At the end is "The accurate accounts published by Authority, of the Siege and Surrender of the Havannah, the chief town of the Island of Cuba."

An Account of the very important Debate in the House of Commons, July 9th, 1782, in which the Great Question of American Independence came under consideration, &c. *London*, 1782. 8vo. 103

Account of the Views and Principles of that Connexion of Whigs, called the Rockingham Party. * * * [*London*] 1782. 8vo, pp. 60. 104

Acevedo. *See* Antunez y Acevedo.

Achenbach (H.) Tagebuch meiner Reise nach den Nordamerikanischen Freistaaten oder, das neue Kanaan. Von H. Achenbach. *Düsseldorf*, 1835. 8vo. 2 Parts. Map and Plates. 105

Achenwall (D. G.) Aanmerkingen wegens Noord-America, en de Engelsche Volkplantingen aldaar. Verhandeling, aangaande de tegenwoordige-Verschillen met de Volkplantingen in Amerika, door Johan Wesley. Uit het Hoogduitsch vertaald. Von D. G. Achenwall. *Utrecht*, 1778. 8vo. 106

Achenwall. Einige Anmerkungen über Nord-Amerika und über dasige Grosbrittannische Colonien. Aus mündlichen Nachrichten des Herrn D. Franklins verfasst. Von Herrn D. Gottfried Achenwall. Nebst H. John Wesleys Schrift von den

Streitigkeiten mit den Colonien in Amerika. *Helmstedt*, 1777. 8vo, pp. 72.+First published at *Stuttgart*, 1769. 8vo. M. 107

Achenwall (Gottfried). Herrn Hofrath Achenwalls in Göttingen Anmerkungen über Nordamerika und über dasige Grosbritannische Colonien aus mündlichen Nachrichten des Herrn Dr. Franklins. *Frankfurt und Leipzig*, 1769. Sm. 8vo, pp. 94. H. 108

Ackermann (F. X.) Das Kaiserreich Brasilien. *Heidelberg*, 1834. 8vo. Map. 109

Aclamacion|y|Pendones|qve levanto|la|mvy noble y coronada|civdad|De los Reyes,|por|el catolico|y|avgvstissimo|Rey. D. Carlos II.|des le. nombre|N. S. con festiva solemnidad.|El.| dia 17, de Octvbre Ano|de 1666|Con licencia.|*En Lima. En la Imprenta de Jvan de|Quevedo y Zarate.* 4to, 6 p. l., and 43 leaves; large plate. 110

Açores. Report of the Isles of Açores, 1591. *See* [Raleigh (Sir W.)]

Acosta (Blas de). Oracion Panegyrica|a las Hon-|ras del Capitan|Martin de Eraso, Secre-|tario de su Excelencia.|Dixola el M. R. P. M. Fr. Blas|Dacosta, de la Orden de Pre-|dicadores, en el Convento insigne de|N. P. S. Francisco de Lima.| Dedicala. al Excelentisimo|Señor don Pedro de Toledo y Leyua, Marques|de Mancera, Señor de las cinco Villas, y su iuris-|dicion, Comendador de Esparragal, en la Or-|den de Alcantara, Gentilhombre de la Camara|de su Magestad, del Consejo de Guerra,|Virrey, y Capitan General|destos Reynos.|Con Licencia, *En Lima, Por Iorge Lopez de|Herrera, Año|de* 1642. 4to, 4 p. l., text, 12 l. 111

Acosta (Blas de). Sermon|a las exeqvias|del ilvstrissimo| señor Don Fr Gabriel de|Zatate de la Orden de Predicadores| Obispo electo de Guamanga.|Celebro las el insigne con|uento de nuestra Señora del Rosario de Lima|assistio a ellas|El Excel^mo, señor Conde de Chin-|chon del Consejo de Estado, Gentilhombre de la Ca|mara de su Magestad, Virrey del Pirù.|La real Avdiencia.|El Ilvstrisimo Senor Don Fer|nando Arias de Vgarte, Arçobispo Metropolitano.|Cabildos, y Nobleza deste Reyno.|Predicole el Maestro, Fr. Blas de Acos-|ta de la misma orden a 27. de Octubre, año de 1637.|*Impresso en Lima por Geronymo|de Contreras, Año de* 1637. 4to, 14 leaves. 112

Acosta (Christoval). Tratado de las Drogas, y medicinas de las Indias Orientales, con sus Plantas debuxadas albivo. Por Christoval Acosta, Medico y Cirujano que las vio ocularmente. *Burgos*, 1578. 4to, Title, &c., 12 leaves, pp. 448; Table, &c., pp. 39. 113

Acosta. Trattato di Christoforo Acosta . . . della Historia, Natura e Virtv delle Droghe Medicinali, & altri Semplici rarissimi, che vengono portati dalle Indie Orientali, in Europa . . . Nuov. rec. della Spagnuola . . . *In Venetia, F. Ziletti*, 1585. 4to, 26 p. l., pp. 342. A. 114

Acosta. Histoire des drogues, épiceries et de certains médicamens simples qui naissent ès Indes, mis en franc. du latin de Ch. l'Écluse par Ant. Colin. *Lyon*, 1602. 8vo. 115

Another Edition. 1619. 8vo. For a Latin Translation, see Garcia d'Orta.

Acosta (Francisco). Vida de Maria de Jesus de Puebla de los Angelos. 1648. 4to. 116

Acosta (Joaquin). Compendio historico del Descubrimiento y Colonizacion de la Nueva Granada en el siglo decimo sexto. *Paris, M. de Beau.* 8vo, pp. 460. Map. 117

Acosta (Joseph de). De Natvra|Novi Orbis|Libri dvo,| et|de Promvlgatione|Evangelii, apvd|Barbaros,|sive|de Procvranda|Indorvm salvte|Libri sex. Avtore Iosepho Acosta presbytero societatis Iesv. *Salmanticæ, Apud Guillelmum Foquel*, M.D.LXXXIX. 8vo, 8 p. l., pp. 640. 118

The original Edition. Mr. Rich observes of Acosta, that he is one of the earliest writers who have treated philosophically of America and its productions. Dr. Robertson pronounces him a standard authority, and Backer, in his Bibliothèque des Écrivains de la Compag. de Jésus, observes: "Joseph de Acosta, né à Medina del Campo, vers l'an 1539, passa, après avoir professé la théologie, à Ocana, en 1571 aux Indes occidentales, et fut le second Provincial de l'ordre des Jésuites au Pérou oú il séjourna pendant 17 ans. Il mourut recteur à Salamanque, le 11 février 1600. Son ouvrage, estimé à juste titre, a été réimprimé assez souvent et traduit dans presque toutes les langues." Pinelo, however, alleges that the work is taken from the MSS. of Diego Duran, a Dominican Monk. See, also, Camus, p. 103. Clement Bibl. Curieuse. Priced in the Nuggets, £2. 2. 0. Salva, 10s. 0d.

Acosta. Editio Altera. *Salmanticæ*, M.DXCV. 8vo. 119

Acosta. Iosephi|A costa,|societatis|Iesv,|de natvra novi orbis|libri dvo.|Et|de promvlgatione|evangelii apvd|barbaros,| siue,|de procvranda indorvm|salute, Libri sex.||¶ *Coloniæ Agrip-*

pinae,|In officina Birckmannica. Sumpti-|bus Arnoldi Mylij.| CIↃ.IↃ.XCVI.| 8vo, 8 p. l., pp. 581. 120

This text was changed, and inserted without the Author's name, in De Bry's Collection. The first two books of this work are nearly the same as the same books of the "Historia Natural." The other six are different.

Acosta. Historia|natvral|y|moral delas|Indias,|en qve se tratan las cosas|notables del cielo, y elementos, metales, plantas, y ani-|males dellas: y los ritos, y ceremonias, leyes, y|gouierno, y guerras de los Indios.|Compuesta por el Padre Ioseph de Acosta Religioso|de la Compañia de Iesus.|Dirigida a la serenissima|Infanti Doña Isabella Clara Eugenia de Austria.|| ¶ Con Privilegio.|*Impresso en Seuilla en casa de Iuan de Leon.|Año de* 1590.||[Colophon.] ¶ Hispali,|Excudebat Ioannes Leonius.| Ano, 1590.| Sm. 4to. Title and 'Tabla,' 18 l., pp. 535. N. 121

First Edition in Spanish. Quaritch, £1. 5s.; Nuggets, £1. 11. 6.; Fleurieu, 20 fr.; Huzard, 22 fr.

Acosta. El mismo. *Barcelona, Coudret*, 1591. Sm. 4to. +*Seville*, 1591. Sm. 4to. + El mismo. Año 1608.|Con Licencia.|*Impresso en Madrid en casa de Alonso Martin.* 4to. Title, 1 l. Tassa y Errata, 1 l. Licencias, etc., 5–12. Text, 13. — 535. Tabla, 21 l. + El mismo. *Madrid*, 1610. 4to. 122

Priced: Nuggets, 1. 11. 6.; Brunet, 8 c. 10 fr.

Acosta. El mismo. Data a luz en esta sexta edicion. D.A.V.C. *Madrid*, 1792. 4to. 2 vols. N. 123

This is the best Spanish Edition. $12 to $15.

Acosta. Historia|Natvrele, e Morale|delle Indie;|Scritta| Dal. R. P. Gioseffo di Acosta|Della Compagnia del Giesu;|Nellaquale si trattano le cose notabili del Cielo, & de gli|Elementi, Metalli, Piante, & Animali di quelle:|i fuoiriti, & ceremonie: Leggi, & gouerni,|& guerre degli Indiani.|*Nouamente tradotta della lingua Spagnuola nella Italiani*|Da Gio. Paolo Galvcci Salodiano|Academico Veneto.|Con Privilegii.|*In Venetia,|Presso Bernardo Basa*, All 'insegna del Sole, M,D,XCVI. 4to. 24 p. l. Text, 173 leaves. N. 124

The only Italian version, printed with the types of Aldus. Priced: Nuggets, £1. 11. 6. Sold in New York, 1865, for $5.

Acosta. Histoire|Natvrelle|et Moralle|des Indes, tant Orientalles|qu' Occidentalles.|Où il est traité des choses remarquables du Ciel,|des Elémens, Métaux, Plantes & Animaux|qui sont propres de ces pais. Ensemble des|mœurs, cérémonies,

loix, gouuernmens &|guerres des mesme Indiens.|Composée en Castilian par Ioseph Acosta, &|traduite en François par Robert |Regnault Cauxois|.Dedié av Roy.|*A Paris,|Chez Marc Orry*, M.D.XCVIII. 8vo. 8 p. l., pp. 375. Table, 17 l. 125

Sold at Puttick's, 1860, £1. 15. 0. Graesse quotes an edition 1597. Reprinted *Paris, Marc Orry*, 1600. Sm. 8vo, 6 p. l., pp. 375. Table, 17 l.+*Paris, Marc Orry*, 1606. Sm. 8vo, 8 p. l., pp. 352. Table, 18 l.+*Paris, Adrian Tiffainè*, 1616. 8vo, 8 p. l., pp. 375. Table, 16 l.+*Paris, Adrian Tiffainè*, 1617. 8vo, 8 p. l., pp. 375. Table, 16 l.+Also reprinted 1619 and 1621.

Acosta. Historie Naturael|ende Morael van de We-|stersche Indien:|Waer inne ghehandelt wordt van de|merckelijckste dinghen des Hemels, Elementen,|Metalen, Planten ende Ghedierten van dien: als oock|de Manieren, Ceremonien, Wetten, Regeeringen|ende Oorloghen der Indianen.|Ghecomponeert door Iosephum de|Acosta, der Jesuitscher Oorden:|Ende nu eerstmael uyt den Spaenschen in onser|Nederduytsche tale overgheset: door Ian Huyghen|van Linschoten.||¶ *Tot Enchuysen,| By Jacob Lenaertsz. Meyn. Boeckvercooper,|woonende op den hoeck van de Kerck brugghe,|int Schrijfboeck. Anno* 1598.|[Colophon.] ¶ Ghedruckt t'Haerlem,|By Gillis Rooman, woo-|nende in de Jacobijne-strate,|in de vergulde Parsse.|Anno 1598.|8vo, 7 p. l., pp. 389. Table, 8 l. 126

This Dutch translation, by Linschoten, formed the basis of the version in De Bry's Collection. It was reprinted in 1624, with the following title:

Acosta. Historie Naturael en Morael|van de Westersche Indien.|Waer inne ghehandelt wort van de merckelijckste dinghen|des Hemels, Elementen, Metalen, Planten ende Gedierten|van dien: Als oock de Manieren, Ceremonien, Wetten,| Regeeringen, ende Oorlogen der Indianen.|Ghecomponeert door Iosephum de Acosta, der|Iesuytscher Oorden:|Uyt den Spaenschen in onse Nederduytsche tale overgheset:|Door Ian Huyghen van Linschoten. De tweede Editie||¶ *t'Amsterdam,|By Broer, Iansz.* Anno 1624. 4to, 4 p. l., pp. 177. Table, 3 l. Gothic Letter. 127

Another Dutch version will be found in Vander Aa's Voyages, Vol. xx.

Acosta. Geographische vnd historische Beschreibung der überauss grossen Landschafft America: welche auch West-India, vnd jhrer grösse halben die Newe Welt genennet wird. Gar artig vnd nach der Kunst in 20 Mappen oder Landtafeln verfasset, etc. *Cölln, Joh. Christoffel*, 1598. Folio. 128

Boucher, Vol. 1, p. 276, refers to an edition in 8vo, 1599, and Mr. J. C. Brown's Catalogue contains the following:

Acosta. New Welt, Das ist: Volkommen Beschreibung von Natur, Art und gelegenheit der Newen Welt, die man sonst America oder West-Indien nennet. *Cölln, Iohan Christoffel*, 1600. Folio, pp. 51. Gothic Letter. 129

Acosta. America oder wie man es zu teutsch nennt die Neuwe Welt oder West India. *Ursel*, 1605. Folio. 130

Title as given by Ternaux, No. 293. Mr. J. C. Brevoort's List of Editions of Acosta includes one "Frankfurt, 1617." Folio; quoted, from Meusel, Vol. III., p. 228, who remarks that the German version was made from the Dutch by Johannes Humberger.

Acosta. The|natvrall|and Morall Historie of the|East and West|Indies.|Intreating of the remarkeable things of Heaven, of the|Elements, Mettalls, Plants and Beasts which are pro-|per to that Country: Together with the Manners,|Ceremonies, Lawes, Governements, and Warres of the Indians.|Written in Spanish by Joseph Acosta, and translated|into English by E. G. ¶ *London|Printed by Val: Sims for Edward Blount and William|Aspley* 1604.|4to, 3 p. l., pp. 590, 7 l. 131

Some copies have the Initials "R. F." before the author's name. The Translator is supposed to be Edward Grimestone. Priced: Nuggets, £2. 2. 0.; North, £3. 7. 0.

Acosta y Perez. Album universal. Periodico semanal de ciencias y artes, con retractos, vistas, costumbres y biografias. Bajo la direccion de los Sres. Acosta y Perez. *Habana*, 1860. 4to, pp. 400, and 37 Lithographic Plates. 132

Acquest of Dominion. *See* [Bollan].

Acrelius. Beskrifning Om De Swenska Församlingars Forna och Närwarande Tilstand, Uti det saa kallade Nya Swerige Sedan Nya Nederland, Meri nu för tiden Pensylvanien, samt nästliggande Orter wid Alfven De La Ware, Wäst-Yersey och New-Castle County, uti Norra America; utigifven af Israel Acrelius. *Stockholm, Harberg & Hesseberg*, 1759. 4to, 10 p. l., pp. 534.

A portion of this work was included in the New York Hist. Coll., Vol. 1, Second Series, under this title: New Sweden, or the Swedish Settlements on the Delaware. Translated from the original Swedish by the late Nicholas Collin, of Philadelphia. See N. A. R., LIV., p. 328.

Across the Atlantic. By the Author of Sketches of Cantabs. *London, Earle*, 1851. Post 8vo. 134

Act Encouraging the Importation of Naval Stores from Her Majesty's Plantations in America. *London*, 1705. Folio. 135

Act for a Company Trading to Africa and the Indies, June 26, 1695. *Edinburgh*, 1696. Folio, pp. 7. 136

Relates to the Darien Expedition. See Darien.

An Act for Disposing of certain Estates and Banishing certain Persons therein named. 1782. 4to. 137

Act for Granting and Applying certain Stamp Duties, and other Duties in the British Colonies and Plantations in America, towards further Defraying the Expenses of Defending, Protecting and Securing the same. *London*, 1765. Folio. + Reprinted, *Boston*, 1765. Folio. + *Same. London, Baskett*, 1765. 8vo, pp. 66. 138

Mr. Rich characterizes this 8vo as "the Original Edition of the celebrated Stamp Act." I am inclined to think it first appeared in folio, with the following title: "Anno Regni Georgii III. Regis Magna Britanniæ Franciæ & Hiberniæ, &c."

An Act for repealing Certain Parts of an Act postponing the Payment of Government Securities. *Boston*, 1781. 8vo, pp. 7.

Act of Parliament appointing Commissioners to inquire into the Losses and Services of those [Loyalists] who have suffered by the late Unhappy Disturbances in America. *London*, 1783. Folio. W. 140

An Act of Parliament for Encouraging the Scots African and Indian Company. *Edinburgh, June* 26, 1695. 4to, pp. 8. 141

Relates to the Darien Colony.

Act of Parliament for Repealing the Stamp Duties and other Duties in the British Colonies and Plantations in America. *London*, 1766. Folio. 142

Act of Parliament relating to the Government of Her Majesty's Ships, Vessels, and Forces by Sea. *London*, 1780. 4to.

Act for Registering Ships to prevent Fraud and Abuses in the Plantation Trade. 1698. Folio. 144

An Act Prohibiting Trade with the Barbada's, Virginia, Bermudas, and Antego. Ordered to be Printed and Published *die Jovis, 3. Octob.*, 1650. Folio, half sheet. 145

Acte d'Independence des Etats-Unis et constitution des républiques française cisalpine et ligurienne. Paris [1778]. 8vo.

In French, German, English and Italian.

Actes et Memoires concernant les Negociations qui ont eu lieu entre la France et les Etats Unis de l'Amerique depuis 1793, jusqu' à la conclusion de la Convention du 30 Septembre, 1800. *Londres, J. B. C. Vogel*, 1807. 12mo. 3 vols. pp. 368, 451, 481. C. 147

All the documents in these volumes are in the respective languages in which they were originally written by the persons acting under the authority of the French and American governments. "If they do not display much of the address for which French diplomacy claims credit, some important points of public law are discussed with ability and spirit, and though they are offensive in their nature, they form precious materials for the annalist. Collections of this kind which render state documents more accessible to historians and statesmen, are of great utility, and entitle the compilers of them to public acknowledgments."—M. R.

The Acts of the Elders, commonly called the Book of Abraham; containing a revelation made to him at a pròtracted meeting, to which is appended a chapter from the Book of Religious Errors, with notes of explanation and commentation, from commencement to termination. Calculated for the meridian of Rhode Island; but will answer for the New England States. Written by Himself. *Providence, Printed for the purchaser*, 1842. Square 12mo, pp. 160. 148

"This curious book relates to the dissensions among various religious denominations in Rhode Island."—Bartlett.

Acugna (Christopher). *See* Acuna (Christoval de).

Acuna (Ant. Gonç. de). Informe à N. R. P. M. General de el orden de Predicadores, Fr. Jhoan Baptista de Marinis. Le Orfrece el Press^do F. Antonio Gonçalez de Acuña, Dr. Cathedratico de prima de moral, Procurador de la Real Universidad de los Reyes. Diffinidor de la Provincia de S. Jhoan Baptista de el Peru en su nombres. 1659. 4to. 149

"With an engraved title, but no printer's name. Evidently printed exclusively for the use of the order of Preachers, and consequently of great rarity. The author appears to have made a voyage from Lima to Spain, to give this account of the state of the religion of his order in South America, to his superiors. It is not mentioned by Nicolas Antonio; and Barcia, who collected every thing relating to America, evidently never saw the book."—Rich.

Acuna (Christoval de). Nvevo Descvbrimiento del Gran Rio de las|Amazonas.|Por el Padre Christoval|de Acuña, Religioso de la Suprema General Inquisicion,|Al qval sue, y se luzo por Orden|de su Magestad, el año de 1639|Por la Provincia de Qvito|en los Reynos del Perù|Al Excelentissimo Señor Conde| Duque de Oliuares|Con Licencia: *En Madrid, en la Imprenta de Reyno,|año de* 1641.|Sm. 4to, 6 p. l.; viz.: Title, etc., pp.

3; Al Lector, 1 p.; Certificates, 2 l.; Clavsvla, etc., 1 l.; Text, 46 l. 150

This little volume is highly prized by collectors of rare books, and has sold as high as £16; but, according to Barcia, its rarity is not owing to a rigid suppression of the work by order of Philip IV., as is stated by most bibliographical writers, but from a very small number of copies having been printed. "It was probably not intended for sale, as it is not furnished with the licenses and privileges usually prefixed to books published at the time. Acuña was accompanied by Artieda, a brother Jesuit, and the object of their voyage was to ascertain whether the treasures of Peru might not be brought to Europe by way of the river Amazon, without going through the South Sea (at that time much infested by pirates) and round Cape Horn."—Rich. The work was suppressed by the Court of Spain, on the ground that it might prove advantageous to the Portuguese, who had wrested from Spanish dominion the Brazils, and the Colony of Para, on the mouth of the Amazon. Peignot says: "On connait trois ou quatre exemplaires, tout au plus, de l'edition originale."

Acuna (Cristoval d'). Relation de la Rivière des Amazones. Tradvite sur l'original Espagnol, par feu Mr. de Gomberville; avec une dissertation sur la Rivière des Amazones, pour servir de préface. *Paris*, *Claude Barbin*, 1682. 12mo, pp. 238. Map. c. 151

Faribault (No. 3) and Brunet quote this edition as in 2 vols. There is an edition with the following imprint: *Sur la Copie imprimée à Paris*, 1682. + Another Edition, 1682, 3 vols., and another with the Voyage of Grillet and Bechamel to Guiana in 1674. 12mo, 4 vols.

Acuna (Christoval de). Voyages and Discoveries in South-America—The First up the River of Amazons to Quito in Peru, and back again to Brazil, By Christopher d'Acvgna—The Second up the River of Plata, and thence by Land to the Mines of Potosi, By Mons. Acarete—The Third from Cayenne into Guiana, in search of the Lake of Parima, reputed the richest place in the world, By M. Grillet and Bechamel. Done into English from the Originals, being the only Accounts of those Parts hitherto extant. *London*, *for S. Buckley*, 1698. 8vo. 152

Pp. viii.; Map; Text, 190 pp.; Title, "An Account of a Voyage, etc. By Mons. Acarete du Biscay, 1698." Map, etc. Text, 79 pp.; Title, "Travels of Grillet and Bechamel, etc., 1698." A Letter, 1 leaf, and Text, 68 pp. Acarete's Relation is in Thevenot's Collection. The Original of Grillet and Bechamel's Voyage has not yet been discovered.

Acuna. Bericht von dem Strom derer Amazonen. *Wien*, 1729. Sm. 8vo. 153

Acushnet. Reports of the Selectmen of Acushnet on the Financial Affairs of the Town. *New Bedford*, 1860, and continued. 8vo. 154

Adair (James). The History of the American Indians;

particularly those Nations adjoining to the Mississippi, East and West Florida, Georgia, South and North Carolina and Virginia: Containing an Account of their Origin, Language, Manners, Religious and Civil Customs, Laws, Form of Government, Punishments, Conduct in War and Domestic Life, their Habits, Diet, Agriculture, Manufactures, Diseases and Method of Cure, and other Particulars, sufficient to render it a Complete Indian System. With Observations on Former Historians, the Conduct of our Colony Governors, Superintendents, Missionaries, &c. Also an Appendix, containing a Description of the Floridas and the Mississippi Lands, with their Productions—The Benefits of colonizing Georgiana, and Civilizing the Indians—And the way to make all the colonies more valuable to the mother country. By James Adair, Esq., A Trader with the Indians and Resident in their Country for Forty Years. *London*, *Edward and Charles Dilly*, MDCCLXXV. 4to, 6 p. l., pp. 464. Map. 155

"Mr. Adair points out various customs of the Indians, having a striking resemblance to those of the Jews; and the great object of his work appears to be, to prove that the aborigines of America are descended from that race. Some distrust appears to have fallen upon his statements, although he himself says that his account is neither disfigured by fable nor prejudice."—Allen. See, also, Faribault, No. 5, Volney and Pinkerton.

Adair. Geschichte der Amerikanischen Indianer. Aus dem Engl. [Von S. H. Ewald.] *Breslau*, 1782. 8vo. 156

Adair (J. M.) Unanswerable Arguments Against the Abolition of the Slave Trade. With a defence of the proprietors of the British sugar colonies, &c. Published for the benefit of the starving tin-miners in Cornwall. *By James Makittrick Adair*. *London*, 1790. 8vo. 157

Adair (R.) Biographical Sketch of General Robert Adair. *Washington*, 1830. 8vo. 158

Adalbert. Aus meinem Tagebuch. Von Adalbert Prinzen von Preussen. *Berlin*, 1847. 4to. 10 Plates. 159

Adalbert. Skizzen zu meinem Tagebuch. *Berlin*, 1847. Folio. 45 Plates, some of which are colored. 160

"Ouvrage de luxe executé par d'habiles artistes, et dont on n'a tiré que *cent* exemplaires qui ont été distribués aux nobles amis de l'auteur."—Friedlander.

Adalbert. Bericht über das Mosquitoland im Auftrag des Prinzen von Preussen, &c. *Berlin*, 1845. 8vo, pp. 274. 2 Maps. 161

Adalbert. Travels in the South of Europe and in Brazil, with a voyage up the Amazon and its Tributary the Xingu. By Heinrich Wilhelm Adalbert, Prince of Prussia. Translated by Sir Robert H. Schomburgk and John E. Taylor. With Introduction by Baron Von Humboldt. *London*, 1849. 2 vols., 8vo, pp. 732. Maps. 162

"If human civilization should ever penetrate into these fastnesses, the structure of this great net of rivers from north to south, may open channels of communication such as are unknown in any other part of the world."—Humboldt's Introduction.

Adam (L.) La Question Américaine de l'Abolition de l'Esclavage aux Etats Unis. Par L. Adam, Magistrat. *Nancy*, 1861. 8vo, pp. 72. 163

Adam (Thomas). The Missionary's appeal to the religious public . . . the Mission in the Island of Trinidad . . . *London*, 1824, 8vo. 164

Adam (Thomas). Missionary's Farewell Sermon: Island of Trinidad. *London*, 1823. 8vo. 165

Adam (W.) Genealogy of the Adam family. By William Adam, of Canaan, Litchfield Co., Conn. *Albany*, 1848. 8vo, pp. 16. 166

Adam (W. J.) Journal of Voyages to Marguaritta, Trinidad, and Maturin, with Travels across the Llaneros and descent of the Orinoco, in 1819–20, comprising Interviews with Bolivar, and characteristic anecdotes. By W. J. Adam. *Dublin*, 1824. 8vo. 167

Adams (Abigail). Journal and Correspondence of Miss Adams, daughter of John Adams, second President of the United States; Written in France and England, in 1785. Edited by her Daughter. *New York*, 1841–2. 12mo. 2 vols. *Plate of the Battle of Trenton and Portrait of Washington*. 168

Adams (Amos). The Character of a Christian's Life and Death illustrated. A Sermon upon the Death of Mrs. Lucy Dudley, Oct. 24, 1756. Preached at Roxbury, Oct. 31, 1756. By Rev. Amos Adams. *Boston*, 1756. 8vo, pp. 26. 169

Adams. Concise Historical View of the Difficulties, Hardships, and Perils, which attended the Planting and Progressive improvements of New England. With a particular account of its long and Destructive Wars, Expensive Expeditions, &c. With reflections, principally moral and religious. In two discourses,

preached at Roxbury on the general fast, April 6, 1769 . . . By Amos Adams, A.M. Pastor of the first church in Roxbury ***. *Boston*, *Kneeland & Adams*, 1769. 8vo, pp. 66.+Same. *Boston printed. London reprinted for Edward and Charles Dilly*, 1770. 8vo, Title, 1 l., pp. 68. 170

For an account of this rare work, see the "Massachusetts Historical Collection," Vol. XXVIII., p. 280; M. R., XLII., p. 156.

Adams. Expediency and Utility of War in the present State of Things. Discourse before Ancient and Honorable Artillery Company, June 4, 1759. By Amos Adams. *Boston*, 1759. 8vo, pp. 32. 171

Adams. Religious Liberty an invaluable Blessing. Two Thanksgiving Discourses, preached at Roxbury, Dec. 3, 1767. By Amos Adams. *Boston*, 1768. 8vo, pp. 57. 172

Adams†. Songs of Victory directed by human compassion and qualified with Christian benevolence; in a Sermon delivered at Roxbury, October 25, 1759, on the general thanksgiving for the success of His Majesty's arms, more particularly in the reduction of Quebec . . . By Amos Adams, A.M. Pastor . . . Roxbury. *Boston*, *Edes & Gill*, 1759. 8vo, pp. 29. 173

Mr. Adams also published Sermons on the Ordination of Jonathan Moore, Samuel Kingsbury, Caleb Prentice and John Wyeth, A Dudleian Lecture, 1770, and other tracts.

Adams (Arthur). *See* Gray (J. E.)

Adams (A. C.) Waiting upon God, the Way to secure our Country's Welfare. A Sermon. *Portland*, 1845. 8vo. 174

Adams (C. B.) Catalogue of Shells collected at Panama, with Notes of their Synonymy, Station and Geographical Distribution. By Charles Baker Adams. *New York*, *privately printed*, 1852. 8vo, pp. 342. 175

Adams. Contributions to Conchology. By C. B. Adams. *New York*, 1849–52. 176

Adams. First Annual Report on the Geology of the State of Vermont. By Charles B. Adams. *Burlington*, 1845. 8vo, pp. 92.+Second, 1846. 8vo, pp. IV., 267.+Third, 1847. 8vo, pp. 32.+Fourth, 1848. 8vo, pp. 8. 177

Adams. Fresh Water and Land Shells of Vermont. [*No imprint.*] 8vo, pp. 19. 178

Adams (Charles Francis). An Address delivered before the Members of the Schools and the Citizens of Quincy, July 4, 1856. By Charles Francis Adams. *Boston*, *Little*, *Brown & Co.*, 1856. 8vo, pp. 36. 179

Adams. An Address on the Opening of the new Town Hall in Braintree, July 29, 1858. By C. F. Adams. *Boston*, 1858. 8vo, pp. 86. 180

[Adams.] An Appeal from the New to the Old Whigs, by a Whig of the Old School. *Boston*, 1835. 8vo, pp. 52. 181

[Adams.] Further Reflections upon the State of the Currency in the United States. *Boston*, 1837. 8vo, pp. 41. 182

Adams. The Life of John Adams, Second President of the United States. *Boston*, 1856. 8vo, pp. 684. 183

Also on large paper. Forms Vol. I. of John Adams' Works, 10 vols., 8vo.

Adams. An Oration delivered before the City Council and Citizens of Boston, July 4, 1843. By C. F. Adams. *Boston*, 1843. 8vo, pp. 39. 184

[Adams.] Reflections upon the Present State of the Currency in the United States. *Boston*, 1837. 8vo, pp. 36. 185

[Adams.] Speech of Charles Francis Adams on the Union. Delivered in the House of Representatives, January 31st, 1861. 8vo, pp. 8. 186

Adams. Texas and the Massachusetts Resolutions. By Charles Francis Adams. *Boston*, 1844. 8vo, pp. 54. 187

Adams. What makes Slavery a Question of National Concern? A Lecture delivered at New York, January 30, 1855. By Charles Francis Adams. *Boston*, *Little*, *Brown & Co.*, 1855. 8vo, pp. 46. 188

Adams. The Charles F. Adams Platform; or, a Looking-glass for the Worthies of the Buffalo Convention. *Washington*, [n. d.] 8vo, pp. 8. 189

Adams (D.) Oration at Fitchburg, Oct. 12, 1801, at a meeting of the Militia Officers of the Fourth Regiment. By Daniel Adams. *Leominster*, 1802. 8vo. 190

Adams. An Oration, Sacred to the Memory of Gen. George Washington, Delivered at Leominster, Feb. 22, 1800. By

Daniel Adams, M.B. [Motto.] *Leominster (Mass.)*, *Printed by Adams & Wilder*, 1800. 8vo, pp. 25. 191

This Author also published a Geography, of which the Fourth Edition was issued, *Boston*, 1819, 12mo, pp. 336; and a Medical and Agricultural Register for 1806–7.

Adams. Government and Rebellion. A Sermon delivered in the North Broad Street Presbyterian Church, Sunday Morning, April 28, 1861. By Rev. E. E. Adams. Published by Request. *Philadelphia*, *Henry B. Ashmead*, 1861. 8vo, pp. 23. 192

Adams. The Temple and the Throne, or the True Foundation. A Sermon, Preached in the North Broad Street Presbyterian Church, September 26th, 1861. By Rev. E. E. Adams. *Philadelphia*, *H. C. Peck*, 1861. 8vo, pp. 28. 193

Adams. (E. G.) An Historical Discourse in Commemoration of the One Hundredth Anniversary of the formation of the First Congregational Church in Templeton, Massachusetts. With an Appendix, embracing a survey of the Municipal affairs of the Town. By Edwin G. Adams, Junior Pastor. *Boston*, *Crosby*, *Nichols & Co.*, 1857. 8vo, pp. VIII., 175. 194

Adams (E.) Connecticut Election Sermon. By Eliphalet Adams. *New London*, 1710. 16mo. + Another. May 10, 1733. *New London*, *T. Green*, 1733. 12mo. 195

Adams. A Discourse putting Christians in mind to be ready for every Good Work. As it was delivered in Boston, Octob. 20, 1706. By Eliphalet Adams. *Boston*, *N. E.*, *Printed by B. Green*, 1706. 8vo, pp. 60. 196

Adams. A Discourse occasioned by the late Distressing Storm, Feb. 20, 1716–17, delivered March 3. By Eliphalet Adams. *New London*, 1717. 12mo, pp. 31. 197

Adams. Discourse on the Death of the Hon. Gordon Saltonstall, Governor of Connecticut. By Eliphalet Adams. With Appendix from the Boston News Letter. *New London* [1724]. 12mo, pp. 60. 198

Adams. Eminently Good and Vseful Men, the Glory and Defence of the Places where they live. As it was set forth in a Sermon at Stonington, on the Death of Rev. James Noyes. *New London*, *T. Green*, 1720. 12mo, pp. 46. 199

Adams. God sometimes answers his People by terrible Things in Righteousness. Sermon on the Meeting-house in

New London being struck by Lightning, Aug. 31, 1735. By Eliphalet Adams. *New London*, 1735. 16mo, pp. 46. M. 200

Also, Sermons at the Ordination of William Gager, John Owen and Thomas Clap, and on the Death of J. J. Fabyan, Mrs. L. Adams and Mrs. M. Bulkley.

Adams. Manual Pereira, or, The Sovereign Rule of South Carolina. With Views of Southern Laws, Life, and Hospitality. By F. C. Adams. *Charleston*, 1853. 12mo, pp. 303. 201

This was printed in Washington, 1853, and some copies have that imprint.+Reprinted. *London*, 1854. 12mo, pp. 400.

Adams. The Story of a Trooper, with much of interest concerning the Campaign on the Peninsula, not before written. By F. Colburn Adams. *New York*, *Dick and Fitzgerald*, 1865. 12mo, cloth, pp. 616. 202

Adams. Uncle Tom at Home. A Review of the Reviewers and Repudiators of "Uncle Tom's Cabin," by Mrs. Stowe. By F. C. Adams. *Philadelphia*, 1853. 12mo. + Reprinted, *London*, *Clarke & Co*, 1853. 12mo. 203

Adams. Justice in the Bye Ways. By F. C. Adams. *New York*, 1856. 12mo. 204

Adams (G.) Genealogy of the Adams Family of Kingston, Mass. By George Adams. *Boston*, 1861. 8vo, pp. 64. 205

Adams (G. W.) An Oration delivered at Quincy, Mass., 5th July, 1824. By George Washington Adams. *Boston*, 1824. 8vo, pp. 24. 206

Adams (H.) An Abridgment of the History of New England, for the use of Young Persons. By Hannah Adams. *Boston*, 1805. 12mo, pp. IV., 185.+Same. Second Edition. *Boston*, *Belcher & Armstrong*, 1807. 12mo, pp. VI., 5–188. 207

Adams. An Alphabetical Compendium of the Various Sects which have appeared in the world from the beginning of the Christian Era to the present day, etc. By Hannah Adams. *Boston*, 1784. 8vo. 208

Adams. A View of Religions . . . Second Edition. *Boston* [1791]. 8vo. 209

Adams. A View of Religions, . . . Third Edition, with large additions. * * * *Boston*, 1801. 8vo, pp. 504.+Same. A New Edition. *London*, 1805. 8vo. 210

Adams. A Dictionary of all Religions and Religious Denominations, Jewish, Heathen, Mahometan, and Christian, ancient and modern. . . . Fourth Edition, with large additions. *New York*, 1817. 8vo. 211

Reviewed by S. Willard, in the North American Review, Vol. VI., p. 86.

Adams. An Appeal to the World on the Controversy respecting the Revolution of Harvard College. By Hannah Adams. *Charlestown*, 1814. 8vo. 212

Adams. A Memoir of Miss Hannah Adams, written by herself. With Additional Notices, by a Friend. *Boston*, *Gray*, 1832. 12mo, pp. IV., 110. Portrait. 213

Adams. A Narrative of the controversy between the Rev. Jedediah Morse, D.D., and the Author. By Hannah Adams. *Boston*, 1814. 8vo, pp. 31. 214

Adams. A Summary History of New England, from the first Settlement at Plymouth, to the Acceptance of the Federal Constitution. Comprehending A General Sketch of the American War. By Hannah Adams. *Dedham*, *Printed for the Author*, M.DCC.XC.IX. 8vo, pp. 513; List, 1 l. 215

Adams. (H. G.) God's Image in Ebony: a Series of Sketches demonstrative of the Mental Powers and Intellectual Capacities of the Negro Race. Edited by H. G. Adams. With a Sketch by F. W. Chesson, and a Chapter by Wilson Armistead. *London*, *Partridge & Okey*, 1854. 12mo, pp. 188. 216

Adams (Israel). A Narrative of the Life of Israel Adams, by Himself. 8vo, pp. 36. s. 217

A conjectural title, as the only copy known lacks the title-page. The author served in the War of 1812.

Adams (Jasper). Characteristics of the Present Century. A Baccalaureate Address to the Graduates of the College of Charleston, delivered 31st October, 1834. By Jasper Adams, D.D. *Charleston*, 1836. 8vo, pp. 11. 218

Adams. An Eulogium pronounced 23d January, 1835, before the College of Charleston, on the Life and Character of the late Elias Horry, Esq. By Jasper Adams, D.D. *Charleston*, 1835. 8vo, pp. 26. 219

Adams. The Moral Causes of the Welfare of Nations. An Oration delivered 1st November, 1834, before the Society of

Graduates of the College of Charleston. By the Rev. J. Adams. *Charleston*, 1834. 8vo, pp. 40. 220

ADAMS. The Relation of Christianity to Civil Government in the United States. A Sermon before the Convention of the Protestant Episcopal Church of the Diocese of South Carolina, Charleston, February 13, 1833. By Rev. Jasper Adams, D.D. *Charleston*, 1833. 8vo, pp. 56.+Second Edition. *Charleston*, 1833. 8vo, pp. 64. 221

Dr. Adams delivered other Orations and Sermons at Geneva, Charleston, &c., on the Appearance of a Comet; the Eclipse of the Sun, &c.

ADAMS (John). Poems on Several Occasions, Original and Translated. By the Rev. John Adams, M.A. *Boston*, 1745. 12mo, pp. 176. M. 222

ADAMS. Flowers of Modern History, comprehending the most remarkable revolutions and events of modern times, to the Conclusion of the American War. By the Rev. John Adams. *London*, 1796. 223

ADAMS. The Flowers of Modern Travels, being elegant, entertaining, and instructive extracts, selected from the works of the most celebrated travellers. By John Adams, M.A. *London*, 1788. 12mo.+*Boston*, 1797. 12mo.+*London*, 1799. 3 vols., 12mo.+*Boston*, 1816. 2 vols., 12mo.+Baltimore [n. d.] 8vo. 224

ADAMS. Choix de Voyages modernes, &c. Traduit par J. F. André. *Paris*, 1799. 2 vols., 8vo. 225

ADAMS. View of Universal History, from the creation to the present time; including an account of the celebrated Revolutions in France, Poland, Sweden, &c. By Rev. John Adams. *London*, 1795. 3 vols., 8vo. 226

Includes the British Colonies in America.

[ADAMS (John)]. A Collection of the Speeches of the President of the United States to both Houses of Congress, at the Opening of every Session, with their Answers, etc. *Boston, Manning & Loring*. 12mo, pp. 282. 227

[ADAMS.] A Collection of State Papers relative to the first acknowledgment of the Sovereignty of the United States of America, and the Reception of their Minister Plenipotentiary,

by their High-Mightinesses the States-General of the United Netherlands. *At the Hague*, 1782. 8vo, pp. 96. M. 228

Republished in England, by Mr. Hollis, with the following title:

[ADAMS.] A Collection of State Papers relative to the first acknowledgment of the Sovereignty of the United States of America, and the reception of their Minister Plenipotentiary by their High Mightinesses the States-General of the United Netherlands. To which is prefixed the political character of John Adams, ambassador. . . . By an American. Likewise an Essay on canon and feudal law, by John Adams, esq. *London, Fielding*, 1782. 8vo, pp. 100. 229

This edition also contains the division in Parliament on peace with America, Feb 27, 1782.

ADAMS. Consideratien op de Memorie aan H. H. M. M. geadresseerd door John Adams. *Leide*, 1781. 8vo. 230

ADAMS. Correspondence of the Late President Adams; originally published in the Boston Patriot, in a Series of Letters. *Boston, Everett and Munroe*, 1809. 8vo, pp. iv., 36. 231

ADAMS. Correspondence between Hon. John Adams and the late Wm. Cunningham, Esq., commenced in 1803, and ending in 1812. *Boston*, 1823. 8vo. pp. 219. 232

See "Jefferson's Memoirs," by Randolph, Vol. iv., p. 389.

ADAMS. A Defence of the Constitutions of Government of the United States of America. By John Adams, LL.D. *London, C. Dilly*, M.DCC.LXXXVII. 8vo, pp. XXXI., 392. 233

First published in this form as a complete work. Reprinted, *Boston*, 1787. 12mo +*New York*, 1787.+*Philadelphia, Hall & Sellers*, M.DCC.LXXXVII. 12mo, pp. XX. 3-390. The following year the author wrote the second and third volumes, and the work was published with the following title:

ADAMS. A Defence of the Constitutions of Government of the United States of America against the Attack of M. Turgot. By John Adams, LL.D. *London, C. Dilly*, MDCCLXXXVII–VIII. 8vo, Vol. I., pp. XXXI., 392; Vol. II., Title, 1 l., pp. 451; Vol. III., Title, 1 l., pp. 528, Index, 18 l. 234

ADAMS. A Defence of the Constitutions of Government of the United States of America, Against the Attack of M. Turgot in his Letter to Dr. Price Dated the Twenty-Second day of March, 1778. By John Adams, LL.D. . . . . In Three Volumes. A New Edition. *London, John Stockdale*, 1794. 8vo, pp. 8,

XXXII., 392; 2 p. l., pp. 452; 2 p. l., pp. 528. Index, 18 l. Portrait. 235

This was reprinted as a Third Edition: *Philadelphia, W. Cobbett*, 1793. 3 vols., 8vo. Stockdale re-issued his edition with the following title:

ADAMS. History of the Principal Republics of the World; a Defence of the Constitutions of government of the United States of America against the attack of M. Turgot . . . *London, J. Stockdale*, 1794. 3 vols., 8vo, pp. XXXVIII., 392, 451, 528 and Index, 18 l. 236

"This work is not, as its title states, a defence of the *American Constitution*, but a warm defence of the Constitution of *Great Britain*. It is the best anti-democratic treatise that we have seen; for Dr. Adams appears to dread that *that* is the extreme to which his countrymen will naturally lean, and he has exerted his best endeavours to obviate that evil."—*Monthly Review*. This writer has not distinguished between republicanism and democracy. The work did much to familiarize the European mind to the novel state of things then taking place in America. It includes the opinions of eminent writers on various republics of the world.

ADAMS. Défense des Constitutions Américaines ou de la nécessité d'une balance dans les pouvoirs d'un gouvernement libre par M. John Adams. Avec des Notes de M. de la Croix. *Paris*, 1792. 2 vols., 8vo. 237

ADAMS. Correspondence of John Adams, Esq., late President of the United States, concerning the British doctrine of Impressment, and many interesting things which occurred during his administration. *Baltimore, H. Niles*, 1809. 12mo, pp. 72. 238

[ADAMS.] Discourses on Davila. A series of papers on Political History. Written in the Year 1790, and then published in the Gazette of the United States. By an American Citizen. *Boston, Printed by Russell and Cutler*, 1805. 8vo, pp. 148. 239

[ADAMS.] A Dissertation on the Canon and Feudal Law. *London* [1782?] 240

ADAMS. Essay on Canon and Feudal Law; with the Political Character of the said John Adams. By an American. *Philadelphia, Robert Bell*, 1783. 8vo, pp. 62. 241

The same as No. 239, with another title. It was published with another tract: "Observations on the Commerce of the American States." It was first published in the *Boston Gazette* in 1765, reprinted in the *London Chronicle*, afterward by Almon, at the end of a tract entitled "True Sentiments of America in 1768."

ADAMS. Four Letters: Being an interesting Correspondence between those Eminently Distinguished Characters, John Adams,

late President of the United States, and Samuel Adams, late Governor of Massachusetts, on the Important Subject of Government. *Boston*, 1802. 8vo, pp. 32. 242

ADAMS. History of the Dispute with America, from its Origin in 1754. Written in the Year 1774. By John Adams, Esq. *London, J. Stockdale*. 8vo, pp. 89. N. 243

"The avowed design of this pamphlet is to pursue the tories through all their dark intrigues and wicked machinations, and to show the rise and progress of their schemes for enslaving America. The Conduct of Bernard and Hutchinson is treated with great freedom and asperity; nor is the indignant author less sparing of some eminent statesmen in England, under whose influence they projected and pursued the inauspicious system of American Taxation."—M. R., LXX., p. 477. The work is an abridgment of the Letters of Novanglus, which first appeared in the *Boston Gazette*. 1774, which were reprinted in another form in Almon's *Remembrancer* for 1775, then translated into Dutch, with the following title:

ADAMS. Geschiedenis van het Geschil tusschen Groote-Britannie en Amerika, zedert deszelfs oorsprong, in den jaare 1754, tot op den tegenwoordigen tijd. Door zijne excellentie, den Heere John Adams, *Schildknaap*, gevolmagtigden staatsdienaar der dertien vereenigde staaten van Noord-Amerika, bij de Republijk der vereenigde Nederlanden. *Te Amsterdam, Bij W. Holtrop*, 1782. 8vo, pp. VIII., 156. *Portrait by Vinkeles*. N. 244

ADAMS. The Inadmissible Principles of the King of England's Proclamation of Oct. 16, 1807, considered. Originally published in the Boston Patriot. *Boston*, 1809. 8vo, pp. 20. M. 245

ADAMS. Letters of John Adams, addressed to his wife. Edited by his grandson, Charles Francis Adams. *Boston*, 1841. 2 vols., 12mo. pp. XXXII., 286; XX., 282. Portrait. 246

ADAMS. Memoir to their High Mightinesses the States General of the United Provinces. *Leyden, April* 19, 1781. 8vo, pp. 14. 247

ADAMS. Mémoire à leurs Hautes-Puissances les Seigneurs Etats-Généraux des Provinces-Unies des Pays-Bas. ——, 1781. 8vo, pp. 15. 248

ADAMS. Speech of the President of the United States to both Houses of Congress, delivered in the Representative Chamber on Thursday, November 23, 1797. *Philadelphia, Joseph Gales*. 8vo, pp. 8. 249

[ADAMS.] An Address in answer to the Speech of the President of the United States to both Houses of Congress, at the

Commencement of the present Session, Reported by a Select Committee on Monday, Nov. 27, 1797. *Philadelphia, Joseph Gales*. 8vo, pp. 6. 250

[ADAMS.] Thoughts on Government: applicable to the present state of the American colonies. In a letter from a gentleman to his friend [George Wythe, of Virginia]. *Philadelphia*, [*John Dunlap*], MDCCLXXVI. 12mo, pp. 28+Reprinted, *Boston, J. Gill*, 1776. 12mo, pp. 16.+Same. Abridged. *Boston*, 1788, &c. 251

ADAMS. Twenty-Six Letters, Upon Interesting Subjects Respecting the Revolution of America. Written In Holland, In the Year 1780. By his Excellency John Adams, While he was sole Minister Plenipotentiary from the United States of America. For Negociating A Peace, and a Treaty of Commerce, with Great-Britain. [*London*], *Printed for the Subscribers* [1786]. 12mo, Advt., 1 l., pp. 87.+Reprinted, *New York, J. Fenno*, 1789. 12mo, pp. 64. 252

These Letters were addressed to Dr. Calkoen, of Amsterdam, and were printed for private circulation.

ADAMS. The Works of John Adams, Second President of the United States; with a Life of the Author, Notes and Illustrations, by his Grandson, Charles Francis Adams. *Boston, Little, Brown & Co.*, 1856. 10 vols., 8vo, pp. XII., 684; XII., 542; 2 p. l., 576; VII., 588; 2 p. l., 496; 2 p. l., 550; XX., 675; XXI., 691; XX., 643; XI., 520; 18 Plates and Fac-similes. 253

Three hundred copies printed on large paper. *See* N. A. Rev., LXXI., p. 407; Liv. Age., XXI., p. 11.

ADAMS. Address to the Federal Republicans of Burlington County, on the Re-election of President Adams and Governor Howell. *Trenton, Sherman*, M.DCCC. 8vo, pp. 32. 254

ADAMS. Brief Consideration of the Services, &c., of Mr. Adams. *See* [Gardner, John].

ADAMS. Deeds and other Documents relating to the several Pieces of Land, and to the Library, presented to the Town of Quincy, by John J. Adams. With a Catalogue of Books. *Cambridge*, 1823. 8vo, pp. 67. M. 255

ADAMS. Facts and Official Documents, Relative to the fitness of General Jackson and Mr. Adams for the office of Presi-

dent, and to the conduct of the parties supporting them. [No imprint.] 8vo, pp. 16. 256

ADAMS. Political Sketches inscribed to His Excellency John Adams, Minister Plenipotentiary, from the United States to the Court of Great Britain. By a Citizen of the United States. *London, C. Dilly*, MDCCLXXXVII. 8vo, pp. IV., 96. 257

"These Sketches are written with much spirit, and that zeal for America and its cause, which has animated her numerous authors and defenders."—*Critical Review*.

ADAMS. A Selection of Eulogies Pronounced in the Several States in Honor of those Illustrious Patriots and Statesmen, John Adams and Thomas Jefferson. *Hartford, D. F. Robinson & Co.*, 1826. 8vo, pp. 426. 258

ADAMS. A Selection of the Patriotic Addresses to the President [John Adams] of the United States, together with the President's Answers, presented in the year 1798. *Boston*, 1798. 12mo, pp. 360. 259

ADAMS. Sketches of the Public Services of Adams, Clay and Crawford . . . . By a New-York Republican. *New York*, 1823. 260

ADAMS. Vindication of the Conduct and Character of John Adams, Esq. In Reply to the Letter of General Hamilton. *New York*, 1800. 8vo. 261

ADAMS. Vindication of the President's Nomination of a new Embassy to France, 1799. 8vo. 262

[ADAMS (John)] and [LEONARD (Daniel)]. Novanglus and Massachusettensis; or, Political Essays, published in the years 1774 and 1775, on the Principal Points of Controversy between Great Britain and her Colonies. The former by John Adams late President of the United States, the latter by Jonathan Sewall, then King's Attorney General of the province of Massachusetts Bay. *To which are added* a number of Letters, lately written by President Adams to the Honourable William Tudor Some of which were never before published. *Boston, Hews & Goss*, 1819. 8vo, pp. 312. 263

Notwithstanding the positive statement on the title, it is satisfactorily settled that Daniel Leonard was the author of Massachusettensis' Letters. Some of the papers signed Novanglus were reprinted in London. *See* Nos. 243 and 244.

ADAMS (Mrs. John). Letters of Mrs. Adams, the wife of John Adams. With an introductory memoir by her grandson,

Charles Francis Adams. *Boston*, 1840. 12mo.+Fourth Edition, revised and enlarged. *Boston*, 1848. 12mo. 264

ADAMS (John, *of Waltham-Abbey*). *See* Juan y Santacilia, J.

ADAMS (J. J.) The Charter Oak, and other Poems. By John Jay Adams. *New York, Samuel Colman*, 1839. 12mo, pp. 60. 265

ADAMS (John G.) Our Country, and its Claims upon us, An Oration delivered before the municipal authorities and citizens of Providence, July 4, 1863. By Rev. John G. Adams. *Providence, Knowles, Anthony & Co.*, 1863. 8vo, pp. 30. 266

ADAMS (John Q.) An Address delivered at the request of a committee of the citizens of Washington; on the occasion of reading the Declaration of Independence on the fourth of July, 1821. By John Quincy Adams. *Washington, Davis and Force*, 1821. 8vo, pp. 31.+Second Edition. *Cambridge*, 1821. 8vo, pp. 34. M. 267

ADAMS. Remarks on the Address. *See* [Fendall (P. R.)]

[ADAMS.] Review of the Address delivered by Hon. John Q. Adams at Washington, 4th July, 1821. *Boston*, 1821. 8vo, pp. 28. 268

[ADAMS.] A Vindication of Mr. Adams's Oration. *Concord, N. H.*, 1821. 8vo. 269

See, also, Niles' Register, Vol. XX., p. 326.

ADAMS. Address of John Quincy Adams to his Constituents of the Twelfth Congressional District, at Braintree, Sept. 17, 1842. *Boston*, 1842. 8vo, pp. 63. 270

ADAMS. An Address to the Members of the Charitable Fire Association of Boston, May 28, 1802. By John Quincy Adams. *Boston*, 1802. 8vo, pp. 25.+Second Edition. *Boston*, 1802. 8vo, pp. 25. 271

Includes a handsome tribute to the memory of Geo. R. Minot, which is reprinted in the Mass. Coll., VIII., 105–110.

[ADAMS.] The Administration and the Opposition. Addressed to the Citizens of New Hampshire. By Algernon Sidney. *Concord*, 1826. 8vo, pp. 20. 272

[ADAMS.] American Principles. A Review of the Works of

Fisher Ames, compiled by A Number of his Friends. *Boston, Everett & Munroe*, 1809. 8vo, pp. 56. 273

ADAMS. Remarks on J. Q. Adams's review of Ames. *See* [Lowell, John].

ADAMS. Argument before the Supreme Court of the United States, in the Case of the United States, Appellants, *vs.* Cinque and others, Africans, captured on the Schooner Amistad, with a Review of the Case of the Antelope, delivered on the 24th February and 1st March, 1841. *New York*, 1841. 8vo, pp. 135. N. 274

ADAMS. Correspondence between John Quincy Adams and several Citizens of Massachusetts, concerning the Charge of a Design to dissolve the Union. With An Appeal to the Citizens of the United States. By Franklin Dexter. *Boston*, 1829. 8vo, pp. 80.+Second Edition. *Boston*, 1829. 8vo, pp. 48.+Same. *Washington*, 1829. 8vo, pp. 56. 275

ADAMS. The Duplicate Letters, the Fisheries and the Mississippi. Documents relating to transactions at the negotiation of Ghent. Collected and published by John Quincy Adams, one of the Commissioners of the United States at the Negotiation. *Washington, Davis and Force*, 1822. 8vo, pp. 256. 276

ADAMS. The Treaty of Ghent and the Fisheries; or, The Diplomatic Talents of John Quincy Adams candidly examined. *Boston*, 1824. 8vo. 277

ADAMS. An Eulogy on the Life and Character of James Madison, Fourth President of the United States. Delivered at the request of the Mayor, Aldermen and Common Council of the City of Boston, September 27th, 1836. By John Quincy Adams. *Boston*, 1836. 8vo, pp. 90. 278

ADAMS. Eulogy on the Life and Character of James Monroe. Boston, August 25, 1831. By John Quincy Adams. *Boston*, 1831. 8vo, pp. 100. 279

ADAMS. Notice of Mr. Adams' Eulogium on the life and character of James Monroe. *Washington*, 1832. 8vo, pp. 36. C. 280

ADAMS. The Jubilee of the Constitution: a Discourse delivered at the request of the New York Historical Society, in the City of New York, on Tuesday, the 30th of April, 1839;

being the Fiftieth Anniversary of the Inauguration of George Washington as President of the United States, on Thursday, the 30th of April, 1789, by John Quincy Adams. *New York, Samuel Colman*, MDCCCXXXIX. 8vo, pp. 136. Plate. 281.

See N. Am. Rev., LIV., p. 211.

ADAMS. A Letter to the Hon. Harrison Gray Otis, A Member of the Senate of Massachusetts, on the Present State of our National Affairs. With Remarks upon Mr. Pickering's Letter to the Governor of the Commonwealth. By John Quincy Adams. *Boston*, 1808. 8vo, pp. 32.+Second Edition. *Boston*, 1808. 8vo, pp. 32.+ *Albany, Printed by John Barber* [1808]. 8vo, pp. 32.+ *New York*, 1808. 8vo.+ *Hallowell*, 1808. 8vo, pp. 24.+ *Sag Harbor*, 1808. 8vo.+ *Boston, Printed; London, Reprinted, R. J. Johnson*, 1808. 8vo, pp. 32. 282

ADAMS. A Letter to the Hon. John Quincy Adams, occasioned by His Letter to Mr. Otis. By Alfred. Printed in America. [*New York*], 1808. 8vo, pp. 43. 283

ADAMS. Verdict of Condemnation. By an Old Citizen of New York. On the Appeal of H. G. Otis & Co. to the People of the United States, in grand Inquest; for the decision of their Controversy with John Quincy Adams. *New York*, 1829. 8vo. 284

ADAMS. Remarks and Criticisms. *See* [Coleman, William].

ADAMS. Letters from John Quincy Adams to his constituents in the Twelfth Congressional district of Massachusetts; to which is added his Speech in Congress, Feb. 9, 1837. *Boston*, 1837. 12mo. 285

ADAMS. Letters from Hon. John Quincy Adams, read at the recent Celebration of West-India Emancipation in Bangor, Me. ——, 1843. 8vo, pp. 8. 286

ADAMS. Letters on the Masonic Institution. By John Quincy Adams. *Boston*, 1847. Rl. 8vo. 287

ADAMS. Lives of celebrated statesmen, by John Quincy Adams, LL.D.; with a sketch of the author, by the Rev. Charles W. Upham. *New York, W. H. Graham*, 1846. 8vo, pp. 105.

James Madison, Lafayette, and James Monroe are the statesmen referred to.

ADAMS. The Lives of James Madison, Fourth President of the United States, And James Monroe, Fifth President of the

United States. By John Quincy Adams. With Historical Notices of their Administrations. *Buffalo*, 1850.+ Reprinted, *Philadelphia, J. L. Gihon*, 1854. 12mo, pp. 432. 289

ADAMS. The New-England Confederacy of MDCXLIII. A Discourse delivered before the Massachusetts Historical Society, May 29th, 1843. By John Quincy Adams. *Boston*, 1843. 8vo, pp. 47. 290

Also, in the Mass. Hist. Collection, Vol. IX., Third Series.

ADAMS. An Oration delivered before the Cincinnati Astronomical Society, on the occasion of laying the Corner-stone of the Observatory. By John Quincy Adams. *Cincinnati*, 1843. 8vo, pp. 72. 291

ADAMS. An Oration addressed to the Citizens of the Town of Quincy, on the Fifty-fifth Anniversary of the Independence of the United States of America. By John Quincy Adams. *Boston*, 1831. 8vo, pp. 40. 292

ADAMS. Oration delivered at Plymouth, Dec. 22, 1802, at the Anniversary Commemorative of the First Landing of our Ancestors at that Place. *Boston*, 1802. 8vo, pp. 31.+ Reprinted, *Plymouth*, 1820. 293

ADAMS. An Oration delivered before the Inhabitants of the Town of Newburyport, at their request, on the Sixty-first Anniversary of the Declaration of Independence, July 4, 1837, by John Quincy Adams. *Newburyport*, 1837. 8vo, pp. 68. 294

ADAMS. Oration on the Life and Character of Gilbert Motier de Lafayette, at Washington, on the 31st December, 1834. By John Quincy Adams. *Washington, Gales and Seaton*, 1835. 8vo, pp. 104.+ Another Edition. *New York*, 1835. 295

ADAMS. An Oration, pronounced July 4th, 1793, at the Request of the Inhabitants of the Town of Boston, in Commemoration of the Anniversary of American Independence. By John Quincy Adams. *Boston, Edes & Son*, 1793. 8vo, 2 p. l., pp. 16.+ Second Edition. *Boston*, 1793. 8vo. G. 296

ADAMS. Poems on Religion and Society, by John Quincy Adams: with notices of his life and character, by John Davis and Thomas H. Benton. *New York*, 1848. 18mo.+ Reprinted, *Auburn*, 1854. 18mo. 297

ADAMS. Present State of our National Affairs. By John Quincy Adams. *Albany*, 1821. 8vo. B. 298

ADAMS. Report on the Apportionment Bill, House of Representatives, July 16, 1842. [*Washington*, 1842.] 8vo, pp. 12. 299

ADAMS. Report on the Massachusetts Resolutions: House of Representatives, April 4, 1844. *Washington*, 1844. 8vo, pp. 23. 300

ADAMS. Six Letters from John Quincy Adams to Edward Livingston, on Masonry. *Philadelphia, C. T. Jones*, 1833. 8vo, pp. 32. 301

ADAMS. The Social Compact Exemplified in the Constitution of the Commonwealth of Massachusetts. With Remarks on the Theories of Divine Right of Hobbes and others, concerning the Origin and Nature of Government; a Lecture delivered before the Franklin Lyceum, Providence, R. I., November 25th, 1842. *Providence, Knowles & Vose*, 1842. 8vo, pp. 32. 302

ADAMS. Speech of John Quincy Adams on the Case of Alexander McLeod, House of Representatives, Sept. 4, 1841. *Washington*, 1841. 8vo, pp. 12. 303

ADAMS. Speech of John Quincy Adams on the Causes of the Failure of the Fortification Bill, &c.; delivered Jan. 22, 1836. *Washington*, 1836. 8vo, pp. 16. 304

ADAMS. Speech of John Quincy Adams on War with Great Britain and Mexico; with the Speeches of Messrs. Wise and Ingersoll, &c. *Boston*, [n. d.] 8vo, pp. 36. 305

ADAMS. Speech of Mr. John Quincy Adams (suppressed by the Previous Question) on the Removal of the Public Deposites, and its Reasons. *Boston* [n. d.] 8vo. pp. 32.+ Another Edition. *Washington, Gales and Seaton*, 1834. 8vo, pp. 43. 306

ADAMS. Speech of John Quincy Adams upon the Right of the People to Petition; on the Freedom of Speech and of Debate in the House of Representatives of the United States; on the Resolution of Seven State Legislatures, and the petitions . . . relating to the Annexation of Texas to this Union. *Washington*, 1838. 8vo, pp. 131. 307

ADAMS. Speech of John Quincy Adams on the Joint Reso-

lution for distributing Rations to Fugitives from Indian Hostilities in Alabama and Georgia; House of Representatives, May 25, 1836. *Washington*, 1836. 8vo, pp. 8. 308

ADAMS. Speech of John Quincy Adams in relation to the Navy Pension Fund; delivered in the House of Representatives, 28th December, 1840. [*Washington*, 1840.] 8vo, pp. 8. 309

ADAMS. Substance of the Speech of John Quincy Adams, with Part of the Debate, in the House of Representatives, upon the Bill relating to the Collection of Duties on Imports. *Boston*, 1840. 8vo, pp. 30. 310

ADAMS. Texas. Extracts from the address of John Quincy Adams to his Constituents, at Braintree, Sept. 17, 1842. Translated into French and Spanish from the National Intelligencer of Oct. 22, 1842. *Washington*, 1842. 8vo, pp. 32. 311

ADAMS. Tariff—Manufactures. May 23, 1832. Mr. Adams from the Committee on Manufactures made the following report: 8vo, pp. 36. 312

Report No. 28, 22d Congr., 1st Session.

ADAMS. Vindication of Gen. Jackson's Invasion and Occupation of Florida, etc. [*Washington*, 1818.] 8vo. B. 313

ADAMS. Address of the Central Committee friendly to the Election of John Quincy Adams as President, 1828. 8vo, pp. 24. 314

ADAMS. Facts and Opinions respecting Mr. John Quincy Adams; and a fair view of the Militia-men Story. [No imprint.] 8vo, pp. 8. 315

ADAMS. The life and public services of John Quincy Adams. With the eulogy before the legislature of New York. By Wm. H. Seward. *Auburn*, 1849, &c. 12mo. 316

ADAMS. The political character of John Quincy Adams delineated. Being a reply to certain observations in the address of Gen. Peter B. Porter and others. *Albany, Printed for the Albany Argus, by D. M'Glashan*, 1828. [*Reprint from the Argus.*] 8vo, pp. 30. 317

ADAMS. Principles of Mr. [J. Q.] Adams' Administration. 1828. 318

ADAMS. Proceedings of the City Council [of Roxbury] on

the Death of John Quincy Adams. *Roxbury*, 1848. 8vo, pp. 7. 319

ADAMS. Sketch of the Life of John Quincy Adams. *Washington*, 1824. 8vo. 320

ADAMS. Sketch of the Life of John Quincy Adams. *New York, Sickels*, 1828. 8vo, pp. 16. 321

ADAMS. The striking similitude between the Reign of Terror of the Elder Adams and the Reign of Corruption of the Younger Adams. An address adopted by the Albany Republican County Convention: together with resolutions expressing their sentiments on the Presidential Question, and nominating the Hon. John Taylor for Presidential Elector. *Albany, Printed for the Albany Argus, by D. M'Glashan*, 1828. 8vo, pp. 8. 322

ADAMS. Testimonials of respect to the Memory of John Quincy Adams by the Legislature of Massachusetts. [No imprint.] 8vo, pp. 28. 323

ADAMS. Tokens of a Nation's Sorrow. Addresses in the Congress of the United States, and Funeral Solemnities on the Death of John Quincy Adams. *Washington, J. & G. S. Gideon*, 1848. 8vo, pp 40. Portrait.+ Second Edition. 1848. 8vo, pp. 40. Portrait. 324

ADAMS & CONDICT. Report of the Minority of the Committee on Manufactures, submitted to the House of Representatives of the United States, Feb. 28, 1833. By J. Q. Adams and Lewis Condict. *Boston*, 1833. 8vo. 325

ADAMS. (J. S.) Town and Country; or, Life at Home and Abroad, Without and Within us. By John S. Adams. *Boston*, 1855. 12mo. 326

ADAMS (J. M.) Address to the People of Cumberland County. By John Milton Adams. *Portland*, 1853. 8vo, pp. 24. 327

ADAMS (Joseph). The Death of the Righteous to be lamented. Sermon on the Death of John Fabyan, Esq., March 30, 1756. By Rev. Joseph Adams, A.M. *Portsmouth, N. H.*, 1757. 8vo, pp. 16. M. 328

ADAMS. A Letter from Mr. *Joseph Adams*, to the Rev. Mr. *Thomas Barnard*, of *Newbury*, with Mr. Barnard's Answer

thereto. *Boston*, 1743. 8vo, pp. 15.+ The Second Edition. *Boston, Thomas Fleet*, 1743. 8vo, pp. 16. 329

ADAMS. The Necessity and Importance of Rulers, Civil and Ecclesiastical, &c. Sermon at Newington, March 13, 1769. By Joseph Adams, A.M. *Portsmouth*, 1769. 8vo, pp. 24. N. 330

ADAMS (Josiah). Address at Acton, July 21, 1835, the first Centennial Anniversary of that Town; with an appendix and map of the Concord Fight. *Boston*, 1835. 8vo, pp. 24. 331

ADAMS. The Genealogy of the Descendants of Richard Haven, of Lynn, Massachusetts, who emigrated from England about 200 years ago. By Josiah Adams. *Boston*, 1843. 8vo, pp. 54. 332

ADAMS. Genealogy &c. . . . being a Republication of the first edition. With Additions. *Boston*, 1849. 8vo, pp. 54, 50. 333

ADAMS. Letter to Lemuel Shattuck, Esq., of Boston . . . in Vindication of the Claims of Capt. Isaac Davis, of Acton, to his just share in the Honors of the Concord Fight. Also depositions of witnesses, &c. *Boston*, 1850. 8vo, pp. 24. 334

Written in answer to Shattuck's "History of Concord."

ADAMS (J. W.) Letter to the Honorable Secretary of War, on the examination of officers for colored troops. By Julius W. Adams. *Brooklyn, Sept. 1st*, 1863. 8vo, pp. 16. 335

ADAMS (Mr.) Speech of Mr. Adams, of Mississippi. On the Bill to Remove the Indians West of the Mississippi, delivered in the Senate of the United States, April, 1830. *Washington*, 1830. 8vo, pp. 31. 336

ADAMS (N.) Annals of Portsmouth, comprising a period of Two hundred Years from the First Settlement of the Town; With Biographical Sketches of a few of the most respectable inhabitants. By Nathaniel Adams. *Portsmouth, Published for the Author*, 1825. 8vo, pp. 400. 337

See N. A. R., xxii., 215.

ADAMS (Neh.) The Life of John Eliot, with an account of the early Missionary efforts among the Indians of New England. By Nehemiah Adams. *Boston*, 1847. 12mo. 338

ADAMS. A Sermon preached to the Congregation at the

Essex Street Church, October 31, 1852. The Sabbath After the Interment of Hon. Daniel Webster. By Nehemiah Adams, D.D. *Boston*, 1852. 8vo, pp. 23.+ Second Edition. *Boston, Press of Geo. C. Rand*, 1852. 8vo, pp. 23. 339

ADAMS. The Sable Cloud; A Southern Tale with Northern Comments. By Rev. Nehemiah Adams. *Boston, Ticknor & Fields*, 1861. 8vo, pp. 275. 340

ADAMS. A South-Side View of Slavery; or, Three Months at the South, in 1854. By Rev. Nehemiah Adams, D.D. *Boston, T. R. Marvin*, 1854. 12mo, pp. 214. 341

ADAMS (S.) On the Conduct of the Society for Propagating the Gospel. By Samuel Adams. *London*, 1765. 8vo 342

ADAMS (R. S.) Nineveh Threatened—A Sermon preached in St. Andrew's Church, Brooklyn, Dec. 30, 1860. By Rev. R. S. Adams. *New York, Mann & Stearns*, 1861. 8vo, pp. 16. 343

Relates to the Southern Rebellion.

ADAMS (S.) An Oration delivered at the State House in Philadelphia, to a very numerous Audience; on Thursday, the 1st of August, 1776, by Samuel Adams, Member of the *** **** ******* the General Congress of the ****** ****** of America. *Philadelphia, Printed; London, Reprinted, Johnston*, MDCCLXXVI. 8vo, Title, 1 l., pp. 42. 344

An undelivered oration. *See* Wells' Life of Adams, Vol. II., p. 439, Vol. III., p. 403. There is no Philadelphia edition. "Mr. Adams, the American Cicero, declaims with warmth and energy against kingly government and hereditary succession. There are passages in this oration which would have done honour to a Roman tribune, when the republican spirit of that mistress of the world was at its greatest height."—M. R., LV., p. 397. *See*, also, Anal. Mag., III., p. 231; Am. Quar. Reg., XIII., p. 269.

ADAMS (Thos.) Democracy Unveiled, in a letter to Sir Francis Burdett, Bart., M.P. By T. Adams, Esq., lately a resident in the United States. *London, Chapple*, 1813. 8vo, pp. 521. 345

The *Monthly Review*, Vol. LXX., p. 275, says that the title of this bulky volume should have been "The Evils of Democracy exemplified in the case of the United States of America."

ADAMS (T. M.) Cool Address to the People of England on the Slave Trade. By T. M. Adams. *London*, 1788. 8vo. 346

ADAMS (W.) God's Eye|on the|Contrite|or a|Discourse|shewing|That True Poverty and Contrition of Spirit and Trembling at God's Word is the Infallible and only way for the Obtain-

ing and Retaining|of Divine Acceptation.|As it was made in the Audience of the General Assembly of the|Massachusetts Colony at Boston in New-England;|May 27. 1685. being the Day of Election there.|By Mr. William Adams|*Boston* in New England.|*Printed by Richard Pierce for Samuel Sewall*, 1685.| 4to, Title, 1 l., pp. 41. 347

ADAMS. The Necessity of the Pouring-out of the Spirit from on High. Upon a Sinning Apostatizing People, set under Judgment, in order to their merciful deliverance and Salvation. Fast Sermon, 21, 9, 1678. By Rev. William Adams. *Boston*, 1679. 4to, pp. 48. M. 348

ADAMS. A|Discourse|Delivered at New-London,|October 23d A.D. 1760.|On the|Thanksgiving|(Ordered by Authority)| For the Success of the British Arms, in|the reduction of Montreal, and the conquest of all Canada.|By William Adams.| *New-London:|Printed and sold by Timothy Green*,|MDCCLXI.| Small 8vo, pp. 25. H. 349

ADAMS (Sir W.) The actual State of the Mexican Mines, and the reasonable expectations of the Shareholders of the Anglo-Mexican Mine Association, being the substance of a letter addressed to the Directors of that Company; with a Supplement, containing additional Data, confirmed by recent intelligence from Mexico; and an Appendix of Original Mexican Documents. By Sir William Adams. *London, Sherwood*, MDCCCXXV. 8vo, pp. IV., 87. 350

ADAMS (W.) An Address before the New-England Society of New York, Dec. 22, 1852. By Rev. William Adams, D.D. *New York*, 1853. 8vo, pp. 56. 351

ADAMS. Christian Patriotism by William Adams, Pastor of Madison Square Presbyterian Church, New York City. *New York, Anson D. F. Randolph*, 1863. 12mo, pp. 21. 352

ADAMS. Christianity and Civil Government. By Rev. William Adams. *New York*, 1851. 8vo, pp. 48. 353

ADAMS. Madison Square Church: Jan. 1, 1858, 1859. 12mo, pp. 12, 16. 354

ADAMS. Prayer for Rulers, a duty of Christian Patriots. A discourse preached in the Madison Square Presbyterian Church, Jan. 4, 1861. By Rev. William Adams, D.D. *New York, Rudd & Carlton*, 1861. 12mo, pp. 41. 355

ADAMS (W. E.) The Slaveholder's War. An Argument for the North and the Negro. By W. E. Adams. *Manchester, Un. and Emanc. Soc.*, 1863. 8vo, pp. 24. 356

[ADAMS (W. T.)] Brave Old Salt, or Life on the Quarter-Deck. A Story of the Great Rebellion. By Oliver Optic (W. T. Adams). *Boston, Lee & Shepard*, 1866. 16mo, pp. 330. 357

[ADAMS.] Fighting Joe; or, The Fortunes of a Staff Officer. A Story of the Great Rebellion. By Oliver Optic. *Boston, Lee & Shepard*, 1866. 16mo, pp. 326. 358

ADAMS. The Yankee Middy; or, The Adventures of a Naval Officer. A Story of the Great Rebellion. By Oliver Optic. *Boston, Lee & Shepard*, 1866. 16mo, pp. 332. 359

ADAMS (Z.) Answer to a Pamphlet, lately published, entitled, "A Treatise on Church Government." By Zabdiel Adams. *Boston*, 1773. Sm. 8vo, pp. 87. 360

ADAMS. Sermon before his Excellency John Hancock, Esq., Governor, etc., May 29, 1782. By Zabdiel Adams. *[Boston], Fleet & Gill* [1782]. 8vo, pp. 59. 361

ADAMS. The Duty and Importance of Making the Scriptures the Rule and Standard of Preaching, delivered at Westford in presence of the Pastors and Deacons convened to confer with the Rev. Mr. Scribner relative to certain Doctrines he had been charged with Preaching. By Zabdiel Adams, of Lunenburgh. *Boston*, 1782. 8vo. 362

ADAMS. The Evil Designs of Men made subservient by God to the Public Good; particularly illustrated in the Rise, Progress, and Conclusion of the American War. A Sermon Preached at Lexington on the Nineteenth of April 1783: Being the Anniversary of the Commencement of the War between Britain and America, which broke out in that Town on the 19th of April 1775. By Zabdiel Adams, A.M. *Boston, Benjamin Edes & Sons*, M,DCC,LXXXIII. 8vo, pp. 39. 363

ADAMS. The Happiness and Pleasure of Unity in Christian Societies, considered. Sermon in Boston, August 26, 1772. *Boston*, 1772. 8vo, pp. 44. 364

ADAMS. Masonic Sermon at Lancaster [Mass.] June 24, 1778. *Worcester*, 1778. Sm. 4to. W. 365

ADAMS. The Nature, Pleasure, and Advantages of Church Musick. Sermon Preached at a Lecture, Lancaster, April 4, 1771. By Zabdiel Adams. *Boston*, 1771. 8vo, pp. 38. 366

Also, Sermons at the ordination of Ch. Stearns, J. Foster, Kingsbury, Noyes, and E. Whipple, and other discourses.

ADAMSON (J.) Memoirs of the Life and Writings of Luis de Camoens. By John Adamson. *London*, 1820. 2 vols., crown 8vo. Portrait. 367

Also on large paper. "An elaborate performance."—LOWNDES.

ADAMSON. Bibliotheca Lusitana; or Catalogue of Books and Tracts, relating to the History, Literature and Poetry of Portugal; forming part of the library of John Adamson. *Newcastle-on-Tyne, Hodgson*, 1836. 12mo, 6 *fasciculi*, pp. 115. 368

Includes some Brazilian Bibliography.

ADAMSON. Catalogue of a valuable collection of rare Editions and Translations of the works of Camoens. *London*, 1856. 8vo, pp. 24. 369

ADAMSON (M.) [Pseud]. A Friendly Epistle to Neighbour John Taylor of Norwich. Containing an earnest invitation to him to join the Quakers, and not attempt to raise up a New Sect, when there are so many in the world. By M. Adamson. To which is added a Short Dialogue between Timothy Tell-Truth, and Obadiah Friendly. Third Edition. *Boston, Re-printed*, 1758. 8vo, pp. 23. M. 370

ADAMSON (T.) A Reply to "Considerations and Arguments proving the Inexpediency of a National Copyright Law, by John Campbell." By Thomas Adamson. *New York*, 1844. 8vo, pp. 20. 371

ADAMSON (W. A.) A Sermon preached at Quebec, in 1854, on the day set apart for humiliation and fasting on account of the war between our Country and Russia. By Rev. W. Agar Adamson. *Quebec*, 1854. 8vo, pp. 14. 372

ADDERLEY. Letter to the Rt. Hon. Benjamin Disraeli, M.P., on the Present Relations of England with the Colonies. By the Right Hon. C. B. Adderley, M.P. With an Appendix of Extracts from Evidence taken before the Select Committee on Colonial Military Expenditure. *London, Parker*, 1862. 8vo. 373

ADDEY (M.) The Life and Military Career of Thomas

Jonathan Jackson, Lieutenant-General in the Confederate Army. By Markinfield Addey. With Portrait. *New York*, 1863. 12mo. 374

ADDEY. "Little Mac," and How he became a Great General. A Life of George Brinton McClellan, for Young Americans. By Markinfield Addey. *New York, J. G. Gregory*, 1864. 16mo, pp. 352. 375

ADDINGTON (Right Hon. Henry). *See* Crisis of the Sugar Colonies.

ADDISON (Alexander). Charge to the Grand Juries of the County Court of the Fifth Circuit of the State of Pennsylvania at December Session, 1798. [On the Alien Act.] By Alex. Addison. *Washington [Pa.]*, 1799. 8vo. 376

ADDISON. The Liberty of Speech and of the Press. A charge to Grand Juries. By Alexander Addison. *Washington [Pa.]*, 1798. 8vo.+Another Edition. *Albany* [n. d.] 8vo. 377

ADDISON. Observations on the speech of Albert Gallatin on the Foreign Intercourse Bill. By Alexander Addison. *Washington, Pa.*, 1798. 8vo. 378

ADDISON. An Oration on the Rise and Progress of the United States of America, to the Present Crisis: And on the Duties of the Citizens. Delivered at Washington, May 15, 1798. By Alexander Addison, Esq. *Philadelphia*, 1798. 8vo, pp. 41. 379

In relation to the impending war with France.

ADDISON. Rise and Progress of Revolution: A Charge to the Grand Juries of the County Courts of the Fifth Circuit of the State of Pennsylvania, At December Sessions, 1800. By Alexander Addison, President of those Courts. *Philadelphia*, 1801.+Another Edition. *Whitehall, Wm. Young*, 1801. 12mo, pp. 36. 380

ADDISON. Trial of Alexander Addison, President of the Courts of Common Pleas, in the Circuit, consisting of the Counties of Westmoreland, Fayette, Washington, and Alleghany, on an Impeachment, by the House of Representatives, before the Senate of the Commonwealth of Pennsylvania. Taken in Short-hand by Thomas Lloyd. *Lancaster*, 1803. 8vo, pp. 154.+Second Edition, with Additions. *Lancaster*, 1803. 8vo.

Additional Facts, Remarks, and Arguments, illustrative of the Advantage to the People of the United States, of a National Circulating Medium. *Washington, E. D. Krafft*, 1822. 8vo, pp. 22. 382

An Additional Number of Letters from the Federal Farmer to the Republican, etc. *Printed in the United States*, 1788. Sm. 8vo. M. 383

Additions to Plain Truth. *See* Plain Truth.

ADDOMS (J. S.) On the malignant fever, which prevailed in the city of New York, 1791. *New York*, 1792. 8vo. 384

Address. *See* [Brown, C. B.], [Dalrymple, Sir J.], [Livingston, Wm.], [Reed, Wm.], [Tucker, Dean], [Webster (Noah)].

An Address and Recommendations to the States, by the United States in Congress Assembled, with sundry papers referred to in the Address. *Philadelphia, Claypole*, 1783. Title, 1 l., pp. viii., 26.+Same. *Hartford, Reprinted*, 1783. 8vo.+Same, with the Newburgh Letters. *Boston*, 1783. 8vo, pp. 62.+*London, Stockdale*, 1783. 8vo, pp. 91. 385

"Should we now think ourselves little interested in the subjects of these American State Papers, we may, however, be much gratified in perusing them, as pieces of fine, energetic writing, and masterly eloquence. It would be a curious speculation for the philosophical enquirer, to account for the perfection to which the English language has been carried in our late colonies, amidst the clamours and horrors of war."—M. R., XLVIII.

Address at Havre de Grace, on a Pamphlet denouncing June 4, 1812, as the day of awful Visitation of the Almighty. *Baltimore*, 1812. 8vo. 386

An Address from the Brethren's Society for the furtherance of the Gospel among the Heathen, to the Members of the Congregations and Societies of the Brethren, and to all those Friends who wish Success to the Missions of the Church of the Brethren. *London*, 1781. 8vo, pp. 16 and 4. 387

Gives an account of the hurricanes at Jamaica and Barbadoes in 1780.

An Address from the clergy of New York. *See* [Cooper, Myles].

An Address from the Members of the Constitutional Body to

their S——, on the Change of the Ministry. By an American Loyalist. *London, Bladon*. 4to. 388

"A feeble attempt at obscene allegory."—M. R., lxviii., p. 540.

An Address in regard to the Memorial of the Surviving Officers of the Revolutionary Army, now before the Representatives of the Nation. *Washington*, 1828. 8vo, pp. 11. 389

Address of a Back Settler to the Impartial Public, *dated Keowee*, Sept. 25th, 1774. 4to. 390

An Address of Christian Counsel and Caution to Emigrants to newly settled Colonies. *London*, 1841. 8vo, pp. 7. 391

No. 6 of Tracts relative to the Aborigines.

Address of Democratic Members of Congress to the Democracy of the United States. 8vo, pp. 8. 392

Address of Members of H. of R., 1812. *See* [Quincy (Josiah)].

An Address of Members of the House of Representatives of the Congress of the United States, to their Constituents, on the Subject of the War with Great Britain. *Alexandria, S. Snowden*, 1812. 8vo, pp. 35.+Same. *Philadelphia* [n. d.] 8vo, pp. 24. +Same. *Northampton, William Butler*, 1812.+Same. *Hartford*, 1812. 8vo.+Same. *Boston*, 1812. 8vo, pp. 29.+Same. *Baltimore*, 1812. 8vo, pp. 35+Same. *London, Longman & Co.*, 1813. 8vo. 393

See the Monthly Review, vol. lxx., p. 64.

Address of the American Society for the Encouragement of Domestic Manufactures to the People of the United States. *New York, Van Winkle*, 1817. 8vo, pp. 32. N. 394

Address of the Congress to the People of the Confederate States. (*Issued from Richmond*, 1864.) 395

Address of the General Assembly of the Presbyterian Church in the Confederate States of America, to all the Churches throughout the earth, as reported by the Rev. J. H. Thornwell, from a Council appointed to prepare it, by the Assembly at Augusta, Ga., Dec. 1, 1861. 396

Address of the Free Constitutionalists to the People of the United States. *Boston, Thayer & Eldridge*. 8vo, pp. 54. 397

Address of the Friends of Domestic Industry, assembled in Convention, at New-York, October 26, 1831, to the People of the United States. *Baltimore*, 1831. 8vo, pp. 44. 398

Address of the Home League to the People of the United States. *New York*, 1841. 8vo. 399

The Address of the People of Great Britain to the Inhabitants of America. *London, T. Cadell*, MDCCLXXV. 8vo, Title, 1 l., pp. 60. 400

"This address is said and believed to have been written by Sir J. D. (Sir John Dalrymple), and printed at the public expense, to be distributed in America, where the greatest part of a large impression has been sent apparently to co-operate with a late conciliatory resolution of the House of Commons. It is replete with expressions of tender affection for the inhabitants of the colonies, and paints the measures and intentions of government toward them in the softest and most pleasing colours."—*Monthly Review*, LIV.

The Address of the Society of the Constitutional Republicans. *Philadelphia*, 1805. 8vo. 401

Principally relating to Pennsylvania.

The Address of the Southern Delegates in Congress to their Constituents. [No imprint.] 8vo, pp. 15. 402

An Address of the Twelve United Colonies of North-America, by their Representatives in Congress, to the People of Ireland. *Philadelphia, Bradford*, 1775. 8vo, pp. 10. 403

Address of the Twelve United Colonies to the Inhabitants of Great Britain, July 8, 1775. *[Philadelphia*, 1775.] 8vo, pp. 8. 404

Address on the Past, Present and Eventual Relations of the United States to France. By Anticipation. *New York*. 8vo, pp. 20. C. 405

An Address to an Assembly of the Friends of American Manufactures. *Philadelphia, Aitken*, 1787. 8vo, pp. 30. 406

An Address to Christians of every Denomination in the United States, on the subject of the ensuing Presidential Election. 1800. 8vo. N. 407

Address to Christians throughout the World, by the Clergy of the Confederate States of America. [1862.] 8vo, pp. 16. 408

Address to a Provincial Bashaw. *See* [Church, B.]

Address to Manufacturers, Traders, and others, on the Importance of Preserving the Colonies. *London*, 1832. Sm. 8vo.

Address to Men of all Parties in the United States by an American Constitutionalist. *Philadelphia*, 1804. 8vo. 410

Address to Persons of Fashion relating to Balls, etc. *Boston*, 1767. 8vo, pp. 56. 411

An Address to Protestant Dissenters. *See* [Priestley, Joseph].

An Address to the City of London, with Continuation. 1762. 8vo. 412

Partly relates to the Conquest of Canada.

Address to the Clergy, 1814. *See* [Plumer, William].

Address to the Congress of the United States, on the Utility and Justice of Restrictions upon Foreign Commerce. With Reflections on Foreign Trade in General and the Future prospects of America. *Philadelphia*, 1809. 8vo, pp. VII., 97. 413

Address to the Democracy and the People of the United States, by the National Democratic Executive Committee. *Washington, McGill & Witherow*, 1860. 8vo, pp. 16. 414

Address to the Democracy of the United States, on the Duty of the Democratic Party at this Crisis [1862]. 8vo, pp. 26. 415

An Address to the Electors, and other Free Subjects of Great Britain, occasion'd by the Late Secession, in which is contain'd a Particular Account of all our Negociations with Spain, and their Treatment of Us, for above Ten Years past. *London*, 1739. 8vo. 416

Address to the Fair Daughters of the United States, calling on them for their advice and interest in the present important Crisis. *New York*, 1811. 8vo, pp. 14. 417

An Address to the Government, the Merchants, Manufacturers, and the Colonists in America, on the Present State of Affairs. *London*, 1775. 8vo. P. 418

Address to the Inhabitants, &c. *See* [Rush (Benj.)]

Address to the Inhabitants of New Mexico and California, on the omission by Congress to provide them with Territorial Governments, and on the Social and Political Evils of Slavery. *New York, Am. Anti-Slavery Society*, 1849. 12mo, pp. 56. 419

An Address to the Inhabitants of the New Settlements in the

Northern and Western Parts of the United States. *New Haven, T. and S. Green*, [*July 2d*, 1793]. 12mo, pp. 6. 420

An Address to the Interior Cabinet on the Affairs of America. *London*, 1782. 4to. 421

Address | to the | Members of the Congress | to be held | At Philadelphia | on | The first of September, 1774. | *Boston*, | *Reprinted and Sold by Mills and Hicks*, | 1774. | 422

Address to the Merchants of Great Britain, or a Review of the Conduct of the Administration, with regard to our Trade and Navigation, with a Justification of the Convention concluded between Great Britain and Spain. By a Merchant Retir'd. 1742. 8vo. 423

Address to the People of America on the Prospect of a War with France; recommended to the perusal of the People of Great Britain. By a True Friend to his Country. *London*, 1798. 8vo. C. 424

An Address to the People of Great Britain, containing thoughts entertained during the Christmas Recess, on the Independence of America. *London, Milne*, 1783. 8vo. 425

"A strenuous advocate for that British Declaration of American Independence that has lately taken place, as well on the ground of policy as of necessity."—M. R. LXVIII., p. 363.

An Address to the People of Great Britain in general, the Members of Parliament, and the leading gentlemen of opposition, in particular, on the present Crisis of American Politics. *Bristol, Newberry*, 1776. 8vo, pp. 79. 426

"This writer professes to have substituted persuasion for argument, and gentle reproof for bitter invective; the Americans, however, will think him bitter enough. He reasons, nevertheless, well on some points, and throws out many sensible remarks."—RICH. *See* M. R., LIV., p. 327.

An Address to the People of Great Britain. *London, Cadell*, 1779. 8vo. 427

"A warm and seasonable exhortation."—M. R., LXI., p. 231.

An Address to the People of Great Britain, on the Meeting of Parliament. *London, Cadell*, 1779. 8vo. 428

M. R., LXI., p. 467.

Address to the People of Great Britain on the Propriety of Abstaining from West India Sugar and Rum. Ninth Edition. *Boston*, 1792. 8vo. 429

An Address to the People of the American States who choose electors . . . To which is added a short sketch of the biography of Gen. George Clinton, and several essays. *Washington*, 1808. 8vo, pp. 54. s. 430

An Address to the "People" of the Several Sovereign States of the United States, on the Frauds committed on their Elective Franchise, under Official Orders, and the Danger of the People being reduced to mere Serfs to a Tyrant Despot, under the Pretext of Negro Freedom, Military Necessity, Union and Liberty. [1861.] 8vo, pp. 16. 431

Address to the People of the United States. *Providence, October* 21, 1844. 12mo, pp. 15. 432

Relates to the Constitution adopted by Rhode Island in 1842.

An Address to the People of the United States, drawn up by order of the National Institution for the Promotion of Industry, established June 1820, by delegates from New-York, New-Jersey, Pennsylvania, Connecticut, Massachusetts, Rhode Island, Ohio, and Delaware. *New York, J. Seymour*, 1820. 8vo, pp. 22. 433

Address to the People of the United States in behalf of the American Copyright Club. 1843. 8vo. 434

An Address to the People, on the Subject of the Contest between Great Britain and America. By ***** ********* *London, Wilkie*, 1776. 8vo. 435

"A zealous invective against the Americans."—M. R., LIV., p. 156.

An Address to the People of the United States on the subject of the Presidential Election. *New York*, 1828. 8vo. P. 436

Address to the People, Representatives, and President of the United States, on a National Education connected with the Militia System. *Washington*, 1826. 8vo, pp. 8. 437

An Address to the Public. *Philadelphia*, 1768. 12mo. P. 438

An Address to the Public, containing some Remarks on the present Political State of the American Republics. *Exeter* [1787]. 8vo, pp. 36. M. 439

An Address to the Representatives in Parliament, upon the State of the Nation. * * * *London, Almon*, 1779. 8vo, pp. 38. 440

See M. R., LXI., p. 467.

An Address to the Republicans and People of New York, Pennsylvania and Virginia, upon the state of Presidential Parties. By a Citizen of New York. To which are added, Questions and Answers on the Presidential Elections. *New York and Philadelphia*, 1824. N. 441

An Address to the Roman Catholics of the United States of America. By a Catholic Clergyman. *Annapolis, printed by Frederick Green; and Worcester, reprinted by J. Tymbs, at the Cross*, MDCCLXXXV. 8vo, 2 p. l., pp. 120. 442

An Address to the Rulers of the State; in which their Conduct and Measures, the Principles and Abilities of their Opponents, and the real Interest of England with regard to America, and her natural enemies, are freely canvassed. By a Friend to Great Britain. *London, Bew*, 1778. 4to. 443

"This writer recommends most earnestly an effectual reconciliation with the Americans, by the most ample and unreserved concessions on our part, even the granting them (what they are already in possession of) their favourite independency."—M. R., LIX., p. 73.

Address to the Soldiers of New Hampshire, from the Granite State Lincoln Club of Washington, D. C. *Washington, L. Towers*, 1864. 8vo, pp. 8. 444

The Addresses and Messages of the Presidents of the United States to Congress, to the Year 1837. *New York*, 1837. 8vo. 445

The Addresses and Messages of the Presidents of the United States, from 1789 to 1839. Together with the Declaration of Independence and Constitution of the United States. With Portraits of the Presidents. *New York*, 1839. 8vo, pp. 632. 446

The Addresses and Messages of the Presidents of the United States, from Washington to Harrison. To which is prefixed the Declaration of Independence, and Constitution of the United States, together with a Portrait and Memoir of W. H. Harrison. *New York and Boston*, 1841. 8vo, pp. 732. 447

Addresses and Messages of the Presidents of the United States, from Washington to Tyler, embracing the Executive Proclamations, Recommendations, Protests and Vetoes, from 1789 to 1843, together with the Declaration of Independence and Constitution of the United States. Fourth Edition. *New York*, 1843. 8vo, pp. 794. 448

Addresses of the Successive Presidents of the United States to

Houses of Congress, at the Opening of each Session, with their Answers; from the Commencement of the present Government to January, 1805; with the Inaugural Addresses during the same period, and the Farewell Address of George Washington. *Washington City*, 1805. 449

Addresses on the Presidential Election. *New York and Charleston*, 1812. 8vo. C. 450

Addresses, Remonstrances, and Petitions, Commencing the 24th of June, 1769, Presented to the King and Parliament, from the Court of Common Council, and the Livery in Common Hall, assembled, with His Majesty's Answers. Likewise The Speech to the King, Made by the late Mr. Alderman Beckford, when Lord Mayor of the City of London. *Printed by Henry Fenwick*. 12mo, pp. 151. 451

Includes some notice of the Quebec Bill, The Declaration of Independence, Dr. Price's Works, &c.

ADELA. Extract from a Despatch to Mr. Stewart, her Majesty's Chargé des Affaires at Washington, respecting the seizure of Mail Bags on board the "Adela." *Br. Parl. Papers, N. Amer. London*, 1864. Folio, pp 3. 452

ADELUNG. Mithridates oder allgemeine Sprachenkunde mit dem Vater Unser als Sprachprobe in beinahe fünfhundert Sprachen und Mundarten, von Johann Christoph Adelung, Churfürstl. Sächsischem Hofrath und Ober-Bibliothekar. *Berlin*, 1806–1817. 5 vols., 8vo, pp. XXII. and VII., 686; XXIV., 808; XII., 708; VI., 474; XII., 530. 453

Vols. 2–5 were written by J. S. Vater. This is a history of all known languages and dialects, with an account of all the books printed in or relating to them. The second and third parts of the third volume—1813–1816—contain the languages of America.

ADELUNG. Geschichte von Californien. *See* Venegas.

ADET. Authentic Translation of a Note from the Minister of the French Republic to the Secretary of State of the United States. *New York*, 1796. 8vo, pp. 38. N. 454

ADET. Notes addressées par le Citoyen Adet, Ministre Plénipotentiaire de la République Française près les États Unis d'Amérique, *Au Secretaire d'Etat des Etats Unis. Philadelphia, B. F. Bache*, 1796. 8vo, pp. 95. 455

ADET. Notes from Citizen Adet, Minister Plenipotentiary

of the French Republic, near the United States of America, *To the Secretary of State of the United States*. [In French and English.] *Philadelphia, B. F. Bache*, 1796. 8vo, pp. 95. 456

Adfywiad cvefydd Lloegr Newdd. *Carmarthen*, 1800. 12mo.

Account of the Revival in New England; in the Welsh Language.

ADGER (J. B.) Christian Missions and African Colonization. By Rev. John B. Adger. *Columbia, S. C.*, 1857. 8vo, pp. 53.

ADGER. A Review of the Reports to the Legislature of South Carolina on the Revival of the Slave Trade. By Rev. John B. Adger. *Columbia, S. C.*, 1858. 8vo, pp. 36. s. 459

Adirondack Iron and Steel Company [Circular]. *New York*, 1854. 8vo, pp. 47, and plans. 460

The Opening of the Adirondacks. With a Map and Illustrations. *New York, Hurd & Houghton*, 1865. 12mo, pp. 82. 461

ADIS (H.) A Letter from Syrranam to Lord Willoughby, General of the Western Isles and of the Continent of Guiana, 1664. *London*, 1664. 8vo. 462

This title is taken from an English Sale Catalogue. I find no other account of the book.

ADLAM (Rev. S.) The First Church in Providence not the Oldest of the Baptists in America. Attempted to be shewn by S. Adlam. *Newport, Cranston*, 1850. 8vo, pp. 28. 463

ADLARD. The Sutton-Dudleys of England, and the Dudleys of Massachusetts in New England, from the Roman Conquest to the Present Time. By George Adlard. *New York, Richardson*, 1863. 8vo, pp. 160. 464

Administration Dissected. In which the Grand National Culprits are laid open for the Public Inspection. *London, Barker*, 1779. 8vo. 465

"A review of the present circumstances and situation of Great Britain, so far as both have been obviously affected by the conduct of government since the commencement of the unfortunate war with the American Colonies."—M. R., LXII., p. 82.

Administration of the Colonies. *See* [Pownall (T.)]

ADOLPHUS. History of England, from the Accession of

George the Third, to the Conclusion of Peace in the Year 1783. By John Adolphus. *London*, 1802. 3 vols., 8vo. 466

Other editions, 1805, 1816, the last continued to the Death of the King, 1840–45. 8vo, 7 vols. The work contains a copious account of the American Revolution. The Political State of the British Empire, *London*. 1818, by the same author, contains some references to the British Colonies in America.

ADRIAN (Dr.) Reise-Scenen aus Amerika. Herausgegeben von Dr. Adrian. Erster Theil. *Frankfurt*, 1836. 16mo, pp. 366. 467

ADRIAN. Chapin's Adrian City Directory and Advertiser for 1865–6. With a List of the principal Post-Offices in Michigan. *Adrian City, Chapin & Bros.*, 1866. 8vo, pp. 172. 468

Adrift in Dixie. *See* [Estabrooks (H. L.)].

Advantages of the Definite Treaty to the People of Great Britain demonstrated, to which is added a copy of our Treaty of Commerce with Spain in the year 1715. *London*, 1749. 8vo. 469

The Advantages of the Revolution Illustrated, being a View of the present State of Great Britain. *London*, 1753. 8vo. 470

Advantages to Great Britain from the approaching War, to which is added two curious plans of the Port and Bay of Havanna, and of Porto-Bello. *London*, 1727. 8vo. 471

Advantages which America derives from her Commerce, Connection and Dependance on Britain, addressed to the People of America. *New York*, 1775. 8vo. 472

Advantages which Ministers in the Colonies may enjoy by conforming to the Church of England. 1762. 8vo. 473

The Adventures of a Bale of Goods from America, in Consequence of the Stamp Act. *London, J. Almon*, 1766. pp. 23.

"A strange attempt at humour. What the author would be at is best known to himself, and, no doubt, will ever remain so."—M. R., XXXIV., p. 157.

Adventures of Hunters and Travellers, and Narratives of Border Warfare. *Philadelphia*, 1852. 12mo. 475

Adventures of a Gold Finder. Written by Himself. *London*, 1850. 3 vols., post 8vo, pp. 910. 476

The Adventures of Jonathan Corncob, Loyal American

Refugee. Written by Himself. *London, Robinson*, 1787. 12mo. 477

"The prototype of the *Halls* and the *Trollopes*, who, as the *Monthly Reviewer* says, 'thought that his ridicule of the *Jonathans* would render his work the more acceptable in England.'"—RICH. *See* M. R., LXXVII., p. 342.

The Adventures of Pomponious, a Roman Knight; or, the History of our own Times, made English by Mr. Macky. *London, E. Curll*, 1726. 2 vols., 12mo. 478

A satire on the celebrated John Law, his schemes and supporters.

Adventures of Uncle Sam in search of his lost honour. *Middletown*, 1816. 12mo. 479

Adventures in the South Pacific. By a Roving Printer. *New York*, 1861. 12mo. 480

"Advertisement, and not a joke." *Philadelphia, Oct.* 1, 1764. 8vo. P. 481

A doggerel electioneering address.

Advice to the Officers of the British Army. *New York*, 1783. 12mo. P. 482

Advice to the Inhabitants of the Northern Colonies, on the Present Situation of Affairs. *New York*, 1755. 8vo. P. 483

Advijs van den | Raedt | van Staten, | Voort-ghebracht aen | de Ho: Mo: Heeren | Staten Generael | der Vereenighde Nederlanden. | Den 8 October, 1650. ¶ *In 's Gravenhage, | By Gerret Pietersz*, 1650. | 4to, 2 l. 484

This advice of the Counsel of State to the States General relates to Brazil.

ADYE. A Treatise on Courts-Martial, etc. By Stephen Payne Adye. *Philadelphia*, 1779. 18mo. s. 485

Aen de | Hoogh Moog: Heeren Staten Generael | der Vereenighde Nederlanden. | 4to, pp. 16. 486

Address of the Agents of the West India Company to the States General. Relates to New Netherland.

Aengemerckte voorvallen | Op de | Vredens Articulen | Met | Portugael. ¶ Anno 1663. | 4to, pp. 15. 487

Important incidents in the negotiations with Portugal concerning Brazil.

Aenmerkenswaardige en Zeldzame West-Indische, Zee-en Land-Reizen door de Caribische Eylanden, Nieuw-Nederland, Virginien, en de Spaansche West-Indien. 1705. 8vo. Plates.

Æolus, or the Constitutional Politician. 1770. 8vo. 489

Æsop, Junior, in America: Being a series of Fables, written especially for the people of the United States of North America. *New York, Printed for the Author*, 1834. 12mo, pp. VIII., 3–238, Engraved Frontispiece and Title. 490

Affaires de l'Angleterre et de l'Amérique. *Anvers*, 1776–9. 8vo, 24 cahiers, divided into 8 tomes, usually bound in 17 vols.

"This work appears to have been an imitation or translation of Almon's Remembrancer, and appears to have extended to fifteen volumes. Among its editors, according to Barbier, were Franklin, Count de Gebelin, Robinet, &c. Harvard College library possesses a copy of this scarce work."—RICH. Mr. Rich was mistaken as to the contents of this work. It is quite different from the Remembrancer, and was probably printed at Paris. It is essential for the Revolutionary period.

An Affecting Narrative. *See* Anson (Lord).

An Affectionate Address to the Inhabitants of the British Colonies in America. By a Lover and Friend of Mankind. *New York*, 1776. 8vo. Title, 1 l.; Introduction, 2 l.; Text, 55 pp.+Another Edition. *Philadelphia*, 1776. 8vo. P. 492

Affiches Américaines. *De l'Imprimerie Royale, Port au Prince*, 1777–83. 4to, 7 vols. 493

"I have in my possession a copy of this French journal, from 1777 to 1783, both inclusive, in seven volumes. As they comprise the greater part of the American war, they contain many interesting articles relating to it, which probably are not to be found elsewhere."—RICH.

Affiches de Brunswick. Anno 1778. 8vo. 494

Includes Beschreiburg von Carolina in Nord-America.

The African Company's Property to the Forts and Settlements in Guiana, in America, considered, and the Necessity of Establishing a Trade in a Regulated Company. [1750.] 8vo.

African Institution, Report. 1803, &c. 496

A Review of the Colonial Slave Registration Acts, in a Report to the African Institution, Feb. 22, 1820. 8vo, pp. 139. s. 497

The African Repository and Colonial Journal. 1826, &c.

The African's Right to Citizenship. *Philadelphia, James S. Claxton*, 1865. 8vo, pp. 31. 499

African Servitude: when, why and by whom instituted? By whom and how long shall it be maintained? Read and consider. *New York, Davies & Kent*, 1860. 8vo, pp. 54. 500

The African Trade, the Great Pillar and Support of the British Plantation Trade in America: Shewing that our Loss, by being beat out of all the Foreign Markets for Sugar and Indigo by the French, has been owing to the Neglect of our African Trade; which only can supply our Colonies with Negroes, for the making of Sugars, and all other Plantation Produce: That the Support and Security of the Negroe-Trade depends wholly on the due and effectual Support of the Royal African Company of England, which has hitherto preserved this invaluable Trade to these Kingdoms: That the Difficulties and Discouragements which the said Company labours under, threaten the absolute Loss of the Negroe Trade to this Nation; and consequently the total Ruin of all the British Plantations in America, And also, What the Royal African Company have a natural Right to hope for this Session of Parliament from their Country, in order to enable them to support and maintain the British Interest, Rights and Privileges in Africa, against the French, and all other Rivals in the same most valuable Trade. In a Letter to the Right Honourable * * * * * * * * * * * *London, J. Robinson*, 1745. 4to, Title and pp. 44. 501

Affidavits and Depositions relative to the Commencement of Hostilities at Concord and Lexington, April 19, 1775. [No imprint.] 8vo. C. 502

AGASSIZ (A.) Illustrated Catalogue of the Museum of Comparative Zoology at Harvard College. Published by order of the Legislature of Massachusetts. No. II. North American Acalephæ. By Alexander Agassiz. *Cambridge*, 1865. 4to, pp. XIV., 234; with 360 Woodcuts in the Text. 503

AGASSIZ (L.) Contributions to the Natural History of the Acalaphæ of North America. *Cambridge*, 1849. 4to. 504

Part I. On the Naked-eyed Medusæ of the Shores of Massachusetts. 4to, pp. 96. 8 Plates. Part II. On the Beroid-Medusæ of the Shores of Massachusetts. pp. 62. 8 Plates.

AGASSIZ. Contributions to the Natural History of the United States of America. By Louis Agassiz. *Boston, Little, Brown & Company*, 1857–62. 4to. 505

To be completed in 10 vols., 4to. Sold to subscribers only. One of the most valuable works ever undertaken by any one editor. Its contents are of too strictly a scientific character to warrant an extended notice here. Let it suffice to observe that in all the essential elements of superiority of execution, it is equally meritorious. Contents: First Monograph. In Three Parts. I. Essay on Classification. II. North American Testudinata. III. Embryology of the Turtle; with thirty-four Plates. Vol.

III. Part I. Acalephs in General. Part II. Ctenophoræ. Part III. Discophoræ. Vol. IV. Second Monograph. In Five Parts. I. Acalephs in General. II. Ctenophoræ. III. Discophoræ. IV. Hydroidæ. V. Homologies of the Radiata; with forty-six Plates. *Boston*, 1862. The volumes are illustrated by Mr. A. Sourel, who, for twenty-three years, has been exclusively engaged in making illustrations for the successive works of Prof. Agassiz. The further publication of this work is suspended for the present [1867].

AGASSIZ. Lake Superior: its Physical Character, Vegetation and Animals, compared with those of other and similar regions. By Louis Agassiz. With a narrative of the tour by J. Elliot Cabot, and contributions by other scientific gentlemen. *Boston, Gould, Kendall & Lincoln*, 1850. 8vo, pp. 428. 506

The most complete work on this comparatively unknown region. Now scarce. *See* Chr. Ex., XLIX., p. 9; Sou. Q. R., XIX., p. 420.

AGASSIZ. Notice of a Collection of Fishes from the Southern Bend of the Tennessee River, Alabama. By L. Agassiz. *New Haven*, 1854. 8vo. 507

Extracted from Silliman's *Journal of Science*, &c., Vol. XVII., Second Series.

AGASSIZ. On Extraordinary Fishes from California, constituting a New Family. *New Haven*, 1853. 8vo, pp. 12. 508

From Silliman's *Journal*, Vol. XVI., Second Series.

The Age of Error; or, A Poetical Essay on the Course of Human Action. By a Philadelphian. *Philadelphia, Printed for the Author*, 1797. 8vo, pp. 16. G. 509

Age of Inquiry; or, Reason and Revelation in Harmony with each other, operating against all tyranny and infidelity: intended as a clue to the present Political Controversy in the United States. To which is added, some Remarks upon the Report of the Committee of the Legislature of Connecticut, upon the Baptist Petition, presented May, 1802. By a True Baptist. *Hartford*, 1804. 8vo, pp. 96. 510

AGG. History of Congress; exhibiting a classification of the proceedings of the Senate and House of Representatives. Vol. I. From March 4, 1789, to March 3rd, 1793, embracing the first term of the Administration of Washington. By John Agg. *Philadelphia*, 1834. 8vo. 511

This publication was not continued.

Aggregate Amount of Persons in the United States and their Territories, according to the Census of 1820, together with a list of Taxable Inhabitants, &c. in the State of Pennsylvania;

also a Summary of the Census of the State of New York, in 1821. *Philadelphia*, 1821. 4to. P. 512

AGIA. Tratado y parcero sobre el servicio personal de los Indios del Peru. Por Fr. Miguel de Agia. *Lima, Antonio Ricardo*, 1604. Folio. 513

"L'auteur était de Valence et religieux minime à Guatémala."—TERNAUX, No. 274. Ricardo was the first printer at Lima. *See* Harrisse, p. 372.

AGLIO (A.) *See* Kingsborough (Lord).

AGNEW (D.) Our National Constitution. Its Adaptation to a State of War or Insurrection. A Treatise by Daniel Agnew, President Judge, Pennsylvania. *Philadelphia, C. Sherman*, 1863. 8vo, pp. 39. 514

AGNEW (J. H.) Reply to Prof. Tayler Lewis' Review of Rev. Henry J. Van Dyke's Sermon on Biblical Slavery; also to his other articles on the same subject, published in "The World." By J. Holmes Agnew. *New York, D. Appleton & Co.*, 1861. 8vo, pp. 63. 515

AGNEW (M.) The Conspiracy Explained and Defended, in a letter to W. W. Phillips. By M. Agnew. Second Edition. *New York*, 1832. 8vo. 516

The Agricultural Interest, as affected by the Reciprocity Treaty, the Tariff, and the Coastwise Trade. *Philadelphia* [n. d.] 8vo, pp. 16. 517

Agriculture, Commerce and Manufactures. *Boston, Nov.* 11, 1826. 8vo, pp. 22. 518

AGÜERO (P. De). Biografías de Cubanos Distinguidos. Por P. De Agüero. I. Don José Antonio Saco. *London, Trubner*, 1860. 8vo, pp. 88. 519

AGUERO (D. G. E. de). Gazophilatium regium Perubicum. Opus sane pulcrum, a plerisque petitum & ab omnibus, in universum, desideratum non sine magno labore & experientia digestum, providèque, & accuratè illustratum. In quo omnes materiae spectantes, ad administrationem calculationem & conservationem, jurium regalium Regni Peruani latissimé discutiuntur & plena manupertractantur, Editum a D. Gaspare de Escalona Aguero, &c. *Matriti*, 1775. 520

The first edition was printed in 1647 and reprinted Matriti, 1675. The second part is in Spanish, and is entitled Gazofilacio Real de Peru. Of the edition of 1775,

some copies are on large paper. The official position of the author gave him access to the best authorities, and the book is reliable. Brunet, p. 115-116, thus notices the previous editions: "Cet ouvrage, qui fait connaître l'administration du gouvernement espagnol au Pérou est porté à 130 fr. sous le nº 32 du LXI Catal. de A. Asher, Berlin 1858, où on le donne comme un livre parfaitement inconnu aux Bibliographes, et même à Antonio: ce dernier, il est vrai, n'a pu parler dans sa Bibliotheca nova imp. en 1672, de cette édition de 1675 mais il en a cité une plus ancienne sous ce titre:"

AGUERO. Arce limesis gazophilacium regium Peruvicum, administrandum, calculandum, conservandum. *Matriti*, 1647. Folio. 521

AGUERO. Miscellaneo Espiritual en Idioma Zapoteca. Por Fray Christobal Aguero. *Mexico, Bernardo Calderon*, 1666. 4to. 522

The Zapoteca is the language spoken by the Indians of Oajaca, Mexico. *See* Ludewig, p. 207.

AGUERO (J.) Exposicion de Don José de la Riva Aguero acerca de su conducta Politica en el tiempo que ejercio la Presidencia de la Republica del Peru. [*Privately Printed.*] *London*, 1824. 8vo. Portraits. 523

AGUEROS. Descripcion Historial de la Provincia y Archipielago de Chilóe, en el Reyno de Chile, y Obispado de la Concepcion: dedicada á Nuestro Católico Monarca Don Cárlos IV. (Que Dios guarde) Por el Padre Fray Pedro Gonzalez de Agueros, de la Regular Observancia de nuestro Padre San Francisco, de la Provincia de la Purísima Concepcion en Castilla la Vieja, Predicador General Apostólico, Ex-Guardian del Colegio de Propaganda Fide de Santa Rosa de Santa María de Ocopa en el Perú, y Arzobispado de Lima, y su Procurador en esta Corte de Madrid. Año de MDCCXI. *En la Imprenta de Don Benito Cano.* 4to, 4 p. l., pp. 318. Map and plate. 524

The plate represents the "Verdadera effigie" of a tree in the valley of Limache, growing in the form of a cross, with the image of the crucified Saviour thereon.

AGUIAR Y ACUÑA. Svmarios de la Recopilacion general de las Leyes, Ordenanças, Provisiones, Cedvlas, Instrucciones y Cartas Acordadas, que por los Reyes Catolicos de Castilla se han promulgado expedido y despachado para las Indias Occidentales, Islas y Tierra Firme del mar Oceano desde el año 1492 que se descubrieron, haste el presente de 1528. Por el Licenciado Don Rodrigo de Aguiar y Acuña. *Madrid, Juan Gonzales*, 1628. Folio, 8 p. l., pp. 178; 4 l.+Reprinted, *Mexico*, 1677. 8 p. l. and 385 l. 525

A book of the greatest rarity, having been printed only for the use of the members of the Council of Indias. *See* Pinelo Bibliotheca (1629); Rich, No. 183; Ternaux, No. 500.

AGUILAR (Jose de). Sermones Varios, predicados en la Ciudad de Lima. Por Jose de Aguilar. Corte de los Reynos del Peru. *Bruselas*, 1704. 4to. 526

AGUILAR. Relacion de las cosas de Iucatan y informe contre los idolatros del obispado de Iucatan. Por Sanchez de Aguilar. *Madrid*, (?) 1639. 527

See Ternaux, No. 591.

AGUIRRE (J.) Collectio Maxima Conciliorum Hispaniæ et Novi Orbis. Cura J. Sanchez de Aguirre. *Romæ*, 1693–94. 4 vols., folio. 528

AGUIRRE. Conciliorum omnium Hispaniæ et Novi Orbis, epistolarumque, decretalium, etc., Collectio maxima; cum notis et dissertationibus illustrata, cura J. S. de Aguirre. Editio locupletata, cura et labore Jos. Catalani. *Romæ*, 1753. 6 vols., folio. 529

AGUIRRE. Collectio Maxima Conciliorum Hispaniæ a Jos. Aguirre edita cum adnotationibus Sylvestri Puego. *Madrid*, 1781. Folio. 530

AGUIRRE. Synopsis Collectionis Maximæ Conciliorum omnium Hispaniæ, et Novi Orbis. *Romæ*, 1695. 18mo. 531

The large collection of Aguirre is highly esteemed and rare. This synopsis seems little known; it is not mentioned by Salmon sur l'Etude des Conciles, where the larger work is analyzed, nor is either of the two noticed by Antonio.

AGUIRRE (Miguel de). Poblacion | de Baldivia. Mo- | tivos, y medios para | aqvella Fvndacion. Defen- | sas del Reyno del Perv; para resistir | las inuasiones enemigas en mar, y | tierra. | Pazes pedidas por los In- | dios rebeldes de Chile, acetadas, y capitv- | ladas por el Gouernador: y estado que tienen hasta nueue | de Abril del año de 1647. | A.D. Philipo IIII. N. S. el Pia- | doso, Rey Catolico de las Españas. y Em- | perador de las Indias. | Por el Padre Maestro Fray Miguel | de Aguirre, del Orden de S. Agustin, Calificador del Santo Ofi- | cio, Catedratico de Prima de Teologia Escolastica en la Real | Vniuersidad de los Reyes. | Año de 1647. | *Impresso en Lima, en casa de Iulian Santos de Saldaña, Por Iorge | Lopez de Herrera.* | Folio, 2 p.l., and 57 folioed leaves, followed by 1 blank leaf and 4 unnumbered leaves. 532

Sold at Puttick's, in 1854, for £3 3s. od.

AGUTTER (W.) The Abolition of the Slave Trade considered in a Religious Point of View. By William Agutter. *London*, 1788. 8vo. 533

AIGREMONT (Jean de Laon, Sieur d'). *See* Laon, Sieur d'Aigremont (Jean de).

AIKEN (John). Labor and Wages at Home and Abroad. *Lowell*, 1849. 8vo, pp. 29. 534

AIKEN (P. F.) Lectures on the British and American Constitutions. A Comparative View of the Constitutions of Great Britain and the United States of America. In six lectures. By P. F. Aiken, Advocate. *London, Longman & Co.*, 1842. Fcap. 8vo. 535

AIKEN (Silas). Posthumous Influence. A Sermon on the Death of Hon. Samuel Hubbard, LL.D. Preached Jan. 2, 1848. *Boston*, 1848. 8vo, pp. 40. 536

AIKEN (Sol.) Address to Federal Clergymen on the Subject of the War Proclaimed by the United States against Great Britain. By Solomon Aiken. *Boston*, 1813. 8vo. W. 537

AIKEN. An Oration delivered before the Republican Citizens of Newburyport, July 4, 1810. By Rev. Solomon Aiken. *Newburyport*, 1810. 8vo, pp. 15. 538

AIKIN (John). Annals of the Reign of King George the Third; from its commencement in the year 1760, to the general peace in the year 1815. By John Aikin, M.D. *London*, 1816. 2 vols., 8vo.+Another Edition. To the Death of His Majesty in the Year 1820. *London*, 1820 *and* 1825. 539

Includes details of the Revolutionary War. *See* M. R., LXXXIII., p. 208.

AIKMAN. Discourse delivered in . . . Newark, N. J., on Thanksgiving Day, November 27, 1851. By Rev. William Aikman. *Newark*, 1851. 8vo, pp. 23. 540

AIKMAN. The Future of the Colored Race in America; being an article in the Presbyterian Quarterly Review, of July, 1862. By William Aikman. *New York, A. D. F. Randolph*, 1862. 8vo, pp. 35.+Another Edition. *Philadelphia, W. S. Young*, 1862. 541

AIKMAN. Government and Administration. A Sermon preached July 19, 1863, succeeding the secession riots in New York. By William Aikman. *Wilmington, Henry Eckel*, 1863. 12mo, pp. 12. 542

AIMARD (Gustave). Les Trappeurs de l'Arkansas. Cinquième Edition. *Paris*, MDCCCLIX. 12mo, pp. xii., 455. 543

Trappers of Arkansas. *London, Ward*, 1864. 12mo. This writer has published about twenty other fictions illustrative of American life.

AIMÉ. Déportation et Naufrage de J.-J. Aimé, ex-législateur, suivi du tableau de vie et de mort des déportés à son départ de la Guyane. Avec quelques observations sur cette Colonie et sur les Nègres. *Paris*, 1800. 8vo, pp. 270. 544

AIMÉ. Narrative of the Deportation to Cayenne, and Shipwreck on the Coast of Scotland, of J. J. Aimé; written by himself. With observations on the present state of that colony, & of the negroes; and an account of the situation of the deported persons at the time of his escape. *London, Wright*, 1800. 8vo, pp. 282. 545

AINSWORTH (W. H.) John Law the Projector. *London, Chapman*, 1864. 3 vols., post 8vo. 546

AISLABIE. Case of the Right Hon. J. Aislabie, as concerned in the great South-Sea Scheme; with his two Defensive Speeches, made in the House of Lords, against the Bill for raising Money upon the Estates of the South-Sea Directors. *London*, (1721.) 4to, pp. 42. C. 547

AISLABIE (John). Speech of the Hon. J. Aislabie, esquire, upon his defence made in the House of Lords, against the bill for raising money upon the estates of the South-Sea Directors. *London*, 1721. 4to.+Second Speech, July 24. *London*, 1721. 4to. S. 548

AITKIN (W. B.) Remarks, N. Y. Assembly, on the Proposition to impose a mill-and-an-half Tax for the Support of Government, 1854. S. 549

AITKEN (James). *See* John the Painter.

AITKEN (R.) Aitken's general American Register, and the Gentleman's and Tradesman's complete Annual Account Book, and Calendar, for the Pocket or Desk; for the Year of our Lord, 1773. *Philadelphia, Joseph Crukshank, for R. Aitken*, 1773. 8vo. 550

2 pl. l., Text A to N, followed by second title, "Aitken's General American Register for the Year of our Lord 1773," etc. Title and 64 pp. The first attempt of its kind in the American Colonies; also published in 1774. *See* Allibone's Dictionary, p. 42.

AKERLY. An Essay on the Geology of the Hudson River, and the Adjacent Regions; Illustrated in a Geological Section of the Country, from the Neighbourhood of Sandy-Hook, in New Jersey, Northward, through the Highlands in New York, towards the Catskill Mountains: Addressed to Dr. Samuel L. Mitchill, by Samuel Akerly. Read before the Lyceum in August, 1819. 1820. 12mo, pp. 69. Map. 551

AKINS. Prize Essay on the History of the Settlement of Halifax, at the Mechanics' Institute, on 18th April, 1839. By Thomas Beamish Akins. *Halifax, N. S.* 18mo, pp. 62. 552

AKINS. Sketch of the Rise and Progress of the Church of England in the British North-American Provinces. By T. B. Akins. *Halifax, N. S.*, 1849. 12mo. M. 553

AKTENSTÜCKE, Gesammelte, des Vereins zum Schutze deutscher Einwanderer in Texas. *Mainz*, 1845. 8vo. Map.

ALABAMA. Acts passed at the First Session of the First General Assembly of the Alabama Territory, 1818. *St. Stephen's* [n. d.] 12mo, pp. 112.+Second Session. *St. Stephen's, A. T.*, 1818. 12mo, pp. 79. 555

Alabama Anti-Masonic Convention. Proceedings of the adjourned meeting at Cahawba. *Selma, Ala.*, 1830. 8vo.+Proceedings and Address at the meeting in Tuscaloosa Co. *Tuscaloosa*, 1830. 8vo. 556

Constitution of the State of Alabama, adopted Aug. 2, 1819. *Huntsville*, 1819. 8vo, pp. 26. 557

Journal of the Convention of the Alabama Territory, begun July 5, 1819. *Huntsville*, 1819. 8vo. 558

Journal of the House of Representatives of the Alabama Territory, at the First Session of the First General Assembly, in the Forty-Second Year of American Independence. *St. Stephen's*, 1818. 4to. 559

Journal of the Legislative Council of the Alabama Territory, at the First Session of the First General Assembly, in the Forty-Third Year of American Independence. *St. Stephen's*, 1818. 8vo. 560

Journal of the Second Biennial Session of the House of Representatives of the State of Alabama, Session 1849–50. *Montgomery*, 1850. 8vo. 561

Journal of the Second Biennial Session of the Senate of Alabama, Session 1849–50, held in the city of Montgomery. *Montgomery*, 1850. 8vo. 562

Journal of the Proceedings of the Baptist State Convention, in Alabama, at its nineteenth anniversary. *Marion, Alabama*, 1842. 8vo. 563

Laws of the State of Alabama, 1819, &c. *Huntsville*, 1820 8vo. 564

Letter to the Legislature of Alabama, on Chartering a Bank like the Union Bank of Louisiana. *New-York*, 1832. 8vo. 565

Protest of the Alabama Delegates. *Charleston* [1861 ?]. 8vo, pp. 4. 566

Report of the Commissioners appointed by the Governor to examine the Southern Bank of Alabama. *Montgomery*, 1851.

Several pamphlets on the State Bank of Alabama are described in Stevens' "Catalogue of American Books in the British Museum."

Report of the House of Representatives on the subject of Direct Trade. *Montgomery*, 1852. 8vo. 568

Transactions of the Alabama Historical Society, at its First Annual Meeting, held at the University of Alabama, July 14, 1851. *Tuscaloosa*, 1852 8vo, pp. 55.+At the Annual Meeting, July 9 and 10, 1855. *Tuscaloosa*, 1855. 8vo, pp. 65. 569

University of Alabama. Report of the Trustees to the General Assembly of Alabama, 1837. *Tuscaloosa*, 1837. 8vo, pp. 7.

Catalogue of the Library of the University of Alabama; with an Index of Subjects. By W. G. Richardson. *Tuscaloosa*, 1848. 8vo. 571

Alabama, Florida and Georgia Railroad Company. Report of Comm. on Naval Affairs: U. S. H. of R. Feb. 18, 1845. [*Cong. Doc.*] 8vo, pp. 15. Map. 572

The Alabama. Correspondence respecting the "Alabama"; also respecting the Bark "Maury," at New York, during the Crimean War; and the temporary Act of Congress, passed by the United States, at the instance of Great Britain, in 1838, to meet the case of the Rebellion in Canada. 8vo, pp. 56. 573

Correspondence respecting the "Alabama." *London, Parl. Papers, N. America*, 1863. Folio, pp. 48. 574

Correspondence respecting the "Alabama." (In continuation of Correspondence presented to Parl. in March, 1863.) *London, Parl. Papers, N. America*, 1864. Folio, pp. 57. 575

Correspondence respecting the "Alabama." (In continuation of Papers presented to Parliament in Feb., 1864.) *London, Parl. Papers, N. America*, 1864. Folio, pp. 18. 576

Narrative of the Cruise of the Alabama, and a list of her officers and men. By One of her Crew. *London*, 1864. 8vo, pp. 16. 577

Proceedings of the Chamber of Commerce of the State of New York, on the Burning of the Ship Brilliant, by the Rebel Pirate Alabama, Tuesday, October 21, 1862. *New York*, 1862. 8vo, pp. 22. 578

ALAMAN. Diccionario universal de Historia y de Geografia; contieno: Historia, propiamente dicha, Biografia universal, Mitologia, Geografia antigua y moderna. Obra dada a luz en España por una Sociedad de literatos distinguidos, con noticias historicas, geograficas, estadisticas, y biograficas sobre las Americas en general, y especialmente sobre Republica Mexicana, por los Sres. D. Lucas Alaman, D. Jose Maria Andrade, D. Jose Maria Basoco, etc. Apendice al Diccionario Universal. Coleccion de artículos, relativos á la Republica Mexicana, recogidos y coordinados por D. Manuel Orozco y Berra. *México*, 1853–56. 4to, 10 vols., pp. iv., 828; iv., 726; 792; 866; 1024; 862; 646; 778; 936; 1142. 579

ALAMAN. Disertaciones sobre la Historia de la República Megicana, desde la epoca de la conquista que los Españoles hicieron a fines del siglo XV. y principios del XVI. de las Islas y Continente Americano hasta la independencia. Por Lucas Alaman. *Mégico*, 1844–1849. 3 vols., 8vo. c. 580

ALAMAN. Historia de Mejico desde los primeros movimientos que prepararon su independencia en el Ano de 1808, hasta la época presente. Por Don Lúcas Alaman. *Méjico*, 1849–1852. 5 vols., 4to, pp. xii., 598; 668; 692; viii., 832; xii., 1108. Frontispiece and Maps. c. 581

ALAMAN. Proceso Instructivo Formado por la Seccion del Gran Jurado de la Cámara de Diputados del Congreso General, en Averiguacion de los Delitos de que fueron Acusados los Ex-Ministros D. Lucas Alaman, D. Rafael Mangino, D. José

Antonio Facio, y D. José Ignacio Espinosa. *México*, 1833 4to. c. 582

Alarm; or, a Plan of Pacification with America, and New-York Freeholder, Nos. 1–7. *New York* [n. d.] 16mo, pp. 64.

The Alarm Bell. No. 1. By a Constitutionalist. *New York, Baker & Godwin*, 1863. 8vo, pp. 16. 583

Alasco; an Indian tale; Two Cantos; with other Poems. *Philadelphia*, 1857. 12mo. 584

Founded on Bartram's Travels in Florida.

ALBACH (James R.) Annals of the West; embracing a Concise Account of Principal Events which have occurred in the Western States and Territories, from the Discovery of the Mississippi Valley to the year Eighteen hundred and fifty-six. Compiled from the most authentic sources and published by James R. Albach. *Pittsburgh, W. S. Haven*, 1856. Rl. 8vo, pp. 1016.

ALBANY. Address of the Albany Republican Corresponding Committee, containing the Documents and Correspondence transmitted by the late Gov. Tompkins to the Committee of Ways and Means and to the House of Assembly. [1820.] 8vo, pp. 22. 586

Address to the Governor, Council, and Assembly of Albany, for establishing an Insurance Company. 1690. Sm. 4to. 587

This title is taken from a MS. list of books relative to America, in the possession of the late Dr. Hawks. It is probably an error as to the date.

Albany Academy. Celebration of the Semi-Centennial Anniversary, Albany, June 23, 1863. *Albany*, 1863. 8vo, pp. 188. Plate. 588

Statutes of the Albany Academy, 1816.+Same, with Amendments. *Albany*, 1831. 12mo.+Same. *Albany*, 1843. 12mo, pp. 36. 589

Albany and Harlem Railroad Company. Proceedings of the Directors, etc. June 19, 1840. 8vo. 590

Albany and Schenectady Railroad Company. Report, &c. 1848. 8vo. 591

Address by the Directors of the Albany and Susquehanna R.R. Co. *Albany*, 1856. 8vo. 592

Address to the Citizens of Albany, on the Albany & Susquehanna R.R., May, 1852. 8vo, pp. 24. s. 593

Some Considerations respecting the proposed Construction of the Albany and Susquehanna Railroad. *Albany*, 1852. 8vo.

Albany and West-Stockbridge R. R. Company: Report of the Superintendent, &c., July 9, 1836. *Albany*, 1836. 8vo. s. 595

Albany Annual Register for 1849–50. *Albany, J. Munsell*, 1850. 4 vols, 12mo. s. 596

Albany Basin and Erie Canal, in which some Important Improvements are suggested. *Albany*, 1836. 8vo. s. 597

Abany Atlas Extra, Oct. 1849. The Syracuse Convention; its Spurious Organization. 8vo, pp. 16. s. 598

Albany City Guide. *Albany*, 1845. 12mo, pp. 112. Map and Plates. 599

Albany Democratic Reformer: Vol. 1, 1844. s. 600

Albany Directory. The first, collected and arranged by J. Fry, 1813. 12mo.+Reprinted 1853. 12mo. The subsequent years have been edited and published respectively by Packard & Van Benthuysen, B. Pearce, Klinck, W. Cammeyer, E. B. Child, W. H. Shiffer, G. J. Loomis, T. G. Wait, S. Wilson, L. G. Hoffman, W. Hunt, Whitney & Bliss, J. Munsell, and Geo. Adams. 601

Albany Federal Committee. Anti-Federal Objections Refuted. *Albany* [n. d.] 12mo. 602

Albany Gallery of Fine Arts. Catalogue of the First Exhibition, 1846. *Albany*, 1846. 8vo. 603

Albany Institute. Report of the Committee appointed to continue the Meteorological Observations on the 21st of March, June, September, and December. Accepted November, 1836. [*Albany*, n. d.] 8vo, pp. 32. 604

Catalogue of the Albany Institute Library, founded 1793. Prepared by George Wood. With Index *Albany*, 1857. 8vo, pp. 454. 605

Albany Institute. First Annual Report. 1825. 8vo. 606

Transactions of the Albany Institute. Vol. 1, 1830; Vol. 2, 1833; Vol. 3. 607

See Trubner's American Bibliographical Guide, p. 22, for a detailed list of the contents of each volume.

Albany Liberty National Nominating Convention. Proceedings and Address. *Albany*, 1841. 8vo. 608

Albany Northern Railroad Company: Report, 1852, &c. 8vo.

Albany Pocket Almanack for the Year 1784. *Printed by R. Balentine*. 18mo. s. 610

Albany Ratification Meeting. The United Democracy for Regular Nominations. Speeches of D. A. Ogden and J. Van Buren, Sept. 27, 1853. 8vo, pp. 16. s. 611

Annual Report of the Trade and Commerce of the City of Albany for the Year 1862, and continued. 8vo. 612

Charter of the City of Albany, printed by order of the Mayor, Aldermen, and Commonalty of the City aforesaid. *New York, Hugh Gaine*, 1771. 4to.+Charter, and act to amend the several acts relating to the city, and to combine the same into one act. *Albany*, 1826. 8vo. 613

Constitutionality of a Bridge at Albany, as shewn in the Remarks of D. Buel, Jr., and Benjamin F. Butler, and the Opinion of Chief Justice Savage in the Troy Bridge Case, decided in the Superior Court of New York in 1836. With an Abstract of the Testimony. *Albany*, 1845. 8vo, pp. 20. 614

Several tracts on the Bridge at Albany are described in the catalogue of the New York State Library.

Correspondence in relation to the Public Meeting at Albany, with Letter from Pres. Lincoln, dated June 12, 1860. [1860.] 8vo, pp. 9. 615

To the Members of the First Presbyterian Church, Albany. [Signed A. March, and others.] March 11, 1847. 8vo, pp. 47.+Another. March 22, 1847.+Another. March 29, 1847. 8vo, pp. 18.+Minutes of a Meeting, March 24, 1846. 8vo, pp. 60. s. 616

This controversy in the First Presbyterian Church was respecting a change of location.

A Geological Survey of the County of Albany, taken under

the direction of the Agricultural Society of the County. *Albany*, 1820. 8vo, pp. 55. 617

Historical Sketch of the Sunday-School connected with the Second Presbyterian Church of the City of Albany. *Albany*, 1857. 8vo, pp. 18. s. 618

Impartial Address to the Citizens of the City and County of Albany; or the thirty-five Anti-federal objections Refuted: by the Federal Committee of the City of Albany. 12mo. s. 619

Laws and Ordinances of the Mayor, Recorder, Aldermen and Commonalty of the City of Albany. *Albany, printed by Alexander and James Robertson*, 1773. 4to. 620

Laws and Ordinances of the Common Council, 1791. 4to.+Same, with the Charter. *Albany*, 1800. 4to.+Same. *Albany*, 1808. 8vo.+Same. *Albany*, 1812. 8vo.+Same. *Albany*, 1838. 8vo. s. 621

Laws and Ordinances of the Common Council of the City of Albany, revised and revived, Dec., 1841; to which are prefixed the charter of the city of Albany, and the several laws and extracts from the Revised Statutes, relating to said City. *Albany*, 1842. 8vo, pp. 333. 622

Presbytery of Albany: Narrative of the Revival of Religion, 1820. *Schenectady*, 1821. 8vo. s. 623

Order of Exercises Seventy-seventh Anniversary of American Independence. *Albany*, 1853. 8vo. 624

Origin of Sunday Schools in Albany. 8vo, pp. 23. 625

Proceedings of the Republican meeting of the citizens of Albany and Colonie, at Jared Skinner's Long Room, March 13, 1810. *Albany*, 1810. 8vo. 626

Proceedings of a Meeting held at Albany [to promote the election of Clinton and Tallmadge]. 1824. 8vo. 627

Propositions Made by the Sachems of the three Maquas Castles, to the Mayor, Aldermen, and Commonality of the City of Albany, and Military Officers of the said City, and County in the City Hall, February 25, 1689–90. Peiter Schuyler Mayor, with ten more gentlemen, then present. Interpreted by Arnout & Hille. [Colophon.] *Boston, Printed by S. Green. Sold by*

Benjamin Harris, at the London Coffee House, 1690. 4to, pp. 12. 628

This exceedingly rare tract relates to the burning of Schenectady.

The Public Schools in Albany, inadequate to meet the Wants of the Public; and the Necessity of Reform. From Albany Morning Express. *Albany*, 1855. 8vo, pp. 45. s. 629

Random Recollections of Albany. *See* [Worth (Gorham, A.)].

Report of the Select Committee of the Senate, showing the Frauds and Peculations of Edwin Croswell, Theodore Olcott, John L. Crew and others, by which the Canal Bank was ruined. *Albany*, 1849. 8vo, pp. 64. 630

Review of the Trade and Commerce of Albany, for 1861. 8vo. s. 631

Return of the Commissioners under the Acts to Improve the Navigation of the Albany Basin, and to Extend the Opening of the Albany Pier; made to the City Council, October 1842. *Albany*, 1842. 8vo, pp. 91. 632

Some Account of Acts in relation to the Construction of the Albany Basin, with the Opinion of a Member of the Albany Bar as to the Rights of Parties Interested. *Albany*, 1848. 8vo, pp. 35. 633

St. Andrew's Society of Albany. Memorial of the Great Sanitary Fair held in the City of Albany, N. Y., February and March. *Albany*, 1864. 8vo. 634

St. Peter's Church. The Answer of "The members of the Congregation of Saint Peter's Church, in the City of Albany," to the Pamphlet lately addressed to them, by the Hon. Lt.-Governor Taylor, and others. *Printed for the Congregation, February*, 1816. 8vo, pp. 100. 635

Controversy in St. Peter's Church, between Rev. Mr. Clowes and Part of his Congregation, in 1816. *Albany*. 8vo. s. 636

Report to the Vestry of St. Peter's Church, Albany, of the Lay Delegates to the Diocesan Convention, &c., New York, 23d September, 1845. *Albany*, 1845. 8vo, pp. 42. 637

St. Peter's Church. Statement of the Finances, with a Plan of Revenue and Support. *Albany*, 1842. 8vo. 638

Song of the Sexton . . . . after the Dedication of Albany Cemetery. 8vo. s. 639

Speeches in behalf of the University of Albany, by Messrs. Ruggles, Tabor, and Rev. Drs. Kennedy and Palmer. *Albany*, 1852. 8vo, pp. 44. s. 640

Statistical Report of the County of Albany for the year 1820. *Albany*, 1823. 8vo. 641

Supplement to the Albany Register, April 20, 1813: Address to the Republican Citizens of New York. *Albany, Southwick*, 1813. 8vo. 642

Trinity Church, Albany: To the Parishioners. 8vo. s. 643

A large collection of the annual reports of the various public institutions, religious societies of Albany, &c., will be found in the New York State Library.

ALBAREZ. Copia de la Espantosa Carta, Escrita por el | P-Fr. Domingo Albarez de Toledo, Procurador General de Corte, del | Orden de N. P. S. Francisco, embiada desde la Ciudad de Lima, al | Reverendissimo P. Commissario General en Estecharque, que su fecha es | de 29. de Octubre de 1687. años, dandole cuenta de los lastimosos estragos | y desgracias que han sucedido en dicha Ciudad. | [Colophon.] Con licencia: *En Barcelona, en casa Vicente Surià*, | *à la calle de la Paja, Año* 1688. | *Vendese el Flos Sanctorum del Padre Ribadeneyra*, | *aumentado con los Santos nuevos, en la* | *misma Imprenta*. | 4to, pp. 4. 644

ALBARRACIN. Apuntes sobre las islas del Delta Arjentino por M. Santiago Albarracin. *Buenos-Aires*, 1860. 8vo, pp. 148.

ALBEMARLE. Letter from the Secretary of the Navy in regard to the Rebel Ram "Albemarle," which recently participated in the rebel attack on Plymouth. *House, Ex. Doc., No.* 53, 38*th Cong.*, 1864. 8vo, pp. 12. 646

ALBENINO (N.) Verdadera | relacion: de lo sussedido | en los Reynos e prouin- | cias d'l peru | desde la y da | a ellos d'l vi Rey Blasco | nuñes vela | hasta el des | barato y muerte de gon | calo Picarro. (*sic*) | [*Colophon*:] Acaboze la presente obra enla muy noble y memorable ciudad ó Seuilla a dos dias del mes de Enero del año de Christo de . M . D . xlix . En casa de Juan de Leon. Siédo primero manda da ver y examinar por los muy reuerendos y muy magnificos Señores inquisidores: y con su licencia mandada imprimir. Small 8vo. 647

ALBERDI. Bases y puntos de parleda para la organizacion politica de la Republica Argentina. Par Juan Bautista Alberdi. *Valparaiso*, 1852. 8vo. 648

ALBERDI. De la integridad nacional de la Republica Arjentina bajo todos sus Gobiernos. A proposito de sus recientes, tratados con Buenos-Aires. Por Juan B. Alberdi. *Parana*, 1855. 8vo, pp. 88. 649

ALBERDI. España y las Repúblicas de la América del Sur. Por J. B. Alberdi. *Paris, Kugelman*, 1861. 650

ALBERDI. Estudios sobre la Constitucion Argentina de 1853, en que se restablece su mente alterada por comentarios hostiles. Por J. B. Alberdi. *Valparaiso*, 1853. 8vo, pp. 104. 651

ALBERDI. Memoria descriptiva sobre Tucuman. Por J. B. Alberdi. *Buenos-Aires*, 1834. 8vo, pp iv., 30. 652

ALBERDI. Organizacion Politico y Economico de la Confederacion Argentina. Por J. B. Alberdi. Nueva edicion correg. y revis. *Besançon*, 1856. 8vo, pp. 870. 653

ALBERDI. Organizacion de la Confederacion Argentina. Por J. B. Alberdi. *Besançon, Jacquin*, 1858. 2 vols., 8vo. 654

ALBERDI. Sistema Economico y rentistico de la Confederacion Argentina segun su Constitucion de 1853. Por J. B. Alberdi. *Valparaiso*, 1854. 8vo. 655

ALBERS (J. A.) Americanische annalen der Arzneykunde Naturgeschichte Chemie und Physick . . . Zweites Heft. *Bremen*, 1802. 8vo. 656

ALBERT EDWARD. The Tour of H. R. H., Albert Edward, the Prince of Wales, through British America and the United States. By a British Canadian. *Montreal*, 1860. 8vo, pp. 271. 657

ALBERT EDWARD (Prince). Relation du voyage de son altesse royale le Prince de Galles en Amérique, reproduite du "Journal de l'Instruction Publique du Bas-Canada," avec un appendice contenant diverses adresses, correspondances, etc. *Montreal*, 1860. pp. 148, xxx. 658

ALBERTI. Descrittione | di Tvtta Italia | di I. Leandro Alberti Bolognese, Nella quale si contiene il Sito | di essa, l'Origine, & le Signorie delle Citta, & delle Castilla, | coi Nomi Antichi &

Moderni, i Costumi de Popolo, le Condicioni de Paesi : | et piv-gli hvomini famosi che l'hanno | Illustrata, i Monti, i Laghi, i Fiumi, le Fontane, | i Bagni, le Minere, con tutte l'opre marauigliose in lei | dalla Natura prodotte. | Con Priuilegio | In Bologna per Anselmo Giaccarelli | M.D.L. | Folio; Title, &c., 4 p. l.; Text, 469 l.; Index, 28 l. 659

"This work is quoted by the *Nova Acta Eruditorum* in reference to the alleged claims of Vespuccius to the discovery of the New World."—HARRISSE.

ALBERTI. Descrizzione di tutta Italia. *Venice*, 1553, 1568, *and* 1581. 4to. 660

ALBERTINIS. De Mirabilibus novæ & veteris Urbis Romæ. Opus editum à Francisco de Albertinis Clerico Florentino, tribus Libris divisum, dicatumque Julio II. Pontif. Max.; Romæ per Joannem de Besichen An. 1505. 661

Title as given by Negri, and quoted, with doubts as to its authenticity, by Harrisse, p. 78.

ALBERTINIS. De Mirabilibus novæ & veteris Urbis Romæ. Libri III. ex Edit. Andr. Fulvii Praenestini, *Romæ*, 1508. 4to.

"Clement gives this title on the authority of the *Bibliotheca Menkeniana*, page 196, and seems to disbelieve its authenticity. Panzer calls the edition of 1510 '*Editio prima*.'"—HARRISSE.

ALBERTINIS. Opvscvlvm de Mirabi- | libus Nouæ & ueteris Vrbis Romæ edi- | tum a Fra*n*cisco de Albertinis Clerico Flore*n* | tino dedicatumq3 Iulio secundo Pon. Max. &c. [Colophon.] Impressum Romæ per Iacobum Mazochium | Romanæ Academiæ Bibliopolam qui in- | fra paucos dies epythaphioru*m* opusculu*m* | in iuce*m* ponet año Salutis. M.D.X. Die. iiii. Febr. | Sm. 4to; Title, 1 l.; Text, 102 l. 663

For a full account of this edition, *see* Harrisse's Bibl. Am. Vet., pp. 120.

ALBERTINIS. Opvscvlvm de Mirabi- | libus Nouæ & ueteris Vrbis Romæ edi- | tum a Fra*n*cisco de Albertinis Clerico Flore*n* | tino dedicatumcq*ue* Iulio secundo Pon. Max. | [*Colophon*:] Impressum Romæ per Iacobum Mazochium | Romanæ Academiæ Bibliopolam qui in- | fra paucos dies epythaphioru*m* opusculu*m* | in luce*m* ponet año Salutis, M.D.X. Die | III. Febr. | Sm. 4to; Title, 1 l.; Text, 102 unnumbered leaves. 664

The reference to Vespuccius is quoted by Harrisse, Bib. Am. Vet., p. 121.

ALBERTINIS. De mirabilibus novæ & veteris Urbis Romæ,

& de Laudibus Civitatum Florentiæ & Sauonæ. Romae 1515 ap Jac. Mazochium in 4to. 665

Title as quoted from Clement by Harrisse, p. 140.

ALBERTINIS. Opusculum de mirabilibus novæ & veteris Urbis *Romæ*: industriâ & impensâ Thomæ Wolff *Chalcographiæ gnari exaratum nuper 4to. ex propriâ Officinâ Urbis* Basileæ, 1519. 666

Title quoted from Maittaire's Annales, by Harrisse.

ALBERTINIS. Mirabilia Rome | Opusculu*m* de Mirabilibus | Noue et Ueteris urbis | Rome editu*m*. a Fran | cisco Albertino | Florentino | Cum Priuilegio. | [*Colophon*:] Imp*r*essu*m* Lugd.⁹ p Ioan. mario*s* su*m*ptib⁹ & expe*n*sis Romani morin bi- | bliophile eiusde*m* ciuitatis. a*n*no dni M.D.XX. die vero. xxviii, martii. | 667

4to, title 1 l. + sixty leaves numbered, repeating 56; on the verso of the last leaf two wood-cuts.

ALBERTINIS. Opusculu*m* de Mirabilibus novæ et veteris Urbis Romæ. *Bononiæ*, 1520. 4to. 668

Title quoted from the Bibliotheca Heberiana, Part vi., No. 128.

ALBERTO. Carta Pastoral que el Illust° S°r D. Fray Joseph Antonio de San Alberto, arzobispo de la Plata, dirige à todos Josque en el pasado concurso han sido nombrados y elegidos para curas. *Buenos Ayres*, 1791. 4to. 669

ALBERTO. Coleccion de Instrucciones Pastorales. Por Jos. Antonio de San Alberto Arzobispo de la Plata en América. *Madrid*, 1786. 2 vols., 4to. 670

ALBERTUS. Habes in hac pagina. Amice le, | ctori Alberti Magni | Germani principis philosophi. | De natura locoru*m*. Librum mira | eruditio*ne* & singulari fruge re, | pertu*m*, & iam primu*m*, summa diligétia reuisum, in lucem | æditu*m*, qué legis dilige*n*, | tius, si uel Cosmogra, | phia uel Phisica p.fecisse te uo- | lueris. | [*Colophon*:] Excusum Viennæ Austriæ. Mens. Mar. M.D. XIIII. | Opera Hieronymi Victoris & Ioan. Sin, | grenii Socioru*m*, diligentiu*m* impressoru*m*. Impe*n*- | sis uero Leonhardi & Lvcæ Alantse | fratrum Ciuium Viennensiu*m*. | Imperante Diuo Maximiliano Cæsare Aug. | P. F. P. P. | 4to, 52 l. 671

Interesting to the American collector on account of a marginal note relating to Vespuccius, which seems to have been inserted with movable type, on the recto of the last leaf in signature e, after the book had been printed. *See* Harrisse, p. 138.

ALBERTUS. De Natura Locorum, edente Georg. Faunstelter (*sic*). *Ed.* II Argentorati, Math. Schurer, &c., 1514. 4to, pp. VI., 73, 389. 672

See Kloss Catalogue, No. 70.

ALBERTUS. Habes in hac pagina. Amice lector. | Al- | berti Magni Germani pri*n*cipis | philosophi, De natura locorum Li | brum mira eruditione, & singula | ri fruge refertu*m*, & iam primum | summa dilige*n*tia reuisum, in | luce*m* editum, quem leges dilige*n*tius, vel si Cosmo | graphia vel Physica | profecisse te vo- | lueris. | [*Colophon*:] Argentorati. Ex Aedibus Matthiæ Schutverij | Mense Ianuario, MD.XV. | Ductu Leonhardi, & Lucæ Alantse fratrum. | 4to, 43 l. 673

See Humboldt Examen Critique, Vol. I., p. 57.

ALBION: in Twelve Books. *Bath*, *Henry Gye*, 1822. 8vo, pp. 234. 674

A remarkable rhodomontine and ridiculous laudation of Great Britain, in which the old French War and the American Revolution are disposed of to the satisfaction of the writer if not to the reader.

ALBRO. The Life of *Rev.* Thomas Shepard. By John A. Albro. *Boston*, *Mass. Sab. School Society*, 1847. 18mo, pp. 324.

ALBUQUERQUE. Memorias Diarias de la Guerra del Brazil, por Discurso de nueve años, empeçando desde el de MDCXXX. Escritas por Duarte de Albuquerque Coello Marques del Basto. *Madrid*, *Diego Diaz de la Carrera*. 1654. 4to, 8 p. l.; Text, 287 l. 676

ALBUQUERQUE (Antonio de). Relaçao breve e verdadeira da memoravel victoria que ouvo o capitâo mor da capitania de Paraiba, Antonio de Albuquerque, dos rebeldes de Olanda, que sâo vinte naos de guerra, e vinte e sete lanchias pretenderâo occupar esta praça de S. Magestad, trazando nella para o effeito dous mil homens de guerra fora a gente do mar. *Lisboa*, *J. Rodriguez*, 1632. 4to. 677

Title as given by Ternaux, No. 537.

ALBUQUERQUE. Relatorio da repartiçao dos negocios estrangeiros apresentado á assembléa geral legislativa na primeira sessâo da decima primeira legislatura pelo resp. ministro A. C. de Sa e Albuquerque. *Rio de Janeiro*, 1861. 4to. 678

ALCAFARADO (Francisco). Rélation Historique de la Décou-

verte de l'Isle de Madère, traduite du Portugais. *Paris*, 1671. 12mo. 679

The Portuguese original is unknown. *See* Graesse, p. 60; Machado Bibl. Lusit., Vol. II., p. 96.

ALCAFARADO (Francisco). An | Historical | Relation | Of the First | Discovery | of the | Isle | of | Madera. | Written originally in Portugueze by Don Francis- | co Alcafarado (gentleman of the Bed-Chamber | to the Infant Don Henry younger | Son of John the First King of | Portugal;) | Who was one of the First Discoverers, thence transla- | ted into French, and now made English. | *London*, | *Printed for William Cademan at the sign of the* | *of the Popes-Head at the entrance into the* | *New Exchange in the Strand.* 1675. | 8vo, Title, pp. 37. 680

Priced, in the Nuggets, No. 57, £1 11s. 6d.

[ALCALA-GALIANO.] Relacion del viage hecho por las Goletas Sutil y Mexicana en 1792, para reconocer el Estrecho de Fuca: con una introduccion en que se da noticia de las expediciones executadas anterior mente por los Españoles en busca del paso del noroeste de la America. *Madrid*, *Imprenta Real*, 1802–1806. Sm. 4to, pp. 168 and 185; Appendix, pp. 120; Atlas of 17 Maps and Plates, sm. folio. 681

"The commander of this expedition was Don Dionysio Alcala-Galiana, said to be also the author of the work."—RICH. *See* Dicco. de Biog.; Barcelona, 1830.

ALCEDO (A.) Diccionario Geográfico-Histórico de las Indias occidentales ó América: es á saber: de los Reynos del Perú, Nueva España, Tierra Firme, Chile, y Nuevo Reyno de Granada. Con la Descripcion de sus Provincias, Naciones, Ciudades, Villas, Pueblos, Rios, Montes, Costas, Puertos, Islas, Arzobispados, Obispados, Audiencias, Vireynatos, Giobiernos, Corregimientos, y Fortalezas, frutos y producciones; con expresion de sus Descubridores, Conquistadores y Fundadores: Conventos y Religiones; ereccion de sus Catedrales y Obispos que ha habido en ellas; y noticia de los sucesos mas notables de varios lugares; incendios, torremotos, sitios, é invasiones que han experimentado; y hombres ilustres que han producido. Escrito por el Coronel D. Antonio de Alcedo, Capitan de Reales Guardias Espanolas. *Con Licencia en la Imprenta de Benito Cano. En Madrid Año de* MDCCLXXXVI. 4to, 5 vols; 2 p. l., xvi., 791; 2 p. l., 636; 2 p. l., 496; 2 p. l., 609; 2 p. l., 461; Resumen, 7; Vocabulario, 186 pp. 682

ALCEDO. The Geographical and Historical Dictionary of America and the West Indies. Containing an Entire Transla-

tion of the Spanish Work of Colonel Don Antonio de Alcedo, . . . with Large Additions and Compilations from Modern Voyages and Travels, and from Original and Authentic Information. By G. A. Thompson, Esq. In Five Volumes. *London*, *James Carpenter*, 1812–1815. 4to, xx., 574; 597; 512; 636; xvi., 462; Errata and Appendix, 105 pp. 683

"Thompson's edition, for its additions, etc., is infinitely superior to the original."—LOWNDES. Copies are sometimes found with an atlas of 19 large maps by Arrowsmith, but they are rare.

ALCEDO. Bibliotheca Americana. Catalogo de los autores que han escrito de la America en diferentes idiomas, y noticia de su vida y patria, años en que vivieron y obras que escrivieron. Compuesta por el mariscal de campo, D. Antonio de Alcedo, Governador de la plaza de la Coruña, año de 1807. 684

"Quarto, about 1000 pages MS. very neatly written, being the original work by the author of the Diccionario de America, and has not been printed."—RICH. Now in the possession of John Carter Brown, Esq., of Providence.

ALCEDO Y HERRERA. Aviso Historico, Politico, Geographico con las Noticias del Peru, Tierra Firme, Chile, y Nuevo Reyno de Granada, en la relacion de los successos de 205 años, por la chronologia de los adelantados, etc., desde el año 1535, hasta el de 1740. Y razon de toda lo Obrado por los Ingleses en aquellos reynos por las costas de los dos mares del norte y del sur, desde el año de 1567, hasta el de 1739. Por D. Dionisio de Alcedo y Herrera. *Madrid*, 1740. Sm. 4to. M. 685

ALCEDO Y HERRERA. Compendio Historico de la Provincia, Partidos, Ciudades, Astilleros, Rios y Puerto de Guayaquil en las Costas de la Mar del Sur. Dedicado al Rey Nuestro Señor en su Real, y Supremo Consejo de las Indias, Por Don Dionysio de Alsedo y Herrera, Presidente, que fue de la Real Audencia de Quito, Governador, y Capitan General de las Provincias de su Distrito. Con Licencia. En *Madrid*, Por Manuel Fernandez . . . Año de M.DCC. 4to, 16 p. l., Text, 99 pp. Plan of Guayaquil. 686

ALCEDO. Memorial informativo del consulado de la Ciudad de los Reyes y la junta general del comercio de las provincias del Peru, sobre diferentes puntos tocantes al estado de la real hazienda y del comercio, etc. Por D. Dionysio de Alsedo y Herrera [Lima?] 1726. Folio, pp. 148. 687

The author of the three preceding works was the father of the author of the "Diccionario."

ALCOCK (T. St. L.) Observations on the Poor Relief Bill for Ireland, and its bearing on . . . emigration . . *and* the British North American Colonies. By T. St. Leger Alcock. *London*, 1847. pp. 30. s. 688

ALCON. Diario de la expedicion del Mariscal de Campo D. Juan Ramirez sobre las Provincias interiores de la Paz, Puno, Arequipa y Cuzco. Por Juan José Alcon. *Lima*, 1815. 4to.

ALCOTT. Hospital Sketches. By Louisa M. Alcott. *Boston*, *James Redpath*, 1863. 8vo, pp. 102. 690

ALCOTT. On Picket Duty, and Other Tales. By Louisa M. Alcott. *Boston*, 1864. 16mo. 691

Relates to the Rebellion.

ALDÁMA. Arte de la Lengua Mexicana, dispuesto por D. Joseph Augustin de Aldáma y Guevára, Presbytero de el Arzobispado de Mexico. *Mexico, en la Imprenta nueva de la Biblioteca Mexicano*, 1754. Sm. 4to. 692

This rare volume is priced 75 fr. by Techener, 100 fr. by Nodier, and £3 3s. 0d. by Thorp, in 1843.

ALDEN (EBENEZER). The Early History of the Medical Profession in the County of Norfolk, Mass. An Address delivered before the Norfolk District Medical Society. By Ebenezer Alden. *Boston*, *May* 10, 1853. 8vo, pp. 48. 693

ALDEN. Historical Sketches of the Origin and Progress of the Massachusetts Medical Society. By Ebenezer Alden, M.D., Fellow of the Society. *Boston*, 1838. 8vo. 694

ALDEN. Memoir of Bartholomew Brown, Esquire, read at a Meeting of the New England Historic-Genealogical Society, February 5, 1862, by Ebenezer Alden, M.D. 1862. 8vo, pp. 8.

ALDEN (E. K.) Memorial of Albert Drake, containing a Funeral Address and Discourse by Rev. Edward K. Alden. *Boston*, *Wright & Potter*, 1865. 12mo, pp. 52. Portrait. 696

ALDEN (John). Lines upon the Death of John Alden, Esq., who died Sept. 12, 1687. *Broadside.* ——, *Reprinted*, 1806. M.

ALDEN (Joseph). The Example of Washington. By Joseph Alden. *New York*, *M. W. Dodd*, 1856, &c. 18mo. 698

ALDEN. The Old Revolutionary Soldier. By Joseph Alden. *New York*, *Gates.* 18mo. 699

ALDEN. The Science of Government in Connection with American Institutions. By Joseph Alden, D.D., LL.D. *New York*, 1866. 12mo, pp. 248. 700

ALDEN (Timothy). An Account of Sundry Missions performed among the Senecas and Munsees; in a Series of Letters, with an Appendix. By Rev. Timothy Alden. *New York*, *printed by J. Seymour*, 1827. 18mo, pp. 180. N. 701

ALDEN. An Account of the Several Religious Societies in Portsmouth, N. H., and of the Ministers of each, from their first establishment to the 1st of January, 1805. By Rev. Timothy Alden, Jun. *Boston*, 1808. 8vo, pp. 40. 702

Also included in the Mass. Hist. Coll., vol. x.

ALDEN. An Address to such as wish to avail themselves of the Advantages to be derived from a Removal into the Western Country. By Timothy Alden, Jr. *New York*, 1813. 12mo, pp. 4. 703

ALDEN. Affection for the House of God recommended. Sermon delivered at Yarmouth, Jan. 1, 1795; occasioned by the opening of a New Meeting-House. By Rev. Timothy Alden, A.M. *Boston*, 1795. 8vo, pp. 22. 704

ALDEN. A Collection of American Epitaphs and Inscriptions, with Occasional Notes. By Rev. Timothy Alden. Pentade I. *New York*, 1812–14. 5 vols., 18mo; pp. 292. 288, 288, 288, 288; List of Patrons, 4 l.; 5 Portraits. 705

The only extensive collection on the subject, and now scarce. The first edition of vol. i. was printed in 4 parts, in 1812; the second edition of vol. i., which usually accompanies the sets, is dated 1814.

ALDEN. The Glory of America. A Century Sermon Delivered at the South Church, in Portsmouth, New Hampshire, January, MDCCCI. Together with a number of Historical Notes, and an Appendix, containing an account of the Newspapers printed in the State. By Timothy Alden, Jr., A.M., Colleague Pastor with the Reverend Samuel Haven, D.D. Presented to the public, at the solicitation of a number of the hearers, to whom it is respectfully dedicated. *Portsmouth*, *William Treadwell & Co.*, 1801. 8vo, pp. 47.; Appendix, 5 pp. 706

ALDEN. Historical Notes, in reference to the Crawford County [Penn.] Sabbath School Union. 1826. 12mo. W. 707

ALDEN. A Sermon delivered at the South Church in Portsmouth [N. H.], on the v. January, MDCCC., Occasioned by the sudden and universally lamented Death of George Washington, Commander of the American Armies, and late President of the United States. By Timothy Alden, Jun., A.M., colleague pastor with the Rev. Samuel Haven, D.D. Published at the desire of a respectable number of the Hearers, to whom it is affectionately dedicated. *Portsmouth*, *New-Hampshire*, *Printed at the United States Oracle Office*, M.DCCC. 8vo, pp. 23. + Same. *Portsmouth*, *New-Hampshire*, *Printed at the United States Oracle Office in January*, *and Re-printed in February*, MDCCC., *by Charles Peirce.* 8vo, pp. 24. 708

ALDEN. A Valedictory Discourse, delivered at the South Church in Portsmouth, New Hampshire, Aug. 12, 1805. By Timothy Alden, Jr. *Portsmouth*, *W. & D. Treadwell*, 1805. 8vo, pp. 16. N. 709

ALDENBURGK. West-Indianische Reisze und Beschreibung der Belæg-und Eroberung der Statt S. Salvador in der Bahie von Todos os Sanctos inn dem Lande von Brasilia, Welches von anno 1623, bis ins 1626. Verzichtet worden. Durch Johann. Gregor. Aldenburgk. *Coburgk*, 1627. 4to. Engraved Title, 50 l. 710

ALDERSON (J.) An Essay on the Rhustoxicodendron, pubescent poison Oak or Sumach; with cases, shewing its efficacy in the cure of paralysis and other diseases of extreme debility. By John Alderson, M.D. *London*, *Johnson*, 1794. 8vo, pp. 34.

ALEGAMBE [P.] Bibliotheca Scriptorum Societatis Jesu, post excusum anno 1608, catalogum ad 1642. Cura Ph. Alegambe. | *Antverpiæ*, 1643. Folio. + Another Edition. *Romæ*, M.DC.LXXVI. Folio. 712

Contains an extensive bibliography of the early Jesuit writers.

ALEGAMBE [P.] Mortes illustres et gesta eorum de societate Jesû qui in odium fidei, pietatis, aut cujuscunque virtutis, occasione missionum sacramentorum administratorum, fidei aut virtutis propugnatæ; ab Etnicis, hæreticis, vel aliis, veneno, igne, ferro, aut morte alia necati, ærumnisve confecti sunt. Auctore Philippo Alegambe. Extremos aliquot annos, mortesque illustres usque ad annum 1655, adjecit Joannes Nadasi. *Romæ*, 1667. Folio. 713

This rare book contains much curious and interesting matter respecting the missionaries of Canada and other parts of America. *See* Charlevoix.

Alegre. Historia de la Compañia de Jesus en Nueva-España, al tiempo de su espulsion. Por Francisco Javier Alegre. Publicala Carlos Maria de Bustamante. *México*, 1841–42. c. 714

Aleman [M.] Ortografia Castellana. Por Mateo Aleman. *Mexico, typis Hieronymi Balbi*, 1609. 4to, 83 l., and Portrait. 715

Priced, Thorpe, 1843, £3, 3s., od. An early specimen of Mexican printing. Brunet gives the date 1606, which is an error.

Alembert. Flanerie Parisienne aux Etats-Unis. Par Alfred D'Alembert. *Paris, Libraire Théatrale*, 1856. 16mo, pp. 278.

Alemparte. Breve exposicion que hace Jose Antonio Alemparte de algunos excesos y abusos cometidos por El Ministro de Justicia Don Mariano Egana. *Santiago de Chile*, 1837. 8vo.

Aleutian Abecedarium. [*St. Petersburg*, 1839?] 718

The Indian language of the Aleutian Islands in Russian America.

Alexander. Life of Alexander Alexander. Written by Himself. *London*, 1830. 2 vols., 12mo. 719

Includes campaigns in South America during the Revolutionary War.

Alexander (Archibald). Biographical Sketches of the Founder and Principal Alumni of the Log College, together with an account of the revivals of religion under their ministry. Collected and edited by A. Alexander, D.D. *Princeton*, 1845. 12mo, pp. 369.+Same. *Philadelphia*, 1851. 12mo, pp. 12. 720

Alexander. Discourse occasioned by the Burning of the Theatre in Richmond (Va.), delivered in Philadelphia, January 8, 1812. By Archibald Alexander. With the Proceedings of the University of Pennsylvania. *Philadelphia*, 1812. 8vo. N.

Alexander (A.) An Address to the Inhabitants of Charleston, South Carolina. *Philadelphia, Kimber, Conrad & Co.*, 1805. 8vo. 722

Alexander (C.) A Sermon occasioned by the Death of His Excellency, George Washington, Lieutenant General of the American Army, and late President of the United States, who departed this life December 14, 1799, æt. 68. Published by desire. By Caleb Alexander, A.M., Pastor of the Church in Meriden, [Mass.] *Boston*, 1800. 8vo, pp. 23. 723

Alexander (C. A.) The Fall of Aztalan; and other Poems. By Charles A. Alexander. *Washington*, 1839. Rl. 8vo.

Relates to the destruction of an early Mexican city.

Alexander (G. W.) Letter addressed to Edward Smith, of Sheffield, on the introduction of Slave-grown Sugar into the British Market. By G. W. Alexander. *London*, 1844. Folio.

Alexander. Letters on the Slave Trade, Slavery, and Emancipation, with a reply to objections made to the Liberation of the Slaves in the Spanish Colonies; addressed to the Friends on the Continent of Europe, during a visit to Spain and Portugal. By George William Alexander. *London, Charles Gilpin*, 1842. Fcap 8vo. 726

Alexander. Remarks on the Theatre, and on the late Fire at Richmond, in Virginia. By G. W. Alexander. *York, Thomas Wilson & Son*, 1812. 8vo. 727

Alexander. Liberté immédiate et absolue, ou Esclavage. Observations sur le Rapport de M. le duc de Broglie, Président de la Commission instituée par décision Royale du 26 Mai 1840, pour l'examen des questions relatives à l'Esclavage et à la Constitution politique des colonies Françaises; adressées a tous les Français Amis de la Liberté et de l'humanité. Par Geo. W. Alexander et John Scoble, de Londres. *Paris, Librairie de Firmin Didot Frères*, 1844. 8vo. 728

Alexander. The Complaint of J. Alexander and W. Smith, to the Committee of the Colony of New York. *New York, J. P. Zenger*, 1735. Folio, pp. 19. s. 729

Alexander. The Report of the Committee of His Majesty's Council, appointed to make inquiry touching a Letter found in the house of Mr. Alexander, in New York, February 1, 1733–4. With other Papers relating to the said Letter. *New York*, 1734. Folio. P. 730

Alexander. The Vindication of James Alexander, one of His Majesty's Council, and of W. Smith, from the matters charged and suggested against them in two Pamphlets lately published . . . . With Supplement containing Case of W. Trusdell *vs.* F. Harrison, for illegal imprisonment. *New York, J. P. Zenger*, 1733. Folio, pp. 20. s. 731

Alexander. New York, March 24, 1735–6. Folio broadside. s. 732

Signed James Alexander. In it he declares he had not consented to George Clarke's doing any act of Government whatsoever. Probably from Zenger's Press.

Alexander (J. E.) L'Acadie; or, Seven Years' Explorations in British America. By Sir James Edward Alexander. *London, Colburn*, 1849. Post 8vo, 2 vols., pp. 684.+Re-issued, *London*, 1853. Post 8vo, 2 vols. 733

Alexander. Salmon-Fishing in Canada. By a Resident Edited by Colonel Sir James Edward Alexander. With Illustrations. *London, Longman*, 1860. Post 8vo, pp. xvi., 350. 734

Alexander. Transatlantic Sketches, comprising Visits to the most interesting Scenes in North and South America and the West Indies; with Notes on Negro Slavery and Canadian Emigration. By Capt. J. E. Alexander. *London, R. Bentley*, 1833. 8vo, 2 vols. Plates by Heath, and Maps.+Same Reprinted, *Philadelphia, Kay & Biddle*, 1833. 8vo, pp. 378. 735

Alexander (J. H.) Index to the Calendar of Maryland State Papers. By John Henry Alexander. *Baltimore*, 1861. 8vo.

Alexander. International Coinage for Great Britain and the United States. By J. H. Alexander. *Baltimore* [*Privately printed*], 1855. 12mo. 737

Alexander (J. W.) The Life of Archibald Alexander, D.D., first Professor in the Theological Seminary at Princeton, N. J. By James W. Alexander, D.D. *New York*, 1854. 8vo. 738

Alexander (Sir W.) An Encouragement to Colonies. By Sir William Alexander, Knight. *London, Printed by William Stanley*, 1624. Sm. 4to, 3 p. l., pp. 47. Map and Portrait. 739

"A very curious work, containing an account of the first settling of the northern parts of America, particularly of the French in Canada. The map contains the coast from Cape Cod to Labrador. Sir William Alexander first settled and gave name to Nova Scotia. A copy of this tract was sold a few years ago for four guineas."—Rich. The map is reproduced in Purchas, Vol. iv. Re-issued in 1630, with the following title:

Alexander (Sir William.) The | Mapp and | Description of | New-England; | Together with | A Discourse of Plantation, and | Colonies: | Also, | A Relation of the nature of the Climate, | and how it agrees with our owne Country | England. | How neere it lyes to New-found-Land, Virginia, | Noua Francia, Canada, and

other Parts of | the West-Indies. | Written by | S^r. William Alexander, Knight. | *London*, | *Printed for Nathaniel Butter.* | *An. Dom.* 1630. | Sm. 4to, Title, 1 l., pp. 47, and Map. 740

Priced, in the Nuggets, No. 59, £21.

Alexander. Copies and Translations of the Royal Charters (confirmed in parliament) by which the Territories of Nova Scotia and Canada, with the Islands and Seas adjacent, and Dignities were granted in 1621, 1625 and 1628, to the Rt. Hon. Sir William Alexander, afterwards Earl of Stirling, &c. *London*, 1831. Folio. N. 741

Title; Prefatory observations, 3 pp. Charter of Nova Scotia, 34 pp. Translation of the Novodamus of Nova Scotia, 1625, 18 pp. Charter of Canada, 6 pp. Charter of the Lordship of Canada, 6 pp.

[Alexander (W.)] Collectitia; or, Pieces, Religious, Moral, and Miscellaneous, adapted to the Society of Friends. Volume First [all published]. *York, W. Alexander & Son*, 1824. 8vo. 742

Includes Fowler's Voyage to New England, and several other articles on American subjects.

Alexander. Dominion of the Prince of Peace; with its application to the Slave Trade and Slavery. By William Alexander. *York*, 1840. 8vo. 743

Alexander (W.) Elements of Discord in Secessia. By William Alexander, Esq., of Texas. *New York, L. P. S., No.* 14. 8vo. 744

Alexander VI. A printed broadside in Gothic type, being a contemporary publication of the celebrated Bull of 1493, dividing the World between the Portuguese and the Spaniards, giving to the former the East Indies, and to the latter America or the West Indies. 1493. Folio. 745

The above broadside sold at Puttick and Simpson's in May, 1854, for £4 8s. od. This description is taken from their catalogue. The famous bull referred to bears the following title: "Exemplar Bullo sive donationis authoritate cujus Episcopus Romanus Alexander ejus nominis Sextus concessit et donavit Ferdinando et Elizabetho Regi et Regino Castello Legionis &c. et suis successoribus Regiones et Insulas novi orbis &c." In Latin and English in Purchas' Pilgrim, Vol. I., B. 2, Ch. 1, p. 14. Purchas follows up his translation of this most arrogant and blasphemous bull of Alexander with an invective, in his best manner, most spirited and able, forcibly depicting the cruel atrocities perpetrated under this instrument, saying that "had not the piety and pity of some eye-witnesses excited the royal provision of the Catholic Kings in this case, even *Hell* itself had been loosed on earth, under the pretext of Heaven, and the prince of *darkness*, had effected his blackest and cruelest designs in habit of an angel of *light*. *Tantum religio poterat suadere malorum*, may we say of this religious, irreligious Bull."

Alexandria. Address to the Inhabitants of Alexandria, and other Seaports in the United States, from a Proprietor of Lands on the Scioto. 1790. 12mo. 746

Alexandria Tammany Society. Long Talk at the First Anniversary Meeting. *Alexandria*, 1804. 8vo. 747

Report from the Joint Committee on the Conduct of the War, on the "Military Administration in the City of Alexandria," and whether punishments of "a cruel and unusual character" are not inflicted without authority of law, in a place known as "the Slave Pen," in that city. *Senate, Report of Committee, No.* 54, 38*th Congress*, 1864. 748

Letter from the Mayor of Alexandria . . (E. C. Dick), inclosing sundry Resolutions of the Citizens of . . Alexandria, expressive of their disapprobation of a motion now depending before the House [of Representatives of the United States of America] to recede to the States of Virginia and Maryland . . parts of the . . District [of Columbia], etc. *Washington*, 1804. 8vo. 749

Alexo de Orrio. Solucion | del gran problema | acerca de la poblacion | de las Americas, | en que sobre el fundamento de los Libros | Santos se descubre facil camino á | la transmigracion de | los Hombres del uno al otro Continente; y como pudieron | pasar al Nuevo Mundo, no solamente las Bestias de servicio, | sino tambien las Fieras, y nocivas. | Y con esta ocasion se satisface | plenamente al delirio de los Pre-Adamitas, apoyado con | esta dificil objecion hasta ahora no bien desatada. | Por el P. Francisco Xavier Alexo | de Orrio, de la Sagrada Compañia de Jesus. | Sacala a luz | Don Francisco Carmona, Godoy, | y Bucareli, Corregidor, Juez de Minas de la Ciudad de | Nuestra Señora de los Zacatecas: Quien la dedica | a el M. Il^{tre}. Sr. Coronèl de los Reales Exercitos | Don Pedro Montesinos de Lara, | Gobernado, que hà sido de la Puebla de los Angeles, | y actual Capitàn General, Gobernador del Nuevo Reyno | de la Galicia, y Presidente de la Real Audiencia, que | reside en la Ciudad de Guadalaxara. | *En Mexico: En la Imprenta Real del Superior Gobierno, y del* | *Nuevo Rezado, de los Herederos de Doña Maria de Ribera*; | *Calle de San Bernardo. Año de* 1763. | 4to, 22 p. l., and 72 pp. 750

Alfieri (V.) L'America Libera: Odi di Vittorio Alfieri da Asti. *** *Dalla tip. di Kehl*, 1784. 8vo, pp. 44. 751

Alfonso. Memorias de un Matancero. Apuntes para la

Historia de la Isla de Cuba, con relacion a la ciudad de San Cárlos y San Severino de Matanzas, principiados en 1838 y continuados para ofrecer un presente al Bazar Matancero. Por Pedro Antonio Alfonso. *Matanzas*, 1854. 8vo, pp. 242. Map.

Algarotte (Count). Letters to Lord Harvey on the following subjects, namely: War between the Russians and Turks; Remarks on the Baltic and Caspian Seas; Dissertation on the Seven Kings of Rome and another on the Empire of *Peruvian Incas*. By the Count Algarotte. Translated into English. *Glasgow, R. Urie*, 1770. 12mo, pp. 232. 753

Alger (H.) The Church Record; being a Concise Sketch of the Origin and History of the West Church in Marlborough. By Rev. Horatio Alger. *Boston*, 1850. 12mo, pp. 22. 754

Alger (W. R.) A Brief Tribute to the Life and Character of Dr. Kane. By Rev. William R. Alger. *Boston*, 1857. 12mo, pp. 11. 755

Alger. The Charities of Boston; or, Twenty Years at the Warren-street Chapel. An Address delivered Jan. 27, 1856. By Rev. William R. Alger. *Boston*, 1856. 8vo, pp. 28. 756

Alger. The Genius and Posture of America: An Oration, delivered before the Citizens of Boston, July 4th, 1857. By William Rounseville Alger. With Preface and Appendix. *Boston*, 1857. 8vo, pp. 60.+*Boston, J. E. Farwell & Co.*, 1864. 8vo, pp. 53. s. 757

Alger. Inferences from the Pestilence and the Fast. A Discourse . . . . Roxbury, Mass. By Rev. William R. Alger. *Boston*, 1849. 8vo. 758

Alger. Lessons for Mankind, from the Life and Death of Humboldt. A Discourse . . . . By Rev. William R. Alger. *Cambridge*, 1859. 12mo, pp. 26. 759

Alger. Our Civil War, as seen from the Pulpit. A Sermon preached in Bulfinch St. Church, Boston, April 28, 1861. By William R. Alger. *Boston, Walker, Wise & Co.*, 1861. 8vo, pp. 20. 760

Alger. Public Morals; or the True Glory of a State. A Discourse delivered before the Legislative Departments of Massachusetts, at the Annual Election, January 1, 1862. By W. R. Alger. *Boston, William White*, 1862. 8vo, pp. 55. 761

Algiers. Information relative to the Commencement of War by the Dey of Algiers against the United States. February 9, 1808. Cong. Doc. 8vo. 762

The Algerine Spy in Pennsylvania; or, Letters written by a Native of Algiers on the Affairs of the United States in America, from the close of the year 1783 to the meeting of the convention. *Philadelphia*, 1787. 12mo, pp. 129. P. 763

Information that the late Differences between the United States and the Dey of Algiers have been Amicably Adjusted. February 15, 1808. Cong. Doc. 8vo. 764

A short Account of Algiers and of its several Wars, etc.; with a Concise View of the Origin of the Rupture between Algiers and the United States. Also an Appendix containing letters from Penrose, McShane, and other American Captives. Second edition. *Philadelphia*, 1794. 8vo, pp. 46. Map. 765

Short History of Algiers, with the Origin of the Rupture with the United States. *New York*, 1805. 18mo. 766

Algora. Arte y Diccionario de la Lengua Tarasca, por Illmo. D. Fr. Juan Algora. 767

"Mentioned by Antonio and quoted by Sousa."—Ludewig, p. 183.

Ali Bey. Extracts from a Journal of Travels in North America, consisting of an account of Boston and its vicinity. *Boston*, 1818. 12mo. 768

Alida. *See* [Sedgwick (Mrs. T.)]

Alison (A.) New Reformation in Europe and America. By Alexander Alison. *London, G. H. Nichols*, 1861. 8vo. 769

Alison (A.) Essays, Political, Historical and Miscellaneous. By Archibald Alison. *Edinburgh*. 3 vols., 8vo. Frequently reprinted. 770

Includes Essays on Negro Emancipation, Colonial Government and the West-India Question, Ships, Colonies and Commerce, and Humboldt.

Alison (F.) Peace and Union Recommended. Two Sermons Preached before the Synods of New York and Philadelphia, May 24 and 25, 1758. By Rev. F. Alison and Rev. D. Bosthwick. *Philadelphia, Printed by W. Dunlap*, 1758. 12mo. 771

Alison (W. P.) Letter to Sir John M'Neil, on Highland

Destitution, and the Adequacy . . . of Emigration as a Remedy. By W. P. Alison. *Edinburgh*, 1851. 8vo, pp. 62. s. 772

All Round the World; an Illustrated Record of Voyages, Travels and Adventures, Edited by W. H. Ainsworth. Vol. I., 1861;—Vol. III., April, 1862. 773

All the Memorials of the Courts of Great Britain and France since the Peace of Aix la Chapelle, relative to the Limits of the Territories of both crowns in North America, and the right to the Neutral Islands in the West Indies. To which are annexed Two maps, one delineating the Right of Great Britain and the other the Claim of France. The French Memorials are Translated and the whole is printed in English. *London*, 1756. 4to.

See Monthly Review, XIV., p. 264.

All the Treaties between the United States and Great Britain, from the Treaty of Paris, 1783, to the Treaty of Ghent, 1814. *Boston*, 1815. 8vo, pp. 48. 775

Allaire. Rapport sur les Voyages pour la Naturalisation des Arbres Forestiers des Etats Unis, fait à la Société d'Agriculture. Par M. M. Allaire, Bosc, etc. *Paris*, 1809. 8vo. 776

Allan. Memorial of John Allan. *New York*, 1864. *See* [Duyckinck (E. A.)]

Alleghany. By-Laws, and System of Education, established at Alleghany College, Meadville, Pa. *Meadville*, 1834. 12mo, pp. 15.+Catalogue of the Library. *Meadville*, 1823. 8vo.+Catalogue of the Officers and Students. *Meadville, Pa.*, 1846, &c. 8vo. 777

Alleghany Portage Railroad. Superintendent's Report. *Harrisburgh*, 1854. 8vo. 778

Alleghany Railroad and Coal Company. Report. *Philadelphia*, 1854, &c. 8vo. 779

Alleghany Magazine; or Repository of Useful Knowledge. Conducted by Timothy Alden, Vol. I. *Meadville*, 1816. 8vo.

The Allegations made against Proprietary Governments. *See* [Penn (William)].

Allen. Ten Years in Oregon. Travels and Adventures of

Doctor E. White and Lady, West of the Rocky Mountains, with Incidents of Two Sea Voyages via Sandwich Islands around Cape Horn, containing also a brief History of the Missions and Settlement of the Country, Origin of the Provisional Government, Number and Customs of the Indians, Incidents witnessed whilst traversing and residing in the Territory, Description of the Soil, Production and Climate. Compiled by Miss A. J. Allen. *Ithaca, N. Y., Andrus, Gauntlett & Co.* 1850. 12mo, pp. 430. 781

Allen (A.) The Claim and Answer; with the subsequent Proceedings in the Case of Andrew Allen, Esq., against the United States. *Philadelphia*, 1799. 4to, pp. 50. M. 782

Allen (B.) The Battle of Valparaiso. A Poem. By B. Allen, Jr. *New York*, 1814. 12mo. 783

Allen (B. F.) An Oration pronounced before the Students of Brown University, in the College Chapel, July 4, 1817, in Commemoration of the Anniversary of American Independence. By Benjamin F. Allen. *Providence, Jones & Wheeler*, 1817. 8vo, pp. 16. 784

Allen (B.) Sketch of the Eastern Coast of Central America. Compiled from Notes of Captain Richard Owen and the Officers of H. M. S. Thunder and Schooner Lark. By Bird Allen. *London*, 1841. 8vo. c. 785

Allen (C.) Speech of Hon. Charles Allen in the H. of R. on the Mexican Indemnity Bill, Jan. 23, 1852. *Washington*, 1852. 8vo. 786

Allen. Speech of Hon. Charles Allen at Worcester, Oct. 5, 1850. [On the Fugitive Slave Law.] *Worcester* [n. d.] 8vo, pp. 8. 787

Allen (D. H.) The Life and Services of Rev. Lyman Beecher, D.D., as President and Professor of Theology in Lane Seminary. A Commemorative Discourse, delivered at the Anniversary, May 7, 1863. By Rev. D. Howe Allen, D.D., Professor of Systematic Theology. *Cincinnati, Johnson, Stephens & Co.*, 1864. 8vo, pp. 30, 5. 788

Allen (E.) Reprint of a Short Biography of Colonel Ebene-

zer Allen, known in the New Hampshire Grants, as Captain or Major, A.D. 1777, before and after. Also, short Biographies of Lieutenant Samuel Allen and Dr. Jacob Roebeck. In addition, some reminiscences of Lake Champlain, reprinted in part. *Plattsburgh, J. W. Tuttle*, 1852. 8vo, pp. 32. s. 789

Title from Hall's Bibl. of Vermont, p. 12.

Allen (E. G.) [*Sale*] Catalogue of Books relating to America. *London*, 1857. 8vo, pp. 28. + Old Books relating to America prior to 1800. *London*, 1858–9. + Since 1800: 1858–9, &c. 790

Allen (Ethan). An Animadversory Address to the Inhabitants of the State of Vermont, with Remarks on a Proclamation, under the hand of his Excellency George Clinton, Esq., Governor of the State of New York. By Ethan Allen. *Hartford, Printed by Watson & Goodwin*, M.DCC.LXXVIII. 8vo, pp. 24. 791

Allen. A Brief Narrative of the Proceedings of the Government of New York, relative to their obtaining the Jurisdiction of that large District of Land to the Westward from Connecticut River, which, antecedent thereto, had been patented by his Majesty's Governor and Council of the Government of New Hampshire. And also of the monopolizing Conduct of the Government of New York, in their subsequently patenting Part of the same Land, and oppressing the Grantees and Settlers under New Hampshire. Together with Arguments demonstrating that the Property of those Lands was conveyed from the Crown to the New-Hampshire Grantees, by Virtue of their respective Charters. With Remarks on a Pamphlet entitled, "A State of the Right of the Colony of New York," &c., and on the Narrative of the Proceedings subsequent to the Royal Adjudication, concerning the Lands to the Westward of Connecticut River, lately usurp'd by New Hampshire. Intended as an Appendix to the General Assembly's State of the Right of the Colony of New York (with Respect to it's Eastern Boundary on Connecticut River, so far as concerns the late Encroachments under the Government of New Hampshire), Published at their Session, 1773. By Ethan Allen. Bennington, 23d September, 1774. *Hartford, Printed by Eben Watson, near the Great Bridge.* 8vo, pp. 211. 792

Referred to in Ira Allen's Hist. Vt., 52; also in a letter of E. Allen in Slade's Vt. State Papers, at p. 93.

Allen. A Narrative of Colonel Ethan Allen's Captivity, From the Time of his being taken by the British, near Montreal, on the 25th Day of September, in the Year 1775, to the Time of his Exchange on the 6th day of May, 1778, Containing, His Voyages and Travels, With the most remarkable Occurrences respecting himself, and many other Continental Prisoners of different Ranks and Characters, which fell under his Observation, in the Course of the same; particularly the Destruction of the Prisoners at New York, by General Sir William Howe, in the Years 1776 and 1777. Interspersed with some Political Observations. Written by Himself, and now Published for the Information of the Curious of all Nations. [Motto.] Price Ten Paper Dollars. *Philadelphia, Printed and Sold by Robert Bell, In Third Street*, M.DCC.LXXIX. 8vo, Title, 1 l., pp. 46. In double columns. 793

This is the first edition. Sold March, 1866, for $56. It was reprinted with the same title, but in single columns, *Philadelphia, Printed; Boston, Reprinted by Draper and Folsom* [1779]. 8vo, pp. 40. M. + Another edition. Same title. *Philadelphia, Printed for and sold by William Mentz, in Cherry Alley*, 1779. 12mo, pp. 64. N. The editor of the Bibliography of Vermont calls this the first edition. I think it is the third.

Allen. [Same Title.] *Newbury, Printed by John Mycall, for Nathaniel Coverly, of Boston, and Sold at his Shop, between Seven-Star Lane and the Sign of the Lamb*, 1780. 8vo, pp. 80. 794

Allen. [Same Title.] *Norwich, Printed by John Trumbull*, 1780. 12mo, pp. 47. 795

It was also reprinted in the appendix to the second volume of "Particulars of the Capture of the ship Olive Branch." *See* Allen, Ira.

Allen. [Same Title.] To which are now Added a considerable number of Explanatory and Occasional Notes, together with an Index of Reference to the most remarkable Occurrences in the Narrative. *Walpole, N. H., Thomas and Thomas*, 1807. 12mo, pp. 158; Subscribers, 1 l. + Another Edition. *Albany, Published by Pratt & Clark*, 1814. 12mo, pp. 144. + Another, erroneously called the "Third Edition." *Burlington, Vt., Chauncey Goodrich*, 1838. 796

Allen. Ethan Allen's Captivity, being a Narrative of Col. Ethan Allen, containing his voyages, travels, etc., Interspersed with Political Observations. Written by Himself. [Edited by F. W. E.] *Boston*, 1845. 12mo, pp. 126. 797

This title is copied from Stevens's Catalogue of American Books in the British Museum.

Allen. A Narrative of Col. Ethan Allen's Captivity. Written by Himself. Fourth Edition, with Notes. *Burlington, Chauncey Goodrich*, 1846. 12mo, pp. 120. 798

Allen. Ethan Allen's Narrative of the Capture of Ticonderoga, and of His Captivity and Treatment by the British. Written by Himself. Fifth Edition, with Notes. *Burlington, C. Goodrich & S. B. Nichols*, 1849. 8vo, pp. 50. 799

Allen. A Narrative of the Captivity of Colonel Ethan Allen, from the time he was taken by the British, near Montreal, September 25th, 1775, to the time of his exchange, May 6th, 1778. 8vo. *Dayton*, 1849. 800

[Allen (E.)] The Present State of the Controversy between the States of New-York and New-Hampshire on the one part, and the State of Vermont on the other. *Printed by Hudson & Goodwin*, M.DCC.LXXXII. 8vo, pp. 16. 801

"Dated, 'State of Vermont, January 17, 1782,' and although it appeared anonymously, is accredited with certainty to Ethan Allen."—Hall's Bib. of Vt.

Allen. Reason the only Oracle of Man, or a Compendious System of Natural Religion. Alternately Adorned with Confutations of a variety of Doctrines incompatible to it; Deduced from the most exalted Ideas which we are able to form of the Divine and Human Characters, and from the Universe in General. By Ethan Allen, Esq. *Bennington, State of Vermont, Printed by Haswell and Russell*, M,DCC,LXXXIV. 4to, pp. 477. 802

This singular book is the rarest of Allen's publications, and is remarkable as being the first work published in America in direct opposition to the Christian religion. An abridgment of it was published in New York in 1836, with the following title: Reason, the only Oracle of Man; or a Compendious System of Natural Religion. By Col. Ethan Allen. *Published by G. W. and A. I. Matsell, 94 Chatham St., New York*, 1836. 12mo, pp. 106, including table of contents and index. "The first edition of this work was printed by Mr. Haswell of Bennington, Vt. Not long after its publication, a part of the edition, comprising the entire of several signatures, was accidentally consumed by fire: whether Mr. Haswell deemed this fire a judgment upon him for having printed the work or not, is unknown—but, the fact is, he soon after committed the remainder of the edition to the flames, and joined the Methodist Connection; so that but few copies were circulated."—Introduction to Matsell's edition, p. 1.

Allen. A Vindication of the Opposition of the Inhabitants of Vermont to the Government of New York, and of their right to form an Independent State, humbly submitted to the consideration of the Impartial World. By Ethan Allen. *Printed by Alden Spooner*, 1779. 8vo, pp. 172. c. 803

"This work was published in obedience to a resolve of the Governor and Council of Vermont, passed August 23d, 1779."—Hall.

Allen. Report of the Committee under the act providing for the erection of a Monument over the grave of Ethan Allen. Printed by order of the Senate, 1858. *Montpelier* [n. d.] 8vo, pp. 7. 804

Allen. Ethan Allen; or, the King's Men, an Historical Novel. By Melville. *New York*, 1836. 8vo. 805

Allen and Fay. A Concise Refutation of the claims of New-Hampshire and Massachusetts Bay to the Territory of Vermont; with occasional Remarks on the long disputed Claim of New York to the same. Written by Ethan Allen and Jonas Fay, Esq'rs. And published by order of the Governor and Council of Vermont. Bennington, the first day of January, 1780. Joseph Fay, Sec'ry. *Hartford, Printed by Hudson & Goodwin.* 8vo, pp. 29. 806

"Published by order of the Governor and Council of Vermont, and exceedingly rare."—Hall. Notices of Allen in the "Remembrancer," Vol. II., p. 51, 108, 129; IV., p. 18; VI., p. 50-53.

Allen (Rev. Ethan). Clergy in Maryland, of the Protestant Episcopal Church since the Independence of 1783. By Rev. Ethan Allen, D.D. *Baltimore, James S. Waters*, 1860. 8vo, pp. 106. 807

Allen. A Discourse prepared for the National Fast Day, June 1st, 1865, on Account of the Murder of our late President, and Preached at St. Thomas's Church, Homestead, Baltimore County, Md. By Ethan Allen, Rector. Published at the request of its hearers. *Baltimore, Wm. K. Boyle*, 1865. 12mo, pp. 12. 808

Allen. Historical Notices of St. Ann's Parish in Ann-Arundel County, Maryland, extending from 1649 to 1857 .... By Rev. Ethan Allen. *Baltimore*, 1857. 12mo, pp. 131. 809

Allen. Maryland Toleration; or, Sketches of the Early History of Maryland, to the Year 1650. By the Rev. Ethan Allen. *Baltimore*, MDCCCLV. 8vo, pp. 64. 810

Allen. A Sermon preached in Baltimore, Thanksgiving Day, August 6, 1863. [On Civil Government.] By Ethan Allen. 12mo, pp. 11. 811

Allen. Who were the Early Settlers of Maryland? a Paper read before the Maryland Historical Society .... October 5th,

1865. By the Rev. Ethan Allen, D.D. *Baltimore*, 1866. 8vo, pp. 18. 812

[Allen (George)]. Address to the Freemen of Massachusetts. By a Freeman. *Worcester*, 1832. 8vo. 813

[Allen (Rev. George)]. Resistance to Slavery every Man's Duty. A Report on American Slavery, read to the Worcester Central Association ... [By Rev. George Allen.] *Boston*, 1847. 8vo, pp. 40. 814

Allen. Thoughts on "The Excitement," in Reply to a Letter to Hon. Edward Everett. (From the Ægis & Yeoman.) By Rev. George Allen. *Worcester*, 1833. 8vo. 815

Allen (H.) Monograph of the Bats of North America. By H. Allen, M.D. *Washington, Smithsonian Institution*, 1864. 8vo, pp. xxiii., 85. 816

Allen (Ira). Miscellaneous Remarks on the Proceedings of the State of New York against the State of Vermont, &c. By Ira Allen. *Hartford, Printed by Hannah Watson*, MDCCLXXVII. 8vo, pp. 15 to 20. 817

Allen. Miscellaneous Remarks, Vindicating the Rights of the people to Form a State, and in Answer to a Pamphlet published by the Convention of New York, dated October 2d, 1776. By Ira Allen. *Hartford, Printed by Hannah Watson*, 1777. 8vo. 818

"This title is not literal, but conjectural, embracing an account of the topics discussed in the pamphlet." Hall's Bibl. Vermont, Slade's Papers, &c.

Allen. The Natural and Political History of the State of Vermont, one of the United States of America. To which is added, An Appendix, containing Answers to Sundry Queries, addressed to the Author. By Ira Allen, Esquire, Major-General of the Militia in the State of Vermont. *London, Printed by J. W. Myers for W. West*, 1798. 8vo, pp. vii., 300. Map. 819

See M. R., XXIX., New Series, p. 260.

Allen. Particulars of the Capture of the Ship Olive Branch, laden with a Cargo of Arms, &c. the property of Major-General Ira Allen, destined for supplying the Militia of Vermont, and captured by His Britannic Majesty's Ship of War, Audacious: together with the Proceedings and Evidence before the High Court of Admiralty of Great Britain. Vol. I. By Ira Allen,

Esq., of Vermont, in the United States of America, the Claimant in this Cause. *London, Printed by J. W. Myers*, 1798. 8vo, pp. vi., 406. s. 820

Pages 1 to 368 of a second volume were printed and distributed without a title—the want of documents having then stopped the publication. Finally, another volume was published as a second, with the following title:

Allen. Particulars of the Capture of the Ship Olive Branch, laden with Arms, the Property of General Ira Allen, captured by the British, and an Account of his Imprisonment in France, and Persecutions by a Conspiracy of the Two Hemispheres: with an Appendix, proposing a Ship Canal from Lake Champlain to the River St. Lawrence; the Evacuation of Ticonderoga, and Events of the War in 1777 .. Truce in 1780, to the end of the War ..... and a Narrative of Colonel Ethan Allen's Captivity, from 1775 to 1778. By Ira Allen of Vermont, the Claimant in this Cause. Volume II. *Philadelphia, Printed for the Author*, 1805. 8vo, pp. xxx., 551. s. 821

This volume includes a resumé of the first, and in some respects may be considered a complete work.

Allen. Statement Applicable to the Case of the Olive Branch, which Has a Cargo of Cannon and Arms for the Vermont Militia, and Captured on its Passage from France to the United States, by an English Man-of-War, in 1796, which are for the Consideration of the Governments and Rulers of Great Britain, France, and the United States. By Ira Allen. *Philadelphia, July*, 1807. 8vo. 822

[Allen.] Twenty Thousand Muskets!!! Particulars of the Capture of the Ship Olive Branch, in November 1796, laden with Cannon, Muskets, &c., by His Majesty's Ship Audacious, in which the destination of the said Ship, and the use of the said Arms, &c., are discovered. *London*, 1797. 8vo, pp. 106. 823

"This pamphlet was written by Gen. Ira Allen. It relates to the capture of the ship Olive Branch (laden by him in France with arms for the use of the Vermont militia) by a British ship of war, on suspicion of being destined for Ireland."—Rich. The above and the following are evidently abridgments of the "Olive Branch" case.

Allen. Concise Summary of the Second Volume of the Olive Branch .... with Letters and Memorials. *Philadelphia, Printed for the Author*, 1804. 8vo, pp. 24. 824

Allen. A Vindication of the Conduct of the General Assembly of the State of Vermont, held at Windsor, in October, 1778, against Allegations and Remarks of the protesting Members;

with Observations on their Proceedings, at a Convention held at Cornish, on the 9th day of December, 1778. By Ira Allen. Arlington, 9th Jan., 1779. *Dresden, Printed by Alden Spooner*, 1779. 12mo, pp. 48. 825

See Allen's Hist. Vt., p. 117, and Williams's Hist. Vt., 2d ed., Vol. II., p. 180.

Allen (James). Neglect of Supporting | and | Maintaining the Pure | Worship of God, | By the Professing People of God: is a God-Provoking and | Land-Wasting Sin. | And Repentance with Reformation of it, the only way to | their Outward Felicity: Or, | The Cause of New-Englands Scarcity: And right way to its | Plenty. | As it was Discovered and Applied in a Sermon Preached at Roxbury, | on a Fast-Day: July 26, 1687. | By James Allen, Teacher to the First Gathered Church in Boston. | *Boston*: | *Printed for Job How, and John Allen: And are to be Sold* | *at Mr. Samuel Greens by the South Meeting* | *House*, 1687. | 4to, 3 p. l., pp. 16. 826

Priced, in Stevens' Nuggets, No. 68, £4 4s.

Allen. New-Englands | choicest Blessing | And the Mercy most to be desired by | all that wish well to this People. | Cleared in a | Sermon | Preached before the | Covrt of Election | At Boston on May 28. | 1679. | By James Allen, | Teacher to the first Gathered Church therein. | *Boston*, | *Printed by John Foster*, 1679. | 4to, 2 p. l., pp. 14. 827

Allen. The Principles of the Protestant Religion Maintained; and Churches of New England, in the profession and exercise thereof, Defended against all the Calumnies of one George Keith, a Quaker, in a book lately published at Pennsylvania, to undermine them both. By James Allen, J. Moodey, Sam'l Willard, and Cotton Mather, Ministers of the Gospel in Boston. *Boston, in New England*, 1690. 12mo, pp. 82. N. 828

Allen. Serious Advice to Delivered Ones from Sickness, &c., or, the Healed One's Prophulacticon. By James Allen. *Boston*, 1678. 4to, pp. 30. 829

Mr. Allibone quotes a sermon, "Healthful Diet," which I have not seen.

Allen (Rev. James, Brookline). A Letter to a Friend in the Country [on the Memorial of Roland Cotton, &c.] By James Allen. *Boston*, 1740. 4to, pp. 11. 830

Allen. Magistracy an Institution of Christ upon the Throne. A Sermon preached in the Audience of His Excellency William

Shirley, Esq.; The Honourable His Majesty's Council And House of Representatives of the Province of the Massachusetts-Bay in New England, On the Day of Election of Counsellors for said Province. By James Allen, V.D.M., Pastor of the Church in Brookline. *Boston, J. Draper, Printer*, 1744. 8vo, pp. 54. 831

ALLEN. Two Discourses on Providence, from Ezek. I. 15, 16, Luke XVII. 10–12. By Rev. James Allen. *Boston*, 1727. 12mo. 832

Mr. Allibone quotes some other books by this author, which have not come under my notice.

[ALLEN (James)]. The Poem which the Committee of the Town of Boston had voted to be published with the late [Warren's 5th of March] Oration; with Observations, &c. *Boston, E. Russell*, 1772. 4to, pp. 30. + Reprinted in *Boston*, 1785. 12mo. 833

[ALLEN (James)]. Considerations on the Present State of the Intercourse between His Majesty's Sugar Colonies and the Dominions of the United States of America. James Allen, Secretary. *London*, 1784. 8vo, pp. 54. 834

"Published by the West India merchants and planters for distribution to the members of Parliament, &c., and not sold."—M. R., LXX., p. 434.

ALLEN (James). Narrative of the Life of James Allen, alias Burby Grove. The Highwayman. Being his Death-Bed Confession. *Boston, Harrington & Co.*, 1837. 835

The Boston Athenæum has a copy, bound in a piece of the skin of the deceased highwayman.

ALLEN (John). An Oration upon the Beauties of Liberty; or, the Essential Rights of the Americans. By John Allen. *Boston*, 1773. 8vo, pp. 31. 836

ALLEN (John). Speech of John Allen, Esq., in the House of Representatives, Friday, 20th Day of April, 1798, relative to employing the Armed Vessels as Convoys. *Philadelphia, W. Cobbett, May* 3, 1798. 8vo, pp. 32. 837

[ALLEN (Rev. John)]. An Essay on the Policy of appropriations Being made by The Government of the United States, for Purchasing, Liberating and Colonizing without the Territory of the said States, the Slaves thereof. In Numbers, some of

which have been Published in the Baltimore American, and the whole of them in the Genius of Universal Emancipation. By a Citizen of Maryland. *Baltimore*, 1826. 8vo, pp. 40. 838

[ALLEN (John)]. The Cause of the Heavy burdens of Great Britain, and of her National Debt; comprising a rapid survey of some of the great events, connected with British History, during the last hundred and fifty years. *London, Darton and Harvey*, 1836. 12mo. + Same. Second Edition. Revised. *London, Darton and Harvey*, 1843. 839

ALLEN (J. F.) Victoria Regia; or, the Great Water Lily of America. With a brief account of its Discovery and Introduction into Cultivation. With illustrations by William Sharp, from Specimens grown at Salem, Mass., U. S. A. By John Fisk Allen. *Boston*, 1854. Folio, pp. 18. C. 840

ALLEN (Jonathan). A Poem, on the Existence of God, An Ode on Creation, To which are added Several Hymns, and an Eulogy on General George Washington. By Jonathan Allen, A.M. *Haverhill, Printed by Galen H. Fay, for the Author*, 1803. 12mo, pp. 36. 841

Also a sermon at the ordination of Rev. Ebenezer Allen, Wolfborough, 1792 *Portsmouth*, 1793. 8vo, pp. 38. And funeral sermon on Eliphalet Kimball. *Newbury Port*, 1786.

ALLEN (Joseph, Junr.) An Oration on the Character of the late Gen. George Washington: Pronounced Before the Inhabitants of the Town of Western, on Saturday the 22d of February, 1800. By Joseph Allen, Junr. *Brookfield, Mass., March*, 1800. 12mo. W. 842

ALLEN. The Day of Small Things. A Centennial Discourse delivered in Northborough, June 1, 1846, in Commemoration of the First Congregational Church in this place, and the ordination of the first minister. By Rev. Joseph Allen. With an Appendix. *Boston*, 1846. 8vo, pp. 64. M. 843

ALLEN. A Discourse. New Year's Day at Shrewsbury, Mass. By Rev. Joseph Allen. *Worcester*, 1822. 8vo. W. 844

ALLEN. Oration at Worcester, July 4, 1795. By Joseph Allen, Junr. *Worcester*, 1795. 4to, pp. 12. M. 845

ALLEN. Sermon at Northborough, Fast Day, April 9, 1829. By Rev. Joseph Allen. *Worcester*, 1829. 8vo. W. 846

ALLEN (J.) Battles of the British Navy from A.D. 1800 to 1840. By Joseph Allen. *London*, 1842. 2 vols., 12mo. 847

Contains some accounts of naval engagements during the War of 1812. Re-issued with new title. *London. Bohn*, 1852.

ALLEN. Memoir of the Life and Services of Admiral Sir William Hargood, compiled from Authentic Documents under the Direction of Lady Hargood. By Joseph Allen, Esq. *Privately printed*, 1841. Rl. 8vo. Portraits and Plates. 848

Contains an account of his services in the American War.

ALLEN (J. H.) The Statesman and the Man. A Discourse on the Death of Hon. John Quincy Adams, delivered Feb. 27, 1848. By Joseph Henry Allen. *Washington*, 1848. 8vo, pp. 23. M. 849

ALLEN. The Public Man. A Discourse on the Death of Hon. John Fairfield, delivered in Washington, Dec. 26, 1847. By Rev. Joseph Henry Allen. *Washington*, 1848. 8vo, pp. 27. M. 850

ALLEN (L. L.) The Island of Cuba, or Queen of the Antilles. By Rev. L. Leonidas Allen. *Cleveland; Harris, Fairbanks & Co.*, 1852. 8vo, pp. 26. 851

ALLEN. Pencillings of Scenes upon the Rio Grande. Originally published in the St. Louis American. By L. Leonidas Allen. *New York*, 1848. 12mo. N. 852

ALLEN (M. O.) The History of Wenham, Civil and Ecclesiastical, from its Settlement in 1639, to 1860. By Myron O. Allen. *Boston, Bazin & Chandler*, 1860. 12mo, pp. 220. 853

ALLEN (P.) A History of the American Revolution; comprehending all the Principal Events, both in the Field and in the Cabinet. By Paul Allen, Esq. To which are added the most Important Resolutions of the Continental Congress, and many of the most Important Letters of General Washington. By Paul Allen, Esq. In Two Volumes. *Baltimore, Printed for John Hopkins*, 1819. 8vo. + Also, *Baltimore, F. Bell*, 1822. 2 vols., 8vo, pp. XI., 592; XIII., 510. 854

"Although the name of Paul Allen is on the title, this work was written by John Neal and Mr. Watkins."—ALLEN'S BIOG. DICT'Y.

ALLEN. History of the Expedition under the Command of Captains Lewis and Clark, to the Sources of the Missouri, thence across the Rocky Mountains and down the River Colum-

bia to the Pacific Ocean; performed during the years 1804–'5–'6, by order of the Government of the United States. Prepared for the Press by Paul Allen, Esq. [?] *Philadelphia, Bradford & Inskeep*, 1814. 2 vols., 8vo, pp. 470, 522. 855

ALLEN. [Same Title.] With the Life of Captain Lewis. By T. Jefferson, President of the United States of America. In Two Volumes. *Dublin, J. Christie*, 1817. 8vo, XXVII., Contents, 4 l., Subscribers, 2 l., pp. 588; Title, 1 l., XII., 643. 7 Plates and Map. 856

Also, printed in London, with the title somewhat altered, and with a preface signed Thomas Rees. *London*, 1814. 4to. And *London*, 1815. 3 vols., 8vo. *See* under Lewis and Clark. Mr. S. G. Drake states in his catalogue that the work was really written by Nicholas Biddle, Esq.

ALLEN. [The Same.] Abridged by M. McVickar. *New York, Harpers*, 1842, &c. 2 vols., 18mo. 857

ALLEN. An Oration on the Necessity of Political Union at the Present Day; delivered in Providence, at the Commencement of Rhode Island College, A.D. 1797. By Paul Allen, Junr., A.B. *Providence, Carter & Wilkinson*, 1797. 8vo, pp. 8.

Also, orations before the Federal Adelphi, 1798, 1800, on the death of R. W. Howell, &c. *See* Bartlett's Bibl. of R. I., p. 46.

ALLEN (R.) Extract from a Discourse delivered Sunday, December 29, 1799, in the African Methodist Episcopal Church of Philadelphia. By the Rev. Richard Allen, of the African Race, before the Church under his Pastoral Care. [*Printed in several newspapers of the day.*] N. 859

This discourse is on the death of George Washington. Title quoted from Hough's Washingtoniana, p. 222.

ALLEN (R. L.) Analysis of the principal Mineral Fountains at Saratoga Springs, embracing their History, their Chemicals and Curative Properties, and directions for their Use; also the Natural History and Objects of General Interest in the County of Saratoga. By Richard L. Allen, M.D. *New York*, 1858. 18mo, pp. 114. Plates. 860

ALLEN. A Historical, Chemical and Therapeutical Analysis of the principal Mineral Fountains at Saratoga Springs. By R. L. Allen, M.D. Second Edition. *Saratoga*, 1848. 18mo, pp. 72. S. 861

ALLEN (R.) An Essay on the Nature and Methods of carrying on a Trade to the South-Sea. By Robert Allen, Who

Resided some Years in the Kingdom of Peru. *London, John Baker*, 1712. 8vo, Title, 1 l., pp. 37. 862

Also, on large paper. A new edition was printed, with the following title:

ALLEN. The Great Importance of the Havanna, set forth in an Essay on the Nature and Methods of carrying on a Trade to the South Sea and the Spanish West-Indies. By Robert Allen, Esq., who resided some years in the Kingdom of Peru. *London, Hinxman*, 1762. 8vo. 863

ALLEN (S.) A Short Narrative of the Claim, Title, and Right of the Heirs of the Hon. Samuel Allen, Esq., to the Province of New Hampshire. [*No imprint.*] 4to, pp. 13. M. 864

ALLEN (S). Address on Intemperance, at Northfield (Mass.) on Fast Day, April, 1833. By Samuel Allen. *Greenfield*, 1833. 8vo. W. 865

ALLEN (S.) The Bible and National Prosperity: a Thanksgiving Discourse at Waterville, Nov. 27, 1851. By Rev. S. Allen. *Waterville*, 1851. 8vo, pp. 24. 866

ALLEN (S. C.) Eulogy on Hon. John Wheelock, LL.D., late President of Dartmouth University, who died April 4, 1817, pronounced in the University Chapel, August 27, 1817, Commencement Day. By Hon. Samuel C. Allen. *Hanover*, 1817. 8vo, pp. 19. N. 867

ALLEN. Oration at Petersham, Mass., July 4, 1806. By Samuel C. Allen. *Boston* [1806.] 8vo. W. 868

ALLEN (Stephen). Observations in opposition to the project of Prohibiting, or Greatly Augmenting, the Duties on Foreign Manufactured Articles, &c. By Stephen Allen. *New York*, 1827. 8vo. N. 869

ALLEN (S. T.) An Address delivered at the Centennial Celebration in Merrimack [N. H.], April 3, 1846. By Stephen T. Allen. Concord. *Boston*, 1846. 8vo, pp. 64. M. 870

ALLEN (Thaddeus). An Inquiry into the Views, Principles, Services, and Influences of the Leading Men in the Origination of our Union, and in the Formation and Early Administration of our Present Government. By Thaddeus Allen. *Boston*, 1847. Vol. I., 8vo, pp. 553. + The Same. *Boston*, 1848. Vol. II., No. I., 8vo, pp. 555–662. N. 871

This work was not completed.

A[LLEN] T[homas]. A Chaine of Scripture Chronologie from the Creation of the World to the Death of Jesus Christ, in seven periods. *London*, 1659. 4to. Engraved Title by Hollar.

"Thomas Allen fled to New England in 1638, and was a pious and painful minister at Charles-Town."—COTTON MATHER.

ALLEN (T.) An Historical Sketch of the County of Berkshire and Town of Pittsfield. Written in May, 1808. By Rev. Thomas Allen. *Boston*, 1808. 8vo, pp. 14. S. 873

ALLEN. Massachusetts Election Sermon, May 25, 1808. By Rev. Thomas Allen. *Boston* [1808]. 8vo, pp. 20. N. 874

ALLEN (T. Junr.) Oration at Pittsfield, Mass., July 4, 1803. By Thomas Allen, Junr. *Pittsfield*, 1803. 8vo. S. 875

ALLEN (Thomas). Report on the Commerce and Navigation of the Mississippi . . . for Chicago Convention of July 5, 1847. By Thomas Allen. *St. Louis, Mo.* [1847]. 8vo, pp. 32. N. 876

ALLEN. Japan, and the Expedition thereto of the United States: a Discourse delivered before the Missouri Historical Society, December 22, 1852. By Thomas Allen. *St. Louis*, 1853. 8vo, pp. 34. N. 877

[ALLEN.] Annual Review. History of St. Louis, Commercial Statistics . . . From the Missouri Republican of January 10, 1854. *St. Louis*, 1854. 8vo, pp. 52. N. 878

ALLEN (T. G.) Letter from Thos. G. Allen to Col. Thomas B. Florence: Representative in the XXXIVth Congress from the First Congressional District, Pennsylvania. *Philadelphia*, 1856. 8vo, pp. 16. 879

Concerning Fremont and the Presidential election.

ALLEN (Timothy). Salvation for all Men, Put out of all Dispute. By Timothy Allen, A.M. & V.D.M. Granville, Massachusetts. *Hartford, Printed by Nathaniel Patten* [1782.] 8vo, Title, 1 l.; "Escapes of the Press," 1 leaf, pp. 56. 880

ALLEN. Answer to Pilate's Question [What is Truth?] By Timothy Allen. *Providence, R. I.*, 1765. 8vo. W. 881

ALLEN (Wilkes). Divine Favours Gratefully Recollected. Thanksgiving Discourse at Chelmsford, Nov. 29, 1810. By Wilkes Allen, A.M. *Cambridge*, 1811. 8vo. W. 882

ALLEN. History of Chelmsford, from its Origin in 1653 to

the Year 1820. To which is added A Memoir of the Pawtucket Tribe of Indians. By Wilkes Allen, A.M., Pastor of the Church in Chelmsford. *Haverhill*, 1820. 8vo, pp. 192. 883

ALLEN (William). The American Crisis: A Letter, addressed by permission to The Earl Gower, Lord President of the Council, &c. &c. &c. On the present alarming Disturbances in the Colonies. Wherein Various important Points, relative to Plantation Affairs, are brought into Discussion; as well as several Persons adverted to of the most distinguished Characters. And an Idea is offered towards a complete Plan of restoring the Dependence of America upon Great Britain to a State of Perfection. By William Allen, Esq. *London, T. Cadell*, MDCCLXXIV. 8vo, pp. IV., 72. 884

"There is an unhappy affectation of fine writing in this pamphlet; and it contains many illiberal passages; but any particular attention to them would be doing honour to a performance which will reflect none upon its author."—M. R., Vol. L., p. 234.

[ALLEN (William)]. Accounts of Shipwreck and of other Disasters at Sea, designed to be interesting and useful to Mariners, . . . Compiled by a Friend of Seamen. *Brunswick*, 1823. 12mo. 885

ALLEN. An Account of the Separation in the Church and Town of Pittsfield; with Remarks on some ecclesiastical proceedings which seem to have violated the principles of the Congregational and Independent Church of New England. By Rev. William Allen, D.D. *Pittsfield*, 1809. 4to, pp. 96. M. 886

ALLEN. Address delivered at Northampton, Mass., October 29, 1854, in commemoration of the Close of the Second Century since the Settlement of the Town. *Northampton*, 1855. 8vo, pp. 56. 887

ALLEN. An American Biographical and Historical Dictionary, containing an Account of the Lives, Characters, and Writings of the most Eminent Persons in North America from its First Discovery to the present time, and a Summary of the History of the several Colonies and of the United States. By William Allen. *Cambridge*, 1809. 8vo, pp. 632. Portrait of Washington. 888

ALLEN. [The Same.] Second Edition. *Boston, William Hyde*, MDCCCXXXII. 8vo, pp. VIII., 800. 889

ALLEN. The American Biographical Dictionary: containing

an Account of the Lives, Characters, and Writings of the most Eminent Persons, deceased in North America, from its First Settlement. By William Allen. Third Edition. *Boston, J. P. Jewitt*, 1857. 8vo, pp. IX., 905. 890

See "Historical Magazine." Vol. I., p. 40.

ALLEN. A Decade of Addresses at Bowdoin College, to which is added a Dudleian Lecture at Cambridge, 1830. By Rev. William Allen. *Concord*, 1830. 12mo. 891

ALLEN. Election Sermon, Mass, May 26, 1813. By Rev. William Allen. *Boston*, 1813. 8vo, pp. 23. 892

ALLEN. An Historical Discourse, delivered in Dorchester, Jan. 2, 1848, on occasion of the Fortieth Anniversary of the Gathering of the Second Church. By Rev. William Allen. *Boston*, 1848. 8vo, pp. 30. S. 893

ALLEN (William). The History of Norridgewock, Maine. Comprising the Memorials of the Aboriginal Inhabitants and Jesuit Missionaries, Hardships of the Pioneers, Biographical Notices of the Early Settlers, and Ecclesiastical Sketches. By William Allen. *Norridgewock, E. J. Peet*, 1849. 12mo, pp. 252.

ALLEN. A Sermon preached before the Council and Legislature of New Hampshire, June 4, 1818, Being the Anniversary Election. By Rev. William Allen. [With List of Preachers.] *Concord*, 1818. 8vo, pp. 44. 895

ALLEN (William). Speech of Hon. William Allen on the Bill to Separate the Government from the Bank; delivered in the Senate, . . . Feb. 20, 1838. *Washington*, 1838. 8vo. 896

ALLEN. Speech of Hon. William Allen on the Report of the Select Committee in Relation to the Assumption of the Debts of the States by the Federal Government, Senate . . . Feb. 11, 1840. *Washington*, 1840. 8vo. 897

ALLEN. Speech of Hon. William Allen in the Senate, March 15, 1842 [On the State of the Public Finances]. [*Washington*, 1842.] 8vo. 898

ALLEN (Capt. W.) A Plan for the Immediate Extinction of the Slave Trade. By Capt. W. Allen. *London*, 1849. 8vo, pp. 36. 899

Allen (William). Wunnissoo, or the Vale of Hoosatunnuk. A Poem, with Notes. *Boston*, 1856. 12mo. 900

Allen (W.) Speech of Hon. William Allen, of Ohio, on Confiscation and Emancipation, delivered in the House of Representatives of the United States, April 24, 1862. *Washington, McGill, Witherow & Co.*, 1862. 8vo, pp. 16. 901

Allen (W.) United we Stand, Divided we Fall: a Poem. By W. Allen. *New York*, 1812. 24mo. 902

Allen (W. G.) The American Prejudice against Colour: an Authentic Narrative, showing how easily the Nation got into an Uproar. By William G. Allen. *London*, 1854. Fcap 8vo.

Allen (W. H.) Eulogy on the Character and Services of the late Daniel Webster, pronounced at the request of the Select and Common Councils of the City of Philadelphia, January 18, 1853. By William H. Allen. *Philadelphia*, 1853. 8vo, pp. 51. N. 904

Allen. Our Country's Mission in History. An Address delivered at the Anniversary of the Philomathæan Society of Pennsylvania College, Sept. 19, 1855. By Wm. H. Allen. *Philadelphia*, 1855. 8vo, pp. 38. M. 905

Allen. Tendencies of the Age to Peace. An Address delivered before the American Peace Society, Boston, May 29, 1854. By Wm. H. Allen. *Boston*, 1854. 8vo, pp. 32. M. 906

Allen. Speech of Hon. William J. Allen, of Illinois, upon the President's Message, delivered in the House of Representatives, January 27, 1864. *Washington*, 1864. 8vo, pp. 14. 907

Allen (W. S.) An Oration delivered in Newburyport, on the Fifty-fourth Anniversary of the Declaration of American Independence, July 4, 1830. By William S. Allen. *Newburyport*, 1830. 8vo, pp. 20. M. 908

Allen Prescott; or the Fortunes of a New England Boy. *New York*, 1834. 2 vols., 12mo. 909

Alleränlteste Nachricht von der Neuen Welt, welche dieser Erfinder derselben ehemals ertheilt, von neuem edirt. *Berlin*, 1722. 8vo. 910

This appears, from Meusel (III., I., 265), to be a translation, by Michael Herr, of Vespucius' account of his voyage, edited by Martin Frederick Voss.

Allerneuester Kriegsstaat oder gründliche Nachrichten von den heutigen Kriegsbegebenheiten. *Leipzig*, 1731, &c. 14 vols., 8vo. 911

Contains notices of the Spanish War in America.

Alley. A Vindication of the Principles and Statements advanced in the Strictures of the Rt. Hon. Lord Sheffield on the Necessity of inviolably maintaining the Navigation and Colonial System of Great Britain: With Tables and an Appendix. * * * By Jerome Alley. *London*, 1806, 8vo, pp. 90. 912

Alley (John B.) Speech of Hon. John B. Alley, of Mass., on the Principles and Purposes of the Republican Party. Delivered in the House . . . April 30, 1860. [*Washington* (?), 1860.] 8vo, pp. 8. 912*

Allgemeine Historie der Reisen zu Wasser und zu Lande, oder Sammlung aller Reisebeschreibungen. *Amsterdam, Arkstee*, 1747–1774. 21 vols., 4to. Maps and Plates. 913

This valuable repertory contains translations of many of the early voyages and travels in America, and some Indian vocabularies, &c., mostly by J. Jo. Schwabe. A detailed list of the contents is given in the Supplement to the Index of Books in the Bates Hall of the Public Library, Boston. Some copies bear the imprint Leipzig, 1747, &c.

Allibone (S. A.) A Critical Dictionary of English Literature, and British and American Authors, Living and Deceased, from the Earliest Accounts to the Middle of the Nineteenth Century. Containing Thirty Thousand Biographies and Literary Notices, with Forty Indexes of Subjects. By S. Austin Allibone. Vol. I. *Philadelphia, Childs & Peterson*, 1858. Imp. 8vo, pp. 1005.

Vol. II. is now [1867] in the press. The industrious author of this useful book has devoted many years of unwearied patience to the examination of the various literary journals and reviews, and the result is a cyclopedia of varied opinion. In it the reader will find the titles of many American books, which from their nature are inadmissible in this work.

The Allies and the Late Ministry Defended against France, and the Present Friends of France. In Answer to a Pamphlet, entitled, The Conduct of the Allies. [By Jonathan Swift.] [*In four parts.*] Part I. Shewing the Necessity of England's entering into the Grand Alliance; and that by it we are oblig'd to insist on the Restitution of Spain and the Indies to the House of Austria. With a particular Vindication of the Eight Article from the gross Corruptions, with which the Author of the Conduct has falsify'd the two Clauses of it that relate to England

and the West-Indies. [By Francis Hare, Bishop of Chichester.] The Third Edition, Corrected. *London, Egbert Sanger*, 1711. 8vo, Part I., pp. 48; Part II., 2 p. l., pp. 71; Part III., 2 p. l., pp. 74; Part IV., 2 p. l., pp. 84. 915

Allin (A.) Home Ballads. A Book for New Englanders. By Abby Allin. *Boston, Munroe & Co.*, 1851. 16mo. 916

Allin (James). The Eternity of God, and the Short Life of Man considered. A Sermon on occasion of the Decease of Mr. Samuel Aspinwal, who died August 13 1732. In the 37th Year of his Age. By James Allin, M.A., Pastor of the Church in Brookline. *Boston in New-England, Printed for D. Henchman*, 1732. 12mo, pp. 26. M. 917

Allin. Thunder and Earthquake. A Loud and Awful Call to Reformation. Fast Sermon at Brookline (Mass.), Nov. 1, 1727. By James Allin. *Boston*, 1727. 16mo. W. 918

Allin. Two Practical Discourses. I. The Wheels of the World Govern'd by a Wise Providence. II. The Doctrine of Merit Exploded, And Humility recommended. By James Allin, A.M., Pastor of the Church of Christ in Brookline. Published at the desire of some that heard them Preach'd. *Boston, N. E., Printed for Samuel Gerrish*, 1727. 919

Also, an Artillery Election Sermon, 1731, which I have not seen.

Allin (John). Animadversions | upon the | Antisynodalia Americana | A Treatise printed in old England, | In the name of the | Dissenting Brethren | In the Synod held at Boston in New England 1662. Tending to clear the Elders and Churches of | New England from those Evils and Declinings charged upon many | of them in the two Prefaces before the said Book. | Together with | An Answer | unto | The Reasons alledged for the opinion of the Dissenters. | And a Reply to such Answers as are given to the | Arguments of the Synod. By John Allin, Pastor of the Church of Christ | at Dedham in N. England. *Cambridge, Printed by S. G. and M. J. for Hezekiah Usher | of Boston*, 1664. Sm. 4to, pp. 82. 920

Allin (John) and Shepard (Thomas). A | Defence | of the | Answer made unto the Nine Questions | or Positions sent from New-England, | Against the | Reply thereto | by That Reverend servant of Christ, | Mr. John Ball; | Entituled, | A Tryall of the New Church-way in | New-England and in Old. | Wherein, beside

a more full opening of sundry particulars | concerning Liturgies, Power of the Keys, matter of | the visible Church, &c. is more largely handled, that | controversie, concerning the Catholick visible | Church; tending to cleare up the | Old-way of Christ in New- | England Churches. | By Iohn Allin, Pastor of Dedham, [and] Tho. Shepard of Cambridge in New-England |. *London, Printed by R. Cotes for Andrew Crooke, and are to be sold at the Green | Dragon in Pauls Church yard*, 1648. | 4to, pp. 211. W.

Allin. The Spouse of Christ coming out of Affliction. By John Allin. *Cambridge*, 1672. 4to. W. 922

Allin (John). *See* [Byam (William)].

Alline (H.) Sermon at Fort Midway, Feb. 19, 1783. By Rev. Henry Alline. *Dover, N. H.*, 1797. 8vo. W. 923

Alline (H.) The Life and Journal of the Rev. Mr. Henry Alline. *Boston, Printed by Gilbert & Dean* [*for Hayden & Sheaa*], 1806. 12mo, pp. 180. 924

Alling (J.) A Register of the Weather . . . for the last Twenty-five Years, ending March 31, 1810 . . . By Jeremiah Alling. *New Haven*, 1810. 8vo, pp. 80. S. 925

Allison (J.) The Slavery Question. Speech of Hon. John Allison, of Pa., delivered in the House of Representatives, April 1, 1856. 8vo, pp. 8. 926

Allison (J.) An Eulogy upon the Life, Character and Public Services of General Zachary Taylor, delivered at the Commissioners' Hall, Spring Garden, July 29, 1850. By Joseph Allison, Esq. *Philadelphia, J. H. Jones*, 1850. 8vo, pp. 24. 927

Allison (P.) A Discourse Delivered in the *Presbyterian Church*, in the *City of* Baltimore, on the 22d February, 1800,—the Day Dedicated to the Memory of Gen. George Washington. By the Reverend Patrick Allison, D.D. *Baltimore, Printed by Wm. Pechin for the Editor of the American* [1800]. 8vo, pp. 24.

Allison. Thoughts on the Examination and Trials of Candidates for the Sacred Ministry. By Rev. Patrick Allison. *Parthenopoli*, 1766. 8vo, pp. 24. 929

Allison (W. B.) Homesteads for Soldiers and Sailors in the Rebellious States. Speech of Hon. William B. Allen, of Iowa,

delivered in the House of Representatives, May 4, 1864. *Washington, Gibson* [1864]. 8vo, pp. 8. 930

Allouez (Claude). *See* French's Louisiana.

Allsop (R.) California and its Gold Mines. Being a series of recent Communications from the Mining Districts upon the condition and future prospects of Quartz Mining, with an account of the richer deposits, and incidental notices of the climate, scenery, and mode of life in California. Edited by Robert Allsop. *London, Groombridge*, 1853. 8vo, pp. 149. 931

Allston (R. F. W.) Essay on Sea Coast Crops; read before the Agricultural Association of the Planting States, on occasion of the Annual Meeting, held at Columbia, the Capital of South-Carolina, December 3d, 1853. By R. F. W. Allston. *Charleston, S. C.*, 1854. 8vo. 932

Allston. Report on the Free School System in South Carolina. By R. F. W. Allston. *Charleston, S. C.*, 1847. 8vo, pp. 26. 933

Allyn (John). Sermon delivered at Plymouth, [Mass.], December 22, 1801, Commemorative of the Pious Ancestry who first immigrated to that Place. By John Allyn, S. H. M., Pastor at Duxboro'. *Boston, Munroe & Francis*, 1802. 8vo, pp. 35. H. 934

Allyn. New Year's Sermon: delivered at Duxborough, Jan. 1, 1806. By Rev. John Allyn. *Boston*, [1806]. 12mo. 935

Allyn. A | Sermon, | Delivered on the 29th of November, 1798, | The Day | of | Public Thanksgiving | in the | State of Massachusetts. | By John Allyn, | Pastor of the Church in Duxborough. *Boston, Printed by Samuel Hall*, 1799. 8vo, pp. 21. 936

Allyn. A Sermon, preached in the Audience of His Excellency Caleb Strong, Esq. Governor, The other Members of the Executive, and The Honorable Legislature of the Commonwealth of Massachusetts, on the Anniversary Election, May 29, 1805. By John Allyn, Congregational Minister of Duxborough. *Boston, Young & Minns*, 1805. 8vo, pp. 37. 937

Allyn. Sermon at the Ordination of Alden Bradford. By Rev. John Allyn. *Boston*, 1794. 8vo. 938

Alm. Plantæ Surinamenses. Cura Jacobiæ Alm. *Upsal*, 1775. 4to, pp. 18. Plate. 939

Republished in Linnæus' "Amœnitates academicæ," VIII., 249–267. [Diss. acad. Præs. C. Linnæus.]

Almanac of Celestial Motions, viz., of the Sun and Planets, &c., for the Year 1674. 16mo. *Cambridge*, 1674.+Of Celestial Motions, for the Year 1680. 16mo. *Boston*, 1680.+Of the Cœlestiall Motions, &c., for the Year of our Lord God M.DC.XCIV. *Boston*, 1694. 16mo. M. 940

These are some of the earliest American almanacs. Thomas' History of Printing gives the titles of some of earlier dates, which will be noticed hereafter.

Almanach Américain, *ou* État physique, politique, ecclésiastique & militaire de l'Amérique; ouvrage qui comprend les forces, la population, les loix, le commerce & l'administration de chaque Province de cette partie du monde; le tableau de ceux qui y figurent par leurs charges & par leurs dignités; celui de la Marine des Peuples Européans [*sic.*] qui y ont des Possessions et le nom des Officiers qui sont employés dans cette partie de l'administration publique. Par M. P. D. L. R ...C. A. L. T. de M. *Paris, Chez l'auteur* [*et chez*] *Lamy*, 1783. 12mo. 941

It appears by a note on the back of the title that this work was edited by M. [Poncelin] de la Roche-Tillac. It was continued annually. The work published in 1782, 1783 and 1785, under the title "État physique, politique, ecclésiastique et militaire de l'Asie, de l'Afrique et de l'Amérique, ouvrage," etc., as above, and with the half-title, "Almanach américain, asiatique et africain, ou État," etc., apparently belongs to the same series. I have seen no volume later than 1787. Barbier implies that it continued to be published till 1791.

Almanach des Colonies, 1788. *Paris*, 1788. 12mo. 942

Almanach et directorum français des États-Unis, pour l'année 1852–1858. *New York*, 1852–58. 7 vols., 12mo. 943

Almanaque Universal Hispano-Americano. *Paris*, 1855. 8vo.

Almaraz. Memoria de los trabajos ejecutados por la comision cientifica de Pachuca en el ano de 1864, dirigida por el Ingeniero Ramon Almaraz. Mandada publicar de orden de S. M. I. por el ministerio de fomento. *Mexico*, 1865. 4to, pp. 358. Plates and Plans. 945

Almbert (Alfred d'). Flanerie parisienne aux États-Unis . . . *Paris, librairie théatrale*, 1856. 16mo, pp. 278 (1). 946

Almeida e Albuquerque (Francisco de Paula d'). Breves reflexoes retrospectivas, politicas, moraes e socides sobre o im-

perio do Brazil, e suas relaçoes com as outras naçoes. *Paris, impr. de Remquet*, 1854. 12mo. 947

Almeida (Gregoria de). *See* [Escobar Manoel de)].

[Almodovar]. *See* Raynal (Abbé).

Almoguerra. Instruccion a curas y ecclesiasticos de las Indias. Por Joannes de Almoguerra. *Madrid*, 1671. 4to.

See Ternaux, No. 883.

Almon (John). Anecdotes of the Life of the Right Hon. William Pitt, Earl of Chatham, with his Speeches. *London, J. Almon*, 1792, 4 vols., 8vo.+*London*, 1797. 3 vols., 8vo.+Seventh Edition, *London*, 1810. 3 vols., 8vo. S. 949

[Almon.] Biographical, Literary, and Political Anecdotes; of several of the most Eminent Persons of the Present Age, with an Appendix, consisting of Original, Explanatory and Scarce Papers. Never before printed. *London, Longman*, 1797. 3 vols., 8vo. 950

Contains numerous articles on American history and politics, account of the controversy about Gov. Hutchinson's Letters, &c. Lowndes characterizes the work as partial and interesting.

[Almon]. A Collection of interesting, authentic Papers, relative to the Dispute between Great Britain and America; shewing the Causes and Progress of that Misunderstanding, from 1764 to 1775. *London, J. Almon*, M.DCCLXXVII. 8vo, pp. 280; Index, pp. 3. N. 951

Usually called, by its running title, "Prior Documents," and intended to accompany the Remembrancer.

Almon. Collection of the most interesting Tracts, lately published in England and America, on the subjects of Taxing the American Colonies and regulating their Trade. *London, Almon*, 1766–1779. 6 vols., 8vo. C. 952

These tracts were published separately, and are described under their respective titles in this Dictionary. Almon merely issued them collectively with the above title in vols. 1 and 2. The titles to the other volumes differ.

[Almon.] The History of the late Minority; Exhibiting the Condvct, Principles, and Views of that Party, dvring the Years 1762, 1763, 1764, and 1765. [By John Almon and H. Cotes.] The third impression. *London*, 1765. 8vo.+The fourth impression. *London, Reprinted*, 1766. 8vo, pp. 332. 953

[Almon.] Memoirs of a late eminent Bookseller. *London, Printed in the year* 1790. 954

Almon was the active pamphleteer and publisher during the American contest, and in close connection with the liberal party and prominent men in the Colonies.

[Almon.] The Remembrancer; or, Impartial Repository of Public Events, from 1775 to 1784. 17 vols., 8vo. *London* [*J. Almon and J. Debrett*], MDCCLXXV. to 1783. 955

Vol. I., pp. 260. 2 Maps of Boston.+Second Edition, 1775. Rl. 8vo.+Third Edition, 1775. Rl. 8vo.+Fourth Edition, 1775. Rl. 8vo.+Vol. II. Part I. For the year 1776. Title and pp. 5–371; Index ii.–iv. Vol. III. Part II. For the year 1776. Title and pp. 356. Vol. IV. Part III. For the year 1776. Title and pp. 350; Index, pp. 6. Map at page 261 and at page 290. Vol. V. For the year 1777. Portrait of Franklin; Title and pp. 314; Index, pp. 8. Vol. VI. For the year 1778. Title and pp. 374; Index, pp. 7. Vol. VII. For the year 1778 and beginning of 1779. Title and pp. 400; Index, pp. 6. Vol. VIII. For the year 1779. Title and pp. 386; Index, pp. 4; Catalogue of Books, &c., pp. 8. Vol. IX. For the year 1780. Title and pp. 384; Index, pp. 6. Vol. X. For the year 1780. Part II. iv. and pp. 380; Catalogue of Books, &c., pp. 8. Vol. XI. For the year 1781. Part I. 2 p. l., pp. 375. Vol. XII. For the year 1781. Part II. Title and pp. 3–394; Index, pp. 2; Catalogue of Books, &c., pp. 8. Vol. XIII. For the year 1782. Part I. Title and pp. 380; Index, pp. 2. Vol. XIV. For the year 1782. Part II. 2 p. l., pp. 378. Vol. XV. For the year 1783. *Printed for J. Debrett*, 1783. Title and Index, 2 l., pp. 378. Vol. XVI. For the year 1783. Part II. 2 p. l., pp. 380. Vol. XVII. For the year 1784. Title and Contents, 4 l., pp. 376. This work contains every authentic paper relative to the American Revolution, whether published in England or America, by the British Ministry or the American Congress. The Prior Documents (No. 900 ante) should be added. Almon states that the plan of the work is "to select from all the public prints the best account of every material public event; to print it in octavo; and at the end of the volume to give a copious index to the whole." "There are several editions of the first volume, all except the first, in royal 8vo, while the remainder are in demy 8vo. The first edition of the first volume is also deficient of several papers contained in the succeeding editions.'—Rich. Prof. Smyth, in his lectures, says, "The great magazine of information is the Remembrancer." "Mr. Almon was assisted by George Pownall in this work, which has now become exceedingly scarce."—Nichol's Lit. Anec.

Almonte (J. N.) Guia de Forasteros y Repertorio de Conocimientos Utiles. *Mexico*, 1852. Sm. 8vo. Maps and Plates.

Almy (J.) and Bostwick (E. B.) State of Michigan. 1845. To Emigrants. [*New York, Isaac J. Oliver, Printer*, 1845.] 16mo, pp. 6 (1). Map. 957

Alnambay 1858. Almanac. *New York, Lith. by T. W. Strong* [1857?]. Broadside. 958

At the bottom of the sheet: "Eugir. Vetromile Datlias." In the Penobscot dialect of the Abnaqui Indians, at Old Town.

Aloncle (Antoine Félix). Renseignements sur l'artillerie navale de l'Angleterre et des États-Unis. Traduit d'après les derniers documents officiels par A. F. Aloncle. *Paris, A. Bertrand,* 1865. 8vo. 3 Plates. 959

Also published in connection with two other works by the same author, under the title: "Études d'artillerie navale de l'Angleterre et des États-Unis." *Paris,* 1865. 8vo.

A'LORD. A short Narrative and Military Experience of Corp. G. A'Lord, Formerly a Member of Co. G. ... 125th Reg't N. Y. V. ... . Containing a Brief Sketch of the War ... . *n. p.* [186–]. 16mo, pp. 64. 960

Alphabetical Army Register: giving the Names, Dates of Present and Original Commissions, Rank, Place of Nativity, and from whence appointed, of all the Officers of the U. S. Army, as shown by the Official Army Register, May, 1863. *New York, Van Nostrand,* 1863. 8vo, pp. 64. 961

ALPHONSE DE XANTOIGNE (Jean). *See* Xantoigne (Jean Alphonse de).

ALSEDO Y HERRERA. *See* Alcedo y Herrera.

ALSINET. Nuevas Utilidades de la Quina, demostradas, confirmadas, y añadidas, por el Doct. D. Josef Alsinet ... . *Madrid, Antonio Munoz del Valle,* 1774. Sm. 8vo, pp. (18), 168 (2).

ALSOP (George.) A | Character | of the Province of | Mary-Land, | wherein is Described in four distinct | Parts (*viz.*), | I. The Scituation, and Plenty of the Province. | II. The Laws, Customs, and natural Demea- | nour of the Inhabitant. | III. The worst and best Usage of a *Mary-* | *Land* Servant, opened in view. | IV. The Traffique, and vendable Commodities | of the Countrey. | Also | A small Treatise on the Wilde and | Naked *Indians* (or *Susquehanokes*) | of *Mary-land*, their Customs, Man- | ners, Absurdities, Religion. Together with a Collection of Histo- | rical Letters. By George Alsop. | *London, Printed by T. J. for Peter Dring,* . . 1666. Sm. 8vo, 10 p. l., pp. 118. Portrait and Map. H. 963

One of the rarest of books. Dr. Bliss' copy sold for £4 10s. The author was a native of Maryland, and published "An Orthodox Plea for the Sanctuary of God, Common Service and White Robe of the House, written for the good of all." *London,* 1669.

ALSOP (R.) A Poem; Sacred to the Memory of George Washington, Late President of the United States, and Commander in Chief of the Armies of the United States. Adapted to the 22d of Feb. 1800. By Richard Alsop. ... *Hartford, Printed by Hudson and Goodwin,* 1800. 8vo, pp. 23. 964

[ALSOP (Richard)]. The Political Green-House, for the Year 1798. Addressed to the Readers of the Connecticut Courant, January 1st, 1799. *Hartford, Hudson & Goodwin* [1799?]. 12mo, pp. 24. 965

Written by R. Alsop, Lemuel Hopkins, and Theodore Dwight, in unequal proportions. *See* Everest's Poets of Connecticut, p. 94.

[ALSOP (Richard) and DWIGHT (Theodore)]. The Echo, with other Poems. [*New York*], 1807. 8vo, pp. xv., 331 (10).

Chiefly a political satire. *See* Duyckinck's Cyclopædia of Amer. Literature, I., 495.

ALSTON (W. J.) The Slavery Question. Speech of Hon. William J. Alston in the House of Representatives, April 18, 1850. *Washington* [n. d.] 8vo, pp. 8. 967

The Altar of Baal thrown down. *See* [Sullivan (James)].

ALTON. Memorial to Congress upon the subject of a National Armory, with the Preamble and Resolutions adopted by the Common Council of the City of Alton, December 2, 1861. ... *Alton, Ill., L. A. Parks & Co.,* 1861. 8vo, pp. 8. 968

ALTON (Davis). Address ... before the Working Man's National Union League ... June 23, 1863, at New Orleans. By Davis Alton. *New Orleans,* 1863. 8vo, pp. 12. 969

Alton Riots. *See* Lincoln (W. S.)

ALTOWAN. *See* [Stuart (Lord)].

ALVA. Catecismo en Lengua Mexicana y Castellana. Por B. de Alva. *Mexico,* 1634. 970

See Ternaux, No. 551. Ludewig does not mention this, but refers to a MS. by Don Bartolini Alva.

ALVARADO (Francisco). Vocabulario del Idioma Misteco. Por Fray Francisco Alvarado. *Mexico, Pedro Balli,* 1593. 4to.

ALVARADO (Pedro de). *See* Barcia, Historiadores, Vol. x., and Ternaux Voyages.

ALVARES. Copy van een Brief aen den Commissaris generael berinen dese Provincie, aengaende het verdestrueren der Stadt Lima in America. Von Domingo de Alvares. 1688. 4to.

ALVAREZ (F.) Puren Indomito. Poema. Por El Capitan F. Alvarez de Toledo. Publicado bajo la direccion de Don Diego

Barros Arana. *Paris and Leipzig, A. Franck,* 1862. 12mo, pp. 111, 485. [Barros Arana Biblioteca Americana.] 973

Three hundred and twenty copies printed, of which twenty are on large paper. From a MS. in the Madrid Library. Narrates the Indian insurrection of 1598, in Chile. Father Ovalle made use of the MS. for his History of Chile.

ALVAREZ (Francisco). Ho Preste Joam das Indias. Verdadera Informaçam das terras do Preste Joam segundo vio y escreveo ho padre Francisco Alvarez capellan del Rey nosso señhor. [*Lisboa,* 1540.] 974

Original edition, of great rarity. For a very full and accurate account of this voyage, see Navarrete, who does not quote this original Portuguese, but the Spanish translation by Padilla. Alvarez acted as secretary to the embassy. The work deserves particular notice, as it contains the first detailed narrative of travels in India, and incidentally of America. A Spanish version. *Anvers,* 1557. 8vo.+*Toledo,* 1538. 8vo.+ Italian in Ramusio, Vol. I., p. 189.+German. Eisleben, 1566. Folio.+1571. Folio.

ALVAREZ (Francisco). Noticia del establecimiento y poblacion de las colonias inglesas en la America septentrional; Religion, orden de gobierno, leyes y costumbres de sus naturales y habitantes; calidades de su clima, terreno, frutos, plantas y animales; y estado de su industria, artes, comercio y navigacion: sacada de varios autores, por Don F. Alvarez ... . *Madrid, Antonio Fernandez,* 1778. Sm. 4to, pp. 196. S. 975

There is an edition, falsely dated 1608, and assigned in the Catalogue of the British Museum to the year 1764.

ALVAREZ (J. J.) and DURAN (R.) Itinerarios y Derroteros de la Republica Mexicana. *Mexico,* 1856. 8vo. 976

ALVAREZ (José). Contestacion, ou la Carta del Indus Patriota, con alguns reflexiones sobre el Dialogo, entre El Entusiasta Liberal, y El Filosofo Rancio, y sobre las notas anonymas con que La Salido reimpreso el manifesto de Dr. José Alvarez de Toledo. *Philadelphia,* 1812. 8vo. 977

[ALVAREZ.] Manifiesto ó satisfaccion pundonorosa, á todos los buenos Españoles Europeos y á todos los pueblos de la America, por un diputado de las Cortes reunidas en Cadiz. [*Philadelphia,* 1811.] 8vo, pp. 83 (1). H. 978

"The author, Don José Alvarez de Toledo, was a deputy in the Cortes of Cadiz, for the island of Santo Domingo."—RICH.

ALVAREZ (J. M.) Instituciones | de derecho real | de Castilla y de Indias. | Por El Dr. D. Jose Maria Alvarez, | Catedratico de Instituciones de Justinia | no en la Universidad de Guatemala. | Obra nuevamente revista, corregida y aumentada con arreglo á la actual Legislacion. | *Guatemala,* 1820. | +*Mexico, Reimpresa en*

la oficina a Cargo de Rivera, 1826. 4 vols., 12mo. | +*Habana,* 1834. 2 vols., sm. 4to. 979

ALVAREZ (Nicolas). Noticias sagradas de Sant. Madre del Rosario en esta Ciudad de los Angeles de Puebla, en esta Nueva Espana. Por ... Nicolas Alvarez. *Puebla* [1650?].

ALVAREZ (R.) Guia de Nueva York. Por R. Alvarez y J. G. Grediaga. *New York,* 1863. 12mo. 981

ALVAREZ DE ABREU. *See* Abreu. No. 76.

ALVEAR (Carlos). Exposicion que hace el señor brigadier D. Carlos Alvear general en xefe del exercito sitiador de Montevideo, de su conducta en la rendicion de esta plaza. Vulnerada por las falsas imputaciones de su gobernador D. Gaspar Vigodet. *Buenos-Ayres, Imprenta de niños expositos,* 1814. Folio, pp. 42 (1). 982

ALVEAR. Observaciones sobre la defensa de la provincia de Buenos-Aires. Amenazada de una invasion espanola al mando del teniente General D. Pablo Morillo. Por Brig.-Gen. Carlos de Alvear. *Buenos-Aires,* 1865. 4to, pp. 86. 983

Fifty copies printed.

ALVEAR (Diego de). Relacion geografica e historica de la provincia de Misiones, del brigadier D. Diego de Alvear ... . Primera edicion. *Buenos-Aires, Imprenta del estado,* 1836. Folio, pp. 106, "tabla corografica" (folded), iii. 984

Forms part of Vol. IV. of the *Coleccion,* etc., of Pedro de Angelis.

ALVES. Ode to Britannia (for the year 1780), Occasioned by our late Successes. By Robert Alves, A.M. *Edinburgh, Creech,* 1780. 4to. 985

"Partly relates to America."—M. R., LXII., p. 246.

ALVIREY. Puntual descripcion de la regia pompa conque in la S. Iglesia de la ciudad de los Reyes mandó solemnias les reales exequias de la S. D. Mario Josepho de Austria regna de Portugal D. J. Mario de Velasco, virrey de los Reinos del Peru y Chile. Por Alexo de Alvirey. *Lima,* 1756. 4to. 986

ALVORD (Benjamin). Address before the Dialectic Society of the Corps of Cadets, in Commemoration of the Gallant Conduct of the Nine Graduates of the Military Academy, and other Officers of the United States' Army, who fell in the Battles ... in Florida, on the 28th of December, 1835, and the

25th December, 1837; the former called Dade's Battle, the latter, the Battle of Okee-cho-bee. Delivered at West Point, N. Y., on the 29th December, 1838. By Lieutenant Benjamin Alvord, U. S. A. ... *New York, Wiley & Putnam,* 1839. 8vo, pp. 62. H. 987

ALVORD (J. W.) Historical Address delivered in the first Congregational Church in Stamford, Ct., At the Celebration of the Second Centennial Anniversary of the First Settlement of the Town. By Rev. J. W. Alvord, Dec. 22d, 1841. *New York, S. Davenport,* 1842. 8vo, pp. 40. 988

ALZATE. Gacetas de Literatura de Mexico. Por D. José Antonio de Alzate Ramirez. No. 1, 15th January, 1788, No. 44, Vol. III., 22d Oct., 1795. *Mexico,* 1788–1795, 3 vols., 4to.

ALZATE. Gacetas de Literatura de Mexico: por D. José Antonio Alzate Ramirez. *Puebla,* 1831. 4 vols., 4to, pp. viii., 450, 486, 478, 456, con laminas. Portrait. 990

ALZATE. Memoria en que se trata del Insecto G.ano ó Cochinilla, de su naturaleza y serie de su vida, escrita en Mexico en 1777. Por D. Josef Antonio de Alzate. *Madrid,* 1795. 8vo, pp. 226. 3 Plates. 991

Am I not a Man, and a Brother? With all Humility addressed to the British Legislature. *London, Payne and Son,* 1788. 8vo.

On the slave trade. *See* M. R., LXXX., p. 69.

AMAMA (Nicolaus ab). Dissertationum Marinarum Decas. In quâ Præter Marina Problemata, varia passim fundamentalia, & Solidioris Philosophiæ Principiis deducta Dogmata discutiuntur. Autore Nicolao ab Amama. Cum Indice Capitum & Articulorum. *Franckeræ, Excudit Idzardus Alberti,* 1651. 8vo, pp. 596. 993

AMANDUS. Chronica | compendiosissima ab | exordio mundi vsque ad annum Domini | Millesimum, quingentesimum, trigesimum | quartum: per venerandum patrem. F. | Amandum Zierixeensem, ordinis Fra | trum Minorum, regularis obseruan- | tiæ, virum in Diuinis & huma | nis rebus peritissimum. | ¶ Eivusdem tractatvs de | septuaginta hebdomadibus Danielis. | Adiectae svnt episto | læ quæ Christiani regis Aethiopiæ, Dauidis, ad | Clementem septimum Rhomanum pontificem, | anno Domini 1533 destinatæ, cum articulis quibus | dam de fide & moribus Aethiopum Christiano- | rum. ¶ Aliæ quoque tres epistolæ, ex noua maris | Oceani Hispania ad

nos transmissæ, de fructu | mirabili illic surgentis nouæ Ecclesiæ, | ex quibus animus Christianus | merito debeat lætari. ¶ *Antuerpiæ apud Simonem Cocum. Anno Do- | mini.* M. CCCCC. XXXIIII. Mense Maio. | Sm. 8vo, 8 p. l., 128 leaves.+Another Edition. 1553. 8vo.+Also, 1624. Folio. 994

The most interesting portion of this compendious chronicle consists of the Letters of Peter of Ghent, alias De Mura, which have been translated into French by Ternaux, in his "Recueil des pièces relatives à la Conquête du Mexique, 1838," pp. 193–203. *See* Troemel and Bib. Am. Vet.

AMARAL. Compilaçao das leis, decretos, regulamentos, instrucçoes, regimentos, consultas e avisos do governo sobre a arrecadaçao, administraçao, e fiscalisaçao dos bens e dinheiros dos orphaos. Em tres partes. Por Antonio Luiz do Amaral e Silva. Parte I., II. *Pernambuco,* 1864 4to, pp. viii., 392, 34.

AMARO. Doctrina extractada de los catecismos Mexicanos de los Padres Paredes, Carochi y Castano, autores muy selectos: traducida al castellano para mejor instruccion de los Indios, en las Oraciones y Misterios principales de la Doctrina cristiana, por el Presbitero Capellan Don Juan Romualdo Amaro, va añadido en este catecismo, el Préambulo de la confession para la mejor disposicion de los Indios en el Santo Sacramento de la Penitencia, y para las personas curiosas que fueren aficionadas al idioma, con un Modo Práctico de contar, segun fuere el número de la materia, para el mismo fin. *Mexico, Luis Abadiano y Valdez,* 1840. Sm. 8vo, pp. 4, 79. 996

AMATI (G.) Viaggi di Cristoforo Colombo tratti dall' opera Ricerche storico-crit.-scientifiche, etc. Di G. Amati. *Milano,* 1830. 8vo. Map. 997

AMAZON. A Relation of the Great River of the Amazons. *See* [Pagan (Count de)].

Amazon. Colonizacion y Navegacion del Amazonas. *Lima,* 1853. Sm. 4to. 998

AMBERTEUIL (H.) Essais historiques et politiques sur les anglo-américains. Par H. Amberteuil. *Bruxelles,* 1781. 2 vols., 8vo. 999

AMBOY. Proposals by the Proprietors of *East Jersey* in *America,* for the building of a Town on Ambo-Point, and for the Disposition of Lands in that Province; and also for the Encouragement of Artificers and Labourers that shall Transport themselves

thither out of *England, Scotland* and *Ireland.* *London, Printed for Benjamin Clarke,* 1682. 4to, pp. 6. 1000

AMBOYNA. A Trve Relation of the Vnivst, Crvell, and Barbarovs Proceedings against the English at Amboyna, in the East Indies, by the Netherlandish Governour and Councel there ... . *London, H. Lownes for N. Newberry,* 1624. 4to, pp. 38. 1001

Frequently reprinted. Many tracts relative to this cruel massacre can be found in the Library of the Massachusetts Historical Society. The True Relation is introduced here on account of the following:

The Second Part of the Tragedy of Amboyna: or a True Relation of a most Bloody, Treacherous, and Cruel design of the Dutch in the New Netherlands in America for the total ruining and murdering of the English Colonies in New England. *London, for T. Matthews,* 1653. 4to. 1002

AMBROSE (Paul). *See* [Kennedy (J. P.)]

AMEMATEGUI. La Dictadura de O'Higgins en Chile. Por Miguel Luis Amemategui. *Santiago,* 1855. 8vo, pp. 495.

Amendments of the Constitution submitted to the consideration of the American People. *Loyal Publication Society, No.* 83. 8vo, pp. 89. 1003*

Amendments proposed to be added to the Federal Constitution, by the Congress of the United States, held at New York, March 4, 1789. *Boston,* 1790. 8vo, pp. 8. P. 1004

Amendments to our National Constitution, Respectfully submitted to the Citizens of the United States. [About 1820.] 8vo, 1 leaf. 1005

AMENT. De Cultuur en behandeling der West-Indischkoffij en indigo beschreven en vergelijkt met die derzelfde producten in Oost-Indië. *Kampen,* 1836. 8vo. 1006

AMERICA. Translated from the French. *London, Printed for the Translator,* 1750. 2 vols., 8vo. 1007

A scarce and interesting privately printed book, chiefly relating to the Aborigines.

America. An Epistle in Verse, with other Poems. *London,* 1820. 12mo. 1008

America: A Dramatic Poem. *See* [Torrey (John)].

America, an Ode; To the People of England. *London, Almon,* 1776. 4to. 1009

"Poetical, and its author a warm friend to America."—*London Magazine.*

America. Correspondence of the Marquess Wellesley, The Earl of Liverpool, and Viscount Castlereagh, with the American Ministers in London. January, 1810, to July, 1812. A. Presented to Parliament, by Command of His Royal Highness the Prince Regent, February, 1813. Folio, 2 p. l., pp. 59. G. 1010

America. Correspondence between The Marquess Wellesley and Mr. Morris, July, 1810, to March, 1811. B. Folio, 2 p. l., pp. 29. G. 1011

America. Correspondence between The Marquess Wellesley and Mr. Foster, April, 1811, to December, 1811. C. Folio, 2 p. l., pp. 73. G. 1012

America. Correspondence between Viscount Castlereagh, and Messrs. Foster and Baker. March to August, 1812. D. Folio, pp. 114. G. 1013

America. Correspondence Relative to the French Decrees and the Orders in Council. Subsequent to 20th May, 1812. Folio, pp. 35. G. 1014

America and Africa. *London, Cassell,* 1856. 12mo. 1015

America and France. The entire Message of the President of the United States [John Adams] to both Houses of Congress; covering the full powers to, and dispatches from, the Envoys Extraordinary of the United States, to the French Republic. *Boston, B. Russell,* 1798. 8vo, pp. 71. 1016

Reprinted in London, with the title of "American State Papers," 1798. 8vo.

America and the Americans. *See* [Boardman (James)].

America and the West Indies. *See* Long (G.)

America as I Found It. By the Author of Memoir of Mary Lundie Duncan. *London, Nisbet,* 1852. 12mo.+Same. *New York, Carters,* 1852. 12mo, pp. 440. 1017

America Compared with England; the respective Social Effects of the American and English Systems of Government and Legislation, and the Mission of Democracy. *London, E. Wilson,* 1848. 12mo. P. 1018

Ausz America, das ist, ausz der | Newen Welt. | Vnderschidlicher Schrei- | ben Extract, von den Jaren 1616, 1617, 1618. | Was gestalt Acht Patres Societatis, vnd zwo andere | Ordenspersonen, von desz Christlichen Glaubens wegen Ihr Blut | vergossen. Was auch sonst die Patres Societatis Gott zu Ehren, | vnnd zu | ausbreittung seines heiligsten Namens, auff | sich genommen. | Ausz Frantzösischer Sprach in die Teutsche | vbergesetzt. | [Motto.] *Getruckt zu Augspurg, bey Sara Mangin* | *Wittib.*, 1620. | 4to, 2. p. l., pp. 91. 1019

America Discovered. A Poem, In Twelve books. By an American. *New York, J. F. Trow*, 1850. 12mo, pp. 283 (1). 1020

America Dissected. *See* [Macsparran (James)].

America, Disputatio Publica. 1. Quæ sit Origo Gentis Americanæ? 2. An America Veteribus quoquè fuerit cognita? *Rinthelii*. [s. a.] 4to. C. 1021

L'America | Geografico-Storico | Politica, | Ovvero | Descrizione, e nome d'ogni Provincia; sua | estensione, confini, proprietà de' climi, fer- | tilità de' terreni; e Stato politico, utile, ed | economico di ciascuno stabilimento Europeo. | Tomo Primo. | *In Venezia*, | MDCCLXXXV. | *Presso Antonio Zatta e Figli*, | *Con Licenza de' Superiori, e Privilegio.* | 3 vols., 4to, pp. xvi., 322; pp. viii., 288; pp. xii., 236. H. 1022

America in Arms. A Short and Faithful Account of the Conduct of Great Britain towards the American States which forced them to declare themselves Free and Independent, . . . *Printed in the Year* 1781. 8vo. 1023

America Invincible. An Heroic Poem, in Two Books; . . . To which is prefixed, A concise History of the Former Wars in America. Dedicated to his Excellency Horatio Gates, Esq. By an Officer of Rank in the Continental Army. Number I. *Danvers, near Boston*, 1777. 8vo, pp. 40. 1024

Book II. ends with the death of Montgomery. The poem was "to be continued."

La America Lloranda por la temprana muerte de su amado, su padre, su bien y sus delicias el E. S. D. Bernardo de Galvez, Conde de Galvez, &c. Capitan Genl. de la Luisiana y dos Floridas, &c. Humilde rasgo del Lic[o]. D. Agustin Pomposa Fernandez de San Salvador Abogado, &c. *Mexico* [n. d.] Sm. 4to, pp. 25, 6. 1025

America Lost. A Poem of Condolence. Addressed to Britannia. *London, Lewis*, 1778. 4to. 1026

See Monthly Review, First Series, Vol. LVIII., p. 469.

America, or a General Survey. *See* [Everett (Alex. H.)]

America Poetica. Colleccion escojida de Composiciones en Verso escritas por Americanos en el presente siglo. *Valparaiso*, 1846. Rl. 8vo, 13 parts, pp. 820. 1027

America Pois'd in the Balance of Justice. Ornamented with an Elegiac Frontispiece, and a Reconciliatory Tail-piece. In this Research the Mother Country and her Colonies is considered in a New Light, and supported by arguments quite different from those held forth by the Parliamentary Speakers and Polemical Writers on either side of the question. By P—oplicola H—istoricus. *Printed for the Author*, 1776. 4to, pp. 40. 2 Plates. 1028

America und seine jetzige Bewegung. Nach einem Vortrag gehalten im vorstädtischen Handwerkerverein. *Berlin, Reinhold Schlingmann*, 1861. 16mo, pp. 32. 1029

La America Vindicada. *See* [Sanchez Valverde].

America Vindicated from the High Charge of Ingratitude and Rebellion: with a Plan of Legislation Proposed to the Consideration of Both Houses, For Establishing a Permanent and Solid Foundation, For a just constitutional Union, between Great Britain and her Colonies. By a Friend to Both Countries. . . . *Devizes, T. Burrough*, M.DCC.LXXIV. 8vo, Title, pp. 48. 1030

"Written by a warm advocate for the Americans, who proposes that a free constitution should be confirmed to North America, similar to that of Ireland."—*Monthly Review*, Vol. L., p. 325.

America. A most singular woodcut or broadside, measuring about 13½ in. by 8½ in. with 4 lines of letterpress beneath, in German, purporting to be a representation and description of the natives discovered by the Portuguese on the northern coast of South America. The following is a literal translation of the inscription, viz.—"This figure represents to us the people and island which have been discovered by the Christian king of Portugal or by his subjects. The people are thus naked, handsome, brown, well shaped in body, their heads, necks, arms, private parts, feet of men and women, are a little covered with feathers. The men also have many precious stones in their faces and breasts. No one else has anything, but all things are in common.

And the men have as wives those who please them, be they mothers, sisters, or friends, therein make they no distinction. They also fight with each other. They also eat each other, even those who are slain, and hang the flesh of them in the smoke. They become a hundred and fifty years of age. And have no government." 1031

The cut attempts to represent the minutiæ of the foregoing inscription. It is believed to be the earliest xylographic print relating to America, and unique. Its date is, doubtless, very shortly subsequent to the letters of Columbus announcing his discovery. In Stevens' Am. Bibliographer, pp. 7, 8, it is reproduced in fac-simile, and described at greater length.

De Americaansche Mercurius behelsende drie . . . Geschiedenissen van Liefdens Hartstochten, Onkuysche Rampspoeden en Rampsalige Minnedriften . . . in America voorgevallen. *Amsterdam*, 1678. 12mo. Plates. M. 1032

An interesting and curious book, now very rare.

Les Américains, ou, la preuve de la Religion Chrétienne. Par les Lumières Naturelles. 1811. 6 vols., 8vo. 1033

American Academy of Arts and Sciences. Memoirs of the American Academy of Arts and Sciences. Vol. I., *Boston*, 1785. Vol. II., Part I., *Boston*, 1793; Part II., *Boston*, 1804. Vol. III., *Cambridge*, 1809–15. Vol. IV., *Cambridge*, 1818–20. New series, Vol. I.–VIII., *Cambridge*, 1833–1861. 1034

A list of the articles contained in these volumes is inserted in Trübner's Bibl. Guide, pp. 7–17.

Proceedings of the American Academy of Arts and Sciences, 1846–1865, &c. *Boston and Cambridge*, 1848–1866. 6 vols., 8vo. 1035

American Adventure by Land and Sea; being remarkable instances of enterprise and fortitude among Americans; Shipwrecks, Indian Captivities, &c. *New York, Harpers*, 1841, &c. 2 vols., 18mo. 1036

The American Alarm, or the Bostonian Plea, for the Rights and Liberties of the People. Humbly addressed to the King and Council, and to the Constitutional Sons of Liberty in America. By the British Bostonian. *Boston, Printed and Sold by D. Kneeland and N. Davis, in Queen Street*, 1763. 8vo, pp. 52. W. 1037

American Almanac. *New Brunswick, N. J.*, 1801. 12mo. 1038

The American Almanac and Repository of Useful Knowl-

edge for the Year 1830–1862. *Boston*, 1829–'62. 33 vols., 12mo. 1039

The volume for 1830 was edited by Jared Sparks; from 1831 to 1842 the work was conducted by Joseph E. Worcester; from 1843 to 1847 by Francis Bowen, subsequently by George P. Sanger. The volumes for 1839, 1849 and 1859 contain general indexes to the volumes for 1830–39, 1840–49 and 1850–59, respectively. This valuable work, which is, in fact, a compendious annual register, terminated in 1862, is well worthy of being preserved as a book of reference. It was succeeded by the National Almanac.

The American and British Chronicle of War and Politics; being an Accurate and Comprehensive Register of the most memorable Occurrences in the last ten Years of His Majesty's Reign: in which will be found above Eighteen Hundred Interesting Events, During the late War between Great Britain and America, France, Spain and Holland; From May 10, 1773, to July 16, 1783. The whole carefully collected from Authentic Records, and correctly arranged in Chronological Order. Multum in Parvo. This compendium, or Political System of Foreign and Domestic Affairs, is a faithful Diary of Civil and Military Transactions, extracted from Government Dispatches and Official Papers, Votes of the House of Commons and Lords, Resolutions of Congress, Acts of Council, Royal Proclamations, Edicts, &c. Provincial Considerations, Debates, Petitions, Addresses, Meetings, and Determinations. Every Engagement by Sea and Land, Military Operations, Civil Establishments, Changes in Administration, Political Struggles, and Principal Appointments; Treaties of Alliance, Commerce, and Peace; Constitutional and Financial Reform; Land and Marine Force of the Belligerent Powers; Public Revenue, Debt, and Expenditure, &c. &c. &c. To the Recapitulation of Public Occurrences during the late War in America and in Europe, is added a general Table of Prior Events; British Governors in America at the Commencement of Hostilities; Members of the first Congress; Constitution and Form of Government of the several States, and Population in each; Ships of War taken, lost, or destroyed; Roads in America; and a copious Abridgement of the Treaties of Peace. *London, Printed for the Author* [1783]. 8vo, 60 unnumbered leaves. S. 1040

The dedication is signed E. J. S. Faribault, No. 926, quotes a book with a similar title, 4 vols., 4to, London, 1801, which is probably an error.

American and English Oppression, and British and American Abolitionists: a Letter addressed to R. D. Webb, Esq. By an American in his Fatherland. *London*, 1853. 8vo. 1041

American and West-Indian Gazetteer, containing an Authentic Description of the Colonies and Islands in that part of the Globe. *London*, 1778. 12mo. 1042

American Anecdotes: Original and Select. By an American. In Two Volumes. *Boston, Putnam & Hunt*, 1830. 12mo, pp. 300 and 300. 1043

Contains four hundred and eighty-seven anecdotes, mostly relating to the American Revolution, with an index. Attributed to Freeman Hunt.

American Annals, 1775. *See* [Pennant (Thos.)]

The American Annual Cyclopædia, and Register of Important Events of the Year 1861. ... *New York, D. Appleton & Co.* [1862]. Rl. 8vo. Continued annually. 1044

The American Annual Monitor for 1858; or, Obituary of the Members of the Society of Friends in America for the Year 1858. *New York, Wm. Wood*, 1859, and continued. 1045

The American Annual Register for 1796. *See* [Callender (J. T.)]

The American Annual Register; for the Years 1825–6; 1826–7; 1827–8–9; 1827–8–9. Second Part; 1829–30; 1830–31 ... For 1825–9, *New York*; 1829–31, *Boston*, 1827–32. 8vo. 1046

Each volume has a double paging. A second edition of the volume for 1826–7 was published in 1835. The work was continued, with the following title:

Fessenden & Co.'s Series. The American Annual Register of Public Events; for the Year 1831–32. ... *Brattleboro', Vt., Fessenden*, 1833. 8vo.+The American Annual Register for the Year 1832–3. *New York, Wm. Jackson*, 1835. 8vo. 1047

Complete sets in eight volumes are rather scarce.

American Antiquarian Society. Address to the Members ... together with the Laws and Regulations of the Institution, and a List of Donations to the Society .... *Worcester, William Manning, March*, 1819. 8vo, pp. 38. 1048

Archæologia Americana. Transactions and Collections of the American Antiquarian Society. Published by Direction of the Society. Vol. I. *Worcester, Mass.*, MDCCCXX. 8vo, pp. 436. Vol. II. [Indian Dialects of North America.] *Cambridge*, 1836. pp. xxx., 573 (1). Vol. III. *Boston*, 1857. pp. cxxxviii., 378. Vol. IV. *Boston*, 1860. pp. viii., 355 (1). 1049

A list of the contents of each volume will be found in Trübner's Bibl. Guide, pp 246–248.

A Catalogue of Books in the Library of the American Antiquarian Society, in Worcester, Massachusetts. [By C. C. Baldwin.] *Worcester*, 1837. 8vo, pp. 571 in all. 1050

This catalogue is replete with the rarest of American pamphlets, as the reference mark W in this dictionary will abundantly testify.

Catalogue of Officers and Members of the American Antiquarian Society, May 29, 1839. ... With the Laws of the Society, as revised. *Worcester*, 1839. 8vo. W. 1051

Communication from the President of the American Antiquarian Society to the Members, October 24th, 1814. *Worcester* [n. d.] 8vo, pp. 12, 6. 1052

Proceedings of the American Antiquarian Society. ... Vol. I., May, 1846, to May, 1848. Vol. II. (pp. 1–160). Vol. III. *Boston*, 1846–49. 8vo (pp. 105–184). Proceedings at the Annual Meeting, Worcester, Oct. 23, 1843. *Worcester*. 8vo. Continued semi-annually. 1053

The American Apollo, containing the Publications of the [Massachusetts] Historical Society, Essays, Moral, Political, and Poetical, and the daily Occurrences in the Natural, Civil, and Commercial World. ... Part I. and II. in 39 Nos. *Boston*, 1791–92. 8vo. 1054

American Archives. *See* Force (Peter).

American Arguments for British Rights. *See* [Hamilton (Alex.)].

American Art. *See* [Waterston (R. C.)]

Transactions of the American Art-Union. For the Year 1844–49. *New York*. 8vo.+ Bulletin, 1848–1851, and Supplementary Bulletin, May 1, 1853. *New York*. 8vo and 4to. 1055

American Association for the Advancement of Science. Report on the History and Progress of the American Coast Survey up to ... 1858. By the Committee of Twenty appointed by the ... Association ... August, 1857. [n. p., 1858.] 8vo. pp. 88. 1056

The composition of the report was begun by Judge J. K. Kane, and, after his death, completed by F. A. P. Barnard.

Proceedings ... . First Meeting, held at Philadelphia, September, 1848. *Philadelphia*, 1849. 8vo, pp. 156. 1057

Continued annually.

Constitution, Addresses and List of Members of the American Association for the Promotion of Social Science, with the questions proposed for discussion, to which are added, Minutes of the Transactions of the Association, July, 1866. *Boston*, 1866. 8vo, pp. 64. 1058

American Atlantic and Pacific Ship Canal Company. Charter and Act of Incorporation ... and Treaty of Protection Negociated between the United States and Great Britain. *New York*, 1850. 8vo, pp. 30.+Charter and Act of Incorporation ... as amended: also Treaty [as above]; ... and Charter granted by the State of Nicaragua to the Accessory Transit Company. *New York*, 1852. 8vo, pp. 28. 1059

American Atlas, consisting of Twenty One Large Maps, viz. a Map of each State and Province, as well as the British Provinces and the West Indies. *Philadelphia*, 1795. Folio. 1060

This is the first native American Atlas. The maps were engraved for the American edition of Guthrie's Geography. A doubtful title; from a bookseller's catalogue.

The American Atlas; containing the following Maps.—viz— 1. North-America 2. South-America 3. United States 4. New-Hampshire 5. Province of Maine 6. Massachusetts 7. Vermont. 8. Rhode-Island 9. Connecticut 10. New-York 11. New-Jersey 12. Pennsylvania 13. Delaware and Maryland 14. Virginia 15. Kentucky, with the adjoining Territories 16. North-Carolina 17. South-Carolina 18. Georgia 19. Tennessee 20. West-Indies. *New-York, Published by John Reid, Bookseller and Stationer, No.* 106, *Water-Street.* 1796. Folio. H. 1061

American Atlas. A Complete Historical, Chronological and Geographical American Atlas; being a Guide to the History of North and South America, and the West Indies: exhibiting an accurate Account of the Discovery, Settlement and Progress of their various Kingdoms, States, Provinces, &c., Together with the Wars, celebrated Battles and remarkable Events, to the year 1822, According to the plan of Le Sage's Atlas, and intended as a Companion to Lavoisne's Improvement of that celebrated Work. *Philadelphia, Carey & Lea*, 1822. Folio. 53 Maps. 1062

For a French translation of this work, *see* Buchon (J. A.)

American Atlas. *See* Jefferys (Thos.)

The American Bard; or, Select Poems of various Times and Countries ... . No. 1., containing: ... "The Land of the

Aztecs," translated from the Mexican Poet, Heredia ... . *New York*, 1860. 8vo, pp. 16. H. 1063

American Bards. *See* [Waln (Robert)].

The American Bee, a Collection of Entertaining Histories. *Leominster, Mass.*, 1797. 12mo. 1064

The American Biography, containing Biographical Sketches of the Officers of the Revolution and of the principal Statesmen of that period, to which are added the Life and Character of Benedict Arnold, and the Narrative of Major Andre, compiled from authentic sources. *Wheeling, F. Kenyon*, 1833. 8vo. 1065

The American Bloody Register, containing the History of the Lives, Last Words and Dying Confession of three most noted Criminals, Richard Barrick and John Sullivan, Highway Robbers, and Confession of Alexander White, Murderer and Pirate. *Boston, Printed and sold by E. Russell*, 1784. 12mo, pp. 30. 1066

The American Bureau of Mines. Union Pacific Railroad. A Geological and Agricultural Survey of 100 miles West of Omaha. By the American Bureau of Mines. *New York*, 1866. 8vo, pp. 44. 1067

American Bravery. *See* [Butler (James)].

American Candour, in a Tract lately published at Boston, entitled "An Analysis of the late Correspondence between our Administration and Great Britain and France," with an attempt to show what are the real causes of the failure of the Negociations between France and America. *London*, 1809. 8vo. 1068

American Charters; granted by Charles II., William and Mary, and George II.; viz., Connecticut, Rhode Island, Pennsylvania, Massachusetts Bay, and Georgia. *London* [n. d.] Folio, pp. 10, 14, 12, 21, 18. C. 1069

A conjectural title from the catalogue of the library of Congress.

The American Christian Record; containing the History, Confession of Faith and Statistics of each Religious Denomination in the United States and Europe; a list of all the Clergymen, with their Post-office Address, etc. *New York*, 1860. 12mo, pp. 696. 1070

American Chronological Tablets, exhibiting in a Methodical

Manner the most Remarkable Occurrences from the Creation of the World to the Present Period. *Baltimore*, 1812. 18mo.

American Chronology: or a Summary of Events relating to the United States, from 1492 to 1813. *Philadelphia*, 1813. 12mo. 1072

The American Citizen's Manual of Reference. *New York*, 1840. 8vo, pp. 102. 1073

The American Citizen's sure Guide: being a Collection of most important State Papers: such as The Declaration of Independence: Articles of Confederation and Perpetual Union: The Constitution of the United States: All the Treaties now in force which the United States have ever made: Merchants' and Seamen's Acts: Duties on Goods, Wares and Merchandize: Census as taken in 1800, &c. ... *Printed for Charles Peirce of Portsmouth, N. H., by S. Sewall, Kennebunk*, 1804. 12mo, pp. 356 (2).+And *Trenton*, 1813. 12mo. H. 1074

The American Civil War, as seen by an Englishman. [*London?* 186–.] 16mo, pp. 4. 1075

American Claim of Rights, addressed to the Deputies of North America, in General Congress. *Charles-Town, S. C.*, 1774. 4to.

American Colonization Society. *See* Slavery.

American Commissioners of Claims at Paris. Statement, Correspondence, Conjectural Notes, &c. *Philadelphia*, 1807. 8vo.

American Congregational Union. The Year Book of the ... Union for the Year 1854. [Vol. I.] *New York*, 1854. 8vo. Continued. 1078

The American Crisis. *See* [Paine (T.)]

The American Crisis, by a Citizen of the World, inscribed to those Members of the Community vulgarly called Patriots. *London, Flexney*, 1777. 8vo. 1079

"The Citizen of the World takes for granted a speedy triumph over the colonists, and accordingly recommends, in the strongest manner, clemency towards the vanquished."—M. R., LVI., p. 400.

The American Crisis; its Causes, Significance, and Solution. By Americus. *Chicago, Ill., J. R. Walsh*, 1862. 1080

American Destiny: what shall it be, Republican or Cossack?

An Argument addressed to the People of the late Union, North and South. *New York, Columbian Association*, 1864. 8vo, pp. 44.

American Dialogues of the Dead and Dialogues of the American Dead. 1814. 8vo. 1081*a*

American Educational Year-Book, for 1857: comprising an Almanac, Educational Statistics, Teacher's Directory, etc. [Edited by the Rev. Augustus Russell Pope. Vol. I.] *Boston, James Robinson and Company*, etc., 1857. 12mo, pp. 192. Continued. H. 1082

American Discovery and Conquest. *London*, 1857. 12mo.

American Encroachments. *See* [Atcheson (Nath.)]

Transactions of the American Ethnological Society. Vols. I.–III. *New York*, 1850–1853. 8vo. 1084

A list of the contents will be found in Trübner's Bibl. Guide.

American Exports and Imports; Calculations and Tables of Corresponding Equivalents, at different Rates of Exchange, of American Exports and Imports; adapted to the Commerce of Great Britain and the United States, as a Manual for Merchants and Manufacturers. Second Edition. *London*, 1851. 4to, pp. 84.

The American Freedman. A Monthly Journal ... . Vol. I. No. I. April, 1866. *New York*, 1866. 8vo. 1086

American Freedmen's Inquiry Commission. Preliminary Report touching the Condition and Management of Emancipated Refugees; made to the Secretary of War ... June 30, 1863. ... *New York, John F. Trow, Printer*, 1863. 8vo, pp. 40. H. 1087

The American Gazette; Being a Collection of all the Authentic Addresses, Memorials, Letters, Petitions and other Papers, which relate to the Present Disputes between Great Britain and her Colonies, containing also many original Papers never before Published. *London, G. Kearsley*, 1768–1770. 8vo. Nos. I to 6, and an Appendix. 1088

The title-page of some copies varies from the above. It includes a Journal of Transactions and Correspondence of Bernard Gage. *See* M. R., Vol. XXXIX., p. 326; XLII., p. 485. A London sale Catalogue quotes an edition with a Boston imprint.

American Gardener's Magazine, and Register of Useful Discoveries and Improvements in Horticulture and Rural Affairs. Vol. I.–II. ... Conducted by C. M. Hovey and P. B. Hovey,

Jr. *Boston: Russell, Shattuck and Williams; and Hovey and Company*, 1835–36. 8vo. Continued as the Magazine of Horticulture. H. 1089

The American Gazetteer; containing a distinct Account of all the Parts of the New World: Their Situation, Climate, Soil, Produce, Former and Present Condition; Commodities, Manufactures, and Commerce. Together with An accurate Account of the Cities, Towns, Ports, Bays, Rivers, Lakes, Mountains, Passes, and Fortifications: The whole intended to exhibit the Present State of Things in that part of the Globe, and the Views and Interests of the several Powers who have Possessions in America. Illustrated with proper Maps. In three volumes. *London, J. Millar*, 1762. 12mo, pp. xxiv., 324; 348; 348.

A meritorious work. *See* M. R., XXV., p. 155. Translated into Italian in 1763. *See* "Il Gazettiere Americano."

American Geographical and Statistical Society. Annual Report ... . For ... 1857. *Society's Rooms, New-York University*, 1850. 8vo, pp. 50 (1). Continued.+Bulletin. Vol. I., for ... 1852. *New York, G. P. Putnam*, 1852. 8vo, pp. 79 (1). Continued.+Catalogue of the Library ... . Compiled by E. R. Straznicky. *New York, G. B. Teubner, Printer*, 1857. 8vo, pp. 32.+Charter and By-Laws. *New York*, 1852. 8vo.+Also, 1860. 8vo, pp. 31.+Proceedings ... . Vol. I. *New York* [1863]. 8vo. +Statement of the Objects and Organization. *New York*, 1856. 8vo, pp. 21.+Also, *New York*, 1857. 8vo, pp. 14. 1091

American Geographical and Statistical Society. The Polar Exploring Expedition. A Special Meeting ... held March 22, 1860. *New York*, 1860. 8vo, pp. 40. Map. H. 1092

The American Gift-Book, containing Washington's Farewell Address, the Constitution of the United States, Sketches of Washington, &c. *New York*, 1859. 12mo. 1093

American Glory. *See* Free Trade.

The American Guide Book; being a Hand-Book for Tourists and Travellers through every part of the United States. *New York and Philadelphia*, 1846. 12mo. 1094

The American Historical Magazine. Vol. I. Nos. I to 6.

January to June, 1836. *New Haven, William Storer, Jr.*, 1836. 8vo, pp. 240. 1095

No more published. It contains much matter relating to New England not to be found elsewhere; among other things a life of Gov. Eaton.

American Historical Magazine. Vol. I. No. I. January, 1850. *New York*, 1850. 1096

Transactions of the American Historical Society. Vol. I. *Washington*, 1839. 8vo. 1097

American Historical Tales. *New York, Appleton*, 1850. 12mo.

American Historical Tales for Youth. *New York*, 1831, &c. 18mo, pp. 204, 177, 174. 1099

The Lives of John Smith, Boone, and Randolph, in one volume.

American History and Biography, etc. *New York, C. Lohman*, 1838. 18mo, pp. vi., 258. 1100

American Home Missionary Society Report. *New York*, 1826. Continued. 1101

American Homestead Association. Proposals to establish the ... Association. [*Washington*, 1865.] Broadside. H. 1101*a*

The American Hunter, a Tale, from Incidents which happened during the War with America. To which is annexed a Somersetshire Story. *London, Kearsley*, 1788. 12mo. 1102

See the M. R., LXXIX., p. 170.

American Husbandry. *See* [Young (Arthur)].

The American in Algiers, or the Patriot of '76 in Captivity; A Poem. *New York*, 1797. 12mo. 1103

The American in Algiers. A Poem. Canto II. [No imprint.] 12mo. M. 1104

American Independence the Interest of Great Britain. *See* [Cartwright (John)].

American Institute. Journal ... a Monthly Publication devoted to Agriculture, Commerce, Manufactures, and the Arts, accompanied with Public Documents. *New York*, 1836–40. 4 vols., 8vo. 1105

Transactions of the American Institute. Annual Report made to the Legislature. *Albany*, 1842. 8vo. Continued. 1106

Alphabetical and Analytical Catalogue of the American Institute Library. With the Rules and Regulations, &c. *New York, W. L. S. Harrison, Printer*, 1852. 8vo, pp. 8, 212. H.

American Institute of Instruction, Act of Incorporation, By-Laws, &c. *Boston*, 1831. 12mo.+Introductory Lectures. *Boston*, 1831. 8vo. 1108

Continued annually. The later volumes include "The Journal of Proceedings, and a List of the Officers."

American International Relief Committee for the Suffering Operatives of Great Britain. Report ... 1862–63. *New York, Printed by C. A. Alvord*, 1864. 8vo, pp. 72. H. 1109

Relates to the cotton famine.

The American Jest Book, containing a Choice Selection of Jests, Anecdotes, Bon Mots, Stories, &c. *Printed at Harrisburgh, for C. Carey, of Philadelphia*, 1796. 8vo. 1110

This scarce book is one of the earliest publications of its kind in the United States.

American Journal of Conchology. Edited by G. W. Tryon, Junr. Vol. I. *Philadelphia*, 1865. 8vo, pp. viii., 387. 30 Plates. 1111

American Journal of Education. For ... 1826–1829. Vol. I.–IV. *Boston*, 1826–29. 8vo. 1112

Monthly. Edited by W. Russell. Continued in the "American Annals of Education."

The American Journal of Education and College Review. Published monthly. Editors: Absalom Peters, D.D., Henry Barnard, LL.D. Vol. I. August, 1855–January, 1856. No. 1–2. *New York, N. A. Calkins* [1855–56]. 8vo. 1113

After these two numbers the editors separated, and established independent journals, Mr. Peters taking as associate editor Hon. S. S. Randall, and also in No. 8, sqq., Alexander Wilder, M.D. Mr. Barnard's Journal dropped the words "and College Review" from the title. Nos. 1 and 2 also appeared as

The American Journal of Education. Published bi-monthly. Edited by Henry Barnard, LL.D. Vol. I. 1856. Nos. I and 2. Second Edition. Originally issued as Nos. I. and II. of the American Journal of Education and College Review. *Hartford, F. C. Brownell* [1856]. 8vo. Continued. 1114

With numerous biographies and portraits. Vol. XI. is also "New Series. Vol. I."

American Journal of Geology and Natural Science. Con-

ducted by G. W. Featherstonhaugh, 1831. *Philadelphia*, 1831. 8vo. 1115

American Journal of Improvements in the Useful Arts, and Mirror of the Patent Office in the United States. By I. L. Skinner. Assisted by Uriah Brown. *Washington*, 1828. 8vo.

Vols. I.–II., New Series. Vol. I., 1831.

American Journal of Indigenous Materia Medica, and Repertory of Medical Science. Conducted by B. Keith, M.D. Vol. I. No. I. November, 1860. *New York*, 1860. 8vo.

The American Journal of Insanity, edited by the Officers of the New York State Lunatic Asylum, Utica. Volume I. *Utica*, 1844–5. 8vo, pp. 396. Continued. H. 1118

Vol. IV., sqq., "*Printed at the Asylum.*"

American Journal of Numismatics and Bulletin of the American Numismatic and Archæological Society. *New York, Edward Cogan*, 1866. Rl. 8vo. 1119

The American Journal of Science, more especially of Mineralogy, Geology, and the other branches of Natural History ... . Conducted by Benjamin Silliman ... . *New York* (I.–L.), *New Haven*, 1818–[47]. 50 vols. Second Series. Vol. I. *New Haven* [1846]. 8vo. Continued. 1120

Conducted by Prof. B. Silliman to January, 1838; to October, 1845, by Profs. B. Silliman and B. Silliman, Junr.; afterward by Profs. B. Silliman, B. Silliman, Junr., and J. D. Dana, aided subsequently to May, 1851, by Prof. A. Gray, Prof. L. Agassiz, Dr. W. I. Burnett, and Dr. W. Gibbs. Vol. 50 is "General Index to Vol. 1–49," and the Preface contains a history of the work; No. 30 of "Second Series" is "General Index to Vol. 1–10;" No. 60 is "General Index of Vol. 11–20;" No. 90 is "General Index to Vol. 21–30." The First Series was quarterly, the Second is bi-monthly.

The American Journal of the Medical Sciences. Edited by Isaac Hays, M.D. Vol. I. *Philadelphia*, 1827. 8vo. 1121

First Series, Vol. I.–XXVI. New Series, continued.

The American Kalendar, or United States Register for the year 1794. To be continued annually. *Philadelphia*, 1794. 12mo, pp. 187.+*London, Reprinted for J. Debrett*, 1794. 12mo, pp. 187. 1122

Highly commended in the *Monthly Review*, Vol. XV., p. 338. The last of which I find a notice is dated 1798.

The American Keepsake ... with a Steel-Plate Engraving of

all the Presidents of the United States, and containing the Declaration of Independence ... Constitution of the United States ... Washington's Inaugural Address, First Annual Message, and his Farewell Address ... . To which is added Date of Formation of State Constitutions, Qualifications of Voters ... in each State; Qualifications for Governors, Senators and Representatives in the Different States. ... To which is appended the New Postage Law of 1845, Entire. *Boston*, 1845. 12mo, pp. 75. H. 1123

The American Laborer: Devoted to the cause of Protection to Home Industry. Vol. I. *New York*, 1842–3. 8vo. 1124

The American Landscape, No. I. Containing ... Views ... . Engraved from Original and Accurate Drawings ... and from well authenticated Pictures; with Historical and Topographical Illustrations. *New York, Elam Bliss*, 1830. 4to, pp. 16. 6 Plates. H. 1125

American Legal Association. Manual of the ... Association: containing its Plan, Constitution and Secretary's Report, together with the Catalogue of its Members, embracing the ... Address of at least one ... Lawyer at almost every Village and City in the Union. Also, The Legal Forms for the acknowledgment of Deeds and the Rates of Interest in every State. *New York, June*, 1851. 8vo, pp. 31 (1). H. 1126

American Liberty, A Poem. [Mottoes.] *New York, Printed by J. Anderson, at Beekman Slip*, MDCCLXXV. 8vo. P. 1127

American Literary Association. Constitution. *Philadelphia*, 1809. 16mo, pp. 16. P. 1128

The American Literary Gazette. *See* American Publishers' Circular.

The American Literary Magazine.—Monthly—By T. Dwight Sprague. Vol. I. *Albany, Printed by Joel Munsell*, 1847. 8vo, pp. iv., 392. Continued. H. 1129

Vol. III., &c., *Hartford, Printed by J. Gaylord Wells*. Contains many biographies and portraits.

American Lyceum of Science and the Arts, Composed of Associations for Mutual Instruction, &c. *Worcester*, 1827. 8vo. 1129*a*

American Lyceum, or Society for the Improvement of Schools,

and Diffusion of Useful Knowledge. [Prospectus.] *Boston, T. R. Marvin, Printer*, 1829. 8vo, pp. 16.+Proceedings of the Convention held in New-York, 1831, 32, to organize the National Department of the Institution. *Boston*, 1831. 8vo.+Also, Proceedings July, 1832. No. I. *New York*, 1832. 8vo.

The American Magazine, a Monthly Miscellany, devoted to Literature, Science, History, Biography, and the Arts; including also State Papers and Public Documents, with ... Public News, and Passing Events ... . Vol. I. *Albany*, 1815. 8vo. H.

The American Magazine and Historical Chronicle. ... *Boston, Rogers and Fowle*, 1743–46. 3 vols., 8vo. M. 1132

The American Magazine and Monthly Chronicle for the British Colonies. Volume I. Containing From October 1757 to October 1758 inclusive. By a Society of Gentlemen. ... *Philadelphia, William Bradford* [1757–58]. 8vo, pp. 656 (6). H. P.

The American Magazine and Repository of Useful Literature. Edited by John S. Wood, M.D., and Barnabas Wood, assisted by several Literary Gentlemen. *Albany*, 1841–42. 8vo. Vol. I; Vol. 2, 3 nos. 1134

American Magazine. Containing a Miscellaneous Collection of Original and other Valuable Essays ... . [Edited by Noah Webster.] *New York, Printed by Samuel Loudon, Dec.* 1787 *to Nov.* 1788. 8vo, pp. 882. H. 1135

The American Magazine for [the Year] 1769. *Philadelphia*, 1769. 8vo. P. 1136

Edited by Lewis Nicola. Nine numbers only published. "The Transactions of the American Philosophical Society" for 1768, 8vo, pp. 118, are usually added.

American Magazine of Useful and Entertaining Knowledge. ... *Boston, John L. Sibley and James B. Dow*, 1834–37. 3 vols., 8vo. Woodcuts. H. 1137

The American Magazine of Wit. A Collection of Anecdotes, Stories, and Narratives, Humorous, Marvellous, Witty, Queer, Remarkable, and Interesting. Partly Selected, and Partly Original. With Plates, By A Judge Of the Convivial Court of Dover, Aided by a Jury of Odd Fellows. *New York, H. C. Southwick*, 1803. 12mo, pp. 346. Frontispiece folded, and plate.+Another Edition. *New York*, 1808. 12mo, pp. 332.

American Magazine; or, Monthly View of the Political State of the British Colonies: for March, 1741. 8vo. C. 1139

The American Mail-Bag; or, Tales of the War. *London, Ward & Lock*, 1863. Fcap 8vo, pp. 348. 1140

American Mariners. *See* [Davis (John)].

American Mechanics' Magazine: containing Useful Original Matter ... as well as Selections ... Conducted by Associated Mechanics. [A weekly paper.] *New York, Published by James V. Seaman*, 1825, 1826. Vols. I., II. pp. 412, 299. P.

Only two volumes published.

American Medical Association. Laws and Regulations ... with a Short Account of the Educational and Benevolent Institutions of Philadelphia. ... *Philadelphia, Printed by T. K. and P. G. Collins*, 1855. 18mo, pp. 127. Map.+With a Sketch of Detroit, and a Brief History of the University of Michigan, and of the Development of the Resources of the State. ... *Detroit, Printed by R. F. Johnstone*, 1856. 12mo, pp. 92. Plate. H.

There are probably other similar volumes. The Sketch of Detroit "is made up of extracts from 'Sketches,' etc., by Robert E. Roberts."

American Medical Association Transactions. Vol. I. *Philadelphia*, 1850. 8vo. Continued. 1143

American Medical Recorder. Conducted by J. Eberle, G. S. Pattison, H. W. Ducachet [etc.] Vol. I. *Philadelphia*, 1818. 8vo. Continued. 1144

American Medical Register. *See* Hosack (Dr.)

American Medical Times. Being a Weekly Series of the New York Journal of Medicine. Vol. I. No. I. June 2, 1860. *New York*, 1860. 8vo, pp. 18. 1145

American Memoranda. *See* [Lumsden (James)].

American Military Biography; containing the Lives, Characters and Anecdotes of the Officers of the Revolution, who were most Distinguished in Achieving our National Independence. Also The Life of Gilbert Motier Lafayette, Major General in the Continental Army, &c. *Printed for Subscribers*, 1825. 12mo, pp. xxiii., 240, 184. Plates. + Another Edition. *Cincinnati*, 1831. 12mo. 1146

The American Military Pocket Atlas; Being an approved Collection of Correct Maps, both General and Particular, of The British Colonies, Especially those which now are, or probably may be, The Theatre of War. Taken principally from the Actual Surveys and judicious Observations of Engineers De Brahm and Romans; Cook, Jackson and Collet; Maj. Holland, and other Officers, Employed in His Majesty's Fleets and Armies. *London, R. Sayer and J. Bennet* [1776]. 8vo, pp. viii.; List of Maps, 1 leaf; 6 Maps, folded. 1147

There are copies in which the title varies from the above, but the collation is the same. *See* Stevens's Nuggets, Nos. 86, 87.

American Mineralogical Journal. Conducted by Archibald Bruce, M.D., &c. *New York*, 1810. Vol. I, 8vo. 1148

The American Miscellany of Popular Tales, Essays, Sketches of Character, Poetry, and Jeux d'Esprit. *London*, 1840. 8vo.

History of the American Missionary Association: its Constitution and Principles, Third Edition, revised and enlarged. *New York*, 1860. 24mo, pp. 72. H. 1149*a*

The American Mock-Bird, a Collection of the most Familiar Songs now in Vogue. *New York*, 1760. 12mo. 1150

The American Monitor. A Political, Historical and Commercial Magazine, Devoted to the Affairs of South America. 1824–25. 2 vols., 8vo. 1151

Includes, also, military and mining information.

American Monitor, or the Republican Magazine for Oct. 1785. *Boston*, 1785. Vol. I. No. I. 4to. 1152

American Monthly Magazine. *New York*, 1833–38. 12 vols., 8vo. 1153

First series, six volumes, edited by H. W. Herbert and A. D. Patterson. Second series, six volumes, edited by Charles F. Hoffman and Park Benjamin.

American Monthly Magazine and Critical Review. *New York*, 1817–18. 4 vols., 8vo. H. 1154

Vol. I. was edited by H. Biglow; II. and III. by H. Biglow and O. L. Holley; IV. by O. L. Holley. De Witt Clinton, Dr. Mitchell, J. K. Paulding, and other eminent men, contributed to this magazine.

American Monthly Magazine and Review. *New York*, 1799–1800. 2 vols., 8vo. 1155

The American Monthly Magazine. [Edited by Jas. McHenry.] *Philadelphia*, 1824. 2 vols., 8vo. 1156

American Monthly Magazine: edited by N. P. Willis. Vol. I.–III. *Boston*, 1829–31. 3 vols., 8vo. 1157

American Monthly Review. *Cambridge and Boston*, 1832–1833. 4 vols., 8vo. 1158

The American Monthly Review; or Literary Journal, from January to April, inclusive, 1795, with an appendix. *Philadelphia*, 1795. Vol. I., 8vo. 1159

American Moral and Sentimental Magazine: Edited by T. Kirk. *New York*, 1797. Vols. I. and II., 8vo. 1160

Includes a long dissertation on the Welch Indians.

The American Museum: Antiquities, Curiosities, Beauties and Varieties of Nature and Art in America. 1823. 18mo.

The American Museum, or Repository of Ancient and Modern Fugitive Pieces, Prose and Poetical. ... *Philadelphia, Printed by Mathew Carey*, M.DCC.LXXXVII.–M.DCC.XCII. 12 vols., 8vo. H. & M. 1162

Vol. I., 2 p. l., pp. xvi., 576. Vol. II., pp. 600, 22 published in 1787. Vol. III., pp. xvi., 603 (1). Vol. IV., pp. 592, published in 1788. Vol. V., The American Museum, or Universal Magazine: containing, Essays on Agriculture—Commerce—Manufactures—Natural and Civil History and Biography—Law Information—Public Papers—Intelligence—Moral Tales—Ancient and Modern Poetry, &c. &c. For the Year 1789. First Part, From January to June. *Philadelphia, Carey, Stewart & Co.*, 1789. pp. 628. Vol. VI., returned to the first title, pp. 492; Proceedings of Congress, pp. 46, Index, pp. (6); published in 1789. Vol. VII., with same title as Vol. VI., pp. 344, and Appendices 44, 44, 44, 40, and Index (4). Vol. VIII., pp. 288 and App. 40, 80, 20, 52, in 1790. Vol. IX., pp. 344 and App. 48, 40, 48. Vol X., pp. 308, App. 36, 48, 44, in 1791. Vol. XI., pp. 308, App. 36, 92, 48 (8). Vol XII., pp. 352 and App. 36, 44, 40. "This work was printed and edited by Mathew Carey. 'I was much attached to this work, and had great reluctance to abandon it, unproductive and vexatious as was the management of it; but at length I sang its requiem, at the close of the year 1792. That it had considerable merit is universally acknowledged; and there is no vanity in the declaration, as the work did not contain a single essay of my own. The whole of my labour consisted in the selection of its contents, and the addition occasionally of a few notes, of little importance.'—*M. Carey's Autobiography*, in *New Eng. Mag.* Washington said that a more useful literary plan had never been undertaken in America, or one more deserving of public encouragement."—RICH. Resumed as:

The American Museum: or, Annual Register of Fugitive Pieces, Ancient and Modern. For the Year 1798. [Motto.] *Philadelphia, Mathew Carey, June* 20, M.DCC.XCIX. 8vo, pp. 416 (5); Table, folded. Not continued. H. 1162*a*

American Musical Miscellany: a Collection of the Newest and most Approved Songs, set to Music. *Northampton, Mass.*, 1798. 12mo. 1163

Contains "Major André's Song to Delia." *See* page 198.

American Nationality. From the Biblical Repertory and Princeton Review, for October, 1861. *Philadelphia, Peter Walker.* 8vo, pp. 37. 1164

American Naval Battles: Being a Complete History of the Battles Fought by the Navy of the United States from its Establishment in 1794 to the Present Time, including the Wars with France, and with Tripoli, the Late Wars with Great Britain and with Algiers: with an Account of the Attack on Baltimore, and of the Battle of New Orleans. With Twenty-one Elegant Engravings, Representing Battles, &c. *Boston, J. J. Smith, Jr.*, MDCCCXXXI. 8vo, pp. 278.+ Same. *Boston, Charles Gaylord*, 1837. 8vo. 1165

Attributed to H. Kimball. Some copies are dated 1840.

The American Nepos: a Collection of the Lives of the most Remarkable and the most Eminent Men, who have contributed to the Discovery, the Settlement, and the Independence of America. ... *Baltimore, G. Douglas*, 1805. 12mo, 2 p. l., pp. xi. (1), 384. Portrait. + Same. Second Edition. *Baltimore, John Vance & Co.*, 1811. 12mo, pp. 408. H. 1166

American Normal School Association. American Normal Schools: Their Theory, their Workings, and their Results, as embodied in the Proceedings of the First Annual Convention of the ... Association, held at Trenton, New Jersey, August 19 and 20, 1859. *New York, A. S. Barnes & Burr*, 1860. 8vo, pp. 113. Illustrations. H. 1167

American Notes and Queries. [Nos. I to 4. *Philadelphia, W. Brotherhead*, 1857.] 8vo, pp. 160. 1168

The first edition of No II. was canceled and reprinted. The work died, as it deserved, at the fourth number.

American Numismatic Society. Constitution and By-Laws ... . Adopted September, 1858. *New York*, 1858, 32mo, pp. 8.

The American Odd-Fellows Museum ... to which is prefixed a concise view of the Origin, Character, and Extent of the Order in America. *New York*, 1856. 2 vols., 8vo. 1170

American Orator: containing Two Hundred Specimens of American Eloquence, with the Declaration of Independence. *Worcester, Z. Baker & Co.*, 1855. 1171

American Orator's Own Book, being Selections from the ablest English and American Orators. *New York*, 1855, &c. 12mo, pp. 250. 1172

American Oratory, or Selections from the Speeches of Eminent Americans. Compiled by a Member of the Philadelphia Bar. *Philadelphia, Biddle*, 1842. 8vo, pp. viii., 531.+ 1836. 8vo.+ 1853. 1173

American Peace Society. Petition in behalf of stipulated arbitration ... to the Senate of the United States, 1853. 8vo, pp. 4.+Annual Reports, 1829, &c. 1174

American Philosophical Society, for promoting Useful Knowledge. Celebration of the Hundredth Anniversary, on the 25th May, 1843; with a Discourse by Dr. Patterson, on the Origin, Progress and Labours of the Society, followed by the Proceedings at a special meeting held on the 26, 27, 29 and 30th May, in further celebration of the occasion, with abstracts of scientific papers then read, &c. *Philadelphia*, 1843. 8vo, pp. 232.

Included in Vol. III. of the Proceedings.

Catalogue of the Library of the American Philosophical Society, held at Philadelphia for promoting Useful Knowledge. Published by order of the Society. *Philadelphia, Joseph R. A. Skerrett*, 1824. 8vo, pp. xv., 290. 1176

Catalogue of the American Philosophical Society Library. Part I., II. ... *Philadelphia, Caxton Press of C. Sherman, Son & Co.* [1863–66]. 8vo, pp. 634. H. 1177

Laws and Regulations of the American Philosophical Society. *Philadelphia*, 1814.+Laws and Regulations adopted June 21, 1833. *Philadelphia*, 1833. 8vo, pp. 46 (1).+As finally amended and adopted, December 16, 1859. Together with the Charter of the Society, and a List of its Members. *Philadelphia*, 1860. 8vo, pp. 80. H. 1178

American Philosophical Society, &c. List of the Members ... [*Philadelphia*, 1865?]. 8vo, pp. 56, 6 (2). H. 1179

Proceedings of the American Philosophical Society, held at

Philadelphia, for promoting Useful Knowledge. *Philadelphia*, 1840–65. 9 vols., 8vo. H. 1180

Transactions of the American Philosophical Society, held at Philadelphia, for promoting Useful Knowledge. Vols. I.–VI., 1769–1809. 6 vols., 4to. *Philadelphia*, 1771–1809.+Vol. I. Second edition, corrected. *Philadelphia*, 1789. 4to. 1181

Transactions of the American Philosophical Society, held at Philadelphia, for promoting Useful Knowledge. New Series. Vol. I. *Philadelphia*, 1818. 4to. Continued. 1182

Transactions of the Historical & Literary Committee of the American Philosophical Society, held at Philadelphia, for promoting Useful Knowledge. *Philadelphia*, 1819, '38 '43. 3 vols., 8vo, pp. iv., 464 (1); xxii., 375 (1); 99. 1183

Contents: Preliminaries, pp. 54. 1. An account of the History, Manners and Customs of the Indian Nations, who once inhabited Pennsylvania and the neighbouring States, by the Rev. John Heckewelder, pp. 348 (N. A. R., ix., p. 155). 2. Correspondence between Mr. Heckewelder and Mr. Duponceau, on the languages of the American Indians, pp. 351–448. 3. Words, Phrases, and Short Dialogues in the Language of the Lenni Lenape, by Mr. Heckewelder, pp. 451–464. Vol. II. has the title-page: A Dissertation on the Nature and Character of the Chinese System of Writing ... . By Peter S. Duponceau ... A Vocabulary of the Cochinchinese Language, by Father Joseph Morrone ... with Notes ... by M. de la Paleen ... and A Cochinchinese and Latin Dictionary ... . Vol. III. contains, 1. Historical Sketch of Continental Paper Money. By Samuel Breck. pp. 40. 2. The Social and Intellectual State of the Colony of Pennsylvania prior to the year 1743. By Job R. Tyson. . pp. 41-63. 3. Biographical Notice of Edward Livingston. By Henry D. Gilpin. pp. 65-84. 4. The Effects of Secluded and Gloomy Imprisonment on Individuals of the African Variety of Mankind in the Production of Disease. By Benjamin H. Coates, M.D. pp. 85-99.

The American Pioneer. A Monthly Periodical, devoted to the Objects of the Logan Historical Society, or to Collecting and Publishing Sketches relative to the Early Settlement and Successive Improvement of the Country. Illustrated. Second Edition. *Cincinnati*, 1842–43. 2 vols., 8vo, pp. 448, 480.

Edited by John S. Williams. The first edition of Vol. I. was published at Chillicothe, 1842.

The American Pioneer: with a New and Useful Plan to establish Free Labor, in the United States. By an American. *Boston, Allen & Co.*, 1854. 12mo, pp. 24. H. 1185

American Poems. Original and selected. Vol. I. *Litchfield*,

Printed by Collier and Buel [1793]. 12mo, pp. viii., 304; List, 3 l.; Errata, 1 l. 1186

"Said to be Dr. E. H. Smith's collection. That keen piece of satire on Gen. Ethan Allen (page 142) is by the celebrated Dr. Lemuel Hopkins."—KILBOURNE.

American Poetical Miscellany. Original and Selected. *Philadelphia, R. Johnson*, 1809. 2 vols., 12mo, pp. 300, 304. 1187

Contains "A Sketch of the Life of Gen. Greene," by Mathew Carey.

American Political and Military Biography. ... Part I. The Political Lives and Public Characters of the Presidents of the United States, and other Distinguished Public Men. Part II. The Lives, Characters, and Anecdotes of the Military and Naval Officers of the Revolution ... . [n. p.], 1825. 12mo, pp. 424. H.

American Political Manual, containing the Constitution of the United States, Declaration of Independence, and Washington's Farewell Address, with copious Index. *Philadelphia* [n. d.] 12mo. 1189

The American Preacher. *See* [Austin (David)].

American Principles. *See* [Adams (J. Q.)]

American Publishers' Circular and Literary Gazette. Vol. I. September, 1855. *New York*, 1855–61. 7 vols., 4to. 1190

Continued as the *American Literary Gazette.*

The American Quarterly Church Review and Ecclesiastical Register. *New Haven*, afterward *New York*, 1858, etc. 8vo.

Previously *The Church Review.*

American Pharmaceutical Association. History of its Formation. [*Philadelphia*, 185–]. 8vo, pp. 10. H. 1192

American Pharmaceutical Association. Proceedings at the [Second]—Thirteenth Annual Meeting. *Philadelphia, Merrihew and Thompson* (1864–65, *Merrihew & Son*), *Printers*, 1853–65. 8vo. H. 1193

The "National Pharmaceutical Convention," held at Philadelphia, Oct. 6, 1852, is considered as the *first* meeting of the Association.

American Pulpit: Sermons by Eminent Orators. *London, Hamilton*, 1852. 8vo. 1194

American Quarterly Observer. Vol. I., July, 1833; Vol. III., Oct. 1834. *Boston.* 8vo. 1195

American Quarterly Observer. Vol. I., No. I., July. *Boston*, 1838. 8vo. 1196

The American Quarterly Register and Magazine. ... Conducted by James Stryker. May, 1848, to December, 1849. Vol. I.–III. ... *Philadelphia, E. C. & J. Biddle* [1848–49]. 3 vols., 8vo. H. 1197

For remaining volumes, *see* Stryker (J.)

The American Quarterly Register. ... Vol. IV.–XV. *Boston, Perkins and Marvin* (afterwards *T. R. Marvin*), 1832–43. 12 vols., 8vo. H. 1198

Vols. I. and II. were entitled "Quarterly Register and Journal of the American Education Society." *Andover, Flagg and Gould*, 1829. Vol. III., "The Quarterly Register of the ... Society." *Bostor, Perkins & Marvin*, 1831. Vols. I. and II., conducted by Rev. E. E. Cornelius and B. B. Edwards; IV.–XI., by Edwards; XII., XIII., by Edwards and W. Cogswell; XIV., by Edwards and S. H. Riddel; XV., by Rev. Samuel H. Riddel.

The American Quarterly Review. *See* Walsh (R.)

American Quarterly Review of the American Protestant Association. Edited by R. W. Griswold. Vol. I. *Philadelphia*, 1844. 8vo. 1199

The American Querist. *See* [Cooper (Myles)].

American Question. A Letter from a Calm Observer to a noble Lord, on the subject of the late Declaration relative to the Orders in Council. *London, Gale and Curtis*, 1812. pp. 16, 8vo. H. 1200

The American Question, and How to Settle It. *London, Sampson Low & Co.*, 1863. Post 8vo, pp. 313. 1201

The American Question. Secession. Tariff. Slavery. *Brighton, Harry Taylor*, 1862. 8vo, pp. 74—*i. e.*, 73 (1). H. 1202

American Rail-Road Journal. *New York*, 1832, &c. 11 vols., 8vo. Continued in 4to. 1203

Henry V. Poor, editor. Assistant editors: James T. Hodge, for mining and metallurgy. Charles T. James, for manufactures and the mechanic arts. M. B. Hewson, for civil engineering.

American Railway Guide, 1851. *New York, C. Dinsmore.* Sm. 4to. 1204

Continued. Published monthly.

The American Rebellion. By an American Citizen. *See* [Victor (O. J.)]

American Register. *See* Walsh (R.)

The American Register: or General Repository of History, Politics, and Science. *Philadelphia*, 1807–1811. 7 vols., 8vo. S.

Edited by C. Brockden Brown. Includes many valuable state papers and letters by eminent persons not to be found elsewhere.

The American Register for 1775. *New York*, 1775. 8vo.

The first book of the kind printed in the *Colony of New York*.

American Register, or Summary Review of History, Politics and Literature. *Philadelphia*, 1817. 2 vols., 8vo. 1207

The American Remembrancer; or, An Impartial Collection of Essays, Resolves, Speeches, &c., Relative, or having Affinity, to the Treaty with Great Britain. *Philadelphia, Mathew Carey*, 1795. 3 vols., 8vo, pp. 288, 288, 312. H. 1208

American Repertory of Arts, Sciences and Manufactures: Edited by J. J. Mapes. *New York*, 1840–42. 4 vols., 8vo.

The American Repository of Useful Information ... . To be continued Annually. *Philadelphia, B. Davies*, 1795. 18mo, pp. 42, and 12 blank leaves, each headed with a vignette appropriate to a month. H. 1210

Afterward entitled "The American Repository, and Annual Register of the United States," etc. The latest volume I have seen is dated 1803.

American Resistance Indefensible: a Sermon on the day appointed for a General Fast, Dec. 13, 1776. By a Country Curate. *London, Gardner*, 1776. 1211

"Contains a brief, but clear and consistent state of our present unhappy conflict in America, with strong deductions in favor of the measures of government."—M. R., LV., p. 487.

American Review. A Whig Journal of Politics, Literature, Science and Arts. *New York*, 1845–47. 6 vols., 8vo.+New series, Vol. I. to X. *New York*, 1848–52. 10 vols. 1212

The title of the second series is *American Whig Review*.

The American Review, and Literary Journal, for the Year 1801–1802. *New York, T. & J. Swords*, 1801–02. 2 vols., 8vo. H. 1213

Edited by C. Brockden Brown and others. A continuation of "The Monthly Magazine and American Review."

The American Review of History and Politics, &c. *See* Walsh (R.)

The American Revolution; written in the Style of Ancient History. *See* [Snowden (Richard)].

American Sketches. *Concord, N. H.*, 1822. 8vo. W. 1214

American Sketches. By a Native of the United States. *London*, 1827. 12mo. 1215

American Sketches, Farmer's Fireside, A Poem. 1823. 12mo. 1216

American Slavery and the Kansas Question, from the "Edinburgh Review." *London, Longman*, 1856. 8vo. 1217

American Society for promoting National Unity. ... [Programme, Constitution, and Proposed Members.] *New York, John F. Trow, Printer*, 1861. 8vo, pp. 10, 6. H. 2218

American Society for the Encouragement of Domestic Manufactures. Address to the People of the United States. *New York*, 1817. 8vo, pp. 32. 1219

American Society for the Promotion of Temperance. *See* American Temperance Society.

The American Songster: being a select Collection of the most celebrated American, English, Scotch and Irish Songs. *New York, S. Campbell*, M,DCC,LXXXVIII. 8vo, pp. xii., 204. 1220

The American Spectator, or Matrimonial Preceptor. Adapted to the State of Society in the American Republic. *Boston*, 1797. 12mo. 1221

The American Spy: Letters written in London, 1764–65. *London*, 1786. 12mo. 1222

The American Spy, a Collection of XXXVI Letters written to various persons resident in the Sister Land. *London, Printed for the Author*, 1791. 12mo. 1223

The American Star, being a Choice Collection of the most approved Patriotic and other Songs. Never before published. Second Edition. *Richmond*, 1817. 16mo. 1224

American State Papers. *See* Washington (George).

American State Papers, and Correspondence between Messrs. Smith, Pinkney, Marquis Wellesley, General Armstrong, M. Champagny, M. Turreau, Messrs. Russell, Monroe, Foster, &c. Containing also, Papers relative to the Annexation of Holland to France; Repeal of the Berlin and Milan Decrees; English and Irish Budget; French State Papers, &c. ... *Philadelphia, Printed; London, Reprinted for Longman, Hurst, Rees, Orme, and Brown, and J. M. Richardson*, 1812. 8vo, pp. 187, 116; 3 Tables, folded. H. 1225

See M. R., N. S., LXIX., p. 269.

American State Papers: containing authentic Documents relating to the History, Politicks, Statisticks, &c., of the United States of America. Communicated to Congress by the President. *Boston*, 1808. 8vo, pp. 95, 80. 1226

American State Papers, containing the Correspondence between Messrs. Smith, Pinkerton, Marquis Wellesley, &c. *London*, 1811. 8vo, pp. 60. 1227

American State Papers. Documents, Legislative and Executive, of the Congress of the United States, from the First Session of the First to the Second of the Twenty-Second Congress, inclusive ... . Selected and edited, under the authority of Congress, by Walter Lowrie, Secretary of the Senate, and Matthew St. Clair Clarke, Clerk of the House of Representatives. *Washington, Gales and Seaton*, 1832–1861. Folio. First Series, 21 vols.; Second Series, 17 vols. 1228

This important publication is classified as follows, namely: I. Foreign Relations, including the Annual Messages of the Presidents (1789–1828), 6 vols. II. Indian Affairs (1789–1827), comprising, 1st. All Documents accompanying Indian Treaties; 2nd. Indian Massacres and Depredations; 3rd. Indian Wars; 4th. Efforts made for their benefit in Civilization, Agriculture and the Mechanic Arts, 2 vols. III. Finance (1789–1828), embracing, 1st. Public Debt and Public Credit; 2nd. Revenue, direct and indirect Taxation; 3rd. The Currency; 4th. The Mint; 5th. Bank of the United States; 6th. Annual Estimates; 7th. Expenses of Collecting Revenue; 8th. Table of Receipts and Expenditure, 5 vols. IV. Commerce and Navigation (1789–1823), embracing, 1st. Imports and Exports; 2nd. Fisheries; 3rd. Lighthouse Establishment; 4th. Improvement of Harbours, Rivers, Roads, and Canals; 5th. Tonnage; 6th. Coasting Trade, 3 vols. V. Military Affairs (1789–1838), 1st. Army; 2nd. Military Academy; 3rd. Fortifications; 4th. Armaments, Arms; 5th. National Armories; 6th. Militia, 7 vols. VI. Naval Affairs (1789-1836), 4 vols. VII. Post-Office Department (1789-1833), 1 vol. VIII. Public Lands (1789-1837), 8 vols. IX. Claims (1789-1823), 1 vol. X. Miscellaneous (1789-1823), 2 vols. This valuable work was printed by order of the United States Government, and distributed through the Members of Congress. It contains reprints, not only of all the

early occasional publications of the Congress that could be found, but many important papers from the Archives of the Government never before published. The Second Series having been published several years after the first, is often found separately, and consists of the following:

American State Papers. Second Series. *Washington*, 1858–61. 17 vols., folio. 1229

Foreign Relations, Vols. 5 and 6. Finance, Vols. 4 and 5. Military Affairs, Vols. 3–7. Naval Affairs, Vols. 2–4. Public Lands, Vols. 4–8. The foregoing, with the Annals of Congress, Register of Debates, and Congressional Globe, form a tolerably complete series of American State Papers to the year 1860. For a list of the sources of information, *see* Hickey's Constitutions, Chapter XI.

American State Papers. Important Documents and Dispatches, which accompanied the Message of the President [John Adams] of the United States of America, to both Houses of Congress, April 3rd 1798, respecting the difference between America and France, including the Instructions to the American Envoys, &c. &c. *London, Wright*, 1798. Sm. 4to, pp. 30.

Same as America and France, No. 1016, with a new title.

American Statesman Extra Sheet. Substance of a Discussion in the Senate, on the Report of a Committee in favor of incorporating Amherst College. [n. p., 1824.] 8vo, pp. 18. H.

The American Statesman's Kalendar, and Register, for 1813. ... *New-York, D. Longworth*, 1813. 36mo, pp. 80. H. 1232

American Statistical Association. Collections of the American Statistical Association. *Boston*, 1847. ——[1854]. 2 vols., 8vo.+Constitution and By-Laws of the American Statistical Association. ... *Boston*, 1840; also 1844. 8vo, pp. 24.+Constitution and By-Laws ... with a List of Officers, Fellows, and Members, January 1862. *Boston, Press of T. R. Marvin & Son*, 1862. 8vo, pp. 12. H. 1233

The American Struggle. Appeal to the People of the North. *London*, 1862. 8vo, pp. 32. 1234

American Sunday School Union. The Charter; being a Plain Statement of Facts, in relation to an Application to the Legislature of Pennsylvania, to grant a Charter to the ... Union. With the Statement of the Resident Members of the Board of Managers, belonging to the Methodist Episcopal Church, in reference to Charges made against the Union by the Christian Advocate and Journal. *Philadelphia*, 1828. 8vo, pp. 24. H.

Historical Sketch of the American Sunday School Union, and

of its Contributions to Popular Education in the United States. [n. p., 1865.] 12mo, pp. 45. H. 1236

The American System. *See* [Hale (Nathan)].

The American System. *Baltimore, Lucas & Deaver*, 1828. 8vo, pp. 42. 1237

American Tears. *See* [Mather (Cotton)].

American Telegraph Magazine. *New York*, 1852. Vol. I., No. I. 8vo. P. 1237*a*

American Temperance Society. First Annual Report of the Executive Committee of the American Society for the Promotion of Temperance. For the Year ending Nov. 1827. *Andover, Printed for the Society by Flagg and Gould*, 1828. 8vo, pp. 67 (1). Continued. H. 1238

American Temperance Union. Ellsworth and his Zouaves. [*New York*, 1861.] 12mo, pp. 4. H. 1239

American Temperance Union. Permanent Temperance Documents. *New York*, 1852–53. 3 vols., 8vo. H. 1240

Vol. I. was published by the Amer. Temp. *Society*, and contains its Annual Reports (IV.-IX.) for 1831-36. Vols. II. and III. contain Reports I.-XVI. of the Amer. Temp. *Union*, for 1837-52. To Vol. III. are appended John Marsh's "Half Century Tribute to the Cause of Temperance," "Proceedings of the Fourth National Temperance Convention," and "Letters from Prof. Stuart of Andover," and others, on the Maine Liquor Law—all three published in 1851.

American Text Book, containing the Declaration of Independence, Articles of Confederation, Constitution of the United States and Washington's Farewell Address. *Cincinnati*, 1850. 48mo.+Another Edition. *Philadelphia, J. E. Potter & Co.*, 1865. 18mo. 1241

The American Thanksgiving Celebration in Paris, Thursday Evening, December 7, 1865. Published by the Committee of Arrangements. *Paris, Printed by E. Brière*, 1865. 8vo, pp. 33. H. 1242

American Thanksgiving Dinner at St. James's Hall, London, Thursday, November 26, 1863. *London, William Ridgway*, 1863. 8vo, pp. 94. H. 1243

The American Times, a Satire, In Three Parts, In which are delineated the Characters of the Leaders of the American Rebellion. Amongst the principal are, Franklin, Laurens, Adams,

Hancock, Jay, Duer, Duane, Wilson, Pulaski, Witherspoon, Reed, McKean, Washington, Roberdeau, Morris, Chase, &c. By Camillo Querno, Poet-laureat to the Congress. *London, Richardson*, 1780. 4to, pp. 40. 1244

M. R., LXII., p. 495. Reprinted, with André's Cow Chace. *See* No. 1449.

The American Tract Society, Boston. *See* [Whipple (C. K.)]

American Tract Society, Boston. A Brief History of the Organization and Work of the ... Society. ... *Boston*, 1855. 16mo, pp. 32. H. 1245

A Brief History of the American Tract Society, instituted at Boston, 1814, and its Relations to the American Tract Society at New York, instituted 1825. *Boston, Press of T. R. Marvin*, 1857. 12mo, pp. 48. H. 1246

Address of the Executive Committee of the American Tract Society to the Christian Public, with a Brief Account of the Formation of the Society. *New York*, 1825. 8vo.+Annual Report. *New York*, 1826. 8vo. Continued. 1247

American Tract Society, Boston. Proceedings of the First Ten Years of the American Tract Society, instituted at Boston, 1814. ... [*Andover*], *Flagg & Gould*, 1824. 12mo, pp. 215. H.

American Tract Society, New York. Ten Years of Colportage in America. *New York*, 1851. 8vo, pp. 32. H. 1249

The American Traveller; being a new Historical Collection, carefully compiled from original Memoirs in several languages, and the most Authentic Voyages and Travels, containing a compleate account of that Part of the World, now called the West Indies, from its Discovery by Columbus to the Present Time. *London, Fuller*, 1743. 8vo, pp. 396. Portraits. C. 1250

Mr. Rich gives 1741 as the date of the first issue, and repeats the title under 1745. I have a memorandum of one dated 1751. "This work was published in [18] numbers, and appears to be the commencement of an extensive work, but of which no more than this volume appeared. It commences with a long introduction on the rise, progress and improvement of navigation, which is followed by book I., divided into two chapters: one on the peopling of America, and the other, which concludes the book, containing an account of the voyages of Columbus."—RICH.

American Traveller. *See* [Cluny (Alex.)]

American Turf Register and Sporting Magazine. *Baltimore*, 1830. Vols. I., II. 8vo, pp. 643, 624. P. 1251

The American Union Commission: its Origin, Operations and Purposes. Organized to aid in the Restoration of the Union upon the basis of Freedom, Industry, Education and Christian Morality, October, 1865. *New York, Sanford, Harroun & Co., Printers*, 1865. 8vo, pp. 24. H. 1252

American Union Commission. Speeches of Hon. W. Dennison, Postmaster-General, Rev. J. P. Thompson, D.D., President of the Commission, Col. N. G. Taylor, of East Tennessee, Hon. J. R. Doolittle, U. S. Senate, Gen. J. A. Garfield, M.C., in the Hall of Representatives, Washington, Feb. 12, 1865. *New York, Printed by Sanford, Harroun & Co.*, 1865. 8vo, pp. 43. H. 1253

American Union Commission. To the Honorable, the Committee of the House of Representatives ... upon Military Affairs. [n. p., 1865?]. 8vo, pp. 4. H. 1254

Facts and suggestions concerning the condition of the refugees.

The American Union shown to be the New Heaven. *See* [Hunt (J.)]

American Unitarian Association. The Quarterly Journal of the ... Association. Vol. I.–VII. *Boston*, 1853–59. 12mo.+Continued as The Monthly Journal ... . Vol. I. *Boston*, 1860. 12mo. H. 1255

Vol. II., No. 10 (Oct., 1861), of the Monthly Journal was an "Army Number," devoted to hymns and patriotic songs for the soldiers.

American Unitarian Biography. *See* Ware (W.)

American Universal Magazine. *Philadelphia*, 1795–98. 4 vols., 8vo. Portraits. 1256

The American Village, and other Poems. [About 1780.]. Sm. 4to, pp. 28. 1257

The American Wanderer through Various Parts of Europe, in a Series of Letters to a Lady. Interspersed with a Variety of interesting Anecdotes. By a Virginian. *London, Printed for J. Robson*, MDCCLXXXIII. 8vo, pp. xvi., 422.+Reprinted. *Dublin, B. Smith*, MDCCLXXXIII. 12mo, pp. xxiii., 288. 1258

By a Loyalist refugee. *See* M. R., LXIX., 182.

The American War. A Letter to an English Friend. *New York*, 1863. 8vo. 1259

The American War, a Poem. *See* [Cockings (George)].

American Weekly Messenger; or, Register of State Papers, History and Politics. Vol. I., II. *Philadelphia*, 1813–15. 8vo.

Edited by John Conrad, and abounding with documents relating to the War of 1812.

The American Whig Review. ... Vol. I.–XIII. *New York*, 1845–51. 8vo. 1261

Vols. I.-X. are entitled "The American Review; a Whig Journal," &c. *See* No. 1212. Vol. VII.-XIII. are also designated, "New Series. Vol. I.-VII."

American Wit and Humor. Illustrated by J. McLenan. *New York, Harper & Bro's* [1859]. 8vo, pp. 206. H. 1262

Gathered mainly from the Drawer of Harper's Magazine.

American Young Man's Best Companion. *Worcester*, 1785. 12mo.+Same. *Walpole, N. H.*, 1794. 12mo. 1263

Die Americanische Seeräuber. *See* Exquemeling.

Americano, Argonauta de las Costas de Nueva-Espana y Tierra-Firme. [n. p., 17–.] 8vo. 1264

A very suspicious title, from one of Stargardt's catalogues.

The Americans, by an "American in London." *See* [Colton (C.)]

Americans against Liberty. *See* [Serle (Ambrose)].

The Americans as they are; described in a Tour through the Valley of the Mississippi. By the Author of "Austria as it is." *London, Hurst, Chance and Co.*, 1828. 12mo, 2 p.-l., pp. vi., Contents, 2 l., pp. 218, Table, 2 l. H. 1265

See N. A. R., XXVIII., 415. "This work is written in a similar spirit to 'The United States of North America as they are.'" The preface appears to have been copied from it. "There is a petulant, cynical, dissatisfied tone about his details of American life, which creates a suspicion that he does not mean to deal fairly by them."—M. R., Vol. CXV., 448. The *North American Review* gives rather a favorable opinion of it.

Americans at Home; or Byeways, Backwoods, &c. *London, Hurst*, 1850. 3 vols., post 8vo. 1266

Americans Defended by an American; being a Letter in Answer to Inquiries concerning the late Imputations of Dishonour upon the United States. *London*, 1844. 8vo. 1267

The American's Dream; or, Partial Downfall of Liberty and

its Ultimate Triumph over Tyranny. By Thomas The Seer. [1862.] 12mo, pp. 24. 1268

American's Guide; comprising the Constitution of the United States and Constitutions of the several States composing the Union, etc. *Philadelphia*, 1864. 12mo. 1269

American's Guide. Comprising the Constitution of the United States, with the Latest Amendments. Also, the Declaration of Independence, Articles of Confederation, with the Federal Constitution, and Acts for the Government of the Territories. *Philadelphia*, 1813. 12mo, pp. 380. + *Trenton*, 1813. 12mo. + *Philadelphia*, 1828. + 1830. + 1832. 12mo. + 1833. 12mo, pp. 402. + 1840. + 1849. 1270

The American's Guide: Comprising the Declaration of Independence; The Articles of Confederation; the Constitution of the United States, and the Constitutions of the several States composing the Union, viz. Maine, Massachusetts, New Hampshire, Vermont, Rhode Island, Connecticut, New York, New Jersey, Pennsylvania, Delaware, Maryland, Virginia, North Carolina, South Carolina, Georgia, Kentucky, Tennessee, Ohio, Indiana, Louisiana, Mississippi, Illinois, Alabama, Missouri. *Philadelphia, Hogan and Thompson* [n. d.] 12mo, pp. 380.

An American's Offering: A Recitative Poem, on events of Revolutionary times, dedicated to the American people, with Historical Notes and Memoranda, illustrative of the truth of the Poem, In five Cantos. *Philadelphia, M. Crosland*, 1849. 8vo, pp. 40. 1272

American's Own Book. The Declaration of Independence; Lives of the Signers, etc. *New York*, 1856. 12mo. 1273

The Americans Roused, in a Cure for the Spleen. Or Amusement for a Winter's Evening; Being the Substance of a Conversation on the Times, over A Friendly Tankard and Pipe. Between Sharp, A Country Parson. Bumper, A Country Justice. Fillpot, An Inn-keeper. Graveairs, A Deacon. Trim, A Barber. Brim, A Quaker. Puff, A late Representative. Taken in Short-Hand, by Sir Roger de Coverley. *New-England, Printed; New York, Reprinted by James Rivington* [1774]. 8vo, pp. 32. S. 1274

Published by the Tories of New York to ridicule the American Congress.

AMERICANUS, *pseudonym*. *See* [Evans (Caleb)].

Americanus examined, and his Principles compared with those of the Approved Advocates for America. By a Pennsylvanian. *Philadelphia*, 1774. 8vo. 1275

America's | Appeal | to | The Impartial World. | Wherein the Rights of the Americans, as | Men, British Subjects, and as Colo- | nists; the Equity of the Demand, and of the Man- | ner in which it is made upon them by Great Britain, | are stated and considered. And, | The opposition made by the Colonies to Acts of Parlia- | ment, their resorting to Arms in their necessary | Defence, against the Military Armaments, | employed to enforce them, Vindicated, | ... *Hartford*, | *Printed by Ebenezer Watson*, 1775. 8vo, pp. 72. N. & H. 1276

... America's Future. [*Edinburgh*, 1864.] 18mo, pp. 3. H.

Signed "An American."

AMERICUS, *pseudon*. The Executive Power of Appointment and Removal: Abuses and needed Checks. [n. p., 1866.] Broadside. 1277*a*

AMERICUS *pseudon*. Thoughts for the Times: addressed to the Considerate People of the Northern States. By Americus. *London, the Author*, 1862. 8vo, pp. 125. H. 1278

AMERIGO VESPUCCI. *See* Vespucci.

Amerika dargestellt durch sich selbst, eine Zeitschrift herausgegeben von Georg Joachim Göschen. *Leipzig, Zeitschrift*, 1818–20. 3 vols., 4to. 1279

Amerika, in alle zyne byzonderheden beschouwd, ter verkryging eener naauwkeurige kennis van dat thans zo veel gerucht maakend waerelddeel. Met twee Kaarten van Zuid en Noord-Amerika opgehelderd. *Amsterdam, Pieter Meijer*, 1780–1782. 4 vols., 8vo. H. 1280

Om Amerika samt om emigrant-föreningen i Stockholm. *Stockholm, In Karta*, 1841. 1281

America and the Stockholm Society for Emigrants. This is something more than an emigrant's guide. The introduction gives an account of the Swedish settlements in North America, and some new particulars of Nova Swecia. On pages 7–10 is an account of the emigration of Norwegians and Swedes from 1821 to 1835.

... Amerika. [Brasilien (Mitte Dezember). Šklaven-Auf-

stände.—Montevideo, 27. Dezember. Kriegsnachrichten. Zustände. Besonderer Abdruck aus Nr. 36. und 37. der Haude und Spener'schen Zeitung vom 11. und 12. Februar 1865.] *Berlin* [1865]. Broadside. H. 1282

Amerika! Treuer Rathgeber und Führer des deutschen Auswanderers nach den Vereinigten Staaten von Nordamerika. *Kreuznach, Voigtländer*, 1849. 8vo, pp. iv., 96. Map, 4to.

Amerika und die Auswanderung dahin. ... In Briefen an einen Freund von einem Weimaraner. *Leipzig, Steinacker*, 1835. 8vo. 1284

Amerika. Zeitschrift für Auswanderer nach Amerika und alle Diejenigen, welche sich über Auswanderung nach jenem Welttheile und amerikanische. Verhältnisse Belehrung verschaffen wollen. Hrsg.: C. Hoffmann. 1. Heft. April 1847. *Stolberg, a. H., Hoffmann*, 1847. 12mo, pp. 48. 1285

Der Amerikaner. *See* [Sauerwein (Wilhelm)].

Amerikanishe Anekdoten aus den neuesten Zeiten. Ein Auszug aus dem Französichen. *Leipzig, in der Weygandschen Buchhandlung*, 1789. 8vo, pp. 290. H. 1285*a*

Amerikanisches Archiv, herausgegeben von J. A. Remer. *Braunschweig*, 1777–78. 3 vols., 8vo. 1286

Amerikanisches Magazin oder Authentische Beiträge zur Erdbeschreibung, Staatskunde und Geschichte von Amerika, besonders aber der vereinten Staaten. Herausgegeben von Professor Hegewisch in Kiel and Professor Ebeling in Hamburg. Erster Band, Hamburg, 1797. *Hamburg, Carl Ernst Bohn*, 1797. H. 1287

The first *Stück* was published in 1795; the first *Band* in 1797; after which I cannot find that the work was continued.

Amerikanisches Magazin. Herausgegeben von Karl Neidhard. I' Heft. [1. Mai 1835.] *Altona und Leipzig, Hammerich*, 1835. 8vo. 4 colored lithographs. 1288

L'Américquain aux Anglois, ou Observations d'un membre des États Unis de l'Amerique, à divers ministres d'Angleterre, Traduit par M. D. B***. *Philadelphia*, M.DCC.LXXXI. 8vo, 2 p. l., pp. 108. H. 1288*a*

L'Amérique Anglaise. *See* [Blome (R.)]

L'Amérique d'après les voyageurs les plus célèbres, par un homme de lettres. *Lille, Lefort*, 1850. 12mo. + 3^{e} édition. *Lille, Lefort*, 1859. 12mo, pp. 190. Plate. + 4^{e} édition. *Lille, Lefort*, 1864. 12mo, pp. 191. Plate. 1289

L'Amérique découverte. *See* [Laureau].

L'Amérique délivrée, esquisse d'un poëme sur l'indépendance de l'Amérique. *Amsterdam, J. A. Crajenschot*, MDCCLXXIII. 2 vols., 8vo, pp. xxiv., 726; Errata 1. H. & S. 1290

An epic poem on the Revolutionary War, with copious historical notes, dedicated to Monsieur John Adams. Signed L. C. D. L. G.

Amérique du Nord; ou, le Correspondant des Etats-Unis. *Paris* [n. d.] 8vo. M. 1291

L'Amérique en 1826. *See* [Zenouwitz (G.)]

De l'Amérique et des Américains, ou Observations curieuses du philosophe La Douceur, qui a parcouru cet Hémisphère pendant la dernière guerre, en faisant le noble métier de tuer les hommes sans les manger. *Berlin, Samuel Pitra*, 1771. Sm. 8vo, pp. 80. H. 1292

"A lively and humorous defence of the American Indians against the attacks of De Pauw, attributed by Meusel to M. Poivre, but Barbier says that it is either by M. Bonneville or Dom Pernetty. Now, Poivre was never in America: he was employed in the East Indies at the time this discussion was going forward. It appears that M. Bonneville was only eleven years of age at the time. As it is not probable that Dom Pernetty wrote two works on the subject, in the same year, all these conjectures as to the authorship of this work are apparently erroneous."—RICH; who gives the imprint, *Berlin*, 1772, 8vo, pp. 116; Heinsius, and also Kaiser, have *Berlin, Rottmann*, 1774, 8vo.

Amérique Méridionale, Iles diverses de l'Océan et Régions circompolaires. *Paris*, 1840. 8vo. A. 1293

L'Amérique, ou Guide utile aux Personnes qui veulent connoitre ce pays et y faire un Voyage heureux et avantageux. *Belfort*, 1824. 4to, pp. 28. 1294

L'Amérique Septentrionale et Méridionale; ou, Description de cette Grande Partie du Monde, comprenant l'Amérique Russe, La Nouvelle Bretagne, la Baie de Hudson, le Labrador, Terre-Neuve, le Canada, les Etats Unis du Nord, les Etats Mexicains, le République de Guatimala, les Antilles, les Lucayes, les Républiques de Colombie, du Pérou, du Chili, la Patagonie, Buénos-Ayres ou La Plata, le Paraguay, l'Empire du Brésil, les Guyanes, un Extrait des Voyages au Pôle Boréal; et

enfin l'Islande, le Groënland, le Spitzberg, avec un précis de la Découverte, de la Conquête et de l'Origine des anciens Peuples, leurs Mœurs, Usages, Coutumes, et Religions. Les arts, sciences, commerce, manufactures, et gouvernemens divers dans leur état actuel; les productions naturelles, les curiosités, etc., Tiré ou traduit des Historiens et des Voyageurs Français et Étrangers les plus célèbres, jusqu'à nos jours, et mis en ordre, par une Societé de Géographes et de Gens de Lettres. *Paris, Ledoux*, 1835. Rl. 8vo, pp. 666. 13 Plates. 1295

AMES (B.) An Oration, pronounced at Bath, in the District of Maine, on the Fourth of July, A.D. 1808. in Commemoration of the American Independence. By Benjamin Ames. [Motto.] *Portland, Argus Press*, 1808. 8vo, pp. 18. H. 1296

AMES (C. G.) Stand by the President! An Address delivered before the National Union Association, of Cincinnati, March 6, 1863. By Rev. Charles G. Ames. *Published by order of the Association, Cincinnati, Johnson*, 1863. 8vo, pp. 14. + *Philadelphia, King & Baird, Printers*, 1863. 8vo, pp. 15. H. 1297

AMES (Ellis). Descendants of William Ames. ... *Caused to be printed and gratuitously distributed, by Messrs. Oliver Ames & Sons, Easton, Massachusetts, July*, 1851. Broadside. H. 1298

[AMES (Fisher)]. The Influences of Democracy on Liberty, Property, and the Happiness of Society, considered. By an American, formerly Member of Congress. With Introduction and Notes by Henry Ewbank, Esq. *London*, 1835. Post 8vo.

AMES. An Oration on the Sublime Virtues of General George Washington, Pronounced at the Old South Meeting-House, in Boston, before His Honor the Lieutenant-Governor, the Council, and the Two Branches of the Legislature of Massachusetts, at their Request, on Saturday, the 8th of February, 1800. By Fisher Ames. *Boston, Young & Minns, Printers to the State* [*n. d.*] 8vo, pp. 31. + Another Edition. *Philadelphia, John Ormrod*, 1800. 8vo, pp. 51. + Another. *New York, Printed for Charles Smith and S. Stephens*, 1800. 8vo, pp. 31. H. 1300

For another edition, *see* Mason (J. M.)

AMES (F.) A Sketch of the Character of Alexander Hamilton. [*Boston*, 1804.] 8vo, pp. 15. H. 1301

Reprinted from the Repertory.

AMES. The Speech of Mr. Ames in the House of Representatives of the United States, when in Committee of the Whole, on Thursday, April 28, 1796, in Support of the Following Motion: Resolved, That it is expedient to pass the Laws necessary to carry into effect the Treaty lately concluded between the United States and the King of Great Britain. *Philadelphia, John Fenno*, M.DCC.XCVI. 8vo, pp. 59. + Same. *Boston, Jno. & J. N. Russell* [n. d.] 8vo, pp. 52. H. + Second Edition. *Boston*, 1796. 1302

AMES. Works of Fisher Ames. Compiled by a Number of his Friends. To which are prefixed, Notices of his Life and Character [by J. T. Kirkland]. ... *Boston, T. B. Wait & Co.*, 1809. 8vo, pp. xxxi., 3 l., pp. 519. Portrait. 1303

AMES. Works of Fisher Ames. With a selection from his Speeches and Correspondence. Edited by his Son, Seth Ames. *Boston, Little, Brown and Company*, 1854. 2 vols., 8vo, pp. xvi., 406; viii., 442. H. 1304

Life of Ames by John Thornton Kirkland, I. 1–28.

Remarks on the Hon. John Q. Adams's Review of Mr. Ames's Works. *See* [Lowell (John)].

[AMES (Julius R.)] The Guardian Genius of the Federal Union. *New York*, 1839. 12mo. 1305

[AMES.] "Liberty:" [Extracts on Slavery.] *New York*, 1837. 8vo, pp. 238. 1306

AMES (Levi). The Last Words and Dying Speech of Levi Ames, who was executed at Boston, on Thursday, the 21st day of October, 1773, for Burglary. Taken from his own Mouth, and Published at his desire, as a Solemn Warning. ... . *Worcester, Seth Clapp*, 1836. 8vo, pp. 8. H. 1307

First printed at Boston, 1773, with Eliot's sermon at his execution.

[AMES (Nathan)]. The Baby and the Bards. Childe Harvard, a Romance of Cambridge. By Señor Alguno. New Edition. And The Bards of Lind: to wit, Longfellow, Bryant, Whittier, Percival, Sprague, Halleck, Lowell, Dana, Holmes, and Willis. ... By the same. *Boston, Redding & Company*, 1851. 16mo, pp. 186. H. 1308

"The Bards" consists of ten parodies, purporting to be "expressly written for 'The Greeting to America' of Jenny Lind."

AMES (Nathaniel). An Astronomical Diary; or, An Almanack for the Year 1726 [to 1775]. *Boston*, 1726-75. 8vo and 16mo. M. 1309

After 1740, frequently reprinted at New London, Hartford, New Haven, Portsmouth, N. H., etc.

AMES (Samuel). Remarks of Hon. Samuel Ames, Reporter of the Decisions of the Supreme Court, in explanation of his Report of the Case, Robert H. Ives *vs.* Charles T. Hazard, *et al.* *Providence, Knowles, Anthony & Co., State Printers*, 1859. 8vo, pp. 25. H. 1310

AMHERST (Jeffrey). Commissary Wilson's Orderly Book. Expedition of the British and Provincial Army, under Maj.-Gen. Jeffrey Amherst; against Ticonderoga and Crown Point, 1759. *Albany, N. Y., J. Munsell*, 1857. Sm. 4to, pp. xi., 230. 1311

No. 1 of Munsell's Historical Series. 110 copies printed, of which 10 are on large paper. The title-page was first printed *Dritish* for British, and the edition was partly distributed before the error was discovered. The notes are by Dr. O'Callaghan. The original MS. is in the possession of Gen. J. Watts de Peyster.

Amherst College. Catalogue of the Library, and Names of Members, of the Athenean Society, from its Formation in 1821, to 1836. *Boston, Printed by John Ford*, 1836. 12mo, pp. 43. H. 1312

Amherst Collegiate Institution. March 1, 1823. To the Public. [n. p. 1823]. 8vo, pp. 6. H. 1313

Amherst Collegiate Institution. A Plea for a Miserable World. I. An Address, delivered at the Laying of the Corner Stone of the Building erecting for the Charity Institution in Amherst, Massachusetts, August 9, 1820, by Noah Webster, Esq. II. A Sermon, delivered on the same Occasion, by Rev. Daniel A. Clark, Pastor of the First Church and Society in Amherst. III. A Brief Account of the Origin of the Institution. *Boston, Printed by Ezra Lincoln*, 1820. 8vo, pp. 48. H. 1314

Amherst Institution. ... January 17, 1825. Petition of the Founders and Proprietors. Presented June 5, 1823. [*Boston*, 1825]. 8vo, pp. 4. Petition to the Legislature for Aid, &c. 1832. 8vo. W. 1315

Annals of Amherst College. The Soil, the Seed, the Sowers, the Presidents and Professors, together with a Popular Guide to the College Buildings and Various Cabinets. *Northampton, Trum-*

bull & Gere; Amherst, J. S. & C. Adams, 1860. 12mo, pp. (2), 70. Plate. H. 1316

Catalogue of Books in the Library of Amherst College. 1827. 8vo. 1317

Catalogue of Amherst College Library. *Amherst*, 1855. 8vo.

Catalogue of the Officers and Students of the Collegiate Institution, Amherst, Mass., November, 1824. *Northampton, Printed by H. Ferry*, 1824. 8vo, pp. 12. Continued. H. 1319

Catalogus Senatus academici, eorum qui Munera et Officia gesserunt quique alicujus Gradus Laurea donati sunt. ... . *Amherstiæ, J. S. et C. Adams, Typographis*, MDCCCXXVIII. 8vo, pp. 8. Continued triennially. H. 1320

Causes of the Growth and Decline of Amherst College. [n. p., 1847.] 12mo, pp. 12. H. 1321

A Constitution and System of By-Laws, For the raising and managing a permanent Charitable Fund, as the basis of an Institution in Amherst, ... for the Classical Education of indigent young men of piety and talents, for the Christian Ministry. [n. p., 1818.] 8vo, pp. 8. H. 1322

Discourses and Addresses at the Installation and Inauguration of the Rev. William A. Stearns, D.D., as President of Amherst College, and Pastor of the College Church. *Amherst, Printed by J. S. & C. Adams*, 1855. 8vo, pp. 107. + Second Edition. 1855. 8vo, pp. 94. 1323

Laws of Amherst College. [n. p., n. d.] 8vo, pp. 27. H.

Obituary Record of Graduates of Amherst College, For the Academical Year, ending July, 1863. [n. p., 1863.] 8vo, pp. 4. Continued. H. 1325

Remarks on the Amherst Collegiate Charity Institution. [n. p., 182–.] 8vo, pp. 11. H. 1326

Report of the Committee appointed to inquire into Facts relative to the Amherst Collegiate Institution, January 8, 1825. [No imprint.] 8vo, pp. 39. H. 1327

Report of the Committee of the Legislature on the Petitions of Amherst and Williams Colleges. 1827. 8vo. W. 1328

Songs of Amherst. ... Published by the Class of '62. *Northampton, Printed by Metcalf & Company*, 1860. 12mo, pp. 72. H.

Statement of the Affairs of Amherst Institution. *Pittsfield*, 1824. 8vo. W. 1330

[Statement in reference to the Petition and Memorial, &c., for Incorporation. *Boston, Printed by Crocker & Brewster, Jan.*, 1824.] 8vo, pp. 15. 1331

The Substance of Two Reports of the Faculty of Amherst College, to the Board of Trustees, with the Doings of the Board thereon. *Amherst, Carter and Adams, Printers*, 1827. 8vo, pp. 22. 1332

Amherst. Mount Pleasant Classical Institution, Amherst, Mass. Catalogue ... . January, 1828. *Amherst*, 1828. 8vo, pp. 16. Continued. 1333

AMHERSTBURG. Minutes and Proceedings of the General Convention, for the Improvement of the Colored Inhabitants of Canada, held by Adjournments in Amherstburgh [*sic*], C. W., June 16th and 17th, 1853. *Windsor, C. W., Bibb & Holly*, 1853. 8vo, pp. 24. H. 1334

[Testimonies in Favor of the Amherstburg Missionary Society.] [n. p., 1853.] 24mo, pp. 10. H. 1335

[AMHURST (Nicholas)]. Some Remarks on a late Pamphlet, entitled, Observations on the Conduct of Great Britain: particularly with relation to the Spanish Depredations & Letters of Reprisal, in a Letter to the Craftsmen. To which is added, A Postscript in Vindication of the West Indian Merchants, against a late Charge of Theft & Pyracy. By Caleb D'Anvers of Gray's Inn Esqre. *London*, 1729. 8vo, pp. 38. 1335*a*

AMICUS PATRIÆ, *pseudon.* *See* A Friendly Check; and Massachusetts.

AMICUS REIPUBLICÆ, *pseudon.* An Address to the Public, containing some Remarks on the Present Political State of American Republicks, &c. By Amicus Reipublicæ. *Exeter, Lamson and Ranlet* [1786]. 8vo, pp. 36. H. 1336

AMIGORENA (José Francisco de). Diario de la expedicion, etc. *See* Angelis (Pedro de).

Amistad Captives. The African Captives. Trial of the prisoners of the Amistad on the Writ of Habeas Corpus ... . *New York*, 1839. 8vo, pp. 47. 1337

Amistad Captives. Africans taken in the Amistad. Congressional Document, containing the Correspondence, &c., in relation to the Captured Africans. *New York, Anti-Slavery Depository*, 1840. 8vo, pp. 48. 1338

See, also, Adams (J. Q.), Barber (J. W.), Giddings (J. R.)

AMMANS. Reisz in das Gelobte Land Von Hans Jacob Ammans. *Zürich, Michel Schauffelbergen*, 1678. Sm. 8vo, 8 p. l., pp. 192, 174. Gothic letter. 1339

"In this volume, at p. 177, is 'Neue Beschreibung der Insel Jamaica in America,' by Hans Jacob Zeller; and at p. 192 is 'Americanische Reisz Beschreibung nach den Caribe Inzeln und New Engelland,' by F. C. Spori. The latter is separately paged, 1 to 90, and is followed by travels in Africa, pp. 93 to 174."—BARTLETT.

AMOR PATRIÆ, *pseudon.* A Comparison of Slavery with Abolitionism; together with Reflections deduced from the Premises, touching the Several Interests of the United States. By Amor Patriæ. ... *New York*, 1848. 8vo, pp. 16. H. 1340

AMOR PATRIÆ, *pseudon.* The Blasphemy of Abolitionism exposed: Servitude, and the Rights of the South, vindicated. A Bible Argument. Together with Reflections ... touching the several interests of the United States, and the evil consequences ... to the Northern States in case of Division ... . By Amor Patriæ. A New Edition, revised, corrected and enlarged. ... *New York*, 1850. 8vo, pp. 24. H. 1341

Amor Patriæ; or, the Disruption and Fall of These States. A Tragedy in Five Acts. ... *St. Louis, George Knapp & Co., Printers*, 1860. 12mo, pp. 103. H. 1342

AMORETTI (Carlo). *See* Maldonado and Pigafetta.

AMORY (Thomas Coffin). The Argument of Thomas C. Amory, against the Proposed Metropolitan Police Bill, before the Joint Special Committee of the Legislature, Monday, March 16, 1863. *Boston, J. E. Farwell and Company, Printers*, 1863. 8vo, pp. 31. H. 1343

AMORY. Life of James Sullivan. With Selections from his Writings. By Thomas C. Amory. Vols. I. II. *Boston, Phillips, Sampson and Company*, 1859. 8vo, pp. xii., 414; v., 424. Portrait. 1344

AMORY (Thomas Coffin, Jr.) An Address delivered at the Dedication of the City Hospital, May 24, 1864, by Thomas C. Amory, Jr. *Boston, J. E. Farwell and Company, Printers*, 1864. 8vo, pp. 45. H. 1345

AMOS (Andrew). Report of Trials in the Courts of Canada, relative to the Destruction of The Earl of Selkirk's Settlement on the Red River; with Observations. By A. Amos, Esq., Barrister at Law, and Fellow of Trinity College, Cambridge. *London, John Murray*, 1820. 8vo, pp. xxx. (2), 388, iv. H.

AMPÈRE (J. J.) Promenade en Amérique. États-Unis, Cuba, Mexique. Par Jean Jacques Ampère. *Paris*, 1855. 2 vols., 8vo, pp. 421, 425.+3[e] édition. *Paris, Lévy frères*, 1860. 2 vols., 8vo. 1347

Amphi-Theatrum, Worinnen III. Aus dem gantzen America alle Nationen nach ihrem Habit in saubern Figuren repraesentirt: Anbey die Laender nach ihrer Situation, Climate, Fruchtbarkeit aufgeführet, etc. *Erffurth*, 1723. Folio. 1348

Georgi dates the American part of this work 1725 (31 sheets); Heinsius speaks of the Asia and America as published together in 1728. It is illustrated with a number of curious woodcuts.

AMPHLETT (Wm.) The Emigrant's Directory to the Western States of North America; including a Voyage out from Liverpool; the Geography and Topography of the whole Western Country, According to its latest Improvements; with Instructions for descending the Rivers Ohio and Mississippi; also, A Brief Account of a New British Settlement on the Head-Waters of the Susquehanna, in Philadelphia. By William Amphlett, formerly of London, ... now Resident on the Banks of the Ohio River. *London, Longman, Hurst, Rees, Orme, and Brown*, 1819. Post 8vo, pp. viii., 208. H. 1349

"The present small volume appears to contain the most impartial account of the Western States that we have yet seen. The author, disclaiming all intention of offering advice on the subject of emigration to the American continent, confines himself to a description of the country; and he does not appear to be one of those speculators who have land to sell, and are, therefore, interested in one particular State."—*M. R.*, XCI., p. 315.

Ampliatio Oder Erweiterung. 1633. *See* Usselincx.

AMPZING (S.) West-Indische | Trivmph-Basvyne, | Tot Godes ere, ende roem der Batavieren gesteken, van we- | gen de veroveringe der Spaensche Silver-vlote van Nova | Hispania, inde Baij van Matanca, door de Schepen vande Ge- | octroijeerde West-Indische

Compagnie, onder het beleyd | vande E. Manhafte Heren See-Helden Pieter | Pieterszen Heyn, Generael, ende Heyn- | rick Korneliszen Lonk, Admirael, geschied den 8. Sept. 1628. | Door | Samvel Ampzing, | Bedienaer des Goddelijken Woords inde Gemeynte des Heren binnen Haerlem. ¶ *Tot Haerlem, by Adriaen Rooman, Ordinaris Stads-Boek-drucker*, cIↄ Iↄ c XXIX. 4to, 6 p. l., pp. 44. 2 Plates. 1350

Amsterdams | Dam-Praetje, | Van | Wat Outs en wat Nieuws. | En | Wat vreemts. ¶ *Tot Amsterdam*, | *By Ian van Soest, Boeckverkooper op de Kalver-Dijck, Anno* 1649. 4to, 20 leaves. 1351

This and the three following relate to Brazil, the New Netherlands, &c.

Amsterdams | Tafel-Praetje, | Van | Wat goets en wat Quaets | En | Wat Noodichs. ¶ *Tot Gouda*, | *By Iasper Cornelisz, Boeckverkooper woonende op de Cingel*, | *Anno* 1649. | 4to, 16 leaves. 1352

Amsterdams | Vuur-Praetje, | Van | 't Een ende 'tander datter | nu om gaet. ¶ *t'Amstelredam*, | *Gedruckt by Claes Pietersz Boeckverkooper*, | *Anno* 1649. 4to, 18 leaves. 1353

Amsterdamsche | Veerman | op | Middelburgh. ¶ *Tot Vlissingen*, | *Gedruckt by my Jacob Jansz Pieck, in't jaer ons* | *Heeren*. 1650. | 4to, pp. 12. 1354

Discourse between John, Pieter, Klaes and Paulus, concerning the West India Company and the Brazils.

The Amulet; a tale of Spanish California. *London*, 1865. 12mo. 1355

Amusemens géographiques. *See* [Navarre (P.)]

ANABLE (C. W.) Order of Services at the Recognition of the Rev. Cortland W. Anable, as Pastor of the Old Cambridge Baptist Church, ... June 21, 1863. [*Cambridge*] *John Ford, Printer* [1863]. 8vo, pp. 4. H. 1356

ANAHUAC. Resumen historico de las principales nationes que poblaron el pais de Anahuac, o virreynato de nueve Espagna. 8vo, pp. 155. Plates. 1357

The Analectic Magazine and Naval Chronicle. *Philadelphia*, 1813–20. 16 vols., 8vo.+New Series. Vol. I. *Philadelphia, J. Maxwell*, 1820. 8vo. Continued. 1358

Among the contributors were Washington Irving, G. C. Verplanck, J. K. Paulding and Paul Allen; the Biography was principally by Irving. It includes a copious and authentic history of the second war with Great Britain.

Anales del Ministerio de Fomento, Colonizacion, Industria y Comercio de la Republica Mexicana. *Mexico*, 1854–55. 8vo.

Analyse de la Carte Générale de l'Océan Atlantique ou Occidental, Dressée au Dépôt des Cartes, Plans and Journaux de la Marine, et Publiée par Ordre du Roi, pour le service des Vaisseaux de Sa Majesté, Sous le Ministère de M. le Maréchal des Castries, Ministre & Secrétaire d'Etat ayant le départment de la Marine & des Colonies, en 1786. *A Paris, de l'Imprimerie Royale*, M.DCCLXXXVI. 4to, title and pp. 42. 1360

Analyse de l'Histoire philosophique et politique des établissements et du commerce des Européens dans les deux Indes. *Leyde*, 1775. 8vo, pp. 255. 1361

"Barbier and Quérard attribute a work with a similar title, printed at Paris in the same year, to Fr. Bernard, a Dutchman. This is probably another edition of the same."—RICH.

Analyse des notes des conseils coloniaux, Ir. législature. Part I. (Martinique, Guadeloupe, Guyane Française, Isle Bourbon.) *Paris*, 1838. 4to. 1362

The Analysis of Patriotism; or, an Inquiry whether Opposition to Government, in the Present State of Affairs, is consistent with the Principles of a Patriot. *London, Keeble*, &c., 1777. 12mo. 1363

Relates to the American Revolution. The author determines his question in the negative.—*See M. R.*, LIX., 155.

Analysis of the late Correspondence, 1809. *See* [Lowell (John)].

ANANIA (G. L. d') L'Universale Fabrica del Mondo overo Cosmografia, diuisa in quattro Trattati. ... Di Gio. Lorenzo d'Anania. *In Venetia, Ad instantia di Aniello San Vito di Napoli*, MDLXXVI. 4to, 12 p. l., pp. 336 (31). *Reprinted* 1582. 4to. +1596. 4to. B. 1364

Trattato quarto relates to America.

The Anarchiad, A New England Poem, written in concert by David Humphreys, Joel Barlow, John Trumbull, and Dr. Lemuel Hopkins. *New Haven*, 1861. 16mo, pp. 120. 1365

[ANBUREY (Thomas)]. Travels through the Interior Parts of America. In a Series of Letters. By an Officer. ... *London, William Lane*, MDCCLXXXIX. 8vo, half title, title, pp. vii. (21), 467; half title, title, pp. 558. Map and 7 Plates. H. 1366

[ANBUREY.] Travels through the interior parts of America. In a Series of Letters. By an Officer. A New Edition. *London, Printed for William Lane*, MDCCXCI. 2 vols., 8vo, pp. XII., 2 leaves of fac-similes; pp. 414; pp. 492. 7 Plates. 1367

Reprinted, with the author's name, in 1792. *See* M. R., LXXXI., p. 61. "Mr. Thomas Anburey, the author of the travels, was an officer under General Burgoyne, and whose conduct, in his unfortunate campaign, one object of this publication appears to have been to vindicate. The *Monthly Reviewer* says: 'He sometimes diverts us with anecdotes concerning the speeches or customs or manners of the people, as he passed among them, which, though droll, or even ridiculous enough, are of that kind to which something similar may be met with in all countries, as may be easily imagined by those who have travelled in England.' How different from the *great* reviewers of 1832! The *Critical Reviewer* pronounces 'this work, in its most essential parts, to be an ill-digested plagiarism from Gen. Burgoyne's Narrative, and from the account of the prosecution of Colonel Henley.'"—RICH. "Anburey copies verbatim from Burnaby and Peters, also very impudently from Smyth."—*From a MS. note by* C. D. EBELING.

[ANBUREY.] Voyages dans les parties intérieures de l'Amérique, pendant le cours de la dernière guerre; Par un Officier de l'Armée Royale. Traduit de l'Anglois [par P. L. Lebas]. *Paris, Briand*, 1790. 2 vols., 8vo, pp. 396, 470. Map. H. 1368

[ANBUREY.] Journal d'un voyage fait dans l'intérieur de l'Amérique septentrionale. Ouvrage dans lequel on donne des détails précieux sur l'insurrection des Anglo-Américains, et sur la chute désastreuse de leur papier-monnoie. Traduit de l'Anglois et enrichi de notes par M. Noël, ancien Professeur de belles-lettres au Collége de Louis-le-grand. Avec carte & figures. *Paris, La Villette*, 1793. 2 vols., 8vo, pp. 336, 453. Map and Plates. H. 1369

See Le Redacteur, Boucher Bibliothèque, and Faribault, p. 4.

ANBUREY. Reisen im Innern von Nord Amerika; imgleichen die Geschichte des Feldzugs und der Uebergabe des Generals Bourgoyne. Aus dem Englischen mit Anmerkungen. *Berlin, Voss*, 1792. 8vo. Plates. C. 1370

Forms part of Bd. VI. of J. R. Forster's Magazin von neuen Reisebeschreibungen.

ANCHIETA (José de). Arte de Grammatica da Lingoa mais usada na Costa do Brasil. Por Feyto pelo Padre Joseph de Anchieta da Copanhia de Jesu. *Coimbra, Antonio de Mariz*, 1595. Sm. 8vo, pp. 120. 1371

Extracts from this rare book will be found in Marcgravius, "Historiæ rerum naturalium Brasiliæ," Chap. VIII., and in Relandus, "Dissert. miscell.," III., 173. Wolf, *Literature de Bresil*, mentions a play in the Indian language by this author.

ANCHIETA (Joseph de). De Lingua Brasiliensium ex ejus Grammatica. *Amstelodami*, 1658. Folio. 1371*a*

ANCHIETA. Vida de ven. P. Joze de Anchieta de Companhia de Jesus, thaumaturgo de nouo Mundo na provincia de Brasil. *Lisboa, J. da Costa*, 1672. Folio. 1372

ANCHIETA. Vida del padre Joseph de Anchieta de la Compañia de Jesus y provincia del Brasil, traducida de latin en castellano por el P. Estevan de Paternina. *Salamanca*, 1618. 12mo.

Title as given by Ternaux Compans, No. 399. *See also* Beretari (Seb.)

ANCHIETA. Vita del P. Guiseppe Anchieta detto l'Apostolo del Brasile, cavata da' Processi formati per la sua Beatificazione. *Romæ*, 1738. 8vo. 1374

Lives of Father Joseph Anchieta, S. J., the Ven. Alvera von Virmundt, Religions of the Order of the Holy Sepulchre; and the Ven. John Berchmans, S. J. *London, Richardson and Son*, 1849. 8vo. 1375

Joseph Anchieta, a native of Teneriffe, left Portugal in the suite of Acosta, in the year 1553, in his twentieth year, and died in Brazil in 1597. He established the College of Perataningo.

Ancient Records. [n. p., 183–?] 8vo, pp. 8. 1376

Purporting to be the "Book of Chronicles, Part I." A burlesque description of some trial "in the reign of Andrew the Farmer," for violation of the Massachusetts Laws restricting the sale of intoxicating liquors.

ANCHOR, *pseudon.* *See* [De Peyster (J. W.)]

Ancient Right of the English Nation to the American Fishery. *See* [Bollan (Wm.)]

ANCIZAR. Peregrinacion por las provincias del norte de la Nueva Granada en 1850 y 51. *Bogotá*, 1853. 12mo, pp. 524. Portrait. 1377

ANCONA. Proceedings of a court martial in the Case of Capt. S. E. Ancona, held at Reading, Pa., May 10, 1854. 8vo. P.

Anderde Discovrs. By Forma van Messieve. *See* West Indies.

ANDERS (Rudolph). Der Weg zum Glück, oder: die Kunst Millionair zu werden. Aus den hinterlassenen Papieren des kürzlich verstorbenen Amerikanischen Millionairs Abbot Law-

rence im Original. Deutsch bearbeitet von Rudolph Anders. *Berlin, G. A. Hoevel*, 1856. 16mo, pp. 28. H. 1379

"Good, moral advice, arranged under forty-four heads. No part of it is unworthy the character of Mr. Lawrence, but undoubtedly no part of it was ever seen by him."—*Boston Courier.* (Art. by George Ticknor.)

ANDERSON. The History of the Life and Adventures of Mr. Anderson, containing his strange varieties of Fortune in Europe and America. Compiled from his own papers. [Motto.] *London, Owen*, 1754. 12mo, pp. 228. + Same. *Dublin*, 1754. 12mo. + Same. *Berwick, W. Pherson*, M.DCC.LXXXII. 12mo, pp. 263. Frontispiece. 1380

The author was kidnapped in London, taken to America, and sold to a planter at Senupexen Inlet, Md., for £10, and afterwards joined the Virginia Rangers against the French Indians, &c. *See* M. R., X, p. 147.

ANDERSON. Eastern Coast of Central America. Mr. Anderson's Report. *London* [1849]. 8vo, pp. 138. 1381

This pamphlet has no regular title, not having been printed for sale. It is addressed to the Directors of the Eastern Coast of Central America Commercial and Agricultural Company.

[ANDERSON (Adam)] An Historical and Chronological Deduction of the Origin of Commerce, from the Earliest Accounts to the present Time. ... To which is prefixed, An Introduction, Exhibiting ... the Importance of our Colonies ... . *London, A. Millar, etc.*, MDCCLXIV. 2 vols., folio. (H.)+Same. Carefully revised, corrected, and continued to the present Time. ... *London*, 1787–'89. 4 vols., 4to.+Same. Carefully Revised, Corrected, and continued to the Year 1789, by Mr. Coombe. *Dublin*, 1790. 6 vols., 8vo. Maps. H. 1382

The author was a clerk in the South-Sea House, London. It contains a most accurate account of the South-Sea Company, and the very extraordinary actions of the year 1720.

ANDERSON (Alexander). Life and Confession. *See* Rockafield (H. A.)

ANDERSON (A.) A General History of Quadrupeds. The Figures engraved on Wood, chiefly copied from the Original of T. Bewick. By A. Anderson. First American Edition, With an Appendix, containing some American Animals not hitherto described. *New-York*, 1804. 8vo, pp. x., 531. H. 1383

Dr. Anderson introduced wood engraving into the United States, and has been called the Bewick of America. He was born in 1775, and still lives—1867.

ANDERSON (C.) This pamphlet is humbly dedicated to the

Ladies and Gentlemen who may please to visit Lundy's Lane, by the author, Charles Anderson, late lieutenant in His Majesty's Provincial Royal Artillery Drivers, who fought in all the actions on the Niagara frontier, and at Stoney Creek, of which he gives a true and impartial account, and is now a guide to the Battle Ground at Lundy's Lane. *Niagara, Chronicle Office.* 12mo, pp. 35. 1384

Anderson (C.) An Address delivered before the Society of Alumni of Miami University, at their Anniversary, August 13th, 1840: by Charles Anderson. *Oxford, Ohio, Printed by John B. Peat*, 1840. 8vo, pp. 37. H. 1385

"Upon the history, condition and prospects of the University."

Anderson (C.) An Address on the Anglo Saxon Destiny ... . By Charles Anderson, Esq. *Cincinnati, Printed by John D. Thorpe*, 1850. 8vo, pp. 48. H. 1386

The title on the cover reads: "The Anglo Saxons: their Origin, History, Character, Identity, and Connection with the English and American People; and their Destiny."

Anderson. A Funeral Oration, on the Character, Life, and Public Services of Henry Clay. Delivered in Cincinnati, Nov. 2, 1852, at the Request of the Clay Monumental Association of Ohio. By Charles Anderson. *Cincinnati, Ben. Franklin Office Print*, 1852. 8vo, pp. 38. H. 1387

Anderson (C.) Thanksgiving for Victory, Peace, and our Country Saved. A Proclamation by Charles Anderson, Governor of the State of Ohio. [*Columbus?* 1865.] Broadside. H.

Anderson (C.) Loyal Publication Society ... . No. 17. The Cause of the War; Who brought it on, and for What Purpose? Speech of Col. Charles Anderson, late of Texas, now of U. S. Volunteers. *New York, Wm. Bryant & Co., Printers*, 1863. 8vo, pp. 16. H. 1389

Anderson (C.) Loyal Publication Society, ... No. 21. Letter addressed to the Opera House Meeting, Cincinnati. By Col. Charles Anderson. *New York, Wm. C. Bryant & Co., Printers*, 1863. 8vo, pp. 15. H. 1389*a*

[Anderson (Charles Frederick)]. Architect's Report and Plans for the Improvement of the Lighting, Heating, Ventilation, and Acoustics of the Senate Chamber, and Hall of the

House of Representatives ... December 2, 1864. *Washington, D. C., McGill & Witherow, Printers*, 1864. 8vo, pp. 36. H.

Anderson (D.) Canada: or a View of the Importance of the British American Colonies; shewing their Extensive and Improveable Resources and pointing out the Great and Unprecedented Advantages which have been allowed To the Americans over our own Colonists; together with the Great Sacrifices which have been made by our late Commercial Regulations of the Commerce and Carrying-Trade of Great Britain to the United States ... . By David Anderson. *London, J. M. Richardson*, 1814. 8vo, pp. xxxi., 355. Map. B. 1391

Anderson. A Charge to the Clergy of the Diocese of Rupert's Land at its Primary Visitation. By David Anderson, D.D., 1852. 8vo. 1392

Anderson. Notes of the Flood at the Red River, in 1852. By David Anderson, D.D., Bishop of Rupert's Land. *London*, 1852. 12mo, pp. 124. C. 1393

Anderson (E.) The Ultimatum of a Free Ministry to the Demands of Politicians. A Discourse, by Rev. Edward Anderson, Pastor of the First Baptist Church, Milford, N. H., July 13, 1856. *Milford, Garfield's Press*, 1856. 8vo, pp. 31. H. 1394

Anderson (F.) Addresses delivered before the Virginia State Convention by Hon. Fulton Anderson, Commissioner from Mississippi, Hon. Henry L. Benning, Commissioner from Georgia, and Hon. John S. Preston, Commissioner from South Carolina, February, 1861. *Richmond, Wyatt M. Eliott, Printer*, 1861. 8vo, pp. 64. H. 1395

Anderson (G. W.) Slavery and Slaveholding in the United States. By Geo. W. Anderson, Pastor of the Lower Merion Baptist Church, Penn'a. *Philadelphia, American Baptist Publication Society* [185–?] 24mo, pp. 67. H. 1396

Anderson (Hugh). A True and Historical Narrative. *See* Tailfer (Patrick).

Anderson. Historical Narrative of the Colony of Georgia. (In Georgia Historical Society's Collections, Vol. II.)

[Anderson (James)]. The Constitutions of the Free-Masons Containing the History, Charges, Regulations, &c., of that most

Ancient and Right Worshipful Fraternity. For the Use of the Lodges. *London, Printed* [1723]; *Philadelphia, Reprinted by B. Franklin*, 1734. 4to.+*London*, 1723.+Republished, Fac-simile, *by Jno. W. Leonard and Co.*, 1855. 4to, 4 p. l., pp. 108. H. 1397

Mr. Corwin's copy of the edition of 1734 sold in 1856 for $9.25.

Anderson (James). Royal Genealogies: or, The Genealogical Tables of Emperors, Kings and Princes, from Adam to these Times; In Two Parts. Part I. ... the Genealogies of the earliest great Families, and most ancient Sovereigns of Asia, Europe, Africa and America ... . The Second Edition. With new Addenda and Corrigenda ... . By James Anderson, D.D. *London, Charles Davis*, M,DCC,XXXVI. Folio, pp. (22), 812 (18). H. 1398

The first edition appeared in 1732.

[Anderson (James)]. Free Thoughts on the American Contest. ... *Edinburgh*, M,DCC,LXXVI. 8vo, pp. 59. H. 1399

First published in the *Edinburgh Weekly Magazine*, over the signature of "Timoleon." Takes the side of Great Britain, and concludes with some severe strictures on Paine's *Common Sense*.

Anderson. The Interest of Great-Britain with regard to her American Colonies, considered. To which is added An Appendix, containing the Outlines of a Plan for a General Pacification. By James Anderson, M.A., Author of Observations on the Means of exciting a Spirit of National Industry, &c. *London, T. Cadell*, M.DCC.LXXXII. 8vo, pp. vii., 136, Appendix 36. H.

The object of the author of this pamphlet is to show "that the American Colonies, instead of promoting the trade and manufactures of Great Britain, have tended in a most powerful manner to depress them. That, instead of adding strength and stability to the empire, they have necessarily weakened it to a great degree, and exposed it to the most imminent danger. That, therefore, the settling of these colonies at first was unwise, and the subsequent encouragement that was given them highly impolitic."—*M. R.*, lxvi., 428. The cotton famine of 1862 is a practical commenton this writer.

Anderson. Observations on Slavery, particularly with a view to its effects on the British Colonies in the West Indies. By James Anderson. *Manchester*, 1789. 4to, pp. 38. P. 1401

Anderson (James). A Few Facts and Observations on the Yellow Fever of the West Indies, by which is shewn, that there have existed two species of Fever in the West India Islands for several years past, indiscriminately called Yellow Fever, but which have proceeded from very different causes; with the success attending the method of cure. By James Anderson, M.D.,

Late Surgeon of the 60th Regiment of Foot. *London, Robinson*, 1799. 8vo. 1402

See *M. R.*, New Series, xxix., 454.

Anderson. Account of the Importation of American Cochineal Insects into Hindostan. *Madras*, 1795. 8vo, pp. 9. 1402*a*

Anderson (James). Memorable Women of the Puritan Times. By the Rev. James Anderson ... . *London, Blackie and Son*, [also] *Glasgow and Edinburgh*, 1862. 8vo, pp. viii., (1), 408; (1), 408. H. 1403

Contains, among others, lives of Margaret Tindal, wife of John Winthrop, Anne Dudley, wife of Simon Bradstreet; Anne Marbury, wife of Wm. Hutchinson; and Mary Dyer.

Anderson (James Stuart Murray). The History of the Church of England in the Colonies and Foreign Dependencies of the British Empire. By the Rev. James S. M. Anderson, M.A. *London*, 1845–56. 3 vols., 8vo, pp. xxviii., 482; xvi., 769; xxiv., 807.+Second Edition. *London, Rivingtons*, 1856. Fcap 8vo, pp. xl., 512, Table and Map; xix., 582; xx., 654. H. 1404

Anderson (Johann). Nachrichten von Island, Grönland und der Strasse Davis, zum wahren Nutzen der Wissenschaften und der Handlung. *Hamburg, Holle*, 1746. 8vo. Plates.+Same. *Frankfurt u. Leipzig*, 1747. 8vo. Map and Plates. 1405

The appendix contains a brief grammar and vocabulary of the Esquimaux language explained in German and Danish.

Anderson. Efterretninger om Island, Grönland og Strat Davis. *Kiöbenhavn*, 1748. 8vo. Map and Plates. Bm. 1406

Anderson. Beschryving van Ysland, Groenland en de Straat Davis. Uit het hoogduitsch vertaalt. Door J. D. J. *Amsterdam*, 1750. 4to. Map and Plate.+Waar by gevoegt zyn de Verbeteringen door Niels Horrebow. *Amsterdam*, 1756. 4to, Map and Plates. 1407

The first part of this edition is the same as the preceding. The second part is Horrebow's Iceland.

Anderson (J.) Histoire Naturelle de l'Islande et du Groënland, traduit de l'allemand par Sellius. *Paris, Séb. Cramoisy*, 1750. +*Paris, Jorry*, 1754. 2 vols., 12mo. 1408

Anderson (J.) Histoire Naturelle de L'Island du Groën-

land, du Detroit de Davis, et d'autres Pays Situes sous le Nord, traduite de l'Allemande. Par M*** [J. P. Rousselot de Surgy]. *Paris, Jorry*, 1750. 2 vols., 8vo. Map and Plates.+*Paris*, 1764. 2 vols., 12mo. 1408*a*

See Boucher, Vol. I., pp. 392.

Anderson (John). Speech of Mr. Anderson, of Maine, on the Proposed Increase of the Tariff: delivered in the House of Representatives of the U. States, March 5, 1828. [n. p., 1828.] 8vo, pp. 8. H. 1409

Anderson (John J.) A Pictorial School History of the United States. ... By John J. Anderson. *New York, Clark & Maynard*, 1864. 12mo, pp. 313, 38. H. 1410

Anderson (Joseph). Judge Anderson's Speech. Delivered in the Senate of the United States. On Thursday the 1st. day of December, on the resolution offered by Mr. Hillhouse, to repeal the several embargo laws. [n. p.], *Dinmore and Cooper, Printers* [1808]. 8vo, pp. 18. H. 1411

Anderson (L.) Speech of the Hon. Lucien Anderson, of Kentucky, on the Democracy of Kentucky and their Allies in the North. House of Representatives, March 5, 1864. 8vo, pp. 15. 1412

Anderson (M. E.) Scenes in the Hawaiian Islands and California. By Mary E. Anderson. *Boston*, 1865. 16mo. 1413

Anderson (O. P.) A Voice from Harper's Ferry. A Narrative of Events at Harper's Ferry; with Incidents Prior and Subsequent to its Capture by Captain Brown and his Men. By Osborne P. Anderson, One of the Number. *Boston, the Author*, 1861. 12mo, pp. 72. H. 1414

Anderson (R.) ... Concurrent Resolutions of the Legislature of New York, in relation to Gen. Robert Anderson. *Washington*, 1864. 8vo, pp. 2. (38th Cong., 1st Sess., House, Misc. Doc., No. 65.) 1415

[Anderson (R. W.)] Hon. Senators and Representatives ... 1st Session, 32nd Congress. ["A few suggestions with regard to non-intervention between European States, a change in our naturalization law, and the revision, concretion and perfection of the jurisprudence of the Confederacy and the Several States." n. p., 1851 or 1852.] 4to, pp. 2. H. 1416

Anderson (R.) Two Discourses, delivered on the Public Fast in Massachusetts, April 8, 1802. By Rufus Anderson, of Wenham, Mass. *Portland*, 1802. 8vo, pp. 40. 1417

Anderson. American Board of Commissioners for Foreign Missions. Report to the Prudential Committee of a Visit to the Missions in the Levant. By Rufus Anderson ... . Also, A Letter to the Committee from the Rev. Dr. Hawes. ... *Boston, Printed for the Board, by T. R. Marvin*, 1844. 8vo, pp. 54. H.

Anderson (R.) The Hawaiian Islands: their Progress and Condition under Missionary Labors. By Rufus Anderson, D.D., Foreign Secretary of American Board of Commissioners for Foreign Missions. With Illustrations. *Boston, Gould and Lincoln*, 1864. 12mo, pp. 450. H.+Second Edition. *Boston*, 1864. 12mo.+Third Edition. *Boston*, 1865. 12mo. H. 1419

Anderson. Memoir of Catherine Brown, a Christian Indian of the Cherokee Nation. By Rufus Anderson, A.M. *Boston*, 1825. 18mo, pp. 180.+*London*, 1825. 16mo. B. M.+*Philadelphia, American Sunday School Union* [1831]. 24mo, pp. 138. H.+*Philadelphia*, 1832. 12mo.+*Cincinnati*, 1827.+*York* [*England*], *W. Alexander & Son*, 1827. 12mo, pp. 202. Plate.

Anderson (T. D.) A funeral oration, delivered before the City Government and Citizens of Roxbury, on the Occasion of paying Funeral Honors to Zachary Taylor, late President of the United States; July 31, 1850. By Rev. Thomas D. Anderson. Together with the other Services. Printed by order of the City Council. *Roxbury*, 1850. 8vo, pp. 40. 1421

Anderson. The Home and the Nation. A Sermon delivered before the Executive and Legislative Departments of the Government of Massachusetts, at the Annual Election, ... Jan. 4, 1860. By Thomas D. Anderson, D.D., Pastor of Dudley St. Baptist Church, Roxbury. *Boston, William White, Printer*, 1860. 8vo, pp. 38. H. 1422

Anderson (W. C.) The National Crisis. An Address delivered before the Young Men's Christian Association of San Francisco, Cal., at their Eighth Anniversary, Aug. 12, 1861. By Rev. W. C. Anderson. *San Francisco*, 1861. 8vo, pp. 10.

Anderson (W.) Liberty and Union! Speeches delivered at the Eighteenth Ward Republican Festival, in Commemoration

of the Birth of Washington, held at the Gramercy Park House, New York, February 22, 1860. Reported phonographically by William Anderson. *New York, Baker and Godwin, Printers*, 1860. 8vo, pp. 40. H. 1424

Anderson (W. J.) Life and Narrative of William J. Anderson, Twenty-four Years a Slave; sold Eight Times! in Jail Sixty Times!! whipped Three Hundred Times!!! ... Also, A Simple and Easy Plan to abolish Slavery in the United States, together with An Account of the Services of Colored Men in the Revolutionary War ... . Written by himself. *Chicago, Daily Tribune Book and Job Printing Office*, 1857. 12mo, pp. 81. H. 1425

Anderson (W. W.) Canada and Jamaica: Two Addresses delivered before the Colored Citizens of New-York, by William Wemyss Anderson, Esq., of Jamaica, and John Scoble, Esq., of London; on the 16th and 23d of October, 1851. Reported ... by John Mullaly, Esq. *New-York, Wm. Harned*, 1851. 12mo, pp. 16. H. 1426

Anderson. A Description and History of the Island of Jamaica, comprising an Account of its Soil, Climate, and Productions, shewing its Value and Importance as an Agricultural Country, and a desirable place of residence for certain Classes of Settlers. Reprinted (it is believed for the first time,) from the great Work, "An Account of America, or the New World," by John Ogilby, Esq., Master of the Revels in Ireland; first published in the year 1671, with preliminary chapter and notes, to connect the Work with our own times; By William Wemyss Anderson, Esq. (With a Map of the Island.) Jamaica and the other West India Islands are destined to be the true and final homes of the civilized Coloured Races. *Kingston, Jamaica, George Henderson*, 1851. 8vo, pp. 46, Errata 9 lines, on a slip. Map. 1427

Anderson. Jamaica and the Americans. By William Wemyss Anderson. *New York*, 1851. 8vo, pp. 30. 1428

Andersonville. *See* [Smith (Gerrit)].

A List of the Union Soldiers buried at Andersonville. Copied from the Official Record in the Surgeon's Office at Andersonville [by Dorence Atwater]. ... *New York, Tribune Association*, 1866. Rl. 8vo, pp. viii., 74. H. 1429

Quartermaster General's Office, General Orders, No. 70

[69½]. The Martyrs who, for Our Country, gave up their Lives in the Prison Pens in Andersonville, Ga. *Washington, Government Printing Office*, 1866. 8vo, pp. 225. H. 1430

The Andover Husking; a Political Tale, suited to the Circumstances of the Present Time, and dedicated to the Whigs of Massachusetts. ... *Boston, J. H. Eastburn, Printer*, 1842. 8vo, pp. 27. H. 1431

Andover. Catalogue of the Library belonging to the Theological Institution in Andover. *Andover, Printed by Flagg and Gould*, 1819. 8vo, pp. 161. H. 1432

Catalogue of the Library of the Theol. Seminary in Andover, Mass. By Oliver A. Taylor, M.A. *Andover, Printed by Gould & Newman*, 1838. 8vo, pp. 531.+First Supplement. *Andover, Printed by J. D. Flagg & W. H. Wardwell*, 1849. 8vo, pp. 66, (1). H. 1433

Catalogue of the Officers and Students of the Theological Seminary, Andover, January, 1818. [n. p., 1818.] Broadside. Continued. H. 1434

Began to be printed in 8vo in 1822, or earlier.

Catalogue of the Teachers' Seminary, Andover, Mass., October, 1836. *Andover, Printed by Gould and Newman*, 1836. 8vo, pp. 14. H. 1435

Catalogue of those who have been educated at the Theological Seminary in Andover. Sept. 27, 1815. *Andover, Printed by Flagg and Gould* [1815]. 8vo, pp. 12. Continued triennially. H.

The Constitution and Associate Statutes of the Theological Seminary in Andover; with a Sketch of its Rise and Progress. [By E. Pearson.] *Boston, Farrand, Mallory, and Co.*, 1808. 8vo, pp. 68.+*Andover, Printed by Flagg and Gould*, 1817. 8vo, pp. 40. H. 1437

The Constitution of Phillips Academy, in Andover. *Andover*, 1817. 8vo, pp. 14. 1438

Laws of the Theological Institution in Andover. *Andover, Printed by Flagg and Gould*, 1817. 8vo, pp. 16.+*Andover*, 1827. 8vo, pp. 31. H.+*Andover, Printed by Gould and Newman*, 1837. 8vo, pp. 31. H.+*Andover, Printed by Allen, Morrill and Wardwell*, 1846. 8vo, pp. 30. H. 1439

A Memorial of the Semi-Centennial Celebration of the Founding of the Theological Seminary at Andover. [Edited by the Rev. John L. Taylor.] *Andover, Warren F. Draper*, 1859. 8vo, pp. 8, 242. H. 1440

Review of the "Constitution and Associate Statutes," &c. From the Monthly Anthology, November, 1808. *Boston*, 1808. 8vo, pp. 35. 1441

Statistics of the Class of 1859, in Andover Theological Seminary. Compiled by the Class Secretary [Charles Ray Palmer]. *Andover, Printed by Warren F. Draper*, 1862. 8vo, pp. 40. H.

Andover and Wilmington Railroad. First Report of the Directors, &c., with that of the Engineer, October, 1834. *Andover*, 1834. 8vo, pp. 24. 1443

ANDRADA E SILVA (José Bonifacio de). Réfutation des calomnies relatives aux affaires du Brésil, insérées par un sieur de Loy dans *l'Indépendant* de Lyon; par MM. Jose Bonifacio d'Andrada, Antonio Carlos-Ribeiro d'Andrada et Martin Francesco-Ribeiro d'Andrada ... . *Paris, imprimerie de Béraud*, 1826. 8vo. 1444

ANDRADA E SILVA. Representaçao à assemblea geral constituente e legislativa do imperio do Brasil, sobre a escravatura, por José Bonifacio Andrada e Silva deputado à dita assemblea de la provincia di S. Paulo. *Paris, imprimerie de F. Didot*, 1825. 8vo. 1445

ANDRADA E SILVA. Memoir addressed to the General, Constituent and Legislative Assembly of the Empire of Brazil, on Slavery! By Jose Bonifaciod 'Andrada e Silva ... . Translated from the Portuguese by William Walton. *London, Butterworth, etc.*, 1826. 8vo, pp. 60. H. 1446

ANDRADE (Alonzo de). Varones ilustres en santidad, letras, y zelo de las almas. De la Compañia de Jesus. Tomo Quinto [and Sexto] a los quatro que saco a luz el Venerable, y Erudito Padre Juan Eusebio Nieremberg, de la Compañia de Jesus. Por el Padre Alonso de Andrade, de la misma Compañia de Iesus, natural de Toledo, Calificador del Consejo Supremo de la Santa y General Inquisition. *Madrid, Joseph Fernandez de Buendia*, 1666–67. 2 vols., folio, 6 p. l., pp. 863; 6 p. l., pp. 754. 1447

For a continuation, *see* Cassani; for the previous volumes, *see* Nieremberg.

ANDRADE E SILVA (J. M. de). Reinado e ultimos momentos de sua magestade o Senhor D. Pedro V. Por José Maria de Andrade e Silva. *Maranhao*, 1862. 8vo, pp. 222. 1448

ANDRÉ (John). The Cow Chace, In Three Cantos, Published on Occasion of the Rebel General Wayne's Attack of the Refugees' Block-House On Hudson's River, on Friday the 21st of July, 1780. *New York, Printed by James Rivington*, MDCCLXXX. 8vo, pp. 69. 1449

"The Cow Chace" occupies twenty-six pages—the remainder is a reprint of "The American Times." *See* No. 1244. The following is the last stanza of this mock-heroic poem; founded on the defeat of Generals Wayne, Irving, and Proctor, to which subsequent events gave a melancholy interest:

And now I've clos'd my epic strain,
I tremble as I show it,
Lest this same warrior-drover, Wayne,
Should ever catch the poet.

First published in Rivington's *Royal Gazette*. *See* M. R., LXVI., 72; Niles's *Reg.*, XX., 386.

ANDRÉ. The Cow Chace: an Heroick Poem, in Three Cantos. Written at New-York, 1780, By the late Major André, With Explanatory Notes, by the Editor. [Motto.] *London, Printed for John Fielding*, 1781. 4to, pp. 32. H. 1450

ANDRÉ. The Cow Chace. In Three Cantos. Written in the Year 1780; By Major John André, Adjutant-General to the British Army, in North America, a few Weeks previous to his Capture by the Americans. *New York, Printed in the Year* 1789. 12mo, pp. 22. 1451

ANDRÉ. The Cow Chace, A Poem in Three Cantos. By Major John André, Adjutant General to the British Army in New York, in 1780. *Albany, N. Y., J. Munsell*, 1866. 8vo, pp. 69. 1452

This edition was suppressed by the editor, Dr. Hough.

ANDRÉ. Case of Major John André, Adjutant-General to the British Army, who was put to death by the rebels, October 2nd, 1780. Candidly represented; with remarks on the Case. *New York, J. Rivington*, 1780. 4to, pp. 28. 1453

ANDRÉ. Proceedings of a Board of General Officers, Held by order of His Excellency Gen. Washington, Commander in Chief of the Army of the United States of America. Respecting Major John André, Adjutant General of the British Army. September 29, 1780. *Philadelphia, Printed by Francis Bailey, in Market-*

Street, M.DCC.LXXX. 8vo, Half Title, 1 l.; pp. 21. H.+ *Hartford, Reprinted by B. Webster*, M.DCC.LXXX. 12mo, pp. 32.

ANDRÉ. Proceedings of a Board of General Officers, Held by order of His Excellency General Washington, Commander in Chief of the Army of the United States of America Respecting Major John André, Adjutant General of the British Army. September 29, 1780. *Philadelphia Printed; New York, Reprinted by James Rivington*, MDCCLXXX. 4to, pp. 13. 1455

See The Royal Gazette, Wednesday, November 1, 1780, No. 427, where it is advertised as the "Proceedings of a Board of *Rebel* Officers," &c.

ANDRÉ. [Another Edition.] To which are appended, The several Letters which passed to and from New York on the Occasion. Published by Order of Congress. *Providence, Printed and Sold by John Carter* [n. d.] 8vo, pp. 16. N. 1456

Also included in the *New York Gazette*, Monday, Nov. 6, 1780, No. 1516. It was afterwards privately reprinted for Mr. John F. McCoy of New York, with an introduction by Dr. F. B. Hough, under the following title:

ANDRÉ. Minutes of a Court of Inquiry upon the case of Major John André, with accompanying documents published in 1780 by order of Congress, with an additional Appendix containing copies of the papers found upon Major André when arrested, and other documents relating to the subject. *Albany, J. Munsell*, 1865. 4to, pp. 66. 1457

One hundred copies printed, of which ten are on large paper.

Andreana. Containing the Trial, Execution, and various matters connected with the History of Major John André, Adjutant-General of the British Army in America, A.D. 1780. *Philadelphia, H. W. Smith*, 1865. 8vo, pp. iv., 67, 4. 12 Plates.

175 copies printed—25 in folio, 50 in 4to, and 100 in 8vo.

André: a Tragedy. *See* [Dunlap (Wm.)]

Vindication of the Captors of Major André. *See* [Benson (E.)]

ANDRÉ (—, *le Père*). Découverte du Nouveau-Monde. Histoire d'Amérique. *Paris, imprimerie de Sétier*, 1832. Broadside.

ANDRÉ. Description des quatre parties du monde: Europe, Asie, Afrique, Amérique. Les productions ...; lettre adressée au peuple français. *Paris, imprimerie de Sétier*, 1832. Folio.

ANDREE (Karl). Amerika in Geographischen und Geschichtlichen Umrissen. Von Dr. Karl Andree ... . Erster Band:

Nord-Amerika. *Braunschweig, George Westermann*, 1851. 8vo, pp. xiii., 810.+2e Auflage. Mit in den Text gedruckten Holzschnitten und einem Kartenwerk von 18 Blättern qu. Fol. von H. Lange. *Braunschweig*, 1854. 8vo. 1461

With the second title: "Nord-Amerika in ... Umrissen. Mit besonderer Berücksichtigung der Eingeborenen und der indianischen Alterthümer, der Einwanderung und der Ansiedlungen, des Ackerbaues, der Gewerbe, der Schifffahrt und des Handels. ... Mit Abbildungen. ..."

ANDREE. Buenos Ayres und die Argentinischen Provinzen. Nach den neuesten Quellen. Von Karl Andree. *Leipzig, C. B. Lorck*, 1856. 12mo, pp. xx., 426. C. 1462

Hausbibliothek für Länder und Völkerkunde, Band 10.

ANDREE. Geographische Wanderungen. Von Karl Andree. *Dresden*, 1859. 2 vols., 8vo, pp. xiv., 762. 1463

Vol I., pp. 74–329, contains Sketches of New York, Illinois, Kentucky and California. Vol. II., pp. 1–87, The Mormons, Discoveries in the West, and the Red River; pp. 88–120, A Glance at Central America.

ANDREE. Kartenwerk zu Nord-Amerika. ... Andree's Nach den neuesten Materialien, mit besonderer Rücksicht auf physikalische Verhältnisse und genauer Angabe der County-Eintheilung, der Eisenbahnen, Canäle, Poststrassen und Dampfschifffahrt, in 18 Blättern mit erläuterndem Texte herausgegeben von Henry Lange. ... *Braunschweig, George Westermann*, 1854. Folio, pp. 28. 1464

ANDREW (J. A.) An Address delivered before The New England Historic-Genealogical Society, at the Annual Meeting Held in Boston, Mass., January 2, 1867. By John A. Andrew, LL.D., President of the Society. To which is added a Report of the Proceedings at Said Meeting. *Boston, Printed by David Clapp & Son*, 1867. 8vo, pp. 11 (1). H. 1465

ANDREW. An Address on the Occasion of dedicating the Monument to Ladd and Whitney, Members of the Sixth Regiment, M. V. M., killed at Baltimore, April 19, 1861. Delivered at Lowell, Massachusetts, June 17, 1865. By John A. Andrew, Governor of the Commonwealth. *Boston, Wright & Potter, State Printers*, 1865. 8vo, pp. 31. H. 1466

ANDREW. Address of His Excellency John A. Andrew, to the Two Branches of the Legislature of Massachusetts, January 5, 1861. *Boston, William White, Printer*, 1861. 8vo, pp. 48. (Senate Doc. No. 2.)+May 14, 1861. Extra Session. *Boston, William White, Printer*, 1861. 8vo, pp. 24. (Senate

Doc. No. 1.)+January 3, 1862. *Boston, William White, Printer*, 1862. 8vo, pp. 75. (Senate Doc. No. 1.)+January 9, 1863. *Boston, Wright & Potter*, 1863. 8vo, pp. 80. H.+November 11, 1863. *Boston, Wright and Potter*, 1863. 8vo, pp. 24.+January 8, 1864. *Boston, Wright & Potter, Printers*, 1864. 8vo, pp. 88. (Senate Doc. No. 1.) H.+January 6, 1865. *Boston, Wright & Potter, Printers*, 1865. 8vo, pp. 140. (Senate Doc. No. 1.) H. 1467

These and the following addresses mostly relate to the Rebellion.

ANDREW. [Address to the Legislature on the Reception of the News of the Occupation of Richmond by Gen. Grant. Dated April 4, 1865. *Boston*, 1865.] 8vo, pp. 3. (Senate Doc. No. 173.) H. 1468

ANDREW. Addresses by His Excellency Governor John A. Andrew, Hon. Edward Everett, Hon. B. F. Thomas, and Hon. Robert C. Winthrop, delivered at the Mass Meeting in Aid of Recruiting, held on the Common under the Auspices of the Committee of One Hundred and Fifty, on Wednesday, August 27, 1862. *Boston, J. E. Farwell and Company, Printers*, 1862. 8vo, pp. 16. H. 1469

[ANDREW.] Commonwealth of Massachusetts [Message of the Governor], Executive Department, April 17, 1865. 8vo, pp. 8. (House Document, No. 227.) 1470

Relates to the assassination of President Lincoln.

ANDREW. The importance of relying on the efforts of the People instead of the machinery of a Bureau. Correspondence concerning the System of recruiting Volunteers now prescribed by the U. S. Provost-Marshal-General. *Boston, Wright & Potter, Printers*, 1865. 8vo, pp. 23. H. 1471

ANDREW. ... [Letter to] S. F. Wetmore, Esq., Indianapolis, Indiana. [Dated Feb. 3, 1863. n. p., 1863.] 8vo, pp. 8. H.

This letter was written in answer to the question raised in the popular branch of the Legislature of Indiana, "Why Massachusetts has not sent to the field during the present war as many men as have been sent by Indiana."

ANDREW. ... A Proclamation to the People of Massachusetts. [November 18. *Boston*, 1863.] 8vo, pp. 11. H. 1473

Explanation of the bounties offered by the State and by the United States.

ANDREW. Opinion In the Case of Edward W. Green. [*Boston*, 1866.] 4to, pp. 20. H. 1474

ANDREW. Letter to the Governor of Massachusetts [J. A. Andrew], on occasion of his Late Proclamation, Of August 20, 1861. *Boston, A. K. Loring*. 8vo, pp. 12. H. 1475

ANDREW. Speeches of John A. Andrew at Hingham and Boston ... with his Testimony before the Harper's Ferry Committee of the Senate, in relation to John Brown. ... [*Boston*, 1860.] 8vo, pp. 16. H. 1476

ANDREW. ... To the ... Senators and Representatives of ... Massachusetts in ... Congress ... . [Representations of the Anomaly existing in the Organization of the Light Artillery Arm of the Volunteer Forces of the United States. *Boston*, 1864.] 4to, pp. 4. H. 1477

ANDREW. [Two letters to Rev. Edw. E. Hale, dated Oct. 7 and 11, declining the Presidency of Antioch College. *Boston*, 1865.] 16mo, pp. 3. H. 1478

ANDREW. ... Valedictory Address of His Excellency John A. Andrew, to the Two Branches of the Legislature of Massachusetts, January 4, 1866. *Boston, Wright & Potter, Printers*, 1866. 8vo, pp. 42. (Senate Doc. No. 2.) H. 1479

ANDREW (J. A.) and BROWNE (A. G., Jr.) Circuit Court of the United States, Massachusetts District, ss. In Admiralty. The United States of America, by Information, *versus* the Schooner Wanderer, and Cargo, G. B. Lamar, Claimant. John A. Andrew, A. G. Browne, Jr., Proctors for the Claimant. The Claimant's Points. *Boston, Prentiss & Deland, Printers*, 1860. 4to, pp. 27. H. 1480

ANDREW (J. A.) and BUTLER (B. F.) Correspondence between Gov. Andrew and Maj. Gen. [Benjamin Franklin] Butler. *Boston, J. J. Dyer & Co.*, 1862. 8vo, pp 86. H. 1481

ANDREW (W.) Constitution of Nature. By W. Andrew. *Milwaukie, Jermaine*, 1864. 8vo. 1482

Relates to the Rebellion.

Andrew College. Catalogue of the Officers and Students of Andrew College, Trenton, Gibson County, Tennessee. First Session. *Trenton, Printed at the Banner Office*, 1854. 8vo, pp. 15. Continued. 1483

ANDREWS (Charles). The Prisoners' Memoirs, or Dartmoor

Prison; Containing a Complete and Impartial History of the entire Captivity of the Americans in England, from the Commencement of the late War between the United States and Great Britain, until all prisoners were released by the Treaty of Ghent. Also a Particular Detail of all Occurrences relative to that Horrid Massacre at Dartmoor, on the fatal evening of the 6th of April, 1815. The whole carefully compiled from the Journal of Charles Andrews, a prisoner in England, from the commencement of the War until the release of all the Prisoners. *New York, Printed for the Author*, 1815. 12mo, pp. 283. Plate.

ANDREWS (C.) Speech of Mr. Charles Andrews, of Maine, in the House of Representatives, February 25, 1852, on the Resolutions of the Legislature of ... Maine tendering Sympathy to Louis Kossuth, Condemning the ... intervention of Russia in the affairs of Hungary, and asking the influence of the United States against all such intervention in future. [n. p., 1852.] 8vo, pp. 7. H. 1485

ANDREWS (C. C.) Reflections on the Operation of the Present System of Education. By Christopher C. Andrews, Counsellor at Law. ... *Boston, Crosby, Nichols and Company*, 1853. 8vo, pp. 29. 1486

ANDREWS (C. C.) History of the New York African Free Schools, from their Establishment in 1787, to the Present Time; ... Also a brief account of the successful labours of the New York Manumission Society, with an appendix, &c. By Charles C. Andrews. *New York*, 1830. 12mo. 1487

ANDREWS. Minnesota and Dacotah. In Letters descriptive of a Tour through the North West, In the Autumn of 1856. With Information Relative to Public Lands, and A table of Statistics. By C. C. Andrews. *Washington*, 1857. 8vo. Map. +Second Edition. *Washington, Robert Farnham*, 1857. 12mo, pp. 215.+Third Edition. *Washington*, 1857. 12mo. H. 1488

ANDREWS (C. C.) History of the campaign of Mobile ... By Brevet Major-General C. C. Andrews ... Maps and Illustrations. *New York*, 1867. 8vo. P. 1489

[ANDREWS (C. W.), D.D.] An Apology. The Protestant Episcopal Society for the Promotion of Evangelical Knowledge: its Origin, Constitution, Tendencies, and Work. *New-York, Printed by John A. Gray*, 1854. 8vo, pp. 44. H. 1490

ANDREWS (David). The Sure and Only Foundation, with Historical Notices. A Centennial Discourse, delivered before the Church of Christ and Second Parish, in Pepperell, Mass., January 29, 1847. By David Andrews, Pastor of the Church. *Boston, A. J. Wright, Printer*, 1847. 8vo, pp. 48. H. 1491

ANDREWS (D.) Truth and Character vindicated; being a Review of Hon. Caleb Butler's History of Ecclesiastical Affairs in Pepperell. By Rev. David Andrews and others. *Boston*, 1849. 8vo, pp. 49. M. 1492

ANDREWS (E. B.) A Funeral Discourse on the Occasion of the Death of Hon. Ephraim Cutler, Delivered at Warren, Washington Co., O., July 24, 1853, by Prof. E. B. Andrews, of Marietta College. ... *Marietta, O., Printed at the Intelligencer Office*, 1854. 8vo, pp. 28. H. 1493

ANDREWS (E. Wigglesworth). An Address before the Washington Benevolent Society, in Newburyport, ... on the 22d. of Feb., 1816. By Edward W. Andrews, A.M. ... *Newburyport, William B. Allen & Co.*, 1816. 8vo, pp. 15. H. 1494

In verse.

ANDREWS (E.) A Sermon, delivered at the Funeral of Mr. Samuel Phillips, at Athol, February 6th, 1810. By Elisha Andrews, A.M., Pastor of the Baptist Church in Templeton. *Worcester, Printed by Henry Rogers*, 1810. 8vo, pp. 18. H. 1495

ANDREWS (Erastus). Historical Discourse at North Leverett, Mass., Aug. 18, 1847. By Erastus Andrews. *Boston*, 1847.

ANDREWS (Ethan Allen). Slavery and the Domestic Slave-Trade in the United States. In a series of letters addressed to the Executive Committee of the American Union for the Relief and Improvement of the Colored Race. By Prof. E. A. Andrews. *Boston, Light & Stearns*, 1836. 12mo, pp. xii., 9–201. H. 1497

ANDREWS (I. D.) ... Communication from the Secretary of the Treasury, transmitting ... the Report of Israel D. Andrews, Consul of the United States for Canada and New Brunswick, on the Trade and Commerce of the British North American Colonies, and upon the Trade of the Great Lakes and Rivers; also, Notices of the Internal Improvements in Each State, of the Gulf of Mexico and Straits of Florida, and a Paper on the Cotton Crop of the United States. *Washington, Robert Arm-*

strong, Printer, 1853. 8vo, pp. xix., 906 (1). Maps. (32d Cong., 1st Sess. Senate. Ex. Doc. No. 112.) H. 1498

ANDREWS (I. W.) Why is Allegiance Due? and Where is it Due? An Address delivered before the National Union Association of Cincinnati, June 2, 1863, by Israel W. Andrews, President of Marietta College. *Cincinnati, Moore, Wilstach, Keys & Co., Printers*, 1863. 8vo, pp. 30. H. 1499

ANDREWS (John). Essay on Republican Principles, and on the Inconveniences of a Commonwealth in a Large Country and Nation, with reflections on the present situation of Great Britain. By John Andrews, LL.D. *London*, 1783. 8vo, pp. 96. M. 1500

ANDREWS. History of the War with America, France, Spain, and Holland; commencing in 1775 and ending in 1783. By John Andrews, L.L.D. In Four Volumes with Portraits Maps and Charts. *London, John Fielding and John Jarvis*, MDCCLXXXV–MDCCLXXXVI. 4 vols., 8vo, pp. iv., 448; Title, 1 l., pp. 449; Title, 1 l., pp. 445; Title, 1 l., pp. 416; Index, 30 l.; List of Subscribers, pp. xiv. 31 Plates. H. 1501

See M. R., LXXV., 466. "Compiled chiefly from the newspapers and the proceedings of the House of Commons."—RICH. "A judicious compilation."—LOWNDES. Highly commended by Dr. Boucher. Includes portraits of Gens. Washington, Greene, Clinton, Burgoyne, Cornwallis, Lafayette, De Grasse, Count D'Estaing, and Capt. Asgill.

ANDREWS (John). Letters of John Andrews, Esq., of Boston, 1772–1776. Compiled and edited from the Original MSS., with an Introduction, By Winthrop Sargent. Reprinted from the Proceedings of the Massachusetts Historical Society. *Cambridge, Press of John Wilson and Sons*, 1866. 8vo, pp. 100. H. 1502

ANDREWS (John). A Discourse delivered before the Merrimack Humane Society, at their Anniversary Meeting, September 1, 1812. By John Andrews, A.M., Minister of the First Church and Religious Society in Newburyport. [Motto.] [With Appendix.] *Newburyport, Press of E. W. Allen*, 1812. 8vo, pp. 32. H. 1503

ANDREWS. An Eulogy on General George Washington: Who departed this life December 14th, 1799, in the 68th year of his age. Delivered before the First Religious Society, in Newburyport, February 22d. 1800. By John Andrews, A.M. Colleague Pastor with the Rev. Thomas Cary. [Motto.] *From*

the Press of Angier March, Newburyport. [1800]. 8vo, pp. 21. H. 1504

ANDREWS. A | Sermon, | delivered February 19, 1795, | being a Day | of | Public Thanksgiving, | throughout the | United States of America. | By John Andrews, A.M. | Junior Pastor of the First Church in Newburyport. | *Printed at Newburyport by | Blunt & March* | [1795]. 8vo, pp. 22. H. 1505

ANDREWS. A Sermon delivered October 1, 1801: at the Dedication of a new House for Public Worship, erected by the First Religious Society in Newburyport. By John Andrews, A.M., Colleague-Pastor with the Rev. Thomas Cary. *Newburyport, Press of Allen & Stickney*, 1801. 8vo, pp. 28. H. 1506

ANDREWS. A Sermon delivered November 26, 1808, at the Interment of the Rev. Thomas Cary, A.M. Senior Pastor of the First Religious Society in Newburyport. By John Andrews, A.M., Surviving Pastor. ... *Newburyport, Edward Little*, 1808. 8vo, pp. 31, Appendix (15). H. 1507

ANDREWS (John L.) Pension, Bounty, and Prize Money Manual. John L. Andrews, Government Claim Agent ... Boston. [*Boston, J. E. Farwell & Co., Printers*, 1862 or 1863.] 32mo, pp. 16. H. 1508

ANDREWS (Joseph). Journey from Buenos Ayres, through the Provinces of Cordova, Tucuman, and Salta, to Potosi, thence by the Deserts of Caranja to Arica, and subsequently, to Santiago de Chili and Coquimbo, undertaken on behalf of the Chilian and Peruvian Mining Association, in the Years 1825–26. By Captain Andrews, late Commander H. C. S. Windham. ... *London, John Murray*, 1827. 2 vols., 16mo, pp. xxxii., 312; viii., 321. H. 1509

"Captain Andrews was sent out during the Mining mania, by one of the numerous London Associations, and in these two volumes, gives a very clear, sensible, and modest account of his journey and subsequent proceedings in execution of his trust. They are well worth any one's reading, both for the entertainment to be derived from them, and the information they occasionally convey."—*Ed. Rev.* *See*, also, M. R., CXIV., 233; Museum, XI., 526.

ANDREWS (Rufus F.) Letter of Rufus F. Andrews, Lately Surveyor of the Port of New York, to Thurlow Weed, Lately Editor of the Albany Evening Journal. *New York*, 1864. 16mo, pp. 14. H. 1510

ANDREWS (Samuel). A Discourse on St. Mark xvi., 15, 16, "And he said unto them, Go ye," &c. By Samuel Andrews, A.M., Late Missionary at Wallingford, from the venerable Society for the Propagation of the Gospel in foreign Parts: and now Missionary at St. Andrews (New-Brunswick). *New Haven, Printed by Daniel Bowen, in Chapel-Street, near the College* (M.DCC.LXXXVII). 4to, pp. 34. S. 1511

[ANDREWS]. A Sermon Preached at Litchfield in Connecticut, before a Voluntary Convention of the Clergy of the Church of England, of Several Provinces in America, June 13, 1770. By —— ——, a Native of the Province. ... Published with Notes, to gratify the very respectable assembly before whom it was delivered, and a copy given, July 1770. 4to, pp. 15. S. 1512

Mr. Andrews published several other tracts and sermons, one of which was on the occasion of a Fast, 1775.

ANDREWS. The True Means to avert National Judgments. A Sermon upon the Solemn Fast ordered through the States of America, May 9th, 1798. Delivered at the House of John Brewer, Esq., in Robins-Town, upon the River Schodick, At His, and the Desire of others of its Inhabitants, Citizens of the United States; and published at their Request. By Samuel Andrews, A.M., Rector of Saint Andrew's Church, in the Parish of Saint Andrews, and Province of New-Brunswick; and Missionary from the Society, &c. *Printed at Boston*, 1798. 8vo, pp. 22. S. 1513

ANDREWS (Samuel). Genealogical Chart of the Sargent Family. Designed and compiled by Samuel Andrews of Boston, A.D. 1851. [*Boston*, 1851.] Broadside. H. 1514

ANDREWS (Samuel G.) The Lecompton Constitution. Speech of Hon. S. G. Andrews, of New York. Delivered in the House ... February 23d, 1858. [Colophon] *Washington, D. C., Buell & Blanchard, Printers*, 1858. 8vo, pp. 8. H. 1515

ANDREWS (Sidney). The South since the War: as shown by Fourteen Weeks of Travel and Observation in Georgia and the Carolinas. By Sidney Andrews. *Boston, Ticknor and Fields*, 1866. 16mo, pp. viii., 400. H. 1516

Consists, for the most part, of letters written to the *Boston Advertiser* and *Chicago Tribune*. The writer sees everything through Northern eyes.

ANDREWS (W. S.) Illustrations of the West Indies. Sailing directions for the Caribbean sea, Gulf of Mexico, and Florida. By W. S. Andrews. *London, Day & Son*, 1861. 2 vols., oblong 4to. 1517

ANDREWS (W. W.) *See* Smith (John Cotton).

ANDREWS (William W.) A Sermon on withdrawing from the Congregational Ministry. Preached in Kent, Conn., May 20, 1849. With statement of reasons ... . 2d edition, with an Introductory Preface. By Rev. William W. Andrews. *New York*, 1851. 8vo. S. 1518

ANDREWS (Wm. W.) The Work of the Church in America, Especially in the West. An Address, Marietta (O.), July 28, 1855. By William W. Andrews. *New York*, 1856. 8vo.

Vol. I. Fourth Year, No. 4. Andrews & Co.'s Stranger's Guide in the City of Boston. 1851. ... *Boston, Andrews & Company* [1851]. Sq. 16mo, pp. 78, (2). H. 1520

ANDROS or ANDROSSE (Sir E.) *See* Stoughton's New England.

ANDROS. Commission of King James the Second to Sir Edmund Andros, June 3, 1686. MSS. [*sic.*] 8vo, pp. 14. 1521

Forms No. 8 of Force's Tracts, Vol. IV. *See*, also, Mass. Hist. Coll., 3d Series, Vol. VII.; R. I. Col. Records, Vol. III.; N. Y. Col. Rec., Vol. III.; Public Records of Conn., Vol. III., pp. 402-436.

ANDROS. Matters objected against Sir Edmund Androsse, &c. [n. d.] 8vo, pp. 56. 1522

See Mass. Hist. Soc. Coll., 2d Series; Vol. VIII.

ANDROS. By His Excellency a Proclamation. ... Given at Fort Charles, at Pemaquid, 10th January, 1688. Signed, E. Andros. [*Printed at Boston in New England*, 1688.] A Broadside. + Reprinted. [n. d.] 1523

ANDROS (Rh. S. S.) Chocorua and other Sketches. By R. S. S. Andros. *Fall River*, 1838. 8vo. 1524

ANDROS. The United States Customs Guide. ... . By R. S. S. Andros, late Deputy Collector of the Customs, Boston. *Boston, T. R. Marvin; New York, D. Appleton & Co.*, 1859. 12mo, pp. 316. H. 1525

ANDROS (Thomas). The grand era of ruin to nations from

foreign influence. A Discourse, delivered before the Congregational Society in Berkley, Nov. 26, 1812. ... By Thomas Andros, A.M. *Boston, Samuel T. Armstrong*, 1812. 8vo, pp. 18. B.

ANDROS. The Old Jersey Captive; or a Narrative of the Captivity of Thomas Andros, (now Pastor of the Church in Berkley,) on board the Old Jersey Prison Ship, at New York, 1781, in a series of letters to a Friend, suited to inspire Faith and Confidence in a particular Divine Providence. *Boston, Wm. Peirce*, 1833. 16mo, pp. 80. 1527

ANDRUS (A.) The Emancipation Proclamation. By Hon. A. Andrus and W. H. Brand. *Albany*, 1863. 1528

ANDRUS (Albert). Report of the Majority of the Committee on Banks, to the Legislature of the State, made April 1, 1864. Private Edition. *Albany, Printed by C. Van Benthuysen*, 1864. 8vo, pp. 13. H. 1529

Signed by Albert Andrus, Alexander Olcott, Edward D. White, James B. Murray.

ANDUEZA. Isla de Cuba, Pintoresca, Historica, Politica, Literaria, Mercantil é Industrial. Por D. J. M. de Andueza. *Madrid*, 1841. 4to. 12 Plates. 1530

Anecdotes Américaines. Histoire Abrégée des évènements du Nouveau Monde, etc. *See* [Hornot (Ant.)]

Anecdotes anglaises et américaines. Années 1775 a 1783. ... *Paris, Delaunay* [*and*] *Brunot-Labbe*, 1813. 2 vols., 8vo, pp. 298; 324. H. 1531

Anecdotes, Historical and Literary: or, miscellaneous selections of passages from eminent authors. *Boston*, 1808. 12mo.

Anecdotes of the American Revolution. *New York*, 1844. 18mo, pp. 252. 1533

Anecdotes Secrètes sur la Révolution du 18 Fructidor; et Nouveaux Mémoires des Déportés à la Guiane, écrits par eux-mêmes: contenant des Lettres du Général Murinais, de Barthélemy, de Tronçon du Coudray, de Laffond Ladebat, de De La Rue, &c.—Relation des Evénemens qui suivirent à la Guiane l'Evasion de Pichegru, Ramel, &c.—Tableau des Prisons de Rochefort, par Richer-Sérisy.—Narration de la Captivité et de l'Evasion de Sir Sidney Smith de la Prison du Temple.—Mémoire de Barbé Marbois, &c. &c. Faisant suite au Journal du

Général Ramel. Seconde Edition, revué, corrigée et augmentée. *Paris, Giguet et Co., Imprimeurs-Libraires; et se trouve a Londres, J. Wright*, 1799. 8vo, Title and Table, 2 l.; Text, pp. 215.

Anecdotes sur les Indiens de l'Amérique du Nord, leurs mœurs et leurs habitudes. *Paris, Delay*, 1845. 16mo. 1 fr. 1535

Anent the North American Continent. "What is that hath been? the same thing shall be. ..." *London, William Ridgway, March*, 1864. Post 8vo, pp. 15. H. 1535*a*

Anent the United States and Confederate States of North America. "... Thoughts of peace and not of affliction." *London, James Ridgway*, 1862. 8vo, pp. 7. H. & P. 1535*b*

ANGEL (William G.) Speech of W. G. Angel in the H. of R. U. S. on the Bank of the United States, 1832. 8vo. 1536

ANGELIS (Pedro de). Coleccion de obras y documentos relativos A la Historia Antigua y Moderna de las Provincias del Rio de la Plata. Ilustrados con notas y disertaciones por Pedro de Angelis. *Buenos Aires, Imprenta del Estado*, 1836–37. 7 vols., 4to. 1537

Printed at the expense of the Argentine Republic, and not for sale. It is a most important collection, embodying all the early travels in Buenos Ayres, Patagonia, and other parts of South America. *See Edin. Rev.*, LXV., 87–109. Trübner's *American Record*, Nov. 21, 1865, contains a complete list of the contents of Vols. I.–VI.

ANGELIS. Biografia del Señor General José Arenales. *Buenos Aires*. 1832. 8vo. Map. 1538

ANGELIS. Historical Sketch of Pepys' Island, in the South Pacific Ocean. *Buenos Aires*, 1842. 8vo, pp. 9, xvii. 1539

ANGELIS. Memoria Historica sobre los Derechos de Soberania y Dominio de la Confederacion Argentina. *Buenos Aires*, 1852. 8vo, pp. lviii. 1540

ANGELIS. De la Navigation de l'Amazone. Réponse a un Mémoire de M. Maury, officier de la marine des Etats-Unis par M. de Angelis ... . *Montevideo, Imprimerie du Rio de la Plata*, 1854. 8vo, pp. 218 (2). H. 1541

ANGELIS. Prospecto de una segunda Serie de Documentos, etc. *Buenos Aires*, 1841. 8vo, pp. iii. 1542

ANGELL (J. K.) A Essay on the Right of a State to tax A Body Corporate, considered in relation to the present Bank Tax

in Rhode-Island. By Joseph K. Angell. ... *Boston, Hilliard, Gray, Little & Wilkins*, 1827. 8vo, pp. 44. H. 1543

ANGELL (J. K.) Reports of Cases. *See* Rhode Island.

ANGELO. Sketches of Travel in Oregon and Idaho, with Map of South Boise. By C. Aubrey Angelo. *New York, the Author*, 1866. 8vo, pp. 181. 1544

ANGELONI (Batista), *pseudon.* *See* [Shebbeare (John)]

Ein Angenehmer Geruch der Rosen und Lilien Die im Thal der Demuth unter den Dornen hervor gewachsen Alles aus der Schwesterlichen Gesellschaft in Saron. *In Jahr des Heils*, 1756. 4to, pp. 26. P. 1545

This and the following are from Mr. Winthrop Sargent's MS. List of Americana.

Ein Angenehmer Geruch der Rosen und Lilien Die im Thal der Demuth unter den Dornen hervor gewachsen Alles aus der Brüderlichen Gesellschafft in Bethania. *In Jahr des Heils*, 1756. 4to, pp. 30. P. 1546

ANGHIERA (Pietro Martire d'). Libretto de tutta la navigazione dei Rei di Spagna delle isole e terreni nuovamente trovati. *Stampato in Venezia per Alberto Vercellese de Lisona nel* 1504. 4to. 1547

This exceedingly rare tract is a translation into the Venetian dialect of the first decade of Anghiera, by Angelo Trivigiano. *See* a curious note on this subject by J. Morelli, following his edition of Columbus' Letter, Bassano, 1810, 8vo, and again in his Works, I., 290. This voyage also forms the fourth book of the collection published by Monte Alboddo, *Vicenze*, 1507, and frequently reprinted. *See* Vespucci.

ANGHIERA. P. Martyris angli | mediolanensis opera | Legatio babylonica | Oceani decas | Poemata | Epigrammata | cum preuilegio | [Colophon] Impressum Hispali cu*m* summa diligencia per Jacobu*m* corum | berger alemanu*m*. Anno. Millessimo quingentessimo, xi. me*n*se vero | Aprili. Folio, 74 leaves. 1548

The above title is from the Bib. Am. Vet., No. 66. Brunet gives the title as follows:

ANGLERIUS. Opera, scilicet legationis babylonicæ libri tres; Oceani decas; Carmina, Janus, Inachus, Pluto furens, et reliqua poemata, hymni et epigrammata; cura Ælii Ant. Nebrissensis. *Hispali, per Jacobum Crumberger*, 1511. Folio, 74 leaves.

Now, as both of these titles were doubtless taken from the books themselves, they were probably two editions in the same year, especially as Harrisse describes the Map as being on the recto of the forty-fifth leaf, and Brunet "au recto de l'avant-dernier feuillet une carte curieuse des découvertes de Colomb." They are both books of ex-

treme rarity.—both editions contain only the first nine books of the first decade and a portion of the tenth. Heber's copy sold for £8 8s. Brunet, in his description of this work, refers to Panzer, IV., 339, and Hain, 10863, concerning an edition of poems of "P. Martyr d'Anghiera (Anglerius), una cum prima decade Oceanicarum, *Hispali*, 1500, in fol. Et effectivement le livre est annoncé sous cette même date dans la Biblioth. uilenbroukiana, pars II., p. 238, No. 1181; mais l'errata placé à la suite de la préface de ce catal. nous previent qu'il faut lire 1511 au lieu de 1500." Respecting this work, I find in Thorpe's Catalogue [about 1842], No. 1895: "Poemata, 4to, s. a., circa 1490," which is there said to be "Unknown to all bibliographers." The conjecture as to the date is probably erroneous.

ANGHIERA. Ioannes ruffus foroliuiensis Archiepus Co*n*senti | n: legat⁹ apo. ad lectore*m* de orbe nouo. | Accipe non noti præclara uolumina mundi | Oceani: & magnas noscito lector opes. | Plurima debetur typhis tibi gratia: gentes | Ignotas: & aues qui uehis orbe nouo. | Magna quoq*ue* autori referenda est gratia nostro: | Qui facit hæc cunctis regna uidenda locis. | Autor. | Siste pedem lector: breuibus compacta libellis | Hæc lege: principibus uariis decimoq*ue* leoni | Pontifici summo inscripta. hic noua multa uidebis. | Oceani magnas terras: uasta æquora: linguas | Hactenus ignostas: atq*ue* aurea sæcula nosces: | Et gentes nudas expertes seminis atri: | Mortiferi nummi: gemmisq*ue* auroq*ue* feracem | Torrentem zonam: parcat ueneranda uetustas. | De orbe nouo Decades | [Colophon] Cura & diligentia uiri celebris Magistri Antonii Ne- | brissensis historici regii fuerunt hæ tres protono | tarii Petri martyris decades Impressæ in | contubernio Arnaldi Guillelmi in | Illustri oppido carpetanæ p*r*oui | *n* ciæ co*m*pluto quod uulgari | ter dicitur Alcala p*erfe* | ctu*m* est nonis No | ue*m*bris An. | 1516. Folio, 63 leaves, Ad lectorem 1 l.; Vocabula barbara, 3 leaves; Incipitur Legatio Babylonicæ, 16 leaves. 1550

"Belle Edition."—Brunet, who, under this title, gives his reasons for placing the author's name in the position he has assigned him. This is the first edition containing the three decades. Priced in the Nuggets, £10 10s. Concerning this edition, *see* Brunet, I., 293; Bib. Am. Vet., 151–153; Bibliotheca Grenvilliana, &c.

ANGHIERA. De orbe novo decades. *Compluti, apud Michaelem d'Egina*, 1530. Folio, pp. 117 (3). 1551

Contains eight decades, and has the "Præfatio Æ. Antonii Nebrissensis."

ANGHIERA. De | orbe novo | Petri Martyris An- | glerii Mediolanensis, Pro- | tonotarij, & Caroli quinti Senatoris | Decades octo, diligenti temporum ob- | seruatione, & vtilissimis annotationibus | illustratæ, suòque nitori restitutæ, | Labore & industria Richardi Haklvyti | Oxoniensis Angli. | Additus est in vsum lectoris accuratus | totius operis index. | [Vignette.] Parisiis, |

Apud Gvillelmvm Avvray, via D.|Ioannis Bellouacensis, sub insigni|Bellerophontis coronati.|M.D.LXXXVII.|Cum priuilegio Regis.| 8vo, 8 p. l., pp. 605, 12 l. Map engraved on copper.

The map is frequently deficient. "This and that of 1530 are the only complete editions of Peter Martyr's Decades. The volume commences with an epistle from Hakluyt to Sir Walter Raleigh, of ten pages."—RICH. Priced, Muller, $15.

ANGHIERA. De nvper|svb D. Carolo reper-|tis Insulis, simulatq*ue* incolarum|moribus, R. Petri Marty-|ris, Enchiridion, Domi-|næ Margaritæ, Diui|Max. Cæf. filiæ|dicatum.|*Basileæ, Anno*|M.D.XXI. 4to, pp. 43. H. 1553

This is an extract from the fourth Decade. It is included in the Novus Orbis, and in Brocard's Desc. Terræ Sanctæ. *See* Bib. Am. Vet., p. 187, 8. Priced, in the Nuggets, £2 2s.

ANGHIERA. Extraict ov recveil des|Isles nouuellem*e*nt trouuees en la grand mer Oce-|ane ou temps du roy Despaigne Ferna*n*d & Eliza|beth sa femme, faict premierement en latin par|Pierre Martyr de Millan, & depuis translate en|languaige francoys.|Item trois Narrations: dont la premiere est de|Cuba, & commence ou fueillet 132.|La seconde, qui est de la mer Oceane, commence|ou fueillet 155.|La tierce, qui est de la prinse de Tenustitan, com|mence ou fueillet 192.|On les vend a Paris rue sainct Iehan de Beau-|uais, chez Simon de Colines au soleil dor.|Cum priuilegio.| [Colophon.] Imprime a Paris par Simon de Colines libraire iure de|luniuersite de Paris, Lan de grace Mil cinq ce*nt*s trente-|deux, le douziesme iour de Ianuier.| 4to, Title and 7 unnumbered l., 207 numbered l. H. 1554

This rare volume contains an abridgment of the first three Decades of Peter Martyr, and is dedicated to the Duke of Angouleme by the translator. On folio 132 there is a new dedication of "Trois Narrations" to Marguerite of France, in which he observes, that the first of the three narrations that follow, an account of Cuba, is translated from Peter Martyr. "Les deux narrations suyuantes faictes en latin par Pierre Sauorguan de Foruile docteur es loix ont este dediees au Pape present Clement septiesme." *See* Bibliotheca Grenvilliana, and Brunet, I., 294.

ANGHIERA. Opvs Epi|stolaru*m* Petri Marty|ris Anglerij Mediola|ne*n*sis Protonotarij|Apl'ici atq*ue* a co*n*si-|lijs reru*m* Indica|ru*m*: nu*n*c p*r*imu*m* et|natu*ra* & medio|cri cura excu|sum: quod|q*uidem* pr*ae*-|ter stili venustate*m*, nostroru*m* q*uoque*| te*m*po*rum* historiae loco esse poterit.|Co*m*pluti Anno d*o*m*i*ni M.D.xxx.|Cu*m* priuilegio C*ae*sareo.| [Colophon.] ℂ Excusum est hoc volu|men Epistolarum Petri Martyris Mediola|nensis citra controversia*m* eruditissimi|in celeberrima & in omni literaru*m*|genere maxime florenti Aca|demia Complutensi in|

Aedibus Michae|lis de Eguia|Anno a|Christo|nato.|M.D.XXX. Folio, Title and 11 p. l.; Text, pp. 199. H. 1555

There is a mistake in the pagination after folio 198, so that there are really 205 leaves. A rare and beautiful edition. Heber's copy sold for £3; La Valliere, 61 fr. Concerning this work, *see* Humboldt's *Examen critique*, Vol. II.; Brunet, I., 294, and Bib. Am. Vet., 280.

ANGHIERA. Opus|Epistolarum|Petri Martyris|Anglerii Mediolanensis,|Protonotarii Apostolici, Prioris Archiepiscopatus Granatensis, atque à|Consiliis Rerum Indicarum Hispanicis, tanta cura excusum, ut|præter styli venustatem quoque fungi possit vice Luminis|Historiæ superiorum temporum.|Cui accesserunt|Epistolæ|Ferdinandi de Pulgar|Coætanei Latinæ pariter atque Hispanicæ cum Tractatu Hispanico de|Viris Castellæ Illustribus.|Editio Postrema.|Amstelodami, Typis Elzevirianis.|Veneunt|Parisiis,|Apud Fredericum Leonard, Typographum Regium,|cIↄ Iↄc LXX. Folio, 14 p. l., pp. 486; 1 l., pp. 32, 62, 1 l. H. 1556

Pulgar's Epistolæ and Varones' have each a separate title and paging. Libri's copy [m. r.] sold for 70 fr.; Raetzel's, 13 fr.; Audry's, 20 fr. Many of these letters relate to the discovery of America and the affairs of the New World, and being published out of Spain, escaped the hands of the Expurgators.

ANGHIERA. Petri Martyris|ab Angleria Mediolanen. Oratoris|clarissimi, Fernandi & Helisabeth Hispaniarum quondam regum|à consilijs, de rebus Oceanicis & Orbe nouo decades tres: quibus|quicquid de inuentis nuper terris traditum, nouarum rerum cupi-|dum lectorem retinere possit, copiose, fideliter, eruditeq*ue* docetur.|Eivsdem praeterea|legationis babylonicae li|bri tres: vbi praeter oratorii mvneris|pulcherrimum exemplum, etiam quicquid in uariarum gentium mori-|bus & institutis insigniter pr*ae*clarum uidit, queq*ue* terra mariq*ue* acciderunt,|omnia lectu mirè iucunda, genere dicendi politissimo traduntur.| [Printer's mark.] *Basileae,|apud Ioannem Bebelium*|M.D.XXXIII.| Title and 11 p. l.; Text, 92 l. 1557

A reprint of the edition of 1517 contains Decades I., II., III., and an abridgment of Decade IV. Priced, Nuggets, £1 11s. 6d. Sold at Puttick's, 1860, for £2 5s. Ternaux, No. 47 *bis*, Brunet and Graesse, quote an edition, *Lut. Paris*, 1536, which does not exist. *See* Bib. Am. Vet., No. 214. I have a MS. list of books on the West Indies, by the late Mr. Ludewig, in which he quotes an edition, *Compluti*, 1540, which is probably an error. *See* No. 1551.

ANGHIERA. De Rebvs|Oceanicis|et Novo Orbe, de-|cades tres, Petri Mar-|tyris ab Angleria|Mediolanensis.|Item eivsdem,|de Babylonica|Legatione, Libri III.|et item|de Rebvs Æthiopicis,|Indicîs, Lusitanicis & Hispanicis, opuscula qu*ae*da*m*|

Historica doctissima, quæ hodiè non facilè|alibì reperiuntur, Damiani|A Goes Equitis|Lusitani.|Quæ omnia sequens pagina latiùs demonstrat.|Cum duplici locupletissimo Indice.|*Coloniæ,| Apud Geruinum Calenium & hæredes|Quentelios.* M.D.LXXIIII.| *Cum gratia & Priuilegio Cæsareo.*| 8vo, 24 p. l., pp. 655; Index, pp. 30. H. 1558

This edition of Martyr was made use of by Robertson in compiling his history. Priced, in the Nuggets, £1 10s. 6d; Muller, $10.

ANGHIERA. Relationi|del S. Pietro Martire|Milanese.|Dell cose notabili della prouincia dell' E-|gitto scritte in lingua Latina alli Sereniss,|di felice memoria Re Catolici D. Fernando,|e D. Isabella, & hora recate nella Italiana.|Da Carlo Passi.|Con Privilegio.|*In Venetia appresso Giorgio de' Caualli* 1564. Sm. 8vo. 7 p. l., viz.: Title, 1 l., "All' Illustriss. et Eccellentiss. Signora Givlia Sforza Pallavicina," etc., 3 l.; "Discorso di Carlo Passi," etc., 3 l.; Text, 71 leaves; "Tavola," etc., 6 l.; "Errori fatti nello stamparsi," etc., 3 l. 1559

Priced, in the Nuggets. £1 1s.

ANGHIERA. Die schiffung mitt dem Lanndt der Gulden Insel gefunde*n* durch H. Johan vo*n* Angliara, Hawptman des Ku*n*nigs vo*n* Hispania, mit allen yren leben vnd sitten. 4to, 4 ff., s. l. e. a. (vers 1520). 1560

"Première édition allemande de la première décade de Pierre Martyr, sur la découverte du nouveau Continent, très rare." This title is from a German catalogue. I find no other mention of this edition, but Mr. C. Welford, in one of his catalogues, lot 354, says: "Unique early tract in German, on the First Discovery of 'The Golden Islands or America.' The date is marked by Mr. Rich in MS., 1560."

ANGHIERA. The Decades|of the newe worlde or|west India,|Conteynyng the nauigations and conquestes|of the Spanyardes, with the particular de-|scription of the moste ryche and large landes|and Ilandes lately founde in the west Ocean|perteynyng to the inheritaunce of the kinges|of Spayne. In the which the diligent reader|may not only consyder what commoditie may|hereby chaunce to the hole christian world in|tyme to come, but also learne many secreates|touchynge the lande, the sea, and the starres,|very necessarie to be know*n*e to al such as shal|attempte any nauigations, or otherwise|haue delite to beholde the strange|and woonderfull woorkes of|God and nature.| Wrytten in the Latine tounge by Peter|Martyr of Angleria, and trans-|lated into Englysshe by|Rycharde Eden.|*Londini.*|*In ædibus Guilhelmi Powell.*|*Anno.* 1555.| 4to, 24 p. l., 361 l.;

"Contentes," "Thinterpretours excuse" in verse, and "Fautes escaped in the pryntynge," 13 l. Portrait. H. & P. 1561

Leaves 1–166 contain three Decades of Peter Martyr; then follow Alexander VI.'s famous Bull; Oviedo's Hystorie of the weste Indies; The vyage abowte the worlde, gathered oute of Pygafetta; The stryfe betwene the Spanyardes and Portugales, for the division of the Indies and the trade of Spices, by Fr. Lopez de Gomara, ending at leaf 244. The remainder of the book does not relate to America. Bellero's map is found in some copies. *See* Rich, No. 30. "Eden was the first Englishman who undertook to present, in a collective form, the astonishing results of the spirit of maritime enterprise, which had been everywhere awakened by the discovery of America. Nor was he a mere compiler. In point of learning, accuracy, and integrity, he is certainly superior to Hakluyt. This work is rendered more precious by information scattered through it, derived from the great seamen of the day, with whom the author's turn of mind led him to associate. In one chapter, he speaks of 'The Voyages of that worthy owlde man, Sebastian Cabote, yet lyvinge in Englande.'"—BIDDLE.

ANGHIERA. The|History of Trauayle|in the|West and East Indies, and other|countreys lying eyther way,|towardes the frutefull and rych|Meluccaes.|As|in Muscouia, Persia, Arabia, Syria, Ægypte,|Ethiopia, Guinea, China in Cathaye and|Giapan: With a discourse of|the Northwest pas-|sage. [Motto] Gathered in parte, and done into Englyshe by|Richarde Eden.|Newly set in order, augmented, and finished,|by Richarde Willes. *Imprinted at London, by Richarde Jugge*, 1577.|Cum privilegio. Sm. 4to, 10 p. l., 466 l., Errata and Table, 6 l. H. 1562

Besides four Decades of Peter Martyr, and "An Abridgment of ... his 5. 6. 7. and 8. Decades," this work contains Oviedo's "West Indies." *See* also an extended notice of this edition, Rich, No. 15.

ANGHIERA. De Nouo Orbe,|or|the Historie of|the West Indies, Contayning the actes|and aduentures of the Spanyardes, which haue|conquered and peopled those Countries,|inriched with varietie of pleasant re-|lation of the Manners, Ceremonies,| Lawes, Gouernments, and|Warres of the Indians.|Comprised in eight Decades.|Written by Peter Martyr a Millanoise of Angleria, Cheife|Secretary to the Emperour Charles the fift,|and of his Priuie Councell.|Whereof three, haue beene formerly translated in-|to English, by R. Eden, whereunto the other|fiue, are newly added by the Industrie, and|painefull Trauaile of M. Lok Gent.| [Motto, 2 l.] *London*|*Printed for Thomas Adams.*|1612.| 4to, 5 p. l.; Text, 318 leaves. H. 1563

Some copies are without date. It was re-issued with the following title:

ANGHIERA. The|famovs|Historie of|the Indies:|Declaring the aduentures of|the Spaniards, which haue conque-|red these

Countries, with varietie of Relations|of the Religions, Lawes, Gouernments, Manners,|Ceremonies, Customes, Rites, Warres,| and Funerals of the People.|Comprised into sundry Decads.|Set forth first by M[r] Hackluyt, and now pub-|lished by L. M. Gent.|The Second Edition.|*London: Printed for Michael Sparke dwelling at the signe|of the blue Bible in Green-Arbor.* 1628.| 4to, 3 p. l.; Text, 318 l. 1564

Priced, in the Nuggets, £4 14s. 6d.

ANGHIERA E OVIEDO. Libro Primo|della Histo|ria de l'In|die Oc|ciden|tali.| [Verso] Svmmario de la Generale| Historia de l'Indie Occi-|dentali cavato da li-|bri scritti dal Si-|gnor Don Pietro|Martyre del consi|glio della Maesta|de l'Imperadore,|et da molte|altre par-|ticvla-|ri rela-|tioni.| *Title and* 79 *leaves and* 1 *blank.* Libro Secon|do delle In|die Oc|ciden|tali|MDXXXIIII.|Con gratia & priuilegio.| [Verso] Svmmario de la|Natvrale et General Histo|ria de l'Indie occidentali, composta da Gonzalo ferdi-|nando del Ouiedo, altrimenti di valde, natio de|la terra di Madril: habitatore & rettore de|la citta di santa Maria antica del Darien,|in terra ferma de l'Indie: il qual fu riue|duto & corretto per ordine de la Maesta del Imperadore, pelo suo|real consiglio, de le dette In|die. & tradotto di lingua castigliana in Italia-|na. Co*n* priuilegio|de la Illustriss.|Signoria di Vinegia,|per a*n*ni XX.| *Title*, 64 *leaves*, *Tavola* 1 *leaf*, *and description of the* 2 *Maps*, 1 *leaf.* Libro vltimo del svmma|rio delle|Indie Occiden|tali|MDXXXIIII.| [Colophon] ℂ In Vinegia, Del mese d'Ottobre.|MDXXXIIII.| Title, 15 leaves and one blank. 2 Maps. 1565

The three parts complete constitute a work of unusual rarity. The last is a relation of Pizarro's Conquest of Peru. Priced, in the Nuggets, £2 12s. 6d. Libri's copy sold for £2 4s.

ANGIER (A.) Spiritual Anatomizing: or, A few Characteristical notes of a Godly State Offered under Ten Heads of Tryal. By Ames Angier. *Boston*, 1714. 12mo. W. 1566

ANGIER (John). A Sower going forth to Sow the Seed|of God's Word.|A|Sermon|Preached December 23d, 1767.|At the Ordination of the Reverend|Mr. Samuel Angier, to the Pastoral Care of|the Third Church in Bridgewater.|Colleague with his Father,|By his Father, Pastor of said Church.|...|...|...|*Boston, Printed by William M[c]Alpine* ...|... .|M,DCC,LXVIII.| Narrow 4to, pp. 26. H. 1567

ANGIER (Joseph). The Order of Services at the Installation

of Rev. Joseph Angier, as Pastor of the First Congregational Parish in Milton, on Wednesday, Sept. 13, 1837. *Boston, Torrey & Blair, Printers*, 1837. 8vo, pp. 4. H. 1568

ANGIER. A Eulogy, on the Occasion of the Death of William Henry Harrison, late President of the United States: delivered at Milton, May 14th, 1841. By Joseph Angier, Minister of the First Parish in Milton. *Boston, William H. S. Jordan*, 1841. 8vo, pp. 32. H. 1569

ANGIOLELO (G. M.) *See* Montalboddo (Fr. de) and Vespucci.

ANGLERIUS. *See* Anghiera (Pietro Martire d').

ANGLIVIEL DE LA BEAUMELLE (Victor Laurent Suzanne Moïse). De l'empire du Brésil, considéré sous ses rapports politiques et commerciaux. Par Angliviel de la Beaumelle. *Paris, Bossange frères*, 1823. 8vo, pp. iv., 260. 1570

Anglo-American Church Emigrants' Aid Society. No. 1. Occasional Paper ... . (Continued from the "Statement.") ... February, 1856. *London, Rivingtons* [etc., 1856]. 8vo, pp. 17–51. H. 1571

No. 3 is "January, 1859."

The Anglo-American Magazine. July 1852 to Dec. 1855. *Toronto, Thomas Maclear.* 7 vols., 8vo. 1572

ANGLO-CALIFORNIAN, *pseudon.* The National Crisis. A Letter to the Hon. Milton S. Latham, Senator from California, in Washington, by Anglo-Californian. From the San Francisco Bulletin, Feb. 4th, 1861. *San Francisco, Towne & Bacon, Printers*, 1861. 8vo, pp. 21. H. 1573

ANGUIANO. Vide de el Capuchino Español, Francisco de Pamplona, primer Missionario para el Reyno del Congo en Africa, y para los Indios en la America. *Madrid*, 1704. Sm. 4to. Portrait. 1574

Anhang zwoer Reisen. Die Erste|e. Moscov. Gesandten Feod. Iskowitz Bäckhoffs. Die Andere|Herrn Z. Wagners durch ein grosz Theil d. Welt ... . *Berlin, Runge* [16–]. 4to.

Wagner visited America.

ANICETUS, *pseudon.* Our Modern Athens. *See* [Clark (W. A.)]

Animadversions on a Reply to a Letter from a Gentleman in New York. 1750. 8vo. P. 1576

ANNA. Schaduwbeelden uit Suriname. *Amsterdam, Gebruders Binger*, 1858. 8vo, pp. viii., 102. Plate.+*Dordrecht, C. Morks, Jzn*, 1862. 8vo, pp. 8, 103. 1577

Annaes maritimos e coloniaes. Publicaçao mensal redigida sobra direçao da Associaçao maritima e colonial. *Lisboa, Imp. nac.*, 1840–46. 6 vols., 8vo, pp. 533; 587; 643; 458; 514; 135. 1577*a*

The last volume was not completed. Contains a memoir on the priority of Portuguese discoveries in North America, etc.

Annales de l'Association de la propagation de la foi, recueil périodique des lettres des évêques et des missionnaires des missions des deux mondes, et de tous les documens relatifs aux missions ... . Collection faisant suite à toutes les éditions des Lettres Edifiantes. ... *Paris, Lyon,* [*afterwards*] *Lyon* [*alone*], 1827–63. 35 vols., 8vo. B. 1578

Of great value for the information which it conveys respecting manners, customs, literature, arts and sciences of countries in both hemispheres, where missions have been established by the Propaganda Society. A partial analysis of the contents is inserted in the Catalogue of the Library of Parliament, Toronto, 1858. A portion of this work was translated, with the following title:

Annals of the Propagation of the Faith, a periodical collection of letters from the bishops and missionaries employed in the missions of the old and new world: and of all the documents relating to those missions and the Institution for the Propagation of the Faith. This collection serves as a continuation of the "Lettres edifiantes." Vol. I. From July 1839 to Nov. 1846. *Paris*, 1841. Vol. II.–VI. *London*, 1841–1845. 6 vols., 8vo.

There is also a German translation, entitled:

Annalen der Verbreitung des Glaubens. ... Aus dem Französischen. Band I. *Einsiedeln, Benziger*, 1840. 8vo. Continued. 1579*a*

According to the "Thesaurus Librorum Rei Catholicæ, *Würzburg*, 1848," the Jahrbücher der Gessellschaft zur Verbreitung des Glaubens, *Cöln*, is also a translation of this work. There is also an edition in Italian, "Annali della propagaziones della fede, *Lyon*," 8vo, apparently published simultaneously with the French.

Annales d'horticulture et de botanique ou Flore des jardins du Roy des Pays Bas, des Possessions Néerlandaises aux Indes Orientales et Occidentales et du Japon. Publiées par P. F. de Siebold et W. H. de Vriese. 1858–60. 3 vols., 8vo. 1580

Annales de l'Histoire de l'Institution des Religieuses Hospitalières de St. Joseph, sous la Règle de St. Augustin. *Saumur, Degony*, 1829. 8vo. 1581

Pages 438 to 492 relate to the religious establishments in Canada.

Annales de philosophie chrétienne. *Paris*, 1830, etc. 1582

Vol. LVI. contains "De la parenté de la langue japonaise avec les idiomes américains, par M. de Charency." I.–LIX. also contain fifty-five other articles on American topics.

Annales des Voyages. *See* Eyriès, Malte-Brun, and Voyages.

Annales du Muséum d'histoire naturelle, par les professeurs de cet établissement. ... and Table des auteurs [et] des matières, 1827, 4to. Continued as Mémoires du Muséum, etc., 1814–32, 4to, and as Nouvelles annales, etc., 1832–1835 and Archives, 1840 to date. *Paris.* 4to. 1583

Contains many articles relating to the French Colonies.

Annales maritimes et coloniales. [Par Labaothe.] *Paris, an* VII. 8vo. 1584

Annales maritimes et coloniales ou Recueil de lois et ordonnances royales, règlements ministériels, mémoires, observations, notices particulières, et generalement tout ce qui peut intéresser la marine et les colonies sous les rapports militaires, administratess, judiciaires, nautiques, consulaires et commerciaux, publié avec l'approbation de M. le ministre de la marine et des colonies par M. Bajot. *Paris*, 1816–1847. Text, 104 vols., and Tables, 2 vols., 8vo. 1585

Indispensable for the History of the French Colonies. Continued monthly, as "Nouvelles Annales de la Marine et des Colonies, 1849," &c.

Annales Philosophiques, Politiques, et Literaires: ouvrage utile aux Amateurs de la verité, par un habitant de Louisiane. *Philadelphia*, 1807. 8vo. 1586

Refers to the Aborigines of America, the Illinois River, the formation of Lower Louisiana, the Orinoco River, &c.

Annales Scientifiques d'Auvergne. *Paris*, 1826, &c. 8vo.

Some articles relate to French Guyane.

Annals of a Western Missionary. Edited by the Rev. C. C. Townsend ... . Vol. I. No. I. October, 1863. *New York*, 1863. 18mo, pp. 18. Continued. H. 1588

No. 2 was published at *Cedar Rapids, Iowa*; later numbers at *Iowa City*.

The Annals of Administration: containing the genuine History of Georgiana the Queen-Mother, and Prince Coloninus her son. A Biographical Fragment, written about the Year 1575. Inscribed by the Proprietor of the Authentic Papers, to Edmund Burke, Esq. *London, Bew,* 1775. 8vo. c. 1589

"Intended to be an allegorical explanation of the origin of our American disputes."—M. R., LII., 263.

Annals of Europe for 1739. *London,* 1740, &c. 6 vols., 8vo. 1590

Includes many chapters on American affairs.

Annals of Great Britain. *See* [Campbell (Thomas)].

Annals of Liberality, Generosity, Public Spirit, &c. [*Philadelphia,* 1823.] 8vo. 1591

No. 6 of the 3d Series was published in 1837.

Annals of the American Revolution: or, a Record of the Causes and Events, which produced and terminated in the Establishment and Independence of the American Republic; also, a Summary Account of the first Settlement of the Country, and some of the principal Indian Wars, and Biographies of the Principal Military Officers. *Hartford,* 1824. 8vo. 1592

Annals of the Army of the Cumberland. *See* [Webster (B. F.)]

Annals of the Colonial Church. *London, Parker,* 1857, &c. 5 vols., 18mo. 1593

Comprise the annals of Fredericton, Toronto and Quebec.

Annals of the Congress of the United States. *See* Gales (J.)

ANNAPOLIS. Annual Register of the United States Naval Academy, at Annapolis, Md. 1865–'66. *Washington, Government Printing Office,* 1866. 8vo, pp. 37. H. 1594

Annapolis. Catalogue of the Library of the U. S. Naval Academy, Annapolis, Maryland, June 30, 1860. *Annapolis, Robert F. Bonsall, Printer,* 1860. 8vo, pp. vi., 1 l., pp. 251 (1). H. 1594*a*

Rules and Regulations for the Government of the Naval Academy at Annapolis, Md. ... *Washington,* 1850. 8vo, pp. 46. 1594*b*

Annapolis. The first annual Report of the Directors of the Annapolis and Elkridge Rail Road Company. [Reports upon the Surveys, Location, and Progress of Construction of the Annapolis and Elkridge Rail-road by G. W. Hughes.] *Annapolis,* 1839. 8vo. 1595

ANNE ARUNDEL CO. AND BALTIMORE CO., *Md.* ... Memorial of Farmers, Mechanics, and Others, of Anne Arundel and Baltimore Counties, against an Increase of Duty on Imported Manufactures. ... *Washington, Printed by Gales & Seaton,* 1828. 8vo, pp. 5. (20th Cong., 1st Sess., House Doc. No. 188.) H. 1596

ANNEKE (Fritz). Der zweite Freiheitskampf der Vereinigten Staaten von Amerika. Erster Band. *Frankfurt,* 1861. 12mo, pp. vii., 368. 3 Maps. c. 1597

ANNEKE (Mathilde Franziska). Das Geisterhaus in New-York. Ein Roman. *Jena, Costenoble,* 1864. 8vo, pp. 307.

[ANNESLEY.] Memoirs of an Unfortunate Young Nobleman, Return'd from a Thirteen Years Slavery in America, Where he had been sent by the Wicked Contrivances of his Cruel Uncle. A Story founded on Truth, and address'd equally to the Head and Heart. ... *London, Printed for J. Freeman,* M DCC XLIII. 2 p. l., pp. 277; Books, pp. 7. H. 1599

[ANNESLEY.] Memoirs of an Unfortunate Young Nobleman, In which is Continued the History of Count Richard, Concluding with a Summary View of the Tryal. Part the Second. By the Author of the First. *London, Printed for J. Freeman,* M DCC XLIII. 12mo, 2 p. l., pp. 235. H. 1600

ANNESLEY. The Case of the Honourable James Annesley, Esq. Being a Sequel to the Memoirs of an Unfortunate Young Nobleman. *London, Printed for W. Bickerton,* MDCCXLV.+ Another Edition. 1756. 12mo, 2 p. l., pp. 215. 1601

The true history of the heir of the Earldom of Anglesey, from which Scott took the plot of Guy Mannering. For full particulars respecting the most mysterious and celebrated Anglesea case and trial, *see* Collins's Peerage; "Notes and Queries," 2d Series, Vol. II., 373; "Gentlemen's Magazine," May, 1840; and Smollett's "Peregrine Pickle." This (which is the third volume) is very scarce.

ANNESLEY. The Trial in Ejectment between Campbell Craig, Lessee of James Annesley, Esq., and others, Plaintiffs, and the Rt. Hon. Richard, Earl of Anglesey, Defendant, before

the Barons of the Exchequer in 1743. *Dublin,* 1744. 12mo, pp. 377. Portrait. 1602

Another edition has this title: "Trial of Richard Earl of Anglesey, Francis Annesley, and John Jans, Gent. for Assault on the Hon. James Annesley, Daniel Mac Kercher, Hugh Kennedy, and W. Goostry, 1744."

ANNESLEY. Fortune's Favourite; Containing Memoirs of the many Hardships and Sufferings, together with the surprizing Deliverance and Advancement to Plenty and Happiness, of Jacobo Anglicano [James Annesley], a young Nobleman; in which will be inserted the Hard Usage of his cruel Uncle, by whose means he was trepann'd into Slavery, which he suffer'd for thirteen Years [in America], with the Manner of his Escape from it. *Printed for the Author,* 1744. 8vo. 1603

[ANNET (Peter)]. A Collection of the Tracts of a certain Free Inquirer, noted for his Sufferings for his Opinions. *London,* 1739. 8vo, pp. 460. 1604

The piece called "Social Bliss carried out" contains the speech of Miss Polly Baker, before a Court of Judicature in Connecticut. *See* Allibone's Dictionary, p. 63.

The Anniversary Week at Bloomington. The Agricultural Convention; Annual Meeting of the Illinois Natural History Society, and Commencement Exercises of the State Normal University. ... *Chicago, July,* 1860. 8vo, pp. 67. H. 1605

Anno Regni | Georgii III. | Regis | Magnæ Britanniæ, Franciæ, & Hiberniæ, | Quinto. | At the Parliament begun and holden at | Westminster, the Nineteenth Day of | May, Anno Dom. 1761, in the First | Year of the Reign of our Sove- | reign Lord, George the Third, | by the Grace of God, of Great Britain, | France, and Ireland, King, Defender | of the Faith, &c. | And from thence continues by several Prorogations to | the Tenth day of January, 1765, being the Fourth | Session of the Twelfth Parliament of Great Britain. | *London: | Printed by Mark Baskett, Printer to the King's most | Excellent Majesty; and by the Assigns of Robert Baskett,* M.DCC.LXV. | 8vo, pp. 66. H. Also in folio.+ *Reprinted by William Dunlap, at the newest Printing Office, in Market Street, Philadelphia.* 8vo, pp. 40. P. + Reprinted. *Boston,* 1765. Folio. 1606

The celebrated Stamp Act. The title given (No. 138) in this Dictionary was copied from Rich.

Annvæ Litteræ Societatis Jesu Anni 1581. Ad Patres et

Fratres eiusdem Societatis. *Romæ, in Collegio eiusdem Societatis,* 1583. 8vo. Continued to 1654, omitting 1615–49. 1607

The imprint varies for the different years to *Florentiæ, Neapoli, Lugduni, Antverpiæ, Moguntiæ, Duaci,* etc. A detailed list is given by Carayon, Bib. hist. de la Comp. de Jésus. Each year contains letters from the South American missions.

Annuaire de la marine et des colonies, 1856. *Paris, Dumaine, Mallet-Bachelier, Ledoyen,* 1857. 8vo, pp. 652. Continued.

Annuaire des Deux Mondes Histoire générale des divers états. 1850. *Paris, au bureau de la Revue des Deux Mondes,* 1851. 8vo. Continued. 1609

Annuaire historique universel, pour 1818 ... . Par C. L. Lesur ... . *Paris,* 1819. 8vo. Continued. 1610

Annuaire des Voyages et de la Géographie. *Paris, Gide & Co.,* 1844. Continued. 1611

Annuaire Oriental et Américain. Publié avec le concours et sous les auspices de la Société d'Ethnographie Américaine et Orientale; par Léon de Rosny, secrétaire perpetuel. *Paris, Challamel ainé,* 1860. 12mo, pp. 143. Continued. c. 1612

The Annual Biography and Obituary, for the Year 1817–1837. *London, Longman* [etc.], 1817–37. 21 vols., 8vo. 1613

Includes a few Americans.

The Annual Register, or a View of the History, Politicks, and Literature, of the Year 1758. *London, Printed for R. and J. Dodsley,* 1759. 8vo. Continued annually. 1614

Some of the earlier volumes were reprinted, and "A New Edition Corrected" of the fifteen volumes for 1758–1772 was published in 1774, by H. Saunders and others. This most valuable record and chronicle of historical and political events for over a hundred years contains accurate accounts of the Revolutionary War, as well as of the revolutions in South America, the Second War with Great Britain, and many other American subjects. It was edited by Burke, Campbell, Allen and others. As there are *spurious* sets, the following memoranda from Lowndes will aid the intending purchaser: "Some time after the year 1791, the copyright and stock from 1758 to 1790 were purchased by Otridge and other booksellers. After which period Messrs. Rivingtons, who had for a short time previously (during the illness of Mr. Dodsley) been agents for the work, published a rival continuation, which lasted from 1791 to 1812, and again from 1820 to 1824, when the two merged by arrangement into one. Some sets of the work have been made up by substituting Rivington's continuation with fictitious titles. How to distinguish the substitution may be ascertained by referring to the preface of the General Index, published by Baldwin & Co. in 1826. 8vo. A general index (1758–80) was published by Dodsley in 1783; another (1781–90) by the Rivingtons in 1799; and a third, superseding the previous ones, from the commencement to 1819, in 1826. And, as this complete index is only applicable to the original, or Dodsley series, the volumes published by the Rivingtons are generally rejected."

The Annual Register, and Virginian Repository, for The Year 1800. [Motto.] *Petersburg, Ross and Douglas* [1801]. 12mo, pp. xii., 208. B. 1615

Annual Retrospect of Public Affairs for 1831. Vol. I. *Boston,* 1831. 12mo. N. 1616

Another Cry of the Innocent for Justice, or a Second Relation of the Unjust Proceedings at Hicks's Hall against the Quakers, with a Short Summary of the Sentencing of Thirty-Six more of the aforesaid people, in scorn called Quakers, all sentenced to be transported to the Island of Jamaica, 1664. 4to, pp. 32. 1617

John Otter, who had been "i'the stocks five times," was sold as a slave to Virginia. *See* p. 25.

Another Cry of the Innocent and Oppressed for Justice; or a Third Relation ... *Printed in the Year* 1665. 4to, pp. 16.

"Relating to Forty-five of the People of God, whom the world in scorn calls Quakers, of which 34 *were sentenced to be transported to the Island of* GAMAICA, *for the space of seven years,*" etc.

Another High Road to Hell. An Essay on the Pernicious Nature and destructive Effects of the Modern Entertainments from the Pulpit. Occasioned by a Pamphlet, entituled The Stage the High Road to Hell, &c. [Motto.] *London, Printed; Boston, Reprinted, Ezekiel Russell,* M,DCC,LXVIII. 8vo, pp. 21. B. 1619

ANQUETIL (Louis Pierre). Motifs des Guerres et des Traités de Paix de la France ... depuis la Paix de Westphalie, en 1648, jusqu'à celle de Versailles, en 1783. Par le Cen. Anquetil. *Paris, Lesguillez frères* [and], *Desenne, an* 6 [1797]. 8vo. 1620

Contains L'Assiento, Brouillerie des Anglais et des Anglo-Americains, Traité de paix pour l'Amérique, etc.

Anschauungen und Erfahrungen in Nord-Amerika. Monatsschrift, herausgegeben von H. Bosshard. 1.–3. Jahrgang. *Zürich,* 1853–55. 8vo. 1621

Ansiedelungen in den Urwäldern von Canada. Ein Wegweiser für Auswanderer nach Amerika von einer Emigrantin. Aus dem Englischen von Dr. F. A. Wiese. *Leipzig, Baumgärtner,* 1837. 8vo. Illustrations. 1622

Die deutsche Ansiedelung in Mittel-Amerika. Dargestellt und herausgegeben von dem Comité der Berliner Colonisations-

Gesellschaft für Central-Amerika. *Berlin, Hempel,* 1850. 8vo, pp. 34. 2 Maps, folio. 1623

Der Ansiedler im Westen. Monatsschrift des Berliner Vereins [in later vols., Gesellschaft] für die deutsche [later, deutsch-evangelische] Mission in Nordamerika [later, Amerika] Red.: W. Eichler. 1. Jahrgang. 1863. *Berlin, Wiegandt & Grieben,* 1863. 4to, pp. 96. Continued. 1624

ANSON (George, *Lord*). A voyage round the World, in the years MDCCXL, I, II, III, IV. By George Anson, Esq; Commander in Chief of a Squadron of His Majesty's Ships, sent upon an Expedition to the South-Seas. Compiled from Papers and other Materials of the Right Honourable George Lord Anson, and published under his Direction. By Richard Walter, M.A. Chaplain of his Majesty's Ship the Centurion, in that Expedition. Illustrated with Forty-two Copper-Plates. *London, T. Osborne,* MDCCXLVIII. 4to, pp. (18), 417. Also in 8vo. 1625

ANSON. A voyage round the World, in the years MDCCXL, I, II, III, IV. By George Anson, Esq; Commander in Chief of a Squadron of His Majesty's Ships, sent upon an Expedition to the South-Seas. Compiled from Papers and other Materials of the Right Honourable George Lord Anson, and published under his Direction. By Richard Walter, M.A. Chaplain of his Majesty's Ship the Centurion, in that Expedition. Second Edition. With Charts of the Southern Part of South America, of Part of the Pacific Ocean, and of the Track of the Centurion round the World. *London, John and Paul Knapton,* MDCCXLVIII. 8vo, 12 p. l., pp. 548. 3 Charts. 1626

Third, fourth and fifth editions, each same date and collation as the second, with some trifling differences in the title of the third edition. It was reprinted in quarto in 1749.

ANSON. A Voyage [etc.] By George Anson, Esq.; now Lord Anson, etc. The Sixth Edition. *London,* MDCCXLIX. 8vo, 12 p. l., pp. 548. 3 Charts. 1627

ANSON. A Voyage [etc.] The Seventh Edition. Illustrated with Charts, Views, &c. *Dublin, Printed for G. and A. Ewing.* 8vo, 9 p. l., pp. 350. 8 Plates. 1628

ANSON. A Voyage [etc.] The Seventh Edition. *London,* MDCCLIII. 8vo.+ The Eighth Edition. *London,* MDCCLIV.+ The Ninth Edition. *London,* MDCCLVI. 4to, pp. (18), 417.

Also in 8vo.+ The Tenth Edition. *London,* MDCCLXII. 8vo. + The Eleventh Edition. *London,* MDCCLXV. 8vo.+ The Twelfth Edition. *London, T. Osborne,* MDCCLXVII. 4to, pp. (18), 417.+ The Thirteenth Edition. *London,* MDCCLXVIII. 8vo.+ The Fourteenth Edition. *London,* MDCCLXIX. 8vo, 12 p. l., pp. 536. 3 Charts.+ The Fifteenth Edition. *London,* MDCCLXXX. 8vo, pp. xxiv., 536. 3 Charts. Also on large paper, rl. 8vo, and in 4to. 1629

Most of the quarto editions were also printed on large paper, and contain 42 plates; that of 1748 is the most desirable. The work has been repeatedly reprinted, often in an abridged form. Those that have come under my notice are quoted below. It is partly reprinted in Callander's Voyages, Vol. III., and in Harris's and other collections. *See* Ret. Rev., X., 285; M. Rev., XXV., 234. In regard to the authorship, *see* Davis's "Olio," pp. 1–4. Rich writes as follows: "Walter had prepared an account of this voyage for the press, but it was found so badly executed, that Benjamin Robins, the mathematician, was employed to re-write it, although, for some reason or other, the worthy chaplain's name was allowed to remain on the title-page. It is called by some English writers a masterpiece of composition; but it appears to have been made amusing at the expense of truth. The progress of science formed no part of this expedition, which was prepared for attacking, unawares, the Spanish possessions and shipping in the South Sea, and which was so successful, that the prize-money divided amongst the officers and crews amounted to more than a million sterling. The *Biographie Universelle* says, that the views, charts and plans deserve praise for their exactness; but Dr. Dibdin says, that the 'plates are in truth barbarously bad, and that to read the text without the plates must be a comfort.' He adds, moreover, that the volume is unworthy, in every respect, of the intrepid Anson. The doctor had, apparently, seen only the *fifth* edition, printed in 1749; in which, of course, the plates must have been nearly worn out. The copies of the first edition, on royal paper, of which I now have one before me, were superior to any book of the kind which had been hitherto published, and were unequalled until Cook's voyages appeared. Of the large paper copies, 350 were taken by subscription."

ANSON. A Voyage round the World. Compiled from his papers, &c., by Richard Walter, M.A. *Edinburgh,* 1781. 2 vols., 12mo. 1630

Other editions at Edinburgh, 1800, 1804, 1807, 1812; at Dublin, 1825. Perhaps the latest reprint of Anson is the edition of Wm. Smith. *London,* 1842. Rl. 8vo. Re-issued, *London, R. Griffin & Co.,* 1853.

ANSON. An Authentic Account of Commodore Anson's Expedition, containing all that was Remarkable, Curious, and Entertaining, during that Long and Dangerous Voyage, Taken from a Private Journal. *London, Cooper,* 1744. 8vo, pp. 60.

ANSON. A Voyage to the South Seas and to other Parts of the World. By George Anson, Esq. *London,* 1744. 12mo.

Published in numbers, with coarse woodcuts.

ANSON. Anson's Voyage to the South Seas, with Appendix containing summary Account of the Discovery of the East

Indies, China, and principal Islands, by the Europeans. *London, R. Walker,* 1745. 8vo. Portrait and Plate. 1633

This is a different relation from Walter's.

ANSON. An Affecting Narrative Of the Unfortunate Voyage and Catastrophe Of his Majesty's Ship Wager, One of Commodore Anson's Squadron in the South Sea Expedition. Containing A full Account of its being cast away on a desolate Island, and of the strange Proceedings of the Officers and private Men, after that unhappy Event: More especially, of those important Incidents, the Shooting of Mr. Henry Cosins, and the imprisoning of Capt. C—p for that Action. The Whole compiled from authentic Journals, and transmitted, by Letter, to a Merchant in London, from a Person who was an Eye-Witness of all the Affair: Exhibiting a compleat View of the Perils and terrible Disasters which the Crew underwent; the wonderful adventure of near an hundred of them, in their Boat, along the vast southern Coast of Patagonia, and thro' the Streights of Magellan, for above a thousand Leagues, during which the greatest Part of them perish'd by Cold and Famine; the Arrival of those few that surviv'd in the miserablest Condition at Rio Grand; their hospitable Reception and Entertainment at that Place; their Passage from thence to Rio Janeiro, next to Lisbon, and finally to England. Intermix'd with several entertaining Passages and Remarks. *Printed for John Norwood, and sold by the Booksellers of London, Bristol, and Liverpool,* MDCCLI. 8vo, Title and pp. 160. 1634

ANSON. Lord Anson's Voyage round the World. *London,* 1759. 12mo, pp. 96. M. 1635

A chap-book edition, with portrait and copper-plates.

ANSON. The History of Commodore Anson's Voyage round the World, at the Commencement of the late Spanish War. Performed in three Years and nine Months, viz. from September 1740 to June 1744. By a Midshipman on Board the Centurion. *London, M. Cooper,* MDCCLXVII. 8vo, Title and Contents, 2 l.; Text, pp. 192. Copper-Plate Portrait of Anson. 1636

ANSON. Voyage autour du monde, fait dans les années 1740, 41, 42, 43 and 44. Par George Anson ... . Orné de Cartes & de Figures en Taille-douce. Traduit de l'anglois. [Par Élie de Joncourt.] *Amsterdam,* 1749. 4to, pp. 331. 37 Plates.+ *Genève,* 1750. 3 vols., 8vo, and Atlas in 4to.+ *Genève,*

1750. 4to, pp. xxiv., 363 (1). 34 Plates. + Seconde Edition. ... *Paris, Par la Compagnie des Libraires*, M.DCC.LXIV. 4 vols., 24mo. Maps and Plates. H. 1637

ANSON. Voyage autour du monde fait dans les années 1740, 41, 42, 43 et 44. Par George Anson. Tires des journaux, etc. par R. Walter. Orné de carte et figures. Traduit de l'anglois par Gua de Malves. *Paris, Quillau*, 1750. 4to. + *Paris*, 1750. 4 vols, 12mo. + *Paris*, 1754. 4 vols., 12mo. 1638

ANSON. Voyage à la Mer du Sud, fait par quelques officiers commandant le vaisseau le Wager. Pour servir de suite au Voyage de Georges Anson. Traduit de l'Anglois. *Lyon*, 1756. 4to. + *Lyon*, 1756. 5 vols., 12mo. + *Paris*, 1764. 5 vols., 12mo. 1639

"This volume is composed, rather than translated, from the Journals of Messrs. Bulkely and Cummins, *London*, 1713; of Alexander Campbell, *Dublin*, 1747; Anonymous, *London*, 1751; and of Isaac Morris, *Dublin*, 1752."—RICH.

ANSON. Des Herrn Admirals, Lord Ansons Reise um die Welt, welche er als Oberbefehlshaber über ein Geschwader von Sr. Grossbritannischen Majestät Kriegschiffen, die zu einer Unternehmung in die Südsee ausgeschickt worden, in den Jahren 1740, 41, 42, 43, 44, verrichtet hat, aus dessen Aufsätzen und Urkunden zusammengetragen und unter seiner eigenen Aufsicht an das Licht gestellet von M. Richard Waltern, Capellan auf Sr. Majestät Schiffe, dem Centurion in diesem Kriegszuge, aus dem Englischen in das Deutsche übersetzt. Nebst vielen Kupfertafeln und Landkarten. Mit Königl. Pohlnischer und Churfürstl. Sächsischer allergnädigster Freyheit. *Leipzig und Göttingen, Abraham Vanderhoeck*, 1749. 4to, pp. xliv., 382; Erklärung, &c., 14 l. 34 Plates. 1640

ANSON. Reis rondom de Weereld. *Amsterdam, Jan Ten Houten*, 1754. 4to. Plates. + *Amsterdam, S. J. Baalde*, 1765. 4to. Plates. 1641

There was also an Italian translation. *Livorno*, 1756. 4to.

Letter to the Right Hon. Lord Anson, in relation to his conduct in America. *London*, 1757. 8vo. 1642

ANSON. De reis van het Schip de Wager. *Amsterdam, S. J. Baalde*, 1766. 4to. Plates. 1642*a*

ANSPACH (F. R.) A Discourse, pronounced on Sabbath Evening, July 4, 1852, in the Lutheran Church of Hagers-

town, on the Death of Henry Clay, by the Rev. F. R. Anspach, A.M. *Hagerstown, Printed by Mittag & Sneary*, 1852. 8vo, pp. 12. H. 1643

ANSPACH (L. A.) A History of the Island of Newfoundland: containing a Description of the Island, the Banks, the Fisheries, and Trade of Newfoundland, and the Coast of Labrador. Illustrated with Two Maps. By the Rev. Lewis Amadeus Anspach, late a Magistrate of that Island and Missionary for the District of Conception Bay. *London, T. and J. Allman, and J. M. Richardson*, 1819. 8vo, pp. xxviii., 512. Map. H. + Second Edition. *London*, 1827. 8vo. 1644

See M. R., New Series, XCVI, 61.

ANSPACH (L. A.) Geschichte und Beschreibung von Newfoundland und der Küste von Labrador. Aus dem Englischen übersetzt. *Weimar*, 1822. 8vo. 2 Maps. 1645

Band XXX. of F. J. Bertuch's Neue Bibliothek der wichtigsten Reisebeschreibungen.

ANSPACH. A Summary of the Laws of Commerce and Navigation, adapted to the present State, Government, and Trade of the Island of Newfoundland. By the Rev. Lewis Amedeus Anspach. Recommenced for Publication by Vice Admiral J. Holloway, Governor and Commander in Chief of Newfoundland, and its Dependencies. *London, Printed by Henney and Haddon*, 1809. 8vo, pp. 140. 1646

ANSTED (D. T.) The Gold-Seeker's Manual; being a Practical and Instructive Guide to all Persons emigrating to the Newly-Discovered Gold Regions of California. By David T. Ansted. *London, Van Voorst*, 1849. 12mo, pp. 176. + *New York, D. Appleton & Company*, 1849. 12mo, pp. 96. H. 1647

ANSTED. Scenery, Science, and Art, being extracts from the note-book of a Geologist and Mining Engineer, by Prof. D. T. Ansted. *London, John Van Voorst*, M.DCCC.LIV. 8vo, pp. viii., 323. 1648

Pages 241 to 311 relate to America.

The Answer of the Assembly of Divines by Authority of Parliament Now sitting at Westminster. Unto the Reasons given into this Assembly by the Dissenting Brethren, Of their not bringing in a Model of their Way. And since Published in Print, under the Title of *A Copy of a Remonstrance*. Which Answer was humbly presented to the Right Honorable the House

of Peers Assembled in Parliament. *London, John Field for Ralph Smith*, 1645. 4to, Title and pp. 24. 1649

Mr. Stevens includes this in his Nuggets. What it has to do with America is not apparent. Perhaps it relates to the Brownists.

An Answer of the Company of Royal Adventurers of England trading into Africa, to the Petition and Paper of certain Heads and Particulars thereunto relating and annexed, exhibited to the Honourable House of Commons by Sir Paul Painter, Ferdinando Gorges, Henry Batson, Benjamin Skutt, and Thomas Knight, on the behalf of themselves and others concerned in his Majesty's Plantations in America. *London, Anno Dom.* 1667. 4to, pp. 18. 1650

Answer of the Elders and other Messengers of the Churches assembled at Boston, 1662, to the Questions propounded by the General Court, with the answer of the dissenting brethren. *Boston*, 1662. 4to, pp. 18. M. 1651

Answer of the States General of the United Provinces of the Low Countries to the Declaration of War of the King of Great Britain. *At the Hague*, 1674. 4to. 1652

Contains an interesting account of Surinam; also some notices of other American colonies.

Answer to a Calumny, with some remarks upon an anonymous Pamphlet on the Assiento Trade, as exercised by the South Sea Company, &c. By the Factor to the South Sea Company, at whom the calumny was aimed. In Two Parts. *London*, 1728. 8vo. 1653

The Answer to a Colonel's Letter. By a Wooden-legged Soldier. Wherein some American matters are slightly touched upon. *London, Main*, 1766. 8vo, pp. 36. 1654

"This wooden-legged soldier is by no means a wooden-headed one. Corporal Oaktree is really a very clever, facetious fellow."—M. R., XXXIV., 162.

Answer to "A Dialogue between a Federalist and a Republican." *Charleston, S. C.*, 1800. 8vo. M. 1655

Answer to a letter from a Gentleman in the Country to his Friend in Town. *New York*, 1756. 12mo. 1656

Answer to a pamphlet. *See* [Shebbeare (John)].

An Answer to a Pamphlet, entitled Taxation no Tyranny.

28

Addressed to the Author, and to Persons in Power. *London, J. Almon*, MDCCLXXV. 8vo, pp. 63. 1657

Written in reply to Dr. Samuel Johnson.

Answer to a Piece entitled "An Appeal to the Impartial Publick by an Association" calling themselves Christian Independents. *Salem*, 1785. 8vo, pp. 23. M. 1658

Answer to "An address to all reasonable Americans," &c. *See* [Cooper (Myles)].

An Answer to an invidious Pamphlet. *See* [Cross].

Answer to the Budget inscribed to the Coterie. *London*, 1764. 4to, pp. 15. 1659

An Answer to the Declaration of the American Congress. *See* [Lind (Dr.)]

Answer to the Exposition of a Pamphlet entitled Papers relative to the Rupture with Spain. 1762. 8vo. 1660

An Answer to the Letter to Two Great Men, containing Remarks and Observations on that Piece, and Vindicating the Character of a Noble Lord from Inactivity. *London, Henderson*, 1760. 8vo. 1661

See M. R., XXII., 71.

Answer to the Observations on the Papers relative to a Rupture with Spain. *London, Hinkxman*, 1762. 8vo, pp. 35. 1662

An Answer to the Pamphlet entitled the Conduct of the Paxton Men, impartially represented: Wherein the Ungenerous Spirit of the Author is Manifested, &c. and the spotted Garment pluckt off. [Motto.] *Philadelphia, Printed by Anthony Armbuster, in Moravian Alley*, 1764. 12mo, pp. 28. 1663

Relates to the Lancaster Massacre.

An Answer to the Questions, Why are you a Federalist, etc. *See* [Quincy (Josiah)].

An Answer to the Reasons against an African Company Humbly Submitted to the Consideration of the Patriots of Great-Britain, in this Present Parleament Assembled. *London, Printed in the Year* 1711. 8vo, pp. 31. 1664

Partly relates to the American Plantations.

An Answer to The Tears of the Foot Guards upon their Departure for America; a Poem. *London*, 1776. 4to. 1664*a*

Answer to the White-Washing Committee, 1831. Broadside.

Relates to a pamphlet entitled "Examination of certain charges against Lemuel H. Arnold," of Rhode Island.

Answer to War in Disguise. *See* [Morris (Gouverneur)].

Antagonisme et solidanté des etats orientaux et des etats occidentaux de l'Amérique du Sud. Ouvrage traduit et précédé d'une introduction par Th. Mannequin. *Paris, Dentu*, 1866. 8vo, pp. 203. 1665*a*

ANTARCTICUS, *pseudon.* A Letter to the President of the Royal Geographical Society of London, on Antarctic Discovery. By Antarcticus. *London, Murray*, 1837. 8vo, pp. 132, 133.

Noticed in *The Athenæum*, 1837. Advocates a British Expedition to rival that of Lieut. Wilkes.

ANTEPARA (José Maria). South American Emancipation. Documents, Historical and Explanatory, shewing the Designs which have been in progress, and the Exertions made by General Miranda, for the South American Emancipation, during the last Twenty-five Years. By J. M. Antepara, a Native of Guayaquil. *London, J. Richardson, B. Dulau, L. N. Pannier*, 1810. 8vo, pp. x., 299 (1). Portrait. H. 1667

Noticed at great length in the M. R., New Series, LXIV., 367.

ANTEQUERA Y CASTRO (Joseph de). Coleccion General de Documentos, que contiene los sucesos tocantes á la segunda época de las conmociones de los Regulares de la Compañia en el Paraguay, y señaladamente la persecucion, que hicieron a Don Josef de Antequera y Castro. Vá añadido en esta edicion el Informe de Don Mathias Angles y Gortari. Tomo Tercero. *Madrid*, M.DCC.LXIX. 4to, 7 p. l., pp. 239, 374, 64 (4). 1668

ANTERSEN (Johann Peter von). Fataler Schiffs-Capitain, oder Erzehlung dessen Reisen nach denen bis dass noch unbekannten Südlichen Welt-Theilen und anderer Merkwürdigkeiten. *Erfurt, Jungnickel*, 1742. 8vo, 18 sheets. 1669

Included in a list of books relating to America. How much it has to do with it I know not.

ANTHOINE DE SAINT-JOSEPH (Baron François). Concordance entre les codes de commerce étrangers et le code de commerce

français: contenant le texte des codes et des lois commerciales des états suivants; Amerique du Sud, ... Etats-Unis, ... Haiti ... Mexique. ... . Nouvelle Édition augmentée ... . *Paris, Videcoq*, 1851. 4to. C. 1670

The first edition was published in 1843.

ANTHOINE DE SAINT-JOSEPH. Concordance entre les codes civils étrangers et le code Napoléon. 2e édition entierement refondue et augmentée. Ouvrage terminé et publié par M. Antoine de Saint-Joseph fils. *Paris, Cotillon*, 1856. 4 vols., 8vo. C. 1671

"C. J. B. Amyot codified the laws of the following countries: South America, United States, Brazil," etc.—LORENZ.

ANTHOINE DE SAINT-JOSEPH. Concordance entre les lois hypothécaires étrangères et françaises. *Paris, Videcoq*. 8vo.

Anthology of New Netherland. *See* [Murphy (H. C.)]

ANTHON (George C.) Narrative and Documents connected with the Displacement of the Professor of the Greek Language and Literature in the University of the City of New York, April 2d, 1851: by George C. Anthon, A.M. *New York, J. R. Winser, Printer*, 1851. 8vo, pp. 72. H. 1672*a*

ANTHON. Parish Annals. A Sermon giving Historical Notices of St. Mark's Church in the Bowery, N. Y., (from A.D. 1795 to A.D. 1845.) Delivered in said Church, May 4, 1845. By Henry Anthon, D.D., Rector of the same. Published by the request of the Vestry. *New York, Stanford and Swords*, 1845. 8vo, pp. 58. Woodcut. H. 1673

ANTHON. The Subject and Spirit of the Christian Minister. A Sermon, preached by Request in St. Peter's Church, Twentieth-Street, New-York, on Palm Sunday, April 1st, 1849. Being the Sunday after the Decease of the Rev. Hugh Smith, D.D., late Rector of said Church. By Henry Anthon, D.D. ... . *New-York, Stanford and Swords*, 1849. 8vo, pp. 22. H. 1674

ANTHON. The Wise and Faithful Steward. A Sermon preached in St. Stephen's Church, New-York ... September 19, 1830, being the Sunday after the Decease of the Right Rev. Bishop Hobart. By Henry Anthon, Rector ... . *New-York, T. and J. Swords*, 1830. 8vo, pp. 19. H. 1675

ANTHON. Tributes to the Memory of the Rev. Henry

Anthon, D.D., late Rector of St. Mark's in the Bowery, New-York. With a Brief Sketch of his Life, by the Rt. Rev. Manton Eastburn, D.D., Bishop of Massachusetts. *New-York, Protestant Episcopal Society for the Promotion of Evangelical Knowledge*, 1862. 8vo, pp. 80 (1). Portrait. H. 1676

ANTHON (John). American Precedents of Declarations, collected chiefly from Manuscripts of Chief Justice Parsons and other Accomplished Pleaders in the State of Massachusetts, digested ... . By John Anthon, Esquire, Counsellor at Law. ... *New York, Stephen Gould*, 1810. 8vo, pp. 570. B. 1677

ANTHON. Oration before the Washington Benevolent Society, and the Hamilton Society in the City of New York, July 4, 1812. By John Anthon. *New York*, 1812. 8vo, pp. 22.

ANTHON. Proceedings on Occasion of the Death of John Anthon, President of the New York Law Institute; with the Address of James W. Gerard. *New York, Bryant & Co., Printers*, 1865. 8vo, pp. 20. 1679

ANTHON (W. H.) Argument of William Henry Anthon, Esq., in behalf of the Defendants, Messrs. Ray Tompkins, and John C. Thompson, on Motion to discharge from Arrest on a Charge of Arson, arising from the Destruction of the Quarantine Hospitals, before Judge Metcalfe ... October 7th, 1858. Reported ... by Joseph L. Blundell. *New York, Wm. C. Bryant & Co., Printers*, 1858. 8vo, pp. 34. H. 1680

ANTHONY (Elliott). Is a Constitution Convention a Legislature? A Speech delivered in the Constitution Convention of Illinois, February 17, 1862. By Elliott Anthony. [*Springfield*, 1862.] 8vo, pp. 13. S. 1681

Relative to the abolition of slavery by Congress.

ANTHONY. The Outlawry of a Race. A Speech delivered in the Constitutional Convention of Illinois, February 12, 1862, on the proposition to forever prohibit negroes or mulattoes from migrating into or settling in the State. By Elliott Anthony. [*Springfield*, 1862.] pp. 8. S. 1682

ANTHONY. Shall the Privilege of the Writ of Habeas Corpus ever be Suspended in this State? A Speech delivered in the Constitutional Convention of Illinois, 1862. By Elliott Anthony. [*Springfield*, 1862.] 8vo, pp. 9. S. 1683

ANTHONY (J.) Trial of James Anthony, for the Murder of Joseph Green: before the Honourable Supreme Court of the State of Vermont, at their Adjourned Term in the County of Rutland, February 28, A.D. 1814. *Rutland, Fay & Davison* [1814]. 8vo, pp. 39. H. 1684

Anti Abolition Tracts. *See* Slavery.

Anticipation. *See* [Tickell (Richard)].

Anticipation continued. Containing the substance of The Speech Intended to be delivered from The T---------e to both H------s of P--r---m---t, On the Opening of the ensuing Session. To which is added, A Sketch of the Debate which will take Place in the H—e of L—ds on the Motion for an Address and Amendment. *London, Printed for the Editor*, MDCCLXXIX. 8vo, pp. 57. 1685

Anticipation: (For the Year MDCCLXXIX.) Containing the Substance of His M——y's Most Gracious Speech to both H----e of P----l-----t, on the Opening of the approaching Session. Together With a full and authentic Account of the Debate which will take place in the H--e of C---s on the Motion for the Address, and the Amendment. With Notes. (First published Five Days before the Opening of the Session.) The Second Edition. *London, S. Bladon*, MDCCLXXIX. 8vo, pp. viii., 51. 1686

See M. R., 1st Series, Vol. LXI., 466.

Anticipation of Marginal Notes on the Declaration of Government of The 9th of January, 1813. In the American National Intelligencer. [Motto.] *London, Printed by A. J. Valpy, Sold by Underwood*, 1813. 8vo, pp. iv., 31. H. + [Second Edition.] (In the Pamphleteer, I., pp. 487–538; II., 249–279.) H. 1687

Anticipation; or the Voyage of an American to England, in the year 1899. In a Series of Letters. *London*, 1781. 12mo. W. 1688

This curious book consists of "Letters supposed to be written towards the close of the 18th [19th] Century, by a young American, stimulated by curiosity to pay a visit to the Country of his Ancestors. The Seat of Government is transferred to America, and England is an almost deserted, depopulated nation; the condition of which, and the manners of the Inhabitants, he describes in the following Letters to his Friends in America."—*Preface.*

Anticipations of the Future, to serve as Lessons for the Present Time. In the form of Extracts of Letters from an English

Resident in the United States, to the London Times, from 1864 to 1870. With an Appendix, on the Causes and Consequences of the Independence of the South. ... *Richmond, Va., J. W. Randolph*, 1860. 12mo, pp. ix., 416. c. 1689

Antidote to the Merino-Mania, now progressing through the United States; or, The Value of the Merino Breed, placed by Observation and Experience, upon a Proper Basis. ... *Philadelphia, J. & A. Y. Humphreys*, 1810. 8vo, pp. 52. H. 1690

The Antigallican; or, The Lover of his own Country: in a Series of Pieces partly heretofore published and partly New, wherein French Influence, and False Patriotism, are fully and fairly displayed. By a Citizen of New England. *Philadelphia, William Cobbett, December*, 1797. 8vo, pp. 82. H. 1691

Antigua. A Poem addressed to a Young Lady. In Three Parts. Part I. Descriptive and Moral. II. Love and Friendship. III. The Caution. Written at Antigua. *Boston*, 1773. 8vo. 1692

Antigua and the Antiguans: a Full Account of the Colony and its Inhabitants, from the Time of the Caribs to the Present Day, Interspersed with Anecdotes and Legends. Also, an Impartial View of Slavery and the Free Labour Systems; the Statistics of the Island, and Biographical Notices of the Principal Families. ... *London, Saunders and Otley*, 1844. 2 vols., post 8vo, pp. xiv., 8, 345; viii., 355. H. 1693

An Act of Assembly, Passed in the Island of Antigua, 1766. [Royal Arms.] *Antigua, Printed (by order of the Council ana Assembly of the said Island), by Alexander Shipton.* Folio, pp. (xiii.), 83. 1694

A handsomely printed book. The act is one ordaining the various courts, regulating forms of procedure, &c.

Acts of Assembly, passed in the Island of Antigua, from 1725 to 1760. *London*, 1764. Folio, pp. 141. 1695

The Case of the Neglected and Deserted Negroes in the Island of Antigua. *W. Phillips, Lombard Street* [n. d.] 4to.

Collection of Exotics from the Island of Antigua. By a Lady. *London, White*, 1800. Folio. Colored Plates. 1697

See M. R., New Series, Vol. XXX., 333.

Immigration (Antigua) ... Correspondence between the Secretary of State for the Colonies and the Legislature of Antigua, relating to an Act passed by them for the purpose of Immigration. ... Ordered by the House of Commons to be printed, 20 April, 1863. Folio, pp. 13. P. 1697*a*

A Genuine Narrative of the intended Conspiracy of the Negroes at Antigua. Extracted from an authentic copy of a Report made to the Chief Governor of the Carabee Islands, By the Commissioners appointed to try the Conspirators. *Dublin*, 1737. Sm. 8vo. 1698

Laws of Antigua, consisting of the Acts of the Leeward Islands from November 1690 to April 1798; and the Acts of Antigua from April 1668 to May 1804; with Analytical Tables of the Acts and an Index. *London*, 1805–18. 3 vols., 4to.

ANTILLES. Derrotero de las islas Antillas, de las costas de tierra firme y de las del seno mexicano, formado en la Direccion de trabajos hidrográficos para inteligencia y uso de las cartas que ha publicado. De órden superior. *Madrid, en la imprenta real*, 1810. 4to, pp. viii., 455. + Segunda edicion, corregida y aumentada con noticias muy recientes y con un Apendice sobre las corrientes del Oceano Atlantico. *Madrid*, 1820. 4to, pp. 591. H. 7000

Histoire et commerce des Antilles. *See* [Butel-Dumont (G. M.)]

Routier des Iles Antilles, des côtes de terre-ferme et de celles du Golfe du Mexique. Troisième édition. Traduit de l'Espagnol par C. F. Chauchéprat. (Supplément. Sur les courans de l'océan Atlantique.) *Paris*, 1829. 8vo. BM. 1701

Souvenirs des Antilles. *See* Montlezun.

ANTILLON (Is.) Dissertacion sobre el origen de la esclavitud de los Negros. *Mallorca*, 1811. 12mo. 1702

Anti-Masonic and Anti-Masonry. *See* Masonry.

Anti-Ministerial | Objections Considered, | or The Unreasonable Pleas | Made by some against their Duty | to their | Ministers, | With Respect to their Maintenance | Answered. | Together | With an Answer to that Question, | Who are Oblig'd to Endeavour a Reformation | In this Case? | In a Letter to Richard Kent, Esq; one | of His Majesty's Justices of the Peace | for the County of Essex, and a Mem- | ber of the Honourable House of | Representatives. | [Mottoes.] *Boston, N. E.* | *Printed by B. Green, Jun. for Samuel* | *Gerrish, at his Shop in Corn-Hill.* | 1725. | Sm. 8vo, Title, pp. 45. H. 1703

Antinomians and Familists condemned. *See* [Welde (Thomas)].

Antioch College. [Its Parentage, Organization, Finances, Claims on Unitarians, etc. n. p., 18–.] 8vo, pp. 4. H. 1704

Antioch College. [Faculty, Requisites for Admission, Terms, &c. n. p., 1853.] 16mo, pp. 16. H. 1705

Appeal in Behalf of Antioch College, with a Statement of its Financial History, Condition, and Prospects. New-York, November, 1858. *New-York, John A. Gray, Printer*, 1858. 12mo, pp. 12. H. 1706

Catalogue ... for the Academical Years, 1853–4 & 1854–5. ... *Cincinnati, Printed by C. F. Bradley & Co.*, 1855. 8vo, pp. 55. Continued. H. 1707

ANTI-PATER. Den | Portugaelsen Donder-slagh, | Tot | Ontwakinge van alle trou- | hertighe Neder-landtsche Regenten ende | Ondersaten. | Om de Balance vanden Gheunieerden Staet | wel te maken, tot voor-cominghe van alle onheyl, | en bevestinghe van onse groot-beroemde | Republijcke. | Door Theophilus Anti-Pater. | *Tot Groeningen, By de Erffghenamen van Nathanael* | *Roman, Anno* 1641. | 4to, 2 p. l., pp. 36. 1708

Relates to the truce between Holland and Portugal concerning the Brazils.

Antiquitates Americanæ. *See* [Rafn (C. C.)]

Antiquités Mexicaines. *See* Lenoir (Alexandre).

The Antiquarian and General Review, edited by Wm. Arthur. Vol. I. *Schenectady*, 1845. 8vo. 1709

Antiquarian, *pseudon.* *See* [Phillips (Henry), *Jr.*]

Proceedings of the Anti-Sabbath Convention, held in the Melodeon, March 23d and 24th, 1848. (Reported by Henry M. Parkhurst.) *Boston, Published by order of the Convention*, 1848. 12mo, pp. 168. + 36mo, pp. 18. H. 1710

Catalogue of the Anti-Secret Confederation, 1847. ... *Troy, N. Y., Press of J. C. Kneeland and Co.*, 1847. 8vo, pp. 32. H.

Anti-Slavery. *See* Slavery.

ANTISELL (Th.) Geology of Southern California. By Thomas Antisell. With Report on the Palaeontology by T. A. Conrad. *Washington*, 1856. 4to, pp. 204. 2 Maps and 24 Plates.

Anti-Synodalia Americana. *See* [Chauncy (Charles)].

The Antithelemite. *See* [Maurice (Henry)].

ANTOINE (A.) Histoire des émigrés français depuis 1789 jusqu' en 1828. Par A. Antoine de Saint Jervais. *Paris, Hivert*, 1828. 3 vols., 8vo. 1713

In this and later works, Antoine added "de Saint-Jervais" to his name. Some of the Émigrés came to America.

ANTONET (C. M.) Sylvino et Anina, mœurs brésiliennes. Par C. M. Antonet. *Paris, Magen et Comon*, 1840. 8vo. 1714

ANTONII (Andre Joao). Cultura e opulencio do Brasil, por suas drogas e minas. Con varios noticias curiosas do modo de haser o assucar, plantar e beneficiar o tabaco, tirar ouro das minas, e descobrir as da prata; e dos grandes emolumentos que esta conquista da America meridional dá ao Reino de Portugal con estes e outros generos e contractos reaes. *Lisboa*, 1711. 4to. + *Reprinted, Rio de Janeiro*, 1841. 8vo. 1715

Quoted by Handelmann in his "Geschichte von Brasilien," *Berlin*, 1860.

ANTONIO (Joseph). Theatro Americano Descripcion General de los Reynos y Provincias de la Nueva Espana y sus jurisdicciones. *Mexico*, 1746. 2 vols., folio. Plate. 1716

ANTONIO (Nicolas). Bibliotheca Hispana Vetus, complectens Scriptores qui ab Octaviani Augusti Imperio, usque ad annum M. floruerunt, studio et curis Josephi Saenz, Cardinalis de Aguirre. *Romæ*, 1696, 2 vols., folio. 1717

The title-page contains a misprint. As the work comprises the authors until the year 1500, the title ought to read, "usque ad annum MD" (1500), instead of M (1000). Antonio died without the means for printing the book. They were furnished by the Cardinal de Aguirre, who intrusted the editorship to Emmanuel Mars, a learned Valentian. The authors are arranged in chronological order; tables are added to facilitate the use of the work. The "Bibliotheca Nova," although published first, is but a sequel of the "Bibliotheca Vetus," of which a reprint likewise has appeared at Madrid, in 1788, under this title:

ANTONIO. Bibliotheca Hispana vetus, sive Hispani Scriptores qui ab Octaviani Augusti Ævo ad annum Christi MD. floruerunt. Auctore D. Nicolao Antonio Hispalensi I.C. Ordinis S. Jacobi equite, patriæ Ecclesiæ canonico, regiorum negotiorum in Urbe & Romana curia Procuratore generali, Consiliario regio. Curante Francisco Perezio Bayerio, Valentino, Sereniss. Hisp. Infantum Caroli III. Regis filiorum Institutore primario, Regiæ Bibliothecæ Palatino-Matritensis Præfecto, qui Et prologum, & Auctoris vitæ epitomen, & notulas adiecit. ... *Matriti, apud Viduam et Heredes D. Joachimi Ibarræ*, MDCCLXXXVIII. 2 vols., folio, pp. xxvii., 556, viii.; xxii., 467. 2 Portraits and Plate. Also on Large Paper. H. 1718

ANTONIO. Bibliotheca Hispana sive Hispanorvm, qvi vsqvam vnqvamve sive Latinâ sive populari sive aliâ quâvis linguâ scripto aliquid consignaverunt Notitia, his qvæ præcesservnt locvpletior et certior brevia elogia, editorum atque ineditorum operum catalogum dvabvs partibvs continens, qvarvm haec ordine qvidem rei posterior, conceptu verò prior duobis tomis de his agit, qvi post annvm secvlarem MD. usque ad præsentem diem floruere. ... Avthore D. Nicolao Antonio Hispalensi, I.C. Ordinis S. Iacobi Eqvite, Patriæ Ecclesiæ Canonico, Regiorum negotiorum in Vrbe & Romana Curia Procuratore generali. *Romæ ex Officina Nicolao Angeli Tinassii*, MDCLXXII. *Svperiorvm Permissv.* Folio, Engraved Frontispiece and 40 p. l., pp. 633; Vol. II., Engraved Frontispiece, pp. 690. 1719

"Nicolas Antonio was born in 1617, at Sevilla, studied at Salamanca, and returned to Sevilla, composed his Bibliotheca Hispana in the convent of the Benedictines, where the abbot, Benedict de La Serra, had accumulated a splendid library. When it was sufficiently advanced, he took it to Rome, where he completed it. He died at Madrid, in 1684. Antonio, agreeable to the custom prevalent at that time, arranged the names of the authors according to the alphabetical order of their Christian names. This is a great inconvenience, which is only partially removed by the addition of a number of tables." Dibdin, in his "Bibliomania," calls the labors of Antonio models of composition in their way. Morhof considers it one of the best works of the kind. A new edition was published at Madrid, by Franc. Perez Bayer, a learned Valentian; the title of which is,

ANTONIO. Bibliotheca Hispana nova sive Hispanorum Scriptorum qui ab Anno MD. ad MDCLXXXIV. floruere Notitia. Auctore D. Nicolao Antonio Hispalensi I.C. Ordinis S. Iacobi equite, patriæ Ecclesiæ canonico, Regiorum negotiorum in Urbe & Romana curia procuratore generali, consiliario Regio. Nunc primum prodit, recognita emendata aucta ab ipso Auctore. ... *Matriti, apud Joachimum de Ibarra*, MDCCLXXXIII–VIII. 2 vols., folio, 5 p. l., pp. xxiii., 830; 669 (1). Also on Large Paper. H.

A[NTROBUS] (B[enjamin]). Some Buds and Blossoms of Piety, also, some Fruit of the Spirit of Love which directs to the Divine Wisdom. *London, Andrew Sowle*, 1684. 4to, pp. 80. + Second Edition, with Additions. *London, for Th. Northcott*, 1691. 8vo, 3 p. l., pp. 128. + *London, Assigns of J. Sowle*, 1716. 8vo. + *London, T. Sowle Raylton, and L. Hinde*, 1743. 8vo. + 5th Edition. *London, Luke Hinde*, 1766. 8vo. 1721

Includes "A Complaint against New England Professors." "Bibl. Anglo-Poetica," No. 897. Priced, £1 5s. The author was a Quaker.

The Ants. A Rhapsody. 1767. 2 vols., 12mo. 1722

"A burlesque on the [French] American War."—CHALMERS.

[ANTONY (Henry B.)] The Fancy Ball. A Sketch. Printed for private circulation. Pulaski House, Savannah, March 31st. [*Savannah, W. T. Williams*], 1837. 8vo, pp. 12. H. 1723

In a copy in Harvard College Library the names are supplied in MS.

ANTUNEZ Y ACEVEDO (R.) Memorias históricas sobre la legislacion y gobierno del comercio de los Españoles con sus colonias en las Indias Occidentales. Recopiladas por el Sr. D. Rafael Antunez y Acevedo, Ministro togado del Supremo Consejo de Indias. *Madrid, En la imprenta de Sancha*, M.DCC.XCVII. Sm. 4to, 2 p. l., pp. xv. (1), 330 (2), cv. H. 1724

ANUNCIACION (*Fr.* Dominga de la). Doctrina Christiana en Castellano y Mexicano, su autor el P. Fr. Domingo de la Annunciation Dominico. *Mexico*, 1565. 4to. 1725

Title from Ternaux-Compans, No. 93.

Anunciation (*Fr.* J. de la). Sermonario en lengua Mexicana. *Mexico*, 1577. 4to. 1726

APALACHICOLA. Annual Report of the Apalachicola Land Company for the year 1838. *New York*, 1838. 8vo. Continued. 1727

APARICIO. Epilogo metrico de la vida de fray Sebastian de Aparicio, con un compuesto de aromas espirituales. *Pueblo da los Angelos*, 1689. 4to. 1728

Title as given by Ternaux-Compans, No. 1035.

Apéndice a la Relacion del Viage al Magallanes de la Fragata de Guerra Santa Maria de la Cabeza, que contiene el de los paquebotes Santa Casilda y Santa Eulalia para completar el reconocimiento del estrecho en los años de 1788 y 1789. Trabajado de Orden Superior. *Madrid*, MDCCLXXXIII. *En la imprenta de la Viuda de D. Joaquin Ibarra.* 4to, 2. p. l., pp. 128. Map. H. 1729

Aperçu de la situation. *See* [Poletika (Pierre)].

Aperçu des dernières Révolutions de la République des Provinces unies de Sud-Amérique. *Paris*, 1820. 8vo, pp. 48. 1730

Aperçu des États-Unis, au Commencement du XIX Siècle, depuis 1800 jusqu'en 1810. *Paris*, 1814. 8vo. Map. 1731

Aperçu sur le chemin de fer de Galveston à Houston en vue de la prochaine réunion des porteurs d'obligations.—Kort overzigt omtrent den ijzeren spoorweg van Galveston naar Houston en Henderson, in verband tot de aanstaande vereeniging der aandeelhouders. *Amsterdam, Weytingh & Brave*, 1862. 8vo, pp. 12, 12. 1732

Title from the *Alphabetische Naamlijst*, etc. It does not appear whether the French and Dutch have separate title-pages.

Apperçu hazardé. *See* [Estaing (C. B., *Count* d')].

APES. A Son of the Forest. The Experience of William Apes, a Native of the Forest. Comprising a Notice of the Pequod Tribe of Indians, Written by Himself. *New York, Published by the Author*, 1829. 18mo, pp. 216. H. + Second Edition. *New York, G. F. Bunce*, 1831. 18mo, pp. 214.

APES. Eulogy on King Philip, as pronounced at the Odeon, in Federal Street, Boston, by the Rev. William Apes, an Indian. ... *Boston, the Author*, 1836. 8vo, pp. 60. Woodcut. + Second Edition. *Boston*, 1837. 8vo, pp. 48. Woodcut. H. 1734

In the second edition the author spells his name "Apess." *See* also No. 1738.

APES. The Increase of the Kingdom of Christ, a Sermon: by William Apes, a Missionary of the Pequod Tribe of Indians. *New York, Printed for the Author by G. F. Bunce*, 1831. 12mo, pp. 24. H. 1735

"The Indians, the Ten Lost Tribes," pp. 21–24.

APES. Indian Nullification of the Unconstitutional Laws of Massachusetts, relative to the Marshpee Tribe: or, The Pretended Riot explained. By William Apes, an Indian and Preacher of the Gospel. *Boston, Press of Jonathan Howe*, 1835. 12mo, pp. 168. Woodcut. G. 1736

The real author of this work is said to be William J. Snelling.

APESS. Experience of Five Christian Indians of the Pequod Tribe. Published by William Apess, Missionary of that Tribe ... . *Boston, Printed for the Publisher*, 1837. 12mo, pp. 47. + Second Edition. *Boston*, 1837. 12mo, pp. 47. 1737

APIANUS (Peter). Cosmogra | phicus Liber Petri Apiani Ma- | thematici studiose collectus. | [Colophon] Excusum Landshutae Typis ac formulis | D. Joannis Weyssenburgers: impensis | Petri Apiani. Anno Christi Sal- | uatoris omnium Millesimo | | quingentesimo | vicesimo- | quarto | Mense Ja- | nu: Phebo Sa | turni domi- | cilium | possidente. | 1524. 4to, Title, 1 l., 5 p. l., pp. 103. Two Revolving Diagrams. 1738

Bienewitz is the German name for which Apianus was used as the Latin equivalent. *See* Bib. Am. Vet., p. 238 seq. Brunet, p. 342. Chapter IV. relates to America; also pages 103, 104. For an account of the author, *see* Clement, I., 404.

APIANUS. Cosmographicus Liber Petri Apiani Mathematici, studiose correctus, ac ab erroribus vindicatus per Gemmam Phrysium. Veneunt Antuerpiae in aedibus Rolandi Bollaert. [Colophon] Excusum Antuerpiae impensis Rolandi Bollaert, Typis Joannis Graphei, Anno a Christo nato 1529. mense Febr., in 4to, Feuilles 56. BM. 1739

Title from Clement. Second edition, with the valuable additions of Gemma Frisius, the pupil of Apianus.

APIANUS. Cosmo- | graphiae introdvctio: cvm | quibusdam Geometriæ ac Astronomiæ prin- | cipijs ad eam rem necessarijs. | Excvsm Ingoldstadii. | M.D.XXIX. | [Colophon] Ingolstadij, Anno M.D.XXXI. | 12mo, 32 l., numbered to 16, after which the enumeration ceases. 1740

APIANUS. [Editio Altera; Colophon] Excusum Iogolstadij [*sic*] | An. M.D.XXXIII. | Mense Ianuario. | 12mo, 32 l. L. 1741

"Title, one leaf + leaves numbered from 2–16 + five unnumb. ll. marked *c*, *c ij*, *c* 3, *c* 4, *c* 5, + three ll. unnumbered and without signatures + five unnumb. ll. marked *d*, *d* 2, *d* 3, *d* 4, *d* 5, + three unnumb. ll. without sig. + five ll. marked *e*, *e* 2, *e* 3, *e* 4, *e* 5 + three ll. without sig., verso of the last of which is blank."—*Bib. Am. Vet.*

APIANUS. Cosmographi- | cvs Liber Petri Apiani Ma- | thematici, iam denuo integritati restitutus | per Gemmam Phrysium. | Item eiusdem Gemmæ Phrysii Libellus de Locorum de- | scribendorum ratione, & de eorum distantiis in- | ueniendis, nunq' antehac visus. | Væneût Antuerpie sub scuto Basiliêsi p' Gregoriû Bontiû. | [Colophon] Ioan. Grapheus typis cudebat Antuerpiæ, | Anno M.D.XXXIII. | mense Febr. | 4to, 66 l. + *Paris*, 1533. 4to. + *Frib. Brisg.*, 1533. 4to. 1742

APIANUS. Cosmo | graphiæ Introdvctio | cum quibusdam Geometriæ ac Astro- | nomiæ principijs ad eam | rem necessarijs. | [Colophon] *Venetijs per Io. Antonium de Nicolinis de Sabio, sumptu & requisitione D. Melchioris | Sessæ. Anno Domini.* | MDXXXV. *Mensis Ianuarij.* | Sm. 8vo, 32 l. 1743

APIANUS. Petri Apiani | Cosmographia, per Gemmam | Phrysium, apud Louanienses Medicum ac Mathema- | ticum insignem, restituta. Additis de adem re ipsius | Gemmæ Phry. libellis, vt sequens pagina docet. | *Væneunt Antuerpiæ in pingui gallina Arnoldo Berckmâno.* | I.5.3.9. | [Colophon] Absolutum Antuerpiae per Aegidium Coppenium, | cura & impensis Arnoldi Berckman, | Anno Christiano. 1539. | 4to, pp. 61, 1 l. 1744

APIANUS. Petri Apiani | Cosmographia, per Gemmam | Phrysium, apud Louanienses Medicum ac Mathematicarum | insignem, Denuo restituta. Additis de eadem re ipsius | Gemmæ Phry. libellis, quos sequens pagina docet. | M.D.XL. | *Væneunt Antuerpiæ in pingui gallina Arnoldo Berkmâno.* | [Colophon] *Excusum Antuerpiæ opera Aegidij Copenij.* | *Anno à Christo nato.* 1540. | 4to, 61 leaves. Map. 1745

APIANUS. Cosmogra- | phiae Introdvctio | cvm qvibsdam Geome- | triae ac Astrono- | miæ principiis | ad eam rem | necessa- | riis. | [Colophon] *Venetijs per Io. Antonium de Nicolinis de Sabio. Sumptu & | requisitione D. Melchioris Sessæ. Anno Domini.* | MDXXXXI. *Mensis Iulij.* | Sm. 4to, Title, 1 l., and 23 l. 1746

Melchior's device of a cat holding a mouse on the verso of the last leaf.

APIANUS. Cosmographia per Gemmam Frisium correcta. Norimb. 1541. 4to. 1747

APIANUS. Cosmographia | Petri Apiani, per Gemmam Frisivm | apud Louanienses Medicum & Mathematicum, insignem, | iam demum ab omnibus vindicata mendis, ac non- | nullis quoque locis aucta. Additis eiusdem argu- | menti libellis ipsius Gemmæ Frisii. | M.D.XLV. | *Væneunt Antuerpiæ sub scuto Basiliensi, Gregorio Bontio.* | [Colophon] *Excusum Antuerpiæ, opera Aeg. Diesthemij.* | *Anno à Christo humanæ salutis | Authore nato,* | .1545. | 4to, Title and 1 l.; Text, 66 l. J. C. B. 1748

APIANUS. Cosmographia | Petri Apiani, per Gemmam Frisivm | apud Louaniensis Medicum & Mathematicum insignem, | iam demum ab omnibus vindicata mendis, ac non- | nullis quoque locis

aucta. Additis eiusdem ar- | gumenti libellis ipsius Gemmæ Frisij. | *Væneunt Antuerpiæ sub scuto Basiliensi, Gregorio Bontio.* | M.D.L. | [Colophon] *Antuerpiæ excusum Gregorio Bontio | typis Deisthemij, anno à Christo* 1550. | Sm. 4to, 2 p. l., 64 l. (2 l.) Map. J. C. B. 1749

Graesse quotes an edition, *Basil*, 1550, 4to, which is probably an error. There are other Latin editions, Paris, 1551, 1553, and Antwerp, 1564.

APIANUS. Cosmographia | Petri Apiani, per Gemmam Fri- | sivm apvd Lovanienses Medicvm et Mathe | maticvm insignem, iam demvm ab omnibvs vindi- | cata mendis, ac nonnullis quoque locis aucta, & annotationi- | bus marginalibus illustrata. Additis eiusdem argumen- | ti libellis ipsius Gemmæ Frisij. | *Coloniæ Agrippinae,* | *Apud Hæredes Arnoldi Birckmanni.* cIↄ Iↄ LXXIV. 4to, 2 p. l. and 58 folioed leaves. 1750

APIANUS. Cosmographia, | sive | Descriptio | Vniversi Orbis, | avctoribvs | Petro Apiano, et Gemma Frisio, | Mathematicorvm Insignivm. | Cuius huic editioni additus est de Astrolabo Catholico libellus, | nunc primum à Martino Euerartho in Epitomen contractus. | Cætera vide pagina quinta. | *Antverpiae,* | *Ex officina Arnoldi Coninx.* | M.D.LXXXIIII. | 4to, 8 p. l.; Text, 480 pp. Map.

The map forms pages 73–81. Clement pronounces this the best edition.

APIANUS. La Cosmographie de Pierre | Apian, libure tresutile traictant de toutes les regions & pays | du monde par artifice Astronomicque, nouuellement traduict | de Latin en François. Et par Gemma Frison Mathema- | ticien & Docteur en Medicine de Louuain corrige. | Auecq aultres libures du mesme Gemma Fr. appartenantz | audict artifice, côme la page ensuyuante la declaire. | M.D.XLIIII. | On les vend en Anuers sur le pont de chambre chez Gregoire Bonte | a l'escu de Basle, imprimez en Latin, François, & Flameng. | [Colophon] Absolut est cest œuure Cosmographicque de Peere Apian, auecq aul | tres liures de la mesme science, Aux despens communs de Gemma | Frison, & Gregoire Bonte. Imprimes en Anuers | par Gillis de Diest, au moys Daoust. | .1544. | 4to, LXV. leaves. 1752

Another French edition, *Paris*, 1533, and *Anvers*, 1581. 4to.

APIANUS. Libro dela | Cosmographia | De Pedro Apiano, el qual trata la descripcion del Mun- | do, y sus partes, por muy claro y lindo artificio augmêta- | do por el doctissimo varon Gemma Frisio, doctor en Me | decina, y Mathematico excellentissimo: con otros | dos libros del dicho Gemma, de la Materia mesma. |

Agora nueuamête traduzidos en Româce Castellano. | M.D.XLVIII. | *Vendese en Enveres en casa de Gregorio Bontio enel | escudo de Basilea. Cum Gratia & Priuilegio.* | Sm. 4to, 2 p. l., 68 l.; Table, 2 l. Map. 1753

APIANUS. Cosmographie, | oft Beschrijuinghe der gheheelder Werelt van | Petrus Apianus, derde werf ghecorrigeert van | Gemma Frisio Mathematicien ende Doctoor in | Medicinen. Metten zeecompasse ende anderen | boecxkens by den seluen Gemma daer toegedaen. | M.D.LXI. *Men vercooptse Tantwerpen inden witten valck by Jan Verwithaghen.* | 4to, 76 l. 1754

APIANUS. Cosmographie. | Ofte beschrijvinge der ghe- | heelder Werelt, begrijpende de gelegentheyt | ende bedeelinghe van elck Landtschap ende contreye | der selver, gheschreven in Latijn door Petrus Apianus. | Gecorrigeert ende vermeerdert door M. Gamma Frisius, excellent | Geographijn ende Mathematicijn, met sommighe andere tractaten van | de selve materie, ghemaect van den voorseyden Gamma, ende hier | by gevoeght, waer af d'inhout staet in't navolgende bladt. | *Tot Amstelredam,* | *By Cornelis Claesz. Boecvercooper, woonende op't Water* | *in't Schrijf-boeck. Anno* 1609. | 4to, 6 p. l., 121 (2) l. 1755

Another edition, *Antwerp*, 1592.

APIANUS. La Cosmographia de Pedro Apiano, corregida y añadida por Gemma Frisio, Medico y Mathematico. ... El Sitio y Descripcion delas Indias y Mundo Nueuo, sacada dela Historia de Francisco Lopez de Gomara, y dela Cosmographia de Ieronymo Giraua Tarragonez. *Anvers, Juan Bellero,* M.D.LXXV. 4to, ff. (2), 68 (14). H. 1756

APIANUS. Introductio Geographica in Verneri Annotationes. Adjuncta est Espitola J. de Regiomonte. *Ingolstadii,* 1533. Folio. A. 1757

[APLIN (John)]. Address to the People of New England; occasioned by the preaching and Publishing of Certain Doctrines, destructive of their Rights and Liberties, both Religious and Civil (by James Macsparran), in a sermon entituled The Sacred Dignity of the Christian Priesthood Vindicated. By a Native of New England. *Newport,* 1753. 8vo, pp. 31. 1758

L'Apocalypse Britannique. *Paris,* 1782. 8vo. 1759

A scarce tract relating to the American Revolution.

APOLLINARIO DA CONCEIÇAO (*Fr.*) Ecco sonoro da clamorosa

voz que deu a cidade do Rio de Janeiro ... na saudosa despedida do irmao Fr. Fabiao de Christo, enfermeiro do convento de S. Antonio da mesma cidade. *Lisboa, por Ignacio Rodrigues,* 1748. 4to. 1759*a*

APOLLINARIO DA CONCEIÇAO (*Fr.*) Primasia serafica na regiao da America. Novo descobrimento de sanctos e veneraveis religiosos de Ordem serafico que ennobrecem o novo mundo com suas virtudes e acçoes Esento par Fr. Apollinario da Conceiçao chronista da provincia de Conceiçao de Rio de Janeiro. *Lisboa Occidental, na officina de Antonio de Sousa da Silva,* 1733. 4to, pp. xxxii., 366. 1759*b*

Transactions of the Apollo Association for the Promotion of the Fine Arts in the United States, at the First Annual Meeting, December 16th, 1839. *New York,* 1839. 8vo, pp. 24. Continued. H. 1760

The last report appeared in 1843, when the Association became "The American Art Union."

APOLLONIUS. Levini Apol- | lonii, Gandobrv- | gani, Mittelbvrgensis, | de Peruuiæ, Regionis, inter Noui Orbis prouincias, celeberrimæ, inuentione: & rebus in | eadem gestis, | libri V. | Ad Iacobvm Clarovtivm Mal- | deghemmæ ac Pitte- | miæ Dominvm. | Breuis, exactaq'ue Noui Orbis, & Peruuiæ | regionis chorographia. | *Antverpiæ,* | *Apud Ioannem Bellerum* ·*sub* | *Aquila aurea.* | M.D.LXVI. | [Colophon] *Antverpiæ,* | *Typis Amati Ta-* | *vernerii.* | 8vo, 236 l.; Index, 7 l.; Colophon, 1 l. Map. H. 1761

Priced, in the Nuggets, £3 13s. 6d.; Raetzel, 10 fr.; Eyriès, 19 fr. Also issued with a new title-page, 1567. Rich (No. 44) and Ternaux (No. 97) quote an edition 1565, which is an error.

APOLLONIUS. De Navigatione Gallorum in terram Floridam, deque clade anno 1565 ab Hispanis accepta. *Antuerpiæ,* 1568. Sm. 8vo. 1761*a*

A rare volume. *See* Camus, p. 45. Boucher quotes the title incorrectly as to the date, and then enters into an argument to show that the date should be 1568. Perhaps some copies read anno 1555.

APOLLONIUS. Dritte Theil der Newen Welt des Peruanischen Königreichs, welches das Mechtigste vnd Fruchtbareste ist, vnder allen andern Landtschafften oder Provintzen des Indianischen Nidergängischen Reichs ... . Item von dem Frantzosen Schiffarth in die Landschafft Floridam, vnd jhrer schröcklichen Niderlag im Jar 1565. Aus dem Latein verteutschet durch Nic. Höninger. *Basel,* 1583. Folio. 1762

APOLLONIUS. Dritte Theil | der Newen Welt | Des Peru- | uischen Königreichs, welches das | Mechtigste und Fruchtbareste ist, vnder allen anderen Landte- | schafften oder Prouintzen des Indianischen Nidergängischen Reichs: | wie vnd durch welche Personen dasselbig zum ersten erfunden, vnd was sich | von der ersten Erfindung an, bisz auff vnsere jetzige zeit, für schröckliche Krieg | vnd Blutuergiessungen, eyns thiels gegen den Peruuischen Einwohnern, an- | der theils zwischen den Spanischen Landtpflägern vnd Vögten, allein von | wegen Ehrgeytzes vnd Eygennutzes verloffen vnd zugetragen haben. Auch | von derselbigê Völckern Sitten, Regiment, Aberglauben, Ceremonien, Got- | tesdienst, Gebräuch in Essen vnd Trincken, Handthierungen, Ge- | werbschafften vnd vnerschöpfflichen Goldtgruben | vnd Reichthumben, so in diesem Kö- | nigreich gefunden werden. | Item, | Von der Frantzosen Schiffarth in die Landtschafft | Floridam, vnd jhrer schröcklichen Niderlag die sie von den Spa- | niern im Jar M.D.LXV. darinn erlitten. Mit angehenckter | Supplication an König Carol den IX. in Franckreich, der Erschlagnen Frantzosen | Witwen, Waysen, Verwandten vnd Einwohnern in der Landtschafft Florida, | darinn sie jhr Vnschuld gegen den Spaniern vor Königlicher | May. gründtlich erkläret vnd geoffenbaret. | Alles | Durch Glaubwürdige Personen, vnd fürnemblich durch den Hoch- | berhümbten Geschichtschreiber Levinvm Appollonivm Gandobrv- | ganvm, in Lateinischer Sprach wahrhafftig beschrieben, und zum theil | selbs Persönlich erfahren. | Erst jetz aber | Ausz dem Latein, zu Nutz allen Regenten vnd Oberherren, Ehrgeytz vnd | Eygennutz zuuermeiden: Auch Liebhabern der Historien, mit höchstem | Fleisz vnd Mühe verteutschet, | Durch | Nicolaum Höniger von Tauber Königshofen. | Getruckt zu Basel. | [Colophon] *Getruckt,* | *zu Basel, Durch Sebastian Henricpetri,* | *im Jar nach Vnser Erlösung,* | M.D.LXXXIII. | *im Hertzen.* | Folio, 6 p. l., pp. 306; Colophon, 1 l. 1762*a*

An Apology. The Protestant Episcopal Society for the Promotion of Evangelical Knowledge: its Origin, Constitution, Tendencies, and Work; submitted to the Impartial Judgment of the Members of the Protestant Episcopal Church. [By C. C. Andrews, D.D.] *New-York, Printed by John A. Gray,* 1854. 8vo, pp. 44. H. 1763

An Apology for Great Britain, in allusion to a pamphlet, intituled "Considerations, &c., par un Canadien, M.P.P." *Quebec,* 1809. 8vo, pp. 31. 1764

Ascribed to Ross Cuthbert, Esq.

An Apology for the Builder; or, a Discourse shewing the Cause and Effects of the Increase of Building. *London, Printed in the Year* MDCLXXXIX. 4to, 37 pp. N. 1765

Includes several references to America. Stevens's Nuggets, No. 132, contains a curious extract.

An Apology for the Times; a Poem addressed to the King. *London,* 1778. 4to. 1766

An Apology for the United States of America. *Liverpool, Published by Melling and Co.,* 1829. 8vo, pp. 16. N. 1767

Apostolicos afanes de la Compañia de Jesus, escritos por un padre de la misma sagrada religion de su provincia de Mexico ["que saca à publica luz Francisco Xavier Fluviá"]. *Barcelona, Pablo Nadel Impressor,* 1754. 4to, 6 p. l., pp. 452, 5 l. H. 1768

An Appeal for a union of Parties on the principles of Washington, Jefferson, Madison and Munroe, By a Republican of 1800. 1850. 8vo. 1769

Appeal for Rectitude in Politics. *See* [Wright (Charles)].

An Appeal for the Union, By a Philadelphia Whig. [*Philadelphia,* 1856.] 8vo, pp. 16. 1770

In favor of Buchanan. First published in the Philadelphia *Evening Journal.*

Appeal from a Countryman. *See* [Howe (R. H.)]

An Appeal from the Twenty eight Judges to the Spirit of Truth and True Judgment in all Faithful Friends, called Quakers, that meet at this Yearly meeting at Burlington the Seventh month 1692. [By George Keith. *Philadelphia,* 1692.] 4to.

Printed by William Bradford, for which he was imprisoned upon the charge of "*uttering and spreading a malicious and seditious paper;*" and this was the beginning of the persecution which drove him from Philadelphia to New York.

The Appeal of Civilization and Liberty in behalf of the Mechanic. [*Washington? Towers, Printer,* 1863?] 8vo, pp. 7. H. 1772

On the required hours of labor of the government printers.

The Appeal of the Religious Society of Friends in Pennsylvania, New Jersey, Delaware, etc., to their Fellow-Citizens of the United States, on behalf of the Colored Races. *Philadelphia, Friends' Bookstore,* 1859. 8vo, pp. 48. P. 1773

An Appeal to Banks. *See* [Brewster (Abel)].

An Appeal to Congress and to the People of the United States ... On the Financial Condition of the Country ... the ... Policy of the Secretary of the Treasury and the Speech of the Hon. Henry G. Stebbins. [*New York,* 1864.] 8vo, pp. 12. H. 1774

An Appeal to Honest Inquirers. *Auburn, Printed by Wm. J. Moses,* 1855. 8vo, pp. 13. H. 1775

Contains an account of the causes which led to the separations within the limits of the New York and New England yearly meetings of Friends.

Appeal to Knowledge, or Candid Discussion of the Preliminaries of Peace, signed at Fontainebleau and laid before both Houses of Parliament. 1763. 8vo. 1776

An Appeal to Reason and Justice, in Behalf of the British Constitution, and the Subjects of the British Empire. In which the present important Contest with the Revolted Colonies is impartially considered, the Inconsistency of Modern Patriotism is demonstrated, the Supremacy of Parliament is asserted on Revolution Principles, and American Independence is proved to be a manifest Violation of the Rights of British Subjects. To which is added, An Appendix, containing Remarks on a Pamphlet intitled, Thoughts on the Present State of Affairs with America, by William Pulteney, Esq. [Motto.] *London, W. Nicoll,* MDCCLXXVIII. 8vo, Half Title, Title, pp. 176. 1777

"The writer of this elaborate appeal traverses again the beaten ground of this exhausted controversy, in order to demonstrate the injustice and ingratitude of the *rebellious* Americans toward their very loving and indulgent parent. He was not probably aware that the *pamphlet* on which he animadverts has generally been considered a ministerial production, and the harbinger of conciliatory proposals."—M. R., LIX., p. 150.

Appeal to the British Nation on the Affairs of South America, particularly as regards New Grenada. *Printed for the Author,* 1819. 1778

An Appeal to the candour and justice of the people of England, in behalf of the West India Merchants and Planters, founded on plain facts and incontrovertible arguments. *London, J. Debrett,* 1792. 8vo, pp. xvi., 118. 1779

An Appeal to the Conservative Men of all Parties. The Presidential Question. An important question: Shall the subject of Slavery forever prevent all useful Legislation, or shall it

be settled by the doctrine of Non-Intervention? The Question fairly stated. 8vo, pp. 16. 1780

An Appeal to the Good Sense of the Democrats. *See* [Phillips (Willard)].

An Appeal to the Government and Congress of the United States, against the Depredations committed by American Privateers on the Commerce of Nations at Peace with us. By an American Citizen. *New-York,* 1819. 8vo, pp. 100. C. 1781

An Appeal To the Government of the United States, in behlf [*sic*] of the people of Louisiana and Arkansas. [n. p., 1862?] 4to, 1 page. 1782

An Appeal to the Justice and Interests of the People of Great Britain, in the Present Disputes with America. By an Old Member of Parliament. *London, J. Almon,* M DCC LXXIV. 8vo, Half Title, Title, pp. 63. + Second Edition. *London, J. Almon,* MDCCLXXV. 8vo, pp. 68. + The Third Edition. *London, J. Almon,* MDCCLXXV. 8vo, pp. 32. + The Fourth Edition, Corrected. *London, J. Almon,* M DCC LXXVI. 8vo, pp. 46. H. + *London Printed; Reprinted at Newcastle upon Tyne,* MDCCLXXVI. 8vo, pp. 72. 1783

"The author of this Appeal is an able advocate for the Colonists, not as composing distinct States, but as having, in common with British subjects, an indefeasible right to an *exclusive* disposal of their own property; after denying the *right*, he proceeds to expose the *impolicy* of raising a revenue in America against the will of the people; and this leads him to severe reprehension of the late measures, and alarming prediction of their consequences."—M. R., LI., 474. The authorship has been attributed to Arthur Lee (*see* R. H. Lee's Life of A. Lee, I., 19), also to Lord Chatham, Mr. Glover, and Dr. Franklin. A Second Appeal was published in 1775.

An Appeal to the People. *See* [Coleman (Wm.)] also [Lowell (John)].

Appeal to the People of the North. [Dated *Louisville, Ky., Jan.,* 1861. n. p. 1861.] 8vo, pp. 16. 1783*a*

Appeal to the People of the United States, By a Freeholder. *Boston,* 1831. 8vo. C. 1784

Appeal to the Public, 1774. *See* Quebec.

An Appeal to the Public in behalf of the Church of England in America. *New York,* 1767. 12mo. 1785

An Appeal to the Public for Religious Liberty against the Oppressions of the present Day. *Boston*, MDCCLXXIII. 8vo, pp. 62. 1786

An Appeal to the Sense of the People, on the Present Posture of Affairs. Wherein the Nature of the late Treaties are inquired into, and the Conduct of the M—i—y with Regard to M—n—ca, A—r—ca, &c., is considered; With Some Remarks upon the Light in which these, and other Publick affairs have been lately represented. *London, David Hookham*, MDCCLVI. 8vo, Title and pp. 54. 1787

See M. R., Vol. xv., 408.

An Appeal to the Unprejudiced, Concerning the present Discontents Occasioned by the late Convention with Spain. *London, T. Cooper*, 1739. 8vo, pp. 32. S. 1788

An Appeal to the Unprejudiced; or, a Vindication of the Measures of Government, with Respect to America. *Oxford*, 1777. 8vo. 1789

See M. R., Vol. LVI., 66.

An Appeal to Thinking Men. From the Natchez (Miss.) *Daily Courier*, 1860. 8vo. 1790

Appel des étrangers. *See* [Turmeau de la Morandière].

An Appendix containing, Abstracts of Such Parts of the Acts of Parliament relating to the Army, as concern the Colonies of North America. [Royal Arms.] *Woodbridge; Reprinted by Order of the General Assembly of the Province of New Jersey, by James Parker, Printer to the Province*, MDCCLX. Folio, pp. 64. P.

Designed as an appendix to the Laws of New Jersey, published in 1752; but when, in 1761, Vol. II. of the N. J. Laws appeared, it was substituted as an appendix to the volume, and is generally so found.

The Appendix: or, some Observations on the Expediency of the Petition of the Africans, living in Boston, &c. lately presented to the General Assembly of this Province. With the Petition. Likewise Thoughts on Slavery. With a useful extract from the Massachusetts Spy of Jan. 28, 1773, &c. By a Lover of Constitutional Liberty. *Boston* [1773]. 12mo. 1792

Appendix in answer to a Pamphlet, entitled The Constitutional Right of the Legislature of Great Britain to Tax the British Colonies in America. *Boston*, 1769. 8vo. 1792*a*

Appendix to a late Essay, on the Rights and Duties of Nations relative to Fugitives, &c. being, a Key to Universal Demonstration: discovered and illustrated in a "Supplementary" Argument. By "Our Writers." ... Fifty-sixth American Edition ... . To which is added, The Embargo, (on common sense) "taken off." By Us. [Motto.] *Boston, Printed by David Carlisle*, 1808. 8vo, pp. 32. H. 1793

An Appendix to the "Considerations on the measures carrying on with respect to the British Colonies in North America." *Philadelphia, Benj. Towne*, 1775. 8vo, pp. 19. P. 1794

An Appendix to the Impartial Statement of the controversy respecting the decision of the late Committee of Canvassers. *New York*, 1792. 8vo, pp. 22. S. 1795

An Appendix to the present State of the Nation. *See* [Grenville (G.)]

Appendix. *See* [Everett (David)], [Secker (Thomas)].

Appleton (D. & Co.) Appleton's Literary Bulletin. *New York*, 1843–46. 39 Nos. 1796

Appleton's Railway and Steam Navigation Guide. June, 1858. Continued. M. 1797

Appleton's United States Postal Guide: containing the Chief Regulations of the Post Office, and a Complete List of Post Offices throughout the United States, with other Information for the People. Published Quarterly. No. 1. *New York, Appletons*, 1863. 16mo, pp. 211. Continued. 1798

See Hall (E. H.), Hawks (F. L.), Richards (T. A.), and Williams (W.)

Appleton (Frank Parker). A Sermon on the Character of Dr. Andrew Nichols, preached in Danvers, Mass., April 3, 1853. By F. P. Appleton, ... *Boston, Printed by John Wilson & Son*, 1853. 8vo, pp. 15. H. 1799

Appleton (J. H.) Piety and Patriotism, The Demand of the Times, Sanctioned and Enjoined by Christ: A Discourse delivered before the Union Baptist Church, Jersey City, N. J., on Sabbath morning, August 24th, 1862. By J. H. Appleton. *New York, C. S. Westcott & Co.*, 1862. 12mo, pp. 28. 1800

Appleton (J.) The Missouri Compromise; or, the Extension of the Slave Power. By General James Appleton. *New-England Antislavery Tract Association, No.* 3. 12mo. 1801

Appleton (Jesse). Addresses by Rev. Jesse Appleton, D.D. late President of Bowdoin College. Delivered at the Annual Commencements, from 1808 to 1818; with a Sketch of his Character. [By Ichabod Nichols, D.D.] *Brunswick* [*Me.*], *Joseph Griffin, Printer*, 1820. 8vo, pp. xxxi., 176. H. 1802

Appleton. Discourse delivered June 20, 1813, before the Officers and Students of Bowdoin College, occasioned by the Death of Tutor Frederick Southgate, A.B. *Boston*, 1813 8vo, pp. 24. 1803

Appleton. The Immensity of God. A Sermon, delivered to the Congregational Society in Hampton, November 14, 1797; at the Dedication of their New House for Public Worship. By Jesse Appleton, A.M. Minister of the Congregational Church in Hampton. [Motto.] *Newburyport, Printed by Edmund M. Blunt*, 1797. 8vo, pp. 32. H. 1804

History of the church, pp. 26–31.

Appleton. A Sermon preached in Boston, at the Annual Election, May 25, 1814, before His Excellency Caleb Strong, Esq. Governour, His Honor William Phillips, Esq. Lieutenant Governour, the Honorable Council, and the Legislature of Massachusetts. By Jesse Appleton, DD. President of Bowdoin College. *Boston, Benjamin Russell*, 1814. 8vo, pp. 29. H. 1805

Appleton. A Sermon, delivered at Brunswick, April 13, 1815, appointed as a Day of National Thanksgiving, by the President of the United States, on account of the Peace recently established between this Country and Great Britain. By Jesse Appleton, D.D. President of Bowdoin College. *Hallowell, Printed by Ezekiel Goodale*, 1815. 8vo, pp. 24. H. 1806

Appleton. Sermon delivered at Portland, Nov. 19, 1818, at the Formation of the Maine Branch of the American Society for educating Pious Youth for the Gospel Ministry. By Jesse Appleton, D.D. *Hallowell*, 1819. 8vo, pp. 28. 1807

Appleton. Works of Jesse Appleton, embracing his Course of Theological Lectures, his Academic Addresses, and a Selection from his Sermons: with a Memoir of his Life and Character [by Prof. A. S. Packard]. *Andover*, 1837. 2 vols., 8vo. Portrait. 1808

Also, by the same, Address before the Mass. Soc. for Sup of Intemperance. *Boston*, 1816. 8vo, pp. 28, and 12mo, pp. 28. Discourse before the Portsmouth Female Asylum. *Portsmouth*, 1806. 8vo, pp. 28. Sermon at the Ordination of Reuben Nason. *Portland*, 1810. 8vo, pp. 19. Lectures and Sermons. *Brunswick*, 1822. 8vo, pp. xx., 421. Perpetuity of the Sabbath. *Portland*, 1814. 8vo, pp. 30. Sermon at Ordination of Benj. Tappan. *Augusta*, 1811. 8vo. Ordination of E. P. Bradford. *Amherst*, 1806. 8vo, pp. 32. Ordination of J. Cogswell. *Portland*, 1810. 8vo, pp. 17. Ordination of Enos Merrill. *Portland*, 1817. 8vo, pp. 28. Ordination of Asa Rand, of Gorham. 1809. Sermon before the Cumberland Society for the Suppression of Public Vices. 1816. Sermon before the Society of Bath and Vicinity for the Suppression of Public Vices. 1816.

Appleton (John, *M.D.*) "Journal de Castorland." By John Appleton. Reprinted from the Proceedings of the Massachusetts Historical Society. *Boston, Printed by John Wilson & Son*, 1864. 8vo, pp. 15. H. 1809

Appleton. Monumental Memorials of The Appleton Family. [Arms.] *Boston, Privately Printed*, mdccclxvii. 4to, ff. 30. 1810

One hundred and fifty copies printed.

Appleton. Pedigree of Appleton. By John Appleton, M.D. [n. p.], 1864. Broadside. H. 1811

Appleton (John). Oration delivered before the Democratic Republicans of Portland and Vicinity, July 4, 1838. By Hon. John Appleton. *Portland*, 1838. 8vo, pp. 16. 1812

[Appleton (Nathan)]. An Examination of the Banking System of Massachusetts, in reference to the Renewal of the Bank Charters. *Boston, Stimpson and Clapp*, 1831. 8vo, pp. 48. H. 1813

Appleton. Introduction of the Power Loom, and Origin of Lowell. By Nathan Appleton. Printed for the Proprietors of the Locks and Canals on Merrimack River. *Lowell, Massachusetts, Printed by B. H. Penhallow*, 1858. 8vo, pp. 36. H.

Appleton. Labor, its Relations in Europe and the United States compared. By Nathan Appleton. *Boston, Eastburn's Press*, 1844. 8vo, pp. 16. H. 1814*a*

Another edition printed as a broadside.

Appleton. Letter to the Hon. Wm. C. Rives, of Virginia, on Slavery and the Union, by Nathan Appleton, of Boston, Mass. *Boston, J. H. Eastburn's Press*, 1860. 8vo, pp. 17. H.

Appleton. Memoir of the Hon. Abbott Lawrence, prepared for the Massachusetts Historical Society, by Hon. Nathan Appleton. *Boston, J. H. Eastburn's Press*, 1856. 8vo, pp. 21. H.

See also Hunt's "Lives of American Merchants," Vol. II.

Appleton. Remarks on Currency and Banking; having reference to the Present Derangement of the Circulating Medium in the United States. By Nathan Appleton. *Boston, Charles C. Little and James Brown*, MDCCCXLI. 8vo, pp. 73. + Second Edition. *Boston*, MDCCCXLI. 8vo, pp. 52. + Third Edition. With an Appendix. *Boston*, 1857. 8vo, pp. 63. H. 1817

Appleton. Remarks upon Mr. Appleton's Remarks on Currency and Banking. By a Disinterested Witness. *Boston*, 1841. 8vo, pp. 64. 1818

Appleton. Remarks on Mr. Bouldin's Resolution of Inquiry into the Nature of Minimum Duties; House of Representatives, Jan. 21, 1832. *Washington*, 1832. 8vo, pp. 12.

Appleton. Speech of Mr. Appleton, of Massachusetts, in Reply to Mr. McDuffie, of South Carolina, on the Tariff. Delivered in the House of Representatives U. S. on the 30th of May, 1832. *Washington, Printed by Gales and Seaton.* 8vo, pp. 22. H. 1820

Appleton. Speech of Mr. Appleton, of Massachusetts, on the Bill to reduce and otherwise alter the Duties on Imports. Delivered in the House of Representatives, in Committee of the Whole, Jan. 23, 1833. *Washington, Printed by Gales and Seaton*, 1833. 8vo, pp. 31. H. 1821

Appleton. Speech of Mr. Appleton, of Mass., on the Tariff and Compromise Act, delivered In the House of Representatives, July 5, 1842. *Washington, Printed at the National Intelligencer Office*, 1842. 8vo, pp. 10. H. 1822

Appleton. What is a Revenue Standard? and a Review of Secretary Walker's Report on the Tariff. By Nathan Appleton. *Boston, Eastburn's Press*, 1846. 8vo, pp. 23. H. 1823

Appleton. Correspondence between Nathan Appleton and John A. Lowell in relation to the Early History of the City of Lowell. *Boston*, 1848. 8vo, pp. 19. H. 1824

Appleton. Correspondence between Nathan Appleton and John G. Palfrey, intended as a Supplement to Mr. Palfrey's Pamphlet on the Slave Power. *Boston, Eastburn's Press*, 1846. 8vo, pp. 20. H. 1825

Appleton (Nathaniel). ... . A Discourse On Psal. cxii. 7. Delivered Feb. 24, 1760. The Lord's Day after the Funeral of Henry Flynt, Esq; Who deceased Feb. 13. Ætatis 85. Having been a Tutor 55, and a Fellow of the Corporation of Harvard-College 60 Years. By Nathaniel Appleton, A.M. Pastor of the First Church in Cambridge. [Motto.] *Boston, New-England, Fowle & Draper*, M.DCC.LX. 8vo, pp. 25. H. 1826

Appleton. ... A Discourse occasioned by the Death of that pious and afflicted Gentlewoman, Mrs. Martha Gerrish. ... By Nathaniel Appleton, M.A. To which are annexed some of Mrs. Gerrish's Letters. *Boston*, 1736. 12mo, pp. 34, 91.

Appleton. ... Discourses ... delivered at the Thursday-Lecture in Boston, January 13, 1742, 3. By Nathanael Appleton, M.A. ... *Boston, D. Henchman*, 1743. 12mo, Title, pp. vii. (1), 215. H. 1828

Appleton. ... A Discourse Occasioned by the much lamented Death of the Rev. Edward Wigglesworth, D.D. Hollis Professor of Divinity in Harvard College, Cambridge; Who departed this Life, January 16. 1765. In the 73d Year of his Age. Having ... discharged the Office of Professor, for more than 42 Years. By Nathaniel Appleton, A.M. ... *Boston, New-England, Printed by Richard and Samuel Draper, and Thomas and John Fleet*, 1765. 8vo, pp. 40. H. 1829

Appleton. A Funeral Sermon: occasion'd By the Death of the Honourable Spencer Phips, Esq; Late Lieutenant-Governour and Commander in Chief, in and over His Majesty's Province of the Massachusetts-Bay, in New-England. Who departed this Life April 4. 1757. Æt. 73. Preach'd at the Publick Lecture in Boston, Thursday April 14. At the Desire of the Honourable His Majesty's Council; And in the Audience of The General Assembly. By Nathaniel Appleton, M.A. ... *Boston, Printed by John Draper*, MDCCLVII. 8vo, pp. 43. 1830

Appleton. Gospel Ministers Must be fit for The Master's Use, and Prepared to every Good Work, if they would be Vessels unto Honour; Illustrated in a Sermon Preached at Deerfield, August 31. 1735. At the Ordination of Mr. John Sargent, To the Evangelical Ministry, with a special Reference to the Indians of Houssatonnoc, who have lately manifested their desires to receive the Gospel. By Nathanael Appleton, M.A. ... *Boston, S. Kneeland & T. Green*, MDCCXXXV. 8vo, Title, pp. xiv., 33. + *Edinburgh*, 1736. H. 1831

With a long historical preface.

Appleton. ... Funeral-Discourse, Preached after the Death of the honorable Francis Foxcroft, Esq; Who died Dec. 31. 1727. In the 71st. Year of his Age. By Nathaniel Appleton, A.M. ... With a Preface, by Mr. Flynt, Fellow of Harvard-College. [Mottoes.] *Boston, in New-England, S. Gerrish*, 1728. 8vo, 2 p. l., pp. iv., 31. H. 1832

Appleton. The Origin of War examin'd and applied, in a Sermon Preached at the Desire of the Honourable Artillery Company In Boston, June 4. 1733. Being the Day of their Election of Officers. By Nathanael Appleton, A.M. ... *Boston, Daniel Henchman*, 1733. 8vo, pp. 27. H. 1833

Appleton. ... A Sermon Preached at Cambridge, The Lord's-Day after the Death of the Reverend & Learned John Leverett, Late President of Harvard-College. By Nathanael Appleton, M.A. ... *Boston, S. Gerrish*, 1724. Sm. 8vo, Title, pp. 36. H.

Appleton. ... Sermon Preach'd March 27. 1737. Being the Lord's Day after the Funeral Of That worthy and faithful Servant of Christ Mr. Benjamin Wadsworth, President of Harvard College. By Nathanael Appleton, A.M. ... *Boston, D. Henchman*, 1737. 8vo, pp. 36. H. 1835

Appleton. ... A Sermon Preached before His Excellency William Shirley, Esq; Governour, His Honour the Lieutenant Governour, The Honourable His Majesty's Council, and House of Representatives Of the Province of the Massachusetts-Bay, in New-England, May 26. 1742. Being the Day for the Electing His Majesty's Council for said Province. By Nathaniel Appleton, A.M. ... *Boston, S. Eliot*, 1742. 8vo, 1 p. l., pp. 60. H. 1836

Appleton. Sermon Preach'd before the Ministers of the Province of the Massachusetts-Bay, in New-England, at their Annual Convention in Boston. May 26. 1743. By Nathanael Appleton, A.M. ... *Boston, Samuel Eliot*, 1743. 8vo, pp. 56. H.

Appleton. ... Sermon From 1 Tim. ii. 4. Preached in Boston, March 27. 1753. at the Ordination of the Rev. Mr. Stephen Badger, as a Missionary with special Reference to the Indians at Natick. ... By Nathanael Appleton, A.M. ... Charge, by ... Dr. Sewall: and the Right Hand of Fellowship, by ... Mr. Abbot. ... *Boston, S. Kneeland*, 1753. 8vo, Title, pp. 34. H.

Appleton. A Sermon preached October 9. Being A Day of public Thanksgiving, Occasioned by the Surrender of Montreal and All Canada, September 8th. 1760. To His Brittanic Majesty. Effected by The British and Provincial Troops under the Command of General Amherst. By Nathaniel Appleton, A.M. Pastor of the First Church in Cambridge. [Motto.] *Boston, New-England, Printed by John Draper*, MDCCLX. 8vo, pp. 36. H.

Appleton. A Thanksgiving Sermon on the Total Repeal of the Stamp-Act. Preached In Cambridge, New-England, May 20th, in the Afternoon preceding the public Rejoicings of the Evening upon that great Occasion. By Nathaniel Appleton, M.A. ... Published by the Desire of the Audience, and at the Expence of the Honourable Brigadier General Brattle. [Mottoes.] *Boston, Edes & Gill*, 1766. 8vo, pp. 32. H. 1840

Appleton. ... Two Discourses, From 1. Cor. iii. 6. Occasioned by the late powerful and awakening Preaching of the Rev^d Mr. Whitefield. ... By Nathaniel Appleton ... . *Boston, S. Eliot*, 1741. 8vo, pp. 44. H. 1841

Appleton. ... Two Discourses from Isaiah vii. on January 28th. 1747, 8: Which was set apart by the Government for Fasting and Prayer, in Consideration of the remarkable Judgments of God upon the Land; and more especially the Destruction of the Court-House by Fire on the 9th of December last. By Nathaniel Appleton, A.M. ... *Boston, New-England, J. Draper*, 1748. 8vo, pp. 51. H. 1842

Appleton. ... Two Discourses preached at Lexington, December 17th. 1752. Being the Lord's Day after the Funeral of their late venerable and aged Pastor, the Reverend Mr. John Hancock, who going to Bed as well as usual the Night after the 5th of December, and awaking some time after Midnight with a great Pain in his Stomach, died in a few Minutes. In the 82d Year of his Age, and 54th of his Ministry. By Nathanael Appleton, A.M. ... *Boston, Printed by S. Kneeland*, 1752. 8vo, Title, pp. 39. H. 1843

APPLETON. ... Two Discourses, On June 11. 1769. Being the Lord's-Day after the Funeral of the Reverend Mr. Edward Holyoke, The late Worthy and Faithful President of Harvard-College: Who deceased June 1. 1769, in the 80th Year of his Age and in the 32d Year of his Presidentship. By Nathaniel Appleton, A.M. ... *Boston, Printed by Richard Draper*, MDCCLXIX. 8vo, pp. 52. H. 1844

APPLETON. ... Two Discourses on April 5, 1770, being the Day of General Fasting and Prayer through the Provinces, in the Time of the Session of the General Court, at Cambridge. *Boston*, 1770. 8vo, pp. 69. W. 1845

Dr. Appleton published several other discourses and sermons, including Exposition of Romans III., 20, 21, 22, 23. *Boston*, 1749. 8vo, pp. 26. Sermon at the Ordination of Josiah Cotton, Oct. 23. 1728. *Boston*, 1728. Sm. 8vo, pp. 31. Ordination of Oliver Peabody, Nov. 7, 1750. *Boston*, 1751. 8vo, pp. 36. Ordination of Matthew Bridge, Feb. 19, 1745, 6. *Boston*, 1746. 8vo, pp. 42. Ordination of John Sparhawk, Dec. 8, 1736. *Boston*, 1737. 8vo, pp. 51. Sermon from Zech. VII., 10. *Boston*, 1741. 8vo, pp. 63. Thursday Lecture. *Boston*, M,DCC,LXIII. 8vo, pp. 33. Sermon at Newton [Mass.], Aug. 9, 1741. *Boston*, 1741. 8vo. Testimony against the fashionable Vice of Swearing. *Boston*, 1765. 8vo, pp. 63. Wisdom of God in the Redemption of Man. *Boston*, 1728. Sm. 8vo, pp. iv., 414.

[APPLETON (Nathaniel), *of Boston*]. Considerations on Slavery, in a Letter to a Friend. *Boston*, 1767. 8vo, pp. 20. 1846

APPLETON (Samuel). The Will of Samuel Appleton; with Remarks, by One of the Executors [Nathaniel Ingersoll Bowditch]. *Boston, Printed by John Wilson & Son*, 1853. 8vo, pp. 32. H. 1847

APPLETON (W. H.) [Petition to Congress for a "Repeal of the Internal Revenue Tax on Books." n. p., 1865.] 4to, pp. (3). 1848

Signed by Wm. H. Appleton and four others. Mr. Appleton also signs a circular n. p., n. d., 4to, pp. 2, relating to the same subject.

An Application Of some General Political Rules, to the Present State of Great-Britain, Ireland and America. In a Letter To the Right Honourable Earl Temple. [Motto.] *London, J. Almon*, 1766. 8vo, pp. 86. P. 1849

Appropriation to Western Rivers [urged. *Washington*, 1836]. 8vo, pp. 16. H. 1850

APPUN (Carl Ferdinand). Über die Behandlung von Sämereien und Pflanzen des tropischen Süd-Amerika, besonders Venezuela's. *Bunzlau Appun*, 1858. 8vo, pp. 40. 1851

APTHORP (East). The Character and Example of a Christian Woman. A Discourse at Christ-Church, Cambridge, on the Death of Mrs Anne Wheelwright. By East Apthorp, M.A. Missionary at Cambridge. [Motto.] *Boston, Green and Russell*, MDCCLXIV. 4to, pp. 32. H. 1852

APTHORP. Considerations on the Institution and Conduct of the Society for the Propagation of the Gospel in Foreign Parts. By East Apthorp, M.A. Missionary at Cambridge. [Motto.] *Boston, New-England, Printed by Green & Russell, and Thomas & John Fleet*, MDCCLXIII. 8vo, pp. 24. H.+Same, forming pp. 149–164 of Dr. Jonathan Mayhew's Observations on the Charter, etc. *London*, M DCC LXIII. 8vo. H. 1853

This tract gave rise to the able expositions of Dr. Jonathan Mayhew.

APTHORP. The Constitution of a Christian Church illustrated in a Sermon at the Opening of Christ-Church in Cambridge, on Thursday 15 October, MDCCLXI. By East Apthorp, M.A. late Fellow of Jesus College in the University of Cambridge. [Motto.] *Boston, Printed by Green and Russell*, MDCCLXI. 4to, pp. (4), iv., 27. H. 1854

APTHORP. The Felicity of the Times. A Sermon preached at Christ-Church, Cambridge, on Thursday, XI August, MDCCLXIII. being a Day of Thanksgiving for the General Peace. By East Apthorp, M.A. ... *Boston, Printed by Green and Russell*, MDCCLXIII. 4to, pp. (2), viii., 26. B. 1855

APTHORP. A Review of Dr. Mayhew's Remarks on the Answer to his Observations on the Charter and Conduct of the Society for the Propagation of the Gospel in Foreign Parts. By East Apthorp, M.A. [Motto.] *London, John Rivington*, M.DCC.LXV. 8vo, Title, pp. 65. H. 1856

See Mayhew (J.), and M. R., XXXII., 472.

APTHORP. A Sermon preached December 13th, 1776, being the Day appointed for a Public Fast, on account of the Troubles in America. By East Apthorp, Vicar of Croydon. *London, Robson*, 1776. 4to, pp. 28. 1857

"We do not believe that this discourse was preached. It is dedicated by the Author to his Parishioners of Croydon, for whose instruction he says it was *written*."—M. R., VI., p. 75. Dr. Apthorp also published: Of Sacred Poetry and Music. Discourse at Christ-Church, Cambridge, Aug. 21, 1764. ... *Boston*, 1764. 4to, pp. 22. Discourses on Prophecy. *London*, 1786. 2 vols., 8vo, and other works. He

was the son of a merchant at Boston, Mass., and founded a church at Cambridge in that State, but meeting with much opposition from the Congregationalists, he left for Great Britain.

Apuntes para la historia de la guerra entre México y los Estados-Unidos. *México*, 1848. 8vo. 1858

Apuntes sobre los principales sucesos, que han influido en el actual estado de la America del Sud. [n. d.] 8vo. 1859

Apuntes historicos de la Defensa de la Republica, Colleccion de noticias, de Hechos autenticos y de documentos, etc. Tomo I. *Montevideo*, 1845. 4to. 1860

ÁQUINO (Thomas de). Elogios dos reverendissimos padres DD. Abbades geraes da Congregaçao Benedictina do reino de Portugal e principado do Brasil. *Porto, na officina de Francisco Mendes Lima*, 1767. 4to, pp. (31), 456. 1861

ARAGO (Dominique François Jean). Rapport fait à l'Academie des Sciences, sur les Travaux Scientifiques exécutés pendant le Voyage de la Frégate la Vénus, Commandé par M. le Capitaine de Vaisseau, Du Petit-Thouars. Arago, rapporteur. *Paris*, 1840. 8vo, pp. 88. 1862

Included in Tome IXe of his "Œuvres complètes," *Paris, Gide*, 1857, where may be found also notices of the voyages of "La Coquille" and "La Bonite."

ARAGO (Jacques Étienne Victor). Deux océans; par M. Jacques Arago. *Paris*, 1854. 2 vols., 18mo, 19½ sheets. 1863

ARAGO. Zwei Oceane. Eine Reise nach Chili, Californien, Taiti und Brasilien. Frei nach dem Französischen. *Cassel*, 1855. 8vo. + *Leipzig und Magdeburg, Gebr. Baensch*, 1857. 8vo, pp. iv., 218. + Im Auszuge deutsch bearbeitet von A. Kretzschmar. *Leipzig, Löschke*, 1854. 8vo, pp. x., 206. Woodcut. (Löschke, J. T. Die neuesten und interessantesten Reisen, II^er^ Bandchen.) 1864

ARAGO. Narrative of a Voyage round the World, in the Uranie and Physicienne Corvettes, commanded by Captain Freycinet, during the years 1817, 1818, 1819, and 1820; on a Scientific Expedition undertaken by order of the French Government. In a Series of Letters to a Friend, by J. Arago, Draftsman to the Expedition. With Twenty-Six Engravings. To which is prefixed, the Report made to the Academy of Sciences, on the General Results of the Expedition. *London*,

Treuttell [etc.], 1823. 4to, pp. vi. (2), xxvii. (5), 285 (3), 297 (2). H. 1865

"A frivolous and worthless narrative, full of ridiculous blunders."—*Quarterly Review*. Pages 36–101 of Part I., and 265–267 of Part II. relate to Brazil (where Arago died in 1855); pp. 256–265 to Montevideo. The Report to the Academy is by François Arago, the father of Jacques. The original French fills pp. 135–175 of Tome IXe of his "Œuvres."

ARAGO. Souvenirs d'un aveugle, voyage autour du monde. Enrichie de 60 délicieux dessins exécutées par Mairin ... et de notes scientifiques par M. F. Arago. *Paris, Hertet et Ozanne*, 1838. 2 vols.+ Troisième édition. *Paris*, 1840. 4 vols., 8vo.+ Nouvelle édition. Illustrée par 20 grandes vignettes et 200 gravures imprimées dans la texte. *Paris, Lebrun*, 1843. 2 vols., 8vo.+Sixième édition, revue, augmentée ... . *Paris*, 1850. 2 vols., 8vo. 25 Vignettes and 150 Woodcuts. 1866

The introduction to this amusing work is by Jules Janin.

ARAGO. Promenade autour du monde pendant les années 1817, 1818, 1819 et 1820, sur les corvettes du roi l'Uranie et la Physicienne, commandées par M. Freycinet, par J. Arago, dessinateur de l'expédition. ... *Paris, Leblanc*, 1822. 2 vols., 8vo. Atlas of 26 Plates. Also on Vellum Paper. 1867

Arancel general de Aduanas Maritimas y Fronterizas. *México*, 1842, 43, 53. 8vo. Published annually? 1868

ARANGO (D. A. J. d'). Poesias offerandos as Senhoras Brasileiras. *Rio de Janeiro*, 1830. 12mo. 1869

ARANGO (F. de.) Al Publico imparcial de esta Isla, Francisco de Arango. *Habana*, 1821. 1870

ARANGO. Contestacion al Manifesto que ha dado el Escmo. Sr. D. Francisco de Arango sobre la Junta Proyestada en la Habana en Julio del año de 1808. *Habana*, 1821. 4to, pp. 31 (1). 1871

ARANGO. Contestacion que dá el Conde de Casa Barreto al papel del Escmo. Señor D. Fr. de Arango: Contrayendose en parte a los publicados por el Señor D. Jose del mismo apellido. *Habana*, 1821. 4to, pp. 18. 1872

ARANGO. Manifiesto del Ayuntamiento de la Habana á la Junta Central, por D. Francisco de Arango. *Imprenta del Gobierno*, 1812. 1873

ARANGO (José de). Acuerdo de la Real Sociedad Patriótica de la Habana, manifestando su reconocimiento al Excmo. Sr. D. Luis de las Casas. Propuesto por D. José de Arango. *Habana*, 1797. 4to, pp. 8. 1874

ARANGO. Breve análisis de la volundad popular y bosquejo del falso patriotismo, por D. José de Arango. *Imprenta de D. Antonio Gil*, 1812. 4to. 1875

ARANGO. Contestacion apacible al ataque brusco del Pbro. Dr. D. Tomas Gutierrez de Piñeres, por D. José de Arango. *Habana*, 1813. 4to, pp. 8. 1876

ARANGO. Demostracion de las facultades coactivas y represivas con que los gefes políticos no pueden ni deben conocer contra los empleados del poder judicial, escrita por D. José de Arango. *Imprenta de Arazoza y Soler*, 1821. Folio, pp. 20. 1877

ARANGO. Deseos patrióticos de un habanero, por D. José de Arango. Se vendió para el socorro de las viudas y huérfanos por los sucesos de 10 y 11 de Marzo de 1820. *Imprenta del Gobierno*, 1820. 4to. 1878

ARANGO. Elogio del Sr. D. Ignacio Montalbo, Conde de Casa Montalbo Caballero del Orden de Santiago &c. ... Pronunciado por D. José de Arango. *Habana*, 1795. 4to, pp. 5. 1879

ARANGO. Examen de los derechos con que se establecieron los gobiernos populares en la Peninsula, y con que pudieron por cautiverio del Sr. D. Fernando VII establecerse en la América Española, donde hubieran producido incalculables ventajas, entre otras la de precaver las sediciones: escrito por el Tesorero de ejército jubilado D. José de Arango, para probar la injusticia de la oposicion que malogró la junta proyectada en la Habana en Julio de 1808. *Habana, oficina de Arazoza y Soler*, 1813. 4to, pp. 18. 1880

ARANGO. Exhortacion patriótica á los habitantes de la isla de Cuba para un alistamiento general proyectado por el gobierno, escrito por D. José de Arango. *Habana*, 1812. 4to, pp. 12. 1881

ARANGO. Exposicion del orígen y naturaleza de mi deuda al tesoro público y de mi conducta patriótica en 1808 y 1809, por D. José de Arango. *Boloña*, 1821. 4to, pp. 37. 1882

[ARANGO.] Manifiesto de las interesantísimas públicas tareas

del Sr. D. Alejandro Ramirez, Intendente de Ejército de la Habana y Superintendente de la Isla de Cuba desde su venida á América. Escrito por un habanero. *Oficina de Arazoza y Soler*, 1820. 8vo, pp. 36. 1883

ARANGO. Nadie se asuste por la segunda y ultima esplicacion mia sobre la Independencia de la isla de Cuba. 4to, pp. 42. 1884

ARANGO. Refutacion del tercer manifiesto de D. Gabriel Claudio Sequeira por D. José de Arango. *Oficina de Arazoza y Soler*, 1821. Folio, pp. 18. 1885

ARANGO. SS. de la Junta Censoria interina de esta ciudad, por D. José de Arango. *Habana, Imprenta de Palmer*, 1811. 4to. 1886

ARANGO. Suplemento del Diario de la Habana n° 689, por D. Francisco Arango, en 1812. Explica su conducta política en el año de 1808 y es interesante para la Historia. 1812. Folio, pp. 8. 1887

Some other works by this author are named by Bachiller.

ARANGO Y PARREÑO. Breve rasgo de los méritos y servicios del Sr. D. Francisco Arango y Parreño. *Imprenta del Gobierno*, 1814. 4to. 1888

ARAUJO (Antonio de). Cathecismo na lingua brasileira, em que se contém a summa da Doutrina Christã, com tudo o que pertence á nossa sancta fé e bons costumes: composto a modo de dialogos por Padres doutos e boas linguas da Companhia de Jesus. *Lisboa, Pedro Craesbeeck*, 1618. 8vo. 1889

Sotwel says that there is no better catechism than this. "Rarissima edição."—DA SILVA.

ARAUJO. Catechismo brasilico da doutrina christã, com o ceremonial dos sacramentos, e mais actos parochiaes, composto por padres doutos da Companhia de Jesus; aperfeiçoado e dado á luz pelo P. Antonio de Araujo; emendado n'esta segunda edição pelo P. Bartholomeu de Leam, da mesma Companhia. *Lisboa, Miguel Deslandes*, 1686. 12mo. 1890

Sold, Langlès, 1825, for 30 fr. *See* Ternaux, 1011.

ARAUJO COSTA (S. O. d'). Codigo commercial do Imperio do Brasil. *Rio de Janeiro*, 1864. 8vo. 1891

ARAUJO E SILVA. Diccionario historico e geographico da provincia de S. Pedro ou Rio Grande do Sul contendo a historia

e a descripçao da provincia em relaçao aos tres reinos da natureza, etc. Por Domingos de Araujo e Silva. *Rio de Janeiro*, 1865. 8vo, pp. vi., 192. 1892

ARBRISSELLE (J. B. d'). Sur l'Amérique méridionale. *Paris, Imprimerie d'Abel Lanoë*, 1820. 8vo, pp. 8. 1893

ARBUTHNOTT (Alexander). Report Of the Committee on Military Affairs, to whom was referred so much of the President's Message, of 17th November last, as relates to the proceeding of the Court Martial, in the Trial of Arbuthnott and Ambrister, and the conduct of the Seminole war, January 12, 1819. [*Washington*, 1819.] 8vo, pp. (2), 4. (15th Cong., 2d Sess. House, No. 82.) 1894

ARBUTHNOTT. Views of the Minority of the Committee ... . January 12, 1819. [*Washington*, 1819.] 8vo, pp. 12. (15th Cong., 2d Session. House, No. 86.) 1895

See also Munroe (James).

ARBUTHNOT. The Trials of A. Arbuthnot & R. C. Ambrister, charged with exciting the Seminole Indians to War against the United States of America. From the Official Documents which were laid by the President before Congress. *London, James Ridgway*, 1819. 8vo, 2 p. l., pp. 80. 1896

ARCE. Illustracion de la Rosa del Peru. *Lima*, 1670. 4to. 1897

The only account I find of this book is in the second appendix to Mr. Rich's Bibliotheca, p. 7.

ARCE (J. D. de). Libro de la Vida del P. Bern. Alvarez, martyr en esta nueva España, Por J. Dias de Arce. *Mexico*. 1762. 4to. 1898

ARCE (M. J.) Memoria de la conducta publica y administrativa de Manuel Jose Arce durante el Periodo de su Presidencia escrita in defensa de las calumnias que contra su persona, han vertido los mismos que se rebelaron contra el Gobierno y la Nacion de Centro America. *Mexico*, 1830. 4to. 1899

ARCE. Proclamacion a los Salvadoreños, March 24, 1827. M. 1900

ARCH (John). Memoir of John Arch, a Cherokee Young Man, compiled from Communications of Missionaries in the Cherokee Nation. Revised by the Committee of Publication. Fifth Edition. *Boston, Massachusetts Sabbath School Society*, 1844. 18mo, pp. 36. H. 1901

Archælogia Americana. *See* American Antiquarian Society.

ARCHAIOS (Mathetees). *See* Mathetees.

ARCHDALE (John). A New | Description | of that | Fertile and Pleasant Province | of Carolina: | With a | Brief Account | of its | Discovery, Settling, | and the | Government | Thereof to this Time. | With several Remarkable Passages of Divine | Providence during my Time. | By John Archdale: Late | Governour of the same |. *London: | Printed for John Wyat, at the Rose in St. Paul's | Church-Yard*. 1707. | 4to, Half Title, Title, "To the Courteous Readers," 2 l.; Text, pp. 32. C. 1902

Reprinted *Charleston, S. C., A. E. Miller*, 1822. 8vo, pp. 33; followed by notices of the Early History of South Carolina, pp. 14; also included in Carroll's collection, Vol. II., 85–120. "Gov. Archdale introduced the cultivation of rice into Carolina"—RICH.

ARCHDEACON (P.) Sketch of the Passaic Falls of Paterson, N. J. By Peter Archdeacon. *New York*, 1845. 12mo. 1903

ARCHENHOLTZ (Johann Wilhelm von). Geschichte der Flibustier. *Tübingen, Cotta*, 1803. 8vo. (II^er^ Band of his Kleine historische Schriften.) 1904

ARCHENHOLTZ. Histoire des Flibustiers, Traduite de l'allemand de M^r^. J. W. d'Archenholtz; [par J. F. Bourgoing]. Avec un Avant-Propos et quelques Notes du Traducteur. *Paris, Henrichs*, 1804. 8vo, pp. xvi., 355. H. 1905

See M. R., New Series, XLV., 459.

ARCHENHOLTZ. History of the Pirates, Freebooters, and Buccaneers of America. Translated from the German of J. W. von Archenholtz, by George Mason. *London*, 1807. 12mo. 1906

ARCHER (Armstrong). Compendium of Slavery as it exists in the United States. *London*, 1844. 12mo. 1907

ARCHER (Thomas). Mems. of America, and Reminiscences at home and abroad; a Series of Tales, by Thomas Archer, Comedian. *London*, 1839. 3 vols., 8vo. 1908

ARCHER (Wm. S.) Speech of Mr. Archer, of Virginia, on the Tariff Bill, delivered in the House of Representatives of the United States, April 26, 1820. [n. p., n. d.] 12mo, pp. 21. H. 1909

ARCHER. Speech of Mr. [W. S.] Archer, on the Proposition to amend the Constitution of the United States, respecting the

Election of President and Vice President. Delivered in the House of Representatives, February 20, 1826. [n. p., n. d.] 12mo. pp. 39. H. 1910

Archer. Speech of Hon. William S. Archer on the Question of the Removal of the Deposites from the Bank of the United States, delivered in the House of Representatives, January 29, 1834. *Washington*, 1834. 8vo, pp. 21. 1911

Archives diplomatiques, 1821–36. *See* Diplomatisches Archiv.

Archives diplomatiques Recueil de diplomatie et d'histoire Tome premier janvier, février, mars 1861. *Paris, Amyot* [1861]. 8vo, 2 p. l., pp. 479. H. 1912

Edited by F. Amyot. Continued monthly. Contains French translations of all American diplomatic documents of importance.

Archives du Muséum d'histoire naturelle, publiées par les professeurs-administrateurs de cet établissement. Tome I. *Paris, Gide*, 1839. 4to. Continued. C. 1913

Contains many articles on American subjects, particularly the French colonies.

Archives littéraires de l'Europe; ou, Mélanges de littérature, d'histoire, et de philosophie. Tome I. *Paris*, 1804, &c. 8vo.

Continued, 4 vols. a year. Contains some Indian vocabularies.

... Archivo americano y espiritu de la prensa del mundo. Tomo I. *Buenos-Aires, Imprenta de la Independencia*, 1843. Folio.

Continued. The new series, beginning in 1847 (?), is in 8vo. The latest which I have seen is "Nueva Serie No. 27, Octubre 31 de 1851." A very important collection of documents.

Archontologia Cosmica, das ist Beschreibung aller Kaiserthümer, Königreiche, und Republiquen der Welt, biss auf das Jahr 1694 continuiret durch M. Merians Erben. *Frankfurt a. M.*, 1695. 1917

Page 308, "Von der Neuen Welt oder West-Indianischen Landen."

Arctic Despatches. Discovery of the North-West Passage. *London, Potter*, 1853. 8vo. 1918

Arctic Discovery and Adventure. By the Author of "Brazil, &c." With Map. *London, Religious Tract Society*, 1863. Fcap 8vo, pp. vii., 387. 1919

Arctic Expeditions. Report of the Committee appointed by the Lords Commissioners of the Admiralty to inquire into and

report on the Recent Arctic Expeditions in search of Sir John Franklin, ... with the Minutes of Evidence ... and Papers connected with the Subject. ... *London*, 1852. Folio, pp. lix. (3), 199. 2 Maps. + Additional Papers relative to the Arctic Expedition under the Orders of Captain Austin and Mr. William Penny. ... *London*, 1852. Folio, pp. iii. (1), 368. Maps and Woodcuts. + Arctic Expedition. Further Correspondence and Proceedings ... . *London*, 1852. Folio, pp. 216. Maps and Woodcuts. + [Additional Papers. *London*, 1852.] Folio, pp. 17, 9 (1), Map, 11, 38. C. 1920

These together form Vol. L. of the Parliamentary Accounts and Papers for 1852. *See* also the Accounts and Papers for 1847-48, Vol. XLI.; 1849, XXXII.; 1850, XXXV.; 1852-53, LX.; 1854, XLII.; 1854-55, XXXV.; 1856, XLI.; and Reports of Committees, 1834, XVIII. (Expedition of Capt. John Ross); 1854-55, VII., where may be found long and interesting papers, generally accompanied by maps and illustrations.

Arctic News. Facsimile of a Journal on board H. M. Ship "Resolute." *London, Ackerman*, 1852. Folio. C. 1921

The Arctic Queen. [A Poem dedicated to Dr. Kane. n. p., 185–.] 8vo, pp. 62. H. 1922

The Arctic Regions: a Narrative of Discovery and Adventure. *New York*, 1840. 16mo. 1923

A digest of the voyages of early and of modern navigators, including an account of the Franklin expedition.

Arctic Miscellanies; a Souvenir of the late Polar search; by the officers and seamen of the expedition. *London, Colburn*, 1851. 8vo, pp. 312. + Second Edition. *London, Colburn*, 1852. 8vo. C.

Arctic Rewards, and their Claimants. *London, Hatchard*, 1856. 8vo, pp. 31. 1925

Arctic Searching Expeditions. Papers and Dispatches. *London, Rivington*, 1852. 8vo. C. 1926

Arcturus, a Journal of Books and Opinion. *New York*, 1841–2. 3 vols., 8vo. 1927

Edited by C. Mathews and Evert A. Duyckinck.

Ardoino (Antonio). *See* Barcia, Historiadores Primitivos. V. I.

Ardouin (B). Études sur l'histoire d'Haïti, suivies de la vie du général J. M. Borgella. Par B. Ardouin, ancien ministre d'Haïti près le gouvernement français. *Paris, Dezobry et E.*

Magdeleine, 1853–54. 5 vols., 8vo. Portrait. + *Paris*, 1855. 2 vols., 8vo. 1928

Ardouin. Géographie de l'Ile d'Haïti, précédée du précis et de la date des événements les plus remarquables de son histoire. Par B. Ardouin. *Port-au-Prince*, 1832. 4to, pp. 184.

Arenales (José). Memoria Histórica sobre las Operaciones e Incidencias de la Division Libertadora, a las órdenes del Gen. D. Juan Antonio Alvarez de Arenales, en su segunda campaña a la sierra del Peru en 1821. Por José Arenales. *Buenos-Aires*, 1832. Portrait and Maps. 4to, pp. xviii., 142. C. 1930

Arenales. Noticias históricas y descriptivas sobre el Gran Pais del Chaco y Rio Bermejo; con observaciones relativas á un plan de Navegacion y Colonizacion que se propone. Por José Arenales. *Buenos-Aires*, 1833. 8vo, pp. v., 421; Errata (1 page), and Map. C. 1931

Arenas (*Padre*). Causas que se han seguido y terminado contra los comprendidos en la conspiracion llamada del Padre Arenas ... Tomo primero. *Mexico*, 1828. 12mo, pp. 117. S.

Arenas (Pedro de). Guide de la conversation en trois langues, français, espagnol et mexicain, contenant un petit abrégé de la grammaire mexicaine, un vocabulaire des mots les plus usuels et des dialogues familiers. Revu et traduit en français par M. Charles Romey. *Paris, Maisonneuve et Cie*, 1862. 12mo.

Arenas (Pedro de). Vocabulario Manual de las dos Lenguas Castellana y Mexicano. Compuesto por Pedro de Arenas. *En la Puebla de los Angeles* (*Mexico*), 1583. 1934

Boturini Catalogue, p. 55.

Arenas. Vocabulario manual de las lenguas Castellana, y Mexicana. Por Pedro de Arenas. *Mexico, Henrico Martinez* [1611]. Sm. 12mo. 1935

A volume of great rarity. The privilege is dated 1611. A complete copy is scarcely known. *See* Ternaux, 340, and the Bibliotheca Grenvilliana. Reprinted with the following title:

Arenas. Vocabvlario | Manual | de las Lengvas | Castellana, y Mexicana. | En qve se contienen las | palabras, preguntas, y respuestas mas comunes, | y ordinarias que se suelin ofrecer en el | trato, y comunicacion entre | Españoles, è Indios. | Enmendado en esta vltima impression. | Compuesto por Pe- | dro de

Arenas. | Impresso con licencia, y Aprobacion. | *En Mexico, Por la Viuda de Francisco Rodriguez Supercio; en la puente de Palacio. Año de* 1690. Sm. 8vo, 4 p. l., pp. 120. 1936

Arenas. Vocabulario Manual de las Lenguas Castellana y Mexicana, en que se contienen las palabras, preguntas y respuestas mas communes, y ordinarias, que se suelen offrecer en el trato, y communicacion entre Espanoles, è Indios, compuesto por Pedro de Arenas. *Mexico*, 1700. 12mo. + *Mexico*, 1728. 8vo. 6 p. l., pp. 140. + *En la Puebla de los Angeles* [*Mexico*], 1793. 12mo. + *Reimpreso en Puebla, en la Imprenta del Hospital de S. Pedro a cargo del C. Manuel Buen Abad. Ano de* 1831. 12mo, pp. 11, 131. 1937

A copy in the library of Harvard College has the following imprint: *Mexico, en la imprenta de Francisco de Rivera Calderon* [n. d.], 6 p. l., pp. 140, but dated, in MS., 1611.

Arends (Fr.) Schilderung des Mississippithales, oder des Westen der Vereinigten Staaten von Nordamerika. Nebst Abriss meiner Reise dahin. *Emden*, 1838. 8vo, pp. 648. 1938

Arey (Henry W.) Digest of the Acts of Assembly and Ordinances of Councils relating to the Girard College for Orphans: with the By-Laws of the Board of Directors, the Rules and Regulations of the Institution, and the Will of Mr. Girard. Prepared for the Use of the Board by H. W. Arey, Secretary of the Girard College. *Philadelphia, Crissy & Markley, Printers*, 1851. 8vo, pp. 72. H. 1939

Arey. The Girard College and its Founder: containing the Biography of Mr. Girard, the History of the Institution, its Organization and Plan of Discipline, with the Course of Education, Forms of Admission of Pupils, Description of the Buildings, &c. &c. and The Will of Mr. Girard. By Henry W. Arey. ... . *Philadelphia, C. Sherman, Printer*, 1852. 12mo, pp. 85 (2). Portrait and View. + *Philadelphia*, 1854. 12mo. + 1860. 12mo. H. 1940

Arfwedson (Carl David). De Colonia Nova Svecia in Americam Borealem deducta Historiola. Quam ... Præside Mag. Erico Gust. Geijer ... p. p. Auctor Carolus David Arfwedson, Vestrogothus. In Audit. Gust. Die XIX Nov. MDCCCXXV. ... *Upsaliæ, Excudebant Regiæ Academiæ Typographi* [1825]. 4to, 2 p. l., pp. 34. Map. H. 1941

This dissertation contains a number of extracts from original documents preserved in the Palmsköld collection in the Upsala University Library. The most extensive is

on pages 23-30, giving an account of the "unexpected hostile attack made upon the Swedish colonies in Nova Suecia by the Dutch, under the command of Peter Stuyvesant, Gov. of New Netherland." The map is after Lindström, corrected in its outline.

Arfwedson. Förenta Staterna och Canada, Åren 1832, 33, 34. *Stockholm, Hjerta*, 1835. 2 pt., 12mo. 1942

Arfwedson. The United States and Canada, in 1832, 1833, and 1834. By C. D. Arfwedson, Esq. ... *London, Richard Bentley*, 1834. 8vo, pp. vii., 433; vii., 418. 2 Plates. H.

Argais (Gregorio de). Vida y Escritos del Venerable Varon Gregorio Lopez dispuesto por diligencia del maestro F. Gregorio de Argaiz para los devotos y doctos. *Madrid, Antonio Francisco de Zafra*, 1678. 4to, 15 p. l., pp. 131; Table, 4 pp. 1944

Argander (F.) Trauerrede auf die ersten Helden und Opfer des Vaterlandes, gehalten am 17. Sept. 1823 in der Metropolitankirche zu Mexico ... . Aus dem Spanischen übersetzt und mit einem Vorworte, über die wichtigsten Ereignisse der mexikanischen Revolution, versehen von E. Buschmann. *Berlin, Bethge*, 1829. 8vo, pp. 80. 1945

Argensola (B. L.) Conqvista | de las | Islas Malvcas | Al Rey Felipe III. N.° S.or | Escrita por el Licen.do Bartolome | Leonardo de Argensola capellan | de la Magestad de la Emperatriz | y Retor de Villahermosa. | [*En Madrid por Alonso Martin, año* M.DC.IX.] Folio, Engraved Title, 5 p. l., and pp. 407. H. 1946

"Few narratives of [East] Indian affairs are written with so much judgment and elegance as his history of the conquest of the Molucca Islands."—Bouterwek.

Argensola. Histoire | de la | conquête | des isles | moluques | par les Espagnols, | par les Portugais, | & par les Hollandois. | Traduite de l'Espagnol d'Argensola, | et | Enrichie des Figures & Cartes Géographiques, | pour l'intelligence de cet Ouvrage. | *A Amsterdam*, | *Chez Jaques Desbordes*. | M.D.CCVI. 3 vols., 12mo, 7 p. l., pp. 405; 2 p. l., pp. 402, Table, 15 l.; 3 p. l., pp. 388, Table, 10 l. Maps and Plates. + *A Amsterdam*, | *Chez Jaques Desbordes*. | M.D.CCVII. 3 vols., 12mo, 4 p. l., pp. 405; Title, pp. 202 [402], Table, 15 l.; Title, pp. 388; Table, 10 l. Maps and Plates. H. 1947

Argensola. The Discovery and Conquest of the Molucco and Philippine Islands; containing their History Ancient and Modern, Natural and Political; Their Description, Product, Religion, Government, Laws, Languages, Customs, Manners,

Habits, Shapes and Inclinations of the Natives. With an Account of many other adjacent Islands, and several remarkable Voyages through the Streights of Magellan, and in other Parts. Written in Spanish by Bartholomew Leonardo de Argensola, Chaplain to the Empress, and Rector of Villa Hermosa. Now translated into English; and illustrated with a Map, and several Cuts. *London, Printed in the Year* 1708. Sm. 4to. 4 Plates. A.

The first work in Stevens's collection of voyages.

Argensola. Beschreibung der Moluckischen Inseln. *Leipzig*, 1738. 2 vols., 8vo. 1949

Argensola. Primera parte de los Anales de Aragon que prosigue los del Segretario Geronimo Zurita, desde el año M.D.XVI [—1520] del nacimiento de nuestro Redemtor. *Zaragoza, Juan de Lanaja*, 1630. Folio. 1950

Contains some particulars concerning Cortez, Magellan. &c.

Argentine Republic. Constitucion de la Republica Argentina, sancionada por el Congreso General constituyente el 24 de Diciembre de 1826. Y el Manifiesto, etc. *Buenos-Ayres*, 1826. 8vo, pp. 55. S. 1951

Almanaque Agricola, pastoril é industrial de la República Argentina y de Buenos-Ayres. *Buenos-Ayres*, 1865. 4to, pp. 184. 1952

Exposicion agrícola-rural Argentina en 1859. *Buenos-Aires*, 1859. 4to, pp. 78. 1953

Foreign Affairs of the Argentine Confederation; ... (in French and English.) *Buenos Ayres*, 1838. 8vo. 1954

Ley del presupuesto general de la nacion Argentina en el ejercicio de 1865. *Buenos-Aires*, 1864. 8vo, pp. 122. 1955

Memoria en que el ministro de la confederacion Argentina en las córtes de Inglaterra, Francia y Espana da cuenta á su gobierno de los trabajos de su mision, desde 1855, hasta 1860. 1860. 8vo, pp. xxx., 128. 1956

Memorias y noticias para servir á la historia antigua de la republica Argentina. Compiladas y publicadas por los fundadores de la Revista de Buenos-Aires. *Buenos-Aires*, 1865. 8vo, pp. vi., 172. 1957

Tarifa de avalúos y de derechos de almacenaje y eslingaje para las aduanas de la República Argentina para el ano de 1866. *Buenos Aires*, 1866. 8vo, pp. 166. 1958

Rejistro nacional de la República Argentina. Ano 1862. *Buenos-Aires*, 1862. 4to, pp. 492. Continued. 1959

Report of the Argilite and Greenup Coal and Iron Company. *Boston, Printed by Dakin and Metcalf*, 1865. 8vo, pp. 17. Map.

Includes an examination of the Company's mineral lands in Greenup County, Kentucky, by A. A. Hayes.

Argonaut, *pseudon.* *See* [Etches (J.)]

Argonavtica Gvstaviana. *See* [Usselincx].

Arguelles. Cuestion, Dulce-Zulueta-Arguelles. [*Habana*, 1865.] 4to, pp. 39. C. 1962

Concerning this, *see* Bartlett Bibl. of the Rebellion, No. 162.

Argüelles (J. G.) Memoria sobre la renta de tabaco, por D. José Ganga Argüelles. *Reimpresa en la Habana en* ... 1812. 4to, pp. 20. 1663

[Arguelles (J. V.)] Manifiesto de los reparos en algunos artículos del reglamento formado por el Excmo. Ayuntamiento, modo de abolir el que habla de la construccion de sumideros, y otras reflexiones para mayor comodidad del público, por J[osé] V[azquez] A[rgüelles]. Por Palmer. 1820. 4to, pp. 8.

An Argument against the Abolition of the Constitution of the United States. *Sangamon, "Tribune" office*, 1864. 8vo, pp. 12.

An Argument against War with Great Britain. *See* [Lowell (John)].

Argument at a Court of Grand Sessions, and Oyer and Terminer in one of his Majesty's Islands. By a Member of the Inner Temple. 1765. *Privately printed*. 4to. 1966

An Argument Delivered on the Part of New-York, at the Hearing Before His Majesty's Commissioners, appointed by his Royal Commission under the Great Seal of Great-Britain, bearing Date the 7th October, 1767, to Settle and determine the Boundary Line, between the Colonies of New-York and New-Jersey. [*New York?*], *Printed in the Year* MDCC.LXIX. 4to, pp. 80. G. B. 1967

An Argument in Defence of the Exclusive Right claimed by the Colonies to tax themselves, With a Review of the Laws of England relative to Representation and Taxation. To which is added, An Account of the Rise of the Colonies; and the Manner in which the rights of the subjects within the realm were communicated to those that went to America, with the exercise of those rights from their first settlement to the present time. *London, Printed for the Author*, M DCC LXXIV. 8vo, pp. vii., 163. 1968

"Another solid and judicious advocate for the colonies has employed his pen to no farther purpose than to render the contrast between equity and power more glaring."—M. R., LI., 148. Attributed to a Mr. Parker.

Arguments in Support of the Supremacy of the British Legislature and their Right to tax the Americans, Addressed to the Citizens of London. By a Liveryman. *London*, 1775. 8vo.

"Most of these arguments are extracted from a pamphlet published seven years ago, under the title of 'A Review of the Controversy.'"—Rich.

Arguments proving the Inconsistency and Impolicy of Granting to Foreigners the Right of Voting: abstracted from a Pamphlet published in the Year 1810, by A Disciple of the Washington School, and one who is personally a warm friend of the Irish. Revised by the Author. *Philadelphia, T. G. Auner*, 1844. 8vo, pp. 8. 1970

Argus, *pseudon.* A Tale of Lowell. Norton: or, The Lights and Shades of a Factory Village: wherein are developed some of the Secret Incidents in the History of Lowell. By "Argus." *Lowell, "Vox Populi Office,"* 1849. 8vo, pp. 80. H. 1971

Arias. Manifiesto al público de D. Anselmo de Paula Arias. [*Habana*], *Imprenta de Soler é hijo*, 1820. 4to. 1972

Arias (F. G.) Diario de la expedicion reduccional del año de 1780, mandada practicar por orden del virey de Buenos Aires, a cargo de su ministro D. Francisco Gavino Arias, coronel del regimiento de caballeria, San Fernando. Primera edicion. *Buenos-Aires, Imprenta del Estado*, 1837. Folio, Title, pp. viii., 50. (Angelis, Pedro de. Coleccion, tom. VI.) H. 1973

Arias (P.) Lettere di Pietro Arias Capitano generale, della conquista del paese del Mar Occeano Scripte alla Maesta Cesarea dalla Cipta di Panama delle cose ultimamente scoperte nel Mar Meridiano decto el Mar Sur. [n. p.], MDXXV. 16mo. 1974

A poem. Notices the departure of Pizarro for Peru in 1525. *See* Bib. Am. Vet., p. 245.

ARISPE. *See* Ramos de Arispe (Miguel).

ARISTIDES, *pseudon.* An Examination of Charges against Burr. 1804. *See* [Van Ness (Wm. P.)]

ARISTIDES, *pseudon.* Remarks on the Proposed Plan of a Federal Government, addressed to the Citizens of the United States of America, and particularly to the People of Maryland. By Aristides. *Annapolis*, 1788. 8vo, pp. 42. N. 1975

ARISTIDES, *pseudon.* Observations upon the Late Proceedings of the House of Assembly in this Province. *From the Press of The Montreal Herald, April*, 1814. 4to, pp. 17.+Supplementary Observations ... . *Montreal Herald, May*, 1814. 4to, pp. 19. H. 1976

ARISTIDES, *pseudon.* Letter to the Secretary of the Treasury on the Commerce and Currency of the United States. By Aristides. *New York*, 1819. 8vo. 1977

ARISTIDES, *pseudon.* Essays on the Spirit of Jacksonism, as exemplified in its deadly hostility to the Bank of the United States, and in the odious calumnies employed for its destruction. By Aristides. *Philadelphia*, 1835. 8vo. 1978

ARISTIDES, *pseudon.* An Address to the Country, by Aristides. ... *Washington*, 1862. 8vo, pp. 12. H. 1979

Urges the immediate abolition of slavery.

Aristocracy. An Epic Poem. [In Two Books.] *Philadelphia, Printed for the Editor*, 1795. 8vo, pp. 16, 17. S.

Aristocracy exposed; a Candid Appeal To the Citizens of Massachusetts. [Motto. n. p.], *October*, 1804. 12mo, pp. 12. H. 1981

Aristocracy in America. *See* Grund (F. J.)

ARIZONA. [Correspondence between Senor A. Ainsa of Arizona, W. H. Seward, Secretary of State, etc., relative to the schemes of the rebels in that territory and in Sonora.] Privately printed. 8vo, pp. 6. 1982

The Acts, Resolutions and Memorials adopted by the Arizona

Legislature at the session ending November 10, 1864. *Prescott*, 1865. 8vo, pp. 79. C. 1983

Charter, Constitution and By-Laws of the Arizona Historical Society. Incorporated and Organized November, 1864. *Prescott*, 1864. 8vo, pp. 16. 1984

ARJONA (Francisco de). Sermon en la muerte de Fr. Julian Chumillas, comisario general de las Indias. Por Francisco de Arjona. [n. p.], 1697. 4to. 1985

ARKANSAS! The Home for Immigrants. [Circular of the Arkansas Immigrant Aid Society, dated Little Rock, Oct. 1865. n. p., 1865.] 4to, pp. 3. 1986

Acts of the General Assembly of Arkansas. 1840. 8vo. Continued. C. 1987

Constitution of the State of Arkansas, done by the People of Arkansas, in Convention assembled, at Little Rock, in the Territory of Arkansas. Published by Authority. *City of Little Rock, Pike, Printer*, 1836. 8vo, pp. 22. H. 1988

Correspondence relating to the Hypothecation of Five Hundred Bonds of the State of Arkansas. *New York*, 1842. 8vo.

Laws of the Territory of Arkansas: comprising the Organic Laws of the Territories of Missouri and Arkansas, with their Amendments and Supplements annexed; all Laws of a General Nature, passed by the General Assembly of the Territory of Missouri, at the Session in 1818; with the Laws of the Territory of Arkansas, for 1819–'20–'21, 1823 and 1825. *Arkansas and Little Rock*, 1821–26. 12mo. C. 1990

Laws of Arkansas Territory, compiled and arranged by J. Steele and J. McCampbell. *Little Rock*, 1835. 8vo. C. 1991

Memorial of the Legislature of the Free State of Arkansas to Congress, and a Letter from W. D. Snow, Senator Elect, to Hon. S. C. Pomeroy, showing the Origin and History of the Re-organized Government of Arkansas—the Loyalty of the State—the Vote, and the Present Legislative Representation in the State. *Washington, Chronicle Print*, 1865. 8vo, pp. 11. H.

Proceedings of the Democratic Whig State Convention, March, 1840. 1840. 8vo. 1993

Report of the Committee on Elections, and the Credentials of T. M. Jacks and J. M. Johnson, claiming seats in the House of Representatives from Arkansas, 1865. [*Washington*, 1865.] 8vo, pp. 9. (38th Congress, 2d Session, House Report, No. 18.) 1994

Report of the Committee on Federal Relations (to the Arkansas Legislature), December, 1860. 1995

Arkansas. This Chart shows the undevelloped Resources of & General Condition of the State of Arkansas, constructed for the Benefit of the Political Wreckers thereof. Broadside. 1996

ARLACH (H. de T. d'). Souvenirs de l'Amérique centrale; par H. de T. d'Arlach, vice consul de France. *Paris, Charpentier*, 1850. 8vo. 1997

ARLEGUI (Joseph). Chronica de la Provincia S. Francisco de Zacatecas, por Navarrete. *Mexico*, 1737. 4to. 1998

A doubtful title from a London catalogue.

ARMAND, *pseudon.* *See* [Strubberg (F. A.)]

ARMAND-AUBERT. Résultats de la Liberté des noirs à Cayenne de 1794 à 1803. *Saint-Pierre-Martinique*, 1837. 4to.

ARMAS (D. F. de). Como los Perros á la luna ladran ... por D. Francisco de Armas. *Imprenta de José Minuese.* 2000

A defence of Dr. Piñeres, of Havana.

ARMAS Y CÉSPEDES (F. de). De la esclavitud en Cuba. Por Francisco de Armas y Céspedes. *Madrid, Duran*, 1866. 4to, pp. 482. 2001

ARMATEUR (L. M. B.) *See* [Prudhomme (Louis)].

ARMIN (Th.) Das heutige Mexico. Land und Volk unter Spaniens Herrschaft, sowie nach erlangter Selbständigkeit. Unter Benutzung der zuverlässigsten und neuesten Quellen herausgegeben von Th. Armin. Mit 150 in den Text gedruckten Abbildungen, nebst 6 Tonbildern. *Leipzig, O. Spamer*, 1864. 8vo, pp. xii., 428. (Jugend und Hausbibliothek, III. Serie, 8. Band.) 2002

ARMIN. Das alte Mexico und die Eroberung Neuspaniens durch Ferd. Cortez. Nach W. Prescott und Bernal Diaz, sowie unter Benutzung der Schriften von Alex. v. Humboldt &c.

Bearbeitet von Th. Armin. Mit über 120 in den Text gedruckten Abbildungen., 6 Tonbildern, 1 Frontispice, sowie 1 Karte von Anahuac. *Leipzig, O. Spamer*, 1864. 8vo, pp. xvi., 376. (Jugend etc. III. Serie, 7. Band.) 2002*a*

ARMING (Friederich Wilhelm). Weiss und Schwarz. Historische Erzählung aus der ersten Zeit des Sonderbundkrieges in Nord-Amerika. *Leipzig, Haefele, jun.*, 1865. 8vo, pp. 489.

ARMISTEAD (W.) A 'cloud of witnesses' against Slavery and oppression. Containing the acts, opinions and sentiments of individuals and societies in all ages. Selected. ... by Wilson Armistead ... *London*, 1853. 12mo, pp. 154. 2003*a*

ARMISTEAD. Memoir of James Logan, a Distinguished Scholar and Christian Legislator, founder of the Loganian Library, &c. Including Correspondence now first printed. By Wilson Armistead. *London*, 1851. 12mo, pp. 192. P. 2004

ARMISTEAD. Memoir of Paul Cuffe, a Man of Colour, compiled from Authentic Sources. By Wilson Armistead. *London*, 1840. 18mo. Portrait. 2005

ARMISTEAD. Select Miscellanies, chiefly illustrative of the History, Christian Principles, and Sufferings of the Society of Friends. ... By Wilson Armistead: *London, Bennett*, 1851. 6 vols., 18mo. + 2d edition. *London, Bennett*, 1852. 6 vols., 18mo. P. 2006

Includes many Americans.

ARMISTEAD. A Tribute for the Negro: being a Vindication of the Moral, Intellectual, and Religious Capabilities of The Coloured portion of Mankind; with Particular Reference to the African Race. Illustrated by numerous Biographical Sketches, Facts, Anecdotes, etc. and many Superior Portraits and Engravings. By Wilson Armistead. *Manchester, William Irwin*, 1848. 8vo, pp. xxxv., 564. H. 2007

ARMITAGE (J.) The History of Brazil, from the Period of the Arrival of the Braganza Family in 1808, to the Abdication of Don Pedro the First in 1831. Compiled from State Documents and other Original Sources. Forming a Continuation to Southey's History of that country. By John Armitage, Esq. In Two Volumes. *London, Smith, Elder & Co.*, 1836. 8vo, pp. xv. (1), 371; viii., 297. Two Portraits. H. & P. 2008

ARMITAGE (T.) The Past, Present, and Future of the United States. A Discourse, delivered by Rev[d] Thomas Armitage, D.D., Pastor of the Fifth Avenue Baptist Church, On Thanksgiving Day, Nov. 27, and Repeated by Request, December 18, 1862. *New York, Printed and Published by T. Holman*, 1862. 8vo, pp. 31. G. 2009

ARMITAGE (W. E.) Unselfish Patriotism. A Sermon preached in St. John's Church, Detroit, Feb. 23, 1862. By Rev. William E. Armitage. *Detroit: Richmond & Backus*, 1862. 8vo, pp. 16. 2010

ARMRISCH (E.) Blondin, der Held vom Niagara. Ein wahrheitsgetreues Lebensbild. Mit 12 Illustrationen. 2. Auflage. *Wien, Schönewerk in Comm.*, 1864. 8vo, pp. 46. 2011

[ARMROYD (George)]. A Connected View of the whole Internal Navigation of the United States, natural and artificial; present and prospective. With Maps. *Philadelphia*, 1826. 8vo, pp. 192. S. 2012

[ARMROYD.] A Connected View ... corrected and improved from the edition of 1826 ... with a sheet map, and numerous engraved profiles ... and with various authentic statistical details. By a Citizen of the United States. *Philadelphia*, 1830. 8vo, pp. 617. C. 2013

ARMROYD. Report of the Committee of Commerce and Manufactures, on the Petition of George Armroyd, & Co. February 21, 1810. ... *Washington, A. & G. Way*, 1810. 8vo, pp. 14. C. 2014

ARMS (H. P.) The Mystery of Providence. A Discourse, occasioned by the Death of Hon. Jabez W. Huntington, United States Senator, Delivered in the First Church in Norwich, November 7, 1847. By Hiram P. Arms. *Norwich, J. Dunham's Press*, 1847. 8vo, pp. 26. H. 2015

ARMSBY (J. H.) Hospitals of the United States; an Address. *New York*, 1853. 8vo, pp. 24. C. 2016

ARMSTRONG (A.) A Personal Narrative of the Discovery of the North West Passage, with numerous Incidents of Travel and Adventure during nearly Five Years continuous Service in the Arctic Regions while in Search of the Expedition under Sir

John Franklin. By Alexander Armstrong. *London, Hurst & Blackett*, 1857. Maps and Plates. 8vo, pp. xxiv., 616. C.

ARMSTRONG (E.) Address delivered at Chester, before the Historical Society of Pennsylvania, on the 8th November, 1851. By Edward Armstrong ... in celebration of the one hundred and sixty-ninth Anniversary of the Landing of William Penn at that place. *Philadelphia, J. Pennington*, 1852. 8vo, pp. 33. 2018

Contains a list of the persons who accompanied Penn.

ARMSTRONG. The History and Location of Fort Nassau upon the Delaware. A paper read before the New Jersey Historical Society, January 20th, 1853, by Edward Armstrong, Esq., ... *Newark, N. J.*, 1853. 8vo, pp. 21. S. 2019

ARMSTRONG (G. D.) The Christian Doctrine of Slavery. By George D. Armstrong, D.D., Pastor of the Presbyterian Church, Norfolk, Va. *New York, Charles Scribner*, 1857. 12mo, pp. 148. 2020

ARMSTRONG. The Summer of the Pestilence; a History of the Ravages of the Yellow Fever in Norfolk, Virginia, A.D. 1855, by George D. Armstrong, D.D., Pastor of the Presbyterian Church, in Norfolk. *Philadelphia, J. B. Lippincott & Co.*, 1856. 12mo, pp. 192.+Second Edition. *Philadelphia*, 1856. 12mo, pp. 192. 2021

ARMSTRONG (Jacob D.) Life and Adventures of Captain Jacob D. Armstrong. *New York, Dewitt and Davenport*, 1852. 8vo, pp. 72. C. 2022

An apocryphal narrative of voyages, masking a political satire.

[ARMSTRONG (John, *M.D.*)] The Art of Preserving Health: A Poem. *London, Printed: Philadelphia, Reprinted, and Sold by B. Franklin*, M.DCC.XLV. 4to, pp. 88. G. 2023

ARMSTRONG (*Gen.* John). Notices of the War of 1812. By John Armstrong, late a Major-General in the Army of the United States, and Secretary of War. *New York*, 1836–1840. 2 vols., 12mo, pp. 260; iv., 244. C. 2024

"Some copies are dated 1840."—N. A. R., LIII., 211. *See also* Sparks' Libr. of Am. Biog., I. and IV.

ARMSTRONG. Papers relating to French Affairs communi-

cated by General Armstrong to Mr. Monroe. *Washington, A. & G. Way*, 1808. 8vo, pp. 21. 2025

General Armstrong also published "A Review of General Wilkinson's Memoirs," and was the author of the Newburgh Letters.

ARMSTRONG. The Life and Letters of George Mortimer, Rector of Thornhill, in the Diocese of Toronto. By John Armstrong, B.A., British Chaplain of Monte Video, South America. *London*, 1847. 8vo. 2026

ARMSTRONG (J. J.) An Oration delivered at Flushing, L. I., 4th of July, 1862. By Rev. John J. Armstrong. *New York, Edwin O. Jenkins*, 1862. 8vo, pp. 24. 2027

ARMSTRONG. An Oration delivered at Queens, L. I., July 4, 1861. By Rev. John J. Armstrong. *Jamaica (L. I.), J. J. Brenton*, 1861. 8vo, pp. 28. 2028

ARMSTRONG (J. W.) Oration delivered at Lowville, N. Y., July 4, 1861. By Rev. J. W. Armstrong. 8vo, pp. 28.

ARMSTRONG (Kosciusko). Review of T. L. M[c]Kenney's Narrative of the Causes which, in 1814, led to General Armstrong's Resignation of the War Office. By Kosciusko Armstrong. *New York, R. Craighead, Printer*, 1846. 8vo, pp. 20. H. 2030

ARMSTRONG (L.) A Sermon, delivered in Northampton, (Montgomery Co.) March 6, 1828, on the Death of Governor Clinton. By Lebbeus Armstrong, Pastor of the Presbyterian Church of Northampton and Edinburgh. *Saratoga Springs, Printed by G. M. Davison*, 1828. 8vo, pp. 24. B. 2031

ARMSTRONG. The Signs of the Times, comprised in ten lectures on the origin, nature, tendency, and alliances of the present popular efforts for the abolition of Capital Punishment. By the Rev. Lebbeus Armstrong. *New York*, 1848. 12mo, pp. 312. S. 2032

ARMSTRONG. The Temperance Reformation of this XIX Century, the Fulfilment of Divine Prophecy. A Sermon. *New York*, 1845. 8vo. 2033

ARMSTRONG. The Temperance Reformation; its History from the Organization of the First Temperance Society to the adoption of the Liquor Law of Maine, 1851 ... and the Influ-

ence of the promulgation of that Law on the Political Interest of the State of New-York, 1852. By Rev. Lebbeus Armstrong. *New York*, 1853. 12mo, pp. 408. S. 2034

ARMSTRONG. ... William Morgan abducted and murdered by Masons, in conformity with Masonic Obligations; and Masonic Measures, to conceal that Outrage against the Laws ... proved in a Sermon, by Lebbeus Armstrong, A seceding mason ... . Delivered in Edinburgh, Saratoga County, Sept. 12, 1831. ... *New York, Printed by L. D. Dewey & Co.*, 1831. 8vo, pp. 32. B. 2035

ARMSTRONG (P.) The Jawbone of an Ass examined. Being a Dialogue between Mr. Sneerhim Speakplain and Mr. Surface Shallowbrain, on the merits of a late publication, by A. H., called "General Censure, or Sampson with a Jawbone in his Hand." By Price Armstrong. *New York*, 1811. 8vo, pp. 51, XXX. S. 2036

"Personal, literary, theological, queer, and a little on America."—H. A. HOMES.

ARMSTRONG (Robert). The Influence of Climate, and other Agents, on the Human Constitution ... with ... an Account of the Epidemic Fever of Jamaica, by Robert Armstrong, M.D., F.L.S., Deputy Inspector of Hospitals and Fleets, &c. [Motto.] *London, Longman*, 1843. 8vo, pp. xv., 207. 2037

ARMSTRONG (R. G.) Memoir of Hannah Hobbie, By Rev. Robert G. Armstrong, A.M. *New York, John S. Taylor*, 1838. 24mo, pp. 255 B.+*New-York, American Tract Society* [n. d.] 24mo, pp. 255. H. 2038

[ARMSTRONG (William)]. Stocks and Stock-Jobbing in Wall Street, with sketches of the brokers, and fancy stocks ... By a reformed stock gambler. *New York*, 1848. 8vo. 2039

ARMSTRONG (W.) Petition of William Armstrong and others relating to the Coinage for the Settlement in America. [About 1700.] Broadside. 2040

ARMSTRONG (W. C.) Life and Adventures of Captain John Smith, by W. C. Armstrong. *Hartford*, 1855. 12mo. 2041

Army and Navy Chronicle, and Scientific Repository: W. Q. Force, Editor. *Washington*, 1843–44. 3 vols., 8vo. 2042

The Army and Navy Chronicle. Edited and Published by B. Homans. Vol. I. 1835. *Washington*, 1836. 4to. + Continued in large 8vo. 2043

Army and Navy Gazette. Journal of the Regular and Volunteer Forces. *New York*, 1862. Folio. Continued.

Army and Navy Journal. *See* The United States Army and Navy Journal.

The Army and Navy Official Gazette. Containing Reports of Battles; also, Important Orders of the War Department, Record of Courts-Martial, etc. Published by Authority of the War Department. *Washington, Printed at the Office of John C. Rives*, 1864. 4to. Continued. 2045

The Army and Navy Prayer Book. *Richmond, Diocesan Missionary Society, Chas. H. Wynne, Printer*, 1864. 32mo, pp. 96.

The Army Hymn Book. *Richmond, Presb. Com. of Publication*, 1863. 18mo, pp. 88. + Second Edition. 18mo, pp. 128.

Army Life; or, Incidents from the Prayer Meeting and the Field. *New York, Bd. of Pub. Ref. Pr. Dutch Church*, 1863. 18mo, pp. 179. 2048

Catalogue of the Army Medical Museum, Surgeon General's Office, Washington, D. C. January 1, 1863. *Washington, Government Printing Office*, 1863. 8vo, pp. 58. H. 2049

Army Meteorological Register ... from 1831 to 1842 inclusive ... . Prepared under Direction of Bvt. Brig. Gen'l Thomas Lawson, Surgeon General in the United States Army. *Washington, C. Alexander, Printer*, 1851. 8vo, pp. 324. 2050

Army Meteorological Register, for Twelve Years, from 1843 to 1854, inclusive, compiiled [*sic*] from Observations made by the Officers of the Medical Department of the Army, at the Military Posts of the United States. Prepared under the Direction of Brevet Brigadier General Thomas Lawson, Surgeon General United States Army. Published by Authority of Hon. Jefferson Davis, Secretary of War. *Washington, A. O. P. Nicholson, Public Printer*, 1855. 4to, pp. xi., 763 (3). Map. 2051

Army of the Potomac. History of its Campaigns. The Peninsular, Maryland, Fredericksburg. Testimony of its three

Commanders, Maj. Gen. McClellan, Maj. Gen. Burnside, and Maj. Gen. Hooker, before the Congressional Committee on the Conduct of the War. *New York, Tribune Association*, 1863. 8vo, pp. 30. 2052

Army of the Potomac. The Defence of Richmond against the Federal Army under General McClellan. By a Prussian Officer in the Confederate Service. Translated from the *Koelnische Zeitung*. *New York, George F. Nesbitt & Co.*, 1863. 8vo, pp. 16. 2052*a*

The Army Register of the United States. ... Corrected up to the 1st of June, 1814. Published by Authority. *Boston, Printed by Chester Stebbins*, 1814. 12mo, pp. vi., 112. H. + *Philadelphia*, 1814. 12mo. Continued. C. 2053

After a few years called "Official Army Register."

Army Regulations, Adopted for use of the Army of the Confederate States, in Accordance with late acts of Congress. Revised from the Army Regulations of the old United States Army, 1857; Retaining all that is Essential for officers of the Line. To which is added, an Act for the Establishment and Organization of the Army of the Confederate States of America. Also Articles of War, For the Government of the Army of the Confederate States of America. *Richmond, Va., West & Johnston*, 1861. 8vo, pp. 198. 2054

[ARNAUD (A.)] Histoire de D. Jean Palafox, eveque d'Angelopolis. [Par M. A. Arnaud. n. p.], 1690. 18mo. 2055

Title as quoted by Ternaux-Compans, No. 1044.

ARNAUD (Achille). Abraham Lincoln Sa naissance, sa vie, sa mort avec un récit de la guerre d'Amérique d'après les documents les plus authentiques par Achille Arnaud Rédacteur à l'Opinion nationale. *Paris, Charlieu frères et Huillery*, 1865. Large 8vo, pp. 96. Illustrations. H. 2056

ARNAUD (Leopold). La vérité vraie sur le conflit entre le Brésil, Buenos-Ayres, Montevideo; réponse à M. Charles Expilly. *Marseille, Boy-Estelon*, 1865. 12mo, pp. 69. 2057

ARNGRIME. Gronlandia edur Grænland saga ur Islendskum Sagna Bookum og Annalum samantekinn og a Latinskt maal Stritsud as heim heidurliga & halaerda Manni Syra. Arngrime Jonssjne Fordum Officiali Nola Stiftis og Soknarpreste ad Mel-

stad. En a Narrœnu utlogd as Ejnare Ejolfssine. *Skalhollte [Iceland], Hendrick Kruse*, 1688. 4to, pp. 45. J.C.B. 2058

The Latin original was never published. Several other works on Greenland were appended to a German version, published at Kopenhagen, 1732. 8vo.

ARNOLD (Benedict). To the | Inhabitants | of | America [Dated] New York October 7. 1780 [Signed] B Arnold. *Printed by James Rivington, Printer to the King's Most Excellent Majesty*. Broad-side, 16⅞ × 12½ inches. T.A.E. 2059

This proclamation, issued after his desertion to the British, was also published in "The Royal Gazette," New York, October 11, 1780.

ARNOLD. Proceedings | of a | General Court-Martial, of the Line, | held at | Raritan, in the State of New-Jersey, | By Order of His Excellency | George Washington, Esq. | General and Commander in Chief of the Army of | The United States of America, | for the Trial of | Major General Arnold, | June 1 1779, | Major General Howe, President. | Published by order of Congress. | *Philadelphia: | Printed by Francis Bailey, in Market Street* | M.DCC.LXXX. Folio, pp. 55. C.M. 2060

The introduction to the following *reprint* of this work (p. xxix.) states that fifty copies were printed, which will account for its extreme rarity.

ARNOLD. Proceedings of a General Court Martial for the Trial of Major General Arnold, with an Introduction, Notes and Index. *New York: Privately Printed*, 1865. 8vo, pp. xxix., 182. Portrait. 2061

Edition, 100 copies 8vo; 35 4to. Printed for F. S. Hoffman. An elegant volume.

ARNOLD. Proceedings of the Supreme Executive Council of the State of Pennsylvania, in the Case of Major General Arnold. *Philadelphia, Printed by Hall & Sellers*, 1779. 4to, pp. 11. M.

ARNOLD. Stories about Arnold, the Traitor, Andre, the Spy, and Champe, the Patriot: for ... Children ... . Second Edition. *New Haven, A. H. Maltby*, 1831. Sq. 16mo, pp. 72. Woodcuts. H. 2063

ARNOLD. Complot d'Arnold et de Sir Henry Clinton. *See* Barbé-Marbois (*Count* Fr.)

ARNOLD (C. H.) The New and Impartial Universal History of North and South America, and of the Present Trans-Atlantic War. ... By Charles Henry Arnold, Esq. Late of Philadelphia,

now of Burlington-Street. *London, Alex. Hogg* [1782]. 12mo, pp. xi., 25–276. + Also 1790 and 1796. H. 2064

"A catchpenny work, with a very long title not worth transcribing."—RICH. *See* M. R., LXVII., 73.

ARNOLD (E. G.) Persecution of the Volunteer Naval Officers ... *Providence, A. Crawford Greene, Printer*, 1863. 8vo, pp. 30.

ARNOLD (G. B.) Mr. Arnold's First Semi-Annual Report, of his Service as Minister at Large, in New-York. Published by the Book and Tract Society of the First Congregational Church. *New-York, Printed by Jas. Van Norden*, 1834. 12mo, pp. 20. Continued, at least 7 having been published. H. 2066

ARNOLD (I. N.) Argument before the United States Supreme Court, in the Case of Arthur Bronson, a citizen of the State of New-York, Complainant, and John H. Kinzie, (*et al.*) citizens of the State of Illinois, Defendants, involving the Constitutionality of the Act of ... Illinois, passed 17th February, 1841, ... the "Appraisal or Two-Thirds Valuation Law." By Isaac N. Arnold, (of Chicago Illinois,) Counsel for Complainant. [n. p., 184–.] 8vo, pp. 16. H. 2067

ARNOLD. Congressional Legislation. Speech of Hon. Isaac N. Arnold, July 14, 1864. [n. p., 1864.] 8vo, pp. 16. H.

ARNOLD. The History of Abraham Lincoln and the Overthrow of Slavery. By Isaac N. Arnold. *Chicago*, 1867. 8vo, pp. 736. C. 2069

ARNOLD. The Power, Duty, and Necessity of destroying Slavery in the Rebel States. Speech of Hon. Isaac N. Arnold, of Illinois. Delivered in the House of Representatives, January 6, 1864. 8vo, pp. 15. + Another Edition. [*Washington*], *Towers, Printers* [1864]. 8vo, pp. 8. H. 2070

ARNOLD. Ship Canal from the Mississippi to Lake Michigan. Speech of Hon. Isaac N. Arnold, of Ill., in the House of Representatives, June 30th, 1862. [n. p., 1862.] 8vo, pp. 8. H. + Delivered in the House ... January 15, 1863. [*Washington, L. Towers & Co., Printers*, 1863.] 8vo, pp. 8. 2071

ARNOLD. Reconstruction; Liberty the Corner-Stone, and Lincoln the Architect. Speech of Hon. Isaac N. Arnold, of Illinois. Delivered in the House of Representatives, March

19, 1864. *Washington, Printed by Lemuel Towers*, 1864. 8vo, pp. 14. H. 2072

ARNOLD. Slavery the Cause of the War and all its Evils. Speech of Hon. I. N. Arnold, of Ill., in the House ... February 17, 1862. [*Washington, D. C., Scammell & Co., Printers*, 1862.] 8vo, pp. 8. H. 2073

ARNOLD (J. L.) Poems. By the late Josias Lyndon Arnold, Esq; of St. Johnsbury (Vermont) formerly of Providence, and a Tutor in Rhode-Island College. *Printed at Providence by Carter & Wilkinson*, M.DCC.XCVII. 8vo, pp. 141. S. 2074

Edited by James Burrill, Jun. Contains many curious pieces relative to local history, &c.; "Elegy on the Death of Mr. Moses Brown, Jr." For a memoir of the author, *see* "The Rural Magazine and Vt. Register," Vol. II., 428–430.

ARNOLD (L. H.) Letter from Lemuel H. Arnold, in reply to the Letter of John Whipple, Esq. [Dated South Kingstown, May 1, 1845. n. p., 1845.] Broadside. H. 2075

ARNOLD. Attempted Speculation of Lemuel H. Arnold and James F. Simmons, upon the funds of the State, while they were members of the General Assembly. *Providence, Herald Office*, 1831. 8vo, pp. 23. 2076

"Relates to the proposition to unite the two Pawtucket Turnpikes."—BARTLETT.

ARNOLD. Examination of certain charges against Lemuel H. Arnold, Esq., the National Republican Candidate for Governor, being a Report of a Committee appointed April 12, 1821. *Providence*, 1831. 8vo, pp. 28. 2077

ARNOLD (R. A.) History of the Cotton Famine, from the Fall of Sumter to the Passing of the Public Works Act. By R. Arthur Arnold. *London, Saunders & Otley*, 1864. 8vo, pp. xiv., 570. + Same. With a Postscript. New Edition. *Saunders & Otley*, 1865. Post 8vo, pp. viii., 350. C. 2078

ARNOLD (Samuel). David serving his Generation, | or | a Discourse | Wherein is shewed that the great Care and | Endeavour of every Christian ought | to be, that he may be Serviceable | unto God and to the present Generation, | Delivered in a | Sermon | Preached to the General Court of the Co- | lony of New-Plimouth in New-England on the 3d. | Day of June 1674. Being the Day of Election | there. | By Samuel Arnold Teacher of the Church | of Christ at Marshfield in New England. | [Mottoes

and imprimatur 9 lines.] *Cambridge, Printed by Samuel Green*, 1674. | 4to, pp. (4), 18. B. 2079

ARNOLD (S. G.) Biographical Sketches of Distinguished Jerseymen, by S. G. Arnold. *Trenton, N. J.*, 1845. 8vo, pp. 61. C. 2080

ARNOLD. The Life of George Washington, first President of the United States. By S. G. Arnold. *New York*, 1840. 18mo, pp. 228. 2081

ARNOLD. The Life of Patrick Henry, of Virginia. By S. G. Arnold. *Auburn*, 1854. 16mo, pp. 270. C. 2082

ARNOLD. History of the State of Rhode Island and Providence Plantations. By Samuel Greene Arnold. *New York, D. Appleton & Co.*, 1859–60. 8vo, pp. xii., 574; 592. C. 2083

ARNOLD. The Spirit of Rhode Island History. A Discourse delivered before the Rhode-Island Historical Society, on the Evening of Monday January 17, 1853. By Samuel Greene Arnold, Lieut. Governor of Rhode-Island. *Providence, George H. Whitney*, 1853. 8vo, pp. 32. H. 2084

ARNOLD (Seth S.) A Sermon preached at Alstead, on the first Sabbath in January, 1826. With historical sketches of the Town. By Seth S. Arnold, Pastor of the First Congregational Church and Society, it being ten years since his Ordination. *Alstead, N. H.*, 1826. 8vo, pp. 48. 2085

ARNOLD (Thomas D.) Speech of Mr. Arnold, of Tennessee, in Committee of the Whole, in favor of "American Industry." Delivered in the House of Representatives U. S. January 24th and 25th, 1833. *Washington, Printed by Gales and Seaton*, 1833. 8vo, pp. 35. H. 2086

ARNOT (Dav. H.) Animadversions on the Proceedings of the Regents of the Smithsonian Institution in their Choice of an Architect for their Edifice at Washington. ... By David Henry Arnot, Architect. *New York*, 1847. 8vo. 2087

ARNOT (G. A. W.) *See* Beechey (Capt. W. F.)

ARNOULD (Ambroise Marie). De la balance du commerce et des rélations commerciales extérieures de la France, dans toutes les parties du globe, particulièrement à la fin du règne de Louis XIV. ... ; le tout appuyé de notes et tables raisonnées ...

Par M. Arnould. ... *Paris*, 1791. 2 vols., 8vo, and 1 vol., Tables, folded in 4to. + Seconde édition. *Paris, Buisson*, 1795. 2 vols., 8vo, and Atlas; 1 vol., 4to S. 2088

ARNOULD. Système maritime et politique des Européens, pendant le dix-huitieme siecle; fonde sur leurs traités de paix, de commerce et de navigation. Par le citoyen Arnould, chef du Bureau du Commerce, et de la Balance du Commerce. [Motto.] *Paris, Imprimerie d'Antoine Bailleul, an* V (1797). 8vo, Half Title, Title, pp. viii., 341 (3). H. 2089

"Les États-Unis de l'Amérique," pp. 232–245. Various other parts of the volume treat of commerce with America.

ARNOULD. System der Seehandlung und Politik Europa's während des 18ⁿ und als Einleitung in dem 19ᵉ Jahrhundert ... . Aus dem Französischen mit Anmerkungen [von J. Dominikus]. *Erfurt, Keyser*, 1798. 8vo. 2090

ARNOULD. Frankreichs Handlung-Bilanz und auswärtige Handlungs-beziehungen ... . [Aus dem Französischen von A. Wittenberg.] *Lübeck*, 1792. 2 vols., 8vo. 2091

ARNOULT (N. E.) Notice of the Sale of New Metz, an Estate on the Ohio River; with Plan. By N. E. Arnoult. *New York*, 1840. 8vo, pp. 14. 2092

ARNSTEDT (Fr.) Werth der gangbarsten Gold- und Silbermünzen in Europa und Nordamerika. 39 Goldmünzen. 64 Silbermünzen. Für jede dieser 103 Geldsorten ist der Werth in 20 Haupt-Staaten von Europa und Nordamerika berechnet. *Hamburg, B. S. Berendsohn*, 1854. 8vo, pp. 16. 2093

Also published with the same imprint, in French, "Évaluation des espèces," etc., and English, "Tables shewing the Value," etc.

AROSEMENA. Examen sobre la franca Communicacion entro las dos Oceanos, por el Istmo de Panama. Su Autor Juste Arosemena. *Bogota*, 1846. 8vo, pp. 48. 2094

Around the World; a Narrative of a Voyage in the East India Squadron under Com. George C. Read. By an officer of the United States Navy. *New York*, 1840. 2 vols., 12mo, pp. 336, 344. 2 Plates. 2095

AROZARENA. Informe presentado á la Junta de Gobierno del Real Consulado de la isla de Cuba, sobre el estado de la agricultura y elaboracion y beneficio de los frutos coloniales en

Jamaica, por D. Ramon Arozarena y D. Pedro Bauduy comisionados por la misma. *Imprenta Fraternal*, 1828, 4to, pp. 54. 2069

Arrangement, for the Grand & Solemn Funeral Procession. Which is to take place on the 25th May inst. 1808, at the Interment of the Remains of Eleven Thousand five hundred American Seamen, Soldiers, and Citizens, who have suffered martyrdom on board the Jersey and other British Prison Ships, in the harbour of New York, during the American Revolution. Folio, Broadside, 1 l. 2097

ARAWAK. Die Geschichte von der Marterwoche, Auferstehung und Himmelfahrt unsers Herrn und Heilandis Jesu Christi. Uebersetzt in die Aruwackische Sprache und erklärend umschrieben. *Philadelphia: Gedruckt bey Carl Cist.* 1799. Wadaijahun Wuussada-goanti, Wapussida-goanti baddia Jesus Christus &c. *Philadelphia, mun* 1799. 8vo, pp. 213. 2098

ARRAWACK. The Acts of the Apostles, translated into The Arrawack Tongue. By the Rev. Theodore Schultz, in 1802. *London*, 1807. 18mo. + *New York, American Bible Society*, 1850. 16mo, pp. 119. B. 2099

ARRAWAK. Gospels of Matthew and John in Arrawak. *London*, 1850. 12mo. 2100

ARREDONDO (N. de). Informe del virey D. Nicolas de Arredondo a su sucesor D. Pedro Melo de Portugal y Villena sobre el estado de la cuestion de limites entre las cortes de España y Portugal, en 1795. Primera Edicion. *Buenos-Aires, Imprenta del estado*, 1836. Folio, Title, pp. iii., 38, ii. (Angelis, Colección, Tomo IV.) 2101

Arrest du Conseil d'Etat du Roi. *Paris, 11 Aug.*, 1716. 4to, pp. 4. 2102

Arrest du Conseil d'Etat &c. *Paris, 9 May*, 1720. 4to, 4 l.

Relates to Louisiana.

Arrest du Conseil d'Estat du roy du 12 février 1726, qui casse une ordonnance de l'intendant du Canada, et condamne la dame Pascal et le sieur Caillaud, capitaine du vaissaud le Comte de Toulouse ... . *Paris*, 1726. 4to. 2103

Arrêt du conseil d'Etat du Roi, portant á cinq livres par

quintal, la taxe impose sur la morue de Pêche Étrangère qui sera importée aux Iles de l'Amerique du Vent & sous le Vent. Du 25 Septembre 1785 ... *A Paris, de l'Imprimerie Royale*, 1785. 4to, pp. 4. Rare. 2104

Arrêt du Roi concernant l'Établissement des Paquebots pour les Colonies Françaises et les États-Unis de l'Amérique, 1786.

The following "Arrests" relate mostly to the French colonies. Many of them are apparently privately printed, and they are all very rare. Arrest [&c.] Conseils [&c. Mdze, Col. Françaises]. *Paris*, 26 *March*, 1722. 4to, pp. 4. Arrest [&c. 5 grosses fumes &c.] *Paris*, 9 *June*, 1722. 4to, pp. 8. Arrest [etc. perception du droit]. *Paris*, 4 *July*, 1722. 4to, pp. 8. Arrest [etc. Sr de la Jaudre]. *Paris*, 15 *July*, 1722. 4to, pp. 3. Arrest [etc. Casse Ordonnance de Martinique]. *Paris*, 13 *Oct.*, 1722. 4to, pp. 4. Arrest [etc. Pour faire passer aux Marchands]. *Paris*, 13 *Oct.*, 1722. 4to, pp. 4. Arrest [etc.] 15 *Déc.*, 1722. 4to, pp. 12. Arrest, [etc. Casse sentence Elus d'Augers]. *Déc.* 22, 1722. 4to, pp. 8. Arrest [Exemption des Communités Religieuses &c.] *Paris*, 6 *Sept.*, 1723. 4to, pp. 4. Arrest [etc.] *Paris*, 27 *Fév.*, 1731. 4to, pp. 3. Arrest [etc. St. Louis, Alex. de Barbillon]. *Paris*, 6 *May*, 1731. 4to pp. 4. Arrest [etc. Sieur Hamel.] *Paris*, 8 *May*, 1731. 4to, pp. 3. Arrest [etc. Qui ordonne les deniers &c.] *Paris*, 22 *May*, 1731. 4to, pp. 3. Arrest [&c.] *Paris*, 29 *May*, 1736. 4to, pp. 4. Arrest [&c. Qui permet aux Armateurs &c.] *Paris*, 21 *May*, 1741. 4to, pp. 4. Arrest [etc. Qui permet aux negocians &c.] *Paris*, 30 *Sept.*, 1741. 4to, pp. 4. Arrest [etc. Commerce Colo. Franç. in Amérique &c.] *Paris*, 1 *March*, 1744. 4to, pp. 7. Arrest [etc. Qui suspend pendant la guerre &c.] *Paris*, 20 *April*, 1744. 4to, pp. 3. Arrest [etc. Lettres]. *Paris*, 14 *Aug.*, 1744. 4to, pp. 11. Arrest [&c. Qui, en interpretante celui du 20 Avril 1744 &c.] *Paris*, 19 *June*, 1745. 4to, pp. 3. Arrest [&c. Qui prorage pour 3 années &c.] *Paris*, 30 *Nov.*, 1745, 1746. 4to, pp. 2.

ARRIAGA (J. de). Extirpacion de la idolatria de los Indios del Peru y medios para la conversion de ellos; Por P. Pablo Joseph de Arriaga. ... *Lima, Geronymo de Contreros*, 1621. 4to, 8 p. l., pp. 148. 2106

ARRICERITA. Cronica serafica del colegio de prop. fide de la S. Cruz de Gueretaro 2da parte. *Mexico*, 1792. 2107

ARRILLAGA (Basilio José). Recopilacion de Leyes, Decretos, Bandos, Reglamentos, Circulares y Providencias de los Supremos Poderes y otras autoridades de la República Mexicana; formada de orden del supremo gobierno, de Enero de 1828 a Diciembre de 1838. *México*, 1838–1842. 13 vols., 8vo. Continued. C.

[ARRINGTON (A. W.)] The rangers and regulators of the Yanaha: or, life among the lawless. A tale of the Republic of Texas. By Charles Summerfield [A. W. Arrington], late Judge of the Rio Grande District. Author of "Sketches of the South-west." *New York* [1856]. 12mo, pp. 397. P. 2108*a*

ARRÓNIZ (M.) Manual de biografia mejicana, ó galeria de hombres célebres de Méjico; por Márcos Arróniz. *Paris, Rosa, Bouret et Cie*, 1857. 18mo, pp. 317. 2109

ARRÓNIZ. Manual de historia y cronología de Méjico. ... . *Paris, Rosa et Bouret*, 1858. 18mo, pp. 426. 2110

ARRÓNIZ. Manual del viajero en Méjico, ó Compendio de la historia de la ciudad de Méjico. *Paris*, 1858. 12mo. Map.

An Arrow against Profane and Promiscuous Dancing, drawn out of the quiver of the Scriptures. By the Ministers of Christ at Boston in New England. *Boston, Printed by Samuel Green, and are to be Sold by Joseph Brunning*, 1688. 16mo, pp. 30. M.

ARROWSMITH (A.) Neuer Zeitungsatlas von Amerika. Nach den besten Originalquellen und den letzten politischen Verträgen entworfen. *Leipzig, Er. Fleischer*, 1832. 7 sheets, sm. folio. Also with an English title, "A New General Atlas," etc. 2113

ARROWSMITH (A.) Outlines of the Physical and Political Divisions of South America, delineated by A. Arrowsmith. *London*, 1840. Folio. 2114

ARROYO Y DAZA (Diego de). Relacion de | las Vitorias qve Don Diego Arroyo y Daza, | Gouernador y Capitan General de la Prouincia de Cuma- | na, tuuo en la gran Salina de Arraya a 30. de Nouiembre del | año passado de 622. y a treze de Enero deste año, contra | ciento y quatro nauios de Olandeses. | [Colophon] *Con Licencia en Madrid, por la viuda de Alonso Martin*. | 1623.] Folio, 2 l. 2115

Reprinted the same year, the arrangement of title only varying.

ARROYO. Grammar of the Mutsun Language, spoken at the Mission of San Juan Bautista, Alta California. By Father Felipe Arroyo de la Cuesta, of the Order of St. Francis. *New York, Cramoisy Press*, 1861. Rl 8vo, pp. 48. H. 2116

Forms No. IV. of "Shea's Library of American Linguistics." 100 copies printed. The Spanish title is as follows:

ARROYO. Extracto de la gramatica mutsun, ó de la lengua de los naturales de la mision de San Juan Bautista, compuesta por el Rev. Padre Fray Felipe Arroyo de la Cuesta, del orden serafico de N. P. San Francisco, ministro de dicha mision en 1816. *Nueva-York*, 1861. 2117

ARROYO. A Vocabulary or Phrase Book of the Mutsun Language of Alta California. By the Rev. F. Felipe Arroyo de la Cuesta, of the Order of St. Francis. *New York, Cramoisy Press*, 1862. Imp. 8vo, pp. 96. H. 2118

Forms No. VIII. of "Shea's Library of American Linguistics." 100 copies printed. The Latin title is "... Alphab. Rivulus obeundus, Exprimationum Causa horum Indorum Mutsun Missionis Sanct. Joann. Baptistæ, exquisitarum a Fr. Philipp. ab Ar.Yo. de la Cuesta, supradictæ Missionis Indion. Minist. ... Año de 1815, con privilegio de ......"

ARSCOT. Some | Considerations | Relating to the Present State | of the | Christian Religion, | Wherein the Nature, End and Design | of Christianity, as well as the Principal Evidence | of the Truth of it, are explained and recommended out of the Holy Scriptures; with a ge- | neral Appeal to the Experience of all Men for | Confirmation thereof. | By Alexander Arscot. | [Motto.] *London, Printed: Reprinted by B. Franklin at the New | Printing-Office, in Philadelphia*, 1732. Sm. 8vo, pp. 112. 2118*a*

ARSCOT. Some Considerations | Relating to the Present State | of the Christian Religion. | Part II. | Wherein the Principal Evidence of | the Christian Religion is explain'd and defended | upon the principles of Reason as well as Revela- | tion; With Observations on some Passages in the | Book intituled, Christianity as old as the Creation, so far as concerns the Doctrine herein advanced. | By Alexander Arscot. [Motto.] *London, Printed: Reprinted by B. Franklin, | at the New | Printing Office in Philadelphia*, 1732. Sm. 8vo, pp. 140; Contents, 1 l.; Advt., 1 l.

Art of Domestic Happiness, and other Poems. By the Recluse. *Pittsburgh, Robert Patterson*, 1817. 12mo, pp. 316; Errata, 1 l. 2119

Some of these poems are descriptive of Western life.

The Art of Making Common Salt. Particularly adapted to the American Colonies ... Detached from the Pennsylvania Magazine for March 1776. *Philadelphia, Printed for R. Aitken*, M.DCC.LXXVI. 8vo, pp. 7. Plate. + *Boston*, 1776. 8vo, pp. 15.

The Art of making Sugar: Under the Heads of I. The Natural History ... II. The Culture of the Sugar-Cane. III. The Mills ... and Furnaces, Coppers, &c. ... [etc.] *London, R. Willock*, M.DCC.LII. 4to, Title, pp. 34 (1.) H. 2120*a*

Art of Pleading. In Imitation of part of Horace's Art of Poetry. *New York, James Parker*, 1751. 8vo, pp. 16. N. 2121

Art of Speaking and holding one's Tongue in and out of Doors, earnestly recommended, at this time, to the Serious Perusal of all Candidates and Electors. *London*, 1761. 8vo.

Principally relating to America.

Art of Speaking. ... *Philadelphia, R. Aitken* ... M.DCC.LXXV. 12mo, pp. 299 (10). 2123

Art de vérifier les dates. *See* Warden (D. B.)

Arte de la lengua névome, que se dice pima, propia de Sonora; con la doctrina christiana y confessionario añadidos. *San Augustin de la Florida*, 1862. 8vo, pp. 97, 32. H. 2124

With another title: "Grammar of the Pima or Névome, a Language of Sonora, from a Manuscript of the XVIII Century, edited by Buckingham Smith. *New York, Cramoisy Press*, 1862." The "Doctrina y confessionario" has a separate title-page. Forms No. V. of "Shea's Library of American Linguistics." 160 copies printed.

ARTEMUS WARD, *pseudon.* *See* [Brown (C. F.)]

ARTETA DE MONTESEGURO (Ant.) Discurso instruct. sobre las ventajas que puede conseguir la industria de Aragon, con la nueva ampliacion de puertos concedida por para el comercio libre de America ... . *Madrid, Imp. Real*, 1783. 4to. 2125

ARTHAUD. Discours prononcé à l'ouverture de la première séance publique du cercle des Philadelphes, tenue au Cap-François le 11 mai 1785; avec une description de la ville de Cap, pour servir à l'histoire des maladies que l'on y observe ... . Par M. Arthaud ... . *Paris*, 1785. 8vo. Bm. 2126

ARTHAUD. Recherches sur la constitution des naturels de Saint Domingue, sur leur arts, leur industrie, et leurs moyens de subsistance. Par M. Arthaud. *Cap François*, 1786. 4to.

ARTHUR (A. H.) Report of Alex. H. Arthur, Commissioner, to Gov. M'Willie, on the Two and Three per cent. Trust Funds and Graves' Defalcation. Printed by Order of the Governor. *Jackson, Mississippian Steam Power Press Print*, 1858. 8vo, pp. 54. H. 2128

ARTHUR (John). The Genealogy of Jesus Christ, according to St. Matthew and St. Luke; Examined, Illustrated, and Vin-

dicated ... By John Arthur, Gent. *New York, James Parker and Company*, 1762. 8vo, pp. 16. 2129

ARTHUR (O. R.) The Three Sisters: or, The Life, Confession, and Execution of Amy, Elizabeth, and Cynthia Halzingler, Who were Tried, Convicted, and Executed, at Elizabethtown, Ark., Nov. 30, 1854, for the Awful and Horrible Murder of the Edmonds Family, consisting of Seven Members, together with the Speech of the Eldest Sister, Amy, on the Gallows Edited by Rev. O. R. Arthur. *Baltimore* [etc.], *A. R. Orton*, 1855. 8vo, Title, pp. 21–50. 4 Woodcuts. H. 2130

ARTHUR. A Sermon Preached at the Ordination of the Rev. Mr. Daniel Thane, at Connecticut-Farms, in New Jersey, August 29th, 1750. By T. Arthur, M.A., Pastor of the Presbyterian Church in the City of New Brunswick. Together with an exhortation, delivered to the people, by C. Smith, A.M. *New York, Printed by James Parker*, 1750. 8vo, pp. 48. P. 2131

ARTHUR (Timothy Shaw). The History of Georgia, from its Earliest Settlement to the Present Time. By T. S. Arthur and W. H. Carpenter. *Philadelphia, Lippincott, Grambo & Co.*, 1853. 12mo, pp. 331. Portrait and Engraved Title. H. 2132

ARTHUR. The History of Kentucky, from its Earliest Settlement to the Present Time. By T. S. Arthur and W. H. Carpenter. *Philadelphia, Lippincott, Grambo & Co.*, 1853. 12mo, pp. 316. Portrait and Engraved Title. H. 2133

ARTHUR. The History of New York from its Earliest Settlement to the Present Time. By T. S. Arthur and W. H. Carpenter. *Philadelphia, Lippincott & Co.*, 1853. 16mo, pp. 336. C. 2134

ARTHUR. The History of Virginia, from its Earliest Settlement to the Present Time. By T. S. Arthur and W. H. Carpenter. *Philadelphia, Lippincott & Co.*, 1852. 12mo, pp. 332.

ARTHUR. Loyal Publication Society, ... No. 57. Growler's Income Tax. By T. S. Arthur. [*New York*, 1864.] 8vo, pp. 4. 2136

ARTHUR. Home Heroes, Saints and Martyrs. By T. S. Arthur. *Philadelphia*, 1865. 12mo, pp. 296. 2137

ARTHUR (W.) The American Question I. English Opinion on the American Rebellion. By the Rev. William Arthur ... II. Slavery the ground of Southern Secession. Extract from a speech of the Hon. A. Stephens ... *London, Sampson Low, Son & Co.*, 1861. 12mo, pp. 12. F. 2138

Another edition of Arthur's tract was published by the Manchester Union and Emancipation Society.

ARTHUR CARRYL. *See* [Osborn (Laughton)].

ARTHUS (Gotard). Historia | Indiae | Orientalis, | ex variis Avctori- | bvs collecta, et ivxta | Seriem Topographicam Regno- | rum, Prouinciarum & Insularum, per Africæ, | Asiæque littora, ad extremos vsque Ia- | ponios deducta, | Qva Regionvm et Insvlarvm | situs & commoditas; Regum & populorum mores & | habitus; Religionum & superstitionum absurda varie- | tas; Lusitanorum item Hispanorum & Batauorum res | gestæ atque Commercia varia, cum rebus admira- | tione & memoratu dignissimis alijs, iucun- | da breuitate percensentur atq; | describuntur. | Avtore | M. Gotardo Arthvs | Dantiscano. | *Coloniae Agrippinae*, | *Sumptibus VVilhelmi | Lutzenkirch*. | *Anno* M.DC.VIII. | Sm. 8vo, 10 p. l., pp. 616. 2139

This is an abridgment of the Petits Voyages of De Bry. Arthus assisted in the compilation of Hulsius's Voyages.

Articles agreed on by the Archbishops and Bishops of both Provinces and the whole Clergy in the Convocation holden at London in 1562, for the Avoiding of Diversities of Opinions, and for the Stablishing of Consent touching true Religion. *Boston, N. E., Richard Pierce*, 1688. 4to, Title, pp. 14. W.

Articles of Agreement, for carrying on an Expedition, by Hudson's Straights, for the Discovery of a North-West Passage to the Western and Southern Ocean of America. Dated March 30, 1745. *Dublin: Printed in the Year* MDCCXLVI. 8vo, pp. 16.

The expedition was undertaken at the instance of Arthur Dobbs. *See* Ellis's Voyage to Hudson's Bay, 1748.

Articles of Confederation and Perpetual Union between the States of New-Hampshire, Massachusetts-Bay, Rhode Island and Providence Plantations, Connecticut, New York, New Jersey, Pennsylvania, Delaware, Maryland, Virginia, North Carolina, South Carolina, and Georgia. *Lancaster, Printed by Francis Bailey*, 1777. Folio, pp. 26. + *New London* [*Conn.*], 1777. Folio, pp. 11. + *Boston*, 1777. Folio, pp. 16. + *Newbern, Re-*

printed, James Davis, 1777. Folio, pp. 9. + *Williamsburg, Printed by Alexander Purdie*. [n. d.] Folio, pp. 4. H. + *Annapolis, Printed by Frederick Green*. [n. d.] 8vo, pp. 15. + *Exeter, N. H., Printed by Zechariah Fowle*, 1777. Folio, pp. 8. + *Williamsburg, Printed by J. Dixon and W. Hunter*, 1778. 4to, pp. 15. C. 2142

Also printed as a broadside folio.

Articles for the better government of the Troops of the Twelve united Colonies of North America. *Philadelphia, W. & T. Bradford*, 1775. 8vo, pp. 16. P. 2143

Articles of Peace and alliance between the most Serene and Mighty Prince Charles II. ... And the most Serene and Mighty Prince Lewis XIV. the most Christian King, concluded the 21–23 day of July, 1667. ... *Printed by the Assigns of John Bill and Christopher Barker* [1667]. 4to, pp. 46. C. 2144

Containing articles for restoring to Great Britain. St. Christopher, Acadia, Antigua, Monsarat, etc. *See* Kennett's Bib. Am. Primordia, p. 121.

Articles of Peace between the most Serene and Mighty Prince Charles II. ... And several Indian Kings and Queens, &c. Concluded the 29th day of May, 1677. Published by his Majesty's command. *London, Printed by John Bill, Christopher Barker, &c.*, 1677. 4to. 2145

Articles of Peace between ... Charles II ... and the ... States General of the United Netherlands; Concluded at Westminster the $\frac{9}{19}$ day of February, $167\frac{3}{4}$. ... *Printed by the Assigns of John Bill and Christopher Barker*, $167\frac{3}{4}$. 4to, pp. (2) 12. B. 2146

Also published in Latin, "Articuli Pacis," etc. *Hagae Comitum, J. Scheltus*, 1674. 4to, pp. 16. Also in Dutch, "Articulen van de Vreede," etc. [n. p., n. d.] pp. 8; and "Translaet uyt het Latijn. Articulen," etc. *S'Gravenhage, J. Scheltus*, 1674. 4to, pp. 20. + *Middelb., Pt. v. Gætthem*, 1674. 4to, pp. 20. The Fifth Article relates to the colony of Surinam.

Articles of Peace and Alliance between the most Serene and Mighty Prince Charles II. ... And the most Serene and Mighty Lords the States General of the United Netherlands; Concluded at Breda the 21–31 day of July, 1667. ... *In the Savoy*, 1667. 4to, pp. 31. C. 2147

Partly relates to the Nieuw Netherlands. Also in Dutch, "Tractaet," n. p., n. d. 4to, pp. (2), 38.

Articles of Peace between William III. and Louis XIV. Sept. 1697. *London*, 1697. 4to. 2148

Refers to Hudson's Bay. In Dutch, "Tractaet," etc., *'sGrav.*, 1697. 4to.

Articles of Peace, Friendship and Entercourse, concluded and agreed between the Protector and Common-wealth of England, and the Queen and Kingdom of Sweden: with reference had to a peculiar Treaty, or Contract, for what concerns Commerce to be exercised in America. Dated May 19, 1654. 2149

Title from Kennett's Bib. Am. Prim., 106. A Dutch version "Articulen van het Tractaet," etc. [n. p.], 1654. 4to, pp. 8. Another version in Aitzema, III., 1088–91, is dated April 11.

Articles of Peace made between the Common-wealth of England, and that of the United Provinces of the Netherlands, with a Proclamation of it by his Highness the Lord Protector. Given at Whitehall 26, April, 1654. 4to. 2150

Another edition, translated from the Dutch, and published at London, May 2, 1654. 4to, pp. 17.

Articles of the Treaty of Peace betwixt England and France, and a particular Reference of the Controversie betwixt both Parties, touching the Forts of Penitacot, St. John, and Port-Royal, lately taken in America. With a Proclamation of the Said Peace, by Oliver, Lord Protector. Given at Whitehall 20th of November 1655. 4to. 2151

See also Tractatus Pacis, and Bib. Am. Prim., pp. 46, 75, 105, 106, 120, 121, 243. A Dutch translation, "Artikelen von Vrede," etc. *s'Gravenhaga, A. Vlacq*, 1655. 4to, pp. 8.

The Articles of War of the Confederate States of America. *Charleston, S. C.*, 1861. 8vo. 2152

Articles of War for the Government of the Armies of the Confederate States. *Charleston*, 1861. 8vo. 2153

Articles touching Navigation and Commerce between ... Charles II. ... And the High and Mighty Lords the States General of the United Netherlands, concluded the 21–31 day of July, 1667. ... *Printed by the Assigns of John Bill and Christopher Barker*, 1667. 4to, pp. 75. 2154

Pages 8 and 9 refer to the trade and navigation of Africa and America.

Articul-Brief van de Generael Nederlandsche Geoctrooirde West-Indische Compagnie ... by de ... Staten Generael ... op den 12 April 1675 geapprobeert ... . *s'Gravenhage, J. Scheltus*, 1675. 4to, pp. 40. 2154*a*

Articuli Pacis et Confoederationis inter ... Lusitaniae Regem

... et ... Foederati Belgii Ordines ... conclusae. *Hagae Comitum, Hill. à Wouw*, 1663. 4to, pp. 24. 2154*b*

This treaty between Portugal and the States General relates to Brazil.

Articuli Pacis inter ... Carolum ... II. ... et ... Ordines Gener. Foeder. Belgii Provinc. ... conclusae [31 Julii]. *Hagæ Comitum, H. à Wouw*, 1667. 4to, pp. 44. 2154*c*

Artikel ... tusschen Carel de II. ... Koninck van Engeland ... ende de ... Staten Generael ... om de geschillen der Engelsche ... en Nederlandsche Oost-Indische Compagnien te voorkomen, Gesl. den 8 Martii 1675 O. St. *Gedruckt*, 1675. 4to, pp. 8. 2155

Articulen ende conditien gemaeckt by het overleveren van Brasilien, als mede het Recif, Maurits Stadt ende Forten ende sterckten daer aen dependerende gesl. den 26 Jan. 1654. *'s Gravenhage, Jan Pietersz* [pseudon.], 1654. pp. 8. 2155*a*

Articulen van Vrede ende Confederatie Tusschen de Republique van Engelandt, Ende de Staten Generael van de Vereenighde Nederlantsche Provintien. *Tot Harderwijck, Vor Ryckaert de Vrede, in 't Jaer ons Heeren* 1654. 4to, 8 l. 2156

Some copies have *s'Gravenhaga*, and others *Wtrecht* instead of *Harderwijck*. *Ryckaert de Vrede* is a pseudonym. This was translated and published at London, May 2, 1654. 4to, pp. 17. *See* No. 2150 *supra*.

Articulen van Vrede | ende Confœderatie, | Gheslooten tusschen den | Doorluchtighsten Coningh van Portugael | ter eenre, Ende de Hoogh Mogende Heeren | Staten Generael der Vereenighde Neder- | landen, ter andere zyde. | *In 'sGraven-Hage, | By Hillebrandt van Wouw, Ordinaris Drucker vande Ho: Mo: | Heeren Staten Generael der Vereenighde Nederlanden.* | *Anno* 1663. Met Privilegie. | 4to, 14 l. 2157

Articulen van Vrede | Ende Verbondt, tusschen | den Doorluchtighsten, Grootmachtighsten Prins ende | Heere, Heere Karel, de tweede van dien naem, | Koningh van Groot Britannien, ter eenre; ende de | Hoogh Mogende Heeren Staten Generael der Veree- | nighde Nederlantsche Provintien, ter andere zijde ge- | slooten. | *Na de Copye, | In 'sGravenhage, | By Hillebrant van Wouw, Ordinaris Drucker van de Hoog | Mogende Heeren Staten Generael der Vereenighde Nederlanden.* | *Anno* 1667. Met Privilegie. | 4to, 12 l. 2158

The original of the treaty of Breda, July 31st, 1667, relates to the New Netherlands. Another edition was published with the same imprint. Imp. 4to, pp. 40

As It Is. [Manners and Customs in Washington recently.] *Albany*, 1860. 12mo, pp. 260. 2159

As the great business of the polite world is the eager pursuit of amusement, and as the Public diversions of the Season have been interrupted by the hostile parade in the capital, the exhibition of a new farce may not be unentertaining. The Group, as lately acted and to be re-acted to the wonder of all superior intelligences, nigh head quarters to Amboyna. The author has thought proper to borrow the following spirited lines from a late celebrated poet, and offer to the public by way of Prologue, which cannot fail of pleasing at this crisis. [Quotation, 12 lines from Pope.] *Boston: Printed and Sold by Edes and Gill*, 1775. 8vo, pp. 22. + *Philadelphia: Reprinted, James Humphreys, Junr.*, 1775. 2160

As you were! A Word of Advice To Straight-Haired Folks: addressed to the Freemen of Connecticut, by One of their Number. To which is subjoined a Nomination for Assistants, and a List of Candidates for Election, as Representatives to Congress. [*New-Haven, T. G. Woodward, Print.*, 1816.] 8vo, pp. 16. H. 2161

ASBURY (Francis). Journal of Francis Asbury, Bishop of the Methodist Episcopal Church in America, from August 7th, 1771, to December 29th, 1778. *Philadelphia*, 1792. + August 7, 1771, to December 7, 1815. *New-York, N. Bangs and T. Mason, for the Methodist Episcopal Church*, 1821. 3 vols., 8vo, pp. viii., 400; 400; 420. B. 2162

ASBURY. Extract from the Journal of Francis Asbury, from Jan. 1, 1779, to Sept. 3, 1780. *Philadelphia*, 1802. 12mo.

Ascot Mining Company, Lower Canada. Reports on Condition and Prospects ... *Boston*, 1864. 8vo, pp. 23. H. 2164

ASCHENFELDT (Friedrich). Memoiren aus meinem Tagebuche, geführt während meiner Reisen und meines Aufenthaltes in Brasilien in den Jahren 1843 bis 1847. *Oldenburg, H. Fränckel*, 1848. 8vo, pp. iv., 156. 2165

ASCHLUND (Arent). Iver Beres Grönlands Beskrivelse, med et Kaart og Forerindring. *Kjöbenhavn*, 1832. + 2[det] forbedrede Oplag. *Kjöbenhavn*, 1832. + A German translation. *Kjöb.*, 1833. 8vo. 2166

ASCHMANN (Rudolf). Drei Jahre in der Potomac-Armee oder eine Schweizer Schützen-Compagnie im nordamerikanischen Kriege. *Richtersweil, Lang*, 1865. 8vo, pp. iv., 228.

ASH (JOHN). The | Present State of Affairs | in Carolina. | By John Ash, Gent. | Sent by several of the Inhabitants of that Colony, to | deliver their Representation thereof to, | and seek Redress from the Lords Proprietors of that Prov- | ince: Together with an Account of his Reception, | by the Honourable the Lord Granville, their Palatine, | President, or Chief of the Proprietors. [*London*, 1706.] 4to, Half-Title, and pp. 29–67 of Appendix to "The Case of the Protestant Dissenters in Carolina," *London*, 1706. C. 2168

[ASH (John)]. Charters of Carolina, and appendix of documents. *London*, 1706. Numbered from No. 1 to No. 14, forming 67 pp., 4to. C. 2169

"The above tract, now rare, is said by Oldmixon [who wrote contemporaneously] to have been drawn up by John Ash, on his mission to the proprietary government of Carolina in London. It is usually found appended to "The Case of the Protestant Dissenters in Carolina," *London*, 1706, and is on the same subject. Sometimes also found separately, but without title-page."—A. R. S.

ASH (St. George). A Sermon Preach'd before the Incorporated Society for the Propagation of the Gospel in Foreign Parts; at their Anniversary Meeting in the Parish-Church of St. Mary-le-Bow; on Friday the 18th of February, 1714. By the Right Reverend Father in God, St. George, Lord Bishop of Clogher in Ireland. *London, J. Downing*, 1715. 8vo, pp. 62. M.

ASH (S.) A Letter of many Ministers in Old England, requesting the judgment of their reverend Brethren in New England concerning nine positions. Written A.D. 1637. Together with their answer thereunto returned, anno 1639, and the reply unto the said answer sent over unto them, anno 1640. Now published by Simeon Ash and William Rathband. *London, for Thomas Underhill*, 1643. Sm. 4to, 5 p. l., pp. 90. 2171

A[SH] (T[homas]). Carolina; | Or | A | Description | Of the Present State of that | Country, | and | The Natural Excellencies thereof; viz. The | Healthfulness of the Air, Pleasantness of the Place, | Advantage and Usefulness of those Rich Commo- | dities there plentifully abounding, which much | encrease and flourish by the Industry of the Plan- | ters that daily enlarge that Colony. | Published by T. A. Gent. | Clerk on Board His Majesties Ship the Richmond, which was | sent out in the Year 1680, with

particular Instructions to | enquire into the State of that Country, by His Majesties | Special Command, and Return'd this Present Year, 1682. | *London, | Printed for W. C., and to be Sold by Mrs. Grover* ... | ... 1682. 4to, pp. (2), 40. C. & H. 2172

Reprinted in Carrol Coll. II., pp. 59–84.

ASHBURNHAM, *Mass.* Annual Report of the School Committee, of Ashburnham, 1849–50. *Fitchburg, Printed by C. C. Curtis*, 1850. 12mo, pp. 11. Continued; 1851–52, and later reports, 8vo. 2173

A Copy of the Valuation and Taxes of the Town of Ashburnham, for the Year 1857. *Fitchburg, Printed by E. & J. F. D. Garfield*, 1857. 8vo, pp. 30. H. 2174

Prospectus and Reports on the Ashburton Coal Company's Estate, in Schuylkill and Luzerne Counties, Penn. Office, No. 39 William Street, New York. *New York, Dodge & Grattan, Printers*, 1864. 8vo, pp. 16. Map. H. 2175

ASHBURTON (*Lord*). *See* Baring (Alexander).

ASHCROFT. Ashcroft's Railway Directory for 1866, containing an Official List of the Officers and Directors of the Railroads in the United States and Canada, together with their Financial Condition and Amount of Rolling Stock. Compiled from Official Reports by John Ashcroft. *New York, John Ashcroft*, 1866. 8vo, pp. 172. 2176

ASHE (Thomas). A Commercial View, and Geographical Sketch, of the Brasils in South America, and of the Island of Madeira ... . By T. Ashe, Esq. Who travelled the Continent of America several Years. *London, Allen & Co.*, 1812. 8vo, Title, pp. 160. H. 2177

According to the "Monthly Review," LXX., pp. 219, a compilation of no merit whatever.

ASHE. Memoirs and Confessions of Capt. Ashe. Written by Himself. *London*, 1815. 3 vols., post 8vo. P. 2178

ASHE. Memoirs of Mammoth and various other Extraordinary and stupendous bones of non-descript animals found in the vicinity of the Ohio, Wabash, Illinois, Mississippi, Missouri, Osage and Red Rivers ... [and now in the Liverpool Museum]. By Thomas Ashe. *Liverpool*, 1806. 8vo, pp. 60. 2179

ASHE. Travels in America, performed in 1806, For the Purpose of exploring the Rivers Alleghany, Monongahela, Ohio,

and Mississippi, and Ascertaining the Produce and Condition of their Banks and Vicinity. By Thomas Ashe, Esq. In Three Volumes. *London, Phillips*, 1808. 12mo, pp. iv., iv., 328; 2 p. l., 292; 2 p. l., 310. + *Newburyport, Re-printed for William Sawyer & Co.*, 1808. 12mo, pp. 366. H. 2180

Some copies have the imprint, *New York*, 1808. Also included in Phillips' Voyages, v. X., and Pinkerton. "An unmeasured hatred of the Americans pervades the whole of Mr. Ashe's narrative. His account of the Atlantic States forms the most comprehensive piece of national abuse we ever recollect to have perused. Their inhabitants it seems are all abominably vicious; but in degrees very nicely distinguished; the middle states being bad—the northern very bad—and the southern execrable."—Ed. Rev., XV., 349. *See also* Quar. Rev.

ASHER (Adolph). A short Bibliographical Memoir of the Collection of Voyages and Travels published by Levinus Hulsius, at Nuremberg and Francfort, from 1598 to 1650. By A. Asher. [s. l.], 1833, 8vo, pp. 16. 2181

This was extracted from Asher's "Monthly List of Old Books," afterwards reprinted, with the following title:

ASHER. Bibliographical Essay on the Collection of Voyages and Travels, edited and published by Levinus Hulsius and his Successors at Nuremberg and Francfort from Anno 1598 to 1660. By A. Asher. *London and Berlin, A. Asher*, 1839. 4to, 3 p. l., pp. 118. H. 2182

One hundred and twenty copies printed.

ASHER (C. W.) Über die deutschen Handelsverhältnisse zu den Ländern des westlichen Amerika. Ein Vortrag, gehalten am 8. Mai 1850 im Verein zur Centralisation deutscher Auswanderung und Colonisation zu Berlin. *Berlin*, 1850. 8vo, pp. 37. 2183

With an official report "Über Californien," by Butler King.

ASHER (G. M.) Henry Hudson the Navigator, the original Documents in which his career is recorded, collected, partly translated, and annotated with an introduction. By G. M. Asher. *London, Hakluyt Society*, 1860. 8vo. 2184

Mr. Hannah, librarian of the Long Island Historical Society, has printed a Sketch of Henry Hudson, the Navigator. By Dr. G. M. Asher, of Heidelberg. *Brooklyn, Reprinted for Private Circulation.* 8vo. pp. 23.

ASHER. Prospectus of a Bibliographical and Historical Essay on the Dutch Books and Pamphlets relating to New-Netherland, and to the Dutch West-India Company, as also on the Maps, Charts, &c. of New-Netherland. Compiled from the Dutch

public and private libraries, and chiefly from the collection of Mr. Frederick Muller in Amsterdam. By G. M. Asher. *Amsterdam*, 1854–55. 4to, 2 l., pp. 120; a List of the Maps and Charts of New-Netherland, pp. 22.; List of Names, pp. 23. Map. N. 2185

Also on large paper. Owing to a dispute between the author and the publisher this work was not completed. It terminates abruptly at page 120, followed by three pages of additions and corrections, which, *prima facie*, convey the idea that the work is complete. Trömel, in his Bib. Amer., evidently had access to the unpublished MS., as he refers to numbers as high as 300, whereas this work describes only 117. *See* Bib. Am. Vet., xxxvi.

ASHER (J.) Incidents in the Life of the Rev. J. Asher, Pastor of Shiloh (Coloured) Baptist Church, Philadelphia, U. S., and A Concluding Chapter on Facts illustrating the Unrighteous Prejudice existing in the Minds of American Citizens toward their Coloured Brethren, with an Introduction by Wilson Armistead ... . *London, Charles Gilpin*, 1850. 16mo, pp. (4), 80. H. 2186

ASHLEY (Chester). Speech ... on the Oregon Question. ... April 3, 1846. *Washington, ... Blair and Rives*, 1846. 8vo, pp. 16. H. 2187

ASHLEY (F. B.) Mormonism: an Exposure of the Impositions adopted by the sect called "The Latter-day Saints." By the Rev. F. B. Ashley. *London*, 1851. 8vo, pp. 36. 2188

ASHLEY (James M.) The Rebellion—Its Causes and Consequences. A Speech delivered by Hon. J. M. Ashley, at College Hall in the City of Toledo, Tuesday Evening, Nov. 26, 1861. *Toledo, Pelton and Waggoner, Printers*, 1861. 8vo, pp. 21. + [*Washington, Towers, Printers*, 1861.] 8vo, pp. 16. H.

ASHLEY. Success of the Calhoun Revolution: the Constitution changed and Slavery nationalized by the Usurpations of the Supreme Court. Speech of Hon. James M. Ashley, of Ohio. Delivered in the U. S. House of Representatives, May 29, 1860. *Washington, D. C., Buell & Blanchard, Printers*, 1860. 8vo, pp. 30. H. 2190

ASHLEY. Protection and Freedom in Arizona. Speech of Hon. J. M. Ashley, of Ohio. Delivered in the House of Representatives, May 8, 1862. [*Washington, Printed by L. Towers & Co.*, 1862.] 8vo, pp. 8. H. 2191

Also, Speeches: "Initiate Emancipation." *April* 11, 1862. 8vo, pp. 8. Protection and Freedom in Arizona. *May* 8, 1862. 8vo, pp. 8. The Liberation and Resto-

ration of the South. *March* 30, 1864. 8vo, pp. 15. Speech, Jan. 6, 1865, on the Constitutional Amendment for the Abolition of Slavery. *New York*, 1865. 8vo, pp. 22. Another Edition. 8vo, pp. 8. Impartial Suffrage. *May* 29, 1866. 8vo, pp. 15.

ASHLEY (John). Memoirs and Considerations concerning The Trade and Revenues of the British Colonies in America. With Proposals for rendering those Colonies more Beneficial to Great Britain. By John Ashley Esq; *London, C. Corbett* [etc.] 1740. 8vo, pp. vi., 154. H. 2192

"This pamphlet relates principally to the Produce of Sugar in the West Indies, and the markets for it."—RICH.

ASHLEY. The Second Part of Memoirs and Considerations Concerning the Trade and Revenues of the British Colonies in America; Tending to shew How the Trade and Interest of those Colonies are interwoven with the Interest of Great Britain, and that the Traffick, Wealth and Strength of the whole British Empire may thereby be greatly increased. By John Ashley, Esq; Late Deputy-Surveyor and Auditor-General of all his Majesty's Revenues arising in Barbados, and the Windward Caribbee Islands in America, and a Member of his Majesty's Council in the said Island of Barbados. *London, Printed by H. Kent for E. Comyns*, MDCCXLIII. 8vo, pp. xii., 127. H. 2193

ASHLEY. A Supplement to the Second Part of the Memoirs of the Trade and Revenues of the British Colonies in America. By John Ashley. 1744. 8vo. 2194

[ASHLEY.] Some Observations on A Direct Exportation of Sugar, from the British Islands. With Answers to Mr. Toriano's Objections to it. In a letter from a Gentleman in Barbados, to his Friend in London. [Signed John Ashley.] *London*, M.DCC.XXXV. 4to, pp. 23. H. 2195

[ASHLEY.] The Sugar Trade, with the Incumbrances thereon, Laid Open. By A Barbadoes Planter. *London, J. Peele*, 1734. 8vo, pp. (8), 22, and 2 folded leaves. W. & H. 2196

ASHLEY (Jonathan). A Letter From the Reverend Mr. Jonathan Ashley, To the Reverend Mr. William Cooper. In Answer to his Objections to Mr. Ashley's Sermon; as publish'd in the Boston Gazette, January 11th. 1743. [*Boston, S. Eliot*, 1743.] 4to, pp. 7. H. & W. 2197

ASHLEY. ... Sermon at Gathering of a Church at New

Salem, and Ordination of Rev. Samuel Kendall, Dec. 15, 1742. By Rev. Jonathan Ashley. *Boston*, 1743. 8vo, pp. 36. M.

ASHLEY. ... A Sermon Preach'd at Deerfield, Nov. 25. 1741. Upon the gathering a Church for Fall-Town [now Bernardstown], and the Ordination of Mr. John Norton ... . By Jonathan Ashley ... . *Boston, Printed by S. Kneeland and T. Green*, 1742. 8vo, Title, pp. 28. H. 2199

ASHLEY. ... A Sermon Preached at Northfield, Jan. 11. 1748. the Day before the Interment of the Remains of the Reverend Benjamin Doolittle, Pastor of the Church there. Who died January 9. 1748, in the 54th Year of his Age, and 30th of his Ministry. By Jonathan Ashley, A.M. ... *Boston, Printed by Rogers and Fowle*, 1749. 8vo, pp. 26. H. 2200

Mr. Ashley also published "The Great Duty of Charity ... A Sermon ... *Boston, S. Eliot*, 1742." 8vo, pp. (4), 25. "A Sermon at the Ordination of Samuel Kendall, at New Salem, 1742." "An humble Attempt," etc. *Boston*, 1753. 4to, pp. 26. "Churches consisting of Saints. Two Sermons. *Boston*, 1753." 8vo, pp. 26.

ASHLEY (S. S.) Present Duty. An Address delivered before the Worcester & Middlesex Temperance Union, at Ashland, Mass., November 11, 1862. By Rev. S. S. Ashley, of Northborough. *Published by the Worcester and Middlesex Temperance Union*, 1863. 8vo, pp. 8. H. 2201

In favor of a prohibitory liquor law.

ASHMEAD (J. W.) Opening Speech of John W. Ashmead, United States District Attorney, in the Case of the United States vs. Castner Hanway, indicted for Treason, in the Circuit Court of the United States for the Eastern District of Pennsylvania, Delivered November 28, 1851. *Philadelphia, B. Mifflin, Printer*, 1851. 8vo, pp. 24. H. 2202

ASHMEAD (William). A Sermon, preached in the Second Presbyterian Church, Charleston, May 24, 1829, on assuming the Pastoral Charge ... . By William Ashmead. ... *Charleston, Observer Office Press*, 1829. 8vo, pp. 47. H. 2203

ASHMUN (J.) History of the American Colony in Liberia, from December 1821 to 1823. By J. Ashmun. Compiled from the Authentic Records of the Colony. *Washington, Printed by Way & Gideon*, 1826. 8vo, pp. 42. Map. H. 2204

ASHMUN (George). Speech of Mr. Geo. Ashmun of Mass.

on the Mexican War, Feb. 4. 1847. *Washington*, 1847. 8vo, pp. 16. 2205

Also, Speeches, July 27, 1846, on the Bill for additional Fortifications. 8vo, pp. 7. Reply to the attack of C. J. Ingersoll upon Daniel Webster, April 27, 1846. 8vo, pp. 16. Speech of Emancipation in [the French] Colonies. 8vo, pp. 16. Speech upon the Texas Boundary, Aug. 14, 1850. 8vo, pp. 15.

ASHMUN. Memoir of the Life and Character of the Rev. Samuel Bacon, A.M. late an Officer of Marines in the United States' Service: afterwards Attorney at Law in ... Pennsylvania: and subsequently a Minister of the Episcopal Church, and Principal Agent Of the American Government for persons liberated from Slave-Ships, on the Coast of Africa; Where he [died] ... May, 1820. By J. Ashmun. *Washington City* [etc.], *Jacob Gideon, junior, Printer*, 1822. 8vo, pp. viii., 288. B.

ASHTON. Ashton's Memorial. An History of the Strange Adventures, and Signal Deliverances, of Mr. Philip Ashton, Who, After he had made his Escape from the Pirates, liv'd alone on a Desolate Island for about Sixteen Months, &c. With A short Account of Mr. Nicholas Merritt, who was taken at the same time. To which is added, A Sermon on Dan. 3. 17, by John Barnard, V.D.M. [Mottoes.] *Boston, N. E., Samuel Gerrish*, 1725. 8vo, pp. (4), 66. H.+*London; Printed for Richard Ford and Samuel Chandler*, 1726. 12mo, 4 p. l., pp. 148. N. 2207

Ashton was taken prisoner by the pirate Low, at Port Rossaway, Cape Sable, and carried into the West Indies, Central America, etc.

ASHWORTH (Henry). Recollections of a Tour in the United States of America, Canada, and Cuba; delivered before the Members of the Bolton Mechanics' Institute. ... By Henry Ashworth. Reprinted from "The Bolton Chronicle." *Bolton, James Hudsmith* [1859]. 8vo, pp. 45. H. 2208

Asie et Amérique, ou Tableau intéressant de la religion, des mœurs, usages et coutumes divers des populations de ces deux parties du monde. *Paris, Lehuby*, 1855. 12mo. 2 Engravings.

ASPDEN. Supreme Court of the United States. No. 160. John A. Brown, Adm'r of John Aspden, of London ... et al., Appellants, vs. Matthias Aspden's Adm'r D. B. N. C. T. A., et al. On Appeal from the Circuit Court, U. S., for the Eastern District of Pennsylvania. [*Washington, Gideon, Print.*, 1851.] 8vo, pp. vii., 1209. H. 2210

ASPEN. Letters and other Documents, Produced in the Case of the Succession of Matthias Aspden, and Ordered to be Printed. *Philadelphia* [*Privately printed*], 1837. 8vo, pp. 316.

The Aspect of the Times, a Political Poem, &c. By a Native of Newark. *Newark*, 1831. 12mo. 2212

The Aspects of Religion in the United States of America. By the Author of "The Englishwoman in America." *London, Low*, 1859. 12mo, pp. 190. 2213

ASPINALL (Joseph). The Transit Question. Transportation to the Seaboard. The Enormous Charges on Western Produce. Letter from Joseph Aspinall, Esq., President of the Detroit Board of Trade, in Reply to Hon. N. S. Benton ... [n. p., 1865.] 8vo, pp. 12. H. 2214

ASPINWALL (Thomas). Catalogue of Books relating to America, in the Collection of Colonel Aspinwall, Consul of the United States of America at London. [*Paris*, 1831?] 8vo, 2 p. l., pp. 66. C. & H. 2215

The collection comprises 771 rare and valuable articles, collected by its worthy possessor during his long residence at London as Consul-General. They were subsequently purchased by Mr. S. L. M. Barlow, of New York, but unfortunately about 3500 of the 4000 volumes which the library contained were destroyed by fire. It is gratifying to add that the portion saved included the rarest of the books.

ASPINWALL. [Letter to Col. Aspinwall, accompanying a Service of Plate, offered to him, on his Return to America, by Baring Brothers and 35 others; with his Reply. *London, Lithographed in imitation of MS.*, 1853.] 4to, pp. 4. H. 2216

ASPINWALL. Remarks on the Narragansett Patent. Read before The Massachusetts Historical Society, June, 1862, by Thomas Aspinwall. *Boston, John Wilson and Son*, 1863. 8vo, pp. 41. H.+Second Edition. *Providence, S. S. Rider*, 1865. 8vo, pp. 40. 2217

ASPINWALL (William). A Brief Description of the Fifth Monarchy, or Kingdome that shortly is to come into the World the Monarch, Subjects, Officers and Lawes thereof. By W. Aspinwall. *London, Printed by M. Simmons for Livewell Chapman*, 1653. 4to. 2218

A[SPINWALL] (W.) The Legislative Power is Christ's peculiar prerogative. Proved from the 9th of Isaiah, vers. 6, 7. By W. A[spinwall.] *London, Livewell Chapman*, 1656. 4to, pp. 39.

Aspinwall resided some time in New England, and edited Cotton's Abstract of Laws. He also published An Explication of the twenty-fourth Chapter of Isaiah. His son, Peter Aspinwall, was the first settler in Brookline, Mass.

ASPLAND (Alfred). On American Prisons. By Mr. Alfred Aspland. Read before the Members of the Manchester Statistical Society December 14, 1864. *Manchester, Cave & Sever, Printers*, 1865. 8vo, pp. 27. 2220

ASPLAND (Robert). An Attempt to delineate the Character of William Ellery Channing. A Sermon ... *London*, 1842. 8vo. 2221

ASPLUND (John). The Annual Register of the Baptist Denomination in North America, to the First of December 1790, containing an Account of the Churches and their Constitutions, Ministers, Members, Associations, their Plan and Sentiments, Rule and Order, Proceedings and Correspondence, ... [Preface dated] *Southampton County, Virginia, July* 14, 1791. 4to, pp. 72. N. 2222

ASPLUND. The Universal Register of the Baptist Denomination in North America for 1790–1–2–3–4. *Boston*, 1794. 12mo. W. 2223

ASSALINI (Paolo). Observations on the ... Plague; ... Trans. from the French by Adam Neale. To which is added, A Letter concerning the Seasoning, or Yellow Fever of the West Indies: By George Pinckard ... *New York, T. and J. Swords*, 1806. 12mo, pp. 281. S. 2224

ASSALL (F. W.) Nachrichten über die früheren Einwohner von Nordamerika und ihre Denkmäler, gesammelt von Friedrich Wilhelm Assall, Berghauptmann des Staates Pennsylvanien. Herausgegeben mit einem Vorberichte von Franz Jos. Mone. *Heidelberg, A. Oswald*, 1827. 8vo, pp. 152. With an Atlas of 12 Lithograph Plates. 2225

Almost a literal translation of Vol. I. of the "Archaelogia Americana."

The Assassination and History of the Conspiracy. A Complete Digest ... *Cincinnati, J. R. Hawley & Co.* 8vo, pp. xi., 21–163. 2226

Relates to the death of Abraham Lincoln.

The Assiento, | or, | Contract | for | Allowing to the Subjects of Great Britain | the Liberty of Importing Negroes | into the Spanish America. | Sign'd by the Catholick King at Madrid, the | Twenty sixth Day of March, 1713. | By Her Majesties special Command. | *London*, | *Printed by John Baskett* ... | ... 1713. | 4to, 2 p. l., pp. 48. H.+*Reprinted*, 1726. 2227

In English and Spanish.

The Assiento Contract Consider'd, as also The Advantages and Decay of the Trade of Jamaica and the Plantations. With the Causes and Consequences thereof. In several Letters to a Member of Parliament. *London, F. Burleigh*, 1714. 8vo, 5 p. l., pp. 50. P. 2228

Assiento que se tomó con Antonio Fernandez Delbas, sobre la renta y prouision general de esclauos negros para las Indias, año de mil y seiscientos y quinze. [*Madrid?*] Folio, pp. 20. S.

Assiento, y Capitvla- | cion que por mandado de su Magestad se | ha tomado con diuersas personas interes- | sadas en el comercio de las Indias, sobre la | cobrança, y administracion del derecho | del aueria por tres años, que comiençan | a correr desde principio deste | de 1618. | Folio, 31 l. 2230

Assiento, | y Capitv- | lacion qve los se- | ñores Presidente y del Conse- | jo Real de las Indias tomaron con los vezinos | de la ciudad de Cadiz, y Vniuersidad de | los mareantes de Seuilla. | Sobre | la cobrança, y administracion | del derecho de la aueria, y despacho de las armadas, y flo- | tas de las Indias, por tiempo de seys años, que | comiençan a correr desde principio | del de 1621. *Año* 1620. | *Impresso* | *en Madrid. Por Fernando Correa de Montenegro.* | Folio, 41. l. J.C.B. 2231

Assiento y | Capitvlacion, qve | los señores Presidente, y del Consejo | Real de las Indias tomaron con Adriano de Legaso, por | si y en nombre del Prior y Consules de la Vniuersidad | de los cargadores a las Indias de la ciudad de Seuilla, y | demas personas interessadas en el comercio dellas, so- | bre la cobrança y administracion del derecho de la Aue- | ria, y despacho de las armada y flotas de las Indias, por | tiempo de seis años, que començaràn acorrer des- | de principio del venidero de 1628. y se | cumpliràn en fin del | de 633. | *En Madrid, Por Iuan Gonçalez.* | *Año de* M.DC.XXVII. | Folio, 44 l. 2232

Assiento y | Capitvlacion, qve | los señores Presidente, y del

Conse- | jo Real de las Indias tomaron con el Prior, y Consu- | les, y Comercio de Seuilla, sobre la cobrança, y ad- | ministracion del derecho de la Aueria, y despacho de | las Armadas, y Flotas de las Indias, por tiempo de | tres años, que comiençan a correr desde prin- | cipio deste de mil y seiscientos, | y quarenta. | *En Madrid, Por Andres de Parra.* | *Año de* M.DC.XXXX. | Folio, 51 l. 2233

Assiento. [*Begins*] En | el Nom- | bre de | Dios, | Amen. | Sepan | qvantos esta | carta viere | como nos Crhis- | toval de Barnvevo Boni- | faz, y Ivan de Vergara Gaviria, | etc. [*Assiento del Aueria de prior y Consules año de* 1618.] Folio, 27 l. 2234

Assimilated Rank of the Civil Branch of the Navy. *See* [Ruschenberger (W. S. W.)]

Association of American Geologists and Naturalists. Reports of the First, Second, and Third Meetings of the Association of American Geologists and Naturalists, at Philadelphia, in 1840 and 1841, and at Boston in 1842. Embracing its Proceedings and Transactions. *Boston, Gould, Kendall & Lincoln*, 1843. 8vo, pp. 544. 21 Plates. H. 2235

Nº 1. Association du sou par semaine en faveur des esclaves. [Compte rendu. *Lausanne, Imp. Georges Bridel*, 1859.] 16mo, pp. 8. H. 2236

The Association of Franklin Medal Scholars. [Its History, with a List of the Scholars.] Printed for the Association from the Annual Report of the School Committee for 1857. *Boston, Geo. C. Rand & Avery, City Printers*, 1858. 8vo, pp. 40. H. 2237

The Association, &c. of the Delegates of the Colonies, at the Grand Congress, held at Philadelphia, Sept. 1, 1774; Versified, and adapted to Music, calculated for Grave and Gay dispositions; with a short Introduction. By Bob Jingle, Esq; Poet Laureat to the Congress. Printed in the Year M,DCC,LXXIV. [*Philadelphia.*] 8vo, pp. 22. N. 2238

Published by the Tories to ridicule the proceedings of Congress. *See* M. R., LII., 263.

[Association for the exhibition of the industry of all nations.] Official Catalogue of the New-York Exhibition of the Industry of all Nations. 1853. *New York, George P. Putnam & Co.*, 1853. 12mo, pp. 192.+First revised Edition. *New York*, 1853. 12mo, pp. 240, 22. N. 2239

Statement made by the Association for the Exhibition of the industry of all Nations in regard to the Organization and Progress of the Enterprise. *New York, Carr and Hicks*, 1853. 8vo, pp. 56. Plate. A. 2240

The Association also published various broadside circulars, and a Description of the Building, broadside.

Association for the Exhibition of the Industry of all Nations. Official Awards of Juries. Professor B. Silliman, Jr., B. P. Johnson, Esq., Samuel Webber, Esq., Commissioners on Juries. ... *New York, Printed by Wm. C. Bryant & Co.*, 1853. 8vo, pp. v., 99. H. 2241

Association of Medical Superintendents of American Institutions for the Insane. [Report of] The Committee on the distribution of Lunatic Hospital Reports ... 1857. 8vo, pp. 8. P.

ASSOLLANT (Alfred). Cannoniers à vos pièces! Par Alfred Assollant. *Paris, E. Dentu*, 1861. 8vo, pp. 30. B. 2243

ASSOLLANT. Scènes de la vie des États-Unis par Alfred Assollant Acacia Les Butterfly Une fantaisie américaine. *Paris, L. Hachette et Cᵉ*, 1859. 12mo, Title, pp. 364. B. 2244

ASTETE DE ULLOA (Gonzalo). Pompa fvnebre, | y Exceqvias, qve | el excelentissimo Señor | D. Pedro de Toledo y Leyba Marques de | Mancera, Virrey destos Reynos hizo en la | muerte de la Reyna nuestra Señora | Doña Ysabel de Borbon. | *A la Ex. S. D. Maria Lvisa* | *de Salazar y Enriquez Virreyna* | *del Perù* | *Por el lic. D. Gonzalo* | *Astete de Vlloa Capellan mayor de la* | *Capilla Real de Lima.* | [1645.] 4to, 126 l. 2245

ASTI (Felice). Memoria o dissertazione sopra la Nuova China China del regno di S. Fè, nell' America meridionale. Seconda edizione ... con lettere de V. Dandolo. *Venezia*, 1791. 4to. 2246

ASTIÉ (J. F.) Histoire de la république des États-Unis depuis l'établissement des premières colonies jusqu'à l'élection du président Lincoln (1620–1860). Par. J. F. Astié. Précédée d'une préface par M. Ed. Laboulaye, de l'Institut. [Motto.] *Paris, Grassart*, 1865. 8vo, pp. xv., 478; 589. B. 2247

ASTIÉ. Le reveil religieux des États Unis (1857–1858), d'après les principales publications américaines et anglaises. *Lausanne, Bridel*, 1859. 12mo. 2248

ASTIÉ (J. F.) De godsdienstige opwekking in Amerika, ten tijde van Jonathan Edwards. Uit het Fransch. *s' Gravenhage, H. J. Gerretsen*, 1866. Post 8vo, pp. 43. 2248*a*

I have not seen the French original.

ASTLEY (Thomas). Collection of Voyages. *See* [Green (John)].

Astor Library, N. Y. Act of Incorporation and By-Laws of the Trustees. *New-York*, 1849. 8vo, pp. 8. 2249

Alphabetical Index to the Astor Library, or Catalogue, with Short Titles, of the Books now collected, and of the Proposed Accessions, as submitted to the Trustees of the Library for their Approval, Jan., 1851. [By Dr. J. G. Cogswell.] *New York, R. Craighead, Printer*, 1851. 8vo, pp. xxx., 446. 2250

Catalogue of Books in the Astor Library relating to the Languages and Literature of Asia, Africa and the Oceanic Islands. *New York, Astor Library Autographic Press*, MDCCCLIV. 8vo, pp. (8), 424. H. 2251

100 copies printed. "Languages of the American Indians," pp. 179–187.

Catalogue or Alphabetical Index of the Astor Library. ... Part I. Authors and Books. [Compiled by J. G. Cogswell.] ... *New York, Printed by R. Craighead*, 1857–61. 8vo, pp. v., 2110.+Supplement ... with an Alphabetical Index of Subjects in all the Volumes. ... *New York*, 1866. 8vo, pp. (4), 605.

With title-pages to divide the work into five volumes.

Concise Classified List of ... Bibliography ... selected ... for the Astor Library. *New York*, 1849. 8vo, pp. 30. 2253

Also prefixed to the Alphabetical Index.

List of Periodicals and Transactions of Societies taken in at the Astor Library, 1855. [*New York*, 1855.] 8vo, pp. 24. Lithographed. 2254

Annual Report of the Trustees to the Legislature, [for 1849]. *Albany, N. Y.*, 1850. 8vo. Continued. 2255

Prospectus of the Astor Mining Company, Eagle River, Lake Superior. *Boston, Wright & Potter*, 1864. 8vo, pp. 16. Map. H. 2256

Astounding Disclosures and Frauds in the Liquor Traffic. Published by P. S. T. S. *Philadelphia, Tract Society*, 1860. 12mo, pp. 24. H. 2257

Astronomical Observations made during the Year 1845 at the National Observatory, Washington: under the Direction of M. F. Maury ... Vol. I. ... *Washington, Printed by J. & G. S. Gideon*, 1846. 4to, pp. v., clvi., 273, 119. Plates. C. 2258

Five volumes were published, covering observations from 1845–50 inclusive. Continued with the title:

Astronomical and Meteorological Observations made at the United States Naval Observatory, during the Year 1861. ... Commander J. M. Gilliss, U. S. N., Superintendent. *Washington, Government Printing Office*, 1862. 4to, pp. xxv., 519 (1). Continued. C. 2259

Four volumes, contains observations from 1861–64 inclusive, had appeared up to 1867.

ASYLUM. Origin of the First Presbyterian Church of Asylum, Bradford Co., Pa. With an Appendix and Notes. And also, A Formula used in Receiving Members. *Towanda, Pa., E. S. Goodrich*, 1843. 12mo, pp. 14. 2260

At Anchor: a Story of our Civil War. By an American. *New York, D. Appleton & Co.*, 1865. 12mo, pp. 311. C. 2261

ATALL (*pseudon.*) *See* [Waln].

ATCHESON. American Encroachments on British Rights; or, Observations on the Importance of the British North American Colonies. And on the Late Treaties with the United States; With Remarks on Mr. Baring's Examination; And a Defence of the Shipping Interest from the Charge of having attempted to impose on Parliament, and of Factious Conduct in their Opposition to the American Intercourse Bill. By Nathaniel Atcheson, Esq. F.A.S. [Motto.] *London, J. Butterworth, and J. M. Richardson*, 1808. 8vo, pp. xiii. (1), cxiii.; 250. 4 Maps and Tables. H., C., & P.+A New Edition, with Considerable Additions. *London*, 1808. 8vo. (In the "Pamphleteer," Vol. VI., pp. 33–98, and 361–98, and 361–400.) 2262

See M. R., LIX., 305.

Atcheson. A Collection of Debates in Parliament on the Navigation and Colonial System, on the Trade between Great Britain and the United States of America, and on the Intercourse between the latter and the British Colonies in North America and the West Indies, &c. &c. from 1783 to 1808, both inclusive, with Prefatory Observations, Notes, and an Appendix, containing ... Documents ... . By Nathaniel Atcheson. *London*, 1808 [or] 1809. 8vo. 2263

[Atcheson.] Collection of Interesting and Important Reports and Papers on the navigation and trade of Great-Britain, Ireland, and the British Colonies in the West Indies and America, with tables of tonnage ... . Printed by order of the Society of Shipowners of Great Britain. Edited by N. Atcheson. *London*, 1807. 8vo, pp. xxviii., 154, ccxcvii. H. & S. 2264

[Atcheson.] A Compressed View of the Points to be discussed, in treating with the United States of America; A.D. 1814. With an Appendix and Two Maps. [Mottoes.] *London, J. M. Richardson*, 1814. 8vo, 2 p. l., pp. 39. 2 Maps. H. & S.

Some copies printed in 4to. Relates to the Boundary Question. *See* M. R., lxxv., 328. Reprinted in the "Pamphleteer," v. 105–139.

Atchison (David R.) Speech of Hon. D. R. Atchison, of Missouri, on the Oregon Question, Delivered in the Senate of the United States, March 12, 1846. [n. p., n. d.] 8vo, pp. 8. H. 2266

Atheos; or the Tragedies of Unbelief. *New York, Sheldon & Company*, 1862. 12mo, pp. 331. 2267

Contains matter relative to Aaron Burr, &c.

Atherton (Booz M.) *See* Wells (Bezaleel).

Atherton (C. G.) Speech of Mr. Atherton of New Hampshire, on the General Appropriation Bill. ... April 23 and 24, 1840. *Washington*, 1840. 8vo, pp. 15. H. 2268

Also: Speech, May 27, 1840, on the Public Revenue. 8vo, pp. 16. Speech on the Twelve Million Loan Bill, July 12, 1841. 8vo. On the Tariff, Dec. 23, 1841. 8vo. On the Proceeds of the Public Lands, March 30, 1842. 8vo. Apportionment Bill, May 3, 1842. 8vo. Speech on the Tariff, May 25, 1844. 8vo.

Atherton (C. H.) An Address delivered at Concord, before the New-Hampshire Historical Society, at their Annual Meeting, June 8, 1831. By Charles H. Atherton, a Member ... . *Concord, Printed by Jacob B. Moore*, 1831. 8vo, pp. 29. N.H.

Atherton. Eulogy on Gen. George Washington, late President of the United States, who died December 14, 1799; Delivered at Amherst, N. H. before the Inhabitants of the Town of Amherst, the Inhabitants of the Town of Milford, and the Benevolent Lodge, on the 22d day of February, 1800, at the Request of the Committee of the Selectmen and other Respectable Citizens of the Town of Amherst, to which was superadded the Request of the Committee of the Benevolent Lodge. By Charles Humphrey Atherton. *From the Press of Samuel Preston, Amherst*, 1800. 8vo, pp. 23. H. 2270

Atherton. Memoir of the Hon. Joshua Atherton. *Boston, Crosby, Nichols, and Company*, 1852. 8vo, pp. 57. H. 2271

Atherton. An Oration, pronounced in the First Parish at Amherst, N. H. ... July 4, 1798. By Charles H. Atherton. [Motto.] *Printed at Amherst, by Samuel Preston, July*, 1798. 8vo, pp. 24. H. 2272

Atherton (W.) Narrative of the Suffering & Defeat of the North-western Army, under General Winchester: Massacre of the Prisoners: Sixteen Months Imprisonment ... with the Indians and British: By William Atherton. *Frankfort, Ky., Printed for the Author by A. G. Hodges*, 1842. 18mo, pp. 152. H. & P. 2273

Atkins (John). A Voyage to Guinea, Brasil, and the West-Indies; In His Majesty's Ships, the Swallow and Weymouth. Describing the several Islands and Settlements, viz. Madeira, the Canaries, Cape de Verd, Sierraleon, Sesthos, Cape Apollonia, Cabo Corso, and others on the Guinea Coast; Barbadoes, Jamaica, &c. in the West-Indies. The Colour, Diet, Languages, Habits, Manners, Customs, and Religions of the respective Natives, and Inhabitants. With Remarks on the Gold, Ivory, and Slave-Trade; and on the Winds, Tides and Currents of the several Coasts. By John Atkins, Surgeon in the Royal Navy. [Motto.] *London, Cæsar Ward and Richard Chandler*, M.DCC.XXXV. 8vo, Title, 1 l., pp. xxv., 265 [pp. 3–18 omitted]; Errata. H. & S. 2274

Atkins. A Voyage to Guinea, Brasil, and the West-Indies; ... Giving a Genuine Account of the Several Islands. ... By John Atkins, Gent. of Plaistow, in Essex. The Second Edition. *London and Scarborough, Cæsar Ward and Richard Chandler*, 1737. 8vo, pp. xxv., 265. S. 2275

This is the previous work, with merely a new title.

Atkins (John). Report of the Evidence in the case, John Atkins, appellant, *vs.* Calvin Sauger & *al.* Executors, relative to the will of the late Mrs. Badger, of Natick. By the appellant. *Dedham* [Ms.], *H. & W. H. Mann* [1822]. 8vo, pp. 84. C. 2276

Atkins. Democracy and Dred Scott. Speech delivered by Smith D. Atkins, Before the Freeport Wide Awakes, at Plymouth Hall ... Aug. 14, 1860 ... [n: p., n. d.] 8vo, pp. 24. H.

Atkins (Thomas). American Slavery. ... A Reply to the Letter of Bishop Hopkins, of Vermont, ... by the Rev. Thomas Atkins ... . *New-York, Scobell, Printer* [n. d.] 8vo, pp. 13. H.

Atkinson (Archibald). Speech of Mr. Atkinson, of Virginia, on the Oregon Question. Delivered in the House ... February 7, 1846. *Washington, Printed at the Union Office*, 1846. 8vo, pp. 8. H. 2279

[Atkinson (Edw'd)]. Cheap Cotton by Free Labor. By A Cotton Manufacturer. *Boston, Williams & Co.*, 1861. 8vo, pp. 52. Second Edition. *Boston*, 1861. 8vo, pp. 54. 2280

Atkinson. ... On Cotton. By Edward Atkinson, Esq., of Boston, Mass., Delivered Dec. 14th, 1865. [n. p., n. d.] 8vo, pp. (12). H. 2281

Lecture II. of a Course "on The Currency, Resources and Indebtedness of the United States, delivered before the American Geographical and Statistical Society."

Atkinson. Report to the Boston Board of Trade on the Cotton Manufacture of 1862, March 1, 1863. By Edward Atkinson. 8vo, pp. 21. Plate. 2282

Mr. Atkinson also published a broadside, "The Cotton Kingdom, *Boston, March*, 1863," and an Article, "The Future Supply of Cotton," in the *North Amer. Rev.*, April, 1864; xcviii., 477-497.

Atkinson (John). The Hermit: Or an Account of F. A. J. Phyle, who lived without the use of fire for upwards of twenty-two years, in a small cave, in the midst of a wood near Mount Holly, in Burlington, N. J., and was found dead in the year 1780. By John Atkinson. *Philadelphia*, 1811. 18mo.

[Atkinson (Joseph)]. A Match for a Widow; or, the Frolics of Fancy. A comic opera; in three acts. As performed at the Theatre-Royal, Dublin. *London: Printed for C.*

Dilly, in the Poultry, MDCCLXXXVIII. 8vo, pp. viii., 61; Epilogue, 1 l. 2284

This rare play was written by Joseph Atkinson, Treasurer of the Ordnance in Ireland. The part of Jonathan was the first attempt to introduce a Yankee character upon the British stage. In it is sung a portion of "Yankee Doodle."—S.

Atkinson (S.) The Effects of the New System of free trade upon our Shipping, Colonies and Commerce ... A Letter to Hon. W. Huskisson. *London*, 1827. 8vo, pp. 63.+A second letter, &c. *London*, 1827. 8vo, pp. 51. S. 2285

Atkinson (Thomas). Address delivered before the Historical Society of the University of North-Carolina, June 6, 1855, by Rt. Rev. Bishop Atkinson. Published by ... the Society. *Raleigh, Holden & Wilson*, 1855. 8vo, pp. 32. B. 2286

Atkinson ... Sermon at the Consecration of Grace Church, Baltimore, Oct. 30. *Baltimore*, 1856. 8vo, pp. 22. 2287

Atkinson (*Rev.* W. Christopher). A Historical and Statistical Account of New Brunswick, B.N.A. With Advice to Emigrants. By the Rev. W. Christopher Atkinson, A.M. Pastor of the Presbyterian Church, Mascreen, St. George's. Third Edition, greatly improved and corrected. *Edinburgh: Printed by Anderson & Bryce*, M.DCCC.XLIV. 12mo, pp. xvi., 284. Map. C.

Atkinson (William King). Oration delivered at Dover, N.H., July 4, 1791. *Dover*, 1791. 4to, pp. 23. 2289

[Atkinson (William P.)] Remarks on an Article from the Christian Examiner, entitled "Mr. Parker and his Views" [by Dr. E. S. Gannett]. *Boston, Wm. Crosby and H. P. Nichols*, 1845. 8vo, pp. 15. 2290

Atlanta. History of the Rebel Steam Ram "Atlanta," now on Exhibition, ... Philadelphia, for the Benefit of the Union Volunteer Refreshment Saloon. With an Interesting account of the Engagement which resulted in her Capture, November, 1863. *Philadelphia, George H. Ives* [1864]. 12mo, pp. 10.+Another edition. *Philadelphia* [1864]. pp. 4. 2291

Address of the Atlanta Register to the People of the Confederate States. One Dollar per Copy. *Atlanta, Ga., J. A. Sperry & Co.; Augusta, Ga., Geo. B. Mitchell* [*Jan.* 1, 1864]. 8vo, pp. 16. H. 2292

Atlantic and Michigan Railway. Sketch of the Geographical Rout[e] of a Great Railway from the Atlantic to the Mississippi. *New York*, 1829. 8vo, pp. 16.+Second edition, with Additions. *New York*, 1830. 8vo, pp. 48. 2293

Atlantic and Pacific Railroad Company Circular ... *New York*, 1855. 8vo, pp. 27. P. 2294

Atlantic and Pacific Telegraph, established under arrangements of Henry O'Reilly. 7000 miles completed and about 4000 additional miles arranged for construction ... . [*New York*, 1852.] 8vo, pp. 16. P. 2295

Atlantic and Mississippi Railroad. Sketch of the Geographical Rout of a Railway to connect the Canals and Navigable Waters of New York, Pennsylvania, Ohio, Indiana, Illinois, Michigan, Missouri ... . Second Edition. *New York*, 1830. 8vo, pp. 48. 2295*a*

Atlantic and St. Lawrence Railroad Company. Report of the President and Directors to the Stockholders, July, 1848. *Portland*, 1848. 8vo, pp. 16. 2296

The Atlantic Club-Book; being Sketches in prose and verse, by Paulding, Halleck, Bryant, &c. *New York*, 1834. 2 vols., 12mo.+Third edition. *New York*, 1847. 2 vols., 12mo.+ *London, Newman*. 2 vols., post 8vo. 2298

Atlantic Magazine. *New York* [1824–5]. 2 vols., 8vo.

The Atlantic Monthly. A Magazine of Literature, Art, and Politics. *Boston, Phillips, Sampson and Company* [1858]. 8vo, pp. iv., 892. Continued. 2299

Vol. IV., etc., *Ticknor and Fields*. In XVI., etc., the title reads: "A Magazine of Literature, Science, Art, and Politics." Edited, for a time, by James Russell Lowell.

Atlantic Navigator: being a nautical description of the coasts of France, Spain and Portugal, the west coast of Africa, the coasts of Brazil and Patagonia, the islands of the Azores, Madeiras, Canaries and Cape Verdes. ... a description of the principal harbours on the coast of North America, etc. 4th Ed. improved and enlarged. *London, James Imray & Son*, 1854. 8vo, pp. xii., vi., 532. C. 2300

Atlantic Telegraph. A History of preliminary experimental proceedings, and a descriptive account of the present state and

prospects of the undertaking. Published by order of the directors of the company, July, 1857. *London, Jarrold & Sons*, 1857. 8vo, pp. 69, 2 plates. C. 2301

Report of Proceedings of a Meeting called to Further the Enterprise of the Atlantic Telegraph, held at the Hall of the Chamber of Commerce, New York, Wednesday, March 4, 1863. Prepared under the Supervision of John Austin Stevens, Jr., Secretary of the Meeting. *New York, W. Amerman, Printer*, 1863. 8vo, pp. 26. C. 2302

The Atlantic Telegraph; its History from the Commencement of the Undertaking in 1854, to the Sailing of the Great Eastern in 1866. ... *London, G. W. Bacon*, 1866. 8vo, pp. 166.+To the final success in 1866. *London, G. W. Bacon*, 1866. 12mo, pp. 116. C. 2303

Atlantis. Amerikanische Erzählungen und Geschichten. Deutsche Ausgabe. I. Theil. *Hamburg*, 1854. 8vo, pp. (6), 154. (Serie II. der Volksschriften des deutsch-amerikanischen Vereins.) 2304

Atlantis. Journal des Neuesten und Wissenswürdigsten aus dem Gebiete der Politik, Geschichte, Geographie, & Statistik, Cultur-Geschichte und Literatur der Nord und Südamerikanischen Reiche, mit Einschluss des westindischen Archipelagus. Herausgegeben von Eduard Florens Rivinus in Philadelphia. [*Leipzig, Hinrichs*], 1826–27. 2 vols., 8vo. C. 2305

Atlantis. Zeitschrift für Leben und Literatur in England und Amerika. Herausgegeben von Karl Elze. *Dessau, Katz* [1853–54]. 2 vols., 4to, about 600 pp. in all. 2306

The Atlanto-Pacific Canal. For all Nations. (The Humboldt line, via the Atrato-Cupica valleys.) Capital £2,500,000. Preliminary statement. *London* [n. d.]. 8vo, pp. 16. 3 Maps.

Atlas Ameriquain. *See* Jeffreys (Thos.)

Atlas Geographicus: or, a compleat System of Geography, (Ancient and Modern) for America. Containing What is of most Use in Bleau, Varenius, Cellarius, Cluverius, Luyts, Baudrand, Sanson, the Royal Commentaries of Peru, &c. With the Discoveries and Improvements of the best Spanish, Dutch, French and English Authors and Travellers, Ancient and Modern, to this Time; with about 30 new Maps, Cuts, San-

son's Tables, &c. as may be seen in the Catalogues thereof annex'd to the Index. The Maps done by Herman Moll, Geographer, in which are all the latest Observations. Europe is two Volumes, Asia the Third, Africa the Fourth, and this the Fifth. Vol. v. To which is added, A Catalogue of the Maps, Cuts, and Sanson's Tables in all the five Volumes, and a Description of Bosnia by Omission left out in Europe. *In the Savoy: Eliz. Nutt*, MDCCXVII. 4to, pp. 807 (4). 24 Maps. C. & P.

Atlas of Battles of the American Revolution, together with Maps, showing the Routes of the British and American Armies, Plans of Cities, Surveys of Harbors, &c., taken during that eventful period, by the Officers attached to the Royal Army. *London*, 1793. Rl. folio. 17 Plates. C. 2309

This being a collection of maps published at various times, with this general title, the number of maps varies from seventeen to twenty-two. A New York firm purchased a large remainder of these maps, and issued them with the above title-page. Their edition is distinguished by the broad letters with which the title is printed, and the omission of the place and date of publication.

An Atlas of the United States of North America; corrected to the present period. *London*, 1832. 4to. 17 Maps fol. 2310

Atlas of the United States for the Use of the Blind. *Boston*, 1837. 4to. S. 2311

Atlas para el viage de las goletas Sutil y Mexicana al reconocimiento del estrecho de Juan de Fuca en 1792, publicado en 1802. Folio. 9 Maps and 8 Views. C. & H. 2312

This Atlas belongs to Alcala Galiano. *See* No. 681.

Atlas zur Entdeckungsgeschichte Amerikas. Aus Handschriften der K. Hof- und Staats-Bibliothek, der K. Universität und des Hauptconservatoriums der K. B. Armee herausgegeben von Friedrich Kunstmann, Karl von Spruner, Georg M. Thomas. Zu den Monumenta saecularia der K. B. Akademie der Wissenschaften ... . München, Nach den Originalen gezeichnet von F. Schleicher, technische Bearbeitung in der lithographischen Anstalt von Seb. Minsinger. *In Comm. bei Asher & Cie in Berlin*, 1859. 4to, letterpress, pp. (4), 151. 13 Colored Maps, folio C. 2313

Atlee (E. P.) An Address delivered before the Female Anti-Slavery Society of Philadelphia. *Philadelphia*, 1834. 8vo, pp. 27. 2314

Atlee. An Address to the Citizens of Philadelphia on the Subject of Slavery, &c. By E. P. Atlee. *Philadelphia*, 1833. 8vo, pp. 15. 2315

Atlee (S. Y.) Essay; submitted ... to the Teachers' Association, of ... Washington, ... October 25th, 1856. [The constitution of the U. States a study for schools.] By Samuel Yorke AtLee, ... *Washington, D. C.*, 1857. 8vo, pp. 15. H.

Atlee (W. L.) Memoir of William R. Grant, M.D., ... With a Notice of his Theory of the Fœtal Circulation. ... By Washington L. Atlee, M.D. ... *Philadelphia, Lippincott*, 1853. 8vo, pp. 22. Portrait of Grant. 2317

Atocha (Alexander J.) Memorial to the Senate and House of Representatives of the United States of America, 1852. 8vo, pp. 21. S. 2318

Atrato. Prospectus of the Atrato and San Juan Canal and Transportation Co. in New Granada, South America. *New York, Baker, Godwin & Co., Printers*, 1851. 8vo, pp. 16. Map.

Prospectus of the Atrato River Mining and Trading Company. *New York, Turnbull & Keech, Printers* [n. d.] 4to, pp. 3. H.

The caption reads, "The Establishment of Protestant Missionaries and Schools in South America, under the Auspices of the ... Company."

Atson (W.) Heart Whispers; or, a peep behind the family curtain, interspersed with sketches of a Tour through Nine Southern States; contained in a series of letters to his wife. By William Atson. *Philadelphia, H. Cowperthwaite*, 1859. 12mo, pp. 368. C. 2321

The Attempt of the North to Subdue the Southerners, and the Attempt of Spain to Subdue the Netherlands. Is there any Analogy between them? An off-hand Enquiry. By the author of "Uncle John's Cabin, next door to Uncle Tom's Cabin." *London, Simpkin, Marshall & Co.*, 1865. 12mo, pp. 16. 2322

Attempt to Elucidate the Pernicious Consequences of a Deviation from the Principles of the Orders in Council. *London, Tipper*, 1809. 8vo, pp. 76. 2323

Attempt to show that America, &c. *See* [Mather (Sam'l)].

Attempt to strip Negro Emancipation of its Difficulties as

well as its Terrors. By a Merchant. *London, G. Woodfall*, 1824. 8vo, pp. 48. C. 2324

Attention, Voters! Address of the National Democratic Committee to the People of the United States. [1864.] 8vo, pp. 4. 2325

ATTERBURY (J. G.) God in Civil Government. A Discourse preached in the First Presbyterian Church, New Albany, November 27, 1862. By Rev. John G. Atterbury. *New Albany, George R. Beach*, 1862. 8vo, pp. 16. 2326

ATTFIELD (W.) The Neptune's Car; a Tale of New York, a Poem. 1857. 8vo. 2327

ATTIBERT (Fr.) Quatre ans à Cayenne. Par Fr. Attibert, déporté. *Bruxelles*, 1849. 2328

[ATTIBERT.] Vier Jahre in Cayenne. Nach den Aufzeichnungen Fr. Attibert's herausgegeben vom Hauptredacteur des Bien-être social. Aus dem Französischen von Fr. X. Lindenberg. *Regensburg, Manz*, 1859. 8vo, pp. 146. 2329

ATTICUS, *pseudon.* Remarks on the Proposed Canal from Lake Erie to the Hudson River. By Atticus. *New-York, Printed by Samuel Wood & Sons*, 1816. 8vo, pp. 14. H. 2330

ATTLEBOROUGH (*Mass.*) Constitution of the Society for the Encouragement of Agriculture, Arts, and Social Intercourse. *Providence* [1805]. 8vo, pp. 15. 2331

ATWATER (Caleb). A Description of the Antiquities discovered in the Western Country, originally communicated to the Antiquarian Society. *Columbus, Ohio*, 1833. 8vo. 2332

Included in Trans. of Amer. Antiq. Soc., Vol. I.

ATWATER. The General Character, Present and Future Prospects, of Ohio. Address at Columbus, Ohio, December, 1826. *Columbus*, 1827. 8vo, pp. 21. C. 2333

ATWATER. A History of the State of Ohio, Natural and Civil, by Caleb Atwater, A.M. First Edition. *Cincinnati: Glezen & Shepard*, 1838. 8vo, pp. 403. C. 2334

See N. A. R., LIII., p. 320. Second Edition. *Cincinnati*, 1838. 8vo, pp. 407. Third Edition. *Cincinnati*, 1858. 8vo.

ATWATER. Remarks made on a Tour to Prairie du Chien; thence to Washington City, in 1829. By Caleb Atwater, late Commissioner employed by the United States to negotiate with the Indians of the Upper Mississippi, for the Purchase of Mineral Country ... . *Columbus, O., Isaac N. Whiting*, 1831. 12mo, pp. vii., 296. C. & H. 2335

Contains a Vocabulary of the Sioux Language. Republished in the following work:

ATWATER. The Writings of Caleb Atwater. Published by the Author. *Columbus, Scott & Wright*, 1833. 8vo, pp. 408. C.

Contains a reprint of 2332 and 2335, with fifteen pages of additional matter.

ATWATER (H. C.) Incidents of a Southern Tour; or, the South seen with Northern Eyes. By the Rev. H. Cowles Atwater. *Boston*, 1857. 8vo, pp. 120. 2337

ATWATER (J.) Considerations on the Approaching Dissolution of the United States Bank. In a Series of Numbers, by Jesse Atwater. *Sidney's Press, New-Haven*, 1810. 8vo, pp. 22. H. 2338

ATWATER (Jeremiah). Sermon preached at Burlington, on the Day of the Anniversary Election, Oct. 14, 1802. *Middlebury*, 1802. 8vo, pp. 39. 2339

ATWATER (Noah). A Sermon, delivered at the Ordination of the Reverend John Taylor, to the Pastoral Care of the Church in Deerfield. February 14th, 1787. By Noah Atwater, A.M. Pastor of the Church in Westfield. *Northampton, Printed by William Butler*, M,DCC,LXXXVII. 8vo, pp. 32. H. 2340

ATWATER. A Sermon ... . By Rev. Noah Atwater, A.M. Late Pastor of the Church in Westfield. Delivered To his People on the 22d of November, 1801, at the close of the 20th year of his ministry, and under a distressing ... disorder of body, which, soon after, terminated his life. *Springfield, Printed by Ashley & Brewer*, 1802. 8vo, pp. 21. H. 2341

ATWOOD. In Memoriam. Discourses in Commemoration of Abraham Lincoln, President of the United States, delivered in the South Church, Salem, April 16th, and June 1st, 1865, By the Pastor, Rev. E. S. Atwood. *Salem, Printed at the Office of the Gazette*, 1865. 8vo, pp. 31. B. 2342

Each sermon has also a separate title-page, beginning, "The Nation's Loss," and "The President's Record."

ATWOOD (Thomas). The History of the Island of Dominica. Containing a Description of its Situation, Extent, Climate, Mountains, Rivers, Natural Productions, &c. &c. Together with an Account of the Civil Government, Trade, Laws, Customs, and Manners of the different Inhabitants of that Island. Its Conquest by the French, and Restoration to the British Dominions. By Thomas Atwood. *London, J. Johnson*, M DCC XCI. 8vo, pp. viii., 285. H. 2343

"Mr. Atwood passed several years in Dominica, and has drawn up a plain and succinct account of this island."—M. R., VII., 15.

ATWOOD. Geschichte der Insel Dominica, aus dem Englischen mit Anmerkungen von G. F. Banecke. *Göttingen, Dieterich*, 1795. 8vo. 2345

ATWOOD. Observations relative to Negro Slaves in the British West India Islands. By Thomas Atwood. *London*, 1790. 8vo. 2345*a*

ATWOOD (W.) The Case of William Atwood, by the late King William ... constituted Chief Justice of the Province of New York ... . With a true Account of the Government and People of that Province; particularly of Bayard's Faction and the Treason for which he and Hutchins stand attainted ... . *London*, 1703. Folio. 2346

AUBANO. *See* Boemo Aubano.

AUBERTEUIL. *See* Hilliard d'Auberteuil.

AUBIN (Penelope). Life of Charlotta Du Pont, an English Lady; taken from her own Memoirs, giving an Account how she was trepan'd by her Stepmother to Virginia, how the Ship was taken by some Madagascar Pirates, of her Marriage in the Spanish West Indies, &c. *London*, 1736. 12mo. 2347

A doubtful title from a London catalogue.

AUBLET (Jean Baptiste Christophe Fusée). Histoire des Plantes de la Guiane Française, rangées suivant la méthode sexuelle, avec plusieurs mémoires sur différents sujets intéressants, relatifs à la culture et au commerce de la Guiane Française, et une notice de l'Ile de France. Ouvrage orné de près de 400 planches en taille douce, etc. Par J. B. Chr. Fusée Aublet. *Paris, Didot*, 1775. 4 vols., 4to. A. 2348

"About 800 plants are described in this work, more than half of them being entirely new. Aublet gave the uncouth Indian names of the plants to his new genera, which have been adopted by most of the French botanists; but Schreber and others have very properly replaced them by others better adapted to the Linnæan nomenclature."—RICH.

AUBONNEAU (— d'). Un mot sur les colonies françaises et particulièrement sur Saint-Domingue. 1800. 8vo. 2349

AUBRE (Paul d'). Colonists and Manufacturers in the West Indies, &c. Translated from the French. 1844. 8vo. Plans.

AUBRÉE (Pierre.) Le royalisme de la Guadeloupe dévoilé, ou Précis historique des trahisons organisées et exécutées par Georges-Henry-Victor Collot, gouverneur. [n. p., an III.] 4to. 2351

Signed, "Les délégués et membres du ci-devant corps représentatif de la Guadeloupe, Pierre Aubrée, Peri, Bresseau, Bouyer." A pamphlet.

AUBRY (—, *avocat.*) Mémoire pour Michel-Jean-Hugues Péan Captaine-Aide-Major des ville et gouvernement de Quebec. *Paris*, 1762. 4to. 2352

"On trouve dans ce mémoire plusieurs détails interessans sur les dernières opérations militaires des Français dans le Canada."—M. DE FONTETTE.

AUBURN. Constitution of the Veteran Association of Auburn. Organized August 23, 1865. *Auburn*, 1865. 12mo, pp. 12. H.

AUBURN. An Account of the Proceedings of the Meeting at Auburn, N. Y. Aug. 23, 1828, in Relation to the Measures taken to enforce the Observance of the Sabbath, and the attempt to establish a Christian Party in Politicks. *Auburn, Richard Oliphant*, 1828. 8vo, pp. 24. W. 2354

AUCAIGNE (Félix). L'alliance Russo-Américaine. Par Félix Aucaigne. *Paris, Dentu*, 1863. 8vo. + 2[e] édition. *Paris, Dentu*, 1863. 8vo. 2355

AUCHINLECK. A History of the War between Great Britain and the United States of America, during the Years 1812, 1813, and 1814. By G. Auchinleck. *Toronto*, 1855. Rl. 8vo, pp. vii., 411. 2356

First appeared in Maclear's "Anglo-American Magazine."

AUCHMUTY (Robert). The Importance of Cape Breton to the British Nation. Humbly represented by Robert Auckmuty, Judge of His Majesty's Court of Vice-Admiralty for the Provinces of Massachusets-Bay and New-Hampshire, in New-England. N. B. Upon the Plan laid down in this Representation, the Island was taken by Commodore Warren and General Pepperill, the 14th of June, 1745. *London, W. Bickerton*, M DCC XLV. Folio, pp. 7. H. 2357

Reprinted in Mass. Hist. Coll., Vol. V., pp. 202-206.

AUCHMUTY (Samuel). Sermon before the Corporation for the Relief of Widows and Children of Clergymen, in the Communion of the Church of England in America, Oct. 2, 1770. With an account, etc. *New York*, 1771. 8vo, pp. 40. 2358

AUCHMUTY. Sermon preached at the Opening of St. Paul's Chapel, in the City of New York, Oct. 30, by Samuel Auchmuty, D.D. *New York, H. Gaine* [1766]. 4to. 2359

AUDAIN (L.) Discours à trois jeunes Haïtiens récemment couronnés au grand concours de la Sorbonne. ... *Paris, Imprimerie de Moquet*, 1858. 8vo, pp. 23. H. 2360

Advocates a European education for Haitians.

Audi alteram partem, or a Counter-Letter to the Right Hon. the E—l of H—ll—gh, on the late and present State of Affairs in the Island of G—n—a, In which is clearly demonstrated, &c. *London, Nicol*, 1770. 8vo, pp. 123, Appendix, 68. 2361

See 'Monthly Review,' XLII., 150.

AUDUBON. The Birds of America from Original Drawings By John James Audubon ... . *London, Published by the Author*, 1827–30. 4 vols., Atlas folio, 435 Colored Plates. H. 2362

First issued in eighty-seven parts; and one of the most sumptuous ornithological works ever published; the coloring of the plumage, and the exact drawing of the birds, can scarcely be surpassed. The birds are represented in action amid the scenes, or on the plants and trees, most common to their habits, presenting a variety of land and marine views of floral and other productions of different climates and seasons. Its great dimensions have permitted eagles and other birds of the largest size to be represented of their natural size, and even in groups. "All is combined to ally," says Brunet, "in the most happy manner, the exactness of individual details with a living and animated representations of general forms." The plates were published without any text, to avoid the necessity of furnishing copies gratis to the public libraries in England, agreeably to the law of copyright. Trübner, p. 174, quotes the work with plain plates. I have never seen one in that condition. Owing to the destruction by fire of the stock and copper-plates the work has become extremely rare, and even small sections command high prices.

AUDUBON. The Birds of America. From Drawings made in the United States and their Territories. By John James Audubon. Reissued by J. W. Audubon. *New York, Roe Lockwood & Son, Publishers*, 1861. 2363

This is a *selection* of one hundred and forty plates, only, from the first edition, reproduced in colored lithographs; much inferior to the former edition. The letter-press to this selection forms 4 vols. royal 8vo, and describes many birds not represented in the volume of plates. Indeed, this reissue is an unfinished publication, and the intelligent collector will only accept it as a cheap substitute for the previous work. The following is a complete work on a smaller scale:

AUDUBON. The Birds of America, from Drawings made in the United States and their Territories. By John James Audubon ... . *New York, J. J. Audubon; Philadelphia, J. B. Chevalier*, 1840–44. 7 vols., rl. 8vo. H. 2364

Chevalier's name does not appear in Vols. VI. and VII. First and most desirable edition in this form published during the author's lifetime, in one hundred parts. It was republished in New York, 1856. In the new edition described below the plates have a tinted background, which is objectionable.

AUDUBON. The Birds of America, from Drawings made in the United States and their Territories. By John James Audubon, F.R.S. Re-issued By J. W. Audubon. *New York, Roe Lockwood & Son*, 1861. 7 vols., impl. 8vo; Vol. I., pp. viii., 246; II. viii., 200; III., viii., 234; IV., viii., 322; V., viii., 346; VI., viii., 456; VII., viii., viii., 372. 500 Colored Plates, each 10 inches by 7. 2365

In a later edition, dated 1865, the pagination is changed, and the work forms eight volumes, but the contents are the same. The edition of seven volumes is preferable for the plates.

AUDUBON. Ornithological Biography, or an Account of the Habits of the Birds of the United States of America; accompanied by Descriptions of the Objects represented in the work, entitled the Birds of America, and interspersed with Delineations of American Scenery and Manners. By John James Audubon ... . *Philadelphia, E. L. Carey and A. Hart*, MDCCCXXXII. 5 vols., rl. 8vo. H. 2366

Vol. I. is often missing. The remaining volumes were published as follows: Vol. II. *Boston, Hilliard, Gray, and Company*, MDCCCXXXV. Vol. III.–V. *Edinburgh, Adam & Charles Black*, MDCCCXXXV.-MDCCCXXXIX. Some copies of Vol. I. have the imprint, *Edinburgh, A. & C. Black*, MDCCCXXXI.

AUDUBON and BACHMAN. The Viviparous Quadrupeds of North America. By John James Audubon ... and the Rev. John Bachman ... . *New York, J. J. Audubon*, 1845–48. 3 vols., Columbier folio. 150 Plates. H. Letterpress, 3 vols., rl. 8vo. 2367

First published in thirty parts, of five plates each (22 x 28). There is another edition (*New York, Roe, Lockwood & Sons*, 1855. Plates, 2 vols., folio. Text, 3 vols., rl. 8vo.), which the publishers say "is precisely the same, in every respect, as that published by Mr. Audubon, and was even printed and colored by the same persons who executed the former under his personal supervision." I cannot endorse this statement. The first edition is by far the best. The following is a reproduction of the work on a smaller scale, matching in size and style the edition of the birds described in No. 2364 *supra*:

AUDUBON and BACHMAN. The Quadrupeds of North America, by J. J. Audubon ... and the Rev. John Bachman, D.D. *New York*, 1851–1854. Rl. 8vo, pp. viii., 384; 334; v., 348. 155 Colored Plates. + *New York, V. G. Audubon*, M DCCC LVI, Rl. 8vo, pp. xv., 383; 334; v., 348. 2368

AUDUBON. A Synopsis of the Birds of North America. By John James Audubon. *Edinburgh, Adam & Charles Black*, MDCCCXXXIX. 8vo, pp. 359. 2369

AUDUBON. Les oiseaux d'Amérique ... . *Paris, Impr. de Renouard*, 1833. 8vo. 2370

A prospectus in French and German.

AUDUBON. Scènes de la nature dans les États-Unis et le nord de l'Amérique. Ouvrage traduit d'Audubon, par Eugène Bazin, avec préface et notes du traducteur. *Paris, P. Bertrand*, 1857. 2 vols., 8vo. 2371

AUDUBON (J. W.) Illustrated Notes of an Expedition through Mexico and California. By J. W. Audubon. *New York*, 1852. With Plates, plain or colored. 2372

The publication of this work was not continued.

AUER (Alois). Das Vater-Unser. *Wien*, 1844–47. 2 pt. oblong folio, 17 leaves. H. 2373

Part I. has the caption, "Das Vater-Unser in mehr als sechshundert Sprachen und Mundarten, typometrisch aufgestellt." Part II. has the title, "Das Vater-Unser in mehr als 200 Sprachen und Mundarten mit Originaltypen." Contains specimens of fifty-seven American languages.

Aufforderung an teutsche Auswanderer zu einer grössern und gemeinschaftlichen Ansiedlung in den Freistaaten von Nordamerika. *Giessen, Ricker, März* 1833. 8vo, pp. 16. 2374

Aufforderung und Erklärung in Betreff einer Auswanderung im Grossen aus Teutschland in die Nordamerikanischen Freistaaten. *Giessen, Ricker, März* 1833. 8vo, pp. 28. + 2[e], mit den Statuten der giessener Auswanderergesellschaft vermehrte Auflage. *Giessen, Ricker, Julius* 1833. 8vo, pp. 56. 2375

AUGER (Édouard). Voyage en Californie par Édouard Auger (1852–1853.) *Paris, L. Hachette et Cie*, 1854. 16mo, 2 p. l., pp. 238. H. 2376

AUGHEY (J. Hill). The Iron Furnace: or, Slavery and Secession. By Rev. John H. Aughey, a Refugee from Mississippi. [Motto.] *Philadelphia, William S. & Alfred Martien*, 1863. 12mo, pp. 296. Portrait. C. & H. 2377

AUGHEY (S.) The Renovation of Politics. A Discourse delivered in St. Paul's Evangelical Lutheran Church, Lionville, Pa., January 4, 1861. By Rev. Samuel Aughey. *West Chester, E. F. James*, 1861. 8vo, pp. 15. 2378

AUGSPURGER (Johann Paul). Kurtze und wahrhaffte Beschreibung der See Reisen von Amsterdam in Holland nacher Brasilien in America und Angola in Africa, Von 4. Novembris 1640 bis 10 Iulii 1642. *Schleusingen, Iohann Michael Schall*, 1644. 12mo, pp. 79. 2379

The Augusta [Ga.] Colonization Society. [Constitution and History. n. p., n. d.] 12mo, pp. 10. H. 2380

AUGUSTA, *Ga.* ... A Tribute of Respect to the Memory of her fallen Heroes, by St. James' M. E. Sabbath School, of Augusta, Ga. Comprising Eulogies, pronounced by Messrs. Martin V. Calvin, Joseph T. Derry and Rev. William M. Crumley; a Full Report of the Action of the Grand Committee of Twenty, an "In Memoriam," by Mr. Henry Cleveland, and an "Oration," ... by Hon. Henry W. Hilliard. *Augusta, Ga.*, 1866. 8vo, pp. 28. H. 2381

Tuther's Augusta Directory For 1861, to which is added a Business Directory ... By T. Tuther, Jr. First Annual Issue. *Augusta, Ga., Press Chronicle & Sentinel*, 1861. 8vo, pp. 26–131. H. 2382

AUGUSTUS (Hieronymus Oliverius). De Imperio Romano Liber, de Partitione Orbis Libri IV. et Epigrammata. *Aug. Vind.*, 1548. 4to. 2383

"The Poem de Partitione Orbis is very interesting to the American collector."—LIBRI'S CATALOGUE, 1861, No. 212.

AUGUSTUS (J.) A Report of the Labors of John Augustus, for the Last Ten Years, in Aid of the Unfortunate: containing a Description of his Method ...; Striking Incidents, and Observations upon the Improvement of some of Our City Institutions ... . *Boston, Wright and Hasty*, 1852. 8vo, pp. 104. H.

AUGUSTUS. Letter concerning the Labors of Mr. John Augustus, the Well-known Philanthropist, From One who knows him. *Boston, Published for Private Circulation, December*, 1858. 8vo, pp. 11. H. 2385

AUGY (— d'). Réflexions sur une lettre écrite le 16 mai par le sieur Peynier à l'assemblée générale de la partie française de Saint-Domingue, séante à Saint-Marc. Du 7 février 1791. [*Paris*], *Impr. de L. Potier de Lille* [n. d.] 8vo. 2386

Signed, "D'Augy."

Aura; or, the Slave. A Poem. *Philadelphia*, 1788. 16mo, pp. 23. 2387

AURELIUS, *pseudon.* *See* [Gardner (John)].

AURIAC (J. B. d'). Les forestiers du Michigan; par Jules B. d'Auriac. *Paris, Brunet*, 1866. 18mo, pp. 18. 2388

AURIAC. ... La guerre noire souvenirs de Saint-Domingue par J. Berlioz d'Auriac *Paris, Putois-Cretté*, 1862. 12mo, 2 p. l., pp. 480. H. 2389

Ausführliche Beschreibung. *See* [Vries (S. Van)].

Ausführliche Beschreibung von der unglücklichen Reise des jüngsthin aus Teutschland nach Carolina und Pensylvanien wandernden Pilgrim, dem übelgegründeten Kocherthalerischen Bericht entgegen gesetzt. *Frankfurt*, 1711. 8vo. 2390

"An account of the journey of some pilgrims from Germany to Carolina and Pennsylvania."—MEUSEL, X., 2, p. 375. Boucher, VI., 56, quotes an edition, *Frankfort*, 1706. 8vo.

Ausführlicher Bericht von der berühmten Landschaft Carolina, an tag gegeben von Kocherthalern. *Frankfurt*, 1709. 8vo.

Meusel, X., 2, p. 375.

Ausilios del Ecuador Solicitados parapasta esponsion Consiguiente y sucesos posteriores. *Quito*, 1841. 4to. 2392

The Auspices of War, an Ode, Inscribed to the Memory of Admiral Boscawen, To which is added, the Prophecy of the Union. A narrative Poem. *London, Dodsley*, 1779. 4to.

M. R., LX., 476.

Auss America. *See* No. 1019.

AUSTIN (A. W.) A Memorandum concerning the Charlestown Post-Office. By Arthur W. Austin, P.M. [n. p., 1835.] 8vo, pp. 23. B. & N. 2394

AUSTIN (Benjamin). Constitutional Republicanism, in opposition to Fallacious Federalism; as published occasionally in the Independent Chronicle, under the Signature of Old-South. To which is added, a Prefatory Address to the Citizens of the United States, never before published. By Benjamin Austin, jun. [Motto.] *Boston, Adams & Rhoades*, 1803. 8vo, pp. 327. C. & H. 2395

AUSTIN. Memorial. To the Legislature of Massachusetts. [Relative to a Charge delivered to the Grand Jury, Nov. Term. 1806, by Theophilus Parsons. With the Report of the Committee on it. n. p., 1808.] 8vo, pp. 11. H. 2396

[AUSTIN.] Observations on the Pernicious Practice of Law. Published occasionally in the Independent Chronicle. By Honestus. *Boston, Printed by Adams & Nourse*, M,DCC,LXXXVI. 8vo, pp. 52. + With an Address never before published. Corrected and amended. ... *Boston, Printed by True & Weston*, 1819. 8vo, pp. 60. H. 2397

Advocates a law reform in Massachusetts, and the abolition of lawyers by profession.

[AUSTIN.] Remarks on a late Proposition [by U. Cotting] from the Boston and Roxbury Mill Corporation ... . [*Boston*, 1818.] 8vo, pp. 8. H. 2398

AUSTIN (C. H.) ... A Discourse, delivered at Rome, N. Y., by Rev. C. H. Austin, on the Death of Lewis Wilcox, who fell at the Siege of Fredericksburgh, Va., December 11, 1862. *Utica, N. Y., Roberts, Printer*, 1863. 8vo, pp. 22. H. 2399

AUSTIN. The Origin of our National Difficulties; examined. By C. H. Austin, Pastor of M. E. Church, Frankfort, N. Y. ... *Utica, N. Y., Keeling & Griffiths, Printers*, 1861. 8vo, pp. 24. H. 2400

The title on the cover is "The Uncultivated Heritage, and the Southern Rebellion. A Sermon ... ."

[AUSTIN (David)]. The American Preacher; or, A Collection of Sermons from some of the most Eminent Preachers, now living, in the United States ... . *Elizabeth-Town (New-Jersey), Printed by Shepard Kollock*, 1791–93. 4 vols., 8vo. + Vol. IV. *New-Haven, Printed by Abel Morse.* 2401

AUSTIN. Republican Festival, Proclamation, and New Jerusalem. New Haven, March 9th, A.D. 1803. [n. p., n. d.] 8vo, pp. 16. H. 2402

AUSTIN. A Discourse delivered on occasion of the death of George Washington, late president, general, and commander-in-chief of the forces of the United States of America, in compliance with the request of the mayor, aldermen, and Common Council of the Borough of Elizabeth, December 25. 1799. Also sketches of a running discourse delivered to the Union Brigade on the same occasion, at their cantonment on Green Brook, in compliance with a request from Colonel Smith, the Commanding officer, December 26, 1799. with an address to the throne of grace, offered at the door of the tabernacle of the cantonment on Green Brook, Feb. 22. the birthday of our national luminary. By David Austin, Jun. *New York, Printed by G. F. Hopkins*, 1800. 4to, pp. 36. Allegorical Plate. 2403

AUSTIN. The National "Barley Cake." or, The "Rock of Offence" a "Glorious Holy Mountain:" in Discourses and Letters. By David Austin, A.M. *Washington, Way & Groff*, 1802. 8vo, pp. 80. C. 2404

Full of warm Federalist politics.

AUSTIN. Downfal of Mystical Babylon, or the Political Operations of 1793–4, a Discourse at Elizabeth Town and New York. By David Austin. 1795. 8vo. 2405

AUSTIN (Elbridge Gerry). Fugitive Slave Case. A Statement of the Facts, connected with the Arrest and Emancipation of George Latimer, a Fugitive Slave. Prepared by E. G. Austin, Counsel for the Claimant. *Boston, John H. Eastburn, Printer*, 1842. 8vo, pp. 11. H. 2406

[AUSTIN (Ivers James)]. An Account of the Origin of the Mississippi Doctrine of Repudiation: with a Review of the Argument which His Excellency Alexander G. McNutt, late Governor of Mississippi, advanced in its Vindication. By a Member of the Boston Bar. ... *Boston, Bradbury, Soden, and Company*, MDCCCXLII. 8vo, pp. 28. H. 2407

AUSTIN. An Address delivered before the Corps of Cadets of the United States Military Academy. By Ivers J. Austin, Esq. a Member of the Board of Visitors. June, 1842. *New York, Wiley and Putnam*, 1842. 8vo, pp. 18 H. 2408

AUSTIN. Argument of Ivers J. Austin, Counsel for the Remonstrants from Watertown, against the Petition for the Incorporation of the Town of Belmont, before the Joint Stand-

ing Committee on Towns. *Boston, Printed by Alfred Mudge and Son*, 1857. 8vo, pp. 58 (1). Map. H. 2409

AUSTIN. An Oration delivered by Request of the City Authorities, before the Citizens of Boston ... July 4, 1839. By Ivers James Austin. *Boston, John H. Eastburn, City Printer*, 1839. 8vo, pp. 36. H. + Second Edition. *Boston*, 1839. 8vo, pp. 36. 2410

AUSTIN (James Trecothick). The Life of Elbridge Gerry. With Contemporary Letters. To the Close of the American Revolution. By James T. Austin, Esq. *Boston, Wells and Lilly*, 1828–29. 2 vols., 8vo, pp. xvi., 520; vii. (1), 408. Portrait. C. & H. 2411

AUSTIN. An Oration pronounced at Lexington, Mass. ... 4th July, 1815. By James T. Austin. *Boston, Printed by Rowe and Hooper*, 1815. 8vo, pp. 21. B. 2412

AUSTIN. An Oration, delivered on the Fourth of July, 1829, ... in the City of Boston. By James T. Austin. *Boston, John H. Eastburn, Printer*, 1829. 8vo, pp. 26. H. 2413

[AUSTIN. Remarks on Dr. Channing's Slavery. By a Citizen of Massachusetts. *Boston, Russell, Shattuck and Co., and John H. Eastburn*, 1835. 8vo, pp. 48. H. 2414

[AUSTIN.] Review of the Remarks on Dr. Channing's Slavery, by a Citizen of Massachusetts. [Austin.] *Boston, James Munroe and Company*, 1836. 8vo, pp. 48. B. 2415

Mr. Austin was also the author of Review of the Rev. Dr. Channing's Letter to Jonathan Phillips on the Slavery Question. *Boston*, 1839. 12mo. An Address, delivered before the Massachusetts Charitable Mechanic Association, ... October 3, 1839. ... *Boston*, 1839. 8vo, pp. 36. Reply to the Centinel Review [relating to the Massachusetts State Prison]. *Boston*, 1824. 8vo, pp. 4. Speech delivered in Faneuil Hall, Dec. 8, 1837, at a Meeting of Citizens. *Boston*, 1837. 8vo, pp. 13.

AUSTIN (Jonathan Loring). An Oration, delivered July 4, 1786, at ... Boston ... . *Boston, Printed by Peter Edes* [1786]. 4to, pp. 19. H. 2416

AUSTIN (Jonathan Williams). An Oration, delivered March 5, 1778, at the Request of the Inhabitants of Boston, to Commemorate the Bloody Tragedy of March 5, 1770. By J. W. Austin. *Boston*, 1776. 4to, pp. 14. P. 2417

AUSTIN (L. A.) Memorial of Mary White Wicker: A

Funeral Sermon delivered at Ticonderoga, N. Y., Aug. 26, 1865, by Rev. L. A. Austin, of Orwell, Vt. ... For Private Circulation. *Andover, Printed by Warren F. Draper*, 1865. 8vo, pp. 60. 2418

AUSTIN (Moses). Summary Description of the Lead Mines in Upper Louisiana. By Moses Austin. *Washington, A. & G. Way*, 1804. 12mo. C. 2419

AUSTIN (Robert F.) Buchananism not Democracy: Speech, New-York Assembly, Feb. 9, 1858. 8vo, pp. 6. S. 2420

AUSTIN (Samuel). An Address, pronounced in Worcester, (Mass.) on The Fourth of July, 1825, being the Forty-ninth Anniversary of the Independence of the United States, before an Assembly convened for the Purpose of Celebrating this Event religiously. By Samuel Austin, D.D. ... *Worcester, Printed by William Manning* [n. d.] 8vo, pp. 23. H. 2421

AUSTIN. The Apology of Patriots, or The heresy of the friends of the Washington and peace policy defended. A Sermon, preached in Worcester, Massachusetts, on the Day of the National Fast ... August 20, 1812. Observed ... in consequence of the Declaration of War against Great-Britain. By Samuel Austin, D.D. Published by Request. *Printed at Worcester, by Isaac Sturtevant*, 1812. 8vo, pp. 32. B. 2422

AUSTIN. An Oration, pronounced at Worcester, on the Fourth of July, 1798 ... . By Samuel Austin, A.M. *Printed at Worcester, by Leonard Worcester*, 1798. 8vo, pp. 38. H. 2423

AUSTIN. An Oration, Pronounced at Newport, Rhode-Island, July 4, 1822. ... By Samuel Austin, D.D. *Newport, William Simons*, 1822. 8vo, pp. 16. 2424

AUSTIN. Protest against Proceedings of the First Church in Worcester. By Samuel Austin, D.D. Member and formerly Pastor of said Church. *Printed by Manning & Trumbull, June*, 1821. 8vo. pp. 16. H. 2425

Mr. Austin also published Discourses at the Dedication of the Calvinist Church, Worcester, Oct. 13, 1823. *Worcester*, 1823. 8vo. An Inaugural Address, pronounced in Burlington, July 26th, 1815, by Samuel Austin, D.D. President of the University of Vermont. ... *Burlington, Printed by Francis G. Fish, August*, 1815. 8vo, pp. 18. H. Examination of Seven Sermons by Rev. Daniel Merrill on Baptism. *Worcester*, 1805. 12mo. The following sermons: Disinterested Love, *New York*, 1791. 8vo; Introductory to his Ministry in Worcester. *Worcester*, 1791. 8vo, pp. 32; At Salem, April 20, 1803, on the Installation of Samuel Worcester. *Worcester*, 1803. 8vo,

pp. 27; Before the Mass. Missionary Soc., May 24, 1803. *Salem*, 1803. 8vo, pp. 32; Incomparable Excellency of Religion. *Catskill*, 1808. 8vo, pp. 17. Also at the ordinations: in Fitchburg, Mass., Sept. 27, 1797, of Samuel Worcester, and again in Granville, N. Y., Oct. 4, of Nathaniel Hall. *Worcester*, 1798. 8vo, pp. 32; of Leonard Worcester, in Peacham, Vt., Oct. 30, 1799. *Peacham*, 1800. 8vo, pp. 32; of John Milton Whiton, Antrim, N. H., Sept. 28, 1808. *Amherst*, 1809. 8vo, pp. 28; of Warren Fay. *Worcester*, 1809. 8vo; of John Nelson, in Leicester, Mass., March 4, 1812. *Worcester*, 1812. 8vo, pp. 28. Sermon at Worcester on the Annual Fast, April 11, 1811. *Worcester*, 1811. 8vo, pp. 32. Sermon delivered at Worcester, on the Day of Public Thanksgiving, observed throughout ... Massachusetts, December 15, MDCCXCVI. By Samuel Austin, A.M.. *Printed at Worcester, by Leonard Worcester*, 1797. 8vo, pp. 24. Sermon preached in Worcester, Mass., on the Occasion of the Special Fast, July 23, 1812. *Worcester*, 1812. 8vo, pp. 28. Sermon preached on the Day of General Election, at Montpelier, Oct. 10, 1816. *Montpelier*, 1816. 8vo, pp. 27. And others.

AUSTIN (S. F.) An Address delivered by S. F. Austin of Texas ... in ... Louisville, Kentucky, On the 7th of March, 1836. *Lexington, J. Clarke & Co., Printers*, 1836. 12mo, pp. 30. H. + An Address of the Honorable S. F. Austin, One of the Commissioners of Texas. [*Louisville*, 1836]. 8vo, pp. 29–47 of some unknown work. B. 2426

AUSTIN SETTLEMENTS. Translation of the Laws, Orders, and Contracts, on Colonization, from January, 1801, up to this time, in virtue of which Col. Stephen F. Austin has introduced, &c., Foreign Emigrants in Texas, with an Explanatory Introduction. *San Felipe de Austin, Texas*, 1829. 8vo. N. 2427

AUSTIN (William). An Oration, pronounced at Charlestown, at the Request of the Artillery Company, on the Seventeenth of June; being the Anniversary of the Battle of Bunker's Hill, and of that Company. [Mottoes.] By William Austin, A.B. *Charlestown, Printed by Samuel Etheridge*, 1801. 8vo, pp. 29. H.

AUSTIN. Harrington's Directory of the City of Austin for the Year 1866. With a Historical and Statistical Review of Austin and the Reese River Mining Region. By Myron Angel. *Austin, Nevada, J. D. Fairchild & Co., Printers*, 1866. 8vo, pp. 119. 2429

AUSTRIA (*Colonel* José de). Bosquejo de la Historia militar de Venezuela en la Guerra de su Independencia. Tomo I. [all published]. *Carácas*, 1855. 8vo, pp. xlvii., 390. 2430

AUSTRO-BOREALIS, *pseudon.* A Platform, etc. *See* [Stearns (E. J.)]

Der Auswanderer am Niederrhein. *Meurs, Dolle*, 1849–50. 8 nos., 8vo, pp. 170 in all. 2431

Contents.—1. Wiskonsin: Manitowac-Rapids. 2. Wiskonsin: Milwaukee. Ebenezer. 3. Iowa: Pella. 4. New-York. 5. Indiana. Wisconsin. Missouri. 6. Wisconsin. [Title on the cover: Wie sieht es in Wisconsin aus? ... Von Wilh. Dames.] 7. Indiana. [Cover-title: Nord-Amerika in seinen verschiedenen Beziehungen, insbesondere der Staat Indiana. Von Pet. Schultze.] 8. Ceresco, Fond du Lac County. [Cover-title: Nordamerika ... . Von Emil Eversz. Menschenhandel in Havre von Le Maitre & Comp. das. u. Washington Finlay in Mainz. Von Louis Eversz.]

Auswanderer-Bibliothek. Verzeichniss der seit den letzten 10 Jahren erschienenen Schriften und Charten für Auswanderer mit Angabe der Stärke, der Verleger, der Preise und einer Uebersicht nach den verschiedenen Ländern und Staaten. *Rudolstadt, Froebel*, 1852. 8vo, pp. 33. 2432

Auswanderer-Calender für 1854 und 1855. 1. Doppel-Jahrgang. *Rudolstadt, Froebel*, 1854. 16mo, pp. 84. 2433

This is the "Ausgabe für Nord-Amerika;" an "Ausgabe für Süd-Amerika," pp. 88, was published; also an edition for North America of the "Calender für 1855 und 1856."

Die Auswanderer in Amerika. Aus den Atlantischen Studien abgedruckt. *Göttingen, Wigand* [1853]. 8vo, pp. 16. 2434

Der Auswanderer, zunächst Organ der sämmtlichen Auswanderungsvereine Sachsens. Mittheilungen aus deutschen Ansiedlungen, Rathgeber für fortziehende Brüder, sowie Besprechungen über geistiges und sittliches Leben transatlantischer Völker. [III.] Jahrgang 1850. *Schneeberg* [*and*] *Leipzig* [1850]. 4to. Continued. 2435

1850. 104 nos. each 4 pp.; 1851, 52 nos. each 8 pp.

Die Auswanderung der Deutschen nach Texas, Nordamerika und Ungarn. Eine Mahnung an die Nation. *München, Franz*, 1844. 8vo, pp. 56. 2436

See also under Mexico, Michigan, and Texas.

Die Auswanderung nach Amerika. *Breslau, Schulz & Co.*, 1850. 8vo, pp. 4. 2437

Über Auswanderungen, überhaupt, über Auswanderungen nach Amerika insbesondere, von dem Standpunkte der Geschichte, der Universalphilosophie, der Moral und Politik. *Rudolstadt*, 1834. 8vo. 2438

Cover-title: "Fluch und Segen der Auswanderungen," etc.

Auswahl kleiner Reisebeschreibungen und anderer statistischen und geographischen Nachrichten. *Leipzig, Schneider*, 1784–95. 22 vols., 8vo. 2439

Auswahl schöner seltener Gewächse als eine Fortsetzung der Amerikanischen Gewächse. Mit 250 illuminirten Kupfertafeln mit Text von Jh. Zorn. *Nürnberg, Bauer u. Raspe*, 1795–98. 5 pt. 8vo. 2440

This is a continuation of Dreyhundert auserlesene Amerikanische Gewächse nach Linnéischer Ordnung. *Nürnberg*, 1785.

Auszüge aus Briefen aus Nord-Amerika, geschreiben von zweien aus Ulm an der Donau gebürtigen, nun im Staate Louisiana ansässigen Geschwistern. Nebst Beschreibung einer Reise durch mehrere der nördlichen und westlichen Staaten von Nord-Amerika. ... *Ulm, Nübling*, 1833. 12mo, pp. 224. Plate.

Ein auszug ettlicher|sendbrieff dem aller durchleüchtigisten| groszmechtigisten Fürsten vnd Herren Herren Carl Römischen vnd|Hyspanischen König &c vnserm gnedigen hern durch ire verordent | Hauptleut | von wegen einer new gefunden Inseln, der selben gelegen|heit vnd jnwoner stitten vn gewonheiten inhaltend vor Kurtzuerschi-|nen tagen zugefandt.| [Colophon] Getruckt in der keiserlichen Stat Nürmberg durch| Fryderichen Peypus | vnd seligklich volend|am. 17. tag Marcij| des jars do man|zalt nach Christi unsers lieben|herren gebvrt. MDXX.| 4to, Title, 1 l., 6 leaves and 1 blank. 2442

Contains an account of the expeditions of Francisco Hernandez de Cordova, Grijalva, and Cortes to Yucatan, from Anghiera.

Autentijck Verhael van 't remarcquabelste is voorgevallen in Brasil, tusschen den Hollandtschen Admirael Willem Cornelisz ende de Spaensche Vloot. Midtsg. de Sententie ende executie over eenighe Schippers, die haren Eedt in't ghevecht niet betracht hadden. *Amsterdam, von J. van Hilten*, 1640. 4to, pp. 12. 2443

"The marks „C 3." and „D" at the foot of two of the pages are evidently misprinted, and instead of A 3. and B."—MULLER.

AUTEROCHE. *See* Chappe d'Auteroche (Jean).

Authentic Account of the Proceedings of the Congress held at New-York, In MDCCLXV, On the Subject of the American Stamp Act. [*London*], MDCCLXVII. 8vo, Title, pp. 37. H. & S.

An Authentic Account of the Rise and Progress of the Present Contest in America. To which is added the Discovery of America by Columbus. *London*, 1776. 8vo. 2445

Authentic Copies of the Correspondence of Charles Cotesworth Pinckney, John Marshall, and Elbridge Gerry, Esqrs. Envoys Extraordinary and Ministers Plenipotentiary to the Republic of France; as Presented to Both Houses of Congress, April 3, 1798. By His Excellency, John Adams. President of the United States of America. *London, Printed for J. Debrett*, 1798. 8vo, pp. 78. 2446

Authentic Copies of the Preliminary Articles of Peace between Great Britain, France, Spain and the United States of America, signed at Versailles, 20th January, 1783. *London*, 1783. 8vo, pp. 32. 2447

Authentic Copies of the Provisional and Preliminary Articles of Peace signed between Great Britain, France, Spain, and the United States of America. ... *London*, 1783. 8vo, pp. 28.

Authentic Copies of the Provisional and Preliminary Articles of Peace between Great Britain and the United States of America, the King of France, and the King of Spain, signed Nov[r] 30, 1782 & Jan. 20, 1783. *London, J. Debrett*, 1783. 8vo. 2449

An Authentic Journal of the Siege of the Havana. By an Officer. To which is prefixed, A Plan of the Siege of the Havana, Shewing the Landing, Encampments, Approaches, and Batteries of the English Army. With the Attacks and Stations of the Fleet. *London, T. Jefferys*, MDCCLXII. 8vo, pp. 44. Plan. C. & H. 2450

An authentic Narrative of Facts relating to the Exchange of Prisoners taken at the Cedars; supported by the Testimonies and Depositions of His Majesty's Officers, with Several Original Letters and Papers. Together with Remarks upon the Report and Resolves of the American Congress on that Subject. *London, T. Cadell*, MDCCLXXVII. 8vo, pp. 50. N. 2451

"These remarks are intended to shew the fallacy of the report of the Congress, and to evince the perfidy of that body, in the resolves."—M. R.

An Authentic Narrative of the Loss of the Doddington Indiaman, and of the Surprising Adventures, and Distresses of those on Board, who survived the Shipwreck, from the Journal of one

of the Surviving Officers. [Motto.] *New-York, Printed by James Parker and Company*, MDCCLXII. 12mo, pp. 28. P. 2452

An Authentic Narrative of the Proceedings of the Expedition under the Command of Brigadier-Gen. Craufurd, until its Arrival at Monte Video; with an Account of the Operations against Buenos Ayres under the Command of Lieut.-Gen. Whitelocke. By an Officer of the Expedition. *London, the Author*, 1808. 8vo, Title, pp. viii., 216. 4 Maps. C. & H.

Authentic Papers from America: submitted to the Dispassionate Consideration of the Public. *London, T. Becket*, 1775. 8vo, Title, pp. 33. S. 2454

This collection contains the several American petitions previous to the repeal of the Stamp Act, contrasted with the petition of the late Congress to the King, and their address to the people of Great Britain. *See* M. R., LII., 87.

Authentic Papers Relating to the Expedition against Carthagena: being the Resolutions of the Councils of War; both of Sea and Land-Officers ... With ... the Letters which passed between Admiral Vernon and General Wentworth; and also between the Goveraor of Carthagena and the Admiral. *London, L. Raymond*, 1744. 8vo, Title, pp. 100. H. 2455

Authentic Papers Relative to the Expedition against the Charibbs, and the Sale of Lands in the Island of St. Vincent. *London, J. Almon*, M DCC LXXIII. 4to, pp. 83. H. 2456

Authentic proceedings of the French King and his parliament against the Jesuits of France, with a preface tracing the artifices of the whole body of Jesuits, and enumerating the various diabolical methods they made use of by Mons. La Valette, their Agent at Martinico, &c. *London, Wilkie*, 1761. 8vo, pp. 61.

Authentic Rebel Papers seized at St. Eustatius, 1781. *London, L. Lambert, G. Kearsly, and J. Bowen*, M.DCC.LXXXI. 4to, Title, pp. vi., 23. H. 2458

The Monthly Reviewer doubts the authenticity of these papers. *See* M. R., LXV., 382.

An Authentic Register of the British Successes, being a Collection of all the Extraordinary Gazettes, from the taking of Louisbourgh, July 26th, 1758, to the Defeat of the French Fleet Nov. 21st 1759. *London*, 1760. 12mo. 2459

Contains particulars of the taking of Louisbourg, Ticonderoga. Fort Duquesne Niagara, and Quebec.

An Authentic Report of the Debate in the House of Commons, June the 23d, 1825, on Mr. Buxton's Motion relative to the Demolition or the Methodist Chapel and Mission House in Barbadoes, and the Expulsion of Mr. Shrewsbury, a Wesleyan Missionary, from that Island. *London, J. Hatchard and Son*, 1825. 8vo, 2 p. l., pp. 119. H. 2459*a*

Authentic Translation of a Note from a Minister of the French Republic to the Secretary of State of the United States, etc. *New York*, 1796. 8vo, pp. 38. 2460

Authentiek Tractaat van Vriendschap, Commercie en Navigatie tusschen zyne Majesteit van Groot-Britanje, en de Vereenigde Staaten van America. [1794.] 8vo, pp. 40. 2461

Avthentische Nachricht Von der Verhandlung, und dem Verlass Der am 14[den] und 15[den], Januarii Anno 174½. In sogenannten Falckner. Schwamm An Georg Hubners Hause gehaltenen Zweyten Versammlung, Sowol Einiger Teutschen Arbeiter Der Evangelischen Religionen Als Verschiedener einzelen treuen Gezeugen und Gottsfurchtiger Nachbarn. Nebst einigen Beylagen. *Philadelphia Gedruckt und zu haben bey B. Franklin* [n. d.] 4to, pp. 19–40. 2462

Avthentische | Relation | Von dem | Anlass, Fortgang und Schlusse | Der am 1[sten] und 2[ten] Januarii, Anno 174½ | In Germantoun gehalten | Versammlung | Einiger Arbeiter | Derer meisten Christlichen Religionen | Vnd | Vieler vor sich selbst Gott-dienenden Christen-Menschen | in Pennsylvania | ausgesetzt | In Germantoun am Abend des 2[ten] Obigen Monats, | *Philadelphia*, | *Gedruckt und zu haben bey B. Franklin*. [1742.] 4to, 8 l. 2463

The Author of Plain Truth strip'd Stark naked. *Philadelphia*, 1764. 12mo. 2464

The Author of Quaker Unmasked, Strip'd Stark Naked, or the Delineated Presbyterian Play'd Hob With. *Philadelphia, Printed in the Year* 1764. 12mo, pp. 12. C. 2464*a*

Autobiography of a Female Slave. *See* [Griffiths (Mattie)].

Autobiography of an English Soldier in the United States Army. *London, Hurst & Blackett* 1853. 2 vols., post 8vo, pp. 306, 313. C. + *Reprinted, New York, Stringer & Townsend*, 1853. 12mo, pp. xii., 9–288. 2 Plates. H. 2465

AUTODICUS. The Critique of the Vision of Rubeta. A Dramatic Sketch, in One Act, By Autodicus. [Motto.] *Philadelphia, Printed for the Trade*, 1838. 8vo, pp. 32. 2466

In answer to Osborne's Poem on New Amsterdam.

Autographs for Freedom. *See* [Griffiths (Julia)].

Autograph Leaves of Our Country's Authors. *Baltimore, Cushing & Bailey*, 1864. 4to, pp. xi., 200. 2467

Published for the Sanitary Fair at Baltimore.

AVALLE. Tableau comparatif des productions des colonies françaises aux Antilles, avec celles des colonies anglaises, espagnoles et hollandaises, de l'année 1787 à 1788. Suivi de l'établissement et mouvement d'une Sucrerie, pendant le cours d'une année. Observations sur l'étendue que ces Habitations doivent avoir ... Par le citoyen Avalle habitant cultivateur de Saint-Domingue. *Paris, Goujon fils, Debray, Fuschs* [n. d.] 4to, Half-title, pp. viii., (2), 5 folded l., 7 l., 1 f. l., 2 l., 1 f. l., pp. 75. Plate. H. 2468

AVALOS Y FIGUEROA (Diego d'). Primera parte de la Miscelanea Austral de D. Diego d'Avalos y Figueroa en varios Coloquios, Interlocutores, Delio, y Cilena, Con la Defensa de las Damas. *Lima, Antonio Ricardo*, 1602. 4to, 22 p. l., pp. 219; Tabla, 8 l. 2469

Relates to the history and antiquities of Peru. *See* Ternaux, 254.

AVE-LALLEMANT (F.) Erinnerungen an Brasilien. *Lübeck v. Rohden*, 1854. 8vo, 2 p. l., pp. 86. 2470

AVÉ-LALLEMANT (Robert C. B.) Reise durch Süd-Brasilien im Jahre 1858. *Leipzig, Brockhaus*, 1859. 2 vols., 8vo, pp. ix., 509; vii., 450. Plates. 2471

AVÉ LALLEMANT. Die Benutzung der Palmen am Amazonen-Strom in der Oekonomie der Indianer. Nach einem im Athenäum zu Hamburg am 19. Nov. 1860 gehaltenen freien Vortrag. *Hamburg, Boyes & Geisler*, 1861. 16mo, pp. vi., 44.

AVÉ-LALLEMANT. Reise durch Nord-Brasilien im Jahre 1859. *Leipzig, Brockhaus*, 1860. 2 parts, 8vo, pp. xxi., 815.

AVÉ LALLEMANT. Tabatinga am Amazonenstrome. Ein Vortrag gehalten am 7. März 1863 im wissenschaftlichen

Verein zu Berlin. *Hamburg, Perthes-Besser & Mauke*, 1863. 8vo, pp. 42. 2474

AVENDAÑO (Diego de). Carta, | que el P. Francisco | Xavier Rector del Colegio | Maximo de S. Pablo, y al presente Preposito | Provincial de la Provincia del Perù. | Remitio a Los Padres Rectores de | los Colegios, y Casas de la Compañia de Iesvs | de la dicha Provincia. | Dandoles vna breve noticia | de la exemplarissima vida, y dichosa muerte | del Venerable P. Diego de Avendaño. | Año. 1689. | *Con licencia en Lima. Por Ioseph de Contreras.* | 4to, 3 p. l., Text, 63 l. 2475

AVENDAÑO. R. P. Didaci de Avendaño Societatis Iesv, Segoviensis, In Pervvio iam pridem publici & primarij S. Theologiæ Professoris, & in Sacro Inquisitionis Sanctæ Tribunali adlecti Censoris, Thesavrus Indicvs, sev generalis Instrvctor pro regimine conscientiæ, in iis quæ ad Indias spectant. Tomvs primvs, Ea continens, quæ ad Ciuilem præsertim conducunt Gubernationem. || Tomvs secundvs Circa spiritualia totus: Sacramenta inquam, Præcepta Ecclesiæ, Priuilegia pro ipsis, Indulgentias, & Sacrorum Hominum status. *Antverpiæ, apud Jacobum Mevrsivm*, M.DC.LXVIII. 2 vols., folio, pp. (16), 347, (17), 41, (3); (8), 369, (19), 66, (5). H. + Auctuarium Indicum, seu Thesauri Indici Tomus tertius || quartus || quintus. *Antverpiæ, Jacob Meursius*, 1675. 3 vols., folio. + Cursus consummatus; seu recognitiones Theologicæ, Expostivæ, Scholasticæ et Morales; utilia multa et specialia continentes generaliter et pro Indiis circa earum thesaurum. *Antverpiæ, Hieron. Verdussen*, 1686. Folio. 2476

AVERAY (*Mr.*) Britannia and the Gods in Council, a Dramatic Poem, wherein Felicity is predicted to Britain, the Causes of the present disputes in Europe and America are debated, and their Issue Prophetically determined. *London*, 1756. 4to. 2477

AVERILL (L. B.) Songs; National and Moral, for the Soldier and Laborer: also, A Wonderful Narrative of an Indian found in a Torpid State, with a Dialogue between an Indian and a White Man. By Leonard B. Averill. *Montpelier, the Author*, 1862. 16mo, pp. 27, (1). H. 2478

AVERY (David). Sermon preached at Greenwich, Conn.,

18th of Dec., 1777, being a General Thanksgiving throughout the United States. *Norwich*, 1778. 12mo, pp. 47. C. 2479

Also: Two Sermons on ... not bridling the Tongue. *Boston*, MDCCXCI. 8vo, pp. 66. A Sermon ... at the Interment of Mr. Walter Moor, ... *Charlestown*, 1799. 8vo, pp. 47.

AVERY. The Lord is to be praised for the Triumphs of his Power. A Sermon Preached At Greenwich, in Connecticut. On the 18th of December, 1777. Being A General Thanksgiving through the United American States. By David Avery, V. D. M. Chaplain to Col. Sherburne's Regiment. *Norwich, Green & Spooner*, 1778. 8vo, pp. 47. C. 2480

AVERY (Edward). Annexation of Roxbury and Boston. Argument on behalf of the Remonstrants, By Edward Avery, Esq. ... *Boston, Press of Geo. C. Rand & Avery*, 1865. 8vo, pp. 44. H. 2481

AVERY (E. K.) The Arguments of Counsel in the Close of the Trial of Rev. Ephraim K. Avery, for the Murder of Sarah M. Cornell ... Hon. Jeremiah Mason, of Boston, for the Prisoner. Albert C. Greene, Attorney General, for the Prosecution. Reported without Abridgement, by Benjamin F. Hallet. Also, a Literal Report of the Medical Testimony of Prof. Walter Channing and Dr. William Turner, revised by the Witnesses, and not before published. ... *Boston, Daily Commercial Gazette and Boston Daily Advocate, June*, 1833. 8vo, pp. 94, (1).

AVERY. A Correct, Full and Impartial Report of the Trial of Rev. Ephraim K. Avery, before the Supreme Judicial Court of the State of Rhode-Island, at Newport, May 6, 1833, for the Murder of Sarah M. Cornell. *Providence, Marshall and Brown* [1833]. 12mo, pp. 178. C. H. 2483

AVERY. Report of a Committee of the New England Annual Conference of the Methodist Episcopal Church, on the case of Rev. Ephraim K. Avery, Member of said Conference. *Boston, Printed by David H. Ela*, 1833. 8vo, pp. 12. H. 2484

AVERY. Strictures on the Case of Ephraim K. Avery, originally published in the Republican Herald, Providence, R. I., with Corrections, Revision and Additions. By Aristides. *Providence, William Simons, Jr.*, 1833. 12mo, pp. 100. C. 2485

AVERY. A Vindication of the Result of the Trial of Rev.

Ephraim K. Avery; to which is prefixed his Statement of Facts relative to the Circumstances by which he became involved in the Prosecution. With a Map. *Boston, Russell, Odiorne and Co.* [and] *David H. Ela*, 1834. 12mo, pp. 74. C. & H. 2486

Several pamphlets concerning this case are described at length in Bartlett's Bibl. R. I., pp. 20, 21.

AVERY (John). The King of the Pirates; being an Account of the famous Enterprises of Captain Avery, the mock King of Madagascar, with his Rambles and Piracies, in two Letters from himself during his stay at Madagascar, and one since his Escape from thence. *London*, 1720. 8vo. 2487

Contains an interesting account of his proceedings, with Captain Sharp, Captain Sawkins, Goiguet, and other pirates, in nearly every part of America.

AVERY (Joseph). An Oration, delivered at Holden, July 4, 1806; being the Anniversary of the Independence of the United States of America. By Joseph Avery. *Boston, Printed by Manning & Loring*, 1806. 8vo, pp. 12. H. 2488

AVERY and HEMPSTEAD. Narrative of Jonathan Rathbun, With Accurate Accounts of the Capture of Groton Fort, the Massacre that Followed, And the Sacking and Burning of New London, September 6 1781, by the British Forces under the command of the Traitor Benedict Arnold. By Rufus Avery And Stephen Hempstead, Eye witnesses of the same. Together with An Interesting Appendix. [No imprint.] 12mo, pp. 80.

AVES (Thomas). Case of the Slave-Child, Med. Report of the Arguments of Counsel, and of the Opinion of the Court, in the case of Commonwealth vs. Aves, ... in the Supreme Judicial Court of Massachusetts. *Boston*, 1836. 8vo, pp. 40. H. + The same. *Boston*, 1836. 8vo, pp. 40. P. 2490

AVEZAC-MACAYA (Marie Armand Pascal d'). Considérations géographiques sur l'histoire du Brésil, examen critique d'une nouvelle histoire génerale du Brésil récemment publ. en portugais à Madrid par M. Fr. Ad. de Varnhagen. Avec 2 cartes. *Paris*, 1857. Rl. 8vo. 2491

AVEZAC-MACAYA. Coup d'œil historique sur la projection des cartes de géographie. ... *Paris, Leiber*, 1863. 8vo, pp. viii., 152. Plates. 2492

From the "Bulletin," etc., April, May, June, 1863.

AVEZAC-MACAYA. Les Voyages de Améric Vespuce au

compte de l'Espagne et les mesures itinéraires employées par les marins Espagnols et Portugais des XVe et XVIe siècles, pour faire suite aux considérations geographiques sur l'histoire du Brésil, ... *Paris*, 1858. 8vo, pp. 188. 2493*a*

From the "Bulletin de la Société de Géographie," Sept., Oct., 1858.

[AVEZAC-MACAYA.] Martin Hylacomylus Waltzemüller ses ouvrages et ses collaborateurs Voyage d'exploration et de découvertes à travers quelques épitres dédicatoires préfaces et opuscules en prose et en vers du commencement du XVIe siècle ... par un géographe bibliophile. *Paris, Challamel ainé*, 1867. 8vo, pp. vi., 176. H. 2493

AVILA (Fr. de). Arte de la lengua Mexicana, y breves platicas de los mysterios de N. Santa Fé catolica, y otras para exortacion de su obligacion á los Indios Compuesta. Por el P. F. Francisco de Avila. ... del orden de los Menores de N. P. San Francisco. *Mexico*, 1717. Sm. 8vo, pp. 98 in all. 2494

Heber's copy sold for £2 14s.; Brunet, 17 fr.

AVILA. Oratio | habita in Ecclesia | cathedrali Limensi ad Domi- | num Bartholomæum Lupum Guerrerum Archiepisco | pum euisdem Ciuitatis, totius Regni Peruani Metropo | litanum, regi- umq; Consiliarium &c. A Doctore Fran- | cisco de Auila Vicario Prouinciæ de Huarocheri, atq; | Parocho ecclesiæ Sancti Damiani in eâdem pro- | uincia. Dominica tertia Aduentus, decima | tertia die mensis Decem b rs [*sic*]. | Anno. 1609. | In qva ipsi Domino Archiepiscopo osten | dit miserrimum statum circa Christianam religionem, in quo Indi huius Me- | tropoleos delitescunt: hocq; vice laudum in aduentu gratissimo ipsius | Domini Archiepiscopi, vice etiam congratulationis illi | offert, remediumq; adhibere persuadet. | Cvm Licentia. | *Limæ. Apud Franciscum à Canto.* | *Anno.* 1610. | 4to, 12 leaves. H. 2495

Avis aux Hessois Et autres peuples de l'Allemagne Vendus par leurs Princes à l'Angleterre. *Cleves, Bertol*, 1777. 8vo, pp. 16. H. 2496

Avis divers, *and* Avis du Cap. *See* Saint-Domingo.

Avis d'un bon patriote. *Paris, imp. de Henri IV.* [n. d.] 8vo.

A pamphlet relating to the affairs of St. Domingo in 1790.

AVITY (Sieur d'). Les | Estats, Empires, | et Principavtez | dv Monde, | Representez par la | Description des Pays, | mœurs des habitans, | Richesses des Prouinces, | les forces, le gouuernement | la Religion, et les Princes | qui ont gouuerné | chacun Estat. | Auec L'origine de toutes les | Religions, et de tous les | Cheualiers et ordres | Militaires. | Par le S^r. D. T. V. Y. gentilhome | ord^re. de la Chambre du Roy. | *A Paris*, M.D.C.XIX. 4to, 10 p. l., pp. 1467, (1). 2498

The notice of the New World occupies sixty-seven pages. Boucher, VI., 171, notices other editions.

AVON. The Mineral Waters of Avon, N. Y. *Rochester*, 1838. 8vo. 2499

AVRIGNY (C. J. Lœuillard d'). Le Départ de la Pérouse, ou les Navigateurs Modernes; Poëme par C. G. L. d'Avrigni, de la Martinique, officier d'administration des colonies etc. *Paris*, 1807. 8vo, pp. 59. S.+In his Poésies nationales. 3e éd. *Paris, Le Normant*, 1812. 8vo. 2500

Away in the Wilderness; or, Life among the Red Indians and Fur Traders of North America. *New York, D. Appleton & Co.*, 1864. 16mo, pp. 117. 2501

Awful Calamities: or, The Shipwrecks of December, 1839, ... on the Coast of Massachusetts; in which were lost more than 90 Vessels, and nearly 200 dismasted, driven ashore or otherwise damaged, and more than 150 Lives destroyed ... Second Edition. *Boston, Press of J. Howe*, 1840. 8vo, pp. 24. Woodcuts. Fifth Edition. 1840. H. 2502

AXMILEN (A. O.) *See* Esquemeling.

AYANQUE (Simon). Lima por dentro y Fuera. Por Simon Ayanque. *Madrid*, 1798. 12mo. 2503

A description of Lima in verse.

AYANQUES (S.) Lima por dentro y fuera. La da a luz Simon Ayanques ... . Nueva edicion. *Paris, Impr. de Fournier; Lima, Joubert-Dubreuil*, 1842. 18mo, pp. 153. 2504

AYCINENA (Juan). Memoria sobre el canal proyectado en el istmo de Nicaragua. Por el ministro general de Guatemala, D. Juan Aycinena. [*New York?* 1836.] 8vo, pp. 16. H. 2505

AYCINENA. Mémoire sur la canalisation projetée de l'isthme de Nicaragua. Par M. J. Aycinena, ministre général du gouvernement de Guatemala. Publié par ordre de M. J. [F.] Cas-

tellon, Ministre plénipotentiaire de Nicaragua près du gouvernement français. *Paris, Imprimerie A. Francois et Compagnie*, 1844. 8vo, pp. 20. H. 2506

AYCRIGG (B.) Report on the Proposed Connection of the West Branch Improvements with the Alleghany River, *Harrisburg*, 1837. 8vo. 2507

AYCRIGG (B. B.) Duties of American Citizens. Position of New Jersey. Dated Passaic, N. J., May 3, 1865. *New York, E. O. Jenkins*, 1856. 8vo, pp. 16. 2508

AYDELOTT (B. P.) The Condition and Prospects of the Protestant Episcopal Church. By B. P. Aydelott, D.D. *Cincinnati, Wm. H. Moore & Co.* [etc.], 1848. 12mo, pp. 176. 2509

AYDELOTT. Our Country's Evils and their Remedy. *Cincinnati*, 1843. 12mo. 2510

AYDELOTT. Prejudice against Colored People. By Rev. B. P. Aydelott. *Cincinnati*, 1863. 24mo, pp. 21. H.+*Cincinnati*, 1863. 8vo, pp. 12. C. 2511

Also: Answer to the Rt. Rev. P. Chase. *Cincinnati* [1832]. 8vo, pp. viii., 45. ... A Discourse, ... on ... the Death of Charles U. Fosdick, January 18th, 1835. *Cincinnati*, 1835. 18mo, pp. 18.

AYER (James C.) Some of the Usages and Abuses in the Management of our Manufacturing Corporations. By J. C. Ayer, M.D. ... *Lowell, C. M. Langley & Co.*, 1863. 8vo, pp. 24. H. 2512

AYER (J. W.) The Great Northwestern Conspiracy in all its Startling Details. By J. Winslow Ayer, M.D. *Chicago, Jno. R. Walsh*, 1865. 8vo. pp. 112. 2513

AYERS (Elisha). Journal of Travel in different parts of the United States, including anecdotes, remarks, adventures, &c. By Elisha Ayers. *Preston* [*Conn.*], 1847. 8vo, pp. 52. C.

AYLLON (*Fr.* Juan de). Relacion de las fiestas que hizo la ciudad de Lima en la cononization de los XXIII Santos martyres del Japon. Por Fr. Juan de Ayllon. *Lima*, 1630. 4to.

AYLMER (F.) A Cruise in the Pacific. Edited by Captain F. Aylmer. *London, Hurst & Blacket*, 1860. 2 vols., post 8vo.

AYLMER (Louisa Anne). Passage of the Pique across the Atlantic. By Lady Aylmer. *London, Hatchard*, 1838. 12mo.

AYLMER (Matthew, 5*th Lord*). Addresses to Lord Aylmer from Public Bodies in Lower Canada on his Removal from the Administration of the Government of that Province, in the Year 1835 With his Answer. 1847. 8vo. Privately printed.

AYLMER. Public Documents relating to Lord Aylmer's Administration of the Government of Lower Canada. 1836. 8vo. Privately printed. 2519

AYMARA. Catecismo en lengua Aymara. *Sevilla*, 1604. 8vo. 2520

AYMÉ (Jean Jacques). Déportation et naufrage de J. J. Aymé, ex-législateur, suivis du tableau de vie et de mort des déportés, à son départ de la Guyane, avec Quelques observations sur cette Colonie et sur les Nègres. *Paris* [1800?]. 8vo, pp. 269, (26). H. 2521

Title given incorrectly in No. 544.

AYMÉ. Johann Aymé's Deportationsreise, Flucht und Schiffbruch; aus dem Französischen mit Karten [von J. J. Brückner]. *Leipzig, Hinrichs*, 1802. 8vo. 2522

A[YNGE] (G. A.) *See* A. (G. A.) No. 2.

AYRAULT (Charles). An Oration delivered at Geneva, July 4th, 1839. *Geneva*, 1839. 8vo. 2523

AYRES (J. A.) The Legends of Montauk. By J. A. Ayres. With an Historical Appendix. *New York, Geo. P. Putnam*, 1849. 8vo, pp. 127. 2524

AYRES DE CAZAL (Manoel). Corografia brazilica ou Relaçao historico-geographica do Reino do Brazil ... . *Rio de Janeiro, na impressao regia* M.DCCC.XVII. 2 vols., 4to, pp. (12), 420; (4), 379, (3). H.+*Rio de Janeiro*, 1838. 2 vols., 8vo.

[AYRES DE CAZAL.] Introducçao da corografia brasilica e a parte della que trata da Bahia. Composta por um presbitero secular do gra priorado do Crato e mandada imprimir por um professor. *Bahia*, 1826. 4to. 2526

[AYSCOUGH (Samuel)]. Remarks on the Letters from an American Farmer; or a Detection of the Errors of M. J. Hector St. John; pointing out the Pernicious Tendency of these Letters to Great Britain. *London*, 1783. 8vo. 2527

The writer of this pamphlet is of opinion "that M. St. John's design, in publishing

his letters, was to diffuse a spirit of migrating to America." He accuses him also of a palpable falsehood, in describing "himself as a native American, descended from Scotch parents, it being a fact, according to this writer, well known, that he is a native of Normandy, and that his chief residence while in America was at New York." *See* M. R., lxviii., 537. The author was the Rev. Samuel Ayscough." *See* NICHOLS, IX., p. 55.

AZAIS (Jean Pierre Hyacinthe). De l'Amérique. Par H. Azais. *Paris, Béchet*, 1818. 8vo, pp. 104. 2528

AZANZA (J. d') and O'FARRILL (G). Memoria de D. José de Azanza y D. Gonz. O-Farill sobra la politica desde Marzo de 1808 hasta abril de 1814. *Paris*, between 1814 and 1820.

AZANZA and O'FARRILL. Exposé des Faits qui justifient leur conduite politique depuis Mars 1808, jusqu'en Avril 1814: traduit de l'espagnol par M. A. Foudras. *Paris*, 1815. 8vo, pp. 325. 2530

AZARA (Felix de). Apuntamientos para la Historia Natural de los Quadrúpedos del Paragüay y Rio de la Plata, escritos por Don Felix de Azara. ... *Madrid, En la Imprenta de la Viuda de Ibarra*, MDCCCII. 2 vols., 4to, 10 p. l., pp. 318; Errata, 1 p.

Mr. Rich (Vol. 2, p. 10) prints a very interesting letter by the author, concerning this work on South America.

AZARA. Apuntamientos para la Historia Natural de los Páxaros del Paragüay y Rio de la Plata. Escritos por Don Felix de Azara. *Madrid, Ibarra*, 1802–1805. 3 vols., sm. 4to. C. 2532

AZARA. Correspondencia oficial e inedita sobre la demarcacion de limites entre el Paraguay y el Brasil, por D. Felix de Azara, primer comisario de la tercera division. ... *Buenos-Aires*, 1836. Folio, pp. 68, ii. 2533

AZARA. Descripcion é historia del Paraguay y del Rio de La Plata, obra póstuma de Don Felix de Azara. La publica su sobrino ... D. Agustin de Azara, marques de Nibbiano, bajo la direccion de D. Basilio Sebastian Castellanos de Losada. *Madrid*, 1847. 2 vols., 4to. Portrait. 2534

AZARA. Diario de la navegacion y reconocimiento del Rio Tebicuari. Obra postuma de D. Felix Azara. ... *Buenos-Aires*, 1836. 4to, Title, pp. v., 47. (Angelis, Coleccion, Tomo II.) H.

AZARA. Diario de un reconocimiento de las guardias y for-

tines, que guarnecen la linea de frontera de Buenos-Aires, para ensancharla; por D. Felix de Azara, capitan de navio de la real armada. ... *Buenos-Aires*, 1837. Folio, Title, pp. iv., 49. (Angelis, Coleccion, Tomo VI.) H. 2536

AZARA. Essais sur l'Histoire Naturelle des Quadrupedes de la Province du Paraguay. Par Don Feliz D. Azara, Captaine du Vaisseau de la Marine Espagnole, etc. Ecrits depuis 1783 jusqu'en 1796: avec une appendice sur quelques reptiles, et format suite necessaire aux œuvres de Buffon. Traduit sur le manuscrit inédit de l'auteur. Par M. L. E. Moreau-Saint-Mery. *Paris*, 1801. 2 vols., 8vo. S. 2537

The original was published in the year following, at Madrid, with additions and corrections by the author. *See* No. 2531.

AZARA. Informes de D. Felix de Azara, sobre varios proyectos de colonizar el Chaco. ... *Buenos-Aires*, 1836. Folio, pp. vi., 11. 2538

AZARA. Memorias sobre el estado rural del Rio de La Plata en 1801, demarcacion de límites entre el Brasil y el Paraguay á últimos del siglo XVIII, é informes sobre varios particulares de la América Meridional española. Escritos póstumos de D. Felix de Azara; los publica su subrino, D. Augustin de Azara, bajo la direccion de D. Basilio Sebastian Castellanos de Losada. *Madrid*, 1847. 4to, pp. 236. Portrait. 2539

AZARA. Natural History of the Quadrupeds of Paraguay and the River la Plata. By Don Felix de Azara. Translated from the Spanish with a Memoir of the Author, a Physical Sketch of the Country, and numerous notes by W. P. Hunter. *London, Longman & Co.*, 1838. 8vo. 2540

Volume I. only published.

AZARA. Voyages dans L'Amérique Méridionale, par Don Félix de Azara, Commissaire et Commandant des limites espagnoles dans le Paraguay depuis 1781 jusqu'en 1801; Contenant la description géographique, politique et civile du Paraguay et de la rivière de La Plata; l'histoire de la découverte et de la conquête de ces contrées; des détails nombreux sur leur histoire naturelle, et sur les peuples sauvages qui les habitent; le récit des moyens employés par les Jésuites pour assujétir et civiliser les indigènes, etc. Publiés d'après les Manuscrits de l'auteur, avec une notice sur sa vie et ses écrits, par C. A.

Walckenaer; enrichis de notes par G. Cuvier ... . Suivis de l'histoire naturelle des Oiseaux du Paraguay et de La Plata, par le même auteur, traduite, d'après l'original espagnol, et augmentée d'un grand nombre de notes, par M. Sonnini; accompagnés d'un Atlas de vingt-cinq planches. *Paris, Dentu, imprimeur-libraire, Rue du Pont-de-Lodi, n^o* 3. 1809. 4 vols., 8vo, and Atlas in 4to, pp. lx., 389; (4), 562, and 3 l. folded; (4), ii., 479; (4), 380. H. 2541

Some copies in vellum paper, others with colored plates. *See* M. R., LXI., 525.

AZARA. Viaggi nell' America meridionale di D. Felice di Azara commissario e comandante de confini nel Paraguay fatti da lui tra il 1781 e il 1801. Pubblicati sulla scorta de suoi manoscritti dal Sig. C. A. Walkenaer, tradotti dal S. P. Gaetano Barbieri. *Milano*, 1817. 2 vols., 12mo. Map and 7 Colored Plates. 2542

AZARA. Viajes por la América del Sud de don Felix de Azara, desde 1789 (1781?) hasta 1801 ... trad. de Walckenaer; con notas de Cuvier. *Monte-Video*, 1850. 8vo, pp. 5, 318.

AŹARA. Reise nach Süd-Amerika in d. J. 1781–1801. Aus dem Span. mit Anmerkungen und einem Leben des Verfassers etc. herausgegeben von Walkenaer. Aus dem Französischen übersetzt von Ch. Weyland. *Berlin, Voss*, 1810. 8vo. Map.

This is an abridgment rather than a translation. There is another version by W. A. Lindau. *Leipzig, Hinrichs*, 1810. 3 vols., 8vo. Maps and Plates.

AZEREDO COUTINHO. *See* Cunha de Azeredo Coutinho.

AZERO Y ALDOVERA (Miguel de). Tratado de los Funerales y de las Sepulturas. *Madrid*, 1786. 4to. 2545

The author refers to the customs among the savages in America, Brazil, California, Mexico, etc.

AZEVEDO. Memorias Historicas do Rio de Janeiro e das provincias annexas a jurisdiçao de Vice-rei do estado do Brazil: por Jozé de Souza Azevedo, Pizarro e Araujo, natural do Rio de Janeiro, &c. *Rio de Janeiro*, 1820. 9 vols., sm. 4to. 2546

B. The Present Attempt, etc. *See* [Morse (S. F. B.)]

B. (A.) An Account of the Late Revolutions in New England; in a Letter from A. B. Dated *Boston, June* 6, 1689. 4to, pp. 7. 2547

[B. (A.)] A Letter from a Merchant in London to his Nephew in North America, relative to the Present Posture of Affairs in the Colonies ... . [Signed A. B.] *London, J. Walter*, M DCC LXVI. 8vo, 2 p. l., pp. 55. H. 2548

B. (A.) Six letters of A. B. on the differences between Great Britain and the United States of America, with a preface by the Editor of the Morning Chronicle. *London, Ridgway*, 1807. 8vo, pp. 48. 2549

See "Monthly Review," New Series, VI., 103.

B..... (A. J.) Notice sur l'île Sainte-Lucie, moyens d'abolir l'esclavage, sans indemnité et sans interruption de travail. Indépendance prochaine des Antilles avec la liberté du commerce et de la conscience. Par A.-J. B..... , colon de Ste-Lucie ... *Paris, Poussielgue-Rusand*, 1841. 8vo. 2550

B. (C. B.) *See* B[rown] (C. B.)

B—— (Mme C—— de la). *See* [Calderon de la Barca (Mme F. E. J.)]

B. (D.) *See* B[audry] (D[es Lozières]).

B. (E.) *See* B[urrough] (E.)

B. (E.) *See* [Engel (Samuel, *le bailli* d')]

B—e (E—d). *See* B[urk]e (E[dmun]d).

B—g—l (E—ce). *See* B[ud]g[e]l (E[usta]ce).

B. (F.) *See* B[ernard] (F[rancis]).

B. (F.) Causes of the Present Distractions in America Explained, by F. B.; 1774. 8vo. 2552

[B. (H.)] The Leaders, etc. *See* [Binney (Horace)].

B. (J.) Plaine and True Relation of the going forth of a Holland fleet to the Coast of Brazil. By J. B. *Rotterdam*, 1623. 4to. 2553

Ternaux, No. 462. Perhaps by J. Baers. *See* Baers.

B. (J.) *See* B[rown] (J[ohn]).

B. (J.) Account of the French Usurpation upon the Trade of England, and what Great Damage the English Yearly sustain by their Commerce, by J. B. *London*, 1679. 4to. 2554

Containing a notice of the disturbances of the English trade by the French on the coast of Newfoundland, and other parts of the East and West Indies.

B. (J.) A Letter to a Member of Parliament, on the Regulation of the Plantation Trade. *London*, 1701. Sm. 4to. 2555

B. (J.) Poem occasioned by the Rise and Fall of South Sea Stock, humbly dedicated to the Merchant-Adventurers trading in the South Seas. By J. B. 1720. 8vo. 2556

B. (L. M.), *armateur*. *See* [Prudhomme (Louis)].

B. (L. M.) *See* Barbé Marbois (F.)

B*** (M.) *See* [Bourgeois], and [Falkner (Thomas)].

B*** (M. de). Histoire. *See* [Behrens (K. F.)]

B. (M. D.) *See* [Dubuisson (P. U.)]

B. (N.) The Constables Pocket Book; or a Dialogue between an Old Constable and a New. *Boston*, 1727. 16mo, pp. 68. M. 2557

B. (R.) *See* B[everly] (R.), and B[urton] (R.)

B. (F.) Observations upon Prince Rupert's White Dogge, called Boye, carefully taken by T. B. for that purpose, imployed by some of quality in the Citty of London. *London*, 1642. 4to.

The above curious satirical tract contains some notices of the witches of New England, etc.

B. (T. T.) Observations on American Independency. [n. p., n. d.] 8vo. 2559

B. (V. D.) *See* B[os] (Van der).

B. (W. B.) Baltimore: or Long Long time ago. By W. B. B. *Baltimore, Murphy & Co.*, 1853. 8vo, pp. 24. 2560

B. (W. D.) *See* B[ickham] (W. D.)

B. (W. S. A.) "The Antigonian and Bostonian Beauties: A Poem. Occasioned by Seeing the Assembly at St. John's, Antigua, on Thursday the 7th of July, and afterwards at Boston, in King Street." By W. S. A. B. *Boston, D. Fowle* [n. d.] 8vo, pp. 8. W. 2561

B. (W. B.) Abraham Lincoln's Character. ... n. p. [1865.] 8vo, pp. 2, (2). 2562

B.....-DUVALLON. *See* [Berquin-Duvallon].

BAADER (Friedrich). Die Bundes-Verfassung der Vereinigten Staaten von Nordamerika. Ein Beitrag zur Lösung der deutschen Verfassungsfrage von Friedrich Baader. *Berlin, Stargardt*, 1848. 8vo, pp. 32. 2563

BAAIJ (G.) Is het vertrek der geloovigen in Nederland naar Noord-Amerika een werk van God of uit den booze? of de geest der Zedige vrijmoed. bedenkingen omtrent het vertrek der geloovigen in Nederl. naar Noord-Amerika beproefd aan de H. S. *Amsterdam, Hoogkamer en Co.*, 1847. 8vo. 2564

BAARS (J.) Beschryving van Brasil. *Amsterdam*, 1651. 4to.

BABBIDGE (C.) The Claims of Congregational Churches. A Centennial Address: being a Plea in Vindication of the Rights of the First Church in Pepperell, Mass. delivered Feb. 9, 1847. By Charles Babbidge, Minister of the First Parish. *Boston, Wm. Crosby and H. P. Nichols*, 1847. 8vo, pp. 44. H. 2566

BABBITT (B. B.) Sermon before the First Annual Convention of the Church Union of the Protestant Episcopal Church, in the Diocese of Massachusetts, delivered ... May 19, 1863, by Rev. Benjamin B. Babbitt, of ... Andover, Mass. ... With the Constitution, Plan of Operation and Organization of the Church Union. *Boston, the Union*, 1863. 8vo, pp. 31, (1). H. 2567

BABBIT (E. B.) The Trial of Lieut. E. B. Babbit, on Charges preferred by Com. Jesse D. Elliott, before a Naval Court Martial ... at ... Charlestown, October 13, 1834. *Boston*, 1835. 8vo, pp. 120. H. 2568

BABBITT (E.) Organization of the House. Speech of Hon.

Elijah Babbitt, of Penn. ... January 20, 1860. [*Washington, Buell and Blanchard, Printers*, 1860.] 8vo, pp. 8. H. 2569

BABBITT. Speech of Hon. Elijah Babbitt, of Pennsylvania, on the Confiscation of Rebel Property. ... In the House ... May 22, 1862. [*Washington*, 1862.] 8vo, pp. 8. H. 2570

BABCOCK (Charles). British Honduras: Central America. A Plain Statement to the Colored People of the U. S. who contemplate Emigration. By Charles Babcock, of Salem, Mass. *Boston, the Author*, 1863. 8vo. pp. 16. H. 2571

BABCOCK (George R.) ... Remarks of Mr. Babcock, of Erie, on the Roman Catholic Church Property Bill: in the Senate, June 24, 1853 ... . *Albany, Cuyler & Henly, Printers*, 1853. 8vo, pp. 12. H. 2572

[BABCOCK (J. S.)]. Memoir of Captain Nathan Hale. ... *New Haven, Printed by S. Babcock*, 1844. 8vo, pp. 16. H.

BABCOCK (Rufus). Forty Years of Pioneer Life. Memoir of John Mason Peck, D.D. Edited from his Journals and Correspondence. By Rufus Babcock. *Philadelphia, Amer. Bapt. Pub. Soc.*, 1864. 12mo, pp. 360. Portrait. 2574

BABCOCK (S. B.) A Discourse on the Death of President Lincoln, preached in the Orthodox Congregational Church, in Dedham, by the Rev. Samuel B. Babcock, in accordance with the Request of a Committee of Citizens, Wednesday, April 19, 1865. *Dedham, Mass., Printed by John Cox, Jr.*, 1865. 8vo, pp. 16. H. 2575

"Not published, but distributed among the families of the town."—S. B. BABCOCK.

BABCOCK. Historical Discourse delivered at the Closing of the Old Episcopal (St. Paul's) Church, Dedham, November 30, 1845, by Rev. Samuel B. Babcock. *Dedham, H. Mann, Printer*. 8vo, pp. 23. H. 2576

BABCOCK. The Rector's Offering, February 11, 1857. [A Historical Sketch of the Episcopal Church in Dedham, Mass. By Rev. S. B. Babcock, D.D.] *Boston*, 1857. 12mo, pp. 23.

BABCOCK (William G.) Farewell Sermon preached at South Natick, Mass. ... Feb. 26, 1860. By Wm. G. Babcock, Minister of the Unitarian Church. *Boston*, 1860. 12mo, pp. 12.

The Parish Committee closed the church because the minister took the part of the workmen of the town, who were on a strike.

The Babcock Family. [*Albany, Munsell*, 1861.] 8vo, pp. 4.

BABIÉ (F.) Voyages chez les peuples sauvages, ou l' homme de la nature; histoire morale des peuples sauvages des deux continents et des naturels des îsles de la Mer du Sud. Par le citoyen F. Babié, d'après les mémoires du Cit. R*** [l'abbé Jérôme Richard]. Avec figures. *Paris, Laurens, Fuchs, Desenne et Lepetit, an* IX [1801]. 3 vols., 8vo. Engravings. S. + Seconde édition. *Paris, Laurens, aîné, Chaumerot*, 1808. 3 vols., 8vo. Engravings. + [Same edition?] *Leipzig, Wolf et Comp.*, 3 vols., 8vo. 2580

"I have not written the *Romance* of the Man of Nature, but his *History*."—*Preface.*

BABO (Franz Joseph Maria). Das Winterquartier in Amerika; ein Original-Lustspiel in 1 Aufzuge. *Berlin* (also *München*), 1778. 8vo. 2581

BABSON (J. J.) History of the Town of Gloucester, Cape Ann, including the Town of Rockport. By John J. Babson. *Gloucester, Procter Brothers*, 1860. 8vo, pp. xi., 610. Map. H.

A considerable portion of the edition was destroyed by fire in February, 1863.

The Baby and the Bards. *See* [Ames (Nathan)].

BACARDI (A.) Apendice al nuevo Colon, ó sea tratado del derecho militar de España y sus Indias, por D. Alejandro Bacardi. *Barcelona*, 1859. 8vo. 2583

[BACELLAR (Antonio Barbosa)]. Relaçao diaria do sitio e tomada da forte praça do Recife, recuperaçao das capitanias de Itamaracá, Paraiba, Rio-Grande, Ciará, e ilha de Fernao de Noronha; por Francisco Barreto Mestre de Campo general do estado do Brasil e Gobernador de Pernambuco. *Lisboa, na off. Craesbeeckiana*, 1654. 4to, pp. (32.) 2584

"Very rare. There is an Italian version"—DA SILVA.

BACH (Moriz). Das Land Otuquis. *See* Kriegk (G. L.)

BACH (M.) Descripcion de la Nueva Provincia de Otuquis en Bolivia. Segunda edicion, corr. y aum. *Buenos Aires*, 1843. 4to, pp. 25. M. 2585

BACH (M.) Die Jesuiten und ihre Mission Chiquitos in Südamerika. Eine historisch-ethnographische Schilderung. Heraus-

gegeben und mit einem Vorworte begleitet von Georg Ludw. Kriegk. *Leipzig, Mittler (Frankfurt, Varrentrap)*, 1843. 8vo, pp. 96. 2586

BACHE (A. D.) Additional Notes of a Discussion of Tidal Observations ... at Cat Island, Louisiana. By Prof. A. D. Bache ... . *New Haven, Printed by B. L. Hamlen*, 1852. 8vo, pp. 15. H. 2587

BACHE. On the Tides of the Atlantic and Pacific Coasts of the United States; the Gulf Stream; and the Earthquake Waves of December, 1854. By A. D. Bache ... . *New Haven, Printed by Ezechiel Hayes*, 1856. 8vo, pp. 43. 7 Plates. H.

Also: Address of ... Bache, President of the American Association for ... 1851, on retiring from the Duties of President. [n. p., n. d.] 8vo, pp. xli.–lx. H. Address ... Franklin Institute ... 1842. 8vo. H. Anniversary Address before the American Institute Of the City of New-York ... October 28th, 1856 ... . *New York*, 1857. 8vo, pp. 60. H. ... Approximate Cotidal Lines of Diurnal and Semi-Diurnal Tides of the Coast of the United States on the Gulf of Mexico. ... . [n. p., 1857.] 8vo, pp. 17. 2 Plates. H. Attempt to fix the date of Dr. Franklin's Observations on North East Storms. *Philadelphia*, 1833. 8vo. Discussion of the Magnetic and Meteorological Observations made at the Girard College Observatory, Philadelphia, in 1840–1845. 6 Parts. 1859–62. 4to, pp. 22, 28, 16. Eulogy on Hon. James Alfred Pearce, of Maryland, ... one of the Regents of the Smithsonian Institution. ... January, 1863. *Washington*, ... 1863. 8vo. pp. 14. H. ... Lecture on the Gulf Stream ... . [n. p., 1860.] 8vo, pp. 71 [17]. 4 Plates. H. ... Navy Yard at Patuxent River. Letter ... relative to the advantages of the Patuxent river ... . [*Washington*, 1866.] 8vo. pp. 2. Map. H. Notes on the Gulf Stream. [With Additional Remarks by G. W. Blunt. [n. p., 1854.] 8vo, pp. 47*–53* of Blunt's American Coast Pilot. 2 Charts. H. Records and Results of a Magnetic Survey of Pennsylvania and Parts of Adjacent States. *Washington City*, 1863. 4to. Report on the Harbor of Charleston, S. C., by ... A. D. Bache ... [and others]. Also Report of Capt. A. H. Bowman ... with Estimate for Deepening the Bar of Sullivan's Island, or Beach Channel. ... With Report of Commissioners appointed by the State ... *Charleston*, 1858. 8vo, pp. 62, (1), 10. H. Report of Experiments to Navigate the Chesapeake and Delaware Canal, by Steam ... *Philadelphia*, 1836. 8vo, pp. 13. P. Report on Education in Europe, to the Trustees of the Girard College for Orphans. *Philadelphia*, 1839. 8vo, pp. 677. Report upon the Sailing Directions for the Port of New-York and its Approaches ... *Cambridge*, 1856. 8vo, pp. 31. Report relative to the New-York Harbor Coast Survey, Dec 28, 1857. N. Y. Sen. Doc. 1858. 8vo, pp. 12. 2 Charts. Reports to Congress of the Progress of the Coast Survey from 1848. *Washington*, 1849. 8vo. Continued. Report to the Controllers of the Public Schools, on the Reorganization of the Central High School of Philadelphia, 1839–40. 8vo. [Two Editions.] Report on ..: a High School for Girls ... [*Philadelphia*, 1840.] Report ... of the Central High School ... *Philadelphia*, 1863. 8vo. Tide Tables for the Principal Sea Ports of the United States, ... *New-York, E. & G. W. Blunt*, 1855. 8vo, pp. 15. H. + Revised Jan., 1857. [*New York*, n. d.] 8vo, pp. 53*–70* of Blunt's "American Coast Pilot." 1 Chart. H. *See also* Boston, etc.

BACHE (B. F.) To the Democratic Republican Electors, of Pennsylvania. By Benjamin Franklin Bache. *Philadelphia*, 1804. 8vo. C. 2589

A broadside, on the Presidential Election.

BACHE (Franklin). Observations and Reflections on the Penitentiary System. A Letter from Franklin Bache, M.D. to Roberts Vaux. *Philadelphia, Jesper Harding*, 1829. 8vo, pp. 13. P. 2590

BACHE (L.) ... Proceedings of a General Court Martial for the Trial of Lieut. Col. Louis Bache ... upon charges of Mutiny, Disobedience of orders, Insubordination [etc.] ... at the Camp Marcus Hook, on the Delaware, in October, 1814. *Philadelphia, Printed by James Wilson*, 1815. 8vo, pp. 66, 12. B. & P.

BACHE (Richard). The Case of Alien Enemies considered and decided, upon a Writ of Habeas Corpus allowed on the Petition of Charles Lochington, an Alien Enemy by Hon. Wm. Tilghman. 22 Nov. 1813. *Philadelphia*, 1813. 8vo.

[BACHE (*Lieut.* Richard)]. Notes on Colombia, taken in the Years 1822–3. With an Itinerary of the Route from Caracas to Bogotá; and an Appendix. By an Officer in the United States' Army. *Philadelphia, H. C. Carey & I. Lea*, 1827. 8vo, pp. 303. Map and 2 Plans. H. 2593

[BACHE.] View of the Valley of the Mississippi; or, the Emigrant's and Traveller's Guide to the West. [By Lieut. R. Bache.] Second edition. *Philadelphia, H. S. Tanner*, 1834. 18mo, pp. ix., 372. 15 Maps. C. 2594

The preface is signed R. B.

BACHE (Richard Meade). The Young Wrecker of the Florida Reef: or the trials and adventures of Fred. Ransom. *Philadelphia, Jas. S. Claxton*, 1866. 16mo, pp. 381. C. 2595

BACHE (W.) Historical Sketches of Bristol Borough, in the County of Bucks, anciently known as "Buckingham:" being the Second Chartered Borough in Pennsylvania; commencing with its Colonial Settlement, in 1681, and closing with the Year 1853. By William Bache. *Bristol, Pa.*, 1853. 16mo, pp. 60. H. 2596

BACHELDER (Samuel). [Vindication of his conduct as agent of the York Manufacturing Company. *Boston?* 1854.] 8vo, pp. 7. H. 2597

BACHELER (O.) Mormonism Exposed, internally and externally. By Origen Bacheler. *New York*, 1838. 12mo, pp. 48. C.

BACHELER. Trial of the Commonwealth, *versus* Origen Bacheler, for a Libel on the Character of George B. Beals, deceased, at the Municipal Court, Boston, March Term A.D. 1829. Before Hon. P. O. Thacher, Judge. Reported by John W. Whitman. [*Boston*], *Published by John H. Belcher*, 1829. 12mo, pp. 47. C. 2599

BACHELER (W.) Debate in the Massachusetts Senate, upon an Act to incorporate the Cambridge Broadway Company ... April 25, 1862. Phonographic Report by W. Bacheler. *Cambridge, Printed by Allen and Farnham*, 1862. 12mo, pp. 43. H.

BACHELET (Louis). Phalanstère du Brésil. Voyage dans l'Amérique méridionale. *Paris, Impr. de Pommeret*, 1842. 8vo, pp. 20. 2601

BACHELIER, *pseudon.* *See* [Durret].

BACHELLER (S.) Remarks on the late printed Answer to Col. Choate's Reasons of dissent from the judgment of a Council in the affair of the Rev. Mr. Bacheller of Haverhill. By the Author of those Reasons. To which is Subjoined a Postscript by Another hand. *Boston, Edes & Gill*, 1761. 8vo, pp. 43. W. 2602

BACHELLER. Twenty Articles of Charge against Rev. Samuel Bacheller, before the council at Haverhill 19th Sep. 1758 with Result of the council; Friendly remarks on Result of council by the aggrieved 17 Apl 1759; also the councils addition to former result with remarks; postcript by Joseph Haynes and Choate's Reasons. *Portsmouth*, 1760. 8vo, pp. 87. M. 2603

BACHELLER. Vindication of an Association from the Charge of Countenancing Heresy in Doctrine, and of Partiality in Conduct in reference to Samuel Bacheller. By One of their Number. *Portsmouth, N. H.*, 1758. 4to. 2604

[BACHELOT DE LA PYLAIE (A. J. M.)] Flore de Terre-Neuve et des îles Saint-Pierre et Miquelon, avec figures dessinées, par l'auteur, sur la plante vivante. Première livraison. *Paris, impr. de F. Didot*, 1829. 4to, pp. 128. 2605

No more published. In the lists of correspondents of the "Société des antiquaries de France," the name is spelled Lapilaye and La Pilaye.

BACHELOT DE LA PYLAIE. Voyage à l'Isle de Terre Neuve, contenant la Description des Isles voisines et des Vues générales

sur leur vegetation. Par M. Bachelot de la Pylaie. *Paris*, 1825. 8vo, pp. 131. 2606

This voyage forms, also, part of Vol. IX. of "Memoires de la Société Linniénne de Paris."

BACHILLER Y MORALES (A.) Antiguedades americanos. Noticias que tuvieron los Europas de la America antes del descubrimiento de Christoval Colon, etc. *Habana*, 1845. 4to.

BACHILLER Y MORALES. Apuntes para la historia de las letras y de la instruccion publica de la Isla de Cuba, por Antonio Bachiller y Morales. *Habana*, 1859–61. 3 vols., 4to, pp. 228, 224, 248. 2608

Contains a list of all the books printed in Cuba from 1724 to 1840.

BACHILLER Y MORALES. Elogio de D. José de Arango y Castillo, escrito por A. Bachiller y Morales. *Habana*, 1852. 8vo, pp. 14. 2609

BACHILLER Y MORALES. Memoria sobre los trabajos de la Caja de Ahorros, descuentos y depositos de la Habana, en 1855–1856, escrita por Antonio Bachiller y Morales. *Habana*, 1856. 8vo, pp. 18. 2610

The publication of these memoirs commenced in 1840.

BACHILLER Y MORALES. Prontuario de agricultura general para el uso de los labradores i hacendados de la Isla de Cuba por Antonio Bachiller y Morales. Edicion ilustrada con laminas. *Habana*, 1856. 8vo, pp. vi., 412. 2611

BACHMAN (J.) An Account of some Experiments made on the Habits of the Vultures inhabiting Carolina, the Turkey Buzzard, and the Carrion Crow. By John Bachman. *Charleston* [1834]. 8vo, pp. 16. C. 2612

Also: The doctrine of the Unity of the human race. *Charleston*, 1850. 8vo. P. An Examination of Professor Agassiz's Sketch of the ... Animal World, and ... the ... Types of Man. 1855. A notice of the "Types of Mankind." *Charleston*, 1854. 8vo, pp. 33. P. *See* Audubon, Quadrupeds of America. No. 2368.

BACK (*Captain Sir* G.) Narrative of the Arctic Land Expedition to the Mouth of the Great Fish River, and along the Shores of the Arctic Ocean, in the Years 1833, 1834, and 1835. By Captain Back, R. N., Commander of the Expedition. Illustrated by a Map and Fourteen Plates. *London, John Murray*, MDCCCXXXVI. 4to, pp. vi., 663. + Same. *London, John*

Murray, 1836. 8vo, pp. vi., 663. + Reprinted. *Philadelphia, E. L. Carey & L. Hart*, 1836. 8vo, pp. 456. Map. + Second Edition. *Philadelphia*, 1837. 8vo. + [In English.] *Paris, Baudry, Amyot* (and some copies) *Galignani*, 1836. 8vo, pp. 338. + Also reprinted at *Brussels*, *Leipsic*, and *Frankfort*, in English. 2613

The plates in the quarto, or admiralty edition, are by Finden. Some copies were printed on large paper, with India proof plates. The "Quarterly Review," LVI., p. 296, says that as a literary composition this work may rank higher than any former volume produced by the northern expeditions. *See also* Ed. Rev., LXIII., 151.

BACK. Voyages dans les régions artiques, à la recherche du capitaine Ross, en 1834 et 1835, et reconnaissance de Rhlwee-Choh, maintenant grande rivière Back; traduit par M. P. Caseaux. *Paris, Arthus Bertrand*, 1836. 2 vols., 8vo. Map.

BACK. Reise durch Nord-Amerika bis zur Mündung des grossen Fischflusses und an den Küsten des Polarmeeres in den Jahren 1833, 34 und 35. Aus dem Englischen von Karl Andrée. *Leipzig, Weber*, 1836. 8vo. Plate and 2 Portraits.

BACK. Wunderbare Reisen und Abentheuer zu Wasser und zu Lande ... 1834–35 ... um ... Capitän Ross aufzusuchen. Nach dem Engl. Reisejournale im Auszuge bearbeitet. *Wien, Gerold*, 1837. 12mo. 2616

BACK. Narrative of an expedition in H. Majesty's Ship Terror, undertaken with a view to Geographical Discovery on the Arctic Shores, in the years 1836–7. By Captain Back, R. N. Illustrated by a Map and twelve Plates. *London, John Murray*, 1838. 8vo. + *Philadelphia*, 1838. 8vo. 2617

BACK. Landreise nach den Küsten des Nordpolarmeeres. Deutsch von K. André. *Leipzig*, 1845. Rl. 8vo. Map. 2618

BACKER. Bibliothèque des écrivains de la Compagnie de Jésus, ou Notices bibliographiques 1° De tous les ouvrages publiés par les membres de la Compagnie de Jésus, depuis la fondation de l'ordre jusqu'a nos jours; 2° Des apologies, des controverses religieuses, des critiques littéraires et scientifiques suscitées à leur sujet. Par Augustin et Alois de Backer, de la même Compagnie. ... *Liége*, 1853–61. 7 vols., large 8vo. H.

An important work for the reliable notices, both biographical and bibliographical, of the Jesuit travelers. An eighth volume will complete the work.

BACKHAUS (Johann Gottlieb). Neue ... Abhandlung vom Tabacksbau, worin die einzige ... Methode gezeigt wird, wie diese Pflanze muss behandelt werden, wenn sie in Teutschland die Stelle des Virginischen Tabacks vertreten soll ... . *Darmstadt*, 1779. 8vo. 2620

BACKHOUSE (Anna.) A Brief Sketch of the Life of Anna Backhouse [daughter of Joseph John Gurney], ... *Burlington, New Jersey, John Rodgers*, 1852. [Privately printed.] 8vo.

BACKUS (Azel). Inaugural Discourse delivered in ... Clinton, December 3, 1812, by the Rev. Azel Backus, D.D. on ... his Induction into the Office of President of Hamilton College, December 3, 1812. *Utica, Printed by Ira Merrell*, 1812. 8vo, pp. 20. 2622

Dr. Backus also published Sermons: At the Funeral of Oliver Wolcott, Governor of Connecticut, Dec., 1797. *Litchfield* [1797]. 8vo. At the Connecticut Election, Hartford, May 10, 1798. *Hartford*, 1798. 8vo, pp. 54.+Reprinted, *New York*, 1798. 8vo. At the Ordination of John B. Whittlesey. *Herkimer, N. Y.*, 1814. 8vo.

BACKUS (Charles). Sermon preached ... At Hartford, on the day of the Anniversary Election, May 9, 1793. *Hartford*, 1793. 8vo, pp. 38. M. 2623

Also: Sermon at the Ord. of Azel Backus, in Bethlem, April 6, 1791. *Litchfield* [1791]. 8vo, pp. 26. At Somers, Conn., Nov., 1793, on the Death of Moses Chapin. *Springfield*, 1794. 8vo. At Wilmington, Mass., Oct 29, 1795, at the Ordination of Freegrace Raynolds. *Boston*, 1795. 8vo. At the Ordination of Timothy Mather Cooly, in Granville, Feb. 3, 1796. *Westspringfield*, 1796. 8vo, pp. 16. At the Ordination of Joseph Russell, in Princetown, Mass., March 16, 1796. *Boston*, 1796. 8vo, pp. 31. Five Discourses on the Truth and Inspiration of the Bible. *Hartford*, 1797. At the Ordination of Thomas Snell, June 27, 1798. *Worcester*, 1798. 8vo. At Pelham, N. H., Oct. 31, 1798, at the Ordination of John Hubbard Church. *Amherst*, 1799. 8vo, pp. 38. At the Ordination of Zephaniah S. Moore. *Worcester*, 1798. 8vo. At Wilbraham, Mass., May 2, occasioned by Six Young Persons being drowned, with Two Discourses on the same Subject by the Rev. Mr. Witter. *Springfield*, 1799. 8vo, pp. 16. Scripture Doctrine of Regeneration. *Hartford*, 1800. 12mo. At Longmeadow, Fast, April 17. *Springfield, Mass.*, 1788. 8vo. At the Ordination of Vinsor Gould, Southampton, Aug. 26, 1801. *Northampton*, 1801. 8vo.

BACKUS (Isaac). All true Ministers of the Gospel are called ... A Discourse shewing the nature and necessity of an internal call to preach the everlasting Gospel; By Isaac Backus. To which is added some short account of the experiences and dying testimony of Mr. Nathanael Shepherd, Pastor in Attleborough, Who died April 14th, 1752. *Boston, D. Fowle*, 1754. 8vo, pp. 115. 2624

[BACKUS.] An Appeal to the Public for Religious Liberty. Against the Oppressions of the Present Day. *Boston, Printed by John Boyle*, MDCCLXXIII. 8vo. pp. 62 (2). 2625

Contains historical notices and extracts from the works of Cotton Mather, John Cotton, Roger Williams, and a list of the author's works.

BACKUS. Church History of New England, from 1602 to 1804, abridged, with a concise History of the Baptists in the Southern parts of America. By Isaac Backus. *Boston*, 1804. 8vo.+With a Memoir ... *Philadelphia, Baptist Tract Dep.*, 1839. 18mo, pp. 250.+*Philadelphia, American Baptist Publication and S. S. Society*, 1844. 18mo, pp. 250. 2626

BACKUS. Discourse concerning the Materials, the Manner of Building, and Power of Organizing, of the Church of Christ; With the True difference and exact limits between Civil and Ecclesiastical Government; and also what are, and what are not just Reasons for Separation. Together with an Address to Joseph Fish, A.M. Pastor of a church in Stonington, occasioned by his late Piece called the *Examiner Examined*. By Isaac Backus. *Boston*, 1773. 8vo, pp. 151. 2627

BACKUS. The Doctrine of Sovereign Grace Opened and Vindicated; two parts, with Appendix, containing a brief Account of the Sentiments of the first Baptist Churches in New England. *Providence, Rhode Island, John Carter*, 1771. 2628

BACKUS. A | Fish caught in his own Net. | An | Examination | of Nine Sermons, from Matt. 16. 18. | Published last Year, by Mr. Joseph Fish of Stonington; | Wherein | He labours to prove, that those called Standing Churches | in New-England are built upon the Rock, and upon | the same Principles with the first Fathers of this | Country: And that Separates and Baptists are joining | with the Gates of Hell against them. | In Answer to which; | Many of his Mistakes are corrected; The Constitution | of those Churches opened; the Testimonies of Prophets | and Apostles, and also of many of those Fathers are | produced, which as plainly condemn his plan, as any | Separate or Baptist can do. | By Isaac Backus. | Pastor of a Church of Christ in Middleborough. | *Boston: Printed by Edes and Gill, in | Queen-Street*, MDCCLXVIII. 8vo, pp. 130; Errata, 1 p. 2629

BACKUS. Government and Liberty Described, and Ecclesiastical Tyranny Exposed. *Boston*, 1778. Sm. 8vo. 2630

BACKUS. A History of New-England, With particular Reference to the Denomination of Christians called Baptists. Containing The first principles and settlements of the Country; The rise and increase of the Baptist Churches therein; The intrusion of Arbitrary Power under the cloak of Religion; the Christian Testimonies of the Baptists and others against the same, with their Sufferings under it, from the Beginning to the present Time. Collected from most Authentic Records and Writings, both Ancient and Modern. By Isaac Backus, Pastor of the first Baptist Church in Midleborough. Vol. I. *Boston, Printed by Edward Draper*, 1777. 8vo, 4 p. l.; Text, pp. 544; Appendix, pp. 15; Errata, 1 p. Vol. II. *Providence, John Carter*, 1784. Title, pp. 448. Vol. III. *Boston, Manning & Loring*, 1796. pp. 334 S. 2631

Complete sets of this valuable work are rare—the *third* volume being generally deficient. *See* Rich, Bibl. Am., Vol. I., 253; Bartlett's Bibl., R. I.

BACKUS. Policy, as well as Honesty, forbids the use of Secular Force in Religious Affairs. Massachusetts-State. *Boston: Printed by Draper and Folsom, and Sold by Phillip Freeman, in Union-Street*, M,DCC,LXXIX. pp. 26; Index to "Our Baptist History," 2 l. 2632

Contains an index to the History of New England. "Not having time and Room therefor, when our Baptist History was finished, a brief Index to it is inserted here." Dr. Backus was an able and voluminous author of works principally relating to the Baptists, including A Circular Letter in the "Minutes of the Warren Association, Sept. 9 and 10, 1794. *Boston*, 1794." The Atonement of Christ ... . *Boston*. MDCCLXXXVII. 8vo, pp. 28. Doctrine of particular Election and final Perseverance. *Boston*, 1789. 8vo. A door opened for equal Christian Liberty. *Boston* 1783. 8vo. Family Prayer not to be neglected. A Discourse. *Newport*, 1766. 8vo. Godliness excludes Slavery. *Boston*, 1785. 8vo, pp. 14. The Infinite Importance of the obedience of Faith. *Boston*, 1791 8vo. The Kingdom of God described by His Word. *Boston*, MDCCXCII. Sm. 8vo, pp. 24. Letter to the Rev. Mr. Benjamin Lord of Norwich, occasioned by some Harsh Things which he has lately published Against those who have Dissented from his Sentiments about the Ministry, the Church, and Baptism. By Isaac Backus. *Providence*, 1764. 8vo. The Liberal Support of Gospel Ministers Inculcated. *Boston*, 1790. 8vo. A Reply to a piece wrote by Israel Holly, Pastor in Suffield, entitled the New Testament Interpretation of the Old, relative to Infant Baptism. *Newport*, 1772. Sermon at Middleborough, Feb. 5, 1769, upon hearing of the death of a godly Mother, to which is added some Memories of her Life. *Providence*, 1769. A Sermon ... Oct. 30, 1771, at the Ordination of Asa Hunt, in Middleborough. *Boston*, 1772. 8vo, pp. 31. A Short Description of the Difference between the Bond Woman and the Free. Sermon at Middleborough, Mass. *Boston*, 1756. 8vo, pp. (4), 45.+Second edition corrected, to which is added an Answer to Mr. Frothingham's late letter, concerning Baptism. *Boston*, 1770. Spiritual Ignorance causeth Men to counter-act their doctrinal Knowledge. A Discourse from Acts xiii. 27. *Providence*, 1763. True Faith will produce good Works. A Discourse ... With Remarks on the Writings of Mr. Sandeman. *Boston*, 1767. 8vo, pp. 94. The Substance of An Address to an assembly in Bridgewater, March

10, 1779, previous to the administration of baptism. ... *Providence*; also *Boston* [n. d.] 8vo, pp. 8. The Testimony of the Two Witnesses. A Sermon from Rev. 11: 3. *Providence*, 1786. 8vo.+With a few remarks upon the late Writings of Dr. Hemmenway and Dr Lathrop, second edition. *Boston*, 1793. 8vo. Truth is Great, and Will Prevail. *Boston* [1781]. 8vo, pp. 36, (8).

BACKUS (John C.) An Historical Discourse on taking leave of the Old Church Edifice of the First Presbyterian Congregation in Baltimore. By John C. Backus, ... *Baltimore*, 1860. 12mo, pp. 105. 2633

BACKUS. A Discourse Delivered at the Opening of the Westminster Presbyterian Church, Baltimore, July 4, 1852. By John C. Backus, Pastor of the First Presbyterian Church, Baltimore. *Baltimore*, 1852. 8vo, pp. 32. Plate. 2634

BACKUS (J.) The Proclamation of the Honourable Joseph Jenks Deputy Governour, Answered; and the Proceedings Of a Justice's Court held at Norwich, July 26. 1725. therein Refer'd to Vindicated. By Joseph Backus, Esq; *Printed for the Author: Sold at several of the Booksellers' Shops in Boston, and N. London*, 1726. 8vo, pp. (2), 32. 2635

BACKUS (J. S.) Backus and Kenyon on Secret Societies: being a discourse delivered by Rev. J. S. Backus, of Auburn, and a Reply to the same, by Rev. H. B. Kenyon, of Ira, Cayuga County, N. Y. *Albany*, 1850. 12mo, pp. 44. 2636

BACKUS (S.) A Dissertation on the Right and Obligation of the Civil Magistrate to take care of the Interest of Religion etc; By Simon Backus. *Middletown*, 1804. 8vo. N. 2637

Backwoods of Canada. *See* Canada.

[BACON (Anthony)]. A Short Address to the Government, the Merchants, Manufacturers, and the Colonists in America and the Sugar Islands, on the Present State of Affairs. *London*, 1775. 8vo. 2638

BACMEISTER (Hartwig Ludwig Christian). Russische Bibliothek zur Kenntniss des gegenwärtigen Zustandes der Literatur in Russland. *St. Petersburg, Riga and Leipzig*, 1772–89. 11 vols., 12mo. 2638*a*

A valuable bibliography of works published either in Russia, or relating to all parts of the Russian Empire, including Russian America.

BACON (B. C.) Statistics of the Colored People of Phila-

delphia. Taken by Benjamin C. Bacon. ... . *Philadelphia, T. Ellwood Chapman*, 1856. 8vo, pp. 16. H. 2639

BACON (David Francis). Essays on Slavery. *New York*, 1846. 12mo. 2640

BACON (E.) Abstract of a Journal of E. Bacon, Assistant Agent of the United States to Africa. With an Appendix, containing interesting accounts. Second Edition. *Philadelphia*, 1822. 8vo. N. 2641

BACON (*Mrs.* Eliza Ann Munroe). Memoir of Rev. Henry Bacon. By Mrs. E. A. Bacon. [Motto.] *Boston, A. Tompkins*, 1857. 12mo, pp. 361. Portrait. H. 2642

BACON (E.) Address before the Republican Citizens of Berkshire, Pittsfield, July 4, 1810. By Ezekiel Bacon. *Pittsfield*, 1810. 8vo, pp. 24. 2643

BACON. A Lecture ... before the Young Men's Association ... December 15, 1843. ... "Notice of ... James Madison, Albert Gallatin, Joseph Story, and John Pierpont." By Ezekiel Bacon. *Utica, N. Y., R. W. Roberts, Printer*, 1844. 8vo, pp. 48. H. 2644

BACON. Oration delivered at Pittsfield, July 4, 1807. *Pittsfield*, 1807. 8vo, pp. 24. 2645

BACON. Oration delivered at Williamstoun July 4. 1799. *Bennington*, 1799. 12mo. 2646

BACON. Recollections of Fifty Years Since ... A Lecture ... before the Young Men's Association ... . February 2, 1843. [Motto.] By Ezekiel Bacon. *Utica, N. Y., R. W. Roberts, Printer*, 1843. 8vo, pp. 43. H. 2647

Also: A Speech on the Judiciary, February 17. 1807. *See also* Skinner (T. J.)

BACON (G. W.) Bacon's Descriptive Handbook of America. Comprising history, geography, agriculture, manufactures, commerce, railways, mining, finance, government, politics, education, religion, characteristics, public lands, laws, &c. By George Washington Bacon, F.R.G.S., and William George Larkins, B.A. With Maps and Plates. *London, G. W. Bacon*, 1866. Post 8vo, pp. viii., 392. 2648

BACON. Bacon's Guide to American Politics; ... [2d ed.]

London, S. Low, Son & Co., Bacon and Co., 1863. 16mo, Title, pp. 94.+1864. 8vo, pp. 100. 2649

BACON. Life and Administration of Abraham Lincoln. Presenting his Early History, Political Career, Speeches, Messages, Proclamations, Letters, &c., with a General View of his Policy as President of the United States, embracing the leading Events of the War. Also the European Press on his Death. Compiled by G. W. Bacon. *London, S. Low*, 1865. Fcap. 8vo, pp. 120. +Fine edition. *London, S. Low*, 1865. Post 8vo., pp. viii., 183.

BACON. Abraham Lincoln geschetst in zijn leven en daden. Naar het Engelsch van G. W. Bacon. *Amsterdam, Jan Leendertz*, 1865. 2651

BACON. Life and Speeches of President Andrew Johnson. Embracing his Early History, Political Career, Speeches, Proclamations, &c. With a Sketch of the Secession Movement, and his Career in relation thereto; also, his Policy as President of the United States. By G. W. Bacon. *London, G. W. Bacon*, 1865. Post 8vo, pp. v., 106. 2652

BACON (Henry). A Review [of a Memoir of Rev. James M. Cook.] *Philadelphia* (1851?). 12mo, pp. 36. S. 2653

BACON (James). The American Indian; or Virtues of Nature. A Play, in Three Acts with Notes; Founded on an Indian Tale. By James Bacon. *London, Harrison & Co.*, 1795. 8vo. Portrait. 2654

Founded on Mrs. Morton's Ouabi. *See* M. R., XIX., 466.

BACON (J.) Sermon on the death of N. Wattles, Franklin, Delaware Co. By Rev. James Bacon. *Cooperstown*, 1798. 8vo.

BACON (John). A Sermon, preached September 29th, 1771. By John Bacon, A.M. ... after he was installed [*sic*], and the Reverend Mr. John Hunt, A.M. ordained, Collegiate Pastors of the South Church in Boston. *Boston, Kneeland and Adams*, MDCCLXXII. 8vo, pp. 35. H. 2656

BACON. Illustrations Illustrated; containing a Brief Reply to Some Part of the annexed Letters of Friendship. By John Bacon. *Hartford*, 1781. 8vo, pp. 31. 2657

BACON. Speeches of Mr. Bacon & Mr. Nicholson, in the National House of Representatives, in defence of the Bill entitled "An Act to repeal Certain Acts respecting the Organiza-

tion of the Courts of the United States," February, 1802. *Boston*, 1802. 8vo, pp. 44. 2658

BACON (*Rev.* Leonard, D.D.) Address before the New-England Society of the City of New York, on Forefather's day. December 22, 1838. By Leonard Bacon. *New-York, Ezra Collier*, 1839. 8vo, pp. 47. 2659

BACON. Commemorative Discourses; delivered on his Sixty-third Birthday, February 19th, 1865; on the Fortieth Anniversary of his Installation, March 12th, 1865, and on his Retirement from Pastoral Duties, September 9th, 1866. By Rev. L. Bacon, D.D. ... With Extracts and Records of the First Ecclesiastical Society, ... *New Haven, T. J. Stafford, Printer*, 1866. 8vo, pp. 66. 2660

BACON. A Commemorative Discourse, on the Completion of Fifty Years from the Founding of the Theological Seminary at Andover. By Leonard Bacon ... . *Andover, W. F. Draper*, 1858. 8vo, pp. 46. H. 2661

BACON. Conciliation. A Discourse at a Sunday Evening Service, July 20, 1862. By Leonard Bacon. *New Haven, Peck, White & Peck*, 1862. 8vo, pp. 20. 2662

BACON. Discourse on the Death of W. H. Harrison, delivered before the Citizens of New Haven, April 17, 1841. By Leonard Bacon. *New Haven*, 1841. 8vo. B. 2663

BACON. A Discourse on the Early Constitutional History of Connecticut, delivered before the Connecticut Historical Society, Hartford, May 17, 1844. By Leonard Bacon. *Case, Tiffany & Burnham*, 1843. 8vo, pp. 21. 2664

BACON. A Discourse on the Traffic in Spirituous Liquors. With an Appendix, exhibiting the present state and influence of the Traffic in the City of New Haven. By Leonard Bacon. *New Haven*, 1838. 8vo. 2665

BACON. The Duties connected with the present Commercial Distress. A Sermon, ... preached in ... New Haven, May 21, 1837 and repeated May 23. By Leonard Bacon. *New Haven, Hitchcock & Stafford*, 1837. 8vo, pp. 18. H. 2666

BACON. Goodly Heritage of Connecticut. A Discourse on Thanksgiving Day, Nov. 19, 1840. *New Haven*, 1840. 8vo.

BACON. A Historical Discourse delivered at Worcester, in the Old South Meeting House, Sept. 22, 1863, the Hundredth Anniversary of its Erection. By Leonard Bacon, D.D. With Introductory Remarks by Hon. Ira M. Barton, the President on the Occasion. And an Appendix. *Worcester, Edw. R. Fiske, Printer*, 1863. 8vo, pp. 106. 2668

BACON. The Jugglers Detected. A Discourse delivered in New Haven, Dec. 30, 1860. By Leonard Bacon. With an Appendix. *New Haven, Thomas H. Pease*, 1861. H. 2669

A reply to a sermon defending slavery, by H. J. Van Dyke.

BACON. Reply to Professor Parker's Letters, in the Boston Post, to Rev. Leonard Bacon, D.D. by the Rev. Leonard Bacon, D.D. From the "New Englander" for April, 1863. [n. p., n. d.] 8vo, pp. 191–258. 2670

On the interpretation of the Constitution by the clergy, etc.

[BACON.] Review of Pamphlets on Slavery and Colonization, ... *New-Haven*, 1833. 8vo, pp. 24. S. & H. 2671

BACON. Sketches of the Life and Public Services of Hon. James Hillhouse of New Haven. By Rev. Leonard Bacon, D.D. ... *New Haven*, 1860. 8vo, pp. 46. Portrait. H. 2672

BACON. Seven letters to the Rev. George A. Calhoun, concerning the Pastoral Union of Connecticut, and its charges against the ministers and churches. By Leonard Bacon, Pastor, &c. *New Haven*. 1840. 12mo, pp. 131. 2673

BACON. Slavery discussed in Occasional Essays, from 1833 to 1846. By Leonard Bacon ... *New York*, 1846. 12mo, pp. 247. 2674

BACON. Thirteen Historical Discourses, on the Completion of Two Hundred Years, from the Beginning of the First Church in New Haven, with an Appendix. By Leonard Bacon. *New Haven, Durrie and Peck*, ... 1839. 8vo, pp. viii., 400. 4 Portraits. H. 2675

Also: Rev. Dr. Bacon's Address at the Funeral of Mrs. [L. O. B.] Thompson ... Jan. 29, 1852. [With an Obituary by Rev. Joshua Leavitt. n. p., n. d.] 12mo, pp. 12. H. Discourse, death of J. Ashmun. *New-Haven*, 1828. A Discourse before the Alumni of Yale College, Aug. 16, 1848. *New-Haven*, 1848. 8vo. Memorial of Nathaniel W. Taylor, D.D. Three Sermons: by Leonard Bacon, D.D., Pastor of the Center Church; Samuel W. S. Dutton ... George P. Fisher ... . *New-Haven, Thomas H. Pease*, 1858. 8vo, pp. 43. H. Oration before the Phi Beta Kappa Society of Dartmouth College, July 30, 1845. *Hanover*, 1845. 8vo, pp. 23.

A Plea for Africa; delivered in New Haven, July 4, 1825. *New Haven*, 1825. 8vo, pp. 22. A Sermon on Thanksgiving Day, Nov. 27, 1851. *New Haven*, 1851. 8vo, pp. 15, (1). Two Sermons on a Day of Fasting, 10th of April, 1857. *New Haven*, 1857. 8vo, pp. 32. A Discourse on a Day of Thanksgiving, Nov. 24, 1859. *New Haven*, 1859. 8vo, pp. 20. A Plea for Africa ... July 4th, 1825. *New Haven*, 1825. 8vo, pp. 22. Sermon at the funeral of Rev. Lyman Beecher, D.D., Jan. 14, 1863. *New York, Phair & Co.*, 1863. 8vo, pp. 31.

BACON (L. B. Stetson). Biography of Mrs. Lydia B. Bacon. Written for the Massachusetts Sabbath School Society ... . *Boston* [1856]. 12mo, pp. 348. H. 2676

BACON (L. W.) An Historical Discourse, on the Two Hundredth Anniversary of the Founding of the Hopkins Grammar School, New Haven, Connecticut. Delivered ... July 24, 1860, by Leonard Woolsey Bacon. With Notes and an Appendix. ... *New Haven, Printed by T. J. Stafford*, 1860. 8vo, pp. 70. H.

BACON (M.) Relation of the Fearful State of Francis Spira after he turned Apostate from the Protestant Church to Popery. Compiled by Math. Bacon, Esq. *Boston*, 1762. 12mo. 2678

BACON (N.) Strange News from Virginia. Being a full and true Account of the Life and Death of Nathaniel Bacon, Esq., who was the only cause and Original of all the late Troubles in that Country. With a full relation of all the Accidents which have happened in the late War there between the Christians and Indians. *London, Printed for William Harriss*, 1677. 4to, pp. 8.

BACON (N. A.) A Table, showing the Date and Place of Birth; ... of Jabez Bacon, late of Woodbury, deceased, and of his Descendant ... Compiled by Nathaniel A. Bacon ... *New Haven, Printed by Hitchcock & Stafford*, 1845. 4to, pp. 4. 2680

BACON (O. N.) A History of Natick, from its first Settlement in 1651 to the Present Time; with Notices of the First White Families. And also an Account of the Centennial Celebration, Oct. 16, 1851; Rev. Mr. Hunt's Address at the Consecration of Dell Park Cemetery, &c., &c., &c., By Oliver N. Bacon, Attorney at Law. *Boston, Damrell & Moore, Printers*, 1856. 8vo, Title, pp. 261. Plate. H. 2681

BACON (R. C.) Statistics of the Colored People of Philadelphia, By R. C. Bacon. *Philadelphia*, 1856. 8vo. 2682

BACON (Samuel). Memoir of Rev. S. Bacon, A.M., late an officer of Marines, afterwards Attorney at Law in Pennsylvania, subsequently an Episcopal Minister. *Philadelphia*, 1831.

BACON. Laws of Maryland at Large, with proper Indexes, Now first Collected into One Compleat Body, and Published from the Original Acts and Records remaining in the Secretary's Office of the said Province. Together with Notes and other matter relative to the Constitution thereof, extracted from the Provincial Records. To which is prefixed The Charter, with an English Translation. By Thomas Bacon, Rector of All Saints, Paris, in Frederick County ... *Annapolis, Printed by Jonas Green, Printer to the Province*, MDCCLXV. Folio. N. 2684

Also on large paper; handsomely printed.

BACON (T.) Four Sermons, upon the Great and Indispensable Duty Of all Christian Masters and Mistresses To bring up their Negro Slaves in the Knowledge and Fear of God. Preached at the Parish Church of St. Peter in Talbot County, in the Province of Maryland. By the Rev. Thomas Bacon, Rector of the said Parish. [Mottoes.] *London, J. Oliver*, M.DCC.L. 12mo, pp. 142. + Six Sermons [etc.] *London, J. Oliver*, M.DCC.LI. 12mo. H. 2685

BACON. Sermons to Masters and Servants. Republished by Rev. W. Meade. *Winchester* [n. d.] 18mo. 2686

[BACON.] Two Sermons, Preached to a Congregation of Black Slaves, at the Parish Church of S. P. In the Province of Maryland. By an American Pastor. [Motto.] *London, John Oliver*, M.DCC.XLIX. 12mo, pp. 79. H. 2687

BACON (T.) Copy of the Charges made to the United States Senate against Thomas Bacon, Collector of Customs, &c. ... with ... facts in refutation ... . [n. p., 1854.] 8vo, pp. 7. H. 2688

[BACON (William John)son). Memorial of William Kirkland Bacon, late Adjutant of the Twenty-sixth Regiment of New York State Volunteers. By his Father. *Utica, N. Y., Roberts, Printer*, 1863. 12mo, pp. 83, (1). Portrait. H. + Another Edition. *Boston, American Tract Society*, 1865. 18mo, pp. 139. 2689

BACON (W. T.) Poem pronounced before the Senior Class of Yale College, July 5, 1837. By William Thompson Bacon, with the Valedictory Oration by Charles Andrew Johnson. *New Haven*, 1837. 8vo, pp. 42. 2690

BACON DE LACHEVALERIE. Observations, présentées à l'assemblee de MM. les électeurs de la partie du nord de Saint-Dominique le 27 Janvier 1789 au Cap François. [1789.] 8vo. 2691

BACQUEVILLE DE LA POTHERIE. Histoire de L'Amerique Septentrionale. Divisée en quatre Tomes. Tome Premier. Contenant le Voyage du Fort de Nelson, dans la Baye d'Hudson, a l'extrémité de l'Amerique. Le premier établissement des François dans ce vaste païs, la prise dudit Fort de Nelson, la Description du Fleuve de saint Laurent, le gouvernement de Quebec, des trois Rivieres & de Montreal, depuis 1534. jusqu' à 1701. Par Mr. de Bacqueville de la Potherie, né à la Guadaloupe, dans l'Amerique Meridionale, Aide Major de la dite Isle. Enrichie de Figures. *A Paris Jean-Luc Nion et Francois Didot*, M.DCC.XXII. 4 vols., 12mo. Maps and Plates. + *Amsterdam, H. des Bordes*, 1723. 4 vols., 12mo. + *Paris, Nyon fils*, 1753. 4 vols., 12mo. C. 2692

This work entirely relates to Canada and the Iroquois Indians; the plates comprise the earliest views taken in Canada. It is written in the form of letters, except the second volume, which is divided into chapters. It contains several badly written memoirs on a considerable portion of the history of Canada. What the author relates, from his own observation, may be relied upon; but, in other respects, he was not well informed, although apparently sincere and dispassionate. The title-pages to vols. II.–IV. differ from the first. *See* Rich, I., 31; Boucher VI., 22.

The Bad Effects of Speculative Theology, and False Philosophy, on the Religion and Morals of Mankind ... . Third Edition. With the Rise and Progress of Perfectionism in Western New York. *Philadelphia* [1839?] 8vo, pp. 48. 2693

"By a layman."

BADE (T.) Der Scalpjäger. Robinson's Erlebnisse, Abenteuer und Fahrten im Westen Amerika's. Natur- und Sittenschilderungen aus dem amerikanischen Jagd-, Kriegs-, Reise-, und Waldleben. Herausgeber: Th. Bade. ... *Leipzig, Spamer*, 1857. 8vo. + 2e verbesserte Auflage. *Leipzig*, 1858. 8vo, pp. viii., 264. Over 100 Illustrations, 5 colored. + 3e Aufl. 1862. 8vo. (Neue Jugend- und Hausbibliothek, 2 Serie, IV. Band.) 2694

BADEN (*Major* N.) [Obituary. n. p. 183–?] 4to, 1 page. H.

BADGER (B.) The Naval Temple: containing a Complete History of the Battles fought by the Navy of the United States. From its Establishment in 1794, to the Present Time ... .

Second Edition. *Boston, Barber Badger*, 1816. 8vo, pp. 322. Engravings. H. 2696

This is said to be the same work as No. 1165.

BADGER (George E.) American Steam Navigation. Speech of Hon. George E. Badger, of North Carolina, for the Collins Steamers. In Senate of the United-States, May 6, 1852. *Washington*, 1852. 8vo, pp. 13. H. 2697

Also: Speech of Mr. Badger, May 11, 1854, on the President's Veto-Message, *Washington*, 1854. 8vo, pp. 16. H. Speech on the Slavery Question, March 18 and 19, 1850. [*Washington*, n. d.] 8vo, pp. 18. H. Speech on the Territorial Question, August 2, 1850. *Washington* [n. d.] 8vo, pp. 8. H. Speech ... on the Ten Regiment Bill. ... Jan. 18, 1848. *Washington*, 1848. 8vo, pp. 20. + [*Washington*, n. d.] 8vo, pp. 16. H. Speech ... February 16, 1854, on the Nebraska Bill. *Washington, Sentinel Office*, 1854. 8vo, pp. 14.

[BADGER (H. C.)] Brief Statement of the Sanitary Commission's Work. [By Rev. Henry C. Badger.] *San Francisco, September*, 1864. 8vo, pp. 16. 2698

BADGER. ... A Discourse occasioned by the Death of Mr. George Livermore. Preached ... 3d September, 1865, by Henry C. Badger ... . *Cambridge, the Family*, MDCCCLXV. 8vo, pp. 30. H. 2699

BADGER. The Humble Conqueror: a Discourse Commemorative of the Life and Services of Abraham Lincoln, preached to the Cambridgeport Parish, April 23, 1865. By Rev. Henry C. Badger. *Boston, William V. Spencer*, 1865. 8vo, pp. 18. H.

BADGER (Sarah). Statement of Facts, relative to the Last Will of the late Mrs. Badger, of Natick [Mass.], which was disallowed on the Final Hearing. By the Principal Legatees. *Dedham, H. & W. H. Mann*, 1824. 8vo, pp. 63. H. 2701

BADGER. Remarks on the Evidence in the Case relative to the Will of the late Mrs. Badger of Natick. *Dedham*, 1824. 8vo. 2702

BADGER (Stephen). Address of a Minister ... [inquiring] "Whether a Church is obliged ... to require a publick, formal and explicit Confession, of some particular Misdemeanors ... previously ... to a Christian Profession, to Baptism, and to Christian Communion ... . *Boston, E. Battelle*, M,DCC,LXXXIV. 8vo, pp. 44. H. 2703

BADGER. The Nature and Effects of Drunkenness ... Two

Discourses ... at Natick ... October, 1773. By Stephen Badger ... . *Boston, Edes and Gill*, 1774. 8vo, pp. 56. H. 2704

BADGER. The Substance of Two Discourses on Intemperance; delivered at Natick [October, 1773]. *Boston, Samuel T. Armstrong*, 1811. 8vo, pp. 23. H. 2705

BADGER (W. W.) Washington, or A Vision of Liberty: a Poem Delivered Before the Genesee Lyceum, at Lima, N. Y. ... February 22, 1855, by William Whittlesey Badger. ... *Lima, N. Y., Press of S. M. Raymond*, 1855. 8vo, pp. 24. H. + Delivered February 22, 1859. ... *New York, Thatcher & Hutchinson*, 1859. 12mo, pp. 24. H. 2706

BADGER & PORTER's Stage Register ... Stages, Steamboats and Canal Packets, in the New England States and ... New-York ... . *Boston*. 8vo. 2707

Bi-monthly. Vol. III., No. 1, is dated July 3, 1827; Vol. IX., No. 1, July, 1833, pp. 28.

BADGLEY (W.) Remarks on Register Offices. *Montreal*, 1836. 12mo. 2708

BADIA (Marc. Ant.) Compendio della guerra nata per confini in America tra la Francia e l'Inghilterra. *Amsterdam*, 1763. 8vo. Portrait. 2709

[BADIN (S. T.)] Origine et progrès de la mission de Kentucky ... par un témoin oculaire. ... *Paris, Adrien Le Clerc*, 1821. 8vo, pp. 32. H. 2710

BAER (Karl Er. von) and HELMERSEN (Gr. v.) Beiträge zur Kenntniss des Russischen Reichs und der angränzenden Länder Asiens. ... Band I. *St. Petersburg*, 1839. 8vo. Continued.

Band I. has the second title: Statistiche und ethnographische Nachrichten über die Russischen Besitzungen an der Nordwestküste von Amerika. Gesammelt von ... v. Wrangel. Mit den Berechnungen aus Wrangell's Witterungs-Beobachtungen und anderen Zusätzen vermehrt von v. Baer. Mit 1 Karte.

BAERS (J.) Olinda, ghelegen int Landt van Brasil, inde Capitania van Phernambuco met mannelijcke dapperheyt ende groote couragie inghenomen, ende geluckelijck rovert op den 16. Februarij a 1630 ... door den Heere Diederich van Weerdenburg. Cort ende claer beschreben. Door Joannem Baers ... . *Amsterdam, Hendrick Laurentsz*, 1630. 4to, pp. 38. J. C. B.

This rare book relates to the taking of Pernambuco by the Dutch. *See* Grant's History of Brazil, p. 54.

[BAERT (Alexandre Balthasar François de Paule, *Baron de*)]. Tableau de la Grande Brètagne, de l'Irlande, et des possessions anglaises, dans les quatres parties du monde. *Paris, Jansen*, An VIII. [1799]. 4 vols., 8vo, pp. v., 460, 11; 516, 12; 502, 50; 486, 24. Maps. S. 2713

Contains many articles on American subjects, particularly the French Colonies.

BAEYLE (Hyp.) Relation du naufrage de la Palacre Saute "Vigilante." *Buenos Ayres*, 1833. 8vo. 2714

Plate of the shipwreck and map of the mouth of the River Plate.

[BÄGERT (J.)] *See* [Begert (J.)]

BAGOT. Sermon before the Incorporated Society for the Propagation of the Gospel in Foreign Parts, February 19, 1790. By Lewis [Bagot], Lord Bishop of Norwich. *London*, 1790. 4to. 2715

BAHAMA. The Charter of the Bahama Islands. 8vo, pp. 16. H. 2716

The Harvard copy has no title-page. The charter was granted 1st Nov., 22 Charles II., *i. e.* 1670.

Communications on different subjects, addressed to the Bahama Agricultural Society. *Nassau*, 1802. 4to. 2717

Correspondence respecting interference with trade between New York and the Bahamas. 1863. Folio, pp. 65. 2718

A British Parliamentary paper.

Letters from the Bahama Islands. *See* [Hart (*Miss*)].

An Official Letter from the Commissioners of Correspondence of the Bahama Islands, to George Chalmers, Esq. Colonial Agent, concerning the Proposed Abolition of Slavery in the West Indies. *Nassau, New Providence, Royal Gazette Office; London, Re-printed by J. S. Brickwood*, 1823. 8vo, pp. 78. H.

Short account of the Bahamas. *See* [Graves (John)].

Votes and Proceedings of the House of Assembly of Bahama Islands. *Nassau, N. Providence*, 1806. Royal 8vo. Continued. 2721

BAHIA. De tweede wachter. *See* [Teelinck (Ewout)].

[BAILEY (*Mrs.* Abigail Abbot)]. Memoirs. *Boston, Samuel T. Armstrong*, 1815?] 24mo, pp. 275. 2722

Title from a copy which had lost its title-page.

BAILEY (A. H.) Allowing Soldiers to Vote. Speech of Hon. Mr. Bailey. New York Senate, April 1, 1863. 8vo, pp. 4.

Also: Objections to the President's Emancipation Proclamation Considered. Speech ... March 5, 1863. *Albany*, 1863. 8vo, pp. 8. ... Report of the Select Committee of the Assembly on the Library ... . [n. p., 1849.] 8vo, pp. 12. B. Review of Gov. Seymour's Message. *Albany, Weed, Parsons & Co.*, 1863. 8vo, pp. 12.

BAILEY (B. F.) Oration at Burlington, Vt. July 4, 1828. By B. F. Bailey. *Burlington*, 1828. 8vo. 2724

BAILEY (B. H.) A Tribute ... to ... Alvan Lamson, D.D. ... Preached ... July 24, 1864, to the First Church ... in Dedham. By Benjamin H. Bailey ... . *Boston, Printed by John Wilson and Son*, 1864. 8vo, pp. 23. H. 2725

[BAILEY (E.)] Sketch of the Life and Educational Labors of Ebenezer Bailey. *Republished from Barnard's American Journal of Education*, [n. p.], 1861. 18mo, pp. 43. Portrait. B.

BAILEY. Triumphs of Liberty; the Prize Ode, recited by Mr. Finn, at the Boston Theatre, ... February 22. 1825. By Ebenezer Bailey. *Boston, Cummings, Hilliard, & Co.*, 1825. 8vo, pp. 8. B. 2727

BAILEY (G.) Reports on the Reservation System of California, and the Indians of Arizona, addressed to the Commissioner of Indian affairs. By G. Bailey, of the Interior Department. *Washington*, 1858. 8vo, pp. 22. 2728

BAILEY (G.) *Junr.* American Progress: A Lecture Delivered before the Young Men's Mercantile Library Association of Cincinnati, December 3, 1846. By Gamaliel Bailey Jr. *Cincinnati, Edwin Shepard*, 1846. Impl. 8vo, pp. 24. 2729

BAILEY (G. F.) Intervention for Freedom. Address of Hon. G. F. Bailey, at Fitchburg, ... Aug. 24th, 1860. ... [n. p., 1860.] 8vo, pp. 8. H. 2730

BAILEY (G. S.) The Great Caverns of Kentucky: Diamond Cave, Mammoth Cave, Hundred Dome Cave. By Rev. G. S. Bailey. *Chicago, Church & Goodman*, 1864. 16mo, pp. 63.

BAILEY (Isaac). American Naval Biography. Compiled by Isaac Bailey. [Motto.] *Providence*, 1815. 12mo, pp. 257. H.

Contains eighteen memoirs.

BAILEY (J.) History of the Seventh-day Baptist General Conference. By Rev. James Bailey. *Toledo, O., S. Bailey & Co.*, 1866. 12mo, pp. 320. 2733

BAILEY (John). Man's chief End | To Glorifie God, | or | Some Brief | Sermon-Notes | On 1 Cor. 10. 31. | By the Reverend Mr. John Bailey, | Sometime Preacher and Prisoner of Christ | at Limerick in Ireland, | And now Pastor to the Church of Christ | in Watertown in New-England. | [Six lines.] | *Boston Printed by Samuel Green, and | are to be Sold by Richard Wilkins Book- | Seller near the Town-House.* | *Anno.* 1689. Sm. 8vo, 4 p. l., pp. 160. B. 2734

Mr. Corwin's copy sold for $5; priced in Nuggets, £2 2s. There is usually bound with this an address "To my Loving and Dearly Beloved | Christian Friends, in and about | Limerick." | Dated "May. 8. 1684." Sm. 8vo, pp. 40, (3). The same author preached the Artillery Election Sermon for 1672, but I have not seen it.

BAILEY (John). An Oration ... at Natick, July 5, 1824, before the Officers of the Regiment of Militia, Comprising the towns of Natick, Framingham, Hopkinton, Holliston and Sherburn. By John Bailey. *Dedham, H. & W. H. Mann, Printers* [1824]. 8vo, pp. 24. H. 2735

BAILEY (John J.) Waldimar, a tragedy. In Five Acts. [Not published.] *New York*, 1834. 8vo, pp. 124, (6). S.

BAILEY (J. T.) An Historical Sketch of the City of Brooklyn and the Surrounding Neighborhood, including the Village of Williamsburg, and the Towns of Bushwick, Flatbush, Flatlands, New Utrecht and Gravesend, to which is added an interesting account of the Battle of Long Island. Compiled from the best Authorities. By J. T. Bailey. *Brooklyn, Published by the Author*, 1840. 12mo, pp. 72. N. 2737

BAILEY (*Rev.* J. W.) Knox College, by whom founded and endowed; also, A review of a Pamphlet entitled "Rights of Congregationalists in Knox College." By J. W. Bailey. *Chicago*, 1860. 8vo, pp. 131. H. 2738

BAILEY (John Whitman). Microscopical Examination made by the U. S. Coast Survey off the Atlantic Coast of the U. S.

By Prof. J. W. Bailey. *Washington*, 1851. 4to, pp. 16. Plate. 2739

This and the following are also included in the Smithsonian Contributions, Vol. II.

BAILEY. Microscopical Observations off the Atlantic Coast and in South-Carolina, Georgia and Florida. By Prof. J. W. Bailey. *Washington*, 1851. 4to, pp. 48. 3 Plates. C. 2740

BAILEY. On the Infusoria of the Family Bacillaria, with Account of Interesting Species found in the United States. [*New-Haven*, 1841.] 8vo, pp. 22. 2 Plates. 2741

BAILEY (Joseph). Speech of Hon. Joseph Bailey on the Bill for the Issuing of additional Treasury Notes, delivered in the House of Representatives, January 18, 1862. 8vo, pp. 8. 2742

BAILEY (L. W.) Observations on the Geology of Southern New Brunswick, made principally during the Summer of 1864 by Prof. L. W. Bailey, Messrs. Geo. F. Matthew and C. F. Hartt. Prepared and arranged, with A Geological Map, by L. W. Bailey, A.M. Professor of Chemistry, &c. in the University of New Brunswick ... *Fredericton, G. E. Fenety*, 1865. 8vo, Title, pp. 158, (1). 2 Maps. H. 2743

BAILEY (L.) A Sermon ... at Randolph, before the Norfolk Auxiliary Education Society ... June 9, 1824. By Luther Bailey ... Medway. *Boston, Printed by Lincoln and Edwards* [1824]. 8vo, pp. 32. H. 2744

With the Treasurer's Report, a list of members, etc.

BAILEY (M. J.) Report on the Practical Operation of the Law relating to the Importation of Adulterated and Spurious Drugs, Medicines, &c. By M. J. Bailey, M.D. ... *New-York, D. Fanshaw, Printer*, 1849. 8vo, pp. 20. H. 2745

BAILEY (P. J.) The International Policy of the Great Powers. By Philip James Bailey. *London, Otley & Co.*, 1861. 16mo, pp. xv., 275. C. 2746

BAILEY (Richard). Letters from the Health Office, submitted to the Common Council of the City of New York. By Richard Bailey. *New York*, 1798. 8vo, pp. 100. 2747

BAILEY (Robert). The Life and Adventures of Robert Bailey, from his Infancy up to December, 1821, interspersed

with anecdotes, and religious and moral admonitions. Written by Himself. *Richmond*, 1822. 8vo, pp. 348. C. 2748

A notorious gambler, of the Stephen Burroughs school.

BAILEY (R. S.) The Church in the Wilderness. Narrative of a Visit to the Right Rev. Philander Chase, Bishop of Illinois. By Robert S. Bailey, M.D. ... *Charleston, Printed by A. E. Miller*, 1839. 8vo, pp. 8. H. 2749

BAILEY (R. T.) Proposed (Underground) Metropolitan Railway. Report of R. T. Bailey, Civil Engineer. *New York, Clayton & Medole, Printers* [1864]. 8vo, pp. 7. Map. H.

BAILEY (Rufus William). Thanksgiving Sermon at Pittsfield, Massachusetts, December 3, 1824. *Pittsfield*, 1825. 8vo, pp. 20. N. 2751

Also: A Sermon, March 5, 1826, at the Funeral of Josiah and George Guy Moseley. *Pittsfield*, 1826. 8vo, pp. 19. The Issue, Presented in a Series of Letters on Slavery. *New York. John S. Taylor*, 1837. 12mo, pp. 110.

BAILEY (S.) The Moral Significance of War. A Discourse delivered in the Baptist Meeting House, Franklin, Indiana, September 26, 1861. By Rev. Silas Bailey, D.D. *Indianapolis, Dodd & Co.*, 1861. 8vo, pp. 20. 2752

BAILEY (T.) Records of Longevity; with an Introductory Discourse on Vital Statistics. By Thomas Bailey. *London*, 1857. Post 8vo, pp. iv., 399. C. 2753

Includes notices of several Americans.

BAILEY (W. L.) Our Own Birds; or, A Familiar History of the Birds of the United States. By W. L. Bailey. *Philadelphia, Association of Friends*, 1863. 18mo. 2754

BAILEY (William). Records of Patriotism and Love of Country. By William Bailey. *Washington*, 1826. 8vo, pp. xv., 216. C. 2755

BAILEY (W. S.) [Circular relating to the Re-establishment of "The Free South." Signed Wm. Shreve Bailey. *Newport, Ky.*, 1864.] 4to, 1 page. 2756

Also: An Appeal to Loyal Religious People in behalf of Kentucky [for funds for the "Loyal Anti-Slavery Methodist Episcopal Church" in Newport, Ky. n. p.], 1865. 8vo, pp. 3.

BAILEY (Winthrop). Sermon at Greenfield, Mass. Sept. 24,

1826, on the Death of Capt. Isaac Newton. By Winthrop Bailey. *Greenfield* [1826]. 8vo. 2757

Also: Sermon before the Third Congregation in Greenfield. *Greenfield*, 1825. 8vo, pp. 8. Sermon in Greenfield, Massachusetts, October 16, 1825; being the Sabbath following the Installation of the Author, etc. *Greenfield*, 1825. 8vo.

BAILLARD (Edme). Discovrs du Tabac, ov il est traité particulièrement dv Tabac en Poudre. Par le Sr. Baillard. *Paris, Le Prest*, MDCLXVIII. Sm. 8vo, 12 p. l., pp. 125, Table and Privilege, 10 l. C. + 1671. 12mo. + 1693. 12mo. + Histoire du tabac, ou il est, etc. *Paris, Le Prest*, 1677. 12mo. + *Paris, Warin*, 1716. 12mo. 2758

BAILLIE (Hugh). A Letter to Dr. Shebear: containing a Refutation of his Arguments concerning the Boston and Quebec Acts of Parliament: and his Aspersions upon the Memory of King William, and the Protestant Dissenters. By Hugh Baillie, LL.D. ... *London, J. Donaldson*, MDCCLXXV. 8vo, Title, pp. 54. H. 2759

[BAILLIE.] An Appendix to a Letter to Dr. Shebbeare. To which are added, Some Observations on a pamphlet, entitled Taxation no Tyranny ... in which the Sophistry of that Author's reasoning is detected. By a Doctor of Laws. *London, J. Donaldson*, 1775. 8vo, pp. 8. S. 2760

[BAILLIE.] Some Observations on a Pamphlet lately published entitled "The Rights of Great Britain asserted" &c. By the Author of the Answer to Dr. Shebbeare and Dr. Johnson. *London, Donaldson*, 1776. 2761

See Rich, I., 237; M. R., LIV., 231.

BAILLIE (R.) Anabaptism, the True Fountaine of Independency Brownisme Antinomy Familisme, And the rest of the other Errours, which for the time doe trouble the Church of England, Vnsealed. Also The Questions of Pædobaptisme and Dipping Handled from Scripture, In A Second Part of The Disswasive from the Errors of the time By Robert Baillie Minister at Glasgow. [Mottoes.] *London, Printed by M. F. for Samuel Gellibrand*, 1647. 4to, 16 p. l., pp. 179, Contents, 5 l., Anthems, 1 l. 2762

The writings of this author, who was a friend of Roger Williams, contain many interesting particulars nowhere else to be found, respecting the Church of Leyden, and its migration to New England. Sold at Puttick's, 1854, for £2 5s.

BAILLIE (T.) An Account of the Province of New Bruns-

wick; including a Description of the Settlements, Institutions, Soil, and Climate of that important Province; with Advice to Emigrants. By Thomas Baillie, Esq. *London, Rivington*, 1832. 12mo, pp. 134. Map. 2763

[BAILLIO.] L'anti-Brissot; par un petit blanc de Saint-Domingue. [Signed Baillio. *Paris*], *Girardin* [n. d.] 8vo, pp. 40, or less. 2764

[BAILLIO.] Mémoire pour les citoyens Verneuil, Baillio jeune, Fournier et Gervais, déportés de Saint-Domingue, contre Léger-Félicité Sonthonax, commissaire civil, envoyé à Saint-Domingue pour y rétablir l'ordre et la paix. [Signed Baillio l'aîné. (6 mars 1793.)] *Paris, B. Guilhemat* [n. d.] 8vo, pp. 40, or less.

BAILLIO. Un mot de vérité sur les malheurs de Saint-Domingue; par M. Baillio ... [1er décembre 1791. *Paris*], *J. B. Chemin* [n. d.] 8vo, pp. 40, or less. 2766

BAILLOT DE SAINT-MARTIN. L'art du cultivateur et du fabricant de tabac, contenant ... moyen de tirer un parti avantageux des caboches et côtes de Hollande et de Virginie. *Paris, Bachelier*, 1810. 8vo. 2767

BAILLY (Félix.) Carte d'étude pour le tracé et le profil du canal de Nicaragua. Par M. Thomas de Gamond, ingénieur civil. Précédé des documents publiés sur cette question. *Paris*, 1858. 4to, pp. 90. 2768

BAILLY. Note pour servir à la Canalisation du Lac Nicaragua. Par M. Bailly, Ingénieur Anglais. Traduit en Français, par ordre de M. F. Castellan, Ministre Plénipotentiaire de Nicaragua. *Paris*, 1844. 4to, pp. 20. 2769

The map is usually done up in a separate volume. It exhibits all the proposed routes of communication with the Pacific.

BAILLY D'ENGEL. *See* [Engel (S., *le bailli* d')].

BAILY (F.) Journal of a Tour in Unsettled Parts of North America in 1796 & 1797. By the late Francis Baily, Esq., F.R.S., With a Memoir of the Author. [By Sir J. Herschel.] *London, Baily Brothers*, MDCCCLVI. 8vo, pp. xii., 439. C. 2770

BAILY (John). Central America; describing each of the States of Guatemala, Honduras, Salvador, Nicaragua, and Costa Rica; their Natural Features, Products, Population, and Remark-

able Capacity for Colonization. With Three Views. By John Baily .... *London, Trelawney Saunders*, 1850. Post 8vo, pp. xii., 164. 3 Plates and Map. C. & H. 2771

BAILY (J.) Die Staaten Central-Amerika's, Guatemala, Salvador, Honduras, Nicaragua und Costa Rica. Nach dem englischen Werke deutsch bearbeitet von Wilhelm Grimm. *Berlin, Besser's Verlag*, 1851. 8vo, pp. viii., 200. Map, folio.

BAIN (J. W.) National lessons from the Life and Death of President Lincoln. A Sermon, preached in the United Presbyterian Church, Canonsburg, Pa., on Fast-day, Thursday, June 1st, 1865. By Rev. J. W. Bain. *Pittsburgh, W. S. Haven*, 1865. 8vo, pp. 16. 2773

BAINES (E.) History of the Wars of the French Revolution, ... with Notes, and an Original History of the late War between the United States and Great Britain. By Edward Baines. *Philadelphia*, 1824. 4 vols., 8vo. + Edited by William Grimshaw. *New York*, 1852. 2 vols., 8vo, pp. 602; 599. C. 2774

BAINES. Baine's [*sic*] History of the Late War, between the United States and Great Britain: with a Critical Appendix, &c. By Ebenezer Harlow Cummins, A.M. *Baltimore, Printed by Benja. Edes*, 1820. 12mo, pp. 167, Appendix, xlvii. H. 2775

BAINES (Edward), *Jr.* History of the Cotton Manufacture in Great Britain; with a notice of its early History in the East, and in all the Quarters of the Globe. By Edward Baines, Jr. *London, Fisher*, 1835. 8vo, pp. 543, 18 p. l. C. 2776

BAINES (Thomas). Observations on the Present State of the Affairs of the River Plate. By Thomas Baines. *London*, 1845. 8vo. 2777

BAIRD (D.) Confederate Spelling Book. *Macon, Ga., Burke, Boyker & Co.*, 1863. 2778

BAIRD (E. C.) [Letter of Recommendation of Capt. E. C. Baird, for promotion. *Philadelphia*, 1862.] 8vo, pp. 3. 2779

Forty-nine copies privately printed.

[BAIRD (Henry Carey)]. General Washington and General Jackson on Negro Soldiers. *Philadelphia*, 1863. 8vo, pp. 8.

BAIRD. Strictures on an Additional Review of Mr. Carey's Letters to the President, By Henry Carey Baird. 8vo, pp. 8.

From the "Merchants' Magazine" of December, 1859.

BAIRD. Protection for Home Labor and Home Productions necessary to the Prosperity of the American Farmer. By Henry Carey Baird. *New York* [1860]. 8vo, pp. 16. P. & H. 2782

BAIRD (H. M.) The Life of the Rev. Robert Baird, D.D., by his Son Henry M. Baird, Professor in the University of the City of New York. *New York, Anson D. F. Randolph*, 1866. 12mo, pp. 347. Portrait. B. 2783

BAIRD (Robert). The Christian Retrospect and Register; a Summary of the Scientific, Moral and Religious Progress of the First Half of the Nineteenth Century. By Robert Baird, D.D. *New-York*, 1851. 12mo, pp. 420. + With a Supplement bringing the work down to the present time. By Robert Baird, D.D. *New York*, 1855. 12mo, pp. 442. C. 2784

BAIRD. Histoire des sociétés de tempérance des États-Unis d'Amérique, avec quelques details sur celles de l'Angleterre, de la Suède et autres contrées. ... Par R. Baird. *Paris, Hachette, Risler*, 1836. 8vo, pp. 272. 2785

BAIRD. Geschichte der Mässigkeits-Gesellschaft in den Vereinigten Staaten Nord-Amerika's. *Berlin, Eichler*, 1834. 8vo. + 2^e^ Auflage. *Berlin, Thome*, 1838. 8vo. 2786

BAIRD. Geschiedenis der matigheids-gezelschappen in de Vereenigde Staten van Amerika .... Naar het Fransch gevolgd. *Utrecht, J. G. van Terveen en Zoon*, 1837. 8vo. 2787

BAIRD. Impressions and Experiences of the West Indies and North America in 1849. By Robert Baird, A.M. ... *Edinburgh*, 1850. 2 vols. crown 8vo. H. + *Reprinted, Philadelphia, Lea & Blanchard*, 1850 and 1851. 12mo, pp. 354. H. + 1851. C. 2788

BAIRD. Memoir of Mrs. Eliza Astor Rumpff, ... By Rev. Robert Baird, D.D. *New York, American Tract Society* [1739?]. 16mo, pp. 80. Portrait. H. + Transplanted Flowers; or, Memoirs [etc.] *Glasgow*, 1839. 8vo. 2789

BAIRD. The Noblest Freedom; or, the Influence of Christianity upon Civil Liberty. A Discourse, addressed to the Alumni of Jefferson College, Pennsylvania. *New York*, 1848. 8vo. 2790

BAIRD. The Progress and Prospects of Christianity in the

United States of America; with Remarks on the subject of Slavery in America; and on the Intercourse between British and American Churches, by R. Baird, D.D. ... *London, Partridge and Okey* [1851]. 8vo, pp. iv., 72. H. 2791

BAIRD. Religion in the United States of America; or, an Account of the Origin, Progress, Relation to the State, and Present Condition of the Evangelical Churches in the United States, with Notices of the Unevangelical Denominations. By the Rev. Robert Baird ... With a Prefatory Recommendation by the Rev. Drs Welsh, Cunningham, and Buchanan. *Glasgow and Edinburgh*, 1844. 8vo, pp. 756. Map. C. + [*Reprinted*], *New-York, Harpers*, 1844. 8vo, pp. xii., 9–343. + *New York*, 1846. 8vo, pp. xii., 343. + *New York*, 1856. 8vo, pp. 696. C.

See Rich, Vol. II., 374.

BAIRD. La religion aux États-Unis d'Amérique. Origine et progrés des églises évangeliques des États-Unis, leurs rapports avec l'État, et leur condition actuelle, avec des notices sur les communions non évangéliques. Par le Rev. Robert Baird. Traduit de l'Anglais par L. Burnier. *Paris, Delay*, 1844. 8vo, 2 vols. 2793

BAIRD. Kerkelijke geschiedenis, kerkelijke statistiek en godsdienstig leven der Vereenigde Staten van Noord-Amerika. Naar de hoogduitsche uitgave van K. Brandes, bewerkt door A. W. van der Worm en E. B. Swalue, met eene voorrede van N. C. Kist. *Schoonhoven, S. E. van Nooten*, 1846–49. 2 vols, 8vo. Map. 2794

BAIRD. Kirchengeschichte kirchliche Statistik und religiöses Leben der Vereinigten Staaten von Nordamerica Nach dem Englischen bearbeitet von Karl Brandes, mit einem Vorwort von Aug. Neander. *Berlin, Reimer*, 1844. 8vo. 2795

See also Büttner (J. G.)

BAIRD. State and Prospects of Religion in America; being a Report made at the Conference of the Evangelical Alliance, in Paris, August 25th, 1855. By The Rev. Robert Baird, D.D. .... *London, Edward Suter* [etc.], 1855. 8vo, pp. 91. Map. H.

BAIRD. De l'état actuel et de l'avenir de la religion en Amérique. Rapport .... *Paris, Ch. Meyrueis et Ce*, 1856. 8vo, 2 p. l., pp. 80. Map. H. 2797

BAIRD. Zustand und Aussichten der Religion in Amerika. Ein Bericht, erstattet ... 25. August 1855. Auf Veranlassung des Verfassers aus dem Englischen übersetzt und herausgegeben von G. W. Lehmann. *Berlin, W. Schultze*, 1856. 8vo, pp. 104. Map, 4to. 2798

BAIRD. Vie d'Anna Jane Linnard, précédée d'une introduction par l'honor. Théod. Frelinghuisen, et d'une lettre du Rév. W. Neill. *Paris, Risler*, 1840. 12mo. 2799

BAIRD. Erinnerungen aus dem Leben von Anna Jane Linnard. Mit einer Einleitung von Theod. Freilinghausen und einem Briefe des Dr. William Neill. Aus dem Englischen. ... *Hamburg, Perthes-Besser und Mauke*, 1841. 12mo, pp. 96.

BAIRD (Samuel J.) Collection of the Acts, Deliverances, and Testimonies of the Supreme Judicatory of the Presbyterian Church, from its origin in America to the present time, with Notes and Documents, Explanatory and Historical. By Rev. Samuel J. Baird. *Philadelphia*, 1856. 8vo, pp. xxii., 586. P.

BAIRD. A History of the early policy of the Presbyterian Church in the training of her ministry, and of the first years of the Board of Education. ... By Rev. Samuel J. Baird, D.D. *Philadelphia*, 1865. 8vo, pp. 37. P. 2802

BAIRD. Southern Rights and Northern Duties in the Present Crisis. A Letter to Hon. William Pennington. By Rev. Samuel J. Baird, D.D. *Philadelphia, Lindsay & Blakiston*, 1861. 8vo, pp. 32. H. 2803

BAIRD (Sp. F.) Catalogue of North American Birds, chiefly in the Museum of the Smithsonian Institution. By S. F. Baird. 1858. 4to. C. 2804

Reprinted from Vol. IX. of Pacific Railroad Report for the Smithsonian Institution: Reprinted in 8vo, pp. 24, 1859, and included in the Smithsonian Misc., Coll. II. There is also an edition printed for labeling, with one side of each leaf blank.

BAIRD. Mammals of North America. The Descriptions of Species based chiefly on the Collections in the Museum of the Smithsonian Institution. By Spencer F. Baird. With Eighty-seven Plates of Original Figures, illustrating the Genera and Species, and including Details of External Form and Osteology.

Philadelphia, J. B. Lippincott & Co., 1859. 4to, pp. xxxiv., 764. 87 Plates. 2805

Published with plain and colored plates. The following were included in this work, issued separately: Mammals coll. on an explor. expedition from the Missouri to Utah lake. [*Washington*, 1859.] 4to, 3 Plates. Mammals of North America, coll. or observed on the different routes for the Pacific railroad. *Washington*, 1857. Rl. 4to, pp. 757. 43 Plates (irregularly numbered). Mammals of the United States and Mexican Boundary. *Washington*, 1859. 4to, 27 Plates. The most of the following are issued by the Smithsonian Institution: Reptiles coll. on an explor. exped. in Upper-California. [*Washington*, 1859.] 4to. 3 Plates. Reptiles coll. on an explor. exped. from the Sacramento Valley to the Columbia River. [*Washington*, 1859.] 4to, 4 Plates. Reptiles coll. on an explor. exped. from the Missouri to Utah lake. [*Washington*, 1859.] 4to. 4 Plates. Revision of the North American Tailed-Batrachia, w. descr. of new gen. and spec. [*Philadelphia*, 1849.] 4to. Reptiles of the western part of North America. *Washington*, 1859. 4to. 13 Plates. Review of American Birds in the Museum of the Smithsonian Institution. By S. F. Baird. Part I. North and Middle America. *Washington* [*June*, 1864 *to May*, 1865.] 8vo, pp. iv., 320. Report to the Secretary of the Smithsonian Institution on the Fishes of the New Jersey Coast as observed in the summer of 1854. *June*, 1855. pp. 40. Another edition, with alphabetical index added. *See* United States Exploring Expedition.

BAIRD. On the Serpents of New York; with a Notice of a Species not hitherto included in the Fauna of the State. *Albany*, 1854. 8vo, pp. 30. 2 Plates. 2806

BAIRD. On the Ruminating Animals of North America, and their susceptibility of domestication. *Washington*, 1852. 8vo, pp. 24. c. 2807

BAIRD and GIRARD. Catalogue of North American Reptiles in the Museum of the Smithsonian Institution: Part I. Serpents. By S. F. Baird and C. Girard. *Washington*, 1853. 8vo, pp. xvi., 172. c. 2808

BAIRD, CASSIN and LAWRENCE. The Birds of North America; the Descriptions of Species based chiefly on the collections in the Museum of the Smithsonian Institution. By Spencer F. Baird, ... with the Co-operation of John Cassin, ... and George N. Lawrence, with an Atlas of One Hundred Plates. *Philadelphia, J. B. Lippincott & Co.*, 1860. 4to, 2 p. l., pp. lvi., 1005; xii., 100 Plates colored. c. 2809

Some portions of this work have also been issued separately: Birds of the United States and Mexican Boundary. *Washington*, 1859. 4to. 25 Colored Plates. Birds coll. on an explor. exped. from the Missouri to Utah lake. [*Washington*, 1859.] 4to. 7 Colored Plates. *See also* Gillis (J. M.)

BAIRD (Thomas H.) Memorial praying for the enactment of measures to preserve the Constitution and Union of the States,

presented to the House of Representatives, February 7, 1863. *Pittsburg, A. A. Anderson & Sons*, 1864. 8vo, pp. 23. 2810

BAJAMÁR. Discurso exhortatorio pronunciado en el Supremo consejo de las Indias ... 2 de Eners ... 1793. Por el ex^{mo} Señor Marques de Bajamár .... *Madrid, imprenta de la viuda de Ibarra*, MDCCLXXXXIII. 8vo, Title, pp. 58. H. 2811

BAJON. Mémoires pour servir à l'Histoire de Cayenne, et de la Guiane françoise, Dans lesquels on fait connoître la nature du Climat de cette contrée, les maladies ... [avec] des Observations sur l'Histoire naturelle du pays, & sur la culture des terres. ... Par M. Bajon, ancien Chirurgien Major de l'Isle de Cayenne ... *Paris, Grangé, le veuve Duchesne, l'Esprit*, M. DCC. LXXVII–LXXVIII. 2 vols., 8vo, pp. (12), xvi., 162 (462), (1); (12), 416. Plates. H. 2812

BAJON. Herrn Bajon's ... Nachrichten zur Geschichte von Cayenne und dem französischen Guiana. ... Aus dem Französischen. *Erfurt, Georg Adam Keyser*, 1780–84. 2 Theile in 3 Abschn., 8vo, Title, pp. xiv., 114; Title, pp. 156; Title, pp. 135. H. 2813

BAJOT (Louis Marin). Abrégé historique et chronologique des principaux voyages de découvertes par mer, depuis l'an 2000 avant J.-C. jusqu'au commencement du XIXe siècle. *Paris, Arth. Bertrand; Bachelier*, 1829. 8vo, pp. 156. Map. + 1835. 8vo.

BAJOT. Catalogue général des livres composant les bibliothèques du département de la marine et des colonies. *Paris, impr. royale*, 1839–43. 5 vols., 8vo. 2815

The five volumes contain, in one arrangement, the catalogues of eleven libraries in France. The six libraries in Martinique, Guadeloupe, French Guiana, Senegal, Bourbon, and Pondicherry, were to form a separate work. I cannot find that it has ever appeared. The plan of the work and the prefaces are by Bajot; the execution of Vol. I.–II. by Levot, of III.–V. by Solvet.

A Bake-Pan for the Dough-Faces. By One of Them. Try it. *Burlington, Vermont, C. Goodrich*, 1854. 8vo, pp. 64. H.

[BAKER (D.)] Yet one Warning More, To Thee O England: Together, With a very tender Lamentation with bowels of Compassion & Mourning, yet over thee O Land ... which may eccho and ring again in the ears of New-England. ... *London, Robert Wilson*, 1660. 4to, Title, pp. 37. 2817

A Quaker Tract, with a long title. Signed Daniel Baker.

BAKER (D.) Solon: or the Rebellion of 1861. A Domestic and Political Tragedy. By D. Baker. *Chicago*, 1862. 8vo.

BAKER (E. C.) Speech of ... E. C. Baker ... upon the Bill to regulate the Hours of Labor in Incorporated Establishments. ... In the Senate of Massachusetts, April 13, 1855. *Boston, Wm. White*, 1855. 8vo, pp. 8. 2819

BAKER (Edward D.) Speech of Hon. E. D. Baker, of Illinois, on the Oregon Question, delivered in the House of Representatives ... January 29, 1846. [No imp.] 8vo, pp. 7. H.

BAKER. Speech of Hon. E. D. Baker, of Oregon ... in the Senate ... January 2d, and 3d, 1861, upon the Secession Question. *Washington, H. Polkinhorn, Printer* [1861]. 8vo, pp. 31. H. 2821

BAKER. Addresses on the Death of Hon. Edward D. Baker, Delivered in the Senate and House of Representatives, on Wednesday, December 11, 1861. *Washington, Gov. Pr. Office*, 1862. 8vo, pp. 87. 2822

BAKER (George E.) The Life of William H. Seward; with Selections from his Works. *Redfield, New-York*, 1855. 12mo, pp. 410. Portrait. c. 2823

BAKER (George M.) Our Twelve Months' Cruise: a Valedictory delivered before the Mercantile Library Association ... May, 1866. By George M. Baker. *Boston*, 1866. Sm. 4to, pp. 16. H. 2824

BAKER (H. F.) Banks and Banking in the United States. ... By Henry F. Baker ... . *Cincinnati, Printed by C. F. Bradley & Co.*, 1854. 2 Parts. 8vo, pp. 56. c. 2825

BAKER (James). The Life of Sir Thomas Bernard, Baronet, By the Rev. James Baker, His Nephew and Executor. *London, John Murray*, 1819. pp. xiii., 199. Portrait. 2826

Sir Thomas Bernard was of the same family as the Governor of Massachusetts.

BAKER (J. B.) ... Plan for the promotion of foreign trade at this port ... *Philadelphia*, 1859. 8vo, pp. 16. P. 2827

BAKER (J. Loring). Exports and Imports, as showing the Relative Advancement of every Nation in Wealth, Strength, and Independence. ... By James L. Baker. *Philadelphia*, 1859. 8vo, pp. 30. H. & P. 2828

[BAKER.] Hard Times. Important Suggestions to Laborers ... With Some Remarks upon the Proposed Reduction of the Duty upon Railroad Iron, and Coal. *Boston, Wright & Hasty, Printers* [Jan.], 1855. 8vo, pp. 24. H. 2829

Published with additions and changes as:

BAKER. Men and Things; or short essays on various subjects, including Free Trade [Kansas, &c.] By James L. Baker. *Boston*, 1858. 12mo, pp. 287. P. 2830

[BAKER.] A Review of the Tariff of 1846 ... in a Series of Articles contributed to the Evening Transcript ... . *Boston, Redding & Co.* [Feb.], 1855. 8vo, pp. 48. H. 2831

BAKER (J. L.) Slavery: by J. L. Baker. ... *Philadelphia, John A. Norton*, 1860. 8vo, pp. 19. + [n. p., n. d.] 8vo, pp. 16. H. 2832

BAKER (J. L.) The Washingtonian Reform. An [Historical] Address ... June 16, 1844. By James L. Baker. ... *Hingham, Jedidiah Farmer, Printer*, 1844. 8vo, pp. 20. H.

BAKER (J.) Speech of Jehu Baker, of Illinois, on Reconstruction; ... in the House of Representatives, January 27, 1866. *Washington*, 1866. 8vo, pp. 15. H. 2834

BAKER (J. F.) Our Martyr President. [Delivered before the Hamilton Literary Association of Brooklyn.] By John F. Baker. [n. p., 1865.] 8vo, pp. 5. H. 2835

BAKER (J. M.) A View of the Commerce between the United States and Rio de Janeiro, Brazil. By John M. Baker. *Washington*, 1838. 8vo, pp. 118. Map. c. 2836

BAKER. A View of the Commerce of the United States and the Mediterranean Sea-Ports, including the Adriatic and Morea; with maps of the principal harbors in those seas. From the MS. of the late John Martin Baker, by his son, Louis Baker. *Philadelphia*, 1847. 8vo, pp. 112. 13 Maps. c. 2837

[BAKER (J. P.)] An Essay on the Art of making Muscovado Sugar wherein A New Process is Proposed. [Motto.] *Jamaica, Printed by Joseph Weatherby, Kingston*, MDCCLXXV. 4to, 2 p. l., pp. iv., 50. H. 2838

BAKER (Louisa). An Affecting Narrative of Louisa Baker

A Native of Massachusetts Who in Disguise Served Three Years as a Marine on board an American Frigate. *Boston, Nath'l Coverly, Jr.*, 1815. 12mo, pp. 24. W. 2839

BAKER (L. C.) Official Report of Col. L. C. Baker, U. S. A., to the Hon. S. P. Chase, Secretary of the Treasury, in the Case of Stuart Gwynn and S. M. Clarke. Also the Minority Report of the Treasury Investigating Committee, with Accompanying Documents. June, 1864. *New York, Henry A. Oliver, Printer*, 1864. 8vo, pp. 48. H. 2840

BAKER. History of the United States Secret Service. By General L. C. Baker ... *Philadelphia, L. C. Baker*, 1867. 8vo, pp. 693, x. Portrait. 2841

BAKER (Luther). An Address delivered to the Philanthropic Society, ... Feb. 22, 1806. By Luther Baker. *Warren, R. I., N. Phillips*, 1806. 12mo, pp. 16. 2842

BAKER. Letter to the Hon. John Quincy Adams, on the Oregon Question. By Luther Baker. *New-Bedford*, 1846. 8vo, pp. 16. 2843

BAKER (P. C.) Franklin. An Address delivered ... on Franklin's Birth-day, January 17, 1865. By Peter C. Baker. *New York, Baker & Godwin*, 1865. 8vo, pp. 28. 2844

BAKER (R. P.) A Report on Kentucky River. By R. P. Baker. 1836. 8vo. 2845

BAKER (Rachel). Devotional Somnium; or a collection of prayers and exhortations uttered by Miss Rachel Baker, in the City of New-York, in the winter of 1815, during her abstracted and unconscious state. With an account of her life, &c. By several medical gentlemen. *New-York, Printed by S. Marks*, 1815. 12mo, pp. 298. c. 2846

BAKER (Richard). The Marchants' Humble Petition and Remonstrance, with account of their shipping Losses since the War with Spain, and brief Treaty of the King of Spain's West Indies, of the Inquisition, and of the Death of the English Agent, Mr. Askham, and the Persecution of the Murderers. By Richard Baker. *London*, 1659. Folio. 2847

BAKER (S. W.) An Address ... before the Washington Independent Temperance Society of Saccarappa, On the 5th of

July, 1841. By Dr. S. W. Baker. ... *Portland, Holden & Appleton, Printers*, 1841. 8vo, pp. 20. H. 2848

[BAKER (W. D.)] The Saturniad: being a full and true account of the rise, progress and downfall of the University of Quilsylvania [Pennsylvania]. By Hyton Hosmot. Translated by A. Lecutt Esq. ... *Philadelphia*, 1836. 12mo, pp. 63. P.

BAKER (W. G.) The Christian Lawyer: being a Portraiture of the Life and Character of William George Baker. ... *New York, Carlton & Porter*, 1859. 16mo, pp. 320. H. 2850

BAKER (*Rev.* William M.) The Life and Labors of the Rev. Daniel Baker, D.D. ... Prepared by his son, Rev. William M. Baker. *Philadelphia, W. S. & Alfred Martien*, 1858. 12mo, pp. 573. Portrait. C. 2851

BAKER STREET BAZAAR. ... Grand Moving Mirror of American Scenery, painted on 25,000 Feet of Canvas, comprising the Mammoth Cave of Kentucky, the Falls of Niagara ... . [*London* 185-?] 16mo, pp. 16. H. 2852

The Balance and Columbian Repository. *Hudson* [*N. Y.*], 1802. 4to. Continued. C. 2853

Balanço da receita e despeza do imperio no exercicio de 1839–40 e estado da divida publica activa e passiva em 31 de dezembre de 1840. *Rio de Janeiro, Typographia Nacional*, 1843. Folio.

Balanza general del comercio maritimo por los puertos de la republica mexicana en el año de 1826. *Mexico*, 1826. 4to.

BALBI. Atlas ethnographique du globe, ou classification des peuples anciens et modernes d'après leurs langues ... . Par Adrien Balbi. *Paris, Rey et Gravier*, 1826. Folio. C. 2856

"'Table XXV contains the 'Division ethnographique de l'Amérique et tableau général des langues américaines;' and Table XLI, 'Tableau polyglotte des langues américaines;' gives a vocabulary of 26 words in about 120 american languages and dialects."—LUDEWIG.

BALBI. Essai statistique sur le royaume de Portugal et d'Algarve, comparé aux autres états de l'Europe, et suivi d'un coup d'œil sur l'état actuel des sciences, des lettres et des beaux-arts parmi les Portugais des deux hémisphères. ... Par Adrien Balbi

... *Paris, Rey et Gravier*, 1822. 2 vols., 8vo, pp. lii., 480; 272, ccclxviii. C. 2857

Partly relates to Brazil.

BALBI. Introduction à l'Atlas ethnographique du globe ... Tome Premier. *Paris, Renouard; Rey et Gravier*, 1826. 8vo, pp. cxliii., 415. C. & W. 2858

BALBO (J. P.) Constitutions républicaines du globe: France, États-Unis (amendée), Delaware (état), Saint-Domingue (revisée), ... *Paris, Bénard*, 1848. 12mo. 2859

BALBOA (M. C.) Histoire du Pérou, par Miguel Cavello Balboa. Inédite. *Paris, Arthus Bertrand*, M.DCCC.XL. 8vo, pp. viii., 331. (Ternaux. Coll. de voyages, xv.) C. 2860

BALBOA. The Lives of Vasco Nunez de Balboa, Hernando Cortes, and Francisco Pizarro. *New York*, 1847. 12mo, pp. 276. C. 2861

BALBUENA (Bernardo de). Grandeza | Mexicana | del Bachiller Ber | nardo de Balbuena, | Dirigida al Ilvs | trissimo y Reuerendissimo Don Fr. | Garcia de Mendoza y Zuñiga | Arcobispo de Mexico. Del | cõsejo de su Magestad. | *Con previlegio | En Mexico Por Melchior Ocharte.* | *Año De.* 1604. | 12mo, 14 p. l., Text, 9–140 leaves. J. C. B. 2862

See Ternaux, No. 269.

BALBUENA. Siglo do oro y Silvas de Erple. *Madrid*, 1608. 8vo. + *Madrid, Harra*, 1821. 8vo. Portrait. 2863

BALBUENA. El Bernardo, o Victoria de Roncesvalles, Poema heroyco. Por Don Bernardo de Balbuena Abadmajor de la Isla de Jamayca. *Madrid*, 1624. 4to. Engraved Title.

First edition of this esteemed Poetical Romance. *See* Bibliotheca Grenvilliana. Priced: £4 4s., by Thorp, 1843. Reprinted in "Poemas Epicos," Biblioteca de Autores Españoles. *Madrid, Rivadeneyra*, 1851. 8vo, pp. 139–399. C. Segunda Edicion. *Madrid, Sancha*, 1808. 3 vols., 12mo, pp. xxii., 388; 493; 425. C.

BALCARCE. Buenos-Ayres. Sa situation présente, ses lois libérales, sa population immigrante, ses progrès commerciaux et industriels. *Paris, Imprimerie Blondeau*, 1857. 8vo, pp. 80.

BALCH (B.) Discourse delivered at Salisbury, West Church, Mass., Nov. 17, 1802, at Ordination of William Balch. *Dover*, 1803. 8vo, pp. 38. 2866

BALCH (Thomas). A Discourse Delivered at Halifax In the County of Plymouth, February 2^{d} 1757. When the Rev. Mr. William Patten was ordained ... there. By Thomas Balch ... . *Boston, S. Kneeland*, 1757. 8vo, 2 p. l., pp. 25. B. 2867

BALCH. The Happiness of a People illustrated and explained. Sermon delivered in Boston, Nov. 29, 1804—Thanksgiving. *Boston*, 1805. 8vo, pp. 23. 2868

BALCH. ... A Sermon Preached at Edgartown on Martha's-Vineyard, July 29th, 1747. When the Reverend Mr. John Newman Was Ordained ... in the Room of ... Mr. Samuel Wiswall, deceas'd. By Thomas Balch ... . [With a prefatory address by E. Mayhew.] *Boston, S. Kneeland and T. Green*, 1747. 8vo, pp. (4), 36, (4). B. 2869

BALCH. A Sermon, Preach'd At Mendon Third Parish, September the 14th, A.D. 1768, At the Ordination of The Rev. Mr. Benjamin Balch. By Thomas Balch ... . *Providence, Printed by John Carter*, M,DCC,LXIX. Sm. 8vo, pp. 38. H. 2870

Mr. Balch also published an election sermon, *Boston*, 1749. 12mo. An artillery election sermon at Boston, June 6, 1763. *Boston, Edes and Gill*, M,DCC,LXIII. 8vo, pp. 38, (1). B.

[BALCH (Thomas)]. Letters and Papers relating chiefly to the Provincial History of Pennsylvania, with some Notices of the Writers. Privately printed. *Philadelphia*, 1855. 12mo, pp. cxxxviii., 312. C. & H. 2871

These are known as the "Shippen Papers." *See also* Galloway (Joseph).

BALCH. Papers relating chiefly to the Maryland Line during the Revolution. Edited by Thomas Balch. One Hundred and Fifty Copies Printed. *Philadelphia, Seventy-Six Society*, 1857. 8vo, pp. (4), 218, (1). C. 2872

BALCH (W.) ... Sermon Preached before His Excellency William Shirley ... May 31. 1749. Being the Day for Electing His Majesty's Council ... . By William Balch, A.M. ... *Boston*, 1749. 8vo, Title, pp. 28. 2873

Also: The Apostles St. Paul and St. James reconciled ... . A Sermon ... in Bradford, Feb. 2, 1742.3. ... *Boston, J. Edwards*, 1743. 12mo, pp. 31 H. A Sermon ... October 4, 1732, At the Gathering of the Second Church ... in Rowley. *Boston*, 1735. 8vo, pp. (4), 19. A Sermon ... at Bradford East-Precinct, January 23, 1742, 3. ... *Boston*, 1743. 16mo, pp. 36. ... A Sermon ... at the Ordination of Benjamin Parker, in Haverhill, Nov. 28, 1744. *Boston, J. Edwards*, 1744. 8vo, pp. 30. H. A Sermon preached before The annual Convention of Ministers in

Boston, N. E. May 29. 1760. ... *Boston, N. E. Printed by B. Mecom*, M,DCC,LX. 8vo, pp. 40. ... . A Vindication Of some Points of Doctrine ... an Answer To the Remarks of The Rev. Messieurs Wigglesworth and Chipman. *Boston, J. Edwards*, 1746. 4to, pp. 92. H.

BALCH (W. S.) Popular Liberty and Equal Rights. An Oration ... before the Mass Convention of the R. I. Suffrage Association ... in Providence, July Fifth, 1841. By Wm. S. Balch. *Providence, B. F. Moore, Printer*, 1841. 12mo, pp. 23. H. 2874

BALCH. Romanism and Republicanism incompatible. A Lecture ... in review of "The Catholic Chapter in the History of the United States," by J. Hughes, D.D., Archbishop of New York. *New York*, 1852. 8vo. 2875

BALCOM (D. A.) The devil on politics; or the history of political religion. By D. A. Balcom. ... *Printed for the Author*. 12mo, pp. 114. P. 2876

Relates in part to the Second War with England.

BALDRIDGE (S. C.) The Martyr Prince. A Sermon on the occasion of the Assassination of President Lincoln, delivered in the Presbyterian Church Friendsville, Sabbath morning, April 23d, 1865. By the Pastor. *Cincinnati, O., Jos. B. Boyd*, 1865. 8vo, pp. 21. 2877

BALDUC. Mission catholique de le Riviere Columbie. Par Rev. Z. B. Z. Balduc. *Quebec*, 1843. 2878

BALDWIN (C. N.) Trial of Charles N. Baldwin for a Libel, in publishing charges of fraud and swindling in the management of lotteries in the State of New-York. Reported by H. W. Warner. *New York*, 1818. 8vo, pp. 37. C. & S. 2879

[BALDWIN (Charles N.)] Universal Biographical Dictionary ... *Richmond*, 1826. 8vo, pp. 444. Plate. C. 2880

BALDWIN (E.) Annals of Yale College, in New Haven, ... from its Foundation, to the Year 1831. With an Appendix, containing Statistical Tables, and exhibiting the Present Condition of the Institution. By Ebenezer Baldwin. *New Haven, Hezekiah Howe*, 1831. 8vo, pp. viii., 324. H. 2881

BALDWIN. Annals of Yale College, from its foundation, to the year 1831. By Ebenezer Baldwin. To which is Added, an

Appendix, bringing it down to 1838. Second Edition. *New Haven, B. & W. Noyes*, 1838. 8vo, pp. viii., 343. C. 2882

See Am. M. R., I., I.

BALDWIN. Catalogue of the Phenogamous Plants and the Ferns growing without cultivation, within five miles of Yale College, Connecticut. Extracted from the appendix to Mr. E. Baldwin's History of Yale College. *New Haven*, 1831. 8vo.

BALDWIN. Funeral Oration on the Death of Jonathan Lyman, pronounced June 18. 1766, at Hatfield. *New Haven, Samuel Green*, 1767. pp. 19. 2884

BALDWIN. Thanksgiving Sermon at Danbury, Connecticut, November 16, 1775, illustrated with notes. By Ebenezer Baldwin. *New York*, 1776. 8vo, pp. 42. 2885

BALDWIN. Observations on the Physical, Intellectual, and Moral Qualities of our Colored Population: with Remarks on ... Emancipation and Colonization. By Ebenezer Baldwin. ... *New Haven, L. H. Young*, 1834. 8vo, pp. 52. B. 2886

BALDWIN (E. W.) Considerations for the American Patriot. A Sermon delivered on occasion of the Annual Thanksgiving, Dec. 12, 1827. By Elihu W. Baldwin. *New York*, 1828. 8vo. 2887

BALDWIN. An Address ... July 13th, 1836. By Rev. Elihu W. Baldwin, A.M. on Occasion of his Inauguration as President of Wabash College. [With notes.] *Cincinnati, Printed by James & Gazlay*, 1836. 8vo, pp. 33. H. 2888

BALDWIN (Geo. C.) Representative Women. By George C. Baldwin. *New York*, 1860. 12mo. C. 2889

BALDWIN (George R.) Report, shewing the Cost and Income of a Railroad, as surveyed from Toledo, Ohio; to Chicago, Illinois; incorporated as the Buffalo and Mississippi Railroad. *Toledo*, 1847. 8vo. 2890

BALDWIN. Report on supplying the City of Charlestown with Pure Water: Made for the City Council ... By George R. Baldwin and Charles L. Stevenson, Civil Engineers. *Boston, Little, Brown and Company*, 1860. 8vo, pp. 77. Map. H. 2891

BALDWIN (H. A.) Baldwin's Consolidated Business Directory, 1866. New York, Boston, and Philadelphia. *New York, H. A. Baldwin & Co.* Rl. 8vo, pp. 926. 2892

BALDWIN. Baldwin's Handbook of Central Park. *New York, H. A. Baldwin & Co.*, 1866. 16mo, pp. xvi., 64. 2893

BALDWIN (H. and S.) Remonstrance against ... abolishing or regulating tolls on vessels passing through the lock and canal at Baldwinsville. By Henry and Stephen Baldwin. *Albany*, March 23, 1836. 8vo, pp. 31. S. 2894

BALDWIN (Henry). A General View of the Origin and Nature of the Constitution and Government of the United States, deduced from the political history and condition of the Colonies and States, from 1774 until 1788, and the Decisions of the Supreme Court; with opinions in the cases decided at January Term, 1837, arising on the restraints on the powers of the States. By Henry Baldwin. *Philadelphia, John C. Clark*, 1837. 8vo, pp. v., 197. C. 2895

BALDWIN. Opinion of the Circuit Court of New Jersey, on rights of fishing in the Delaware. Delivered by Justice Baldwin. *Philadelphia*, 1831. 8vo, pp. 16. P. 2896

BALDWIN (John D.) State Sovereignty and Treason. Speech of Hon. John D. Baldwin, of Massachusetts, Delivered in the House of Representatives, Washington, March 5, 1864 ... . [*Washington*, 1864.] 8vo, pp. 8. H. 2897

BALDWIN (Joseph G.) The Flush Times of Alabama and Mississippi. A Series of Sketches. By Joseph G. Baldwin. *New-York, D. Appleton and Company*, M.DCCC.LIII. 12mo, pp. x., 330. Woodcuts. H.+Seventh edition. *New York*, 1854. pp. x., 330. 2898

BALDWIN. Party Leaders; Sketches of Thomas Jefferson, Alexander Hamilton, Andrew Jackson, Henry Clay, John Randolph of Roanoke, including notices of many other distinguished American Statesmen. By Joseph G. Baldwin. *New York*, 1854. 12mo, pp. 370. C.+Seventh Edition. *New York*, 1855. 12mo, pp. 370. C. 2899

BALDWIN (Lewis). Candid Development of Facts tending to Exhibit the real grounds of difference Existing between the First Baptist Church of Philadelphia and the Philadelphia Association. By Lewis Baldwin. *Philadelphia*, 1819. 8vo. 2900

BALDWIN (L.) Letter to the Hon. John Pickering, President of the Salem Mill Dam Corporation, upon the Estimates,

&c. of that Work. By L. Baldwin, Engineer ... . *Salem, Printed by Andrews & Foote*, 1826. 8vo, pp. 11. H. 2901

BALDWIN. Report on the Subject of introducing Pure Water into the City of Boston. By Loammi Baldwin ... . *Boston, John H. Eastburn, Printer*, 1834. 8vo, pp. 78. Map. H.+Second Edition, with Additions. *Boston, Hilliard, Gray and Co.*, 1835. 8vo, pp. iv., (1), 143. 3 Maps. 2902

BALDWIN. Report on the Brunswick Canal and Railroad, Glynn County, Ga. With an Appendix. Containing the Charter, and Commissioner's Report. *Boston*, 1836. 8vo, pp. 42. M.+*Boston*, 1837. 8vo, pp. 48. 2903

BALDWIN. Thoughts on the Study of Political Economy, as connected with the Population, Industry, and Paper Currency of the United States. By L. Baldwin ... . *Cambridge, Printed by Hilliard and Metcalf*, 1809. 8vo, pp. 75. H. N. 2904

BALDWIN (M.) ... Sermon preached at Springfield, Dec. 13, 1770, at the Execution of William Shaw. By Rev. Moses Baldwin. *Boston*, 1771. 8vo, pp. 24.+Third Edition. *Boston*, 1771. 8vo. W. 2905

BALDWIN. ... A Sermon ... occasioned by the death of Dr. A. Stone ... *Boston*, 1774. 8vo. 2906

BALDWIN (N. B.) Discourse on Henry Clay and Daniel Webster, delivered by request, in the Bethesda Baptist Church, New-York, Nov. 25, 1852. By Rev. N. B. Baldwin. *New-York*, 1853. 8vo. 2907

BALDWIN (R. S.) Argument of Roger S. Baldwin, of New Haven, before the Supreme Court of the United States, in the Case of the United States, Appellants, *vs.* Cinque, and Others, Africans of the Amistad. *New York, S. W. Benedict*, 1841. 8vo, pp. 32. H. 2908

Also: Remarks on Mr. Mason's speech. Senate, Sept. 26, 1850. 8vo, pp. 4. Speech on territorial compromise bill, U. S. Senate, July 25, 1848. 8vo, pp. 8. Speech ... in favor of the Admission of California into the Union, and on the Territorial Bills, and the Bill in relation to Fugitive Slaves ... . March 27 and April 3, 1850. *Washington*, 1850. 8vo, pp. 20. H. Speech on Texan claim to New Mexico, U. S. Senate, July 25, 1850. 8vo, pp. 8.

BALDWIN (S.) A Sermon preached at Plymouth, Dec. 22, 1775. Being the Anniversary Thanksgiving in commemoration of the first Landing of the Fathers of New England, there

Anno domini 1620. By Samuel Baldwin, A.M. *Boston*, 1776. 8vo, pp. 39. 2909

BALDWIN (Samuel Davies). Armageddon; or, the Overthrow of Romanism and Monarchy; the existence of the United States Foretold in the Bible, its future greatness, &c. By S. D. Baldwin. *Cincinnati, Applegate & Co.*, 1854. 8vo, pp. 480. C.

BALDWIN (S.) An Oration pronounced before the Citizens of New-Haven, July 4th, 1788 ... . By Simeon Baldwin ... . *New-Haven, Printed by J. Meigs*, M.DCC.LXXXVIII. 8vo, pp. 16. H., M. 2911

BALDWIN (Theron). Historical Address delivered in Monticello, Illinois, June 27, 1855, at the Seventeenth Anniversary of Monticello Female Seminary. By Rev. Theron Baldwin, First Principal of the Institution. *New York, John F. Trow, Printer* [1855]. 8vo, pp. 32. H. 2912

Contains a history of the seminary.

BALDWIN (Thomas). A Brief Sketch of the Revival of Religion in Boston, In 1803–5. Written by the late Dr. Baldwin ... . [*Boston*, 1826.] 8vo, pp. 8. H. 2913

BALDWIN. Brief Vindication of the Particular Communion of the Baptist Churches; being a Reply to the Remarks of the Rev. Noah Worcester, A.B. in his "Friendly Letter" to the author. By Thomas Baldwin. *Boston*, 1794. 12mo.+Third Edition. *Suffield, E. Gray*, M,DCC,XCIX. 12mo, pp. 112. 2914

BALDWIN. A Discourse delivered before the Ancient and Honorable Artillery Company, in Boston, June 1, 1807. Being the Anniversary of their Election of Officers. *Boston*, 1807. 8vo, pp. 28. 2915

BALDWIN. Discourse ... in the Second Baptist Meeting-House in Boston ... January, 1824. With ... Historical Sketches of the Church ... . By Thomas Baldwin ... . *Boston, Printed by Lincoln & Edmands* [1824]. 8vo, pp. 32. H.+Second Edition. *Boston*, 1841. 8vo. B. 2916

BALDWIN. A Sermon ... Boston ... April 2, 1799 ... . [With some remarks on the state of religion in the U. S.] *Boston, Printed by Manning & Loring*, 1799. 8vo, pp. 24. H.

BALDWIN. Sermon ... before C. Strong, Esq., Governor ... May 26, 1802. Being the Day of General Election. By

Thomas Baldwin ... *Boston, Young & Minns, Printers*, 1802. 8vo, pp. 36. H.+Second Edition. *Boston, June*, 1802. 8vo, pp. 32. H.+Third edition. *New York*, 1802. B. 2918

BALDWIN. A Sermon delivered February 19, 1795. Being the Day of Public Thanksgiving throughout the United States. By Thomas Baldwin, A.M. *Boston, Printed by Manning & Loring*, 1795. 8vo, pp. 24. 2919

BALDWIN. A Sermon, delivered to the Second Baptist Society in Boston, On Lord's Day, December 29, 1799. Occasioned by the Death of General George Washington, Who Departed this Life the 14th Inst. Æ. 68. By Thomas Baldwin, A.M. Pastor of the Second Baptist Church in Boston. Published by particular Desire. *Boston, Manning & Loring* [1800]. 8vo, pp. 28. H. 2920

BALDWIN. A Sermon Preached February 15, 1802. Before the Honourable Senate and House of Representatives of the Commonwealth of Massachusetts, on the Day of the Interment of his Honor Samuel Phillips, Esq. Lieutenant Governor, who died February 10, 1802. Æ. 50. By Thomas Baldwin, A.M. Chaplain to the House. *Boston, Young and Minns*, 1802. 8vo, pp. 21. B., H. 2921

Also: ... A Sermon ... at Templeton, October 16, 1800, at the Installation of the Rev. Elisha Andrews ... . *Boston*, 1800. 8vo, pp. 24. H. Sermon ... March 30, 1814, in the First Baptist Meeting-House ... at the Installation of the Rev. James M. Winchell. ... *Boston* [n. d.] 8vo, pp. 24. H. Sermon at Boston, July 11, 1799, at the Ordination of William Collier. *Boston*, 1799. 8vo. Sermon at the Ordination of Elisha Williams, at Beverly, Mass. June 15, 1803. *Boston*, 1803. 8vo. At the Ordination of the Rev. Jeremiah Chaplin. *New York*, 1804. 8vo. Of Rev. David Leonard as Evangelist, Bridgewater, Dec. 17, 1794. *Boston*, 1795. 8vo. Of Rev. Daniel Merrill, Sedwick, May 15, 1805. *Boston*, 1805. 8vo, pp. 36. Also Sermons: April, 1799, at a Quarterly Meeting of Several Churches for Special Prayer. *Boston*, 1799. 8vo. Feb. 19th, 1804. *Boston*, 1804. May 30, 1804. *Boston*, 1804. 8vo. A Discourse ... before ... the Boston Female Asylum, September 26, 1806 .... [n. p.], *Russell & Cutler, Printers*, 1806. 8vo, pp. 29, (1). (With "Statement of Expences," etc.) H. ... Discourse ... in Boston, March 16, 1807, at the Interment of the Rev. Samuel Stillman, D.D. ... *Boston* [n. d.] 8vo. H. May 28, 1809. *Boston*, 1829. 8vo. On Jan. 1, 1811, at the Opening of the New Meeting House belonging to the Second Baptist Church in Boston, *Boston*, 1811. 8vo. Sermon at the opening of a new Meeting House, at Cambridge, Mass. Dec. 25, 1817. *Boston*, 1818. 8vo. Sermon, May 7th, 1817. *Boston*, 1817. 8vo. At Boston, Feb. 21, 1819, the Lord's Day after the Execution of the Pirates. *Boston*, 1819. 8vo.

BALDWIN. *See* Clay (Joseph), Stillman (Samuel).

BALDWIN (Thomas). Narrative of the Massacre, by the

Savages, of the Wife & Children of Thomas Baldwin, Who, since the melancholy period of the destruction of his unfortunate family, has dwelt entirely alone, in a hut of his own construction, secluded from human society, in the extreme western part of the State of Kentucky. *New-York, Martin & Perry*, 1835. 8vo, pp. 24. Plate. H. 2922

[BALDWIN (Thomas)]. Historical Sketch of the Origin, Progress, and Wants, of Illinois College. May, 1832. *New-York, John T. West, Printer*, MDCCCXXXII. 8vo, pp. 16. B.

BALDWIN (T.) and THOMAS (J.) A New and Complete Gazetteer of the United States, giving a full and comprehensive Review of the Present Condition, Industry, and Resources of the American Confederacy, embracing also important Topographical, Statistical and Historical Information, from Recent and Original Sources; together with the Results of the Census of 1850, and Population and Statistics in many Cases to 1853. By Thomas Baldwin and J. Thomas, M.D. *Philadelphia, J. B. Lippincott & Co.*, 1854. Rl. 8vo, pp. 1364. C. 2924

BALDWIN. A Universal Pronouncing Gazetteer; ... By Thomas Baldwin. *Philadelphia*, 1845. 12mo, pp. 550.+Eighth edition, with a Supplement. *Boston*, 1849. 12mo, pp. 704.+New edition, with population inserted according to the census of 1850. *Philadelphia*, 1852. 12mo, pp. 692, iv., 55. C. 2925

BALDWIN (W.) *See* Darlington (W.)

BALDWIN SCHOOL. Addresses delivered at the Dedication of the Edifice of the Preparatory Department, of the Baldwin School, Saint Paul, Minnesota Territory; And Catalogue for 1853. *Saint Paul, Owens & Moore, Printers*, 1854. 8vo, pp. 39, (1). H. 2926

BALDWIN. A Plan of Baldwin, Maine, copied and reduced from the original in the Land Office. [*Boston*, 1815.] 8vo.

BALESTIER. The Annals of Chicago; a Lecture delivered before the Chicago Lyceum, January 21, 1840. By J. N. Balestier. 8vo, pp. 24. *Chicago, Edward H. Rudd*, MDCCCXL. 8vo, pp. 24. H. 2928

BALESTIER. Historical Sketches of Holland Lodge, with incidental Remarks on Masonry in the State of New York. By Joseph N. Balestier. *New York*, 1862. 8vo, pp. 101. 2929

BALFOUR (J.) Mémoire du sieur Jean Balfour, habitant de l'ile de Tabago, à MM. les députés à l'Assemblée nationale de France. *Paris, Prault* [n. d.] 4to, pp. 40, or less. 2930

[BALFOUR.] Observations sur le deuxième Mémoire du Sieur Roume ... . [Signed Jean Balfour. *Paris*], *imp. du Patriote français* [n. d.] 8vo, pp. 40, or less. 2931

BALKAM. "The Harper's Ferry outbreak and its Lesson." A Sermon preached in the Pine Street Chapel, Sabbath Afternoon, December 11th, 1859. By Rev. U. Balkam. *Lewiston, Printed at the Journal Office*, 1859. 8vo, pp. 16. 2932

BALL (Benjamin Lincoln). Three Days on the White Mountains; being The Perilous Adventure of Dr. B. L. Ball on Mount Washington, during October 25, 26, and 27, 1855. Written by Himself. *Boston, Nathaniel Noyes*, 1856. 12mo, pp. 72. B. 2933

BALL (Charles). Slavery in the United States. A Narrative of the Life and Adventures of Charles Ball, a Black Man, who lived Forty Years in Maryland, South Carolina and Georgia, as a Slave, under Various Masters, and was One Year in the Navy with Commodore Barney, during the Late War; containing an Account of the Manners and Usages of the Planters and Slaveholders of the South—a Description of the Condition and Treatment of the Slaves, with Observations upon the State of Morals amongst the Cotton Planters, and the Perils and Sufferings of a Fugitive Slave, who twice escaped from the Cotton Country. *New-York, John S. Taylor*, 1837. 12mo, Title, pp. 517.+Third Edition. *J. T. Shryock, Pittsburgh*, ... 1854. 12mo, pp. vi., 9–446. B., C. 2934

BALL (C.) Der Negersclave. Leben und Abenteuer ... . Erzählt von ihm selbst. *Berlin, J. Springer*, 1854. 2 vols., 8vo, 2 p. l., pp. 236; 2 p. l., pp. 196. 2935

BALL (H.) A Sermon delivered at Rutland, Wednesday, January 1st, 1800, Before a numerous Audience assembled to publicly mourn the Death of General George Washington; who departed this life at Mount Vernon, Virginia, on the 14th of December, 1799, Æt. 68. By Heman Ball, A.M. Minister of the Gospel at Rutland, Vermont. *Rutland, Printed for S. Williams, Esq.* [1800]. 8vo, pp. 27. W. 2936

BALL (John). An | Answer | to two | Treatises | Of Mr. Iohn Can, | the Leader of the English Brownists in Amsterdam. | The former called, | A Necessitie of Separation from the Church of England, | proved by the Nonconformists Principles. | The other, | A Stay against Straying: Wherein in opposition to | M. Iohn Robinson, he undertakes to prove the unlaw- | fulnesse of hearing the Ministers of the | Church of England. | Very seasonable for the present times. | By the late learned, laborious and faithfull servant of Jesus Christ, | John Ball. | *London*, | *Printed by R. B. and are to be sold by John Burroughes, at his Shop at* | *the signe of the Golden Dragon neere the Inner Temple gate*, | *in Fleet-street*, 1642 |. 4to, 10 p. l., pp. 144, 92, Table and Errata, pp. 3. H.

BALL. Friendly Triall of the Grounds tending to Separation. *Cambridge*, 1640. Sm. 4to. 2938

Title from Col. Aspinwall's Catalogue.

BALL. A Tryall of the New-Chvrch Way in New-England and in Old ... By ... John Ball, of Whitmore. Penned a little before his Death, and sent over to the New England Ministers, Anno 1637, as a Reply to an Answer of theirs in justification of the said Positions. Now published ... By William Rathband and Simeon Ash. ... *London*, *Thomas Underhill*, 1644. 4to, pp. (12), 90. H. 2939

BALL (J. P.) Ball's ... Mammoth Pictorial Tour of the United States. Comprising Views of the African Slave Trade ... . Compiled for the Panorama. *Cincinnati*, *Achilles Pugh*, *Printer*, 1855. 8vo, pp. 56. Woodcut, folded. H. 2940

BALL (L. C.) War Meeting. Speech delivered at Hoosick Falls, April 24, 1861. By L. Chandler Ball. 8vo, pp. 7.

BALL. Extract from a Speech delivered at South Hoosick, on the Raising of the American Flag, May 25, 1861. By L. Chandler Ball. 8vo, pp. 8. 2942

BALL. Our Federal Relations. Speech in the Assembly of New York. *June* 29, 1861. 8vo, pp. 8. 2943

BALL (M. D.) A Poem by Mott: Dulany Ball, of Virginia, delivered before the Theta Delta Chi Fraternity ... at the University of William and Mary, June Second, 1856. *Norfolk*, *Va.*, *Southern Argus Printing Office*, 1856. 8vo, Title, pp. 21. H.

Defends slavery and the South.

[BALL (Richard)]. The Practicability, Safety, and Advantages of Negro Emancipation. *Bristol*, *Printed by Wright & Bagnall*, 1830. 8vo, 1 sheet. 2945

A Ballad concerning the Fight between the English and French at Lake George. [*Boston*, 1755.] Broadside, in 2 columns. P. 2946

Ballads of the South. *New York*, *T. R. Dawley*, 1864. 32mo, pp. 13–72. 2947

Ballads of the War. *New York*, *T. R. Dawley*, 1864. 32mo, pp. 9–72. 2948

BALLANCE (C.) Speech of Charles Ballance ... in the Wigwam, Peoria, Oct. 5th, 1860. [n. p., n. d.] 8vo, pp. 8. H.

BALLANTINE. The Importance of God's Presence with an Army, going against the Enemy; and the Grounds on which it may be expected. Represented in a Sermon Preached at a Lecture in Westfield, on Wednesday June 2, 1756. Just before Captain John Mosely, and His Company, began their March towards Crown-Point. By John Ballantine, M.A. ... Westfield. ... *Boston*, *Edes and Gill*, 1756. 8vo. M. 2950

BALLANTYNE. Handbook to the New Gold Fields. A full account of the Richness and Extent of the Fraser and Thompson River Gold Mines, with a Geographical and Physical account of the Country, and its Inhabitants, &c. By R. M. Ballantyne. *Edinburgh*, *Strahan*, 1858. 2951

BALLANTYNE. Hudson's Bay; or, Every-Day Life in the Wilds of North America during Six Years' Residence in the Territories of the Hon. Hudson's Bay Company. By Robert Michael Ballantyne. *Edinburgh*, *Nelson*, 1848. 12mo. + Second Edition, 1848. + Third Edition. *Edinburgh*, *Nelson*, 1859. 12mo, pp. 330. + *Boston*, 1859. 12mo. 2952

Also: Martin Rattler; or, a Boy's Adventures in the Forests of Brazil. *New York*, and *Edinburgh*, *Nelson*, 1858. 16mo. Snow Flakes and Sunbeams; or, the Young Fur Traders. *Edinburgh*, *Nelson*, 1856. Crown 8vo, pp. 440. + *Boston*. 1859. 12mo. The Golden Dream; or, Adventures in the Far West. *London*, *J. F. Shaw*, 1854. 12mo, pp. 360. The Wild Man of the West. A Tale of the Rocky Mountains. By R. M. Ballantyne. *Edinburgh*, 1862. 16mo, pp. viii., 419. + *Boston*, *Crosby & Nichols*. Ungava, a Tale of Esquimaux Land. By R. M. Ballantyne. *London*, 1858. 12mo. + *New York*, *Phinney*, *Blakeman & Mason*, 1859. 12mo. The World of Ice; or, Adventures in the Polar Regions. *London*, *Nelson*. 12mo, pp. 320.

BALLARD (E.) Memorial Volume of the Popham Celebration, August 29, 1862; Commemorative of the Planting of the Popham Colony on the Peninsula of Sabino, August 19, O. S., 1607, establishing the Title of England to the Continent. Published under the direction of the Rev. Edward Ballard, Secretary of the Executive Committee of the Celebration. *Portland*, *Bailey & Noyes*, 1863. 8vo, pp. xiv., 9–368. 2 Maps. B. & H. 2953

BALLARD (F. W.) The Huguenot Settlers of New York City and its Vicinity. By Frank W. Ballard. [No imprint.] 12mo, pp. 19. H. 2954

BALLARD. New York City a Mission Field. An Address delivered before the New York Young Men's Christian Association, by Frank W. Ballard, April 27, 1863. ... [*New York*, 1863.] 12mo, pp. 18. H. 2955

BALLARD. The Stewardship of Wealth as Illustrated in the Lives of Amos and Abbott Lawrence. A Lecture. By F. W. Ballard. *New York*, 1866. 12mo. + Second Edition. [*New York*, n. d.] 8vo, pp. 16. H. 2956

BALLARD (J.) A Sermon ... in Lowell, on the Sabbath following the Funeral of Alvah Mansur, Esq., who died ... Nov. 1, 1840. By Joseph Ballard. ... . *Lowell*, *Leonard Huntress*, *Printer*, 1840. 12mo, pp. 12. H. 2957

[BALLARD (William)]. Sketch of the History of Framingham, Mass. *Boston*, 1827. 8vo, pp. 71. W. 2958

BALLARNA (S.) Relacion Circunstanciada de todas las Operaciones de la Escuadra i Ejercito Espedicionario sobre Chiloe. Por Santiago Ballarna. *Santiago*, 1826. 4to, pp. 23. M. 2959

BALLENSTEDT (C. W. T.) Beschreibung meiner Reise nach den Goldminen Californiens. Zur Belehrung und Warnung für Auswanderer. *Schöningen*, 1851. 8vo, pp. 104. 2960

BALLEROY (J. B.) Tarif belge, mis en rapport avec les tarifs des Pays-Bas, d'Allemande, de France, d'Angleterre et des États-Unis, par J. B. Balleroy. *Bruxelles*, 1844. Folio. B. 2961

BALLESTEROS. Ordenanzas del Peru, recogidas y ordenadas por el licenciado D. Tomas de Ballesteros. *Lima*, *J. D. Contreras*, 1685. Folio. 2962

50

The Ballot Box, the Palladium of our Liberties. *New Orleans*, *July*, 1863. *Printed for the Compiler*, 1863. 8vo, pp. 65.

BALLOU (Adin). A Concise Exposition of the Hopedale Community: Descriptive, Statistical, Historical and Constitutional. [n. p., 1853.] 4to, pp. 8. H. 2964

BALLOU. A Discourse on ... American Slavery, delivered in ... Mendon, Mass. July 4, 1837. By Adin Ballou. ... *Boston*, *Isaac Knapp*, 1837. 24mo, pp. 88. H. 2965

BALLOU. Violations of the Federal Constitution in the "Irrepressible Conflict" between the Pro-Slavery and Anti-Slavery Sentiments of the American People. By Adin Ballou. *Milford* (*Mass.*), 1861. 12mo, pp. 48. 2966

BALLOU. The Voice of Duty. An Address delivered at the Anti-Slavery Picnic at Westminster, Mass., July 4, 1843. By Adin Ballou. *Milford* (*Mass.*), *Community Press*, 1843. 8vo pp. 12. 2967

BALLOU (H.) A Sermon ... on Fast Day Morning, April 3, 1828. By Hosea Ballou ... . *Boston*, *Bowen & Cushing*, 1828. 12mo, pp. 12. H. 2968

BALLOU. A Sermon ... at the Dedication of the Universalist Meeting-House At Shirley, Mass. January 9, 1817. By Hosea Ballou. ... *Salem*, *Printed by Warwick Palfray*, *Jun.*, 1817. 8vo, pp. 23. H. 2969

Also: Oration before the Grand Lodge of the State of New Hampshire, June 24th, 1810. *Portsmouth*, 1810. 4to, pp. 16. Sermon at the Dedication of the First Universalist Meeting-house, Roxbury, Jan. 4, 1821. *Boston*, 1821. 8vo. pp. 20. Oration at Windsor, Vt. Dec. 27, 1808. *Windsor*. 8vo. Discourse at Philadelphia, June 2, 1828, at the Ordination of T. Fiske. *Philadelphia*. 8vo. And other Sermons and Discourses.

BALLOU (John). The Lady of the West; or, the Goldseekers. Written for the Great American Nation. By J. Ballou. *Cincinnati*, 1855. 12mo. 2970

BALLOU (Maturin M.) Biography of Rev. Hosea Ballou. By his Youngest Son, Maturin M. Ballou. ... *Boston*, *Abel Tompkins*, 1852. 12mo, pp. 404. Portrait. H. 2971

BALLOU. History of Cuba; or, Notes of a Traveller in the Tropics. Being a Political, Historical, and Statistical Account of the Island, from its First Discovery to the Present Time.

By Maturin M. Ballou. ... *Boston*, *Phillips*, *Sampson and Company* [etc.] 12mo, pp. 230. 6 Plates. C. & H. 2972

BALLSTON SPRINGS. [A Poem.] *New York*, *S. Gould*, 1806. 12mo, pp. 46. 2973

BALLSTON SPA. Catalogue and Circular of the State and National Law School at Ballston Spa, N. Y. *New York*, 1852. 8vo, pp. 14. B. 2974

BALLY (Victor). Du typhus d'Amérique, ou de la fièvre jaune. *Paris*, *Smith*, *et Gabon*, *l'auteur*, 1814. 8vo, pp. 26, 623.

BALMANNO. Romances of the Sea, and Voyage across the Atlantic. By Mrs. Balmanno. *New York*, 1849. 8vo, pp. 8.

BALME. American States, Churches, and Slavery. By Rev. J. R. Balme. *Edinburgh*, *Nimmo*, 1862. Post 8vo, pp. lxviii., 546. + Second Edition. *London*, *Hamilton*, 1863. Post 8vo. + New Edition. With Synopsis of the American War. *London*, *Hamilton*, 1865. Post 8vo, pp. lxviii., 776. C. 2977

BALME. Letters on the American Republic, or, Common Fallacies and Monstrous Errors refuted and exposed. By Rev. Joshua R. Balme. ... *London*, *Hamilton*, *Adams & Co.*, 1863. 12mo, pp. vii., 112. + New Edition. *Ibid*, 1864. 12mo. 2978

BALME. Synopsis of the American War. By J. R. Balme. *London*, *Hamilton*, *Adams & Co.*, 1865. 12mo, pp. 547–776. B.

BALMIS (Francesco Saverio de). Demonstracion de las eficaces virtudes, nuevamente descubiertas en las Raices de dos plantas de Nueva España, especies de Agave y de Begonia, para la cura del vicio venereo, y Ecrofulosa, y de otras graves Enfermedades que resisten al uso de Mercurio, y demas remedios conocidos. Por Francesco Saverio de Balmis. *Madrid*, 1792. 4to. 2 Plates. 2980

BALMIS. Specifico antivenereo nuovamente scoperto nella virtù delle due piante americane, Agave e Begonia, prima traduzione dalla spagnuolo. *Roma*, *Paolo Gianchi*, 1795. 8vo, pp. 149. 2 Plates. 2981

BALMIS (F. X.) Über die amerikanische Pflanzen Agave und Begonia, als Mittel gegen Lustseuche ... . Aus dem Spanischen in's Italienische, und aus diesem ins Deutsche übersetzt von Friedr. Ludw. Kreisig. ... *Leipzig*, *Baumgärtner*, 1797. 8vo, pp. 156. Plates. 2982

BALTASAR (Jean). Noticia de la vida y preciosa muerte del P. Nicolas de Tamaral Jesuita misionero de Californias. *Mégico*, 1752. 4to. 2983

BALTASAR. Relacion de la vida y gloriosa muerte del P. Lorenzo Carranco Jesuita misionero de Californias. *Mégico*, 1751. 4to. 2984

BALTASAR. Vida del esclarecido P. Juan Gumersvac, de la Compañia de Jesus. *Mégico*, 1737. 4to. 2985

BALTASAR. Vida del Ven. P. Francisco Maria Picoli, Jesuita misionero de Californias. *Mégico*, 1730. 4to. 2986

BALTHASAR DE MEDINA. Chronica de la Santa Provincia de San Diego de Mejico de Religiosas Descalços de N. S. P. S. Francisco en la Nueva España, Vidas de Illustres y Venerables Varones etc. *Mexico*, 1682. Folio. 2987

At folio 230 is a map, "Auctor invenit, Antonius Ysartii Execud. Mexici 1682," which is probably the earliest specimen of copperplate engraving in Mexico, hitherto discovered. *Vide* Puttick's Catalogue, May, 1854, Lot 31, where it is said to be one of the rarest works of its class. It sold for £10.

BALTIMORE (*Lord*). *See* Calvert (George).

BALTIMORE. Relation of Lord Baltimore's Plantation. *See* Maryland.

BALTIMORE, A.D. 1862; or How they act in Baltimore. By A Volunteer Zouave. Fourth Edition. *Baltimore*, *James S. Waters*, 1862. 12mo, pp. 12. 2988

Baltimore, A.D. 1862; or the Volunteer Zouave in Baltimore. By an Officer of the "Guard." *Baltimore*, *J. Davis & Co.*, 1862. 12mo, pp. 7. 2989

Baltimore. A Short Account of the Establishment of the See, and of the Consecrating Dr. Carroll First Bishop; with a Discourse delivered on that Occasion ... . *London*, 1790. 8vo.

Baltimore and Ohio Railroad Company. Annual Report of the President, and Directors, to the Stockholders of the Baltimore and Ohio Rail Road Company. *Baltimore*, 1827. 8vo. Continued. 2991

This was one of the first railroad companies organized in the United States. The Annual Reports include much information relative to the country through which the road passes.

A History and Description of the Baltimore and Ohio Rail Road; with an Appendix, containing a full account of the ceremonies and procession attending the laying of the corner-stone, by Charles Carroll, of Carrollton, on the Fourth of July, 1828, and an original and complete report of the great opening celebration at Wheeling, January, 1853; to which is added a supplement. Illustrated by a Map and Six original Portraits. By a Citizen of Baltimore. *Baltimore*, *J. Murphy*, 1853. 8vo, pp. 200. Maps and Portraits. 2992

The following tracts are selected from a large number, as possessing some historical or geographical interest: Address and report of a select Com. of the B. & O. R. R. Co., also, a letter from the Pres't, recommending measures for the immediate prosecution of the road to the Ohio river. *Baltimore*, 1848. pp. 42. Address of Thomas Swann, Esq. (President,) ... on the ... Completion of the Road to the Ohio River, and the Report of B. H. Latrobe, Esq., Chief Engineer. *Baltimore*, 1849. 8vo, pp. 25. Address of Thomas Swann, Esq. May 1, [1850] in relation to ... providing for a Settlement of the Route West of Pile's Fork to the City of Wheeling. *Baltimore*, ... 1850. 8vo, pp. 70. Communication from the President ... to Thomas Donaldson, Esq., Chairman ... 1847. 8vo., pp. 17. Communication from the Balt. and Ohio R. R. Co. to the Mayor and City Council of Balt. *Baltimore*, 1831. pp. 14. Communication from Thomas Swann, Esq. ... on the Cumberland and Knobly Routes. 1849. 8vo, pp. 19. Contract between the City of Wheeling and the B. and O. R. Co., ... *Richmond*, *Printed by Colin*, *Baptist and Nowlan*, 1850. 8vo, pp. 24. Correspondence between the Secretary of War and the President of the B. & O. R. R. Co. in relation to additional routes between Washington and New York *Baltimore*, 1862. 8vo, pp. 14. Documents accompanying a Memorial of the President and Directors of the Baltimore and Ohio Railroad Company. 20th Congress, H. of R. *Washington*, 1828. 8vo. Documents submitted by the Baltimore and Ohio Railroad Company, in behalf of their application to the Legislature of Virginia. (With the reports of J. Knight, chief engineer, etc.) *Richmond*, 1838. 8vo, pp. 20. Laws and Ordinances relating to the B. and O. R. R. Co. *Baltimore*, *Lucas & Deaver*, 1836. 8vo, pp. 124. The Mayor and City Council of Baltimore *vs.* the B. and O. R. R. Co., containing the Bill, Answer, Testimony and Exhibits. *Baltimore*, ... 1857. 8vo, pp. 165. Memorial of the Citizens of Baltimore to the Mayor and City Council, in relation to the B. and O. R. R. 1836. 8vo, pp. 78. Objections to Yielding to Northerners the Control of the Baltimore and Ohio Rail Road, on which depends the Development of the Farms, Mines, Manufactures and Trade of the State of Maryland, By a Marylander. *Baltimore*, 1860. 8vo, pp. 25. Opinion on a portion of the location for the B. and O. R. R.: Addressed to the Rail-Road Committee of the ... City of Wheeling; by J. H. Alexander, Civil Engineer. *Baltimore*, 1850. 8vo, pp. 54. Reply of the Chief Engineer of the B. and O. R. R. Co. to the Review of his Report of February 15, 1849, on the Grave Creek and Fish Creek Routes by the Engineer of the City of Wheeling. *Richmond*, 1850. 8vo, pp. 51. Report and Documents submitted by the Committee appointed to confer with the Authorities of the City of Wheeling, respecting the late Law of Virginia, granting the right of way to the B. & O. R. R. Company. ... *Baltimore*, 1847. 8vo, pp. 67. 2 Maps. Report of the Engineers on the reconnoissance and surveys made in reference to the Baltimore and Ohio Railroad. *Baltimore*, *W. Woody*, 1828. 8vo, pp. 189. Report upon the surveys for the extension of the B. & O. R. R., from its present termination near Harper's Ferry, to Wheeling and Pittsburgh. *Baltimore*, *Lucas & Deaver*, 1838. pp. 138. Report of the Select Com. of B. & O. R. R. Co. appointed to prepare an exposition in reference to the Governor's message of January

4, 1840. *Baltimore*, *J. Murphy*, 1840. pp. 26. Reports of the Majority and Minority of the Committee on Western Connections of the B. and O. R. R. *Baltimore*, ... 1857. 8vo, pp. 21. Testimony taken before a Special Committee of the House of Delegates of Maryland, ... to inquire into the Allegations of Discriminations against the Citizens of Maryland, by the B. and O. R. R .... *Baltimore*, 1863. 8vo, pp. 32. "Viator," on the Baltimore & Ohio Rail Road Co. An Analysis of their Reports since 1848. Their Misrepresentations Sifted and Exposed, in a series of chapters. [1854.] 8vo, pp. 120.

Baltimore and Susquehannah Railroad Company. Memorial of the President and Directors. [*Baltimore*, 1835.] 8vo. 2993

Report and Proceedings in relation to the Baltimore and Susquehannah Railroad, Aug. 3, 1827. Report of president and directors. *Baltimore*, 1825. 8vo. Continued. 2994

Correspondence between the Honorable E. Louis Lowe, Governor of Maryland, and Robert Clinton Wright, President of the B. and S. R. R. Co., on the subject of the Future Prospects of the Road. *Baltimore*, 1853. 8vo, pp. 44. 2995

Baltimore as it Is. *Baltimore*, *J. W. Woods*, 1857. 12mo, pp. 185. 2996

The Baltimore Book: Edited by W. H. Carpenter and T. S. Arthur. *Baltimore*, 1839. 12mo. 2997

Baltimore Directory for 1796. By Thompson and Walker. *Baltimore*. 12mo. 2998

For 1799 ... By John Mullin. With Map. pp. 144. For 1802. C. W. Stafford. 12mo. For 1804 ... By James Robinson. 12mo, pp. 192. Continued at intervals, and afterwards annually, by various editors and publishers.

Baltimore Address Directory ... to which is prefixed a statistical article. By W. G. Lyford. *Baltimore*, 1836. 12mo, pp. 142. 2999

Baltimore Business Directory ... for 1853. 18mo. 3000

Baltimore Literary and Religious Magazine, for 1835; conducted by R. T. Breckinridge and A. B. Cross. *Baltimore*, 1835–37. 7 vols., 8vo. 3001

Baltimore Literary Monument, edited by J. M. McJilton and T. S. Arthur. Vol. I. 3002

Baltimore Phœnix and Budget: Monthly Magazine, April 1, 1841–March, 1842. *Baltimore*. 8vo. 3003

The Baltimore Repertory of Papers on Literary and other Topics, etc. *Baltimore*, 1811. 8vo. N. 3004

Baltimore Weekly Magazine. *Baltimore*, 1801. 4to. Continued. 3005

Baltimore Southern and Western Commercial Convention, Held in Baltimore, December 18th, 1852, under the Auspices of the Board of Trade. Full Report ... . (From the Baltimore American, Dec. 20.) [n. p., n. d.] 8vo, pp. 20. B. 3006

An Account of the Great Whig Festival, held in the City of Baltimore, November 12th, 1835. *Baltimore*, 1835. 8vo, pp. 40. 3007

An Act for the Establishment and Support of Public Schools, in the City of Baltimore. [n. p., n. d.] 8vo, pp. 16. 3008

Address of the Candidates of the American Party to the People of Baltimore. [n. p., n. d.] 8vo, pp. 4. 3009

Address of the City of Baltimore to the Citizens of Maryland, made in pursuance of resolutions passed in Town meeting ... friendly to internal improvements. *Baltimore*, 1836. 8vo, pp. 8.

Address of the Grand Jury to the Court of Oyer and Terminer for Baltimore County; and the Reply of the Court to that Address *Baltimore*, 1813. 8vo. N. 3011

First Annual Report of the Baltimore Association, for the Moral and Educational Improvement of the Colored People. [n. p.], *November*, 1865. 8vo, pp. 31. H. 3012

The Annual Report of the Baltimore Humane Impartial Society and Aged Women's Home, ... 1852. *Baltimore*, 1852. 8vo, pp. 12. H. 3013

Annual Report of the Board of Trade. *Baltimore*, 1851. 8vo. Continued. 3014

Annual Report of the Commissioners of Public Schools.

First Annual Report of the Ladies' Union Relief Association, of Baltimore. *Baltimore, Printed by W. M. Innes*, 1862. 8vo, pp. 13. H. 3016

Annual Report of the Executive Committee of the Union Relief Association of Baltimore, Made June 26th, 1862, with

Constitution and List of Officers and Members. *Baltimore*, 1862. 8vo, pp. 20. H. 3017

Continued till 1866.

Appeal for the establishment of a Free Library in Baltimore. 1856. 8vo. 3018

An Authentic Account of all the Proceedings on the 4th of July, 1815, with regard to laying the Corner Stone of the Washington Monument in Baltimore. *Baltimore*, 1815. 8vo, pp. 44. P. 3019

An Authentic Narrative of the Baltimore Mob of 1812. 1812. 12mo. 3020

Brief Account of the Origin and Services of the first Union Relief Association of Baltimore. 8vo, pp. 4. 3021

A Brief History of the Establishment of the Floating School of the City of Baltimore. *Baltimore, Bull & Tuttle*, 1860. 8vo, pp. 87. 3022

Catalogue of Books, &c. belonging to the Library Company of Baltimore. *Baltimore*, 1809. 8vo. + A Supplement, &c., 1816. *Baltimore*, 1816. 8vo, pp. 36. + Circular of the Shareholders of the Baltimore Library. 1854. pp. 60. 3023

Charter, Constitution, and Regulations of the Mercantile Library Association of Baltimore ... . Established November 14th, 1839. *Baltimore*, 1864. 8vo, pp. 9, (1). H. 3024

Citizen Soldiers at North Point and Fort McHenry, September 12th and 13th, 1814. Resolves of the citizens in town meeting. Particulars relating to the battle, official correspondence, &c. *Baltimore* [n. d.] 12mo. 3025

A Complete View of Baltimore, with a Statistical Sketch of its Institutions. *Baltimore*, 1831. 18mo. 3026

Communication from the Mayor of Baltimore with the Mayor and Board of Police of Baltimore City. *Frederick*, 1861. 8vo, pp. 8. 3027

Constitution & By-Laws of the Church Home Society ... . *Baltimore* [1855]. 32mo, pp. 15. H. 3028

Constitution and By-Laws of the Clerical Benevolent Asso-

ciation of the Diocese of Baltimore, Instituted September 29th, 1857. ... *Baltimore*, 1858. 8vo, pp. 12, (4). H. 3029

Constitution of the Young Men's Christian Association ... adopted December, 1864. ... *Baltimore*, 1865. 12mo, pp. 10. H.

Dedication of Green Mount Cemetery. *Baltimore*, 1839. 8vo, pp. 36. 3031

Dedicatory Services at the opening of Mount Olivet Cemetery. *Baltimore, Armstrong & Berry*, 1849. 8vo, pp. 20. 3032

Description of Washington Monument, and of the Public Buildings in Baltimore. *Baltimore, Printed by Hanzsche & Brother* [n. d.] 18mo, pp. 14. 3033

An Exact and Authentic Narrative of the events which took place in Baltimore on the 27th and 28th of July last ... To which is added a Narrative of Mr. John Thomson ... *Sept.* 1, 1812. 18mo, pp. 71. S. 3034

Expose of the Baltimore Custom House Frauds. By Honestus. 1849. 8vo. 3035

Historical Sketch of the Central High School, Baltimore, its wants and claims. *Baltimore*, 1850. 8vo, pp. 62. 3036

Inauguration Ceremonies and Address of Hon. Thos. Swann on the opening of Druid Hill Park, October 19th, 1860. *Baltimore*, 1860. 8vo, pp. 40. 3037

Interesting Papers relative to the Recent Riots at Baltimore. *Philadelphia*, 1812. 8vo, pp. 89. S. 3038

Journal of the Internal Improvement Convention ... in Baltimore ... December, 1834. *Baltimore*, 1835. 8vo, pp. 93, (1). H. 3039

List of Families and other Persons residing in Baltimore in 1752. 3040

Probably the first directory.

Memoranda concerning Baltimore City and surroundings. Dedicated to the Western Editors who visited Baltimore on an Editorial Excursion, in May and June, 1860. *Baltimore*, 1860. 12mo. Maps. 3041

Memorial of Chas. Howard, Wm. H. Gatchell, John W.

Davis, Police Commissioners of the City of Baltimore, to the Senate and House of Representatives of the United States. [1861.] 8vo, pp. 16. 3042

The Memorialists were prisoners in Fort McHenry.

Memorial of sundry Tallow Chandlers, of Baltimore, Maryland. *Washington, Gales & Seaton*, 1824. 8vo, pp. 5. 3043

Memorial of the Mayor and City Council of Baltimore to Congress, with accompanying Documents. *Baltimore, Wm. M. Innes*, 1861. 8vo, pp. 20. 3044

Relates to the suspending of the functions of the Board of Police.

The Memorial of the Merchants and Traders of the City of Baltimore. *Baltimore*, 1806. 8vo, pp. 49. 3045

Memorial of the Merchants of Baltimore, on the violation of Neutral Rights. *January* 29, 1806. Cong. Doc. 3046

Memorial of the Underwriters and Merchants of the city of Baltimore to Congress. [1823.] 12mo. 3047

Mercantile-Library Association of Baltimore. Annual Report of the Board of Directors. 1839. Continued. 8vo.

Minutes of the Baltimore Baptist Association. 1808. 8vo. Continued. 3049

Narrative of the Religious Fracas in the German Reformed Church, of Baltimore. 1804. 8vo. 3050

An Ordinance for the general Valuation and Assessment of Property in the City of Baltimore. Approved May 26, 1858. 8vo, pp. 18. 3051

Ordinances of the Corporation of the City of Baltimore, from February, 1797, to May, 1798. *Baltimore*, 1798. 8vo. P.

Ordinances of the Corporation of the City of Baltimore, with the Act of Incorporation and Supplement ... . *Baltimore, Printed by Warner and Hanna*, 1801. 8vo, pp. 329, xxxii., (42). B. + Added ... such Acts of the State Legislature ... as relate to ... Baltimore ... compiled ... by Samuel Young. *Baltimore, Printed by William Warner*, 1816. 8vo, pp. 305, 37. 3053

The Ordinances of the Mayor and City Council of Baltimore; to which is prefixed a Collection of Acts and Parts of

Acts of Assembly, relating to the Corporation. ... *Baltimore, Printed by John D. Toy*, 1838. 8vo, pp. 630. B. 3054

Other ordinances of the Corporation were published for the various and extra sessions, in 1803, 1804, and subsequent years.

Outline of a Plan to Unite the Baltimore Library Company with the Historical Society of Maryland. 8vo. 3055

Picture of Baltimore, Containing A Description of all Objects of Interest in the City; and Embellished with Views of the Principal Public Buildings. *Baltimore, F. Lucas, Junr.* [1832]. 18mo, pp. 249. Map, 2 Plates and Plan. 3056

The Poor in Baltimore: Three Classes. ... Eleventh Annual Report of the Baltimore Association for the Improvement of the Condition of the Poor. *Baltimore, John W. Woods, Printer*, [1860]. 8vo, pp. 32. 3057

Proceedings and Speeches at a Public Meeting of the Friends of the Union, in the City of Baltimore, held at Maryland Institute January 10th, 1861. *Baltimore, John D. Toy*, 1861. 8vo, pp. 56. 3058

Proceedings of sundry citizens of Baltimore, convened for the purpose of devising the most Efficient Means Of Improving the Intercourse between that City and the Western States. *Baltimore, Printed by William Woddy*, 1827. 8vo, pp. 38. 3059

Proceedings of the Joint Standing Committee on Water of the City Council, to whom was referred the Subject of a Supply of Water for the City of Baltimore. *Baltimore*, 1855. 8vo, pp. 56. H. 3060

Prospectus of the South Baltimore Company, with the Acts of Incorporation, 1832–1854–1856. *Baltimore, John W. Woods, Printer*, 1856. 8vo, pp. 15. 3061

Proceedings, Statements and Resolutions of a meeting of the Methodist Episcopal Church opposed to the late proceedings against members of the Baltimore Union Society. 1828. 8vo.

Remarks on the Intercourse of Baltimore with the Western Country, with a view of the Communications proposed between the Atlantic and the Western States. *Baltimore*, 1818. 8vo, pp. 30. Map. M. 3063

Report of a Committee of the Baltimore Young Men's Society on Lotteries, May 13th, 1834. *Baltimore*, 1834. 8vo, pp. 24. 3064

Report of the Baltimore Christian Association, Auxiliary to the Christian Commission, for the Year Ending, May 1st, 1863. ... *Baltimore, J. W. Woods*. 12mo, pp. 12. 3065

Report of the Commissioners appointed to examine into the practicability of a Canal from Baltimore to the Potomac, Together with the Engineer's Report. *Baltimore, J. Lucas*, 1823. 8vo, pp. 69. 3066

Report of the Committee of Internal Improvement made to the Trade Convention of the City of Baltimore. *Baltimore, Sands & Nelson*, 1835. 8vo, pp. 20. 3067

Report of the Committee of the Stockholders of the Canton Company of Baltimore, in Boston and its Vicinity, June 13, 1838. *Boston*, 1838. 8vo, pp. 15. Map. B. 3068

Report of the Baltimore Christian Association, auxiliary to the Christian Commission, for ... 1863. ... *Baltimore* [1863]. 12mo, pp. 12. 3069

Report of the Board of Commissioners to the Mayor and City Council, relative to the city boundaries, avenues, etc. *Baltimore, J. Lucas*, 1852. 8vo, pp. 16. 3070

[First Annual] Report [for 1829] of the Commissioners of Public Schools, to the City Council of Baltimore. [No imprint. 1830.] 8vo, pp. 17. Continued. H. 3071

Report of the Committee of Grievances and Courts of Justice of the House of Delegates of Maryland, on the subject of the recent Mobs and Riots in the city of Baltimore; together with the depositions taken before the Committee. *Annapolis, Jonas Green*, 1813. 8vo, pp. v., 346, Deposition, 1 l. + *Baltimore, Reprinted*, 1813. 8vo, pp. 88. 3072

Report of the Maryland Commissioners on a proposed Canal from Baltimore to Conewago. *Baltimore, T. Lucas*, 1823. 8vo, pp. 84. 3073

Report of the Engineer appointed by the Commissioners of the Mayor and City Council of Baltimore upon the subject of the Maryland Canal. *Baltimore, Lucas & Deaver*, 1837. 8vo.

Report of the Police Commissioners of Baltimore City, with accompanying Documents. *Baltimore*, 1861. 8vo. 3075

Relative to the scenes in Baltimore during the Civil War.

Report of the Visitors of the Jail ... . *Baltimore*, 1846. 8vo, pp. 19. H. 3076

Report to the Legislature on the State of Affairs in Baltimore. 1860. 8vo. 3077

Reports and Resolutions of the Joint Committee of Senate and House of Delegates of Maryland upon the reports and memorials of the Police Commissioners and the Mayor and City Council of Baltimore. *Frederick G. S. Riley*, 1861. 8vo, pp. 26. 3078

Review of a Correspondence between the Archbishop and the Mayor of Baltimore. 1839. 8vo. 3079

Resolutions passed by The Citizens of Baltimore, in Mass Meeting assembled, January 31, 1866, against "The Sunday Law" ... . [n. p., n. d.] 8vo, pp. 3. 3080

Rules and Regulations for the Government of the Baltimore Club [n. d.] 12mo, pp. 8. 3081

Rules of Order and Regulations, adopted by the Board of Commissioners of Public Schools ... . May, 1864. *Baltimore*, 1846. 8vo, pp. 19. H. 3082

A Series of Letters and other Documents relating to the late Epidemic or Yellow Fever in Baltimore. By a Baltimore Physician. ... *Baltimore*, 1820. Sm. 8vo, pp. 211. P. 3083

Sketch of Loudon Park Cemetery: its Dedication, and Address of the Hon. Charles F. Mayer, delivered on that occasion. *Baltimore*, 1853. 8vo, pp. 23. 3084

The Stranger's Guide in Baltimore, showing the easiest and best mode of seeing all the Public Buildings and places of note in and around the City, and in the neighborhood; together with some brief observations on its Trade, Resources, Prosperity, Commercial Advantages, and Future Prospects. Embellished with a Map of the City and Views of the Principal Public Buildings. By a Baltimorean. *Baltimore, John Murphy & Co.* [n. d.] 18mo. 3085

To Capitalists and Citizens of Baltimore. The Western Maryland Rail Road. [n. d.] 8vo, pp. 19. 3086

To the Citizens of Baltimore. *Baltimore*, 1829. 8vo, pp. 21.

Relates to the affair of Los damos Argentinos.

To the Pewholders and other Contributors of St. Paul's Church, Baltimore. 1804. 8vo. 3088

A Voice from the "Aged Guard of '62" of the City of Baltimore. [n. d.] 3089

Baltzell (John). An Essay on the Mineral Properties of the Sweet Springs of Virginia, and Conjectures respecting the Processes of their Production by Nature. ... *Baltimore, Werner and Hanna*, 1802. 8vo, pp. 30. 3090

Baluffi (G.) L'America, un tempo spagnuola riguardata sotto l'aspetto religioso dall' epoca del suo discuoprimento sino al 1843 di monsignore Gaetano Baluffi arcivescovo di Camerino ... . *Ancona, per Gustavo Sartorj Cherubini*, 1844. 2 vols., 8vo, pp. xxxiii., 274, 3 l.; 335, (1), 2 l. folded, 2 l. 3091

Translated into German, with the following title:

Baluffi. Das vormals Spanische Amerika aus dem religiösen Gesichtspunkte betrachtet, vom Zeitraume seiner Entdeckung an bis 1843. Aus dem Italienischen verdeutscht und mit Anmerkungen und Citaten begleitet von F. M. M. 1. Bd. 1. Hälfte. *Wien, Mechitharisten-Congregat-Buchandlung*, 1848. 8vo, pp. xxiv., 140. 3092

Banchero (G.) La tavola di bronzo, il pallio di Seta ed il codice Colombo-americano nuovamente illustrati. *Genova*, 1857. 4to. Plates. 3093

Bancroft (Aaron). The Committees vindicated. An Examination of The Rev. Mr. Barstow's "Remarks on the Preliminary History of Two Discourses, by Rev. A. Bancroft." *Keene, N. H.*, 1822. 8vo, pp. 22. H. 3094

Bancroft. A Discourse ... before the Second Congregational Society in Worcester ... April [8], 1827 ... [after] the Ordination of Rev. Alonzo Hill. By Aaron Bancroft ... . *Worcester*, 1827. 8vo, pp. 20. H. 3095

Bancroft. An Essay on the Life of George Washington, Commander in Chief of the American Army, through the Revolutionary War; and the First President of the United States. By Aaron Bancroft, A.A.S. Pastor of a Congregational Church in Worcester. *Worcester, Printed by Thomas & Sturtevant, October*, 1807. 8vo, 2 p. l., pp. vii., 552. Portrait. H. 3096

See Ecl. Rev., Series IV., Vol. IV., 489. Reprinted with the following title:

BANCROFT. Life of George Washington, Commander in Chief of the American army through the Revolutionary War, and the First President of the United States. By Aaron Bancroft. *London, John Stockdale*, 1808. 8vo, pp. xii., 560. + Second Edition. *Boston*, 1826. 2 vols., 12mo. + Also, 183. 2 vols., 12mo, pp. 223; 218. + *Boston, Phillips, Sampson, and Company*, 1855. 12mo, pp. 218. 3097

BANCROFT. An Eulogy on the Character of the Late Gen. George Washington. Delivered before the Inhabitants of the Town of Worcester, Commonwealth of Massachusetts, on Saturday the 22d of February 1800. By Aaron Bancroft. Printed according to a Vote of said Town, requesting a Copy for the Press, and directing that each Head of a Family should be furnished with one. *Worcester, Printed by Isaiah Thomas, Jun., March*, 1800. 8vo, pp. 21. H. 3098

BANCROFT. The Nature and Worth of Christian Liberty ... a Sermon ... in Worcester ... June [23], 1816. With ... Strictures on the Attempt to establish Consociation in Massachusetts. By Aaron Bancroft ... . Second Edition. *Worcester, Printed by William Manning, July*, 1816. 8vo, pp. 35. + *September*, 1816. 8vo, pp. 35. H. 3099

BANCROFT. A Sermon, Preached before his Excellency Caleb Strong ... May 27, 1801, the day of General Election. ... *Boston, Young & Minns*, 1801. 8vo, pp. 29. H. 3100

BANCROFT. Sermon preached Feb. 15, 1802, before the Senate and House of Representatives of Massachusetts, on the Day of the Interment of Lieut.-Gov. Samuel Phillips. By Aaron Bancroft. *Boston*, 1802. 8vo, pp. 21. 3101

BANCROFT. A Sermon [at Worcester] ... July 9th, 1826 ... [on] the Death of the Hon. John Adams, a Former President of theUnited States. ... *Worcester, Charles Griffin*, 1826. 8vo, pp. 15. H. 3102

BANCROFT. ... A Sermon, delivered before the Second Christian Church and Society in Worcester, on the Sixth Day of January, 1811. *Worcester, Printed by Isaac Sturtevant*, 1811. 8vo, pp. 24. H. & W. 3103

Contains notes on the history of the town.

BANCROFT. A Sermon delivered in Worcester, January 31, 1836, by Aaron Bancroft, D.D. at the Termination of Fifty Years of his Ministry. ... *Worcester, Clarendon Harris*, 1836. 8vo, pp. 44. H. 3104

BANCROFT. A Vindication of the Result of the late Mutual Council convened in Princeton. By Aaron Bancroft, D.D. *Worcester, Printed by William Manning, June*, 1817. 8vo, pp. 63. H. 3105

Also: A Discourse ... at Windsor ... Vermont, on the 23d of June, MDCCXC. at the Ordination of the Rev. Samuel Shuttlesworth ... . *Worcester, Printed by Isaiah Thomas*, MDCCXC. 8vo, pp. 24. H. A Sermon delivered at Brimfield on the 20th of June, 1798, at the Installation of the Rev. Clark Brown. ... *Worcester*, 1798. 8vo, pp. 23. Masonic Sermon at Worcester, June 11, 1793. *Worcester*, 1793. 8vo. Sermon occasioned by the Execution of Samuel Frost, at Worcester, Oct. 31. 1793. *Worcester*. 8vo. ... An Oration ... before the ... Leicester Academy, on the Fourth of July, 1806; At Opening of a New Building ... . *Worcester, Printed by Thomas & Sturtevant, July*, 1806. 8vo, pp. 20. H. Sermon at the Ordination of Nathan Parker. *Portsmouth*, 1808. 8vo, pp. 31. Sermon at Worcester, Jan. 1817, on the Duties of the 4th Commandment. 2d Ed. *Worcester*. 8vo. Discourse on Conversion. *Worcester*, 1818. 8vo. ... Sermon [at Worcester], ... November 22, 1818, the Sunday following the Interment of Mrs. Mary Thomas. ... *Worcester, Printed by William Manning, December*, 1818. 8vo, pp. 23. H. A Sermon ... at the Installation of the Rev. Luther Willson, ... in Petersham, June 23, 1819. *Worcester, Printed by William Manning, July*, 1819. 8vo, pp. 28. H. Sermon at Keene, N. H., 15 August, 1819. *Worcester*, 1821. 8vo. A Discourse Delivered before the Convention of Congregational Ministers of Massachusetts, ... June 1, 1820. ... *Boston, Printed by Wells and Lilly*, 1820. 8vo, pp. 32. H. Sermons on the Doctrines of the Gospel. *Worcester, May*, 1822. 8vo, pp. 429, (1). H. Discourse at Worcester, April 28, 1824, before the Worcester Auxiliary Society for ameliorating the Condition of the Jews. *Worcester*. 8vo. A Sermon at the Installation of Rev. Andrew Bigelow ... in Medford, July 9, 1823. *Boston*, 1823. 8vo, pp. 23. H. A Sermon ... in Shrewsbury, at the Interment of the Rev. Joseph Sumner, D.D. December 13, 1824. ... *Worcester, S. B. Manning, Printer, April*, 1825. 8vo, pp. 15. H. A Sermon ... at the Dedication of the Second Congregational Church in Worcester, Aug. 20, 1829. ... *Worcester, Griffin and Morrill, Printers*, 1829. 8vo, pp. 24. B. Compare, also: Letters and Remarks, occasioned by a Sermon, delivered by the Rev. Aaron Bancroft, A.M., November 30, MDCCXCV., in Opposition to the Doctrine of Election. *Worcester, L. Worcester*, MDCCXCV. 8vo, pp. 30. B. Review (extracted from the Panoplist.) of Dr. Bancroft's Discourse, against Conferences. *Boston, Samuel T. Armstrong*, 1817. 8vo, pp. 16. H. Review of Dr. Bancroft's Appendix to the 2d Edition of his Discourse on the 4th Commandment. *Worcester*, 1817. 8vo.

[BANCROFT (Edward)]. An Essay on the Natural History of Guiana, In South America. Containing A Description of many Curious Productions in the Animal and Vegetable Systems of that Country. Together with an Account of The Religion, Manners, and Customs of several Tribes of its Indian Inhabitants. Interspersed with A Variety of Literary and Medical Observations. In Several Letters from A Gentleman of the Medical Faculty, During his Residence in that Country. ... *London, T. Becket and P. A. De Hondt*, MDCCLXIX. 8vo, pp. (4), iv., 402, Contents, 1 l. Plate. H. 3106

"A very useful and entertaining work."—RICH.

BANCROFT. Naturgeschichte von Guiana in Süd-Amerika. ... Aus dem Englishen. ... *Frankfurt und Leipzig, J. Dodsley und Compagnie*, 1769. 8vo, pp. x., (2), 248. Plate. H. 3107

BANCROFT. Proeve over de natuurlyke geschiedenis van Guana. *Utrecht, A. van Paddenburg en J. M. van Vloten*, 1782. 8vo. 3108

BANCROFT. Beschryving van Guiana, en een bericht van de rivieren en plantagien Berbice, Essequebo en Demerary. In Brieven. *Amsterdam*, 1794. 8vo. 3109

BANCROFT. Facts and Observations briefly stated in support of an intended application to Parliament. [n. p.], 1798. 8vo.

"Relates to Quercitron Bark."—RICH.

[BANCROFT (Edward)]. Remarks on the Review of the Controversy between Great Britain and her Colonies. In which The Errors of its Author are exposed, and The Claims of the Colonies vindicated, Upon the Evidence of Historical Facts and authentic Records. To which is subjoined, A Proposal for terminating the present unhappy Dispute with the Colonies; Recovering their Commerce; Reconciliating their Affection; Securing their Rights; And establishing their Dependence on a just and permanent Basis. Humbly submitted to the Consideration of the British Legislature. *London, T. Becket and P. A. De Hondt*, MDCCLXIX. 8vo, Half Title, Title, pp. 126. C.

Reprinted with the above title and the author's name, as: By Edward Bancroft. [Motto.] *London; Printed in the Year* 1769. *New-London, in New-England; Re-printed and Sold by T. Green*, M,DCC,LXXI. 8vo, pp. 130. B. "The Review of the American Controversy [by William Knox] is here sharply and successfully attacked, by an able hand; who, attending to the obvious import of words in the charters of the principal colonies, and the general tenor of those transactions wherein they have been concerned, proves them to be distinct dependencies, not included within the realm of England, but having constitutions framed after the same model."—M. R., XLI., 49. *See also* Rich I., 171 and 505.

BANCROFT (E. Nathaniel). An Essay on the Disease called Yellow Fever. ... . By Edward N. Bancroft, M.D. *London*, 1808. 8vo. + Second Edition. *London*, 1811. 8vo, pp. 811. + Third Edition, with Notes by B. Davidge. *London*, 1820. 8vo. + *Baltimore*, 1820. 8vo. 3112

See Edinb. Med. and Surg. Jour., July, 1812, VIII., 324–344.

BANCROFT. A Sequel to An Essay on the Yellow Fever, principally intending to prove by Incontestable Facts and Important Documents that the Fever called Bulam or Pestilential, has no Existence as a Distinct or a Contagious Disease. *London, Callow*, 1817. 8vo, pp. 487. 3113

See Lond. Med. Repos., Nov., 1817; VIII., 401–417.

BANCROFT (George). Address at Hartford before the Delegates to the Democratic Convention of the Young Men of Connecticut, on the Evening of February 18, 1840, by George Bancroft. ... [No title-page.] 8vo, pp. 16. H. 3114

BANCROFT. Fellow Citizens ... . [Attack upon him in reference to his intention to deliver a "Democratic Address." *Boston*, 1839?] 4to, 1 page. H. 3115

BANCROFT. History of the United States, from the Discovery of the American Continent to the Present Time. By George Bancroft. *Boston, Little, Brown & Co.*, 1834. 8vo, Vol. I., pp. xii., 469, 1834; II., viii., 468, 1837; III., viii., 477, 1840; IV., with Portrait of John Adams, and Maps, x., 462, 1852; V., ix., 459, 1852; VI., xix., 528, 1854; VII., 1858; VIII., with Portrait of Jefferson, 475, 1860; IX., 1776 to 1778, with Portrait of La Fayette (4), 506, 1866. 3116

The above are the dates of the first edition of each volume. Vols. I.–III. have also title, "History of the Colonization of the United States. Vols. I.–III." Vols. IV.–VI. have also half title, "The American Revolution. Epoch First. ... 1748–1763; Epoch Second. ... 1763–1774; The Crisis." Vols. VII. and VIII. have also title, "The American Revolution. Vols. I.–III." Fifty copies of Vols. I.–VIII. are printed on large paper. *New York, Charles B. Richardson & Co.*, 1861. H. Repeatedly reprinted both in Boston and London. The English edition, by *Bentley*, also by *H. G. Bohn*, is in 8vo and 12mo; *Routledge*, in 12mo.

The variations between the first and later editions are so considerable as to make it desirable to possess them both. The additions concerning De Soto first appeared as * * * pages in the large paper edition.

BANCROFT. History of the United States, from the Discovery of the American Continent. *London, Routledge*, 1851–1867. 8 vols, 12mo. + New Edition. *London*, 1859–61. 7 vols., 8vo. 3117

Vols. I., II. and III. of the American edition, are included in Vols. I. and II. of this.

BANCROFT. History of the American Revolution. By George Bancroft. *London, R. Bentley*, 1852–54. 3 vols., 8vo. C. 3118

These volumes are a reprint of Vols. IV.–VI. of the History.

BANCROFT. History of the United States from the Discovery of the American Continent to the War of Independence. *London, W. S. Orr & Co.*, 1843. Rl. 8vo. pp. 584. 3119

See N. A. R., XL., 99; LII., 75. Ed. Rev., LXXXV., 61. Am. Q. R., XVI., 200. For. Q. R., XXVII., 327.

BANCROFT. History of the Colonization of the United States. *London, Fullarton* [n. d.] Rl. 8vo. 3120

BANCROFT. History of the Colonization of the United States. By George Bancroft. Abridged by the Author. ... *Boston, Charles C. Little and James Brown*, 1841. 2 vols., 16mo, pp. xvi., 332, Map; xv., 316, Plate. H. 3121

BANCROFT. History of the United States. *London, Fullarton* [n. d.] Rl. 8vo. 3122

BANCROFT. Histoire des États-Unis depuis la découverte du continent américain, traduite de l'anglais par Mlle Isabelle Gatti de Gamond. *Bruxelles, Lacroix, Verbœckhoven et Cie*, 1862–64. 9 vols., 8vo. 3123

BANCROFT. Geschichte der Vereinigten Staaten von Nordamerika ... . Nach der 9. Aufl. des Originals deutsch von A. Kretzschmar. *Leipzig, O. Wigand*, 1845–64. 8 vols., 8vo. + Ier Band., 2^e Aufl. 1847. 3124

BANCROFT. Geschichte der amerikanischen Revolution von Georg Bancroft. Aus dem Englischen von W. E. Drugulin Mit einem Vorworte von Fr. Bülau. ... *Leipzig, Lorck*, 1852–54. 3 vols., 8vo, pp. xx., 386, Plan, 4to; xii., 404; xx., 434. (Moderne Geschichtschreiber, herausg. von Friedrich Bülau, Ier Bd.) 3125

BANCROFT. Storia degli Stati Uniti, volgarizzata con note da C. Carenzi. *Losanna et Torini*, 1847. 8vo. A. 3126

BANCROFT. De Forenede Staters Historie oversat af. Chr. Wulff. *Kjöbenhavn, Lose and Delbanco*, 1853–55. 6 vols. 3127

BANCROFT. Joseph Reed: a Historical Essay. By George Bancroft. ... *New York, W. J. Widdleton*, 1867. 8vo, pp. 64. H. 3128

BANCROFT. The League for the Union. Speeches of the Hon. George Bancroft, and James Miliken, Esq. *Philadelphia, William S. & Alfred Martien*, 1863. 8vo, pp. 20. 3129

BANCROFT. ... Letter on the Exchange of Prisoners during the American War of Independence. [*New York*, 1862.] 8vo, pp. 7. H. 3130

BANCROFT. Literary and Historical Miscellanies. By George Bancroft. *New York, Harper and Brothers*, 1855. 8vo, pp. 517. 3131

BANCROFT. Memorial Address on the Life and Character of Abraham Lincoln, delivered, at the Request of both Houses of the Congress of America, before them, in the House of Representatives at Washington, on the 12th of February, 1866. By George Bancroft. *New York*, 1866. 8vo, pp. 69. + *Washington, Government Printing Office*. 8vo, pp. 69. Portrait. H. 3132

Of this edition 50 copies were printed on large paper imperial 4to, with an addition to the Appendix (pp. 71–80), "Correspondence relating to the Memorial Address." H.

BANCROFT. Éloge funèbre du President Lincoln, prononcé en séance solennelle du Congrès des États-Unis d'Amérique. Traduction de l'Anglais par Gustave Jottrand. *Bruxelles, Verbœckhoven et Cie*, 1866. 8vo, pp. 43. 3133

BANCROFT. The Merits of Thomas W. Dorr, etc. *See* [Curtis (G. T.)]

BANCROFT. New-York Historical Society. Mr. Bancroft's Letter on the Exchange of Prisoners, during the American War of Independence. [*New York*, 1862.] 8vo, pp. 7. H. 3134

BANCROFT. Mr. Bancroft and his Boston Critics. [*New York?* 1862.] 8vo, pp. 4. H. 3135

Relative to the exchange of prisoners.

BANCROFT. The Necessity, the Reality, and the Promise, of the Progress of the Human Race. Oration delivered before the New York Historical Society, November 20, 1854. *New York*, M DCCC LIV. 8vo, pp. 5–37 of the "Semi-Centennial Celebration ... of the New York Historical Society." H. 3136

Has a separate title-page.

BANCROFT. ... Oration by George Bancroft, on the Twenty-second of February, 1862. To which is added Washington's Farewell Address. *New York, E. D. Baker, April 15th*, 1862. 12mo, pp. 103–126. B. 3137

Pulpit and Rostrum, No. 29.

BANCROFT. Review of the Report of the Committee of Ways and Means; and of the Message of the President of the United States, relative to the United States Bank. From the American Quarterly Review—March, 1831. *Philadelphia, Carey and Lea*, 1831. 8vo, pp. 38. H. 3138

BANCROFT. Oration Pronounced in Union Square, April 25, 1865, at the Funeral Obsequies of Abraham Lincoln in the City of New York. By George Bancroft. *New York, Schermerhorn & Co.* 12mo, pp. 23. Portrait. 3139

Forms Nos. 34 and 35 of The Pulpit and Rostrum.

BANCROFT. An Oration delivered on the Fourth of July, 1826, at Northampton, Mass. By George Bancroft. *Northampton, T. Watson Shepard, Printer*, 1826. 8vo, pp. 26. H., W. 3140

BANCROFT. Oration delivered before the Democracy of Springfield, and Neighboring Towns, July 4, 1836. *Springfield*, 1836. 8vo, pp. 40. + Second edition, with Prefatory Remarks, *Springfield*, 1836. 8vo. 3141

BANCROFT. Poems. By George Bancroft. *Cambridge, Hilliard & Metcalf*, 1823. 12mo, pp. 77. A. 3142

W. J. Davis' copy sold for $40 in 1862. It has since (1867) sold for $2.50.

BANCROFT (H. H.) Bancroft's Hand-Book Almanac, Official Register and Business Directory for the Pacific States and Territories, etc., etc., for the year 1864. Edited by Wm. H. Knight. (Third year.) 18mo, pp. 440. 3143

Contains an Historical Memoir on the past and present condition of the Indian Tribes of the two Californias, by R. Taylor.

BANCROFT (Joseph). Census of the City of Savannah ... with Statistics ... Historical Notices, and a Commercial Directory ... . Second Edition. *Savannah, Edward J. Purse, Printer*, 1848. 12mo, pp. 96. Map. B. 3144

BANCROFT (Luther S.) Address to the Prescott Guards, and to the Inhabitants of Pepperell, June 17, 1830. By Luther S. Bancroft. *Groton, Mass.*, 1830. 8vo. 3145

BANCROFT (W. L.) A New Railway Outlet from Chicago to the Seaboard. Port Huron and Lake Michigan Railroad Company — Chicago and Michigan Grand Trunk Railway Company. ... By W. L. Bancroft ... *Port Huron, Michigan*, 1866. 8vo, pp. 52. H. 3146

BANDINEL (J.) Some Account of the Trade in Slaves from Africa as connected with Europe and America. By James Bandinel, Esq. *London, Longman*, 1842. 8vo, pp. xv., 323. C. 3147

BANDINEL. Der afrikanische Sklavenhandel ... . Aus dem Englischen von Alex. Hechsel. *Berlin, Hermes*, 1843. 8vo, pp. 184. 3148

BANDINI. Vita e lettere di Amerigo Vespvcci gentilvomo fiorentino raccolte e illvstrate dall' abate Angelo Maria Bandini. *Firenze*, MDCCXLV. 4to, pp. lxxvi., 128, (1). Genealogical Table. H. 3149

This is an elaborate panegyric of Vespucius, in which he is called the Discoverer of America. The researches of later Spanish authors have shown Bandini's dates to be incorrect. *See* Rich, I., 81, "Journal étranger," Sept., 1756.

BANDINI. Americus Vespucci eines florenzischen Edelmannes, Leben und nachgelassene Briefe ... . Aus dem Italienischen des Herrn Abts Angelus Maria Bandini übersetzet, und mit Anmerkungen erläutert. *Hamburg, Georg Christian Grund, und Leipzig, Adam Heinrich Holle*, 1748. 8vo, pp. (10), 299, (9). Engraving. H. 3150

BANGOR (*Bp. of*). *See* Egerton (John), Herring (Thomas).

The Bangor Directory ... . *Bangor, Samuel S. Smith*, 1859. 12mo, pp. 142. Continued. H. 3151

The Bangor City Directory ... . To which is added a Directory of Brewer. *Bangor, W. F. Stanwood*, 1864. 12mo, pp. 215. 3152

BANGOR Journal of Literature, Science, Morals, and Religion, from June 1, 1837, to May 24, 1838. Ed. by Rev. Thomas Curtis. *Bangor*, 1837–38. 4to. 3153

Act to incorporate the Bangor and Piscataquis Canal and Railroad Company [Me.] [n. p.], 1833. 12mo, pp. 11. 3154

The City Charter and Ordinances of the City of Bangor. *Bangor, Printed by James Burton, Jr.*, 1834. 12mo, pp. 67. H.

The Charter and Ordinances of the City of Bangor, with the Acts of the Legislature relating to the City. ... *Bangor, Smith & Sayward, Printers*, 1851. 8vo, pp. 7, 208. B. 3156

Catalogue of the Theological Institution, Bangor, Maine. 1833–34 [etc.] *Bangor*, 1834 [etc.] 8vo. Continued. 3157

General Catalogue of the Theological Seminary, Bangor, Me., 1854. *Bangor*, 1854. 8vo, pp. 22. 3158

Report on the Affairs of the Bank of Bangor. *Boston*, 1822. 8vo. 3159

A Survey of the Theological Seminary, at Bangor, Me. Published ... by the Trustees. *Bangor, Burton & Carter, Printers*, 1830. 8vo, pp. 20. 3160

Bangs (Edward), *Esq.* An Oration delivered at Worcester, ... fourth of July, 1791. ... By Edward Bangs, Esq. *Worcester, Isaiah Thomas*, 1791. 4to, pp. 16. H. 3161

Bangs. An Oration ... at Worcester, July 4, 1800. By Edward Bangs, Esq. *Worcester, Isaiah Thomas, Jun.*, 1800. 8vo, pp. 30, (1). H. 3162

Bangs (E. Dillingham). An Oration pronounced at Springfield, Mass. on the Fourth of July, 1823 ... . By Edward D. Bangs, Esq. ... *Springfield*, 1823. 8vo, pp. 16. W., H. 3163

Bangs. An Oration, pronounced at Sutton, Massachusetts, July 5th, 1813 ... . By Edward D. Bangs, Esq. ... *Boston, Printed by J. Belcher, for Henry Rogers, Worcester*, 1813. 8vo, pp. 16. H. 3164

Bangs (Nathan). An Authentic History of the Missions under the care of the Missionary Society of the Methodist Episcopal Church. By Nathan Bangs, D.D. ... *New-York*, 1832. 12mo. S. 3165

Bangs. A History of the Methodist Episcopal Church, from its Origin in 1776, to the General Conference in 1840. By Nathan Bangs, D.D. *New York*, 1838–1840. 4 vols., 12mo. + Third Edition, revised and corrected. *New-York*, 1845–53. 4 vols., 12mo, pp. 371; 430; 447; 461, 44. 4 Portraits and 1 Plate. C. 3166

The third and fourth volumes are not noted as of a second or third edition, but they are copyrighted in 1840 and 1841. The tenth edition of Vol. I. appeared in 1857.

Bangs. Life of Rev. Freeborn Garrettson. By Nathan Bangs, D.D. Third Edition. *New York*, 1832. 12mo. + Fifth Edition. *New-York, Carlton & Porter* [n. d.] 16mo, pp. 294. Portrait. B. 3167

Bangs. The Present State, Prospects, and Responsibilities of the Methodist Episcopal Church, with an Appendix of Ecclesiastical Statistics. By N. Bangs, D.D. *New York*, 1850. 12mo. 3168

Also: The errors of Hopkinsianism detected and refuted. ... . *New-York*, 1815. 12mo, pp. 324. A Vindication of Methodist Episcopacy. *Cincinnati*, 1821. 12mo, pp. 166. The Substance of a Sermon preached on the opening of the Methodist Episcopal Church in John St., N. Y., Jan. 4, 1818. *New York*, 1818. 8vo, pp. 32. Emancipation, its necessity and means of accomplishment calmly Submitted to the Citizens of the United States. *New York*, 1846. 8vo, pp. 101. The Growth of the New York Conference, being the Substance of a Sermon delivered before that body, at its late Session in the City of Brooklyn, June 14, 1848. *Ne v York*, 1848. 8vo, pp. 24. A Centenary Sermon, preached in the Vestry St. Church in the City of New York, Oct. 25, 1839, on the 100th year of Methodism. *New York*, 1840. 8vo, pp. 26. A Discourse on the Death of Wilbur Fish, D.D., delivered in the Greene St. M. E. Church, N. Y., on the ... 29th March, 1839. *New York*, 1839. 8vo, pp. 24.

[Banister (Thomas)]. Britain and her Colonial Dependencies; and their Right to be represented in Parliament. *London, J. Hatchard and Son*, MDCCCXLIV. 8vo, pp. 24. H. 3169

The copy in Harvard College Library has fifty-two pages of MS. memoranda in reference to the same subject, signed Thomas Banister.

[Banister.] Letter to the Right Hon. the Lords Commissioners of Trade and Plantations; or, an Essay on the Principal Branches of Trade in New England. *London*, 1715. 8vo, pp. 19. 3170

Banister. Memoranda relating to the Present Crisis as regards our Colonies, our Trade, our Circulating Medium, and Railways. ... By Thomas Banister. Second Edition. *London, John Ollivier*, 1848. 8vo, pp. 8, (1). H. 3171

Banister (William B.) An Oration at Newburyport ... [July 4, 1809]. By William B. Banister, Esq. *Newburyport, Press of E. W. Allen*, 1809. 8vo, pp. 20. H. 3172

Bank Bills, or Paper Currency, and the Banking System of Massachusetts: with Remarks on Present High Prices. By a Conservative. *Boston, Little, Brown and Company*, 1856. 8vo, pp. 16. C. & H. 3173

The Bank Dinner; an Exposé of the Court Party of Kentucky. *Louisville*, 1825. 8vo, pp. 61. 3174

Bank Secrets of the Bank of Columbia. [n. p.], 1801. 4to. C.

Bank Tax and Bank Currency. An Appeal to the Congress of the United States, by a Committee of New Jersey State Bank Officers. *Trenton (N. J.), American Office*, 1864. 8vo, pp. 18. 3176

Banks and Paper Currency; Their effects upon Society, by a Friend of the People. [No imprint.] 8vo, pp. 12. 3177

First Annual Report of the Board of Managers of the Association of Banks, for the Suppression of Counterfeiting. *Boston, Prentiss & Sawyer, Printers*, 1854. 8vo, pp. 36. Continued. H.

Letter from the Secretary of the Treasury, transmitting Reports as to the condition of Banks throughout the United States, March 3, 1857. *Washington*. 8vo. + *Washington*, 1850. 8vo.

Observations on incorporating New Banks. *Philadelphia*, 1812. 8vo. 3180

Proceedings of the Friends of a National Bank, at their Public Meeting, held in Boston, Fifteenth July, 1841. ... *Boston*, 1841. 8vo, pp. 32. H. 3181

Reasons against a National Bank. *New York*, 1841. 8vo.

Reflections excited by the present state of Banking Operations in the United States. By a Virginian. *Washington*, 1818. 8vo. 3183

Remarks on Banks and Banking, and the Skeleton of a Project for a National Bank. By a Citizen of Boston. *Boston*, 1840. 8vo, pp. 62. 3184

Remarks on Currency and Banking. *See* Appleton (N.), No. 1817.

Remarks on Private Banking, addressed to Hon. Isaac Pierson. *Albany*, 1818. 8vo, pp. 28. 3185

Remarks on the Banks and Currency of the New England States; ... To show the Public Benefits resulting from the System pursued by the Allied Banks in Boston. ... *Boston, William L. Lewis, Printer*, 1826. 8vo, pp. 40. H. 3186

Report from the Secretary of the Treasury on the present System of Keeping and Disbursing the Public Money, 1834. C.

Report of the Tax Committees of the New York, Boston, and Philadelphia Clearing House Associations, upon the Acts of Congress Relating to Banks organized by or under the State Authorities. *New York, C. S. Westcott & Co.*, 1863. 8vo, pp. 16. 3188

Bank of the United States *vs.* Osborn and others. State of the Case and Argument for the Apellants, in the Case of the Bank of the United States *versus* the Auditor and Treasurer of the State of Ohio and others, in the Supreme Court of the United States. *Cincinnati*, 1823. 8vo. C. 3189

A large number of pamphlets were issued relating to the Bank of the United States. The following are among the more important that have come under my notice: An Act to incorporate the Subscribers to the Bank of the United States. *Philadelphia*, 1816. 18mo, pp. 56. Brief Review of the Origin, Progress, and Administration of the Bank of the United States. *Philadelphia*, 1819. 12mo, pp. 44. Considerations on the Bank of the U. States, 1832. *See* [Young (S.)] ... April 13, 1830. ... Report: [of] the Committee of Ways and Means ... [on] the Bank of the United Stetes ... . [*Washington*, 1830.] 8vo, pp. 31 (1), 2 l. folded. H. Examination of the President, Cashiers and Directors of the United States Bank, to which is prefixed the Report of the Committee appointed to investigate its proceedings, etc. *New York*, 1816. 8vo. Judicial Decisions, upon the Cases of Habeas Corpus, brought by the late officers of the Bank ... *Philadelphia, J. Perry*, 1842. 8vo, pp. 45. The Memorial of Henry D. Gilpin, John T. Sullivan, and Peter Wager, of Pennsylvania, and Hugh M'Elderry, of Maryland, Directors of the Bank of the United States: appointed by the President, by and with the advice and consent of the Senate. [1841]. 8vo, pp. 55. Narrative and Correspondence concerning the Removal of Deposits, and Occurrences connected therewith. *Philadelphia*, 1838. 8vo, pp. 175. Observations on the Bank of the United States. *Annapolis* [n. d.] 8vo. C. Proceedings of the stockholders of the Bank of the United States, preparatory to the creation of a trust for closing the concerns. *Philadelphia*, 1811. 8vo, pp. 39. P. Proceedings of the Stockholders ... 28th Oct. 1816 and 6th Jan. 1817. *Philadelphia*, 1817. pp. 12. Remarks upon the Bank of the U. S., 1831. *See* [Henshaw (David)]. Report of the committee of the House of Representatives of United States, appointed 30th Nov. 1818, on the Bank of the United States. *Washington*, 1819. 8vo. Report of Committee ... to inspect the Books of the Bank ... Read Jan. 16, 1819. 8vo, pp. 166, 19 Tables. (H. of Rep. Doc't). Report of the Joint Committee ... of the General Assembly of Ohio, on the Communication of the Auditor of State Upon the ... proceedings of the Bank of the United States, against the Officers of State, in the United States' Circuit Court. ... *Concord* [*N. H.*], *June*, 1821. 8vo, pp. 64. H. Report of the Condition of the Bank of the United States, by the Committee of inspection and investigation, &c., appointed 1822. Adopted by the Stockholders. *Philadelphia*, 1822. 8vo, pp. 88. Report of the Proceedings of the Triennial Meeting of the Stockholders of the Bank of the United States. ... First Day of September, 1828. *Philadelphia*, 1828. 8vo, pp. 18. H. + Also, 1831. Report of the Bank of the United States. Sept. 1831. *Philadelphia*, 1831: 8vo. Reports of the Committee of Inquiry appointed March 14, 1832, by the H. of R. at Washington, concerning the Bank of the United States. [No imp.] 8vo, pp. 112. Reports of the Minority of the Committee, and of Mr. Adams, (one of the Members of the Committee,) appointed to examine the Books

and Proceedings of the Bank of the United States. *Washington*, 1832. Large 8vo, pp. 29. H. 22d Congress 1st Session [31] Report of the Secretary of the Treasury ... transmitting [the names of the foreign stockholders of the Bank of the U. States]. *Washington*, 1832. 8vo, pp. 103. P. Report of the Bank of the United States to the Committee of Ways and Means of the H. of R. Jan. 28, 1833. [*Philadelphia*, 1833.] 8vo, pp. 23. P. Report of a Committee of Directors of the Bank of the United States. [n. p., 1833.] 8vo, pp. 48. H. + [n. p., 1833.] 8vo, pp. 36. H. ... Report [of] ... the Committee of Ways and Means ... . [*Washington*, 1833.] 8vo, pp. 184. (22d Cong. 2d Sess. House Rep. No. 121.) B. & H. ... Report: [of] The Committee of Finance ... [on] the Bank of the United States ... . [*Washington*, 1834.] 8vo, pp. 48. (23d Cong., 2d Sess. Senate Doc. No. 17.) H. Report of the Committee of Investigation Appointed at the Meeting of the Stockholders of the Bank .. Jan. 4, 1841. *Philadelphia*, 1841. 8vo, pp. 79. Report of the Investigating Committee, April, 1841. *Boston*, 1841. 8vo. Report of a Committee of Directors of the Bank of the United States. [No imprint.] 8vo, pp. 41. Report of the Committee of Directors of the Bank of the United States. 8vo, pp. 52. Report of the Joint Committee of Valuation of the Bank ... 8vo, pp. 27. Rules and Regulations for the Government of ... *Philadelphia*, 1817. 18mo, pp. 16. A view of the principal causes that have produced the present extraordinary advance of the stock of the U. S. Bank ... [*Philadelphia*, 1818.] 8vo, pp. 24. P. Vindication of the Constitutional power to repeal the Charter of the Bank of U. S. *Philadelphia*, 1837. The War on the Bank of the United States. *See* [Gordon (T. F.)]

Bankers' Magazine and Statistical Register: Ed. by J. S. Homans. 1846. New series, 1852, &c. *Baltimore, Boston and New York*. 8vo. Continued. 3190

Banking Association and Uniform Currency Bill with Extracts from Reports of Secretary of the Treasury, Submitted to Congress in December, 1861, and December, 1862. 8vo, pp. 36. 3191

An Act to Provide a National Currency, secured by a Pledge of the United States Stocks, and to provide for the Circulation and Redemption thereof. Approved February 25, 1863. *Washington, Government Printing Office*, 1863. 8vo, pp. 38. 3192

Bankrupt Law of the United States, etc. *Philadelphia*, 1841. 8vo, pp. 48. 3193

Act to establish an uniform system of Bankruptcy throughout the United States; enacted April 4, 1800. *Philadelphia*, 1800. 8vo, pp. 33. 3194

A Letter to the Senate and House of Representatives of the United States upon the Expediency of an Uniform System of Bankruptcy. ... *Boston*, 1821. 8vo, pp. 31. H. 3195

Banks (Henry). A Memorial to the Congress of the United States, relative to Revolutionary Events. By Henry Banks. *Frankfort, Ky.*, 1827. 12mo, pp. 71. 3196

Banks. A Review of Political Opinions, published for the benefit of the People of Kentucky. By Henry Banks, of Virginia. *Frankfort, Ky.*, 1822. 8vo, pp. 88. P. 3197

On the subject of the Bank of the Commonwealth.

Banks. Reply to a Scurrilous Publication in the Kentucky Whig. By Henry Banks. [n. d.] 8vo, pp. 60. 3198

Banks. Sketches Recommending an Independent System of Banking, &c. By Henry Banks. *Richmond*, 1811. 8vo. C.

Banks (John). The Vindication of John Banks of Virginia, against foul Calumnies published by Judge Johnson, of Charleston, S. C., and Dr. Charles Caldwell, of Lexington, Ky. Also the Vindication of Gen. Henry Lee, of Virginia; with Sketches and Anecdotes of many Revolutionary Patriots and Heroes. By Henry Banks. *Frankfort, Ky.*, 1826. 8vo, pp. 86. W. 3200

Banks (Joseph). Journal d'un voyage autour du monde en 1768, 1769, 1770, et 1771 ... traduit d l'Anglais MM. Banks et Solander par M. de Fréville. *Paris*, 1773. 12mo, pp. 287.

Probably an abridged translation, with some additions, of the English edition of 1772.

Banks. Supplément au voyage de M. de Bougainville; ou journal d'un voyage autour du monde fait par MM. Banks et Solander, Anglois, en 1768, 1769, 1770, et 1771 Traduit de l'Anglois par M. de Fréville. *Paris*, 1772. 8vo, pp. 287.

Frequently bound up as a third volume of Bougainville's Voyages. Quérard gives the imprint, *Paris*, 1793. 8vo. Nos. 3201 and 3202 are evidently the same. Probably the *date* of 3202 is a mistake. And Quérard's date is perhaps an error for 1773.

Banks. Neueste Reise-Beschreibungen und Entdeckungen des fünften Welttheils, welche sowohl in Gesellschaft der Herren Banks und Solander, als nachher unternommen worden. *Nürnberg*, 1786. 2 vols., 8vo. 3203

This title is from Boucher, Vol. I., p. 146, but it is not found in Kayser.

Banks. An Epistle from Oberea, Queen of Otaheite, to Joseph Banks, Esq. Translated by T. Q. Z. Esq. ... with historical and explanatory Notes. *London, J. Almon*, 1773. 4to.

Banks. A Second Letter from Oberea, Queen of Otaheite, to Joseph Banks, Esq. ... *London, Johnson*, 1745. 4to. 3205

A Satire upon Banks' Voyage. *See* M. R., XLIX., 503, and LI., 394.

Banks (N. P.) ... Address of Hon. N. P. Banks ... from the Steps of the Merchants' Exchange on Political Questions affecting Commercial Interests, September 25th, 1856. [*New York*, 1856.] 8vo, pp. 24. B. & H. 3206

Also: An Address delivered By Maj. General N. P. Banks, at ... New Orleans, on the Fourth of July, 1865. [n. p., n. d.] 8vo, pp. 15. H. Address of His Excellency Nathaniel P. Banks, to the ... Legislature of Massachusetts, January 7, 1858. *Boston*, 1858. 8vo, pp. 21. + January 7, 1859. *Boston*, 1859. 8vo, pp. 48. lxvii. + January 6, 1860. *Boston*, 1860. 8vo, pp. 36, xxiv. B. Address of Hon. N. P. Banks ... [at New York] September 25th, 1856. [n. p., n. d.] 8vo, pp. 24. H. American Republican Politics. Remarks of Mr. Banks, of Mass. [*Washington*, 1856.] 8vo, pp. 8. H. Emancipated Labor in Louisiana [n. p., 1864?] 8vo, pp. 45. H. The Great Questions of National and State Politics. Speech ... at Worcester .. September 8th. *Boston*, 1857. 12mo, pp. 12. Letter to Samuel B. Ruggles ... . [In Defence of his Wall Street Speech of Sept. 25, 1856. No imprint.] 8vo, pp. 8. B. Questions propounded to the Candidates for Speaker, and their responses: U. S. H. of R., Jan. 21, 1856. 8vo, pp. 8. The Reconstruction of States. Letter of Major-General Banks to Senator Lane. *New York, Harper*, 1865. 8vo, pp. 23. + Another Edition. 8vo, pp. 12. Speech of Mr. Banks ... In the House of Representatives May 23, 1854, on the Nebraska and Kansas Bill. ... *Washington*, 1854. 8vo, pp. 15. B. Speech of N. P. Banks, Jr., of Mass., on the Employment of Army Officers in National Armories. ... July 17, 1854. 8vo, pp. 16. H. Speech ... on the Representation of the United States at the Exhibition of the World's Industry, Paris, 1867; ... in the House ... March 14, 1866. ... *Washington*, 1866. 8vo, pp. 24. Suggestions presented to the Judiciary Committee of the Senate of the U. S., relating to the State of Louisiana. 38th Congress, Senate Miscellaneous Document, No. 9, 1865. 8vo, pp. 8.

Banks. Expédition du Général Banks dans la Rivière Rouge. Traduit de l'Anglais par Abraham Moivre. *Paris*, 1866. 8vo, pp. 13. P. 3206*a*

A translation of Gen. Banks' report.

Banks (T. C.) Baronia Anglia Concentrata; or a Concentrated Account of all the Baronies called Baronies in Fee ... By C. T. Banks. *Ripon*, 1843–44. 2 vols., 4to. B., C. 3207

Includes an Historical Account of the First Settlement of Nova Scotia, Nova Scotia Baronets, the Charters in favor of Sir William Alexander, &c.

Banks. An Analytical Statement of the Case of Alexander Earl of Stirling and Dovan ... his Official Dignities, and Peculiar Territorial Rights and Privileges in the British Colonies of Nova Scotia and Canada, ... with ... Notes and Observations. By Sir Thomas C. Banks ... . *London*, 1832. 8vo, pp. xlix., 123, 2 l. folded. H. 3208

Bannantine (J.) Memoirs of Colonel Edward Marcus Despard. By James Bannantine, his Secretary when King's Superintendent of Honduras, &c. *London, J. Ridgway*, 1799. 8vo. 3209

See M. R., New Series, Vol. XXVIII., 233.

Bannard (W.) Moral Aspect and Destitution of the City of New-York: A Discourse at the opening of the Presbytery of New-York, ... Oct. 13, 1851. By Rev. William Bannard, D.D. *New-York*, 1851. 8vo, pp. 31. S. 3210

Banneker (B.) Copy of a Letter from Benjamin Banneker, to the Secretary of State [Thos. Jefferson], with his Answer. *Philadelphia, Daniel Lawrence*, M.DCC.XCII. 4to, pp. 15. H.

This writer was a free black man, and this is one of the earliest works published by an American negro. Pages 13–15 contain an account of the author, "taken from Banneker's Almanac."

De banneling. Schetsen uit, Noord-Amerika. Uit het Hoogduitsch door H. Picard. *Gouda, G. B. van Goor*, 1847. 2 pt., 8vo. 3211*a*

Banner of the Constitution, devoted to General Politics, Political Economy, State Papers, foreign and domestic News, &c. *Philadelphia*, 1829. 3 vols. 3212

Continued to 1832. Edited by Conoly Ragnet.

The | Banners | Of Grace and Love | displayed | In the farther Conversion of the Indians | In New-England: | Held forth in sundry Letters from divers Ministers to | the Corporation established by Parliament, for Promoting | the Gospel amongst the Heathen in New-England; | and farther attested by | Edm. Callamy | Simon Ashe | VVill. Spurstow | Lazarus Seaman | George Griffith | Phil. Nye | VVilliam Bridge | Henry Whitfield | Joseph Carryll | Ralph Venning. | *London*, | *Printed by W. Godbid, for Edw. Farnham, and are to | be sold at his Shop in Popeshead-Alley*, | M. DC. LVII. | 4to, 8 p. l., pp. 40. H. 3213

This is a reprint of "Strength out of Weakness."

[Bannister (John W.)] Sketch of a Plan for Settling in Upper Canada a Portion of the Unemployed Labourers of England. By a Settler. *London, Harding*, 1821. 8vo. + Sketches of Plans for Settling in Upper Canada a portion of the unemployed labourers of Great Britain and Ireland. Second edition with additions. By a Settler. ... *London, Harding*, 1822. 8vo, pp. 53. + Third Edition. *London, Marshall*, 1826. 8vo, pp. 39. Map. + A new Edition, with Additions on Nova Scotia, &c. *London*, 1831. 8vo. Map. 3214

Bannister (N. H.) Putnam, the Iron Son of '76. A national military drama ... By N. H. Bannister ... *New York* [n. d.] 12mo, pp. 29. P. 3214*a*

BANNISTER (Saxe). British Colonization and Coloured Tribes. By S. Bannister ... . *London, William Ball*, 1838. 12mo, pp. xii., 323. H. 3215

BANNISTER. Humane Policy, or Justice to the Aborigines essential to a due Expenditure of British Money. By Saxe Bannister. *London, Underwood*, 1830. 8vo. A. 3216

BANNISTER. Humane Policy; or, The Civilization of African and other Barbarous People, Attainable by Wise Measures, and Just and Amalgamated Colonization. By S. Bannister ... . Second Edition. *London, Fisher, Son, & Co.* [n. d.] 8vo, 2 p. l., pp. xii., 50. Map. H. 3217

BANNISTER. ... The Jurisdiction of the Privy Council in Appeals by, and against Public Officers in the Colonies. [Signed S. Bannister. From Fisher's Colonial Magazine, for March, 1843. n. p., 1843.] 8vo, pp. 8. H. 3218

BANNISTER. Records of British Enterprise beyond Sea. *London, Longman*, 1850. 8vo. 3219

[BANNISTER.] Remarks on the Indians of North America in a Letter to an Edinburgh Reviewer. *London*, 1822. 8vo.

BAÑOS Y SOTOMAYOR (Diego de). Constituciones synodales del Obispado de Veneçuela, y Santiago de Leon de Caracas. Hechas en la santa iglesia cathedral de dicha Ciudad de Caracas, en el Año del Señor de 1687. Por ... Don Diego de Baños y Sotomayor, Obispo del dicho Obispado ... . *Madrid, Lucas Antonio de Bedmar, y Narvaez* [1698]. Folio, 8 p. l., Engraved Title, pp. 474. H. 3221

Banques coloniales. Martinique, Guadeloupe, Réunion, Guyane, Sénégal. Lois, statuts, documents principaux. Nouvelle édition, amendée et mise à jour. *Paris, à l'Agence centrale des banques coloniales*, 1867. 8vo, pp. 234. 3222

BANVARD (John). Description of Banvard's Panorama of the Mississippi River, painted on Three Miles of Canvas ... . *Boston, John Putnam, Printer*, 1847. 8vo, pp. 43 (1). H. 3223

BANVARD. Description of Banvard's Geographical Painting of the Mississippi River, extensively known as the "Three Mile Picture," with new additions of the Naval and Military Operations on that River, exhibiting a view of country 1,500 miles in

length from the Mouth of the Missouri to the Balize. *New York, Bigelow, Printer*, 1862. 8vo, pp. 38. 3224

BANVARD. Banvard ou les aventures d'un artiste. *Paris, typographie Dondey-Dupré*, 1850. 12mo, pp. 22. H. 3225

BANVARD (Joseph). The American Statesman; or Illustrations of the Life and Character of Daniel Webster. Designed for American Youth. By Rev. Joseph Banvard ... . *Boston, Gould and Lincoln*, 1853. 16mo, pp. 334. H. 3226

BANVARD. A Guide to Providence River and Narragansett Bay, from Providence to Newport. By Joseph Banvard. *Providence*, 1858. 18mo. 3227

BANVARD. A Memorial Sermon of Rev. Job Borden Boomer. Preached in South Sutton ... March 12, 1865. *Boston*, 1865. 8vo, pp. 36. H. 3228

BANVARD. Novelties of the New World; or, The Adventures and Discoveries of the First Explorers of North America. By Joseph Banvard ... . With Illustrations. *Boston, Gould and Lincoln*, 1852. 18mo, pp. 324. H. 3229

BANVARD. Plymouth and the Pilgrims; or Incidents of Adventure in the History of the First Settlers. By Joseph Banvard. *Boston, Gould and Lincoln*, 1851 *and* 1853. 18mo, pp. 288. Illustrations. C. & H. 3230

BANVARD. Priscilla; or, Trials for the Truth. An Historic Tale of the Puritans and the Baptists. By the Rev. Joseph Banvard ... . *Boston, Heath and Graves*, 1854. 18mo, pp. 405. 8 Illustrations. H. 3231

BANVARD. Romance of American History, as illustrated in the Early Events connected with the French Settlement at Fort Carolina; the Spanish Colony at St. Augustine, and the English Plantation at Jamestown. By Joseph Banvard ... . With Illustrations. *Boston, Gould and Lincoln*, 1852. 18mo, pp. 306. H. 3232

BANVARD. Tragic Scenes in the History of Maryland and the Old French War. With an Account of various Interesting Contemporaneous Events which occurred in the Early Settlement of America. By Joseph Banvard ... . *Boston, Gould and Lincoln*, 1856. 18mo, pp. 239. Illustrations. H., S. 3233

Baptist Memorial and Monthly Record, devoted to the history of the denomination. *New York*, 1841. 8vo. 3234

A new series, commenced and continued, Vol. VIII.

The Baptists of the North on the State of the Country. *Brooklyn: (N. Y.) May* 27, 1861. 8vo, pp. 11. 3235

Act of Incorporation, Constitution and By-Laws, of the Northern Baptist Society. *Boston, Lincoln & Edwards*, 1830. 8vo, pp. 20. H. 3236

Also Annual Reports, from 1824.

An Address from the Baptist Church in Philadelphia to the Sister Churches throughout the Confederated States of North America. *Philadelphia, Aitken*, 1781. Sm. 8vo, pp. 16. P.

General Convention of Baptists, being their second Triennial Meeting. *Philadelphia*, 1820. 8vo. 3238

Minutes of the Eighth Session of the Baptist Convention of Nova Scotia, New Brunswick, and Prince Edward Island ... Sept. 17th, 19th, & 20th. *Halifax, N. S.*, 1853. 18mo, pp. 56. H. 3239

Minutes of the Warren Association, held at the South Baptist Meeting-House in Middleborough, September 10 and 11, 1799. *Boston*, MDCCXCIX. 8vo, pp. 11. H. 3240

See Philadelphia, also Warren Association, and other local headings.

Proceedings of the Southern Baptist Convention, held in Augusta, Georgia, May [8–12] ... 1845. *Richmond, H. K. Ellyson, Printer*, 1845. 8vo, pp. 20. 3241

Also: Twelfth Annual Report of the Baptist General Tract Society ... . January 1836. *Philadelphia*, 1836. 8vo, pp. 40. Also for other years; and Reports of the American Baptist Home Mission Society, 1826, &c. Other historical Baptist tracts, under the names of states, cities or towns.

BAPTISTA (Juan). Advertencias. Para los Confessores de los Naturales. Compvestas por el padre fray Juan Baptista, de la Orden del Seraphico Padre Sancto Francisco, Lector de Theologia, y Guardian del Conuento de Sanctiago Tlatilulco: de la Prouincia del Sancto Euangelio. *En Mexico, en el Conuento de Sanctiago Tlatilulco, por M. Ocharte, año* 1600. 8vo, Primera Parte, 15 p. l., 112, 58 l.; Segunda Parte, 113–443, Index Locorum, 104 ff. 3242

The verso of the last leaf reads: "Excudebat Ludouicus Ocharte Figueroa, Mexici, in Regio Collegio sancte crucis, sancti Jacobi de Tlatiluco. Anno domini 1601."

54

BAPTISTA. Platicas morales de los Indios para la doctrina de sus hijos, en lengua Mexicana intitulado huehuetlatolli. Por Fr. Juan Bautiste franciscano. *Mexico*, 1601. 3243

Title from Ternaux, 253. *See* Ternaux, No. 252, concerning the press at which No. 3242 was printed. Consult also Pinelo, Antonio and Wadding.

BAQUEIRO. Ensayo historico sobre las revoluciones de Yucatan desde el ano de 1840 hasta 1864, por Serapio Baqueiro. *Merida*, 1865–66. 8vo, Entrega, 1 to 17, containing pp. 1 to 280. 3244

BARADERE. Refutation du manifeste du général Oribe contre les agens français. Par Juan Maria Raymond Baradere. *Montevideo*, 1839. 8vo. 3245

In French and Spanish.

BARADÈRE. Lettre à M. Laisné de Villevêque. *Paris, impr. de Tastu*, 1830. 8vo. 3245*a*

Relates to the colonization of Guazacoalco, in Mexico.

BARADÈRE. Réponse à la brochure de M. Dubouchet sur le Guazacoalco. *Paris, impr. de Tastu*, 1830. 3245*b*

BARAGA (F.) Abrégé de l'Histoire des Indiens de l'Amérique septentrionale, par F. Baraga. Traduit de l'allemand. *Paris*, 1837. 12mo. 3246

BARAGA. A Dictionary of the Otchipwe Language, explained in English. This language is spoken by the Chippewa Indians, as also by the Otawas, Potawatamies, and Algonquins, with little difference. For the use of Missionaries and other persons living among the above mentioned Indians. By the Rev. Frederick Baraga ... *Cincinnati, Printed for Jos. Heemann*, 1853, 12mo, pp. vii., 662. 3247

In Ojibwe-Eng., and Eng.-Ojibwe.

BARAGA. Jesus obimadisiwin ōma aking, gwaiakossing anamiewin ejitwatjig mi sa catholique enamiadjig gewabandangig. *Paris, impr. de Bailly*, 1837. 18mo. Map. 3247*a*

This and the next are in the Ottawa language.

BARAGA. Otchipwe anamie masinaigan. Gwaiakossing anamiewin ejitwatjig mi sa catholique enamiadjig gewabandangig. *Paris, impr. de Bailly*, 1837. 18mo. 3247*b*

BARAGA. A Theoretical and Practical Grammar of the Otchipwe Language. By Rev. Fred. Baraga, Missionary at L'Ange, Lake Superior. *Detroit, Printed by Jabez Fox*, 1851. 12mo, pp. 576. 3248

BARALT (R. M.) Resumen de la Historia de Venezuela, desde el descubrimiento de su Territorio por los Castellanos en el siglo xv. hasta el año de 1797 ordenado y compuesto con arreglo à Muñoz, Navarrete, etc. por Rafael Maria Baralt. Ha cooperado a él en la parte relativa à las guerras de la conquista de la Costa-Firme el señor Ramon Diaz, el cual le ha añadido los apéndices ... *Paris, H. Fournier y compía*, 1841. 8vo, Title, pp. 448 (1). 5 Portraits. B. 3249

BARALT. Resumen de la historia de Venezuela, desde el año de 1797 hasta el de 1830, por Rafael Maria Baralt y Ramon Diaz. Tiene al fin un breve bosquejo historico ... 1831. hasta 1837. *Paris, H. Fournier y compía*, 1841. 2 vols., 8vo, 2 p. l., pp. 398 (1); Half Title, 370 (1). 38 Portraits. B. & C. 3250

The most complete work on Venezuelan history.

BARALT and URBANEJA. Catecismo de la historia de Venezuela, desde el descubrimiento de su territorio en 1498, hasta su emancipacion politica de la monarquia espanola en 1811. Compuesto por Rafael M. Baralt y Manuel M. Urbaneja. *Caracas*, 1865. 18mo, pp. 94. 3251

BARAZE (Cypriano). Compendio de su Vida y muerte a de Manos los Barbaros Moxos en la Provincia del Peru. *Madrid*, 1711, 12mo. 3252

BARAZE. Entrada del Padre Cypriano Baraze, en la mission de los Moxos [n. p., n. d.] 8vo. 3252*a*

"Après 1702, époque de la mort du P. Baraze."—CARAYON.

BARBA (A. A.) Arte de los metales, en que se enseña el verdadero beneficio de los de oro y plata por açogue: el modo de fundirlos todos, y como se han de refinar y apartar unos de otros. Compuesto por el Licenciado Alvaro Alonso Barba. *Madrid, Imp. del Reyno*, 1640. 4to. + *Madrid* [1729]. 4to. + *Madrid*, 1790. 4to. + Nuevamente ahora añadido con el tratado de las antiguas minas de España, que escribió Don Alonso Carrillo y Laso ... . Reimpreso por el real tribunal de mineria de esta capital ... . *Lima*, 1817. 4to, 2 p. l. pp. 271 (7). H.

In the Catalogue of the Royal Library at Upsala, an edition is cited, *Madrid*, 1630, 4to; in that of the London Institution, Vol. I., 113, an edition, *Madrid*, 1639, 8vo. The sale of this work was prohibited by the Inquisition.

BARBA. The First [- Second] Book of the Art of Metals, in which is declared the Manner of their Generation, and the Concomitants of them. Art of Refining Silver by Quicksilver. Translated by Edward [Montagu] ... Earl of Sandwich. *London*, 1674. 2 vols., sm. 8vo. 3254

Reprinted in "A Collection of valuable Treatises upon Metals, Mines, and Minerals. *London*, 1738." 12mo. + "Second Edition. 1740." 12mo.

BARBA. Traité de l'art métallique extrait d'Alvar Alfonse Barba ... . Traduite de l'espagnole [par Ch. Hautin de Villars]. *Paris, Prault*, 1730. 12mo. Plates. 3255

BARBA. Metallurgie, ou l'art de tirer et purifier les métaux, Traduite de l'Espagnol d'Alphonse Barba [par l'abbé Nic. Lenglet du Fresnoy] avec Les Dissertations les plus rares sur les Mines & les Opérations Métalliques. ... *Paris, Pierre-Alexandre Le Prieur*, M. DCC. LI. 2 vols., 12mo, pp. xliv. (12), 456 (16), 2 Plates; (12), 456 (20). H. 3255*a*

The translator signs the "Epistre" with the *pseudonym*, "Gosford."

BARBA. Berg-Büchlein von den Metallen und Mineral. Ursprung. Deutsch von J. L. M. C. *Hamburg, Schultz*, 1676. 8vo, 13 sheets. + *Frankfurt, Fleischer*, 1726. 2 Theile, 8vo. + [Ibid.], 1739. 8vo, 14 sheets. 3255*b*

BARBA. Docimasia, oder Probier- und Schmelzkunst. Aus dem Französischen, mit einem Anhang vermehrt, herausgegeben von M. Godar. Mit Karten. *Wien, Kraus*, 1775. 8vo. 3255*c*

I have seen mention of editions at *Wien*, 1749, 8vo, and 1767, 8vo, but they are not noted in Georgi, Heinsius, or Kayser, and perhaps are due simply to typographical mistake.

BARBA. Verhandeling over de Mynen, Metalen en Mineralen. *'s Hertogenbosch, A. Palier*, 1735. 8vo. 3255*d*

BARBADOES (Thomas), *Bp. of. See* Parry (Thomas).

The Barbadoes Packet; Containing Several Original Papers: giving an Account of the Most Material Transactions that have lately happened in a certain Part of the West-Indies. In a Letter from a Gentleman of the said Island to his Friend in London. *London, S. Popping*, 1720. 8vo, 6 p. l., pp. 68.

BARBADOES. An account of the Donations for the Relief of the Sufferers by Fire, at Bridge Town in the Island of Barbadoes, in May and December, 1766, and of the Application of the Same. *London, S. Goadby* [1769]. 4to, 2 p. l., pp. 40 (1).

An Account of the Fatal Hurricane by which Barbadoes suffered, August, 1831. *Bridge Town*, 1831. 8vo, pp. 150.

Acts and Statutes | Of the Island of | Barbados | Made and Enacted since the Reducement of | the same, unto the Authority of the | Common-wealth of England. | And | Set forth the seventh day of September, in the | year of our Lord God, 1652. By the Ho- | nourable Governour of the said Island, | the Worshipfull the Council, and | Gentlemen of the Assembly. | Together with the Charter of the said Island, | or Articles made on the Surrender, and | Rendition of the same. | Published for the publick good. | *London, Printed by Will. Bentley, and are to be | ssuld by him at the India Bridge.* [1654.] Sm. 8vo, 8 p. l., pp. 176. P. 3259

Acts of Assembly, passed in the Island of Barbadoes, From 1648, to 1718. *London, Printed by John Baskett* [etc.] MDCCXXI. Folio, pp. xxxii., 314. H. + Part II., from 1717–18 to 1738. *London*, 1730–39. Folio. C. 3260

An Address to the Committee. *See* [Dickinson (J.)]

An Authentic Report of the Debate in the House of Commons, June the 23d, 1825, on Mr. Buxton's Motion relative to the Demolition of the Methodist Chapel and Mission House in Barbadoes, and the Expulsion of Mr. Shrewsbury, a Wesleyan Missionary, from that Island. *London, J. Hatchard and Son*, 1825. 8vo, pp. (4), 119. H. 3261

Candid Observations on Two Pamphlets lately published, viz. "An Address to the Committee of Correspondence in Barbadoes"—By a North American And "An Essay toward the Vindication of the Committee of Correspondence" By a Barbadian. By a native of Barbados. *Barbados, Printed by George Edward and Comp.*, M.DCC.LXVI. 8vo, pp. 37. P. 3262

The Case of Barbados, for Indemnification of Losses in the Late Insurrection. *Westminster*, 1819. 8vo, pp. 6. 3263

A Declaration of the Inhabitants of Barbadoes, respecting the demolition of the Methodist Chapel. With an Appendix. *Barbados, Printed at the Barbadian Office*, 1826. 8vo, pp. 20. 3263*a*

A Defence of the Conduct of Barbadoes, During the late Expedition to Martinique and Guadaloupe. In a letter to the Right Hon. Gen. Barrington. By a Native, Resident in the Island. ... *London, R. & J. Dodsley*, M DCC LX. 8vo, pp. 88. H.

A Detection of the State and Situation of the Present Sugar Planters, of Barbadoes and the Leward Islands; With an Answer to this Query, Why does not England, or her Sugar Islands, or both, make and settle more Sugar Colonies in the West-Indies? Written in the Month of December 1731, by an Inhabitant of one of His Majesty's Leward Caribbee Islands; and humbly Dedicated to the Right Honourable Sir Robert Walpole. *London, J. Wilford*, 1732. 8vo, 2 p. l., pp. viii., 99.

Desultory Sketches and Tales of Barbados. ... *London, Henry Washbourne*, 1840. 16mo, pp. viii., 264. B. 3266

An Essay towards the Vindication of the Committee of Correspondence. By a Barbadian. [*Circa* 1766.] 3267

This title is inferred from the "Candid Observations." *See* No. 3262.

Examination of statements respecting Barbados, made by Messrs. Wilberforce, Stephen, &c. *London*, 1824. 8vo, pp. 7.

Extracts from the Votes and Proceedings of the Hon. the Assembly for the Island of Barbados, 1730. [n. d.] 8vo, pp. 8. M. 3269

Great News from the Barbadoes, Or, A True and Faithful Account of the Grand Conspiracy of the Negroes against the English, and the happy Discovery of the same. With the number of those that were burned Alive, Beheaded, and otherwise Executed for their horrid Crimes. With a short Description of that Plantation. With Allowance. *London, Printed for L. Curtis*, 1676. 4to, pp. 14. J. C. B. 3270

The | Groans of the | Plantations: | Or | A True Account | of their | Grievous and Extreme Sufferings | By the Heavy | Impositions | upon | Sugar, | And other Hardships. | Relating more particularly to the | Island of Barbados. | *London, | Printed by M. Clark in the Year* M DC LXXXIX. 4to, Title, pp. 35. H. + *London, | Printed by M. Clark in the Year* 1689, | *and Reprinted* 1698. 4to, Title, pp. 31. 3271

Instructions for the Management of a Plantation in Barbadoes, and for the Treatment of Negroes &c. [Privately printed.] *London*. 1786. 8vo. 3272

Joint Letter from the Proprietors of the Island of Barbadoes to Col. Richard Scot, and others. 1700. Folio. 3273

Laws and Acts of Barbadoes from 1643 to 1763 edited by Richard Hall. *London*, 1764. Folio. 3274

Laws of Barbadoes collected in one volume by William Rawlin, Clerk of the Assembly of the said Island. *Printed for W. Rawlin, Esq.*, 1699. Folio. 3275

Laws of Barbadoes. 1855. 8vo. 3276

Letter from a Gentleman at Barbados. 1740. *See* [Baxter (Th.)]

A Letter to the North American. 1766. *See* [Dickenson (John)].

Letters on the Laboring Population of Barbadoes. *London*, 1858. 8vo. 3277

Memoirs of the First Settlement Of the Island of Barbados, and other the Carribbee Islands, with the Succession of the Governors and Commanders in Chief of Barbados to the Year 1742. Extracted from Ancient Records, Papers and Accounts taken from Mr. William Arnold, Mr. Samuel Bulkly, and Mr. John Summers, some of the First Settlers, the last of whom was alive in 1688, aged 82. Also some Remarks on the Laws and Constitution of Barbados. *London, E. Owen*, M.DCC.XLIII. Sm. 8vo, Title, the Publisher to the Reader, and Introduction, 3 p. l., pp. 84, Appendix, pp. 15. 3278

Contains a list of the inhabitants of Barbadoes, in 1638, who then possessed more than ten acres of land. First printed with the title, "Some Memoirs." *See* No. 3290.

On recent Proceedings of the Legislature of Barbados. *London*, 1826. 8vo, pp. 43. 3279

Public Acts in Force, passed by the Legislature of Barbadoes from May 11, 1762 to April 8, 1800. By Samuel Moore, *London*, 1800. Rl. 8vo. 3280

Remarks Upon a Book, intitled, A Short History of Barbados: in which the Partial & unfair Representations Of the Author upon the Subjects of his History in general, And upon that of the Demand of Privileges in Particular, Are Detected and Exposed. *Barbadoes*, 1768. 8vo. + *Reprinted, London, J. Almon*, M.DCC.LXVIII. 8vo, pp. 88. H. 3281

Report of a Debate in Council, on a Despatch from Lord Bathurst to ... Sir Henry Warde, Governor of Barbados. *London*, 1823. 8vo. 3282

A Report of a Committee of the Council of Barbadoes, appointed to inquire into the Actual Condition of the Slaves in this Island, with a view to refute certain Calumnies respecting their Treatment; and also to take into Consideration certain Measures ... lately agitated in the House of Commons. ... *London, W. Sior*, 1824. 8vo, Half Title, pp. 127. H. 3283

The Report from a Select Committee of the House of Assembly, appointed to inquire into the Origin, Causes, and Progress of the late Insurrection. ... *Barbados, W. Walker* [1816]. 8vo, Half Title, pp. 63. H. + *London*, 1818. 3284

A Representation of the Miserable State of Barbadoes, Under the Arbitrary and Corrupt Administration of his Excellency, Robert Lowther, Esq; the present Governor. Humbly offer'd to the Consideration of His Most Sacred Majesty, and the Right Honourable the Lords of His Majesty's most Honourable Privy-Council. With A Preface, containing Remarks on an Address, printed in the Postman, and in the Whitehall Evening-Post of May 14, 1719. *London, Bernard Lintot* [1719]. 8vo, 2 p. l., pp. 44. 3285

The Seaman's Practical Guide for Barbadoes and the Leeward Islands ... *London*, 1832. 8vo. 3286

A Short | Account | of the | Manifest Hand of God | That hath Fallen upon Several | Marshals and their Deputies | Who have made Great Spoil and Havock of the | Goods of the People of God called | Quakers, | in the | Island of Barbadoes, | For their Testimony against Going or Sending | to the Militia. | With a Remarkable Account of some others of the Perse- | cutors of the same People in the same Island. Together | with an Abstract of their Sufferings. | *London, Printed and Sold by T. Sowle, near the | Meeting-house in White-hart-Court in Gracious-street.* 1696. | 4to, pp. 23, Abstract, a folded sheet. 3287

A Short History of Barbados, from its First Discovery and Settlement, to the End of the year 1767. *London, J. Dodsley*, M DCC LXVIII. 12mo, pp. viii., 121 (2). C. & H. 3288

A Short History of Barbados, from its first Discovery and Settlement to the Present Time. A new edition corrected and enlarged. *London: Printed for J. Dodsley*, 1768. 18mo, pp. xiii., 132. 3289

Attributed to H. Frere. *See* M. R., XXXIX., p. 13. I find an edition, dated 1761, in a London bookseller's catalogue.

Some | Memoirs | of the first Settlement of the | Island of Barbados | and other the | Carribbee Islands | with the Succession of the | Governours and Commanders in Chief | of Barbados to the Year 1741. | Extracted from Antient Records, Papers, | and Accounts taken from Mr. William | Arnold, Mr. Samuel Bulkly, and Mr. | John Summers, some of the first Settlers, | the last of whom was alive in 1688 aged | 82. | Also some Remarks on the Laws and Con- | stitution of Barbados [By Wm. Duke] | *Barbados. Printed by Wm. Beeby*, 1741. | Sm. 8vo, 2 p. l., pp. 84, 15. H. 3290

A rare and interesting volume. Priced, Thorp, 1843, £1 11s. 6d. Reprinted as "Memoirs ... to the Year 1742." *See* No. 3279.

A Supplement to the Detection of the State and Situation of the Sugar Planters of Barbadoes and the Leeward-Islands; Shewing, among other New Matters, That the surest Way for England to command the Sugar-Market Abroad, is to contract rather than inlarge her Sugar Colonies. In a Letter from an Inhabitant of one of His Majesty's Leeward Caribbee Islands, to a Member of the House of Commons in England. To which is added, a Letter from a Traveller in the Caribbees to his Friend in London. *London, J. Wilford*, 1733. 8vo, 2 p. l., pp. 84. 3291

Tabular Statements as to the Diocese of Barbados, 1842, &c. [v. d.] 3292

BARBACENA. A Expoçicaõ do Marquez de Barbacena commentada por hum Brasileiro Nato. *Anvers*, 1831. 8vo. 3293

BARBACENA. Remarques sur la déclaration du marquis de Barbacena relativement au retour de la princesse du Gram-Para à Rio-Janeiro. *Paris, Delaforest*, 1830. 8vo, 3 sheets. 3294

BARBARÁ. Usos y costumbres de los Indios Pampas y algunos apuntos históricos sobre la guerra de la Frontera por F. Barbará. *Buenos Ayres, Bernheim*, 1856. 8vo, pp. 98. 3295

This rare book contains specimens of the dialect spoken by the Maiká tribe at Tapalqué. pp. 92–98.

Barbarities of the Enemy, exposed in a Report Of the Committee of the House of Representatives of the United States. ... appointed to enquire into the spirit and manner in which the war has been waged by the enemy. And the Documents, accompanying said Report. *Troy, Francis Adancourt*, 1813. 12mo,

pp. 178, Errata, 1 l. B. + [Another E tion.] *Printed at Worcester By Isaac Sturtevant*, 1814. 12mo, pp. 192. C. 3296

Barbarities of the Rebels at Manassas. [No imprint; *circa* 1861.] 8vo, pp. 8. 3297

BARBAROSSA, *pseudon.* *See* [Scott (John)].

BARBAROUX (Charles Ogé). Résumé de l'Histoire des États-Unis de l'Amérique. Par Charles Ogé Barbaroux. *Paris*, 1824. 18mo. + Seconde édition. *Paris, Lecointe et Durey*, 1824. 12mo, pp. 356. + 3^e^ édition. *Paris*, 1826. 18mo. S. + L'histoire des États-Unis d'Amérique. ... *Boston*, 1832. 12mo. + Édition revue ... . *Philadelphia, Parrish, Dunning, & Mears* [cop. 1832.] 24mo, pp. 304. H. + Continuée depuis l'année 1825 jusqu'à nos jours, par T. Séron. *Philadelphia*, 1854. 24mo. C. 3298

BARBARY STATES. Message of the President on the relations existing between the United States and the Barbary Powers. February 24, 1815. 8vo. Cong. Doc. 3299

See also 24th Cong., 2d Sess., House, Ex. Doc. No. 69; 25th Cong., 2d Sess., House, Ex. Doc. No. 149; 26th Cong., 1st Sess., House, Ex. Doc. No. 78.

BARBAULD (*Mrs.* A. L. Aikin). Epistle to William Wilberforce, Esq. on the Rejection of the Bill for Abolishing the Slave Trade. By Anna Letitia Barbauld. *London, J. Johnson*, 1791. 4to, pp. 14. P. + Second Edition. *London*, M.DCC.XCI. 4to, pp. 14. H. 3300

In verse. *See* M. R., New Series, VI., 225.

BARBAZ (A. L.) Washingtons overgang ter onsterfelijkheid, lofzang, door A. L. Barbaz. *Amsterdam, A. Balster*, 1800. 8vo, pp. 12. 3301

[BARBÉ-MARBOIS.] Complot D'Arnold et De Sir Henry Clinton contre Les Etats-Unis d'Amérique et contre Le Genéral Washington Septembre 1780. *Paris, Didot l'ainé*, MDCCCXVI. Sm. 8vo, pp. 44, 184. Portraits of Washington and Arnold, and Plan of West Point. C. 3302

Reprinted in 1831. A translation by Robert Walsh, Esq., is contained in the second volume of the "American Register" for 1817.

BARBÉ-MARBOIS. De la Guyane Francaise, de son Etat physique, de son Agriculture, de son Régime intérieur et du Projét de la peupler avec des Laboureurs Européens: ou Examen d'un écrit de M. le Marquis de Barbe-Marbois sur le même

sujet. Suivi de considérations sur le commerce Colonial de la France, et sur l'Administration spéciale de ces Colonies. *Paris, Trouvé*, 1827. 8vo, pp. 232. 3303

BARBÉ-MARBOIS. État des finances de Saint-Domingue, contenant le résumé des recettes et dépenses de toutes les caisses publiques, depuis le 10 Nov. 1785, jusqu'au 1er Janv. 1788. *Au Port-au-Prince, de l'imprimerie de Mozard*, 1788. 4to, 2 p. l., pp. 64, Table, xii. in xi. 3304

BARBÉ-MARBOIS. État des finances de Saint-Domingue, contenant le résumé des recettes et dépenses de toutes les caisses publiques depuis le 1er Janvier 1788 jusqu'au 31 Decembre de 1788 la même année; par M. Barbe de Marbois, intendant des Isles Françoises sous le veut. *Au Port-au-Prince, de l'imprimerie de Mozard*, 1789. 4to, 2 p. l., pp. 58, Tables, xiii. in xi. C.

Quérard also gives the title: "État de la partie espagnole de Saint-Domingue." Nos. 3304, 3305, were published with a third part (Jan. 1–Dec. 31, 1789, by the chevalier de Proisy), with the imprint, *Paris, imp. royale*, 1790. 3 pts. in 1 vol., 4to.

BARBÉ-MARBOIS. Histoire de la Louisiane et de la cession de cette colonie par la France aux États-Unis de l'Amérique Septentrionale; précédée d'un discours sur la constitution et le gouvernement des États-Unis. Par M. Barbé-Marbois, avec une carte relative à l'étendue des pays cédés. *Paris, imp. de Firmin Didot*, 1829. 8vo, 3 p. l., pp. 485. Portrait and Map. H. 3306

BARBÉ-MARBOIS. The History of Louisiana, particularly of the Cession of that Colony to the United States of America; with An Introductory Essay on the Constitution and Government of the United States. By Barbé-Marbois ... . Translated from the French by an American Citizen [Wm. B. Lawrence]. *Philadelphia, Carey & Lea*, 1830. 8vo, pp. xviii., 15–455 (1). C., H. 3307

See N. A. R., XXVIII., 389; XXX., 551.

[BARBÉ-MARBOIS.] Journal d'un déporté non jugé ou déportation en violation des lois décrétée le 18 Fructidor an V (4 Septembre 1797). *Paris, Didot*, 1834. 2 vols., 8vo. (Only 300 copies printed.) + *Paris, Chatel*, 1835. 2 vols., 8vo. 3308

At the end of the second volume are several pieces by the same author, under the title of "Annexes;" and also a "Voyage dans l'intérieure du Continente de l• Guyane, chez les Indiens Rocouyens, par Claude Toug, mulatre, en 1769." It appears that only a few copies were printed, and those not intended for sale.—Cat. Mar. 15016.

BARBÉ-MARBOIS. Journal d'un déporte non jugé, ou déportation en violation des lois, décrétée le 18 fructidor an V (4 septembre 1797). Par M. le Comte de Barbé-Marbois ... . *Bruxelles*, 1835. 2 vols., 18mo, pp. 305; 301. H. 3309

BARBÉ-MARBOIS. Mémoire et observations du sieur Barbé de Marbois ... sur une dénonciation signée par treize de MM. les députés de Saint Domingue, et faite à l'Assemblée nationale au nom d'un des trois comités de la colonie [18 juin 1790]. *Paris, Knapen et fils* [n. d.] 4to. 3310

BARBÉ-MARBOIS. Mémoire laissé par M. Barbé de Marbois, intendant à Saint-Domingue, à l'ordonateur, en conformité des ordres du roi. [Colophon:] *Imprimé par Mozart, au Port-au-Prince, le 26 Octobre 1789, et réimprimé depuis à Paris.* 4to, pp. 15. 3311

BARBÉ-MARBOIS. Observations personnelles à l'intendant de Saint Domingue, pour être jointes aux états imprimés des finances de la colonie. [Signed Barbé de Marbois. 20 mars 1790. *Paris, Knapen*, 1790. 4to, pp. 40 or less. 3311*a*

[BARBÉ-MARBOIS.] Réflexions sur la colonie de Saint-Domingue, ou examen approfondi des causes de sa ruine, et des mesures adoptés pour la rétablir; terminées par l'exposé rapide d'un plan d'organisation propre à lui rendre son ancienne splendeur; adressées au commerce et aux amis de la prosperité nationale. *Paris*, 1796. 2 vols., 8vo. 3312

Rich remarks, "On the fly-leaf of this work is found the following notice of a book, which is not mentioned in any list of the author's works: 'On trouve chez le même libraire, l'ouvrage suivant du même auteur, Histoire des désastres de Saint Domingue, précédée d'un tableau du régime et des progrès de cette colonie depuis sa fondation jusqu' à l'époque de la révolution Français. 1 vol. 8vo avec carte.'"

BARBÉ-MARBOIS. Remontrances de M. de Marbois, intendant de Sainte-Domingue, contre l'arrêt d'enregistrement de l'acte intitulé: "Ordonnance de M. le gouverneur général, concernant la liberté du commerce pour la partie du sud de Saint Domingue." [11 mai 1789. n. p.], *Louis* [n. d.] 8vo, pp. 40 or less. 3312*a*

BARBEE. The Cotton Question. The Production, Export, Manufacture, and Consumption of Cotton. A Condensed Treatise on Cotton in all its aspects: Agricultural, Commercial, and Political. Illustrated. By William J. Barbee, M.D., of De Soto County, Mississippi. *New York*, 1866. 12mo, pp. 251. 4 Plates. 3313

BARBER (Daniel). History of My Own Times. By Rev^d^. Daniel Barber. Parts 1 and 2. *Washington, S. C. Ustick*, 1827–28. 8vo, pp. 48, 32. W. 3314

BARBER (E. D.) An Address before the Anti-Masonic Convention of the County of Addison at Middlebury, on the 12th March, 1829. By E. D. Barber. *Vergennes, Gamaliel Smith*, 1829. 12mo, pp. 36. B. 3315

BARBER. "Popular Excitements." An Address delivered before the Anti-Masonic Convention holden at Middlebury, Vt. Feb. 26th, 1830. By E. D. Barber. *Middlebury*, MDCCCXXX. 8vo, pp. 19. B. 3316

BARBER (John Warner). Connecticut Historical Collections, containing a General Collection of Interesting Facts, Traditions, Biographical Sketches, Anecdotes, &c., relating to the History and Antiquities of every Town in Connecticut, with Geographical Descriptions. Illustrated by 190 Engravings. By John Warner Barber. *New Haven, Durrie & Peck*, 1836. 8vo, pp. 568. C. + [Second edition.] *New Haven, Durrie & Peck and J. W. Barber* [1846]. 8vo, pp. 576. Map. H. 3317

BARBER. Elements of General History. By John Warner Barber. *New Haven*, 1866. 18mo. 3318

BARBER. Historical Collections; being a general Collection of interesting Facts, Traditions, Biographical Sketches, Anecdotes, &c., relating to the History and Antiquities of every Town in Massachusetts; with Geographical Descriptions. Illustrated by 200 Engravings. ... By John Warner Barber. *Worcester, Dorr, Howland & Co.*, 1841. 8vo, pp. viii., 632. + *Worcester, Warren Lazell*, 1844. 8vo, pp. 631. Map. H. 3319

First published in 1839. Another edition, dated 1848.

BARBER. Historical Scenes in the United States ... By J. W. Barber. *New-Haven, Monson and Co.*, 1827. 18mo, pp. 120. Map and 16 Plates. B. 3320

Reprinted as Historical, Poetical and Pictorial American Scenes. *New Haven* [n. d.], 12mo, and again reprinted with the following title:

BARBER. Historical, Poetical and Pictorial American Scenes; principally Moral and Religious: Being a selection of interesting incidents in American History: to which is added a Chronological Table of Important Events, in the Secession War. By John W. Barber. *New Haven* [n. d.] 12mo, pp. 190. 3321

BARBER. The History and Antiquities of New England, New York, and New Jersey ... . Illustrated by numerous Engravings. *Worcester, Dorr, Howland & Co.*, 1840. 8vo, pp. 576. H. + *Hartford*, 1846. 8vo, pp. 576. C. 3322

BARBER. History and Antiquities of New Haven, (Conn.) from its Earliest Settlement to the Present Time. Collected and Compiled from the most Authentic Sources. By J. W. Barber. ... *New Haven, J. W. Barber*, 1831. 12mo, pp. 120. Map, 6 Plates Colored, and Woodcuts, Plain. H. + 1846. C.

The plates include a view of New Haven and Fort Hale, etc.

BARBER. A History of the Amistad Captives: being a Circumstantial Account of the Capture of the Spanish Schooner Amistad, by the Africans on board; their Voyage, and Capture near Long Island, New York; with Biographical Sketches of each of the Surviving Africans Also, an Account of the Trials had on their Case, before the District and Circuit Courts of the United States, for the District of Connecticut. Compiled from Authentic Sources, by John W. Barber ... . *New Haven, Ct., E. L. & J. W. Barber*, 1840. 8vo, pp. 32. Folded Plate and Woodcuts. H. & C. 3324

BARBER. History of the United States. By J. W. Barber. *New-Haven*, 1832. 12mo. S. 3325

BARBER. Interesting Events in the History of the United States: Being a Selection of the Most Important And Interesting Events Which have Transpired Since the Discovery of this Country to the Present Time. Carefully Selected from the most approved Authorities. By J. W. Barber. *New Haven, J. W. Barber*, 1828. 12mo, pp. v., 216. + *Boston* [n. d.] 12mo.

Reproduced, and the title changed to "Incidents in American History, relating to the Discovery and Settlement of the Country. Third edition. *New York, George F. Cooledge & Bro.*, 1847." 12mo, pp. 404.

BARBER. Hauptbegebenheiten der Amerikanischen Geschichte. Bearbeitet von Ernst Grünewald, bevorwortet von Heinrich Künzel. *Darmstadt, Leske*, 1849. 8vo, pp. viii., 288. 3327

BARBER. Pictorial History of the State of New-York. *Cooperstown*, 1846. 8vo. 3328

This is a new title to the Historical Collections. *See* No. 3331.

BARBER. Views in New-Haven and its Vicinity, with a Particular Description to each View. Drawn and Engraved by J. W. Barber. *New-Haven*, 1825. 18mo, pp. 11 and 6 Plates.

BARBER and HOWE (H.) Historical Collections of the State of New Jersey, relating to its history and antiquities, with Geographical description of every Township in the State, with 120 engravings. By J. W. Barber and Henry Howe. *New York*, 1845. 8vo. + 1846. 8vo, pp. 512. H. + *Newark, N. J.* [1852]. + *Newark*, 1857. 8vo. C. 3330

BARBER and HOWE. Historical Collection of the State of New York; containing a General Collection of the most Interesting Facts, Traditions, Biographical Sketches, Anecdotes, &c., relating to its History and Antiquities, with Geographical Descriptions of every Township in the State. Illustrated by Two hundred and thirty wood Engravings. By J. W. Barber and Henry Howe. *New York*, 1841. 8vo, pp. 608. + *New York*, 1844. 8vo, pp. 616. + *New York*, 1845. 8vo. H. + *Cooperstown*, 1846. 8vo. + *New York*, 1851. C. 3331

BARBER and HOWE. Our whole Country, or the past and present of the United States, historical and descriptive. By J. W. Barber and H. Howe. *Cincinnati*, 1861. 2 vols., 8vo.

BARBER and PUNDERSON (L. S.) City Guide to New Haven ... By J. W. Barber and L. S. Punderson ... . *New Haven*, 1860. 18mo, 1 p. l., pp. 36. Map. H. 3333

BARBER and PUNDERSON. History and Antiquities of New Haven, Conn., from its earliest settlement to the present time. With Biographical Sketches and Statistical Information of the Public Institutions, &c., &c. By John W. Barber and Lemuel S. Punderson. Second Edition. *New Haven*, 1856. 12mo, pp. 180. 5 Plates and numerous Woodcuts. M. 3334

[BARBEU-DUBOURG (Jacques)]. Calendrier de Philadelphie, ou Constitutions de Sancho-Pança et du bonhomme Richard en Pennsylvanie. *Philadelphie et Paris, Esprit*, 1778. 12mo.

BARBEY (Théodore). Le Texas; par Théodore Barbey, consul du Texas, à Paris. *Paris, l'auteur*, 1841. 8vo, Title, pp. 22. Map. 3336

BARBICHON (P. M.) Dictionnaire complet de tous les lieux de la France et de ses colonies. Ouvrage entièrement neuf ... . *Paris, Tétot*, 1831. 2 vols., 8vo. 3337

BARBIER (Jean). Retour du Brésil Naufrage du jeune Léon, du Havre; poëme en trois chants par Jean Barbier. 2e édition. *Alger, Dubos*, 1867. 8vo, pp. 38. 3337a

BARBINAIS (L. G. de la). *See* La Barbinais (L. G. de).

BARBOSA. *See* Cunha Barbosa.

BARBOSA MACHADO. *See* Machado.

BARBOT (J.) Tryal of John Barbot, Attorney-at-Law, for the Murder of Mathew Mills, Esq., at a Court of Oyer and Terminer, at Basseterre, in and for the Island of St. Christopher, Friday, January 5, 1753, before the Hon. Wm. M. Burt, with the Prisoner's narrative. 1753. Folio. 3338

BARBOUR (B. J.) An Address delivered before the Literary Societies of the Virginia Military Institute, at Lexington, On the 4th of July, 1854. By B. J. Barbour ... . *Richmond, Macfarlane & Fergusson*, 1854. 8vo, pp. 32. H. 3339

BARBOUR (I. R.) Barbour's Temperance Table. By I. Richmond Barbour. *Boston*, 1831. 12mo, pp. 24. H. 3340

The caption is, "Statistical Table, showing the influence of Intemperance on the Churches."

BARBOUR (J.) Eulogium upon the Life and Character of James Madison. By James Barbour ... . *Washington*, 1836. 8vo, pp. 29. H. 3341

BARBOUR. Speech of Mr. J. Barbour ... on the Restriction of Slavery in Missouri. Delivered in the Senate, Jan. 31, 1820, *Washington* [1820]. 12mo, pp. 26. H. 3342

BARBOUR (John S.) Notes to the Senators and Representatives from the State of Virginia, in relation to the Claim of Virginia for Money advanced to the General Government. [Signed J. S. Barbour. n. p., 1852.] 8vo, pp. 23. H. 3343

BARBOUR (L.) Kansas Contested Election. Speech of Hon. Lucian Barbour, of Indiana, in the House of Representatives, March 18, 1856. ... On the ... Contested Election Case from the Territory of Kansas, ... [No imprint.] 8vo, pp. 8. 3344

BARBOUR (O. R.) Reports of Cases ... in the Court of Chancery of the State of New York. By Oliver L. Barbour ... *New-York, Banks, Gould & Co.*, [also] *Albany*, 1847–49. 3 vols., 8vo. 3344a

BARBOUR. Speech of Hon. P. P. Barbour ... on Internal Improvements. ... In the House ... January 15, 1824. *Washington*, 1846. 8vo, pp. 8. H. 3345

BARBOUR (Philip P.) Speech of Mr. P. P. Barbour, of Virginia ... in the House of Representatives ... February 10, 1820, On the ... Bill authorising the people of Missouri to form a Constitution ... . *Washington* [1820]. 12mo, pp. 28. H. 3346

BARBOUR. Speech of Mr. P. P. Barbour, of Vir. on the Tariff Bill. Delivered in the House of Representatives U. S. March 26, 1824. *Washington*, 1834. 12mo, pp. 38. H. 3347

BARCENA (Alonzo de). Arte y Vocabulario de la Lengua de los Indios Abipones y Quiranguis. pp. 210. 3348

Printed, according to Loçano, Descripcion Chorographica del gran Chaco; and Barcia, in his edition of Leon Pinelo. Title from Ludewig Lit. of Ab. Lang.

[BARCIA (Andres Gonzalez)]. Ensayo cronologico, para la historia general de la Florida. Contiene los descubrimientos, y principales sucesos, acaecidos en este Gran Reino, à los Españoles, Franceses, Suecos, Dinamarqueses, Ingleses, y otras Naciones, entre sì, y con los Indios: cuias Costumbres, Genios, Idolatria, Govierno, Batallas, y Astucias, se refieren: y los Viages de algunos Capitanes, y Pilotos, por el Mar de el Norte, à buscar Paso à Oriente, ò vnion de aquella Tierra, con Asia. Desde el Año de 1512. que descubriò la Florida, Juan Ponce de Leon, hasta el de 1722. Escrito por Don Gabriel de Cardenas z Cano Dedicado al Principe Nuestro Señor. Con Privilegio: *En Madrid. En la Oficina Real, y à Costa de Nicolas Rodriguez Franco, Impresor de Libros. Año de* CIↃ IↃCCXXIIJ. *Se hallaràn en su Casa, en la Calle de el Poço, y en Palacio.* Folio, pp. (40), 366, 1 folded l., pp. (56). C., H. 3349

Though called a chronological history of Florida, it comprises nearly the whole continent of America north of Mexico. It is appended to Garcilaso de la Vega's "La Florida." Severely criticised in Joseph de Salazar's "Crisis," etc. Gabriel Cardenas z Cano is an anagram of the author's name.

BARCIA. Historiadores primitivos de las Indias Occidentales, que juntó, traduxo en parte, y sacò à luz, ilustrados con eruditas Notas, y copiosos Indices, el illustrissimo Señor D. Andres Gonzales Barcia ... . Divididos en tres tomos. *Madrid*, MDCCXLIX. 3 vols., folio. C., H., P. 3350

Mr. Rich devotes nearly two pages of his Bibliotheca (Vol. I., 95–97) to an analysis of this highly valuable collection of works relative to the early settlement of this country. The following is a collation and list of the contents: Vol. I. 2 l. La His-

toria del Almirante Don Christoval Colòn, que compuso en Castellano Don Fernando Colòn, su hijo, y traduxo en Toscano Alfonso de Ulloa, vuelta à traducir en Castellaño, por no parecer el original. 128 pp.—Quatro Cartas de Hernan Cortès, dirigidas al Emperador Carlos V. (pp. 1–156).—Dos Relaciones hechas al mismo Cortès, por Pedro de Alvarado (pp. 157–166).—Otra Relacion hecha al mismo Hernan Cortès, por Diego de Godoy (pp. 166–173).—Relacion sumaria de la Historia Natural de las Indias ... por ... Gonzalez Fernandez de Oviedo. 57 pp., indice 9 l.—Examen Apologetico de la Historica narracion de los Naufragios, Peregrinaciones, y Milagros de Alvar Nuñez Cabeza de Baca, contra la Censura del Padre Honorio Filopono, por Don Antonio Ardoino, Marquès de Lorito. (*Madrid, Juan de Zuñiga*, 1736). 50 pp.—Relacion de los Naufragios del Gobernador Alvar Nuñez Cabeza de Baca. 43 pp., 9 l.—Comentarios del mismo de lo sucedido durante su gobierno del Rio de la Plata. 70 pp., 2 l. Vol. II. Historia General de las Indias, por Francisco Lopez de Gomara. 226 pp. 30 l.—Chronica de la Nueva-España, ò Conquista de Mexico, por el mismo. 214 pp., 23 l. Vol. III. Historia del Descubrimiento, y Conquista de la Provincia del Peru ... por Agustin de Zarate, 4 l., 176 pp. 14 l.—Verdadera Relacion de la Conquista del Perù, y Provincia del Cuzco, embiada al emperador Carlos V. por Francisco de Xerèz, (pp. 179–237, 7 l.)—Historia, y Descubrimiento del Rio de la Plata, y Paraguay, por Hulderico Schmidèl, traducida del Latin. 31 pp., 9 l.—Argentina, y Conquista del Rio de la Plata, con otros acaecimientos de los Reynos del Perù, Tucumàn, y Estado del Brasìl, por el Arcediano Don Martin del Barco Centenera, Poema compuesto de veinte y ocho Cantos. 107 pp., 17 l.—Viage del Mundo, de Simòn Perez de Torres. (pp. 1–45).—Epitome de la Relacion del Viage de algunos mercaderes de San Malò à Moka, en Arabia, en el Mar Bermejo, hecho por los años de 1708. 1709. y 1710. formado, y puesto en Castellano por el Alferez Don Manue. de Grova, natural de la Gran Canaria. (pp. 45–48). In 1853, Dr. Hawtrey's copy sold for £7 10s.; 1859, Lady Webster's, £16; Santander's, 116 fr.; Rætzel's, 157 fr.; Meerman's, 62 florins.

BARCIA-PINELO. *See* Pinelo-Barcia.

BARCLAY (A.) Effects of the late Colonial Policy of Great Britain described. By Alexander Barclay. *London*, 1830. 8vo.

BARCLAY. A Practical View of the Present State of Slavery in the West Indies; or, An Examination of Mr. Stephen's "Slavery of the British West India Colonies:" ... particularly ... the Actual Condition of the Negroes in Jamaica: with Observations on the Decrease of the Slaves since the Abolition of the Slave Trade, and on the Probable Effects of Legislative Emancipation: also, Strictures on the Edinburgh Review, and on the Pamphlets of Mr. Cooper and Mr. Bickell. By Alexander Barclay, lately, and for Twenty-one Years Resident in Jamaica. *London, Smith, Elder & Co.*, 1826. 8vo, pp. (2), xxv., 462. H. + Second Edition. *London*, 1827. 8vo, pp. (4), xxv., 462. C.

BARCLAY. Remarks on Emigration to Jamaica; addressed to the Coloured Class of the United States. By Alexander Barclay, Esq., Commissioner of Emigration for Jamaica. *London*, 1840. 8vo, pp. 16. 3353

BARCLAY (Anthony). Proceedings of the Meeting held ... May 26th, 1845. in Furtherance of the Establishment of A Free Church for British Emigrants at the Port of New-York. [Signed by Anth. Barclay and three others. n. p., n. d.] 8vo, pp. 6. H.

BARCLAY (Captain). *See* Barclay (R.)

BARCLAY (C.) Letters from the Dorking Emigrants who went to Upper Canada, in 1832. Edited by Charles Barclay. *London*, 1833. 8vo, pp. 44. 3355

BARCLAY (C. C.) Sermon on the Times ... A Sermon preached in St. Thomas' Church, Bethel, on the National Fast Day, January 4th, 1860. By Rev. Cuthbert C. Barclay. *New Haven, Tuttle, Morehouse & Co.*, 1861. 8vo, pp. 19. H.

BARCLAY (D.) An Account of the Emancipation of the Slaves of Unity Valley Pen, in Jamaica. By David Barclay. *London, William Phillips*, 1801. 8vo, pp. 20. P. + Second Edition, with an Appendix. *London*, 1801. 8vo, pp. 20. + *Dorking, printed; sold by J. and A. Arch, Cornhill*, 1825. 8vo, pp. 20.

See M. R., 2d Series, XXXVII., 445.

BARCLAY (David). Speech of Hon. D. Barclay on the President's message; House of Representatives of the United States, January 7, 1857. [n. p., 1857.] 8vo. 3358

BARCLAY (H.) Memorial of Henry Barclay, Late Sexton of St. Luke's Church, Philadelphia, July 13, 1858. [n. p., n. d.] 8vo, pp. 8. 3359

BARCLAY (J. J.) An Address, delivered at the Laying of the Corner Stone of the House of Refuge for Colored Juvenile Delinquents ... July 1, 1848. By James J. Barclay, ... *Philadelphia*, 1848. 8vo, pp. 15 (1). H. 3360

BARCLAY. An Address delivered at the Organization of the Normal School ... the 13th of January, 1848 ... . By James J. Barclay ... . *Philadelphia*, 1848. 8vo, pp. 23 (1). C. & H.

Mr. Barclay is the author of other addresses.

BARCLAY (P.) The Universal Traveller or, a Complete Account of the most Remarkable Voyages and Travels of the Eminent Men of our own and other Nations to the present Time. Containing A Relation of the Successes or Misfortunes that attended them in their various Attempts and many entertaining

Descriptions of the Curiosities in Art and Nature, The Manners, Customs &c. observable in the Countries they visited. Collected from the best Authorities, Printed or Manuscript. By Patrick Barclay, D.D. *Dublin: R. Reilly*, MDCCXXXV. Folio, vii., 858; Index, 10 l. P. 3362

Contains copious accounts of the Spanish colonies in North America, planting of Virginia, New England, &c., the travels of Columbus, Cortez, Pizarro, &c. .

BARCLAY (Robert). The Anarchy of the Ranters, and Other Libertines; the Hierarchy of the Romanists, and other Pretended Churches, equally refused and refuted, in a two-fold Apology for the Church and People of God, called in Derision, Quakers. Wherein They are vindicated from those that accuse them of Disorder and Confusion on the one hand, and from such as calumniate them with Tyranny and Imposition on the other; shewing, that as the true and pure Principles of the Gospel are restored by their Testimony; so is also the antient Apostolick Order of the Church of Christ re-established among them, and settled upon its right Basis and Foundation. By Robert Barclay. *Philadelphia, Reprinted, and Sold by B. Franklin, and D. Hall*, 1757. 8vo, pp. viii., 112. + *Philadelphia, Joseph Crukshank*, 1770. 8vo, pp. viii., 111. + *Wilmington* [*Del.*], 1783. 8vo, pp. 111. 3363

BARCLAY. An Apology for the True Christian Divinity, As the same is Held Forth, and Preached, by the People, called in Scorn Quakers: Being A full Explanation and Vindication of their Principles and Doctrines; by many Arguments, deduced from Scripture and Right Reason, and the Testimonies of Famous Authors, both Ancient and Modern: With a full Answer to the strongest Objections usually made against them. ... By Robert Barclay ... . The Sixth Edition in English. ... *Newport, Printed by James Franklin*, 1729. 8vo, 6 p. l., pp. 524 [574], 31. + *Philadelphia*, 1775, 1780, 1789, 1805, and 1855. + *New York*, 1827. 8vo. + *Providence*, 1840. 8vo. 3364

First published in Latin in 1676. The first edition in English, *London*, 1678; second, 1678; fourth, 1701; fifth, 1703; sixth, 1736; seventh, 1765; eighth, 1780. Many other editions; also translations into Dutch, German, French, Spanish, Danish, and, in fact, into Arabic. *See* J. Smith's "Catal. of Friends' Books," pp. 179–184, where the foreign titles are incorrect.

BARCLAY. Apologie Oder Vertheidigungs-Schrift der wahren Christlichen Gottesgelahrtheit Wie solche unter dem Volk, so man aus Spott Quaker, das ist, Zitterer nennet, vorgetragen und

gelehret wird. ... ins Deutsche ubersetzt. *Germantown, Gedrucht bey Christoph Saur*, 1776. 8vo, pp. 797 (25). C. 3365

Books printed by Sower are not common. At the battle of Germantown this printer's property was destroyed. The British used the poor fellow's books for making cartridges!

B[ARCLAY] (R.) A Catechism and Confession of Faith, Approved of and Agreed into by the General Assembly of the Patriarchs, Prophets, and Apostles, Christ himself chief Speaker In and Among them, ... By R. B. a Servant of the Church of Christ. *London, Printed, and Re-printed and Sold by Samuel Keimer*, 1726. 12mo, pp. vi., 1 l., 99. + *New York*, 1752. 12mo. + The Eighth Edition. By R. B. ... *London, Printed; Philadelphia, Reprinted and Sold by James Chattin*, 1753. 12mo, pp. viii., 200. P. + *Philadelphia*, 1773. 12mo, pp. x., 150, 64. + *Philadelphia*, 1788. 12mo. + Eleventh Edition. *Philadelphia*. 1793. 12mo. + [Id.], 1843 .12mo + To which is added, The Ancient Testimony of the said People, revived. *Wilmington, Del., James Wilson*, 1821. 12mo. 3366

BARCLAY. Truth triumphant through the Spiritual Warfare, Christian Labours, and Writings of that able and faithful servant of Jesus Christ, Robert Barclay, Governor of East Jersey. *London, T. Northcott*, 1692. Folio, pp. lv., 908; 8 l. + To which is prefixed an account of his Life and Writings. *Philadelphia*, 1831. 3 vols., 8vo. 3367

Although appointed Governor of East Jersey, he never resided there. His intellectual superiority placed him at the head of his sect. Smith records an edition, *By B. C. Stanton, of Springborough, Ohio.* 3 vols., 8vo, and queries whether it is the same as the edition of 1831.

BARCLAY (Robert). Agricultural Tour in the United States and Upper Canada, with Miscellaneous Notices. By Captain Barclay, of Ury. *Edinburgh, Blackwood*, 1842. Post 8vo, pp. xxiii., 181. C. 3368

The author was the celebrated walking captain, a descendant of the Apologist. Reprinted in *The New World*, March 4, 1843. 4to, pp. vi., 251–265.

BARCLAY (Robert), *pseudon.* Address to the Society of Friends in the United States. [n. p., n. d.] 8vo. pp. 8. N.

Relates to the Harrison and Tyler campaign.

BARCLAY (Sidney), *pseudon.* *See* [Post (Lydia Minturn)].

BARCO CENTENERA. Argentina y Conquista del Rio de la Plata, con otros acaecimientos de los Reynos del Peru, Tucu-

man, y estado del Brasil ... Por El Arcediano Don Martin del Barco Centenera. *Lisboa, Pedro Crasbeeck*, 1602. 4to, 4 p. l., Text, 230 l. J. C. B. 3370

The author passed twenty-eight years in America, where he took part in the conquest of La Plata. He gives accounts of the expeditions of Pedro Mendoza, Alvar Nuñez Cabeça de Vaca, and Thomas Candish. Reprinted in Barcia Historiadores Primitivos, v. 3.

BARCO CENTENERA. La Argentina ó la conquista del Rio Plata. de la Poema histórico. Por el Arcediano D. Martin del Barco Centenera. *Buenos-Aires*, 1836. 4to, pp. 312. 3371

BARD (S. A.), *pseudon.* *See* [Squier (E. G.)]

BARD (W.) Address, delivered before the Alumni of Columbia College, on the Third Day of May, 1826 ... . By William Bard, A.B. *New-York, G. & C. Carvill*, 1826. 8vo, pp. 36. H.

Contains information on education in the State of New York.

BARDWELL (H.) Memoir of Rev. Gordon Hall. By Horatio Bardwell. *Andover*, 1834. 12mo. 3373

BARÈRE DE VIEUZAC (Bertrand). Convention nationale. Rapport fait au nom du Comité de salut public Par Barère, Sur les Colonies Françaises Isles du Vent. Dans la Séance du 19 thermidor, l'an 2 ... . [*Paris*, 1794.] 8vo, pp. 3. H. 3374

BARHAM (H.) An Essay upon the Silk Worm. By Henry Barham. *London*, 1799. 8vo. 3375

Contains an account of its cultivation in Virginia on pp. 52–100.

BARHAM. Hortus Americanus: containing an account of the Trees, Shrubs, and other Vegetable Productions, of South-America and the West-India Islands, and particularly of the Island of Jamaica; Interspersed with many curious and useful Observations, respecting their Uses in Medicine, Diet, and Mechanics. By the late Dr. Henry Barham. To which are added, a Linnæan Index, &c. &c. &c. *Kingston, Jamaica: Alexander Aikman*, MDCCXCIV. 8vo, 4 p. l., pp. 212; Index, 18 l.

BARHAM (J. T.) Considerations On the Abolition of Slavery. By J. T. Barham. 1823. 8vo. 3377

BARHAM (W.) Descriptions of Niagara, selected from various Travellers; with original additions. By William Barham ... *Gravesend, Houlston* [1847]. 8vo, pp. 180; 2 Plates. C. 3378

Barhydt (D. P.) Industrial Exchanges and Social Remedies, with a Consideration of Taxation. By Dav. Parish Barhydt ... *New York, George P. Putnam*, 1849. 12mo, 2 p. l., pp. 238. c., H. 3379

Baril. L'empire du Brésil. Monographie complète de l'Empire sud-américain, orné du portrait de dom Pedro II. Par V. L. Baril, comte de la Hure. *Paris, Sartorius*, 1862. 8vo, pp. xv., 576. 3380

Baril. Le Mexique. Résumé géographique, statistique, industriel, historique et social ... Par V. L. Baril, comte de la Hure. *Douai, Ve Céret-Carpentier*, 1862. 8vo, pp. xviii., 271.

Baril. Les peuples du Brésil avant la découverte de l'Amérique. Par V. L. Baril, comte de la Hure. *Douai, Ve Céret-Carpentier*, 1861. 4to, pp. 14. 3382

Baril. Voyage sur le Rio Parahyba. Par V. L. Baril, comte de la Hure. *Douai, Ve Céret-Carpentier*, 1861. 4to, pp. 17 3382a

[Barinetti (Charles)]. A Voyage to Mexico and Havana, with some observations on the United States. By an Italian. *New York, C. Vinten*, 1841. 8vo, pp. x., 139 c., 3383

Baring (A.) An Inquiry into the Causes and Consequences of the Orders in Council, and an Examination of the Conduct of Great Britain towards the Neutral Commerce of America. By Alexander Baring, Esqr, M.P. *London, J. M. Richardson*, 1808. 8vo, pp. 183. + Second Edition. *London, Richardson*, 1808. 8vo, 2. p. l., pp. 179. + Third Edition. 1808. 8vo, pp. iv., 179. + *New-York, Hopkins & Bayard*, 1808. 8vo, pp. 104 + *New-York, Re-printed from the London Edition, John Bleecker*, 1808. 8vo, pp. 104. c. & H. + Second American Edition. *New-York*, 1808. 8vo, pp. 104. c., H. 3384

Baring. A letter to the Hon. Baron Ashburton, on the Importance of the corn and flour trade with England, via the River St. Lawrence and on the advantages of introducing Maize into Great Britain. *New York*, 1842. 8vo. P. 3385

Baring. Mr. Alexander Baring's Speech in the House of Commons, on the 15th Day of May, 1823, on Mr. Buxton's Motion for a Resolution Declaratory of Slavery in the British Colonies being Contrary to the English Constitution and to Christianity. *London, Marchant, Printer*, 1823. 8vo, pp. 17. H.

Baring. Speech of Lord Ashburton on the Second Reading of the Canada Government Bill. *London*, 1838. 8vo. 3387

Several Parliamentary papers on the Ashburton Treaty are included in the Lord's papers in the Canadian Parliamentary Library. *See also* the numerous Parliamentary papers referred to in the Boston Public Library's Index, Upper Hall, p. 832, "North-eastern Boundary." *See also* N. Am. R., Vol. LVI., p. 452. Q. R., Vol. LXXI., p. 560. Fraser's Mag., Vol. XXVI., p. 579; Vol. XXVII., p. 272. *See also* Webster (Daniel).

Baring, Brothers, & Co. [Statement of their transactions with S. Jaudon, agent of the Bank of the United States. *London?* 1840.] 8vo, pp. 70. H. 3388

Barker (C.) The Golden Belt, or, The Carib's Pledge. By Colin Barker. *New York, Beadle*, 186–[?]. 12mo. 3388a

The scene is laid in the tropics, just after the discovery of this country by Columbus.

Barker (D.) An Address ... at Rochester, July 4, 1828, by David Barker, Jr. ... *Dover, D. W. Ela and Co., Printers*, 1828. 8vo, pp. 25 or 26? H. 3389

Barker. Jacob Barker to the Electors of the First Senatorial District of the State of New-York. [n. p., 1828.] 8vo.

[Barker.] The Ballot Box the Palladium of our Liberties. By Jacob Barker. *New Orleans, For the Compiler, July*, 1863. 8vo, pp. 65. 3391

Barker. Incidents in the Life of Jacob Barker of New Orleans, Louisiana; with Historical Facts, his Financial Transactions with the Government, and his Course on Important Political Questions, from 1800 to 1855. *Washington*, 1855. 8vo, pp. v., 285; 2 plates. c. 3392

Mr. Barker's public life has been checkered by numerous trials. The following pamphlets are partly historical: Mr. J. Barker's Speech in the Case of Barker vs. Barker, ... against a claim preferred by H. Barker for damages. [*New York*, 1843.] 8vo. Brief and Speech in the U. S. Court of Claims. *Washington*, 1857. 8vo. c. Further Remarks, &c., on The late Trials for Conspiracy. Jacob Barker to the Public. [Dated August, 1819.] 8vo, pp. 50. B. The Speeches of Mr. Jacob Barker and his Counsel, on the Trials for Conspiracy, etc. *New York*, 1827. Letters developing the Conspiracy formed in 1826, for his ruin. 8vo. New Orleans, January 14, 1830. To the ... Members of the U. S. Senate from La. Signed Jacob Barker. [Against Hugh Maxwell.] 8vo, pp. 18. Trial of Jacob Barker, Thomas Vermilyea, and Matthew L. Davis, for Alleged Conspiracy, New York, Aug., 1827, before Judge Ogden Edwards. Reported by Hugh Maxwell. *New York*, 1827. 8vo, pp. 332. c. Report of the Trial of Henry Eckford, Jacob Barker and others, Sept. 25, 1826; Jacob Barker's Speech in the Court of Gen. Sessions, June 6, 1822; Third Trial of Jacob Barker for conspiracy. *New-York*, 1827. *See also* Ward (R. R.)

Barker (James N.) The Indian Princess an Operatic Melo-Drama. Founded on an Incident in Smith's Virginia. By J. N. Barker. *Philadelphia*, 1808. 18mo, pp. iv., 74. 3393

Barker. An Oration, Delivered at Philadelphia Vauxhall Gardens, on the Forty-First Anniversary of American Independence. By James N. Barker. *Philadelphia, J. Binns*, 1817. 8vo, pp. 11. 3394

Barker. Sketches of the Primitive Settlements on the River Delaware. A Discourse delivered before the Society for the Commemoration of the Landing of William Penn, On the 24th of October, 1827. By James N. Barker. Published by Request of the Society. *Philadelphia, Carey, Lea and Carey*, 1827. 8vo, pp. 62. 3395

Barker (J.) Address delivered at Halifax, July 4, 1803. By Rev. Joseph Barker, A.M. *Boston* [1803]. 8vo, pp. 16.

Barker. A Discourse delivered in Middleboro', Mass., Aug. 20, 1812, being the day of the National Fast. By Rev. Joseph Barker, A.M. *Boston*, 1812. 8vo. 3397

Barker. A Sermon delivered at the Ordination of the Rev. Otis Thompson ... [over] the Second ... Church in Rehoboth, September 24th, 1800. By Joseph Barker ... *Providence, B. Wheeler*, 1801. 8vo. 3398

Barker. The Stability of Christ's Church. A Century Sermon Preached at Middleboro', Mass. Jan. 6, 1795. By Joseph Barker. *Boston*, 1796. 8vo, pp. 31. 3399

Barker (J.), *Esq.* John Brown, or the True and False Philanthropist, Lecture by Joseph Barker, Esq., at Concert Hall. *Philadelphia, G. W. Taylor*, 1859. 8vo, pp. 28. 3400

Barker. Slavery and Civil War, or the Harper's Ferry Insurrection, with a Review of Discourses on the subject, by Rev. W. H. Furness, Hon. J. R. Giddings, and Wendell Phillips, Esq. A Lecture, By Joseph Barker. [No imprint.] 8vo, pp. 24. 3401

Barker (R.) Narrative of the Sufferings of Robert Barker, Carpenter on board the Thetis Snow, of Bristol, in her Voyage to the Coast of Guinea and Antigua. 1755. 8vo. 3402

Reprinted with the following title:

Barker. The Unfortunate Shipwright, or Cruel Captain, being a Faithful Narrative of the unparalleled Sufferings of Robert Barker on board the Thetis Snow of Bristol, in a Voyage to Guinea and Antigua. [1762.] 8vo. 3403

Barker. The Second Part of the Unfortunate Shipwright, or the Unparalleled Sufferings of Robert Barker, late Carpenter on board the Thetis-Snow of Bristol, on a voyage to the Coast of Guinea and Antigua. *London*, 1773. 8vo. + 1776. 8vo.

Barker (T. H.) Union and Emancipation: a Reply to the 'Christian News' Article on 'Emancipation and War.' By Thos. H. Barker ... *Manchester, Union and Emancipation Society*, 1863. 12mo, pp. 23. H. 3405

Barker (W. T.) Speech of Hon. W. T. Barker, upon the Right of Legislative Supervision over Railroad Corporations, delivered in the House of Representatives, February 24, 1866. ... *Des Moines*, 1866. 8vo, pp. 15 (1). H. 3406

Barkshire (*Earl of*). *See* Guiana.

Barlæus, *or* Baarle, *or* Baerle (Caspar). Casparis Barlæi ... Poemata. Editio IV, Altera plus parte auctior. Pars I. Heroicorvm. || Pars II, Elegiarvm et miscellaneorvm Carminvm. *Amstelodami, Apud Ioannem Blaev*, M D C XLV–XLVI. 2 vols., sm. 12mo, pp. (22), 731 (1); (8), 576. H. 3407

"Argo Batava. Sive Epinicium in captam classem Mexicanam," I., 200–210; "Triumphus super capta Olinda, Pernambuci urbe, Brasiliæ Metropoli," I., 244–250; "Mavritivs Redvx ... ex Orbe Americano," I., 333–340. Other editions, *Amst., Elzev.*, 1628 and 1630, 8vo, which contain only the first part. Pars II. was first published in an "Editio nova ... altera parte auctior. ... *Lugdv. Batav.*, Ex officina Elzeviriana, cIↄ Iↄc XXXI." Sm. 12mo, 8 p. l., pp. 511 (1). B. There is an Ed. v., *Amst., Blaev*, M D C LV., 2 vols., 12mo, H., and an ed., *Francof., Folginer.*, 1689, 2 vols.? 12mo. The "Triumphus super capta Olinda" appeared separately, *Lugd. Bat.*, 1630, folio.

Barlæus. Casparis Barlæi, | Rervm per Octennivm | in | Brasilia | Et alibi nuper gestarum, | Sub Præfectura Illustrissimi Comitis | I. Mavritii, | Nassoviæ, &c. Comitis, | Nunc Vesaliæ Gubernatoris & Equitatus Fœderatorum | Belgii Ordd. sub Avriaco Ductoris, | Historia. | *Amstelodami*, | *Ex Typographeio Ioannis Blaev*, M D C XLVII. Folio, 6 p. l. (including an Engraved Title), pp. 340, Index, 4. l. 30 Plates, 24 Maps, and Portrait of Maurice of Nassau. H. 3408

Clement (*Bibl. cur.*, II., 430) calls this work "*fort rare*," most of the copies having been consumed by a fire, which destroyed the warehouses of Bleau, the publisher. It is a magnificent work, illustrated with [55] maps, views, and portrait of Prince Maurice. Heber's copy sold for £1 1s.; Tross', 30 fr. A Chilian vocabulary will be found on pages 283–289. Copies are sometimes found on large paper.

Barlæus. Casparis Barlæi, | Rervm per Octennivm | in | Brasilia | Et alibi gestarum, | Sub Præfectura Illustrissimi Comitis | I. Mauritii | Nassaviæ &c. Comitis, | Historia. | Editio secunda. | Cui accesserunt | Gulielmi Pisonis Medici | Amstelædamensis | Tractatvs | 1. De Aeribus, aquis & locis in Brasilia. | 2. De Arundine saccharifera. | 3. De Melle silvestri. | 4. De Radice altili Mandihoca. | Cum Grat. & Pvivil. [*sic*] Sac. Cæsar. Majest. | *Clivis, ex Officinâ Tobiæ Silberling*, | M. DC. LX. | 8vo, 8 p. l., including the Titles, one of which is engraved, Portrait and Arms of Prince Maurice, pp. 664, Index, 11 l. 7 Plates and 2 Maps. H. & J. C. B. 3409

Priced, by Muller, $7.50. Contains a Chilian and Latin vocabulary, on pp. 474-491. This second edition in Latin contains the natural history of the country, by G. Piso. The plates and maps are the same as those in the German version, described *infra*, with one added, of the eclipse of Nov. 12, 1640. The place of publication is misprinted *CLIVIS*. Reissued, with the following title:

Barlæus. Descriptio totivs Brasiliæ, in qua agitur de natura et indole Regionis et incolarum, de regimine politico, regum successione, de rebus privatis, de arundine saccharifera, de melle silvestri, de aquis et locis, de moribus, legibus, et ritibus istarum gentium. *Clivis, Tobiæ Silberlingii*, 1689. 8vo, 5 p. l., pp. 664, 11 l. 2 Maps, 6 Plates and Portrait. 3410

Barlæus. Brasilianische | Geschichte, | Bey Achtjähriger in selbigen Landen | geführeter Regierung | Seiner Fürstlichen Gnaden | Herrn | Johann Moritz, | Fürstens zu Nassau etc. | Erstlich in Latein durch Casparem | Barlæum beschrieben, | Vnd jetzo in Teutsche Sprach vbergesetzt. | [Vignette.] | Cum Grat. & Privil. Sac. Cæsar. Majest. | *Cleve, Gedruckt bey Tobias Silberling*, | *Im Jahr* 1659. | 8vo, Engraved and Printed Title, Portrait, Arms, &c., 4 l., Dedication, 10 l., pp. 848, Register, 10 l. 8 Maps and Plates. H. 3411

Barlæus. Brasilianische Geschichte. Erstlich in Latein beschreiben; und kurtze und wahre Beschreibung der funffjährigen harten Befängnüs, durch Nicolaus Schmidt. *Leipzig*, 1684. 8vo. P. 3412

See Boucher, v., 276.

Barlow (E.) An Exact Survey of the Tide. Explicating its Production and Propagation, Variety and Anomaly, in all Parts of the World; Especially near the Coasts of Great Britain and Ireland. With a Preliminary Treatise concerning the Origin of Springs, Generation of Rain, and Production

of Wind. The Second Edition, with Curious Maps. By E. Barlow, Gent. *London, John Hooke*, 1722. 8vo, 8 p. l., pp. 122, 2d Title, pp. 212. 12 Maps. 3413

Barlow (Joel). Advice to the Privileged Orders in the several States of Europe, resulting from the necessity and propriety of a General Revolution in the Principle of Government. Part I. By Joel Barlow. *Paris, Barrois*, 1792. 8vo. + *London, J. Johnson*, 1792. 8vo, 2 p. l., pp. 156. + *Reprinted at New York*, 1792. 8vo, pp. 178. + Third Edition. *London, J. Eaton*, 1793. 8vo. + Part II. *Paris, Barrois*, 1793. 8vo, pp. 101. + *London*, 1793. 8vo. *Re-printed, New York*, 1794. 8vo. + Second Edition. *London, Eaton*, 1795. 8vo, pp. 64. H. 3414

See M. R., VII., 313; XVIII., 300; Anal. Mag., IV., 130, 263.

Barlow. Avis aux Ordres privilégiés dans les divers états de l'Europe. *Paris*, 1794. 2 Parts, 8vo. 3415

Barlow. The Columbiad a Poem. By Joel Barlow. [Motto.] *Printed by Fry and Kammerer for C. and A. Conrad and Co., Philadelphia*, 1807. 4to, pp. xvi., 454. Portrait by Fulton, and 11 Plates by Smirke. H., P. + *Philadelphia, Condict, Conrad and Co.*, 1809. 2 vols., 12mo. + *London, Richard Phillips*, 1809. Rl. 8vo, pp. 426. 3416

The quarto edition was printed at the expense of Robert Fulton, to whom it was dedicated. It is "a new edition with great alterations of the Visions of Columbus, beautifully printed, and illustrated with fine engravings."—Rich. Some copies were issued with proof impressions of the plates. The last edition, which was also issued on large paper, has the following title:

Barlow. The Columbiad. a Poem. With the Last corrections of the Author. By Joel Barlow. [Motto.] *Paris, F. Schoell*, 1813. Rl. 8vo, pp. xl., 448. 4 Plates. H. 3417

Barlow. The Conspiracy of Kings; a Poem; Addressed to the Inhabitants of Europe, from another quarter of the World. By Joel Barlow. *London*, 1792. 8vo. + *Paris, Barrois, Senior, and R. Thompson*, 1793. 8vo, pp. 32. H. + *Newburyport, Robinson & Tucker*, 1794. 8vo, pp. 30. 3418

[Barlow.] An Elegy on the late Honorable Titus Hosmer, Esq; one of the Counsellors of the State of Connecticut ... *Hartford, Hudson & Goodwin* [1780]. 16mo, pp. 15. B. 3419

[Barlow.] "The Hasty Pudding;" A Poem, in three cantos, Written at Chambery, in Savoy, Jan. 1793. *New York*,

1796. 8vo, pp. 15. + *Salem, J. Cushing*, 1799. 12mo, pp. 21. + *Canandaigua, N. Y.* 12mo. + *Caldwell*, 1821. 12mo, pp. 18. B. + With a Memoir [on] Maize, or Indian Corn; compiled by D. J. Browne. *New York*, 1847. 12mo. + *New York* [n. d.] 12mo. 3420

Barlow. Letter to Henry Gregoire, ... in Reply to his Letter on the Columbiad. By Joel Barlow ... *Washington City, Printed by Roger Chew Weightman*, 1809. 8vo, pp. 15. H.

Barlow. Joel Barlow to his Fellow Citizens of the United States of America. Letter I. On the system of policy hitherto pursued by their Government. [Dated *Paris* 4 *March*, 1799.] 8vo, pp. 55. H. + Letter II. On certain political Measures proposed to their consideration. [With an appendix. Dated *Paris* 20 *december* 1799.] 8vo, pp. 102. H. + *Philadelphia* 1801. 8vo.

Republished in England, with the following title:

Barlow. Letters from Paris, to the Citizens of the United States of America, on the System of Policy hitherto pursued by their Government relative to their Commercial Intercourse with England and France, &c. By Joel Barlow. *London, James Ridgway*, 1800. 8vo, pp. 116. H. 3423

The Massachusetts Historical Society Catalogue describes an edition, 1799. 8vo, pp. 32, 36. Also: A Letter to the National Convention of France, on the Defects in the Constitution of 1791. To which is added the Conspiracy of Kings: a Poem. *New York* [n. d.] 8vo. A letter addressed to the people of Piedmont. Translated from the French by the author. *London*, 1795. 8vo, pp. 48. + *New York*, 1795. 12mo. Notice sur la vie et les Ecrits de Joel Barlow. [By Dumont Lee.] 1813. 8vo.

Barlow. An Oration, delivered at the North Church in Hartford, at the meeting of the Connecticut Society of the Cincinnati, July 4th, 1787. In Commemoration of the Independence of the United States. By Joel Barlow, Esquire. *Hartford, Printed by Hudson & Goodwin* [1787]. 4to, pp. 20. B.

Barlow. Oration delivered at Washington, July Fourth, 1809; at the Request of the Democratic Citizens of the District of Columbia. By Joel Barlow. *Washington City, R. C. Weightman*, 1809. 8vo, pp. 14. H. 3425

Barlow. The Political Writings of Joel Barlow. Containing Advice to the Privileged Orders. Letter to the National Convention. Letter to the People of Piedmont. The Conspiracy of Kings. A New Edition Corrected. *Printed at New-*

York, by Mott & Lyon, for Fellows & Adam, Thomas Greenleaf, and Naphtali Judah, 1796. 12mo, pp. 258. H. 3426

Some copies have the following imprint: *New York, Printed by Mott & Lyon, at their Printing Office No. 71, Barclay St. and Sold by them at their Store No. 70, Vesey Street*, 1796.

[Barlow.] Poem spoken at the Public Commencement at Yale College, New Haven, Sep. 11 (or 12), 1781. *Hartford* [n. d.] 8vo, pp. 16. 3427

Barlow. The Prospect of Peace; a Poetical Composition delivered in Yale College, July 23, 1778. By Joel Barlow. *New Haven*, 1788. 12mo, pp. 12. 3428

[Barlow.] Prospectus of a National Institution, to be established in the United States. *Washington, printed by Samuel H. Smith*, 1806. 8vo, pp. 44. H. 3429

Barlow. A Second Letter to his Fellow-Citizens of the United States, on certain Political Measures proposed to their consideration. *New York*, 1801. 8vo. 3430

Dated *Paris*, 10 *Dec.*, 1799.

[Barlow.] The Second Warning; or Strictures On the Speech of John Adams, President of the United States, at the Opening of Congress in November last. *Paris*, 1798. 8vo, pp. 28. M. 3431

Barlow. A Translation of Sundry Psalms which were omitted in Dr. Watts's version; to which is added a number of hymns. By Joel Barlow. *Hartford, Barlow & Babcock*, 1785. 12mo, pp. 14. 3432

Barlow. Two Letters to the Citizens of the United States, and one to General Washington—written from Paris, in the year 1799, on our Political and Commercial Relations. By Joel Barlow. *New Haven*, 1806. 12mo, pp. 119. c. 3433

Barlow. The Vision of Columbus; A Poem in Nine Books. By Joel Barlow, Esquire. *Hartford, Printed by Hudson and Goodwin for the Author*, M.DCC.LXXXVII. 8vo, pp. 248, Subscribers, 6 l. H. 3434

The subscribers' names include His Most Christian Majesty [Louis XVI.], 25 copies; His Excellency George Washington, Esq., 20 copies; Maj.-Gen. le Marquis de la Fayette, 10 copies, etc. Afterwards amplified into the Columbiad.

Barlow. The Vision of Columbus [etc.] Second Edition. *Hudson and Goodwin*, M.DCC.LXXXVII. 12mo, pp. 258, Subscribers, pp. 5. + *London*, *C. Dilly*, 1787. 12mo. 3435

In this edition the dedication to the French king is omitted. *See* M. R., LXXVIII., 248.

Barlow. The Vision of Columbus. A Poem, in Nine Books. By Joel Barlow. The Fifth Edition, corrected. [Motto.] To which is added, The Conspiracy of Kings: a Poem, by the same author. *Paris*, *Barrois*, *Senior*, *and R. Thomson*, 1793. 8vo, 2 p. l., pp. 304. Portrait. H. 3436

The author calls this the fifth edition. I have not seen what would constitute a fourth, if the English reprint is to be accounted a third. This Paris edition was reprinted. [n. d.] 8vo.

Barlow. The Vision of Columbus: a Poem, in Nine books. With explanatory notes. By Joel Barlow. From a revised edition of the Author. *Baltimore*, *W. D. Bell and J. D. Fry*, 1814. 16mo. 3437

Barlow (N.) A Vision Seen by Nathan Barlow, of Freetown, (Called so by the Inhabitants) Adjacent to the North End of Harlem, in the County of Kennebeck, District of Maine, January 8, 1801. ... *Greenfield*, *Mass.*, 1802, 12mo, pp. 11. W.

Barlow (P. W.) Niagara Suspension Railway Bridge. By Peter W. Barlow. *London*, *J. Weale*, 1860. 8vo. 3439

Barlow (S. L. M.) Bibliotheca Barlowiana. *New York*, MDCCCLXIV. 8vo, pp. 35. 3440

Four copies privately printed. Mr. Barlow's collection of books relating to America is probably, with one exception, the finest in New York.

Barlow (William). An Address on the Duties of Government in reference chiefly to public instruction, with the outlines of a plan for the application of the Smithsonian Fund to that object. By Rev. William Barlow. *New York*, 1847. 8vo.

Barlow. ... A Funeral Discourse Commemorative ... of the Late Hon. Stephen Van Rensselaer. Delivered at Ogdensburgh, February 17, 1839, by the Rev. William Barlow ... . *Albany*, *Printed by Packard*, *Van Benthuysen and Co.*, 1839. 8vo, pp. 47. H. 3442

[Barnard (C. F.)] The Life of Collin Reynolds, the Orphan Boy and Young Merchant. ... *Boston*, *Samuel G. Simpkins*, 1835. 24mo, pp. 32. H. 3443

Barnard. Report to the Delegates of the Benevolent Societies of Boston, Nov. 8, 1836. By Rev. Charles F. Barnard. *Boston*, 1836. 8vo. H. 3444

Barnard (C. H.) Narrative of the Sufferings and Adventures of Captain C. H. Barnard in a Voyage Round the World, during the years 1812, 1813, 1814, 1815, and 1816: embracing an account of the seizure of his vessel at the Falkland Islands. *New-York*, 1829. 8vo. 6 Plates. C. 3445

Barnard (Daniel D.) The Anti-Rent movement and Outbreak in New York. By Daniel D. Barnard. *Albany*, 1846. 8vo, pp. 27. 3446

Barnard. A Discourse on the Character of Daniel Webster, delivered at a Meeting of Americans in Paris, On the 16th Nov., 1852. By Daniel D. Bernard. 8vo. + Daniel Webster — Speech of Mr. Barnard ... at a Meeting of Americans in Paris ... . *Berlin*, *Printed by C. & F. Unger*, 1852. 8vo, pp. 21. B. 3447

Barnard. A Discourse on the Life, Character, and Public services of Ambrose Spencer, late Chief Justice, before the Bar of the City of Albany. *Albany*, 1849. 8vo. S. 3448

Barnard. A Discourse on the Life, Services, and Character of Stephen Van Rensselaer, delivered before the Albany Institute, April 15, 1839. With an Historical Sketch of the Colony and Manor of Rensselaerwyck in an Appendix. By Daniel D. Barnard. *Albany*, *Hoffman & White*, 1839. 8vo, pp. 144. H., S.

Barnard. Lecture on the Character and Services of James Madison ... . By Daniel D. Barnard. *Albany*, 1837. 8vo, pp. 47. B., C., H. 3450

Barnard. An Oration delivered before the ... Corporation and the Military and Civic Societies of ... Albany, on the Fourth of July, 1835. By Daniel D. Barnard. ... *Albany*, 1835. 8vo, pp. 51. B. 3451

Barnard. Speeches and Reports in the Assembly of New-York, at the Annual Session of 1838. By Daniel D. Barnard. *Albany*, *Oliver Steele*, 1838. 12mo, pp. xi., 228. H. 3452

Barnard. Speech of Mr. Barnard, of New York, on the Annexation of Texas. Delivered ... Jan. 24, 1845. *Washington*, 1845. 8vo, pp. 16. H. 3453

Barnard. Speech ... on the Report and Resolutions of the Committee on Elections, relative to the elections by General Ticket in the four recusant States of New Hampshire, Georgia, Mississippi, and Missouri. ... Feb. 13, 1844. [*Washington*, n. d.] 8vo, pp. 16. H. 3454

Also the following: An address delivered September 6, 1831 ... Williams' College: ... *Williamstown*, 1831. 8vo, pp. 36. Address before the ... Societies of Rutgers College ... July 18th, 1837. ... . *Albany*, 1837. 8vo, pp. 46. H. Anniversary Address ... before the American Institute ... 20th October, 1843. ... *New-York*, 1843. 8vo, pp. 28. H. A discourse ... at Burlington before the Literary Societies of the University of Vermont, August 1st, 1838. *Albany*, 1838. 8vo, pp. 56. H. Discourse before the Senate of Union College, On the 24th day of July, 1843. ... *Albany*, 1843. 8vo, pp. 55. H. A Letter from the Hon. D. D. Barnard ... to the Hon. Erastus Brooks ... on the Proceedings against Trinity Church, now pending in the Senate of the State. *Albany*, 1857. 8vo, pp. 43. H. Man and the State. Social and Political. An Address. *New Haven*, 1846. 8vo. B. A Plea for Social and Popular Repose ... . *New-York*, 1845. 8vo, pp. 22. Remarks ... on the Bill in relation to Duties and Drawbacks. ... July 28, 1841. *Washington*, 1841. 8vo, pp. 7. The Social System. An Address pronounced before the House of Convocation, of Trinity College, Hartford, August 2, 1848. ... *Hartford*, 1848. 8vo, pp. 29. Speech ... on the Tariff bill. ... March 17, 1828. *Washington*, 1828. 8vo, pp. 16. Speech ... in relation to the Contest for Seats from the State of New Jersey: ... December 4, 1839. *Washington*, 1839. 8vo, pp. 11. B. Speech ... on the Proposition to refuse the Oath to Five Members returned from New Jersey: December 18, 1839. *Washington*, 1839. 8vo, pp. 15. Speech against abandoning corsuspending the Prosecution of Works of Internal Improvement. ... February 14, 1840. *Washington*, 1840. 8vo, pp. 16. B. Speech ... on the Treasury Note Bill ... March 25, 1840. *Washington*, 1840, 8vo, pp. 16. B. Speech ... on the Sub-Treasury Bill. ... June 12, 1840. *Washington*, 1840. 8vo, pp. 22. B. Speech ... on the Loan Bill, ... July 9, 1841. *Washington*, 1841. 8vo, pp. 12. B. Speech ... in opening the Debate on the Bankrupt Bill ... also, his Speech in Reply on the same subject. Delivered ... August 10 and 17, 1841. *Washington*, 1841. 8vo, pp. 20. H. Speech ... in relation to the Destruction of the "Caroline," and the Case of McLeod. ... August 31, 1841. *Washington*, 1841. 8vo, pp. 15. B. Speech ... in Favor of a Uniform System of Electing Representatives by Districts throughout the United States. ... In the House ... April 28, 1842. *Washington*, 1842. 8vo. B. Speech ... on the Veto of the Provisional Tariff Bill. ... In the House ... July 1, 1842. *Washington*, 1842. 8vo, pp. 12. B. Speech ... on the Policy of a Protective Tariff. ... July 6, 1842. *Washington*, 1842. 8vo, pp. 14. B Speech on the 'Remedial Justice Bill.' [n. p.], 1842. 8vo, pp. 7. B. Speech ... on the President's Exchequer Plan: ... January 25, 1843. *Washington*, 1843. 8vo, pp. 12. Speech ... Dec. 29, 1843, and Jan. 2, 1844. On the Bill to refund the Fine imposed upon Gen. Jackson. *Washington*, 1844. 8vo, pp. 20. Speech ... on the Tariff Bill ... May 14, 1844. *Washington*, 1844. 8vo, pp. 32. B. Truths for Voters. ... [*Boston*, 1860.] 12mo, pp. 12. H.

Barnard (E.) A Sermon Preached before his Excellency Francis Bernard, Esq; Governor and Commander in Chief, The Honourable His Majesty's Council, And the Honourable House of Representatives, Of the Province of the Massachusetts-Bay in New-England, May 28th. 1766. Being the Anniversary for the Election of His Majesty's Council for said Province. By Edward Barnard, A.M. Pastor of the First Church in Haverhill. *Boston*, *Printed by Richard Draper*, MDCCLXVI. 8vo, pp. 39. H.

Barnard. A Sermon ... before the Annual Convention of Ministers of the Massachusetts-Bay, in Boston. May 27th. 1773. By Edward Barnard ... . *Boston*, *Thomas Leverett*, M,DCC,LXXIII. 8vo, pp. 32. B., H. 3456

Also: A Fast Sermon, 12 April, 1764. *Portsmouth*, 1764. 8vo. Sermon ... at the Ordination of the Rev. Mr. Henry True, to the Pastoral care of a Church in Hampstead in the Province of New Hampshire, June 24, 1752. 8vo, pp. 31. A Sermon Preached at the Ordination of the Rev. Mr. Gyles Merrill ... In Plastow and the North Part of Haverhill, March 6. 1765. ... *Boston*, 1765. 8vo, 2 p. l., pp. 26. H. A Sermon Preached at the Ordination of the Rev. Mr. Thomas Cary, ... Newburyport, May 11th, 1768. *Boston*, *Edes & Gill*, MDCCLXVIII. 8vo, pp. 47.

Barnard (Frederick Augustus Porter). Art Culture: its Relation to National Refinement and National Morality. An Oration ... before the Alabama Alpha of the ... Phi Beta Kappa ... July 11th, 1854: by Frederick A. P. Barnard A.M. ... *Tuscaloosa*, 1854. 8vo, pp. 25. H. 3457

[Barnard.] A Letter to the President of the United States. By a Refugee. *New York*, *C. S. Westcott & Co.*, 1863. 8vo, pp. 32. H. 3458

Barnard. Letters on College Government, and the Evils inseparable from The American College System in its Present Form ... . By Frederick A. P. Barnard ... . *New York*, *D. Appleton & Co.*, 1855. 8vo, pp. 104. N., H. 3459

Also: Improvements Practicable in American Colleges. ... *Hartford*, *F. C. Brownell*, 1856. 8vo, pp. 30. H. Letter to ... the Board of Trustees of the University of Mississippi. ... *Oxford*, *University of Mississippi*, 1858. 8vo, pp. 112, Errata (1). H. Report on a Proposition to modify the Plan of Instruction in the University of Alabama, made to the Faculty of the University. Read to the ... Trustees, Sept. 26, 1854. *New York*, 1855. 8vo, pp. 104. Proceedings at the Inauguration of Frederick A. P. Barnard ... as President of Columbia College, ... October 3, 1864. ... *New York*, *Hurd and Houghton*, 1865. 8vo, pp. 106. H.

Barnard (F. C.) Life of a Negro Slave. By Mrs. F. C. Barnard. *London*, *H. Washbourne*, 1835. 12mo. + 1846. 12mo. 3460

Barnard (Frederick Lamport). Three Years' Cruise in the Mozambique Channel, for the Suppression of the Slave Trade. By Lieut. Barnard. *London*, 1848. Post 8vo, pp. 334. C.

Barnard (G. N.) Photographic Views of Sherman's Campaign from Negatives taken on the Field, by George N. Barnard, Official Photographer of the Military Division of the Mississippi. *New York*. Plates in folio, Text, 8vo, pp. 30. 3462

Barnard (*Mrs.* H. Jenkins). A Narrative of the Proceedings in America, of the Society called Quakers, in the Case of Hannah Barnard. With a Brief Review of the Previous Transactions in Great Britain and Ireland: intended as a Sequel to an Appeal to the Society of Friends. ... *London*, *J. Johnson*, 1804. 8vo, pp. xvi., 145, Errata, 1 p. 3463

Barnard (H.) Biographical Sketch of Ezekiel Cheever; with Notes on the Early Free Schools and Early School-Books of New England. By Henry Barnard. (Reprinted with additions from the American Journal of Education for March, 1856.) 8vo, 2 p. l., pp. 32. + Second edition. *Hartford*, 1856. 8vo. H. 3464

Also, in his Educational Biography, Vol. I.

Barnard. Educational Biography. Memoirs of Teachers, Educators, and Promoters and Benefactors of Education, Literature, and Science. Reprinted from the American Journal of Education. Edited by Henry Barnard, LL.D. ... Part I. Teachers and Educators. *New York*, *F. C. Brownell*, 1859. 8vo, pp. 524. 31 Portraits. + Second Edition. [Ibid.], 1861. 8vo, pp. 524. Portrait. H. 3465

Barnard. History and Condition of Common Schools and other Institutions of Education in Connecticut. By Henry Barnard, LL.D. Second Edition. *Hartford*. 8vo, pp. 62.

[Barnard.] Memoir of Cornelius Conway Felton. Republished from Barnard's American Journal of Education, for March, 1861. [n. p., n. d.] 8vo, pp. 265–296. Portrait. H. 3467

Barnard. Report on the Condition and Improvement of the Public Schools of Rhode Island, submitted Nov. 1, 1854, by Henry Barnard, Commissioner of Public Schools. *Providence*, 1854. 8vo, pp. 255. 3468

Barnard. Tribute to Gallaudet; a Discourse in Commemoration of the Life, Character and Services of the Rev. Thomas H. Gallaudet, LL.D., delivered before the Citizens of Hartford, Jan. 7th, 1852. With an appendix: Containing History of Deaf-Mute Instruction and Institutions, and other Documents. By Henry Barnard. *Hartford*, *Brockett & Hutchinson*, 1852. 8vo, Title, pp. 267 (1). Portrait. B. 3469

Also: Educational Tracts, by Henry Barnard. No. 1 to No. 8. *Hartford*, 1842–6. 8vo. Legal Provision respecting the Education and Employment of Children in Factories and Manufacturing Establishments; with an Appendix on the Influence of Education on the Quality and Pecuniary Value of Labour, and its connection with Insanity and Crime. *Hartford*, 1842. 8vo, pp. 52, 32. Normal Schools, and other Institutions, Agencies, and Means designed for the Professional Education of Teachers, ... Part I. United States and British Provinces. Part II. Europe. *Hartford*, 1851. 8vo, pp. 600. Practical Illustrations of the Principles of School Architecture ... 2nd edition. With 163 Woodcuts. *New York*, 1854. 8vo, pp. 176. School Architecture; or, Contributions to the Improvement of School-Houses in the United States. *New York*, 1848. 8vo. + Fourth Edition. *New York*, 1850. 8vo. + Fifth Edition. *New York*, 1854. 8vo, pp. 464. Woodcuts. H. + 5th edition. *Hartford*, 1854. 8vo, pp. 464. 300 Cuts. *See* American Journal of Education; Connecticut; Journal of the Rhode Island Institute of Instruction.

Barnard (John). A Proof of Jesus Christ His being the ancient promised Messiah: a Sermon preach'd in the Chapel of Harvard-Colledge ... June 23. 1756. By John Barnard, A.M. ... *Boston*, *J. Draper*, 1756. 8vo, pp. 55 (2). H. 3470

With a dedication to Lucy Dudley, relict of Paul Dudley, founder of the lecture, and an appendix, containing an extract from his will. The second Dudleian lecture preached, and the first published.

Barnard. The Throne Established by Righteousness. A Sermon Preach'd Before His Excellency Jonathan Belcher, Esq; ... May 29. 1734. Being the Day for the Electing His Majesty's Council there. By John Barnard ... . *Boston*, MDCCXXXIV. 8vo, pp. 60. H. 3471

Also: A Call to Parents, and Children. Or, The Great Concern of Parents; and The Important Duty of Children. ... [Sermons.] *Boston*, 1737. 8vo, pp. (4) 70. H. The Certainty, Time, and End of the Birth of our Lord and Saviour ... . Jesus Christ ... A Sermon, at the Lecture, in Marblehead, December 25. 1729. ... By John Barnard. *Boston*, 1731. 8vo, pp. (4), 66. ... Dudleian Lecture. 1768. *Salem*, 1768. 8vo, pp. 28. The Imperfection of the Creature, and the Excellency of the Divine Commandment ... Nine Sermons on Psal. cxix. 96. *Boston*, *Rogers and Fowle*, *and D. Gookin*, MDCCXLVII. 8vo, 4 p. l., pp. 248. H. Janua Coelestis. Or, the Mystery of the Gospel in the Salvation of a Sinner, Opened and Explained ... In several Discourses on Acts xvi. 30. By John Barnard ... . *Boston*, *Rogers and Fowle*, 1750. 8vo, pp. 442 (1). H. The Lord Jesus Christ the ... Supream Head of the Church. A Sermon ... at ... [the] Anniversary Convention, in Boston; which was followed with a collection for the Propagation of the Gospel. June 1. 1738. ... *Boston*, *H. Foster*, 1738. 8vo, Title, pp. 34. H. A New Version of the Psalms of David; Fitted to the Tunes used in the Churches: With several Hymns Out of the Old, and New, Testament. ... *Boston*, *T. Leverett*, 1752. 12mo, 2 p. l., pp. 278 (1). The copy in Harv. Coll. Lib. has MS. corrections by the author. ... Sermon on the Death of John Atwood, who died Aug. 26, 1714. *Boston*, 1714. 16mo. ... Sermon ... at Salem ... after the Death of the Reverend, Mr. George Curwin ... Novemb. ... 1717. ... *Boston*; *Samuel Gerrish*, 1717. Sm. 8vo, 2 p. l., pp. ii., 42. H. ... A Sermon Preached at the Funeral of ... The Reverend Mr. Samuel Cheever, Pastor of a Church ... in Marblehead; who deceased May 29, 1724. ... *Boston*, 1724. 12mo, 2 p. l., pp. 41. H. ... A Sermon Delivered at the Lecture in Boston, Sept. 18. 1729. *Boston*, 1729. ... 8vo, Title, pp. 49, Errata, 1 l. H. Sermons on Several Subjects ... . By John Barnard, A.M. ... . *London*, *Printed for Samuel Gerrish*, *and Daniel Henchman*, *Boston*, MDCCXXVII. 8vo, pp. 190. H., W. Also on large paper. The True Divinity of Jesus Christ; ... a Discourse at The Public Lecture in Boston, ... July 16, 1761. *Boston*, MDCCLXI. 8vo, pp. 38. H., N. Two Discourses Addressed to Young Persons: To which is added, A Sermon Occasioned by the Earthquake, ... October 29. 1727. By John Barnard ... . *Boston*, MDCCXXVII. 12mo, 2 p. l., pp. iv., 99. H. Two Sermons: The Christian's Behavior under Severe and Repeated Bereavements, and the Fatal Consequence of a People's Persisting in Sin, Preached in the Time of Measles. By John Barnard, A.M. *Boston*, *N. E.*, 1714. 12mo, pp. 68. W. A Zeal for Good Works Excited and Directed; In a Sermon At the publick Thursday Lecture, in Boston, March 25th 1742. ... By John Barnard, A.M. ... *Boston*, *S. Eliot*, 1742. 8vo, pp. 43. H. *See* Ashton's Memorial, No. 2207.

Barnard (John), *of Andover*, *b.* 1690, *d.* 1758. ... A Sermon ... After the ... Earthquake Which occur'd ... Between the 29th and 30th of October, 1727. By John Barnard ... . *Boston*, *John Phillips*, 1727. Sm. 12mo, pp. 132. B. 3472

Barnard. ... A Sermon ... before ... May 28th. 1746. Being the Day for the Election of His Majesty's Council ... By John Barnard ... . *Boston*, *Daniel Gookin*, 1746. 8vo, pp. 30. 3473

Barnard. ... A Sermon, delivered, in Publick, to the Assembly of Ministers, at their Anniversary Convention, in Boston, ... June 1, 1738. By John Barnard. *Boston*, *S. Kneeland & T. Green*, 1738. 8vo, Title, pp. 34. 3474

Barnard. ... Sermon occasioned by the Death of Mr. Abiel Abbot, 18th May, 1739. Preface by Rev. Samuel Phillips. ... May 28th. *Boston*, *Daniel Gookin*, 1739. 8vo, pp. xviii., 24. H. 3475

Barnard. ... A Sermon Preach'd at the Gathering of a Church, and the Ordination of the Reverend Mr. Timothy Walker to the Pastoral Office at the New Plantation called Pennicook [now Concord, N. H.], Nov. 18th 1730. By John Barnard, M.A. ... *Boston*, *in New England*, *Printed by B. Green for John Phillips*, 1739. 8vo, pp. (4), 42. B. 3476

Barnard (Jonathan G.) The C. S. A. and the Battle of Bull Run. A Letter to an English Friend. By J. G. Barnard ... . With Five Maps. *New York*, *D. Van Nostrand*, 1862. 8vo, Title, pp. 136. H. 3477

Barnard. The Dangers and Defences of New York. Addressed to the Hon. J. B. Floyd, Secretary of War, By Major J. G. Barnard ... . Published by order of the Chamber of Commerce, by Permission of the Secretary of War. *New York*, *D. van Nostrand*, 1859. 8vo, pp. 62. C., H. 3478

Barnard. Eulogy on the Late Brevet Major-General Joseph G. Totten, late Chief Engineer, United States Army. By J. G. Barnard ... . Reprinted from the Annual of the National Academy of Sciences for 1866. *Washington*, 1866. 8vo, pp. 38. + *New York*, *D. Van Nostrand*, 1866. 12mo, pp. 82. H.

Barnard. The Isthmus of Tehuantepec; being the Results of a survey for a Railroad to connect the Atlantic and Pacific oceans, made by the scientific commission under the direction of Maj. J. G. Barnard, U. S. Engineers, with a Resume of the Geology, Climate, local Geography, production, industry, Fauna and Flora of that region. Illustrated with numerous maps and engravings, arranged and prepared for the Tehuantepec Railroad Company of New-Orleans, by J. J. Williams, principal assistant Engineer: with a volume of maps. *New York*, *D. Appleton & Co.*, 1852. 8vo, pp. 295. Plates. 3480

Barnard. Notes on Sea-Coast Defences: consisting of Sea-Coast Fortification, the Fifteen-Inch Gun, and Casemate Embrasures. By Major J. G. Barnard ... . *New York*, 1861. 8vo, pp. 110 (1). Plate. H. 3481

Barnard. Letter to the Editors of the National Intelligencer, in answer to the Charges against the United States Military Academy, in the Report of the Secretary of War, of July, 1861. *New York*, *D. Van Nostrand*, 1862. 8vo, pp. 18. 3482

Barnard. The Peninsular Campaign and its Antecedents, as developed by the Report of Maj.-Gen. Geo. B. McClellan, and other Published Documents. By J. G. Barnard, ... *New York*: *D. Van Nostrand*, 1864. 8vo, pp. 96. Map. + *Washington*, *D. C.*, *Union Congressional Committee*, 1864. 8vo, pp. 15. H.

Barnard and Barry. Report of the Engineer and Artillery Operations of the Army of the Potomac, from its Organization to the close of the Peninsular Campaign. By Brig.-Gen. J. G. Barnard, Chief Engineer, and Brig.-Gen. W. F. Barry, Chief of Artillery. Illustrated by Eighteen Maps, Plans, etc. *New York*, *D. Van Nostrand*, 1863. 8vo, pp. 230. B., H. 3484

BARNARD (R.) The Isle of Man, or the Legal Proceeding in Manshire against Sin. By Richard Barnard. *Boston, re-printed by J. Franklin for B. Eliot, and sold at his shop in King Street.* 1719. 12mo, pp. 126. 3485

BARNARD (Thomas), *the elder*, *d.* 1776. A Sermon Preached in Boston ... Before the Society For encouraging Industry, And employing the Poor, September 20. 1758. By Thomas Barnard ... . *Boston, S. Kneeland*, MDCCLVIII. 8vo, pp. (4), 25 (2). H., B. 3486

BARNARD. A Sermon preached to the Ancient and Honorable Artillery Company in Boston New England, June 5, 1758, Being the Anniversary of their election of officers, By Thomas Barnard, A.M. Pastor of the First Church in Salem. *Boston, Edes & Gill*, 1758. 8vo, pp. 32. 3487

BARNARD. A Sermon Preached at the Ordination of the Rev. William Whitwell, To the Joint Pastoral Care of the First Church ... in Marblehead ... August 25. 1762. ... followed by an historical Account of the First Church ... . *Boston, Printed by J. Dpaper* [*sic*], MDCCLXII. 8vo, pp. (4), 51. H. 3488

BARNARD. A Sermon Preached before ... Francis Bernard, Esq; Governor ... May 25th. 1763. Being the Anniversary for the Election of His Majesty's Council ... . By Thomas Barnard, A.M. *Boston*, MDCCLXIII. 8vo, pp. 45. H. 3489

Also: ... A Discourse ... at the Funeral Of the Reverend Mr. Peter Clarke, Late Pastor ... in Danvers, June 16, 1768. ... *Salem, Samuel Hall*, 1768. 8vo, pp. 23. H. ... Dudleian Lecture ... May 11th, 1768. *Salem*, M.DCC.LXVIII. 8vo, pp. 28. H. ... Sermon at the Ordination of Josiah Bayley, at Hampton Falls, N. H. Oct. 19, 1757. *Portsmouth, Daniel Fowle*, 1757. 4to, pp. 35. ... A Sermon preach'd at the Ordination of Edward Barnard, to the pastoral care of the First Church in Haverhill, April 27, 1743. *Boston*, 1743. 8vo.

BARNARD (Thomas), *the younger*, *d.* 1814. A Discourse delivered before the Humane Society of ... Massachusetts ... June 10, 1794. ... *Boston*, MDCCXCIV. 8vo, pp. 25. H., N.

With lists of officers and members.

BARNARD. A Discourse before the Society for Propagating the Gospel among the Indians and Others in North America ... November 6, 1806. ... *Charlestown, Samuel Etheridge*, 1806. 8vo, pp. 39. H. 3491

With the usual historical appendix.

BARNARD. A Sermon, preached at the Ordination of the Rev. Aaron Bancroft, ... Worcester, February 1, MDCCLXXXVI. By Thomas Barnard ... . *Worcester, Isaiah Thomas*, MDCCLXXXVI. 8vo, pp. 52. H. 3492

BARNARD. A Sermon, preached December 29, 1799, in the North Meeting House, Salem, the Lord's Day after the Melancholy Tidings were received of the Death of General George Washington, who died Dec. 14, 1799. By Thomas Barnard, D.D., Minister of the North Church and Congregation. Published by Desire of the Town. *Salem, Printed by Thomas C. Cushing* [1800]. 8vo, pp. 27. H. 3493

Also: A Discourse on Natural Religion ... September 3, 1795, at the Lecture founded by ... Paul Dudley ... . *Boston*, 1795. 8vo, pp. 24. H. A Sermon ... June 1, 1789 ... [at the Artillery Election]. *Boston*, M,DCC,LXXXIX. 8vo, pp. 29. H. A Sermon, delivered before the Congregational Ministers of ... Massachusetts, at their Annual Convention in Boston, May 30, 1793. ... *Boston, Samuel Hall*, MDCCXCIII. 8vo, pp. 23. H. A Sermon, delivered on the Day of National Thanksgiving, February 19, 1795. ... *Salem*, MDCCXCV. 8vo, pp. 25. H. A Sermon, delivered on the Day of Annual Thanksgiving, December 15, 1796. ... *Salem* [n. d.] 8vo, pp. 22. H. A Sermon, delivered at Salem, on March 31, 1796, the Day of General Fasting ... . *Printed at Newburyport, for John Dabney, Salem*, 1796. 8vo, pp. 20. H. A Sermon preached before the Salem Female Charitable Society, ... July 6th, 1803. ... *Salem*, 1803. 8vo, pp. 22, (Subscribers, etc.) 8. H. A Sermon ... June 7th, 1809. at the Ordination of the Rev. Ichabod Nichols ... Portland. ... *Portland, printed by J. M'Kown*, 1809. 8vo, pp. 23. B. H. & A Sermon ... before the Bible Society of Salem and Vicinity. ... April 20, 1814. *Salem*, 1814. 8vo, pp. 16.

BARNAVE (Antoine Pierre Joseph Marie). Rapport fait a l'Assemblée Nationale sur les Colonies, au nom des Comités de Constitution, &c Marine, d'Agriculture, de Commerce et des Colonies, le 23 Septembre 1791. Par M. Barnave. Imprimé par ordre de l'Assemble Nationale. *A Paris, de l'Imprimerie Nationale*, 1791. 8vo, pp. 12. 3494

BARNBY. The American Savage, or Orab and Phœbe. By Mrs. Barnby. *London*, 1808. 2 vols., 12mo. 3495

A doubtful title, from an auctioneer's catalogue.

BARNES (Albert). Albert Barnes On the Maine Liquor Law. The Throne of Iniquity; or Sustaining Evil by Law: a Discourse in behalf of a Law prohibiting the Traffic in Intoxicating Drinks. ... By Rev. Albert Barnes. [*Springfield*, 1852.] 12mo, pp. 24. H. + *New York*, 1852. 12mo, pp. 24. + *Harrisburg*, 1852. 8vo, pp. 11. H. + *Philadelphia* [n. d.] 12mo, pp. 28. H.

BARNES. The Church and Slavery. By Albert Barnes.

Philadelphia, 1856. 12mo, pp. 196. + *Philadelphia, Parry & McMillan*, 1857. 12mo, pp. 196. + Third Thousand,—with an Appendix. *Philadelphia, Parry & McMillan*, 1857. 16mo, pp. 204. H. 3497

BARNES. Church Manual, for the Members of the Presbyterian Church, Morris-Town, N. J. Compiled by Albert Barnes, Pastor ... . *Morris-Town, Printed by Jacob Mann*, 1828. 12mo, pp. 47. 3498

Contains Sketch of the History of the Presbyterian Church, Morristown, list of ministers, elders and deacons.

BARNES. The Conditions of Peace. A Thanksgiving Discourse ... November 27, 1862. By Albert Barnes. *Philadelphia*, 1863. 8vo, pp. 63. H. 3499

BARNES. Doeg, the Edomite; or, The Informer. A Lecture on the Fifty-Second Psalm, delivered ... Philadelphia, January 6, 1861, by Albert Barnes. Not published. *Philadelphia*, 1861. 8vo, pp. 46. H. 3500

Bears on the execution of the Fugitive Slave Law.

BARNES. Exclusivism. By Albert Barnes. Extracted from the Presbyterian Quarterly Review for March and June, 1857. *Philadelphia, Henry B. Ashmead, Printer*, 1857. 12mo, pp. 76. H. 3501

Contains considerable information on the state of sects in the United States.

BARNES. Home Missions. A Sermon in behalf of the American Home Missionary Society ... May, 1849; by Albert Barnes. *New York*, 1849. 8vo, pp. 48. H., B. 3502

BARNES. An Inquiry into the Scriptural Views of Slavery. By Albert Barnes. ... *Philadelphia, Perkins & Purves*, 1846. 12mo, pp. 384. H. + *Philadelphia*, 1855. 12mo, pp. 384.

BARNES. The Love of Country. A Sermon ... April 28, 1861. By Albert Barnes. ... *Philadelphia, C. Sherman & Son*, 1861. 8vo, pp. 48. B. 3504

BARNES. Our Position. A Sermon, preached before the General Assembly of the Presbyterian Church in the United States ... May 20, 1852. By Albert Barnes. *New York, Newman & Ivison*, 1858. 8vo, pp. 39. B. 3505

BARNES. Plea in behalf of Western Colleges. A Discourse delivered before the Society for promoting Collegiate and Theological Education at the West, in ... Newark, New Jersey, October 29, 1845, and in ... Philadelphia, February 22, 1846 By Albert Barnes. *Philadelphia, William Sloanaker*, 1846. 8vo, pp. 28. H. 3506

BARNES. The State of the Country, A Discourse, Delivered in the First Presbyterian Church, Philadelphia, June 1, 1865. On the Day appointed as a Day of "Humiliation and Mourning" in view of the Death of the President of the United States, by Albert Barnes. *Philadelphia, Henry B. Ashmead, Printer*, 1865. 8vo, pp. 74. B. 3507

BARNES. Thanksgiving Sermon. The Virtues and Public Services of William Penn: ... a Discourse ... November 27, 1845, by Albert Barnes. *Philadelphia*, 1846. 8vo, pp. 24. H., P.

Also: A Sermon, Occasioned by the Death of the Rev. James Patterson. *Philadelphia*, 1838. 8vo, pp. 44. A Sermon ... October 19, 1845 on ... the Death of Henry Mill, M.D. ... *Philadelphia*, 1845. 8vo, pp. 28. ... A Sermon ... November 13, 1858, on ... the Death of Mr. Thomas P. Sparhawk. By Albert Barnes. *Philadelphia*, 1858. 8vo, pp. 24. H. Life at Three-Score: a Sermon ... in ... Philadelphia, November 28, 1858. *Philadelphia*, 1859. + Second Edition. *Philadelphia, Parry & McMillan*, 1859. 12mo, pp. 78. H. ... A Sermon preached in ... Philadelphia February 11, 1866, on the Death of Mr. James Crowell ... . *Philadelphia, Pa., Ashmead*, 1866. 8vo, pp. 24. Also several theological works.

BARNES. Debates in the Presbytery of Philadelphia on the case of Albert Barnes ... *Philadelphia*, 1831. 8vo, pp. 80. 3509

BARNES (David). Discourse Delivered at South Parish in Scituate, February 22, 1800. The Day assigned by Congress, To mourn the Decease and venerate the Virtues of General George Washington. ... By David Barnes, D.D. Published by Desire. *Boston, Manning & Loring, Printers* [1800]. 8vo, pp. 16. H. 3510

BARNES. A Sermon Preached at the Ordination of the Rev. Mr. Abiel Leonard, ... Woodstock, June 23. 1763. By David Barns [*sic*] ... . *Boston, Printed by Thomas and John Fleet*, 1764. 8vo, pp. 34. H. 3511

BARNES. Sermons by the Late David Barnes, D.D. of Scituate. *Boston, Munroe, Francis and Parker*, 1815. 18mo, pp. 142. H.

"Character of Dr. Barnes." pp. 138–142. Also: ... A Discourse ... at Barnstable, Sept. 30, 1801, on the Ordination of the Rev. Jotham Waterman ... . *Boston, Jan.* 1802. 8vo, pp. 27. H. A Discourse on Education, delivered before the

Trustees of the Derby Academy, At Hingham, April 5th, 1796. ... *Boston*, 1803. 8vo, pp. 27. H. ... A Sermon ... at the East Church in Pembroke, November 2, 1800, soon after the Decease of their Pastor, Rev. James Hawley, Æt. 30. ... *Boston*, 1801. 8vo, pp. 20. H. Thoughts on the Love of Life and Fear of Death: In a Sermon. *Boston*. 1795. 8vo, pp. 23.

BARNES (D. M.) The Draft Riots in New York, July, 1863. The Metropolitan Police: their Services during Riot Week. Their Honorable Record. By David M. Barnes. *New York, Baker & Godwin*, 1863. 8vo, pp. 117 (1). H. 3513

BARNES (Edward). Hanes o Fasnach y Caethglud yn Africa. *Wrexham*. 12mo. 3514

A history of the slave-trade, in Welsh.

BARNES (Isaac O.) An Address, delivered at Bedford, New Hampshire, on the One Hundredth Anniversary of the Incorporation of the Town, May 19th, 1850. By Isaac O. Barnes. *Boston, printed by Alfred Mudge*, 1850. 8vo, pp. 45. H. 3515

BARNES. Letter of Isaac O. Barnes, ... to the Hon. Elisha Whittlesey ... relating to Certain Bills of Costs on Indictments in the District Court [of Massachusetts], March Term, 1849; and Affidavits ... [etc.] *Boston, printed by John Wilson & Son*, 1852. 8vo, pp. 6, 12, 15 (1), 4 (32). H. 3516

BARNES (J.) The Green Mountain Traveler. By J. Barnes. *New York*, 1856. 12mo, pp. 360. 3517

BARNES. Jefferson Medical College ... in relation to John Barnes, M.D. ... *Philadelphia*, 1828. 8vo, pp. 38. P. 3518

BARNES (J. H.) Tariff or Rates of Duties for the Year 1828, with all the Alterations made in the Year 1830 on Tea, Cocoa, Coffee, Salt, and Molasses. To which is added a Correct Woollen Table ... also a Cotton Table ... . Compiled by J. Harbeson Barnes & Elijah A. Carroll. *Philadelphia*, 1830. 8vo, pp. viii. (2), 7–131, also *54 and *82. B. 3519

BARNES. Tariff or Rates of Duties, from March 3, 1833, on Importations: Collated by J. H. Barnes and E. A. Carroll. *Philadelphia*, 1832. 12mo. S. 3520

BARNES (Joseph). Remarks on Mr. John Fitch's Reply to Mr. James Rumsey's Pamphlet, by Joseph Barnes, formerly Assistant, and now Attorney in fact to James Rumsey. *Philadelphia, Printed by Joseph James*, M, DCC, LXXXVIII. 8vo, pp. xvi., 16. P. 3521

BARNES. Treatise on the Justice, Policy, and Utility of establishing an effectual system for promoting the progress of Useful Arts, by assuring property in the products of Genius. By Joseph Barnes. *Philadelphia, Francis Bailey*, 1792. 8vo, pp. 34.

BARNES (Jos. K.) Annual Report of the Surgeon General, United States Army. 1865. [*Washington*] *Surgeon General's Office* [1865]. 8vo. Continued. 3523

BARNES (Melvin). A Circular, or Short Biography of Col. Ebenezer Allen, known as Captain or Major, in the New Hampshire Grants, and its Rangers, A.D. 1777, and after. [n. p., 1851.] 8vo, pp. 16. H. 3524

[BARNES (Melvin)]. Reprint of a Short Biography of Colonel Ebenezer Allen ... . Also Short Biographies of Lieutenant Samuel Allen and Dr. Jacob Roebeck. In addition Some Reminiscences of Lake Champlain ... . *Plattsburgh, J. W. Tuttle, Printer*, 1852. 8vo, pp. 32, Errata (1). H. 3525

BARNES (S. W.) Mississippi Extension of the Watertown & Madison R. R. Remarks of Hon. S. W. Barnes, in the Senate, February 19th, 1857. Bill to amend the Charter ... . Adverse Memorials ... . *Madison*, 1857. 8vo, pp. 16. 3526

BARNES (T.) At the Supreme Judicial Court, May Term, 1810, in Cumberland. ... Thomas Barnes *vs.* the Inhabitants of the First Parish in Falmouth. [Opinion of the Justices.] [No imprint.] 8vo, pp. 16. H. 3527

For the recovery of certain ministerial taxes.

BARNES (W.) The Settlement and Early History of Albany. A Prize Essay, By William Barnes Esq. *Albany, Gould, Banks & Gould*, 1851. 8vo, Title, pp. 25. B. 3528

BARNES. The Settlement and Early History of Albany. By William Barnes. *Albany, N. Y.: J. Munsell*, 1864. 8vo, pp. 100. Plates. B. 3529

Two hundred and fifty copies printed.

BARNES (W. H.) The Body Politic [of the United States.] By William H. Barnes. *Cincinnati*, 1866. 12mo, pp. 309.

BARNES. The Drama of Secession, or, Scenes from American History. By William H. Barnes A.M. *Indianapolis, Merrill & Company*, 1862. 16mo, pp. 60. B. 3531

BARNES. History of the Thirty-Ninth Congress. By W. H. Barnes. *Indianapolis, Macaulay & Co.*, 1867. 8vo, pp. 613. Portrait. 3532

BARNET. The Martyrs and Heroes of Illinois in the Great Rebellion. Biographical Sketches. Edited by James Barnet. *Chicago, J. Barnet, printer*, 1865. 8vo, pp. xvi., 9–263. Portraits. 3533

BARNETT (F.) The Hero of No Fiction: or, Memoirs of Francis Barnett the Lefevre of "No Fiction:" and a Review of that Work. With Letters and Authentic Documents. *Boston, C. Ewer and T. Bedlington*, 1823. 2 vols., 18mo, pp. 384; 360. B. 3534

"No Fiction" was by Rev. Andrew Reed. He represented Lefevre as coming to Canada, and drew some very fanciful pictures of that country.

BARNETT (H. N.) The Late Theodore Parker: A Discourse delivered in ... Finsbury ... June 3, 1860, By Henry N. Barnett. ... *London, George Manwaring*, MDCCCLX. 8vo, pp. 16.

BARNEY (C.) Recollections of Field Service with the 20th Iowa Infantry Volunteers, or what I saw in the Army; embracing Accounts of Marches, Battles, Sieges, and Skirmishes in Missorri, Arkansas, Mississippi, Louisiana, Alabama, Florida, Texas, and along the Northern Border of Mexico. By Captain C. Barney. *Davenport*, 1866. 12mo, pp. 323. 3536

[BARNEY (C. W.)] Dedicated to the Genius of War of Delaware. Inscribed to the Officers and Privates of the First Troop Delaware Light Dragoons, by the Author. 8vo, pp. 8.

BARNEY (John). [Notes of Travel in various parts of the U. S. n. p., 1834?] 8vo, pp. 19. H. 3538

BARNEY. To ... Congress ... : The Memorial and Petition of John Barney, in behalf of ... the co-heirs of Joshua Barney, who was an officer of the Navy ... during the whole ... Revolution ... . [n. p., n. d.] 4to, pp. (3). H. 3539

BARNEY. [Two Letters on Political subjects and one describing a visit to Massachusetts. *Baltimore?* 1838?] 8vo, pp. 14. H. 3540

BARNEY (Joshua). A Biographical Memoir of the Late Commodore Joshua Barney: from Autographical Notes and Journals

in possession of his Family, and other Authentic Sources. Edited by Mary Barney. ... *Boston, Gray and Bowen*, 1832. 8vo, pp. xvi., 328. Portrait. C., H. 3541

See Nat. Mag. and Am. Q. R., XIII., 1.

BARNEY (J.) Report on the Survey of the Portsmouth & Newburyport Rail Road. By Joshua Barney, Civil Engineer. [Imprint torn off the copy before me.] 12mo, pp. 12. H. 3542

BARNEY (Mary). Mrs. Barney's Letter to President Jackson. [Dated Baltimore, June 13th 1829. n. p., n. d.] 8vo, pp. 4. H.

BARNEY (Wm. C.) The Ocean Monopoly and Commercial Suicide. To ... Congress. *New York*, 1855. 8vo, pp. 16. S.

BARNICOU. La république d'Haïti renaissant de ses cendres, sujet allégorique d'un tableau nationale. Par Barnicou fils, peintre d'histoire. *Paris, impr. de Renaudière*, 1821. 8vo.

BARNITZ (J.) State of the Accounts of Jacob Barnitz, Esquire, Collector of Excise, York County, from November 20th 1782, to the 1st of May 1784. In which is exhibited, The Excise accruing within said time the monies received by the said Collector on account thereof. And the Sums yet due. Together, With the Payments made to the Treasurer of the State. *Philadelphia, Printed by Robert Aitken*, ... M, DCC, LXXXIV. 8vo, pp. 8. P. 3546

BARNITZ. State of the Accounts of Jacob Barnitz, Esq. Collector of Excise, York County, from the 1st of May, 1784, to 1st of May, 1785. *Philadelphia, Printed by John Steele*, M, DCC, LXXXV. 8vo, pp. 6. P. 3547

BARNITZ. State of the Accounts of Jacob Barnitz, Esquire, late Collector of Excise, for the County of York; From the 1st of May, 1785, until the 24th of December, 1785, being the time he ceased to act. *Philadelphia, Printed by Robert Aitken*, ... M. DCC. LXXXVI. 8vo, pp. 6. P. 3548

BARNOIN (T.) Rapport de M. Théophile Barnoin, arbitre-juge dans l'affaire de Gernon, négociant américain à Philadelphie, et François-Hippolyte Lecomte, ci-devant négocian, français, et maintenant propriétaire du domaine de Sceaux. *Paris, impr. de Bailleul*, 1817. 4to. 3549

Only 100 copies printed.

Barns (D.) *See* Barnes (D.), No. 3511.

Barns (T.) Oration delivered at Freeport, Me., July 4, 1807. By Thomas Barns. *Portland* [1807]. 8vo, pp. 12.

The Barnstable Conference of Evangelical Congregational Churches: comprising the Constitution ... with a Concise Historical Sketch of the several Churches ... . By a Committee ... . *Boston*, 1846. 12mo, pp. 44. H. 3551

... Memorial of the Manufacturers of Salt, of Barnstable, Massachusetts, praying that the Duty on Imported Salt may not be repealed. ... *Washington*, 1828. 8vo, pp. 3. (20th Cong., 1st Sess., Doc. 131.) H. 3552

Minutes of the Barnstable Baptist Association, at its Twenty-seventh Anniversary ... . *Boston*, 1858. 8vo, pp. 20. Continued. H. 3553

Barnstable County. *See* [Davis (Wendell)].

The Declaration of Ministers in Barnstable County relating to the Late Practice of Itinerant Preaching. *Boston*, 1745. 12mo, pp. 8. 3554

Proceedings of the Centennial Celebration, September 3, 1839. *Barnstable*, 1840. 8vo, pp. 92. 3555

Transactions of the Barnstable County Agricultural Society, for ... 1856. ... *Press of the Barnstable Patriot*, 1837. 8vo, pp. 47. H. 3556

Barnuevo. Señor Rodrigo Barnueuo, de la Compañia de Jesus, y su Procurador general de la prouincia del Perú, dize: Que la dicha su prouincia ha mas de setenta años, que por orden de la Real corona administra, y tiene a su cargo las doctrinas de los Indios del pueblo de Juli, en la Prouincia de Chucuyto ... [*Imprimé à Lima*, 16 ...] 4to, 2 l. 3557

Title from Le Clerc, Bib. Am.

Barnuevo (Pedro de Paralto). *See* Paralto-Barnuevo.

Barnum (E. M.) The gold and silver fields of Oregon & Idaho. A Statement of the Yield ... By E. M. Barnum [1866]. 8vo, pp. 13. 3585

Barnum (H. L.) The Spy Unmasked; or, Memoirs of Enoch Crosby, alias Harvey Birch, the Hero of Mr. Cooper's

Tale of the Neutral Ground: being an authentic account of the Secret Services which he rendered his Country during the Revolutionary War, (Taken from his own lips, in short-hand.) Comprising many interesting Facts and Anecdotes, never before published. By H. L. Barnum. Embellished with Engravings. *New York, J. & J. Harper*, 1828. 8vo, pp. 206. 6 Plates. c.

Reprinted in London, with the following title:

Barnum. The Spy Unmasked or Memoirs of Enoch Crosby, Alias Harvey Birch. The Hero of the Spy, a tale of the Neutral Ground, By Mr Cooper. By H. L. Barnum. In Two Volumes. *New York, J. & J. Harper. London, A. K. Newman & Co.*, 1828. 12mo, pp. 234; 222. + *London*, 1829. 2 vols., 8vo. 3560

Barnum. [Same Title as No. 3562.] Embellished with a correct Likeness of the Hero, with a Fac-simile of his signature. Second Edition. *Cincinnati, A. B. Roff*, 1831. 12mo, pp. 216. Portrait. 3561

Barnum. The Spy Unmasked. Adventures of Enoch Crosby *alias* Harvey Birch, the Hero of Cooper's Tale of the Neutral Ground. By H. L. Barnum. *New York, G. P. Putnam*, 1864. 16mo, pp. 312. 3562

This edition was edited (?) by Frank Moore, who omitted the notes and abridged the work.

Barnum (P. T.) The Humbugs of the World. An Account of Humbugs, Delusions, Impositions, Quackeries, Deceits, and Deceivers generally, in all Ages. By P. T. Barnum. ... *New York, Carleton*, 1865. 12mo, pp. 424. + 1866. 12mo, pp. 424. H. 3563

Contains "Personal Reminiscences," "The Spiritualists," "The Peter Funks," etc.

Barnum. The Life of P. T. Barnum. Written by Himself. *New York, Redfield*, 1854. 12mo, pp. 404. + 1855. 12mo. H. *London, S. Low & Co.*, 1854. Fcap 8vo, pp. 372. + *London, Ward & Lock*, 1854. 12mo. + *London, Knight*, 1855. Post 8vo, pp. 308. Plate. And other editions. c. 3564

Barnum. Mémoires de Barnum illustrés par Janet-Lange. Traduction Raoul Bourdier. ... *Paris, Gustave Barba* [n. d.] Large 8vo, Title, pp. 96. H. 3565

Barnum. Barnum's Leben. Von ihm selbst geschildert. Deutsch von W. E. Drugulin. *Leipzig, Kollmann*, 185–. 4

vols., 8vo, pp. viii., 187; 214; 156; 216. (Amerikanische Bibliothek, Bd. 130–133.) 3566

Barnum. Leben und Abenteuer P. T. Barnum's ... . Von ihm selbst beschrieben. Aus dem Englischen. *Wien, Hartleben*, 1855. 3 vols., 8vo, pp. 192; 171; 155. (Amerikanisches Lese-Cabinet, Lfg. 25–32.) 3567

Barnum. Leven en avonturen von P. T. Barnum ... zijne uitgestrekte ondernemingen en kunstreizen met Jennij Lind, Tom Thumb, etc. ... . *Rotterdam, H. Nijgh*, 1856. 8vo. Plates.

Barnum. Barnum, der Kaufmann, Journalist und Raritätenmann. Oder So macht man Geschäfte und so wird man reich. Eine Selbstbiographie. Deutsch von A. Kretzschmar. *Leipzig, O. Wigand*, 1855. 8vo. pp. 315. 3569

Barnum. To Republicans. [Extracts from "The Nation," New York Herald, etc. against his election to Congress. n. p., 1867.] Tall 8vo, pp. 4. H. 3570

Barnum's American Museum, Illustrated. A Pictorial Guide to that far famed Establishment; containing much interesting matter, and highly useful to visitors. *New York*, 1850. 8vo.

Barnum's Parnassus. *See* [Butler (W. A.)]

Barnwell (John). An | Account | of the | Foundation, and Establishment | Of a Design, now on Foot, for a | Settlement | on the | Golden Islands, | To the South of | Port Royal | in | Carolina. | By Authority of a Royal Charter. | *London*: | *Printed in the Year* MDCCXX. | 4to, pp. 8. H. 3572

Barnwell (R. G.) The New-Orleans Book. Edited by Robert Gibbes Barnwell ... *New Orleans*, 1851. 12mo, pp. xii., 384. B. 3573

A collection of poems, many of them relating to Louisiana.

Barnwell (William H.) ... A Sermon, for the Day of Thanksgiving, Humiliation & Prayer, appointed by the Governor of South-Carolina, November 21, 1851, by Rev. W. H. Barnwell ... . *Charleston, printed by Edward C. Councell*, 1851. 8vo, pp. 23. H. 3574

Barnwell, *pseudon.* *See* [Roosevelt (R. B.)]

Baron (A.) Voyages autour du monde de Cook; par A. Baron. *Limoges et Isle, E. Ardant et Thibaut*, 1867. 12mo, pp. 72. Engravings. 3575

Baron (Rich.) Californien in der Heimath. Eine Erzählung ... . Mit 4 Stahlstichen. *Breslau, E. Trewendt*, 1858. 8vo, pp. 120. 3576

Baron. Der Deutsche Knabe in Amerika. Hold-Else's Wanderungen. Zwei Erzählungen ... . *Breslau, Trewendt & Granier*, 1851. 8vo, pp. 149. 4 Engravings. + Zweite Auflage. *Breslau*, 1866. 8vo, pp. 151. 3577

Baroncourt (M. Petit de). *See* Petit de Baroncourt (M.)

Baroux (L.) Notice sur la mission des Pottowatomies dans l'Etat du Michigan, par M. l'abbé Baroux, missionnaire apostolique. *Caen, Hardel*, 1859. 8vo, pp. 48. 3578

Barr (J.) A Correct and Authentic Narrative of the Indian War in Florida, with a description of Maj. Dades Massacre, ... By Capt. James Barr. *New York, J. Narine*, 1834. 12mo, pp. 32. 3579

Barr (J. M.) ... Choice Extracts from a Speech of Joseph M. Barr, recently appointed Post Master at Wilmington, Del. ... October 6th, 1866. [n. p., n. d.] Broadside. H. 3580

Barr (Mary). Memoir of Mrs. Mary Barr. Printed for private distribution. *Cincinnati, Gazette Company Print*, 1863. 8vo, pp. 10. c. 3581

Barr (T. H.) A Discourse delivered by the Rev. T. H. Barr, at Canaan Center, April 19, 1865, on the occasion of the Funeral Obsequies of our late President, Abraham Lincoln. Published by special request. *Wooster, Ohio, Republican Press*, 1865. 12mo, pp. 11. 3582

Barral (L. M.) Renseignements sur la côte méridionale du Brésil et sur le Rio de la Plata, recueillis dans la campagne hydrographique de la gabare l'Émulation, pendant les années 1830–1832. *Paris, Ledoyen*, 1850. 8vo. (Extrait des "Annales maritimes" de 1832.) 3583

Barrande (J.) Documents anciens et nouveaux sur la faune primordiale et le système Taconique en Amérique. *Paris, imprimerie Martinet*, 1861. 8vo, pp. 119. 2 Plates. 3584

Barratt (B. F.) ... A Sermon preached at the Dedication of the New Church Temple, in Providence, R. I., Oct. 14, 1843. By B. F. Barratt. *New York, John Allen*, 1843. 12mo, pp. 47.

Barratt (Joseph). Key, etc. *See* Tenesles (Nicola).

Barratt. Report on the Season of 1846, with table showing the flowering of Fruit Trees. *Middletown*, 1846. 8vo. B. 3586

Barratt. ... On the Tracks of Large Birds, found at Middletown, Conn., by Joseph Barratt, M.D. [*Middletown, July*, 1846.] Broadside. 3587

Barrault (E.) Les inventeurs et la loi des États-Unis modifiée en 1861. Texte, documents, et commentaires de la législation des brevets d'invention, dessins et modèles de fabrique aux États-Unis, par Émile Barrault ... . *Paris, E. Lacroix*, 1864. 18mo, pp. 54. 3588

Barré. Discours de Nicolas Barré, sur la navigation du chevalier de Villegagnon en Amérique. *Paris, Le Jeune*, 1558. 8vo. 3589

See Lelong, No. 39769; Ternaux-Compans, No. 82. Boucher, v. 286, gives the title differently.

Barre (W. L.) Life and Public Services of Millard Fillmore. By W. L. Barre, of Kentucky. *Buffalo* [1856]. 12mo. Portrait. c. 3590

Barre. Lives of Illustrious Men of America. By W. L. Barre. *New York*, 1859. 8vo. 3591

Barré Saint-Venant (Jean). Des colonies modernes sous la zone torride, et particulièrement de celle de Saint-Domingue, ouvrage dans lequel on decouvre les causes de leurs malheurs, et ou l'on developpe les veritables principes du gouvernement qui leur convient; les moyens economiques de les faire arriver promptement à la plus grande prosperité et de rendre le sort des negres preferable à celui d'aucun peuple de l'Europe. Par M. Barré Saint-Venant. ... *Paris, Brochot* [1802]. 8vo, pp. 516. Maps. 3592

Catalogue of Barre Academy, Barre, Vt. *Montpelier*, 1852. 8vo, pp. 16. H. 3593

Barreda (*Br. D.* Nicholas de la). Doctrina christiana en lengva Chinanteca, añadida la explicacion de los principales mys-

terios de la fee. Modo de baptizar en caso de necessidad, y de ayudar á bien morir, y methodo de administracion de sacramentos. *Mexico, Por los herederos de la viuda de Franc. Rodriguez Lupercio*, 1730. 4to. 3594

"7 fnc., 95 pp. (chiff. 85) à 2 colonnes. Cette doctrine chrétienne est sans nul doute le seul livre qui existe maintenant sur la langue chinanteca ou chinacanteqna; puisque la grammaire de Fr. de Cepeda, impr. à Mexico en 1560, in-4°, n'existe dans aucune biblioth. connue (Cf. Ludewig, Bibliotheca glottica, p. 40). Cette langue est parlée par les Indiens de Oaxaca, Mexique, dans les districts de Quiechapa, Jalalog et Chuapan. Une note mss. collée sur la couverture indique que ce vol. a été donné à M. Melchior Verheyen, voyageur, par le curé de Jalapillio. M. Mendoza." Title and note from Leclerc, Bib. Am., No. 117.

Barreiros. Commentarius de Ophira Regione apud Divinam Scripturam commemorata et ad eam Navigatione. *Conimbricæ*, 1561. 4to. 3595

Bossi (Vita di Colombo, p. 61) says: "Gaspare Varrerio ... scrittore di un libro eruditissimo de Ophyra regione, dedicato nel 1550 al re di Portogallo, composto forse molto tempo prima." A second dedication, however, dated 1560, shows that it was not published before the date given above, when it was appended to:

Barreiros. Chorographia de alguns logares que stam em hum caminho que fez Gaspar Barreiros em o anno de M.D.XXXXVI começando na cidade de Badajoz ... tee a de Milam ... con algunas outras obras. *Coimbra, Ioao Aluarez*, 1561. 4to.

The Commentarius is also appended to A Canisii De Locis S. Scripturæ Hebraicis Commentarius, *Antverpiæ*, 1600, 8vo; and, with the following title, to the "Novus Orbis:"

Barreiros. Casparis Varrerii Lvsitani Commentarius de Ophyra Regione, In sacris litteris Lib. III. Regum & II. Paralipomenon. *Roterodami, Apud Ioannem Leonardi Berevvout*, 1616. 8vo, (42) l. H. 3597

Also to Joh. Is. Pontani Discussionum Historicarum Libri Duo, *Harderovici Gelrorum*, 1637, 8vo; and it is included in Criticorum Sacrorum Tomus Secundus, *Amstelodami*, fol., II. 1163–1182. (H.) Georgi mentions an edition, "*Harderwici*, 1627, 8vo," which is perhaps an error for 1637, as above. In catalogues, Barreiros almost uniformly appears under the Latin form Varrerius. "In this dissertation the author disproves the then reigning opinion that the Ophir of King Solomon was America. He tried to show, that Ophir was not far distant from Iudæa, and certainly in Asia. His reasoning is ingenious and learned."

Barrell (Charles, Henry F., George, and Samuel Brown). Statement of Facts relative to the Conduct of Mr. Benjamin Joy, Executor ... of the Late Joseph Barrell, Esq. of Charlestown. [n. p.] *August*, 1816. 8vo, pp. 20. H. 3598

Barrell (J.) The State of Gerrish and Barrell's Accounts and Disputes, delivered Mr. Robert Sanderson and Mr. Nathaniel

Bethune, June, 1751. By John Barrell. *Boston*, 1751. 8vo, pp. 46. 3599

Barrenechea (*D.* Juan de). Nueva obseruacion astronomica del periodo tragico de los temblores grandes de la Tierra. Exactamente arreglada à Europa, y Assia, y de la America, à los Reynos del Perù, Chile, y Guathemala. *Lima, J. Gonzales de Cossio*, 1734. 4to, (14), 36 (3) l. 1 Table, 1 Plate. 3600

Title from Leclerc, Bib. Am., No. 118.

Barrera. Epistola a los missionarios de Mexico, por Alonso de la Barrera. *Madrid*, 1631. 3601

Title from Ternaux, No. 529.

Barrere (B.) Emigration à Monte Video y à Buenos Ayres. Par B. Barrere. *Paris*, 1842. 8vo, pp. 52. 3602

"Sur la nombreuse emigration des Basques."

Barrère (P.) Essai sur l'histoire naturelle de la France Equinoxiale. Ou dénombrement Des Plantes, des Animaux & des Minéraux, qui se trouvent dans l'Isle de Cayenne, les l'Isles de Remire, sur les Côtes de la Mer, & dans le Continent de la Guyane ... . Par Pierre Barrère ... . *Paris, Piget*, M. DCC. XLI, 12mo, pp. xxiv., 215. + *Paris, Veuve Piget*, M.DCC.XLI.X. 12mo, pp. xxiv., 315 (7). H. 3603

There are copies of the first edition on large paper. "In this little work the author gives but a very imperfect idea of the natural treasures of those countries. The plants are arranged alphabetically, under the names given them by Plumier & Tournefort."—*Biog. Univ.*

Barrère. Nouvelle relation de la France Equinoxiale, contenant La Description des Côtes de la Guiane; de l'Isle de Cayenne; le Commerce de cette Colonie; les divers changemens arrivés dans ce Pays; & les Mœurs & Coûtumes des différens Peuples Sauvages qui l'habitent. Avec Des Figures dessinées sur les lieux. Par Pierre Barrere, Correspondant de l'Académie Royale des Sciences de Paris, Docteur & Professeur en Médicine dans l'Université de Perpignan; Médecin de l'Hôpital Militaire de la même Ville, ci-devant Médicin-Botaniste du Roi dans l'Isle de Cayenne. *Paris, Piget, Damonneville, Durand*, M. DCC. XLIII. 12mo, 4 p. l., pp. 250 (1). 16 Plates, 3 Maps. C., H. 3604

"Barrere a décrit la manière dont les Espagnols cultivent le riz, dans *l'Histoire de l'Académie des sciences* (1743)."—Quérard.

Barrere. Neue Reisen nach Guiana, Peru und durch das südliche Amerika ... aus dem Französischen der Herren Barrere, Bouguer und de la Condamine übersetzt. Mit vielen Kupfertafeln und Landkarten. *Goettingen, Abram Vandenhöecks Wittwe.* 1751. 8vo, pp. (14), 380 (12). (Sammlung neuer ... Reisen, IIter Theil.) H. 3605

Barres (F. W. Des). The Atlantic Neptune published for the Use of the Royal Navy of Great Britain. By Joseph F. W. Des Barres, Esq., under the directions of the R. H. Lords Commissioners of the Admiralty. *London*, 1777. 2 vols., Atlas folio. 146 Maps. 3606

See Rich's Bibl. Am., Vol. I., 249, where three pages are occupied in describing this Atlas, and it is justly termed "The most splendid collection of charts, plans and views ever published. It was executed at the expense of the British Government, for the use of the British navy, and no expense spared in its execution in order to render it a monument worthy of the nation." The coast of Nova Scotia was surveyed by J. F. W. Des Barres, Esq.; the coasts, harbors, &c., of St. Lawrence, in North America, by Major Holland; those of New England, &c., by S. Holland, G. Sproule, C. Blascowitz, J. Grant, and T. Wheeler; and those of North America, from New York south-westward to the Gulf of Mexico, from various surveys.

Barres. Remarks on Des Barres' Chart of Boston Harbor. 1775. 4to. 3607

Title from Col. Aspinwall's Catalogue, No. 453.

Barres. The Sea Coast of Nova Scotia; exhibiting the diversities of the Coast, the banks, rocks, &c., with Remarks and Directions for Navigation and Pilotage. Surveyed by Joseph F. W. Des Barres, Esq. *London*, 1777. Folio. 3608

Barret (J. R.) Speech ... In the House ... May 29, 1860. *Washington* [n. d.] 8vo, pp. 8. H. 3609

Barreto (Francisco). Relaçam diaria do sitio e tomada da forte praça do Recife, recuperaçao das capitanias de Itamaraca, Paraiba, Rio-Grande, Ciara é ilha de Fernando de Noronha, por Francisco Barreto mestre de campa general do estado do Brasil e gobernador de Pernambuco. *Lisboa, Craesbeeck*, 1654. 4to, 16 l. 3610

Title from Ternaux-Compans, No. 736.

Barreto (Nicholas). Contestacion al Manifesto que ha dado el Escmo. S. D. Francisco de Arango sobre la Junta proyectada en la Habana en Julio del año de 1808. *Habana*, 1821. 8vo, pp. 31, Errata, 1 l. 3611

BARRETO. Contestacion que dá el Conde de Casa Barreto, al papel de Escmo. Señor D. Francisco de Arango; contrayendose en parte a los publicados por el Señor D. Jose del mismo appellido. *Habana*, 1821. 8vo, pp. 18. 3612

BARRETT (B. F.) Love toward Enemies and the Way to Manifest it. A Sermon ... June 12th 1864. By B. F. Barrett ... *Philadelphia, J. B. Lippincott & Co.*, 1864. 12mo, pp. 24. 3613

[BARRETT (Jonathan Fay)]. Concord: a Poem, delivered before the Lyceum, Concord, Mass., January 22, 1851 ... . *Boston, Ticknor, Reed, and Fields*, M DCCC LI. 16mo, pp. 32. H.

BARRETT (Joseph C.) The Soldier Bird. A History of "Old Abe," the Live War Eagle of the Eighth Wisconsin Regiment. By Joseph C. Barrett. *Chicago, A. L. Sewell*, 1865. 8vo, pp. 61. 3615

BARRETT (Joseph H.) Life of Abraham Lincoln; with a condensed view of his most important speeches. Also, a sketch of the life of Hannibal Hamlin, of Maine. By Joseph H. Barrett. *Cincinnati*, 1860. C. 3616

BARRETT. Life of Abraham Lincoln; presenting his Early History, Political Career, and Speeches, in and out of Congress; also, a General View of his Policy as President of the United States, with his Messages, Proclamations, Letters, etc., and a Concise History of the War. By Joseph H. Barrett. *Cincinnati: Moore, Wilstach & Baldwin*, 1864. 12mo, pp. 518. + [with] A History of his Eventful Administration, and of the Scenes attendant upon his Tragic and Lamented Demise. *Cincinnati, Moore, Wilstach & Baldwin*, 1865. 8vo, pp. 842.

Of this work 100,000 copies have been sold.

BARRETT. Das Leben und Wirken Abraham Lincoln's. Aus dem Englischen frei übersetzt von J. L. C. Eggers. *Cincinnati, Moore, Wilstach & Co.*, 1864. 8vo. + *Cincinnati*, 1866. 8vo.

BARRETT-LENNARD. *See* Lennard.

BARRETT (S.) A Discourse, delivered before the Ancient and Honorable Artillery Company, June 6, 1831 ... . By Samuel Barrett ... . *Cambridge*, 1831. 8vo, pp. 19. B., C. 3619

BARRETT. A Discourse delivered ... Boston, on Fast Day, April 10, 1851, by Samuel Barrett. ... *Boston*, 1851. 8vo, pp. 15. H. 3620

BARRETT. ... A Sermon, preached ... March 4, 1838. In Consequence of the Late Duel in Washington. By Samuel Barrett ... . [*Boston*], 1838. 8vo, pp. 18. B. 3621

BARRETT. Two Discourses, preached ... February 10, 1850, on the Completion of the Twentyfifth Year of his Ministry, by Samuel Barrett. ... *Boston, printed by Tuttle & Dennett*, 1850, 8vo, pp. 40. H. 3622

Also: A Sermon ... at the Ordination of the Rev. Moses G. Thomas ... Concord, N. H. February 25, 1829. ... . *Boston, Leonard C. Bowles*, 1829. 12mo, pp. 25. H. Afterwards published as a tract on religious experience. A Sermon ... at the Installation of the Rev. George R. Noyes ... in Petersham, Oct. 15, 1834. *Boston, Charles Bowen*, 1834. 12mo, pp. 24. H. A Sermon, preached ... August 9, 1832, the Day appointed for fasting ... on account of the Approach of the Cholera. By Samuel Barrett ... . *Boston*, 1832. 8vo, pp. 18. H.

BARRETT (S. A.) Maintonomah, and other Poems. By S. A. Barrett. *New-York, Cady & Burgess*, MDCCCXLIX. 12mo, pp. 209. B. & H. 3623

BARRETT (Walter), *pseudon. See* [Scoville (Joseph A.)]

BARRETT (W. G.) Baptist Mission in Jamaica. A Reply to the Circular of the Committee of the Baptist Missionary Society. By William Garland Barrett ... . *London* [1842]. 8vo, pp. 16. H. 3624

BARRICK (Richard). The Life and Dying Confessions of Richard Barrick, and John Sullivan, Highway Robbers, together with the last words of Alexander White, Murderer and Pirate, ... Executed at Cambridge, ... November 18. 1784. *Printed and Sold at Worcester. Sold also by Edward Houghton, Post-Rider*, 1784. 12mo, pp. 12. 3625

BARRILLON. Politique de la France et de l'humanité dans le conflit américain par Barrillon ... . *Paris, Guillaumin et Cie*, 1861. 8vo, pp. 40. H. 3626

BARRINGER (D. M.) Speech of Mr. D. M. Barringer, of North Carolina, on the Tariff ... in the House ... July 1, 1846. [*Washington*, n. d.] 8vo, pp. 15. H. 3627

BARRINGTON (D.) Miscellanies by the Honourable Daines Barrington. ... *London, B. White, and J. Nichols*, M DCC LXXXI. 4to, pp. iv., viii., 557 (1). 2 Maps and 4 Tables. H. 3628

Contains the celebrated "Tracts on the possibility of approaching the North-Pole." In these tracts are laid down the results of numerous inquiries addressed to whaling captains, especially to those who frequented the coasts of Labrador and Greenland. A large part of Dr. Scoresby's "Arctic regions" is devoted to a discussion of the facts collected by Barrington. Also contains, "Whether the Turkey was known before the Discovery of America," and Francisco Antonio Maurelle's "Journal of a Spanish Voyage in 1775, to explore the Western Coast of N. America."

BARRINGTON. The Possibility of reaching the North Pole asserted. By the Hon. D. Barrington. A New Edition. With an Appendix, containing Papers on the Same Subject, and on A North West Passage. By Colonel Beaufoy, F.R.S. Illustrated with a Map of the North Pole, according to the Latest Discoveries. Second Edition. *London, T. and J. Allman*, 1818. 8vo, pp. xxiv., 258. Map. H. + The possibility of approaching the North Pole [etc.] *New-York, James Eastburn & Co.*, 1818. 8vo, pp. 187. Map. B. + *New York*, 1819. 8vo, pp. 187. Map. C. 3629

See Monthly Review, New Series, LXXXV., 418.

BARRINGTON. Instances of Navigators who have reached High Northern Latitudes. Read at a Meeting of the Royal Society, May 19, 1774. [Signed Daines Barrington, F.R.S. *London, Benjamin White*, 1774.] 4to, pp. 8. H. 3630

BARRINGTON. Additional instances of Navigators who have reached High Northern Latitudes lately received from Holland. [1776.] 4to, pp. 2. 3631

[BARRINGTON.] The Probability of reaching the North Pole discussed. ... *London, C. Heydinger*, M.DCC.LXXV. 4to, Title, pp. 155. H. 3632

Page 91 is a half title, "A Supplement to the Probability," etc., and page 93 a title, "Additional Instances," etc.; page 113 is a half title, "A Second Supplement," etc.; and page 115, a title, "Observations on the Floating Ice which is Found In High Northern and Southern Latitudes. To which are added Experiments on the Freezing of Sea Water. By B. Higgins, M.D.," etc. *London*, M. DCC. LXXVI. This work caused the memorable voyage undertaken by Captain Phipps.

BARRINGTON (Shute), *Bishop*. The Political Life of William, Viscount Barrington, Compiled by his Brother. *London*, 1814. 4to, pp. 207, Index, 2 l. Portrait. 3633

Includes his letters on American affairs.

BARRINGTON (W. L.) Reflections on Some of the Results

of the Late American War: being A Lecture, delivered in the Friends' Institute ... March 29th, 1866. By William L. Barrington ... . *Dublin*, 1866. 8vo, pp. 43. H. 3634

BARRIO. Noticia sobre el terreno carbonifero de Coronel i Lota, sobre los trabajos de esplotacion [*sic*] en el emprendidos [*sic*] por Don Paulino del Barrio, injeniero de minas. *Santiago*, 1857. Imp. 8vo, pp. 107. 5 Plates. 3635

BARRIOS (G.) Manifesto of Don Gerardo Barrios, Captain General and President of the Republic of San Salvador, to his Fellow Citizens. Translated from the Spanish. *Nueva York, S. Hallet*, 1864. 8vo, pp. 52. H. 3636

BARRITT (F. F.) East and West; or, The Beauty of Willard's Mill. By Mrs. Frances Fuller Barritt. *New York, Beadle and Company*. 12mo. 3637

"A romance of western life and adventure."

BARRITT. The Land-Claim: a Story of the Upper Missouri. By Mrs. F. F. Barritt. *New York, Beadle and Company*. 12mo. 3638

BARROILHET. Consideraciones sobre la requeza del Peru; por Carlos Barroilhet. *Paris, impr. d'Aubusson et Kugelmann*, 1859. 8vo, pp. 33. 3639

BARROILHET (C.) Grandeza ó decadencia del Perú; por Carlos Barroilhet. *Paris, impr. d'Aubusson et Kugelmann*, 1858. 8vo, pp. 30 3640

BARROILHET. Opusculo sobre el Huano, dedicado a la nacion peruana, por Carlos Barroilhet. *Paris, impr. Walder*, 1857. 8vo, pp. 104. 3641

BARROILHET. Examen critico de un opusculo sobre el huano; por Carlos Barroilhet. *Paris, impr. Kugelmann*, 1860. 8vo, pp. 31. 3642

BARRON (J.) Proceedings of a Court of Inquiry, Held at the Navy yard, Brooklyn, New York, upon Captain James Barron of the United States' Navy, in May, 1821. *Washington, J. Gideon*, 1822. 8vo, pp. 111. 3643

BARRON. Proceedings of the General Court Martial convened for the Trial of Commodore James Barron, Captain Charles Gordon, Mr. William Hook, and Captain John Hall of the

United States Ship Chesapeake, in the month of January 1808. Published by order of the Navy Department. *Washington, Printed by Jacob Gideon, Jr.*, 1822. 8vo, pp. 496. 3644

BARRON. Correspondence. *See* Decatur (Stephen).

[BARRON (William)]. History of the Colonization of the Free States of Antiquity, applied to the Present Contest between Great Britain and her American Colonies. With Reflections concerning the Future Settlement of these Colonies. *London, T. Cadell*, M DCC LXXVII. 4to, pp. vii. (1), 151. C., H. 3644*a*

BARROS (*P.* André de). Vida do apostolico padre Antonio Vieyra da Companhia de Jesus, chamado por antonomasia o grande: acclamado no Mundo por principe dos oradores evangelicos, prégador incomparavel dos reys de Portugal, Varao esclarecido em virtudes, e letras divinas, e humanas; restaurador das missones do Maranhao, e Pára. ... Pelo P. André de Barros da companhia de Jesus. *Lisboa, na nova Officina Sylviana*, 1746. Folio, 12 p. l., pp. 686. Portrait of Vieyra. 3645

"Le P. André de Barros, né à Lisbonne en 1697, supérieur de la maison professe de cette ville, fut chargé par l'Académie royale de l'histoire du Portugal d'écrire les mémoires ecclésiastiques de l'évêché d'Algarve. Il mourut à Lisbonne en 1794."—LE CLERC. I have a MS. catalogue of books relating to Brazil, compiled by the late Mr. Ludewig, in which he quotes an edition, *Lisboa, officina de Miguel Rodriguez*, 1736, 4to. "Father Vieyra was most zealous in converting the Indians of Brazil, but was much persecuted by the Portuguese inhabitants for opposing their making slaves of them as fast as they became Christians, which, it appears, they had previously done, as a thing of course."—RICH.

BARROS ARANA. *See* Alvarez de Toledo (F.), (No. 973), Yves d'Evreux, and Perrot (N.)

BARROS E SOUSA DE MESQUITA DE MACEDO LEITÃO E CARVALHOSA (Manuel Francis de.) *See* Santarem (*Viscount de*).

BARROS (Joam de). Asia de Joam de Barros dos|fectos que os Portugueses fize-|ram no descobrimento & conquista dos ma-|res & terras do|Oriente.|*Impressa per Germano Galharde em|Lixboa: a* xxviij. *de Junho|anno de* m. v. lij.| 2 p. l., Text folioed 1 to 128. Segunda decada da Asia de Joam|de Barros dos feitos que os|Portugueses fizeram no|descobrimento & conquista dos mares & ter-|ras do oriente.|*Impressa per Germano Galharde em|Lixboa. aos.* xxliiij. *dias de|Março de* M. D. L. iij. 2 p. and 143 l. Decada Terceira|da Asia de|Ioamo de Barros:|dos feitos qve os Por-|tvgveses fezeramo no descobri-|mento & conquista dos mares & terras|do Oriente.|Dirigida ao Senado da

Cama-|ra desta cidade de Lisboa. [Vignette] *Em Lisboa|Com todas as licenças necessarias.|Impressa per Iorge Rodriguez. Anno de* 1628.|*Aa custa de Antonio Gonçaluez mercador de liuros.*| Folio, 10 p. l., Text, 262 l. 3646

This is a most important collection, consisting of eight decades in all. Decades II. and III. contain some particulars concerning Magellan, the discovery of America, Brazil, etc. Diego do Couto assisted in the compilation, and a complete set of these "Autores Dignos de Eterna Fama," is certainly "one of the rarest and most important in the whole range of Portuguese literature." I have not thought it necessary to describe the other decades. A perfect copy of the Decada VI. is of the greatest rarity, nearly all the copies having been destroyed by fire. Concerning this work, *see* Da Silva Diccionario Bibliographia Portuguez, III., 322; Oliveyra, Mémoires Historiquos y Littéraires de Portugal; Bibliotheca Grenvilliana, Vol. I., 60; and Meuselius, Vol. II., Part II., 28. Brunet remarks that the original editions are presque introuvables. An imperfect set sold at Puttick's, in 1860, for £19 15s. There was an Italian translation of Decades I. and II., with the following title:

BARROS. L'Asia del Sig. Giovanni di Barros, consigliero del christianissimo Re di Portogallo, de fatti dei Portoghesi nello scoprimento e conquiste de mari e terre di Oriente. *Venetia*, 1561–62. 2 vols., 4to. 3647

BARROS. Da Asia de Ioao de Barros e de Diogo de Couto nova ediçao ... . *Lisboa, Na Regia Officina Typografica*, MDCCLXXVIII.-M.DCCLXXXI. 15 vols., sm. 8vo. Portrait. H.

The work of Barros fills eight volumes. Vol. IX. is a "Vida ... de Barros por Manoel Severim de Faria e indice geral ... ."

BARROS (Jose Mauricio Fernandes Pereira). Apontomentos de Direito financeiro brasileiro. *Rio de Janeiro, Typ de E. & H. Laenimert*, 1855. 8vo, pp. 431. 3649

BARROS (Joao Borges de). Relaçao summara dos funebres obsequios, que se fizeram na cidade da Bahia a memoria do sr. dr. Manuel de Mattos Botelho, provisor e governador do bizpaeto de Marianna. *Lisboa, na Reg. Off. Silviana*, 1745. 4to.

BARROT. Piezas Officiales relativas à los Acontecimientis de Cartajena en Julio i Agosto del presente año conexionados con la persona del Sr Adolfo Barrot, Consul Frances en aquella plaza. *Bogotà*, 1833. 8vo, pp. 120, Supplement (1834), 39.

BARROW (Alexander). Speech ... on the Oregon Question. Delivered in the Senate of the U. S., on the 30th of March, 1846. [*Washington*, 1846.] 8vo, pp. 16. H. 3652

BARROW (C.) On the Affairs of the West Indies. By C. Barrow. *London*, 1830. 8vo, pp. 16. 3653

[BARROW (John).] A Chronological Abridgment or History of Discoveries made by Europeans in different parts of the world. *London*, 1756. 3 vols., 12mo. 3654

Republished, with the following title:

BARROW. A Collection of Authentic, Useful and Entertaining Voyages and Discoveries. By John Barrow, Esq. *London, G. Knox*, 1764, 1765. 3 vols., 12mo. + Also *London*, 1783.

Includes Columbus, Vasco de Gama, Drake, Raleigh, Cavendish, etc. *See* M. R., XXXII., 481.

BARROW. Abrégé chronologique, ou Histoire des découvertes des Européens dans les differentes parties du monde: extraite des Relations les plus exacte et des voyages les plus véridiques, par. M. Barrow, traduite de l'anglois par M. Targe. *Paris, Saillant-Desaint et Panckoucke*, 1766. 12 vols., 12mo. S. 3656

"Cet abrégé, fait avec une méthode qui manque à l'Histoire générale des Voyages, de l'abbé Prévost, a dû avoir du succès avant la publication de l'abrégé de cette histoire, par la Harpe."—QUÉRARD.

BARROW. A Voyage to Cochinchina, in the Years 1792 and 1793 ... . By John Barrow ... . With several Engravings by Medland, coloured ... . *London, T. Cadell and W. Davies*, 1806. 4to, pp. xviii. (2), 447. H. 3657

Pages 72–136, with two plates and a map, relate to "Rio de Janeiro" and "The Brazils."

BARROW. Voyage à la Cochinchine par les îles de Madère, de Ténériffe, le cap Vert, le Brésil et l'île de Java, en 1792–93, traduit de l'anglais, par Malte-Brun, avec des notes. *Paris, Buisson*, 1807. 2 vols., 8vo, and Atlas, 4to. 3658

BARROW (*Sir* John). An Auto-Biographical Memoir of Sir John Barrow, Bart. ... including Reflections, Observations, and Reminiscences at home and abroad, from Early Life to Advanced Age. ... *London, John Murray*, 1847. 8vo, pp. xi., 515. Portrait. C., H. 3659

"A Voyage to the Greenland Whale Fishery," pp. 16–28; War and Peace with America; The Arctic Voyages, 325–334. *See* N. A. R., LXVI., 348.

BARROW (John). A Chronological History of Voyages into the Arctic Regions; undertaken chiefly for the purpose of discovering a North-East, North-West, or Polar Passage between the Atlantic and Pacific, from the Earliest Periods of Scandinavian Navigation to the Departure of the Recent Expeditions under the orders of Captains Ross and Buchan. ... By John Bar-

row, F.R.S. *London, John Murray*, 1818. 8vo, pp. (6), 379, 48. Map and 3 Woodcuts. C., H. 3660

Another edition, brought down to 1848, contains a translation of Maldonado's famous voyage from the Atlantic to the Pacific, with cuts. An elaborate work, written while the author was Secretary to the Admiralty, with full command of the needful materials. *See* Monthly Review, LXXXVIII., 62; Q. R., III., 194.

BARROW. Histoire Chronologique des Voyages vers le pôle arctique ... depuis les premierès navigations des Scandinaves jusqu'a l'expedition faite en 1818. Traduit ... par ... [de Fauconpret]. *Paris, Gide fils*, 1819. 2 vols., 8vo. Maps. 3661

[BARROW.] The Eventful History of the Mutiny and Piratical Seizure of H. M. S. Bounty; its Cause and Consequences. Illustrated by Six Etchings, from Original Drawings by Lieut.-Colonel Battey. *London, John Murray*, MDCCCXXXI. 16mo, pp. ix., 356. H. 3662

Reprinted, with the following title:

[BARROW.] A Description of Pitcairn's Island and its Inhabitants. With an authentic Account of the Mutiny of the Ship Bounty, and of the subsequent Fortunes of the Mutineers. *London, John Murray*, 1839. + [Reprinted.] *New York, Harpers*, 1839. 18mo. + *London*, 1847. 16mo. S. 3663

The two preceding books scarcely belong to "Americana," except that the object of the Bounty's voyage was to convey the bread-fruit tree to the West Indies. *See* Bligh (W.)

BARROW. The Geography of Hudson's Bay: being the remarks of Captain W. Coats, in many Voyages to that Locality, between the years 1727 and 1751. With an Appendix, containing extracts from the Log of Capt. Middleton on his Voyage for the Discovery of the North-West Passage, in H. M. S. "Furnace" in 1741–2. Edited by John Barrow, Esq. *London, Printed for the Hakluyt Society*, M DCCC LII. 8vo, 4 p. l., pp. x., 146. 3664

BARROW. The Life of George Lord Anson, Admiral of the Fleet; Vice-Admiral of Great Britain; and First Lord Commissioner of the Admiralty, previous to, and during, the Seven-Years' War. By Sir John Barrow ... . *London, Murray*, MDCCCXXXIV. 8vo, pp. xxxix., 484. Portrait. C. & H. 3665

BARROW. The Life of Richard, Earl Howe, K.G., Admiral of the Fleet and General of Marines. By Sir John Barrow,

Bart., F.R.S. *London, Murray*, MDCCCXXXVIII. 8vo, pp. xvi., 432. Portrait and Fac-similes. C. & H. 3666

Contains an account of his services in command of the American fleet, engagement with Count D'Estaing's squadron, &c. *See* Ed. and Qu. Reviews.

BARROW. Life, Voyages, and Exploits of Admiral Sir Francis Drake, with numerous Original Letters from him and the Lord High Admiral to the Queen and great Officers of State. Compiled from MSS. in the State Paper Office, British Museum, and the Archives of Madrid, never before published. By John Barrow, Esq. *London, John Murray*, 1843. 8vo, pp. 440. C.

Reprinted and abridged. *London*, 1842. 12mo, pp. 200.+1844. 12mo.+*New York*, 1846. 12mo.

BARROW. Memoirs of the Naval Worthies of Queen Elizabeth's Reign; of their Gallant Deeds, Daring Adventures, and Services in the Infant State of the British Navy, with brief Biographical Notices of the respective Commanders: illustrated by numerous Autograph Letters and other unpublished Documents. By John Barrow, Esq. F.R.S. *London, John Murray*, 1845. 8vo, pp. 512. 3668

Comprising accounts of the American voyages of Frobisher, Davis, Gilbert, Hawkins, Drake, Cavendish, and others, from unpublished sources.

BARROW. Voyages of Discovery and Research within the Arctic Regions, from the Year 1818 to the Present Time: under the command of the several Naval Officers employed by Sea and Land in search of a North-west Passage from the Atlantic to the Pacific, with Two Attempts to reach the North Pole. Abridged and arranged from the Original Narratives, with Occasional Remarks, by Sir J. Barrow, Bart. *London, John Murray*, 1846. 8vo, pp. 544. Portrait and Plates.+*New York, Harpers*, 1846. 12mo. 3669

BARROW. A Letter to John Barrow, Esq., on the subject of Polar Expeditions; or the Reviewer Reviewed. *London, Ridgway*, 1819. 8vo, pp. 16. 3670

BARROW. A Letter to John Barrow, Esq. F.R.S. on the late Extraordinary and Unexpected Hyperborean Discoveries [of Ross, Parry, &c.] For Private Perusal only. *London, W. Pople*, 1826. 8vo, pp. 46. H. 3671

"Another edition, with some alterations, was printed in the same year, and with the addition to this title 'made by a Quarterly Reviewer and Captain Parry.'"—O. RICH.

BARROW (John). Facts relating to North Eastern Texas, condensed from Notes made during a Tour through that portion of the United States. By John Barrow. *London, Simpkin & Co.*, 1849. 8vo, pp. 68. Map. P. 3672

BARROW (Robert). *See* [Dickinson (Jonathan)].

BARROW (Robert Ruffin). ... A Miscellaneous Essay on the Political Parties of the Country, the Rise of Abolitionism and the Impolicy of Secession. By R. R. Barrow. *New Orleans, L. Marchand, Printer*, 1861. 8vo, pp. 20. H. 3673

BARROW (W.) Speech of Mr. Washington Barrow, of Tennessee, on the Reference of the Presidents Annual Message, delivered in the House. ... January 24, 1848. *Washington*, 1848. 8vo, pp. 15. H. 3674

BARROWS (E. P.) A View of the American Slavery Question. By E. P. Barrows, Jr. ... *New York, John S. Taylor*, 1836. 24mo, pp. 114. 3675

BARROWS. The High School Policy of Massachusetts, by Rev. W. Barrows ... . From the New Englander for November, 1858. *New Haven*, 1858. 8vo, pp. 22. B., H. 3676

BARROWS. Honor to the Brave. A discourse delivered Aug. 23, 1863. By Rev. William Barrows. *Boston, John M. Whittemore & Co.*, 1863. 8vo, pp. 19. 3677

BARROWS. Our War and our Religion: and their Harmony. A Discourse delivered in the Old South Church, Reading, Mass., March 2, 1862. By William Barrows, Pastor. *Boston, J. M. Whittemore & Co.*, 1862. 8vo, pp. 19. B. 3678

BARROWS. Shall we legislate? Alcohol and the Commonwealth ... By Rev. W. Barrows. *Boston*, 1851. 8vo, pp. 42.

BARROWS. The War and Slavery; and their Relations to each other. A Discourse, delivered in the Old South Church, Reading, Mass., December 28, 1862. By Rev. William Barrows. *Boston*, 1863. 8vo, pp. 18. H.+Second Edition. *Boston, John M. Whittemore & Co.*, 1863. 8vo, pp. 18. B. 3680

BARRUEL-BEAUVERT (P. A. de). Bombardement et entière destruction de Grey-Town. 2me lettre du délégué de la population française de Grey-Town (Royaume mosquite, Amérique

Centrale) ... . [Signed Philippe Auguste de Barruel-Beauvert.] *Paris*, 20 *Septembre*, 1856. 8vo, pp. 41 (1). H. 3681

BARRY (E. D.) A Discourse delivered in St. Matthew's Church, Jersey City, December, 1845. By the Rev. Edmund D. Barry ... containing Historical Notices of the ... Parish ... . *New-York, Stanford & Swords*, 1846. 8vo, pp. 24. H. 3682

[BARRY (*Lieut.* Henry)]. The Advantage which America derives from her Commerce, Connexion, and Dependance on Britain. Addressed to the People of America. 1775. 8vo, pp. 16. M. 3683

[BARRY (Henry)]. Answers to Strictures on a Pamphlet entitled a "Friendly address to all reasonable Americans, on the subject of our Political confusions". *Boston*, 1774. 8vo.

The Strictures are attributed to General Henry Lee. The Friendly Address is by Dr. Thomas Cooper.

BARRY (J. S.) A Genealogical and Biographical Sketch of the Name and Family of Stetson; from the Year 1634, to the Year 1847. By John Stetson Barry. ... *Boston, the Author*, 1847. 8vo, pp. 116. H. 3685

BARRY. A Historical Sketch of the Town of Hanover, Mass., with Family Genealogies. By John S. Barry ... . *Boston, Samuel G. Drake*, 1853. 8vo, pp. 448. Woodcuts. H. 3686

BARRY. The History of Massachusetts. ... By John Stetson Barry ... . *Boston, the Author*, 1855–57. 8vo, pp. xii., 516; xii., 514; xii., 468. H. 3687

Vol. I. The Colonial Period, *Phillips, Sampson, and Company*, 1855; II. The Provincial Period, 1857; III. The Commonwealth Period, 1857. *See* North American Review, LXXXV., 266.

BARRY (P.) The Theory and Practice of the International Trade of the United States and England, and of the Trade of the United States and Canada; with Tables of Federal Currency, Canadian Currency and Sterling, Exchange Formulas, &c., by P. Barry. *Chicago, D. B. Cooke & Co.*, 1858. C.

BARRY (Pat.) American and Indian Transit. *London*, 1859. 8vo. 3689

BARRY (T.) Narrative of the Singular Adventures and Captivity of Mr. Thomas Barry among the Munsipi Indians, in the unexplored regions of North America, during the years 1797,

1798, and 1799; including the manners, customs, &c. of that tribe; also a particular account of his escape, accompanied by an American Female; the extraordinary hardships they encountered, and their safe arrival in London. Written by Himself. *London, Neil*, 1800. 12mo, Colored Plate. 3690

"Probably a fictitious narrative."—RICH. *See* M. R., XXXV., 214.

BARRY (W.) A History of Framingham, Massachusetts, including the Plantation, from 1640 to the Present Time, with an Appendix, containing a Notice of Sudbury and its First Proprietors; also, a Register of the Inhabitants of Framingham before 1800, with Genealogical Sketches: By William Barry ... *Boston, James Monroe and Company*, 1847. 8vo, pp. iv., 456. C. & H.

BARRY (W. T.) Address of William T. Barry, ... to the People of the United States. *Washington*, 1834. 8vo, pp. 24. H.

BARRY. Letter of William T. Barry, Postmaster General, to the House of Representatives of the United States; Reviewing the Report of the Select Committee of that House, appointed to investigate the affairs of the Post Office Department. March 2, 1835. *Washington, printed by Blair and Rives*, 1835. 8vo, pp. 30. H. 3693

BARSTOW (A. C.) Speeches of Hon. A. C. Barstow, Rev. Geo. T. Day, Rev. A. Woodbury, Hon. Thomas Davis, and Resolutions adopted at a Meeting ... in Providence, R. I., December 2d, 1859, on the ... Execution of John Brown. *Providence*, 1860. 8vo, pp. 32. H. 3694

BARSTOW (B.) A Letter to the Hon. James Buchanan, President Elect ... . By Benjamin Barstow, of Salem, Mass. *Concord, N. H.*, 1857. 8vo, pp. 16. H. 3695

BARSTOW. Speech of Benjamin Barstow, of Salem, on the Abolition Propensities of Caleb Cushing. Delivered at the Massachusetts National Democratic Convention, held at Boston, Sept. 22, 1853. ... *Boston*, 1853. 8vo, pp. 16. H. 3696

BARSTOW (G.) The History of New Hampshire from its Discovery, in 1614, to the Passage of the Toleration Act, in 1819. By George Barstow. *Concord, I. S. Boyd, June* 4, 1842. 8vo, pp. iv., 456, Errata, 1 slip. Portraits. H.+Second Edition. *Boston, Little, Brown & o., Jan*. 20, 1853. 8vo, pp. iv., 456. C. 3697

BARSTOW. War the Only Means of preserving our Nationality. An Oration, delivered at San Jose ... Cal. July 4, 1864, By George Barstow. *San Francisco*, 1864. 8vo, pp. 16. H.

BARSTOW (Wm. A.) The trial in the Supreme Court ... on the relation of Alex. Bashford *vs* Wm. A. Barstow contesting the right to the office of Governor of Wisconsin ... *Madison, Wis.*, 1856. 8vo, pp. 368. P. 3699

BARSTOW (Z. S.) Remarks on the "Preliminary History" of Two Discourses by the Rev. Aaron Bancroft, D.D. By Zedekiah S. Barstow. ... *Bellows Falls*, 1821. 8vo, pp. 24. H., M.

Also: ... A Sermon ... at Acworth, N. H. October 14, 1829, at the Installation of Rev. Moses G. Grosvenor ... . *Boston*, 1829. 8vo, pp. 27 (1). H. ... A Sermon ... Nov. 5, 1857, at the Ordination of the Rev. Charles Greenwood ... in Weitmoreland. ... *Keene*, 1858. 8vo, pp. 16. H.

BART (T. M.) Considérations philosophiques et politiques sur le régime des colonies. *Bordeaux*, 1801. 8vo. C. 3701

BARTH (Christian Gottlieb). Der Negerkönig Zamba. Eine Sklavengeschichte. Seitenstück zu „Onkel Tom's Hütte." Nach dem Englischen bearbeitet. Zweite Auflage. *Stuttgart, J. F. Steinkopf*, 1865. 8vo, pp. 232. Engraving. 3702

BARTH. Unipkautsit 52git maggoertorlugit Bibelemit. Illinniarringnut kittorngarenullo illingajut. *Calev, Barthib sonnalauktangit; Stuttgart, J. F. Steinkopfib nelilauktangit*, 1852. 12mo, pp. vi., 205. Woodcuts. 3703

Bible stories in the Esquimaux language.

BARTHE (J. G.) Le Canada Reconquis par la France. Par J.-G. Barthe. Suivi de Pièces Justificatives Ouvrage illustré de six Gravures et une Carte. *Paris, Ledoyen*, 1855. 8vo, 8 pl. l., pp. 416, Table, 1 l. C. 3704

BARTHE. Lettre sur le Canada. À M. de Monmerqué, conseiller à la Cour royale de Paris ... . *Paris, impr. de Remquet*, 1854. 8vo. 3705

BARTHÉLEMY (Auguste Marseille). À M. J. K. Polk, président des États-Unis. L'Amérique. *Paris, impr. de Lange-Lévy*, 1848. 8vo. 3706

BARTHELEMY (Peter). Supreme Court. In Error. P. Barthelemy & L. de Bullion for Conspiracy and Libel against the Rev. A. Verren, *versus* the People. ... 1st.—Opening Argu-

ment for the Plaintiffs in Error. 2d—Argument of J. R. Whiting ... for the Maintenance of the Trial—the Charge of the Recorder ... The Sentence and Execution complained of. 3d.—Closing Argument for the Reversal of the whole Proceeding, by H. M. Western & Clinton Dewitt, of Counsel for the Defence ... . [n. p., 1841.] 8vo. pp. 98. H. 3707

BARTHELEMY. Letter to the Right Reverend Benjamin T. Onderdonk, D.D. ... in reply to his Congratulations to the Rev. Antoine Verren, Tried and Acquitted for ... Perjury. By P. Barthelemy. *New York, Casserly and Sons*, 1842. 8vo, pp. 14. H. 3708

BARTHÉLEMY-HADOT (*Mad.* Marie Adèle). Guillaume Penn, ou les premiers colons de la Pensylvanie. *Paris, Pigoreau*, 1816. 3 vols., 12mo. 3709

This and the following are probably fictions:

BARTHÉLEMY-HADOT. La révolte de Boston, ou la jeune hospitalière. *Paris, Lecointe et Durey*, 1820. 3 vols., 12mo.

BARTHELMESS. Bibliographie der Freimaurerei in Amerika, zusammengestellt von R. Barthelmess, M.D. *New York*, 1856. 8vo, pp. 48. 3711

BARTHEMA. *See* Varthema.

BARTHOLOMEW (Andrew). A Dissertation on the qualifications necessary to a lawful profession, and enjoying special ordinances, &c. *Hartford* [1769]. 12mo, pp. 47. 3712

BARTHOLEMEW. Sermon before the Association of Litchfield County, Goshen, October 2, 1766. By Andrew Bartholomew. *Hartford*, 1767. 8vo, pp. 32. 3713

BARTHOLOMEW (E.) State of the Accounts of Edward Bartholomew, Collector of Excise for the City and County of Philadelphia, From the time of his Appointment, Nov. 21, 1782, to the 22d of Nov. 1783. In which is exhibited, the Amount of the Monies received by him, on account of Excise accrued before his Appointment; and the Amount of Monies received on account of Excise accruing within the period aforesaid; together with a list of the Persons by whom the same were paid. Also the Payments thereof to the Treasurer. Likewise the Excise accruing since the time of his Appointment, which is represented to be still outstanding. And the amount of the

Quantity exported. *Philadelphia, Printed by J. Bailey*, ... M,DCC,LXXIV. 8vo, pp. 25. P. 3714

Title misprinted 1774 for 1784.

BARTHOLOMEW. State of the Accounts of Edward Bartholomew, Esq. Collector of Excise for the City and County of Philadelphia, From the 22d of Nov. 1783, to the 22d of Nov. 1784. ... *Philadelphia, Printed by J. Bailey*, ... M.DCC.LXXXV. 8vo, pp. 27. P. 3715

BARTHOLOMEW. State of the Accounts of Edward Bartholomew, Esquire; Collector of Excise, Philadelphia City and County; From the time to which his Accounts were last settled, to the 31st December, 1785, inclusive. *Philadelphia, Printed by Robert Aitken*, ... M,DCC,LXXXVI. 8vo, pp. 23. P. 3716

BARTHOLOMEW (J.) Black's Atlas of North America. A Series of Twenty Maps constructed and engraved by John Bartholomew. With Introductory Letter-Press and a Complete Index. *Edinburgh, Adam and Charles Black*, MDCCCLVI. Folio, pp. 39. 20 Maps. H. 3717

BARTHOLOMEW (J. G.) The Hour of Peril. A Sermon ... in Roxbury ... April 21, 1861. By Rev. J. G. Bartholomew. *Boston*, 1861. 8vo, pp. 20. H. 3718

BARTHOLOMEW (Orlo). An Address: delivered at Augusta, [Oneida County, N. Y.] September 7th, 1847, on the Fiftieth Anniversary of the Formation of the Congregational Church. By Orlo Bartholomew. *Hamilton* [*N. Y.*], 1849. 8vo, pp. 25. S. 3719

BARTLET (W. S.) The Frontier Missionary: a Memoir of the Life of the Rev. Jacob Bailey, A.M., Missionary at Pownalborough, Maine; Cornwallis and Annapolis, N. S.; with Illustrations, Notes, and an Appendix. By William S. Bartlet, A.M., ... With a Preface by Right Rev. George Burgess, D.D., .. *Boston, Ide and Dutton*, 1853. 8vo, pp. ix., 365 (1). Portraits and Woodcuts. H. 3720

Contains interesting details of eastern border life during the Revolutionary War.

[BARTLETT (Bailey?)]. Remarks on the Proceedings of the Episcopal Conventions for forming an American Constitution. Addressed to the Publick. With Proposals for them in Future Conventions. And an Account of the Plan proposed for an

American Church. By a Layman. *Printed by S. Hall, Boston*, MDCCLXXXVI. 8vo, pp. 8. H. 3721

"Mr. Bartlett of Haverhill."—*MS. note on the copy in Harv. Coll. Library.*

BARTLETT (C. R.) An Account of the rise and progress of the Malignant Fever, commonly called the Yellow Fever! which lately appeared in Newport;— ... By Charles R. Bartlett, M.D. To which is added some Remarks on the Conduct of the Author, and others immediately concerned in this first transaction of this unfortunate affair. *Newport, Dion Farnsworth*, 1801. 8vo, pp. 43. 3722

"At the end is Moses Brown's account of those who died in Providence of the disease."—J. R. BARTLETT.

BARTLETT (D. W.) ... The Life of Gen. Franklin Pierce, of New-Hampshire, the Democratic Candidate for President of the United States. By D. W. Bartlett. Thirteenth Thousand. *Auburn, Derby & Miller*, 1852. 16mo, pp. 300. Portrait. H. +New Edition. 1855. 12mo, pp. 304. 3723

BARTLETT. The Life and Public Services of Hon. Abraham Lincoln. To which is added a Biographical Sketch of Hon. Hannibal Hamlin. By David W. Bartlett. *New York*, 1860. 12mo. 3724

BARTLETT. Modern Agitators; or, Pen Portraits of living American Reformers. By David W. Bartlett. *New York*, 1856. 12mo, pp. 396. 6 Portraits. C. 3725

See Putnam's Magazine, Vol. v., p. 547.

BARTLETT. Presidential Candidates: containing Sketches, Biographical, Personal, and Political, of Prominent Candidates for the Presidency in 1860. By D. W. Bartlett. *New York, A. B. Burdick*, 1859. 12mo, pp. 360. C. & H. 3726

BARTLETT (E.) A Brief Sketch of the Life, Character, and Writings of William Charles Wells, M.D., F.R.S. ... By Elisha Bartlett ... . *Louisville, Ky., Prentice and Weisinger*, 1849. 8vo, pp. 32. B. 3727

BARTLETT. The History, Diagnosis and Treatment of the fevers of the United States. By Elisha Bartlett, M.D. *Philadelphia, Lea & Blanchard*, 1847. 8vo, pp. 547.+Third Edition, Revised. *Philadelphia*, 1852. 8vo, pp. xxv., 1 l. 49–595. B. +Fourth Edition, Revised by A. Clark, M.D. *Philadelphia*, 1856. 8vo, pp. xxxii., 610. C. 3728

BARTLETT. An Oration ... [at] Lowell, July 4, 1848, by Elisha Bartlett. ... *Lowell, James Atkinson, Printer*, 1848. 8vo, pp. 38. H. 3729

BARTLETT. A Vindication of the Character and Condition of the Females employed in the Lowell Mills, against the Charges contained in The Boston Times, and the Boston Quarterly Review. By Elisha Bartlett, M.D. *Lowell, Leonard Huntress, Printer*, 1841. 8vo, pp. 24. H. 3730

BARTLETT (Ichabod). Speech of Mr. Bartlett, of New-Hamp. on the Proposition to amend the Constitution of the United States. Delivered in the House of Representatives, 30th March, 1826. *Washington City*, 1826. 8vo, pp. 28. H.

BARTLETT. Speech of Mr. Bartlett, on the subject of Retrenchment. Delivered in the House of Reps., Feb. 6, 1828. Second Edition. *Washington*, 1828. 8vo, pp. 24. B., H. 3732

BARTLETT (I.) Oration at Nottingham, N. H. Dec. 27, 1800. By Israel Bartlett. *Portsmouth* [1801]. 8vo. W. 3733

BARTLETT (John). A Discourse, on ... Animation ... before the Humane Society of ... Massachusetts, June 11, 1792. By John Bartlett. ... . *Boston, printed by Isaiah Thomas and Ebenezer T. Andrews*, MDCCXCII. 4to, pp. 40. H., W. 3734

With the Act of Incorporation, Catalogue of Members, etc. Also: A Discourse before the Roxbury Charitable Society, Sept. 19, 1796. 4to. W. Discourse at Marblehead, Mass. June 20, 1819. *Salem*. 8vo. W. Discourse ... Marblehead, Feb. 27, 1825. *Salem*, 1825. 8vo. W.

BARTLETT (J. R.) Bibliography of Rhode Island. A Catalogue of Books and other Publications relating to the State of Rhode Island, with Notes, Historical, Biographical, and Critical. By John Russell Bartlett. Printed by order of the General Assembly. *Providence, Alfred Anthony, Printer*, 1864. 8vo, pp. 287. B. 3735

One hundred and fifty copies printed on large paper.

BARTLETT. Bibliotheca Americana. A Catalogue of Books relating to North and South America in the Library of John Carter Brown of Providence, R. I. Part I. 1493 to 1600 || Part II. 1601 to 1700. With Notes by John Russell Bartlett. *Providence*, 1866. Imp. 8vo, 2 p. l., pp. 79; 249. 3736

A splendid and almost unrivalled collection, rich in the epistles of Columbus, Vespuccius and Cortes, colonial and revolutionary pamphlets, and the whole range of Americana. Mr. Bartlett has appended many very interesting bibliographical notices. Fifty copies printed. The third part, 1700 to 1800, is now [1868] in preparation.

BARTLETT. Census of the Inhabitants of the Colony of Rhode Island and Providence Plantations, taken by order of the General Assembly, in the year 1774; and by the General Assembly of the State ordered to be printed. Arranged by J. R. Bartlett. *Providence, Knowles, Anthony & Co.*, 1858. 8vo, pp. 239. 3737

BARTLETT. Dictionary of Americanisms. A Glossary of Words and Phrases, usually regarded as Peculiar to the United States. By John Russell Bartlett ... . *New York, Bartlett and Welford*, 1848. 8vo, pp. xxvii., 412. H. 3738

Ten copies of this edition were printed on large paper. Second edition, greatly improved and enlarged. *Boston, Little, Brown and Company*, 1859. 8vo, pp. xxxii., 524. H. Totally different from the first, and certainly nearly double the number of words. *See* Preface. A third edition. *Boston, Little, Brown & Co.*, 1860. 8vo, pp. xxxii., 524.

BARTLETT. Woordenboek van Americanismen Een lijst van woorden en zinnen, gewoonlijk als eigenaardig aan de Vereenigde Staten beschouwd: door John Russell Bartlett. Bewerkt door M. Keijzer. *Gorinchem, J. Noorduyn en Zoon*, 1854. 12mo. 3739

There is also a German translation in the British Museum, the title of which I have not seen.

BARTLETT. A History of the Destruction of His Britannic Majesty's Schooner Gaspee, in Narragansett Bay, on the 10th June, 1772; accompanied by the Correspondence connectfd [*sic*] therewith; the Action of the General Assembly of Rhode Island thereon, and the Official Journal of the Proceedings of the Commission of Inquiry appointed by King George the Third, on the Same. By John Russell Bartlett, Secretary of State. *Providence, A. Crawford Greene, Printer to the State*, 1861. Imp. 8vo, pp. 140. H. 3740

One hundred and twenty-five copies printed for private distribution. This is also included in Vol. VII. of the Rhode Island Colonial Records.

BARTLETT. Index to the printed Acts and Resolves of, and of the Petitions and Reports to, the General Assembly of the State of Rhode Island and Providence Plantations from 1758 to 1850. By J. R. Bartlett. *Providence, Knowles, Anthony & Co.*, 1856. 8vo, pp. xiii., 424. + Supplement to Index 1850 to 1862. *Providence, Alfred Anthony*, 1863. 8vo, pp. xxxiv., 103. 3741

BARTLETT. [A Letter to the Hon. Alexander H. H. Stuart, Secretary of the Interior, in Defence of the Mexican Boundary

Line. *Washington*, 1853.] 8vo, pp. 173. (Special Session 1853. Senate Ex. Doc. No. 6.) 3742

BARTLETT. The Literature of the Rebellion. A Catalogue of Books and Pamphlets relating to the Civil War in the United States, and on Subjects growing out of that Event, together with Works on American Slavery, and Essays from Reviews and Magazines on the Same Subjects. Compiled by John Russell Bartlett. ... *Boston, Draper and Halliday; Providence, S. S. Rider & Bro.*, 1866. Rl. 8vo, pp. 477. H. 3743

Two hundred and fifty copies printed in octavo, and sixty copies on large paper. It describes six thousand and seventy-three different books, pamphlets, and magazine articles; also three hundred eulogies, sermons, poems, etc., on the death of Abraham Lincoln.

BARTLETT. Memoirs of Rhode Island Officers who were engaged in the Service of their Country during the great Rebellion of the South. By J. R. Bartlett. Illustrated with 34 Portraits. *Providence: S. S. Rider & Brother*, 1867. 4to, pp. 448. 34 Portraits and 1 Plate. 3744

Edition, five hundred and fifty copies, of which twenty-five are on large paper.

BARTLETT. [Official Despatches, Correspondence and Reports connected with the Commission to run and mark the boundary between the United States and Mexico, 1850–1851. *Washington*, 1852.] 8vo, pp. 515. 7 Maps. (32d Cong., 1st Sess. Senate. Ex. Doc. No. 119.) 3745

BARTLETT. Personal Narrative of Explorations and Incidents in Texas, New-Mexico, California, Sonora and Chihuahua, connected with the United States and Mexican Boundary Commission, during the Years 1850, '51, '52, and '53. By John Russell Bartlett, United States Commissioner during that Period. In Two Volumes, with Map and Illustrations. *New York, D. Appleton & Company*, M.DCCC.LIV. 8vo, Half Title, pp. xxii., 506; Half Title, xvii., 624. 3746

Also, republished with this imprint: *London, George Routledge & Co.*, 1854; and with this title: American Exploring Expedition: a Personal Narrative, etc.

BARTLETT. The Progress of Ethnology, an Account of Recent Archeological, Philological and Geographical Researches in Various Parts of the Globe, tending to elucidate the Physical History of Man, by John R. Bartlett. *New York*, 1847. 8vo, pp. 151. + Second Edition. *New York*, 1847. 8vo, pp. iv., 151. H. 3747

BARTLETT. Records of the Colony of Rhode Island and Providence Plantations in New England. Printed by order of the Legislature. Transcribed and Edited by John Russell Bartlett, Secretary of State. *Providence, R. I., A. Crawford Greene and Brother* [and others], *State Printers*, 1856–1865. 3748

10 vols., 8vo, pp. 549; 609; 595; 622; 594; 629; 643; 661; 763; 527. Fifty copies printed on large paper.

BARTLETT. Reminiscences of Albert Gallatin. *New York*, 1849. 8vo. 3749

BARTLETT. ... Report on the subject of the Boundary Line between the United States and Mexico. [*Washington*, 1853.] 8vo, pp. 31 (1). 5 Maps. (32d Cong., 2d Sess. Senate. Ex. Doc. No. 41.) 3750

BARTLETT. Report to the General Assembly of the State of Rhode Island, on the Soldier's National Cemetery at Gettysburg, January, 1865. 8vo, pp. 6. 3751

BARTLETT. Report on the State Beneficiaries; including the Deaf and Dumb, the Blind and Insane. Presented to the General Assembly, January, 1863. *Providence, Alfred Anthony*, 1863. 8vo, pp. 15. Continued annually. 3752

Mr. Bartlett has collected and described, in his "Literature of the Rebellion," an extraordinary assemblage of newspaper cuttings concerning the Civil Wars, commencing in September, 1860, and continuing to the end of the year 1865, forming seventy volumes folio.

BARTLETT and WELFORD'S Catalogue, Part II. American History, &c. *New York* [n. d.] 8vo, pp. 37. 3753

[BARTLETT (J. E.)] The Boston and Maine Railroad: a Statement showing the Result of its Management for the Last Ten Years. April, 1866. *Boston*, 1866. 8vo, pp. 16. H.

Signed, "In behalf of the petitioners for a stockholders' meeting, J. E. Bartlett, W. B. Dodge, Committee."

BARTLETT (J. S.) Maize, or Indian Corn. Its Advantages as a Cheap and Nutritious Article of Food. With Directions for its Use. By John S. Bartlett, M.D. ... *London, Wiley & Putnam*, MDCCCXLVI. 12mo, pp. 24. H. 3755

BARTLETT (J. S.) Report of the Evidence in the Case of John Stephen Bartlett, M.D. *versus* the Mass. Medical Society,

as given before a Committee of the Legislature, at the Session of 1839. ... *Boston*, 1839. 8vo, pp. 55. H. 3756

Also: A Letter to the ... Massachusetts Medical Society ... May 31, 1837. By John Stephen Bartlett, M.D. formerly Fellow ... . *Boston*, 1837. 12mo, pp. 12. H.

BARTLETT (Joseph). ... An Address, delivered at the Exchange Coffee-House Hall ... Third of July, 1823. Also,—including—a Poem—an Ode—and the New Vicar of Bray. ... By Joseph Bartlett ... . *Boston*, 1823. 8vo, pp. 20. H. 3757

BARTLETT. Oration delivered before the Republican Citizens of Portsmouth, N. H., 4th July, M.DCCC.IX. By Joseph Bartlett. *Portsmouth* [n. d.] 8vo, pp. 16. 3758

BARTLETT. Oration at Biddeford, Me. July 4, 1805. By Joseph Bartlett. *Saco*, 1805. 4to. 3759

BARTLETT. Physiognomy a Poem; delivered ... in the Chapel of Harvard University, ... July 18, 1799. By Joseph Bartlett. *Boston, J. Russell*, 1799. 4to, pp. 16. 3760

Also in his Aphorisms ... Physiognomy ... and the Blessings of Poverty. ... *Boston, printed by Jonathan Howe*, 1823. 12mo, pp. 148, 16, 16. H.

BARTLETT. A Narrative of the Captivity of Joseph Bartlett among the French and Indians. *Printed for the Purchaser*, 1807. 12mo, pp. 12. W. 3761

BARTLETT (Josiah). A Dissertation on the Progress of Medical Science, in ... Massachusetts. Read at the annual meeting of the Massachusetts Medical Society, June 6th, 1810. By Josiah Bartlett. *Boston, printed by T. B. Wait and Co.*, 1810. 8vo, pp. 48. H. 3762

Also in Mass. Hist. Col., 2d Series, Vol. I.

BARTLETT. An Historical Sketch of Charlestown, ... Massachusetts, read ... at the Opening of Washington Hall, Nov. 16, 1813. By Josiah Bartlett, M.D. *Boston, printed by John Eliot*, 1814. 8vo, pp. 24. H. 3763

Also in the Mass. Hist. Soc. Collections, 2d Series, Vol. II., pp. 163–184.

BARTLETT. A Memoir of the Hon. Josiah Bartlett, of Stratham, N. H. who died April 16, 1838, aged Seventy Years. By Josiah Bartlett, M.D. *Gilmanton, N. H., printed by Alfred Prescott*, 1839. 8vo, pp. 7. H. 3764

BARTLETT. Address before the Washington Benevolent Society. *Charlestown*, 1813. 8vo. 3765

BARTLETT. An Address: delivered at Warren Hall, in Charlestown ... [before] King Solomon's Lodge, February 22, 1797. ... By Josiah Bartlett ... . *Charlestown* [1797]. 8vo, pp. 16. H. 3766

BARTLETT. Discourse on the Origin, Progress, and Design of Freemasonry, Charlestown, June 24, 1793. *Boston*, 1793. 8vo, pp. 20. 3767

BARTLETT. Oration at Charlestown, June 17, 1794. Before the Artillery Company. *Boston*, 1795. 8vo, pp. 15. W. 3768

BARTLETT. Oration at Charlestown, at the Dedication of Warren Hall. *Charlestown*, 1786. 12mo. 3769

BARTLETT. An Oration occasioned by the Death of John Warren, M.D. Past Grand Master. Delivered in the Grand Lodge of Massachusetts, ... in Boston, June 12, 1815. In Presence of The Supreme Executive of the Commonwealth. *Boston, Printed for Russell, Cutler & Co.*, 1815. 8vo, pp. 24. B. 3770

BARTLETT. An | Oration, | on the Death of | General George Washington, | delivered at the request of the | Selectmen and Parish Committee, | before the | Inhabitants of Charlestown, | in the County of Middlesex, and Commonwealth of | Massachusetts, on Saturday Feb. 22, 1800. | Being the day set apart by the | Congress of the United States, | to testify the | Grief of the Citizens, on that melancholy Event. | By Josiah Bartlett, Esq. | Fellow of the Massachusetts Medical Society, and Member | of the Historical Society. | *Charlestown*: | *Printed by Samuel Etheridge.* | M,DCCC. 8vo, pp. 15. 3771

BARTLETT. Speech ... at the Republican Convention (of the County of Rockingham) at Kingston Plains. Sept. 10, 1812; with the Address and Resolutions adopted by the said Convention. *Portsmouth* (*N. H.*), 1812. 8vo. 3772

BARTLETT. Speech on Retrenchment. *Washington City*, 1847. 8vo. B. 3773

BARTLETT (M. R.) Statistical and Chronological View of the United States of North America. By M. R. Bartlett. *New York*, 1833. 12mo. W. 3774

BARTLETT (R.) Remarks and Documents relating to the Preservation and Keeping of the Public Archives. By Richard Bartlett. *Concord, N. H.*, 1837. 8vo. 3775

Also included in the New Hampshire Hist. Coll., Vol. I.

BARTLETT (Robert). A Sermon delivered on the day of general election, ... Oct. 13, before the, ... Legislature of Vermont: By Robert Bartlett. *Montpelier*, 1825. 8vo. 3776

BARTLETT (S. C.) Duties of Educated Men [especially in America]. An Address ... before the Alumni Association ... of Dartmouth College ... July 20, 1864. By Samuel C. Bartlett ... . *Boston*, 1865. 8vo, pp. 34. H. 3777

BARTLETT (S. R.) The Concord Fight. *Boston*, 1860. 8vo, pp. 34. 3778

BARTLETT (T.) An Epistolary Disquisition on College Morality, by the Hon. Thomas Bartlett, Jun. ... with a Review of the Letter. [n. p.] 1851. 8vo, pp. 8. H. 3779

Relates to a disturbance at the celebration at St. Johnsbury, Vt., July 7, 1851.

BARTLETT (W. A.) Defence of Washington A. Bartlett before the Naval Court of Inquiry. *New York*, 1857. C. 3780

BARTLETT. Reply of Washington A. Bartlett, to the Testimony taken before the Naval Committee of the Senate ... . With ... Official Documents ... . May, 1856. *Washington*, 1856. 8vo, pp. 71 (1). H. 3781

BARTLETT. A Portion of the Evidence submitted to the Senate, in the Case of W. A. Bartlett, formerly of the Navy of the United States. [n. p., *July*, 1856.] 8vo, pp. 32. H. 3782

BARTLETT (W. E.) Defence of the Religious Society of Friends, who constitute the Yearly Meeting of Baltimore, against certain Charges circulated by Joseph John Gurney. *Baltimore*, 1839. 8vo, pp. 18. B. 3783

"Signed by direction ... Wm. E. Bartlett, Clerk."

BARTLETT (William Henry). American Scenery; or Land, Lake, and River Illustrations of Transatlantic Nature. From Drawings by W. H. Bartlett, Engraved in the first style of the Art by R. Wallis, J. Cousen, Willmore, Brandard, Adlard, Richardson, &c. The literary department by N. P. Willis, Esq. *London, George Virtue*, MDCCCXL. 4to, Vol. I., Engraved

Title, pp. iv. (2), xii., 140, 65 Plates, Map and Portrait; II., Engraved Title, iv., 106, 53 Plates. B. 3784

First issued in thirty parts. Some proof copies of the plates were printed in folio without letter-press. This work has been frequently reprinted, without date. The intelligent buyer will get the first edition. It was also issued, with the letter-press, in French and in German.

BARTLETT. Gezigten in Amerika, naar afbeeldingen op de plaats zelve geteekend. Uit het Engels vertaald door C. J. Zweerts. *Amsterdam, G. J. A. Beijerinck*, 1841. 8vo. A.

BARTLETT. Canadian Scenery, Illustrated from drawings, by W. H. Bartlett. The literary department by N. P. Willis, Esq. ... *London, James S. Virtue* [1842]. 4to, 3 p. l., pp. 128, 54 Plates; 3 p. l., 116, 64 Plates. 3786

This, also, has been reissued without a date, and a few copies of the plates were issued as proofs before letter-press, on India paper, folio size. It is the finest of Mr. Bartlett's works. It was also issued with a French title, as follows:

BARTLETT. Le Canada Pittoresque, faisant suite aux voyages en Amérique, en Suisse, en Ecosse, etc., enrichi de gravures faites sur les dessins de M. Wm. H. Bartlett, et exécutées avec le plus grand soin, par MM. R. Wallis, J. Cousen, Willmore, Brandard, Bentley, Richardson, etc. La partie littéraire par N. P. Willis. *Londres et Paris*, 1857. 2 vols., 4to. 3787

BARTLETT. The History of the United States of North America; from the Discovery of the Western World to the Present Day. By W. H. Bartlett ... . Continued by B. B. Woodward ... . *New York* [*London*, 1856?] 3 vols., rl. 8vo, pp. iv., (3), 698; 2 p. l., pp. 720; 2 p. l., pp. 726. 3788

BARTLETT. The Pilgrim Fathers; or, The Founders of New England in the Reign of James the First. By W. H. Bartlett ... . *London, Arthur Hall, Virtue & Co*, 1853. Rl. 8vo, pp. 240. 28 Plates. H. + Second Edition. [1854.] + New Edition. *Edinburgh, Nelson*, 1866. 8vo, pp. 230. 28 Plates. C. 3789

The principal merit of this work is in the fine plates in the early editions.

BARTLEY (J.) Lays of Ancient Virginia, and other Poems. By James Avis Bartley. *Richmond*, 1855. 12mo, pp. 206.

BARTOL (C. A.) A Discourse ... on Theodore Parker. By C. A. Bartol. *Boston*, 1860. 8vo, pp. 28. B., H. 3791

BARTOL. The Hand of God in the Great Man: a Sermon delivered in the West Church, Boston, occasioned by the Death of Daniel Webster. By C. A. Bartol, Junior Minister. Published by Request. *Boston, Crosby, Nichols, and Company*, 1852. 8vo, pp. 28. H.+Second Edition. *Boston*, 1852. 8vo, pp. 22. B. 3792

[BARTOL.] Influence of the Ministry at Large in the City of Boston. By a Spectator. *Boston, James Munroe & Co. and S. G. Simpkins*, 1836. 12mo, pp. 72. H. 3793

BARTOL. The West Church and its Ministers. Fiftieth Anniversary of the ordination of Charles Lowell, D.D. *Boston*, 1856. 8vo, pp. 242. M. 3794

Also: Address ... in Groton, at the Funeral of ... Rev. George W. Wells, March 21, 1843. *Boston*, 1843. 8vo, pp. 12. H. Conditions of Peace: A Discourse ... in memory of David Kimball Hobart, June 14, 1863. ... *Boston*, 1863. 8vo, pp. 28. H. Congregational Freedom. A Discourse, after Thirty Years' Ministry, preached in the West Church ... March 3, 1867, with ... Proceedings of the Parish, March 10. *Boston*, 1867. 8vo, pp. 23. H. A Discourse on the Life and Character of Samuel Putnam ... Late Judge of the Supreme Court of Massachusetts ... . *Boston*, 1853. 8vo, pp. 20. H. ... A Discourse ... on ... the Death of Dr. George C. Sha tuck. ... *Boston*, 1854. 8vo, pp. 30. B., H., S. Extravagance: A Sermon for the Times ... on Fast Day, April 7, 1864. ... *Boston*, 1864. 8vo, pp. 12. H. The Fall: a Sermon ... Nov. 27, 1864, the Sunday after the Decease of Mrs. Sarah Putnam. ... *Boston*, 1865. 8vo, pp. 14. H. Individual and Public Reform. A Discourse on Fast Day, April 2, 1846. *Boston*, 1846. 8vo, pp. 16. B. The Duty of the Time. A Discourse ... April 28, 1861. ... *Boston*, 1861. 8vo, pp. 16. B., H. The Memorial of Virtue: A Sermon ... Jan. 22, 1865, after the Death of Edward Everett. ... *Boston*, 1865. 8vo. pp. 13. The Nation's Hour: A Tribute to Major Sidney Willard, ... December 21 ... . *Boston*, 1862. 8vo, pp. 58. H. Our Sacrifices. A Sermon ... November 3, 1861 ... the Sunday after the Funeral of Lieut. William Lowell Putnam. ... *Boston*, 1861. 8vo, pp. 23. H. Public Causes for Gratitude, A Sermon ... on Thanksgiving Day, November 25, 1847 ... . *Boston*, 1848. 8vo, pp. 16. B. The Purchase by Blood: A Tribute to Brig.-Gen. Charles Russell Lowell, Jr. ... Oct. 30, 1864. ... *Boston*, 1864. 8vo, pp. 21. H. The Recompense. A Sermon for Country and Kindred, ... August 24. ... *Boston*, 1862. 8vo, pp. 23 (1). H. Religion in our Public Schools. A Discourse ... . *Boston*, MDCCCLIX. 12mo, pp. 23. B. The Remission of Blood: a Tribute to our Soldiers and the Sword ... . *Boston*, 1862. 8vo, pp. 20. H. ... A Sermon ... at the Ordination of ... George M. Bartol ... in Lancaster, Mass. ... August 4, 1847. ... *Lancaster*, 1847. 8vo, pp. 50. H. ... A Sermon on the Character of Rev. Ephraim Peabody, D.D. Delivered ... December 7, 1856 ... . *Boston*, 1857. 12mo, pp. 16. B., H. A Sermon ... on Fast-day, April 10. *Boston*, 1851. 8vo, pp. 20. Traveller's Report; or, Abroad and at Home: Sermon ... Nov. 19, 1854. ... *Boston*, 1854. 8vo, pp. 25. H. The Unspotted Life: a Discourse in Memory of Rev. Thomas Starr King ... . March 6, 1864. ... *Boston*, 1864. 8vo, pp. 15. H. The Voice of Twenty Years: a Discourse on ... the Twentieth Anniversary of his Ordination ... . *Boston*, 1857. 8vo, pp. 19. H.

BARTOL (G. Murillo). An Inheritance to Children's Children: a Discourse occasioned by the Death of Mrs. Sarah Thayer. Preached at Lancaster, June 28, 1857, ... By George M. Bartol. ... *Boston*, 1857. 8vo, pp. 19. H. 3795

BARTOLACHE (J. I.) Manifiesto satisfactorio anunciado en la Gazeta de Mexico (Tom. I. Núm. 53.) Opusculo guadalupano compuesto por el doctor D. Joseph Ignacio Bartolache, natural de ... Santa Fé ... . *México, Impreso por D. Felipe de Zúñiga y Ontiveros*, M.DCC.XC. 4to, pp. 14 (14), 105, 16 (12). H.

On the apparitions of the Virgin of Guadalupe, with bibliographical accounts of nineteen books on the same subject, and extracts from them.

BARTOLOMEI (G.) L'America poema eroico di Giralamo Bartolomei Già Smedvcei. Al cristianissimo Lvigi XIV. Re di Francia ... . *Roma Lodouico Grignani*, MDCL. 4to, pp. (18), 564 (11). Plate. H. 3797

"Poeme en quarante chants, dont Améric Vespuce est le héros."—TERNAUX, No. 692. Priced, Trois, 40 fr. *See* Biog. Univ.

BARTOLOMEIDES (Ladislaw). Historie ō Americe, ukazující, kterak byla skrze Krist. Kolumbusa wynalezena. Sepsal Lad. Bartolomeides. *W. Prešpurce u Webra*, 1794. 8vo, pp. 169

BARTOLOZZI (F.) Apologia delle Ricerche istorico-critiche circa alle scoperte d'Amerigo Vespucci alle quali può servire d'aggiunta, scritta da Francesco Bartolozzi in confutazione della lettera seconda allo stampatore data col nome del padre Canovai delle cuole pie. *Firenze, Gaetano Cambiagi*, MDCCLXXXIX. 8vo, pp. 40. H. 3799

Also on large paper. Usually found with the following work:

BARTOLOZZI. Ricerche istorico-critiche circa alle scoperte d'Amerigo Vespucci con l'aggiunta di una relazione del medesimo fin ora inedita. Compilate da Francesco Bartolozzi. *Firenze, Gaetano Cambiagi*, MDCCLXXXIX. 8vo, pp. 182; Errori, 1 page. H. 3800

BARTON (A.) The Disappointment: or, the Force of Credulity. A new American Comic Opera, of two Acts. By Andrew Barton, Esq. [Motto.] *New York, Printed in the Year* M,DCC,LXVII. 8vo, pp. v., 58. P.+Second edition, revised and corrected, with large additions, by the Author. *Philadelphia, Francis Shallus*, 1796. 12mo, pp. iv., 94, 1. P. 3801

The Philadelphia Library has a copy of this very rare book, with a MS. key to the Characters, who were Philadelphians ... Air No. IV. is Yankee Doodle (1767).

BARTON (B. S.) Additional Facts, Observations, and Conjectures relative to the Generation of the Opossum of North America. In a Letter ... By Benjamin Smith Barton. *Philadelphia*, 1813. 8vo, pp. 24. P. 3802

BARTON. Archæologiæ Americanæ Telluris Collectanea et Specimina; or, Collections with Specimens for a Series of Memoirs on certain Extinct Animals and Vegetables of North America; together with Facts and Conjectures relative to the Ancient Condition of the Lands and Waters on the Continent. By B. S. Barton. Part I., with Plates. *Philadelphia*, 1814. 8vo.

BARTON. Collections for an Essay towards a Materia Medica of the United States ... By Benjamin Smith Barton ... . Part I. *Philadelphia, Carr & Way*, 1798. 8vo, pp. vii., 49. B.+Second Edition, *Philadelphia*, 1801. 8vo., pp. xii., 64.+Third Edition. *Philadelphia*, 1810. 8vo.+Part II. 1804, pp. 53. C. 3804

BARTON. A Discourse on some of the Principal Desiderata in Natural History, and on the Best Means of promoting the Study of this Science, in the United-States. ... By Benjamin Smith Barton. ... . *Philadelphia, printed by Denham & Town*, 1807. 8vo, pp. 90. B., C. 3805

BARTON. Elements of Botany, or Outlines of the Natural History of Vegetables. By Benjamin S. Barton, M.D. *Philadelphia*, 1803. 8vo.+Revised ... with ... Notes ... . *London, Gold*, 1804. Rl. 8vo, pp. 344, 35. 30 Plates.+Second Edition. *Philadelphia*, 1817. 8vo, pp. 302, 168; Appendix, 16; Explanation of the Plates, &c., pp. 40. 30 Plates. 3806

Pritzel describes a Second Edition, enlarged. *Philadelphia*, 1812–14. 8vo, pp. xviii., 324 and Index; pp. iv., 180, 4. 40 Plates.

BARTON. Facts, Observations, and Conjectures relative to the Generation of the Opossum of North America. By Professor Barton, in a Letter to M. Roume. *Philadelphia*, 1806. 8vo, pp. 14. 3807

BARTON. Flora Virginica, sive Plantarum præcipue indigenarum Virginiæ Historia inchoata, Iconibus illustrata, Studio e Cura B. S. Barton, M.D. *Philadelphia*, 1812. 8vo, pp. 78. P.

BARTON. Fragments of the Natural History of Pennsylvania. By B. S. Barton, M.D. Part First. *Philadelphia, Way & Graff*, 1799. Folio, pp. xviii., 24. P. 3809

"This work has never yet been published ... . It is nothing more than an enlarged and new modified edition of the Flora Virginica of Clayton and Gronovius."—*William Barton*.

BARTON. Hints on the Etymology of certain English Words, and on their Affinity to Words in the Language of different Euro-

pean, Asiatic and American [Indian] Nations, in a letter from Dr. Barton to Dr. Thomas Beddoes. [*Philadelphia*, 1803.] 4to, pp. 14. W. 3810

BARTON. Inquiry into the Question whether the Apis Mellifica, or True Honey Bee is a Native of America. [n. p., n. d.] 4to, pp. 21. M. 3811

BARTON. A Memoir concerning an Animal of the Class of Reptilia or Amphibia which is known in the United States by the name of Alligator and Hellbender. *Philadelphia*, 1812. 8vo. 1 Plate. 3812

BARTON. A Memoir concerning the Disease of Goitre, as it prevails in different Parts of North America. By Benjamin Smith Barton ... . *Philadelphia, the Author*, 1800. 8vo, pp. viii., 94. B. 3813

Translated into German with the following title:

BARTON. Abhandlung über den Kropf, wie er sich in Nord-Amerika häufig findet. Aus dem Englischen, mit Anmerkungen von W. Liebsch. *Göttingen, Dieterich*, 1802. 8vo. 3814

And into Spanish, with the title:

BARTON. Memoria sobre a bronchocele ou papo da America Septentrional, por Benjamin Smith Barton, traducida em portuguez por Hypolito José da Costa Pereira Furtado de Mendonça. *Lisbon*, 1801. 8vo. 3815

BARTON. A Memoir concerning the Fascinating Faculty which has been ascribed to the Rattle-Snake, and other American Serpents. By Benjamin Smith Barton ... . *Philadelphia, the Author*, 1796. 8vo, pp. 70. H. 3816

This and the Supplement (No. 3825) were printed only for private distribution. *See* Trans. Am. Phil. Soc., Vol. IV.

BARTON. Memoir concerning the Fascinating Faculty which has been ascribed to various species of Serpents. By B. S. Barton. A New Edition, greatly Enlarged. *Philadelphia*, 1814. 8vo, pp. 76. 1 Plate. C. 3817

BARTON. Abhandlung über die vermeinte Zauberkraft der Klapperschlange. Aus dem Englischen, mit Anmerkungen von E. A. W. v. Zimmermann. *Leipzig, Hinrichs*, 1798. 8vo.

A translation also appeared in the Amerikanisches Magazin, Hamburg, 1797. I., 1–13, "Von der bezaubernden Kraft," etc.

BARTON. New Views of the Origin of the Tribes and Nations of America. By Benjamin Smith Barton ... . *Philadelphia, for the Author, by John Bioren*, 1797. 8vo, pp. xii., cix., 83. H. +[Second Edition.] *Philadelphia*, 1798. 8vo, Title, pp. xxviii., cix., 133, 32. C. & H. 3819

This Edition has an Appendix, containing Notes and Illustrations. It is the first philosophical treatise on American Philology by an American Author. *See* Murray.

BARTON. Observations on some Parts of Natural History: to which is prefixed, an Account of several Remarkable Vestiges of an Ancient date, which have been discovered in different parts of North America. Part I. By Benjamin Smith Barton ... *London, C. Dilly*, [1787.] 8vo, 2 p. l., pp. 76. Plate. C. 3820

"A prefixed advertisement to this work informs us that it is the production of a very young man, written chiefly as a recreation from the laborious studies of medicine. It is, however, a curious tract; we have here only the first part; the other three, which will complete the work, are to be published in a few months."—*Monthly Review*.

This part, the only one ever published, relates entirely to antiquities, giving an account of the Indian ruins in the Mushingum, and remarks on the first peopling of America, &c.

BARTON. Papers relative to certain American Antiquities. *Philadelphia, Thomas Dobson*, 1796. 4to, pp. iv., 39. 2 Plates.

BARTON. The Philadelphia Medical and Physical Journal, arranged by Benjamin S. Barton, M.D. *Philadelphia*, 1805–6. 8vo. Vols. I. & II. 3822

Each volume has two parts, with independent title-pages and pagings. Includes papers on the Falls of Niagara, Mohawk Indians, American Mammoth, Welsh Indians, White Negroes, &c.

BARTON. Remarks on the Speech attributed, by Mr. Jefferson, to Logan. By Benjamin Smith Barton. [*Philadelphia*, 1806.] 8vo, pp. vii., 24. C. 3823

Reprinted from Phil. Med. Trans.

BARTON. Some Account of the Siren Lacertina, and other Species of the same Genus of Amphibious Animals. *Philadelphia*, 1808. 8vo. C. 3824

Fifty copies only printed. Reprinted with the following title:

BARTON. Some Account of the Siren Lacertina, and other Species of the same Genus of Amphibious Animals. In a letter from Professor Barton, of Philadelphia, to Mr. J. G. Schneider, of Saxony. *Philadelphia*, 1821. 8vo, pp. 33. Plates. 3825

BARTON. Specimen of a Geographical View of the Trees and Shrubs, and many of the Herbaceous Plants of North-Amer-

ica, between the Latitudes of Seventy-one and Twenty-five. ... [*Philadelphia*,] 1809. 4to, pp. 10, 26. Plates. 3826

BARTON. Supplement to a Memoir concerning the Fascinating Faculty which has been ascribed to the Rattlesnake and other American Serpents, in a Letter from Prof. Barton to Prof. Zimmermann, of Brunswick in Germany. [*Philadelphia*, 1800.] 8vo, pp. 40. 3827

Also "The Article America, corrected and considerably enlarged, by Dr. Barton," in John Pinkerton's Modern Geography. *Philadelphia*, 1804. 8vo, II., 394–554. M.

BARTON (C. C.) Manifest of the Charge preferred to the Navy department, and subsequently to Congress, against Jesse Duncan Elliott Esq. a Captain in the Navy of the United States, for unlawful conduct while Commodore of the late Mediterranean Squadron, and a refutation of the recrimination raised by that officer: by Charles Crillon Barton, of the U. S. Navy. [No imprint,] 1839. 8vo, pp. 46 & 24. 3828

BARTON (Clara). Roll of Missing Men. No. I. [*Washington*, 1865.] Broadside. 4 or more numbers have been published.

BARTON (C.) ... Defence of Cyrus Barton, Against the attacks of Hon. Isaac Hill upon the Establishment of the New-Hampshire Patriot and State Gazette. [n. p., September 7, 1840.] 8vo, pp. 16. H. 3830

BARTON (C.) An Address delivered before the Republicans of Newport, and vicinity, July 4, 1828. *Newport, (N. H.) published by Dunbar Aldrich*, 1828. 8vo, pp. 16. C. 3831

BARTON (D.) Speech of Hon. David Barton on Mr. Foot's Resolution relative to the Public Lands, U. S. Senate, Feb. 9, 1830. [No imprint.] 8vo, pp. 42. B. 3832

BARTON. Speech of Mr. Barton, of Missouri, upon the power of the President to remove Federal Officers; and upon the Restraining Power and Duty of the Senate ... *Washington*, 1830. 8vo, pp. 28. 3833

BARTON. Speech of Mr. Barton of Tuscaloosa in the House of Representatives of Alabama on the Land Bill. *Tuscaloosa*, 1829. 8vo, pp. 16. 3834

BARTON (E. H.) The Cause and Prevention of Yellow Fever, contained in the Report of the Sanitary Commission of New Orleans, by E. H. Barton, M.D., A.M., Chairman of the Sanitary

Commission, &c.; with a large Plan of New Orleans. *Philadelphia*, 1855. 8vo, pp. 348.+Third edition; with the addition of upwards of seventy pages of "Prefatory Remarks," and a Supplement. *New York*, 1857. 8vo. C. 3835

BARTON. A Discourse on Temperance, and of the Applicability of Stimulants in a Warm Climate ... by E. H. Barton ... . *New Orleans*, 1837. 8vo, Title, pp. 32. H. 3836

With statistics of intemperance in the United States, and especially in New Orleans.

BARTON. Report of the Sanitary Commission of New Orleans on the Epidemic Yellow Fever of 1853. Published by authority of the City Council of New Orleans. *New Orleans*, 1854. 8vo. C. 3837

BARTON. Report to the Louisiana State Medical Society, on the Meteorology, Vital Statistics and Hygiène of the State of Louisiana. By E. H. Barton ... . To which is added, an Appendix, Showing the Experience of Life Insurance Companies in Louisiana, With Tables of Mortality ... . By H. G. Heartt ... . *New Orleans*, 1851. 8vo, Title, pp. 66; Table, 1 l. folio. H.

BARTON (E.) Trial of Elijah Barton and Six others for the Murder of Paul Chadwick, at Malta, in Maine, on September 8th, 1809. Taken in Short Hand by John Merrick. *Hallowell*, 1810. 8vo. 3839

BARTON (Hull). Discourse delivered in Boston, March 1, 1826, for the Relief of the Boston Bard [Robert S. Coffin]. *Boston*, 1826. 8vo, pp. 20. 3840

BARTON. An Exposition of Facts, in a Letter to Stephen Gould, an Elder of the Society of Friends. By Hull Barton. ... *New Bedford, Printed by Benj. Lindsey*, 1823. 12mo, pp. 34.

BARTON (I.) Eulogy, delivered in the Chapel of Brown University, on Mr. Ezra Bailey ... who died October 7, 1818. By Ira Barton ... *Providence, Miller & Hutchens*, 1817. 8vo, pp. 16. B. 3842

BARTON. An Oration, delivered at Oxford, on the Forty-sixth Anniversary of American Independence. By Ira Barton . ... *Cambridge*, 1822. 8vo, pp. 24. H. 3843

BARTON (James). Dissertatio de Dysenteria contagiosae, præcipue de illa Specie, quæ in Indiis Occidentalibus observatur ... . *Lugduni Batavorum*, 1788. 8vo, pp. 57. 3844

BARTON (James L.) Address on the Early Reminiscences of Western New-York, and the Lake Region of Country. Delivered before the Young Men's Association of Buffalo. February 16, 1848. By James L. Barton. *Buffalo*, 1848. 8vo, pp. 69. B.+Second Edition. *Buffalo*, 1848. 8vo. 3845

BARTON. Commerce of the Lakes. A Brief Sketch of the Commerce on the Great Northern and Western Lakes for a Series of Years; ... added, ... the Business done through Buffalo on the Erie Canal, for ... 1845 and 1846. Also, Remarks as to the True Canal Policy of the State of New-York. By James L. Barton. *Buffalo*, 1847. 8vo, pp. 80, and Table, folded.+Second Edition. *Buffalo*, 1847. 8vo. B. 3846

BARTON. Commerce of the Lakes, and Erie Canal. By James L. Barton. *Buffalo*, 1851. 8vo, pp. 51. B. 3847

BARTON. Lake Commerce. Letter to the Hon. Robert M'Clelland ... in relation to the Value and Importance of the Commerce of the Great Western Lakes. By James L. Barton. *Buffalo*, 1846. 8vo, Table, pp. 34. H.+Second Edition. With additional Notes. *Buffalo, Jewett, Thomas & Co.*, 1846. 8vo, pp. 32; Table, folded, 1 l.+Third Edition. With additional Notes. 3848

BARTON (T.) Unanimity and Public Spirit. A Sermon, Preached at Carlisle, And some other Episcopal Churches, in the Counties of York and Cumberland, soon after General Braddock's Defeat. Published by particular Request. By the Reverend Mr. Thomas Barton, Missionary to the said Churches. To which is prefixed, A Letter from the Reverend Mr. Smith, Provost of the College of Philadelphia, concerning the Office and Duties of a Protestant Ministry, especially in Times of public Calamity and Danger. *Philadelphia: Printed and Sold by B. Franklin and D. Hall, at the New-Printing-Office; by W. Dunlap, in Lancaster; and in York County by the Author*, 1755. 8vo, pp. xx., 16. H. 3849

BARTON (T. T.) A Fast Sermon, Preached at Fitchburg, July 23, 1812. By Titus T. Barton, A.B. ... *Leominster, Mass., printed by Salmon Wilder, August*, 1812. 8vo, pp. 24. H. 3850

BARTON. A Sermon, preached at Tewksbury, February, 22, 1800. On Account of the Death of General George Washington.—By the Reverend Titus Theodore Barton.—Published at the request of the hearers.—*Printed at Medford*, (Massachusetts.) 1800. 8vo, pp. 8. 3851

[Barton (William), a.m.] The Constitutionalist, addressed to Men of all Parties in the United States. *Philadelphia*, 1804. 8vo, pp. 49. 3852

Barton. A Dissertation on the Freedom of Navigation and Maritime Commerce, and such Rights of States relative thereto, as are founded on the Law of Nations: adapted more particularly to the United States … . By William Barton, m.a. … . *Philadelphia, Baltimore, and Washington City*, 1802. 8vo, pp. 339, xlv., (3). c. & h. 3853

Barton. Observations on the Trial by Jury, with Remarks on Legislation and Jurisprudence, and the Profession of the Law, Address to the Citizens of Pennsylvania. By William Barton, a.m. *Strasburg*, 1803. m. 3854

Barton. Memoirs of the Life of David Rittenhouse, ll.d. f.r.s. Late President of the American Philosophical Society, &c. Interspersed with various Notices of many Distinguished Men: with an Appendix, containing Sundry Philosophical and other Papers, most of which have not hitherto been Published. By William Barton, m.a. … *Philadelphia, Edward Parker*, 1813. 8vo, Title, pp. 614. Portrait. c. & h. 3855

Barton (W. P. C.) A Biographical Sketch, read pursuant to appointment before the Philadelphia medical society, … 16th February, 1816, of their late President; Professor Barton. By Wm. P. C. Barton, m.d. *Philadelphia, J. Maxwell*, 1810. 8vo, pp. 32. Portrait. 3856

Barton. Compendium Floræ Philadelphicæ: containing a Description of the Indigenous and Naturalized Plants found within a Circuit of Ten Miles around Philadelphia. By Wm. P. C. Barton, m.d. In Two Volumes. … *Philadelphia, M. Carey and Son*, 1818. 2 vols., 12mo, 4 p. l., pp. 251; 234. b.

See N. A. R., xiii., 119.

Barton. A Flora of North America. Illustrated by Coloured Figures, drawn from Nature. By William P. C. Barton … . *Philadelphia, M. Carey & Sons* … 1821–23. 3 vols., 4to, pp. xix., (5), 138; x., 107; vii., (1), 100. 106 Plates. b., h.

Pritzel speaks of a second edition, 1825, "verosimiliter eadem impressio."

Barton. Floræ Philadelphicæ Prodromus … . Auctore W. P. C. Barton, m.d.; or, Prodromus of the Flora Philadelphica, exhibiting a List of all the Plants to be described in that Work, which have as yet been by him collected. *Philadelphia, Maxwell*, 1815. 4to, pp. 96. 3859

Barton. Hints for Naval Officers cruising in the West Indies. By William P. C. Barton, m.d. *Philadelphia*, 1830. 12mo, pp. 222. c. 3860

Barton. Outlines of Lectures on Materia Medica and Botany, delivered in Jefferson Medical College. By William P. C. Barton. *Philadelphia*, 1827. 2 vols., 24mo. 3861

Barton. A Treatise containing a Plan for the Internal Organization and Government of Marine Hospitals, in the United States; with … a Scheme for amending and systematizing the Medical Department of the Navy. By William P. C. Barton, m.d. … *Philadelphia*, 1814. 8vo, pp. xxvi., 244.+Second Edition, with Emendations and Additions. *Philadelphia, the Author*, 1817. 8vo, pp. (2), viii., (1), 240, xix.–xxv., (1). Plate. c., h.

Barton. Vegetable Materia Medica of the United States, or Medical Botany, containing a Botanical, General, and Medical History of the Medicinal Plants indigenous to the United States. Illustrated with nearly 100 colored engravings, carefully drawn from nature by the author. By William P. C. Barton, m.d. … *Philadelphia, Cary*, 1817–1825. 2 vols., 4to., pp. xv., 273; xvi., 243. 50 Plates. 3863

N. A. R., vi., p. 344. Issued with plain and colored plates. Also: Some Account of a Plant used in Lancaster County, Pennsylvania as a Substitute for Chocolate, Holcus Bicolor Willd. *Philadelphia, Palmer*, 1816. 8vo, pp. 8. Most of the works of Professor Barton are out of print.

Barton (W. S.) Epitaphs from the Cemetery on Worcester Common, with Occasional Notes, References, and an Index. By W. S. Barton. *Worcester, printed by Henry J. Howland*, [1848.] 8vo, pp. 36. h. 3864

Bartow (R.) Exposition of the Failure of the Franklin Bank, N. Y. By Robert Bartow. *New York*, 1831. 8vo. s.

Bartram (A.) and others. Apology for having imported some stockings. *Philadelphia, July* 14, 1770. Broadside, 1 page. b. 3866

Bartram (John). A Catalogue of Trees, Shrubs, and Herbaceous Plants indigenous to the United States of America, cultivated and disposed of by John Bartram & Son, at their Botanical Garden, Kingsess, near Philadelphia. … *Philadelphia*, 1807. 8vo.

Bartram. Observations on the Inhabitants, Climate, Soil, Rivers, Productions, Animals, and other matters worthy of Notice. Made By Mr. John Bartram, In his Travels from Pensilvania To Onondago, Oswego and the Lake Ontario, In Canada. To which is annex'd, a Curious Account of the Cataracts at Niagara. By Mr. Peter Kalm, A Swedish Gentleman who travelled there. *London, J. Whiston and B. White*, 1751. 8vo, Title, pp. 94. Map. c. & h. 3868

Also various papers in the "Philosophical Transactions." *See* [Stork (W.)]

Bartram. Account of the Bartram Garden, published in "The Horticulturist" in 1850. Revised and corrected by the Author and now printed for the Central Fair in aid of the U. S. Sanitary Commission. *Printed by C. Sherman, Son & Co.*, 1864. 12mo, pp. 11. h. 3869

Bartram (William). Travels through North and South Carolina, Georgia, East & West Florida, the Cherokee Country, the Extensive Territories of the Muscogulges, or Creek Confederacy, and the Country of the Chactaws; containing an Account of the Soil and Natural Productions of those Regions, together with Observations on the Manners of the Indians. Embellished with Copper-Plates. By William Bartram. *Philadelphia, Printed by James & Johnson*, m,dcc,xci. 8vo, pp. (2), xxxiv., 522. Portrait of Mico Chlucco, Map, and 7 Plates. h. +*London, Reprinted for J. Johnson*, 1792. 8vo, pp. xxiv., 520, (12). Portrait, Map, and 7 Plates. h.+*Dublin, J. Moore* [*etc.*], 1793. 8vo, 12 p. l., 526 pp.; Index 3 l., Directions, 1 p. Portrait, Map and 7 Plates.+The Second Edition in London. *Philadelphia, Printed by James and Johnson*, 1791; *London, Reprinted for J. Johnson*, 1794. 8vo, pp. xxiv., 520, Index and Directions, 4 l. 8 Plates and Map. 3870

In this second edition the title page only is new. Unequalled for the vivid picturesqueness of its descriptions of nature, scenery, and productions. "It is written in the spirit of the old travellers."—Coleridge. There are copies of the English edition on large paper. *See* Rich, i., 357; Boucher, Vol. vi.; M. R., x., 13, 130.

Bartram. Voyage dans les parties sud de l'Amérique septentrionale; Savoir: les Carolines septentrionale et méridionale, la Georgie, les Florides orientale et occidentale, le pays des

Cherokées, le vaste territoire des Muscogulges ou de la confederation Creek, et le pays des Chactaws. Contenant des détails sur le sol et les productions naturelles de ces contreés, et des observations sur les mœurs des Sauvages qui les habitent. Par William Bartram. Imprimié à Philadelphie, en 1791, et à Londres, en 1794, et trad. de l'ang. par P. V. Benoist. *Paris, Cartaret et Brosson, Maradan*, an vii. [1799–1801].+*Paris, Maradan, an IX.* 2 vols., 8vo, 2 p. l., pp. 457, (1); 2 p. l., pp. 436, (1). Portrait, Map, and 4 Plates. h. 3871

Bartram. Reisen durch Nord- und Süd-Karolina, Georgien, Ost- und West-Florida, das Gebiet der Tskerokesen, Krihks und Tschaktahs. Aus dem Englischen mit Anmerkungen von E. A. W. v. Zimmermann. *Berlin, Voss*, 1793. 8vo. Plate. (Magazin von merkwürd. Reisebeschreib. Bd. x.) 3872

Bartram. Reizen door Noord- en Zuid-Carolina, Georgie, Oost- en West-Florida; de Landen der Cherokees, des Muscogulges, of het Creek bondgenootschap en het land der Chactaws. Uit het Engelsch vertaald, door J. D. Pasteur. *Haarlem*, 1794–97. 8vo. Map. 3873

J. de Jong's "Alphabetische Naamlijst" gives the imprint, *Amsterdam, H. Mooleneizer*, 1797. 3 parts, 8vo. Plate and Map.

Bartreau (C. K.) What has been done in Tennessee; the kind of Government we are under; the kind of Government our Fathers gave us; Tennessee and the Institution of African Slavery—How shall we maintain it? *Nashville*, 1861. 8vo.

Barzena (Alfonso). Lexica et præcepta grammatica, item liber confessionis et precum, in quinque Indorum Linguis, quarum usus per Americam australem, nempe Puquinica, Tenocotica, Catamareana, Guaranica, Natixana, sive Mogaznana. *Peruviæ*, 1590. Folio. 3875

"Livre très rare, cité par Sotwel, *Biblioth. Soc. Jesu, p.* 33, qui n'en marque ni la date ni bien positivement le lieu d'impression, et qui probablement en a composé arbitrairement le titre. Ce n'est pas, comme l'ont cru plusieurs bibliographes, le premier livre impr. au Pérou, car au mot Vocabolario nous citons une édition faite à Lima (*Los Reyes*) en 1586."—Brunet.

Basalenque (Diego). Arte de la lengua tarasca, dispuesto con nuevo estilo y claridad; sacado a luz P. Nicolas de Quixas. *Mexico*, 1714. 8vo.+*Mexico*, 1805. 16mo. 3875a

Basalenque. Chronica de la provincia de S. Nicholas de Polentino de Mechoacau de la orden de S. Augustin. Por Fr. Diogo Basalenque. 1673. 4to. 3876

Basanier (Martin). *See* Laudonniere.

Bascom (E. L.) A Masonic Discourse, Spoken at Greenfield, Massachusetts, before the Officers and Brethren of the Republican Lodge of Free and Accepted Masons, in that Town, on the Festival of St. John the Evangelist, January 1st, a.l. 5800. By Brother Ezekiel L. Bascom. Published by the United Request of the Brethren. *Printed at Greenfield*, (*Mass.*) *by T. Dickman* 1800. 8vo, pp. 14. w. 3877

Also: A Masonic Address at Leicester, Mass., June 24, 1817. *Leicester*, 1817. 8vo.

Bascom (*Rev.* H. B.) Methodism and Slavery; with other matter in Controversy between the North and the South; being a Review of the Manifesto of the Majority in reply to the Protest of the Minority of the late general conference of the Methodist Episcopal church, in the Case of Bishop Andrew. By H. B. Bascom. *Frankfort* (*Ky.*), 1845. 8vo, pp. 165. c. 3878

Bascom. The little Iron Wheel … despotism of Episcopal Methodism. By J. H. Bascom. … *Nashville*, 1856. 16mo, pp. 307. 3879

Bascom (*Rev.* Jonathan). A Sermon preached at Eastham, Thanksgiving-Day, December 15, 1774. By Jonatham Bascom, v.d.m. … *Boston, Edes and Gill*, m,dcc,lxxv. 8vo, pp. 20.

Bascom (Jonathan). An Oration, delivered February 22, 1800. The Day of Public Mourning For the Death of General George Washington. By Rev. Jonathan Bascom, Of Orleans, To the People of his Charge. … *Printed by Samuel Hall, Boston*, 1800. 8vo, pp. 15. h. 3881

Bascom (William). Sermon at Leominster, Mass., May 14, 1815. *Leicester* [1815]. 8vo. w. 3882

Bashford *vs.* Barstow. The Trial in the Supreme Court, of the Information in the Nature of a Quo Warranto filed by the Attorney General, on the Relation of Coles Bashford *vs.* Wm. A. Barstow, contesting the Right to the Office of Governor of Wisconsin. … *Madison, Wis.*, 1855. 8vo, pp. 368. h. c., 3883

[Basket (*Sir* James)]. History of the Island of Saint Domingo from its first Discovery by Columbus to the present period. *London, Printed for Archibald Constable & Co., Edinburgh*, 1818. 8vo, pp. xiv., 426.+*New York*, 1825. 8vo, pp. 206. 3884

[Basket]. Histoire de l'Ile de Saint-Domingue, depuis l'Époque de sa découverte par Christophe Colomb Jusqu'a l'Année 1818. Publiée sur des documents authentiques, et suivie de Pièces justificatives, Telles que la Correspondance de Toussaint-Louverture avec Buonaparte; le Cérémonial de la Cour d'Haïty; la Constitution de ce royaume; l'Amanach royal d'Haïty; la Correspondance du comte de Limonade, et le Manifeste du roi Christophe. *A Paris, Delauney*, 1819. 8vo, Half-title, pp. ii., 390. 3885

Bason's Country Almanack, for 1821 … calculated for North and South Carolina, by Joshua Sharp. *Charleston, W. P. Bason* [n. d.] 12mo, pp. (36). 3885a

With the usual local information.

Basque. Discourse delivered at Newport, R. I. By Rev. Benjamin Basque. *Boston*, 1726. 12mo, pp. 40. m. 3886

Bass (E.) Masonic Sermon at Newburyport, December, 1779. By Bp. Edward Bass. *Newbury*, 1780. 12mo.

Also: A Sermon before the Merrimac Humane Society, at Newburyport, Sept. 6, 1803. [n. p.] 1803. 8vo, pp. 23.

Bass (J.) Letter to the Rev. Mr. Niles, of Braintree, Mass containing some Remarks on his Dying Testimony. By John Bass, a.m. *Boston*, 1753. 12mo. 3888

Bass. A True Narrative of an Unhappy Contention in the Church at Ashford [Connecticut]: and the Several Methods used to bring it to a Period. By John Bass, a.m., Late Pastor of Said Church. *Boston; New-England, Printed for D. Gookin*, 1751. Small 4to, pp. 28. m. 3889

Basse-Terre. Historiquc des événements qui se sont passés à la Basse-Terre … depuis la revolution. *Guadeloupe, imp. de V. Bénard*, 1791. 8vo. 3889a

Basse-Terre. Memoire historique et politique pour la ville de la Basse-Terre. *Marseille, imp. de F. Brebion*, 1791. 8vo.

Bassett (A.) … A Sermon Preached at the Anniversary Election in Hartford, May 14, 1807. By Amos Bassett, a.m. … *Printed by Hudson & Goodwin, Hartford*, 1807. 8vo, pp. 34.

Bassett (Francis). An Oration, delivered on … the Fifth of July, 1824. By Francis Bassett. … *Boston*, 1824. 8vo, pp. 24.

Bassett (G. W.) A Discourse on the Wickedness and Folly of the Present War. Delivered in the Court House at Ottawa, Ill. … Aug. 11, 1861. By Geo. W. Bassett … . [Ottawa, 1861.] 8vo, pp. 24. h. 3893

Bassett. A Northern Plea for the Right of Secession. By Geo. W, [*sic*] Bassett … *Ottawa*, 1861. 8vo, pp. 24. 3893a

Bassett. Slavery examined by the Light of Nature. Sermon … by Rev. Geo. W. Bassett, at Washington, D. C. … February 28, 1858. [n. p., 1858]. 8vo, pp. 8. b. 3894

Bassett. A Warning for the Crisis. Or Popular Errors involved in the Present War. An Address … February 2nd, 1863. By Geo. W. Bassett. *Ottawa, J. H. Leggett, Printer*, 1863. 8vo, pp. 32. h. 3895

Bassett (W.) Letter to a Member of the Society of Friends, in reply to objections against joining Anti-Slavery Societies. By William Bassett. *Boston, Isaac Knapp*, 1837. 12mo, pp. 44.

Basterot. De Québec à Lima journal d'un voyage dans les deux Amériques en 1858 et en 1859 par le vicomte de Basterot *Paris, L. Hachette et Cie*, 1860. 18mo, 2 p. l., pp. vii., 338. b. 3897

Bastide (Jean François de). Mémoire historique Sur la négociation de la France & de l'Angleterre, depuis le 26 Mars 1761 jusqu' au 20 Septembre de la même année, avec les Pièces justificatives. *Paris, de l'imprimerie royale*, m.dcclxi. 8vo, Title, pp. iv., 196. h. 3898

Relating to Canada.

The Bastille in America: or Democratic Absolutism. By an Eye-Witness. *London, Robert Hardwicke*, 1861. 8vo, pp. 39.

The Bastiles of the North. *See* [Sangston (Lawrence.)]

Bastos (José de Reveira). Roteiro do Cidade do Santa Maria di Belem do Grao Pará, pelo rio Tocouton a cinea até a Porto Real do Pontrol da Caputaria do Gogaz. *Rio de Janeiro, imprenta regia*, 1811. 8vo, pp. 19. 3900

Bastos do Solitario. Estudos sobre Reforma administrativa, Ensino religioso, Africanos livres, Trafico de escravos, Liberdade de cabotagem, Abertura do Amazonas, Communicaçoes com os Estados Unidos, &c. Dr. A. C. Tavares Bastos. Segunda ediçao. *Rio de Janeiro*, 1863. 8vo, pp. xiv., 438.

Basuyne des Oorloghs,|Ofte|Waerschouwinghe, aen de| Vereenichde Nederlanden, dat de selvige|in den Oorloge met den Coninggh van Spaen-|gien moeten Continueren.|Ghestelt door een Oprecht Liefhebber der selver Landen.|*Gedruckt voor Pieter Walschaert, Anno* 1625. 4to, 12 leaves. 3902

This "Call to arms, or demonstration to the United Provinces, that they should continue the war with the King of Spain," relates to Brazil.

Batalla de Yanacocha canto Heroico al triunfo de las Armas Pacificadoras. *Arequipa*, 1835. 8vo. 3903

Batbie (Anseleme Polycarpe). Traité théorique et pratique de droit public et administratif, contenant … la comparaison de notre législation avec les lois politiques et administratives de l'Angleterre, des États- Unis … etc. Par A. Batbie … . *Paris, Cotillon*, 1861–68. 7 vols., 8vo. 3903a

Vol. i. is entitled, "Introduction générale au droit public," etc.

Batchelder (E.) Border Adventures; or, The Romantic Incidents of a New-England Town; and other Poems. With an Appendix. By Eugene Batchelder … . *Boston*, 1851. 12mo, pp. 48. 3904

Relates to New Ipswich, N. H. *See* N. E. Gen. Reg., v., 266.

[Batchelder]. Brother Jonathan's Welcome to Kossuth. A Poem. … *Boston*, [1852]. 8vo. pp. 27. 3905

[Batchelder]. A Romance of the Sea-Serpent, or the Icthyosaurus. Also, a Collection of the Ancient and Modern Authorities, with Letters from Distinguished Merchants and Men of Science. *Cambridge, John Bartlett*, 1849. 12mo, pp. (4), 172.+[2d Ed. *Ibid.*] h. 3906

Also: A New Fremont Song … . [*Cambridge*, 1856.] 16mo, pp. (3).

Batchelder (J.) Memorial to the Massachusetts Legislature. By Hon. John Batchelder, President of the New England Female Medical College. Presented … May 17, 1866. Being a Reply to the Report of the Judiciary Committee of the House … . *Boston*, 1866. 8vo, pp. 11. h. 3907

[Batchelder (John M.)] Comparison of Products, Population, and Resources of the Free & Slave States. [n. p.] 1861. Broadside, lithographed.+*Cambridge*, 1861. Bd., lith.

Batchelder (J. P.) Second edition of "An Advertisement," by C. B. Coventry, with a "Candid Exposition of Facts," by J. P. Batchelder, m.d … . *Utica*, 1829. 8vo, pp. 16.

BATCHELDER (Samuel). Introduction and Early Progress of the Cotton Manufacture in the United States. ... *Boston, Little, Brown and Company*, 1863. 16mo, pp. iv., 108. B. & H. 3910

[BATCHELDER]. Statistics of the Cotton Manufacture. From the Seventh Annual Report of the Boston Board of Trade. *Boston*, 1861. 8vo, pp. 16. H. 3911

BATCHELDER, *Jr.* (Samuel). The Young Men of America ... . Prize Essay: By Samuel Batchelder, Jr. ... . *New York, Boston*, 1858. 8vo, pp. 32.+1860. 12mo, pp. 70. H. 3912

BATCHELDER (W.) Masonic Discourse at Danvers, Mass., Sept, 26, 1810. By William Batchelder ... . *Salem*. [n. d.] 8vo. 3913

BATCHELDER. A Sermon ... at Buxton, A.D. 1802, at the Ordination of Abner Flanders ... By William Batchelder ... . *Portsmouth, N. H., printed by N. S. & W. Peirce*, 1803. 8vo. pp. 17. H. 3914

BATCHELLER (D.) Sermon at Oxford, Mass., Oct. 7, 1818, at the funeral of Maj. Archibald Campbell. By David Batcheller. *Worcester*, 1818. 8vo. W. 3915

BATCHELOR (G.) Aux Français. Le parti républicain, ses doctrines et ses hommes. [*New York, Octobre*, 1860.] 12mo, pp. 24. H. 3916

BATCHELOR (G.) By George Batchelor ... History of all the Teachers' Associations ever established in the City of New-York ... . *New-York*, 1861. 12mo, 1 p. l., pp. 48. H. 3917

BATEMAN (Edmund). A Sermon Preached before the Honourable Trustees For establishing the Colony of Georgia, in America, and the Associates of ... Dr. Bray; at their Anniversary Meeting, March 19, 1740–1, at the Parish Church of St. Bride, ... London. By Edmund Bateman D.D. ... *London, John and Henry Pemberton*, M.DCC.XLI. 4to, *pp.* 21. C. 3918

BATEMAN (J.) The Orchidaceæ of Mexico and Guatemala. By James Bateman, Esq. *London, Ridgway*, 1837–1842. Elephant folio, pp. 16. 40 Colored Plates. C. 3919

Of this splendid work 125 copies only were printed for subscribers price £21. Priced: H. G. Bohn, £12 12s.

BATEMAN (N.) School Laws of Illinois, as amended February 16, 1865, with official and judicial decisions, [and with remarks]. By Newton Bateman. *Springfield*, 1866. 8vo.

BATES (Barnabas). A Brief Statement of the Exertions of the Friends of Cheap Postage in the City of New York. By Barnabas Bates ... . *New York*, 1848. 8vo, pp. xxvi., (1), 52.

BATES (Benjamin). A Letter addressed to a Member of the Legislature of Virginia. By Benjamin Bates. ... *New York, printed by Mahlon Day*, 1821. 12mo, pp. 12. 3922

On militia fines. This was also appended to a "Memorial of ... Friends to the Legislature of Virginia, on the Milita Laws." ... *New-Bedford*, 1813. 16mo, pp. 18. H.

BATES (D. B.) Incidents on Land and Water, or Four Years on the Pacific Coast. Being a Narrative of the Burning of the Ships Nonantum, Humayoon, and Fanchon ... . By Mrs. D. B. Bates. Second Edition. *Boston*, 1857. 12mo, pp. 336. B.+Third Edition. 1857.+Fourth Edition. *Boston, James French and Company*, 1858. 12mo, pp. 336. Woodcuts. H.

BATES (E.) In the Supreme Court of the U. States. In Prize. Causes Nos. 134, 163, 170, 261, 262, 263. Brief for the United States, Respondents in the Several Appeals. Edward Bates, Attorney General. C. Eames, of Counsel. [n. p.] *Gideon & Pearson, Printers*, [1863]. 8vo, pp. 9. H. 3924

BATES. Opinion of Attorney-General Bates on Citizenship. *Washington, Government Printing Office*, 1863. 8vo, pp. 27.

BATES. Opinion of Hon. Edward Bates, Attorney General ... on the Validity of the Acceptances given by John B. Floyd, Secretary of War, to Russell, Majors, & Waddell, now held by Peirce & Bacon. *Washington, Government Printing Office*, 1862. 8vo, pp. 17. H. 3926

BATES. Opinion of the Attorney General (Edward Bates) on the Suspension of the Writ of Habeas Corpus. [1861.] 8vo, pp. 12. 3927

BATES. The Rights of Citizens. Important Opinion of Attorney General Bates. *Hartford*, 1863. 12mo, pp. 34.

BATES (Edward). Edward Bates against Thomas H. Benton. *St. Louis, Mo., Charless & Paschall*, 1828. 12mo, pp. 12. 3929

BATES (Elisha). An Examination of Certain Proceedings

and Principles of the Society of Friends, called Quakers. By Elisha Bates. ... *St. Clairsville, the Author*, 1837. 8vo, pp. 309 (2). H. 3930

BATES. The Miscellaneous Repository. A Periodical Publication. By Elisha Bates. *Mountpleasant* [*Ohio*,] 1827–36. 5 vols., 8vo. 3931

Contains numerous articles relating to Friends in America.

BATES (H. W.) Contributions to an Insect Fauna of the Amazon Valley. Coleoptera-Longicornes. Part I. Lamiares. *London*, 1867. 8vo, pp. 258. 3932

BATES (H. W.) The Naturalist on the River Amazons; a Record of Adventures, Habits of Animals, Sketches of Brazilian and Indian Life, and Aspects of Nature under the Equator, during Eleven Years of Travel. By Henry Walter Bates. With Map and Illustration. *London, John Murray*, 1863. 2 vols., post 8vo, pp. xiv., 774.+Second Edition. *London, Murray*, 1864. 12mo, pp. xii., 466. 1 Map. S. 3932*a*

BATES. The River Amazons; a Record of Adventures, with Sketches of Brazilian and Indian Life, during Eleven Years of Travel. By Henry Walter Bates ... . *London, John Murray*, 1867. Post 8vo. 3933

BATES. Der Naturforscher am Amazonenstrom. ... Aus dem Englischen. ... *Leipzig, Dyk*, 1866. 8vo, pp. viii., 416. Woodcuts, Lithograph Map, and 8 Plates. 3934

BATES (Isaac C.) An Oration pronounced at Northampton, July 4, 1805. ... By Isaac C. Bates. *Northampton, Thomas M. Pomroy*, 1805. 8vo, pp. 30 (1). H. 3935

BATES. An Oration Pronounced before the Washington Benevolent Society of the County of Hampshire, on their First Anniversary, 1812. In Commemoration of the Nativity of Washington. By Isaac C. Bates ... . *Northampton, printed by William Butler* [1812]. 8vo, pp. 24. H. 3936

Also, Speech ... on the Tariff Bill. ... March 26, 1828. *Washington*, 1828. 8vo, pp. 26. H. Speech ... on the Indian Bill. House of Representatives. May, 1830. [n. p., n. d.] 8vo, pp. 24. B. Speech ... in Defence of the Protective System: Delivered February 21, 1844. *Washington*, 1844. 8vo, pp. 18.+[n. p., n. d.] 8vo, pp. 16. H.

BATES (Joseph). A Vindication of the Seventh Day Sabbath ... with a further History of God's Peculiar People, from

1847 to 1848. By Joseph Bates. *New Bedford, Mass.*, 1848. 8vo, pp. 116. 3937

BATES (Joshua), *D.D.*, *d.* 1854. Address of Rev. Joshua Bates, D.D. at the Semi-Sentennial [*sic*] Celebration of Middlebury College. 1850. [n. p., n. d.] 8vo, pp. 24. H. 3938

BATES. An Anniversary Discourse, delivered at Dudley, Massachusetts, March 20, 1853. With Topographical and Historical Notices of the Town. By Joshua Bates, D.D. *Boston, Press of T. R. Marvin*, 1853. 8vo, pp. 58. H. 3939

BATES. Address ... in Castleton December 2, 1823, at the Commencement of the Vermont Academy of Medicine, connected with Middlebury College. ... [n. p.] 1824. 8vo, pp. 16. H. 3940

With "An Historical Sketch," etc.

BATES. A Sermon delivered before the Society for Propagating the Gospel among the Indians and Others in North America, Nov. 4, 1813. By Joshua Bates ... . *Boston, Cummings and Hilliard*, 1813. 8vo, pp. 44. H. 3941

Also: Brief Account of the Happy Death of Mary Ann Clap ... who died July 15, 1816 ... . *Dedham, Abel D. Alleyne*, 1816. 18mo, pp. 36. H.+Second Edition. *Dedham*, 1816. 18mo, pp. 36. H. Discourse at Castleton on the Organization of the Mount Vernon Institution, Middlebury, Vt., 1818. 8vo; pp. —. A Discourse ... at Middlebury, on the Annual Fast: April 15, 1818. ... *Middlebury* (*Vt.*), 1818. 8vo, pp. 28. H. A Discourse delivered Feb. 15, 1818, Being the Sabbath Preceding the Dissolution of the Pastoral Relation between the Author and the First Church in Dedham. *Dedham*, 1818. 8vo, pp. 23. A Discourse, delivered March 4, 1814, at the Interment of the Rev. Thomas Prentice, D.D., Pastor of the Church in Medfield. *Dedham*, 1814. 8vo, pp. 24. H. A Sermon, preached, January 11, 1804. at the Ordination of the Rev. James Thompson ... in Barre. ... *Worcester*, 1804. 8vo, pp. 32. H. Sermon at the Ordination of Rev. Wm. Bates in Northbridge, Mass., Nov. 5, 1845. *Andover*, 1846. 8vo, pp. 26. H. Two Sermons on Temperance on the Annual Fast, April 8, 1813. *Boston*, 1813. 8vo, pp. 36.+Second Edition. *Dedham*, 1814. 12mo, pp. 38. Discourse at Castleton, Vt., Sept. 16, 1818, at the organization of the Vermont Juvenile Missionary Society. *Middlebury*, 1818. 8vo. Inaugural Address as President of Middlebury College, Vt., March 18, 1818. *Middlebury*, 1818. 8vo, pp. 40. H.+An Inaugural Oration ... . Second Edition. *Middlebury*, 1818. 8vo, pp. 24. H. A Sermon ... Feb. 26, 1817, at the Ordination of the Rev. Rufus Hurlburt ... at Sudbury. *Dedham*, 1817. 8vo, pp. 40. H. Sermon at Boston, Jan. 4, 1816, before the Society for Foreign Missions of Boston and Vicinity. *Dedham*, 1816. 8vo. Sermon at the Ordination of Federal Burt. *Dover*, 1817. 8vo Sermon at the Ordination of Ira Ingraham. *Middlebury*, 1821. 8vo.

BATES (Joshua), *d.* 1864. A Memorial of Joshua Bates, from the City of Boston. *Boston, City Council*, MDCCCLXV. Rl. 8vo, pp. 58. Portrait and Plates. 3942

BATES. Proceedings of the City Council in Relation to the Death of Joshua Bates, Esq. *Boston*, 1864. 8vo, pp. 10.

BATES. Tribute of Boston Merchants To the Memory of Joshua Bates, October, 1864. *Boston, printed by John Wilson and Son*, 1864. 8vo, pp. 49. 3944

BATES (Mary). The Private Life of John C. Calhoun. ... [From] the "International Magazine" ... . By Miss Mary Bates. *Charleston: Walker, Richards and Co.*, MDCCCLII. 8vo, pp. 31. H. 3945

BATES (S. P.) A Discourse on the Life and Character of John Barker, D.D. by Samuel P. Bates. *Lancaster, Wm. B. Wiley, Printer*, 1860. 8vo, pp. 16. H. 3946

BATES (Walter). Mysterious Stranger; or, Memoirs of Henry More Smith, alias Henry F. Moon, alias Wm. Newman, who is now confined in Simsbury Mines, in Connecticut, for Burglary, &c., By Walter Bates. *New Haven*, 1816. 18mo, pp. 108. 3947

BATES. Narrative of the Conduct and Adventures of Henry Frederic Moon, a native of Brighthelmstone, Sussex, now under sentence of Imprisonment in Connecticut; an Account of his Artifices, Impostures, Mechanical Ingenuity, &c. By W. Bates, Sheriff of New Brunswick. 1817. 8vo. Portrait. 3948

BATES (William). [An Oration, delivered in Fairhaven July 4, 1821.] By Wm. Bates, Esq. *New Bedford*, 1821. 8vo.

[BATES (W. C.)] The Stars and Stripes in Rebeldom. A Series of Papers written by Federal Prisoners (Privates) in Richmond, Tuscaloosa, New Orleans, and Salisbury, N. C. With an Appendix. *Boston, T. O. H. P. Burnham*, 1862. 12mo, pp. 137. H. 3950

The successive editors of the paper as it originally appeared were George T. Childs, J. W. Dickins, Leroy Warren, and Wm. C. Bates.

BATES COLLEGE. Catalogue of the Officers and Students of Bates College, Lewistown, Me., for 1864. *Lewistown*, 1864. 8vo, pp. 38. H. 3951

BATH. The City Charter: with the Joint Rules and Orders of the City Council ... . *Bath* [*Me.*,] 1848. 16mo, pp. 40.

Also: Addresses of the Mayor, Statements of the Appropriations, Receipts and Expenditures, Reports of the School Committee, for various years.

BATH. French's Village in Bath. Building Lots at Auction. *Albany*, 1857. 8vo. S. 3953

BATHER. Full and Faithfull Account of the Life of James Bather, late Boatswain of the Nightingale Brig, written by himself, containing narrative of the steps taken by John Lancey, master of the ship, for wilfully burning and sinking the said Vessel, in order to defraud the Insurers, and relation of the discovery made, &c. London [1746]. 8vo. 3954

Containing some interesting notices of the author's proceedings at Newfoundland, Carolina, Charlestown, Boston, the Bermudas, Jamaica, Maryland, Philadelphia, and other parts of America. Title from Thorpe's catalogue, for 1842.

Bath-kol. A Voice from the Wilderness. Being an humble attempt to support the Truth of God, against some of the principal errors raging at this time. By the first Presbytery of the Eastward. *Boston, Printed by N. Coverly between the Sign of the Lamb and the White-Horse*, 1783. 12mo, pp. 360. 3955

This singular New England production is signed at the end by William Davidson, Moderator, and Simon Williams, Pros. Clerk.

BATHURST (Edward). Hispaniola, Hayti, Saint Domingo. [*Privately printed*] 1851. 8vo. 3956

The Canadian Parliamentary Library contains the following: Memorial of the Colonial Agents to Earl Bathurst, 25th February, 1824. pp. 3. Letter from Earl Bathurst to the Colonial Agents, February, 1824. pp. 3. Letter from the Colonial Agents to Earl Bathurst, 1st March, 1824. pp. 2. Another, 9th March, 1824. pp. 4. Report of a Debate in [the Colonial] Council [Barbados,] and a Despatch from Lord Bathurst to the Governor to ... Sir Henry Wande, Governor of Barbados. *Barbados. London, Re-printed* 1823. 8vo, Title, pp. 40 (1). B.

BATHURST (H.) Sermon before the Incorporated Society for the Propagation of the Gospel in Foreign Parts, February 16, 1810. By Henry, Lord Bishop of Norwich. *London*, 1810. 8vo, pp. 76. 3957

BATON ROUGE. List of Premiums to be given by the Baton Rouge Industrial Fair Association ... the Second Monday of March, 1860. *Baton Rouge*, 1860. 8vo, pp. 15. H. 3958

Also Annual Reports of the Female Orphan Asylum. Incorporated Feb. 5, 1850.

BATOPILAS MINING CO. The Articles of Association of the Batopilas Mining Co. 1826. 8vo. P. 3959

BATTEL (Andries). De gedenkwaardige Voyagie van Andries Battel van Leigh in Essex, na Brasilien, en desselfs wonderlijke avontuuren, zijnde gevangen gebragt van de Portugijsen na An-

gola ... A° 1589 en vervolgens. Door hem selfs in het Engels beschreven ... . *Leyden, Vander Aa*, 1706. 8vo, pp. 46 and Register. Map and Plates. S. 3960

Forms part of Vander Aa's Naaukeurige versameling. (*See* No. 3.)

A Battle! a Battle! a Battle a Squirt; | Where no Man is kill'd, and no Man is hurt! | To the Tune of | Three new blue Beans, in a new blue blown Bladder; | rattle Bladder rattle Bladder!! To which is added, | The | Quaker's Address, versify'd; | and | King Wampum, or Harm watch Harm | Catch | ... . *Printed and Sold at the Blue-Nose, near | Brazen-Nose-College, Germantown* [*Phil.*, 1764]. 16mo, pp. 12. P. 3961

This curious and very rare poem relates to the Paxton Boys.

Battle Field of Shiloh. [n. p., n. d.] 8vo, pp. 8. 3962

Battle Fields of the South. From Bull Run to Fredericksburgh: With Sketches of Confederate Commanders, and Gossip of the Camps. By an English Combatant, Lieutenant of Artillery on the Field Staff. *London: Smith, Elder & Co.*, 1863. 2 vols., post 8vo, pp. xliii., 339; 399. 2 Maps.+*New York, John Bradburn*, 1864. 8vo, pp. 517. 2 Maps. 3963

The Battle Grounds of America, illustrated by Stories of the Revolution. With Fourteen Engravings. *Auburn, J. C. Derby*, 1846. 12mo. 3964

The Battle of Bunker's Hill. *See* Bunker's Hill.

The Battle of Chancellorsville, and the Eleventh Army Corps. *New York, G. B. Teubner*, 1863. 8vo, pp. 48. 3965

The Battle of Fort Sumter, and first Victory of the Southern Troops. Compiled chiefly from the detailed reports of the Charleston Press. *Evans & Cogswell, Charleston*, 1861. 8vo.

BATTLE OF LAKE ERIE MONUMENT ASSOCIATION. An Account of the Organization & Proceedings of the Battle of Lake Erie Monument Association. And Celebration of the 45th Anniversary of the Battle ... at Put-in-Bay Island, on September Tenth, 1858. *Sandusky*, 1858. 8vo, pp. 49. B., H. 3967

Battle of New Orleans; or, Jackson's Victory. By a Citizen of Baltimore. *Baltimore*, 1825. 16mo, pp. 36. 3968

Battle of Niagara, a Poem without notes, and Goldau the Maniac Harper. By John O'Cataract. *Baltimore, N. G. Maxwell*, 1818. 12mo, pp. 143. 3969

Battle of the Thames, October 5, 1813; from an unpublished Poem, entitled Tecumseh. By a Young American. *New York*, 1840. 12mo. 3970

... Battles during the Great American Rebellion, A.D. 1861–1862. [From the N. Y. Sunday Times of August 24. n. p., 1862.] Broadside. H. 3971

BATWELL (D.) A Sermon preached at York-Town, before Captain Morgan's and Captain Price's Companies of Riflemen, on Thursday, July 30, 1775. Being the Day recommended by the Honourable Continental Congress for a General Fast throughout the Twelve United Colonies of North America. By Daniel Batwell M.A. Published by request. *Philadelphia, printed by John Dunlap*, M.DCC.LXXV. 8vo, pp. 20. P. 3972

BAUCHE and ZEVALLOS. Disertaciones sobre la navigacion à las Indias Orientales por el Norte de la Europa. Escritas, la primera, por M. Bauche, de la Academia de Ciencias de Paris; y la segunda, por el Capitan de Fragata, de la Real Armada, D. Ciriaco de Zevallos. *Isla de Leon* (*Cadiz*), 1798. Sm. folio, pp. xxii., 14. 3973

"These dissertations relate to the practicability of a *North West* passage to the East Indies, and not to a passage by the North of Europe, as the title would lead one to believe. The dissertation of M. Bauche relates principally to the supposed discoveries of Ferrer Maldonado."—RICH.

BAUDISSIN (*Graf* Adelbert). Der Ansiedler im Missouri-Staate. Den deutschen Auswanderern gewidmet. *Iserlohn, Bädeker*, 1854. 8vo, 2 p. l., pp. 181, and Lithographed Map, folio. 3974

BAUDISSIN. Zustände in Amerika illustrirt von Graf A. Baudissin. *Altona, A. Mentzel* [and] *New-York* [and] *Saint-Louis*, 1862. 8vo, pp. vi., 273. B.+Peter Tütt. Zustände in Amerika. Zweite Auflage. *Altona*, 1862. 8vo, pp. vi., 273.+Dritte Auflage, *Altona*, 1866. 8vo, pp. vi., 273. 3975

"A worthless book; relating the supposed adventures of a German in America."—*Ch. Rau.*

BAUDISSIN (Ulrich). Cora oder die Sklavin. Amerikanisches Charakterbild in 5 Aufzügen. Nach vorhandenen Stoffen frei bearbeitet. *Altona, Mentzel*, 1862. 8vo, pp. 122. 3976

Baudouin (A.) La mort de Maximilien (vers); par Alphonse Baudouin. *Bar-sur-Aube, imp. Mme Jardeaux*, 1867. 4to, pp. 4. 3977

[Baudouin (Jean Marie Théodore)]. Washington, ou l'Orpheline de la Pensylvanie, mélodrame en trois actes. *Paris, Fages*, 1815. 8vo. 3978

Published under the pseudonym of d'Aubigny.

[Baudous (Wilhelmus de)]. Lof-dicht van alle de voornaemste exployten, ghedaen onder het bewint van de Gheoctr. Westind. Compagnie, door het cloeck beleyt van ... P. Pz. Heyn, beginn. van den Jare 1624, 1625, 1626, 1627 ende 1623. *Dordrecht, gedr. by Franç. Bosselaer*, 1629. 4to, pp. 16. 3978a

The dedication is signed Γουλελμος δέ Βαυδοῦς, χιρογγος [*sic*].

B[audry] d[es Lozières (Louis Narcisse)]. Voyage à la Louisiane, et sur le continent de l'Amérique Septentrionale, fait dans les années 1794 à 1798; Contenant un Tableau historique de la Louisiane, des observations sur son climat, ses riches productions, le caractère et le nom des Sauvages; des remarques importantes sur la navigation; des principes d'administration, de législation et de gouvernement propres à cette Colonie, etc. etc. Par B*** D***. Orné d'une belle carte. ... *Paris, Dentu, An* xi.-1802. 8vo, pp. iv., 382. Map. H. 3979

Contains vocabularies of the Dacotah and Chippeway Indians.

Baudry des Lozières. Second Voyage à la Louisiane, faisant suite au premier de l'auteur de 1794 à 1798. Contenant la vie militaire du général Grondel ... . Par Baudry des Lozieres. *Paris, Charles, An* xi.-1803 (Mars). 2 vols., 8vo, 1 p. l., pp. xvi., 414 (1); 2 p. l., pp. 410 (1). 3980

Contains the military life of General Grondel, commander of the French armies in Louisiana, and his services against the English and Indians, &c., and a Congo vocabulary. "These volumes have no other pretensions to their title of a voyage to Louisiana, than that the author published the previous work in 1802. It is in fact a miscellany relating to the whole colonial affairs of France." *See* M. R., xlii., 479.

Bauer (Edm.) Einige Bemerkungen über den Handels- und Schiffahrts-Verkehr Triest's mit Ostindien, China, Brasilien und andern transatlantischen Ländern. Zweite Auflage. *Triest, Münster*, 1864. 8vo, pp. 71. 3981

Bauer (Franz). Some experiments on the Fungi which constitute the Colouring Matter of the Red Snow discovered in Baffin's Bay. *London*, 1820. 4to, pp. 9. 3982

Reprinted from the "Philosophical Transactions."

Bauer (Johann Chr. August). Alexander Selkirchs Schicksale zu Wasser und zu Lande ... . Erster Theil. *Berlin, Dunker*, 1806. || Zweiter-Vierter Theil. *Leipzig, Wienbrack*, 1807-10. 8vo. 3983

Bauer. Alex. Selkirchs sällsamma äfventyr i fremmande verldsdelar. *Stockholm, Hægeström*, 1819-28. 4 vols., 12mo. 3984

Bauer. Franklin und Washington, oder Sammlung der merkwürdigsten bekannten Züge aus dem Leben dieser Männer. *Berlin, Fröhlich*, 1806. 8vo. 3985

Baugher (H. L.) The Christian Patriot. A Discourse addressed to the Graduating Class of Pennsylvania College, September 15, 1861. By H. L. Baugher, d.d., President of Pennsylvania College. *Gettysburgh, A. D. Buehler*, 1861. 8vo, pp. 25. 3986

Baumann (Ludwig Adolph). Abriss der Staatsverfassung der vornehmsten Länder in America. Nebst einem Anhange von den nördlichen Polarländern. *Brandenburg, Heffenland*, 1776. 8vo. Map. 3987

Baumbach, (L. von). Briefe aus den Vereinigten Staaten von Nordamerika in die Heimath, mit besonderer Rücksicht auf deutsche Auswanderer. *Cassel, Fischer*, 1851. 12mo, pp. iv., 192. 1 Lithograph, 4to.+Neue Briefe ... . *Cassel, Fischer*, 1856. 8vo, pp. xiv., 336. C. 3988

Baumgarten (Siegm. Jac.) Allgemeine Geschichte. *See* [Schröter (J. F.)]

Baumont (Simon van). Pertinente beschryvinge van Guiana, gelegen aen de vaste kust van America. *Amsterdam*, 1676. 4to. 3989

Baury (A. L.) Historical Sketch of St. Mary's Church, Newton Lower Falls Massachusetts. A Sermon, preached in St. Mary's Church, Newton Lower Falls, on the Fourth Sunday after Easter, 1847: being the Twenty-fifth Anniversary of the Incumbent's first officiating in that Church. By Alfred L. Baury, Rector. *Boston, James B. Dow*, 1847. 8vo, pp. 34. 3990

Baury. ... A Sermon, preached in ... Newton Lower Falls, Mass., ... December 24, 1840, at the Funeral of Zibeon Hooker, an Officer of the American Revolutionary Army. By Alfred L. Baury ... . *Boston, James B. Dow*, 1841. 8vo, pp. 28. H. 3991

Bausset-Roquefort. Notice historique sur l'invention de la navigation par la vapeur. Par M. le marquis de Bausset-Roquefort. *Lyon, Girard et Josserand*, 1864. 8vo, pp. 39. 3992

Bautista (E. de San J.) Advertencias á los Confesores de Indios. Por Fr. Elias de San Juan Bautista. *Mexico*, 1600. 2 vols., 8vo. 3993

Bautista. Confessionario en lengua Mexicana por Fr. Elias de San Juan Bautista. *Mexico*, 1599. 8vo. 3994

Bautista. Diálogos en Lengua Mexicana, por Fr. Elias de San Juan Bautista. *Mexico*, 1598. 8vo. 3995

Bautista. Miseria y brevedad de la vida del hombre, en lengua Nahuatl. Por Fr. Juan Bautista, Franciscano. *Mexico*, 1604. 4to. 3996

Bautista. Platicas antiquas que en la excellentissima lengua Nahuatl, enmendo y crecento el ... P. Juan Bautista, Franciscano. *Mexico*, 1599. 8vo. 3997

Bautista. Platicas morales de los Indios para la doctrina de sus hijos, en lengua Mexicana intitulado huehuetlatolli. Por Fr. Juan Bautista, Franciscano. *Mexico*, 1601. 8vo. 3998

Bautista. Sermonario en lengua Nahuatl. Por. Fr. Juan Bautista, Franciscano. *Mexico*, 1606. 4to. 3999

Except No. 3998, these titles are from Ternaux, Nos. 234, 253, 275 and 298.

Bauzá (Felipe). Über den gegenwärtigen Zustand der Geographie von Süd-Amerika, von Don Philipp Bauzá ... . Uebersetzt durch Wilhelm Friedrich Freyherrn von Karwinsky 4000

Published in German and Spanish in the "Denkschriften d. K. Akad. d. Wiss., München, 1824." 4to, Band viii., pp. 87-124. I do not know that it has ever been separately printed.

Bavier's (Fr. Urban), des See-Capitäns, merckwürdige Reisen und Begebenheiten, seine Kriegsdienste zu Lande, Seefahrten nach Ost- und Westindien von ihm selbst beschrieben. *Franckfurt und Linz*, 1752. 8vo.+*Nürnberg, Monath*, 1752. 8vo. 4001

Kayser and Heinsius give this name as Bavier; I have seen it spelled Bawier.

Baxley (H. W.) What I saw on the West Coast of South and North America, and at the Hawaiian Islands. By H. Willis Baxley, m.d. *New York, D. Appleton & Company*, 1865. 8vo, pp. 632. Woodcuts. B. 4002

Baxter. Mr. Baxter Baptiz'd in Bloud,| or,| A Sad| History| of the| Unparallel'd Cruelty| of the| Anabaptists| In New-England.| Faithfully Relating the Cruel, Barbarous, and| Bloudy Murther of Mr. Baxter an Orthodox| Minister, who was kill'd by the Anabaptists, and his| Skin most cruelly flead off from his Body.| With| An Exact Account of all the Circumstances and Parti| culars of this barbarous Murther.| Published by his mournfull Brother Benjamin Baxter| Living in Fen-Church-Street, London. With Allowance.| *London,| Printed in the Year*, 1673.| 4to, Title and 6 pp. 4003

A fictitious narrative—the "allowance" was withdrawn after an examination of the pretended case.

Baxter (G. A.) An Essay on the Abolition of Slavery. By G. A. Baxter, d.d. *Richmond*, 1836. 8vo. S. 4004

Baxter (J.) Discourse ... Delivered at George-Town in Arowsick upon the death of John Watts, Esq., who departed this Life Nov. 26th, 1717. By Joseph Baxter. *Boston*, 1718. 16mo, pp. 34. 4005

Baxter. Journal of several Visits to the Indians on Kennebec River, 1717-1721. By Rev. Joseph Baxter. *Boston*, 1867. 8vo. 4006

Baxter. ... A Sermon Preached before the Honourable the Lieutenant Governour, the Council, and Representatives of the Province of the Massachusetts-Bay, in New-England, May 31. 1727. Being the Day for the Election of his Majesty's Council. By Joseph Baxter ... . *Boston, Samuel Gerrish*, 1727. 8vo, 2 p. l., pp. 36. H., M. 4007

Baxter (M.) Louis Napoleon the Destined Monarch of the World, ... subsequently to become completely supreme over England and most of America, ... With Seven Diagrams and Two Maps. Third Edition, enlarged. By the Rev. M. Baxter. *W. S. & A. Martien, Philadelphia*, 1858. 12mo, pp. 344.+New Edition. *London, Macintosh*, 1865. 12mo. 4008

Also: End of the World about 1864-69. ... Predictions of Coming Calamities are verified by the Present American Commotions ... . *Boston, E. Dutton* [etc.], 1861. 8vo, pp. 16. H. "The Coming Battle" relates somewhat to America.

Baxter (R.) Certainty of the World of Spirits: and Cotton Mather's Wonders of the Invisible World. *London*, 1834. 18mo. 4009

Baxter. Geschichten aus der Geisterwelt ... und: Die Wunder der unsichtbaren Welt, von Dr. Cotton Mather. Aus dem Englischen übersetzt von Eduard Binder. Mit einer Vorrede von Justinus Kerner. *Reutlingen, Ensslin und Laiblin*, 1828. 12mo. 4010

Baxter. Baxter's Directions to Slaveholders Revived. ... To which is subjoined A Letter from the Worthy Anthony Benezet, To the celebrated Abbe Raynal. With his Answer. *Philadelphia, F. Bailey*, mdcclxxxv. 24mo, pp 8, 16, 12. 4011

Baxter. Wehkomaonganooa asquam Peantogig Kah asquam Quinnuppegig, Tokonogque mahche woskeche Peantamwog. Onk woh sampwutt:ahae Peantomwog. Wu[t]ankausuonk wunneetou noh nohtompeantog. Ussowesu Mr. Richard Baxter. Kah yeuyeu qushkinnummun Indiane Wuttinnontœwaonganit. Wussohsumœwontamunat œwesuonk God ut Christ Jesus ut, kah œneneheonat Indiansog. ... *Cambridge, Printed by S. G. for the Corporation in London for the Indians in New England*, 1688. Sm. 8vo, pp. 188. B. 4012

A book of extreme rarity, printed by Samuel Green. Thomas' "Hist. Printing," I., 257, quotes an edition, 1664, but does not mention this. *See* Eliot (John).

Baxter. Reliquiæ Baxterianæ: or, Mr. Richard Baxter's Narrative of The most Memorable Passages of his Life and Times. Faithfully Publish'd from his own Original Manuscript, by Matthew Sylvester. ... *London, T. Parkhurst* [etc.] m dc xc vi. Fol., 14 p. l., pp. 448, 200, 132 (8). Portrait. B. 4013

Contains original correspondence with Gov. Endicott, John Norton, and John Eliot, of New England, pp. 290-298.

Baxter. Vindiciæ Anti-Baxterianæ, or some Animadversions on a Book, entituled Reliquiæ Baxterianæ, or the Life of Mr. R. Baxter. 1696. 12mo. 4014

Baxter (S.) Tyrannicide Proved Lawful, a Discourse delivered in the Mines at Symsbury, in Connecticut, to the Loyalists confined there, by order of Congress, Sept. 19, 1781. By Simeon Baxter. *London*, 1782. 8vo. 4015

[Baxter (Th.)] A Letter from a gentleman at Barbadoes, to his friend now in London, concerning the administration of the late Gov. B——g. *London, Roberts*, 1740. 8vo, pp. 44. 4016

Baxter (W.) Pea Ridge and Prairie Grove; or, Scenes and Incidents of the War in Arkansas. By Wm. Baxter. *Cincinnati, Poe & Hitchcock*, 1864. 16mo, pp. 262. 4017

Baxter (William Edward). America and the Americans. By W. E. Baxter, Esq., m.p. *London* [and] *New York, Geo. Routledge & Co.*, 1855. 16mo, 2 p. l., pp. 224. B. 4018

Baxter. Discours sur la guerre civile aux États-Unis, prononcé par M. Baxter ... en janvier 1865. Traduction de M. J. H. Livingstone. *Avranches, Hambis*, 1865. 8vo, pp. 15. 4019

Baxter. The Social Condition of the Southern States of America. A Lecture delivered in the Corn Exchange Hall, Dundee, on November 5, 1862. By W. E. Baxter, Esq., m.p. for the Montrose District of Burghs. *London, James Nesbitt and Co.*, m.dccc.lxii. 12mo, pp. 28. B. 4020

The Bay Fight, Mobile Bay, August 5, 1864. Reprinted from Harper's Monthly. *New York*, 1864. 12mo, pp. 18. 4021

Bayard (F. M.) Voyage dans l'intérieur des États-Unis, à Bath, Winchester, dans la vallée de Shenandoha, etc. etc. etc. Pendant l'Été de 1791. Par Ferdinand-M. Bayard. ... *Paris, Cocheris*, 1797. 8vo, pp. xvi., 336. H.+Seconde édition, Augmentée de descriptions et d'anecdotes sur la vie militaire et politique de Georges Washington. Par Ferdinand-M. Bayard ... . *Paris, Batilliot* [etc.], *an VIe* [1798]. 8vo, pp. xxv. [xxiii.], 349. Map. 4022

Bayard (James). A Brief Exposition of the Constitution of the United States, With an Appendix, containing the Declaration of Independence and the Articles of Confederation. *Philadelphia, Hogan & Thompson*, 1833. 12mo, pp. 178.+*Philadelphia*, 1834. 12mo.+Second Edition. 1840. 12mo, pp. 178. +1845. 12mo. pp. 178. H. 4023

Bayard (James A.), *the elder, d.* 1815. Address of Ajax to James A. Bayard, Esq., March 25, 1802. [n. p.] 8vo, pp. 7. 4024

On the election of Jefferson.

Bayard. Speech of Mr. Bayard on the Foreign Intercourse Bill. Delivered in the House of Representatives ... On the third Day of March, 1798. [n. p., n. d.] 8vo, pp. 16. 4025

Bayard. Speech of the Hon. Mr. Bayard. Member of the National Legislature from the State of Delaware. On the Bill received from the Senate, ... entitled "An Act to repeal certain Acts respecting the Organization of the Courts of the United States." Delivered in the House of Representatives February

19th and 20th, 1802. [No imprint.] 12mo, pp. 60.+[No imprint.] 8vo, pp. 34. H.+*Hartford, Hudson & Goodwin*, 1802. 8vo, pp. 48. *Worcester, Isaiah Thomas, Junior, April*, 1802. 12mo, pp. 48. 4026

See also Giles (W. B.)

Bayard. Mr. Bayard's Speech, upon his Motion to amend the Resolution offered by Mr. Giles [relative to the Embargo], by stricking [*sic*] out that Part which is in Italics. Delivered in the Senate ... February 14, 1809. [n. p., n. d.] 8vo, pp. 21. H.+... Striking ... . [*Portland*, n. d.] 12mo, pp. 24. H. 4027

Bayard. Speech of the Hon. James A. Bayard, In the Senate of the United States, Upon his motion made on the 16th of June, to postpone the further consideration of the bill declaring War against Great Britain, to the 31st of October. [*Exeter, N. H., C. Norris & Co., Printers*, 1812.] 8vo, pp. 16. H.+[1812.] 8vo, pp. 30. 4028

Bayard (James A.), *the younger*. Abolition, and the Relation of Races. Speech of Hon. James A. Bayard, of Delaware, delivered in the Senate, April 2 and 3, 1862. [*Washington*, 1862.] 8vo, pp. 15 and 18. 4029

Bayard. Remarks in the Senate of the United States, Jan. 31, 1855. Vindicating the late James A. Bayard, of Delaware, from the Charges in the "Anas" of Thomas Jefferson, aspersing his Character. *Washington*, 1855. 8vo. 4030

Also, ... Condition of the Country. Speech ... In the Senate of the United States, March 20, 21 and 22, 1861. *Washington, H. Polkinhorn.* 8vo, pp. 43. Executive Usurpation: Speech ... July 19, 1861. 8vo, pp. 24. Speech ... March 22, 1858, on the Admission of Kansas into the Federal Union under the Lecompton Constitution. *Washington*, 1858. 8vo, pp. 40. H. Speech on the Expulsion of Mr. Bright, February 5, 1862. [n. p., n. d.] 8vo, pp. 16. Speech ... January 19, 1864, against the Validity of the Test Oath ... [of] July 2, 1862, with the subsequent Proceedings in the Senate, and his final Remarks before the resignation of his Seat. Also, a Letter addressed by Mr. Bayard to a Constituent, December 22, 1860. *Philadelphia*, 1864. 8vo, pp. 38. Two Speeches ... February 28th and March 3, 1863, in opposition to the Conscription Bill, and the Bill to appoint a Dictator, entitled "An Act relating to Habeas Corpus, and regulating Judicial Proceedings in certain cases." *Baltimore, W. M. Innes*, 1863. 8vo, pp. 32.

Bayard (Lewis P.) Sermon in Trinity Church, Newark, January 26, 1817, at the Institution of a Church Missionary Society. By Lewis P. Bayard. *New York*, 1817. 8vo, pp. 20. 4031

Bayard. Memorial of the Rev. Lewis P. Bayard, d.d.; containing a Discourse ... by Rt. Rev. Dr. Onderdonk ... Edited by J. W. Brown ... *New-York*, 1841. 12mo, pp. 272. 4032

Bayard (Nicholas). An Account of the Commitment, Arraignment, Tryal, and Condemnation of Nicholas Bayard, Esq., for High Treason: in endeavouring to subvert the Government of the Province of New York, by signing and procuring others to sign scandalous libels called petitions, to his late Majesty King William, the Parliament of England, and the Lord Cornbury ... With a copy of the Libels or Addresses. *New York, William Bradford*, 1703. Folio. 4033

Bayard. An Account of the Illegal Prosecution and Tryal of Coll. Nicholas Bayard, in the Province of New York, for supposed High Treason in the Year 170½. Collected from several Memorials taken by divers Persons privately, the Commissioners having strictly prohibited the taking of the Tryal in open Court. *Printed and Sold by William Bradford at the Sign of the Bible in New-York*, mdccii. Folio, pp. (11), 44. P. 4034

See White Kennet, Bib. Am. Prim., pp. 154 and 184.

Bayard. A| Journal| of the| Late Actions| of the| French at Canada.| With| The Manner of their being Repuls'd, by His| Excellency, Benjamin Fletcher, Their Majesties| Governour of New-York.| Impartially Related by Coll. Nicholas Reyard [*sic*], and Lieutenant Coll.| Charles Lodowick, who attended his Excellency, during the whole| Expedition.| To which is added.| I. An Account of the present State and Strength of Canada,| given by Two Dutch Men, who have been a long Time Pri-| soners there, and now made their Escape.| II. The Examination of a French Prisoner.| III. His Excellency Benjamin Fletcher's Speech to the Indians.| IV. An Address from the Corporation of Albany, to His Excellen-| cy, Returning Thanks for His Excellency's early Assistance for| their Relief.| Licensed, Sept. 11th. 1693. Edward Cooke.| *London, Printed for Richard Baldwin, in Warwick-Lane*, 1693.| 4to, pp. iv., 22. 4035

Reprinted with the following preliminary title:

Bayard. Journal of the Late Actions of the French at Canada, by Col. Nicholas Beyard, and Lieut. Charles Lodowick. *New York, Reprinted for Joseph Sabin*, 1868. 4to, 2 p. l., pp. 55. 4036

Bayard (R. H. and J. A.) Documents relating to The Presidential Election in the Year 1801: containing a Refutation of Two Passages in the Writings of Thomas Jefferson, Aspersing the Character of the Late James A. Bayard, of Delaware. *Philadelphia*, 1831. 8vo, pp. 14. H., S. 4037

BAYARD (S.) An Address delivered before the Washington Benevolent Societies of Princeton & Cranbury, in the State of N. Jersey, on Monday, the Twenty-Second day of February, 1813, in the Presbyterian Church at Princeton, in commemoration of the Birth-day of Washington. By Samuel Bayard. *New Brunswick, Printed and Published by Lewis Deary*, 1813. 8vo, pp. 22.

[BAYARD.] Address to the well disposed, reflecting, and unprejudiced freeholders of West Chester Co. recommending the support of Stephen Van Rensselaer as Governor and James Watson as Lieutenant Governor etc. *New York*, 1801. 8vo.

BAYARD. A Funeral Oration, Occasioned by the Death of Gen. George Washington; and Delivered on the First of January, 1800, In the Episcopal Church; at New-Rochelle, in the State of New York. By Samuel Bayard, Esq. *New-Brunswick, Printed by Abraham Blauvelt*, 1800. 8vo, pp. 24. P. 4040

BAYARD (W.) An Exposition of the Conduct of the Two Houses of G. G. & S. Howland, and Leroy, Bayard & Company, in Relation to the Frigates Liberator and Hope, in Answer to A Narrative on that Subject, by Mr. Alexandre Contostavlos. By William Bayard. *New-York*, 1826. 8vo, pp. 47. 4041

BAYARD. Memorial of Wm. Bayard & Co. to Congress praying for a charter for a Railroad from the Mississippi River to California. *Washington*, 1849. 8vo. 4042

BAYER (Wolfgang). Herrn P. Wolfgang Bayers ... Reise nach Peru. ... Herausgegeben von C. G. von Murr. *Nürnberg, Johann Eberhard Zeh*, 1776. Sm. 8vo, pp. 214. H. 4043

Also published by Murr in his "Journal," *Nürnberg*, 1776, III., 115–326, and in his "Nachrichten," *Halle*, 1809, 8vo, I., 380–387. P. Stöcklein's Welt-Bott, Bd. xxxviii., No. 778, contains "Concio de Passione D. N. J. C. in Lingua Aymarensi Indica, in Missione Juliensi in Regno Peruano publice prolata a P. Bayer ... Latine reddita," which is also in Murr's "Journal," I., 277–334, III.; 55–104.

BAYER. Reis naar Peru door P. W. Bayer. *Amsterdam, W. Holtrop*, 1782. 8vo. 4044

BAYFIELD (Henry Wolsey) Sailing directions for the Gulf and River St. Lawrence; being the result of a survey made by order of the Lords Commissioners of the Admiralty. By Captain H. W. Bayfield. [Vol. I., 2d Ed.] *London*, 1843–47. 2 vols., 8vo. 4045

BAYFIELD. St. Lawrence Pilot, for the Gulf and River. Fourth Edition. *London*, 1860. 2 vols., 8vo. 4046

BAYFIELD. Pilote du golfe et du fleuve Saint-Laurent. Par H. W. Bayfield ... . 1e, 2e partie. ... Traduction par A. Legras. | 3e partie. ... Traduction par A. Mac-Dermott. ... *Paris, G Bossange et Cr*, 1863–65. 3 Parts. 8vo. 4047

BAYFIELD: Lake Superior. Early History, Situation, Harbor, &c. Ocean Commerce, Mineral & Agricultural Resources, Rail Roads, Stage Roads, &c. Climate of Lake Superior, Pre-Emption Lands, Invitation to Settlers. An Account of a Pleasure Tour to Lake Superior, Its Climate, Scenery, Pictured Rocks, Sailing Days of the Steamboats, Fare, &c. [*Philadelphia*], *May*, 1858. 8vo, pp. 14. S. 4048

BAYLEY (Abner). Sermon at the Ordination of the Rev. Mr. John Page Hawke, in Kingston, N. H., December 21, 1763. *Portsmouth*, 1764. 4to. 4049

BAYLEY (Daniel). The Essex Harmony; containing a collection of Psalm Tunes. Engraved. *Boston*, 1771. 12mo. + *Newburyport*, 1772. 12mo. *Newburyport*, 1785. + New Harmony of Zion, 1788. 8vo. 4050

Also: New and Complete Introduction to the Grounds and Rules of Music. *Newburyport*, 1764. 16mo. Psalm-Singer's Assistant ... . *Newbury-Port, the Author* [n. d.] Sm. 8vo, pp. 8, 16. (Music, engraved.) H. The Universal Harmony; or, a Compendium of Church Musick. *Newburyport*, 1773. 8vo. These are among the earliest American music books.

BAYLEY (F. W. N.) Four Years Residence in the West Indies. By F. W. N. Bayley. ... *London, William Kidd*, MDCCCXXX. 8vo, pp. xiii, 693. Plates. H. + Third Edition, enlarged. ... Added ... the Dreadful Hurricanes in Barbados, St. Vincent, and St. Lucia, in August, M.DCCC.XXXI. *London, Kidd*, M.DCCC.XXXIII. 8vo, pp. xiii., 1 l., 1 folded l., pp. 742. H. 4051

BAYLEY (J. R.) Memoirs of the Right Rev. Simon Wm. Gabriel Bruté, D.D. First Bishop of Vincennes, with Sketches describing his recollections of Scenes connected with the French Revolution, and Extracts from his Journal. By the Rt. Rev. James Roosevelt Bayley, D.D. Bishop of Newark. *New York, John Gilmary Shea*, MDCCCLX. 4to, pp. xi., 9–323. 9 Plates.

Fifty copies on large paper. Also a cheaper edition. *New York*, 1861. 12mo.

BAYLEY. A brief Sketch of the History of the Catholic Church of the Island of New York. *New-York, Dunigan & Bro.*, 1853. 18mo, pp. 156. C. 4053

BAYLEY (Kiah). ... A Sermon, preached at the Ordination of the Rev. Nathan S. S. Beman ... [over] the Third Congregational Church in Portland: March 14th, A.D. 1810. By Kiah Bayley ... . [n. p., n. d.] 8vo, pp. 24. H. 4054

Also: A Discourse on the Necessity and Importance of Wisdom and Knowledge, delivered at the opening of the Lincoln Academy in New-Castle, Oct. 1st, 1805. *Wiscasset*, 1805. 8vo. A Sermon Delivered before the Maine Missionary Society, ... June 23, 1813. By Kiah Bayley, Pastor of the Church in Newcastle. *Hallowell*, 1813 8vo, pp. 32. Two Discourses in Consequence of the War. *Hallowell*, 1812. 8vo.

BAYLEY (N.) English and Latine Exercises for School-Boys. ... By N. Bayley, School-master. The Fifth Edition, newly improv'd and Revis'd by several hands. *Boston, Printed by T. Fleet, for Samuel Phillips*, 1720. 12mo, pp. 208. 4055

One of the earliest American school-books.

BAYLEY (R.) An Account of the Epidemic Fever which prevailed in the City of New-York, during part of the Summer and Fall of 1795. By Richard Bayley. *New York*, 1796. 8vo, pp. 160. B. 4056

BAYLEY. Letters from the Health Office, submitted to the Common Council of the City of New York. By Richard Bayley. *New York*, 1798. 8vo, pp. 100. 4057

BAYLEY (S.) A Narrative of some remarkable Incidents in the Life of Solomon Bayley, formerly a Slave, in the State of Delaware, North America; written by himself, ... to which are prefixed, A Few Remarks by Robert Hurnard. *London, Harvey and Darton*, 1825. 12mo, pp. 68. + Second Edition, 1835. 12mo, pp. 68. 4058

BAYLIE (R.) A Dissvasive from the Errours Of the Time: Wherein the Tenets of the principall Sects, especially of the Independents, are drawn together in one Map ... . By Robert Baylie ... . *London, Samuel Gellibrand*, 1645. 4to, 12 p. l., 252.

The author was a friend of Roger Williams, and part of this interesting volume relates to the men and affairs of New England.

BAYLIES (Francis). Address before the Members of the Taunton Lyceum, delivered July 4, 1831. By Francis Baylies. *Boston*, 1831. 8vo, pp. 37. 4060

[BAYLIES.] Albany Argus Extra. Friday Oct. 23, 1828. ... A reply to the address of Gen. Peter B. Porter and others, to the Republican citizens of the State of New York. Part II., No. I. 8vo, pp. 9. 4061

Refers to Adams' administration.

BAYLIES. Eulogy on Lafayette, delivered in the Masonic Temple, Boston, October 9, 1834, at the request of the Grand Lodge of Freemasons in Massachusetts. By Francis Baylies. *Boston*, 1834. 8vo, pp. 48. B., H. 4062

BAYLIES. Eulogy on the Hon. Benjamin Russell, delivered before the Grand Lodge ... of Massachusetts, March 10, 1845. By Brother Francis Baylies. *Boston*, 1845. 8vo, pp. 66. 4063

BAYLIES (F.) An Historical Memoir of the Colony of New Plymouth. Vol. I. Part the First. From 1620 to 1641. || Vol. II. Parts II. III. IV. || By Francis Baylies. *Boston, Hilliard, Gray, Little, and Wilkins*, M DCCC XXX. 2 vols., 8vo, pp. xii., 321 (1); ix., 286, 2 l., 193, 2 l., 170. B. 4064

Reissued with the following title:

BAYLIES. An Historical Memoir of the Colony of New Plymouth, from the Flight of the Pilgrims into Holland in the Year 1608, to the Union of that Colony with Massachusetts in 1692. By Francis Baylies. With some Corrections, Additions, and a Copious Index, by Samuel G. Drake. ... *Boston, Wiggin & Lunt*, 1866. 2 vols., 8vo, Title, pp. xii., 321 (1), iii.–ix., 286; 4 p. l., 193, 2 l., 170, 145. 2 Portraits, 2 Maps, 1 folding l. 4065

This reissue of an old work, with new title-page, contains a Fifth Part by the editor, which is new matter. Parts I. and II. form Vol I.; Parts III. to V. form Vol. II.

BAYLIES. A Narrative of Major General Wool's Campaign in Mexico, in the Years 1846, 1847 & 1848. By Francis Baylies. ... *Albany, Little & Company*, 1851. 8vo, pp. 78. Portrait of Wool. S., H. 4066

BAYLIES. Nineteenth Congress. First Session. North West Coast of America. May 15, 1826. ... Mr. Baylies made the following Report. [*Washington*, 1826.] 8vo. 4067

BAYLIES. Some Remarks on the Life and Character of General David Cobb, ... delivered at the Taunton Lyceum. July 2d, 1830. By Hon. Francis Baylies. *Albany, J. Munsell*, 1864. 8vo, pp. 18. Portrait. 4068

One hundred copies printed.

BAYLIES. Speech of the Hon. Francis Baylies, before the Whigs of Taunton, on the 13th of Sept., 1837. *Taunton, Bradford & Amsbury*, 1837. 8vo, pp. 16. H. 4069

BAYLIES (William). An Oration ... at Middleborough, (Mass.) at a Meeting of the Federal Republicans, of the County of Plymouth ... July 4, 1808. By William Baylies. *Boston*, 1808. 8vo, pp. 24. H. 4070

BAYLIES. A View of the Proceedings of the House of Representatives of the United States in the Case of the Plymouth Election. ... By William Baylies. *Boston, printed by Greenough and Stebbins*, 1809. 8vo, pp. 44. H., S. 4071

BAYLOR (C. G.) "Direct Trade." Speech of C. G. Baylor, Esq., U. S. Consul, Amsterdam, delivered at the Invitation of ... the Legislature of ... Georgia, in the Hall of the House of Representatives, December, 1851. ... *Washington*, 1852. 8vo, pp. 31 (1). 4072

Annual Catalogue of ... Baylor University. Male Department. Independence, Texas ... . *Anderson*, 1852. 8vo. Continued. 4073

[BAYLY (James)]. A Brief Narrative Of some of the Brethren Of the second Church in Bradford: Aggrieved with the Rev. Mr. Balch's Doctrine & Administration; Containing Reasons why they Desire Advice of Neighbour Churches. *Boston; Rogers and Fowle*, 1746. 8vo, pp. 14. B. 4074

Signed "James Bayly, Jonathan Hale, Thomas Merrill, Jonathan Hopkinson."

BAYLY (Lewis), *Bishop of Bangor*. Practice of Piety. *Boston*, 1716. 12mo. 4075

This was translated into French, Italian, Dutch, German, Swedish, Welsh, Hungarian, and Polish. I cannot find the date of the first edition; the 11th was published in 1619, and the 71st in 1792. It was also translated into the language of the Massachusetts Indians, by John Eliot, with the following title:

BAYLY. Manitowompae | Pomantamoonk. | Sampwshanau | Christianoh | Uttoh woh an | Pomantog | wussikkitteahonat | God. | *Cambridge*, 1665. Sm. 8vo, pp. 397 (3). + *Cambridge.* | *Printed for the right Honerable Corperation in London* | *for the Gospelizing the Jndins, in New-England* [*sic*]. | 1685. | Sm. 8vo, pp. 333 (2).

Thomas' "History of Printing," I., 258 and 262, quotes a second edition, 1667, and a fourth edition, 1687.

BAYLY (Thomas Henry). Slavery in the Territories. Speech of Hon. T. H. Bayly, of Virginia, in the H. of R., May 16, 1848 ... . [1848]. 8vo, pp. 15. 4077

BAYLY. Speech of Mr. Bayley, of Virginia, on the Annexation of Texas; ... January 7, 1845. *Washington*, 1845. 8vo, pp. 15. 4078

Also: Speech ... on the Oregon Question ... in the House ... January 27, 1846. *Washington*, 1846. 8vo, pp. 15. H. Speech ... on the Harbor Bill, and in Reply to Hon. C. Hudson, of Massachusetts, on the Corn Trade of England ... March 11, 1846. *Washington*, 1846. 8vo, pp. 22. H. Speech ... on the Bill ... amendatory of the Tariff law of 1842. [*Washington*, n. d.] 8vo, pp. 16. H. Speeches ... on the French Resolutions, and upon the Question of Privilege. ... April 3, 10, 11, & 21, 1848. *Washington*, 1848. 8vo, pp. 24. H. The Mexican Treaty. Speech ... June 20, 1854. [n. p., n. d.] 8vo, pp. 7. H.

BAYLY (W.) The Original Astronomical Observations made in the Course of a Voyage to the Northern Pacific Ocean for the Discovery of a North East or North West Passage: wherein The North West Coast of America and North East Coast of Asia were explored. In ... the Resolution and Discovery, In ... [1776–80]. By Captain James Cooke ... and Lieutenant James King; and Mr. William Bayly ... . *London, P. Elmsly, and Mess. Mount and Page*, M DCC LXXXII. 4to, 6 p. l., pp. 351 (1). H. 4079

[BAYMAN.] Notes [by Robert Bayman] and Letters [by Mrs. A. Phelps Bayman] on the American War. By an English Lady. *London, William Ridgway*, 1864. 8vo, Title, pp. 82. H. 4080

BAYNE (P.) The Christian Life Social and Individual. By Peter Bayne, M.A. ... *London, Groombridge*, 1855. Post 8vo. + *London, Hogg & Sons*, 1859. Post 8vo. + *Boston, Gould and Lincoln*, 1857. 12mo, pp. 528. H. 4081

"Wilberforce," pp. 158–204.

BAYNE (Thomas). A Sermon delivered at Irasburgh, Vt., May 2, 1866, on the Occasion of the Death of the Hon. Ira Hayden Allen. By the Rev. Thomas Bayne. *Montpelier*, 1866. 8vo. 4082

BAYNE (W. M.) Description of Bayne's Gigantic Panorama of a Voyage to Europe, comprising Views of Boston; the Harbor; Halifax ... . *Boston*, 1848. 8vo, pp. 34. H. + *Philadelphia*, 1849. 8vo, pp. 46. 4083

BAZANCOURT (C. de). Le Mexique contemporain Par le baron de Bazancourt Domination espagnole et guerre d'indépendance 1519–1824 Histoire complète de ses révolutions 1824–1861 Campagnes du général américain W. Scott 1847 Cause de la guerre actuelle 1861–1862 *Paris, Amyot*, 1862. 12mo, 2 p. l., pp. 388. Map. B. 4084

BAZILE (L.) Le conseil des colons de Saint-Domingue, de leurs créanciers et ayans cause ... . *Paris, l'auteur*, 1826. 18mo. 4085

BAZLEY (Thomas). Cotton as an Element of Industry, its confined supply, and its extending consumption by increasing and improving agencies. By Thomas Bazley. *London*, 1852. 12mo, pp. 70. C. 4086

BAZY (S.) De la fabrication des sucres en France et aux colonies. *Paris, l'impr. de J. Didot aîné*, 1829. 8vo, pp. 80.

Be Patient! *See* [Clark (*Rev.* T. G.)]

BEACH (A. B.) Our Children: their Dangers, and our Duties. A Sermon ... in ... New York ... October 31, 1858. By the Rev. Alfred B. Beach ... . *New York*, 1858. 8vo, pp. 17. H. 4088

BEACH (D.) A Statement of Facts, concerning the Death of Samuel Lee, and the Prosecution of David Sanford, for Murder. By David Beach. ... *New-Haven, the Author* [1807]. 8vo, pp. 14. H. 4089

BEACH (G.) George Beach, and the Northampton [Mass.] Town Meeting. [n. p., 1825]. 8vo, pp. 8. 4090

BEACH (John). A Calm and Dispassionate Vindication of the Professors of the Church of England, against the abusive Misrepresentations and falacious Argumentations of Mr. Noah Hobart, in his late Address to them. Humbly offered to the Consideration of the good People of New-England, With a Preface by Dr. Johnson, and an Appendix containing Mr. Wetmore's and Mr. Caner's Vindication of their own Cause and Characters from the Aspersions of the same Author. By John Beach, A.M. Minister of the first Church of Christ in Reading. *Boston, Printed and Sold by J. Draper in Newbury-street*, 1749. 4to, Title, pp. viii., 75. 4091

BEACH. A Continuation of the Calm and Dispassionate Vindication of the Professors of the Church of England, against ... Mr. Noah Hobart, in his second Address to them. Humbly offered to ... the good People of New England. ... *Boston, D. Fowle*, 1751. 8vo, pp. 91 (3.) H. 4092

BEACH. A Friendly Expostulation, with all Persons concern'd in publishing A late Pamphlet, Entitled, The real Advantages which Ministers and People may enjoy, especially in the Colonies, by conforming to the Church of England. [Motto.] By John Beach, A.M. *New York, Printed and Sold by John Holt*, 1763. 8vo, 2 p. l., pp. 48. 4093

BEACH. Animadversions, Critical and Candid, on Some Parts of Mr. Beach's Late "Friendly Expostulation" in A Letter From a Gentleman in New England to his Friend in Pennsylvania. *New York, B. Mecom*, 1763. Sm. 8vo, pp. 12.

BEACH. Sermon at New Haven, Con. June 4, 1760, before the Clergy of the Church of England, at their Annual Convention. *Boston, James Parker & Co.*, 1760. 8vo, pp. 44, Appendix, xi. 4095

Also: Appeal to the unprejudiced From the injurious and uncharitable reflections of Mr. Jonathan Dickinson. *Boston, Printed in the Year* 1737. 12mo, pp. 106. An Attempt to prove that God is a Rewarder of all those who diligently seek him. Letter to Jedidiah Mills. *Boston*, 1748. 8vo, pp. 23. God's Sovereignty and his Universal Love to the Souls of Men reconciled; in Reply to Jonathan Dickinson's Remarks. *Boston*, 1747. 12mo. A Modest Enquiry into the State of the Dead. ... *New London, T. & J. Green*, 1755. 8vo, pp. (4), 43. B. Second Familiar Conference upon some Antinomian Tenets, Occasioned by Mr. David Judson's Remarks upon the first. *New York*, 1765. 8vo. A Second Vindication of God's Sovereign Free Grace Indeed. In a fair and candid examination of the last Discourse of the late Mr. Dickinson, ... With a Preface by Dr. Johnson. *Boston*, 1748. 8vo, pp. 82. N. A Sermon on the Duty of Loving our Enemies. 1738. Sermon upon the Decease of the Rev. Dr. Samuel Johnson, etc., who died January 6, 1772. *New-haven* [1772]. A Sermon, shewing, that Eternal Hope Is God's Free Gift, ... *Newport, Printed by the Widow Franklin*, 1745. 12mo, pp. 38. + *Reprinted.* 12mo, pp. 25. W.

BEACH (L.) A Word or two about the War. By Lewis Beach. *New York, John F. Trow* [n. d.] 8vo, pp. 28. 4096

BEACH (M. S.) The Letter List Advertising in New York City. Competition between The Sun and The Herald. *New York, Proprietors of the Sun*, 1858. 8vo, Title, pp. 16. H. 4097

BEACH (S. B.) Escalala, an American Tale, by Samuel B. Beach. *Utica, Wm. Williams*, 1824. 12mo, pp. 109. 4098

[BEACH (S. F.)] Argument. *See* [Wells (H. H.)]

Beach (W.) ... Rise ... of the New York Medical Institution and Reformed Medical Society of the United States. By W. Beach. *New-York*, 1830. 12mo, pp. 49. s. 4099

Beacon Hill. *See* [Morton (*Mrs.* S. W. A.)]

Beadle (D. W.) The American Lawyer ... containing a Map and Seal for each State in the Union. By Delos W. Beadle ... . *New York*, *Phelps & Fanning*, 1851. 12mo, pp. 358. 4100

Beadle. Der Amerikanische Sachwalter ... . *New York*, 1852. 12mo, pp. 360. Woodcuts. 4101

Among the "Dime Publications" of Irwin P. Beadle and Beadle and Company, the following deserve mention here: Dime Knapsack Songster; containing the choicest Patriotic Songs ... . *New York.* 18mo, pp. 72. Dime Military Song Book. ... Edited by Wm. Ross Wallace. *New York*, 18mo, pp. 72. Dime Military Song Book and Songs for the War. ... *New York.* 18mo, pp. 76. Dime Patriotic Speaker: ... Together with Poems for the Hour. *Beadle and Company*, *New York* [n. d.] 12mo, pp. 99. Dime Songs for the War ... *New York and London.* 18mo, pp. 72. Beadle's Dime Speakers Nos. 1 & 2. *New York.* 12mo, pp. 100. + Dime Patriotic Speaker, No. 3. *New York*, 12mo. + Dime Comic Speaker, No. 4. *New York.* 12mo. + Dime Song Book ... . *New York*, *Irwin P. Beadle* [1856]. 12mo. pp. 72. Dime Tales, Traditions, and Romance of Border and Revolutionary Times. Edward S. Ellis, Editor. 12mo, pp. 60. Dime Union Song Book. *New York.* 18mo, pp. 74.

Beadle (W. A.) Narrative of the Life of William Beadle, of Wethersfield, in the State of Connecticut. Containing, I. The Particulars of the "horrid Massacre" of himself and Family. II. Extracts from the Rev. Mr. Marsh's Sermon at the Funeral of his Wife and Children. *Hartford*, *Bavil Webster*, 1783. 12mo, Woodcut Title, pp. 24. + *Reprinted by Alden Spooner*, *Windsor*, *Vt.*, 1795. 12mo, pp. 24. W. 4102

I find the following title in one of Bumstead's catalogues: Letter from a Gentleman in Wethersfield, to his Friend, containing a Narrative of the Life of W. Beadle, and the Particulars of the Massacre of Himself and Family. 8vo.

Beadon (Richard). Sermon before the Incorporated Society for the Propagation of the Gospel in Foreign Parts, February 19, 1796. By Richard, Lord Bishop of Gloucester. *London*, 1796. 8vo, pp. 88. 4103

Beale (C. L.) Executive Protest, Prerogatives, and Patronage. Speech of Hon. Chas. L. Beale, of New York. Delivered in the House ... June 13, 1860. *Washington*, 1860. Large 12mo, pp. 12. H. 4104

Beale (E. F.) The Presidency. Speech of Lieut. E. F. Beale, Delivered at ... Chester ... November 7th, 1864. [n. p., n. d.] 8vo, pp. 9. H. 4105

Beale and **Heap.** Central Route to the Pacific from the Valley of the Mississippi to California. With numerous Engravings. By E. F. Beale and Gwin Harris Heap. *Philadelphia*, *J. B. Lippincott & Co.*, 1824. 8vo, pp. 136. 4106

Beale (S. T.) Trial and conviction of Dr. Stephen T. Beale, with the letters of Chief Justice Lewis, and Judges Black and Woodward, on his case. Interesting Ether cases, and letters of Professor Gibson, Professor Wiltbank, W. Badger, esq., W. L. Hirst, esq., Rev. Albert Barnes, Dr. Henry A. Boardman, &c. *Philadelphia*, 1855. 8vo. 4107

Beale (T.) A few observations on the Natural History of the Sperm Whale, with an Account of the Rise and Progress of the Fishery, and of the Modes of Pursuing, Killing, and "Cutting in" that Animal, with a List of its Favorite Places of Resort. By Thomas Beale ... . *London*, *Effingham Wilson*, 1835. 8vo, pp. 58 (2). B. 4108

Republished with the following title: ... Natural History of the Sperm Whale; its Anatomy and Physiology, Food, Spermaceti, Ambergris, Rise and Progress of the Fishery, "Cutting in" and "Trying out," description of Ships, Boats, &c. To which is added, a Sketch of a South-Sea Whaling Voyage. By Thomas Beale. *London*, 1839. Post 8vo. B. & C.

Beale. Trial of John Y. Beall, as a Spy and Guerrillero, by Military Commission. *New York*, *D. Appleton and Company*, 1865. 8vo, pp. 94. H. 4109

Beall. John Y. Beall, the Pirate Spy. By Lieut. Col. ——. *New York*, *T. R. Dawley*, 1865. 12mo, pp. 106. 4110

Beals (William). Trial of William Beals & Charles G. Greene, for an alleged Libel, published in the Boston Morning Post, on Alfred W. Pike, Preceptor of the Topsfield Academy, at the November Term of the Sup. J. Court, at Salem, before ... Judge Putnam. ... *Boston*, *Beals & Greene*, 1835. 8vo, pp. 52. H. 4111

Beaman (C. C.) A Poem: delivered ... January 17, 1831. Being the Birth-Day of Franklin. By Charles C. Beaman. ... *Boston*, *John H. Eastburn*, 1831. 8vo, pp. 12. H. 4112

Beaman (F. C.) Provisional Governments over the Districts of Country now in Rebellion against the Lawful Authority of the United States. Speech of F. C. Beaman of Michigan in the House of Representatives, April 4, 1862. 8vo, pp. 7. 4113

Beaman. Reconstruction. Speech of F. C. Beaman ... in the House of Representatives, March 22, 1864, on the Bill to guarantee to certain States, whose Governments have been usurped or overthrown, a Republican form of Government. *Washington*, 1864. 8vo, pp. 15. H. 4114

Beaman. Representation of Rebellious States. Speech of Hon. F. C. Beaman, of Michigan, in the House ... February 24, 1866. [*Washington*, n. d.] 8vo, pp. 8. H. 4115

Beames of Eternal Brightness, or Branches of Everlasting Blessings, to be spread over India and all Nations of the Earth, by John, who is called a Quaker. 1661. 4to. 4116

The India referred to includes America.

Beamish. The Discovery of America by the Northmen, In the Tenth Century, with Notices of the Early Settlements of the Irish in the Western Hemisphere. By North Ludlow Beamish ... . *London*, *T. & W. Boone*, 1841. 8vo, 8 p. l., pp. 239 (11), 1 l., 4to, folded. 2 Maps, and Plate. B., C., H.

This is a translation of a portion of Prof. Rafn's Antiquitates Americanæ.

Bean (C.) Report of the Committee of Claims, on the Petition of Charles Bean, Captain of Militia in Massachusetts. April 9th, 1810. Read. *Washington City*, 1810. 8vo, pp. 4. H.

Bean (J.) A Sermon Delivered at Wrentham, October 26, 1773, on compleating the first Century since the Town was incorporated. By Joseph Bean, A.M. ... *Boston*: *John Boyle*, MDCCLXXIV. 8vo, pp. 36. M. + [n. p., *Dec.*, 1834.] 8vo, pp. 16. H. 4119

Bear Valley. Report to the Legislature of Pennsylvania, containing a description of Bear Valley coal basin ... . *Harrisburg*, 1839. 16mo. 4120

"Bear Valley Coal Company." Reports of Prof. William F. Roberts ... [etc.] *Boston*, 1865. 8vo, pp. 73. Map. H.

Statistics connected with the Bear Valley Coal Region ... [n. p., n. d.] 8vo, pp. 32. 4121a

Bearcroft (Philip). A Sermon Preached before the Honorable Trustees For Establishing the Colony of Georgia in America, ... at their Anniversary Meeting. March 16, 1737–8. ... at London. By Philip Bearcroft, D.D. *London*, *Printed by John Willis*, M.DCC.XXXVIII. 4to, pp. 22. 4122

Bearcroft. Sermon preached before the Incorporated Society for the Propagation of the Gospel in Foreign Parts, at their Anniversary Meeting in the Parish Church of St. Mary-le-Bow, On Friday February 15. 1744. By Philip Bearcroft, D.D. Chaplain in Ordinary to His Majesty, and Secretary of the Society. *London*, MDCCXLIV. 4to, pp. 73. N. 4123

Beard (J. R.). ... A Discourse in Commemoration of the Extinction of Slavery in the British Colonies, On the 1st of August, 1838. By John R. Beard. *London*: *Smallfield and Son*, 1838. 12mo, pp. 18. H. 4124

Beard. The Life of Toussaint L'Ouverture, the Negro Patriot of Hayti: comprising an Account of the Struggle for Liberty in the Island, and a Sketch of its History to the Present Period. By the Rev. John R. Beard, D.D. ... With numerous Engravings. *London*, MDCCLIII. 12mo, pp. xi. (1), 335. 7 Plates, and Map. B., C. 4125

Beard. Toussaint l'Ouverture, de bevrijder der negers op Haïty. Naar het Engels door J. B. Rietsap. *Utrecht*, *N. de Zwaan*, 1853. 8vo. 4126

Beard (T.) Life of Mr. Thomas Beard, Wrote by Himself: With Some Account of his Death, Sept. 15, 1710. Soon after he had Compleated the 17th Year of his Age. *Printed first at London.* + *Boston*: *Reprinted for T. Hancock*, 1735. Title, pp. xvi., 47. 4127

Beardslee (G. W.) Rejection of the Application for a Reissue upon New and Amended Claims of the Letters Patent originally issued in 1838 to Barnabas Langdon ... . By George W. Beardslee. *Albany*; *Weed*, *Parsons and Company*, 1852. 8vo, pp. 39. H. 4128

Beardsley (E. E.) An Address delivered in St. Peter's Church, Cheshire, October 1, 1844, on occasion of the Fiftieth Anniversary of the Episcopal Academy of Connecticut. By Rev. E. E. Beardsley, M.A. *New Haven*, 1844. 8vo, pp. 46. H.

Beardsley. ... An Anniversary Discourse, delivered in St. Thomas' Church, New Haven, Easter Sunday, 1858. By Rev. E. E. Beardsley, D.D., Rector. *New Haven*: *Peck*, *White & Peck*, 1858. 8vo, pp. 16. 4129a

Beardsley. ... An Anniversary Discourse, delivered in ... New Haven, Easter Sunday, 1858. By Rev. E. E. Beardsley ... . *New Haven*: *Peck*, *White & Peck*, 1858. 8vo, pp, 16. H.

Beardsley. Commemorative Discourse, delivered in St. Thomas's Church, New Haven, the Sunday following the death of Bishop Brownell. By E. E. Beardsley, D.D. *New Haven*, *T. J. Stafford*, 1865. 8vo, pp. 20. 4130a

Beardsley. ... A Discourse, Commemorative of the Life and Services of the Rev. Stephen Jewett ... in ... New Haven, Conn. ... September 1, 1861, by Rev. E. E. Beardsley ... . *New Haven*: *Peck*, *White and Peck*, 1861. 8vo, pp. 16. H. 4131

Beardsley. ... A Discourse delivered at the Re-opening of St. Peter's Church, Cheshire, after Extensive Improvements, November 9th, 1864, By E. E. Beardsley, D.D., ... *New Haven*: *Thomas J. Stafford*, *Printer*, 1865. 8vo, pp. 15. 4131a

Beardsley. ... A Discourse delivered to the Pupils of the Episcopal Academy of Connecticut, (at Cheshire,) Friday Evening, November 20, 1863, by E. E. Beardsley, D.D., ... *New Haven*: *Thomas J. Stafford*, *Printer*, 1862. 8vo, pp. 20. 4131b

Beardsley. Historical Sermon delivered in St. Peter's Church, Cheshire, July 28th, 1839. By E. E. Beardsley. *Hartford*: *Case*, *Tiffany & Co.*, 1839. 8vo. pp. 16. 4131c

Beardsley. An Historical Address pronounced before the House of Convocation of Trinity College, in Christ Church, Hartford, July 30th, 1851, on occasion of the twenty fifth annual commencement of that Institution. By the Rev. E. E. Beardsley, M.A. ... *Hartford*, 1851. 8vo, pp. 31. 4132

Beardsley. The History of the Episcopal Church in Connecticut, from the Settlement of the Colony to the Death of Bishop Seabury. By E. Edwards Beardsley, D.D. ... *New York*, *Hurd & Houghton*, 1865. 8vo, pp. xxix., 470. B., C. 4133

Vol. II., bringing the history forward to the death of Bishop Brownell in 1865, is in press.

Beardsley. ... A Sermon, preached at the Consecration of Christ Church, Stratford, July 29th, 1858, by Rev. E. E. Beardsley ... . *New Haven*, 1858. 8vo, pp. 28. B., C. 4134

Beardsley. ... The Sermon at the Closing Services in St. Thomas' Chapel, New Haven ... March 12, 1854. By Rev. E. E. Beardsley ... *New Haven*, *George B. Bassett & Co.*, 1854. 8vo, pp. 12. H. 4135

Beardsley. ... A Sermon, Preached at the Consecration of Christ Church, Stratford, July 29th, 1858, by Rev. E. E. Beardsley, D.D., ... *New Haven*: *Peck*, *White & Peck*, 1858. 8vo, pp. 28. 4135a

Beardsley. A Sketch of William Beardsley: one of the original Settlers of Stratford, Conn., and a Record of his Descendants to the third generation; and of some who bear his name to the present time. By E. Edwards Beardsley, D.D. *New Haven*, *Bassett & Barnett*, 1867. 8vo, pp. 32. 4136

Beardsley (Levi). Remarks of Mr. L. Beardsley, in the Senate, in committee of the whole, on the bill to expediate the construction of the New-York and Erie Rail-road, April 20th, 1836. [n. p., n. d.] 8vo, pp. 9. 4137

Beardsley. Remarks of Mr. Beardsley, of New York, on the Right of Petition: delivered in the House ... January 5, 1844. *Washington*, 1844. 8vo, pp. 8. H. 4138

Beardsley (L.) Reminiscences; Personal and other Incidents; Early Settlement of Otsego County; Notices and Anecdotes of Public Men; Judicial, Legal, and Legislative Matters; Field Sports; Dissertations and Discussions. By Levi Beardsley ... . *New-York*, *printed by Charles Vinten*, 1852. 8vo, pp. x., 575. Portrait. 4139

Beardsley (S.) Opinion of the Hon. Samuel Beardsley, late chief justice of the State, and letter from Hon. William L. Marcy on the Canal Bill. *Albany*, 1851. 8vo, pp. 1 5. 4140

Also: Remarks ... on the Right of petition, delivered in the House of Representatives, January 5, 1844. *Washington*, 1844. 8vo, pp. 8. Speech ... on the resolution proposing to examine into the affairs of the Bank of the United States. ... March 7, 1832. 8vo, pp. 8. Speech ... May 9 and 10, 1832, upon the power of the House to punish for an alleged contempt and breach of privilege. 8vo, pp. 16. Speech ... 16th of January, 1834, on the subject of the Removal of the Public Deposites from the Bank of the United States. *Washington*, 1834. 8vo, pp. 15. Speech ... on a memorial from the inhabitants of the city of Utica and of the County of Oneida, New York, relative to the removal of the deposites, ... May 5, 1834. *Washington*, 1834. 8vo, pp. 6. Speech on the right of members to their Seats in the House of Representatives, ... February 8, 1844. *Washington*, 1844. 8vo, pp. 7. Report of the Beardsley Divorce Case. *New York* [n. d.] 8vo.

Beasley (*Rev.* Frederic), *A.M.* Sermon delivered before the Convention of the Protestant Episcopal Church in the State of New York, Oct. 4, 1808. *New York*, 1808. 8vo, pp. 32.

Beasley (M.) Elements of Geographical and Astronomical Science; with Alterations adapted to the Modern Divisions of Europe and South America, by T. Beasley. *London*, 1826. 8vo. 4142

Beasley (R. E.) A Plan to stop the Present and prevent Future Wars. By Rob't E. Beasley ... . Containing a Proposed Constitution for the General Government of the Sovereign States of North and South America. ... Published for the Author in English and Spanish. *Río Vista*, *Cal.*, 1864. 12mo, pp. 24. H.

Beatson (John). A Sermon, occasioned by that Branch of British Commerce which extends to the Human Species. By John Beatson. *Hull*, 1789. 8vo, pp. 64. S. 4144

Beatson (Robert). Naval and Military Memoirs of Great Britain, from the Years 1727 to the Present Time. By R. Beatson, Esq. *London*, *Strachan*, 1790. 3 vols., 8vo. + From 1727 to 1783. *London*, *Longman* [etc.], 1804–06. 6 vols., 8vo.

"Contains the whole series of naval and military events which occurred during the American Revolution."—Faribault. *See* M. R., IV., 198, 323; XLIX., 284.

Beatson (R. S.) The Plains of Abraham: Notes Original and Selected. By Lt. Col. R. S. Beatson. *Gibralter*, 1859. 8vo, pp. 48. Portraits of Wolfe and Montcalm. 4246

Beatty (Charles). Double Honor due to the Laborious Gospel Minister. Represented in a Sermon Preached at Fairfield in New Jersey the 1st of December, 1756. At the Ordination of the Reverend Mr. William Ramsey. Published at the Desire of the Hearers, By Charles Beatty. *Philadelphia*: *William Bradford*, 1756. 8vo. 4147

Beatty. ... Sermon Preached at Fairfield, in New-Jersey, the 1st of December, 1756. At the Ordination Of the Reverend Mr. William Ramsey. By Charles Beatty, Minister of the Gospel at Nishanung. *Philadelphia*, *William Bradford* [n. d.] 8vo, Half Title, pp. 56. 4148

Beatty. The Journal of a Two Months Tour; with a view of Promoting Religion among the Frontier Inhabitants of Pennsylvania, and of Introducing Christianity among the Indians to

the Westward of the Alegh-geny Mountains. To which are added, Remarks on the Language and Customs of some particular Tribes among the Indians, with a brief Account of the various attempts that have been made to civilize and convert them, from the first Settlement of New England to this Day; By Charles Beatty, A.M. ... *London*: *William Davenhill and George Pearch*, M DCC LXVIII. 8vo, pp. 110. C., H. 4149

Reprinted at the end of "Brainerd's Journal." *Edinburgh*, 1798. 8vo. This journal, though chiefly of a religious cast, is enlivened with many agreeable notes and circumstances relating to the manners and customs of the Delaware Indians, who, from certain similar customs and some traditions among them, the author conjectures to be the descendants of the ten tribes of Israel.

Beatty. Tagebuch einer Zween Reise ... Herausgegeben aus dem Englischen Von Carl Beatty A.M. und übersetzt. *Frankfurt und Leipzig*, *In Joh. Georg. Fleischers Buchhandlung*, 1771. 8vo, pp. 157. H. 4150

Beatty (M.) The Monitor; or, an address to the People of Great Britain, America, and Ireland, on the present Situation of affairs. By M. Beatty. *London*, *J. Debrett*, 1786. 8vo.

"A strange jumble of piety and politics."—M. R., LXXV., 256.

Beaty. The trial of Robert Beaty, (who was tarred and feathered), on an indictment for perjury. *Baltimore*, *Printed for the Proprietor*, 1809. 8vo, pp. 51. P. 4152

Beau. Catalogue des coquilles recueillies à la Guadeloupe et ses dépendances; par M. Beau ... précédé d'une introduction par M. P. Fisher. *Paris*, *imp. Paul Dupont*, 1858. 8vo, pp. 27.

Reprinted from the "Revue Coloniade," Dec., 1857.

Beau (C. le). *See* Le Beau.

Beauchamp (A. de). Histoire du Brésil, depuis sa découverte en 1500 jusqu' en 1810, contenant L'origine de la monarchie portugaise; le tableau du règne de ses rois, et des conquêtes des Portugais dans l'Afrique et dans l'Inde; la découverte et la description du Brésil, ... enfin, l'histoire civile, politique et commerciale, les révolutions et l'état actuel de cette vaste contrée. Par M. Alphonse de Beauchamp ... . *Paris*, *Alexis Eymery*, 1815. 3 vols., 8vo, pp. 39, 388; Title, pp. 500; Title, pp. 516 (1). Map, and 2 Plates. H. 4154

Some copies were printed on vellum paper. *See* M. R., LXXXV., 461.

Beauchamp. Histoire de la conquête et des révolutions du Pérou, par Alphonse de Beauchamp. Avec Portraits. *Paris*,

M. DCCC. VIII. 2 vols., 8vo, 2 p. l., pp. 280; 2 p. l., 272. H. + *Paris*, 1813. 2 vols., 8vo. + *Paris*, 1835. 2 vols., 8vo.

This work is said to be plagiarised from Southey's History of Brazil. Translated into Portuguese by the Abbe Ignacio Felizardo Fortes, with the following title:

BEAUCHAMP. Historia do Brasil, desde a sua descoberta im 1500 até 1810 escripta em francez, por M. de. Beauchamp. *Rio de Janerio, impressa regia*, 1818–19. 2 vols., 8vo. 4156

BEAUCHAMP. L'indépendance de l'empire du Brésil, présentée aux monarques européens; Par M. Alphonse de Beauchamp .... *Paris, Delaunay, juin*, 1824. 8vo, 2. p. l., pp. xv., 138 (1). S., H.

BEAUCHAMP. Réfutation de l'escrit intitulé: Coup d'œil sur l'état politique du Brésil au 12 Novembre 1825, considéré dans ses divers rapports avec le Portugal; publié à Londres en mars 1824. *Paris, Delaunay*, 1824. 8vo. 4158

BEAUCHAMP (Jeroboam O.) The Confession of Jeroboam O. Beauchamp, who was executed at Frankfort, Ky., 7th July, 1826, for the Murder of Col. Solomon P. Sharp, late att'y gen'l of Ky.; with Some Poetical Pieces by [his Wife] Mrs. Ann Beauchamp. *Bloomfield, Ky.*, 1826. 8vo. + *Kentucky, H. T. Goodsell* [1854]. 8vo, pp. 100. 4159

The Beauchamp Tragedy, in Kentucky. As detailed in the Confession of Jereboam O. Beauchamp; to which is added A Biographical Sketch of Col. Solomon P. Sharp, and a historical account of the Old Court and New Court Controversy, etc. The whole presenting a narrative of many exciting incidents in Kentucky life some thirty years ago. *New York, Dinsmore & Co.*, 1858. 12mo, p. x., 134. 4160

[BEAUCHAMP.] Kentucky Tragedy, Letters of Ann Cook, late Mrs. Beauchamp, to her Friend in England. Containing a short History of that remarkable Woman. *Washington*, 1826. 12mo, pp. 91. 4161

BEAUCHAMP. Kentucky Tragedy. A Full and Particular Account of the Lives and Tragical Deaths of Jeroboam O. Beauchamp, and Ann, his Wife, the Murderers of Col. Sharp. *Philadelphia* [n. d.] 18mo, pp. 32. 4162

BEAUCHAMP (*Lord*). *See* Lygon (W.)

BEAUCHENE. Les aventures de Monsieur Robert Chevalier dit de Beauchêne, capitaine de flibustiers dans la Nouvelle-

France, rédigées par monsieur Le Sage. *Paris, Est. Ganeau*, 1732. 2 vols., 12mo. + *Maestricht; Dufour et Roux*, 1783. + *Lille, Ch. F. J. Lehoucq*, an II. [1794]. 3 vols., 18mo. + Édition stéréotype, d'après le procédé d'Herhan. *Paris, Mme Dobo*, 1824. 2 vols., 18mo. 4163

"Ce n'est point une fiction, mais l'histoire singulière d'une capitaine de flibustiers, qui fut tué à Tours, par des Anglais, en 1731, rédigé d'après les mémoires fournis par sa veuve."—QUÉRARD.

BEAUCLERK. Lithographic News of military operations in Canada, under Sir John Colborne, during the late insurrection. By Lord Charles Beauclerk. *London*. 1840. 4to. S. 4164

[BEAUDRY (Hercules)]. Le Conseiller du Peuple ou Reflexions adressées aux Canadiens Français, par un Compatriote. *Montreal*, 1861. 12mo, pp. 281. 4165

BEAUFORT, *S. C.* Remonstrance of the Citizens of Beaufort District, S. C. against any further Increase of the Duties on Imports. ... *Washington*, 1828. 8vo, pp. 7. (20th Cong., 1st Sess., House, Doc. No. 28.) 4165a

BEAUFOY (Henry). The Speech of Mr. Beaufoy ... 18th June, 1788, in a Committee of the Whole House, on a Bill for Regulating the Conveyance of Negroes from Africa to the West-Indies. To which are added Observations on the Evidence adduced against the Bill. *London, J. Phillips*, M,DCC,LXXXIX. 8vo, 2 p. l., pp. 37. H. 4166

BEAUFOY. The Substance of the Speech of Henry Beaufoy, Esq. to the British Society for extending the Fisheries, &c. ... March 25, 1788. ... *London, T. Cadell* [etc.], 1788. 8vo, pp. 109. 4167

Relates only to the British fisheries; but there are some remarks strongly discouraging emigration to America.

[BEAUFOY.] Tour through parts of the United States and Canada. By a British Subject. *London, Longman*, 1828. 8vo, pp. 141. Map and Plates. 4168

"Henry Beaufoy, esq. sent me a copy of this book with a note stating that it was written by his brother, who had a few copies printed for distribution among his friends."—RICH.

BEAUFOY (M.) Mexican Illustrations, founded upon Facts; Indicative of the Present Condition of Society, Manners, Religion, and Morals, among the Spanish and Native Inhabitants of

Mexico: With Observations upon the Government and Resources of the Republic of Mexico, as they appeared during Part of the Years 1825, 1826, and 1827. Interspersed with Occasional Remarks upon the Climate, Produce, and Antiquities of the Country, Mode of Working the Mines, &c. By Mark Beaufoy .... *London; Carpenter and Son*, 1828. 8vo, pp. xii., 310. Map and 6 Plates. B., P. 4169

BEAUFOY (*Mr.*) Memoire au Soutien de l'appel de la fabrique de N. D. de Montréal. *Montréal*, 1867. 8vo, pp. 29.

BEAUGÉ. Lettre écrite par M. Beaugé, habitant au Limbé, dépendance de la partie du nord de Saint-Domingue, à M. de Montdion, citoyen de Paris, en date du 5 août 1790. [n. p., n. d.] 8vo, pp. 40, or less. 4171

BEAUJOUR (*Baron* Louis Philippe Félix de). Aperçu des États-Unis, au commencement du XIXe. siècle, depuis 1800 jusqu'en 1810, avec des tables statistiques. Par le Chevalier Félix de Beaujour .... *Paris, L. G. Michaud*, [also] *Delaunay*, M. DCCC. XIV. 8vo, pp. 274. Map, 17 Plates, folded. H. 4172

BEAUJOUR. Sketch of the United States of North America, at the Commencement of the Nineteenth Century, from 1800 to 1810; with Statistical Tables, and a New Map, by the Author; containing all the Late Discoveries, and exhibiting the Division of Territorial Zones, Boundary Lines, &c. By le Chevalier Felix de Beaujour .... Translated from the French. With Illustrative Notes and Appendix. By William Walton, Esq. *London; J. Booth* [etc.], 1814. 8vo, pp. xx., 363, 17 l., 4to, folded. Map. C., H. 4173

See N. A. R., II., 68.

[BEAULIEU (Charles Gillston de)]. De la nécessité de rendre nos colonies francaises indépendantes, et de supprimer notre acte de navigation; par C.-G.-D.-B. *Paris* [n. d.] 12mo. 4174

BEAUMARCHAIS (Emélie Eugénie). The Daughter of Pierre Augustin de Beaumarchais, to the Hon. the members of the Senate and House of Representatives of the United States. *Paris, Oct.* 20, 1822. 4to, pp. 4. 4175

BEAUMARCHAIS. Report of the Committee on Claims, on the Petition of E. E. Beaumarchais, March 10, 1806. 8vo, pp. 113. [Congressional Document.] 4176

[BEAUMARCHAIS (Pierre Auguste Caron de)]. Influence du despotisme de l'Angleterre sur les deux mondes. *Boston, Londres et Paris*, 1781. 8vo. 4177

"Attributed to Beaumarchais by Chardon de la Rochette, but not included in the 'Œuvres' of Beaumarchais."—QUÉRARD.

[BEAUMARCHAIS.] Le vœu de toutes les nations, et l'intérêt de toutes les puissances, dans l'abaissement et l'humiliation de la Grande-Bretagne. Seconde édition, corrigée par l'Auteur. [n p., 1778.] 8vo, Half Title, pp. 74. H. 4178

BEAUMARCHAIS. Claim of De Beaumarchais' Heir Against the United States. *Paris, J. Smith*, 1822. 8vo, pp. 56. W.

BEAUMARCHAIS. Memorial and Claim of Amélie Eugénie Caron de Beaumarchais, wife of André Toussaint De La Rue, heir and representative of Caron de Beaumarchais, for a balance due his estate for sundry arms, ammunition, &c. furnished the United States during the war between Great Britain and America. *Richmond*, 1801. Sm. 4to, pp. 34. C. 4180

BEAUMARCHAIS. Memorial on the subject of the claim of Caron Beaumarchais. February 1807. (Cong. Doc., 1807.)

BEAUMARCHAIS. Observations sur le Memoire justicatif de la cour de Londres (ou Apologie de la conduite de la France, relativement à l'insurrection des colonies anglaises). Par P. A. Caron de Beaumarchais, Armiteur et Citoyen Français. *A Londres, à Philadelphie et se trouve par tout*, 1779. 4182

Also included in his "Œuvres," of which there are many editions.

BEAUMONT (Arthur J.) An American's Defence of his Government, in an appeal to the Common Sense of the nations of Europe. By Arthur J. Beaumont, a citizen of the United States of North America. *London*, 1831. 8vo, pp. 36. + *Paris, printed by Fain*, 1831. 8vo, pp. 68. C. 4183

BEAUMONT. De la Constitution américaine, et de quelques calomnies dont elle a été l'obiet de nos jours. Par A. J. Beaumont. *Paris; Bennis, Papinot*, 1831. 8vo, pp. 60. C. 4184

BEAUMONT (*Baron* de). Lettre à M. le comte Molé, sur la question mexicaine. *Paris, Bohaire*, 1839. 8vo, pp. 36. 4185

BEAUMONT. Resumé et solution de la question mexicaine, pour servir de discussion sur les crédits supplémentaires. Par le Baron de Beaumont. *Paris, Bohaire*, 1839. 8vo, pp. 40.

BEAUMONT (G. A. O.) Eulogy on the Life and Character of Wm. Henry Harrison ... delivered at ... Chicago, in the Presbyterian Church ... on the 14th Day of May, 1841. By Geo. A. O. Beaumont, Esq. *Chicago*, 1841. 12mo, pp. 12. H.

BEAUMONT (Gustave de la Bonninière de). Marie, ou l'esclavage aux États-Unis: tableau des mœurs américaines. Par Gustave de Beaumont ... *Paris*, 1835. 2 vols., 8vo. + *Bruxelles, L. Hauman*, 1835. 2 vols., 12mo, pp. 390; 2 p. l., pp. 324 (2). + Seconde édition, revue et corrigée. *Paris*, 1835. 2 vols., 8vo. + Troisième édition, corrigee. *Paris*, 1836. 2 vols., 8vo. + Quatrième édition. *Paris, Charles Gosselin*, 1840. 2 vols., 18mo. + Cinquième édition. *Paris, Ch. Gosselin*, 1842. 12mo. + *Bruxelles*, 1844. 2 vols., 8vo. 4188

Highly commended in the "Quarterly Review," LIII., 289. *See*, also, Rich, II., 273.

BEAUMONT. Nordamerikanische Bilder und Zustände. Deutsch von Spazier. *Weimar, Voigt*, 1836. 2 vols., 8vo. 4189

BEAUMONT and TOCQUEVILLE (A. de). Du système pénitentiaire aux États-Unis, et de son application en France; suivi d'un appendice sur les colonies pénales et de notes statistiques. Par MM. G. de Beaumont et A. de Tocqueville. ... *Paris, H. Fournier jeune*, 1833. 8vo, 2 p. l., pp. viij., 439. 5 Plates. H. + Seconde édition, entièrement refondue et augmentée d'une introduction .... *Paris, Ch. Gosselin*, 1836. 2 vols., 8vo, 49¾ sheets. 5 Plates. + Troisième édition. *Paris, Ch. Gosselin*, 1845. 12mo, 18¾ sheets. + [Another] Troisième édition ... augmentée. *Bruxelles; Hauman, Cattoir et compa*, 1837. 2 vols., 12mo. B. 4190

BEAUMONT. On the Penitentiary System in the United States, and its Application in France; with an Appendix on Penal Colonies, and also, Statistical Notes. By G. de Beaumont and A. de Tocqueville .... Translated from the French, with an Introduction, Notes and Additions. By Francis Lieber. *Philadelphia: Carey, Lea & Blanchard*, 1833. 8vo, pp. xlvii., 301. H. 4191

BEAUMONT. Amerika's Besserungs-System, und dessen Anwendung auf Europa mit einem Anhange über Straf-Ansiedelungen und zwei und zwanzig Beilagen, Aus dem Französischen der Herren G. v. Beaumont und A. de Tocqueville nebst Erweiterungen und Zusätzen von Dr. N. H. Julius. *Berlin*,

Theod. Ch. Fried. Enslin, 1833. 8vo, pp. xxxviii., 458 (1). 4 Plates and 1 Table. B. 4192

BEAUMONT. Om Bodssystemet i de Forenede Stater og om dets Anvendelse i Frankrige, overs. af N. A. Colban. *Christiania, Dahl*, 1839. 8vo. 4193

BEAUMONT (J. A. B.) Travels in Buenos Ayres, and the Adjacent Provinces of the Rio de la Plata. With Observations intended for the Use of Persons who contemplate Emigrating to that Country; or, Embarking Capital in its Affairs. By J. A. B. Beaumont, Esq. *London, James Ridgway*, MDCCCXXVIII. 8vo, pp. xii., 270. Map. H. 4194

[BEAUMONT DE BRIVAZAC.] L'Europe et ses colonies, en décembre 1819. *Paris, Brissot-Thivars*, 1820. 2 vols., 8vo. + Seconde édition. *Paris, Chasseriau*, 1822. 2 vols., 8vo. 4195

BEAUMONT (S. van). Pertinente beschrijvinge van Guiana, gelegen aan de vaste kust van Amerika. *Amsterdam*, 1676. 4to.

BEAUPORT. Report of the Commissioners of the Temporary Lunatic Asylum, at Beauport, January, 1849. [n. p.] 1849. 8vo, pp. 29. 4197

BEAUREGARD. Gen. Beauregard's Official Report of the "Battle of Manassas." *Richmond*, 1861. Sm. 8vo, pp. 29.

BEAUREGARD. Report of General G. T. Beauregard of the Defense of Charleston, Published by order of Congress. *Richmond, R. M. Smith, Public Printer*, 1864. 8vo, pp. 93. 4199

These two reports are very scarce, having been mostly destroyed by fire.

The Beauregard Songster, being a collection of Patriotic, Sentimental and Comic Songs. Arranged by Hermann L. Schreiner. *Published by John C. Schreiner & Son, Macon and Savannah, Ga.*, 1864. 18mo, pp. 36. 4200

BEAUREPAIRE. *See* Quesnay de Beaurepaire.

BEAUREPAIRE-ROHAN (*M.* de) Viagem de Cayabâ ao Rio de Janeiro, pelo Paraguay, Corientes. *S. Paulo*, 1847. 8vo, pp. 19. 4201

Title from Demarsay Hist. Paraguay, p. 147.

Beautes de L'Histoire d'Amérique, d'apres les plus celèbres voyageurs et géographes qui ont écrit sur cette partie du monde

par G*** .... *Paris, Alexis Eymery*, 1818. 2 vols., 12mo, Half Title, Front., Eng. Title, pp. 315; Half Title, Front., Eng. Title, 392. + *Paris*, 1828. 2 vols., 12mo. Engravings.

The Beauties and Deformities of Fox, North, and Burke, selected from their Speeches, from the Year 1770 down to the Present Time, 1784. 12mo. 2 Plates. + Third Edition. *London*, 1784. + Seventh Edition. *London*, 1784. 12mo, pp. 83. 2 Plates. 4203

Chiefly relative to American affairs.

The Beauties of American History. By the Author of Evenings in Boston, etc. *Hartford*, 1850. 12mo. 4204

The Beauties of Brother Bull-us. By his Loving Sister, Bull-a. *New York, James Eastburn*, 1812. 24mo, pp. (2), 93. B. 4205

"I propose to extract the most excellent effusions of the 'Diverting History of John Bull and Brother Jonathan,' and accompany them with suitable comments."—*Preface*.

Beauties of Poor Richard's Almanack, for the Year 1760. *Boston* [1760]. 12mo. W. 4206

Beauties of the British Senate; taken from the Debates of the Lords and Commons. *London*, 1782–1784. 2 vols., 8vo, pp. xvi., 307; viii., 351. 4207

American Affairs, Vol. I., 91–109. Another edition, to the end of the 2d session of the administration of W. Pitt. *London*, 1786.

BEAUVAIS (J. A.) A statement of Facts respecting a contract made with Rev. Wheelock Craig, Pastor of the Trinitarian Church, New Bedford. By Jos. Arthur Beauvais. 1863. *New Bedford*, 1863. 8vo, pp. 8. 4208

BEAUVALLET (Léon). Rachel et le nouveau monde, promenade aux États-Unis et aux Antilles. Par Léon Beauvallet. *Paris, A. Cadot*, 1856. 16mo, pp. viii., 304. 4209

BEAUVALLET. Rachel and the New World. A Trip to the United States and Cuba. Translated from the French of Léon Beauvallet. *New York: Dix, Edwards & Co.*, 1856. 12mo, pp. xiv., 404. H. 4210

BEAUVOIS (A. M. F. J.) Catalogue Raisonné du Museum de Mr. C. W. Peale. *Philadelphia*, 1800. 8vo. 4211

BEAUVOIS (Eugène). Découvertes des Scandinaves en Amérique, du dixième aux treizième et quatorzième siècles, fragments de sagas irlandaises, traduits pour la première fois en français, par E. Beauvois .... *Paris, Challomel aîné*, 1860. 8vo, pp. 77.

From the "Revue orientale et américaine."

BEAVEN (J.) Recreations of a Long Vacation, or a Visit to Indian Missions in Upper Canada. By James Beaven, D.D. *Toronto*, 1846. 12mo. + *London, Burns*, 1847. 12mo, pp. 196. S. 4213

BEAVEN (Samuel). The Religious Liberties of the Christian Laity Asserted. By Samuel Beaven. *Newport, R. I.*, 1753. 16mo. W. 4214

BEAVER MEADOW Railroad and Coal Co. Reports. *Philadelphia*, 1845, and continued. P. 4214a

BEAVER (B.), *pseudon*. Adventures of Dick Onslow among the Red Skins. *London, Dean*, 1862. 12mo. 4215

BECERRA TANCO (L.) Felicidad de México, en el principio y milagroso origen que tuvo el Santuario de la Virgen Maria Nrâ. Srâ. de Guadalupe extramuros: en la Aparicion admirable de esta Soberana Señora y de su prodigiosa Imagen. Sacada a luz y añadida, por el Br. Luis Becerra Tanco .... *Sevilla, por Tomás Lopez de Haro*, 1685. 4to, less than 30 l. 4216

The first edition was probably published before 1672, when the author died. A second edition was published in *Mexico* about 1675, with a preface and posthumous additions from the author's papers, and edited by Antonio Gama. It was reprinted in the "Coleccion" of Torres Tuñon, *Madrid*, 1785. *See* Bartolache's "Manifiesto," pp. 8–12, 55.

BÉCHAMEL. Voyage to Guiana. *See* Acuña.

BÉCHARD (Ferdinand). Lois municipales des républiques de la Suisse et des États-Unis. Par Ferdinand Béchard. *Paris, Giraud et Dagneau*, 1852. 18mo, 12 sheets. 4217

BECHER (A. B.) The Landfall of Columbus on his First Voyage to America with a Translation of the Baron Bonnefoux's History of his Previous Life also a Chart showing his Track from the Landfall to Cuba and an Outline of his Subsequent Voyages By A. Becher ... *London, J. D. Potter*, 1856. 8vo, pp. xxvi. (1), 376. Plate, and Maps. B. 4218

See New Q. R., October, 1856, 468.

Becher. Navigation of the Pacific Ocean, ... being a Brief Account of the Winds, Weather, and Currents ... by A. B. Becher ... . *London, J. D. Potter*, MDCCCLX. 8vo, pp. viii., 132. 2 Maps. H. 4219

Becher (C. C.) Mexico in den ereignissvollen Jahren 1832 und 1833 und die Reise hin und zurück, aus vertrautlichen Briefen, mit einer Anhange über die neuesten Ereignisse ... nebst mercantileschen und statistischen Notizen. Von C. C. Becher. *Hamburg [Perthes, Besser und Maucke]*, 1834. 8vo. Plate, and Map. 4220

Becher (Johann Joachim). Politische Discvrs von den eigentlichen Ursachen des Auf- und Abnehmens der Städte, Länder, und Republicken. *Franckfurt*, 1668. 8vo.+[*Id.*] 1673. 8vo. + *Franckfurt, Zunner*, 1688. 8vo, 82 sheets.+Vierdte Auflage, *Leipzig*, [also] *Jena, Bielck*, 1721. 8vo, 82 sheets.+Neuvermehrte und durch Herr Cammerrath Zincken verbesserte Auflage. *Zell, Gsellius*, 1753. 8vo.+Aufs Neue edirt von E. G. H. Zink. *Leipzig*, 1754. 8vo.+*Marburg, Krieger*, 1759. 8vo. 4221

Bechler (G. R.) Atlas showing Battles, Engagements, and Important Localities connected with the Campaigns in Virginia, completing the Campaign Map designed, engraved, and published by Gustavus R. Bechler. *Philadelphia, F. Leypoldt* [1864]. Oblong 8vo, pp. 7. 18 Plates. C. 4222

Bechteln. Kurzer | Catechismus | Vor etliche | Gemeinen Jesu | Aus der | Reformirten Religion | In Pennsylvania, | Die sich zum alten Berner Synodo halten : | Herausgegeben von | Johannes Bechteln, | Diener des Worts Gottes. | *Philadelphia*, | *Gedruckt bey Benjamin Franklin*, 1742. | 24mo, pp. 42. 4223

In the Nuggets, No 496, this book is priced at £10 10s., and is said to be unique. I have sold five copies, at about five dollars each.

Beck (Abraham). Western Land Agency and Commission Office, St. Louis, Mo. *St. Louis*, 1820. 16mo, pp. 32. 4224

Beck (J. B.) An Historical Sketch of the state of Medicine in the American Colonies, from their First Settlement to the Period of the Revolution ... by John B. Beck, M.D. ... . *Albany, J. Munsell*, 1842. 8vo, pp. 35.+Second Edition. *Albany*, 1850. 8vo, pp. 63. H. 4225

Also in the Transactions of the Medical Society of the State of New York, 1830. 8vo, pp. 41–99. H.

Beck. A Letter on the Establishment of a New Medical School in connection with Columbia College, 1832. By John B. Beck ... . *New York*, 1832. 8vo, pp. 8. B. 4226

Beck (Lewis C.) An Account of the Salt Springs at Salina, in Onondaga County, State of New York ... . By Lewis C. Beck, M.D. ... . *New-York*, 1826. 8vo, pp. 36. B., S. 4227

Reprinted from "New York Med. and Phys. Journal," No. 18.

Beck. Botany of the Northern and Middle States ... . arranged according to the Natural System. By Lewis C. Beck ... . *Albany, printed by Webster and Skinner*, 1833. 12mo, pp. lv., 471. H. 4228

Beck. Botany of the United States of America, arranged according to the Natural System. By Lewis C. Beck, M.D. *New York*, 1848. 12mo. 4229

Beck. Botany of the United States north of Virginia; comprising descriptions of the flowering and fernlike Plants hitherto found in those States. By Lewis C. Beck. Second Edition. *New York, Harpers*, 1848. 12mo, pp. xiii., 480. C.+Third edition, revised and enlarged. *New York*, 1856. 12mo, pp. 471. C. 4230

Beck. A Gazetteer of the States of Illinois and Missouri; containing a General View of each State—a General View of their Counties and a Particular Description of their Towns, Villages, Rivers, &c. &c. With a Map, and other Engravings. By Lewis C. Beck, A.M. ... *Albany, Charles R. and George Webster*, 1823. 8vo, pp. 352. Map and 5 Plates. H. 4231

Beck. Geographical Botany of the United States. By Lewis C. Beck, M.D. [*New York*], 1828. 8vo. P. 4232

Beck. Mineralogy of New-York ... . By Lewis C. Beck ... . *Albany*, 1842. 4to, pp. xxiv., 1 l., pp. 536, 2 l. Woodcuts, and 8 Plates. B. 4233

With a second title-page, engraved, "Natural History of New York. ..." Usually lettered "Natural History of New York. Part 3."

Beck. Report on the Breadstuffs of the United States, made to the Commissioner of Patents, by Lewis C. Beck, M.D. *Washington*, 1849. 8vo, pp. 31. B. 4234

[Beck (Nicholas F.)] Considerations in Favour of the Construction of a Great State Road, from Lake-Erie to the Hudson-River. By a Citizen of New-York. *Albany*, 1827. 8vo, pp. 48. B. 4235

[Beck (Paul), *Jr.*] A Proposal for altering the Eastern Front of the City of Philadelphia, with a view to prevent the recurrence of Malignant Disorders, on a Plan conformable to the Original Design of William Penn. By a Citizen of Philadelphia. *Philadelphia, W. Fry*, 1820. 8vo, pp. 11. Plan.

Beck (T.) Eulogium on the Life and Services of Simeon De Witt, Surveyor General of the State of New-York, Chancellor of the University, &c. &c. &c. By T. Romeyn Beck, M.D. *Albany, E. W. and C. Skinner*, 1835. 8vo, pp. 29. B., H., S. 4237

Beck (Theodoric R.), *M.D.* Statistics of the Medical Colleges of the United States. By T. Romeyn Beck, M.D. 1839. *Albany, Joel Munsell*, 1839. 8vo, pp. 64. B. 4238

Beck (R.) Sermon at Amherst, Oct. 2, 1782, at the Ordination of David Parsons. By R. Beck. *Springfield*, 1783. 8vo.

Beck-Bernard (*Mme* Amélie Lina). La Rio-Parana; cinq années de séjour dans la république argentine. *Paris, Grassart*, 1864. 12mo. 4240

Beck-Bernard (Charles). La république argentine. *Lausanne: Delafontaine et Rouge*, 1865. 12mo. 4241

Becker (Abraham). Address delivered at Worcester, N. Y., July 26, 1852, on the occasion of the burial of Capt. Leslie Chase, of the United States Army, by Abraham Becker, Esq., and Poem delivered on the same occasion by Robert F. Queal. *Albany*, 1852. 8vo, pp. 23. S. 4242

Becker. Address before the ... Citizens of Charlotteville, N. Y., July 5, 1852, at their celebration of the seventy-seventh anniversary of American Independence. By Abraham Becker. *Albany*, 1862. 8vo. C. 4243

Becker (George.) Speech delivered at the Freshman Prize Debate ... Yale College, Jan. 17, 1857, by George Becker ... . ["Ought Politics to be Discussed in the Pulpit?"] *Albany*, 1857. 4to, pp. 11. H. 4244

[Becker (Gottfried Wilhelm)]. Südamerika wie es war und wie es jetzt ist; oder Ursprung und Fortgang der Revolution daselbst bis 1819. *Leipzig, Rein*, 1820. 8vo. 4245

Becket (Thomas). Journal of a Voyage round the World in His Majesties Ship Endeavour, In the Years 1768, 1769, 1770 and 1771; undertaken in Pursuit of Natural Knowledge, at the Desire of the Royal Society, containing all the various occurrences of the voyage; With Descriptions of several new Discovered Countries in the Southern Hemisphere, and accounts of their Soil and Productions; and of many singularities in the Structure, Apparel, Manners, Customs, Policy, Manufactures &c. of their Inhabitants. To which is added a concise vocabulary of the Language of Otahitee. *London*, MDCCLXXI. Rl. 4to, pp. 133. 4246

Beckett (S. B.) Guide Book of the Atlantic and St. Lawrence, and St. Lawrence and Atlantic Railroads, including a Full Description ... of the White Mountains, by S. B. Beckett ... . *Portland: Sanborn & Carter*, 1853. 18mo, pp. vi. (3), 8–180. Map and Woodcuts. B. 4247

Beckford (Wm.) A Descriptive Account of the Island of Jamaica: with Remarks upon the Cultivation of the Sugar-Cane, throughout the different Seasons of the Year, and chiefly considered in a Picturesque Point of View; also, Observations and Reflections upon what would probably be the Consequences of an Abolition of the Slave-Trade, and of the Emancipation of the Slaves. By William Beckford, Esq. ... *London: T. and J. Egerton*, M,DCC,XC. 2 vols., 8vo, 2 p. l., pp. lx., 404; 2 p. l., 405. H. 4248

"The Author resided for several years in Jamaica, and was largely concerned in its plantations and traffic; his work, in consequence, contains much valuable information."—Rich, I., 362.

Beckford. Vues pittoresques de la Jamaïque, avec une description détaillée de ses productions, surtout des cannes à sucre, des travaux, du traitement et des mœurs des nègres, etc. Traduit de l'anglois par J. S. P. *Genève, Barde*, 1792. 2 vols., 8vo.+*Lausanne*, 1793. 2 vols., 12mo.+*Paris, La Villette*, 1793. 2 vols., 12mo, pp. 190; 224. 4249

Beckford. Mahlerische Beschreibung der Insel Jamaica aus dem Englischen. *Berlin, Voss*, 1790. 2 vols., 8vo. 4250

Heinsius has the date 1790; Kayser, 1791.

Beckford. Remarks upon the Situation of Negroes in Jamaica, impartially made From a local Experience of nearly Thirteen Years in that Island, by W. Beckford, jun. ... *London, T. and J. Egerton*, MDCCLXXXVIII. 8vo, pp. viii., 99. H. 4251

See Rich, I., 348; M. R., LXXIX, 69.

Beckley (Hosea). The History of Vermont; with Descriptions, Physical and Topographical. By Rev. Hosea Beckley, A.M. *Brattleboro, Geo. H. Salisbury*, 1846. 12mo, pp. 396.

Beckmann (Joh.) Litteratur der älteren Reisebeschreibungen. Nachrichten von ihren Verfassern, von ihrem Inhalte, von ihren Ausgaben und Uebersetzungen. ... Von Johann Beckmann ... . *Göttingen, Johann Frederick Röwer*, 1807–10. 8 Bde in 8 Stücke, 8vo, pp. xii., 750; vi., 756. H. 4253

This is the title of the Stücke; the title of the Bände reads: "... Reisebeschreibungen. Von Johann," etc.

Beckmann (Johann). Voyages dans les Colonies du melieu de L'Amérique-Septentionale, par Jean Beckmann; traduits de l'Allemand. *Lausanne*, 1798. 8vo. 4254

Beckmann or Becmann (Johann Christoph). Historia Orbis Terrarum, geographica et civilis ... . *Francofurti ad Oderam*, 1673. 4to. + Editio tertia correctior. *Francofurti ad Oderam et Lipsiæ, Zimmermann*, 1685. 4to, 107 sheets.+Editio quinta. *Francofurti et Lipsiæ, apud Henr. Joh. Meyeri Hered.*, 1698. 4to.+[*Id.*] 1707. 4to. 4255

Like all the general geographies, has some chapters on the New World.

Beckwith (C.) Arguments in the Case of Isaac H. Burch vs. Mary W. Burch. By C. Beckwith, Esq., and Hon. O. W. [H.?] Browning. *Chicago: Scott & Company, Printers*, 1861, 8vo, 2 p. l., pp. 162, 91. B. 4256

Beckwith (E. G.) Explorations on a Voyage from Great Salt Lake to California. With geological report and description of organic remains by J. Schiel. *Washington*, 1854. Imp. 4to, pp. 114. 4 Plates. 4257

Beckwith. Report of Exploration of a Route for the Pacific Railroad, near the 38th and 39th Parallels of Latitude, from the Mouth of the Kansas to Sevier River, in the Great Basin. By Lieut. E. G. Beckwith ... . [*Washington*, 1854 or

1855.] 8vo, 2 p. l., pp. 149. 2 Maps. 33d Cong., 1st Sess. House Doc., 129.) B., H. 4258

Also, in the same document: Report of Explorations of a Route for the Pacific Railroad, on the Forty-first Parallel of North Latitude. pp. 136. And in 33d Cong., 2d Sess., Ex. Doc., Vol. XI., Part 2, the same reports are printed in 4to, one with colored, the other with uncolored plates. H.

Beckwith (G.) ... A Sermon Preached before the General Assembly of ... Connecticut, May 13th, 1756. Being the Day of the Anniversary Election there. By George Beckwith ... . *New London, T. Green*, 1756. Sm. 8vo, pp. 64. H. 4259

Also: The Invalidity or Unwarrantableness Of Lay Ordination ... . *New-London, Printed by Timothy Green*, 1763. Sm. 8vo, pp. 79. H. (*See* especially pp. 56–76.)+ Second Letter on the subject of Lay Ordination. *New London, Conn.*, 1766. 12mo.

Beckwith (G.) Number 20. 1867 ... . Beckwith's Almanac. Calculated for Connecticut and Adjacent States. By George Beckwith, Phonographer. ☞ Survivor of Beers, Middlebrook and Prindle. ☜ ... *New Haven, Conn., H. C. Peck* [n. d.] 18mo, pp. (72). H. 4260

Beckwith (G. C.) Eulogy on William Ladd, late President of the American Peace Society. By George C. Beckwith. ... *Boston, Whipple & Damrell*, 1841. 8vo, pp. 23. H. 4261

Beckwith. The Peace Manual, or War and its Remedies. By G. C. Beckwith. *Boston*, 1847. 18mo. C. 4262

Beckwith. A Universal Peace Society, with the Basis of co-operation in the cause of Peace. [A Letter to John Lee L.L.D., President of the London Peace Society.] *Boston*, 1844? 8vo. 4263

Beckwith. The History of Block Island. By Henry T. Beckwith. Read before the Rhode Island Historical Society, Nov. 1856. *Historical Magazine, April*, 1858. 4to, pp. 8.

A few copies printed separately.

Beckwourth (J. P.) The Life and Adventures of James P. Beckwourth, Mountaineer, Scout, and Pioneer, and Chief of the Crow Nation of Indians. With Illustrations. Written from his own Dictation, by T. D. Bonner. *New York, Harper & Brothers*, 1856. 12mo, pp. 537. 4265

Beckwourth. Le Chasseur. Scènes de la vie sauvage en Amérique. Traduit de l'anglo-américain par Noblet. *Paris, Dentu*, 1860. 18mo, pp. x., 504. Vignette. 4266

Bécourt (R. E.) Au roi sur la necessité et la possibilité de reconquérir les colonies de l'Amérique du Sud, du Mexique et de Saint-Domingue; par R. de Bécourt. [13 février 1824.] *Paris, Dentu; Petit*, 1824. 8vo, pp. 16. 4267

Bedard (P. H.) Lettre à M. Chaboillez, Cur de Longueil, relativement à ses "Questions sur le Gouvernement Ecclsiastique du district de Montral" par P. H. Bedard. *Montreal*, 1823. 8vo, pp. 40. 4268

Bedard (Thomas). Observations sur le Projet du Changement des Tenures dans cette Province. Par Thomas Bedard. [Eng. and French.] *Québec*, 1791. 8vo, pp. 11. 4269

Bedard. Observations on the Report respecting a Change in the Tenures of this Province. By Thomas Bedard. [English and French.] *Québec*, 1791. 8vo, pp. 11; M. 4270

Bedell (G. T.) Fellow Workers. Two Sermons Preached by the Rev. Gregory Thurston Bedell, D.D., ... 2d Day of October, 1859, being the Close of his Ministry in the Church of the Ascension, New-York. Also, Notitiæ Parochiales. *New-York, Printed by the Vestry*, 1859. 12mo, pp. 106. H. 4271

Bedell. Notitiæ parochiales. Parish Statistics of the Church of the Ascension. ... Prepared by the Rector ... . *New-York: Baker, Godwin & Co.*, 1851. 12mo, pp. 24. View. H.

Also: *New York*, 1860. 12mo, pp. 62. H. And for other years?

Bedell. Sermons by Rev. Gregory T. Bedell, D.D. ... . With a Biographical Sketch of the Author, by Stephen H. Tyng. *Philadelphia, William Stavely, John C. Pechin*, 1835. 2 vols., 8vo, pp. 7, memoir ccli, 308; 3 p. l., pp. 502. B. 4273

Bedell. A Votive Pillar. A Discourse Commemorating the Anniversary of the Church of the Ascension, N. Y. Preached on the Occasion of the 10th anniversary of his Pastorate on Sunday March 20, 1853. By Rev. G. Thurston Bedell, Rector ... *New-York: A. D. F. Randolph*, 1853. 12mo, pp. 48. 4274

Bedenckinge | Over d'Antwoordt der Heeren Bewint- | hebbers vande Oost-Indische | Compagnie : aen | d'Edele Gr : Mog : Heeren | Staten van Hollandt en West-Vrislant, | in twee Schrift-

en, overgelevert, belan- | ghende de Combinatie der twee | Compagnien. | Concordiâ res parvæ crescvnt. | [Vignette.] | *In s' Graven-Haghe, | By Jân Veeli, Boeck-verkooper in t' Gorstraetjen, | Anno* 1644. | 4to, 4 p. l., pp. 32. 4275

Prefixed is the "Antwoordt," for the title of which, *see* Consideratie.

Bedford (G. S.) Address, Introductory to a Course of Lectures delivered in ... New York, November 8, 1834, by Gunning S. Bedford ... . Second Edition. *New York*, 1835. 8vo, pp. 29. H. 4276

Bedford. An Address ... November 15, 1835, By Gunning S. Bedford ... . *New York*, 1836. 8vo, pp. 32. H. 4277

Both addresses criticise severely the management of the New York College of Physicians and Surgeons.

Bedford. Reports of the School Committees of Bedford, Mass., presented April, 1847, and April, 1848. *Boston*, 1848. 8vo, pp. 18. H. 4278

The report for 1847 reproaches the citizens for a want of interest in the schools, in an unusually pungent style.

Bedford (*Duke of*). *See* Russell.

Bedford, *N. H.* History of Bedford, New-Hampshire, being Statistics, compiled on the occasion of the One Hundredth Anniversary of the Incorporation of the Town; May 19th, 1850. *Boston, Alfred Mudge*, 1851. 8vo, pp. 364. Map. H.

Peter P. Woodbury, Thomas Savage, and William Patten were the publishing committee.

Bedford, *N. Y.* Circular Letter from the Committee of the Society for the Suppression of Vice in the Town of Bedford, etc. 8vo, pp. 8. 4280

Bedford, *Pa.* The Bedford Mineral Springs with an Analysis of its Waters ... . *Philadelphia*, 1857. 12mo, pp. 12.

END OF VOLUME ONE.

A Dictionary of Books

RELATING TO AMERICA.

BEDINGER (Daniel). A Letter from Daniel Bedinger, late Navy Agent at Norfolk, to Robert Smith, Esq., Secretary of the Navy. With an Appendix. *Norfolk.* 1808. 8vo. c. 4282

BEDINGER (Henry). Speech of Henry Bedingeron the War with Mexico; delivered. ... Jan. 6, 1847. *Washington.* 1847. 8vo. 4283

Bedlam, a Ball, and Dr. Price's Observations on Civil Liberty. A Poetical Miscellany. *London; Dodsley.* 1775. 4to.

Ridicules the saints of New England. *See* M. R., LIV, 421.

The Bee, No. 1. By William Honeycomb. Tuesday, February 12th, 1765. [*Philadelphia*]; *Printed in the Year* M,D,CC,LXV. 12mo, pp. 16. P. 4285

Against the Pennsylvania Government. Three numbers only published.

BEEBE (G. J.) A Sure Cure for the Tetotal Mania, and a Quietus for the Maine Liquor Law. Second Edition. By G. J. Beebe. *Middletown; N. Y.* 1852. 8vo, pp. 29, (1). H.

BEEBE (G. J.) *See* McNeir.

BEEBEE (S.) An Answer to Mr. Wadsworth's Book "The Lord's Day Proved to be the Christian Sabbath." Also, Poems. By Samuel Beebee. *America.* 1722. 18mo. 4287

BEECH (E. D.) The Hoosac Mountain Tunnel. Speech of Hon. E. D. Beech ... on the ... Loan of the Credit of Massa-

chusetts to the Amount of Two Millions ... to the Troy and Greenfield Railroad, in the Senate, April 11 and 12, 1851. *Boston.* 1851. 8vo, pp. 17. H. 4288

[BEECHER (Catharine Esther)]. The Duty of American Women to their Country. *New York; Harper & Brothers.* 1845. 24mo, pp. 164. H. 4289

BEECHER. An Essay on Slavery and Abolitionism, with reference to the Duty of American Females. *Philadelphia, Henry Perkins: Boston, Marvin & Perkins.* 1837. 18mo, pp. 152. H. + 2d Ed. *Philadelphia.* 1837. 18mo. B. 4290

BEECHER. The Evils suffered by American Women and American Children: the Causes and the Remedy. ... By Miss C. E. Beecher. *New York*, [1846]. + The Evils .... Also, An Address to the Protestant Clergy of the United States. *New York*, [1846]. 8vo, pp. 36. H. 4291

BEECHER. Suggestions respecting Improvements in Education, presented to the Trustees of the Hartford Female Seminary ... . By Catharine E. Beecher. *Hartford; Packard & Butler.* MDCCCXXIX. 8vo, pp. 84. H. 4292

With a list of the officers and pupils of the Seminary.

BEECHER. ... To the Board of National Popular Education. [*Hartford; Conn.* 1849.] 8vo, pp. 25, (1). H. 4293

Gives an account of the operations of the Board.

BEECHER. The True Remedy for the Wrongs of Woman; with a History of an Enterprise having that for its object. By Catharine E. Beecher. *Boston; Phillips, Sampson & Co.* 1851. 12mo, pp. viii, 263. H. 4294

BEECHER. Truth stranger than Fiction: a Narrative of Recent Transactions, involving Inquiries in regard to the Principles of Honor, Truth, and Justice, which obtain in a Distinguished American University [Yale College]. By Catharine E. Beecher. ... *New York; the Author.* 1850. 12mo, 2 l., pp. 296. H. 4295

Relates to Miss Delia Bacon, author of "The Philosophy of the Plays of Shakespeare," and a "Mr. A."

BEECHER (Ch.) The Antichrist of New-England. A Sermon, preached at the Opening of the Essex North Conference, Haverhill, Mass., Sept. 9, 1860. By Charles Beecher, George-

town, Mass. *Boston; Crosby, Nichols, Lee & Co.*, 1860. 12mo, pp. 35. H. 4296

BEECHER. The Duty of Disobedience to Wicked Laws. A Sermon on the Fugitive Slave Law. By Charles Beecher, Newark, N. J. *Newark, N. J.; J. McIlvaine: New-York, Wm. Harned.* 1851. 8vo, pp. 22. B., H. 4297

This is the imprint on the cover; on the title-page it is *New-York, John A. Gray, Printer.*

BEECHER. The God of the Bible against Slavery. By Rev. Charles Beecher. Antislavery Tracts, No. 17. 12mo, pp. 11.

BEECHER. Historic Fire: address to Calliopean Society of Wabash College, July 18, 1849. *Indianapolis.* 1849. 8vo, pp. 27. 4299

BEECHER. A Review of the "Spiritual Manifestations." ... *New York; G. P. Putnam.* M.DCCC.LIII. 12mo, pp. 75. H. + *London; Bosworth.* 1853. 12mo. 4300

BEECHER. Sermon on the Nebraska Bill. *New York.* 1854. 8vo, pp. 16. 4301

BEECHER (E.) A Narrative of Riots at Alton: in connection with the Death of Rev. Elijah P. Lovejoy. By Rev. Edward Beecher. *Alton; George Holton.* 1838. 12mo, pp. 159.

BEECHER. The Papal Conspiracy exposed, and Protestantism defended, in the Light of Reason, History, and Scripture. By Rev. Edward Beecher, D.D. *Boston; Stearns & Co.* 1855. 12mo, pp. 420. H. + With a Preface by Dr. Begg. *London; Nesbit*, 1856. 12mo. 4303

Contains "Cautions to Americans," "The Treason of the Romish Bishops in America," etc.

BEECHER. The Question at Issue. A Sermon, delivered at Brooklyn, New York, before the Society for the Promotion of Collegiate and Theological Education at the West. By Edward Beecher, D.D. *Boston.* 1850. 8vo, pp. 32. H. + Second Edition. *Boston.* 1851. 8vo, pp. 23. B. 4304

BEECHER (E. and C.) The Result Tested. A Review of the Proceedings of a Council at Georgetown, Mass., Aug. 15, 16, and 22, 1863. By Rev. Edward Beecher, D.D., and Rev. Charles Beecher. ... *Boston; Wright & Potter.* 1863. 8vo, pp. 38. B., H. 4305

BEECHER (G.) The Biographical Remains of Rev. George Beecher, late pastor of a church in Chillicothe, Ohio, and former pastor of a church in Rochester, New York. *New York; Leavitt, Trow & Co.* 1844. 16mo, pp. 345. S. 4306

BEECHER (H. W.) Address to the Society for Promotion of Collegiate Education at the West. Boston, May 28, 1856. By Henry Ward Beecher. *New York.* 1856. 8vo, pp. 18.

BEECHER. The American Cause in England. An Address by the Rev. Henry Ward Beecher, on "The American War," Delivered at Free Trade Hall, Manchester, England, ... October 9, 1863. *New York; Coutant & Baker.* 1863. 8vo, pp. 15. + *Boston; James Redpath.* 1863. 12mo, pp. 39. 4308

BEECHER. American Rebellion. Report of the Speeches of the Rev. Henry Ward Beecher, delivered at Public Meetings in Manchester, Glasgow, Edinburgh, Liverpool, and London. *Manchester, Union and Emancipation Society. London; Sampson, Low & Son*, [etc.], 1864. 8vo, 2 l., pp. 175. Plate. B. 4309

BEECHER. Defence of Kansas. By Henry Ward Beecher. [*Washington.* 1856.] 8vo, pp. 8. H. 4310

BEECHER. A Discourse delivered at ... Brooklyn, N. Y., upon Thanksgiving Day, November 25th, 1847. By Henry Ward Beecher. *New York; Cady & Burgess.* 1848. 8vo, pp. 27. B. 4311

BEECHER. England and America: Speech of Henry Ward Beecher, at the Free-Trade Hall, Manchester, [England], October 9, 1863. ... *Boston; James Redpath.* 1863. 12mo, pp. 39.

BEECHER. Eyes and Ears. By Henry Ward Beecher. *Boston; Ticknor and Fields.* 1862. 12mo, pp. vii., 419. H + .*London, Low.* 1862. 8vo. 4313

A collection of articles from the "New York Ledger" and the "New York Independent." Many of them relate to America.

BEECHER. Freedom and War. Discourses on Topics suggested by the Times. By Henry Ward Beecher. *Boston; Ticknor and Fields.* 12mo, pp. iv, (1), 445. H. 4314

BEECHER. ... Henry Ward Beecher and Theodore Parker. Mr. Beecher's Reasons for lecturing in the "Fraternity Course;" being a Reply to Certain Criticisms ... . *Boston; A. Williams and Company.* 1859. 16mo, pp. 20. H. 4315

BEECHER. Life Thoughts gathered from the Extemporaneous Discourses of Henry Ward Beecher, by one of his Congregation [Edna Dean Proctor]. *Boston.* 1858. 12mo, pp. xviii, 299. + With Biography. *London; Simpkin.* 1863. 18mo. 4316

BEECHER. Norwood: or, Village Life in New England. By Henry Ward Beecher. *New York; C. Scribner & Co.* 12mo, pp. 549. 4317

BEECHER. Notes from Plymouth Pulpit: a Collection of Memorable Passages from the Discourses of Henry Ward Beecher. With a Sketch of Mr. Beecher and the Lecture-Room. By Augusta Moore. New Edition. Revised and Greatly Enlarged. *New York; Harper & Brothers.* 1865. 12mo, 2 l., pp. 374. B. 4318

BEECHER. Presentation Memorial to Working Men. Oration at the Raising of "the Old Flag," at Sumter; and Sermon at the Death of Abraham Lincoln, President of the United States. By the Rev. Henry Ward Beecher. [Also, a Sketch of Mr. Lincoln by J. H. Estcourt.] *Manchester*, [*Eng.*]; *Alexander Ireland and Co.* 1865. 8vo, pp. 55 (2). H. 4319

BEECHER. ... Oration at Raising the Old Flag over Fort Sumter, April 14, 1865. By Rev. Henry Ward Beecher. *New York; Schermerhorn, Bancroft & Co.* 1865. 12mo, pp. 24.

BEECHER. Royal Truths. By Henry Ward Beecher. Sixth Edition. *London; Strathan.* 1862. + *Boston.* 1866. 12mo, pp. v, 324. Portrait. 4321

BEECHER. Thanksgiving Sermon, 25 November, 1847. *New York*, 1848. 8vo, pp. 27. 4322

BEECHER. Universal Suffrage; an Argument. By Henry Ward Beecher ... . *New York; Published by Wm. E. Whiting.* 8vo, pp. 15. 4323

BEECHER. War and Emancipation. A Thanksgiving Sermon, preached in ... Brooklyn, N. Y. ... November 21, 1861. By Henry Ward Beecher. ... *Philadelphia; T. B. Peterson & Brothers*, [1861]. 8vo, pp. 31. B., H. 4324

BEECHER. Woman's Influence in Politics: an Address Delivered by Henry Ward Beecher ... Feb. 2d, 1860. *Boston; R. F. Wallcut.* 1860. 12mo, pp. 18. H. 4325

Also: Woman's Duty to vote. Speech ... May 10, 1866. *New York, American Equal Rights Association.* 1867. 12mo, Title, pp. 31. H.

BEECHER *and* HUGHES. Civil War: Its Causes, Its Consequences, Its Crimes, and Its Compromises. Series Number 1, By H. W. Beecher and Archbishop Hughes. ... *New York; Reuben Vose*, [1861]. 8vo, pp. 37. 4326

A series of imaginary conversations.

[BEECHER (*Mrs.* Henry Ward)]. From Dawn to Daylight; or, the Simple Story of a Western Home. By a Minister's Wife. *New York*, 1859. 12mo, pp. 339. 4327

BEECHER (Lyman.) Autobiography, Correspondence, etc., of Lyman Beecher, D.D. Edited by Charles Beecher. With Illustrations. In Two Volumes. *New York; Harper & Brothers.* 1864. 12mo, pp. 563; 587. + *London; Low.* 1863–65. 2 vols.

BEECHER (Lyman). The Design, Rights, and Duties of Local Churches. A Sermon delivered at the Installation of the Rev. Elias Cornelius ... in Salem, July 21, 1819. ... *Andover.* 1819. 8vo, pp. 54. H. 4329

BEECHER. The Ballot Box a Remedy for National Crimes. A Sermon, entitled 'The Remedy for Duelling,' By Rev. Lyman Beecher, D.D.; appplied to the Crime of Slaveholding. By One of his Former Parishioners. *Boston; Isaac Knapp.* 1838. 16mo, pp. 36. H. 4330

BEECHER. The Faith once delivered to the Saints. A Sermon at Worcester, Mass. Oct. 15, 1823, at the Ordination of Rev. Loammi Ives Hoadly ... . *Boston.* 1823. 8vo, pp. 48. H. + Second Edition. *Boston*, 1824. 8vo, pp. 40. H. 4331

BEECHER. The Government of God desirable. A Sermon delivered at Newark, during the Session of the Synod of New-York and New-Jersey, October, 1808. By Lyman Beecher, A.M. ... *New-York; Printed by Smith & Forman.* 1809. 8vo, pp. 26. + Second Edition. *New-York.* 1809. 8vo, pp. 24. B. + Second Edition. *Sutton, Mass.* 1811. 8vo. W. + Seventh Edition. *Boston.* 1827. 8vo, pp. 27. 4332

BEECHER. The Memory of our Fathers. A Sermon at Plymouth, on the Twenty-second of December, 1827. By Lyman Beecher, D.D. *Boston.* 1828. 8vo, pp. 30. + Second Edition. *Boston.* 1828. 8vo, pp. 30. B., H. 4333

BEECHER. ... On the Importance of assisting Young Men ... in Obtaining an Education for the Gospel Ministry. [2d. Edit. 6000. *Andover.* 1816.] 12mo, pp. 20. H. 4334

Contains information respecting the religious condition of the United States.

BEECHER. A Plea for the West. By Lyman Beecher, D.D. *Cincinnati; Truman & Smith.* 1832. 18mo, pp. 172. H. + Second Edition. *Cincinnati.* 1835. 12mo, pp. 190. C. 4335

BEECHER. A reformation of morals practicable and indispensable. A Sermon delivered at New-Haven ... October 27, 1812. By Lyman Beecher ... . Second Edition. *Andover.* 1814. 8vo, pp. 32. H., W. 4336

BEECHER. The Remedy for Duelling. A Sermon delivered before the Presbytery of Long-Island, at the Opening of their Session at Aquebogue, April 16, 1806. By Lyman Beecher ... . Re-published by subscription. To which is annexed the Resolutions and Addresses of the Anti-Duelling Association of New-York. *New York; Williams and Whiting.* 1809. 8vo, pp. 48. H. + Second Edition. *New York.* 1809. B. + *Boston.* [n. d.] 8vo, pp. 16. H. 4337

[BEECHER.] The Rights of the Congregational Churches of Massachusetts. The Result of an Ecclesiastical Council, convened at Groton, Massachusetts, July 17, 1826. *Boston.* 1827. 8vo, pp. 63. H. + Second Edition. [*Ibid.*] 8vo, pp. 47. H.

See Lowell (John) for a review of the above.

BEECHER. ... Sermon, delivered in Park Street Church, Boston, Sept. 3, 1817, at the Ordination of Mr. Sereno Edwards Dwight, as Pastor of that Church; and of ... Elisha P. Swift, Allen Graves, John Nichols, Levi Parsons, & Daniel Buttrick, As Missionaries to the Heathen. ... *Andover.* 1818. 8vo, pp. 51. H. 4339

BEECHER. ... A Sermon ... Sept. 17, 1828, at the Installation of Rev. Bennet Tyler in Portland, Maine. ... *Boston*; 1829. 8vo, pp. 48. H. 4340

BEECHER. A Sermon, containing a General History of the Town of East-Hampton (L. I.), From its First Settlement to the Present Time. Delivered at East-Hampton, Janu. 1, 1806. By Rev. Lyman Beecher. *Sag-Harbor, N. Y.; Alden Spooner.* 1806. 8vo, pp. 40. 4341

See N. Y. Med. Repos., 1807, X., 51–53.

BEECHER. A sermon delivered at the funeral of Henry Obookiah, a native of Owhyhee. By Lyman Beecher. *Elizabethtown, N. J.* 1819. 12mo. 4342

BEECHER. Six Sermons on the Nature, Occasions, Signs, Evils, and Remedy of Intemperance. By Lyman Beecher, D.D. *Boston*, 1827. 12mo, pp. 107.+ Seventh Edition. *New York.* 1833. 12mo. + Tenth Edition. *Boston.* 1830. 16mo. B. 4343

These sermons were chiefly instrumental in the formation of numerous temperance societies. There is a Swedish version, Sex predikningar ... . *Norrköping*, 1831, 8vo, and one in modern Greek, *λογοι περι της φυσεως, των αφορμων ... της ακρασιας. ὑπο Λυμανου Βηχερου.* Εν Αθηναις, εκ της τυπογραφίας Αγγελου Αγγελιδου, 1841. 12mo, 2 l., pp. 141. H.

BEECHER. The Works of Lyman Beecher, D.D. ... . 2 vols., 12mo. *Boston; Jewett & Co.* 1852. 4344

Also: A Sermon at Woolcot (Con.) Sept. 21, 1814, at the Installation of the Rev. John Keyes ... . *Andover.* 1815. 8vo, pp. 34. H. Sermon at Worcester, Oct. 15, 1823, at the Ordination of Loammi Ives Hoadley. *Boston.* 1824. 8vo. + 2d Ed. *Boston.* 1824. 8vo. Review of the foregoing, [from the Christian Examiner.] *Boston.* 1824. 8vo. Reply to the Review, [from the Christian Spectator.] *Boston.* 1825. 8vo. ... A Sermon delivered at the Installation of the Rev. Elias Cornelius as Associate Pastor ... in Salem, July 21, 1819. *Andover.* 1819. 8vo, pp. 54. B. + Sermon at Andover, July 16, 1832. 8vo.

BEECHER *and* NETTLETON. Letters of the Rev. Dr. Beecher and Rev. Mr. Nettleton, on the "New Measures" in conducting Revivals of Religion. With a Review of a Sermon, by Novanglus. ... *New-York; G. & C. Carvill.* 1828. 8vo, pp. 104. B. 4345

BEECHER (T.) Sermon on the Death of Gov. Noah Noblet. *Indianapolis*, 1844. 8vo, pp. 27. 4346

BEECHEY (F.) Narrative of a Voyage to the Pacific and Beering's Strait, to co-operate with the Polar Expeditions: performed in his Majesty's Ship Blossom, under the Command of Captain F. W. Beechey, R. N. ... In the Years 1825, 26, 27, 28. ... In Two Parts. *London; Henry Colburn and Richard Bentley.* MDCCCXXXI. 4to, pp. xx, (2), Errata 1 slip, 392; vii, (1), Errata 1 slip, 393–742. 3 Maps and 21 Plates. H. + *London, John Murray.* 1831. 2 vols., 8vo. Maps and Plates. + *Philadelphia.* 1832. 8vo, pp. 493. 4347

Captain Beechey and Sir John Franklin had arrived within fifty leagues of each other, when the latter was compelled by the weather to return. One of the most valuable of modern voyages, containing a most interesting visit to Pitcairn's Island, the coast of California, etc. *See* Q. R., XLV, 57. Also, Hooker (J. W.), and Richardson (J.)

BEECHEY (F. W.) Reise nach dem Stillen Ocean und der Beeringstrasse ... in den Jahre 1825–28. Aus dem Englischen übersetzt. *Weimar.* 1832. 2 vols., 8vo. Map and Plate. (Bibl. d. neuesten Reisebeschreibungen, Bd. LIX., LXI.) 4348

BEECHEY. A Voyage of Discovery towards the North Pole, performed in His Majesty's Ships Dorothea and Trent, under the Command of Captain David Buchan, R. N., 1818; to which is added a Summary of all the Early Attempts to reach the Pacific by way of the Pole. By Captain F. W. Beechey, R. N., F.R.S., One of the Lieutenants of the Expedition. Published by order of the Lords Commissioners of the Admiralty. *London; R. Bentley.* 1843. 8vo, pp. iv, (1), 351. 5 Plates. + *London.* 1849. 8vo. 4349

Also reprinted as extra series, No. 77, of the New World. *New York; J. Winchester.* 1843. 4to, pp. 32. Of the Voyage to Pacific there is a French version in Albert-Montémont. Bibliothèque universelle des voyages. *Paris.* 1833–36. 46 vols., 8vo, Vol. XIX.

BEEDE (Thomas). An Oration, delivered at Roxbury, July 4, 1799 ... . By Thomas Beedé. *Boston; Ebenezer Rhoades.* 1799. 8vo, pp. 15. H. 4350

Also: Masonic Discourses at Lexington, Mass., June 24, 1803. *Amherst.* 1803. 8vo. Discourse at Washington, N. H. Sept. 28, 1803. 8vo. *Amherst.* 1804. Discourse, Portsmouth, June 24, 1806, before the Grand Lodge of the State of New Hampshire. *Portsmouth.* 1806. 4to., pp. 13. A Discourse delivered in Dublin, N. H., at the Consecration of Altemont Lodge ... Sept. 18, 1816. *Keene.* 1817. 8vo.

BEEDE. A Sermon, preached at Concord, before ... the Governor, ... of the State of New-Hampshire, June 6, 1811. By Thomas Beede, A.M. ... *Concord; printed by I. and W. R. Hill.* ... 1811. 8vo, pp. 20. H. 4351

BEEK (J. ter). Dissertatio de elephantiasi Surinamensi. *Lugduni Batavorum.* 1841. 8vo. 4352

Beelden uit Amerika. Naar het Hoogduitsch door H. G. Hartman, jr. Uitgegeven ten voordeele van een weldadig doel ... . *Rotterdam; W. Wenk.* 1859. Sm. 8vo, pp. 6, 136. 4353

BEERS' Almanack for ... 1818 ... . By Andrew Beers, Philom. *New-Haven; Maltby, Goldsmith & Co.,* [n. d.] 12mo, pp. 24. H.

There are Beers' almanacks as early as [*Hartford*] 1798. 12mo.

BEERS (F. W.) Atlas of the Oil Region of Pennsylvania from Actual Surveys under the Direction of F. W. Beers, C.E. Assisted by Beach Nichols, J. M. Beers, A. Leavenworth, C. S. Peck, C. A. Curtis & Geo. Stewart With a few facts relating to Petroleum ... by Ivan C. Michels ... . *New York; F. W. Beers,* [etc.] 1865. Oblong folio, Title, Map folded, pp. 48 (of which 36 contain maps, and are printed on one side only). 4355

BEERS. Atlas of Licking Co., Ohio. *New York.* 1866. 4to.

BEERS. Atlas of Muskingum Co., Ohio. *New York.* 1866. 4to. 4357

BEERS (S. P.) *See* Connecticut.

BEERS (W. P.) An Oration on the Death of General Washington; pronounced Before the Citizens of Albany, ... January 9th, 1800. By William P. Beers, Esquire. *Albany; Printed by Charles R. and George Webster,* [1800]. 8vo, pp. 17. H.

BEESON (John). ... An Address to the People of the United States [in behalf of the Indians] by John Beeson. [n. p. 1859.] 8vo, pp. 8. H. 4359

BEESON. A Plea for the Indians; with Facts and Features of the late War in Oregon. By John Beeson. ... *New York; John Beeson.* 1857. 12mo, pp. 143, (1). + [Second Edition. *Ibid.*] B. + *New York; John Beeson.* 1858. 12mo, pp. 143, (1). H. 4360

BEESON. A Sequel to the Plea for the Indians. *New York.* 1858 [?]. 12mo. 4361

BEETS (N.) De bevrijding der slaven. Redevoering, gehouden in de openbaaren vergadering van de Nederl. maatschappij tot bevordering van de afschaffing der slaven. *Haalem; de Erven F. Bohn.* 1856. 8vo. 4362

[BEGERT (Jakob)]. Nachrichten von der amerikanischen Halbinsel Californien: mit einem zweyfachen Anhang falscher Nachrichten. Geschrieben von einem Priester der Gesellschaft Jesu, welcher lang darinn diese letztere Jahre gelebt hat. ... *Mannheim; Löffler.* 1772. 8vo, pp. 358. + 1773. 8vo. Map.

Chapter twenty relates to the language of the Indians of California. There is a translation of the ethnological portions, by Prof. Charles Rau, in the Smithsonian Report for 1863, pp. 352-369; 1864, 378-399.

Begin ende Voortgang. *See* [Commelin (Isaac)].

The Beginning and the End—Dedicated to the Army of the Potomac. By your Humble Wagoner. *New York; John A. Gray & Green.* 1863. 8vo, pp. 41. 4364

The Beginning, Progress, and Conclusion of the Late War; with other Interesting Matters considered; and a Map of the Lands, Islands, Gulphs, Seas, and Fishing-Banks, comprising

the Cod Fishery in America, annexed for the Better Explanation of several Proceedings Relative to it.. [Motto:] *London; J. Almon.* M DCC LXX. 4to, Title, pp. 32. Map. H. 4365

See Rich, I, 180; M. R., XLIII, 398.

The Beginning, Progress and Conclusion of Bacon's Rebellion in Virginia, In the Years 1675 and 1676. *Washington;* 1835. 8vo, pp. 26. (Force's Tracts, Vol. I.) H. 4366

First printed in the "Richmond Enquirer," Sept. 1, 5, 8, 1804. Signed "T. M."

BEGRISS der Mirakelen, Met de welcke Godt de onsterffelijcke Glorio van de H. Rosa ... Heeft gheweerdight ... *Brussels; Phillips Olengaent.* 1671. 18mo, pp. 52, Table, etc., 4 l.

In Gothic letter. This title is from J. R. Bartlett's catalogue of J. C. Brown's library.

BEGUERIE (J. M.) Histoire de la fièvre, qui a regné, sur la flotille française, sortée du Port du Tarente, dans la mer Ionienne, pendant l'an x, allant au Cap-François, Ile St. Domingue ... . *Montpellier.* 1806. 8vo, pp. 104. 4368

See N. Y. Med. Repos., 1807, x, 390–394.

BEHN (A.) The Dramatic Works of Mrs. Aphra Behn. *London.* 1702. 2 vols., 8vo. + Second Edition. *London; W. Meadows.* 1716. 2 vols., 8vo, Portrait, Title, pp. 583, 4 l., (1); 403, (1). H. + *London.* 1724. 4 vols., 12mo. 4369

BEHN. The Histories and Novels of Mrs. Aphra Behn, together with her Life. *London.* 1696. 8vo. + *London.* 1718. 8vo. + *London.* 1722. 2 vols., 8vo. + Eighth Edition, with Life by Gildon. 1735. 2 vols., 12mo. + *London,* 1751. 2 vols., 18mo. H. 4370

Contains Oroonoko.

BEHN. Oroonoko; or, the Royal Slave. A true History. By Mrs. Behn. *London.* 1688. 8vo. + *London.* 1800. 12mo.

The scene is laid in Surinam. Southern borrowed the plot of his tragedy from this.

BEHN. The | Widdow Ranter | or, | The History of | Bacon in Virginia. | A | Tragi-comedy, | Acted by their Majesties Servants. | Written by Mrs. A. Behn. | *London; Printed by James Knapton at the | Crown in St. Paul's Church-Yard.* 1690. | 4to, pp. 56. 4372

Founded on the story of Col. Bacon's "Insurrection in Virginia," on which obscure part of history it throws much light, exhibiting strongly the mismanagement of the colony, the incompetence of the authorities, etc., and the state of affairs which led to the outbreak.

BEHN. Oronoko, ou le royale esclave traduit de l'Anglois de Mad. Behn, [par de Laplace]. *Amsterdam.* 1745. 12mo. + *La Haye.* 1745. 12mo. 4373

BEHR (Ottomar von). Guter Rath für Auswanderer nach den Vereinigten Staaten von Nordamerika, mit besonderer Berücksichtigung von Texas. Vorzüglich für Landleute und Handwerker. *Leipzig; Friese.* 1847. 8vo, pp. iv, 107. 4374

BEHR. Goode raad voor landverhuizers naar de Vereenigde Staten van Noord-Amerika, ook met betrekking tot Texas. Met eene voorede van O. G. Heldring. *Arnhem; J. W. Swaan.* 1849. 8vo. 4375

BEHREND (Fr. J.) Geschichte der Gefängnissreform. [Erster Theil.] Vereinigte Staaten; Grossbritannien; Irland. *Berlin; Brigl & Lobeck.* 1859. 8vo, pp. viii, 182. 4376

B[EHRENS (Karl Friedrich)]. Reise nach den unbekandten Sud-Ländern und rund um die Welt. In einem Send-Schreiben, mit Poetischer Feder entworffen. *Hamburg.* 1735. 16mo, pp. 48. 4377

[BEHRENS.] Reisebeschreibung um die Welt Carl. Fridr. Behrens der wohlerfahrne Südländer. *Leipzig; Monath.* 1738. 8vo, pp. 132. Plates. 4378

This title is given by Boucher in a more probable form, as follows: "Wohlversuchte Sud-Länder, d. i. ausführliche Reise-Beschreibung um die Welt unter Roggewein, von 1721 bis 1723, von Carl Friedr. Behrens. *Leipzig* 1739. 8vo.

[BEHRENS.] Histoire de l'expédition [de Roggewein] de trois vaisseaux, Envoyés par la Compagnie des Indes Occidentales des Provinces-Unies, aux terres australes en MDCCXXI. Par Monsieur de B***. *La Haye; la Compagnie.* M. D. CC. XXXIX. 2 vols., 18mo, 5 l., pp. 224; 2 l., 254. C., H. 4379

"Two relations were published of Roggewein's voyage round the world, one in Dutch, printed at Dort in 1728, in 4to, with the title, 'Twee Jaarige reyze rondom de Wereld;' the other in German. The author of this last was Charles Frederic Behrens, a native of Mecklenburgh, serjeant and commander of marines with Roggewein. 'It is a very poor performance, written with much ignorance, though with the parade of knowledge. It appears to me that Behrens kept no journal, and wrote from memory; but his narrative seems to be faithful in the recital of the things he saw.'—*Dalrymple.*"—RICH.

BEIJER (M.) *See* Beyer.

BEIL (J. A.) Stand und Ergebnisse der Europäischen und

Amerikanischen Eisenbahnen bis zu dem J. 1847. *Wien.* 1847. Imp. 4to, pp. 296, and 15 sheets, (Tables). 4381

Beiträge zur Kenntniss der Spanischen Besitzungen in Amerika. Aus dem Spanischen von Ch. A. Fischer. *Dresden; Beger.* 1802. 8vo. 4382

Beiträge zur Kenntniss des amerikanischen Mühlenwesens und der Mehlfabrikation. *Berlin.* 1832. 4to, and Atlas, folio.

Beiträge zur Kenntniss des Russischen Reichs. *See* Baer.

BEKFORD (W.) *See* Beckford (W.)

Beknopte en zakelyke beschryving van de voornaamste Engelsche volk-plantingen in Noord-Amerika; neffens aanmerkingen over den oorsprong en voortgang der tegenwoordige geschillen, en des oorlogs, tusschen Groot-Brittanie en deszelfs kolonisten. *Amsterdam; P. Conradi.* 1776. 2 vols., 8vo. 4385

BELANGER. Jardin botanique de Saint-Pierre (Martinique); rapport de M. Belanger sur la situation d'ensemble de cet établissement. *Paris; imp. Paul Dupont.* 1857. 8vo, pp. 23. 4386

Reprinted from the "Revue Coloniale," March, 1857.

BELANI (H. E. R.), *pseudon.* *See* [Haeberlin (C. L.)]

BELARIUS of Cymbeline, *pseudon.* Work, etc. *See* [Evans (E.)]

BELCHER (C. H.) Belcher's Farmer's Almanack, For ... 1843 ... . Calculated for Halifax ... . *Halifax, N. S.; C. H. Belcher,* [n. d.] 12mo, pp. 104. Continued. H. 4388

BELCHER (E.) The Last of the Arctic Voyages; being a Narrative of the Expedition in H.M.S. Assistance, under the Command of Captain Sir Edward Belcher, C.B., in search of Sir John Franklin, during the Years 1852–53–54. With Notes on the Natural History, by Sir John Richardson, Professor Owen, Thomas Bell, J. W. Salter, and Lovell Reeve. In Two Volumes. ... *London; Lovell Reeve.* 2 vols., rl. 8vo, 1 l., pp. xviii, 383; vii, 419. Maps and Plates, some colored. B. 4389

BELCHER. Narrative of a Voyage Around the World. ... in Her Majesty's Ship Sulphur, during the Years 1836–1842, including Details of the Naval Operations in China, 1840–41.

London; Henry Colburn. ... 1843. 2 vols., 8vo, Title, pp. xxii, 1 l., and more than 386; vi, (1), 474. Maps and Plates. B.

Botany and Zoology of Belcher's Voyage, *see* Hinds. "Among the countries visited by the Sulphur may be mentioned California, the Columbia River, and the N. W. Coast."—RICH.

BELCHER (Jonathan). A Conference of ... Jonathan Belcher, Esq; Captain General and Governour in Chief of His Majesty's Province of the Massachusetts-Bay ... with Edewakenk Chief Sachem of the Penobscut Tribe, Loron ... , Toxus Chief Sachem of the Norridgewock Tribe, Adiawando Chief Sachem of the Pigwacket Tribe, and Medaganesset Chief Sachem of the Ameresccoggin Tribe, with other Chief Men of the said Indian Tribes, at Falmouth in Casco-Bay, July 1732 ... . [No title-page.] 4to, pp. 23. H. 4391

BELCHER. The Laws of Nova Scotia. 1767. 8vo. 4392

BELCHER (Joseph), *b.* 1719, *d.* 1790. ... a Brief Sermon Preached to the Great & General Assembly of the Province of the Massachusetts Bay, Convened at Boston ... May 28th, 1701. The Stated day for their Anniversary Election of Counsellors. By Mr. Joseph Belcher ... . *Boston; Samuel Sewell. Junior.* 1701. Sm. 8vo, pp. 47. B., H. 4393

BELCHER. Copy of a Letter found in the Study of the Reverend Mr. Joseph Belcher, since his Decease. *Boston.* 18mo, pp. 4. 4394

BELCHER. The Life of Faith, Exemplified and Recommended, in a Letter found in the Study of the Reverend Mr. Joseph Belcher, late of Dedham in New-England, since his Decease. An Answer to this Question, How to live in this World, so as to live in Heaven? To which is added, A few Verses by the late Reverend Mr. Killinghall, upon reading of it. *London; J. Oswald.* MDCCXLI. 8vo, pp. 8. 4395

BELCHER. ... An Ordination Sermon, Preached at Bristol, N. E. Aug. 30. 1721. when Mr. Nathanael Cotton Was Ordained ... there. By Joseph Belcher ... . *Boston; B. Green.* 1722. Sm. 8vo, 2 l., pp. iv, 38. H. 4396

BELCHER. Two Sermons, one on a Fast Day, the other to a Collection of Young People, preached in Dedham, N. E. *Boston.* 1710. 16mo, pp. 28. 4397

BELCHER. The Worst Enemy Conquered. A Brief Discourse on the Methods and Motives to pursue A Victory over those Habits of Sin, which War against the Soul. Delivered on June 6th, 1698, the Day for Election of Officers in the Artillery-Company, at Boston. By Mr. Joseph Belcher, Pastor of the Church in Dedham. [Preface by C. Mather.] *Boston, in New England; Printed by Bartholomew Green and John Allen.* 1698. 12mo, pp. 38. 4398

BELCHER (Joseph). The Clergy of America: Anecdotes illustrative of the Character of Ministers of Religion in the United States. By Joseph Belcher. *Philadelphia.* 1849. 12mo, pp. 478. + *Philadelphia.* 1855. 12mo, pp. 478. 4399

BELCHER. The Baptist Pulpit of the United States: Eloquent and Instructive Passages from the Sermons of 250 Baptist Ministers. *New-York.* 1850. 12mo. Many Portraits. 4400

BELCHER. George Whitefield: a Biography, with Special Reference to his Labors in America. Compiled by Joseph Belcher, D.D. ... *New York; American Tract Society,* [n. d.] 12mo, pp. 514. Portrait. 4401

BELCHER. The Religious Denominations in the United States, their History, Doctrine, Government, and Statistics; with a Preliminary Sketch of Judaism, Paganism, and Mohammedanism. By Rev. Joseph Belcher, D.D. *Philadelphia.* 1854. 8vo. + New Edition. *Philadelphia.* 1855. Rl. 8vo, pp. xii, 1024. Also, crown 8vo. 4402

BELCHER (Samuel). Concio ad Magistratum. Or An Assize Sermon Preached before the Honourable Her Majesties Superiour Court of Judicature, Court of Assize, and general Goal Delivery, at Ipswich in New-England the 21. May, 1702. ... By Samuel Belcher ... . *Boston.* 1707. Sm. 8vo, pp. 13. 4403

BELCHER. An Essay Tending to Promote the Kingdom of our Lord Jesus Christ, ... in a Sermon Preached before ... the Governour ... May 28. 1707. ... the Anniversary Day for the Election of Her Majesties Council, for that Province. By Samuel Belcher ... . *Boston in N. E.; Printed by B. Green.* 1707. Sm. 8vo, Title, pp. 20. H. 4404

BELCHERTOWN. Report of the Case of Belchertown Election; with the Documents and Minutes of the Arguments in the Case. Published under the direction of D. Everett, Esq. *Boston.* 1811. 8vo, pp. 49. 4405

BELCOURT (George Antoine). Catechism and Sacred Hymns in the Chippewa or Santeux language. By G. A. Belcourt ... *Anamihe-Masinahigan, Kebekong, Otenang.* 1839. 18mo. 4406

BELCOURT. Principes de la langue des sauvages appelés Sauteux. Par le G. A. Belcourt. *Québec; Imprimerie de Frechette and Co.* 1839. 12mo, pp. 146. 4407

BELCOURT. Traduction du catéchisme et de cantiques dans la langue des Sauteux. *Québec.* 1839. 18mo. 4408

[BELDEN (E. P.)] New-York—as it is; being the Counterpart of the Metropolis of America. ... *New-York; printed by Prall, Lewis & Co.* 1851. 12mo, 2 l., pp. 18. 4409

An account of his model of New York.

BELDEN. New York: Past, Present, and Future; comprising a History of the City of New-York, a Description of its Present Condition, and an Estimate of its Future Increase. *New York; G. P. Putnam.* 1849. 12mo, pp. 125, 24, and 180 of Advertisements. + Second Edition. *New-York.* 1849. 12mo. + Third Edition. *New-York.* 1850. 12mo. + Fourth Edition. *New-York; Prall, Lewis & Co.* 1851. 12mo, pp. 141. Map, and Plates. + [Another Edition.] *New-York.* 1851. 12mo, pp. 153, (26), Advertisements, 332. 4410

BELDEN (W. L.) An Account of Jane C. Rider, the Springfield Somnambulist. The Substance of which was delivered as a Lecture before the Springfield Lyceum, Jan. 23, 1832. By L. W. Belden, M.D. *Springfield; Meriam.* 1834. 12mo, pp. 134, Errata, 1 l. + *London,* 1834. 12mo, pp. 134. S., H. 4411

See Lond. Med. Gaz., Oct., 1834, XV, 52; Johnson, Med. Chir. Rev., Oct., 1834, XXV, 440–444.

[BELDENE (W. W.)] ... A Tribute to the Memory of Gen. George B. Boomer, of the Army of the Mississippi, who fell before Vicksburg, May 22, 1863. 32mo, pp. 20. H. 4412

The dedication is signed "W. W. B."

BELDING (A.) An Elegy, On the Death of Mrs. Anne Belding, Late Wife of the Reverend Mr. Joshua Belding, Of Newington; Who died October 29, 1773. ... by a Youth of his Parish. *Hartford; Printed by Eben Watson.* 1774. 8vo, pp. 8.

BELDING. United States Bonds and Securities. What they are—their Cost—and the Interest they pay. With ... . other ... Information concerning American Finances and Exchange. By Belding, Keith & Co. ... . *London.* 1867. 8vo, pp. 11, (12.)

BELDING'S Northwestern Review, devoted to Agriculture, Commerce ... and general Statistics. Ed. by H. H. Belding: Monthly. *Keokuk. Iowa.* 8vo. Vol. I., Nov., 1857; Continued to April, 1858. 4418

BELENA (Eusebio Bentura). Recopilacion sumaria de todos los Autos acordados de la Real Audiencia y Sala del Crimen de esta Nueva España, y providencias de su superior Gobierno; de varias Reales Cédulas y Ordenes que despues de publicada la Recopilacion de Indias, etc. *México; Don Felipe de Zúniga.* 1787. 2 vols., folio, Title, pp. xxxvi; 2d Title, Recopilacion sumaria, 100; 3d Title, Recopilacion de algunos, 114; 4th Title, Recopilacion sumaria, 373. Vol. II. Title, Capias a la Letva afrecidas en el Primer Tomó, etc., Erratai, 1 l., Indice, 1 l., Text, pp. 420, Articulos, lxxxvi. 4419

BELFAST. Ireland & America, *viâ* Galway. Memorial to ... Lord John Russell, from the Town Council, Harbour Commissioners, and Chamber of Commerce of Belfast, and Statement in support thereof ... . *London; James Madden.* 1852. 8vo, pp. 16.

Belgische Compagnie zur Colonisation des Districts Santo Thomas, Staat Guatemala. *Dresden.* 1842. 8vo, 4 sheets. 2 Maps. 4421

Die Belgischen Colonien in Guatemala und in Brasilien. Versuch einer Darstellung des Thatsächlichen, mit einem Hinblick auf die Hoffnungen, welche sich daran knüpfen. *Köln,* 1844. 8vo, 9¾ sheets. C. 4422

BELGROVE (Wm.) A Treatise upon Husbandry or Planting. By William Belgrave. A regular bred, and long experienc'd Planter, Of the Island of Barbados. And may be of great Use to the Planters of all the West-India Islands. *Boston, New-England; D. Fowle.* 1775. Sm. 4to, Title, pp. 86. H. 4423

BÉLIÈRES. Vie d'Anne Gertrude, pieuse créole de Cayenne; par J. J. Bélières, missionnaire apostolique. *Avignon, imp. Aubanel frères.* 1857. 18mo, pp. 89. + Seconde édition. [*Ibid*] 18mo, pp. 158. + Quatrième édition ... augmentée. *Nyons; Pénable frères.* 1859. 12mo, pp. 180. 4424

BELISARIO (A. M.) A Report of the Trial of Arthur Hodge ... at the Island of Tortola ... April, 1811 ... for the Murder of his Negro Man Slave named Prosper. Stenographically taken by A. M. Belisario ... . *Middletown,* [*Conn.*]; *printed by Tertius Dunning.* 1812. 12mo, Title, pp. 186. H. 4425

BELISLE (D. W.) The American Family Robinson; or, the Adventures of a Family lost in the great Desert of the West. By D. W. Belisle. *Philadelphia.* 1854. 12mo. 4426

BELISLE. History of Independence Hall: from the Earliest Period to the Present Time. Embracing Biographies of the Immortal Signers of the Declaration of Independence, with Historical Sketches of the Sacred Relics preserved in that Sanctuary of American Freedom. By D. W. Belisle. ... *Philadelphia; James Challen & Son.* 1859. 12mo, pp. 396. Plate, and 4 Woodcuts. C., H. 4427

"More popular than historical."—*H. Mag.*, IV, 31.

BELISLE (Orvilia S.) The Archbishop; or Romanism in the United States. *Philadelphia.* 1853. 12mo. + Fourth Edition. *Philadelphia.* 1859. 12mo. 4428

BELKNAP (Jeremy). American Biography: or, An Historical Account Of those Persons who have been distinguished in America, as Adventurers, Statesmen, Philosophers, Divines, Warriors, Authors, And other Remarkable Characters. Comprehending a Recital of The Events connected with their Lives and Actions. ... By Jeremy Belknap, D.D. ... *Boston; Isaiah Thomas and Ebenezer T. Andrews.* MDCCXCIV–VIII. 2 vols., 8vo, pp. 416; 476, (1). 4429

BELKNAP. American Biography. By Jeremy Belknap, D.D. With Additions and Notes, by F. M. Hubbard. *New York; Harpers.* 1843. 3 vols., 18mo, pp. 370; 333; 315. + *New York.* 1857. 4430

Also, reprinted in Knapp's Library of American History.

BELKNAP. A Discourse, intended to commemorate the Discovery of America by Christopher Columbus; delivered at the Request of the Historical Society in Massachusetts on the 23d day of October, 1792, being the Completion of the Third Century since that Memorable Event. To which are added, Four Dissertations, Connected with various parts of the Discourse, viz. 1. On the cicumnavigation of Africa by the ancients. 2. An Ex-

amination of the pretensions of Martin Behaim to a discovery of America prior to that of Columbus, with a Chronological detail of all the Discoveries made in the 15th Century. 3. On the question, whether the Honey-bee is a native of America? 4. On the colour of the native Americans and the recent Population of this Continent. By Jeremy Belknap, D.D. ... *Boston; Belknap and Hall.* MDCCXCII. 8vo, pp. 132, Advertisements, 2 l.

BELKNAP. An Election Sermon, preached before the General Court, of New-Hampshire, at Portsmouth, June 2, 1785. By Jeremy Belknap. ... *Portsmouth. Printed by Melcher and Osborne.* M,DCC,LXXXV. 8vo, pp. 48. H. 4432

[BELKNAP.] The Foresters; An American Tale: being a Sequel to the History of John Bull the Clothier. ... *Boston.* 1792. C. + The Second Edition, revised and considerably enlarged. *Boston; I. Thomas and E. T. Andrews,* [etc.] *Nov.*, 1796. 16mo, pp. 240. H. 4433

An historical allegory, in which the whole of the occurrences of the War of Independence are dramatized. Virginia figures under the name of Walter Pipeweed, whose grandson George is Washington.

BELKNAP. The History of New-Hampshire. Volume I. Comprehending the Events of One Complete Century from the Discovery of the River Piscataqua. By Jeremy Belknap, A.M. ... *Philadelphia; Printed for the Author by Robert Aitken.* M.DCC.LXXXIV. 8vo, pp. viii, 361, lxxxiv. + *Boston; re-printea for the Author.* M.DCC.XCII. 8vo, pp. viii, 362, ciii. H. || Volume II. Comprehending the Events of Seventy Five Years, from MDCCXV to MDCCXC. ... *Boston; Isaiah Thomas and Ebenezer T. Andrews,* MDCCXCI. 8vo, pp. 493, (1). Map. || Volume III. Containing a Geographical Description of the State; with Sketches of its Natural History, Productions, Improvements, and Present State of Society and Manners, Laws and Government. ... *Boston; Belknap and Young.* MDCCXCII. 8vo, pp. 480, Subscribers, 7 l., and Errata, (1). 4434

There are copies in which the imprint varies. Vol. II., *Printed at Boston, for the Author. by Isaiah Thomas and Ebenezer T. Andrews, Fausts' Statue, No. 56 Newbury St.* MDCCXCI. *Boston; Printed for the Author by Thomas & Young.* 1792; and Vol. III, *Printed at Boston for the Author, by Belknap & Young, State St.* MDCCXCIII.

BELKNAP. The History of New-Hampshire; Comprehending the Events of one complete Century and seventy-five years, from the Discovery of the River Piscataqua to the Year One thousand seven hundred and ninety. Containing also, A Geo-

graphical Description of the State, with Sketches of its Natural History, Productions, Improvements, and Present State of Society and Manners, Laws and Government. By Jeremy Belknap, D.D. The Second edition, with large additions and improvements. Published from the Author's last manuscript. Illustrated by a Map. *Boston; Bradford and Read.* 1813. 3 vols., 8vo, pp. 351, Map; 377; 354. 4435

There are copies of this edition with the following title:

BELKNAP. The History of New-Hampshire. Comprehending the Events of one complete Century from the Discovery of the River Piscataqua. By Jeremy Belknap, A.M. ... [*Dover*]; *Printed for O. Crosby and J. Varney, by J. Mann and J. K. Remick.* 1812. 3 vols., 8vo, pp. 351; 377; 354. Map. 4436

The titles to Vol. II and III of this date read the same as in No. 4434.

BELKNAP. The History of New-Hampshire. By Jeremy Belknap, D.D. ... From a Copy of the Original Edition, having the Author's last Corrections. To which are added Notes, containing various Corrections and Illustrations of the Text, and Additional Facts and Notices of Persons and Events therein mentioned. By John Farmer. ... Vol. I. *Dover; S. C. Stevens and Ela & Wadleigh.* 1831. 8vo, pp. xvi, 512. Portrait. H.

This edition was not completed. This is the fourth edition of Vol. I; *see* supra. For an extensive notice of this work, *see* M. R., XII, 158; LXXIII, 278.

BELKNAP. A Sermon, delivered before the Convention of the Clergy of Massachusetts, In Boston, May 26, 1796. By Jeremy Belknap ... . *Boston.* 1796. 8vo, pp. 29. S., H. 4438

BELKNAP. A Sermon on Military-Duty, preached At Dover, [N. H.], November 10, 1772 ... At a Review of the Second Regiment of Foot ... . By Jeremy Belknap ... . *Salem,* [*Mass.*] MDCCLXXIII. 8vo, pp. 27. H., W. 4439

BELKNAP. A Sermon, Delivered on the 9th of May, 1798, the Day of the National Fast ... . By Jeremy Belknap ... . *Boston; Printed by Samuel Hall.* 1798. 8vo, pp. 29. B., H.

BELKNAP. Life of Jeremy Belknap, D.D. the Historian of New Hampshire. With Selections from his Correspondence and Other Writings. Collected and arranged by his Grand-Daughter. *New York; Harper and Brothers.* 1847. 16mo, pp. 253. Portrait. 4441

Also: A Sermon preached at the Installation of Rev. Jedidiah Morse ... in Charlestown, On the 30th of April 1789. By Jeremy Belknap ... . *Boston.* 1789. 8vo, pp.

32. H. Two Sermons, delivered April 27, 1788, on the Institution and Observation of the Sabbath. ... *Boston; S. Hall, and Manning & Loring. April,* 1801. 8vo, pp. 38. H. And other sermons and addresses. Concerning Belknap and his works, *see* N. H. Hist. Coll., Vol. I, pp. 284–288; and the indexes to the first three series of the Mass. Hist. Coll.; N. A. Rev., XVIII, 34; XLVI, 480; and Polyanthea.

BELKNAP (Rufus R.) The Fire Marshal Almanac and Reference Book for the Year 1859. Containing ... a Memoranda [*sic*] Of past Fires ... . Also, the Ordinances of the City in relation to Fires, together with an account of several Large Fires ... . By Rufus R. Belknap ... . [*New York.* 1858.] 36mo, pp. 70.

This was the first number published. The author asserts that it had a circulation of 243,000 copies. The next number was entitled:

BELKNAP. The Fireman's Almanac ... . By Rufus R. Belknap ... . *New York; H. Dexter & Company,* [etc., 1859.] 12mo, pp. (70). Continued. H. 4443

BELKNAP. Fire Marshal Rufus R. Belknap's Semi-Annual Report of ... Fires in ... Brooklyn, W. D. ... ending April 30th, 1860, with ... Full Particulars ... . *Brooklyn; printed by Andrew R. Rome.* [1860]. 8vo, pp. 16. H. 4444

BELL (A. N.) Malignant Pustule in the United States. By A. N. Bell ... . *Albany.* 1862. 8vo, pp. 25. H. 4445

BELL (A. W.) State Register; comprising an Historical and Statistical account of Louisiana, from its earliest Settlement as a Territory down to its present period as a State; with a list of all State and Parish Officers. By A. W. Bell. *Baton Rouge.* 1855. 8vo. C. 4446

[BELL (Andrew)]. Men and Things in America. *London; Longman.* 1838. 12mo. 4447

From an advertisement in another book, in which he is described as author of "Thomason's Men," etc.

BELL (B.) An Impartial History of the Trial of Benjamin Bell for the pretended crime of Extortion, etc. *Windsor.* 1797. 12mo, pp. 155. N. 4448

BELL. A Sermon Preached at Steuben April 1813, in which are shewn the Evil effects of War and when it may be Lawful and Expedient to go to War. By Rev. Benjamin Bell, A.M. *Plainfield. March,* 1814. 8vo, pp. 86. 4449

Also: A Discourse, delivered at Cornish (N. H), 1792. *Windsor,* (*V.*) [1792.] 8vo, pp. 51. And other discourses.

BELL (C.) Facts relating to the Early History of Chester, N. H., from the Settlement in 1720, until the Formation of the State Constitution in the Year 1784. Collected By Charles Bell. MDCCCLI. *Concord; for the N. H. Historical Society by G. Parker Lyon.* 1863. 8vo, pp. 73. H. 4450

BELL (D.) A Short Journal of the Labours and Travels, in the Work of the Ministry, of that Faithfull Servant of Christ, Deborah Bell. [Edited by Robert Bell.] *London; Luke Hinde.* 1762. 8vo, 5¾ sheets. + *London; James Phillips.* 1766. 8vo, 8 sheets. 4451

There is also a life of Deborah Bell in "The Friend's Library," *Philadelphia,* 1841. Vol. V.

BELL (H.) Speech of Hon. Hiram Bell, of Ohio, in the House ... March 11, 1852, on the Public Domain and the Tariff. [*Washington.* 1852.] 8vo, pp. 7. H. 4452

BELL (James). A System of Geography, Popular and Scientific, or a Physical, Political, and Statistical Account of the World. ... By James Bell, ... *Glasgow; A. Fullerton & Co.* MDCCCXXXII. + [*Ibid*]. MDCCCXXXVI. 6 vols., 8vo. 4453

Volumes five and six relate to America. There is a new edition, corrected and revised to 1847, 6 vols., 8vo, pp. 3700, atlas, maps, and illustrations.

BELL. An epistle to Friends in Maryland, Virginia, Barbadoes, and the other Colonies, and Islands in the West Indies, where any Friends are. [Dated *Brownley, near London, 3rd month,* 1741.] Folio, 1 sheet. 4454

BELL (John), *b.* 1762, *d.* 1820. An Inquiry into the Causes which produce, and the Means of preventing Diseases among British Officers, Soldiers, and Others in the West Indies. Also Notes, relating to some particulars in the Army in ... the West Indies. By John Bell, M.D. ... *London; J. Murray.* M.D.CCXCI. 8vo, pp. xv, 180. H. 4455

BELL (J.) On Baths and Mineral Waters. ... Part 2. A History of the Chemical Composition and Medical Properties of the Chief Mineral Springs of the United States and of Europe. *Philadelphia; Porter.* 1831. 12mo, pp. 18, 532. 4455*a*

BELL. The Mineral and Thermal Springs of the United States and Canada. By John Bell, M.D. ... . *Philadelphia; Parry and McMillan.* 1855. 12mo, pp. xx, (1), 14–394. C., H.

BELL. Report on the Importance and Economy of Sanitary Measures to Cities. *New-York.* 1860. 8vo, pp. 243. (City Document.) C. 4457

There are some notices of American physicians in his Medical Heroism. Address ... February 24, 1859. ... *Philadelphia.* 1859. 8vo, pp. 38. H.

BELL (J.) An Address, delivered before the Alumni Society of the University of Nashville, October 3, 1843, by the Hon. John Bell, A.M. With ... a Catalogue of the Alumni and certain Proceedings of the Society. *Nashville; W. F. Bang & Co., Printers.* 1844. 8vo, pp. 42. H. 4458

BELL. Mr. Bell's Suppressed Report in relation to difficulties between the Eastern and Western Cherokees. [n. p., 1840.] 8vo, pp. 23. S. 4459

BELL. Speech of John Bell, of Tennessee, on Slavery in the United States, and the Causes of the present Dissensions between the North and South. Delivered in the Senate, ... the 5th and 6th of July, 1850. *Washington; Gideon & Co.* 1850. 8vo, pp. 30. 4460

Another edition is entitled:

BELL. The Compromise Bill. Speech of the Hon. John Bell, of Tennessee, in the Senate, ... July 3 and 5, 1850, On the Bill for the Admission of California ... [etc.] *Washington,* [1850.] Large 12mo, pp. 24. H. 4461

Also: An Address delivered at Nashville, Oct. 5, 1820, at the University of Nashville. *Nashville.* 1830. 8vo, pp. 37. Speech ... at Vauxhall Garden, Nashville, on the 23rd of May, 1835. *Nashville; printed by W. Hasell Hunt & Co.* 1835. 8vo, pp. 37. H. Speech ... on Naval Appropriation Bill; ... March ... 1836. *Washington.* 1836. 8vo. Speech ... on the Bill to secure the Freedom of Elections. House ... January 25, 1837. [*Washington.* 1837.] 8vo, pp. 16. H. Speech ... on the Bill making Appropriations for the Suppression and Prevention of Indian Hostilities. ... May 31, 1838. *Washington.* 1838. 8vo, pp. 16. Speech ... on the Message of the President of the United States. ... December 26, 1838. 8vo, pp. 23. H. Speech of Mr. Bell ... on his Bill to secure the Freedom of Elections. ... April, 1840. *Washington.* 1840. 8vo, pp. 39. B. Speech ... on the Sub-Treasury Bill. ... June 16 and 17, 1840. *Washington.* 1840. 8vo, pp. 23. B. Speech ... on the Mexican War. ... February 2 and 3, 1848. [*Washington.* 1848.] 8vo, pp. 32. H. Speech ... on Non Intervention, April 13, 1852. 8vo, pp. 32. + *Washington.* 1852. 8vo, pp. 16. ... Speech ... March 3, 1854. On the bill to establish the Nebraska and Kansas Territories, and to repeal the Missouri Compromise. [*Washington.* 1854.] 8vo, pp. 16. Speech ... On the Nebraska and Kansas Bill, May 24, 25, 1854. 8vo, pp. 24. Speech ... delivered at a Mass Meeting of the American Party, held at Knoxville, Tenn., Sept. 22, 1855. 8vo, pp. 22. Speech, Upon our Relations with Great Britain, Feb. 26, 1856. *Washington.* 1856. 8vo, pp. 15. Lieut. M. F. Maury. Speech ... on the Naval Retiring Board; ... April 28 and 29, 1856. *Washington.* 1856. 8vo, pp. 13. H.

Speech ... On the Acquisition of Cuba, Feb. 26, 1858. 8vo, pp. 16. Speech ... on the Admission of Kansas under the Lecompton Constitution. ... March 18, 1858. [*Washington.* 1858.] 8vo, pp. 32. H. Speech on the Fifteen-million Loan Bill ... May 26, 1858. *Washington.* 1858. 8vo, pp. 31.

BELL. ... The Life, Speeches, and Public Services of John Bell, Together with a Sketch of the Life of Edward Everett. ... *New York; Rudd & Carleton.* M DCCC LX. 16mo, pp. 118. Portrait. H. 4462

BELL. Who is John Bell? [n. p., 1860.] 4to, pp. 4. H.

BELL (J. C.) Addresses on the Occasion of the Death of the Hon. John C. Bell, Assemblyman from El Dorado County: delivered in the Assembly and Senate of California, Seventeenth and Eighteenth of April, 1860. *Sacramento; printed by Charles T. Botts.* 1860. 8vo, pp. 29. H. 4464

BELL (J. G.) American Revolutionary War. Catalogue of an Extraordinary Collection of Original Documents connected with the British Army ... containing also a few Autograph Letters, &c., of the Leaders of the American Army. On Sale by John Gray Bell ... . *Manchester.* 1857. 8vo, pp. 44. N.

In 1860, this collection belonged to Thomas Phillips, Bart., Middle Hill, Worcestershire.

BELL (James H.) [Declaration of his Political Views. *Austin; Texas.* 1866?] Broadside. H. 4466

BELL (J. M.) A Poem: delivered August 1st, 1862. By J. Madison Bell, at the Grand Festival to commemorate the Emancipation of the Slaves in the District of Columbia, and ... the British West Indian Isles. *San Francisco; B. F. Sterett.* 1862. 8vo, Title, pp. 10. H. 4467

BELL. A Poem entitled The Day and the War, delivered January 1, 1864 ... by J. Madison Bell, at the Celebration of the First Anniversary of President Lincoln's Emancipation Proclamation. *San Francisco.* 1864. 8vo, pp. 27. H. 4468

BELL (Joshua F.) Speech of Mr. F. Bell, of Kentucky, on the Oregon Question, delivered in the House ... February 4, 1846. *Washington.* 1846. 8vo, pp. 14. H. 4469

BELL (Luther V). An Address ... Derry, N. H. July 4, 1832. By Luther V. Bell ... . *Concord.* 1832. 8vo, pp. 22.

Contains some notice of the temperance movement.

BELL. Design for the Butler Hospital for the Insane at Providence, Rhode Island. By Luther V. Bell. [n. p., n. d.] 8vo, pp. 22. 4471

BELL. ... Dr. Bell's Letter. [On the Heating and Ventilation of the Proposed City Prison.] *Boston.* 1845. 8vo, pp. 17. (City Doc., No. 36.) H. 4471*a*

BELL. Eulogy on General Zachary Taylor, late President of the United States, delivered ... Cambridge, August 13, 1850. By Luther V. Bell. *Cambridge.* 1850. 8vo, pp. 43. H. 4472

BELL. Medical Opinion in the Parish Will Case. By Luther V. Bell ... . *New York.* 1857. 8vo, pp. 69. B. 4473

BELL. Memoir of Dr. Luther V. Bell, of Massachusetts. Reprinted from the American Journal of Insanity, October, 1854. *Utica, N. Y.* 1854. 8vo, pp. 27. Portrait. H. 4474

BELL. ... What Diet can be selected which will ensure the Greatest Probable Health and Strength to the Laborer in the Climate of New England? ... By Luther V. Bell, M.D. *Boston; D. Clapp, Jr.* 1836. 8vo, pp. 46, (1). H. 4475

The V is not the initial of any name, but a letter assumed by Mr. Bell to distinguish himself from another Luther Bell.

BELL (M. A.) ... South side View of Cotton is King; and the Philosophy of American Slavery, By Manuel A. Bell; Atlanta, Ga. *Atlanta.* 1860. 8vo, pp. 47. 4476

BELL (R.) Hispanicarum Rerum Scriptores aliquot ex Bibliotheca clarissimi viri Dr. Roberti Bell, Angli nunc accuratius emendatiusque recusi ... . Cum Indice copiosissimo. *Francofurti*, 1579–80. 2 vols., folio. 4477

In the breviate of the reign of Philip II, particular mention is made of the missions to Florida, Mexico, and Peru. For the title of the third volume, *see* Potthast, Bib. Hist. Med. Ævi.

BELL (R.) Bell's Address to Every Free-Man; but especially to the Free Citizens of Pennsylvania, Concerning, A Tyrannical Embargo, now laid upon the Free-Sale of Books by Auction. ... *Philadelphia; Robert Bell.* M,DCC,LXXXIV. 8vo, pp. 7, (1). C., H.

BELL. Illuminations for Legislators, and for Sentimentalists; containing, I. Sentiments on what is Freedom, and what is Slavery, By a Farmer [J. Dickinson]. II. Sentiments on Lib-

erty, exhibited in Observations on the Revolution of America, By Abbe [*sic*] Raynal. ... IV. ... Re-published by Robert Bell ... Provedore to the Sentimentalists in America. *Philadelphia; Robert Bell.* M,DCC,LXXXIV. 8vo, 2 l., pp. 52. H. 4479

BELL. Bell's Memorial on the Free Sale of Books: To which are added Sentiments on what is Freedom ... . By a Farmer. *Philadelphia; Robert Bell.* M,DCC,LXXXIV. 4480

This is the second title-page of his "Illuminations."

BELL (S. B.) Sermon delivered by the Rev. Samuel B. Bell, D.D., ... New York City, on Thanksgiving Day, Nov. 24, 1864. *New York; Baptist & Taylor.* 1864. 8vo, pp. 24.

BELL (S. S.) Colonial Administration of Great Britain. By Sidney Smith Bell ... . *London; Longman*, [etc.] 1859. 8vo, pp. (1), xi, 470. C., H. 4482

BELL (T.) *See* Belcher (C.)

BELL (W.) Hints to Emigrants, in a Series of Letters from Upper Canada. By the Rev. William Bell ... . *Edinburgh; Waugh and Innes.* M.DCCC.XXIV. 12mo, pp. iv, 236. Map, and Plans. H., P. 4483

BELLAMONT (*Earl of*). *See* Coote (R.)

BELLAMY (George Anne). Apology for the Life of Mrs. Bellamy. Written by herself ... Second Edition. *London.* 1785. 6 vols., 12mo. Portrait, and Frontispieces. 4484

"Vol. VI was published subsequently, and is frequently wanting."—LOWNDES. Contains some particulars concerning General Braddock. There is a French version: Mémoires ... traduites de l'anglais par P.-V. Benoist et Delamarre. *Paris; H. Nicolle*, an VII [1799]. 2 vols., 8vo. Portrait. + Nouvelle édition, publiée avec une notice sur l'auteur, par Thiers. *Paris; Ponthieu.* 1824. 2 vols., 8vo. The latter edition forms part of a "Collections des mémoires sur l'art dramatique." Also in German: Merkwürdiges Leben ... von ihr selbst beschrieben. Aus dem Englischen. *Hamburg.* 1786–87. 3 vols., 8vo.

BELLAMY (Joseph). A Blow at the Root of the Refined Antinomianism of the Present Age. *Boston*, 1763. 8vo, pp. 46.

BELLAMY. A Careful and Strict Examination of the External Covenant, a Reply to Rev. Moses Mather's "The Visible Church in covenant with God further illustrated." A Vindication of the Plan on which the Churches of New England were originally formed, &c. *New Haven*, [n. d.] 8vo, pp. 186.

[BELLAMY.] Dialogue on the Christian Sacraments wherein the Nature and Import of an Attendance on them are inquired into, from the Scriptures. *Boston.* 1762. 8vo. 4487

Written on occasion of the dismissal of the Rev. Jonathan Edwards from his pastoral office at Northampton.

BELLAMY. Essay on the Nature and Glory of the Gospel of Jesus Christ, etc. By Joseph Bellamy, A.M. ... *Boston, N. E.* 1762. 12mo. + *Worcester; Isaiah Thomas.* 1797. 12mo. *London.* M,DCC,LXXXIV. 12mo, pp. viii, 227, (2). + *London*, [n. d.] 8vo. W. 4488

A supplement to Theron, etc.

BELLAMY. The Great Evil of Sin, as it is committed against God: A Sermon preached at Goshen, before the Consociation of Litchfield County, Conn., May 30, 1753. By Joseph Bellamy. *Boston; S. Kneeland.* 1753. 8vo, pp. 36. M. 4489

BELLAMY. The Half-way Covenant. A Dialogue. By Joseph Bellamy, D.D. [Motto:] *Boston; Re-printed and Sold by Kneeland and Adams.* MDCCLXIX. 8vo, pp. 16. H. 4490

BELLAMY. The Half-way Covenent, A Dialogue, Between Joseph Bellamy, D.D. And a Parishioner, Continued. By the Parishioner. Correcting Some Errors Contained in the former Dialogue. *New London; Timothy Green.* 1769. 12mo, pp. 17.

BELLAMY. The Inconsistence of Renouncing the Half-way Covenant, and yet retaining the Half-way Practices, a Dialogue. *New Haven*, [n. d.] 4to. S. 4492

BELLAMY. The Law our School-Master, A Sermon preached at Litchfield before the Association of Litchfield County, June 8th, 1756, and published with great enlargements. *New Haven.* 1756. 8vo. 4493

BELLAMY. Letters and Dialogues between Theron, Paulinus, and Aspasio. Upon the Nature of Love to God, Faith in Christ, and Assurance of a Title to eternal Life. With some Remarks on The Sentiments of the Rev. Messrs. Hervey and Marshall, on these Subjects. Published at the Request of many. By Joseph Bellamy, A.M. of Bethlem in New England. *Boston.* 1750. 12mo. + *Boston; S. Kneeland.* 1759. 16mo, 2 l., pp. v, 227. B., C. + *London.* 1761. 12mo. + *Washington, Conn.* 1798. 12mo. 4494

BELLAMY. Reply to the Rev. Moses Mather's piece entitled the Visible Church in Covenant with God, further illustrated, &c., a Vindication of the plan on which the Churches in New England were originally formed, interspersed with Remarks upon some things advanced by Mr. Sandeman on some of the important points in debate. *New Haven*, [n. d.] 4495

BELLAMY. A Sermon Delivered before the General Assembly Of the Colony of Connecticut, at Hartford, On the Day of the Anniversary Election, May 13th, 1762. By Joseph Bellamy ... . *New London; Timothy Green*, [1762]. 8vo, pp. 43.

BELLAMY. The Works of Joseph Bellamy, D.D. First Pastor of the Church in Bethlem, Conn. With a Memoir of his Life and Character [by Tryon Edwards]. ... *New York.* 1811–12. 3 vols., 8vo. + *Boston; Doctrinal Tract and Book Society.* 1853. Large 12mo, pp. lxxiii, 613; v, 731. H. 4497

Mr. Bellamy was an active controvertialist, and published many works not noted in the above list. Among them are: The Millenium; or, the Thousand Years of Prosperity promised to the Church of God ... shortly to commence, ... *Elizabethtown.* 1794. 8vo, pp. 321. Remarks on the Rev. Mr. Croswell's Letter To the Reverend Mr. Cumming. ... *Boston; S. Kneeland.* M,DCC,LXIII. 8vo, pp. 36. H. A Second Dialogue, between a Minister and his Parishioner, concerning the Half-Way Covenant. *Hartford.* 1769. 12mo, pp. 15. Sermons Upon the Divinity of Jesus Christ. The Millenium. The Wisdom of God, in the Permission of Sin. ... *Boston.* M,DCC,LVIII. 12mo, pp. vi, 209, (2). N. + *Northampton, England.* 1780 or 1783? 12mo. That there is but one Covenant, ... viz., The Covenant of Grace, proved from the Word of God, and the Doctrine ... Advanced by the Rev. Moses Mather ... shewn to be an Unscriptural Doctrine; prefixed is an Answer to a Dialogue concerning the Half Way Covenant lately printed at New London. *New Haven.* 1769. 8vo. N. True Religion delineated. ... In Two Discourses. The whole adapted to the weakest capacities, and designed for the Establishment, comfort and quickening of the People of God, in these evil Times. By Joseph Bellamy, A.M., with a Preface by the Rev. Mr. Edwards. *Boston.* 1750. 8vo. + Second Edition. *Edinburgh; M. Gray.* 1788. 12mo, Title, pp. xii, 390. + *Morristown.* 1804. 8vo. M. The Wisdom of God In the Permission of Sin, Vindicated; In Answer to a late Pamphlet, Intitled, An Attempt, &c. ... *Boston; S. Kneeland.* 1760. 12mo, Title, pp. iii, (3), 87. H.

BELLAMY. An Attempt to point out the fatal and pernicious Consequences of the Rev[d]. Mr. Joseph Bellamy's Doctrines respecting Moral Evil. *Boston; Edes & Gill.* 1759. 8vo, pp. 31. 4498

The MS. from which this was printed, as is supposed, is in the library of Harvard College.

BELLARDI (Luigi). Saggio di Ditterologia Messicana. 2 parti ed appendice. *Torino.* 1860–62. 4to, pp. 215. 5 Plates.

BELLARMINO. Declaracion Copiosa de las Quatro Partes Mas Essenciales, y Necessarias de la Doctrina Christiana compvesto

por orden del Beatissimo P. Clemente Octaus de Felice Memoria. Por el Eminentissimo Cardenal Roberto Belarminio, de la Compania de Iesvs, con las adiciones del Maestro Sebastian de Lirio, Catedratico de Prima de Griego en la Vniversidad de Alcala. Tradvcida de Lengva Castellana en la General del Inga Por el Bachiller Bartolomé Ivrado Palomino Natural de la cuidad del Cuzco, Beneficiado de la Doctrina de Cauana, y Guandoual, Vicario, Iuez Ecclesiastico, y Comissaria de la Santa Cruzada de la Provincia de Conchucos, Predicador general enla dicha lengua en este Arçobispado, y Visitador general de la Idolalatria Dirigida al Illmo Señor Dod. D. Pedro de Villagomez, Arzobispo de la Civdad de los Reyes, del Consego de su Magestad. *Con Licencia, Impresso en Lima, por Iorge Lopez de Herrera, en la Calle de la Carcel de Corte, Año de* 1694. 4to, 12 p. l., Text, 136 leaves, pp. 3. 4500

Originally published in Italian. *Roma; Luigi Zanetti.* 1603. 12mo or 4to. For a list of the numerous editions and translations, *see* Backer, I, 74–77; VII, 87–91. Except the Bible and the Imitation of Christ, no work, says Backer, has been translated into so many languages. This edition contains both the Spanish and Peruvian versions.

BELLE BOYD. *See* [Hardinge (*Mrs.* B.)]

BELLE BRITTAN on a Tour. *See* [Fuller (H.)]

BELLE SCOTT; or, Liberty Overthrown! A Tale for the Crisis. ... *Columbus; D. Anderson: Cincinnati; Geo. S. Blanchard.* 1856. 12mo, pp. 426. C., H. 4501

BELLECOMBE (André de). Discours prononcé à la séance d'ouverture du Congrès d'archéologie américaine, le 23 juillet 1863, par A. de Bellecombe, président. *Paris; au local du Comité* 1864. 8vo, pp. 22. 4502

BELLEFONTAINE *and* INDIANA RAILROAD Co. First Annual Report. 1851. *Cleveland*, 1851. 8vo. Continued. 4503

Exhibit of the Affairs of the Bellefontaine and Indiana Railroad Company, July, 1851. *New-York.* 1851. 8vo. 4504

Bellefontaine Railroad Line. Third Joint Annual Report ... for 1858. *Cleveland, O.* 1859. 8vo. 4505

Bellefontaine Cemetery. Annual Report. *St. Louis.* 1862. 8vo. Continued. 4505*a*

BELLE-FOREST (François de, *comingeois*). L'histoire | vniverselle | dv monde, | contenant l'entiere descri- | ption & situation des quatre parties de la terre, la diuision | & estenduë d'vne chacune Region & Prouince d'icelles. | Ensemble l'origine & particulieres mœurs, loix, coustumes, | religion, & ceremonies de toutes les nations, & peuples | par qui elles sont habitées. | Diuisée en quatre liures. | Par François de Belle-forest Comingeois. | Marque typogr. | *A Paris: | Chez Geruais Mallot, à l'Aigle d'or, ruë S. | Iean de Beauuais.* 1570. | Avec Privilege dv Roy. | 4to, 18 l., pp. 317, 13 l. 4506

A curious compilation. Pages 245–317, relate to America. For Belleforest's "Cosmographie," *see* Munster (S.)

BELLEGARDE (H. L.) *See* Neimeyer Bellegarde (H. L. de).

BELLEGARDE (Jean Baptiste Morvan de). Histoire Universelle des Voyages faits par Mer et par Terre, dans l'Ancien et dans le Nouveau Monde. Pour éclairer le géographie ancienne et moderne. Par L'Abbe J. B. M. de Bellegarde. *Amsterdam.* 1708. 24mo. C. 4507

BELLEGARDE. A complete collection of Voyages made into North and South America, in due order as they happen'd, beginning from Christopher Columbus, and Americus Vespucius, and descending to this present time. By M. L'Abbé Bellegarde of the Royal Academy. Translated from the French original printed at Paris. Adorn'd with cuts. *London.* 1711. 8vo, pp. 364. B. 4508

"Published in French at Paris in 1707, under the name of *Du Perier.*" *See* infra. "It is the same book as Du Perier's, printed in 1708, with a new title-page, in which the name of the Abbé Bellegarde is substituted for that of Du Perier."—RICH. Bellegarde also translated Las Casas.

BELLEGARRIGUE (A.) Les femmes d'Amérique par A. Bellegarrigue. *Paris; Blanchard.* 1853. 32mo, pp. 96. H. 4509

BELLE ISLE. Arrest du Conseil d'Etat du Roy qui ordonne l'Infeodation de l'Isle, Terre et Marquisat de Belle Isle au profit de la Compagnie des Indes, du 17 Mars 1720. *Paris.* 1720. 4to. 4510

Belleisle. An impartial Narrative of the Reduction of Belleisle. Containing a Detail of the Military Operations, and every interesting Anecdote, since the first landing of our Forces on the Island, to the Surrender of the Citadel of Palais. In a Series of

Letters, Written by an Officer, employed on the Expedition. *London; Printed for J. Burd, at the Temple Exchange, Fleet-street.* 1761. 8vo, Half Title, Title, pp. 48. 4511

Belle Isle. Lettres Patentes du Roy portant confirmation du Contrat d'Infeodation de la Terre de Belle Isle. *Paris.* 1720. 4to. 4512

BELLEMARE. A MM. les membres de la Chambre des députés. Résumé de le dernière époque de la question française dans la Plata. Par Alfred Gustave Bellemare. *Paris; impr. de Brière.* 1841. 8vo, pp. 60. 4513

The three following tracts are signed A. G. Bellemare.

[BELLEMARE.] Affaire de la Plata. Notes statistiques et commerciales sur le commerce français dans la Plata. *Paris; impr. de Brière.* 1841. 4to, pp. 4. 4514

[BELLEMARE.] Affaires de la Plata. Réfutations des nouvelles allégations du ministère. *Paris; impr. Brière.* 1841. 8vo, pp. 16. 4515

[BELLEMARE.] Affaires de la Plata; Compte-rendu du délégué de la population française de la rive gauche de la Plata, à ses commettans. *Paris; impr. Brière.* 1841. 4to, pp. 60. 4516

BELLEMARE. Question internationale. Recours à S. M. l'empereur. Capture et confiscation du brick anglais The Fame et de sa cargaisson, aussi de propriété anglaise. Blocus de Buenos-Ayres de 1847 à 1848. *Paris; impr. de Vignancour.* 1853. 4to. 4517

BELLEMARRE (Louis de). Costal, l'indien. Roman historique. Scènes de la guerre de l'indépendance du Mexique. Par Gabriel Ferry (Louis de Bellemarre). Ouvrage posthume. *Paris; Vve Lecou.* 1852. 12mo, 20½ sheets. + Seconde édition. *Paris; Hachette et Cie.* 1855. 16mo, 14¼ sheets. + Troisième édition. [*Ibid.*] 1862. 18mo, pp. 438. 4518

[BELLEMARRE.] Costal der Indianer. Historischer Roman. Scenen aus dem mexicanischen Befreiungskriege. Hinterlassenes Werk. Ins Deutsche übertragen von W. L. Wesché. *Leipzig. Kollmann.* 1853 [1852–53]. 4 vols., 8vo, pp. 179; 180; 190; 189. + Zweite Auflage. [*Ibid.*] 1855. 4 vols., 8vo, pp. 738. 4519

[BELLEMARRE.] Uit Amerika. Krijgsavonturen tijdens den Mexikaansche vrijheidsoorlog in het jaar 1811. Door G. Ferry. Naar het Fransch. *Amsterdam; de weduwe D. Kunst.* 1862. 8vo, pp. 2, 255. 4519*a*

[BELLEMARRE.] Costal, de Indiaan. Schetsen en tooneelen uit den Mexicaanschen vrijheidsoorlog. Uit het Fransch von G. Ferry vertaald door L. C. Cnopius. Nieuwe uitgave. *Leiden; van den Heuvel & van Lanten.* 1863. 2 parts, 8vo. 4519*b*

[BELLEMARRE.] Le dragon de la reine, ou Costal, l'indien. Roman historique; par Gabriel Ferry. *Paris; De Potter.* 1855. 4 vols., 8vo, 82 sheets. 4520

[BELLEMARRE.] Le coureur des bois, ou les chercheurs d'or; par Gabriel Ferry. *Paris; Cadot.* 1853. 7 vols., 8vo, 144 sheets. + Troisième édition, revue et corrigée avec soin sur des notes posthumes de l'auteur. *Paris; Victor Lecou.* 1853. 2 vols., 18mo, 24⅞ sheets. + Nouvelle édition. *Paris; Hachette et Cie.* 1860. 2 vols., 18mo, pp. 950. 4521

Originally published in the journal "L'Ordre."

[BELLEMARRE.] Die Blume der Prairie oder die deutschen Colonisten an den Ufern des Colorado. Von Gabriel Ferry. *Grimma; Verlags-Comptoir.* 1852. 2 vols., 8vo, pp. 228; 178. (Europäische Bibliothek, 646., 647. Band.) 4522

[BELLEMARRE.] Les révolutions du Mexique. Par Gabriel Ferry. Préface de George Sand. *Paris; Dentu.* 1864. 18mo, pp. xx., 257. 4523

[BELLEMARRE.] Scènes de la vie Méxicaine. Par Gabriel Ferry. *Paris, Lecou*, 1854. 12mo, 10 sheets. + Nouvelle édition. *Paris; Hachette et Cie.* 1856. 16mo, 10⅝ sheets. 4524

[BELLEMARRE.] Scenes de la Vie militaire au Mexique. Par Gabriel Ferry. *Paris; L. Hachette et Cie.* 1858. 12mo, pp. 295, Table, 1 l. + Seconde édition. *Paris; Hachette.* 1860. 18mo, pp. 228. 4525

First published in the "Revue des Deux Mondes" for 1850 and 1851.

[BELLEMARRE.] Aus dem Soldatenleben in Mexico. Ins Deutsche übertragen von L. Th. Fort. *Halle; Heynemann.* 1860. 2 Thle. in 1 Bde. 8vo, pp. 320. 4526

[BELLEMARRE.] Der Schwur. Historischer Roman aus dem mexicanischen Unabhängigkeitskriege von Gabr. Ferry. *Berlin: Sacco.* 1860. 2 vols., 16mo, pp. 719. (Novellen-Sammlung, Bdchn. 573–582.) 4527

[BELLEMARRE.] Die Helden des Südens. Mexikanische Kriegsbilder. Aus dem Französischen des Gabr. Ferry. *Berlin: Sacco.* 1854. 16mo, pp. 319. (Novellen-Sammlung, Bändchen. 222–226.) 4528

[BELLEMARRE.] De helden van het zuiden. Naar het Fransch. *Leiden: weduwe D. Kunst.* 1866. 8vo, pp. 142. 2 Lithographs. 4528*a*

[BELLEMARRE.] Neue transatlantische Bilder von Gabriel Ferry. *Grimma: Verlags-Comptoir.* 1851. 5 vols., 8vo, pp. 252; 214; 207; 234; 218. (Europäische Bibliothek, 472.–475., 490. Band.) 4529

[BELLEMARRE.] Scènes de la vie sauvage au Mexique. Par Gabriel Ferry. *Paris: Charpentier.* 1856. 16mo. + Troisième édition. [*Ibid.*] 1856. 12mo, pp. 347. + Quatrième édition. [*Ibid.*] 1860. 18mo, pp. vi, 347. + Sixième édition. [*Ibid.*] 18mo, pp. xii, 354. C. 4530

[BELLEMARRE.] Les sqatters. La clairière du bois des hogues. Par Gabriel Ferry. *Paris: Hachette et Cie.* 1858. 18mo, pp. 264. 4531

[BELLEMARRE.] Die Squatter oder Erlebnisse eines jungen Auswanderers in Virginien und Californien. *Sondershausen: Neuse.* 1860. 16mo, pp. 239. 4532

[BELLEMARRE.] De squatters, avonturen in de wouden en prairiën van Amerika. Door G. Ferry. *Amsterdam: de weduwe D. Kunst.* 1861. 8vo, pp. 230. Colored Vignette. 4432*a*

[BELLEMARRE.] The Tiger Hunter, by Capt. Mayne Reid. *London; Darton.* 1862. 12mo. 4533

[BELLEMARRE.] Vagabond Life in Mexico. By Gabriel Ferry. *London:* [*J. Blackwood*], 1856. Crown 8vo, pp. 450. + *New York*, 1856. 12mo. C. 4534

[BELLEMARRE.] Voyage et aventures au Mexique. Par L. de B. G. Ferry. *Paris: Charpentier.* 1864. 18mo, pp. 355. S.

[BELLEMARRE.] Der Waldgänger. Roman aus Amerika's Urwäldern von Gabr. Ferry. Deutsch von W. L. Wesché. *Leipzig: Kollmann.* 185–. 8 vols., 8vo, pp. 230; 207; 189; 208; 208; 184; 176; 199. + Zweite Auflage. [*Ibid.*] 8vo, pp. 1601. (Amer. Bibl., Bd. 175–182.) 4536

[BELLEMARRE.] The Woodrangers, by Capt. M. Reid. *London: Hurst and Blackett.* 1860. 3 vols., post 8vo. + *H. Lea.* 1860. 12mo. + *London: C. H. Clarke.* 1861. 12mo. 4537

[BELLEMARRE.] Amerikanische Reisenovellen. Nach dem Französischen von A. Diezmann. *Leipzig: Teubner.* 1847. 16mo, pp. 398. (Die belletristische Welt, 35.–40. Bändchen.)

[BELLEMARRE.] Der Waldläufer. Scenen aus dem mexicanischen Waldleben. Aus dem Französischen von G. Füllner. *Halle: Knapps Sortement-Buchhandlung.* 1851. 8 vols., 8vo, pp. 192; 200; 168; 164; 175; 155; 180; 124. + Aus dem Französischen von Chr. Fr. Grieb. *Stuttgart: Franckh.* 1851. 18 Bändchen, 8vo, pp. 259; 254; 322; 336. (Das belletristische. Ausland, 1575.-1592. Bändchen.) + Für die Jugend bearbeitet von Julius Hoffmann. *Breslau: Trewendt & Granier.* 1852. 2 vols., broad 8vo, pp. iv, 566. 12 colored Plates. + Zweite Auflage. [*Ibid.*] 1854 [1853]. + Dritte Auflage. [*Ibid.*] 1856. 2 vols., 8vo, pp. iv, 308; 1 l., 259. 12 Lithographs. 4539

[BELLEMARRE.] De woudlooper; schetsen en tafereelen uit de wouden en prairiën van Amerika. Door G. Ferry. Met eene voorede van J. J. A. Goeverneur. *Utrecht: B. Dekema.* 1856. Post 8vo. 12 colored Plates. + Naar de tweede Hoogduitsche uitgave van Julius Hoffmann. Derde druk, met eene voorede van J. J. A. Goeverneur. *Utrecht: B. Dekema.* 1864. 2 vols., 8vo, pp. 8, 316; 4, 262. 12 colored Copperplates. 4540

Bellemarre perished, in 1852, in the shipwreck of the packet "Amazon." I do not know whether his "Capitaine Pillavidas, *Paris, De Potter*, 1856," 3 vols., 8vo, and his "Le Vicomte de Châteaubrun, *Paris, De Potter*, 1856," 2 vols., 8vo, and 1861, 12mo, relate to America. His "Nouvelles mexicaines par Gabriel Ferry. Seconde édition revue et augmentée" forms the first Lieferung of the first Series of Van Muyden and Rudolph's "Collection d' auteurs français. *Berlin; Janke.* 1865. 8vo. He also published in the "Revue des Deux Mondes," between April, 1846, and Aug., 1851, thirteen articles on California, Mexico, etc., some of them extending through several numbers.

BELLENGER (*Rev.* J. M.) Catéchisme dans la langue des Abénakis. *Québec.* 1832. 12mo. 4541

BELLERS. Essays about the Poor, Manufactures, Trade, Plantations ... &c. By John Bellers. *London: T. Sowle.* 1699. 4to, 4 sheets. 4542

Included in an English catalogue of books relating to America. I have not seen it.

The Belles-Lettres Repository; and Monthly Magazine. *New York.* 1819. 4 vols., 8vo. 4543

Contains some historical articles.

BELLET (L.) La vérité sur les obligations mexicaines; par M. Louis Bellet. *Paris: Guérin.* 1867. 8vo, pp. 14. 4544

[BELLEVUE.] Courte Réponse à Gros Mémoire. *A Paris: de l'imprimerie Nationale.* 1790. 8vo, pp. 15. 4545

By M. Blanchetierre Bellevue, deputy from Martinique. It relates to colonial affairs, and is in reply to a memorial of the deputies of Saint-Pierre, presented to the National Assembly, but not, so far as I can learn, printed.

BELLEY. Belley de Saint-Domingue, représentant du peuple, à ses collègues. [6 fructidor an II. *Paris:*] *imp. de Pain.* [n. d.] 4to, pp. 48 or less. 4546

BELLEYME (A. de). La France et le Mexique par Adolphe de Belleyme ... . *Paris: Dentu.* 1863. 8vo, pp. 23. B. 4547

BELLIDO (Joseph). Vida de la Ven. Maria Ana Agreda de S. Ignacio, fundadora, y Prelada de las Religiosas Dominicas Recoletas de Sta Rosa de la Puebla de los Angeles. *Megico.* 1759. 8vo. 4548

Also: Elegia in Laudem S. Virginis Cristinæ. *Mexici.* 1749. 8vo.

Belligerent Rights Asserted and Vindicated against Neutral Encroachments. Being an answer to an Examination of the British Doctrine which subjects to capture a neutral trade not open in time of Peace. *London.* 1806. 8vo, pp. vii, 91. 4549

BELLIN (Jacques Nicolas). Description géographique de l'Amérique Septentrionale [sur-tout du Canada] avec des Remarques sur la navigation du Détroit de Belle-Isle; par M. Bellin. *Paris.* 4to. 4550

Title taken from Lelong, No. 2202.

BELLIN. Déscription Géographique de la Guyane. Contenant les Possessions et les Etablissemens des François, des Espagnols, des Portugais, des Hollandois dans ces vastes Pays. Le Climat les Productions de la Terre et les Animaux Leurs Habitans, leurs Mœurs, leurs Coutumes. et le Commerce qu'on y peut

faire. Avec des Remarques pour la Navigation et des Cartes, Plans et Figures. Dressées au dépost des Cartes et Plans de la Marine ... . Par le S. Bellin Ingenieur de la Marine. ... [*Paris; Imprimerie de Didot.* M. D. CC. LXIII.] 4to, 2 Titles, one engraved, pp. xiv, (2), 294, (1). 20 Maps, and 10 Plates. 4551

The author's name appears only on the engraved, the imprint only on the printed title. The latter is included in the pp. xiv.

BELLIN. Description géographique des debouquemens qui sont au nord de l'isle de Saint Domingue Avec des Cartes et des Plans des Isles qui forment ces Passages, Et des Dangers qui s'y trouvent. Pour le service des Vaisseaux du roy. ... Par N. Bellin ... . *Paris.* M. DCC. LXVIII. 4to, 5 l., pp. 152. 34 Maps and Plans. B., H 4552

Rich, I. 165, gives the date as above. Quérard, I. 165, says, 1766. This is the engraved title, on which alone the author's name appears. The printed title reads: Description des débouquemens qui sont au nord de l'isle de Saint-Domingue. ... *Versailles.* M. DCCLXXIII.

BELLIN. Déscription géographique des isles Antilles possedées par les Anglois. Sçavoir La Jamaïque, la Barbade, Antigue, Montserrat, S. Christophle, Nieves, l'Anguille, et les Vierges, Isles Lucayes et Bermudes. Pour joindre aux Cartes de ces Isles qui ont eté dressées au depost des Cartes et Plans de la Marine. Par le S. Bellin ... . [*Paris: Didot.*] M DCC LVIII. 4to, engraved and printed Title, pp. xij, 171. 15 Maps, and 7 Views. H.

The author's name appears only on the engraved title; the imprint only on the printed title. The latter is included in the pp. xij. I have seen a catalogue which describes a 12mo edition, *Amsterdam*, 1759.

BELLIN. L'Hydrographie Françoise; ou recueil des cartes générales et particulières qui ont été faites pour le service des vaisseaux du Roy, par ordre des ministres de la marine, depuis 1737, jusqu'en 1765. *Paris.* 1737–1765. 2 vols., folio. + 1804. 2 vols., folio. 80 Maps. C. 4554

Parts IX., X., XI., and XII., relate to America. Full particulars of this highly important marine atlas will be found in the "Catal. de Cartes comp. l'Hydrographie française." *Paris.* 1847.

BELLIN. Le petit atlas maritime recueil de cartes et plans des quatre du monde, en Cinq Volumes. I. Volume. Amerique Septentrionale et Isles Antilles. II. Volume. Amérique Meridionale. Mexique Terre-Ferme, Bresil, Perou, Chily. III. Volume. Asie et Afrique. IV. et V. Volumes. Europe et les Etats qu'elle contient. ... Par le S. Bellin ... . [n. p.] 1764. *Paris.* 1764. 5 vols., 4to. 575 Maps and Plans. 4555

BELLIN. Recueil des memoires qui ont été publiés avec les cartes hydrographiques, Que l'on a dressées au Dépôt des Cartes Plans de la Marine, pour le service des Vaisseaux du Roi par ordre du Ministere, depuis l'année 1737. jusqu'en 1751. Par le Sieur Bellin, Ingénieur ordinaire de la Marine. [*Paris.* 1851.] 4to. H. 4556

"A volume of these appeared, *Paris, Didot*, 1756, but M. Bellin has since written others as he published new maps."—LELONG. The memoirs were separately published; they are independently paged, and have no title-pages, but merely captions, and sometimes colophons.

BELLIN. Remarques sur le détroit de Belle-Isle, et les côtes septentrionales de la Nouvelle France, depuis la rivière S. Jean, jusqu'au cap Charles. *Paris: Didot.* 1758. 4to, pp. 16. 4557

BELLIN. Remarques sur la carte réduite de l'Océan septentrional, compris entre l'Asie et l'Amérique. *Paris: Didot.* 1766. 8vo. pp. 8. 4558

BELLIN (M.) Remarques sur la carte de l'Amérique Septentrionale, Comprise entre le 28e et le 72e dégré de Latitude, avec une description geographique de ces parties; Par M. Bellin ... . *Paris: Didot.* M. DCC. LV. 4to, pp. 131. H. 4559

BELLINI (B.) La Colombiade Poema eroico di Bernardo Bellini Professor ... *Micheli e Bellini.* 1826. 2 vols., 8vo.

BELLO (Andres). Silva Americana. La Agricultura de la Zona torrida. *Carácas.* 1863. 16mo, pp. 15. 4561

"One of the finest specimens of Spanish didactic poetry."—TRÜBNER.

BELLOC. Histoires de l'Amérique, et de l'Océanie, depuis l'époque de leur découverte jusqu'en 1839. Par M. Belloc. *Paris: P. Duménil.* 1839. 8vo, pp. 492. 31 Plates, and 2 Maps. 4562

Quérard says "488 pag." Forms Vol. X. of "Le Monde." Reprinted with the following title:

BELLOC. Histoires de l'Amérique, et d'Océanie, depuis les temps les plus reculés jusqu' à nos jours. Ouvrage orné de planches. *Paris.* 1846. 8vo. 4563

BELLOMONT (*Earl of*). *See* Coote (R.)

[BELLON DE SAINT-QUENTIN (J.)] Dissertation sur la traite des negrès. *Paris.* 1764. 12mo. 4564

BELLORO (Giovanni Tommaso). Notizie d' atti esistenti nel publico archivio de' notaj di Savona, concernenti la famiglia di Cristoforo Colombo. *Torino.* 1810. 8vo, pp. 14. + *Genova.* 1821. 4565

"This pamphlet having become very scarce, I had it reprinted in 1821."—G. B. SPOTORNO. Unfortunately, Spotorno does not give any title, and I have only been able to obtain one, conjecturally, from the following sentence of Harrisse (Notes on Columbus, p. 68): "Belloro's essay [in Zach, *see* below] seems to have been published in a different form, and as early as 1809, since we find a refutation in an anonymous pamphlet (by Giuseppe Nervi): Il Sig. Tommaso Belloro Avv. Savon. Vedi notizie d'atti esistenti nel pubb. arch. de' Notaj. di Savona, concernenti la famiglia di Cristoforo Colombo, stampate a Torino l'anno, 1810. ... 8vo, 14 pp." It is plain that Harrisse has confounded Giambattista and Tommaso Belloro, and apparently, in preparing his MS. for the press, he has mistaken a note found in some pamphlet of Nervi's for the title of the pamphlet. By Belloro's essay he means a long letter in Baron Zach's "Correspondance astronomique, *Gênes*, 1818, foll., Vol. XIV., by Giam Battista Belloro, expressing doubts whether Christopher Columbus was a Savonese. It is severely criticised by G. B. Spotorno, pp. 298–306 of Tom. IV. of his "Storia letteraria Della Liguria, *Genova*, 1824–58," 5 vols., 8vo. H. After mentioning a pamphlet on the same subject by Isnardi, Harrisse continues: "Thereupon Giambattista Belloro penned a powerful reply: 'Appendice dell' avvocato Giambattista Belloro alla revista critica sopra la patria di Cristoforo Colombo, contra la riposta di un academico di Cogoletto. *Genoa*, 1839, 8vo,' which, it is hardly necessary to add, silenced Cogoletto and Isnardi forever." It is difficult, in this whole account, to determine how much is the result of Harrisse's personal examination, and how much rests on the authority of others, or on conjecture.

BELLOT (J. R.) Memoirs of Lieutenant Joseph René Bellot ... . With his Journal of a Voyage in the Polar Seas in Search of Sir John Franklin. ... *London: Hurst and Blackett.* 1855. 2 vols., post 8vo, pp. vii, 391; Title, pp. 403. B. 4566

BELLOT (R.) Journal d'un Voyage aux mers polaires, executé à la recherche de Sir John Franklin, en 1851 et 1852–1854. Par J. R. Bellot, avec la précédé d'une notice sur sa vie et les travaux de l'Auteur, par M. Julien Lemer. *Paris: Perrot.* 1854. 8vo, pp. lvi, 414. Plate, Map, and Facsimile. C. + Avec une introduction par M. Paul Boiteau ... Seconde édition. *Paris: Perrotin.* 1866. 18mo, pp. xliv, 363. Map, and Portrait. 4567

BELLOT DES MINIÈRES (Ernest). La question américaine; suivie d'un appendice sur le coton, le tabac, et le commerce général des anciens États-Unis, par Ernest Bellot des Minières. *Paris: Dentu.* 1861. 8vo, pp. 48. + Deuxième édition. [*Ibid.*] 1861. 8vo, pp. 48. + Troisième édition. [*Ibid.*] 8vo, pp. 64. B. + Quatrième édition. [*Ibid.*] 8vo, pp. 74. C. + Cinquieme édition. [*Ibid.*] 1862. 8vo, pp. 96. 4568

BELLOWS (H. Whitney). Discourse Occasioned by the Death of William Ellery Channing, D.D., pronounced before the Uni-

tarian Societies of New-York and Brooklyn ... October 13th, 1842. By Henry W. Bellows. ... *New-York: Charles S. Francis and Company.* 1842. 8vo, pp. 28. H. 4569

BELLOWS. Historical Sketch of Col. Benjamin Bellows, Founder of Walpole: an Address, on occasion of the Gathering of his Descendants to the Consecration of his Monument, at Walpole, N. H., Oct. 11, 1854. By Henry W. Bellows. With an Appendix, containing an Account of the Family Meeting. *New-York: John A. Gray, Printer.* 1855. 8vo, 1 l., pp. 125, (1). 3 Plates, and Genealogical Chart. H., S. 4570

BELLOWS. The Leger and the Lexicon: or, Business and Literature in Account with American Education. An Oration ... July 26, 1853. By Henry W. Bellows. *Cambridge: John Bartlett.* 1853. 8vo, pp. 53. 4571

BELLOWS. Public Life in Washington, or the Moral Aspects of the National Capital and the apparent Tendencies of Political Thought and Feeling in Congress and Cabinet. An Address, to his own Congregation, May 7, 1866 ... by Henry W. Bellows. *New York: James Miller.* 1866. 8vo, pp. 26. B. 4572

BELLOWS. ... A Plea for Unbroken Fealty on the Part of the Loyal States to the Constitution and the Union, despite the offences of the Rebel States. A Discourse, given on ... National Fast, Sept 26, 1861 ... by Henry W. Bellows. *New York: H. B. Price.* 1861. 8vo, pp. 25. B., H 4573

BELLOWS. Unconditional Loyalty. By Henry W. Bellows, D.D. *New York: Anson D. F. Randolph.* 1863. 8vo, pp. 16. H. + [*Ibid.*] 12mo, pp. 12. 4574

BELLOWS. The War to end only when the Rebellion ceases. [Discourse on the National Fast, April 30.] By Henry W. Bellows, D.D. *New-York: Anson D. F. Randolph*, [1863]. 8vo, pp. 16. H. 4575

Also: Address at the Funeral of Robert C. Goodhue, at All Soul's Church, April 9th, 1862. *New York: J. A. Gray, Printer.* 1862. 8vo, pp. 12. The Advantage of Testing our Principles, Compensatory of the Evils of Serious Times. A Discourse ... Feb. 17th, 1861, [in] ... Philadelphia, ... *Philadelphia: C. Sherman & Son.* 1861. 8vo, pp. 20. H. ... Discourse ... on occasion of the Death of Jonathan Goodhue. ... . *New York: C. S. Francis & Co.* 1848, 8vo, pp. 24. H. ... A Discourse at the Installation of Rev. William Henry Channing as Pastor ... in Washington, D. C., December 9th, 1861; ... *Washington, D. C.:* [n. d.] 8vo, pp. 30. H. Duty and Interest identical in the present Crisis. A Sermon preached in All Soul's Church, April 14, 1861. *New York: Wynkoop, Hallenbeck & Co.* 1861. 8vo, pp. 16. Letter ...

to Gov. Morgan of New York, relative to the Plans and Wants of the United States Sanitary Commission, Oct. 22, 1861. [Letter ... to S. G. Perkins, relative to the future of Disabled Soldiers, August 15, 1862.] Sanitary Commission, No. 49. [n. p., n. d.] 8vo, pp. 8. Letter ... to J. S. Newberry, M.D. Secretary of the Western Department, November 5, 1862. U. S. San. Com'n, 1862. 8vo, pp. 10. U. S. Sanitary Commission. No. 63. Letter to the Women of the North-West ... Oct. 29, 1863. [n. p., n. d.] 8vo, pp. 7. Memorial of William Ware. A Sermon preached to his Old Flock ... February 29, 1852, by his Successor, Henry W. Bellows. *New-York.* 1852. 8vo. The Moral Significance of the Crystal Palace: a Sermon, preached October 30, 1853 ... . *New York: G. P. Putnam & Co.* M. DCCC. LIII. 12mo, pp. 24. H. The New Man for the New Times. A Sermon preached ... on New-Year's Day, 1865, ... *New York: James Miller.* 1865. 8vo, pp. 16. H. Pensions required for the Relief and Support of Disabled Soldiers and Sailors and their Dependents. A Report to the Standing Committee, United States Sanitary Commission. By H. W. Bellows, D.D., President, New York, December 15, 1865. 8vo, pp. 26. Religious Liberty. ... A Sermon preached ... at Washington, on Washington's Birth-Day, February 22, 1852. ... *Washington: Printed by Kirkwood & McGill.* 1852. 8vo, pp. 15. Sermon preached November 26, 1843, at the Ordination of Mr. Dexter Clapp ... at Savannah, Ga. ... . *New York.* 1843. 8vo, pp. 32. B. A Sermon preached at the Installation of Adams Ayer, as Associate Pastor in Charlestown, N. H. June 7, 1855. ... . *Brattleboro: O. H. Platt, Printer.* 1855. 8vo, pp. 32. H. ... Sermon ... at the Ordination of Stephen Barker ... in Leominster, Mass., September 2, 1857. *Boston.* 1857. 8vo, pp. 42. H. ... A Sermon preached at the Ordination of Mr. Frederick N. Knapp ... Brookline, Mass. ... October 6, 1847. ... . *Boston.* 1847. 8vo, pp. 47. H. A Sermon occasioned by the late Riot in New York. *New York.* 1849. 12mo. Services at the Funeral of the late Professor James J. Mapes, Saturday, Jan. 13th, 1866. Conducted by the Rev. Dr. Bellows. *New York.* 1866. 8vo, pp. 14. Speech ... at ... Philadelphia, ... Feb. 24, 1863. ... *Philadelphia: C. Sherman, Son & Co., Printers.* 1863. 8vo, pp. 32. H. The State and the Nation—Sacred to Christian Citizens. A Sermon preached in ... New York, April 21, 1861. *New York: James Miller.* 1861. 8vo, pp. 16. H. Statement from Dr. Bellows, with Letters on Battles and Relief Work in Maryland, Sept. 24, 1862. [n. p.] 8vo, pp. 18. Sanitary Commission, No. 54. [Statement ... as to the Labor and Wants of the Commission. October 22, 1862.] [n. p., n. d.] 8vo. pp. 7. H. The Work of the Sanitary Commission. Address ... at Philadelphia, October 29, 1863. 8vo, pp. 8. B.

BELLOY (Auguste), *Marquis de.* Christophe Colomb et la découverte du nouveau monde. Par M. le marquis de Belloy. Compositions et gravures par Léopold Flameng. *Paris: E. Ducrocq.* 1864. 4to, pp. 208. 4576

BELLY (Felix). Apertura del istmo americano. Canal de Nicaragua; por el Sor Dr Felix Belly. *Paris: imp. Paul Dupont.* 1859. 8vo, pp. 15. 3 Maps. 4577

BELLY. Percement de l'isthme de Panama, par le canal de Nicaragua. Exposé de la question. Par Félix Belly. *Paris: Librairie nouvelle.* 1858. Rl. 8vo, pp. 178. 2 Maps. + Seconde édition. *Paris.* 1859. 8vo, pp. 114. 3 Maps. 4578

See Petermann's Geog. Mitth., 1859, pp. 360, 361. "Résumé d'un travail plus complet dont la publication est retardée par des causes materielles."

BELLY. Durchstich der amerikanischen Landenge. Kanal von Nicaragua ... Uebersetzt von K. Schibel. *Paris.* 1859. Large 8vo, pp. v, 104, and 3 lithographed Maps, folio. 4579

BELLY. À travers l'Amérique centrale Le Nicaragua et le canal interocéanique. Par Felix Belly publié avec une carte originale du Nicaragua ... . *Paris: librairie de la Suisse romande.* 1867. 2 vols., 8vo, 4 l., pp. 430; 2 l., pp. 480. 4580

See Thomé de Gamond.

BELMANN (E.) Erindringer om mit Ophold og mine Reiser i Brasilien fra Aaret 1825 til 1831. *Kjöbenhavn* [?]: *Schovelin.* 1833. 8vo, pp. viii, 240. 4581

BELMONT (Augustus). The Belmont Gallery, on Exhibition for the Benefit of the U. S. Sanitary Commission ... April 4th, to ... 9th. ... *New-York,* [1864]. Large 12mo, pp. 12. H.

Belmont Coal Mining Company. Reports of Prof. George I. Chace ... [etc.] Articles of Agreement, and By-Laws of the Company. *Boston.* 1863. 8vo, pp. 47. Map. H. 4583

The Transactions of the Belmont Medical Society. For 1851–52. ... *Bridgeport,* [*Ohio*]: *printed by J. G. Affleck.* 1852. 8vo, pp. 67. Continued. H. 4584

BELMONTE (B. E. C.) Neêrlandsch West-Indiê in zijne belangen, en Dr. W. R. van Hoëvell in zijn „Slaven en vrijen". Slavernij.—Emancipatie.—Kolonisatie. *Leiden: P. H. v. d. Heuvell.* 1855. 8vo. 4585

BELMONTE. Over de hervorming van het regerings-stelsel in Nederlandsch West-Indië. *Leiden: P. H. van den Heuvell.* 1857. 8vo, pp. (6), xiv, 244. 4586

Brinkman's "Alphabetische naamlijst" gives the author's name as B. E. Dolaço Belmonte.

BELMONTE BERMUDEZ. Algunas hazañas de las muchas de D. Garcia Hurtado de Mendoza, marques de Cañete. Por Luis Belmonte Bermudez. *Madrid: por Diego Flamanco.* 1622. 8vo.

"Comédie très rare."—TERNAUX, No. 443. "A poor attempt at flattery, which, on its title-page, professes to be the work of Luis de Belmonte, but, in a sort of table of contents, is ascribed chiefly to eight other poets, among whom are Antonio Mira de Mescua, Luis Velez de Guevara, and Guillen de Castro."—TICKNOR, Hist. Span Lit, 3d Ed., II, 470 *n.*

BELMONTET (L.) La tragédie mèxicaine. Maximilien, ode élégiaque; par Louis Belmontet. *Paris: imp. Kugelmann.* 1867. 8vo, pp. 4. H. 4588

BELOIT. First Annual Report of the Trustees of Beloit College. January, 1849. *Beloit: Wisconsin.* 1849. 8vo, pp. 20.

Catalogue of the Officers and Students of Beloit College and Seminary for the Academical Year 1849–50. *Beloit.* 1851. 8vo, pp. 19. Continued. A. 4590

BELOT (C.) La fièvre jaune à la Havane, sa nature et son traitement. Par Charles Belot ... . *Paris: J. B. Baillière et fils.* 1865. 8vo, pp. 166. 4591

BELOT (G.) La république du Salvador. Par Gustave de Belot. *Paris: Dentu.* 1865. 8vo, pp. 95. 4592

BELOT. Utilité pour Bordeaux d'un dock de marchandises au Centre-Amérique; par G. de Belot, directeur des monnaies de l'État de Salvador. *Bordeaux: imp. Dme Crugy.* 1862. 8vo, pp. 53. 4593

BELOT *and* LINDEMANN (C.) Amérique centrale. La république du Honduras et son chemin intérocéanique. Par Gustave de Belot et Charles Lindemann. *Paris: Dentu.* 1867. 8vo, pp. 72. 4594

BELSHAM (J.) Canadia, Ode Επινικιος. *London: Dodsley.* 1760. 4to. P. 4595

See "Monthly Review," 1st Series, Vol. XXII. 439. The author signs the dedication.

BELSHAM (T.) American Unitarianism or a Brief History of "the Progress and Present State of the Unitarian Churches in America." Compiled, from Documents and Information communicated by the Rev. James Freeman, D.D. and William Wells Jun. Esq. of Boston, ... [etc.] by Rev. Thomas Belsham ... . Extracted from his "Memoirs ... of the Reverend Theophilus Lindsay," printed in London, 1812 ... . *Boston: Nathaniel Willis.* 1815. 8vo, pp. 48. H. + Second Edition. *Boston.* 1815. 8vo, pp. 48. H. + Third Edition. *Boston.* 1815. 8vo. H. + Fourth Edition. *Boston.* 1815. 8vo, pp. 48. B. + Fifth Edition. *Boston.* 1815. 8vo, pp. 48. H. 4596

The fourth edition, and a review of it by Jedidah Morse, are included in "Tracts on the Unitarian controversy. *Boston.* 1816." 8vo. H.

BELSHAM. A Discourse on the Death of the Rev. Joseph Priestley, with a brief Memoir of His Life and Writings. By Thomas Belsham. *London.* 1804. 8vo. + *London.* 1808. + *Boston.* 1809. 12mo. 4597

BELSHAM. Memoirs of the Late Reverend Theophilus Lindsey, M.A. ... also a General View of the Progress of the Unitarian Doctrine in England and America. By Thomas Belsham. ... . *London: J. Johnson and Co.* 1812. 8vo, pp. xxiii, 544. Portrait. H. 4598

BELSHAM. A Sermon occasioned by the Death of Rev. Theophilus Lindsay, M.A. ... To which is added a Brief Biographical Memoir by Thomas Belsham. *London: T. Johnson.* 1808. 8vo, 2 l., pp. 72. H. 4599

BELSHAM (W.) Memoirs of the Reign of George III. to the Session of Parliament ending A.D. 1793. By W. Belsham. ... *London:* 1795. 4 vols., 8vo. H. + Second Edition. *London.* 1795. 4 vols., 8vo. H. + Third Edition. *London.* 1796. 6 vols., 8vo. + *Dublin.* 1796. 2 vols., 8vo. + To the commencement of the year 1799. *London.* 1801. 6 vols., 8vo. + Fifth Edition. *London.* 1801–5. 7 vols., 8vo. 4600

Contains many particulars concerning the American Revolution. *See* M. R., XVII. 121; XXXVII. 75. The "History of Great Britain, 1688–1802," 12 vols., 8vo, by the same author, contains many references to America.

BELSHAM (W. J.) Chronology of the Reigns of George III. and IV.; including every important fact ... with a General Chronology from the Earliest Records. *London.* 1828. 32mo.

BELT (E. W.) Reform Conspiracy, a Letter Addressed to Bradley T. Johnson. *Baltimore.* 1858. 8vo. 4602

BELTRAMI (Giacomo Costantino). Appeal on the Contemptible and Malignant Article in LXXIV of the Quarterly Review, on Beltrami's "Pilgrimage in America, &c. 8vo. 4603

Not published.

BELTRAMI. La découverte des sources du Mississippi et de la Riviere Sanglante. Description Du Cours entier du Mississippi, Qui n'était connu, que partiellement, et d'une grande partie de celui de la Riviere Sanglante, presque entièrement inconnue; ainsi que du cours entier de l'Ohio. ... Observations critico-philosophiques, Sur les Mœurs, la Religion, les Superstitions, les Costumes ... le Dénombrement, l'Origine, &c., &c., de plusieurs nations indiennes. ... Coup-d'œil, sur les Compagnies Nord-ouest, et de la Baie d'Hudson, ainsi que sur la Colonie Selkirk. Preuves evidentes, Que le Mississippi est la première Rivière du Monde. Par J. C. Beltrami ... . *Nouvelle-Orléans: Imprimé par Benj. Levy.* 1824. 8vo, pp. v, 1 l., (Errata), 1 slip, 327, (1). 4604

"Relation curieuse et très-interéssante."—LECLERC. The author accompanied Major Long in his second expedition, who remarks: "An Italian whom we met at Fort St. Anthony, attached himself to the expedition, and accompanied us to Pembina. He has recently published a book which we notice merely on account of the fictions and misrepresentations which it contains." The "Revue encyclopédique," 1826, XXIX. 457, criticised the work severely, and doubted the discovery. The author replied in a "Lettre sur la découverte d'un manuscrit mexicain," which was printed in Tome XXXII of the Revue, and in the English edition of his "Pilgrimage." *See*, also, N. A. R., XXVII. 89, 90.

BELTRAMI. A Pilgrimage in Europe and America, leading to the Discovery of the Sources of the Mississippi and Bloody River; with a Description of the Whole Course of the former, and of the Ohio. By J. C. Beltrami, Esq. formerly Judge or a Royal Court in the Ex-Kingdom of Italy. ... *London; Hunt and Clarke.* 1828. 2 vols., 8vo, pp. lxxvi, 471, 2 l., Errata, 1 slip; Title, 545, 2 l. Portrait, Plan, Map, and 3 Plates. H. 4605

The "Revue encycl.," XXXIX. 657, announced a French translation, "but," says Quérard, "it has never come to our knowledge that it was published."

BELTRAMI. To the Public of New York and of the United States, the author of "The Discovery of the Sources of the Mississippi ... Dec. 1825. *New York: Joseph Drake,* [1825]. 8vo, pp. 36. C. 4606

This is a defence and explanation of the previous work.

BELTRAMI. Le Mexique. Par J. C. Beltrami. *Paris; Crevot: Delaunay.* 1830. 2 l., pp. xxx, 11, 443, Table, 1 l.; 2 l., pp. 431. C. 4607

See a review, by Depping, in Tome XLV. of the "Revue Encyclopédique." On Beltrami's life and writings, *see* "Minnesota Hist. Soc. Coll. for 1867," pp. 13–20.

BELTRAN. Arte de el idioma Maya reducido a succinctas reglas y semilexicon Yucateco. Por el R. J. Fr. Pedro Beltran de Santa Rosa Maria, ex custodio, hijo de esta Recoleccion franciscana de Merida. *Mexico: por la viuda de José Bernardo de Hogal.* 1746. 4to, 8 l., pp. 188. 2 Plates. N. 4608

Very scarce. Priced, by Thorp, in 1843, £4 4*s*. Selections from this will be found in Norman's Yucatan, and in the Transactions of the American Ethnological Society.

BELTRAN. Arte del idioma maya reducido a sucintas reglas, y semilexicon yucateco. Por el R. P. J. Fr. Pedro Beltran de Santa Rosa Maria ... . Segunda edicion. *Merida de Yucatan: imprenta de J. D. Espinosa. Julio,* 1859. 4to, 8 l. pp. 242. H.

BELTRAN. Declaracion de la doctrina cristiana en el idioma yucateco por el Reverendo padre Fr. Pedro Beltran de Santa Rosa anadiendole el acto de contricion en verso y prosa. *Mérida de Yucatan.* 1860. 12mo, pp. 24. 4610

BELU (C.) Des colonies et de la traite des nègres. Par C. Belu. ... *Paris: Debray. an* IX. 1800. 8vo, 2 l., pp. 72. H.

BELVIDERE, *N. J.* An Act to Incorporate the Town of Belvidere, N. J. [n. p., n. d.] 8vo. 4612

BELVILLE (J.) Address at the Inauguration of the Hatborough Monument, Commemorating the Battle of the Crooked Billet, Delivered in Toller Academy, December 5, 1861. By Rev. Jacob Belville. *Doylestown, Pa.: J. D. Mendenhall.* 1862. 8vo, pp. 12. 4613

BEMAN. An Address, delivered in ... Troy ... February 23, 1824, in Commemoration of Washington's Birth-Day. By Nathan S. S. Beman ... . *Troy: printed by Francis Adancourt.* 1824. 8vo, pp. 15. B. 4614

BEMAN. Antagonisms in the Moral and Political World. A Discourse delivered in the First Presbyterian Church, Troy, New York, on Thanksgiving Day, November 18, 1858. By Nathan S. S. Beman, D.D. *Troy, N. Y.: A. W. Scribner & Co.* 1858. S. 4615

BEMAN. Characteristics of the Age: a discourse delivered in ... Troy, N. Y. on Thanksgiving Day, December 12, 1850, by Nathan S. S. Beman, D.D. *Troy, N. Y.* 1851. 8vo, pp. 32.

BEMAN. Our Civil War. The Principles involved. Its Cause and Cure; being a Discourse delivered November 27, 1862. By N. S. S. Beman, D.D. *Troy, N. Y.: A. W. Scribner & Co.* 1863. 8vo, pp. 52. 4617

BEMAN. Thanksgiving in the Times of Civil War; being a Discourse delivered in the First Presbyterian Church, Troy, N. Y., November 28, 1861 By N. S. S. Beman, D.D. *Troy: A. W. Scribner & Co.* 1863. 8vo, pp. 46. 4618

Also: The Crisis and the Triumph: or the History and Present Attitude of the Temperance Cause ... . *Troy, N. Y.* 1846. 8vo, pp. 31. H. ... A Discourse

before the Society for the Promotion of Collegiate and Theological Education at the West ... at Springfield, Mass., Oct. 28, 1846. *New York.* 1847. 8vo, pp. 24. B. Discourse delivered in Stephentown and Troy, before the Temperance Societies of those towns. *Troy.* 1820. 8vo. B. Fast Sermon at Portland, Me. Aug. 20, 1812. *Portland: Hyde, Lord & Co.* 1812. 8vo, pp. 16. The Influence of Freedom on Popular and National Education: a Lecture, ... Troy, February 24, 1846. ... *Troy, N. Y.: Young & Hartt.* 1846. 8vo, pp. 32. H. ... The Influence of Sunday-Schools at the West. ... *Philadelphia: American Sunday-School Union.* [etc. 1845?] 16mo, pp. 8. H. The Intellectual Position of our Country: ... Lecture ... in ... Troy, December 10th, 1839. ... *Troy: N. Tuttle, Printer.* 1839. 8vo, pp. 23. H. Oration before the Alumni of Middlebury College. *Troy.* 1825. 8vo. A Plea for the Swiss Mission in Canada: a Discourse, delivered in ... Troy, October 15, 1843. *Troy, N. Y.: Young & Hartt.* 1843. 8vo, pp. 36. H. ... The Roman Catholic Population of our World, scattered abroad everywhere, as furnishing a Missionary Field. A Sermon, ... May the 8th, 1859. ... *New York.* 1859. 12mo, pp. 24. H. The Western Continent: a Discourse, delivered In ... Troy, July Fourth, 1841. ... *Troy, N. Y.* 1841. 8vo, pp. 27. H.

BEMBO (Pietro), *Cardinal.* Historiæ Venetiæ. L. XII. *Venetiis: apud Aldi filios.* 1551. Folio. + *Lutetiæ; Parisiis: ex officina Michaelis Vascosani.* 1551. 4to. 4619

Contains some reference to Columbus. Also, with the other Latin works of Bembo. *Basileæ.* 1556. 8vo. + [*Ibid.*] 1567. 8vo. + *Argentorati.* 1602. 8vo, + [*Ibid.*] 1611. 8vo. + [*Ibid.*] 1652. 8vo. + *Venetiis, apud Dominicum Lovisam.* 1718. 4to; and in Latin and Italian, in Vol. I of his "Opere," *Venezia.* MDCCXXIX. Folio. H.; and, in Latin, in "J. J. Grævii Thesavrvs' Antiq. et Hist. Ital." *Lvdg. Bat.* 1704–25. Fol., Tom. V, Pars I. H.

BEMBO. Della Istoria Vinitiana di M. Pietro Bembo Card. volgarmente scritta, libri dodici. *Vinegia: Gualtero Scotto.* 1552. 4to, (14), 180 l. + Aggiuntovi di nuovo la Tavola delle cose piu notabili ... per M. Alemanio Fino. *Venezia: Giordano Ziletti e Comp.* 1570. 4to. 4620

"L'Imprimeur vénitien Giord. Ziletti en a changé le frontispice et la dédicace et a ajouté des tables pour faire croire que c'est une nouvelle édition: *Ven.* 1570. (28 ff. non ch. et 180 ff.)"—GRAESSE.

BEMBO. Istoria Veneziana, pubbl. da Jac. Morelli, *Venezia: Zatta.* 1790. 2 vols., 4to. Portrait. + *Milano; Società Tipografica de' Classici Italiani.* 1809. 2 vols., 8vo. H. 4621

In this edition, pp. 347–354 of Vol. I. relate to America.

BEMENT (E. M.) An Appeal to the Citizens of New York for the Organization of the Andrew Johnson Cavalry, for special service in East Tennessee. By Ernest M. Bement. *New York: Wyncoop & Hallenbeck.* 1863. 8vo, pp. 12. 4622

BEMIS, *pseudon.?* Clay and Frelinghuysen. Whig Songs for the Great Mass Convention on Boston Common, Sept. 19, 1844. By Bemis. [*Boston.*] 1844. 18mo, pp. 18. H. 4623

BEMIS (G.) American Neutrality: its Honourable Past, its Expedient Future. A Protest against the Proposed Repeal of the Neutrality Laws, and a Plea for their Improvement and Consolidation. By George Bemis. *Boston; Little, Brown and Company.* 1866. 8vo, pp. vi, (1), 211, (1). H. + *London: Sampson, Low & Co.* 1867. 8vo. 4624

BEMIS. Hasty Recognition of Rebel Belligerency, and Our right to complain of it. By George Bemis. *Boston: A. Williams & Co.,* [1865]. 8vo, pp. viii, (1), 57. H. 4625

BEMIS. Precedents of American Neutrality, in Reply to the Speech of Sir Roundell Palmer, Attorney-General of England, in the British House of Commons, May 13, 1864. By George Bemis. *Boston: Little, Brown and Company.* 1864. 8vo, pp. viii, 83. B., H. 4626

BEMIS. Report of the Case of John W. Webster ... Professor ... in Harvard University; indicted for the Murder of George Parkman ... before The Supreme Judicial Court of Massachusetts; including the Prisoner's Confessional Statements ... and an Appendix ... . By George Bemis ... . *Boston: Charles C. Little and James Brown.* 1850. 8vo, pp. xii, 628. Illustrations. H., S. 4627

BEMIS (S.) ... A Discourse, occasioned by the Death of Mrs. Susan Bemis, Consort of the Reverend Stephen Bemis, and delivered at Harvard Oct. 21, 1810. By Stephen Bemis. ... *Cambridge.* 1810. 8vo, pp. 19. H. 4628

BEMIS. The first of Patriots gathered to his grave in peace; and the Evil since brought upon his Country. An Address, delivered before the Washington Benevolent Society of Lancaster and Sterling, Feb. 22, 1815. By Stephen Bemis. ... *Worcester: printed by William Manning.* 1815. 8vo, pp. 20. H.

BEMIS. Two Discourses, delivered at Harvard, the One, August 20, 1812, the Day of the National Fast on account of the War with Great Britain; the Other, May 29, 1813, on ... taking Leave of the People of his Charge; Together with the Result of Council, &c. By Stephen Bemis ... . *Harvard: Printed by Sewall Parker.* 1814. 8vo, pp. 46. 4630

BENADUCI. *See* Boturini Benaduci.

BENAMATI (Guid 'Ubaldo). Delle due trombe i primi fiati, cioè tre libri della vittoria navale, e tre libri del mondo nuovo, poemi eroici di Guidubaldo Benamati. *Parma: Anteo Viotti* 1622. Sm. 12mo. 463[illegible]

Priced, in Tross' Catal., VIII, 1862, 20fr.

[BENARD (T. N.)] Banque française de l'Amérique et des Indes. [Signed T. N. Benard.] *Paris.* 1856. 8vo, ½ sheet

Reprinted from the "Journal du Havre," June 18, 1856.

BENAVENTE (D. J.) Memoria sobre las primeras campañas en la guerra de la independencia de Chile. *Santiago.* 1845. 8vo pp. viii, 200. C. 463[illegible]

BENAVENTE (J.) Memorial sobre las cosas de la nueva España. Por Fr. Juan de Benavente. *Mexico.* 1630. Folio.

See Ternaux Bibl. Am., No. 1630.

BENAVIDES (*Fray* Alonso). Memorial|qve Fray Ivan|de Santander de la|Orden de san Francisco, Comissario General|de Indias, presenta a la Majestad Catolica| del Rey don Felipe Qvarto|nuestro Señor.|Hecho por el Padre Fray Alonso|de Benauides Commissario del Santo-oficio, y Custodio que ha|sido de las Prouincias, y conuersiones del|Nueuo-Mexico.|Tratase en el de los tesoros es-|pirituales, y temporales, que la diuina Magestad ha manifestado|en aquellas conuersiones, y nueuos descubrimientos, por|medio de los Padres desta serafica Religion.|*Con licencia*|*En Madrid en la Imprenta Real. Año* M. DC. XXX.| 4to, Title, pp. 10 [103]. J. C. B., H. 4636

"Ouvrage curieux et devenu rare."—BRUNET. *See* Duyckinck's Cyclopædia, Suppl., p. 11; Ternaux, No. 518.

BENAVIDES. Requeste Remonstrative au Roy d'Espagne sur la conversion du Nouveau-Mexico; traduite de l'Espagnol ne François par un Religieux de l'Ordre de S. François. *Bruxelles: Francois Vivien.* 1631. 12mo, 6 l., pp. 120. J. C. B. 4637

A translation of the preceding. In the "Catalogue de la Bibl. de Lille," the title reads differently, as follows, but no imprint is given: "Reqveste remonstrative que le Reuerendissime père, frère Jean de Santander ... présente à ... Philippe IV, par le R. P. frère Alphonse de Benauides ... traduite de l'espagnol en françois par un religieux de l'ordre de St François [le frère Francois Paludanus]."

BENAVIDES. Relatio quam Philippo IV. ... per modum Memorialis, sive Libelli supplicis exhibuit Rev. P. F. J. de Santander ... Per manus Adm R. P. F. Alphonsi de Benavides, eiusdem Ordinis, Custodis Provinciæ et Conversionis Novi Mexici nec non Sanctæ Inquisitionis Commisarii ... in qua agitur de magnis Thesauris spiritualibus et temporalibus Deo adjuvante in

Novo Mexico detectis. *Salisburgi. Christ° Katzenberger.* 1634. Sm. 8vo, pp. 158. J. C. B. 4638

This is a Latin translation of No. 4635, by Jean Gravendonc. *See* Bartlett's Cat. of J. C. Brown's library, II, 54, 65. This rare and interesting relation of Benavides contains an account of each of the nations or tribes of Mexico. I have never seen a second copy.

BENAVIDES (Pedrarias). Secretos de Chirurgia, especial de las enfermedades de Morbo galico y Lamparones y Mirrarchia, y asi mismo la manera como se curan los Indios de llagas y heridas y otras passiones en las Indios ... Compuesto por el doctor Pedrarias de Benavides. *Valladolid: Fernandez de Cardova.* 1567. 12mo, 165 l. J. C. B. 4639

Concerning this rare little book, *see* Ternaux, No. 103.

BENAVIDES Y DE LA CERDA (Bort de). Sermon en la Dedicacion del nuevo y famosa Templo de S. Pablo de la Comp. de Jesus de Lima. *Lima.* 1639. 4to. 4640

Title from Puttick's catalogue, 1860. The book sold for 8s.

BÉNARD DE LA HARPE. *See* La Harpe.

BENAZECH (J.) Les États-Unis et autres pays du nord de l'Amérique ... Par J. Benazech ... *Toulouse; Éd. Privat: Paris; Delagrave et Cᵉ.* 1866. 8vo, pp. viii, 440. B. 4641

The Bench and Bar of Cayuga County, New York. A Poem. [n. p., n. d.] 12mo, pp. 42. 4642

BENDEL (A.) Aufsätze betreffend das Eisenbahnwesen in Nord-Amerika. Nach Reise-Notizen des Geh. Regier.-Rath Henz bearbeitet ... *Berlin; Ernst & Korn.* 1862. 4to, pp. v, 74. Woodcuts, 2 Plates engraved on copper and 5 on stone, 4to and folio. 4643

BENDENIUS. Relatio triplex de rebus Indicis; J. R. P. Cornelii Bendenii dicti Godines (in Mexicana provincia 1650 interfecti) Caaiguarum (Paragueriae) gentis mores, coepta conversio R. P. A. Kunddi, dicta Crespi, elogium. *Antwerpiæ; J. Meursius.* 1658. Sm. 8vo. Portrait. 4644

See Tross' catalogue, No. 913, where it is priced 25fr.

BENDER (H. R.) Oration delivered before the Washington Benevolent Society, of the County of Cortland in Homer ... February 22, 1813. By Hastings R. Bender. *Homer; Printed by John W. Osborn.* 1813. 12mo, pp. 16. 4645

BENEDICT (D.) An Abridgment of the General History of the Baptist Denomination in America and other parts of the World. By David Benedict, A.M. *Boston.* 1820. 12mo, pp. 448. 4646

BENEDICT. An Address before the Grand Lodge of Rhode Island, June 24, 1830. *Pawtucket: Meacham & Fowler.* 1830. 8vo, pp. 21. 4647

BENEDICT. A General History of the Baptist Denomination in America, and other Parts of the World. By David Benedict, A.M. ... In Two Volumes. *Boston: the Author.* 1813. 8vo, pp. 606; 556, Subscribers Names (24). H. + Fifth Thousand. *New York: Lewis Colby and Company.* 1848. Rl. 8vo, pp. viii, 970. Portrait. H. + Sixth Edition. *New York.* 1849. Rl. 8vo, pp. viii, 970. C. 4648

The first edition contains matter omitted in the others.

BENEDICT. Fifty Years among the Baptists. By David Benedict, D.D. *New York: Sheldon & Co.* 1860. 12mo, pp. 437. C. 4649

BENEDICT. A History of All Religions. Providence, 1824. By David Benedict, A.M. 12mo. 4650

BENEDICT (E. C.) Address at the First Anniversary of the Free Academy ... New York, July 24, 1850. *New York.* 1850. 8vo. 4651

BENEDICT. The Beginning of America a Discourse delivered before the New-York Historical Society ... November 17 1863 by Erastus C. Benedict ... *New-York.* MDCCCLXIV. 8vo, pp. 64. C., H. 4652

BENEDICT. The Constitutional Amendment. [n. p., 1866?] 8vo, pp. 8. H. 4653

[BENEDICT.] New York and the City Travel: Omnibus and Railroad. What shall be done? [*New York. June,* 1851.] 8vo. 4654

BENEDICT. Religion in Public Schools: a Paper read before the American Association for the Advancement of Education ... at Pittsburgh, Pa., August, 1853. *Newark, N. J.* 1854. 8vo. 4655

BENEDICT. The War. Speech of Hon. E. C. Benedict, in the Assembly of the State of New York, April 6, 1864. *Albany: Weed, Parsons & Co., Printers.* 1864. 8vo, pp. 16. 4656

BENEDICT (G. G.) The Battle of Gettysburgh, and the Part taken therein by Vermont Troops. By G. G. Benedict. *Burlington.* 1867. 12mo, pp. 24. 4657

BENEDICT (J.) Speech of Hon. J. Benedict, delivered in the Assembly, February 19, 1851, on the Compromise Resolutions, offered by Mr. Varnum of New York. [n. p., 1851.] 8vo, pp. 15. S. 4658

BENEDICT (Joel). ... A Sermon, delivered at the Funeral of the Rev. Levi Hart, D.D. Pastor ... in ... Preston, who died October 27, 1808, Aged 70 Years. By Joel Benedict ... *Norwich.* 1809. 8vo. H. 4659

BENEDICT (Kirby). Anniversary Address delivered before the Historical Society of New Mexico at Santa Fe, December 31, 1860, by Kirby Benedict ... *Santa Fé, N. M.: Manderfield & Tucker, Printers,* [1860]. 8vo, pp. 20. H. 4660

BENEDICT. Correspondence relating to Chief Justice Kirby Benedict, of New Mexico. [n. p., 1864.] 4to, 1 p. H. 4661

BENEDICT (Lewis). A Memorial of Brevet Brigadier General Lewis Benedict, Colonel of 162d Regiment N. Y. V. I., who fell in Battle at Pleasant Hill, La., April 9, 1864. *Albany, N. Y.: J. Munsell.* 1866. 4to, pp. 155. Portrait. H. 4662

BENEDICT (*Rev.* Noah), *A.M.* ... Sermon at the Funeral of Rev. Joseph Bellamy, D.D., Bethlem, March 9, 1790. By Noah Benedict. With Appendix. *New Haven.* 1790. 8vo, pp. 44. 4663

[BENEDICT.] The Watery War; a Poetical Description of the existing Controversy between the Pedobaptists and Baptists on the Subjects and Mode of Baptism. By John of Enon. *Boston: Manning & Loring.* 1808. 12mo, pp. 34. 4664

BENEDICT (Thomas). A Genealogy of the Benedict Family, taken from a Manuscript kept by James Benedict, Esq. of Ridgefield. [*Albany.* 1849.] Folio, pp. 4. S. 4665

BENESKI (Charles de). Narrative of the last moments of the Life of Don Augustin de Iturbide, ex-Emperor of Mexico, by

Col. Chas. de Beneski; Translated from the Spanish. *New York: Tyrell & Tompkins.* 1825. 8vo, pp. 41. C. 4666

BENEZET (Anthony.) Avertissement à la Grande-Bretagne et à ses colonies, ou Tableau abrégé de l'état misérable des negres esclaves dans les dominations anglaises. 1767. 8vo. 4667

[BENEZET.] Brief Considerations on Slavery, and the expediency of its abolition. With some hints on the means whereby it may be gradually effected. Recommended to the serious attention of All, and especially of those entrusted with the Power of Legislation. [Motto.] *Burlington: printed and sold by Isaac Collins.* M.DCC.LXXIII. 8vo, pp. 16. P. 4668

[BENEZET.] The Case of our Fellow Creatures, the Oppressed Africans, Respectfully recommended to the serious consideration of the Legislature of Great Britain. By the people called Quakers. *London: Phillips.* 1784. 8vo. + *London Printed; Philadelphia reprinted; Joseph Crukshank.* M.DCC.LXXXIV. 8vo, pp. 13. 4669

See M. R., LXXII. 470.

BENEZET. A Caution and Warning to Great-Britain and Her Colonies, in A short Representation of the Calamitous State of the Enslaved Negroes in the British Dominions. Collected from various Authors, and submitted to the Serious Consideration of all, more especially of Those in Power. By Ant. Benezet. *Philadelphia: Henry Miller.* M DCC LXVI. 8vo, pp. 35, (4). C. + [Title abridged.] *Philadelphia; printed: London; reprinted.* 1767. 8vo, pp. 46. + [Full title.] To which is added, An Extract of a Sermon, preached by the Bishop of Gloucester, before the Society for the Propagation of the Gospel. By Anthony Benezet. *Philadelphia: Printed by D. Hall, and W. Sellers.* MDCCLXVII. 8vo, Table, pp. 52. H. + *London reprinted: James Phillips.* 1784. 8vo, pp. 46. + *London.* 1785. 8vo, pp. 46. 4670

BENEZET. A Collection of Religious Tracts. *Philadelphia: Printed by Joseph Crukshank.* 1773. 12mo. 4671

Includes a Life of David Brainard, Wesley's Thoughts on Slavery, etc. Smith's catalogue attributes, with an interrogation, "A Collection of Religious Tracts ... *Philadelphia: Printed by Enoch Story.* 1784." 12mo, 5 sheets, to Benezet.

BENEZET. Considerations on War, Slavery, and the Nature and Bad Effects of Spirituous Liquors. By Anthony Benezet. *Philadelphia: Joseph Crukshank.* 1778. 18mo, pp. 48. 4672

[BENEZET.] An Extract from a Treatise on the Subject of Prayer, [by William Law]. With some Thoughts on War; Remarks on the Nature and bad effects of the use of Spirituous Liquors. And considerations on Slavery. [By Anthony Benezet.] *Philadelphia: Printed by Joseph Crukshank.* 1780. 12mo, pp. 90. 4673

[BENEZET.] The | Mighty Destroyer | Displayed, | In some Account of the | Dreadful Havock made by the mistaken Use as | well as Abuse of | Distilled Spirituous Liquors. | By a Lover of Mankind. | *Philadelphia: | Printed by Joseph Crukshank, between Second | and Third Streets, in Market-Street.* | M.DCC,LXXIV. | Sm. 12mo, pp. 48. + [*Reprinted.* n. p., n. d.] 12mo, pp. 48. 4674

This is usually followed by Wesley's Thoughts on Slavery, pp. 83.

[BENEZET.] Notes on the Slave Trade, &c. [n. p., n. d.] 12mo, pp. 8. + [Reprinted. n. p., n. d.] 12mo, pp. 8. P. 4675

[BENEZET.] Observations on the Inslaving, Importing and Purchasing of Negroes. With some advice thereon Extracted from the Yearly Meeting Epistle of London for the present Year. ... *Germantown: Printed by Christopher Sower.* 1759. 8vo, + The Second Edition. *Germantown: Printed by Christopher Sower.* 1760. 8vo, pp. 16. 4676

BENEZET. The Plainness and Innocent Simplicity of the Christian Religion. With Its salutary Effects, compared to the corrupting Nature and dreadful Effects of War. With Some Account of the blessing which attends on a Spirit influenced by divine Love, producing Peace and Good-Will to Men. Collected by Anthony Benezet. *Philadelphia: Joseph Crukshank.* MDCCLXXXII. 12mo, pp. 48. + *Philadelphia.* 1793. 12mo. W. + *London: Darton and Harvey.* 1800. 12mo, pp. 48. 4677

Frequently reprinted.

[BENEZET.] The | Potent Enemies | of | America | laid open: | being | Some account of the baneful effects attending the use of | Distilled Spirituous Liquors, | and the | Slavery | of the | Negroes; | [Motto.] *Philadelphia: | Printed by Joseph Crukshank in Market- | Street, between Second and Third Streets.* | [1774.] 12mo, Title, pp. 48, 83, 16. P., H. 4678

Consists of an original tract by a "Lover of Mankind" [A. Benezet], a reprint of Rev. J. Wesley's Thoughts on Slavery, and a brief sketch of David Brainard, with a letter by him, etc. A reprint of part of the Collection of Religious Tracts.

[BENEZET.] Remarks on the nature and bad effects of Spirituous Liquors. [n. p., n. d.] 12mo, pp. 12. H., A. 4679

[BENEZET.] Serious Considerations on Several Important Subjects: viz On War ... Observations on Slavery, and remarks on ... Spirituous Liquors. *Philadelphia: Joseph Crukshank.* 1778. 8vo, pp. 48. 4680

BENEZET. Serious Reflections on the Times. By Anthony Benezet. *Philadelphia.* 1778. 18mo, pp. 4. P. 4681

BENEZET. A Short Account of the People called Quakers; ... their Rise, Religious Principles and Settlement in America, Mostly collected from different Authors, for the Information of all serious Inquirers, particularly Foreigners. By Anthony Benezet. *Philadelphia: Joseph Crukshank.* M,DCC,LXXX. 8vo, pp. 27. H. + Second Edition. *Philadelphia,* [1780]. 12mo, pp. 36. S. + The Third Edition. ... *Philadelphia: Printed by Enoch Story.* ... MDCCLXXXIII. Sm. 8vo, pp. 40. H. + *New-Bedford: Printed by Abraham Shearman, jun.* 1799. 8vo, pp. 28. H. 4682

Reprinted with the title:

BENEZET. A Short Account of the Religious Society of Friends commonly called Quakers. By Anthony Benezet. *Philadelphia: Kimber and Conrad.* 1814. 8vo, 1½ sheets. 4683

BENEZET. Observations sur l'origine, les principes, et l'etablissement en Amerique, De la Societé Connue sous la Denomination de Quakers ou Trembleurs: Extrait de divers Auteurs. Redigés, principalement, en faveur des Etrangers. Par Antoine Benezet [*sic*]. *Philadelphie: Chez Joseph. Crukshank.* MDCCCLXXX. 8vo, pp. 36. H. + *Philadelphie: l'imprimé à Londres par Jacques Phillips.* M DCC LXXXIII. 12mo, pp. 48. H. + Nouvelle édition. *A Londres; De l'imprimerie de Guillaume Phillips.* 1817. 12mo, pp. 48. H. + Nouvelle édition. *Paris: impr. de Cellot.* 1822. 12mo., pp. 48. 4684

Translated into German, with the following title:

BENEZET. Kurzer Bericht von den Leuten, die man Quäker nennet; ihrem Ursprung, ihren Religionsgründen, und von ihrer Niederlassung in Amerika. Durch Anton Benezet. *Philadelphia: Gedruckt bei Melchier Steiner.* 1783. 12mo, 2 sheets. 4685

[BENEZET.] A Short Account of that part of Africa Inhabited by the Negroes, With Respect to the Fertility of the Country; the good Disposition of many of the Natives, and the Manner by which the Slave Trade is carried on. Extracted

from several Authors, in order to shew the Iniquity of that Trade, and the Falsity of the Arguments usually advanced in its Vindication. With a Quotation from George Wallis's System of the Laws etc. and a large Extract from a Pamphlet, lately published in London, on the subject of the Slave Trade. *Philadelphia: Printed in the Year* M,DCC,LXII. 8vo, pp. 56. 4686

[BENEZET.] A Short Account ... With Quotations from the Writings of several Persons of Note, viz. George Wallis, Francis Hutcheson, and James Foster, and a large extract from a Pamphlet lately published in London, On the subject of the Slave Trade. The Second Edition, with large Additions and Amendments. *Philadelphia: printed by W. Dunlap, in the Year* MDCCLXII. 8vo, pp. 80. P. + The Third Edition in *London, Reprinted by W. Baker and J. W. Galabin.* 1768. 8vo, pp. 80. 4687

[BENEZET.] Short Observations on Slavery, Introductory to some Extracts from the writings of the Abbé Raynal, on that important Subject. [n. p., n. d.] 12mo, pp. 8. S. 4688

BENEZET. Some Historical Account of Guinea, its Situation, Produce, and the General Disposition of its Inhabitants, with an Inquiry into the Rise and Progress of the Slave Trade, its Nature, and Lamentable Effects. Also, a Republication of the Sentiments of Several Authors of Note on this subject, particularly an Extract from a Representation of the injustice of Slavery, by Granville Sharp. *Philadelphia.* MDCCLXXI. 8vo. + *Philadelphia.* M,DCC,LXXII. 8vo. + *Philadelphia; Printed* M,DCC,LXXI. *London: Owen. Reprinted* M,DCC,LXXII. 8vo, pp. 198, 6. + Third Edition. 1784? + A New Edition. *London: J. Phillips.* M. DCC. LXXXVIII. 8vo, pp. xv, 131. H. 4689

The edition of 1788 has a vignette of a negro, by Bewick. *See* M. R., LXXVII. 73; LXVIII. 343.

BENEZET. Relation historique de la Guinée, avec une recherche sur l'origine et les progrès de la traite des nègres, sur sa nature et ses déplorables effets. Quatrième édition. *Londres.* 1788. 8vo. 4690

The first edition appeared in 1762.

[BENEZET.] Some Observations on the Situation, Disposition, and Character of the Indian Natives of this Continent. *Philadelphia: Joseph Crukshank.* 1784. Sm. 8vo, pp. 59. 4691

[BENEZET.] Thoughts on the Nature of war, &c. By Anthony Benezet. [*Philadelphia.* 1776.] 4692

BENEZET. Views of American Slavery, taken a Century ago. Anthony Benezet. John Wesley. ... *Philadelphia.* 1858. 24mo, pp. 138. H. 4693

BENEZET. Anthony Benezet. From the Original Memoir: Revised, with Additions, by Wilson Amistead. *London: A. W. Bennett.* 1859. 8vo, pp. 160. 4694

This author was a Protestant refugee, who established a school for the education of negroes in Philadelphia, and, in addition to the long list of books here enumerated, published several school-books, including: A First Book for Children. *Philadelphia: J. Crukshank.* 1778. 16mo, pp. 32. + Reprinted. *London: James Phillips and Son.* 1798. 16mo, pp. 32. The Pennsylvania Spelling-Book. Second Edition ... enlarged. *Philadelphia: Joseph Crukshank.* 1779. 12mo, pp. 168. Smith, in his Catalogue of Friend's Books, to which the reader is referred for a more extended list of Benezet's works, attributes to him, with a query: A Serious Address to the Rulers of America. 1783, in which supposition I think he is mistaken. I incline to think that "A Mite cast into the Treasury: or, Observations on Slave-Keeping. *Philadelphia: Joseph Crukshank,* [1785]," is by Benezet.

BENHAM (Ashbel). Federal Harmony; Containing in a Familiar Manner, the Rudiments of Psalmody, &c. Sixth Edition. *Middletown,* [n. d.] Oblong 4to. 4695

Also: Social Harmony. *Wallingford.* 1798. 8vo.

BENINGTON (James.) Sketch of the Life of James Benington. ... *Boston: Publishing Fund.* 1824. 12mo, pp. 11. H. 4696

BENITO. *See* Fernandez (Benito).

BENIAMENOFF. *See* Veniaminov (Ivan).

BENJAMIN (Jonathan). Harmonia Cœlestis; a Collection of Church Music. *Northampton.* 1799. 8vo. 4697

BENJAMIN (J. J.) Drei Jahre in Amerika 1859–1862. *Hannover.* 1862. 3 Theile, 8vo, pp. xxxiv, 684. Portrait. 4698

BENJAMIN (Judah P.) Address delivered before the Public Schools of Municipality Number Two, of the City of New Orleans, on the 22nd February, 1845, by J. P. Benjamin, Esq. *New Orleans.* 1845. 8vo, pp. 14. H. 4699

BENJAMIN. Address upon the General Changes of the Practical Operation of our Constitution Compared with its Theory, &c. By J. P. Benjamin. *San Francisco.* 1860. 8vo, pp. 25. 4700

BENJAMIN. Defence of the National Democracy against the Attack of Judge Douglas Constitutional Rights of the States.

Speech of Hon. J. P. Benjamin, of Louisiana. Delivered in the Senate ... May 22, 1860. [*Washington.* 1860.] 8vo, pp. 24. H. + [n. p., n. d.] 8vo, pp. 16. 4701

BENJAMIN. In the United States District Court, Northern District of California. The United States *vs.* Andres Castillero. On Cross Appeal. Claim for the Mines and Land of New Almaden—Argument of Hon. J. P. Benjamin ... 24th, 25th and 26th October, and 5th November, 1860, in Reply to the Government's Special Counsel. Reported by Sumner & Cutter. *San Francisco.* 1860. 8vo, pp. 247. H. 4702

BENJAMIN. Intercepted Instructions to L. Q. C. Lamar, Styled Commissioner, etc. The African Slave Trade. The Secret Purpose of the Insurgents to Revive it. *Philadelphia; C. Sherman & Son.* 1863. 8vo, pp. 34. 4703

BENJAMIN. Relations of States. Speech of Judah P. Benjamin delivered in the Senate of the United States, May 8, 1860, on the Resolutions submitted by the Hon. Jefferson Davis, March 1, 1860. *Baltimore; Murphy & Co.* 1860. 8vo, pp. 8.

BENJAMIN. Kansas Bill. Speech of Hon. J. P. Benjamin, of La., delivered in the Senate ... March 11, 1858. Slavery protected By the Common Law of the New World. Guarantied by Constitution. Vindication of the Supreme Court of the U. S. *Washington: G. S. Gideon, Printer.* 1858. 8vo, pp. 29.

BENJAMIN. Speech of Hon. J. P. Benjamin ... on the Kansas Question. Delivered in the Senate, May 2, 1856. *Washington.* 1856. 8vo, pp. 28. H. 4706

BENJAMIN. Extracts from the Speech ... on the Kansas Question: showing the True Meaning of the Kansas Law, and his Reasons for joining the Democratic Party. Delivered in the Senate, May 2, 1856. *Washington.* 1856. 8vo, pp. 8. 4707

BENJAMIN. Speech of the Hon. J. P. Benjamin ... on the Acquisition of Cuba. Delivered in the Senate of the U. S., Feb. 11, 1859. [n. p., n. d.] 8vo, pp. 16. 4708

BENJAMIN. Speech of the Hon. J. P. Benjamin on the Right of Secession. Delivered in the Senate of the United States, December 31, 1860. [n. p., n. d.] 8vo, pp. 16. 4709

BENJAMIN (L. N.) The St. Albans Raid; or, Investigation into the Charges against Lieut. Bennett H. Young and Command, for their Acts at St. Albans, Vt., On the 19th October, 1864. Being a Complete and Authentic Report of all the Proceedings on the Demand of the United States for their Extradition, under the Ashburton Treaty. Before Judge Coursol, J.S.P., and the Hon. Mr. Justice Smith, J.S.C. ... By L. N. Benjamin, B.C.L. *Montreal.* 1856. 8ov, 2 l., pp. 480. 4710

Some copies have the imprint, *Boston, A. Williams & Co.*, 1865. H.

BENJAMIN (Park). Shakings. Etchings from the Naval Academy By a Member of the Class of '67 Engraved by John Andrew. *Boston; Lee & Shepard.* Oblong 8vo, 61 l. B. 4711

BENJAMIN (S. G. W.) Ode on the Death of Abraham Lincoln. By S. G. W. Benjamin. *Boston; William V. Spencer.* 1865. 16mo, pp. 15. 4712

BEN JESSE. A Letter to the Independent Reflector. By David Marin Ben Jesse, Pastor of Aquenouka. 1753. 4713

BENNER (Enos). Lebensbeschreibungen sämmtlicher Unterzeichner der Unabhängigkeits Erklärung der Vereinigten Staaten von Nord-Amerika. *Sumnytown, Penn.* 1858. 12mo, pp. x, 550. C. 4714

Mostly a translation from C. A. Goodrich's "Lives of the Signers."

BENNET (R. G.) Nederlandsche Zeereizen in het laatst der XVI, XVII en in het begin der XVIII eeuw, met aanteekeningen, uitgegeven door R. G. Bennet en J. van Wijk Roelandsz. *Amsterdam; Schalekamp en van de Grampel.* 1828. 3 vols., 8vo. + *Amsterdam; H. Bakker, Czn.* 1828–32. 5 vols., 8vo. 4715

BENNET *and* VAN WIJK. Verhandeling over de Nederlandsche ontdekkingen in Amerika, Australië, de Indiën en de Poollanden, en de namen, welke weleer aan dezelve door Nederlanders zijn gegeven, door R. G. Bennet en J. van Wijke ... . *Utrecht; Johannes Altheer.* MDCCCXXVII. 8vo, Title, pp. 215, 8 l. folded, and Atlas, folio. B. 4716

BENNET (W.) ... Sermon before the Society in Scotland for propagating Christian Knowledge, 1799. With Appendix. By Rev. William Bennet. *Edinburgh.* 1800. 8vo, pp. 78, and Appendix, 51. M. 4717

BENNET [*sic*] *and* WALTON'S Almanac, for 1813 ... . Calculated by Joshua Sharp. ... *Philadelphia: Bennett & Walton*, [n. d.] 12mo, pp. 47. H. 4718

BENNETT (A.) Adventures in the Far West and the Far South West. By Alfred Bennett. *Philadelphia.* 1852. 8vo.

BENNETT (A. H.) An Address delivered at the Dedication of the New School House In East Jaffrey, N. H., July 4, 1854, by the Hon. A. H. Bennett. Also ... description of the New School House. *Peterborough: E. H. Cheney, Printer.* 1854. 8vo, pp. 31. H. 4720

BENNETT (B.) Address on American Independence at Middletown, July 4, 1802. By Benjamin Bennett. *New York.* 1802. 24mo. 4721

BENNETT (D. K.) Chronology of North Carolina. Showing when the most remarkable events connected with her History took place, from the Year 1584 to the Present Time; with explanatory Notes. By D. K. Bennett. *New-York.* 1858. 12mo. C. 4722

BENNETT (E.) Clara Moreland; or adventures in the South-West. By Emerson Bennett. *Philadelphia.* 1853. 12mo.

BENNETT. Clara Moreland ... (Fortsetzung von „Viola") von Emerson Bennett. Aus dem Englischen übersetzt. *Leipzig: Kollmann.* 1856. 3 vols., 8vo, 2 l., pp. 160; 2 l., 160; 2 l., 168. (Amerikanische Bibliothek, 225.–227. Bändchen.)

Bennett has written a large number of stories bearing on Western life. The following have come under my notice: Ella Barnwell; an historical Romance of Border Life. *Cincinnati.* 1854. 8vo.—Die Flüchtlinge. Eine Indianergeschichte aus dem Jahre 1812. Von Emerson Bennett. Aus dem Englischen übersetzt von Marie Heine. *Leipzig: Kollmann.* 1858. 2 vols., 8vo, pp. 232; 252. (Amerikanische Bibliothek, 301., 302. Bändchen.)—Forest Rose; a Tale of the Frontier. New Edition. *Cincinnati.* 1852. 8vo.—Leni Leoti; or, Adventures in the Far West: a Sequel to the "Prairie Flower." New Edition. *Cincinnati, O.* 1850. 8vo.—Mike Fink, a Legend of the Ohio. *Cincinnati: J. A. and U. P. James.* 1853. 8vo, pp. 100.—The Prairie Flower, or adventures in the Far West, by Emerson Bennett, New Edition, revised and corrected by the Author. *Cincinnati: J. A. and U. P. James.* 1850. 8vo. pp. 120.—The Phantom of the Forest: a Tale of the Dark and Bloody Ground. Author's Revised Edition. *Philadelphia: J. E. Potter & Co.* 1867. 12mo, pp. 503.—Viola; or, Adventures in the Far South-West.—Viola oder Abenteuer im fernen Südwesten von Emerson Bennett. Aus dem Englischen übersetzt. *Leipzig: Kollmann.* 1856. 2 vols., 8vo, 2 l., pp. 148; 172. (Amerikanische Bibliothek, 223., 224. Bändchen.)—Wild Scenes on the Frontiers, or Heroes of the West. *New York.* 1859. 12mo.—Die Waldesbraut von Emerson Bennett. Aus dem Englischen. *Leipzig: Kollmann.* 1857. 3 vols., 8vo, pp. 151; 156; 160. (Amerikanische Bibliothek, 277.–279. Bändchen.)—Walde-Warren. Eine amerikanische Criminalgeschichte. Aus dem Englischen übersetzt von Marie Heine. *Leipzig: Kollmann.* 1864. 8vo, pp. 224

BENNETT (E. T. B.) Songs of the Rivers. By Emily T. B. Bennett. *New York.* 1865. 12mo, pp. 262. 4725

BENNETT (F. D.) Narrative of a Whaling Voyage round the Globe, from the year 1833 to 1836; comprising Sketches of Polynesia, California, the Indian Archipelago, etc. With an account of southern whales, the Sperm Whale-Fishery, and the natural history of the climates visited. By Frederick Debell Bennett, Esq., F.R.G.S. ... In Two Volumes. *London: R. Bentley.* 1840. 8vo, pp. xv, 402; 395. Plates. C. 4726

According to Herman Melville, this is one of the only two works on the whale fishery of any value. Rich differs. The title in Rich, Vol. II., differs.

BENNETT (A.) Speech of Hon. Henry Bennett, of New-York, on the Admission of California, delivered in the House of Representatives, Monday, May 27, 1850. *Washington.* 1850. 8vo, pp. 16. 4727

Also: Speech ... on the Public Lands. ... February 25, and March 3, 1852. *Washington.* 1852. 8vo, pp. 12. H.—Speech ... on Equal Grants of Land to the several States for Public Purposes. ... In the House ... July 5, 1854. [n. p., n. d.] 8vo, pp. 16. H.—Speech ... against the repeal of the Missouri Compromise, and upon the Political effect of Slavery, delivered ... May 17, 1854. *Washington: J. T. & L. Towers.* 1854. 8vo, pp. 16.

BENNETT (J. G.) The Life and Writings of James Gordon Bennett, Editor of the New York Herald. *New York*, 1844. 8vo, pp. 64. 4728

This work is said to have been suppressed.

BENNETT. Memoirs of James Gordon Bennett and his Times. By a New York Journalist. *New York.* 1855. 12mo. 4729

BENNETT (John). Essay for regulating and improving the Trade and Plantations of Great Britain. *London.* 1736. 8vo.

Title taken from Watt, "Biblioth. Brit.," who puts it under the name Bennet. Perhaps this is the first edition of the "Two Letters," No. 4732.

BENNETT. A Memorial of the Difficulties, Hardships and Perplexities, which Mr. Bennet hath, and doth still labour under. Humbly submitted to the ... Court of Directors of the South-Sea Company. To which is added ... Numb. 1. A Petition to His ... Majesty from the General Assembly of Barbadoes, passed ... 21st of August, 1733. Numb. 2. A State of the Case; and ... Judge Reeves's Opinion thereon, in relation to the South-Sea Company's Negroes sold by Mr. Woodbridge ... . Numb. 3. A State of the Licensees Case, who traded under the South Sea Company's Powers, and are Sufferers by

Spanish Seizures and Confiscations. *London: J. Roberts.* 1734. 4to, 2 l., pp. 40. H. 4731

BENNETT (John). Two Letters and Several Calculations on the Sugar Colonies and Trade; addressed to Two Committees nominated by the West-India Merchants, &c. With ... 1. Four Letters concerning the flourishing Condition ... of the French Sugar Colonies ... . 2. Some Proposals ... for the ... Advancement of the British Sugar Colonies ... . By Mr. Bennett ... . The Second Edition. *London: R. Montagu.* 1738. 8vo, Title, pp. xxxi, (1), 73. H. 4732

The author mentions having published, "about two years ago ... a few Sheets relating to Trade and Colonies ... The 'National Merchant,'" of which I find no account elsewhere.

BENNETT (J. C.) The History of the Saints; or, an Exposé of Joe Smith and Mormonism. By John C. Bennett. *Boston.* 1842. 12mo, pp. 344. + Third Edition. *Boston: Leland & Whiting.* 1842. 8vo, pp. ii, 344. Woodcuts, and 2 Portraits.

BENNETT (Joseph). An Oration, pronounced July 4th, 1808, before the Inhabitants of New-Bedford ... . By Joseph Bennett, A.B. *New-Bedford: printed by Benjamin Lindsey.* 1808. 8vo, pp. 15. H. 4734

The Address is followed by an Ode to Liberty, by Elihu Doty.

BENNETT. ... A Sermon, delivered in Woburn, January 4, 1846, being the Twenty-Fifth Aniversary of the Author's Ordination. By Joseph Bennett, ... *Boston: B. Perkins & Co.* 1846. 8vo, pp. 22. H. 4735

BENNINGTON and its Surroundings. [n. p., n. d.] 8vo, pp. 16. Plate. H. 4736

BENOIT (P. J.) Voyage a Surinam Description des possessions néerlandaises dans la Guyane Par P. J. Benoit. Cent dessins pris sur nature par l'auteur lithographiés par Madou et Lauters. *Bruxelles: Société des Beaux Arts.* 1839. Folio, Title, pp. 76. 100 Plates. B. + [*Bruxelles: Bruylant Christophe et Cie.*] 1858. 4to. 50 Plates. 4737

The plates are in two tints. Published at 100fr. There are copies on India paper. *See* Petermann's Mittheilungen, 1859, pp. 489, 490.

BENOÎT (*Mlle* Eulalie). Brésil et France, ou l'Album d'Éléonore. *Tournai: Casterman.* 1853. 18mo. 4738

BENQUE (W.) *and* RAWOLLE (C.) Sketches for laying out Central Park. *New York.* 1858. 8vo. 4739

BEN SADDI (Nathan), *pseudon.* *See* [Dodsley (Robert).]

BENSON (A. G.) Memorial of Alfred G. Benson to the Senate and House of Representatives of the United States [asking Compensation for his Losses in obtaining Guano from the Lobos Islands, under the Promised Protection of the American Government. n. p., 1855]. 8vo, pp. 28. H. 4740

[BENSON (Egbert).] Brief Remarks on the "Wife" of Washington Irving. ... *New York: printed by Grattan and Banks.* 1819. 8vo, pp. 16. H. 4741

[BENSON.] Cases and Queries submitted to every Citizen of the United States, etc. *New York.* 1809. 8vo, pp. 24. 4742

BENSON. Memoir, read before the Historical Society of the State of New-York, 31st December, 1816; by Egbert Benson. *New York: Printed by William A. Mercein.* 1817. 8vo, pp. 72. H. 4743

I have seen it with the imprint T. & W. Mercein. There are several copies existing, with numerous MS. notes and additions by the author; one is it Harvard. It was reprinted with the following title:

BENSON. Memoir, read before the Historical Society of the State of New-York, December 31, 1816. By Egbert Benson. ... Second Edition—with Notes. *Jamaica: Henry C. Sleight, Printer.* 1825. 12mo, pp. 127. H. 4744

Also reprinted in N. Y. H. S. Coll., II., pp. 77–148, and with a separate title, as below. The Society objected to the printing of the work at the time of its delivery.

BENSON. Memoir read before the Historical Society of the State of New York, December 31, 1816. By Egbert Benson. Re-printed from a copy, with the Author's last corrections. *New York: Bartlett and Welford.* 1848. 8vo, pp. 72. 4745

[BENSON.] Vindication of the Captors of Major Andre. *New York: Kirk & Mercein.* 1817. 12mo, pp. 99. H. 4746

Chiefly made up with letters of Washington, Arnold, Robinson, Sir H. Clinton, Major André and C. Thomson. This edition is now very scarce. A copy sold, in March, 1866, for $41. Reprinted with the following title:

BENSON. Vindication of the Captors of Major Andre, By Egbert Benson, LL.D. With Introduction and Appendix. [By

C. I. Bushnell.] *New York: Privately Printed, [for Francis S. Hoffman].* 1865. 8vo, pp. ix, 134. 4747

Edition, 115 copies, of which 35 are on large paper, and 6 on drawing paper. It was reprinted the same year *verbatim et literatim*, as below:

BENSON. Vindication of the Captors of Major Andre. By Egbert Benson, LL.D. *New York: Reprinted for Joseph Sabin.* 1865. 8vo, pp. 84. 4748

250 copies printed, of which 50 are on large paper. Forms No. III. of Sabin's Reprints, 8vo Series.

BENSON (H.) A Biographical Sketch of the late Rev. Schuyler Hoes, Wesleyan Minister. By Rev. H. Benson. *Syracuse, N. Y.: Wesleyan Methodist Book Room.* 1853. 12mo, pp. 21.

BENSON (H. C.) Life among the Choctaw Indians, and Sketches of the South-West. By Henry C. Benson, A.M., of Placerville, California; with an Introduotion by Rev. T. A. Morris, D.D., Senior Bishop of the M. E. Church. *Cincinnati: Swormstedt & Poe.* 1860. 12mo, pp. 314. C. 4750

BENSON (M.) A Sermon Preached before the Incorporated Society for the Propagation of the Gospel in Foreign Parts ... February 15, 1739–40. By Martin Lord Bishop of Glocester. *London: J. & H. Pemberton.* 1740. 8vo, pp. 100. B. 4751

BENSON (S. A.) Stephen Allen Benson, President of Liberia. [n. p., 1855?] 12mo, pp. 12. Woodcut Portrait and View.

BENT (*Rev.* Joseph), *Jr.* A Discourse Delivered at the Dedication of the North Meeting House in Weymouth, Mass., Nov. 28, 1832. By Rev. Joseph Bent, Jr. *Hingham.* 1833. 8vo, pp. 27. 4753

Contains many historical notes.

BENT (N. T.) A Discourse, Historical of St. Thomas' Church, Taunton, Mass. ... By Rev. N. T. Bent ... . *Taunton, Mass.: Hack and Bradbury, Printers.* 1844. 8vo, pp. 33. H.

BENT. The Signs of the Times, or the Moral Meaning of our Present Commercial Difficulties. A Sermon preached in ... Philadelphia ... Nov. 17. 1839. By Rev. T. N. Bent ... . *Philadelphia.* MDCCCXXXIX. 8vo, pp. 22. H. 4755

[BENT.] The Past: a Fragment. Written for the Ladies Fair, at Mechanics Hall, February, 1840. *New Bedford: Printed by Benj. Lindsey.* 1840. 8vo, pp. 10. 4756

BENT (Silas). A Paper on the Kuro-Siwo, or Japan Stream; read before the American Geographical and Statistical Society, by Silas Bent ... January 24th, 1856. *New York*, [n. d.] 8vo, pp. 8. Map. H. 4757

Touches upon the influence of the stream on the western coast of North America.

[BENTALOU (Paul).] Pulaski vindicated from an Unsupported Charge, Inconsiderately or Malignantly introduced in Judge Johnson's Sketches of the Life and Correspondence of Major Gen. Nathaniel Greene. *Baltimore: printed by John D. Toy.* 1824. 8vo, pp. 34, iii. H. 4758

BENTALOU. A Reply to Judge Johnson's Remarks on an Article in the North American Review, relating to Count Pulaski. By Paul Bentalou. ... *Baltimore.* 1826. 8vo, pp. 41.

See N. A. R., XX. 375; XXIII. 414.

[BENTHAM (Ed.)] De Tumultibus Americanis deque eorum Conciliatoribus Meditatio Senilis. *Oxonii: J. Fletcher, and D. Prince; B. White: Londini.* M DCC LXXVI. 8vo, 2 l., pp. 36. H.

"Occasioned by the sarcastic observations on the conduct of the University of Oxford respecting their address to the King. The author extols the University, praises the ministry, and reviles the Americans."—*Monthly Review*, LIV. 332.

[BENTHAM.] The Honor of the University of Oxford defended, against the Illiberal Aspersions of E——d B——e, Esq; with Pertinent Observations on the Present Rebellion in America. Translated from the Original Latin of E. B——, D.D. ... *London: Geo. Kearsley; and Oxford: J. and J. Fletcher*, [1776]. 8vo, Title, pp. ii, 36. H. 4761

A translation of the "De tumultibus." *See* M. R., LIV. 410.

BENTHAM (George). The Botany of, etc. *See* Hinds (R. B.)

BENTHAM. Plantas Hartwegianas imprimis Mexicanas adjectis nonnullis Grahamianis enumerat novasque describit Bentham. *Londini.* 1839–46. 8vo, pp. 283 Continued. 4762

BENTHAM. Observations on Some Genera of Plants connected with the Flora of Guyana. 1838. 4to. 3 Plates. 4763

BENTHAM *and* ORSTED (A.) Plantæ Centroamericanæ. 8vo.

Bentham (Jeremy). Canada. Emancipate your Colonies, an unpublished Argument. *London.* 1830. 8vo. + *London.* 1838. 4765

This fills pp. 407–418 of Vol. iv. of his "... Works ... published under the Superintendence of ... John Bowring. *Edinburgh: William Tait.* MDCCCXLIII." 11 vols., 8vo. H.

Bentham. Codification Proposal, addressed by Jeremy Bentham to all Nations professing Liberal Opinions ... . [n. p.?] 1822. 4766

Contains some letters from the "Anglo-American United States" on the reception of his proposal in New Hampshire and other states. Reprinted in Bowring's edition, iv. 535–594.

Bentham. Jeremy Bentham to the National Convention of France. [n. p. 17—.] 8vo, pp. 48. H. 4767

"Emancipate your Colonies."

Bentham. Papers relative to Codification and Public Instruction: including Correspondence with the Russian Emperor, and divers Constituted Authorities in the American United States. Published by Jeremy Bentham. *London: Payne and Foss, and R. Hunter.* 1817. 8vo. 4768

Bentham. Supplement to Papers ... [as above]. *London.* [Same.] 4769

Reprinted, differently arranged, in his works, published by Bowring, iv. 451–533.

Bentley (Charles). Twelve Views in the Interior of Guyana, from Drawings by Charles Bentley, with descriptive letterpress by R. H. Schomburgk, and illustrations on Wood. *London.* 1841. Folio. 4770

Twelve plates colored, to imitate the original drawings.

Bentley (John). An Inroad upon the Sacred Trial by Jury; or, the Case of John Bentley, Gaoler of Baltimore County Gaol, &c. *Baltimore.* 1811. 8vo. 4771

Bentley (W.) An Address delivered in the Essex Lodge ... at the Induction of the Officers, ... December 27, 1798. By William Bentley. *Salem.* 1799. 8vo, pp. 31. H. 4772

Bentley. A Funeral Discourse, delivered in ... Salem ... after the Death of Major General John Fiske, who died September 28, 1797, Æt. 53. By William Bentley ... . *Salem: printed by Thomas C. Cushing.* 1797. 8vo., pp. 37. B., H. 4773

Bentley. A Sermon, delivered in ... Salem ... March 13: occasioned by the Death of Jonathan Gardner, Esq. Master of the Marine Society in Salem; who died March 2, 1791. Æt. 63. By William Bentley ... . *Salem.* MDCCXCI. 8vo, pp. 32. H.

Bentley. A Sermon, before the Governor ... [etc.] of Massachusetts, on the Day of General Election, May 27, 1807. By William Bentley ... . *Boston: printed by Adams and Rhodes.* 1807. 8vo, pp. 25. H. 4775

Bentley. A Sermon, preached before the Ancient and Honourable Artillery Company, in Boston, June 6, 1796, being the Anniversary of their Election of Officers. By William Bentley ... . *Boston: printed by Manning & Loring.* 1796. pp. 23. H.

Also: A Charge delivered before the Morning Star Lodge, in Worcester, Massachusetts ... June 25, A.L. 5798. ... *Worcester: Press of Brother Isaiah Thomas, Jun. June, A.L.* 5798. 8vo, pp. 36. H.—A Discourse, Delivered at Amherst, August 10, 1797 ... at the Installation of the Benevolent Lodge ... . [n. p.] *Samuel Preston, Printer.* 1797. 8vo, pp. 24. H.—A Funeral Discourse, delivered in ... Salem ... 15th April, 1804 ... [on] Benjamin Hodges, A.B. ... Aged XIX. ... *Salem.* 1804. 8vo, pp. 23. H.—A Sermon, delivered July 2, 1806. at the Ordination of Mr. Joseph Richardson ... in Hingham. ... *Boston.* 1806. 8vo, pp. 24. H.—A Discourse Delivered in Roxbury, October 12, 5796 ... at ... [the Consecration] of Washington Lodge ... . *Boston: William Spotswood,* 1797. 8vo, pp. 21.—A Discourse, delivered ... September 2, 1807, at the Annual Meeting of the Salem Female Charitable Society. ... *Salem: printed by Pool & Palfray.* 1807. 8vo, pp. 27. H.—A Sermon, preached at the Stone Chapel in Boston, September 12, 1790. ... *Boston: printed by Samuel Hall.* MDCCXC. 8vo. pp. 24. B., H.

Bentley's Miscellany. Vol. i. *London: Richard Bentley.* 1837. 8vo, pp. (8), 636. Continued. + *New-York.* 1837, [etc.] 8vo. 4777

The early volumes contain "Wolfert's Roost," by Irving, "Uncle Sam's Peculiarities," etc.; and there are numerous other articles relating to America.

Bentom (C.) A Statement of Facts and Law relative to the Persecution of the Rev. Clark Bentom, Protestant Missionary from the London Missionary Society, for the Assumption of the Office of a Dissenting Minister of the Gospel, in Quebec, by the King's Attorney General of Lower Canada. *Troy, [N. Y.]: Printed for the author* ... 1804. 8vo, pp. 32. M., S. 4778

Benton (C.) *and* Barry (S. F.) A Statistical View of the Number of Sheep in the several Towns and Counties in ... [the New England States] ... New York, Pennsylvania ... and Ohio: a Partial Account of the Number of Sheep in Virginia, Maryland, New Jersey, Delaware, and Kentucky, in 1836. And

an Account of the Principal Woolen Manufactories in said States. ... By C. Benton and S. F. Barry. *Cambridge: Folsom, Wells, and Thurston.* 1837. 18mo, pp. 143. H. 4779

Benton (C. S.) Speech of Mr. Benton, of New York, on the Tariff. ... In the House ... June 30, 1846. *Washington.* 1846. 8vo, pp. 15. H. 4780

Benton (J.) An Address to the People of the United States On the Presidential Election. By Jesse Benton. *Nashville: Printed by Joseph Norvell for the Author.* 1824. 12mo, pp. 34.

This is a severe attack upon General Jackson, and incidentally on John Q. Adams.

Benton (Nathaniel S.) A History of Herkimer County, including the Upper Mohawk Valley, from the Earliest Period to the Present Time: with a Brief Notice of the Iroquois Indians, the Early German Tribes, the Palatine Immigrations into the Colony of New York, and Biographical Sketches of the Palatine Families, the Patentees of Burnetsfield in the year 1825. Also Biographical Notices of the most Prominent Public Men of the County: with Important Statistical Information. By Nathaniel S. Benton. *Albany: J. Munsell.* 1856. 8vo, pp. v, (2), 6–497. Map and Plates. B., C. 4782

[Benton (Thomas Hart).] Abridgment of the Debates of Congress, from 1789 to 1856. From Gales and Seaton's Annals of Congress; from their Register of Debates; and from the Official Reported Debates, by John C. Rives. By the Author of the Thirty Years' View. *New York: D. Appleton & Company.* 1857–61. 16 vols., 8vo. 4783

Contents.—Vol. i. 1789–'96; ii. 1796–1803; iii. 1803–'08; iv. 1808–'13; v. 1813–'17; vi. 1817–'21; vii. 1821–'24; viii. 1824–'26; ix. 1826–'28; x. 1828–'30; xi. 1830–'32; xii. 1832–'36; xiii. 1836–'59; xiv. 1839–'43; xv. 1843–'46; xvi. 1846–'50. This forms a good substitute for the works abridged, occupying, as they do, seventy volumes in octavo, and nearly fifty in quarto.

Benton. ... Discourse of Mr. Benton, of Missouri, before the Maryland Institute, On the physical geography of the country between Missouri and California, with a view to ... settlement, and the construction of a Railroad. Delivered ... December 5, 1854. [n. p. n. d.] 8vo, pp. 16. H. + Delivered [with Slight Additions] ... at Boston ... December 20, 1854. *Washington.* 1854. 8vo, pp. 24. H. 4784

[Benton.] Historical and Legal Examination of that part of the Decision of the Supreme Court of the United States in the

Dred Scott Case, which declares the unconstitutionality of the Missouri Compromise Act and the Self-Extension of the Constitution to Territories, carrying Slavery along with it. With an Appendix. Containing: i. The Debates in the Senate in March, 1849, between Mr. Webster and Mr. Calhoun ... . ii. The Inside View of the Southern Sentiment, in relation to the Wilmot Froviso ... . iii. Review of President Peirce's Annual Message ... of December, 1856. By the Author of the "Thirty Years' View." *New-York: Appleton.* 1857. + 1858. + 1860. 8vo, pp. 4, 3–193. B., C. 4785

Benton. Letter from Col. Benton to the People of Missouri. Central National Highway from the Mississippi River to the Pacific. [n. p. 1853.] 8vo, pp. 24. H. 4786

[Benton Thirty Years View; or, a History of the Working of the American Government for Thirty Years, from 1820 to 1850. Chiefly taken from the Congress Debates, the Private Papers of General Jackson and the Speeches of Ex-Senator Benton, with his Actual View of Men and Affairs: with Historical Notes and Illustrations, and some Notices of Eminent Deceased Cotemporaries: by a Senator of Thirty Years. ... *New York: D. Appleton & Coompany.* 1854–56. Rl. 8vo, pp. ix, 739; 788. Portrait and Plate. H. 4787

Subsequently reprinted without alterations, and dated 1860, 1861, 1865, etc. Mr. Benton was a veteran politician and an industrious representative. His speeches have been most numerous, and are usually characterized by more strength than elegance. The following are among those of public interest: The Admission of California. Speech ... in the Senate ... April 8, 1850. On the Compromise Resolutions of Mr. Bell, of Tennessee ... . [*Washington.* n. d.] 8vo, pp. 8. H.— ... Anti-Compromise Speech ... of Mr. Benton ... in the Senate ... June 10, 1850. On his motion to postpone until the 4th day of March, 1851 ... the Compromise Bill. [n. p. n. d.] 8vo, pp. 15. H.—A Letter ... to Commodore Stewart, on the Action of the Navy Board. [n. p.] 1856. 12mo, pp. 10. H.—Highway from the Mississippi to the Pacific Ocean. Speech ... in the Senate ... February 7, 1849 ... . [*Washington.* n. d.] 8vo. pp. 8. H.—Nebraska and Kansas. Speech ... in the House ... April 25, 1854. [*Washington.* 1854.] 8vo, pp. 8. H.—Remarks ... on the annual Expenditures of the Government. In Senate, ... May 1 [1840. *Washington.* 1840.] 8vo, pp. 8. —Speech ... on The Amendment of the Constitution ... in the Senate ... January 30, 1824. *Washington.* 1824. 12mo, pp. 47. H.—Speech ... in the Senate of the United States, ... on the Mission to Panama, March 13, 1826. *Washington.* 1826. 8vo, pp. 47. + Another Edition. [n. p. n. d.] 12mo, pp. 59.— ... Speeches on the Public Lands, Delivered in the Senate ... First Session of the 20th Congress, ... *Washington.* 1828. 8vo, pp. 44.—Speech ... on the Resolutions submitted by him, Dec. 23. 1828, on The Public Debt, [etc.], ... in the Senate ... January 6, 1829. *Washington.* 1829. 8vo, pp. 12.—Speech ... in the Senate ... January 6, 1829, on his resolution in relation to the Public Debt, &c. &c. *Washington.* 1829. 8vo, pp. 14. —Speech ... in Reply to Mr. Webster; The resolution offered by Mr. Foot relative to The Public Lands being under consideration, delivered in the Senate, Session

1829–30. *Washington: Gales and Seaton.* 1830. 12mo, pp. 14.—Speech ... on the Bill to Abolish the duty on Alum Salt. Delivered in the Senate Feb. 8, 1830. *Washington.* 1831. 8vo, pp. 46.—Speech ... On introducing a Resolution against the Renewal of the Charter of the Bank of the United States ... February 2, 1831. *Washington.* 1831. 8vo, pp. 23.—Speech ... in the Senate of the United States, Jan. 20, 1832, on the State of the Currency. *Washington.* [1832]. 8vo. W.—Speech ... on the Resolutions offered by Mr. Clay, on 26th December, relative to the Removal of the Public Deposits from the Bank of the United States. ... January 2d, 3d, 6th and 7th, 1834. *Washington.* 1834. 8vo, pp. 47. S. + *Albany.* 1834. 8vo, pp. 3. B. + *Boston.* 1834. 8vo, pp. 44. H.—Speech ... on the Motion of Mr. Webster for Leave to bring in a Bill for prolonging the Charter of the Bank of the United States; ... in the Senate ... March 21, 1834. *Washington: printed by Francis Preston Blair.* 1834. 8vo, pp. 24. H.—Speech ... on the Resolution of Mr. Ewing, for rescinding the Treasury Order [of July 11, 1836, for excluding Paper Money from the Land Offices, etc.] delivered in the Senate, Dec. 1836. *Washington.* 1837. 8vo.—Speech ... on the Expunging Resolution. Delivered in the Senate, January 12, 1837. [n. p. n. d.] 8vo, pp. 7. H.—Speech ... on the Bill designating and limiting the Funds receivable for the Revenues of the United States; delivered in the Senate, Jan. 27. 1837. *Washington.* 1837. 8vo.—Speech ... on the Bill to separate the Government from the Banks. Delivered in the Senate ... March 14, 1838. *Washington.* 1838. 8vo, pp. 31. H.—Speech ... . In Senate, January 6, 1840—On Mr. Benton's resolutions against ... assuming, or providing for the payment of the State debts .. . [n. p. n. d.] 8vo, pp. 16. H.—Speech ... on the Case of McLeod. [n. p. 1841.] 8vo, pp. 8. H.—Speech ... on his Motion to postpone the operation of the Bankrupt Act; delivered in the ... Senate, December 27, 1841. [*Washington.* 1841.] 8vo.—Speech ... on his motion to Expunge from the Journal the sentence pronounced against President Jackson, for violating the laws and constitution. [n. p. n. d.] 8vo, pp. 32.—Speech ... on the Cabinet Plan for a Federal Exchequer. ... In the Senate, January 13, 1842. [n. p. n. d.] 8vo, pp. 16. H.—Speech ... on the Tariff. Delivered in the Senate of the United States, March 25, 1844. *Washington.* 1844. 8vo, pp. 16. H.—Speech ... on the Tariff. Delivered in the Senate ... March 25, 1844. *Washington.* 1844. 8vo, pp. 16. H.—Speech ... delivered in the Senate ... May 16, 18, and 20, in Secret Session on the Treaty for the Annexation of Texas ... . *Washington.* 1844. 8vo, pp. 21. H. + [Continued.] *Washington.* 1844. 8vo, pp. 8. H.—Speech ... on the Oregon Question. Delivered in the Senate of the United States, May 22, 25, & 28, 1846. *Washington: Blair and Rives.* 1846. 8vo, pp. 39.—Speech ... on the California Claims. Delivered in the Senate ... April 11, 1848. *Washington.* 1848. 8vo, pp. 12. H.—Speech. ... on the adjudication of land titles and sale of Gold Mines in New Mexico and California. Delivered in the Senate of the United States, January 15, 1849. [n. p. n. d.] 8vo, pp. 16.—Speech ... against ceding Seventy Thousand Square Miles of New Mexico to Texas ... July 15, 1850. 8vo, pp. 8.— ... Extract from Senator Benton's Speech ... in St. Louis ... November 9th. General Taylor. [*New York.* 1850.] Folio, 1 p. H.—Speech ... On the Bill to appropriate ten millions. Delivered in the House of Representatives, June 26, 1854. *Washington.* 1854. 8vo, pp. 14.—Texas Annexation Bill. Speech ... in Reply to Mr. McDuffie. Delivered in the Senate ... June 15, 1844. *Washington.* [n. d.] 8vo, pp. 16. H.—Three Speeches of the Honorable Thomas H. Benton, Senator from ... Missouri, Two delivered in the Senate of the United States, and one at Boonville, Indiana, on the Subject of the Annexation of Texas ... . *New York.* 1844. 8vo, pp. 48. H.

Benwell (J.) An Englishman's Travels in America: his Observations of Life and Manners in the Free and Slave States. By J. Benwell. *London and Bath: Binns and Goodwin.* [1853.] Fcap 8vo, pp. vii, 231. + *London: Ward and Lock.* 1857. 8vo.

Benzenberg (Johann Friedrich). Das Anleihen in Frankreich, England und Nordamerika vom J. 1792 bis zum J. 1836. *Düsseldorf.* 1836. 8vo, 4 sheets. 4789

Benzoni (Girolamo). La Historia del | Mondo Nvovo | di M. Girolamo Benzoni | Milanese. | La qval tratta dell'Isole, | & Mari nuouamente ritrouati, & delle nuoue | Città da lui proprio vedute, per acqua | & per terra in quattordeci anni. | Con Privilegio della Illustrissima Signoria | di Venetia, Per anni xx. | [Colophon:] *In Venetia, | appresso Francesco | Rampazetto.* | M D LXV. Sm. 8vo, 4 l., (Text) 175 l. Portrait on the title, and other Woodcuts. H.

Sold, in 1830, £1 1s.; priced, by Asher, 20fr. Reprinted with the following title:

Benzoni. La Historia del | Mondo Nvovo | di M. Girolamo Benzoni | Milanese. | La qval tratta delle | Isole, & mari nuouamente ritrouati, et delle | nuoue Città da lui proprio vedute, | per acqua, & per terra in | quattordeci anni. | Nuouamente ristampata, et illustrata con la giunta d' alcune | cose notablie dell' Isole di Canaria. | Con Privilegio. | [Colophon:] *In Venetia, ad instantia di Pietro & Francisco Tini.* 1572. 8vo, 4 l., (Text) 179 l., 1 l. Woodcuts. S. 4791

"Benzoni was born at Milan about 1519. At the age of twenty-two he left his country to visit the New World, and, after fourteen years of travel, returned and published this work. Its style is inelegant, but it deserves to be perused by those interested in the history of the first establishment of the Europeans in America from other than Spanish sources."—Trovenal.

Benzoni. Novae Novi | Orbis Historiæ, | Jd est, | Rerum ab Hispanis in India Occidentali ha- | ctenus gestarum, & acerbo illorum | in eas gentes dominatu, | Libri Tres, Vrbani Calvetonis | opera industriàque ex Italicis Hieronymi Benzo- | nis Mediolanensis, qui eas terras xiiii. anno- | rum peregrinatione obijt, commentarijs descripti, | Latini facti, ac perpetuis notis, argumentis et locu | pleti memorabilium rerum accessione, illustrati. | His ab eodem adiuncta est, | De Gallorum in Floridam expeditione, & insigni Hispanorum | in eos sæuitiæ exemplo, Breuis Historia. | Anchora | [Woodcut of an anchor] | Sacra. | [*Genevæ,*] *Apvd Evstathivm Vignon.* | M.D.LXXVIII. | 8vo, Title, (Epistola) 5 l., (Præfatio) 8 l., (Epigrammata) 1 l., (Primi Libri Svmma) 1 l., (Text) pp. 480, (Elenchvs) 6 l., (Mendas ... emendato) 1 l. B. & C. 4792

It is said that, from this work, Kotzebue obtained the foundation of his famous play of "Pizarro." Priced, by Asher, 20fr.; Tross, 15fr.; Puttick, 1860, 11s. This edition was issued with a new title-page, dated M. D. LXXXI.—the collation being precisely the same. Priced, in Köhler's catalogue, 4 thalers. In Mr. Bartlett's catalogue

of Mr. J. C. Brown's library, another edition of this date is described; the only difference seems to be in the collation—this one containing only 15 l., (text) pp. 480, but no index. *See* Bartlett's Cat., Vol. i., Nos. 182 and 183.

Benzoni. Historia | Indiae Occidentalis, | Tomis duobus comprehensa. | Prior, res ab Hispanis in India Occidentali ha- | ctenus gestas, acerbum illorum in eas Gentes do- | minatum, insignéque in Gallos ad Floridam In- | sulam sæuitiæ exemplum describit. | Alter verò, Brasiliæ (quæ & America dicitur) re- | rúmque in ea obseruatione dignarum a nobis pe- | nitus incognita descriptionem continet. | Hieronymo Benzone Italo, & Ioanne | Lerio Burgundo, testibus oculatis, autoribus. Ex eo- | rum autem idiomate in latinum sermonem Vrbani | Calvetonis & G.M. studio conversi: perpetuis notis, | argumentis, Figuris, Indicibus, & locupleti memorabilium | rerum accessione illustrati. | Addita est Totius Indiæ Occidentalis, seu orbis illius noui breuis | descriptio, quæ maximam hanc mundi partem vno velut | intuitu perlustrandam oculis subiicit. | [Vignette.] *Excvdebat | Evstathivs Vignon.* | M. D. LXXXVI. 8vo, 16 l., pp. 480, (Index) 6 l.; (Lerius) Title, 30 l., pp. 341, (Errata) 1 l., (Index) 8 l. Folded Woodcut at p. 178. H., S.

Benzoni. Novae Novi | Orbis Historiæ, | Jd est, | Rerum ab Hispanis in India Occidentali ha- | ctenus gestarum, & acerbo illorum | in eas gentes dominatu, | Libri tres, | Vrbani Calvetonis | opera industriáque ex Italicis Hieronymi | Benzonis Mediolanêsis, qui eas terras xiiii. | annorum peregrinatione obijt, commentariis | descripti, Latini facti, ac perpetuis notis, ar- | gumentis & locupleti memorabilium rerum | accessione illustrati. | His ab eodem adiuncta est, | De Gallorum in Floridam expeditione, & insigni | Hispanorum in eos sæuitiæ exemplo, | breuis Historia. | [*Genevæ:*] *Apud Hæredes Eustathij Vignon | Anno* M.DC. 8vo, Title, (Epistola) 5 l., (Præfatio) 8 l., (Epigrammata) 1 l., (Primi Libri Svmma) 1 l., (Text) pp. 480, (Index) 6 l. 4794

More scarce than the first edition. One of the rare "anchor" books, having that device on the title.

Benzoni. Histoire | Novvelle | dv Novveav | Monde, | Contenant en somme ce que les Hespa- | gnols ont fait iusqu' à present aux Indes | Occidentales, & le rude traitement | qu'ils font à ces poures peuples-la. | Extraite de l' Italien de M. Hierosme Benzoni Milanois, qui ha | voyagé xiiii. ans en ces pays-la: & enrichie de | plusieurs Discours & choses dignes de memoire. | Par M. Vrbain Chavveton. | Ensemble, | Vne petite Histoire d'vn Massacre commis par les He- | spagnols sur quelques François en la Floride. |

Auec vn Indice des choses les plus remarquables. [*Genève:*] *par Evstace Vignon.* 1579. 8vo, 12 l., pp. 726, (Floride) pp. 104, (Indice) 7 l. C. 4795

Sold at Puttick's, 1860, for $1 2s. The pp. 104 have the title: Brief discovrs et histoire d'vn voyage de quelques François en la Floride: et du massacre autant iniustement que barbaremēt executé sur eux par les Hespagnols, l'an mil cinq cens soixante cinq ... M. D. LXXIX. "There are copies of this French translation with the date 1589. Charlevoix [and Fevret de Pontette] think that the part of the book relating to Florida is taken from the work of Le Challeux on the same subject printed in 1566."—Leclerc. Faribault mentions an edition of this version published in 8vo in 1690; perhaps a misprint for 1590.

Benzoni. Novæ novi orbis historiæ. Das ist Aller Geschichten So in der newen welt Occidentalis India, das ist India, nach Abendwerts genent wird vnd etwa anno 1492. Von Christophoro Colombo gefunden worden by den Einwöhnern derselbigen vnd den Spanien mehrers so darin auch denn Frantzosen eins theils bisz aust, annum 1556, etc. *Hamburg: in verlegung Bernd Arens.* 1648. 4to, 14 l., pp. 537 (for 527). J. C. B. 4796

Benzoni. Der | Newen | Weldt vnd In- | dianischen Königreichs, newe vnnd | wahrhaffte History, von allen Geschichten, Handlungen, | Thaten, Strengem vnnd Ernstlichem Regiment der Spanier gegen den | Indianern, vngläublichem grossem Gut von Goldt, Sylber, Edelgestein, | Peerlin, Schmaragdt, vnnd andern Reichtumb, so die Spanier darinn erobert: sambt von den | sorglichen Schiffarthen, Kriegen, Schlachten vnnd Streit, Eroberung vnd verher- | gung vieler Prouintz, Landtschafften, vnd Königreich, so sich bey | vnser Gedächtnuss haben darinn verloffen | vnd zugetragen. | Dessgleichen, | Von der Indianer wunderbarlichen Sitten, Statuten, Glauben, | Religion, Gottesdienst, Ceremonien, Gebräuch in Essen vnd Trin- | cken, Kleidung, Handthierung vnnd Gewerbschafft, etc. Item von ihrer Eygenschafft, | Natur, seltzamen Gewächss der Früchten, Bäwmen, Metallen, Specerey vnd andere | vnbekandtliche ding mehr, so von jhnen in vnsere landt- | schafft geführt werden. | Erstlich, | Durch Hieronymum Bentzon von Meyland in Welscher Spraach | wahrhafftig beschrieben, vnnd selbs persönlich in xiiii, Jaren durchwanderet. | Vorhin nie in Teutscher Spraach dessgleichen gesehen: Erst jetzt mit sonderm Fleiss | allen Regenten vnd Oberherrn, sambt liebhabern der Historien | zuo nutz auss dem Latein in das Teutsch | Durch, | Nicolaum Höniger von Königshofen an der Tauber. | gebracht. | Getruckt zu Basel, durch Sebastian | Henricpetri. | [Colophon:] *Getruckt | Zu Basel, durch Sebastian Henricpetri, im*

|*jhar nach vnser Erlösung vnd Selig-|machung Jesu Christi.*| M. D. LXXIX.|Folio, 4 l., pp. ccxix. C. 4797

Priced, Weigel, 6 thalers. Georgi, in his first supplement, mentions an edition of this version, dated 1575, but he had evidently not seen the book, for he does not give the number of sheets.

BENZONI, MARTYR, *and* APOLLONIUS. Der|Newenn|Weldt vnd In-|dianischen Nidergängischen König-|reichs, Newe vnd Wahrhaffte History ... . Auch Liebhabern der Historien, ausz dem Latein in das|Teutsch gebracht,|Durch,|Nicolaum Höniger von Königshofen|an der Tauber.|*Getruckt zu Basel. Sebastian Henricpetri.* M.D.Lxxxij. 10 l., pp. ccxliii, Ander Theil, (Peter Martyr) 12 l., pp. ccxlv.-dcij., (Colophon) 1 l., (Dritte Theil, Apollonius) 6 l., pp. cccvi, (Colophon) 1 l. J. C. B. 4798

BENZONI. Novæ novi orbis historiæ. das ist aller Geschichten so inder newen Welt, welche India Occidentalis genent wird sich zugetragen. ... Deszgleichen von der Frantzosen Meerfahrt in das Land Floridam, zusamt beschreibung der Canarischen Insuln, etc., Durch Abel Scherdigern Pharrern zu Wasungen ausz dem Latein in Deutsch bracht Anno 1589. *Helmsdadt durch. Jac. Lucium.* 1590–91. 4to, 15 l., pp. 517, 6 l. + *Franckfort.* 1595. 4799

BENZONI. Historie der Neue Welt. *Hamburg.* 1608. 4to.

Title as quoted by Ternaux, No. 676, who, I think, is in error as to the date.

BENZONI. Eigentliche Fürbildung aller newen fremden seltsamen Historien und Geschichten so sich wahrhaftig in dem mächtigen Königreiche Peru zu Zeiten als die Spanier erstmals dasselbe Land erfunden, zugetragen haben. *Francfurt.* 1597. Folio. 4801

BENZONI. De Historie|vande|Nieuwe werelt|Te weten, de| Beschrijvinghe van West-Indien.|Waer in verhaelt wert, van de Eylanden eñ Zeen|nieuwlicx ghevonden, ende den nieuwen| Steden die hy daer zelfs ghezien-heeft, ende|'tghene daer is ghebeurt te water ende|te lande, in veertien jaren tijds|die hy aldaer ghe-|weest is.|Door Ieronimus Benzonius van|Milanen.|Wt het Italiaens over-ghezet in Nederduyt|door Karel vander Mander Schilder.|*Tot Haerlem, by Paschier van Wes-|bus, Boecverkooper inden beslagen Bybel.*|*Anno* 1610.|8vo, 10 l., pp. 404. J. C. B.

Sold for 7s. at Puttick's, 1860; priced, Muller, $1.50. This title differs from that given by Tiele, "Journaux des navig. néerl.," p. 292, so much, I have thought it best to give both, as there may have been two editions in the same year. Tiele's is as follows:

BENZONI. De Historie, van|De nieuwe weerelt,|te weten, de|Beschrijvinghe van West-Indien.|Daer in verhaelt wert van de Eylanden ende Zeen nieulicx|gevonden, ende van den nieuwen Stedê die hy daer selfs|ghesien heeft, ende tghene daer is ghebeurt te water ende|te lande, in veerthien Jaren tijts, die hy aldaer geweest is.|Door Ieronimus Benzonius van Milanen.| Wt het Italiaens overgheset in Nederduyts, door|Carel vander [*sic*] Mander Schilder|[Woodcut.]|*Tot Haerlem, by Paeschier van Wesbus* [*sic*] *Boeckvercooper*,|*in den beslaghen Bybel.* 1610|8vo, 10 l., pp. 404. 17 Woodcuts in the text. 4803

BENZONI. Beschryvinghe van|West-Indien,|Waer in verhaelt wordt, de eerste vindingh|van de Eylanden, Steeden, Plaetsen, en Rivieren,|van het selve, als mede hoe de Spangiaerts het Landt verwoest,|verbrandt ende ingenomen hebben.|Mitsgaders:|De Natuer, Zeden, Huysen, en Kleedingh der Indianen,| oock van de Goudt en Silvermijnen, ende haer Levens-middelen.| Beschreven door Jeronimus Benzonius van Milanen;|En uyt het Italiaens overgeset door Carel Vermander.|[Woodcut.]| *t'Amsterdam, Gedruckt*|*By Gillis Joosten Saeghman, in de Nieuwestraet*|*Ordinaris Drucker van de Journalen der Zee- en Landt-Reysen.*|4to, pp. 56. 19 Woodcuts in the text. 4804

The text of Benzoni, printed in double columns, fills pp. 3–48; pp. 49–56 contain "Beschryvinge van de Regeeringh van Peru, beschreven door ... Pedro de Madriga." The two additional cuts belong to this. After the death of Van Mander (1606), his friend Passchier van Westbusch found this version among his papers, and published it. *See* Tiele, "Journ. des navig. neerl." pp. 292–294.

BENZONI. History of the New World, by Girolamo Benzoni, of Milan. Shewing his Travels in America, from A.D. 1541 to 1556: with some Particulars of the Island of Canary. Now first translated, and edited by Rear-Admiral W. H. Smyth ... . *London: printed for the Hakluyt Society.* M.DCCC.LVII. 8vo, 3 l., pp. iv, 3 l., 280. B. 4805

See, also, Purchas' Pilgrim, IV. 1445.

BENZONI. De gedenkwaardige West-Indise Voyagien, Gedaan door Christoffel Columbus, Americus Vesputius, En Lodewijck Hennepin. Behelzende een naaukeurige en waarachtige Beschrijving der eerste en laatste Americaanse ontdekkingen. *Leyden.* 1704. 4to. 6 Plates. 4806

Also in Van der Aa's Naaukeurige Versameling. *See* No. 3.

BENZONI. Scheeps-togt na West-Indien van Hieronymus

Benzo in het Jaar 1541. Nu aldereerst uyt het Italiaans vertaald. *Leyden.* 1706. 4to. BM. 4807

Included in Van der Aa's Naaukeurige Versameling. *See* No. 3. For other editions of Benzoni, *see* Bry (T. de).

BERARD (A. B.) School History of the United States. By A. B. Berard. 12mo, pp. 224. 4808

BERBICE. Kort Historisch verhaal van den eersten aanleg., enz. der Colonie Rio de Berbice. gelegen in het Landschap Guiana in Zuid-Amerika. *Amsterdam: C. Sepp, Jz.* 1807. 8vo. Plates of Nieu Amsterdam a Rio de Berbice. 4809

Beschryvinge van de rivier en colonie van Berbice. *Amsterdam.* 4to. 4810

Title from Boucher, VI. 259.

Kortbondige beschryvinge van de colonie de Berbice ... . Verrijkt Met Merkwaardige Berichten wegens de ... Opstandt door de Negers ... . Uit de Aantekeningen van een voornaam Heer opgemaakt, die eenige Jaaren op de Colonie zyn verblyf gehouden heeft. ... *Amsteldam: S. J. Baalde.* MDCCLXIII. 4to, 3 l., pp. 40 [misprint for 50]. Map and Plate. H. + Tweede druk. *Amsterdam: S. J. Baalde.* 1763. 4to. Plates. 4811

Priced, Muller, No. 992, $4; Nijhoff, fr.2.50.

Kort verhaal van de rebellie der Negers in de Colonie de Berbice in 1763. *Amsterdam.* 1763. 4to. 4812

Requeste, met Memorie en Bijlagen van P. Pama, c. s. eigenaars van plantagien in de colonie de Berbice. 1741. Folio, pp. 188. 4813

Resolutie van de Staten-Generaal in d. 4 Oct. 1764, betr. de expeditie van den Hert. ven Brunswijk naar de Berbices. Met Bijlagen en eene Kaart. [n. p. n. d.] Folio, pp. 80. 4814

BERBREUGGER. Essai historique sur la révolution du Paraguay et le gouvernement dictatorial du docteur Francia. 8vo. 4815

BERCHON (E.) Des services à vapeur transatlantiques et de ceux d'Europe aux États-Unis en particulier; par M. le docteur Ernest Berchon ... . *Le Havre.* 1866. 8vo, pp. 23. 4816

BERCHON. En steamer D'Europe aux Etats-Unis Histoire, Souvenirs, Impressions de Voyage Par le Dr Ernest Berchon ... . *Havre: imprimerie Lepelletier.* 1867. 16mo, pp. xv, 287, (1). 3 Maps. 4817

BERDUGO (Nicolas). Reducciones de plata, y oro, a las leyes de 11. Diner. y 22. Quilat. valores de una. Y otra especie por marcos, onzas, ochav. tomin. y gran. como S. Mag. lo manda en sus novissimas reales ordenanzas, expedidas en 1. de Agosto de 1750, [etc.] *Mexico: Doña Mariu de Rivera.* 1752. 8vo, 14 l., pp. 324. 4818

BERE (Iver.) Gronlands Beskrivelse, med et Kort og Forerindring of Arent Aschlund. *Kjöbenhavn.* 1832. 8vo, pp. 12. Map.

No. 2166 should have been entered under this head.

BERE. Beschreibung von Grönland, mit einer Karte und Vorrede von Arent Aschlund. Aus dem Dänischen. *Kopenhagen: Schubothe.* 1833. 8vo. 4820

BERENGER (J. H. de). Letter to the Right Hon. W. Pitt, from John Henry de Berenger, de Beaufain, of South Carolina, claiming compensation as an American Loyalist. 1792. 4to.

BERENGER (J. P.) Collection de tous les voyages faits autour du monde Par les différentes Nations de l'Europe, Redigée par M. Berenger; avec figures. ... *A Lausanne: J. Pierre Heubach; Geneve: François Dufart.* M. DCC. LXXXVIII.–LXXXIX. 9 vols., 8vo. Map, and 9 Plates. H. 4822

"The 'Voyages Interessans' sometimes form a tenth volume of this collection."—RICH.

BERESFORD (J.) Thoughts on the Discontents of the People Last Year, respecting the Sugar Duties. With an Appendix, containing A Report from the Committee of the British House of Commons ... . *Dublin: William Wilson.* M.DCC.XXXI. 8vo, Title, pp. 95, 66. B. 4823

Beretning om de norske Setlere i Amerika. *Bergen, C. Rudolf.* 1848. 8vo. 4824

Beretning om Californien og dets Guldrigdom. Med et Kart over Californien. *Christiania.* 1849. 16mo, pp. 125. 4825

BERETTARI (Sebastiano). Josephi Anchietæ soc. Jesv sacerdotis in Brasilia defvncti Vita. Ex iis, qvæ de eo Petrvs Roterigivs soc. Jesv Præses Prouincialis in Brasilia quatuor libris Lusitanico idiomate collegit, aliísque monumentis fide dignis, à Sebastiano Beretario descripta. Prodit nunc primum. *Lvgdvni: sumptibus Horatij Cardon.* 1617. 8vo, 3 l., pp. 277. 4826

BERETTARI. Vita R. P.|Iosephi|Anchietae Socie-|tatis Iesv Sacerdo-|tis in Brasilia|defuncti.|Ex iis qvæ de eo Petrvs|Roterigvs Societatis|Iesv Præses Prouincialis in Brasilia|quatuor libris Lusitanico idiomate|collegit, alijsq*ue* monumentis|fide dignis à|Sebastiano Beretario|ex eadem Societate descripta.|Prodit nunc primùm in Germania.|[Seal of the Society.]|*Coloniae Agrippinae,*|*Apud Ioannem Kinchivm. sub*|*Monocerote.*|M. D. C. XVII.| *Permissu Superiorum & priuil.*|12mo, 2 l., pp. 427, (2). J. C. B. & H.

Priced, Trübner, £1 1s.; Butsch, fl.5.20. The Portugese original from which Berettari made his translation exists only in MS. The book gives an account of the first mission of the Jesuits to the Brazils.

BERETTARI. Vida del Padre Joseph de Ancheta [*sic*] de la Compañia de Jesvs, y provincial del Brasil. Tradvzida de latin en castellano por el P. Esteuan de Paternina de la misma Compañia, y natural de Logroño. *Salamanca: Antonia Ramirez.* 1618. 8vo, 7 l., pp. 430, 1 l. 4828

BERETTARI. La vie miraculeuse du P. Joseph Anchieta, de la Compagnie de Jésus: Escrite en Portugais par le Père Pierre Roderiges, puis en latin, augmentée de beaucoup par le P. Sebastien Beretaire, finalement traduite du latin en françois par un religieux de la mesme Compagnie. *Douay: de l'imprimerie de Marc Wyon.* 1619. 12mo, pp. 462. 4829

Dedicatory epistle signed by "P. J. d'O." [Outreman], a Jesuit.

BERETTARI. Vita del P. Gioseppo Anchietto, Religioso della Compagnia di Gesù Apostolo del Brasile. Composta in latino, dal P. Sebastiano Berettario, e nel volgare Italiano ridotta da un divoto religioso ... . *Torino, eredi di Gio. Domenico Torino.* 1621. 8vo. 4830

BERETTARI. Vita del Padre Gioseffo Anchieta della Compagnia di Giesù. Scritta da un Religioso della medesima Compagnia. ... *Bologna: l'herede del Benacci.* 1651. 24mo, pp. 227.

Taken from the Latin life. Melzi says that Rosotti, "Syllabus Script. Pedemontii," thinks this written by the Jesuit Gio. Battista Astria. Perhaps it was translated by him.

BERETTARI. Vita del padre Gioseffo Anchieta della Compagnia di Giesv'. Scritta da vn Religioso della medesima Compagnia. *Bologna: per l'heredo del Benacci.* 1658. 16mo, pp. 227.

This edition is dedicated to "G. B. Gargiaria, président de la chambre ducale de Parme. L'épître dédicatoire est signée Alessandro Calui, qui doit en être le traducteur." —LECLERC.

[BERETTARI.] Compendio|de la vida de el apostol|de el

Brasil, nvevo thavmatvrgo,|y grande obrador|de maravillas|V. P. Joseph|de Anchieta,|de la Compañia de Jesvs,|natural de la Ciudad de la Laguna, en la Isla|de-Tenerife vna de las de| Canaria.|Ponese â el fin de el vna delineacion de los Ascendientes, y descen-|dientes de su linage en dicha Isla, que prueva su antigua|patria, contra vna nueva, y Lusitanica|conjetura.| Dalo a la estampa|Don Baltasar de Anchieta,|Cabrera, y Samartin su sobrino.|...|...|...|...|*En Xerez de la Frontera, por Iuan Antonio Taraçona. Año* 1677.|4to, 4 l., Portrait of Anchieta, pp. 65. H. 4833

"Le P. Berettari publia son ouvrage d'après le mss. du P. Pierre de Rodrigues né à Evora en 1542, ce religieux entra dans la Compagnie à l'âge de quatorze ans et fut recteur des collèges de Madère et de Bragance, et depuis visiteur à Angola et au Brésil. Il mourut à Fernambouc en 1614 à l'âge de 72 ans. (Les PP. de Backer fixent l'époque de sa mort en 1628, ce qui ne s'accorde pas avec la date de 1556 qu'ils donnent comme étant celle de son entrée dans la Compagnie.) Ce fut pendant son séjour au Brésil qu'il composa la vie du P. Joseph de Anchieta. Elle n'a jamais été imprimée; le manuscrit se conservait dans la bibliothèque du collège de Lisbonne.—*Cf.* BARBOSA. *Bibl. Lusitana.*" —LECLERC.

BERG (Albert). Physiognomie der tropischen Vegetation Süd-Amerika's, dargestellt durch eine Reihe von Ansichten aus den Urwäldern am Magdalenen-Strome und der Anden von Neu-Granada; nebst dem Bruchstück eines Briefes von Alexander von Humboldt an den Verfasser, und einer Vorrede von Friedrich Klotzsch. *Düsseldorf: Jul. Buddeus.* 1854. Folio, pp. xxx, 36. 14 Lithographs. 4834

Has also the titles, "Physiognomy of tropical vegetation," etc. — "Études physiognomiques sur la vegetation," etc. *See* Petermann's "Mittheilungen," 1856, p. 124. Priced, Asher, 75fr.

BERG (J. F.) Catholicism Compatible with Republican Government. Lecture by Rev. Joseph F. Berg. *Philadelphia.* 1860.

BERG. Loyalty a Christian Obligation. A Sermon preached on Thanksgiving day, November 24, 1859, by Joseph F. Berg, D.D. *Philadelphia: Hayes & Zell.* 1859. 8vo, pp. 22. 4836

BERG. A Review of the Speech of Hon. Joseph R. Chandler, of Pennsylvania, in the House of Representatives of the United States. By Joseph F. Berg. *Philadelphia.* 1855. 8vo. 4837

BERG. The Stone and the Image; or, the American Republic the Bane and Ruin of Despotism; an exposition of the fifth kingdom of Daniel's Prophecy. By J. F. Berg. *Philadelphia.* 1856. C. 4838

"The Jesuits; a Lecture ... Dec. 23, 1850 ... . *Philadelphia: E. S. Jones.* 1851." 8vo, pp. 16. H., also deserves mention here.

BERG (Olof). Nordamerikas Stellung zum Quintupel-Tractat vom 20. December 1841. Eine Beleuchung der Sklaven- und Handelsverhältnisse der Vereinigten Staaten, als Versuch eines Commentars zur Note des General Cass d. d. Paris 13. Februar 1842. ... *Königsberg: Gräfe und Unzer.* 1842. 8vo, 12 sheets.

BERG (O.) Revisio Myrtacearum Americae hucusque cognitae. [*Halis.* 1856.] 8vo, pp. 472. 4840

BEBG. Ad Myrtacearum Americanarum Aequinoctialium Revisionem Mantissae Tres. [*Linn.* 1858–62.] 8vo, pp. 131.

BERG. Sklaverei, Seeherrschaft und die Preussische Staatszeitung. Ein Nachtrag zu meiner Schrift: "Nordamerikas Stellung ... ." *Königsberg: Gräfe und Unzer.* 1843. 8vo, $5\frac{1}{2}$ sheets. 4842

BERG *and* ORSTED. Myrtaceae Centroamericanae. [*Havniae.* 1857. 8vo. 4842*a*

BERG VAN DUSSEN MUILKERK (W. E. J.) Bijdragen tot de Geschiedenis onzer Kolonisatie in Noord-Amerika. A. Van de oprigting der West-Indische Compagnie in 1621, tot aan de inbezitneming van Nieuw Nederland in December 1623. 8vo.

From "De Gids," June, 1849. Apparently not published separately. I have not seen the part.

BERGAMO. *See* Foresti (J. P.)

BERGAÑO Y VILLEGAS. Dedicatoria que ofrece D. Juan de Cabrera y Palma en obsequio del Illmo. Sr. Diocesano, en la cual procura y desea satisfacer la dignidad del pastor y ministros del culto, licenciosamente vulnerada por D. Simon Bergaño y Villegas. [*Habana:*] *Imprenta del Gobierno.* 1812. 4844

BERGEN (T. G.) The Bergen Family: or, The Descendants of Hans Hansen Bergen, one of the Early Settlers of New York and Brooklyn, L. I. With Notes on the Genealogy of some of the Branches of the Cowenhoven Voorhees, Eldert, Stoothoof, Cortelyon, Stryker, Suydam, Lott, Wyckoff, Barkeloo, Lefferts, Martense, Hubbard, Van Brunt, Vanderbilt, Vanderveer, Van Nuyse, and other Long Island Families. By Teunis G. Bergen, *New York: Bergen & Tripp.* 1866. 8vo, pp. 302. C. 4845

BERGEN. Genealogy of the Van Brunt Family 1653–1867. By Teunis G. Bergen, Bay Ridge, New Utrecht, N. Y. *Albany: Joel Munsell.* 1867. 8vo, pp. 79. 4846

BERGEN, *N. J.* A Traveller's Sketch. *Bergen Point, N. J.* 1859. 12mo, pp. 11. Map. 4847

Describes the La Tourette House.

BERGER (Frederich Ludwig von). Gründliche Erweisung dass Ihro K. Kais. Maj. in Dero Oesterreichischen Niederlanden nach Belieben Commercia zu stabiliren, und zu Aufrichtung einer Ost- und Westindischen Compagnie Privilegia zu ertheilen berechtiget. *Regensburg und Leipzig: Seidel.* 1723. 4to, 8 sheets. 4847*a*

"Also in the 'Europ. Staatskanzelley,' Thiel XLIII." — ADELUNG.

BERGER. Grondig Bewijs dat Syne Roomsch-Keiz. Maj. in zijne Oostenr. Nederlanden bevoegd is koophandel te vestigen, als ook tot opregting van eene Oosten West-Ind. Compagnie privilegien kan geeven. *s'Gravenhage.* 1724. 4to, pp. 52.

BERGERON (J. J.) Du mal rouge observé à Cayenne, et comparé à l'éléphantiasis. *Paris.* 1823. 4to, pp. 26. 4849

See "Journ. univ. des sc. méd.," déc. 1823; and Gerson u. Julius, "Mag. d. ausl. Heilk.," 1829, XV. 663.

BERGERON (Pierre). Traicté de la navigation et des voyages de descovverte et conqueste modernes et principalement des François. *Jean de Hevqveville et Michel Soly.* 1629. 16mo, 5 l., pp. 303. 4850

Usually found with Bethencourt (J. de), Histoire des Canaries. *Paris.* 1630.

BERGH (Henry). "Married Off." [A Newport Sketch.] *New York: Carleton.* 1862. 12mo, pp. 75. 8 Plates. 4851

BERGH (L. Ph. C. van den). Nederlands Aanspraak op de Ontdekking van Amerika voor Columbus. [n. p. n. d.] 8vo, pp. 11. S. 4852

Probably from some periodical.

BERGHAUS (Heinrich Karl Wilhelm). Abriss einer Geschichte der geographischen Entdeckungen von den ältesten Zeiten bis zur Gegenwart. *Berlin: Hasselberg'sche Verlagsbuchhandlung.* 1857. 8vo, pp. 208. 4853

BERGHAUS. Allgemeine Länder und Völkerkunde, nebst einem Abriss der physicalischen Erdbeschreibung. ... *Stuttgart: Hoffmann.* 1837–44. 7 vols., 8vo. S. 4853*a*

Vol. VI. Das amerikanische Staatensystem. In Rayser this is dated 1836–46.

BERGHAUS. Chart of the Approaches of Rio de Janeiro. *Potsdam.* 1843. Imp. folio. 4854

BERGHAUS. Die vereinigten Staaten von Nordamerika, geographish-statistisch vorzugsweise nach Van der Straten-Ponthoz geschildert. Mit besonderer Rüchsicht auf die deutsche Auswanderung. ... *Gotha: J. Perthes.* 1848. 8vo, pp. viii, 98. 2 colored Maps by Fr. von Stülpnagel, folio. 4855

BERGHAUS. Physikalischer Atlas, oder Sammlung von Karten, von Heinrich Berghaus. *Gotha: J. Perthes.* 1838–40. 5 Lfrg., folio. 31 Maps and (Text) 14 sheets. + [*Ibid.*] 1845. 2 vols., folio. 4856

BERGHAUS. Dr. Heinrich Berghaus' physikalischer Atlas: Eine, unter der fördernden Anregung Alexander's von Humboldt verfasste Sammlung von 93 Karten, auf denen die hauptsächlichsten Erscheinungen der anorganischen und organischen Natur nach ihrer geographischen Verbreitung und Vertheilung bildlich dargestellt sind. ... Zweite ... verbesserte Auflage. *Gotha: Justus Perthes.* 1852. 2 vols., folio. 4857

In eight Abtheilungen, with separate title-pages, dated 1849-52.

BERGHAUS. Die Völker des Erdballs nach ihrer Abstammung und Verwandtschaft und ihre Eigenthümlichkeiten in Regierungsform, Religion, Sitte und Tracht geschildert. Mit 150 naturgetreuen colorirten Abbildungen. *Brüssel und Leipzig: Muquardt.* 1845–47. 2 vols., 8vo, 50 sheets and 150 colored Engravings on wood. + Zweite Ausgabe. [*Ibid.*] 1852–53. 2 vols., 8vo, pp. 462; viii, 336. + Neue wohlfeile Ausgabe. [*Ibid.*] 1861–62. 2 vols., 8vo, pp. 462; viii, 386. 4857*a*

Also: Allgemeine See-Atlas, oder Sammlung hydrographischer Karten und Beschreibungen der europäischen und amerikanischen Meere. *Berlin: Reimer.* 1832. Imp. folio. 10 Maps. (Apparently no map of American seas was ever published.) — Grundlinien der physikalischen Erdbeschreibung. ... *Stuttgart: Hallberger'sche Verlagshandlung.* 1847. 8vo, 1 l., pp. viii, 439. + Zweite Ausgabe. [*Ibid.*] 1856. [*Ibid.*] — Grundriss der Geographie ... . *Breslau: Grass Barth und Comp.* 1840–43. 11 Lfrg., 8vo, 83 sheets. 3 Maps — Kabinets-Bibliothek der neuesten Reisen und Forschungen im Gebiete der Länder- Völker- und Staatenkunde. Herausgegeben von Heinrich Berghaus. *Berlin: Reimer.* 1834–35. 2 vols., 8vo. (Vol. I. has the second title: Ausgewählte Schriften der Königl. geographischen Gesellschaft zu London. Erster Theil.) — Lehrbuch der Erdbeschreibung. Erster Kursus. ... *Berlin: Reimer.* 1831. 8vo, 26 sheets. — Physikalischer Schul-Atlas ... . *Gotha: J. Perthes.* 1859. 4to, 12 sheets, and 28 Maps. — Was man von die Erde weiss. Ein Lesebuch zur Selbstbelehrung ... . *Berlin: Hasselberg'sche Verlagshandlung.* 1856–61. 4 Thiele, 8vo, pp. 208; xix, 894; xii, 549; vi, 382. — Berghaus also edited the "Annalen der Erd- Völker- und Staatenkunde, *Berlin.* 1829," etc. 8vo; and an "Almanach ... . Den Freunden der Erdkunde gewidmet. *Stuttgart: Hoffmann.* 1837," etc. 16mo.

BERGHAUS *and* [GEBAUER (August)]. Bibliothek der Länder- und Völkerkunde, nach den neuesten politischen Gestaltungen ... . *Stuttgart.* 1849. 3 vols., pp. viii, 454; xx, 476; 404.

Contents: I. Allgemeine Geographie ... von Heinrich Rebau [pseudonym]. II. Allgemeine Staatenkunde ... von ... Berghaus. Zweite ... verbesserte Auflage. + Zweite [dritte] Ausgabe. *Stuttgart: Hallberger'sche Verlagshandlung.* 1856. 8vo, pp. xx, 476. III. (with the separate title:) Grundlinien der Ethnographie. Enthaltend eine allgemeine Völkertafel oder Nachweisung aller Völker der Erdbodens, nach Sprachstämmen und Sprachfamilien ethnographisch und geographisch geordnet; und eine vergleichende, übersichtliche Beschreibung ihrer Sitten, Gebräuche und Gewohnheiten. Herausgegeben von Heinrich Berghaus. + Zweite Ausgabe. *Stuttgart: Hallberger'sche Verlagshandlung.* 1856. 8vo, 1 l., pp. 404.

BERGK (J. K.) Reise in Brasilien, Peru und Caracas. Nach Lindley, Barrow, Tuckey, Depons und andern Reisebeschreibern ausgearbeitet ... von J. A. Bergk. Mit sechs Kupfern. *Leipzig: in der Baumgärtnerschen Buchhandlung.* 1808. 8vo, pp. iv, 122. H. 4858*a*

BERGMAN (G.) Herinneringen uit zijne genees- en heelkundige praktijk in de kolonie Suriname, benevens een juist verslag der procedure contra C. J. van West. *Amsterdam: P. J. G. Diederich.* 1850. 8vo. 4859

BERGOMAS *or* BERGOMENSIS (J. P.) *See* Foresti (J. P.)

Bergordnung für Neuspanien, welche in allen Theilen der vormaligen königlichen Spanischen Besitzungen America's noch kraftbeständig ist. Aus dem Spanischen von J. Nöggerath und J. P. Pauls. *Bonn: Weber.* 1828. 8vo, 12 sheets. 4860

BERGSTRÆSSER (W.) Die königlich sächsischen Strafanstalten mit Hinsicht auf die amerikanischen Pönitentiarsysteme. Insbesondere die Strafanstalten zu Hubertusburg ... von Wilhelm Bergsträsser ... . *Leipzig: Leopold Voss.* 1844. 8vo, pp. viii, 327. Plan. B. 4861

[BERGUIN (H. K.)] Considerations relative to a Southern Confederacy, with Letters to the North, on the Preservation of the Union, and a Note from the Secret History of the Emancipation in the English West Indies. By a Citizen of North-Carolina. *Raleigh.* 1860. 8vo, pp. 40. H. 4862

Bericht der Association für die Ausstellung der Industrie-Erzeugnisse aller Nationen in New-York im Jahr 1853 über die Organisation und den Fortschritt der Unternehmung. ... *Stuttgart: Druck der K. Hofbuchdruckerei Zu Guttenberg.* [n. d.] 8vo, pp. 44. Plate. H. 4863

Bericht eines Englischen Amerikaners von Philadelphia an seinen Freund in Engelland über den dermahligen Krieg Gross-Brittaniens mit seinen Amerikanischen Colonien vom 15 December 1776. Nach dem Englischen Original. *Frankfurt una Leipzig: [Perrenon].* 1777. Sm. 8vo, pp. 48, (1). H. 4864

Bericht von Gröhnland gezogen aus zwo Chroniken: Einer alten Ihslandischen und einer neuen Dänischen; Jetzo aber deutsch gegäben von Henr. Sivers. *Hamburg.* 1674. 4to. Plates and Map. 4865

Bericht von Beschaffenheit ... desz in America zwischen dem Rio Orinoque und Rio de las Amazones, an der vesten Küst in Guiana gelegenen Landes, welchen die West-Indische Compagnie der Staten General an den Grafen zu Hanaw ... überlassen hat. *Frankfurt.* 1669. 4to. Map. 4866

Bericht von der Landschafft Carolina im Englischen America. *Franckfurt: Oehrling.* 1709. 8vo, 5 sheets, 1 l. 4867

Bericht über die im höchsten Auftrage, etc. *See* [Fellechner.]

Berigt door Directeurs van de Societeit van Suriname aan de Staten Generaal der Vereenigde Nederlanden tot jusificatie van derzelver gehoudene conduites. [n.-p.] 1731. Folio, pp. 56.

Berigt van Bewinthebberren der geoctroyeerte West Indische Compagnie ter Kamer Zeeland, nopens de begeving van ampten op Essequebo en Demerary en het verkoopen van 's Compagnies plantagien. Met Bylagen. 1772. Folio, pp. 52. 4869

Berigt van de moederlijke vereenigingen in Amerika en Engeland. *Rotterdam: Mensing en van Westreenen.* 1838. 8vo.

BERISTAIN DE SOUZA (José Mariano). Biblioteca Hispano-Americana Septentrional ó Catálogo y Noticia de los Literatos, que ó nacidos, ó educados, ó florecientes en la America Septentrional Española, han dado a luz algun escrito, ó lo han dexado preparado para la prensa. La escribia, el Doctor D. Jose Mariano Beristain de Souza, del claustro de las Universidades de Valencia y Valladolid, Caballero de la Orden Española de Carlos III. y Comendador de la Real Americana de Isabel la Católica, y Dean de la Metropolitana de Mexico. *En México: Calle de Santo Domingo y Esquina de Tacuba Año de* 1816–21. 3 vols., 4to, 2 l., pp. xviii, 540; 1 l., 525; 1., 1366. 4871

Vol. II. has, in addition to the above title, "Y la publica Don José Rafael Enriquez Trespalacios Beristain, Sobrino del Autor. *Officina de D. Alexandro Valdés.* 1819.'

"De Souza, is by far the most important work for the literature of New Spain that has ever been composed. It comprises 3687 biographies, and although, like most Spanish works of the kind, singularly uncritical, yet it is a perfect treasure as regards the cultivation of science and literature in Mexico and the adjacent countries. The work is extremely scarce, and appears to be altogether unknown in Europe."—LUDEWIG. *See also* [Harrisse] Bib. Am. Vet., pp. xx, xxi. Señor Icazbalceta, of the city of Mexico, announced a new edition, but I believe it has not been published.

BERISTAIN DE SOUZA. Cantos de las musas mexicanas, con motivo de la colocacion de la estatua equestre de bronce de Carlos IV. *Mexico: M. de Zuniga y Ontiveros.* 1804. 4to, 5 l., pp. 138. 4872

This is a collection of pieces by various authors. *See* Leclerc, No. 149.

BERISTAIN DE SOUZA. Oracion panegirico-eucaristica, que en la solemne accion de gracias por la instalacion de la soberana junta de gobierno de España y de sus Indias, celebrada por los caballeros de la orden de Carlos III, residentes en Mexico, dixo en la iglesia metropolitana el dia 8 de diciembre de 1808. *Mexico: Doña Maria Fernandez Jauregui.* 1809. 4to. pp. 47. 4873

BERKEL (Adriaan von). Amerikaansche | Voyagien, | Behelzende een Reis na | Rio de Berbice, | Gelegen op het vaste Land van Guiana, | aande Wilde-kust van America, | Mitsgaders een andere na de Colonie van | Suriname, | Gelegen in het Noorder Deel van het gemelde | Landschap Guiana. | Ondermengd met alle de byzonderheden noopende de Zeden, | Gewoonten, en Levenswijs der Inboorlingen, Boom-en Aard- | gewassen, Waaren en Koopmanschappen, en andere | aanmerkelijke zaaken. | Beschreven door | Adriaan van Berkel, | Vercierd met kopere Plaaten. | *Tot Amsterdam,* | *By Johan ten Hoorn, Boekverkooper tegen over* | *het Oude Heeren Logement, inde Historischryver,* 1695 | 4to, 4 l., pp. 139, (Table) 2 l. 2 Plates, engraved and printed Titles.

BERKEL. Adrian van Berkel's Beschreibung seiner Reisen nach Rio de Berbice und Surinam. Aus dem Holländischen übersetzt. *Memmingen: bey Andreas Seyler.* 1789. 8vo, 8 l., pp. 5–278. 4875

BERKELEY (George). Abstract of Bp. Berkeley's Treatise on Tar Water, adapted to Diseases Frequent in America. *New York.* 1745. 12mo. 4876

BERKELEY. Account of the Life of. *See* [Stock (Joseph).]

BERKELEY. A Miscellany, containing Several Tracts on

Various Subjects. By the Bishop of Cloyne. ... *London: J. and R. Tonson and S. Draper.* M DCC LII. 8vo, pp. vi, 267. B. + *Dublin.* 1752. 4877

Contains, "A Proposal For the better Supplying," etc., and, "A Sermon Preached before the ... Society." Includes the stanzas, of which the last begins: "Westward the course of empire takes its way."

[BERKELEY.] A Proposal For the better Supplying of Churches in our Foreign Plantations, and for Converting the Savage Americans to Christianity, By a College to be erected in the Summer Islands, otherwise called the Isles of Bermuda ... *London: Printed by H. Woodfall.* 1725. 8vo, pp. 24. H. 4878

Reprinted 1731, and again with the Miscellany in 1752. *See* M. R., VII. 318.

BERKELEY. A Sermon Preached before the Incorporated Society for the Propagation of the Gospel in Foreign Parts ... 18th of February, 1731. ... By George Berkeley ... . *London: Printed by J. Downing.* M. DCC. XXXII. 8vo, pp. 78, (1). B.

Dean Berkeley refers to his favorite province, Rhode Island, and makes some allusions to Slavery. *See* Hist. Mag., I. 312. N.

BERKELEY. A Word to the Wise: or, the Bishop of Cloyne's Exhortation to the Roman Catholick Clergy of Ireland. Fourth Edition. *Boston.* 1750. 8vo, pp. 16. 4880

BERKELEY. The Works of George Berkeley, D.D. late Bishop of Cloyne. To which is added an account of his Life, and several of his Letters. *Dublin.* 1784. 2 vols., 4to. Portrait. + *London.* 1820. 3 vols., 8vo. B. + *London: Thomas Tegg and Son.* 1837. 2 vols., 8vo. B., H. 4881

BERKELEY. Memoirs of George Berkeley, D.D., late Bishop of Cloyne in Ireland, containing letters on the Bermuda Project, and from Newport in Rhode Island, &c. 1784. 8vo. 4882

BERKELEY (George Charles Grantley Fitz-Hardinge). The English Sportsman in the Western Prairies. By the Hon. Grantley Berkeley. *London: Hurst and Blackett.* 1861. Rl. 8vo, pp. 430. Illustrations. C. 4883

Catalogue of the Berkeley Divinity School [incorporated 1854], Middletown, Conn. 1857. *Middletown, Conn.* 1857. 8vo, pp. 23. Continued. H. 4884

BERKENHOUT. Lucubrations on Ways and Means, addressed to Lord North. By J. Berkenhout, M.D. *London.* 1780. 8vo.

BERKENMEYER (W. C.) Consilium in Arena, oder Mitleidens volle Antwort auf das Bitt-Schreiben der Hoch-Teutsch-Luthrischen Gemeinde im Camp. *Nieuw-York.* 4to. 4886

BERKENMEYER. Willem Christoffel Berkenmeyers ... Herder- en Wachter-Stem, Aan de Hoog- en Neder-Duitsche Lutheriaanen in dese Gewesten, eenstemmig te zyn vertoont met twe Brieven en andere Redenen Lutherscher theologanten: aangaande 't Van Dierensche Beroep, en De Henkelsche Bevestiging. *Nieuw-York: J. Peter Zenger.* MDCCXXVIII. 4to, 2 l., pp. 150, (1), (Post-script, 12). H. 4887

BERKLEY. The Naval History of Britain, from the Earliest Periods of which there are Accounts in History, to the Conclusion of the Year M.D.CCLVI, Compiled from the Papers of the Late Honorable Captain George Berkley, ... and Illustrated with a Great Number of Figures, and Folio Copper-Plates, of Sea Charts, Heads, Engagements, and other Subjects. *London.* MDCCLVI. Folio, 5 l., pp. 706, (Index) 1 l. 4888

Includes many articles relating to America.

BERKLEY (*Sir* William). A Discourse and View of Virginia. By Sir William Berkley the Governour. *London.* 1663. 4to, pp. 12. 4889

Watt mentions "A Description of Virginia, in Francis Moryson's edition of the Laws of Virginia. *London.* 1662. Fol." Moryson says that Berkley was the author of the most and best of the said laws. *See* Bliss's Wood's Athenæ, III. 1111, 1112.

BERKLEY. A List of those that have been executed for the Late Rebellion in Virginia, by Sir William Berkeley, Governor of the Colony. Copied from the Original Manuscript ... in the ... British Museum ... by Robert Greenhow ... . *Washington: Peter Force.* 1835. 8vo, pp. 4. (Force's Tracts, Vol. I. No. I.) H. 4889*a*

BERKLEY, *Mass.* "Better Edification" a Good Plea. Proceedings of an Ecclesiastical Council, in the Town of Berkley, October 19, 1831. And the Documents connected therewith. *Taunton: James Thurber, Printer.* 1831. 8vo, pp. 26. H. 4889*b*

BERKS COUNTY. State of the Accounts of the Collectors of Excise, for Berks County, from the 4th of August 1774, (to which time they were settled by the Committees of Accounts of Assemblies) until the 24th of November 1781. In which is exhibited, The Account of the Monies received by them respec-

tively, and accounted for; Also, Lists shewing the names of Persons from whom Excise became due, and was received. Likewise, the Payments made thereof to the Treasurer. *Philadelphia: Printed by Robert Aitken, three Doors above the Coffee-House, in Market Street.* M,DCC,LXXXIII. 8vo, pp. 7. P. 4890

BERKSHIRE. A History, etc. *See* [Field (D. D.)]

Berkshire Baptist Association, [Mass.] 30th Anniversary held in Egremont, 1857 ... *North-Adams.* 1857. 8vo, pp. 20.

Berkshire Baptist Association [N. Y.] Minutes, 27, 28 Sept. 1826, with the Owego Creek Church. *Printed Cortland Village.* 1826. 8vo, pp. 10. Continued. 4892

The Berkshire Jubilee, celebrated at Pittsfield, Mass. August 22 and 23, 1844. *Albany: Weare. C. Little; E. P. Little, Pittsfield.* 1845. 8vo, pp. 244. Woodcuts. C., H. 4893

Address to the Inhabitants of the County of Berkshire, Mass., respecting their present Opposition to Civil Government. *Hartford, Conn.: Watson & Goodwin.* 1778. 8vo, pp. 28. 4894

Catalogue of the Members and Licentiates of the Berkshire Association, from 1763 to 1848. ... *North Adams: printed by Henry Chickering.* 1849. 8vo, pp. 8. H. 4895

Catalogue of the Trustees, Overseers, Faculty and Students, of the Berkshire Medical Institution, for the Year 1853, and of the Alumni and Honorary Graduates, Since its Incorporation in 1823. Pittsfield, Mass., October, 1853. *Pittsfield.* 1853. 8vo, pp. 40. View. + Catalogues and Announcements for other years. H. 4896

Remonstrance and Petition to the Honble. the General Court of the Commonwealth of Massachusetts. *Hudson.* 1787. 4to.

Transactions of the Berkshire County [Mass.] Agricultural Society: during ... 1854. *Pittsfield.* 1854. 8vo, pp. 62. Continued. H. 4898

There are also various catalogues, circulars, etc., of the "Berkshire Family School," the "Berkshire County Mutual Life Insurance Company," and the "Berkshire Medical Institution," which do not deserve fuller description.

Berlin-Falls Manufacturing Company of New Hampshire. [Charter, etc.] *Boston: T. R. Holland.* 1864. 8vo, pp. 10.

BERLIOZ D'AURIAC (J.) La caravane des Sombreros. Par Jules B. d'Auriac. *Paris: Brunet.* 1867. 18mo, pp. 225. 4900

The "Bibliogr. de la France" enters this author's works under Auriac, under which head I gave two titles (Nos. 2388, 2389). Lorenz, however, puts him under Berlioz d'Auriac, and I take this opportunity to include his recent publications. They all belong to the series entitled, "Les drames du Nouveau-Monde."

BERLIOZ D'AURIAC. L'esprit blanc. Par Jules B. d'Auriac. *Paris: Brunet.* 1866. 18mo, pp. 221. 4901

BERLIOZ D'AURIAC. Les forestiers du Michigan. Par Berlioz d'Auriac. *Paris: P. Brunet.* 1866. 8vo, pp. 231. 4902

BERLIOZ D'AURIAC. Jmi l'Indien. Par Jules B. d'Auriac. *Paris: Brunet.* 1867. 18mo, pp. 227.

BERLIOZ D'AURIAC. Le mangeur de poudre. Par Jules B. d'Auriac. *Paris: Brunet.* 1866. 18mo, pp. 229. 4903*a*

BERLIOZ D'AURIAC. Œil-de-Feu. Par Jules B. d'Auriac. *Paris: Brunet.* 1867. 18mo, pp. 323. 4903*b*

BERLIOZ D'AURIAC. Les pieds fourchus. Par Jules B. d'Auriac. *Paris: Brunet.* 1866. 18mo, pp. 227. 4903*c*

BERLIOZ D'AURIAC. Rayon-de-Soleil. Par Jules B. d'Auriac. *Paris: Brunet.* 1866. 18mo, pp. 227. 4903*d*

BERLIOZ D'AURIAC. Le scalpeur des Ottavas. Par Jules B. d'Auriac. *Paris: Brunet.* 18mo, pp. 225. 4903*e*

BERLIOZ D'AURIAC. Les terres d'or. Par Jules B. d'Auriac. *Paris: Brunet.* 1867. 18mo, pp. 231. 4903*f*

BERMEJO. Estudios recreativos, historicos y morales. Por D. Ildefonso Bermejo. *Buenos Ayres.* 1855. 8vo, pp. 322.

BERMINGHAM (Thomas). The Thames, the Shannon, and the St. Lawrence, or the Good of Great Britain, Ireland, and British North America identified & promoted: in the Development of the Vast Resources of Ireland and British North America, by the Employment, for the Next Ten Years, of 250,000 Families of the Destitute Peasantry of Ireland ... . By Thomas Bermingham ... . *London: Messrs. Fores.* 1847. 8vo, pp. (2), 31, (4), 1 sheet folded. H. 4905

Bermuda. Acts of Assembly, Made and Enacted in the Bermuda, or Summer-Islands, From 1690, to 1713–14. *London: Printed by John Baskett* [etc.] M DCC XIX. Folio, Title, pp. v, 79. C., H. + Continued to 1736. *London.* 1737. Folio. N.

Bermuda: A Colony, a Fortress, and a Prison; or Eighteen Months in the Somers' Island. (With a Map and Illustrations.) By a Field Officer. ... *London: Longman, Brown, Green & Roberts.* 1857. 8vo, pp. x, (2), 287. Map. C. 4907

The Bermuda Pocket Almanack for ... 1861 ... . *Bermuda: Printed by D. M'Phee Lee.* 1861. 16mo, pp. 62 [64]. H. 4908

Bermuda. A Plaine Description of the Bermvdas. *See* (C. W.)

Bermuda ... . Report of the Committee ... [on] the Origin and Spread of the Yellow Fever, by which Bermuda was visited in 1864, together with the Appendices. ... [*London.* 1866.] Folio, pp. 112. Map and Diagram, folded. (Parl. Papers, Sess. 1866, Vol. XLIX. No. 477.) B., H. 4909

A Sketch of the Bermudas or Somers Islands. *London.* [1852 or 54.] 12mo. 4910

Bermudez (Joseph Manuel). Fama Postuma del Excell. Senor Doctor Don Juan Domingo Gonzalez de la Regura y Oracion Funebre. *Lima.* 1805. 4to. Portrait, Monument and curious folded View of the Cathedral of Lima. 4911

Bermudez. Oracion funebre del excelent. señor Conde de La Union: que en las exequias celebradas por el ilustre Cabildo y regimiento de esta ciudad de los Reyes, dixo en la iglesia catedral el dia XXVII. de Noviembre de 1795. *Lima: Imprenta Real.* 1796. 8vo, 4 l., pp. 89, 11. 4912

"Le comte De La Union mourut le 20 novembre 1794, à l'âge de 42 ans et 3 mois, il en avait employé 29 au service du roi. Son nom était: Don Luis Fermin de Carbajal y Vargas, conde De La Union." — Leclerc.

Bermudez. Oracion funebre del Señor Don Vincente Morales Duarez: presidente del soberano congreso nacional. Que dixo ... en VII. de noviembre ... Jose Manuel Bermudez. *Lima: Bernardino Ruiz.* M DCCC XII. 4to, pp. 51, (1). H. 4913

Bermudez (L. B.) *See* Belmonte Bermudez.

Bermudez (Silverio). Longevidad de la Tierra, su pro contra, ó sea Ensayos sobro estudios de literatura i ciencias. *Carácas.* 1866. 8vo, pp. 52. 4914

Bermudez de Castro. Bombardment of Valparaiso. Speech of the Spanish Minister for Foreign Affairs; together with the Diplomatic Circulars, Report of the Spanish Admiral, &c. &c. &c. referred to therein. *London: printed by T. H. Schrader.* [1866.] 8vo, Title, pp. 39. H. 4915

The Bermudian. A Poem. *Williamsburg, Va.: Alexander Purdie & John Dixon.* 1774. 4to, pp. viii, 15. 4916

Bernal Diaz Del Castillo. *See* Diaz del Castillo (Bernal).

Bernal (Ralph). Speech of Ralph Bernal, M.P., May 19th, 1826, on a Motion touching the Condition of Slaves. 8vo, pp. 16. 4917

Bernaldez (Andrès). Historia de los Reyes Católicos D. Fernando y Da. Isabella. Cronica inedita del Siglo XV, escrita por El Bachiller Andres Bernaldez ... . *Granada: José Maria Zamorra.* 1856. 2 vols., 4to. 4918

See Prescott's "Ferdinand and Isabella," II. 108; Harrisse's "Notes on Columbus," pp. 7–9. Contains some particulars concerning Columbus. A copy of the MSS. is in Harvard College Library.

Bernard (*Rev.* David). Light on Masonry: a Collection of all the most important Documents on the subject of Speculative Freemasonry, the Abduction of William Morgan, &c. By Rev. David Bernard. *Utica.* 1829. 12mo, pp. 570. C. 4919

[**Bernard** (*Sir* Francis).] The Causes of the Present Distractions in America Explained: in Two Letters to a Merchant in London. By F—— B——. [*Boston:*] *Printed in the Year* 1774. 8vo, pp. 16. S. 4920

Bernard. Copies of Letters from Sir Francis Bernard to the Earl of Hillsborough. [n. p. n. d.] 8vo, pp. 28. M. + [Another Edition. n. p. n. d.] 4to, pp. 16. W. + *Boston.* 1769. Folio. W. 4921

Bernard. Copy of the Complaint Of the House of Representatives of Massachusetts-Bay against Sir Francis Bernard: With Sir Francis Bernard's Answer. [*Boston.* 1770?] 4to, pp. 15. P. 4922

See Tudor's "Otis," Chap. 21; Bancroft, Vol. v. Chap. x.

Bernard. Letters to the Ministry from Governor Bernard, General Gage, and Commodore Hood. And also Memorials to the Lords of the Treasury, From the Commissioners of the Customs: With Sundry Letters and Papers annexed to the said Memorials. *Boston: Edes and Gill.* 1769. 8vo, pp. 108. P. + *London: Re-printed for J. Wilkie.* [n. d.] 8vo, pp. 146.

Bernard. Letters to the Right Honorable the Earl of Hillsborough, from Governor Bernard, General Gage and the Honorable His Majesty's Council for the Province of Massachusets-Bay. With an Appendix containing divers Proceedings referred to in the said Letters. *Boston, New England: Printed by Edes and Gill,* ... 1769. Folio, pp. 83. C., W. + *Salem.* 1769. 4to. + *London: Re-Printed for J. Almon.* [n. d.] 8vo, pp. 165.

"These two collections of letters commence in January, 1768, and reach to July, 1769. So that the two contain a complete view of the political contests and dissensions in the colony of Massachusetts Bay during that period. The copies were obtained and sent to Boston by William Bollan, at the time agent for the council of Massachusetts. 'In our opinion, the gentlemen of the council have greatly the advantage over the governor and the general, with respect to the solidity and force of the arguments used by them, and have completely vindicated themselves from the charges brought against them by the officers of the crown, in their letters to Lord Hillsborough.' — M. R.," XLI. pp. 320 and 398.

Bernard. Select Letters on the Trade and Government of America; and the Principles of Law and Polity, applied to the American Colonies. Written by Governor Bernard, at Boston, In the Years 1763, 4, 5, 6, 7, and 8. Now first published: To which are added The Petition of the Assembly of Massachuset's Bay against the Governor, his Answer thereto, and the Order of the King in Council thereon. *London: T. Payne.* M DCC LXXIV. 8vo, Title, pp. vii, 130. B., H. + The Second Edition. *London: T. Payne.* 1774. 8vo, Half Title, Title, pp. vii, 130. C. 4925

These letters, published by the Governor himself, throw great light on the affairs of New England at that period. The trial was said to be partial, because the assembly had never been suffered to meet, and consequently could not support the charge, so the Governor was honorably acquitted. *See* Ann. Reg. 1770. 76; M. R., L. 412; Rich, I. 202.

[**Bernard.**] An Elegy to the Infamous Memory of Sr. F—— B——. "Auri cœcus Amore, Vendidit Hic Patriam." [*Boston:*] *Printed in the Year* M,DCC,LXIX. 4to, pp. 14. 4926.

Verses on Sir Francis Bernard. The reverse of title exhibits the famous woodcut of a broken snake, of which N. E. represents the head, etc., and seven other colonies the remaining fragments, with the motto: Join or Die. For "An Address to a Provincial Bashaw," *see* [Church (B.)]

Bernard. A third Extraordinary Budget of Epistles and Memorials between Sir Francis Bernard, of Nettleham, Baronet, some Natives of Boston, New England, and the present Ministry, against N. America, the True-Interest of the Empire and the Rights of Mankind. [1769.] 8vo, pp. 8. P. 4927

No imprint. Probably printed by Edes & Gill, Boston.

[**Bernard** (Fr.)] Analyse de l'Histoire philosophique et politique des établissemens et du commerce des Européens dans les deux Indes. *Leyde.* 1775. 8vo, pp. viii, 245. S. 4928

A review of Raynal's work; and perhaps one-fourth touches on paragraphs in his account of America. *See* Vol. I., No. 1361, of this Dictionary.

Bernard (John). Recollections of the Stage. By John Bernard, formerly of the Federal Street Theatre, Boston. *Boston: Frederick S. Hill.* 12mo. 4929

Announced in 1831. The Philadelphia Library Company has a title, "Retrospections of the Stage. By the late John Bernard. *London and Boston.* 1830. 2 vols.," 12mo.

Bernard (J. A.) A Geographical Dictionary. In which are Represented The Present and Antient Names of all the Countries, Provinces, Remarkable Cities, Towns, Ports, Seas, Streights, Fountains, Rivers, Mountains, Universities, &c. of the Whole World. *London:* 1692. Folio, pp. 6, 437. W. 4930

[**Bernard** (J. F.)] Ceremonies et coutumes religieuses ... . *Amsterdam.* 1723–43. 8 tom. in 9 vols., folio. Also: Superstitions anciennes et modernes et préjugés vulgaires ... . *Amsterdam: J. F. Bernard.* 1733–36. 2 vols., folio. 4931

Nearly all the success of this work is owing to its 266 fine engravings. It is a compilation from the writings of R. Simon, J. Abbadie, Boulainvilliers, etc., and "was edited by J. F. Bernard, the minister Bernard, Bruzen de la Martinière, and others. The first volumes were reprinted in 1735 and 1739, with some additions to the text, but the first edition is preferred, because it contains the early impressions of the engravings. A very fine copy sold, St.-Mauris, 3191 fr. Ordinary copies cost from 200 to 250 fr." — Brunet. Reprinted with the title:

Bernard. Histoire générale des cérémonies ... représentées en 243 figures dessinées par B. Picart, avec des explications par les abbés Banier et la Mascrier. *Paris.* 1741. 7 vols., folio.

A few of the plates and the vignettes were newly engraved at Paris by Duflos and others. Bernard reprinted the new dissertations in this edition as Tome VII, 2e partie of his own, and also added an eighth volume. The Cérémonies reappeared, edited by Poncelin, *Paris, Laporte,* 1783, 4 vols., folio, to which was added Superstitions orientales, *Paris,* 1785, folio. Also:

Bernard. Cérémonies ... . Nouvelle édition ... Corrigée; augumentée. ... *Paris: L. Prudhomme.* M. DCCC. VIII.–X. 12 vols. in 13 pts., folio. H. 4933

The additions are by Count Henri Grégoire, F. H. S. de l'Aulnaye, and Théophile Mandar. "Finally," says Brunet, "these everlasting engravings again figure in a reimpression of the 'Histoire des religions,' with changes and additions. 'Des mœurs et coutumes religieuses de tous les peuples du monde et de l'idolâtrie. *Paris.* 1816–1819.'" 6 vols., 4to. 638 Plates. There is also an edition, *Amsterdam.* 1729. 4 vols., folio. It was translated into English, with the following title:

Bernard. The Religious Ceremonies and Customs of the Several Nations of the Known World. Represented in above an Hundred Copper-Plates designed by the Famous Picart. Together with Historical Explanations, and several curious Dissertations. Written Originally in French; and now Published in English, with very Considerable Amendments and Additions ... *London: Nicholas Prevost.* M DCCXXXI–M DCCXXXIX. 7 vols., folio, pp. 223. Plates. 4934

There are copies with the titles differing, and copies on large paper. Some have the imprint, "*London: Claude Du Bosc.* MDCCXXXIII," etc.

[**Bernard.**] Recueil de Voiages au Nord, Contenant divers Mémoires tres utiles au Commerce et à la navigation. *Amsterdam: J. F. Bernard.* 1715–18. 4 vols., 12mo. 4935

Contents: Vol. I. 3 l., (Discours) pp. xliv, 2 l., title engraved. — Relation de l'Islande [par La Peyrère]. pp. 84. Map. — Relation du Groenland [par La Peyrère]. pp. 85–188. Map and Plate. — Addition aux mémoires. pp. 189–200. Map. — Essai d'instructions pour voyager utilement. pp. 116. Plate. Vol. II. 2 l. — Journal d'un voyage au Spitzbergen et au Groenlandt. Contenant une relation exacte de tout ce qu'on a remarqué dans ce voyage depuis le 15. Avril jusqu'au 21. Août 1671. Translated from the German of Friedr. Martens. pp. 205. 14 Plates. — Journal du capitaine Jean Wood, allant à la découverte d'un passage pour les Indes Orientales par le Nord-Est. En l'année 1676. pp. 206–237. — Journal à bord du Prospère, commandé par le cap. Guill. Flawes, depuis la Nouvelle Zemble jusqu'en Angleterre. pp. 238–266. — Supplément aux voyages du capitaine Wood et de Fr. Martens vers le Nord-Est. Contenant des observations, touchant le Nord-Oüest de Groenland, etc. Traduit de l'anglois. pp. 267–298. Vol. III. 1 l. — Relation de terre-Neuve, par White, qui y a été en 1700, trad. de l'original anglois. pp. 1–31. Map. — Lettre de Mr. de Liste sur la question, si le Japon est une ile. pp. 32. — Relation de la découverte de la terre de Jesso, ou d'Eso, au nord du Japon, par le vaisseau Castricom en 1643. pp. 44–56. Map. — Relation concernant l'empire et le gouvernement du Japon. Par Fr. Caron. pp. 57–141. — Relation de la Tartarie Orientale par le P. Martini. pp. 142–185. Map. — Memoire pour l'établissement du commerce au Japon, dressé suivant l'ordre de Colbert par Caron. pp. 186–256. — Lettre de M. Delisle à M. Cassini, sur l'embouchure de la rivière de Missisipi. pp. 257–267. — Lettre de Delisle touchant la Californie. pp. 268–277. — Mémoire touchant la Californie. Extrait de la relation des missions établies par les RR. PP. Jésuites et présenté au conseil roial de Mexique, traduit sur l'original espagnol, pp. 278–287. This memoir is signed F. M. Picolo, and dated *Guadalaxara, le* 10 *février,* 1703. — Relation d'une descente des Espagnols dans la Californie en 1683. Traduit du castillan. pp. 288–300. — Voyage de l'Empereur de la Chine dans la Tartarie. Ecrit par le P. Verbiest en l'année 1682

et 1683. pp. 301–336. — Addition qui appartient au voyage précédent. pp. 337-340. Vol. IV. Part I. Frontispiece. pp. lxii. — Relation du naufrage d'un vaisseau hollandois, sur la côte de l'isle de Quelpaerts: avec la description du royaume de Corée. [Etc.] 2 Plates. Part II. 7 l. — Voyage de Jean Huyghen de Linschoten, au nord par le détroit de Nassauw et iusqu'à l'embouchure du fleuve Oby, en 1594. pp. 15–148. — Second voiage de Linschoten au detroit de Nassau, ou passage de Waigatz. pp. 149–245. 3 Plates. — Catalogue, pp. 246-248. This collection was reprinted, with additions, as below:

[**Bernard.**] Recueil de Voiages au Nord, Contenant divers mémoires très utiles au Commerce et à la Navigation. *A Amsterdam: Chez Jean Frederic Bernard.* M. DCC. XV.–M. DCCXXVI. 9 vols., 12mo. 4936

The contents of Vols. I. to IV. are the same as No. 4935. Vol. V. 1 l. — Relation de la Louisiane ou Mississipi, écrite à une dame par un officier de marine. pp 1-34. Map. — Relation de la Louisiane, et du Mississipi. Par le Chev. de Tonti, Gouverneur du fort Saint Louis, aux Islinois. pp. 35-195. — Voyage en un pays plus grand que l'Europe, entre la mer glaciale et le Nouveau Mexique par le P. Hennepin. pp. 197-370. — Relation des voyages de Gosnol, Prince et Gilbert, à la Virginie en 1602 et 1603. Traduite de l'anglois. pp. 371-395. — Relation du détroit et de la baie de Hudson, à M***. Par M. Jeremie. pp. 396-432. — Les trois navigations de Martin Frobisher, pour chercher un passage à la Chine et au Japon par la mer Glaciale, en 1576-78. Écrites à bord du vaisseau de Frobisher. Traduites de l'anglois. pp. 433-494. Vol. VI. 5 l. — La conqueste de l'empire de la Chine par les Tartares. pp. 477. Vol. VII. 1 l. — Histoire des deux conquérans Tartares qui ont subjugué la Chine. pp. 89-135. [Etc.] Vol. VIII. — Voyage de Moscou à la Chine, par Evert Isbrands Ides. — Negociations du Sieur Lange à la Chine. — Mœurs et usages des Ostiackes, par Muller. 12 l., pp. 429. 2 Maps. Vol. IX. Relation des Natchez, par le P. Lepetit, missionaire. — Raisons de la Grande Bretagne d'avoir formé une colonie dans la Georgie: traduit de l'anglois du Chev. Benj. Martin. — Decouverte d'un pays plus grand que l'Europe dans l'Amérique Septentrionale. [By Hennepin.] A catalogue of J. C. Hotten's describes a set in ten volumes.

Bernard. Recueil ... . Nouvelle edition, Corrigée & mise en meilleur ordre. [Vignette.] *Amsterdam: Jean Fre'de'ric Bernard.* M. DCC. XXXI.–XXXVII. 9 vols., 8vo. H. 4937

The titles of Vols. V. and VI., in the set before me, read "Troisième Edition;" and Vol. VII.–IX., which are dated XXV., XXVII., and XXXVII., have no note of the edition.

[**Bernard.**] Recueil de voyages dans l'Amérique Méridionale, contenant diverses observations remarquables touchant le Pérou, la Guiane, le Brésil, etc. Traduits de l'espagnol et de l'anglois. *Amsterdam: Fréd. Bernard.* 1728. 3 vols., 12mo. 4937a

Contents: Vol. I. Relation des voyages de François Coréal aux Indes Occidentales, contenant une description exacte de ce qu'il y a vû de plus remarquable pendant son séjour, depuis 1666. jusques en 1697. pp. 332, 2 l. 12 Maps and Plates. Vol. II. Voyages de Coréal. Troisième partie. pp. 1–150. — Relation de la Guiane, du lac de Parimé, et des provinces d'Emeria, d'Arromaia et d'Amapaia découvertes par le Chev. Walter Raleigh. Traduites de l'original anglois. pp. 153–260. — Relation de la Guiane, traduite de l'anglois du Capitaine Keymis. pp. 261–288. — Relation en forme de journal, de la découverte des iles de Palaos, ou Nouvelles Philippines. pp. 291–302,

1 l. 5 Plates and Maps. Vol. III. Journal du voyage du capitaine Narbrough, à la mer du Sud, par ordre de Charles II. pp. 1-200. — Relation d'un voyage aux Terres Australes inconnues, tirée du journal du capitaine Abel Jansen Tasman. pp. 203-223. Lettre du P. Nyel sur la mission des Moxes, peuples de l'Amérique Méridionale. pp. 224-235. — Relation espagnole, de la mission des Moxes dans le Pérou. Imprimée à Lima, par ordre de Mgr. Urbain de Matha, évêque de la ville de la Paix. [By le P. Nyel.] pp. 236-278, 1 l. Map.

Bernard. La Guyane française et l'ordre de Saint-Joseph de Cluny; par Mme Laure Bernard. *Paris: imp. de Ducessois.* 1834. 8vo. 4938

Bernard (Louis). Coup-d'œil sur la situation agricole de la Guyane française, par M. le général Louis Bernard. *Paris.* 1842. 8vo, pp. 68. 4939

Bernard. Mémoire sur les moyens d'appliquer le travail des Européens à la culture des terres de la Guyane française. *La Rochelle.* 1827. 8vo. 4940

Bernard. Mémoire sur la culture du poivrier à la Guyane française, depuis son introduction, en 1787, jusqu'à la présente année 1843. *Paris.* 1843. 8vo. 4941

Bernard. Projet d'établissement d'une sucrerie centrale sur la rivière de Cayenne, à la Guyane française, par le général Louis Bernard, ancien élève de l'École polytechnique. 1843. 8vo.

Bernard (M.) A Lecture on Alleged Violations of Neutrality by England in the Present War. By Mountague Bernard ... June ... . *London: William Ridgway.* 1863. 8vo. pp. 45. B., H. 4943

Bernard. On the Principle of Non-intervention. A Lecture delivered in the Hall of AllSouls' College. By Mountague Bernard. *Oxford and London: J. H. & Jas. Parker.* 1860. 8vo, pp. 36. 4944

Bernard. Two Lectures on the present American War. By Mountague Bernard ... . November, M DCCC LXI. *Oxford and London.* [n. d.] 8vo, pp. 95. B. 4945

[**Bernard** *and* **Poussin.**] Message of the President in relation to the Survey of a Route for a Canal between the Gulf of Mexico and the Atlantic Ocean; with the Report of the Board of Internal Improvement on the same, February 28, 1829. pp. 52. Map. B. 4946

The report is by M. Bernard and M. Poussin. *See* a notice in the "Southern Review," Vol. VI., pp. 410-420.

[**Bernard** (T.)] Appeal to the Public, stating and considering the Objections to the Quebec Bill. 1774. 8vo. 4947

[**Bernard.**] A Letter to the Right Honourable Lord Camden, on the Bill for restraining the Trade and Fishery of the Four Provinces of New England. *London: T. Cadell.* MDCCLXXV. 8vo, Title, pp. 44. W. 4948

"This writer, by suppressing and misrepresenting facts, endeavors to defend the expediency, justice, and humanity of the bill, which is the subject of his letter, in opposition to the noble lord to whom the letter is addressed." — M. R., LII. 452.

Bernardes (Diogo). Rimes Varias, Flores do Lima; Varias Poezias do Fr. Ag. da Cruz. *Lisboa.* 1770–71. 3 vols., 4to.

This collection of the works of South American poets is scarce.

Bernardes (I. de R.) Description Breve de la Muy Noble, y leal Ciudad de Zacatecas, su situacion, su estuario y minas que la ... . Por Don I. de Rivéra Bernardes. *Mexico.* 1732. Sm. 4to. C. 4950

Bernardin de Cardenas. *See* Cardenas (Bernardin de).

Bernardino. Relacion de la Victoria que han tenido las armas de su magestad en la ciudad de S. Domingo ... contra las armada Inglesa de Guillermo Pen. Embiada por el Señor D. Bernardino de Meneses Bracamonte, etc. *Sevilla: Juan Gomez de Blas.* 1655. Folio, pp. 4. J. C. B. 4951

Bernardo de Nantes (*Fr.*) *See* Nantes (Bernando de).

Bernau (J. H.) Missionary Labours in British Guiana; with Remarks on the Manners, Customs, and Superstitious Rites of the Aborigines. By Rev. J. H. Bernau. *London: J. F. Shaw.* 1847. Post 8vo. 16 Plates. C. 4952

Bernhard (Karl), *Duke of* Sachsen-Weimer-Eisenach. Reise Sr. Hoheit des Herzogs Bernhard zu Sachsen-Weimar-Eisenach durch Nord-Amerika in den Jahren 1825 und 1826. Herausgegeben von Heinrich Luden. *Weimar: Wilhelm Hoffmann.* 1828. 2 vols., 8vo, Title, pp. XXX, (2), 317; iv, (1), 323. 4 Maps, 4 Plates, 4 Plans, and 25 Vignettes. B., C. 4953

Also on fine paper. A Dutch translation was published at Dordrecht, 1829, 8vo.

Bernhard. Travels through North America, during the Years 1825 and 1826. By His Highness, Bernhard, Duke of Saxe-Weimar-Eisenach. *Philadelphia.* 1828. 2 vols., 8vo, pp. iv, 9–212; 238. H. 4954

BERNHARDI (W.) Blondin, der Held des Niagara. Seine Fahrten und Abenteuer zu Wasser und zu Lande. Von Wolfgang Bernhardi. Vierte Auflage. *Berlin: Uthemann & Müller.* 1865. 8vo, pp. 16. (Theatrum Mundi, Bd. IV.) 4955

BEROA (Diego de). Litteræ Annvæ | Provinciæ | Paraqvariæ | Societatis Iesv | Ad admodùm R. P. Mvtivm | Vitellescvm ejusdem Socie- | tatis Prepositum Generalem | Missæ à R. P. Jacobo de Beroa Para- | quariæ Præposito Provinciæ. | Ex Hispanico autographo Latinè | redditæ à P. Francisco de Hamal | Belgâ Societatis ejusdem. | *Insvlis:* | *Typis Tossani Le Clercq.* | *Anno* M. DC. XLII. | 8vo, Title, 3 l., pp. 347, (Errata, 1). 4956

The Bakkers mention "Epistola de Vita et Morte P. Alphonsi Aragonii Societatis Jesu, qui in Collegio Assumptionis in Provincia Paraquaria Diem obiit Anno 1629. En Espagnol;" but they give no imprint. The author was a Spanish Jesuit, and spent most of his life in Paraguay. Antonio does not mention the work. Pinelo quotes it under the name of Hamal. It relates to the years 1635 to July 1637.

BERQUEN (R. de). Les Merveilles des Indes Orientales et Occidentales, ou Nouveau Traité des Pierres précieuses et perles, contenant leur vraye nature, dureté, coleurs et Vertus, &c. *Paris: C. Lambin.* 1661. 4to, 5 l., pp. 112. Portrait. + *Paris:* [*C. Lambin*]. 1669. 4to. J. C. B. 4957

Dedicated to Mlle. d'Orleans, whose portrait forms the frontispiece.

BERQUIN (M.) Lettre d'un colon de Saint Domingue à un journaliste français, en réponse aux provocations anti-coloniales de quelques folliculaires anglais, et autres. Par M. Berquin (de Saint-Domingue). *Paris: Panckoucke.* 1814. 8vo, pp. 23.

[BERQUIN-DUVALLON.] Aurélien et Astérie, ou Les malheurs des préjugés; aventure coloniale. *Paris.* 1804. 12mo.

BERQUIN-DUVALLON. De Saint-Domingue, considéré sous le point de vue de la restauration prochaine ... . *Paris: Panckoucke.* 1814. 8vo, pp. 44. 4960

BERQUIN-DUVALLON. Sentiments des colons de Saint-Domingue envers leur monarque et leur patrie. *Paris: Panckoucke.* 1814. 8vo, pp. 32. 4961

[BERQUIN-DUVALLON.] Vue de la colonie espagnole du Mississipi, ou des provinces de Louisiane et Floride occidentale. En l'année 1802. Par un observateur résident sur les lieux ... . B......-Duvallon, Éditeur. *Paris. An* XI. 1803. 8vo, pp. xx, 318, 5, (4). 2 colored Maps. C., H. 4962

Attributed by Barbier and Quérard to Berquin-Duvallon as the author.

[BERQUIN-DUVALLON.] Vues de la Colonie Espagnole du Mississippi, ou des Provinces de la Louisiane et Floride Occidentale, en l'an 1802. Seconde édition. *Paris.* 1804. + *Paris:* 1805. 8vo. 4963

The edition of 1805 has the author's name on the title-page.

BERQUIN-DUVALLON. Schilderung von Louisiana. Aus dem Franszösischen des von Duvallon herausgegeben Werkes abgekürtzt. Mit einer Anleitung und Zusätzen herausgegeben von T. F. Ehrmann. ... *Weimar: Industrie comptoirs.* 1804. 8vo, pp. xxviii, 344. Map. (Bibliothek der neuesten und wichtigsten Reisebeschreibungen ... Zehnter Band.) C. S. 4964

[BERQUIN-DUVALLON.] Travels in Louisiana and the Floridas in the Year 1802. Giving a Correct Picture of those Countries, Translated from the French, with Notes, &c. By John Davis. *New York: J. Riley & Co.* 1806. 12mo, pp. viii, 181. 4965

BERQUIN-DUVALLON. Vœux des colons de Saint-Domingue, portés au pied du trône ... par un de ces colons agissant au nom de tous. *Paris: Panckoucke.* 1814. 4to, pp. 16. 4966

BERREDO (B. P. de). Annaes Historicos do Estado do Maranhao, em que se da noticia do seu descobrimiento, e tudo o mais que n'elle tem succedido desde o anno em que foy descoberto até o de 1718. Por Bernardo Pereira de Berredo. *Lisboa: Francisco Luiz Ameno.* 1749. Folio, 12 l., pp. 710. 4967

The author was appointed governor of Maranham in the year 1718. His death took place March 13th, 1748, while preparing this work for the press. He was distinguished amongst his countrymen for his valor, but "has left for himself a more durable remembrance in his historical annals of the state over which he presided."—SOUTHEY. Quoted by Silva, I. 383, at 1.600 reis.

BERRIAN (H.) A Brief Sketch of the Origin and Rise of the Workingmen's Party in the City of New York. By Hobart Berrian. ... *Printed at the Office of the "Workingman's Advocate," Washington City, by Wm. Greer.* 8vo, pp. 16. H. 4968

BERRIAN (R.) The American Telegraph and Signal Book. By Richard Berrian. *New York.* 1823. 12mo, pp. 44. 4969

BERRIAN (S.) An Oration delivered before the Tammany ... [and other] Societies, in the City of New-York, on the Fourth

of July, 1811. By Samuel Berrian. ... *New York: Joseph Harmer.* 1811. 8vo, pp. 22, (1). B. 4970

BERRIAN. An Oration delivered before the Tammany ... [and other] Societies, in the City of New-York, on the Fourth Day of July, 1815. By Samuel Berrian ... . *New York: John Low.* 1815. 8vo, pp. 32. B. 4971

BERRIAN (W.) Facts against Fancy; or, a True and Just View of Trinity Church. By the Rev. William Berrian, D.D., the Rector ... . *New York: Pudney & Russell, Printers.* 1855. 8vo, pp. 74. H. 4972

BERRIAN. "The Rector rectified." In Reply to "Facts Against Fancy, by Rev. Wm. Berrian ... ." from the Protestant Churchman. *New-York: Anson D. F. Randolph.* 1856. 8vo, pp. 46. H. 4973

BERRIAN. An Historical Sketch of Trinity Church, New-York. By the Rev. William Berrian, D.D. ... *New York: Stanford and Swords.* 1847. 8vo, 2 l., pp. 9–386. 6 Plates. B., C.

BERRIAN. Recollections of Departed Friends, or the Lives of Sixteen New York Citizens. By William Berrian. Second Edition. *New York.* 1850. 12mo, pp. 219. 4975

BERRIAN. Report to the Vestry of Trinity Church on the State of the Parish, by William Berrian ... . *New York.* 1856. 8vo, pp. 55. H. 4976

BERRIAN. Semi-Centennial Sermon, by the Rev. William Berrian, D.D., Rector of Trinity Church, New-York ... . *New-York.* 1860. 8vo, pp. 31. H. 4977

BERRIEN (J. M.) Eulogy on the Life and Character of William Henry Harrison, Late President of the United States; delivered ... [in] Savannah ... May 12th, 1841. By the Hon. John Macpherson Berrien. *Savanhan* [*sic*]: *W. T. Williams.* 1841. 8vo, pp. 26. H. 4978

BERRIEN. An Oration delivered at the Baptist Church in the City of Savannah, on Friday the 22nd. of February, 1822; at the request of the Georgia Hussars; By John Macpherson Berrien, Commander of the Corps. Published by their Desire. *Savannah: W. T. Williams.* 1822. 8vo, pp. 24. 4979

The oldest militia in the United States.

BERRIEN. Remarks of Mr. Berrien, of Georgia, on the Compromise Bill. ... Jan. 16, 1850. 8vo, pp. 16. 4980

BERRIEN. Speech of Mr. Berrien, of Georgia ... in the Senate ... on the Mission to Panama, March, 1826. *Washington City.* 1826. 8vo, pp. 28. H. 4981

BERRIEN. Speech ... on the Joint Resolution to annex Texas to the United States: delivered in the Senate ... Feb. 1845. *Washington.* 1845. 8vo. B. M. 4982

BERRIEN. Speech of Mr. Berrien, ... on the Bill appropriating Three Millions of Dollars to be expended under the Direction of the President in negociating a Peace with Mexico. ... In the Senate ... February 5, 1847. *Washington,* 1847. 8vo, pp. 32. H. 4983

BERRIEN. Speech of Mr. Berrien, of Georgia, on the Ten Regiment Bill. ... In the Senate ... March 17, 1848. *Washington.* 1848. 8vo, pp. 16. H. 4984

BERRIEN. Speech of Mr. Berrien, of Georgia, on the Subject of Slavery in the Territories, delivered in the Senate of the United States, February 11 and 12, 1850. [n. p. n. d.] 8vo, pp. 32. 4985

BERRIMAN (W.) A Sermon Preach'd before the Honourable Trustees for Establishing the Colony of Georgia in America, and the Associates of the late Reverend Dr. Bray; at their Anniversary Meeting, March 15, 1738–9. In the Parish Church of St. Bridget, alias St. Bride, in Fleetstreet, London. By William Berriman, D.D. Rector of St. Andrew's Undershaft, and Fellow of Eton College. Published at the Desire of the Trustees and Associates. *London: John Carter.* M.DCC.XXXIX. 4to, pp. 24.

BERRIO. Informe sobre las minas de Tasco y modo de beneficiarlas. Por D. Luis Berrio de Montalvo. 1634. Folio.

See Ternaux-Compans, No. 554.

BERRO. Ideas de fusion. Coleccion de cartas escritas por el Ciudadano Presidente D. Bernardo Berro. *Montevideo.* 1860. 8vo, pp. xvi, 44. 4988

BERRY (G.) The Gold of California: a Short Inquiry into its Probable Effects ... . By George Berry. ... *London.* 1849. 8vo, pp. 16. 4988*a*

BERRY (H.) Slavery and Abolitionism, as viewed by a Georgia Slave. By Harrison Berry, The Property of S. W. Price, Covington. *Atlanta, Georgia: M. Lynch & Co.* 1861. 8vo, pp. 41, (1). Woodcut of Berry. B. 4989

BERRY (Henry). The Speech of Henry Berry, (of Jefferson,) in the House of Delegates of Virginia, on the Abolition of Slavery. [n. p. 1832.] 8vo, pp. 8. 4990

BERRY (J. R.) Christian Patriotism. A Sermon delivered in the Reformed Dutch Church of Kinderhook, June 23, 1861. By Rev. J. Romeyn Berry, Pastor. *Albany: Weed, Parsons and Company.* 1861. 8vo, pp. 34. H. 4991

BERRY (P.) A Review of the Bishop of Oxford's Counsel to the American Clergy, with reference to ... Slavery. Also ... Remarks on the Relation of the Wilmot Proviso to the Interests of the Colored Class. By the Rev. Philip Berry ... . *Washington: William M. Morrison* [etc.] 1848. 8vo, pp. 26. H. 4992

BERRY. Review of the Mexican War on Christian Principles: and an Essay on the Means of preventing War. By the Rev. Philip Berry ... . (Reprinted from the "Southern Presbyterian Review.") *Columbia, S. C.* 1849. 8vo, pp. ix, 87.

BERRY (R. T.) A Discourse Commemorative of the History of the Bridge Street Church, Georgetown, D. C., delivered September 8, 1848. By R. T. Berry, the pastor of the Church. Published by the ladies of the Congregation, for the benefit of the Church. *Washington.* 1848. 8vo, pp. 24. S. 4994

BERRY. A National Warning; a Sermon preached ... as an improvement of the calamity that occurred on board ... the Steam Frigate Princeton, etc. By R. T. Berry. *Philadelphia.* 1844. 12mo. B. M. 4995

BERRY, SALTER & Co.'s Railway Business Directory for 1866–7: embracing the Louisville and Nashville, Nashville and Chattanooga, Nashville and Decatur, Memphis and Charleston, and Western and Atlantic Railroads. *Louisville: Berry, Salter & Co.* 1866. 8vo, pp. 382. 4996

BERRYER (Pierre Antoine). Discours de M. Berryer sur les emprunts mexicains contractés en France, prononcés le 22 et le 23 juillet dans la discussion du budget de 1868 au Corps législatif. *Paris: imp. Raçon et Ce.* 1867. 16mo, pp. 62. 4996*a*

Reprinted with the title:

BERRYER. Discours prononcés ... les 22 et 23 juillet 1867; par M. Berryer: la dette du Mexique et les obligations mexicaines. *Paris: Douniol.* 1867. 18mo, pp. 63. 4996*b*

The Berry-Pickers of Wisconsin. Illustrated. *Philadelphia: Presb. Pub. Com.* 1865. 16mo, pp. 245. 4997

BERT (Pierre). *See* Bertius (Petrus).

BERTAL (A. J.) La famille Need, ou Les établissements philanthropiques aux États-Unis; par A. Bertal. *Paris: Cherbuliez.* 1855. 18mo, 9 sheets. 4998

BERTAL (A. J.) *See* Bescherelle.

BERTAUD (C. F. J.) Dissertation sur la maladie que les médecins de Saint-Domingue ont appelée fièvre jaune ou fièvre de Siam. *Paris: impr. de Didot jeune, an* XIII [1804]. 4to.

BERTELLI E FORLANI, Tavole moderne di Geografia de la maggior parte del Mondo. *Roma.* 1558–80. Imp. folio, engraved Title, and 71 large Maps. 5000

"This series of maps, of which sets or copies vary considerably in their extent, was the best, most complete, and most correct atlas that had till then appeared. In the number, there are three large special maps of America, North and South, besides three maps of the World, in which America also appears. It is remarkable, as shown in these maps, how far the chorography of the regions now comprised in Canada and the States was developed seventy years after the discovery of America. Even the quite recent researches of Jacques Cartier were already utilized."

BERTHELOT (Amable). Dissertation sur le Canon de Bronze, trouvé en 1826, sur un banc de sable, dans le Fleuve Saint-Laurent, au-devant de la paroisse de Champlain, dans le District des Trois-Rivières. *Québec.* 1827. 12mo. 5001

"Dans la première partie de cet écrit, l'auteur entreprend de prouver, que Jacques Cartier ne fit pas naufrage sur un rocher, auquel une tradition erronée a conservé en Canada, le nom de 'La Roche de Jacques Cartier.' Dans la seconde partie, l'auteur conjecture que le Canon de Bronze ainsi trouvé, a dû appartenir à Verrazzani, et que c'est ce dernier qui fit naufrage dans ce même endroit."—FARIBAULT, No. 56.

BERTHELOT (Sabin). Essai historique sur l'île de Cuba à l'époque de la découverte et pendant les premières années de la colonisation; suivi de l'analyse de M. Ramon de La Sagra; par S. Berthelot. *Paris: impr. de Bourgogne.* 1846. 8vo, 3 sheets.

BERTHET (E.) Les émigrants; (la colonie du Kansas); par Elie Berthet. *Paris: de Potter.* 1860. 5 vols., 8vo, pp. 1602 in all. + *Paris.* 1861. 4to, pp. 158, with double columns.

+ *Paris.* 1862. 4to, pp. 158. + *Paris.* 1864. 4to, pp. 158. + *Paris.* 1865. 4to, pp. 158. 5003

BERTHET. Les missionnaires du Paraguay par Élie Berthet ... . *Paris: Boisgard.* 1853. 18mo. + [*Ibid.*] 1858. 4to, pp. 48. Illustrations. 5004

BERTHOLD (Arnold Adolf). Ueber verschiedene neue oder seltene Reptilien aus Neu-Granada und Crustaceen aus China. *Göttingen: Dieterich.* 1846. 4to, 4 sheets. 3 Plates. 5005

BERTIE (Willoughby). Speech of the Earl of Abingdon, on His Lordship's Motion for postponing the Further Consideration of the Question for the Abolition of the Slave Trade; with Some Strictures on the Speech of the Bishop of St. David's. *London: Debrett;* [also] *Sewel* [etc. n. d.] 8vo, pp. 23. H.

BERTIE. Thoughts on the Letter of Edmund Burke, Esq; to the Sheriffs of Bristol, on the Affairs of America. By the Earl of Abingdon. *Oxford, Printed: Lancaster, Re-printed And Sold by John Dunlap.* M,DCC,LXXVIII. 8vo, pp. 30. B. 5007

For other editions, *see* Vol. I., Nos. 61-64. The Second Edition (H.) has pp. 64, and not, as there stated, pp. 68.

BERTIE. A Dissertation on the Political Abilities of the Earl of Abingdon, &c. &c. By a Gentleman of the Inner Temple. *London: Fielding and Co.* 1780. 8vo. 5008

See M. R., LXIII. 144.

BERTIER (*Comte* Ferdinand de). Opinion de M. Bertier sur le project de loi relatif à l'indemnité des colons de Saint-Domingue, prononcée le 8 mars 1826. *Paris: impr. de Boucher.* 1826. 8vo, pp. 44. 5009

BERTIN (Antoine de). Epitre à M. Desforges Boucher sur les productions de l'Amérique. [n. p.?] 1778. 8vo. 5010

Probably reprinted in his "Œuvres," of which Quérard mentions twelve editions, published at Paris, between 1785 and 1826.

[BERTIN.] Des moyens de conserver la santé des blancs et des nègres aux Antilles ou climats chauds et humides de l'Amérique, contenant un exposé des causes des maladies propres à ces climats et à la traversée ... les procédés à suivre, soit pour les éviter, soit pour les détruire; et le traitement en particulier de quelques maladies communes chez les nègres, telles que le pian, le mal d'estomac et la lèpre. *S.-Domingue; et à Paris: chez Méquignon l'aîné.* 1786. 8vo. 5011

BERTIUS (Petrus). Beschreibung der gantzen Welt abgebildet mit sehr schönen Cosmographischen Land-Tafeln. *Amsterdam.* 1650. Oblong 8vo. 168 Maps. 5012

Lib. v. contains "Geographische Tabellen, in welchen America vnnd Magellanica Beneben ihren Tabeln gantz klärlich werden vorgebildet vnd beschrieben."

BERTIUS. Breviarium Totius Orbis Terrarum. *Francofurti.* 1627. 12mo. BM. + *Francofurti.* 1640. 12mo. BM. + *Lipsiæ: Gross.* 1664. 12mo. + *Amsterodami: apud Janssonio Waesbergios.* 1676. 4to, Title, pp. 32. 5013

America, New England, Maryland, Virginia, Carolina, Barbadoes, and New Spain occupy about a page in all. This Breviarium is also contained in Cluverius's "Introductio in Geographiam. *Lugd. Bat.* 1641." 12mo.

BERTIUS. P. Bertij Tabvlarvm Geographicarvm contractarvm Libri septem. In quibus Tabulæ omnes gradibus distinctae, ... *Amsterodami.* 1616. 4to. BM. + *Amsterodami Sumptibus et typis æneis Iodoci Hondij. anno* 1618. Oblong 8vo, pp. viii, 830, (Appendix) 4. J. C. BT. 5014

This edition has 176 maps and plates, by Iodocus Hondius printed on the reverse of the pages. Livre septiesme des tables geographiqves, auquel est continue L'Ameriqve, &c. ... contains twelve maps and plates relating to America, and a map of the world. The text is in French. The date on the engraved title-page is altered from 1616, and served, probably, for a Latin edition. The "Privilège" is dated 1617. A Latin edition is before me, with different maps, and divided into five books, the last with twelve maps and plates relating to America. The title is lost, but the dedication is dated Leyden, 1600. There was a German edition published in Frankfort in 1612, containing only the first five books. The other editions are: *Amst.* 1600. 4to. BM. + *Amst.: Laurent.* 1605. 8vo. + [*Ibid.*] 1613. Folio. + Cum Mappis. *Amst.: Elzev.* 1620. 8vo. Herrera's "Novvs Orbis. *Amst.* 1622," folio, contains "Brevis ... Americæ ... descriptio, Excerpta è Tabulis Geographicis P. Bertii," 11 l. The "Description de l'Amérique" is included in Herrara, pp. 229-254, and Linschoten. Bertius also edited "Ptolemy." *Amst.* 1618. 2 vols., folio. *See also* Hondius and Mercator.

BERTOLONI (A.) Antonii Bertolonii ... Florula Guatimalensis sistens Plantas nonnullas in Guatimala Sponte nascentes *Bononiæ: ex Typographaeo Emygdii ab Ulmo. A.* MDCCCXL. 4to, pp. 43, (2). 12 colored Plates. B. 5015

BERTON (Henri Montan). Ponce de Léon, opéra bouffon en trois actes. [Paroles et musique.] *Paris: Migneret, an* VI [1798]. 8vo. 5016

BERTONI *or* BERTONIO (L.) Arte Breve de la Lengua Aymara, para introduction del arte grande de la misma lengua. Por P. Ludovico Bertonio. *Roma: Zannetti.* [?] 1603. 8vo.

BERTONIO. Arte y Grammatica copiosa de la Lengua Aymara. Por el P. Ludovico Bertonio. *Roma: Zannetti.* 1608. 8vo.

BERTONIO. Arte de la Lengua Aymara, con una sylva de phrases de la misma lengua, y su declaracion en romance. *Impressa en la casa de la Compañia de Jesus en Juli Pueblo, en la Provincia de Chucuyto, por Francisco del Canto.* 1612. Sm. 4to, pp. x., 1618. 5019

Title and collation from Ludewig's Lit. Am. Abor. Lang.

BERTONIO. Arte y vocabulario en la lengua general del Peru llamada Quichua, y en la lengua española. *Lima: Impr. por Franc. del Canto.* 1614. 12mo. 5020

This exceedingly rare book is wanting in most of the celebrated collections of books of its class. Neither Ludewig nor Brunet credit the authorship of this to Bertonio. Sold at Puttick's, 1860, £4 4s.

BERTONIO. Confessionario | mvy copioso | en dos Lengvas, Aymara, | y Española, con vna instruccion a cerca de los siete | Sacramentos de la Sancta Yglesia, y otras | varias cosas, como puede verse por la | Tabla del mesmo libro. | Por el Padre Lvdovico Ber | tonio Italiano de la Compañia de Iesus en la Prouincia | del Peru natural de Rocca Contradæ dela | Marca de Ancona | Dedicado al Padre Ioan | Sebastian Prouincial dela mesma | Compañia y Prouincia. | [Vignette.] | *Impresso enla casa dela Copañia de Iesus de Iuli | enla Prouincia de Chucuyto. Por Francisco | del Canto.* 1612. | *Esta tassado este Confessonario, a Real el pliego.* | Sm. 8vo, 8 l., pp. 351. J. C. B. 5021

BERTONIO. Libro | de la Vida y | Milagros de Nvestro Señor | Iesu Christo en dos Lenguas, Aymara, y Romance, | traducido de el que recopilo el Licenciado Alon | so de Villegas, quitadas, y añadidas algunas | cosas, y acomodado ala capacidad | de los Indios. | Por el Padre Lvdovico Bertonio Ita- | liano dela Compañia de Iesus enla Prouincia de el Piru natural | de Rocca Contrada dela Marca de Ancona. | Dedicado al Illvstrissimo y Reve- | rendissimo Señor don Alonso de Peralta primer Arço- | bispo de los Charcas. | *Impresso enla Casa de la Compañia de Iesus de Iuli Pueblo enla | Prouincia de Chucuyto por Francisco del Canto.* 1612. | *Esta tassado esta libro a Real cada pliego en papel.* | [Colophon:] *Impresso en el Pueblo de Iuli, de | la Prouincia de Chucuyto, con la | emprêta de Francisco del Canto.* | *Año* M. DC. XII. 4to, 8 l., pp. 660, and 3 (?) l. 5022

"This very rare volume must be of considerable use to a student of the Indian dialect of Aymara, from its unusual bulk, and the consequent number of words and phrases employed, as compared with other works of a like nature." An imperfect copy sold at Puttick's, 1860, for £3 16s.; Chaumette, 25fr.

BERTONIO. Vocabulario en la Lengua Aymara. *Impresso en*

la casa de la Compania de Jesus en Juli Pueblo, en la Provincia de Chucuito, por Francisco del Canto. 1612. 4to. BD. 5023

Graesse, I. 351, expresses an opinion that this is detached from the "Arte." *See* catalogue "Chaumette des Fossés," Nos. 66, 78, and 576. Also: Lud. "Lit. Ab. Lang."

BERTRAN (*D.* Felipe), *obispo de Salamanca, inquisidor general.* Carta instructiva a un predicador moderno, para formar con acierto un sermon; proponiendole por modelo el que en alabanza de S. Tomas de Aquino, predicó en Madrid año de 1770, el señor D. F. Bertran. *Mexico: Felipe de Zuñiga, y Ontiveros.* 1779. 8vo, pp. 22. 5024

"Sermon, que en alabanza de S. Tomas de Aquino predicó en el colegio de Rev. padres dominicos de Madrid, etc." *Reimpreso en México, por Fel. de Zuñiga y Ontiveros.* (1779). pp. 68. Title from Leclerc, No. 156.

BERTRAND. Lettre Missive touchant la conversion du Grand Sagamos de la Nouvelle-France, qui en était auparavant l'arrivée des Français le Chef et le Souverain, contenant sa promesse d'amener ses sujets à la même conversion ou les y contraendre par la force des armes. ... Datée du 28 juin 1618. [Signed, Bertrand.] *Paris: J. Regnoul.* 1610. 8vo, pp. 48 or less.

BERTRAND (Henri Gratien, *Comte* de). Sur la détresse des colonies françaises en général, de l'île de la Martinique en particulier, et de la necessité de diminuer la taxe exorbitante établie sur le sucre exotique. Par le général Bertrand. *Paris: imp. de F. Didot.* 1839. 8vo, 3 sheets. 5026

BERTRAND (L. A.) Autorité divine, ou Réponse à cette question: Joseph Smith était-il envoyé de Dieu? suivie du Credo de l'église de Jésus-Christ, par l'Elder L. A. Bertrand, président de la conférence de Paris. *Paris: impr. de Ducloux.* 1853. 8vo, 2 sheets. 5027

BERTRAND. Discours de M. de Bertrand, Ministre de la Marine, à l'Assemblée Nationale, le 19 Décembre, 1791, sur l'état actuel de la colonie de St. Domingue. [1791.] 8vo. 5028

BERTRAND. Mémoires d'un Mormon; par L. A. Bertrand. *Paris: Jung-Treuttel.* 1862. 18mo, pp. 329. 5029

BERTULUS (É.) De l'importation de la fièvre jaune en Europe et de la possibilité de son développement par 48° 25′ 14″ de latitude boréale. Mémoire qui établit, sur des faits authentiques, le danger des relations avec les Antilles ... . Par Évariste Bertulus ... . *Toulon: imp. de E. Aurel.* 1840. 8vo. 5030

BERVILLE (Saint-Albin). Rapport fait par M. Berville, au nom du jury chargé de prononcer sur les resultats du concours ouvert pour célébrer le voyage du général La Fayette aux États-Unis. *Paris: Baudouin frères.* 1826. 8vo, pp. 24. 5031

BERWICK. Catalogue of the Officers and Students of Berwick Academy, for the Academical Year 1847 & 8. *Dover.* 1848. 12mo, pp. 12. + For other years. H. 5032

BESANÇON (L. A.) Besançon's Annual Register of the State of Mississippi, for the Year 1838. Compiled from Original Documents — being a full Exhibit of all the Tabular and Statistical Information which it was possible to obtain from Authentic Sources. Vol. I. *Natchez: L. A. Besançon.* 1838. 12mo, pp. 232. Map. M. 5033

BESCHERELLE (Louis Nicolas) *and* BERTAL (A.) Histoire de la fondation des colonies espagnoles et anglaises en Amérique; par M. Bescherelle âiné ... et par M. A. Bertal. *Paris: Borrani et Droz.* 1857. Oblong 4to, pp. 100, of four columns each. 5034

BESCHKE (W.) Memorial to the Congress ... Concerning several great Inventions of National Importance, and the Infringements of a U. S. Patent in building Ironclad Vessels and Iron Turrets. ... by William Beschke ... . [n. p. 1865.] 8vo, pp. 38, (1), 15. H. 5035

BESCHKE. Memorial to the United States' Congress ... concerning European Navies and the American Navy; the Breech-Loading and Steady Ship-Gun, and the Improved War-Steamer with Submerged Propellers invented by William Beschke ... *Philadelphia.* 1852. 12mo, pp. 64. H. 5036

Beschlüsse des Kongresses der Vereinigten Staaten zur Regulation der Auswanderung auf Kauffahrteischiffen. Uebersetzt von einem Ausgewandertem. *Rastadt: Hanemann.* 1854. 8vo, pp. 22. 5037

Beschouwing van het adres, ingediend door P. C. Bosch Reitz aan de Zee Kamer c. s. op 21 Febr. 1845, betrachtend de Kolonie Suriname, door einige inwooner der kolonie Suriname. *Amsterdam.* 1845. 8vo. 5038

"Behelzende verzoek om hooge grondwett tuschenkomst."

Beschreibung Americæ 9. Thiele mit Kupffern. *Franckfurt: Wechel.* 1591. Folio, 13 sheets. 5039

Title from Georgi. Perhaps an edition of Acosta.

Beschreibung der Antill-Insul. *Frankfurt: Serlin.* 1668. 12mo, 41 sheets, 4 l. 5040

Beschreibung der dreizehn unabhängigen Nordamerikanischen Staaten; aus dem englischen Quellen. *Köln.* 1783. 8vo.

Beschreibung der neuerfundenen pensylvanischen Kamine oder Oefen. *See* Pennsylvania.

Beschhreibung der Spanischen Macht in Nord-amerika. *Sorau: Hebold.* 1767. 4to. 5042

Beschreibung und Geschichte vom Westindien. *See* Förster (T.)

Beschreibung der Europaischer Kolonien in Amerika. *See* [Burke (Ed.)]

Beschreibung der Provinz Carolina. *See* [Oldmixon (John).]

Beschreibung von der unglücklichen Reise. *See* [Höen (M. W.)]

Beschreibung des Welt-teils Amerika und des Süd Landes. *Amsterdam.* 1673. Folio. Maps and Plates. 5043

Beschryving der Zee en Landreizen naar de Oost- en West-indiën. *Amsterdam.* 1683. Folio. 5044

Beschryving van de Kaap-Breton. *See* Cape Breton.

Beschryving van de kolonie Suriname. *See* Suriname.

Beschryving van de nieuw uitgevonden Pensilvanische. *See* Pennsylvania.

Beschryving van de kolonie Berbice. *See* Berbice.

Beschryving van oud en nieuw Groenland. *See* Greenland.

Beschrijving van Guiana. *See* Guiana.

Beschrijving van ... Curaçao. *See* Hering (Y. H.)

Beschrijvinghe | Van | Virginia, | Nieuw Nederlandt, | Nieuw

Engelandt, | En d'Eylanden | Bermudes, | Barbadoes en S. Christoffel. | Dienstelyck voor elck een derwaerts handelende, en alle voort-planten | van nieuw Colonien. | Met koperen Figuren verciert. | *'tAmsterdam, | By Joost Hartgers, Boeck-verkooper op den Dam, bezyden 't Stadt-huys, | op de hoeck vande Kalver-straet, inde Boeck-winckel, Anno* 1651. 4to, pp. 88. Map. 5045

This "Description of Virginia, New Netherland, New England and the islands of Bermuda, [etc.] which is very useful for all trading thither and all founders of new colonies, is a reprint of some parts of the 'Vertoogh,' and of the second edition of De Laet." Asher, No. 6, describes it as having sixty pages. "The van of New Amsterdam contained in this book appears to be taken from the same engraving as that in the first edition of Van der Donck." *See* Muller's Catal., No., 4544.

Beschryvinge | van eenige voorname Kusten in | Oost- en West- | Indien: | Als Zueriname, Nieuw-Nederland, | Florida, van 't Eyland Kuba, Brazil, | Suratte, Madagascar, Ba- | tavia, Peru en Mexico. | Van haar Gelegentheid, Aart en Gewoonte dier Vol- | keren; hun koophandel, Gods-dienst, | en zelzaame Voor-vallen. | *Door verscheidene Liefhebbers gedaan.* | *Te Leeuwarden, | By Meindert Injema, Boek-drukker en Verkoper | in de St. Jakobs-straat, by de Waags-Piep.* 1716. | 4to, Title, pp. 150. H. 5046

In a copy described by Asher, an additional engraved title reads: "Beschryvinge van. Oost en West-Indien: Te Leeuwarden by Jan Clasen." The description of New Netherland, pp. 50–76, is a reprint of three chapters of Melton, pp. 138–162.

Beskrifning ofver de Engelska Colonierne i Nordamerica, utdragen af de tilförlätigaste Anbeten, Ofversatuing. *Stockholm.* 1777. Map. 5047

Beskrivelse over Eylandet St. Croix. *See* St. Croix.

BESOLDUS (Christophorus). Discursus Politicus | de | Incrementis | Imperiorum, eorum- | que amplitudine | procurandâ. | Cvi inserta est | Dissertatio singularis, De No- | vo Orbe. | Auctore, | Christoforo Besoldo, JCto. | *Argentorati, | Impensis Hæredum Lazari Zetzneri.* | *Anno* M DC XXIII. 4to, pp. 65. 5048

BESOLDUS. De novo orbe conjectanea. *Tubingæ.* 1694. Sm. 4to. 5049

BESSIÈRE (J. F.) Franklin Comédie historique en cinq actes et en prose. Par J. F. Bessièrre. *Paris: l'auteur.* 1838. 8vo, 6 sheets. 5050

BEST (George). A True Discourse of the late Voyages of discouerie for the finding of a Passage to Cathaya by the North-Weast Under the Conduct of Martin Frobisher, Generall; ...

With a particular Card thereunto adjoyned of Meta Incognita so farre forth as the secretes of the voyage may permit. *London: Bynneman.* 1578. 4to, 8 l., pp. 52, 39, 68. 2 Maps. J. C. B. H.

The maps are usually deficient. Reprinted in Pinkerton's "Voyages," Vol. XII., and Hakluyt, 1849, p. 630. The author sailed with Frobisher 1576–8, and this is the first account of these three voyages. *See* Bibliotheca Grenvilliana, Bartlett's Cat. of J. C. Brown's Library. *See also* Kennett's Bib. Am. Prim., p. 22, No. 2. Jude's copy, with fac-simile drawings of the two maps, sold for £8 10s. Heber's copy sold for £8 5s. A book of great rarity. The third and last voyage into Meta Incognita was also printed in 16mo, and reprinted in Hakluyt's Collection. *See* Ellis (T.)

BEST. La Navigation du Captaine Frobisher ez-régions d Est et Nord-Ouest, en l'anne 1577, par Antoine Chappin. *Geneves.* 1577. 8vo. 5652

BEST. Historia Navigationis anno 1577, ex Anglia in Septentrionisis et Occidentales traetum susceptæ. 8vo. *Nuremberg.* 1589. 8vo. 5053

According to Faribault, this Latin version, by T. Freigius, is from the French translation of the English original.

BEST (William). ... A Sermon Preached before the Honourable Trustees for Establishing the Colony of Georgia in America, ... at their Anniversary Meeting, March 18. 1741–2. ... In which some Notice is taken of a late abusive Pamphlet, intituled, A true and historical Narrative of the said Colony. By William Best, D.D. ... *London: W. Innys.* M DCC XLII. 4to, pp. 32. H.

BEST. The Relief of the Persecuted Protestants of Saltzburgh, and the Support of the Colony of Georgia, a Sermon. By William Best, D.D. *London.* 1734. 4to. 5055

BESTE (J. R.) The Wabash: or Adventures of an English Gentleman's Family in the Interior of America. ... By J. Richard Beste. ... *London: Hurst aud Blackett.* 1855. 2 vols., 12mo, Title, pp. viii, 329; viii, 352. 2 colored Lithographs.

BETAGH (William). A Voyage round the World. Being an Account of a Remarkable Enterprize, begun In the Year 1719, chiefly to cruise on the Spaniards in the great South Ocean. Relating the True historical Facts of that whole Affair: Testifyd by many imployed therein; and confirmed by Authorities from the Owners. By William Betagh, Captain of Marines in that Expedition. *London: T. Combes, J. Lacy, and J. Clarke.* MDCCXXVIII. 8vo, 8 l., pp. 342, (3). Map. H. + *London.* 1737. 8vo. 5057

The author was captain of marines in Capt. Shelvocke's Voyage. He says "His (Shelvocke's) pretended narrative is entirely a deception, and his whole conduct an

indignity to his country." "Betagh tells his own story very differently, and his lively manner gives his narrative much beauty and spirit." — KERR's *Collection*. This was about the last of the buccaneering expeditions. Included in Pinkerton's Voyages, Vol. XVI., and Harris' Coll., Vol. I.

BETANCOURT (A.) La Cartilla del Pueblo. *Carácas.* 1855. 8vo, pp. 45. 5058

BETANCOURT (G.) ... Addresses delivered at the Celebration of the Third Anniversary in Honor of the Martyrs for Cuban Freedom. By Jaspar Betancourt, Esq., President of the Cuban Revolutionary Junta, and J. S. Thrasher, Esq., at ... New Orleans, Sept. 1, 1854. *New Orleans.* 1854. 8vo, pp. 8. H.

BETANCOURT (J. R.) Una feria de la caridad en 183 ... Cuento comagüeyano. Escrito en 1841 por J. Ramon de Betancourt. *Habana.* 1858. 8vo, pp. 238. 5060

BETANCOURT (J. V.) Aguinaldo matanzero. Editores Jose Victoriano Betancourt, Miguel T. Tolon. *Matanzas.* 1847, Sm. 8vo, pp. 184, (3). B. 5061

A collection of poems by various writers. Some relate to America.

BETANCUR (S. G.) Storia della Vita, virtu, donni, e grazzi del Pietro di S. Giuseppe Betancur. Fondatore dell' ordine Betlemitico nelle Indie occidentali. *Romae.* 1739. 4to. 5062

With a curious vignette of the sun rising over America, and other plates.

BETANCURT (Fr. Augustin de). *See* Vetancurt (Fr. A. de).

BETANCUR I FIGUEROA (Luis de). Derecho de las Iglesias Metropolitanas de las Indias sobre que sus prelacias sean proveidas en las capitulares dellus, y naturales de sus provincias. *Madrid.* 1635. 4to. 5063

BETANCURT (Luis de). Derecho | de las Iglesias | Metropolitanas, i | Catedrales de las | Indias, | sobre | qve svs Prelacias sean | proveidas en los Capitulares dellas, i Natu- | rales de sus Provincias. | Al Rei Nvestro Señor, | En su Real i Supremo Consejo | de las Indias. | Por el Doctor Don Lvis de | Betancurt i Figuerora, Consultor del Santo Oficio de la In- | quisicion, i Fiscal de la de Canaria, Chantre de la santa Iglesia | de san Francisco del Quito en las Provincias del Peru, i | Procurador general de las de Indias. | *Año* [Motto.] 1637. *Con Licencia.* | *En Madrid. Por Francisco Martinez.* 4to. C 5064

A very scarce book, not mentioned by Nicolas Antonio. *See* Rich's Catalogue, Nos. 209 and 217; Ternaux, Nos. 552, 560, and 575, where are also cited editions of 1634 and 1635.

BETENDORF (Joao Filippe). Compendio da doutrina christaa na lingua portugueza, e Brasilica. Composto pelo P. J. F. Betendorf, antigo Missionario de Brasil. Reimpresso de ordem de S. Alteza real, por Fr. José Mariano da Conceiçao Vellozo. *Lisboa.* 1800. 12mo, pp. viii, 131, 2 l. 5065

"Cette doctrine chrétienne qui selon la préface, aurait été composée en 1681, n'est pas mentionnée par Antonio et Pinelo. Barbosa Machado, cite un catéchisme en brésilien, composé par le P. Antonio de Araujo, imprimé en 1618. Réimprimé avec des augmentations de F. Bartholameu de Leao, en 1686. Ne serait-ce pas le même que celui qui est announcé dans la préface de notre volume?"—LECLERC, No. 158.

BETETA (Gregorio de). *See* Ternaux Recueil, Vol. XX.

BETHANY COLLEGE. Catalogue and certain Details of Bethany College. Session First. July 4th, 1842. *Bethany, Va.* 1842. 12mo, pp. 11. Continued. H. 5066

BETHEL COLLEGE. Sixth Annual Catalogue of the Officers and Students of Bethel College, Russellville, Kentucky. For the Collegiate Year 1859–'60. ... *Nashville, Tenn.* 1860. 8vo, pp. 32. H. 5067

BETHEL FEMALE COLLEGE. Catalogue of Bethel Female College, Hopkinsville, Ky., for the [First] Collegiate Year ending June 10, 1858. *Hopkinsville, Ky.* 1858. 8vo, pp. 15. H.

BETHEL (J.) The Living Temple: a Brief Memoir of Jane Bethel. ... *Philadelphia Sunday-School Union.* [1854.] 24mo, pp. 83. Woodcuts. H. 5069

"This is a real life and not a picture."

BETHEL. Official Report of the Battle of Bethel, June 10th, 1861. *Richmond.* 1862. 8vo, pp. 31. B. 5070

BETHEL TEMPERANCE SOCIETY. An Account of a Temperance Meeting, held in the Seamen's Bethel, Boston, being the Anniversary of the Bethel Temperance Society, December 25, 1836. ... [*Boston.* n. d.] 12mo, pp. 24. H. 5071

Minutes of the Bethel Association, held at the Baptist Church, on Jamey's Creek, Spartanburgh County, South Carolina, begun on Saturday, August 10, 1793, with their Circular Letter. [*Charlestown.* 1793.] 4to. 5072

Other Minutes were published in 1791, and sequent years.

BETHENCOURT. (Galien). *See* Bontier.

BETHENCOURT. Traicté de la Navigation et des Voyages de Descouverte et Conquestes modernes et principalement des Francois, avec une exacte et particuliere description des toutes les Isles Canaries, les preuves du temps de la conqueste d'icelles et la Genealogie des Bethencourts et Braquemons. *Paris.* 1629–30. 8vo. Portrait by Moncornet. 5073

BETHUNE (A. N.) Sermon on the duty of Loyalty. By Rev. A. N. Bethune. *Cobourg.* 1849. 8vo, pp. 16. 5074

BETHUNE. Thoughts upon the Clergy Reserve question as now agitated: in a Letter to the Hon. R. Baldwin, H. M's. Attorney General, U. C. By Rev. A. N. Bethune. *Toronto.* 1850. 8vo, pp. 16. 5075

BETHUNE (G. W.) The Claims of our Country on its Literary Men. An Oration before the Phi Beta Kappa Society of Harvard University, July 19, 1849. By George W. Bethune. *Cambridge: John Bartlett.* 1849. 8vo, pp. 52. H. 5076

BETHUNE. Discourse on the Death of W. H. Harrison, late President of the United States. By Geo. W. Bethune. *Philadelphia.* 1841. 8vo, pp. 22. 5077

BETHUNE. A Discourse on the Duty of a Patriot, with some allusion to the Life and Death of Andrew Jackson. ... By George W. Bethune. *Philadelphia.* 1845. 8vo, pp. 36. 5078

BETHUNE. The Duties of Educated Men; an Oration before the Literary Societies of Dickinson College, Carlisle, Pa., July, 1843. By George W. Bethune ... . *Philadelphia: the Societies.* 8vo, pp. 40. H. 5079

BETHUNE. Memoirs of Mrs. Joanna Bethune. By her Son, the Rev. George W. Bethune, D.D. With an Appendix, containing Extracts from the Writings of Mrs. Bethune. *New York: Harper & Brothers.* 1863. 12mo, pp. 250. 2 Woodcuts. 5080

BETHUNE. Orations and Occasional Discourses by George W. Bethune, D.D. *New-York: George P. Putnam;* [also] *London.* 1850. 12mo, pp. viii, 428. H. 5081

BETHUNE. The Prospects of Art in the United States. An Address ... May 1840. By George W. Bethune. ... *Philadelphia: J. Clark, Printer.* 1840. 8vo, pp. 45. 5082

BETHUNE. Reasons for preferring a Union with the Reformed Dutch Church of North America. A Discourse preached at the Installation of the Rev. John Gosman, D.D. As Pastor of the Second Reformed Dutch Church, Philadelphia. By George W. Bethune ... . *Philadelphia.* 1836. 8vo, pp. 24. H. 5083

BETHUNE. The Relation of the Sunday-school System to our Christian Patriotism. Annual Sermon, in behalf of the American Sunday-School Union. Delivered at Philadelphia, May 16, 1847. By Geo. W. Bethune ... . *Philadelphia.* [n. d.] 12mo, pp. 26. H. 5084

BETHUNE. ... A Sermon ... February 3d, 1839 on ... the Death of Stephen Van Rensselaer. By Geo. W. Bethune. ... *Philadelphia.* 1839. 8vo, pp. 24. H. 5085

Also: "A Sermon on our Liberties. 1835," and other sermons and discourses, and "Lays of Love and Faith," with other fugitive poems.

BETHUNE (J.) Letter to the Parishioners of Christ's Church, respecting a Tract intituled: "Lent Usages." *Montreal.* 1847. 8vo, pp. 8. 5086

BETHUNE. Sermon on the occasion of the Death of the late Chief Justice Reid. By Rev. John Bethune. *Montreal.* 1847. 8vo, pp. 17. 5087

BETHUNE. A Sermon preached in 1852, on the Occasion of the Primary Visitation of the Right Reverend Francis Fulford, Lord Bishop of Montreal. By Rev. J. Bethune. *Montreal.* 1852. 8vo, pp. 21. 5088

Betoog over het nadeel eener belasting op den publiek verkoop van koloniale en buitenlandsche producten. *Middelburg.* 1818. 8vo. 5089

Betrachtungen über den gegensärtigen Zustand, etc. *See* [Hilliard d'Auberteuil.]

Betrachtungen ueber das Laenderei-Vertheilungs-Gesetz und die Colonisation in Brasilien. *Rio de Janeiro.* 1854. 4to, pp. 8.

BETTENCOURT (José de sá). Memória sobre a plantaçao dos Algodœs, e sua exportaçao. *Lisboa.* 1798. 8vo. 5091

First printed in the Brazilian Journal "O Auxiliador," Tom. IX. No. 9. *See* Varnhagen's Brasil, II. 284; Silva, V. 118.

BETTINGER (J. B.) *See* Guide.

BETTLE (J.). Extracts from the Memorandums of Jane Bettle [of Pennsylvania], with a Short Memoir respecting her. Reprinted from the American Edition. *London: C. Gilpin.* 1845. 12mo, 4 sheets. 5092

BETTONI (Nicolas). Discours et faits mémorables du général La Fayette. [Prospectus.] *Paris: Bettoni.* 1834. 8vo, 2 l.

There were to be two editions,—one in 8vo, with three portraits (and also with fifteen portraits), and one in 12mo.

BETTRIDGE (W.) A Brief History of the Church in Upper Canada, with an exhibition of its spiritual wants, and Notes on the Clergy Reserves Question. By William Bettridge, Rector of Woodstock, U. C. *London: Groombridge.* 1838. 8vo, pp. 143. C. 5094

BETTS (Samuel R.) District Court of the United States for the Southern District of New York. The United States *vs.* the Bark Springbok and her Cargo. In Prize. Opinion of the Court, by Judge Betts. *New-York.* 1863. 8vo, pp. 36. H.

BETTS. District Court ... [as above]. The United States *vs.* the Schooner Stephen Hart and her Cargo. In Prize. Opinion of the Court, by Judge Betts. *New-York: John W. Amerman, Printer.* 1863. 8vo, pp. 58. H. 5096

BETTS. District Court ... [as above]. The United States *vs.* the Steamer Peterhoff and her Cargo. In Prize. Opinion of the Court, by Judge Betts. With an Appendix, containing the Opinions of Judge Marvin, in the District Court of the United States for the Southern District of Florida, in the cases of the Dolphin and the Pearl. *New-York: John W. Amerman, Printer.* 1864. 8vo, pp. 116. H. 5097

BETTS (W.) The Causes of the Prosperity of New-York. An Anniversary Address delivered before the St. Nicholas Society of New-York, December 3d, 1850. By William Betts, LL. D. ... *New-York: Stanford and Swords.* 1851. 8vo, pp. 27, (1). H. 5098

BETTZIECH-BETA (H.) Benjamin Franklin. Sein Leben, Denken und Wirken. Von Heinr. Bettziech-Beta. *Leipzig: F. A. Brockhaus.* 1853. 8vo, 2 l., pp. 108. (Unterhaltende Belehrungen, 18. Bändchen.) 5099

BEUCKELAER (C.) Spiegel voor de Jeucht, daer in Oude en Jonghe konnen sien de wreede Tyrannijen, en moordadigheden ghepleeght in meest alle de deelen vande Wereldt, dic alleen in Hoogh-Duytslandt ... maer oock in West-Indien ... en insonderheyt in de Valleyen van Piemont ... Door Cornelis Beuckelear ... . *Middelburg: Joh. de Somer.* 1664. 4to. 5100

BEUDIN. Relatio triplex | de rebvs indicis: | I R. P. Cornelij Beudinij, dicti | Godinez, martyrium. | II. Caaiguarum gentis mores, | cœpta conuersio. | III R. P. Adriani Knudde, dicti | Crespi, Elogium. | *Antverpiæ | Apud Iacobvm Mevrsivm | An.* CIↃ IↃCLIV. | 16mo, pp. 70. Portrait of Cornelius Beudin. 5101

This rare collection includes: I. (pp. 7–31.) Elogium R. P. Cornelii Beudin dicti Godinez Gravelingani Belgæ e Societate Jesu, in Mexicana Provincia à barbaris in odium fidei interfecti. Anno CIↃ. IↃ CL, IV Junij. II. (pp. 32–47.) Relatio de Caaiguarum gente, cœpta ad fidem adduci, ex litteris R. P. Nicolai del Techo, alias du Toict, Insulensis, datis ex Residentiâ S. Mariæ Maioris ad Uruaicam fluvium provinciæ Paraquariæ, anno 1651. III. (pp. 48–70.) Elogium R. P. Adriani Knudde dicti Crespi, Brugensis Belgæ, e Societate Jesu insignis operarii in missione Paraquariensi, ibique defuncti an. 1651, Februarij 25, Hispanice scriptum à R. P. Nicolao del Techo, Latine ex autographo versum. *See* Backer, II. 646.

BEUGHEM (Cornelius van). Bibliographia Historica, Chronologica & Geographica Novissima ... sive Conspectus primus. Catalogi Librorum ... quotquot ... ab Anno ... MDCLI. per Universam Europam, in quavis Lingua ... Aut Novi aut Emendatiores & Auctiores Typis prodierunt. Opera ... Corneli à Beughem ... *Amstelædami: Apud Jansonio-Waesbergios.* 1685. 12mo, 8 l., pp. 788. 5102

This early bibliography contains notices of books relating to America.

BEUKMA (K. Jz.) Brieven van K. Jz. Beukma ... verhuisd naar de Vereenigde Staten van Noord-Amerika, in den Jare 1835, aan deszelfs achtergelaten familie in de provincie Groningen. *Groningen: W. Zuidema.* 1835. Map and Plate. + *Groningen:* [*Ibid.*] 1836. 2 vols., 8vo. 5103

BEULLOCK. Le Mexique en 1823. *See* Bullock (W.)

BEVAN (M. L.) Report of the Bank of the United States, to the Committee of Ways and Means of the House of Representatives, January 28, 1833. [Signed Matthew L. Bevan, Chairman. n. p. n. d.] 8vo, pp. 50. B. 5104

BEVAN (W.) The Operation of the Apprenticeship System in the British Colonies. By Rev. William Bevan. A State-

ment adopted by the Liverpool Antislavery Society, Dec. 19, 1837. *Liverpool.* 1838. 8vo, pp. 61. M. 5105

BEVAN. The Pilgrim Fathers, the Defenders of the Congregational Order, the true Successors of the Apostles, the first Anglican Reformers. A Lecture by the Rev. William Bevan. *London: Partridge & Okey.* 1854. 8vo, pp. 28. 5106

BEVANS. Sketch of the Trial of William Bevans, for the Murder of Peter Lunstrum, on board the United States' Ship Independence, On the 6th of November, 1816. *Boston: Thomas G. Bangs.* 1816. 8vo, pp. 39. H. 5107

BEVERIDGE (J.) Epistolæ Familiares et Alia Quædam Miscellanea. Familiar Epistles, and other miscellaneous pieces, Wrote originally in Latin Verse, By John Beveridge, A.M. Professor of Languages in the Academy of Philadelphia. To which are added several Translations into English Verse, by different Hands. ... *Philadelphia: Printed for the Author by William Bradford.* M, DCC, LXV. 8vo, pp. xi, 88. P. 5108

[BEVERIDGE.] In Obitum Magnæ Spei Juvenis, Nathanaelis Smiberti. *Hartford.* 1757. 8vo, pp. 4. M. 5109

BEVERIDGE (W.) A Sermon Preached before the Society for the Propagation of the Gospel in Foreign Parts ... Feby 21, 1706–7. By the Right Reverend William Lord Bishop of St. Asaph. *London: Joseph Downing.* 1707. 4to, pp. 24. 5110

BEVERLEY *or* BEVERLY (John.) Unio Reformantium sive Examen Hoornbecki de Independentismo ... . Per Johannem Beverley ... . *Londini: S. Thompson.* 1659. 8vo, pp. (16), 1 l. folded, 185 [183]. B. 5111

Contains numerous references to American authors, especially to Cotton and Norton.

B[EVERLEY] (R[obert]). The History and Present State of Virginia, In Four Parts. I. The History of the First Settlement of Virginia, and the Government thereof, to the present Time. II. The Natural Productions and Conveniences of the Country, suited to Trade and Improvement. III. The Native Indians, their Religion, Laws, and Customs, in War and Peace. IV. The present State of the Country, as to the Polity of the Government, and the Improvements of the Land. By a Native and Inhabitant of the Place. *London: Printed for R. Parker, at the Unicorn, under the Piazza's of the Royal-Exchange.*

MDCCV. 8vo, Frontispiece, 6 l., (Text) pp. 104; 40; 64; 83, folded sheet after p. 50, (Tables and Errata) pp. 16 and 2 l. 14 Copperplates. H. 5112

Contains frontispiece of the arms of Virginia, and this title: "The History and Present State of Virginia. By R: B: gent:" It has also fourteen fine engravings, by Gribelin, copied from De Bry's Latin edition of Hariot's "Admiranda Narratio." Reprinted with the following title:

[BEVERLEY.] The History of Virginia, In Four Parts. I. The History of the First Settlement of Virginia, and the Government thereof, to the Year 1706. II. The natural Productions and Conveniences of the Country, suited to Trade and Improvement. III. The Native Indians, their Religion, Laws, and Customs, in War and Peace. IV. The Present State of the Country, as to the Polity of the Government, and the Improvements of the Land, the 10th of June 1720. By a Native and Inhabitant of the Place. The Second Edition revis'd and enlarg'd by the Author. *London: Printed for B. and S. Tooke in Fleetstreet; F. Fayram and J. Clarke at the Royal-Exchange, and T. Bickerton in Pater-Noster Row,* 1722. 8vo, Frontispiece, Title, (Preface) 3 l., pp. 284, (Table) 12 l. 14 Plates. C., H. 5113

Some copies have the imprint: *London: Printed for F. Fayram and J. Clarke at the Royal-Exchange, and T. Bickerton in Pater-Noster Row,* 1722. The dedication in the first edition of 1705 is omitted here, and the preface is entirely different, and there are many suppressions and additions. The author spells his name Bevereley on page 72. *See* Jefferson's Notes on Virginia, Ques. 222. It was again reprinted as below:

BEVERLEY. The History of Virginia, in Four Parts. I. The History of the First Settlement of Virginia, and the Government thereof, to 1706. II. The Natural Productions and Conveniences of the Country, suited to Trade and Improvement. III. The Native Indians, their Religion, Laws, and Customs, in War and Peace. IV. The Present State of the Country, as to the Polity of the Government, and the Improvements of the Land, the 10th of June, 1720. By Robert Beverly ... . Reprinted from the Author's Second Revised Edition, London, 1722. With an Introduction by Charles Campbell, Author of the "Colonial History of Virginia." *Richmond, Va.: J. W. Randolph.* 1855. 8vo, pp. xx, 264. B. 5114

[BEVERLEY.] Histoire de la Virginie; contenant, I. L'Histoire du premier Etablissement dans la Virginie, & de son Gouvernement jusques-à-présent. II. Les Productions naturelles & les Commodités du Païs, avant que les Anglois y négociassent, & l'améliorassent. III. La Religion, les Loix, & les Coûtumes des Indiens Naturels, tant dans la Guerre, que dans la Paix. IV.

L'Etat present du Païs, tant à l'égard de la Police, que de l'Amelioration du Païs. Par un Auteur natif & habitant du Païs. Traduite de l'Anglois. Enrichie de Figures. *Imprimé à Orleans, & se vend à Paris, Chez Pierre Ribou* ... M DCCVII. 12mo, (engraved Title) 1 l., (Title and Preface) 4 l., pp. 416, folded sheet, (Table and Aprobation) 9 l. 14 Plates. H. 5115

There is a ship on the engraved title-page. Another edition of this date reads:

[BEVERLEY.] Historie de la Virginie, [as before.] *Amsterdam: Chez Thomas Lombrail.* M D CC VII. 12mo, (engraved Title) (6), pp. 432, 1 l. folded, (Tables) 8 l. 14 Plates. H. 5116

[BEVERLEY.] Histoire de la Virginie, [as in No. 5115]. *Amsterdam: Claude Jordan.* 12mo. 5117

The same impression as the preceding, with a new title-page. I have seen in English catalogues, editions dated 1718 and 1722; probably errors as to date. "A work of considerable merit, particularly relative to the numerous Indian tribes, then resident in the State, but now extirpated or greatly diminished."—PINKERTON. Beverley is the best authority concerning the particular subjects delineated in his quaint and agreeable pages; and his work affords the most vivid, comprehensive, instructive, and entertaining picture of Virginia at the date of his writing that is to be found. *See* N. A R., I. 158–161.

BEVERLEY (T.) A Discourse upon Evangelical Repentance unto Salvation not to be Repented of, upon the late Solemn Occasion of the late Dreadful Earthquake in Jamaica. 1693. Sm. 8vo. 5118

[BEVERLEY (William).] An Abridgment of the Publick Laws of Virginia, in force and use, June 10, 1720. Second Edition. *London: Printed for F. Fayram & J. Clarke.* 1728. 12mo, 4 l., pp. 184, Index, 8 l. C. 5119

BEVERLY, *Mass.* Catalogue of the Public Library of ... Beverly. *Salem: T. J. Hutchinson.* 1856. 8vo, pp. 38. + Supplement. [n. p. 1860.] 8vo, pp. 8. H. 5120

Catalogue of the Public Library, of the Town of ... Beverly. *Boston: printed by C. P. Moody.* 1862. 8vo, pp. 108. H. 5121

Regulations of Beverly Second Social Library. *Salem: printed by Joshua Cushing.* 1806. Sm. 8vo, pp. 21. H. 5122

"I. The Library shall contain no novels, romances, nor plays; but consist principally of the serious productions of Calvinistic Divines."

Remarks on the Recent Ordination at Beverly. By "Another Layman." *Salem: Warwick Palfray, Jun. Printer.* 1824. 8vo, pp. 24. H. 5123

Also: "Annual Report of the School Committee," "Annual Report of the Receipts, Expenditures, &c."

BEY (Ali), *pseudon.* *See* [Knapp (Samuel L.)]

BEYARD (Nicholas). *See* Bayard (Nicholas).

BEYER (E.) Beyträge zur Kenntniss des gegenwärtigen Zustandes der Colonie Surinam. *Nürnberg: Schrag.* 1823. 8vo.

BEYER (Ed.) Album of Virginia: or the Old Dominion, Illustrated. *Richmond.* 1857. Oblong folio. 40 Views. 5125

BEYER (Mor.) Das Auswanderungsbuch oder Führer und Rathgeber bei der Auswanderung nach Nordamerika und Australien, mit Berücksichtigung von Texas und Kalifornien, in Bezug auf Ueberfahrt, Ankunft und Ansiedelung nebst einer Schilderung der geographischen, politischen und geselligen Zustandes jener Länder ... . Grossentheils nach eigner Auffassung während eines zwölfjährigen Aufenthalts in Amerika ... . *Leipzig: Baumgärtner.* 1846. 8vo, pp. xii, 236. Woodcut + Zweite unveränderte Auflage. 1846. + Dritte verbesserte und stark vermehrte Auflage. *Leipzig: Baumgärtner.* 1850. 8vo, pp. xii, 297. 5126

This is the title of the third edition; that of the first is apparently much shorter, and contains no mention of Australia and California.

BEYER. Het boek der landverhuizers, of gids en raadsman bij de verhuizing naar Noord-Amerika, ten opzigte van den overtogt, de aankomst, de vestiging aldaar ... . Naar het Hoogduitsch vrij bewerkt ... . Met houtsneêfiguren. *Amsterdam: Hoogkamer en Co.* 1846. 8vo. 5127

BEYER, KOCH (Louis), *and* KOCH (Albert). Lebensbilder und Reisen in Amerika. Für Auswanderer und alle Interessenten der Zustände und Verhältnisse in Nordamerika herausgegeben von Mor. Beyer. Neue Ausgabe. *Leipzig: Müller.* 1850. 2 vols., 12mo, pp. x, 447; iv, 437. 5128

First edition, 1839.

BEYER *and* KOCH (L.) Amerikanische Reisen. *Leipzig: Imm. Müller.* 1839. 4 vols., 12mo, 38 sheets. 5129

Beylage zum 150ten Stück des Philadelphischen Staatsboten. Protestation gegen die Bestellung Herrn Benjamin Franklins zu einem Agentem fur diese Provinz. Folio, pp. 4. (Oct. 20–Nov. 5, 1764.) P. 5130

Beytrag zur Geschichte von Paraguay. *See* [Nusdorfer (B.)]

BEZERRA E LIMA (Joao Ant.) Elogio do padre D. Luiz Caetano de Lima. *Lisboa.* 1759. 4to, 19 l. 5131

Bezono (H.) *See* Benzoni (H.)

Biancani (Giuseppe). Sphæra Mundi, seu Cosmographia Demonstrativa, ac facili Methodo tradita: in qua totius mundi Fabrica, una cum novis, Tychonis, Kepleri, Galiliæ, aliorumque Astronomorum inventis continetur, etc. Accesserunt Brevis Introductio ad Geographiam, Apparatus ... . *Bononiæ: typis Sebastiani Bonomii.* 1620. 4to. + *Mutinæ: typis Juliani Cassiani.* 1630. Folio. + [*Ibid.*] 1635. Folio. + [*Ibid.*] *Typis And. Cassiani.* 1653. Folio. 5132

Bianchetti (Giuseppe). Elogio a Cristoforo Colombo. Letta nell' Ateneo di Treviso. *Venezia: Franc. Andreola.* 1820. 4to, pp. 27. 5133

[Bianchi (Isidoro).] *See* Carli (G. C.)

Biard (François). Deux années au Brésil, par F. Biard. Ouvrage illustré de 180 vignettes dessinées par. E. Riou, d'après les croquis de M. Biard. *Paris: Hachette et Cie.* 1862. 8vo, pp. 684. 5134

Biard. Voyage au Brésil par François Biard. L'Amazone. *Berlin: Janke.* 1863. 8vo, pp. 146. (Muyden, G. van, and Rudolph, Ludwig. Collection des auteurs français, II. Serie, 6., 7. Lief.) 5135

Biard (Pierre). Relation de la Nouvelle France, de ses terres, naturel du païs et de ses habitans; item du voyage des pères Jésuites au dictes contrées et de ce qu'ils y on faict jusques à leur prinse par les Anglois. Par Pierre Biard, de Grenoble, Jésuite. *Lyon: Louis Muguet.* 1612. 16mo. + *Lyon: L. Muguet.* 1616. 12mo. 5136

Biarnès (Adolphe). Le droit des gens La France et les Yankees. Par Adolphe Biarnès. ... *Nantes: imprimerie V. de Courmaceul.* 1866. 8vo, pp. 98, Errata (1). H. 5137

Biart (L.) Le Bizco. Une passion au Mexique Par Lucien Biart. *Paris: Hetzel.* 1867. 18mo, pp. 353. + Seconde édition. *Paris: Hetzel.* 1867. 18mo, pp. 354. + Troisième édition. [*Ibid.*] 5138

Biart. Les mexicaines, poésies. *Paris: imprimerie de Chaix.* 1853. 18mo. 5139

Biart. Le Mexique d'hier et le Mexique de demain. Par Lucien Biart. *Paris: E. Dentu.* 1865. 8vo, pp. 34. 5140

Biart. La terre chaude, scènes de mœurs mexicaines. Par Lucien Biart. *Paris: Claye.* 1862. 18mo, pp. 337. 5141

Biart. La terre tempérée, scenes, de la vie mexicaine. Par Lucien Biart. *Paris: Hetzel.* 1866. 18mo, pp. iv, 311. 5142

[Bias (C.)] The Sweet Chalybeate Springs [Virginia], commonly known as the Red Sweet Springs, with a Synopsis of the Routes by which they are reached ... . *Philadelphia: J. B. Lippincott & Co.* 1860. 12mo, pp. 24. Lithograph. H. 5143

Bibaud (François Marie Uncas Maximilien). Bibliothèque Canadienne. *See* Bibliothèque Canadienne.

Bibaud. Biographie des Sagamos illustres de l'Amérique Septentrionale. Précédée d'un index de l'histoire fabuleuse de ce continent. Par F. M. Maximilien Bibaud ... . *Montréal: imprimerie de Lovell et Gibson.* 1848. 8vo, pp. 309. B., C. 5145

Bibaud. Catéchisme de l'histoire du Canada. Par Maximilien Bibaud. *Montréal.* 1853. 32mo. 5146

Bibaud. Le Charlatanisme dans l'histoire, ou revue critique de l'histoire du Canada de F. X. Garneau. *Montréal.* 1855.

Bibaud. Commentaires sur les Lois du Bas-Canada, ou Conferences de l'Ecole de Droit liée au Collége des RR. PP. Jésuites, suivis d'une notice Historique. *Montréal.* 8vo, pp. 595. 5148

Bibaud. Dictionnaire historique des hommes illustres du Canada et de l'Amérique. Par Bibaud, Jeune ... . *Montréal: Bibaud et Richer.* 1857. 8vo, pp. 389. 5149

Bibaud. Les Institutions de l'Histoire du Canada ou annales canadiennes jusqu'à l'an MDCCCXIX, suivies D'un précis jusqu'à nos jours, d'un tableau historique des progrès, et biographique des hommes illustres du Canada, et accompagnées de synchronismes de l'histoire générale de l'Amérique. Livre II, où l'on développe l'économie de la constitution de la France Septentrionale. Par Bibaud, jeune ... . *Montréal: imprimé par Senécal et Daniel.* 1855. 8vo, pp. 440. H. 5150

Livre I. was to be published hereafter.

Bibaud. La Confédération du Sud. *Montréal.* 1864. 8vo, pp. 119. 5151

Bibaud. Les Machabées Canadiens. *Montréal.* 1859. 8vo, pp. 28. 5152

Bibaud. Opuscules. *Montréal.* 1857. 12mo, pp. 70.

"Cette brochure nous est venue avec la continuation du 'Dictionnaire Biographique,' et du 'Supplément aux Travaux sur l'Histoire du Canada,' par le même auteur, ouvrages dont nous parlerons très au long lorsqu'ils seront terminés. Les opuscules se composent d'essais lus à l' 'Œuvre des bons livres' ou à la 'Société Philotechnique.' Ils ont pour titre, 1° Système politique des Jésuites au Paraguay, 2° Droits des gens 3° Géologie, 4° Le Code Napoléon." — *Journ. de l'Inst. Pub. L. C.*

Bibaud. Le Panthéon Canadien, (Choix de Biographies.) Dans lequel on a introduit les hommes les plus célèbres des autres Colonies Britanniques. *Montréal.* 1858. 8vo, pp. 364.

Bibaud. Tableau Historique des Progrès Matériels et Intellectuels du Canada. *Montreal.* 1858. 8vo, pp. 50. 5155

Bibaud. Tablettes Historiques Canadiennes. *Montréal.* 1859. 8vo, pp. 39. + Seconde édition. *Montréal.* 1861. 8vo, pp. 46. 5156

Bibaud. La société historique de Montreal. *vs* Maximilien Bibaud. [n. p.] 12mo, pp. 28. H. 5157

Bibaud (Michael). Epitres, Satires, Chansons, Epigrammes, et autres pièces de vers. *Montréal.* 1830. 12mo. 5158

Bibaud. Histoire du Canada, sous la domination française. Par M. Bibaud. *Montréal: John Jones.* 1837. 12mo, pp. 370. B. + Seconde Edition. *Montréal.* 1843. 8vo. 5159

Bibaud. Historie du Canada et des Canadiens sous la domination anglaise. Par Michel Bibaud. *Montréal.* 1844. 2 vols., 8vo. 5160

Bibb (George M.) An Exposition of the Meaning of the Clause in the Constitution of the United States, that "No State shall pass any *ex post facto* Law." Blair *vs.* Williams, and Lapsley *vs.* Brashear. [n. d.] 8vo, pp. 24. 5161

Bibb. Speech of the Honorable George M. Bibb of Kentucky: delivered in the Senate of the United States, April 28, 1834, on the President's Protest. *Washington.* 1834. 8vo. S.

Relates to the removal of the deposites. Also: Opinion in the Case of Applegate [*et al.*] *vs.* Lexington and Ohio Railroad Company, Louisville Chancery Court, November, 1838. *Louisville.* [n. d.] 8vo, pp. 31. — An Oration commemorative of Laying the Corner-stone of the College of the Louisville Medical Institute, Feb. 22, 1838. [*Louisville.*] 1838. 8vo, pp. 29. B.

Bibb (H.) Life of an American Slave, by Himself. *New York.* 1849. 12mo. 5163

Bibelingoak. *Havniame: Missionscollegium.* 1849. 8vo, pp. 62.

An abstract of Bible history in the Greenland language, founded on the earlier work of Fabricius.

The | Holy Bible | Containing the Old and New | Testaments; | Newly translated out of the | Original Tongues: | And with the former | Translations | Diligently compared and revised. *Philadelphia: | Printed and Sold by R. Aitken ...* M. DCC. LXXX II. 12mo, 2 l., A[2] to Aaaa 5 in 12's, New Testament, A[2] to Dd in 6's. Not paged. 5165

"The first Bible printed in English in this country with an American imprint." — O'Callaghan. Concerning another, *see* Thomas' Hist. of Printing, I. 305.

Holy Bible translated from the Latin Vulgate: Diligently compared with the Hebrew, Greek, and other editions, in divers languages; And first published by the English College at Doway; Anno 1609. &c. *Phildelphia: Cary, Stewart & Co.* 1790.

The first Douay Bible, and believed to be the first *quarto* Bible in English printed in the United States. *See* O'Callaghan, page 35.

Holy Bible Abridged; or, the History of the Old and New Testament, illustrated with Notes, and adorned with Cuts, For the Use of Children. *Boston: for N. Coverly.* [1782]. Sm. 18mo, pp. 107. 5167

These early specimens of American woodcuts are rather coarse.

Holy Bible. *Philadelphia: Printed by W. Young.* 1790. 12mo, A to Ll, 12's, not paged. 5168

The Holy Bible Abridged; or, the History of the Old and New Testament. Illustrated with Notes and adorned with Cuts. For the Use of Children, &c. *New York: Hodge, Allen & Campbell.* 1790. 24mo, pp. 180. 5169

The woodcuts are coarse, and include one engraved by Maverick, in his ninth year.

Holy Bible. *Trenton: Isaac Collins.* 1791. 4to, 4 l., Text, B to R[2]; Apocrypha, A to U; New Testament, etc., A[2] to Hh[2]; Concordance, A to I[4]. 5170

"The first Bible printed in New Jersey." — O'Callaghan.

Holy Bible. *Philadelphia: W. Young.* 1791–2. 2 vols., 18mo, not paged. 5171

The Holy Bible ... with the Apocrypha. ... With an Index. *Worcester: Isaiah Thomas.* MDCCXCI. 2 vols., folio, 2 l., pp. 460; Title, pp. 461–1012, and an Alphabetical Table. 50 Engravings and Woodcuts. H. 5172

"Other copies have been issued in one volume." — O'Callaghan.

The Holy Bible ... with the Apocrypha ... and ... an Index, and an Alphabetical Table Of all the Names ... . *Worcester: Isaiah Thomas.* MDCCXCI. 4to, pp. 1310. Plate. H. 5173

Holy Bible. *New York: Hodge & Campbell.* 1792. 4to, not paged. 5174

The same edition is announced with twenty copperplates.

Holy Bible. *New York: Hugh Gaine.* 1792. 12mo, not paged. 5175

"This Bible is said to have been imported by Gaine." — O'Callaghan.

Holy Bible. *Philadelphia: Wm. Young.* 1792. 18mo. 5176

Holy Bible ... with the Apocrypha. *Worcester: Isaiah Thomas.* 1793. 8vo, pp. 960; Apocrypha not paged. 5177

There was also an edition without the Apocrypha.

Holy Bible. *Trenton: Isaac Collins.* 1793. 8vo, not paged.

Holy Bible ... and the Apocrypha: With Marginal References. *Philadelphia: Berriman & Co.* 1796. Folio, B to 8z[2] not paged. 18 Plates. 5178

The same edition was printed with another title, and without plates.

Holy Bible Abridged, &c. With Cuts. The Second Worcester Edition. *Worcester: Thomas, Son, & Thomas.* 1796. 32mo, pp. 171, List of Books, 3. 5179

Holy Bible. *Worcester: Isaiah Thomas.* 1797. 12mo, A to Kk[11] in 12's, not paged. 5180

Holy Bible. *Worcester: Isaiah Thomas.* 1798. 12mo. + Same. *Worcester: Isaiah Thomas.* 1799. 12mo. 5181

"Thomas' 'Standing' edition of 1797, with a new date." — O'Callaghan.

Holy Bible ... with the Apocrypha. *Philadelphia: Printed for John Thompson and Abraham Small.* M.DCC.XCVIII. Folio, 2 l., B to 10F[2]; Apocrypha A to Ll[2]; New Testament, etc., A to 3T[2]. Frontispiece. 5182

"The first hot-pressed edition of the Bible printed in America." — O'Callaghan. A beautiful edition, and very well printed. The device on the title is the American

eagle below an open Bible; the whole surrounded by a lustre and fifteen stars. Vol. I. contains the Old Testament to the end of Psalms, with a handsome copperplate (*Baralet fecit.—Lausen sculp.*) Vol. II. contains the rest of the Old Testament, the Apocrypha (in italics, but with no separate title-page) and the New Testament, with a separate title-page; and concludes with the usual Scriptural tables, etc.; and some copies have a list of subscribers (two pages) at the end. The foregoing twenty numbers are believed to include all the American editions of the Bible in English printed before 1800. Further information respecting other American Bibles will be found in O'Callaghan's list of Bibles.

Holy Bible. *See* (Eliot) John.

Indian versions of parts of the Bible will generally be found under the name of the books, sometimes under the name of the translator, and occasionally under the initiatory word; this irregular arrangement has become necessary, as it was not my intention, at the commencement of this work, to include them. The index will generally indicate the location.

The Bible and the Sword; or, the Appointment of the General Fast Vindicated, in an Address to the Citizens of America, etc. *Baltimore.* 1812. 8vo. N. 5183

Bible Association of Friends in America: First Report. *Philadelphia.* 1830. 8vo. Continued. 5184

The Bible in the Army; a Statement of the Distribution of the Scriptures among the Military and Naval Forces of the Union, by the New York Bible Society, 1861. *New York: Bible Society.* 1862. 8vo, pp. 31. 5185

The Bible of Every Land. A History of the Sacred Scriptures in every Language and Dialect into which Translations have been made: Illustrated with Specimen Portions in Native Characters; Series of Alphabets; Coloured Ethnographical Maps, Tables, Indexes, etc. ... *London: Samuel Bagster.* [1848–51?] 4to, pp. lxiv, 3 l., 406, 1 l., pp. 12. Maps and Plates. H. + New Edition. *London.* [1860]. 4to. C. 5186

"American Languages," Map and pp. 359–393.

The Bible on the Present Crisis. The Republic of the United States, and its Counterfeit Presentment; the Slave Power of the Confederacy; the Copperhead Organization and the Knights of the Golden Circle; the Civil War in which they are involved; its Duration and Final Results, described in Daniel and the Revelations, and other Prophecies of the Old and New Testaments. *New York: Sinclair & Tousey.* 1863. 8vo, pp. 104. H. 5187

The copyright is taken out by C. Bowen, who is perhaps the author.

Bible View of Polygamy. [n. p. n. d.] 8vo, pp. 4. 5188

A defence of Mormonism, signed Mizpah.

Bible View of Slavery; or, Bishop Hopkins reviewed. By a Layman. [n. p.] 1864. 8vo, pp. 8. H. 5189

Bible View of Slavery reconsidered. A Letter to the Rt. Rev. Bishop Hopkins. Second Edition, enlarged. [Signed, Biblicus.] *Philadelphia: H. B. Ashmead.* 1863. 8vo, pp. 15.

Biblia, | Das ist: | Die Heilige Schrift | Altes und Neues | Testaments, | Nach der Deutschen Uebersetzung | D. Martin Luthers, | Mit jedes Capitels kurtzen Summarien, auch | beygefügten vielen und richtigen Parllelen [*sic*]; | Nebst einem Anhang | Des dritten und vierten Buchs Esrä und des | dritten Buchs der Maccabäer. *Germantown: Gedruckt bey Christoph Saur.* 1743. 4to, 2 l., pp. 995, (Das Neue Testament) 277 (including a title-page), (Register) 3, (Kurtzer Begriff, etc.) 4. H. 5191

After Eliot's Indian version, this is the first Bible printed in this country, and it is the first in a European language. It is no part of the design of this work to state the reason; it may, however, be briefly observed, that the Bibles could be produced more cheaply abroad, and that their publication in the Colonies was supposed to be interdicted by the patents to the Royal Printers. The type from which the Bible was printed was imported from Frankfort-on-the-Main. One thousand copies were printed, and bound in wooden boards. The volume is very scarce. *See* "Hist. Mag.," Nov., 1859; III. 325–328.

Biblia, das ist heilige Schrift, Altes und Neues Testaments, nach der teutschen Uebersetzung D. M. Luthers. ... *Germantown: Gedruckt bey Christoph Saur.* 1763. 4to, 2 l., pp. 992; (New Testament) 277, (Register) 3. 5192

Biblia, Das Ist: Die ganze Heilige Schrift [etc.] *Philadelphia: zu finden bey Ernst Baisch.* 1775. 8vo, 16 l., pp. 909; New Testament, 265, Anweizung, etc., 4. 5193

D. O'Callaghan infers, from the imprint, that this edition was imported in sheets from Germany.

Biblia, Das ist: Die ganze Göttliche Heilige Schrift ... . Dritte Auflage. *Germantown: Christoph Saur.* 1776. 4to, 2 l., pp. 992; (New Testament) 277 (including a title), (Register) 3.

Of this edition three thousand copies were printed, but the greater part was used for cartridge paper at the battle of Germantown. Sowe doubting the capacity of the Colonists to secure their independence, removed to Philadelphia when in possession by the British; his estate was confiscated by the Colonists, and his books were sold.

The Bibliographical Miscellany. Nos. 1–5. *London: John Petheram.* 1853–54. 8vo. 5195

Contains "Voyage of Sir Thomas Button for the Discovery of a North-West Passage in 1612," etc.

Bibliographical Tracts. Number One. Spurious Reprints of Early Books. *Boston.* 1865. 4to, pp. 19. H. 5196

"From the Boston Daily Advertiser of March 24, 1865. With Additions and Corrections." This is a caustic and deserved critique, by Mr. Charles Deane, on a reprint of Mather and Calef on the Salem Witchcraft. 131 copies printed, a few of which are on large paper. No. II. has not yet appeared.

La Biblioteca Americana, por una sociedad de Americanos. Vol. I. *Paris: H. Bossange.* 1823. 5197

"Appears to be all that was published." — Rich, II. 155.

Biblioteca Peruana, 1861–4. *See* Fuentes (Manuel A.)

Bibliotheca Americana; or, a Chronological Catalogue of the most Curious and Interesting Books, Pamphlets, State Papers, &c. upon the Subject of North and South America, from the Earliest Period to the Present, in Print and Manuscript; for which Research has been made in the British Musæum, and the most Celebrated Public and Private Libraries, Reviews, Catalogues, &c. With an Introductory Discourse on the Present State of Literature in those Countries. *London: Printed for J. Debrett* [etc.] M DCC LXXXIX. 4to, 2 l, pp. 271, Errata, 1 l.

This book, which has been variously ascribed to Dalrymple, Homer, Long, and with more probability, by Homer himself, to Reid, was the fullest English work on the subject up to its date; but its complicated arrangements, errors of date, unintelligible abbreviations, and frequent repetitions mar its utility. Some of the remarks in the introduction are curious, if not true. The errata, if all printed, would fill a dozen pages. *See* M. R., II. 474; Rich, I. 354.

Bibliotheca Americana. A Catalogue of Books relating to the History and Literature of America. ... Sold by Puttick and Simpson. *London. March,* M.DCCC.LXI. 8vo, pp. vi, 273.

Also on large paper, royal 8vo. This catalogue contains 2415 lots, with collations, etc., and will be useful to the collector. It is, in fact, an *abridgment* of Stevens' "Historical Nuggets," although the latter was not *published* till 1862.

Bibliotheca Americana. *See* Bartlett (John Russell) and Smith (John Russell).

Bibliotheca Americana Vetustissima. *See* [Harrisse (H.).]

Bibliothecæ Americanæ Primordia. *See* [Kennett (White).]

Bibliotheca Americo-Septentrionalis. *See* [Warden (D. B.)]

Bibliotheca Inlustris. *See* Kingsborough (*Lord*).

Bibliotheca Mexicana Catalogue d'une collection de livres rares (principalement sur l'histoire et la linguistique) réunie au Mexique par M. *** attaché a la cour de l'empereur Maximilien dont la vente se fera Le Mardi 3 Novembre 1868 ... *Paris: librairie Tross.* 1868. 8vo, pp. (vi), 47. 5200

Bibliotheca Sacra and Theological Review. ... Vol. I. *London: Wiley and Putnam.* 1844. 8vo. Continued. H. 5201

Bibliotheca Sacra. Index to the Bibliotheca Sacra and American Bibilical Repository, Volumes I. to XIII. containing an Index of Subjects and Authors, a Topical Index, and a List of Scripture Texts. By W. F. Draper. *Andover: W. F. Draper.* 1857. 8vo, pp. 223, 13. H. 5202

The imprints of the different volumes vary. Andover, at which it has always been printed, appears on the title-page of all but the first volume. In Vols. VIII.–XIX., the title reads: Bibliotheca Sacra and American Biblical Repository, in XV.–XX., and Biblical Repository; after XX. these words are omitted. Many of the volumes contain valuable articles relating to this country.

Die Bibliothek für meine Kinder. Drittes Bändchen. Waldleben in Amerika. ... *Leipzig: O. Wigand.* 1848. 8vo, pp. 60. 10 Illustrations. 5203

Bibliothek klassischer Schriftsteller Nordamerika's. *Frankfurt: Sauerländer.* 1837–41. 12 vols., 16mo. 5204

Bibliothèque américaine, Contenant des Mémoires sur l'Agriculture, le Commerce, les Manufactures, les Mœurs et les Usages de l'Amérique; L'Analyse des Ouvrages scientifiques de ce pays, ainsi que de ceux des Européens qui y ont voyagé; Et des Extraits des journaux publiés en Amérique, sur tout ce qui peut intéresser le Commerçant et l'homme d'état; Par une Société de Savans et d'Hommes de Lettres. ... *Paris: H. Caritat, et Barrois fils.* 1807. 3 vols., 8vo. C. 5205

The first four numbers appeared under the title of "L'Amérique du Nord."

La Bibliothèque Canadienne, ou Miscellanées historiques, scientifiques, et littéraires. ... Tome II. M. Bibaud, editeur et proprietaire. *Montreal: De l'Imprimerie de J. Lane.* 1825–26. 8vo, pp. 240. H. 5206

After Vol. IX. continued as:

L'observateur, ci-devant La Bibliothèque Canadienne, journal

historique, littéraire et politique. ... Tome I. M. Bibaud, editeur et proprietaire. *Montreal: de l'imprimerie de Ludger Duvernay.* 1830. 8vo. H. 5207

At least one more volume was published.

Bibliothèque portative des voyages; traduite de l'anglais par MM. Henry et Breton. *Paris.* [v. d.] 42 vols., 18mo. With Plates. 5208

BIBRA (Ernst, *Baron* von). Die Algodon-Bay in Bolivien, naturhistorisch geschildert. ... *Wien.* 1853. Folio, pp. 42. 3 colored Plates. 5209

Separately published from the "Denkschriften d. k. Akad. d. Wiss.," math.-naturw. Classe, IV. 75–116. H.

BIBRA. Beiträge zur Naturgeschichte von Chile. ... *Wien: Gerold.* 1853. Large 4to, 1 l., pp. 70. 5 Plates, folio. 5210

Separately published from the "Denkschriften d. k. Akad. d. Wiss.," math.-naturw. Classe, V. 73–142. H.

BIBRA. Aus Chili, Peru und Brasilien. *Leipzig: Costenoble.* 1862. 3 vols., 8vo, pp. 845. 5211

BIBRA. Erinnerungen aus Süd-Amerika. *Jena: Costenoble.* 1861. 3 vols., 8vo, pp. xv, 718. 5212

BIBRA. Hoffnungen in Peru. Ein Roman. *Jena: Costenoble.* 1864. 3 vols., 8vo, pp. 720. 5213

BIBRA. Ein Juwel. Südamerikanischer Roman. *Jena: Costenoble.* 1863. 3 vols., 8vo, pp. 827. 5214

BIBRA. De zwarte diamant. Zuid-Amerikaansche roman. Uit het Hoogduitsch. *Amsterdam: B. Eisendrath.* 1866 [1865]. 2 vols., 8vo, pp. (2), 250; (2), 217. Lith. title-vignette. 5215

BIBRA. Reise in Südamerika. *Mannheim: Bassermann.* 1854. 2 vols., 8vo, 2 l., pp. 291; 1 l., pp. 357. 5216

BIBRA. Über Chile. (Aus d. Sitzungsberichten d. k. Akad. d. W.) *Nürnberg.* 1853. 8vo, pp. 12. 5217

BICKELL (R.) The West Indies as they are; or a Real Picture of Slavery: but more particularly as it exists in the Island of Jamaica. In Three Parts. With Notes. By the Rev. R. Bickell ... . *London: J. Hatchard and Son, and Lupton Relfe.* MDCCCXXV. 8vo, pp. xvi, 256. B., H., P. 5218

An extended notice of this work appeared as No. XIV. of a series of tracts, entitled "Negro Slavery," 8vo, pp. 133–148.

BICKER *and* HEEMSKERCK. *See* Ottsen (Hendrick).

BICKERSTAFF (Isaac), *pseudon.* A Letter from a Gentleman in Transilvania to his Friend in America, giving some account of the late disturbances that have happened in that Government, with some Remarks upon the political revolutions in the Majistracy, and the debates that happened about the Change. Humbly inscribed to Counsellor Quondam by his Friend Isaac Bickerstaff, of the Middle Temple. [Motto.] *New-York: printed in the Year* 1764. 12mo, pp. 12. P. 5219

Transilvania means Pennsylvania. The tract ridicules all parties.

BICKERSTAFF'S Boston Almanack, For ... 1768 ... . *Boston: John Mein.* [n. d.] 8vo, pp. (39). Continued. H. 5220

With the usual local information. The number for 1769 contains the celebrated "Liberty Song," which was the joint production of John Dickinson and Arthur Lee, with the music. *See* Tudor's "Life of Otis," page 322, 531–533. There is an almost entirely different version of the song in the number for 1770, from which it is copied by Lossing, in his "Field Book of the Revolution," I. 486, 487, where he also gives a fac-simile of the title-page. It is entitled "The Massachusetts Song of Liberty," and, acccording to Lossing, "is believed to have been written by Mrs. Mercy Warren."

[BICKFORD (James).] The Authentic Life of Mrs Mary Ann [Dunn] Bickford, who was murdered in ... Boston, on the 27th of October, 1845. ... Fourth Edition. *Boston.* [1846?] 12mo, pp. 23. H. 5221

BICKHAM (G.) The British Monarchy, or a New Chorographical Description of all the Dominions subject to the King of Great Britain, comprehending the British Isles, the American Colonies, ... By George Bickham. *London: G. Bickham.* 1748. Folio. 190 Plates. C. 5222

This work is entirely engraved. The American Colonies occupy twenty-one folios. There are copies dated 1749.

B[ICKHAM] (W[illiam] D.) Rosecrans' Campaign with the Fourteenth Army Corps, or the Army of the Cumberland: a Narrative of Personal Observations, with an Appendix, consisting of Official Reports of the Battle of Stone River. By "W. D. B.," Correspondent of the Cincinnati Commercial. *Cincinnati: Moore, Wilstach, Keys & Co.* 1863. 12mo, pp. 476. Map. B. 5223

BICKLEY (G. W. L.) Adalaska; or, the Strange and Mysterious Family of the Cave of Genreva. *Cincinnati.* 1853. 8vo. 5224

BICKLEY Address to the People of the Southern States. By George W. L. Bickley, President of the Knights of the Golden Circle. *Richmond.* 1860. 8vo. 5225

BICKLEY. History of the Settlement and Indian Wars of Tazewell County, Virginia. With A Map, Statistical Tables, and Illustrations. By Geo. W. L. Bickley ... . *Cincinnati: Morgan & Co.* 1852. 8vo, pp. 267. B., C. 5226

BIDDEFORD, *Me.* General Directory of Biddeford and Saco, with Business Directory of York County, for 1866. *Biddeford: J. E. Butler & Co.* 1866. 18mo, pp. 131. C. 5227

Also: Mayor's Address and ... Annual Report for various years, — the 12th is for 1866–67.

BIDDLE (C.) Communicaciones entre el Señor Carlos Biddle, Coronel de los E. Unidos del Norte i la Sociedad amigos del Pais. *Panama.* 1836. 8vo. 5228

BIDDLE (C. John). The Alliance with the Negro. Speech of Hon. Charles J. Biddle of Pennsylvania, delivered in the House of Representatives of the United States, March 6, 1862. *Washington.* 8vo, pp. 8. H. 5229

BIDDLE. Eulogy upon the Hon. George Mifflin Dallas, delivered before the Bar of Philadelphia, February 11, 1865. By Charles J. Biddle. *Philadelphia: McLaughlin.* [1865.] 8vo, pp. 51. 5230

BIDDLE. Speech ... in the House of Representatives, June 2, 1862, [on the Bill to appoint Diplomatic Representatives to the Republics of Hayti and Liberia]. [n. p. n. d.] 8vo, pp. 8. *See also* Pennsylvania.

BIDDLE (Clement). *See* Philadelphia Directory.

BIDDLE (G. W.) Contribution among Terre Tenants. A Lecture read May 6, 1863, before the Law Academy of Philadelphia. By George W. Biddle, Esq. *Philadelphia.* 1863. 8vo, pp. 31. 5232

[BIDDLE (James).] To the Freeholders ... of ... Pennsylvania. [*Philadelphia.* 1765.] Folio, broadside, 1 l. P. 5233

This is an Address read by James Biddle, Esq., Sept. 26, 1765, charging B. Franklin and Gov. Franklin with having promoted the Passage of the Stamp Act, &c

BIDDLE (J. C.) An Address delivered before the Philomathean and Phrenakosmian Societies of Pennsylvania College. By James C. Biddle, July 4, 1838. *Gettysburg.* 1838. 8vo, pp. 31.

BIDDLE. A Statement, by James C. Biddle and William M. Meredith, of the Philadelphia Bar. *Philadelphia. June,* 1822. 8vo, pp. 35. H. 5235

In relation to their imprisonment for contempt of court.

BIDDLE (N.) Address at laying the Corner Stone of the Girard College for Orphans in Philadelphia; By Nicholas Biddle, with an Account of the Proceedings, July 4, 1833. *Philadelphia.* 1833. 8vo. W. 5236

BIDDLE. An Address ... before the Alumni Association of Nassau-Hall, ... September 30, 1835. By Nicholas Biddle, LL.D. ... Second Edition. *R. E. Hornor, Printer.* 1835. 8vo, pp. 24. + Third Edition. *Princeton, N. J.: Robert E. Hornor.* 1835. 8vo, pp. 20. + *Philadelphia: John C. Clark.* 1836. 8vo, pp. 24. 5237

BIDDLE. Address delivered before the Philadelphia Society for promoting Agriculture ... on the Fifteenth of January, 1822. By Nicholas Biddle, Esq. ... *Philadelphia: Clark & Raser, Printers.* 1822. 8vo, pp. 39. H. 5238

On the condition of agriculture in Pennsylvania; very interesting.

[BIDDLE.] Commercial Regulations of the Foreign Countries with which the United States have Commercial Intercourse, Collected, Digested, and Printed under the direction of the President ... *Washington.* 1819. 8vo, pp. 528. P. 5239

BIDDLE. An Eulogium on Thomas Jefferson, delivered before the American Philosophical Society, April 11, 1827. By Nicholas Biddle ... . *Philadelphia.* 1827. 8vo, pp. 55. P. 5240

BIDDLE. An Ode to Bogle. By Nicholas Biddle, July 16, 1829. *Philadelphia: Privately printed for Ferdinand J. Dreer.* 1865. 8vo and 4to, pp. 8. 5241

BIDDLE. Oration Delivered before the Pennsylvania State Society of Cincinnati on the Fourth of July, MDCCCXI. By Nicholas Biddle, Esq. *Philadelphia: C. and A. Conrad and Co.* 1811. 8vo, pp. 28. 5242

BIDDLE. Two Letters ... embracing a History of the Re-Charter of the Bank of the United States, and a View of the Present Condition of the Currency. By Nicholas Biddle ... . *London.* 1837. 8vo, pp. 20. 5243

BIDDLE (O.) Oration delivered Mar. 2, 1781, before the American Philosophical Society for promoting Useful Knowledge. By Owen Biddle. *Philadelphia.* 1781. 4to, pp. 36. 5244

[BIDDLE.] A Plan for a School and an Establishment similar to that of Ackworth, in Yorkshire, Great-Britain, varied to suit the Circumstances of the Youth within the Limits of the Yearly Meeting for Pennsylvania and New-Jersey, Introduced with the Sense of Friends in New-England, on the Subject of Education; and an Account of some Schools in Great-Britain: To which is added Observations and Remarks, intended for the consideration of Friends. *Philadelphia: Printed by Joseph Crukshank.* M.DCC.XC. 8vo, pp. 53. P. 5245

[BIDDLE (Richard).] Captain Hall in America. By an American. *Philadelphia: Carey & Lea.* 1830. 8vo, pp. 120.

Reprinted in England with the following title:

[BIDDLE.] A Review of Capt. Basil Hall's Travels in North America, in the years 1827 and 1828. By an American. *London: Kennett.* 1830. 8vo, 149. + Second Edition. *London.* 1830. 8vo. 5247

[BIDDLE.] Memoir of Sebastian Cabot, with a Review of the History of Maritime Discovery. Illustrated by Documents from the Rolls, now first published. *Philadelphia.* 1831. 8vo, pp. viii, 327. C. + [Reprinted as] A Memoir [etc.] *London: Hurst, Chance & Co.* 1831. 8vo, pp. viii, 333. H. + Second Edition. *London.* [*Ibid.*] 1832. 8vo. C. 5248

Concerning this able work, *see* N. A. R., XXXIV. 405–428. "The author has accomplished his task with signal ability, and has dispelled the darkness which prejudice and carelessness had suffered to gather over the fair fame of a great navigator." Brunet, I. 1446, erroneously remarks: "Cet ouvrage intéressant est de M. D.-B. Warden."

BIDDLE. Remarks of Mr. Biddle of Pennsylvania, on the Bill to postpone the Fourth Instalment payable under the Deposite Act. Delivered in the House ... September, 1837. *Washington.* 1837. 12mo, pp. 10. H. 5249

BIDDLE. Speech of Mr. Biddle, on the Bill to authorize the

Issue of Treasury Notes. Delivered in the House ... May 15, 1838. *Washington.* 1838. 8vo, pp. 19. H. 5250

BIDLACK (Benjamin A.) Address delivered by B. Alden Bidlack, 25 Feb. 1839, at Wilkes-Barre, Penn., in Vindication of the Patriotism and Military Services of the first Settlers of Wyoming. *Washington,* [*D. C.*]: 1842. 8vo, pp. 16. C. 5251

BIDLAKE (J.) The Slave Trade. A Sermon by John Bidlake. *Plymouth.* 1789. 4to, pp. 32. P. 5252

[BIDWELL (Barnabas).] Commonwealth of Massachusetts. The Attorney-General's Report respecting Claims for Confiscated Debts. *Boston.* 1808. 8vo, pp. 22, (1). H. 5253

BIDWELL. An Oration, at the Celebration of American Independence, in Stockbridge, July, 1795. By Barnabas Bidwell, Esquire. ... *Stockbridge, printed by Loring Andrews.* 1795. 4to, pp. 21. 5254

BIDWELL. Oration at Sheffield, Mass. July 4, 1805. By Barnabas Bidwell. *Pittsfield.* 1805. 8vo. S. 5255

BIDWELL. Oration at Yale College, Conn. on the death of Roger Newton, Jun. who died Aug. 10, 1789. By Barnabas Bidwell. *New Haven.* [1789.] 8vo. W. 5256

BIDWELL (C. T.) The Isthmus of Panama. By Charles Toll Bidwell, F.R.G.S., British Vice Consul at Panama. *London: Chapman and Hall.* MDCCCLXV. 8vo, pp. vii, 418. Colored Plate. B. 5257

BIDWELL (Marshall Spring). Sir F. B. Head and Mr. Bidwell. The Cause and Circumstances of Mr. Bidwell's Banishment by Sir F. B. Head, correctly stated and proved by a United Empire Loyalist. .... *Kingston: Printed by T. H. Bentley.* 1838. 8vo or 4to, pp. 16. H. 5258

BIDWELL. A Compilation and Digest of the Laws relating to Common Schools, applicable to the City and County of New-York, with Observations on the same. Prepared by Marshall S. Bidwell, Esq. ... . *New-York: Press of M. Day & Co.* 1842. 8vo. 5259

BIEDMA (Lus Hernandez de). Conquest of Florida. *See* Soto (H. de) and French (B. F.)

BIENEWITZ (Peter). *See* Apianus, Nos. 1738–57.

The title of No. 1739, quoted from Clement, is slightly incorrect — it is as follows:

[BIENEWITZ.] Cosmographicvs Liber Petri Apiani Mathematici, studiose correctus, ac Erroribus vindicatus per Gemmam Phrysium. *Væneunt Antuerpiæ in Ædibus Rolandi Bollaert* [Colophon] *Excusum Antuerpiæ Impensis Rolandi Bollaert: Typis Joannis Graphei, Anno à Christo nato* M. D. XXIX. *mense Febr.* 4to, lv, (1) l. 5260

Biennial Register of all Officers and Agents in the Service of the United States. *Washington.* 1838. 12mo. Continued.

First published as the "U. S. Register," and known as the "Blue Book."

BIER (George Henry). Defence of Passed-Midshipman G. H. Bier, U. S. Navy, delivered before the Court of Inquiry ... at the Navy Yard, New-York, Feb. 4, 1851. ... *New-York: John F. Trow.* 1851. 8vo, pp. 11, (1). H. 5262

BIERCE (L. V.) Historical Reminiscences of Summit County. By Gen. L. V. Bierce. *Akron, Ohio: T. & H. G. Canfield.* 1854. 12mo, pp. 158. 5263

BIERCE. On Presidential Arrests. (Ohio Senate, 31, 3, '63.) *Columbus: "Fact" Office.* 1863. 8vo, pp. 4. 5264

BIERFREUND (Fr. Ludvig). Revolutionen i det Spanske Amerika, med en Kort Fremstill af dette Lands Opdagelse og Historie. *Odense: S. Hempel.* 1820. 8vo, pp. 492. 5265

BIERSTADT (A.) The Rocky Mountains. [A Description of the Picture.] By Albert Bierstadt. [n. p. 1863.] 4to, pp. 3.

BIERVLIET (P. van). Études sur l'esclavage aux État-Unis, par Paul van Biervliet ... . *Louvain-Bruxelles: typographie de C.-J. Fonteyn.* 1857. 8vo, pp. 144. B. 5267

BIESEN (*Dr.* J. J. van den). Een Amerikaansche hefboom tot opbeuring van ons lager onderwijs. *Amsterdam: C. L. van Langenhuysen.* 1868. 8vo, pp. 58. 5268

BIET (Antoine). Voyage|de la France|Eqvinoxiale|en l'Isle de Cayenne,|entrepris par les Francois|en l'Année M. DC. LII.| Diuisé en trois Livres.|Le Premier, contient l'établissement de la Colonie,|son embarquement, & sa route iusques à son arriuée| en l'Isle de Cayenne.|Le Second, ce qui s'est passé pendant quinze mois que|l'on a demeuré dans le païs.|Le Troisiesme, traitte du temperament du païs, de|la fertilité de sa terre, & des mœurs & façons de faire|des Sauuages de cette contrée.|Avec vn Dictionnaire de la Langue du mesme Païs.|Par Me Antoine Biet, Prestre, Curé de Ste Geneviéve|de Senlis, Superieur des Prestres qui ont passé dans le Païs.| [Vignette.] *A Paris,|Chez François Clovzier, dans la Cour du Palais,|proche l'Hostel du Premier President.*|M. DC. LXIV.|*Avec Privilege dv Roy.*| 4to, 12 l., pp. 432. B., C., H. 5269

"Adelung, in his Mithridates (III. 684), says that the vocabulary of Biet is, with a few exceptions, the same as the one given by Boyer."—LUDEWIG. *See* Rich, No. 334; Faribault, No. 64; Boucher, VI. 253; Leclerc, No. 165, 31fr. Sold at Puttick's, 1860, for £2 5s.; Techener, 10fr.

Les Bigarures d'un Citoyen de Genève, et ses Conseils Republicains, dediés aux Américains; avec quantité d'anecdotes amusantes, interessantes & autres pour servir à terminer l'histoire des Jésuites. Vol. I. de l'Imprimerie du Congres Général. *Philadelphie*, [*i. e. London*]. || Vol. II. aux depens du Congrès-Général en Amérique. [*Ibid.*] 1776–77. 2 vols., 12mo, pp. xii, 308; xii, 316. C. 5270

Contains some curious particulars relative to the Court of King George and the American Colonies: a chapter on the Irish Catholics sent to fight the Americans, etc. John Wilkes is supposed to have assisted in the authorship.

BIGELOW (Abijah). Political Queries and Statements. [n. p. n. d.] 8vo, pp. 15. 5271

BIGELOW. The Voters' Guide: or, the Power, Duty, Privileges of the Constitutional Voters in the Commonwealth of Massachusetts. To which are added, Original remarks, with various extracts from Historians, and the writings and public Speeches of eminent political characters in this and other countries, tending to explain the causes of the Rise and Fall of Republican Governments. By Abijah Bigelow, Attorney at Law. ... *Leominster*, (*Mas.*): *Printed by S. & J. Wilder. Feb.* 4, 1807. 18mo, pp. 156. C., H. 5272

BIGELOW (A.) ... A Discourse ... May 14th, 1841, the Day of the National Fast ... [for] the Death of William Henry Harrison ... . By Andrew Bigelow ... . *Taunton.* 1841. 8vo, pp. 28. B., H. 5273

BIGELOW. ... A Discourse delivered in Eastport, on the Dedication of the First Congregational Meeting-House ... January 13, 1820. By Andrew Bigelow, M.A. *Eastport: printed by Benjamin Folsom.* 1820. 8vo, pp. 16. H. 5274

BIGELOW. A Farewell Discourse ... in Eastport ... May 27, 1821, by Andrew Bigelow. ... *Boston.* 1821. 8vo, pp. 32.

BIGELOW. Mr. Bigelow's Farewell Address to his Flock in Taunton ... November 20th, 1842. ... With an Appendix. *Boston: printed by Isaac R. Butts.* 1843. 12mo, pp. 24. H.

BIGELOW. Mr. Bigelow's Letter to sundry disaffected Individuals in his Congregation. [Dated Taunton, November 30th, 1841. n. p. n. d.] 4to, 2 l. H. 5277

BIGELOW. An Oration, delivered before the Washington Benevolent Society at Cambridge, July 4, 1815. By Andrew Bigelow, A.B. *Cambridge: Hilliard and Metcalf.* 1815. 8vo, pp. 16. H. 5278

BIGELOW. Pastoral Memorial. A Discourse ... in Taunton ... April 10, 1842, on the Ninth Anniversary of the Preacher's Settlement. ... *Boston.* 1842. 12mo, pp. 20. B., H. 5279

BIGELOW. A Pastor's Retrospect. Two Discourses ... in Taunton ... April 7, 1840, on the Completion of a ... Seven Years' Ministry ... . [n. p. n. d.] 12mo, pp. 31, (1). B., H.

BIGELOW. Two Sermons ... Chelsea, October 21, 1827, *Boston.* 1827. 12mo. 5281

Also other sermons and discourses.

BIGELOW. ... A Sermon preached before ... the Legislature of Massachusetts, at the Annual Election ... January, 6, 1836. By Andrew Bigelow ... . *Boston.* 1836. 8vo, pp. 78. B., H.

Contains a list of all those who have preached at the anniversary from 1631.

BIGELOW. ... A Sermon preached in Norton ... 15th February, 1835, at the Interment of the Rev. Pitt Clarke, Pastor of the First Congregational Parish ... . By Andrew Bigelow ... . Added ... Extracts from the Diary of the Deceased. *Taunton.* 1835. 8vo, pp. 29, (1). B. 5283

BIGELOW. Signs of the Moral Age. Sermon preached in Reading, North Parish ... January 6, 1828. With Sundry Notes. By Andrew Bigelow. *Boston: Bowles and Dearborn.* 1828. 12mo, pp. 42. B. 5284

[BIGELOW (*Mrs.* Eliza Tappan).] Memoire of Lucy Maria

Bigelow, Daughter of Rev. J. Bigelow, who died ... October 23, 1832 ... . Fourth Edition. *Boston.* 1841. 12mo, pp. 52. 5285

BIGELOW (Erastus Brigham). Internal Taxation Simplified. [A Letter to] Hon. Thaddeus Stevens, Chairman of the Committee of Ways and Means. [Signed E. B. Bigelow. Dated Washington, March 19, 1862. n. p. n. d.] 8vo, pp. 6. B., H. 5286

BIGELOW. The Provision and Grain-Growing Interests, as affected by the Repeal of the British Corn Laws, and the American System of Protection. *Boston: Press of John Wilson and Sons.* 1866. 4to, 7 l. H. 5287

Extracts from his "Tariff Question."

BIGELOW. Remarks on the Depressed Condition of Manufactures in Massachusetts, with Suggestions as to its Cause and its Remedy. By E. B. Bigelow. *Boston: Little, Brown, and Company.* 1858. 8vo, pp. 28. H. 5288

BIGELOW. A Statement of Facts in relation to the Lancaster Mills ... . By E. B. Bigelow. *Boston.* 1851. 8vo, pp. 29, (1).

BIGELOW. The Tariff Question considered in regard to the Policy of England and the Interests of the United States. With Statistical and Comparative Tables. By Erastus B. Bigelow. *Boston: Little, Brown, & Company.* 1862. 4to, pp. x, (1), 103, 242. 5290

BIGELOW. A Memoir of Erastus Brigham Bigelow, (now Candidate for Congress,) reprinted from Hunt's Merchants' Magazine for February, 1854. ... *Boston.* 1860. 8vo, pp. 16. H.

BIGELOW (G. T.) *and* BEMIS (George). Report of the Trial of Abner Rogers, Jr. indicted for the Murder of Charles Lincoln, Jr. late Warden of the Massachusetts State Prison; before the Supreme Judicial Court of Massachusetts; holden at Boston ... January 30, 1844. By George Tyler Bigelow and George Bemis ... . *Boston: Charles C. Little and James Brown.* MDCCCXLIV. 8vo, pp. 286, (2). H. 5292

BIGELOW (H. Jacob). Ether and Chloroform; their Discovery ... . By Henry J. Bigelow ... . *Boston.* 1848. 8vo, pp. 18. 5293

Contrasts the cold reception of the American discovery south of Boston with the attitude of European surgeons.

BIGELOW (Jacob). American Medical Botany, being a Collection of the Native Medicinal Plants of the United States, containing their Botanical History and Chemical Analysis, and Properties and Uses in Medicine, Diet and the Arts, with Coloured Engravings. By Jacob Bigelow ... . *Boston: Cummings & Hilliard.* 1817–20. 3 vols., 8vo, pp. 197, (1); 199, (1); 197, (1). 60 Plates. H. P. 5294

See N. A. R., VI. 344; XII. 100.

[BIGELOW.] Eolopoesis. American Rejected Addresses. ... *New York: J. C. Derby.* [1855.] 16mo, pp. 240. H. 5295

Parodies on famous American poets, purporting to have been written for the directors of the New York Crystal Palace.

BIGELOW. Facts Serving to shew the Comparative Forwardness of the Spring in Different Parts of the United States. By Jacob Bigelow, M.D. ... *Cambridge: University Press, Hilliard and Metcalf.* 1818. 4to, pp. 11. B., P. 5296

BIGELOW. Florula Bostoniensis. A Collection of Plants of Boston and its Environs, with their Generic and Specific Characters, Synonyms, Descriptions, Places of Growth, and Time of Flowering, and Occasional Remarks. By Jacob Bigelow, M.D. *Boston: Cummings and Hilliard.* 1814. 8vo, pp. viii, 268. H., P. + Second Edition, greatly Enlarged. To which is added a Glossary of the Botanical Terms employed in the Work. *Boston: Cummings, Hilliard, & Co.* 1824. 8vo, pp. 5, (1), 422, (1). H. + Third Edition Enlarged, and containing a Glossary of Botanical Terms. *Boston: Charles C. Little and James Brown.* 1840. 8vo, pp. vi, (1), 468. C., H. 5297

See N. A. R., October, 1840.

BIGELOW. A History of the Cemetery of Mount Auburn. By Jacob Bigelow ... . *Boston and Cambridge: James Munroe and Company.* M DCCC LX. 16mo, pp. xii, 2 l., 263. B., H., S. 5298

BIGELOW. Inaugural Address, ... at Cambridge, December 11, 1816. By Jacob Bigelow ... . *Boston.* 1817. 8vo, pp. 24, (2). H. 5299

Contains a history of the Rumford Professorship, and the Rules and Statutes.

BIGELOW. Modern Inquiries: Classical, Professional, and Miscellaneous. By Jacob Bigelow, M.D., late President of the American Academy of Arts and Sciences, and late a Professor

in Harvard University. ... *Boston: Little, Brown, and Company.* 1867. 8vo, pp. xi, 379. H. 5300

The Life and Works of Count Rumford, Chap. III.; On ... Mount Auburn Cemetery, Chap. V.; Cattle Disease in Massachusetts, Chap. XV.; Aphorisms of the War, Chap. XVIII., XIX., etc.

BIGELOW. Some Account of the [White] Mountains of New Hampshire. By Jacob Bigelow ... . (From the New-England Journal of Medicine and Surgery, for October, 1816.) [*Boston.* 1816.] 8vo, pp. 18. BA., C. 5301

[BIGELOW (John).] Constitutional Reform, in a Series of Articles contributed to the Democratic Review, upon Constitutional Guaranties in Political Government ... with a History of Constitutional Reform in New Jersey, Louisiana ... and New York ... . To which are added Two Letters of [*sic*] the Hon. Michael Hoffman, ... on a Reorganization of the Judiciary ... . Also the Correspondence of Thomas Jefferson on Constitutional Reform. Edited by Thomas Prentice Kettell. *New York.* 1846. 8vo, pp. vi, 77. S. 5302

BIGELOW. Les États-Unis d'Amérique en 1863, leur histoire politique; leurs ressources minéralogiques, agricoles, industrielles et commerciales, et de la part pour laquelle ils ont contribué à la richesse et à la civilisation du monde entier. Par John Bigelow, consul des États-Unis à Paris. *Paris: L. Hachette et Cie.* 1863. 8vo, pp. xxiv, 555. 5303

BIGELOW. ... Gli Stati Uniti nel 1863; traduzione con proemio. *Milano: Corona e Caimi.* 1863. 12mo, pp. 470. (Collana di storie e memorie contemporanee diretta da Cesare Cantù, Vol. II.) 5304

BIGELOW. Jamaica in 1850: or, the Effects of Sixteen Years of Freedom on a Slave Colony. By John Bigelow. *New York & London: George P. Putnam.* 1851. 12mo, Title, pp. iii, iv, 214. BA. 5305

BIGELOW. Memoir of the Life and Public Services of John Charles Fremont, including an Account of his Explorations, Discoveries, and Adventures on Five Successive Expeditions across the North American Continent; Voluminous Extracts from his Private and Public Correspondence; his Defence before the Court-Martial, and Full Reports of his Principal Speeches in the Senate of the United States. By John Bigelow. *New*

York: Derby and Jackson. 1856. 12mo, pp. 480. Portrait and Woodcuts. H. 5306

BIGELOW. The Farewell Banquet to Mr John Bigelow ... Minister ... Plenipotentiary of the United States to France Given ... December 19th 1866 by the American Residents of Paris *Paris: typographie de Henri Plon.* 1867. 8vo, pp. 50. H. 5307

Mr. Bigelow was, from 1849 to 1861, one of the editors and proprietors of the "New York Evening Post," and subsequently Minister to France, in which capacity he was the author of many despatches concerning the civil war in the United States, which are included in the Diplomatic Correspondence for 1861–65. *See* Franklin (B.)

BIGELOW (J. F.) The Hand of God in American History. A Discourse delivered in the Baptist Church, Keeseville, N. Y., July 7, 1861; also before the United Literary Societies of New Hampton Institution, Fairfax, Vt., July 15, 1861. By Rev. John F. Bigelow. ... *Burlington: W. H. & C. A. Hoyt & Co., Printers.* 1861. 8vo, pp. 42. H. 5308

BIGELOW (J. M.) Botanical Profile representing the geographical distribution of the Forest Trees along a route from Arkansas to Mexico. [*Washington.*] 1856. 1 large sheet. 5309

BIGELOW. Description of the Botanical Character of the West of North-America. [*Washington.* 1856.] Imp. 4to, pp. 26. Colored Plate. 5310

BIGELOW. Florula Lancastriensis: or a Catalogue comprising nearly all the flowering and filiocid Plants growing naturally within the limits of Fairfield County. By John M. Bigelow, M.D. ... *Lancaster, O.:* 1841. 8vo, pp. 22. S. 5311

BIGELOW (J. P.) Abstract of Massachusetts School Returns, for 1836. By John P. Bigelow. *Boston.* 1837. Oblong 4to.

BIGELOW. ... Address of John Prescott Bigelow, Mayor ... on ... retiring from Office: January 3, 1852. *Boston.* 1852. 8vo, pp. 11. B. 5313

BIGELOW. ... Inaugural Address ... by John Prescott Bigelow, Mayor ... January 1, 1849. *Boston.* 1849. 8vo, pp. 17. + [Same.] January 7, 1850. *Boston.* 1850. 8vo, pp. 19. B.

BIGELOW. Statistical Tables: exhibiting the Condition and Products of certain Branches of Industry, in Massachusetts for the Year ending April 1, 1837. Prepared ... by John P. Bigelow, Secretary of the Commonwealth. *Boston.* 1838. 8vo, pp. viii, 207, (2). BA., C. 5315

BIGELOW (J. R.) The American's Own Book, containing the Constitutions of the several States of the Union, embracing the Declaration of Independence, Constitution of the United States, and of each State, with the Amendments, and much other matter of general interest, from authentic Documents. Embellished with Seals of the different States. By John R. Bigelow. *New York.* 1847. 8vo, pp. 515. + Second Edition. *New York.* 1848. 8vo, pp. 515. + [Third Edition.] *New York: Gates, Stedman, & Co.* [*and*] *B. G. St. John.* 1849. 8vo, pp. 8, ix, (1), 10–536. Map and Plates. BA., C. 5316

BIGELOW (J.) ... A Sermon, delivered March 12, 1828, at the Ordination of Rev. Asahel Bigelow ... in Walpole, Mass. By Jonathan Bigelow ... . *Boston: T. R. Marvin.* 1828. 8vo, pp. 20. H. 5317

[BIGELOW (Josiah).] Review of "An Address to the Working-Men of New-England ... . By Seth Luther. ..." By a Factory Hand, of Waltham. *Cambridge: the Author.* 1832. 12mo, pp. 31. H. 5318

BIGELOW (L.) Address ... before the Worcester Agricultural Society, October 12, 1820, being their Anniversary Cattle Show and Exhibition of Manufactures. By Hon. Lewis Bigelow. ... *Worcester. Feb.* 1821. 8vo, pp. 32, (2). H. 5319

With an account of the show, list of officers, etc.

BIGELOW. An Oration, pronounced at Templeton, [Mass.,] July 5, 1813. in commemoration of ... American Independence, before the Washington Benevolent Societies, [etc.] By Lewis Bigelow. *Worcester: Isaac Sturtevant.* 1813. 8vo, pp. 28. W.

[BIGELOW (L.)] Copy of Affidavit [Signed Liberty Bigelow. n. p. 1855.] 8vo, pp. 2. H. 5321

Relating to the ice business of the Fitchburg Railroad.

BIGELOW (T.) An Address, delivered at the Opening of Williams Hall, ... March 8, 1853. By Timothy Bigelow. *Boston: B. H. Greene.* 1853. 8vo, pp. 32. B., H., S. 5322

On the early history and present position of Boston, the Pilgrim Fathers, etc.

BIGELOW. An Address delivered on the Third Anniversary of the Washington Benevolent Society, April 30, 1814. By the Hon. Timothy Bigelow. *Boston: C. Stebbins.* 1814. 8vo, pp. 19. H. 5323

[BIGELOW.] Documents respecting the Resolutions of the Legislature of Massachusetts, passed Feb. 15, 1812. [*Boston.* 1812.] 8vo, pp. 14. M. 5324

Relating to the embargo.

BIGELOW. An Eulogy on the Life, Character, and Services of Brother George Washington, Deceased. Pronounced before the Fraternity of Free and Accepted Masons, ... At ... Boston, ... Feb. 11. 1800, Being the Day set apart by them to pay Funeral Honors to their Deceased Brother. By Brother Timothy Bigelow. To which are added, Two Addresses to the Deceased, when President of the United States, and his Answers ... . *Boston: Printed by F. Thomas and E. T. Andrews.* [1800.] 8vo, pp. 26. H. 5325

BIGELOW. An Oration delivered before the Municipal Authorities of the City of Boston, July 4, 1853. By Timothy Bigelow. Together with the Speeches at the Dinner in Faneuil Hall ... . *Boston: J. H. Eastburn.* 1853. 8vo, pp. 80. B., H.

BIGELOW. Oration at Amherst, N. H., April 4, 1798, at the Interment of Hon. Samuel Dana. By Timothy Bigelow. *Amherst: Samuel Preston.* 1798. 8vo, pp. 12. W. 5327

BIGELOW. An Oration, Pronounced at Cambridge before the Φ. B. K. ... July 21, 1796. ... . *Boston.* 1797. 8vo, pp. 15.

Gives a history of the society.

BIGELOW. Ceremonies at the Dedication of the Bigelow Monument, Worcester, Massachusetts, April 19, 1861. *Boston: printed by John Wilson and Son.* 1861. 8vo, pp. 37. Plate. B.

Erected to the memory of Colonel Timothy Bigelow by his great-grandson, Col. T. Bigelow Lawrence.

BIGELOW (Tyler). Address, delivered at the Eighth Anniversary of The Massachusetts Peace Society, Dec. 25, 1823. By Tyler Bigelow, Esq. *Boston: printed by John B. Russell.* 1824. 8vo, pp. 24. B., H. 5330

BIGELOW (W. E.) The Boston Tragedy. An Expose of the Evidence in the Case of the Parkman Murder! ... Compiled by W. E. Bigelow. *Boston.* 1850. 8vo, pp. 32. Portrait of Webster. B. 5331

BIGGS (A.) Speech of Hon. Asa Biggs, of North Carolina ... in the House ... June 24, 1846. ... on the Bill ... amendatory of the Tariff law of 1842. [*Washington?* n. d.] 8vo, pp. 7. H.

[BIGGS (J.)] The History of Don Francisco de Miranda's Attempt to Effect a Revolution in South America, in a Series of Letters. By a Gentleman who was an Officer under that General, to a friend in the United States. To which are annexed sketches of the Life of Miranda and Geographical Notices of Caraccas. *Boston.* 1808. 12mo. + *Boston.* 1809. 12mo. C. + Second Edition. *Boston: Edward Oliver.* 1810. 12mo, pp. xi, 312. H. + Third Edition. *Boston.* 1811. 12mo. 5333

Reprinted in London, with the following title:

BIGGS. The History of Don Francisco de Miranda's Attempt to Effect a Revolution in South America. In a Series of Letters. By James Biggs. Revised, corrected, and enlarged. To which are annexed, Sketches of the Life of Miranda, and Geographical Notices of Caraccas. ... *London: the Author.* 1809. 8vo, pp. xv, (1), 312. C., H. 5334

BIGGS (J.) A Concise History of the Kehukee Baptist Association, from its original rise to the present time ... . In Two Parts. By Elder Joseph Biggs ... *Printed and Published by George Howard: Tarborough, N. C.* 1834. 12mo, pp. 300.

BIGGS (Wm.) Military History of Europe, &c., from the Commencement of the War with Spain, in 1739, to the Treaty of Aix-la-Chapelle in 1748. *London.* 1755. 8vo. 5336

Included in J. R. Smith's catalogue of books relating to America.

BIGHAM (T. J.) Address, delivered before the Philological Institute, on the Eighth December, 1842 ... . By T. J. Bigham ... . *Pittsburgh: printed by A. Jaynes.* 1842. 8vo, pp. 24.

"Our theme, the Character of the Pioneers in the Valley of the Ohio."

BIGLAND (John). A Geographical and Historical View of the World: exhibiting a Complete Delineation of the Natural and Artificial Features of each Country; and a Succinct Narrative of the Origin of the Different Nations, their Political Revolutions and Progress in Arts, Science, Literature, Commerce, &c. ... By John Bigland ... . With Notes, correcting and improving the Part which relates to the American Continent and Islands. By Jedediah Morse ... . *Boston: Thomas B. Wait and Co.* [etc.] 1811. 5 vols., 8vo. H. + Second American Edition. *Boston.* 1812. 5338

BIGLAND. Letters on the Study and Use of Ancient and Modern History. By John Bigland. *London.* 1805. 8vo. + *Philadelphia.* 1806. 8vo. + Second Edition. *London.* 1808. 8vo, pp. xx, 23–615. Portrait. H. + *Philadelphia.* 1814. 12mo.

Contents: Character of Columbus. — Colonization of America. — Simplicity of the Indians. — Slavery in South America. — Reflections on Slavery, etc.

BIGLER (W.) Address of Hon. William Bigler, delivered at New Hope, Bucks County [Pennsylvania], September 17, 1863. *Harrisburg, Pa.* [1863.] 8vo, pp. 13. H. 5340

BIGLER. Addresses delivered at the Opening of the Pennsylvania Female College, at Harrisburg, by Governor Bigler, Professors Waugh and Tiffany: with a List of the Officers. *Harrisburg.* 1853. 8vo, pp. 42, (2). H. 5341

BIGLER. State of the Union: Speech of Hon. Wm. Bigler ... Delivered in the Senate of the United States, January 21, 1861. [*Washington.* 1861.] 8vo, pp. 16. H. 5342

[BIGLOW (William).] Classology: an Anacreontic Ode ... . *Boston: Thurston, Torry, and Emerson.* 1843. 8vo, pp. 8. H.

Written in 1792, but the last stanza added in 1842. Introduces all the names of the class of 1794.

[BIGLOW.] Commencement, a Poem: or rather Commencement of a Poem. Recited before the Phi Beta Kappa Society ... in Cambridge, Aug. 29, 1811. By a Brother. ... *Salem, printed by Thomas G. Cushing.* 1811. 8vo, pp. 8 H. 5344

BIGLOW. History of Sherburne, Mass. from its Incorporation, M DC LXXIV, to the End of the Year M DCCC XXX; including that of Framingham and Holliston, so far as they were Constituent Parts of that Town. By William Biglow ... . *Milford, Mass.: Ballou & Stacy.* 1830. 8vo, pp. 80. C., H. 5345

BIGLOW. History of the Town of Natick, Mass. from the Days of the Apostolic Eliot, M DC L, to the Present Time, M DCCC XXX. By William Biglow. *Boston: Marsh, Capen, & Lyon.* M DCCC XXX. 8vo, pp. 87, (1). C., H. 5346

[BIGLOW.] Re-Commencement ... called also, Censure, Scandal ... and Things in General, or What you please. ... *Boston: printed by J. Belcher.* 1811. 8vo, pp. 11. H. 5347

[BIGLOW.] Re-Re-Commencement: a Kind of Poem: Calculated to be recited before an "Assemblage" of New-England Divines, of all the various Denominations ... . *Salem: printed by Thomas C. Cushing.* 1812. 8vo, pp. 8. H. 5348

BIGLOW. Sawney, Redivivus et Restauratus; or, Miscellaneous Verses. By William Biglow. ... Nos. 1, 2. *Boston: the Author.* 1816. 12mo. (No. 2, pp. 36.) W. 5349

Also: Education, a Poem ... . *Salem: Joshua Cushing.* 1799. 8vo, pp. 17. B., H. A Poem on Intemperance. ... *Cambridge Press.* 1834. 12mo, pp. 12. H.

BIGLY (C. A.), *pseudon.* Aurifodina: or, Adventures in the Gold Region. By Cantell A. Bigly [*i. e.*, Can tell a big lie]. *New York: Baker and Scribner.* 1849. 12mo, pp. 103. C. 5350

A satiric extravaganza, based upon the discovery of gold in California.

BIGNEY (M. F.) The Forest Pilgrims, and other Poems. By M. F. Bigney. *New Orleans: James A. Gresham. New York: M. Doolady.* 1867. 12mo, pp. 258. B., C. 5351

Many of the poems relate to this country.

BIGOT (J.) Copie d'vne lettre escrite par Le Père Jacques Bigot de la Compagnie de Jésus, pour accompagner Un collier de pourcelaine envoiée par les Abnaquis de la Mission de Saint François de Sales dans la Nouvelle France du tombeau de leur Saint Patron à Annecy. *Manate: Jean-Marie Shea.* M. DCCC. LVIII. Sm. 8vo, pp. 8, (1). H. 5352

BIGOT. Copie d'vne lettre escrite par Le Père Jacques Bigot de la Compagnie de Jésus, l'an 1684, Pour accompagner un collier de pourcelaine envoiée par les Abnaquis de la Mission de Sainct François de Sales dans la Nouvelle France au tombeau de leur Sainct Patron à Annecy. *Manate: Jean-Marie Shea.* M. DCCC. LVIII. Sm. 8vo, pp. 9, (1). H. 5353

This is a Second Edition. Besides the insertion of "l'an 1684," and the substitution of "Sainct" for "Saint," in the title, there are various corrections in the body of the work.

BIGOT. Relation de ce qvi s'est passé de plvs remarqvable dans la Mission Abnaquise de Sainct Joseph de Sillery, Et dans l'Establissement de la Nouuelle Mission De Sainct Francois de Sales, l'annéз 1684. Par le R. P. Jacques Bigot, de la Compagnie de Jésus. *Manate: Jean-Marie Shea.* M. DCCC. LVII. Sm. 8vo, pp. 61, (1). BA. H., 5354

No. II. of Shea's Cramoisy Series.

BIGOT (J.) Relation de ce qvi s'est passé de plus remarqvable Dans la Mission Abnaquise de Sainct Joseph de Sillery et de Sainct François de Sales, l'Année 1685. Par le R. Père Jacque Bigot, de la Compagnie de Jésus. *Manate: Jean-Marie Shea.* M. DCCC. LVIII. Sm. 8vo, pp. 21, (1). H. 5355

No. III. of Shea's Cramoisy Series.

BIGOT. Relation de Mission Abnaquise de St. François de Sales L'Année 1702. Par le Père Jacques Bigot, De la Compagnie de Jésus. *Nouvelle-York: Presse Cramoisy de Jean Marie Shea.* M.DCCC.LXV. Sm. 8vo, pp. 26. 5356

Forms part of No. XIX. of Shea's Cramoisy Series.

BIGOT (V.) Relation de ce qvi s'est passé de plvs remarqvable dans la Mission des Abnaquis à L'Acadie, L'Année 1701. Par le Père Vincent Bigot, de la Compagnie de Jésus. *A Manate: Jean-Marie Shea.* M. DCCC. LVIII. Sm. 8vo, pp. 34, (1). H.

No. IV. of Shea's Cramoisy Series. One hundred copies only of each of these Cramoisy Series were printed.

BIGSBY (J. J.) Notes on the Geography and Geology of Lake Huron. By John J. Bigsby, ... From the Transactions of the Geological Society of London. [Vol. VI.] *London: Printed by Richard Taylor.* 1824. 4to, pp. 175–209. 6 Plates, and Map.

BIGSBY. Notes on the Geography, and Geology, of the Countries bordering on Lake Superior, by Dr. J. J. Bigsby. *London.* 1824. 4to. Map. 5359

Bigsby published two articles with this title in the Quart. Journ. of Sci., 1825, XVIII. 1–34, 228–269. Perhaps this was not separately published.

BIGSBY. The Shoe and Canoe; or, Pictures of Travel in the Canadas. Illustrative of their Scenery, and of Colonial Life; with facts and opinions on Emigration, State Policy, and other points of public interest. By John J. Bigsby, M.D. With numerous plates and maps. *London: Chapman & Hall.* 1851. 2 vols., post 8vo, pp. 352; 341. C. 5360

Bijdragen ter gedachtniss van G. Washington, met het portret. *Haarlem: weduwe A. Loosjes Pz.* 1801. 8vo. 5361

Bijdragen tot de kennis der Nederlandsche en vreemde koloniën, bijzonder betrekkelijk de vrijlating der slaven. Eerste- vierde iaargang. *Utrecht: C. van der Post Jr.* 1844–47. 4 vols., 8vo. each in 6 pts., Map. 5362

Bijzonderheden uit de geschiedenis van Amerika, na de ontdekking van Columbus. Nieuwe uitgave. *Nijmegen: D. J. Haspels.* 1832. 8vo. 5363

BILBAO (F.) Obras completas de Francisco Bilbao. Edicion hecha por Manuel Bilbao ... . *Buenos Aires.* 1866, 65. 8vo, 4 l., pp. (1), xi–ccv, 443, (1); 2 l., pp. (1), 8–551, (1). Portrait.

Many of the works relate to South America.

BILBO (W. N.) ... Brownlow Republicanism vs. Etheridge Conservatism. Etheridge's Record exposed. ... Delivered at the State House, June 4th, 1867. By Colonel W. N. Bilbo. [*Nashville.* 1867.] 8vo, pp. 16. H. 5365

BILBO. The Past, Present and Future of the Southern Confederacy. An Oration delivered in the City of Nashville, October 12, 1861. By Col. W. N. Bilbo. *Nashville: J. D. W. Green & Co.* 1861. 8vo, pp. 47. 5366

Bilder aus dem geselligen [*or* gesellschaftlichen] Leben der Nord-Amerikaner. Von einem Deutschen ... *Reutlingen.* 1835. 8vo, pp. 16. Lithograph. 5367

Bilder aus Rio de Janeiro und Umgebung. Aus dem Portugiesischen. *Hamburg: Kittler.* 1861. 8vo, pp. 95. 5368

Bilder zum Anschauungs-Unterricht für die Jugend. Dritter Theil. Enthaltend: Ausländische, nach geographischen Rücksichten geordnete Natur-Gegenstände. Zweite Hälfte. ... *Esslingen: Schreiber.* 1844. Sm. folio, 7½ sheets. 15 colored Plates, of which 7 relate to America. 5369

BILDERDIJK (Willem). Avondschemering. *Brussel.* 1828.

Contains a poem, "America," which is also in his ... Dichtwerken ... . *Haarlem: A. C. Kruseman.* 1856–59. 15 vols., 8vo, IX. 355–358. H.

BILES-ISLAND LOTTERY. 1771. The Scheme. [*New York.* 1771.] Folio broadside. P. 5371

A List of the Numbers that Came up Prizes in Biles-Island Lottery, for the Benefit of a Place of Worship in Borden-Town. [May, 1775.] Folio broadside. P. 5372

BILL (L.) History of the Bill Family. Edited by Ledyard Bill. *New York.* 1868. 8vo, pp. 367, (1). Portrait, and 12 Photographs. B. 5372*a*

Issued for the family, with and without photographic portraits.

BILL. Pen-Pictures of the War. Lyrics, Incidents, and Sketches of the Rebellion; comprising a Choice Selection of Pieces by Our Best Poets. To which is added, Current and well-Authenticated Anecdotes and Incidents of the War. Together with a Full Account of many of the Great Battles, also, a Complete Historical Record of all Events, both Civil and Military, from the Commencement of the Rebellion. Compiled by Ledyard Bill. *New York: L. Bill.* 1864. 8vo, pp. 344. + Sixth Edition. *New York.* 1866. 8vo, pp. 368. Plate. B., C.

A Bill for repealing several Subsidies and an Impost now Payable on Tobacco of the British Plantations, and for Inland Duty in lieu thereof. *London: W. Webb.* MDCCXXXIII. 8vo, pp. 39.

A Bill concerning the Judicial System of the United States; proposed for the Relief of the Supreme Court, and some of the Circuit Courts, with Remarks ... . [n. p. 184–?] 8vo, pp. 7, (1).

A Bill for Repealing several Subsidies and an Impost now Payable on Tobacco of the British Plantations and for granting an Inland Duty in lieu thereof. *London.* 1733. 8vo, pp. 39.

A Bill for Re-uniting to the Crown the Government of several Colonies and Plantations in America. [n. p. *Circa* 1720.] Folio, pp. 2. 5377

A Bill in the Chancery of New-Jersey. At the Suit of John Earl of Stair, and others, Proprietors of the Eastern-Division of New-Jersey; against Benjamin Bond, and some other Persons of Elizabeth-Town; distinguished by the Name of the Clinker Lot Right Men. With Three large Maps ... . To which is added; The Publications of The Council of Proprietors of East New-Jersey, and Mr. Nevill's Speeches to the General Assembly, concerning The Riots committed in New-Jersey, and The Pretence of the Rioters, and their Seducers. These Papers will give a better Light into the History and Constitution of New-Jersey, than any Thing hitherto published, the Matters whereof have been chiefly collected from Records. Published by Subscription: *Printed by James Parker, in New-York,* 1747; *and a few Copies are to be Sold by him, and Benjamin Franklin, in Philadelphia; Price bound, and Maps, coloured, Three Pounds; plain and stitcht only, Fifty Shillings, Proclamation Money.* Folio, pp. 124, (Appendix) 39, (4). 3 Maps. C., H. 5378

The three maps consist of: I: The coast and the country adjoining from Boston to Cape Hatteras; II. A map of New Jersey; III. A map of the property in dispute.

Concerning this dispute, *see* Sedgwick's Livingston, page 69. Ludewig, following Rich, says some copies are dated 1748, which is doubtful.

A Bill in the Chancery of New-Jersey, at the suit of John Hunt; against William Earl of Stirling And Others, Proprietors of the Eastern Division of the Province of New-Jersey. *Philadelphia: Printed By William Goddard.* M.DCC.LXVII. Folio, pp. 21. E. 5379

A Bill to be entitled An Act for the Sequestration of the Estate, Property and Effects of Alien Enemies, and for the Indemnity of Citizens of the Confederate States, and persons aiding the same in the Existing War with the United States. September 3, 1861. [n. p. n. d.] 8vo, pp. 8. 5380

The Confederate Confiscation Bill.

A Bill to establish an uniform system of Bankruptcy throughout the United States. Doc. H. R., 14 December, 1798. *Philadelphia:* 1798. 8vo, pp. 32. C. 5381

Bill to provide for Organizing, Arming, and Disciplining the Militia of the United States. *Philadelphia.* 1798. 8vo, pp. 18.

Le Bill Seigneurial exposé sous son vrai jour, et quelques avis d'un Cultivateur aux Censitaires du Bas-Canada. *Québec.* 1855. 8vo, pp. 41. CP. 5383

Bill Arp so called. A Side-show from the Southern Side of the War. Illustrated by M. A. Sullivan. *New York.* 1866. 12mo, pp. 204. C. 5384

Bill, regelende de Afschaffing der Slavernij, benevens de Schadevergoeding aan de Eigenaars der Slaven, in de Gezamenlijke Kolonien van het Britsche Rijk. *Amsterdam.* 1833. 8vo. 5385

BILLARD (E.) La vérité sur l'invention américaine de la vulcanite (caoutchouc durci). Par Ed. Billard fils. *Paris: impr. Gaittet.* 1860. 8vo, pp. 8. 5386

BILLARDON DE SAUVIGNY (L. Edme). Abjir, drame en 4 actes. *Paris.* 1785. 8vo. 5387

"C'est le sujet d'Asgill, tiré de l'histoire de la révolution américaine." — QUÉRARD.

BILLARDON DE SAUVIGNY. Hirza, ou les Illinois, tragédie en 5 actes. *Paris.* 1767. 8vo. 5388

"The poetry, says Palissot, was as rude as the scene. Although the author changed the denouement three or four times, the piece was damned." — QUÉRARD.

BILLARDON DE SAUVIGNY. Washington, ou la liberté du Nouveau-Monde, tragédie en 4 actes. *Paris: Maillard.* 1791. 8vo. 5389

"All the rules of art are violated in this piece." — QUÉRARD.

BILLAUD-VARENNES (Jacques Nicolas). Memoires écrits au Port-au-Prince en 1818, contenant la relation de ses voyages et aventures dans le Mexique depuis 1805, jusqu'en 1817; avec des notes historiques et un précis de l'insurrection américaine depuis son origine jusqu'en 1820. *Paris: Plancher; Domère.* 1821. 2 vols., 8vo. C. 5390

"Ces mémoires sont apocryphes." — QUÉRARD.

BILLAUD-VARENNES. Question du droit des gens: Les républicains d'Haiti possèdent-ils les conditions requises pour obtenir la ratification de leur indépendence? par un Observateur philosophe. *Port-au-Prince.* 1818 (an 15 de l'indépendance). 4to. 5391

BILLAULT (Auguste Adolphe Marie). Expédition du Mexique. Discours de S. Exc. M. Billault, ministre sans portefeuille. Corps législatif. Séance du 26 juin 1862. *Paris: impr. Panckoucke et Cᵉ.* 1862. 8vo, pp. 115. 5392

From the "Moniteur," 27 juin 1862. Also a Spanish version, *Paris,* 1862.

BILLAULT. Expédition du Mexique. Discours de Son Exc. M. Billault, ministre sans portefeuille. Corps législatif. Séance du 7 février 1863. *Paris: impr. Panckoucke et Cᵉ.* 1863. 8vo, pp. 72. 5393

From the "Moniteur univ.," 8 fév. 1863.

BILLAULT. Speech on the French in Mexico. *London.* 1863. 8vo. 5394

BILLBERG (J.) Plantarum Brasiliensium Decas I et 2. 5395

Title from the catalogue of the Astor Library. On application for it, the book was not to be found. No such work is mentioned among the writings of the Swedish botanist Gustaf Johan Billberg, in the Svenskt biog. Lex., ny följd.

BILLE (Steen Andersen), *b.* 1781. Explanatory Letter to the Honorable Burgher Council of St. Croix, and to Messrs. Baring Brothers & Comp. of London and Messrs. Hope & Comp. of Amsterdam, on the Plan proposed by Him for the Relief of the Island of St. Croix. *St. Croix* [*Christiansted*]. 1822. 8vo, pp. 68. 4396

BILLE. Reply to Lawyer G. F. Borch, from Mr. Steen Bille, in consequence of a Paper presented to him by Mr. Borch, on the 30th, of June 1824, relative to the Sale of Clairmount Estate, and pursuant to a Notice given by that Gentleman, on the 10th of January preceding. 8vo, pp. 22. 5397

BILLE. The Sale of the Estate Clairmount in the Island of St. Croix, discussed in Vindication of Mr. Steen Bille's Honour and Character, scandalously vilified and slandered by Mr. Isaac M. Heyliger. Taken from the Government Gazette of the St. Croix and republished ... as a Supplement to the Author's Explanatory Letter ... . *St. Croix [Christiansted]: printed by Elisabeth James.* 1824. 8vo, pp. 64. 5398

BILLE (Steen Andersen), *b.* 1797. Beretning om Corvetten Galathea's Reise omkring Jorden i Aarene 1845, 46 og 47. *Kjöbenhavn: Reitzel.* 1849–51. 3 vols., 8vo. 19 Lithographs, 5 Maps, and a Facsimile. + Anden, forkortede Udgave, efter Overeenskomst med Forfatteren besörget ved W. v. Rosen ... . *Kjöbenhaven: Reitzel.* 1853. 2 vols., 8vo. 12 Lith. and 2 Maps. 5399

BILLE. Bericht über die Reise der Corvette Galathea um die Welt in den Jahren 1845, 46 und 47. Aus dem Dänischen übersetzt und theilweise bearbeitet von W. von Rosen. *Kopenhagen: Reitzel.* 1852. 2 vols., 8vo, pp. xiv, 465; x, 518. 14 Plates and 2 Maps. H. 5400

BILLECOCQ (Jean Baptiste Louis Joseph). L'ancien avocat soussigné ... . *Paris: impr. de J. Tastu.* [n. d.] 4to, pp. 48 or less. 5401

"Consultation au sujet des quarante-un déportés de la Martinique."

BILLECOCQ. Mémoire sur les effets désastreux pour les colonies françaises, du système de fiscalité appliqué à leur commerce. Par M. Billecocq, avocat. *Paris: Charles Gosselin.* 15 *Janvier* 1825. 8vo, Title, pp. 40. H. 5402

M. Billecocq also translated J. Long's and J. Meares' "Voyages" into French.

BILLERICA, *Mass.* Celebration of the Two Hundreth Anniversary of the Incorporation of Billerica, Massachusetts, May 29th, 1855: including the Proceedings of the Committee, Address, Poem, and Other Exercises of the Occasion. With an Appendix. ... *Lowell.* 1855. 8vo, pp. 152, B., H., S. 5403

... Statement of the Expenses of ... Billerica, for ... 1847–8. *Lowell.* 1848. 8vo, pp. 11. H. 5404

Annual Report of the Receipts and Expenditures of the Town of Billerica. March 1852. *Lowell.* 1852. 8vo, (6) l. H. 5405

Also: "Annual Report of the School Committee" for various years.

BILLET (H.) De l'histoire, comment il conviendrait de la faire. La guerre de l'indépendance américaine Washington. ... Par M. Billet ... . *Montreuil-sur-Mer: Duval-Barbet.* 1852. 8vo, 1 sheet. 5406

BILLIARD (François Jacques Marie Auguste). Abolition de la traite et de l'esclavage dans les colonies françaises. Mémoire présenté aux chambres. Par A. Billiard ... . *Paris: Brière.* 1827. 8vo, 8¼ sheets. + Deuxième édition. *Paris.* 1827. 8vo. 5407

BILLIARD. Les vrais principes sur la question des sucres français et étrangers, ou nouvelles observations en faveur des colonies, présentées à MM. les membres de la commission d'enquête. *Paris: impr. de Doyen.* 1829. 8vo, pp. 24. 5408

BILLINGS (E.) Catalogues of the Silurian Fossils of the Islands of Anticosti: with Descriptions of some new Genera and Species. By E. Billings, F.G.S., Palæontologist of the Geological Survey of Canada. *Montreal.* 1866. Rl. 8vo, pp. 93. 5409

BILLINGS. Geological Survey of Canada. Palæozoic Fossils. Vol. I., containing Descriptions and Figures of New and Little-known Species of Organic Remains from the Silurian Rocks. By E. Billings, F.G.S. *London: Baillière.* 1866. Rl. 8vo, pp. 426. 400 Woodcuts. 5410

Some copies have the imprint, *Montreal.* 1865. Morgan's Bibl. Canad. contains an extended list of the author's contributions to serial literature.

BILLINGS (*Mrs.* E. A.) The Female Volunteer; or the Life, Wonderful Adventures and Miraculous Escapes of Miss Eliza Allen ... of Eastport, Maine. [n. p. 1851.] 8vo, 2 l., pp. 7–68. H. 5411

Miss Allen followed her lover, W. Billings, in the Mexican war and to California, in disguise. The autobiography ends with her marriage.

BILLINGS (F). An Address delivered at the Dedication of the School House in the Fifth District of San Francisco, September 23, 1854. By Frederick Billings, Esq. *San Francisco.* 1854. 8vo, pp. 20. BA. 5412

This and the following are partly historical:

BILLINGS. Address delivered at the Fifth Anniversary of the Orphan Asylum Society of San Francisco, Feb. 5, 1856. By Frederick Billings, Esq. *San Francisco.* 1856. 8vo, pp. 22. 5413

BILLINGS (J.) Expedition. *See* Sauer (Martin) *and* Savytchev.

BILLINGS (John). Oration, 4th July, 1808, on board the Sloop "William," of Portsmouth Harbor. By John Billings. *Portsmouth.* 1808. 8vo. N. 5414

BILLINGS (Josh.), *pseudon.* *See* [Shaw (Henry W.)]

BILLINGS (W.) The Continental Harmony, containing A Number of Anthems, Fuges, and Chorusses, in several Parts. ... By William Billings ... . *Boston: Isaiah Thomas and Ebenezer Andrews.* 1794. Oblong 8vo, pp. (1), 199, (1). H. 5415

BILLINGS. Music in Miniature, containing a Collection of Psalm Tunes of Various Metres, set in score by W. Billings. *Boston.* 1779. 12mo. 5416

BILLINGS. The New-England Psalm-singer, or American Chorister. *Boston.* [1770.] 4to. 5417

BILLINGS. The Psalm Singer's Amusement ... composed by William Billings ... . *Boston.* 1781. Oblong 8vo, pp. 103, (1). H. 5418

BILLINGS. The Singing Master's Assistant, or Key to Practical Music. Being An Abridgement from the New-England Psalm-Singer ... . Composed by William Billings ... . *Boston: Printed by Draper and Folsom.* 1778. Oblong 8vo, pp. 32, 104. 5419

BILLINGS. The Suffolk Harmony ... composed by William Billings ... . *Boston: the Author.* MDCCLXXXVI. Oblong 8vo, pp. (2), 56, (4), 8. H. 5420

BILLROTH (A.) Ein Evangelist in Brasilien. Aus dem Nachlasse Hermann Billroth's des vormaligen Pfarrers der deutsch-evangelischen Gemeinde in Rio de Janeiro vom Pred. Alb. Billroth. ... *Bremen: C. Ed. Müller.* 1867. 8vo, pp. viii, 488. Portrait of H. B., and Map. 5421

See W. Hauck's Theol. Jahresbericht, II. 546, 547.

Billyke beweegreedenen om aen Spanje den oorlog aen te doen voorgestelt in eene brief eenes koopmans te Londen, handelende op Amerika. ... In 't Hollands overgezet. ... *Amserdam [sic]: By Gerrit de Grott.* 1738. 8vo, pp. 30. 5422

This is perhaps a translation of "Strenuous motives for an immediate war with Spain. *London.* 1738."

BILTON (Thomas). Captain Bilton's Journal of his Unfortunate Voyage from Lisbon to Virginia, In the Year 1707. Giving an Account of the Miraculous Preservation of Himself and Nine other Persons; who ... reduc'd to a small Boat ... for 31 Days ... At length ... were Cast upon ... Anguilla, a small Island in the West-Indies; An Exact Description thereof; Their Reception ... and ... the Strange Creatures found in those Parts. *London: A. Bettesworth, and E. Curll.* 1715. 8vo, 2 l, pp. 28. H. 5423

"Merely a journal of winds, weather, &c., extracted from the Log-book, with a few occasional observations." — RICH, Vol. I. 428.

BILUAO. Sermon de la Fe, en el solene y General Auto, que su Tribunal Santo celebrò en la Ciudad de Lima. Por Luys de Biluao. *Lima.* 1626. 4to. 5424

BIMBO, *pseudon.* The Pleasures of Yachting; addressed to Col. W. P. Winchester, by his Friend Bimbo. *Boston: Eastburn's Press.* 1849. 8vo, pp. 10. H. 5425

In a copy in Harv. Coll. Libr. the names of the yachting-party are supplied in MS.

BINCKES (Jacob). Missive van den Commandeur Binckes, geschrieven aen S. H. Prince van Orange ... aen 't Eylant Tabago, den 22 Mrt., 1677. *'s Gravenhage: J. Scheltus.* 1677. 4to, pp. 4. 5426

BINDER (Chr.) Mærkværdigt Brev om Mormonernes Skjændigheder. *Kiöbenhavn: Gandrup.* 1854. 8vo. 5427

BINET (G.) Neuf mois aux Etats Unis d'Amérique. Par M. G. Binet. *Geneve: Joel Cherbuliez.* 1862. 12mo, pp. 184. 5428

A sketchy account of a rapid run through the United States, with a few trivial remarks upon politics.

BINGHAM (A.) Ojibwa Spelling-Book, according to the Improved Orthography of Edwin James. By A. Bingham. *Albany.* 1825 or 1829. 8vo. 5429

BINGHAM (Caleb). The American Preceptor. Ninth Edition. *Boston.* 1801. 12mo. 5430

BINGHAM. The Columbian Orator, original and selected Pieces, with Rules for the Art of Eloquence. *Boston.* 1797. 12mo. + 15th Edition. *Boston. April,* 1812. 12mo, pp. 300. 5431

Frequently reprinted. The last I have seen is *New York and Baltimore.* 1841.

BINGHAM (H) A Residence of Twenty-one Years in the Sandwich Islands; or, the Civil, Religious, and Political History of those Islands; comprising a Particular View of the Missionary Operations connected with the Introduction and Progress of Christianity and Civilization among the Hawaiian People. By Hiram Bingham. *Hartford.* 1847. 8vo, pp. 616. Map and Plates. + Second Edition. *Hartford.* 1848. 8vo. + Third Edition ... . To which is added a Table of Missionaries of the American Board ... . *Hartford: Hezekiah Huntington.* 1849. 8vo, pp. 616, (4). Portrait, 6 Woodcuts, and Map. H. + *Canandaigua.* 1855. 8vo, pp. 616, (4). 5432

Probably the best work on the Sandwich Islands. Scarcely relates to America, except that the missionary operations were chiefly by Americans.

BINGHAM (J. C.) The Spoiler Spoiled. A Sermon preached in the Free Presbyterian Churches of Neshanock and Hopewell, Thursday, June 1st, 1865. By Rev. J. C. Bingham. Published by the Congregation. *Mercer: Office of the Whig and Dispatch.* [1865.] 12mo, pp. 13. 5433

On the death of Abraham Lincoln.

BINGHAM (J. F.) Bright Republic. A Song and Chorus Written for the National Jubilee, July 4th, 1865. By Rev. J. F. Bingham. Music by William Krauskopp. [*Buffalo, N. Y.* 1865.] 8vo, pp. 4. 5434

BINGHAM. Great Providences toward the Loyal Part of this Nation. A Discourse delivered at the United Service of the Seven Presbyterian Congregations of Buffalo, Nov. 24, 1864, on the occasion of the Annual Thanksgiving of the State and the Nation. *Buffalo: Breed, Butler & Co.* 1864. 8vo, pp. 59. 5435

BINGHAM. The Hour of Patriotism. A Discourse. ... at Buffalo, November 27, 1862, the day of the Annual Thanksgiving in the State of New York. By Joel F. Bingham, Pastor of Westminster Congregation. *Buffalo: Franklin Press.* 1862. 8vo, pp. 39. 5436

BINGHAM. National Disappointment. A Discourse occasioned by the Assassination of President Lincoln delivered in Westminster Church, Buffalo, Sunday Evening, May 7th, 1865. By Joel F. Bingham, Pastor of the Congregation. *Buffalo: Breed, Butler and Company.* 1865. 8vo, pp. 36. 5437

BINGHAM (J. A.) Argument of John A. Bingham, Chairman of the Managers on the Part of the House, before the Senate of the United States, sitting for the Trial of Andrew Johnson, President of the United States, impeached ... May 4, 5, and 6, 1868. *Washington: F. & J. Rives & Geo. Bailey.* 1868. 8vo, pp. 59. H. 5438

BINGHAM. Bill and Report of John A. Bingham, and Vote on its Passage, repealing the Territorial New Mexican Laws establishing Slavery and authorizing Employers to whip "White Persons" and others in their Employment, and denying them Redress in the Courts. [n. p. 1860?] 8vo, pp. 7. H. 5439

BINGHAM. Bingham's Bill and Report on the New Mexican Slave Codes. [n. p. 1860.] 8vo, pp. 8. H. 5440

BINGHAM. "The Constitution as it is." Speech of Hon. J. A. Bingham, of Ohio, in reply to Mr. Norton of Missouri. Delivered ... January 9, 1863. [n. p. n. d.] 8vo, pp. 8. 5441

BINGHAM. Kansas Contested Election. Speech of Hon. J. A. Bingham, of Ohio, in the House ... March 6, 1856. ... *Washington, D. C.: Buell & Blanchard.* 1856. 8vo, pp. 12. H. 5442

BINGHAM. The Lecompton Conspiracy. Speech of Hon. John A. Bingham ... in the House ... January 25, 1858. [*Washington.* 1858.] 8vo, pp. 8. H. 5443

BINGHAM. Policy of the President. Speech of Hon. John A. Bingham ... January 9, 1866. [n. p. n. d.] 8vo, pp. 8. 5444

BINGHAM. The Power and Duty of Congress to Provide for the Common Defence and the Suppression of the Rebellion. Speech of Hon. John A. Bingham. ... January 15, 1862. [n. p. n. d.] 8vo, pp. 8. 5445

BINGHAM. The Treasury Note Bill. Speech of Hon. Jno. A. Bingham ... In the House ... February 4, 1862. [*Washington.* 1862.] 8vo, pp. 8. H. 5446

BINGHAM. Self-Preservation the Right and Duty of the General Government. The Rebel States but Organized Conspiracies—not Constitutional States, nor entitled to State Rights. Speech of the Hon. John A. Bingham ... In the House ... March 12, 1862. [n. p. 1862.] 8vo, pp. 8. H. 5447

BINGHAM. Shall the Government surrender to the Rebellion? Speech of Hon. John A. Bingham in Reply to Hon. C. L. Vallandigham ... January 14, 1863. [n. p. n. d.] 8vo, pp. 16. 5448

BINGHAM. Speech of Hon. Jno. A. Bingham ... in reply to Hon. John J. Crittenden ... in the House ... April 11, 1862, on the Bill to emancipate Slaves ... . [*Washington.* 1862.] 8vo, pp. 8. H. 5449

BINGHAM. Speech of Hon. John A. Bingham ... on the Civil Rights Bill; delivered in the House ... March 9, 1866. *Washington.* 1866. 8vo, pp. 8. H. 5450

BINGHAM. Trial of the Conspirators for the Assassination of President Lincoln, &c. Argument of John A. Bingham, Special Judge Advocate ... . Delivered June 27 and 28, 1865, before the Military Commission, Washington, D. C. *Washington: Government Printing Office.* 1865. 8vo, pp. 122. H. 5451

BINGHAM. Reply of the Judge Advocate, John A. Bingham, to the Defence of the Accused, before a General Court Martial for the Trial of Surgeon General Hammond. *Washington: Government Printing Office.* 1864. 8vo, pp. 64. 5452

BINGHAM (K. S.) The Rise and Fall of the Democratic Party. Speech of Hon. Kinsley S. Bingham, of Michigan, ... in the ... Senate, May 24, 1860. [*Washington.* 1860.] 8vo, pp. 16. H. 5453

BINGHAM. Territorial Governments. Speech of Hon. Kinsley S. Bingham, of Michigan. ... In the House ... August 7, 1848. *Washington.* 1848. 8vo, pp. 8. H. 5454

[BINGHAM (L. D.)] The Little Drummer-Boy; a Sketch of the Life of Clarence D. McKenzie, the child of the 13th Regt. N. Y. S. M. *New York: Wm. Ferris.* 1862. 5455

[BINGHAM (L. G.)] The Young Christian Soldier [Luther M. Bingham]: his Life and Death. *Boston: Army Committee of the Young Men's Christian Association.* [n. d.] 32mo, pp. 15, (1). H. 5456

BINGHAM. The Young Quartermaster. The Life and Death of Lieut. L. M. Bingham of the 1st So. Ca. Vols. *New York: Bd. of Pub. Ref. Pr. Dutch Ch.* 1864. 18mo, pp. 216. Portrait. 5457

[BINGHAM (William).] A Letter from an American, Now resident in London, to a Member of Parliament, on the Subject of the Restraining Proclamation; and containing Strictures on Lord Sheffield's Pamphlet, on the Commerce of the American States. *London: J. Stockdale.* MDCCLXXXIV. 8vo, 2 l., pp. 52. H. 5458

Reprinted with the following addition to the title:

BINGHAM. A Letter from an American [as in No. 5458]. Said to be written by William Bingham, Esquire; late Agent for the Congress of the United States of America, at Martinico. To which are added, Mentor's Reply to Phocion's Letter; with some Observations on Trade, addressed to the Citizens of New-York. *Philadelphia: Robert Bell.* M.DCC.LXXXIII. 8vo, pp. 24. + *Philadelphia: Robert Bell.* M,DCC,LXXXIV. 8vo, pp. 24. H., P. 5459

This also forms No. 1 of M. Carey's "Miscellaneous Pamphlets, chiefly on American Affairs." Both Allen and Allibone attribute a description of Maine to this author, which is an error. *See* Lincoln (Benjamin).

BINGLEY (W.) An | Epistle of Love | and Tender Advice, | to | Friends and Brethren | in | America, | Or elsewhere; | To live in the Truth, that they may shew | forth the Virtue and Effects of it in | Holy Life. | By your Friend and Brother in the Truth, who Travels | for Sion's Prosperity, | William Bingley. | [*London*] *Printed by Andrew Sowle: And sold at the three-Keys in | Nags-Head-Court in Grace-Church-Street,* 1689. | 4to, pp. 14. 5460

BINGLEY (*Rev.* W.) Biographical Conversations on Celebrated Travellers; comprehending Distinct Narratives of their Personal Adventures. By Rev. William Bingley. *London: J. Sharpe.* 1819. 16mo, pp. x, 360. C. + Second Edition. [*Ibid.*] 1821? 12mo. + Third Edition. [*Ibid.*] 1826. 12mo. B. 5461

BINGLEY. Biographical Conversations on the most eminent Voyagers of different Nations from Columbus to Cook. By Rev. William Bingley. *London: J. Sharpe.* 1818. 16mo, pp. xii, 348. C. + Second Edition. [*Ibid.*] 1821? 12mo. + *London.* 1826. 5462

BINGLEY. Travels in North America, from Modern Writers. With Remarks and Observations; exhibiting a Connected View of the Geography and Present State of that Quarter of the Globe. By the Rev. William Bingley ... . *London: Harvey and Darton.* 1821. 12mo, 6 l., pp. 346. 3 Plates. H. 5463

BINGLEY. Travels in South America. From Modern Writers, with Remarks and Observations; exhibiting a Connected View of the Geography and Present State of that Quarter of the Globe. By the Rev. William Bingley ... . *London: John Sharpe.* 1820. 12mo, 6 l., pp. 346. 2 Plates. BA. 5464

BINNEY (Amos). Documents relative to the Investigation, By Order of the Secretary of the Navy, of the Official Conduct of Amos Binney, United States Navy Agent at Boston, upon the Charges made by Lieutenant Joel Abbot and others. Published by the Accused. *Boston: printed by Phelps and Farnham.* 1822. 8vo, pp. iv, 260. C., H. 5465

[BINNEY.] Remarks made at the Annual Meeting of the Boston Society of Natural History, June 2, 1845; showing the Origin and History of the Society, its Influence on the Cultivation of the Natural Sciences in New England ... . By the President. *Boston: Freeman and Bolles.* 1845. 8vo, pp. 16. H. 5466

BINNEY. The Terrestrial Air-Breathing Mollusks of the United States, and the Adjacent Territories of North America: described and illustrated by Amos Binney. Edited by Augustus A. Gould, Vols. I.–III. Plates. *Boston: Charles C. Little ana James Brown.* MDCCCLI–LVII. 3 vols., 8vo, pp. xxix, 1 l., 9–266; 4 l., 362; 40. C. 5467

Vol. III. consists chiefly of plates, which are published plain and colored. Some copies have the plates on India paper, and a few were issued on large paper, with the plates in duplicate, *i. e.*, plain on India paper, and colored on ordinary paper. Imp. 8vo. H. For Vol. IV., *see* Binney (W. G.)

BINNEY (B.) An Oration delivered on the late Public Commencement at Rhode-Island College, in Providence, September 1774. Being A Plea, for the Right of Private Judgment in Religious Matters; or, For the Liberty of choosing our own Religion, corroborated By the well-known consequences of Priestly Power. To which, are annexed, The Valedictions of the Class then first graduated. By Barnabas Binney, A.B. ... *Boston: John Kneeland.* MDCCLXXIV. 4to, pp. 44. H. 5468

BINNEY (C. J. F.) The History and Genealogy of the Prentice or Prentiss Family, in New England, from 1631 to 1852. Collected by C. J. F. Binney. *Boston: the Author.* 1852. 8vo, pp. iv, 272, 8. Lith. Plates and Portraits. B , C., H. 5469

BINNEY (H.) Address to Contributors at Centennial Meeting of the Philadelphia Contributionship for the Insurance of Houses from Loss by Fire. *Philadelphia: ... C. Sherman, Printer.* 1852. 8vo, pp. 77. 5470

[BINNEY.] The Alienigenæ of the United States under the Present Naturalization Laws. *Philadelphia: C. Sherman, Printer.* 1853. 8vo, pp. 32. + Second Edition. [*Ibid.*] H. 5471

BINNEY. Argument of Horace Binney, Esq., in the Case of Vidal *vs.* the City of Philadelphia, in the Supreme Court of the United States, February, 1844. *Philadelphia: C. Sherman, Printer.* 1844. 8vo. 5472

[BINNEY.] Bushrod Washington. [Motto.] *Philadelphia: printed by C. Sherman.* 1858. 8vo, pp. 29. BA. 5473

BINNEY. Correspondence and Remarks in regard to Bishop Doane's Signature of the name of Horace Binney as a Subscriber to the new Church Edifice in Burlington. *Philadelphia.* 1849. 8vo, pp. 87. S. 5474

BINNEY. An Eulogium upon the Hon. William Tilghman, late Chief Justice of Pennsylvania. By Horace Binney. *Philadelphia: C. Sherman & Son.* [1827.] 8vo, pp. 50. P. + *Philadelphia: Philip H. Nicklin.* 1827. 8vo, pp. 46. H. 5475

BINNEY. An Eulogy on the Life and Character of John Marshall, Chief Justice of the Supreme Court of the United States. Delivered at the Request of the Councils of Philadelphia, on the 24th September, 1835. By Horace Binney. *Philadelphia: printed by J. Crissy and G. Goodman.* 1835. 8vo, pp. 70, and Erratum. H. 5476

[BINNEY.] An Inquiry into the Formation of Washington's Farewell Address. ... *Philadelphia: Parry & McMillan.* 1859. 8vo, pp. 250. C., H. 5477

[BINNEY.] The Leaders of the Old Bar of Philadelphia. ... *Philadelphia: printed by C. Sherman and Son.* 1859. 8vo, pp. 120. H. + *Philadelphia: H. B. Ashmead.* 1866. 5478

One hundred copies of the edition (1866) printed.

BINNEY. Letter from Horace Binney. ... To the General Committee of Invitation and Correspondence of the Union League of Philadelphia ... . [n. p. 1863.] 8vo, pp. 4. H.

[BINNEY.] Obituary. Horace Binney Wallace. *Philadelphia: C. Sherman, Printer.* 1853. 8vo, pp. 12. 5480

[BINNEY.] The Privilege of the Writ of Habeas Corpus under the Constitution. *Philadelphia: T. B. Pugh.* 1862. 12mo, pp 52. + Second Edition. *Philadelphia: C. Sherman & Son, Printers.* 1862. 8vo, pp. 58. B. 5481

[BINNEY.] Second Part. The Privilege of the Writ of Habeas Corpus under the Constitution. *Philadelphia: C. Sherman & Son, Printers.* 1862. 8vo, pp. 50. H. + *Philadelphia: John Campbell.* 1862. 8vo, pp. 50. B. 5482

Forty-nine copies printed on large paper in 4to.

[BINNEY.] Third Part. The Privilege of the Writ of Habeas Corpus under the Constitution. *Philadelphia: Sherman & Co., Printers.* 1865. 8vo, pp. 74. C. 5483

BINNEY. Presidential Power over Personal Liberty. A Review of Horace Binney's Essay on the Writ of Habeas Corpus. [n. p.] *Imprinted for the Author.* 1862. 8vo, pp. 94. B., C. 5484

Attributed to Isaac Myer, Jr.

BINNEY. Remarks on Mr. Binney's Treatise on the Writ of Habeas Corpus. By a Member of the Philadelphia Bar. *Philadelphia.* 1862. 8vo, pp. 29. C. 5485

BINNEY. A Reply to Horace Binney's Pamphlet on the Habeas Corpus. *Philadelphia.* 1862. 8vo, pp. 40. C. B. 5486

Attributed to Charles H. Gross. *See also* [Brown (D. B.)], Bullitt (J. C.), Jackson (T.), [Montgomery (J. T.)], Nicolas (S. S.), and [Wharton (G. M.)] The controversy respecting the privilege of the writ of habeas corpus grew out of some arrests made in the North during the Civil War, in the year 1862.

BINNEY. The Writ of Habeas Corpus and Mr. Binney. [*Philadelphia.* 1862.] 8vo, pp. 35. + Second Edition. *Philadelphia: John Campbell.* 1862. 8vo, pp. 29. C. 5487

BINNEY. Opinion of Horace Binney, Esq. on the Right of Councils to Subscribe for Stock in the Pennsylvania Railroad Company. *Philadelphia.* 1846. 8vo. P. 5488

BINNEY. Opinion of Horace Binney, Esq. on the Columbia Bridge Company. *Columbia, Pennsylvania.* 1820. 12mo. P.

BINNEY. Remarks to the Bar of Philadelphia, on the occa-

sion of the Deaths of Charles Chauncey and John Sergeant. By Horace Binney. *Philadelphia: C. Sherman, Printer.* 1853. 8vo, pp. 39. C. 5490

BINNEY. Remarks upon Mr. Binney's Letter, of January 3, 1840, to the Presidents of the Councils of the City of Philadelphia. By the Writer of the Letter. *Philadelphia: C. Sherman & Co., Printers.* 1840. 8vo, pp. 31. H., P. 5491

I have not seen the letter refered to. It is "A short Letter to the Councils of Philadelphia.

BINNEY. ... Removal Public Deposites. Report Of the Minority of the Committee of Ways and Means. Submitted by Mr. Binney. March 4, 1834. ... [*Washington.* 1834.] 8vo, pp. 34. (23d Cong., 1st Sess., House Rep. No. 313.) H. 5492

BINNEY. Reply to part of the Report to the Diocesan Convention of New Jersey, in the case of Bishop Doane. By Horace Binney. *Philadelphia.* 1852. 8vo. 5493

[BINNEY.] A Review of Hamilton's Edition of the Federalist. Philadelphia, 1864. [*Philadelphia: Sherman, Printer.* 1864.] 8vo, pp. 8. 5494

BINNEY. Speech delivered by Horace Binney, Esq., at the Anti-Jackson Meeting, held in the State House Yard, Philadelphia, October 20, 1832. [*Philadelphia.* 1832.] 8vo, pp. 8.

BINNEY. Speech of Mr. Binney, of Pennsylvania, on the Contested Election of Letcher and Moore. Delivered in the House ... May, 1834. *Washington.* 1834. 8vo, pp. 23. BA.

BINNEY. Speech of the Hon. Horace Binney, on the Question of the Removal of the Deposites. Delivered in the House ... January, 1834. *Washington.* 1834. 8vo, pp. 56. B., H.

Mr. Binney also published "Reports of Cases adjudged in the Supreme Court of Pennsylvania," and other law tracts.

BINNEY (T.) A Study for Young Men; or, A Sketch of Sir Thomas Fowell Buxton. By Rev. Thomas Binney. *Boston: Wm. Crosby and H. P. Nichols.* 1851. 18mo, pp. 149. H.

BINNEY (William). Oration on the Death of Abraham Lincoln. *See* Providence, *R. I.*, Proceedings.

BINNEY (William G.) ... Bibliography of North American Conchology, previous to the Year 1860. Prepared for the Smithsonian Institution, by W. G. Binney. Part I. American Authors. *Washington.* 1863. 8vo, pp. iv, 2 l., 650. (Smiths. Misc. Coll., Vol. V.) H. + Part II. Foreign Authors. *Washington.* 1864. 8vo, pp. 298. C. 5499

BINNEY. Description of American Land Shells. 4 parts. [*Philadelphia.*] 1857. 8vo, pp. 32. C. 5500

BINNEY. List of North-American Gasteropoda. Second Edition. [*Washington.* 1860.] 8vo. 5501

BINNEY. Land and Fresh-Water Shells of North America. Part II. Pulmonata Limnophila and Thalassophila. By W. G. Binney. *Washington. September*, 1865. 8vo, pp. ix, 161. 261 Woodcuts. (Smithsonian Misc. Col., Vol. VII.) H. 5502

"Part I, now ready for the press."—*Preface*, dated August, 1865.

BINNEY. ... Land and Fresh-Water Shells of North America. Part III. Ampullariidæ, Valvatidæ, Viviparidæ, Fresh-Water Rissoidæ, Cyclophoridæ, Truncatellidæ, Fresh-Water Neritidæ, Helicinidæ. By W. G. Binney. *Washington. September*, 1865. 8vo, pp. viii, 120. (Smithsonian Misc. Coll., Vol. VII.) H.

BINNEY. Notes on American Land Shells. No. 4. By W. G. Binney. 8vo, pp. 33. C. 5504

BINNEY. The Terrestrial Air-Breathing Mollusks of the United States, and the Adjacent Territories of North America. Vol. IV. By W. G. Binney ... . *Boston: from the Boston Journal of Natural History, Vol. VII. New York: B. Westermann.* M DCCC LIX. 4to, pp. viii, 207. 6 Plates. B. 5505

For vols. I–III, *see* Binney (Amos). For other papers, *see* Royal Society's "Cat. of Scientific Papers. (1800–1863.)"

BINNS (J.) An Oration, on American Independence, July 4, 1810. By John Binns. *Philadelphia.* 1810. 8vo, pp. 11. P.

BINNS. Recollections of the Life of John Binns; Twenty-nine years in Europe, and Fifty-three in the United States. Written by himself, with Anecdotes; Political, Historical, and Miscellaneous. *Philadelphia.* 1854. 12mo, pp. 349. Portrait.

BINNS (William). A Sermon on the Death of President Lincoln, Preached by the Rev. W. Binns, in the Unitarian Chapel,

Birkenhead, On Sunday Evening, April 23rd, 1865. Reprinted from the "Birkenhead & Cheshire Advertiser." *Birkenhead: J. Oliver, Printer.* 1865. 18mo, pp. 13. 5508

Biographia Americana. *See* [French (B. F.)]

The Biographical Annual: containing Memoirs of Eminent Persons Recently deceased. Edited by R. W. Griswold. ... *New-York: Linen and Fennel.* 1841. 12mo, Title, pp. ix–307. 2 Portraits, and a title-vignette. C., H. 5509

The Biographical Magazine containing Portraits of Eminent and Ingenious Persons of every age and nation. With their Lives and Characters. *London.* 1794. + Second Edition. *London: E. Wilson.* MDCCCXIX. 2 vols., rl. 8vo. 5510

Includes Columbus, Drake, and Rawleigh.

Biographical Memoirs of Washington. *See* [Condie (J.)], [Corry (John)], and Washington (G.)

Biographical Sketches of Eccentric Characters. *Boston.* 1832. 18mo. C. 5511

Biographie de deux Indiens de la haute Californie. Helba, chef de la tribu des Nemchas, âgé de 24 ans. Walpouté, sa femme en quatrième noces, âgée de 14 ans, d'une tribu plus éloignée. *Paris: impr. de Gaittet.* 1855. 18mo, 1 sheet. 5512

Biographie etrangère: ou galerie universelle, historique, civile, militaire, politique et littéraire; Contenant les portraits politiques de plus de trois mille personages célèbres ... parmi lesquels on distingue surtout les indépendans espagnols de l'Amérique méridionale ... . Par une Société de Gens de Lettres. *Paris: Alexis Eymery.* 1819. 2 vols., 8vo, 2 l, pp. ii, 470; 2 l., pp. 452. B.

Biographies of Successful Philadelphia Merchants. *Philadelphia: J. K. Simon.* 1864. 8vo, pp. 245. 5514

BIONDELLI (Bern.) *See* Evangeliarium epistolarium.

[BIONDELLI (B.)] Scoperta dell' America fatta nel secolo x da alcuni scandinavi *Milan.* 1839. 8vo, Title, pp. 20. H.

Signed "B. Biondelli. Dalla Rivista europea 28 febbraio 1839."

BIONDELLI. Sunto di alcune lezioni sulle antichitá Americane. *Milano.* 1853. 8vo. 5516

BIONDO (Michaele Angelo). De ventis et navigatione libellus, cum accuratissima descriptione, a Gadibus ad Novum Orbem. *Venetiis: apud Commum de Tridino.* 1544. 8vo. 5517

"Annoncé comme un des livres les plus rares sur l'Amerique."—BRUNET. Libri's copy, 1859, sold for £2 8s.

BIONDO. De Ventis et Naviga- | tione, Libellvs | Avttore Michaele | Angelo Blondo | inqvo Navigationis Vtilis- | sima continetvr Doctrina cvm | Pixide nouo, & diligenti examine | uentorum, et tempestatum. | Cvm Accvrantissima Descriptione | distantiæ locorum interni maris, & Oceani, a Gadibus ad | nouum orbem, vtique valde necessaria, Nam | seruantes doctrinam hanc, cum citius | tum securius vtrunq*ue* mare | transfretabunt. | Opus Recentissmvm. | Cum Priuilegio Summi Pontificis atq: Illustrissim | Senatus Venetiarum in Decennium. | [Colophon:] *Venetijs Apud Cominum de | Tridino Montisferrati* | M . D . XLVI. | 4to, 18 l. BM.

Contains "Woodcut diagrams showing the cardinal points. On the recto of leaf 16 begins: 'De nauigatione oceani ad nouû orbem. Cap. XXV.'"—HARRISSE. Pinelo cites an edition, 1648. Probably an error. "Traité fort rare relatif à l'Amérique et dans lequel on trouve aussi un traité du compas."—LECLERC.

BIONNE (H.) La question du percement de l'isthme de Panama, devant un congrès international. Par M. Henry Bionne, lieutenant de vaisseau. *Paris: E. Lacroix.* 1864. 8vo, pp. 16. Map. C. 5519

BIOREN (J.) Bioren's Town and Country Almanack, (formerly published by Mr. Zachariah Poulson.) for ... 1808 ... . *Philadelphia: John Bioren.* [1807.] 12mo, pp. 48. H. 5520

BIOT (Édouard Constant). Mémoire sur la condition de la classe servile au Mexique avant la conquête des Espagnols. *Paris: B. Duprat.* 1840. 8vo. 5521

Quérard merely mentions a "Note sur la condition des esclaves au Mexique avant l'invasion des Espagnols.—Impr. dans le Journal de la morale chétienne, t. XX [1841]." The title above, taken from a bookseller's catalogue, perhaps belongs to the same work, which may never have been separately published. It is not mentioned in the "Bibliog. de la France," 1840–41. The "Uber die Anlegung," by this author, has the word America in the title, but there is nothing in the work to justify its insertion here.

BIOT (Jean Baptiste). Mélanges scientifiques et littéraires par J.-B. Biot ... . *Paris: Michel Lévy freres.* 1858. 3 tom., 8vo. H.

"Franklin," III. 57–91; a notice of Irving's "Astoria," III. 333–386; and of Wilkes' expedition, III. 387–461.

BIRCH (A. N.) *See* The Colonial Office List.

BIRCH (E. P.) The Refined Poetry of the South. (From

the Southern Confederacy.) The Devil's Visit to "Old Abe." By Rev. E. P. Birch, of La Grange, Ga. [n. p. n. d.]. 8vo, pp. 4. 5523

BIRCH (J. H.) Address in Commemoration of ... William Henry Harrison. Delivered ... at Fayette, Missouri ... the Third Day of May 1841. By James H. Birch. *Benson & Green, Boon's Lick Times.* [n. d.] 8vo, pp. 23. BA. 5524

[BIRCH.] Letters to the President of the United States, exposing the Official Malversations of the Commission of the General Land Office, and the Secretary of the Interior, as shown in Senate Committee Report, No. 289. *Saint Joseph, Mo.: F. M. Posegate & Co., Printers.* 1858. 8vo, Title, pp. 39, (1). H.

Signed James H. Birch.

BIRCH. Review of Senate Committee Report, No. 289. ... [*St. Joseph, Mo.* 1858.] 8vo, pp. 21, (1). H. 5526

BIRCH. Speech of James H. Birch, delivered in the House of Representatives, June 1, 1864, in the Contested Election Case with Austin A. King. [n. p. n. d.] 8vo, pp. 12. 5527

BIRCH (T. E.) Virginian Orator; being a Variety of Original and Select Poems, Orations, and Dramatic Scenes ... By Thomas E. Birch. *Richmond.* 1808. 16mo. C. 5528

BIRCH (T. L.) Seemingly Experimental Religion or War against the Gospel by its Friends. Being the Examination and Rejection of Tho. Ledie Birch, a Foreign ordained Minister, by the Rev. Presbytery of Ohio, under the very Rev. General Assembly's Alien Act; The Trial of the Rev. John M'Millan, ... and Injustice in permiting the Rev. John M'Millan to escape Church Censure. With Remarks ... By the Rev. Thomas Ledie Birch, A.M. *Washington: Printed for the Author.* MDCCCVI. 8vo, pp. 144. 5529

BIRCH (W.) The City of Philadelphia, in the State of Pennsylvania, North America, as it Appeared in the Year 1800, consisting of 28 Plates. Drawn and Engraved by W. Birch and Sons. *Philadelphia.* 1800. Oblong 4to. C. 5530

BIRCH. The Country Seats of the United States, with some Scenes connected with them. By W. Birch. *Springfield, Pa.* 1808. Oblong 4to. Part I. 20 Plates. 5531

BIRCKHEAD (J.) and Co. Pro-Forma Sales and Invoices of Imports and Exports at Rio de Janeiro, with Tables, Remarks, etc.; James Birckhead and Co. *Rio de Janeiro: Printing Office of P. Plancher.* 1827. 8vo, pp. 59. 5532

BIRD (Francis W.) Address of Hon. F. W. Bird, to his Constituents, upon the Provisions of the New Constitution, delivered at South Walpole, October 29th, 1853. ... *Boston.* 1853. 8vo, pp. 20. H. 5533

BIRD. "The Existing Vacancy" (which never existed) "in the 7th Councillor District." By F. W. Bird. ... *Boston.* 1865. 8vo, pp. 34. H. 5534

BIRD. The Hoosac Tunnel: its Condition and Prospects. By F. W. Bird. ... *Boston.* 1865. 8vo, pp. 28. H. 5535

BIRD. The Hoosac Tunnel: our Financial Maelstrom. By F. W. Bird. ... *Boston.* 1866. 8vo, pp. 69. H. 5536

BIRD. The Last Agony of the Great Bore [the Hoosac Tunnel]. By F. W. Bird. *Boston: E. P. Dutton & Co.* 1868. 8vo. H. 5537

BIRD. "Let my People go." Originally published in Norfolk Co. Journal, of December 14th, 1861. With some slight additions and corrections, is republished ... . By F. W. Bird. *Boston.* 1862. 8vo, pp. 8. H. 5538

BIRD. Review of Gov. Banks' Veto of the Revised Code, on account of its authorizing the Enrolment of Colored Citizens in the Militia. ... By F. W. Bird. *Boston.* 1860. 8vo, pp. 58, iv. B., H. 5539

BIRD. The Road to Ruin: or, the Decline and Fall of the Hoosac Tunnel. ... By F. W. Bird. Third Edition. *Boston.* 1862. 8vo, pp. 46. H. 5540

BIRD *and* GRIFFIN (J. Q. A.) The Election Case in the Eleventh (Norfolk) District. Arguments before the Committee on Elections, by Hon. F. W. Bird and J. Q. A. Griffin, Esq., February 14 and 16, 1866. *Boston.* 1866. 8vo, pp. 29. H.

[BIRD (H. M.)] A View of the relative Situation of Great Britain and the United States of North America. By a Merchant. *London: J. Debrett.* M, DCC, XCIV. 8vo, 2 l., pp. 43. C.

Attributed to H. M. Bird in the Catal. of the Canadian Parliament. *See* M. R., XIV. 212.

BIRD (Isaac). Genealogical Sketch of the Bird Family, having its origin in Hartford, Conn. By Isaac Bird. *Hartford: Elihu Geer.* 1855. 24mo, pp. 8. S. 5543

[BIRD (*Miss* Isabella).] Aspects of Religion in the United States of America. By the author of "The Englishwoman in America." *London: S. Low and Co.* 1859. 12mo, pp. 190. C.

[BIRD.] The Englishwoman in America. *London.* 1856. 12mo. C. 5545

BIRD (James). Francis Abbot, the Recluse of Niagara; and Metropolitan Sketches, Second Series. *London.* 1837. 8vo.

BIRD (J.) A Discourse delivered to the Freemen collected in the Second Society in Saybrook, April 11th, A.D. 1803. By Jonathan Bird, A.M. ... *Middletown: printed by T. & J. B. Dunning.* [n. d.] 8vo, pp. 16. H. 5547

"It has excited much warmth, and many illiberal observations among the Demo's in this town." — *Advertisement.*

BIRD (Joseph). Fires and Fire Systems. [*Cambridge?* 1858.] 8vo, pp. 16. H. 5548

BIRD (R. M.) Abdalla the Moor, and the Spanish Knight. A Romance of Mexico. *London: A. K. Newman.* 1835. 4 vols., 12mo. BM. 5549

BIRD. Calavar; or the Knight of the Conquest; a Romance of Mexico. *Philadelphia.* 1834. 2 vols., 12mo. + New Edition. *Philadelphia.* 1847. + *New York.* 1854. 2 vols., 12mo.

BIRD. Cortes; or the Fall of Mexico. A Romance. *London: R. Bentley.* 1835. 3 vols., post 8vo. 5550*a*

BIRD. The Hawks of Hawk Hollow; a Tradition of Pennsylvania. *Philadelphia.* 1835. 2 vols., 12mo. C. + *London: A. K. Newman.* 1837. 3 vols., 12mo. + *London: Ward & Lock.* 1856. Fcap 8vo 5551

BIRD. De valken uit het valkenhol. Eene geschiedenis uit Pensylvanië. Uit het Engelsch. *Deventer: A. ter Gunne.* 1843. 2 vols., 8vo. 5552

BIRD. The Infidel; or the Fall of Mexico. A Romance. ... *Philadelphia: Carey, Lea & Blanchard.* 1835. 2 vols., 12mo, pp. (3), 14–254; (3), 14–228. H. 5553

BIRD. Nick of the Woods or Jibbenainosay. A Tale of Kentucky. By R. M. Bird. *Philadelphia.* 1837. 2 vols., 12mo. + A New Edition. *New York: Redfield.* 1853. 12mo, pp. xii, 391. + *London: R. Bentley.* 1837. 3 vols., post 8vo. + *London: Ward & Lock.* 1860. Fcap 8vo. + A New Edition, revised by the Author. *New York: W. J. Widdleton.* 1864. 12mo, pp. 392. 5554

BIRD. Ausgewählte Amerikanische Romane. *Frankfurt, a. M.: Sauerländer.* 1840–41. 6 vols., 16mo. (Bibliothek klassischer Schriftsteller Nordamerika's, Band VII.–XII.) 5555

There are two novels, each in 3 vols., and with a second title-page, viz.: "Die Falken aus der Falken-Höhle. Eine Geschichte aus Pensylvanien," and "Der Waldteufel. Ein Roman aus Kentucky."

BIRD. Nathan der Quäker, oder der Satan des Urwaldes. Nordamerikanischer Roman, herausgegeben von W. Harrison Ainsworth. Aus dem Englischen übersetzt von Joh. Sporschil. *Leipzig: Kollmann.* 1838. 3 vols., 8vo. 5556

BIRD. Die Gefahren der Wildness. Eine Erzählung ... . Nach dem Englischen des Dr. Bird bearbeitet von F. Hoffmann. ... *Stuttgart: Stoppani.* 1847 [1846]. 8vo. 16 Illustrations.

BIRD. Skovdjævelen. Fortælling af det amerikanske Colonistliv. Oversat. *Kjöbenhaven: Jordan.* 1847–50. vols., 8vo.

Perhaps his Peter Pilgrim. *London.* 1839. 2 vols., 8vo, relates to America.

BIRD (S.) The Importance of the Divine Presence with our Host. Sermon delivered at New Haven, April 27, 1759, to Col. David Wooster and his Company, at the request of the Colonel. By Rev. Samuel Bird. *New Haven.* 1759. 12mo, pp. 24. 5559

BIRD (W. A.) The Boundary Line between the British Provinces and the United States. A paper read before the Buffalo Historical Society, February 1st, 1864. By William A. Bird, Esq. *Buffalo: Wheeler,* [etc.] 1864. 8vo, pp. 8. 5560

BIRDSALL (Ausburn). The Wilmot Proviso—Martin Van Buren. Speech of Hon. A. Birdsall ... in the House ... July 24, 1848 ... . [*Washington.* 1848.] 8vo, pp. 8. H. 5561

BIRDSEYE (G. W.) Woman and the War. A Poem. By George W. Birdseye. *New York: J. Dickson.* 1865. 8vo, pp. 24. 5562

BIRKBECK (M.) An Address to the Farmers of Great Britain: with an Essay on the Prairies of the Western Country. By Morris Birkbeck. To which is annexed the Constitution of the State of Illinois. *London: James Ridgway.* 1822. 8vo, pp. 52.

BIRKBECK. An Appeal to the People of Illinois, on the Question of a Convention. By Morris Birkbeck. *Shawnetown. July,* 1823. 8vo, pp. 25. BA. 5564

BIRKBECK. Extracts from a Supplementary Letter from the Illinois; an Address to British Emigrants; and a Reply to the Remarks of William Cobbett, Esq. By Morris Birkbeck. *London: James Ridgway.* MDCCCXIX. 8vo, 2 l, pp. 36. H. + Second Edition. *New York.* 1819. 8vo. C. 5565

BIRKBECK. Letters from Illinois. By Morris Birkbeck ... . *London.* 1818. 8vo, pp. xv, 114. H. + Second Edition. *London.* 1818. 8vo. + Third Edition. *London: Taylor and Hessey.* 1818. 8vo. C. 5566

BIRKBECK. Letters from Illinois. By Morris Birkbeck ... . Illustrated by a Map of the United States, shewing Mr. Birkbeck's Journey from Norfolk to Illinois and a Map of English Prairie and the Adjacent Country, by John Melish. ... *Philadelphia: Carey and Son.* 1818. 12mo, pp. 154. 2 Maps. H. 5567

See North American Review, VIII. 347; XLIV. 97–125; Edinb. Rev., XXX. 120; Q. R., XIX. 54.

BIRKBECK. Lettres sur les nouveaux établissemens qui se forment dans les parties occidentales des États-Unis d'Amérique. Par Morris Birkbecks. Traduit sur l'édition originale de Philadelphie. ... *Paris: L'Huillier* [and] *Delaunay.* 1819. 8vo, Title, pp. xvj, 156. Map. H. 5568

BIRKBECK. Notes on a Journey in America, from the Coast of Virginia to the Territory of Illinois, with Proposals for the Establishment of a Colony of English. By Morris Birkbeck. ... *Philadelphia: Caleb Richardson.* 1817. 12mo, pp. 189. C. + *London.* 1818. 8vo, pp. iv, 144. Map. H. + The Second Edition. *London: James Ridgway.* 1818. 8vo, pp. 163. Map. BA. + The Third Edition. *London: Ridgway.* 1818. 8vo, pp. 156. + The Fourth Edition. *London: Ridgway.* 1818. 8vo, Title, pp. 156. Map. + Fifth Edition. *London: Ridgway.* 1819. 8vo. + *Dublin.* 1818. 8vo. Map. + *Cork.* 1818. 8vo. + *Philadelphia.* 1819. 12mo. C. 5569

"One of the most interesting and instructive books that have appeared for many years." — *Edinb. Rev.* XXX. 120. *See also* M. R., LXXXV. 146; Q. R., XIX. 54.

BIRKBECK. Bemerkungen auf einer Reise in America von der Küste von Virginien bis zum Gebiete von Illinois. Nebst einer vollständ. geograph.-statist.-politisches Uebersicht von d. Vereinigten Staaten von Nordamerika. Aus dem Englischen. *Jena: Bran.* 1818. C. 5570

BIRKENHEAD IRON-CLADS. Correspondence between Her Majesty's Government and Messrs. Laird Brothers; and an Appendix, containing the Correspondence between Officers of H. M.'s Customs and Capt. Inglefield, R. N., and Mesars. Laird Brothers, respecting the Iron-Clad Vessels building at Birkenhead, 1863–4. *London: Vacher & Sons.* [1864.] 8vo, pp. 69.

BIRKETT (Mary). A Poem on the African Slave Trade. Addressed to her own Sex. By M. Birkett. ... [First Part.] *Dublin: J. Jones.* 8vo, 1½ sheets. + The Second Edition. *Dublin: printed by J. Jones.* M, DCC, XCII. 8vo, 3 l, pp. 19.‖ [Second Part.] *Dublin: printed by J. Jones.* 1792. 8vo, 2 sheets. H. 5572

BIRKINSHAW. The Chevaliers: A Tale. With a True Account of An American Revival. By Maria Louisa Birkinshaw. *London: Simpkin, Marshall, and Co.* 1860. 8vo, 2 l. pp. 416.

BIRKS. The Gospel in Canada, and its relation to Huron College. With Introduction by Rev. T. R. Birks, M.A. *London: W. Hunt.* 1865. Post 8vo. 5574

BIRNEY (J. G.) Correspondence between James G. Birney, of Kentucky, and several Individuals of the Society of Friends [on colonization]. *Haverhill.* 1835. 8vo, pp. 8. BA. 5575

BIRNEY. Examination of the Decision of the Supreme Court of the United States, in the Case of Strader, Gorman and Armstrong *vs.* Christopher Graham, delivered at its December Term, 1850: concluding with an Address to the Free Colored People, advising them to remove to Liberia. By James G. Birney. *Cincinnati: Truman & Spofford.* 1852. 8vo, pp. 46, (1). H.

BIRNEY. Letter on Colonization, addressed to the Rev. Thornton J. Mills ... . By Hon. James G. Birney ... . *Boston.* 1834. 12mo, pp. 46. + *New York: Anti-Slavery Reporter.* 1834. 18mo, pp. 46. 5577

BINNEY. Letter to Hon. John F. Driggs, August, 1863. 8vo, pp. 23. 5577*a*

BIRNEY. Mr. Birney's Letter to the [Presbyterian] Churches ... in Kentucky [on Slavery. n. p.] 1834. 12mo, pp. 24. H.

BIRNEY. Mr. Birney's Second Letter. To the Ministers and Elders of the Presbyterian Church in Kentucky. [n. p.] 1834. 16mo, pp. 16. H. 5579

BIRNEY. Birney's Vindication of Abolitionists. Protest of the American Anti Slavery Society. Outrage upon Southern Rights, etc. *Boston: Isaac Knapp.* 1836. 12mo, pp. 80. 5580

BIRNEY. Sinfulness of Slaveholding In all Circumstances, Tested by Reason and Scripture. By James G. Birney. *Detroit: Charles Wilcox.* 1846. 8vo, pp. 60. 5581

[BIRON (Claude).] Curiositez de la nature et de l'art, apportées dans deux voyages, l'un aux Indes d'occident en 1698 et 1699 ... . *Paris.* 1703. 12mo, pp. xxxiii, 282, and Index. Plates. 5582

BIRT (J.) Official Responsibility affirmed and enforced. In a Letter to Sir George Grey ... on the Administration of the Act for the Abolition of ... Slavery. By John Birt. ... *London.* 1837. 8vo, pp. 16. 5883

The Birth and Death of Nations. *See* [McKaye (J.)]

The Birth, Parentage and Education of Praise-God Barebone, To which is added An Election Ballad, Or the Lamentation of Miss *******. A true and doleful Ditty. *Printed for Jack Northwester, at the Sign of the White Oak in Heart of Oak Street.* MDCCLXVI. 8vo, pp. 17. P. 5584

A satire on John Dickinson.

BISBE (J.) An Oration pronounced July 4, 1821 ... in Southbridge, Mass ... By John Bisbe, Jun. ... Subjoined ... the ... Proceedings of the Day. *Worcester.* 1821. 8vo, pp. 29. BA.

BISBE. A Sermon delivered in ... Portland, on the Annual Thanksgiving, November 29, 1827. By John Bisbe, Jun. ... . *Portland: printed by Thomas Todd.* 1828. 8vo, pp. 20. H. 5586

BISBEE (J. H.) A Sermon delivered before ... the Legislature of Massachusetts, at the Annual Election ... Jan. 6, 1847. By John H. Bisbee ... . *Boston.* 1847. 8vo, pp. 35. B., H.

BISBEE. Ecclesiastical History of the Town of Worthington. *See* [Price (J. C.)]

BISBEE (N.) An Oration delivered in Newport on the Fourth of July, 1805. By Noah Bisbee, Junr. *Newport: Asa Barber.* 1805. 8vo, pp. 52. 5588

BISBIE (D. T.) Appeal for Water Line from Norfolk, Va., Westward. *Norfolk.* 1857. 8vo. 5589

BISHOP (A.) Connecticut Republicanism. An Oration on the extent and power of Political Delusion. Delivered in New-Haven, on the Evening preceding the Public Commencement, September, 1800. By Abraham Bishop. *New Haven.* [1800.] 8vo, 2 l., pp. 64, (Appendix) 6 l. C. + Second Edition. ... *Newark: Printed by Pennington and Gould,* M,DCCC. 8vo, pp. 71. B. + *Philadelphia: Mathew Carey. Nov.* 13, 1800. 8vo, pp. 80. H. + *Albany: Printed by John Barber.* 1801. 8vo, pp. xi, (1), 68. B. 5590

BISHOP. Three Letters to Abraham Bishop, Esq.; containing Some Strictures on his Oration pronounced September, 1800. *Hartford.* 1800. 8vo, pp. 36. C. 5591

BISHOP. Church and State. A Political Union, formed by the Enemies of Both Illustrated by Correspondence between the Rev. Stanley Griswold, And the Rev. Dan. Huntington, And between Col. Ephraim Kirby, And the Rev. Joseph Lyman. [Motto. n. p.] 1802. 8vo, pp. iv, 60. 5592

BISHOP. Georgia Speculation Unveiled; in Two Numbers. By Abraham Bishop. *Hartford: printed by Elisha Babcock.* 1797. 8vo, pp. 39. H. 5593

BISHOP. Georgia Speculations Unveiled. In Two Parts. *Hartford: Elisha Babcock, and Hudson & Goodwin.* 1797–98. 8vo, pp. 144. C. 5594

The second part was issued separately, and is different from the second number.

BISHOP. Oration delivered in Wallingford, On the 11th of March 1801, before the Republicans of the State of Connecticut, at their General Thanksgiving, for the Election of Thomas Jefferson To the Presidency and of Aaron Burr To the Vice Presidency of the United States of America. By Abraham Bishop. ... *New Haven: Printed by William W. Morse.* 1801. 8vo, pp. 111, (1). B., C., H. 5595

BISHOP. Oration, in honor of the Election of President Jefferson, and the Peaceable Acquisition of Louisiana, delivered at the National Festival, in Hartford, on the 11th of May, 1804. By Abraham Bishop. [*Hartford:*] *General Committee of Republicans.* 1804. 8vo, pp. 24. B., H. 5596

BISHOP. Proofs of a Conspiracy, against Christianity, and the Government of the United States; exhibited in Several Views of the Union of Church and State in New-England. By Abraham Bishop. *Hartford: John Babcock, Printer.* 1802. 8vo, pp. 166. B., C. 5597

[BISHOP.] Rod for the Fool's Back; or, Abraham Bishop unmask'd. By a Citizen of Connecticut. *Reprinted: Bennington.* 1800. 16mo, pp. 15. B. 5598

BISHOP (A. W.) Loyalty on the Frontier, or Sketches of Union Men of the South-West; with Incidents and Adventures in Rebellion on the Border. By A. W. Bishop, Lieut. Col. First Arkansas Cavalry Volunteers. *St. Louis: R. P. Studley & Co., Printers.* 1863. 12mo, pp. 228. C. & H. 5599

BISHOP. An Oration delivered at Fayetteville, Kansas, July 4, 1865. By Brig. Gen. Albert W. Bishop. *New York: Baker & Godwin.* 1865. 8vo, pp. 27. 5600

BISHOP (*Mrs.* A.) Travels of Anna Bishop in Mexico, in 1849. *Philadelphia.* 1852. 12mo. 5601

[BISHOP (Francis A.)] Report of the Chief Engineer on the Survey and Cost of Construction of the San Francisco & Washoe Railroad ... . January, 1865. *San Francisco: printed by Towne & Bacon.* 1865. 8vo, pp. 20. H. 5602

BISHOP (G.) Manual of the Common Council of the City of Brooklyn, for 1858–9. By G. Bishop, Jr. *Brooklyn.* 1859. 12mo. Continued. 5603

BISHOP (George). *See* Bishope (G.)

BISHOP (H. E.) Floral Home; or, First Years of Minnesota: Early Sketches, Latter Settlements, and Further Developments. By Harriet E. Bishop. *New York: Sheldon & Co.* 1857. 12mo, pp. 342. Portrait and Woodcuts. C. 5604

BISHOP (H. F.) The Rise, Progress and Present Status of Dentistry [especially in the United States]. By H. F. Bishop ... . *Worcester.* 1868. 8vo, pp. 19. H. 5605

Bishop (J. L.) A History of American Manufactures from 1608 to 1860: exhibiting the Origin and Growth of the Principal Mechanic Arts and Manufactures, from the Earliest Colonial Period to the Adoption of the Constitution, and comprising Annals of the Industry of the United States in Machinery, Manufactures and Useful Arts, with a Notice of The Important Inventions, Tariffs, and the Results of each Decennial Census. By J. Leander Bishop, M.D. To which is added, Notes on the Principal Manufacturing Centres, and Remarkable Manufactories at the Present Time. In Two Volumes. ... *Philadelphia: Edward Young & Co.* 1861–64. 8vo, 2 l., pp. 7–11, 642, (1); Portraits, Title, 11–826. H. + Vol. III. *Philadelphia.* 1867. 8vo, pp. 437. With Portraits. C. 5606

The title of Vol. II. reads: "are added Statistics of the Principal Manufacturing Centres, and Descriptions of Remarkable," etc.

Bishop (J. P.) Commentaries on the Criminal Law. Third Edition. By Joel P. Bishop. *Boston: Little, Brown, & Co.* 1865. 2 vols., 8vo. + Fourth revised and enlarged Edition. *Boston: Little, Brown, & Co.* 1868. 2 vols., 8vo, pp. xxxii, 778; xii, 809. C. 5607

"Embraces much that is applicable to the late Rebellion, and matters that have grown out of it." — Bartlett.

Bishop. Secession and Slavery: or, the Effect of Secession on the Relation of the United States to the Seceded States and to Slavery therein; considered as a Question of Constitutional Law, chiefly under the Authority of Decisions of the Supreme Court; embracing also a Review of the President's Plan of Reconstruction. By Joel Prentiss Bishop .... *Boston: A. Williams & Co.* 1864. 8vo, pp. 112. B., H. 5608

Harvard College Library has also a copy, with the imprint: *Boston: Proof Sheet, not published.* 1863. 8vo, pp. 108. Republished with the following title:

Bishop. Secession and Slavery: or the Constitutional Duty of Congress to give the Elective Franchise and Freedom to all Loyal Persons, in Response to the Act of Secession. By Joel Prentiss Bishop ... Second Edition. *Boston: Williams.* 1866. 8vo, pp. 112. H. 5608*a*

Bishop. Thoughts for the Times. By Joel Prentiss Bishop. *Boston; Little, Brown, and Company.* 1863. 8vo, pp. 36. B., H.

Bishop (John). A Sketch of the Life of John Bishop. *Boston: the Author.* 1859. 12mo, pp. 23. Portrait. H. 5610

Signed "John Bishop, the Reformed Drunkard."

Bishop (J. S.) A Concise History of the War, Designed to Accompany Perrine's New War Map of the Southern States, with An Introduction and Statistical Appendix, Compiled from Authentic Sources. By Capt. John S. Bishop. *Indianapolis.* [1864.] 18mo, pp. 132, Appendix, 6 l. Map. 5611

Bishop (J. W.) History of Fillmore County, Minnesota. By J. W. Bishop. *Chatfield.* 1858. 8vo. S. 5612

Bishop (M.) The Life and Adventures of Matthew Bishop, of Deddington, in Oxfordshire, containing an Account of several Actions by Sea, Battles and Sieges by Land, in which he was present, from 1701 to 1711, interspersed with many curious Incidents ... written by himself. *London. J. Brindley.* 1744. 8vo.

An amusing piece of autobiography, by a common sailor, containing an account of his expedition to Canada, New England, and other parts of America. *See* "Retrospective Review," 2d Ser., II. 42–55.

Bishop (N. H.) A Thousand Miles' Walk across the Pampas and Andes of South America. By Nathaniel H. Bishop. *Boston: Lee and Shepard.* 1868. 12mo, pp. 310. 5614

Bishop (P. B.) Liberty's Ideal. By Putnam P. Bishop. *New York: Sheldon & Co.* 1864. 16mo, pp. 128. 5615

Bishop (P. E.) Sermon on the Death of Rev. William B. Davies. By Rev. P. E. Bishop. ... *Charleston: printed by A. J. Burke.* MDCCCLVI. 8vo, pp. 24. H. 5616

Bishop (R.) Instructions and Observations Relative to the Navigation of the Windward and Gulf Passages As laid down in two large Charts .... By Robert Bishop, Many Years a Master in the Royal Navy. *London: the Author.* M. DCC. LXI. 8vo, Title, pp. ii, 54. H. + The Second Edition. *London: the Author.* MDCCLXV. 8vo, pp. 128. 5617

Bishop (R. H.) Outline of the History of the Church in Kentucky, during a period of forty years [1783–1823]. By Robert H. Bishop ... ; containing memoirs of Rev. David Rice, [with his two Epistles to Presbyterians, and a Tract in opposition to Slavery]. *Lexington, Ky.: Thomas T. Skillman.* 1824. 16mo, pp. 420. C. 5618

Bishop. A Tribute of Respect to Departed Friends, and a Word of Encouragement to their Sons. ... By R. H. Bishop, D.D. *Oxford: R. H. Bishop, Jun.* 1837. 8vo, pp. 17. H. 5619

Two sermons, with "Biographical Notices," pp. 14–17.

Bishop (S. C.) Petition of Samuel C. Bishop, and the Boston Cutta [*sic*] Percha Co., in the Matter of Petition of George P. [B.] Simpson, for Relief. *New York: Bloom & Smith, Printers.* 1862. 8vo, pp. 13. H. 5620

Bishop (S. G.) An Eulogium on the Death of Gen[l] George Washington Commander in Chief of the Armies of America, Pronounced Feb. 22[d] A.D. 1800. at the Meeting House in Pittsfield, Rockingham County, State of New Hampshire. By Samuel G. Bishop, Preacher of the Gospel. [Motto.] Published to please the Author, that the reader may know what a good and virtuous example is, and be excited to copy it. *Printed at Gilmanton, By E. Russell, for the Author, March,* 1800. 8vo, pp. 16. 5621

One of the rarest of the Washington eulogies; reprinted with the following title:

Bishop. Eulogium on the Death of George Washington. By Samuel G. Bishop. *Roxbury: privately printed for W. E. Woodward.* 1866. 8vo, pp. 16. 5622

One hundred copies printed, six of which are on drawing paper.

[Bishop (W.)] To the Voters of the Second Electoral District of the State of Missouri. [Signed William Bishop. n. p. 1860.] 8vo, pp. 7. H. 5623

Bishop (W. S.) Speech on the Bill in relation to Church Tenures, by Hon. William S. Bishop, of the County of Monroe, delivered in the Senate, February 25, 1855. *Rochester.* 1855. 12mo, pp. 12. B., H., S. 5624

Bishop (W. W.) A Journal of the Twelve Months Campaign of Gen. Shields' Brigade, in Mexico, in the Years 1846–7. Compiled from Notes of Lieutenants J. J. Adams & H. C. Dunbar. By Capt. W. W. Bishop ... *St. Louis: Cathcart, Prescott, & Co., Printers.* 1847. 8vo, pp. 48. H. 5625

Bishops' College. Proceedings of the Annual Convocation of the University of Bishops' College, Lennoxville ... the 25th Day of June, 1863 .... *Montreal: printed by M. Longmoore & Co.* 1863. 8vo, pp. 39. H. 5626

The Bishops' Council: with Reminiscences of an annual Conference of the Methodist Episcopal Church. By an ex-presiding Elder. *St. Louis: P. M. Pinckard.* 1867. 12mo, pp. 338. C. 5627

The Bishop's Bonus. *See* Toleration, *pseudon.*

The Bishop's Fund and Phœnix Bonus. *See* Hamilton, *pseudon.*

Bishope (G.) New England Judged, | Not by Man's, but the Spirit of the Lord: And | The Summe sealed up of New England's | Persecutions. | Being | A Brief Relation of the Sufferings of the People called Quakers in | those Parts of America, from the beginning of the Fifth | Moneth 1656. (the time of their first Arrival at Boston from | England) to the later End of the Tenth Moneth, 1660. | Wherein | The Cruel Whippings and Scourgings, Bonds and Imprisonments, Beat- | ings and Chainings, Starvings and Huntings, Fines and Confiscati- | on of Estates, Burning in the Hand and Cutting of Ears, Orders of Sale | for Bond-men, and Bond-Women, Banishment upon pain of | Death, and Putting to Death of those People, are Shortly touched; | With a Relation of the Manner, and Some of the Other most Ma | terial Proceedings; and a Judgement thereupon | In Answer | To a Certain Printed Paper, intituled, A Declaration | of the General Court of the Massachusetts holden at Boston, the | 18 October, 1658. Apologizing for the same. | By George Bishope. | ... [Motto.] | *London: Printed for Robert Wilson, in Martins le Grand.* 1661. | Sm. 4to, pp. 147. 5628

There is an error in the pagination, at pp. 97–104.

Bishope. An | Appendex | to the Book, Entituled, | New England Judged: | being | Certain Writings, (never yet Printed) | of those Persons which were there | Executed. | Together | with a short Relation, of the Tryal, | Sentence, and Execution, | of William Leddra. | Written by them in the time of their Imprisonment, in the | Bloody Town of Boston. | *London, | Printed for Robert Wilson, at the sign of the Black-spread- | Eagle and Windmil, in Martins Le Grand.* | 1661. | 4to, pp. 177–208. 5629

Pages 191–198 should read 199–208.

Bishope. New England | Judged. | The Second Part. | Being, | A Relation of the cruel and Bloody Sufferings of the People | called | Quakers, in the Jurisdiction chiefly of the Massa- | chusets; Beginning with the Sufferings of William Ledra, | whom they murthered, and hung upon a Tree at Boston, the | 14th of the first month, 166⁰⁄₁. barely for being such a one as | is called a Quaker, and coming within their Jurisdiction; | And ending with the Sufferings of Edward Wharton, the 3d | month, 1665. And

the remarkable Judgements of God | in the Death of John Endicot Governour, John Norton, | High Priest, and Humphrey Adderton, Major General. | By George Bishope. | [Motto.] *London, Printed in the Year,* 1667. | 4to, pp. 147, Errata, 9 lines. 5630

These three works should go together to form a complete book, and, when complete, they constitute a volume of great rarity. The following is an abbreviation:

Bishope. New-England Judged, | by the | Spirit of the Lord. | In Two Parts. | First, Containing a Brief Relation of the Sufferings | of the People call'd Quakers in New-England, from the | Time of their first Arrival there, in the Year 1656, to | the Year 1660. Wherein their Merciless Whippings, | Chainings, Finings, Imprisonings, Starvings, Burning in | the Hand, Cutting off Ears, and Putting to Death, with | divers other Cruelties, inflicted upon the Bodies of In- | nocent Men and Women, only for Conscience-sake, are | briefly described. In Answer to the Declaration of their | Persecutors Apologizing for the same, MDCLIX. | Second Part, Being a farther Relation of the Cruel and | Bloody Sufferings of the People call'd Quakers in New- | England, Continued from anno 1660, to anno 1665. Be- | ginning with the Sufferings of William Leddra, whom | they put to Death. | Formerly Published by George Bishope, and now | somewhat Abreviated. | With an Appendix, | Containing the Writings of several of the Sufferers; | with some Notes, shewing the Accomplishment of their Pro- | phecies; and a Postscript of the Judgments of God, that | have befallen divers of their Persecutors. | Also, | An Anfwer to Cotton Mather's Abuses of the said People, | in his late History of New-England, Printed anno 1702. | The whole being at this time Published in the said Peoples | Vindication, as a Reply to all his Slanderous Calumnies. | ... | ... Rev. 12. 11. | *London, Printed and Sold by T. Sowle, in White- | Hart-Court in Gracious Street,* 1703. 8vo, Title, pp. (6), 498, 212, Index and Errata, 6 l. C. & H. 5631

The following work forms the latter part, pp. 212; it is sometimes found separately: Truth and Innocency | Defended; | against | Falshood and Envy: | And the Martyrs of Jesus, and | Sufferers for his sake, | Vindicated. | In Answer to Cotton Mather (a Priest of | Boston) his Calumnies, Lyes and Abuses | of the People called Quakers, in his late | Church-History of New-England. | With Remarks and Observations on several Pas- | sages in the same, and his Confessions to the | Just Judgments of God on them. | By John Whiting. | [Motto, 8 lines.] | *London: Printed and Sold by T. Sowle* ... | ... 1702. | The address "To the Unprejudiced Reader" is signed by Joseph Grove. For an extended list of Bishope's writings, *see* Smith's "Catalogue of Friends' Books," I. 277–283. Perhaps his "Epistle of Love," *London,* 1661, relates to America.

Bisschop-Grevelink (A. H.) Bemerkingen betreffende de

Nederlandsche West-Indische eilanden. *Rotterdam: H. A. Kramers.* 1848. 2 pts., 8vo, pp. 37; 30. 5632

Bisse (Philip), *Bishop of Hereford.* Sermon preached before the Society for the Propagation of the Gospel in Foreign Parts, at their anniversary meeting in the Parish of St. Mary-le-Bow, 21st February, 1717. By Philip, Lord Bishop of Hereford. *London.* 1718. 4to, pp. 32. 5633

Bissell (C.) A Poem before the Phi Beta Kappa Society of Yale College. By Champion Bissell. July 24, 1861. ... *New Haven: printed by E. Hayes.* 1861. 8vo, pp. 18. H. 5634

Bissell (J.) Genealogy of the Bissell Family. *Albany.* 1859. 8vo. 5635

From Stiles' "History of Ancient Windsor," with a new paging.

Bissell (Johann), *translator. See* [Victoria (Pedro Gove de).]

Bissell (S.) Education of Indian Youth: Letter of Rev. Samuel Bissell, and appeal of A. J. Blackbird, a Chippewa Indian. *Philadelphia: Wm. Geddes.* 1856. 16mo, pp. 15.

Bissell (W. H.) The Slave Question. Speech of Mr. William H. Bissell, of Illinois, in the House ... February 21, 1850 ... . [*Washington.* n. d.] 8vo, pp. 8. H. 5637

Bisset (C.) Medical Essays and Observations. By Charles Bisset, M.D. *New-Castle-upon-Tyne, Printed; sold by A. Millar and D. Wilson, and J. Dodsley* [*London*]. 1766. 8vo, 4 l., pp. 304. H. 5638

Pages 1–46 relate to the West Indies.

Bisset (George). Honesty the Best Policy in the Worst Times: A Sermon intended to have been preached at Newport, R. I. the Sunday preceding the Evacuation of that Garrison by his Majesty's Troops. *London: W. Richardson.* 1784. 4to, pp. 20. W. 5639

Bisset. [Masonic] Sermon at St. John's, N. B. Dec. 27, 1786. *St. John: Christopher Sower.* [1787.] 4to, pp. 12.

The same Sower who formerly printed at Germantown, Pa.

Bisset. A Sermon at Newport, R. I. Oct. 24, 1773. *Newport.* [1773.] 8vo. W. 5641

Bisset. A Sermon Preached in Trinity-Church, Newport, Rhode-Island ... June 3, 1771; At the Funeral of Mrs. Abigail Wanton, Late Consort of The Hon. Joseph Wanton, jun. Esq; Who departed this Life ... May 31, 1771, in the 36th Year of her Age. By George Bisset, M.A. ... *Newport: Printed by S. Southwick.* MDCCLXXI. 4to, pp. 20. H. 5642

Bisset. Abridgment and Collection of the Acts of Assembly Of the Province of Maryland, At present in Force. With A small choice Collection of Precedents in Law and Conveyancing. Calculated for the use of the Gentlemen of the Province. By James Bisset, Attorney at Law. [Motto.] *Ppiladelphia* [*sic*]: *the Author.* 1759. 8vo, 4 l., pp. 566. H. 5643

[Bisset (John).] A Letter, &c. 8vo, pp. 112. B. 5644

Criticises a Scotch apologist for Whitefield, with many remarks on Whitefield's course in America. The copy I have seen wanted its title-page.

Bisset (R.) Sermon for the relief of the Widows and Children of the Protestant Episcopal Church in Maryland, at Baltimore, June 19, 1791. By the Rev. Richard Bissett. With an Appendix. *Philadelphia.* 1791. 8vo, pp 22, Appendix, 17. P.

Bisset (R.) History of the Negro Slave Trade in its connection with the Commerce and Prosperity of the West Indies, and the Wealth and Power of the British Empire. By Robert Bisset, LL.D. ... *London.* 1805. 2 vols., 8vo. 5646

Bisset. The History of the Reign of George III. to the Termination of the Late War. To which is prefixed, a View of the Progressive Improvement of England, in Prosperity and Strength, to the Accession of His Majesty. In Six Volumes. By Robert Bisset, LL.D. ... *London: T. N. Longman and O. Rees.* 1803. 8vo. C., H. + A New Edition. Vol. I.–III. *Philadelphia: Levis & Weaver.* 1810–11. ‖ Vol. IV. *Baltimore: Edward J. Coale.* 1811. 4 vols., 8vo. Portrait. H. + Reprinted. *Albany.* 1816. 2 vols., 8vo. + The Second Edition, completed to the Death of the King. In Six Volumes. *London: Longman.* 1820. 8vo, pp. xxiv, 460; xii, 474; xvi, 478; xix, 494; xix, 485; xv, 640. + Reprinted. *Philadelphia.* 1822 & 1828. 3 vols., 8vo. 5647

In common with other histories of the period, it contains much relating to the Stamp Act and the American Revolution. *See* M. R., New Series, XXVII. 23; XLV. 135.

Bisset. The Life of Edmund Burke, comprehending an

Impartial Account of his Literary and Political Efforts, and a Sketch of the Conduct and Character of his most eminent Associates, Coadjutors, and Opponents. By Robert Bisset LL.D. *London: Cawthorne.* 1798. 8vo, pp. 592. + Second Edition. *London.* 1800. 2 vols., 8vo. B. & C. 5648

See M. R., New Series, XXVI. 361.

Bisset. Edmund Burkes Leben in hist.–litt.–polit. Hinsicht. Aus dem Englischen von J. G. C. Fick. *Gera: Heinsius.* 1799. 8vo. 5649

Bissette (Cyrille Charles Auguste). Lettre au ministre de la marine et des colonies sur la nécessité d'arrêter la réaction aux Antilles françaises. *Paris: impr. de A. Mie.* 1831. 8vo, pp. 48 or less. 5650

"M. Bissette was challenged on account of this letter by two colonists of Martinique, in the name of the whites in the colonies. He fought with one of them, and was wounded." — Quérard.

Bissette. Lettre de M. Bissette à maître L. Cicéron, avocat à Saint-Pierre [Martinique]. *Paris: imp. d'Auffray.* 1833. 8vo, pp. 8. + *Paris: impr. d'Herban.* 1834. 8vo. 5651

This letter occasioned a law-suit and a duel, in which duel M. Cicéron was wounded.

Bissette. Mémoire justicatif des hommes de couleur de la Martinique. Par C. A. Bissette. *Paris:* 1825–29. 5 vols., 8vo. 5652

Also: A mes compatriotes. *Paris: impr. de Mie.* 1831. 8vo, pp. 4. — A mes compatriotes. *Paris: impr. de Poussielgue.* 1850. 8vo. — A M. le baron de Mackau ... ministre de la marine et des colonies. *Paris: impr. de Poussielgue.* 1845. 8vo. — Au clergé français. Emancipation des esclaves. *Paris: Sirou et Desquers.* 1847. 8vo. — (Anon.) Calomnies devenues vérités, ou réponse au pamphlet de MM. Lacharrière et Foignet, délégués des colons de la Guadeloupe. *Paris: impr. de Mie.* 1831. 8vo, pp. 24. — Une cause célèbre coloniale. Mme Marlet, de la commune Robert, Martinique, [Signed Bissette]. *Paris: impr. de Poussielgue.* [1850.] 8vo. — C. C. A. Bissette homme de couleur de la Martinique, à un colon, sur l'émancipation civile et politique appliquée aux colonies françaises. *Paris: Ledoyen.* 1830. 8vo, pp. 32. — Colonies. Esclavage. Lettre à M. le ministre de la marine et des colonies. *Paris: impr. de Poussielgue.* 1845. 2 pts., 8vo. — Déclaration de M. Bissette au sujet de sa dernière brochure sur l'ouvrage de M. Schœlcher. *Paris: impr. de Schneider.* 1843. 8vo. — Deux mots sur une note de M. V. Schœlcher. *Paris: Ebrand.* 1843. 8vo. + Post-scriptum au Deux mots ... . *Paris: impr. de Poussielgue.* 1843. 8vo. — Discours prononcé dans la discussion du projet de loi sur la presse dans les colonies. Séance du 7 août 1850. *Paris: impr. de Panckouke.* 1850. 8vo. (From the "Moniteur," 8 août.) — Les esclaves des colonies françaises au clergé français. Par C. A. Bissette. *Paris:* 1844. (Suppressed.) — Examen rapide des deux projets de loi relatifs aux colonies, adressé à la chambre des députés. *Paris: impr. d'Everat.* 1833. 8vo, pp. 16. — Lettre à M. Agènor de Gasparin ... sur son discours, prononcé dans la séance du 4 mai en faveur de l'abolition de l'esclavage. *Paris: impr. de Dupont.* 1844. 8vo. — Lettre à M. V. Schœlcher. *Paris: Ebrard.* 1843. 8vo. — Lettres politiques sur les colonies, sur l'esclavage et sur les questions qui s'y rattachent. *Paris: Ebrard.* 1843. 3 letters, 8vo. + Quatrième lettre. *Paris: l'auteur.* 1846. 8vo. + [The four letters together.] 1848. 8vo. — Liberté de la presse confisquée à la Martinique au profit des propriétaires d'esclaves. ... Par C. A. Bissette. *Paris: Ebrard.* 1845. 8vo, pp. 48 or less. — Mémorie au ministre de la marine et des colonies, et à la commission de législation coloniale, sur les améliorations législatives et organiques à apporter au régime des colonies françaises. *Paris: impr. de Mie.* 1831. 8vo, pp. 48. — Notes sur le projet de loi relatif au régime législatif des colonies. *Paris: impr. de Dupont.* 1833. 8vo, pp. 8. — Observations sur les projets de lois coloniales présentées à la chambre des députés. *Paris: impr. de Mie.* 1832. 8vo, pp. 36. — Pétition à la Chambre des Députés [contre l'administration coloniale de la Martinique. 5 jan. 1846.] Par C. A. Bissette. *Paris: impr. de Poussielgue.* [n. d.] 8vo, pp. 48 or less. — Polémique sur les événements de la Grand' Anse [Martinique. Signed Bissette.] *Paris: impr. de J.-S. Cordier.* 1834. 8vo, pp. 12. — Du projet Mackau, tendant à violer la loi du 24 avril 1833 sur le régime législatif des colonies. *Paris: impr. de Dupont.* 1844. 8vo. — Réfutation du livre de M. Victor Schœlcher intitulé: Des colonies françaises. *Paris: impr. de Breton.* 1843. 8vo. — Réfutation du livre de M. V. Schœlcher sur Haïti. *Paris: Ebrard.* 1844. 8vo. — Réponse à la brochure de M. Fleuriau, délégué des colons de la Martinique. *Paris: impr. de Mie.* 1831. 8vo, pp. 24. — Réponse au factum de M. Schœlcher intitulé: La verité aux ouvriers et cultivateurs de la Martinique. *Paris: impr. de Poussielgue.* 1850. 8vo. Perhaps, also, the following relate to the West India colonies: A M. Dupin, député de la Nièvre ... . *Paris: impr. de Poussielgue.* 1845. 8vo. — Lettre à MM. les électeurs du premier collége électoral de Rennes ... . *Paris: impr. de Sirou.* 1846. 8vo. — Lettre à M. Granier (de Cassagnac). *Paris: impr. de Bailly.* 1842. 8vo. Bissette also edited the "Revue des colonies."

BISSETTE *and* FABIEN. A la Chambre de Pairs. Plainte des mandataires des hommes de couleur de la Martinique contre M. le contre-amiral Dupotet, gouverneur de cette colonie. [Signed Bissette, Fabien.] *Paris: imp. de P. Dupont et Gaultier-Laguionie.* 1833. 8vo, pp. 48 or less. 5653

Also: Demande en grâce pour Adèle, jeune esclave de la Martinique, condamnée à la peine du fouet pour avoir chanté "La parisienne." [Signed Bissette and Fabien. 19–28 juillet 1831.] *Paris: impr. de A. Mie.* [n. d.] 8vo, pp. 4. + Another edition, with the same imprint. — Dénonciation contre M. le comte de Peyronnet ... pour détention prolongée pendant vingt-un mois par suite de rétention frauduleuse et de mauvaise foi, de pièces à lui adressées par les hommes de couleur de la Martinique pour être transmises à la cour de cessation. [Signed Bissette et Fabien fils.] *Paris: de E. Duverger.* 1828. 8vo, pp. 16. + Dénonciation contre ... Peyronnet ... et ... le marquis de Clermon-Tonnerre ... pour détention ... par suite de rétention ... de pièces à eux adressées par MM. Bissette, Fabien et Volny ... . [Signed Bissette, Fabien.] *Paris: imp. de E. Duverger.* 1829. 8vo, pp. 48 or less. — Pétition des hommes de couleur de la Martinique, déportés aux colonies étrangères par M. le général Donzelot, en décembre 1823 et janvier 1824. [Signed Bissette, Fabien fils.] *Paris: imp. de E. Duverger.* 1828. 8vo, pp. 48 or less. — Réponse de MM. Bissette et Fabien, de la Martinique, à MM. de la Charrière et Foignet, de la Guadeloupe. *Paris: impr. de A. Mie.* 1831. 8vo. + À M. de Lac Charrière. Paris, ce 25 juillet 1831. *Paris: Mie.* [n. d.] 8vo. pp. 48 or less. This or another reply was appended to a "Lettre de M. Foignet," etc. *Paris.* 1831. 8vo, pp. 4.

BISSETTE, FABIEN, *and* RICHARD. Pétition à la Chambre des

députés, relative à l'amélioration du sort des esclaves aux colonies. [Signed Bissette, Fabien, et Mondésir Richard.] *Paris: impr. de Dupont.* 1833. 8vo, pp. 12. 5654

BISSETTE, FABIEN, *and* VOLNY. Pétition des hommes de couleur libres de la Martinique, qui depuis deux ans attendent dans les prisons de Brest l'envoi de la procedure à la suite de laquelle ils ont été condamnés aux galères perpétuelles. ... 22 mars 1826. [Signed Brissette, Fabin fils, Volny. *Paris:*] *imp. de E. Duverger.* [n. d.] 8vo, pp. 48 or less. + A la Chambre des Pairs. Pétition additionnelle pour Bissette, Fabien fils et Volney ... avril 1826. [*Paris:*] *imp. de E. Duverger.* [n. d.] 8vo, pp. 48 or less. 5655

BISSETTE, FABIEN, *and* VOLNY. Réponse des condamnés de la Martinique à ce qui les concerne dans le discours prononcé à la Chambre des Députés par S. Exc. le ministre de la marine, le 6 juin 1826. [Signed Bissette, Fabien fils, Volny. *Paris:*] *imp. de Duverger.* [n. d.] 8vo, pp. 48 or less. 5656

BISSING (Friedrich). Das Verfassungsrecht der vereinigten Staaten Nord-Amerika's nach James Kent, nebst der Verfassungsurkunde und einer statistischen Tabelle. *Heidelberg.* 1836. 8vo, 7½ sheets. 5657

BITTINGER (J. B.) An Address at the Laying of the Corner-stone of the Lake Erie Female Seminary at Painesville, O., July 4, 1857. By J. B. Bittinger. ... *Cleveland.* 1857. 8vo, pp. 23.

A biographical sketch of Mary Lyon.

BITTINGER. A Plea for Humanity. A Sermon preached in ... Cleveland, Ohio, by Rev. J. B. Bittinger. ... *Cleveland.* 1854. 8vo, pp. 28. H. 5659

The half-title is, "Nebraska. A Plea," etc.

BITTINGER. A Sermon preached before the Presbyterian Churches of Cleveland, on the National Fast Day, September 26, 1861. By Rev. J. B. Bittinger. *Cleveland: E. Cowles & Co.* 1861. 8vo, pp. 21. 5660

BIVEN (Rarey). An Oration, July 4, 1838. *Schenectady.* 1838. 12mo, pp. 6. 5661

Les bivouacs de Vera-Cruz à Mexico; par un zouave. Avec une carte spéciale de l'expédition dressée sur plan par l'auteur. Préface par Aurélien Scholl. *Paris: libraire centrale.* 1865. 18mo, pp. xiv, 252. + Seconde édition. [*Ibid.*] 18mo. 5662

BIZARI (P.) Senatvs Popvliqve Genvensis Rervm domi foriqve gestarvm Historiæ atqve Annales ... . Avctore Petro Bizaro Sentinati. *Antverpiæ: Ex officina Christophori Plantini.* M.D.LXXXIX. Folio, pp. 802, (35). 5663

"We think [this] may be consulted with some little profit, as it is quoted by Bossi and others." — HARRISSE, *Notes on Columbus*, page 49.

BJORCK (T. Er.) Dissertatio Gradualis, de Plantatione Ecclesiae Svecanae in America quam ... d. 14 Jun. An. MDCCXXXI. examinandam ... sistit Tobias E. Biorck, Americano-Dalecarlus. *Upsaliae: Literis Wernerianis.* [1731.] 4to, pp. 34. Map. 5664

BLACHFORD (M.) Sailing Directions for the Coasts and Harbours of North America ... from Nova Scotia to the Gulf of Florida ... . *London: R. Blachford.* 1836. 8vo, (3) l., pp. 75. B. 5665

BLACHFORD. Sailing Directions for the Gulph and River of St. Lawrence, giving a particular description of all the Harbours, Islands, Anchorages, Rocks, Shoals and other dangers. *London.* 1842. 4to, pp. 95. 5666

BLACK, (Adam *and* Charles). *See* Bartholomew (J. G.), No. 3717.

BLACK (J.) Unity of Mankind — A Lecture. By Rev. James Black. *Caledonia, U. C.* 1865. pp. 26. 5667

BLACK (J. S.) The Doctrines of the Democratic and Abolition Parties Contrasted, Negro Equality, The Conflict between "Higher Law" and the Law of the Land. Speech of Hon. Jeremiah S. Black. ... Philadelphia October 24, 1864. [n. p. n. d.] 8vo, pp. 8. 5668

BLACK. Eulogy on the Life and Character of General Andrew Jackson. Delivered at Bedford, Pa., July 28, 1845. By Jeremiah S. Black. *Chambersburg.* 1845. 8vo, pp. 23. S. 5669

BLACK. Observations on Senator Douglas's Views of Popular Sovereignty, as expressed by Harper's Magazine, for September, 1859. By J. S. Black. *Washington: Thomas McGill.* 1859. 8vo, pp. 24. C. 5670

BLACK. Speech of Hon. Jeremiah S. Black, at the Democratic Mass Convention in Lancaster City, September 17, 1863. [n. p. n. d.] 8vo, pp. 7. 5671

BLACK (J.) An Authentic Narrative of the Mutiny on board the (Transport) Ship Lady Shore; with Particulars of a Journey through Part of Brazil: in a Letter, dated "Rio Janeiro 18th January 1708," to the Rev. John Black, Woodbridge, Suffolk, from Mr John Black one of the surviving Officers of the Ship. *London: Robinson.* 1798. 8vo. 5672

In the catalogue of the Bodleian library a copy is cited, *Ipswich.* [n d.] *See* M. R., XXVIII. 232.

BLACK (J.) A Sermon on National Righteousness and Sin. Delivered ... Pittsburgh, April 3, 1827, before a large assembly, convened for the purpose of adopting Resolutions against Duelling. By Rev. John Black, D.D., Pastor ... With the, Anti-Duelling Resolutions. *Pittsburgh.* 1827. 18mo, pp. 16. 5673

BLACK (John) *and others.* Address to the Federal Republicans of Burlington county [N. J.] recommending them to support the present members in the Legislature from that county, at the ensuing Election, as are friendly to the re-Election of President Adams and Governor Howell. *Trenton: Sherman, Mershon, and Thomas.* 1800. 8vo, pp. 36. C. 5674

BLACK HAWK. Life of Ma-ka-tai-me-shi-kia-kaiak; or, Black Hawk, Embracing the Tradition of his Nation — Indian Wars in which he has been engaged — Cause of joining the British in their late War with America, and its History — Description of the Rock-River Village — Manners and Customs — Encroachments by the Whites, contrary to Treaty — Removal from His Village in 1831. With an account of the cause and general History of the late War, his surrender and confinement at Jefferson Barracks, and travels through the United States. Dedicated by Himself. J. B. Patterson, of Rock Island, Ill., Editor and Proprietor. *Boston: Russell, Odiorne, & Metcalf.* 1834. 12mo, pp. 155. Portrait. + *Boston: Theodore Abbot.* 1845. 12mo, pp. 155. Portrait. C. 5675

First Edition. *Cincinnati.* 1833. *See* N. A. R., XL. 68.

BLACK HAWK. An Account of the Indian Chief Black Hawk, and his tribes, the Sac and Fox Indians, with the affecting narrative of a Lady who was taken prisoner by the Indians. Also an account of other depredations. The Capture of Black Hawk and his Party. *Philadelphia: S. E. Corner.* 1834. 8vo, pp. 26. 5676

BLACK HAWK. Life and Adventures of Black Hawk, The Great Indian Chief of the West. *Cincinnati.* 1858. 12mo. + [*Ibid.*] 1858. 12mo. 5677

Perhaps this is by Daniel Drake, M.D.

Black Hawk, and Scenes in the West. *See* [Smith (Elbert H.)]

Black Hawk Gold Mining Company. Report of Colonel Crosby. November, 1865. *New-York.* 1865. 8vo, pp. 18. H.

Black List. A List of those Tories who took part with Great Britain In the Revolutionary War, and were attainted of High Treason, commonly called the Black List! To which is prefixed the legal opinions of Attorney Generals McKean & Dallas, &c. *Philadelphia: Printed for the Proprietor.* 1802. 8vo, pp. 16. C. + *New York: Privately Reprinted.* 1865. 4to, 2 l., pp. 16. C. 5679

Thirty copies [re-]printed.

Black Republican Imposture Exposed! Fraud upon the People. Fremont and his Speculations. *Washington.* 1856. 8vo, pp. 16.

Black River and Utica Rail Road Company. Report of the Chief Engineer to the Directors, June 1, 1854. *Utica.* 1854. 8vo, pp. 92. Map. 5681

Black River Baptist Association, N. Y. Minutes, June 14, 1820. *Watertown.* 1820. 8vo. Contiuued. S. 5682

Also: Minutes of the 51st Anniversary, Belleville, 1859. *Watertown.* 1859. 8vo.

Black River Marble and Soapstone Manufacturing Company's Report. 1838. 8vo. 5683

BLACK'S EDDY, *on the Delaware.* A Review of the Question of the Outlet Lock at Black's Eddy. [n. p. n. d.] 8vo, pp. 12. Map. H. 5684

Blackbeard. A Page from the Colonial History of Philadelphia. *New York.* 1835. 2 vols., 12mo. 5685

BLACKBURN. Report of Mr. Blackburn on the Memorial of the Sandy and Beaver Canal. *Harrisburg.* 1835. 8vo, pp. 11.

BLACKBURN (W. M.) The Crime against the Presidency, A Sermon delivered Sunday, April 16, 1865, in the Fourth Presby-

terian Church, Trenton, N. J., by the Pastor, Rev. William M. Blackburn. *Trenton, N. J.: Murphy & Bechtel, Printers.* 1865. 8vo, pp. 24. B. 5687

Five hundred copies printed.

BLACKBURN. Thanksgiving for Victory; a Sermon delivered, in accordance with the late Proclamation of the President of the United States, August 6, 1863, in the Park Presbyterian Church, Erie, Pa., by the Pastor, the Rev. W. M. Blackburn. *Erie: Dispatch Presses.* [1863]. 8vo, pp. 24. 5688

[BLACKBURNE (Francis).] A Critical Commentary on Archbishop Secker's Letter to the Right Honourable Horatio Walpole, concerning Bishops in America. ... *London: E. and C. Dilly.* M DCC LXX. 8vo, pp. 111. C. & H. + *Philadelphia: John Dunlap.* 1771. 8vo, pp. 72. C. & S. 5689

Reprinted in Blackburne's Works. *London.* 1804. 7 vols., 8vo, II. 1–99. H.

[BLACKBURNE.] Memoirs of Thomas Hollis, Esq. F.R. and A.S.S. [Motto.] *London.* MDCCLXXX. 4to, pp. viii, 1–506; ii, 507–841; Index, by John Disney, printed between 1804 and 1807, 12 l. 29 Plates, and Portraits. C. & H. 5690

"Archdeacon Blackburne, the learned and nervous writer who compiled it." — DISNEY'S *Memoirs of Brand-Hollis.* This privately printed work is now rather scarce. The plates are by Bartolozzi, Cipriani, and others. Between pp. 532 and 533 come pp. 533¹–576*, 577†–584, 579**–580. These pages are sometimes deficient. Heath's copy sold for £4 7s.; Brockett's for £6. The subject of this memoir was a liberal benefactor to Harvard College.

BLACKFORD (D. de). Précis de l'état actuel des colonies angloises Dans l'Amérique Septentrionale [avec la "réponse de M. Franklin A l'interrogatoire qu'il a subi devant la Chambre des Communes, au mois de Février 1766. lorsque la révocation de l'Acte du Timbre y fut mise en délibération" traduit de l'Anglais] par M. Dominique de Blackford. *Milan: les Freres Reycends.* MDCCLXXI. 12mo, pp. 99. H. 5691

"Part of this work is a compilation from Douglas and Kalm, and the remainder consists of a translation of the examination of Dr. Franklin, 1767. It is generally found with a translation of Toreen's Voyage to Surat, &c." — RICH. *See* Torén (O.)

BLACKIE (W. G.) The Imperial Gazetteer; a General Dictionary of Geography, Physical, Political, Statistical, and Descriptive, compiled from the latest and best authorities. 700 illustrations. *Glasgow.* 1855. 2 vols., imp. 8vo, pp. xii, 1308; 1288, 61. 5692

Includes copious notices of American localities.

BLACKLEY (*Rev.* F. R.) The Greenland Minstrel; A Poem, in six cantos; with Introductory Narrative, illustrated from Drawings taken on the spot, during a Voyage to Greenland, in 1826. By Rev. Frederick R. Blackley. *London: Simpkin & Marshall.* 1839. 16mo, pp. xxxv, 148. 9 Plates. C. 5693

BLACKMAN (L.) Louisa Blackman's Escape from the Mormons. Written by Herself. *Indianapolis: Ben. Franklin Printing House.* 1867. 8vo, pp. 23. C. 5694

BLACKMORE (R. D.) The Fate of Franklin. A Poem. *London: Hardwicke.* 1860. Fcap 8vo. 5695

BLACKSTONE (*Sir* William). Blackstone's Commentaries, with Notes of Reference to the Constitution and Laws of the Federal Government of the United States, and of the Commonwealth of Virginia; with an Appendix to each volume, containing short tracts upon such subjects as appeared necessary to form a connected view of the Laws of Virginia as a member of the Federal Union. By St. George Tucker, Professor in the University of William and Mary. *Philadelphia: Published by William Young Birch, and Abraham Small.* 1803. 5 vols., 8vo.

BLACKSTONE. An Interesting Appendix to Sir William Blackstone's Commentaries on the Laws of England, etc., containing ... I. Priestley's Remarks, ... [Six Parts] etc. ... *Philadelphia: R. Bell.* MDCCLXXII. 4to, pp. iv, 276. C. & P. 5697

Some copies of this volume were issued with a different title, viz.: "The Palladium of Conscience; or, the Foundation of Religious Liberty displayed, asserted, and established, etc."

BLACKSTONE. Catalogue of the Blackstone Library Association. Organized Oct. 4, 1855. ... *Woonsocket: S. S. Foss, Printer.* 1856. 8vo, pp. 51. H. 5698

BLACKSTONE. Report of the School Committee of the Town of Blackstone, For the Year ending April, 1854 . ... *Woonsocket, R. I.* 1854. 8vo, pp. 15. Continued. H. 5699

Appears to be the first published.

BLACKSTONE CANAL. Account of the Proposed Canal from Worcester to Providence, containing the Report of the Engineer; together with some Remarks upon Inland Navigation. Published by order of the Committee for the County of Worcester. *Worcester: Wm. Manning.* 1822. 8vo, pp. 18. + *Providence: John Miller.* 1825. 8vo, pp. 16. + Report of the Board of Com-

missioners of Internal Improvements in relation to a Route for a Canal, from Boston to the Blackstone Canal, and thence to the line of Connecticut, &c. *Boston: Dutton & Wentworth.* 1828. pp. 18. C. + Charter, By-Laws, &c., of the Blackstone Canal Corporation. *Providence: Cranston & Hammond.* 1835. 8vo, pp. 39. 5700

Blackstone Family; Being Sketches, Biographical and Genealogical, of William Blackstone, and his Descendants. *Norwich, Conn.* 1857. 8vo, pp. 43. 5701

Blackstone Monument. An Address delivered at the Formation of the Blackstone Monument Association, together with the Preliminaries and Proceedings at Study Hill, July 4, 1855. ... *Pawtucket, R. I.: James L. Estey.* 1835. 8vo, pp.39. 5702

The Blackwater Chronicle. *See* [Kennedy (J. P.)]

BLACKWELL (R.) Original Acrostics on some of the Southern States, and most Eminent men of the Southern Confederacy, and on various other subjects, Political and Personal. By Robert Blackwell. *Published by Z. F. Milbourn of Loudoun Co., Va.* 1863. 12mo, pp. 24. C. 5703

BLACKWELL (R. S.) A Practical Treatise on the Power to Sell Land for the Non-Payment of Taxes assessed thereon, embracing the Decisions of the Federal Courts, and of the Supreme Judicial Tribunals of the Several States. By Robert S. Blackwell, of the Illinois Bar. *Chicago: D. B. Cooke & Co.* 1855. 8vo, pp. xxxiii, 776. C. + Second Edition, Revised and Enlarged. *Boston: Little, Brown & Co.* 1864. 8vo, pp. xxxii, 668.

BLACKWOOD (I.) A Description of the Province and Bay of Darien, giving a full account of all its Situation, inhabitants, way of living and religion ... being vastly rich with gold, silver and other commodities, etc. By Isaac Blackwood. *Edinburgh: Andrew Anderson.* 1699. 4to, pp. 16. J. C. B. 5705

[BLACKWOOD (Thomas).] Remarks on the Constitution of the Canadas, Civil and Ecclesiastical, with a View to its Amendment. By a Layman of the Church of Scotland. [n. p. n. d.] 8vo. CP. 5706

BLACKWOOD (T.) Nullification considered and defended on the Principle of Abstract Right, and as necessary to the Preservation of Popular Freedom in a Confederation of Republics. By Thomas Blackwood. *Charleston: the Author.* 1833. 8vo, pp. 24. H. 5707

Blackwood's Edinburgh Magazine. Vol. I. April–September, 1817. *Edinburgh: William Blackwood; and T. Cadell and W. Davies, London.* 1817. 8vo. Continued. An American reprint. *New York.* 5708

Contains many articles relating to America — generally unfriendly — especially so to the North during the late Civil War. The articles, "Spence's American Union," and "The Convulsions of America," were reprinted, *New York: Leonard Scott & Co.* 1862.

Blada (V.), *pseudon.* Sketches from the Civil War in North America, 1861, '62, '63. By V. Blada. *London.* 1863. 4to.

A series of forty-five sketches, chiefly of scenes in the Confederate army, really published in Baltimore. Only twelve copies were struck off for friends, when the plates were destroyed, for fear of exposing the artist, who is a German dentist in Baltimore.

Bladensburg. A Narrative of the Battle of Bladensburg; in a Letter to Henry Banning, Esq. By an Officer of Gen. Smith's Staff. [n. p. 1814?] 8vo, pp. 16. Map. C. & H. 5710

Bladensburg Races, written shortly after the Capture of Washington City, 1814. 12mo. C. 5711

A satirical poem on Madison and his administration, in imitation of John Gilpin. Reprinted in 4to about 1865.

Bladh (C. E.) Republiken Chile åren 1821–28. *Stockholm: Hjerta.* 1837. 8vo. 5712

Bladh. Resa till Montevideo och Buenos Ayres. *Stockholm.* 1839. 8vo. 5713

Blaeu *or* Blaaw (Johan). Atlas Maior, sive Cosmographia Blaviana, qua Solvm, Salvm, Cœlvm, accvratissime describvntur. [*Amstelædami.* 1662.] 11 vols., folio. 5714

This is a general half-title, each volume has a special title; that of Vol. XI. is: America, qvæ est Geographiæ Blavianæ Pars Qvinta; Liber Vnvs. Volvmen Vndecimvm. *Amstelædami: Labore & Sumptibus Ioannis Blaev.* M DC LXII. Folio, Title, pp. 287, (2). Engraving and 27 Maps. H. Vol. I. includes the Arctic Regions. For a detailed account of Blaeu's atlases, *see* Clément, "Bibl curieuse," IV. 267-276. J. Jansson and J. Blaeu, who have been confounded by some writers, were rival publishers of atlases at Amsterdam. The chronology of these atlases, according to M. Duve, is briefly this: Willem Bleau, who died in 1638, following Gerardus Mercator and Jodocus and Cornelis Hondius, published not long before his death an atlas in 2 vols., to which the brothers Johan and Cornelis Blaeu added a IIId. vol. in 1640 (changing the date of I. and II. to 1640), a IVth in 1646, a Vth in 1654, and a VIth in 1656. The Atlas Major followed in 1662, and was reprinted in 1665.

Blaeu. Le Grand Atlas, ou Cosmographie Blauiane, en laquelle est exactement descritte la Terre, la Mer et le Ciel.

[*Amsterdam: J. Blaeu.* MDCLXIII.] 12 vols, folio. + [*Ibid.*] 1667. [*Ibid.*] 5715

This should be accompanied by "L'Atlas du mer, ou monde aquatique, représentant toutes les côtes de mer connues en l'univers. *Amst.* 1667. Folio." Vol. XII. contains "L'Amérique."

Blaeu. Grooten Atlas oft Wereltbeschrijving in welcke 't aerdryck, de zee en hemel wort vertoont en beschreven. *Amsterdam.* 1664. 9 vols., folio. 5716

There are 24 maps of parts of America

Blaeu. Atlas Universal y Cosmographico de los Orbes Celestes y Terrestre ... . *Amsterdam.* 1659–72. 11 vols., folio.

Clément gives this title as follows: Atlas Mayor, Geographia Blaviana, que contiene las Cartas, y Descripciones de todas las partes del mondo. *Amsterdam: Juan Blaeu.* 1659-72. Grasse gives the title in a third form, and mentions only ten volumes, which is the number in the printed catalogue of the British Museum. "L'édition espagnole, *Amsterd.* 1659-72, 10 vol. a été en grande partie détruite dans l'incendie qui réduisit en cendres les magasins de Blaeu, en février 1672." — Brunet. This large Atlas, though common formerly, is now becoming scarce. The maps are all on a very large and comprehensive scale, and are taken from early and authentic surveys. The volume relating to America contains a complete digest of the early travels of the Spaniards and English. The map of Bermuda is very curious, giving the names of the English shareholders, amongst whom the native tribes were divided. Priced, in English catalogues, from £7 to £10.

Blaeu (Willem Jansz.) Atlas Magnus sive Geographia et Cosmographia Blaviana, qua solum, salum, coelum accuratissime describuntur. *Amst.* 1650. 11 vols., folio. With 563 Maps. 5718

"Cette première édition du célèbre atlas de Blaeu est moins recherchée que la suivante en français ["Le Grand Atlas"], quoiqu'elle renferme nombre de pièces qui y manquent." — *Grasse.*

Blaeu (Willem Jansz. *and* Johan). Novvs Atlas, das ist, Weltbeschreibung, Mit schönen newen aussführlichen Land-Taffeln in Kupffer gestochen vnd an den Tag gegeben Durch Gvil. vnd Iohannem Blaev. *Amsterdami: Apud Iohannem Guilielmi F. Blaeu.* CIↃ IↃC XLVIIII, XLVII, XLVII, XLVI. 4 vols., folio. About 400 colored Maps. H. 5719

At the end of Vol. II. is "America," 35 l., including 15 maps.

Blaeu. Theatrum Orbis Terrarum, sive Atlas Novus. *Amsterdam.* 1649. 9 vols., folio. BD. 5720

In the catalogue of Carl Ritter's library is cited an edition of this: "Tom. I–V. *Amst.* 1640–54. Folio." Grässe gives the imprint: *Amst.: Blaeu.* 1645. 4 vols., folio.

Blaeu. Toonneel des aerdriicx, Ofte nievwe atlas, Dat is beschryving van alle Landen; Nu nieulycx uytgegeven, Door Wilhelm: en Iohannem Blaeu. ‖ Tweede deel van't toonneel ... . *Amsterdami: Apud Guiljelmum et Iohannem Blaeu* CIↃ IↃC XXXV. 2 vols., folio. Colored Maps. H. + *Amsterd.* 1650. 4 vols., folio. 5721

"America, ofte de nievwe wereld," at the end of Deel II., occupies 40 leaves, including 14 maps.

Blagden. A Discourse occasioned by the Death of Mrs. Elizabeth Livingston Budington, preached in ... Charlestown, January 14, 1855. By George W. Blagden, D.D. *Boston: S. K. Whipple & Co.* 1855. 8vo, pp. 26. B. 5722

Blagden. Great Principles associated with Plymouth Rock. An Address delivered before the Pilgrim Society of Plymouth, December 22, 1834. By Geo. W. Blagden. *Boston: Light & Horton.* 1835. 8vo, pp. 30. H. 5723

Blagden. Pastor's Memorial. Twenty-fifth Anniversary of the Installation of George W. Blagden, D.D. as Pastor of the Old South Church and Society in Boston. [n. p.] 1862. 12mo, pp. 118. H. 5724

Blagden. Remarks, and a Discourse on Slavery, by G. W. Blagden. *Boston: Ticknor, Reed, & Fields.* M DCCC LIV. 8vo, pp. 30. B., H., M. 5725

Blagden. A Sermon, preached at the Ordination of Mr. James H. Means ... Dorchester, Mass., July 13, 1848. By Rev. George W. Blagden ... . *Boston.* 1848. 8vo, pp. 43. H.

Blagdon (F. W.) The Modern Geographer; being a General History and Descriptions of The Empires, Kingdoms, States, and Colonies of the World, their Revenues, Commerce, Laws, Manners, Religions, &c. By Francis William Blagdon. *London.* [n. d.] 5 vols., 8vo. 60 Plates, and Maps. 5727

Vol. I. comprises America, and contains a full account of the United States, with curious extracts from travelers, etc.

Blaikie (A.) The Philosophy of Sectarianism; or, a Classified View of the Christian Sects in the United States; with Notices of their Progress and Tendencies. Illustrated by Historical Facts and Anecdotes. ... By the Rev. Alexander Blaikie ... . *Boston: Phillips, Sampson, & Co.* 1854. 12mo, pp. 362. C. + *London: Low.* 1854. 8vo. + *Boston: Phillips, Sampson, and Company.* 1855. 12mo, pp. 362. S., H. 5728

[Blaikie.] The Schools; or, a Comparative Statement of the Relative Position and Distinctive Principles of the New, Old, Older, and Oldest, Schools of Presbyterians, in the United States. By a Presbyterian. *Boston: Alexander Moore.* 1860. 12mo, pp. 59. H. 5729

Blaine (J. Gillespie). Are the Five-Twenty Bonds Redeemable in Coin? Speech of J. G. Blaine ... in the House ... November 26, 1867. ... [*Washington?* n. d.] 8vo, pp. 8. H.

Blaine. Mr. Blaine's Letter of Acceptance [of a nomination for re-election as representative in Congress. Dated Augusta, Aug. 20th, 1864. [n. p. n. d.] 4to, p. (1). H. 5731

[Blaine.] Memoir of Luther Severance. ... [Preface signed Jas. G. Blaine.] *Augusta, Me.* 1856. 8vo, pp. 33. H. 5732

Blaine. Reimbursement of Loyal States for Expenses incurred in the War for the Union. Speech of Hon. James G. Blaine ... in the House ... March 21, 1866. [*Washington.* 1866.] 8vo, pp. 8. H. 5733

Blaine. Speech of Mr. Blaine of Augusta in Reply to Mr. Gould of Thomaston, on the Confiscation Resolves, March 7, 1862. *Augusta: Journal Office.* 1862. 8vo, pp. 12. 5734

Blaine. ... Speech of Mr. Blaine ... In favor of amending the Federal Constitution, by striking out the clause which prohibits the taxing of Exports. Delivered in the House ... March 2, 1865. [n. p. 1865.] 8vo, pp. 4. H. 5735

Blaine. Speech of Hon. James G. Blaine ... January 8, 1866, on his Proposition to Amend the Constitution with respect to the Basis of Representation in Congress. [n. p. n. d.] 8vo, pp. 4. 5736

Blair (D.) Some Account of the last Yellow Fever Epidemic of British Guiana. By Daniel Blair. Edited by John Davy. Third Edition, with Illustrations and Supplementary Documents. *London: Longman & Co.* 1852. 8vo, pp. 246.

Blair (F. P.), *Jun.* Confiscation of Rebel Property. Speech of Francis P. Blair, Jr. ... in the House ... February 5, 1864. *Washington, D. C.* 8vo, pp. 16. H. 5738

Blair. The Destiny of the Races of this Continent. An Address delivered before the Mercantile Library Association of Boston, Massachusetts. On the 26th of January, 1859. By Francis P. Blair, Jr. ... *Washington, D. C.: Buell & Blanchard, Printers.* 1859. 8vo, pp. 38. H. 5739

Blair. "Frémont's Hundred Days in Missouri." Speech of Hon. F. P. Blair, Jr. ... on Frémont's Defense ... in the House ... March 7, 1862. *Washington.* 1862. 8vo, pp. 16.

Blair. The Case of General Fremont. Remarks Suggested by the Speech of the Hon. F. P. Blair, Delivered in the House of Representatives, March 7th, 1862. 8vo, pp. 32. C. 5741

Also: The Jacobins of Missouri and Maryland. Speech ... delivered in the House ... February 27, '64. [n. p. n. d.] 8vo, pp. 14. H. — ... Letter ... . To my Neighbors. [*New York.* n. d.] 8vo, pp. 8. — Letter ... to the Republican Association of Washington, D. C., Dec. 10, 1855. [On the Government of the Territories, Slavery, etc. n. p. n. d.] 8vo, pp. 8. — Brief des Herrn Francis P. Blair an den Republikanischen Verein von Wahington [*sic*], D. C. [*Washington.* 1855.] 8vo, pp. 8. — Remarks ... in Joint Session of the General Assembly of Missouri, upon the Subject of the Senatorial Election. [Also Remarks ... Jan. 10, 1855, in Reply to Mr. Stewart. n. p. n. d.] 8vo, pp. 16. H. — Secretary Chase scheming for the Presidency. His intrigues and official Abuses. Speech ... April 23, 1864. [n. p.] 8vo, pp. 15. — Speech ... on the Acquisition of Territory in Central and South America, to be colonized with Free Blacks, and held as a Dependency by the United States. ... Delivered in the House ... On the 14th day of January, 1858. With An Appendix. *Washington.* 1858. 8vo, pp. 31. H. — Speech ... on the Policy of the President for the Restoration of the Union and Establishment of Peace. ... in the House ... April 11, 1862. [n. p. n. d.] 8vo, pp. 8. — Message of the President of the United States, in relation to a Military Appointment of the Hon. Francis P. Blair, Jr., representing the First Congressional District of Missouri. pp. 2. (House of Representatives Ex. Doc., No. 77, 38th Cong., 1st Sess.) — Military appointment of Francis P. Blair, Jr. (Report No. 110, 38th Congress, 1st Session, 1864.)

... Blair Investigation Case. Report of the Special Committee ... to ... investigate the charge made by the Hon. J. W. McClurg, of Missouri, against F. P. Blair, jr., ... of violating the laws in the matter of an alleged Liquor Speculation ... . [*Washington.* 1864.] pp. 75. (House of Representatives, 38th Congress, 1st Session, Report No. 61.) C. 5742

Blair (H.) ... A Sermon preached before The Society for propagating Christian Knowledge ... in ... Edinburgh ... January 1. 1750. ... By Hugh Blair ... . To which is subjoin'd A short Account of the Present State of the Society. *Edinburgh: A. Kincaid.* M.DCC.L. 8vo, Title, pp. 50. H. 5743

Blair (J. B.) Admission of West Virginia. Speech of Hon.

Jacob B. Blair, of Virginia, in the House ... July 16, 1862. [n. p. n. d.] 8vo, pp. 8. H. 5744

Blair (J.) Our Saviour's Divine Sermon on the Mount, contained in the Vth, VIth, and VIIth Chapters of St. Mathew's Gospel, explained; and the Practice of it recommended in divers Sermons and Discourses. To which is prefixed a Paraphrase on the whole Sermon on the Mount. *London.* 1722. 5 vols., 8vo. + *London.* 1740. 4 vols., 8vo. C. 5745

"Best edition of these valuable sermons, with a recommendatory preface by Dr. Waterland." — Lowndes. Mr. Blair was unremitting in his exertions for the spiritual benefit of the Colonists; it is of him that the well-known anecdote is recorded, that once pleading their cause energetically to a noble Secretary of State, the only answer he obtained was: "D—n their souls! let them make tobacco." *See* Hartwell (J.)

Blair (J.) Animadversions on a Pamphlet entitled "Thoughts on the Examination and Trials of Candidates for the sacred Ministry," in a Letter to the unknown author. By Rev. John Blair, M.A. *Philadelphia.* 1766. 12mo, pp. 44. S. 5746

Also: Essays on ... the Sacraments ... . On Regeneration ... . On ... the Means of Grace. ... *New-York: Printed by John Holt.* M,DCC,LXXI. 8vo.

Blair (John). Blair's Chronological and Historical Tables, from the Creation to the present time. With additions and corrections from the most authentic writers. *London: Longman.* 1851. Rl. 8vo. + Revised and enlarged. ... To ... April, 1856. By J. Willoughby Rosse. *London: H. G. Bohn.* MDCCCLVI. Post 8vo, pp. xiii, 788. H. 5747

General in its character, but grouping important facts in American history.

Blair (J. D.) A Sermon on the Death of Lieutenant-General George Washington, delivered in the Capitol in Richmond. By John D. Blair, Chaplain of the House of Delegates. *Richmond.* 1800. 18mo, pp. 18. 5748

Title from Hough's Washingtoniana. Probably incorrect.

Blair (M.) Comments on the Policy inaugurated by the President, in a Letter and Two Speeches, By Montgomery Blair, Postmaster-General. *New York: Hall, Clayton & Medole, Printers.* 1863. 8vo, pp. 20. H. 5749

Blair. Gov. Blair's Speech. Political issues before the people. Views and assumptions of the Radicals, — and comments upon them, and upon the Proposed Amendments to the Constitution. A Compromise necessary. [n. p. n. d.] 8vo, pp. 12. 5750

Blair. Letter of Montgomery Blair to the Meeting at Cooper-Institute, March 6, 1862. 5751

Also: Speech ... at the Cooper Institute, N. Y., to ratify the Union. Nominations. *New York: D. W. Lee,* 1864. 8vo, pp. 16. — Speeches ... 1. On the Monroe Doctrine. [At Hagerstown, Md., 12th July, 1865, Exposing the alliance of the American Secretary of State with Louis Napoleon to overthrow the Monroe Doctrine and establish a despotism on this Continent. 2. Defence of the People of the Southern States. [*Washington.* 1865.] 8vo, pp. 23. H. — Speech ... on the Revolutionary Schemes of the Ultra Abolitionists, and in Defence of the Policy of the President, delivered at the Unconditional Union Meeting, held at Rockville, Montgomery Co., Maryland, ... October 3, 1863. *New York: D. W. Lee, Printer.* 1863. 8vo, pp. 20. B., H. + *Baltimore.* 1863. 8vo, pp. 18. — Speech ... on the Causes of the Rebellion and in Support of the President's Plan of Pacification, delivered before the Legislature of Maryland ... 22d of January, 1864. *Baltimore: Printed by Sherwood & Co.* 1864. 8vo, pp. 22. B. — Supreme Court of the United States. No. 7. December Term, 1856. Dred Scot, (A Colored Man,) vs. John F. A. Sandford. Argument of Montgomery Blair, of Counsel for the Plaintiff in Error. *Washington, D. C.* [n. d.] 8vo, pp. 40. H.

Blair (S.) Animadversions on the reasons of Mr. Alexander Creaghead's receding from the judicatures of this Church. Together with its Constitution. By Samuel Blair. [Motto.] *Philadelphia: printed by William Bradford.* [1742]. 12mo. P.

Blair. A Discourse delivered in the first Presbyterian Church of Philadelphia, May 9th, 1798. By Samuel Blair. *Philadelphia: J. Walters.* 1798. 8vo, pp. 31. 5753

Blair. The | Doctrine | of | Predestination | Truly & Fairly Stated; | Confirmed from clear Scripture-Evidence, and | Defended against all the material Arguments | and Objections advanced against it | By Samuel Blair, late Minister of the Gospel at | Shrewsbury in New-Jersey, now at London-derry | in Pennsylvania. | *Philadelphia:* | *Printed by B. Franklin for the Author.* M. DCC. XLII. | Sm. 8vo, pp. 79, and Advertisement. G. 5754

Blair. A [Fast-day Sermon.] By the Rev. Samuel Blair. *Philadelphia.* 1798. pp. 31. 5755

Blair. An Oration pronounced at Nassau Hall, January 14, 1761: on occasion of the Death of His late Majesty King George II. By Samuel Blair, A.B. *Woodbridge in New Jersey: James Parker.* MDCCLXI. 4to, pp. 8. C. 5756

Blair. A funeral Discourse delivered in the third Presbyterian Church in the city of Philadelphia, on the 17th day of November, on occasion of the death of the Rev. Dr. John B. Smith, late pastor of said church, who departed this life, on the

22d of August 1799. By the Rev. Dr. Samuel Blair. ... Published at the desire of the congregation. *Philadelphia: W. W. Woodward.* 1799. 8vo, pp. 38. C. 5757

Blair. A Particular Consideration of ... The Querists: Wherein ... Mr. Whitfield's Soundness in ... Doctrine [is] maintained ... . By Samuel Blair. ... *Philadelphia: B. Franklin.* 1741. 8vo, pp. 63. B. 5758

Blair. A Short and faithful Narrative, of the late remarkable revival of religion in the Congregation of New-Londonderry, and other parts of Pennsylvania. As the same was sent in a letter to the Rev. Mr. Prince of Boston. By Samuel Blair, Minister of the Gospel at New Londonderry, in Pennsylvania. [Motto.] *Philadelphia: William Bradford.* [1744.] 12mo, pp. 46. P. 5759

Blair. A Vindication of The Brethren who were unjustly and illegally cast out of the Synod of Philadelphia ... against The Charges of the Rev. Mr. John Thompson in his ... Government of the Church of Christ, &c. By Samuel Blair ... . *Philadelphia: Printed by B. Franklin for the Author.* MDCCXLIV. 8vo, pp. 63. B. 5760

Blair. The Works of the Reverend Samuel Blair, Late Minister of the Gospel at Frogs-Mannor, in Chester County, in Pennsylvania ... . *Philadelphia: W. Bradford.* 1754. 8vo. 5761

Blair (T.) Some Short and Easy Rules, teaching the true Pronunciation of the French Language. By Thomas Blair. *Boston.* 1720. 8vo, pp. 12. M. 5762

Blake (A. V.) The American Booksellers' Complete Reference Trade-List, and Alphabetical Catalogue of Books published in this country; with the Publishers' and Authors' names and prices, arranged in classes ... . Compiled by Alexander V. Blake. To which is added an article [by P. T. Washburn] on the law of copyright. *Claremont, N. H.* 1847. 4to, pp. 224. + Supplement ... . *Claremont.* 1848. 4to, 4 l., pp. 224, 235–351. B., S.

"A trade-list ... without ... pretensions to bibliographical accuracy." — Trübner.

Blake (C.) A Historical Account of the Providence Stage. By Charles Blake. Being a Paper read before the Rhode Island Historical Society, October 25th, 1860. (With additions.) *Providence, R. I.: George H. Whitney.* 1868. 12mo, pp. 297.

Edition, two hundred copies.

BLAKE (D. T.) Historical Treatice of the Practice of the Court of Chancery of the State of New-York; containing all the Proceedings of a suit, as well in the Court of Chancery as in the Court for the Trial of Impeachments and Correction of Errors. *New York.* 1818. 8vo. + Second Edition. *Albany.* 1824. 8vo. 5765

BLAKE (Francis). An Examination of the Constitutionality of the Embargo Laws; comprising a View of the Arguments ... in the case of the United States *vs.* Brigantine William, Tried ... at Salem, (Mass.) September Term, 1808. By Francis Blake ... . Added, the Opinion pronounced by the Court ... . *Worcester: printed by Goulding and Stow.* 1808. 8vo, pp. 61. H.

BLAKE. An Oration, pronounced at Worcester, (Mass.) ... July 4, 1812. By Francis Blake. ... *Worcester.* [n. d.] 8vo, pp. 36. B., H. 5767

BLAKE. An Oration, Pronounced at Worcester, on the Anniversary of American Independence; July 4, 1796. By Francis Blake, Esq. *Worcester: Thomas, Son, & Thomas. July,* 1766. 4to, pp. 18. H. 5768

BLAKE (George). A Masonic Eulogy, on the Life of the Illustrious Brother George Washington, pronounced before the Brothers of St. John's Lodge, on the Evening of the 4th Feb. 5800. ... By Brother George Blake. [Motto.] *Boston: printea by Brother John Russell.* 5800. 8vo, pp. 23. H. + Second Edition ... . 5800. [1800]. 8vo, pp. 23. C. 5769

BLAKE. An Oration pronounced July 4th, 1795, at the Request of the Inhabitants of the Town of Boston. ... By George Blake. ... *Boston: Benjamin Edes.* 1795. 8vo, pp. 28.

[BLAKE.] Sketch of the Proceedings and Trial of William Hardy, for Murder of an Infant, Boston, Nov. 27, 1806. *Boston: Oliver J. Munroe.* 1807. 8vo, pp. 47. C. 5771

BLAKE (H. G.) Freedom takes no step backwards. Speech of Hon. Harrison G. Blake of Ohio, delivered in the House of Representatives, Feb 19, 1861. 8vo, pp. 7. 5772

BLAKE. Our Country before Party. Speech of Hon. H. G. Blake of Ohio, on the State of the Union. Delivered in the House ... Feb. 28, 1863. [n. p. n. d.] 8vo, pp. 32. 5773

BLAKE. Slavery in the District. Speech of Hon. H. G. Blake, of Ohio, delivered In the House ... April 11, 1862, on the Bill for the Release of certain Persons held to Service or Labor in the District of Columbia. [n. p. n. d.] 8vo, pp. 8.

BLAKE (Henry N.) ... Report ... as to the Expediency of employing Foreign Artists to decorate our National Edifices. [Signed Henry N. Blake. *Cambridge.* 1857.] 16mo, pp. 4. H.

BLAKE. Three Years in the Army of the Potomac. By Henry N. Blake, late Captain 11th Regiment Massachusetts Volunteers. *Boston: Lee & Shepard.* 1865. 16mo, pp. 319. C.

BLAKE (J.) ... Annals of the Town of Dorchester. By James Blake. [1630–]1750. *Boston: David Clapp, Jr.* 1846. 12mo, pp. 95. Facsimile, 2 pp. C. & H. 5777

Forms Number Two of the "Collections of the Dorchester Antiquarian and Historical Society."

BLAKE (J. F.) A Sermon on the Services and Death of Abraham Lincoln, preached in Christ Church, Bridgeport, Conn. Easter Sunday April 16, 1865. Repeated in the North Congregational Church, Bridgeport, April 19, 1865. By Rev. John Falkner Blake. *New York: W. H. Kelly & Bro.* 1865. 8vo, pp. 29. 5778

BLAKE (J. L.) American Universal Geography, for Schools and Academies. Illustrated by Maps. *Boston.* 1833. 4to.

BLAKE. Anecdotes of the American Indians. [n. p. n. d.] 18mo. + *Hartford: C. M. Welles.* 1850. 18mo, pp. 252. C.

BLAKE. A General Biographical Dictionary, comprising a Summary Account of the most distinguished persons of all Ages, Nations and Professions, including more than one thousand articles of American Biography. By Rev. J. L. Blake, D.D. *New York.* 1835. Imp. 8vo, pp. 1060. + Second Edition. *New York.* 1839. Imp. 8vo. + Fourth Edition. *Philadelphia.* 1840. Rl. 8vo. + Eighth Edition. *Boston.* 1850. Rl. 8vo. + Twelfth Edition. Including more than Two Thousand Articles of American Biography. 1854. Imp. 8vo. + Thirteenth Edition. *Philadelphia: H. Cowperthwait & Co.* 1856. pp. 1366. H., C. 5781

BLAKE. The Family Encyclopædia of Useful Knowledge and General Literature, &c. *New York.* 1834. Imp. 8vo.

Scissors and paste. Contains twenty-two woodcuts of American views.

[BLAKE.] History of the American Revolution. *London.* 1834. 8vo. + First American Edition with Notes. *Columbus, O.* 1834. 12mo. + *New York.* 1844. + 1846. + 1847. + 1854. 18mo, pp. 252. 4 Maps. C. + The American Revolution, including also the Beauties of American History. *New York.* 1860. 8vo, pp. 504. 5783

Published under the superintendence of the Society for the Diffusion of Useful Knowledge.

BLAKE (Joseph), *Jun.* An Oration, Pronounced July 4th, 1792, at the Request of the Inhabitants of the Town of Boston ... . By Joseph Blake, jun. ... *Boston: printed by Benjamin Russell.* MDCCXCII. 4to, pp. 16. H. 5784

BLAKE (J. M.) Speech of Hon. Joseph M. Blake, upon the report of the case, Ives *vs.* Hazard, made to Chief Justice Samuel Ames, State Reporter. [n. d.] 8vo, pp. 16. 5785

BLAKE. Libel Suit of Chief Justice Ames against Thomas R. Hazard. Hon. Joseph M. Blake's argument for defendant upon plaintiff's demurrer. *Providence: A. C. Greene.* 1862. 8vo. 5786

BLAKE (M.) A Centurial History of the Mendon Association of Congregational Ministers, with the Centennial Address, delivered at Franklin, Mass., Nov. 19, 1851, and Biographical Sketches of the Members and Licentiates. By Rev. Mortimer Blake. *Boston: for the Association by Sewall Harding.* 1853. 12mo, pp. 348. B., S. 5787

BLAKE. The First Quarter Century of the Winslow Church: containing a Historical Discourse, preached January 12, 1862, and an Appendix. By Mortimer Blake, Pastor. *Taunton, Mass.* [n. d.] 8vo, pp. 67. H. 5788

BLAKE. The Issues of the Rebellion. A Sermon preached before the Taunton and Raynham Volunteers ... June 2, 1861, by Rev. Mortimer Blake ... . *Taunton: Republican Office.* 1861. 8vo, pp. 13. H. 5789

BLAKE (Nancy). Letters to a Western Cousin. *New York.* 1864. 8vo. 5790

BLAKE (R.) The History and Life of Robert Blake, Esq.; of Bridgewater, General and Admiral of the Fleets and Naval Forces of England. Containing a full Account of his Glorious

Atchievements by Sea and Land, more especially by Sea; where he obtained many Surprising Victories over Dutch, French, Spaniards, and others, Turks as well as Christians. To which is added a Sketch of a Comparison between the two Great Actions against the Spaniards at Sancta Cruz and Porto Bello. Written by a Gentleman bred in his Family. *London: for J. Millan and R. Davis.* [n. d.] 12mo, 8 l., pp. 128. 5791

A life of this celebrated admiral [by John Gorton], is included in "Lives of Eminent Persons." *London.* 1834. 8vo.

BLAKE. Blake's Remarks on Com. Johnstone's Account of his Engagement with a French Squadron, under the Command of Mons. de Suffrein, on April 16, 1781, in Port Praya Road, in the Island of St. Jago. A New Edition. To this Edition is prefixed a Letter from Blake to the Commodore, and a Plan of the Harbour, &c. *London: J. Debrett.* M DCC LXXXII. 8vo, Title, pp. 38. Plan. H. 5792

The Manchester Free Library has an edition, *London,* 1781. 8vo, pp. 21.

BLAKE. An Order of Parliament for a Day of Thanksgiving, for the Great Success of General Blake against the Spaniard, at Sancta Cruz. 1657. Folio. 5793

BLAKE (S.) Blake Family. A Genealogical History of William Blake, of Dorchester, and his Descendants, comprising all the Descendants of Samuel and Patience (White) Blake. With an Appendix, containing Wills, &c. of Members of the Family, and other Interesting Matter. By Samuel Blake ... . *Boston: Ebenezer Clapp, Jr.* 1857. 8vo, pp. 140. B., H. 5794

BLAKE (S. H.) An Address, delivered before the Association of Teachers, and Friends of Popular Education, at Exeter, Dec. 28, 1836. By S. H. Blake. *Bangor: the Association.* 1837. 8vo, pp. 23, (2). H. 5795

BLAKE (S. J.), *or* JEX-BLAKE. A Visit to some American Schools and Colleges. By Sophia Jex Blake. *London: Macmillan and Co.* 1867. Crown 8vo, pp. xii, 250. B. & C. 5796

BLAKE (W.) America, a Prophecy. *Lambeth: Printed by William Blake in the Year* 1793. Folio, pp. 20. 5797

The American Revolution is the theme. It is one of the most curious and scarce of the works of this gifted but eccentric artist. Sold at Puttick's, May, 1854, for £5. Copies are sometimes found with colored plates, and a few were printed in blue and white. *See* Gilchrist's Life of Blake, I. 109.

BLAKE (W. H.) Separate Report of Mr. Blake's Speech on the Rebellion Losses. *Montreal.* 1849. 5798

Title from Morgan's Bibl. Canadensis.

BLAKE (W. J.) The History of Putnam County, N. Y.; with an Enumeration of its Towns, Villages, Rivers, Creeks, Lakes, Ponds, Mountains, Hills, and Geological Features; Local Traditions; and Short Biographical Sketches of Early Settlers, etc. By William J. Blake ... . *New York: Baker & Scribner.* 1849. 12mo, pp. iv, 13–368. B., C., H. 5799

BLAKE (W. O.) History of Slavery and the Slave Trade, ancient and modern, and of the Political History of Slavery in the United States. By W. O. Blake. *Columbus, O.: J. & H. Miller.* 1858. 8vo. + 1861. 8vo, pp. 866. 2 Plates. C. 5800

BLAKE (W. P.) Annotated Catalogue of the Principal Mineral Species hitherto recognized in California and the adjoining States and Territories: being a Report to the California State Board of Agriculture. By William P. Blake. March, 1866. *Sacramento: the Author.* 1866. 8vo, pp. 31. 5801

BLAKE. Description of the Fossils and Shells collected in California by William P. Blake ... . *Washington.* 1855. 8vo, pp. 34. (33d Cong., 1st Sess., House Doc. 129.) H. 5802

BLAKE. Description of the various Silver Ores and Minerals, with notices of the principal Silver Mines of Europe, and North and South America, together with Papers on the Metallurgy of Silver. *New Haven.* 1861. 8vo. 5803

BLAKE. The Gold Placers of the Vicinity of Dahlonega, Georgia. Report of William P. Blake ... and of Charles T. Jackson ... with a ... Historical Notice of Gold Mining in Georgia. *Boston.* 1859. 8vo, pp. 63, (1). 2 Maps and Woodcut. BA. 5804

BLAKE. Prospectus of the Chestatee Hydraulic Company, and Report of William P. Blake ... upon the Gold Placers, of a Part of Lumpkin County, Georgia ... . *New York.* 1858. 8vo, pp. 39. H. 5805

BLAKE. Report of a Geological Reconnaissance in California; made in connection with the Expedition to Survey Routes in California to connect with the Surveys of Routes

for a Railroad from the Mississippi River to the Pacific Ocean, under the command of Lieut. R. S. Williamson, Corps Top. Engrs., in 1853. By William P. Blake, Geologist and Mineralogist of the Expedition. With an Appendix, containing descriptions of portions of the Collection by Professor Louis Agassiz, [and others]. *New York: H. Bailliere.* 1858. 4to, pp. xvii, 370, xiii. 5 Maps, 14 Sections, 14 Views, and 72 Plates. 5806

BLAKE. Report upon the Gold Placers in the Vicinity of Dahlonega, Georgia, which may be washed by Water from the Yuhula River. By William P. Blake ... . *New York.* 1858. 8vo, pp. 14. Map. H. 5807

BLAKE. Review of a Portion of a Geological Map of the United States and British Provinces, by J. Marcou. *London.* 1856. 8vo. 5808

BLAKE. ... Routes in California, to connect with the Routes near the Thirty-fifth and Thirty-second Parallels ... . Geological Report, by William P. Blake ... . *Washington, D. C.* 1857. 4to, pp. xvi, (1) l., pp. 370, (1) l., pp. xiii. 4 Geol. Maps, 14 Tinted Plates, 30 Plates, and many Woodcuts. (33d Cong., 2d Sess., House Ex. Doc., Vol. XI. Pt. 5.) H. 5809

For his report on the route east of the Rocky Mountains, *see* Vol. XI. Pts. 2 and 3, Pacific Railroad Report, or, the same matter in Senate Ex. Doc., Vol. XIII. Pts. 2 and 3.

BLAKE. Observations of the Physical Geography and Geology of the Coast of California from Bodega Bay to San Diego. With Colored Plates. *New York.* 1858. 4to. C. 5810

Reprinted from the U. S. Coast Survey Report for 1855, pp. 376–398.

BLAKE, BROTHERS & Co. To ... Congress ... . [n. p. 1864.] Fol., pp. (4). H. 5811

Relates to a claim on the Government for interest on certain lost certificates of indebtedness.

BLAKSLEE (Solomon). An Oration, delivered at East-Haddam, Feb. 22, 1800, agreeable to the Proclamation of the President of the United States; on the Death of the late General George Washington. By Solomon Blakslee, B.M. *Hartford: Printed by Hudson and Goodwin.* 1800. 8vo, pp. 15. 5812

BLANC (Edmond Adolphe). Affaires de La Plata. Le traité

Le Prédour et les intérêts de la France dans l'Amérique du Sud. Par M. Edmond Blanc ... . *Paris: Goujon.* 1849. 8vo, 1 sheet.

BLANC (Hippolyte). Le merveilleux dans le jansénisme, le magnétisme, le méthodisme et le baptisme américains ... par Hippolyte Blanc *Paris: Henri Plon.* 1865. 8vo, pp. x, (1), 445.

"Methodistes et baptistes américains," pp. 253–278.

BLANC-GILLY (Matth.) Observations impartiales sur les troubles de Saint-Domingue. *Paris.* 1791. 8vo. 5815

Also: Éloge de capitaine Cook. *Paris: Morin.* 1787. 8vo.

BLANC (Vincent Le). *See* Le Blanc (Vincent).

BLANCHARD (A.) An Address delivered at the Consecration of the Lowell Cemetery, June 20, 1841. By Amos Blanchard ... . *Lowell: Leonard Huntress.* 1841. 8vo, pp. 23. H. 5816

[BLANCHARD (Calvin).] A Crisis Chapter on Government. [Signed. *New York.* 1865.] 8vo, pp. 4. H. 5817

[BLANCHARD.] An Eye-Opener! A Real Liberty Song. [*New York.* 1862.] 24mo, pp. 18. + [Second Edition, with an Appendix. *New York.* 1862.] 24mo, pp. 22. H. 5818

[BLANCHARD.] Life of Thomas Paine. By the Author of the Religion of Science. *New York.* 1860. 12mo. C. 5819

BLANCHARD. Tracts of The Society for Abolishing Humbug! No. 1. [*New York.* 1864.] 12mo, pp. 4. H. 5820

BLANCHARD (C.) Chief Justice Caton's Seymour Letter. Remarks by Charles Blanchard, of Ottawa, Illinois. *Ottawa Republican.* 1863. 8vo, pp. 12. 5821

BLANCHARD (Émile). Insectes d'Amérique. *See* Orbigny (Alcide d').

BLANCHARD (I. H. T.) A Discourse delivered by Rev. I. H. T. Blanchard, in South Natick, December 9, 1834. Occasioned by the Death of John Atkins, Esq. *Boston: Joseph Dowe.* 1835. 8vo, pp. 20. H. 5822

BLANCHARD (J.) Speech of Mr. John Blanchard ... on the Tariff. Delivered in the House ... June 29, 1846. *Washington.* 1846. 8vo, pp. 16. 5823

BLANCHARD (J.) Public Men, and Public Institutions of the Church. Discourse before the Literary and Moral Society of Ripley College, Ohio, September 29, 1842. By J. Blanchard. [n. p. n. d.] 8vo, pp. 8. 5824

BLANCHARD (J.) *and* RICE (N. L.) A Debate on Slavery, held in the City of Cincinnati, October, 1845, upon the Question: Is Slaveholding in itself Sinful, and the Relation between Master and Slave a Sinful Relation? Affirmative: J. Blanchard. Negative: N. L. Rice. *Cincinnati.* 1846. 12mo. S. + Fourth Edition. *Cincinnati.* 1857. 12mo. C. 5825

BLANCHARD (J. Pollard). Journal of my Forty-Fifth Ascension. Being the first performed in America, on the Ninth of January, 1793. ... By J. P. Blanchard. *Philadelphia: Charles Cisk.* 1793. 8vo, pp. 27. Plate. W. 5826

[BLANCHARD.] Circular. To the Members of the Convention for amending the Constitution of Massachusetts. [Signed Joshua P. Blanchard. n. p. 1853.] 12mo, pp. 28. B., H.

[BLANCHARD.] Plan for terminating the War, by Division of the United States, without Concession of Principle or Right on the Part of the North. [Signed J. P. B. n. p. 1861.] 4to, (1) l. H. 5828

BLANCHARD. Principles of the Revolution: showing the Perversion of them and the Consequent Failure of their Accomplishment. By J. P. Blanchard. *Boston: Press of Damrell and Moore.* 1855. 8vo, pp. 24. H. 5829

BLANCHARD. To the Members of the American Peace Society. [The Recent History of the Society. *Boston.* 1851.] 16mo, pp. 8. H. 5830

[BLANCHARD.] The War of Secession. [n. p. n. d.] 12mo, pp. 23. B., H. 5831

Also: Address delivered at the Thirteenth Anniversary of the Massachusetts Peace Society, December 25, 1828. *Boston.* 1829. 8vo, pp. 15. H.

BLANCHARD (P.) San Juan de Ulúa ou Relation de l'expédition française au Mexique, sous les ordres de M. le contre-amiral Baudin; par MM. P. Blanchard et A. Dauzats. Suivi de notes et documents, et d'un aperçu général sur l'état actuel du Texas, par M. E. Maissin ... . *Paris: Gide.* 1839. Rl. 8vo, pp. xii, 591. 18 Plates. 34 Woodcuts. B. 5832

Published at 45fr., or without vignettes, 25fr.

BLANCHARD. Merkwaardige lotgevallen van vermaarde reizigers en zeelieden; naar het Fransch. ... *Rotterdam: J. Immerzeel, Jun.* 1821. 12mo. Plates. 5833

BLANCHARD. Reisje rondom de wereld, geschikt om jonge lieden tot de aardrijkskunde op te leiden; naar het Fransch. ... *Rotterdam: J. Immerzeel Jun.* 1821. 12mo. Plates. 5834

BLANCHARD. Reise om de wereld. Nieuwe uitgave. *Amsterdam: G. J. A. Beijerinck.* 1835. 8vo. Plates. 5835

BLANCHARD (R.) Hand-Book of Iowa; describing its Agricultural, Commercial, and Manufacturing Resources ... also, its Physical Geography and Geology. By Rufus Blanchard. *Chicago: Blanchard & Cram.* 1867. 18mo, pp. 92, (2). Map and Woodcuts. H. 5836

BLANCHARD. Hand-book of Minnesota: describing its Agriculture, Commercial and Manufacturing Resources, etc. By Rufus Blanchard. *Chicago: Blanchard & Cram.* 1867. 18mo, pp. 64. 5837

BLANCHARD (Victor). Voyages de La Pérouse autour du monde. *Limoges et Paris: Ardant.* 1848. 12mo. 5838

BLANCHARD. Voyages de Magellan, Byron, Wallis, Bougainville, Surville, Marion, autour du monde. *Limoges et Paris: Ardant.* 1848. 12mo. Vignette. 5839

BLANCHARDIÈRE. *See* Courte de la Blanchardière (l'Abbé).

[BLANCHE (*Madame*).] Discours sur les Américains [par madame Blanche, ancienne habitante de Saint-Domingue]. ... 1784. 5840

BLANCHELANDE. Copie de la lettre de M. Blanchelande; gouverneur de Saint-Domingue, à M. de Bertrand, ministre de la marine, contenant le récit des malheurs affreux arrivés au Cap. [2 sept. 1791.] *Paris: imp. des affiches.* [n. d.] 8vo, pp. 48 or less. 5841

BLANCHELANDE. Lettre de M. de Blanchelande aux commissaires nationaux civils. Au Cap, 15 février, 1792. *Le Cap-Français: Dufour de Rians.* [n. d.] 4to, pp. 48 or less. 5842

BLANCHELANDE. Mémoire de M. de Blanchelande sur son administration à Saint-Domingue. [28 nov. 1791.] *Le Cap-Français: Dufour de Rians.* [n. d.] 4to. 5843

BLANCHELANDE. Nouvelles de Saint-Domingue ... 26 septembre et 10 octobre, extraites de quatre lettres de M. de Blanchelande ... au ministre de la marine, et de la déclaration faite à la municipalité de Bordeaux par le capitaine Dupin ... . [n. p. 1791.] 8vo, pp. 48 or less. 5844

BLANCHELANDE. Précis de Blanchelande sur son accusation. [*Paris:*] *imp. de N.-H. Nyon.* 1793. 8vo, pp. 40 or less. 5845

BLANCHET (*Madame*). Plaidoyer de Me Blanchet ... contre le président de la république d'Haïti, devant le tribunal civil du Havre, audience du 3 mai 1827 ... . *Paris: impr. de Gaultier-Laguionie.* 1827. 8vo, 6 sheets. 5846

BLANCHET (*Dr.* François). Appel au Gouvernement Impérial et aux Habitans des Colonies Anglaises dans l'Amérique du Nord, sur les prétentions exorbitantes du Gouvernement Exécutif et du Conseil Législatif de la Province du Bas-Canada; par un Membre de la Chambre d'Assemblée. *Quebec: Imprimerie Canadienne.* 1824. 8vo. 5847

BLANCHETIÈRE-BELLEVUE. Courte Réponse à gros mémoire. [Signed Blanchetière-Bellevue.] *Paris: Imp. nationale.* 1790. 8vo, pp. 48 or less. 5848

Answer to "Mémoire des officiers municipaux de la ville de Sainte-Pierre île Martinique."

BLANCHETIÈRE-BELLEVUE. Récit des événements arrivées à la Martinique depuis le 3 juin jusqu'au 9, contradictoirement à la relation publiée par MM. Ruste et Corio, députés de St Pierre. [Signed Blanchetière-Bellevue, député extraordinaire de la Martinique.] *Paris: Imp. nationale.* 1790. 8vo, pp. 48 or less.

BLANCHETIÈRE-BELLEVUE. Réfutation complète des accusations portées par MM. Ruste et Corio ... contre M. de Damas. [Signed Blanchetière-Bellevue. *Paris: imp. de G.-A. Rochette.* n. d.] 4to, pp. 48 or less. 5850

BLANCKE (G.) Verzameling van eenige belangrijke stukken wegens de plantagien Waterland, Adrichem, Palmeneribo en Surinombo [in de kolonie Suriname]. Met een toelichtend berigt uitgegeven. *Amsterdam.* 1834. 8vo. 5851

"Contains 23 letters of the widow Wiërdels, and all the other documents relative to her debt." — MULLER.

BLANCO (M. R.) Conversion | de Piritv. | De Indios Cvmanagotos, | Palenqves, y Otros. | Svs Principios, y Incrementos | que oy tiene, con todas las cosas mas singu- | lares del Pais, politica, y ritos de sus natura- | les, practica que se observa en su Re- | duccion, y otras cosas dignas | de memoria. Sacalas nvevamente a luz | el P. Fr. Matias Rviz Blanco, de la | Observancia de N. P. S. Francisco, Lector de Theologia, Examinador del Obispado de Puerto Rico, y Comissario | Prouincial que ha fido dos vezes en dicha | Conversion. Dedicalas | al Excellentissimo Señor Marqves de | los Velez, dignissimo Presidente del Supremo, | y Real Consejo de las Indias. | Con Privilezio. | *En Madrid: Por Iuan Garcia Infançon Año* 1690. | Sm. 8vo, 7 l., pp. 160, Index, 3 l. 5852

Ternaux, No. 1105, cites an edition, *Madrid*, 1698, 12mo, which I have not seen.

BLANCO. Introduction de la Conversion del Piritu, trata de la tierra, provincia y moradores. por Fr. Mathias Ruix Blanco, franciscano. 1690. 8vo. 5853

Title from Ternaux, No. 1043.

BLANCO. Manval | para Catekizar, | y administrar los | Santos Sacramentos à los Indios | que habitan la Prouincia de la nue- | ua Andaluzia, y nueua, Barcelona, | y San Christoval de los | Cumanagotos. | Dirigido a la Santis- | sima Trinidad. | Por el Padre Fr. Mathias | Ruiz Blanco, de la Regular Obser- | vancia de nuestro Padre San Fran- | cisco, hijo, de la Santa Prouincia de | Andaluzia, Lector de Theologia, y | Predicador Apostolico en las Santas | Missiones de Piirtu, y Exami- | nador Synodal en este Obis | pado de Puerto Rico. | *En Burgos: Por Juan de Viar. Año.* 1683. | Sm. 8vo, 8 l., pp. 101. J. C. B. 5854

Priced, in Tross' Catalogue, 1861, No. 888, at fr.140.

BLANCO SOLANA (Juan). España y la republica de Méjico. 1861. 5855

Les blancs et les noirs en Amérique et le coton dans les Deux Mondes, par l'auteur de La paix en Europe par l'alliance anglo-française. *Paris: Dentu. Londres: Barthès et Lowell.* 1862. 8vo, pp. 43. C., H. 5856

"Advises the South to free the slaves and return to the Union." — BARTLETT.

BLAND (*Colonel*). An Abstract of Military Discipline, from Col. Bland. *Boston.* 1747. 16mo. W. 5857

BLAND. Principles of the Revolution. *Boston.* 1855. 8vo, pp. 24. 5858

BLAND (Edward). *See* Discovery of New Brittaine.

BLAND (R.) An Enquiry into the Rights of the British Colonies; intended as an Answer to "The Regulations lately made concerning the Colonies, and the Taxes imposed upon them considered," in a letter addressed to the author of that Pamphlet. By Richard Bland, of Virginia. *Williamsburgh: Printed by Alexander Purdie and Co.* [1766.] 8vo, pp. 23. + [Colophon:] *London: Re-printed for J. Almon.* MDCCLXIX. 8vo, pp. 5–19. H.

"Mr. Bland is by no means a bad advocate for his countrymen on the other side of the Atlantic." — M. R., XL. 256. "The best writer in Virginia." — TUCKER's Jefferson, I. 64. *See also* Bancroft, v., Chap. XXIV.

BLAND. A Letter to the Clergy of Virginia in which the Conduct of the General Assembly is Vindicated, against the Reflexions contained in a Letter to the Lords of Trade and Plantations, from the Lord-Bishop of London. By Richard Bland, Esq; one of the Representatives in Assembly from the county of Prince George. [Motto.] *Williamsburgh: Printed by William Hunter.* MDCCLX. 8vo, pp. vi, 20. P. 5861

The Bishop's Letter is reprinted in the preface, and relates to the celebrated disputes that grew out of the legislative attacks upon the church property in Virginia.

BLAND (Theodoric). Memorial of Chancellor Bland to the Legislature of Maryland. *Baltimore.* 1825. 8vo, pp. 73. 5862

BLAND. The Opinion of Judge Bland on the Right of the Judiciary to Declare an Act of Assembly Unconstitutional. *Baltimore.* 1816. 8vo. 5863

BLAND. Message from the President ... Report of Theodoric Bland, Esquire, on South America. *Washington.* 1819. 8vo. pp. 107. P. 5864

Reprinted with the following title:

BLAND. Present State of Chili, from the Report laid before Congress, by Judge Bland, the Commissioner sent to that country by the Government of the United States, in 1818. *London: Richardson.* 1820. 8vo, pp. 83. 5865

[BLAND.] The Voter's Text-book; or, the Maryland Citizen's Companion to the Polls. [n. p. n. d.] 8vo, pp. 52.

The Bland Papers: being a Selection from the Manuscripts of Colonel Theodorick Bland, Jr. of Prince George County, Virginia. To which are prefixed an Introduction, and a Memoir of Colonel Bland. ... Edited by Charles Campbell. In Two Volumes. ... *Petersburg: printed by Edmund & Julian C. Ruffin.* 1840–43. 2 vols., 8vo, pp. xxxi, 160; 2 l., 9–130. 5867

A collection of papers relating to the Revolution — now scarce.

BLAND (T.) Remarks on North-American species of Helicidae. By Thomas Bland. [*New York.*] 1858–60. Rl. 8vo, pp. 96. Plate. C. 5868

BLAND *and* COOPER (J. C.) On North-American Helicidae and on the geographical distribution of West-India Land-shells. *New-York.* 1862. 8vo, pp. 23. Plate. C. 5869

BLAND *and* HAINES. On new terrestrial Mollusks and Shells from the West-Indies and Siam. [*New York.*] 1855. 8vo, pp. 8. Colored Plate. 5870

The three preceding works were printed by the New York Lyceum of Natural History.

[BLANE (Gilbert).] A Short Account of the most Effectual Means of preserving The Health of Seaman. [n. p. 1780?] 4to, 3 l., pp. ii, 20. H. 5871

Contains some "Remarks on the West-India Station."

[BLANEY (*Captain*).] An Excursion through the United States and Canada during the Years 1822–23. By an English Gentleman. *London: Baldwin, Cradock, & Joy.* 1824. 8vo, 2 l., pp. 511, 2 Maps, and Statistical View folded, Errata, 1 l. C. H.

The author of this poor book speaks of the total want of all those games and sports that obtained for his own country the appelation of "Merry England," to which Mr. Rich replies in an indignant note. *See* Rich, II. 158.

BLANQ-DEISISLES. Zélénie, ou l'orpheliee américaine, comédie. Par M. Blanq-Desisles. *Lausanne et Paris.* 1787. 8vo. + Dernière edition. *Besancon: Neuve Charmet.* 1790. 5873

BLAQUIÉRE (E.), *translator.* *See* Lavaysse (J. J. Danxion).

BLASCHKE (Ed.) Topographia medica portus Novi-Archangelscensis [?], sedis principalis coloniarum Rossicarum in septentrionali America. Accedunt tabulæ. *Petropoli.* 1842. Rl. 8vo. 5874

BLASQUEZ (Pedro é Ignacio). Memoria sobre el Magrey Mexicano (Agave Maximilianea). *Mexico: Andrade y Escalante.* 1865. 8vo, pp. 32, 1 l. 2 colored Plates. 5876

BLATCHFORD (John). Narrative | of | Remarkable Occurrences, | In the Life of | John Blatchford, | Of Cape-Ann, Commonwealth of Massachusetts. | Containing, | His treatment in Nova-Scotia ... the West-Indies ... Great- | Britain ... France, and the East-Indies, as a prisoner in the | late war. | Taken from his own mouth. | *New-London: Printed by T. Green.* | M,DCC,LXXX,VIII. | ... 8vo, pp. 22. H., M. + Second Edition. *New London: Timothy Green.* 1794. 12mo, pp. 22. + Reprinted with Introduction and Notes by Charles J. Bushnell. *New York: Privately Printed.* 1865. 8vo, pp. 127. 2 Plates.

BLATCHFORD (R. M.) Extract from a Report to the Trustees of the Apalachicola Land Company, by Richard M. Blatchford, Esq., President of the Board of Directors, and Special Agent of said company ... Made May 17, 1837. 8vo, pp. 16. Map. 5878

BLATCHFORD (S.) Reports of Cases in Prize, Argued and Determined in the Circuit and District Courts of the United States, for the Southern District of New York. 1861–65. By Samuel Blatchford. *New York: Baker, Voorhis, & Co.* 1865. 8vo, pp. viii, 729. C. 5879

Most of these cases arose out of the civil war.

BLATCHFORD. An Address delivered to the Oneida Indians, September 24, 1810, by Samuel Blatchford, D.D. Together with the Reply, by Christian, a Chief of Said Nation. ... *Albany.* 1810. 8vo, pp. 11. B. 5880

BLATCHFORD. A Farewell Address delivered in ... Waterford, [on] the Departure for the Frontiers of Three Detached Companies of Artillery, of the Militia ... 21st of September, 1812. By Samuel Blatchford ... . *Albany: printed by Websters and Skinners.* 1812. 8vo, pp. 17. B. 5881

BLATCHFORD. A Sermon delivered ... April 13, 1815: being the day of National Thanksgiving. ... By Samuel Blatchford, D.D. *Albany.* [1815.] 8vo, pp. 20. S. 5882

BLATCHFORD. The Validity of Presbyterian ordination maintained. In a letter to the Rev. William Smith, D.D., occasioned

by the publication of his Sermon, Preached at the consecration of Bishop Jarvis, at New-Haven, on the 18th October 1797. Together with Strictures on said Sermon. By Samuel Blatchford. A.M. Pastor of a Church at Stratfield, Connecticut. ... *New-Haven.* 1798. 8vo, pp. 32. S. 5883

BLATCHFORD (T. W.) Eulogy on Samuel McClellan, M.D. ... read ... February 3, 1857, by Thomas W. Blatchford, M.D. *Albany.* 1857. 8vo, pp. 23. H. 5884

BLATCHFORD. Our Alma Mater Fifty Years Ago. An Oration delivered before the Alumni Association, of the College of Physicians and Surgeons, Medical Department of Columbia College, ... March 14, 1861. By Thos. W. Blatchford ... . *Troy, N. Y.* 1861. 8vo, pp. 44. H., S. 5885

BLATCHLY (A.) Mining and Milling in the Reese River Region of Central and Southeastern Nevada. By A. Blatchly, M.E. *New York: Slote & Janes.* 1867. 12mo, pp. 48. C. 5886

[BLAUVELT (—).] Fashion's Analysis, or the Winter in Town, a Satirical Poem, by Sir Anthony Avalanche, with Notes, Illustrations, etc. *New York.* 1807. 12mo. 5887

BLEBY (H.) Death Struggles of Slavery: being a Narrative of Facts and Incidents, which occurred in a British Colony, during the Two Years immediately preceding Negro Emancipation. By Henry Bleby ... . *London: Hamilton, Adams, and Co.* 1853. 12mo, pp. iv, 304. C. 5888

BLEBY. Der Negeraufstand in Jamaica oder Todeskämpfe des Sclaventhums. ... Actenmässige Darstellung der Bedrückungen, Ungerechtigkeiten, Verfolgungen und Grausamkeiten gegen die Sclaven und ihre weissen Beschützer. Nach einem 17jährige Aufenthalte auf Jamaica ... . Nach dem Englischen frei bearbeitet von Ludwig von Alvensleben. ... *Weimar: Voigt.* 1855. 8vo, pp. iv, 281. 4 Lithographs. 5889

BLEBY. Scenes in the Caribbean Sea. By Henry Bleby. *London: Hamilton.* 1854. 18mo, pp. 210. 5890

BLEBY. Speech of Rev. Henry Bleby, Missionary from Barbadoes, on the Results of Emancipation in the British W. I. Colonies, Delivered at the Celebration of the Massachusetts Anti-Slavery Society, held at Island Grove, Abington, July 31st, 1858. ... *Boston: R. F. Walcutt.* 18mo, pp. 36. H. 5891

BLEDSOE (A. T.) An Essay on Liberty and Slavery. By Albert Taylor Bledsoe, LL.D. *Philadelphia: J. B. Lippincott & Co.* 1856. 12mo, pp. 383. + 1857. 12mo. C. 5892

BLEDSOE. Is Davis a Traitor; or Was Secession a Constitutional Right previous to the War of 1861. By Albert Taylor Bledsoe, ... *Baltimore: Printed for the Author, by Innes & Company.* 1866. 12mo, pp. vi, 263, Errata, 1 p. C. 5893

BLEDSOE. Is Slavery a Blessing? A Reply to Professor Bledsoe's Essay on Liberty and Slavery. With Remarks on Slavery as it is. By a Citizen of the South. *Boston: John P. Jewett.* 1857. 8vo, pp. 120. 5894

BLEDSOE (J.) Masonic Oration, delivered by Jesse Bledsoe, Esq. at Frankfort, (Kentucky,) ... December 27, 1811, in Honor of the Late Grand Master Joseph H. Daviess, Esq. And others, who fell in the recent Engagement with the Indians on the Wabash. ... [And] an Ode, entitled, The Battle of Tippecanoe ... . *Albany: Register Office.* 1812. 8vo, pp. 16. B.

BLEECKER (A. E.) Posthumous Works of Ann Eliza Bleecker, in Prose and Verse. To which is added, A Collection of Essays, Prose and Poetical, by Margaretta V. Faugeres. *New York: T. & J. Swords.* 1793. 12mo, pp. xvii, 375. Portrait by Tiebout. 5896

Mr. Corwin's copy sold (1846) for $11. "The Memoirs of Miss Bleecker and her poems were published many years ago; but I have sought in vain among the libraries and the Bleeckers to obtain a copy." — W. L. STONE, Life of Brant, Vol I. 207. Mr. Allibone says, reprinted, 1809, which is an error.

BLEECKER (A. J.) Documents of Anthony J. Bleecker. U. S. Asssessor Eight District, New York. ... vouchers for his fitness to receive and retain office. ... *New York.* [1868.] 12mo, pp. 12. H. 5897

BLEECKER. [Testimonies of his Devotion to the Principles of the Republican Party. *New York.* 1861. 12mo, pp. 12. H.

BLEEKER (L.) The | Order Book | of | Capt. Leonard Bleeker, | Major of Brigade | in the Early Part of the | Expedition under Gen. James Clinton, | against the | Indian Settlements of Western New York, | in the | Campaign of 1779. | *New York:* | *Joseph Sabin* ... . | 1865. | 4to, pp. 138. 5899

Two hundred and fifty copies printed, of which fifty are on large paper. The introduction and notes are by F. B. Hough.

BLEEKER (P.) Description des espèces de Silures du Suriname. *Haarlem.* 1864. 4to. 16 colored Plates. 5900

BLEEKROD. Notice sur la gutta-percha de Surinam. Par M. le professeur Bleekrod, de l'Académie de Delft. *Paris: imp. Martinet.* 1858. 8vo, pp. 10. 5901

Reprinted from the "Annales des sci. nat.," 4e sér., t. VII.

BLEFKEN (Ditmar). Islandia sive populorum et mirabilium quæ in ea Insula reperiuntur accuratior descriptio, cui de Gronlandia sub finem quædum adjecta. *Lugduni Batavorum: ex typographio Henrici ab Haestens.* 1607. Sm. 8vo, pp. 71. 5902

See Beckmann, "Lit. d. ält Reisebeschr.," I. 114–123.

BLEFKEN. Beschryvingh van Yslandt en Groenlandt. *t'Amsterdam.* 1665. 8vo. 5903

BLEFKEN. Een corte ende warachtige beschrigvinge der twee Eylanden. Ijslandt ende Groenlant, ... Door Dithmarum Blefkenium. *Gorinchem: Adriaen Helmichsz.* 1608. 18mo, pp. 14, 48. J. C. B. 5904

BLEFKEN. Scheeps-togt na Ysland en Groenland gedaan door Dithmarum Blefkenium in 't jaar 1563. Nu aldereerst vertaald. *Leyden.* 1706. 8vo. BM. 5905

Forms Vol. 57 of Vander Aa's Naaukeurige versameling. *See* No. 3. Stuck cites, also, a Dutch version, *Leuwarden.* 1716. 8vo, of which Beekman says he could find no other mention. There is a German version, with a map, in Hieron. Megiser's "Septentrio novantiquus oder die newe Nortwelt. *Leipzig.* 1613." 8vo, pp. 473, and *Leipzig.* 1653; and also, without a map, in F. M's "Neu entdecktes Norden. *Frankfurt und Leipzig.* 1727." 8vo, pp. 302. There is an English version, with a map, in Purchas's "Pilgrims," 1625, folio, III. 643.

The Blennerhassett Papers, Embodying the Private Journal of Harman Blennerhassett, and the hitherto unpublished Correspondence of Burr, Alston, Comfort Tyler, Devoreaux, Dayton, Adair, Miro, Emmett, Theodosia Burr Alston, Mrs. Blennerhassett, and others, their contemporaries; developing the purposes and aims of those engaged in the attempted Wilkinson and Burr Revolution; embracing also the first account of the "Spanish Association of Kentucky," and A Memoir of Blennerhassett, By William H. Safford. *Cincinnati: Moore, Wilstach, & Baldwin.* 1864. 8vo, pp. 665. 3 Portraits. B. C. 5906

BLEYNIE (Léon). Provence et Brésil. *Toulon: imprimerie Laurent.* 1854. 12mo, 10½ sheets. 5907

BLICKE (C.) An Essay on the Bilious or Yellow Fever of Jamaica: Collected from the Manuscript of a late Surgeon. By Charles Blicke. *London: T. Becket and Co., and E. and C. Dilly.* M.DCC.LXXII. 8vo, 2 l., pp. vii, 71. H. 5908

BLIGH (W.) A Narrative of the Mutiny, on board his Britanic Majesty's Ship Bounty, and the subsequent voyage of Part of the Crew, in the ship's boat, from Tofoa, one of the Friendly Islands, to Timor, a Dutch settlement in the East Indies. By Lieut. William Bligh. *London: G. Nichol.* 1790. 4to, pp. 88. Maps. P. + *Philadelphia.* 1790. + *Dublin: Printed for L. White.* ... 1790. 8vo, pp. vii, 144. C. 5908*a*

BLIGH. Relation de l'enlèvement du navire le Bounty: ... traduit par D. Lascallier ... *Paris.* 1790. 8vo, pp. xvi, 171. + Seconde édition. *Paris.* 1792. 8vo. 5909

The only relation this book bears to America is indicated in the following title, which Rich includes in his Bibliotheca Americana, and Stevens in his Nuggets. The mutineers settled in Pitcairn's Island, off the coast of South America:

BLIGH. A Voyage to the South Sea, undertaken by Command of His Majesty, for the purpose of conveying the Bread-Fruit Tree to the West Indies, in His Majesty's Ship the Bounty, commanded by Lieutenant William Bligh. Including an Account of the Mutiny on board the said Ship, and the subsequent Voyage of part of the Crew, in the Ship's Boat, From Tofoa, one of the Friendly islands, To Timor, a Dutch settlement in the East Indies. The whole Illustrated with Charts, etc. Published by permission of the Lords Commissioners of the Admiralty. *London: George Nichol.* M.DCC.XCII. 4to, 10 l, pp. 264. 8 Plates. Portrait by Conde. C. + Reprinted. *Dublin.* 1792. 8vo. 5910

Some copies on large paper. The Fonthill copy sold for £2 11s.; Roxburgh, £1 1s. Lord Byron's poem, "The Island," is based on this narrative. Included in Mavor's Voyages, Vol. XIII.

BLIGH. Voyage à la mer du Sud, entrepris pour introduire aux Indes occidentales l'arbre à pain et d'autres plantes utiles; avec une relation de la révolte à bord de son vaisseau, etc. Traduit de l'anglais par F. Soulés. *Paris.* 1792. 8vo. 5911

BLIGH. Reise in das Südmeer. Nebst J. F. de Sürville's Reise in das Südmeer. Aus dem Englischen mit Anmerkungen von G. Forster. ... *Berlin: Voss.* 1793. 8vo. Plates, and Map. 5912

BLIGH. Captain Bligh's Answer to the Assertions contained in the Appendix to a Pamphlet entitled "Minutes of the Proceedings of the Court-martial, held at Portsmouth, August 12th, 1792." *London.* 1794. 4to. P. 5913

Blik op den vroegeren en tegenwaardigen toestand van het eiland Curaçao. *Rotterdam: H. V. Gogh.* 1847. 8vo. + 1848. 8vo, pp. 28. 5914

BLISMON, *pseudon.* *See* [Blocquel (S.)]

BLISS (C. R.) Deliverance from the Furnace. A Thanksgiving Sermon, delivered at South Reading, December 7, 1865, by Rev. Charles R. Bliss ... . *Boston: Press of T. R. Marvin & Son.* 1865. 8vo, pp. 25. H. 5915

BLISS (Daniel). The Gospel hidden to them that are lost; being the Substance of Two Sermons preached at Concord. ... By Daniel Bliss, A.M. ... Published at the repeated Request, and free cost, of some who heard them. ... *Boston: P. Kneeland.* 1755. 8vo, pp. 44. 5916

BLISS (E.) A Brief History of the New Gold Regions of Colorado Territory; together with Hints and Suggestions to Intending Emigrants. By Edward Bliss. ... *New York: John W. Amerman, Printer.* 1864. 8vo, pp. 31. S. 5917

BLISS (G.) An Address to the Members of the Bar of the Counties of Hampshire, Franklin and Hampden, ... at Northampton, September 1826, By George Bliss. *Springfield: Tannatt & Co., Printers.* 1827. 8vo, pp. 85. B., H. 5918

This might have been entitled, A History of the Hampshire Bar.

BLISS. An Address, delivered at the Opening of the Town-Hall in Springfield, March 24, 1828. Containing Sketches of the Early History of that Town, and those in its Vicinity. With an Appendix. By George Bliss. ... *Springfield: Tannatt & Co., Printers.* 1828. 8vo, pp. 68. H. 5919

BLISS. Historical Memoir of the Springfield Cemetery, read ... May 23, 1857. By George Bliss ... . Accompanied by an Address delivered at the Consecration of the Cemetery, September 5, 1841, by Rev. Wm. B. O. Peabody. *Springfield, Mass.: Samuel Bowles and Company, Printers.* 1857. 8vo, pp. 23. H.

BLISS. Historical Memoir of the Western Railroad. By George Bliss. *Springfield, Mass.* 1863. 8vo, pp. 190, (1). B.

BLISS. Letter to the Majority of the Joint Committee of the Legislature on the Affairs of the Western Railroad. By George Bliss. *Boston.* 1843. 8vo, pp. 26. 5922

BLISS. Letter to the Stockholders of the Michigan Southern & Northern Indiana Railroad Company. By George Bliss, (President ... .) ... *New York.* 1860. 8vo, pp. 13. H. 5923

[BLISS (Henry).] Consideration of the Claims and Conduct of the United States respecting their North Eastern Boundary, and of the Value of the British Colonies in North America. *London: John Hatchard and Son.* 1826. 8vo, 2 l, pp. 112, and Table, folded. H. 5924

BLISS. Letter to Sir Henry Parnell ... on the New Colonial Trade Bill. By Henry Bliss, Esq. *London.* 1831. 8vo, pp. 37.

BLISS. On Colonial Intercourse; with an Appendix, containing a Memorial to the Right Honourable the Board of Trade against opening the West Indies to Ships of the United States ... By Henry Bliss, Esq. *London.* 1826. 8vo, pp. 111. + *London:* 1830. 8vo. 5926

BLISS. The Colonial System: Statistics of the Trade, Industry, and Resources of Canada, and the other Plantations in British America. By Henry Bliss, Esq. *London.* 1833. 8vo, pp. 169. 5927

BLISS. An Oration, delivered at the Baptist Meeting-House in Colebrook, (Con.) On the National Thanksgiving ... By Henry Bliss. [n. p. 1815.] 8vo, pp. 16. S. 5928

BLISS. Thanksgiving. A Poem. In Two Parts. By Henry Bliss. *Pittsfield, Mass.: Phinehas Allen. May,* 1815. 8vo, pp. 24. W. 5929

BLISS (L.), *Jun.* The History of Rehoboth, Bristol County, Massachusetts; comprising a History of the Present Towns of Rehoboth, Seekonk, and Pawtucket, from their Settlement to the Present Time; together with Sketches of Attleborough, Cumberland, and a part of Swansey and Barrington, to the Time that they were severally separated from the Original Town. By

Leonard Bliss, Jr. ... *Boston: Otis, Broaders, and Company.* 1836. 8vo, pp. v, 294, Errata, 1 p. C., H. 5930

A work of much merit, written when the author was a young man. He was subsequently assassinated at Louisville, Ky. *See* N. A. R., XLIII. 534–537.

BLISS (P.) Citizenship: State Citizens, General Citizens. Speech of Hon. Philemon Bliss, of Ohio ... in the House ... January 7, 1858. [*Washington, D. C.* 1858.] 8vo, pp. 8. H.

BLISS. Success of the Absolutists. Their Idealism; what and whence is it? Speech of Hon. Philemon Bliss ... in the House ... May 24, 1858. *Washington, D. C.*, 1858. 8vo, pp. 15. H. 5932

BLISS (P. C.) The Ethnography of the Gran Chaco, being the Results of a Voyage of Exploration in the River Bermejo in 1863. By Porter Cornelius Bliss. *Buenos Aires.* 1864. 4to, pp. 16. 5933

BLISS (S. A.) Memoir of Sarah Ann Bliss, who died at Stockbridge, Mass. aged Eighteen Years. ... Third Edition. *Boston: Massachusetts Sabbath School Society.* 1843. 24mo, pp. 54. H.

[BLISS (*Rev.* Seth).] Letters to the Members, Patrons and Friends of the Branch American Tract Society in Boston, Instituted 1814; and to those of the National Society in New York, Instituted 1825. By the Secretary of the Boston Society. *Boston: Crocker and Brewster.* 1858. 8vo, Title, pp. 3, 3–112. + [Second Edition.] *Boston:* [*Ibid.*] 1858. 8vo, Title, pp. 2, 3, 3-112. H. + Third Edition. *Boston.* 1858. 8vo. pp. 112.

These letters relate to the slavery question.

BLISS (S.) A Geography of New England: being a Descriptive Key, to accompany the "Outline Map of New England." By Sylvester Bliss ... . *Boston: John P. Jewett & Co.* 1847. 18mo, pp. 96. H. 5936

BLISS. Memoirs of William Miller, generally known as a Lecturer on the Prophecies, and the Second Coming of Christ. By Sylvester Bliss ... . *Boston: Joshua V. Himes.* 1853. 12mo. pp. vi, 426. Portrait. H. 5937

BLISS (T. E.) Clarum et Venerabile Nomen. A Discourse, commemorative of the Life and Character of Abraham Lincoln, late President of the United States, Delivered April 23, 1865. By Rev. T. E. Bliss, Pastor of the Union Church of Memphis. *Memphis, Tenn.: W. A. Whitmore, Printer.* 1865. 8vo, pp. 16.

BLISS. Popular Education indispensable to the Life of a Republic. An Address before the State Teacher's Association, and the Legislature, Nashville, Nov. 15, 1866. By Rev. T. E. Bliss. *Memphis.* 1866. 8vo, pp. 11. 5939

BLISS (W. S.) ... Sketches of the Life and Character of William Starkie Bliss, formerly of Newburyport. Well known in Boston by the Cognomen of the Nice Young Man: in New York by the Cognomen of the Hotel Swindler. By his First Wife. *New York* [etc.] 1851. 8vo, pp. 40. H. 5940

BLISS (Z.) The Extinction of Slavery a National Necessity, before the present conflict can be ended. By Rev. Z. Bliss. 8vo, pp. 8. 5941

BLOCIUS *or* BLOY (Johann). Historiæ per Saturam ex Novi Orbis Scriptoribus excepta memorabilia. Studio J. Blocii. *Rostochii.* 1627. 12mo. 5942

The date is from a Paris catalogue, Dec. 17, 1860. Georgi gives the date 1625.

BLOCKADE. North America. Papers relating to the Blockade of the Ports of the Confederate States. *London: Harrison and Son.* [1861.] Folio, pp. 126. C. 5943

The Blockheads, or, Fortunate Contractor. An Opera, in Two Acts, as it was performed at New York [during the Revolution] ... *Printed at New York. London: Reprinted for G. Kearsley.* M.DCC.LXXXII. 8vo, pp. v, 43. 2 Plates. 5944

The Blockheads; or, the Affrighted Officers. A Farce. *Boston.* 1776. 8vo, pp. 19. M. 5945

Blockley Alms-house. *See* Philadelphia.

[BLOCQUEL (Simon).] Beaux traits de l'historie des voyages, ou anecdotes curieuses sur différents peuples des cinq parties du monde. Édition revue par Buqcellos ... . *Lille: Castiaux; et Paris: Delarue.* 1825. 18mo, 6 sheets. 8 Engravings. 5946

[BLOCQUEL.] Le jeune voyageur dans les cinq parties du monde. Ouvrage contenant le portrait, le caractère, la religion, les mœurs ... des différents peuples de l'univers. ... *Paris: Delarue.* 1829. 4 vols., 16mo. 72 Plates. 5947

Some copies have the title: "Beautés de l'histoire des voyages." Each of the parts of the world, with 18 plates, was sold separately. Published under the *pseudonym*, Blismon.

[BLOCQUEL.] Nouvel abrégé du Voyageur français dans les cinq parties du monde ... . *Paris: Delarue.* 1829. 2 vols., 12mo. 8 Plates. 5948

Published under the *pseudonym*, Buqcellos.

BLODGET. (L.) ... Climate of the Summer of 1853, in its Relation to the Agricultural Interests of the United States. (A Report to the Secretary of the Smithsonian Institution). By Lorin Blodget ... . *Washington. November,* 1853. 8vo, pp. 26. C. H. 5949

BLODGET. Climatology of the United States, and of the Temperate Latitudes of the North-American Continent. Embracing a Full Comparison of these with the Climatology of the Temperate Latitudes of Europe and Asia. And especially in regard to Agriculture, Sanitary Investigations, and Engineering, with Isothermal and Rain Charts for Each Season, the Extreme Months, and the Year, including a Summary of the Statistics of the Meteorological Observations in the United States, condensed from Recent Scientific and Official Publications. By Lorin Blodget ... . *Philadelphia: J. B. Lippincott and Co.* 1857. 8vo, pp. 536. B., C. 5950

Highly eulogized by Humboldt.

BLODGET. The Commercial and Financial Strength of the United States, as shown in the Balances of Foreign Trade and the Increased Production of Staple Articles. By Lorin Blodget. *Philadelphia: King & Baird.* 1864. 8vo, pp. 39. H. + [Second Edition.] 8vo, pp. 56. H. 4951

BLODGET. Die commerzielle und finanzielle Stärke der Vereinigten Staaten. ... Nach dem Englischen von Konsul C. Gilbert Wheeler. *Nürnberg: Korn.* 1865. 8vo, pp. vi, 33.

BLODGET. On the Climatic Conditions of the Summer of 1853, most directly Affecting its Sanatary Characters ... . By Lorin Blodget ... . *New York.* 1853. 8vo, pp. 23. B. 5953

BLODGET. Proposed Navy Yard at League Island. By Lorin Blodget. *Philadelphia.* 1862. 8vo, pp. 27. C. 5954

BLODGET (S.) A Prospective-Plan of the Battle near Lake George, on the Eighth Day of September, 1755. With an Explanation thereof; Containing A full, tho' short, History of that important Affair. By Samuel Blodget, Occasionally at the

Camp, when the Battle was fought. *Boston; N. E.: Richard Draper.* MDCCLV. 4to, Title, pp. 5. Plan. C. W. + *London: T. Jefferys.* MDCCLVI. 4to, pp. (2), 5. H. 5955

[BLODGET (Samuel), *Jun.*] Economica: a Statistical Manual for the United States of America. ... *City of Washington: the Author.* 1806. 8vo, pp. viii, 202, Appendix, xiv. H. + With Additions to Beginning of the Year 1810. ... *City of Washington.* 1810. 8vo, pp. vii, (1), 202, xiv, 8. C., H. 5956

Contains, among other valuable information respecting the population and general wealth of America, a brief chronology from its discovery, in 1492, to 1806. The author takes out the copyright.

[BLODGET.] Economy. Thoughts on a Plan of Economy (suited to the Crisis of 1808) for the United States of America. [Signed S. B. n. p. n. d.] 8vo, pp. 8. H. 5957

[BLODGET.] Thoughts on the increasing wealth and national economy of the United States of America. By Samuel Blodget. *City of Washington: Way & Groff.* 1801. pp. 40, Table, 1 l. C. 5958

[BLODGET (William).] Facts and Arguments respecting the Great Utility of an Extensive Plan of Inland Navigation in America. ... *Philadelphia: printed by Wm. Duane.* 1805. 8vo, pp. 61, (1). 1 Map. C. H. 5959

BLODGET CANAL. Statements concerning the Blodget Canal at Amoskeag Falls, on Merrimac River, N. H. *Merrimac. June,* 1806. 8vo, pp. 8. W. 5960

BLODGETT (J. W.) AND Co. A Catalogue of Notes, Accounts, and Securities Due and Belonging to the Estate of J. W. Blodgett & Co. to be sold at Public Auction ... March 2, 1858 ... . *Boston.* 1858. 8vo, pp. 141. H. 5961

BLOIS (J. T.) Gazetteer of the State of Michigan, in Three Parts, containing a General View of the State, a Description of the Face of the Country, Soil, Productions, Public Lands, Internal Improvements, Commerce, Government, Climate, Education, Religious Denominations, Population, Antiquities, &c. &c. With a Succinct History of the State from the Earliest Period to the Present Time. Also a Particular Description of the Counties, Towns, Villages, Post Offices, Water Courses, Lakes, Prairies, &c., alphabetically arranged; with an Appendix, containing the usual Statistical Tables, and a Directory for Emigrants, &c. By John T. Blois. *Detroit: Sidney L. Rood & Co. New York: Robinson Pratt & Co.* 1838. 12mo, pp. 418, Errata, 1 l. B., H. + Reprinted. 1840. C. 5962

BLOM *or* BLOME (Anth.) Verhandeling over den landbouw, in de colonie Suriname, volgens eene negentien-jaarige ondervinding zamengesteld, door Anthony Blom: ... met ... ophelderingen en bewysredenen voorzien door, Floris Visscher Heshuysen ... . *Haarlem: Cornelis van der Aa* MDCCLXXXVI. 8vo, 4 l., pp. xxiv, 448, (4). + *Amsterdam.* 1787. 8vo. 5963

These editions are entirely different," says Muller; and apparently that of 1787 was not edited by Heshuysen.

BLOM. Vervolg van den Surinaamschen landman. Eerste deel. n°. 1–12. *Paramaribo.* 1801. 8vo. 5964

BLOME (R.) Britannia; or a Geographical Description of the Kingdoms of England, Scotland, and Ireland, with the Isles and Territories thereto belonging, with an account of the Nobility and Gentry. *London.* 1673. Folio. Maps, and 12 Plates.

Taken from Camden and Speed. Pages 422–493 relate to America. There are copies on large paper.

BLOME. A | Description | Of the Island of | Jamaica; | With the other Isles and Territories | in America, to which the | English are Related, viz. | Barbadoes, | St. Christophers, | Nievis, or Me- | vis, | Antego, | St. Vincent, | Dominica, | Montserrat, | Anguilla, | Barbada, | Bermudes, | Carolina, | Virginia, | Maryland, | New-York, | New-England, | New-Found- | Land. | Taken from the Notes of Sr. Thomas | Linch Knight, Governour of Jamaica; | and other Experienced Persons in the | said Places. Illustrated with Maps. | Published by Richard Blome. | *London:* | *Printed by T. Milbourn, and sold by* | *I. Williams Junior, in Cross-Keys-* | *Court, in Little Brittain* [*sic*]. 1672. | Sm. 8vo, 4 l., pp, 192. 3 Maps. C., H. 5966

Reprinted with the following title:

BLOME. A | Description | of the Island of | Jamaica; | With the other Isles and Territories | in America, to which the | English are Related, viz. | Barbadoes, St. Christophers, Nievis, or Mevis, Antego, St. Vincent. Dominica, Montserrat, Anguilla. Barbada, | Bermudes, | Carolina, | Virginia, | Maryland, | New-York, | New-England, | New-Found- | Land. | Published by Richard Blome. | Together | With the Present State of | Algiers. | *London,* | *Printed by J. B. for Dorman Newman, at the Kings-Arms in the*

Poultrey. 1678. Sm. 8vo, 3 l., pp. 88, followed by separate Title, pp. 17, and 2 l. Portrait of De Ruyter by Vaughan, and 4 Maps. 5967

BLOME. Description de l'Isle de la Jamaique. *See* Bernard (J. F.) Recueil de Divers Voyages, Vol. II., No. 4937*a*.

BLOME. A Geographical Description Of the Four Parts of the World Taken from the Notes & Workes Of the Famous Monsieur Sanson ... and other Eminent Travellers and Authors. ... By Richard Blome Gent. ... *London: R. Blome.* 1670. Folio, 5 l., pp. 113, (5), 82, (3), 138, (6), 56, (2), 55, (1). Maps.

America, pp. 56, (2).

[BLOME.] L'Amerique | angloise, | ou | description | des | isles et terres | du | roi d'Angleterre, | dans | l'Amerique. | Avec de nouvelles Cartes de cha- | que Isle & Terres. | Traduit de l'Anglois. | *A Amsterdam,* | *Chez Abraham Wolfgang,* | *prés la Bourse.* | M. DC. LXXXVIII. 12mo, 2 l., pp. 331, (Table) 1 l. 7 Maps.

Reprinted with the following title:

[BLOME.] Description des isles et terres Que l'Angleterre possede en Amerique Avec de nouvelles Cartes de chaque Isle & des Terres. Traduit de l'Anglois. *Amsterdam: Estienne Roger.* MDCCXV. 12mo, 2 l., pp. 331, (1). 7 Maps. H. 5970

BLOME. Englisch America. *Leipzig: Gross.* 1697. 12mo, 34 sheets, 1 l. 5971

[BLOME.] The Present State Of His Majesties Isles and Territories in America, viz. Jamaica, Barbadoes, S. Christophers, Mevis, Antego, S. Vincent, Dominica, New-Jersey, Pensilvania, Monserat, Anguilla, Bermudas, Carolina, Virginia, New-England, Tobago, New-Found-Land, Mary-Land, New-York. With New Maps of every Place. Together with Astronomical Tables, Which will serve as a constant Diary or Calendar, for the Use of the English Inhabitants in those Islands; from the Year, 1686, to 1700. Also a Table by which, at any time of the Day or Night here in England, you may know what Hour it is in any of those parts. And how to make Sun-Dials fitting for all those Places. Licens'd, July 20. 1686. Roger L'Estrange. *London: Printed by H. Clark, for Dorman Newman,* 1687. 8vo, 4 l., pp. 262, (Tables) 18 l. Portrait, Plate, and 7 Maps. C., H. 5972

BLOMFIELD (E.) A General View of the World, Geographical, Historical and Philosophical, on a Plan entirely New. By Rev. E. Blomfield. *Bungay.* 1807. 2 vols., 4to. 5973

"Very little on America. Less than might have been expected." — H. A. H.

BLONDEEL VAN CUELEBROUK. Colony de Santo-Tomas. Enquête de M. Blondeel van Cuelebrouk, Chargé d'Affaires, Commissaire Extraordinaire du Gouvernement. Deposé sur le Bureau de la Chambre des Representants, le 10 Juin 1846. *Bruxelles.* 1846. + Suite de l'Enquête de M. Blondeel. 25 Nov. 1846. Folio, pp. 240, 136. 6 Maps. S. 5974

This colony, situate on the Bay of Honduras, was settled by Belgians.

BLONDUS (M. A.) *See* Biondo, Vol. II., Nos. 5517, 5518.

BLOOD. The Colonnades. A Poem. By B. Blood. *Amsterdam, N. Y.: The Author.* Rl. 8vo, pp. 113. 5975

BLOOD (C.) A Discourse dilivered [*sic*] July 11, 1811, at the Opening of the New Meeting-House belonging to the First Baptist Church ... in Portland. By Caleb Blood, Pastor ... . *Portland: John McKown, Printer.* 1811. 8vo, pp. 32. H. 5976

BLOOD (H. A.) The History of Temple, N. H. By Henry Ames Blood. ... *Boston: printed by Geo. C. Rand & Avery,* 1860. 8vo, pp. v, (2), 352. 28 Plates. C. H. 5977

BLOOD (M.) A Sermon delivered at Thomastown, June 26, 1820; before the Maine Missionary Society ... . By Mighill Blood ... . *Bangor: printed by J. Burton, Jr.* 1820. 8vo, pp. 40.

"The Report of the Trustees. Treasurer's Statement," pp. 25–40.

BLOOD (W.) A Mission to the Indians of Orialla, South America. To which is added a Narrative of the Destruction of the "Amazon." By the Rev. William Blood. *London: Partridge & Oakey.* [1853.] 12mo, pp. 190. 6 Plates. C. 5979

In some copies the title reads:

BLOOD. A Mission to the Indians of Orialla, in South America: with, Two Sermons, on the Destruction by Fire of the Steamship "Amazon," on 2nd January, 1852. *London.* [1853.] 12mo. CP. 5980

BLOOD. La perte de l'Amazone vaisseau à vapeur parti d' Angleterre pour les États-Unis ... le 2 janvier 1852, incendié en pleine mer ... . *Paris: Meyrueis.* 1860. 18mo, pp. 35.

BLOODGOOD (Abraham) *and* HAMMOND (Judah). A Circular letter from the General Republican Committee, of the City of New York, to their Republican Fellow Citizens, throughout the State, in vindication of the measures of the General Government. *New York: Frank White & Co.* 1809. 8vo, pp. xxiii, 105. C.

[BLOODGOOD (F. A.)] Statement of Facts in relation to the Claims of the Inhabitants of the County of Tompkins, for a Bank in Ithaca. *Albany: printed by D. M'Glashan.* 1829. 8vo, pp. 11. B. 5983

Signed Francis A. Bloodgood, "For himself and his associates."

BLOODGOOD (S. De Witt). The Crisis. An Economic View of the Present Contest. From the American Railroad Journal, October 25, 1862. By S. De Witt Bloodgood. *New York.* [n. p.] 8vo, pp. 4. H. 5984

[BLOODGOOD.] The Sexagenary; or, Reminiscences of the American Revolution. *Albany: W. C. Little and O. Steele.* 1833. 12mo, pp. 283. C. + *Albany: J. Munsell.* 1866. 8vo, pp. 234. 3 Portraits. 5985

The edition of 1866 forms No. 5 of Munsell's Series of Local American History, o. which fifty copies are on large paper.

BLOODGOOD. A Treatise on Roads, their History, Character and Utility, By S. De Witt Bloodgood. *Albany: Oliver Steele.* 1838. 12mo, pp. 228. C. 5986

The Bloody Week! Riot, Murder, & Arson, Containing A full Account of this Wholesale Outrage on Life and Property, Accurately Prepared from Official Sources, By Eye Witnesses. With Portraits of "Andrews," the Leader and "Rosa," his Eleventh Street Mistress. *New York: Coutant & Baker.* [1863.] 8vo, pp. 32. 5987

Relates to the draft riots in the city of New York.

The Bloody Tribunal, or an antidote against Popery, and a History of the Cruelties of the Inquisition in Spain, Portugal, East and West Indies, &c. *London.* 1746. 8vo. Plates.

Title from a doubtful source, — an auctioneer's catalogue.

BLOOMFIELD (B.) The Quartermaster's Guide; being a Compilation from the Army Regulations and other Sources. By B. Bloomfield ... . *Richmond: West & Johnston.* 1862. 12mo. B.

BLOOMFIELD (J.) Laws of the State of New Jersey, from 1800 to 1811; compiled and published under the Authority of the Legislature. By Joseph Bloomfield. *Trenton.* 1811. 8vo.

BLOOMFIELD (O. B. F.) The Life and Adventures of Obadiah Benjamin Franklin Bloomfield, M.D. a native of the United States of America, now on the tour of Europe. Written by himself. *Philadelphia: Published for the Proprietor.* 1818. 12mo. pp. xi, 210. C. 5991

BLOOMFIELD, *Me.* Council at Bloomfield. Result, and Proceedings of the Mutual Ecclesiastical Councils. Convened at Bloomfield, October 19th, 1848. *Skowhegan.* 1848. 16mo, pp. 14. 5992

BLOOMFIELD, *N. J.* Constitution of the Benevolent Society of Bloomfield; Instituted in 1810. *Newark.* 1811. 8vo, pp. 16.

BLOOR (Alfred J.) How the Sanitary does its Work. A Visit to Belle Plain. (From the Boston Daily Advertiser, May 23.) [*Boston.* 1864.] Broadside. H. 5994

BLOOR. Letters from the Army of the Potomac, written during the Month of May, 1864, to several of the Supply Correspondents of the U. S. Sanitary Commission, by Alfred J. Bloor ... . *Washington, D. C.: McGill & Witherow, Printers.* 1864. 8vo, pp. 67. H. 5995

BLOSS (W. C.) ... Map of the United States and Territories, showing the Possessions and Aggressions of the Slave Power. By William C. Bloss ... . [Fourth Edition.] *Rochester, N. Y.* [185–.] Large broadside. H. 5996

Bloudy newes from the Barbadoes, being a true relation of a ... fight between the parliament navie, commanded by Sir George Ayscue, and the king of Scots forces ... . 1652 [1651]. 4to.

BLOUET (Abel). Rapport sur les Pénitenciers des États-Unis. Par M. Abel Blouet, Architecte du gouvernement. *Imprimerie Royale.* 1837. Folio, pp. 114, 1 l. 45 Plates. C.

Principally devoted to the architecture of American prisons.

BLOUNT (*Sir* T. P.) Essays on Several Subjects. By Sir Thomas Pope Blount. *London.* 1692. 12mo. 5999

Contains some curious notices. The following is a specimen: "Those Americans, who kill their old decrepit parents, instead of believing themselves parricides, call us cruel for letting ours continue so long in the miseries of old age. And as for that practice of theirs, of eating their own parents, they think they do thereby give them the most noble sort of sepulture, by burying them in their own bodies," &c.

BLOUNT (W.) Further Report of the Committee appointed 8th July [1797] to prepare and report Articles of Impeachment against William Blount. [*Philadelphia.* 1797.] 8vo, pp. 4. M. + Further Report. [*Philadelphia:*] *John Fenno.* 1798. 8vo, pp. 11. C. 6000

BLOUNT. Message of the President of the United States Relative to the Affair of William Blount; and the Report of a Committee of Congress containing the evidence relative thereto. Proceedings on Impeachment. *July,* 1797. 8vo. C. 6001

BLOUNT. Proceedings on the Impeachment of William Blount, a Senator of the United States from the State of Tennessee, for High Crimes and Misdemeanors. *Philadelphia: printed by Joseph Gales.* 1799. 8vo, pp. 102. C., H. 6002

BLOUNT. Report of the Committee of the House of Representatives of the United States appointed to prepare and report Articles of impeachment against William Blount, a Senator of the United States, impeached of High Crimes and Misdemeanors ... . [*Philadelphia:*] *printed by John Fenno.* [Dec. 16, 1797.] 8vo, Title, pp. vi, (1), 4, 16, (Appendix) clx, 4. B., C., H.

The crime was, arranging an expedition with the Indians and British to take the Floridas and establish a British government in the Spanish dominions on the Mississippi.

BLOUNT. A Catechetical Exposition of the Constitution of the State of Tennessee, intended principally for the Use of Schools. By Willie Blount, Esq. *Knoxville: printed by George Roulston.* [n. d.] 12mo, pp. 24. 6004

BLOW (*Hon.* Henry T.) Missouri Question. A Freedom Policy and Reconstruction. Speech delivered in the City of Washington, December 16, 1863, on the Invitation of the National Union League. [n. p. n. d.] 8vo, pp. 13. 6005

BLOW. Speech of Hon. Henry T. Blow, of Mo., in Reply to the Charges of Hon. F. P. Blair, and the Postmaster General. Delivered In the House ... February 23, 1864. [*Washington.* 1864.] 8vo, pp. 16. H. 6006

A Blow at ... Aristocracy. *See* Phileleutheros, *pseudon.*

BLOWE (D.) A Geographical, Commercial, and Agricultural View of the United States of America; forming a complete Emigrant's Directory, with an Account of Canada. By Daniel Blowe. *Liverpool: H. Fisher.* [*About* 1820.] 8vo, pp. xxxvi, 758. Portrait of Washington, and 2 Maps. C. 6007

BLOWERS (T.) Artillery Election Sermon. By Rev. Tho. Blowers. *Boston.* 1717. 8vo. 6008

BLOWERS. Sermon on the Death of the Rev. J. Green. *Boston.* 1715. 8vo. 6009

Blue Book. *See* Disturnell (J.), Register, *and* United States.

The Blue Laws of New Haven Colony, usually called Blue Laws of Connecticut; Quaker Laws of Plymouth and Massachusetts; Blue Laws of New York, Maryland, Virginia and South Carolina. First Record of Connecticut; Interesting Extracts from Connecticut Records; Cases of Salem Witchcraft; Charges and Banishment of Roger Williams, &c.; and other Interesting and Instructive Antiquities. Compiled By an Antiquarian [Royal R. Hinman]. *Hartford: printed by Case, Tiffany & Co.* 1838. 12mo, pp. 336, (Errata) 1 slip. H. 6010

"The execution of the editorial department of this work is most deplorable. Mistakes and blunders meet the reader at every turn." — N. A. R., XLVIII. 50. There are other editions, dated *Hartford,* 1825, 1828, 1833, and 1836, and a so-called new edition, edited by S. M. Smucker, *New York,* 1860, 12mo; and another bears the imprint, *Cincinnati.* [n. d.] 12mo. Plate. *See* Code *and* Connecticut.

The Blue Shop. *See* [Cobbett (William).]

BLUETT. Some Memoirs of the Life of Job, son of Solomon, the High Priest of Boonda, in Africa, who was a Slave about Two Years in Maryland, in the Years 1731, 2, and afterwards being brought to England, was set free and sent to his Native Land, in the Year 1734. By Thomas Bluett, who was intimately acquainted with him. *London.* 1734. 8vo. 6011

[BLUMEAU (J.)] Remarks On Several Acts of Parliament Relating More especially to the Colonies abroad; As also on diverse Acts of Assemblies there: Together with A Comparison of the Practice of the Courts of Law in some of the Plantations, with those of Westminster-Hall: And a modest Apology for the former, so far as they materially differ from the latter. Wherein is likewise contain'd, A Discourse concerning the 4½ per Cent. Duty paid in Barbados, and the Leeward Islands. ... *London: T. Cooper.* 1742. 8vo, pp. vij, signed T. M., 125. + The Second Edition. [*Ibid.*] C., H. 6012

Attributed to Jonathan Blumeau, Attorney General of Barbadoes, by Rich, I. 68.

BLUMENAU (Hermann). Deutsche Kolonie Blumenau in der Provinz Santa Catharina in Süd-Brasilien. Bericht bis Juni 1855

und Aufforderung zum Anschluss. Nebst Bemerkungen über deutsch-brasilianische Kolonisation im Allgemeinen, Beschreibung des Itajahy-Gebietes und 1 Karte. *Rudolstadt: Fröbel.* 1856. 8vo, 2 l., pp. 60, and 1 l., 4to. + Jahresbericht ... 1856. Nebst einem Anhang, enhalten: Aufsätze, Zeitungscorrespondenzen und Briefauszüge von Ansiedlern ... . *Hamburg: Kittler.* 1857. Folio, pp. 16. + ... Bericht ... 1857 von Dr. H. Blumenau. *Rudolstadt: G. Froebel.* 1858. 8vo. Map.

BLUMENAU. Die deutsche Kolonie in der südbrasilischen Provinz Sta. Katharina. Eine genaue Beschreibung für Auswanderungslustige. *Rudolstadt: Froebel.* 1851. 8vo, pp. 39.

BLUMENAU. Südbrasilien in seinem Beziehungen zu deutscher Auswanderung und Kolonisation. Abgerissene Nachrichten, Bemerkungen und Winke, besonders für Auswanderer. Nebst einem Anhange, Auszüge aus der brasilischen Reichsverfassung und verschiedene Gesetze enthaltend. *Rudolstadt: Froebel.* 1850. 8vo, pp. iv, 101. 6015

BLUMENAU. Leitende Anweisungen für Auswanderer nach der Provinz Sta. Catharina in Südbrasilien. *Rudolstadt: Froebel.* 1851. 8vo, pp. iv, 59. 6016

BLUMHARDT (Christoph Gottlieb). Versuch einer allgemeinen Missions-geschichte der Kirche Christi. ... *Basel: Neukirch.* 1829–33. 3 vols., 8vo. 6017

BLUMHARDT. Christian Missions; or a Manual of Missionary Geography and History: Heathen Asia, West Indies and America. Edited by Dr. Barth. *London.* 1846. 8vo. 6018

BLUMHARDT. Histoire générale de l'établissement du christianisme dans toutes les contrées où il a pénétré depuis le temps de Jésus-Christ. Traduit de l' allemand par A. Bost. *Genève.* 1838. 8vo. 6019

BLUNDELL (B.) The Contributions of John Lewis Peyton to the History of Virginia and of the Civil War in America 1861–65. Reviewed by B. Blundell. ... *London: John Wilson.* 1868. 8vo, pp. 46. H. 6020

BLUNDELL (J. L.) Arguments of Counsel in the West Washington Market Case ... [City of New-York *vs.* Taylor and Brennan]. With the Opinion of Judge Ingraham ... . Reported by Joseph L. Blundell ... . *New York.* 1860. 8vo, pp. 279. B. 6021

Blundeville (T.) Description of Universal Mappes and Cardes, and of their use necessarie for Travellers by Land or Sea. By Thomas Blundeville, of Newton-Flotman, in Norfolk. *London.* 1589. 4to. Black Letter. 6022

Contains curious notices of the situation of America, the Isles of Azores, etc.

Blundeville. His Exercises, containing eight Treatises on Arithmeticke; Cosmographie; the Use of the Globes; the Universal Map of Petrus Plancius. *London.* 1592. 4to. + *London: Printed by John Windet.* 1594. 4to. 6023

Blundeville. M. Blvndeville|His|Exercises,|Contayning eight Treatises, the Titles where-|of are set downe in the next Printed Page: which Treati-|ses are very necessary to be read and learned of all yong Gentlemen|that haue not beene exercised in such Disciplines, and yet are|desirous to haue knowledge as well in Cosmographie, Astrono-|mie, and Geographie, as also in the Art of Navigation,|in which Art, it is impossible to profit|without the helpe of these, or such|like Instructions.|To the furtherance of which Art of Navigation, the sayd|Master Blvndevile specially wrote the said Treatises,|and of meere good will doth dedicate the same to|all young Gentlemen of this|Realme.|The sixth Edition corrected and augmented. *London:|Printed by William Stansby, and are to be sold by Richard|Meighen, at his shop vnder Saint Clements Church without|Temple Barre.* 1622.|4to, 7 l., pp. 799. + *London.* 1636. 4to. 6024

"Contains an account of Sir Francis Drake's First Voyage unto the West and East Indies; both outward and homeward; the Voyage of M. Candish, unto the West and East Indies; a Description of Peter Plancius's Universal Map, set forth in the year 1592, containing places newly found, as well in the East and West Indies, as also towards the North Pole, which no map made heretofore hath."

Blunt (E. M.) The American Coast Pilot; containing the Courses and Distances ... from Passamaquoddy through the Gulf of Florida ... describing the Soundings, Bearings of the Light-Houses and Beacons from the Rocks, Shoals, Ledges, &c. together with the Courses and Distances From Cape-Cod and Cape-Ann to Georges' Bank ... . By Capt. Lawrence Furlong. Corrected and improved by the most Experienced Pilots in the United States ... Third Edition. *Newburyport (Massachusetts): Printed by Edmund M. Blunt, (Proprietor).* 1800. 8vo, pp. 251. c., h. + Fourth Edition. [*Ibid.*] 1804. 8vo, pp. 386. ba. + Sixth Edition. [*Ibid.*] *June*, 1809. 8vo. ba. + Seventh Edition. *New York.* [1812.] 8vo, pp. 311, Appendix of Laws, 63. + Ninth Edition. *New York.* 1817. 8vo, pp. xvi, 328, 84,

17. 17 Maps. + Eleventh Edition. *New York.* 1827. 8vo, pp. xvi, 696, 4. + Thirteenth Edition, improved by E. & G. W. Blunt. *New York. June*, 1837. 8vo, pp. xix, 720. b. + Sixteenth Edition. *New York: E. and G. W. Blunt.* 1850. 8vo, pp. 642. c. + Twenty-first Edition. By George M. Blunt. *New York.* 1867. 8vo, pp. vi, 841. c. 6025

The first edition was published at *Newburyport, Mass.*, 1796, 8vo.

Blunt. Analysis of the Authorities upon which the Dangers have been inserted in Blunt's New Chart of The Atlantic ... . Added ... the Variations of the Magnetic Needle, as observed in Different Parts ... and ... the progress of Ice Islands from Greenland to Newfoundland, &c. &c. Compiled by Edmund M. Blunt ... . *New-York: William Hooker.* 1819. 8vo, 1 l., pp. 76. h. 6026

Blunt. Le guide du navigateur dans l'Océan Atlantique, ou tableau des bancs, récifs, brisants, gouffres et autres écueils qui s'y trouvent, avec l'examen des documents qui établissent et constatent leur existence ... . Traduit de l'anglois. *Paris: Mme Seignot.* 1821. 8vo, pp. 205. 6027

Quérard cites an edition, 1822, 8vo, pp. 208.

[Blunt.] Le pilote américain, contenant la description des côtes orientales de l'Amérique du Nord, depuis le fleuve Saint-Laurent jusqu'au Mississipi; suivi d'une notice sur le Gulf-Stream; traduit de l'anglais Par P. Magré ... . *Paris: imprimerie royale.* 1826. 8vo, pp. vij, 359. h. 6028

This is a translation of parts only of the original. *See* a notice by Francœur in the "Revue ency.," Vol. xxxii.

Blunt. Renseignements sur la partie de la côte comprise entre la Trinité espagnole et Maranham. Traduit du Pilote américain par P. Magré. *Paris: imprimerie royale.* 1827. 8vo.

From the "Annales maritimes."

Blunt. Renseignements sur la partie comprise entre l'île Sainte-Catherine et Buenos-Ayres. Traduit du Pilote américain, par P. Magré. *Paris: impr. royale.* 1827. 8vo. 6030

Blunt (E. *and* G. W.) Le Pilote côtier des États-Unis de Edmund and G. W. Blunt. Traduit de l'anglais et annoté d'après les travaux hydrographiques les plus récents, par Ch. Pigeard ... . *Paris: Ledoyen.* 1854. 8vo. 6031

Blunt. Sailing Directions for the West Coast of North America, from Bodega to Cape San Lucas. *New York: E. & G. W. Blunt.* 1849. 8vo. 6032

Blunt (E. M.) Blunt's Stranger's Guide to the City of New-York ... . To which is prefixed an Historical Sketch, General Description, Plan and Extent of the City, with an Appendix ... a Plan of the City, and Engravings of Public Buildings. *New-York: Edmund M. Blunt.* 1817. 12mo, pp. xv, (2), 14–305, (1). b., c., h. + Also 1818 and 1822. 6033

One of the earliest guide books to the city of New York.

Blunt (George W.) The Way to avoid the centre of our violent Gales. *New York: G. W. Blunt.* 1866. 8vo, pp. 31. Chart. c. 6034

Blunt (Henry). Zee- en land -voyagie van H. Blunt, na de Levant in het Jaar 1634. Door den reysiger aangetekent, en nu aldereerst uyt het Engelsch vertaalt. *Leyden.* 1707. 8vo. bm.

Forms Vol. cxv of Van Aa's "Naaukeurige versameling." *See* No. 3.

[Blunt (*Sir* John).] The True State of the South Sea Scheme. [About 1720.] 8vo. 6036

Blunt (J.) An Anniversary Discourse, delivered before the New-York Historical Society ... Dec. 13, 1827. By Joseph Blunt. *New York: G. and C. Carvill.* 1828. 8vo, pp. 52. b.

See "American Annual Register," Nos. 1046, 1047, and "National Advocate," 1820.

Blunt. Brief Examination of the Relations between the Cherokees and the Government of the United States. By Joseph Blunt. *New York: Clayton & Van Norden.* 1832. 8vo, pp. 15.

[Blunt.] An Examination of the Expediency and Constitutionality of Prohibiting Slavery in the State of Missouri. By Marcus. *New York.* 1819. 8vo. 6039

Blunt. A Historical Sketch of the Formation of the Confederacy, particularly with reference to the Provincial Limits and the Jurisdiction of the General Government over Indian Tribes and the Public Territory. By Joseph Blunt. *New-York: Geo. & Chas. Carvill.* 1825. 8vo, pp. 6, 116. c., h. 6040

See N. A. R., xxii. 460.

Blunt. Remarks of Joseph Blunt, Esq., ... At a Public Meeting, held at Albany, September 2d, 1841. [n. p. n. d.] 8vo, pp. 8. h., s. 6041

On the Tariff Question.

Blunt. Report to the National Convention of the Home League, held in the City of New-York, October 13, 1842. By Joseph Blunt, Esq. [No imprint.] 8vo, pp. 15. ba. 6042

[Blunt.] Sketches of the Resources of the City of New York ... . *New York.* 1827. 8vo. 6043

Blunt. Speeches, Reviews, Reports, &c. By Joseph Blunt. *New-York: James Van Norden & Co.* 1843. 8vo, 2 l., pp. 274.

Blyden (E. W.) Address at the Annual Meeting of the Maine Colonization Society, June, 1862. By Rev. E. W. Blyden. [n. p. n. d.] 8vo, pp. 4. 6045

Blyden. A Vindication of the African Race, etc. By Edward W. Blyden. *Monrovia, Africa.* 1857. 8vo, pp. 37. 6046

Blyden. A Voice from Bleeding Africa, on Behalf of her Exiled Children. By Edward W. Blyden. ... *Liberia: G. Killian, Printer.* 1858. 8vo, pp. 33. h. 6047

"Mr. Blyden is a full black, educated entirely in Liberia, understands, besides Latin, Greek, and Hebrew, five of the European languages, a professor of Mathematics, and now qualifying himself to teach Arabic."

Blydenburgh (S.) Oration intended to have been delivered at Springfield, Mass. July 4, 1811. By Samuel Blydenburgh. *Brookfield: E. Merriam & Co.* [n. d.] pp. 26. 6048

Blyth (J.) An Oration on the Death of General George Washington, delivered at All Saint's Parish (S. C.), on the 22d of February, 1800. By Dr. Joseph Blyth. *Boston.* 1800. 8vo.

Blyth (S[tephen C.)] History of the War between the United States and Tripoli and other Barbary Powers. *Salem: Printed at the Salem Gazette Office.* 1806. 12mo, pp. 144. c.

Blythe (J.) Discourse on the Present State and Duty of the Church, delivered at the Opening of the Synod of Kentucky, October, 1824. By James Blythe. *Lexington.* 1824. 8vo, pp. 32. 6051

Also: "A Sermon delivered at Pisgah, on the resignation of the Pastoral Charge after a Connection of Forty Years," which I have not seen.

Boadicea: The Mormon Trip: Life Scenes in Utah. 8vo.

Board of Treasury, 1786. *See* [Osgood (Samuel).]

Report of the Board of Education for Freedmen, Department of the Gulf, for the Year 1864. *New Orleans: printed at the Office of the True Delta.* 1865. 8vo, pp. 25, (2). Continued?

First Annual Report of the General Agent of the Board of National Popular Education, with the Constitution of the Board. *Cincinnati.* 1848. 8vo, pp. 32. Continued. h. 6054

Board of State Charities. *See* Massachusetts.

Boardman (C. A.) The Agency of God, illustrated in the achievement of the Independence of the United States: a Sermon delivered July 4, 1826 ... . By Charles A. Boardman. *New Haven.* 1826. 8vo. 6055

Boardman. ... A Sermon addressed to the Legislature of the State of Connecticut, at the Annual Election in New Haven, May 5, 1830. By Charles A. Boardman, ... *New-Haven: L. Huntington Young, Printer.* 1830. 8vo, pp. 20. 6056

Boardman (D. S.) Sketches of the Early Lights of the Litchfield Bar. By Hon. David S. Boardman. *Litchfield, Conn.: James Humphrey, Jr.* 1860. 8vo, pp. 38, (1). h. 6057

Boardman (G. D.) Addresses delivered in ... Philadelphia, April 14th, 16th, and 19th, 1865. By the Reverend George Dana Boardman ... . h. 6058

This is the title on the cover; the following are the separate titles:

Boardman. An Address in Commemoration of the Re-Establishment of the National Flag at Fort Sumter, April 14, 1865. Delivered ... On the Same Day, by the Reverend George Dana Boardman ... . *Philadelphia: Sherman & Co., Printers.* 1865. 8vo, pp. 26. 6059

Boardman. Death, the Law of Life. A Discourse, delivered on the Sunday Morning after the Murder of President Lincoln ... April 16, 1865. By the Rev. George Dana Boardman ... . *Philadelphia: Sherman & Co., Printers.* 1865. 8vo, pp. 27–45. 6060

Boardman. An Address in Commemoration of Abraham Lincoln, President of the United States, delivered in the Meeting-House of the First Baptist Church of Philadelphia, on the Day of his Funeral at the National Capital, April 19, 1865. By the Reverend George Dana Boardman, Pastor. *Philadelphia: Sherman & Co., Printers.* 1865. 8vo, pp. 47–64. 6061

Boardman. Civil Government, a Divine Ordinance. A Discourse delivered in ... Philadelphia, November 6th, 1864, by the Rev. George Dana Boardman ... . *Philadelphia: Ringwall & Brown, Printers.* 1864. 8vo, pp. 32. h. 6062

Also: "Re-Establishment of the Flag. 1865." 8vo.

Boardman (G. N.) Repentance of Sin and Restoration from Calamity. A Sermon preached in the Presbyterian Church, Binghamton, September 26, 1861. By the Rev. George N. Boardman. *Binghamton, N. Y.: G. W. Reynolds.* 1861. 8vo, pp. 18. 6063

Boardman. The Death of President Lincoln. A Sermon preached in the Presbyterian Church, Binghamton, April 16, 1865. By Rev. George N. Boardman. *Binghamton, N. Y.: F. N. Chace.* 1865. 8vo, pp. 16. 6064

Boardman (H. A.) The American Union. A Discourse delivered ... December 12, 1850, the Day of the Annual Thanksgiving in Pennsylvania, and repeated ... December 19, ... By Henry A. Boardman, d.d. *Philadelphia: Lippincott, Grambo and Co.* 1851. 8vo, pp. 56. + Third Thousand. [*Ibid.*] b. Fourth || Fifth Thousand. [*Ibid.*] h. Sixth Edition. *Philadelphia: J. B. Lippincott & Co.* 1851. + Seventh Edition. *Philadelphia: J. B. Lippincott & Co.* 1860. 8vo, pp. 58. 6065

Boardman. A Discourse Commemorative ... of the Late Rev. Samuel Miller, d.d. of Princeton, New Jersey. Delivered January 27th, 1850 ... . By the Rev. H. A. Boardman, d.d. *Philadelphia: William S. Martien.* 1850. 8vo, pp. 40. b. 6066

Boardman. A Discourse on the Life and Character of Daniel Webster. By H. A. Boardman, d.d. *Philadelphia: Joseph M. Wilson.* 1852. 8vo, pp. 64. b., h. 6067

Boardman. The Federal Judiciary. A Thanksgiving Discourse, by Henry A. Boardman, d.d. [Nov. 27, 1862.] *Philadelphia: William S. & Alfred Martien.* 1862. 8vo, pp. 54.

Boardman. The General Assembly of 1866. By H. A. Boardman, d.d. *Philadelphia: J. B. Lippincott & Co.* 1866. 8vo, pp. 124. 6069

Boardman. God's Providence in Accidents. A Sermon occasioned by the Death of the Rev. John Martin Connell, Mr. John Field Gillespie, and Miss Susan Gillespie, Three of the Victims of the Railroad Catastrophe at Burlington, New Jersey, on the 29th day of August, 1855. By Henry A. Boardman, d.d. *Philadelphia: Parry & McMillan.* 1855. 8vo, pp. 43. h. 6070

Boardman. Healing and Salvation for our Country from God alone. A Sermon Preached in ... Philadelphia, on Thanksgiving Day, Nov. 24, 1864. By Henry A. Boardman, d.d. *Philadelphia: William S. and Alfred Martien.* 1864. 8vo, pp. 24.

Boardman. The Importance of Religion to the Legal Profession: with some Remarks on the Character of the late Charles Chauncey, Esq. A Discourse delivered ... September 30th, and ... October 14th, 1849, in ... Philadelphia. By Henry A. Boardman, d.d. *Philadelphia: Wm. S. Martien.* 1849. 8vo, pp. 40. h. 6072

Boardman. Is there any ground to apprehend the Extensive and Dangerous Prevalence of Romanism in the United States? By H. A. Boardman, d.d. *Philadelphia.* 1841. 12mo, pp. 69.

Boardman. The Low Value set upon Human Life in the United States: A Discourse delivered on Thanksgiving-Day, November 24th, 1853, by H. A. Boardman, d.d. *Philadelphia: Joseph M. Wilson.* 1853. 8vo, pp. 32. h. 6074

Boardman. The New Doctrine of Intervention, tried by the Teachings of Washington: An Address ... in ... Philadelphia, on the 23d and 24th of February, 1852. By H. A. Boardman, d.d. *Philadelphia: Lippincott, Grambo and Co.* 1852. 8vo, pp. 63. + Second Edition. [*Ibid.*] 6075

With the half-title: "Kossuth or Washington."

Boardman. Not "this *or* that" but "this *and* that." The Union Principle though *Un*-denominational not *Anti*-denominational. [n. p. 1858.] 8vo, pp. 16. h. 6076

A defence of the "Appeal for the American Sunday-School Union," published by Dr. Boardman and others, in Nov., 1857.

Boardman. The Peace-Makers. A Sermon ... on Sunday, April 9, 1865. Appointed by the Governor of Pennsylvania as a Day of Thanksgiving for the Recent Victories of the National Forces in Virginia. By Henry A. Boardman, d.d. *Philadelphia: James S. Claxton.* 1865. 8vo, pp. 31. 6077

Boardman. The Peace We Need, and How to Secure it. A Sermon Preached in the Tenth Presbyterian Church, Philadelphia, on the Day of National Humiliation, June 1, 1865. By Henry A. Boardman, d.d. *Philadelphia: James S. Claxton.* 1865. 8vo, pp. 32. 6078

Boardman. A Quarter Century Discourse. Delivered in the Tenth Presbyterian Church, Philadelphia. By H. A. Boardman, d.d. *Philadelphia: Parry & McMillan.* 1858. 8vo, pp. 106. 6079

Boardman. A Reformed and Revived Christianity, our Country's Great Necessity: A Sermon preached on Thanksgiving Day, November 28, 1867, in ... Philadelphia, by Henry A. Boardman, d.d. *Philadelphia: J. B. Lippincott & Co.* 1867. 8vo, pp. 27. h. 6080

Boardman. A Sermon occasioned by the Death of William Henry Harrison, the Late President ... preached ... April 11, 1841 ... . By H. A. Boardman ... . *Philadelphia: William S. Martien.* 1841. 8vo, pp. 28. 6081

Boardman. The Sovereignty of God, the Sure and Only Stay of the Christian Patriot in our National Troubles. A Sermon ... Sept. 14 and ... September 28, 1862. By Henry A. Boardman, d.d. *Philadelphia: William S. & Alfred Martien.* 1862. 8vo, pp. 31. b., h. 6082

Boardman. Suggestions to Young Men engaged in Mercantile Business. A Discourse occasioned by the Death of Mr. Archibald Sloan, ... Philadelphia, October 9th, 1851. By Henry A. Boardman, d.d. *Philadelphia.* 1851. 8vo, pp. 31. s.

Boardman. Thanksgiving in War: A Sermon Preached in ... Philadelphia, on the 28th Day of November, 1861. By Henry A. Boardman, d.d. *Philadelphia: C. Sherman & Son.* 1861. 8vo, pp. 28. 6084

Boardman. What Christianity Demands of Us at the Present Crisis: a Sermon Preached on Thanksgiving Day, Nov.

29, 1860: by Henry A. Boardman, D.D. *Philadelphia: J. B. Lippincott & Co.* 1860. 8vo, pp. 28. H. 6085

BOARDMAN. A Word of Friendly Counsel to Young Men. A Sermon on the Death of George M. Ramsaur, of North Carolina, Delivered in ... Philadelphia ... Feb. 24, 1856. By Henry A. Boardman, D.D. *Philadelphia: Hayes & Zell.* 1856. 8vo, pp. 30. 6086

[BOARDMAN (James).] America and the Americans. "Audi alteram partem." By a Citizen of the World. *London: Longman.* 1833. 8vo, pp. 430. 6087

See Vol. I., No. 4018, for another work with a similar title.

BOARDMAN (J.) The presence of Christ the Glory of his House. A Sermon delivered at the Dedication of the New Brick Meeting house in West Boylston, Aug. 22, 1832. By John Boardman. *Salem.* 1832. 8vo. 6088

BOARDMAN (S. L.) The Agriculture and Industry of Kennebec County, Maine. With notes upon its History and Natural History. By S. L. Boardman. *Augusta, Maine: printed for the Author.* 1868. 8vo, pp. viii, 200. Portrait. 6089

BOARDMAN. Agricultural Survey of Somerset Co., Me. *Augusta.* 1860. 8vo. 6090

BOARDMAN. General View of Kennebec, Me. 8vo, pp. 83.

[BOARDMAN (William W.)] A Plan ... for Insurance against Fire for the City of New-Haven ... . *New-Haven: printed by Baldwin & Peck.* 1834. 8vo, pp. 16. H. 6092

Contains a list of the fires in New Haven between 1800 and 1833.

The Boatswain's Whistle. Published at the National Sailors' Fair. *Boston. November* 9–19, 1864. Folio, pp. 80. H. 6093

Bob's Letter. [*Cowan, Tennessee. Aug.* 23, 1862.] 8vo, pp. 6.

Concerning the campaign in Tennessee

BOBIN. The Letters of Isaac Bobin, (1718–24) Private Secretary of George Clarke afterwards Lieutenant Governor of the Colony of New York, with Introduction and Notes, By E. B. O'Callaghan, LL.D. *Albany: J. Munsell.* [Announced 1868]. 6095

BOCANEGRA (J. P.) Ritval | Formvlario, e | Institvcion de Cvras, para | Administrar a los Natvrales de | este Reyno, los santos Sacramentos del Baptismo, Con- | firmacion, Eucaristia, y Viatico, Penitencia, Extre- | mavncion, y Matrimonio, con aduertencias | muy necessarias. | Por el Bachiller Ivan Perez Bo- | canegra, Presbitero, en la lengua Quechua general: examinador en | ella, y en la Aymara en este Obispado. Beneficiado propieta- | rio del pueblo de san Pedro de Antahuaylla | la chica. | Al Insigne Señor Licenciado Fran- | cisco Calderon de Robles y Peñafiel, Arcediano de la Ca- | tedral de la Ciudad del Cuzco, Prouisor, y | Vicario General del. | Con Licencia. *Impresso en Lima: por Geronymo | de Contreras, Iunto al Conuento de santo Domingo | Año de* 1631. | 4to, 16 l., pp. 720, Table, 4 l. J. C. B. 6096

This rare volume, in the Spanish and Quichuan [native Peruvian] languages, is not noticed by Brunet, Ternaux, or Ludewig.

BOCANEGRA (Matea de). Historia del Auto publico y general de Fé, celebrado en Mégico en 11 de Abril 1649. *Mégico: Calderon.* 1649. 4to. 6097

"Sotwel and Antonio cite a different date: 'Historia del auto general de la Fee, celebrado en Mexico el año de 1652. *Megico* ... .'" — BACKER.

BOCANEGRA. Sermon predicado en la fiesta de la solenne colocacion de la Cruz de Picara hallada en Tepeapulco. *Mégico.* 1648. 4to. 6098

BOCANEGRA. Sermon de la Publicacion de la Bula de la Sta Cruzada en Mégico el dia de S. Miguel de año 1649. *Mégico.* 1649. 4to. 6099

BOCANEGRA. Teatro gerarquico de la Luz, Pira cristiano-politica del Gobierno erigida por la M. N. y M. L. Ciudad de Mégico a la entrade de su Virey, el Conde de Salvatierra. *Mégico: Ruiz.* 1642. 4to. 6100

BOCANEGRA. Viage del Marqués de Villena por Mar y Tierra à Mégico, en verso Castellano. *Mégico.* 1640. 4to. 6101

Also: Sermon predicado en la fiesta de la solenne colocacion de la Cruz de Picara hallada en Tepeapulco. *Mégico.* 1648. 8vo — Sermon de la publicacion de la Bula de la Sta Cruzada en Mégico el dia de S. Miguel del año 1649. *Mégico.* 1649. 4to.

BOCCAGE (*Md.* Du). *See* Du Boccage.

BOCCHI (Francesco). Libri duo Elogiorum quibus Viri aliqui Clarissimi Florentini & alii decorantur. *Florentiæ: ex Officina Sermartelliana.* 1607. 4to. 6102

Contains some particulars concerning Vespucius. Harrisse's Bib. Am. Vet. gives the erroneous date 1667.

BOCK (Carl Wilhelm). Erklärung des Baues der berühmtesten und merkwürdigsten älteren und neueren Sprachen Europa's, Asien's, Afrika's, Amerika's und der Südsee-Inseln. *Berlin: Plahn:* 1853. 8vo, pp. viii, iv, 98, iii.–viii., 172, 24. 1 Lithograph, and 4 Tables, 4to. 6103

A part of this, not relating to America, appeared in 1844, under the title, "Analysis Verbi."

BOCK (Friedrich Samuel). Einleitung in die Kenntniss der Reiche und Staaten der Welt, nach der ältern, mittlern und neuern Zeit. *Königsberg.* 1745. 8vo. + Zweite Auflage. [*Id.*] 1750. 8vo. 6104

BOCK. Kurzgefasste Missionsgeschichte, oder Nachrichten von den in neuern Zeiten angewandten Bemühungen, die Heiden zum christlichen Glauben zu bekehren. *Königsberg: Hartung.* 1743. 8vo. 6105

Meusel gives the imprint as *Züllichau.*

BOCKETT (Elias). A Determination of the Case of Mr. Thomas Story, and Mr. James Hoskins, relating to an affair of the Pennsylvania Company, &c. *London: J. Roberts.* 1724. 4to, pp. 12 + The Second Edition. [Title differing.] *London: T. Smith.* 1724. 8vo, pp. 16. 6106

BOCKETT. A Poem to the Memory of Aquila Rose, who dy'd at Philadelphia, August the 22d, 1723. Ætat. 28. By Elias Bockett. *London: the Author.* 172¾. 8vo, pp. 12.

Keimer wrote a poem on this subject, and gives a different date for his death. *See* Hazard's Pa. Reg., Nov., 1828, p. 268.

BOCKETT. The Wit and Honesty of James Hoskins, &c. consider'd in Remarks on their late Pamphlet, call'd "The Pennsylvania Bubble." By the Translator of the Pattern of Modesty. *London: J. Smith.* 1726. 8vo, pp. 96. 6108

BOCOCK (*Mr.*) Admission of California. Speech of Mr. Bocock, of Virginia, ... Jan. 3, 1850. ... 8vo, pp. 8. 6109

BODEMANN (F. W.) Hans Egede, der Apostel der Grönländer. Nach seinem Leben und Wirken dargestellt von Friedrich Wilhelm Bodemann. *Bielefeld: Velhagen und Klasing.* 1853. 8vo, pp. 84. (Sonntags-Bibliothek, von A. Rische, VIer Band, 2es Heft.) 6110

BODDILY (J.) A Sermon delivered at Newburyport, on the

22d of February. By Rev. John Boddily, Minister of Second Presbyterian Society in said town, [on the Death of George Washington]. (Published by Request.) *Printed at Newburyport: Edmund M. Blunt.* 1800. 8vo; pp. 15. 6111

BODINE (M.) The Early Life and Complete Trial of Mary, alias Polly Bodine, For the Murder of Emeline Houseman and her Child, &c. *New York.* 1846. 12mo, pp. 60. 6112

BODLEY (T.) Address of Thomas Bodley, to the People of Kentucky, Concerning Humphrey Marshall; with Documents. *Lexington.* 1808. 8vo, pp. viii, 27. C. 6113

BODWELL (J. C.) Address delivered at the Consecration of The Lake Grove Cemetery, Holliston, Mass., June 1, 1860, by The Rev. J. C. Bodwell, of Framingham. *Holliston: E. G. Plimpton, Printer.* 1860. 8vo, pp. 19. H. 6114

BOEHM (Ant.) *See* Sepp (Ant.)

BOEHM (H.) Reminiscences, Historical and Biographical, of Sixty-four Years in the Ministry. By Rev. Henry Boehm, Bishop Asbury's Traveling Companion and Executor of his Last Will and Testament. ... Edited by Rev. Joseph B. Wakeley. *New York: Carlton & Porter.* 1865. 12mo, pp. 493. BA.

BOELEN (J.), *Jz.* Reize naar de Oost- en Westkust van Zuid-Amerika en, van daar, naar de Sandwichs- en Philippijnsche Eilanden, China enz. gedaan, in de jaren 1826, 1827, 1828 en 1829, met het koopvaardijschip Wilhelmina en Maria. *Amsterdam: ten Brink en de Vries.* 1835.–36. 3 pts, 8vo. 6116

BOEMUS, *Germ.* BOEM (Joannes). Omnivm Gentivm Mores, Leges, et Ritvs, ex mvltis Clarissimis Rervm Scriptoribus a Ioanne Boemo Aubano Sacerdote Teutonicæ Militiæ Deuoto nuper collectos ... . [Colophon:] *Augustæ Vindelicorum excusa in officina Sigismundi Grimm ac Medici, Marci Vnirsung. Anno* ... M. D. XX. *mense Iulio.* Folio, 6 l., lxxi numbered l. C. 6117

Reprinted: *Friburgi Brisgoiæ: excudebat Joannes Faber Emmeus.* 1536. 8vo. + 1538. 8vo. + 1540. 8vo. + *Lugduni: apud Franciscum Justum.* 1536. 8vo. *Pariisis: apud Ambrosium Girault.* 1536. 8vo. + *Antuerpiæ: in æd. Joan. Steelesii.* 1537. 8vo; 1538. 8vo. + *Venetiis.* 1542. 8vo. + *Lugduni: apud S. Gryphium.* 1541. 8vo; 1556. 12mo. + *Lvgdvni: Apud Bartholomæum Vincentium.* M. D. LXXVI. 16mo. (H.) + *Lugdvni: Apud. Ioan* [sic] *Tornæsium.* 1582. 8vo. (H.); 1591. 12mo; also without place, but probably *Lugduni.* 1604. 12mo; 1620. 12mo. These editions have nothing to do with America, but are cited here on account of one printed at *Geneva,* with the following title:

BOEMUS. Mores, leges, | et ritvs omnivm | gentivm, | Per I. Boëmum Aubanum, Teutonicum, ex mul- | tis clarissimis rerum scriptoribus collecti. | Ex Nicol. Damasceni historia excerpta quædam | eiusdem argumenti. | Itidem & ex Brasiliana I. Lerij historia. | Fides, religio, & mores Æthiopum, ac deploratio | Lappianæ gentis, Damiano à Goes auctore | De Æthiopibus etiam nonnulla ex Ios. Scaligeri | lib. VII. de Emendatione temporum. | Cum Indice locupletissimo. | *Genevæ.* | *Apvd I. Tornæsivm.* | CIↃ. IↃ. CXX. | 16mo, pp. 504, 12 l. 6118

BOEMUS. Gli costumi, le Leggi, et l'usanze di tutti le genti; raccolte da molti illustri Scrittori per Giovanni Boemo Aubano Alemano, tradotti per Lucio Fauno. Aggiontovi di nuovo gli costumi e l'usanze dell' Indie Occidentali, overo Mondo Nuovo, da P. Gieronimo Giglio. *Venetia: Francisco Lorenzini.* 1560. 12mo, 1 l., Text, 236 l. J. C. B. + *Venetia: Giacomo Cornetti.* 1585. 8vo, 240 l. 6119

Priced: J. R. Smith, 7s. 6d.; Tross, 1862, 20fr.; Leclerc, No. 178, 2fr. The part relating to America occupies leaves 193–240. The other Italian versions are Tradotti per il Fauno. *Venezia: Tramezzino.* 1543; *also Vineggia: per Mich. Tramezino.* 1549. 8vo. (BD.), 1558, 1564, and 1566. According to Brunet, the fourth book, treating of the Americans, first appeared in the Venice edition of 1543. Another authority says 1564. For a Spanish translation, *see* Tamara (Francisco). There are French versions: Discours des pais ... . [*Lyon.*] 1544. 12mo. + *Lyon: J. de Tournes.* 1552. 16mo. Whether either of them contains the fourth book, I do not know. The translations, entitled, Recueil ... . *Paris,* 1539, 1542, and *Anvers,* 1540 of course do not. *See* Ziegler (Jacob).

BOEMUS. The Manners, Lawes and Customs of all Nations. Collected out of the best Writers by Joannes Boemvs Avbanvs a Dutch Man. With many other things of the same Argument, gather'd out of the Historie of Nicholas Damascene. The like also out of the Historie of America or Brasill, written by John Lerius. ... Written in Latine, and now neuly translated into English. By Ed. Aston. *At London, Printed by G. Eld.* 1611 4to, pp. 589. 6120

BOEN (W.) Anecdotes and Memories of William Boen a Coloured Man, who Lived and Died near Mount Holly, New Jersey. ... *Philadelphia: John Richards.* 1824. + *Manchester Reprinted by John Harrison.* 1846. 12mo, pp. 12. 6121

Reprinted in Comly's Miscellany, I. 385, and V. 269.

BOERO (Giuseppe). Relazione della gloriosa morte di ducento e cinque beati martiri nel Giappone. *Roma.* 1867. 6122

BOERO. Les deux cinq cent Martyrs du Japon, béatifiés par

Pie IX en 1867. Par le Père Boero ... . Traduite de l'italien par le Père Aubert ... . *Paris: Albanel.* 1868. 18mo, pp. viii, 280. 6123

Contains sketches of B. Peter de Zuñiga, Laurel and B. Bartholomew Gutierrez, Mexicans, as well as of some who had been on American missions.

BOESCHE. *See* Bösche (Eduard Theodor).

For other names of the same class, *see also* Bö.

[BOESNIER.] Le Mexique conquis ... . [Poëme.] *Paris: Desaint et Saillant [et] Durant le Prieur. Rouen: L'allemant.* M. DCC. LII. 2 vols., 16mo, 3 l., pp. xvj, 216; 3 l., 249, (1). 2 Maps. C. & H. 6124

BOGARDUS (W. E.) Sermon on the Death of our late President, preached by the Rev. W. E. Bogardus, April 30, 1865, in the R. P. D. C. at Unionville, Westchester Co., New York. *New York: Isaac J. Oliver.* 1865. 8vo, pp. 16. 6125

BOGART (D. S.) The Voice of Gratitude: a Discourse delivered on 22d November, 1804; being the Anniversary Thanksgiving in the Presbyterian Church at South Hampton, L. I. By David Schuyler Bogart. *Sag Harbor.* 1805. 8vo, pp. 24. 6126

BOGART (William H.) Daniel Boone and the Hunters of Kentucky. By W. H. Bogart. *Auburn and Buffalo: Miller, Orton & Mulligan.* 1854. 16mo, pp. 390. Woodcuts. H. + *New York and Auburn.* 1856. 12mo. + [*Ibid.*] 1857. 12mo.

BOGART. Index to the Documents of the Legislature of New York, from 1842 to 1854 inclusive. *Albany.* 1855. 8vo. C.

[BOGART.] Who Goes There? or Men and Events. By "Sentinel." *New Yerk.* 1866. 12mo, pp. 288. C. 6129

Many reminiscences of the great men of America, from Washington to Zachary Taylor.

BOGEN (F. W.) L'empire francais et les États-Unis. Réponse à la lettre d'un homme da la race latine à sa Majesté l'empereur Napoleon III. Par F. W. Bogen, citoyen adoptif des États-Unis. *New York: D. Appleton & Co.* 1859. 8vo, pp. 15. H. 6130

BOGEN. The German in America; or Advice and Instruction for German Emigrants in United States ... . Also, a

Reader for Beginners in the English and German Languages. By F. W. Bogen. *Boston.* 1851. 16mo. + Second Edition. *Boston: B. H. Greene,* [etc.] 1851. 16mo, pp. 177. B. & C.

This has also a German title-page, "Der Deutsche in Amerika," etc., and is printed in German and English, on alternate pages.

BOGEN. Report of Rev. F. W. Bogen ... [of his Labors among the German Emigrants in New-York and Neighborhood]. For the Year, from May 1, 1853–1854. [n. p. n. d.] 8vo, pp. 8. B. 6132

BOGGS (J.) The Southern Christian Exemplified, in the Memoirs of Anthony J. Pearson. By J. Boggs. *New York.* 1838. 18mo. 6133

BOGOTA. Almanaque de Bogota i Guia de Forasteros pora 1867. Por T. M. Vergara i T. B. Gaitan. *Bogata: Gaitan.* 1866. 32mo, pp. xx, 384. C. 6134

BOGOTA. Exposicion de los sentimientos de los funcionarios publicos, asi nacionales como departamentales y municipales, y demas habitantes de la ciudad de Bogota, hecha para ser presentada al libertador presidente de la republica. *Bogota?* 1826? + *Reimpresa en New-York.* 1827. 8vo, pp. 26, (1). H. 6135

BOGOTA. Reglamento para el rejimen y policia interior de la municipalidad de Bogotá. *Bogotá.* 1866. 18mo, pp. 42. 6136

BOGUE (David) *and* BENNETT (James). History of Dissenters, from the Revolution in 1688, to ... 1808. ... By David Bogue & James Bennett. *London: the Authors.* 1808–12. 4 vols., 8vo. C. 6137

"State of Religion in America," II. 424–456; III. 85–105; Vol. III. contains, also, much on Wesley's mission to Georgia, and Vol. I. a few notices of the Quakers.

BOGUSLAWSKI (B. von). Über deutsche Colonisation in Mexico. Ein Bericht an den Berliner Verein zur Centralisation deutscher Auswanderung ... . *Berlin: Hempel.* 1851. 8vo, pp. viii, 120. 6138

BOGY (Lewis V.) Defence of Mr. Commissioner Bogy before The Committee on Indian Affairs of the House of Representatives ... . [Jan. 12, 1867. n. p. n. d.] 8vo, pp. 38. H.

... The Bohemian. No. 1. [*Richmond, Va.* 1863 or 64.] 8vo, pp. 40. B. 6140

A periodical

BOHEMIAN MINING CO. Charter and By-Laws of the Bohemian Mining Co., with letters from the Mines. *Philadelphia.* 1851. 8vo, pp. 12. 6141

Also: Report ... . *Philadelphia.* 1854. 8vo, pp. 12. And others?

BOHN (H. G.) A Pictorial Handbook of Modern Geography, on a Popular Plan, Compiled from the best authorities, English and Foreign, and completed to the present time; ... By Henry G. Bohn, ... *London: H. G. Bohn.* 1861. Post 8vo, pp. x, (11), 529. 5 Maps. + Second Edition. [*Ibid.*] 1863. 6143

BOHN (Casimir). Bohn's Hand-Book of Washington. Illustrated with Twenty Engravings ... . *Washington: Cassimir* [*sic*] *Bohn, and Taylor & Maury.* 1852. 18mo, pp. ix–97, (1). H. + *Washington.* 1860. C. + With a Supplement. Prepared by Charles Lanman, Esq. *Washington: Casimir Bohn.* 1861. 18mo, pp. 134. Map, and Engravings. C. & H. 6142

In the second edition, Mr. Bohn has recognized the "Confederate States."

BOHUN (E.) The Diary and Autobiography of Edmund Bohun, Esq. ... Licenser of the press in the reign of William and Mary, and subsequently Chief Justice of South-Carolina; with an Introductory Memoir, Notes and Illustrations by S. Wilton Rix. ... *Privately printed at Beccles [England], by Read Crisp.* 1853. 4to, pp. xxxiv, 148. Plates. S. 6144

Also on large paper. Judge Bohun died in South Carolina, 1696. "This autobiography is in the highest degree curious and interesting." — MACAULAY's England, Vol. IV.

BOHUN. A Geographical Dictionary, [etc.] *London.* 1688. 8vo. + A Geographical Dictionary ... of the whole World ... . Begun by Edmund Bohun ... . Continued, Corrected, and Enlarged ... By Mr. Bernard . ... *London: Charles Brome.* MDCXCIII. Folio, 4 l., pp. 437, 11 l. H. + Fourth Edition, continued, and with Additions, by John Augustine Bernard. *London.* 1695. Folio. B. 6145

BOHUN (R.) Discourse concerning the Origin and Properties of Wind, with an Historicall Account of Hurricanes. *Oxford.* 1671. 8vo. 6146

Some of the hurricanes referred to were in America.

BOIES (Charles Alfred). Poem [by Boies] and Valedictory Oration [by Joseph Leonard Daniels] pronounced before the Senior Class in Yale College, Presentation Day, June 13, 1860. ... *New Haven: printed by Tuttle, Moorhouse & Taylor.* 1860. 8vo, pp. 32, 2 l. H 6147

Boies (J.) Report of the Trial of John Boies, for the Murder of his Wife, Jane Boies, [before] ... the Supreme Judicial Court ... at Dedham ... June 2, 1829. *Dedham: H. & W. H. Mann, Printers.* [n. d.] 12mo, pp. 36. H. 6148

Boies (Patrick). Oration ... Blandford, Mass., 4th July 1814 ... By Patrick Boies. *Springfield.* 8vo, pp. 18. 6149

Boigne (C. P. J. Leborgne de). *See* Leborgne de Boigne (C. P. J.)

The Boiler Explosion of the Martin Boiler on Board the U. S. "Double-Ender" Chenango. The Coroner's Inquest, a Full Report of the Testimony, the Charge of Dr. Norris to the Jury, and the Two Verdicts. *New-York: Hurd & Houghton.* 1864. 8vo, pp. 141. H. 6150

Boilieu (L. de). Recollections of Labrador Life. By Lambert de Boilieu. *London: Saunders, Otley & Co.* 1862. Post 8vo, pp. 251. 6151

Based on the experiences of a residence of many years, with notices of the Esquimaux, and the record of a visit to Newfoundland.

[Boimare (A. L.)] Notes Bibliographiques et raisonnées sur les principaux ouvrages publiés sur La Floride et l'ancienne Louisiane, depuis leur découverte jusqu'à l'epoque actuelle, accompagnées de trois Cartes, de Guillaume Belisle, publiée en 1703 et 1712. Folio, pp. 60, Liste, 1 l. [Privately Lithographed.] 6152

Boisduval (Jean Alphonse). Faune entomologique de l'Océan Pacifique, avec l'illustration des insectes nouveaux recueillis pendant le voyage de l'Astrolabe, sous le commandement du vice-amiral Dumont d'Urville. *Paris.* 1832–35. 2 vols., 8vo.

Boisduval. Lépidoptères de la Californie. Par le docteur J. A. Boisduval. *Paris:* [Malteste]. 1852. 8vo, 3½ Sheets.

Republished from the "Annales de la Société entomologique de France," août 1852.

Boisduval *and* Lecomte (John). Histoire générale et iconographique des lépidoptères et des cheniles de l'Amérique septentrionale. Par M. J. A. Boisduval et M. John Lecomte de New York. *Paris: Méquignon-Marvis,* [et ensuite] *Roret.* 1829, etc. 8vo. 6155

Was to be published in about fifty numbers of text, each with three colored plates. Livr. 28 appeared in March, 1843.

Boishébert (Sieur de). Mémoire dans l'Affaire du Canada. *Paris: Moreau.* 1763. 4to. 6156

Boislecomte (André Olivier Ernest Sain de). De la crise américaine et de celle des nationalités en Europe par M. Sain de Boislecomte ... *Paris: E. Maillet.* 1862. 8vo, 2 l., pp. 155.

[Bois-Meslé (Jean-Baptiste Torchet de).] Histoire générale de la marine. *Paris: Prault.* 1744–58. + Seconde édition. *Paris.* 1759. 3 vols., 4to. Illustrations. 6158

Relates "les expéditiones anciennes et modernes," etc.

Boisrond-Tonnerre. Mémoires pour servir à l'histoire d'Hayti. Par l'adjudant général Boisrond-Tonnerre. *Dessalines: de l'imprimerie centrale du gouvernement.* 1804. 8vo, pp. 104. H.

Boisrond-Tonnerre. Mémoires pour servir à l'histoire d'Haïti, par Boisrond-Tonnerre; précédés de différents actes politiques dus à sa plume, et d'une étude historique et critique, par Saint-Remy, des Cayes (Haïti). *Paris: chez France.* 1851. 12mo, 5½ sheets. 6160

Boissard (Jan. Jac.) Icones quinquaginta Virorum illustrium, Doctrina et Eruditione; omnia in Aes incisa a Theodoro de Bry. *Francoforti.* 1597–99. 4 vols., 4to. 6161

Includes Columbus, with a biography of twenty-three pages. *See* the note in Graesse's "Trésor." The "Bibliotheca" is a second edition of this, and Graesse describes a third, fourth, and fifth.

Boissard. Bibliotheca | siue | Thesavrvs Virtvtis | et Gloriæ: | In quo continentur | Illvstrivm Erv- | ditione & doctrina Virorum Effi- | gies & Vitæ, summa diligentia | accuratè descriptæ, | Et in Centurias duas distributæ | Per | Ian. Iacobum Boissardum. | Artificiosissimè in æs incisæ | à Ioan. Theodor. de Bry. | Accesserunt Clariss. aliquot Virorum effi- | gies & vitæ nunc recens conscriptæ. | *Francofvrti,* | *Sumtibus Gvilielmi Fitzeri.* | *Anno* M.DC.XXVIII. 5 Pts., 4to, pp. 299, Index, 4 l.; 3 l., 206; 4 l., 197, Index, 5; 4 l., 299, Index, 5; 8. 237 Portraits. 6162

Contains a biography of Columbus, Lindschoten, etc. *See* Bolton Corney's "Curiosities of Literature."

Boissier de Sauvages de la Croix (Pierre Augustin de) *and* Pullien (Samuel). Directions for the Breeding and Management of Silkworms, Extracted from the Treatises of the Abbé Boissier de Sauvages and Pullien. With a Preface giving some Account of the Rise and Progress of the scheme for

encouraging the Culture of Silk in Pennsylvania and the adjacent Colonies. *Philadelphia: Printed by Joseph Crukshank, and Isaac Collins.* M. DCC. LXX. 8vo, pp. xv, 32. C. P. 6163

See A. Q. R., Dec., 1831.

Boistel d'Exauvillez (André Philippe Octave). *See* [Solis (A. de).]

Boisthibault (*M.* Doublet de). *See* Doublet de Boisthibault (*M.*)

Boisneuf (Payen de). *See* Payen de Boisneuf.

Boissiere. *See* Tanguy de la Boissiere.

Boitel (Pierre), *sieur de Gaubertin.* Tableau des merveilles du monde. *Paris.* 1616 [or 1617]. 8vo. 6164

Boitel (Amédée). Du pin maritime, de sa culture dans les dunes, de la pratique du résinage ... suivi d'une notice sur la culture des dunes de Cap-Breton ... . *Paris: Mme Huzard.* 1848. 8vo. 2 Plates. 6165

Republished with the following title:

Boitel. Mise en valeur des terres pauvres par le pin maritime ... suivie d'un appendice sur ... les vignes de Cap-Breton. Par Amédée Boitel. Seconde Édition ... . *Paris: Masson.* 1857. 8vo, pp. 244. Illustrated. 6166

Boitel (Ch.) Quelques mois de l'existence d'un fonctionnaire public aux colonies de la Guadeloupe et de la Martinique, Par Ch. Boitel. *Paris: Bohaire.* 1832. 8vo, pp. 280. A. 6167

Bokee (D. A.) Oration Delivered By Hon. David A. Bokee, in the First Baptist Church, Brooklyn, July 4th, 1851, on the occasion of the Seventy-Sixth Anniversary of our National Independence. *Brooklyn: Lees & Foulkes, Printers.* 1851. 8vo, pp. 11. 6168

[Boker (G. Henry).] Hymn for the Eighty-Seventh Anniversary of American Independence. *Philadelphia.* [1863.] 12mo, pp. 2. (Union League.) 6169

Boker. Our Heroic Themes. A Poem read before the Phi Beta Kappa Society of Harvard University, July 20, 1865. By George H. Boker. *Boston: Ticknor & Fields.* 1865. 16mo, pp. 20. H. 6170

Boker. Poems of the War. By George H. Boker. *Boston: Ticknor and Fields.* 1864. 16mo, pp. 200. C. & H. 6171

Boker. The Second Louisiana. [A Black Regiment.] May 27th, 1863. [A Poem.] By George H. Boker. *Union League of Philadelphia.* + [n. p. n. d.] 16mo, 1 page. + [n. p. n. d.] 16mo, 2 l. H. 6172

Boker. Das Zweite Louisiana Regiment ... . Frei übersetzt von Carl Theodor Eben. [n. p. n. d.] 16mo, 1 page. H. + [Ubersetzt von Friedrich Leypoldt? n. p. n. d.] 16mo, 1 page. H. 6173

[Boker.] Tardy George [McClellan]. 1862. 8vo, 1 l. + *New York: Privately printed* [*for F. S. Hoffman.*] 1866. 4to, pp. 4. 6174

Fifty copies reprinted. Several short pieces in his "Plays and Poems ... . *Boston: Ticknor and Fields,* M DCCC LVI," 2 vols., 16mo, relate to America.

Bokum (H.) A Discourse on the State of the German Population in the United States. By Rev. Hermann Bokum. *New York.* 1836. 8vo, pp. v, 267. 6175

Bokum. The Stranger's Gift. A Christmas and New Year's Present. Edited by Hermann Bokum ... . *Boston: Light and Horton.* 1836. 12mo, pp. 103. Engraving. H. 6176

Contents: The American Germans; The American Dutch; The Mohawk; New England; The German Emigrant.

Bokum. The Tennessee Handbook and Immigrant's Guide. Giving a description of the state of Tennessee, its agricultural and mineralogical character, railroads, etc. By Hermann Bokum, Commissioner of Immigration. *Philadelphia: J. B. Lippincott & Co.* 1868. 16mo, 2 l., pp. 164. Map. C. 6177

Bokum. The Testimony of A Refugee from East Tennessee. By Hermann Bokum, Chaplain, U. S. A. *Philadelphia:* [*Union League*]. 1863. 8vo, pp. 24. H. 6178

Bokum. Das Zeugniss eines Flüchtlings von Ost-Tennessee. Von Hermann Bokum, Kaplan der Vereinigten Staaten *Philadelphia.* 1863. 8vo, pp. 23. 6179

Bokum. Wanderings North and South. [A Refugee's Testimony. Sketches of East Tennessee Life. Life and Death of a Christian Soldier. The Turner's Lane Hospital.]

By Hermann Bokum ... . *Philadelphia: King & Baird, Printers.* 1864. 8vo, 3 l., pp. 73. H. 6180

The bracketted words are from the title on the paper cover.

Bolduc (J. B. Z.) Mission de la Colombie Lettre et Journal. *Quebec.* 8vo, pp. 95. 6181

Boletin de las Leyes del Imperio Mexicano. *See* Mexico.

Boletin de la Sociedad Mexicana. *See* Mexico.

Bolingbroke (Henry). A Voyage to the Demerary, containing a Statistical Account of the Settlements there, and of those of the Essequebo, the Berbice, and other Contiguous Rivers of Guyana. By Henry Bolingbroke, Esq. of Norwich, Deputy Vendue Master at Surinam. *London: Richard Phillips.* 1807. 4to, 6 l., pp. 400. Map. H. + *Philadelphia.* 1813. 8vo, pp. 260. C., BA. 6182

Also concluded in Phillips's Voyages, Vol. x. "Notwithstanding its transcripts, its trifling, and its repetitions, this volume contains a respectable portion of new information, and much sound sense." — *Edinb. Rev.,* XII. 410. *See also* M. R., LVIII. 1.

Bolingbroke (H.) Reise nach dem Demarary nebst eine Beschreibung der Niederlassungen daselbst so wie jener am Essequebo, Berbice u. s. w. Aus dem Englischen übersetzt. *Leipzig: Rein.* 1812. 8vo. Map. 6183

Bolingbroke (*Lord*). *See* St. John, Henry, Lord Bolingbroke.

Bolivar. Bolivar's Denkwürdigkeiten, herausgegeben von seinem General-Adjutanten Ducudray-Holstein; die Charakterschilderung und Thaten der Süd-Amerikanischen Helden, die geheime Geschichte der Revolution in Colombia und eine Sittengemälde des Colombischen Volkes enthaltend. Deutsch bearbeitet von C. N. Röding. *Hamburg, Hoffmann und Campe.* 1830–31. 2 vols., 12mo, 14 and 8½ sheets. 6184

Bolivar. Colleccion de documentos relativos a la vida publica del Libertador de Columbia y del Peru. *Caracas.* 1826. 4 vols., 8vo. 6185

See N. A. R., XXVIII. 203; XXX. 26.

Bolivar. Correspondencia general del Libertador Simon Bolívar. Enriquecida con la insercion de los manifiestos, menságes, exposiciones, proclamas, etc. publicados por el Heroe Colombiano, desde 1810 hasta 1830. (Precede á esta coleccion

interesante la vida de Bolívar). Tomo primero. *Nueva York.* 1865. 8vo, pp. xiiii, 616. Portrait and Facsimile. + Segunda Edicion. *Nueva York: Jenkins, Pr.* 2 vols., 8vo. 6186

Bolivar. Ensayo sobre la conducta del general Bolivar. Reimpreso de los números 11, 13 y 14 del Duende de Buenos Ayres. *Santiago de Chile.* 1826. 6187

Bolivar. Proclamas de Simon Bolivar, libertador de Colombia. 1862. 8vo, pp. 74. 6188

Bolivar. South American Independence. Speech of Simon Bolivar, President Liberator of the Republic of Colombia, on the Installation of the Second National Congress of Venezuela, with an Account of the Proceedings on this Occasion. *London.* 1819. 8vo. 6189

Bolivar. Union latino-americana, ó pensamiento de Bolivar de formar una liga, etc. *Paris: Rosa et Bouret.* 1865. 8vo.

Bolivar i Washington. *See* [Urdaneta (Amenodore).]

Bolivia. Calendario y Guia de forasteros de la republica Boliviana para el año de 1834. *Paz de Ayacucho: Imprenta del colejio des Artes.* 1857. 12mo, pp. 195, 3 l. 6191

Codigo civil, Sante-Cruz Presidente. *Paz de Ayacucho.* 1831. Sm. 4to. 6192

Codigo penal Boliviano. *Paz de Ayacucho.* 1830. Sm. 4to.

Constitucion Politica de la Republica Boliviana. *Paz de Ayacucho.* 1831. Sm. 4to, pp. 30. 6194

Constitucion Politica de la Republica Boliviana sancionada por la asemblea general constituyente de 1831. Y reformada en algunos de sus articulos, con arreglo á ella misma por el congreso constitucional de 1834. *Paz de Ayacucho: Imprenta del colegio des artes.* [1834.] 4to, 1 l., pp. 35. 6195

Dated: "Palacio del gobierno Boliviano en Chuquisaca à 20 de Octubre de 1834 — 25° de la Independencia," and signed "Andres de Santa Cruz."

Constitucion Politica de la Republica Boliviana sancionada por el Congreso Jeneral constituyente de 1839. *Imprenta de la Ciudad Sucre.* 1839. Sm. 4to, pp. 40. 6196

Disposiciones commerciales vijentes en Republica Boliviana. *Sucre.* 1840. 4to, pp. 30. 6197

Memoria del ministro de estado en el despacho de la guerra a la convencion nacional en 1843. Republica Boliviana. *Sucre: Beeche y Compañia.* 4to, pp. 8. 6198

Dated: "Sucre à 23 de Abril de 1843," and signed "Manuel Sagarnaga.

Memoria que presenta el ministro de relaciones esteriores de la Republica de Bolivia à la convencion nacional reunida en Abril de 1843. *Imprenta de Beeche y Cia.* [n. d.] 4to, pp. 9.

Dated: "Sucre à 23 de Abril de 1843," and signed "M. de la Cruz Mendez."

Memoria que presenta el ministro de la guerra a las camaras lejislativas en el año de 1810. *Imprenta de la libertad.* [n. d.] folio, pp. 8. 6200

Dated: "Ciudad Sucre, à 5 de Agosto de 1840," and signed "Manuel Dorado."

Memoria que presenta el ministro de la Guerra a las cameras Legislativas del Pueblo Bolivano en el año de 1840. *Ciudaa Sucre.* 1840. 4to. 6201

Mensaje del Presidente de Bolivia, al congreso estraordinario de 1828. [Colophon:] *Valparaiso.* [n. d.] 4to, pp. 12. H.

Mensaje que El Presidente de la Republica dirijedo al Congreso Extraordinario de Bolivia. *Paz de Ayacucho.* 1838. Sm. 4to, pp. 12. 6203

Ojeada al Proyecto de Constitucion. *See* [Guzman (Antonio Leocadio).]

Presupuesto jeneral de los gastos de la República Boliviana, decretado por el congreso constitucional para el año de 1841. *Imprenta de la libertad.* 4to, pp. 26. 6204

Dated: "Sucre à 11 de Noviembre de 1840."

Proyecto de Constitucion para la República, de Bolivia y Discurso del Libertador. *Bogotá.* 1826. 4to, pp. 16, 31. 6205

N. A. R., XXX. 26, gives the imprint, *Guayaquil.*

Project of the Constitution for the Republic of Bolivia, with Addresses of the Liberator; Translated. 1826. 8vo. 6206

Bollaert (W.) Antiquarian, Ethnological and other Researches in New Granada, Equador, Peru and Chile, with Observations on the Pre-Incarial, Incarial, and other Monuments

of Peruvian Nations. By William Bollaert, F.R.G.S. ... With Plates. *London: Trübner & Co.* 1860. 8vo, Title, pp. 279.

Also, articles in the "Memoirs of the Anthropological Society of London." (H.), Vols. I. and II., on the Anthropology and Palæography of the New World, and on the Astronomy of the Red Man. C.

[Bollan (W.)] The Ancient Right of the English Nation to the American Fishery; and its Various Diminutions; examined and stated. With A Map of the Lands, Islands, Gulfs, Seas, and Fishing-Banks comprising the whole. Humbly Inscribed to the sincere Friends of the British Naval Empire. ... *London: S. Baker.* MDCCLXIV. 4to, Title, pp. 105. Map. C., H.

See M. R., XXX. 325. An English catalogue describes a large paper copy.

[Bollan.] Coloniæ Anglicanæ Illustratæ; Or, the Acquest of Dominion, and the Plantation of Colonies made by the English in America, with the Rights of the Colonists, Examined, stated, and illustrated. Part I. Containing I. The Plan of the whole Work, including the Proposition, asserting the Rights of the Colonists, intended to be established. II. A brief History of the Wars, Revolutions, and Events which gave Rise to all the marine Discoveries and foreign Acquisitions made by the Modern Europæans. III. A Survey of the Knowledge and Opinions, which the Europæans had of the Earth in Times preceding these Discoveries; with other matters relating to this Subject. IV. The Particulars of the Progress made by the Portuguese, from their beginning these Discoveries, to the death of King John II, and an Account of the Grants made to the kings of Portugal of the Countries that were or might be discovered, by the Bulls of several Popes, with one of them set forth at large. ... *London: S. Baker.* MDCCLXII. 4to, pp. viii, (1), 141, (1). C., H. 6209

A very learned work, but of which, unfortunately, no more was published. The author was William Bollan, the Massachusetts agent in England from 1745 to 1762. *See* M. R., XXVII. 220.

[Bollan.] Continued Corruption, Standing Armies, and Popular Discontents Considered; And the Establishment of the English Colonies in America, With Various subsequent Proceedings, and the Present Contests, examined, with Intent to promote their cordial and perpetual Union with their Mother-Country, for their mutual Honour, Comfort, Strength and Safety. ... *London: J. Almon.* MDCCLXVIII. 4to, pp. 82. Plate by Bartolozzi. C. 6210

"An important tract." — Rich. *See* M. R., XXXIX. 493.

[BOLLAN.] Epistle from Timoleon to all the Honest Freeholders, and other Electors of Members of Parliament; wherein the great mischief and danger of corruption are set forth and proved from its operations in Greece and Rome. By William Ballon. *London.* 1768. 4to, pp. 23. 6211

[BOLLAN.] The Free Briton's Memorial, to all the Freeholders, Citizens and Burgesses, who elect the Members of the British Parliament, presented in order to the Effectual Defence of their Injured Right of Election. *London: J. Williams.* MDCCLXIX. 4to, Title, pp. 35. C., H. 6212

See especially pp. 21, etc.

[BOLLAN.] The Free Briton's Supplemental Memorial to the Electors of the Members of the British Parliament; wherein the Origin of Parliaments in Europe, and other Interesting Matters are considered. ... *London: J. Williams.* MDCCLXX. 4to, Title, pp. 61. C. 6213

BOLLAN. The Freedom of Speech and Writing upon Public Affairs, considered ... . *London: S. Baker.* MDCCLXVI. 4to, Title, pp. 160. B., H. 6214

Pages 139–160 relate to America.

[BOLLAN.] The Importance and Advantage of Cape Breton, Truly Stated, and Impartially Considered. With Proper Maps. ... *London: John and Paul Knapton.* MDCCXLVI. 8vo, pp. vi, (2), 156. 2 Maps. C. H. 6215

Taken principally from Charlevoix's "Nouvelle France." Attributed to Bollan, by Eliot and Allen. This must not be confounded with "The Importance of Cape Breton consider'd; in a Letter to a Member of Parliament, From an Inhabitant of New-England. *London: R. Dodsley, and M. Cooper.* MDCCXLVI." 8vo, Title, pp. 73. H.

[BOLLAN.] Beschryving van de importantie en door-deeligheit van Kaap Breton. *Delft: R. Boitet.* 1717. 8vo. 6216

[BOLLAN.] Die Wichtigkeit und Vortheil des Kap-Breton, in einer richtigen Beschreibung dieser berufenen Insel, welche nach der Erzählung eines gewissen berühmten französischen Scribentens mehr werth ist, als die Goldbergwerke in Peru, vorgestellt, und durch Anmerkungen und zwo richtige Landcharten erläutert. Ins Deutsche übersetzet. *Leipzig: bey Peter Schenken.* 1747. 8vo, pp. 174. H. 6217

[BOLLAN.] The Mutual Interest of Great Britain and the American Colonies considered, With respect to an Act passed

last Sessions of Parliament for laying a Duty on Merchandise, &c. With Some Remarks on a Pamphlet, intitled, "Objections to the Taxation of the American Colonies, &c. considered." In a Letter to a Member of Parliament. ... *London: W. Nicoll.* MDCCLXV. 4to, pp. 12. H. 6218

This author animadverts on the foregoing pamphlet "with plain good sense, and a becoming zeal for the liberties of his fellow-subjects of North America. He is not an elegant writer, but appears to be well acquainted with the mutual interest and natural connection between this country and her colonies." — M. R., XXXII. 309.

BOLLAN. The Petitions of Mr. Bollan, Agent for the Council of the Province of Massachusetts Bay, lately presented to the Two Houses of Parliament; With a brief Introduction relating to the Law of Nature, the Authority of Human Rulers, and the Subject's common Right of Defence; with Subsequent Observations, respecting the Nature of the Principalities established in Europe by the Northern Conquerors, and of the English Constitution; to which is subjoined the Council's Defence against the Charge of certain Misdemeanours. ... *London: J. Almon.* MDCC LXXIV. 4to, Title, pp. 49. C., H. 6219

See M. R., LI. 323.

BOLLAN. The Petition of Mr. Bollan, Agent for the Council of the Province of Massachusetts Bay, to the King in Council, dated January 26, 1774. Published with Illustrations, in order briefly to shew to the Impartial and Considerate the Importance of perfect Harmony between Great Britain and the Colonies, their Merits, the Benefits thence accrued to this Kingdom in Point of Empire, Manufactures, Commerce, Wealth and Naval Strength; and the Origin and Progress of their present unhappy Difference; with intent to promote their cordial and perpetual Union, for their mutual Safety and Welfare, with which their Dissention is Incompatible. *London; J. Almon.* MDCCLXXIV. 4to. 6220

In the Mass. Hist. Soc.'s Coll., 1st Ser., VI. 41–48; 129–138, are two letters by Bollan, and a Petition to the Duke of Bedford, relative to the French Encroachments, 1748. He was also the author of "Britannia Liberia; a Defence of the Free State of Man in England, &c." "The Right of every Man in a Free State to Speak and Write freely in Defence of Public Rights." Mr. Rich, on the authority of Allen, credits a pamphlet, entitled, "The Importance of the Colonies of North America. ... *London.* 1766," to Mr. Bollan, which is an error. The tract in question is by Nicholas Ray. *See* M. R., L. 233.

BOLLER (H. A.) Among the Indians. Eight Years in the Far West: 1858–1866. Embracing Sketches of Montana and Salt Lake. By Henry A. Boller. *Philadelphia: T. Elwood Zell.* 1868. 12mo, pp. 428. Map. B. 6221

BOLLES (J. A.) The Episcopal Church Defended, with an Examination into the Claims of Methodist Episcopacy; in a series of letters addressed to the Rev. Allen Steele. By James A. Bolles. With his Replies. *Batavia: Genesee Co., N. Y.* 1842 [or] 3. 12mo, pp. 198. 6222

BOLLES. The Church of the Advent. A Salutatory Sermon preached ... on ... the Fifteenth Anniversary of the Foundation of the Parish. By the Rev. James A. Bolles, D.D., Rector. *Boston.* 1859. 8vo, pp. 26. H. 6223

Also: The Anniversary Sermon and Report ... Sixteenth Anniversary," and so on.

BOLLES. The Church of the Future in America. ... By Rev. James A. Bolles, D.D. ... *New York: Daniel Dana, Jr.* 1859. 12mo, pp. 22. H. 6224

BOLLES (John), *of New London, born before* 1700. To Worship God in Spirit, & in Truth, is to Worship Him in the True Liberty of Conscience ... . John Bolles ... . With an Answer thereto; by Jacob Johnson ... . [n. p.:] *the Author.* MDCCLVI. 8vo, pp. 127, (1), 29, (1), 74, (1). B. 6225

John Bolles was a Baptist, from Rhode Island, and his treatise is directed against the Cambridge and Saybrook platforms, with an account of the sufferings of Quakers and Baptists in Massachusetts and Connecticut. Johnson's "Answer" is followed by "A Reply ... By J. Bolles," addressed "To the General Court at Boston, May 29th 1754," opposing their Confession of Faith, on "Your first Day Sabbath," "Swearing," "Baptism," and "Civil Government," with much matter on the persecution of the Quakers.

BOLLES. The following treatise contains A Brief Account of Persecutions in Boston and Connecticut Governments. By John Bolles of New London. [*New London:*] *Printed for the Author.* 1758. 16mo, pp. 30. M. 6226

BOLLES. Answer to a Book entituled The Christian Sabbath. By Mather Byles [jun., of New London. n. p.] 1759. 8vo, pp. 23. M. 6227

BOLLES (J. A.) Genealogy of the Bolles Family in America. By John A. Bolles. *Boston: H. W. Dutton & Son.* 1865. 8vo, pp. 64. 6228

BOLLES. An Oration, delivered before the Inhabitants of Winchester, Mass. July 4, 1860. By John A. Bolles. *Boston: Press of T. R. Marvin & Son.* 1860. 8vo, pp. 19. BA. 6229

BOLLES. United States *vs.* B. S. Osbon. Argument of the

Judge Advocate, Major John A. Bolles, A.D.C., Before a General Court Martial, in New York City, May 8, 1865. [n. p. n. d.] 8vo, pp. 14. H. 6230

BOLLES (J. R.) A Reply to Bishop Hopkins' View of Slavery, and a Review of the Times, by John R. Bolles. [Motto.] *Philadelphia: J. W. Daugaday.* 1865. 8vo, Title, pp. 36. H. 6231

BOLLES (L.) A Discourse ... before the Members of the Salem Female Charitable Society, September 27, 1810 ... . By Lucius Bolles ... . *Salem.* 1810. 8vo, pp. 16. B. 6232

BOLLES. Sermon at the Dedication of the First Baptist Meeting-house, Salem, Jan. 1, 1806. By Rev. Lucius Bolles, D.D. *Boston.* 1806. 8vo, pp. 20. 6233

BOLLES. A Sermon ... at Newburyport ... December 9, 1818, at the Ordination of the Rev. Hosea Wheeler ... [over] the Baptist Church ... . By Lucius Bolles ... . *Newburyport: printed by W. & J. Gilman.* 1819. 8vo, pp. 24. H. 6234

BOLLIN (J.) Geografisk politisk Beskrivelse over de forenede nordamerikanske Stater, isærdeleshed for Emigranter. Udarb. nærmest efter Comminister J. Bollins „Beskrifning øfver førente Staterna etc. Wexiø 1853." *Christiania: Kom. h. Feilberg & Landmark.* 1853. 12mo, pp. 112. 6235

BOLLMAN (Erick). A Letter to Thomas Brand, Esq., M.P., etc., on the Practicability and Propriety of a Resumption of Specie Payments. *Philadelphia. Reprinted.* 1819. 8vo. 6236

BOLLMAN. Paragraphs on Banks. By Erick Bollman, M.D. Second Edition. *Philadelphia.* 1811. 12mo. P. 6237

BOLLMAN. Plan of an Improved System of the Money Concerns of the Union. By Erick Bollman, M.D. *Philadelphia.* 1816. 8vo, pp. 52. 6238

BOLLMAN (L.) Copy of a Letter from Lewis Bollman, of Indiana, to Senator H. S. Lane [on the Department of Agriculture. n. p. 1862.] 8vo, pp. 7. H. 6239

BOLLMAN. The Industrial Colleges. The Nature of the Instruction to be given in them; their several Kinds and Courses of Instruction considered. By Lewis Bollman. ... Added A Communication ... By Richard Owen ... . [n. p. 1864.] 8vo, pp. 40. H. 6240

BOLOIX (D. P.) Sucinta noticia del ramo de la cera en la isla de Cuba á fines de Marzo de 1815, por D. Pablo Boloix. *Habana: imprenta de Arazoza y Soler.* 1816. Folio. 6241

BOLTON (E. C.) *and* WEBBER (H. H.) The Confederation of British North America. By Edward Chichester Bolton and Horace H. Webber. With Maps. *London: Chapman & Hall.* 1866. Post 8vo, pp. 149. C. 6242

BOLTON (James). Brook Farm: the Amusing and Memorable of American Country Life. By Rev. J. Bolton. With an Illustration. *London: Macintosh.* 1863. 16mo, pp. viii, 183.

BOLTON (J.) Account of the Loss of the [American] Ship Omartal [on "The Banks"]. By ... One of the Crew ... John Bolton ... . [n. p. 1860?] 8vo, pp. (4). H. 6244

BOLTON (R.) Genealogical and Biographical Account of the Family of Bolton in England and America. Deduced from an early period, and continued down to the present time, Collected chiefly from Original Papers and Records; with an Appendix. By Robert Bolton, A.M. ... *New York: John A. Gray, Printer.* 1862. 8vo, pp. viii, 223. Table folded. 6245

Fifty copies printed. One of the best works of its class. "Contains also a short pedigree of the Woodhull Family, of Long Island, to which the author's second wife belongs." — WHITMORE.

[BOLTON.] A Guide to New Rochelle and its Vicinity. *New York: A. Hanford.* 1842. 18mo, 2 l., pp. 67. Plate. C. 6246

BOLTON (R.) A History of the County of Westchester, from its First Settlement to the Present Time. By Robert Bolton, Jr. ... *New York: printed by Alexander S. Gould.* 1848. 8vo, pp. xxxii, 559; Title, 582. Map, folded Tables, and Woodcuts. 6247

This work is out of print. Mr. Bolton is now (1869) preparing a new edition.

BOLTON. History of the Protestant Episcopal Church, in the County of Westchester, from its Foundation, A.D. 1693, to A.D. 1853. By Robert Bolton ... . *New York: Stanford & Swords.* 1855. 8vo, pp. xxiii, 749. Woodcuts, and 2 Portraits. H. 6248

BOLTON (T.) An Oration delivered March Fifteenth 1775, at the Request of a Number of the Inhabitants of the Town of

Boston. By Dr. Thomas Bolton. ... [n. p.] M, DCC, LXXV. 8vo, pp. 8. BA. 6249

This oration was delivered from the balcony of the British Coffee-House, by a gentleman disguised, to a crowded audience of officers, Tories, etc., in ridicule of that delivered by Dr. Warren. "I cannot boast," said the orator, "the ignorance of Hancock, the insolence of Adams, the absurdity of Rowe, the arrogance of Lee, the vicious life and untimely death of Mollineux, the turgid bombast of Warren, the treasons of Quincy, the hypocrisy of Cooper, nor the principles of Young." — p. 3.

BOLTON (W.) A Narrative of the last Cruise of the U. S. Steam Frigate Missouri; from the day she left Norfolk, until the arrival of her Crew in Boston; including a full and circumstantial detail of the General Conflagration, which took place at Gibralter, resulting in her total Loss. Interspersed with explanatory notes and remarks. By William Bolton, one of the Crew. *Boston.* 1843. + *Philadelphia.* 1844. 8vo, pp. iv, 32.

BOLTON (W. C.) The Trial of Capt. William C. Bolton, for an alleged violation of the orders of Commodore Hull, in returning from the Mediterranean to the United States, in May, 1841. *Philadelphia.* 1841. 8vo, pp. 16. P. 6251

BOLTON. A Historical Sketch of the First Congregational Church in Bolton. Printed by Vote of the Church. *Clinton: printed by Ballard & Messinger.* 1851. 12mo, pp. 28. H. 6252

BOLTON, *Mass.* Result of an Ecclesiastical Council convened at Bolton, Aug. 3, 1773, at the desire of Thomas Goss and his Church in Bolton. *Boston.* 1773. 8vo, pp. 11. 6253

Result of an Ecclesiastical Council at Bolton, 1773. A Second Treatise on Church Government, in Three Parts. By a Neighbour. *Boston.* 1773. 8vo, pp. 78. 6254

[BOLTWOOD (L. M.)] Genealogies of Hadley Families, embracing the early Settlers of the Towns of Hatfield, South Hadley, Amherst and Granby. *Northampton: Metcalf & Company, printers.* 1862. 8vo, pp. 168. 6255

"This is a reissue of a portion of Judd's History of the Town, pp. 445–608; but all this part was the work of Hon. Lucius M. Boltwood." — WHITMORE. *See* Judd (Sylvester), *the elder.*

BOLZIUS (*Rev. Mr.*) Journals in Georgia in 1734. *See* Reck (P. G. F. von), *also* Force's Tracts, Vol. IV., No. 5.

BOM (J.) Verslag wegens zijne en verschied. Burgers van Demerarij geweldadige en tijranike Verwoering, Lotgevallen, Schipbreuk, Gevangenis ... . *Amsterdam.* 1799. 8vo. 6256

Bombardement de Valparaiso (documents officiels), suivi du combat du Callao. Seconde édition, corrigée et augmentée. *Paris: imprimerie Vallée.* 1865. 8vo, pp. vi, 182. 6257

Bombardement de Valparaison. Destruction d'une ville sans défense. Documents officiels. *Paris: impr. Vallée.* 1866. 8vo, pp. 168. 6258

BON (*Mme* Élisabeth de). La voyageur moderne, ou Extrait des voyages les plus récents dans les quatre parties du monde, publiés en plusieurs langues jusqu'en 1821. *Paris: A. Eymery.* 1821–22. 6 vols., 8vo. 36 Engravings. + [*Ibid.*] 12 vols., 12mo. Engravings. 6259

A miserable compilation, according to Depping, "Rev. encyc.," XIV. 375.

BON HARBOR, *Ky.* An Account of Bon Harbor, in the State of Kentucky, on the Ohio River, one hundred and sixty miles below the falls, possessing extensive coal mines ... *London.* 1849. 8vo, pp. 39. 6260

Some of the papers signed "Robert Triplet;" the object, to dispose of the lands.

BONA (F. de). Cuba, Puerto Rico y Santo Domingo. Folleto. *Madrid: Bailli-Baillière.* 1862. 6261

BONAFOUS (Matthieu). Traité du maïs, ou Histoire naturelle et agricole de cette céréale. ... *Paris: Mme Huzard.* 1833. 8vo, pp. 190. 3 Plates. 6262

This was the first sketch of the following:

BONAFOUS. Histoire naturelle, agricole et économique du maïs. *Paris: de l'imprimerie de Mme Huzard. Turin: Bocca.* 1836. Folio, pp. 181. 19 Plates, and 11 Engravings in the text. 6263

Published at 100 fr. "Magnifique ouvrage. Quelques exemplaires seulement ont un beau portrait de l'auteur, par M. Maurin. L'ouvrage est divisé en sept chapitres: le premier consiste en recherches sur la patrie du mais. M. Bonafous conclut que le mais était connu dans l'ancien monde, en Chine ou en d'autres contrées orientales avant la découverte de l'Amérique." — QUÉRARD. The work was translated into Arabic, and into Dutch; also, by Dr. Lomeni, into Italian, *Milan: Visay.* 1836. 8vo. 3 Plates.

BONAPARTE (Charles Jules Laurent Lucien). American Ornithology; or, the Natural History of Birds inhabiting the United States, not given by Wilson. With Figures drawn, engraved, and coloured, from Nature. By Charles Lucian Bonaparte. *Philadelphia: published by Samuel Augustus Mitchell, sola by Anthony Finley.* 1825–1833. Rl. 4to, Vol. I. pp. vi, (1), 105,

22 Plates, 1825; II. vii, (1), 95, 14 Plates, 1828; III. 2 l., 60, 9 Plates, 1828; IV. 2 l., pp. 142, 15 Plates, 1833. C. H. 6264.

A necessary adjunct to Wilson's Ornithology; now very scarce. Reprinted in part in Sir Wm. Jardine's edition of Wilson's Ornithology. *London.* 1832. 3 vols. 8vo. Also, at *Edinburgh*, 1834. 4 vols., fcap 8vo. *See* Quérard's note, quoted from the "Rev. encycl.," t. XXIX.

BONAPARTE. A Geographical and Comparative List of the Birds of Europe and North America. By Charles Lucian Bonaparte, Prince of Musignano. *London: John Van Voorst.* 1838. 8vo, pp. vii, 67. B., C., P. 6265

BONAPARTE. Observations on the Nomenclature of Wilson's Ornithology. By Charies Lucien Bonaparte. *Philadelphia: A. Finley.* 1826. 8vo, 128 l. C. 6266

See Quérard's note, from the "Rev. encycl.," t. XXXII.

BONAPARTE. Ornithology of North America, by Charles Lucien Bonaparte. *New York.* 1826. 8vo. C. 6267

From the "Annals of the Lyceum of Natural History of New York," vol. II. Nos. 1, 2, and 3. *See* Quérard's note, quoted from the "Rev. encycl.," t. XXXII.

BONAPARTE (J. N.) Cour impériale de Paris. Première chambre Appel Du jugement de la première Chambre du Tribunal de première instance de la Seine, du 15 fevrier 1861. M. Jérome-Napoléon Bonaparte et Mme Élisabeth Patterson contre S. A. I. le prince Napoléon. [n. p. n. d.] 8vo, pp. 139. B. & C.

On the back of the title-page is the imprint: *Baltimore: Jas. S. Waters.* If this applies to anything beyond the title-page, the book is probably a reprint.

BONAPARTE (L.) Révolution de Brumaire ... . Par Lucien Bonaparte ... . Suivie d'une notice nécrologique sur ce prince et d'une ode: "l'Amerique." *Paris: Charpentier.* 1845. 8vo, $18\frac{3}{4}$ sheets. 6269

Bonaparte in the West Indies. *See* Toussaint-Louverture (François-Dominique).

BONAVENTURA (F. G. de San). *See* San Bonaventura (F. G. de).

BOND (A.) The Christian awaiting his last Change. A Discourse occasioned by the Death of Hon. John A. Rockwell. ... Norwich, Ct. February 17, 1861. By Alvan Bond, D.D. ... *Boston.* 1861. 8vo, pp. 36. 6270

Bond. A Discourse on the Life and Character of Dea. Joseph Otis, delivered in ... Norwich, Conn., March 19, 1854. With an Appendix, by ... Alvan Bond, D.D. ... *Norwich: Andrew Stark, Printer.* 1855. Sm. 12mo, pp. 75. H. 6271

Bond. ... A Discourse, occasioned by the Death of Mr. Russell Hubbard, delivered in ... Norwich, Ct. June 14, 1857. By Alvan Bond ... . *Boston.* 1857. 8vo, pp. 44. H. 6272

Bond. ... A Discourse, occasioned by the Death of Hon. John A. Rockwell, delivered in ... Norwich, Ct. February 17, 1861. By Alvan Bond ... . *Boston.* 1861. 8vo, pp. 38. H.

Bond. A Historical Discourse, delivered at the Hundredth Anniversary of the Organization of the Second Congregational Church, Norwich, Conn. July 24, 1860. With an Appendix. By Alvan Bond, D.D. *Norwich.* 1860. 8vo, pp. 64. Plan.

Bond. Memoir of the Rev. Pliny Fisk ... . By Alvan Bond ... . *Boston: Crocker and Brewster. New-York: Jonathan Leavitt.* 1828. 12mo, pp. 437. Portrait. H. + *Edinburgh.* 1828. 8vo.

Bond. The Memory of the Fathers; a Discourse ... in Norwich, January 1, 1843. By Alvan Bond. *Norwich: J. Dunham's Press.* 1843. 8vo, pp. 20. H. 6276

Bond ... Plinius Fisk von Alvan Bond. Aus dem Englischen übersetzt. *Erlangen: Heyder.* 1835. 8vo, pp. vi, 473. (Leben evang. Heidenboten. Herausg. von G. P. Heller, 1er Band.) 6277

Bond. ... A Sermon occasioned by the Death of Hon. Jabez W. Huntington, United States Senator, who died in Norwich, Nov. 2, 1847, Aged 59 Years. By Alvan Bond ... . *Norwich: J. Dunham's Press.* 1847. 8vo, pp. 24. H. 6278

Bond. ... A Sermon preached in ... . Norwich, Conn. October 23d, 1853, the Sabbath after the Funeral of Erastus Perkins. By ... Alvan Bond ... . *Norwich: Charles B. Platt, Printer.* 1853. 8vo, pp. 19. H. 6279

Bond. Two Discourses delivered on the Annual Fast, April 1, 1836. *Norwich, [Conn.]* 1836. 8vo. 6280

Bond (H.) An Address delivered before the New England Society of Philadelphia; at its Semi-annual Meeting, in May,

1824. By Henry Bond, M.D. *Philadelphia: the Society.* 1824. 8vo, pp. 23. H., P. 6281

Bond. Biographical Notice of the Late John Ruan, M.D.; read ... before the College of Physicians ... By Henry Bond, M.D., September 2, 1845, and published in the Transactions of the College. *Philadelphia.* 1845. 8vo, pp. 8. H. 6282

Bond. Family Memorials. Genealogies of the Families and Descendants of the Early Settlers of Watertown, Massachusetts, including Waltham and Weston; to which is appended the Early History of the Town. With Illustrations, Maps, and Notes. By Henry Bond, M.D. ... *Boston: Little, Brown & Company.* 1855. 2 vols., 8vo, pp. viii, 672; 2 l., 673–1094. Map, Plates, and Portraits. H. + Second Edition. With a Memoir of the Author, by Horatio Gates Jones, A.M. ... *Boston.* 1860. 8vo, pp. xv, iii–viii, 1094. Map and Portraits. B., C.

"The largest and most important town-history yet issued." — Whitmore.

Bond (J. W.) Minnesota and its Resources, to which are appended Camp-Fire Sketches or Notes of a Trip from St. Paul to Pembina and Selkirk Settlement on the Red River of the North. By J. Wesley Bond. *New York: Redfield.* 1853. 12mo, pp. 364. Map and 2 Plates. C. + *Chicago: Keen and Lee.* 1856. 12mo, pp. 400. Map and 2 Plates. H. + *Chicago: Keen & Lee. Philadelphia: Charles Desilver.* 1856. 12mo, pp. 412. Woodcuts. C. 6284

Bond (Samson). A Publick Tryal of the Quakers in Barmudas upon the First Day of May, 1678. *Boston in New England: printed by Samuel Green, upon Assignment of Samuel Sewall.* 1682. 4to, pp. 100. M., W. 6285

Bond (T.) Anniversary Oration, delivered May 21, [1782,] before the American Philosophical Society. By Thomas Bond. *Philadelphia.* [1782.] 8vo, pp. 34. P. 6286

Bond (W.) Sermon preached in St. George's Church, Montreal, on the 9th April, 1854, on behalf of the Ladies' Benevolent Institution. By the Rev. William Bond. *Montreal.* 1854. 8vo, pp. 19. S. 6287

Bond (W. C.) History and Description of the Astronomical Observatory of Harvard College. By William Cranch Bond,

A.M., Director ... . *Cambridge: Metcalf and Company.* 1856. 4to, 3 l., pp. cxci. Woodcuts. B., H. 6288

This forms Vol. I., Part I., of "Annals of the ... Observatory." Prof. Bond had previously written a "Description of the Observatory ...," for the "Memoirs of the American Academy of Arts and Sciences," N. S., I. 177–188, with 6 Plates.

Bond (W. K.), *of Ohio.* Speech ... upon the Resolution to correct Abuses in the Public Expenditures, and to separate the Government from the Press. Delivered in the House of Representatives, April, 1838. [n. p. n. d.] 8vo, pp. 16. + Second Edition. *Keene.* [n. d.] 8vo, pp. 16. H. + [n. p. n. d.] Folio, pp. 2. 6289

Bond. Speech of Mr. Bond ... on the Treasury Note Bill. ... In the House ... March 18, 1840. [*Washington.* 1840.] 8vo, pp. 32. B. 6290

Bondage a Moral Institution, sanctioned by the Scriptures ... . By a Southern Farmer. *Macon: printed by Griffin & Purse.* 1837. 8vo, pp. 78. H. 6291

Bondrye (L. N.) Historic Records of the Fifth New York Cavalry, First Ira Harris Guards; with Observations of the Author by the way, giving Sketches of the Armies of the Potomac and of the Shenandoah. Also Interesting Accounts of Prison Life and of the Secret Service. Complete Lists of its Officers and Men. By the Rev. Louis N. Bondrye, Chaplain of the Regiment. *Albany: S. R. Gray.* 1866. 16mo, pp. 358. C. 6292

Bondt (Nic.) Dissertatio medica de cortice Geoffreae Surinamensis. *Lugduni Batavorum.* 1788. 8vo, Preface, pp. 106. Plate. + *Amstelodami.* 1788. 8vo. 6293

I have seen this dated, in some catalogues, 1768, which I suppose to be a misprint.

Bondt. Verhandeling over de uitmunt. eigenschappen van den bast der Surinaamsche Geoffraea in de geneeskunde; vertaald en vermeerdrd door H. A. Bake. *Leyden: A. en J. Honkoop.* 1790. 8vo. Illustrations. 6294

Bonduel (Fl. S. J.) Souvenir d'une mission indienne. Nakam et son fils Nigabianong, ou l'enfant perdu, précédé d'une notice historique. Par le R. P. Fl. S. J. Bonduel ... . *Tournai: Castermans et fils.* 1856. 8vo, 2¾ sheets. Portrait, Map, and 3 Engravings. 6295

Bonduel. Souvenir Religieux | d'une mission Indienne | ou recueil de Prieres, | Le premier qui fut jamais écrit dans cette langue, pour l'usage des néophytes, | de la mission des Indiens | Mennomonies de St. Michel-Archange, fondée le 15 Decembre 1852, | au nord du lac Shawanow, Etat du Wisconsin, diocese de Milwaukie, | par le Réverénd Père F. S. J. Bonduel, &c. *Tournai: | Imprimerie de Malo et Levasseur.* | 1853. 16mo, pp. 16. 6296

Bonduel. Tableau comparatif entre le condition morale des tribus indiennes de l'État de Wisconsin, considérée sous l'influence de paganisme, et celle de leur état actuel, envisagée sous l'influence du catholicisme, ou Mémoire partiel de l'État des missions indiennes du diocèse de Milwaukie. Par le R. P. Fl. S. J. Bonduel ... . *Tournai: Castermans et fils.* 1856. 8vo, 2 sheets. 2 Plates. 6297

Bone (J. H. A.) Petroleum and Petroleum Wells. ... With a Complete Guide Book and Description of the Oil Regions of Pennsylvania, West Virginia, Kentucky, and Ohio. By J. H. A. Bone. *New York: American News Company. Philadelphia: J. B. Lippincott & Co.* 1865. 16mo, pp. 95. BA. + Second Edition, revised and enlarged. *Philadelphia: J. B. Lippincott & Co.* 1865. 16mo, pp. 153. C. 6298

A Bone to Gnaw for the Democrats. *See* [Cobbett (Wm.)]

Bonelli (L. Hugh de). Travels in Bolivia; with a Tour across the Pampas to Buenos Ayres, &c. *London.* 1854. 2 vols., post 8vo. C. 6299

Bonham (J. E.) Remarks of Hon. J. Ellis Bonham, on the Bank Question, together with Governor Bigler's Veto on the Bank-Bills, and the Debate on the same. *Harrisburg: McKinley & Lescure.* 1852. 8vo, pp. 36. 6300

Bonham (M. L.) Speech of Hon. Milledge L. Bonham ... on the Election of Speaker. ... In the House ... December 16, 1859. [n. p. n. d.] 8vo, pp. 8. H. 6301

Bonilla. Dia 5 de Julio del año 14 en la Habana; por D. Alejandro Bonilla. *Imp. de Boloña,* 1820. 4to. 6302

"Contiene relaciones curiosas para la historia de ese dia en que se tuvo noticia de la Constitucion." — Bachiller.

Bonilla. Felicitacion á sus estimados conciudadanos &c..

por D. Alejandro Bonilla. *Imprenta de D. José S. Boloña.* 1820. 4to. 6303

"Se regocija con la publicacion de la Constitucion y celebra el Patriotismo del Marqués Veitia que le regaló una cinta con letras para el sombrero y el alusivo lema de la época." — Bachiller.

Bonilla (J. Z.) Arte de Lengua Totonaca, conforme al Arte de Antonio Nebrija. Compuesto por D. Joseph Zambrano Bonilla, Cura beneficiado, etc. ... Lleva añadido una doctrina de la Lengua Naolingo, con algunas voces de la Lengua de aquella Sierra y de esta de Aca, que por orden de su Illustrmo. se imprimo. Su autor el Lic. D. Francisco Dominguez, Cura de Xalpam de los Angelos. *Puebla.* 1752. 8vo, pp. 134, 79.

The Naolingo is the dialect generally called Tatimolo, the Indian language of Vera Cruz. *See* Adelung's "Mithridates," Vol. III. Part 3, pp. 46–59.

Bonilla y San Juan (A.) Representacion que dirige a S. M. las cortes generales D. Alexand. Bonilla y San Juan; manifestando el acto tan tiránico como violento que ha experimentado, acompañada de todos los documentos necesarios, legalizados en toda forma, para acreditar la increible injusticia con que se le ha degradado por el general de este apostadero el excmo. señor D. Ign. Maria de Alava, y los individuos que componian el anterior consejo de regencia. *Habana: Arazoza y Soler.* 1812. 4to, pp. 34. 6305

Bonin (T.) Mila, ou le dernier wigwam des Pawnies, épisode d'un voyage en Californie, suivi des 1re et 2e parties de Mon voyage autour du monde ... . Par Th. Bonin. *St-Germain-du-Bois: l'auteur.* 1855. 32mo, 3⅜ sheets. 6306

Bonin. Mila or the Last Wigwam of the Pawness [*sic?*], an Episode of a Journey through California. By Theodore Bonin. Translated from the French by Alpha. *Lons-le-Saulnier: impr. Damelet.* 1865. 32mo, pp. 106. 6307

Bonne-Maison (Alonzo de). *See* Esquemeling (John).

Bonner (John), *A.M.* An Essay on the Registry Laws of Lower Canada. *Quebec.* 1852. 8vo. 6308

Bonneau (Alexandre). Haïti, ses progrès — son avenir avec un précis historique sur ses constitutions, le texte de la constitution actuellement en vigueur et une bibliographie d'Haïti. Par Alexandre Bonneau *Paris: E. Dentu.* 1862. 8vo, pp. 176.

Bonneau. Les intérêts français et européens à Santo-Domingo, par Alexandre Bonneau. *Paris: Dentu.* 8vo.

A pamphlet published in 1861 or 1862. Not mentioned in the "Bibliog. de la France."

Bonnechose (François Paul Emile Boisnormand de). Bolivar.. *Paris: Mesnier, Ladvocat.* 1831. 8vo, 1 sheet. 6311

Bonnechose. Channing en face de la nouvelle école théologique. Par Émile de Bonnechose. *Paris: impr. Meyrueis.* 1865. 8vo, pp. 28. 6312

Republished from the "Revue chrétienne," 5 mai 1865.

Bonnefoux (*Baron* de L.) Vie de Christophe Colomb, Par M. le Baron de Bonnefoux ... . *Paris: Arthus-Bertrand.* [1853.] 8vo, pp. 468. C. 6313

See "Revue contemporaine," x. 484; "Athenæum français," 1854, 258; "Putnam's Magazine," II. 468. For a translation, *see* Becher (A. B.), Vol. I. No. 4218.

Bonnefoux (L.) The Constitution Expounded, Respecting its Bearing on the Subject of Slavery. By L. Bonnefoux. In Two Parts. Second Edition. *New York: Wilmer & Rogers.* 1850. 8vo, pp. 26. 6314

Bonnefoux. The Constitution. No. 9. By L. Bonnefoux. ... November, 1864. *New York.* 1864. 8vo, pp. 26. H. 6315

Bonnefoux. Extracts from a Treatise on the Constitution of the United States. By L. Bonnefoux. *New York: W. C. Bryant & Co.* 1863. 8vo, pp. 31. 6316

Bonnell (G. W.) Topographical Description of Texas. To which is added an Account of the Indian Tribes. By Geo. W. Bonnell. *Austin: Clark, Wing, & Brown.* 1840. 16mo, pp. viii, 7–150. BA. 6317

Bonnemain (A.) Régénération des colonies, ou moyens de restituer graduellement aux hommes leur état politique ... et Moyens pour rétablir promptement l'ordre dans les colonies Françaises. Par A. Bonnemain ... . *Paris: Girod et Tessier.* 1er. *mars* 1792. 8vo, pp. 111, 1 l. folded. H. 6318

Bonner (J.) Child's History of the United States of America; upon the Plan of Charles Dickens's "Child's History of England," by J. Bonner. *New York.* 1855–66. 3 vols., 12mo.

Vol. III. Part 2, is "History of the Great Rebellion. *New York: Harper & Bros.* 1866." 12mo, pp. 367.

Bonner (T. D.) *See* Beckwourth (J. P.), Vol. I, No. 4265.

Some copies have a London imprint, *S. Low, Son & Co.* 1856.

Bonnet (Auguste). Considérations sur les systèmes pénitentiaires en général, et en particulier sur celui de Philadelphie, dont la regle est actuellement suivie à Bordeaux. Par Auguste Bonnet, D.M.P. *Bordeaux: Gazay.* 1844. 8vo, 3¼ sheets. 6320

Also: Question pénitentiaire. De l'influence que le système de Pennsylvanie exerce sur le physique et le moral des prisonniers ... . Par Aug. Bonnet, D.M.P. *Bordeau: imprimerie de Balarac jeune* 1845. 8vo, 4½ sheets.

Bonnet (E.) Souvenirs de Guy-Joseph Bonnet, général de division des armées de la République d'Haïti, ancien aide de camp de Rigaud. Documents relatifs à toutes les phases de la révolution de Saint-Domingue, recueillis et mis en ordre par Edmond Bonnet. *Paris: Auguste Durand.* 1864. 8vo, pp. xxiii, 502. Portrait. 6321

Bonnet (G. J.) Paris, la 10 fructidor an 6 de la République française une et indivisible. Guy-Joseph Bonnet Aide-de-Camp du Géneral Rigaud Commandant la department du Sud de Saint-Domingue: Au Directoire Exécutif et au corps Legeslatif ... &c. *L'Imprimerie de J. F. Saby, rue du Bacq. No.* 149. [1798.] 8vo, pp. 32. 6322

Bonnet. États-Unis de l'Amérique à la fin du XVIIIe siècle. Par J. E. Bonnet. ... *Paris: Maradan.* [1802.] 2 vols., 8vo, pp. xij, 7–24, lxij, 312, (1); 2 l., 469, (1). 6323

"L'ouvrage que j'ai l'honneur d'offrir au public fut imprimé hors de France, sous un titre different de celui qu'il porte aujourd'hui. Des raisons qui me sont particulières, et qui sont entièrement indifferentes pour le lecteur m'obligent à ce petit changement." — *Avert. de l'auteur. See* M. R., XIX. 575.

[Bonnet.] Réponse aux principales questions qui peuvent être faites sur les États-Unis de l'Amérique, par un habitant de la Pennsylvanie. *Lausanne.* 1788. 2 vols., 8vo. + Par un citoyen des États-Unis. ... *Lausanne: Luquiens.* M. DCC. XCV. 2 vols., 8vo, pp. 311, (1); 1 l., 469. H. 6324

An answer to the leading questions which apply to the United States of America, by an adopted citizen of Pennsylvania. "These two volumes undertake to answer 137 questions, for the information of those who think of migrating to North America." — M. R., XIX. 575. Reprinted with the following title:

Bonnet. Tableau des États-Unis de l'Amérique, au commencement du XIXe siècle. Par M.-E. Bonnet, ancien Professeur du Droit de la Nature et des Gens ... . *Paris: Testu et Ce. Dentu.* 1816. 8vo, pp. vii, (1), 175. Map. H. 6325

Bonnet (Stede). The Tryals of Major Stede Bonnet, and other Pirates, viz. Robert Tucker, Edward Robinson, Neal Paterson, William Scot, Job Bayley, John-William Smith, Thomas Carman, John Thomas, William Morrison, William Livers *alias* Evis, Samuel Booth, William Hewet, John Levit, William Eddy *alias* Nedy, Alexander Annand, George Ross, George Dunkin, John Ridge, Matthew King, Daniel Perry, Henry Virgin, James Robbins, James Mullet *alias* Millet, Thomas Price, John Lopez, Zachariah Long, James Wilson, John Brierly, and Robert Boyd. Who were all condemn'd for Piracy. As also The Tryals of Thomas Nichols, Rowland Sharp, Jonathan Clarke, and Thomas Gerrat, for Piracy, who were Acquitted. At the Admiralty Sessions held at Charles-Town, in the Province of South Carolina, on Tuesday the 28th of October, 1718. and by several Adjournments continued to Wednesday the 12th of November, following. To which is Prefix'd, An Account of the Taking of the said Major Bonnet, and the rest of the Pirates. *London: Printed for Benj. Cowse, at the Rose and Crown in St. Paul's Church-Yard.* M. DCC. XIX. Folio, pp. vi, 50. H. 6326

[Bonneville (C. de).] De l'Amérique ... . *Berlin [Lyon]: Samuel Pitra.* 1771. 8vo, pp. 80. H. 6327

See No. 1292 and the note. "Rich is mistaken in saying that Bonneville was 'only eleven years of age' in 1771. He confounds C. de Bonneville, born about 1710, with Nic. de Bonneville, born in 1760. Ersch gives the name as Bonneville (Zacherie de Pazzi de) and Quérard, as Bonneville (Zach. de Pazzi de). I have followed Hoefer's 'Biog. gén.,' which attributes the work, without hesitation, to Bonneville. It has been wrongly attributed to Ant. Jos. Pernety or Pernetti, who *defended* Pauw." — C. A. C.

Bonneville (B. L. E.) *See* Irving (W.)

Bonnycastle (R. H.) The Canadas in 1841. By Sir Richard H. Bonnycastle ... . *London: Henry Colburn.* 1841. 2 vols., post 8vo, pp. xii, (1), 348; viii, 338. Map, Woodcuts, and 2 Plates. H. 6328

Bonnycastle. Canada and the Canadians, in 1846. By Sir Richard Henry Bonnycastle ... . *London: Henry Colburn.* 1846. 2 vols., post 8vo, pp. viii, 313; viii, 293. B. 6329

Bonnycastle. Canada and the Canadians. By Sir Richard Bonnycastle. New Edition. In Two Volumes. *London: Henry Colburn.* 1849. Post 8vo, pp. viii, 313; viii, 293. C. 6330

Bonnycastle. Canada as it was, is, and may be. By

Lieutenant-Colonel Sir Richard H. Bonnycastle. With considerable Additions, and an Account of Recent Transactions, By Sir James Edward Alexander, K.L.S., etc. ... *London: Colburn and Co.* 1852. 2 vols., post 8vo, pp. xiv, 315; Title, 320. Two Maps. BA., C. 6331

BONNYCASTLE. Newfoundland in 1842: a Sequel to "The Canadas in 1841." By Sir Richard Henry Bonnycastle, Knt. ... *London: Henry Colburn.* 1842. 2 vols., post 8vo, pp. x, 367; iv, (1), 351. Map, and 5 Illustrations. C., H. 6332

"Prepared under the sanction of the British Government."—*Advertisement.*

BONNYCASTLE. Spanish America; or a Descriptive, Historical, and Geographical Account of the Dominions of Spain in the Western Hemisphere, Continental and Insular; illustrated by a Map of Spanish North America, and the West-India Islands; a Map of Spanish South America, and an Engraving, representing the Comparative Altitudes of the Mountains in those Regions. By R. H. Bonnycastle, Captain in the Corps of Royal Engineers. ... In Two Volumes. *London: Longman,* [etc.] 1818. 8vo, pp. xxxix, (2), 336; v, (1), 359. Map and Plate. H. + *Philadelphia: Abraham Small.* 1819. 8vo, pp. 482. Map and Plate. C. 6333

See M. R., LXXXIX. 166.

BONPLAND (Aimé). Plantes équinoxiales, recueillies au Mexique, à l'ile de Cuba, dans les provinces de Caracas, de Cumana, aux Andes de Quito, sur les bords de l'Orinoque et des Amazones. *Paris.* 1805. 2 vols., folio. 140 Plates. 6334

BONPLAND. *See* Humboldt (F. H. A. von).

BONREPOS (de). Description du Mississippi, le nombre des villes et colonies établies par les Français, les îles, rivières et territoires qui le bordent ... les mœurs et négoces des sauvages qui y habitent, la manière de se faire la guerre et la paix, la fertilité du pays et la chasse ... . Par M. le chevalier de Bonrepos ... . *Paris: Gyrin.* 1720. 8vo, less than 48 pp. + *Rouen.* 1772. 12mo. 6335

Lelong gives the imprint: *Rouen.* 1720. 12mo.

BONT (J.) *and* ZAS (N.) Oost- en Westindische warande, vervattende de leeswys en geneeskonst daar gebruikt. *Rotterdam.* 1674. 8vo. 6336

BONTEKOE (Willem Ysebrantsz). Journael ofte gedenck-

waerdige beschrijvinge van de Oost- Indische Reyse ... 18 [28?] dec. 1618–16 nov. 1625. Waer by ... Journael van Dirk Az. Raven kommandeur op 't schip Spitsbergen, gedestineert naer Groen-landt. 1639. *Amsterdam: J. Hartgers.* 1648. 4to. + *Utrecht: L. de Vries.* 1649. 4to. Engravings. + *Amsterdam: G. J. Saeghman.* [About 1663]. 4to. Engraving. + *Amsterdam: Weduwe G. de Groot.* 1716. 4to. Woodcuts. + Bontekoe's avontuurlijke Reyze en Raven's reyze na Groenland. *Amsterdam.* 1789. 4to. Woodcuts. + *Amsterdam: Erven de Weduwe J. van Egmont.* [n. d.] 4to. Woodcuts. + *Amsterdam: S. en W. Koene.* [n. d.] 4to. Woodcuts. + [With some variations.] *Amsterdam: B. Koene.* [n. d.] 4to. Woodcuts. 6337

BONTEKOE. Journael oft gedenckwaerdige beschrijvinge vande O. I. reysen waerby het journael van Dirck Alberts Raven naer Groenland enz. *Utrecht: L. de Vries.* 1655. 4to. 6338

BONTEKOE. Journaal van de Oost-Indische Reyze, 1618–25: en't Journaal van Dirk Alberts Raven. *Amsterdam.* 1756. 4to.

BONTEKOE *or* BONTEKUHE VAN HORN. Die denckwürdige Reyse nach Ost Indien, vorgenommen den 28 [18?] Dec. 1618. und vollbracht den 16 Nov. 1625. Eine andere Reyse durch den Commandeur Türck Alberts Raven nach Spitzbergen, im Jahr 1639 ... . *Franckfurt am Mayn.* 1648. 4to. 6340

BONTIUS (J.), PISO (G.), *and* MARKGRAEF (G.) Oost en West Indische warande, vervattende aldaar de leef- en geneeskonst. Met een verhael van de speceryen, etc. in Oost- en West-Indien voorvallende. *Amsterdam.* 1694. 8vo. 6341

BONYNGE (F.) The Future Wealth of America: being a Glance at the Resources of the United States, and the Commercial and Agricultural Advantages of cultivating Tea, Coffee, and Indigo, the Date, Mango, Jack, Lechee, Guava and Orange Trees, etc. With a Review of the China trade. By Francis Bonynge ... . *New York: the Author.* 1852. 12mo, pp. 242, and (Errata) 1 slip. C., H. 6342

A Circular of the Book and Pamphlet Society. *Boston.* 1841. 18mo, pp. 18. 6343

The Book Buyer a Summary of American & Foreign Literature. Vol. I. No. I. *New York:* [*Scribner, Welford, & Co.*] *October* 15, 1867. 8vo, pp. 8. Continued. H. 6344

BOOK. 283

A Book for every Soldier's Knapsack. *See* [Dodge (Robert)].

The Book for the Nation and Times. By a Citizen U. S. N. A. *Philadelphia: William S. & A. Martien.* 1864. 8vo, pp. 64. H. 6345

Book of Anecdotes, and Joker's Knapsack. Including Witticisms of the late President Lincoln, and Humors, Incidents, and Absurdities of the War. *Philadelphia: J. E. Potter.* 1866. 12mo, pp. 350. 6346

The Book of Bubbles. A Contribution to the New York Fair, in aid of the Sanitary Commission. *New York: Endicott & Co., Lithographers.* 1864. Oblong 8vo, pp. iv, 68. Plates.

The Book of Commerce by Sea and Land. To which are added, a History of Commerce, and a Chronological Table, a map and numerous engravings. *Boston,* 1834. 4to. 6348

The Book of Common Prayer, And Administration of the Sacraments, And other Rites and Ceremonies As revised and proposed to the Use of The Protestant Episcopal Church, At a Convention of the said Church in the States of New York, New Jersey, Pennsylvania, Delaware, Maryland, Virginia, and South Carolina. Held in Philadelphia, from September 27th to October 7th 1785. *Printed by Hall & Sellers: Philadelphia.* 1786. 8vo. + *London: reprinted for J. Debrett.* M, DCC, LXXXIX. 8vo. 6349

Known as the proposed prayer book. Reprinted in Hall's "Reliquæ Liturgicæ. 1841." *See* M. R., LXXX. 387.

The Book of Common Prayer, And Administration of the Sacraments, and other Rites and Ceremonies of the Church, according to the use of the Protestant Episcopal Church in the United States of America: together with the Psalter, or Psalms of David. *Philadelphia: Printed by Hall & Sellers.* MDCCXC. 12mo. 6350

The Psalter alone is paged (pp. 221), and has a separate title. This is the first edition of the book now in use. The chief difference between it and the subsequent editions is, that the words, "He descended into Hell," in the creed, are in italics and between brackets, and to be totally omitted, at the discretion of the user, and the words, "which we now offer unto thee," in the Communion Service, are in capitals. *Vide* Bp. White's Mem. Prot. Ep. Ch. (ed. 1836), pp. 148–160. The other editions, up to the year 1800, are as follows: *Philadelphia: Hall & Sellers.* 1791. 12mo. + *New York: Hugh Gaine.* M,DCC,XCIII. 8vo. + M,DCC,XCIII. 12mo. + MDCCXCIV. 8vo. + *Boston.* 1794. 12mo. + *Philadelphia: Printed by Hall & Sellers.* MDCCXCIV. 12mo, pp. 221, (iii). + M,DCC,XCV. Folio. + *Philadelphia: W. Young and J. Ormrod.*

1795. 12mo, pp. xxxiv, 370. This is the first correctly printed edition. With The Whole Book of Psalms, in Metre; with Hymns, &c. + *New York: Printed for T. Allen.* 1797. 12mo. pp. xxxiv, 238. + With The Whole Book of Psalms, in Metre, with Hymns, Suited to the Feasts and Fasts of the Church and other Occasions of Public Worship. *New York: Printed for T. Allen.* 1797. pp. 168, (ii). + *Philadelphia: Printed by Hall & Sellers.* MDCCC. 12mo, pp. xxxvi, 327. *See* Hist. Mag., I. 158, 219, 281, 308; II. 396.

The Book of Common Prayer, And Administration of the Sacraments, aud other Rites and Ceremonies of the Church, according to the use of the Church of England: Together with a Collection of Occasional Prayers, and divers Sentences of Holy Scripture, necessary for Knowledge and Practice. Formerly collected, and translated into the Mohawk Language under the direction of the Missionaries of the Society for the Propagation of the Gospel in Foreign Parts, to the Mohawk Indians. A New Edition: To which is added The Gospel according to St. Mark, Translated into the Mohawk Language, by Captn. Joseph Brant, An Indian of the Mohawk Nation. *London: C. Buckton:* 1787. Ne Yakawea Yondereanayendaghkwa Oghseragwegouh, neoni yakawea ne orighwa dogeaghty Yondatnekosseraghs neoni Tekarighwagehhadont, oya oni Adereanayent, ne teas nikariwake Raditsihuhstatsygowa Ronaderighwissoh Goraghgowa a-onea Rodanhaouh. Oni, watkanissaaghtoh Oddyake Adereanayent, neoni tsiniyoghthare ne Kaghyadoghseradogeaghty, Newahòeny Akoyendarake neoni Ahhondatterihhonny. A-onea wadiròroghkwe, neoni Tekaweanadènnyoh Kanyenkehàga Tsikaweanondaghko, ne neane Raditsihuhstatsy ne Radirighwawakoughkgòwa ronadanhà-outh, Kanyenkewaondye tsi-radinakeronnyo Ongwe-oewe, Keagaye ase yondereanayendaghkwa. Oni tahoghsonderoh St. Mark Raorighwadogeaghty, Tekaweanadennyoh Kanyenkehàga Rakowànea T'Hayen danegea Roewayats. *London: C. Buckton.* 1787. 8vo, 2 Titles, pp. iii, 506. 18 Copperplates. 6351

For the first edition, *see* the Order for morning and evening prayer. Concerning this version, *see* Doc. Hist., N. Y., Vol. IV. 321, 326, 330, 340, 343, 364, 417. The frontispiece represents the reception of the Mohawk delegation by George III.

The Book of Common Prayer, according to the use of the Church of England, translated into the Mohawk Language, compiled from various translations, revised, corrected and prepared for the press, under the direction of the Rev. Abraham Nelles, Chief Missionary, &c. The Collects, &c. &c. translated by John Hill, Junr. appear in Mohawk for the first time in this Edition of the Prayer Book. *Hamilton: Ruthven.* 1842. 8vo, pp. 456. Ne Kaghyadonhsera ne yadereanayeadagwha,

tsiniyouht ne yontsha ne skanyaderatcha onouhsadokeaghty tekaweanatonyouh Kanyeakehaka kaweenoetaghkouh, &c. ne halse Abraham Nelles, &c. &c. *Oghroeirakouh: Ruthven.* 1842. 8vo. 6352

The Book of Common Prayer, and Selections from the Psalms and Hymns, according to the use of the Protestant Episcopal Church in the United States of America. Translated into the Mohawk or Iroquois language, by the request of the Domestic Committee of the Board of Missions of the Protestant Episcopal Church. By the Rev. Eleazer Williams, V.D.M. Revised edition of his former translation. *New York.* 1867. 12mo, pp. 101, 38. 6353

Book of Common Prayer, and Administration of the Sacraments and other Rites and Ceremonies of the Church ... in the Confederate States of America; together with the Psalter. ... *Richmond,* [*Virginia*]: *J. W. Randolph.* MDCCCLXIII. 18mo and 24mo, not paged. 6354

In this edition, really printed by Eyre & Spottiswoode, London, the prayers for the President of the United States are altered to "The President of the *Confederate States.*" But, by a curious omission, the prayer to be used at sea remains unchanged, and the Almighty is asked to be a safeguard unto the *United States.* The greater part of the edition was captured from the *Anglo-Rebel* blockade-runner *Minna,* by the Government dispatch ship *Circassian,* off Wilmington, Dec. 6, 1863.

Selections from the Book of Common Prayer in use in the Protestant Episcopal Church, in the Confederate States of America. *Charlottesville,* [*Va.*]: *J. Alexander.* 1861. 8vo.

Ye Book of Copperheads. Pictures and Rhymes. *Philadelphia: Frederick Leypoldt.* 1862. Oblong 8vo, 16 leaves of Woodcuts. 6356

Book of Mormon. *See* Mormon, *pseudon.*

The Book of Nullification. By A Spectator of the Past. *Charleston.* 1830. 8vo, pp. 31. 6357

Written in Scriptural style.

The Book of Peace; a Collection of Essays on War and Peace. *Boston.* 1845. 12mo. 6358

Consisting of sixty-four tracts, with independent title-pages and pagings.

Book of Revelations: A Companion to the New Gospel of Peace. *New York: J. F. Feeks.* 1863. 12mo. 6359

The Book of the Constitution; containing the Constitution of the United State, a synopsis of the several State Constitutions, with other Important Documents, ... *New York.* 1833. 12mo. 6360

A Book of the | Continuation of Forreign Passages. | That is, | Of the Peace made between this Common-wealth, | and that of the united Provinces of the Netherlands, | with all the Articles of that Peace. Apr. 5. 1654. | And the | Articles of Peace, Friendship and Entercourse agreed | between England and Sweden, in a Treaty at Vpsall. | May 9, 1544. | As also | The substance of the Articles of the Treaty of Peace | betwixt England and France. Given at White Hall | the 20 of Novemb: 1655. | From Generall Blakes Fleet, | The Turks in Argier do consent to deliver up all the | English slaves, and desire a firme Peace for ever: | And in Tunnis Road we battered their Castle of | Porta-serina, and set on fire their fleet in the Har- | bour. April 9. 1655. | Moreover, | An attempt on the Island of Jamaica, and taking the Town of St. Jago de la viga, | beating the Enemy from their Forts and Ordnance, being a body of 3000 men, and | so took possession of the Island, May 10. 1655. With a full Description thereof. | With a true Narrative of the late Successe which it hath pleased God to Give | to some part of the Fleet of this Common-wealth, the Speaker, the Bridg- | water, the Plimouth Frigots, against the King of Spains West India Fleet: | the value of what is taken and posessed by the calculation of the Spaniards | about nine millions of pieces of eight, and 350 prisoners and all this with- | out che [*sic*] losse of one vessell of the English, 1656. | *London: Printed by M. S. for Thomas Jenner at the South entrance of the Royal Exchange.* 1657. | 4to, Title, pp. 61. Illustrated. J. C. B.

A curious historical tract, with plates by Pass, of the taking of the Spanish West India fleet. Townley's copy sold for $5 5s.

Book of the Prophet Stephen, Son of Douglas. Wherein Marvellous Things are foretold of the Reign of Abraham. *New York: Feeks & Bancker.* 1863. 12mo, pp. 48. + Book Second. *New York: J. F. Feeks.* 1864. 16mo, pp. 48. 6362

Book of the Signers. *See* Brotherhead (W.)

Book of the United States, exhibiting its Geography, Divisions, Constitution, Government, Natural History, Institutions, Literature, Biography, Statistics, &c. ... *New York.* 1839. 8vo. + *New York.* 1841. + *Hartford.* 1845. 6363

Book of Truth, or Medley of Facts relating to the American War. *Edinburgh.* 1781. 8vo. 6364

Title from a bookseller's catalogue.

The Book of Trade. Vol. I. [to Vol. III.] *New York.* 1851–52. 6365

Booksellers' Advertiser, and Monthly Register of New Publications. American and Foreign. January 1–December, 1834. Volume I.—No. 1–12. *New York: West & Trow.* 4to. H.

No more was published. The editor was George Palmer Putnam.

Booksellers' Trade List and Publisher's Register. No. 1. *April.* 1854. 4to. Continued to July, 1854, or longer. 6367

The Booksellers' and Stationers' Trade List: containing the Names of the Booksellers in the United States and Canada. Published, under the Auspices of the New York Trade Sale Association, by Miller & Hopkinson. *New York City. May,* 1863. 8vo, pp. 64. 6368

BOOLE (*Rev.* Wm. H.) Antidote to Rev. H. J. Van Dyke's Pro-Slavery Discourse. A Sermon Delivered in the M. E. Church, Mount Vernon, N. Y., January 13, 1861. By Rev. Wm. H. Boole. ... *New York: E. Jones & Co.* 1861. 8vo, pp. 34. 6369

BOONE (D.) Life and Adventures of Colonel Daniel Boon, the First White Settler in the State of Kentucky.—Comprising—An account of his first excursion to Kentucky in 1769, then a wild Wilderness, inhabited by no other human being but Savages—his remove there with his family in 1773—and of his various encounters with the Indians, from the Year 1769 to 1782. Written by himself. To which is added, A narration of the most important incidents of his life from the latter period, until the period of his death, June 27, 1821, at the advanced age of 90 Years—comprising an account of his many extraordinary excursions and hair-breath [*sic*] escapes, while in the pursuit of the wild beasts of the forests, his favourite amusement until the day of his Death. Annexed, Is an Eulogy on Col. Boon, and choice of life, by Lord Byron. *Providence: Printed by H. Trumbull.* 1824. 12mo, pp. 36. Fine Portrait of Boon.

A very rare pamphlet. The publisher was probably the author.

BOONE. Report of the Committee, appointed on the Petition of Daniel Boon February 1st, 1810. ... *Washington City.* 1810. 8vo, pp. 4. H. 6371

BOONE. The Adventures of Daniel Boone, the Kentucky Rifleman. By the Author of Uncle Philip's Conversations. [F. L. Hawks, D.D.?] *New York.* 1844. 18mo, pp. 174.

BOONE. Life of Daniel Boone. The Pioneer of Kentucky. *Boston: E. O. Libby & Co.* 1858. 6373

BOONE. Life and Times of Daniel Boone. Including an account of the Early Settlement of Kentucky. *Philadelphia: G. G. Evans.* [n. d.] 12mo. 6374

A reproduction of some anonymous book, with a new title-page.

BOONE (H. H.) *See* Harlow (S. R.)

[BOONE (Nicholas).] Military Discepline; the Compleat Souldier, and Expert Artilleryman ... . To which is added the Military Laws of the Province of Massachusetts Bay. *Boston: Nicholas Boone.* 1701. 16mo. + Second Edition with Additions. Being a Collection from several Author's By N. Boone. *Boston: Nich. Boone.* 1706. 8vo, 2 l., pp. 124. B. 6375

One of the first books on military science printed in the colonies. *See* Hist. Mag., IV. 146, 147.

BOONE (W. T.) D'Arcy Dunn ... . By Rev. W. T. Boone. Also ... The American Anachron, or Senator Sumner's Dream, Ulysses Redivivus, or the Next Presidential Election, &c. ... *Windsor, New Publishing Library:* [*printed by William Macnab, Halifax, N. S.*] 1867. 8vo, pp. iv, 106, (Errata) 1 slip. H. 6376

Anachron is used for anachronism, and applied to President Johnson.

BOON-ISLAND. Abstract of a Printed Newspaper called The Boston-News-Letter, from New-England. Published by Authority; giving an Account of the sad Sufferings of the Seamen who had been Shipwreckt on Boon-Island. Publlshed in the Supplement. September 10, 1711. Folio, 1 sheet. 6377

Relates to the wreck of the *Nottingham* galley.

BOORMAN (J.) Trinity Church. A Letter from Mr. James Boorman to the Rector, Church Wardens and Vestrymen of Trinity Church ... . *New-York. February,* 1855. 8vo, pp. 32.

Boorn. Sketches of the Trial of Stephen and Jesse Boorn, for the Murder of Russel Colvin ... To which is added ... Said Colvin's ... Return to Manchester, After the Conviction & Sentence of the Boorns ... . *Boston: printed by Nathaniel Coverly.* 1820. 12mo, pp. 24. H. 6379

This differs somewhat from the Rutland pamphlet.

Boorn. Trial of Stephen and Jesse Boorn, for the Murder of Russel Colvin, with the subsequent wonderful discovery of Colvin alive, and an account of his return to Manchester, where the murder was alleged to have been commited, with other interesting particulars, relative to this mysterious affair in addition to the trial. Second Edition. *Rutland, Vermont.* [1820.] 8vo. C. 6380

The Boot on the Other Leg; or, Loyalty above Party. *Philadelphia: [Union League.]* 1863. 8vo, pp. 16. + [In German.]

The Boot and Shoe Trade containing a List of the Boot and Shoe Manufactures and Dealers in the United States. *New York: Wm. F. Bartlett,* 1859. 18mo, pp. 195. B. 6382

Booth (A.) Commerce in the Human Species. A Sermon on the Slave Trade. By Abraham Booth. *London.* 1792. + *Philadelphia: Reprinted by D. Lawrence.* 1792. pp. 40. + Third Edition. *London.* 1792. 8vo. P. 6383

Booth (J. C.) Letter to the Hon. Millard Fillmore, President of the United States. In Reply to Charges of Prof. R. S. M'Culloh, by James C. Booth, Melter and Refiner in the U. S. Mint. Jan. 17, 1853. *Philadelphia.* [1853.] 8vo, pp. 42.

Booth. Memoir of the Geological Survey of the State of Delaware: including the Application of the Geological Observations to Agriculture. By James C. Booth, A.M. ... *Dover: printed by S. Kimmey.* 1841. 8vo, pp. 188. B., C. 6385

Booth. Report of the Examinations and Survey of the Coal Lands, &c. Belonging to the Boston Purchase, near Cumberland, ... Maryland. By James C. Booth ... . *New-York.* 1836. 8vo, pp. 8. B. 6386

Booth (J. W.) Confession de John Wilkes Booth, assassin du président Abraham Lincoln: publiée d'apres le manuscrit original. Traduit de l'anglais. *Paris: E. Dentu.* 1865. 18mo, pp. 270. 6387

Booth. The Life, Crime, and Capture of John Wilkes Booth, and the Pursuit, Trial and Execution of his Associates. *New York: Dick & Fitzgerald.* [1865.] 8vo, pp. 64. 6388

Booth (M. L.) History of the City of New York, from its Earliest Settlement to the Present Time. By Mary L. Booth ... . Illustrated with over One Hundred Engravings. *New York: W. R. C. Clark & Meeker.* MDCCCLIX. 8vo, pp. 846. B. + [*Ibid.*] MDCCCLX. 8vo, pp. 850. 6389

The engravings are poor woodcuts. It was also issued with a new date, *New York: W. R. C. Clark.* 1865 [and] 1866, and in 1867, with the following title:

Booth. History of the City of New York. By Mary L. Booth. *New York: W. R. C. Clark.* 1867. 2 vols., 8vo, pp. 892. Illustrated. C. 6390

This edition, in two volumes, is the same as the others, up to page 753 [?] From this point the authoress has made some additions and alterations, and *omitted* the Charter. One hundred copies were printed on large paper.

Booth. New and Complete Clock and Watchmakers' Manual ... . Compiled from the French. With an Appendix, containing a History of Clock and Watchmaking in America. By M. L. Booth ... . *New York: John Wiley.* 1860. 12mo, pp. xvii, 288. 6 Plates in 12 Parts. B. + New Edition, with Full Index. 6391

Booth (R. R.) The Nation's Crisis and the Christian's Duty. A Sermon preached ... New York, May 12, 1861. By Robert Russell Booth, D.D. *New York: A. D. F. Randolph.* 1861. 8vo, pp. 24. 6392

Booth. Personal Forgiveness and Public Justice. A Sermon preached in ... New York, April 23, 1865. By ... Robert Russell Booth, D.D. ... *New York: Anson D. F. Randolph.* 1865. 8vo, pp. 23. 6393

Also reprinted in the "National Preacher," Vol. XXXIX., 1865. Relates to the assassination of Abraham Lincoln.

Booth (S. M.) Glover Rescue Trials. [Their Number, Results, Costs, etc. Dated Milwaukee, February 25, 1856. n. p. n. d.] 4to, 1 page. H. 6394

Booth. Justice Essential to National Prosperity. Address before the National Equal Suffrage Association. By Sherman M. Booth, Washington, D. C., June 6, 1866. *Washington.* 1866. 8vo, pp. 12. 6395

Booth (W.) Speech of Hon. Walter Booth, of Connecticut, ... June 4, 1850 ... on the ... Constitution of California. [*Washington.* 1850.] 8vo, pp. 7. 6396

Booth *and* **Rycraft.** *See* Fugitive Slave Law.

Act of Incorporation and By-Laws of the Boott Cotton Mills. *Boston.* 1843. 16mo. pp. 7. H. 6397

Bor (Pieter). Historie de Nederland oorlogen. *Amsterdam.* 1684. Folio. 6398

Title from Netscher, XXIII. Relates to the Dutch Wars in Brazil.

Borch (Gerhard Frederik). Defence, against King's Attorney and Judge Advocate Bille's Insidious Attack on Mr. Borch, in his Publications of the 4th, 8th, and 15th of December last. *St. Croix [Christiansted.]* 1824. 8vo. 6399

Borch. Mr. G. F. Borch's Answer to King's Attorney and Judge Advocate Bille's Publication, dated the 6th of July last. [n. p. 1824.] 8vo. 6400

Borchardt (S.) *See* Brazil.

Borcke (Heros von). Memoirs of the Confederate War for Independence by Heros von Borcke lately Chief of Staff to General J. E. B. Stuart *Edinburgh: William Blackwood and Sons.* MDCCCLXVI. 2 vols., post 8vo, pp. x, 323; vii, 318. Map. B. + *Philadelphia: J. B. Lippincott & Co.* 1867. 12mo, pp. 438. Map. B. 6401

Borda (A. de). Pratica de Confessores de Monjas, en que se explican los quatro votos de Obediencia, Pobreza, Castidad, y Clausura, por modo de Dialogo. Dispuesta por el R. P. M. F. Andres de Borda. *Mexico.* 1708. 16mo, 11 l., pp. 88.

Borda (J. C.) Calendario arreglado al meridiano de Bogotá por José Cornelio Borda, seguido de la guia oficial i descriptiva de Bogotá, para el ano de 1859. *Bogotá.* 1858. 8vo, pp. 60.

Borda y Orosco. Relacion de les Reales Exequias a la Memoria de la Reyna Doña Isabel Farnesio. *Lima.* 1768. 4to.

Borde (*Sieur* de la). *See* La Borde (*Sieur* de).

Bordeaux. Adresse de MM. les maire et officiers muni-

cipaux de Bordeaux à l'Assemblée nationale, du 6 novembre 1790. *Bordeaux: M. Racle.* 1790. 8vo, less than 48 pp.

Relates to St. Domingo.

Borden (N. B.) Address of Hon. Nathaniel B. Borden, Mayor ... At the Last Regular Meeting of the Board of Aldermen, for ... 1858. *Fall River: William S. Robertson, Printer.* 1858. 8vo, pp. 18. B. 6406

Borden (S.) Deposition of Simeon Borden, 1843. [*Washington:*] *J. & G. S. Gideon.* 1844. 8vo, pp. 54. 6407

Relates to the Rhode Island boundary.

Borden. Report of Simeon Borden to the Commissioners of the States of Massachusetts and Rhode Island, for determining the Boundary Line between said States. *House Document of Massachusetts.* 1847. 8vo. 6408

Borden (T.) ... A Sermon, preached in ... Sandwich, Mass., September 15, 1856. At the Funeral of Seth F. Nye, Esq. By T. Borden ... . *Boston: A. Tompkins.* 1856. 8vo, pp. 14. H. 6409

Bordentown. Catalogue of the Officers and Students of the Bordentown Female College, of Bordentown, N. J. Chartered by the Legislature ... . Rev. John H. Brakeley, A.M. President and Proprietor. *Philadelphia.* 1860. 8vo, pp. 20. View. H. 6410

See also Vol. II., No. 5372, of this Dictionary.

Border and Bastile. *See* [Lawrence (G. A.)]

The Border Ruffian Code in Kansas. [*New York: Tribune Office.* 1856.] 8vo, pp. 15, (1). H. 6411

The Border States, their Power and Duty in the present Disordered Condition of the Country. [1860.] 8vo, pp. 46.

Bordier (Jacques), *Jesuit.* Relation | de ce qvi s'est passé | de plvs remarqvable | avx Missions des Peres | de la Campagnie de Iesvs, | en la | Novvelle France, | aux années mil six cent soixante cinq, | & mil six cent soixante six. | Envoyée au R. P. Jacqves Bordier | Provincial de la Province de France. | [Vignette.] | *A Paris,* | *Chez Sebastien Cramoisy, & Sebastien* | *Mabre Cramoisy, Imprimeurs ordinai-* | *res dv Roy, ruë S. Jacques aux Cicognes.* | M.DC.LXVII. | *Avec Privilege du Roy.* 8vo, 4 l., pp. 47. J. C. B.

One of the rarest of the Jesuit Relations.

Bordley (J. B.) Essays and Notes on Husbandry and Rural Affairs, with Plates. By J. B. Bordley. *Philadelphia.* 1799. 8vo, pp. 591. + Second Edition. *Philadelphia.* 1801. 8vo.

Bordley. Sketches on Rotations of Crops, and other Rural Matters. To which are Annexed, Intimations on Manufactures; On the Fruits of Agriculture, And on New Sources of Trade, interfering with Products of the United States in Foreign Markets. By J. B. Bordley. *Charles Cist: Philadelphia.* 1796. 8vo, pp. (2), 76. C. + *Philadelphia.* 1797. 8vo, pp. (2), 76. S.

Bordley. View of the Course of Crops in England and Maryland, with Comparison of Products. *Philadelphia.* 1794. 4to, pp. 22. B. 6416

Bordley. *See* Parkinson (Sidney).

Bordone (B.) Libro di Bene- | detto Bordone | Nel qual si ragiona de tutte l'Isole del mon- | do con li lor nomi antichi & moderni, | historie, fauole, & modi del loro u | uere, & in qua'l parte del ma | re stanno, & in qual pa | rallelo & clima | giacciono. | Con il breve di papa | Leone. Et gratia & priuilegio della | Illustrissima Signoria com' | in quelli appare. | M.D.XXVIII. | [Colophon:] *Impresse in Venegia per Nicolo d'Aristotile, detto Zoppino, nel mese di Giu* | *gno, del.* M.D.XXVIII. Folio, Title, 1 l., 8 unnumbered l., containing 3 Maps, 73 l. J. C. B. 6417

Concerning the author and the book, *see* [Harrisse] "Bib. Am. Vetus.," p. 266, etc.; and Lelewell, "Géogr. du Moyen-Age," II. 114 and 162; *and, per contra,* Lenglet du Fresnoy, "Méthode pour étudier la Géographie," Vol. I. Part I. p. 419; *also,* Renouard, "Annales des Alde," I. 142.

Bordone. Isolario, ... con la giunta del Monte dell' oro nuovamente ritrovato. *Vinegia, Zoppino.* 1532. Folio. Maps.

This title is from Graesse's "Trésor."

Bordone Isolario | di Benedetto Bordone | Nel qual si ragiona di tutte l'Isole del mon- | do, con li lor nomi antichi & moderni, | historie, fauole, & modi del loro vi | uere, & in qual parte del ma- | re stanno & in qual pa | rallelo & clima | giaciono. | Con la gionta del Monte del Oro | nouamente ritrouato. | Con il breve del papa. | Et gratia & priuilegio della Illustrissi | ma Signoria di Venetia co- | me in quelli appare. | MDXXXIIII. | [Colophon:] *Impresse in Venegia per Nicolo de Aristotile, detto Zoppino, nel mese* | *di Giugno, del.* M.D.XXXIIII. | Folio, 10 l., Text, 74 leaves. J. C. B., BM. 6419

A woodcut plan of the City of Mexico before its destruction by Cortes, adorns the 10th page.

Bordone. Isolario | di Benedetto | Bordone nel qval si | ragiona di tvtte le isole | Del mondo, con li lor nomi antichi & | moderni, historie, fauole, & modi | del loro viuere, & in qual parte | del mare stanno, & in qual | parallelo & clima | giaciono. | Ricorretto et di | nvovo ristampato | Con la gionta del Monte | del Oro nouamente | ritrouato. | [Vignette.] *In Venetia.* [Colophon:] *Stampato in Venetia per Francesco di Leno.* | [1537.] Folio, 10 l., Text, lxxiiii l. 6420

"This edition was probably published before 1540. At the end is a copy of a letter from the Prefetto of New Spain, giving an account of the conquest of Peru, by Pizarro, in 1533. At page 10 is a plan of the great city of Temistitan (Mexico)." — Rich, No. 19.

Bordone. Isolario | diBenedetto Bordone | Nel qual si ragiona di tutte l'Isole del mondo, | con li lor nomi antichi & moderni, historie, | fauole, & modi del loro viuere, & in qual | parte del mare stanno, & in qual pa- | rallelo & clima giaciono. Ri- | coreto, & di Nuouo | ristampato. | Con la gionta del Monte del Oro | nouamente ritrouato. | Con il breve del papa | Et gratia & priuilegio della Ilustrissi- | ma Signoria di Venetia co- | me in quelli appare. | M. D. [Vignette.] XLVII. | [Colophon:] *In Vinegia ad instantia, & spese del Nobile huomo* | *M. Federico Toresano.* M. D. XLVII. Folio, 4 l., lxxiiii l., 6 l. of Plates, Maps, etc. J. C. B., BD., BM., H. 6421

Printed by Paulus Manutius Aldus. *See* Renouard, "Annales," I. 338, 339. The six leaves at the end are sometimes bound at the beginning. A large map also covers f. xxix *b* and xxx *a*, and there are 108 in the volume.

Bordonova (S.) Cónducto del Obispo de Puebla D. Pelagio Antonio de Lavastida manifestada en sus notas al Gobierno de Mejico antes y despues de su destierro ejecutado el 12 de mayo de 1856. Con documentos. *Paris.* 1857. 8vo, pp. 104.

[**Boré.**] Faits relatifs aux troubles de Saint-Domingue. [*Paris:*] *imp. du Patriote français.* 1792. 8vo, less than 48 pp.

The caption reads "présentés au comité colonial, en vertu d'un décret de l'Assemblée nationale, par M. Boré."

Boreas, *pseudon.* Slave Representation, by Boreas. Awake! O Spirit of the North. 1812. [n. p. n. d.] 8vo, pp. 28. BA.

Boreel Hofman (J. L. V.) Intrede te St. Croix in Amerika, over 1 Thess. v. 12. 13. *Leiden: L. van Egmond.* 1766. 4to.

Borges (A. C.) Primeiro livro de leitura para uso da infancia brasileira; composto pelo Dr Abilio Cesar Borges, director do

Gymnasio bahiano. *Paris: Ve Aillaud, Guillard et Ce.* 1866. 18mo, pp. 36. 6426

Borgman (C.) Bezoek in de Vereenigde Staten van Noord-Amerika, in het jaar 1850. *Groningen: A. L. Scholtens.* 1854. 8vo. 6427

[**Borland** (*Rev.* Francis).] Memoirs | of | Darien | Giving a short Description of that Countrey, | with an Account of the Attempts of the | Company of Scotland, | To Settle a Colonie in that Place. | With a Relation of some of the many Tragical | Disasters, which did attend that Design. | Written mostly in the Year 1700. while the Author was in the | American Regions. | [Mottoes, 5 lines.] | *Glasgow: Printed by Hugh Brown.* M. DCC. XV | Price Eihgt-pence [*sic*]. | 8vo, pp. 102. Map. BA. 6428

"An exceedingly rare pamphlet. Mr. Rich, I. 23, from his description, had evidently never seen it, although he may be right as to the author's name. It is a very interesting narration, with a coarse woodcut plan of Caledonia Harbor on page 9. The author says, 'what passages he did not see himself, these he relates as he had them delivered by credible persons, who were eye-witnesses of them when they occurred; and the author being the only person of all the ministers who were sent abroad upon the service of Caledonia, that lived to return to his native country. Another surviving minister, was the Rev. Archibald Stobo, who settled at Charles Town in Carolina.'" — J. R. Smith. Sold, 1863, $2.15. Reprinted as a "History of Darien," [&c.] *Glasgow.* 1779.

Borland (S.) Speech of Hon. Solon Borland, of Arkansas, upon the Deficiency Bill ... exposing the Lawless and Wasteful Extravagance of the Whig Administration. ... . In the Senate ... May 27, 1852. ... *Washington.* 1852. 8vo, Title, pp. 16. H.

Borland. Second Speech of Solon Borland ... against the Monopoly of the Collins Line of Steamers. ... In the Senate ... May 27, 1852. ... *Washington.* 1852. 8vo, Title, pp. 8. H.

Borneck (Adolar). Treuherz und Fröhlich. Eine Erzählung aus dem amerikanischen Wald- und Indianer-Leben. In freier Bearbeitung [nach Aimard?] für die Jugend. ... 1861. + Zweite Auflage. *Dresden: Meinhold & Söhne.* 1862. 8vo, pp. 188. 8 colored Lithographs, after designs by Bernh. Schmelzer.

Borrero (Eugenio). Informe del secretario de relaciones esteriores i mejoras internas al congreso constitucional de 1846. *Bogota: Jose A. Cualla.* [1846.] 4to, pp. 15, 17 Tables. 6432

Borrett (G. T.) Out West: a Series of Letters from Canada and the United States. By George Tuthill Borrett, M.A. *London: Groombridge.* 1866. Post 8vo, pp. 294. C.

Borthwick (J. D.) The Battles of the World. By Rev. J. Douglas Borthwick. *Montreal.* 1866. 8vo, pp. 500. 6434

Includes notice of the old French War, the American Revolution, War of 1812 and the Civil War of 1861–6.

Borthwick. The British American Reader. By J. Douglas Borthwick. *Montreal.* 1860. 12mo, pp. 288. 6435

Compiled with the object of providing for Canadian youths, reading lessons which would convey information as to the history, geography, geology, botany, natural history, productions, climate, and scenery of the British possessions in North America.

Borthwick. Three Years in California. By J. D. Borthwick. With eight Illustrations by the Author. *Edinburgh: W. Blackwood & Sons.* 1857. 8vo, pp. 384. C. 6436

Also: "Cyclopedia of History and Geography. *Montreal.*" 1859. 8vo, pp. 251, in which the British American possessions are prominently treated.

[**Bory** (Gabriel de).] Mémoires sur l'administration de la marine et des colonies ... . *Paris: Pierres.* 1789. 2 vols., 18mo.

Contains three essays: "Mémoire sur les établissements d'un conseil de marine;" "Essai sur la population des colonies à sucre," published in 1776 and in 1780; "Mémoire sur le système à suivre dans une guerre purement maritime avec l'Angleterre," published in 1780.

Bory de St. Vincent (J. B. G. M.) Essais sur les Isles fortunées et l'antique Atlantide, ou Précis de l'histoire générale de l'Archipel des Canaries. Par J. B. G. M. Bory de St. Vincent. *Paris: Boudouin.* 1801. 4to, pp. 522. 3 Maps, and Illustrations. A. 6438

Contains curious researches on the knowledge of the ancients respecting America, the Island Atlantis, etc. "L'Homme," by the same author, merely relates in a general way to man in America.

[**Bos** *or* **Bosch** *in Latin* **Sylvius** (Lambertus van den).] Leeven en Daden | Der Doorluchtighste | Zee-Helden | En | Ontdeckers van Landen, | deser eeuwen. | Beginnende met Christoffel Colombus, | Vinder van de Nieuwe Wereldt. | En eyndigende met den Roemruchtigen Admirael | M. A. de Ruyter, Ridd. &c. | Vertoonende veel vreemde Voorvallen, dappere Verrichtingen, | stoutmoedige Bestieringen, en swaere Zee-slagen, &c. | Naeukeurigh, uyt veele geloofwaerdige Schriften, en Authentijcke | Stucken, by een gebracht, en beschreven, | Door V. D. B. | *t'Amsterdam.* | *By Jan Claesz. ten Hoorn, en Jan Bouman,* | *Boeckverkoopers. Anno* 1676. | *Mit Privilegie voor* 15. *Jaren.* 2 vols, 4to, 4 l., pp. 350; 1 l., 303, 7 l. Map, and 30 Plates.

B[os]. Leeven en Daaden | Der Doorluchtigste | Zee-Helden, | Beginnende met de Tocht na | Damiaten, | Voorgevallen in den Jare 1217. | En eindigende met den beroemden Admirael | M. A. de Ruyter, Hartog, Ridd. &c. | Vertoonende alle de voornaemste Zeedaden die de Hollanders en Zee- | landers &c. van haer begin aen, loffelijck tegens hun vyanden ver- | richt hebben; nevens veel vreemde Voorvallen, dappere Helde- | daden, stoutmoedige Bestieringen, en swaere Zee-slagen, &c. | Naeukeurigh, uyt veele geloofwaerdige Schriften, en Authentijcke | Stucken, by een gebracht, en beschreven, | Door V. D. B. | Met veele curieuse koopere Plaeten verciert. | t'Amsteldam, | By *Jan ten Hoorn, en Jan Bouman*, | *Boekverkoopers, in Compagnie. Anno* 1683. | 4to, 8 l., pp. 784, 4 l. + Deuxième édition du No. 366, augmentée de text et de gravures. *Amst. Jan ten Hoorn, en Jan Bouman.* 1683. 4to, 8 l., pp. 784, 7. 28 Plates, and Portraits. 6440

This work, divided into two parts, gives interesting biographies, accompanied with portraits of Cristofero Colombo, Amerigo Vespucci, Ferd. Magellan, Vasco de Gama, Francisco and Lorenzo d'Almeida, Alfonso d'Albuquerque, Andrea Doria, Horusce and Hareaden Barbarossa, Dragut Rais, Don Juan d'Austria, Uluccialy, Francis Drake, Thomas Candish, Jacques Mahu, Olivier van Noort, Joris van Spilbergen, Willem Schouten, Le Maire, Jacques l'Hermite, Schapenham, Hendrick Brouwer, Elias Herckmans, George Clifort, John Norris, Robert Devereux. — Part II. Jacob van Heemskerck, Nicolo and Antonio Zeni, Sebastian Cabot, Gasper Cortereal, Gomez, Martin Frobisher, John Davis, Jan Huygen van Linschoten, Pieter Pietersz Heyn, Hendrik Loncque, Marten Herbertsz Tromp, Jacob van Wassenaer, and Michiel Adriaensz de Ruyter.

B[os]. Leben | und | Tapffere Thaten | der aller-berühmtesten | See-Helden, | Admiralen und Land-Erfinder | unserer Zeiten, | angefangen mit | Cristoforo Colombo | Entdeckern der Neuen Welt, | und geendigt mit dem | Welt-berühmten Admiral | M. A. de Ruyter, Rittern, etc. | Worinnen | Viel seltsame Geschichten, Ritterliche Verrichtungen, klüglich-tapffere | Anschläge, und blutige See-Treffen, aus beglaubten Schrifften und Originalien | beurkundet, und mit schönen Kupffer-Figuren beleuchtet, zu finden sind: | Unlängst in Nider-Teutscher Sprache aufgesetzt, | durch V. D. B. | Anjetzo aber in unsere Hoch-Teutsche reinlich überbracht, | Von | Matthia Krämern, Sprachmeistern. | Samt einem Anhange, | Vieler Denckwürdigkeiten, welche der Niderländische Author den | Helden-Thaten Almeyda, Albuquerque, und Acuniæ, entweder ausge- | lassen, oder nur kürtzlich gerührt, beygetragen und erstattet, | Durch | Erasmum Francisci. | *Nürnberg*, | *In Verlegung Christoph Endters Seel. Handlungs-Erben.* | *Anno* M DC LXXXI. | 4to, Engraved Title, Title, 4 l., pp. 1090, 18). Portraits, Plates, and Map. H. 6441

The appendix (pp. 1009–90), by Erasmus Francisci, contains additions to the lives of Francisco and Lorenzo d'Almeida, Alfonso d'Albuquerque, Tristan and Nuno d'Acuna.

Bos. 'T oude nieuws der ontdeckte weereld: vervaetende een duydelycke beschryvingh van uytstekende en aloude, steden, gebouwen ... . *Amsterdam.* 1667. 16mo. Plates. 6442

Bosanquet (C.) Thoughts on the Value, to Great Britain, of Commerce in General; and on the Value and Importance of the Colonial Trade in particular. By Charles Bosanquet, Esq. *London: Richardson.* 1807. Crown 8vo, pp. 83. 6443

See M. R., New Series, LIV. 93.

Bosanquet. Letter to W. Manning, Esq., M.P., on the causes of the Rapid and Progressive Depreciation of West-India Property. By Charles Bosanquet. Second Edition. *London.* 1807. 12mo, pp. 54. 6444

Boscana (Geronimo) *See* [Robinson (A.)]

Boscawen, *N. H.* The Constitution, with the Names of the Present Members of the Boscawen Moral Society; established April 12, 1815. ... *Concord: printed by George Hough.* 1816. 8vo, pp. 8. H. 6445

Also various town reports.

Boscawen. A Report of the Proceedings of an Ecclesiasti cal Council held in Boscawen, N. H. *Concord, N. H.* 1833. 12mo, pp. 44. 6446

Bosch (D. W.), *Dzn.* Geschied- en aardrijkskundige beschrijving van Neêrlands Oost- en West-Indische bezittingen. *Amsterdam: Schalekamp, van de Grampel en Bakker.* 1844. 8vo. + 2e druk. *Amsterdam: [Id.]* 1856. 8vo. 6447

Bosch (G. B.) Reizen in West-Indië en door een gedeelte van Noord- en Zuid-Amerika. *Utrecht.* 1829. 2 pts., 8vo. + *Utrecht: L. E. Bosch en Zoon.* 1833–43. 3 pts., 8vo. 6448

Bosch. Reizen in West Indië, en door een gedeelte von Zuid- en-Noord-Amerika. *Utrecht.* 1829–43. 3 vols., 8vo.

Relates principally to Dutch Guiana and Curaçao.

Bösche (Eduard Theodor). Portugiesisch-brasilianischer Dolmetscher ... . Für Auswanderer nach Brasilien ... Nebst ... Vergleichungen der Münzen, Masse, Gewichte etc. *Hamburg: Kittler.* 1853. 8vo, pp. iv, 257. 6450

Bosch Spencer (H.) Commerce de la cote occidentale de l'Amérique du Sud. Statistique commerciale du Chili, de la

Bolivie, du Pérou, de l'Equateur, de la Nouvelle-Grenade, de l'Amèrique centrale et du Mexique. Importations et exportations ... . Industrie agricole et minière du Chili, de la Bolivie et du Pérou; par M. H. Bosch Spencer ... . *Bruxelles: imprimerie et lithographie de D. Raes.* 1848. 8vo, pp. xxvij, xxi, 429, (1), and Atlas of 17 Plates, folio. B., C. 6451

Bosch Spencer. Inlichting over de Huano of Guano van Peru en Bolivia, en over het gebruik dezer meststof in Amerika en Europa. Naar het Fransch door C. J. Vorsterman van Oijen. *s'Hertogenbosch: Lutkie en Cranenburg.* 1853. 8vo.

[Bosch (— van den).] Bedenkingen wegen de nieuwe reglement onlangs ingevoerd in Suriname [door v. d. Bosch. 1822?] 8vo, pp. 15. 6453

Bosch (J. van den). Nederlandsche bezittingen in Azia, Amerika en Afrika in derzeloer toestand en aangelegenheid voor dit Ryk, wysgeerig, staatshuishoudkundig en geographisch beschouwd, met byvoeging der noodige sabellen, en eenen atlas van nieuwe kaarten door J. van den Bosch, general major. *'sHage en Amsterdam: de Gebroeders van Cleef.* 1818. 2 vols., 8vo. 6454

Bosque (*Sieur*). Memorie adressé a l'Assemblée Nationale, contenant les persecutions éprouvées par les Français, à Tabago, & notamment par le sieur Bosque, pour avoir donné des preuves de civisme, & dont l'impression a été ordonnée par la Section de la Bibliothèque. Deuxième Édition. *A Paris: De l'imprimerie de L. Potier de Lille, rue Favart, No.* 5. 1791. 8vo, pp. 160.

A curious and rare book.

Bosquejo ligerísimo de la Revolucion de Méjico, por un verdadero mejicano. *Philadelphia: imprenta de Teracrouef [Rocafuerte] y Naroajeb [Bejarano].* 1822. 8vo, pp. 300. 6456

"Severisimo escrito contra Iturbide que termina con un poema de Heredia, que no lo firma. (Aunque aparece impreso en Filadelfia lo fué en la Habana.)" — Bachiller.

Bosquejo de la Marcha de la Republica y de la influencia Militar en sus destinos. *Santiago de Chile.* 1841. 4to, pp. 16.

Bosquejo del Comercio en esclavos, y reflexiones sobre este trafico considerado, moral, politica, y cristianmente. *London.* 1814. 8vo. Plate. 6458

Title from a London catalogue; probably incorrect.

Bosquejo, historico de la revolucion de tres dias en la capital de los Estados-Unidos Mexicanos. *Mexico.* 1828. 12mo, pp. 13. 6459

Boss (P.) The Tryals of Peter Boss. 1693. *See* Keith (George).

Bossange (H.) Ma Bibliothéque Américaine. *Paris: H. Bossange.* [about 1862.] 12mo. 6460

A list of books relating to America in M. Bossange's library.

Bossart (J. J.) *See* Oldendorp (C. G. A.)

Bossert (G.) Das Wanderbüchlein nach Nordamerika. oder Schilderung der Auswanderung nach Nordamerika. Verfasst nach ungedruckten Briefen ausgewanderter Württemberger. *Rotweil: Herder.* 1842. 12mo, 2 sheets. 6461

Bossi (B.) Viage pintoresco por los Rios Paraná, Paraguay, Sn Lorenjo, Cuyaba y el Arino tributario del grande Amaonas, con la descripcion de la provincia de Mato-Grosso, bajo u aspecto fisico, géografico, mineralojico y sus producciones naturales. Por el C. Bartolomé Bossi. *Paris: Dupray de la Mahérie.* 1863. 4to, pp. xii, 155. 6462

Bossi (L.) Vita di Christoforo Colombo scritta e corredata di nuove osservazioni di note storico-critiche e di un' appendice di documenti rari o inediti dal cavaliere Luigi Bossi ... . Con tavole incise in rame. *Milano: Dalla Tipografia di Vincenzo Ferrario.* 1818. 8vo, 4 l., pp. 255, (1). Portrait and 5 Plates. C., H.

Bossi. Histoire de Christophe Colomb suivie de sa correspondance, d'éclaircissemens et de pièces curieuses et inédites, traduite de l'italien du Chevalier Bossy, par C. M. Urano, Ornée du portrait de Columb et de plusieurs gravures dessinées par lui-même. *Paris: Carnevillier ainé, [et] Peytieux.* M.DCCC.XXIV. 8vo, Title, pp. xij, 368. Portrait of Columbus. 4 Plates. H. + Seconde édition. *Paris: Boulland, H. Jeannin.* 1825. 8vo. 6464

Contains facsimiles of the wood engravings, from a very rare edition of Columbus' first letter. The revised second edition is unchanged.

Bossu (N.) Nouveaux voyages aux Indes Occidentales Contenant une Relation des differens Peuples qui habitent les environs du grand Fleuve Saint-Louis, appellé vulgairement le Mississipi; leur Religion, leur gouvernement, leursmœurs [*sic*];

leurs guerres & leur commerce. Par M. Bossu, Capitaine dans les Troupes de la Marine. ... Seconde édition. *Paris: Le Jay.* M. DCC. LXVIII. 2 vols., 12mo, pp. xx, 244; Title, 264. 4 Plates. C., H. + *Amsterdam: D. T. Changuin.* MDCCLXIX. 2 vols., 12mo, pp. xx, 187; 193, 3 l. 4 Plates. + *Amsterdam* [i. e. *Paris*]. 1777. 8vo, Part I., pp. xx, 187; Part II., Half-Title, pp. 193, 3 l. 4 Plates. 6465

I find no record of the first edition.

Bossu. Travels through that Part of North America formerly called Louisiana. By Mr. Bossu, Captain in the French Marines. Translated from the French, By John Reinhold Forster, F.A.S. Illustrated with Notes relative chiefly to Natural History. To which is added by the Translator a Systematic Catalogue of all the known Plants of English North-America, or, a Flora Americæ Septentrionalis. Together with An Abstract of the most useful and necessary Articles contained in Peter Loefling's Travels through Spain and Cumana in South America. Referred to the Pages of the original Swedish Edition. ... *London: T. Davies.* M DCC LXXI. 2 vols., 8vo, pp. viii, 407; Half-Title, Title, 432. C., H. 6466

Valuable for the botanical information which it contains. The catalogue of plants was issued separately. *See* Rich, I. 186; M. R., XLVI. 56.

Bossu. Nieuwe Reizen naer Nord-Amerika. Behelzendee eene beschryving van de onderscheidene volken en stammen, die de landen omtrent de groote rivier Saint Louis, gewoonlyk de Mississipi genaamd, bewoonen. ... En volgens den Parysschen druk in 't Nederduitsch vertaald. *Amsterdam: S. van Esveld.* 1769. 2 vols., 8vo. 4 Plates. 6467

Bossu. Neue Reisen nach West-Indien Darinnen Nachrichten ... der Völker enthalten, die an dem grossen Flusse Saint Louis, der gemeiniglich der Mississippi genannt wird, wohnen. Aus dem Franzósischen übersetzt. 2 Bde. *Frankfurt, Leipzig, und Helmstädt.* 1771–74. 8vo. 6468

Bossu. Neue Reisen nach Westindien. Aus dem Französchen des M. Bossy. *Helmstadt: Fleckeisen.* 1776. 8vo. 6469

Bossu. Noveaux Voyages dans l'Amérique Septentrionale, contenant Une collection de Lettres écrites sur les lieux par l'Auteur, à son ami, M. Douin ... ci-devant son camarade dans le nouveau Monde. Par M. Bossu, Chevalier ... . *Amsterdam*

[i. e. *Paris*]: *Changuion.* M. DCC. LXXVII. 8vo, pp. xvj, 392. 4 Plates. H., P. 6470

"Bossu's account of his *two first* voyages to Louisiana was printed in 1768; after which he made a *third* voyage, the account of which is given in this volume — which, not having been reprinted, nor translated into any other language, is a much scarcer work than the former. There are copies with the date of 1778, and with 'nouvelle édition,' on the title-page, but the edition is the same." — Rich, I. p. 260.

Boston *or* Sampson (P.) The Confession, Declaration, Dying Warning and Advice of Patience Sampson, alias Boston, Who was Executed at York, July 24th. 1735. for the Murder of Benjamin Trot ... a Child of about Eight Years of Age. [Colophon:] *Boston: S. Kneeland and T. Green.* 1735. 8vo, pp. 8. B. 6471

Boston. A Faithful Narrative of the Wicked Life and Remarkable Conversion of Patience Boston, alias Sampson, who was executed for Murder at York, July 24, 1735, with Preface by Samuel and Joseph Moody. *Boston.* 1738. 8vo, pp. 35. M.

Boston, *Massachusetts.* In arranging the numerous titles under this head, it has been thought most convenient to put, first, certain general works published by the town or city, together with general anonymous works relating to Boston; and afterwards to group together the publications of particular branches of the municipal government, and of societies, churches, etc., each followed by the anonymous publications relating to it, and some anonymous works relating to particular events, as the massacre.

Boston. Address of the Committee appointed by a Public Meeting, held at Faneuil Hall, September 24, 1846, for the Purpose of considering the Recent Case of Kidnapping from our Soil, and of taking Measures to prevent the Recurrence of Similar Outrages. With an Appendix. *Boston: White & Potter, Printers.* 1846. 8vo, pp. 8, 42. 6473

Address of the Gentry and Merchants of Boston &c. giving an Account of the unfortunate Expedition to Quebec in Canada. *London.* 1691. 8vo. 6474

Address to the Citizens of Boston, and Memorials to the City Government, in behalf of the Massachusetts Anti-Liquor Law. *Boston.* [1853.] 12mo, pp. 24. H. 6475

An Address to the Citizens of Boston and Vicinity on the Subject of a Rural Cemetery [Mount Hope Cemetery]. *Boston: Eastburn's Press.* 1850. 8vo, pp. 7. 6476

Addresses by His Excellency Governor John A. Andrew, Hon. Edward Everett, Hon. B. F. Thomas, and Hon. Robert C.

Winthrop, Delivered at the Mass Meeting in aid of Recruiting, held on the Common under the Auspices of the Committee of One hundred and Fifty, on Wednesday, August 27, 1862. *Boston.* 1862. 8vo, pp. 16. 6477

An Appeal to the World; or a Vindication of the Town of Boston, from Many false and malicious Aspersions contain'd in certain Letters and Memorials, written by Governor Bernard, General Gage, Commodore Hood, the Commissioners of the American Board of Customs, and others, and by them respectively transmitted to the British Ministry. Published by order of the Town. *Printed and Sold by Edes and Gill, in Queen Street: Boston.* 1769. 8vo, pp. 37. S. + Reprinted. *London: J. Almon.* 1770. 8vo, Title, pp. 58. H., S. 6478

"Copies of this book were ordered at a town meeting, to be sent to Col. Isaac Barré, Governor Pownal, Doctor Franklin, William Bollan, Dennys de Berdt, and Alderman Trecothick." — Rich. Often attributed to William Cooper, but really by Samuel Adams. *See* Wells' Adams, I. 282–289; Tudor's Otis, Chap. XXII.

The Aristocracy of Boston; who they are, and what they were, being a History of the Business and Business Men of Boston, for the Last Forty Years. By one who knows them. *Boston: the Author.* 1848. 8vo, pp. 32. H. 6479

Copyrighted by Thomas L. V. Wilson, who is probably the author.

Boston. A Poem. *Boston: J. Nancrede.* 1803. 8vo, pp. 16.

Boston Almanack for the Year of our Lord God 1692. By H. B. *Boston.* 1692. M. 6481

The Boston Almanack, for the Year 1836. *Boston.* [1835.] 32mo. Continued. 6482

Boston and Albany Road-Book. A Directory for all the Rail Road and Stage Routes connecting the Boston and Worcester, and Western Rail Roads, and a Compendium of the Statistics, Historical Associations and other Matters of Interest of every Town ... . *Springfield.* 1847. 18mo. H. 6483

Boston and its Environs; a Poem. *Boston.* 1832. 12mo.

Boston and its Vicinity, Past and Present. *Boston.* 1851. 16mo, pp. 358. 120 Engravings. 6484

Boston and the West. [By "the friends of the Troy and Greenfield Rail Road." *Boston.* 1851.] 8vo, pp. 11. H. 6485

The Boston Assemblage, or A Peep at Caucus Hall, most respectfully inscribed to the Boston Rebel. By Tristram Trap 'em Esq. *Boston.* 1812. 8vo, pp. 12. B. 6486

Boston before the Revolution. *Boston.* 1825. 12mo. 6487

The Boston Book. Being Specimens of Metropolitan Literature, Occasional and Periodical. *Boston: Light and Horton.* 1836. 12mo, Engraved Title, pp. 312. H. + Edited by B. B. Thatcher. *Boston: Light & Stearns.* 1837. 12mo, Engraved Title, pp. 360. H. + *Boston.* 1841. 12mo. + *Boston: Ticknor, Read, and Fields.* MDCCL. 12mo, Engraved Title, pp. vii, 364. H. 6488

Vol. I. was edited by Henry T. Tuckerman, II. by Benj. B. Thacher, III. by George S. Hillard.

Boston By-Ways to Hell. A Visit to the Dens of North Street. *Boston: J. M. Usher.* 1867. 12mo, pp. 23. H. 6489

Boston City Measured by the Author of the "Philippiad." [*Boston: T. Wiley, Jr.*] 1849. 12mo, pp. 60. 6490

Boston Courier Report of the Union Meeting in Faneuil Hall, Thursday, December 8th, 1859. *Boston.* [1859.] 8vo, pp. 32. 6491

Boston Ephemeris. An Almanack for the Year M.DC.LXXXIII. *Boston.* 1683. 16mo. M. 6492

Boston Journal of Philosophy and the Arts; intended to Exhibit a view of the progress of Discovery ... conducted by Dr. John W. Webster, Dr. John Ware and Daniel Treadwell. [1823 to 1826]. *Boston.* 1824–26. 3 vols., 8vo. 6493

The Boston Literary Magazine. Edited by W. G. Hanaford and H. Bourne. Volume I. *Boston.* 1832. 8vo. 6494

The Boston Magazine. *Boston: Norman & White.* [1783–89]. 8vo. 6495

The Boston Magazine, Vol. I. No. I. October 26, 1805. [*Boston: Belcher & Armstrong.* n. d.] 4to, pp. 4. Continued.

The Boston Medical and Surgical Journal. Volume I. February, 1828 — February, 1829. *Boston.* 1829. 8vo, pp. vii, 832. Continued. H. 6497

Boston Memorial on the Cotton Manufacture. [12th March, 1846. Also "Extracts from the Boston Memorial of 1842 ... ." *Boston.* 1846.] 8vo, pp. 11. H. 6498

Boston Miscellany of Literature and Fashion. Edited by Nathan Hale, Jr. Volume I. January to July, 1842. *Boston and New York: Bradbury, Soden & Co.* [1842.] Rl. 8vo, Engraved Title, pp. iv, 284, etc. Continued. H. 6499

The title of Vol. III. is "The Boston Miscellany and Lady's Monthly Magazine, edited by H. T. Tuckerman."

The Boston Mob of Gentlemen of Property and Standing. Proceedings of the Anti-Slavery Meeting held in Stacy Hall, Boston, on the Twentieth Anniversary of the Mob of October 21, 1835. Photographic Report by J. M. W. Yerrington. ... *Boston: R. F. Wallcut.* 8vo, pp. 76. H. 6500

The Boston Opposition to the New Law [the "Fifteen Gallon Law"] for the Suppression of Rum Shops and Grog Shops, fully detected and plainly exposed ... . *Boston.* 1838. 12mo, pp. 32. H. 6501

Boston Prize Poems, and other Specimens of Dramatic Poetry. *Boston: J. T. Buckingham.* 1824. 12mo. 6502

The Boston Quarterly Review. Volume I. [Edited by O. A. Brownson.] *Boston: Benjamin H. Greene.* 1838. 8vo, pp. iv, 516. Continued. H. 6503

After Vol. v., 1842, incorporated with the "United States Magazine and Democratic Review;" in 1844, resumed and continued as "Brownson's Quarterly Review;" Mr. Brownson having, in the interval, become a Catholic.

The Boston Review. Vol. I. No. I. January, 1861. *Boston.* 1861. 8vo. Continued. 6504

Boston Slave Riot, and Trial of Anthony Burns. Containing the Report of the Faneuil Hall Meeting; the Murder of Batchelder; Theodore Parker's Lesson for the Day; Speeches of Counsel; ... Judge Lorings's Decision; and Detailed Account of the Embarkation. *Boston: Fetridge and Company.* 1854. 8vo, pp. 86. 6505

The Boston Spectator; devoted to Politicks and Belles-Lettres. *Boston.* 1814. Large 4to. B. 6506

Edited by John Park; and includes many articles relative to the War of 1812. Sixty-one or more numbers published.

Boston Traveller Extra. Incomes of the Citizens of Boston, and other Cities and Towns in Massachusetts. ... *Boston.* 1866. 8vo. Continued. 6507

The Boston Weekly Magazine. No. I. *Boston: Rogers & Fowle.* 1743. 8vo. 6508

Three numbers were published.

The Boston Weekly Magazine; devoted to Morality, Literature, Biography, History, the Fine Arts, Agriculture, &c. &c. Volume I 1802–3. ... *Boston: Gilbert and Dean.* 1803. 4to, pp. vii, 212. Continued. H. 6509

The Boston Weekly Messenger, a Journal of Politics, Agriculture, Literature, and Miscellaneous Intelligence. *Boston: Published by Nathan Hale.* 1815. Contiuned. 6510

The Bostonian Ebenezer. *See* [Mather (Cotton).]

The Bostonian Prophet. An Heroi-comico-serious-parodical-pindaric Ode, in Imitation of The Bard. With Notes critical, satirical and explanatory, by the Editor. *London: J. Etherington.* 1779. 4to. 6511

"Not a bad parody of Mr. Gray's celebrated ode, and yet not good enough to entitle its author to much praise." — M. R., LXX. 479.

The Catholic Question at Boston; by Amana. With Three Letters, by Rev. James Hervey. *Boston.* 1815. 8vo. B. 6512

The Changery. An Allegorical Memoir of the Boston Exchange Office. By Perspective. *Boston.* 1805. 12mo. 6513

The Citizens' and Strangers' City Guide ... . [*Boston:*] *William Hamilton.* 1852. 12mo, pp. 36. K. 6514

Defence of the Exposition of the Middling Interest. *See* [Sullivan (George).]

Description of the Daily Evening Traveler Building, and Great Power Press. *Boston.* 1853. 32mo. B. 6515

Description of the Town and Harbour of Boston. ... Given (gratis) with M. Armstrong's Plan of the Country, Thirty Miles round Boston. Folio, 1 l. 6516

Description of Tremont House. *See* [Eliot (W. H.)]

Discourse at the Thursday Lecture, March 16, 1797. With

an Appendix, containing an Account of several daring Attempts to set Fire to the Town. *Boston.* 1797. 6517

Title from the "Genealogical Register," XX. 147, probably incorrect.

The Distressed State of the Town of Boston. *See* [Colman (John).]

Documents of the City of Boston, for ... 1838 ... . *Boston.* 1838. 8vo. Continued. 6518

The Eighty second Anniversary of American Independence: being a Full Report of the Events of the Day in the City of Boston, together with the Revised Orations of R. Choate and J. S. Holmes. ... July 5, 1858. *Boston: William White.* 8vo, pp. 127. 6519

Entertainment for a Winter's Evening. *See* [Church (B.)]

An Exposition of the Principles and Views of the Middling Interest in the City of Boston. *Boston.* 1822. 8vo, pp. 8. N.

Facts for the Consideration of the Legal Voters of Boston. [Foreign Immigration, &c. n. d.] 8vo, pp. 4. 6521

History of Boston, From 1630 to 1856. Illustrated with One Hundred and Twenty Engravings. *Boston: F. C. Moore & Company.* 1856. 18mo, pp. 246. 6522

Probably the same as No. 6484, with a new title.

Letter to a Friend. *See* [Chauncey (Charles).]

Letter to the Freeholders and Qualified Voters, relating to the ensuing Election. *Boston.* 1749. 4to, pp. 12. M. 6523

Local Loiterings. *See* [Ross (J. Dix).]

Memorial of the Merchants of ... Boston [relative to the Violation by Great Britain of the Rights of Neutrals]. January 20. 1806. *Washington.* 1806. 8vo. 6524

Memorial of Merchants of Boston on the Non-Importation Act. *Washington.* 1812. 8vo. 6525

Memorial of the Merchants of the Town of Boston, in the State of Massachusetts, 3d Feb. 1806, referred to the Committee of the Whole House on the State of the Union. *Washington.* 1806. 8vo. 6526

A Memorial to the Congress of the United States, on the

Subject of restraining the Increase of Slavery in New States to be Admitted into the Union. Prepared in pursuance of a Vote of the Inhabitants of Boston and its Vicinity, assembled at the State House, on the Third of December, A.D. 1819. [Daniel Webster, Chairman of Committee.] *Boston.* 1819. 8vo, pp. 22.

Memorials of Citizens of Boston to the Legislature, for a Bank of Ten Millions. 1833. 8vo. 6528

Miscellaneous Remarks on the Police of Boston; as respects Paupers, Alms and Work Houses, Classes of Poor and Beggars ...; Charitable Societies; Foreign and Domestic Missionary Societies; Evils of the Justiciary ... . *Boston: Cummings & Hilliard.* 1814. 8vo, pp. 42. H. 6529

Names of the Streets, Lanes, and Alleys within the Town of Boston, in New England. 1708. *Boston.* 1708. M. 6530

Names of the Streets, Lanes and Alleys in the Town of Boston. ... [Containing also a description of the Town.] *Boston: Printed by Benjamin Edes & Son.* 1800. 18mo. 6531

Narrative of the Martyrdom at Boston in 1659. 1851. 4to.

This title is from one of B. Quartich's catalogues, in which a lot of rare pamphlets are grouped. I am unable to find any account of the book.

The New Custom House. Strictures on an Article in the North-American Review, April, 1844, entitled Architecture in the United States. *Boston.* 1844. 12mo, pp. 23. M. 6533

Notices of the Histories of Boston. By Sigma. 1857. *See* [Sargent (L. M.)]

Notification to persons desiring to leave the Town, 24th July, 1775. [n. p. n. d.] Folio, 1 l. M. 6534

Notification of Town Meeting, March 14, 1785. [n. p. n. d.] Broadside. 6535

Observations of the Merchants At Boston, in New-England, upon Several Acts of Parliament, made In the fourth, sixth, and seventh Years of his Majesty's Reign Respecting American Commerce and Revenue, and their Military and Civil Execution. [n. p.] MDCCLXX. 8vo, 2 l., pp. 37. H. + *London: G. Kearsley.* 1770. 8vo. 6536

Official Papers printed for the Common Council, of the City of Boston, comprising the Constitution of the United States, and the Constitution of Massachusetts, with the Amendments. City and Police Acts; Acts relating to the Board of Health, Overseers of the Poor, and Firewards. Together with an Act providing for the Assessment of Taxes. *Boston: Russell and Gardner.* 1822. 8vo, pp. 138, 1 l. 6537

Opinions of the Press in Relation to the Liquor Traffic, and the Morals of Boston. 16mo, pp. 63, (1). *Boston.* 1846. H.

Order of Exercises at the Festival of the Pilgrims, Dec. 22, 1842. *Boston.* [1842.] Folio, 1 l. 6539

The Ordinances of the City of Boston, passed since ... 1834, ... with the Acts of the Legislature relating to the City, since that Period ... . *Boston.* 1843. 8vo, pp. 75, iv. H. 6540

Plain Facts addressed to the inhabitants of Boston, on the City Expenses ... 1834. *Boston.* 12mo, pp. 8, 28. 6541

The Present Condition of Boston, in Relation to Railroad Facilities, Foreign Commerce, ... &c. *Boston.* 1851. 8vo, Map. 6542

Proceedings of a Convention of Delegates from several of the New-England States, Held at Boston, August 3–9, 1780, to advise on Affairs necessary to promote the most Vigorous Prosecution of the War, and to provide for a Generous Reception of our French Allies. Edited from an Original Manuscript Record in the New York State Library, with An Introduction and Notes. By Franklin B. Hough. *Albany, N. Y.: J. Munsell.* 1867. Sm. 4to, pp. 80. Plate. 6543

Proceedings of a Great Whig Meeting of Citizens of Boston ... Oct. 10th, 1838. *Boston.* 1838. 8vo, pp. 19. H. 6544

Proceedings of the Constitutional Meeting at Faneuil Hall, November 26th, 1850. *Boston: Printed by Beals & Greene.* 1850. 8vo, pp. 46. H. 6545

Proceedings of the Inhabitants of the Town of Boston at Town Meeting in Faneuil Hall, 28th October, 1772, printed by Order of the Town. *Boston.* 1772. 6546

Proceedings of the Temperance Convention held in Boston, 23d September, 1835. With Address. *Boston.* 1836. 8vo, pp. 45. M. 6547

The Proceedings of Two Meetings, held in Boston, on the 7th & 14th July, to protest against the Nomination of Gen. Scott, for the Presidency, and to recommend Hon. Daniel Webster for that Office. *Boston.* 1852. 8vo. H. 6548

Recruiting System of the City of Boston ... . Published by Order of the Recruiting Committee. *Boston.* 1863. 16mo, pp. 47. H. 6549

Register of the City of Boston. *Boston.* 1851. 8vo. 6550

Remarks on the Project of establishing a Line of Packets between Boston and Liverpool. *Boston.* [n. d.] 8vo, pp. 20. W.

Report and Proceedings at a Town Meeting, 6th September, 1782, on an Illicit Trade with the Enemy. [*Boston.* 1782.] Folio, 1 sheet. 6552

Resolutions of the Republican Citizens of Boston, December, 1808. *Boston.* 1808. 12mo. C. 6553

Selections from the Chronicle of Boston, and from the Book of Retrospections & Anticipations. Compiled in the Last Month of the Last Year of the Town, and the First Month of the First Year of the City, being ... *Boston.* MDCCCXXII. 8vo, pp. 132. H. 6554

Shawmut or the Settlement of Boston by the Pilgrims. *Boston.* 1847. 18mo, pp. 136. + Second Edition. *Boston.* 1848.

Sketches of Boston. *See* [Homans (J. S.)]

A Sketch of the Recent Improvements at East-Boston, together with the Act of Incorporation and By-Laws. January, 1836. *Boston.* 1836. 8vo, pp. 14. 6556

Songs for the Whig Celebration, July 4, 1834. *Boston.* 1834. 8vo, pp. 8. 6557

State of the Importations from Great Britain into the Port of Boston, from January, 1769, to Aug. 17, 1769; with the Advertisements from the Boston Chronicle. [Preface by John Mein.] *Boston.* 1769. 4to. W. 6558

A State of Importations from Great-Britain, into The Port of Boston, from the beginning of January 1770: Taken from the Cockets and Manifests, sworn to by the Masters of the several Vessels. *Boston.* M DCC LXX. 8vo, pp. 48. H. 6559

State of Importation from Great Britain into the Port of Boston, from January 1770—also an account of all the goods that have been reshipt from this above Port for Great Britain, since January 1769. Taken from the Custom-house of Boston. *Boston.* 1770. 8vo, pp. 87. M. 6560

The Stranger's Guide in the City of Boston. *Boston.* 1848. 16mo, pp. 94. S. 6561

The Strangers's Guide in the City of Boston, No. 2, 1849. *Boston.* 1849. 16mo. W. 6562

Testimony of a Club Convened at Boston respecting the Times. *Boston.* 1748. 4to. 6563

Tri Mountain; or, The Early History of Boston. *Boston: Heath & Graves.* 1855. 18mo, pp. 136. 6564

A Trip to Boston. 1838. *See* [Wines (E. C.)]

A Vindication of the Ministers of Boston from the Abuses and Scandals lately cast upon them in divers Printed Papers. By some of their People. *Boston.* 1722. 12mo, pp. 14. N. 6565

Vindication of the Town of Boston from many False and Malicious Aspersions, contained in certain Letters and Memorials, written by Gov. Bernard, Gen. Gage, Com. Hood, the Commissioners of the American Board of Customs, and others, and by them respectively transmitted to the British Ministry. *Published by order of the town Boston.* 1769. 8vo, pp. 37. 6566

The Votes and Proceedings of the Freeholders and other Inhabitants Of the Town of Boston, In Town Meeting Assembled, According to Law, the 5th and 18th days of November. 1773. (Published by Order of the Town.) *Boston: Joseph Greenleaf.* M,DCC,LXXIII. 8vo, pp. 15. H., W. 6567

The | Votes and Proceedings | of the | Freeholders and other Inhabitants | of the | Town of Boston, | In Town Meeting assembled, | According to Law. | (Published by order of the Town.) |

To which is prefixed, as Introductory, | An attested Copy of a Vote of the Town | at a preceding Meeting. | *Boston: Printed by Edes and Gill ...* | *And T. and J. Fleet ...* . | [1772]. 8vo, pp. iv, 43. H. 6568

The meetings were Oct. 28 and Nov. 2 and 20, 1772.

The Votes and Proceedings ... [as in No. 6568]. The whole containing a particular Enumeration of those Grievances that have given Rise to the present alarming Discontents in America. *Boston, Printed: London, reprinted: J. Wilkie.* MDCCLXXIII. 8vo, Half-Title, Title, pp. viii, 43. 6569

The meeting was in November 20, 1772. The London editor [Dr. Franklin?] has added a preface, giving an account of the discontent arising from the tax on tea, &c. "In the report of the committee to the town meeting at Boston we have a concise system of politics, adapted to their situation as colonists, which is drawn up with great good sense and mature judgment." — M. R., XLVIII. 67.

Votes and Proceedings of the Town of Boston, June 17, 1774. [*Boston.* 1774.] 8vo, pp. 2. 6570

A Voyage to Boston: a Poem. [Motto.] By the Author of American Liberty, A Poem, General Gage's Soliloquy, &c. *New York: Printed by John Anderson, at Beekman's Slip.* [1775.] 8vo, pp. 24. P. + Reprinted. *Philadelphia.* 1775. 6571

Working Men of Boston. Report of a Committee. [n. p. n. d.] 8vo, pp. 4. 6572

Academy of Music. First Annual Report of the Boston Academy of Music, read ... May, 1833. *Boston: Perkins, Marvin, & Co.* 1835. 8vo, pp. 16. Continued. H. 6573

Association of Delegates from the Benevolent Societies of Boston. First Annual Report, Oct. 13, 1835. *Boston.* 1835. 12mo, pp. 48. 6574

Association of Franklin-Medal Scholars. *Boston.* 1858. 8vo, pp. 40. 6575

Asylum for Indigent Boys. An Account of the Boston Asylum for Indigent Boys, the Act of Incorporation, Bye-Laws, and the Rules and Regulations adopted By the Board of Managers. Also, an Extract from the First Anniversary Sermon, by the Rev. Mr. Lowell. *Boston: Printed by Nathaniel Willis.* 1816. 12mo, pp. 32. + Second Edition. *Boston.* 1823. 12mo, pp. 36. + *Boston.* 1831. 12mo, pp. 24. + Third Edition. *Boston.* 1832.

12mo, pp. 38. H. + ... A Statement of the Present Depressed Condition of the Funds of that Institution ... . *Boston. March*, 1831. 12mo, pp. 12. H. 6576

A Report of the Directors of the Boston Farm School, on the Proposed Union of this Institution with the Boston Asylum for Indigent Boys. May, 1834. [*Boston.* 1834.] 8vo. 6577

Back Bay. Report of the Joint Special Committee on the Back Bay Streets, with reference to their Direction, Sewerage, and Grade. *Boston.* 1863. 8vo, pp. 90. H. 6578

Baptist Auxiliary Education Society. Sketch of the History of the Baptist Auxiliary Education Society of the Young Men of Boston, with the Constitution and List of Members. *Boston.* 1833. 12mo. 6579

Benevolent Society. Report of the Committee of Delegates from the Benevolent Societies of Boston. *Boston.* 1834. 12mo, pp. 32. 6580

Board of Trade. Annual Report of the Boston Board of Trade. 1856. *Boston.* 1856. Continued. 6581

The Reciprocity Treaty between the United States and Great Britain, of June 5, 1854. Report of a Special Committee of the Boston Board of Trade ... . *Boston.* 1865. 8vo, pp. 23. H.

Report to Boston Board of Trade, and A Memorial to Congress, on the Subject of Seamen and Marine Disasters. *Boston.* 1855. 8vo, pp. 20. H. 6583

Report of a Committee of the Boston Board of Trade upon the Cotton Tax. *Boston.* 1867. 8vo, pp. 16. H. 6584

Report of the Committee of the Boston Board of Trade, appointed ... "to make ... Investigation into the Causes of the Recent Monetary Difficulties and Mercantile Embarrassments ... . *Boston.* 1858. 8vo, pp. 20. H. 6585

... Report on the Northern Pacific Railroad ... . *Boston.* 1865. 8vo, pp. 22. H. 6586

Steam Communication between Boston and New Orleans. [*Boston: James French for the Board of Trade.* 1860.] 8vo, pp. 8. H. 6587

Boston, Eng. Message of the Mayor, transmitting Seals and Documents from the Borough of Boston, England, Dec. 4, 1851. [*Boston.* 1851.] 8vo, pp. 9. 6588

Boston Athenæum. Catalogue of the Books in the Boston Athenæum. [*Boston.* 1810.] 8vo, 2 l., pp. 266. H., B. 6589

Catalogue of Books in the Boston Atheneum; To which are added the By-Laws of the Institution. And a List of its Proprietors & Subscribers. *Boston.* 1827. 8vo, Title and Advertisement, pp. 356. + ... Books added ... since ... 1827. [To Oct., 1829.] [*Boston.* n. d.] 8vo, pp. 64. + In 1830–1833. *Boston. January*, 1834. 8vo, pp. 80. + *Boston.* 1840. 8vo, pp. 178, (1). + *Dec.* 1, 1854, *to Dec.* 15, 1865. 8vo. Continued. 6890

A Catalogue of the First Exhibition of Paintings, in the Athenæum Gallery. ... *Boston. May* 10, 1827. 4to, Title, pp. 8, 1 l. Continued; in 1829, etc., in 8vo. 6591

... Catalogue of the First Exhibition of Sculpture in the Athenæum Gallery. MDCCCXXXIX. *Boston.* [n. d.] 8vo, pp. 9. + Second. + Third. 6592

Afterwards included in the "Catalogue of ... Paintings."

Memoir of the Boston Athenæum. [Written by John T. Kirkland.] With the Act of Incorporation, and Organization ... . *Boston. May*, 1807. 8vo, Title, pp. 30. H. 6593

Poetical Illustrations of the Atheneum Gallery. *Boston: True & Greene.* 1827. 6594

Report to the Proprietors of the Boston Athenæum, in relation to the issuing of New Shares. *Boston.* 1853. 8vo, pp. 22.

Bridges. An Answer to a Pamphlet, entitled "Considerations on the Public Expediency of a Bridge from one Part of Boston to the other." *Boston: printed by E. Lincoln.* 1806. 8vo, pp. 31, (8). H. 6596

An Appeal to the Good Sense of the Legislature and the Community, in favor of a New Bridge to South Boston. By a Citizen. *Boston: printed by True and Greene.* 1825. 8vo, pp. 22. H. 6597

Collection of Facts and Documents relative to the Project of a Bridge from South Street in Boston to Dorchester Neck, and

the Annexation of that Peninsula to the Town of Boston. *Boston: printed by E. Lincoln.* 1805. 8vo, pp. 62, (1). H. 6598

Concise View of some Facts and Arguments respecting another Bridge to South Boston. [n. p. n. d.] 8vo, pp. 20.

Considerations on the Public Expediency of a Bridge from one Part of Boston to the other. *Boston. Jan.*, 1806. 8vo, pp. 33.

See "An Answer," etc. No. 6596.

Observations concerning the Canal Bridge. [n. p. n. d.] 8vo, pp. 6. + [n. p.] 1819. 8vo. 6601

Opinions of the Judges of the Supreme Court of the United States in the Case of the Proprietors of Charles-River Bridge *vs.* the Proprietors of Warren Bridge *et als.*, January Term, 1837. *Boston.* 1837. 8vo. 6602

Reasons, principally of a Public Nature, against a New Bridge from Charlestown to Boston. *Boston.* 1825. 8vo, pp. 35.

Report and accompanying Documents on the Petition of Lot Wheelwright and Others for a Free Bridge to South Boston. [*Boston.* 1826.] 8vo, pp. 16. M. 6604

The Report on the ... Subject of the Free Bridge ... . *Boston.* 1826. 8vo, pp. 23. H. 6605

Review of the Case of the Free Bridge, between Boston and Charlestown. In which the Expediency and Constitutionality of that Measure are considered; with a Statement of the Legislative Proceedings upon it at the Late January Session. Including the Public Documents. *Boston.* 1827. 8vo, pp. vi, 106. H.

By-Laws. Several Rules, Orders, and By-laws, made and agreed upon by the Freeholders and Inhabitants of Boston of the Massachusetts, May 12 and Sept. 22, 1701. *Boston.* 1702. 4to, pp. 44. 6607

The By-Laws and Orders Of the Town of Boston ... now in Force. Revised in the Year 1758. *Boston: Green & Russell.* M. DCC. LVIII. 4to, pp. 16. H. 6608

The By-Laws and Town-Orders of The Town of Boston, Made and passed at several Meetings in 1785 and 1786. ... *Boston: Printed by Edmund Freeman.* M, DCC, LXXXVI. 8vo, pp. 158, (7). H. 6609

The By-Laws and Orders of the Town of Boston, Passed at a legal Town-Meeting, May 22, 1801 ... together with The Rules and Regulations of the Board of Health. Also, Sundry Laws of the Commonwealth relating to Town Affairs. *Boston: Printed by Manning & Loring.* 1801. 12mo, pp. 82, (2). H.

Abstract of the By-laws of the Town of Boston, April, 1817. [n. d.] 8vo, pp. 8. 6611

The By-Laws and Orders of the Town of Boston, passed at several Legal Town Meetings, and duly approved by the Court of Sessions: together with Rules and Orders passed by the Selectmen. The Rules and Regulations of the Board of Health. Also, Sundry Laws of the Commonwealth, and other Important Information relating to the Town of Boston. Published under the Direction of the Selectmen. *Boston: Andrew J. Allen.* 1818. 12mo, pp. 244. B., H. 6612

By-Law, Rules and Regulations, Acts and Resolves. *Boston.* 1856. 8vo. 6613

Census, etc. Report and Tabular Statement of the Censors appointed by the Board of Mayor and Aldermen, to obtain the State Census of Boston, May 1. 1850. Also; A Letter from Jesse Chickering, M.D. in reference to the Same. *Boston: John H. Eastburn, City Printer.* 1850. 8vo, pp. 79. 6614

At A Legal Meeting of the Freeholders and other Inhabitants of the Town of Boston, Holden on the 14th Day of January, A.D. 1822: Voted—That the Selectmen ... cause to be published ... a Correct list—stating the amount of Real and Personal Estate on which the Inhabitants have been ... assessed ... 1821. ... *Boston: Printed by True & Greene.* 1822. Rl. 8vo, pp. 206. 6615

List of Persons supposed to be worth one hundred thousand dollars. Revised edition. *Boston.* 1846. 8vo, pp. 48. 6616

List of Persons, Copartnerships, and Corporations, who were taxed twenty-five dollars and upwards, in the City of Boston, in ... 1829. ... *Boston.* 1829. 8vo. Continued. 6617

List of Persons, ... taxed on Six thousand dollars and upwards .. in the Year 1849, ... *Boston.* 1850. 8vo. Continued.

List of Persons ... who were taxed on Ten thousand Dollars

and upwards ... in the Year 1858, ... *Boston: J. E. Farwell & Co.* 1863. 8vo, pp. 202. Continued. 6619

List of Persons ... who were taxed on twenty thousand dollars and upwards ... in the Year 1864. ... . *Boston: J. E. Farwell & Co., Printers.* 1865. 8vo. Continued. 6620

A List of Stockholders in the National Banks of Boston, May 1, 1866. ... *Boston: Mudge & Son, City Printers.* 1866. 8vo, pp. 524. H. 6621

List of Wealthy Persons in Boston in 1852. *Boston: J. H. Eastburn.* 1853. 8vo. 6622

Our First Men; a Calendar of Wealth, Fashion and Gentility. *Boston.* 1846. 8vo. 6623

Report of the City Registrar of the Births, Marriages and Deaths, in the City of Boston, for the Year 1849. *Boston: E. H. Eastburn, printer.* 1850. 8vo. Continued. 6624

Report of the Committee of the City Council appointed to obtain the Census of Boston for the year 1845. *Boston.* 1846. 8vo. Map. 6625

Report of the Joint Special Committee on the Census of Boston, May, 1855, including the Report of the Censors, with Analytical and Sanitary Observations. By Josiah Curtis, M.D. *Boston.* 1856. 8vo, pp. xiv, 104. H. 6626

Report of the Committee of Valuation, 1793. [1793.] 8vo, pp. 15. + 1801. [1801.] 8vo, pp. 18. 6627

Chamber of Commerce. Rules and Regulations of the Boston Chamber of Commerce, established March 17, 1794. *Boston: Printed by Ezra W. Weld and William Greenough.* 1794. 8vo, pp. 16. H. 6628

Charter. Charter of the City of Boston. *Boston.* 1827. 8vo.

The Charter and Ordinances of the City of Boston, together with the Acts of the Legislature relating to the City. Collated and revised By Thomas Wetmore and Edward G. Prescott, Commissioners. Second Edition. *Boston.* 1834. 8vo. + Collated and Revised pursuant to an Order of the City Council. By Peleg W. Chandler. *Boston.* 1850. 8vo, pp. 582. B. + With Appendix. *Boston.* 1856. 8vo. B. 6630

Proposed Amendments of the City Charter, submitted to the Citizens, to be accepted or rejected, February, 1838. *Boston.* 1838. 8vo, pp. 24. 6631

Report of the Committee appointed to revise the City Charter, October, 1837. [*Boston.* 1837.] 8vo, pp. 24. 6632

The Revised City Charter, to be submitted to the Citizens ... November, 1854. *Boston.* 1854. 8vo, pp. 43. 6633

Report of the Committee of Internal Health on the Asiatic Cholera, together with a Report of the City Physician of the Cholera Hospital. *Boston.* 1849. 8vo, pp. 180, (2). 6634

With numerous engravings of localities; map, etc.

The following are arranged in the alphabetical order of the usual names of the churches:

Churches. A Manifesto or Declaration Set forth by the Undertakers of the New Church Now Erected in Boston ... November 17th. 1699. [n. p. 1699?] Folio, pp. 3. H. 6635

Catalogue of Members of the Baldwin Place Baptist Church. ... August ... *Boston.* 1846. 12mo, pp. 24. H. + Alphabetical and Chronological Catalogue ... . January, 1863. *Boston.* 1863. 16mo, pp. 32. H. 6636

The Articles of Faith ... of the Bowdoin Street Church ... with a List of the Members ... *Boston.* 1837. 12mo, pp. 57. + *Boston.* 1843. 12mo, pp. 63. + Members of the Bowdoin-Street Church, Feb. 1, 1841. [n. d.] 12mo, pp. 8. + Feb. 1, 1849. [n. d.] 12mo, pp. 11. 6637

Catalogue of the Members of the Charles Street Baptist Church. Together with a Brief History of the Church. *Boston.* 1851. 24mo, pp. 23, (2). H. 6638

A Statement of the Affairs of the Parish of Christ Church, Boston, Published by the Vestry. *Boston.* 1855. 8vo, pp. 18.

Correspondence between the ... Bishop of Massachusetts and the Rectors of the Parish of the Advent. Boston, A.D. 1845 to A.D. 1856. Printed, not Published. *Boston: John Wilson and Son.* 1856. 8vo, 4 l., pp. 123. H. 6640

Essex Street Church and Society. Memorial Volume to Commemorate the twenty-fifth Anniversary of the Installation of

Nehemiah Adams. March 28, 1859. *Boston.* 1860. 12mo, pp. 128. B. 6641

A Memorial of Federal Street Meeting House. *Boston.* 1860. 8vo. S. 6642

A Brief History of the First Baptist Church in Boston; with a List of its Members, 1839. *Boston.* 1839. 12mo, pp. 36. + *Boston.* 1843. 12mo, pp. 36. 6643

Brief History of the First Free Congregational Church; with the Articles of Faith, Covenant, &c. *Boston.* 1840. 12mo, pp. 48. 6644

Origin and Foundation of the Franklin Street Church ... with ... Rules, Articles of Faith ... and Names of Members. *Boston.* 1836. 12mo, pp. 23, (1). H. 6645

Form of Admission, Articles of Faith and Covenant, Rules, and List of Members, of Garden-Street Church. *Boston.* 1842. 32mo, pp. 31. 6646

Address to the Friends of Grace Church, Boston. *Boston.* 1847. 16mo, pp. 8. 6647

Address to the Members of the Congregation of Grace Church, Boston, May, 1842. *Boston.* 1842. 12mo, pp. 22. 6648

The Recent Attempt to defeat the Constitutional Provisions in favor of Religious Freedom, Considered in reference to the Trust conveyances of Hanover Street Church. By a Layman. *Boston.* 1828. 8vo, pp. 24. + Second Edition. *Boston.* 1828. 12mo. 6649

Review of a Pamphlet on a Trust Deed of the Hanover Street Church. *Boston.* 1828. 8vo, pp. 37. H. 6650

Hollis Street Society. Correspondence between a committee and the Pastor upon the subject of a second Ecclesiastical Council. *Boston.* 1840. 8vo, pp. 23. 6651

Proceedings of an Ecclesiastical Council, in the case of the proprietors of Hollis-street Meeting House and the Rev. J. Pierpont, their pastor. Prepared by ... S. H. Lothrop ... *Boston.* 1841. 8vo, pp. 385. 6652

Correspondence between the Committee and the Rev. J. Pierpont, which terminated in his resignation, May 10, 1845. *Boston.* 8vo, pp. 16 6653

Letter ... to their Unitarian brethren, with the documents, relating to a recent call of a minister, by that Society. *Boston.* 1846 8vo. 6654

Remarks on a Letter from the Hollis-street Society to their Unitarian Brethren. *Boston.* 1846. 8vo, pp. 22. 6655

Report of the Committee of the Proprietors upon the "Result" of the late Mutual Ecclesiastical Council. [n. p. n. d.] 8vo, pp. 21. 6656

Articles of Faith and Covenant of the Maverick Church. With Rules, and Names of Members. *Boston.* 1839. 16mo, pp. 12. + With a List of the Members. *Boston.* 1844. 12mo, pp. 24. M. 6657

The Confession of Faith and Covenant of the New [Mount-Vernon] Congregational Church in Boston. *Boston.* 1842. 12mo, pp. 16. 6658

A Sketch of the History of the Boston Society of the New Jerusalem, with a List of its Members. ... *Boston: Wm. Carter and Brother.* 1863. 12mo, pp. 66. H. 6659

Historical Notices of the New North Religious Society in the Town of Boston, with Anecdotes of the Reverend Andrew and John Eliot, &c. &c. *Boston: Phelps and Farnham.* 1822. 8vo, pp. 51. 6660

A Vindication of the New-North-Church ... From several Falshoods spread in ... An Account of the Reasons why a considerable Number belonging to the New-North Congregation in Boston, could not consent to Peter Thacher's Ordination there, &c. ... *Boston: Printed by J. Franklin, for D. Henchman.* 1720. 8vo, Title, pp. 14. 6661

Chronicles of the Old South Church. *Boston.* 1863. 8vo, pp. 10. 6662

The Confession of Faith, and Form of Covenant, of the Old-South Church, in Boston, Mass. With Lists of the Founders, the Pastors, the Ruling Elders and Deacons, and the Members. *Boston.* 1841. 12mo, pp. 85. + *Boston.* 1855. 8vo, pp. 119.

Exercises at the Consecration of the Flag of the Union, by the Old South Society in Boston, May 1st, 1861. *Boston.* 1861. 8vo, pp. 16. H. 6664

The Form of Covenant of the Old-South Church, Boston; with Lists of the Founders, the Pastors, the Ruling Elders and Deacons, and the Members. *Boston.* 1833. 12mo, pp. 29

Old-South Chapel Prayer Meeting. Its Origin and History; with Interesting Narratives, and Instances of Remarkable Conversions in Answer to Prayer. *Boston: J. E. Tilton & Co.* 1859. 12mo. 6666

Reasons for the Appointment of a Committee, to Investigate the Prudential Affairs of the Old South Church in Boston. [By Joseph Ballard.] To which are added Copies of Mrs. Norton's Deeds. [*Boston. Jan.* 1, 1859.] 8vo, pp. 46 6667

The Articles of Faith, and the Covenant, of Park-street Church, Boston; with a List of Members. *Boston.* 1841. 12mo, pp. 34. 6668

Semi-Centennial Celebration of Park Street Church and Society, February, 1859. *Boston.* 1861. 12mo, pp. 166. Portrait.

The Articles of Faith and Covenant of the Pine-street Church, Boston; with List of Members. *Boston.* 1833. 12mo, pp. 30.

The Declaration of Faith, with the Church Covenant, and List of Members, of the Rowe-Street Baptist Church. Fifth Edition. *Boston.* 1848. 16mo, pp. 71. 6671

The Sears Fund connected with St. Paul's Church, in Boston. Report of a Committee of the Proprietors, by their Chairman [B. F. Hallett], Easter, 1854. *Boston.* 1854. 8vo, pp. 32. H.

The Affairs of the Second [Old North] Church in Boston. [Christian Examiner, November, 1850. *Boston.* 1850.] 8vo, pp. 7. 6673

A Brief Statement of the Causes which led to a Division of the Christian Church in Summer Street, and the Establishment of another Meeting at the Lyceum Hall in Hanover Street, etc. [*Boston.* 1837.] 12mo, pp. 12. H. 6674

Appendix to the Report on the Accounts of the Treasurer of Trinity Church, containing Farther Correspondence. ... *Boston.* 1846. 8vo, pp. 29. H. 6675

Correspondence between the Wardens and Vestry and the Rector and Assistant Minister of Trinity Church. ... [*Boston.* 1846.] 8vo, pp. 40. H. 6676

Proceedings of the Proprietors and of the Vestry of Trinity Church, at Several Successive Meetings. [*Boston.* 1846.] 8vo, pp. 8. H. 6677

Proceedings of the Trustees of the Greene Foundation in relation to the Election of an Assistant Minister of Trinity Church. ... *Boston.* 1847. 8vo, pp. 24. H. 6678

Proceedings of the Trustees of the Greene Foundation, relative to the Resignation of the Rev. J. L. Watson, as Assistant Minister of Trinity Church. ... *Boston.* 1846. 8vo, pp. 10, (1).

Protest of the Laity of Trinity Church ... against the Election of any Assistant Bishop for the Eastern Diocese. *Boston: Munroe & Francis.* 1838. 8vo, pp. 15. H. 6680

Warren Street Chapel. Proceedings of the Annual Meeting. *Boston.* 1837. 12mo. 6681

First Annual Report, Jan. 1, 1837. [n. d.] 12mo, pp. 20.

Report of a Committee to the Contributors, April 15, 1837. [n. d.] 12mo, pp. 12. 6683

City Hall. Proceedings on the Occasion of laying the Corner Stone of the City Hall ... December 22, 1862. *Boston.* 1862. 8vo, pp. 55, and Facsimile of the Subscription Paper for the first Town-House in Boston, folio, pp. (4). 6684

The City Hall, Boston. ... *Boston.* MDCCCLXVI. 8vo. 6685

Common. Appeal of the old Elm on Boston Common. [In verse.] *Boston.* 1866. Slip. 6686

Boston Common. *Boston: William D. Ticknor and H. B. Williams.* 1842. 12mo, pp. 63. H. 6687

Boston Common. [Opinions of Jeremiah Mason and Franklin Dexter as to the Right of the City to sell certain Lands, originally Part of the Boston Common.] *Boston.* 1843. 8vo, pp. 19. 6688

The Boston Common, or Rural Walks in Cities. By a Friend of Improvement. ... *Boston.* 1838. 12mo, pp. 62. Engravings. 6689

Common Council. Rules and Orders of the Common Council of the City of Boston, City Charter, the City Ordinances, &c. *Boston.* 1833. 12mo. Continued. 6690

Proceedings at the Dedication of the City Hall, September 18, 1865. ... *Boston: City Council.* 1865. 8vo, pp. 36. 6691

City Hospital. A Description of The City Hospital of Boston. ... Plans of the Building, etc. etc. *Boston: J. E. Farwell & Company, Printers.* 1865. 8vo, pp. 129, (2). 8 Plates. H.

Also: First Annual Report of the Trustees ... . January 1, 1865. *Boston.* 1865. 8vo. — Act of the Legislature and Ordinances of the City Council relating to the City Hospital ... . *Boston.* 1864. 8vo.

... Proceedings at the Dedication of the City Hospital, May 24, 1864. *Boston.* 1864. 8vo, pp. 61, (3). H. 6693

Directory. The Boston Business and Copartnership Directory: Containing the Names and Location of all Firms and Individuals doing Business in Boston ... . *Boston: Compiled and published by Dean Dudley.* 1863-4. 16mo, pp. 355, (1). Map. Continued. 6694

Boston Business-Street Directory, for 1858, by Damrell & Moore, and George Coolidge. ... [*Boston.* 1857.] 32mo, pp. 94. H. + *Boston: G. Coolidge.* 1867. 24mo, pp. 343. 6695

The | Boston Directory. | Containing, | A List of the Merchants, Mechanics, | Traders, and others, of the Town of Boston; | in Order to enable Strangers to find the Residence | of any Person. | To which is added, | Publick Offices ... | Barristers and Attorneys at Law ... | Physicians, Surgeons ... | ... the Bank. | Names and places of Abode of all the Engine-men. | Illustrated with a Plan of the Town of Boston. | *Boston: Printed and sold by John Norman, at Oliver's-Dock.* | 1789. 16mo, pp. 56. H. + Reprinted. *Boston.* 1852. 12mo, pp. 63. 6696

"The Boston Directory was first published in 1789 *by John Norman*; next, in 1796, 1798, 1800, and 1803, *by John West*; in 1805, '07, '09, '16, and '18, *by Edward Cotton*; in 1820-23, '25, and '26, *by John H. A. Frost and Charles Stimpson, Jr.*; in 1827, *by Hunt and Stimpson and John H. A. Frost*; in 1828, *by Hunt and Stimpson*; from 1829 to 1846, *by Charles Stimpson, Jr.* In 1846 began "Adams's New Directory of the City of Boston ... . *Boston: George Adams.* 1846." 8vo. Continued. For a history of the work, *see* Adams's Boston Directory for 1852, Appendix, p. 60. Pages 61-76 contain a reprint of the Directory of 1789." — C. A. C.

Complete Business Directory of Boston, for the Year 1857. ... Volume I. [*Boston:*] *Published annually by Damrell & Moore and George Coolidge.* [n. d.] 8vo, pp. 196. H. 6697

Boston Dispensary. Institution of the Boston Dispensary, for the Medical Relief of the Poor. Incorporated 1801. *Boston: Press of James Loring.* 1837. 12mo, pp. 15, (1). 6698

History of the Boston Dispensary, 1859. *See* [Lawrence (William R.)]

East Boston. Description of and Statement of the Property of the East Boston Company. *Boston.* 1836. 8vo, pp. 18. 6699

Episcopal Charitable Society. Constitution, Act of Incorporation, and By-Laws, of the Boston Episcopal Charitable Society, instituted in ... 1724: with a List of the Officers and Members; and an Historical Memoir of the Society, by Isaac Boyle, D.D. ... *Boston.* 1860. 8vo, pp. 34. H. 6700

Laws and Regulations of the Boston Episcopal Charitable Society, Instituted in the Year 1724. ... *Boston: Printed by H. Sprague.* 1805. 8vo. pp. 14. 6701

Faneuil Hall. Observations on the "Remarks on the Constitutionality of the Memorial for and Extension of Faneuil-Hall Market." *Boston.* [1824.] 8vo, pp. 8. 6702

Also: Remarks on the Constitutionality of the Memorial of the City Council for an Extension of Faneuil Hall Market. [n. p. n. d.] 8vo. — Report of the Committee of both Branches of the City Council, on the Extension of Faneuil Hall Market, giving an Account of the whole Expense of the same. [*Boston.* 1826.] 8vo.

Female Anti-Slavery Society. Annual Report of the Boston Female Anti-Slavery Society; being a Concise History of the Cases of the Slave Child, Med, and of the Women demanded as Slaves of the Supreme Judicial Court of Mass. ... *Boston: the Society.* 1836. 12mo, pp. 90. H. 6703

With the half-title: "Right and Wrong in Boston in 1836."

Ninth Annual Report of the Boston Female Anti-Slavery Society. ... *Boston: Oliver Johnson.* 1842. 8vo, pp. 46, (1). H.

With the half-title: "Ten Years of Experience."

Female Asylum. An Account of the Rise, Progress, and Present State, of the Boston Female Asylum. Together with the Act of Incorporation. Also, the Bye-Laws, and Rules and Regulations, adopted by the Board of Managers. *Boston: Printed by Russell and Cutler.* 1803. 8vo, pp. 28. H. + *Boston: Printed By Russell and Cutler.* 1810. 12mo, pp. 40. + *Boston:* 1833. 12mo, pp. 24. H. 6705

Female Missionary Society. A Brief Account of the Origin and Progress of the Boston Female Society for Missionary Purposes. With Extracts from the Reports of the Society, In May, 1817 and 1818 ... . *Boston:* [n. d.] 8vo, pp. 24. H.

Franklin Fund. A Sketch of the Origin, Object and Character of the Franklin Fund, for the Benefit of Young Married Mechanics of Boston. ... *Boston.* 1866. 8vo, pp. 38. H. 6707

Land Bank. A Letter from a Country Gentleman at Boston, To his Friends in the Country. [Dated, June 10, 1740. n. p. n. d.] Sm. 8vo, pp. 12. B. 6708

On the subject of a bank.

A Letter, From One in Boston, To his Friend in the Country. In Answer to a Letter directed to John Burril, Esqr. Speaker to the House of Representatives, for the Province of the Massachusetts-Bay in New-England. [n. p.] 1714. Sm. 8vo, Title, pp. 37. B. 6709

Signed F---l. B---t.

A Projection For Erecting a Bank of Credit In Boston, New-England, Founded on Land Security. [*Boston.*] 1714. Sm. 8vo, pp. 22. B. 6710

A Vindication of the Bank of Credit Projected in Boston from the Aspersions of Paul Dudley, Esqr. in a Letter By him directed to John Burril Esqr. Late Speaker to the House of Representatives for the Province of the Massachusetts-Bay in New-England. [n. p.] 1714. Sm. 8vo, Title, pp. 20. B. 6711

Gas Light Company. Trial. Boston Gas Light Company versus William Gault, containing the Arguments of Counsel, and the Charge of the Judge. ... *Boston.* 1848. 8vo, pp. 119. Woodcuts. 6712

Girls' High School. An Account of the High School For Girls, Boston. With A Catalogue of the Scholars February, 1826. *Boston: Thomas B. Wait and Son.* 1826. 8vo, pp. 20.

Government. Two Plans for forming the Town of Boston into an Incorporated City. *Published by order of the Town for the Perusal and Consideration of the Inhabitants.* [1784.] 4to, pp. 8. H. 6714

Report of the Town Convention [on Alterations in the County and Town Government. *Boston.* 1804.] 8vo, pp. 62, (1). H. 6715

... [Report of a Committee on a System of Municipal Government for the Town, December, 1821. *Boston.* 1821.] 8vo, pp. 8. H. 6716

Boston, February 22, 1792. Incorporation. An Antiquarian ... found the following Original Paper, whereby it appears that Seventy Years ago the Subject ... was agitated ... . [*Boston.* 1792.] Broadside. H. 6717

Proposed Amendments of the City Charter, submitted by the City Council ... . *Boston.* 1838. 8vo, pp. 24. H. 6718

... The Revised City Charter, to be submitted to the Citizen's ... 1854. *Boston.* 1854. 8vo, pp. 43. H. 6719

Report, 16th October 1815, of the Committee appointed to take into Consideration the Expediency of making an Alteration in the Municipal Government of the Town. 8vo. 6720

Report of the Committee on Amendments to the City Charter. [*Boston.* 1865.] 4to, 63 l., printed on one side only. H. 6721

... [Report of the Joint Committee instructed to revise the City Charter. Dated Oct. 16, 1837. *Boston.* 1837.] 8vo, pp. 24. H. 6722

Harbor. Communications and Reports in relation to the Surveys of Boston Harbor by the United States Commissioners, Joseph G. Totten ... A. D. Bache ... C. H. Davis ... . *Boston: J. E. Farwell & Co., Printers.* 1862. 8vo, pp. 204 in all. 18 Maps and Diagrams. + [With two new reports. *Ibid.*] 1863. 8vo, pp. 272 in all. 23 Maps, and Diagrams. 6723

Report of the Commissioners in Relation to the Flats in Boston Harbor, January, 1850. 8vo, pp. 72. Map. (Mass. Senate Doc., No. 3.) 6724

Report of the Joint Standing Committee on Boston Harbor for the year 1852. *Boston: J. H. Eastburn.* 1853. 8vo, pp. 79. 2 Plates. C. 6725

Report on the Relation of Mystic Pond and River to Boston Harbor. *Boston.* 1861. 8vo, pp. 95. B. 6726

House of Refuge. Remarks on a Report ... on the Subject of the House of Reformation. ... By the Directors. *Boston: printed by Samuel N. Dickinson.* 1833. 8vo, pp. 64. H. 6727

Relates to a "... Report of the Standing Committee of the Common Council on ... the House of Reformation ... ." [*Boston.* 1832.] 8vo, pp. 84. H.

Howard Benevolent Society. Historical Sketch of the Howard Benevolent Society, organized 1812. With the Forty-Second Annual Report ... . *Boston.* 1852. 12mo, pp. 20. H. 6728

Immigrant Society in Boston. Information for Immigrants to the New-England States. *Boston.* 1795. Folio, 1 l. M. 6729

Library. Catalogue of the Boston Library, Jan. 1, 1795. 8vo. + Nov. 1, 1807. *Boston.* 12mo. + *Boston.* 1815. 8vo, pp. 64. + [*Boston.* 1817.] 8vo, pp. 16. + *Boston.* 1824. 8vo. + *Boston: T. M. Marvin.* 1844. 8vo, pp. 335, 73. + Supplemental Catalogue ... 1849. [*Boston.* 1849.] 8vo, pp. 72.

Long Wharf. Boston Pier, or Long-Wharf, incorporated ... July 14, 1772. Additional Act Passed ... June 24, 1824. Also, Rules and By-Laws, ... *Boston.* 1825. 12mo, pp. 25.

Markets. Some Reasons and Arguments offered to the Good People of Boston and adjacent places for the setting up of Markets in Boston. *Boston, N. E.: Printed by J. Franklin.* 1719. 12mo, pp. 14. M. 6732

See, before, Faneuil Hall, No. 4702.

By-law for setting up and regulating a Public Market. *Boston.* 1734. 4to, pp. 7. 6733

Marine Society. Constitution and Laws of the Boston Marine Society, instituted in 1742. *Boston.* 1792. 12mo. + Constitution and Laws of the Boston Marine Society, instituted in the year 1742. Incorporated in the year 1754. *Boston.* 1809. 18mo, pp. 47. + With a Brief History of the Society for One Hundred Years: and a Full Account of the Centennial Celebration, June 17, 1842. *Boston.* 1842. 12mo, pp. 84. H. 6734

Massacre. A fair Account of the late Unhappy Disturbance At Boston in New England; extracted From the Depositions that have been made concerning it by Persons of all Parties. With an Appendix, containing Some Affidavits and other Evidences relating to this Affair, not mentioned in the Narrative of

it that has been published at Boston. *London: B. White.* M DCC LXX. 8vo, pp. 28, Appendix, 31. H. 6735

"A defence of the massacre at Boston. The author is a zealous advocate for the soldiers, and endeavors to prove that their firing upon their assailants was, if not wholly unavoidable, at least highly excusable; that they were provoked to it by the most unsufferable insults, and that the people were entirely the aggressors. He supports his representations by the affidavits of twenty-nine persons; most of whom, however, it will be observed, are officers in the army." — M. R., XLIII. 68.

Letters from the Town of Boston to C. Lucas, Esq., inclosing a Narrative of the Massacre perpetrated there March 5, 1770, by the Soldiers of the 29th Regiment, &c. *Dublin, Reprinted.* [1770.] 6736

Title from one of Puttick and Simpson's catalogues, about 1860.

Orations delivered at the Request of the Inhabitants of the Town of Boston, to commemorate the Evening of the Fifth of March, 1770; When a Number of Citizens were killed by a Party of British Troops, quartered among them, in a Time of Peace. *Boston: Printed by Peter Edes, in State-Street.* [1785?] 16mo, pp. 200, (Errata) 1 slip. H. + Second Edition. *Boston.: Wm. T. Clap.* 1807. 12mo, pp. 198, (Index) 1 l. C.

The orations are by James Lovell, A.M., Dr. Benj. Church, Dr. Joseph Warren (of Bunker Hill fame), Benj. Hichborn, William Tudor, Jonathan Mason, Jr., Thos. Dawes, Jr., and John Hancock. Also an oration by Perez Morton, on the reinterment of the remains of Joseph Warren, April 8th, 1776.

The Poem which the Committee of the Town of Boston had voted unanimously to be Published with the late Oration; with Observations relating thereto; Together with some very pertinent Extracts from an ingenious Composition never yet published. *Boston: E. Russell.* M, DCC, LXXII. 4to, pp. 30. P. + *Boston.* 1785. 12mo. 6738

An ironical piece, which completely imposed on the committee, who unanimously voted to print it with Warren's Oration on 5th March, and Mr. Samuel Adams carried it to the printer; but, it leaking out that the author was a warm Tory, the committee reconsidered the matter, and discovered the jest. The author was James Allen, concerning whom *see* Duyckinck, I. 235. *See also* Vol. I., No. 833, in this Dictionary.

A Short Narrative of the Horrid Massacre in Boston, perpetrated in the Evening of the Fifth Day of March, 1770. By Soldiers of the XXIXth Regiment; which with the XIVth Regiment were then Quartered there: With some Observations on the state of things prior to that Catastrophe. *Printed by Order of the Town of Boston, and Sold by Edes and Gill, in Queen-Street, And T. & J. Fleet, in Cornhill.* 1770. 8vo, pp. 38, Appendix, 81 for 83 pp., pp. 79 and 80 being repeated. Plate. 6739

A Short Narrative ... . To which is added, an Appendix, containing The several Depositions referred to in the preceding Narrative; and also other Depositions relative to the Subject of it. *Boston, Printed, Re-printed for W. Bingley, London.* MDCCLXX. 8vo, pp. 48, 83. Plate. + *London: E. and C. Dilly, ana J. Almon.* M. DCC. LXX. 8vo, pp. 166. Plate. H. + *New York: re-published with Notes and Illustrations by John Doggett, Jr.* 1849. 8vo, pp. 122. Plate and Plan. H. + *Boston.* 1840.

This edition contains a few more facts than the preceding. Said to have been written by James Bowdoin. *See* a note in Rich, I. 180.

Additional Observations to A Short Narrative of the Horrid Massacre in Boston, perpetrated In the Evening of the 5th of March 1770. *Printed by Order of the Town of Boston.* M DCC LXX. 8vo, pp. 12. 6741

Forms a supplement to the Short Narrative. *See* the following note: "The copies of this narrative sent to England and other parts, conclude with the foregoing page. Since they were sent, it has appeared necessary to add a few pages to the remaining copies: to do which an opportunity has been given by the restraint laid on the publishing of the said narrative here. The reason of that restraint will appear by the following vote of the town, passed at the town-meeting held on the 26th of March, namely: 'The committee appointed to prepare a true state of facts relating to the execrable massacre perpetrated on the evening of the 5th instant, in order that the same be transmitted to Great Britain, having accordingly reported, and the report being accepted by the town, and ordered to be printed: And whereas the publishing of the said narrative with the depositions accompanying it, in this country, may be supposed by the unhappy persons now in custody for trial, as tending to give an undue bias to the minds of the jury who are to try the same. Therefore voted, That the committee reserve all printed copies in their hands excepting those to be sent to Great Britain, till the further order of the town.'"

Mayor. An Address ... on the Organization of the City Government, January 5, 1829. By Harrison G. Otis, Mayor. ... . *Boston.* 1829. 8vo, pp. 15. 6742

This is not the first, but the first I have seen, and perhaps the first printed. Continued annually.

Mechanics' Institution. First Annual Report of the Board of Managers, &c., 1828; with Constitution. *Boston.* 1828. 8vo, pp. 24. M. 6743

Mercantile Library Association. Annual Report. ... *Boston.* 1821. 8vo. Continued. 6744

A Catalogue of Books ... with a History of the Institution, Constitution, By-Laws, etc. ... *Boston: the Association.* 1844. 8vo, pp. 100. H. + [*Ibid.*] 1848. 8vo. + [*Ibid.*] 1850. 8vo, pp. 135, (Supplement), 35. H. + [By Wm. Fred. Poole.] *Boston.* 1854. 8vo, pp. xxiii, 298. + Supplement. [*Ibid.*] 8vo, pp. (4), 52. H. 6745

Report of the Board of Directors from 1820 to 1845. *Boston.* 1845. 8vo, pp. 51. 6746

Mills, Mill-Dam. Contract between the Town of Boston and the Mill Corporation, July 24, 1807. *Boston.* [1807.] 8vo, pp. 12. 6747

The Boston and Roxbury Mill Corporation. *See* [Cotting (Uriah)].

Report of the Town's Committee On the Petition of Isaac P. Davis and Others, for Liberty to build a Mill Dam and Turnpike Road, from the bottom of Beacon-Street ... . [No imprint.] 8vo, pp. 28. H. + [*Boston.* 1814.] 8vo, pp. 7. 6748

Municipal Register. Municipal Register, Rules and Orders of the City Council, Recent Ordinances and Laws, and a List of the Officers of the City of Boston, for 1841. *Boston.* 1841. 12mo, pp. 104. Continued. 6749

The previous volumes are called "Rules and Orders."

Police. Remarks on the Police of Boston. *Boston.* 1814. 8vo, pp. 42. 6750

Port Bill. The Alarming Boston Port-Bill Act, which prohibited the Entrance and Clearance of all Vessels whatsoever at that Port from the ensuing 1st Day of June, 1774, and transfers the seat of Government and the Custom House to the Town of Salem. 4to, pp. 4. P. 6751

No title-page, printer's name, or year, but probably printed at *Boston*, 1774.

The Boston Port Bill; with Gov. Johnstone's Speech in the House of Commons. [n. p. n. d.] Folio, 1 l. 6752

Port Society. An Account of the Port Society of the City of Boston and its Vicinity, and of the Proceedings at its Third Anniversary Meeting. ... *Boston.* 1832. 8vo, pp. 24. H. 6753

In 1867, two societies, united under the name of "Boston Port and Seamen's Aid Society," and published a "First Annual Report ... . *Boston.* 1868." 8vo, pp. 42, (1). H. Other reports.

Public Garden. Report of the Joint Committee on Public Lands in relation to the Public Garden, July, 1850. *Boston.* 1850. 8vo, pp. 52. Map. 6754

Public Lands. Report of the Committee chosen by the Inhabitants of ... Boston ... [on] the Expediency of authorizing the

City Council to make sale of the Uplands and Flats, lying west of Charles Street. [*Boston.*] 1824. 8vo, pp. 21, (1). H.

Public Latin School. Materials for a Catalogue of the Masters and Scholars who have belonged to the Public Latin School, Boston, Massachusetts, From 1635 to 1846. ... *Boston: Wm. Crosby and H. P. Nichols.* 1847. pp. vii, 72. H. 6756

This school publishes annual catalogues.

Prize Book Of the Public Latin School. No. 1. *Boston.* 1820. 8vo. + No. 4. *Boston.* 1823. 6757

Boston Prize Poems, and other Specimens of Dramatic Poetry. *Boston.* 1824. 12mo. 6758

Public Library. Advertisement of the Commissioners for Designs for a Library Building, January, 1855. [*Boston.* 1855.] 8vo, pp. 4. 6759

Also: Annual Report of the Public Library of the City of Boston ... 1852. *Boston.* 1852. 8vo. Continued. — Catalogue of Books. *Boston: J. Wilson & Son.* 1854. 8vo, pp. iv, 180. — Communication from Hon. Edward Everett; with Catalogue of Books presented by him to the City of Boston. *Boston.* 1851. 8vo, pp. 27. — First Report of the Commissioners, March, 1855. [*Boston.* 1855.] 8vo, pp. 9. — Index to the Catalogue of Books in the Upper Hall of the Public Library of the City of Boston. ... *Boston.* 1861. Imp. 8vo, pp. vii, 902. — First Supplement. *Boston.* 1866. Imp. 8vo, pp. v, 718, Index to the City Documents, 21. — Index to the Catalogue of a Portion of the Public Library of the City of Boston, arranged in the Lower Hall. ... *Boston.* 1858. Rl. 8vo, pp. iv, 204. — Proceedings at the Dedication of the Building for the Public Library ... January, 1858. *Boston.* 1858. Rl. 8vo, pp. 194. Plate. — Proceedings on the occasion of Laying the Corner-Stone of the Public Library ... 17 September, 1855. *Boston: Moore & Crosby.* 1855. 8vo, pp. 72. — Report of the Trustees ... July, 1852. *Boston.* 1852. 8vo, pp. 24. — Report of the Committee on the Library, in relation to the Donations received from the City of Paris ... with the Proceedings of the City Government upon the Subject of International Exchanges. *Boston.* 1849. 8vo, pp. 72. — First Annual Report of the Trustees, 1853. [*Boston.* 1853.] 8vo, pp. 9. Continued. — ... Report upon opening the Reading Room ... on Sundays. 1867. 8vo, pp. 6.

Public Schools. Report of a Special Committee of the Grammar School Board, presented August 29, 1849, on the Petition of Sundry Colored Persons, praying for the Abolition of the Smith School [for Colored Children]. With an Appendix. *Boston.* 1849. 8vo, pp. 71. 6760

First Semi-Annual Report of the Superintendent of Public Schools of the City of Boston. Second Edition. *Boston: J. H. Eastburn, City Printer.* 1852. 8vo, pp. 48. Continued. 6761

Review of the Reports of the Annual Visiting Committees of

the Public Schools of the City of Boston, for 1845. *Boston: Charles Stimpson.* 1846. 8vo, pp. 58. 6762

The Scholiast Schooled. An Examination of the Review of the Reports of the Annual Visiting Committee, &c., by Scholiast. *Cambridge.* 1846. 8vo, pp. 65. 6763

Some Observations ... on Public Education based upon a Report of the Superintendent of the Boston Schools. By a Citizen. *Boston: Alfred Mudge & Son.* 1865. 12mo, pp. 44.

Triumph of Equal School Rights in Boston. Proceedings of the Presentation Meeting held in Boston, Dec. 17, 1855; including Addresses by John T. Hilton, Wm. C. Nell, Charles W. Slack, Wendell Phillips, Wm. Lloyd Garrison, Charles Lenox Remond. *Boston: R. F. Wallcut.* 1856. 12mo, pp. 24.

Railroads. The Railroad Jubilee. An Account of the Celebration commemorative of the Opening of Railroad Communication between Boston and Canada, September 17th, 18th and 19th, 1851. *Boston: J. H. Eastburn.* 1851. 8vo, pp. 288. Map. 6766

Brief Statement of Facts in Relation to the Proposed Railroad from Boston to Fitchburg. *Charlestown.* 1842. 8vo, pp. 22.

A Tabular Representation of the Present Condition of Boston, in relation to Railroad Facilities, Foreign Commerce, Population, Wealth, Manufactures, &c. &c. Also, a few statements relative to the commerce of the Canadas, prepared for the Railroad Celebration. *Boston.* 1851. 8vo, pp. 28. Map. P. 6768

Also: Remonstrance of the Boston and Lowell Railroad Corporation in the Matter of Petitions for Leave to construct Railroads, 1845. [n. p.] 1845. 8vo, pp. 6. — Report of a Committee on the Boston and Lowell Railroad. *Boston.* 1831. 8vo. — Report of the Directors, 1844. *Boston.* 1845. Continued. — Charter of the Boston and Lowell Railroad, and Report of the Directors, 1848. *Boston.* 1849. 8vo, pp. 36. — Report of the Committee of Investigation appointed by the Stockholders of the Boston and Maine Railroad, at a Meeting at Exeter, N. H., May 28, 1849. *Boston.* 1849. 8vo, pp. 79. Maps. B. — Report of the Directors to the Stockholders, September, 1849. 8vo. Continued. — Report of a Committee of Stockholders of the Boston and Portland Railroad. *Andover.* 1840. 8vo, pp. 7. — Report on a Railroad from Boston to the Hudson River, and from Boston to Providence. *Boston.* 1829. 8vo. P. — Boston and Providence Railroad Corporation. Report of the Board of Commissioners of Internal Improvement in Relation to the Examination of different Routes. *Boston.* 1828. 8vo, pp. 72. — First Annual Report of the Directors of the Boston and Providence Rail Road Corporation. *Boston.* 1833. 8vo. Continued. — Report of the Board of Directors to the Stockholders of the Boston and Providence Railroad Company. *Boston.* 1832. 8vo. — Report of the Grantees of

the Boston and Providence Railroad Company and Lowell Railroad Corporation, with the Report of the Engineer. 8vo. — Report of the Committee for investigating the Affairs of the Boston and Providence Railroad Corporation, appointed January, 1856. *Boston.* 1856. 8vo, pp. 31. — Report of the Directors; with Reports of Engineer, and Plans, 1832. *Boston.* 1832. 8vo, pp. 87. — Report of the Directors, June, 1849. *Boston.* 1849. 8vo, pp. 22. Continued. — Statement by the Boston and Providence Railroad Corporation in Explanation of their Proceedings in Relation to the Steamboats. *Boston.* 1838. 8vo, pp. 11. — Act of Incorporation and By Laws of the Boston and Worcester Rail Road Corporation. *Boston.* 1831. 12mo. — The Act to establish the Boston and Worcester Railroad Corporation. *Boston.* 1833. 12mo, pp. 29. — Report of the Directors at a Special Meeting of the Boston and Worcester Rail Road, Jan. 18, 1833. *Boston.* 1833. 8vo, pp. 23. W. — Report of the Directors of the Boston and Worcester Rail Road Corporation to the Stockholders; together with the report of John M. Fessenden, Esq., Civil Engineer, and a Plan and Profile of the Location of the Railroad. *Boston.* 1832. 8vo, pp. 40. — Annual Report of the Boston & Worcester Rail-Road Corporation, ... 1831, ... *Boston.* 1832. 8vo. Continued. — Report of the Committee of the Boston and Worcester and Western Railroad Corporations on the Subject of uniting the two Railroads. *Boston.* 1846. 8vo, pp. 54.

Roxbury. Report of the Committee in Favor of the Union of Boston and Roxbury. *Boston: Eastburn's Press.* 1851. 8vo, pp. 35. 6769

Reports in relation to the Annexation of Roxbury to Boston, and the Act of the Legislature to unite said Cities. *Boston.* 1867. 8vo, pp. 35. H. 6770

Sailor's Snug Harbor. Proceedings on the Occasion of Laying the Corner-Stone of the Sailor's Snug Harbor of Boston, On July 14, 1856. *Boston.* 1857. 8vo, pp. 30. H. 6771

Also: "Report ... . *Boston.* 1861." 8vo, pp. 23, (1). H.

Seamen's Aid Society. First Annual Report of the Seamen's Aid Society, of the City of Boston. *Boston.* 1834. 12mo, pp. 18. Continued in 8vo. 6772

Social-Law Library. Rules and Catalogue of the Social Law Library. *Boston.* 1814. 8vo, pp. 24. + *Boston.* 1824. 8vo, pp. 32. + Third Edition. *Boston.* 1865. 8vo, pp. vi, 281. C.

Society of Natural History. Annual Report of the Boston Society of Natural History 1868–69. I ... . *Boston: the Society.* 1868. 16mo, pp. 127, (1). H. 6774

Contains (pp. 26–48) "Sketch of the History and Present Operations of the Society."

Boston Journal of Natural History, containing Papers and Communications read to the Boston Society of Natural History, 1833–1837. *Boston: Hilliard, Gray, and Company.* MDCCCXXXVII. 8vo, Title, pp. 536. Plates. Continued. H.

A list of the contents of Vol. I.–VI. will be found in Trübner's "Bib. Guide."

Proceedings of the Boston Society of Natural History. *Boston. the Society.* 1844. 8vo, Title, pp. 221, (Corrections) 1 slip. Continued. 6776

Superior Court. Remarks on "An Act to establish the Superior Court of the City of Boston" ... . By a Citizen. *Boston.* 1849. 8vo, pp. 39. + Supplement. *Boston.* 1849. 8vo, pp. 14.

Tea Party. A Retrospect of the Boston Tea Party, with a memoir of G. R. T. Hewes. By a citizen of New York. [J. Hawkes?] *New York.* 1834. 12mo. 6778

Tontine. Constitution of the Boston Tontine Association. *Boston.* M.DCCXCI. 12mo, pp. 19. N. 6779

Water. ... An Act for supplying the City of Boston with Pure Water. [*Boston.* 1846.] 8vo, pp. 12. H. 6780

Address of the Faneuil Hall Committee, on the Project of a Supply of Pure Water ... May 5, 1845. *Boston.* [n. d.] 8vo, pp. 32. H. 6781

Arguments and Statements addressed to the Members of the Legislature, in relation to the Petition of the City of Boston for Power to bring into the City the Water of Long Pond. ... *Boston.* 1845. 8vo, pp. 25. 6782

Bericht der Cochituate-Wasserleitungs-Commission an den Stadtrath von Boston im J. 1852. ... Aus dem Englischen übersetzt von Ingen. Alfr. Lenz. *Wein: Gerold's Sohn.* 1866. 8vo, pp. vii, 47. 6783

Boston Aqueduct and the City of Boston. [From the Daily Evening Transcript, July and Aug. 1849. *Boston.* n. d.] 12mo, pp. 48. H. 6784

Celebration of the Introduction of the Water of Cochituate Lake into the City of Boston. October 25, 1848. *Boston.* [1848.] 8vo, pp. 48. 6785

History of the Introduction of Pure Water into ... Boston. 1868. *See* [Bradlee (N. J.)]

Also: Communication to the City Council [from the Mayor, Theodore Lyman, jun.], on the Subject of Introducing Water into the City. ... *Boston.* 1834. 8vo, pp. 39. H. — Document. No. 9. Papers relating to the Introduction of Pure Water. *Boston.* 1838. 8vo, pp. 28, 26, 16, 13. H. — Hints to the Honest Tax Payers ... . [*Boston.* 1844?] 8vo, pp. 8. H. — How shall we Vote on the Water Act? [n. p. 1845.] 8vo, pp. 24. — Inquiry into the best Mode of supplying the City of Boston with Water ... in reply to

... Mr. Wilkins and Mr. Shattuck ... [etc.] By a Member of the Late Board of Water Commissioners. *Boston.* 1845. 8vo, pp. 70. H. — ... Memorial ... presented to the Board of Common Councilmen ... by the Boston Aqueduct Corporation. ... March 19, 1838. [n. p. n. d.] 8vo, pp. 8. H. — Report of the Commissioners appointed ... March 16, 1837, to devise a Plan for supplying the City of Boston with Pure Water. *Boston: John H. Eastburn, City Printer.* 1837. 8vo, pp. 83. H. + [*Id.*] 8vo, pp. 95. 2 Maps. H. — Report of the Commissioners appointed ... August 26, 1844, to report the best Mode and Expense of bringing the Water of Long Pond into the City of Boston. *Boston.* 1844. 8vo, pp. 32. — Report of the Commissioners appointed ... to examine the Sources from which a Supply of Pure Water may be obtained for the City of Boston. *Boston: J. H. Eastburn, City Printer.* 1845. 8vo, 2. l., pp. 128, xxxii. Map. — Statement of Evidence before the Committee of the Legislature, at the Session of 1839, on the Petition of the City of Boston, for the Introduction of Pure Soft Water. *Boston.* 1839. 8vo, pp. 62. H. — Proceedings before a Joint Special Committee of the Massachusetts Legislature, upon the Petition of the City of Boston, for Leave to introduce a Supply of Pure Water into that City, from Long Pond. February and March, 1845. Reported ... by Nathan Hale, Jr. *Boston.* 1845. 8vo, pp. viii, 144. H. — Arguments and Statements addressed to the ... Legislature, in relation to the Petition of the City of Boston for Power to bring into the City the Water of Long Pond. By a Remonstrant. *Boston.* 1845. 8vo, pp. 25. H. — Thoughts about Water. [*Boston.* Aug. 31, 1844.] 8vo, pp. 16.

Widows' Society. Constitution of the Widows' Society ... with some Account of ... its Proceedings to the Present ... [and] a List of its Members. *Boston.* 1823. 8vo, pp. 16. H.

Young Men's Christian Association. Third Annual Report of the Army Committee of the Boston Young Men's Christian Association. ... [*Boston.* 1864.] 8vo, pp. 36. H. 6787

BOSTWICK (D.) A Fair and Rational Vindication of the Right of Infants To the Ordinance of Baptism. By David Bostwick ... . *New-York. London: Re-printed for Edward and Charles Dilly.* MDCCLXV. 8vo, pp. 54. H. + *New Brunswick.* 1790. 8vo, pp. 63. 6788

The preface contains "Some Strictures of his Person and Character." — pp. v–viii.

BOSTWICK. Self Disclaimed and Christ Exalted; a Sermon preached at Philadelphia, before the Reverend Synod of New York, May 25th, 1758. By David Bostwick, A.M. Published at the Request of the Members of the Synod. [Mottoes.] *Philadelphia: Printed by W. Dunlap.* M.DCC.LVIII. 12mo, pp. 54. + *London: reprinted.* 1759. 8vo, pp. 43. + *London.* 1776.

Concerning this sermon, *see* Allen's "Biographical Dictionary."

BOSTWICK (E.) A Genealogical Register of the Name of Bostwick, with the Families in their respective Generations, Births, Marriages and Deaths, as far as obtained, from 1668 to 1850. By Erastus Bostwick. *Burlington: Printed by Tuttle & Stacy.* 1851. 12mo, pp. 50. 6790

BOSTWICK (E. B.) *See* Almy (J.) and Bostwick. Vol. I., No. 957.

BOSTWICK (Henry). Lectures upon Portions of History, with Historical Outlines for the Use of Schools. *New York.* 1838. 8vo, pp. 154. 6791

BOSWORTH (B.) Signs of Apostacy | Lamented. [A Poem. Signed] Benjamin Bosworth, | of New England. | In the 81st Year of my Age, 1693. | 12mo, pp. 4. 6792

The following opinion on perriwigs possess more force than elegance:

"Art thou a Christian, O then why dost wear
Upon thy Sacred Head, the filthy Hair
Of some vile wretch, by foul Disease that fell,
Whose Soul perhaps is burning now in Hell?"

BOSWORTH (N.) Hochelaga Depicta: the Early History and Present State of the City and Island of Montreal. With Numerous Illustrative Engravings. Edited by Newton Bosworth, ... *Montreal: William Greig.* MDCCCXXXIX. 8vo, 7 l., pp. 9–284. 16 Plates and 2 Maps. C. + *London: Simpkin.* 1840. 12mo. + *Montreal.* 1846. 8vo. + New Edition. 1867. 6793

BOTELER. Speech of Hon. Alexander R. Boteler, of Virginia, on the Organization of the House, delivered in the House of Representatives January 25, 1860. *Washington, D. C.: William H. Moore.* 1860. 8vo, pp. 16. + [*Washington: printed by Lemuel Towers.* n. d.] 8vo, pp. 8. H. 6794

BOTELHO (José de S. Bernardino). Epistola ao serenissimo sr. D. José, principe do Brasil, no dia 21 de Augusto de 1778. *Lisboa na Regia Offic. Typ.* 1788. 8vo, pp. 10. (In verse.)

BOTELHO. Oraçao de serenissimo Sr D. José, principe do Brasil, pronunciado nas exequias solemnes que fez celebrar o Senado da Camara da villa de Torres-novas. *Lisboa, na Regia Offic. Typ.* 1788. 8vo. 6796

BOTELLO DE MORAES Y VASCONCELOS (F.) El Nuevo Mundo. | Poemma heroyco de D. Francisco Botello | de Moraes y Vasconcelos; | con las Alegorias de Don Pedro de | Castro, Cavallero Andaluz. | Dedicalo sv Avtor | a la | Catholica Magestad | de | Philippo Qvinto, | Avgvsto, piadoso, feliz Rey de las | Españas, y Indias. | Por mano del Ilvstrissimo Señor | D. Manvel de Toledo | General de Batalla en los exercitos | de su Magestad, &c. | Con licencia: *Barcelona*, | *en la Imprenta de* | *Ivan Pablo Marti*, *por* | *Francisco Barnola Impressor*, *Año* 1701. | *Vendese en su misma Casa, en la Plaça de San Iayme, y à su Costa*. 4to, 16 l., pp. 476.

BOTELLO. El Colon; poema de D. Francisco de Moraes Vasconcelos y Botello. *Madrid*. 1716. 4to. 6798

"The foundation of this poem is the 'Nuevo Mundo' described above. A few cantos only were printed, and are sometimes met with, without title or preliminaries, and it is only from Barcia's edition of Pinelo (1737) that the time and place of publication are ascertained." — RICH. Silva, II. 359, makes no mention of this work.

BOTERO (G.) Commentariolus Parallelvs, sive Libellus Assertorius (quo Principum Scilicet et Indiarum Regis Augustissimi, Regis Philippi inquam Secundi, et Turcici Magni Imp. Mahumetis Tertii Vires, Opes, Provinciæ, atque forma eas bene administrandi et regendi tempore belli atque pacis Explicantur, armaq. et arcana deteguntur). *Col. Agrip.* 1597. 4to. 2 Maps.

Contains a description of New Spain. One of the maps indicates "America sive India nova anno Dei. 1492 a Christ. Colombo detecta."

BOTERO. Relationi vniversali, nella quale si contiene la descrittione di tutta la terra: i monti, laghi, fiumi, minere, et opre marauigliose in essa dalla natura prodotte: L'isole, et penisole de l'Oceano, et del Mediterraneo: Le prouincie, le città i costumi de' popoli, et le conditioni de' paesi. *Bergamo: Comin Ventura*. 1594–95. 2 pts., 8vo, 3 l., pp. 408; 10 l., 214.

"Deuxième édition de ces deux premières parties, non citée par Haym. Cet ouvrage qui a eu un grand succès, a été supprimé a cause d'un passage dans la 2e partie, au chapitre intitulé: 'Forze del regno di Francia.' pp. 16–23." — LECLERC, No. 188.

BOTERO. Delle | relationi | vniversali | di Giovanni Botero | Benese. | Parte Prima. | Nella qvale si da | raguaglio de' Continenti, e dell' Isole sino | al presente scouerte. | Revista dall' avtore, e | di nuouo arricchita in infiniti luoghi di cose | memorabili, e curiose. | ... | *In Roma*, | ... *Appresso Giorgio Ferrari*. | M. D. XCV. | 3 vols., 4to, 4 l., pp. 403. 6 l.; Title ("Relatione ... del Mondo nuouo"), 2 l., 98, 3 l.; Title, 2 l., 161, 3 l. BA. 6801

The last paging but one has the title:

BOTERO. Relatione | vniversale | De' Continente del Mondo nuouo. | Di Giovanni Botero | [6 lines.] | [Imprint, 3 lines, as before.] 6802

BOTERO. Delle | relationi | vniversali | ... | ... | Parte seconda.

| [3 lines.] | *In Roma*, | ... *Georgio Ferrari*. M. D. XCII. | [2 lines.] | 4to, 2 l., pp. 282, (14). BA. 6803

"Mondo nvovo," pp. 257, 258. A catalogue of Puttick's (1860) cites editions, *Brescia*. 1598. 4to. + *Venetia*. 1600. 4to.

BOTERO (Giovanni). Le | Relationi | Vniversali | di Giovanni Botero | Benese, | Divise en Qvattro Parti. | Nella Prima Parte si contiene la descrittione dell' Europa, dell' Asia, | e dell' Africa; & i costumi, ricchezze, negotij, & industria di cia- | scuna natione. Et si tratta del Continente del Mondo Nuouo. | etc. *In Venetia: Nicolò Polo*. M.D.XCVII. | 3 pts., 4to, 16 l., pp. 240, 80, 4 Maps; 10 l., 152; 183, Tables, 9 l., 79. 6804

BOTERO. Le relationi universali divise in quattro parti; nella prima ... si tratta del continente del Mondo Nuovo; ... nella quarta delle superstizioni in che vivevano già le genti del Mondo Nuovo. *Venetia*. 1602. 4 vols., 4to. 6805

BOTERO. Le relationi vniversali di Giovanni Botero, Benese, divise in sette parti. ... Con le Figure, & due copiosissime Tauole. ... Nuouamente ristampate, & ricorrette. *Venetia: Alessandro Vecchi*. M DC XVIII. 8 pts., 4to, 15 l., pp. 208, 72; Title, 9 l., pp. 131; Title, pp. 156, (8); Title, 7 l., pp. 68; Title ("Aggivnta ... . Di Mostri, & Vsanze ... con le sue Figure ... . Raccolte ... da ... Vecchi"), 31 l; Title, 3 l., pp. 56; Title, 3 l., pp. 52; ("Saggio dell' opera, De' prencipi ... Del Sig. ... Botero ... . *Venetia: Alessandro Vecchi*. MDCXVII."), pp. 22. BA. 6806

[BOTERO.] Le Relationi ... Et si tratta del Continente del Mondo nuevo et dell' Isole & Penisole sino al pres. scoperte ... delle superstitione in che viuevano già le gente del Mondo nuevo, e delle difficoltà, e mezi, co' quali si è quiui introdotta la religione christiana &c. *Venetia*. 1622. 4to. + *Venetia*. 1640. 4to.

BOTERO. Allgemeine historische Weltbeschreibung. Ioannis Boteri desz Benesers. In vier Bücher abgetheilt. Im ersten wirdt beschrieben Europa, Asia, Affrica, dessgleichen die Newe Welt. Aus dem Italian durch Aeg. Albertinum übersetzt Mit künstlichen Landtafeln gezieret. *München: Nicollas Henry*. 1611. Folio, 10 l., pp. 471. 5 Maps. J. B. C. + *München*. 1612. Folio. + *München*. 1661. Folio. 6808

BOTERO. Relaciones | vniversales | Del mundo de Iuan Botero Benes, Primera, | y Segunda Parte, Traduzidas ... | ... | ... por su Magestad: por el Li- | cenciado Diego de Aguiar ... | ... |

... | ... | ... | *Año* 1603 | *Impresso en Valladolid por los herederos de Diego* | *Fernandez de Cordoua*. | *Vendase en casa de Martin de Cardoua*. Folio, (4). 24, 207, 110 l. H. 6809

The colophon of "la segunda parte" has the date M.D.XCIX. *See* Rich's Catalogue, No. 96.

BOTERO. Description de todas las provincias, reynos, estados, y ciudades principales del mundo [trad.] por Fr. Jayme Rebullosa de la orden de Predicadores. *Gorona: por Jayme Brò*. 1748. 4to, 5 l., pp. 456. 6810

The description of America occupies pp. 276–340.

BOTERO. An | Historicall description | of the most famous kingdomes and | Common-weales in the | Worlde. | Relating their situations, man- | ners, customes, ciuill gouernment, and | other memorable matters. | Translated into English, and enlarged, with an Addition | of the Relation of the states of Saxony, Geneua, | Hungary and Spaine; in no language | euer before imprinted. | *Printed at London for Iohn Iaggard*, 1603. | 2 l., pp. 268. 6811

On page 11, the author remarks: "Mexicana is, on all sides, surrounded by the sea, saving that nigh unto Nombre de Dios, it is ioyned by a necke of land to Peruana, &c.," 17 lines; on p. 32, "New Worlde," 4 pages.

BOTERO. Relations of the Most Famous Kingdoms and Common-Wealths thorowout [*sic*] the World. Translated out of the Italian, by R. J.; now once againe inlarged. *London: John Partridge*. 1630. 4to. C. 6812

The map contains portraits of Sir F. Drake, F. Magellan, T. Cavendish, and O. Vander Noort, by Vaughan. I have seen this work described as "Englished by R. Peterson." Sold at Puttick's, 1860, for £2 6s.

Both Sides of the Question, or a Candid and Impartial Enquiry into a Certain Doubtful Character lately whitened by a C——t. M——l in a Letter to a General Officer, acquitted by Court Martial. [n. p.] 1749. 8vo. 6814

Relating to Georgia, South Carolina, and the seige of St. Augustine.

Both Sides; or, a Short Chapter of Facts. [*Boston*. 1848.] 8vo, pp. 4. H. 6815

States the anti-slavery record of Martin Van Buren, and of Gen. Taylor and his supporters.

Both Sides, or The Real State of Parties. 8vo, pp. 8. 6816

Signed, "Jefferson." Relates to the tariff.

Botschafft des Groszmechtigsten. *See* Zummaraga (J.)

Botschaft über den Vertrag zwischen den Vereinigten Staaten Amerikas und der schweizerischen Eidgenossenschaft. [*Bern?* 1851?] 8vo, pp. 43. 6817

BOTTA (C.) Storia della guerra dell' independenza degli Stati Uniti d'America. Scritta da Carlo Botta. *Parigi: D. Colas*. 1809. 4 vols., 8vo, 2 l., pp. xj, viij, 363; 2 l., pp. 543; 2 l., pp. 553; 2 l., pp. 477. H. + Terza edizione, con alcune correzione dell' autore. *Milano*. 1819. 4 vols., 8vo, pp. lxxxiv, 348; 511; 523; 479, Lista, viii. 4 Portraits, and 2 Maps. + *Milano*. 1820. 4 vols., 8vo. + *Firenze*. 1822. 4 vols., 8vo. + *Milano*. 1822. 3 vols., 8vo. + *Milano*. 1824–25. 6 vols., 16mo. + *Livorno: Pietro Meucci*. 1825–26. 7 vols., 8vo, pp. 215; 180; 208; 236; 220; 276; 227. + *Firenze*. 1825. 10 vols., 24mo. + *Milano*. 1827. 4 vols., 8vo. + *Milano*. 1830. 4 vols., 18mo. + *Torino*. 1832. 8 vols., 18mo. (Biblioteca popolare.) + *Padua*. 1833. 6 vols., 16mo.. + *Torino*. 1833. 5 vols., 8vo. + *Livorno: Bertani, Antonelli, e c.* 1836. 8vo, pp. viii, 568. Portrait, and 13 Plates. H. + *Livorno*. 1837 [or 1839 or both?] 8vo. Plates. + *Milano*. 1841. 8vo, pp. 580. + *Milano: Borroni e Scotti*. 1844. 2 vols., 8vo. Frontispiece. + *Milano*. 1850. 2 vols., 8vo. + *Firenze: Felice Le Monnier*. 1856. 2 vols., 8vo, 2 l., pp. lxii, 556; 2 l., pp. 634. B. + *Torino*. 1858. 2 vols., 12mo. 6818

The plates in the Livorno edition of 1836 are very amusing; the scenery and architecture are entirely Italian.

BOTTA. Histoire de la guerre de l'indépendence des États-Unis d'Amérique. Par Mr Charles Botta ... . Traduite de l'italien et précédée d'une introduction, par Mr L. D. Sevelinges. Ouvrage orné de plans et cartes géographiques. *Paris: J. G. Dentu*. 1812–13. 4 vols., 8vo, 3 l., pp. xc, 409; 2 l., pp. 593; 2 l., pp. 603; 2 l., pp. 550. Atlas, Portrait, Maps, and Plans. 6819

See N. A. R., XIII. 169.

BOTTA. History of the War of the Independence of the United States of America. Written by Charles Botta. Translated from the Italian, by George Alexander Otis. ... *Philadelphia: Printed for the Translator*. 1820. 3 vols., 8vo, pp. 448; v, 567; xii, 503. H. 6820

See N. A. R., XIII. 163. Frequently reprinted, with the following title:

BOTTA. History of the War of the Independence of the United States of America. By Charles Botta. Translated

from the Italian, by George Alexander Otis, Esq. Second Edition, in Two Volumes, Revised and Corrected. *Boston: Published by Harrison Gray*. 1826. 2 vols., medium 8vo, pp. viii, 6-414; 455. + *Glasgow: Fullarton & Co.* 1844. Rl. 8vo, pp. 584. Map and Plates. + Seventh Edition, In Two Volumes, Revised and Corrected. *New Haven: Nathan Whiting*. [n. d.] 2 vols., 8vo, pp. 472; 468. Maps and Plate. + Eighth Edition ... . *New-Haven*. 1838. 2 vols., 8vo, pp. 472; 468. Map, Woodcuts, and 2 Plates. BA. + Ninth Edition. *New Haven*. 1839. 2 vols., 8vo. + *New Haven*. 1840. 2 vols., 8vo. + *Cooperstown*. 1845. 2 vols., 8vo, pp. 472, 468. + *Cooperstown*. 1848. 2 vols., 8vo. + Tenth Edition. *Buffalo*. 1852. 2 vols., 8vo. + *Buffalo*. 1854. 6821

BOTTA (V.) Resolutions on the Death of President Lincoln, offered By Professor Vincenzo Botta, at the Meeting of the Italian Residents of New York ... April 23, 1865 ... . [n. p. n. d.] 8vo, pp. (4). H. 6822

Botta wrote "La questione americana" in the "Revista contemporanea," 1861, pp. 241–255.

BOTTARELLI (Giovanni Gualberto). The Conquest of Mexico, an Opera, Italian and English. [Probably] *London*. 1767. 8vo. 6823

BOTTEN-HANSEN (Paul). Mormonismens Historie tilligemed en kort Oversigt over Sektens Troeslaerdomme og Kirkeforfatning. ... *Christiania*. 1853. 8vo, pp. vi, 52. 6824

"Isaer efter det Tydske." Republished from "Illustreret Nyhedsblad" for 1853.

BÖTTGER (Adolf). Habana. Lyrisch-epische Dichtung. 1853. + Zweite Auflage. *Leipzig: Costenoble*. 1854. 16mo, pp. x, 1 l., pp. 210. 6825

BÖTTGER (C.) Einige wichtige Ansiedelungsgebiete in Texas, nach Original-Aufnahmen ... entworfen. [Beilage zur Allgem. Auswanderungs-Zeitung.] *Rudolstadt: Fröbel*. 1848. Folio. A colored Lithograph. 6826

BOTTS (J. M.) Address to the Citizens of Richmond on the Subject of constructing a continuous Railroad Communication from their City to the Waters of the Ohio. *Richmond: printed by Colan and Nowen*. 1852. 8vo, pp. 14. H. 6827

Signed by John M. Botts and eight others.

BOTTS. The Great Rebellion: its Secret History, Rise, Progress, and Disastrous Failure. By John Minor Botts, of Virginia. The Political Life of the Author Vindicated. ... *New York: Harper & Brothers*. 1866. 12mo, pp. 402. Portrait.

BOTTS. Letter of Hon. John M. Botts to Hon. Edward Bates. [Dated] Richmond, April 19, 1861. [n. p. n. d.] 8vo, pp. 8. H. 6829

BOTTS. Letters of John Minor Botts ... . on the Nebraska Question. *Washington*. 1853 [1854]. 8vo, pp. 16. BA. 6830

BOTTS. The Past, the Present, and the Future of our Country. ... Correspondence between the Opposition Members of the Legislature of Virginia and Hon. John Minor Botts, January 17, 1860. *Washington*. [n. d.] 8vo, pp. 16. H. 6831

BOTTS. ... Report prepared by Mr. Botts ... [on the Bill to raise Ten Additional Regiments for the War with Mexico] for Presentation, but ... precluded by the Treaty of Peace. [*Washington*. 1848.] Large 12mo, pp. 23. H. 6832

Also: Speech ... on the New-Jersey Contested Election. ... In the House ... January 9, 1840. *Washington*. 1839. 8vo, pp. 16. B., H. — Speech ... at a Dinner at Powhatan Court-House, Va., June 15, 1850. 8vo, pp. 15. — Speech ... on the Objections of the President [Tyler] to the Bill to establish a Fiscal Corporation, House of Representatives, Sept. 10, 1841. *Washington*. 1841. 8vo, pp. 16. — Speech ... on the Political Issues of the Day, delivered at Richmond, Aug. 8, 1856. *Richmond*. 1856. 8vo, pp. 31. — Speech ... at the Academy of Music, New York, on the 22d February, 1859. *New York*. [1859.] 8vo, pp. 40. — Substance of the Remarks made by John Minor Botts, On ... the Entertainment given to him ... in ... Richmond ... 2d December, with some additions ... . *Washington*. [1848.] 8vo, pp. 16. H. — To the Whigs of Virginia. [*Washington*.] 1848. 8vo, pp. 15. H. — To the Whole Whig Party of the United States. [*Washington*. 1848.] 8vo, pp. 16. H.

BOTURINI BENADUCI. (L.) Catalogo del museo historico indiano del Cavallero Lorenzo Boturini Benaduci ... quien llegò a la Nueva España por Febrero del año 1736 ... . [n. p. n. d.] 4to, pp. 96. 6833

BOTURINI BENADUCI. Idea de una nueva historia general de la America Septentrional. Fundada sobre material copioso de figuras, Symbolos, Caractères, y Geroglificos, Cantares, y Manuscritos de Autores Indios, ultimamente descubiertos. Dedicala al Rey N.tro Señor en su Real, y Supremo Consejo de las Indias el Cavallero Lorenzo Boturini Benaduci, Señor de la Torre, y de Hono. Con Licencia. *En Madrid: En la Imprenta de Juan de Zuñiga*. *Año* M. D. CC. XLVI. 4to, engraved

Frontispiece and Portrait, 20 l., pp. 167, Catalogo, 4 l., pp. 96. H. 6834

"The curious and learned author of this work arrived in Mexico in 1750; and, desirous of writing the history of that kingdom, he made, during eight years he remained there, the most diligent researches into its antiquity; acquired a considerable mastery of the Mexican language, entered into friendship with the Indians to obtain their ancient pictures from them, and procured copies of many valuable manuscripts which were in the libraries of the monasteries." — CLAVIGERO. And *see* Bartolache's "Manifiesto," pp. 42, 43, Prescott's "Mexico," Bustamente (C. M.), etc. The appendix to this work is of the highest bibliographical interest. It contains a catalogue of a rich collection of books, MSS., and maps, relating to the early history of Mexico, which Boturini made during his travels in the middle of the last century, and which, unfortunately, is now lost. In consequence of a legal process, in which Boturini was cast, the whole of his museum was confiscated by the Viceroy of Mexico (1743), and has been given up, since that period, to the destroying hand of time. It was first deposited in the Office of the Secretary Viceroy, where it sustained heavy damages by the neglect of its keepers. What remained was transferred, at a later period, to the library of the university, and reduced there, by the same unfortunate circumstances, almost to nothing. The last remains of the collection were kept, in 1853, in the Museo Nacional of Mexico. *See* Icazbalzeta's "Notice on the Life and Writings of Boturini" in the "Diccionario universal de historia y de geografia," Vol. I., pp. 666. *Mexico*. 1853. "Ce livre est rare en Europe. ... Vendu avec le 'Catalogo del Museo,' 100 flor. Meerman; seul, 43 fr. et 20 fr. Raetzel." — BRUNET. Lord Rothesay's Copy sold for £3 3s.

BOTURINI BENADUCI. Tezcoco en los ultimos tiempos de sus antiguos reyes, ó sea Relacion tomada de los manuscritos ineditos de Boturini; redactados por el Licenciado D. Mariano Veytia, publicalos con notas y adiciones ... Don Carlos Maria de Bustamante. *Mexico: imprenta de Mariano Galvan Rivera*. 1826. Sm. 4to, 4 l., pp. 276, Table, 4 l. C. 6835

BOUCARUT (A.) Manuel de la navigation dans le Rio de la Plata; d'après les documents nautiques les plus récents ... par A. Boucarut ... . *Paris: Ledoyen*. 1857. 8vo, pp. 128. 6836

Reprinted from the "Annales hydrographiques," 1856.

BOUCHACOURT. Notice industrielle sur la Californie par M. Ch. Bouchacourt ... . *Paris: F. Mathias*. *Lyon: Ch. Savy jeune*. 1849. 8vo, pp. 72. 6837

BOUCHARD DE LA POTERIE (Claude Florent). A Pastoral Letter, From the Apostolic Vice-Prefect, Curate of the Holy Cross at Boston. [*Boston*. 1789.] 4to, pp. 24, (1). H. 6838

Also: To the Publick. [Dated Boston, January 29, 1789. An Appeal for aid in paying the debts of the Catholic Church of the Holy Cross in Boston. n. p. n. d.] 4to, 1 page. H. — To the Publick. Vindication and credentials. n. p. 1789. 4to, pp. 4. H.

BOUCHER (J.) A View of the Cause and Consequences of

the American Revolution, in Thirteen Discourses, Preached in North America, between the Years 1763 and 1775: with an Historical Preface. By Jonathan Boucher ... Vicar of Epsom ... Surrey. *London: G. G. & A. J. Robinson*. M.DCC.XCVII. 4 l., pp. xcv, 596. C. H. 6839

"Dedicated to Washington. The author was a refugee, who returned to England, on account of his political principles, in 1775, and died there, in 1804. In the preface, he passes in review the different histories of the American Revolution, all of which are censured as partial and defective, not even excepting the account in the Annual Register, said to be written by Burke." — M. R., XXIX. 369.

[BOUCHER.] Histoire de la dernière guerre entre la Grande-Bretagne, et les Etats-Unis de l'Amérique, la France, l'Espagne et la Hollande depuis son commencement en 1775, jusqu'à sa fin en 1783. ... Ornée de Cartes géographiques & marines. *A Paris: Chez Brocas*. M. DCC. LXXVII. 4to, pp. xxiv, (ii), 357, (3). 7 Maps, 2 folded sheets. C. + *Paris: Brocas*. 1787. 4to, pp. xxxiv, (2), 357, (3), 2 Tables, folded. H. + *Paris*. 1788. 2 vols., 8vo. 6840

[BOUCHER.] Historia de la última guerra entre la Inglaterra, los Estados-Unidos de América, la Francia, España, y Holanda, desde 1775 hasta 1783. Version del frances al castellano. *Alcala*. 1793. 2 vols., 4to. 6841

BOUCHER (Philippe) *and* GAVET (D.) Jakaré-Ouassou, ou les Tupinambas, chronique brésilienne. *Paris: Debay*. 1830. 8vo, pp. 448. 6842

[BOUCHER (Pierre).] Histoire | véritable | et | natvrelle | des | mœvrs et prodvctions | dv pays | de la Novvelle-France, | vvlgairement dite | le | Canada. | *Paris: Florentin Lambert*. M. DC. LXIV. Sm. 12mo, 12 l., pp. 168. + *Réimprimée à Quebec, par E. Fréchette, en* 1849. 8vo. 6843

"Ce petit ouvrage passe pour être fort exact. 16 fr. 50c. Eyries." — BRUNET. The author avows that the work contains nothing new; it is extracted from the Relations of the Jesuits and the Voyages of Champlain.

BOUCHER. Relation de la Novvelle-France. 1659–60. *Paris*. 1661. 8vo. 6844

BOUCHER DE LA BRUÈRE, *fils*. Le Canada sous la domination Anglaise par Boucher de la Bruère, fils. *St. Hyacinthe*. 1863. 8vo, pp. 80. 6845

BOUCHER DE LA BRUÈRE, *fils*. St. Hyacinthe: a Lecture. *St. Hyacinthe*. 1859. 12mo, pp. 16. 6846

BOUCHER DE LA RICHARDERIE (G.) Bibliothèque universelle des voyages, ou Notice complete et raisonnée de tous les Voyages anciens et modernes dans les differentes parties du monde, publiés tant en langue française qu'en langues étrangères ... classés par ordre de pays dans leur série chronologique; avec des extraits plus ou moins rapides des Voyages les plus estimés de chaque pays, et les jugements, motivés sur les Relations anciennes qui ont le plus de célébrité. Par G. Boucher de la Richarderie ... . *Paris: Treuttel et Würtz, et à Strasbourg.* 1808. 6 vols., 8vo, 2 l., pp. xxx, 495; viij, 531; vij, 503; viij, 542; vij, 527; viij, 485. 6847

In the matter of dates and titles very incorrect, but valuable for the extracts it contains from the voyages of the last century. Vol. vi. relates to America. Dibdin pronounces it "an indispensable performance."

BOUCHETTE (J.) The British Dominions in North America; or a Topographical and Statistical Description of the Provinces of Lower and Upper Canada, New Brunswick, Nova Scotia, The Islands of Newfoundland, Prince Edward, and Cape Breton. Including Considerations on Land-Granting and Emigration. To which are annexed, Statistical Tables and Tables of Distances, &c. By Joseph Bouchette, Esq., Surveyor General of Lower Canada ... Embellished with Views, Plans of Towns, Harbours, &c. ... *London: Longman, Rees, Orme, Brown, Green, and Longman.* 1832. 2 vols., 4to, pp. xxvi, (2), 498; xi, (1), 296, (1). 33 Plates. H. 6848

BOUCHETTE. A Topographical Description of the Province of Lower Canada, with Remarks upon Upper Canada, and on the Relative Connexion of both Provinces with The United States of America. By Joseph Bouchette, Esq., Surveyor-General of Lower Canada ... . *London: W. Faden.* 1815. 8vo, pp. xv, 640, lxxxvi, (2). Portrait, 8 Maps, 6 Views, 2 engraved Tables, and a large Map on 10 sheets, in two cases. C., H. 6849

BOUCHETTE. Description Topographique de la Province du Bas Canada avec des remarques sur le Haut Canada et sur les relations des deux provinces avec les Etats Unis de l'Amerique. Par Joseph Bouchette. ... Enrichie de plusieurs vues, plans de ports, de batailles, etc. *Londres: Davidson.* 1815. Rl. 8vo, pp. 664, Appendix, 86. 18 Plans, etc. 6850

BOUCHETTE. A Topographical Dictionary of the Province of Lower Canada. *London: Longman,* [etc.] 1832. 4to, pp. xii, (384). H. 6851

Usually found with No. 6848, making 3 vols., 4to.

BOUCHOT (A.) Histoire du Portugal et de ses colonies. Par Auguste Bouchot ... . *Paris: L. Hachette et Cie.* 1854. 18mo, 2 l., pp. xvi, 470, (1). 2 Maps and 2 Plans. (Hist. univ. pub. sous la direction de V. Duruy.) C., H. 6852

BOUDIN (J. Ch. M.) Statistique de la population de la France et de ses colonies, d'après les derniers recensements. Par J. Ch. M. Boudin ... . *Paris: J. B. Baillière.* 1852. 8vo, 3½ sheets. 6853

From the "Annales d'hygiène publique," Tom. XLVIII.

BOUDINOT (Elias). Life of the Rev. William Tennent, late pastor of the Presbyterian Church at Freehold, N. J. By Elias Boudinot, LL.D. Improved Edition. *Trenton: E. B. Adams.* 1833. 18mo, pp. 78. + [Another Edition.] In which is contained, among other interesting particulars, an account of his being three days in a trance and apparently lifeless. *New York: Carter* 1847. 18mo, pp. 128. 6854

[BOUDINOT.] A Memoir of the Rev. William Tennent, Minister of Freehold, Monmouth County, N. J. first published in the Evangelical Magazine ... . *Springfield: G. W. Callender.* 1822. 18mo, pp. 67. H. 6855

BOUDINOT. A Star in the West; or, A Humble Attempt to discover the long lost Ten Tribes of Israel, preparatory to their Return to their Beloved City Jerusalem. By Elias Boudinot, LL.D. [Mottoes.] *Trenton, N. J.: D. Fenton, S. Hutchinson, and J. Dunham.* 1816. 8vo, pp. iv, 312. C., H. 6856

Pages 89–107 are devoted to an enquiry into the language of the American Indians. The appendix includes "Historical Sketches of Louisiana."

BOUDINOT. Oration at Elizabeth Town, before the Society of Cincinnati in New Jersey, July 4, 1793. *Elizabeth Town.* 1793. 4to, pp. 32. W. 6857

BOUDINOT (Elias), *a Cherokee Indian.* An Address to the Whites. Delivered in the First Presbyterian Church, on the 15th of May, 1825. By Elias Boudinot, a Cherokee Indian. *Philadelphia: Printed by William F. Geddes.* 1826. 8vo, pp. 16.

This Cherokee Indian took the name of Dr. Boudinot, by his permission. *See* Allen's "Biogr. Dict," and "Cherokee Phœnix."

BOUDINOT. Letters and other Papers relating to Cherokee Affairs; being in Reply to sundry publications authorized by

John Ross. By E. Boudinot, formerly Editor of the Cherokee Phoenix. *Athens: printed at the Office of the "Southern Banner."* 1837. 6859

BOUDINOT. Poor Sarah, or the Indian Woman, in Indian Charactesr. *New Echota.* 1833. 18mo. 6860

BOUDRY DE LOZIÈRE. *See* Baudry de Lozière, Vol. I., Nos. 3979–80.

BOUDRYE. Historic Records of the Fifth New York Cavalry, First Ira Harris Guard: its Organization, Marches, Raids, Scouts, Engagements and General Services, during the Rebellion of 1861–1865, with Observations of the Author by the Way, giving Sketches of the Armies of the Potomac and of the Shenandoah. Also Interesting Accounts of Prison Life and of the Secret Service. Complete Lists of its Officers and Men. By Louis N. Boudrye, Chaplain of the Regiment. Illustrated with Steel Portraits and Wood Cuts. *Albany: S. R. Gray.* 1865. 12mo, pp. 358. 11 Plates. + Second Edition. *Albany: S. R. Gray.* 1865. 12mo, pp. 358. 11 Plates. B., C. 6861

BOUÉ (A.) Einige Bemerkungen über amerikanisch-mexikanische Geographie und Geologie ... . *Wien.* 1866. 8vo, pp. 12. 6862

From the "Sitzungsberichte der k. Akad. d. Wiss."

BOUET-WILLAUMEZ (*Le comte* Louis Édouard). Les colonies françaises en 1852. Par le comte Bouët-Willaumez ... . *Paris: imp. de Gerdès.* 1852. 8vo, 2 sheets. 6863

Republished from the "Revue des Deux Mondes," 1 juin, 1852, XIV. 929–952.

BOUGAINVILLE (Louis de). Voyage autour du monde, par la frégate du roi La Boudeuse et la Flûte L'Etoile; En 1766, 1767, 1768 & 1769. *Paris: Saillant & Nyon.* M. DCC. LXXI. 4to, 3 l., pp. 417, (3). Maps. B. + [*Ibid.*] 2 vols., 8vo. + Nouvelle édition, avec le journal d'un voyage autour du monde, par Banks et Solander. Traduit de l'anglais par Fréville. *Paris.* 1793. 3 vols., 8vo. Maps. 6864

BOUGAINVILLE. Voyage autour du monde, par la frégate du Roi La Boudeuse, et la flûte L'Etoile; En 1766, 1767, 1768 & 1769. Seconde édition, augmentée. ... *Paris.* M. DCC. LXXII. 2 vols., 8vo, 4 l., pp. xliij, 336; 2 l., 453, (3). Maps. H. 6865

Contains a vocabulary of the Island of Tahiti, and a short explanation of sea terms used in the work. For what is often called a third volume, *see* No. 6867. Reprinted in A. Montémont's "Biblioth. univ.," Vol. IV.

BOUGAINVILLE. Voyage autour du monde ... en 1766–69. *Neuchâtel.* 1772. 2 vols., 8vo. 6866

BOUGAINVILLE. Supplément au voyage de M. de Bougainville; ou Journal d'un voyage autour du monde, Fait par MM. Banks & Solander, Anglois, en 1768, 1769, 1770, 1771. Traduite de l'Anglois, par M. de Fréville. ... *Paris.* M. DCC. LXXII. 8vo, Half-Title, pp. xvj, 362, (3). 6867

The supplement was compiled and translated from an annonymous account of Banks and Solander's voyage with Captain Cooke in the *Endeavour.*

BOUGAINVILLE. Voyage ... 1766 à 1769. Nouvelle édition ... précédée d'une notice sur Bougainville ... . *Paris: Bibliothèque des communes.* 1861. 12mo, pp. viii, 312. Map. 6868

BOUGAINVILLE. A Voyage round the World. Performed by Order of His Most Christian Majesty, In the Years 1766, 1767, 1768 and 1769. By Lewis de Bougainville, Colonel of Foot, and Commodore of the Expedition in the Frigate La Boudeuse, and the Store-ship L'Etoile. Translated from the French. By John Reinhold Forster, F.A.S. *London: J. Nourse, and T. Davies,* M DCC LXXII. 4to, pp. xxviii, 476. 5 Maps. C., H. + *Dublin.* 1772. 8vo, pp. xxxii, 480. Map and Plate.

BOUGAINVILLE. The History of a Voyage to the Malouine (or Falkland) Islands, Made in 1763 and 1764, Under the Command of M. de Bougainville, in order to form a Settlement there; and of Two Voyages to the Streights of Magellan, with an Account of the Patagonians: Translated from Dom Pernety's Historical Journal written in French. Illustrated with Copper Plates. *London: T. Jefferys.* MDCCLXXI. 4to, 2 l., pp. xvii, 294. + *London.* 1773. 4to. 6870

First printed at Berlin, in French, in 1763. The translator has omitted the detail of ordinary occurrences which are common to every voyage, retaining whatever seemed, in any view, peculiar to this expedition. Several charts and plans are also added, which are not in the original. The copies with the date 1773 are probably the same, with a new title-page. *See* M. R., XLV. 413; XLVI. 204; XLVIII. 402. *See also* Walpole's Correspondence, V. 312. Reprinted in Pinkerton's Voyages, Vol. XIII. *See also* Pernety.

BOUGAINVILLE. Reise um die Welt, welche mit der Fregatte la Boudeuse in den Jahren 1766–69 gemacht worden. Aus dem Französischen. *Leipzig: Fritsch.* 1772. 8vo, pp. 330. Map and Plate. + Zweite Auflage. *Leipzig.* 1783. 8vo. 6871

BOUGAINVILLE. Reis rondom de weereldt ... . Uit het Fransch

vertaald, en met eenige Aenteekeningen verrijkt, door Pieter Leuter. *Te Dordrecht: A. Blussé en Zoon.* 1772. 2 pts., 4to, pp. (4), xxvi, 414. 20 Maps. + Tweede druk. *Amsterdam: Schalekamp en van de Grampel.* 1796. 2 pts., 4to. Maps and Plates. 6872

Le Bougainville de la jeunesse, ou Voyages dans l'Amérique. *Limoges [et] Paris: F. F. Ardant frères.* 1860. 16mo, pp. 128. Engraving. 6873

BOUGAINVILLE (*Baron* Louis Antoine de). Album pittoresque de la frégate la Thétis et de la corvette l'Espérance: collection de dessins relatifs à leur voyage autour du monde, en 1824, 1825 et 1826, sous les ordres de M. le Baron de Bougainville, recueillis et publiés par M. le vicomte de Latouanne, Lieut. de vaisseau abord de la Fregate la Thetis. *Paris: Bulla.* Rl. 4to. 35 Lithographs. 6874

"84 fr. Pap de Chine, 165 fr." — BRUNET.

BOUGAINVILLE. Journal de la navigation autour du globe de la frégate La Thétis et de la corvette L'Espérance, executé pendant les années 1824, 1825 et 1826 publié par ordre du rois sous les auspices du departement de la marine par M. le Baron de Bougainville, capitaine de vaisseau ... chef de l'expédition publié par ordre du Roi sous les auspices du departement de la Marine, etc. *Paris: Arthus Bertrand.* M DCCC XXXVIII. 2 vols., rl. 4to, pp. viij, 742; xvi, 165, 1 l., with a folio Atlas, containing 12 Plates of Natural History, 27 other Plates, and 9 large Maps. B., C.

Also on "papier vélin, 225 fr., avec doubles figures coler 350 fr."

BOUGUER (Pierre). La Figure de la Terre, déterminée par les observations de Messieurs Bouguer, et de la Condamine, envoyés par order du Roy au Pérou, pour observir aux environs de l'équateur. Avec une relation abregée de ce voyage, que contient la description du pays dans lesquels les operations ont été faites. Par M. Bouguer. *Paris.* 1749. 4to, pp. cx, 396. Plates. C.

BOUGUER. Justification de plusieurs faits qui concernent les operations des académiciens au Perou. *Paris.* 1752. 4to. Large Map. 6877

Quérard gives the title: "Justification des Mémoires de l'Académie des sciences de 1744, et du livre de la figure de la terre. *Paris.* 1752. 4to, pp. 54."

BOUGUER. *See* Barrère (P.), Vol. I, No. 3605, and Pinkerton's Voyages, Vol. XIV.

BOUILLÉ (François Claude Amour, *Marquis* de). Chanson militaire, sur le prise de Dominique, Sept. 1778, par M. le Marquis de Bouillé 1778. 18mo. 6878

Bouillé is the subject, not the author of this poem.

BOUILLÉ (René, *Marquis* de). Essai sur la vie du marquis de Bouillé (François Claude Amour) ... gouverneur général des îles du Vent pendant la guerre d'Amériqué ... . Par son petit-fils René de Bouillé. *Paris: Amyot.* 1853. 8vo. 6879

BOUILLÉ. Une commission ... [etc.] *Paris: imp. de P. Dupont.* [1862.] 8vo, less than 48 pp. 6880

A report by Bouillé, representative of Guadeloupe on "Le choix définitif du point d'escale des transatlantiques."

BOUIS (Amédée Théodore). Biographie du général Andrew Jackson, ancien président des Etats-Unis. *Paris: imp. de Fournier.* 1842. 8vo, pp. 32. Portrait. 6881

"Second edition. The first was anonymous." — QUÉRARD.

BOUIS. Le bivouac aux prairies d'Amérique. Par M. Amédée Bouis, Américain. *Paris: l'auteur.* 1847. 8vo, 3¾ sheets. + Seconde édition. [*Ibid.*] 6882

"A fragment of an unpublished novel, entitled: 'Les pionniers de l'Orégon.'" — *Bibliog. de la France.*

BOUIS. Le Whip-Poor-Will, ou les pionniers de l'Orégon. Par Amédée Bouis. *Paris: Comon.* 1847. 8vo, 28 sheets.

[BOULANGER (Nicolas Antoine).] Recherches sur l'origine du despotisme oriental. Ouvrage posthume de Mr. B. I. D. P. E. C. ... *Paris.* 1761. 12mo, pp. 104. + [*Paris: libraries associés.*] M. DCC. LXIII. 12mo, 2 l., pp. xix, 180. H. + [n. p.] MDCCLXVI. Sm. 8vo, 2 l., pp. 332. H. 6884

I have seen, in a London bookseller's catalogue, an edition dated 1764, possibly by misprint. Quérard mentions an edition: "*Amsterdam: Rey.* 1766. 12mo."

[BOULANGER.] The Origin and Progress of Despotism. In the Oriental and other Empires of Africa, Europe, and America ... . *Amsterdam,* i. e. *London: [the private press of John Wilkes.]* M.DCC.LXIV. 8vo, Title, pp. 285. C., H. 6885

The references to America are very slight.

BOULIGNY. Address of Hon. John E. Bouligny, of Louisiana, to his Constituents, in Reply to Mr. Henry St. Paul. [n. p. 1860.] 8vo, pp. 4. H. 6886

BOULTER (Hugh). A Sermon Preached before the Incorporated Society for the Propagation of the Gospel in Foreign Parts; ... 16th of February, 1721. By ... Hugh, Lord Bishop of Bristol. *London: J. Downing.* 1722. 8vo, pp. 61, (1). H., N.

BOULTON (D'Arcy). A Sketch of His Majesty's Province of Upper Canada. By D'Arcy Boulton, Barrister at Law. *London: Nornaville and Fell.* 1805. 4to, pp. xi, 99. Map. H., P. 6888

BOULTON (H. J.) A Short Sketch of the Province of Upper Canada, for the Information of the Labouring Poor throughout England. To which is prefixed Thoughts on Colonization. By Henry John Boulton, Esq. *London.* 1826. Sm. 8vo. 6889

Also: "The Drainage of Land [in] Canada. *Toronto.* 1859." pp. 12. "On thorough drainage ... in Canada. *Toronto.* 1860." pp. 8. And a "Communication to Lord Monteagle, respecting Emigration to Canada."

[BOULTON (Richard).] A Compleat History of Magick, Sorcery, and Witchcraft. *London: Printed for E. Curll.* 1715–16. 2 vols., 12mo. Frontispiece. 6890

The second volume contains "The Tryalls of several Witches, at Salem, in New England," etc. There is, perhaps, something on the same subject in his "Possibility and reality of ... witchcraft, demonstrated ... . *London.* 1720." 8vo, and his "Vindication of a Compleat history of magick ... . *London.* 1722." 12mo.

BOUMANN (C. C.) Creolinden, et Billede of Livet i Vestindien. *Kjöbenhavn: Seidelin.* 1838. 8vo, pp. 160. 6891

BOUNIOL. Les marins français ... vies et récits dramatiques, d'après les Documents originaux. Par M. Bathild Bouniol. *Paris: Bray.* 1868. 2 vols., 18mo, pp. 828. 6892

Probably contains accounts of the early French explorers.

BOUQUET (*Chevalier* Henry). *See* [Smith (William)].

BOURBOURG (*L'Abbé* Brasseur de). *See* Brasseur de Bourbourg (C. E.)

BOURDIOL (H.) Exploration dans l'isthme de Darien (Amérique Central), au point de vue d'une communication interocéanique, racontée à la Société de géographie de Paris ... 16 décembre. 1864, par M. H. Bourdiol ... . *Paris: imp. Martinet.* 1865. 8vo, pp. 22. 6893

Taken from the "Bulletin" of the Society, Dec., 1864.

[BOURDON (Louis Gabriel).] Voyage d'Amérique, dialogue en vers, avec des notes. *Paris.* 1786. 12mo. 6894

BOURGEOIS (Auguste Anicet) *and* DUGUÉ (Ferdinand). Les pirates de la Savane, drame à grand spectacle en cinq actes et six tableaux. Par MM. Anicet Bourgeois et Ferdinand Dugué. *Paris: librairie théâtrale.* 1859. 18mo, pp. 108. + [*Ibid.*] 4to, pp. 30, in double columns. Vignette. + *Paris: Michel Lévy frères.* 1864, 1865, [and] 1867. 4to, pp. 30, in double columns.

[BOURGEOIS.] Christophe Colomb, ou l'Amérique découverte: poëme en XXIV chants, par un Américain. *Paris: Moutard.* 1773. 2 vols., 8vo. S. 6896

[BOURGEOIS.] Voyages interessans dans differentes colonies françaises, espagnoles, anglaises, &c.; contenant des observations importantes relatives à ces contrées; et un memoire sur les maladies les plus communes à Saint Domingue, leurs remèdes et le moyen de s'en preserver moralement et phisiquement. Avec des anecdotes singulières, qui n'avaient jamais été publiées. Le tout rédigé et mis au jour, d'après un grand nombre de manuscrits, par M. N. ... . *A Londres et Paris: Bastian.* 8vo, pp. vii, 507. 6897

With a different title, this forms Vol. X. of Bérenger's "Collection abrégé des voyages." It is taken from the papers of M. B * * * (Bourgeois), "secretary of the chamber of Agriculture of the Cape," by his nephew M. N. (Nougaret). Richardiere says that "the most interesting part of the work is that which relates to the islands of Portorico, Curassoa, Grenada, and the Bermudas, and to New Mexico: about which places it would be difficult to find such interesting and satisfactory details in any other work." It bears sufficient evidence, in typographical execution, of having been printed in France. The "Monthly Review," LXXX. 1789, says "the work is ill written. We should suspect Monsr. N. not to be a native of France. His remarkable anecdotes are neither amusing nor instructive. Compared with the pompous title, this work is one illustration, among many, of the *parturient montes.*" *See also* Boucher.

BOURGEOIS. Reisen durch einige französische, englishe, holländische, spanische Besitzungen, in der neuen Welt. Mit eingestreuten historischen, statistischen, und andern Bemerkungen, welche die Sitten und Naturgeschichte dieser Länder betreffen. *Leipzig: Weygand.* 1789. 8vo. 6898

BOURGEOIS. Voyage aux États-Unis d'Amérique, et description des mœurs, coutumes et usages de ses habitans. Traduit de l'Anglais, avec notes et additions. *Paris.* 1834. 8vo. 6899

BOURGEOIS (J.) La question d'Amérique en 1864 Par M. J. Bourgeois *Paris: Dentu.* 1864. 8vo, pp. 45, 1 l. B. 6900

BOURGEOYS *or* BOURGEOIS. Sa vie. *See* [Fallon (*L'Abbé*)] and [Montgolfier (M.)]

Bourges (Florentin de). Voyage aux Indes Orientales par le Paraguay, le Chili, le Pérou, &c. [1713–14.] 6901

See "Lettres édifiantes," xiii. 228–299.

Bourgoing (J. Fr.) Relation d'un Voyage récent des Espagnols sur les Côtes Nord-ouest de l'Amérique Septentrionale. *Paris.* 1789. 3 vols., 8vo. + Séconde Édition. *Paris.* 1792. + Troisième Édition. *Paris.* 1803. 6902

Translated into German, *Jena*, 1789, and reprinted in Archives Littéraires de l'Europe. *Paris et Tubingue*, 1804–1818, No. iv., 1804. 8vo.

Bourgoing (P.) Vertus et bienfaits des missionnaries, ou Histoire abrégée des missions de l'Amérique. *Paris.* 1854. 2 vols., 8vo. + *Lille: impr. de Lefort.* 1827. 2 vols., 18mo. + *Lille: Lefort.* 1828. 18mo, pp. 216. Plate. + *Lille: Lefort.* 1840. 18mo, pp. 216. 6903

Bourguignat (Auguste). Question de La Plata. Les traités Le Prédour. Notice au point de vue du droit international. *Paris: impr. de Chaix.* 1849. 8vo. 6904

Bourguignat. Question de La Plata. Seconde notice et nouveaux documents. Les traités Le Prédour doivent être ratifiés. Réponse à M. Edmond Blanc. *Paris: impr. de Chaix.* 1850. 8vo. 6905

Bourguignat. Question de La Plata. Troisième notice. La général Rosas devant la France, esquisse impartiale. *Paris: impr. de Lacour.* 1851. 8vo. 6906

Bourinot (J. G.) Confederation of the Provinces of British North America. By John George Bourinot. *Halifax.* 1866. 8vo, pp. 18. 6907

Bourkarsson (N.) Tre år i Mormonlandet. Berättelser efter egna iakttagelser. 1868. 8vo, pp. 196. 6908

Bourne (A.) ... A Narrative of the Wonderful ... Case of Ansel Bourne, of Westerly, Rhode Island, who in the Midst of Opposition to the Christian Religion was suddenly struck Blind, Dumb and Deaf; and after Eighteen Days was suddenly and completely restored ... in the Christian Chapel ... 15th of November, 1857 ... . *Irvington, N. J.: Moses Cummings.* 1858. 24mo, pp. 47. H. 6909

Bourne (B. Franklin). The Captive in Pa[tagonia] ... , the among the Giants. A Personal Narrative. Benjamin F. Bourne. With illustrations. *Boston: Gould & Lincoln.* 1853. 12mo, pp. 233. C. 6910

Reprinted in England, with the following title:

Bourne. The Giants of Patagonia: Captain Bourne's Account of his Captivity amongst the extraordinary Savages of Patagonia. With Six fine Engravings. To which is added, the painfully interesting Narrative of the Fate of the Patagonian Society's Mission in Terra del Fuego. *London: J. Vizetelly.* 1853. 12mo, pp. 233. + [Another Edition.] *London: Ingram, Cooke & Co.* 1853. 12mo, 5 l., pp. 160. C. 6911

Bourne (C.) The Proceedings in the Court of King's Bench, on the Indictments against Charles Bourne, Gent. on the prosecution of Sir James Wallace, for a Libel and for an Assault; containing the evidence, ... Taken in short hand by Joseph Gurney. *London: Sold by M. Gurney.* MDCCLXXXIII. 4to, pp. 41. C. 6912

The assault was in consequence of Wallace's ill treatment of Bourne on a voyage to Jamaica. Mr. Bourne had served, and had been wounded during the American Revolution.

Bourne (E. E.) An Address on the Character of the Colony founded by George Popham, at the Mouth of the Kennebec River August 19th (o. s.) 1607: Delivered in Bath, on the Two hundred and fifty-seventh Anniversary of that Event. By Hon. Edward E. Bourne ... . *Portland: Brown Thurston.* 1864. 8vo, pp. 60. BA., H. 6913

Two hundred copies printed.

Bourne (George). The Picture of Quebec. *Quebec.* 1829. 18mo. + [Another Edition.] Revised. *Quebec.* 1831. 18mo.

Bourne. Life of John Wesley with Memoirs of the Wesley family, to which are subjoined Whitehead's funeral sermon and a comprehensive history of American Methodism. By George Bourne. Also a preface and portrait of J. Wesley engraved by Tiebout. *Baltimore.* 1807. 8vo. 6915

[Bourne.] An Address to the Presbyterian Church enforcing the Duty of Excluding all Slaveholders from the "Communion of Saints." *New York.* 1833. 8vo, pp. 16. H. 6916

Bourne. The Book and Slavery Irreconcilable. By George Bourne. *Philadelphia.* 1816. 12mo. S. 6917

[Bourne.] The Condensed Anti-Slavery Bible Argument; by a Citizen of Virginia. ... *New York: printed by S. W. Benedict.* 1845. 8vo, pp. 91. H. 6918

Bourne. Lorette. The History of Louise, Daughter of a Canadian Nun, exhibiting the Interior of Female Convents. ... Sixth Edition. *New York: Charles Small.* 1834. 18mo, pp. 208. H. 6919

Bourne. Man stealing and Slavery denounced by the Presbyterian and Methodist Churches, together with an Address to all the Churches. By the Rev. George Bourne. *Boston: Garrison and Knapp.* 1834. 8vo, pp. 19. 6920

[Bourne.] Picture of Slavery in the United States of America. *Middletown, Con.: Edwin Hunt.* 1834. 18mo, pp. 227, (1). Woodcuts. B. + *Boston: Isaac Knapp.* 1838. 18mo, pp. 227, (1). C. H. 6921

[Bourne (Geo.), *Editor.*] The Spirit of the Public Journals: or, beauties of the American newspapers for 1805. *Baltimore: Dobbin & Murphy.* 1806. 12mo, pp. 300. C. 6921a

Bourne (H. R. F.) English Merchants: Memoirs in Illustration of the Progress of British Commerce. By H. R. Fox Bourne ... . *London: Richard Bentley.* 1866. 2 vols., 8vo, 10 l., pp. xiv, (1), 427; x, (1), 434. C. B. 6922

Contains interesting notices of commerce with America, especially the early commerce.

Bourne. English Seamen under the Tudors. By H. R. Fox Bourne ... . *London: Richard Bentley.* 1868. 2 vols., 8vo, pp. xii, (1), 304; ix, (1), 314. 5 Maps. B. 6923

Treats of the Cabots, Frobisher, Sir Humphrey Gilbert, Raleigh, John Davis, Hawkins, Drake, Cavendish, and others.

Bourne (H.) History of the Primitive Methodists. By Hugh Bourne. *Cincinnati.* 1833. 8vo, pp. 107. 6924

I find this title in a Western catalogue of Americana. It is probably a reprint of an English work, with some American additions.

[Bourne (*Miss*).] The British West India Colonies in Connection with Slavery, Emancipation, etc. By a Resident in the West Indies for Thirteen Years. With an Introduction and Concluding Remarks by a Late Stipendiary Magistrate in Jamaica [Stephen Bourne]. *London: Thomas Bosworth.* 1853. 8vo, Title, pp. 42. BA. 6925

Bourne (S.) A Sermon occasioned by the death of Rev. Alexander Phœnix, Preached to the Congregational Church of Harlem, N. Y., September 13th, 1863, by Rev. S. Bourne, Jr. With one of the Sermons of Mr. Phœnix. Printed for Private Distribution. *New York: Baldwin and Jones, ... Printers.* 1864. 8vo, pp. 32. Portrait. 6926

[Bourne (Silvanus).] The Dangers of Vice. A Poetical Fragment, By a Gentleman formerly of Boston. *Columbia.* 1789. 4to, pp. 16. 6927

Bourne (W. O.) ... The Irrepressible Platform. [Signed Wm. Oland Bourne. *New York.* 1860.] 4to, pp. (4). H. 6928

Bourne. Letter to Hon. J. J. Crittenden. [Dated] New-York, February 22, 1861. [n. p. n. d.] Sm. folio, 1 page.

Bourne. The Rebellion and its Purposes. *New York.* 1862. Folio, 1 l. (Also in German.) 6931

Bourne. Poems of the Republic. By Wm. Oland Bourne, A.M. A Contribution to the Metropolitan Fair. *New York: Edward O. Jenkins, [Printer]* ... . 1864. 12mo, pp. 48.

B[ourne]. Reconstruction. [Signed B. *New York.* 1862.] 12mo, pp. 11. 6933

Bourne. The Republic; a Poem. By Wm. Oland Bourne. *New York: R. Brinkerhoff.* [1862.] 12mo, pp. 8. + [With 4 other poems.] *N. Y.: Office of the "Soldiers-Friend."* [n. d.] 8vo, pp. (8). H. 6934

Bours (John). An Appeal to the Public, in which the Misrepresentations and Calumnies, contained in a Pamphlet, entitled, A Narrative of Certain Matters relative to Trinity Church, in Newport, in the State of Rhode Island, by a very extraordinary man, the Rev. Jamey Sayere, A.M., late Minister of said Church, are pointed out, and his very strange conduct during the time of his Ministration at Newport, faithfully related. By John Bours, Merchant, and one of the Vestry of Said Church. *Newport: Peter Edes.* 1789. 8vo, pp. 39, Appendix, v. W. 6935

Boursier (Adolphe). Le cousin d'Amérique. Par Adolphe Boursier. *Paris: Hipp. Souverain.* 1852. 8vo, 22 sheets.

A novel?

Bouse (*Sir* L.), *pseudon.* Adventures of Sir Lyon Bouse, Bart., in America, during the Civil War. *New York.* 1867. 16mo, pp. 67. C. 6937

Attributed to Richard Grant White, of New York.

Bousell (J.) ... Message unto the King, ... to set at liberty the African Slaves. By John Bousell ... *London. John Dennis* ... [1790.] 8vo, pp. 24. 6938

La boussole morale et politique des hommes et des empires; traitant de Carthage moderne Boston etc. *Boston.* 1780. 12mo.

Boussingault (A.) La nouveau theatre du monde. *Paris.* 1668. 5 vols., 12mo. 6940

Boussingault *and* Roulin. Viajes cientificos à los Andes ecuatoriales, ó coleccion de memorias sobre fisica, quimica é historia natural de la Nueva Granada, Ecuador y Venezuela. Traducidas por J. Acosta. *Paris.* 1849. 8vo. 6941

I suspect some error in this title, as I do not find any mention of the work in the "Bibliog. de la France," in Quérard, or in Lorenz.

Boussingault (M.) *See* Orbigny (Alcide d').

Boutelle (J. A.) A Brief Genealogy of the Whipple Family; compiled for Oliver M. Whipple, Esq., of Lowell, Mass. By John A. Boutelle, of Woburn. *Lowell: E. D. Green & Co.* 1857. 8vo, pp. 36. 6942

Boutelle. The Burke and Alvord Memorial. A Genealogical Account of the Descendants of Richard Burke of Sudbury, Mass. [and Alexander Alvord of Windsor, Conn.]. Compiled by John Alonzo Boutelle of Woburn, Mass., for William A. Burke of Lowell, Mass. *Boston: printed by Henry W. Dutton and Son.* 1864. 8vo, pp. 239. H. 6943

Boutillier (T.) Etat des sommes dépensées à même l'octroi de £30,000, voté dans le but d'aider à l'établissement des terres vacantes de la Couronne dans le Bas-Canada. Rapport de M. T. Boutillier. *Québec.* 1855. 8vo, pp. 58. 6944

Boutillier. Report on the progress of Settlement in the Townships of Lower Canada during the Year 1855. By T. Boutillier. *Toronto.* 1856. 8vo, pp. 72. 6945

Bouton (J. B.) A Memoir of General Louis Bell, late Col. of the Fourth N. H. Regiment, who fell at the Assault on Fort Fisher, N. C., January 15, 1865. By John Bell Bouton. ... *New York.* 1865. 8vo, pp. 53. H. 6946

Privately printed. Also: (anonymous), Round the Block. An American Novel. ... *New York: D. Appleton and Company.* 1864. 12mo, pp. 468. Woodcuts. H.

Bouton (J. W.) No. 16. Bibliotheca Americana. Catalogue of ... Books relating to America ... for Sale ... by J. W. Bouton ... . [*New York.* 1863?] 4to, pp. 24. 6947

Bouton (le P. Jacques). Relation de l'establissement des François depvis l'an 1635. En l'isle de la Martinique, l'vne des Antilles de l'Ameriqve. Des mœurs des Sauuages, de la situation, et des autres singularitez de l'isle. Par le pere Jacques Bouton, de la Compagnie de Jesu. *Paris: Sebastien Cramoisy.* 1640. 8vo, 3 l., pp. 141. 6948

"Cet ouvrage est la plus ancienne relation de la Martinique que l'on possède. Elle mérite d'être recherchée pour les renseignements qu'elle nous donne sur les mœurs et usages des Caraibes, avant l'établissement des Français dans cette île. Très-bel exempl. provenant de la bibliothèque des Jésuites de Caen."—Leclerc. *See also* Rich's Catalogue, No. 228.

Bouton (Nathan). *See* Virgil, Cortland County, N. Y.

Bouton (Nathaniel). An Account of the New Hampshire Historical Society. By Rev. Nathaniel Bouton, D.D. *Concord: Asa McFarland.* 1850. 8vo. C. 6949

Bouton. Centennial Discourses. *Concord: Jacob B. Moore.* 1830. 8vo. C. 6950

Bouton. Christian Patriotism. An Address Delivered at Concord [N. H.], July the Fourth, 1825. *Concord: printed by Sheppard and Bannister.* 1825. 8vo, pp. 24. H. 6951

Bouton. A Commemorative Discourse, delivered at Boscawen, N. H. on occasion of the Fiftieth Anniversary of the New-Hampshire General Association, August 25, 1859. By Nathaniel Bouton, Pastor of the First Church in Concord. *Concord: Steam Printing Works of McFarland & Jenks.* 1859. 8vo, pp. 78, Pastors' Names, 1 l. H. 6952

Bouton. "Days of Adversity" or Admonitions Against Disunion. A New Year's Sermon preached in Concord, N. H., January 6, 1861, by Nathaniel Bouton. ... *Concord: Cogswell, Printer.* 1861. 8vo, pp. 22. 6953

Bouton. Discourse, Commemorative of Forty Years Ministry at Concord, N. H. *Concord.* 1865. 8vo. 6954

Bouton. A Discourse on the Death of President Harrison, delivered in Concord, N. H. on the ... Annual State Fast, April 15, 1841. By Rev. Nathaniel Bouton ... . *Concord.* 1841. 8vo, pp. 19. B. 6955

Bouton. The Fathers of the New Hampshire Ministry. An Historical Discourse, preached before the General Association of N. H. Manchester, Aug. 22, 1848. By Rev. Nathaniel Bouton. *Concord: Asa McFarland.* 1848. 8vo, pp. 43. S.

Bouton. The Good Land in which we Live. A Discourse ... at Concord, N. H., on the Day of Public Thanksgiving, November 28, 1850. By Nathaniel Bouton ... . *Concord.* 1850. 8vo, pp. 30. H. 6957

Chiefly on the Fugitive Slave Law.

Bouton. An Historical Discourse in Commemoration of the Two-Hundredth Anniversary of the Settlement of Norwalk, Ct, delivered July 9, 1851. *New York.* 1851. 8vo. 6958

Bouton. The History of Concord, from its First Grant in 1725, to the Organization of the City Government in 1853, with a History of the Ancient Penacooks. The whole interspersed with Numerous Interesting Incidents and Anecdotes, down to the Present Period, 1855; embellished with Maps; with Portraits of Distinguished Citizens, and Views of Ancient and Modern Residences. ... By Nathaniel Bouton ... . *Concord: Benning W. Sanborn.* 1856. 8vo, pp. (4), 786. C., H. 6959

Bouton. History of Education in New Hampshire. A Discourse delivered before the New Hampshire Historical Society, at their Annual Meeting in Concord, June 12, 1833. By Nathaniel Bouton. *Concord: Marsh, Capen & Lyon.* 1833. 8vo, pp. 36. 6960

Bouton. History of the Temperance Reform in Concord. A Discourse ... December 10, 1843. By Nathaniel Bouton ... . *Concord: Press of Asa McFarland.* 1843. 8vo, pp. 23. H. 6961

Bouton. List of Pastors, Deacons and Members of the 1st Congregational Church in Concord, from 18 November, 1730, to 18 November, 1830. *Concord: Asa McFarland.* 1830. pp. 21. 6962

Bouton. A Memorial Discourse on Occasion of the Fiftieth Anniversary of the Concord Female Charitable Society ... January 26, 1862. By Nathaniel Bouton ... . *Concord.* 1862. 8vo, pp. 40. H. 6963

Bouton. Permanence amid Changes. A Discourse preached on the Twenty-Fifth Anniversary of his Settlement over the First Congregational Church and Society in Concord, N. H. By Nathaniel Bouton. *Concord: McFarland & Jenks.* 1850. 8vo, pp. 54. 6964

Bouton. Provincial Papers. Documents and Records relating to the Province of New-Hampshire, from the Earliest Period of its Settlement: 1623–1686. Published by Authority of the Legislature ... . Volume I. Compiled and edited by Nathaniel Bouton ... . *Concord: George E. Jenks, State Printer.* 1867. 8vo, pp. x, (1), 629. C. H. 6965

Bouton. The Responsibilities of Rulers. A Sermon ... at Concord, June 5, 1828, before the ... Authorities of ... New-Hampshire. By Nathaniel Bouton ... . *Concord.* 1828. 8vo, pp. 31. H. 6966

Bouton. ... A Sermon ... March 12, 1829, at the Installation of the Rev. John Smith ... in Exeter. By Nathaniel Bouton ... . *Concord: Asa M'Farland, Printer.* 1829. 8vo, pp. 29. H. 6967

Bouton. Thanksgiving Sermon, at Concord, Nov. 23, 1826, *Concord: Repository & Observer Office.* 1826. 8vo, pp. 24.

Bouton. Two Sermons, preached 21st November, 1830, in Commemoration of the Organizing of the First Church in Concord, and the Settlement of the First Minister, on the 18th November, 1730. By Nathaniel Bouton. *Concord: printed by M'Farland.* 1831. 8vo, pp. 102. Map. H., N. 6969

Historical "Notes," pp. 57–102.

Boutron-Charlard (A. F.) *and* Henry. Recherches ... sur les causes de l'âcreté de l'huile de ricin d'Amérique. *Paris: impr. de Fain.* 1842. 8vo. 6970

Only fifty copies printed.

Boutwell (E. B.) Statement of Commander E. B. Boutwell, of the United States Navy [on his resignation of his command]. [*Washington?* 1859.] 8vo, pp. 8. H. 6971

Boutwell (G. S.) Address of Gov. Boutwell at the Dedication of the Davis Monument, at Acton, October 29, 1851. [n. p. n. d.] 8vo, pp. 8. H. 6972

Boutwell. Address of Governor Boutwell at the Dedication of the Monument to the Memory of Capt. Wadsworth, at Sudbury, Mass., Nov. 23, 1852. [*Boston.* 1852.] 8vo, pp. 8.

Boutwell. Eulogy on the Death of Abraham Lincoln, delivered before the City Council and Citizens of Lowell ... April 19th, 1865, by the Hon. George S. Boutwell. ... *Lowell: City Council.* 1865. 8vo, pp. 17. H. 6974

Boutwell. A Manual of the Direct and Excise Tax System of the United States; including the Forms and Regulations established by the Commissioner of Internal Revenue, the Decisions and Rulings of the Commissioner, together with Extracts from the Correspondence of the Office. By George S. Boutwell. Late Commissioner of Internal Revenue. *Boston: Little, Brown & Company.* 1863. 8vo, pp. x, 500. B. + Fourth Edition. *Boston: Little, Brown & Company,* [etc.] 1864. 8vo, pp. x, 333. C., BA. 6975

Boutwell. Speeches and Papers relating to the Rebellion and the Overthrow of Slavery. By Geogre S. Boutwell. *Boston: Little, Brown and Co.* 1867. Crown 8vo, pp. vii, 628.

Boutwell. The Tax-Payer's Manual; containing the Entire Internal Revenue Laws, with the Decisions and Rulings of the Commissioner, Tables of Taxation, Exemption, Stamp-Duties, &c., and ... Index. ... By George S. Boutwell ... . *Boston: Little, Brown and Company.* 1865. 8vo, 2 l., pp. 197.

Also: An Address ... before the Franklin County Agricultural Society ... October 4, 1855. ... *Greenfield: printed by Charles A. Mirick,* 1855. 8vo, pp. 21. H. (A Comparison of the East and the West.) — Address before the Housatonic Agricultural Society [on the Profits and Wastes of Agriculture in Massachusetts] ... at Great Barrington, September 1854. *Pittsfield: printed by Reid, Hull & Peirson.* 1853. 8vo, pp. 21. H. — System of Agricultural Education. ... [n. p. 1857.] 8vo, pp. 15. H. — Address before the Hillsborough Agricultural and Mechanical Society. September 30, 1852. *Boston: Phillips, Sampson and Company.* 1853. 8vo, pp. 24. BA. — Address ... to the People of Berlin, upon the Provisions of the New Constitution [of Massachusetts], October 3, 1853. *Boston.* 1853. 8vo, pp. 16. H. — Address ... September 18, 1850, before the Middlesex Society of Husbandmen and Manufacturers [on the Importance of Farmers to New England]. ... *Boston.* 1850. 8vo, pp. 28. H. — An Address upon Secession. Delivered at Charleston, Mass., on the Eve of the 8th of January, 1861. ... . *Boston: Ticknor and Fields.* 1861. 8vo, pp. 30. B., H. — Argument on the Petitions for the Division of Middlesex and Worcester Counties,

before the Legislative Committee, March 25, 1855. [*Boston.* n. d.] 8vo, pp. 12. + *Boston.* [n. d.] Folio, pp. (2). H. + Worcester and Middlesex Counties, made ... April 23d, 1856. [n. p. n. d.] Large 12mo, pp. 12. H. — Confiscation of Rebel Property. Speech ... in the House of ... January 19, 1864. [*Washington.* 1864.] 8vo, pp. 8. H. — Decisions on the Tax Law. *New York: D. Appleton & Co.* 1863. 8vo, pp. 24. — Emancipation: Its Justice, Expediency and Necessity, as the means of securing a Speedy and Permanent Peace. An Address delivered ... in Tremont Temple, Boston, under the Auspices of the Emancipation League, December 16, 1861. [*Boston.*] 1861. 8vo, pp. 12. H. — Impeachment. Speech ... in the House ... December 5 and 6, 1867. [*Washington.* 1867.] 8vo, pp. 16. H. — Reconstruction. Speech ... in the House ... January 17, 1868. [*Washington.* n. d.] 8vo, pp. 8. H. — Reconstruction and its Relations to the Business of the Country. An Address ... before the Old Bay State Association, Boston, December 27, 1866. [*Washington.* 1866.] 8vo, pp. 7. H. — Reconstruction: Its True Basis. Speech ... at Weymouth, Mass. July 4, 1865. *Boston: Wright & Potter, Printers,* 1865. 8vo, pp. 45. H. — Remarks of Hon. G. S. Boutwell, B. F. Butler, and Thomas Williams, on the President's Veto of the Reconstruction Bill; ... in the House ... July 19, 1867. *Washington.* 1867. 8vo, pp. 8. H. — ... Speech ... before the National Union League Association. Washington, D. C., June 16, 1863. *Washington.* 1863. 8vo, pp. 8. H. — Speech ... upon the "Bill to Guarantee to certain States, whose Governments have been usurped or overthrown, a Republican form of Government." Delivered in the House of Representatives, May 4, 1864. 8vo, pp. 16. Speech ... on Suffrage in the District of Columbia; ... in the House ... January 18, 1866. *Washington.* 1866. 8vo, pp. 7. H. — Speech ... on the Constitutional Amendment reported from the Joint Committee on Reconstruction; ... in the House ... May 9, 1866. *Washington.* 1866. 8vo, pp. 7. H. — Speech ... on the Admission of Tennessee ... in the House ... July 20, 1866. *Washington.* 1866. 8vo, pp. 7. H. — Thoughts on Educational Topics and Institutions. ... *Boston: Phillips, Sampson and Company.* MDCCCLXIX. 12mo, pp. 365. C., H. — Wadsworth Monument. Date of Sudbury Fight. (Communicated to the New England Historical and Geological Register for April, 1866. *Boston.* 1866. 8vo, pp. 11. H. — An Oration ... in Acton, Mass., on the 29th of October, 1851, by His Excellency George S. Boutwell ... and a Poem, ... by Rev. John Pierpont ... [on] the Completion of the Granite Monument ... on Acton Common, over the Remains of Captain Isaac Davis, and Privates Abner Hosmer and James Hayward, with ... an Account of the Proceedings ... and a few Revolutionary Facts ... . *Boston.* 1852. 8vo, pp. 69. B.

Bouvet de Cressé (Auguste Jean Baptiste). Histoire de la Catastrophe de Saint-Domingue, avec la correspondence des généraux Leclerc ... Henry Christophe ... Hardy, Vilton, etc., certifiée conforme aux originaux ... publiées par A.-J.-B. Bouvet de Cressé ... . *Paris: Peytieux.* 1824. 8vo. 6978

The "Advertisement" of the author is signed J....e Ch......e.

Bouvet de Cressé. Histoire de la marine de tous les peuples, depuis la plus haute antiquité, jusqu'à nos jours. Par A. J. Bouvet de Cressé ... . *Paris: A. André.* 1824 2 vols., 8vo, pp. xvi, 560, 576. S. 6979

Bouvet de Cressé. Précis des victoires et conquêtes des Français dans les deux mondes, de 1792 à 1813 ... . Par A. J

B. Bouvet de Cressé. *Paris: Tenon.* 1823. 2 vols., 12mo, 34⅜ sheets. 2 Plates. 6980

Bouvier (J.) A Law Dictionary adapted to the Constitution and Laws of the United States of America, and of the several States of the American Union, with References to the Civil and other systems of Foreign Law. By John Bouvier. *Philadelphia.* 1839. 2 vols., 8vo, pp. 559; 628. + Second Edition. *Philadelphia.* 1843. 2 vols., 8vo. + Third Edition. *Philadelphia.* 1848. 2 vols., 8vo, pp. 756; 757. + *London: Stevens.* 1853. 2 vols., 8vo. + Twelfth Edition, revised and greatly enlarged. *Philadelphia: G. W. Childs.* 1867. 2 vols., rl. 8vo, pp. viii, 780; 732. 6981

Also: Institutes of American Law. *Philadelphia.* 1851. 4 vols., 8vo. — A Brief Memoir of John Bouvier. [From the National Portrait Gallery.] *Philadelphia.* 1852. 8vo, pp. 12. [Portrait.] P.

Bouyer (F.) La Guyane française, notes et souvenirs d'un voyage exécuté en 1862–1863; par Frédéric Bouyer, capitaine de frégate. Ouvrage illustre de types, de scènes et de paysages par Riou, et de figures d'histoire naturelle par Rapine et Delahaye, d'après les croquis de l'auteur ... . *Paris: L. Hachette et Cᵉ.* 1867. 4to, pp. 322. 6982

Reviewd in the "Annales des voyages," Dec., 1867, pp. 104–201.

Bovell (J.) Constitution and Canons of the Synod of the Diocese of Toronto, with Explanatoiy Notes and Comments. By James Bovell, M.D. ... *Toronto.* 1858. 8vo, pp. 52. 6983

Bovell. A Plea for Inebriate Asylums: commended to the Consideration of the Legislators of the Province of Canada. *Toronto.* 1862. 4to, pp. 50. 6984

Also: Outline of the History of the British Church. *Toronto.* 1860. 18mo, pp. 156; and sundry contributions to Canadian scientific journals. *See* Morgan's "Bibl. Canad."

Bovis (de). Essais sur l'esprit des lois coloniales. Par M. de Bovis, avocat et propriétaire à la Guadeloupe. *Paris: impr. d'Éverat.* 1820. 8vo, pp. 36. 6985

Bowden (J.) The History of the Society of Friends in America. By James Bowden. *London: Charles Gilpin.* 1850–54. 2 vols., 8vo, pp. viii, 426; 416. Maps, Plates, and Facsimiles. + *London: Bennett.* 1861. 2 vols., 8vo. 6986

Vol. I. was published in four parts, with a prospectus to each. Vol. II. (Pennsylvania and New Jersey) was published by *W. & F. G. Cash,* 1854.

Bowden. A Letter From John Bowden, A.M., Rector of St Paul's Church, Norwalk, Ct., to the Reverend Ezra Stiles, D.D LL.D., President of Yale-College, Occasioned by some Passages concerning Church Government, in an Ordination Sermon, preached, at New-London, May 17th. 1787. *New-Haven.* M,DCC,LXXXVIII. 8vo, pp. 5, (2). H. 6987

Also: A Second Letter ... *New Haven: Printed by T. & S. Green.* 1789. 8vo, pp. 108. H. Strictly speaking, these do not relate to America further than they bear on the question of Episcopacy in the United States.

Bowditch (H. I.) An Address on the Life and Character of James Dean, M.D., of Greenfield, Mass. By Henry I. Bowditch, M.D. August 4, 1858. *Greenfield: H. D. Mirick & Co., Printers.* 1858. 8vo, pp. 45. H. 6988

Bowditch. ... A Valedictory Address to the Graduating Medical Class of Harvard University, March 11, 1863. With Additional Remarks on a Topic of Importance at the present hour [the Rebellion]. By H. I. Bowditch, M.D. *Boston.* 8vo, pp. 52. 6989

Bowditch. A Brief Plea for the Ambulance System for the Army of the United States, as drawn from the Extra Sufferings of the Late Lieut. Bowditch and a Wounded Comrade. By Henry I. Bowditch, M.D. *Boston: Ticknor and Fields.* 1863. 1863. 8vo, pp. 28. B., H. 6990

Also: ... Abuse of Army Ambulances. [*Boston.* 1862.] 8vo, pp. 4.

Bowditch. Consumption in New England: or, Locality One of its Chief Causes. An Address ... . By Henry I. Bowditch, M.D. *Boston: Ticknor & Fields.* 1862. 8vo, pp. 104. Map. H. 6991

Reprinted with the following title:

Bowditch. Consumption in New England and elsewhere, or Soil-Moisture one of its Chief Causes. ... By Henry I. Bowditch. Second Edition. *Boston.* 1868. 8vo, pp. 17, 59–154. Maps. B. 6992

Pages 59-154 are merely sheets 8–19 of a volume of the Medical Communications of the Mass. Med. Soc.; but the prefatory matter is new.

Bowditch. Memoir of Amos Twitchell, M.D. with an Appendix, containing his Addresses, etc. By Henry I. Bowditch, M.D. *Boston: printed by John Wilson and Son.* 1851. pp. v, 1 l., pp. 212. Portrait. H. 6993

[Bowditch.] Memorial [of Nathaniel Bowditch, who fell at Kelly's Ford, 1863]. ... *Boston: privately printed by John Wilson & Son.* 1865. 4to, pp. vi, (1), 134 Map and Photographs. B. 6994

[Bowditch.] Sketch of the Life and Character of Nathaniel Bowditch, LL.D. made at the Dedication of the Bowditch School, January 7, 1862. *Boston.* 1863. 8vo, pp. 17. H. 6995

Bowditch (N.) Directions for sailing into the Harbours of Salem, Marblehead, Beverly and Manchester. By Nathaniel Bowditch, A.M., A.S.S. *Newburyport: Printed by Edmund M. Blunt.* 1806. 8vo, pp. 26. H. 6996

Dr. Bowditch's MSS., in 19 vols., 4to, and 12 vols., folio, are in the Public Library of Boston.

Bowditch (N. Ingersoll). An Argument for a Catholic Church on the Jail-Lands. *Boston.* 1853. 8vo, pp. 15, (Erratum) 1 line. H. 6997

Bowditch. The Ether Controversy. Vindication of the Hospital Report of 1848. By N. I. Bowditch. *Boston.* 1848. 8vo, pp. 32. H. 6998

Bowditch. A History of the Massachusetts General Hospital. By N. I. Bowditch. ... Not Published. *Boston: Printed by John Wilson & Son.* 1851. 8vo, pp. xi, 442, (1). 2 Portraits, and 2 Plates. C., H. 6999

Bowditch. Memoir of Nathaniel Bowditch, by his Son Nathaniel Ingersoll Bowditch, originally prefixed to the fourth volume of the Mécanique Céleste. Second Edition. *Boston: Charles C. Little and James Brown.* MDCCCXL. 4to, pp. 172. 2 Portraits. 7000

The first edition consisted of some extra copies of the memoir in the "Mécanique Céleste," with the title-page of Vol. IV., pp. 168. BA., H.

[Bowditch.] Memoir of Nathaniel Bowditch. *Boston: James Munroe & Co.* 1841. 12mo, pp. xiii, 158. 7001

Bowditch. Suffolk Surnames. By N. I. Bowditch. ... Not Published. *Boston: Printed by John Wilson and Son.* 1857. 8vo, pp. 108. + Second Edition, enlarged. *Boston: Ticknor and Fields.* 1858. 8vo, pp. xv, 383. + Third Edition. *London: Trübner and Co. Boston, U. S.: Ticknor and Fields.* 1861. 8vo, pp. xxv, 757. Portrait. C., H. 7002

Bowditch. To the Public. [Defence of his Conduct, in the Case of Latimer, a Fugitive Slave, against the Charges of J. B. Gray.] *Boston.* 1842. 12mo, pp. 11. B. 7003

[Bowditch.] Wharf Property; or, The Law of Flats; being Remarks before the Judiciary Committee of the Senate of Massachusetts, April 14, 1852. *Boston.* 1852. 8vo, pp. 40. Woodcuts. H. 7004

With much historical matter on the wharf property of Boston.

Bowditch (W. Ingersoll). The Anti-Slavery Reform, its Principle and Method. By William I. Bowditch. *Boston: Robert F. Wallcut.* 1850. 8vo, pp. 19. H. 7005

[Bowditch.] Cass and Taylor on the Slavery Question. ... *Boston: Damrell & Moore.* 1848. 12mo, pp. 23. H. 7006

[Bowditch.] The Constitutionality of Slavery. ... Reprinted from the Massachusetts Quarterly Review. *Boston.* 1848. 8vo, pp. 48. H. 7007

[Bowditch.] God *or* Our Country. Review of the Rev. Dr. Putnam's Discourse, delivered on Fast Day, entitled God *and* Our Country. ... *Boston: I. R. Butts.* 1847. 8vo, pp. 23.

Bowditch. The Rendition of Anthony Burns. By W. I. Bowditch. *Boston.* 1854. 8vo, pp. 40. H. 7009

Bowditch. Slavery and the Constitution. By William I. Bowditch. *Boston: Robert F. Wallcut.* 1849. 8vo, 2 l., pp. 156. H. 7010

Bowditch. The United States Constitution, a Pro-Slavery Instrument according to the necessary meaning of its terms. By William I. Bowditch. *American Anti-Slavery Society.* [n. d.] 16mo, pp. 12. 7011

Bowditch Library. Report of the Proprietors of the Bowditch Library. *Boston: printed by I. R. Butts.* 1841. 8vo, pp. 16. H. 7012

Bowdler (T.) Anecdotes of the late Lieut.-Gen. Villettes, Commander of the Forces, and Lieut. Governor of the Island of Jamaica. By Thomas Bowdler. [*Jamaica? Privately printed.*] 1808. 4to. 7013

Bowdler. A Short View of the Life and Character of Lieu-

tenant-General Willets, late Lieutenant-Governor and Commander of the Forces in Jamaica. By Thomas Bowdler. *Bath.* 1815. 8vo. Portrait. 7014

[Bowdoin (James).] Opinions respecting the Commercial Intercourse between The United States of America, and The Dominions of Great-Britain, including Observations Upon the Necessity and Importance of an American Navigation Act. By a Citizen of Massachusetts. ... *Boston: Samuel Hall.* 1797. 8vo, pp. 61, (1). B. 7015

Bowdoin. A Philosophical Discourse, Addressed to The American Academy of Arts and Sciences, ... On the Eighth of November M,DCC,LXXX, After the Inauguration of the President into Office. By James Bowdoin, Esq; ... . *Boston: Printed by Benjamin Edes and Sons.* M,DCC,LXXX. 8vo, pp. 35. Portrait. + *London: John Stockdale.* 1785. 8vo, pp. 30. 7016

Bowdoin. A Philosophical Discourse, addressed to the American Academy of Arts and Sciences; to which are added three memoirs on philosophical subjects. The whole extracted from the first volume of the Memoirs of the Academy lately published. By James Bowdoin, Esquire, ... *Boston: printed by Adams and Nourse.* M. DCC. LXXXVI. 4to, pp. 71. Plate. 7017

Handsomely printed; probably for private distribution.

Bowdoin (James), *Editor.* *See* Boston, No. 6739.

Bowdoin College. Acts relative to Bowdoin College, and the Standing Rules and Orders of the Overseers of the College. [n. p. n. d.] 8vo, pp. 16. 7018

Also: ... An additional Act to alter the Law establishing Bowdoin College. [n. p. 1832.] 8vo, pp. 2. H.

Annual Circular [*afterwards* Announcement] of the Medical School of Maine, at Bowdoin College ... . *Brunswick.* 1842. 8vo, pp. 7. Continued. 7019

Bowdoin Port-Folio. M DCCC XXXIX. Conducted by the Undergraduates ... . *Brunswick: Press of Joseph Griffin.* [n. d.] 8vo, 4 l., pp. 248. H. 7020

Catalogue of the Athenæan Library, Bowdoin College. 1861. [Classed.] *Brunswick.* 1861. 8vo, pp. 86. 7021

Catalogue of the Athenæan Society of Bowdoin College. ... Instituted 1817. Incorporated 1828. *Brunswick.* M DCCC XXXVIII. 8vo, pp. 24. Continued. H. 7022

Bowdoin College Catalogue of the Fraternity of ΦBK, Alpha of Maine. Bowdoin College ... . *Brunswick.* 1834. 8vo, pp. 14. H. 7023

Catalogue of the Library of Bowdoin College ... . [Classed.] *Brunswick.* 1821. 8vo, pp. iv, 120. H. 7024

A Catalogue of the Library of Bowdoin College, to which is added an Index of Subjects. *Brunswick: Printed for the College.* M.DCCC.LXIII. 8vo, pp. vi, (1), 832. H. 7025

Catalogue of the Library of the Medical School of Maine, at Bowdoin College. February, 1823. *Brunswick.* 1823. 8vo, pp. 24. H. + Appendix. ... December, 1823. *Brunswick.* 1823. 8vo, pp. 16. + February, 1825. *Brunswick.* 1825. 8vo, pp. 82. + February, 1830. *Brunswick.* 1830. 8vo, pp. 84. + February, 1834. *Brunswick.* 1834. 8vo, pp. 73, (1). H. 7026

Catalogue of the Peucinian Library. Bowdoin College. 1859. *Lewiston.* 1859. 8vo, pp. 86. 7027

Catalogue of the Officers and Members of the Peucinian Society. Bowdoin College ... . *Hallowell.* 1818. 8vo, pp. 11. + Instituted 1805, reorganized, 1814. *Exeter: printed by Charles Norris. September,* 1826. 16mo, pp. 16. + For other years. H. 7028

Catalogue of the Officers and Students of Bowdoin College, Brunswick. October, 1815. *Hallowell: N. Cheever, Printer.* [n. d.] Broadside. Continued. + Bowdoin College, and the Medical School of Maine. February, 1822. *Brunswick.* 1822. 8vo, pp. 16. Continued. H. 7029

From "April, 1830," to the first catalogue for "1837–8," the form is 12mo.

Catalogus Senatus Academici et eorum qui Munera et Officia gesserunt, quique alicujus Gradus Laurea donati sunt in Collegio Bowdoinensi, Brunsvici ... . *Portlandiæ: e Typis Johannis McKown.* 1810. 8vo, 4 l. Continued triennially. H. 7030

For 1813, '16, and '19, *Hallowell;* 1822, etc., *Brunsvici;* 1813, *e Typis Nathanielis Cheever;* 1816 and '19, *Ezechielis Goodale;* 1822, *Griffin et Weld;* 1825, '31–64, *Josephi Griffin;* 1828, *Georgii Griffin.*

Charter of Bowdoin College, together with various Acts of the Legislature, and the Decision of the Circuit Court, and the By-Laws of the Overseers. *Brunswick: printed by J. Griffin.* 1850. 8vo, pp. 60. 7031

College Roll of Honor. [n. p. 1867.] 8vo, pp. 36. H. 7032

The cover-title is "Bowdoin in the War."

Laws of Bowdoin College. *Hallowell.* 1817. 8vo, pp. 29. + *Brunswick.* 1824. 8vo, pp. 30. + [*Id.*] 1825. 8vo, pp. 28. + [*Id.*] 1832. 8vo, pp. 30. + [*Id.*] 1837. 8vo, pp. 30. + [*Id.*] 1844. 8vo, pp. 30. + [*Id.*] 1855. 8vo, pp. 30. 7033

Medical Institution at Bowdoin College. *Brunswick.* 1821. 8vo, pp. 4. 7034

Order of Commencement Exercises. *Portland.* 1806. Broadside. Continued to 1812. + *Hallowell.* 1813. 8vo, pp. 3. Continued. + *Brunswick.* 1822. 4to, pp. 4. Continued annually. + [Programme of] Commencement Week. *Brunswick.* 1837. Broadside. Continued annually. 7035

Proceedings of the Board of Trustees of Bowdoin College in the Case of William Allen *vs.* Joseph McKeen, Treasurer; with Opinion of J. Story. *Augusta.* 1834. 12mo, pp. 30. 7036

Roll of Honor. List of Members of Bowdoin College, who have served in the U. S. Army or Navy during the War of the Rebellion. *Brunswick: for the Benefit of the Soldiers' Memorial Fund.* 1865. 8vo, pp. 12. H. 7037

Rules and Regulations relating to several Laws of Bowdoin College. [*Brunswick.* 1858.] 8vo, pp. 31–37. 7038

There are some other college publications, not of sufficient importance for description.

The Bowdoin Poets, Edited by Edward P. Weston. *Brunswick.* 1840. 8vo. 7039

BOWDOINHAM. Minutes of the Bowdoinham Baptist Association, held at Hartswell, 1790. *Bowdoin.* 1792. + At Readfield, August 28 and 29, 1793, with their Circular Letter. *Portland: Printed at T. B. Wait's Office.* [1793.] 8vo. Continued.

BOWDON. Course of Study, Rules and Regulations of Bowdon Collegiate Institution, Bowdon, Carroll County, Georgia. *Atlanta, Geo.* 1858. 8vo, pp. 8. H. 7041

BOWEN (Abel). Bowen's Boston News-Letter, and City Record. Vol. I. From Nov. 5, 1825, to June 17, 1826 ‖ Vol. II. ... To January 1827. ‖ Jerome V. C. Smith, Editor. *Boston: Abel Bowen.* 1826. 2 vols., 8vo, each 2 l., pp. 312, (104). C. B. 7042

BOWEN. Bowen's Picture of Boston, or The Citizens and Stranger's Guide to the Metropolis of Massachusetts, and its Environs. Embellished with Engravings. *Boston: Abel Bowen.* MDCCCXXIX. 18mo, pp. 252. Map and Plates. H. + To which is prefixed the Annals of Boston [by Alonzo Lewis]. ... Second Edition, enlarged ... . *Boston: Lilly Wait & Co. and Lorenzo H. Bowen.* MDCCCXXXIII. 18mo, pp. 316. Maps and Plates. C. B. + Embellished with Engravings. Third Edition. *Boston.* 1838. 18mo, pp. 304. C. 7043

BOWEN. Illustrations to Bowen's Picture of Boston ... . *Boston: Abel Bowen.* MDCCCXXIX. 4 l., 2 Maps, 9 l. of Plates, 2 l. of Woodcuts. H. 7044

[BOWEN.] The Naval Monument, containing Official and other Accounts of all the Battles fought between the Navies of the United States and Great Britain during the Late War; And an Account of the War with Algiers, with Twenty-five Engravings. To which is annexed a Naval Register of the United States. *Boston: A. Bowen.* 1816. 8vo, pp. xvi, (2), 316, (2), Errata, 1 slip. 25 Plates. H. + *Boston.* 1830. 8vo. N. + Revised and Corrected, and Brought down to the Year 1836. + *New York.* [1837.] C. + *New York.* 1838. 8vo. C. + *Boston: George Clark.* 1840. 8vo, pp. viii, 326, Index, 1 l. 23 Plates. C. 7045

BOWEN (Benjamin B.) A Blind Man's Offering: by B. B. Bowen. ... *Boston: the Author.* M DCCC XLVII. 12mo, pp. 432. H. + Fourth Edition. *New York.* M DCCC LX. 12mo, pp. 432.

Mentioned here for "Biographical Sketch of the Author;" "Our Country;" and "A Journey across the Alleghanies."

BOWEN (C. S. C.) The 'Alabama' Claims and Arbitration. Considered from a Legal Point of View. By Charles S. C. Bowen ... . *London: Longmans, Green, and Co.* 1868. 8vo, pp. 77. C. B. 7047

[BOWEN (D.)] A History of Philadelphia, With a Notice of Villages, in the Vicinity ... ; with an Historical Account of the Military Operations of the Late War, including the Names of over Two Thousand Patriotic Officers, and Citizen Soldiers, who volunteered their Services in defence of this City, when threatened by an Hostile Army. In 1812–13, & 14. *Philadelphia.* 1839. 8vo, Title, pp. iv, 200, (2). Woodcuts. H., P.

BOWEN. Coal and Coal Oil; or, the Geology of the Earth. Being a Popular Description of Minerals and Mineral Combustibles. By Eli Bowen. *Philadelphia: T. B. Peterson and Brothers.* [1865.] 12mo, pp. iv, 494. B. C. 7049

"About seven years ago ... I wrote most of the matter of the present work, under the title of the "Physical History of the Earth." — p. iii.

BOWEN. Coal and the Coal Trade. *Philadelphia.* 1862. 8vo.

BOWEN. The Coal Regions of Pennsylvania, being a General, Geological, Historical, & Statistical Review Of the Anthracite Coal Districts. Illustrated with Colored Maps and Engravings, and containing numerous Statistical Tables. Edited by Ele [*sic*] Bowen. *Pottsville, Pa.: E. N. Carvalho & Co.* 1848. Rl. 8vo, pp. (4), 72, 32. C., H. 7051

BOWEN. The McGinnes Theory of the Schuylkill Coal Formation, together with the Proceedings on the Presentation of a Tea Service of Silver at the Mount Carbon House; and the Remarks of Messrs. Hughes, Fraley, McGinnes, Cresson, Ford, Carey, Adam, &c., &c. Reported, with Comments, by Mr. Ele [*sic*] Bowen. *Pottsville, Pa.: B. Bannan, Printer.* 1855. 8vo, pp. 56. 7052

BOWEN. ... The Pictorial Sketch-Book of Pennsylvania. Or its Scenery, Internal Improvements, Resources, and Agriculture, popularly described, by Eli Bowen. ... Illustrated with over 200 Engravings, and a Colored Map. *Philadelphia: J. W. Moore.* 1852. + *Philadelphia.* 1853. C. + Eighth Edition, revised and greatly enlarged. *Philadelphia: W. White Smith.* 1854. 8vo, pp. 309, and (Pedestrian Sketches) 207. H. + Ninth Edition, revised and enlarged. *Philadelphia.* 1854. 7053

The engravings are poor woodcuts.

BOWEN. Rambles in the Path of the Steam Horse. *Philadelphia.* 1855. C. 7054

A description of the Baltimore and Ohio Railroad, with a catch-penny title.

BOWEN. United States Post Office Guide, Review of the Post Office Establishment in the United States, Exposition of the Scheme of Distribution, List of all the Post Offices in the United States, the Mail, Railroad, Canal, and Steam Boat Routes. By Eli Bowen. *New York.* 1851. Rl. 8vo. Map. C. 7055

BOWEN (F.) Documents of the Constitution of England and America, from Magna Charta to the Federal Constitution of 1789. Compiled and edited, with Notes, by Francis Bowen ... . *Cambridge: John Bartlett.* 1854. 8vo, pp. vii, (1), 142. C., H.

BOWEN. Memoir of Edmund Dwight. Written by Francis Bowen ... . Reprinted from Barnard's American Journal of Education for September, 1857. [n. p. n. d.] 8vo, pp. 22. H.

BOWEN. The Principles of Political Economy applied to the Condition, the Resources, and the Institutions of the American People. By Francis Bowen ... . *Boston: Little, Brown, and Company.* 1856. 8vo, pp. xxv, 546. H. + Second Edition. [*Id.*] 1859. C. H. 7058

Prof. Bowen contributed memoirs of Lincoln, Otis, Phips, and Steuben, to Sparks' "American Biography."

BOWEN (G.) Report of the Trial of George Bowen, for the Murder of Jonathan Jewett, Who committed suicide on the 9th of November, 1815, while ... in ... Gaol ... under Sentence of Death for the Murder of his Father. ... *Northampton,* [*sic*]. 1816. 8vo, pp. 56. H. 7059

BOWEN (H. L.) Memoir of Tristram Burges; with Selections from his Speeches and Occasional Writings. By Henry L. Bowen. *Providence: Marshall, Brown & Company. Philadelphia: W. Marshall and Company.* MDCCCXXXV. 8vo, pp. 404. Portrait. C., H. 7060

BOWEN (J. L.) Scouting Dave; or, The Winnebago Renegade. A Story of the Black Hawk Wars. By James L. Bowen. *New York: American News Company.* 8vo, pp. 44. 7061

Also: The Doomed Hunter. *London: Routledge.* 1867. 12mo. — The Maid of Wyoming. *London: Routledge.* 1867. 12mo. — The Mohegan Maiden; or, The Stranger of the Settlement. *New York: Beadle & Co.* 1867. 18mo, pp. 99. + *London: Routledge.* 1867. 12mo. — The Yankee Scout; or, Haps and Mishaps of the Border. ... *New York: American News Company.* 1865. 8vo, pp. 41.

BOWEN (J. B.) Memorials of John Bowen, LL.D., Late Bishop of Sierra Leone. Compiled from his Letters and Journals, by his Sister. *London: James Nisbet & Co.* 1861. Post 8vo, pp. 633. 7062

Includes the story of his life as a settler in Canada.

[BOWEN (Nathan).] The New-England Diary, or Almanack, for the Year 1725. *Boston.* 1725. 16mo. Continued. 7063

BOWEN (Nathaniel). A Discourse, delivered at the Request of the American Revolution Society ... on the Death of Gen. Christopher Gadsden, September 10, 1805. By Nathaniel Bowen ... . *Charleston: printed by W. P. Young.* [n. d.] 8vo, pp. 21.

BOWEN (N. H.) An Historical Sketch of the Isle of Orleans, being a paper read before the Literary and Historical Society of Quebec. By Noel H. Bowen. *Quebec.* 1860. 8vo, pp. 40.

BOWEN (P.) A Discourse occasioned By the Death of the Rev. Samuel Checkley, M.A. Late Colleague-Pastor of the New South-Church ... in Boston: Who departed this Life On the First of December, 1769 ... . By Penuel Bowen, A.M. Surviving Pastor ... . Dec. 1, 1769. *Boston: Printed by Edes and Gill.* M, DCC, LXX. 8vo, pp. 42. H. 7066

BOWEN (W. W.) Calumny refuted: an Answer to the Exposition of Thomas H. Lewis, by William W. Bowen. *New Orleans: printed by John Gibson.* 1839. 8vo, pp. 64, 27, (1). H.

BOWENS (Charles de). *See* Teumer (F. M.)

BOWERS (Bath). An Alarm Sounded To prepare the Inhabitants of the World To meet the Lord in the way of his Judgement, by Bath Bowers. [1709.] Sm. 4to, pp. 23. 7068

Dated at the end, *Philadelphia, July 17,* 1709, but probably printed by Bradford, at New York.

BOWERS (J.) A Discourse on the Occasion of the Death of General George Washington, delivered in St. Ann's Church, Pittston, on Saturday, 22nd February, 1800, By James Bowers. Published at the request of the Wardens and Vestry of the Episcopal Parish in said town. *Hallowell.* 1800. 8vo, pp. 18.

BOWES (John). Notes on the Colonial Empire of Great Britain. *London: Simpkin.* 1867. 12mo. 7070

BOWIE (R. I.) Speech of Hon. Richard I. Bowie, of Maryland, on the California Question. ... June 6, 1850. *Washington.* 1850. 8vo, pp. 15. 7071

BOWKER (J.) Wreck-elections of a Busy Life. [A parody on Horace Greeley's autobiography "Recollections of a Busy Life."] *Hartford: Kellogg & Bulkeley.* 1868. Oblong 4to. 22 lithographic Plates. C. 7072

BOWLER (M.) A Treatise on Agriculture and Practical Husbandry. By Metcalf Bowler. *Providence, R. I.: B. Wheeler.* 1786. 8vo, pp. 88. C. 7073

One of the earliest works of its class printed in Rhode Island.

BOWLES (B. F.) A Sermon ... at the Funeral of Helen Hanchett ... in ... Natick ... December 7, 1856. By Rev. B. F. Bowles. *Natick.* 1857. 8vo, pp. 27. B. 7074

BOWLES (C.) Life, Labors and Travels of Elder Charles Bowles; with Essay on the African Race, and Fugitive Slave Law. [n. p. n. d.] 8vo, pp. 286. 7075

BOWLES (Ch. S. P.) European Branch of the United States Sanitary Commission. ... Report of Mr. Ch. S. P. Bowles, Delegate to England. [*Paris.* 1864.] 4to, pp. 14, (16). H.

Lithographed in imitation of writing.

BOWLES (S.) Across the Continent: a Summer's Journey to the Rocky Mountains, the Mormon and the Pacific States, with Speaker Colfax. By Samuel Bowles, Editor of "The Springfield Republican." *Springfield, Mass.: Samuel Bowles & Company. New York: Hurd & Houghton.* 1866. 8vo, pp. xx, 452.

BOWLES. Von Ocean zu Ocean. ... Nach den Reisebriefen des Verfassers frei bearbeitet von Robert Schweichel. *Leipzig: Schlicke.* 1868. 8vo; pp. vii, 231. 7078

BOWLES. Our New West. Containing the results of two Journeys to the Rocky Mountains. Announced in 1869. 7079

BOWLES. Genealogical and Historical Notes of the Bowles Family. By Samuel Bowles ... . [Second Issue, revised.] January 1, 1851. [n. p. n. d.] 8vo, pp. 8. H. 7080

BOWLES (W.) Suggestions for the Speedy and Secure conveyance of our Reinforcements to Canada. By Captain W. Bowles, R.N. *London.* 1837. 8vo, pp. 12. 7081

BOWLES (W. A.) Authentic Memoirs of William Augustus Bowles, Esquire, Ambassador From the United Nations of Creeks and Cherokees, to the Court of London. *London: R. Faulder.* M. DCC. XCI. 12mo, Title, pp. vi, 79. H. P. 7082

"Mr. Bowles was a native of Maryland; and, being of an unsettled, roving, and enterprising disposition, attached himself to one of the Indian nations, became enamored of a savage life, and married a savage girl; then settled among her friends, and became by adoption an Indian Warrior." — RICH, I. 368. The pamphlet does not state the object of his errand to England.

BOWLES. The Life of General W. A. Bowles, A Native of America — Born of English Parents, in Frederick County, Maryland, in the Year 1744. From "Public Characters, for 1802." *London. New York: Re-printed by Robert Wilson.* 1803. 8vo, pp. 31. 7083

BOWLES (W. L.) The Ancient Missionary of Chili. A Poem Descriptive of South America. By Rev. W. L. Bowles. *London: Bulcock.* 1835. 12mo. 7084

BOWLES. The Missionary of the Andes. *London.* 1822. 12mo. 7085

A poem. Perhaps a reprint of "The Missionary; a Poem. Second Edition, enlarged. *London.* 1815. 8vo. BD. + *Philadelphia.* 1815. 12mo. + Third Edition. *London.* 1816. 16mo, pp. vii, 205. MN.

BOWLES. The Spirit of Discovery; or, the Conquest of Ocean. A Poem, in Five Books: with Notes, Historical and Illustrative. By the Reverend Wm. Lisle Bowles ... . *Bath printed: sold by Cadell and Davies, and J. Mawman, London.* 1804. 12mo, Title, pp. xxii, (1), 254. 2 Plates. + *London.* 1806. 8vo. + *London.* 1809. 7086

Pages 161–166, 209–216 relate to America.

BOWLIN (J. B.) The Judiciary System. Speech of Hon. James B. Bowlin ... in the House ... March 6, 1848. [*Washington.* n. d.] 8vo, pp. 7. H. 7087

BOWLIN. Railroad to the Pacific. Speech of Hon. James B. Bowlin of Missouri ... March 19, 1850 ... [n. p. n. d.] 8vo, pp. 7. 7088

Also: Speech ... on the Naturalization Laws. ... In the House ... December 18, 1845. *Washington.* 1846. 8vo, pp. 6. H. — Speech ... on the Oregon Question, ... in the House ... January 6. 1846. [n. p. n. d.] 8vo, pp. 8. — Speech ... on the Bill to reduce and graduate the Price of the Public Lands to Actual Settlers ... . in the House ... July 6, 1846. [n. p. n. d.] 8vo, pp. 7. H.

BOWLING (W. K.) Historical Address to the Graduating Class of 1868, University of Nashville. By W. K. Bowling, M.D. *Nashville: W. N. F. Lyon, Printer.* 1868. 8vo, pp. 31.

BOWLING. Lecture Introductory to the Second Course in the Medical Department of the University of Nashville ... Nov. 1st ... . By W. K. Bowling, M.D., Prof. ... *Nashville, Tenn.* 1853. 8vo, pp. 23. H. 7090

With historical remarks on the school.

BOWLY (Samuel). A Speech delivered on the 1st of Oct. 1830. At a Public Meeting in Gloucester, on the Abolition of Slavery. 1831. 12mo. 7091

BOWMAN (A.) Bear-hunters of the Rocky Mountains. By Anne Bowman ... . Illustrated by Zwecker. *London: Routledge, Warne & Routledge.* 1861. 16mo. + *Boston: Crosby & Nichols.* 1862. 12mo, pp. 474. + Illustrated. [*Ibid.*] 16mo. + [*Ibid.*] 1864. 12mo. 7092

BOWMAN. Clever Jack, and other Tales, By Anne Bowman ... . *New York: James Miller.* 1865 [1864]. 12mo. B. 7093

One of the tales is: "The Indians and the Gold Mines."

BOWMAN. Esperanza: or, the Home of the Wanderers. By Anne Bowman. *London: Routledge.* 1854. 12mo, pp. 435.

BOWMAN (J.) Remarks on the Result of an Ecclesiastical Council which met at Dorchester 14 Nov 1773 with some reflections on the proceedings of the Church as set forth in the Narrative and on the reasons of the dismission of Jonathan Bowman. *Boston.* 1774. 8vo, pp. 39. S. 7095

BOWMAN (Samuel M.) *and* IRWIN (R. B.) Sherman and his Campaigns: a Military Biography. By Col. S. M. Bowman and Lt.-Col. R. B. Irwin. *New York: Charles B. Richardson* [etc.] 1865. 8vo, pp. 520. 8 Portraits, and 4 Maps. C. H. 7096

Re-issued in 1868, under the name of S. M. Bowman only. 8 l., pp. 512. 5 Maps.

BOWNAS (S.) An Account of the Life Travels and Christian Experiences in the Work of the Ministry of Samuel Bownas. [Edited by J. Besse.] *London: Luke Hinde.* 1756. 8vo, pp. 216. C. + *London Printed. Philadelphia: Re-printed by Wm. Dunlap.* 1759. 8vo, pp. (2), 242. + The Second Edition. *London: Luke Hinde.* 1761. 8vo, pp. 216. + *London: James Phillips.* 1795. 12mo, pp. 204. + *Stamford: Henry and John F. Hull.* 1805. 12mo, pp. 306. + New Edition. *London: Charles Gilpin.* 1846. Fcap 8vo, pp. 288. 7097

Reprinted in the "Friend's Library," Vol. XII. *London.* 1836. And Vol. III. *Philadelphia.* 1839. 12mo. Bownas landed in Maryland, 1702. Soon after he arrived he held a public dispute with George Keith; also with William Bradford, and suffered imprisonment for his belief. His account of the *Labadies*, a community resembling the Shakers, is very amusing. A statement on page 58 of the first edition conveys the idea that his answer to George Keith was printed at Philadelphia.

BOWNAS. An Account of Elizabeth Hanson. *See* Hanson (E.)

BOWRIE (Thomas). A Dictionary of the Hudson's Bay Indian Language. [n. p. About 1776.] Folio, pp. 8. 7098

Title from Ludewig's Lit. Ab. Lang. Allibone gives the author's *name* Bowrey, and the *date* 1701.

BOYCE (*Capt.*) Seizure of the Ship Industry, by a Conspiracy, and the consequent sufferings of Captain James Fox and his companions, their captivity among the Indians in North America, etc. ... By Captain Boyce. *London.* [n. d.] 8vo, pp. 287. Plate. 7099

BOYCE (William W.) The Annexation of Cuba. Speech of Hon. W. W. Boyce, of S. Carolina, delivered in the House of Representatives, January 15, 1855. [*Washington.* n. d.] 8vo, pp. 7. H. 7100

BOYD (Adam). A discourse, sacred to the memory of George Washington, the father of his country. Delivered in Nashville, 22d of February, 1800. *Nashville* (*Tenn.*) 1800. 8vo, pp. 22.

BOYD (A.) State of the Accounts of Andrew Boyd, Esq. late a Sub-Lieutenant of Chester County. From March 1777, to March 1780. In which is exhibited, The amount of the Monies received by him for Fines incurred within that Time in the 8th Battallion of militia, and accounted for. Together with Lists shewing by whom the same were paid, ... *Philadelphia: Printed by F. Bailey.* MDCCLXXIV. 8vo, pp. 12. P. 7102

Title misprinted 1774 for 1784.

BOYD (Andrew). Business Directory and Gazetteer of the towns and villages on the Albany and Susquehanna railroad; and of Cooperstown, Delhi, Norwich, Oxford, Franklin, etc., 1868–9. *Albany: C. Van Benthuysen & Sons.* 1868. 8vo, pp. 220. C. 7103

Boyd's Auburn Directory, [with] Business Directory of Cayuga Co., 1867–68. Compiled by A. & W. H. Boyd. *Auburn: A. & W. H. Boyd.* [1867.] 12mo, pp. 286. 1 Map. C. 7104

Boyd's Business Directory of the Counties of Berks, Lebanon, Lehigh, Northampton, and Schuylkill, Pa. 1860. [n. p. n. d.] 8vo, pp. 1–48, 149–232, 49–123. H. 7105

BOYD (A. H.) Thanksgiving Sermon delivered in Winchester,

Va., November 29, 1860. By A. H. Boyd, D.D. *Winchester: J. H. Crum & Co.* 1860. 8vo, pp. 20. 7106

BOYD. [Vindication of his conduct as agent of the York Manufacturing Company. n. p. 1854.] 8vo, pp. 13. H. 7107

BOYD (Belle). *See* [Hardinge (*Mrs.* B.)]

BOYD (G.) A Pastoral Letter addressed to the Members of St. John's Church ... Philadelphia, on ... abolishing the System of Pew Rents, and making their Place of Worship Free. By the Rev. George Boyd. *Philadelphia: Wm. Stavely.* MDCCCXXXVI. 8vo, pp. 8. H. 7108

BOYD (H.) Miscellaneous Works of Hugh Boyd ... the Author of the Letters of Junius. *London.* 1800. 2 vols., 8vo, pp. xiii, 291, 323; 495. C. 7109

Includes abstracts of the two great speeches of Earl Chatham on the American War. If the title-page is to be believed, an important and vexed question is settled as to the identity of Junius.

BOYD (J.) Address ... before the Charitable Irish Society in Boston at ... their Centennial Anniversary, March 17, 1837. By James Boyd, President ... . *Boston: James B. Dow.* 1837. 8vo, pp. 40. H. 7110

On the conduct of the Irish here, the naturalization laws, etc.

BOYD (J). The Vision, and Other Poems, in Blank Verse, By John Boyd, A Man of Colour, ... Preliminary Observations by C. R. Nesbitt, Esq. *Exeter.* 1834. 12mo, pp. xix, 23.

The author was a native of New Providence.

BOYD (John). Railways in New Brunswick, published by the Chamber of Commerce. *St. John, N. B.* 7112

This imperfect title is from Morgan's "Bib. Canadensis."

BOYD (J. A.) A Summary of Canadian History: from the time of Cartier's Discovery to the Present Time. By John A. Boyd, M.A. *Toronto.* 1860. 8vo, pp. 123. 7113

The eighteenth thousand was published in 1865.

BOYD (J. P.) Documents and Facts, relative to Military Events during the late War. By John P. Boyd, Brig. Gen. in the U. S. Army. [n. p. 1816.] 8vo, pp. 28. C. H. 7114

BOYD. ... Col J. P. Boyd's New Orleans and Carrollton Mass Meeting Speeches. ... August 5, 1867, and ... 29th ... . [*New Orleans: N. O. Republican Office.* n. d.] 8vo, pp. 8. H.

BOYD (L.) Biographical Sketch of Hon. Linn Boyd of Kentucky, the present speaker of the House of Representatives of the United States. By a Virginian. *Washington.* 1852. 8vo, pp. 16. 7116

BOYD. Speeches and Proceedings upon the Announcement of the Death of the Hon. Linn Boyd, in the Senate and House of Representatives of Kentucky ... December 20, 1859. *Frankfort, Ky.: Jno. B. Major, State Printer.* 1860. 8vo, pp. 52. Portrait. H. 7117

[BOYD (S. S.)] Considerations on the Appointment of a Justice of the Supreme Court of the United States ... addressed to the President and Senate. By Jurisconsult. [*Natchez?*] 1852. 8vo, pp. 14. H. 7118

BOYD (W.) God's Way the Best Way. Briefly and Plainly demonstrated in a Sermon preach'd at the Lecture in Boston. March 19, 1718–1719. By William Boyd, A.M. *Boston.* 1719. 12mo, pp. 22. M. 7119

BOYD. An Oration, on the Death of Mr. John Russell, Senior Sophister, at Harvard University. Delivered November 25, in the College Chapel; By William Boyd. *Boston: Printed by John W. Folsom, for the Author.* M,DCC,XCV. 8vo, pp. 18. H.

Also: Woman: a Poem. *Boston: J. W. Folsom.* 1796. 4to, pp. 15. H.

BOYD. ... (From the Montreal Transcript.) Swartzen. Model of an Advertisement for a Canadian Furrier. [Signed] William Boyd, Typ. Montreal, January 1859. [n. p. n. d.] Tall 8vo, pp. 3. H. 7121

In the metre of "Hiawatha."

BOYD (W. H.) Business Directory of Essex, Hudson and Union Counties, N. J. *New York.* 1859. 12mo. 7122

BOYD. New York City Tax Book, being a List of Persons, Corporations, and Co-partnerships, Resident and Non-Resident, who were taxed according to the Assessor's Books, 1856–57. By W. H. Boyd. [*New York.* 1857.] 12mo, pp. 248. S. 7123

BOYD. Pictorial Directory of Broadway, in which will be found an Alphabetical, a Business, and a Numerical or Street Directory, giving the Names of the Occupants of every Building on Broadway. Illustrated with Views of Public Buildings and Places of Business. *New York: William H. Boyd.* 1859. 8vo. 7124

BOYD. Pennsylvania Business Directory. ... *Philadelphia.* 1861. 8vo. 7125

See also Delaware, Kingston, Newark, Newport, Norwich, Paterson, Pawtucket, Philadelphia, Rome, Rondout, Schenectady, etc.

BOYDEN (E.) The Epidemic of the Nineteenth Century. [The Anti-Slavery Mania.] By E. Boyden, Of Hopedale ... Va. *Richmond: Chas. H. Wynne, Printer.* 1860. 8vo, pp. 25.

BOYDEN (J. W.) The Evidence of the Validity of the Will of Oliver Smith, and the Arguments of Messrs. Choate and Webster in the Supreme Judicial Court at Northampton. With A Biographical Sketch, and a Copy of the Will and Probate Proceedings. By James W. Boyden ... . *Amherst: H. B. Nims.* 1847. 8vo, pp. 60. H. 7127

BOYE (Emmanuel de). Vita et Obitus Ven. P. Henrici Wenceslai Richter, S. J., ex Provincia Bohemiæ in Americam missi, et ibi trucidati. *Pragæ.* 1675. 8vo. 7128

BOYE (J.) America, Om af de Gamle kiendt: Af de Nyere hvorledes opdaget: og i sin Natur tildeels hvorledes befundet. Ap Johannes Boye, Professor. *Kiöbenhavn: J. Rüse.* 1829. Sm. 8vo, pp. 54. C. 7129

"This is merely the commencement of a great work interrupted by his death."—ESSLEW.

BOYER (B. M.) Admission of Alabama. Speech of Hon. Benjamin M. Boyer ... in the House ... March 17, 1868. *Washington: F. & J. Rives & Geo. A. Bailey.* 1868. 8vo, pp. 8. H. 7130

BOYER. Impeachment of the President. Speech of Hon. Benjamin M. Boyer ... in the House ... February 22, 1868. *Washington.* 1868. 8vo, pp. 8. H. 7131

BOYER (*Lieut.*) A Journal of Wayne's Campaign; Being an Authentic Daily Record of the most Important Occurrences during the Campaign of Major General Anthony Wayne, against the Northwestern Indians; Commencing on the 28th Day of July, and Ending on the 2d Day Nov. 1794, including an Account of the Great Battle of August 20th. By Lieutenant Boyer. *Cincinnati, O.: William Dodge.* 1866. 4to, pp. 23.

Usually found with Jacob's "Life of Cresap. *Cincinnati.* 1866."

BOYER (Paul). Veritable|Relation|de tovt ce qvi|s'est fait

et passé|au voyage que Monsieur de|Bretigny fit à l'Amérique|Occidentale. Auec vne Description des Mœurs, & des|Prouinces de tous les Sauuages de cette|grande partie du Cap de Nord: vn Diction-|naire de la Langue [Galibienne], & vn aduis tres-neces-|saire à tous ceux qui veulent habiter ou faire|habiter ce Païs-là, ou qui desirent d' y esta-|blir des Colonies.|Le tout fait sur les lieux, par Pavl Boyer,|Escuyer, Sieur de Petit-Puy.|*A Paris, Chez Pierre Rocolet* ...|...|...|M. DC. LIV.|...| Sm. 8vo, 10 l., pp. 463, (1). H. S. 7133

Also on large paper. Priced, Trosse, 1866, 110 fr. Sold at Puttick's, 1854, £1 8s. Contains an account of the first establishment of the French in Guyane, in 1653. "Bretigny—un homme feroce, qui, ayant egalement declaré la guerre aux colons et au sauvages, fut massacré."—RAYNAL.

BOYER-PEYRELEAU (Eugène Édouard). Événements de la Guadeloupe en 1814 et pendant les Cent jours, avec une relation du procès du contre-amiral Linois, gouverneur, et de l'adjudant général Boyer-Peyreleau, commandant en second. Extrait de l'Histoire générale des Antilles ... . Précédé d'une Déclaration de l'auteur à ses concitoyens, et d'une Notice biographique par l'éditeur. *Alais: Martin.* 1849. 8vo. 7134

BOYER-PEREYLEAU. Les Antilles françaises, particulièrement la Guadeloupe, depuis leur découverte jusqu'au 1er janvier 1823. *Paris: Brissot-Thivars.* 1823. 3 vols., 8vo, pp. viii, 420. Map. 446. 14 Plates. 530. + Jusqu'au 1er novembre 1825, par Le colonel Boyer Peyreleau (Eugène Édouard) ... . Deuxième édition. *Paris: Ladvocat.* 1826. 3 vols., 8vo, pp. xvi, 420, Map; 2 l., pp. 466; 3 l., 11 folded l., pp. 530. H. 7135

"The last volume does not extend beyond 1816."—QUÉRARD. The "Cat. de l'hist. de France," published by the Bibliothèque imperiale, dates the 2e éd. 1825.

BOYLE (F.) A Ride Across a Continent: a Personal Narrative of Wanderings in Central America. By Frederick Boyle, F.R.G.S. *London: Strahan & Co.; and Richard Bentley.* 1868. 2 vols., Post 8vo, pp. 620. Illustrations. 7136

BOYLE (H.) Chronology of the Eighteenth and Nineteenth Centuries, comprehending every important transaction from the year 1700 to the close of the year 1825. By Henry Boyle. *London: Sherwood, Gilbert & Piper.* 1826. 8vo, pp. iv, 688. C.

BOYLE (I.) An Historical Memoir of the Boston Episcopal Charitable Society. By Isaac Boyle, D.D. ... *Boston: the Society.* 1840. 8vo, pp. 31. H. 7138

BOYLE (*Captain* Robert). *See* [Chetwood (W. R.)]

BOYLE (R.) General Heads for the Natural History of a Country Great or Small; Drawn for the Use of Travellers and Navigators. *London.* 1692. 12mo. 7139

Chapter VIII. relates to Virginia; IX., to Guiana and Brasil; X., to the Antilles and Carribbe Islands.

BOYLSTON (T.) The Will of Thomas Boylston, Esq. Late of London. [With Remarks of Ward Nicholas Boylston on his Bequest to the Town of Boston. *Boston.* 1816.] 8vo, pp. 16. H. 7140

BOYLSTON (Z.) An Historical Account of the Small-Pox inoculated in New England, Upon all Sorts of Persons, Whites, Blacks, and of all Ages and Constitutions. With some Account of the Nature of the Infection in the Natural and Inoculated Way, and their different Effects on Human Bodies. With some short Directions to the Unexperienced in this Method of Practice. Humbly dedicated to her Royal Highness the Princess of Wales, By Zabdiel Boylston, F.R.S. *London: Printed for S. Chandler, at the Cross-Keys in the Poultry.* M.DCC.XXVI. 4to, pp. 62. + The Second Edition, Corrected. *Re-Printed at Boston in N. E. for S. Gerrish in Cornhil, and T. Hancock at the Bible and Three Crowns in Annstreet.* M. DCC. XXX. 8vo, pp. vi, vi, 53.

Dr. Boylston was the first person to introduce this practice into New England. *See* Allen's "Biog. Dict."

BOYLSTON. A Letter to Dr. Zabdiel Boylston, occasioned by a late Dissertation concerning Inoculation. *Boston.* 1730. 8vo, pp. 14. 7142

See Allen's "Biog. Dict.," article Boylston.

BOYLSTON. Some Account of what is said of Inoculating or Transplanting the Small-Pox, by Dr. Emanuel Timonius and Jacobus Pylarinus. With Remarks. By Zabdiel Boylston. *Boston.* 1721. 16mo, pp. 22. M. 7143

See "Analytical Magazine," VI. 69.

Boylston Medical Society of Harvard University. Catalogue of the Members. *Boston.* 1819. B. + ... Catalogue of the Officers and Students, and Course of Instruction in the Boylston Medical School. Fifth Year, 1851–52. *Boston.* 1852. 8vo, pp. 16. Continued. H. 7144

A Reply to the Remonstrance to the Legislature of the Faculty of the Massachusetts Medical College, against the Petition of the Boylston Medical School for Power to confer Medical Degrees. [*Boston.* 1854.] 4to, pp. 2. 7145

BOYNTON (C. B.) English and French Neutrality, and the Anglo-French Alliance, in their Relation to the United States, & Russia, including an Account of the Leading Policy of France and of England for the Last Two Hundred years—the Origin and Aims of the Alliance—the Meaning of the Crimean War—and the Reason of the Hostile Attitude of these Two Powers towards the United States, and of the Movement on Mexico; with a Statement of the General Resources—the Army and Navy of England and France—Russia and America—showing the Present Strength and Probable Future of these Four Powers. By Rev. C. B. Boynton, D.D. *Cincinnati: C. F. Vent & Co.* [also] *Chicago.* 1864. 8vo, pp. 576. B. 7146

BOYNTON. The Four Great Powers: England, France, Russia and America. Their Policy, Resources, and Probable Future. A revision with important modification of the work by the same author, entitled "English and French Neutrality, etc." By Rev. C. B. Boynton, D.D. *Cincinnati: C. F. Vent & Co.* 1866. 8vo, pp. 520.

BOYNTON. "God's Hand in the War." A Sermon, By Rev. C. B. Boynton ... 13th of April, and ... repeated ... on the 27th. *Cincinnati: "Free Nation" Office.* 1862. Large 8vo, pp. 16. B.

BOYNTON. The History of the Navy during the Rebellion. By Charles B. Boynton, D.D. ... Illustrated with numerous engravings. *New York: D. Appleton & Company.* 1867–68. 2 vols., 8vo, pp. 576; 579, (1), 1 l. Portraits and colored Lithographs.

See "The Saturday Rev.," XXIV. 577–579.

BOYNTON. History of West Point, and its Military Importance during the American Revolution; and the Origin and Progress of the United States Military Academy. By Captain Edward C. Boynton, A.M. *New York: D. Van Nostrand.* 1863. 8vo, pp. xviii, (1), 9–408. 35 Illustrations, including Maps. B.

One hundred copies printed on large paper. Also: The Navies of England, France, America, and Russia [extracted from No. 7247 *supra*] ... *New York: John F. Trow, Printer.* 1865. 8vo, pp. 72. H.—Oration, delivered on the Fifth of July, 1847, before the Native Americans of Cincinnati. ... *Cincinnati: Tagart & Gardner, Printers.* 1847. 8vo, pp. 24. H.—Oration delivered before the New England Society of Cincinnati, on the Anniversary of the Landing of the Pilgrims, December 22d, 1847. ... *Cincinnati: the Society.* 1848. 8vo, pp. 32. H.—Our Country, the Herald of a new Era; a lecture delivered before the Young Men's Mercantile Library Association, of Cincinnati. ... *Cincinnati.* 1847. 8vo.

BOYNTON *and* MASON (T. B.) A Journey through Kansas; with sketches of Nebraska; describing the country, climate, soil, mineral, manufacturing, and other resources. By Rev. C. B. Boynton and T. B. Mason, committee from the "Kansas League" of Cincinnati. With a new and authentic map. *Cincinnati: Moore, Wilstach, Keys & Co.* 1855. 8vo, pp. 216. Map. C. 7151

A third edition has been published.

BOYNTON (T. J.) Oration delivered at Key West, Florida, July 4, 1861. By Thomas J. Boynton. *Key West.* 1861. 8vo, pp. 23. 7152

The Boys and Girls Stories of the War. Contents: General Stonewall Jackson, Commodore Foot and Colonel Small, etc. etc. *Richmond: West & Johnston.* [n. d.] 32mo, pp. 32. H.

BOZMAN (J. L.) The History of Maryland, from its First Settlement, in 1633, to the Restoration, in 1660, with a Copious Introduction, and Notes and Illustrations. By John Leeds Bozman. *Baltimore: James Lucas & E. K. Deaver.* 1837. 2 vols., 8vo, pp. xii, 9–314; 728. C., H. 7154

BOZMAN. A Sketch of the History of Maryland, during the Three First Years after its Settlement: to which is prefixed, a Copious Introduction. By John Leeds Bozman. *Baltimore: Edward J. Coale.* 1811. 8vo, pp. 387, (1). Portrait of Geo. Calvert. C., H. 7155

BRACE (Charles L.) Address upon the Industrial School Movement, delivered ... November, 1857, by C. L. Brace ... . *New York.* 1857. 8vo, pp. 27. H. 7156

BRACE. The Best Method of disposing of our Pauper and Vagrant Children. C. L. Brace ... . *New York: Wynkoop, Hallenbeck & Thomas, Printers.* 1859. 8vo, pp. 36. H. 7157

BRACE. Short Sermons to Newsboys: with a history of the formation of the Newsboys' Lodging House. By Charles Loring Brace. Illustrations. *New York: C. Scribner & Co.* 1866. 16mo, pp. vi, 244. C. 7158

BRACE (Jonathan). Half-Century Discourse. History of the Church in Newington [Conn.] ... in the Discourse delivered ... 16th of January, 1855 ... by J. Brace, D.D. ... *Hartford.* M. DCCC. LV. 8vo, pp. 75. Portrait. H. 7159

Brace (J. P.) The Fawn of the Pale Faces; or, Two Centuries ago. By J. P. Brace. *New York: D. Appleton & Company.* MDCCCLIII. 12mo, pp. 288. 7160

Bracht (Viktor). Texas im Jahre 1848. Nach mehrjährigen Beobachtungen dargestellt von Viktor Bracht. Mit verschiedenartigen Zugaben Auszügen aus Briefen. *Elberfield: Jul. Bädeker.* 1849. 8vo, pp. xii, 322. (Neueste Länderkunde, Bd. 1.) c. 7161

Brackenridge (Henry M.) Early Discoveries by Spaniards in New-Mexico; containing an account of the Castles of Cibola, and the Present appearance of their Ruins. By H. M. Brackenridge ... . *Pittsburgh, Pa.: H. Miner.* 1857. 8vo, pp. 48. s.

Brackenridge. History of the Late War, Between the United States and Great-Britain. Containing a Minute Account of the various Military and Naval Operations. Illustrated with Plates. By H. M. Brackenridge Esq. Second Edition. *Baltimore: Joseph Cushing.* 1817. 12mo, pp. 363. 6 Plates. + Third Edition. Revised and Corrected. *Baltimore: Cushing & Jewett.* 1817. 12mo, pp. 360. 5 Plates. c. + Fourth Edition Revised and Corrected. *Baltimore: Cushing & Jewett.* 1818. 12mo, pp. xxiv, 348. + *Philadelphia.* 1839. 12mo, pp. 298. Plates. + [*Ibid.*] *Philadelphia: James Kay, Jun. and Brother.* 1844. 12mo, pp. 298. c. + [*Ibid.*] 1845. + [*Ibid.*] 1846. pp. 298. c. 7163

Brackenridge. Histoire de la Guerre entre les Etats-Unis d'Amerique et l'Angelterre, pendant les années 1812, 1813, 1814, et 1815. Par H. M. Brackenridge, citoyen Americains traduite sur la seconde edition par A. de Dalmas avec une carte du théâtre de la guerre par A. de Delmas. *Paris: Corbet.* 1820. 2 vols., 8vo, 2 l., pp. 310; 2 l., 317. Map. c. + Nouvelle édition, augumentée de la carte du théâtre de la guerre et du traité de paix entre Sa Majesté britannique et les Etats-Unis. *Paris: Brissot-Thivars [et] Corbet.* 1822. 2 vols., 8vo. Map.

Brackenridge. Istoria della guerra fra gli Stati-Uniti d' America e l'Inghilterra, negli anni 1812–15. Tradotta da G. Borsieri. *Milano: Bettoni.* 1821. 8vo. 7165

Brackenridge. History of the Western Insurrection in Western Pennsylvania, commonly called the Whiskey Insurrec-

tion. 1794. By H. M. Brackenridge ... . *Pittsburgh: Printed by W. S. Haven.* 1859. 8vo, pp. 336. c., H. 7166

The author's father defended the insurgents; in this work, the father is defended. *See* "Hist. Mag.," III. 377; also, Craig (N. B.)

Brackenridge. North American Pamphlet on South American Affairs. *London.* 1818. 8vo, pp. 35–83. c., H. 7167

This is a reprint of No. 7172 *infra* in "The Pamphleteer," Vol. XIII., No. XXV.

Brackenridge. Journal of a Voyage up the River Missouri; performed in Eighteen Hundred and Eleven, by H. M. Brackenridge, Esq. *Baltimore: Coale and Maxwell.* 1815. 12mo, pp. 247. + Second Edition, Revised and Enlarged by the Author. *Baltimore: Coale and Maxwell.* 1816. 12mo, pp. viii, 246. H.

First published with the "Views of Louisiana." *See* N. A. R., IV. 112–128.

Brackenridge. Letters to the Public, relating to the President's removing him from office, as one of the Judges of Florida. 1832. 8vo. W. 7169

Brackenridge. Mexican Letter. *Washington.* 1850. 8vo.

Brackenridge. Recollections of Persons and Places in the West. By H. M. Brackenridge, a Native of the Ohio. *Philadelphia: James Kay, Jun. and Brother.* [1834.] 12mo, pp. 244. H. + Second Enlarged Edition. *Philadelphia: J. B. Lippincott & Co.* 1868. 12mo, pp. 331. c. 7171

There are editions, dated 1836, 1838, and 1840.

[**Brackenridge.**] South America. A Letter to J. Monroe, President U. S. A. on the present state of that Country. *Washington.* 1817 or 1818. 8vo, pp. 52. 7172

Republished in "The Pamphleteer." Translated into French, by De Pradt.

Brackenridge. Speech on the Tariff, delivered in Broadhurst's Grove, 6th Oct. 1843. *Pittsburgh.* 1843. 8vo. 7173

Brackenridge. A Speech delivered by H. M. Brackenridge, in the Presidential Campaign of 1864. Sixty Years in the North and Twenty Years in the South. *Pittsburgh.* 1865. 8vo, pp. 74. H. 7174

Brackenridge. The Spirit of the Public Journals; or, Beauties of the American Newspapers for the Year 1805. *Baltimore: Printed by George Dobbin & Murphy.* 1806. 12mo, pp. 300. c. 7175

Brackenridge. Views of Louisiana; together with a Journal of a Voyage up the Missouri River, in 1811. By H. M. Brackenridge, Esq. *Pittsburgh, Cramer, Spear and Eichbaum.* 1814. 8vo, pp. 304. BA., C., H. 7176

Reprinted with the following title:

Brackenridge. Views of Louisiana; containing Geographical, Statistical and Historical Notices of that Vast and Important Portion of America. By H. M. Brackenridge, Esq. *Baltimore: Schaeffer & Maund.* 1817. 12mo, pp. 323. 7177

This does not include the "Journal," which was published separately. *Baltimore.* 1817. *See* No. 7168 *supra.*

Brackenridge. Ansichten von Louisiana nebst einem Tagebuche einer im Jahre 1811 den Missouri-Fluss aufwärts gemachtete Reise. Von H. M. Brackenridge. Aus dem Englischen. *Weimar: Ind.-Compt.* 1818. 8vo. 7178

"Readers may get some idea of the difficulties which attend the compilation of such a work as the present by comparing the title above with the form in which I first found it, in one of the catalogues published by Charles B. Norton, New York, 1858, from which it has been restored by conjectural emendation. 'Anfichter von Louisiana nebt einen Jozebudre einer, inr Zahre, 1811, den Missouri. Flup answurts gemadote Reize. Von H. M. Brackeridge. *Weimar.* 1818. 8vo.' The words 'Aus dem Englischen' and '*Ind.-Compt.*' are taken from another source, which, however, gave only the first three words of the title. It is but fair to add that this is an unusually bad case." — C. A. C.

Brackenridge. Voyage to South America, performed by Order of the American Government, in the Years 1817 and 1818, in the Frigate Congress. By H. M. Brackenridge, Esq. Secretary to the Mission ... In Two Volumes. ... *Baltimore: the Author.* 1819. 8vo, pp. 351, (1), 381. Map. H. + *London: Printed for T. and J. Allman.* 1820. 8vo, pp. xix, 331, Appendix, 40; 2 l., pp. 317. c. 7179

Another English edition has the following title:

Brackenridge. Voyage to Buenos Ayres, performed in the Years 1817 and 1818, by order of The American Government. By H. M. Brackenridge, Secretary to the Mission. *London: R. Phillips.* 1820. 8vo, pp. 116. 7180

"An extraordinary mass of information, replete with philosophic views." — Baron Humboldt. *See* M. R., XCIII. 82.

Brackenridge. Reise nach Südamerika, in den Jahren 1817–18. Aus dem Englischen. *Leipzig: Göschen.* 1821. 2 vols., 8vo. Map. 7181

[**Brackenridge.**] Strictures on a Voyage to South America, as Indited by the "Secretary to the (late) Mission" to La Plata; including Observations on the Capability of the Spanish Americans for Civil Liberty ... By a Friend of Truth and Sound Policy. *Baltimore.* 1820. 8vo, pp. 175. s. 7182

Brackenridge *and others.* Speeches on the Jew Bill, in the House of Delegates of Maryland, by H. M. Brackenridge, Col. W. G. D. Worthington, and John S. Tyson, Esquire. Together with an Argument on the Chancery Powers, and an Eulogy on Thomas Jefferson, and John Adams, &c. By H. M. Brackenridge. *Philadelphia: J. Dobson (Agent).* 1829. 8vo, 2 l., pp. 236. BA. C. 7183

[**Brackenridge** (Hugh Henry).] The Battle of Bunkers Hill. A Dramatic Piece of Five Acts, in Heroic Measure. By a Gentleman of Maryland. *Philadelphia: Printed and Sold by Robert Bell.* MDCCLXXVI. 8vo, 2 l., pp. 49. Plate. H., N. 7184

The frontispiece prefixed to this book, "The Death of Warren," engraved by Norman, is said to be the earliest known specimen of engraving in Brirish America by a native artist. The drama appears to have been actually represented on the stage. I have seen it attributed to John Burk, who wrote a piece with a somewhat similar title. *See* Burk (John). Sold at Puttick's, 1860, for £1 15s.

[**Brackenridge.**] The Death of General Montgomery, at the Siege of Quebec. A Tragedy. With an Ode, in honour of the Pennsylvania Militia, and the small band of regular Continental Troops, who sustained the Campaign, in the depth of Winter, January, 1777, and repulsed the British Forces from the Banks of the Delaware. By the Author of a Dramatic Piece on the Battle of Bunker's-Hill. To which are added, Elegiac Pieces, Commemorative of distinguished Characters. [Motto.] *Philadelphia: Robert Bell.* M,DCC,LXXVII. 8vo, pp. 79, (5). H. 7185

With a curious frontispiece on copper (Norman sc.) of the death of Montgomery, and an explanatory fly-leaf.

Brackenridge. An Eulogium of the Brave Men who have Fallen in the Contest with Great Britain; Delivered on Monday July 5, 1779. Before A Numerous and Respectable Assembly of Citizens and Foreigners in the German Calvanist Church, Philadelphia. By Hugh H. Brackenridge, A.M. *Philadelphia: Printed by F. Bailey.* [1779.] 4to, pp. 25. P. 7186

Brackenridge. Eine Lobrede auf diejenigen tapfern Männer, welche in dem Streit mit Gross-Brittanien gefallen ... . Von

Hugh H. Brackenridge, A.M. ... *Philadelphia: Gedruckt bey Steiner und Cist.* [n. d.] 12mo, pp. 23. H. 7187

Brackenridge. Gazette Publications. By H. H. Brackenridge. *Carlisle: Printed by Alexander & Phillips.* 1806. 12mo, pp. 348. c. 7188

Apparently privately printed. "It will serve to give some idea of what the town of Pittsburgh was at an early period, and the state of society at that time," July, 1786. — *Preface.*

Brackenridge. Incidents of the Insurrection in the Western Parts of Pennsylvania, In the Year 1794. By Hugh H. Brackenridge. *Philadelphia: John McCulloch.* 1795. 8vo, Title, 1 l., pp. 5–124; [Vol. II.], pp. 84; [Vol. III.], pp. 154.

A scarce book, in defence of the author and the subject. "It was at first intended to publish this work in three vols., with an appendix to each vol., &c. ... But this plan was relinquished, and it was judged best to publish the whole in one vol." (pp. 154.) This accounts for the three paginations; that the second and third begin with page 5 is, perhaps, owing to title-pages, etc., being dropped. *See* Brackenridge (H. M.), No. 7166 *supra.*

[**Brackenridge.**] A Poem on Divine Revelation; being an Exercise delivered at the Public Commencement at Nassau-Hall, September 28, 1774. By the same person who ... September 25, 1771, delivered a small Poem on the Rising Glory of America. *Philadelphia: R. Aitken.* 1774. 8vo, 2 l., pp. 22. s. 7190

The poem on the "Rising Glory of America," was the joint production of Freneau and Brackenridge. *See* Freneau (P.)

Brackenridge. Six Political Discourses, founded on Scripture. By H. H. Brackenridge, Esq. *Lancaster.* 1777. 12mo, pp. 88. P. 7191

These sermons were preached in the camp of the Revolutionary army. "Modern Chivalry," by the same author, is a work of much originality, and one of the earliest works of humor by an American author; it was first printed, *Philadelphia*, 1792–97. Reprinted, 1807, 1815, 1846, and 1851. This last edition is abridged, but contains a memoir of the author.

[**Brackenridge.**] The Standard of Liberty, an occasional paper. By Democritus. [*Philadelphia: Neely & Jones.* About 1802.] 8vo, pp. 55. c. 7192

Brackenridge (William D.) Botany: Cryptogamia: Filices: including Lycopodiaceæ and Hydropterides. *Philadelphia: Printed by C. Sherman.* 1854–6. 4to, pp. viii, 357, with Atlas, folio. 46 Plates. c. 7193

Forms vol. XVI. of the "U. S. Exploring Expedition." One hundred copies printed.

Bracket (A. N.) An Address delivered before the Coos Agricultural Society. By Adino N. Bracket. *Concord.* 1821. 8vo. c. 7194

Brackett (A. G.) History of the United States Cavalry, from the Formation of the Federal Government to the 1st of June, 1863. To which is added a List of all the Cavalry Regiments, with the Names of their Commanders, which have been in the United States Service since the Breaking out of the Rebellion. By Albert G. Brackett, Major ... . *New York: Harper & Brothers.* 1865. 12mo, pp. 337. B. C. 7195

Brackett. General Lane's Brigade in Central Mexico. By Albert G. Brackett, late an Officer in the United States Volunteer Service. *Cincinnati: H. W. Derby.* 1854. 12mo, pp. 366. Portrait. c. 7196

Brackett (Edward A.) Twilight Hours: or Leisure Moments of an Artist. By E. A. Brackett. ... *Boston: printed by Freeman and Bolles.* 1845. 12mo, pp. 95. H. 7197

Several of these essays are on American themes.

Brackett (J.) An Oration, pronounced in the Chapel, Dartmouth College, on the Fourth of July, 1805. ... By James Brackett ... . *Hanover, (N. H.): printed by Moses Davis.* [n. d.] 8vo, pp. 12. H. 7198

Brackett (J. W.) The Ghost of Law, or Anarchy and Despotism; a Poem, delivered before the Phi Beta Kappa Society, of Dartmouth College, at their Anniversary, August, 1803. By J. Warren Brackett. *Hanover: M. Davis.* 1803. 4to, pp. 24. N. 7199

Brackett. Oration delivered July Fourth, 1810, before the Washington Benevolent Society, and the Hamilton Society, of the City of New-York. By J. W. Brackett. ... *Brooklyn.* 1810. 8vo, pp. 16. H., N. 7200

Bradburn (G.) A Statement, by George Bradburn, of his Connection with the "True Democrat," and John C. Vaughan. *Cleveland: the Author.* 1853. 8vo, pp. 20. H. 7201

Bradburn (S.) An Address to the people called Methodists concerning the Evil of Encouraging the Slave Trade. By Samuel Bradburn. *Manchester.* 1792. 8vo, pp. 24. P. 7202

Reprinted with the following title:

Bradburn. An Address to the People called Methodists,

concerning the Criminality of Encouraging Slavery. By Samuel Bradburn. Fifth Edition. *London: M. Gurney.* [n. d.] 8vo, pp. 16. W. 7203

Bradbury (C.) History of Kennebunk Port, from its First Discovery by Bartholomew Gosnold, May 14, 1602, to A.D. 1837. By Charles Bradbury. *Kennebunk: printed by James K. Remich.* 1837. 12mo, pp. 301. Plate. BA., C., H., M. 7204

See N. A. R., XLVII. 259–261.

Bradbury (J. W.) Removals and Appointments to Office. Speech of Hon. J. W. Bradbury ... in the Senate ... April 23, 1850. [*Washington.* n. d.] 8vo, pp. 16. H. 7205

Bradbury. Speech of Hon. James W. Bradbury ... on the Bill providing for the Payment of Claims for French Spoilations previous to the Year 1800. Delivered in the Senate ... April 15, 1852. *Washington.* 1852. 8vo, pp. 20. H. 7206

Bradbury (J.) Travels in the Interior of America, in the Years 1809, 1810, and 1811; including a Description of Upper Louisiana, together with the States of Ohio, Kentucky, Indiana, and Tennessee, with the Illinois and Western Territories, and containing Remarks and Observations useful to Persons Emigrating to those Countries. By John Bradbury, F.L.S. ... *Liverpool: printed for the author, by Smith and Galway. London: published by Sherwood, Neely, and Jones.* 1817. 8vo, pp. xii, (Errata) 1 slip, pp. (1), 10–364. H. + Second Edition. *London: Sherwood, Neely & Son.* 1819. 8vo, pp. 346. Map. c. 7207

Osage vocabulary on pp. 215–219.

Bradbury (T.) The Necessity of Contending for Revealed Religion: with a Sermon on the Fifth of November, 1719. By Thomas Bradbury. To which is Prefix'd, A Letter from the Reverend Cotton Mather D.D. on the late Disputes about the Ever-Blessed Trinity. *London: H. Woodfall.* M.DCC.XX. 8vo, pp. xxiv, 88. W. + Reprinted. *Boston.* 1740. 7208

I find the following in a catalogue of Americana: The Ass: or, the Serpent. A Comparison between the Tribes of Issachar and Dan, in their Regard for Civil Liberty. November 5, 1712. By Thomas Bradbury. ... Third Edition. *London.* 1712. 12mo. + *Boston: printed by Edes and Gill.* M,DCC,LXVIII. 8vo, pp. 22. BA. C. + *Newburyport.* 1774. 8vo, pp. 29.

Braddock's Defeat; or, the First Field of the West; a Poem. By a Citizen of the West. With Historical Notes. *St. Louis.* 1839. 12mo. 7209

For other poems on this event, *see* Tilden's "Miscellaneous Pieces," also the "Pennsylvania Gazette, Sept. 30, 1756."

The Expedition of Major General Braddock to Virginia; with The Two Regiments of Hacket and Dunbar. Being Extracts of Letters from an Officer in one of those Regiments to his Friend in London, describing the March and Engagement in the Woods. Together With many little Incidents, giving A lively Idea of the Nature of the Country, Climate, and Manner in which the Officers and Soldiers lived; also the Difficulties they went through in that Wilderness. *London: Printed for H. Carpenter.* MDCCLV. 8vo, Half-Title, pp. 29. H. P. 7210

A rare tract, and "a vile misrepresentation of everything that the worthless, unknown scribbler undertakes to describe." M. R., XIII. 306. *See* [Chauncy (Charles)]. The Phil. Library possesses a broadside, entitled, "Advertisement. *Philadelphia, the 22d of May,* 1775. For 200 men to open the Cumberland road to Gen. Braddock:" to which a German translation is appended.

The History of an Expedition against Fort du Quesne, in 1755 under Major-General Edward Braddock, Generalissimo of H. B. M. Forces in America. Edited from the Original Manuscripts, by Winthrop Sargent, M.A., ... *Philadelphia: Lippincott, Grambo & Co.* 1855. 8vo, pp. 423. 21 Plates. 7211

Six Plans | Of the Different | Dispositions | of the | English Army, | Under the Command | of the | Late General Braddock, | in | North America. | I. Line of March with the whole | Baggage. | II. Plan of the Disposition of the | advanced Party, of four hun- | dred Men to protect the | Workers while clearing the | Road. | III. Encampment of the Detachment | sent from the Little Meadows. | IV. Line of March of the Detach- | ment sent from the Little Mea- | dows. | V. Plan of the Field of Battle on | the 9th of July 1755. | VI. A Map shewing the Rout and | Encampments of the Army. | By an Officer. | *London: | Printed for T. Jefferys at Charing Cross.* MDCCLVIII. | Folio. C. D. R. 7212

This series of plans is extremely rare. I know of but two perfect copies — one in the possession of Mr. John A. Rice, of Chicago; the other, with Mr. William M. Darlington, of Pittsburgh, Pa.

Bradford (A.) Anniversary Sermon at Plymouth, Mass. Dec. 21, 1804. By Alden Bradford. *Boston: Gilbert & Dean. Jan.*, 1805. 8vo, pp. 24. W. 7213

Bradford. Biographical Notices of distinguished Men in New England: Statesmen, Patriots, Physicians, Lawyers, Clergymen, and Mechanics. By Alden Bradford, LL.D. *Boston: S. G. Simpkins.* 1842. 12mo, pp. 464. C., H. 7214

See N. A. R., October, 1842.

BRADFORD. Biography of the Hon. Caleb Strong, several Years Governor of the State of Massachusetts. By Alden Bradford. *Boston: West, Richardson & Lord.* 1820. 8vo, pp. 30. C. H. 7215

BRADFORD. Complete and Authentic History of the Battle of Bunker Hill, June 17, 1775, derived from the Best Authorities. By Alden Bradford, Esq. *Boston: Bradley & Co.* 8vo, pp. 14. B. 7216

BRADFORD. A Discourse delivered at Hallowell, at the Opening of the Academy in that Place, May 5, 1795. By Alden Bradford ... *Hallowell.* 1795. 8vo. 7217

BRADFORD. A Discourse before the Society for Propagating the Gospel among the Indians and Others, in North America, November 4, 1830. By Alden Bradford ... . *Boston: Press of John Putnam.* 1830. 8vo, pp. 51. H., S. 7218

BRADFORD. Eulogy in Commemoration of the Sublime Virtues of General George Washington, Wiscasset, February 22, 1800. By Alden Bradford. *Wiscasset.* 1800. 8vo, pp. 16. BA.

BRADFORD. History of Massachusetts, From 1764, to July, 1775: when General Washington took Command of the American Army. By Alden Bradford ... *Boston: Richardson and Lord.* 1822. 8vo, pp. vii, pp. 414. BA., C., H. 7220

BRADFORD. History of Massachusetts, from July, 1775, when General Washington took Command of the American Army, at Cambridge, to the Year 1789, (Inclusive,) When the Federal Government was established under the Present Constitution. By Alden Bradford ... . *Boston: Wells and Lilly.* 1825. 8vo, pp. 376. BA., C., H. 7221

BRADFORD. History of Massachusetts, from the Year 1790, to 1820. By Alden Bradford. *Boston: the Author.* 1829. 8vo, pp. 327. BA., C. H. 7222

"The work of a gentleman, with whom New England history has been the study of a life, and who, from the official relation which he long sustained as Secretary of the Commonwealth, enjoyed peculiar advantages for its prosecution." — N. A. R., XLIV. 536; XXX. I. *See* Farmer and Moore's Coll., II. 129–143. The above 3 Nos. form a continuous series of three volumes.

BRADFORD. History of Massachusetts, for Two hundred Years: from the Year 1620 to 1820. By Alden Bradford ... . *Boston: Hilliard, Gray & Co.* 1835. 8vo, pp. 480. Map.

BRADFORD. History of the Federal Government for Fifty Years: from March 1789, to March, 1839. By Alden Bradford ... . *Boston: Samuel G. Simpkins. First of July,* 1840. 8vo, pp. 480. Portrait of Adams. BA., C., H. 7224

See N. A. R., October, 1842.

BRADFORD. Memoir of the Life and Writings of Rev. Jonathan Mayhew, D.D., Pastor of the West Church and Society in Boston, from June, 1747 to July, 1766. By Alden Bradford ... . *Boston: C. C. Little & Co.* 1838. 8vo, pp. iv, 484. Portrait. BA., C., H. 7225

See N. A. R., July, 1838.

BRADFORD. New-England Chronology: from the Discovery of the Country, by Cabot, in 1497, to 1800 [1820]. By Alden Bradford ... . *Boston: S. G. Simpkins.* 1843. 12mo, pp. 202.

BRADFORD. An Oration pronounced at Wiscasset, on the fourth of July, 1804, in commemoration of American Independence. By Alden Bradford. *Wiscasset.* 1804. 8vo, pp. 19. S.

[BRADFORD.] A Particular Account of the Battle of Bunker or Breed's Hill, on the 17th June, 1775. By a Citizen of Boston. *Boston.* 1825. 8vo, pp. 26. S. + Second Edition. *Boston.* 1825. S. 7228

BRADFORD. A Sermon delivered before The Congregational Society at Thomastown (Maine) November 2, 1806; being the Lord's day after the Interment of the Hon. Henry Knox, Who died, October 25th, Ætat: 56 Years. By Alden Bradford ... . [n. p.:] *Babson and Rust.* [n. d.] 8vo, pp. 16. C. H. 7229

BRADFORD. A Sermon delivered at Plymouth, December 21st, 1804; the Anniversary of the Landing of Our Fathers In December, 1620. By Alden Bradford ... . With Notes. *Boston. Jan.,* 1805. 8vo, pp. 24. H. 7230

BRADFORD. A Sermon delivered at the Ordination of the Rev. Nathan Tilton, to the Pastoral Care of the Church and Society in the Second Parish in Scarborough, December 10, 1800: by Alden Bradford ... . *Portsmouth: Printed by Charles Peirce.* 1801. 8vo, pp. 27. H., M. 7231

BRADFORD. Two Sermons delivered in Wiscasset (Pownalborough), 9th May, 1798, National Fast. *Wiscasset.* 1808. 8vo, pp. 20. W. 7232

Mr. Bradford also edited a collection of speeches. *See* under *Massachusetts.*

BRADFORD (A. W.) American Antiquities, and Researches into the Origin and History of the Red Race. By Alexander W. Bradford. *New York: Wiley & Putnam.* 1841. 8vo, pp. 435. C. 7233

Some copies have the imprint: *New York: Dayton and Saxton. Boston: Saxton and Pierce.* 1841. 8vo, pp. 435. H. An able investigation of the subject. A desirable companion to the works of Stephens and others, on the ruins of Central America. *See* N. A. R., LIV. 283, and "Athenæum," May 21, 1842.

BRADFORD. A Discourse delivered before the New York Historical Society ... November 20, 1845. By Alexander W. Bradford. *New York.* 1846. 8vo, pp. 31. C. N. 7234

BRADFORD. An Oration delivered at Portchester, in the Town of Rye, County of Westchester, on the Fourth Day of July, 1865, by Alexander W. Bradford. *New York: Bradstreet Press.* 1866. 8vo. pp. 42. 7235

BRADFORD (A. W.) Inaugural Address of Hon. Augustus W. Bradford, Governor of Maryland. Delivered in the Senate Chamber. Annapolis, January 8th, 1862. *Annapolis: Sipley & Co., Printers.* 1862. 8vo, pp. 15. 7236

This and the following relate to the Civil War.

BRADFORD. Message of Gen. Bradford to the General Assembly of Maryland; with Documents. January Session, 1864. *Annapolis: Bull & Supple, Printers.* 1864. 8vo, pp. 87. + January Session, 1865. *Annapolis: Bayly, Printer.* 1865. 8vo, pp. 32. 7237

BRADFORD (E.) Discourse at Hopkinton, Mass. Oct. 5, 1791, at the Ordination of Nathaniel Howe. By Ebenezer Bradford. *Newburyport.* 1791. 8vo. W. 7238

BRADFORD. The Duty of a Minister ... illustrated. A Sermon at the Installation of the Rev. John H. Stevens in the Church in Stoneham, Sept. 11, 1795. By Ebenezer Bradford, A.M. *Newburyport.* 1795. 8vo, pp. 31. 7239

BRADFORD. ... A Sermon, delivered on the Day of National Thanksgiving. February 19, 1795. By Ebenezer Bradford ... . *Boston.* M,DCC,XCV. 8vo, pp. 23. H. M. 7240

BRADFORD. ... A Sermon, delivered on the Day of Public Humiliation and Prayer ... April 2, 1795: with an ... Answer to Dr. Tappan's Remarks on his Thanksgiving Sermon, dated February 19, 1795. By Ebenezer Bradford ... . *Boston.* 1795. 8vo, pp. 40. H. 7241

BRADFORD. ... A Sermon delivered at the Ordination of the Rev. Moses Bradford, to the Pastoral Care of the Church in Francis Town, September 8, 1790. By Ebenezer Bradford. *Newburyport.* MDCCXCI. 8vo, pp. 32. 7242

BRADFORD. Sermon at the Ordination of Daniel Gould. *Newburyport.* 1795. 8vo. 7243

BRADFORD. Strictures on the Remarks of Dr. Samuel Langdon on the leading Sentiments in Dr. Hopkins's System of Doctrines. By Ebenezer Bradford, A.M. *Boston: J. Thomas.* 1794. 8vo, pp. 47. W. 7244

BRADFORD (E. P.) A Sermon preached at Concord, before ... the Legislature of ... New-Hampshire, June 7, 1821. By Ephraim P. Bradford ... . *Concord: printed by Hull & Moore.* 1821. 8vo, pp. 27. H. 7245

BRADFORD. A Sermon, preached at Dunbarton, N. H. December 27, 1843, at the Funeral of Rev. Walter Harris, D.D. First Pastor of the Congregational Church ... who died December 25, 1843, aged 82. By Ephraim P. Bradford ... . *Concord.* 1844. 8vo, pp. 16. H. 7246

[BRADFORD (Gamaliel), *Senior.*] State Prisons and the Penitentiary System vindicated ... . Also, some ... Remarks and Documents relating to the Massachusetts State Prison. By an Officer of this Establishment at Charlestown. *Charlestown: S. Etheridge.* 1821. 8vo, pp. 63. H. 7247

See Mass. Hist. Soc. Coll., 3d Ser., I.

[BRADFORD (Gamaliel), *M.D.*] A Letter to the Hon. Harrison Gray Otis, Peleg Sprague, and Richard Fletcher, Esq. [on Slavery]. ... *Boston: James Munroe and Company.* M DCCC XXXVI. 24mo, pp. 35. 7248

BRADFORD (G. W.) Historical and Biographical Address, delivered before the Cortland County Medical Society, at the fiftieth anniversary meeting, Aug. 10, 1858. By George W. Bradford, M.D., Secretary of the Society ... *Homer, N. Y.* 1858. 8vo, pp. 27. S. 7249

BRADFORD. Memoir of J. Miller. *Albany.* 1862. 8vo.

BRADFORD. The Christian Duty of Patriotism. A Sermon ... in Watertown, on Fast Day, April 16th, 1857 by George Bradford. ... *Boston.* 1857. 8vo, pp. 19. H. 7251

BRADFORD (James). *See* Gage (Thomas).

BRADFORD (John). Address to the Inhabitants of New Brunswick, and Nova Scotia, occasioned by the Mission of two Ministers, John James and Charles William Milton, sent out by the Countess of Huntington from her College in South Wales. By John Bradford. *London.* 1788. 8vo. 7252

BRADFORD (Moses). A Sermon delivered ... before ... the Governor, ... Council, etc., of ... New-Hampshire, June 4. 1812. *Concord.* 1812. 8vo. 7253

BRADFORD (S.) A Sermon Preached before the Incorporated Society for the Propagation of the Gospel in Foreign Parts; at their Anniversary Meeting in the Parish-Church of St. Mary Le Bow; on Friday the 19th of February 1719. By Samuel, Lord Bishop of Carlisle. *London.* 1720. 4to, pp. 72. N. 7254

BRADFORD (S. D.) Letters to the Honorable William M. Meredith, Secretary of the Treasury, on his Recent Treasury Report. The Injurious Effects of Protective and Prohibitory Duties, and the Advantages of Free Trade. ... By S. D. Bradford, Esq. ... *Boston.* 1850. 8vo, pp. 36. H. 7255

BRADFORD. Letters of S. D. Bradford, Esq. to the Hon. Abbott Lawrence, in Reply to those addressed by Mr. Lawrence to the Hon. William C. Rives ... . Also, the Letters of Mr. Lawrence, ... with the Famous Faneuil Hall Proceedings, Resolutions, &c. in favor of Free Trade, in ... 1820. ... *Boston.* 1826. 8vo, pp. 39. H. 7256

BRADFORD. Works of Samuel Dexter Bradford, LL.D. ... *Boston: Phillips, Sampson & Company.* 1858. 8vo, pp. xii, 427. Portrait. H. 7257

Six obituary notices, and some discussions of public concerns.

BRADFORD (S. F.) Impostor Detected, or a Review of some of the Writings of Peter Porcupine, by Timothy Tickletoby, to which is added a Refreshment for the memory of Wm. Cobbet. By Samuel F. Bradford. *Philadelphia.* 1796. 8vo, pp. 51, 23.

BRADFORD (S. H.) The Story of Columbus, simplified for the Young Folks. By Sarah H. Bradford. *New York: C. Scribner.* 1856. 12mo, pp. 255. + *New York: A. D. F. Randolph.* 1864. 16mo, pp. 255. 7259

BRADFORD (Thomas G.) A Comprehensive Atlas, Geographical, Historical & Commercial, by T. G. Bradford. *Boston: William D. Ticknor. New York: Wiley and Long. Philadelphia: T. T. Ash.* [1835.] 4to, pp. 172, 180 l. C. 7260

BRADFORD. An Illustrated Atlas, Geographical, Statistical, and Historical, of the United States and the Adjacent Countries. By T. G. Bradford. *Boston: Weeks, Jordan, and Company.* [1838.] 4to, 3 l., pp. 170. 40 Maps. H. 7261

Reproduced with new titles, 1839 and 1842; also with a Philadelphia imprint.

BRADFORD (*Gov.* Wm.) History of Plymouth Plantation by William Bradford, the Second Governor of the Colony. Reprinted from the Massachusetts Historical Collections. Edited, with Notes by Charles Deane, Member of the Massachusetts Historical Society. *Boston: privately Printed.* M.DCCC.LVI. 8vo, pp. xix, (1), 476. H. 7262

Also forms Massachusetts Historical Society Collections, 4th Series, Vol. III. An edition of fifty copies was privately printed for presentation by Mr. C. Deane. *See* Young (A.) "Chronicles of the Pilgrims," pp. 1–108, 459–470.

[BRADFORD (W.) *and others.*] Mourt's Relation or Journal of the Plantation at Plymouth with an Introduction and Notes by Henry Martyn Dexter *Boston John Kimball Wiggin* M DCCC LXV 4to, pp. xxxi, 8 l., pp. 176. Map. H. 7263

For other works of Gov. Bradford's, *see* Mass. Hist. Soc. Coll., 1st Ser., III. 27–84; 4th Ser., II. 119; III. (History of Plymouth Plantation).

BRADFORD (W.) Fac Simile privately printed for John William Wallace ... of Philadelphia, from originals now in Possession of Arch Street Meeting & of Mr Nathan Kite. Of the First Proposals made in America (So far as known December 1. 1862.) To print the Holy Bible in English. ... [Signed William Bradford. Philadelphia, the 14th of the 1st Month, 1688. [n. p. n. d.] Oblong 4to, pp. (2). Lithographed. H. 7264

On one page are facsimiles of a letter "To the half years Meeting of ffriends held at Burlington," relating to the proposals.

BRADFORD (Wm). *See* Budd (Thomas) and Keith (George).

The catalogue of the American Antiquarian Society quotes an "Account of his Trial at Philadelphia," as by Bradford. It is more probably by George Keith, under whose name we give the title correctly. The following notice is from Joseph

Smith's Catalogue of Friends' books, and is here introduced on account of the interest attached to his name: "William Bradford was born in Leicester, about the year 1659. He was placed as an apprentice to learn the printing business with Andrew Sowle in London. Whilst in this situation, he appears to have been convinced of Friends' principles, and was admitted into membership among them. Shortly after he was of age he married Elizabeth Sowle, a daughter of his late master, and then went over to America. This was in 1682 or 1683. A Certificate of Devonshire House Monthly Meeting, recommending William Bradford and Elizabeth his wife, as members of the Society of Friends, was read in Philadelphia Monthly Meeting, held the 4th of the 11th month, 1685, and accepted. They were not, however, settled in Philadelphia, but in Oxford township; and belonged to Oxford Monthly Meeting. His press was probably at Burlington, or at Chester, or at Kensington. Having received his printing materials from England, William Bradford was now ready to carry on business. The first work that he printed appears to have been 'An Epistle of John Burnyeat's, in 1686.' In the year 1687, he issued a prospectus for publishing by subscription a folio Bible with notes, but not receiving sufficient encouragement, the work was relinquished. In the year 1691, he joined with George Keith in his controversy with the Society, and in 1692 wished to be discharged from the engagement as Friends' printer. He removed to New York with his press in 1693, and was appointed printer to the government. There he continued to reside until 5th month 23rd, 1752, when he suddenly deceased, aged 94 years." He signed many books and papers during the Keithian controversy. It is scarcely necessary to add, that Bradford being the first printer in the Middle Colonies, books printed by him are eagerly sought for by the American collector; many of them are printed without a separate title-page, but their completeness is ascertained by the paging and signatures. For a list of books printed by Bradford, *see* the index to this work, and J. W. Wallace's "Address."

BRADFORD (W.) An Enquiry how far the Punishment of Death is Necessary In Pennsylvania. With Notes and Illustrations. By William Bradford, Esq. To which is added, an Account of the Gaol and Penitentiary house of Philadelphia, and of the Interior Management thereof. By Caleb Lownes ... . *Philadelphia: Printed by T. Dobson.* M,DCC,XCIII. 8vo, pp. 43–108, (1), Errata, 1 l., Table at page 72. H. + *London: J. Johnson.* M,DCCC,XCV. 8vo, pp. 114. BM. 7265

See Rich, I. 394, for a notice of this work from the "Monthly Review."

BRADFORD (W. M.) Expulsion of Free Negroes from the State. Remarks of Wm. M. Bradford ... in the Senate ... [of Tennessee] February 11, 1860. [n. p. n. p.] 8vo, pp. 4. H.

BRADFORD (William John Alden). Notes on the Northwest, or Valley of the Mississippi. Comprising the Country between Lakes Superior and Michigan, East; the Illinois and Missouri Rivers, and the Northern Boundary of the United States; — including Iowa and Wisconsin, Part of Michigan Northwest of the Straits of Mackinaw, and the Northern Illinois and Missouri. By Wm. J. A. Bradford. *New York and London: Wiley and Putnam.* 1846. 12mo, pp. vi, (1), 302. C., H. 7267

BRADFORD, *Mass.* Letters from the First Church in Gloucester to the Second in Bradford; with their Answers; and Appendix. *Boston.* 1744. 4to, pp. 32. G. 7268

Also: "Report of the School Committee."

Vindication of the Second Church in Bradford against a late piece entitled a "Brief Narrative," &c. By James Baily. *Boston: Rogers & Fowle.* 1746. 8vo, pp. 24. 7269

BRADFORD CLUB. *See* Drake (J. R.), [Duyckinck (E. A.)], Grasse (*Count de*), Hough (F. B.), Murphy (H. C.), Papers relating to Hatfield, and Soto (de).

The Bradford Club was first known as "The Club," and consisted of six gentlemen, who printed "Washington's Diary" and "Melvin's Journal." One of "The Club" having sold his books, the remaining five formed the "Bradford Club," whose publications will be described under the headings to which we have referred. The publications are limited to 75 "Club" copies, and 75 subscriber's copies. The verso of each title-page conveys the idea that 75 only are printed. Of the "Papers relating to Hatfield and Deerfield," only 100 copies in all were printed.

BRADISH (Luther). Mr. Bradish's Remarks in Assembly, on the Preamble and Resolutions offered by him, relative to a Distribution of the Proceeds of the Public Lands, May 25, 1836. *New York: printed by James Van Norden.* 1836. 8vo, pp. 25.

BRADISH. Proceedings of the New York Historical Society on the Death of Hon. Luther Bradish. *New York.* 1865. 8vo.

[BRADISH (L.)] Reply to the Remonstrance of the Corporation of Trinity Church. *New York.* 1848. 8vo, pp. 15. H.

Signed by Luther Bradish and fourteen others.

[BRADISH.] A Statement and Declaration of Views. *New-York.* 1846. 8vo, pp. 6. H. 7273

Relates to Trinity Church. Signed by Luther Bradish and twelve others.

BRADLEE (C. D.) A Sermon Delivered by Request before the Third Religious Society in Dorchester, the First Sabbath after the Decease of Rev. Richard Pike, February 22, 1863. By Rev. Caleb Davis Bradlee. *Boston: Walker, Wise and Company.* 1863. 8vo, pp. 15. H. 7274

BRADLEE. A Sermon for the Church of the Redeemer; by Rev. C. D. Bradlee of Roxbury. Preached Sunday, April 23d, 1865. [n. p. n. d.] 8vo, pp. 8. B. 7275

Refers to the death of President Lincoln. Only ten copies printed.

BRADLEE (J. E.) Bradlee's Pocket Guide to the White Mountains, Lake Winnipiseogee, and Lake Memphremagog. With Maps. *Boston: John E. Bradlee.* 1862. 16mo, pp. 120. Map. H. 7276

[BRADLEE (N. J.)] History of the Introduction of Pure Water into the City of Boston, with a Description of its Cochituate Water Works. ... Compiled by ... [N. J. Bradlee]. *Boston: Alfred Mudge & Son, City Printers.* 1866. 8vo, pp. xxi, (1), 299. 15 Plates, Maps, and Plans. B. C. 7277

BRADLEY (C.) The Connecticut Register; or Official State Calendar of public Officers and Institutions in Connecticut, for 1847. *Hartford.* 1847. 18mo. C. 7278

BRADLEY. (G. S.) The Star Corps; or, Notes of an Army Chaplain during Sherman's Famous "March to the Sea." Rev. G. S. Bradley, Chaplain 22d Wisconsin. *Milwaukee: Germain & Brightman, Printers.* 1865. 12mo, pp. 304. Portrait. BA.

BRADLEY (J.) Narrative of Two Excommunications upon Jesse Bradley (for Conscience Sake), by the Congregational Church in Lee. *Stockbridge.* 1796. 8vo, pp. 22. M. 7280

BRADLEY. Accounts of Religious Revivals in many Parts of the United States from 1815 to 1818. ... By Joshua Bradley, A.M. ... . *Albany: printed by J. G. Loomis & Co.* 1819. 24mo, pp. 300. H. 7281

BRADLEY (J. P.) Progress Its Grounds and Possibilities An Address By J. P. Bradley. *New Brunswick.* 1849. 8vo. B.

BRADLEY (*Hon.* J. P.) The Constitutional Amendment. Letter from Hon. Joseph P. Bradley, of New Jersey, to Mr. Charles Knap, on the Question of the Number of States requisite to ratify an Amendment to the Constitution. [*Washington.* 1865.] 8vo pp. 4. 7283

BRADLEY (M. E.) Douglas Farm; a juvenile story of Life in Virginia. By Mary E. Bradley. *New York.* 1857. 12mo.

BRADLEY (Micah). Oration at Portsmouth, N. H. July 5, 1813. *Portsmouth, N. H.: W. Weeks, Printer.* [1813.] 8vo, pp. 24. 7284

BRADLEY (S. R.) Vermont's Appeal to the Candid and Impartial World. Containing, a fair stating of the claims of

Massachusetts-Bay, New-Hampshire, and New-York. The Right the State of Vermont has to Independence. With an Address to the Honorable American Congress, and the Inhabitants of the Thirteen United States. By Stephen R. Bradley, A.M. *Hartford, Conn.: Hudson & Goodwin.* [1780.] 8vo, pp. 51. C. S. 7286

See Thompson's "Hist. Vt.," Part II. 107. Reprinted in the "Brattleboro' (Semi-weekly) Eagle," 1851. "A faithful and well-written account of the controversy; now very scarce."

BRADLEY (W. C.) Oration at Westminster, Vt. July 4, 1799. By William C. Bradley. *Walpole: Printed by David Carlisle, for Thomas & Thomas.* 1799. 4to, pp. 16. 7287

BRADMAN (A.) Narrative of the Extraordinary Sufferings of Mr. Robert Forbes, his Wife and five Children, during an unfortunate Journey through the Wilderness from Canada to Kennebeck River, in 1784: In which three of their Children were starved to death. Taken partly from their own mouths, and partly from an imperfect journal; and published at their request. By Arthur Bradman. *Philadelphia: Printed for M. Carey.* 1794. 8vo, pp. 16. C. S. 7288

The Worcester Ant. Soc. Catalogue describes an edition printed at *Portland, Me.,* 1791.

BRADSHAW (G.) Bradshaw's Railway Manual and Directory, for 1856: a Hand-Book, giving the History and Position of each Company; with Statistics ... . *London.* 1856. 12mo.

Includes companies in British North America, the West Indies, South America, and the United States.

BRADSHAW (T.) The Slave Trade inconsistent with Reason and Religion. A Sermon Preached in the Parish Church of Tottenham, Middlesex, March 16, 1788. By Thomas Bradshaw, D.D. *London. Richardson.* 1788. 4to. 7290

See M. R., LXXVIII. 446.

BRADSHAW (W.) The Angel of the Battle-Field. A Tale of the Rebellion. By Wesley Bradshaw. *New York: American News Company.* 1865. 8vo, pp. 96. 7291

BRADSHAW. General Sherman's Indian Spy; Narrative of Wenonah while Scouting from Atlanta through Georgia and South Carolina. By Wesley Bradshaw. *Philadelphia.* [1863.]

BRADSHAW. The Volunteer's Roll of Honor. A Collection of the Noble and Praiseworthy Deeds performed in the

Cause of the Union, by the Heroes of the Army and Navy of the United States. By Wesley Bradshaw. ... *Philadelphia: Barclay & Co.* [1864.] 8vo, 2 l., pp. 21–100. 7293

BRADSHAW. Washington Vision. By Wesley Bradshaw. *Philadelphia: C. W. Alexander & Co.* 1865. 8vo, pp. 26. 7294

BRADSHAW (W. S.) Voyages to India, China, and America; with an Account of the Swan River Settlement. By W. S. Bradshaw. *London.* 1857. Crown 8vo, pp. 230. 7295

[BRADSTREET (*Mrs.* Anne).] The | Tenth Muse | Lately sprung up in America. | Or | Severall Poems, compiled | with great variety of VVit | and Learning, full of delight. | Wherein especially is contained a com- | pleat discourse and description of | The Four | Elements, | Constitutions, | Ages of Man, | Seasons of the Year. | Together with an Exact Epitomie of | the four Monarchies, viz. | The | Assyrian, | Persian, | Grecian, | Roman. | Also a Dialogue between Old England and | New, concerning the late troubles. | With divers other pleasant and serious Poems. | By a Gentlewoman in those parts. | *Printed at London for Stephen Bowtell at the signe of the | Bible in Popes Head-Alley,* 1650. | Small 8vo, 7 l., pp. 207. R. 7296

A volume of much rarity. Priced, Thorpe, 1843, 15*s.*; J. R. Smith, 1864, £5 15*s.* Reprinted with additions as:

[BRADSTREET (*Mrs.* Anne).] Several | Poems | Compiled with great variety of Wit and | Learning, full of Delight; | Wherein especially is contained a compleat | Discourse, and Description of | The Four Elements, | Constitutions, | Ages of Man, | Seasons of the Year. | Together with an exact Epitome of | the three first Monarchyes | Viz. The Assyrian, | Persian, | Grecian. | And beginning of the Romane Common-wealth | to the end of their last King: | With diverse other pleasant & serious Poems, | By a Gentlewoman in New-England. | The second Edition, Corrected by the Author, | and enlarged by an Addition of several other | Poems found amongst her Papers | after her Death. | *Boston, Printed by John Foster,* 1678. | 18mo, pp. (14), 255, (1). B., C. 7297

[BRADSTREET.] Several | Poems | Compiled with great Variety of Wit and Learn- | ing, full of Delight; | Wherein especially is contained, a compleat Discourse and | Description of | The Four | Elements, | Constitutions, | Ages of Man, | Seasons of the Year. | Together with an exact Epitome of the three first | Monarchies,

viz. the | Assyrian, | Persian, | Grecian, and | Roman Common | Wealth, from its begin- | ging, to the End of their | last King. | With divers other pleasant and serious Poems. | By a Gentlewoman in New-England. | The Third Edition, corrected by the Author, | and enlarged by an Addition of several other | Poems found amongst her Papers after her | Death. | *Re-printed from the second Edition, in the Year* | M. DCC. LVIII. | 18mo, pp. xiii, 233.

Finally reprinted with copious notes under the following title:

BRADSTREET. The Works of Anne Bradstreet, in Prose and Verse. Edited by John Harvard Ellis. *Charlestown: A. E. Cutter.* 1867. Rl. 8vo, pp. lxxvi, 434. 2 Plates, 1 Facsimile. C. 7299

Of this elegant reprint, two hundred and fifty copies were printed for subscribers. Cotton Mather, in his "Magnalia," remarks, these "poems, divers times printed, have afforded a grateful entertainment unto the ingenious, and a monument for her memory beyond the stateliest marbles," which is higher praise than we can accord them. Ward, author of the "Simple Cobbler of Agawam," says, "The Authoress was a right Du Bartas girle." Some extensive selections from this authoress are included in "Duyckinck's Cycl.," I. 47–52.

BRADSTREET (Benjamin), *died* 1762. Godly Sorrow described, and the Blessing annexed consider'd. A Discourse Deliver'd January 28th, 1741, 2. At a Time of Great Awakenings. *Boston.* 1742. 8vo, pp. (4), iv, 28. B. 7300

Also: "Reduction of Cape-Breton. *Boston.* 1745." 8vo, pp. 23.

[BRADSTREET (John).] An Impartial Account of Lieut. Col. Bradstreets's Expedition to Fort Frontenac. To which are added, A few Reflections on the Conduct of that Enterprize, and the Advantages resulting from its Success. By a Volunteer on the Expedition. *London: T. Wilcox,* [etc.] M.DCC.LIX. 8vo, 2 l., pp. 60. C., H., S. 7301

See Munsell's Historical Series, No. IV., and Bancroft, IV. 308.

BRADSTREET (John M.) AND SON. ... The Commercial Reports of the Principal Cities of the United States and Canadas. [*New York.* 1857.] Folio. Continued. 7302

BRADSTREET. Gazeteer of the Manufactures and Manufacturing Towns of the United States. 1866. Compiled by J. M. Bradstreet & Sons. *New York: J. M. Bradstreet & Sons.* 1866. 4to, 6 l., pp. 172. C. 7303

BRADSTREET (Martha). Judicial Specimens, and brief explanatory Correspondence. *New York.* 1828. 8vo. B. 7304

BRADSTREET. Memorial, praying for the Impeachment of Alfred Conkling, U. S District Judge of the Northern District of New York. *New York.* 1829. C. 7305

BRADSTREET. An Offering at the Altar of Truth, Dedicated to the good sense of A Free People, By Mrs Martha Bradstreet. *New York.* 1827. 8vo, pp. 79. B. 7306

BRADSTREET. Statement of Facts in relation to the Dismissal of Mrs. Martha Bradstreet's Suits, from the District Court of the United States, for the Northern District of New-York, August Term--1832. *Albany.* 1831. 8vo, pp. 27. B. H. 7307

There are many more pamphlets in the State Library at Albany relating to Mrs. Bradstreet's claim to a portion of the city of Utica.

BRADSTREET (N.) A discourse delivered at Hopkinton before the Honorable Legislature of the State of New Hampshire, at the Annual Election, June 4, 1807. By Rev. Nathan Bradstreet. *Amherst.* 1807. 8vo, pp. 24. C. M. 7308

BRADSTREET (S.) Historical Discourse, First Church Marblehead, August 25, 1762. By Simon Bradstreet. *Boston.* 1762. 8vo, pp. 51. 7309

Title from the "N. E. Gen. Reg.," XXI. 328.

BRADSTREET. ... A Sermon Preached in Marblehead, January 12. 1755 ... after the Funeral of Mr. Samuel Bradstreet, Of Charlestown, Who died January 4. Ætat. 43. By Simon Bradstreet ... . *Boston: Printed, By Daniel Fowle.* [n. d.] 8vo, Half-Title, pp. 28. H. 7310

BRADWELL (J. B.) Validity of Slave Marriages. Opinion by Hon. James B. Bradwell, Probate Judge. *Chicago: E. B. Myers & Chandler.* 1866. 8vo, pp. 23. H. 7311

BRADY (Jasper E.) Speech of Mr. J. E. Brady ... on the Late War with Mexico, its Origin, Objects, and Results: delivered in the House ... June 27, 1848. *Washington.* 1848. 8vo, pp. 14. H. 7312

BRADY (J. T.) Speeches of James T. Brady and Hon. Mr. Truman at the Union Mass Meeting. New York, March 6, 1863. [*New York.* 1863.] 8vo, pp. 5. 7313

[BRADY (James T.) *and* BRYAN (John A.).] Trial of Charles B. Huntington for Forgery. Principal Defence: Insanity. Prepared for Publication by the Defendant's Counsel ... . *New York: John S. Voorhies.* 1857. 8vo, pp. xii, 480. H.

BRADY (N.) *and* TATE (N.) A New Version of the Psalms of David. ... By N. Brady, D.D. and N. Tate, Esq. *Boston.* [n. d.] 12mo. 7315

Probably about 1740; other editions, 1755, 1757, 1770, 1771, etc.

BRADY (W.) The Kedge-Anchor; or, Young Sailor's Assistant, etc. By William Brady, Sailing Master U. S. Navy. 9th Edition. *New York: for the Author.* 1857. 8vo, pp. 400. 32 Plates. C. 7316

BRAGA (Bernardo de). Sentimentos publicos de Pernambuco na morte do Serenissimo Infante D. Duarte, na igreja de N. S. da Nazareth. *Lisboa: por Domingo Lopes Rosa.* 1651. 4to.

BRAGA. Sermao que prégou na Sé da Bahia em a nova publicaçao de Bulla da Cruzada, a 18 de Janho de 1644. *Lisboa: por Paulo Craesbeeck.* 1659. 4to, pp. viii, 26. 7318

See Silva, I. 371, 372, for other works by this author.

BRAGANÇA. Exequias do Senhor D. Miguel de Bragança no Rio de Janeiro. *Rio de Janeiro.* 1867. 8vo, pp. 28. 7319

BRAGDON (J. H.) Report of the Proceedings, on the occasion of the Reception of the Sons of Newburyport resident abroad, July 4th, 1854, by the City Authorities and the Citizens of Newburyport. Compiled and reported by Joseph H. Bragdon. ... . *Newburyport: Moses H. Sargent.* 1854. 8vo, pp. 116.

BRAGG (A.) Memoirs of Col. Arial Bragg. Written by Himself. ... *Milford: George W. Stacy, Printer.* 1846. 16mo, pp. 86. C. H. 7321

BRAGG (B.), *pseudon.* A Voyage to the North Pole, by Benjamin Bragg, Accompanied by his Friend Captain Slapperwhack; with An Account of the Dangers and Accidents they experienced in the Frozen Seas of the Polar Circle. Also the manner of their wintering on the Island of Spitzberg, and Discovery of the Polar Continent. Embellished with an Elegant Plate and Map. *London: G. Walker.* 1817. 12mo, 5 l., pp. 211. Map. 7322

BRAGGE (R.) Church Discipline according to its Ancient Standard, as it was practis'd in Primitive Times. By Robert Bragge. *New London, Conn.* 1768. 12mo. 7323

BRAHM (W. G. de). The Atlantic Pilot. Calculated for the safe Conduct of Ships in their navigation from the Gulph of

Mexico along Cuba and the Martieres, through the New Bahama Channel, to the Northern parts of his Majesty's Dominions on the Continent of America, and from thence to Europe. By William Gerard de Brahm, His Majesty's Surveyor General of the District of North America. *London.* 1772. 8vo. 3 Charts.

BRAHM. History of the Province of Georgia: with Maps of Original Surveys. By John Gerar William de Brahm, His Majesty's Surveyor-General for the Southern district of North America. Now First Printed. *Wormsloe.* [*N. C.*] MDCCCXLIX. 4to, pp. 55, (1). 6 Plates. C. BA. 7325

Forty-nine copies privately printed, from a manuscript in the Library of Harvard College, for the editor, George Wymberley-Jones.

BRAHM. Recherches faites par Ordre de S. M. Brit. depuis 1765 jusqu'en 1771, pour rectifier les cartes & perfectionner la navigation du Canal de Bahama. Traduite le l'Anglais de W. Gerard de Brahm, par Ch. Romme. [n. p. 1771.] 4to, pp. 16. Map. + *Paris.* 1788. 4to. 7326

See "American Military Pocket Atlas," Vol. I., No. 1147.

BRAILSFORD (E.) An Experimental Dissertation on the Chemical and Medical Properties of the Nicotiana Tabacum of Linnaeus, Commonly Known by the Name of Tobacco. By Edward Brailsford, of Charleston, South-Carolina. ... *Philadelphia: J. Ormrod.* 1799. 8vo, pp. 78. 7327

BRAILSFORD. Case of Brailsford & others *vs.* James Spalding; also Douglas *vs.* the Executors of Stirk—Decided in the Circuit Court for the District of Georgia. 2nd May, 1792. *Savannah.* 1792. 8vo, pp. 36. S. 7328

BRAINARD (J.) A Genuine Letter from Mr. John Brainard, Employed by the Scotch Society for the Propagating the Gospel, A Missionary to the Indians in America, and Minister to a Congregation of Indians, at Bethel in East Jersey. To his Friend in England. Giving an Account of the Success of his Labours, as well as the Difficulties and Discouragments that attend his Mission among those Savages. *London: Printed for J. Ward.* M. DCC. LIII. 8vo, pp. 16. N. 7329

BRAINARD (J. G.) An Oration Commemorative of the Virtues and Services of General George Washington; spoken in the Presbyterian Church in the City of New London, [Conn.], February 22d, 1800. By J. G. Brainard, Esq. *New London: Printed by Samuel Green.* 1800. 8vo, pp. 14. 7330

BRAINARD (J. G. C.) Fugitive Tales, No 1: Fort Braddock Letters: By John Gardner Calkins Brainard. *Washington: Charles Galpin.* 1830. 18mo, pp. iv, 8–97. C. 7331

BRAINARD. The Literary Remains of John G. C. Brainard, with a Sketch of his Life. ... By J. G. Whittier. *Hartford: P. B. Goodsell.* [Copyright 1832.] 12mo, pp. 228. H. 7332

BRAINARD (W. F.) An Address, in Commemoration of the Sixth of September, 1781. Spoken on Groton Heights, Sept. 6, 1825. By William F. Brainard. *New-London: Printed under the Direction of the Committee.* 1825. 8vo, pp. 32. C. H.

Relates to the burning of New London, Conn.

BRAINERD (C.) The Public School System of New York City; Imperfect, Extravagant, and Inefficient. The True Remedy. Remarks of Cephas Brainerd ... before the Assembly's Committee on Colleges, Academies, and Schools, at Albany, 6th February, 1867. *New York: Trow & Smith, Book Manufacturing Co.* 1868. 8vo, pp. 31. H. 7334

BRAINERD. The Work of the Army Committee of the New York Young Men's Christian Association, which led to the Organization of the United States Christian Commission: ... by Cephas Brainerd. *New York: John Medole, Printer.* 1866. 8vo, pp. 40. H. 7335

[BRAINERD (Cephas) *and* STEARNS (James S.)] Argument on the Constitutionality and Construction of the "Riot Act" of 1855. [Signed.] *New York.* 1864. 8vo, pp. 25. H. 7336

BRAINERD (C. N.) My Diary; or, Three Weeks on the Wing. A Peep at the Great West. By C. N. Brainerd. *New York: Egbert, Bowne & Co., Printers.* 1868. 8vo, pp. 45.

BRAINERD (D. S.) A Sermon preached in Old Lyme, on the Twenty-fifth Anniversary of his Pastorate, July 1, 1866. By D. S. Brainerd. *New Haven: Tuttle, Morehouse & Taylor, Printers.* 1866. 8vo, pp. 20. 7338

BRAINERD (D.) An Abridgment of Mr. David Brainerd's Journal among the Indians. Or, the Rise and Progress of a Remarkable Work of Grace among a Number of the Indians In the Provinces of New-Jersey and Pennsylvania. By David Brainerd, Minister of the Gospel, and Missionary from the Honourable Society in Scotland for propagating Christian Knowledge.

To which is prefix'd a Dedication to the said Society, By P. Doddridge, D.D. [Motto.] *London: John Oswald, and John Trail, and other Booksellers in Edinburgh.* MDCCXLVIII. 12mo, Title, pp. vi, 3–110, Appendix, (iv). C. H. 7339

Brainerd, in his preface, says the name of the abridger was kept studiously secret.

BRAINERD. Mirabilia Dei inter Indicos, or the Rise and Progress Of a Remarkable Work of Grace Amongst a Number of the Indians In the Provinces of New-Jersey and Pennsylvania, Justly represented in A Journal Kept by Order of the Honourable Society (in Scotland) for propagating Christian Knowledge. With some general Remarks. By David Brainerd, Minister of the Gospel, and Missionary from the said Society. Published by the Rev. & Worthy Correspondents of the said Society. With a Preface by them. [Motto.] *Philadelphia: William Bradford.* [1746.] 8vo, pp. viii, 253. BA., H., P.

The paper in some copies is finer than that of others, it is probable that two editions were printed in the same year; the attestation in each is dated August 29, 1746. At page eighty is a second title-page, "Divine Grace display'd or a Continuation and Progress Of a Remarkable Work of Grace," etc., but the paging continues regularly. It appeared again, *Worcester*, 1793, and [n. p. 1798.] 8vo, pp. 355. The running title is, "Life of Mr. David Brainerd," and the preface is signed by Jonathan Edwards. *See* Rich, I. 83.

BRAINERD. Aanmerklyk verhaal van een zonderling werk van Gods genade onder de Indianen. *Utrecht: Weduwe J. J. van Poolsum en A. van Paddenburg.* 1756. 8vo. 7341

BRAINERD. Das Leben von David Brainerd, Missionar unter den Indianern. Nach dem, von Jonathan Edwards herausgegebenen Tagebuche Brainerd's beschrieben. *Neu-York.* 1854. 16mo, pp. 310. Woodcut. 7342

BRAINERD. ... Brainerd's Remarks on the Work of Grace under his Ministry amongst the Indians at Croswicks, N. J. With an Introduction by Talbot W. Chambers ... . *New-York.* 1856. 12mo, pp. 24. H. 7343

BRAINERD. The Life of David Brainerd, Missionary to the North American Indians, A.D. 1742–47. *London: Seeleys.* 1856. 12mo, pp. 320. 7344

BRAINERD. Memoirs of David Brainerd. ... By a Sunday School Teacher. ... *Philadelphia: American Sunday School Union.* [Copyright 1826.] 24mo, pp. 141. H. 7345

Another edition was issued by the New York Tract Society. [n. d.] 18mo, pp. 144.

BRAINERD. Life, Remains and Letters of David Brainerd, with his Journals Complete, &c. *Aberdeen: George & Robert King.* 1845. 18mo, pp. 595. C. BM. 7346

BRAINERD (T.) Good Men the Treasure of Earth. A Sermon on the Death of Levi Eldridge, Esq., delivered in the Third Presbyterian Church, Philadelphia, April 22, 1854, by Thomas Brainerd, D.D. *Philadelphia.* 1854. 8vo, pp. 23. 7347

BRAINERD. Old Pine Street Church. Manual of the Third Presbyterian Church, Philadelphia. *Philadelphia: W. F. Geddes.* 1859. 8vo, pp. 64. 1 Plate. C. 7348

BRAINERD. Our Country Safe from Romanism. A Sermon at ... Philadelphia, April, 1841. By the Rev. Thomas Brainerd ... . [*Philadelphia:*] *L. R. Bailey, Printer.* 1843. 8vo, pp. 45. H. 7349

BRAINERD. Patriotism aiding Piety. A Sermon preached in the Third Presbyterian Church, Philadelphia, on the 30th of April, 1863, the Day Appointed by the President of the United States for Humiliation, Fasting and Prayer. By Rev. Thomas Brainerd, D.D. *Philadelphia: William F. Geddes.* 1863. 8vo, pp. 32. 7350

BRAINERD. Remarks of Rev. Dr. Brainerd at the Funeral of Lieut. John T. Greble, U. S. A. *Philadelphia: G. T. Stockdale.* 1861. 8vo, pp. 7. 7351

BRAINERD. ... A Sermon on the Death of Frederick A. Raybold, Esq. ... Philadelphia, May 11th, 1851. By Thomas Brainerd, D.D. *Philadelphia: L. R. Bailey, Printer.* 1851. 8vo, pp. 22. 7352

BRAINERD. The Life of John Brainerd, brother of David Brainerd, and his Successor as Missionary to the Indians of New Jersey. By Rev. Thomas Brainerd, D.D., Pastor of "Old Pine Street Church," Philadelphia. *Philadelphia: Pbn. Pub. Com.* 1865. 8vo, pp. 492. Illustrated. C. B. 7353

BRAINTREE. Auditors' Annual Report of the Receipts and Expenditures of the Town of Braintree, From Feb. 1, 1858, to Feb. 1, 1859. ... *Boston: William White, Printer.* 1859. 8vo, pp. 30. Continued. 7354

Historical Notices of the First Congregational Church in Braintree, 1707–1830. *Boston.* 1830. 16mo, pp. 24. M. 7355

Report of the School Committee of the Town of Braintree, 1845. [n. p. 1845.] 8vo, pp. 8. 7356

Result of a late Ecclesiastical Council. [First Parish in Braintree, Dec. 5, 1792. n. p. n. d.] 4to, pp. 7. M. W. 7357

Sermon preached 1707, on Gathering a Church at Braintree, from Eph. II. 22, with the Covenant. *Boston.* 1709. 18mo.

BRAITHWAITE (A.). A Letter from Anna Braithwaite to Elias Hicks on the Nature of his Doctrines, ... *Philadelphia.* 1825. 8vo. 7359

Also: The Errors of Anna Braithwaite, in relation to the Doctrines held and preached by Elias Hicks. ... *New York.* 1824. 8vo, pp. 19. N.

BRAITHWAITE (J.) Supplement to Capt. Sir John Ross's Narrative of a Second Voyage in the Victory, in Search of a N. W. Passage; containing all the Suppressed facts necessary to a proper understanding of the causes of the Failure of the Steam Machinery of the Victory, and a just appreciation of Sir John Ross's Character as an Officer and a Man of Science. By John Braithwaite. *London.* 1835. 4to. 7360

BRAITHWAITE (J. B.) Memoirs of Joseph John Gurney; with Selections from his Journal and Correspondence. Edited by Joseph Bevan Braithwaite ... *Norwich: Fletcher and Alexander,* [etc.] 1854. 8vo, pp. xii, 542; vii, 551. 2 Facsimiles. C. BA. + *Philadelphia: Lippincott, Grambo & Co.* 1854. 2 vols., 8vo, Title, pp. 554; 608. 1 Facsimile. C. 7361

Some copies of the American edition have the imprint of *J. Longstreet.* A second edition was published. *Norwich.* 1855. 2 vols., post 8vo, 45½ sheets.

BRAKEL (W. à). Brief aan de Heer N. N. Koopman in Nieuw-Nederland: behelzende een opwekkinge en bestieringe tot en in de bekeeringe, heiligmakinge, ende 't leven door 't geloove op de beloofte. Om des zelfs deftigheid vermeerdert, verbetert en met volkomen schriftuur-plaatzen uitgedrukt. 10e druk. *Groningen* 1730. Sm. 8vo. 7362

BRAKEMAN (N. L.) A Great Man Fallen. A Sermon preached in the Methodist Church, Baton Rouge, La., April 23, On the Death of Abraham Lincoln, president of the United States. By Rev. N. L. Brakeman, Post Chaplain. Preached and Published by Request. *New Orleans: Times Office.* 1865. 8vo, pp. 32. 7363

A third edition, with notes and appendix, was published.

BRAMAN (D. E. E.) Braman's Information about Texas. Carefully Prepared by D. E. E. Braman, of Matagorda, Texas. *Philadelphia: J. B. Lippincott & Co.* 1857. 12mo, pp. 192. C., H. + [*Ibid.*] 1858. H. 7364

BRAMAN (I.) A Discourse, delivered at Topsfield, April 26, 1813. at the Funeral of the Rev. Ashel Huntington, who deceased on the 22d. aged 52. By Isaac Braman ... . Also, a Sermon ... by M. Huntinton ... . *Haverhill: Ms. W. B. and H. G. Allen.* 1813. 8vo, pp. 23. H. 7365

BRAMAN. An Eulogy on the Late General George Washington, who Died Saturday, 14th December, 1799. Delivered at Rowley, Second Parish, February 22, 1800. By Isaac Braman, A.M., Minister of the Gospel in that place. Published by Desire of the Hearers. *Haverhill: From the Press of Seth H. Moore.* [1800.] 8vo, pp. 24. C. 7366

BRAMAN. Union with France a greater evil than union with Britain. A Sermon preached in Rowley, West-Parish, at the Annual Fast, April 5th, 1810. By Isaac Braman. ... *Haverhill, (Mass.): William B. Allen.* 1810. 8vo, pp. 24. H. 7367

Also: A Sermon at the Ordination of Gardner Braman Perry. *Haverhill.* 1814. 8vo. — Sermon at the Ordination of John Boardman. *Worcester.* 1821. 8vo. — Sermon at the Ordination of Milton Palmer Braman. *Salem.* 1826. 8vo.

BRAMAN (M. P.) A Discourse delivered before ... the Legislature of Massachusetts, on the Annual Election, January 1, 1845. By Milton P. Braman ... . *Boston: Dutton and Wentworth, Printers.* 1845. 8vo, pp. 85. H. 7368

BRAMAN. The Mexican War. A Discourse delivered on the Annual Fast, 1847, by Milton P. Braman ... . *Danvers: printed at the Courier Office.* 1847. 8vo, pp. 36. H. 7369

BRAMAN. ... A Sermon, preached at the Dedication of the New Meeting-House, erected by the First Religious Society in North Danvers, November 21st, 1839. By Milton P. Braman ... . *Salem: Ives & Jewett.* 1840. 8vo, pp. 50, (Errata) 1 slip.

BRAMHALL (F. G.) The Military Souvenir; a Portrait Gallery of our Military and Naval Heroes. Edited by Frank G. Bramhall. In Two Volumes. Vol. I. *New York: J. C. Buttre.* 1863–66. pp. ix, 144. Fontispiece, and 75 steel Engravings. 7371

BRAMHAM (J. W.) Correspondence of James W. Bramham with Gov. Williams. *Natchez.* 1808. 12mo, pp. 20. C. 7372

BRAMSTON (W.) Two Sermons at the Parish Church of St. Christopher, By Wm. Bramston, 1713. 4to. 7373

BRAMWELL. The War in America. A Sermon preached August 18, 1861, at St. Peter's Church, Congleton, [England]. *Congleton: W. Burghope.* 1861. 8vo, pp. 15. 7374

[BRANAGAN (T.)] Avenia; or, A Tragical Poem on the Oppression of the Human Species, and Infringement of the Rights of Man, In Six Books, with Notes Explanatory and Miscellaneous. Written in imitation of Homer's Iliad. By Thomas Branagan ... . *Philadelphia.* 1805. 12mo, pp. 353, (1). P. 7375

On slavery in the West Indies.

BRANAGAN. Beauties of Philanthropy. *Philadelphia.* 1808. 18mo. C. 7376

BRANAGAN. Beauties of Philanthropy: and Guardian Genius of the Federal Union. *New York.* 1839. 12mo, pp. 288, 104.

[BRANAGAN.] Concise View of the Principal Religious Denominations in the United States; With Notes. *Philadelphia.* 1811. 12mo. 7378

BRANAGAN. Essay on the Oppression of the Exiled Sons of Africa. To which is added, a letter to Napoleon Bonaparte in 1801. By Thomas Branagan. *Philadelphia.* 1804. 12mo. C.

BRANAGAN. The Flowers of Literature, being a Compendious Exhibition of the most Interesting Geographical, Historical, Miscellaneous and Theological Subjects. *Trenton* 1806. 12mo, pp. 324. + *Philadelphia: J. Rakestraw.* 1810. 12mo. pp. 324.

BRANAGAN. The Guardian Genius of the Federal Union. *New York.* 1840. 12mo. S. 7381

BRANAGAN. The Penitential Tyrant. A Juvenile Poem in Two Cantos, to which is prefixed, Compendious Memoirs of the Author. By Thomas Branagan. *Philadelphia.* 1805. 18mo, pp. 122. 7382

BRANAGAN. The Penitential Tyrant; or Slave Trader Reformed; A Pathetic Poem. In four cantos. By Thomas Branagan. *New York.* 1807. 18mo, pp. 302. P. 7383

BRANAGAN. Serious Remonstrances, addressed to the Citizens of the Northern States, and their Representatives, on the recent revival of the Slave Trade; with a plan for Colonizing the Free Negroes. By Thomas Branagan. *Philadelphia: Thomas T. Stiles.* 1805. 12mo, pp. 133. C., P. 7384

BRANCH (S. H.) A Brief History of Francis Fauvel Gouraud, who is about to bamboozle the (Verdant?) Bostonians with an Exploded System of Artificial Memory. By S. H. Branch. *Boston. January* 1, 1845. 8vo, pp. 12. H. 7385

BRANCH. The Alligator. By Stephen H. Branch. No. 1. *New York.* 1858. 4to. 25 numbers published. 7386

This eccentric, if not insane, author also published "Daily Hand, with Truth and a Heart in it. *New York. September,* 1859." 8vo. 21 numbers. "Weekly Star. *New York.* 1860." 4to. 28 numbers. "Life of Stephen Branch. No. 1. *New York.* 1857."

BRANCH (Wm.), *Jr.* Life: a Poem in Three Books, Descriptive of the Various Characters in Life, the different passions, with their moral influence, &c. Dedicated to the Social and Political Welfare of the People of the United States. By Wm. Branch, Junr. *Franklin Press, Richmond.* 1819. 18mo, pp. xii, 218 C. 7387

BRAND (C.) Journal of a Voyage to Peru: a Passage across the Cordillera of the Andes, in the Winter of 1827, performed on foot in the Snow; and a Journey across the Pampas. By Lieut. Chas. Brand, R.N. *London: Henry Colburn.* 1828. 8vo, pp. xvii, (2), 346. 4 Plates. C., H. 7388

BRAND. Tagebuch einer Reise nach Peru, im Winter 1827. Von Lieut. Brand. Aus dem Englishen. *Jena: Bran.* 1828. 8vo. 7389

Reprinted from the "Ethnograph. Archiv."

BRAND (W. F.) ... The Church viewed in its relation to the State. A Sermon, By W. F. Brand. ... *Baltimore: James S. Waters.* 1862. 8vo, pp. 16. 7390

BRANDAO MONTEZUMA (Francisco Gomes). Memoria politico e historica de revoluçao da provincia da Bahia, principiada a 25 de Junho de 1822 na muito patriotica villa da Cachoeira. Appresentado a S. M. I. o senhor D. Pedro I. *Rio de Janeiro.* 1822. 4to. 7391

"Parece que é hoje rara este opusculo, mesmo no Brasil." — SILVA, II. 387.

BRANDEGEE (A.) Speech of Hon. Augustus Brandegee, of Connecticut ... in the House ... December 12, 1864, on the Bill by the Committee on Naval Affairs, locating the Naval Station for Iron Clads at New London, Conn. *Washington.* 1864. 8vo, pp. 16. H. 7392

BRANDES (Fr.) Reise nach Lima, San Francisco ... . *Plauen.* 1858. 8vo. 7393

BRANDES (K.) Sir John Franklin, die Unternehmungen für seine Rettung und die nordwestliche Durchfahrt. Nebst einer Tabelle der arktischen Temperaturen von Dr. H. W. Dove und Karte von Henry Lange. *Berlin: Nicolaische Verhandlung.* 1854. 8vo, pp. viii, 312, 1 Table, 4to. C. 7394

BRANDHOF Ez. (A. van den). Brief aan de Europesche Kolonisten te Groningen aan Saramacca. *Paramaribo.* 1848. 8vo.

"Antwoord op een aanzoek om meerdere ondersteuning aan het gouvernement gedaan."

BRANDIN (A. V.) L'Amérique Espagnole en 1830. Coup d'œil sur sa situation actuelle et réflexions sur la reconnoissance et la future pacification de ses nouveaux états par Louis Philippe Ier Par A. V. Brandin, D.M. &c. temoin oculaire. *Paris: impr. de Demonville.* 1830. 8vo, pp. 48. 7396

BRANDIN. Annales Medicales del Peru. Por Don Abel Victorino Brandin, M.D. Num. primero. Num. tercero. *Lima.* 1827. 4to. 7397

BRANDIN. De la influencia de los diferentes climas del universo sobre el hombre y en particular, de la influencia de los climas de la America Meridional. Por Don Abel Victorino Brandin ... . *Lima: J. M. Masias.* 1826. Sm. 4to, 8 l., pp. 114, (1). C., H. 7398

BRANDLIGT (C.) Geschiedkundige Beschouwing van de Walvisch-Visscherij. Von C. Brandligt. *Amsterdam.* 1843. 8vo, pp. 38. 8 Plates. B. 7399

BRANDON (C.) David Woodburn, the Mountain Missionary. By Curris Brandon. *Boston: H. Hoyt.* 1865. 16mo, pp. 310.

BRANDON (Lorenço). Señor.| Medios para| V. Magestad ahorrar lo mucho que gasta| cada año en las Armadas del Reyno de| Portugal, y Estado de la India, con mas| fruto y comodidad,

para poder| venir la plata del Pirù con| menos costa y riesgo.| [*Ending*] Suplico, a V. M. sea seruido de mandar consulter en |razon de todo lo que pareciere, &c. [Colophon:] *Madrid* 23. *Diziem|bre* 1622. *D. Lorenço Brandon.* 4to, 7 leaves.

BRANDRETH (G. A.) Speech of Hon. Geo. A. Brandreth, in favor of the "Eight Hours Bill," Delivered in the Assembly of ... New York, at Albany, March 15, 1866. [n. p. n. d.] 8vo, pp. 16. H. 7402

BRANDT (F.) Una Mirada hácia el Porvenir de la Hacienda Nacional de Venezuela. *Carácas.* 1864. 8vo, pp. 27. 7403

BRANDT. Una Mirada retrospectiva sobre la Hacienda de Venezuela. *Carácas.* 1850. 8vo, pp. 47. 7404

BRANDT (G.) Het leven en bedryf van Michiel de Ruiter, L.-Admiraal Gen. van Hollandt en W. Vrieslandt. *Amsterdam.* 1671. 4to. Engravings. + [*Id.*] 1687. + [*Id.*] 1701. 4to. Same Engravings. + [*Id.*] 1732. 4to. Same Engravings. + 4e Druk. *Amsterdam.* 1746. 4to, 4 l., pp. 1065, 12 l. 7 Plates. + Het leven en bedrijf van Michiel de Ruiter, op nieuw uitgegeven. *Dordrecht.* 1835. 5 pts., 8vo. Plates. C. 7405

BRANDT. La vie de Michel de Ruiter ... . Où est comprise l'Histoire maritime Des Provinces Unies, depuis l'An 1652. jusques à 1676. Traduite du Hollandois de Gerard Brandt. Et enrichie de Figures. ... *Amsterdam: De L'Imprimerie de P. & J. Blaeu, Pour Waesberge, Boom, à Someren & Goethals.* M DC XC VIII. 4to, 3 l., pp. 317, (17). Plates. C. H. 7406

BRANDT. Leben und tapffere Thaten der aller berühmtesten Seehelden und Land-Erfinder u. Zeiten angefangen mit Cristoforo Colombo Entdeckern der neuen Welt und geendigt mit dem weltberühmten Admiral M. A. de Ruyter. Mit vielen Portraits u. Kupfertafeln. *Nürnberg.* 1681. 4to, 5 l., pp. 1090, 9 l. C. 7407

BRANDT. Leben und Thaten des fürtrefflichen See-Helden Mich. de Ruiter etc. Worinnen auch der Ost- und West-Indien u. versch. heidn. Länder Beschaffenheit zu finden sind. *Amsterdam.* 1687. 2 pts., 4to. Portrait and Plates. 7408

BRANDT (R. J.) Okalluhtualiæt, nuktérsimarsut, R. J. Brandt-mit Kårsome niüvertuksaugallaomit, ark' iksórsimarsut titârnekartisimarsudlo P. Kragh-mit Lintrupimiut Hjertingimiudlo Pellesiænnit *Kjöbenhavn.* 1839. Sm. 8vo, pp. 118. C. H.

7 dialogues, 9 tales, 5 fables in the Greenland language, edited by Peder Kragh.

Brandt in Brasilien. *See* Brazil.

BRANNAN (B.) State of the Accounts of Benjamin Brannan, Esq. late Sub Lieutenant of Chester County, from the time of his Appointment in March 1777, until the time of his Resignation in December [17] following. 8vo, pp. 3. *Philadelphia.* 1783.] P. 7410

Title printed from bottom to top.

BRANNAN (J.) Official Letters of the Military and Naval Officers of the United States, during the War with Great Britain in the Years 1812, 13, 14, & 15. With some Additional Letters and Documents elucidating the History of that Period. Collected and arranged by John Brannan. *Washington City: the Editor.* 1823. 8vo, pp. 510. BA., C., H. 7411

BRANNAN (William P.) Vagaries of Vandyke Brown, [*pseudon.*] An autobiography in verse. *Cincinnati: R. W. Carroll & Co.* 1865. 12mo, pp. 265. C. 7412

This author acquired considerable reputation as the true author of the sermon called "The Harp of a Thousand Strings."

BRANT (Joseph). Principal Events in the Life of that Indian Chief, with portrait. 8vo. 7413

A very doubtful title, from S. G. Drakes' catalogue, 1867.

BRANT. *See* Mohawk *and* St. Mark.

BRANTLY (W. T.) A Discourse delivered before the Phi Beta Kappa Society of the University of Georgia ... February 22d, 1852. By W. T. Brantly ... . *Athens, Ga.: the Society.* 1852. 8vo, pp. 27. H. 7414

BRANTLY. Our National Troubles. A Thanksgiving Sermon. Delivered in ... Philadelphia ... Nov. 29, 1860. By William T. Brantly ... . *Philadelphia: T. B. Peterson & Brothers.* 1860. 8vo, pp. 32. H. 7415

BRANTLY. ... A Sermon, Delivered at Augusta, Georgia, May 6th, 1821, at the Dedication of the Baptist Church in that place. By the Rev. William T. Brantly, A.M. *Augusta.* 1821. 8vo, pp. 22. 7416

BRANTZ (L.) Meteorological Observations; made in the Vicinity of Baltimore during the years 1817, 1818, 1819, 1820, 1821, 1822, by Lewis Brantz. *Baltimore: Printed at the Office of the Federal Gazette, by William Gwynn.* 87 leaves, Tables. + [The same] for 1823, 1824, 1836, 1837, by Lewis Brantz. *Baltimore: Printed at the Office of the Federal Gazette, by William Gwynn.* 41 folios. 7417

Fifty copies privately printed. Printed only on one side of each folio. *See also* Schoolcraft's Indians, Vol. III. 335.

BRASHEARS (N.) Columbia's Wreath; or Miscellaneous Poems, composed between the Years 1814 and 1830. By Noah Brashears. Second Edition. *Washington: S. A. Elliot.* 1830. 12mo, pp. 120. C., S. 7418

BRASIL. *See* Brazil.

BRASSEUR DE BOURBOURG (E. Charles, *l'abbé*). Antiquités Mexicaines. A propos d'un mémoire sur la peinture didactique et l'écriture figurative des anciens Mexicains, par M. J. M. A. Aubin, publié dans la Revue Archéologique. *Paris.* 1852.

BRASSEUR DE BOURBOURG. Aperçu d'un voyage dans les états de San-Salvador et de Guatemala. Par M. l'abbé Brasseur de Bourbourg. *Paris: imp. Martinet.* 1857. 8vo, pp. 24. 7420

Reprinted from the "Bulletin de la Soc. de Géog.," avril et mai, 1857.

BRASSEUR DE BOURBOURG. Archives des indigèns. Par M. L'Abbe Brasseur de Bourbourg. *Paris: A. Bertrand.* 1857. 2 l., pp. xcii, 440, 2 l., pp. 66. 7421

BRASSEUR DE BOURBOURG. Cartas para servir de introduccion a la Historia Primitiva de las Naciones Civilizadas de la America setentrional. Par Don E. Carlos Brasseur de Bourbourg. *Mexico: M. Murguia.* 1851. 4to, pp. 75. 7422

BRASSEUR DE BOURBOURG. Collection de documents dans les langues indigènes pour servir à l'étude de l'histoire et de la philologie de l'Amérique ancienne . ... [*Paris: A. Bertrand.*] 1861–68. 4 vols., rl. 8vo. 7423

This is the general title to the volumes described in Nos. 7427, 7435, 7437 *infra.* I. Popol Vuh. II. Gramatica. IV. Quatre lettres. For III., *see* Landa (D. de). Relation de Yucatan.

BRASSEUR DE BOURBOURG. Coup d'Œil sur la Nation et la Langue des Wabis, population maritime de la côte de Tehuantepec, publié dans la Revue Orientale et Américaine, tome V. *Paris.* 1861. 7424

BRASSEUR DE BOURBOURG. Esquisse biographique sur Mgr. de Laval. *Quebec.* 1855. 7425

Title from Morgan's "Bib. Canadensis;" perhaps the same as No. 7430 *infra.*

BRASSEUR DE BOURBOURG. Essai historique sur les sources de la philologie mexicaine et sur l'ethnographie de l'Amérique centrale. [*Paris.* 1859.] 2 pts., 8vo. 7426

Extracted from the "Revue américaine et orientale."

BRASSEUR DE BOURBOURG. Gramatica de la lengua Quiche. Grammaire de la langue Quichée espagnole-française mise en parallèle avec ses deux dialectes Cakchiquel et Tzutuhil, Tirée des manuscrits des meilleurs auteurs guatémaliens. Ouvrage accompagné de notes philologiques avec un vocabulaire comprenant les sources principales du Quiché comparées aux langues Germaniques et suivi d'un essai sur la poésie, la musique, la danse et l'art dramatique chez les Mexicaines et les Guatémaltèques avant la conquête; Servant d'introduction au Rabinal-Achi drame indigène avec sa musique originale, texte Quiché et traduction française en regard. Recueilli par l'abbe Brasseur de Bourbourg ... . *Paris: Arthus Bertrand.* 1862. Rl. 8vo, Title, pp. xvii, 246, 122, Music, (12). BA. 7427

The Gramatica is followed by Rabinal-Achi vepu Xahoh-Tun. *Paris: Auguste Bertrand.* 1862. Rl. 8vo, pp. 122, 12, etc., which has a separate title-page, and is perhaps, sold separately. The two works form Vol. II. of the "Collection."

BRASSEUR DE BOURBOURG. De Guatémala à Rabinal, Episode d'un voyage dans l'Amérique Centrale, exécuté dans les années 1854, 1855. Publié dans la Revue Européenne, numéros du 1 et du 15 février 1859. 7428

BRASSEUR DE BOURBOURG. Histoire des Nations Civilisées du Mexique et de l'Amérique-centrale, durant les siècles antérieurs à Christophe Colomb; écrite sur des documents originaux et entièrement inédits, puisés aux anciennes archives des indigènes. Par M. l'abbé Brasseur de Bourbourg. *Paris: Arthus Bertrand.* 1857–59. 4 vols., 8vo. C. 7429

BRASSEUR DE BOURBOURG. Histoire de Mgr. de Lava., premier évèque de Québec. *Québec.* 1845. 8vo. Portrait.

"Cetté brochure n'a pas été mise dans le commerce." — LORENZ.

BRASSEUR DE BOURBOURG. Histoire du Canada, de son église et de ses missions, depuis la découverte de l'Amérique jusqu'à

nos jours, écrit... documents inédits compulsés dans les archives de l'archevêché et de la ville de Québec, etc. Par M. l'Abbé Brasseur de Bourbourg. *Paris: Sagnier et Bray.* 1852. 2 vols., 8vo, pp. iv, 328; 350. 7431

BRASSEUR DE BOURBOURG. Histoire du Commerce et de l'Industrie chez les Nations Aztéques avant la découverte de l'Amérique, par Christophe Colomb, publiée dans les Nouvelles Annales des Voyages. *Paris.* 1858. 7432

BRASSEUR DE BOURBOURG. Lettres pour servir d'introduction à l'histoire primitive des nations civilisées de l'Amérique septentrionale, adressées à Monsieur le duc de Valmy. Par M. l'abbé E. Charles Brasseur de Bourbourg ... . Cartas para servir de introduccion á la Historia primitiva de las naciones civilizadas de la America Setentrional. *Mexico: Imprenta de M. Murguía.* 1851. 4to, pp. 75. H. 7433

In French and Spanish.

BRASSEUR DE BOURBOURG. Monuments anciens du Mexique. Palenqué, Ococingo et autres ruines de l'ancienne civilisation mexicaine, collection de vues, bas-reliefs, morceaux d'architecture, coupes, vases, etc., dessinés d'après nature et relevés par de Waldeck, avec texte explicatif rédigé par M. l'abbé Brasseur de Bourbourg. Livr. 1re. *Paris: A. Bertrand.* 1860. 4to. 7434

BRASSEUR DE BOURBOURG. Monuments anciens du Mexique. Palenqué et autres ruines de l'ancienne civilisation du Mexique Collection de Vues, Bas-Reliefs Morceaux d'Architecture, Coupes, Vases, Terres cuites, Cartes et Plans dessinés d'après nature et relevés par M. de Waldeck texte rédigé par M. Brasseur de Bourbourg ... *Paris: Arthus Bertrand.* 1866. Folio, Title, pp. xxiii, 83, (1), viii. Map and Plates, 3–56. B. 7435

With a second title-page: "Recherches sur les ruines de Palenqué et sur les origine, de la civilisation du Mexique par M. l'abbé Brasseur de Bourbourg ... . *Paris: Arthus Bertrand.* 1866." The text has also been issued separately.

BRASSEUR DE BOURBOURG. Popol Vuh. Le livre sacré et les mythes de l'antiquité américaine, avec les livres héroïques et historiques des Quichés. Ouvrage original des indigènes de Guatémala, texte Quiché et traduction française en regard, accompagnée de notes philologiques et d'un commentaire sur la mythologie et les migrations des peuples anciens de l'Amérique,

etc., composé sur des documents originaux et inédits, par l'abbé Brasseur de Bourbourg ... . *Paris: Arthus Bertrand.* 1861. 8vo, Title, pp. cclxxix, 367, (1). 2 Maps, and Lithograph. C.

Forms Vol. I. of the "Collection," described in No. 7423 *supra.*

BRASSEUR DE BOURBOURG. Quatre lettres sur le Mexique Exposition absolue du système hiéroglyphique mexicain la fin de l'age de pierre. époque glaciaire temporaire commencement de l'age de bronze. origines de la civilisation et des religions de l'antiquité d'après le Teo-amoxtli et autres documents mexicains, etc. Par M. Brasseur de Bourbourg ... . *Paris: Auguste Durand et Pedone. Madrid: Bailly-Baillière.* 1868. 8vo, pp. xx, 463.

Forms Vol. IV. of the "Collection," described in No. 7423 *supra.*

BRASSEUR DE BOURBOURG. Quelques Traces d'une émigration de l'Europe septentrionale en Amérique dans les traditions et les langues de l'Amérique Centrale. Lettre adressée à M. C. Rafn, secrétaire de la Société Royale des Antiquaries du Nord, publiée dans les Nouvelles Annales des Voyages. *Paris.* 1858.

BRASSEUR DE BOURBOURG. Recherches sur les ruines de Palenqué et sur les origines de la civilisation du Mexique, par l'abbe Brasseur de Bourbourg. *Paris: A. Bertrand.* 1867. 4to.

BRASSEUR DE BOURBOURG. S'il existe des sources de l'histoire primitive du Mexique dans les monuments égyptiens et de l'histoire primitive de l'ancien monde dans les monuments américains? *Paris: A. Durand.* 1864. Rl. 8vo, pp. 146. 7440

From the "Relation du Yucatan de Diego de Landa."

BRASSEUR DE BOURBOURG. Voyage sur l'Isthme de Tehuantepec, dans l'état de Chiapas et la république de Guatémala, exécuté dans les années 1859 et 1860. Par M. l'Abbé Brasseur de Bourbourg. ... . *Paris: Arthus Bertrand.* 1861. 8vo, pp. 209, (1). B. + [*Ibid.*] 1862. 8vo. C. 7441

Also in the "Nouvelles Annales des Voyages. *Paris.* 1862." Some copies on thick paper. "The distinguished French traveler and archæologist, Abbé Brasseur de Bourbourg, has recently returned from his last (the sixth) exploring tour in Mexico and Central America. We have reason to believe that he will, ere long, lay before the scientific world the results of his recent investigations, in whieh he was very much aided by his position as one of the members of the Scientific Commission appointed by the Emperor to explore Mexico." — TRÜBNER. *Per contra,* some of the Abbé's works are said to be disfigured by numerous apocryphal relations, which would have been excluded by a more thorough scholar. *See* "The Abbé Brasseur and his Labors," in "Lippincott's Mag.," Jan. 1868, I. 79–86.

BRASSEUR (*General* Le). *See* Le Brasseur.

BRATTLE (William). To the Public. *Boston.* [1774.] 4to.

An address, signed W. Brattle, in justification of his conduct in delivering certain military stores to General Gage.

BRATTLEBORO'. A Description of the Brattleboro' Hydropathic Establishment, with a Report of 563 Cases treated there ... . [By Robert Wesselhœft, the Proprietor.] *Brattleboro': printed by J. B. Miner.* 1848. 8vo, pp. 32. View. H. + With 392 Cases treated in 1848. *Brattleboro'.* 1849. 8vo.

Prospectus of the Lawrence Water-Cure, Brattleboro', Vt. Opened May 15, 1853. *New-York: Printed by Curran Dinsmore & Company.* 1853. 8vo. 7444

BRAUER (Johann Hartwig). Beiträge zur Geschichte der Heidenbekehrung. Mitgetheilt von Johann Hartwig Brauer ... . *Altona: Joh. Friedr. Hammerich.* 1835–39. 3 vols., 12mo.

Each Beitrag has a second title. The first is: Johann Elyot und die Familie Mayhew, die Apostel der Indianer. 1835. + Zweite Auflage. 1847. pp. xii, 100. The third is: Die Heidenboten Friedrichs IV. von Dänemark. II. Thomas von Westen und Hans Egede. ... 1839. pp. x, 144. H.

BRAUN (B.) Carta del P. Bartholome Braun, Visitador de la Provincia Tarahumara a los PP. Superiores de esta Provincia de Nueva-España sobre la apostolica vida, virtudes, y santa Muerte del P. Francisco Hermano Glandorff. *Mexico.* 1764. 4to, pp. 33. 7446

BRAUN. Vida y prodigiosas virtudes del P. Francisco Herman Glandorf, Missionero de la Compañia de Jesus. *Megico.* 1764. 4to. 7447

BRAUN (Georg) *and* HOHENBERG *or* HOGENBERG (Franciscus). Civitates Orbis Terrarum, in Æs incisæ et excusæ, et Descriptione Topographica, Morali, Politica, illustratæ. *Coloniæ Agrippinæ.* 1572–1617. 6 vols. 7448

Contains views of Cusco, Mexico, etc., accompanied with descriptive accounts, indexes, etc. Georgi has a title: Theatrum Urbium Præcipuarum Mundi. *Coloniæ.* 3 vols., folio. + *Antverpiae.* 1522. 3 vols., folio.

BRAUNS (Ernest Ludwig). Amerika und die moderne Völkerwanderung. *Potsdam: Vogler.* 1833 [1832]. 8vo. Portrait.

BRAUNS. Das liberale System oder das freie Bürgerthum. In einem Gemälde des Bundesstaates von Nordamerika. *Potsdam.* 1833. 2 vols., 8vo. 7450

BRAUNS. Europa und Nordamerika im Lichte der Gegenwart. *Grimma: Verlags-Comptoir.* 1851. 8vo, pp. viii, 148. 7451

BRAUNS. Ideen über die Auswanderung nach Amerika; nebst Beitrag zur genauern Kenntniss seiner Bewohner und seines gegenwärtigen Zustandes. Von Dr. Ernst Brauns. *Göttingen: Vandenhöck und R.* 1827. 8vo, pp. 880. Plate of Das Rathhaus zu New York. C., P. 7452

BRAUNS. Neudeutschland in Westamerika. Oder: Welches ist die zur Ansiedelung für auswandernde Deutsche geeignetste Weltgegend ... *Lemgo: Meyer.* 1847. 8vo. pp. xiv, 90. 7453

BRAUNS. Praktische Belehrungen und Rathscläge für Reisende und Auswanderer nach Amerika, von Dr. E. Brauns. *Braunschweig.* 1829. 8vo, 2 Titles, pp. 492, (3). C., H. 7454

With the second title: "Mittheilungen aus Nordamerika, die höhern Lehranstalten und die Englisirung der dortigen Deutschen betreffend. ..."

BRAUNS. Skizzen von Amerika. Zu einer belehrenden Unterhaltung für gebildete Leser, mit besonderer Rücksicht auf Reisende und Auswanderer nach Amerika. *Halberstadt: Vogler.* 1830. 8vo. 7455

BRAUNS (F. W.) Joy in Tribulation. A Sermon preached in Baltimore, November 28, 1861. By Rev. F. W. Brauns. *Baltimore: John D. Toy.* 1861. 8vo, pp. 15. 7456

BRAUNSCHWEIG (Johann Daniel von). Ueber die alt-amerikanischen Denkmäler. Mit einem Vorwort von Carl Ritter. *Berlin: G. Reimer.* 1840. 8vo, pp. 185. BM. 7457

BRAVET. Le Paraguai Jésuitique; ou Description succinte des terres dont les Jésuites Espagnols se sont emparés dans l'Amérique Méridionale, en y portant la foi ... Le tout extrait fidellement des Mémoires du sieur Bravet, Ingénieur à la Martinique, que ces Peres firent Généralissime de leurs troupes dans la guerre contre les Xaraïes en 1718. *Amsterdam.* 1768. 12mo, 3 l., pp. 55. 7458

"Pièce fort rare Dans l'avertissement, on la dit extraite des Mémoires de Bravet, qui, dans une lettre adressée en 1721 au duc d'Orléans, alors régent, raconte l'évènement qui le fit entrer au Paraguay." — LECLERC, No. 1612.

BRAVO (F.) Sermon en las honras de doña Hypolita de Cordova, virreyna del Peru, Por Fr. Fernando Bravo. *Lima.* 1660. 4to. 7459

BRAVO. Qui non intrat per ostium sed ad|cendit aliunde ille fur est.|Veritas et vita ego sum via . Ioan . x .|opera me|dicin-

alia, in quibus|que plurima extant|scitu medico ne . | cessaria in . 4 . ii . [*sic*] di|gesta, quae pagina|versa continentur,|Authore Francis|co Brauo Orsumen|si doctore, ac Me|xicano medico.| 1549.|*Mexici, apud Petrum Ocharte.*|*Cum priuilegio.*| Sm. 4to, 4 l., 303 leaves. Woodcuts. L. 7460

The date of 1549, on the title-page, is an error of the press. Concerning this rare book, *see* "Bib. Am. Vet." pp. 435, 436.

BRAVO (J.) Arte de la Lengua de Michoacan (Tarasca). Por Fr. Juan Bravo. *Mexico.* 1574. 8vo. 7461

"This Grammar formed part of three volumes in 8vo, printed by Pedro Balli, in the same year. It was accompanied by a Confessionario, etc., in the same language. Souza says of the Fr. Bravo, 'fue maestro peritisimo de la lengua Pirinda, llamada Tarasca.'" — LUDEWIG.

BRAVO DE LAGUNAS Y CASTILLA (Joseph de). Discurso histórico jurídico del orígen y fundacion del hospital de S. Lázaro de Lima. *Lima.* 1761. 4to. 7462

BRAVO DE LAGUNAS Y CASTILLA. Voto Consultivo que ofrece al Exc. Señor Don Jos. Ant. Manso de Velasco, Capitan-General de los Reynos del Perù. *Lima.* 1761. 4to. 7463

BRAVO DE RIVERO Y ZAVALA (Diego Miguel). Meritos, y servicios de D. Diego Miguel Bravo de Rivero. *Lima.* 1793. 4to, pp. 24. 7464

BRAWERN. Schiffahrt nach dem Königreich Chili in Westindien verrichtet durch Herrn Heinrich Brawern und Hern Helias Herckman im Jahr 1642 und 1643. *Francfurt an Mayn: C. Leblun.* 1649. 7465

Title as given by Ternaux, No. 688.

BRAWERN (H. H.) *See* Hulsius *and* Churchill, Vol I.

[BRAXTON (C.)] Address to the Convention of the Colony and Ancient Dominion of Virginia, on the subject of Government in general, and recommending a particular form to their consideration. By a native of that Colony. *Philadelphia: John Dunlap.* 1776. 12mo, pp. 25. C. 7466

Attributed to Carter Braxton, in Jefferson's handwriting, in the copy in the Library of Congress.

BRAXTON (Carter M.) Map of the Battle Field of Fredericksburg, explained by extracts from official reports; also, Gen. Rob. E. Lee's report of the Battle. *Lynchburg: Virginian print.* 1866. 8vo, pp. 44. Map. 7467

BRAY (C.) British Empire: a Sketch of the Geography, Growth, Natural and Political Features of the United Kingdom, its Colonies and Dependencies. By Caroline Bray. *London: Longman.* 1863. Fcap 8vo, pp. ix, 552. Map. 7468

BRAY (O.) An Oration pronounced in the brick meeting house, New Haven, at the request of Hiram Lodge of Free and Accepted Masons, on the anniversary of St. John the Evangelist, Jan. 1, 1802. By Oliver Bray. *New Haven.* 1802. 8vo, pp. 32. 7669

BRAY (Thomas). Abstract of the Proceedings of Dr. Bray, Commissary for Maryland, and his Associates, 1823. Account of the Designs of the Associates of the late Dr. Bray *London:* [n. d. No title.] 4to, pp. 4. + Account of the Designs of the Associates of the late Dr. Bray, with an Abstract of their Proceedings. *London.* 1760. 8vo. + 1763. + 1767. + 1770. + *London.* 1794. 8vo. + *London.* 1804. + *New York.* 1804. 12mo. 7470

The catalogue of the Bodleian Library attributes this account to Thomas Bray, D.D., Rector of Exeter College.

BRAY. Account of the Institution established by the late Dr. Bray for founding clerical libraries in England and Wales, and Negro schools in British America. *London.* 1833. 12mo. 7471

BRAY. The Acts of Dr. Bray's Visitation, held at Annapolis in Maryland, May 23, 24, 25, 1700. With Proposals for the Propagation of the Christian Religion, and for the Reduction of the Quakers in Pennsylvania, &c. *London: Printed for W. Downing.* [1700.] 4to, pp. 17. BDL. 7472

BRAY. Apostolick Charity, its Nature and Excellence considered in a Discourse upon Dan. 12: 3. Preached at St Paul's, [Dec 19. 1697] at the Ordination of some Protestant Missionaries to be sent into the Plantations. To which is Prefixt, A General View of the English Colonies in America, with respect to Religion; in order to shew what Provision is wanting for the Propagation of Christianity in those Parts. Together with Proposals for the Promoting the same; And to induce such of the Clergy of this Kingdom, as are Persons of Sobriety and Abilities to accept of a Mission. And to which is subjoin'd The Author's Circular Letter lately sent to the Clergy there. By Thomas Bray, D.D. *London: Printed for William Hawes.* 1699. 4to, pp. xxiv, 30, iv. + *London: Printed by E. Holt.* 1700. 4to, Title, pp. 33. Proposals, 3 l. 7473

BRAY. Bibliotheca Parochialis: |or, a|Scheme|of such|Theological Heads|both|General and Particular, |as are|more peculiarly Requisite to be Well|studied by every|Pastor of a Parish. |Together with a|Catalogue of Books|which may be read upon each of those Points.|Part I. By Thomas Bray, D.D.|*London:*| *Printed by E. H. for Robert Clavel, at the Peacock, in|St. Paul's Church-Yard.* M DC XC VII. 4to, 10 l., pp. 130. S. 7474

"The conclusion, showing the present state of the Protestant religion in Maryland," etc. — pp. 125–130. The author states that the object of this bibliographical treatise was to give those who went to Virginia, Maryland, and the American plantations, an idea of the books they should take. He speaks of having assisted in first founding a parochial library in Maryland. At the end are proposals "to induce persons of sobriety and abilitie to accept of a mission" to the plantations; and regulations that books sent to the Maryland libraries shall have on the cover, "ex gr. E Bibliotheca de Mary-Town; — de James-Town," etc. The work was not completed; but in the second edition the title-page reads: "Bibliotheca Parochialis, &c.; or, a Scheme of such theological and other heads, as seem requisite to be perused or occasionally consulted by the Reverend Clergy: Together with the Books which may be profitably read on each of those points, in order to promote the forming and erecting Libraries of three degrees, viz. General, Decanal or Leading and Parochial Libraries throughout Her Majesty's Dominions, both at Home and Abroad. Vol. I. The Second Edition, with large Additions. *London: R. Wilkin.* 1767." 8vo. 4 l., pp. 412. C.

BRAY. A Circular Letter to the Clergy of Maryland, subsequent to the late Visitation, written by their Affectionate Brother and Faithful Fellow Labourer, Thomas Bray. To which is added, Cursus Catecheticus Americanus. Consisting of Books more particularly fitted to the Use of the three several Classes of Catechumens, in order to Season the growing Generation with the Principles of Piety and Virtue; Pursuant to the Resolutions made to that Purpose the second Day of Visitation at Annapolis. May 4, 1700. [n. p. n d.] 4to, pp. 6. BM. 7475

Title from the "Bib. Am. Prim.," and the collation from an English catalogue, in which the date is said to be 1701.

BRAY. An|Essay|Towards Promoting all|Necessary and Useful Knowledge,|both|Divine and Human,|In all the Parts of|His Majesty's Dominions,| Both at Home and Abroad.| By Thomas Bray, D.D.|*London*,|... | *Robert Clavel* ...|M,DCXCVII. 4to, 4 l., pp. 221. 7476

BRAY. An Introductory Discourse to Catechetical Instruction ... In a Pastoral Letter to the Clergy of Maryland; ... Containing a Course of Catechising to be observed on the Plantations, consisting of Books more particularly fitted for the Use of three several Classes of Catechumens there, pursuant to the Resolutions made to that purpose the 2d day of the Visitation

in Maryland, May 24, 1700. With a Preface ... By Thomas Bray, D.D. *London: printed by J. Brudenell ... for William Hawes* ... 1704. 8vo. 7477

BRAY. A Letter from Dr. Bray to such as have contributed towards the Propagating Christian Knowledge in the Plantations. [1700.] 4to, pp. 3. 7478

BRAY. A Memorial, Representing the present State of Religion on the Continent of North America. By Thomas Bray, D.D. *London: Printed by William Downing for the Author.* 1700. 4to, pp. 15. BM. 7479

"With proposals for the propagation of the Christian religion in the several provinces on the continent of North America." — KENNET.

BRAY. The|Necessity|of an early|Religion|being a|Sermon |Preach'd the 5th of May Before The|Honourable|Assembly of|Maryland|By Thomas Bray D.D.|*Annapolis, Printed by Order of the|Assembly By Tho: Reading, For Evan Jones book-|seller, Anno Domini* 1700.| 4to, pp. 20. 7480

BRAY. The Present State of the Protestant Religion in Maryland, under the Government of Francis Nicholson Esqr. by Dr. Bray, deputed by the Lord Bishop of London, to be his Commissary in that Province. [*London.* 1700.] Half sheet. 7481

BRAY. Several Circular Letters to the Clergy of Maryland, subsequent to their late Visitation, to enforce such Resolutions as were taken therein. By Thomas Bray, D.D. ... *London: Printed by William Downing.* 1701. 4to, pp. 21. 7482

See "Bib. Am. Prim.," pp. 181, 183. Includes "A Course of Catechising," "The Layman's Library," etc.

BRAY. Whole Course of Catechetical Instruction, with an introductory Discourse: being a Pastoral Letter to the Clergy of Maryland. *London.* 1704. 12mo. 7483

BRAY. Publick Spirit, Illustrated in the Life and Designs Of the Reverend Thomas Bray, D.D. Late Minister of St. Botolph without Aldgate. *London: J. Brotherton.* MDCCXLVI. 8vo, pp. 54, (1). + *London.* 1808. 8vo 7484

Replete with interesting particulars relating to America, particularly the province of Maryland.

BRAY (T. W.) Reflection on Death and Eternity: or A Funeral Oration On the Death of Samuel Hyde, Of Norwich, Who died March the 15th, A.D. 1763, Being a Member of Yale-

College, in New Haven: which was pronounced in the College-Hall, on the 21st of June, A.D. 1763. By Thomas Wells Bray, A Class-Mate of the Deceased; and Published at the Request of the bereaved Parents ... *New Haven: Printed by Benjamin Mecom.* 1764. 8vo, pp. 24. 7485

BRAY. Sermon occasioned by the Death of Abel Chittenden, Student of Yale College, September 2, 1770. *New Haven.* [1770.] 4to. 7486

BRAY (*Capt.* William). To the Supreme Authority, the Parliment of the Commonwealth of England: A Serious charge and accusation against Mr. Edw. Winslow one of the Commissioners for compounding at Haberdasher's Hall. *Imprinted at London.* 1652. 4to, pp. 6. J. C. B. 7487

I suppose this was Edw. Winslow, Gov. of Plymouth Colony, who returned to England in 1635.

BRAYMAN (J. O.) Thrilling Adventures by Land and Sea. Being remarkable historical facts. ... Edited by J. O. Brayman. New Edition. *Buffalo.* 1852. 12mo, pp. 504. 7488

BRAYMAN. Daring Deeds of American Heroes, with Biographical Sketches. Edited by James O. Brayman ... . New Edition. *Buffalo.* 1852. 12mo, pp. 450. + *Auburn: Derby & Miller. Buffalo: Derby, Orton & Mulligan.* 1853. 12mo, pp. 499. Woodcuts. B. 7489

BRAYTON (J. A.) Sermon on the occasion of the Funeral of Mrs. Mary Ann Phelps ... . December 6th, 1857. By Rev. J. A. Brayton. *Painesville, Ohio: Commercial Advertiser Print.* [n. d.] 12mo, pp. 11. H. 7490

BRAYTON (J. J.) Our Duty in relation to Southern Slavery. A Discourse delivered at South Hingham, January 29, 1860, by J. J. Brayton ... . *Boston.* 1860. 8vo, pp. 16. H. 7491

BRAYTON (P.) A Short Account of the Life and Religious Labours of Patience Brayton, of Swansey, Mass., mostly selected from her own Minutes. *New-York: Isaac Collins and Son.* 1801. 12mo. 5⅜ sheets. + *New-Bedford: Printed by Abraham Shearman, Jun.* 1801. 12mo. 6 sheets. + *New-York, Printed London: Reprinted, William Phillips.* 1802. 12mo. 6 sheets.

Also reprinted in Vol. x. of "The Friend's Library. *Philadelphia.* 1846."

BRAZ DA COSTA RUBIM. Vocabulario Brasileiro para servir de complemento aos Diccionarios da Lingua Portugueza. Por Braz da Costa Rubim. *Rio de Janeiro.* 1853. 8vo, pp. 84.

BRAZER (J.) A Discourse on the Life and Character of the late Hon. Leverett Saltonstall, delivered in the North Church, Salem, Mass. ... May 18, 1845. By John Brazer ... . *Salem.* 1845. 8vo, pp. 52. H. 7494

The appendix contains biographical notices.

BRAZER. Sermons, by John Brazer, D.D. *Boston: Wm. Crosby and H. P. Nichols.* 1849. 12mo, pp. xvi, 367. H. 7495

"Memoir," by W. S. B., pp. ix–xvi. Also: A Discourse ... delivered ... in Salem ... 4th of April 1829, at the Interment of Edward Augustus Holyoke, M.D. LL.D. &c. &c. ... . *Salem: Foote & Brown.* 1829. 8vo, pp. 34. H., S. — A Discourse preached ... [in] Salem, Mass., August 20, 1843, the Sunday succeeding the Death of Hon. Benjamin Pickman. *Salem.* 1843. 8vo, pp. 25, vi. — A Discourse ... at the Installation of the Rev. Andrew Bigelow, at Taunton, April 10, 1833. ... . *Cambridge: Charles Folsom, Printer.* 1833. 8vo, pp. 38. H. — Discourse before the Society for the Promotion of Christian Education in Harvard University; delivered at Boston, Aug. 28, 1825. *Boston.* 1825. 8vo. — A Sermon ... of the Ordination of the Rev. Jonathan Cole ... in Kingston, January 21, 1829. ... . *Salem: Foote & Brown.* 1829. 8vo, pp. 27. H. — ... A Sermon, on the Anniversary of Ordination, preached to the North Society in Salem, Mass. ... November 19th, 1837. ... *Salem.* 1837. 8vo, pp. 22. H.

BRAZER (Samuel). Address, pronounced at Worcester, on May 12th, 1804, in Commemoration of the Cession of Louisianna To the United States. By Samuel Brazer, Junior. *Printed at Worcester by Sewall Goodridge, May 19th*, 1804. 8vo, pp. 15. + Second Edition. [*Ibid.* n. d.] pp. 15, (1). 7496

BRAZER. Address at Hatfield, Mass. March 4, 1807, in commemoration of the Inauguration of Thomas Jefferson. *Northampton.* [n. d.] 8vo, pp. 16. 7497

BRAZER. Oration at Charlton, Mass. July 4, 1811. *Worcester: Henry Rogers.* [1811.] 8vo, pp. 16. 7498

BRAZER. Oration, pronounced at Lancaster, July 4, 1806 ... By Samuel Brazer, Junior. ... *Worcester: Printed ... By Samuel Cotting. July* 1806. 8vo, pp. 24. B., H. 7499

BRAZIL. Aanmerkingen van eenen Reiziger, over Hollandt ... Braziliё ... Uit het Fransch vertaalt. *Amsteldam.* 1729. 4to. 7500

Pages 176–178 relate to Brazil.

Accoord|Van|Brasilien,|Mede van 't Recif, Maurits-Stadt,| ende de omleggende For-|ten van Brasil.|*t'Amsterdam,*|*By Claes Lambrechtsz. van der Wolf*, 1654.| 4to, pp. 8. J. C. B. 7501

Eeenige Advijscit ende verklaringhen uyt Brasilien. In dato den 19. Mey 1648. *Amsterdam.* 1648. 4to, 4 leaves. 7502

Advys op de Presentatie van Portugal. Het Eerste Deel. [1649.] 4to, pp. 24. 7503

Aen-Spraeck|aen den|Getrouwen Hollander,| Nopende|De Proceduren der Portugesen|in Brasill.|*In 'sGraven-Hage,*|*Gedruckt by Isaac Burghoorn Boeck-drucker,*|*op 'tDelfsche Wage-Veer*, 1645.| 4to, pp. 24. 7504

Discourse to faithful Hollanders on the actions of the Portuguese in Brazil. *See* Asher, No. 206. Trömel mentions a copy on which the name of Dirk Graswinkel is written in a contemporary hand as that of the author.

Aktenstücke Brasilischer Seite, betreffend die Kolonisation des Kaiserreiches. Herausgegeben von J. Hörmeyer. Jahrgang 3. *Rudolstadt.* 1861. 8vo. 7505

A Justiça. *Rio de Janeiro.* 1866. 8vo, pp. 24. 7506

Almanach de lembranças Brasileiras, coordenadas e escritas por Cezar Augusto Marques. 2e anno. 1863. *Maranhao.* 1862. 12mo, pp. 426. 7507

Almanach de lembranças luso-brasilerio para o anno de 1866. Por Alex. Magno de Castilho e Antonio Xav. Rod. Cordeiro. 1866. 18mo, pp. 384. 7508

Almanak do ministerio da guerra organisado na repartiçao de adjudante general 1865. *Rio de Janeiro.* 1865. 8vo. Continued. 7509

Almanak de ministerio da marinha, 1856. *Rio de Janeiro.* 1856. 8vo. 7510

Almanak militar para o anno de 1865. *Rio de Janeiro.* 1865. 8vo, pp. viii, 542. Continued. 7511

... The Anglo-Brazilian Times. Political, Literary, and Commercial Editor and Proprietor William Skully [Semi-weekly] Anno I. *Rio de Janeiro.* 1865. Folio. 7512

Annuario historico Braziliense. Primeiro anno 1821. *Rio de Janeiro: Plancher.* 1824. 8vo, pp. 150. Continued. 7513

Annuario politico, historico y estatistico do Brazil. Primeiro anno. *Rio de Janeiro.* 1846. 8vo. BD. 7514

Antvvoort|Vanden|Ghetrouwen Hol-|lander.|Op den Aenspraeck van den|Heetgebaeckerden|Hollander|Vrienden mogben kijven,|Maer moeten Vrienden blyven.|*Ghedruckt Anno* M.VIc.XLV.| 4to, pp. 16. 7515

Antwoorde|Vande Heeren Staten Generael, op|ende tegens 't versoeck wegens den Koninck|van|Portvgal,|Gadaen om t'hebben restitutie van Couchin, en-|de andere plaetsen, inde Indien de Portugesen afgeno-|men, met het geene verders, ontrent de Portu-|geesche sake, ende 's Nederlants vrye navi-| gatie, op de Brasilien past. *Voor Lambert Lambertsen Schiedam.* 1664.| 4to, pp. 11. 7516

Reply of the states general concerning the restitution of Couchin, and other places.

Ao imperador. Cartas politicas de Erasmo. Segunda ediçao. *Rio de Janeiro.* 1866. 8vo, pp. 92. 7517

Apertura del Amazonas o la clausura fluvial del Brasil. ... *Paris: Dubuisson et Ce.* [n. d.] 8vo, pp. 29. Map. 7518

Articul-| Brief. | Beraemt over het Scheeps-ende Crijgs-| Dolck|Ten dienste van de|Ge-octroyeerde West-Indische Compagnie in|Brasyl, Guinea| Ende vorders de Limiten van den Octroye. — *Tot Groeningen,*|*Gebruckt by Hans Sas Boeckedrucker Ordinaris*|*Anno* M. DC. XL.| 4to, pp. 20. 7519

Articvlen|Ende conditien gemaeckt by het overleveren|van| Brasilien|als mede het Recif, Maurits Stadt ende For-|ten ende sterckten daer aen de|penderende. Gesloten den 28 January 1654.|*In 's Gravenhage,*|*Gedruct by Jan Pietersz. Anno* 1645. [sic]| 4to, pp. 8. 7520

Our title, No. 2155*a*, is slightly incorrect.

Apologie ofte vvaerachtige, &c., 1643. *See* Liebergen (Arnout van).

Avtentyck|Verhael|Van 't gene in Brasiel tot den 15 September is|voorgevallen, geschreven uyt 't Resif|*t'Amsterdam, voor Jan van Hilten inde Beurs-straet, inde gebor-|duyrde Hantschoen.* 1645.| Sm. folio, sheet. 7521

Auctentijck Verhael van 't remarc-|quabelste is voorgevallen in Brasil,|tusschen den Hollandtschen Admirael|Willem Cor-

nelisz. ende de|Spaensche Vloot.|Midtsgaders|De Sententie ende executie over eenighe Schippers,|die haren Eedt in 't ghevecht niet|bretracht hadden. *T'Amsterdam.*|*Ghedruckt voor Ian van Hilten. Anno* 1640.| 4to, 8 leaves. 7522

The marks „C 3" and „D" at the foot of two of the pages are evidently misprinted for A 3 and B. *See* Muller, No. 1041.

Avisa particolari delle Indie di Portugallo riceuuti in questi doi anni del 1551. et 1552. da li Reuerendi Padri de la compagnia de Jesu, doue fra molte cose mirabili, si uede delli paesi, delle genti, et costumi loro et la grande conuersioue [*sic*] di molti populi, che cominciano a riceuere il lume della santa fede et relligione christiana. *Roma: Valerio Dorico, et Luigi fratelli Bressani.* 1552. 8vo. pp. 267 7523

"Imprimée en caractères ronds, cette collection renferme plusieurs notices intéressantes sur le Brésil." *See* Leclerc, No. 93. Sold, in 1868, for 35fr.

Balanço da receita e despeza do imperio no exercicio de 1839–40 e estado da divida publica activa e passiva em 31 dezembre de 1840. *Rio de Janeiro.* 1843. 4to. 7524

Beneficien voor de Soldaten gaende|naer Brasil.|*In 's Gravenhage,* | *Byde Weduwe, ende Erfgenamen van wijlen Hillebrandt Iacobsz van Wouw, Ordi*|*naris Druckers vande Ho. Mo. Heeren Staten Generael. Anno* 1647.| 4to, pp. 4. 7525

Betrachtungen ueber das Laenderei-Vertheilungs-Gesetz und die Colonisation in Brasilien. *Rio de Janeiro.* 1854. 4to, pp. 8. 7526

Bibliotheca litteraria. No. 1–6 [all published]. *San Luiz.* 8vo, pp. 64, 44, 42, 36, 52, 40. 7527

Brandt in Brasilian Gedruck in't Jaer ons Heeren [n. p.] 1648. 4to, pp. 9. B. H. 7528

In Asher's Essay, this account of a conflagration in Brazil is said to occupy twenty pages.

O Brasil historico; escripto pelo Dr. A. J. de Mello Moraes. Primeiro anno. [Jan.–dez.] *Rio de Janeiro.* 1864. 4to. Continued. 7529

O Brasil visto por Cima. Carta a huma senhora sobre as questos do tempo. *Rio de Janeiro: typographia do Diario.* 1822. pp. 46, 1 l. 7530

Brasilianische Geschichte Johann Moritz, Fürsten zu Nassau. *Cleve: Silberl.* 1659. 8vo, 57 sheets, 3 l. 7531

Title from Georgi.

Das Brasilianische Handelsrecht. Nach dem Codigo Commercial do Imperio do Brasil übersetzt und mit Bemerkungen begleitet von S. Borchardt und Hermann Stolp. *Berlin: Decker.* 1856. 8vo, pp. viii, 98. 7532

Über Brasilien, nebst Beobachtungen der Gelb-Fieber-Epidemie in den J. 1848–1852. Herausgegeben von einem practischen Arzte. ... *Hamburg: Th. Niemeyer in Comm.* 1852. 8vo, pp. 32. 7533

De Brasilsche | Breede-Byl; | ofte | t'Samen-Spraek, | Tusschen Kees Jansz. Schott, ko- | mende uyt Brasil, en Jan Maet, | Koopmansknecht, hebbende | voor desen ook in Brasil geweest, | over | Den verloop in Brasil. | *In 't Jaer onses Heeren.* 1647. | 4to, 1 l., pp. 36. J. C. B. 7534

Written in the form of a dialogue between a Scotsman coming from Brazil, and a merchant who had been there, touching the affairs of the country.

Brasilsche | Gelt-Sack, | Waer in dat klaerlijck ver- | toont wort, waer dat de Participanten | van de West-Indische Compagnie haer | Geldt ghebleven is. | *Gedruckt in Brasilien op 't Reciff in de Bree-Bijl. Anno* 1647. | 4to, 14 leaves. 7535

Muller asserts that this is the first book printed in Brazil, and perhaps the first book in the *Dutch* language printed on this continent. "The pamphlet is full of interest, and contains many curious details about the West India Company and New Netherlands." *See* Muller, No. 1050; Trömel, No. 230.

Brasilsche | Oorloghs | overwegingh. | *Gedruckt in 't jaer* 1648. | 4to, 4 leaves. 7536

"Considerations on the War in Brazil," dated Delft 23 July 1643, sold at Puttick's, 1854, for 11s.

Brasilische Reise, 1678. *See* Simon (L.)

Brasyls | Schuyt-Praetjen, | Ghehouden tusschen een Officier, | een Domine, en een Coopman, noopende den | Staet van Brasyl: Mede hoe de Officieren en Sol- | daten tegenwoordich aldaer ghetracteert werden, | en hoe men placht te leven ten tyde doen de Por- | togysen noch onder het onverdraeghlijck Iock | der Hollanderen saten. | Dit door een onpartydich toe-hoorder ghean- | noteert. | *Ghedruckt in de West-Indische Kamer by Maerten, | Daer het gelt soo lustich klinckt alsser zijn Aep-staerten.* | *Anno* 1649. | 4to, 12 leaves. J. C. B. 7537

This scarce tract contains a talk between an officer, a clergyman, and a merchant, on the affairs of Brazil, and the treatment of the Portuguese by the Hollanders. The imprint is curious: "at Martins where the sound of money is as jolly as an apes tail." Tiele suggests the imprint ['s *Hage: J. Breeckevelt*].

De Portogysen goeden Buyrman. Getrocken uyt de Registers van syn goet Gebuerschap gehouden in Lisbona, Maringan, Caep Sint Augustijn, Sint Paulo de Loando, en Sant Tomée. Dienende tot Antwoort op het ongefondeerde Brasyls-Schuyt-praetjen. ... [n. p.] *Ghedruckt ... Anno* 1649, *den* 24 *December.* 4to, pp. 16. 7538

O Brazil agricola, industrial, commercial, scientifico, litterario, e noticioso. Nos. 1–21 (Janeiro, 1863–Agosto, 1864). *Pernambuco.* pp. 336. 7539

Brazil *and* Buenos Ayres. *See* Conder (J.)

Brazil: its History, Natural Productions, Habits and Customs of the Natives, &c. *London: Religious Tract Society.* Fcap 8vo. Map, and numerous Engravings. 7540

Brazil por hum presbitero secular do gram priorado do Crato. *Rio de Janeiro.* 1817. 2 vols., 4to. 7541

Brazilian Improvements, more particularly as regards the Province of Espirito Santo. By a Well-Wisher to Brazilian Independence. *London: Ridgway* [etc.]. 1825. 8vo, 1 l., pp. 29. H. 7542

Breeden-Raedt. *See* [Melyn (Cornelis)].

Brevis repetitio | Omnium que Excellentissimus D. Lega- | tus Portugalliæ ad componendas res Brasilicanas | proposuit vel egit a die 23. Maij. usque ad. 1. No- | vembris hujus anni 1647. Exhibita Celsis Pre- | pontentibus D.D. Ordinibus Generalibus harum | Confœderatarum Provinciarum. ad. 28. diem | ejusdem mensis. | [Vignette.] | *Hagæ-Comitis,* | *Excudebat Ludolphus Breeckevelt,* | *Typographus. Anno* 1647. | 4to, 8 leaves. 7543

"Récapitulation des propositions et transactions de l'ambassadeur du Portugal, faites à l'égard des affaires du Brésil dès le 23 mai jusqu'au 1er novembre 1647."—Trömel.

Briefe über Portugal und Brasilien; aus dem Französischen von M. Chr. Sprengel. *Leipzig: Weygand.* 1782. 8vo. 7544

Bril-gesicht | Voor de verblinde eyghen | baetsuchtige Handelaers op | Brasil. | By Forme van Advijs door een Lief-hebber van 't Vaderlandt geschreven aen synen Vriendt. | *Gedruckt* | *Na de Geboorte ons Heeren en Salighmakers Jesu Chrsiti* | *Op het Jaer* 1638. | 4to, pp. 8. 7345

This "pair of spectacles," for merchants trading with Brazil, is a tract of much rarity.

A Caça no Brazil, ou Manual do Caçador em toda a America tropical acompanhado de um glossario dos termos usuaes de Caça por um Brazileiro devoto de S. Huberto. *Rio de Janeiro.* 1860. 8vo. Frontispiece. 7546

Claar vertooch | Van de | Verradersche en Vyantlijcke Acten | en Proceduren | Van | Poortugaal, | In 't verwecken ende stijven van de Rebellie | ende Oorloghe | In | Brasil. | Beweesen uyt de Brieven en Geschriften van het | selve Rijck ende hare Ministers, door een Lief-hebber by | een versamelt, tot wederlegginge van de Frivole Ex- | cusen tot der Portugijsen onschult voort gebracht. | *t' Amsterdam,* | *Gedruckt by de Weduwe van Ioost Broersz. woonende in de* | *Pijl-steegh, in de Boeck-druckerye* 1647. 4to, 20 leaves. J. C. B., H. 7547

Codigo Brasiliense, ou colleccao das leis, alvaras, decretos, cartas regias, &c; promulgadas no Brasil desde a Feliz Chegada do Principe Regente N. S. a estes estados, desde 1808 até 1821. *Rio de Janeiro.* 1811–1821. 3 vols., 4to. C. 7548

Colleccao das Leis do Imperio do Brasil. *Rio de Janeiro.* 1838. Continued. 7549

Vol. xxxvii. was published 1867.

Collecçao das Leis e Decretos do Imperio do Brazil desde a feliz Epoca da sua Independencia. *Rio de Janeiro.* 1827. 4to.

The Commercial and Constitutional Laws of Brazil. (Now first translated from the Portuguese.) By Thomas Spence ... . *London: Dunn & Duncan. Etc.* 1866. 12mo, pp. xvi, 286. H.

Concept | Van Reglement op Brasil, | Ghenomen by haere Ho. Mo. de Heeren | Staten Generael der Vereenighde Ne- | derlanden, ende de Bewindt-hebberen | der Geoctroyeerde West-Indische | Compagnie. | [Vignette.] | *Ghedruckt in 't Iaer ons Heeren* | 1648. | 4to, 4 leaves. 7552

Consideratie, | Over de tegenwoordige ghe- | legentheydt van Brasil. | In twee Deelen ghestelt: | Int eerste werdt aenghewesen op wat maniere | men aldaer | alles beter coop sal connen | hebben, ende wat voordeelen aldaer | uyt staen te verwachten. | Int tweede deel ofte profijtelijcker is dat, sulx geschiede door de Compagnie selfs, ende | hare Dienaers alleen, ofte door | Particuliere. | Alles met redenen bevesticht, ende de teghenworpinghe die daer | tegen souden connen worden byghebracht, voldaen. | *t'Amstelredam,* |

Ghedruckt by Iohannis Iaquet, woonende inde Nieuwe-Lely-straet. | *Voor Ian van Hilten, Boeck-verkooper woo-* | *nen inde Beurs-straet.* 1644. | 4to, pp. 34. 7553

Considerations relative to the War between the People of Brazil and those of La Plata. *London.* 1826. 8vo. 7554

Constituçao Politica do Imperio do Brasil. *São Paulo.* [n. d.] 16mo. 7555

Constituçao politica do Imperio do Brasil, e carta constitucional do Reino de Portugal. *Paris.* 1830. 8vo. 7556

Constitucao politica do imperio do Brasil seguida do acto addicional. *Paris: Durand et Pedone Lauriel.* 1868. 18mo, pp. 35. 7557

Contestacion de los gefes del Egército Unido de los Andes y Chile al manifiesto del ex-mayor general D. Miguel Brayer, sobre su conducta en el tiempo que permanecíó en Sud-America. [n. p. 1818.] 4to, pp. 21. H. 7558

Copia der Newen Zeytung ausz Presillg Landt. [n. p. n. d.] Sm. 4to, Title, 2 unnumbered l., and 1 blank. J. L., J. C. B.

This copy of a letter from the land of Brazil is described by Harrisse at much length. *See* "Bib. Am. Vet.," pp. 171–175. *See also* Humboldt. A French translation is included in Ternaux's "Archives des Voyages." The following is another edition:

Copia der Newen Zeytung ausz Presillg Landt. [Colophon:] *Getruckt zu Augspurg durch Erhart oglin.* [n. d.] Sm. 4to, Title, 3 unnumbered l. J. L. 7560

"This edition presents differences in the orthography throughout, but not to such an extent as to give new readings, especially of the mysterious passage: 'Und wollen die Ersamen Portugaleser sagen es seien Gezyner, so gen Malagua navigieren,' and of the expression 'Nort Assril,' which so greatly perplexed von Hagen and Humboldt." —*Bib. Am. Vet.,* p. 175.

Copye | Ofte | Cort ende waerachtigh | verhael van 't gene ghepasseert is soo te | Water als te Lande sint de komste | ende vertreck van de Spaensche Vloot in | Brasil overgesonden voor sijn Genade | Heer Graef Mauritz van Nassau | waer van het principael ghesonden is | aen sijn Hoocheyt den Prince van | Oraengien. | *t' Amsterdam,* | *Voor Francoys Lieshout, Boek-verkooper op den Dam in 't* | *Groot Boek. Anno* 1640. | 4to, pp. 16. 7561

Copie | Van een Missive gheschreven by een vry Man, in | Brasil, aen seecker zijnen vrient alhier, gevonden onder de ver-

droncken brie- | ven, uyt het Schip Zeelandia tegen 't Eylant Wicht gestrant, ende de West- | Indische Compagnie ter hant gekomen. | *Voor Francoys Leishout op den Dam.* 1646. Sm. 4to, sheet. 7562

Corografia Brazilica. *See* [Cazal (Manual Ayres de)].

Correio Braziliense ou Armazem Literario. 1808–13. 10 vols., 8vo. 7563

Contains much information about the South American States during the period of their struggle for independence.

Cort, Bondigh ende Waerachtigh | Verhael | Van 't schandelyck over-geven | ende verlaten vande voorname Conquesten | van | Brasil, | Onder de Regeeringe vande Heeren | Wouter van Schonenburgh, | President | Hendrick Haecx, Hoogen Raet, | ende | Sigismondus van Schoppe, | Luytenant Generael over de Militie, 1654. | *Tot Middleburgh,* | *Gedruckt by Thomas Dircksz.* | *van Brouwers-haven.* | *Anno* 1655. | 4to, pp. 28. J. C. B. 7564

Cort ende waerachtich verhael | van der | Portugysen in Brasil | Revolte ende verraderlijcke hostiliteyt, | Voorgenomen | Ende in 't werk gestelt, | Tegens | De Staet deser Landen | Ende de | West Indische | Compagnie | Ende andere goede Ingesetenen ende Ne- | derlanders aldaer woonende. [1647.] | 4to, pp. 8. 7565

Cort verhael, 1640. *See* N. (N.)

Coup d'œil sur l'etat politique du Bresil du 12 Novembre, 1823. *Londres: chez l'Auteur.* 8vo. 7566

Customs, Laws. [Of Brazil.] *New York.* 1861. 8vo.

Die ein vnd zwantzigste Schiffart oder Gründliche vnd vmbständliche fernere Beschreibung der vollkommesten Landschaft Brasilien Americæ ... . *Frankfurt am Mayn: Wolffgang Hoffman.* 1629. 4to, pp. 131. Map, and 4 Plates. 7567

This account of Dutch enterprise in Brazil forms Part xxi. of "Hulsius's Voyages."

Documentos estatisticos sobre o commercio do Imperio do Brasil nos annos de 1845 a 1849, que acompanhao o relatorio da commissao en carregada do revisao da tarifa das alfandaga do imperio. *Rio de Janeiro: typographia nacional.* 1853. 4to, Title, pp. 261, 63, 103, 15, (3), 80, (2), 3, 11, (3), 1 Table folded. BA. 7568

Einige Advijsen uyt Brasilien. *Amsterdam.* 1648. 4to.

Emigration to Brazil. *New York: S. Hallet, Printer.* 1866. 8vo, pp. 68. 7569

The Empire of Brazil at the Paris International Exhibition of 1867. *Rio de Janeiro: E. H. Laemmert.* 1867. 8vo, pp. 197. Map. H. 7570

The Empire of Brazil at the Paris International Exhibition of 1867. With an Appendix: Catalogue of the Articles sent to the Universal Exhibition of Paris in 1867, and a large map. *Rio de Janeiro.* 1867. 8vo, pp. 140, 198. 7571

L'empire du Brésil à l'exposition universelle de 1867 à Paris. *Rio de Janeiro: Laemmert.* 1867. 8vo, pp. 135, 205. Map.

Een cort ende warachtich Verhael | Van de vermaerde See- | strijdt en loffelijcke Victorie | die Godt Al- | machtich verleent heeft de Generale West-Indische | Compagnie onder 't beleyt vanden Manhaften Ad- | mirael Generael Adrien Ianssen Pater, ende Vice-Ad- | mirael Maerten Tyssen, teghen de Spaensche Armade | onder 't veleyt van Don Antonio Doquendo Biscayn, | geschiet op de Cust van Brasil op de hoochte van 17. | Graden omtrent 50 Mijlen bezuyden ofte hoven de | Bahia de todos los Sanctos | indesen Jare 1631. | *Tot Middleburgh,* | *Bij Zacharias Roman, Boeck-verkooper woo-* | *nende op den Burght inden Vergulden Bybel Anno* 1631. | 4to, pp. 8. 7573

This "Short and true account of the glorious sea-fight and laudable victory took place on the coast of Brazil, about fifty miles south of the Bahia do todos los Sanctos." —Asher.

Eenige Advijsen | ende | verklaringhen | uyt Brasilien. | In dato den 19 Mey 1648. | Van 't gepasseerde. | *Tot Amsterdam,* | *By Philips van Macedonien, Drucker* | *in de Druckerije van Ian Roonpoorts Toorn.* | *Anno* 1648. | 4to, pp. 8. J. C. B. 7573

Estatutos do Instituto historico e geographico brasileiro, installado no Rio de Janeiro Em o dia 21 de Outubro de 1838 ... . Reformados ... 10 de Novembro de 1839. *Rio de Janeiro: typographia de J. E. S. Cabral.* 1839. 8vo, pp. 13. H. 7574

Examen | Over het | Vertoogh | Tegen het ongefondeerde ende schadelijck | sluyten der Vryen handel | in Brasil. | Door | Een onder soecker der waerheyt | *In 't Iaer onses Heeren* | M. D. C. XXXVII. | 4to, pp. 16. 7575

Reply to the Vertoogh, reprinted with the following title:

Examen | Over het | Vertoogh | Teghen het onghefondeerde ende scha- | delijck sluyten der Vryen handel | in Brasil. | Door | Een ondersoecker der waerheydt. | *In 't Iaer onses Heeren* | M. D. C. XXXVII. | 4to, pp. 15. 7576

Extract | ende Copye, | Van verscheyde Brieven en Schriften, | Belangende | de | Rebellie der Paepsche Portugesen | van desen Staet in Brasilien. | Tot bewijs | Dat de Kroon van Portugael schuldich is aen de selve. | *Ghedruckt in 't Iaer ons Heeren.* | 1646. 4to, pp. 31 or 32. 7577

An important tract, relating to the insurrection of Joam Fernandez Vieira in Brazil.

Extract | uyt de Missive vanden | President | ende | Raden | aende Ho. Mo. Heeren | Staten | Generael. | Op 't Recif den 22 April 1648. | *In 's Graven-hage,* | *By Ludolph Breeckevelt, Boeckdrucker,* | *woonende inde Pooten inde Vinder vande Druckery. Anno* M. DC. XLVIII. | 4to, pp. 8. 7578

Extract | uyt den Brief vande Po- | litycque Raeden in Brasil aen de Ed. Heeren Ghecom- | mitteerden ter Vergaderinge der Negenthiene vande | Gheoctroyeerde West-Indische Compagnie over | de veroveringe van de Stadt Philippia nu Frederick- | stadt, met alle sijn Forten en Starcken ghelegen in de Capitania van Paraiba | [At the end] *In s'Graven-hage* | *Bij de Weduwe, ende Erfgenamen van wijlen Hillebrant Jacobsz van Wouw, Ordinaris Druckers van de Ho:* *Mo:* | *Heeren Staten Generael. Anno* 1635. | 4to, pp. 4. 7579

Relates to the conquest of the town of Philippia, now Frederickstadt, situated in the Capitania of Paraiba.

Une fete brésilienne. *See* Denis (F.)

Floræ Fluminensis [Regni Brasiliensis] Icones. *See* [Vellozo de Miranda (J.)]

Florilegio da poezia brazileira ou collecçao das mais notaveis composiçoes dos poetas brazileiros falecidos, contendo as biographias de muitos delles, tudo precedido de um ensaio historico sobre as letras no Brasil. *Rio de Janeiro.* 1850. 3 vols., 8vo.

Folhinha de Braz Gomes parao anno de 1866 contendo a chronica nacional noticias curiosas e interessantes e a historia do Brazileiro Braz Gomes, perseguido pela inquisiçao. Anno xxvii. *Rio de Janeiro.* 1866. 18mo, pp. 344. 7583

De ghepretendeerden over- | last van eenighe Ingeboorenen ende In- | ghesetenen voor de Zeeuwen ende | wtheemsche Ameren haer in | Brasil aengedaen. | *Ghedruckt in 't Iaer ons Heeren* 1638. | 4to. pp, 4. 7584

Gründliche und umbständliche fernere Beschreibung der vollkomnesten Landtschafft Brasilien, Americæ; Item, was gestalt der schöne Portus und hafe Totos los Sanctos, sampt der Statt Salvador in an. 1624, von den Hollandern gewunnen, und hernach wider verlassen worden. *Franckfurt.* 1629. 4to. BD.

Forms Part xxi. of Hulsius's "Sammlung."

Haerlems | Schuyt-praetjen, | op't | Redres | vande | West-Indische Compagnie. | [Vignette.] *Gedruckt op't Jaer* 1649. 4to, 12 leaves. 7586

Handbook for Emigrants to Brazil, containing a collection of dispositions of the Brazilian legislation, that most particularly interest those strangers who will make their residence in Brazil, accompanied with some statistics, tables, the Brazilian system of measures and money, and a map of the Empire. *Rio de Janeiro.* 1865. 8vo, pp. viii, 112. 7587

Historia Natvralis | Brasiliae, | Auspicio et Beneficio | Illvstriss. I. Mavritii Com. Nassav. | illivs Provinciæ et Maris svmmi Præfecti Adornata: | In qua | Non tantum Plantæ et Animalia, sed et In- | digenarum morbi, ingenia et mores describuntur et | Iconibus supra quingentas illustrantur. | *Lvgdvn. Batavorvm,* | *Apud Franciscum Hackium,* | *et* | *Amstelodami,* | *Apud Lud. Elzevirium.* 1648. | Folio, 6 l, pp. 293, 7 l. BD. 7588

The History of the Brazils, from the Original Discovery in 1500, to the Emigration of the Royal Family of Portugal, in 1807. *London.* 1808. 8vo. 7589

De Instellinge van de | Generale Compagnie, | ghemaeckt in | Portugael, | Na | Brasil, | toelatinge, met de Acte van Sijn | Maiesteyt, | Gepasseert den 10 Meert, 1649. | *Gedruckt tot Amsterdam,* | *Voor de Weduwe van Francoys Lies-houdt, Boeck-verkoopster op den* | *Dam, in 't Groot Boeck.* | 4to, 12 leaves. 7590

International Relations with Brazil: Proceedings on the reception of H. E. Senhor D'Azambuja, Envoy Extraordinary and Minister Plenipotentiary from Brazil by the Chamber of Commerce of the State of New York, November 2, 1865, with remarks of Rev. James C. Fletcher, on the Mail communication between the United States and Brazil. *New York.* 1865. 8vo, pp. 15. 7591

Journalier verhael ofte copie van sekeren brief geschreven uit Brasijl, nopende de victorie van januarij 1640, aan de Bewindthebberen ter Kamer van de Mase. [*Rotterdam?*] 1640. 4to.

Title from Netscher, p. 16.

Iournael|Ofte|Kort Discours, nopende|de Rebellye ende verradelijcke Desseynen|der Portugesen, alhier in Brasil voorgenomen,|'twelck in Junio 1645. is ontdeckt.|Ende wat voorder daer nae ghepasseert is,|tot den 28. April 1647.|Beschreven door een Lief-hebber, die selfs int begin|der Rebellye daer te Lande is gheweest, ende|aldaer noch is residerende.|*Tot Arnhem,|Ghedruckt by Jan Jacobsz. Boeck-verkooper woonende in|de Backer-straet, in de vergulde Presse. Anno* 1647.| 4to, 40 leaves. 7593

This rare tract relates to the rebellion in Brazil, 1645–47.

Das Kaiserreich Brasilien bei der Pariser Universal Ausstellung von 1867 *Rio de Janeiro: E. & H. Laemmert.* 1867. 8vo, pp. 204. Map. H. 7594

Korte|Observatien|Op het|Vertoogh,|Door een ongenaemden uyt-gegeven.|Aende|Ho: Mo: Heeren Staten Generael|der Vereenighde Nederlanden.|Nopende de voor-gaende ende tegenwoordige|Proceduren van Brasil.|In-gestelt door een Lief-hebber des Vaderlandts.|*t'Amsterdam,|Gedruckt by Pieter van Marel Boeck-verkooper woonende|inde Hemelsche Globe: Anno* 1647. 4to, 4 leaves. 7595

In refutation of the Vertooch described, *infra.*

Legislaçao do Brasil. Consolidaçao das leis civis (publicaçao autoriçada pelo governo). Segunda ediçao mais augmentada. *Rio de Janeiro.* 1865. 4to, pp. clxxxviii, 680. 7596

Lettres sur l'Administration du Brésil sur la Douane de Rio Janeiro. *Paris.* 1826. 8vo. 7597

Liberdade religiosa no Brasil. Estudo de direito constitucional. *Rio de Janeiro.* 1865. 8vo, pp. 62. 7598

The Lobster's Voyage to the Brazils. [In Verse.] Illustrated with Engravings [by W. Mulready?]. *London.* 1808. 16mo. BM. 7599

Lyste van 't ghene de Brasil jaerlijcks can opbrenghen. [n. p. 1648.] 4to, 1 leaf. 7600

Memoria documentada offerecida a naçào brazileira sobre o melhoramento, ou reforma das ordens regulares, e em particular dos Benedictinos no Brazil. *Rio de Janeiro.* 1834. 8vo. BD.

Memorias do Instituto historico e geographico brasileiro. Tomo primeiro. *Rio de Janeiro: typographia de Laemmert.* 1839. 4to, pp. 53. H. 7602

Minerva Brasiliense. Bibliotheca Brasilica, ou Colleçao de obras originaes, ou traduzidas de autores celebres. Tomo I. *Rio de Janeiro: Typographia Austral.* 1844. 8vo. Continued.

Minerva Brasiliense. Jornal de sciencias, lettras e artes, publicado por huma associaçao de litteratos. *Rio de Janeiro: E. S. Cabral.* 1843. 4to. Continued. 7604

Motiven|Die d'E. Officieren der|Militie|in Consideratie hebben ghenomen om|met den Vyandt (namentlick de Portu-|gesen) in Accoord te treden.|Ady 23. Ianuary, Anno 1654.| 4to, pp. 4. 7605

Monarchy v. Republic: or, Has not Constitutional Monarchy in Brazil more tended to prosperity, than Republicanism in the other South American States? A Political Tract for the Times. *Bristol.* 1859. 7606

See "Quart. Review," CVIII. 303–342.

Nachrichten von den k. k. österreichischen Naturforschern in Brasilien und den Resultaten ihrer Betriebsamkeit. Aus den Amtsrelationen der k. k. Gesandtschaft am Hofe von Rio Janeiro an das Ministerium der auswärtigen Angelegenheiten in Wien. *Brünn: Trassler.* 1820–23. 2 pts., 8vo. Map and Plate. 7607

Het Naderste ende Sekerste|Journalier Verhael|ofte|Copye van sekeren Brieff, gheschreven|uyt Brasyl, aen de E: E: Heeren Bewinthebberen|der geoctroyeerde West-Indische Compagnye, ter Ka-|mer van de Mase, nopende de treffelijcke ende langh-|gewenschte Victorye die Godt Al-machtigh ons|verleent heeft, onder 't wijsselijck beleyt van Sijn Excell:|Graef Maurits van Nassau, etc. in Brasyl, tegen de|machtige Vloot des Konings van Spanjen, bestaende in|88. Zeylen, voor-ghevallen in de Maendt van Januario, 1640.|Mits-gaders|Een kort Verhael

van de Justitie welcke ghedaen is|aen eenighe Capiteynen die in desen Scheeps-strijdt|haer devoir niet en hebben gedaen.|*In 's Gravenhage,|Gedruckt by Isaac Burchoorn, Boeckdrucker in|de Speuy-straet inde Nieuwe Druckery* 1640.| 4to, pp. 16. 7608

Noticias curiosas sobre o Bresil. *Rio de Janerio.* 1824. 4to.

Oblaçao do Instituto historico e geographico Brasileiro ó memoria de seu Presidente honorario o Senhor Dom Affonso augusto primogenito de SS. MM. II. *Rio de Janeiro.* 1847. 4to. 7610

Contains poems by Ribeiro, Souza Silva, S. José, and Paula Menezes.

Observaçoes sobre a carta constitucional do reino de Portugal e a constituiçao do imperio do Brasil. *Paris: imp. de Casimir.* 1831. 8vo, 7¾ sheets. 7611

Ontdeckinghe | van | Rijcke Mijnen | in | Brasil. | Luctor & Emergo.|*T'Amsterdam,|Ghedruckt voor Iohan van Hilten.* 1639.| 4to, 4 leaves. 7612

Netscher, pages 192–199, gives a French translation of a portion of this rare work on the mines and commerce of Brazil.

O Patriota Brasileiro: Periodico mensal. Vol. I. *Paris.* 1830. Continued. S. 7613

La politica brasileira en el Rio de la Plata ante las calumnias del partido blanco. *Buenos-Ayres.* 1864. 7614

La politique du Brésil, ou la fermeture des fleuves sous prétexte de l'ouverture de l'Amazone. ... Traduit de l'espagnol. *Paris: Dubuisson et Cie.* 8vo, pp. 30. Colored Map. 7615

Den Portugaelsen Donder-slagh. *See* Anti-Prater, Vol. I., No. 1708.

A Posteridade. Brasil Historico e a Corographia Historica do Imperio do Brasil. Segunda Ediçao por um curioso, com permissao do autor, e feita com notas biblicas. *Rio de Janeiro.* 1867. 8vo, pp. 48. 7616

Projecto de constituiçao para o imperio do Brasil, organizado no conselho de estado sobre as bases appresentadas por sua magestad Pedro I. imp. *London.* 1824. 8vo. BD. 7617

Propositie ghedaen, 1647. *See* Sousa Continho.

Propositio facta celsis. *See* Sousa Continho.

Reflexoes Politicas offerecidas aos Brasileiros Aantes du sua Patria. *Philadelphia.* 1831. 8vo. 7618

Regimento da Navegaçao e conquistas do Brasil, Angola, etc. *Lisboa.* 1655. 7619

Reglement opt Brasil, 1648. *See* West Indische Compagnie.

Relaçao da acclamaçao que se fez na capitania do Rio de Janeiro do Estado do Brazil, e nas mais de sul, ao senhor roi D. Joao IV por verdadeiro roi e senhor do reino de Portugal. *Lisboa: por Rodrigues.* 1641. 4to, pp. 15. 7620

Relaçao da viagem que fez ao Brasil, 1657. *See* [Brito Freire].

Relaçao dos publicos festejos que tiveram logar do 1.º de Abril até 9, pelo feliz regresso de SS. MM. II. e A. I., voltando de Belem á côrte imperial do Rio Janeiro: seguida do sermao prégado em acçao de graças na igreja de S. Francisco de Paula, e de varias peças de poesia, etc. Feita por ordem do conselheiro Intendente geral da Policia, para eterna memoria de tao grandes dias nos fastos brasileiros. *Rio de Janeiro, na Imperial Typ. de Plancher.* 1826. 8vo, pp. 130. 7621

The sermon is by the Canon Januario da Cunha Barbarosa.

Relacion|Verdadera,|de la Gran Vitoria qve han|alcançado en el Brasil la gente de la Baia de|Todos Santos, contra los Olandeses. Dase|cuenta como les mataron dos mil hombres,| y de la grand prassa que les tomaron, haziendo-|los embarcar, y dexar el puerto, quitando-|les todo el bagaje que|Ileuauan.| [Colophon:] *Impressa con licencia en Seuilla, por Nicolas Rodriguez, en calle de Genoua. Año de* 1638.| 4to, 2 leaves. 7622

Relations veritables. *See* [Courbe (Augustin)].

Relatorio apresentado à Assembléa geral legislativa na terceira sessao da decima legislatura, pelo ministro e secretario do estado dos negocios da guerra. *Rio de Janeiro.* 1859. + Pelo ministro ... dos negocios estrangeiros. *Rio de Janeiro.* 1859. 7623

Also: For other years and by other ministers.

Relatorio da commissao de inquerito, nomeada por aviso do Ministerio da Fazenda de 10 de Octubre de 1850. *Rio de Janeiro.* 1860. Folio, pp. 129. 7624

Remarks upon the Objects and Advantages of the Anglo-Brazilian Canal, Road, Bridge and Land Improvement Company. *London.* [1835.] 8vo. BD. 7625

Rémonstrances des Négocians du Brésil, contre les insultes faites au Pavillon Portugais: et contre la saisie violente et tyrannique de plusieurs de leurs navires, par les officiers de la marine anglaise, accompagnées d'autres piéces intéressantes: traduites du Portugais et de l'Anglais, par F. S. Constancio, D.M. etc. *Paris.* 1814. 8vo, pp. 80. S. 7626

Reports of the Directors of the Imperial Brazilian Mining Association, addressed to the Shareholders, with Account of the Produce of the Gold-Washings. 1826–27. 3 vols., 8vo. Maps and Plates. 7627

Title, probably not correct, from a bookseller's catalogue.

Revista Brazileira. Jornal de sciencias, letras e artes, dirigido por Candido Baptista de Oliveira. Publicaçao trimensel. *Rio de Janeiro: Typ. Univ. de Laemmert.* 1857. 8vo. Continued.

See Silva, VII. 149.

Revista contemporanea de Portugal e Brasil Primeiro anno *Lisboa: Typ. do Futuro.* 1859. 4to, pp. 586. Continued. 7629

For an analytical table of the contents of vols. I. to VI. of this monthly journal, *see* Silva, VII. 146–7.

Revista trimensal de historia e geographia ou Jornal da Instituto historico geographico Brasileiro. ... Tomo primeiro. ... N.º 1º Abril de 1839. *Rio de Janeiro.* 1839. 8vo. Continued. C. H. 7630

Tom. XXVIII. was published in 1864. Another series has the title: "Revista do instituto historico e geographico de Brazil. ... Tomo I. *Rio de Janeiro: Laemmert.* 1856." 8vo.

Revista semanaria dos trabalhos legislativos da camara dos senhores deputados dedicada a assembléa legislativa do Brasil. ... Sessao 1828. *Rio de Janeiro: na typographia do Diario.* 8vo, Title, pp 443, (5). Continued. H. 7631

Revista universal Brasileira, jornal de instrucçao e recreio. *Rio de Janeiro.* 1848. 4to. 7632

Reys-boeck van het rijcke | Brasilien | Rio de la Plata ende Magallanes,|Daer in te sien is: | De ghelegentheydt van hare Landen ende|Steden haren handel ende wandel met de|Vruchten ende Vruchtbaerheyt der|selver: Alles met copere pla-|ten

uytghebeelt.|Als oock|De leste reyse van den Heer van Doort, met|het veroveren van de Baeye De todos los|Santos, t'samen ghestelt door N. G.|[Vignette.]|*Ghedruckt in 't Jaer onses Heeren|Anno* 1624.|*By Jan Canin.*| 4to, 34 l., unpaged. 6 folded Maps of Brasil and parts adjacent. C. 7633

Seeckere naedere Missive,|Geschreven uyt Brasilien|aen een seecker goedt Vriendt waer|in Klaerlijck verhaelt wordt het|Ghevecht het welcke tusschen|de Onse ende de Portu-|gijsen op den 19 April|is geschiedt.|*In 's Graven-Hage,|By Ludolph Breeckevelt, Boeck-Drucker|woonende inde Pooten inde Vinder vande Druckery.*|*Anno* M. DC. XLVIII.| 4to, pp. 8. 7634

Seeckere | Remonstrantie | Aen hare Hoogh Moghende de Heeren Staeten Generael der Vereenighde|Nederlanden|overgegeven|Door|De gesamentlijcke aenwesende gedeputeerdens| uyt Brazyl|Tenderende tot behoudenisse van die glo-|rieuse Ronincklycke Conquesten.|*Anno* MDCLVII.| 4to, pp. 8. 7635

Speculatien | Op 't | Concept van Reglement | Op | Brasil. | *t'Amsterdam,|Ghedruct by Samuel Vermeer, op den Nieuwen Dijck.* 1648.| 4to, 1 l., pp. 22. J. C. B. 7636

Speculatien|op't|Concept van Reglement op|Brasil|*Amsterdam.|Ghedruct by Samuel Vermese* ... 1648.| 4to, pp. 14. 7637

Speculations on the draught for the commerce with Brazil.

Het Spel|van|Brasilien,|Vergheleken by een goedt|Verkeer-Spel.|*Ghedruckt in 't Iaer ons Heeren* 1638.| 4to, pp. 7. 7638

A Brazilian satire on the West India Company. Reprinted as a broadside. Asher, No. 149, says pp. 8.

Tractado da Terra do Brasil, ... colleçao de noticias para a historia y e geographia das nacoes ultra marinas. *Lisboa: typ. acad.* 1826. 4to. 7639

Translado de una carta, embiada del Brasil à vn cavallero desta corte, dandole cuente de las vitorias grandes que han tendo las armas catolicas de D. Felide IIII., governadas por el Conde de Castillo. *Madrid.* [n. d.] 4to. BD. 7640

Tydingh uyt Brasil aende Heeren|Bewinthebberen van de West-Indische Com-|pagnie, van wegen den tocht by den Generael Brouwer nae de|Zuyd-Zee gedaen, komende met het Iacht de Zeeusche|Jager, dat den 5 Marty met brieven aen de Heeren

|Bewinthebberen, tot Rochel gearriveert is | *t' Amsterdam by François Leishout, op den Dam,* 1644.| Sm. folio sheet. 7641

This news from Brazil relates to the expedition made by General Brouwer to the South Sea.

Verhael van 't schandelijck over-geven ende verlaten van de voornaemste conquesten van Brasil onder Wouter van Schonenburgh, 1654. *Middleburgh.* 1655. 4to. BM. 7642

Vertooch|aen de|Hoogh en Mogende Heeren Staten Generael|der Vereenichde Nederlanden,|nopende|De voorgaende ende tegenvvoordighe Proceduren|van Brasil.|Midtsgaders|De doccumenten daer toe dienende. | *t'Amsterdam,* | *Gedruckt by Johannes van Marel, Boeckverkooper,|woonende inde Globe. Anno* 1647.| 4to, 3 l., pp. 26. 7643

Discourse addressed to the states general on the past and present events in Brazil, etc.

Viagem da Armada da Companhia do commercio e frotas do estado do Brasil, a cargo do general Francisco do Brito Freire. *Lisboa.* 1656. Folio. 7644

See Silva, VII. 419.

Viagem ao interior do Brazil con una exacto descripçao das Ilha dos Açores. *Lisboa: na Imprenta regia.* 1819. 4to. 7645

Le vrai intérêt des puissances européennes et de l'Empereur du Brésil à l'égard de la situation actuelle du Portugal. Traduit de l' allemand. *Bruxelles: P. J. Voglet.* 1830. 8vo, pp. 40. C.

Voor-looper | Brenghende oprecht bescheyt | uyt Amsterdam| aen een voortreffelijcken Heer in|'sGravenhaghe,|weghens de verraderije in|Brasil|Met het Schip Zeelandia, asgevardicht|den twaelfden December 1645, van|Pharnembuco.|*Gedruckt in 't Iaer ons Heeren* 1646.|Den thienden Februarij| 4to, pp. 4.

Vryheden|Ende|Exemptien|t'Accordeeren ende toe te staen, weghen de Generale Geoctroyeerde West-|Indische Compagnie, uyt krachte van den Octroye by hare Hog. Mog. de|Heeren Staten Generael der Vereenigde Nederlanden deselve verleent, aen alle de-|gene die hun met hare woonstede naer Brasil sullen willen begeven, ofte tegenwoordig daer.woonen.|[25 *Nov.* 1644.] |Sm. folio sheet, 49 lines. 7648

Warhafft,|Umbständ und gründlicher | Bericht,| Aus einem Original|Schreiben hoher Potentaten|extrahiret|Darin referiret wird, wie es eigendlich mit|Einnehmung der vortrefflichen Region Bahia im Kö-|nigreich Brasilien gelegen, daraus der

König in Hispanien Jähr-|lich in die 80 oder 90. Million Goldes intraden sich gema-|chet, und eine gute Zeit gewalthätiger Weise|innen gehabt,|So aber nun die hochmögende Herren Staden Gene-|ral mit einer herrlichen Victori uberweltiget, und in jhre|Gewalt gebracht, zugangen sey.|Jedern zu guter Nachrichtung jetzo in Druck|auszgegeben.|*Gedruckt im Jahr,* 1624.| 4to, 4 leaves. 7649

BREARD. Réponse du sieur Breard, ci-devant contrôleur de la marine à Québec Aux mémoires de M. Bigot, & du sieur Pean. [*Paris.* 1763.] 4to, pp. 42. H. 7650

Signed "Clos, Procureur & Conseil."

Breaking the Line. 1830. *See* [C. (G.)]

BREAZEALE (J. W. M.) Life As It Is; or Matters and Things in General: containing, amongst other things, historical sketches of the Exploration and first Settlement of the State of Tennessee; Manners and Customs of the Inhabitants; their Wars with the Indians; Battle of King's Mountain; History of the Harps, (two noted Murderers;) ... . By J. W. M. Breazeale. *Knoxville: Printed by James Williams.* 1842. 12mo, pp. 256. 7651

BRÉBEUF (Jean de). Relation de ce que les Jésuites ont fait et de ce qui s'est passé chez les Hurons en la Nouvelle-France en l'année 1634. *Paris: Sébastien Cramoisy.* 1634. 8vo. + En l'année 1635. [*Ibid.*] 1635. 8vo. 7652

His catechism in the Huron language is printed in Champlin's "Voyages," 1632. 4to. *See* Faribault, No. 86.

BRÉBEUF. Relation de ce qui s'est passé dans le pays des Hurons. *See* Le Jeune (Paul), at the end of whose "Relation ... 1633," this is printed.

BRECK (J.) West Point; or A Tale of Treason. An Historical Drama, in three Acts, dramatised from Ingraham's Romance of American History. By Joseph Breck, Esq. With a prologue by John H. Hewitt, Esq. Epilogue by R. Horace Pratt, Esq. *Baltimore: Bull & Tuttle.* 1840. 8vo, pp. 22.

BRECK (*Mr.*) Speech of Mr. Breck, of Kentucky on ... California ... March 25, 1850. [n. p. n. d.] 8vo, pp. 16.

[BRECK (R.)] A Letter from the Elders in the Province of the Massachusetts-Bay, Who assisted In the Ordination of the Rev. Mr. John Hubbard, at Meriden, June 22, 1769; in Answer To a Letter from the Reverend Association in the County of

New-Haven. Dated at Bethany, May 29, 1770. *New-Haven: Printed by T. and S. Green.* [n. d.] 8vo, pp. 24. H. 7655

Dated Sept. 10, 1770; signed "Robert Breck, John Ballantine, Joseph Lathrop."

BRECK. A Letter to the Author of the Pamphlet Called, An Answeer [*sic*] to the Hampshire Narrative. *Boston.* 1737. 8vo, 2 l., pp. 84, (Errata) 1 slip. C., B., M. 7656

By ministers of Hampshire County.

BRECK. The only Method to Promote the Happiness of a People and their Posterity. A Sermon Preached before the Honourable the Lieut. Governour, the Council, and Representatives of the Province of the Massachusetts-Bay in New-England, May 29th. 1728. Being the Day for the Election of His Majesty's Council. By Robert Breck M.A. Pastor of the Church in Marlborough. ... *Boston, New-England: T. Hancock.* 1728. 8vo, Title, pp. 42. B. 7657

BRECK. The Departure of Elijah lamented. A Sermon Preached at the Funeral of the Rev. Stephen Williams, D.D. Pastor of a church in Springfield, who departed this Life, June 10, 1782. in the Ninetieth Year of his Age. *Springfield.* 1782. 8vo, pp. 27. 7658

BRECK. Discourse at Amherst, Mass. Jan. 1781, occasioned by the Death of Rev. David Parsons. *Springfield: Babcock & Haswell.* 1783. 8vo, pp. 26. W. 7659

BRECK. A Narrative of the Proceedings Of those Ministers of the County of Hampshire, &c. That have disapproved of the late Measures taken in order to the Settlement of Mr. Robert Breck, In the Pastoral Office in the first Church in Springfield. With a Defence Of their Conduct in that Affair. Written by Themselves. ... *Boston.* 1736. 8vo, 2 l., pp. 93, (1). C., B., H.

BRECK. An Examination of and Some Answer to A Pamphlet, intitled, A Narrative and Defence of the Proceedings of the Ministers of Hampshire, who disapproved of Mr. Breck's Settlement at Springfield. With a Vindication of those Ministers and Churches, that approved of, and acted in the Settlement of said Mr. Breck. ... *Boston: H. Foster.* 1736. 8vo, 2 l., pp. 98. C., B., M. 7661

By a Boston clergyman.

BRECK. Past Dispensations of Providence called to Mind. In a Sermon, Delivered in the first Parish in Springfield, on the

16th of October 1775. Just one hundred years from the burning of the Town by the Indians. By Robert Breck ... . *Hartford: Printed by [Joel] Barlow & Babcock.* M,DCC,LXXXIV. 8vo, pp. 28. H., M. 7662

BRECK (R.), *and others.* An Account Of the Conduct of the Council which dismissed the Rev. Mr. Edwards from the Pastoral Care of the first Church at Northampton; with Reflections on the Protestation accompanying the Printed Result of that Council, and the Letter Published relating to that affair. [n. p. n. d.] 8vo, pp. 8. B. 7663

Signed by Robert Breck and three others.

BRECK. A Letter to the Rev. Mr. Hobby, in answer to his Vindication of the Protest, against the Result of an Ecclesiastical Council, met at Northampton. By Robert Breck and others. *Boston.* 1751. 4to, pp. 26. W. 7664

BRECK (R. L.) The Habeas Corpus and Martial Law. By Robert L. Breck. Prepared for the Danville Quarterly Review for December, 1864. *Cincinnati: R. H. Collins.* 1862. 8vo, pp. 39. C. 7665

BRECK (S.) Address. ... September 20th, 1828, On the Death of the Hon. Richard Peters. By Samuel Breck. *Philadelphia: printed by L. R. Bailey.* 1828. 8vo, pp. 27. H. P. 7666

BRECK. Discourse before the Society of the Sons of New England of the City and County of Philadelphia, on the History of the Early Settlement of their Country; delivered December 21, 1844. By their President, Samuel Breck, being their First Anniversary. *Philadelphia.* 1845. 8vo, pp. 44. C., H. 7667

BRECK. Historical Sketch of Continental Paper Money. By Samuel Breck. *Philadelphia: John C. Clark, Printer.* 1843. 8vo, pp. 40. C. BA. + *Reprinted by A. C. Kline.* 1863. 8vo, pp. 34. 7668

First issued in Vol. III. of the "Transactions of the Historical and Literary Committee of the American Philosophical Society." Fifty copies printed on large paper, folio.

BRECK. Report to the Pennsylvania Legislature on the system of General Education. By Samuel Breck. *Harrisburg.* 1834. 8vo. P. 7669

BRECK. Sketch of the Internal Improvements already made by Pennsylvania; with Observations upon her Physical and

Fiscal Means for their Extension; particularly as they have reference to the Future Growth and Prosperity of Philadelphia. Illustrated by a Map of ... Pennsylvania. By Samuel Breck. *Philadelphia.* 1818. 8vo, pp. 82. + Second Edition Revised and enlarged ... *Philadelphia: M. Thomas.* 1818. 8vo, pp. 81, (1). Map. C. H. 7670

BRECKENRIDGE (J. C.) Address of Hon. John C. Breckenridge ... preceding the Removal of the Senate from the Old to the New Chamber ... January 4, 1859. *Washington.* 1859. 8vo, pp. 7. H. 7671

Also: Address to the People of Kentucky. Dated Bowling Green, Kentucky, October 8, 1861. *Baltimore: "The South Office."* 1862.—Substance of a Speech ... at Frankfort, Kentucky, December 21, 1859. [n. p. n. d.] 8vo, pp. 8.—Gen. Butler; The Democratic Review; Judge Douglas; The Presidency; Speech ... House of R., March 4, 1852. 8vo, pp. 15.—Speech ... Nebraska and Kansas, March 23, 1854. 8vo, pp. 8. (And other speeches in the "Congressional Globe.")

BRECKENRIDGE. Biographical Sketch of Hon. John C. Breckenridge, Democratic Nominee for President, and General Joseph Lane, Democratic Nominee for Vice President. *Washington.* 1860. 8vo, pp. 32. C. 7672

BRECKENRIDGE. Breckenridge and Lane Campaign Documents. *Washington: National Democratic Committee.* 1860. C.

A series of twelve political tracts, etc., published to influence votes in favor of the Democratic presidential candidate, 1861.

BRECKENRIDGE (R. Jefferson). Address delivered before the Colonization Society of Kentucky at Frankfort, on the 6th Jannary, 1831. By Robert J. Breckenridge. *Franckfort.* 1831. 8vo, pp. 24. C. 7674

BRECKENRIDGE. The Civil War; Its Nature and End. Danville Review, December, 1861. By Robert J. Breckenridge. *Cincinnati: Office Danville Review.* 1861. 8vo, pp. 33.

BRECKENRIDGE. A Discourse on the Formation and Developement of the American Mind. ... Lafayette College, At Easton, Pa., on the 20th September, 1837. ... By Robert J. Breckenridge—A.M. ... *Baltimore: Richard J. Matchett, Printer.* 1837. 8vo, pp. 40. BA. 7676

BRECKENRIDGE. Discourse of R. J. Breckenridge, D.D., delivered at Lexington, Ky., January, [*sic*] 4, 1861, the Day of National Humiliation. ... *Cincinnati: Faran & McLean.* 1861. 8vo, Title, pp. 23. H. 7677

BRECKENRIDGE. Dr. Breckenridge's Statement in Reply to the Calumnies of Lt. Gov. Jacob, of Kentucky. [Dated Danville, Ky., February 9th, 1865. n. p. n. d.] Broadside. H.

BRECKENRIDGE. 1. Our Country—its Perils—its Deliverance ... . 2. State of the Country ... . 3. Discourse delivered on the day of National Humiliation, Jan. 4, 1861 ... . 4. The Civil War: its Nature and End ... . Four Articles on the State of the Country and the Civil War: By Rev. Robert J. Breckenridge ... . Reprinted from the Danville Quarterly Review for ... 1861. *Cincinnati: Office of the Danville Review.* 1861. 8vo, 2 l., pp. 73–115, 292–341, 639–672. C., BA. 7679

BRECKENRIDGE. The Great Deliverance and the New Career. An Oration, ... at Schenectady, N. Y., on the 25th July, 1865. By Robert J. Breckenridge, D.D., LL.D. ... *Philadelphia: James S. Claxton.* 1865. 8vo, pp. 32. 7680

Contains reference to the assassination of Mr. Lincoln.

[BRECKENRIDGE.] The Nation's Success and Gratitude. [The Substance of a Discourse delivered in Danville, Kentucky, November 26, 1863.] *Philadelphia: Henry B. Ashmead.* 1864. 8vo, pp. 22. H. 7681

Printed for the Union League of Philadelphia.

BRECKENRIDGE. Our Country: its Peril and its Deliverance. From Advance Sheets of the Danville Quarterly Review, for March, 1861. By the Rev. Robert J. Breckenridge, D.D., LL.D. ... *Cincinnati: Office of the Danville Review.* 1861. 8vo, pp. 43. C., H. 7682

BRECKENRIDGE. Papism in the XIX. Century, in the United States; select Contributions to the Papal Controversy during 1835–40. By Robert J. Breckenridge. *Baltimore: D. Owen & Son.* 1841. 12mo, pp. xii, 343. C. 7683

BRECKENRIDGE. ... Presbyterian Government, not a Hierarchy but a Commonwealth. ... *Baltimore.* 1843. Rl. 8vo, pp. 29. S. 7684

BRECKENRIDGE. "State of the Country," by the Rev. Robert Breckenridge, D.D. LL.D. *Cincinnati: Danville Review Office.* 1861. 8vo, pp. 26. 7685

BRECKENRIDGE. Speech of Robert J. Breckenridge ... at Lexington, Ky. On the 12th day of October, 1840, in reply to

the Speech of Robert Wickliffe, delivered ... 10th day of August ...; and in defence Of his Personal character, his political principles and his religious connexions. *Lexington, Ky.* 1840. 8vo, pp. 32. BA., P. 7686

BRECKENRIDGE. The Second Defence of Robert J. Breckenridge against the Calumnies of Robert Wickliffe; being a reply to his printed speech of November 9th, 1840. *Baltimore.* 1841. 8vo, pp. 67. C. + [Another Edition.] *Louisville, Ky.* 1841. 8vo, pp. 39. C. 7687

BRECKENRIDGE. The Third Defence of R. J. Breckenridge against the Calumnies of Robert Wickliffe ... *Baltimore: R. J. Matchett.* 1843. 8vo, pp. 90. C., P. 7688

BRECKENRIDGE. Two Speeches on the State of the Country, at Cincinnati, May 20, 1862, and during a Debate in the Presbyterian General Assembly, Columbus, May 22, 1862. By Robt. J. Breckenridge, D.D. *Cincinnati: Joseph P. Boyd.* 1862. 8vo, pp. 44. 7689

BRECKENRIDGE. Report of the Trial of Robt. J. Breckenridge, Indicted for Libel on Jas. L. Maguire, &c. *Baltimore.* 1840. 8vo, pp. 36. 7690

For a "Discussion on Slavery," *see* Thompson (G).

BRECKENRIDGE (S. M.) Oration delivered at the Union Celebration, at Hannibal, Mo., July 4, 1862. [n. p. n. d.] 8vo, pp. 15. 7691

BRECKENRIDGE (W. D.) Botany of the United States' Exploring Expedition: Cryptogamia, Filices, including Lycopodiaceæ, and Hydropterides, by William D. Breckenridge. *Philadelphia.* 1854–5. 4to, pp. viii, 357. Atlas of 46 Plates, folio.

100 copies printed. Forms vol. XVI. of the "United States Exploring Expedition."

[BRECKENRIDGE (W. L.)] Hints on Colonization and Abolition, with Reference to the Black Race. [n. p. n. d.] 8vo, pp. 25. 7693

BRECKENRIDGE. Speech of Rev. W. L. Breckenridge, delivered in the First Presbyterian Church, ... June 1, ... In Vindication of his principles and conduct, against ... Rev. Mr. [Edward T.] Taylor ... . *Louisville.* 1841. 8vo, pp. 23. H.

BRECKENRIDGE. Theological Seminaries in the West. By

William L. Breckenridge and Edward P. Humphrey. *Louisville.* 1850. 8vo, pp. 42. S. 7695

BRECKENRIDGE. *See* Brackenridge.

BREDAN (D.) Desengano a los pueblos de Bresil, y demas partes en las Indias Occidentales, para quitarles las dudas y falsas imaginaciones que podrian tener acerca de las declaraciones de los ... Estados Generales y los Administr. de la Compania. Compuesto por Daniel Bredan notario y escrivano publico en Amsterdam. *Amsterdam: P. As. de Ravestein.* 1631. 4to, pp. 14. 7696

BREED'S HILL. *See* Bunker Hill.

BREED (W. P.) Faith and Patience. A Sermon for the Times, by Rev. William P. Breed. Preached [at] ... Philadelphia, Thanksgiving Morning Nov. 27th, 1862. Repeated by Request, February 8, 1863. *Philadelphia: John Alexander.* 1863. 8vo, pp. 25. 7697

BREED. The National Nest-Stirring. A Discourse on the Times. Delivered in the West Spruce St. Presbyterian Church, ... May 5, 1861. By Rev. William P. Breed. *Philadelphia: H. B. Ashmead.* 1861. 8vo, pp. 15. 7698

BREED. The Lights which God hath showed us. A Thanksgiving Discourse, delivered November 28, 1861. ... By Rev. W. P. Breed. *Philadelphia: John Alexander.* 1861. 8vo, pp. 26. 7699

BREEN (H. H.) St. Lucia, Historical, Statistical, and Descriptive. By Henry H. Breen, Esq. Thirteen Years a Resident in the Island. *London: Longman.* 1844. 8vo, pp. xvii. 423. Map. C., BM., S. 7700

BREES (S. C.) A Key to the Colonies; or, Advice to the Million upon Emigration. For the use of all Classes. By S. C. Brees. *London.* 1851. 18mo, pp. 100. 7701

BREESE (S.) Speech of Hon. S. Breese, of Illinois, on the Oregon Question, delivered in the Senate of the United States, Monday, March 2, 1846. *Washington: Blair and Rives.* 1846. 8vo, pp. 22. 7702

BREESE. Speech of Mr. Sidney Breese of Ill., on the Mexican Question, and the Ten Regiment bill, Senate, Feb. 14. *Washington.* 1848. 8vo, pp. 14. 7703

Also: "Report on granting Public Lands to Illinois for Railroads, &c." 8vo.

Bref de nostre S. P. le Pape Innocent X. Sur le differend d'entre l'Euesque d'Angelopolis, ou colonie dite des Anges, en la Nouuelle Espagne dans les Indes Occidentales, et les P. P. Jésuites. Contenant la decision de plusieurs cas importans touchant la jurisdiction episcopale, et les priuileges des reguliers. *Sur l'imprimé à Rome, Ex Typographia Reuerendæ Cameræ apostolicæ.* 1648, 1659. 4to, pp. 16. 7704

An important tract relating to Bishop Palafox and the Jesuits.

BREGA (G. W.) ... Reports by George W. Brega upon Trade with the Provinces of British North America, the Free Navigation of the River St. Lawrence and the Gulf Fisheries. [*Washington.* 1868.] 8vo, pp. 31. (40th Cong., 2d Sess. Ex. Docs. 240 & 295.) C., H. 7705

BRÉHAT (Alfred de), *pseudon.* *See* [Guézenec (Alfred de)].

BREIDFJORD (Sigard Eriksen). Frá Grænlandi. *Kaupmannahöfn.* 1836. 7706

BREITENBAUCH (Georg August von). Religionszustand der verschiedenen Länder der Welt in den ältern und neuern Zeiten, ... herausgegeben von Joh. Elias Lange ... *Leipzig: in der Breitkopfischen Buchhandlung und bey dem Herausgeber.* 1787. 8vo, pp. 114. Map. 7707

BREITENBAUCH. Vorstellung der vornehmsten Völkerschaften der Welt, nach ihrer Abstammung, Ausbreitung und Sprache. *Leipzig: im Chursächsischen Intelligenz-Comtoir und bey Lange.* 1786. 8vo, pp. 98. Large ethnological Map. 7708

A portion is devoted to the Aborigines of America.

BREMER (Frederica). Hemmen i Nya Verlden. Bref under en vesa i Norra Amerika och pä Cuba. *Stockholm.* 1866. 2 vols., 12mo. 7709

BREMER. Die Heimath in der Neuen Welt. Ein Tagebuch in Briefen, geschrieben während zweijähriger Reisen in Nordamerika und auf Cuba. Von Friederike Bremer. Aus dem Schwedischen übersetzt von G. Fink. *Stuttgart.* 1853. 24 pts. in 3 vols., 16mo., pp. x, 462; xiv, 520; xiv, 534. (Das belletristische Ausland, Bdchn. 2009–2023, 2114–2122.) 7710

BREMER. Die Heimat in der Neuen Welt. Ein Tagebuch ... [as above]. Aus den Schwedischen. *Leipzig: Brockhaus.*

1854–55. 9 pts., 12mo, pp. xvi, 131; 2 l., pp. 164; 2 l., pp. 161; 2 l., pp. 176; 2 l., pp. 191; 2 l., pp. 157; 2 l., pp. 170; 2 l., pp. 188; 2 l., pp. 203. 7711

BREMER. De Nieuwe wereld. (Homes of the New World.) Naar Fr. Bremer door S. J. van den Bergh. *Haarlem: A. C. Kruseman.* 1854. 2 pts., 8vo. 2 Plates. 7712

BREMER. Homes of the New World. Impressions of America. By Frederika Bremer. Translated by Mary Howitt. *London: A. Hall,* 1853. 3 vols., post 8vo, pp. 1346. C. + *New York: Harper and Brothers.* 1853. 2 vols., 12mo, pp. xii, 651; 654. C., H. 7713

BREMER. La Vie de famille dans le nouveau monde. Lettres écrites pendant un séjour de deux années dans l'Amérique du Sud et à Cuba. Traduit du suédois par Mlle R. Du Puget. *Paris: Chez Mlle Du Puget.* 1854–55. 3 vols., 16mo. 7714

BREMOND (Marie Auguste). La Martinique. Description en vers. *Toulouse: imprimerie d'Aurel.* 1828. 8vo. 7715

BREMOND (M. F.) Extrait de la lettre de M. F. Bremond, parti du Havre le 27 novembre 1829, à bord du navire l'Amérique ... à M. Besson, correspondant de la colonie de Guazacoalco ... . *Paris: imprimerie de Tastu.* 1830. 8vo, ½ sheet.

BRENAN (D.) Remarks on Education, by Hon. Daniel Brenan. *Charlottetown.* 1856. 8vo, pp. 61. 7717

[BRENT (H. J.)] Was it a Ghost? The Murders in Bussey's Wood. An Extraordinary Narrative. *Boston: Loring.* 1868. 12mo, pp. 143. Woodcut. H. 7718

Preface signed J. B.

BRENT (J. C.) Biographical Sketches of the most Reverend John Carroll, first Archbishop of Baltimore, with Select Portions of his Writings. Edited By John Carroll Brent. *Baltimore: J. Murphy.* 1843. 12mo, pp. 321. Portrait. C. 7719

BRENT. ... Claim of Baron De Kalb and Heirs. [Signed John Carroll Brent, Attorney for the Heirs of De Kalb. Washington, December, 1849. n. p. n. d.] Broadside. H. 7720

BRENT. Letters on the National Institute, Smithsonian Legacy, The Fine Arts, and other Matters connected with the Interests of the District of Columbia. By John Carroll Brent. *Washington.* 1844. 8vo, pp. 90. C., S. 7721

BRENT (Lind). Incidents in the Life of a Slave Girl. Written by herself. Edited by L. Maria Child. *Boston.* 1861.

BRENT (R. J.) Report of Attorney General Brent in relation to the Christiana Treason Trials, &c. *Annapolis.* 1852. 8vo. 7723

BRENT. Speech of Robert J. Brent, Attorney General of Maryland, in the Case of the United States vs. Castner Hanway for Treason. Official Report. [n. d.] 8vo, pp. 24. C. 7724

BRENTANO (Carl August von.) Bilder aus einer Reise nach Amerika 1852. Mit einer Vorrede von H. Russwurm. *Augsburg: Schmid.* 1855. 12mo, pp. xx, 148. 7725

BRENTON (E. P.) The Naval History of Great Britain, from the Year MDCCLXXXIII. to MDCCCXXXVI. By Edward Pelham Brenton, Captain in the Royal Navy. A New and Greatly Improved Edition, Illustrated with Portraits, Plans, etc. In Two Volumes. *London: Henry Colburn.* 1837. 2 vols., 8vo, pp. xxiv, (1), 640; 2 l., pp. 728. 23 Plates. H., C. 7726

First published, *London.* 1822. 5 vols., 8vo and 4to. + *London.* 1824–30. 7 vols., 8vo. Contains some details of the War of 1812.

BRENTON. A Letter to the Rt. Hon. R. W. Horton, shewing the Impolicy, Inefficacy, and Ruinous Consequences of Emigration, and the Advantages of Home Colonies, by Edw. P. Brenton ... . *London: C. Rice.* 1831. 8vo, pp. 37, 1 l. B. 7727

BRENTON. Life and Correspondence of John, Earl of St. Vincent, [Sir John Jervis] Admiral of the Fleet, &c. &c. By Edward Pelham Brenton. *London: H. Colburn.* 1838. 8vo, pp. xvi, 500, xii, 418. Portrait and Map. C. 7728

Lord St. Vincent commanded the squadron which captured Guadeloupe, Martinique, and St. Lucia.

BRENTS (J. A.) The Patriots and Guerillas of Tennessee and Kentucky. The Sufferings of the Patriots. Also the Experience of the Author as an Officer in the Union Army. Including Sketches of Noted Guerrillas and Distinguished Patriots. By Major J. A. Brents. *New York: J. A. Brents.* 1863. 12mo, pp. 171. 2 Plates. C. 7729

BRERETON (John). A | Briefe and true Relation of | the Discouerie of the North | part of Virginia; being a | most pleasant, fruitfull | and commodious | soile: | Made this present Yeere, 1602,

by | Captaine Bartholomew Gosnold, Cap- | taine Bartholowmew [*sic*] Gilbert, and diuers | other gentlemen their associats by the | permission of the honourable knight, | Sir Walter Ralegh, &c. | Written by M. Iohn Brereton | one of the voyage. | Whereunto is annexed a Treatise, | of M. Edward Hayes, conteining important | inducements for the planting in those | parts, and finding a passage that | way to the South Sea, | and China. | With diuers instructions of speciall moment | newly added in this second im- | pression. | *Londini,* | *Impensis Geor. Bishop.* 1602. 4to, pp. 48. H.

A work of the greatest rarity. Jadis' copy sold for £5 15s. 6d. Reprinted in the Mass. Hist. Soc. Collection, 3d Series, VIII. 83–123.

BRERETON (J. A.) Floræ Columbianæ Prodromus, exhibens Enumerationem Plantarum, quæ hactenus exploratæ sunt: or a Prodromus of the Flora Columbiana, exhibiting a List of All the Plants which have as yet been collected. Compiled by John A. Brereton, M.D. ... *Washington. Jonathan Elliot.* 1830. 12mo, pp. 86, (1). C., H. 7731

BREREWOOD (E.) Enqviries Tovching the diuersity of Langvages, and Religions, through the chiefe parts of the World. Written by Edvv. Brerevvood ... . *London: Iohn Bill.* M.DC.XXII. 4to. + *London.* 1635. Sm. 4to. + *London.* MDCLXXIV. 8vo.

The author devotes a portion of the work to the first peopling of America, claiming the Tartars as their forefathers. His account of religion in America is very curious, especially the part where he describes an old priest who baptized 700,000! Chapter XXII. relates to the idolatries practised in America.

BREREWOOD. Recherches curieuses sur la diversité des langues et des religions, mises en françois par J. de la Montagne. *Paris: Olivier la Varenne.* 1640. 8vo. + *Saumur: J. Lesnier.* 1663. 8vo. 7733

BRESSANI (Fr. G.) Breve Relatione d'alcvne Missioni de' PP. della Compagnia di Giesù nella Nuoua Francia. Del P. Francisco Guisippe Bressani. *In Macerata, per H. de Agostino Grisei.* 1653. 4to, 2 l., pp. 127. J. C. B. 7734

Very rare. Priced, £3 3s., by B. Quaritch. *See* Leclerc, No. 209.

BRESSANI. Relation abrégée de quelques missions des S. pères de la Compagnie de Jésus, dans la Nouvelle-France. Par le R. P. F.-J. Bressany ... . Traduit de l'Italien et augmenté d'un avant-propos, de la biographie de l'auteur, et d'un grand nombre de notes et de gravures, par le R. P. F. Martin. *Montreal: des presses de John Lovell.* 1852. 8vo, pp. 336, (Errata) 1 slip. C.

BREST, *France.* Lettre de la municipalité de Brest à MM. de l'assemblée générale de Saint-Domingue, à présent, à Paris. Brest, le 29 septembre 1790. [n. p. n. d.] 8vo, pp. 48 or less.

BREST. Lettre de MM. de la municipalité de Brest à MM. les membres de l'assemblée générale de Saint-Domingue à Paris. Brest, le 27 septembre 1790.—Réponse de l'assemblée générale de la partie française de Saint-Domingue à MM. les maire et officiers de la municipalité de Brest. Paris, 2 octobre 1790. [n. p. n. d.] 8vo, pp. 48 or less. 7737

BRETON. *See* Cape Breton.

BRETON DE LA MARTINIÈRE. *See* Denis (F.)

BRETON (E.) Die Baudenkmäler aller Völker der Erde in getreuen Abbildungen dargestellt und mit Hindeutung aus ihre Entstehung, Bestimmung und geschichtliche Bedeutung geschildert. Nach der zweite Ausgabe von Ernst Breton's Monumens de tous les peuples, herausg. von Heinr. Berghaus. Mit vielen Illustr. im Text und 150 Platten [Holzschnitten] in Tondruck. 2. [Titel-]Ausg. *Brüssel: Muquardt.* 1853–54. 2 vols., 4to, 2 l., pp. 284; 2 l., pp. 242. 7738

BRETON (R.) Dictionaire | Caraibe-François, | Meslé de quantité de Remarques | historiques pour l'esclaircissement | de la Langue. | Composé par le R. P. Raymond Breton, | Religieux de l'ordre des Freres Prescheurs, | & l'vn des premiers Missionnaires Apo- | stoliques en l'Isle de la Gardeloupe & au- | tres circonuoisines de l'Amerique. | *A Auxerre.* | *Par Gilles Bovqvet, Imprimeur* | *ordinaire du Roy.* | M. D. C. LXV. | 8vo, 8 l., pp. 480.

"A lexicographical production of extreme rarity. The author, a Dominican, was subprior of the Monastery of Preaching Friars at Blainville; and one of the first four French missionaries deputed to the Island of Gardeloupe, now called Gaudeloup, and the Caribbee Islands in America"

BRETON. Dictionaire | François-Caraibe, | Composé par le R. P. Raymond Breton, | Religieux de l'ordre des Freres Prescheurs, & l'vn des quatre premiers François | Missonnaires Apostoliques en l'Isle de la | Gardeloupe, & autres circonuoisines de | l'Amerique. | *A Auxerre.* | *Par Gilles Bovqvet, Impimeur* | *ordinaire du Roy.* | M. D. C. LXVI. | 8vo, 5 l., pp. 415. J. C. B. 7740

BRETON. Grammaire | Caraibe. | Composée par le R. P. Raymond Breton | Religieux de l'Ordre des Freres Prescheurs, | & l'vn des quatre premiers Missionnaires | Apostoliques en l'Isle de la

Gardeloupe, | & autres circonuoisines de l'Amerique. | *A Auxerre.* | *Par Gilles Bvqvet, Imprimeur* | *ordinaire du Roy.* | M. D. C. LXVII. | 8vo, pp. 136. J. C. B. 7741

The Carribee Grammar is of especial rarity. Sold at Puttick's, 1840, for £12

BRETON. Petit | Catechisme | ov | Sommaire des trois premieres parties de la Doctrine | Chrestienne. | Traduit du François. en la langue des Ca- | raibes Insulaires, par le R. P. Raymond | Breton Sous-Prieur du Conuent des | Freres Prescheurs de Blainuille. | [Vignette.] *A Auxerre.* | *Par Gilles Bovqvet, Imprimeur or-* | *dinaire du Roy.* [M. D. C. LXIV. | Sm. 8vo, pp. 70. J. C. B.

B[RETON] (W[illiam)]. Militia Discipline. By W. B., Gent. *Printed at London.* 1717. 12mo. + *Boston, N. E.: D. Henchman.* 1733. Title, 1 l., pp. 78. W. 7743

BRETT (W. H.) Indian Missions in Guiana. By the Rev. W. H. Brett. *London: Bell and Daldy.* 1851. 12mo, pp. 300.

BRETT. The Indian Tribes of Guiana. By the Rev. W. H. Brett. *New York: Robert Carter & Brothers.* 1852. 12mo, pp. 352. Woodcuts. C. 7745

Includes Indian vocabularies. The author was a missionary of the Society for the Propagation of the Gospel. Reprinted as below:

BRETT. The Indian Tribes of Guiana: their Condition and Habits; with Researches into their Past History, Superstitions, Legends, Antiquities, Languages, &c. By the Rev. W. H. Brett ... . *London: Bell & Daldy.* 1868. 8vo. Colored Illustrations and Woodcuts. 7746

BREUGEL (G. P. C.) Dagverhaal van eene reis naar Paramaribo en verdere omstr. in de kolonie Suriname. *Amsterdam.* 1842. 8vo. 7747

Breve apostólico y estatutos generales para los misioneros franciscos observantes de propaganda fide en las provincias internas de Nueva-España. *Madrid.* 1781. 4to. 7748

Breve Instruccion, o Arte para entender la lengua comune de los Indios segun que se habla en la provincia de Quito. *Lima: en la Imprenta de la Plazue la de San Christoval.* 1753. Sm. 8vo.

An imperfect copy of this rare book sold at Rætzel's [*i. e.* Ternaux-Compans'] sale for 17fr.

Breve diseño critico de la emancipacion y libertad de la nacion

mexicana, y de las causas que influyeron en suo mas ruidosos sucesos, acaecidos desde el grito de Iguala hasta la espantosa muerte del libertador en la villa de Padilla. *Mexico: Ontiveros.* 1827. 18mo, pp. 16, xviii, 205. 7750

Breve Noticia de las Solemnes Exequias de la Reina Madre Doña Maria Luisa de Borbon, que celebró el ilustrisimo y venerable Señor Presidente y Cabildo de la Santa Iglesia de Valladolid de Michoacan, en los 8 y 9 del Mes de Noviembre de 1819. *Mexico.* 1820. 4to, pp. 21, 27, 32. 7751

Breve Relacion de las Acclamaciones Festivas, plausible celebridad, y expressivas demonstraciones de amorosa y fina lealtad conque solemnizo la nobilissima, y siempre leal Ciudad de Manila la publicacion de la Jura, que en ella se hizo de el Principe de Asturias D. Luis Phelipe Fernando de Borbon. *Mexico.* 1712. 4to. 7752

A rare Mexican imprint. Priced, by Thorp, in 1842, £2 12s. 6d.

Breve relacion del origen y fundacion de los siervos de Maria Santissima. *Mexico.* 1699. 8vo. 7753

Title, as given by Ternaux, No. 1125.

Breve relazione ... Piacenza, 1802. *See* [T. (G. A.)]

BREVOORT (J. C.) History and its Sources An Address read before the Long Island Historical Society at the Annual Meeting May 7th 1868 By James Carson Brevoort President of the Society. *Brooklyn.* MDCCCLXVIII. Imp. 8vo, pp. 23, and facsimile. 7754

Mr. Brevoort is a diligent student of American history; and during his connection with the Bradford Club, assisted in editing their publications—more particularly "De Soto's Narrative," and "Washington's Diary." He also assisted in the compilation of the History of Perry's Expedition to Japan.

BREWER (Daniel). God's Help to be Sought in Time of War. Sermon preached at Springfield, March 26, 1724. By Rev. Daniel Brewer. *Boston.* 1724. 8vo, pp. 19. 7755

BREWER (D. R.) Loss of the San Francisco. A Sermon at Newport, R. I., 22 Jan., 1854. By Rev. D. R. Brewer. *Providence.* 1854. 8vo. 7756

BREWER (J. M.) Prison Life. By John M. Brewer, Late Reading Clerk of the Maryland Senate of 1860–1861, and still later of Fort Delaware and Warren. *Baltimore: S. S. Mills.* [n. d.] 8vo, pp. 31. 7757

BREWER (L.) Adventures of Lucy Brewer, who served as a Marine on Board the U. S. Frigate Constitution. *Boston.* 1815. 12mo. 7758

BREWER (S.) Proceedings of the Trial of Stephen Brewer, before the Presbyterian Church of Cortland Village, March 14th & 15th, 1859. ... *Cortland, N. Y.* 1859. 8vo, pp. 24. H.

BREWER (T. M.) North American Oology; or, Descriptions and Figures of the Eggs of North American Birds, with notices of their Geographical Distribution during the breeding season. By Thomas M. Brewer, M.D. Part I. Raptores et Fissirostres. *Washington.* 1857. 4to, pp. viii, 142. 5 Plates.

See Smithsonian Contributions, Vol. II. Of this work, a small edition was issued with the plates printed in colors and finished by hand. The edition, as published in the Smithsonian Contributions, contains plain plates only, printed from another set of stones.

BREWER (U. C.) The Bible and American Slavery. A Discourse delivered at the Christian Chapel, West Seventeenth St., New York, on January 4, 1863. By Urban C. Brewer. *New York: W. Reid Gould.* 1863. 8vo, pp. 30. 7761

BREWER (William A.) Remarks of Mr. Brewer, of Cambridge, before the Joint Special Committee of the Legislature, on ... the Liquor Law ... March 15, 1853. *Boston.* [n. d.] 12mo, pp. 12. 7762

BREWER. Description of the Mammoth Cave of Kentucky, the Niagara River and Falls, ... in Summer and Winter; the Prairies ... &c. to illustrate Brewer's Panorama. *Boston: J. M. Hewes & Co* 1850. 8vo, pp. 44. H. 7763

BREWER (*Mr.*) Grand Moving Mirror ... comprising the Mammoth Cave of Kentucky, the Falls of Niagara ... . *London.* [n. d.] 12mo, pp. 16. S. 7764

BREWERTON (G. D.) The War in Kansas. A Rough Trip to the Border, among New Homes and a Strange People. By G. Douglas Brewerton ... . *New York: Derby & Jackson.* 1856. 12mo, pp. 400. C., H. 7765

Republished as the "Wars of the Western Border; or, New Homes and a Strange People. By G. W. Douglas Brewerton ... . *New York: Derby & Jackson.* 1860." 12mo, pp. 400. H.

BREWERTON (John). Report of Capt. Brewerton, connected with the Improvement of the Hudson River Navigation. December 26, 1838. *Albany: Printed by H. D. Stone & Co.* 1839. 8vo, pp. 24. S. 7766

BREWSTER (A. O.) Speech of Col. A. O. Brewster, before the Democracy of Concord, N. H. ... February 26th, 1863. ... *Boston.* 1863. 8vo, pp. 35. H. 7767

[BREWSTER (Abel).] An Appeal to Banks in Particular, and the Public in General. [Signed Abel Brewster.] *Hartford.* 1815. 8vo, pp. 40. B., P. 7768

BREWSTER (B. H.) Address delivered the Twenty-eighth June, 1853, before the American Whig and Cliosophic Societies of the College of New Jersey. By Benjamin H. Brewster, Esq, *Philadelphia.* 1853. 8vo, pp. 21. H. 7769

[BREWSTER.] Supreme Court of the United States. Isaac Roach, Treasurer of the Mint of the United States ... Plaintiff in Error, *vs.* the County of Philadelphia. ... Brief of Argument for the Defendant ... . *Philadelphia.* [n. d.] 4to, Title, pp. 28.

BREWSTER. Address delivered before the Alumni of the High School, Philadelphia, by Benj. H. Brewster, February 12, 1863. *Philadelphia: King & Baird.* 1863. 8vo, pp. 8. 7771

BREWSTER. Inauguration of the National Union Club. Speech of Benjamin H. Brewster, delivered at the Musical Fund Hall, Philadelphia, Wednesday Evening, March 11, 1863. As Reprinted for the North American. *Philadelphia.* 1863. 8vo, pp. 8. 7772

BREWSTER. Oration delivered on the Fourth July, 1843. Before the Citizens of New Hope, Bucks County, Pennsylvania. By B. H. Brewster. *Philadelphia: Mifflin & Parry.* 1843. 8vo, pp. 8. 7773

BREWSTER (C. W.) Rambles about Portsmouth. Sketches of Persons, Localities, and Incidents of Two Centuries. Principally from Tradition and Unpublished Documents. By Charles W. Brewster. *Portsmouth, N. H.: C. W. Brewster & Son.* 1859. 8vo, pp. 376. C., H. 7774

BREWSTER (F. C.) Oration Delivered before the Literary Societies of Lafayette College, By F. Carroll Brewster, Esq., of Philadelphia, July 30, 1861. [n. p. n. d.] 8vo, pp. 17. 7775

BREWSTER (F. E.) Philosophy of Human Nature, Slavery, Politics, Governments, &c. *Philadelphia.* 1851. 12mo, pp. 471. P. 7776

"This book, by an original thinker, is patriotic and anti-slavery in its tone."—L. P. S.

BREWSTER. Slavery and the Constitution, both sides of the Question. By Francis E. Brewster. *Philadelphia.* 1850. 8vo, pp. 24. 7777

BREWSTER (*Sir* F.) Essays on Trade and Navigation. *London.* 1695. Sm. 8vo. 7778

Relates in part to the Newfoundland fishery, etc.

[BREWSTER (H. B.)] A Report of the Proceedings of an Ecclesiastical Council; held in Boscawan, N. H. In the Trial and Expulsion of a member of the Second Congregational Church. ... *Concord, N. H.: printed by H. B. Brewster.* 1833. 8vo, pp. 44. H. 7779

BREWSTER (J.) An Address delivered at Brewster's Hall, Wednesday Evening, January 28, 1857, to the Young Men of New Haven, Ct. By James Brewster. ... *New York.* 1857. 8vo, pp. 42. 7780

BREWSTER (J.) An Exposition of the Treatment of Slaves in the Southern States, &c. Together with a System of Reformation Recommended by Jarvis Brewster. *New Brunswick.* 1815. 8vo, pp. 34. 7781

BREWSTER (L. D.) Poem, by Lyman D. Brewster, and the Valedictory Oration [on American Civilization], by Adolphe Bailey, Pronounced before the Senior Class in Yale College, June 13, 1855. *New Haven: the Class.* 1855. 8vo, pp. 46. H.

BREWSTER. The Fifth Annual Address of the Rector of Christ Church, New Haven, Conn., and Parish Statistics. ... *New Haven: printed by George Tuttle.* 1859. 8vo, pp. 16. H.

BREWSTER (M.) Poems on Divers Subjects. By Martha Brewster of Lebanon. *New London: J. Green.* 1757. 4to, pp. 35. M. 7784

BREZ (Guy de). The Rise, Spring, and Foundation of the Anabaptist, or Re-baptized, of our Time. Written in French by Guy de Brez, 1565. Minister of the Word, and Martyr. And Translated for the use of his Countrymen, by J. S. *Cambridge: Printed and sold by Marmaduke Johnson.* 1668. 4to, pp. 52. M., W. 7785

A volume of extreme rarity. The translator was Joshua Scottow.

[BRIALMONT (Alexis Henri).] Le Corpes belge du Mexique,

Considérations en faveur de l'organisation de ce corps, par un officier d'état-major. *Bruxelles: Guyat.* 1864. 8vo. 7786

BRIAND DE VERZE. Nouveau dictionnaire complet géographique, statistique, typographique ... de la France et de ses colonies. Édition refondue en entier par Warin Thierry. *Paris.* 1844. 8vo. 7787

BRIANO (Giorgio). Cristoforo Colombo; tragedia. *Torino.* 1842. 8vo. 7788

BRIANT (L.) Some Friendly Remarks on a Sermon Lately Preach'd at Braintree, 3d Parish, and now Published to the World by the Revd. Mr. Porter of Bridgewater; ... in a Letter to the Author to be communicated to his Attestators. By Rev. Lemuel Briant. *Boston.* 1750. 4to, pp. 31. 7789

Also: Some more Friendly Remarks on Mr. [John] Porter and Company in a Second Letter to him and Mr. [John] Cotton [Plymouth] and Mr. F—xcr—ft. *Boston.* 1751. 8vo, pp. 35. — Some more Friendly Remarks on Mr. Porter and Company. In a Second Letter to him and two of his Abettors, viz. Mr. Cotton, Appendix Writer, and Mr. F—xcr—ft, Marginal-Noter. *Boston.* 1751. 4to. — The Absurdity and Blasphemy of depretiating moral Virtue: a Sermon preached ... in Boston, June 18, 1749. *Boston.* 1749. 8vo, pp. 31.

BRIANT (Timothy). A Receipt from Middleborough, in the Province of the Massachusetts Bay, concerning the Canker, or Throat Distemper. *Boston.* [n. d.] 8vo, pp. 8. 7790

BRICE (A.) A Universal Geographical Dictionary, or Grand Gazetteer; describing Especially the British Dominions and Settlements throughout the World; with maps. By Andrew Brice. *London.* 1759. 2 vols., folio, pp. 1446. P. 7791

BRICE (J. R.) History of the Revolutionary War with England, A.D. 1776. Brief Account of the Captivity and Cruel Sufferings of Captain Deitz, and John and Robert Brice, the latter of whom is still living (formerly of Rensselaerville) in New Scotland, (formerly a part of Bethlehem) Albany Co., N. Y., who were taken Prisoners of War by the British, Indians and Tories. Now First Published over said Robert Brice's own Signature. The Horrible Massacre of the Deitz Family, in Berne, Albany Co., Seventy-one Years Ago. Brief account of an attempt of Sebastian Lewis, Chas. Van Eps and W. H. Lewis and others to defraud said Robert Brice out of his property. ... In three volumes. To be continued. Vol. I. By James R. Brice Esq. ... *Albany.* 1851. 8vo, pp. 48. 7792

Chiefly a trial, with advertisements of a cure for dropsy.

BRICE. Secrets of the Mt. Pleasant State Prison Exposed. By James R. Brice. *Albany.* 1839. 8vo. B. 7793

BRICE (J.) A Selection of all the Laws of the United States, now in Force, relative to Commercial Subjects, with Marginal Notes and References ... . By John Brice ... . *Baltimore: Neal, Wills & Cole.* 1814. 8vo, pp. v, (1), 6–554, xviii, xviii. + A Supplement ... . [*Ibid.*] 1816. 8vo, pp. 80. H. 7794

BRICEÑO (Mariano de). Censura y reforma del codigo de instruccion publica de 1843. Por Mariano de Briceño. *Caracas.* 1857. 8vo, pp. 60. 7795

BRICEÑO. Estudios sobre los partidos. Publicados en el "Diario de avisos de Caracas." Por Mariano de Briceño. *Caracas.* 1855. 8vo, pp. 92. 7796

BRICEÑO. La gran cuestion fiscal de Venezuela. Aranceles — Importaciones — Contrabando — Reforma del sistema aduanero. Por M. de Briceño. *Caracas.* 1864. 4to, pp. lvi, 76. 7797

BRICEÑO. Memoir Justificatory of the Government of Venezuela on the Isla de Aves Question. *Washington.* 1858. 8vo.

BRICEÑO. Mis ausencias. Por M. de Briceño. *Caracas.* 1857. 8vo, pp. 32. 7799

BRICKELL (J.) The Natural History of North Carolina. With an account of the Trades, Manners, and Customs of the Christian and Indian Inhabitants. Illustrated with Copper-Plates, whereon are curiously Engraved the Map of the Country, several strange Beasts, Birds, Fishes, Snakes, Insects, Trees and Plants, etc. By John Brickell, M.D. *Dublin: the Author.* 1737. 8vo, pp. viii, 408. Map, and 2 Plates. + *Dublin.* 1743. 8vo, pp. viii, 408. Map, and 2 Plates. C. H. 7800

The edition, 1743, is the same book with a new title-page [from Lawson's "Carolina"]. A more daring piece of plagiarism was never executed. — N. A. R., XXIII. 288.

The Bride of Fort Edward, Founded on an Incident of the Revolution. *New York: S. Colman.* 1839. 12mo, pp. viii, 174.

BRIDEL (L.) Le pour et le contre ou avis à ceux qui se proposent de passer dans les Etats-Unis d'Amérique. Suivi d'une description du Kentucky et de Genesy, deux des nouveaux

éstablissemens les plus considérables de cette partie du nouveau monde. Avec une carte typométrique. Par Louis Bridel, pasteur de l'église française à Basle. ... *Paris: Levrault, Schoell & Comp. An* XII. 1803. 8vo, 2 l., pp. 162. Map. 7802

The map is a curiosity; it is "composée avec des caractères mobiles par G. Haas à Basle."

BRIDEL. Récits américains, ou Conversions, réveils, expériences chrétiennes et entretiens sur la recherche du salut. Tirés des mémoires et journaux de trois pasteurs presbytériens des États-Unis. *Paris.* 1854. 2 vols., 12mo. 7803

BRIDEL. Verhalen uit Noord-Amerika. Christelijke ervaringen en gesprekken, medegedeeld door drie leeraren uit de Presbyteriaansche Kerk der Vereenigde Staten. Uit het Fransch, door M.W.D. Middelhoven. Eerste aflevering. *Amsterdam: H. Höveker.* 1854. 8vo. 7804

I do not know whether more was published.

BRIDGE (E.) A Sermon Preach'd before ... Francis Bernard, Esq; Governor ... Of the Province of the Massachusetts-Bay in New-England, May 27th, 1767. Being the Anniversary for the Election of his Majesty's Council for the Province. By Ebenezer Bridge, A.M. ... *Boston: Printed by Green and Russel.* MDCCLXVII. 8vo, pp. 60. H., N. 7805

BRIDGE. A Sermon Preach'd to the Ancient and Honorable Artillery Company, In Boston, June 1st. 1752. Being the Anniversary of their Election of Officers. ... *Boston, N. E.: S. Kneeland.* 1752. 8vo, Title, pp. 25. 7806

BRIDGE (James), *and others.* To the Honourable Senate, and the House of Representatives of the commonwealth of Massachusetts. [A memorial from the citizens of Maine on its separation from Massachusetts Proper, and against its incorporation with any other district. *Boston.* 1820.] 8vo. 7807

BRIDGE (Josiah). A Sermon preached before ... the Council, Senate and House of Representatives, of ... Massachusetts, May 27, 1789. Being the Day of General Election. *Boston.* M,DCC,LXXXIX. 8vo, pp. 54. H., M. 7808

BRIDGE. A Sermon, preached November 15, 1786, at the Ordination of the Rev. Jude Damon ... in Truro. By Josiah Bridge ... . *Boston.* M,DCC,LXXXVII. 8vo, pp. 30. H. 7809

BRIDGE (M.) A Sermon Preach'd May 20th 1761. at the Ordination Of the Reverend Mr. Eliab Stone, in Reading, [Mass.] By Mathew Bridge ... . *Boston: Printed by Thomas and John Fleet.* 1761. 8vo, pp. 32. H. 7810

BRIDGE (T.) Jethro's Advice Recommended to the Inhabitants of Boston, in New-England, Viz. To Chuse Well-qualified Men, and Haters of Covetousness, for Town Officers. In a Lecture on Exodus 18. 21. 9th 1st Month 1709. 10. By Thomas Bridge ... . *Boston: Nicholas Boone.* 1710. 8vo, pp. 32. H. + Second Edition, with Preface. *Boston.* 1733. 16mo, pp. 24. 7811

BRIDGE. ... a Sermon, Preached to the Honourable Artillery Company in Boston, On the Day of their Election of Officers, June 4th. 1705. By Mr. Thomas Bridge ... . *Boston: Samuel Phillips.* 1705. 12mo, Title, pp. 55. H. 7812

BRIDGE. What Faith can do. A Brief Essay on the Nature and Power of a True Faith. In some Notes of a sermon taken in short hand, when it was preach'd unto a few Christians in a Neighborhood, meeting in their usual course, at the house of one of their Neighbors; in Boston 15th d. 6th m. 1712. *Boston.* 1713. 16mo, pp. 28. 7813

BRIDGENS (R.) Sketches of West India Scenery, with illustrations of Negro Character, &c., taken during a Voyage to and some years Residence in Trinidad. The Process of Making Sugar there, &c. By Lieut. R. Bridges. *London: Jennings.* 1839. Rl. 4to. 27 Plates. 7814

The Bodleian Library dates this 1836.

Bridgeport and East Bridgeport Directory ... . 1857–8. *Bridgeport, Conn.: Pomeroy & Morse.* [n. d.] 12mo, pp. 175, and numerous colored leaves inserted. Continued. H. 7815

Bridgeport Directory and Annual Advertiser for 1867–8. *Bridgeport: Standard Assoc., Printers.* 12mo, pp. 110, 32. 7816

Bridgeport Library Association. Catalogue of the Library, January 1860. *Bridgeport, Conn.: Pomeroy & Morse.* 1860. 8vo, pp. 88. C. 7817

First Annual Report of the Soldiers' Aid Society, Bridgeport, Conn., July 25, 1863. [n. p. n. d.] 8vo, pp. 19. 7818

Special Report of the Soldiers' Aid Society, Bridgeport, Conn., March 4th, 1864. *Bridgeport: Standard Press.* 1864. 8vo, pp. 39, (1). H. 7819

BRIDGES (G. W.) The Annals of Jamaica. By the Rev. George Wilson Bridges ... . *London: John Murray.* 1827. 2 vols., 8vo. + Second Edition. *London: John Murray.* MDCCCXXVIII. 2 vols., 8vo., pp. xix, 604; xii, 505, (1). C., H. 7820

Includes a chapter on the Mosquito Shore. In the preface to the second volume, the author says he has "completed his design of bringing down the annals of Jamaica, from the first blush of that morning which dawned upon the long night of transatlantic oblivion, to the present evening of its decayed and feeble existence." "The edition of 1827 was suppressed." — QUARITCH.

BRIDGES. Dreams of Dulocracy, or the Puritanical Obituary. "An Appeal," not to the Romantic Sensibility, but to the Good Sense, of the British Public. By Rev. George Wilson Bridges. *Jamaica.* 1824. 8vo. 7821

BRIDGES. Emancipation unmask'd, in a Letter to the Earl of Aberdeen. *London.* 1835. 8vo. BM. 7822

BRIDGES. A Voice from Jamaica, in reply to W. Wilberforce. By Rev. George Wilson Bridges. 1823. 8vo. BD.

BRIDGES (L.) Report to Captain Morton on the Battle of Murfreesboro'. 1863. [n. p. n. d.] 8vo. 7824

BRIDGES (W.) Map of the City of New-York and Island of Manhattan; with Explanatory Remarks and References. By William Bridges, Architect and City Surveyor. ... *New-York: printed for the Author, By T. & J. Swords.* 1811. 8vo, pp. 54, including List of Subscribers, pp. 6. Map. BA., N. 7825

The map was, up to its date, the largest published. It was issued separately.

BRIDGES (S. A.) The Slavery Question. Speech of Hon. Samuel A. Bridges, of Penn., in the House ... February 17, 1849 ... . [*Washington.* n. d.] 8vo, pp. 8. H. 7826

BRIDGE-TOWN. An account of Donations. *See* Vol. I., No. 3256.

BRIDGEWATER, *Mass.* Celebration of the Two-Hundredth Anniversary of the Incorporation of Bridgewater, Massachusetts, At West Bridgewater, June 3, 1856; including the Address by Hon. Emory Washburn, of Worcester; Poem by James Reed,

A.B., of Boston; and other Exercises. With an Appendix. ... *Boston: printed by John Wilson and Son.* 1856. 8vo, pp. 167. View and Portrait. BA., H. 7827

Letter from the Inhabitants of Bridgewater, Somersetshire, England, to the Inhabitants of Bridgewater, Massachusetts ... dated Sept. 10, 1846; with the Reply of the Latter, dated Feb. 10, 1847. *Boston.* 1847. 8vo, pp. 39, (1). H. 7828

Manual of the Scotland Trinitarian Congregational Church, Bridgewater, Mass. containing the History ... [etc.] with a Catalogue of its Members ... . *Boston.* 1863. 12mo, pp. 16. H.

Minutes of Meeting at Bridgewater, Sept. 8 and 9, 1795. *Boston.* 1795. 8vo, pp. 12. 7830

Also: "Annual Report of the Selectmen, etc."

BRIDGHAM (S. W.) An Oration delivered at the Commencement of Rhode Island College, in Providence, Sept. 6, 1797. By Samuel W. Bridgham. *Providence: Carter & Wilkinson.* 1797. 8vo, pp. 7. 7831

BRIDGHAM. An Oration delivered ... in Providence, on the Fourth of July, A.D. 1798. By Samuel W. Bridgham, A.M. ... *Providence: Carter and Wilkinson.* 1798. 8vo, pp. 12. 7832

BRIDGMAN (C. D. W.) Words spoken in ... Albany, May 2, 1864, at the Obsequies of the Late Colonel Lewis Benedict. By the Rev. C. D. W. Bridgman. *Albany: J. Munsell.* 1866. 8vo, pp. 12. H. 7833

BRIDGMAN (Elijah C.) A-me-li-ke ho chung kwo che leo. A Brief History of the United States of America. Part I. *Engraved in the twenty-fourth year of Taou Kwang* (D. 1844). *The blocks are kept at Kwei Keang.* N. 7834

This title of a Chinese work is taken from the catalogue of the New York Historical Society.

BRIDGMAN (L.) Fac Simile of the Handwriting and composition of Laura Bridgman. *Boston.* [n. d.] 4to, p. (1). 7835

BRIDGMAN (T.) Epitaphs from Copp's Hill Burial Ground, Boston. With Notes. By Thomas Bridgman. ... *Boston and Cambridge: James Munroe and Company.* 1851. 12mo, pp. xxiii, (1), 252, (Patrons) 8. Plate. B., H. 7836

The New York Mercantile Library gives the imprint, *Philadelphia.* 1851. 12mo. The introduction is by J. H. Shepard.

BRIDGMAN. Epitaphs from King's Chapel Burial Ground. *Philadelphia.* 1853. 12mo. 7837

Title from the New York Mercantile Library catalogue. But *see* "Memorials," No. 782.

BRIDGMAN. Inscriptions on the Grave Stones in the Grave Yards of Northampton, and of the other Towns in the Valley of the Connecticut, as Springfield, Amherst, Hadley, Hatfield, Deerfield, &c. with Brief Annals of Northampton. Embellished with Portraits of President Edwards and Governor Strong. Transcribed by Thomas Bridgman. *Northampton, Mass.* 1850. 12mo, pp. 227. C., H. 7838

BRIDGMAN. Memorials of the Dead in Boston; containing Exact Transcripts of Inscriptions on the Sepulchral Monuments in King's Chapel Burial Ground, in the City of Boston. With Copious Historical and Biographical Notices of many of the Early Settlers of the Metropolis of New England. By Thomas Bridgman. *Boston: Benjamin B. Mussey & Co.* 1853. 12mo, pp. 339, (Testimonials) 2 l., (Patrons) pp. 17. Portrait and Woodcuts. B., H. 7839

BRIDGMAN. The Pilgrims of Boston and their Descendants: with an Introduction by Hon. Edward Everett, LL.D. Also, Inscriptions from the Monuments in the Granary Burial Ground, Tremont street. By Thomas Bridgman ... . *New York: D. Appleton and Company.* M.DCCC.LVI. 8vo, pp. xvi, 406. Portraits and Woodcuts. C., H. 7840

Bridgewater Baptist Association. Pennsylvania Minutes. *Montrose.* 1827. 7841

BRIE (F.) Considerations sur l'emigration basque à Montevideo; par F. Brie. *Bayonne.* 1841. 8vo, pp. 32. 7842

A Brief Account, 1691. *See* New England.

A Brief Account of Georgia, 1743. *See* Georgia.

Brief Account of the Albany-County Penitentiary. *Albany.* 1848. 8vo, pp. 6. M. 7843

A Brief Account of the Associated Presbyteries; and a General View of their Sentiments concerning Religion and Ecclesiastical Order. *Catskill.* 1796. 12mo. 7844

A Brief Account of the Discoveries and Results of the United States Exploring Expedition: from the American Journal of Science, Vol. XLIV. *New Haven.* 1843. 8vo, pp. 18. 7845

A Brief Account of the Mission established among the Esquimaux Indians, on the Coast of Labrador, by the Church of the Brethren, or Unitas Fratrum, [*sic*]. *London: Brethren's Society for the Furtherance of the Gospel, and M. Lewis.* MDCCLXXIX. 8vo, pp. 33. C., H. 7846

A Brief Account of the Late Revivals of Religion ... in a Number of Towns in the New-England States, and also in Nova Scotia, Extracted chiefly from Letters ... *Boston: Manning & Loring, May,* 1799. 8vo, pp. 8. H. + *Halifax.* 1800. Sm. 8vo. + *Bristol,* [*England*]. 1800. 8vo. + *Clipstone, reprinted.* [n. d.] 12mo. + To which is added a very interesting Letter from a Minister in London to his Friend in Massachusetts. *Boston.* 1799. 12mo, pp. 24. + *Windsor, Vt.: Reprinted by Alden Spooner.* 1800. 12mo, pp. 24. 7847

A Brief Account of the Province of East New Jersey. *See* New Jersey.

Brief Account of the ... Relief Association. *See* Baltimore, Vol. I., No. 3021.

A Brief Account of the Proceedings of the Committee, appointed in the year 1795 by the Yearly Meeting of Friends of Pennsylvania, New-Jersey, &c. for promoting the Improvement and gradual Civilization of the Indian Natives. *Philadelphia printed. London reprinted: Phillips & Fardon.* 1806. 8vo, pp. 50. C. 7848

Followed by

A Brief Account of the proceedings of the Committee appointed by the Yearly Meeting of Friends, held in Baltimore, for promoting the Improvement and Civilization of the Indian Natives. *Baltimore: Coale and Hewes. London reprinted: Phillips and Fardon.* 1806. 8vo, pp. 43. C. 7849

A brief Account of the Revenues, Pomp, and State of the Bishops, and other Clergy in the Church of England. In a Letter, &c. *Boston: Samuel Gerrish.* 1725. 8vo, Title, pp. 13.

Belongs to the controversy excited by J. Checkley's "Modest Proof of the Order," etc.

A Brief Account of the Rise, Progress, and Present State of the Paper Currency in New England. *Boston.* 1749. 8vo, pp. 15. M. 7851

A Brief Account of the Society of the Friendly Sons of St. Patrick; With Biographical Notices of Some of the Members, and Extracts from the Minutes. *Philadelphia: the ... Society.* 1844. 16mo, pp. 112. Frontispiece. 7852

A Brief and Impartial Review of the State of Great Britain, at the Commencement of the session of 1783; humbly addressed to the Right Honourable and Honourable the Lords and Commons of Great Britain. *London: J. Debrett.* MDCCLXXXIII. 8vo, pp. 75. + Second Edition *London: J. Debrett.* M,DCC,LXXXIII. 8vo, pp. 75. + The Third Edition, Corrected. *London: J. Debrett.* M.DCC.LXXXIII. 8vo, pp. 75. c. 7853

Mostly relates to America.

A Brief and perfect | Journal | of | The late Proceedings and | Successe of the English Army in the | West-Indies, | Continued until June the 24th. 1655. | Together with | Some Quæres inserted and answered. | Published for satisfaction of all such who desire truly | to be informed in these particulars. | By I. S. an Eye-witnesse. | *London. Printed* 1665. | 4to, pp. 27. 7854

"An account of the Expedition sent out by Cromwell, under Penn and Venables, when Jamaica was taken from the Spaniards." — RICH.

Brief and True Account of the Persecutions of the Church of England, the beginning and progress of War with the Indians, &c., in Answer to a Scandalous Pamphlet, called "News from New England, by C. D." 1690. 4to, pp. 8. 7855

"Neither this or the 'News from England' appear to be known to American Bibliographers." — J. R. SMITH.

A Brief and True Narration, 1675. *See* New England.

A Brief and True Narrative of the Hostile Conduct of the Barbarous Natives towards The Dutch Nation. Translated by E. B. O'Callaghan. *Albany: J. Munsell.* MDCCCLXIII. 8vo, pp. 48. c. 7856

Fifty copies printed.

Brief Answer to the Principal Objections opposed to the amendment of the Insolvent Law. [n. p. 1823?] 8vo, pp. 13.

Brief aus Amerika; von einem Basler Landmann, an seine Freunde in der Schweiz. Nebst einer kurzen Beschreibung der nordamerikanischen Freistaaten zur Belehrung für alle Auswanderungslustige herausgegeben. *Arau und Basel: in der Samuel Flickischen Buchhandlung.* 1806. 8vo, pp. 127. c., M. 7858

Brief aus Highland im Staate Illinois, an die Freunde in der

Heimath, von Ad. Eug. Bandlier, Frdr. von Graffenried und A. Reitmann. *Bern.* 1850. 8vo, pp. 11. 7859

Brief betreffende de Plantagien Waterland, Adrichem, Palmeneribo en Surinombo, gelegen in de kolonie Suriname. *Amsterdam.* 1834. 15 pts., 8vo. 7860

Briefe aus den Vereinigten Staaten von Nord America. Von ***. *Leipzig.* 1853. 2 vols., 16mo. 7861

Brief Considerations in favor of Mr. Adams, 1796. *See* [Gardner (John)].

Brief Considerations on Slavery, 1773. *See* [Benezet (Anthony)], No. 4683.

Brief, Decent, but Free Remarks, and Observations, on several Laws passed by The ... Legislature of ... Connecticut, since the Year 1775. By a Friend to his Country. ... *Hartford: Printed by Hudson & Goodwin.* M,DCC,LXXXII. 8vo, pp. 55.

A Brief Description of Carolina, 1666. *See* Carolina.

Brief Description of the Skeleton of the Gigantic Mastodon in the Baltimore Museum. 1836. 7863

A Brief Discourse concerning Regular Singing. *Boston.* 1725. 12mo, pp. 18. W. 7864

A Brief Discourse Concerning the Lawfulness of Worshipping God by the Common Prayer. *See* [Williams (John)].

A Brief Discourse Concerning the Unlawfulness of the Common-Prayer Worship. *See* [Mather (Increase)].

A Brief Enquiry into the Causes of, and Conduct pursued by, the Colonial Government, for quelling the Insurrection in Grenada; From its Commencement on the Night of the 2d of March, to the Arrival of General Nichols, on the 14th of April, 1795. In a Letter from a Grenada Planter to a Merchant in London. *London: R. Faulder.* 1796. 8vo, 2 l., pp. 204, Appendix, 20, Errata, 1. Map. 7865

A Brief Enquiry into the True Nature and Character of our Federal Government; being a Review of Judge Story's Commentaries on the Constitution of the United States. By a Virginian. *Petersburg: Printed by Edmund and Julian C. Ruffin.* 1840. 8vo, pp. 132. 7866

A Brief Essay on the Advantages and Disadvantages which respectively attend France and Great Britain, with regard to Trade. With some Proposals for Removing the Principal Disadvantages of Great Britain. *London.* 1750. 8vo. 7867

A Brief Essay on the number Seven. A Poem. By a Wellwisher to Truth. *Newport, R. I.* 1735. 12mo. W. 7868

Not relating to America, but a piece of early American poetry.

A Brief Examination into the Increase of the Revenue, Commerce, and Navigation of Great Britain, since the Conclusion of the Peace in 1783. *Dublin: P. Wogan, [etc.]* M.DCC.XCII. 8vo, 2 l., pp. 52. H. 7869

Brief Examination into the Increase of the Revenue, Commerce and Navigation of Great Britain since the Conclusion of the Peace in 1783. Third Edition. *London.* 1792. 7870

A Brief Examination of the Expediency of repealing the Naturalization Laws Originally published in the Native American Newspaper, New Orleans. *New Orleans.* 1840. 8vo, pp. 19.

A Brief Examination of the Plan and Conduct of the Northern Expedition in America, In 1777. And of the Surrender of the Army under the Command of Lieutenant-General Burgoyne. *London: Printed for T. Hookham.* M DCC LXXIX. 8vo, Half-Title, pp. 52. H., S. 7872

Includes Burgoyne's letter of October 20, 1777, to Lord G. Germaine. *See* M. R., LXIX. 320.

A Brief Examination of Lord Sheffield's Observations. *See* [Coxe (Tench)].

Brief Exposition of the United Society of Believers. *See* Shakers.

A Brief Extract, or Summary of Important Arguments, advanced by some late Distinguished Writers, in support of the Supremacy of the British Legislature, and their Right to Tax the Americans. Addressed to the Freemen and Liverymen of London. ... By a Liveryman. *London: J. Wilkie.* 1775. 8vo, Title, pp. 48. BA., C. 7873

A Brief History of the ... Floating School. *See Baltimore*, Vol. I., 3022.

A Brief History of the Protestant Episcopal Church, known by the Name of Unitas Fratrum, or United Brethren, with the Reasons for and against the Privileges granted them in the British Dominions [of America] in the Year 1749. *London.* 1750. 8vo. 7874

A Brief History of the Church in Boston. *See* Boston, No. 6643.

Brief History of the Pittsburgh and Connellsville Rail Road Company, and its Object in asking the Interposition of Congress to aid in restoring its Vested Rights, assailed by Unjust and Unconstitutional State Legislation. *Baltimore.* 1866. 8vo, pp. 8.

A Brief History of the Rise and Progress of the Charitable Scheme, carrying on by a Society of Noblemen and Gentlemen in London, For the Relief and Instruction of poor Germans, and their Descendants, settled in Pennsylvania, and the adjacent British Colonies in North America. Published by Order of the Gentlemen Appointed Trustees-General, for the Management of the said Charitable Scheme. *Philadelphia: Printed by B. Franklin and D. Hall.* MDCCLV. 4to, pp. 18. P. 7876

A Brief History of the Wars and Treaties in which England has been engaged, from the Restoration of King Charles II. to the Present Time. *London: J. Robinson.* 1796. 8vo. 7877

See M. R., XXII. 206.

A Brief Memorial representing the present state of Religion on the Continent of North America. 1700. Folio. 7878

Title from an English bookseller's catalogue.

Brief Memorials of the Lives and Dying Sayings of several Young Quakers. *London.* 1781. 12mo. 7879

Includes Gulielma Penn, of Pennsylvania; Springett Penn; Robert Barrow; Morgan Cadwallader, of Pennsylvania; Elizabeth Wills, of New Jersey; Cath. Burling, of New York, etc. Title from an English catalogue. I do not find it in Smith's catalogue of Friends' books.

A Brief Narration, 1645. *See* New England.

A Brief | Narrative | and Deduction of the several Remark- | able Cases of Sir William Courten, and Sir Paul | Pyndar, Knights; and William Courten late of London | Esquire, Deceased: Their Heirs, Executors, Admi- | nistrators and Assigns, together with their Surviving | Partners and Adventurers with

them to the East-In- | dies, China and Japan, and divers other parts of Asia, | Europe, Africa and America: Faithfully represented | to both Houses of Parliament. | Reduced under four Principal Heads, viz. | I. The Discovery and Plantation of Barbadoes. | II. Their Vndertakings, and Expeditions to the East- | India, China and Japan. | III. The Denyal of Justice upon their civil Actions | depending in Holland and Zealand. | IV. Their Loanes and Supplyes for the Service of the | Crown, upon the Collection of Fines and Compositi- | ons out of the Popish Recusants Estates, &c. | Recollected out of the Original Writings and Records, | for publick Satisfaction. | *London: Printed in the Year* 1679. Folio, 2 l., pp. 12, 115–118. 7880

Brief Narrative of Incidents in the War in Missouri, and of the Personal Experience of one who has Suffered. *Boston: Press of the Daily Courier.* 1863. 8vo, pp. 28. 7881

A Brief Narrative of the Trial for the Bloody and Mysterious Murder of the Unfortunate Young Woman, in the Famous Manhattan Well. Taken in Short Hand by a Gentleman of the Bar. [n. p. 18—.] 8vo, pp. 16. H. 7882

Brief Notice of an "Account of the True Nature and Object of the Late Protestant Episcopal Clerical Association of the City of New-York ... ." *New-York: T. & J. Swords.* 1829. 8vo, 1 l., pp. 16. H. 7883

A Brief of the Claim, on the Part of the Province of New-Jersey, and of the Proof Offered in Support of it, before the Commissioners Appointed by His Majesty, for Settling the Boundary Line, between the said Province of New-Jersey, and the Province of New-York, From the Station on Hudson's River, to the Station on Delaware River; with Observations upon, and Answer to, the several Objections, made by the Agent on the Part of New-York. [n. p. n. d.] Folio, pp. 44.

Signed by John Stevens, James Parker, Walter Rutherfurd; New York, Sept. 28, 1769. Extremely rare. Except the copy noted above, I know of but one, belonging to Mr. George Brinley.

A Brief Outline for a National Bank. By a Native Citizen. *Cincinnati: Paul & Dodd, Printers. Sept.,* 1837. 8vo, pp. 8.

A Brief Outline of the Rise, Progress, and Failure of the Revolutionary Scheme of the Nineteen Van Buren Electors of the Senate of Maryland, in ... 1836. *Baltimore: Printed by Sands & Neilson.* 1837. 8vo, pp. 90. 7886

A Brief Popular Account of all the Financial Panics and Commercial Revulsions in the United States, from 1690 to 1857: with a more particular history of the two great Revulsions of 1837 and 1857. By Members of the New York Press. *New York: J. C. Haney.* 1857. 12mo, pp. 59. 7887

Brief recit de Canada. *See* [Cartier (J.)]

A Brief Relation of the state of New England, 1689. *See* New England.

Brief Remarks on Scriptural Notices, respecting Bondmen and Plan for the gradual Manumission of Slaves. By a British Planter. *London.* 1823. 8vo. 7888

Brief Remarks on the Defence of the Halifax Libel, on the British-American-Colonies. *Boston: Printed and Sold by Edes and Gill.* M, DCC, LXV. 8vo, pp. 40. C., W. 7889

See Tudor's "Life of Otis," p. 188.

Brief Remarks on the Organization and Action of the Board of Missions of the Protestant Episcopal Church in the United States. By a Member of the Society. ... *New York: Burgess, Stringer & Co.* 1844. 8vo, pp. 15. H. 7890

Brief remarks on the Slavery registering bill; and on a special report of the African Institution. *London.* 1816. 8vo. 7891

Brief Remarks on the "Wife" of Washington Irving. *See* [Benson (Egbert)], No. 4741.

Brief Report of the Services rendered by the Freed People to the United States Army in North Carolina, in the Spring of 1862, after the Battle of Newbern. *New York: Vincent Collyer.* 1865. 8vo, pp. 63. 7892

Brief Reports of Operations in Tennessee, 1862. *See* Tennessee.

Brief Review of the Origin, Progress, and Administration of the Bank of the United States. *Philadelphia.* 1819. 12mo, pp. 44. W. 7893

Brief Review of "Considerations respectfully Submitted to the Citizens of Boston and Charlestown, on the Annexation of their Two Cities." By a Native of Boston. *Boston: Printed by Prentiss & Sawyer.* 1854. 8vo, pp. 15. 7894

Brief review of the Plan and Operations of the Association for the Relief of Maimed Soldiers [of the C. S. A. *Richmond, Va.?* 1865.] 8vo, pp. 10. H. 7895

A Brief Review of the Rise and Progress, Services and Sufferings, of New England, especially the Province of Massachuset's-Bay. Humbly submitted to the Consideration of both Houses of Parliament. *London: J. Buckland.* MDCCLXXIV. 8vo, pp. 32. + *Norwich.* 1774. 8vo, pp. 32. 7896

"Contains a very decent, and, to all appearance, a very fair and impartial statement of facts that ought to have due attention paid to them." — M. R., L. 324.

Brief Sketch of Parties, the American and British, as connected with the American System, with an account of the Extraordinary Doings of the Maine Legislature for 1831. *Portland.* 1831. 8vo. 7897

Brief Sketch of the Military Operations on the Delaware during the Late War: Together with a copy of the Muster Rolls of the several Volunteer-Corps which composed the Advance Light Brigade, as they stood at the close of the Campaign of One thousand Eight Hundred and fourteen. *Philadelphia: R. P. McCulloh.* 1820. 12mo, pp. 96. Map. 7898

A Brief Sketch of the plan and advantages of A Sectional Floating Dry Dock for the use of the United States Navy. *New York.* 1843. 8vo, pp. 27. 7899

Brief Sketch of the Political Importance of the British Colonies. *Edinburgh: Bell & Bradfute.* [1826.] 8vo, pp. 87. C. 7900

A Brief Sketch of the Property of the North American Coal Company; with remarks on Coal Mines. *New York.* 1827. 8vo, pp. 23. P. 7901

Brief State of ... Pennsylvania, 1755. *See* [Smith (William)].

A Brief State of the Controversy between the Colonies of New-York and New-Jersey, respecting their Boundary-line. *London.* 1770. 4to, pp. 8. Map. 7902

A Brief State of the Services, 1766. *See* Massachusetts.

A Brief Statement of Facts, in Support of the Bill authorizing certain Towns in Franklin and Berkshire to take Stock

in the Troy and Greenfield R. R. Company. [n. p. n. d.] 8vo, pp. 4. 7903

A Brief Statement of Opinions given in the Board of Commissioners under the Sixth Article of the Treaty of Amity, Com merce, and Navigation with Great Britain. With an Appendix, containing certain articles of the Treaties with Great Britain; — The Commissions under the said Sixth Article of the Treaty of Amity, and references to opinions delivered by the Judges of the Supreme and Circuit Courts of the United States. By one of the Commissioners under the said Sixth Article. *Philadelphia: Printed By James Humphreys.* 1800. 8vo, pp. viii, 71. N. 7904

A Brief Statement of the Rise and Progress of the Testimony of the Religious Society of Friends, against Slavery and the Slave Trade. ... *Philadelphia.* 1843. 12mo, pp. 59. 7905

Brief Statement of the Sanitary Commission Work. October, 1864. California Branch. [n. p. n. d.] 8vo, pp. 16. 7906

Brief Statement, supported by Original Documents of the Important Grants conceded to the Central American Commercial and Agricultural Company, by the State of Guatemala. *London: Whitaker & Co.* 1839. 8vo, pp. 132. 2 Maps. 7907

Brief Survey of the Great Extent and Evil Tendencies of the Lottery System, as existing in the United States. *Philadelphia:* 1833. 8vo, pp. 48. M. 7908

A Brief Topographical Manual ... of New York, 1811. *See* [Goodenow (Sterling)].

Brief van de Weleerwaarde Classis van Amsterdam, aan de Weleerwaarde Vergaderinge van predikanten, & ouderlingen der herformde kerken in de provincien van Nieuw-York, en Nieuw-Jersey. *Nieuw-York: Gedrukt by John Holt.* 1772. 8vo, pp. iii, 5. 7909

Brief van een burger van Amsterdam tot antwoort van de Wederlegging van de argumenten, opgestelt wegens de Bewinthebbers der Oost en West Indische Compagnie door Neny. *'s Hage.* 1724. 4to. 7910

Brief van een Heer te Londen aan zijn vriend te Amsterdam, waarin: of de Amerikanen van eenige mogendheid van Europa hulp te wachten hebben ... Gevolgen ... regtmatigheid enz. van dezen opstand. *Amsterdam.* 1776. 8vo. 7911

Brief van een Koopman in Amsterdam, aan zyn Vriend in London, wegens de Compagnie van de Zuidzee. Uit het Engels vertaald. *Amsterdam.* 1712. 4to, pp. 12. 7912

Brief van een S[urinam]s Heer aan een Vriend in Zeeland, ter beantwoording van eenige opgegeve vragen. *Utrecht.* 1772. 4to. 7913

Brief van het Algemeene Synode der Hollandsche gereformde kerk van de Vereenigten Staten ... aan de leeraren, kerkenraden enz. d. gereformde kerk in Frankrijk. *Amsterdam.* 1830. 8vo.

Brief van Z. Kon. Maj. van Denemarken, aen ... de Staten Generaal ... Geschr. tot Flensburg, den 24 Aug. 1654. [*'s Gravenhage: W. Breeckevelt.*] 1654. 4to, pp. 4. 7915

A Brief View of Constitutional Powers, showing that the Union consisted of Independent States United. *Philadelphia.* 1864. 8vo, pp. 76. C. 7916

Brief View of Ecclesiastical Jurisdiction, as it is this day practised in England. Addressed to Sir Nathaniel Curzon. *Boston.* 1765. 8vo. 7917

Bears on the controversy about an American Episcopate.

Brief View of the United States, 1810. *See* [Hare (Robert), M.D.]

A Brief Vindication of the Proceedings of the Trustees Relating to the College. Containing a Sufficient Answer to the Late Famous Protest, with its Twenty Unanswerable Reasons. By an Impartial Hand. *New-York: Printed and Sold by H. Gaine, at the Printing-Office in Queen-Street, between the Fly and Meal-Markets.* 1754. pp. 12. P. 7918

Relates to what is now Columbia College.

A Brief Vindication of the Purchassors against the Propritors, in a Christian Manner. *New-York: Printed by J. Zenger, jun.* 1745–6. 12mo, pp. 37. G. B. 7919

This very rare tract relates to the dispute about the boundary between New York and New Jersey. The only copies known are in the possession of Mr. George Brinley, of Hartford, and the English State Paper Office. Thomas does not mention this printer, and I have seen no other specimen.

Derde en vierde brief wegens eene uitstorting des Heiligen Geestes in de Vereenigde Staten van Amerika. *Amsterdam: H. de Hoogh.* 1858. 8vo. 7920

Briefe aus Amerika für deutsche Auswanderer. Mit 5 Ansichten nach der Natur aufgenommen und in Stahlstich ausgeführt. *Darmstadt.* 1852. 5 nos., 12mo, pp. iv, 234. 7921

Briefe aus Columbien an seine Freunde, von einem hannöverischen Offizier; geschrieben in dem J. 1820. *Leipzig: Brockhaus.* 1822. 8vo. 7922

Briefe aus den Vereinigten Staaten von Nord-Amerika. Von * * *. *See* [Jörg Eduard)].

Briefe aus Nord-Amerika von einem kathol Missionär. Zwite. Titel-Auflage der "Skizzen." *Augsburg: Schmid.* 1848 [1845?] 8vo, pp. viii, 296. 7923

Briefe eines Deutschen aus Nord-Amerika an seine Freunde und Verwandte in Deutschland. Eine Lektüre zur belehrenden Unterhaltung. Herausgegeben von E. E. Kutschera. *Saaz.* 1837. 12mo. Map and View. 7924

Briefe in die Heimath, geschrieben zwischen October 1829 und Mai 1830 während einer Reise über Frankreich, England und die Vereinigten Staaten von Nordamerica nach Mexico. *Stuttgart und Tübingen.* 1835. 8vo. 7925

A Briefe Relation, 1602. *See* New England.

A Briefe | Relation | of the Persecvtion lately made | Against the Catholike Christians in the | Kingdome of Iaponia | Deuided into two Bookes. | Taken out of the Annuall Letters of the Fathers of | the Society of Iesvs, and other Authenticall | Informations. Written in Spanish, and printed first at Mexico in the West Indies, the | yeare of Christ M.DC.XVI. | And | Newly translated into English by W. W. Gent. | The first Part. | *Permissu Superiorum* M.DC.XIX. 16mo, pp. 350, Table 2 pp. 7926

Briefe über Brasilien. 1. Sklavenhandel. 2. Behandlung der Sklaven. 3. Auswanderung nach Brasilien und Colonisation daselbst. *Frankfurt a. M.: Hedler.* 1857. 8vo. 7927

Briefe über d. gegenwärtigen Zustand von Nordamerika. *See* [Sprengel (M. C.)]

Briefe über die Vereinigten Staaten von Nord-Amerika. Geschrieben in den Jahren 1832–33. (Aus dem Französichen des Herrn von J. M. B. de *****.) *Berlin: Dümmler.* 1835. 2 vols., 8vo. 7928

Briefe über Portugal, nebst einem Anhang über Brasilien. Aus dem Französischen. Mit Anmerkungen herausgegeben von Matthias Christ. Sprengel, Professor der Geschichte in Halle. *Leipzig: in der Weygand'schen Buchhandlung.* 1782. 12mo, Title, 5 l., pp. 290. 7929

Briefe über die jetzige Uneinigkeit zwischen den Amerikanischen Colonien und dem Englischen Parlament. Aus dem Englischen. *Hannover.* 1776. Sm. 8vo, pp. 108. H. 7930

Kayser gives the imprint: *Berlin: Hamburg.* 1777.

Briefe von Deutschen aus Nord-America, mit besonderer Beziehung auf die Giessner Auswanderer-Gesellschaft vom Jahre 1834. Eine Schrift zur Belehrung über die wahren Verhältnisse der deutschen Einwanderer in den Vereinigten Staaten, nebst Vorsichtsmassregeln und auf Erfahrungen gegründete Rathschläge. *Altenburg: Expedition der Eremiten.* 1836. 8vo.

Briefve Deduction par laquelle est clairement monstré que l'isle de Tabago appartient à Monseigneur le Duc en Livonie etc. *Mitau, (Russia).* 1668. 4to. 7932

In Dutch and French. Extremely scarce. This singular publication exhibits the claim of the Duke of Livonia to the Island of Tabago.

Brier (W. W.) The Opening Sermon before the Synod of Alta California ... by Rev. Wm. Wallace Brier, in ... San Francisco, October 3d, 1860. ... *San Francisco.* 1860. 8vo, pp. 18. 7933

See pp. 12, 13.

Briet (P.) Parallela Geographiæ Veteris et Novæ. Auctore Philippo Brietio ... [Vignette.] *Parisiis: Sebastiani Cramoisy, et Gabrielis Cramoisy.* M. DC. XLVIII–XLIX. 3 vols., 4to, 4 l., pp. 512, (1); 14 l., pp. 508, (4); 10 l., 509–1046, (1). P., H.

Briève et Fidèle Exposition de l'Origine, de la Doctrine, des Constitutions, Usages et Cérémonies de l'Eglise de l'Unité des Freres, connus sous le Nom de Freres de Boheme et de Moravie, tirée de leurs Actes et Titres Autentiques, par un Auteur Impartial, Ami de la Vérité. [n. p.] 1758. 8vo. 16 Plates.

"The plates in this rare and interesting volume are each of the size of two octavo pages, and contain elaborate representations of the ceremonies of ordination, of the different modes of baptizing infants, negroes, Greenlanders, and American Indians, also of the exorcism, prosternation, Eucharist, Agapæ, holy kiss, feet washing, marriage, etc."

Brieven over het bestuur der colonien Essequebo en Demerary, gewisseld tusschen de Heeren Aristodemus en Sincerus. Nevens bylagen, tot deeze briefwisseling, en eene voorreden van den Nederlandschen uitgeever. *Amsterdam: W. Holtrop.* 1785–88. 12 pts., 8vo. H. 7936

Brieven tusschen den Eng. Viceadm. Joung, den Hr. Colpoys en den Hr. J. de Graaff, Gouverneur van St. Eustatius, ter verantwoording van den laatsten. *Amsterdam.* 1777. 8vo. 7937

Briggs (C.) A Sermon delivered at the Installation of the Rev. Artemas B. Muzzey ... Cambridge-port ... January 1, 1834. By Charles Briggs ... . *Cambridge: James Munroe and Company.* 1834. 8vo, pp. 17. H. 7938

Briggs. A Discourse delivered at Concord, [Mass.] October the Fifth, 1825. *Concord.* 1825. 8vo, pp. 34. H. 7939

Briggs (C. F.) *and* Maverick (A.) ... The Story of The Telegraph, and a History of the Great Atlantic Cable; a Complete Record of the Inception, Progress, and Final Success of that Undertaking. A General History of Land and Ocean Telegraphs. Descriptions of Telegraphic Apparatus, and Biographical Sketches of the Principal Persons connected with the Great Work. By Charles F. Briggs, and Augustus Maverick. ... *New York: Rudd & Carleton.* M DCCC LVIII. 12mo, pp. 255. Maps, Portrait, and Woodcuts. C., H. 7940

Briggs (C.) Dissertations on the License System and Maine Liquor Law. By Clinton Briggs, Esq. ... *Auburn: Wm. J. Moses.* 1853. 12mo, pp. 88. H. 7941

Briggs (E.) A Sermon, preached at Dennis, April 30, 1804, at the Interment of the Rev. Nathan. Stone, A.M. who died April 26, 1804, in the Sixty-seventh Year of his Age, and the Fortieth of his Ministry. By Ephraim Briggs, A.M. ... *Boston: printed by William Burdick.* 1804. 8vo, pp. 18, (1). H. 7942

Also, a sermon at the ordination of Ephraim Briggs, Junr.

Briggs (George N.) Address to the Legislature of Mass. Jan, 11, 1848. *Boston: Dutton and Wentworth.* 1848. 8vo, pp. 22. BA. 7943

Briggs (G. Ware). Address at the Funeral of Deacon William P. Ripley, ... at Plymouth ... Nov. 13, 1842. By George W. Briggs. *Plymouth: printed by James Thurber.* 1842. 8vo, pp. 16. BA., C. 7944

Briggs. Address before the City Authorities in Salem, at the Celebration of the Birth-Day of Washington, February 22, 1862. By George W. Briggs ... . *Salem.* 1862. 8vo, pp. 24.

Briggs. Eulogy on Abraham Lincoln, By George W. Briggs, D.D., June, 1865. With the Proceedings of the City Council on the Death of the President. *Salem, Mass.* 1865. 8vo, pp. 48. 7946

One thousand copies printed in octavo, and three hundred in quarto.

Briggs. Memoir of Daniel Appleton White, by George W. Briggs. ... (From the Historical Collections of the Essex Institute.) *Salem: the Institute.* 1864. 4to, Title, pp. 47. H. 7947

Briggs. Two Sermons preached in the First Church in Plymouth, Mass. ... July 4, 1847. By George W. Briggs. ... *Plymouth.* [n. d.] 8vo, pp. 31. H. 7948

Briggs (H. L.) A Lecture on the Moral, Social and Political Condition of Utah Territory, by Hugh L. Briggs, Esq. [n. p.] 1857. 8vo, pp. 18. H. 7949

Briggs (Isaac). Documents accompanying the Bill for the Relief of Isaac Briggs. Presented January 17, 1810. *City of Washington: A. & G. Way, Printers.* 1810. 8vo, pp. 8. H.

Briggs. Statements and Remarks addressed to Thomas Newton, ... on the subject of Agriculture, Manufactures, and Commerce. By Isaac Briggs. *Washington: W. A. Davis.* 1816. 8vo, pp. 18. 7951

Briggs (*Rev.* I.) A Pastoral Address to the Old Colony Association, delivered at New Bedford, April 30, 1855. By Rev. Isaac Briggs. ... *New Bedford: E. Anthony, Printer.* 1855. 8vo, pp. 11. 7952

Briggs (John A. B.) An Oration delivered at the North Meeting House, in Tiverton, on the 11th of February, 1800, on the Death of General George Washington. By the request of the Honorable Town Council of Tiverton. *Newport: Henry Barber.* 1800. 8vo, pp. 10. 7953

Briggs (John). The History of Jim Crow. *London.* 1839. 8vo. 7954

Briggs (L.), *Jr.* Plymouth County Railroad. Remarks in Relation to the Importance of a Railroad through the Eastern

Part of Plymouth County, from S. Weymouth to Duxbury. ... By L. Briggs, Jr. *Boston.* 1848. 8vo, pp. 8. H. 7955

Briggs (W.) The Military History of Europe, &c., from the Commencement of the War with Spain in 1739. *London.* 1755. 8vo. 7956

Included in a London catalogue of "Americana."

Brigham (C. A. G.) Fasts of Nineveh and the Fasts of Connecticut. A Sermon preached on Friday, April 22, 1859. By C. A. G. Brigham. *Enfield, Conn.* 1859. 8vo, pp. 16.

Brigham (C. H.) An Address delivered to the Companies of California Adventurers, of Taunton ... February 4th, 1849, by Rev. Charles H. Brigham. [*Taunton?* 1849.] 8vo, pp. 8.

Brigham. A biographical Sketch of Rev. Simeon Doggett, Pastor of the Second Congregational Church in Raynham. By Charles H. Brigham. *Boston: Crosby, Nichols, and Company.* 1852. 12mo, pp. 45. 7959

Also: "A sermon on the National Fast, 1861."

Brigham (H. H.) A Voice from Nazareth. A Letter ... to the Rev. H. D. Walker, In Reply to a War Sermon preached by him in September, 1864. By H. H. Brigham. ... *Plymouth.* 1865. 8vo, pp. 38. H. 7960

Brigham (W.) An Address delivered before the Inhabitants of Grafton, on the First Centennial Anniversary of that Town, April 29, 1835. By William Brigham. *Boston: Light & Horton.* 1835. 8vo, pp. 40. H., M. 7961

Brigham. The Compact, with the Charter and Laws of the Colony of New Plymouth: together with the Charter of the Council at Plymouth, and an Appendix, containing the Articles of Confederation of the United Colonies of New England, and other Valuable Documents. Published agreeably to a Resolve, passed April 5, 1836. Under the Supervision of William Brigham, Counsellor at Law. *Boston.* 1836. 8vo, pp. 10, (1), 357.

By a resolve of the Legislature, fifteen hundred copies were printed for the use of the Commonwealth. "The volume is chiefly valuable as illustrating the spirit of the Pilgrim Fathers, and exhibiting the manners, wants, and sentiments of those early times." — N. A. R., XLIV. 538.

Brigham. Address delivered before the Worcester Agricul-

tural Society, September 28, 1855. *Worcester: C. B. Webb, Printer.* 1855. 8vo, pp. 12. H. 7963

This is the cover-title; the proper title is, "... Transactions of the ... Society, for ... 1855. ..."

Bright (J. D.) Speech of Hon. Jesse D. Bright ... on the Bill for the Admission of Kansas as a State. ... In the ... Senate, March 20, 1858. *Washington, D. C.: Indianians' Democratic Club.* 1858. 8vo, pp. 15. H. 7964

Also: "Speech on the Resolution proposed for his Expulsion. Senate, February 5, 1862." 8vo, pp. 8; and other speeches.

Bright (John). A Liberal Voice from England. Mr. John Bright's Speech at Rochdale, December 4, 1861, on the American Crisis. (From the Rebellion Record ... .) *New York: G. P. Putnam.* 1862. Rl. 8vo, Title, pp. 13. H. 7965

Bright. Speech of John Bright, Esq., M.P., at Birmingham ... . January 26 1864. ... [*Manchester.* 1864.] 8vo, pp. 8. H.

Bright. Speeches of John Bright, M.P. on the American Question. With an Introduction by Frank Moore. *Boston: Little, Brown, and Company.* 1865. 12mo, pp. xv, 278. Portrait. C., H., S. 7967

Bright (J. M.) An Oration on the Life, Character and Public Services of the Hon. Felix Grundy, by Hon. John M. Bright ... . Delivered ... May 3, 1853 ... . *Nashville: John T. S. Fall, Printer.* 1859. 8vo, pp. 27, 2 l. H. 7968

Bright. Speech of John M. Bright against Know-nothingism, at Flat Creek, Bedford Co. *Nashville, Tenn.* 1855. 8vo, pp. 32. S. 7968

Bright (Jonathan B.) The Brights of Suffolk, England; Represented in America by the Descendants of Henry Bright Jun., who came to New England in 1630, and Settled in Watertown, Massachusetts. By J. B. Bright. ... For Private Distribution. *Boston: printed by John Wilson and Son.* 1858. 8vo, 2 l., pp. xvi, 345. Portrait, Maps, etc. H., S. 7969

Bright (M.) A Report of the whole Trial of Gen. Michael Bright and Others: ... in the Circuit Court, of the United States, on and for the District of Pennsylvania, ... on an indictment for obstructing ... the execution of the writ of arrest issued out of the District Court of Pennsylvania. ... By Thomas Lloyd. *Philadelphia: P. Byrne.* 1809. 8vo, pp. 222, (2). C., P. 7970

Relates to the case of G. Olmstead *vs.* Exec. of D. Rittenhouse.

Brightly (F. C.) An Analytic Digest of the Laws of the United States from the Adoption of the Constitution to the End of the Thirty-fourth Congress. 1789–1857. [Vol. II. 1857–1865.] By Frederick C. Brightly ... . *Philadelphia: Kay & Brother.* 1858–1865. 8vo, pp. lx, 1083; xxii, 525. H. 7971

Brightly. Biennial Digest for 1857 and 1859, on the plan and in continuation of Brightly's Analytical Digest of the Laws of the United States, and completing it to the present date. By F. C. Brightly. *Philadelphia: Kay & Brother.* [1860.] 8vo, pp 1085–1131. 7972

Brighton (J. G.) Admiral Sir P. B. V. Broke, Bart. K.C.B. A Memoir, Compiled by Rev. J. G. Brighton, M.D. *London.* 1866. Rl. 8vo, pp. xvi, 488. 7973

The Admiral was in command of the "Shannon" in the action between that vessel and the "Chesapeake."

Brighton, *Mass.* Annual Report of the Receipts and Expenditures of the Town of Brighton, April, 1841. [n. p. n. d.] 8vo, pp. 7. H. 7974

The first printed.

Report of the School Committee of the Town of Brighton, for the Year 1839....'40. ... [*Printed at the Waltham Press.* 1840.] 12mo, pp. 4. Continued. H. 7975

This is the second report, but the first that was printed.

Treasurer's Report of the Receipts and Expenditures of the Town of Brighton, for the Year ending March 1, 1861. *Cambridge.* 1861. 8vo, pp. 32, (5). Continued. H. 7976

The Brighton [*Mass.*] and Brookline Business Directory ... with an Almanac for 1850. [1st year.] ... By George Adams ... [and Rev. Frederic A. Whitney]. *Boston.* 1850. 32mo. Continued? 7977

Brightwell (C. L.) Annals of Industry and Genius. By C. L. Brightwell. *London: T. Nelson and Sons.* 1863. 12mo, pp. 298. 7978

Contains a biography of Benjamin Franklin.

Brightwell. Byepaths of Biography. By C. L. Brightwell. *T. Nelson and Sons.* [n. d.] 12mo, pp. 278. 7979

Contains a chapter on Captain John Smith.

[Brignoles (*Marquis* de).] Observations critiques sur l'écrit intitulé Christophe Colomb, ou Notice concernant cet illustre navigateur; faisant suite aux étudbs [*sic*] biographiques ... sur ... Arnauld, ... Nicole et ... Necker; par M. le Comte Lanjuinais ... . *Paris: Fantin.* 1824. 8vo, pp. 31. 7980

A refutation of Lanjuinais' pamphlet published in 1823, by the Marquis de Brignoles. *See* Quérard, under Lanjuinais.

Bril-gesicht voor de verblinde eyghen baetsuchtige Handelaers op Brasil. By Forme van Advijs door een Liefhebber van 't Vaderlandt geschrieven aen synen Vriendt. [n. p.] 1638. pp. 8.

BRIMBLECOMB (Nicholas), *pseudon.?* Uncle Tom's Cabin in Ruins. Triumphant Defence of Slavery! in a Series of Letters to Harriet Beecher Stowe. By Nicholas Brimblecomb, Esq. *Boston: Charles Waite.* MDCCCLIII. 8vo, 2 l., pp. 162. H. 7982

An ironical work.

BRIMFIELD, *Mass.* Address to the Selectmen and others of Brimfield. [n. p. n. d.] 8vo. B. 7983

An Authentic Copy of the Result of the Ecclesiastical Council convened at Brimfield, March 12, 1801. *Worcester.* 1801. 8vo, pp. 15. 7984

Popish Hierarchy suppressed by Buonaparte in Italy; and his Holiness exerting his Influence, in a late Ecclesiastical Council at Brimfield, called by Letters Missive to Instal the Rev. Clark Brown. By Agathocles. *Springfield: Francis Stebbins.* 1798. 8vo, pp. 55. W. 7985

BRINCKLÉ (W. D.) Remarks on Entomology, chiefly in reference to an Agricultural Benefit, by W. D. Brincklé, M.D. *Philadelphia.* 1852. 8vo. 7986

BRINGAS (D. M.) Oracion fúnebre de Dona Mar. Josefa de Vergara. *Mexico.* 1815. 4to, 37 l. 7987

BRINGAS. Sermon politico-moral para dar principio á la mision extraordinaria, formada de venerables sacerdotes de ambos cleros, dirigida á la concordia y union de los habitantes de esta America, y el restablecimiento de la paz. *Mexico.* 1813. 4to, 22 l. 7988

BRINGAS. Sermon que en la Reconquista de Guanaxuato, predico extemporaneamente el la Iglesia parroquial de dicha Ciudad, el Padre Fr. Diego Miguel Bringas, Missionero apostolico del Colegio de la Santa Cruz de Queretaro, etc. *Mexico.* 1811. 4to, 2 l., pp. 38. 7989

This sermon was delivered after the expulsion of the insurgents from Guanaxuato.

[BRINGHURST (Joseph), *Junr.*] Copy of a Letter from a Young Man, a Quaker in Pennsylvania, to the late William Cowper, the Poet. *Chester: Broster and Son.* 1800. 12mo.

BRINKERHOFF (Jacob). Speech of Mr. J. Brinkerhoff, of Ohio, on the Annexation of Texas: delivered in the House ... January 13, 1845. ... *Washington.* 1845. 8vo, pp. 8. H. 7991

BRINKERHOFF. Speech ... on the Oregon Question. ... In the House ... January 5, 1846. *Washington.* 1846. 8vo, pp. 8. H. 7992

BRINKERHOFF. The Wilmot Proviso. Speech of Hon. Jacob Brinkerhoff, of Ohio, delivered in the House of Representatives, Feb. 10, 1847. 8vo, pp. 7. S. 7993

BRINLEY (F.) Life of William T. Porter. By Francis Brinley. *New York: D. Appleton and Company.* M.DCCC.LX. 12mo, pp. vii, 273. Portrait. H. 7994

BRINLEY (F.), *Jr.* An Address delivered before the Franklin Debating Society ... January 17, 1830, being the Celebration of their Seventh Anniversary, and the Birth Day of Franklin. By Francis Brinley, Jr. *Boston: the Society.* 1830. 8vo, pp. 16.

BRINSLEY (J.) Consolation for our Grammar Schooles, or Comfortable incouragement, for laying of a sure foundation of all good Learning in our Schooles; more especially for all those of an inferiour sort, and all ruder countries and places; namely for Ireland, Wales, Virginia, with the Sommer Islands, and for the more speedie attaining of our English tongue ... that all may speake one and the same language ... By John Brinsley. *London: Richard Field.* 1622. 4to, 8 l., pp. 84. J. C. B. 7996

Contains a long and very interesting introduction addressed to the Council and Company of Virginia and Sommer Islands.

BRINSMADE (T. C.) Record of Private Practice, For the Years 1858 and 1859; and Mortuary Record of the City of Troy, N. Y. For the Years 1858 and 1859. By Thomas C. Brinsmade, M.D. ... . *Albany.* 1860. 8vo, pp. 43. H. 7997

BRINTON (Daniel Garrison). The Myths of the New World: a Treatise on the Symbolism and Mythology of the Red Race in America. By D. G. Brinton ... . *New York: Leypoldt & Holt.* 1868. 8vo, pp. viii, 307. BA. 7998

Fifty-five copies printed on large paper, quarto.

BRINTON. Notes on the Floridian Peninsula, its Literary History, Indian Tribes and Antiquities. By Daniel G. Brinton, A.B. *Philadelphia: Joseph Sabin.* 1859. 12mo, pp. viii, 13–202.

BRION DE LA TOUR (Louis) *and* MACLOT (Jean Charles). Description générale de l'Europe, de l'Asie, de l'Afrique et de l'Amérique ... . *Paris.* 1795. 4to. 8000

BRION (M.) Almanach intéressant dans les circonstances présentes. Description abrégée des Etats Unis de l'Amérique; des Possessions Anglaises et des Pays qui y sont contigus, dans les Indes Orientales. Par M. Brion ... . *Paris: Desnos.* [n. d.] 18mo, engraved Title, pp. 72. Plate, and 2 Maps. H. 8001

Las Brisas del avila. Periodico quincenal. *Caracas.* 8002

No more published.

BRISBANE (A. H.) Ralphton; or, the Young Carolinian of 1776. A Romance on the Philosophy of Politics. By A. H. Brisbane. *Charleston: Burges and James, Printers.* 1848. 12mo, pp. ix, 242. B. 8003

BRISBANE (A.) Social Destiny of Man; or Association and Reorganisation of Industry. By Albert Brisbane. *Philadelphia.* 1840. 12mo, pp. 480. 8004

BRISBANE (C.) Communication from Sir Charles Brisbane, K.C.B. Governor of St. Vincent, to the House of Assembly of that Colony, ... enclosing Lord Bathurst's Despatch Of the 9th of July, [for ameliorating the condition of the Slaves,] with the Joint Reply of the Council and Assembly; and a Letter depicting the Alarm and Danger excited by the Insurrection in Demerara, September, 1823. *London.* 1823. 8vo, pp. 74. H. 8005

BRISBANE (W. Henry). Amanda: A Tale for the Times. By Dr. W. H. Brisbane. *Philadelphia.* 1848. 32mo. + *New York: Anti-Slavery Society.* 1849. 12mo, pp. 52. 8006

Originally published in the "National Era."

BRISBANE. The Constitution of the United States, versus Slavery. By William H. Brisbane. *Philadelphia.* 1846. 32mo, pp. 24. H. 8007

BRISBANE. An Eulogium on the Life and Character of the late Honorable Thomas Morris. *Cincinnati.* 1845. 8vo. 8008

BRISBANE. Slaveholding examined in the Light of the Holy Bible. By William Henry Brisbane. *Philadelphia.* 1847. 12mo, pp. viii, 222. + *New York: A. & F. Anti-Slavery Society.* 1849. 24mo, 3 l., pp. 222. + *New York.* 1857. 8009

BRISBANE. Speech of the Rev. Wm. H. Brisbane lately A Slaveholder in South Carolina; Containing an Account of the Change in His Views on the Subject of Slavery. Delivered ... Cincinnati, February 12, 1840. *Hartford: S. S. Cowles.* 1840. 8vo, pp. 12. 8010

BRISBIN (J. S.) Speech of Brig. Gen. Jas. S. Brisbin, delivered at Louisville, Ky., July 4, 1865. [n. p. n. d.] 8vo, Title, pp. 11. H. 8011

"The journals of Kentucky refused to publish General Brisbin's speech on account of the extreme radical views he put forth in it."

BRISBIN. Campaign Lives of U. S. Grant and S. Colfax. By Gen. J. S. Brisbin. *Cincinnati: C. F. Vent & Co.* 1868. 12mo, pp. 411. Portraits and Illustrations. 8012

BRISEÑO (Ramon). Estadistica bibliográfica de la literatura chilena. Obra compuesta en virtud de encargo especial del consejo de la universidad de Chile. *Santiago: imprenta Chilena.* 1862. 4to, pp. xiv, 546. C. 8013

BRISSOT DE WARVILLE (Jean Pierre). Adresse à l'assemblée Nationale, pour l'abolition de la Traite des Noirs. Par la Société des Amis des Noirs à Paris. *Paris.* 1790. 8vo. 8014

BRISSOT DE WARVILLE. Affaire de Tabago. Réponse de J.-P. Brissot aux lettres insérées dans le "Journal de Paris" par MM. Dillon, ... et Henrion (de Flozelles), ... sur les réclamations des planteurs de Tabago. [*Paris: imp. du Patriote français.* n. d]. 4to, pp. 48 or less. 8015

BRISSOT DE WARVILLE. The Commerce of America with Europe, particularly with France and Great Britain, comparatively stated and explained, Shewing the importance of the American Revolution to the Interests of France, and pointing out the actual situation of the United States of North America in regard to Trade, Manufactures and Population. By J. P. Brissot de Warville, and Etienne Clavière. Translated from the last French edition, revised by Brissot, and called the Second Volume of his View of America. With the Life of Brissot, and

an Appendix, by the Translator [Joel Barlow]. *London: J. Jordan.* MDCCXCIV. 8vo, pp. lxiv, 348. Portrait. + *New York: T. and J. Swords.* 1795. 12mo, pp. xxxv, 228. Portrait. C.

See M. R., LXXVI. 593; LXXX. 77; New Series, XX. 237. This was also issued as a second volume of Brissot's Travels. *See* No. 8027.

BRISSOT DE WARVILLE. A Critical Examination of the Marquis de Chatellux's Travels in North America, in a Letter addressed to the Marquis; Principally intended as a Refutation of his Opinions Concerning the Quakers, the Negroes, the People, and Mankind. Translated from the French of J. P. Brissot de Warville, with Additions and Corrections of the Author. *Philadelphia: Printed by Joseph James.* M,DCC,LXXXVIII. 8vo, pp. 89. P. + *London.* 1788. 8vo. P. 8017

A translation of No. 8019 *infra*.

BRISSOT DE WARVILLE. Discours sur un projet de décret, relatif à la révolte des noirs, prononcé à l'Assemblée Nationale, le 30 Octobre, 1791, par J. P. Brissot, Député, imprimé par ordre l'Assemblée nationale. [1791.] 8vo, pp. 17. 8018

BRISSOT DE WARVILLE. Examen critique des voyages dans l'Amérique Septentrionale, de M. le Marquis de Cha[s]tellux; ou lettre ... Dans laquelle on réfute principalement ses opinions sur les Quakers, sur les Negres, sur le Peuple, et sur l'Homme. Par J. Brissot de Warville. ... *Londres* [*Paris*]. 1786. 8vo, 2 l., pp. 143. B., C. 8019

"A spirited writer here attacks the Marquis for having, in the publication of his travels, exposed to ridicule, and grossly misrepresented the principles and manners of the Quakers; he also endeavors to show that the Marquis's reflections on the slavery of the negroes, and his thoughts on the condition of mankind, with respect to the ranks in society, are often unjust. M. de Warville's language is forcible, his arguments are striking, if not always conclusive, and his work is replete with liberal sentiments on religious and political subjects." — M. R., LXXVI. 337.

BRISSOT DE WARVILLE. Lettre de J. P. Brissot a M. Barnave, Sur ses rapports concernant les colonies, les décrets qui les ont suivis, leurs conséquences fatales; sur sa conduite dans le cours de la révolution; sur le caractère des vrais démocrates; sur les bases de la constitution, les obstacles qui s'opposent à son achèvement, la nécessité de la terminer promptement, etc. ... *Paris: Dessenne, Bailly.* 20 *Novembre*, 1790. 8vo, 2 l., pp. 104.

BRISSOT DE WARVILLE. L'Indépendence des Anglo-Américains démontrée Utile à la Grande-Bretagne. *Paris.* 1782. 8vo.

BRISSOT DE WARVILLE. The Life of J. P. Brissot, Deputy from Eure and Loire, to the National Convention. Written By Himself. Translated from the French. *London: J. Debrett.* 1794. 8vo, pp. 92. + Second Edition. *London.* 1794. 8vo, pp. 92. S. 8022

This enlightened philosopher and amiable man fell a victim to the fury of the French Revolutionists. Gulliotined, October, 1793. *See* M. R., Second Series, XIV. 237.

BRISSOT DE WARVILLE. Memoire sur les noirs de l'Amérique Septentrionale. Lu à l'Assemblée de la Société des amis des noires le 9 Février, 1789. Par J.-P. Brissot de Warville. ... *A Paris: au bureau de Patriote français.* 1789. 8vo, pp. 56.

BRISSOT DE WARVILLE. Mémoires sur ses Contemporains et sur la Révolution Française. *Paris.* 1830. 4 vols., 8vo.

BRISSOT DE WARVILLE. New Travels in the United States of America. Performed in 1788. By J. P. Brissot de Warville. Translated from the French. *London: J. S. Jordan.* MDCCXCII. 8vo, 2 l., pp. 483, Contents, 2 l. + *Dublin.* MDCCXCII. 12mo, pp. 483. + *New York.* 1792. 8vo. + *Boston: Joseph Bumstead.* 1797. 12mo, pp. 276, and Contents.

BRISSOT DE WARVILLE. New Travels in the United States of America, Including the Commerce of America with Europe; Particularly with France and Great Britain. In two Volumes. To which is prefixed A Sketch of the Life of Brissot, with an Elegant Portrait. *London: J. S. Jordan.* MDCCXCIV. 8vo, pp. lxiv, 348. P. 8026

This was reproduced with a new title and an additional volume, as below:

BRISSOT DE WARVILLE. New Travels in the United States of America, performed in M.DCC.LXXXVIII. Containing The latest and most accurate Observations on the Character, Genius, and present State of the People and Government of that Country — Their Agriculture, Commerce, Manufactures, and Finances — Quality and Price of Lands, and Progress of the Settlements on the Ohio and the Mississippi — Political and Moral Character of the Quakers, and a Vindication of that excellent Sect from the Misrepresentations of other Travellers — State of the Blacks — Progress of the Laws for their Emancipation, and for the final Destruction of Slavery on that Continent — Accurate Accounts of the Climate, Longevity — Comparative Tables of the Probabilities of Life between America and Europe, &c. &c. By J.

P. Brissot de Warville. Second Edition, corrected. *London: J. S. Jordan.* M DCC XCIV. 8vo, pp. xii, 416; [Vol. II.], 1 l., lxiv, 348. C., H. 8027

The author came to the United States just before the French Revolution, for the purpose of selecting a suitable place for establishing a colony of respectable persons, who had determined to abandon the then despotic government of France, and seek an asylum under the mild and equal government of the United States. M. Brissot was commissioned to collect every necessary information, prior to the execution of so important a plan. These volumes contain the result of his assiduous labors, and minute enquiries, and sufficiently manifest that he was qualified to accomplish such an arduous undertaking. The second volume is a new edition of Brissot and Clavière's "De la France, et des Etats-Unis," etc., printed at Paris in 1787, and in English in 1788. *See* No. 8016.

BRISSOT DE WARVILLE. New Travels in the United States of America: including The Commerce of America with Europe; particularly with France and Great Britain. ... 2 vols., 8vo, General Title, pp. xii, 416; General Title, pp. lxiv, 348. Portrait. B., H. 8028

This general title has no imprint. Vol. I. has the 2d title:

BRISSOT DE WARVILLE. New Travels in the United States of America, performed in M.DCC.LXXXVIII. ... By J. P. Brissot de Warville. ... Vol. I. Second Edition, corrected. ... *London: J. S. Jordan.* M DCC XCIV. 8029

Vol. II. has the 2d title:

BRISSOT DE WARVILLE. The Commerce ... [as above]. By J. P. Brissot de Warville, and Etienne Claviere. Translated from the Last French Edition, Revised by Brissot, and called the Second Volume of his View of America. With the Life of Brissot, and an Appendix, by the Translator. *London: J. S. Jordan.* M DCC XCIV. 8030

BRISSOT DE WARVILLE. New Travels in the United States of America ... . By J. P. Brissot de Warville. ... *Boston: Prest of Joseph Bumstead.* 1797. 12mo, pp. 276, (3). B., H. 8031

BRISSOT DE WARVILLE. Neue Reise durch die Vereinigten Staaten von Nord Amerika im Jahre 1788. Aus dem Französischen des Herrn Brissot von Warville verteutscht. ... Neue unveränderte Auflage. ... *Hof: Gottfried Adolph Grau.* 1796. 3 vols., 8vo, pp. ; ; Title, 353, (1). 8032

BRISSOT DE WARVILLE. Neue Reise durch die Nord-Amerikanischen Freistaaten im Jahre 1788, mit Anmerkungen von J. R. Foster, aus dem Französischen. *Berlin.* 1792. 8vo. 8033

BRISSOT DE WARVILLE. Nieuwe Reize in de Vereenigde Staaten van Nord-America. *Amsterdam.* 2 vols. 8vo. 8034

BRISSOT DE WARVILLE. Nouveau voyage dans les États-Unis de l'Amérique Septentrionale, fait en 1788; Par J. B. Brissot (Warville), Citoyen François. ... *Paris: Buisson. Avril*, 1791. 3 vols., 8vo, 2 l., pp. lij, 395; 2 l., pp. 460; 2 l., pp. 448. 8035

The third volume has also the following title: "De la France, et des États-Unis, ou de l'Importance de la révolution de l'Amérique pour le bonheur de la France ... . Par Étienne Clavière, et J. B. Brissot (Warivlle). Nouvelle édition." This was published separately. *See* Clavière (E.)

BRISSOT DE WARVILLE. Oration upon the Necessity of establishing at Paris a Society to co-operate with those of America and London toward the Abolition of the Trade and Slavery of the Negroes, delivered 19th February, 1788. *Philadelphia: F. Bailey.* 1788. 8vo, pp. 25. C. 8036

Preface by the translator, Chas. Crawford.

BRISSOT DE WARVILLE. Réflexions sur le Nouveau Décret rendu pour la Martinique et les Colonies, le 27 novembre 1790. ... . Par J. P. Brissot. [n. p. n. d.] 8vo, pp. 16. BA. 8037

BRISSOT DE WARVILLE. Reise durch die Vereinigten Staaten von Nord-America, im Jahr 1788. Aus dem Französischen von T. F. Ehrmann. *Dürkheim an der Haard: F. L. Pfähler.* 1792. 8vo, pp. lxviii, 628. Table. + *Heidelberg.* 1792. 8vo. C.

This Heidelberg edition is probably the same as the other, with a new title-page only.

BRISSOT DE WARVILLE. Réplique de J. P. Brissot, à la première et dernière lettre de Louis-Marthe Gouy, Défenseur de la Traite des Noirs et de l'Esclavage. ... *Paris: Belin, Desenne, Bailly.* 10 février 1791. 8vo, Title, pp. 54. H. 8039

BRISSOT (M. A.) Voyage au Guazacoalcos, aux Antilles, et aux Etats-Unis. Par M. A. Brissot. Ouvrage précédé de trois lettres de Lafayette. *Paris.* 1837. 8vo, pp. 390. Map, and 2 Plates. 8040

The author was J. P. Brissot's son.

BRISTED (C. A.) The Coward's Convention. By Charles Astor Bristed. *New York Loyal Publication Society.* [1862.] 8vo. 8041

BRISTED. A Few Words of Warning to New Yorkers, on the consequences of a Railroad in Fifth Avenue. ... By Charles Astor Bristed. *New York: W. C. Bryant & Co., Printers.* 1863. 8vo, pp. 33. 8042

BRISTED. The Interference Theory of Government. By Charles Astor Bristed. ... *New York: Leypoldt & Holt.* 1867. 16mo, pp. 109. C. 8043

Treats, in part, of the Mormons, Our War, and The Aquarian [*i. e.*, Temperance] Movement.

BRISTED. A Letter to the Hon. Horace Mann. *New York.* 1850. 18mo. + Second Edition. *New York.* 1850. 12mo.

Relates to Mr. Mann's remarks on the character of J. J. Astor.

[BRISTED.] A Letter to Dr. Henry Halford Jones [Josiah Gilbert Holland], (Editor of the Wintertown Democrat [Springfield Republican],) concerning His Habit of Giving Advice to Everybody, and his Qualifications for the Task, by Carl Benson. *New York.* 1864. 8vo, pp. 45. H. 8045

BRISTED. Now is the Time to Settle it. Suggestions on the Present Crisis. By Charles Astor Bristed. *New York: Martin B. Brown.* 1862. 12mo, pp. 24. C. 8046

BRISTED. The Upper Ten Thousand: Sketches of American Society. By C. Astor Bristed. *New York: Stringer & Townsend.* M.DCCC.LII. + *London: J. W. Parker.* 1852. 12mo, pp. iv, 291. C. 8047

BRISTED. Les États-Unis d'Amérique, ou Tableau de l'Agriculture, du Commerce, des Manufactures, des Finances, de la Politique, de la Littérature, des Arts, et du Caractère moral et religieux du Peuple Anglo-Américain; traduit de l'anglais de John Bristed ... *Paris: Alexis Eymery.* 1826. 2 vols., 8vo, pp. 380; 320. C., H. 8048

BRISTED. Hints on the National Bankruptcy of Britain, and on Her Resources to maintain the Present Contest with France. By John Bristed. *New York.* 1809. 8vo, pp. 700. C. 8049

"In some parts very severe on the Americans." — J. R. SMITH.

BRISTED. The Resources of the United States of America; or, A View of the Agricultural, Commercial, Manufacturing, Financial, Political, Literary, Moral and Religious Capacity and Character of the American People. By John Bristed ... .

New-York: James Eastburn & Co. 1818. 8vo, pp. xvi, 505, (1). BA., C., H. 8050

See N. A. R., VII. 401. Published in London, with the title changed to "America and her Resources, ... *London: H. Colburn.* 1818." 8vo, pp. xvi, 505. Probably a new title-page only printed.

BRISTED. Der Hilfsquellen der vereinigten Staaten von Nord-Amerika, oder Ueberlick des Zustandes und Characters des nordamerikanischen Volks. Aus dem Englischen übersetzt. *Weimar. Lander- Industrie-Comptoir.* 1819. 8vo. 8051

BRISTED. Thoughts on the Anglican and Anglo-American Churches. By John Bristed. *New York.* 1823. 8vo, pp. 500. *London: J. Holdsworth.* 1823. 8vo, pp. 500. A. 8052

See "Eclectic Rev.," 1823, XIX. 53-68. Also: An Oration on the Utility of Literary Establishments, delivered ... at the Opening of the Literary Rooms in New-York, On the eleventh of February, 1814. By John Bristed, Esq. *New-York: Eastburn, Kirk & Co.* 1814. 8vo, pp. 16. M. — An Address, delivered to the Auxiliary New-York Bible Society, on the Fifteenth of November, 1813. ... *New-York: the Society.* 1813. 8vo, pp. 22. Both slightly relate to the United States.

BRISTOL (Hugh), *Bishop of.* 1722. *See* Boulter (Hugh).

BRISTOL (William). An Address intended to have been delivered (in substance) at the late Town Meeting in New Haven, on the Situation of Public Affairs. *New Haven.* 1809. 8vo, pp. 19. N. 8053

BRISTOL. An Account of the Settlement of the Town of Bristol, in the State of Rhode Island; and of the Congregational Church therein; with the succession of Pastors from its origin to the present time; together with the Act of Incorporation of the Catholic Congregational Society, and the Rules established in said Society. *Providence: Printed by Bennett Wheeler.* 1785. 8vo, pp. 16. N. 8054

Ludewig attributes this to Dr. Ezra Stiles. Mr. Geo. Brinley's copy has inscribed upon it, in an old handwriting, "Drawn up by Judge Bourne." Also: "Constitution and List of Officers of the Young Men's Christian Association, Bristol. Organized December, 1863. *Providence: Alfred Anthony.* 1863. 12mo, pp. 14.

Annual Report of the School Committee of the Town of Bristol, for the Year ending April, 1868. *Providence.* 1868. 8vo, pp. 12. H. 8055

BRISTOL, *Conn.* Remonstrance of the Baptist Elders at Bristol to the General Assembly. *Bristol.* 1803. C. 8056

BRISTOL COUNTY AGRICULTRAL SOCIETY. Transactions ... for ... 1852. ... *Boston.* 1853. 8vo, pp. vii, 71. Continued. H.

The Bristol County Almanac for 1852: containing a Sketch of each Town, County and Town Officers, and a Business Directory ... &c. Also Similar Information concerning Nantucket and Dukes Counties. *Boston: George Adams.* 1852. 32mo, pp. 116. H. 8058

BRISTOL COUNTY, *Mass.* Directory and Gazetteer for 1867-68. Compiled by Dudley & Greenough. *Boston: Dudley & Greenough.* 1867. 8vo, pp. 223, 84. C. 8059

Proceedings of a County Convention of Delegates from all the Towns in Bristol County, held at Taunton, October 11th, 1837, [for the nomination of Senators]. *New Bedford: Printed by J. C. Parmenter.* 1837. 8vo, pp. 16. 8060

BRISTOL ACADEMY. *See* Taunton, Mass.

BRISTOL COLLEGE. First Annual Catalogue of the Officers and Students of Bristol College, Bucks County, Pennsylvania. For ... 1834-35. *Philadelphia: Key & Biddle.* 1834. 8vo, pp. 23. B., C. 8061

BRISTOL AND CLIFTON LADIES' ANTI-SLAVERY SOCIETY. Special Report of the ... Society ... from January 1851 to June, 1852; with a Statement of the Reasons of its Separation from the British and Foreign Anti-Slavery Society. ... *London: John Snow. Bristol: W. Whereat.* 1852. 8vo, pp. 68. H. 8062

BRISTOL (T. W.) Lake Superior. *See* Houghton (J.)

Britain: A Poem, in Three Books. *Edinburgh.* 1757. 12mo. 8063

Contains a long note on Braddock's defeat, on page 15.

Britain and her Colonial Dependencies, 1844. *See* [Banister (T.)], Vol. I., No. 3169.

Britain Preserved. A Poem; in Seven Books [with Appendix of Notes]. *London: John Murray.* 1800. 8vo, pp. 376.

The author remarks: "The poem is supposed to commence at the first breaking out of the American commotions, and after describing the principal actions and events, to end about the year 1789, when the war was really finished." *See* M. R., XXXII. 302.

Britain's Mistakes in the Commencement and Conduct of the Present War. By a Merchant and Citizen of London. [*London:*] *T. Cooper.* M,DCC,XL. 8vo, pp. 62. BA. + *Dublin.* 1740.

Chiefly relating to America. *See also* "Supplement to Britain's Mistakes."

Britain's Remembrancer. Being Some Thoughts on the proper Improvement of the present Juncture. The Character of this Age and Nation. A brief View from History, of the Effects of the Vices which now prevail in Britain, upon the greatest Empires and States of former Times. Remarkable Deliverances this Nation has had in the most imminent Dangers: with Suitable Reflections. Some Hints, shewing what is in the Power of the Several Ranks of People, and of every Individual in Britain to do toward securing the State from all its Enemies. *and Sold by B. Franklin, at the New Printing-Office near the Market.* [1746.] Sm. 8vo, pp. 47. + The Sixth Edition. The Fifth Edition. *London: Printed. Philadelphia: Re-printed, London Printed. New York: Reprinted James Parker.* 1748. + The Seventh Edition. *Boston: Reprinted* 1759. 12mo, pp. 51. C., M. 8066

Britannia: A Poem, 1767. *See* [Gough (James)].

Britannia Americana. *See* [Oldmixon (John)].

Britannia and the Gods in Council; a Dramatic Poem on the present Disputes in Europe and America, and their issue Prophetically Determined. *London.* 1756. 4to. 8067

Britannia in Tears: An Elegy occasioned by the Dismission of the Right Honorable William Pitt, and H. Legge, Esqrs., &c. *London.* 1757. 4to. 8068

Britannia Libera, or a Defence of the Free State of Man in England, against the Claim of any Man there as a Slave. Inscribed and submited [*sic*] to the Jurisconsulti, and the Free People of England. ... *London: J. Almon.* M DCC LXXII. 4to, Title, pp. 47. H. 8069

Britannia Major: the New Scheme, or Essay for Discharging the Debts, Improving the Lands, and Enlarging the Trade, of the British Dominions in Europe and America. ... *London: J. Noon.* M.DCC.XXXII. 8vo, pp. viii, 70. H. 8070

Some copies are printed on thick paper.

Britanniæ Speculum; or, A Short View of the Ancient and Modern State of Great Britain, and the Adjacent Isles, and of all other Dominions and Territories now in actual possession of His present Sacred Majesty, King Charles II. *London.* MDCLXXXIII. 12mo. 8071

Britannia to America. [Hieroglyphic letter commencing] My dear Daughter ... [n. p. n. d.] Broadside. 8072

This letter is chiefly expressed and elucidated by emblematical figures of birds, fruits, flowers, instruments, utensils, etc.

Britannia Triumphans: Historical Account of Signal Naval Victories over the Spanish by Drake and others. 1577-1704. 1723. 8073

This and the following title are copied from a bookseller's catalogue, and are probably incorrect:

Britannia Triumphant; or, an Account of the Sea-Fights and Victories of the English Nation, under Drake, Raleigh, Hawke, Howe, Wolfe, &c. *London.* 1777. 8vo. Portraits. 8074

BRITANNICUS, *pseudon.* The Dominican Republic, and the Emperor Soulouque, being remarks and strictures on the misstatements, and a refutation of the calumnies, of M. d'Alaux, in the article under the above title, in the Revue des Deux Mondes; preceded by a concise account of the historical events of the Dominician Republic, and a glance at the peninsula of Samana. By Britannicus. *Philadelphia.* 1852. 8vo, pp. 72. 8075

Britannische ryk, 1741. *See* [Oldmixon (John)].

British Almanac of the Society for the Diffusion of Useful Knowledge; with the Companion to the Almanac, or Year-Book of general Information, for 1830. *London: Charles Knight.* 12mo. Continued. 8076

The Companions are clear and lucid recapitulations and abridgments of all the prominent occurrences of the times, colonial and foreign, as well as British.

British American Association and Nova Scotia Baronets. Report of the Action for Damages for Alleged Libel, Broun (*soi-disant*), Sir Richard, against the "Globe" Newspaper. [n. p.] 1846. 8vo. 8077

Seventy copies printed.

The British American Journal of Medical and Physical Science. Edited by Archibald Hall, M.D., University of McGill College. *Montreal.* 1845. 8vo and 4to. Continued. 8078

BRITISH AMERICAN LAND COMPANY. Emigration to Canada. The Eastern Townships of Lower Canada: An Account of the Peculiar Advantages they offer to Settlers; with Information for Emigrants. To which is appended a Map, Showing the Situa-

tion of the Lands now offered for Sale by the ... Company, and the Course of the Grand Trunk Railway ... . [*London.* 186-?] 16mo, pp. 15. Map. H. 8079

British American Magazine: devoted to Literature, Science, and Art. *Toronto, U. C.* 1863. 8vo. 8080

Minutes of the Proceedings of a Convention of Delegates from the British American League, held at Kingston [Canada West], on the 25th, and by adjournment on the 26th, 27th, 28th and 31st days of July, 1849. *Kingston.* 1849. 8vo, pp. 24. S.

British and American Liturgy: on Modern Politics and Patriotism. *See* Magapica (Magi).

BRITISH AND FOREIGN ANTI-SLAVERY SOCIETY. Annual Report, 1840. *London.* 1840. 8vo. Continued. 8082

Comercio de esclavos en la isla de Cuba. [*London.* 1855.] 8vo, pp. 8. H. 8083

Proceedings of the General Anti-Slavery Convention, called by the Committee of the British and Foreign Anti-Slavery Society, and held in London, from ... June 12th, to ... June 23rd, 1840. *London: British and Foreign Anti-Slavery Society.* 1841. 8vo, pp. xi, 597. H. 8084

Addresses from the Committee of the British and Foreign Anti-Slavery Society to the Women of England. [*London.* 185-?] 8vo, pp. 4. H. 8085

BRITISH AND FOREIGN FREED-MEN'S AID SOCIETY. ... Address. [*London. April,* 1866.] 4to, pp. (2). H. 8086

BRITISH AND NORTH AMERICAN MINING ASSOCIATION. ... Prospectus. *London.* [185-.] Sm. folio, pp. (3). H. 8087

British Barbarity and Piracy!! ... Facts Respecting the treatment of Americans by the commanders of British vessels of war, within the neutral waters of the empire of China, in 1807. [*Boston. March,* 1808.] Broadside. H. 8088

BRITISH COLUMBIA AND VANCOUVER'S ISLAND. A complete Hand-book. With a map. *London: William Penny.* [1858.] 8vo, 2 l., pp. 67. Map. C. 8089

Papers respecting the proposed Union of British Columbia and Vancouver's Island. *London.* 1866. Folio. 8090

This and the following are Parliamentary papers:

Further Papers respecting the union of British Columbia and Vancouver's Island. *London.* 1866. Folio. 8091

The British Columbia Gold Fields. Reprinted from "The Times." *London: Rixon and Arnold.* 1862. 8vo. 8092

British Columbia Mission, Occasional Paper. 1860. 8vo. Maps and Plates. 8093

Guide Book for British Columbia. The Wonders of the Gold Diggings of British Columbia, by a Successful Digger, who has made his Fortune there, and advises others to go and make theirs. *London: Dean.* 1862. 12mo. 8094

The Hand Book of British Columbia and Emigrant's Guide to the Gold Fields. With Map and Illustrations. *London: W. Oliver.* 1862. 12mo. 8095

British Colonial Slavery compared with that of Pagan Antiquity. *London.* 1830. 8vo. 8096

British Cruelty, Oppression, and Murder. *See* Hancock (John).

British Diplomacy in the River Plate. *London.* 1847. 8vo, pp. 56. 8097

The British Emigrant's Guide to the United States, with ample notices respecting various Trades and Professions. *London: C. Knight.* 1847. 18mo, pp. iv, 288. Plates. 8098

First published in 1840, as the "British Mechanic," etc. *See* No. 8111 *infra.*

The British Empire in America, consider'd. In a Second Letter, From a Gentleman of Barbadoes, to his Friend in London. *London: J. Wilford.* M.DCC.XXXII. 4to, Title, pp. 29. C. 8099

The British Empire in America, 1708, and 1741. *See* [Oldmixon (John)].

The British Fisheries. *London.* 1784. 8vo, pp. 60. 8100

National Committee of British Freed-Men's Aid Societies. Report of the Proceedings at the Meetings held ... May 17, 1865. ... *London: S. W. Partridge.* 1865. 8vo, Title, pp. 76.

BRITISH GUIANA. An Address to the Colonists of British Guiana, from a Member of the Court of Policy. *Demerary.* 1833. 4to. 8102

Privately printed.

Nya Sverige i Södra America, jemte Beskrifning om "British Guiana." Sammandrag af Humboldts, Hancocks, Schomburgk's Arbeten. *Stockholm: Fru Ortman.* 1841. 8vo. 8103

Observations on the Climate, Soil, and Productions of British Guiana. ... Second Edition. *London.* 1840. 8vo, pp. 92.

Dialogue or Conversation between a Planter and some Headmen on a Plantation in British Guiana, joined by the Minister and Schoolmaster. By a Well-wisher to the Labouring Classes and the Colony at Large. *Demerara.* 1848. 8vo. 8105

Memorial and other Documents regarding the present condition of the Catholic Church in British Guiana. *London.* 1841. 8vo. 8106

The British Hero, and Ignoble Poltron Contrasted: or, the Principal Actors in the Siege and Defence of Fort St. Phillip, and the Mediterranean Expedition, characterized. With some Strictures on the French Proceedings in America. An Ode. *London: Robinson.* 1756. 4to. 8107

See "Monthly Review," Vol. XV. 319.

The British Hero in Captivity. A Poem. *London: J. Robson.* 1782. 4to. 8108

"A compliment to the gallant Cornwallis, the unfortunate André, and the generous Arnold." — M. R., LXVI. 473.

BRITISH HONDURAS COMPANY. Proposals for the Establishment of Townships and Sale of Lands in British Honduras in Central America. [n. p. 185-?] 8vo, pp. 4. H. 8109

British Honour and Humanity; or, The Wonders of American Patience, As exemplified in the modest publications, and universal applause of Mr. William Cobbet; including a Variety of Anecdotes and Remarks, personal and political, and a survey of the modern State of American Newspapers: by a Friend to Regular Government. *Philadelphia: Robert Campbell.* 1796. 8vo, pp. 58. H., P. 8110

The British Mechanic, and Labourer's Hand Book and True Guide to the United States; with ample notices respecting various Trades and Professions. *London: C. Knight.* 1840. Rl. 18mo, pp. 292. 8111

Republished with the title given above. No. 8098.

British Military Biography, from Alfred to Wellington. *London: Scott & Co.* 1841. 18mo, pp. x, 638, 1 l. c. 8112

British North America. Copies or Extracts of Correspondence relative to the Affairs of British North America. (Presented by Her Majesty's Command.) Ordered, by the House of Commons, to be Printed, 11 February 1839. *London.* 1839. Folio, pp. iv, 400. (Parl. Acc. and Papers, Vol. XXXII.) 8113

British North America; comprising Canada, Columbia, Nova Scotia, Newfoundland, &c. *London: Religious Tract Society.* [n. d.] Fcap 8vo. Map. 8114

Further Correspondence respecting the proposed Union of the British North American Provinces. 1867. Folio. 8115

The British North American Almanac, and Annual Record for 1864. A Hand Book of Statistical and General Information. Edited by James Kirby, M.A. *Montreal.* 1864. 8vo, pp. 368. 8116

"The first American work of the kind relating to the British American Provinces." — *Albion, N. Y.*

British Opinions of the American Colonization Society. *Boston,* 1833. 12mo, pp. 36. 8117

British Opinions on the Protecting System; being a Reply to Strictures on that System ... From the North-American Review, January, 1830. *Boston.* 1830. 8vo, pp. 85. + Second Edition. *Boston.* 1830. 8vo, pp. 43. 8118

British Partizan. *See* [Moragne (*Miss*)].

British Philanthropy and Jamaica Distress. Reprinted from the "Westminster Review" of April 1st, 1853. [*London.* 1853.] 8vo, Title, pp. 37. H. 8119

The British Prize Ship. A Poem; with a Poem on the Death of Captain Biddle. *Philadelphia.* 1781. 12mo. 8120

British Relations with the Chinese Empire in 1832. Comparative Statement of the English and American Trade with India and Canton. *London.* 1832. 8vo. BM. 8121

The British Sailor's Discovery; or the Spanish Pretensions Confuted. Containing A short History of the Discoveries and Conquests of Spain in America, with a particular Account of the illegal and unchristian Means they made Use of to establish their

Settlements there; Proving that the sovereign sole Dominion, claimed by the Crown of Spain to the West-Indies, is founded upon an unjustifiable Possession; ... That America was discovered and planted by the antient Britons 300 years before Columbus conducted the Spaniards thither; ... Also The Declaration of War against Spain by Oliver Cromwell, in 1655, translated from the Latin Original; wherein the English Right to the West-Indies is plainly demonstrated, ... *London: T. Cooper.* 1739. 8vo, 2 l., pp. 72. 8122

Apparently written to excite the English nation against the Spaniards. Relates to the disputes between Spain and England about the limits of Georgia and Carolina. Perhaps the same as the "Proposal for humbling Spain," etc, published the same year.

The British Spy; or, Letters to a Member of the British Parliament, written during a Tour through the United States. By a Young Englishman of Rank. *Newburyport, Mass.: At the Repertory Office.* 1804. 12mo, pp. 105. W. 8123

British Sympathies in the American Crisis. By an Irishman. *Dublin: Porteous & Gibbs.* 1863. 12mo, pp. 15. 8124

BRITISH TEMPERANCE EMIGRATION SOCIETY. Description of the Wisconsin Territory and some of the States and Territories adjoining to it, in the Western Parts of the United States ... . Second Edition, enlarged. Published by the Committee of the British Temperance Emigration Society and Saving Fund. ... *Liverpool.* MDCCCXLIV. 12mo, pp. 48. H. 8125

The British Treaty. [n. p. n. d.] 8vo, pp. 86. BT. 8126

Page 3 commences, "To those members of Congress who have the sense to perceive, and the spirit to pursue the true interests of their country, this pamphlet is dedicated." Probably printed at Philadelphia in 1807. Reprinted with the following title:

The British Treaty with America. With an Appendix of State Papers; which are now first published. *America: Printed unknown where, or by whom sold. Reprinted for John Joseph Stockdale, London.* 1808. 8vo, pp. 147. S. 8127

The appendix contains Jay's Treaty, 1794; Letter from T. Jefferson, Sept. 5, 1793; His Majesty's Explanatory Notes of the new Treaty; and Mr. Merry's Letter.

British Treaty. Debates in the House of Representatives of the United States, during the First Session of the Fourth Congress, upon Questions Involved in the British Treaty of 1794. The Second Edition. *Philadelphia: William Duane.* 1808. 8vo, Part I., pp. 386; Part II., 362. P. 8128

The British West India Colonies in Connection with Slavery. *See* [Bourne (*Miss*)], No. 6925.

Das Brittische Reich in America. *See* [Oldmixon (John)].

BRITO (Bernard Gomes de). *See* Gomes de Brito (B.)

BRITO (F. T. de). Itinerario geographico, com a verdadeira descripçao dos caminhos, estrados, roças, sitios, povoaçoes, logares, villas, rios montes e serras, que ha da cidade de S. Sebastiao do Rio de Janeiro até ás Minas do ouro por Francisco Tavares de Brito. *Sevilha: Offic. de Antonio da Silva.* 1732. 8vo, pp. 26 or 76. 8129

A volume of great rarity. *See* Silva's Dic. bib. port., III. 72.

BRITO FREIRE. Nova|Lusitania,|historia da|guerra|Brasilica|a|purissima alma|e|savdosa memoria|do serenissimo principe|Dom Theodosio|principe de Portvgal,|e|principe do Brasil.|Por|Francisco de Brito Freyre.|Decada primeira.|*Lisboa|na officina de Joam Galram.*|*Anno* 1675.| Folio, engraved and printed title, 7 l., pp. 460. BT. 8130

Meusel, Vol. III., pt. 2, p. 58, seems to be puzzled by the name Freyre, but in the work itself (p. 105), mention is made of an Estevan de Brito Freyre, and of a Joano Machado de Brito, Senhor das Villas de Sanseris and Frieiras. This important work should be consulted for the history of the war between the Portuguese and Dutch. Ternaux, No. 917, remarks: "Ce volume très-rare et qu'Antonio n'avait jamais vu: car il dit en le citant, 'Olyssepone circiter annum 1667 prodiisse dicitur,' ne contient que la première décade; le premier livre rapporte l'histoire de la découverte du Brésil et des premiers établissemens qu'on y fonda; les neuf autres sont consacrés à l'histoire de la guerre contre les Hollandais de 1623 à 1638. Brito joua lui-même un rôle distingué dans cette guerre, car il commanda la flotte en 1655 et 1656." *See* Silva's Dic. Bibl., II. 361, where it is quoted at 3600 to 4000 reis. The following work is usually bound up with it:

BRITO FREIRE. Viage|da armada|Da companhia do|commercio, e frotas|do estado do Brasil.|A cargo do General|Francisco de Brito Freyre.|*Impressa|por mandado de|el rey|nosso|senhor.*|*Anno* 1655.| Folio, Title, 3 l., pp. 64, 20 l. BT. 8131

From the "Decreto," dated 1657, it is evidently printed at Lisbon. No mention is made of this work by Netscher in his "Hollandais du Brésil."

BRITO FREIRE. Relaçao da viagem que fez ao Brasil a armada da Companhia no anno de 1655, a cargo do general Francisco de Brito Freire. *Lisboa: por Henrique Valente de Oliveira.* 1657. 12mo. 8132

BRITO (Joao Rodgigues de). Cartas economico-politicas sobre agricultura e commercio da Bahia. Dadas à luz por I. A.

F. Benavides, etc. *Lisboa: Imp. Nacional.* 1821. 4to, pp. viii, 105. 8133

BRITO (J. Jose Rodrigues de). Memorias politicas sobre as verdadeiras bases de grandeza das naçoes de Portugal. *Lisboa.* 1803. 3 vols., 4to. 8134

BRITO (P. J. M. de). Memoria politica sobre a Capitania de Santa Catherina escripta no Rio de Janeiro em o anno de 1816 por Paulo Joze Miguel de Brito. *Lisboa: typ. de Acad. Real das Sisneros.* 1829. 4to. + 1832. 4to. 8135

Das Brittische Reich in America, Oder Kurzgefasste Beschreibung der Engländischen Pflanzstädte sammt ihrer Macht, Geschichte und Handlung in Nord-America, Nebst zuverlässiger Nachricht von den Gränzstreitigkeiten und Kriege mit Frankreich, durch eine sauber illuminirte Landkarte aller Engländischen Provinzen erläutert. *Sorau: Gottlob Hebold.* 1771. 4to, pp. 48. H. 8136

[BRITTON (John).] Sheridan and Kotzebue. The enterprising Adventures of Pizarro, preceded by a brief Sketch of the Voyages and Discoveries of Columbus and Cortez, &c. *London: Hurst, &c.* 1799. 8vo. 8137

BRIZARD (*l'Abbé* Gabriel). Fragment de Xénophon, nouvellement trouvé dans les ruines de Palmyre par un Anglais; traduit du Grec en Français. *Paris.* 1783. 24mo. 8138

"Cet ouvrage, qu'on pourrait prendre, d'après le titre pour être de Xénophon, n'est qu'une fiction originale de Gabr. Brizard sur la révolution d'Amérique. Sur un exemplaire envoyé à Mlle. Cosson, on a trouvé le clef suivante, écrite de la main de l'auteur: 'Thales,' Franklin. — 'Érugènes,' Vergennes. — 'Tangides,' D'Estaing. — 'Tusinonas,' Washington. — 'Fylaatête,' La Fayette. — 'Olybule,' Bouillé. — 'Cheramos,' Rochambeau. — 'Ucocide,' Couèdic. — 'Usanas,' le prince de Nassau. — 'Chéroiclète,' La Clocheterie. — 'Frusen,' Suffren. — 'Ubatomen,' le vicomte de Beaumont." — *Barbier.*

BROAD (A.) A Discourse, ... 13th September, 1814, to a Detachment of the United States Army at ... Brooklyn. By Amos Broad. *New York.* 1814. 12mo, pp. 16, (2). B. 8139

BROAD. The Trial of Amos Broad and his Wife, On three several Indictments for Assaulting and Beating Betty, a slave, and her little female child Sarah, aged three years. Had at the Court of Special Sessions of the Peace, held in and for the city and county of New-York, at the City Hall, the 28th day of February, 1808. ... *New-York: Printed by Henry C. Southwick.* 1809. 8vo, pp. 31. BA. 8140

BROADDUS (*Rev.* William F.) Centennial Sermon of the Potomac Baptist Association, of Virginia. [*Alexandria?*] 1867. 16mo, pp. 58. C. 8141

A Broadside for the Times. By E. Pluribus Unum. *New York: James O. Noyes.* 1861. 12mo, pp. 24. 8142

A "Broadside into Parker and the Politicians." Nos. 1, 2. [*Albany.* 1858.] S. 8143

Two separate broadsheets, printed on both sides, 19 inches by 11. Published by the Abolitionists, in behalf of Gerrit Smith, for Governor of New York.

The Broadway. *London and New York: Routledge.* 1867. 8vo. Continued. 8144

Broadway Journal. *New York City.* 1845. 2 vols., 4to.

Broadway Railroad. *Boston. June* 18, 1860. 8vo, pp. 8.

BROADWAY TABERNACLE ANTI-SLAVERY SOCIETY. Proceedings of a Meeting to form the ... Society ... . *New-York.* 1838. 18mo, pp. 42. 8147

BROADWELL (S.) An Appeal to ... Congress ... on ... Bank Tax and Bank Currency, by a Committee of New Jersey State Bank Officers. *Trenton, N. J.* 1864. 8vo, pp. 18. H.

BROCA (Philippe de). Étude sur l'industrie huitrière des États-Unis, faite par ordre de Son Exc. M. le ministre de la marine et des colonies, suivie de divers aperçus sur l'industrie de la glace en Amérique, les bateaux de pêche pourvus de glacières, les réserves flottantes à poissons, la pêche du maquereau, etc. *Paris: Challamel aîné.* 1863. + Nouvelle édition, augmentée de divers documents et de notes. *Paris: Challamel aîné.* 1864. 18mo.

BROCARDUS *or* BURCARDUS *and* ANGHIERA. Descri-|ptio terrae sanctae|exactissima, autore Brocardo Mona-|cho libellus diuinarum scriptura-|rum studiosis, multò|vtilissimus.|De Nouis Insulis nuper repertis, & de|moribus incolarum earundem, |per Petrum Martyrem|res lectu digna.|Antverpiae|In ædibus Ioannis Steelsii|Anno à Christo nato|M.D.XXXVI.|[Colophon:] *Typis Ioan Graphei.*|M.D.XXXVI.| Sm. 8vo, 48 l. J. C. B. 8150

Some copies lack the colophon. The extract from Peter Martyr commences on the 29th leaf. *See* "Bib. Am. Vet," pp. 125, 188, 351.

BROCCHUS (P. E.) Letter of Judge Brocchus to Hon. Daniel Webster, upon the Difficulties in the Territory of Utah. *Washington.* 1852. 8vo, pp. 14. H. 8151

BROCK (*Sir* Isaac). The Life and Correspondence of Major-Gen. Sir Isaac Brock, K.B.; interspersed with Notices of the celebrated Indian Chief Tecumseh, and comprising brief Memoirs of Daniel De Lisle Brock, Esq., Lieutenant E. W. Tupper, R.N., and Colonel W. De Vic Tupper. Edited by his Nephew, Ferdinand Brock Tupper, Esq. *Guernsey and London.* 1845. 12mo, pp. 480. + Second Edition. 1847. Post 8vo.

BROCK. Correspondence, Addresses, &c. connected with the Subscriptions of various Indian Tribes in Upper Canada, in aid of the funds for the Re-construction of Brock's Monument on Queenstown Heights. *Toronto.* 1841. 8vo, pp. 32. S. 8153

BROCK. Paper relating to the Reconstruction of the Monument of Major General Sir Isaac Brock. *London and Montreal.* 1839. 8vo. 8154

BROCKENBROUGH (W. H.) Virginia. *See* Martin (J.)

Also: Speech Upon the Course to be pursued in prosecuting the Mexican War. House ... May 11th, 1846. [*Washington.* 1846.] 8vo, pp. 8. H. + Speech ... on the Three Million Bill. ... In the House ... Feb. 13, 1817. *Washington.* 1847. 8vo, pp. 20. H.

BROCKETT. Grant and Colfax: their Lives and Services. By L. P. Brockett. *New York: C. B. Richardson & Co.* 1868. 12mo, pp. 136. Portraits and Maps. 8155

BROCKETT. The Great Rebellion; its History, Biography and Incidents. By L. P. Brockett, M.D. *Auburn: American Publishing Company.* 1865. 2 vols., 8vo. 8156

BROCKETT. The History of the Civil War. By L. P. Brockett, M.D. *Philadelphia: Jones & Brothers.* 1866. Rl. 8vo, pp. 1020. 8157

BROCKETT. The Life and Times of Abraham Lincoln, President of the United States. Including his Speeches, Messages, Inaugurals, Proclamations, etc. ... By L. P. Brockett, M.D. *Philadelphia: Bradley & Co.* 1865. 8vo. 8158

BROCKETT. Men of Our Day; or, Biographical Sketches of Patriots, Orators, Statesmen, Generals, etc. By L. P. Brockett. *Philadelphia: Zeigler, McCurdy & Co.* 1868. 8vo, pp. 653. Portraits. 8159

BROCKETT. Our Great Captains. Grant, Sherman, Thomas, Sheridan, and Farragut. By L. P. Brockett. *New York: C. B. Richardson.* 1866. 12mo, pp. 292. 8160

[BROCKETT.] The Philanthropic Results of the War in America. Collected from Official and other Authentic Sources. By an American Citizen. *New York: Sheldon & Co.* 1864. 18mo, pp. 160. C. 8161

BROCKETT *and* VAUGHAN. Woman's Work in the Civil War: a Record of Heroism, Patriotism and Patience. By L. P. Brockett, M.D. ... and Mrs. Mary C. Vaughan ... . With an Introduction, By Henry W. Bellows, D.D. ... *Philadelphia: Zeigler, McCurdy & Co. Boston: R. H. Curran.* 1867. 8vo, 2 l., pp. 21–799. 16 Engravings. B., BA., C. 8162

BROCKMANN (Karl). Amerikanische Kolonisation im Lichte des Geistes der Zukunft. *Hamburg: Meissner & Schirges.* 1861. 8vo, pp. 48. 8163

BROCKWAY (D.) A Sermon Preached at Hartford before the Honorable General Assembly of the State of Connecticut, on the Anniversary Election, May 11, 1815. By Diodate Brockway, A.M. ... *Hartford: Printed by Hudson and Goodwin.* 1815. 8vo, pp. 29. BA. 8164

BROCKWAY. A Missionary Sermon, delivered in Hartford. ... By Diodate Brockway. *Hartford.* 1812. 8vo, pp. 15.

BROCKWAY (J.) Mr. Brockway's Apology to the Rev. Nathan S. S. Beman, with the Facts in the Case. ... *Troy: the Author.* 1827. 8vo, pp. 55. 8166

BROCKWAY. A Delineation of the Characteristic Features of the Revival of Religion in Troy, in 1826 and 1827. By J. Brockway ... . *Troy: printed by Francis Adancourt.* 1827. 8vo, pp. 64. B. 8167

BROCKWAY (T.) America Saved; or Divine Glory Displayed in the late war with Great Britain. A Thanksgiving Sermon, preached in Lebanon. ... By Rev. Thomas Brockway, A.M. *Hartford.* [n. d.] 8vo, pp. 24. M. 8168

BROCKWAY. A Sermon delivered at the Ordination of the Rev. Bezaleel Pinneo ... in Milford, October 26th, 1796. By Thomas Brockway ... . *New-Haven.* M,DCC,XCVII. 8vo, pp. 30. H. 8169

BROCKWELL (C). Brotherly Love Recommended in a Sermon Preached before the Ancient and Honourable Society of Free and Accepted Masons, in Christ-Church, Boston, on Wed-

nesday, the 27th of December, 1749. By Charles Brockwell, A.M. His Majesty's Chaplain in Boston. Published at the request of the Society. *Boston, in New-England: Printed by John Draper, in Newbury Street.* M,DCC,L. 8vo, 2 l., pp. 7–21. M. 8170

BROCKWELL. The Political and Natural History of Portugal, from its first erection into a kingdom, anno 1090, to the present time. With the history of Brazil, and all other Dominions subject to Portugal, in Asia, Africa, and America. By Charles Brockwell, jr. *London.* 1726. 8vo, pp. 393, Index, 22. Maps and Plates. C. & P. 8171

BROCKWELL (Will.) Reisen Nach der neuentdeckten Insel St. Andreas. [Uebersetzt von Th. Fr. Ehrmann.] *Zittau: Schöps.* 1788. 8vo. 8172

BRODHEAD (J.) A Sermon preached in the Central Reformed Protestant Dutch Church, Brooklyn, ... the 27th day of July, 1851, by Jacob Brodhead, D.D. ... *Brooklyn.* 1851. 8vo, pp. 21, 3. S. 8173

Includes some historical data.

BRODHEAD (J. R.) An Address delivered before the New York Historical Society, at its Fortieth Anniversary, 20th November, 1844. With an Account of the subsequent Proceedings at the Dinner ... By John Romeyn Brodhead. *New York.* 1844. 8vo, pp. 107. 8174

Forms an appendix to Vol. II. of the "Proceedings of the New York Historical Society."

BRODHEAD. Addresses of John Romeyn Brodhead, Esq. and ... Gov. Horatio Seymour, delivered before the Clinton Hall Association, and Mercantile Library Association, at ... the Removal of the Library to Astor Place ... 8th June, 1854. With Reports then submitted. *New York.* 1854. 8vo, pp. 40.

BRODHEAD. [Final Report of the Agent of the State of New York, to Procure and Transcribe Documents in Europe, relative to the Colonial History of said State.] *Albany: E. Mack.* 1845. 8vo, pp. 374, Errata, 1 l. (Senate Doc. No. 47, 1845.) 8176

BRODHEAD. The Government of Sir Edmund Andros over New England, in 1688 and 1689. Read before the New York Historical Society ... 4th December, 1866. By John Romeyn Brodhead. *Morrisania, N. Y.* 1867. 8vo, 2 l., pp. 40. H.

BRODHEAD. The History of the State of New York. First Period, 1609–1664. By John Romeyn Brodhead. *New York: Harper & Brothers.* 1853. 8vo, pp. xv, 801. Map. H. + Second Edition. *New York: Harper & Bros.* 1859. 8vo, pp. xv, 801, Advertisement, 1 l. Map. H. 8178

Illustrated with a map of New Netherlands, according to the Charters granted by the States General, on the 11th of October, 1614, and the 3d of June, 1621. *See* "Westminister Review," New Series, III. 607.

BRODHEAD. Oration on the Conquest of New Netherland. Delivered before the New York Historical Society, Oct. 12, 1864. *New York.* 1864. 8179

See also New York State.

BRODHEAD (R.) Government of the Territories. Speech of Hon. Richard Brodhead, of Penn., in the House ... June 3, 1848 ... Upon ... Slavery in the Territories, and in Support of the ... Baltimore Convention ... . [*Washington.* 1848.] 8vo, pp. 7. H. 8180

Also: Speech ... on the Mexican War and the Wilmot Proviso. Delivered ... February 9, 1847. [n. p. n. d.] 8vo, pp. 16. + Speech ... on the Tariff Bill, containing allusions to our Relations with England and Mexico; Delivered in the House ... June 25; 1846. [*Washington.* 1846.] 8vo, pp. 16. H.

BRODIE (W.) Pitcairn's Island, and the Islanders, in 1850. By Walter Brodie. Together with Extracts from his Private Journal, and A Few Hints upon California. Also the Reports of all the Commanders of H. M. Ships that have touched at the above Island since 1800. *London: Whittaker & Co.* 1851. Post 8vo, pp. 260. Portrait. S. 8181

BRODIE (W.) Modern Slavery and the Slave Trade: a Lecture delivered at the Cheshunt Literary Scientific Institution. By the Rev. William Brodie, M.A., Curate of Cheshunt. *London: J. Hatchard & Son.* 1860. 8vo, Title, pp. 51. BA. 8182

BRODIGAN (Thomas). Botanical, Historical, and Practical Treatise on the Tobacco Plant. *London.* 1830. 8vo. 8183

BROECK (Van den). Journal|ofte|Historiaelse Beschrijvinge |Van Matheus vanden Broeck.|Van 't geen hy selfs ghesien ende waerachtigh ge-|beurt is, wegen 't begin ende Revolte van de Por-|tugese in Brasiel, als mede de conditie et het over-| gaen van de Forten aldaer.|*'tAmstelredam,*|*Voor Gerrit van Goedesbergen, Boeck-verkoo-|per op het water, by de nieuwe-brugh, inde Delfse Bybel. Anno* 1651.| Sm. 4to, pp. 40. Map, and 2 Plates. 8184

"Most curious and very rare." — NETSCHER.

BROGDEN (*Rev.* Wm.) Freedom and Love; A Sermon preached before the Ancient and Honourable Society of Free and Accepted Masons, in the Parish Church of St. Anne, in the City of Annapolis, on Wednesday, 27th Dec., 1749. By Rev. William Brogden. *Annapolis.* 1720. 4to, 10 leaves. 8185

BROGLIE (Achille L. V. C., *Duke* de). Cruautés de la traite des noirs, ou Relation des horreurs commises sur les nègres a bord des vaisseaux le Rodeur et l'Estelle: extraite du discours de M. le duc de Broglie, prononcé a la chambre des pairs le 28 mars 1822. ... By M. le duc de Broglie. [*Paris:*] *Henri Servier.* 1822. 12mo pp. 11. 8186

BROGLIE. Discours prononcée par M. Le duc de Broglie à la chambre des pairs le 28 mars 1822, sur la traite des Négres. [*Paris: L.-É. Herhan, imprimeur-stéréotype.* 1822.] 8vo, pp. 107. BA. 8187

BROGLIE. Le corps législatif, le Mexique et la Prusse. Par Albert de Broglie ... . *Paris: Douniol.* 8vo, pp. 16. 8188

Reprinted from the "Correspondant."

BROKAW (Abraham) *and others.* Reasons assigned by a Number of Ministers, Elders, and Deacons for declaring themselves the true Reformed Dutch Church in the United States of America. *Hackensack, N. J.: printed by John G. Spencer.* 1822. 12mo, pp. 19. B. 8189

[BROKESBY (Francis).] Some Proposals towards Promoting the Propagation of the Gospel in our American Plantations, Humbly offered in a Letter to Mr. Nelson, a worthy Member of the Society for Propagating the Gospel in Foreign Parts. To which is added a Postscript. *London: Printed for G. Sawbridge.* 1708. 4to, pp. 30. BD. 8190

BROME MINING COMPANY. Reports on the Prosperity of the Brome Mining Company, situated in Bedford County, Canada East. [n. p. n. d.] 8vo, pp. 16. H. 8191

BROMFIELD (J.) Reminiscences. *See* [Tracy (A.)]

BROMLEY (T.) The Way to the Sabbath of Rest, Or the Soul's Progress in the Work of the New-Birth. With Two discourses of the Author never before Printed viz. The Journeys of the Children of Israel, as in their Names and historical Pas-

sages, they comprise the great and gradual Work of Regeneration: And A Treatise of Extraordinary divine Dispensations, under the Jewish and Gospel Administrations. By Mr. Thomas Bromley. To which are added A Discourse on Mistakes concerning Religion, Enthusiasm, Experiences, &c. By Thomas Hartley Rector of Winwick. *London Printed. Germantown: Reprinted and sold by Christopher Sower, Also sold by Solomon Fussell and Jonathan Zane in Philadelphia.* 1759. 8vo, pp. viii, 280, 168. C. 8192

Usually followed by "A Discourse on Mistakes concerning Religion, Enthusiasm, Experiences, &c. By Thomas Hartley, A.M. *London Printed. Germantown: reprinted by Christopher Sower.* 1759;" and "Observations on the Inslaving of Negroes. 1760."

BROMLEY (Walter.) An Address delivered at the Free Mason's Hall, Halifax, August 3d, 1813. On the deplorable state of the Indians. *Halifax.* 1813. 8vo, pp. 16. 8193

BROMLEY. An Appeal to the Virtue and Good Sense of the Inhabitants of Great Britain, &c. In Behalf of the Indians of North America. By Walter Bromley. *Halifax.* 1820. 12mo, pp. 57. BA. 8194

The appendix contains letters to the author on the civilization of the Indians.

BROMLEY. Mr. Bromley's Second Address on the Deplorable State of the Indians, delivered in the Royal Acadian School, Halifax, Nova Scotia, March 8, 1814. *Halifax.* 1814. 16mo, pp. 53. M. 8195

BROMLEY. A Catechism of Geography; in Two Parts. *Halifax.* 1822. 8vo, pp. 132. 8196

BROMLEY. General Description of Nova Scotia. *Halifax.* 1825. 8vo. 8197

BROMLEY. Two Addresses on the Deplorable State of the Indians; one delivered at the Free-Masons' Hall, Aug. 3, 1813, the other at the Royal Acadian School, March 8, 1814, at Halifax in Nova-Scotia. By Walter Bromley, Late Paymaster of the 23d Regiment, Welch Fusiliers. *London: Published (for the benefit of the Indians) by T. Hamilton.* 1815. 12mo, pp. 71. 8198

BROMLEY (*Mrs.* Clara Fitzroy). A Woman's Wanderings in the Western World. A Series of Letters addressed to Sir Fitzroy Kelly, M.P. By his Daughter, Mrs. Bromley. *London: Saunders and Otley.* 1861. Post 8vo. Illustrations. C. 8199

BROMME (T.) Alabama und Mississippi, eine geograph.-statist.-topographische Skizze für Einwanderer und Freunde der Lander-und Volkerkunde. *Baltimore: Scheld und Compagnie.* 1838. 8vo. C. 8200

Extracted from his "Wohlfeile Hand-Bibliothek."

BROMME. Atlas zu A. von Humboldt's Kosmos in zwei und vierzig Tafeln, mit erläuternden Texte. Herausgegeben von Traugott Bromme. *Stuttgart: Krais und Hoffmann.* [1851–54.] Oblong folio, pp. 136. S. + Volksausgabe in 42 colorirten Tafeln. [*Ibid.*] 1861. Oblong folio, (Text) pp. 28. C. 8201

[BROMME.] Der freie Auswanderung als Mittel der Abhülfe der Noth im Vaterlande. Nebst Entwurf eines Planes zur Einrichtung einer deutschen Kolonisations-Gesellschaft. Von einem Sachsen. *Dresden: Walther.* 1831. 8vo. 8202

BROMME. Beiträge zur Topographien. Statistik der Vereinigten Staaten von Nord-Amerika. Erstes Bdchn. Mit 1 Postkarte der Vereinigten Staaten und 18 Nebenkärtchen. *Baltimore: Scheld und Comp.* 1836. 12mo. 8203

BROMME. Gemälde von Nord-Amerika in allen Beziehungen, von der Entdeckung an bis auf die neueste Zeit. Eine pittoreske Geographie für alle und ein umfassendes Reisehandbuch für Jene, welche in diesem Lande wandern wollen. *Stuttgart: Scheible, Rieger und Sattler.* 1842. 8vo. 75 Plates. 8204

First published with the title, "Des Universums neue Welt. Nord-Amerika, in allen Beziehungen geschildert. Zweiter Abdruck, zuglich Pendant zu Meyer's Universum. ... *Stuttgart: Scheible.* 1838–42. 8vo. Plates.

BROMME. Illinois und Missouri, Taschenbuch für Einwanderer und Freunde der Länder- und Volkerkunde. *Baltimore: Schele und Compagnie.* 1838. 8vo. Map. 8205

Extracted from his "Wohlfeile Hand-Bibliothek."

BROMME. Leitfaden für Auswanderer nach den Vereinigten Staaten von Nord-Amerika, Texas, Brasilien &c. Oder Wer soll und darf auswandern, wer nicht? Wie soll man auswandern? nebst Vorschriften für Einwanderer und einem Rathgeber in amerikanischen Rechtsangelegenheiten. *Bamberg: Buchner.* 1853. 8vo, 2 l., pp. 232. 8206

Extracted from the "Hand- und Reisebuch für Auswanderer."

BROMME. Louisiana. Ein Taschenbuch für Auswanderer und Freunde der Länder- und Völkerkunde. *Leipzig.* 1837. 8vo. 8207

BROMME. Michigan. Eine Geographisch-Statisch-Topographische Skizze für Einwanderer und Freunde der Länder und Völkerkunde. Von Tr. Bromme. *Baltimore, Md.* 1833. 8vo, pp. 91. Map. 8208

BROMME. Neuester Wegweiser für Auswanderer nach Amerika. Mit grosser Eisenbahn- Post- und Reise-Karte. *Stuttgart: Hoffmann.* 1852. 8vo, pp. 96. 8209

BROMME. Neuestes vollständigstes Hand- und Reisebuch fur Auswanderer aller Klassen und jeden Standes nach den Vereinigten Staaten von Nord-Amerika, Ober-und-Unter Canada, Neu-Braunschweig, Neu-Schottland und Texas. ... Herausgeben von Traugott Bromme. *Bayreuth.* 1840. 8vo. + Zweite vermehrte und verbesserte Auflage. ... *Bayreuth: Verlag der Buchner'schen Buchhandlung.* 1843. 8vo, Title, pp. iv, ii, 358. Map. BA. + Dritte ... Auflage. ... [*Ibid.*] 1845. 8vo. 8210

BROMME. Neuestes vollständigstes Hand- und Reisebuch für Auswanderer nach den Vereinigten Staaten von Nord-Amerika, mit einer Karte. *Bayreuth: Büchner.* 1843. 12mo, pp. 358. + Funfte Auflage. [*Ibid.*] 1848. 8vo, pp. xii, 555. Map by J. E. Worl. + Sechste ... Auflage. [*Ibid.*] 1850. 8vo, pp. xviii, 605. Map. + Siebente Auflage. *Bamberg.* 1853. 8vo. Map. + Siebente, sehr vermehrte und verbesserte Auflage von Büttner. Mit einem Rathgeber in Amerikanischen Rechtsangelegenheiten ... . *Bamberg: Buchner.* 1853. 8vo, pp. xiv, 744. Map. 8211

Apparently the later editions omit the words "Neuestes vollständigstes."

BROMME. Nordamerika's Bewohner, Schönheiten, und Naturschätze in Allgemeinen, und die Brittischen Besitzungen insbesondere. *Stuttgart: Scheible.* 1839. 8vo. S. 8212

BROMME. Nordamerika. *Stuttgart.* 1838–42. 16 pts., 8vo. 2 steel Engravings, and 87 other Plates. 8213

BROMME. Plan einer in Nord-Amerika zu gründern deutschen Kolonie. *Baltimore: Scheld & Comp.* 1834. 8vo. 8214

BROMME. Post-, Kanal- und Eisenbahnkarte der Vereinigten Staaten van Nord-Amerika. Nach Smith, Tanner, Mitchel und den Berichten des General-Postamts bearbeitet. In Stahl gestochen von J. A. Bühler. *Stuttgart: Hoffmann.* 1850. Folio, pp. 24. 8215

BROMME. Rathgeber für Auswanderungslustige. Wie und wohin sollen wir auswandern: nach den Vereinigten Staaten oder Britisch Nord-Amerika — nach dem Land jenseits der Felsengebirge oder dem Freistaat Texas — Santo Thomas oder die Musquitoküste — Sud-Amerika oder Westindien &c. oder ist es besser, unsere Kräfte den weniger kultivirten Theilen des deutschen Vaterlandes zu widmen? Eine umfassende Beleuchtung der bisherigen deutschen Auswanderung. Mit 17 Karten und Plänen. *Stuttgart: Hoffmann'sche Verlagsb.* 1846. 8vo.

BROMME. Reise durch die Florida's, von St. Augustine durch die Halbinsel nach Pensacola. *Leipzig.* 1837. 8vo. 8217

BROMME. Reisen durch die Vereinigten Staaten und Ober-Canada. *Leipzig.* 1834–35. 3 vols., 8vo. C. 8218

"Printed at Dresden, apparently for a German bookseller in Baltimore." — RICH, II. 265.

BROMME. Taschenbuch für Reisende in den Vereinigten Staaten von Nord-Amerika. *Leipzig: Einhorn.* 12mo. + *Baltimore.* 1836. 18mo. 8219

BROMME. Die Verfassungen der Vereinigten Staaten von Nord-Amerika, der Frei-Staaten Pennsylvania und Texas, der Königreiche Belgien und Norwegen, die Bundes-Verfassung der Schweiz und die Englische Staats-Verfassung. Zur Beantwortung der Frage: ob Republik, ob konstitutionelle Monarchie? Von Traugott Bromme. Zweite, mit der Staats-Verfassung Frankreichs und den Grundrechten des deutschen Volks nebst Einführungs-Gesetz vermehrte Aufl. *Stuttgart: Hoffmann'sche Verlags-Buchhandlung.* 1849. 8vo, pp. xiv, 206, 1 l. folded. H.

BROMME. Wegweiser für Einwanderer und Reisende in den Vereinigten Staaten von Nord Amerika und den Canadas. Eine genaue Zusammenstellung aller Eisenbahn-, Post-, und Dampfboot-Routen. Mit einer Karte entworfen von J. E. Woerl. *Bayreuth.* 1848. 8vo, pp. viii, 155. 8221

BROMME. Wohlfeile Hand-Bibliothek für Auswanderer nach den Vereinigten Staaten von Nord-Amerika und Freunde der Kunde fremder Welttheile. *Leipzig und Baltimore: Scheld und Compagnie.* 1838. 6 vols., 8vo. 3 Maps. 8222

BROMWELL (H. R.) The War in America. A Sermon. By Rev. H. R. Bromwell. *Congleton,* [*Englana*]. 1861. 12mo, pp. 15. 8223

[BROMWELL (William).] Locomotive Sketches, with Pen and Pencil, or, Hints and Suggestions to the Tourists over the Great Central Route from Philadelphia to Pittsburg. ... *Philadelphia: J. W. Moore.* 1854. 16mo, Half-Title, pp. 192. Map and Woodcuts. C. & H. 8224

BROMWELL. Off-hand Sketches; a Companion for the Tourist and Traveller over the Philadelphia, Pottsville and Reading railroad. *Philudelphia: J. W. M. Moore.* 1854. 16mo, pp. 194. C. 8225

BROMWELL (W. J.) History of Immigration to the United States; exhibiting the Number, Sex, Age, Occupation, and Country of Birth, of Passengers arriving in the United States by Sea from Foreign Countries, from September 30, 1819, to December 31, 1855: compiled entirely from Official Data; with an Introductory Review of the Progress and Extent of Immigration to the United States prior to 1819, and an Appendix containing the Neutralization and Passenger Laws of the United States, and Extracts from the Laws of the several States relative to Immigrants, the Importation of Paupers, Convicts, Lunatics, &c. By William J. Bromwell. *New York: Redfield.* 1856. 8vo, pp. (3), 12–225. BA., C. 8226

BRONSON (E.) An Inquiry into the Origin, Nature, and Object of the British Order in Council of May 16, 1806. First Published in the United States Gazette June 20, 1811. By E. Bronson. *Philadelphia.* 1811. Sm. 8vo, pp. 26. N. 8227

BRONSON (G. C.) Historical Sketches of the Board of Supervisors of the County of New York. By Hon. G. C. Bronson. *New York.* 1862. 8228

BRONSON. Report of the Select Committee, relative to the Conduct of Elam Lynds, late Keeper of the Sing Sing Prison. [n. p.] 1831. 8vo. B. 8229

BRONSON (H.) Biographical Notice of Prof. William Tully, M.D. By Henry Bronson, M.D. ... [n. p. 1859?] 8vo, pp. 7.

BRONSON. A Historical Account of Connecticut Currency, Continental Money, and the Finances of the Revolution. By Henry Bronson, M.D. ... [n. p. n. d.] 8vo, Half-Title, pp. iv, 192. C. & BA. 8231

Forms one of the "Papers of the New Haven Colony Historical Society. Vol. I. *New Haven.* 1865," but was apparently also issued separately.

BRONSON. The History of Waterbury, Connecticut; the Original Township embracing Present Watertown and Plymouth, and Parts of Oxford, Wolcott, Middlebury, Prospect and Naugatuck. With an Appendix of Biography, Genealogy and Statistick. By Henry Bronson, M.D. *Waterbury: Bronson Brothers.* 1858. 8vo, Title, pp. viii, (2), 582, Errata, 2 l., 2 Plans, 6 Views, 19 Portraits, 1 Plate of Facsimiles. C., H., S.

BRONSON (T.) ... A Sermon ... before the Convention of the ... Episcopal Church in the State of Connecticut, ... Stratford, on the Second Day of June, 1813: occasioned by the Death of the Right Rev. Abraham Jarvis, D.D. Bishop of Connecticut. By Tillotson Bronson ... . *New Haven: printed by Oliver Steele.* 1813. 8vo, pp. 19. B., N. 8233

BRONSON (W. W.) A Memorial of the Rev. Bird Wilson, D.D., LL.D. late Emeritus Professor of Systematic Divinity, in the General Theological Seminary of the Protestant Episcopal Church ... . By W. White Bronson. *Philadelphia: J. B. Lippincott & Co.* 1864. 12mo, pp. 212. Portrait. H. 8234

BROOK (B.) The Lives of the Puritans: containing a Biographical Account of those Divines who distinguished themselves in the cause of Religious Liberty, from the Reformation under Queen Elizabeth, to the Act of Uniformity, in 1662. By Benjamin Brook . ... *London: James Black.* 1813. 3 vols., 8vo, pp. xxviii, 452; viii, 507; xi, 556. C. & P. 8235

This and the following relate incidentally to the early settlers of New England.

BROOK. Memoir of the Life and Writings of Thomas Cartwright, B.D. the distinguished Puritan Reformer; including the principal Ecclesiastical Movements in the Reign of Queen Elizabeth. By the Rev. B. Brook. *London.* 1845. 8vo, pp. 496.

BROOK (J.) Fugitive Slave Laws. A compilation of the Laws of the United States and of States, in relation to Fugitives from Labor. By Jehiel Brooks. *Washington: Taylor & Maury.* 1860. 8vo, pp. 32. 8237

BROOK FARM ASSOCIATION. Constitution of the Brook Farm Association, for Industry and Education, West Roxbury, Mass. with an Introductory Statement. *Boston.* 1844. 8vo, pp. 12. 8238

BROOKE (C. W.) A Reply to the Communication, signed D. H. Mulvany, which appeared in the Norristown Free Press, by C. W. Brooke. *Norristown.* 1835. 8vo. P. 8239

BROOKE (F.) The History of Emily Montague. By Mrs. Frances Brooke. *London.* 1769. 4 vols., 12mo. 8240

This novel contains "A racy description of Canadian scenery, colonial courtships, and Quebec society in olden times." — *Brit. Can. Rev.*

BROOKE (*Mrs.* F. T.) A Narrative of my Life; for my Family. By Francis T. Brooke. ... *Richmond: the Writer.* 1849. 12mo, pp. 90. B. 8241

BROOKE (H.) Gustavus Vasa, the Deliverer of his Country. Inscrib'd to his Excellency General Washington, Commander in Chief of the Forces of the Thirteen United States of America. Written By Henry Brooke, Esq. ... *Philadelphia: Printed and Sold By Robert Bell.* M.DCC.LXXVIII. 8vo, pp. 88, Epilogue, 3 l.

BROOKE (H. K.) Annals of the Revolution: or, a History of the Doans. By H. K. Brooke. *Philadelphia: John B. Perry. New York: Nafis & Cornish.* [n. d.] 18mo, pp. 84. 8243

BROOKE (J. T.) Short Notes on the Dred Scott Case. By J. T. Brooke. *Cincinnati: Moore, Wilstach & Co.* 1861. 8vo, pp. 29. 8244

BROOKE (S.) Slavery, and the Slaveholder's Religion, as opposed to Christianity. By Samuel Brooke ... *Cincinnati: the Author.* 1846. 12mo, pp. 72. BA. 8245

BROOKES (R.) Brookes's Universal Gazetteer, remodelled and brought down to the Present Time. By John Marshall; with Numerous Additions by the American Editor, and the Population ... according to the Census of 1840. *Philadelphia: E. H. Butler.* 1843. 8vo, 2 l., pp. 9–816. B. 8246

BROOKFIELD, *Mass.* A Communication from the Brookfield Association to the Ecclesiastical Council who ordained Loammi Ives Hoadly over "The Calvinistic Society of Worcester," and Report of the Committee of the said Association ... . *Worcester: William Manning, Printer. Feb.* 1824. 8vo, pp. 24.

Report of the School Committee of the Town of Brookfield, for ... 1848–9. *Westbrookfield, Mass: Press of S. Oliver Cooke & Co.* 1849. 16mo, pp. 16. H. 8248

Decision of the Supreme Judicial Court of Massachusetts, in a Case relating to the Sacramental Furniture of a Church in Brookfield; with the Entire Arguments of Hon. Samuel Hoar, Jun. for the Plaintiff, and of Hon. Lewis Strong for the Defendant. *Boston: Peirce and Parker.* 1832. 8vo, pp. 48. BA., S.

Historical Sketch of the Baptist Church in Brookfield. [n. p. 1849 or 5–?] pp. 8. H. 8250

BROOKLINE. The Brookline, Jamaica Plain and West Roxbury Directory, for 1868 ... . Also, Business Directory, &c., ... of Dedham and Brighton. *Boston: Compiled, printed and published by Dudley & Greenough.* 1868. 12mo, Title, pp. 10–204, 68. Map. B. 8251

Answer to Certain Objections to incorporating the Brookline Horse Railroad Co. on the Petition of Wm. Aspinwall and Others. [*Boston.* 1857.] 8vo, pp. 13. H. 8252

By-Laws of the Town of Brookline, adopted March 8, 1847 ... . *Boston.* 1855. 8vo, pp. 12. + Additional By-Laws ... adopted June 3, 1857 ... . *Boston.* 1857. 8vo, pp. 4. H. 8253

History of the Baptist Church, Brookline, Mass. with ... a List of the Officers and Members. ... *Boston.* 1861. 16mo, pp. 39, (1). H. 8254

List of Taxes Assessed in the Town of Brookline. And the Names of the Tax Payers, for the Years 1851, 52, 53. *Boston: Printed by John Wilson and Son.* 1854. 8vo. + For ... 1854. *Boston.* 1855. 8vo, pp. 35. Continued. H. 8255

Report of a Committee of the Town of Brookline, on the Subject of New School-Houses, and their Location. *Boston.* 1853. 8vo, pp. 8. H. 8256

Report of Saint Paul's Church, Brookline, Mass. for the Parochial Year ending June 18, 1864. ... *Boston.* 1864. 16mo, pp. 20. H. 8257

Report of the Committee of the Town of Brookline for building a Road from the End of the Mill-Dam to Washington-Street. [n. p. 1853.] 8vo, pp. 8. H. 8258

Report of the School Committee of the Town of Brookline, March 2, 1840. *Boston.* 1840. 8vo, pp. 15. Continued. H.

Roads, &c. in the Town of Brookline. [n. p. 1844.] 12mo, pp. 12. H. 8260

Special Report of the Board of Trustees of the Brookline Public Library, upon the Library, Lot and Building. March 29, 1867. *Boston.* 1867. 8vo, pp. 10. H. 8261

The Treasurer's Report of the Receipts and Expenditures of the Town of Brookline for the Financial Year ending February 1, 1856. *Boston.* 1856. 8vo, pp. 28. Continued. H. 8262

BROOKLYN. Brooklyn and Long Island Fair in aid of the U. S. Sanitary Commission. *Brooklyn.* 1864. 12mo. 8263

Articles of Association, By-Laws, Rules and Regulations, of the Brooklyn Athenæum and Reading Room, ... *Brooklyn.* 1853. 12mo, pp. 20. + Annual Report, 1854, etc. 8vo. Continued. + A Catalogue of the Library of the Brooklyn Athenæum and Reading Room, with the Rules of the Library Committee. Nov. 1, 1853. *New York.* 1853. 8vo, pp. 64.

The Brooklyn City and Kings County Record: A Budget of General Information; with a Map of the City, An Almanac. And an appendix containing the New City Charter. *Brooklyn: William H. Smith.* 1855. 12mo, pp. 216, Charter, 71. 8265

Act of Incorporation, By-Laws and Catalogue of the Brooklyn City Library ... . *Brooklyn.* 1840. 8vo, pp. 80. H. 8266

The Brooklyn City Register for 1848. By S. H. Cornwell. *Brooklyn.* 1838. 18mo, pp. 203. 8267

Brooklyn Young Men's Christian Association. Report. *Brooklyn.* 1854. 8vo. Continued. 8268

Act of Incorporation of the Village of Brooklyn in the County of Kings. 1816. 8vo. N. 8269

An Act further to amend the Charter of the City of Brooklyn. Passed May 26. 1841. 12mo, pp. 4. 8270

An Act to amend "An Act to Revise and amend the Several Acts Relating to the City of Brooklyn, passed April 4, 1850." Passed June 19, 1851. 8vo, pp. 6. 8271

An Act to Consolidate and Amend the Act Entitled "An Act to incorporate the City of Brooklyn, passed April 8, 1834" and the various acts amendatory thereof. 1846. 8vo, pp. 96. 8272

An Act to Consolidate and Amend the Several Acts Relating to the City of Brooklyn. [n. p. n. d.] 8vo, pp, 16. 8273

An Act to Consolidate the Cities of Brooklyn and Williamsburgh and the Town of Bushwick into one Municipal Government, and to incorporate the Same. *Brooklyn.* 1854. 8vo. 8274

An Act to Incorporate and Vest Certain Powers in the Freeholders and Inhabitants of the Village of Brooklyn, in the County of Kings. *Brooklyn: Printed by A. Spooner.* 1816. 8vo, pp. 12.

An Act to Incorporate the City of Brooklyn. As reported To an Adjourned Meeting of the Freeholders and Inhabitants of the Village of Brooklyn, held on the 10th November, 1825. By the Committee, appointed to prepare the same. *Brooklyn: Printed by Alden Spooner. Nov.*, 1825. 8vo, pp. 32. 8276

"This proposed act was rejected by the people." — G. F.

An Act to Reduce the Law incorporating the Village of Brooklyn, and the Several Acts Amendatory thereof into One Act, and to amend the same. Passed April 3. 1827. *Brooklyn. Printed by A. Spooner.* 1827. 12mo, pp. 37. 8277

An Act to revise and amend the Several Acts Relating to the City of Brooklyn, passed Feb. 19. 1849. 1849. 8vo, pp. 48.

Acts and Ordinances of the City of Brooklyn. *Brooklyn.* 1836. 8vo. 8279

Acts relating to the City of Brooklyn and the ordinances thereof, together with an Appendix containing the Old Charters, Statistical Information, &c. *Brooklyn.* 1840. 8vo, pp. 282.

Annual Report of the Comptroller of the City of Brooklyn, to the Common Council. *Brooklyn, E. D.: Bishop & Kelley.* 1855. 8vo, pp. 111. Continued. 8281

The Battle of Brooklyn, a Farce; as it was performed on Long-Island, 27th of August, 1776. By the Representatives of the Tyrants of America, assembled at Philadelphia. *New York: J. Rivington, in the year of the rebellion.* 1776. 12mo, pp. 27. C.

Brooklyn City Hospital, and the Address of J. C. Hutchinson, M.D. ... *Brooklyn.* 1859. 8vo, pp. 39. 8283

Campaign Document No. 1, of the Central Union Club, of Brooklyn. *Brooklyn.* 1864. 8vo, pp. 16. H. 8284

Campaign Tracts. Published by the Brooklyn Daily Union. [1862.] 8285

No. 1. What our Generals Say. 8vo, pp. 3. 2. Facts which are now History. 8vo pp. 4. 3. What Sort of an Armistice the Rebels will accept. 8vo, pp. 4. 4. The Great Issues. 8vo, pp. 7.

Charter of the City of Brooklyn, and the Laws of the State of New-York relating to said City; with the Ordinances thereof, and an Appendix, containing the Old Charters, Statistical Information, etc. *Brooklyn.* 1846. 8vo, + Communication to the Legislature from the Minority of the Committee appointed to forward a Copy of the proposed New Charter for the City of Brooklyn. 1849. 8vo, pp. 4. + New Charter of the City of Brooklyn Passed April 4, 1850. 8vo. 8286

The Charter of the City of Brooklyn and the special laws relating thereto; together with the Ordinances for the government of the city. Published by order of the Common Council. *Brooklyn: George C. Bennett.* 1857. 8vo. 8287

This was prepared by Mr. Henry C. Murphy, to whom had been entrusted the draught of the original charter, as well as of the subsequent extensive amendments of 1862.

Charters and other Documents relating to the City of Brooklyn. [By Gabriel Furman, Esq.] *Brooklyn: John Douglass.* M DDCC XXXVI. [*sic*]. 8vo, pp. 62. Map. 8288

Directory. Spooner's Brooklyn Directory, for the Year 1822. *Brooklyn, N. Y.: Published by Alden Spooner.* 1822. 12mo, pp. 71. Woodcut Map. 8289

The first Brooklyn directory was published in 1822, and afterwards the publication continued annually for the years 1823 to 1826, and from 1829 to 1833. The city was incorporated in 1834, and the directory has been regularly continued since, and including that year. In the years 1827 and 1828 is was not published.

Explanatory Remarks to a Sectional Plan of Prospect Park, as Suggested by H. A Graef. *Brooklyn.* 1865. 8vo. 8290

Ferries. Memorial to the Legislature of the State of New York concerning the Ferries between New York and Long Island. 8vo, pp. 14. 8291

Also: The Law Papers & Documents relating to the Management of the old, or Fulton Ferry. *Brooklyn.* 1822. 8vo, pp. 80. — A Statement of Facts, ... in relation to the Steam Boat Ferries. *Brooklyn.* 1822. 8vo, pp. 45, (1). The question of a South Ferry to Long Island, stated and argued, in several papers originally published in the New-York American. By a Freeman. *New York.* 1826. 8vo, pp. 63. — All the proceedings in relation to the New South Ferry, between the cities of New York and Brooklyn, from Dec. 1825, to Jan. 1835. *New York.* 1835. 8vo, pp. 12. — Report made by order of the Common Council of the City of Brooklyn, on the

Water Line of that city. By J. G Swift, Engineer. 10th September, 1835. *Brooklyn.* 1835. 8vo, pp. 12. — Union Ferry Company of Brooklyn. Proceeding and Testimony and the Remarks thereon by Mr. Benj. D. Silliman, ... before the Committee of the Assembly. February, 1867. *Brooklyn.* 1867. 8vo, pp. 48. The ferry question is the subject of many pamphlets, to be found in the library of the Long Island Historical Society.

Financial Report of the City of Brooklyn, for the year ending the 28th day of February, 1847. *Brooklyn.* 1847. 4to, pp. 8.

History of the Brooklyn and Long Island Fair, Feb. 22, 1864. *Brooklyn: Union Press.* 1864. 8vo, pp. 189. 8294

Also, with folded plates, printed in colors. 4to, pp. 189. The fair was for the benefit of the United States Sanitary Commission.

A Law to revise and amend the several Acts relating to the City of Brooklyn ... . *Brooklyn.* 1848. 8vo, pp. viii, 5–72. H.

Laws in Relation to the Village of Brooklyn, compiled by order of the Trustees of said Village, May, 1826. *Brooklyn: Printed by Geo. L. Birch,* 110 *Fulton-street.* 1826. 8vo, pp. 27.

Laws and Ordinances of the City of Brooklyn, together with such General Laws of the State as affect the city in its Corporate Capacity. *New York.* 1865. 8vo. 8297

List of Persons Enrolled in Sixth, Ninth, Twelfth and Eighteenth Wards, Brooklyn, N. Y. [1863.] 8vo, pp. 162. 8298

This was the enrollment for the draft of 1863; others were published, but some only exist in manuscript, or the newspapers of the period.

Manual of the Plymouth Church, Brooklyn, L. I. Henry Ward Beecher, Pastor. ... *New York.* 1854. 8vo, pp. 55. Plate. 8299

Manual prepared for the use of the Brooklyn Common Council. ... *Brooklyn: E. B. Spooner, Printer.* 1855. 8vo, pp. 20. + Manual of the Brooklyn Common Council. Prepared by the City Clerk, by order of the Board. *Brooklyn: Bennett & Smith, Printers.* 1856. 12mo, pp. 35. + 1857. 18mo, pp. 108, (4), iii. + For 1858–9. Compiled by William G. Bishop, ... *Brooklyn,* 1858. 12mo, pp. 209. Map. + For 1859–60 ... *Brooklyn.* 1859. 12mo, pp. 375. Map. Continued. 8300

Since 1860, continued in octavo.

Manual of the Park Presbyterian Church of Brooklyn, N. Y. with a Brief Historical Sketch. *New York.* 1860. 24mo.

Memorial of the Revival in Plymouth Church, Brooklyn, [Rev. Henry Ward Beecher,] During the Early Part of the Year 1858: Comprising Incidents and Narratives, and also Fragments of Sermons, Lectures, etc., By the Pastor. By a Member of the Church. *New York: Clark, Austin & Smith.* 1859. 12mo, pp. 144. 8302

Memorial ... to the Legislature ... against ... An Act in relation to Local Assessments, 1858. 8vo, pp. 12. 8303

Mercantile Library Association of the City of Brooklyn. The First Annual Report of the Board of Directors ... January 13, 1859. *Brooklyn.* 1859. 8vo, pp. 38. H. Continued. + Catalogue of the Books in the Mercantile Library of the City of Brooklyn, N. Y. August, 1858. ... *Brooklyn.* 1858. Large 8vo, 2 l., pp. 138. H. + *Brooklyn.* 1859. 8vo, 3 l., pp. 138, 76. C.

Municipal Register. Members of the Common Council, Standing Committees and Officers, of the City of Brooklyn, for the Year 1853. ... . *Brooklyn.* 1853. 8vo, pp. 12. 8305

A Narrative of the Difficulties in the First Presbyterian Church of Brooklyn, N. Y., in the Years 1838, '39, '40. [n. p. n. d.] 8vo, pp. 38, xi. 8306

An Ordinance for the Preservation of the Public Health in the City of Brooklyn. Adopted Dec. 26. 1856. *Brooklyn.* 1857. 8vo. 8307

Ordinances of the Village of Brooklyn Passed in 1828. *Brooklyn.* 8vo. 8308

The Ordinances of the City of Brooklyn collected and indexed by Howard C. Cady: ... . *Brooklyn.* 1850. 8309

A Plain Statement of Matters affecting the Interests of St. Thomas' Church, Brooklyn, L. I. [n. p. 1853.] 8vo, pp. 32.

Proceedings at the Dinner given by the Citizens of Brooklyn to the Hon. Henry C. Murphy, on his Departure as Minister to the Netherlands. *Brooklyn.* 1857. 8vo, pp. 90. 8311

Proposed Act to Consolidate the Cities of Brooklyn and Williamsburgh and the town of Bushwick into one Municipal Government, to be known and called the City of Brooklyn. *Williamsburgh.* 1854. 4to, pp. 69. 8312

Prospect Park. Annual Report of the Commissioners of Prospect Park, January 28th, 1861. *Brooklyn.* 8vo, pp. 80. Plates. Continued. 8327

Prospectus of the Atlantic Dock Company. New York, August 1st, 1840. *New York.* 1840. 8vo, pp. 16. Map.

Remonstrance from the 8th and 9th Wards of the City of Brooklyn, on behalf of the people of said Wards against the proposed New Charter of said City. 1848. 8vo, pp. 16. 8315

Report of a Committee of the Board of Supervisors of the County of Kings, On the subject of a County Poor House, &c. Made March 28, 1829. *Brooklyn.* 1829. 8vo, pp. 12. 8316

Report of the Commissioners appointed under "an Act to provide for the opening of Washington Park, on Fort Green, in the City of Brooklyn," passed April 27th, 1847. *Brooklyn.* 1847. 8vo, pp. 13. 8317

St. Ann's Church, (Brooklyn, New York;) From the Year 1784 to the Year 1845; with a Memorial of the Sunday Schools. To which is added an Appendix, containing a brief Notice of the other Episcopal Churches in Brooklyn. By a Sunday School Teacher. *Brooklyn: F. G. Fish.* 1845. 12mo, pp. 220.

Statement and Appeal of the Trustees of St. Thomas's Church, Brooklyn. *New York.* 1853. 8vo, pp. 39. H. 8319

Suggested Outline of a Plan for a University in Brooklyn. [n. p. n. d.] Rl. 8vo, pp. 17. 8320

Printed for the use of the Committee of Ten.

Water. The Brooklyn Water Works and Sewers. A Descriptive Memoir. Prepared and Printed by Order of the Board of Water Commissioners. With 59 Lithographic Plates. *New York: D. Van Nostrand.* 1867. 4to, pp. xxvi, 160. C. 8321

Charter of the Nassau Water Company, Incorporated April 12, 1855, for the purpose of supplying the Consolidated City of Brooklyn with pure and wholesome Water. *Brooklyn: I. Van Anden's Steam Presses* 1855. 8vo, pp. 34. 8322

Charter of Incorporation of the Long Island Water Works Company. *Williamsburgh: Printed at the Office of the Independent Press.* 1853. 8vo, pp. 14. 8323

Documents and Plans submitted by the Water Committee to the Common Council of the City of Brooklyn, for the year 1854. *Brooklyn: Heighway & Co.* 1854. 4to, pp. 145. 27 Plates. C. 8324

Many other documents on the supply, etc., of water, are in the library of the Long Island Historical Society.

An Examination of the Water Question. ... *New York: Holman, Gray & Co., Printers.* MDCCCLIV. 18mo, pp. 20, 12, 32.

Report of Special Committee on Communication of Henry Ruggles to Supply the City with Water. October 2, 1854. *Brooklyn: I. Van Anden's Steam Press.* 1854. 8vo, pp. 13. 8326

Report of the Water Committee of the Common Council of the City of Brooklyn, and accompanying Documents, presented May 5th, 1856. *Brooklyn.* 1856. 8vo. 8327

And other reports. Also: Review of the New Water Documents, by a Citizen who Pays Taxes. ... A Candid Consideration of the whole Subject. *Brooklyn.* 1856. 8vo, pp. 15.—Answer to a Tax Payer. 8vo, pp. 8.—Tax Payer's Reply to "An Advocate for Water." 8vo, pp. 8.

Report of John S. Stoddard, City Surveyor, on the subject of Supplying Brooklyn with Water by the Well System. *Brooklyn.* 1854. 8vo, pp. 16. 8328

Report of the Standing Committee on Water, and Communications of W. J. M'Alpine and J. B. Jervis, Esqs. Engineers, on the subject of Water, for the City of Brooklyn. Presented December 22, 1851. *Brooklyn.* 1851. 8vo, pp. 24. 8329

Report of the Special Committee of the Common Council, on Supplying the City with Water. Presented December 20, 1847. *Brooklyn.* 1847. 8vo, pp. 139, (1). 8330

A Report on the Extent and Character of the District supplying Water to the City of Brooklyn. By Theodore Weston, C.E. With a Communication in relation to the same, from James P. Kirkwood ... . And an Analysis of the Water of the Jamaica Reservoir, by Prof. A. K. Eaton ... . *Brooklyn, N. Y.* 1861. 8vo, pp. 66, 1 l. folded. Map and Woodcuts. H. 8331

A Treatise relating to the Origin, History, and Present Position ... of the Williamsburgh Water Works Company; embracing an Outline of the various Acts passed for that Company; ... 1855. 8vo, pp. 62. 8332

The Water Question. Report of the Debate in the Common Council, on Monday Evening, January 31st, 1853. 8vo, pp. 12. 8333

Water for Brooklyn and Williamsburgh. A Visit to the Sources of Supply. ... . [n. p. n. d.] 8vo, pp. 4. 8334

Also, reports of the following, and other public institutions: Annual Report of the Health Officer, of the number of Deaths and their Causes, in the City of Brooklyn, during the Year 1851. ... *Brooklyn: E. B. Spooner, Printer.* 1852. 8vo.— ... Brooklyn Industrial School Association, and Home for Destitute Children. Established ... 1854. *Brooklyn.* 1854. Continued.— ... Brooklyn Female Employment Society, Established in 1854. *Brooklyn.* 1854. 8vo. Continued.— ... Nassau Water Department ... . January, 1863. ... *Brooklyn.* 1863. 8vo, pp. 132. H.—First Annual Report of the City Superintendent of Schools of the consolidated city of Brooklyn; for the Year ending January 31, 1856, together with other Documents ... . *Brooklyn.* 1856. 8vo, pp. 80. H.—Fire Marshal Almanac ... for 1859. *Brooklyn.* 18mo. Church Charity Foundation. 2d Report. *Brooklyn.* 1854. 12mo.—Report of the Committee on Public Health. *Brooklyn.* 1857. 8vo, pp. 35.—Report of the Brooklyn Association in aid of the Grande-Ligne Mission, for the Year Ending Dec. 18. 1861. *Brooklyn.* 1862. 8vo.

BROOKS (B. F. C.) Memphis; her Great Men; their Sayings Writings and Doings as Secession Leaders, Editors and Tools. Including an Interior View of Port Hudson, while occupied by the Rebels. By B. F. C. Brooks. *Memphis: Brooks & Co.* 1864. 8vo, pp. 86. 8335

BROOKS (C.) Address delivered in Oak-Grove Cemetry, Medford, Mass. September 6, 1866, at the Consecration of the Monument erected in Honor of the Medford Volunteers. By Charles Brooks. *Boston.* 1866. 8vo, pp. 14. H. 8336

BROOKS. History of the Town of Medford, Middlesex County, Massachusetts, from its First Settlement, in 1630, to the Present Time, 1855. By Charles Brooks. ... *Boston: James M. Usher.* 1855. 8vo, pp. viii, 576. BA., C., H. 8337

BROOKS. Some Reason for the Immediate Establishment of a National System of Education for the United States. By Charles Brooks. *New York: Loyal Publication Society.* 1865. 8vo, pp. 22. + Second Edition. *Boston: Press of John Wilson & Son.* 1869. 8vo, pp. 22. BA. 8338

BROOKS. The Tornado of 1851, in Medford, West Cambridge, and Waltham, Middlesex County, Mass. Being a Report by Rev. Charles Brooks, and Reports by other Committees. *Boston: J. M. Usher.* 1852. 18mo, pp. 72. H. 8339

BROOKS. A Statement of Facts from each Religious Denomination in New-England, respecting Ministers' Salaries. ... By Charles Brooks ... . *Boston: Crocker & Brewster,* [*etc.*] 1854, 8vo, pp. 24. H. 8340

Also: An Appeal to the Legislatures of the United States in relation to Public Schools. ... . *Cambridge.* 1867. 8vo, pp. 15. H.—A Discourse delivered in Cohasset ... October 13, 1835, at the Interment of the Rev. Jacob Flint, Pastor of the First Church ... . *Hingham: Jedediah Farmer.* 1835. 8vo, pp. 20. H.—Elementary Instruction. An Address delivered before the Schools and the Citizens of Quincy, July 4, 1837. *Quincy.* 1837. 8vo, pp. 20. BA.—A Lecture delivered before the American Institute of Instruction, at Montpelier, Vt., Aug. 16, 1849, on the Duties of Legislatures in relation to Public Schools in the United States. By Rev. Charles Brooks ... . *Boston: Ticknor, Reed, and Fields.* 1850. 12mo, Title, pp. 17. H.—Massachusetts Sanitary Survey. (From the Christian Examiner for May, 1851.) *Boston: Wm. Crosby & H. P. Nichols.* 1851. 8vo, pp. 22. H.—Remarks on Europe, relating to Education, Peace, and Labor; and their Reference to the United States. *New York: C. S. Francis and Company.* 1846. 8vo, pp. 42. H.—Memoir of John Brooks, Governor of the State of Massachusetts. ... . [n. p. 1865.] 8vo, pp. 7. Portrait. H.—Two Lectures: I. History of the Introduction of State Normal Schools in America. II. A Prospective System of National Education for the United States. ... . *Boston.* 1864. 8vo, pp. 25. H.

BROOKS (C. Timothy). Aquidneck. A Poem. Pronounced on the one hundredth Anniversary of the Incorporation of the Redwood Library, Newport, R. I., Aug. 24, 1847; with other commemorative pieces. By Rev. Charles T. Brooks. *Providence: C. Burnett, Jun.* 1848. 12mo, pp. 63. 8341

[BROOKS.] The Controversy touching the Old Stone Mill, in the Town of Newport, Rhode-Island. With Remarks, Introductory and Conclusive. *Newport: Charles E. Hammett, Jr.* MDCCCLI. 12mo, pp. 91, (1). Woodcut. H. 8342

Also: A Poem pronounced before the Phi Beta Kappa Society, at Cambridge, August 28, 1845. *Boston: Charles C. Little and James Brown.* 1845. 8vo, pp. 36. H.—Songs of Field and Flood. Printed for the Ladies' Fair at the Ocean House, Newport, August, 1853. *Boston: John Wilson & Son.* 1853. 8vo, pp. 47.

BROOKS (D.) The Religion of the Revolution. A Discourse, delivered at Derby, Conn., 1774; by David Brooks, A.M., upon the Causes that led to the Separation of the American Colonies from Great Britain, and the Establishment of a Free Government. *Rochester, N. Y.* 1854. 8vo, pp. 13. H.

BROOKS (E.) *and* LOWELL (J. A.) A Correspondence between Edward Brooks and John A. Lowell, with Remarks by Edward Brooks, referring to Documents annexed. *Boston.* 1847. 8vo, pp. 177, 72. H. 8344

A controversy on the administration of the Boott Estate.

BROOKS. An Answer to the Pamphlet of Mr. John A. Lowell, entitled "Reply to the Pamphlet recently circulated by Mr. Edward Brooks." With New Facts and Further Proofs. By Edward Brooks. *Boston.* 1851. 8vo, pp. xix, 836. H., S.

BROOKS (Erastus). The Twenty-ninth Congress, Its men and its measures; its professions and principles. What it has done for itself, what for the country, and what against the country. Being a review of the proceedings of the First Session ... . [*Washington.* 1846.] 8vo, pp. 16. BA. 8346

Also: Speech ... Feb. 7th, 8th, and 13th, 1855, The Lemmon Slave Case and Slavery—Secret Societies and Oaths—Grounds of Opposition to Mr. Seward—The Common Schools of New York ... [etc. n. p. n. d.] 8vo, pp. 15. BA.—Speech, at Hartford, Connecticut, July 8, 1856. Mr. Fillmore's Claims on northern men for the Presidency. [*New York.* 1856.] 8vo, pp. 16.—Speech on the Church Property Bill, N. Y. Senate [1855.] 8vo, pp. 11.—Speech ... April 6, 1857, upon the Trinity Church Bill. ... *Albany.* 1857. 8vo, pp. 44. And other speeches.

BROOKS *and* HUGHES. The Controversy between Senator Brooks and "† John," Archbishop of New York. Growing out of the Speech of Senator Brooks on the Church Property Bill. In the N. Y. State Senate, March 6th, 1855. Arranged for Publication, with an Introductory Preface by W. S. Tisdale. *New York: De Witt & Davenport.* [1855.] 8vo, pp. 81. 2 Portraits. H., S. 8347

BROOKS (J.) The Currency, its expansion. The Public Debt, the New National Banks. Speech of Hon. James Brooks, of New York, delivered in the H. of R., March 24, 1864. [n. p. n. d.] 8vo. 8348

Also: Col. Fremont's Romanism. Extracts from an Address before the People of Orange, N. J. [n. p. 1856.] 8vo, pp. 15.—Defence of President Fillmore before a Meeting of the American Party, held at Cincinnati, May 30, 1856. Reported by T. Shinkwin, of Cincinnati, ... [n. p. n. d.] 8vo, pp. 15. BA.—The Galphin Claim. Speech ... May 17, 1850 ... . [*Washington.* 1850.] 8vo, pp. 17. H.—How Massachusetts Reigns and has Reigned. Effect on Negro Race and on Slavery. Border State Co-operation. Cost of Massachusetts Government. ... February 19, 1864. *Washington.* 1864. 8vo, pp. 7.—Reciprocity discussed—Trade with England and her Colonies. Speech ... delivered in the House ... May 14, 1850. *Washington.* 1850. 8vo, pp. 8. H.—Speech ... Jan. 4, 1853, Cuban affairs: Reply to Mr. Polk. 8vo, pp. 6.—Speech ... on the Deficiency Bill. ... March 20, 1852. [n. p. n. d.] 8vo, pp. 15. H.—Report upon Coinage and Seignorage, ... *Washington, July* 29, 1852. 8vo, pp. 15. H.—Speech ... December 30, 1862. [*New York.* 1862.] 8vo, pp. 16.—Speech of ... April 19, 1864 [on the Tax Bill. n. p. n. d.] 8vo, pp. 8.—Speech ... on the President's Message, ... December, 1864. [n. p. n. d.] pp. 24.—Speech ... on the Deficiency Bill. *Washington.* 1852. 8vo, pp. 15.—The Two Proclamations. Speech ... before the Democratic Union Association, Sept. 29th, 1862. [n. p. n. d.] 8vo, pp. 8. And many other speeches in the "Congressional Globe."

BROOKS (J. H.) Subjection to Civil Rulers. The Christian's Duty. A Fast Day Sermon, preached April 30, 1863, at St. Louis. By Rev. James H. Brooks. *St. Louis: Sherman Spencer.* 1863. 8vo, pp. 16. 8349

BROOKS (J. T.) Four Months among the Goldfinders in Alta California; being the Diary of an Expedition from San Francisco to the Gold Districts. By J. Tyrwhitt Brooks, M.D. *London: David Bogue.* 1849. Post 8vo, pp. xviii, 207. Map. + Second Edition. *London.* 1849. Post 8vo, pp. xviii, 207. Map. + *New York: D. Appleton & Company.* M.DCCC.XLIX. 8vo, pp. 94. C., H. + *Paris: Galignani.* 1839. Rl. 8vo, pp. 136. Map.

The Paris edition includes Bryant's California.

BROOKS. Vier maanden onder de goudzoekers in Opper-Californie, of Dagboek eener expeditie van San Francisco naar de gouddistricten. Uit het Engelsch door G. Francken. *Amsterdam.* 1849. 8vo. Map. 8351

BROOKS. Vier Monate unter den Goldsuchern im Sacramento-Thale in Obercalifornien. Tagebuch von J. Tyrwhitt-Brooks ... . *Zürich.* 1849. 8vo, pp. 56. H. 8352

BROOKS. Vier Monate unter Goldfindern in Ober Kalifornien. Tagebuch einer Reise von San Francisco nach den Golddistricten. Deutsch von Fr. Gerstäcker. *Leipzig.* 1849. 8vo. Map. 8353

BROOKS (J.) Commonwealth of Massachusetts. [*Boston.* 1814.] 8vo. 8354

A report on certain proposed alterations in the militia system of the commonwealth, with the draft of a new bill for regulating, governing, and training the militia.

BROOKS. A Discourse delivered before the Humane Society of ... Massachusetts, 9th June, 1795. By John Brooks ... . *Boston: Printed by T. Fleet, Jun.* MDCCXCV. 4to, pp. 32. H., N.

BROOKS. An Eulogy, on General Washington; delivered before the Inhabitants of the Town of Medford, The 13th of January, 1800. By John Brooks, A.M. ... *Boston: Printed by Samuel Hall.* 1800. 8vo, pp. 15. BA., H., N. 8356

BROOKS. An Oration Delivered to the Society of the Cincinnati in the Commonwealth of Massachusetts, July 4th 1787.

By John Brooks, Esq. *Boston: Printed by Edmund Freeman.* ... M.DCC.LXXXVII. Sm. 4to, pp. 16. B.; H. 8357

Also: Message of His Excellency the Governor, to the Legislature of Massachusetts. *Boston.* 1823. 12mo, pp. 12. BA.; and other documents.

BROOKS (J. W.) Letters of John W. Brooks, Esq., Chairman of Commissioners of Troy & Greenfield Railroad, and Hoosac Tunnel, to Hon. Tappan Wentworth, Chairman of Legislative Committee. (Contained in Senate Doc. No. 289.) [n. p. 1866.] 8vo, pp. 36. H. 8358

BROOKS. The Pro Rata Question. What is the True Policy of the State of New York? Discussed by J. W. Brooks, Esq. *Albany.* 1860. 8vo, pp. 21. H. 8359

BROOKS (N. C.) A Complete History of the Mexican War: its Causes, Conduct, and Consequences: comprising an Account of the various Military and Naval Operations from its Commencement to the Treaty of Peace. Illustrated ... . By N. C. Brooks, A.M. ... *Philadelphia: Grigg, Elliot & Co. Baltimore: Hutchinson & Seebold.* 1849. 8vo, pp. xvi, 5-558. Maps, Portraits, etc. C., H. 8360

BROOKS. The History of the Church; a Poem. *Baltimore.* 1841. 18mo. 8361

BROOKS. Vitæ Virorum Illustrium Americæ Columbo ad Jacksonum: Notis Anglicis illustratæ, necnon Vocum Omnium Interpretatione instructæ. [Motto.] Auctore N. C. Brooks, LL.D. *Novi Eboraci: A. S. Barnes et Burr.* MDCCCLXIV. 12mo, pp. 356, Errata, 1 l. 8362

[BROOKS (P. C.) *and* DUTTON (Warren).] ... Report of the Special Joint Committee on the Subject of Warren Bridge. [*Boston.* 1835.] 8vo, pp. 34. (Senate, No. 58.) 8363

BROOKS (P.) The Life and Death of Abraham Lincoln. A Sermon, preached at ... Philadelphia .. April 23, 1865, by the Rev. Phillips Brooks. ... *Philadelphia: Henry B. Ashmead, Printer.* 1865. 8vo, pp. 24. H. 8364

BROOKS. Our Mercies of Re-Occupation, A Thanksgiving Sermon, preached at ... Philadelphia, November 26, 1863. By Phillips Brooks. *Philadelphia: William S & Alfred Martien.* 1863. 8vo, pp. 32. H. 8365

BROOKS (P. S.) Disunion Document, No. 1. Speech of Honorable Preston S. Brooks. Delivered at Columbia, South Carolina, Aug. 29, 1856. *Boston: John P. Jewett & Co.* 1856. 12mo, pp. 12. Portrait. H. 8366

BROOKS. National Politics. Speech of Hon. S. P. [*sic*] Brooks ... on resigning his Seat in Congress. ... In the House ... July 14, 1856. [*Washington.* 1856.] 8vo, pp. 4. H. 8367

[BROOKS (Seth).] A Plowman's Complaint against a Clergyman: being a letter to the Baptist Association at Philadelphia. Written by an alient Baptist Dissenter. [Motto.] *Philadelphia: printed for the Author.* MDCCLXVII. 8vo, pp. vii, 27. P. 8368

An account of the author's expulsion from the church at Cohansey.

BROOKS (T. H.) History of the Island of St. Domingo from its Discovery by the Portuguese to 1823. *London.* 1824. 8vo. Plates. 8369

BROOKS GUARDS. Constitution and By-Laws of the Brooks Guards. 1861. *Charleston: Presses of Evans and Cogswell.* 1861. 12mo, pp. 11. H. 8370

Brooksiana; or the Controversy between Senator Brooks and Archbishop Hughes, growing out of the recently enacted Church Property Bill, with an introduction by the most reverend Archbishop of New York. *New York.* 1855. 12mo, pp. 198. S.

See also No. 8347, *supra.*

BROOKSOP (J.) An | Invitation of Love | unto the | Seed of God, | Throughout the World. | With | a Word | To the Wise in Heart. | And a Lamentation | For New-England. | Given forth from the movings of the Spirit of the | Lord, by one who is known to the World by the | Name of | Jone Brooksop. | *London: Printed for Robert Wilson.* [1662.] 4to, pp. 15. 8372

BROOM (J.) Address delivered at Castle Garden, Feb. 22, 1854, before the Order of United Americans on the Occasion of their Celebration of the One hundred & twenty-second Anniversary of the Birthday of Washington, by Jacob Broom, Esq. ... *New York.* 1854. 8vo, pp. 19. S. 8373

Also: An Address pronounced before the Order of the United Sons of America, ... February, A.D. 1850. ... . *Philadelphia: Jones, Printer.* 1850. 8vo, pp. 19.—Defence of Americanism. ... August 4, 1856. [n. p. 1856.] 8vo, pp. 8. H.

BROOM (W. W.) An Englishman's Thoughts on the Crimes of the South, and the Recompense of the North. *New York: Loyal Publication Society, No.* 84. 1865. 8vo, pp. 24. 8374

[BROOM.] Great and Grave Questions for American Politicians, with a Topic for American Statesmen. By Eboracus. *Boston: Walker, Fuller & Co.* 1866. 8vo. pp. 122. 8375

[BROOM.] Abraham Lincoln's Character, Sketched by English Travellers. [n. p. n. d.] 8vo, pp. 4. 8376

BROOMALL (J. M.) National Currency. Speech of the Hon. J. M. Broomall ... in the House ... February 7, 1865. [*Washington, D. C.* 1865.] 8vo, pp. 16. H. 8377

BROOMALL. On the Reconstruction of the Rebel States. Speech ... in the House of Representatives, April 20, 1864. 8vo, pp. 16. 8378

BROOMALL. Reconstruction. Speech of Hon. J. M. Broomall, of Pa. ... in the House ... Jan. 8, 1867. [*Washington.* 1867.] 8vo, pp. 8. H. 8379

BROOMALL. Speech of Hon. J. M. Broomall of Pennsylvania on the Civil Rights Bill; delivered in the House of Representatives, March 8, 1866. *Washington.* 1866. 8vo, pp. 8.

BROOMALL. Speech of Hon. John M. Broomall ... on the Constitutional Amendment reported from the Joint Committee on Reconstruction ... in the House ... May 9, 1866. *Washington.* 1866. 8vo, pp. 7. H. 8381

BROOMALL *and* MOORHEAD (J. K.) Speeches of Hon. J. M. Broomall, and Hon. J. K. Moorhead ... in the House ... February 24, 1868, on the Resolutions ... for the Impeachment of the President. *Washington.* 1868. 8vo, pp. 7, (1). H. 8382

BROSIUS (N.) State of the Accounts of Nicholas Brosius, Esq. Collector of Excise, Berks County, from the time of his appointment, November 8th, 1783, to the 12th August, 1784. *Philadelphia: Printed by John Steele.* M,DC.,LXXXV. 8vo, pp. 7. P. + From August 1784, till August 1785. *Philadelphia: Printed by Robert Aitken.* M.DCC.LXXXVI. 8vo, pp. 4. P. 8383

BROSS (J. A.) Memorial of Colonel John A. Bross, Twenty-ninth U. S. Colored Troops, who fell in leading the Assault on Petersburg, July 30, 1864. Together with a Sermon by ... Arthur Swazey. By a Friend. *Chicago.* 1865. 8vo, pp. 80. Portrait. H. 8384

Bross (W.) Address of the Hon. William Bross, Lieutenant-Governor of Illinois, on the Resources of the Far West, and the Pacific Railway, before the Chamber of Commerce of the State of New-York at a Special Meeting ... January 25, 1866. *New-York.* 1866. 8vo, pp. 30. H. 8385

Also: Address before the Mechanics' Institute, at the Close of The Sixth Annual Fair, November 14th, 1853, ... *Chicago.* 1853. 8vo, pp. 30. H. — The Toronto & Georgian Bay Ship Canal. Reply to certain Queries of the ... Canal Committee of the Canadian Parliament. ... . *Chicago.* 1864. 8vo. H.

Bross *and* French (J. C.) America as a Field for the Exertions of the Christian Scholar. An Address delivered before the Alumni of Williams College by Hon. William Bross ... July 31, 1866. Song of the old Church at Williamstown: A Poem ... by Rev. J. Clement French ... . *Chicago.* 1866. 8vo, pp. 55. H. 8386

Brossard (A. de). Considérations historiques et politiques sur les republiques de La Plata, dans leurs rapports avec la France et l'Angleterre. Par Alph. de Brossard. *Paris: Guillaumin.* 1850. Rl. 8vo, pp. 470. 8387

Also: Étude sur le droit de visite. *Paris: Dentu.* 1842. 8vo.

[Brosses (Charles de).] Histoire des navigations aux Terres Australes Contenant ce que l'on sçait des mœurs & des productions des Contrées découvertes jusqu'à ce jour ... et des moyens d'y former un établissement. ... *Paris: Durand.* M. DCC. LVI. 2 vols., 4to, Title, pp. xiv, 463, (4); Title, 513, (1). 7 Maps.

Contains the voyages of Vespucius, Magellan, Drake, Sarmiento, Hawkins, De Nort, Spilberg, Nodal, Schouten, the Buccaneers, etc. The "Terra Australis Cognita," by Callandar, 3 vols., 8vo, is principally taken from this work.

Brosses. Vollständige Geschichte der Schiffarthen nach den ... Südländern. Aus dem Französischen übersetzt und mit Anmerkungen und Zusätzen von J. C. Adelung. *Halle: Gebauer.* 1767. 4to. Plates. 8389

Brother Jonathan: or, The New Englanders. *Edinburgh: William Blackwood. London: T. Cadell.* MDCCCXXV. 3 vols., post 8vo, 2 l., pp. 421; 2 l., pp. 451; 2 l., pp. 452. H. 8390

Brother Jonathan's Welcome to Kossuth. ... *See* Batchelder, Vol. I., No. 3905.

Brother Jonathan's Wife. A Lecture ... By a Retired Editor ... *Philadelphia.* 1842. 8vo, pp. 16. P. 8391

Brotherly Love: a Discourse. *Boston.* 1762. 12mo. 8392

Brother Mason, the Circuit Rider; or, Ten Years a Methodist Preacher. *Cincinnati: J. R. Hawley & Co.* 1869. 8vo, pp. 311. 8393

Brotherhead (W.) Autographi Holographiani. *Philadelphia.* 1857. Imp. 4to, pp. 19. 8394

Twenty-five copies privately printed. From the "American Notes and Queries," No. 3. *See* Vol. I., No. 1168, of this Dictionary.

Brotherhead. The Book of the Signers: containing Facsimile Letters of the Signers of the Declaration of Independence. Illustrated also with Sixty-one Engravings from original Photographs and Drawings, of their Residences, Portraits, &c. From the collections of an Association of American Antiquaries. Edited by William Brotherhead. *Philadelphia: William Brotherhead.* 1861. 4to, pp. viii, 114. C. 8395

Ninety-nine copies were printed in folio, on thick paper, with proof plates.

Brotherhead. General Fremont, and the Injustice done him by Politicians and Envious Military Men. By W. Brotherhead ... . *Philadelphia: W. Brotherhead.* 1862. C., H. 8396

A well-meant, but disjointed and ungrammatical performance.

Brothers (T.) Nineteen Numbers of the Radical Reformer, and Working Man's Advocate: a Philadelphia Weekly Publication, edited ... by Thomas Brothers: to which is appended, a Letter, to Mr. Daniel Webster, on his Speech in the Senate of the United States, asking Leave to bring in a Bill to continue, for Six Years, the Charter of the Bank of the United States. *Philadelphia.* 1836. 8vo, pp. vi, 304, 25. H. 8397

Brothers. The United States of North America as they are; not as they are generally described: being a Cure for Radicalism. ... By Thomas Brothers, resident in the United States Fifteen Years. *London: Longman* [etc.] 1840. 8vo, pp. v, 517. BA., C., H., P. 8398

Brouez (P.) Une Colonie belge dans l'Amérique Centrale; ou Relation du voyage et du sejour de M. P. Brouez à Santo Thomas de Guatemala. *Mons.* 1846. 8vo. 8399

Brough (J.) ... Dayton Speech of Hon. John Brough. President Lincoln's Response relative to the Arrest of Vallendigham. *Cincinnati: Moore, Wilstach, Keys & Co., Printers.* 1863. 8vo, pp. 31. 8400

Brough. The Defenders of the Country and its Enemies. The Chicago Platform dissected. Speech of Governor Brough, delivered at Cincinnati, Ohio, Sept. 3. From the Cincinnati Gazette, September 5, 1864. *Cincinnati.* 1864. 8vo, pp. 16.

Brough. Die Dayton Rede des Achtbaren John Brough. President Lincoln's Erwiderung in Bezug auf die Verhaftung Vallendigham. *Cincinnati: Moore, Wilstach & Co.* 1863. 8vo, pp. 31. 8402

Also: Speech ... at the Union Mass Meeting, Marietta, Ohio, June 10, 1863. [n. p. n. d.] 8vo, pp. 8; and sundry messages as Governor of Ohio to the Legislature.

Brough (W ?) On the danger of Emancipation of the Negroes. 1833. 8vo. 8403

Title from an English catalogue.

Brougham (Henry), *Baron Brougham and Vaux.* Appendix to the Concise Statement of the Question regarding the Abolition of the Slave Trade. *London.* 1804. 8vo. 8404

Brougham. Historical and Political Dissertations. By Henry, Lord Brougham ... . *London and Glasgow: Richard Griffin and Company.* 1857. 5 l., pp. 424. H. 8405

Contains "Foreign Relations of Great Britain," and "Right of Search."

Brougham. Historical Sketches of Statesmen who flourished in the Time of George III. To which is added, Remarks on Party, and an Appendix. First Series. || Second Series. || To which are added, Remarks on the French Revolution. Third Series. By Henry Lord Brougham, F.R.S. ... *London: Charles Knight and Co.* MDCCCXXXIX–MDCCCXLIII. 3 vols., 8vo, pp. viii, 404; xiv, (1), 334; ix, 1 l., pp. 406, (1). BA. + *London.* 1839–43. 6 vols., 18mo, pp. 238; 256; 210; 208; 240; 252. + *Paris: Baudry.* 1839. 8vo, pp. viii, 418. H. + *Philadelphia.* 1839–1844. 12mo. + New Edition. *London.* 1844. Rl. 8vo, pp. 418. + *Philadelphia.* 1854. + *London and Glasgow: Richard Griffin.* 1855. 3 vols., post 8vo, 3 l., pp. 442; iv, 497; iv, (2), 444. H. 8406

Contains biographies of George III, Lord Chatham, Lord North, Lord Mansfield, Mr. Burke, Mr. Fox, Mr. Pitt, Lord Grenville, and others.

Brougham. Esquisses historiques des hommes d'État du temps de Georges III, tracées par lord Brougham. Traduites de l'anglais et accompagnées de notices et de réflexions historiques, par Urbain Legeay. *Lyon: Périsse.* 1847. 8vo. 8407

Brougham. Immediate Emancipation. The Speech of Lord Brougham in the House of Lords ... February 20th, 1838, on Slavery and the Slave-Trade. ... *London: J. Haddon,* [*ana*] *G. Wightman.* [1818.] 12mo, pp. 24. H. 8408

Brougham. An Inquiry into the Colonial Policy of the European Powers. ... By Henry Brougham, Jun. ... . In Two Volumes. *Edinburgh: Printed by D. Willison, for E. Balfour, Hauners & Miller. London: T. N. Longman & O. Rees.* 1803. 2 vols., 8vo, 2 l., pp. 588; 3 l., pp. 588. C., P., H. 8409

The larger portion of this scarce work relates to America, and is said to have been written before the author was of age. It contains a resumé of the policy of the Spanish, English, French, and Colonial Governments.

Brougham. Lives of Men of Letters and Science who flourished in the Time of George III. By Henry Lord Brougham, F.R.S. ... With Portraits, engraved on Steel. *London: Charles Knight and Co.* 1845–46. 2 vols., 8vo, pp. xv, 516, (1); xi, (1), 516. + *Philadelphia: Lea & Blanchard.* 1839. 2 series, each in 2 vols., 12mo. BA. + New Edition. *London.* 1846. 8vo, pp. 522. 10 Portraits. + *Philadelphia.* 1848. 8410

Vol. II. has the imprint: *London: Henry Colburn.* 1846. Includes a "Life of Dr. B. Franklin."

Brougham. Lord Brougham's Speech upon the Ashburton Treaty, delivered in the House of Lords ... 7th April, 1843. *London: James Ridgway.* 1843. 8vo, Title, pp. 70. C., H.

Brougham. Opinions of Henry Brougham, upon Negro Slavery. *London.* 1826. 8vo, pp. 47. + *London.* 1830. 8vo, pp. 23. 8412

Brougham. Political Philosophy, By Henry, Lord Brougham, F.R.S. ... Part I. Principles of Government, Monarchical Government. Part II. Aristocracy, Aristocratic Government. Part III. Of Democracy, Mixed Monarchy. *London.* 1842–6. 3 vols., 8vo. + Second Edition. *London.* 1849. 3 vols., 8vo. + Third Edition. *London: H. G. Bohn.* 3 vols., 8vo, pp. xii, 665; xiv, 393; xix, 426. 8413

Brougham. Sketches of Public Characters, Discourses and Essays. ... By Henry Lord Brougham. ... *Philadelphia: E. L. Carey & A. Hart.* 1839. 2 vols., 12mo, pp. ix, 1 l., pp. 13–247; 252. BA. 8414

Vol. I. contains "Orders in Council," pp. 25–48; "Abolition of the Slave Trade," pp. 89–100.

Brougham. The Speech of Henry Brougham, Esq. Before the House of Commons, Friday, April 1, 1808, in support of the Petitions from London, Liverpool and Manchester, against the Orders in Council. Taken in short-hand by Mr. A. Fraser. *London: J. Ridgway.* 1808. 8vo, pp. 84. + *Philadelphia: Hopkins & Earle.* 1808. 8vo, pp. xiii, 65. + *London.* 1808. 8vo, pp. 103. + *Boston: Farrand, Mallory and Co.* 1808. 8vo, pp. xiii, 65. H. 8415

Brougham. Lord Brougham's Speech on the Maltreatment of the North American Colonies. *London.* 1838. 8vo. 8416

Brougham. The Speech of Henry Brougham, Esq., M.P. in the House of Commons, ... June, 1812. Upon the Present State of Commerce and Manufactures; ... *London.* 1812. 8vo, Title, pp. 59. + *Philadelphia.* 1812. 8vo. BA. 8417

Brougham. Speeches of Henry Lord Brougham, upon Questions relating to Public Rights, Duties and Interests, with Historical Introductions, and a Critical Dissertation upon the Eloquence of the Ancients. *Edinburgh.* 1838. 4 vols., 8vo. + *Philadelphia: Lea & Blanchard.* 1841. 2 vols., 8vo, pp. 631; Title, vii–618. H. 8418

Vols. II. and IV. contain speeches on the American Colonies, slave trade, etc.

Brougham. Speeches on Social and Political Subjects, with Historical Introductions. By Henry, Lord Brougham ... . *London and Glasgow: Richard Griffin and Company.* 1857. 2 vols., post 8vo, pp. x, 462; viii, 445. H. 8419

Vol. II. contains "Orders in Council," "The Slave Trade," "Negro Slavery," and "Emancipation of Negro Apprentices."

Brougham. Three Letters to Lord Brougham on the Execution in Upper Canada of the Traitors Lount and Matthews. By a British Subject. [From the London Times.] *London: John Murray.* [1838?] 8vo, pp. 18. C. 8420

Brougham (J.) ... An Original Aboriginal Erratic Operatic Semi-Civilized and Demi-Savage Extravaganza, being a Per-Version of Ye Trewe and Wonderrefulle Hystorie of Ye Rennowned Princesse, Po-ca-hon-tas: or, The Gentle Savage. In Two Acts. By John Brougham, Esq. ... *New York: Samuel French.* [185-.] 12mo, pp. 32. (French's American Drama, No. 28.) H. 8421

[Broughton (Arthur), *M.D.*] Hortus Castensis: or, A Catalogue of exotic Plants cultivated in the Botanic Gardens, in the Mountains of Linguanea, in the Island of Jamaica ... *St. Jago de la Vega.* 1794. 4to, pp. 35. 8422

Broughton (W. R.) A voyage of Discovery to the North Pacific Ocean: in which the Coast of Asia from the Lat. of 35° North to 52° North, the Island of Insu (commonly known under the Name of the Land of Jesso) the North, South, and East Coasts of Japan, the Lieuchieux and the Adjacent Isles, as well as the Coast of Corea, have been examined and surveyed. Performed in His Majesty's Sloop Providence and her Tender, in the Years 1795, 1796, 1797, 1798. By William Robert Broughton. *London: T. Cadell and W. Davies.* 1804. 4to, pp. xx, 393, (1). 9 Charts and Views. C. 8423

See "Monthly Review," LVII. 79.

Broughton. Voyage de découvertes dans la partie septentrionale de l'Océan pacifique, pendant les années 1795, 1796, 1797 et 1798. Traduit par J. R. B. Eyries. *Paris: Dentu.* 1807. 2 vols., 8vo. 6 Maps, and Plans. 8424

Broughton. Entdeckungsreise in das stille Meer, vorsiiglich nach der Nordostkuste von Asien 1795–98 aus dem Engl. *Weimar.* 1805. 4to. Map and Plate. 8425

Broughton. Broughton's Monthly Planet Reader, and Astrological Journal. 1860. 8vo. Continued. 8426

Contains the nativities of W. H. Seward, and other Americans.

Brouwer (Hendrick). Journael|Ende|Historis verhael van de|Reyse gedaen by Oosten de Straet le|Maire naer de Custen van Chili, onder|het beleyt van den Heer Generael|Hendrick Brouwer,|In den Jare 1643 voor gevallen,|Vervatende|Der Chilesen manieren, handel ende ghewoonten.|Als mede|Een beschryvinghe van het Eylandt Eso, ghelegen|ontrent dertigh Mylen van het machtigh Rijcke van|Japan, op de hooghte van 39 graden, 49 minu-|ten, Noorder breete; soo alst eerst in 't selvige jaer door het Schip Castri-|cum bezeylt is.|Alles door een Liefhebber uyt verscheyden Journalen ende|Schriften te samen gestelt, ende met eenighe|Kopere Platen verrijckt.|*Tot Amsterdam,*|*Gedruckt by Broer Jansz, woonende op de Nieu-zijds|Achter-burghwal, in de Silvere Kan.* Anno 1646.| 4to, pp. 104. 3 Plates. + *Tot Amsterdam,*|*Gedruckt by Jan I. Bouman Boeck-*

verkooper, woont op 't|Water, tegen over de Koorn-Marckt, inde Lelye onder de Doornen. [1660.]| 4to, 104. 3 Plates. 8427

Forms the twenty-fifth part of Hulsius' collection. The second imprint is merely a reissue. *See* Ternaux, No. 646; Muller, No. 826; Tiele, pp. 226, 227. There are translations in J. Burney's "Discoveries in the South Seas," Vol. III., and Churchill's "Collection of Voyages," Vol. I.

Brower (R. F.) ... Robert F. Brower, M.D. ... The Corner-Stone of Patriotism, Government, and Nationality, are the Only Practicable Basis for Restored Peace. ... *Danbury, Conn.* 1862. 8vo, Title, pp. 7. H. 8428

Brown (A. V.) Address of Ex.-Gov. Aaron V. Brown, before the Democratic Association of Nashville, June, 24, 1856. *Nashville: printed by G. C. Torbett and Company.* 8vo, pp. 22.

Brown. Agricultural Address of Ex.-Gov. Aaron V. Brown, at Knoxville, Tenn., October 1854. *Nashville.* [n. d.] 8vo, pp. 18. H. 8430

Brown *and others.* The New Jersey contested Election. To the People of the United States [of America: an address from A. V. Brown and others, members of the committee on elections of the House of Representatives. *Washington.* 1840]. 8vo. 8431

Brown. Speeches, Congressional and Political, and other Writings by Ex-Governor Aaron V. Brown of Tennessee. Collected and arranged by the editors of the Union and American. *Nashville, Tenn.* 1854. 8vo, pp. viii, 706. S. 8432

Also: Address delivered before the Two Literary Societies of the University of North Carolina, May 31st, 1854, ... *Raleigh: William C. Doub.* 1854. 8vo, pp. 27. H. — Speech ... on the Right of Members elected by General Ticket to their Seats. ... In the House ... February 9, 1844. *Washington.* 1844. 8vo, pp. 14. H. — Speech ... against receiving, referring, or reporting on Abolition Petitions. ... In the House ... January 10, 1844. *Washington.* 1844. 8vo, pp. 12. H.

Brown (A.) Genealogical History with Short Sketches and Family Records of the Early Settlers of West Simsbury, now Canton, Conn. By Abiel Brown, Esq., with an Introductory and Commendatory Notice by Rev. J. Burt. *Hartford: Press of Case, Tiffany & Co.* 1856. 8vo, pp. 151. 8433

Brown (A. G.) Address of Hon. Albert G. Brown, before the Members of the Legislature of the State of Mississippi, November 8, 1859. *Washington.* 1859. 8vo, pp. 15. H. 8434

Brown. Letter of Albert G. Brown to his Constituents. *Washington.* 1850. 8vo, pp. 8. BA. 8435

Brown. Speeches, Messages, and other Writings of Hon. Albert G. Brown, a Senator in Congress from the State of Mississippi. Edited by M. W. Cluskey ... . *Philadelphia: Jas. B. Smith.* 1859. 8vo, pp. 614. Portrait. H. 8436

Brown. State of the Country. Speech of Hon. A. G. Brown, of Mississippi; In the Confederate Senate, December 24, 1863. [n. p. n. d.] 8vo, pp. 16. 8437

Also: New Mexico and California. Speech ... in the House ... February 10, 1849, On the Proposition of Mr. Preston ... to admit New Mexico and California as a State, and in reply to Mr. Hunt on the general policy of the Administration. [*Washington.* 1849.] 8vo, pp. 7. H. — Relations with Great Britain. Speech ... in the Senate ... March 12–13, 1856 ... [on] the Three Million Appropriation Bill ... . [*Washington.* 1856.] 8vo, pp. 15. H. — Remarks ... on the Bounty Land Bill, and on the Distribution of Printed Documents. ... In the House ... May 8, 1848. *Washington.* 1848. 8vo, pp. 7. H. — Speech ... on the Homestead Bill, and in Vindication of the Policy of providing Homes for the Homeless on the Public Lands. ... [n. p. n. d.] 8vo, pp. 14. H. — Speech ... on the President's Veto Message, and in defence of ... a Grant of Land ... for the ... Indigent Insane. ... In the Senate ... May 17, 1854. *Washington.* 1854. 8vo, pp. 15. H. — Speech ... on the Bill to authorize the People of the Territory of Kansas to form a Constitution ... . On the Senate, April, 28, 1856 [*sic*]. *Washington.* 1856. 8vo, pp. 15. H. — Speech ... on the Slavery Question, ... in the Senate ... December 22, 1856. *Washington.* 1856. 8vo, pp. 30. H. — Speech ... at Hazlehurst ... 11th of September, 1858. [*Washington.* 1858.] 8vo, pp. 8. H. — Speech ... delivered at Crystal Springs, Copiah Co., Miss., September 6th, 1860. *Jackson, Mississippi.* 1860. 8vo, Title, pp. 8, (1). H. And other speeches.

Brown *and* Toombs. Remarks of Senators Brown and Toombs, on the Kansas Conference Bill. ... In the Senate ... April 29, 1858. [*Washington.* 1858.] 8vo, pp. 8. H. 8438

Brown (A. C.) Colony Commerce; or, Reflections on the Commercial System, as it respects the West-India Islands, our Continental Colonies & the United States of America: with some Remarks on the Present High Price of Sugar, and the Means of reducing it. By Alexander Campbell Brown. *London: R. Faulder, and W. and J. Stratford.* [n. d.] 8vo, pp. iv, 83. H. 8439

Brown (A. E.) Address before the American Whig and Cliosophic Societies of the College of New Jersey. June 23d, 1846. By Alexander E. Brown. *Princeton.* 1846. 8vo, pp. 30.

[Brown (A. M.) *and* Ewing (Thomas).] The Judicial Record of Hon. Henry W. Williams, of Allegheny, Candidate for Judge of the Supreme Court, of Pennsylvania, 1867. [n. p. n. d.] 8vo, pp. 8. H. 8441

[Brown (Alfred N.)] Brief Memorials of an Only Son [Alfred Marsh Brown], in a Letter to his Surviving Sister. ... *St. John's College Press.* [1846?] 16mo, pp. 70. H. 8442

Brown (A.) A Discourse delivered before the North-British Society, in Halifax, Nova-Scotia, at their Anniversary Meeting on the 30th of November, 1790. By Andrew Brown, D.D. *Halifax: printed by John Howe.* M.DCC.XCI. 8vo, pp. 20. 8443

Brown. The Perils of the Time, and the Purposes for which they are appointed. A Sermon preached On the last Sabbath of the Year, 1794 ... . By Andrew Brown, D.D. ... *Halifax: printed by Howe and M'Kinstry.* MDCCXCV. 8vo, pp. 40. 8444

Brown. A Sermon on the Dangers and Duties of the Seafaring Life; preached ... at Halifax ... *Boston.* 1793. 8vo, pp. 43. M., N. 8445

Brown. A Letter concerning Family History. By Andrew Brown. 1812. [*Printed at Albany by J. Munsell.* 1860.] pp. 12. 8446

Brown (A. W.) Sam's Fast, January 1, 1863. Awbron's Nationair. Song set for the day. Abe's Policy. Sambo's Call. New York, Dec. 1, 1862. By A. W. Brown, of East Rockport, Ohio. [n. p. n. d.] 8vo. pp. 15. 8447

Brown (A.) Laws of Antigua. By Anthony Brown. *London.* 1806. 8vo. 8448

Brown (A.) Oration at Brixton, July 4, 1808. By Asa Brown. *Portland.* 1808. 8vo. 8449

Brown (B.) An Address delivered before the Two Literary Societies of the University of North Carolina ... in June 1839. By Hon. Bedford Brown. ... *Raleigh, N. C.: Printed by T. Loring.* 1839. 8vo, pp. 39. H. 8450

Brown. Speech of Mr. Brown of North Carolina, on the bill imposing additional Duties, ... Delivered ... Feb. 23, 1838. *Washington.* 1838. 8vo, pp. 19. S. 8451

Brown (B. B.) Meteorological Observations for ... 1841, '2, '3, '4. By B. B. Brown ... . *St. Louis.* 1845. 8vo, pp. 8. 8452

Brown (B. G.) An Address of B. Gratz Brown, Esq. Slavery In its National Aspects as related to Peace and War.

Delivered ... at St. Louis ... September 17, 1862. [n. p. n. d.] 8vo, pp. 8. + (Second Edition.) [*Ibid.*] H. 8453

Also: Emancipation as a State Policy. Letter ... [dated St. Louis, May 30th, 1862. n. p. n. d.] 8vo, pp. 16. H. — Extracts from a Speech ... in the Missouri House of Representatives, Feb. 12, 1857. [*Philadelphia.* 1857.] 8vo, pp. 12. H. — Freedom and Franchise Inseparable. ... [*Washington. Dec.*, 1864.] 8vo, pp. 8. H. — Freedom for Missouri. Letter of ... Brown., [*sic*] to the "Weekly New Era," ... St. Joseph, Missouri. [Dated St. Louis, April 12, 1862. n. p. n. d.] 8vo, pp. 8. H. — Immediate Abolition of Slavery by Act of Congress ... March 8, 1864. *Washington.* 1864. 8vo, pp. 16. H. — Let us have Genuine Freedom in Missouri. *St. Louis, November* 15, 1864. 8vo, pp. 4. — Missouri should be included in the Proclamation. ... [n. p. n. d.] 8vo, pp. 4. H. — Oration ... at the Inauguration of Lyon Monument Association, in Jefferson City, Missouri, January 11, 1866. *Washington.* 1866. 8vo, pp. 12. H. — A Public Letter ... to the People of Missouri. [*Washington.* 1866.] 8vo, pp. 8. H. — The Reconstruction Measures Constitutional. Speech ... at ... Saginaw City Mich, Oct. 22d, 1868. [n. p. n. d.] 8vo, pp. 6. H. — Speech ... on ... Gradual Emancipation in Missouri. ... In the House ... February 12, 1857. *Saint Louis.* 1857. 8vo, pp. 26, (1). H. — Universal suffrage. An Address ... delivered at ... St. Louis, Mo., September 22, 1865. ... *St. Louis: Democrat Office.* 1865. 8vo, pp. 19. H.

Brown (C.) Remarks of Charles Brown ... on the Proposed Mission to Rome. ... In the House ... March 8, 1848. *Washington.* 1848. 8vo, pp. 8. H. 8454

Also: Remarks ... on the Pay of Navy Officers, and Whig Measures; also on the Bankrupt law and Military Academy. (Delivered in the House of Representatives. Feb. 3, 1843.) *Washington.* 1843. 8vo.

Brown (C.) A Narrative of the Expedition to South America, which sailed from England at the close of 1817, for the Service of the Spanish Patriots, &c. ... By C. Brown, late captain of the Venezuelan Brigade. *London: Booth.* 1819. 8vo. 8455

[Brown (Charles Brockden).] An Address to the Congress of the United States, on the Utility and Justice of Restrictions upon Foreign Commerce. With Reflections on Foreign Trade in general, and the Future Prospects of America. *Philadelphia.* 1809. 8vo, pp. 97. C. 8456

[Brown.] Address to the Government of the United States on the Cession of Louisiana. 1803. 8vo. 8457

Mr. Brown also edited "The Literary Magazine and American Register," 1803–1807, "American Register," 1806–1809, and is believed to be the author of "The British Treaty" (*see* No. 8126); and is also the author of "Arthur Merwyn," "Clara Howard," "Edgar Huntly," "Jane Talbot," "Ormond," and "Wieland," all novels of much originality, and which have often been reprinted. *See* "National Portrait Gallery," III. 8; Sparks' "Biog.," I. 117.

Brown (C. C.) Manifest of the Charges preferred to the Navy Department and subsequently to Congress, against Jesse Duncan Elliott, Esq., a Captain in the Navy of the U. S., for

unlawful conduct while Commodore of the late Mediterranean Squadron; and a refutation of the recrimination raised by that officer. By Charles Crillon Brown, U. S. Navy. [*Washington.*] 1839. 8vo, pp. 46, xxiv. 8458

Brown (C. H.) Insurrection at Magellan. Narrative of the imprisonment and escape of Capt. Chas. H. Brown from the Chilian Convicts. By Elizabeth H. Appleton. *Boston: Geo. C. Rand.* 1854. 12mo, 1 l., pp. 228. C. 8459

Brown (C. M.) A Brief Address to the Citizens of West Roxbury, prior to their Annual Meeting, 1858. By Charles M. Brown. *Boston.* 1858. 8vo, pp. 8. BA. 8460

Brown (Clark.) Remarks on the Doings and Result of an Ecclesiastical Council, Holden in Brimfield, From March 12, to March 18, 1801 ... . To which is added, The Rev. Mr. Brown's Request, For a Dismission ... . Also, a Statement of Facts, In a Letter, to a Member of the Council. *Boston.* 1801. 8vo, pp. 20. H. 8461

Also: A Sermon, preached at Wareham, March 31st, [1793,] ... *New Bedford: Printed by John Spooner.* 1793. 12mo? — Sermon at Northfield, Massachusetts, before Harmony Lodge, ... June 24, 1799. *Greenfield.* 1799. 8vo. — Sermon, June 24, 1808, at the Celebration of the Festival of St. John the Baptist, in Danville, Vermont. *Danville.* 1808. 8vo. — Sermon on the Annual Thanksgiving in this State. 1808. *Keene, N. H.* 1809. 8vo, pp. 27.

Brown (C. S.) Memoir of Rev. Abel Brown. *Worcester.* 1849. 12mo. 8462

[Brown (David Boyer).] Reply to Horace Binney on the Privilege of the Writ of Habeas Corpus under the Constitution. By a Member of the Philadelphia Bar. *Philadelphia: James Challen & Son.* 1862. 8vo, pp. 31. + Second Edition. *Philadelphia: James Challen & Son.* 1862. 8vo, pp. 31. H. 8463

Brown (*Mrs.* D. C.) Memoir of Rev. Lemuel Covell, and of his son Rev. Alanson L. Covell. *Brandon, Vt.* 1839. 2 vols. in 1, pp. 174; 226. C. 8464

Brown (D. P.) The Forum; or, Forty Years Full Practice at the Philadelphia Bar. By David Paul Brown. ... *Philadelphia.* 1856. 2 vols., 8vo, 3 l., pp. xi–588, 4 l. of Facsimiles of Autographs; Title, 521, (1). C., H. 8465

Brown. Abstract from David Paul Brown's Speech upon the Higher Law. [n. p. n. d.] Broadside. H. 8466

Also: Discourse before the Societies of St. Mary's College, Baltimore, ... July, 1848. ... *Baltimore.* 1848. 8vo, pp. 52. BA. — Eulogium upon Wilberforce;

with a Brief Incidental Review of the Subject of Colonization, delivered, at the Request of the Abolition Society, March 10. 1834. ... *Philadelphia: T. K. Collins & Co.* 1834. 8vo, pp. 40. — Eulogium upon William Rawle, LL.D. ... 31st of December, 1836. ... *Philadelphia: E. L. Carey & A. Hart.* 1837. 8vo, pp. 45, (1). H. First Speech, ... delivered in 1818, in the Case of the Commonwealth of Pennsylvania against John Binns, for Assault and Battery. ... *Philadelphia.* 1858. 8vo. pp. 30. H. — Oration before the First Troop of City Cavalry [giving a sketch of the History of the Troop]. ... *Philadelphia.* 1829. 8vo, pp. 24. P. — An Oration ... Before the Anti-Slavery Society of New York, on the Fourth of July, 1834, ... *Philadelphia: printed by T. K. Collins & Co.* 1834. 8vo, pp. 30. H. — Speech ... before the Mayor's Court of Philadelphia, September 17, 1825, on the subject of a Riot and Assault and Battery. Taken in Short-Hand, by M. T. C. Gould ... . *Philadelphia.* 1825. 8vo, pp. 38. H. — Speech ... before the Court of Sessions in New York, upon the Trial of Dr. Frost for Manslaughter. December 13, 1837. *Philadelphia.* 1859. 8vo, pp. 51. H. — Speech in the Case of Hinchman *vs.* Ritchie, *et al.* ... Sixth of April ... 1849. *Philadelphia.* 1849. 8vo, pp. 66. H.

Brown (D. S.) America in Fifty Hours; India and Back in a Fortnight: being Suggestions for certain Improvements in the Construction of Steam Vessels. By D. S. Brown. *London.* 1852. 8vo. 8467

Brown (Edward). Notes on the Origin and Necessity of Slavery. ... *Charleston: printed by A. E. Miller.* 1826. 8vo, pp. 48. H. 8468

Brown (E.) Sermon preached at the Ordination of Rev. Mr. Zedekiah Sanger ... in Duxbury, July 3d, 1776. By Elijah Brown, A.M. ... *Boston: Printed by T. and J. Fleet.* 1776. 8vo, pp. 34. 8469

Brown (F.) Sermon delivered July 23, 1812, on the State Fast appointed in Consequence of the Declaration of War against Great Britain. By Francis Brown, D.D. *Portland.* 1812. 8vo, pp. 32. 8470

Also: A Sermon delivered before the Maine Missionary Society ... in Gorham, June 22, 1814. *Hallowell.* 1814. 8vo, pp. 32. — A Fast Sermon ... at North-Yarmouth, April 7, 1814 ... . *Portland.* 1814. 8vo, pp. 27. — A Sermon ... at Concord ... June 3, 1818, before the Convention of Congregational and Presbyterian Ministers ... . *Concord,* [*N. H.*] 1818. 8vo, Title, pp. 25. H.

Brown (F. H.) Roll of Students of Harvard University who served in the Army or Navy of the United States during the War of the Rebellion. Prepared by order of the Corporation. By Francis H. Brown, M.D. *Cambridge: Welch, Bigelow & Co.* 1866. 8vo, pp. 47. H. 8471

Brown (F. G.) Oration delivered by F. G. Brown, before the Enosinian Society of the Columbian College, D. C., July 4th, 1835. *Washington.* 1835. 8vo. C. 8472

Brown (F. T.) An Address delivered in the Central Presbyterian Church, Chicago, July 4th, 1865, by the Pastor, Rev. Frederick T. Brown, D.D. *Chicago: Jameson & Morse, Printers.* 1865. 8vo, pp. 24. 8473

Brown. A Sermon: Giving Thanks for Union Victories, preached [at] Georgetown, D. C. August 6th, 1863, by the Pastor, Frederick T. Brown. ... *Washington: Polkinhorn, Printer.* 8vo, pp. 15. 8474

Brown (*Hon.* G.) The American War and Slavery. A Speech of the Hon. George Brown, at the Anniversary Meeting of the Anti-Slavery Society of Canada, held at Toronto ... February 3, 1863. *Manchester, Eng.: Union and Emancipation Society.* 1863. Sm. 8vo, pp. 16. BA. 8475

Brown (G.) An Obituary Memoir of Robert F. Mott; read before Two Literary Societies to which he belonged, and published at their Joint Request. By Goold Brown. *New York: Samuel Wood & Sons.* 1827. 8vo, pp. 32. 8476

Brown (*Rev.* G.) Recollections of Itinerant Life. By Rev. George Brown, D.D. *Cincinnati.* 1867. 12mo, pp. 456. Portrait. 8477

[Brown (George).] Paläorama. Oceanisch-amerikanische Untersuchungen und Aufklärungen. Mit wesentlicher Berücksichtigung der biblischen Urgeschichten. Aus dem Nachlasse eines amerikanischen Alterthumsforschers. *Erlangen: Eduard Besold.* 1868. 8vo, pp. vi, 530. 8478

Brown (G. H.) Groton Junction Post Office. ... [Dated April 15, 1863. Circumstances attending his Removal from the Post Office and Subsequent Restoration. n. p. n. d.] Broadside. H. 8479

Brown (G. W.) The Origin and Growth of Civil Liberty in Maryland. A Discourse delivered by Geo. Wm. Brown, before the Maryland Historical Society. Baltimore, April 12, 1850, being the Fifth Annual Address to that Association. *Baltimore: Printed by John D. Toy.* 1850. 8vo, pp. 40. C. 8480

Brown (G. W.) *and* Brune (F. W.) In the Court of Appeals The Mayor and City Council of Baltimore ... and Others, Appellants *vs.* Charles Howard ... And Others, Appellees. Appeal from An Order of the Circuit Court for Baltimore City,

Refusing to Grant an Injunction. Reply of Geo. Wm. Brown and Frederick W. Brune, Counsel for ... Appellees ... . *Balt.:* [1863?] 8vo, Title, pp. 20. H. 8481

A suit growing out of the suspension of the Police Commissioners of Baltimore by President Lincoln, June 27, 1861.

Brown. The Old World and the New. An Address delivered by George Wm. Brown ... . Rutgers College, New Jersey, 22d July, 1851. *New York.* 1851. 8vo, pp. 44. BA. 8482

Also: Statement of facts relative to the purchase of property from George W. Brown et al. With the opinion of the Supreme Court. Also the answers filed by the defendants. *Philadelphia.* 1854. 8vo.

Brown (H.) A Narrative of the Anti-Masoick Excitement, in the Western Part of the State of New-York, during the Years 1826, '7, '8, and a part of 1829. By Henry Brown, Esq. Counsellor at Law. *Batavia, N. Y.: Printed by Adams & M'Cleary.* 1829. 12mo, 4 l., pp. 244. BA., C., S. 8483

Brown. The History of Illinois from its First Discovery and Settlement, to the Present Time. By Henry Brown. *New-York: J. Winchester.* MDCCCXLIV. 8vo, pp. x, 492. Map. 8484

Brown (H. S.) ... Speech by Harvey S. Brown ... . California and the Democracy. [*San Francisco.* 1860.] 8vo, pp. 8. 8485

Brown (H. S.) The Pilgrim Fathers: a Lecture by the Rev. Hugh Stowell Brown ... October 25 & 27, 1853, Illustrative of the Government Prize Picture, by Charles Lucy, The Departure of the Pilgrim Fathers, (A.D. 1620.) *Manchester: Thomas Agnew and Sons.* 4to, pp. 46. Plate. H. 8486

Brown (H. S.) An Anti-Slavery State Convention proposed! [Signed H. S. Brown. Milwaukee, Wis. March 22d 1864. n. p. n. d.] 8vo, pp. 4. H. 8487

Brown (H.) A Review of Rev. Dr. Raphael's Discourse on American Slavery as being consistent with the Hebrew Servitude of the Old Testament. A Sermon preached in the Baptist Church, Shusham, March 27, 1861. By Rev. Hugh Brown ... *North White Creek, N. Y.: R. K. Crocker.* 1861. 8vo, pp. 39. 8488

Brown (Ignatus). History of Indianapolis, from 1818 to 1868. *Indianapolis: Logan & Co.* 8vo, pp. 100. 8489

With "Indianapolis Directory," 1868.

Brown (I. V.) Biography of the Rev. Robert Finley, D.D., of Basking-Ridge, N. J. 2d edition, enlarged, with an account

of his agency as the author of the American Colonization Society. Also a Sketch of the Slave Trade, a view of our national policy and that of Great Britain towards Liberia and Africa. With an appendix. By Rev. Isaac V. Brown. *Philadelphia: J. W. Moore.* 1857. 12mo, pp. 336. S. 8490

Brown. A Historical Vindication of the Abrogation of the Plan of Union by the Presbyterian Church in the United States of America. By Rev. Isaac V. Brown. *Philadelphia: W. S. & A. Martien.* 1855. 8vo, pp. 325. C. 8491

Brown. Memoirs of the Rev. Robert Finley, D.D. late Pastor of the Presbyterian Congregation at Basking Ridge, New-Jersey, and President of Franklin College, located at Athens, in the State of Georgia. With Brief Sketches of some of his Cotemporaries, and Numerous Notes. By the Rev. Isaac V. Brown, A.M. *New-Brunswick: Terhune & Letson.* 1819. 8vo, pp. 370, (Errata) 1 slip. Portrait. BA. 8492

Brown. Slavery Irreconcilable with Christianity and Sound Reason; or, an Anti-Slavery Argument. By Rev. Isaac V. Brown, D.D. *New York: Charles Scott & Co.* 1858. 8vo. 8493

Brown (J. F.) Brown's Almanac. 1857. Fitchburg Almanac, Directory and Advertiser. *Fitchburg: Shepley & Wallace.* 18mo, pp. 69. BA. 8494

Brown (J. S.) Catalogue showing the Subject or Title of Every Patent granted by the U. S. Government, Prior to the year 1855; and the Number issued under each Title. By J. S. Brown, A.M. *Washington.* 1855. 8vo, pp. 19. H. 8495

Brown (J.) True Loyalty in a Citizen is Fidelity to his State. By Jacob Brown. [Addressed to Andrew Johnson. *London: Privately Printed.*] 8vo, pp. 20. H. 8496

Brown (J.) The Claim or Title of Mr. James Brown, to a certain Tract or Gore of Land being the Westermost Part of the Lands granted, by the General Assembly of the Colony of Connecticut, to the Proprietors of New Fairfield, etc., stated and vindicated. *New Haven: Printed by B. Mecon.* M.DCC.LXV. 8vo, pp. 32. N. 8497

Brown (J.) The Restitution of all things: an Essay on the important purpose of the Universal Redeemer's Destination. By James Brown, Chaplain of the British Garrison at Savannah in Georgia. 1785. 8vo. 8498

Brown (J.) The Golden Wedding of Col. James Brown and Wife, at Framingham, Mass., Nov. 4, 1857. ... *Holliston: E. G. Plimpton, Printer.* 1857. 8vo, pp. 59. H. 8499

Brown (J.) Third Essay. New Brunswick, as a Home for Emigrants: with the Best means of promoting Immigration, and developing the Resources of the Province. By Hon. James Brown ... *Saint John.* 1860. 16mo, pp. 21. H. 8500

Brown (J. B.) Views of Canada and the Colonists, embracing the Experience of an Eight Years' Residence; Views of the Present State, Progress, and Prospects of the Colony; with detailed and practical Information for intending Emigrants. By James Brown. *Edinburgh.* 1851. Fcap 8vo. + Second Edition. Corrected throughout and greatly enlarged. *Edinburgh.* MDCCCLI. Fcap 8vo. C., S. 8501

Brown (James D.) The Arcade Hotel Guide ... [to] Philadelphia ... . By J. D. Brown, Proprietor Arcade Hotel. *Philadelphia.* 1856. 24mo, Title, pp. 34. H. + [*Id.*] 1857. 24mo, pp. 34, 3 l. H. + [*Id.*] 1859. 18mo, pp. 32. 8502

Brown (James M.) *See* Penn (W.)

B[rown] (J.) The Merchants' Avizo, very necessary for their Sonnes and Servants when they send them beyond the Sea. *London.* 1616. 4to. 8503

Included in an English catalogue of Americana.

Brown (John), *of Hingham.* A Discourse Delivered at the West Church in Boston, August 24, 1766. Six Weeks after the Death of The Reverend Dr. Mayhew. By John Browne A.M. ... *Boston: Printed by R. and S. Draper.* ... 1766. 8vo, pp. 19, 3. 8504

[Brown.] The Examiner examin'd. Or, An Answer to The Rev. Mr. Prescott's Examination of Certain Remarks On ... a Letter relating to the Divisions of the first Church in Salem. ... By the Author of the Remarks. ... *Boston: Printed by T. Fleet.* 1726. 8vo, 2 l., pp. 105, (1). B. 8505

Brown (*Rev.* John). ... A Funeral Sermon Preached At Bedford, Oct. 31. 1725. Some time after the Death Of the Reverend Mr. Thomas Symmes, Pastor ... there ... with A ... Large ... Account of Him ... . By John Brown ... . *Boston: S. Gerrish.* 1726. 8vo, 2 l., pp. 70. C., H. 8506

Also: In what Sense the Heart is Deceitful and Wicked. A Discourse. ... *Boston: Fowle.* 1754. 12mo, pp. 22. N. — Our Great King to be served with our Best. A

Sermon delivered At the Lecture in Newbury-Newtown, Feb. 27. 1727, 8. ... Preparatory to the Lord's Supper. ... *Boston: Samuel Gerrish.* M. DCC. XXIX. 2 l., pp. 23. B. — A Sermon, preached at Arundel, at Ordination of Rev. Thomas Prentice. *Boston.* 1731. 16mo, pp. 30. — Solemn Covenanting with God, one of the best means to prevent fatal Declensions. A Discourse, before the Public Renewal of Covenant in Haverhill On the ... General Fast: March 21. 1727, 8. ... . *Boston: Samuel Gerrish.* M, DCC, XXVIII. 8vo, 2 l., pp. 35. B.

BROWN (John), *of Newcastle.* Sermon at St. Paul's Cathedral on occasion of the Brief for the Establishment of the Colleges of Philadelphia and New York, To which is prefixed an Address to the Principal Inhabitants of the North American Colonies, on occasion of the Peace. By John Brown, Vicar of Newcastle. *London.* 1763. 4to. S. 8507

BROWN (J. H. Hobart). Sermon preached at the Burial of Thomas Powell, Esq., of Newburgh, N. Y. By Rev. J. H. Hobart Brown, Rector ... *Newburgh, N. Y.* 1856. 8vo, pp. 12.

BROWN (John), *of Haddington.* The Christian ... Exemplified; In the Lives of ... Thomas Shepherd, Cotton Mather, and Jonathan Edwards, in America. *Edinburgh.* M.DCC.LXXXI. 12mo, pp. 295. 8509

BROWN. Compendious History of the British Churches in England, Scotland, Ireland, and America. ... *Glasgow.* 1784. 2 vols., 12mo, pp. viii, 340; 368. + *Edinburgh.* 1823. 2 vols., 8vo, pp. xxii, 418; vii, 439. C., S. 8510

BROWN. The Self Interpreting Bible. *New York: Hodge and Campbell.* 1792. Folio, 22 l., A to 8A², Apocrapha, A to TI, New Test. A to 3X²; not paged. 18 Plates. 8511

"This is the earliest edition of the Bible composed and printed in the State of New York." — O'CALLAGHAN.

BROWN (John). Batavia, as delineated in the Intercepted Letters on board the Lisette, with Observations of the Admiralty Prize Courts, and the Justice and Expediency of conciliating the American States By J. Brown, Merchant. *London.* 1812. 8vo. 8512

BROWN. The Mysteries of Neutralization; or, the British Navy Vindicated from the Charges of Injustice and Oppression towards Neutral Flags. By John Brown, of Great Yarmouth. *London: Jordan & Maxwell.* 1806. 8vo, pp. iv, 156. G. 8513

BROWN. Veluti in Speculum; or, A Scene in the High Court of Admiralty: Displaying the Frauds of Neutral Flags,

as Exemplified in the Case of the Silenus, With Remarks on The Prosecution for Libel instituted against the Author by Admiral Montagu. The Application of His Majesty's Licences: Forged American Certificates: Injustice towards Neutrals: and Danger of His Majesty's Dock-Yards. Addressed to Ministers and Parliament. By John Brown, ... *London: Jordan and Maxwell.* 1807. 8vo, pp. 101. G. 8514

"War in Disguise," and "The Danger of the Country," two tracts relating to the War of 1812, are often attributed to this author, but are more probably by Sir John Stephen.

BROWN (John). Select Remains. *Pittsburg, Penn.* 1810. 12mo. W. 8515

BROWN (John). Slave Life in Georgia; being a Narrative of the Life, Sufferings, Adventures, and Surprising Escape from Slavery, of John Brown, a Fugitive Slave, now in England. Edited by L. A. Chamerovzow. *London.* 1855. 12mo. 8516

BROWN (John). The North-West Passage and the Plans for the Search for Sir John Franklin. A Review, with Maps, &c. By John Brown, F.R.G.S. *London: E. Stanford.* 1858. 8vo. + Second Edition, with a Sequel, including the Voyage of the "Fox." *London: Published by E. Stanford.* 1860. 8vo, Half-Title, pp. xiii, 463, 64. BA., C. 8517

BROWN (John). The John Brown Invasion an Authentic History of the Harper's Ferry Tragedy with Full Details of the Capture, Trial, and Execution of the Invaders, and of all the Incidents connected therewith. ... *Boston: James Campbell.* 1860. 8vo, pp. 112. 8518

BROWN. Life, Trial, and Execution of Captain John Brown, known as "Old Brown, of Ossawatomie," with a full account of the attempted Insurrection at Harper's Ferry. Compiled from official and authentic sources, including Cook's Confession, and all the incidents of the Execution. *New York: Robert M. De Witt.* [1859.] 8vo, pp. 108. 8519

BROWN. Sklavenleben in Amerika: oder wunderbare Lebensschicksale eines auf britisches Gebiet entkommenen, ehemaligen Negersklaven, Names John Brown. Nach dessen eigenen Worten deutsch wiedererzählt sowie mit einer Einleitung über den dermaligen Stand der Sklaven-Frage versehen ... von Dr. Chr. Fr. Grieb. *Stuttgart: Chr. Belserschen Buchhandlung.* 1855. Sm. 8vo, pp. xlii, 214. B. 8520

BROWN. Startling Incidents and Developments of Osowottomy Brown's Insurrectionary and Treasonable Movements, &c. By a Citizen of Harper's Ferry. *Baltimore.* 1859. 12mo. 8521

BROWN. Testimonies of Capt. John Brown, at Harper's Ferry, with his address to the Court. *New York: American Anti-Slavery Society.* 1860. 8vo, pp. 16. 8522

BROWN. The Martyrdom of John Brown. The Proceedings of a Public Meeting held in London on the 2nd December, 1863, to commemorate the Fourth Anniversary of John Brown's Death. *London: Emancipation Society.* 1864. 8vo, pp. 22, (1). 8523

BROWN. Speeches of Hon. A. C. Barstow, Rev. George T. Day, Rev. Augustus Woodbury, Hon. Thomas Davis, and Resolutions adopted at a Meeting of Citizens held in Providence, R. I., Dec. 2, 1859, on the occasion of the Execution of John Brown. *Providence: Amsbury & Co.* 1860. 8vo, pp. 32. 8524

See Harper's Ferry. Report of the Senate.

BROWN (J. H.) Minutes and Proceedings of the Division Court Martial, Begun and holden at Charlestown, on the 14th of August 1810. Upon Charges Exhibited by Capt. Lot Pool, Against Ens. John H. Brown. By order of the Hon. Joseph B. Varnum, Maj. Gen. of the 3d Division Massachusetts Militia. *Charlestown.* 1810. 8vo, pp. 131. W. 8525

BROWN (J. M.) Brief Sketch of the First Settlement of the County of Schoharie, by the Germans: Being an Answer to a Circular Letter, addressed to the Author, by "The Historical and Philosophical Society of New-York." By John M. Brown. *Schoharie: Printed by L. Cothbert.* 1823. 8vo, pp. 23. 8526

BROWN (John Thompson). Speech in the House of Delegates of Virginia, on the Abolition of Slavery, January 18, 1832. *Richmond: C. H. Wynne.* 1860. 8vo, pp. 32. 8527

BROWN (J. W.) Safeguards of American Civilization. *New York.* 1847. 8vo. B. 8528

BROWN (J. Y.) Remarks of Hon. John Young Brown of Kentucky, in reply to the Question of Hon. W. C. Anderson, of Kentucky. [n. p. n. d.] 8vo, pp. 8. 8529

BROWN (Jonathan). The History and Present Condition of

St. Domingo. By J. Brown, M.D. ... *Philadelphia: William Marshall and Company.* 1837. 2 vols., 12mo, pp. iv, 307; Title, 289. BA., C., H. 8530

"This work is written with singular clearness and precision." — N. A. R.

BROWN (J. E.) Speech of Governor Joseph E. Brown ... at Marietta, Georgia ... March 18th, 1868. [n. p. n. d.] 8vo, pp. 8. H. 8531

[BROWN (Josephine).] Biography of an American Bondman [Wm. Wells Brown], by his Daughter. ... *Boston: R. F. Wallcut.* 1856. 12mo, pp. 104. H. 8532

BROWN (L.) Poems of the Prairies. By Leonard Brown. *Des Moines: Mills & Co.* 1866. 12mo, pp. 216. + New Edition. *Des Moines: Redhead & Wellslager.* 1868. 16mo, pp. 186. B. 8533

These poems are mostly descriptive of Western scenery, and partake, in a measure, of the freshness and vigor of the scenes described.

BROWN (M.) Speech of Mr. Milton Brown ... On ... the right of the Members from ... New Hampshire, Georgia, Mississippi, and Missouri, who were elected under the General Ticket System ... to retain their seats. ... In the House ... Seventh of February, 1844. [*Washington.* 1844.] 8vo, pp. 16.

BROWN. Speech of Mr. Milton Brown ... on the Bill to protect the Rights of American Settlers in ... Oregon. Delivered in the House ... April 15, 1846. 8vo, pp. 8. H. 8535

BROWN. Speech of Mr. Brown, of Burlington [N. J.], in favor of the Bill incorporating the Camden and Keyport Railroad Company. Made in the House of Assembly, Feb. 18, 1851. *Trenton: printed by Sherman and Harron.* 1851. 8vo, pp. 15. H. 8536

BROWN (Moses). From the Meeting for Sufferings for New-England, to the several Quarterly and Monthly-Meetings belonging to the Yearly Meeting. [Colophon:] *Providence: Printed by John Carter.* [1782] 4to, pp. 19. 8537

BROWN. Brief Notices of the Life and Character of the late Moses Brown. Reprinted from the Providence Journal of October 4, 1841. *Providence.* 1841. 12mo, pp. 15. 8538

Also included in the "Irish Friend," Vol. II., No. 3.

BROWN. Genealogy of a portion of the Brown Family; principally from the Moses Brown Papers, and from other Authentic Sources. *Providence: Press of H. H. Brown.* 1851. 16mo, pp. 16. 8539

BROWN (Mount). Catalogue of British, Colonial, and Foreign Postage Stamps. Fifth Edition. Revised, Augmented, and Corrected. *London: Passmore.* 1864. 16mo, pp. v, 96. 8540

BROWN (N.) An Address ... before the Wayne County Education Society ... in Newark, January 22, 1831. By Nathaniel Brown ... . *Palmyra, N. Y.* 1831. 8vo, pp. 23, (1).

BROWN (O.) Memoranda of the Preston Family. By Orlando Brown. *Albany: J. Munsell.* 1864. 8vo, pp. 26. + *Cincinnati: Wrightson & Co.* 1864. 8vo, pp. 16. 8542

Twenty-five copies of Mr. Munsell's edition printed. First printed for the family at Frankfort, Ky., 1842.

[BROWN (Peter).] The Fame and Glory of England Vindicated. By Libertas. *New York and London.* 1842. 12mo, pp. 306. 8543

Mr. Brown was a contributor to the "Albion" newspaper. This work is a reply to C. E. Lester's "Glory and Shame of England."

BROWN (R.) An Argument in Defence of the Principle of the Navigation Laws ... a Speech ... *Bishopwearmouth.* 1847. 8vo, pp. 32. S. 8544

Contains allusions to American legislation.

BROWN. Calender of State Papers and Manuscripts relating to English Affairs, existing in the Archives and Collections of Venice. ... By Rawdon Brown. *London.* 1864–67. 2 vols., 8vo. 8545

Contains some particulars concerning Columbus.

[BROWN (Rebecca).] Stories about General Warren, in Relation to the Fifth of March Massacre, and the Battle of Bunker Hill. By a Lady of Boston. *Boston: James Loring.* 1835. 32mo, pp. 112. BA. 8546

BROWN (R.) Der englische Held und Ritter Franc. Dracke in einer ausführlichen Beschreibung von dessen Leben, Thaten und Seereisen. *Leipzig.* 1726. 8vo. Portrait. 8547

Possibly a translation of Richard Burton's "English Hero, or Sir Francis Drake." This title is from a French, and the following from a German catalogue. Probably should be under Burton (R.)

BROWN. Lebensbeschreibung des Franz Dracke, nebst einem Anhang über den Schiffbruch des Jagd-Schiffes der Schelling. *Leipz.* 1740. 8vo. 8548

BROWN (*Rev.* Robert C. Lundin). British Columbia. An Essay. *New Westminster: Royal Engineer Press.* [1853.] 12mo, 2 l., pp. 64, xxxiii. S. 8549

BROWN (Robert F.) ... The Corner-stone of Patriotism, Government, and Nationality, and the only Practical Basis for Restored Peace. *Danbury, Conn.* 1862. 8vo, pp. 7. 8550

BROWN (R. T.) The Mission of Nations. A Sermon preached at Greenwood, Indiana, November 27, 1862. 8vo, pp. 15. 8551

BROWN. The Christian Civilization. A Discourse delivered April 30, 1863, at Brownsburg, Indiana. *Indianapolis: Daily Journal.* 1863. 8vo, pp. 15. 8552

BROWN (S.) A Treatise on ... Yellow Fever, ... comprising An Account of the Disease in several of the Capitals of the United States; But more particularly as it has prevailed in Boston. By Samuel Brown ... . *Boston: printed by Manning & Loring. April,* 1800. 8vo, pp. 112. H. 8553

Also: Inaugural Dissertation on the Bilious Malignant Fever, in Harvard College, July 10, 1797. *Boston.* 1797. 8vo, pp. 54.

BROWN (S.) Clerical Directory; Containing a List of the Clergy of New York and Brooklyn, with their residence, 1834. 5. Also a list of Churches, Benevolent and Religious Societies, &c. By S. Brown. *New York.* 1834. 18mo. 8554

BROWN (S. G.) An Address, delivered before the Society of the Alumni of Dartmouth College, at their first Triennial Meeting, July 25, 1855. By Samuel Gilman Brown. With an Account of the Proceedings ... . *Concord, N. H.: Press of McFarland & Jenks.* 1856. 8vo, pp. 69. H. 8555

Also: A Discourse Commemorative of Charles Brickett Haddock, D.D. late Professor of Intellectual Philosophy and Political Economy. Delivered ... [at] Dartmouth College, April 19, 1861. ... . *Windsor, Vt.: Press of Bishop & Tracy.* 1861. 8vo, pp. 30. Portrait. H. — A Eulogy on the Life and Character of Henry Clay, delivered before the Students of Dartmouth College, Oct. 15, 1852, ... *Boston.* 1852. 8vo, pp. 42. — A Discourse Commemorative of John Newton Putnam, Late Professor of the Greek Language and Literature in Dartmouth College: delivered ... July 19, 1864. ... . *Concord: printed by McFarland & Jenks.* 1864. 8vo, pp. 32.

BROWN (S. R.) An Authentic History of the Second War

for Independence: Comprising Details of the Military and Naval Operations, from the Commencement to the close of the Recent War: Enriched with numerous Geographical and Biographical Notes. By Samuel R. Brown. In Two Volumes. *Auburn: J. G. Hathaway.* 1815. 12mo, pp. 228, Appendix, 94, Index, 1 l.; pp. 264, Appendix, 129, Index, 1 l. C., S.

BROWN. Views of the Campaigns of the North-Western Army, &c. comprising Sketches of the Campaigns of Generals Hull and Harrison — A minute account of the Naval Conflict on Lake Erie — Military anecdotes — Abuses in the Army — Plan of a Military Settlement — View of the Lake Coast from Sandusky to Detroit. By Samuel R. Brown. ... *Troy.* 1814. 12mo, pp. 156. S., H. + *Burlington, Vt.* 1814. 12mo, pp. 156. + *Philadelphia: William G. Murphy.* 1815. 12mo, pp. 156. 8557

Probably but one edition, in fact; with a change of imprint.

BROWN. The Western Gazetteer; or Emigrant's Directory. containing a Geographical Description of the Western States and Territories, viz. the States of Kentucky, Indiana, Louisiana, Ohio, Tennessee and Mississippi: And the Territories of Illinois, Missouri, Alabama, Michigan, and North-Western. With an Appendix, containing Sketches of some of the Western Counties of New-York, Pennsylvania, and Virginia; a Description of the Great Northern Lakes; Indian Annuities, and, Directions to Emigrants. By Samuel R. Brown. *Auburn, N. Y.: printed by H. C. Southwick.* 1817. 8vo, pp. 360, Errata, 1 slip. S. + *Belfast.* 1819. 8vo. + A New Edition. *Auburn.* 1820. 8vo, pp. 360. + *London.* 1820. 8vo. 8558

Contains much curious matter relative to the Indians and antiquities. *See* N. A. R., VI. 134–138.

BROWN (S.) An Essay on American Poetry, with several Miscellaneous Pieces, Sentimental, Descriptive, Moral and Patriotic, by Solyman Brown, A.M. *New Haven: Hezekiah Howe.* 1817. 12mo, pp. 191. 8559

BROWN. Pictorial and Business Directory of the City of New York and Vicinity, 1853. Square 12mo, pp. 293. 8560

BROWN. A Second Address to the People of Litchfield County. By Solyman Brown. *New-Haven: Printed by Flagg & Gray.* 1818. 12mo, pp. 24. H. 8561

BROWN. Union of Extremes: a Discourse on Liberty and

Slavery, as they stand related to the Justice, Prosperity, and Perpetuity of the United Republic of North America. By Solyman Brown ... . *New-York.* [185–.] 8vo, Title, pp. 24.

BROWN (S.) An Appeal to the Inhabitants of Her Majesty's Canadian Provinces against ... Imprisonment for Debt in Canada West; in which is embodied a History of the Sufferings and Wrongs of Mr. Sylvester Brown, a prisoner, ... at Chatham, ... By Sylvester Brown, Rochester, N. Y. *Published by the Author.* 1859. 12mo, pp. 143. 25 Woodcuts. 8563

BROWN (T.) Memoirs of Tarleton Brown, a Captain in the Revolutionary Army. Written by Himself. With a Preface and Notes, by Charles I. Bushnell. *New York: Privately Printed.* 1862. 8vo, pp. 64. 8564

Forms No. 4 of Bushnell's "Crumbs for Antiquarians," Vol. I.

BROWN (T.) An Address in Christian Love, to the Inhabitants of Philadelphia; on the Awful Dispensation of the Yellow Fever, in 1798. By Thaddeus Brown. *Philadelphia: Printed for the Author by R. Aitkin.* 1798. 12mo, pp. 71. W. 8565

BROWN (T.) Poems on several occasions. By the late Rev. Thomas Brown. *New York.* 1801. 18mo. 8566

BROWN (T.) An Account of the People Called Shakers: Their Faith, Doctrines, and Practice exemplified in the Life, Conversations and Experience of the Author during the Time he belonged to the Society. To which is affixed a History of their Rise and Progress to the Present Day. By Thomas Brown of Cornwall ... *Troy: Parker & Bliss.* 1812. 12mo, pp. 372.

BROWN (T. C.) Examination of Mr. Thomas C. Brown, A Free Colored Citizen of S. Carolina, as to the Actual State of Things in Liberia in ... 1833 and 1834 ... . *New-York.* 1834. 8vo, pp. 40. BA. 8568

BROWN (T. S.) History of the Grand Trunk Railway. By Thomas Storrow Brown. *Quebec.* 1864. 8vo, pp. 100. 8569

BROWN. Report on Cholera and Emigration. By Thomas Storrow Brown. *Montreal.* 1832. 8570

BROWN (T.) Trip to Jamaica, with a True Character of the People and Island. By Tom Brown. *London.* 1699. Folio.

Interspersed with poetry, and written in the ordinary style of the "facetious author," who is very severe in his observations, especially on the people of Port Royal, whom he describes as scare-crows, and says: "They have this pleasure in drinking that what they put into their bellies, they soon stroke out at their finger ends."

BROWN (W.) The History of the Propagation of Christianity among the Heathen since the Reformation. ... By Rev. W. Brown. *London.* 1814. 4 vols., 8vo. + *London.* MDCCCLIV. 2 vols., 8vo. 8572

Includes copies of details of missions among the Indians.

[BROWN (William?).] The Claims of Thomas Jefferson to the Presidency examined at the Bar of Christianity. By a Layman. *Philadelphia.* 1800. 8vo. 8573

Perhaps by the same author as the following:

BROWN (W.) An Oration, spoken at Hartford, in ... Connecticut ... July 4th, A.D. 1799. By William Brown. *Hartford: printed By Hudson and Goodwin.* 1799. 8vo, pp. 23. H., N.

BROWN (W.) America, a Four Years' Residence in the United States and Canada, with the Manners, Customs, and Character of the Inhabitants. By William Brown. *London.* 1849. 8vo. 8575

An intelligent and interesting description of the places visited by the author.

BROWN (William A.) The Harp of Nature: A Book of Poems. ... *Utica.* 1846. 18mo, pp. 110. S. 8576

BROWN (W. B.) ... A Sermon occasioned by the Death of Mrs. S. Agnes Smith, Wife of John Smith, Esq., delivered ... in Andover, Mass., January 11, 1852. By Rev. William B. Brown ... . *Andover.* 1852. 8vo, pp. 23. H. 8577

BROWN (W. H.) Portrait Gallery of Distinguished American Citizens, with Biographical Sketches and fac-similes of original letters. By William H. Brown. *Hartford.* 1845. Folio, pp. 111. [27 full length silhouette Portraits.] P. 8578

BROWN (*Lieut.* W. H.) Views taken during the Arctic Expedition of the Ships Enterprise and Investigator. By Lieut. W. H. Brown. *London.* 1850. Imp. 4to. 8579

BROWN (W. H.) An Historical Sketch of the early movement in Illinois for the Legalization of Slavery, ... By Hon. William H. Brown, ... *Chicago: Press of Church, Goodman and Donnelly.* 1865. 8vo, pp. 44. 8580

BROWN. Memoir of the Late Hon. Daniel P. Cook: read before the Chicago Historical Society, June 9, 1857, By William H. Brown, Esq. ... . *Chicago: Scripps, Bross & Spears, Printers.* 1857. 8vo, pp. 30. H., S. 8581

BROWN (W. L.) Notes on Artillery — from Robins, Hutton, Chesney, Mordecai. By W. Leroy Brown. *Richmond: West & Johnston.* [1862?] 8582

[BROWN (William Linn).] Scribblings and Sketches, Diplomatic, Piscatory, and Oceanic. By a Fisher in Small Streams. *Philadelphia.* 1844. 8583

BROWN (W. W.) Trial of Col. William W. Brown, of the Providence First Light Infantry Company, on charges preferred by Gen. Joseph S. Pitman, Brigadier General, Second Brigade, Rhode Island Militia; at Providence, August, 1856. *Providence: A. Crawford Greene.* 1856. 8vo, pp. 23. 8584

BROWN. Statement respecting the Court Martial ordered by General Burnside for the trial of Col. W. W. Brown, on charges preferred by General Pitman. *Providence.* 1856. 8vo, pp. 11. 8585

BROWN (W. W.) The American Fugitive in Europe. Sketches of Places and People abroad. By Wm. Wells Brown. With a Memoir of the Author. *Boston: John P. Jewett and Company, [etc.]* 1855. 12mo, pp. 320. Portrait. H. 8586

This is a reprint of his "Three Years in Europe ... . *London.* 185–."

BROWN. Anti-Slavery Harp: a Collection of Songs for Anti-Slavery Meetings. Compiled by William W. Brown. *Boston: Bela Marsh.* 1849. 12mo, pp. 47. BA. 8587

BROWN. Biography of An American Bondman, by His Daughter. *See* Brown (Josephine), No. 8532.

BROWN. The Blackman, his Antecedents, his Genius, and his Achievements. By William Wells Brown. ... *New York: Thomas Hamilton. Boston: R. F. Wallcut.* 1863. 12mo, pp. 288. BA. + *Boston: James Redpath.* 1863. 12mo, pp. 312. H. + New Edition. *Boston: James Redpath.* 1864. 8vo, pp. 310. C. 8589

BROWN. Clotel; or, the President's Daughter: A Narrative of Slave Life in the United States. By William Wells Brown ... . With a Sketch of the Author's Life. ... *London: Partridge & Oakey.* 1853. 16mo, pp. viii, 245. H. 8590

Reprinted as "Clotelle; a tale of the Southern States. ... *Boston: J. Redpath.* 1864." 18mo, pp. 104.

BROWN. A Description of William Wells Brown's Original

Panoramic Views of the Scenes in the Life of an American Slave. *London: Charles Gilpin.* 12mo, pp. 48. BA. 8591

BROWN. The Escape; or, a Leap for Freedom. A Drama. *Boston.* 1858. 12mo, pp. 52. 8592

BROWN. Levensgeschiedenis van den Amerikaanschen slaaf W. Wells Brown, door hem zelven beschreven. Naar de 5e Eng. uitgave vertaald door M. Keyzer. *Zwolle: W. E. J. Tyeenk Willink.* 1850. 8vo. Plate. 8593

BROWN. Narrative of W. W. Brown, a Fugitive Slave. Written by himself. *Boston: Anti-Slavery Office.* 1847. 12mo, pp. 110. Portrait. BA. 8594

A twelfth thousand was published in 1850. *See* No. 8532, *supra.*

BROWN. The Negro in the American Rebellion: his Heroism and his Fidelity. By William Wells Brown. *Boston: Lee and Shepard.* 1867. 12mo, pp. xvi, 380. C. 8595

BROWN. Three Years in Europe; or, what I have seen and people I have met. With a Memoir of the Author, by William Farmer. *London: C. Gilpin* 1852. 16mo, pp. xxxii, 312. C.

BROWN (W. Y.) The Army Chaplain: his Office, Duties, and Responsibilities, and the Means of Aiding him. By Rev. W. Y. Brown, A.M., Hospital Chaplain U. S. Army. *Philadelphia: Wm. S. & A. Martien.* 1863. 18mo, pp. 144. C.

BROWN. The Christian Hero: his Conflicts, Virtues, and Crown. By Rev. W. Y. Brown ... Washington, D. C., Aug. 3, 1862. *Salem, N. J.* 1862. 8vo, pp. 16. 8598

BROWN UNIVERSITY. Act of Congress granting Lands for the establishing of Agricultural Colleges; with the Resolutions passed by the General Assembly of the State of Rhode Island accepting these Lands, and assigning the same to Brown University; also a Resolution providing for State Scholarships in that University. *Providence: Alfred Anthony.* 1863. 8vo, pp. 12.

Brown University under the Presidency of Asa Messer, S.T.D., LL.D. By an Alumnus. *Boston: Crosby & Ainsworth.* 1867. 8vo, pp. 23. H. 8600

Annual Report of the Faculty of Brown University, to the Corporation ... September 3, 1829. ... *Providence: printed by H. H. Brown.* 1829. 8vo, pp. 14. H. 8601

The Brown Paper. Brown University. Vol. I. Nos. 1–7. 1857–1863. Folio. 8602

Published annually, in November. *See* Bartlett's Bib. R. I.

Catalogue of Brown University. *Providence: Walter R. Danforth.* 1826. 8vo, pp. 61. 8603

Catalogue of Books belonging to the Library of Rhode Island College. *Providence: J. Carter.* 1793. 12mo, pp. 38. + *Providence.* 1826. 8vo, pp. 60, (1). H. 8604

A Catalogue of the Library of Brown University ... . With an Index of Subjects. *Providence.* 1843. 8vo, pp. xxvi, (1), 560. H. 8605

Compiled by Prof. C. C. Jewett. It contains a history of the library.

Catalogue of the Books in the Library of the Philermenian Society, together with the Names of its Members; Brown University. *Providence: Jones & Wheeler.* 1810. 16mo, pp. 16. + *Providence: Miller & Hutchens.* 1817. 12mo, pp. 22. + *Providence.* 1829. 8vo. 8606

Catalogue of the Delti Phi Society [connected with Brown University]. *Providence.* 1845. 12mo, pp. 39. + *New York.* 1851. 8vo, pp. 55. 8607

Catalogue of the Fraternity of Φ B K, Alpha of Rhode-Island, Brown University ... . 1839. *Providence.* 1839. 8vo, pp. 15. H. + 1862. 8608

Catalogue of the Library and Members of the Philermenian Society. Founded A.D. 1794. *Boston.* 16mo, pp. 46, (1). Continued triennially. H. 8609

A Catalogue of the Library of the United Brothers' Society of Brown University, with the Names of Members. Founded, A.D. 1806. *Providence: printed by Knowles, Vose & Co.* 1837. 12mo, pp. 40. Continued biennially. 8610

Catalogue of the Officers and Students of Brown University, Providence, Rhode Island, April 1, 1804. 8611

Folio sheet. Continued to 1823 in this form; from 1820 to 1835 in 8vo; 1835 to 1847 in 12mo; 1847 to 1866 in 8vo; and so continued. An edition of the catalogue, 1842–43, was published by the students in 8vo, who disliked the cheap-looking style of the "regular edition."

A Catalogue of the Officers and Students of the Sophomore Class in Brown University, 1845–46. Second Edition. *Providence.* 1845. 8vo, pp. 8. 8612

Catalogus eorum qui in Collegio Rhod. Ins. et Prov. Plant. Nov.-Anglorum, ab anno 1769, ad annum 1775, alicujus Gradus Laurea donati sunt. *Providence: Typis Johannis Carter.* 1775. Sm. folio, broadside. Continued to 1795. 8613

"The first 'Triennial Catalogue,' so called, published in Rhode Island." — BARTLETT.

Catalogus eorum qui in Collegio Rhodiæ Insulæ quod est Providentiæ, ab Anno MDCCLXIX, ad Annum MDCCXCVIII, Alicujus Gradûs Laureâ donati sunt. *Providence: Typis Carter et Wilkinson.* [1798.] 12mo, pp. 22. Continued. H. 8614

The college was afterwards called "Universitas Brownensis" and "Brunensis."

Catalogus Præsidum et Sociorum, cum Professoribus, Tutoribus, et Omnibus, qui in Universitate Brunensi, Providentiæ, in Republica Insulæ Rhodiensis, alicujus Gradus Laurea exornati fuerunt. *Providence: N. Mann & Co.* 1815. 8vo, pp. 22.

Catalogus Senatus Academici, eorum qui munero et officia gesserunt, quique alicujus gradus laurea donati sunt in Universitate Brownensi, Providentia, ... *Providenciæ: Typis H. H. Brown.* 1827. 8vo, pp. 28. Continued. 8616

Catalogus Universitatis Brownensis. MDCCCXVII. *Providence: Hugh H. Brown.* 1817. 8vo, pp. 23. Continued. 8617

Celebration of the One hundredth Anniversary of the Founding of Brown University, September 6th, 1864. *Providence: S. S. Rider & Bro.* 1865. 8vo, 3 l., pp. 178. H. 8618

Fifty copies printed on large paper, with a portrait.

The Charter of Rhode Island College, granted 1764. *Newport: Printed by Samuel Hall. London: Reprinted for Blythe & Beaver.* 8vo, pp. 16. + *Providence: J. Carter.* 1803. 8vo, pp. 12. + The Charter of Brown University. ... *Providence: H. H. Brown.* 1834. 8vo, pp. 15. 8619

Dedication of the New Chapel of Brown University, Wednesday, February 4th, 1835. Being the Order of Exercises, with an original Ode by Albert G. Greene, Esq. 8620

Title from Mr. Bartlett's Bibl. of Rhode Island, from which, indeed, most of these titles are copied.

Exhibition of Rhode Island College and Brown University. Sophomore, Junior and Senior. Order of Exercises. April 20, 1803. Continued. 8621

An Expositor of certain Newspaper Publications relative to the Affairs of Brown University, August, 1826. [Signed X Y Z.] *Providence.* 1826. 8vo, pp. 15. 8622

Historical Sketch of Brown University. 8vo, pp. 8. 8623

Reprinted from the "Rhode Island Schoolmaster." A Sketch of the History of Brown University was published in the seventh number of the Brunonian, 1830. *Providence.* 1830. 8vo, pp. 8.

Historical Sketch of the Library of Brown University. With Regulations. *New Haven: Tuttle.* 1861. 8vo, pp. 20. 8624

From the "University Quarterly," April, 1861.

The Laws of Rhode Island College, enacted by the Fellows and Trustees. *Providence: J. Carter.* 1793. 12mo, pp. 35. + *Providence: J. Carter.* 1803. 8vo, pp. 29. + *Providence: Brown & Danforth.* 1823. 8vo, pp. 16. + *Providence: Walter R. Danforth.* 1827. 8vo, pp. 20. + Revised Edition, 1835. *Providence: H. H. Brown.* 1835. 8vo, pp. 20. + Enacted August 1, 1850. *Providence: Joseph Knowles.* 1850. 8vo, pp. 25. + *Providence: Knowles, Anthony & Co.* 1856. 8vo, pp. 24. + *Providence: A. C. Greene.* 1861. 8vo, pp. 27. 8625

A Letter to the Corporation of Brown University, suggesting certain Improvements in its Academical System. 1815. 8vo, pp. 20. 8626

"Signed Alumnus Brunensis, and dated August 18, 1815." — BARTLETT, Bib. R. I.

Order of Exercises for 1795. 8627

The First Commencement was at Warren, R. I., 1769. Folio to 1812, then continued in octavo, as below:

Order of Exercises and Theses for Commencement, Sep. 2, 1812. *Providence: Jones & Wheeler.* 1814. 8vo, pp. 16. Continued to 1817. 8628

Proceedings of the Corporation and of the Alumni of Brown University, in reference to the Resignation of President Wayland, and the Induction of President Sears. *Providence: Knowles, Anthony & Co., Printers.* 1856. 8vo, pp. 23. 8629

Report of the Committee of the Corporation of Brown University, appointed to raise a Fund of One hundred twenty-five thousand Dollars. *Providence: Knowles, Anthony & Co., Printers.* 1851. 8vo, pp. 16. H., S. 8630

Report to the Corporation of Brown University, on Changes in the System of Collegiate Education. Read March 28, 1850. *Providence: George H. Whitney.* 1850. 8vo, pp. 76. BA., H., P.

A Sketch of the History and Present Organization of Brown University. Published by the Executive Board. *Providence.* 1861. 8vo, pp. 15. View. H. 8632

Supplement to the Laws of Rhode Island College. *Providence.* 1793. 12mo, pp. 7. + *Providence: J. Carter.* 1803. 8vo, pp. 7.

Triennial Catalogue of the Library and Members of the Philermenian Society in Brown University. Founded A.D. 1794. *Providence.* 1849. 8vo, pp. 92. 8634

Triennial Catalogue of the United Brothers' Society of Brown University. Instituted, A.D. 1806. *Providence.* 1848. 8vo, pp. 64. H. + *Providence: A. C. Greene.* 1853. 8vo, pp. 84. 8635

A True and Candid Statement. 1826. *See* [Holroyd (John)].

[BROWNE (Albert Gallatin), *Jr.*] In Memoriam J. W. B. *Boston: Crosby, Nichols, Lee and Company.* 16mo, pp. iv, 90.

Containing Memoir of John White Browne, by J. A. Andrew; Sermon at Hingham on his Death, by C. C. Shackford; Sermon at Salem, by E. Wilson, etc.

BROWNE. Sketch of the Official Life of John A. Andrew, To which is added ... [his] valedictory address on the Subject of Reconstruction ... January 5, 1866. *New York: Hurd & Houghton.* 1868. 16mo, pp. xii, 211. Portrait. B. C. 8637

BROWNE (Alexander E.) Address delivered before the American Whig and Cliosophic Societies of the College of New Jersey, 23d June, 1846. *Princeton.* 1846. 8vo. N. 8638

BROWNE (Ansel). Wonderful Works of God. A Narrative of the Wonderful Facts in the Case of Ansel Browne, of Westerly, Rhode Island, who, in the midst of Opposition to the Christian Religion, was suddenly struck Blind, Dumb, and Deaf; and after 18 days was suddenly and comparatively restored, in the Presence of Hundreds of Persons, in the Christian Chapel, at Westerly, on the 15th Nov. 1857. Written under his Direction. *Irvington. N. J.* 1858. 18mo, pp. 47. Portrait.

BROWNE (A.) The Necessity of Reformation, in Order to avert Impending Judgments. A Sermon, Preached at Ports-

mouth, in New Hampshire, May 6, 1757. Being the Annual Fast. By Arthur Browne, A.M. ... *Portsmouth.* M,DCC,LVII. 8vo, pp. 21. M. 8640

[BROWNE.] Remarks on Dr. Mayhew's Incidental Reflections relative to the Church of England. As contained in his Observations on the Charter, and conduct of the Society, &c. By a son of the Church of England. *Portsmouth.* 1763. 4to, pp. 31. 8641

Also: The Advantages of Unity. A Sermon ... before the Right Worshipful Lodge of Free and Accepted Masons, on the 24th of June 1748. *Portsmouth.* [1748.] 8vo, pp. 41. M. — Doctrine of Election ... a Sermon ... at Portsmouth, ... *Portsmouth: Daniel Fowle.* M.DCC.LVII. 8vo, pp. 23. N. — The Excellency of the Christian Religion; exhibited in a Sermon before the Episcopal Clergy of New England ... Sept. 20, 1738. ... *Boston.* 1738. 8vo. pp. 20. — The Folly and Perjury of the Rebellion in Scotland display'd. ... Feb. 23, 1745–6. *Boston.* 1746. 4to, pp. 18. — [Masonic] Sermon at Boston, Oct. 1, 1755. *Boston: Printed for J. & T. Leverett in Cornhill.* 1755. 4to, pp. 24. — Miscellaneous Sketches, or, Hints for Essays ... *London.* 1798. 2 vols., 8vo. — Religious Education of Children recommended, in a Sermon preached in the church of Portsmouth, [N. H.] Dec. 27, 1739, Being the Day appointed for the Execution of Penelope Kenny. *Boston.* 1739. 8vo, pp. 21.

BROWNE (C.) The United States: Their Constitution and Power. Containing a Popular Summary of the Naval and Military Forces of the Union, as well as the American Idea of Defence. By Charles Browne ... . *Kent and Company.* 1856. 16mo, Title, pp. 86. 8642

[BROWNE (C. F.)] Artemus Ward among the Mormons ... . [Facetious] Programme ... . [*Boston.* 1865?] 8vo, pp. 4.

[BROWNE.] Artemus Ward in London; and other Papers. By C. F. Browne. Illustr. *New York: G. W. Carleton.* 1867. 12mo, pp. 229. C. 8644

[BROWNE.] Artemus Ward; his Travels. Part I. Miscellaneous. Part 2. Among the Mormons. *New York: Carleton.* 1865. 12mo, pp. 231. Illustrations. C. + *Montreal.* 1865. 8vo, pp. 94. 8645

BROWNE. Artemus Ward (his Travels) Among the Mormons. Part I. On the Rampage. Part 2. Perlite Litteratoor. Edited by E. P. Hingston. *London: J. C. Hotten.* 1864. Post 8vo, pp. xxx–192. 8646

Also a cheap edition.

[BROWNE.] Artemus Ward, his Book; Or, the Confessions and Experiences of a Showman, with an Introduction by George

Augustus Sala. *London: Ward & Lock.* 1864. Crown 8vo, pp. 96. 8647

BROWNE (Daniel Jay). The American Bird Fancier. By D. J. Browne. *New York: C. M. Saxton.* [1856.] 12mo, pp. 107. c. 8648

BROWNE (D. J.) The Sylva Americana; or a Description of the Forest Trees indigenous to the United States, Practically and Botanically considered. ... By D. J. Browne. ... *Boston: William Hyde & Co.* MDCCCXXXII. 8vo, pp. 408. Illustrated.

See N. A. R., XLIV. 334.

BROWNE. The Trees of America: Native and Foreign, Pictorially and Botanically Delineated, and scientifically and popularly described; being considered principally with Reference to their Geography and History, Soil and Situation; Propagation and Culture; Accidents and Diseases; Properties and Uses; Economy in the Arts; Introduction into Commerce; and their Application in Useful and Ornamental Plantations. Illustrated by numerous Engravings. By D. J. Brown ... . *New York: Harper & Brothers.* M,DCCC,XLVI. 8vo, pp. xii, 520. C., H., P.

BROWNE (David). A Self-Defence, with a Refutation of Calumnies, Misrepresentations and Fallacies. Respecting the Logierian Diplomatic Institution. *Boston.* 1828. 8vo, pp. 28.

BROWNE (Dunn), *pseudon.* Experiences in the Army. *See* [Fiske (S.)]

BROWNE (G. M.) Remarks of George M. Browne ... in the House ... March 31, and April 21, 1857, on the Kansas Resolves. [*Boston.* 1857.] 8vo, pp. 8. BA. 8652

BROWNE (John), *of Cohasset.* A Discourse delivered on the Day of the Annual Provincial Thanksgiving, Dec. 6, 1770. *Boston.* 1771. 8vo, pp. 15. 8653

BROWNE (John), *of Nevis.* In the Eleventh month, on the Nineth Day of the Moneth, as I was waiting upon the Lord in the Land of my Nativity, the Spirit of the Lord then signified unto me the second time, saying, Arise and take up a Lamentation over New England; and being made willing, have writ as followeth.—With a Warning to the Rulers and Magistrates of Boston in New England—by Margaret Braister. B.—*Printed in the Year,* 1678. Folio broadside. 8654

Also: "The Faith of the Martyrs in New England vindicated."

BROWNE (J.), *of Hingham.* *See* Brown (John).

BROWNE (J.) Brief Survey of the Prophetical and Evangelical Events of the Last Times. By Capt. John Brown of Orpington, Kent. *London.* 1653. 8vo. 8655

Refers to the English plantations in America. *See* p. 38.

BROWNE (J. R.) Adventures in the Apache Country; a Tour through Arizona and Nevada, with Notes on the Silver Regions of Nevada. By J. Ross Browne. Illustrated. *New York: Harper & Brothers.* 1869 [1868]. 12mo, pp. (3), 6–535.

BROWNE. Crusoe's Island: A Ramble in the Footsteps of Alexander Selkirk, with Sketches of Adventures in California and Washoe. By J. Ross Browne, ... *New York: Harper & Bros.* 1864. 12mo, pp. 436. c. 8657

BROWNE. Etchings of a Whaling Cruise, with Notes of a Sojourn on the Island of Zanzibar. To which is appended a brief history of the Whale Fishery, its Past and Present Condition. By J. Ross Browne. *New York: Harper & Brothers* ... 1846. 8vo, pp. xiii, 580. Illustrated. c. 8658

BROWNE. Mineral Resources of the States and Territories West of the Rocky Mountains. Letter from the Secretary of the Treasury, transmitting the Report of J. Ross Browne on the Mineral Resources of the States and Territories West of the Rocky Mountains. *Washington.* 1868. 8vo, pp. 674. c. 8659

BROWNE. Relacion de los Debates de la Convencion de California, sobre la formacion de la Constitution de Estado, en Setiembre y Octubre de 1849: Por J. Ross Browne. *Nueva-York: S. W. Benedict.* 1851. 8vo, pp. 439, xiii. C., S. 8660

BROWNE. Report of the Debates in the Convention of California, on the formation of the State Constitution, in September and October, 1849. By J. Ross Browne. *Washington: printed by John T. Towers.* 1850. 8vo, pp. 479, xlvii, (1). C., H. 8661

BROWNE. Resources of the Pacific Slope. A Statistical and Descriptive Summary of the Mines and Minerals, Climate, Topography, Agriculture, Commerce, Manufactures, and Miscellaneous Productions, of the States and Territories West of the Rocky Mountains. With a Sketch of the Settlement and Exploration of Lower California. With an Index to J. Ross

Browne's Report, and a Sketch of the Settlement and Exploration of Lower California, viz., Historical Summary of Lower California; from its Discovery in 1532 to 1867, by Alexander S. Taylor; also with Historical Memoir of Washington Territory and Sketch of Nevada, etc. *New York: D. Appleton and Company.* 1869 [1868]. 8vo, pp. 678, 200. c. 8662

This is a report to the Secretary of the Treasury, printed apparently at Washington. Pages 1 and 2, which in the official edition contain the letter of the Secretary of the Treasury, are here omitted.

BROWNE. Report of J. Ross Browne on the Mineral Resources of the States and Territories west of the Rocky Mountains. Also, appended, Report of James W. Taylor on the Mineral Resources of the United States east of the Rocky Mountains. *Washington.* 1868. 8vo, pp. 674, 72. c. 8663

BROWNE *and* TAYLOR (J. W.) Reports upon the Mineral Resources of the United States. By Special Commissioners, J. Ross Browne and James W. Taylor. *Washington.* 1867. 8vo, pp. 360. S. 8664

BROWNE (John W.) Dissolution of the Union. Speech at the Anniversary of the New York Young Men's City Anti-Slavery Society. [n. p. n. d.] 8vo. B. 8665

BROWNE (J. H.) Four Years in Secessia: Adventures within and beyond the Union Lines: embracing a Great Variety of Facts, Incidents, and Romance of the War. Including the Author's Capture at Vicksburg, May 3, 1863, while running the Rebel Batteries; his Imprisonment at Vicksburg, Jackson, Atlanta, Richmond, and Salisbury; his Escape and Perilous Journey of Four Hundred Miles to the Union Lines at Knoxville. By Junius Henri Browne, Special War Correspondent of the New York Tribune. With Illustrations. *Hartford: O. D. Case and Company.* 1865. 8vo, pp. vi, 450. Woodcuts.

BROWNE. The Great Metropolis; a Mirror of New York. A Complete History of Metropolitan Life and Society, with Sketches of Prominent Places, Persons and Things in the City, as they actually exist. By Junius Henri Browne. ... *Hartford: American Publishing Company.* 1869. 8vo, pp. 700 Woodcuts.

BROWNE (N. B.) An Address Delivered before the Union League ... Philadelphia, at its Opening Celebration, May 9, 1863, By N. B. Browne, Esq., President ... [*Philadelphia:*] *Published by the League.* 1863. 8vo, pp. 16. 8668

BROWNE. The True Issues now involved. Shall the Republic stand on the Foundation laid by our Patriotic Fathers, or shall the Nation be sacrificed to the Covetousness and Knavery of the Confederates in Treason? Letter of N. B. Browne to C. J. Biddle. pp. 24. 8669

BROWNE (P.) The Civil and Natural History of Jamaica. In Three Parts. Containing, I. An accurate Description of that Island, its Situation and Soil; with a brief Account of its former and present State, Government, Revenues, Produce, and Trade. II. A History of the natural Productions, including the various Sorts of native Fossils; perfect and imperfect Vegetables; Quadrupedes, Birds, Fishes, Reptiles and Insects; with their Properties and Uses in Mechanics, Diet, and Physic. III. An Account of the Nature of Climates in general, and their different Effects upon the human Body; with a Detail of the Diseases arising from this Source, particularly within the Tropics. In Three Dissertations. The Whole illustrated with Fifty Copper-Plates: In which the most curious Productions are represented of the natural Size, and delineated immediately from the Objects. By Patrick Browne, M.D. *London: Printed for the Author.* MDCCLVI. Folio, 7 l., pp. 506. Map, Charts, and 49 Plates. C., P. 8670

Mr. Rich, I. 119, quoting from Mr. Chalmers, says 250 copies only were printed; and that all the copperplates were destroyed. The third part mentioned in the title is not included in the work. *See* the author's apology at the end of the volume. *See also* M. R., XV. 30, 333.

BROWNE. The Civil and Natural History of Jamaica. Containing I. An accurate Description of that Island, its Situation, and Soil; with a brief Account of its former and present State, Government, Revenue, Produce, and Trade. II. An History of the Natural Productions, including the various Sorts of native Fossils; Perfect and Imperfect Vegetables; Quadrupeds, Birds, Fishes, Reptiles, and Insects; with their Properties and Uses in Mechanics, Diet and Physic. By Patrick Browne, M.D. Illustrated with Forty-nine Copper Plates; in which the most curious productions are represented of their natural sizes, and delineated immediately from the objects, By George Dionysius Ehret. There are now added Complete Linnæn Indexes, and a large and accurate Map of the Island. | *London:* | *B. White & Son.* M,DCC,LXXXIX. Folio, 7 l., pp. 503, 23 l. Map, and 49 Copper-plates. c. 8671

With the exception of a few leaves being reprinted, with some alterations, the substitution of a new map of Jamaica, the omission of the chart, and the addition of the four indexes, this edition is the same as the first.

BROWNE (P. A.) An Address, intended to promote a Geological and Mineralogical Survey of Pennsylvania, the Publication of a Series of Geological Maps, and the Formation of State and County Geological and Mineralogical Collections. By Peter A. Brown. *Philadelphia.* 1826. 8vo, pp. 8. 8672

BROWNE. A Lecture on the Oregon Territory. I. The Title of the United States to its Sovereignty. II. Its Capabilities and Value to our Country. III. And the necessity of an immediate settlement of it from the States. By Peter A. Browne. LL.D. *Philadelphia.* 1843. 8vo, pp. 20. BA. 8673

BROWNE. Lecture upon the Naturalization Law of the United States. *Philadelphia.* 1845. 8vo, pp. 24. 8674

BROWNE. Memorial [to the Legislature of Pennsylvania for a Geological Survey of the State]. *Philadelphia.* 1827. 8vo, pp. 20. S. 8675

BROWNE. On the Geological Character of the Beds on which Philadelphia stands. By Peter A. Browne. *Philadelphia.* 1833. 8vo, pp. 23. P. 8676

Also: The Classification of Mankind by the Hair and Wool of their Heads, with the Nomenclature of Human Hybrids. ... *Philadelphia.* 1853. 8vo, pp. 14. C., P.—An Essay on Indian Corn. *Philadelphia.* 1837. 8vo, pp. 31. A.—Essays on the Physical History of the Globe ... *Philadelphia.* 1833. 8vo, pp. 6. P.—A Summary of the Law of Pennsylvania, securing to mechanics and others payment for their labor, etc. *Philadelphia: J. Maxwell.* 1814. 8vo, pp. 25. C.—Trichologia Mammalium: or, a Treatise on the Organization, Properties, and Uses of Hair and Wool; together with an Essay upon the Raising and Breeding of Sheep. ... *Philadelphia.* 1852. 4to, pp. 188.

BROWNE (*Sir* T.) Works of Sir Thomas Brown, containing Enquiries into Vulgar Errors, Religio Medici, Miscellany Tracts, &c. *London.* 1686. Folio. c. 8677

Tract XII. contains a curious poetical prophecy concerning America, with an exposition and notes. In his "... Works ... edited by Simon Wilkin ... . *London: William Pickering.* 1836." 4 vols., 8vo, (BA.), this occupies pp. 231–238 of Vol. IV. Browne's works are reprinted in Bohn's "Antiquarian Library." *London,* 3 vols., 12mo.

BROWNE (*Lieut.* W. H.), *R. N.* Ten Colored Views taken during the Arctic Expedition of Sir James C. Ross, with Summary of the Expeditions in Search of Sir John Franklin. *London: Ackerman & Co.* 1850. Folio, pp. 8. 7 Plates. c. 8678

BROWNE (W. H.) Speech of Mr. Wm. H. Browne ... in the House of Delegates of Virginia, on the Removal from the Commonwealth of the Free Colored Population. Delivered February 23, 1853. *Richmond: printed by Ritchies & Dunnavant.* 1853. 8vo, pp. 12. H. 8679

BROWNE. Browne's Banking and Mercantile Table, Interest Table and Counting-house Almanack, for 126 years, 1794–1901. *New-York.* 1841. 4to. 8680

BROWNELL (C. de Wolf). The Indian Races of North and South America. Comprising an Account of the principal Aboriginal Races, a Description of their National Customs, Mythology and Religious Ceremonies; the History of their most Powerful Tribes, and of their most Celebrated Chiefs and Warriors; their Intercourse and Wars with European Settlers; and a Great Variety of Anecdote and Description, illustrative of Personal and National Character. By Charles De Wolf Brownell. Including the late Sioux War and Indian Massacres in Minnesota. With Numerous and diversified Colored Illustrations from Original Designs. ... *New York: H. & S. Scranton.* 1853. 8vo, pp. 720. 40 Plates. C. + *Hartford: Hurlbut, Scranton & Company.* 1864. 8vo, pp. 763. 8681

BROWNELL (H.) North and South America illustrated ... . By Henry Brownell, A.M. ... *Hartford.* 1863. 2 vols., 8vo.

BROWNELL (H. H.) The Discoverers, Pioneers and Settlers of North and South America, from the earliest period, 982, to the present time: comprising the Lives of the most famous Discoverers, Explorers and Conquerors, of the New World; an account of the Foundation of Colonies, and the settlement of the States and Provinces; the History of the Sufferings and Privations of the Early Settlers, and their Wars with the Native Inhabitants; ... By Henry Howard Brownell, A.M. ... *Cincinnati.* 1853. + *Boston.* 1853. + *Hartford and Cincinnati.* 1857. 8vo, pp. 640. c. 8683

[BROWNELL.] Lyrics of a Day: or Newspaper Poetry. By a Volunteer in the U. S. Service. Second Edition. *New York: Carleton.* M DCCC LXIV. C., H. 8684

END OF VOLUME TWO.

A DICTIONARY OF BOOKS

RELATING TO AMERICA.

BROWNELL (H. H.) People's Book of Ancient and Modern History. *Hartford, Conn.* 1851. 8vo. c. 8685

BROWNELL. The People's Book of American History. *Hartford: L. Stebbins.* 1854. 2 vols., 8vo. c. 8686

BROWNELL. Poems. By Henry Howard Brownell. *New York: D. Appleton & Company. Philadelphia: George S. Appleton.* MDCCCXLVII. 12mo, 4 leaves, pp. 13–208. H.

Includes "The Tomb of Columbus," "Niagara," "Farewell to the Antilles."

BROWNELL. War-Lyrics and other Poems. By Henry Howard Brownell. *Boston: Ticknor and Fields.* 1866. 16mo, pp. viii, 243. C., H. 8688

BROWNELL (T.) Documents in the Case of Thomas Brownell. [n. p. 1855.] 8vo, pp. 14, (1). H. 8689

BROWNELL. A Sermon, addressed to the Legislature of ... Connecticut, at the Annual Election in New-Haven, May 1st, 1822. By Thomas Church Brownell, D.D., LL.D. ... *New-Haven: ... J. Barber, printer.* 1822. 8vo, pp. 16. H. 8690

BROWNELL (T. T.) New Englandism not the Religion of the Bible; examined in a Review of Bishop Brownell's fourth charge to his Clergy. *Hartford.* 1844. 8vo. H. 8691

BROWNING (C.) Appeal to the Citizens of Maryland, one of the United States of America, from the Legitimate Descendents of the Baltimore Family. By Charles Browning, of Horton

Lodge, Epsom, Surrey, and Kingdom of Great Britain. *Baltimore.* 1821. 8vo, pp. 88. S. 8692

BROWNING (M.) Fourty-Four Years of the Life of a Hunter; being Reminiscences of Meshach Browning, a Maryland Hunter, roughly written down by Himself. Revised and illustrated by E. Stabler. *Philadelphia: J. B. Lippincott & Co.* 1859. 12mo.

BROWNING (O. H.) ... An Oration delivered by Hon. O. H. Browning ... at Quincy, Ill., July 4, 1863. *Quincy, Illinois: Whig and Republican Press.* 1863. 8vo, pp. 19. 8694

BROWNING. Speech of Hon. O. H. Browning, of Illinois, on the Confiscation of Property. ... In the Senate ... March 10, 1862. [*Washington.* n. d.] 8vo, pp. 16. H. 8695

BROWNING (S.) Poems. By Samuel Browning. *London.* 1846. 8vo. Portrait. 8696

Includes a Voyage to Quebec, in Two Cantos.

BROWNLEE (W. C.) A Careful and Free Enquiry into the true Nature and Tendency of the Religious Principles of the Society of Friends, commonly called Quakers. In two parts. 1st. The History of their Opinions, the Rise and Progress of the Society. 2d. Dissertations on their Doctrinal Tenets, their Worship, Ministry, &c. By William Craig Brownlee, D.D. *Philadelphia.* 1824. 8vo, pp. 334. 8697

BROWNLEE. Review of W. C. Brownlee on Quakerism. From the Church Examiner. *Boston.* 1825. 8vo, pp. 31. 8698

BROWNLEE. Popery, an Enemy to Civil and Religious Liberty; and Dangerous to our Republic. Fourth Edition. *New York.* 1839. 12mo. 8699

BROWNLEE. Memorial of the Rev. William C. Brownlee, D.D. Published by the Consistory of the Collegiate Ref. Prot. Dutch Church of the City of New-York. [*New York.* 1860.] 8vo, pp. 8. Portrait. H. 8700

BROWNLOW (W. G.) An Address to the Loyal People of Tennesssee -- greeting: ... [Signed W. G. Brownlow. Knoxville, March 18th, 1868. n. p. n. d.] Broadside. H. 8701

BROWNLOW. Parson Brownlow and the Unionist of East Tennessee; with a Sketch of his Life. Comprising the Story of the Experiences and Sufferings of the Unionists of East Tenıessee; the Parson's Remarkable Adventures; Incidents of the Prison-Life of Himself and Coadjutors; Anecdotes of his Daughter; Editorials of the Knoxville Whig; together with an Interesting Account of Buell's Occupation of Tennessee. *New York: Beadle and Company.* 18mo, pp. 96. 8702

BROWNLOW. A Political Register, setting forth the Principles [*sic*] of the Whig and Locofoco Parties in the United States, with the Life and Public Services of Henry Clay. Also an Appendix Personal to the Author; and a General Index. By William G. Brownlow ... . *Jonesborough, Tenn.* 1844. 8vo, Title, pp. v–vii, 9–349. C., H. 8703

BROWNLOW. Portrait and Biography of Parson Brownlow, The Tennessee Patriot. Together with his last Editorial in the Knoxville Whig; also his recent Speeches, Rehearsing his Experience with Secession, and his Prison Life. *Indianapolis: Asher & Co.* 1862. 12mo, pp. 72. 8704

BROWNLOW. Sketches of the Rise, Progress, and Decline of Secession; with a Narrative of Personal Adventures among the Rebels. By W. G. Brownlow ... . *Philadelphia: George W. Childs. Cincinnati: Applegate & Co.* 1862. 12mo, pp. 458. Portrait. BA., C. 8705

Known as Parson Brownlow's Book. *See also* "Pulpit and Rostrum," September 1, 1863.

BROWNLOW. Sufferings of Union Men. An Address by Parson Brownlow ... delivered before the Citizens of New York, at the Academy of Music, May 15, 1862. Reported by Chas. B. Collar. [n. p. n. d.] 12mo, pp. 36. 8706

BROWNLOW. Speech of Governor Brownlow, Delivered in Knoxville. ... March 24th, 1866 ... . [n. p. n. d.] Broadside.

Also: Message and Inaugural Address to the Senate and House of Representatives, Session of 1865. *Nashville, Tenn.: S. C. Mercer.* 1865. 8vo, pp. 23. And other messages and speeches.

BROWNLOW (W. G.) *and* PRYNE (A.) Ought American Slavery to be perpetuated? A Debate between W. G. Brownlow and Rev. A. Pryne, held at Philadelphia, September, 1858. *Philadelphia: J. B. Lippincott & Co.* 1858. 12mo, pp. 305. C.

BROWNSON (O. A.) An Address, delivered at Dedham, on the Fifty-eighth Anniversary of American Independence, July 4, 1834. By O. A. Brownson. ... *Dedham: H. Mann, Printer.* 1834. 8vo, pp. 25. 8709

BROWNSON. An Address on Popular Education. Delivered in Winnisimet Village, ... July 23, 1837. By O. A. Brownson. ... *Boston.* 1837. 8vo, pp. 15. H. 8710

BROWNSON. The American Republic; its Constitution, Tendencies, and Destiny. By O. A. Brownson, LL.D. *New York: P. O'Shea.* 1866. 8vo, pp. xvi, 439. C. 8711

BROWNSON. Constitutional Government. By O. A. Brownson ... *Boston: Benjamin H. Greene.* 1842. 8vo, pp. 35. BA.

BROWNSON. Essays and Reviews chiefly on Theology, Politics, and Socialism. *New York.* 1852. 12mo, pp. xii, 521. C.

See the "Boston Quarterly Review," No. 6.

BROWNSON. The Laboring Classes. An Article from the Boston Quarterly Review. *Boston.* 1840. 8vo, pp. 24. 8714

BROWNSON. Defence of the Articles on the Laboring Classes. From the Boston Quarterly Review. *Boston.* 1840. 8vo, pp. 94. 8715

BROWNSON. An Oration before the Democracy of Worcester and Vicinity, delivered at Worcester, Mass., July 4, 1840, by O. A. Brownson. *Boston: E. Littlefield. Worcester: M. D. Phillips.* 1840. 8vo, pp. 38. H. 8716

BROWNSON. Social Reform. An Address before the Society of the Mystical Seven in the Wesleyan University, Middletown, Conn. August 7, 1844. *Boston.* 1844. 8vo, pp. 42. BA. 8717

BROWNSON. The Spirit-Rapper; an Autobiography. By O. A. Brownson ... . *Boston: Little, Brown and Company. London: Charles Dolman.* M. DCCC. LIV. 12mo, pp. xi, 402. H. 8718

BROWNSON. Brownson's Quarterly Review. National Series. Volume I. *New York: D. & J. Sadlier & Co.* ... [1864.] 8vo.

No more was issued.

BRUCE (A.) An Historical Account of the most Remarkable Earthquakes, and Volcanic Eruptions, from the Beginning of the World. By Rev. Arch. Bruce. *Whitburn.* 1820. 12mo. P.

Includes an account of the destruction of Lima, etc.

BRUCE (Archibald). *See* American Mineralogical Journal, Vol. I., No. 1148.

BRUCE (C. H.) Obituary Notice. Died, in New Orleans, August 23d, Charles Henry Bruce, Esq. formerly of Boston. [n. p. 1817.] 8vo, pp. 3. H. 8721

BRUCE (G.) An Address to the Stockholders and Creditors of the New York and Erie Railroad Company. [*New York.* 1859.] 8vo, pp. 16. H. 8722

BRUCE (H.) The Warehouse Manual and General Custom House Guide, with Forms of Entries, Oaths, Bonds, etc.; Tables of Foreign Weights, Measures, and Currencies reduced to the United States Standard. Schedule of the Rates of Storage, adopted by the Chamber of Commerce of the City of New York, Provisions relative to Drawback, Extracts from Treassury Regulations, etc. Compiled and arranged by Hamilton Bruce ... . *New York: the Author.* 1862. 8vo, pp. 216. 8723

BRUCE (James C.) An Address delivered before the Alumni and Graduating Class of the University of North Carolina, at Chapel Hill, June 3, 1841. *Raleigh.* 1841. 8vo. N. 8724

BRUCE (L.) The Happiness of Man the Glory of God. A Sermon Preached before the Honourable Trustees For Establishing the Colony of Georgia in America, and the Associates of the late Rev. Dr. Bray; at their Anniversary Meeting, March 15, 1743, in the Parish Church of St. Margaret, Westminster. By Lewis Bruce, A.M. Preacher of his Majesty's Chapel, Somerset-House. *London: Printed by Daniel Browne.* MDCCXLIV. 4to, Title, pp. 53. 8725

BRUCE (P. H.) Memoirs of Peter Henry Bruce, Esq., a Military Officer in the service of Prussia, Russia and Great Britain. Containing an Account of his Travels in Germany, Russia, Tartary, Turkey, the West Indies, &c. ... *London: Printed for the Author's Widow.* MDCCLXXXII. 6 l., pp. 446. C. + Reprinted. *Dublin.* 1783. 8vo, pp. xv, 527. P. 8726

Contains adventures among the Creek and Cherokee Indians, in Georgia, etc. *See* M. R., LXVII. 410.

BRUCE. Nachrichten von seinen Reisen in Deutschland, Russland, der Tartarei, Westindien etc. ... Aus dem Englischen. *Leipzig.* 1784. 8vo. 8727

BRUCE (S. D.) American Stud Book: containing full Pedigrees of all the Imported Thorough-bred Stallions and Mares, from the Earliest Accounts of Racing in America, etc. By S. D. Bruce. Illustrated. Vol. I., A to L. *Chicago: E. B. Myers & Chandler.* 1869. 8vo, pp. xi, 649. 8728

BRUCE (V.) The Cloud of Human Experience. A Token of God's Protection. A Sermon delivered in St. Paul's Church, Hoboken, November 2, 1862. By Rev. V. Bruce. *Hoboken: A. O. Evans.* 1863. 12mo, pp. 10. 8729

[BRUCE.] Poems, chiefly in the Scottish Dialect, originally written under the signature of the Scots-Irishman, By A Native of Scotland with Notes and Illustrations. *Washington,* [*Pa.*]: *J. Colerick.* 1801. 12mo, pp. xii, 126, Glossary, 6 l. 8730

Probably the first book printed at that place.

BRÜCKMANN (Franz Ernst). Relatio Historico-Botanico Medica de Avellana Mexicana vulgo Cacao, ejusque balsamo. *Brunsvigæ: Schröter.* 1728. 4to, 2 sheets. A. 8731

BRÜCKNER (G.) Amerikas wichtigste Charakteristik nach Land und Leuten. Mit zahlreichen Holzschnitten und 3 Stahlstichen. *St. Louis: Witter.* [1858.] 8vo, 2 l., pp. 203. + Mit 2 Karten und 36 Stahlstichen. Congress-Ausgabe. [*Ibid.*] 1858. 8vo, 2 l., pp. 203. C. 8732

Die Brüder-Mission auf den Dänisch-Westindischen Inseln. Ein Rückblick auf deren erstes Jahrhundert, zum 21. August 1832. *Gnadau: Burkhard.* 1832. 8vo, pp. 40. 8733

BRUDIEU *and* LIGNIÈRES. Brudieu et Lignières, citoyens arbitrairement déportés au Port-au-Prince, à la Convention nationale. [*Paris.*] 1792. 8vo, pp. 48 or less. 8734

BRUÉ (A. H.) *and* PICQUET (Ch.) Nouvelle carte de l'Amérique septentrionale et meridionale. *Paris.* 1840. 8 parts, eleph. folio. 8735

BRUEN (M.) A Discourse the substance of which was delivered in Woodbridge, Dec. 13, 1821, the Day of public Thanksgiving and Prayer appointed by the Governor of the State of New Jersey. By M. Bruen. ... *New York.* 1822. 8vo, pp. 48. S. 8736

BRUEN. Memoirs of the Life and character of the Rev. Matthias Bruen, late pastor of the Presbyterian church in Bleecker St. New York. *New-York: John P. Haven.* 1831. 8vo, pp. vii, 356. C. 8737

BRUERE. Copies of Letters from Governor Bruere to Lord Dartmouth, and from Lord George Germaine to Sir Basil Keith, relative to the British Army's Proceedings in America. *London.* 1775. 8vo. 8738

Title from one of Th. Thorpe's catalogues.

BRUGGE (J) *See* Segerez van der Brugge (J.)

BRUIN. Omnium pene Europæ, Asiæ, Africæ et Americæ gentium habitus, elegantissime æri incisi: quibus accedunt Romani Pontificis, Cardinalium, Episcoporum, una cum omnium ordinum monachorum et religiosorum habitu. *Antuerp.: cura Abrah. de Bruin.* 1581. Oblong folio. 8739

Fifty-eight copperplates, containing some hundreds of costumes.

BRULIUS (Joachim). Historiæ | Pervanæ | Ordinis Eremitarvm | S. P. Avgvstini | Libri Octodecim | Non tantùm rebus ibi per Augustinianos egregiè gestis, ac præclaris | præceptis exemplisq*ue* vitæ sæcularis non minùs quàm Religiosæ, sed | ubere insuper & amœnâ veteris novæq*ue* Peruviæ notitiâ mirificè | referti, tractatur enim de origine Peruanorum, eorum moribus, regi- | mine, Religione, qualitatibus terræ, de eorum subiectione per Hispa- | nos, ac de Hispanorum bellis civilibus similibusque rebus quàm | plurimis, quarum breviarium Index exhibet. | Avctore | R^do. & Eximio P. M. Ioachimo Brvlio sacræ Theo- | logiæ Doctore, Ordinis Eremitarum S. P. Avgvstini | per Provinciam Coloniensem seu Belgicam | Priore Provinciali. | [Vignette]. *Apud Gvilielmvm Lesteenivm via vulgo Hoogh- | straet dicta, sub Pellicano aureo. Anno* 1651. | *Cum gratia & Privilegio.* | Folio, 2 vols in 1, 4 l., pp. 276; 2 l., pp. 181, Index and Errata, pp. 6. H. 8740

Said to be printed in Holland. "Antonio supposes this to be taken from Calancha's 'Chronica,' No. 226. Some copies have the date 1751." — O. RICH, No. 288.

BRULLEY (C. A.) Essai sur la cochenille et le nopal, pour servir à l'histoire de l'établissement de la première nopalerie française dans l'île de Saint-Domingue. *Paris.* 1795. 8vo.

BRUMAULD DE BEAUREGARD (Jean). Mémoires de Mgr. J. Brumauld de Beauregard, évêque d'Orléans, chanoine de premier ordre au chapitre royal de Saint-Denis, précédés de sa vie écrite sur des notes et des documents authentiques. *Poitiers: impr. de Saurin.* 1842. 2 vols., 12mo. 8742

"Dans le 2e volume se trouve un mémoire intitulé: 'Ma Déportation à la Guyane, 1797–1801.'"

BRUMBY (R. T.) Address before the Philomathic Society of the University of Alabama, Dec. 8, 1838. By R. T. Brumby. *Tuskaloosa.* 1838. 8vo, pp. 25. BA. 8743

BRUMMELKAMP (A.) Holland in Amerika oder die holländische Colonie im Staate Michigan. Mitgetheilt für Auswanderer. Aus dem Hollandischen von G. A. *Mühlheim a. d. Ruhr: Nieten.* 12mo, pp. 26. 8744

BRUMMELKAMP. Stemmen uit Noord-Amerika. *Amsterdam.* 1847. 8vo. + *Arnhem.* 1847. 8vo. 8745

BRUMMELKAMP (A.) *and* VAN RAALTE (A. C.) Landverhuizing, of waarom bevorderen wij de Volksverhuizing en wel naar Noord-Amerika en niet naar Java? *Amsterdam.* 1846. 8vo. 8746

[BRUN (Jean B.)] Le triomphe du nouveau monde; réponses académiques, Formant un nouveau système de Confédération, fondé sur les besoins actuels des Nations Chrétiennes-commerçantes, & adapté à leurs diverses formes de Gouvernement: dédié Aux Souverains, aux académies, à tous les Gens de bien, & envoyé très-respectueusement à la plupart des Gouvernemens Chrétiens, à plusieurs Académies, à quelques Grands Hommes Par l'Ami du Corps Social. ... *Paris: l'Auteur,* [*et*] *la Veuve Herissant.* M. DCC. LXXXV. 2 vols., 8vo, pp. ix, 242; 2 l., pp. 298, 4 l. C., H. 8747

On the same subject, *see* "Blackwood's Mag.," LX. 261. "By Jean Brun, who on account of this work was dismissed from the congregation of the Oratory." — BARBIER.

BRUN (Malthe Conrad). *See* Malte-Brun (Conrad).

BRUNE (F. W.), *Jr.* American Education. An Address ... June 23rd, 1852. By F. W. Brune, Jr. ... *Baltimore: printed by Joseph Robinson.* 1852. 8vo, pp. 19. H. 8748

BRUNE (Frederick W.) *See* Brown (G. W.), Vol. II., No. 8481.

BRUNEL (A.) Observations topographiques, météorologiques et médicales faits dans de le Rio de la Plata, pendant le blocus de Buenos-Ayres. ... Par M. Adolphe Brunel, M.D., Chirurgien major de la Corvette la Perle. *Paris: Desloges.* 1842. 8vo, pp. 56. 8749

BRUNET (O.) Catalogue des plantes canadiennes. Par L'Abbe Ovide Brunet. *Quebec.* 1865. 8vo, pp. 200. 8750

BRUNET. Catalogue des vegetaux ligneux du Canada. Par L'Abbe Ovide Brunet. *Quebec.* 1867. 8vo, pp. 64. 8751

BRUNET. Enumération des genres de plantes de la Flore du Canada, précédée des Tableaux analytiques des Familles, et destinée aux élèves qui suivent le cours de botanique descriptive donné à l'Université Laval. *Quebec.* 1863. 12mo, pp. 45.

BRUNET. Histoire des Picea qui se rencontrent dans les limites du Canada. Par L'Abbe Ovide Brunet. *Quebec.* 1866. 8vo, pp. 16. 3 Plates. 8753

BRUNET. Notice sur les Plantes de Michaux et sur son voyage du Canada et à la Baie d'Hudson d'apres sou journal manuscrit et autres documents. *Quebec.* 1863. 8vo, pp. 44.

BRUNET. Voyage d'André Michaux en Canada. Par L'Abbe Ovide Brunet. *Quebec.* 1861. 8vo, pp. 27. 8755

This was translated into English by Dr. Sterry Hunt in the "Canadian Naturalist;" also published in pamphlet form.

BRUNNERMANN (K.) Geschichte der nordamerikanischen Literatur. Eine literar-historiche Studie von Dr. K. Brunnemann. *Leipzig: Fr. Wilh. Grunon.* 1866. 8vo, pp. iv, 159.

The Brunonian. Edited by Students of Brown University. ... *Providence: H. H. Brown.* 1829–31. 8vo, pp. 386. 8757

In twelve numbers—July, 1829, to March, 1831.

BRUNOT (F. R.) The Soldier's Return. [A Poem.] By F. R. Brunot, Esq. [*Pittsburgh.* 1863.] 24mo, pp. 24. 8758

BRUNS (P. F.) *and* ZIMMERMANN (E. A. W.) Repositorium für die neueste Geographie, etc. *Tübingen: Cotta.* 1792–1793. 3 vols., 8vo. 8759

Contains "Extracts from Journals of Expeditions to the North of California," I. 25.

BRUNSON (Alfred.) Description of Northern Wiskonsan. [*Madison.* 1843.] 8vo, pp. 16. 8760

BRUNSON. Prairie du Chien: its Present Position and Future Prospects. *Milwaukee.* 1857. 12mo, pp. 12. H. 8761

BRUNSON. Communication ... relative to his Travels in the Northwestern Wilderness of Wisconsin. Leg. Doct., Dec. 19, 1843. 8vo, pp. 12. M. 8762

BRUNSWICK, *Ga.* Public Sale, at Brunswick, Georgia. The Brunswick Land Company offer ... from one to two hundred well selected Lots. *Boston.* [1837.] 8vo, pp. 12. Map. H.

BRUNSWICK, *Me.* An Answer to the Remarks of the Plymouth Company, or, as they call themselves, the proprietors of the Kennebeck Purchase, from the late Colony of New Plymouth, published by virtue of their vote of 31st of January last; on the Plan and extracts of deeds published by the Proprietors of the Township of Brunswick. Agreeable to their vote of the 4th of January immediately preceding. Wherein the many trifling cavils against said plan and extracts are answered, many aspersions cast on them wiped off; and their entire consistency with each other fully shown. And also the boundaries of the Plymouth companies' Tract upon Kennebeck River are at large set forth and ascertained. *Boston, N. E.* 1753. 4to, pp. 33. C.

See Plymouth Company.

A Description of Brunswick, Me. *See* [Putnam (Henry)].

Financial and Superintending School Committee's Reports of the Town of Brunswick, from March 1, 1864 to March 1, 1865. [*Brunswick:*] *Press of J. Griffin.* [n. d.] 8vo, pp. 28. H. 8765

Proceedings of the Convention of Delegates held in Brunswick, Maine, 1816. [*Brunswick.* 1816.] 8vo, pp. 20. 8766

Relating to separation from Massachusetts.

Town Accounts, 1846. [n. p. n. d.] 8vo, pp. 8. Continued. H. 8767

Brunswick Antimony Company. Reports by Prof. George I. Chace ... and Wm. Petherick ... . *Boston.* 1864. 8vo, pp. 16. (1). Map. H. 8768

BRUNT (J.) Extracts from Locke and others, containing a Defence of Natural, Judicial, and Constitutional Rights. With a short account of the Publisher's Difficulties, intermixed with some political remarks. By Jonathan Brunt. *Frankfort, Ky.* 1804. 8vo, pp. 36. C. 8769

BRUNTON (W.) ... A Sermon on the Occasion of Fasting and Prayer on Account of the Cholera Morbus. By Rev. William Brunton. *Montreal.* 1832. 8vo. 8770

[BRUSH.] Speech of a Member of the General Assembly of New York, At their Session, in 1775. *New-York.* MDCCLXXV. 8vo, pp. 12. H. 8771

BRUSH (Conklin). Address before the Brooklyn Common Council. *Brooklyn.* 1851. 8vo, pp. 8. 8772

Brush (John C.) A small Tract, entitled, a Candid Exposition of the various opinions on the subject of the character and quality of the Wheat and Flour in the Northern and Southern Sections of the United States. By John C. Brush. *Washington: T. Gideon, Jr.* 1820. 8vo, pp. 52. c. 8773

Brush (S.) An Address delivered At Canandaigua ... February 2, 1866 ... . By Samuel Brush, Esq. ... [On the Taxation of U. S. stocks and on National Banks.] *Canandaigua, N. Y.: Ontario Rep. Office.* 1866. 8vo, pp. 27. c., h. 8774

Brutel de la Riviére. Togt van het Engelsche schip Pagoda naar de zuidpool. [*Amsterdam.*] 1850. 8vo. 8775

Brutus, *pseudon.* The Crisis: or, Essays on the Usurpations of the Federal Government. By Brutus. ... *Charleston: printed by A. E. Miller.* 1827. 8vo, pp. 166. h. 8776

Brutus, *pseudon.* Foreign Conspiracy against the Liberties of the United States: the Numbers of Brutus originally published in the New-York Observer. Revised and corrected with Notes by the Author. ... [With an Appendix.] *New-York: Leavitt, Lord & Co., [etc.]* 1835. 12mo, pp. 188. c., h. 8777

Brutus. Letters of Brutus to certain celebrated Political Characters. *Edinburgh.* 1791. 8vo, 2 l., pp. 72. c. 8778

Relates to Burgoyne, Burke, Pitt, etc.

Brutus (Lucius Junius), *pseudon.* *See* New Haven Remonstrance.

Bruyas (J.) Radices Verborum Iroquæorum. Auctore Jacobo Bruyas Societatis Jesu. *Neo-Eboraci: Typis J. M. Shea.* 1863. 8vo, 2 l., pp. 123. ba., c. 8779

With the 2d title: "Radical Words of the Mohawk Language, with their Derivatives. By Rev. James Bruyas S. J. Missionary on the Mohawk. *Cramoisy Press: New-York.* 1862." Imp. 8vo, pp. 123. Forms No. x. of Shea's "Library of American Linguistics."

Bruyere (J.-B.) Notice sur M. Jean-Baptiste Bruyere. *Montréal.* 1859. 18mo. 8780

Bruyn (H. de). Plan eener trapsgewijze emancipatie der slaven in de Nederlandsche West-Indische kolonien. *Zalt-Bommel: Joh. Noman en Zn.* 1851. 8vo. 8781

Bruzual (Manual E.) A sus compatriotas. *Carácas.* 1864. 8vo, pp. xv. 8782

Bruzen de la Martinière (A. A.) Introduction à l'histoire de l'Asie, de l'Afrique et de l'Amérique. Pour servir de suite à l'introduction à l'histoire du baron de Pufendorff. Par Mr. Bruzen de la Martinière. *Amsterdam: Z. Chatelain.* 1735. 2 vols., 12mo, 1 l., pp. xxii, 504, 2 Maps, and engraved Frontispieces; 1 l., pp. 568. 2 Maps. c. + *Amsterdam: Z. Chatelain.* 1738. 2 vols., 12mo, 1 l., pp. xxii, 504, Map; pp. 427. 3 Maps.

"Dans le second volume de cette continuation (pp. 99–427), l'auteur parle avec beaucoup de précision et d'exactitude des découvertes, et des établissemens des François, Anglois, Hollandois, Suédois et Danois dans les isles et le continent de l'Amérique septentrionale." — Le P. Charlevoix.

THEODOR DE BRY.

After much deliberation, I have determined to content myself with the description contained in Brunet's *Manuel de Libraire*, which has been translated for this work by Mr. Charles A. Cutter, Librarian of the Boston Athenæum. The titles of the first Latin edition have been printed at length; the remainder are abbreviated as in Brunet.

Bry. Collectiones Peregrinationum in Indiam Orientalem et Indiam Occidentalem, xxv Partibus comprehensæ a Theodoro, Joan.-Theodoro de Bry, et a Matheo Merian publicatæ. *Francofurti ad Mœnum.* 1590–1634. 25 Parts, folio.

Such is the made-up title which is ordinarily given in catalogues to the twenty-five parts of the collection of voyages published by the de Bry or De Bry. The collection is divided into two series. The first, known as the "Great Voyages" (*Grands Voyages*), because the pages are a little over an inch taller and wider than in the second series, contains the voyages to the West Indies, and consists, in the Latin edition, of thirteen parts, in the German, of fourteen. The second series, the "Small Voyages" (*Petits Voyages*), contains the voyages to the East Indies, in twelve parts in Latin, and thirteen in German. [The Larger and The Lesser Travels would, perhaps, be more appropriate names, but the terms here adopted have become familiar as translations of the French designations. — Tr.]

To Theodor or Theodoric de Bry, engraver, print-seller, and book-seller, at Frankfort on the Main, the commencement of this collection is due. He conceived the plan after publishing, in 1590, the narration of travels in Virginia, written in English by Thomas Hariot, which had already appeared in London in 1588, in 4to. (*See* Hariot.) In order to get more profit from the plates which he had added to this relation, he had the text printed in four languages, — English, French, Latin, and German, and so had four different editions to offer to the public. The success of this volume decided the publisher to issue, the next year, a second (on the Floridas), which the title designates as *Americæ Secunda Pars*, but he printed the text of this and the ensuing volumes only in Latin and German. At the time of his death, in March, 1598, Theodor de Bry had already issued, from 1590 to 1596, six parts of the Great Voyages. After him, his widow and his two sons, Johann Theodor and Johann Israel, issued the 7th and 8th parts in 1599, the 9th in 1600; and, as the title of this last part bears the words *Postrema Pars*, it appears that they intended to stop there. Nevertheless, Johann Theo-

dor, resuming the interrupted enterprise, printed at Oppenheim, in 1619 and 1620, a 10th and 11th part, and his heirs issued a 12th at Frankfort in 1624; finally, Math. Merian, one of his son-in-laws, published, in 1634, the 13th and last part, which is merely the translation of the 13th and 14th parts of the German text, already published by him in 1628 and 1630. The same year that Merian published this last part of the Latin text, he united under a collective title the thirteen parts of the Great Voyages, of which he possessed the stock, and published a new edition of the First Part, augmented with an *Elenchus*, or table of the different pieces contained in each of the thirteen parts.

The two brothers, Johann Theodor and Johann Israel de Bry, published the eight first parts of the Latin text of the Small Voyages in 1598, 1599, 1601, 1604, 1606, and 1607; they had published, a little before these dates, the eight first parts of the German text. Johann Theodor alone issued the 9th, 10th, and 11th parts of the German text in 1612, 1613, and 1618, and the same parts of the Latin text in 1612, 1613, and 1619. It is to his second son-in-law, William Fitzers, an Englishman by birth, that the 12th part is due. It was printed in 1628, as well as the 12th and 13th parts of the German text, which form a continuation to the German abridgement of the eleven first parts, which the same Fitzers had just published under the title of "Orientalische Indien." ...

Thus forty-four years passed between the publication of the first volume of the Great Voyages and that of the last volume of the Latin text of these relations. Now, during this long interval, the publishers of this great collection must have reprinted, even more than once, the greater part of the volumes, which had become successively out of print; but, before coming to entire reimpressions, they would naturally use the portions either of text or of plates which were on hand. It appears, in fact, that the plates were at first printed only for a part of the two texts of the first volumes, and that, when this first impression was exhausted, it became necessary to have a second, and at the same time, to print on the pages destined to receive the engravings both the numbers indicating their order, and the titles or explanations, which appear above and below those engravings, and that, finally, when the text was entirely exhausted, they reprinted it, at first with the old date, and afterwards with a new date. This explains how it is that one encounters, besides the editions reprinted as a whole, copies of the first edition offering so many various readings that one might think they belonged to different editions. It is certain that before the publication of the sixth volume, many of the first had been already reprinted, and that after that time the publishers could only deliver to the new purchasers of their collection copies formed of parts belonging to different editions. But we must not forget to say that there is only a single edition of the last parts of each of the two sections; and this is what makes them much more rare than the first parts. The reprints of these latter usually contain only plates more or less worn, and even those of these reprints of which the titles bear the address of Math. Merian not only have plates worn out, badly retouched, or re-engraved in counter-proof; but their very paper is detestable, the impression is very bad the text incorrect, and, what is worse, defective in many places; they are to be sought for, therefore, only for the sake of some additions which were made in them, as we shall take care to point out in our description at the proper time. This collection, it must be confessed, has not that importance for geographical science which it has acquired as a bibliographical curiosity, because it is uncritical; it contains very few relations which had not been already published separately; and the reprints or translations which are given of the others are worth infinitely less than the original texts. It is true that numerous plates, many of which are well enough engraved, were added to these texts; but they had been made, for the most part, after fanciful designs, adapted, some well, some ill, to the narrations of the travellers, and multiplied as a mere matter of speculation. The only advantage, then, which this great work has, is that of uniting in the same form a number of curious pieces which could not be procured separately without difficulty, and, moreover, were only to be had in different shapes. This has been enough to cause it to be sought for by opulent lovers of books, to secure it a dis-

tinguished place in nearly all the great libraries of Europe and America; and this has carried its price far above its real value. To form a complete copy of the Great and the Small Voyages, it is not enough to collect the first editions of each part: it is necessary, besides, to add to these the reprints which have any additions in the text, and any noteworthy differences in the plates. This was done, in France, as early as the commencement of the xviiith century by M. de Cisternay Du Fay, an enlightened amateur, whose name is still preserved in the memory of book-lovers. The catalogue of his books, compiled by Gabr. Martin, contains, at No. 2825, a copy of this collection, bound in 5 volumes, in blue morocco, which the epithet *exemplar omni genere perfectum* carried as high as 450 francs, a remarkable price at that time. After this, a lettered bibliophile, equally well known, the Abbé d'Orléans de Rothelin, having succeeded in forming a copy more complete than that of M. Du Fay, described it in a tract of 44 pages, small 4to, of which he had only a few copies printed (*see* the title Observations*), and although his observations are confined to giving the title of each part and some short notes, they served as a guide to collectors, until De Bure the younger had furnished, in his "Bibliographie instructive" ("Histoire," Vol. 1.), a more complete and, moreover, a much more detailed description of the same collection. It is true that the work of this bibliographer leaves much to be desired, both in the data necessary to determine the first impressions of the plates, and in the description of the parts reprinted, and, finally, because some errors have slipped in, and he has entirely omitted the edition with the German text, although several parts of that, in the Great Voyages, and especially in the Small Voyages, contain the first proofs of the plates. In spite of these omissions, his account has hitherto been the most convenient guide in collating the Latin text of this collection. Undoubtedly, the "Mémoire sur la collection des Grands et Petits Voyages," published by Camus, in 1802, is, in a scientific aspect, a work much superior to that of De Bure, as it gives good analyses of all the narrations published by De Bry, and indicates with care a large number of the originals; but it is less satisfactory in details concerning the subject-matter of the book, and is a little behind hand in the historical portion.

In preparing the different editions of our "Manuel," we have often thought of abridging the description given by De Bure, and completing it, but we have always shrunk from the difficulties of an enterprise requiring such minute care, and one that would have required of us much more time than we could have devoted to a single article. Since that, in our leisure moments, we have determined to fill this lamentable gap in our Dictionary. The better to do this we have consulted all the documents hitherto published on this subject, and after having compared them with the three copies in the *Bibliothèque impériale*, including the German text, and with that in the *Bibliothèque Mazarine*, we have prepared a new description, less abundant than that of De Bure in minute details, but, we are inclined to believe, more complete and more exact than his, and containing, in addition, the necessary details in regard to the German texts, for which we have used the "Bibliographische Mittheilungen," published at Leipzig, in 1845, by T. O. Weigel. Nevertheless, we do not flatter ourself that we have met with, or even foreseen, all the modifications that the fancy of collectors can introduce into the formation of a copy of this great collection, for, although the wisest confine themselves to the first editions and those of the reprints which contain some additions, other collectors, less easily satisfied, assemble all the editions which have been made of most of the parts, both in Latin and in German; others, finally, go beyond even these last, constantly seeking all the copies of the same edition that present to their eyes any differences, either in the engraved frontispieces, or in the preliminary matter, or, above

* Under this heading, Brunet gives the title, Observations et détails sur la collection des grands et petits voyages (par l'abbé d'Orléans de Rothelin). 1742. Sm. 4to, pp. 14. A very small edition printed: 24 fr. d'Hangard; 12 fr. 50 c. Parison. This work, which that of Camus, on the same subject, has made almost useless, is reprinted with additions in Lenglet du Fresnoy's *Méthode pour étudier la géographie*, ed. 1768, 1. 324–361.

all, in the plates, whether re-engraved or merely retouched; they do not forget even those which were pasted over others which had been wrongly placed; so that, perhaps, no two copies of this work are exactly alike. That which M. De Bure the elder had formed for himself, which was sold at Paris, in December, 1853, for 11,500 francs (plus 5 per cent. for expenses), contained duplicate plates, and, what is more remarkable, a second edition of the 10th part of the Small Voyages, dated 1633, which is wanting both in the two fine copies at the *Bibliothèque impériale*, and in that still more valuable one which Mr. Thomas Grenville bequeathed, with all his rich library, to the British Museum, and, finally, in the collection of Mr. J. Lenox, at New York, one of the most complete which exist, especially in the first editions of the German text. On the other hand, a well-known Russian book-lover, M. Serge de Sobolewski, honorary member of the Imperial Library at St. Petersburg, boasted, not long since, that his collection had reached 170 parts, all differing from one another in some points, and he flattered himself that he should find means to still further augment it. This learned collector has lately done us the honor to communicate to us, in regard to the different parts of the Latin text of the Great and the Small Voyages, some valuable notes, of which we have made use, to the improvement of our descriptions. As to the original editions of the narrations which the De Bry have reproduced, we shall say nothing here, having taken care to describe them in this "Manuel" under the names of their authors; moreover it is well known that amateurs admit into their collections only those original relations which are in folio.

Our readers will doubtless be glad to find here the opinion of M. Sobolewski on the cause and the effects of the successive modifications which the copies of this great collection have undergone. The learned bibliophile writes to us from Moscow: "It should be remarked, that soon after the publication of the first parts, and while the publication of the following parts was going on, the stock, and even the idea of the brothers de Bry, were parcelled out among their heirs, and then among the different publishers to whom the heirs sold their stock. Owing to these partitions, as the editions were in different hands, each proprietor was more or less obliged to reprint certain parts entirely, or to reprint leaves and sheets; in this latter case, they often could no longer use the old plates, which were in other hands, but employed fresh ones, which they caused to be engraved after those that they did not now possess. All these manipulations, together with the long time during which the publication of these two series lasted, gave, from the very commencement, importance to the original work, and especially to copies which were not only of the same edition, but where each part were free from the mixture of leaves printed at different times. Afterwards collectors and amateurs, in forming copies for their libraries, introduced more confusion into the bibliography of the Great and Small Voyages, by mixing together all that, at first sight, appeared to complete or much enrich their copies. All these causes united, confused the cataloguers; they saw more editions than there really were, and took for differences of edition the result of the printer's inadvertence or forgetfulness, and of the book-sellers necessities; and before long the increasing vanity of collectors, in place of separating the second editions from the first, and the altered reprint of Merian from the two original editions, mingled them all, in order that they might be able to announce that such and such a part of their collection contained so many leaves with variations!!! Or they increased the number of their volumes by adding the original editions of the voyages, which the publishers of the collection had copied, and the editions which had been copied after texts given in the collection. For my own part," adds M. Sobolewski, "I am opposed to this rage for giving variations, and enriching one's copy by mixture of editions. In my opinion," he continues, "a good copy of the Latin collection ought to contain the 25 parts either from the first or the second edition, or from the reprint. If it contains all three, which is to be preferred, each edition should form a part of the work by itself, and in no case should one bind with the plates of the first edition those of the second (and *vice versa*), in order to be able to speak of double or triple plates, as my friends the De Bure have too often done. If the printer has forgotten to print a plate on a place left blank, or if, by mistake, he has printed the wrong one,

I do not consider that a variation to be noted. If some leaves are wanting in any part, I put in white paper rather than the corresponding leaves taken from another edition, or from a reprint. You can see in the catalogue of Langlès that that Orientalist possessed the third part of the Great Voyages, composed of leaves of different editions, and this I have often found to be the case with that part."

Before beginning the detailed description of the collection with which we are now occupied, we must recommend to those persons who have to collate copies not to be content to ascertain the presence of the number of plates which we specify, but to take great care to satisfy themselves that these plates are the ones which belong to the part that they have under their eyes. This precaution is the more essential, because the plates of one of these parts have often been adapted to another, or plates which were wanting in one part, have been replaced by those which bore the same number in another part.

A. — GREAT VOYAGES.

First Part.

Bry. Admiranda Narratio | Fida tamen, de Commodis et | Incolarvm Ritibvs Virginiæ, nvper | admodvm ab Anglis, qvi à Dn. Richardo | Greinvile Eqvestris Ordinis Viro eò in | Coloniam Anno. m.d.lxxxv. dedvcti svnt | inventæ, Svmtvs faciente Dn. VValtero | Raleigh Eqvestris Ordinis Viro Fodinarv*m* | Stanni præfecto ex Avctoritate | Serenissimæ Reginæ Angliæ. | Anglico scripta Sermone | à Thoma Hariot, eivsdem Walteri Domesti- | co, in eam Coloniam misso vt Regionis si- | tvm diligenter observaret | Nvnc avtem primvm Latio donata à | C . C . A . | Cvm Gratia et Privilegio Cæs. Ma[tis] Spec[li] | ad Qvadriennivm | *Francoforti aa Mœnvm* | *Typis Ioannis Wecheli, Svmtibvs vero Theodor* | *de Bry Anno* CIↃ IↃ XC. | *Venales reperivntvr in Officina Sigismvndi Feirabendi.* |

Description.

1. The title given above, engraved, and in an engraved border.

2. Dedicatory epistle to Maximilian, elected king of Poland, at the top of which are engraved the arms of this prince, and lower down five lines, of which the first ends with the word "vestræ," 1 l.

3. Advertisement, "Benevolis coloniae ... promotoribus," with a summary in 4 lines, 1 l., p. 5.

4. Text, in Italics ("Prima pars"), pp. 7–34. The first line of the 3d page ends with the word "pluribus," and the last line of the text has only the figures 1588.

5. Printed title, commencing "Vivæ imagines," undated; it bears an ornament in a lozenge.

6. "Index omnium capitum;" this is the list of the plates.

7. An engraving representing Adam and Eve, with the words "Theodore de Bry fe" at the bottom of the plate.

8. Advertisement, "Benevolo lectori," a leaf printed on one side only; the open letter is a capital in type within an ornament engraved on wood.

9. Map of Virginia, followed by 22 plates on as many leaves, with explanations at the foot of each; the leaves are numbered from ii to xxiii, on the obverse, at the top, and some of the plates in Arabic figures, at the bottom of the plates.

10. A leaf, with the announcement, "Pictonum ... icones;" eight lines underneath, and on the reverse the explanation of the first plate, in 17 lines.

11. Five plates (costume of the ancient Picts), numbered 1 to 5 below the plates; these, with the explanations, occupy 9 leaves.

12. Advertisement, "Interpres lectori," on one leaf, with a triangular tail-piece.

"Index præcipuarum rerum," 2 l.; on the reverse of the second, "Mendæ quæ typographicas operas fugerunt," with the same triangular ornament as the advertisement above.

A last leaf on which is repeated the colophon "Impressum ... " which is at the foot of the first frontispiece, with the date m. d. xc.

Of this first part there are two old editions very distinct from one another, the one the original, the other counterfeit; and there are three varieties of the original edition, presenting differences merely 1° in the title, 2° in pages 29 and 34 of the text, 3° in the explanation of plates iii, iv, v, vi, vii, viii, ix, x, xi, xii, xv, and xxii. All the rest is of the same impression, without any differences. Among the plates which afford variations, three are triplicates, the iiid, viiith, and xth. The others, as well as the pages 29 and 34, are only duplicates. The title presents no other difference than that of Theodor*i* and Feirabend*ii* in place of Theodor and Feirabend*i*. It is to be presumed that Theodori and Feirabendii denote the first impression, for the same orthography is employed on the titles of the French and English editions, and their dedication is dated several days before that of the Latin and German editions. As to the counterfeit of this part, there are two sorts of copies, one reproducing the pages 29 and 34, as well as the explanations of the plates of one of the varieties of the original edition, and the other representing as faithfully the second variety of the original. Until now no one has been able to decide with certainty to which of the varieties of the original edition and of the counterfeit the priority is to be assigned. But one can distinguish at first sight the plates of the first edition from those of the counterfeit, first, by the beauty of the proofs and the superiority of the paper, and more surely still by the height of the capitals employed in the printed title-pages and in the explanation of each plate, and by the Roman letters which indicate their order. In the first edition, these letters are about 9 millimètres* high (a little more than 4 lines); in the second, they are only about 7 *millimètres*† or 3 lines. But it is well to know that there was a second impression of the plates, in which, while preserving the capitals 9 *millimètres* high, a change was made in the typographic arrangement of the explanations of several plates, so that the two impressions differ in the last words of the first lines, as we shall show:—

Plate			*1st impression*	*2d impression*
III.	At the end of the first line,		in publi	pro
IV.	"	"	prode-	decussa
V.	"	"	periti in	ut appa-
VI.	"	"	nisi	memoratæ
VII.	"	"	ver-	instar
VIII.	"	"	lacum	oppidû
IX.	"	"	latere	ab uno
X.	"	"	Roa-	Roanoac
XI.	"	"	sæpenume-	naturæ
XII.	"	"	ferreis	aliis
XV.	"	"	Admodum	Cacia ad

Additional remarks: In the first impression of plate iii, the initial P of the explanation is printed from a type placed in a *passe-partout;* in the second, this P is engraved on wood, together with its ornaments. There is the same difference in the letter S in the explanation of plate iv. Many bibliographers have asserted that in the first edition the field of the scutcheon of the dedicatory epistle should be without the cross-hatching which was added to the plate after the first impression; but we have

* About .354 in. † About .275 in.

not yet been able to verify the accuracy of this remark. The second edition, or counterfeit, bears the same title and the same date as the first, and the description of one will apply to the other, with, however, the following differences:—

The first of the five lines which are at the foot of the scutcheon of the dedicatory epistle ends with the syllable "Ma."

The summary preceding the advertisement "Benevoli" which follows this epistle, is in three lines in place of four.

The first line of the 34th page of the text ends with "pluribus qui," and the last line of the text contains the words "anni 1588."

The printed title ("Vivæ imagines") which precedes the plates has an ornament, of which the centre presents a monster's head.

The vignette placed at the end of the index, which is only about 53 *millimètres* (23 lines) square in the first edition is higher and much broader in the second.

In the title which precedes the costumes of the Picts, there are, at the bottom of the page, only 7 lines in place of 8, and on the reverse, 16 in place of 17.

The errata, which, in the first edition, are on the reverse of the second leaf of the second index, have been retained in a part of the copies of the second, but with a tail-piece, which is not of a triangular form. In other copies these errata have disappeared, and the reverse of the leaf remains blank. The leaf which, in the first edition, contains the colophon and the date, has not been reproduced in the second.

We have seen several copies of this counterfeit edition (with the errata), in which the place of the frontispiece where are engraved the words "Francofurti ... in officina Sigismundi Feirabendii" has remained blank, as in the edition of 1634, of which we have still to speak.

To better characterize the difference of the two editions already described, in regard to the 22 plates of Virginia, we will give the number of lines in the explanations of each plate, in both editions.

Plate	*Original edition.*	*Reprint.*	*Plate*	*Original edition.*	*Reprint.*
II.	19 lines.	17 lines.	X.	6 lines.	7 lines.
III.	19 "	16 "	XI.	8 "	8 "
IV.	12 "	11 "	XII.	16 "	13 "
V.	7 "	7 "	XIII.	17 "	15 "
VI.	8 "	8 "	XIV.	9 "	11 "
VII.	12 "	9 "	XV.	11 "	12 "
VIII.	14 "	11 "	XVI.	5 "	6 "
IX.	8 "	8 "			

Plates xvii, xviii, xix, xx, and xxii, occupying each an entire page, are accompanied by explanations separate from or pasted on the plate.

Plate	*Original edition.*	*Reprint.*	*Plate*	*Original edition.*	*Reprint.*
XIX.	20 lines.	20 lines.	XXII.	21 "	18 lines.
XX.	25 "	20 "	XXIII.	11 "	
XXI.	13 "	10 "			

These plates, beginning with the 3d, occupy signatures A–D.

After the 23d is a blank leaf, which completes sheet D.

The exactitude of the table above has been verified by examination of many copies; but the details which Santander has given on p. 35 of the iiid volume of his catalogue differ from ours in what concerns the second edition, where, according to him, there are only 6 lines to plate v, 7 to pl. vi, 7 to p. ix, 6 to pl. x, 7 to pl. xi, but 14 to pl. xii, and 10 only to pl. xv.

We have mentioned, above, the rather remarkable engraving which represents Adam and Eve in Paradise, below which the engraver has traced his name in this manner

"Theodore de Bry fe." "If there were," says Camus, on p. 38 of his memoir, "'Jo.' before 'Theodore,' it would indicate the second edition." This remark is not entirely exact; for, although, as the author of the memoir rightly says, these two letters were added to the plate, it could not have been done, we think, before the death of Theodore de Bry, in 1597. This is why the plate not only is without the "Jo." in a large number of copies of the second edition of the first part, and even of those which no longer have the name of Feyrabend; but is still to be found (before the retouch) in the first edition of the third part, which was published in 1592; and the plate had been very much worn when the two letters were added. Only in copies which left the store-house of the publisher after 1597 can it be found with the syllable "Jo."

There is in the library at Breslau a copy of this first part which has this peculiarity, — the frontispiece is engraved as usual, but either because the plate was printed with the legend covered, or this legend had been erased, they were able to print in the empty space the words, "Pars prima Americæ, 1600." This might lead to the wholly false supposition that there was an edition different from any that are known.

[Some important corrections of the account given above will be found in a letter of M. Sobolewski which will be given after the description of the German edition of de Bry. — Tr.]

The last edition of this first part was issued by Math. Merian, under the following collective title: —

Bry. Historiæ Americæ sive Novi Orbis, comprehendens in XIII sectionibus exactissimam descriptionem vastissimarum et multis abhinc sæculis incognitarum terrarum, quæ nunc passim Indiæ occidentalis nomine vulgo usurpantur: cum elegantissimis tabulis et figuris æri incisis nec non Elenche sectionum et indice capitum ac rerum præcipuarum. *Francofurti, sumptibus Matthæi Merian, anno* 1634.

At the commencement of this volume is a sheet of ten unnumbered leaves, containing the title given above, printed in the midst of an engraving where are represented thirteen medallions, the voyages collected in the thirteen parts of this collection; a second printed title, fuller than the first, a general preface ("in opus americanum præfatio"), and, finally, an "Elenchus," or table of the different pieces contained in each part. This "Elenchus" directly refers only to the edition which Merian was selling in 1634, and does not indicate the pages where one could find, in each edition, the heads referred to. The general preface, however, which indicates the order in which the pieces collected in the Great Voyages ought to be read, is an essential portion of the work. It is then necessary to unite, as has been ordinarily done, these 10 leaves to the first editions of the first part; this is what gives a value to this edition of 1634, which has become rare. The difficulty of procuring it led an English bookseller, some time ago, to have the introduction, which is the only useful part, reprinted. This reprint has only 9 leaves; but another has been made at Paris, which, though it also does not reproduce the engraved frontispiece, has 10 leaves like the original edition, because the preface, instead of commencing on the reverse of the title-page, commences on the obverse of the second leaf.

After the 10 preliminary leaves, the edition of 1634 has the engraved title of this part (without the address), and then the dedicatory epistle. Both the advertisement "Benevolis" and the privilege have been omitted. The pages of the text are numbered 5–34. The plates, as well as their explanations, are printed on both sides of the leaves. The index of these plates is on the obverse of the leaf, the reverse being blank. This last edition is, moreover, in every respect, very inferior to the two first, and the same can be said of all the parts which Merian has printed.

Exact title and description of the first part of the Great Voyages in the French translation.

Bry. Merveillevx et estrange|rapport, tovtesfois fidele, des|commoditez qui se trovvent en|virginia, des facons des natvrels habi|tans dicelle, laqvelle a esté novvelle|ment descovverte par les anglois que me|sire Richard Greinville chevalier y mena|en colonie lan 1585. a la charge principale|de messire Walter Raleigh chevalier svrinten|dant des mines d'estain, favorisé par la royne|d'Angleterre, et autorisé par|ses lettres patentes|par Thomas Hariot servitevr dv susdit|messire Walter lvn de cevx de la dite colo|nie qvi y a este employé|a descovvrir|tradvit novvellement d'anglois *en* fra*n*cois [*sic*] impr. auec grace & priuil. de la Maiest. Imper. pour quatre Ans.

(This mention of the privilege is printed from type in Roman letters, and pasted on the plate; the rest is engraved in capitals.)

Francoforti ad Moenvm|typis Ioannis Wecheli, svmtibus [sic] *vero Theodori|de Bry anno* CIↃ IↃ XC.|*Venales reperivntvr in officina Sigismondi Feirabendii.*

Title engraved within an engraved frontispiece, as in the Latin edition.

Dedicatory epistle to "Gvillaume conte (*sic*) palatin du rhin," signed "Theodor de Bry, natif de la cité de Liége," 1 l., with the scutcheon of the Count, above the text, pp. 3 and 4.

"Aux adventuriers | bienvveillans et favorisans | l'entreprisse de la colonie et—demevre de Virginia, 1 l., sig. a 2., pp. 5, 6. Text, pp. 7–33, the reverse of the last leaf being blank.

"Les vrays pour | traicts, | et facon de vivre dv peuple dune | partie de l'Amerique | novvellement appellee Virginia ... Recveillis diligemment, et tirez sur le naturel par Jan | With, qui a esté expressement envoyé | au dit païs pour ce faire l'anne (*sic*) susdite 1585. et celle de lan 1588 | puis taillez en cuiure et nouuellement mis en lumiere | par Theodore de Bry a ses propres despens." (1 printed l., the reverse blank.)

"Table de toutes les figures contenues en ce livre," 1 l.

The plate of Adam and Eve, a very fine proof, 1 l.

"Au lecteur," 1 l., the reverse blank.

The map of Virginia, followed by plates II–XXIII. with their explanations in French.

"Avcvns povrtraicts des Pictes ancien | nement habitans vne partie de la grand Bretaigne" (a printed title), with the explanation of the first plate on the reverse. The five plates follow with the explanation *vis-à-vis* (9 l.)

Tables of the principal matters, 2 l., sig. Fd. On the reverse of the second is a list of errata longer than in the Latin edition.

Finally, on a last leaf, this imprint: —

"A Francfort | de l'imprimerie Ian. | Wechel, aux despens de Theodore | de Bry. | M. D. XC."

This edition is tolerably well printed, on a sized paper. The plates are better than those which were in the various copies of the first Latin edition, which we have been able to examine; it is, moreover, of very great rarity, and is worth not less than 1000 to 1200 fr. On this subject I have an anecdote from M. Sobolewski. During a stay in Paris, some years ago, this distinguished bibliophile was offered, for 100 fr., a copy of

the French "Virginie," described above, without a title; but, as he already had three complete copies, he did not think he ought to take it. Now, what came of his refusal? Some months later this same copy was sold for 1000 fr., after a title had been added to it, from which Simonin had cut the Latin inscription, substituting blank paper, on which a skillful penman had written, for 30 fr., after a copy borrowed from M. Sobolewski himself, a facsimile of the French inscription.

English edition of the first part.

Bry. A briefe and true report|of the new foundland of Virginia,|of the commodities and of the nature and man|ners of the naturall inhabitants. Discouered by|the English Colony there seated by Sir Richard|Greinuile Knight In the yeere 1585. Which Remained Vnder the gouernement of twelue monethes, |At the speciall charge and direction of the Honou-|rable Sir Walter Raleigh Knight, lord Warden|of the ſtanneries Who therein hath beene fauoured|and authoriſed by her Maiestie|and her letters patent:|This fore book Is made in Engliſh|By Thomas Hariot ſeruantt to the abouenamed|Sir Walter, a member of the Colony, and there|imployed in discouering. |Cum Gratia et Privilegio, Caes. Ma[tis] specia[lis]|*Francoforti ad Moenvm|Typis Ioannis Wecheli, svmtibvs vero Theodori|De Bry anno* CIↃ IↃ XC|*Venales reperivntvr in officina Sigismvndi Feirabendii*| [Colophon:] *At Franckfort,|inprited* [sic] *by Ihon We|chel, at Theodore de Bry, own|coast and chardges.*|MDXC.| Folio.

[The title above is taken from a copy belonging to Mr. James Lenox, of New York, who has kindly furnished the following collation: —

The English title is engraved on the frontispiece, and the Latin imprint below. I have never heard of, or seen, any other than a Latin imprint. In some copies the English title is on a slip, and pasted over the Latin.

The first and second lines are in large Roman type—no capitals, except "A;" all the rest in italics, except "Sir Walter Raleigh," "Maiestie," "By," "Walter," and "Cum Gratia," etc., and the whole imprint; these are in small, and the imprint in larger capitals.

Title, 1 leaf, verso, blank. Dedication to Sir Walter, with his arms, pp. 3, 4, in italics. "To the Adventvrers," etc., pp. 5, 6. First Part, Roman, pp. 7–12. Second Part, 13–21. Third and Last Part, pp. 22–30. Conclusion, 31–33, 1 blank page. Title, "The trve pictvres and fashions of the People of Virginia," 1 leaf, verso, blank; table of the pictures, including the map, 2 pages. Plate of Adam and Eve, recto blank, 1 leaf. "To the gentle Reader," 1 page, verso, blank. Plates and map, I–XXII, the map, I. Nos. XIII–XVII, XVIII, XIX, XX, and XXII, are on double leaves. Sometimes the description is on the verso of the first, and the plate on the recto of the second leaf; or the plate occupies part of the verso of the first, and the whole of the recto of the second leaf, and the description a portion of the verso of the first leaf. In all the others, the plates occupy a part of the recto of one leaf, with the description below, and the verso of the leaf blank. The map is on a double leaf, without any description. "Some Picture, | of the Pictes ...," 1 page — verso, description of the first plate; second leaf, picture No. I, recto — verso, blank; third leaf, description No. II — recto, blank; fourth leaf; picture No. II — verso, blank; fifth leaf, recto, blank — verso, description of plate No. III;

sixth leaf, plate No. III, recto — verso, blank; seventh leaf, recto, blank — verso, description of plate IIII; eighth leaf, picture No. IIII — verso, blank; ninth leaf, recto, blank — verso, description No. V; tenth leaf, picture No. V — verso, blank; a table of the principal things, etc., 3 pages; fourth page, faults escaped; colophon on recto of next leaf: "At Franckfort, | Inprinted by Ihon We|chel, at Theodore de Bry, owne | coast and chardges" | The first, second, and fifth lines in large capitals; the third and fourth lines in small Roman type.

Collation — a, including title-page, in 4s, b in 6s, c in 4s, d in 10s, to plate II, inclusive; A in 6s, B in 8s, C in 8s, D in 5s, E in 8s, F in 6s, including a blank leaf.]

This English text is so rare, that only five or six copies are known. That which is described in the "Biblioth. Grenvil.," I. 185-186, had been bought by Lord Oxford, at Frankfort, about 1710, for £100. Another brought the same price at the Nassau sale. The copies which were sold for only £47 5s., at the Thomson sale, in 1813, and 31 fr. at Hanrott's, were not perfectly complete.

The volume is in three parts. The first ("The Report") consists of 33 pages, including the title; the second ("The trve pictvres and faschions of the People of Virginia") is in 23 plates, each having its description, with a title, a table, a notice to the reader, and the plate of Adam and Eve; the third part ("Some picture of the Pictes ..."), in 5 plates, with their descriptions, which, with the title, occupy 12 leaves, and are followed by another leaf, bearing the colophon.

Second Part.

Bry. Brevis narratio|eorvm quæ in Florida Americæ provincia |Gallis acciderunt, secunda in illam Nauigatione, du-|ce Renato de Laudoñiere classis Præfecto:|Anno M D LXIIII.|Qvae est secvnda pars Americae.|Additæ figuræ et Incolarum eicones ibidem ad vivum expressæ|brevis item Declaratio Religionis, rituum, vivendique|ratione ipsorum.|Auctore|Iacobo le Moyne, cui cognomen de Morgues, Laudoñierum | in ea Navigatione sequnto.|Nunc primùm Gallico sermone à Theodoro de Bry Leodiense|in lucem edita: Latio verò donata a C.C.A.|Cum gratia & priuil. Cæs. Maiest. ad quadriennium.|*Francoforti ad Mœnvm,|Typis Ioannis Wecheli, sumtibus vero Theodori|de Bry Anno* M D XCI.|*Venales reperiuntur in officina Sigismundi Feirabendii.*|

The title above, engraved and within an engraved frontispiece.

Dedicatory epistle to Christian, Duke of Saxony, with his engraved scutcheon and six printed lines below, 1 l.

Advertisement "benevolo lectori," 1 l.; on the first page is a vignette, representing the Ark of Noah, with 14 lines below.

Privilege of the Emperor, 1 l., the reverse blank.

Text, commencing by this summary, "Gallorum in Floridam ... altera navigatio, duce Laudonniero ...," 30 pp. (the first page has only 25 printed lines). This narration, written by Le Moyne de Morgues, had never been published.

Map of Florida, which is often placed before the text.

"Index capitum" (table of the plates), 1 l.

Engraved frontispiece, and in the middle a title, also engraved ("Indorum Floridam provinciam inhabitantium Eicones"), below the address "Francofurti ad Mœnum ...," and the same date as in the first frontispiece, above.

Forty-two plates, on as many leaves (sig. A2–H), with explanations at the foot of each; the leaves are numbered from 1 to XLII, at the top of the pages, and the engravings, in Arabic figures at the bottom of the plates.

"Libellus sive epistola supplicatoria ... ad Carolum IX ... ," 3 l., of which one is numbered H2; the ornament placed at the head of the first page should represent a winged man.

"De quarto Gallorum in Floridam navigatione," 5 l., including the index. On the reverse of the 5th l., "Parergon de authore et occasione hujus historiæ." The fifth paragraph of this last piece (which is a "monitum" on the "Parergon") should have 5 lines; at the bottom of the page is the catch-word, "mendæ."

"Mendæ quædam," 1 l., the reverse blank.

"Parergon continens ... ," 4 l. On the reverse of the last, "Francofurti ad Mœnum, apud Joannem Wechelum impensis Theodori de Bry. M. D. XCI."

In some copies the same inscription is found printed on a separate leaf, which is placed after the 42 plates. Above the date is a vignette engraved on wood, — a mask with ornaments.

Of this part there has been a first original edition, a second original edition, — in which the title of the engravings bears the date M. D. CIX, — and an edition reprinted under the first date of 1591.

The first impression of the 42 plates is recognized by the number of the lines, and by the words which end some of the lines, as will be seen in the table below.

N. B. The first line which follows the number of each plate indicates the first edition, designated by the letter *a*; and the second line the reprints, designated by the letter *b*.

Plate			
I.	*a*, 12	lines, end of the 1st:	*appulerunt*
	b, 13	" " "	*non*
II.	*a*, 10	" " "	*indo-*
	b, 9	" " "	Indorum
III.	*a*, 9	" " "	navigarunt
	b, 9	" " "	donec
IV.	*a*, 8	" " "	legeris
	b, 8	" " "	nomen
V.	*a*, 17	" " "	nuncuparunt
	b, 17	" " "	nuncu-
VI.	*a*, 14	" end of the 2d:	jubet, ut
	b, 13	"	
VII.	*a*, 16	" end of the 1st:	Propugnaculo
	b, 14	" " "	insu-
VIII.	*a*, 17	"	the capital of the word Appulis on 5 lines.
	b, 17	"	the same capital on 4 "
IX.	*a*, 12	" " "	sententiam, po-
	b, 11	" " "	flumen
X.	*a*, 15	" " "	latus occi-
	b, 14	" " "	objectum &
XI.	*a*, 18	" " "	eorum
	b, 19	" " "	potente
XII.	*a*, 21	" " "	quadragenta
	b, 20	" " "	miliaribus
XIII.	*a*, 10	" end of the 2d:	gesta
	b, 10	" " "	gesta re-
XIV.	*a*, 16	" end of the 1st	sparsi
	b, 14	" " "	discur-
XV.	*a*, 18	" " "	gessit ver-
	b, 17	" " "	num-

Plate			
XVI.	*a*, 12	" end of the 3d:	orbem ante
	b, 12	" " "	in orbem
XVII.	*a*, 13	" end of the 1st:	etiam in
	b, 12	" " "	eorum
XVIII.	*a*, 10	" " "	solent eo
	b, 10	" " "	eo die
XIX.	*a*, 7	" " "	sepul-
	b, 7	" " "	sepulcra
XX.	*a*, 14	" end of the 2d:	sunt na-
	b, 14	" " "	correpti sunt
XXI.	*a*, 11	" " "	mollior est
	b, 11	" " "	*nam mollior*
XXII.	*a*, 9	" end of the 4th:	monte aut
	b, 11	" " "	monte
XXIII.	*a*, 6	" end of the 1st:	coacervant sin-
	b, 6	" " "	coacervant
XXIV.	*a*, 10	" " "	solent. qua
	b, 10	" " "	solent
XXV.	*a*, 10	" end of the 4th:	tempore
	b, 10	" " "	tempo-
XXVI.	*a*, 12	" end of the 1st:	nam
	b, 13	" " "	nam fa-
XXVII.	*a*, 10	" end of the 2d:	volens
	b, 10	" " "	indulgere vo-
XXVIII.	*a*, 14	" " "	adeo exacte
	b, 14	" " "	adeo ex-
XXIX.	*a*, 20	" end of the 3d:	ut ab
	b, 20	" " "	ut
XXX.	*a*, 15	" end of the 1st:	torrentis
	b, 14	" " "	alicu-
XXXI.	*a*, 10	" " "	adve-
	b, 10	" " "	ex-
XXXII.	*a*, 7	" " "	puniuntur
	b, 8	" " "	Rege in-
XXXIII.	*a*, 5	" in the course of the 1st:	feriali
	b, 5	" " "	feciali
XXXIV.	*a*, 11	" end of the 1st:	autem
	b, 11	" " "	die
XXXV.	*a*, 11	" end of the 2d:	sele-
	b, 10	" " "	selectissimi
XXXVI.	*a*, 6	" end of the 1st:	cursu-
	b, 6	" " "	cursuram
XXXVII.	*a*, 13	" end of the 2d:	animalis
	b, 14	" " "	alicujus ani-
XXXVIII.	*a*, 15	" " "	utriusque
	b, 14	" " "	utrim-
XXXIX.	*a*, 17	" end of the 1st:	cum pri-
	b, 17	" " "	cum
XL.	*a*, 10	" end of the 2d:	illius
	b, 10	" " "	jl-
XLI.	*a*, 9	" end of the 5th:	aliquanto-
	b, 9	" " "	ali-
XLII.	*a*, 12	" end of the 1st:	pote-
	b, 12	" " "	po-

Second Edition.

As there is a second edition of the third part, printed in 1605, it is to be presumed that there must have appeared a reprint of the second part, between the edition of 1591 and that of 1609, but we only know this latter, which has the same plate for frontispiece, the same title and the same date, 1591, as the first, but differ in some other points. For example, in the dedication there are only 5 lines below the scutcheon, in place of 6; the notice "Benevoli lectori" ordinarily retains the plate representing Noah's Ark (yet in some copies this vignette has been replaced by the scutcheon of the dedicatory epistle). The ornaments of the initial, below the vignette, represent a man pruning a vine, — they are different in the first edition; — in the second the privilege is generally printed on the reverse of a leaf, of which the obverse has the engraving of the seven scutcheons accompanied by the six virtues, which plate had already served for the first edition of the third part. The copy described in Langlès' catalogue, however, had this privilege printed on the obverse of a leaf, the reverse of which was wholly blank, as in the first edition.

After this privilege, there is in the second edition a piece entitled, "Historia luctuosæ expeditionis Gallorum in ... Florida," on 4 l., not numbered, on the reverse of the last being a notice, "De occasione et authore hujus historiæ;" but this edition, which has been reproduced in the reprint of this part, is the same thing, except a few phrases, as the "Parergon" and the "Monitum," of which we have already spoken, which have been retained in this edition of 1609.

The vignette placed at the head of the first page of "Libellus ... ad Carolum IX," represents a man's head, below which two angels, one on each side, sound trumpets. In the first edition it is a winged man. There is the same difference in the vignettes in the part entitled, "De quarta ... Gallorum navigatione." In the "Parergon de authore," which is on the reverse of the 5th leaf of this same part, the fifth paragraph has only 4 lines in place of 5. The catch-word of this leaf is "Parer." instead of "Mendæ;" there are no errata, and the reverse of the 4th leaf of the "Parergon continens ..." is blank.

The engraved title, dated 1591, which in the first edition comes before the 42 plates, in the second is replaced by a printed title, with this date, "Anno Christi M. D. CIX." (It is printed 1619 in the Langlès catalogue.)

In the second edition the frontispiece has the same engraved cartouch which served for the other two editions, but the title printed in the cartouch is different. It begins thus, "Historiæ Americanæ | secunda pars | continens Navigationes | Gallorum in Floridam ... ." It retains the imprint, "Francofurti ad Mœnum ... M. D. XCI." After this title comes 3 preliminary leaves, as above, and the text commences at page 3, with these words, "Historiæ | luctuosæ Expe | ditionis ... ." It ends at page 52, which is followed by the title of the "Indorum ... Eicones," and the 42 plates of which we have already spoken.

We have seen two different copies of this edition — that of the *Bibliothèque impériale*, which conforms exactly to the present description, and that of the *Bibliothèque Mazarine*, which, although resembling the other in the title and the 52 pages of text, wants the 3 preliminary leaves, and has the plates printed two by two on each leaf, so that these 42 plates and the explanations only occupy 21 leaves. The reverse of the printed title presents the explanation of the two first plates, and the reverse of plates 41 and 42 the index of all these plates. This last impression is probably that which Math. Merian used for the collection of the Great Voyages which he issued, under a collective title, in 1634.

Third Part.

Bry. Americae|tertia pars|memorabilem provinciæ Brasiliæ Historiam|continens, Germanico primùm sermone scriptam à|

Ioanne Stadio Homburgensi Heso, nunc autem|Latinitate donatam à Teucrio Annæo Priuato Col-|chanthe Po: & Med: Addita est Narratio profectionis|Ioannis Lerij in eamdem Provinciam, quæ ille initio|Gallicè conscripsit, postea verò Latinam, fecit. His ac-|cessit Descriptio Morum & Ferocitatis incolarum |illius Regionis, atque Colloquium ipsorum idio-|mate conscriptum.|Omnia recens evulgata, & eiconibus in æs incisis|ac ad vivum expressis illustrata, ad normam exem-|plaris prædictorum Autorum: studio et diligentia | Theodori de Bry Leodiensis, atque | civis | Francofurtensis, *anno* MDXCII. | *Venales reperñitur* [sic] *in officina* | *Theodori de Bry.*|

Title engraved, in an engraved frontispiece.

Dedicatory epistle to William Count Palatine of the Rhine, 1 l. (5 lines below the scutcheon; there are 6 in the edition of 1605.)

Two leaves. On the obverse of the first is an engraved plate, representing seven scutcheons; in the first impression these are without the figures of the seven virtues, which were added to the plate, before the second impression, to fill up the empty space. On the reverse is the notice, "Theod. de Bry lectori," which is continued on the obverse of the second leaf, whose reverse contains the imperial privilege. Map, entitled, "Americæ pars magis cognita." This is sometimes placed after p. 138.

Dedicatory epistle of J. Stadius, 1 l., with a vignette in wood representing a man having wings on his shoulders.

Preface of Johannes Dryander (relating to the same narration), 3 l.; on the reverse of the third the "argumentum totius narrationis." The vignette, at the top of the first page, is narrow and short, not filling the whole width of the page.

Text of Stadius, pp. 134, having on the first an engraving representing a sea-port, with houses at the right of the spectator.

On p. 3 of this narration, the summary of Chapter II, "De ijs quæ acciderunt circa primam naviga | tionem," is in two lines; it is in one line in the edition of 1605, and in that of 1630 it is thus expressed, "De iis quæ acciderunt circa navigationis initium."

At page 7 of the same relation, the summary of the chapter (Chap. III), "De modo obsidendi et obsessos oppu | gnandi," is also in two lines; it is in only one in the edition of 1605; and in that of 1630 is thus expressed, "Lusitani obsessi ab Indis oppugnantur acriter."

There are in this part thirty-four engravings, not including the first, printed on the same pages as the text, and in this number several are repeated.

After page 134 is a second engraved frontispiece, bearing this title, also engraved, "Navigatio in Brasiliam Americæ ... a Joanne Lerio Burgundo ... Venales reperiuntur in officina Sigismundi Fierabendii," without date.

4 leaves of preliminary matter, pp. 137–143. The Greek verses on p. 137 are in large characters, called "Saint Augustin" [pica]; the catch-word "Joan," at the foot of page 140, is in upright letters. Page 143 should have 27 lines (it has only 17 in the edition of 1605, and 16 in that of 1630). Page 144 ordinarily contains the engraving of Adam and Eve, with the mark, "Theodore de Bry fe," as in the first part. In some copies this page has been left blank.

Text of the relation of Lerry, p. 145 to 284, with 10 plates printed in the text. In the plate on p. 151 the vessel is on the right, and has the standard with three fleurs-de-lis; in the plate on p. 248, the man who is carried is on the right of the spectator. In the edition of 1630 these two plates and several others have been re-engraved and reversed

Two letters ("Exemplar duarum litterarum") of Nic. Barré on the expedition of the Chevalier de Villegagnon, which occupy pp. 285 to 295, including a printed frontispiece, "typis Joannis Wecheli, M. D. XCII;" on p. 296 begins an Index, which continues on thirteen unnumbered pages. On the reverse of the last is the inscription, "Impressum Francofurti ... apud Joannem Wechelium, impensis Theodori de Bry. M.D.X.CII."

This third part has had two original editions, and perhaps also two altered editions. There are even two kinds of copies of the edition of 1592. The first agree with the description above; the others differ merely in the plate with seven scutcheons, where the spaces at first left blank have been filled by the figures of the six virtues, and in the two engraved frontispieces, where, after the word "officina," "Sigismundi Feyrabendii" has been substituted for "Theodori de Bry." This change, which appears in the edition of 1605, must have been made about 1597; for, after the publication of the sixteenth part of the Great Voyages in German, with this date, the name of Feyrabend does not appear in the other volumes of the collection.

Second Edition.

The edition of 1605 preserves the first engraved frontispiece of that of 1592, but with the name of J. de Bry substituted for that of Feyrabend. It presents some other differences: on the first page of the dedicatory epistle are six printed lines; the frontispiece which precedes the narration of Jean de Lerry, and takes the place of pp. 135 and 136, is printed from type, and bears the name of Theod. de Bry; the ten Greek verses, commencing at p. 137 are in small characters; p. 143 has only 17 lines; p. 144 is blank, or if it has the print of Adam and Eve, the plate is in the second state, that is to say, with "Jo." before "Theodori."

The printed frontispiece ("Exemplar duarum litterarum"), p. 285, which precedes the two letters of Barré, has the words, "Typis Matthæi Beckeri M.DC.V."; and the colophon, which is on the reverse of the last leaf of the index, is "Impressum Francofurti ad Mœnum apud Matthiam Beckerum. M. DC. V."

Third Edition (*altered edition*).

In the edition dated 1630, the title printed in the middle of the engraved frontispiece differs from that of the two other editions. Here is an extract: —

"Historiæ Antipodum, sive Novi Orbis qui vulgo Americæ et Indiæ occidentalis nomine usurpatur, pars tertia ... . Omnia ab infinitis mendis repurgata et in concinniorem ordinem redacta studio Jo. Ludovici Gottofridi ... . Francofurti, sumptibus Matthæi Meriani, Anno M. DC. XXX."

Notwithstanding the corrections and improvements of which this title speaks, the edition is in every respect far inferior to the two preceding. It wants the preface of J. Dryander; the printed title on p. 135 has neither ornament nor address; the text ends on p. 294; there is no colophon, and the long index which is in the first editions has not been reprinted; the plate on the first page of the text of Stadius, which was very much worn in the edition of 1605, has been re-engraved for this, but reversed, and with differences in the personages; other plates are re-engraved and reversed. Camus, p. 56, remarks that at p. 86 of Merian's edition is a plate representing the Indians eating fish, which is not in the other editions; we have found it not at the page named, but at p. 120, and that in three copies; in one of these copies the plate at p. 248 was wanting, and in the others it was reversed.

Another remark is to be made on this same p. 248. In five copies of the first edition of this part, of which two were those of Rothelin and Camus de Limare, with the vignette of the seven scutcheons, printed before the six virtues were added, we have seen, on the first line of the said page, above the plate, this clause, "tum excavata fossa non oblonga;" but in the edition of 1605, in consequence of resetting the type,

the same clause begins at the end of the last line, *below* the plate, in this manner, "tumum exca-", with the end of the word ("vata") as a catch-word, and repeated on the first line of p. 249. Finally, in the edition of 1630, the first word of this clause, "Tumin," with the n broken, is at the end of the last line of p. 148. Camus, then, is wrong in saying, on p. 57 of his *Mémoire*, that in the first edition the last line of p. 248 has "tumum," and that this mistake was corrected in the second edition. We fear that in correcting this error the editor of the "Bibliotheca Grenvilliana" has committed another, in saying that the first edition has really "tum in" in the last line of this page; at least we know of no copy which justifies his assertion.

The *Bibliothèque Mazarine* has two copies dated 1630; one conforms to the description above; the other appears to be the edition of 1605, in which Merian had inserted the title-page of his own. In a "Catalogue of Rare Books," printed at New York in 1854, mention is made of a copy of the edition of 1630 in which, on p. 86, the title of Chap. XLVI is printed in 2 lines, and the text in 13 lines. Below this text ought to be the plate cited by Camus. At the foot of p. 272 and at the commencement of p. 273 are 6 lines of text printed twice. M. Sobolewski has pointed out to us that this edition of 1630 is often composed of a mixture either of sheets taken from the original editions or of sheets imitated from the two original editions, which has made him suspect that perhaps each of the original editions has had its imitation. According to him, this third part is the most difficult study of any. There are sheets of six different impressions, among which two are such exact facsimiles of one another that their difference can only be perceived with the magnifying glass.

In many copies of the different editions of this third part, there have been added at the end 28 plates, which were published, under the title of "Brevis summa ... ," in 1617, in connection with the second edition of the sixth part, although they belonged to the third.

Fourth Part.

Bry. Americae | pars qvarta | sive, | Insignis & Admiranda Historia de reperta | primùm Occidentali India à Christophoro | Columbo Anno M. CCCCXCII | Scripta ab Hieronymo Bezono Mediolanense, | qui istic a*n*nis XIIII. versatus, dilige*n*ter omnia observa- | vit. | Addita ad singula ferè capita, non contemnenda scholia, | in quibus agitur de earum etiam gentium idololatria. | Accessit præterea illarum Regionum Tabula | chorographica. | Omnia elegantibus figuris in æs incisis expres- | sa à Theodoro de Bry Leodiense, cive | Francofurtensi *Anno* CIↃ IↃ XCIIII. Ad | Invictis. Rudolphus II. Rom. Imperator. | *Cum privilegio S. C. Maiestat.* |

Title engraved, in an engraved frontispiece (with the emblem and device of Th. de Bry, — several marigolds, with these words, "Nul sans soucy").

On a separate leaf, the plate of the seven scutcheons with the six virtues, and on the reverse the imperial privilege.

On another leaf, "Theod. de Bry benevolo lectori." On the first page a plate representing a ship and marine gods; below, 22 lines of text, the first of which ends with the word "Indiæ."

On a third leaf, some Latin and some French verses in honor of Th. de Bry. On the first page a plate, bearing this engraved title, "Americæ retectio;" at the bottom of this page the catch-word, "artes."

146 pages, containing a preface, "Christianis et piis lectoribus;" on p. 7 a note, "De ambiguo Indiæ nomine;" then, pp. 8–10, some verses, the argument of the

book; lastly, the text, pp. 11–145 (the additions on the margin are in round characters); on the reverse of p. 146 the colophon, "Impressum Francofurti ad Mœnum, typis Johannis Feyrabend, impensis Theodori de Bry. Anno M D. LXXXXIIII."

A blank leaf; a second print of the engraved frontispiece, which is at the beginning of the IVth part; a map of occidental America; 24 engraved plates on leaves numbered I to XXIIII.

It appears that there were two impressions of these plates for the first edition of this part. In the first, the plates are not numbered; in the second, they have Arabic numbers, beginning with the third plate; but the explanations printed at the bottom of these pages are the same as in the first impression, while they differ in those of the second edition. On a part of the prints of the frontispiece, the words which follow the date have been corrected thus: "Ad Invictis. Rudolphus [*sic*] Romæ Imperator." (Cat. Santander.)

Second Edition.

The second edition is a repetition of the first, with the same frontispiece and the same date; it can be recognized by the following marks: 1° in the notice "Benevolo lectori," the first line below the plate ends with the first syllable of the word "Indiæ;" the word is complete in the first edition; 2° at the foot of the first page of the third leaf ("Americæ retectio") there is not the catch-word "artes" which is in the first edition; 3° the greater part of the additions in the margin of the text of Benzoni (wrongly called Bezoni) are in italics; 4° the reverse of p. 145 has neither colophon nor date.

The 24 plates are numbered with Arabic figures, and the explanations added at the foot of the plates differ in some points from those of the first edition. For example:—

Plate XIV. The number is XIIII in the 1st, and XIV in the 2d edition (also XIIII in the edition of 1644).

Plate XV. The first line ends with "Carolum V." (only "Carolum" in the 2d edition).

Plate XVII. The 2d line ends with "soluens O-" (only "soluens" in the 2d edition).

Plate XVIII. In the printed title at the top of the page is "alij" ("alii" in the 2d edition).

Plate XIX. The 3d line ends with "spem fu-" (only "spem" in the 2d edition).

Plate XX. The 2d line ends with "duces" ("du-" in the 2d edition).

Plate XXII. The 2d line of the title has "obijcit" ("obiicit" in the 2d edition).

Plate XXIII. The 1st line of the title has "sibijpsis" ("sibi ipsis" in the 2d edition).

Plate XXIV. The last line but one has "mutato" ("mutato con-" in the 2d edition).

We will add, in regard to plate II ("Pisces in mari alati"), that in the 3d edition the ship is entirely different; it has on one of its masts the banner with three fleurs-de-lis, and the engraving is heavily shaded.

Third Edition.

Bry. Historia antipodum sive novi orbis liber quartus ... . *Francofurti in officina Matthæi Meriani.* MDC. XXXXIV (1644).

This third edition contains a title printed in an engraved frontispiece, 1 l.; preface, "Christianis et piis lectoribus," 2 l. (pp. 3–6); "argumentum," p. 7; text, pp. 8–74. The engravings are printed in the text.

The 2d plate has the flag with the three fleurs-de-lis, but it is very much worn.

Fifth Part.

Bry. Americæ | pars qvinta | Nobilis & admiratione plena | Hieronymi Bezoni Mediolanensis, | secundæ sectionis Hia: Hispanorum, tùm in | Nigrittas seruos suos, tùm in Indos crudelita- | tem, Gallorumq*ue* piratar*um* de Hispanis toties | reportata spolia; Aduent*um* item Hispanor*um* | in Nouam Indiæ continentis Hispaniam, | eorumq*ue* contra incolas eius regionis | sæuitiam explicans. | Addita ad singula fere Capita scholia, in quibus | res Indiæ luculentèr exponuntur. | Accessit præterea Tabula Chorographica Nouæ | Hispaniæ in India Occidentalj. | Ad | Invictis. Rvdolph. II. Rom. Imp. Avg. | Omnia elegantibus figuris in aes incisis expressa à | Theodoro de Bry Leod. cive Franc. *Ao.* CIↃ IↃ XCV. | Cum Privilegio S. C. Maiestatis. |

[Brunet adds,] The word "historia," which we have restored above, is wanting in the fourth line of the title in the first impressions of the plate. [The title above, where the word appears in full, is apparently copied from an impression different from either of those described by Brunet.]

Title engraved, in an engraved frontispiece.

2 leaves for the preface and the argument. At the commencement of the preface is the portrait of Columbus, and below the portrait 11 lines. The title of the argument ("secundi libri summa") is in upright letters; the reverse is blank.

Map of New Spain, dated 1595.

Text ("Novæ orbis liber secundus"), the pages numbered 5 to 92; but as the numbers 79–88 are omitted, there are really only 82 pages.

A frontispiece like the one at the commencement of this part; then 22 plates, their order marked by Roman letters at the top of the page. The explanation of these plates presents the same small Roman characters as the notes at the end of the chapters.

We know only these two editions of the fifth part of the Great Voyages, and we are ignorant whether Math. Merian issued a third. The frontispiece of his which has the figure V in many collections formed by him after the death of his father-in-law, really belongs to the 7th part, as Camus has remarked. According to M. Sobolewski there existed an edition of this fifth part, "tertiusquam (or tersusquam) ante hac edita, 1625," of which he had only seen one copy, that of Camus de Limare. Now, that amateur's copy, which the *Bibliothèque impériale* possesses is, according to Camus (p. 81), and in our opinion, a seventh part with the number V (*see* the account of this seventh part below).

The second or counterfeit edition, with the same date as the first, is recognizable: —

1° By the engraved title, in which is added, between the 4th line and the 5th, the word "Hia," an abbreviation of Historia, which had been omitted on the plate before the second impression. (Yet these three letters are also in a part of the copies of the first edition of the text.)

2° By the text of the first page of the preface, which has 13 lines in place of 11. (But I have seen a copy, appearing to be of the second edition, where this page had only 11 lines, and where the leaf of the argument was without the ornament, which in the first edition is at the foot of the page.)

3° By the body of the work, which, being printed in smaller characters than in the first edition, ends at p. 72.

4° By the notes at the end of the chapters, which are in Italics.

5° By the 22 plates, as the leaves are numbered in Arabic figures instead of Roman, and the explanations are in the same characters as the 72 pages of text.

We are able to assert that the author of the "Bibliographie instructive," and after him Camus, have erroneously given as the distinctive mark of the first edition of this 5th part what must apply to the second. So the first impressions of the plates are those which are ordinarily found after the text in 92 (82) pages; and it is by a mistake of the binder that in one of the copies in the *Bibliothèque Mazarine* the plates numbered in Roman figures accompany the text in 72 pages.

Sixth Part.

Bry. Americae | pars sexta. | sive | historiæ ab Hieronymo Be*n*zono | Mediolane*n*se scriptæ, sectio tertia, res no*n* | minus nobiles & admiratione plenas con- | tinens, quàm præcedentes duæ. In hac | enim reperies, qua ratione Hispani opule*n*- | tissimas illas Peruäni regni provincias oc- | cuparint, capto Rege Atabaliba: deinde orta | inter ipsos Hispanos in eo regno civilia bella. | Additus est brevis de Fortunatis insulis Cōmenta- | riolus in duo capita distinctus. | Item additiones ad singula Capita Histo- | riam illustrantes. | Accessit Pervāni regni chorographica Tabula. | Ad | invictis: Rvdolph: H: Rom: im: Avg: | Omnia elegantibus figuris in æs incisis expressa | à Theodoro de Bry Leod: cive autem Franco- furte*n*se. | *Ao* M D XCVI. | Cum privilegio S. C. Matis. |

Title engraved, in an engraved frontispiece. (The copy described in the catalogue of J. J. De Bure had this frontispiece double, with a difference in the title.) "Libri tertii summa et argumentum," 1 l. This summary is printed in 2 lines.

Map of America, forming a half-planisphere. It is also placed at p. 98.

Plan of Cusco, on the same page. Text, pp. 5–108. There are 22 chapters, with notes, as far as p. 77. On p. 78 commences the description of the Canaries, in 2 chapters, numbered 1 and 2.

Frontispiece in all respects like that which is at the head of this sixth part. There are copies, on the title of which a little engraved plate has been pasted with these words, "Sequuntur icones artificiosæ ordine historiam precedentem illustrantes ... ," then 28 plates (numbered at the top of the pages from 1 to 28), with the explanations below printed, some in Italic, some in Roman characters. These last belong to the Nos. 7, 10–19, 21, 22, 27, and 28.

Second Edition.

The summary on the 1st leaf ("Tertii libri summa ...") in three lines.

Text, pp. 5–78. It is in smaller characters than in the edition in 108 pp., and a large part of the notes which were at the end of most of the 22 chapters of the first edition have been suppressed. The description of the Canaries which, in the preceding edition forms two chapters numbered 1 and 2, occupies in this the chapters 23 and 24, pp. 56–59.

The frontispiece which precedes the plates is a printed title, of which we give the beginning and end: —

Bry. Brevis summa earum rerum quæ in tertia Americæ parte continentur ... *Oppeinhemii* [so in Brunet], *ex officina typographica Hieronymi Galleri, sumtibus Joannis Theodori de Bry filii civis et bibliopolæ Oppeinheimensis.* M. DC. XVII.

The explanations of the 28 plates are all printed in Italics, of a smaller font than in the first edition, from which they differ also in the number of the lines; thus, in the 1st edition, for plate 1 there are 12 lines (in the 2d, 8); pl. II, 18 lines (in the 2d 13); pl. III and IV, each 13 lines (in the 2d, 10); pl. V, 14 lines (10 in the 2d); pl. VI, 14 (10 in the 2d); and for all the others similar differences. I have seen a copy of this 2d edition, which contained the plates of the 1st.

In many copies of the 2d edition the 28 plates and their title are placed in the third part, to which they belong.

Seventh Part.

Bry. Americæ pars VII. | Verissima et ivcvn- | dissima descriptio prae- | cipvarvm qvarvndam Indiæ | regionum & Insularum, quæ quidem nullis an- | te hæc tempora visæ cognitæque, iam primum | ab Vlrico Fabro Straubingensi, multo cum periculo inuentæ & ab eodem summa dili- | gentia consignatæ fuerunt, ex Germanico in La- | tinum sermonem conuersa autore M. | Gotardo Artvs Dan- | tiscano. | Illustrata verò pulcherrimis imaginibus, & in | lucem emissa, studio & opera Theodo- | rici de Bry piæ memoriæ, relictæ | viduæ & filiorum. | *Anno Christi*, M. D. XCIX. | *Venales reperiuntur in officina* | *Theodori de Bry.* |

Title printed, in an engraved frontispiece.

"Præfatio ad lectorem" and "lectori benevolo," 2 l., pp. 3–6.

Text printed in long lines, pp. 7–62, finishing with these words, "finis itineris Ulrici Fabri" (a name Latinized from the German Ulrich Schmidel — *see* this name in the *Manuel*). Between the brief title and the first lines of this text is an engraving representing a gate with houses on the right. This plate had been already used.

The plates, three in number, which belong to the text of this part are found with those of the eighth part, at the end of its text; they form the first three numbers.

The second edition has also a printed title within the same engraved frontispiece, but the date is M. DC. XXV. It has not the 2 preliminary leaves; the text printed in 2 columns is paged from 3 to 35; the reverse of the last is blank. The 3 plates are printed in the text on pp. 7, 14, and 20. On p. 1 is a vignette representing a seaport, but in reverse, having the houses on the left of the reader. In a part of the copies of this second edition, the title has "pars V," and the two II which follow this number are traced by the hand; in others, the number VII is plainly printed. This frontispiece retains the words "editio tertia," which, as we have said, relate to the 5th part, for which the plate had already served.

Eighth Part.

Bry. Americæ pars VIII. | Continens | primo, descriptionem | trivm itinervm nobilissimi | et fortissimi eqvitis Francisci Draken, | qvi peragrato primvm vniverso terrarvm orbe, | postea cum nobilissimo Equite Iohanne Havckens, ad expugnan- | dum ciuitatem Panama, in Indiam nauigauit, vbi vitam | suam ambo finierunt. | Secvndo, iter nobilissimi Equitis Thomæ Candisch, qui duorum ferè annorum spa- | cio, 13000. Anglicana miliaria in mari confecit, vbi describuntur quoque omnia quæ in hoc itinere | ipsi

acciderunt & visa sunt. | Tertio, duo itinera, nobilissimi & fortissimi Domoni Gvaltheri Ralegh Equitis | & designati gubernatoris Regij in Anglia præsidij, nec non fortissimi Capitanei Lavrentij | Keyms. | Qvibvs itineribvs describitvr avriferum et po- | tentissimum Regnum Gviana, ad Septentrionem fluminis Orenoqve, aliàs Ore- | gliana dicti, situm, cum metropoli eius Manoa & Macviegvarai, | aliisq*ue*; finitimis regionibus & fluuiis, mercibus item præstantissimis, | & mercatura, quæ in regno hoc exercetur. | Primo qvidem Anglicana lingva partim ab eqvitibvs ipsis, par- | tim ab aliis, qui hisce itineribus interfuerunt, sparsim consignata: Iam verò in vnum Corpus | Redacta, & in Latinum Sermonem conuersa, auctore | M. Gotardo Artvs Dantiscano. | Figuris & imaginibus artificiosè illustrata & in lucem emissa, opera & sumptibus | Theodorici de Bry P. M. relictæ Viduæ & filiorum. | *Anno* M. D. XCIX. |

Printed frontispiece, in the middle of which is a small map of the world.

Map of Guiana. Preface, 1 l.

Text in 2 parts, — the first, pp. 3–78, the second, pp. 1–99 (reverse blank), the whole in long lines. In the greater part of the copies is a small map of the world at the foot of p. 78 of the first part, and another small map at p. 3 of the second part, under the last line of Ralegh's preface.

A printed title, of which we give the beginning and end: —

Bry. Tabulæ et imagines et septimam et octavam Americæ partem ... pertinentes ... *impressæ Francofurti ad Mœnum, per Matteum Becker, sumptibus dictorum Theodorici de Bry viduæ te filiorum*: *Anno* M. D. XCIX.

18 plates, with explanations printed at the foot of the pages. On the last, "Finis Tabularum."

The second or altered edition has a title, at the foot of which is a small square map and the colophon, "Francofurti, typis Erasmi Kempfferi, Anno M. DC. XXV."

The text (except the prefaces and the *pièces justificatives*) is in 2 columns in a single series, paged from 3 to 127. At the foot of this last page is the catch-word "Histo." Page 58, ordinarily blank, is sometimes filled by the engraving of Adam and Eve. There should be, pp. 129–160, a piece entitled, "Historiæ Antipodum sive Novi Orbis partis nonæ liber tertius ... ." This piece (the relation of an expedition made in 1599), illustrated by some engravings, was not in the first edition; but, though it is placed here in the 8th part, it really belongs to the 9th. The nineteen plates are printed with the text, which, with the three of the seventh part, implies four more plates than in the first edition; but, adds Camus, after having made this remark, some are repeated several times; the same plate is to be found on pp. 57 and 72; I have not perceived any that was not in De Bry's collection. The map of Guiana, which ought to be placed immediately after the text, is wanting in some copies. J. J. De Bure's copy had at pp. 57 and 58 two illustrations which are not usually found.

In a "Catalogue of Curious Books," printed at New York in 1854, mention is made of a second edition of this eighth part, dated M. D. XCIX. It has no preface. The text, "Descriptio primi itineris" commences on the reverse of the frontispiece, and is printed in characters smaller than those of the first edition; so that pp. 2, 3, and

4 contain the same matter as pp. 3–6 of the first. The catch-word ("statio") of p. 4 is the same as that of p. 6 (1st edition), and the reader can pass from the 4th to the 7th page without any break. This must be an edition made for Merian after 1625.

Ninth Part.

Bry. Americæ | Nona & postrema Pars. | Qva de ratione elemen- | torvm: de Novi Orbis natv- | ra: de hvivs incolarvm svperstitiosis | cultibus: deq*ue*; forma Politiæ ac Reipubl. ipsorum copiosè per- | tractatur: Catalogo Regum Mexicanorum omnium, à primo | vsq; ad vltimum Moteçumam II. addito: cui etiam ritus eo- | rum coronationis, ac sepulturæ annectitur, cum enu- | meratione bellorum, quæ mutuò | Indi gesserunt. | His accessit | designatio illivs navigationis, qvam | s. naues Hollandicæ Anno 1598. per fretum Magellanum in Moluc- | canas insulas tentarunt: quo modo nimirum oborta tempestate Ca- | pitaneus Sebalt de Weert à cæteris nauibus dispulsus, | postquam plurimis mensibus in freto infinitis ærumnis miserè iacta- | tus fuisset, tandem infecta re post biennium An. 1600. domum re | uersus sit. | Addita est tertio | Navigatio recens, qvam 4. Navivm præ- | fectus Olevier à Noort proximè suscepit: qui freto Ma- | gellanico classe transmisso, triennij spatio vniuersum terræ orbem | seu globum mira nauigationis sorte obiuit: annexis illis, quæ in itine- | re isto singularia ac memorabiliora notata sunt. | Omnia è Germanico Latinitate donata, & insuper elegantissimis figuris æneis coornata, editaq*ue*; sumptibus | Theodori de Bry p. m. viduæ & binorum | filiorum. | *Francof. Apud Matth. Beckervm.* 1602. |

4 l., namely, the title printed in an engraved frontispiece; dedicatory epistle to Christian II, Duke of Saxony (the scutcheon on 1 l., and the epistle on another l.); notice to the reader ("Lectori benevolo").

The body of the volume is divided into 3 parts, namely: —

1° Text of the 7 books, "De Novi Orbis natura," pp. 1–362, and one blank leaf.

2° "Relatio historica ... navigationis Sebalti de Weert ... . Francofurti, excudebat Matthæus Beckerus, M. DC. II."; a printed title bearing the vignette which represents five ships; a map of the Strait of Magellan; text, pp. 3–56. Then 25 engravings on as many leaves (sign. *aaij* to ff. 5, and numbered I–XXIV), with their explanations at the foot of the pages. These plates are preceded by a printed title ("Idæa vera et genuina præcipuarum historiarum ... gentis Indiæ ... "), dated M. DC. II.

3° "Additamentum nonæ partis Americæ, hoc est descriptio ... navigationis quam Olevier a Noort ... confecit ... . *Francofurti, excudebat Matthæus Beckerus,* M. DC. II." Printed title, with the portrait of Olivier de Noort in the middle. Text, pp. 3–100; 14 plates on as many leaves (1 to XIV), with the explanations at the foot of the pages; they are preceded by a printed title ("Vera et genuina, sed brevis tamen designatio insularum ... "), with the same names of city and printer, and the same date as above.

The words "Postrema pars," which are in the first title of this ninth part, seem to indicate that the heirs of Theodore de Bry intended to end their collection there; and, in fact, it was not till seventeen years later, in 1619, that Johann Theodor de Bry continued it by issuing the tenth part. He had published the German text of this same part the preceding year. "This original edition of the ninth part," M. Sobolewski writes to us, "has had two leaves reprinted, namely, the second of the Additamentum, and the second of the Narratio; probably," adds our correspondent, "these impressions were made for two different stocks, and merely distinguish the sets coming from these stocks."

The altered edition of the ninth part has a title considerably different from the first; it begins and ends thus:—

BRY. Americæ|pars decima:|Qua continentur,|I. Duæ Navigationes Dn. Americi Vesputii, sub auspiciis Castellani Regis, hactenus confuse nec suo loco edita: nunc vero sublatis innumeris mendis interpretum ablespia admissis, decenter et ordine accurata; studio et opera Jo. Ludovici Gottofridi Ambergensis. *Francofurti, apud Matthæum Merianum. Anno* M. DC. XXXIII.

This edition is divided into three parts. The first contains the voyage of Sebalt de Weert, the second that of Olivier de Noort, the third the voyage made by the Dutch fleet in 1599, a narrative which is not in the edition of 1602, described above. It is here accompanied by 5 plates printed in the text.

Merian has not reprinted in this volume the seven books "De natura Nova Orbis" of Jos. Acosta, because there was an extract from it in the "Paralipomena Americæ," in the 12th part of the Great Voyages, printed in 1624; he has also not given the plates of these seven books; in this way he has reduced the text of this part to 160 pages, of which part are in two columns. There is between pp. 38 and 41 a second printed title, "Historia Antipodum ... liber secundus ... . *Francofurti, typis Wolffgangi Hoffmanni, anno* 1633." The plates which are printed in the text have in part double numbers, in Arabic figures, which indicate the order of the plates and that of the leaves to which they belong. The latter references are not always correct. The edition of 1633 sold separately 140 fr. (Eyriès), but it is worth much less.

TENTH PART.

BRY. Historia Antipodum sive Novi Orbis qui vulgo Americæ et Indiæ occidentalis nomine usurpatur, Pars nona ... Omnia Ferdinandi|susceptæ.|II. Solida narratio de moderno provinciæ Virginiæ statu, qua ratione tandem pax cum Indianis coaluerit,|ac castella aliquot ad regionis præsidium ab Anglis extructa fuerint: additâ historiâ lectu jucun-|dissimâ, quomodo Pokahuntas, Regis Virginiæ Powhatani filia, primori cuidam Anglo|nupserit; Authore Raphe Hamor .Virginiæ Secretario. | III. Vera descriptio Novæ Angliæ, quæ Americæ pars ad Septentrionalem Indiam spectat, à Capitaneo|Johanne Schmidt, Equite atque Admirali delineata: cui accessit discursus, quomodo in | secunda navigatione à Gallis captus, Anno 1616. demum liberatus fuerit. | Omnia nunc primùm in lucem edita, atque eleganter in æs incisis iconibus illustrata,|Sumptibus ac studio|Johann-Theodori de Bry.|*Oppenheimii*|*Typis Hieronymi Galleri.*|*Anno*|M DC XIX.|

Printed title, in the middle of which is an engraved vignette representing three vessels with a man and woman standing. In a part of the copies there are more vessels, and the man and woman are sitting.

Map of the Philippine Islands, which belongs to the 11th part.

Text, pp. 3-72. Camus has remarked that at p. 21 of the copy which he had under his eyes, the initial H was printed upside down. In one which I have seen it is properly placed.

"Icones sive exactæ ... delineationes ...", with the same date as the printed title above, 12 plates on as many leaves (numbered I–XII, with the explanation. At the foot of the last is, "Finis decimæ partis Americæ."

ELEVENTH PART.

BRY. Americæ | pars vndecima:|Seu|descriptio admirandi| itineris a Guillielmo Schouten|Hollando peracti: qua ratione in meridio-|nali plaga freti Magellanici novum hactenusque incognitum in mare Australe transitum pate-|fecerit: Quas item terras, insulas, gentes, resque mirabiles in dicto Au-|strali Oceano obvias habuerit.|Omnia elegantibus mappis, atque iconibus in æs incisis jam primùm illustrata, | Operâ & Sumptibus | Johann-Theodori de Bry Argentinensis. | *Oppenheimii* | *Typis Hieronymi Galleri.* | *Anno* M. DC. XIX. |

Printed frontispiece. In the middle a map of the world in two hemispheres, below which are the busts of Schouten and Magellan, crowned by Fame; behind them, on the right, the medallions of Candish and Spilberg; on the left those of Drake and Olivier de Noort.

"Procemium," 1 l., numbered 3 and 4.

Map of New Guinea and map of the South Sea.

Text, pp. 5–49, the reverse of the last blank.

Printed frontispiece, with the words, "Sequuntur veræ vivæque rerum ... imagines ...", and the names of the city and the printer, and the date above.

Nine plates, numbered I–IX, with signatures and catch-words, and the names of the places engraved on many of the plates. The small map of the Strait of Magellan, which, according to Guil. Fr. De Bure, should be placed here, must be a duplicate, as it had been already used in the 9th part, and reappears in the 13th.

BRY. Americæ|tomi vndecimi | appendix. | Sev | admirandæ navigationis a Geor-|gio a Spilbergen, classis Belgicæ cvm| potestate Præfecti, per fretum Magellanicum & Mare meridio-|nale, ab Anno 1614. vsq; ad Annum 1618. inclusiuè|peractæ, descriptio.|Qva|Novi per fretvm Magellanicvm et Mare meri-|dionale in Indiam Orientalem transitvs, incognitarvm-|que hactenus terrarum & gentium vt & omnium quæ terra marique acciderunt & visa sunt | memorabilium, explicatio continetur, additis pulcherrimis & nun-|quam antea visis figuris in æs incisis, | Auctore | M. Gothardo Arthvsio Dantiscano. | Francofvrti,| *Typis Ioannis Hoferi, Sumptibus Ioannis-*|*Theodori de Bry.*|*Anno* M. DC. XX. |

(Printed title, having one of the vignettes which are on the frontispiece of the 10th part.)

Preface, 1 l., paged 3 and 4.

Text, pp. 5–34, and 1 blank leaf.

"Sequuntur veræ vivæque imagines incognitarum hactenus regionum ...". (A printed title, with the same date as above.)

Twenty engravings representing views of places and of combats. The plates have no number, and only a few bear the names of the places; but the leaves are numbered from I to XX. At the foot of the last is "Finis."

All the copies of this appendix which we have seen, as well as those which passed under the eyes of Camus, had the paper soiled by the spreading of the bad ink which the printer used. But there are some which are not soiled.

Neither this part nor the preceding have been reprinted; but, for some unknown reason, two different vignettes have been used for the title-pages.

TWELFTH PART.

BRY. Novi Orbis pars dvodecima. | Sive | descriptio | Indiæ occiden-|talis,|Auctore|Antonio de Herrera,|Supremo Castellæ & Indiarum authoritate Philippi|III. Hispaniarum Regis Historigrapho.|Accesservnt et aliorvm In-|diæ Occidentalis Descriptiônes, vti & nauiga-|tionum omnium per Fretum Magel-|lanicum succincta narratio.|Qvibvs cohærent | Paralipomena Americæ, in qvi-|bus res plurimæ memoria & obseruatione dignissima, imprimis regio-|num natura, aeris constitutio, temperamenta elementorum, in-|colarum ingenia quæ in magno opere historico aut omst-|suntur, aut leuiter attinguntur, incunda non|minus quam erudita descriptione|persractantur.|*Francofvrti,*|*Sumptibus Hæredum Iohan. Theodori de Bry.*|*Anno Salutis* M. DC. XXIV.|

Printed title, in an engraved frontispiece. Another printed frontispiece, conceived in the same terms, but without the engraved border.

Dedicatory epistle of J. Th. de Bry, dated 1 Aug. 1623; Herrera's preface, and table of contents, 1 l.

Text, l. 1–154, the reverse of the last blank. In the text of Herrera, ending at l. 44, fourteen maps are inserted at different places where the text shows that they ought to be. These fourteen maps, numbered 1–14, are sometimes placed together at the end of the text. The "Paralipomena Americæ," which commence on the reverse of l. 73, are merely, as we have already said, an extract from Acosta's history, inserted at the beginning of the ninth part of the Great Voyages; and this explains why 14 of the 19 plates which are here printed in the text had been already employed in the said ninth part, as Camus shows, pp. 160, 161 of his *Mémoire*, where he also says that in the greater part of the copies seen by him, at pl. XII on l. 130, a new engraving, representing a triumphal entry, had been pasted on another engraving, which probably was not in its right place.

THIRTEENTH PART.

BRY. Demica Tertia Pars|Historiæ|Americanæ,|qvæ continet exactam|et accvratam de-|scriptionem|I. Novæ Angliæ, Virginiæ, Brasiliæ, Guianæ, & insulæ Bermudæ, quarum|hac-

tenus exigua & imperfecta notitia habita fuit.|II. Terræ Australis incognitæ, cuius chorographia antehac in nullo Itinera-|rio aut Navigatione litteris tradita.|III. Expugnationis vrbis S. Salvatoris & Sinus Omnium Sanctorum ab|Hollandis factæ & quomodo Hispani vrbe & Sinu illo rursus potiti|sint.|IV. Novi Mexici, Cibolæ, Cinaloæ, Quiviræ, rerumq: memo-|rabilium, quæ in|Iucatan, Guatimala, Fonduris & Panama observatæ sint, nec non|aliquot Anglicarum iis locis coloniarum.|V. Navigationis Hollandorum per vniversum orbem, duce Iacobo Eremita.|VI. Classis Hispanicæ prædevitis ab Hollandis, duce Petro Heinio, in portu in-|sulæ, qui Matanza dicitur, interceptæ.|VII. Vrbis Olindæ de Fernambucco in Brasilia ab Hollandis, duce Henrico|Cornelio Lonckio, occupatæ.|Additis passim tabvlis æri incisis, qvi-|bus jam memoratæ descriptiones illustrantur.|*Francofvrti ad Mænvm,*|*Sumptibus Matthæi Meriani ciuis &*|*Chalcographi Francofurtensis.*|M DC XXXIV.|

A printed title in an engraved frontispiece.

Notice to the reader, 1 l.

Text divided into 15 sections, pp. 1–149. This is the translation of the pieces which form the 13th and 14th parts of the German text printed in 1628 and 1630. The engravings which belong to the 13th Latin part are printed in the text, except nine maps or plates, namely:—

1° Large map of America ("America nouiter delineata"); 2° Strait of Magellan (a small map, which is also in the 9th part); 3° "Description de las Indias occidentales" (this is the first of those which accompany the description of Herrera); 4° Map of Virginia, before p. 12; 5° Map of Brazil, before p. 36; 6° Map of Guiana, at p. 46; 7° Map of Bahia de Todos os Sanctos, and of the city of San Salvador; 8° Map of the island of Cuba and of the combat fought in sight of that island, with the portraits of Admiral Lonq and General Hayn, at p. 136; 9° A large plate representing two views of Olinda, at p. 145. These plates are sometimes placed together before the text, and in a different order from that in which we give them.

The pages on which these engravings ought to be found are pp. 4, 5, 11, 18, 25, 28, 87, 102 (view of Terra del Fuego), 108 (numbered 118), 112, 113, 116, 118 (two views), 125, 127, 132, 137 (flying-fishes). In the text, p. 57 is wrongly numbered, and after p. 60 the numbering recommences 51, 52 (numbered 25), 53, etc.

This thirteenth part did not appear till ten years after the twelfth, and forty-four years after the original edition of the first; it may, then, well be believed that very few of the first purchasers of the commencement of this collection would have taken pains to complete it, and many of them may have died before they could do so. It is for this reason that this last part of the Great Voyages is wanting in a number of copies, and that to procure it separately it is necessary to take it, as well as the "Elenchus" of 1634, from copies of the same collection sold by Matthew Merian after this date. It must have been the same with the twelfth and last part of the Small Voyages, which was not published till thirty years after the first, and nine years after the eleventh. These last parts were only printed once, and we think that a much smaller number of copies was printed than of the others.

B.—SMALL VOYAGES.

[OMITTED.]

COPIES OF THE COLLECTION OF THE GREAT AND SMALL VOYAGES WHICH HAVE BEEN SOLD AT AUCTION SINCE 1709.

1. In 6 vols., dated 1624, "Bibliotheca BIGOT.," No. 1946.
2. 5 vols., blue mor., dated 1598 and 1634, DU FAY, No. 2825, 450 fr. The Elenchus of 1634, the double parts of the 2d ed., and those plates which have variations had been added.
3. 25 pts., 1598, etc., 6 vols., COLBERT, No. 2963, 145 fr.
4. 25 pts., 1598–1634, in 6 vols., blue mor., Count D'HOYM, No. 3224, 400 fr.
5. 25 pts. in 6 vols., 1598, etc., LONGUERUE, No. 1098.
6. 25 pts., 1598–1634, in 7 vols., red and citron mor., and also the 9 first pts. of the Great Voyages, 1590–1602, 1st ed., blue mor., ROTHELIN, No. 2820, 750 fr. This was the most complete copy that had yet appeared. It was afterwards in the library of Paris de Meyzieux.
7. 25 pts., 1598–1634, in 6 vols., gr. mor., with many parts doubled, DE BOZE, No. 1513, priced 800 fr.
8. 1590–1634, bound by Derome père, in 12 vols., red mor., a copy said to be more complete than that of Rothelin, GIRARDOT DE PRÉFOND, No. 1060, 985 fr.
9. 25 pts., in 7 vols., 1598–1624, Huet's copy. (Catalogue des JÉSUITES DE LA MAISON PROFESSE, No. 5354.) The copy passed into the *Bibliothèque du roi*, and served to form another.
10. Bd. in 16 vols., blue mor., the copy described in the "Bibliogr. instructive" and in the GAIGNAT catalogue, No. 2602–2623, 1600 fr.
11. Bd. in 10 vols., blue mor., LAURAGUAIS, No. 578, sold at first for 1151 fr., and resold as incomplete for 604 fr.
12. 12 vols., blue mor., 1st ed., RANDON DE BOISSET, No. 1102, 1002 fr.
13. 1st edition in 9 vols., blue mor., with 2 vols. of continuations, in the same binding, first sale of MEL. DE SAINT-CERAN (1780), No. 1395, 1529 fr. 19 sous; and second catalogue (1791), No. 1929, 12 vols., blue mor., complete copy, 1512 fr.
14. The Rothelin copy again, but with 2 vols. composed of duplicate plates added, and some continuations, GOUTARD, Nos. 1040–1042, 2551 fr. This same copy was bought by M. Paris the younger, who added the different continuations described in the "Bibliotheca PARISINA" (*Lond.* 1790), No. 486, when the copy containing these 60 pts., bd. in 24 vols., reached £210. This same copy, in the same condition as in the GOUTARD catalogue, was offered for sale, in 1855, in Paris, by Techener. It was bought for 12,000 fr. by Mr. Lenox, of New-York. It was described in the "Bulletin du Bibliophile," 1855, pp. 38–41.
15. 1st and 2d ed., without the 13th part of the Great Voyages, 16 vols., blue mor., including 2 vols. of continuations, as in the DE GAIGNAT copy, Duke LA VALLIÈRE, Nos. 4508–4510, 1950 fr.
16. 21 vols., violet mor., including the duplicates, the French part, and the continuations, CAMUS DE LIMARE, No. 1380, 4802 fr. Bought for Louis XVI, and to-day in the *Bibliothèque impériale*.
17. 25 pts., in 6 vols., 1590–1634, SOUBISE, No. 5905 *bis*, 602 fr.
18. 13 vols., blue mor., with duplicates and continuations, but without the "Elenchus" of 1634, CREVENNA, No. 5769, no price.
19. 29 vols., red mor., with the Small Voyages in German, announced as the most complete which it is possible to have, LOMENIE DE BRIENNE, in 1792, No. 389, 6300

fr. This copy, which is described in the catalogue of the Count DE BOUTOURLIN, ed. 1805, must have perished when the library of the Count was burnt.

20. 12 vols. complete, with the duplicates and the continuations. Well described in the catalogue of LA SERNA SANTANDER, III. Nos. 3690–3691. Bought for 4000 fr., by Renouard, and afterwards sold by him in London.
21. The Latin edition, with duplicates and continuations, 15 vols., blue mor., with the German text, *Oppenheim*, 1620, in 9 vols., blue mor., the two sets, CAILLARD, Nos. 1840, 1841, 4350 fr.
22. A copy of the 2d ed., without the 13th part of the Great Voyages and the 12th of the Small Voyages, but with the "Appendix Regnum Congo," LANGLÈS, No. 1951, 650 fr.
23. 16 vols., blue mor., 1st and 2d edition, with duplicates and continuations, "Librairie DE BURE," 1834, No. 2810, offered for 4000 fr.
24. 13 vols., green mor., 1st ed., with the first part, duplicates and some continuations, same catalogue, 2d part, No. 2637, sold for 1501 fr.
25. 39 vols., half mor., bl., 1st, 2d, and 3d ed., with duplicate plates and the continuations, sale of J. J. DE BURE, 11,500 fr., and 5 per cent. added. Bought by M. Dutuit, of Rouen.
26. 8 vols., wanting some plates, "Biblioth. WILLETT," in 1813, £126. This is the copy that served as a foundation for that of M. Grenville.
27. 7 vols., blue mor., including the duplicate parts, and a number of plates inserted. Bought at London, by the Duke of Devonshire, for £546.
28. 11 vols., mor., catalogue of the library at FONTHILL (M. BECKFORD), 200 guineas.
29. 13 vols., blue mor. The copy in the library of Lord SPENCER, at Althorp.
30. An incomplete copy, "Biblioth. HEBER," VII, No. 1918, £30 19s. 6d.
31. A copy, in 30 vols., was in the HANROTT library; it included the German text.
32. Another in 11 vols., blue mor., STUARD sale, in 1855. It had the "Elenchus," the "Appendix de Congo," and the six first parts of the Great Voyages in duplicate.
33. 25 pts. in 6 vols., fawn-colored calf, DE JUSSIEU, No. 1423, 730 fr. Some of the first volumes were not of the first impression.

GREAT AND SMALL VOYAGES, WITH THE GERMAN TEXT.

For the description of the Great and Small Voyages in German, we have used: 1°, the copy in the *Bibliothèque impériale*, where the first parts of the Great Voyages are of the second edition; 2°, the "Bibliotheca Grenvilliana;" 3°, more particularly the work published by Weigel, with the title:—

BRY. Bibliographische Mittheilungen über die deutschen Ausgaben von de Bry's Sammlungen der Reisen nach dem abend- und morgenländischen Indien. *Leipzig, T.-O. Weigel*, 1845. 8vo, pp. 52, including the "Fortsetzung," beginning at p. 41.

This pamphlet is extracted from the "Serapeum."

It has been asserted that the plates of this text had been printed before those of the Latin text, but this cannot apply in the Great Voyages to any but the 9th part, printed in 1601 (the Latin in 1602); the 10th part, 1618 (the Latin in 1619); the 12th part, 1623 (the Latin 1624); the 13th and 14th part, 1627, 1628. In regard to the Small Voyages, it is certain that of the 13 parts of the German text eight preceded,

each by about one year, the same parts in Latin. These are parts I–IV, VI–VIII, XI. Part XII, although it has the same date as the Latin edition, must have preceded it by some months. The description which we have given of the plates with the Latin text will serve, with some exceptions, for the German edition.

M. Sobolewski, after having assembled all the parts he could find of this collection, both in Latin and in German, has just finished an essay on the latter, which he designs to print. By comparing the two texts, he has convinced himself that the German edition was made with more care and a better typographical arrangement than the Latin, and that it has experienced fewer transfers from the stock of one bookseller to another. We can add, that the collection of the first editions of all the parts of the German text is very difficult.

A.—GREAT VOYAGES.

I.

BRY. Wunderbarliche, doch Warhafftige Erklärung, von der Gelegenheit vnd Sitten der Wilden in Virginia, welche newlich von den Engelländern, so im Jar 1585. vom Herrn Reichard Greinuile ... ist erfunden worden, In verlegung H. Walter Raleigh, Ritter vnd Obersten desz Zinbergwercks. Erstlich in Engeländischer Sprach beschrieben durch Thomam Hariot, vnd newlich durch Crist. P. in Teutsch gebracht ... *Gedruckt zu Franckfort am Mayn, bey Johann Wechel, in verlegung Dieterich Bry. Anno* 1590. *Werden verkaufft in H. Sigismund Feyerabends Landen.* Folio.

There are copies in which this title gives the address of the bookseller in Latin, as in the first edition of the Latin text of this part.

Description.

The title given above.
Dedicatory epistle to Christian, Duke of Saxony, pp. 3, 4.
Advertisement, pp. 5, 6.
Text, pp. 7–33.
"Warhafftige Contrafacturen ..." (an engraved title with the name of Theodorus de Bry).
"Register," pp. 2.
The plate representing the fall of Adam.
Map of Virginia, counting as No. 1 of the plates.
Address to the reader ("dem günstigen Leser"), 1 page.
Plates II–XXIII.
"Etliche contrafeyt der Völcker ...", 1 page.
5 plates, with their explanations, 9 l.
"Register," pp. 3.
The colophon: "*Gedruckt zu Franckfurt am Mayn, bey Johann Wechel, in verlegung Theodori de Bry.* M.D.XC.," 1 page.

It should be noticed, that the publisher is called "Dieterich Bry" on the first title of this part, and "Theodori de Bry" in the colophon above.

SECOND EDITION, 1600.

The title ends thus: "*Jetzt widerumb vbersehen vnd zum andernmal in Truck gegeben. Gedruckt zu Francfort am Mayn, bey Matthes Becker, in verlegung Dieterich de Bry seliger nachgelassene Wittwe, vnd beyder Söhne,* 1600."

Dedication and advertisement, pp. 3–6; text, pp. 7–31; title, "Warhafftige contrafacturen," engraved; "Register," pp. 2; the plate representing the fall of Adam; map of Virginia; address to the reader, 1 p.; plates I–XXII (not counting the map), "Etliche ...", 1 page, and 5 plates with their explanation, as in the 1st ed., "Register," pp. 3, and the colophon, "*Gedruckt zu Franckfort am Mayn, bey Mattes Becker* ... M. D. C."

THIRD EDITION.

Printed title, in an engraved frontispiece, ending thus: "*Jetzt widerumb, vebersehen, vnd zum drittenmal in Truck gegeben. Gedruckt zu Oppenheim bey Hieronymo Gallern, in Vorlegung Johann.-Theodori de Bry.* M.DC.XX."

The rest as in the 2d ed., only the title ("Warhafftige ...") has, like the frontispiece, the address above, but with the date "M. DC. XIX.," and at the end of the table is the word "Ende," and no colophon.

II.

BRY. Der ander Theyl, der Newlich erfundenen Landtschafft Americæ, von dreyen Schiffahrten, so die Frantzosen in Floridam (die gegen Nidergang gelegen) gethan. Eine vnter dem Häuptmann H. Laudonniere, Anno 1564. Die ander vnter H. Ribald, 1565. Die dritte vnter H. Guorguesio, 1567, geschehen. Ausz dem Frantzösischen in Latein beschrieben, durch C. C. A. Und jetzt ausz dem Latein in Teutsch bracht, durch den Ehrwirdigen H. Oseam Halen. Auch mit schönen und kunstreichen Kupfferstücken und deren angehenckten Erklärung, alles an Tag gegeben, durch Dieterich von Bry, Bürger in Franckfort am Mayn, Anno 1591. *Getruckt zu Francfort am Mayn, bey Johann Feyerabendt, in Verlegung Dieterich von Bry.*

The title given above, on an engraved plate.
Dedication to Wilhelm, Count Palatine, 1 l.
Advertisement (with the plate of the Ark), 1 l.
Privilege, 1 l.
Map of Florida.
Text, pp. I–XLII.
Title in an engraved border, with the imprint, "*Francoforti ad Mœnum typis Joannis Wecheli, sumptibus vero Theodori de Bry. Anno* M.DXCI ... ."
"Register" of the plates, pp. 2.
XLII plates.
"Vnterthänige supplication ... an König Carlen ...," pp. 6.
"Warhafftige ... Beschreibung der vierdent Schiffahrt ...," pp. 9.
"Neben-Bericht von dem Authore," pp. 10.
"Register," with the colophon, "*Gedruckt zu Franckfurt am Mayn, bey Johann Feyerabendt in Verlegung Theodorici von Bry.*"

SECOND EDITION.

Printed title, in an engraved frontispiece, ending thus: "*Jetzung (ou Jetzunder) zum andern mal an Tag gegeben, durch Dieterich de Bry, Bürger in Franckfort am Mayn, Anno* 1603; et plus bas: *Francoforti ad Mænum, typis Joannis Wecheli, sumptibus vero Theodori De Bry, Anno* M.DXCI."

The rest as in the first edition, except that there is no privilege, and that the title which precedes the 42 plates is printed from type, and has the address, "*Franckfort am Mayn, bey Wolffgang Richtern, in Verlegung Dieterichs de Bry seligen Wittib, vnd ihrer zween Söhne. Anno* M. DCIII."

The 42 pl. numbered in Roman figures at the top of the pages, and in Arabic at the foot of the plates, are followed by 13 l. of text as above, sign. M to O five, with the table on the reverse of the last, but without the colophon. This edition of 1603 is enlarged by the translations of the pieces added to the second edition of the Latin text.

III.

BRY. Dritten Buch Americæ, Darinn Brasilia durch Johann Staden von Homberg ausz Hessen, ausz eigener erfahrung in Teutsch beschrieben. Item Historia der Schiffart Joannis Lery in Brasilien, welche er selbst publiciert hat, jetzt von Newem verteutscht, Durch Teucrium Annæum Priuatum, C... Alles von Newem mit künstlichen Figuren in Kupffer gestochen vnd an Tag geben, *Durch Dieterich Bry von Lüttich, jetzt Burger zu Franckfurt am Mayn*, 1593. — *Venales reperiuntur in officina Theodori de Bry.*

The title above.
Dedication to Frederick IV, Palatine of the Rhine, pp. 3.
Preface of de Bry, pp. 2.
"Kaiserliches Wappen" (plates representing the arms of the seven electors).
Map, "Chorographia ... Peruanæ provinciæ."
Text, pp. 1–92.
26 plates printed on pp. 1, 3, 5, 7, 10, 13, 16, 22, 24, 27, 29, 35, 37, 39, 45, 48, 50, 52, 54, 56, 70, 75, 83, 85, 86, and 87.
Engraved frontispiece, "Schiffart in Brasilien in America ... 1593."
"Lobschrifft zu Ehren Johannes Lerio," pp. 2.
"Vorrede Johannis Lerii," pp. 20.
"Plus Videre quam habere" and "Kurtzer inhalt eines jeden Capitels," together, pp. 7.
Plate, the fall of Adam.
Text, pp. 93–285. Pages 136, 175, 261 are wrongly numbered, and Nos. 248, 249, are repeated.
10 plates, which are printed at pp. 97, 103, 150, 155, 189, 193, 195, 215, 221, and 245.
The plates which, in the Latin text, are at chapters 10, 13, 49, 53, etc., do not occur in the German version, nor does the Index which we have mentioned in describing the Latin edition of this 3d part.

SECOND EDITION, WITH THE SAME DATE AS THE FIRST.

This may be recognized first by the title, where the two words, "Teucrium" and "Priuatum" are divided between two lines, thus, "Teu-crium, "Priua-tum," while

in the first they are not divided; and, secondly, by the title after p. 92, which is engraved in the first edition, and printed from type in the second. The rest, as well in the text as the plates, is similar enough to the first edition, only that in the first part of 92 pages, p. 59 is wrongly paged, and in the part, from pp. 93 to 285, pp. 249 and 250 are repeated. In regard to this third part, an edition is described in the "Biblioth. Grenvil.," p. 189, which retains the date 1593 on the frontispiece, but has, in addition, a map dated 1624 (which is perhaps the one which belongs to the eighth part). The copy of the second edition in the *Bibliothèque impériale* does not have this date (1624) anywhere. It has, on the reverse of p. 3 of the preface, the plate of the seven scutcheons, and then 4 l., which contain, "Vorrede ... Herrn Philipsen, Landtgraffen zu Hesen ... Herrn Philipsen, graff zu Nassau." The fall of Adam is not, ordinarily, in the second edition.

IV.

BRY. Das vierdte Buch von der neuwen Welt, oder Neuwe vnd gründtliche Historien, von dem Nidergängischen Indien, so von Christophoro Columbo im Jar 1492 erstlich erfunden. Durch Hieronymum Bentzo von Meyland, welcher 14 Jar dasselbig Land durchwandert, auffs fleissigst beschrieben vnd an Tag geben; Durch Dieterich von Bry, Bürger in Franckfurt am Mayn. (Without date, but 1594 at the foot of page 141).

The title given above.
The plate with the seven scutcheons of the electors on the reverse.
Imperial privilege, 1 l.
Map, "Occidentalis Americæ."
Preface in 2 l. ("an den günstigen Leser"), with a vignette engraved on the first page.
Another preface, "Den Christlichen vnd frommen Lesern ...", 5 l., with a plate on the first page.
Text, pp. 1–141 (pp. 49, 50 are repeated). At the foot of the last, "*Gedruckt zu Franckfort am Mayn bey Johann Feyrabend, in Verlegung Dieterichs von Bry.* M. D. XCIIII."
An engraved title, "Americæ pars quarta ... omnia elegantibus figuris in æs incisis a Theodoro de Bry, Leodiense, cive Francofurtensi. Anno cIↄ. XCIIII. ...", 24 plates, [the last numbered XXIIII and not XXIV].

SECOND EDITION, 1613.

Printed title, in an engraved frontispiece, with no place nor date, and, moreover, in the copy in the *Bibliothèque impériale*, a Latin title, an engraved plate retaining the date, "Anno cIↄ. XCIIII." Both have the device, "Nul sans soucy."
3 p. l. as above.
Map, "America sive Novi Orbis descriptio." In the copy in the *Bibliothèque impériale*, "Orient. Americæ tabula chorographica," date "M.D.XCIIII."
Six unnumbered leaves, sign. E o Cij (as above).
Text in 141 pages; at the foot of the last, "*Zu Francfurt am Mayn bey Matthias Beckers seligen Wittib, in Verlegung Johann Theodors de Bry.* M.DC.XIII."
Engraved Latin title, dated "cIↄ.XIII."
Map, "Occidentalis Americæ" (in some copies only).
24 engravings, with Arabic numbers on the plates.

V.

BRY. Americæ das fünffte Buch, vol schöner unerhörter

Historien, ausz dem andern Theil Joannis Benzonis von Meylandt gezogen ... an Tag geben, durch Dietherich von Bry, Burger in Franckfurt am Mayn.

This first edition is very rare.
Title without date (it is sometimes pasted on the Latin frontispiece, dated "cIↄ Iↄ xcv").
Preface, with the portrait of Columbus, in a vignette, and the argument, 2 l.
Map, "Hispaniæ novæ ... descriptio, 1595."
Text, pp. 7–115 (pp. 92, 93, 114 are wrongly paged).
Title of the plates, "Americæ pars quinta ... Omnia elegantibus figuris in æs incisis expressa a Theodoro de Bry Leod. cive Franc. A° cIↄ Iↄ xcv."
22 Plates, of which the 17th is wrongly numbered.
The second edition has, like the first, a German title, without any date, but some copies have the Latin title dated "cIↄ Iↄ xcv," while the title which precedes the 22 plates is thus expressed: —
"Folgen hernacher Eigentliche vnd Warhafftige Fürbildungen ... an Tag geben, durch Johann Dietherich de Bry ... *Gedruckt zu Franckfurt am Mayn, durch Erasmum Kempffer.* M.DC.XIII."
The rest as in the first edition, except that in the text, pp. 57 and 76 are the only ones wrongly paged.

VI.

BRY. Der sechste Theil der neuwen Welt, oder Der Historien Hieron. Benzo von Meylandt, Das dritte Buch ... an Tag geben Durch Dieterich von Bry, Kunststecher vnd Bürger zu Franckfurt am Mayne ... M. D. XCVII.

Title pasted on an engraved plate.
Dedication to Maurice, Landgrave of Hesse, with his scutcheon, 1 l.
Preface (Vorrede), 1 l.
Map, "America ... 1596."
Text, pp. 1–62 [a misprint; it should be 62 l.]. Page 56 is not numbered. On p. 62 is "*Gedruckt zu Franckfurt am Mayn bey Johann Feyrabendt, in verlegung Dietrichs von Bry. Anno* M. D. XCVII."
Plate, "Cusco urbs nobilissima ...".
Title "Folgen hernacher Eigentliche Fürbildung ... an Tag geben, Durch Diterich de Bry Leodiensem. *Gedruckt zu Franckfurt am Mayn, durch Johann Feyrabendt. Im Jar* M.D.XCVII."
Plates numbered I–XXVIII.

EDITION OF 1619.

Printed title in an engraved frontispiece; it begins, "Der Sechste Theil Americæ oder der Historien ...", and has the date "MDCXIX."
Dedication, preface, the map "America ... 1596," and the plate "Cusco," as in the first edition.
Text, pp. 1–121, in 22 chapters.
Printed title, "Sechster Theil Americæ Eigentliche Fürbildung ... vnd jetzo von newem an Tag geben, durch Dieterich de Bry Leodiensem. Oppenheim, in Vorlegung Johann Theodors de Bry. *Gedruckt bey Hieronymo Gallern.* MDCXVIII."
28 plates.
The map, dated 1596, is wanting in several copies, because it has been used in another part.

VII.

BRY. Das VII. Theil America. Warhafftige vnnd liebliche Beschreibung etlicher fürnemmen Indianischen Landschafften vnd Insulen, die vormals in keiner Chronicken gedacht, vnd erstlich in der Schiffart Vlrici Schmidts von Straubingen, mit grosser gefahr erkündigt, vnd von ihm selber auffs fleissigst beschrieben vnd dargethan. Vnd an Tag gebracht durch Dieterich von Bry, *Anno* M. D. XCVII.

The title given above.
Advertisement of Dietrich de Bry, 1 l.
"Warhafftige Beschreibung ...".
Text, pp. 1–31, the first beginning with an engraving, which is not the same as that in the Latin text.
The Hamburg and the Gotha library each have a copy of this part, in which is found a title for the plates, beginning and ending as follows: —
"Folgen nun die Figuren vnd Kupfferstück, deren etliche ins siebende Theil ... Jetzo new auffs zierlichste zugericht vnd an Tag geben, durch Dieterich de Bry, seligen, nachgelassene Erben. *Gedruckt zu Franckfort am Meyn durch Matthæum Becker.* M.DC."
The plates are numbered XV and I–III in the copy at Hamburg, and XV only in that at Gotha ("Weigel," p. 46), which establishes the existence of a second edition of this 7th part.
[For some corrections of the last two paragraphs, *see* the Appendix.]

THIRD EDITION, 1617.

Printed title, in an engraved frontispiece, and ending thus: "Jetzo zum drittenmal auffgelegt vnd gebessert durch Johan-Theodor de Bry, Bürgern zu Oppenheim ... *Gedruckt bei Hieronymo Gallern.* M DC XVII."
Notice of Theod. de Bry.
Text, pp. 52, the first having an engraving, the fifty-second being blank.
A printed title beginning, "C. Folgen nun die Figuren ...", and ending, "*Franckfurt, in Verlegung Joannis-Theodori de Bry S. Erben.* M DC XXIV."
Three plates, with explanations, at the foot of which is, "Americæ Siebender Theil." In the Latin edition these form the three first of the 18 plates of the eighth volume. They are wanting in some of the copies of the German text. The words "zum dritten mahl an Tag geben," which occur on the title dated 1617, and on that which has the date 1624, confirm the existence of the rare second edition of which we have just spoken.

VIII.

BRY. Americæ Achter Theil, In welchem Erstlich beschrieben wirt das Mächtige vnd Goldtreiche Königreich Guiana ... Item, Ein kurtze Beschreibung der vmbligenden Landtschafften Emereia, Arromaia, Amapaia, Topago, etc ... Alles mit fleisz beschrieben durch ... Walthern Ralegh ... Zum andern, die Reyse desz Edlen vnd vesten Thomas Candisch ... Vnd zum dritten die letzte Reysz der gestrengen, Edlen vnd vesten Frantzen Draeck vnd Johan Havkens ... an Tag gegeben, durch Dieterichen von Bry seligen, hinderlassene Erben. *Gedruckt zu Franckfurt am Mayn, durch Matthæum Becker*, 1599.

The title given above, having at the foot a small square engraved map.
Advertisement, pp. 3.
Another of Sir Walter Ralegh, pp. 2.
"Tabula geographica. Guiana."
Text, "Guiana" in 1595, pp. 1–56.
Notice to the reader in regard to another voyage to Guiana, pp. 1–30. [An error: the notice occupies pp. 1, 2; the text of the voyage, pp. 3–30.]
Title of the voyage of Th. Cavendish, in 1586, etc. ("Reise desz Edlen vnd vesten Thomas Candisch ...", dated "M. D. XCIX."
Text of Th. Candisch, pp. 1–48.
Title for the plates ("Warhafftige vnd Eygentliche Fürbildung ..."), dated "M. D. XCIX."
6 plates.
"Additamentum," title dated "*Anno* M DC."
Advertisement, pp. 3, 4.
Text, pp. 5–73; there is no p. 46.
Title for the plates ("Folgen nun die Figuren ..."), dated MDC.
15 plates.

SECOND EDITION, 1624.

Printed title, longer than in the first edition. Here is the beginning and the end: —

BRY. Achter Theil Americæ, darinnen Erstlich beschrieben wird das Mächtige und Goldtreiche Königreich Guiana zu Norden ... Von Newem vbersehen in ein richtigere Ordnung gebracht, vnd zum ändernmahl vffgelegt, auch mit vielen Kupfferstücken vber vorige vermehrt. *Franckfurt, Bey Caspar Rödtel: in Verlegung Weiland Johannis-Theodori de Bry Seeliger Erben.* M. DC. XXIV.

The two prefaces, 5 l., not numbered. Sometimes there is only the preface of Sir Walter Ralegh.
Map, "Guiana."
Text, pp. 1–130, in 2 columns. The plates, to the number of 20, are placed at pp. 3, 11, 15, 19, 21, 27, 58, 62, 70, 75, 81, 84, 92, 94, 98, 103, 116, 119, 121, 124.
[For corrections, *see* the Appendix.]

IX.

BRY. Neundter vnd Letzter Theil Americæ, Darin*n* gehandelt wird, von gelegenheit der Elementen, Natur ... der Newen Welt: ... Alles auffs trewlichste aus Niederländischer Beschreibung Johan Hugen von Lintschotten, in vnser Hochteutsche Sprache versetzet, durch Johannem Humberger Wetterauium. Ferner auch von der Reise der fünff Schiffe, so im Junio desz 1598. Jahrs, in Hollandt auszgefahren, der meynung, durch das Fretum Magelanum, zu den Moluckischen Inseln zu schiffen ... an Tag geben, durch Dietrichs de Bry seligen Wittib, vndzween Söhne. *Gedruckt zu Franckfurt am Mayn, bey Wolfgang Richter.* (Without date, or with the date 1601, as in Mr. Grenville's copy.)

The title given above.
"Dedication" to Louis, Landgrave of Hesse, with his arms, 1 l.
"Durchleuchtiger hochgeborner Fürst ...", pp. 2.
"An den gutwilligen Leser," pp. 2.
Text, pp. 1–327 (pp. 224, 238, 297 wrongly numbered).
Title, "Historische Relation ... . *Gedruckt zu Franckfurt am Mayn, durch Matthæum Becker.* M. DCI."
Text, pp. 3–72 (the numbers 57 and 58 are doubled, and 61 and 62 are wanting; 71 is incorrect).
Title for the plates ("Warhafftige vnd eygentliche Abconterfeyung vnd Fürbildung ..."), dated "in Jahr M. DC I."
25 plates.
Title, "Additamentum Oder Anhang desz neundten Theils Americæ ... . *Gedruckt zu Franckfurt am Mayn, durch Matthæum Becker,* M. DCII."
Map, "Fretum Magellanicum" (not in the 2d edition).
Text, pp. 3–103, the last numbered 130.
Title of the plates ("Warhafftige ..."), dated "in Jahr 1602."
14 plates.

SECOND EDITION.

The title differs much from that of the first edition. It begins with these three words, "Neundter Theil Americæ," without the words "vnd Letzter" before "Theil," and ends, "Vnd an Tag geben durch Matthæum Merian ... . *Getruckt zu Franckfurt am Mayn, Bey Wolffgang Hoffmann*" in part of the copies "*bey Matheo Rempffern*").
The title given above, printed in an engraved frontispiece, is also undated.
Dedication, with the arms, 1 l.
The two advertisements (the 1st dated 1601), 2 l.
Text, pp. 1–206 (with the mistakes in pagination).
Title, "Additamentum, dated as in the first edition.
Title of the plates ("Warhafftige"), the same.
Plates, numbered I–XIV.
As this second edition was published by Matth. Merian, it could not have appeared before 1620.
The "Additamentum" of this 9th part had been previously published separately with this title: —

BRY. Neur Schiffart. Warhafftige und eygentliche Beschreibung der Langwierigen, sorglichen und gefährlichen Reyse so Olivier van Noort, General Oberster uber vier Schiffe durch das gefährliche Fretum Magellanicum um die gaz Welt gethan hat, verteutscht durch M. Gothard Arthus von Dantzig. *Franckfurt am Mayne, bey Matthias Becker*, 1602. 4to, pp. 119, including the engraved Frontispiece, and 14 Plates.

X.

BRY. Zehender Theil Americæ Darinnen Zubefinden: Erstlich zwo Schiffarten Herrn Americi Vesputii ... Zum andern: Ein gründlicher Bericht von dem jetzigen Zustand der Landschafft Virginien. ... Zum dritten: Ein warhafftige Beschreibung desz newen Engellands ... von Capitein Johann Schmiden ... beschrieben ... *in Vorlegung Johann-Theodor de Bry, Kunst vna*

Buchhändlers. Gedruckt zu Oppenheim bey Hieronymo Gallern, Anno MDXVIII.

The title given above, printed, with an engraved vignette.
Notice to the reader, pp. 2.
Map, "America noviter delineata."
Text, pp. 5–73 (the 66th is wrongly paged in many copies).
Printed title for the plates ("Folgen hernacher Eigentliche ... Fürbildungen ..."), with the date "Anno MDXVIII."
Plates numbered I–XII.

XI.

BRY. Historische Beschreibung, Der wunderbarlichen Reyse, welche von einem Holländer, Wilhelm Schouten genandt, neulicher Zeit ist verrichtet worden: ... ans Tage Liecht gegeben, durch vnd in Verlegung Johann-Dieterich von Bry. *Getruckt zu Franckfurt am Mayn, Durch Paull Jacobi. Im Jahr,* M. DC. XIX.

There are copies in which the title begins thus, "Eylffter Theil Americæ. Beschreibung der ...".
[*See* the Appendix.]
After this title are:
Advertisement, pp. 2.
2 maps, *a.* "Nova Guinea," *b.* "Mappe von der Südsee."
Text, pp. 5–35.
Printed title for the plates ("Folgen ... Fürbildung"), dated "Anno MDCXIX."
9 plates, numbered I–IX.

BRY. Appendix desz eilfften Theils Americæ. ... *Getruckt zu Oppenheim bey Hieronymo Gallern, in Verlegung Johann Theodor de Bry. Anno* M DC XX.

Text, pp. 3–38 (the 36th wrongly numbered).
Another printed title for the plates, dated "Anno MDC. XX."
20 plates, numbered I–XX.
The two maps mentioned above, on Weigel's authority, are not found in most copies.
It is probable that the copies of this eleventh part and the thirteenth, whose titles do not show the order which they hold in the collection, were published separately, and perhaps previously to those copies which were designed to form the continuation of the first parts.

XII.

BRY. Zwölffter Theil der Newen Welt, Das ist: Gründliche volkommene Entdeckung aller der West-Indianischen Landschafften ... Insuln ... entdecket vnd beschrieben, Durch Antonium de Herrera, ... Item Petri Ordonnez de Cevallos Beschreibung der West Indianischen Landschafften. ... *Gedruckt zu Frankfurt, in Verlegung Johann Dietherichs de Bry, Anno* 1623.

Printed title, in an engraved frontispiece.
Herrera's preface, with no table, 1 l.
Map, "America sive novus orbis."
Text in two columns, pp. 1–131 (p. 14 wrongly numbered). The plate "Cusco vrbs nobilissima" occurs at p. 99.

The 14 plates (16 in the copy of Mr. Grenville) which belong to the text of Herrera are placed either in this part or in the 13th.
In place of the "Paralipomena," which in the Latin edition follow p. 73 of the text, this edition has 38 pages on San Salvador and Aldendurg [so in Brunet], with an appendix; in the Latin edition this forms the 7th section of the 13th and last part.

XIII.

BRY. Dreyzehender Theil Americæ; Das ist: Fortsetzung der Historien von der Newen Welt, oder Nidergängischen Indien; Darinnen erstlich ein sattsame und gründtliche Beschreibung desz Newen Engellandts, Virginia, Brasilia, Guiana, und Bermuda. Am Ende ist ein Discurs, von der Statt St. Salvator ... *Franckfurt, Gedruckt bey Caspar Rötel, in Verlegung Matthei Merian. Anno* M. DC. XXVIII.

The copy in the *Bibliothèque impériale* has the title given above; but in other copies this title begins thus, "Continuatio Americæ, d. i. Fortsetzung ...", and the date is "M. DC. XXVII."
The title given above.
Notice to the reader, 1 l.
Text, pp. 1–90 (p. 87 is wrongly numbered). There are 7 pl. in the text, at pp. 5, 7, 15, 37, 42, 60, and 69.
Map of Virginia, for p. 17, and a map of Guiana for p. 67.
Another text, pp. 1–38.
And besides, according to Weigel,
A plate, "Warhafftige Abbildung von Einnehmung der statt S. Salvator."
This part contains the text of the seven first sections of the Latin translation printed in 1634. In Mr. Grenville's copy, at p. 67, is a map of Brazil which is not in the Latin edition.

XIV.

BRY. Vierzehender Theil Americanischer Historien, Inhaltend, Erstlich, Warhafftige Beschreibung etlicher West-Indianischer Landen ... Alsz New Mexico, Cibola, Cinaloa, Quiuira, ... Zum Andern, Eine Schiffart der Holländer vnder dem Admiral Jacob Eremiten vmb die gantze Welt ... Zum Dritten, Historiche [so in Brunet] Erzehlung, welcher gestalt die sehr reiche Spanische Silberflotta durch Peter Hein ... 1628 ertapt vnd heim gebracht worden. Zum Vierdten, Was massen die Statt Olinda de Fernambucco ... erobert worden ... an den Tag gegeben durch Mattheum Merian, Buchhändlern vnd Kunststechern zu Franckfurt am Mayn, *Gedruckt zu Hanaw bey David Aubrj, im Jahr* MDCXXX.

Printed title.
Advertisement, 1 l.
Text, pp. 1–72, with 14 plates printed at pp. 8, 21, 23, 26, 30, 35, 36, 39, 41, 48, 50, 55, 60, and 64.
At p. 69 are two plates on a single sheet, "Olinde" and "Phernanbuco."
The copy described by Weigel has, after the title, 3 maps which are not in that in

the *Bibliothèque impériale*, *a.* "Descripcion de las Indias orientales," *b.* "Fretum magellanicum," *c.* "Virginia."

And after the advertisement two other maps: —

"America noviter delineata,"

"Das Norder Theil des Lands Brasilien."

This 14th German part contains sections 8 to 15, which are in Latin in the 13th volume of the Great Voyages in that language, printed only in 1634.

ABRIDGEMENT OF THE GREAT VOYAGES.

Bry. America, das ist, Erfindung und Offenbahrung der Newen Welt, etc., durch M. Philippum Ziglerum von Würzburg; und in Truck gegeben von Johan Theodoro de Bry, Buchhändlern und Bürgern zu Oppenheim. *Gedruckt zu Franckfurt am Mayn durch Nicolaum Hoffmann*, 1617. Folio.

This volume contains an abridgement of the nine first parts of the Great Voyages, and some other relations already published.

Bry. Historia Antipodum, Newe Welt and Americanische Historien. Inhaltend Beschreibungen aller West-Indianischen Landschafften, Insulen, etc., Durch Johan Ludwig Gottfriedt; mit Landtafeln Kupfferstucken, etc. *Durch Mattheum Merian, Buchhändlern und Kunst-Stechern zu Frankfurt am Mayne, anno* 1631. 3 pts. in 1 vol., folio.

An abridgement of the twelve first parts of the German text of the Great Voyages published by the de Bry. The two first parts form, together, pp. 562, and have, moreover, an engraved frontispiece, a printed title, and 4 preliminary leaves for the dedicatory epistle and the preface; the third part has only 72 pages. The second edition, printed at Frankfort, in 1665, contains some additions.

This work should not be confounded with the three parts of the Great Voyages (the 3d, 4th, and 9th), which, in the editions issued by Math. Merian in 1630, 1644, and 1633, also have the title, "Historia Antipodum."

APPENDIX.

At the end of the volume which contains the article de Bry, Brunet prints a letter received from M. Sobolewski after that article was printed.

Paris, 1 *October*, 1860.

I am proud, Monsieur, to be cited by you, and I regret that I did not arrive in Paris soon enough to communicate to you some observations on the Great and the Small Voyages of De Bry in German, while you were printing your notice. You have here only a single copy, by no means complete, and this has prevented your being as exact and as explicit in regard to the German collection as you are for the Latin. As to the latter, your notice would leave nothing to be desired if you had not accepted, with too much confidence, all that I had the honor to say to you in a former letter. Unhappily I have led you into error in regard to the first part of the Great Voyages (col. 1315),

and I hasten to set right what I then advanced; at Moscow I had not the means of verifying some notes formerly taken on a journey.

There are only two impressions of the original edition (the one which has large numbers printed above the plates). I had thought that there were three varieties of the explanations of plates III, VIII, and X. It was a mistake; there are only two. On the other hand, I had forgotten to tell you that there were also two varieties of the explanation of plate XXII; this should be added to the table which you give in col. 1316. This had escaped MM. De Bure.

There are also two impressions of the second edition of this part (the one with small characters printed above the plates), which reproduce, line by line, — but only for pp. 7–34 of the text, — the two impressions of the original edition. You have indicated perfectly, at the foot of col. 1313, the differences which distinguish the preliminary and supplementary matter of this second edition from the same sheets of the original edition; as to the explanations of the plates, it is again I that have led you into error. The two impressions of the second edition do not reproduce, as you say, following me, the two impressions of the first, although the attempt was made for a few plates. In general the explanations with the small figures are differently arranged from those with the large figures, and are only to be met with in one impression, excepting a single plate, the XXIId. I have a copy where the first line ends, not as usually with "principum se," but with "sepulturam," and contains 18 lines in place of 20. It may be that some other differences have escaped me, in consequence of my not having had occasion to notice them; for this reason I subjoin a table, which rectifies and completes your two tables, and gives to amateurs the means of verifying and establishing such discoveries as are still possible. As to what Santander says, it is erroneous merely because he did not distinctly make up his mind what should be called first and second editions. For my part, I understand by first edition either of the two impressions with large numbers, and by second edition either of the two impressions with small figures (see the remarks after the following table). After having consulted a considerable number of copies, which had remained in their ancient bindings, I am convinced that the two impressions of the first edition are always to be found mingled, whether the title has "Theodor Feirabend*i*" or "Theodor*i* Feyrabend*ii*," and that it is impossible to decide the question of priority.

Table to be substituted for those of columns 1316 and 1317.

II	19	præbant in	19	præbant in	17	regio
III	19	publi	16	*pro*	16	*pro*
IIII	12	prode	10	decussa	11	ma
V	6	periti in	7	appa	7	ap
VI	7	nisi	8	*memoratæ*	8	*memoratæ*
VII	12	ver	10	*instar*	9	*instar*
VIII	14	lacum	11	*oppidum*	11	*oppidum*
IX	7	latere	8	ab uno	8	colligata
X	7	Roa	6	Roanac	7	miliaribus a
XI	8	*sæpenume*	7	naturæ	8	*sæpenume*
XII	16	ferreis	14	*aliis*	13	*aliis*
XIII	17	ratio	17	ratio	15	rationem
XIV	9	illic	9	illic	11	pavan
XV	16	admodum	11	ad	12	capa
XVI	5	meditul	5	meditul	6	me
XVII	11	vel	11	vel	8	bello de
XVIII	22	ma	22	ma	20	magnum
XIX	20	sunt	20	sunt	14	non
XX	25	sunt	25	sunt	20	hæ pi-
XXI	13	ligneo	13	ligneo	10	elabora
XXII	20	*principum se*	21	principum	20	*principum se*
XXIII	11	expres	11	expres	11	has

The first column gives the number of the plates.

The second column gives the number of the lines of explanation below the plate, and the last word of the first line of one of the impressions of the edition with large numbers. Measure of this larger number |

The third column gives the same number and the same word for the other impression with large numbers |

The fourth column marks in the same way the edition with small numbers. Measure of this smaller number |

N. B. To make the differences in the ends of the lines of the different editions more conspicuous, we have printed here several words in Italics, although these words are in Roman in the editions which we have described.

Collection of the de Bry, in German.

Col. 1344. The copy in the *Bibliothèque impériale*, the only one, I believe, that you have at Paris, is very defective. It is, therefore, not astonishing that in using mine, which is perfectly complete, I find several corrections to be made in your article. I will begin by remarking that the titles of the first parts of the Great Voyages in German are, in general, printed separately and pasted on the frontispieces engraved for the Latin edition; but they are sometimes found printed on frontispieces where the legend had been left blank.

Col. 1345–46. *First part, second and third editions.* The title which precedes the engravings is entirely printed from type, while in this it is printed in an engraved cartouch.

Col. 1346. *Second part, second edition.* I add, as distinctive marks of this edition, that the privilege is dated 20 August 1603, and that the text is numbered in Arabic figures 1–42, instead of in Roman numerals I–XLII, as in the first edition.

Col. 1347. *Third part.* The two editions of this part resemble one another perfectly in type and paper, but there are some differences which might easily escape the collater, and are worth while to note: In the first edition the catch-word of p. 7 is "wilden," with a small w, and the word "Referirt" on the second line of p. 285 has a capital R, but the second has "Wilden," with a capital W, and "referirt," with a small r. If p. 136 is wrongly numbered in some copies, it is from an accident during the printing, as I have satisfied myself, and this error is very often to be found corrected. Where the map is dated 1624, it is because, to supply one wanting in that copy, one was taken from a later edition, as this map is to be found repeated in other parts printed later.

Col. 1348. *Fourth part, first edition.* The last plate is numbered XXIIII, and not XXIV.

Col. 1349. *Sixth part, first edition.* The text has 62 leaves and not 62 pages; this is a misprint in your account.

Seventh part. The last seven lines of your col. 1349 and the first seven of col. 1350, contain some errors borrowed from the account given by Weigel, who had apparently used a copy in which the binder had introduced some plates not belonging there. To understand this, it should be known that the three plates of the seventh part of the Great Voyages in German were published at first at the end of the "Additamentum" of the eight part, in 1600, as was done in the Latin edition; they there form Nos. I, II, III, and are preceded by the following general title, "*Folgen nun die Figuren ... deren etliche ins siebende Theil ... etliche ins achte ... jetzo new auffs zierlichste zugericht vnd an Tag geben durch Dieterich de Bry, seligen Erben. Gedruckt zu Francfort am Meyn durch Matthæum Becker*, MDC.;" but afterward, when a second

edition of the eighth part was published in 1624, with illustrations in the text and the "Additamentum" included in the text, as there was no place for these plates, they were struck off again with a title printed *ad hoc*, beginning, "Folgen nun die Figuren, welche ins siebende Theil, zur beschreibung der Reysen Ulrich Schmids von Straubingen gehören," and ending with, "*Francfurt, in Verlegung Joannis Theodori de Bry S. Erben*, M. DC. XXIV." This title and these three engravings, by themselves, ought only to be met with, therefore, in the copies of the collection where the eighth part is of the first edition, and where the "Additamentum" of 1600 is to be found; while they are duplicates in those where the eighth part is of the second edition. The impression of 1624 is distinguished from that of 1600, as you remark further on, by the words, "Americæ siebender Theil," below the explanation of each engraving. No second edition of this part is known, but a third edition is known; it is remarkable that the case is the same with the Latin text of this part.

Col. 1350. *Eighth part, first edition.* You reproduce a slight inaccuracy of Weigel, when you say that the notice to the reader in regard to another voyage to Guiana extends from p. 1 to p. 30. The notice of this second voyage of Raleigh to Guiana occupies pp. 1 and 2; the text of the voyage, pp. 3–30.

The text of the second edition of the eighth part contains all that is in the first edition and the "Additamentum," no more, no less, but arranged in a better order. As to the plates, those which are at pp. 15, 76, 116, are not in the first edition; plate XII of the "Additamentum" of 1600 is wholly wanting, as well as plates I, II, III, for which, as I have said above, there was no longer any place.

Col. 1352. *Tenth part.* The vignette of the title is different in some copies; the case is the same in the Latin edition.

Except in the points that I have mentioned, I find everything perfectly exact and precise. The differences between the plates of the different editions might be pointed out, especially for the Small Voyages in German, but this could be done only by the aid of engravings, which would occupy too much space, and, moreover, would only interest the booksellers and the amateurs in Germany, of whom you are, Monsieur, the guide and the providence.

Receive my thanks for the honor you have done me in associating my name with yours, as well as the assurance of my high and sincere consideration.

Serge Sobolewski.

Bryan (D.) The Appeal for Suffering Genius: a Poetical Address for the Benefit of the Boston Bard; and the Triumph of Truth, a Poem. By Daniel Bryan. *Washington City: the Author.* 1826. 8vo, pp. xiii, 80. c., h. 8785

Bryan. The Lay of Gratitude, consisting of Poems occasioned by the Recent Visit of Lafayette to the United States, by Daniel Bryan. *Philadelphia: H. C. Carey & I. Lea.* 1826. 8vo, pp. 104. ba. 8786

Bryan. The Mountain Muse: Comprising the Adventures of Daniel Boone; and the Power of Virtuous and Refined Beauty. By Daniel Bryan, of Rockingham County, Virginia. *Harrisonburg: the Author.* 1813. 12mo, pp. 252, List of Subscribers, pp. 12. c., h. 8787

Bryan. Thoughts on Education: A Poem. *Richmond, Va.* 1830. 8vo. 8788

Bryan. Tribute to the Memory of Rev. G. G. Cookman, also a Poem on the Loss of the Steamer President. *Alexandria.* 1841. 8vo. 8789

Bryan (G. J.) Life of George P. Barker, with Sketches of some of his Celebrated Speeches; the Proceedings of the Bar of Erie County on the Occasion of his Death, and the Funeral Sermon of John C. Lord, d.d. By George J. Bryan. *Buffalo: O. G. Steele.* 1849. 16mo, pp. 215. Portrait. c., s. 8790

Bryan (Hugh). Living Christianity delineated, in the Diaries and Letters of two Eminently pious Persons lately deceased; viz. Mr. Hugh Bryan, and Mrs. Mary Hutson, Both of South-Carolina. With a Preface by the Reverend Mr. John Conder, and the Reverend Mr. Thomas Gibbons. *London: J. Buckland.* MDCCLX. 12mo, pp. xi, 171. c., p. 8791

See M. R., XXIII. 255.

Bryan (James), *M.D.* A Plea for the Establishment of Veterinary Colleges in the United States, being a Lecture delivered Oct. 24, 1854, before the State Agricultural Society of Pennsylvania. *Philadelphia.* 1855. 8vo, pp. 16. 8792

Bryan. Progress of Medicine during the First Half of the Nineteenth Century. ... Lecture ... . By James Bryan, m.d. ... *Philadelphia: Grattan & M'Lean.* 1851. 8vo, pp. 28. h.

Bryan (J. W.) An Oration on the Completion of the Club-foot and Harlow's Creek Canal, and the Fifty First Anniversary of our Independence, delivered July 4, 1827. By James W. Bryan. *Newbern, N. C.: Watson & Machen.* 1827. 8vo, pp. 12. m. 8794

Bryan (John A.) Letter on the Union of the Atlantic and Pacific Oceans, at or near the Isthmus of Panama. 1845. 8vo.

Bryan. The Ohio Annual Register; containing a condensed history of the State, with a full and complete catalogue of all the public officers in the several counties in Ohio; Officers of State, Members of Congress and the Legislature, Cabinet and other officers of the General Government, etc., etc., since the adoption of the State Constitution; also the names of the Governors, Judges, etc., appointed under Territorial Government; together with a variety of tables and other useful information calculated for the public convenience and general interest. By John A. Bryan. *Columbus.* 1814. 12mo. 8796

Bryan (John H.) Speech in Congress, on the Proposition to Amend the Constitution, Respecting the Election of President and Vice-President, March 13, 1826. [n. p. n. d.] 12mo, pp. 15. w. 8797

Bryan (Jonathan). Letter to the Negroes lately converted in America and particularly those at the plantation of J. Bryan. *London.* 1743. 8vo. 8798

Bryan (Samuel). Proceedings in the Case of Francis Johnson, Esq., prosecuted for Delinquencies as Receiver-general of the Land-office, Pennsylvania. *Lancaster, Pa.* 1799. 8vo, pp. 27. 8799

Bryan. A Statement of measures contemplated against Samuel Bryan, Esq., Register-General of the Commonwealth of Pennsylvania ... the evident motive for them was his spirited prosecution of Francis Johnson, Esq., late Receiver-General ... also a summary account of the late disgraceful fracas. ... *Philadelphia.* 1800. 8vo, pp. 62. p. 8800

Bryan (Thomas). Observations on the Tariff, with reference to the printing of Silk into Handkerchiefs, etc. Addressed to the Secretary of State of the United States. [*New York.* 1827.] 8vo pp. 7. c. 8801

Bryan (T. B.) Stephen A. Douglas on the Cause and Effect of the Rebellion. Letter from Thomas B. Bryan, Esq. [n. p. n. d.] 8vo, pp. 3. 8802

Bryand (Édouard). Histoire de St-Dominigue. *See* [Edwards (Bryan)].

Bryant (C. S.) *and* Murch (A. B.) A History of the Great Massacre by the Sioux Indians in Minnesota [in August, 1862], including the personal narratives of many who escaped. By Charles S. Bryant, a.m., and Abel B. Murch. Eighth Thousand. *Cincinnati; Rickey & Carroll.* 1864. Crown 8vo, pp. 504. c. 8803

Bryant (E.) What I saw in California: being the Journal of a Tour by the Emigrant Route and South Pass of the Rocky Mountains, across the continent of North America. ... in the Years 1846, 1847. ... By Edwin Bryant, Late Alcade of San Francisco. *New York: D. Appleton & Co.* 1848. 12mo, pp. 455. + Second Edition. *New York.* 1848. + Third Edition.

[*Ibid.* and] *Philadelphia: Geo. S. Appleton.* M DCCC XLIX. 12mo, pp. 455. c., h. 8804

A sixth edition was published in 1849. It was reprinted, *London: Routledge.* 1849. 12mo, pp. 144. This was the first of the modern books which drew attention to the large deposits of gold in that country. An edition was published at Paris with J. T. Brooks'. *See* Vol. II., No. 8350.

Bryant. Voyage en Californie. Description de son sol, de son climat, de ses mines d'or. Traduit par X. Marmier. Augmenté de divers renseignements sur l'état actuel de la Californie, et d'une Notice scientifique sur l'or et son exploitation. *Paris: Arthus Bertrand.* [1849.] 8 sheets. Map. 8805

Bryant (J. R. M.) Eulogium on Chief Justice Marshall, delivered ... Washington City, on the 24th of September, 1835, By James R. M. Bryant. ... . *Washington: Jacob Gideon, Jr.* 1835. 8vo, pp. 16. c. 8806

[Bryant (J.)] Account and History of the Oregon Territory, together with a Journal of an Emigrating Party. *London.* 1846. 12mo. 8807

Title from J. R. Smith's Catalogue.

Bryant (J. H.) Poems by John Howard Bryant. *New York: D. Appleton and Company.* M.DCCC.LV. 12mo, pp. vi, 1 l., pp. 7–93. h. 8808

Includes "Indian Summer," "The New England Pilgrim's Funeral," etc.

Bryant (J.) Account of an Insurrection of the Negro Slaves in the Colony of Demerara, August 1823. By Joshua Bryant. *Georgetown (Dem.:) Printed by A. Stevenson.* 1824. 12mo, pp. vii, 125. 2 folded Plates. c. 8809

Bryant (S.) An Oration delivered at Mount Aaron, in West Dedham, July 4, 1839. ... By Samuel Bryant ... . Second Edition. *Dedham: H. Mann's Press.* 1839. 8vo, pp. 12.

Bryant's Songs from Dixie's Land. *New York: R. M. De Witt.* 1865. 18mo. 8811

Bryant (W. C.) An Address to the People of the United States in behalf of the American Copyright Club, adopted at New York, Oct. 18, 1843. *New York.* 1843. 8vo, pp. 20. 8812

Bryant. The American Landscape, No. 1. Engraved from Original and Accurate Drawings. With Historical and Topographical Illustrations. [By W. C. Bryant.] *New York.* 1830. 4to. 8813

Bryant. A Discourse on the Life, Character and Genius of Washington Irving. Delivered before the New York Historical Society, at the Academy of Music in New York, on the 3d of April, 1860. By William Cullen Bryant. *New York.* 1860. 8vo, pp. 46. 8814

Bryant. The Embargo; or, Sketches of the Times. A Satire. The Second Edition, corrected and enlarged. Together with The Spanish Revolution, and other Poems. By William Cullen Bryant. *Boston: Printed for the Author by E. G. House.* 1809. 12mo, pp. 35, (1). c. 8815

This is the first published volume of the eminent poet's verses, and appeared when he was but fourteen years of age. "Thanatopsis" appeared in the "North American Review" in 1816, and was first issued in book form in the edition of his poems published in 1821. *See* No. 8821.

Bryant. A Forest Hymn, by William Cullen Bryant. With Illustrations by John A. Hows. *New York: W. A. Townsend & Co.* [n. d.] 4to, 32 leaves. 8816

Bryant. The Fountain and other Poems. By William Cullen Bryant. *New York & London: Wiley & Putnam.* 1842. 12mo, pp. 100. ba. 8817

Bryant. A Funeral Oration, occasioned by the Death of Thomas Cole, delivered before the National Academy of Design, New-York, May 4, 1848. By William Cullen Bryant. ... *New-York: D. Appleton & Company.* M DCCC XLVIII. 8vo, pp. 42. h. 8818

Bryant. Letters of a Traveller; or, Notes of Things seen in Europe and America. By William C. Bryant. *New York: G. P. Putnam.* 1850. 12mo, pp. 442. c. + Third Edition. *New York.* 1851. 8vo. c. 8819

Also, on large paper, with illustrations on steel. Republished with the following title: "The Picturesque Souvenir. Letters of a Traveller; or, Notes of Things seen in Europe and America. By William Cullen Bryant. With Thirteen Illustrations on Steel. *New York: George P. Putnam.* 1851." 12mo, Title, pp. 442. ba.

Bryant. Letters of a Traveller. Second Series. [Letters from Spain and other countries.] *New-York: D. Appleton & Co.* 1859. 12mo, pp. 277. c. 8820

Bryant. Poems by William Cullen Bryant. *Cambridge: Hilliard and Metcalf.* 1821. 8vo, pp. 44. c., ba. + *New York.* 1832. 12mo. p. + With Illustrations by E. Leutze, engraved by American Artists. *Philadelphia: Carey and Hart.*

1847. 8vo, engraved Title, pp. 378. Plates. + Second Edition. *Philadelphia: Carey and Hart.* 1847. 8vo, pp. 378. 20 Plates. + Sixth Edition. *Philadelphia: A. Hart.* 1850. c.

BRYANT. Poems by William Cullen Bryant. Collected and arranged by the Author. Illustrated with Seventeen Engravings. *New York: Appleton & Co.* [n. d.] Sm. 4to, 7 l., pp. 340. c.

This edition was printed in London by R. Clay, for Griffin & Co. The Appletons purchased a number of copies, and substituted their names as the publishers. Mr. Bryant's poems have been reprinted in many forms in England.

BRYANT. Poems, collected and arranged by the author. Illustrated with seventy-one Engravings, by the brothers Dalziel, from Drawings by eminent artists. *London: Sampson, Low, Son & Co.* 1858. Sm. 4to, pp. xv, 344. Portrait, and 71 Woodcuts. c. 8823

BRYANT. Poems of William Cullen Bryant. Collected and arranged by the Author. ... *New York: D. Appleton and Company.* 1865. 2 vols., 12mo, pp. x, (1), 296; vi, (1), 286. BA.

BRYANT. Thirty Poems William Cullen Bryant. *New York: D. Appleton and Co.* M.DCCC.LXIV. 12mo, pp. 222. c.

BRYANT. Voices of Nature. By William Cullen Bryant. With Illustrations. *New York: D. Appleton & Co.* 1865. 12mo, pp. 91. c. 8826

Consists of selections from the rural poems of the author.

BRYANT (W. M.) A Sermon delivered on Thanksgiving Day, [Dec. 5, 1822,] at Mattapoisett, Rochester. By William M. Bryant. *New Bedford: Printed by Benj. Lindsey.* 1823. 8vo.

BRYDGES (George). Letters from Sir George Brydges, now Lord Rodney, to His Majesty's Ministers ... relative to the Capture of St. Eustatius and its Dependencies and shewing the State of the War in the West Indies at that period, together with a continuation of his Lordship's Correspondence with the Governors and Admirals in the West Indies and America during the year 1781, and until the time of his leaving the command and sailing for England. *London: J. Debrett.* 1789. 4to, pp. 180. 8828

"In one of his letters, Lord Rodney states, that if it had not been for the English merchants settled in St. Eustatius, 'who supplied the American rebels with every necessary and implements of war, the rebellion must have been long since at an end.'" — M. R., II. 472.

BRYDGES (*Sir* Samuel Egerton). Restituta; or, Titles, Extracts, and Characters of Old Books in English Literature,

revived. *London: Longman, Hurst, Rees, Orme, and Brown.* 1814–16. 4 vols., 8vo. BA., S. 8829

Vol. II., pp. 202–225, include a reprint from the excessively scarce original of "A True Report of the Laste Voyage into the West and Northwest Regions, &c., 1577, worthily atchieued by Capteine Frobisher," etc. The "Imaginative Biography," by the same author, contains a notice of Sir Walter Raleigh.

BRYDONE (J. M.) Narrative of a Voyage, with a Party of Emigrants, sent out from Sussex, in 1834, by the Petworth Emigration Committee, to Montreal, thence up the River Ottawa and through the Rideau Canal, to Toronto, Upper Canada, and afterwards to Hamilton. ... By James Marr Brydone, Surgeon R. N. *Petworth, (Eng.)* 1834. 8vo, pp. 66. Map. c.

BUACHE DE LA NEUVILLE (Jean Nicolas). Mémoire sur les pays de l'Asie et de l'Amérique, situés au nord de la Mer du Sud, accompagné d'une carte de comparaison des plans de MM. Engel et de Vaugondy, avec le plan des cartes modernes. Par J. N. Bauche, géorg. ord. du Roi. *Paris.* 1775. 4to, pp. 22. Map. 8831

Also, in the "Mémoires de l'Académie des sciences," "Considérations sur les limites méridionales de la Guyane française" (1797), "Observations sur quelques iles situées entre le Japon et la Californie," Map (1798), "Recherches sur l'île Antillia et sur l'époque de la découverte de l'Amérique" (1806).

BUACHE (P.) Considerations géographiques et physiques sur les nouvelles découvertes au Nord de la grande Mer, appellée vulgairement la Mer du Sud; avec des cartes, qui y sont relatives ... . Par M. Philippe Buache. *Paris,* 1753. 3 pts., 4to.

Reprinted from the "Mém. de l'Acad. des Sciences." *See* Faribault, No. 191.

BUACHE. Nouvelles observations concernant les dernières connoissances venuës de Russie, qui confirment les vuës, indiquées dans les Considerations géographiques, &c. sur le voisinage de l'Amerique et de l'Asie, séparées uniquement par un long détroit, et sur la grande Presqu' Ile supposée; présentée à l'academie des sciences. Par Philippe Buache. *Paris.* 1753. 12mo.

Also, in the "Mém. de l'Acad. des Sciences," "Mémoire sur les différentes idées qu'on a eues de la traversée de la Mer Glaciale arctique ..." (1759), "Considérations géographiques et physiques sur les terres australes ou antarctiques" (1761).

BUACHE. Objets à considerer sur un mémoire qu'il avoit appris qu'on se proposoit de présenter à l'académie contre la relation de l'amiral de Fonte. Par M. Philippe Buache. *Paris.* 1753. 12mo. 8834

The Bubble, a Poem. *London.* 1721. 8vo. 8835

On the South Sea Scheme.

The Bubbles of Canada. *See* [Haliburton (T. C.)]

BUCARELI Y URSUA. Allocutio Exc. D. D. Antonii M. Bucareli, et Ursua, Pro-Regis, Gubernatoris, Ducisque Generalis totius Novæ Hispaniæ, ad Patres Concilij IV. Provincialis Mexicani facta prima die sui ingresus 10 Oct. anni 1777. [*Mexico.* 1777.] Folio, 4 leaves. 8836

The Buccaneer. A Tale. *London.* 1832. 3 vols., 12mo.

The Buccaneers; a Romance of our own Country in its Ancient Days; illustrated with Divers Marvellous Histories, and Antique and Facetious Episodes; gathered from the most Authentic Chronicles of the Settlement of the Nieuw Nederlandts ... [by] Terentius Phlogobombos. [Motto.] In Five Books. *Boston: Munroe & Francis. New York: Charles S. Francis.* 1827. 2 vols., 12mo, pp. 263; 381, (2). H. 8838

Buccaneers of America. *See* Esquemeling (John) *and* Oexmelin (A. O.)

BUCH (Christian Leopold von). Pétrifications recueillies en Amérique par Mr. Alexandre de Humboldt et par Mr. Charles Degenhardt. *Berlin: imprimerie de l'académie des sciences.* 1839. Folio, 2 l., pp. 32. 2 Plates. c. 8839

BUCHAN (David Stewart Erskine, *Earl of*). *See* Erskine (D. S.)

BUCHANAN (A. C.) Emigration practically considered; with detailed Directions to Emigrants proceeding to North America, particularly to the Canadas. By A. C. Buchanan. *London.* 1828. 12mo, pp. 148. c. 8840

Also: Annual Report of A. C. Buchanan, Esq., on the Emigration to Canada, during the Season of 1854. *Quebec.* 1855. 8vo, pp. 35.

BUCHANAN (A.) An Oration, composed and delivered at the request of the Republican Society of Baltimore on the Fourth of July, One thousand seventeen hundred and ninety four. By Archibald Buchanan. *Baltimore: Clayland, Dobbin & Co.* M,DCC,XLV. 8vo, Title, pp. 40. 8841

BUCHANAN (C.) Colonial Ecclesiastical Establishments: being a view of the state of the Colonies of Great Britain, ... Prefaced by some Considerations on the National Duty ... By Rev. Claudius Buchanan, D.D. Second Edition. *London: T. Cadell.* 1813. 8vo. 8842

BUCHANAN (E. Y.) Historical Sketch of the Parish of Trinity Church, Oxford, Philadelphia. Read in the Church, on Sunday, August 2d, 1857. By the Rev. Edward Y. Buchanan, Rector. Printed by Request. Published for Presentation. *Philadelphia: Lindsay & Blakiston.* 1857. 8vo, pp. 56.

[BUCHANAN (Franklin).] In relation to the Claims of the Officers of the Late Texas Navy. *New York.* [n. d.] 8vo, pp. 44. H. 8844

BUCHANAN (G.) An Oration upon the Moral and Political Evil of Slavery. Delivered at a Public Meeting of the Maryland Society for promoting the abolition of Slavery. ... Baltimore, July 4, 1791. By George Buchanan, M.D. ... *Baltimore: Edwards.* 1793. 8vo, pp. 20. P. 8845

Also: Treatise on the Typhus Fever, for the benefit of establishing a Lying-in Hospital at Baltimore. *Baltimore.* 1789. 8vo.

BUCHANAN (Harrison Gray). Asmodeus; or, Legends of New-York. Being a complete exposé of the Upper Ten Thousand. *New York: Munson & Co.* 1848. 8vo, pp. 96. c. 8846

BUCHANAN (I.) Britain the Country, *verses* Britain the Empire. Our Monetary Distresses — their legislative Cause and Cure. By Isaac Buchanan. *Hamilton, C. W.* 1860. 8vo, pp. clxiv, 288. 884-

BUCHANAN. The British American Federation a Necessity; its Industrial Policy also a Necessity. By ... Isaac Buchanan ... . *Hamilton: printed at the "Spectator" Steam Press.* 1865. 8vo, pp. 48. H. 8848

BUCHANAN. A Government Specie-paying Bank of Issue and other Subversive Legislation, proposed by the Finance Minister of Canada. *Hamilton.* 1866. 8vo, pp. 24. 8849

BUCHANAN. Memorial to the Commercial Convention at Detroit. *Hamilton.* 1865. 8vo. 8850

"Printed, but not distributed or published." — H. J. MORGAN.

BUCHANAN. Militia Brochure; our Battalion Organization should not be as Volunteers but as a Militia Force. *Hamilton, C. W.* 1863. 8vo, pp. 15. 8851

BUCHANAN. The Relations of the Industry of Canada, with the Mother Country and the United States, being a Speech by Isaac Buchanan, Esq., M.D., as Delivered at the late Demon-

stration to the Parliamentary Opposition at Toronto — together with a Series of Articles in Defence of the National Sentiments contained therein. ... To which is added a Speech Delivered by him at the Dinner given to the Pioneers of Upper Canada, at London, Canada West, 10th December, 1863. ... . With Copious Notes and Annotations ... and an Appendix containing Valuable Documents. Edited by Henry J. Morgan. ... *Montreal: John Lovell.* 1864. 8vo, pp. 551. H. 8852

BUCHANAN. The True Policy in Canada of a Patriotic Ministry. By Isaac Buchanan. *Quebec.* 1860. Folio, pp. 4.

Also: "The Crisis of Sir Robert Peel's Mission. ... *Hamilton.* 1850." 8vo, pp. 16. *See* Morgan's "Bibl. Canad," pp. 54–56.

BUCHANAN (James). Letter addressed to Sir F. B. Head, Lt. Governor of Upper Canada on the Construction of Railroads in that Province. *Toronto.* [n. d.] 8vo. 8854

BUCHANAN Letter on Free Trade and Navigation of the St. Lawrence, addressed to the Earl of Elgin and Kincardine. By James Buchanan. *Toronto.* 1846. 8vo, pp. 31. 8855

BUCHANAN. Letter to the Rt. Hon. Sir Charles Bagot, Governor General of British North America. With a View to preserve from Contamination and Crime Destitute and Neglected Female Children, containing Plan and Estimate. By James Buchanan, Esq. ... *New York.* 1842. 8vo, pp. 14. c. 8856

BUCHANAN. Observations on the Penitentiary System in the United States ... . By James Buchanan, Esq. ... . *London: Black, Young, and Young.* MDCCCXXIX. 8vo, pp. 32. 8857

BUCHANAN. Plan for the Melioration and Civilization of the British North American Indians: Addressed to the Right Honourable the Earl of Dalhousie, G.C.B. &c. &c. &c. By James Buchanan, Esq. His Majesty's Consul for the State of New-York, Author of "Sketches," &c. *New York: W. E. Dean.* 1824. 8vo, pp. 13. 8858

BUCHANAN. Reasons submitted in favor of allowing a Transit of Merchandize through Canada to Michigan without payment of Duties; with Observations as to the Importance of the River St. Lawrence, for extending the Trade of the Canadas and British Commerce generally. By James Buchanan. *Toronto.* 1836. 8vo. 8859

BUCHANAN. Sketches of the History, Manners, and Customs of the North American Indians, with a Plan for their

Melioration. By James Buchanan, Esq. His Majesty's Consul for the State of New York. *New York: William Borradaile.* 1824. 2 vols., 16mo, pp. xi, 13–182; 156. C., H. + *London: Black, Young, and Young.* MDCCCXXIV. 8vo, pp. xi, 371. Map.

Principally a compilation from Heckewelder and other works. — N. A. R., XIX. 464. "The author is himself absolutely without any qualifications whatever for the task he has undertaken. The literary composition of his volume is below criticism, and its only value consists in the copious extracts from an account of the Indian Nations by John Heckewelder. The compiler's other assistants are a Dr. Jarvis of New York, and a Mr. Duponceau of Philadelphia, etc." — *Quarterly Review,* XXXI. 80. Some copies of the New York edition are dated 1825.

BUCHANAN (James), *President.* Mr. Buchanan's Administration on the Eve of the Rebellion. *New York: D. Appleton and Company.* 1865. 8vo, pp. 296.. BA. 8861

BUCHANAN. Last letter of Mr. Buchanan to Mr. Pakenham, on the American Title to Oregon. *Baltimore: Constitution Office.* 1845. 8vo, pp. 16. 8862

Also: Mr. James Buchanan's Answer to the Misrepresentations of Mr. Davis's Speech; vindicating Himself and the Democratic Party, from the Unfounded Aspersion of designing to Destroy the Banks and reduce the Wages of Labor and the Value of Property. (... In the Senate, ... March 6, 1840.) *Worcester: E. W. Bartlett & Co.* [n. d.] 8vo, pp. 12. — Remarks ... in reply to Mr. Sprague, of Maine, ... on imports. ... *Washington.* 1828. 8vo, pp. 24. — Remarks ... 4th February, 1828, on Mr. Chilton's Resolutions to Retrench the Expenditures. ... *Washington.* 1828. 8vo, pp. 23. — Remarks ... in reply to Mr. Davis, of Massachusetts, against the Independent Treasury Bill, Senate U. S. March 3. 1840. *Washington.* 1840. 8vo, pp. 8 — Speech ... respecting the Fortifications and Defence of the Country, February 1, & 2, 1836. *Washington.* 1836. 8vo, pp. 22. H. — Speech ... on the ... resolution of the twenty-eight of March 1834. Senate Jan. 16. 1837. *Washington.* 1837. 8vo, pp. 13. — Speech ... on the Bill imposing Additional Duties ... on Public Officers. ... September 29, 1837. *Washington.* 1837. 8vo, pp. 22. H. — Speech ... January 22, 1840, On the Independent Treasury Bill, ... [*Washington.* 1840.] 8vo, pp. 16. H. — Speech ... Feb. 14, 1839, on the Bill to prevent the interference of certain Federal Officers with Elections. [n. p. n. d.] 8vo pp. 15. — Speech ... in Defence of the Administration of Mr. Van Buren against the Charge of Extravagance ... January 22, 1841. *Washington.* 1840 [*sic*]. 8vo, pp. 14. H.—Speech ... against the Bill to incorporate the subscribers to the fiscal Bank of the United States. Senate 7 July, 1841. 8vo, pp. 15. — Speech ... in support of the veto power, and in reply to Mr. Clay of Kentucky. U. S. Senate Feb. 2. 1842. 8vo, pp. 16. — Speech ... on the Bill to provide further Remedial Justice in the Courts of the United States: delivered in the Senate of the United States ... May 9, 1842. *Washington.* 1842. 8vo, pp. 16. H. — Speech ... in favor of the Treaty for the Annexation of Texas to the United States, ... June 8, 1844. [n. p. n. d.] 8vo, pp. 15. — Speech ... on the Oregon Question. ... March 12, 1844. [n. p. n. d.] 8vo, pp. 15. — Speech ... July 9, 1860. *Washington City.* 1860. 8vo, pp. 8.

BUCHANAN. Memorial. Impeachment of James Buchanan, President of the United States. [*New York.* 1860.] 16mo, pp. 24. H. 8863

BUCHANAN. James Buchanan, his Doctrines and Policy as exhibited by Himself and Friends. [*New York.* 1856.] 8vo, pp. 16. 8864

The following are a portion of the tracts issued during the Presidential Campaign of 1856: "Justice to Buck." Papers containing several Reasons why James Buchanan should receive the Distinguished Consideration of the People. By One who knows him well. Paper the First. *Philadelphia: Alex. C. Bryson.* [1856.] 12mo, pp. 24. H. — Life and Public Services of Hon. James Buchanan. *New York.* 1856. 12mo. — The Life of the Hon. James Buchanan, as written by himself, and set to Music by an Old Democrat ... . *Lancaster, near Wheatland.* 1856. 18mo, pp. 12. H. — Memoir of James Buchanan, ... *Philadelphia.* 1856. 8vo, pp. 16. — ... Plain Facts and Considerations: ... in Favor of James Buchanan ... and John C. Breckenridge ... . By an American Citizen. ... *Boston: Brown, Bazin, and Company.* 1856. 8vo, pp. 32. BA. — Short Answers to Reckless Fabrications, against the Democratic Candidate for President, James Buchanan. *Philadelphia: William Rice, Printer.* 1856. 8vo pp. 32.

BUCHANAN, KING, *and* BROWN. Remarks of Messrs. Buchanan, King, and Brown, in reply to Messrs Davis, Preston, and Clancy, on the Subject of the Currency. Senate of the U. S., March 6, 1840. *Washington.* 1840. 8vo, pp. 13. 8865

BUCHANAN (J.) State of the Account of John Buchanan, Esquire, Collector of Excise, Cumberland County, from the 20th of January to the 25th of April, 1783. ... *Philadelphia: Printed by Robert Aitken.* M,DCC,LXXXIV. 8vo, pp. 7. P. 8866

BUCHANAN. State of the Accounts of John Buchanan, Esq., Collector of Excise, Cumberland County. From 25th April, 1783, to 21st February, 1785. *Philadelphia: Printed by John Steele.* MDCCLXXXV. 8vo, pp. 3. P. 8867

BUCHANAN (J. R.) Free Collegiate Education. A ... Lecture delivered by Prof. J. R. Buchanan ... Jan. 26, 1852 ... [at] Cincinnati. ... with a Statement of the Measures adopted by the Trustees and Faculty of the E. M. [Eclectic Medical] Institute for the Establishment of a Free Medical College, to be connected with a Public Hospital, and which may serve as the Nucleus of a Free National University. *Cincinnati: W. M. Naudain, Printer.* 1852. 8vo, pp. 16. BA., H. 8868

BUCHANAN (R.) The Life and Adventures of John James Audubon, the Naturalist. Edited from materials supplied by his Widow, by Robert Buchanan. ... *London: Sampson Low, Son, & Marston.* 1868. 8vo, pp. vii [viii], 366. 2 Portraits.

B[UCHANAN] (W. B.) Baltimore: or Long, Long Time Ago. By W. B. B. [Motto.] 1853. *Baltimore: Murphy & Co., Printers.* [1853.] 8vo, pp. 24. H. 8870

BÜCHELE (*Dr.* C.) Land und Volk der Vereinigten Staaten von Nord-Amerika. ... Vorzuglich für Auswanderer. Nach eigenen Beobachtungen und den neuesten Quellen geschildert. *Stuttgart: Halberger.* 1855. 8vo, pp. viii, 622. c. 8871

BUCHER (*Rev.* T. P.) Union National Fast Day Sermon, delivered at Gettysburg, Penn., Friday, Jannary 4, 1861. *Gettysburg: H. C. Neinstadt.* 1861. 8vo, pp. 26. 8872

BÜCHLER (Johann Ulrich). Land- und Seereisen nach Nordamerika und Westindien, über Amsterdam nach Baltimore, Pittsburg, Gallipoli, Sensanetta, Neu-Veveg, die Gegend am Ohio und Missisippi ... . Zweite Auflage. *Chur: Grubenmann.* [183–?] 8vo. 8873

BUCHNER (J. H.) History of the Mission of the United Brethren's Church to the Negroes in the Island of Jamaica, from the Year 1754 to 1854. By J. H. Buchner. *London: Longman.* 1854. 12mo, pp. 175. 8874

BUCHNER (K.) ... Dr. Karl Follen. Mit Benutzung von noch ungedruckten Briefen desselben aus Amerika in die Heimath. Ier-IIer Artikel. [*Altona.* 1841.] 8vo, pp. 59–78, 113–146. H. 8875

BUCHON (Jean Alexandre). Histoire universelle des religions ... . *Paris.* 1844–45. 8vo. 8876

Vol. III. comprises "Religions de l'Océanie et de l'Amérique, par Saint-Germain Le Duc."

BUC'HOZ (Pierre Joseph). Dissertation sur le noisetier de St.-Domingue, un des plus grands arbres de l'Amérique. *Paris: l'auteur.* 1786. Folio. 8877

BUC'HOZ. Dissertation sur le quinquina ... et spécialement sur la nouvelle espèce que'on trouve dans les îles Antilles. *Paris: l'auteur.* 1787. Folio. Colored Plates. 8878

[BUC'HOZ.] Dissertation sur le rocoulier, sur sa culture en Europe et en Amérique ... . *Paris: l'auteur.* 1788. Folio. Colored Plates. 8879

BUCK (A.) Documents accompanying a Bill for the Relief of Anthony Buck. April 3d, 1810. ... . *Washington.* 1810. 8vo, pp. 4. H. 8880

Also: Report of the Committee of Commerce and Manufactures, on The Petition of Anthony Buck. March 23, 1810. ... . *Washington.* 1810. 8vo, pp. 8. H.

Buck (E.) The Drift of the War. By Edward Buck. *Boston: A. Williams & Co.* 1861. 8vo, pp. 20. H. 8881

First published in the Boston "Transcript," 1861.

Buck. Massachusetts Ecclesiastical Law. By Edward Buck, of the Suffolk Bar. *Boston: Gould and Lincoln. New York: Sheldon and Company.* 1866. 8vo, pp. viii, 13–310. H. 8882

Contains many interesting and important facts respecting the past and present state of New England.

Buck (E.) Answers to Rev. Albert Barnes' Questions on Romans 5: 12–21. By Ephraim Buck, M.D. With a Short Sketch [pp. 28–35] of his Character and Last Sickness. *Boston: Franklin Wood.* 1859. 12mo, pp. 35. H. 8883

Buck (W. J.) History of Bucks County from its earliest Settlement to the close of the Eighteenth Century. By William J. Buck. [n. p. n. d.?] 8vo, pp. 118, Appendix, pp. 24. 8884

Buck. History of Montgomery County within the Schuylkill Valley: containing Sketches of all the Townships, Boroughs and Villages in said limits, from the earliest period to the present time; with an account of the Indians, the Swedes, and other early Settlers, and the local events of the Revolution; besides notices of the Progress in Population, Improvements, and Manufactures; Prepared chiefly from Original Materials: By William J. Buck. *Norristown: Printed by E. L. Acker.* 1859. Imp. 8vo, pp. 124, Index and Errata, iv. C. 8885

The author announces a history of Moreland Township.

Buckalew (C. R.) Cumulative Voting. Speech of Charles R. Buckalew, of Pennsylvania, in the United States Senate, July 11, 1867. [*Washington.* 1867.] 8vo, pp. 8. H. 8886

Also: Reconstruction. Speech ... January 29, 1868. [*Washington.* 1868.] 8vo, pp. 16. — Representation in Congress. Speech ... February 21, 1866. [*Washington.* 1866.] 8vo, pp. 16. H. — Representative Reform — The Cumulative Vote. ... Philadelphia ... November 19, 1867; (with an Appendix.) [*Washington.* 1867.] 8vo, pp. 15. H.

[Bucke (Charles).] On the Beauties, Harmonies and Sublimities of Nature, with occasional remarks on the Laws, Customs, Manners and Opinions of Various Nations. Second edition. *London: G. & W. B. Whittaker.* 1823. 4 vols., 8vo, pp. xii, 387; 407; 388; 342. + *London.* 1837. 3 vols., 8vo. + Selected and revised by the Rev. W. P. Page. *New York.* 1841. 12mo. 8887

Several of the articles relate to America.

Buckholtz (L. v.) Infantry Camp Duty, Field Fortifications, and Coast Defence. *Richmond: J. W. Randolph.* 1861. 16mo. 8888

Buckholtz. Tactics for Officers of Infantry, Cavalry and Artillery. Arranged and Compiled by L. v. Buckholtz. *Richmond, Va.: J. W. Randolph.* 1861. 12mo. 8889

Buckingham (E.) An Oration delivered at Trenton Falls, July 4, 1842. ... By Edgar Buckingham. *Utica.* 1842. 8vo.

Buckingham (Henry A.) Harry Burnham, the young Continental; or, Memoirs of an American Officer during the Revolution. *New York: Burgess & Garrett.* 1852. 8vo, pp. 256.

Buckingham (J. S.) America, Historical, Statistic, and Descriptive. By J. S. Buckingham, Esq. *London: Fisher, Son & Co.* [1841.] 3 vols., 8vo, pp. vi, 5 l., pp. 504; 7 l., pp. 563; 6 l., pp. 596, Index, 10 l. Portrait and Woodcuts. C., H. + *New York: Harper & Brothers.* 1841. 2 vols., 8vo, pp. 515; xiv, 9–516. Portrait and Woodcuts. C. 8892

Buckingham. Appeal to the British Nation, on the Greatest Reform yet remaining to be accomplished. By James S. Buckingham. Read and adopted at the World's Convention, held in London, August, 1846. *London: James Ridgway.* 1846. 8vo, pp. 64. H. 8893

This has an appendix, entitled, "... Mr. Buckingham's Travels in the Eastern and Western World." [From the "Colonial Magazine" for April, 1841.] pp. 1–16.

Buckingham. Autobiography of James Silk Buckingham, including his Voyages, Travels, Adventures, Speculations, Successes, and Failures, faithfully and frankly narrated; interspersed with Characteristic Sketches of Public Men with whom he has had intercourse during a period of more than fifty years. *London: Longman.* 1855. Vols. I. and II., post 8vo. C. 8894

Buckingham. Canada, Nova Scotia, New Brunswick, and the other British Provinces in North America, with a Plan of National Colonization. By James S. Buckingham. *London: Fisher, Son, & Co.* [1843.] 8vo, 8 l., pp. 540. 7 Plates, and Map. C., H. 8895

Buckingham. The Eastern and Western States of America. By J. S. Buckingham, Esq. ... . *London: Fisher, Son, & Co.* 3 vols., 8vo, 8 l., pp. 573; 4 l., pp. 536; 5 l., pp. 495. Plates.

Buckingham. History and Progress of the Temperance Reformation in Great Britain and other Countries of the Globe; with Statistical and Documentary Evidence of its Beneficial Results, and a Plea for a Maine Law, to enforce the Suppression of all Traffic in Intoxicating Drinks. By James Silk Buckingham. *London: Partridge, Oakey, & Co.* 1854. 8vo, pp. 160. Table. C., H. 8897

Buckingham. Mr. Buckingham's Address to the People of the United States. New-York, Oct. 25, 1837. [*New-York: D. Fanshaw, Printer.* 1837.] 8vo, pp. 4. BA. + [n. p. n. d.] 8vo, pp. 8. H. 8898

Buckingham. The Slave States of America. By J. S. Buckingham, Esq. *London* [&] *Paris: Fisher, Son, & Co.* [1842.] 2 vols., 8vo, Title, 9 l., pp. 487 [misprint for 587]; 6 l., pp. 588. 8 Steel Engravings. BA. 8899

There are two issues of this work, the second having the collation, 2 l., pp. xvi, 587; 6 l., pp. 600. 8 Plates. H. Here pp. 588–600 contain an index. Mr. Rich commences a long note on this series by characterizing them as "Mr. Buckingham's great work on America." In the sense of being *large*, they may merit the appellation. They are a collection of sketches and extracts, hastily, and often ungrammatically expressed, tolerably impartial, and really containing a fund of statistical and general information on the rise, progress, manners, etc., of the people. The plates are from Bartlett's "American Scenery." *See* Rich, II. 360.

Buckingham (J. Albert). Christian Ambition. A Sermon occasioned by the Death of Rev. Nathaniel Gage. ... Ashby, Mass., ... May 12th, 1861. By John A. Buckingham. *Cambridge: Welch, Bigelow, and Company, Printers.* 1861. 8vo, pp. 16. H. 8900

Buckingham (J. H.) An Address delivered before the Massachusetts Charitable Mechanic Association, on the Occasion of their Fifteenth Triennial Festival, October 1, 1851. By Joseph H. Buckingham ... . *Boston: Press of T. R. Marvin.* 1851. 8vo, pp. 23. H. 8901

Buckingham (J. Tinker). An Address delivered before the Massachusetts Charitable Mechanic Association, at the Public Celebration of their Third Triennial Festival. By Joseph T. Buckingham, Dec. 21, 1815. *Boston.* 1816. 8vo, pp. 23. H.

Also: Address ... at the ... Eighth Triennial Festival, October 7, 1830. By Joseph T. Buckingham. *Boston.* 1830. 8vo, pp. 30, (1).

Buckingham. An Address to Native Americans, by J. T. Buckingham, Esq. together with the Declaration and Principles

of the Native Americans of Boston. Second Edition. *Boston: H. B. Skinner.* 1844. 12mo, pp. 24. H. 8903

Buckingham. Annals of the Massachusetts Charitable Mechanic Association. Compiled by Joseph T. Buckingham. *Boston: Crocker & Brewster.* 1853. 8vo, pp. viii, 432. Portraits. + Supplement. Annals ... 1852 to 1860. [*Boston.* n. d.] 8vo, Title, pp. 427–623. Plate. H. 8904

Buckingham. Miscellanies selected from the Public Journals. *Boston: J. T. Buckingham.* 1822–24. 2 vols., 12mo, pp. xii, 13–268; xi, 13–256. H. 8905

Buckingham. Personal Memoirs and Recollections of Editorial Life. In Two Volumes. By Joseph T. Buckingham. *Boston: Ticknor, Reed and Fields.* M DCCC LII. 2 vols., Title, 1 l., pp. 256; 255. Portrait. BA., C., H. 8906

[Buckingham. Report on the Mexican War.] 8vo, pp. 7. (Mass. Senate Document, Jan., 1848, No. 16.) H. 8907

[Buckingham. Report on the establishment of a State Agricultural School, etc.] 8vo, pp. 9. (Mass. Senate Document, March, 1848, No. 85.) H. 8908

Buckingham. Specimens of Newspaper Literature: with Personal Memoirs, Anecdotes, and Reminiscences. By Joseph T. Buckingham. *Boston: Little & Brown.* 1850. 2 vols., 12mo, 2 l., pp. xii, 348; Title, 1 l., pp. 356. 2 Portraits. H.

Contains many interesting literary anecdotes connected with the early history of this country.

Buckingham. Speeches of Hon. Joseph T. Buckingham, Charles M. Ellis, Esq., and Hon. Anson Burlingame, at the Free Democratic Meeting in Faneuil Hall, October 13, 1852. ... . *Boston: published at the Commonwealth Office.* 1852. 8vo, pp. 16. H. 8910

Buckingham. Trial: Commonwealth *vs.* J. T. Buckingham, on an Indictment for a Libel, ... December Term, 1822. *Boston.* [1822.] 8vo, pp. 60. 8911

The trial was for a libel on the Rev. John N. Maffit. *See* "A Correct Statement and Review of the Trial. *Boston: William S. Spear.* 1822." 8vo, pp. 16. BA.

Buckingham (*Mrs.*) A Winter in Washington. *New York.* 1824. 2 vols., 12mo. 8912

Title from A. G. Greene's catalogue — very doubtful.

Buckingham (Samuel G.) A Memorial of the Pilgrim Fathers. By S. G. Buckingham, Pastor of the South Church, Springfield, Mass. *Springfield: Samuel Bowles & Co., Printers.* 1867. 8vo, pp. 52. H. 8913

Buckingham (*Governor* William A.) *See* Connecticut.

Buckingham (*Rev.* Thomas). *See* Knight (*Madame* Sarah Kemble).

Buckingham and Chandos (*Duke of*). *See* Grenville (R. T. N. B. C.)

Buckington (N.) Serious Considerations on the Political Conduct of Lord North, since his Entry into the Ministry. ... By Nathaniel Buckington, Esq. ... *London: J. Stockdale.* 1783. 8vo. 8914

See M. R., LXIX. 512.

Buckland (C.) Memorial of Cyrus Buckland [to Congress praying for remuneration for his improvements in the manufacture of side arms. *Washington.* 1854.] 8vo, pp. 14, (1). H.

Buckle (J.) Letter to Viscount Melville on the Ordinance of the Earl of Durham, Governor of Canada. By John Buckle. *London.* 1832. 8vo, pp. 32. 8916

Buckler (Thomas H.) A History of Epidemic Cholera, as it appeared at the Baltimore City and County Alms-House, in the Summer of 1849, with some Remarks on the Medical Topography and Diseases of this Region. By Th. H. Buckler ... . *Baltimore: printed by James Lucas.* 1851. 8vo, pp. 46. H. 8917

Buckley (S. B.) A Preliminary Report of the Texas Geological Survey; together with Agricultural Observations, and an Outline of the Mineral Deposits of the State. By S. B. Buckley. *Austin: J. Walker.* 1866. 8vo, pp. 86. C. 8918

Bucklin (S. F.) Semi-Centennial Discourse, Marlborough, Mass. By Sylvester F. Bucklin. *Boston.* 1859. 8vo, pp. 52.

Title from the N. E. G. R., XXI. 328.

Buckminster (Edward). Masonic Address at laying the Corner Stone of St. John's Episcopal Church at Portsmouth, N. H. June 24, 1807. *Portsmouth.* [1807.] 8vo. W. 8920

Buckminster (J.) A Discourse Delivered in the First Church of Christ at Portsmouth on Thursday December 11.

1783, Being the Day recommended by the honourable Congress for a General Thanksgiving ... after the Ratification of a Treaty of Peace ... By Joseph Buckminster, Junr., A.M. ... *New Hampshire, Portsmouth: Printed by Robert Gerrish.* M,DCCLXXXIV. 8vo, pp. 33. N., W. 8921

Buckminster. A Discourse delivered at Portsmouth, New-Hampshire, November 1st, 1789. On the Occasion of the President [George Washington] of the United States honoring that Capital with a Visit. By Joseph Buckminster, A.M. ... *Portsmouth: John Melcher.* 1789. 8vo, pp. 21. BA. 8922

Buckminster (Joseph), *of Rutland.* ... Sermon at Ordination of Rev. Ebenezer Sparhawk, Narraganset No. 6 [Templeton], Nov. 18, 1761. *Boston.* 1762. 8vo, pp. 30. M. 8923

Buckminster (J.), *of Portsmouth.* A Discourse delivered in ... Portsmouth, November 15, 1798. A Day observed as an Anniversary Thanksgiving. By Joseph Buckminster, A.M. ... [Motto.] *Portsmouth, New Hampshire: printed by John Melcher.* 1798. 8vo, pp. 21. H. 8924

Buckminster. Discourse delivered in ... Portsmouth, December 14, 1800, the Anniversary of the Death of George Washington, Late President of the United States, and Commander in Chief of their Armies. By Joseph Buckminster, A.M. *Portsmouth, New Hampshire: Printed ... by Charles Peirce, Dec.* 1800. 8vo, pp. 21. N. 8925

Buckminster. A Discourse occasioned by the late Desolating Fire. Delivered in Portsmouth the Lord's Day succeeding that Event. By Joseph Buckminster, A.M. ... *William & Daniel Treadwell: Portsmouth, N. H. Jan.,* 1803. 8vo, pp. 39.

Buckminster. The Duty of Republican Citizens in the Choice of their Rulers. The Substance of Two Discourses, delivered in ... Portsmouth, February 28, 1796. By Joseph Buckminster, A.M. [Motto.] *Portsmouth, New-Hampshire: Printed by Charles Peirce,* ... 1796. 8vo, pp. 22. BA., N. 8927

Buckminster. A Sermon preached before ... the ... Council and ... House of Representatives of ... New Hampshire, June 7, 1787. By Joseph Buckminster, A.M. ... *Portsmouth: Robert Gerrish.* M,DCC,LXXXVIII. 8vo, pp. 30. BA., W. 8928

Buckminster. A Sermon, delivered in the First Church in Portsmouth, on the Lord's day after the melancholy tidings of The Death of George Washington, the Father, Guardian and Ornament of His country. By Joseph Buckminster, A.M. *Portsmouth: Printed by John Melcher.* 1800. 8vo, pp. 17. 8929

The two following sermons form part of the work: A Sermon, delivered in the First Church in Portsmouth, January 5th, 1800. The house being dressed in mourning in token of respect to the memory of General Washington. 8vo, pp. 19–29. — A Second Sermon, delivered Lord's day, January 5, 1800. 8vo, pp. 31–45.

Buckminster. Religion and Righteousness the Basis of National Honor and Prosperity. A Sermon Preached to the North and South Parishes in Portsmouth, Fraternally united in Observance of the 22d February, 1800; The day appointed by Congress to pay tributary respect to the Memory of General Washington. By Joseph Buckminster, A.M. *Portsmouth, New Hampshire: Charles Peirce.* 1800. 8vo, pp. 28. 8930

Also: A Discourse at York, September 3, 1792, the day on which Joseph Abbott, Jr. received a Pardon, etc. 1792. 8vo. — A Discourse delivered before the Members of the Portsmouth Female Charity School, October 14, 1803. *Portsmouth: Printed by W. C. & W. Peirce.* 1803. 8vo, pp. 12. H. — A Discourse delivered in the North Church of Christ, in Portsmouth. [*Portsmouth.* 1803.] 8vo, pp. 20. — A Discourse delivered at the Ordination of the Rev. J. S. Buckminster to the Pastoral Charge of the Church in Brattle Street, ... Boston. *Boston: printed for Young & Minns,* 1805. 8vo, pp. 37. BA. — A Discourse, ... at the Interment of the Rev. Samuel Haven, D.D., and of his Wife Mrs. Margaret Haven, who survived her Husband about thirty-six hours. Also a Monody ... by Rev. James A. Neal. *Portsmouth: Printed by W. & D. Treadwell.* [1808.] 8vo, pp. 40. H. — Sermon delivered at the Interment of Mrs. Susannah Porter, consort of Rev. Mr. Porter, at Rye, N. H. Feb. 7, 1794. *Portsmouth.* 1794. 8vo, pp. 27. N. — A Sermon ... at Exeter, October 15. 1798. At the Interment of Mrs. Sarah Rowland, Consort of the Rev. William F. Rowland, and Eldest Daughter of Col. Eliphalet Ladd. ... *Portsmouth, New Hampshire: Printed by John Welcher.* 1798. 8vo, pp. 16. W. — Sermon before the Ecclesiastical Convention of New Hampshire, Concord, June 5, 1799. *Concord.* 1799. 8vo. N. — Sermon at the Installation of the Rev. James Miltimore, ... in Newbury ... *Newburyport: Printed by W. & J. Gilman ... for William Sawyer & Co. May,* 1808. 8vo, pp. 35. — Sermon at the Installation of James Thurston; ... *Portsmouth.* 1809. — Sermon at the Interment of the Rev. Moses Hemminway, D.D., at Wells, Me. *Kennebunk.* 1811. 8vo, pp. 24. BA. — The Substance of Three Discourses delivered in Park Street Church, Boston. By Joseph Buckminster, D.D. ... August 11, 1811. *Boston: Samuel J. Armstrong.* 8vo, pp. 38. BA.

Buckminster. Observations on Mr. Buckminster's Sermon Delivered February 28, 1796, on the duty of Repulican Citizens in the choice of their Rulers. *Portsmouth: Charles Pierce.* 1796. 8vo, pp. 23 or 24. W. 8931

Buckminster. Extract from a Discourse by the Rev. J. S. Buckminster, preached in the Church in Brattle Square, Boston,

October, 1811, the Sabbath after the Interment of Hon. James Bowdoin. *Albany: J. Munsell.* 1848. 8vo, pp. 8. H., S. 8932

Buckminster. A Sermon preached at ... Boston, Dec. 18th, 1808. The Lord's Day after the Public Funeral of His Excellency James Sullivan, Governour of Massachusetts. By Joseph S. Buckminster ... . *Boston: J. Belcher, Printer.* 1809. 8vo, pp. 41. Portrait. B. 8933

Buckminster. A Sermon, delivered at the Interment of the Reverend William Emerson, Pastor of the First Church of Christ in Boston, who died May 12, 1811 ... . By Joseph Stevens Buckminster ... . *Boston: printed by Joseph T. Buckingham.* 1811. 8vo, pp. 24. H. 8934

Buckminster. Sermons by the late Rev. J. S. Buckminster. With a Memoir of his Life and Character. *Boston: ... John Eliot.* 1814. 8vo, pp. lxii, Half-Title, 430. Portrait. + Second Edition. [*Ibid.*] 1815. + Third Edition. [*Ibid.*] 1821. 8vo. 8935

Buckminster. Sermons by the Late J. S. Buckminster, now first published from the Author's Manuscript. *Boston:* 1829. 8vo. + Works; with Memoirs of his Life. *Boston.* 1839. 2 vols., 12mo. 8936

[Buckminster (*Mrs.* L. N. H.)] The Hastings Memorial. A Genealogical Account of the Descendants of Thomas Hastings of Watertown, Mass. From 1634 to 1864. With an Appendix and Index. *Boston: Samuel G. Drake.* 1866. 8vo, Title, pp. 183. H. 8937

Bucknam (*Rev.* Nathan). Ability to, and Fidelity in, the Ministry derived from Christ. A Sermon preach'd at Shrewsbury, North Precinct Oct. 26. 1743. When the Reverend Mr. Ebenezer Morse was ... ordained Pastor of the second Church of Christ in Shrewsbury. By Nathan Bucknam. A.M. ... *Boston: S. Eliot.* 1743. 8vo. BA., M. 8938

Bucknam. A Monitor for Gospel Ministers. A Sermon preached at Brookfield, Mass. Sept. 13, 1749, at the Ordination of the Reverend Mr. Elisha Harding. By Nathan Bucknam. *Boston.* 1749. 12mo, pp. 32. M. 8939

Buckner (A.) Speech of Aylett Buckner, of Kentucky, on the Propriety of organizing Governments for the Territories.

Delivered in the House of Representatives, Feb. 17, 1849. [*Washington: Towers, Printer.* 1849.] 8vo, pp. 16. H. 8940

BUCKNER (H. F.) A Grammar of the Maskwke, or Creek Language. To which are prefixed Lessons in Spelling, Reading, and Defining. By H. F. Buckner ... assisted by his Interpreter G. Herrod. *Marion, Ala.* 1860. 12mo, pp. 139. 8941

BUCKNER. Maskoke Hymns, Original, collected and revised. By H. F. Buckner ... and G. Herrod, interpreter. *Marion, Ala.: Mission Board.* 1860. 32mo, pp. 160. 8942

Also: The Gospel, according to John, in the Creek Language. *Marion: Ala.* 1860. 24mo, pp. 190.

BUCKNER (John), *Bishop of Chichester.* Sermon before the Incorporated Society for the Propagation of the Gospel in Foreign Parts ... February 19, 1802. *London.* 1802. 4to. N. 8943

BUCKNER (Samuel). The American Sailor: a Treatise on practical Seamanship ... . *Newport, R. I.: Edes.* [1790.] 4 l., pp. 96. 8944

One of the earliest American treatises on the subject.

BUCKS COUNTY, *Pa.* A Narrative of the Measures pursued at the Anniversary Election for Representatives, in the County of Bucks, October, 1770. *Philadelphia.* 1771. 8vo, pp. 7. P.

State of the Accounts of the Collectors of Excise for Bucks County, From the 1st of July, 1776 (to which Time the Accounts of the Excise of said County, have been settled and paid) to the 21st of November, 1783. In which is exhibited, the Excise accruing within said time the monies received by the respective Collectors on account thereof. And the sums yet due. Together, with the Payments made to the Treasurer of the State. *Philadelphia: Printed by F. Bailey.* M,DCC,LXXXIV. 8vo, pp. 18. P. 8946

State of the Accounts of Joshua Anderson, Esq. Late Sub-Lieutenant of Bucks County. From March 1780, to April 1783. In which is set forth the Amount of the Fines received within that Period from Delinquents of the Fourth Batallion, for non-performance of Militia Duty and Exercises. ... *Philadelphia: Printed by F. Bailey.* M,DCC,LXXIV. 8vo, pp. 38. P. 8947

The date should be 1784. The Philadelphia Library contains many similar documents.

BUCQUOY (J. de). De waterwereld beschouwd, en de byzonderheden langs de kusten aangeweezen ... byzonderlijk voor de Oost- en West-indise handel. *Haerlem.* 1752. 4to. Map.

BUDAN (A.) La Guadeloupe pittoresque. Texte et dessins. *Paris: Noblet et Baudry.* 1863. Folio. 12 Plates. 8949

BUDD (*Rev.* Henry). Anniversary Sermon and Report of Committee of Proceedings of the Society for Educating the Poor of Newfoundland. *London.* 1825. 8vo. 8950

Title from J. R. Smith's catalogue.

BUDD (Thomas). A Brief answer to two papers procured from Friends in Maryland, the one concerning Thomas Budd's favouring John Lynam, &c. the other concerning his owning George Keith's Principles and Doctrines. [*Philadelphia:*] *Printed* [*by William Bradford*] *in the Year*, 1692. 4to, pp. 4. 8951

BUDD (T.) Good Order Established | in | Pennsilvania & New-Jersey | in | America, | Being a true Account of the Country; | With its Produce and Commodities there made. | And the great Improvements that may be made by | means of Publick Store-houses for Hemp, Flax, and | Linnen-Cloth; also the Advantages of a Publick- | School, the Profits of a Publick-Bank, and the Proba- | bility of its arising, if those directions here laid down are | followed. With the advantages of publick Granaries. | Likewise, several other things needful to be understood by | those that are or do intend to be concerned in planting in | the said Countries. | All which is laid down very plain, in this small Treatise; it | being easie to be understood by any ordinary Capacity. To | which the Reader is referred for his further satisfaction. | By Thomas Budd. | [*London:*] *Printed in the Year* 1685. | 4to, pp. 40. J. C. B. 8952

Priced, in the Nuggets, £6 16s. 6d.; Willis & Sotheran, £3 3s. Reprinted with the following title:

BUDD. Good Order Established in Pennsylvania and New Jersey, in America, being a True Account of the Country; with its Produce and Commodities there made in the year 1685. By Thomas Budd. A new edition, with Introduction and Notes by Edward Armstrong. *New York: W. Gowans.* 1865. 8vo, pp. 111. C. 8953

Sixty copies on large paper. Forms No. 4 of Gowans' "Bibliotheca Americana."

BUDD. A Just Rebuke to several Calumnies, Lyes and Slanders Reported against Thomas Budd. [*Printed by William Bradford, Philadelphia, about* 1692.] 4to, pp. 8. 8954

BUDD. A True and Perfect account of the disposal of the one hundred Shares or Proprieties of the Province of West-New-Jersey, by Edward Bylling, dated the 13th of July, 1685. 8955

"This paper he unadvisedly published in print." — SMITH'S "Friends' Books," I. 330.

[BUDD.] A True Copy of Three Judgments given forth by a Party of Men, called Quakers at Philadelphia, against George Keith and his Friends. With two answers to the said Judgments. [*Philadelphia: Printed by William Bradford.* 1692.] 4to, 2 sheets. 8956

BUDD, *and others.* An Expostulation with Thomas Lloyd, Samuell Jennings, and the rest of the Twenty-eight unjust Judges and Signers of the Paper of Condemnation against George Keith and the rest of his Friends. And Complaint for a Public Hearing and Tryal before all impartial People. [*Printed by William Bradford: Philadelphia.* 1692.] 4to. 8957

This is signed by Thomas Budd, Richard Hilliard, John Hart, Thomas Paschall, William Bradford, James Cooper, and Elizabeth Keith. Reprinted in the "True Copy."

BUDD (T. A.) An Oration before the Washington Benevolent Society of Pennsylvania ... on the 22nd of February, 1828. By Thomas A. Budd, Esq. *Philadelphia: printed by John Clarke.* 1828. 8vo, pp. 25. BA. 8958

BUDDINGH (D.) De kerk, school en wetenschap in de Vereenigde Staten van Noord-Amerika. Door D. Buddingh. *Utrecht: Kemink en Zoon.* 1853.—De Hervormde, Hollandsche kerk in de Vereenigde Staten van Noord Amerika ... . *Utrecht.* 1852. pp. xi, 167.—De school ... . *Utrecht.* 1852. pp. vi–xx, 275.—De wetenschap ... . *Utrecht.* 1853. pp. iii–xii, 344. 3 pts., 8vo. S. 8959

BUDEIUS (S. P.) De Navigatione Illustris ac Magnanimi Equitis Aurati Humfredi Gilberti ad deducendam in Novum Orbem Coloniam suscepta Carmen ἐπιβατικόν. Cura Stephani Parmenii Budei. *Londonii: apud T. Purfutium.* 1582. 4to, 8 leaves. BM. 8960

BUDGE (R.) Case of the Petitioner, Richard Budge, late Commander and Part Owner of the Ship "Hope," and Sole

Owner of her Cargo of Logwood, respecting Condemnation of the said Ship and Cargo at New Jersey. [1708.] Folio, pp. 3.

B[UD]G[E]L (E[usta]ce). Vindication of E—ce B—g—l, Esq., from the Imputation of his being the Author of a Printed Speech, said to be Spoken at a General Court of the South-Sea Company in Merchant-Taylor's Hall, Sep. 30th, 1720. *London.* 1720. 8vo. 8962

Budget général des dépenses du ministère de la marine et des colonies pour l'exercice 1839. *Paris.* 1838. 4to. 8963

The Budget. Inscribed to the Man, who thinks himself Minister. ... *London: J. Almon.* MDCCLXIV. 4to, pp. 23. With an Appendix. *April*, 1764. 4to, pp. 7. + Third Edition. *London: J. Almon.* MDCCLXIV. 4to. + Fourth Edition. *London: J. Almon.* MDCCLXIV. 4to, pp. 23. S. 8964

See "Answer to the Budget," Vol. I., No. 1659.

The Budget. *See* [Torrens (*Colonel*)].

BUDGETT (S.) The Model Merchant, or Memoir of Samuel Budgett. *Philadelphia:* [n. d.] 12mo, pp. 187. 8965

BUDINGTON (W. E.) A Memorial of Giles F. Ward, Jr., late First Lieutenant 12th N. Y. Cavalry. By William Eves Budington, D.D. *New York: A. D. F. Randolph.* 1866. 16mo, pp. 99. 8966

BUDINGTON (W. I.) Capital Punishment: A Discourse, occasioned by the Murder of the late Warden of the Mass. State Prison, ... Charlestown. By William I. Budington ... . *Boston: Press of T. R. Marvin.* 1843. 8vo, pp. 32. H. 8967

BUDINGTON. A Farewell Discourse, preached in the First Church, Charlestown, Mass., September 17, 1854. By William I. Budington. *Philadelphia: printed by Isaac Ashmead.* 1854. 8vo, pp. 24. H. 8968

BUDINGTON. The History of the First Church, Charlestown, in nine lectures, with notes. By William I. Budington ... . *Boston: Charles Tappan.* 1845. 8vo, pp. 258. Plate. C. 8969

BUDINGTON. Our Puritan Fathers our Glory: A Sermon preached in Commemoration of the 220th Anniversary of the Founding of the First Church, in Charlestown, Mass. ... No-

vember 14, 1852. By William I. Budington, Pastor. *Charlestown: McKim & Cutter. Boston: B. H. Greene.* 1852. 8vo, pp. 32. H., M. 8970

Buds and Flowers, of Leisure Hours. ... By Henry Hawser, Sailor, &c. *Philadelphia: printed for the Author, by Geo. W. Loammi Johnson.* 1844. 8vo, pp. 132. BA. 8971

Poems, by a prisoner in the Eastern State Penitentiary, Pennsylvania.

BUÉE (W. U.) Narrative of the successful manner of cultivating the Clove Tree, in the Island of Dominica, one of the Windward Charibbee Islands, by William Urban Buée. *London.* 1797. 8vo. 8972

BUEL (A. W.) Speech of the Hon. Alexander W. Buel in defence of the Constitution and the Union, delivered at a Public Dinner given to him by his Fellow Citizens at Detroit, November 19, 1850. *Washington: Union Office.* 1850. 8vo, pp. 13.

Also: Free Navigation of the St. Lawrence; A Report made to the House of Representatives. *Washington.* 1856. 8vo.

BUEL (D.), *Jr.* Address, delivered at the Consecration of Oakwood Cemetery, Oct. 16, 1850. By Hon. David Buel, Jr. *Troy, N. Y.* 1850. 8vo, pp. 15. S. 8974

BUEL. Troy for Fifty Years: A Lecture, delivered before the Young Men's Association of the City of Troy. By David Buel, jun. ... On the 21st December, 1840. *Troy: N. Tuttle, Printer.* 1841. 8vo, pp. 35. 8975

BUEL (Jesse). The Farmer's Companion. *Boston: Marsh, Capen, Lyon and Webb.* 1839. 12mo, pp. 303. H. + Second Edition. ... *Boston.* 1840. 12mo. + Sixth Edition, with Eulogy by Amos Dean. *New York.* 1847. 12mo. 8976

Also: Address delivered before the Agricultural and Horticultural Societies of New Haven County, Sep. 25, 1839. *New Haven.* 1839. 8vo, pp. 35.

BUEL (S.) Address, delivered on the Occasion of the Opening of the Marshall Cemetery, May, 2, 1839. By Samuel Buel ... . *Marshall: printed by H. C. Bunce.* 1839. 8vo, pp. 13. H.

BUELL (A. H.) Obituary Addresses on ... the Death of Hon. Alexander H. Buell ... delivered in the Senate and House of Representatives, January 31, 1853. [*Washington.* 1853.] 8vo, pp. 8. BA. 8978

BUELL (D. C.) Statement of Major General Buell, in Review of the Evidence before the Military Commission, appointed by the War Department, in November, 1862. Campaign in Kentucky, Tennessee, Northern Mississippi and North Alabama in 1861 and 1862. [n. p. 1862.] 8vo, pp. 72. H. 8979

BUELL (P. L.) The Poet-Soldier: a Memoir of J. K. Gibbons. By P. L. Buell. With introduction by Nelson Sizer. *New York.* 1868. Fcap. 8vo, pp. 48. Portrait. 8980

BUELL (Samuel). A Copy of a Letter, from the Rev. Mr. Buell. Of East-Hampton, on Long-Island, to the Rev. Mr. Barber, of Groton, in Connecticut ... giving an Account of a most extraordinary Work of God, begun and carrying on in that Place. [Vignette.] *London.* 1764. 8vo, pp. 8. H. 8981

BUELL. A Faithful Narrative Of the Remarkable Revival of Religion in the Congregation of East-Hampton, on Long Island, in the Year of our Lord 1764, with Some Reflections. By Samuel Buell, A.M., &c. ... *New York: Samuel Brown.* 1766. 16mo, Title, pp. xi, 2 l., pp. 87. + *Glasgow.* 1768. 12mo. 8982

Reprinted with the following title:

BUELL. A Faithful Narrative of the Remarkable Revival of Religion, in the Congregation of Easthampton, on Long-Island, ... in the year 1764. By Samuel Buell, D.D. ... To which are added, Sketches of the Author's Life—memoirs of his daughter, Mrs. Conklin, and his son, Samuel Buell. ... Also, an Account of the Revival ... in Bridgehampton & Easthampton, In ... 1800. *Sag-Harbor: printed by Alden Spooner.* 1808. 12mo, pp. 144. Portrait of Buell. 8983

BUELL. Sermon at East Hampton, at the Ordination of Mr. Samson Occum, a Missionary among the Indians, with a Letter from Mr. Bostick, giving some account of Mr. Occum's Education, Character, &c. *New York.* 1761. 8vo. 8984

BUELL. A Sermon, delivered at the Ordination of the Reverend Aaron Woolworth, A.M. To the Pastoral Charge of the Church in Bridge-Hampton, on Long-Island, August 30, 1787. By Samuel Buell, A.M. Pastor of the Church at East-Hampton, Long-Island. *Elizabeth-Town, (New Jersey): Printed by Shepard Kollock, on Golden-Hill.* M, DCC, LXXXVIII. 8vo, pp. 46.

Also: Sermon at the Funeral of his Son in the 16th year of his age, with Memoirs of his Life. *New London.* 8vo.—A Sermon preached at Enfield, May

16, 1771, ... *New London.* 1771. 12mo.—Sermon at Bridge Hampton on the Funeral of Saml. Buell Woolworth. *Sag Harbour.* 1794. 8vo.—Sermon on the Death of Rev. Chas. J. Smith at East Hampton, L. I., 1770. *New London: T. Green.* 1770. 8vo, pp. 42.—Sermon at the Ordination of Rev. Joseph Hasard, Southold, June 7, 1797. *New London.* 1797. 8vo, pp. 30.

BUELL, HAZARD, *and* PRIME. An Account of the late Success of the Gospel, in the Province of New-York, North-America: Contained in Letters from the Rev. Messrs. Buell, Hazard, and Prime. *Coventry: T. Luckman.* M,DCC,LXV. 8vo, pp. 16. S. 8986

BUENA-MAISON. *See* Oexmelin (J.)

BUENAVENTURA (Gabriel de San). *See* San Buenaventura (Gabriel de).

BUENO (C.) Descripcion de las Provincias de el Peru. Por el Cosmographo mayor del Virreynato, Don Cosme Bueno. *Lima.* 1763. 8vo, pp. 262. 8987

"This work appears to have been published with the Guia or Calendario of Lima annually, during seventeen years, and is probably the most correct geographical account of Peru and Chili extant; the author says it required all that time to obtain the necessary information from the different provinces. In point of rarity, the book may be considered as almost unique, as few persons will have taken the trouble to have collected together these separate accounts published in such a length of time, and to have formed them into a volume. The title is MS.; nor is it probable there ever was a separate printed one."—RICH, I. 141. The following is perhaps the same work:

BUENO. El conocimiento de los tiempos ... Calculado por las tablas de Cassini y Halley, para el meridiano de esta muy noble, muy leal ciudad de Lima. 1767–96. 12mo. 8988

Leclerc, No. 226, describes 13 volumes of this series, commencing in 1767.

BUENO (José Antonio Pimenta). Direito publico brasileira, e analyse da Constituçao do imperio. *Rio de Janeiro.* 1857. Rl. 8vo. 8989

BUENOS AYRES. Account of the Viceroyalty of Buenos-Ayres, on the Rio de la Plata: including its Geographical Position, Climate, Aspect of the Country, Natural Productions, Commerce, Government, and State of Society and Manners. *London.* [n. d.] 8vo. Map. 8990

Actas capitulares desde el 21 hasta el 25 de Mayo de 1810, en Buenos-Aires. *Buenos Aires.* 1836. Folio, pp. 56. 8991

Almanak y kalendario general diario de quartos de luna, segun

el meridiano de Buenos-Ayres. Para el año de 1795. *Buenos-Ayres: imprenta de niños expósitos.* [1795.] 8vo. 8992

Contains an account of Buenos Ayres, and is one of the earliest books printed in that city.

Anales de la Academia de Medicina de Buenos Ayres. Agosto de 1823. *Buenos Ayres.* 1823. 4to. No. 1., continued.

Anales del Museo público de Buenos Aires, para dar á conocer los objetos de la historia natural nuevos ó poco conocidos conservados en este establecimiento. Por German Burmeister. ... . Entrega primera. *Buenos-Aires: Imprenta de Bernheim y Boneo.* 1864. 4to, pp. iv, 85, 1 l. 4 Plates. H. 8993

El Aniversario de la Sociedad literaria de Buenos Aires. *Buenos Aires.* 1823. 4to, pp. 24. 8995

Anexos a la Memoria del Ministerio de relaciones exteriores. *Montevideo.* 1863–64. 4to, pp. 508. 8996

A list of the contents of this volume is inserted in Trübner's "Am. Record."

Anuario de la Administracion General de Correos presentado al Exc. Gobierno Nacional por el Administrador General. 1863–66. Rl. 8vo. 8997

Anuario de correos de la republica arjentina presentado al Exmo. Gobierno nacional por el Director jeneral. Séptima publicion. *Buenos Aires.* 1865. 8vo, pp. 101, iii. Lithograph and Map. 8998

Archivo Americano. *See* Vol. I., No. 1915.

An authentic and interesting Description of the City of Buenos Ayres, and the adjacent Country; situate on the River Plate, on the East side of South America, shewing the Manners, Customs, Produce, and Commerce, of that most important and valuable Country; including an Account of the Capture of Buenos Ayres, July 2, 1806. Illustrated with a Map of South America. *London: J. Fairburn.* [1806.] 16mo, pp. 60. Map. + Second Edition, with Additions. [n. d.] 12mo. Map. C. 8999

An authentic narrative of the proceedings of the expedition under the command of Brigadier General Crauford, until its arrival at Monte Video; with an account of the Operations against Buenos Ayres, under the command of Lieutenant General Whitelocke. By an officer of the expedition. *Egerton.* 1808. 8vo, pp. 220. 2 Maps. 9000

Banda Oriental. Victoria obtenida sobre los Imperiales en las Costas de Sarandí. [Oct. 12, 1825. *Buenos Ayres.* 1825.] pp. 2. 9001

Buenos Ayres: Truth and Reason, *versus* Calumny and Folly: in which the leading Circumstances of General Whitelocke's Conduct in South America are explained. With an Appendix in answer to an expensive Publication of last Week, refuting every Personality therein advanced. *Kerby.* 1808. 8vo. 9002

The publication referred to is the Authentic narrative, No. 9000.

Coleccion de Documentos Officiales sobre la Mission de los Ministros de S. M. Britannica y S. M. el Rey de los Franceses cerca del Gobierno de Buenos-Aires, encargado de las Relaciones Exteriores de la Confederacion Argentina. *Buenos-Aires.* 1845. 4to. C. 9003

In Spanish, French, and English.

Coleccion de leyes y decretos sobre justicia nacional 1863. *Buenos Aires.* 1863. 4to, pp. 118. 9004

Constitucion de la Republica Argentina. *Buenos Ayres.* 1826. 4to. 9005

Correspondence sustained between the Government of Buenos-Aires, charged with the Foreign Affairs of the Argentine Confederation, and Capt. John B. Nicholson, Commander of the United States Naval Forces on the Coast of Brazil and River Plate, respecting the Questions produced by the Agents of France. *Buenos-Aires.* 1839. 8vo. 9006

In French and English.

Correspondencia con los Ministros de Inglaterra y de Francia sobre los asuntos de las Pacificacion, presentada a la H. Sala de Representantes por el Gobierno de Buenos-Aires. *Buenos Ayres.* 1846. Folio. 9007

In Spanish, French, and English. *See* Rich, II. 286 and 297.

Debates de la Camara de Senadores de Buenos Aires sobre el proyecto que autoriza al Gobernador de la Provincia a convocar e instalar el Congreso nacional. Edicion oficial. *Buenos Aires.* 1862. 4to, pp. 192. 9008

Departamento del interior. Notas conjeadas entre el gobierno de la confederacion Argentina y el de la provincia de Buenos Aires en los meses de Febrero, Marzo y Abril de 1858. *Parana.* 1858. 4to, pp. 20. 9009

Diario de la segunda division de limites, al mando de Diego de Alvear, con la descripcion de su viage desde Buenos-Aires. *Buenos-Aires.* 1837. 4to, pp. 48. 9010

Diario de sesiones de la Camara de Senadores del estado de Buenos Aires, 1857. *Buenos Aires.* 1858. 4to, pp. 674. 9011

Diario de sesiones de la convencion del estado de Buenos-Aires encargada del examen de la constitucion federal. *Buenos-Aires.* 1860. 4to, pp. 544. 9012

Estatuto provisional pàra la direccion y administracion del estado formado por la Junta de Observacion nuevamente establecida en Buenos Ayres a 5 de Mayo de 1815. [*Buenos Aires.* 1815.] 8vo, pp. 42. H. 9013

A Five Years' Residence in Buenos Ayres, during the years 1820 to 1825; containing remarks on the Country and its Inhabitants; and a visit to Colonia del Sacramento. By an Englishman. With an Appendix, containing Rules and Police of the Port of Buenos Ayres, Navigation of the River Plate, &c. &c. *London: G. Herbert.* 1825. 8vo, pp. viii, 176. P. + Second Edition. *London: G. Herbert.* 1827. 8vo, pp. viii, 176. BD.

After the title is a leaf inserted, dated Buenos Ayres, Feb., 1826, by the author, apologizing for his book.

El gobernador de la provincia y el excelentisimo Cabildo. [Proclamation. Dated Buenos-Ayres 26 de Marzo de 1820.] *Buenos-Ayres: Imprenta de la Independencia.* [n. d.] 4to, 1 page.

Impugnacion á la requesta dada al Mensage del Gobierno, de 14 de Setiembre ultimo. Por un Observador. *Buenos Aires.* 1827. 4to, pp. 200. 9016

Informe de la comision de cuentas de los anos 1854 y 1855, presentado á la asamblea general legislativa del estado de Buenos Aires. *Buenos Aires.* 1857. 4to, pp. 40, and Tables. 9017

El labrador argentino, revista de Agricultura, pastoreo economía rural y doméstica, artes y oficios. Segunda edicion ... aumentada ... . Hecha bajo los auspicios del Exmo. Gobierno de la Provincia de Buenos Aires. *Buenos Aires.* 1867. 8vo. B.

Legacion de Buenos Aires en Montevideo, Publication Oficial. *Buenos Aires.* 1856. Folio. 9019

Letters from Buenos Ayres and Chili. *See* [Davie (J.)]

Manifesto de la diputacion de Buenos Aires y documentos a ella referentes. *Buenos-Aires.* 1861. 8vo, pp. 16. 9020

Memorandum del gobierno de la provincia de Buenos Aires, sobbe [*sic*] los tratados celebrados por los ministros de Francia, Inglaterra y Estados Unidos, con el general D. Justo Jose de Urquiza. Sobre la lirre [*sic*] navegacion de los rios Parana y Uruguay. *Buenos Aires: Imprenta de la Tribuna.* 1853. Large 8vo, pp. 37. H. 9021

Also: Memoria de la municipalidad de la ciudad de Buenos Aires correspondiente a los anos 1856 y 1857, 1858, 1859. *Buenos Aires.* 1858–60. 4to, pp. 92, 156, 152. —Memoria presantada por Don José Portugués bajo la direccion de su abogado D. Miguel Navarro Viola. *Buenos Aires.* 1866. 8vo, pp. 108. — Memoria presentada por el ministro de estado en el departamento de guerra y marina al congreso nacional de 1865. *Buenos Aires.* 4to, pp. 178, and Tables. — Memoria presentada por el ministro de estado en el departamento de justicia, culto é instruccion pública al congreso nacional de 1865. *Buenos Aires.* 1865. 4to, pp. xiv, 180. — Memoria presentada por el ministro de estado en el departamento de relaciones exteriores el congreso nacional de 1865. *Buenos-Aires.* 1865. 4to, pp. 274. — Memoria del ministerio del interior de la republica argentina presentada al congreso nacional de 1863, 64. *Buenos Aires.* 1863, 64. 2 vols., 8vo. — Memoria de la municipalidad de la ciudad de Buenos Aires ... Contiene ademas todas las ordenanzas y acuerdos dictados desde el año 1856. *Buenos Aires.* 1861. 8vo, Title, pp. 200, iv. Lithographs. — Memoria presentada por el ministro de estado en el departamento de hacienda al congreso nacional de 1865 *Buenos Aires.* 1865. 8vo, pp. xlvi, 3 l., 10 l. folded, pp. 14, 1 l. folded. — Memorias y noticias para servir á la Historia Antigua de la Republica Argentina, compiladas y publicadas por los Fundadores de la Revista de Buenos Aires. *Buenos Aires.* 1865. 4to.

Mensage del encargado del poder ejecutivo nacional al soberano Congreso de la República, 1862. *Buenos Aires.* 1862. 4to, pp. xxii, 128. Tables. 9022

Also: Mensage del Gobierno Argentino presentado al congreso de la nacion, el 1. de Mayo de 1865. *Buenos Aires.* 1865. 4to, pp. 20. — Mensage del Gobierno de la provincia de Buenos Aires, a la honorable asamblea general legislativa 1. de Mayo de 1865. *Buenos Aires.* 1865. 4to, pp. 264. —Mensage del gobierno de Buenos Aires a la ... Legislatura. *Buenos Aires.* [v. d.] Continued annually.— Mensage del gobierno provisorio del estado de Buenos-Aires á la hon. asamblea lejislativa. *Buenos-Aires.* 1860. 4to, pp. 74 — Mensaje del Gobierno provisorio del estado de Buenos Aires, á la Honorable Asamblea Lejislativa 1° de May de 1860. Publicacion oficial. *Buenos Aires.* 1860. 4to, pp. viii, 70. — Mensage del poder ejecutivo a la ... legislatura constitucional del estado de Buenos-Aires. *Buenos-Aires.* 1855. 8vo, pp. 32. Continued. — Message du gouvernement de Buenos Aries a la vingt-septieme legislature — *Buenos Ayres: imprimerie de l'Independance.* 1849. Large 8vo, pp. 241. H.

Message of the Government of Buenos Ayres to the Twenty-second Legislature. *Buenos Ayres.* 1844 & 1845. 8vo, pp. 31. Continued. 9023

Monarchial Projects; or a Plan to place a Bourbon King on the Throne of Buenos Ayres, in Opposition to British Interests;

being the Proceedings instituted against the Late Congress and Directory, for the Crime of High Treason, &c. with Preliminary Remarks, Illustrative of the Subject in Question, and explanatory of the Causes which led to the Recent Revolution in that Country. ... *London: Ridgway and Booth.* 1820. 8vo, pp. lv, 89. H. 9024

Movimento general de la aduana de Buenos Aires en los meses de Julio, Agosto y Setiembre de 1860. *Buenos Aires.* 1860. 4to, pp. 34. 9025

Narrative of the Expedition to, and the Storming of, Buenos Ayres. 1807. 8vo. 9026

Oficio del Consul encargado interinamente del Consulado General de Francia en Buenos-Aires, al Sr. Ministro de Relaciones Exteriores de la Confederacion Argentina, Reclamando a nombre del derecho de gentes, para que los Franceses, que publica y notoriamente se hallen establecidos en la Republica con los mismos goces y libertades civiles que los ciudadanos Argentinos, no sean considerados como domiciliaros del lugar en donde estan establecidos. Contestacion del Sr. Ministro, y otros Documentos relativos al mismo asunto. *Buenos-Aires: Imprenta del Estado.* 1838. 4to, pp. 114. 9027

Also: Note Officielle du Consul chargé par interim du consulat general de France à Buenos-Aires, a Mr. Le Ministre de Relations Exterieures de la Confederation Argentine, Reclamant, au nom du droit des gens, pour que les Français, qui d'une maniere publique et notoire sont ètablis dans la Republique et y jouissent des memes libertes civiles que les citoyens Argentins, ne soyent pas consideres comme domicilies des lieux ou ils sont etablis. Reponse de Mr. Le Ministre, et d'autres documents sur la meme matiere. *Buenos-Aires.* 1838. 8vo, pp. 265. [With French and English title-page, and text on opposite pages.] In Trübner's "Am. Record," this is said to contain 130 pages.

Official Note from the Consul charged ad Interim of the General Consulate of France in Buenos Ayres, to the Minister for Foreign Affairs to the Argentine Confederation, Reclaiming on the authority of international law, that the French, who notoriously and publicly have established themselves in the Republic with the same enjoyments and civil liberties as the Argentine Citizens, be not considered as domiciled in the Place in which they have established themselves. The Answer from the Minister and other Documents upon the same subject. *Buenos-Aires: State Printing Office.* 1838. 4to, pp. 229. 9028

In French and English.

Ordenzas provisionales del excmo. cabildo justicia y regimiento

de la ciudad de Buenos-Ayres *Buenos-Ayres: imprenta de niños expósitos.* 1814. Folio, Title, pp. 32. H. 9029

El Protector nominal de los pueblos libres, D. José Artigas, clasificado por el Amigo del órden. *Buenos Ayres.* 1818. 4to, pp. 68. 9030

Real Cedula de Ereccion del Consulado de Buenos-Ayres, expedida en Aranjuez a XXX de Enero de M DCC XCIV. *Madrid.* M DCC XCIV. Folio, Title, pp. 36. (En la Oficina de Don Benito Cano.) 9031

An official paper, probably privately printed.

Recopilacion de leyes y decretos de aduana desde Mayo de 1810. *Buenos Aires.* 1860. 4to, pp. 306. 9032

Registro diplomatico del Gobierno de Buenos Aires. *Buenos Aires.* 1835. 4to, pp. 118. 9033

Registro estadistico del estado de Buenos Aires. *Buenos Aires.* 1854–1863. 19 vols., folio, pp. 52; 110; 120; 130; 126; 134; 182; 154; 158; 181; 169; 206; 158; 215; 124; 170; 192; 182; 164. 3 Maps. 9034

Registro estadistico de Buenos Aires, 1864. Tomo primeiro. *Buenos Aires.* 1864. Folio, pp. 120. Continued. 9035

Registro Oficial del Gobierno de Buenos Aires. Libro Primero. Agosto, 1821. *Buenos Ayres.* 1821. 4to. Continued.

Report of the Committee of the British Merchants, elected at the last general meeting, held 27th May, 1852. *Buenos-Aires.* 1853. 8vo, pp. 8. 9037

A Relation of Mr. R. M's Voyage to Buenos Ayres. *See* M (R.)

Relation d'un voyage fait récemment dans les provinces de La Plata, par L. C., ex-agent supérieur du service des hôpitaux militaires des armées françaises; et description de Buenos-Ayres, de son gouvernement, de son indépendance, et des troupes d'Artigas opposées à l'armée portugaise de Montevideo, etc. etc. *Paris: Delaunay.* 1818. 8vo, pp. 65. H. 9038

La república argentina, sus colonias agrícolas, ferro-carriles, navigacion, comercio, riqueza territorial, &. &. Por La Comision de Inmigracion de Buenos Aires. *Buenos Aires.* 1866. 8vo, 2 l., pp. 68. 2 Maps. B. 9039

La Revista de Buenos Aires. Periodico mensual de historia Americana, literatura y derecho. Destinado a la Republica Argentina, la Oriental del Uruguay y la del Paraguay, publicado bajo la direccion de Miguel Navarro Viola y Vicente G. Quesada (Abogados). *Buenos Aires.* 1859. 8vo, pp. 648. Continued. 9040

A summary account of the Vice-royalty of Buenos-Ayres, or, La Plata: including its Geographical Position, Climate, Aspect of the Country, Natural Productions, Commerce, Government, and State of Society and Manners. ... *London: R. Dutton.* [1806.] 8vo, Title, pp. 59. Map. S. 9041

Supplemento a la Correspondencia Oficial con el Consul encargado interinamente del Consulado General de Francia en Buenos-Aires. *Buenos-Aires: Imprenta del Estado.* 1838. 4to, Title, pp. 69–114. 9042

Trübner's "Record" quotes this at 130 pages.

Supplement to the Private Correspondence between the Governor and Capt. General of Buenos Ayres and the Rear Admiral of the French Naval Forces on the Station of Brazil and South Seas. *Buenos Ayres.* 1838. Sm. 4to. 9043

In French and English.

Tesoro de comerciantes real cédula ereccional del consulado de Buenos Aires. Reimpresa por Justo Maeso. *Buenos-Aires.* 1856. 8vo, pp. 24. 9044

Ultimatum del Sr. Consul de Francia Mr. Aimé Roger, dirigido al Gobierno de Buenos-Aires, encargado de las relaciones exteriores de la Confederacion Argentina, con la correspondiente contestacion y Documentos que le son Relativos. *Buenos-Aires: Imprenta del Estado.* 1838. 4to, pp. 97. 9045

Ultimatum of Mr. Aimé Roger, Consul of France, Addressed to the Government of Buenos Ayres, charged with the Foreign Affairs of the Argentine Confederation, its Answer and relative Documents. *Buenos Ayres: State Printing Office.* 1838. 4to, pp. 189. 9046

In French and English. Apparently a translation of No. 9045; both were probably printed only for official use.

BUENDIA (Joseph de), *Cathedralico de Filosofia en su Maximo de San Pablo de Lima.* Vida Admirable y Prodigiosas Virtudes

del Ven. y Apostolico Padre Francisco del Castillo, Natural de Lima, Ciudad de los Reyes en la Provincia del Perù. *Madrid.* 1693. 4to. 9047

BUFFALO. Annual Statement of the Trade and Commerce of Buffalo, for the year 1851. 8vo. Continued. 9048

A Brief Summary of Christian doctrine and a form of covenant adopted by the First Presbyterian Church, Buffalo. To which a historical sketch of the church is prefixed. ... *Buffalo.* 1838. 12mo, pp. 48. + Enlarged edition. *Buffalo.* 1852. 12mo, pp. 63. 9049

Astronomical Calendar, or Western Almanac for ... 1824. *Buffalo.* 12mo. 9050

Buffalo Business Directory, with Alphabetical and Classified Index. Vol. 1., 1855. *Buffalo.* 1855. 8vo. 9051

Buffalo in 1825. Containing Historical and Statistical Sketches. *Buffalo.* 1825. 12mo, pp. 14. Map and Plate. GB. 9052

The Commercial Advertiser Directory for the city of Buffalo, 1854. *Buffalo: Jewett, Thomas & Co.* 1854. 12mo, pp. 482. Continued. 9053

The Commercial Advertiser's Twentieth Annual Statement of the Trade and Commerce of Buffalo, for 1857. Including Statistics, showing the Whole Export of Flour and Grain from the Lake Regions. ... with a Brief Notice of the Manufactures of the City. *Buffalo.* 1858. 8vo, pp. 40. H. 9054

A Directory for the Village of Buffalo, containing the names and residence of the heads of families and householders in said Village on the first of Jan. 1828. To which is added a sketch of the history of the Village from 1801 to 1828. *Buffalo: Pub. by L. P. Crary.* 1828. 18mo, pp. 55. 9055

The first directory. After 1840, the directory was published annually, except in 1843, 1845, and 1846. Some late issues contain additional matter, as below:

Thomas' Buffalo City Directory for 1863. To which is prefixed "Buffalo, Past and Present." An Address ... By Guy H. Salisbury, Esq. Followed by a Sketch of the Climatory of Buffalo. By Wm. Ives, Esq. ... *Buffalo: E. A. Thomas.* 1863. 8vo, pp. viii, 17–394. + For 1864. To which is prefixed The Physiognomy of Buffalo, by Rev. George W. Hosmer, D.D. and

"The History of our Lake Commerce," by E. P. Dorr ... . *Buffalo: G. A. Thomas.* 1864. 8vo, pp. 382. B. + For 1865. To which is prefixed "The Old Ferry at Black Rock," by Charles D. Norton, Esq., [etc.] *Buffalo: C. F. S. Thomas.* 1865. 8vo, pp. 376. C. + For 1867. To which is prefixed ... History of Grain-Elevators, by J. Dart; and Early History of Grand Island and Ararat, by L. F. Allen. *Buffalo: Thomas, Howard & Johnson.* 1867. 8vo, pp. 461. 9056

First Annual Report of the General Aid Society for the Army. Buffalo, N. Y., January 1, 1863. *Buffalo: Franklin Press.* 1863. 8vo, pp. 15. 9057

The First Unitarian Church in Buffalo: its History and Progress. Rev. Dr. Hosmer's Quarter Centennial Discourses: The Parish — The Pulpit. An Account of the Quarter Centennial Celebration, on Wednesday Evening, October 16th, 1861. Printed for Private Circulation. *Buffalo.* 1861. 8vo, pp. 94. H., S. 9058

The Manufactories of Buffalo in 1859. *Buffalo: E. R. Jewett.* 1859. 8vo, pp. 46. 9059

Report of the Harbor Committee in relation to an Increase of Harbor Facilities at the City of Buffalo. Approved at a General Meeting held Aug. 21, 1847. And Approved by the Common Council, Aug. 24, 1847. *Buffalo: Steam Press of Jewett, Thomas & Co.* 1847. 8vo, pp. 54. Map. H., S. 9060

Report of the Select Committee of the Common Council, on the Subject of the Harbour and Business of the City of Buffalo. Made to the Common Council June 1, 1841. *Buffalo.* 1841. 8vo, pp. 16. H. 9061

Report on the Vessels, Commerce and Trade of the Lakes and Erie Canal and of the Commercial Business of Buffalo, for the Year 1861. Published by Direction of the Buffalo Committee of Public Defense. *Buffalo.* 1862. 8vo, pp. 15. H.

Revised Charter of the City of Buffalo, with the By-laws and Ordinances. *Buffalo.* 1863. 8vo. S. 9063

The following tracts and reports relate to Buffalo. (The New York State Library at Albany contains many others.) Buffalo Association for the Relief of the Poor. Address, by G. W. Hosmer, 1852. + Address, Constitution, 1853. 12mo. — Buffalo Gas Light Company. Rules and Regulations for the Introduction of Gas ... Buffalo, 1848; Buffalo, 1852: — Revised, 1855. *Buffalo.* 1855. — Buffalo General Hospital. Articles of Association, 1855. *Buffalo*, 1856. + Dedicatory Exercises ... *Buffalo.*

1858. 8vo. — Buffalo Horticultural Society. Constitution. Exhibition, 1845. Address by Hon. G. W. Clinton. *Buffalo*, 1846. + Report, 1847. *Buffalo*. 1848. 8vo. Continued. — Buffalo Juvenile Asylum. Act to Incorporate ... *Buffalo*. 1856. 8vo. — Buffalo Orphan Asylum. Report, 1843. *Buffalo*. 1843. 8vo. Continued. — Buffalo Presbytery. Alleged Relations of the American Board of C. F. Missions to Slavery Examined. By a Committee of Presbytery. *Buffalo*. 1845. 12mo, pp. 32. — Buffalo Trust Company. Charter and By-laws ... *Buffalo*. 1852. 8vo. — Buffalo, Warren and St. Louis Railroad. Preliminary Report. ... *Buffalo*. 1854. 8vo. Map. —Buffalo, Corning and New-York Railroad Company. Statement. *New York*. 1852. 8vo. — Buffalo Female Acadamy. Circular and Catalogue, 1852. Proceedings First Annual Commencement, July 1852. *Buffalo*. 1852. 8vo. Continued. — Buffalo Harbor: Letter from the Secretary of War, relative to the different Plans for its improvement, Jan. 6, 1849. *Washington*. 1849. 8vo, pp. 19. (Cong. Doct.) S. — Buffalo Medical Journal and Monthly Review of Medical and Surgical Science; Edited by Austin Flint and Sanford B. Hunt. Vol. I. *Buffalo*. 1845–6. 8vo. — By-Laws and Ordinances. *Buffalo*. 1855. pp. 77. — Celebration of the Fourth of July at Buffalo, 1865. 8vo S. — Charity Foundation of the Protestant Episcopal Church in ... Buffalo ... *Buffalo*. 1858. 12mo, pp. 16. — St. Louis Church, Buffalo. Documents. *Buffalo*. 1852. 8vo. + Affairs. *Buffalo*. 1853. 8vo. S. — A Summary Declaration of the Faith and Practice of the Washington Street Baptist Church of ... in Buffalo, N. Y. (With a List of Members.) *Buffalo: Press of Thomas & Co.* 1839. Sm. 16mo, pp. 15. H. — Annual Announcement of the Medical Department, University of Buffalo. *Buffalo*. 1845. 8vo. Continued. — Annual Announcement and Catalogue of the Medical Department of the University of Buffalo, June, 1850. *Buffalo: Jewett, Thomas & Co.* 1850. 8vo, pp. (13). Lithograph. Continued. H. — Annual Circular of the Medical Department of the University of Buffalo, October, 1846. *Buffalo: Jewett, Thomas & Co., Printers*. 1846. 8vo, pp. (11). Continued. H. — Young Men's Association of Buffalo. Celebration of the Quarter-Century Anniversary. *Buffalo*. 1861. 8vo. — Annual Report of the ... Young Men's Association of the city of Buffalo; ... *Buffalo*. 1836. 8vo. Continued. — Address, Constitution and By-Laws ... of the Young Men's Christian Union, of the city of Buffalo. ... . *Buffalo: Geo. Reese & Co., Printers*. 1852. 16mo, pp. 16. H.

BUFFIN (J.) The true Quaker reproveing [*sic*] the false one. Or them that would be counted Quakers and are not: So set forth by John Buffin, former Bookseller in the Jerseys, and Pennsylvania. ... *Philadelphia: printed for the Author according to Copy*. 1764. 12mo, pp. 17. P. 9064

"It was enough, formerly, in New England, if one said *thee* to one person, to send him to prison, and whip him also." — Page 13.

BUFFINTON (J.) Kansas — The Lecompton Constitution. Speech of Hon. James Buffinton, of Mass. Delivered in the House of Representatives, March 24th, 1858. [*Washington*. 1858.] 8vo, pp. 7. H. 9065

Also: Position of Massachusetts on the Slavery Question. ... April 30. 1856. [No imp.] 8vo, pp. 7.

BUFFON. Lettres | à un Amériquain | sur l'histoire naturelle, générale et par- | ticuliere de monsieur de Buffon, | troisième partie. | *à Hamburg* | 1.7.5.1. | Sm. 8vo, Title, pp. 31, 96, 69.

"The title is a curious specimen of typography." Priced, in Stevens' Nuggets, 10s. 6d.

BUFFUM (E. G.) Six Months in the Gold Mines; from a Journal of three years' Residence in Upper and Lower California, 1847–8–9. By E. Gould Buffum, Lieutenant First Regiment New York Volunteers. *Philadelphia: Lea and Blanchard*. 1850. 12mo, pp. 172. + *London*. 1850. 12mo, pp. 256.

BUFORD (N. B.) African Colonization. [Dated Washington, December 19, 1862. Signed N. B. Buford, Brig. Gen. U. S. Vols. n. p. n. d.] 16mo, pp. (3). + (Letter No. 2.) [Dated Cairo, Ills, Feb. 12, 1863. Signed. n. p. n. d.] 16mo, pp. (3). H. 9068

[BUGBEE (James).] A Memorial of Edward Everett, from The City of Boston. *Boston: Printed by order of the City Council*. MDCCCLXV. 4to, pp. 315. Steel Portrait and Lithograph. BA.

BUGBEE (S.), *Jr*. An Oration, pronounced at Wrentham, July 4, 1803 ... . By Samuel Bugbee, Jun. *Dedham: Printed by H. Mann*. M DCCC III. 8vo, pp. 16. H. 9070

[BUGG (Francis).] News from Pensilvania, or a Brief Narrative of Several Remarkable Passages in the Government of the Quakers of that Province. Touching their Proceedings in their Pretended Courts of Justice, their Way of Trade and Commerce; with Remarks and Observations upon the whole. Published by the Author of the Pilgrim's Progress. Together with a Postscript, ... *London*: ... . 1703. 8vo, pp. 36. 9071

BUGG. The Picture of Quakerism Drawn to Life in 2 Parts. The First, Shewing the Vanity of the Quakers' pretence of their being the One only Catholic Church of Christ, &c. — The Second, Containing a Brief History of the Rise, Growth, and Progress of Quakerism; being a modest correction of the General History of the Quakers, wrote in Holland by Gerrard Croese. By Francis Bugg, Sen. *London: W. Kittleby*. 1697. 8vo, 22 sheets. 9072

Contains an "Account of the Persecution of G. Keith, in Pennsylvania in America, by the Quakers," "Croese's Mistake concerning W. Penn," etc. For a list of other works by this author, *see* Smith's "Catalogue of Friends' Books," I. 332–347. Doubtless others, besides those quoted here, relate to America. About 1680, Bugg "turned an envious and contentious apostate."

A Bugle Blast from the Army. What the Soldiers think of Northern Traitors. They will remember them when they return. The Voice of Loyal Democrats in the Army to Traitor Democrats at Home. *Michigan*. 1863. 8vo, pp. 8. 9073

The Bugle Call. Devoted to the cause of our Sick and Wounded Soldiers. *Chicago*. 1865. 4to. 9074

BUHLE (M.) Reisen durch die Vereinigten Staaten von Nord-Amerika. *Nürnberg: Bauer und Raspe*. 1808 2 vols., sm. 8vo. 9075

This forms the second and third parts of his "Erholungen für die gebildete Jugend," and has two title-pages.

BUHOUP (J. W.) Narrative of the Central Division of the Army of Chihuahua, commanded by General Wool. By Jonathan W. Buhoup. *Pittsburgh*. 1847. 12mo. S. 9076

Building Associations of Connecticut and other States Examined, with a Review of the New York and Massachusetts Systems. Also a Complete Review of all the Building Associations established in Connecticut. *New Haven*. 1856. 4to

BUISOT (J. P.) Discours sur la nécessité de maintenir le décret rendu le 15 mai, 1791, en faveur des hommes de couleur libres, par J. P. Buisot. [n. p. n. d.] 9078

A doubtful title; perhaps by J. P. Brissot.

[BUISSON (Jean Francois).] Relation de la mission du Missisipi du Seminaire de Québec en 1700. Par MM. de Montigny, de St. Cosme, et Thaumur de la Source. [Vignette.] *Nouvelle York: a la presse Cramoisy de Jean-Marie Shea*. M DCCC LXI. 8vo, pp. 66, 1 l. H. 9079

B[UISSON (*M.* Du.)] Abrégé de la revolution de l'Amérique Angloise, depuis le commencement de l'année 1774, jusqu'au premier Janvier 1778. Par M. ***, Américain. [Motto.] *Paris: Cellot & Jombert*. 1778. 12mo, Title, pp. 452, 1 l. + *Yverdun*. M.DCC.LXXIX. 12mo, pp. xii, 345. 9080

The author (M. du Buisson, according to Barbier) says, in his preface, that "the French nation knew so little of the people with whom their sovereign had just formed an alliance, that they applied the name of *Bostonian* to all the inhabitants of the thirteen provinces, when of right it belonged only to those of the province of Massachusetts." At the end of the work is a copy of the treaty with France, which was made in this year.

[BUISSON.] Historischer Abriss der in Nord-Amerika vorgefallenen Staatsveränderung, von 1774 bis 1778, von M..., einem Amerikaner. Aus dem Französischen. *Bern: Haller*. 1779. 8vo, pp. 365. 9081

B[UISSON]. Nouvelles considérations sur Saint-Domingue, en réponse a celles de M. H. Dl. Par M. D. B. ***. [Motto.]

Paris: Cellot & Jambert. 1780. 2 pts., 8vo, Half-Title, Title, pp. 178, 2 l.; Title, Half-Title, pp. 164. 9082

"An answer to M. Hilliard D'Auberteuil by M. Du Buisson." — BARBIER.

BUIST (G.) A Discourse, occasioned by The Death of Brigadier General M'Pherson, who was lost in the Ship Rose in Bloom, Shipwrecked on her passage from Charleston to New York, August 24th, 1806; Delivered, by desire, in the Presbyterian Church of Charleston, S. C. November 30th, 1806. By the Rev. George Buist, DD. *Charleston: Printed by William P. Young*. 1807. 12mo, pp. 42. N. 9083

BUIST. An Oration delivered at the Orphan-House of Charleston, South-Carolina, October 18th, 1795, being the Sixth Anniversary of the Institution. By the Reverend George Buist, D.D. ... . *Charleston: printed by Markland & M'Iver*. MDCCXCV. 8vo, pp. 25, 1 l. H. 9084

Het Buitenland. *Arnhem: J. van Eymond Jr*. 1866. 12mo.

Twelve numbers appear in a year. No. 3 is "De vorst der Peons, of de avonturen von Putnam-Pomfret in Mexico. Naar het Engelsch door J. B. Rietstap."

BULDEREN. Gedenckwaerdighe Voyagie naer West-Indiae, onder het beleydt van den Comm. Jacob Binckes, nevens desselfs Voorval met de France op Tabago. Beschr. en by-gewoont door H. v. B. *Amsterdam*. 1677. pp. 8. 9086

"Onderteekend: Bulderen, bekend rijmelaar. Dit verhaal is echter grootendeels in proza." — TIELE.

BULFINCH (B. S.) Georgia, a Poem. To which are added, other Metrical Compositions. By Benjamin S. Bulfinch, An American Traveller. *Printed at the University Office, Mt. Zion, Ga*. 1820. 8vo. W. 9087

BULFINCH (Charles). ... A Concise Statement of the Construction and of the Physical and Moral Effects of Penitentiary Prisons, On the Auburn Principle ... . [n. p.] 1829. 8vo, pp. 8. H. 9088

BULFINCH (John). The Trial of Moses Adams, High Sheriff of the County of Hancock, ... for the Murder of his Wife, June, 1815. Second Edition. *Boston*. 1815. 8vo, pp. 32. M.

BULFINCH (S. Greenleaf). Christian Patriotism; a Discourse ... in Augusta, Geo. February the 7th, 1836. soon after the De-

parture of Two Companies of Volunteers, For the Seminole War. By S. G. Bulfinch. ... *Augusta, Georgia*. 1836. 8vo, pp. 16. BA. 9090

BULFINCH. Honor; or, The Slave-Dealer's Daughter. By Stephen G. Bulfinch. [Motto.] *Boston: William V. Spencer*. 1864. 12mo, pp. 238. H. 9091

Also: Discourse ... on the Day of Humiliation and Prayer. *Charleston*. 1833. Sm. 8vo. — Farewell Discourse ... Washington, May 12, 1844, ... *Washington*. 1844. 8vo, pp. 20. BA. — Sermon ... Augusta, Geo., Sunday, July 4, 1830. *Augusta*. 1830. 8vo, pp. 27. — Sermon on the Death of Wm. H. Harrison. By S. G. Bulfinch. *Washington*. — ... A Sermon ... at ... Dorchester, on Sunday, Feb. 2, 1862, on ... the Decease of Mrs. Sarah Cushing, Wife of Hon. Abel Cushing. ... [n. p.] *Samuel P. Brown, Printer*. 1862. 8vo, pp. 15. H.

[BULFINCH (Thomas).] ... The Boy Inventor; a Memoir of Matthew Edwards, Mathematical-Instrument Maker. [Motto.] *Boston: Walker, Wise, & Co*. 1860. 18mo, pp. 109, 2. Portrait. H. 9092

BULFINCH. Oregon and Eldorado; or, Romance of the Rivers [Columbia and Amazon]. By Thomas Bulfinch ... . *Boston: J. E. Tilton and Company*. 1866. 12mo, pp. xiv, 1 l., pp. 464. C., H. 9093

BÜLICH (J. D. von). Orbis Terrarum Veteribus Cogniti Typus in binnis Tabulis à Jo. Strubio, antehac exhibitus et brevi Epitome illustratus à Jo. Bunone. Nunc denuò plurimis locis adauctus, cum delineatione Novi Orbis sive Veteribus incognitæ Americæ. *Helmstadii*. 1694. 4to. 9094

Title from Fischer's catalogue, who remarks that it is unmentioned by Brunet, Stevens, Rich, etc.

BULKELEY (G.) The People's | Right to Election | Or Alteration of Goverment [*sic*] in Connecticott, | argued | In a Letter; | By Gershom Bulkeley Esq; one of their Majesties Justices of the peace | In the County of Hartford. | Together with a Letter to the said Bulkeley, | from a Friend of his in the Bay. | To which is added, The Writing delivered to James Russell of Charlestown | Esq; warning him and others concerned, not to meet to Hold a Court | at Cambridge, within the County of Middlesex. | By Thomas Greaves Esq; Judge of their Majesties Inferior Court of Pleas | and one of their Majesties Justices of the peace within the said County | And also his Answer to Mr. Broadstreete and the Gentlemen mett at the | Town-house in Boston concerning the same. | Published for the Information & Satisfaction of their

Majesties loyall | (but abused) Subjects in New-England. | *Philadelphia: Printed by Assignes of William Bradford, Anno* 1689. | 4to, pp. 18. BA. 9095

Printed without a separate title-page. Reprinted in the "Con. Hist. Soc. Collections," Vol. I. In the "Historical Magazine," III. 255, a tract, entitled "Some seasonable considerations for the Good People of Connecticut," is attributed to Bulkeley. I have not been able to find a copy of this work.

BULKELEY (P.) The Gospel-Covenant; | or | the Covenant | of Grace Opened. | Wherein are explained; | 1. The differences betwixt the Covenant of grace and Covenant | of workes. | 2. The different administration of the Covenant before and | since Christ. | 3. The benefits and blessings of it. | 4. The Condition. | 5. The properties of it. | Preached in Concord in Nevv-England | by Peter Bulkeley, sometimes fellow | of Saint Johns College in Cambridge. | Published according to Order. | *London: Printed by M. S. for Benjamin Allen, and are to be sold | at the Crowne in Popes-head Alley*. 1646. 4to, 8 l., pp. 383, Table, 4 l.

The first minister of Concord, Mass.; came to New England in 1635.

BULKELEY. The Gospel-Covenant; | or | the Covenant | of Grace opened. | Wherein are explained; | 1. The differences betwixt the Covenant of grace and Covenant | of workes. | 2. The different administration of the Covenant before and since | Christ. | 3. The benefits and blessings of it. | 4. The Condition. | 5. The properties of it. | Preached in Concord in New-England | by Peter Bulkeley, sometimes fellow | of Saint Johns Colledge in Cambridge. | Gen. 17. 1. 7. | ... | ... | ... | ... . | Isai. 55. 3. | ... | ... . | The second Edition, much enlarged, and corrected by the Author. | And the chiefe heads of Things (which was omitted in the former) | distinguished into Chapters. | *London: | Printed by Matthew Simmons, dwelling in Aldersgate-street | next doore to the Golden Lyon*. 1651. | 4to, 7 l., pp. 432, Table, 5 leaves. H., N. 9097

For some Latin poetry by this author, *see* Mather's "Magnalia."

BULKLEY (C.) The Signs of the Times, Illustrated and Improved. In a Sermon preached at the Evening-Lecture in the Old-Jewry, on Sunday, October 21, 1759. On Occasion of the Surrender of Quebec to his Majesty's Forces, September 18, 1759. By Charles Bulkley. *London*. M DCC LIX. 8vo, pp. 30, 1 l. 9098

BULKLEY (C. H.) Removal of Ancient Landmarks; or the Causes and Consequences of Slavery Extension. A Discourse preached at West Winsted, Conn., March 5, 1854. *Hartford: Case, Tiffany & Co*. 1854. 8vo, pp. 23. 9099

BULKLEY (C. H. A.) A Five Years' Ministry. (No. 1.) An Anniversary Sermon ... Winsted, Conn., December 5th, 1858, by C. H. A. Bulkley. ... *Winsted*. 1859. 8vo, pp. 27. + ... (No. 2.) A Parting Sermon ... Winsted, Conn., May 22, 1859, by C. H. A. Bulkley. *Winsted*. 1859. 8vo, pp. 24.

BULKLEY. Niagara. A Poem. By Rev. C. H. A. Bulkley. *New-York: Leavitt, Trow & Co*. MDCCCXLVIII. 12mo, pp. 191, (1). B., H. 9101

BULKLEY (E. A.) A Farewell Sermon ... Geneva, N. Y., On February 24th, 1850, by Rev. Edwin A. Bulkley. ... [*Geneva:*] *E. Van Volkenburgh, Printer*. 1850. 8vo, pp. 16.

BULKLEY. The Uncrowned Nation. A Discourse commemorative of the Death of Abraham Lincoln, Sixteenth President of the United States: preached in the First Presbyterian Church of Plattsburgh, N. Y., April 19, 1865, by the Pastor, Rev. Edwin A. Bulkley. *Plattsburgh. N. Y.: J. W. Tuttle, Printer*. 1865. 8vo, pp. 16. H. 9103

BULKLEY. Wars and Rumors of Wars. A Sermon preached at ... Groton, Mass., ... April 21st, 1861, by the Pastor, Rev. Edwin A. Bulkley. *Cambridge: printed by Miles and Dillingham*. 1861. 8vo, pp. 16. 9104

BULKLEY (J.) An Impartial Account of a late Debate at Lyme, in the Colony of Connecticut, (On ... Baptism ... And III. The Maintenance of the Ministers of the Gospel.) Giving a Summary of what was there Delivered, on both Sides. ... Also giving some Account of the Rise of the Antipedo-Baptist Perswasion [*sic*]. By John Bulkley, A.M. To which is added, A Narrative of one lately Converted from Dreadful Errors: By Another Hand. *N. London: T. Green*. M, DCC, XXIX. Sm. 8vo, pp. (1), Title, 199, (1). B. 9105

"Contains some remarks on the theological tenets of Mrs. Hutchinson, Samuel Gorton, and Roger Williams." — BARTLETT'S "Bib. R. I."

BULKLEY. The Necessity of Religion in Societies ... . A Sermon Preach'd before the General-Assembly of the Colony of Connecticut, at Hartford, May 14. 1713. By John Bulkley, A.M. ... [n. p.:] *Timothy Green*. 1713. 8vo, Title, pp. 70.

BULKLEY. ... Sermon preached at Colchester, at Ordination of Rev. Judah Lewes, Dec. 17, 1729. *New London*. 1730. 8vo, pp. 48. 9107

BULKLEY (J.) A Voyage to the South-Seas, In the Years 1740–1. Containing A faithful Narrative of the Loss of his Majesty's Ship the Wager on a desolate Island, in the Latitude 47 South, Longitude 81:40 West: With the Proceedings and Conduct of the Officers and Crew, and the Hardships they endured on the said Island for the space of five Months; their bold Attempt for Liberty, in Coasting the Southern Part of the vast Region of Patagonia; setting out with upwards of Eighty Souls in their Boats; the Loss of the Cutter; their Passage through the Streights of Magellan; an Account of their Manner of living on the Voyage on Seals, Wild Horses, Dogs, &c. and the incredible Hardships they frequently underwent for Want of Food of any Kind; a Description of the several Places where they touch'd in the Streights of Magellan, with an Account of the Inhabitants, &c., and their safe Arrival to the Brazil, after sailing one thousand Leagues in a Long-Boat; their Reception from the Portuguese; an Account of the Disturbances at Rio Grand; their Arrival at Rio Janeiro; their Passage and Usage on Board a Portuguese Ship to Lisbon; and their Return to England. Interspersed with many entertaining and curious Observations, not taken notice of by Sir John Narborough, or any other Journalist. The Whole compiled by Persons concerned in the Facts related, viz. John Bulkeley and John Cummins, Late Gunner and Carpenter of the Wager. [Motto.] *London: Jacob Robinson*. M.DCC.XLIII. 8vo, pp. xx, 220. H. + *Dublin*. 1743. 12mo. + *London*. 1752. 8vo. 9108

"The Wager was one of the ships which sailed from England, under Commodore Anson, on a voyage round the world." — RICH, I. 72. Another edition was printed anonymously. *London: J. T.* 1743. 16mo, pp. 11, 104. Reprinted as below:

BULKLEY. A Voyage to the South Seas, In the Years 1740–1. ... By John Bulkeley and John Cummins ... . The Second Edition, with Additions. ... *London: Printed. Philadelphia: Reprinted by J. Chattin, for the Author*. 1757. 8vo, pp. xxxii, 306. BA., P. 9109

Contains a narrative of the loss of the ship Wager on a desolate island, etc. A dedication to the Hon. Wm. Denny, Lieut. Governor of Pennsylvania, and additions by the authors (who had emigrated to Pennsylvania), and a subscription list of all the distinguished names in the colonies (over 1200).

BULL (P.) A Wolf in Sheep's Clothing; or an old Jesuit Unmasked, Containing an Account of the Wonderful Apparition of Father Petre's Ghost, in the form of the Rev. John Wesley. With some conjectures concerning the Secret cause that moved him to appear at this very critical juncture. By Patrick Bull, Esqr. *Dublin: Printed. London: Reprinted by Trickett.* 1775. 12mo. 9110

"The author insinuates that Mr. Wesley had solicited an American bishoprick." — M. R., LIII. 440.

Bulla Confirmationis et Novæ Concessionis Privilegiorum omnium Ordinum Mendicantium, cum Certis Declarationibus Decretis et Inhibitionibus S. D. N. D. Pij Papæ V. *Mexici, apud Antonium Spinosa, Anno,* 1568. 4to. 9111

"An extremely rare specimen of the early typography of the New World." — AUG. FISCHER.

BULLARD (A.) The Peculiarities of the Age. A Sermon, preached before the General Assembly of the Presbyterian Church of the United States, at their Meeting at Washington City, May, 1852. By Artemas Bullard, D.D. ... *Boston: Press T. R. Marvin.* 1852. 8vo, pp. 31. H. 9112

BULLARD (E. F.) The Nation's Trial: the Proclamation: Dormant Powers of the Government: the Constitution a Charter of Freedom, and not "a Covenant with Hell:" By Edward F. Bullard ... [Motto.] *New York: C. B. Richardson.* 1863. 8vo, pp. 62. H. 9113

BULLARD (*General*). Temperance and Popery: an Address delivered before the Saratoga County Convention, at Ballston Spa, October 10, 1854, by Gen. Bullard. *Albany: J. Munsell.* 1854. 8vo, pp. 10. H. 9114

BULLARD (H. Adams). A Discourse on the Life and Character of the Hon. François Xavier Martin, Late Senior Judge of the Supreme Court, of the State of Louisiana, pronounced at the request of the Bar of New-Orleans, by Henry A. Bullard ... [Motto.] *New-Orleans: printed by J. B. Steel.* 1847. 8vo, pp. 35. H. 9115

BULLARD. A Discourse delivered before the Historical Society of Louisiana January 13, 1836. By Henry A. Bullard ... *New Orleans: Benjamin Levi.* 1836. 8vo, pp. 30. 9116

Reprinted in French's "Historical Collections," I. 1–23. Full of authentic and curious information respecting the early history of Louisiana. *See* N. A. R., XLIII. 281.

[BULLARD.] The History of Don Francisco de Miranda's Attempt to effect a Revolution in South America ... By ... an Officer under that General ... To which are annexed,

Sketches of the Life of Miranda, and Geographical Notices of Caraccas. ... *Boston: Oliver and Munroe.* 1808. 12mo, pp. xi, 300. BA. 9117

BULLARD. Speech of Mr. Bullard, of Louisiana. On the Tariff, in the Committee of the Whole House on the State of the Union, June 15, 1832. [n. p. n. d.] 8vo, pp. 16. 9118

BULLARD *and* CURRY. A New Digest of the Statute Laws of the State of Louisiana, from the Change of Government to the Year 1841, inclusive: Compiled by Henry A. Bullard, one of the Judges of the Supreme Court of Louisiana, and Thomas Curry, late Reporter ... and now Judge ... Vol. I. *New Orleans: E. Johns & Co.* 1842. 8vo, pp. 876. C. 9119

BULLARD (O. A.) Views in New York City, embracing many of the most celebrated Public Buildings in the Empire City, with a Description of each. [n. p. n. d.] 8vo, pp. 96.

BULLARD. "The Diamond Point." A National Poem. *Camp Utley, Racine County, Wis.* 9121

Bullarium Latino-Hispanicum Ord. Fratrum Bethlemitarum in Indiis Occidentalibus in quo comprehenduntur omnes Apostolicæ Litteræ à Summis Pontificibus editæ ab Anno 1672, usque ad Annum 1773. *Romæ.* 1773. 4to. 9122

BULLART (I.) Academie des sciences et des arts, Contenant les Vies ... & les Eloges Historiques des Hommes Illustres ... Par Isaac Bullart. *Amsterdam.* 1682. 2 vols., folio, 279 sheets. + *Brusselles: François Foppens.* M. DC. XCV. 2 vols., folio. BA. 9123

Portraits and biographies of Columbus, Vesputius, Magellan, Cortes, Drake, and Candish (2d ed.), II. 265–284.

BULLEN (Christians). Christians Bullen eines seefahrenden journal was auf der Schiffahrt nach der Nordsee und denen Insuln Groenland und Spitzbergen täglich vorgefallen ist im Iahr Christi 1667. *Bremen: Wessel.* 1668. 4to, 12 leaves.

"Exceedingly rare." — TERNAUX, 862.

BULLER (Ch.) Responsible Government for Colonies. By Charles Buller, M.P. *London.* 1840. 9125

The author was secretary to Lord Durham in Canada, and is supposed to have written Lord Durham's report.

Bulletin colonial, supplément à la Revue du dix-neuvième siècle. *Paris: Avril,* 1836–27 *septembre,* 1840. Folio. 9126

In the titles of some numbers were also the words, "France et colonies, journal politique, littéraire, maritime." — HATIN.

Bulletin de la Société Philomatique. 9127

The volume for 1817 contains "Note sur une nouvelle espèce d'ours de l'Amérique du Nord, 'Ursus griseus,'" and "Note sur le Wapiti, espèce de cerf de l'Amérique septentrionale," by H. M. Ducrotay de Blainville.

Bulletin de Société de Géographie. Année 1822. *Paris.* 1822. Continued. 9128

Includes numerous articles relating to America — especially the French colonies; also Indian vocabularies, etc. *See* Ludewig's Lit. Ab.

Bulletin historique et littéraire de la Société de l'histoire du protestantisme français. *Geneva?* 9129

"The 'Bulletin' is now (1868) in the seventeenth year of its existence, and contains matter of deep interest to ... the descendants of the French Protestant refugees who came hither to escape persecution." — E. T. FISHER.

BULLIONS (A. B.) Sermon on the Death of Gen. Taylor. By Rev. A. B. Bullions. *Waterford.* 1850. 8vo. 9130

BULLITT (J. C.) A Review of Mr. Binney's Pamphlet on "The Privilege of the Writ of Habeas Corpus under the Constitution." By J. C. Bullitt. *Philadelphia: C. Sherman & Son.* 1862. 8vo, pp. 56. C. 9131

Fifty copies printed on large paper, in 4to, for John Campbell.

BULLIVANT (B.) Letter from Benj. Bullivant, of Boston, NA., to Mr. James Petiver, of the Museum in London, on the Natural History of Boston. 1697. 4to, 1 l. 9132

A manuscript? Title from an English catalogue.

BULLOCK (A. H.) Abraham Lincoln: the Just Magistrate, the Representative Statesman, the Practical Philanthropist. Address by Alex. H. Bullock, before the City Council and Citizens of Worcester, June 1, 1865. *Worcester: printed by Charles Hamilton.* [1865.] 8vo, pp. 49. H. 9133

Also: Massachusetts and the War Tax. Speech ... in the Massachusetts House of Representatives, April 10, 1862. *Boston: Wright & Potter, Printers.* 1862. 8vo, pp. 30. H. — The Mechanic Arts Favorable to Liberty and Social Progress. Address ... September 20, 1865. ... *Boston: Wright & Potter, Printers.* 1865. 8vo, pp. 28. H. — The Relations of the Educated Man with American Nationality. Address ... Williams College, August 1, 1864. *Boston: Wright & Potter, Printers.* 1864. 8vo, pp. 32. H.

BULLOCK (C.) Washington and other Poems. By Cynthia Bullock. *New York.* 1847. 12mo, pp. 108. 9134

BULLOCK (J. R.) Report of J. R. Bullock, Commissioner for adjusting the Claims of Rhode Island against the U. S., Jan., 1863. *Providence.* 1863. 8vo, pp. 11. M. 9135

BULLOCK (W.) Catalogue of the Exhibition, called Modern Mexico; containing a Panoramic View of the City, with Specimens of the Natural History of New Spain, and Models ... now open ... at the Egyptian Hall, Piccadilly. By W. Bullock, F.L.S. &c. &c. *London.* 1824. 8vo, pp. 27. Plate. BA.

BULLOCK. Description of the Panorama of the superb City of Mexico, and the surrounding scenery. Painted ... by R. Burford, Esq. By Mr. W. Bullock, Junior. *Mexico.* 1830. 8vo, pp. 16. + *Philadelphia.* 1833. 8vo, pp. 16. 9137

BULLOCK. A Description of the Unique Exhibition, called Ancient Mexico; collected on the Spot in 1823, by the Assistance of the Mexican Government, and now open for Public Inspection at the Egyptian Hall, Piccadilly. By W. Bullock, F.L.S. &c. &c. *London.* 8vo, Title, pp. 50. Plate. BA. 9138

BULLOCK. Sketch of a Journey through the Western States of North America, from New Orleans, by the Mississippi, Ohio, City of Cincinnati, and Falls of Niagara, to New York, in 1827. By W. Bullock, F.L.S., &c. With a Description of the New and Flourishing City of Cincinnati, by Messrs. B. Drake, and E. D. Mansfield. And a Selection from Various Authors on the Present Condition and Future Prospects of the Settlers, in the Fertile and Populous State of Ohio, containing Information useful to Persons desirous of Settling in America. ... *London: John Miller.* 1827. 12mo, pp. xxxi, viii, 135. 2 Maps. CN., H. 9139

"Mr. Bullock's journey occupies 31 pp., followed by a reprint of Drake and Mansfield's 'Cincinnati in 1826,' 92 pp., and an appendix of extracts from various works, 36 pp.; with a plan of Mr. Bullock's proposed settlement called Hygeia." — RICH, II. 194.

BULLOCK (W.), *F.L.S.* Six Months' Residence and Travels in Mexico; containing Remarks on the Present State of New Spain, its Natural Productions, State of Society, Manufactures, Trade, Agriculture, and Antiquities, &c. With Plates and Maps. By W. Bullock, F.L.S. Proprietor of the late London Museum. *London: John Murray.* 1824. 8vo, pp. xii, 532.

17 Plates. + Second Edition. *London: John Murray.* 1825. 2 vols., 18mo, pp. xvi, 255; vii, 264. Map, Table, and 10 Plates. C. 9140

This author was the first English traveller in Mexico since Father Gage, in 1640. There is a French translation in Tome XLI., as well as the following of Albert-Montémont's "Bibliothèque universelle des voyages," *Paris,* 1835. 8vo.

BULLOCK. Le Mexique en 1823, ou relation d'un voyage dans la Nouvelle-Espagne, contenant des notions exactes et peu connues sur la situation physique, morale et politique de ce pays. Ouvrage traduit de l'anglais par M***, précédé d'une introduction, et enrichi de pièces justificatives et de notes; par Sir John Byerley. *Paris: A. Eymery.* 1824. 2 vols., 8vo, pp. lxxii, 364; 368, 1 l., Atlas, pp. 11. 20 Plates, and Portrait. + Voyage au Méxique. ... *Paris: Lebigre.* 1831. 2 vols., 8vo, and Atlas.

The "Voyage" is merely the remainder sheets of the preceding work, with a new title-page.

BULLOCK. Mexico in 1823 of Beschrijving eener Reis door Nieuw-Spanje, voorafgegaan door eene Inleiding van Sir John Byerley, en verrijkt met historische bescheiden en aanteekeningen, zoo van den Vertaler, als van den Schrijver. Uit het Engelsch. *Delft, Weduwe: J. Allart.* 1825. 8vo. Plate.

BULLOCK. Reise nach Mexico im Jahre 1823. Aus dem Englischen. (Aus dem ethnogr. Archiv abgedr.) *Jena: Bran.* 1824. 8vo. 9143

BULLOCK. Sechs Monate in Mexiko, oder: Bermerkungen über den gegenwärtigen Zustand Neu-Spaniens. Aus dem Englischen übersetzt von Friedrich Schott. *Leipzig.* 1825. 2 pts., 8vo. + *Dresden: Hilscher.* 1825. 2 pts., 8vo. 9144

BULLOCK (W.) Virginia | Impartially examined, and left | to publick view, to be considered by all Judi- | cious and honest men. | Under which Title, is compre- | hended the Degrees from 34 to 39, wherein | lyes the rich and healthfull Countries of Roanock, | the now Plantations of Virginia | and Mary-land. | Looke not upon this Booke, as | those that are set out by private men, for private | ends; for being read, you'l find, the publick | good is the Authors onely aime. | For this Piece is no other then the Adventurers | or Planters faithfull Steward, disposing the Ad- | venture for the best advantage, advising | people of all degrees, from the highest | Master, to the meanest Servant, | how suddenly to raise their | fortunes. | Peruse the Table, and you shall

finde the | way plainely layd downe. | By William Bvllock, Gent. | 19 April, 1649. Imprimatur, Hen: Whaley. | *London: Printed by John Hammond, and are to be sold at his house | over-against S. Andrews Church in Holborne.* 1649. Sm. 4to, 6 l., pp. 66. H.

This rare book is dedicated to "the Earle of Arundell and Surrey, and the Lord Baltimore." Reprinted in Force's Tracts, Vol. III. *See* Ternaux, No. 685, and Rich, No. 271. Poulson's copy sold for \$80. Priced, by J. R. Smith, £6 16s. 6d.; Nuggets, £10 10s.

BULLOCK (W. H.) Across Mexico in 1864–65. Maps and Illustrations. *London: Macmillan and Co.* 1866. Post 8vo.

BULLUS (O.) Memorial to the Congress of the U. States, with the Documents accompanying the same, of Oscar Bullus, Commander, U. S. N. *New York: H. Cassidy, Printer.* 1856. 8vo, pp. 26. H. 9147

BULNES (M.) Biografica del Jeneral Don Manuel Bulnes, Presidente de la Republica de Chile. *Santiago.* 1846. 8vo.

BULOSE (M.) La république de Nicaragua dans l'Amérique Centrale. Par M. Bulose. *Berlin.* 1849. 8vo. 9148*a*

BÜLOW (Adm. Heinrich Dietrich). Der Freistaat von Nordamerika in seinem neuesten Zustand von D. von Bülow. *Berlin: Johann Friederich Unger.* 1797. 2 vols., 16mo, Title, 2 l., pp. 309; 286. H. 9149

"The free States of North America, described by Von Bülow, who attacks, 'with a sort of ecclesiastical hatred, the praisers of America, treating them as men systematically perverse and deceitful, of misanthropic hearts or insane minds, and as a designing sect of deluders, rather than as dupes.' He visited America twice between the years 1791 and 1796, and gives, on the whole, the most unfavorable account that had hitherto been published by any European traveller." — RICH, I. 407.

BÜLOW (*Baron* Alex. von). Auswanderung und Colonisation im Interesse des deutschen Handels. *Berlin: Mittler & Sohn in Comm.* 1849. 8vo, pp. xvi, 404. Map. 9150

BÜLOW. Der Freistaat Nicaragua in Mittel-Amerika, und seine Wichtigkeit für den Welthandel, den Ackerbau und die Colonisation. Nach eigener Anschauung und mit besonderer Bezugnahme auf die Berliner Colonisations-Gesellschaft für Central-Amerika dargestellt. Nebst einer Karte von Nicaragua und einer Colonisations-Plan. *Berlin: Hempel.* 1849. 8vo, pp. xii, 139. C. 9151

BÜLOW. Karte des Isthmus von Nicaragua und Panamá in Mittel-Amerika, mit den verschied. Canal Projecten zur Ver-

bindung des Atlantischen und Stillen Oceans nach J. Baily und den besten Quellen zusammengestellt. *Berlin: Besser's Verl.* 1851. Folio. 9152

BUMA (Johannes Acronius van). Argo Belgica, sive de Expeditione Belgica in Africa et America, sub Propraefectura Celeberrimi Herois Michaelis Ruteri, Carmen Chronicum, Annum Congruum MDLXV Literis Chronicis accurate designans. *Daventriæ.* 1688. 8vo. 9153

BUMPUS (A.) A Series of Letters, written by Amaziah Bumpus, and addressed to Gov. John Davis. Originally published in the Norfolk Democrat. ... *Dedham.* 1842. 8vo, pp. 40. H. 9154

BUMSTEAD (Geo.) [Sale] Catalogue of Books, &c. relating to ... America. Chronologically Arranged. *London.* 1856. 8vo, pp. 23. + [Another Catalogue.] *London.* 1864. 8vo. 9155

BUMSTEAD. ... A Catalogue of ... Books and Pamphlets relating to ... America, ... containing many Curious Articles Unknown to American Bibliographers, Chronologically Arranged. On Sale, ... by George Bumstead, ... *London.* MDCCCLXVI. 8vo. 9156

BUNCE (O. B.) Reconstruction. By Oliver B. Bunce. *New York.* 1862. 8vo, pp. 11. 9157

BUNCE. The Romance of the Revolution; being a History of the Personal Adventures, Heroic Exploits, and Romantic Incidents, as enacted in the War of Independence. Edited by Oliver B. Bunce. With Plates. *New York.* 1852. 8vo, pp. 454. 9158

BUNCH (*Mr.*) North America. Correspondence respecting the Withdrawal by the Government of the United States of Mr. Bunch's Exequatur as Her Majesty's Consul at Charleston. *London: Harrison and Sons.* Folio, pp. 27. 9159

[BUNDY (J. M.)] State Rights and the Appellate Jurisdiction of the Supreme Court of the United States. A Constitutional Argument. By a Member of the Rock County Bar. *Beloit: Journal and Courier Print.* 1860. 8vo, pp. 50. H.

BUNGAY (G. W.) The Bobolink Minstrel: or, Republican Songster, for 1860. Edited by George W. Bungay, ...

"Lincoln and Liberty." ... *New York: O. Hutchinson.* 1860. 24mo, pp. 72. H. 9161

BUNGAY. Crayon Sketches and Off-Hand Takings of Distinguished American Statesmen, Orators, Divines, Essayists. Editors, Poets, and Philanthropists. By George W. Bungay, *Boston: Stacey & Richardson.* 1852. 12mo, pp. 408. Portraits.

Reprinted as "Off-hand Takings; or Crayon Sketches of the Noticeable Men of our Age. By George W. Bungay. Embellished with Twenty Portraits on Steel." *New York.* [1854.] 12mo, pp. 408. B.

BUNGAY. Pen and Ink Portraits of the Senators, Assemblymen, and State Officers of the State of New York. *Albany: J. Munsell, Printer.* 1857. 8vo, pp. 83. 9163

BUNGENER (F.) Lincoln — sa vie son œuvre et sa mort par F. Bungener. *Lausanne: Georges Bridel.* 1865. 12mo, pp. 49.

BUNGENER. Lincoln. Zijn leven, werk en dood. Naar het Fransch. *Utrecht: J. J. H. Kremer.* 1866. Post 8vo, pp. 4, 118. 9165

BUNGENER. Abramo Lincoln Com' ei visse, qual'opera compiè, qual fu la sua morte *Firenze tipografia Claudiana.* 1866. 16mo, pp. 88. H. 9166

BUNKER (E. S.) A Reply to "The Proceedings and Minutes" of the "New York and Boston Steam-boat Company." By Elihu S. Bunker. [Motto.] *New-York: printed by George F. Nesbitt.* 1831. 8vo, pp. 24. H. 9167

Bunker's Hill. Extract from the Third Book of 'Washington,' a national Poem, awaiting Publication. [*Boston: J. H. Bang, printer.*] n. d. 8vo, pp. 8. H. 9168

Bunker Hill Monument. *Boston.* 1844. 16mo, pp. 8. 9169

Bunker Hill Declaration. September 10, 1840. [n. p. n. d.] 8vo, pp. 12. H. 9170

An Account of Bunker Hill Battle and Monument. *Boston: John Sey.* 1843. 12mo, pp. 36. 9171

Annual Addresses and Reports read before the Bunker Hill Soldiers' Relief Society. April 19, 1862, & April 20, 1863. [Vignette.] *Charlestown: William H. De Costa.* 1863. 8vo, pp. 26. 9172

Bunker Hill. The Monument. [A description of the Monument, and an account of the battle it commemorates.] ([*New York*] *Weekly Herald, June* 10, 1843.) H. 9173

Bunker Hill Monument Association. Act of Incorportion, By-Laws, and a List of the Original Members. ... with a Statement shewing the Magnitude and Progress of the Work. *Boston: printed by Samuel N. Dickinson.* 1830. 8vo, pp. 74. H.

Also: Address of the Bunker Hill Monument Association, to the Selectmen of the several Towns in Massachusetts. *Boston: A. Sampson, ... Printer.* 1824. 18mo, pp. 12. H. + Address to the Public Relative to the Progress of the Monument. *Charlestown.* [1830.] 8vo, pp. 17. — Ceremonies ... on the Displaying of the National Flag from the Monument, June 17, 1861. With the Annual Proceedings of the Association. [Vignette.] *Boston: George C. Rand & Avery, Printers.* 1861. 8vo, pp. 44. H. — Celebrations, ... of the Anniversary of the Battle of Bunker Hill, in 1850 and 1857. *Boston.* 1858. 8vo. Portraits. + Circular of the Directors. *Boston.* 1824. 8vo. B. — Inauguration of the Statue of Warren, by the Bunker Hill Monument Association. *Boston.* 1858. 8vo, pp. viii, 224, 3. Plate. + Petition ... to the Mayor and Aldermen of Charlestown to lay out a Street from City Square to Monument Square, with a Plan of the same. [*Boston.*] ... MDCCCLXVIII. 8vo, pp. 12. Plan. H. + Proceedings ... June 17, 1862. *Boston: Geo. C. Rand & Avery, Printers.* 1862. 8vo, pp. 20. H. + Proceedings ... on the Occasion of their Fortieth Anniversary, June 17, 1863. [Vignette.] *Boston: Press of Geo. C. Rand & Avery.* 1863. 8vo, pp. 23. H. — Proceedings of ... On the occasion of their Forty-first Anniversary, June 17, 1864. [Vignette.] *Boston: Press of Geo. C. Rand & Avery.* 1864. 8vo, pp. 31. — Proceedings of ... at the Annual Meeting, June 17, 1865; with the President's Address, ... and other Incidents of the Anniversary. *Boston:* ... MDCCCLXV. 8vo, pp. 82. H. — Proceedings of ... at the Annual Meeting, June 17, 1867; ... And the Reception of the President of the United States. *Boston:* ... M DCCC LXVII. 8vo, pp. 64. H. — [Report and Address of] a Committee of the Bunker Hill Monument Association [signed] Joseph E. Sprague, Sec'y. *Salem, (Mass.) February* 15, 1829. Folio, pp. (3). H. — Report of the President, Vice-Presidents, and several Directors, ... From June 1831 to June 1832. *Boston.* 1832. 8vo, pp. 15.

Battle of Bunker Hill. A Dramatic Poem. *See* [Brackenridge (H. H.)], Vol. II., No. 7184, and [Burk (John)], Vol. III, No. 9269.

In the catalogue of A. G. Greene's library, I found the following title: "Battle of Bunker's Hill. By a Lieutenant Colonel in the Continental Army."

Circular [respecting the Bunker-Hill Monument, Sept. 20, 1824. *Boston.* 1824.] 8vo, pp. 8. 9175

Colonne de Bunker Hill, Monument élevé à la Memoire des Patriotes Americains, morts sur le champ de Bataille ou fut remportée le premiére victoire de l'Independance. *Paris.* 1825. 8vo, pp. 40. 9176

"This pamphlet is composed of a Discourse by Mr. Webster, and another by M. Keratry." — RICH.

A Full and Correct Account of the Battle of Bunker Hill, Fought June 17, 1775. *Boston: June* 17, 1825. pp. 8. 9177

History of Bunker Hill Battle and Monument. *Charlestown.* 1843. 8vo, pp. 16. 9178

Names of Subscribers to the Bunker Hill Monument, 1830.

A Particular Account of the Battle of Bunker, or Breed's Hill, on the 17th of June, 1775. By a Citizen of Boston. Second Edition. *Boston: Cummings, Hilliard & Company.* 1825. 8vo, pp. 27. 9180

By Alden Bradford. *See* Vol. II., No. 7228.

Panoramic View from Bunker Hill Monument. Engraved ... from a drawing by R. P. Mallory. [A folded Engraving, with Letterpress description.] *Boston: Redding & Co.* ... 1848. 4to, pp. 16. BA. 9181

Services on Bunker Hill, for 17 June, 1825. [n. p. 1825.] 8vo, pp. 4. 9182

Sketches of Bunker Hill Battle. *See* [Ellis (George E.)]

BUNKLEY (J. M.) The Testimony of an Escaped Novice from the Sisterhood of St. Joseph, Emmetsburg, Maryland, the Mother-House of the Sisters of Charity in the United States. By Josephine M. Bunkley. *New York: Harper & Brothers.* 1855. 12mo, pp. 338. C. 9183

BUNN (A.) Old England and New England, in a Series of Views taken on the Spot. By Alfred Bunn. *London: Richard Bentley.* 1853. 2 vols., post 8vo, pp. xxi, 313; viii, 328. + *Philadelphia: reprinted by A. Hart.* 1853. 12mo, pp. xv, 13–315.

BUNN (M.) Short Narrative of the Life and Sufferings of Matthew Bunn after his Arrival at the British Garrison at Detroit, April 30, 1792, from his Indian Captivity. 1797. 12mo.

Reprinted as below:

BUNN. Narrative of the Life and Adventures of Matthew Bunn, (of Providence, R. I.) In an Expedition against the North-Western Indians, in the years 1791, 2, 3, 4, and 5. [7th edition, revised — 4000 copies.] *Batavia: Printed for the Author, by Adams and Thorf.* 1828. 12mo, pp. 59. 9186

BUNNELL (D. C.) The Travels and Adventures of David C. Bunnell, During twenty-three years of a Sea faring Life; Containing an Accurate Account of the Battle of Lake Erie. Under the Command of Com. Oliver H. Perry: Together with Ten Years' Services in the Navy of the United States. Also Service Among the Greeks. Imprisonment Among the Turks, &c., &c. Written by Himself. *Palmyra, N. Y.: E. B. Grandin.* 1831. 12mo, pp. 199. Map. 9187

BUNNER (E.) History of Louisiana, from its First Discovery and Settlement to the Present Time. By E. Bunner. *New York: Harpers.* 1841. 12mo, pp. xxxi, 14–267. BA. + *New York.* 1846. 12mo. 9188

Forms Vol. 176 of Harper's "Family Library."

BUNNER (R.) A Discourse ... on the 8th Day of October, 1834, ... on the Genius and Spirit of the People, and the Age that colonized the Free States of North America. By R. Bunner. *New-York: G. F. Hopkins & Son. December,* 1834. 8vo, pp. 22. B., C., H. 9189

BUNSEN (C. C. J.) The Law of Slavery in the United States. By Christian Charles Josias Bunsen ... . *Boston: Little, Brown and Company.* 1863. 12mo, pp. 12. BA. 9190

Extracted from his "Hippolytus and his Age. *London.* 1854."

BUNSTER (G.) Observations on Capt. F. B. Head's Reports, Relating to the Failure of the Rio de la Plata Mining Association. By Lieut. Grosvenor Bunster, R. N. *London.* 1827. 8vo. 9191

BUNTING (R. F.) The Mysteries of Providence. A Fast-Day Discourse, delivered August 21st, 1863, in Camp on Silver Creek, near Rome, Georgia. By Rev. R. F. Bunting, Chaplain Terry's Texas Rangers (Eighth Texas Cavalry). *Atlanta, G.: J. J. Toon & Co.* 1864. 8vo, pp. 23. 9192

BUNTLINE (Ned), *pseudon.* *See* Judson (E. Z. C.)

BUONAPARTE in the West Indies. *See* Louverture (Toussaint).

BUONFIGLIO COSTANZO (Giuseppe). Historia Siciliana ... . *Venetia: Ciera.* 1604. 2 pts., 4to, 22 l., pp. 692. + *Messina: Chiaramonte.* 1738. 3 pts., folio, 4 l., pp. 463, 472, 10 l.

Containing an account of Columbus and his discoveries in America, including the story of the Egg.

BUQCELLOS, *pseudon.* *See* [Blocquel (S.)], Vol. II., No. 5946.

BURBANK (C.) Speech of Judge Burbank, in the Senate of California, February 7th, 1861, on the Union Resolutions. *Sacramento: J. Anthony & Co., printers.* 1861. 8vo, pp. 19. H.

BURBANK. Speech of Judge Burbank, in the Senate of California, Febuary 27, 1861, on the Crittenden Compromise Resolutions. *Sacramento: J. Anthony & Co.* 1861. 8vo, pp. 16.

BURBANK. Defence of Maj. Gen. Caleb Burbank, ... before the General Court-Martial ... at Worcester, on the 8th day of Sept., 1818. ... *Worcester: Wm. Manning.* 1819. 8vo, pp. 60.

BURBANK (Gardner). Defence of [Lieut. Col.] Burbank before a Court Martial, at Worcester, Sept. 8, 1818. *Worcester: Wm. Manning.* 1819. 8vo, pp. 44. 9197

BURCH (S.) A Digest of the Laws of the Corporation of the City of Washington, to the First of June, 1823; With an appendix, containing the Acts of Cession from Maryland and Virginia, the Laws of the United States relating to the District of Columbia, &c. Compiled by Samuel Burch. *Washington: James Wilson.* 1823. 8vo, pp, 364, Index, vii. 3 Tables.

BURCH. General Index to the Laws of the United States, from March 4th, 1789, to March 3d, 1827, including all Treaties entered into between these periods. ... Compiled by Samuel Burch. ... *Washington City.* 1828. 8vo. C. 9199

BURCHARD (C.) A Statement of Facts in Relation to the Case of Rev. Jacob Knapp. By Charles Burchard ... . *New York: the Author.* 1846. 8vo, pp. 45. B., H. 9200

BURCHARD (J.) Sermons, Addresses & Exhortations, by Rev. Jedediah Burchard: With an Appendix, containing some account of Proceedings during Protracted Meetings, held under his Direction, in Burlington, Williston, and Hinesburgh, Vt., December, 1835, and January, 1836. By C. G. Eastman. *Burlington: Chauncey Goodrich.* 1836. 12mo, pp. vi, (1), 119, (1).

"Burchardism" made a religious epoch in the history of portions of Vermont.

BURCHARD (N.) Address on Agriculture: ... 6th Sept., 1847, by Hon. Nathan Burchard ... . Accompanied by Remarks on the Establishment of an Agricultural College, ... by Charles L. Fleischman ... . *New York.* 1847. 8vo, pp. 28.

BURCHARD (S. D.) Causes of National Solicitude. A Sermon preached in the Thirteenth Street Presbyterian Church, New York, on Thanksgiving Day, Nov. 25, 1847. By Rev. Samuel D. Burchard. *New York: S. W. Benedict.* 1848. 8vo, pp. 23. H. 9203

BURCHELL (W. F.) Memoir of Thomas Burchell, Twenty-two years a Missionary in Jamaica. By his Brother, Wm. Fitzer Burchell. *London.* 1849. 12mo, pp. 428. P. 9204

BURCHETT (J.) A Complete History of the most remarkable Transactions at Sea, from the Earliest Accounts of Time to the Conclusion of the last War with France, including the most considerable Naval Expeditions, Sea Fights, Stratagems, Discoveries, and Maritime Occurrences, by Josiah Burchett. *London: J. Waltoe.* 1720. Folio, 28 l., pp. 799, 17 l. 8 Maps, 1 Plate. C. 9205

BURCHETT Memoirs of Transactions at Sea during the War with France; Beginning in 1688, and Ending in 1697. ... By Josiah Burchett Esq; Secretary to the Admiralty. *London.* 1703. 8vo, 22 l., pp. 408. BA., N. 9206

Contains an account of various expeditions to the West Indies.

BURCHETT. Mr. Burchett's Justification of his Naval Memoirs, in answer to the reflections of Col. Lillingston on that part which relates to Cape François and Port de Paix. With some short Observations on our West India Expedition. *London.* 1704. 8vo, pp. 166. 9207

BÜRCK (August). Magellan, oder die erste Reise am die Erde. Nach den vorhanderen Quellen dargestellt. Mit Magellan's Bilde. *Leipzig: B. Tauchnitz jan.* 1844. 8vo.

BURCK (Wm.) *See* [Burke (Edmund)].

BURCKE. La Intolerancia Politico-Religiosa Vindicada ó Refutacion del Discurso que en favour de la Tolerancia Religiosa Publicó D. Guil. Burcke, en la Gaceta de Caracas del Martes 19 de Febrero, 1811. *Reimpresso in Mexico.* 1826. 8vo.

The Burdell Case. Closing Argument of Charles Edwards, advocate for infant next of kin of Harvey Burdell, and in opposition to the claim of Emma Augusta Cunningham, for letters of Administration. *New York: J. S. Voorhies.* [1857?] 8vo, pp. 66. Map. 9210

BURDER (G.) The Welch Indians; or, a Collection of Papers, respecting a people whose Ancestors emigrated from Wales to America, in the year 1170, with Prince Madoc, (three hundred years before the First Voyage of Columbus), And who are said now to inhabit a beautiful Country on the West Side of the Mississippi. Dedicated to the Missionary Society by George Burder. *London: T. Chapman.* [1797.] 8vo, pp. 35. 9211

No date on the title, but the dedication is dated March 10, 1797.

BURDETT (C.) The Beautiful Spy. An exciting story of Army and High Life in New York in 1776. By Charles Burdett. *Philadelphia: J. E. Potter.* 1865. 12mo, pp. 437.

BURDETT. Life and Adventures of Christopher Carson, the celebrated Rocky Mountain Hunter, Trapper, and Guide. Also, his services to the United States government, as guide to the expeditions under Colonel J. C. Fremont and others. By Charles Burdett. *Philadelphia.* 1860. 12mo. C. 9213

BURDETT. Margaret Moncrieffe; the first love of Aaron Burr. A romance of the Revolution. With an appendix containing the letters of Colonel Burr to "Kate" and "Eliza," and from "Leonora," etc. By Charles Burdett. *New York: Derby & Jackson.* 1860. 12mo, pp. 497. C. 9214

BURDICK (W.) Massachusetts Manual: or Political and Historical Register; and Almanac. ... By William Burdick. No. 1. January 1, 1814. *Boston: Charles Callender.* [1814.] 12mo, pp. 67. + Vol. I. 1814. 12mo, pp. 219. 9215

BURDICK. An Oration on the Nature and Effects of the Art of Printing. Delivered in Franklin-Hall, July 5, 1802, before the Boston Franklin Association. By William Burdick ... . *Boston: Printed by Munroe & Francis.* 1802. 8vo, pp. 31. H.

Bureau of Refugees, Freedmen, and Abandoned Lands, 1867. Fourth Semi-Annual Report on Schools for Freedmen, July 1st, 1867. By J. W. Alvord. *Washington.* 1867. 8vo, pp. 96.

BURFORD (Robert). Description of a View of the Falls of Niagara. Now Exhibiting at the Panorama, Charles Street, Boston. *Boston.* 1837. 8vo, pp. 12. 9218

BURFORD. Description of the Panorama of the Superb City of Mexico, by Robert Burford. *New York.* 1828. 8vo, pp. 16. + *Boston.* 1828. W. 9219

BURGAIN (Luis Antonio). Fernandes Vieira, ou Pernambuco libertado: drama em quatro actos, e em verso ... . *Rio de Janeiro: typ. Austral.* 1845. 4to, pp. 32. 9220

BURGAIN. O vaticinio: drama allegorico em um acto, e em verso. *Rio de Janeiro* (?) 9221

"Refers to the minority of the Emperor of Brazil. Was first printed in the journal 'Despertador,' and afterwards separately." — DA SILVA.

BURGE (William). Extract from Mr. Burge's Printed Letter to the Rt. Hon. Sir George Murray, and Observations thereon; intended as a Short Exposition of the Proceedings of the Government, and the Supreme Court of Jamaica, in the case of Lecesne and Escoffery. [n. p. n. d.?] 8vo. 9222

BURGE. Jamaica. The Speech of W. Burge ... Agent for Jamaica, at the Bar of the House of Commons, against the Bill entitled "An Act to provide for the Enactment of certain Laws in the Island of Jamaica." ... 7th June, 1839. From Hansard's Parliamentary Debates, Session 1839. [n. p.] 1839. 8vo, pp. 40. H. 9223

BURGE. Jamaica. The Speech of W. Burge ... at the Bar of the House of Commons, against the Bill intituled "An Act to make Temporary Provision for the Government of Jamaica." Monday, 22nd April 1839. *London: Calkin & Budd,* [*etc.*]. 1839. 8vo, pp. 89. BA. 9224

BURGE. A Reply to the Letter by the Marquis of Sligo to the Marquis of Normanby, relative to the Present State of Jamaica, &c. By William Burge, Esq., One of her Majesty's Counsel and the Agent for Jamaica. *London: Calkin & Budd.* 1839. 8vo, pp. 64. 9225

BÜRGER (Ernest Moritz). Sendschreiben und die evangelischen Gemrinde, zunachst in Wisconsin Missouri, Preussen und Sachsen. *Leipzig: Kössling,* 1846. 8vo. 9226

[BURGER (Louis).] Report of the Committee appointed to investigate the Capacities and Advantages of the New McCarty Gun. *New York: S. S. Motley, Printer.* 1862. 8vo, pp. 10.

BURGES (B.) A Short Account of the Solar System, and of Comets in General; together with a Particular Account of the Comet that will appear in 1789. By Bartholomew Burges. *Boston: B. Edes & Son.* 1789. 16mo, pp. 16, 2 l. H., N. 9228

BURGES (T.) Battle of Lake Erie, with Notices of Commodore Elliot's Conduct in that Engagement. By Hon. Tristam Burges. *Providence: Brown & Cady.* 1839. 12mo, pp. xv, 132. Diagrams. + *Philadelphia: W. Marshall & Co.* 1839. 12mo, pp. xv, 117. 9232

[BURGES.] Reasons why the Hon. Elisha R. Potter should not be a Senator in Congress. By One of the People. *Providence.* 1834. 8vo, pp. 12. 9233

BURGES. The Valley of Alvarado, or the Spy of Tennessee; a Legend of Mexico. [A poem.] By Tristam Burges. *Providence, R. I.* 1847. 8vo, pp. 25. S. 9234

BURGES. War Necessary, Just and Beneficial. An Oration pronounced on Commencement at Rhode Island College, Sept. 4, 1799. By Tristam Burges, a Candidate for the Second Degree. *Providence: B. Wheeler.* 1799. 8vo, pp. 8. W. 9235

Also: Address before the Rhode Island Peace Society, June 29, 1819. *Providence: Joseph Knowles.* 1849. 8vo, pp. 20. — Address to the Rhode-Island Society for the Encouragement of Domestick Industry ... at Pawtuxet, October 17, 1821. ... *Providence: Miller and Hutchens. August,* 1822. 8vo, pp. 29, 1 l. BA. — Address to the Landholders and Farmers of Newport County, delivered at a meeting of the friends of Messrs. Pearce and Burges, ... August 7, 1829. Third edition. *Providence: Daily Advertiser.* 1829. 8vo, pp. 22. — The Art of Excelling; an Oration ... September 5, 1798. *Providence: John Carter, Jun.* 1799. 8vo, pp. 22 — A Brief of the Remarks made before the Committee on Rail-ways and Canals, on the Petition of the Seekonk Branch Rail-road Co. [n. p. n. d.] 8vo, pp. 37. H. — A Brief Sketch of the Remarks delivered at East Greenwich at a Convention of National Republicans, on the 23d August, 1832. *Providence: Wm. Marshall & Co.* 1832. 8vo, pp. 15. — The Cause of Man; an Oration, together with Valedictory Addresses, pronounced at the Commencement of Rhode Island College, Sept. 7, A.D., 1796. *Providence: Carter & Wilkinson.* 1796. 8vo, pp. 17. — Liberty, Glory and Union or American Independence: an Oration, pronounced before the People of Providence, July 4th, A.D. 1810. ... *Providence: Dunham & Hawkins. Printers.* [1810.] 8vo, pp. 22. H. — An Oration, delivered in ... Providence, on the Fourth of July, 1801 ... . *Providence: John Carter.* [1801.] 8vo, pp. 22. H., N. — An Oration, delivered before the Rhode Island Federal Adelphi, Sept. 9, 1831. *Providence: Weden & Knowles.* 1831. 8vo, pp. 36. — An Oration pronounced before the Citizens of Providence, on the Fourth of July, 1831. ... *Providence: W. Marshall & Co.* 1831. 8vo, pp. 32. — The Plough and the Sickle, or Rhode Island in the War of the Revolution of 1776. *Providence: B. T. Albro, for the author.* 1846. 8vo, pp. 28. [Relates to the State Debt.] — Remarks sent to the People who Celebrated the Fourth of July, 1835, at Woonsocket Falls. *Woonsocket Falls: Sherman & Wilder,* 1835. 8vo, pp. 16. — Remarks ... at the Celebration of the Fourth of July in Clayville, R. I., in Reply to a Sentiment expressed at the Dinner given on that Occasion. ... *Providence: Daily Advertiser Office.* 1829. 8vo, pp. 31. — Report ... From the Select Committee of the House of Representatives of the United Saates, to which was referred the Memorial of the Officers and Soldiers of the Rhode Island Brigade ... February 25, 1835. *Washington.* 1835. 8vo, pp. 40. — Speech ... on the Judiciary Bill. ... Jan. 23, 1826. *Washington: printed by Gales & Seaton.* 1826. 12mo, pp. 24. — Speech ... on the

Amendatory Bills for Relief of the Survivors of the Revolutionary Army, ... January 4, 1827. *Washington: printed by Gales & Seaton.* 1827. 8vo, pp. 31. H. — Speech ... Jan. 11. 1827, on Revolutionary Claims. *Providence.* [1827.] 8vo. W. — Speech ... on the State of the Union, March 29, 1828, on Mr. Mallory's Motion. ... [*Washington.* 1828.] 8vo, pp. 37. H. + Second Edition. *Washington.* [1828.] 8vo, pp. 42. W. — Speech ... April 21st, A.D. 1828. on the Tariff. *Washington: Way and Gideon.* 1828. 8vo, pp. 88. — Speech ... May 10, 1830. on the Bill for the more Effectual Collection of the Duties on Imports, ... *Providence.* 1830. 8vo. — Speech ... on the ... the Salary appropriated for the Minister to Russia. ... February 3, 1831. *Washington: printed by Gales & Seaton.* 1831. 8vo, pp. 53. H. — Speech ... at the Public Dinner given him by the Citizens of New York, March 30, 1831. [1831.] 12mo, pp. 31. — Speech ... in the Case of Samuel. Houston, charged with a Violation of the Rights and Powers of the House, by assaulting the Hon. William Stanberry, a Member from Ohio, for Words spoken in Debate. Delivered ... May 11, 1832. *Washington: printed by Gales and Seaton.* 1832. 8vo, pp. 32. H., S. — Speech ... on the Bill to reduce and otherwise alter the Duties on Imports. ... Jan. 28 and 29, 1833. *Washington: printed by Gales and Seaton.* 1833. 8vo, pp. 52. H. — ... Speech delivered ... in the House of Representatives, March 18, 20, & 26, 1834, when ... Reasons for Removing the Public Money, were under Consideration ... . *Washington: printed by Gales and Seaton.* 1834. 8vo, pp. 83. H. — Speech ... delivered at a Meeting of his Fellow Citizens, in the Town House in Providence, on Friday Evening, March 3, 1835. [*Providence.*] 1835. 8vo, pp. 16. — The Spirit of Independence: An Oration, delivered before the Providence Association of Mechanics and Manufacturers, at their Annual Election, April 14, 1800. With Odes. *Providence.* 1800. 8vo, pp. 28. — A Statement of some Leading Principles adopted by General Jackson, and of the Effects of these Principles and Measures on the Union, Prosperity and Constitution of the American People. An Address to the Citizens of Rhode Island, in Answer to their Call on the Delegation of this State in Congress. *Providence: Wm. Marshall.* 1832. 8vo, pp. 12.

BURGESS (C.) The Life and Character of Abraham Lincoln. With some lessons from his Death. A Discourse delivered in the M. E. Church at a Union Meeting of the Baptist, Methodist, and Presbyterian Congregations of Panama, April 30th, 1865. By Rev. C. Burgess, Pastor of Presbyterian Church. Published by request. *Jamestown, N. Y.: Bishop Bro's.* 1865. 8vo, pp. 20. 9236

BURGESS (D.) The Craftsman; a Sermon. Composed by the late Daniel Burgess, and intended to be preached by him in the High Times [*sic*], but prevented by the Burning of his Meeting House. *Philadelphia: Printed by S. Keimer.* [*about* 1725.] Sm. 4to, pp. 21. P. 9237

At the end: "Now in the Press, a Dialogue betwixt a Quaker and a Hirling Priest. Printed in England, and now to be reprinted, to prevent (if possible), the Spreading of the Contagion of the Priestly Delusions in America."

BURGESS. Rules for Hearing the Word of God. ... . By Daniel Burgess ... . The Third Edition. *Boston: Thomas Fleet.* 1742. 8vo, 2 l., pp. 18. 9238

[BURGESS (Ebenezer), *D.D.*] Address to the American Society

for colonizing the Free People of Colour of the United States. ... *Washington: printed by Davis and Force.* 1818. 8vo, pp. 56.

BURGESS. Burgess Genealogy. Memorial of the Family of Thomas and Dorothy Burgess, who were settled at Sandwich, in the Plymouth Colony, in 1637. *Boston: Press of T. R. Marvin & Son.* 1865. 8vo, Title, pp. 196. Portraits. H. 9240

[BURGESS.] Dedham Pulpit: or, Sermons by the Pastors of the First Church in Dedham, in the XVIIth and XVIIIth Centuries; with a Centennial Discourse by the Present Pastor. *Boston: Perkins & Marvin.* 1840. 8vo, pp. viii, 517. 9241

[BURGESS (George).] Pages from the Ecclesiastical History of New England, during the Century between 1740 and 1840. *Boston: James B. Dow.* 1847. 16mo, pp. 126. + *Boston: Dutton & Co.* 1864. 12mo. M. 9242

BURGESS. Poems of the Rt. Rev. George Burgess, D.D. Bishop of Maine. With An Introduction by [A. C. Coxer]. *Hartford: Brown & Gross.* 1868 [1867]. 16mo, pp. viii, (2), 276. B. 9243

"Patriotic Poems," pp. 226–235. Also: Address at the Funeral of Bishop T. C. Brownell, D.D., LL.D. ... *Cambridge.* 1865. 4to. — A Discourse delivered before the Maine Historical Society, at Brunswick, August 2, 1854. By George Burgess, D.D., Bishop of the Protestant Episcopal Church in Maine. 8vo, pp. 25. (Included in the Maine Historical Collections, Vol. IV.) — A Sermon at the Consecration of St. John's Church, Hartford, April 20, 1842. *Hartford.* 1842. 8vo, pp. 24. — ... A Sermon, Oct. 28, 1853, ... at the Consecration of the Rev. W. Ingraham Kip, D.D., as Missionary Bishop of California. By the Right Rev. George Burgess, D.D. *Albany.* 1853. 8vo, pp. 25. S. — A Sermon ... September 12, 1860, at the Admission of the Rev. Frederic D. Huntington, D.D. to the Holy Order of Deacons. ... . *Boston: E. P. Dutton and Company.* 1860. 8vo. — Sermon on the Death of Hon. Robert H. Gardiner, delivered at Christ Church, Gardiner, Me. ... April 3, 1864. *Boston: printed by John Wilson and Son.* 1864. 8vo, pp: 20. H.

BURGESS (Wilson) *and* CANDLER (John). Narrative of a Recent Visit to Brazil, ... to present an Address on the Slave Trade and Slavery, issued by the Religious Society of Friends. *London: Edward Marsh.* 1853. 8vo, 5¾ sheets. 9244

[BURGH (James).] An Account of the First Settlement, Laws, Form of Government, & Police of the Cessares, a People of South America. In Nine Letters, from Mr. Vander Neck, one of the Senators of that Nation to his Friend in Holland. With Notes by the Editor. *London.* 1764. 8vo. C. 9245

"The Cessares are a race of white Indians in Chile, about whom, however, very little is known. The present work adds nothing to our information respecting them, being

merely a new version of Sir Thomas More's 'Utopia.' It was written, according to Nichols, by the celebrated author of the 'Dignity of Human Nature,' Mr. Burgh." — RICH. The book is not worth the space it occupies here; it is as veracious as "Peter Wilkins," but not so imaginative.

BURGH. Political Disquisitions; or an Enquiry into public Errors, Defects, Abuses, Illustrated by and established upon Facts and Remarks, extracted from a Variety of Authors, Ancient and Modern. Calculated to draw the timely Attention of Government and People, to a due Consideration of the Necessity, and the Means, of Reforming those Errors, Defects, and Abuses; of Restoring the Constitution, and Saving the State. By J. Burgh. ... *London.* 1774. 3 vols., 8vo. + *Philadelphia: Robert Bell.* M,DCC,LXXV. 3 vols., 8vo, pp. xxiii, (viii), 486; vii, (vii), 477; xii, 460, Index, (53). BA., S. 9246

"Burgh's Political Disquisitions are said so have produced a great effect upon the mind of the American colonists during the Revolution." — W. GOWANS.

BURGOA (Francisco de). Historia Geográfica descripcion de la parte Septentrional, del polo ártico de la America, y nueva Iglesia de las Indias Occidentales. *Mexico.* 1674. Folio.

BURGOA. Palestra historial de virtudes, y exemplares apostolicos, fundada del zelo de heroes de la orden de Predicadores en el nuevo mundo de la América en las Indias Occidentales. *Mexico: Imprenta de Juan Ruyz.* 1670. Folio, Frontispiece, 11 l., text, 269 l., Index, 4 l. 9248

A very rare book. The author was a native of Antequera de Oaxaca, and, during his early life, was missionary amongst the Indians, and afterwards Provincial of his Province.

BURGOYNE (J.) Condolence; | An | Elegiac Epistle | from | Lieut. Gen. B–rg–yne, | Captured at Saratoga, Oct. 17. 1777, | To | Lieut. Gen. Earl. C–rnw–ll–s, | Captured at York-Town, Oct. 17. 1781. | With | Notes by the Editor. | *London:* | *Printea for T. Evans,* ... MDCCLXXXII. | 4to, pp. 32. 9249

BURGOYNE. The Dramatic and Poetical Works of the Late Lieut. Gen. J. Burgoyne; to which is prefixed Memoirs of the Life of the Author. Embellished with Copper-Plates. *London: printed by C. Whittingham.* 1808. 2 vols., 12mo, pp. 235; 244. 5 Plates. BA., P. 9250

Also on large paper, 8vo. The Memoirs include a sketch of the author's campaign in America. *See* M. R., LVII. 99.

BURGOYNE. A Letter from Lieut. Gen. Burgoyne to his Constituents, upon his late Resignation; with the Correspond-

ences between the Secretaries of War and him, relative to his return to America. *London: J. Almon.* MDCCLXXIX. 8vo, Title, pp. 37. + Second Edition. C., H. [*Ibid.*] + The Fourth Edition. [*Ibid.*] + The Fifth Edition. [*Ibid,*]. H. + The Sixth Edition. *London: J. Almon.* MDCCLXXIX. 8vo, Title, pp. 37. 9251

After General Burgoyne's surrender, he was allowed to return to England on parole. Thinking himself ill treated by the government, and having been elected Member of Parliament for Preston, he joined the opposition; whereupon an official order was sent to him, signifying that it was the King's pleasure that he should return to America and rejoin his captive army. He remonstrated, and was again ordered, and, in consequence, resigned all his civil and military employments. In this letter he gives an explanation of his conduct. *See* M. R., LXI. 389; Rich, I. 278.

BURGOYNE. The Military Opinions of General Sir John Burgoyne. Collected and edited by Captain the Hon. George Wrottesley. *London: Bentley.* 1859. 8vo, pp. 480. 9252

BURGOYNE. Orderly Book of Lieut. Gen. John Burgoyne, from his Entry into the State of New York until his Surrender at Saratoga, 16th Oct., 1777. From the Original Manuscript deposited at Washington's Headquarters, Newburgh, N. Y. Edited by E. B. O'Callaghan, M.D. [Motto.] *Albany, N. Y.: J. Munsell* M.D.CCC.LX. 4to, pp. xxxiv, 221. 6 Plates.

Munsell's Historical Series, No. VII. One hundred copies printed on fcap 4to, and ten copies on large paper.

[BURGOYNE.] The Speech of a General Officer in the House of Commons, February 20, 1775. [n. p. n. d.] 4to, pp. 8. W.

BURGOYNE. A State of the Expedition from Canada, as laid before the House of Commons, by Lieutenant-General Burgoyne, and verified by Evidence; with a Collection of Authentic Documents, and an Addition of many Circumstances which were prevented from appearing before the House by the Prorogation of Parliament. Written and Collected by Himself, and dedicated to the Officers of the Army he commanded. *J. Almon.* MDCCLXXX. 4to, pp. viii, 140, Appendix, pp. 62, 1 l. Maps and Plans. H. + The Second Edition. *London: J. Almon.* MDCCLXXX. 8vo, pp. ix, (2), 191, Appendix, cix. 6 Maps and Plans. 9255

"General Burgoyne writes well. His very interesting story is told in a masterly manner, and the materials of which it is composed will be held in great estimation by historians, who shall record the events of the unhappy war, to which they owe their birth." — M. R., LXII. 247.

BURGOYNE. A Supplement to the State of the Expedition

from Canada, containing General Burgoyne's Orders, respecting the Principal Movements, and Operations of the Army to the Raising of the Siege of Ticonderoga. *London: J. Robson.* MDCCLXXX. 4to, Title, pp. 26. + *New York: Privately Reprinted* [*for F. S. Hoffman*]. 1865. Rl. 4to, pp. 26. 9256

The New York edition was printed mostly for presentation. The work was originally published without Gen. Burgoyne's authority. *See* M. R., XLII. 492.

BURGOYNE. The Substance of General Burgoyne's Speeches, on Mr. Vyner's Motion, on the 26th of May; and upon Mr. Hartley's Motion, on the 28th of May, 1778. With an Appendix, containing General Washington's Letter to General Burgoyne. &c. *London: J. Almon.* MDCCLXXVIII. 8vo, 2 l., pp. 42, Appendix, 3 l. + The Second Edition. [*Ibid.*] + The Third Edition. [*Ibid.*] + The Fourth Edition. [*Ibid.*] 8vo, 2 l., pp. 42, Appendix, 3 l. + The Fifth Edition. [*Ibid.*] + The Sixth Edition. [*Ibid.*] MDCCLXXVIII. + *Dublin.* 1778. 8vo. C. 9257

See M. R., LVIII. 476.

BURGOYNE. A Brief Examination of the Plan and Conduct of the Northern Expedition in America, in 1777. And of the Surrender of the Army under the Command of Lieutenant-General Burgoyne. *London: T. Hookham.* M DCC LXXIX. 8vo, pp. 52. 9258

See Monthly Review, First Series, LIX. 320.

BURGOYNE. Briefe des Generals Lee, und des Generals Burgoyne bey Gelegenheit der Ankunft des letztern in Boston. *Braunschweig.* 1777. 8vo, pp. 8. C. 9259

BURGOYNE. An Enquiry into, and Remarks upon the Conduct of Lieutenant General Burgoyne. The Plan of Operation for the Campaign of 1777, the instructions from the Secretary of State, and the Circumstances that led to the Loss of the Northern Army. *London: Matthews.* 1780. 8vo, pp. 50, Advertisement, 1 l. 9260

See M. R., LXII. 174. A poetical piece, called the "Blockade of Boston," has been attributed to General Burgoyne. *See* McFingal, c. IV. For Burgoyne's Original Letters, *see* Mass. Hist. Coll., v. 2; for a Proclamation dated July 10, 1777, *see* N. Hamp. Hist. Soc. Coll., v. 2.

BURGOYNE. Essay on Modern Martyrs: With a Letter to General Burgoyne. [Motto.] *London: Messrs. Paynes and R. Faulder.* M DCC LXXX. 8vo, Half-Title, Title, pp. 52. BA.

Supposed to be written by a Mr. Dallas.

BURGOYNE. The Lamentations of General Burgoyne, After he became the Prisoner of the Rebels. [n. p. n. d.] 18mo, pp. 8. 9262

A satirical poem.

BURGOYNE. A Letter to Lieut. Gen. Burgoyne, on his Letter to his Constituents. *London: T. Becket.* 1779. 8vo, Title, pp. 35. BA. 9263

"Instead of the liberal manner of a gentleman, this writer attacks Mr. Burgoyne with the ferocity of one of his own savages, reeking and hot from the murder of poor Miss McRay" [*sic*]. — M. R. LXI. 389.

BURGOYNE. A Letter to Lieut. Gen. Burgoyne, occasioned by a Second Edition of his State of the Expedition from Canada. *London: G. Kearsley.* 1780. 8vo, pp. 32. H. 9264

"The great object of this letter is to defend Lord G. Germaine, and Government in general, from the charges brought against them, in the prefatory speech to the state of the expedition. The general is attacked with great severity, and Sir William Howe comes in for a share of the author's keen animadversion." — RICH, I. 285. *See* M. R., January, 1781.

BURGOYNE. Remarks on General Burgoyne's State of the Expedition from Canada. [Motto.] *London: G. Wilkie.* MDCCLXXX. 8vo, pp. 60. BA. 9265

"A criticism in defence of the ministry." — M. R., LXI. 322.

BURGOYNE. A Reply to Lieutenant General Burgoyne's Letter to his Constituents. ... [Motto.] *London: J. Wilkie.* MDCCLXXIX. 8vo, Half-Title, Title, pp. 46. + The Second Edition. *London: J. Wilkie.* MDCCLXXIX. 8vo, 2 l., pp. 46. + The Third Edition. *London: J. Wilkie.* MDCCLXXIX. 8vo, 2 l., pp. 46. C. 9266

"This writer merits commendation for the decent and candid strains in which he writes. He does not, like the general's antagonist above mentioned, assail with a blunted tomahawk. He cuts up like a skillful surgeon, and dissects his subject with the dexterity of an able anatomist." — M. R., LXI. 389. Attributed to Sir John Dalrymple, but with more probability to George Germaine, Lord Sackville, who was colonial secretary during the American Revolution.

BURGOYNE. Reponse à un des Articles des Annales Politique de M. Linguet concernant la Defaite du Gen. Burgoyne en Amérique. *Londres, l'Auteur,* 1788. 8vo. 9267

[BURGWIN (H.)] Address to the Parishioners of St. Peter's Church, Pittsburg. [n. p.] *W. G. Johnston & Co., Printers.* 8vo, pp. 15. H. 9268

BURGY (J. J.) Recueil de tares et usages des principales villes de commerce de l'Europe, des États-Unis d'Amérique et d'Égypte. *Mulhausen: Risler.* 1825. 8vo. 9269

[BURK (Edward).] The Hurricane: a Poem, by an Eyewitness. .Also, Historical Notices of St. Domingo, from the seizure of Toussaint l'Ouverture to the Death of Christophe. With illustrations. *Bath.* 1844. 8vo, pp. 75. C. 9270

BURK (J.) Bunker Hill; or, the Death of Gen. Warren: an Historic Tragedy. In Five Acts. By John Burk ... . As performed at the Theatres in America, for fourteen nights, with unbounded applause. *New York: P. Greenleaf.* 1797. 12mo, pp. 55. + *New York: D. Longworth.* 1817. 12mo, pp. 44.

Another edition has the following title:

BURK. Bunker-Hill; or the Death of General Warren; an American Historical Play in Five Acts. By John Burke [*sic*], Author of the History of Virginia, etc. *Baltimore: Printed by Richard D. Rider.* 1808. 12mo, pp. 39. 9272

BURK. The History of Virginia, from its First Settlement to the Present Day. By John Burk. *Petersburg, Virginia: the Author.* 1804. Vol. I., 8vo, 2 l., pp. iv, 348; Vol. II., *Petersburg,* 1805, pp. 335, Appendix, lxii; Vol. III., pp. 469. The History of Virginia, commenced by John Burk, and continued by Skelton Jones, and Louis Hue Girardin; Vol. IV., *Petersburg, Virginia, Printed by M. W. Dunnavant, for the Proprietors,* 1816, 8vo, pp. 538, xv, [1 l.] H., N. 9273

Complete sets are very scarce — the greater portion of Vol. IV. having been destroyed by fire. Sold, at New York, in 1864, for $90. The following is by the same author, who assumed the name of Daly.

BURK (J. Daly). Oration at Petersburg, March 4, 1803, to Celebrate the Election of Thomas Jefferson. By John D. Burk. [n. p.] 1803. 8vo. C. 9274

BURKART (Joseph). Aufenthalt und Reisen in Mexico in den Jahren 1825 bis 1834. Bemerkungen über Land, Produkte, Leben und Sitten der Einwohner und Beobachtungen aus dem Gebiete der Mineralogie, Geognosie, Bergbaukunde ... . Mit einem Vorworte von J. Nöggerath. *Stuttgart: Schweizerbart.* 1836. 2 vols., 8vo. 11 Plates. 9275

BURKART. Description du filon et des mines de Veta-Grande près de la ville de Zacatecas dans l'État du même nom au Mexique. *Paris: impr. de Fain.* 1835. 8vo, pp. 35. 9276

BURKART. Report, containing the Result of the Preliminary Examination of the Mines in the possession of the Real Tlalpuxahua Mining Association, and Sketch of the Mining Operations of the Company. By Joseph Burkart. *London.* 1826. 8vo. 9277

BURKE (Ædanus). An Address to the Freemen of the State of South-Carolina. Containing Political Observations on the following Subjects I. On the Citizens making a temporary Submission to the British Arms, after the reduction of Charlestown [*sic*] in 1780. ... By Cassius. Supposed to be written by Ædanus Burke Esquire, one of the Chief Justices of the State of South-Carolina. [Motto.] *Philadelphia: Robert Bell.* M DCC-LXXXIII. 8vo, pp. 32. BA., H., P. 9278

[BURKE.] Considerations on the Society, or Order of Cincinnati; lately instituted by the Major-Generals, Brigadier-Generals, and other Officers in the American Army. Proving that it creates a race of Hereditary Patricians, or Nobility. Interspersed with Remarks on the Consequences to the Freedom and Happiness of the Republic. Addressed to the People of South-Carolina and their Representatives. By Cassius. Supposed to be written by Ædanus Burke Esq. One of the Chief-Justices of the State of South-Carolina. *Philadelphia: Robert Bell.* M.DCC.LXXXIII. 8vo, pp. 16. + *New York.* 1783. 8vo, pp. 16. P. + *Hartford: Basil Webster.* 1783. 8vo, pp. 23. + *Hartford: Hudson & Goodwin.* 1784. 8vo. N. 9279

BURKE. Observations upon a late Pamphlet entitled "Considerations upon the Society or Order of the Cincinnati," clearly evincing the Innocence and Propriety of that Honourable and Respectable Institution. In answer to Vague Conjectures, False Insinuations and unfounded Objections. By an Obscure Individual. ... *Philadelphia: R. Bell.* M.DCC.LXXXIII. 8vo, pp. 28.

[BURKE (A.)] Burke's Guide, or, the Visitor's Companion to Niagara Falls, its Strange and Wonderful Localities. By an Old Resident. *Buffalo: Andrew Burke.* 1850. 12mo, pp. 106. Woodcut. 9281

[BURKE (Edmund).] An Account of the European Settlements in America. In Six Parts. I. A short History of the Discovery of that Part of the World. II. The Manners and Customs of the original Inhabitants. III. Of the Spanish Settlements. IV. Of the Portuguese. V. Of the French, Dutch, and Danish. VI. Of the English. Each Part contains An accurate Description of the Settlements in it, their Extent, Climate, Productions, Trade, Genius and Disposition of their Inhabitants: the Interests of the several Powers of Europe with respect to those Settlements; and their Political and Commercial Views with regard to each other. In Two Volumes. *London: Printed for R. and J. Dodsley in Pall-Mall.* MDCCLVII. 2 vols., 8vo, 5 l., pp. 3–312, Map; 2 l., pp. 3–300, Contents, 10 l., Map. BA., C. + The Second Edition, with Improvements. *London: R. and J. Dodsley.* MDCCLVIII. 2 vols., 8vo, pp. viii, 3–324, Contents, 5 l; pp. xii, 13–308. 2 Maps. C. + The Third Edition, with Improvements. *London: R. and J. Dodsley.* M DCC LX. 2 vols., 8vo, 5 l., pp. 324, 5 l.; 6 l., pp. 308. 2 Maps. H. + The Fourth Edition, with Improvements. *London: J. Dodsley.* MDCCXLV. 2 vols., 8vo, pp. xx, 3–324; xii, 308. + [Another.] *Dublin: Printed for Peter Wilson.* M.DCC.LXII. 2 vols., 12mo, pp. xiv, 319; viii, 301 + A New Edition. *London: R. Dodsley.* 1766. 2 vols., 12mo. + The Fifth Edition, with Improvements. *London: J. Dodsley.* MDCCLXX. 2 vols., 8vo, 4 l., pp. xii, 3–324; xii, 3–308. 2 Maps. + The Sixth Edition, with Improvements. *London: J. Dodsley.* M.DCC.LXXVII. 2 vols., 8vo, 4 l., pp. i–xii, 324; i–xii, 308. 2 Maps. H. Some copies on large paper. + [Reprinted.] *Dublin.* 1777. 2 vols., 8vo. + A New Edition, illustrated with Maps *London.* 1808. 2 vols., 8vo. Also on large paper, rl. 8vo. + A New Edition. *London: J. Stockdale.* 1808. 4to, pp. 482. 2 Maps. 9282

Stockdale's edition was printed to complete Burke's works in quarto and octavo.

BURKE. An Account of the European Settlements in America, ... First American Edition. *Boston.* 1835. 8vo. + Also his Correspondence with Dr. French. *Boston.* 1851. 8vo, pp. 687. 9283

The authorship of this book has been attributed to Soame Jenyns, Richard Burke, and afterwards to Wm. Bourke, but it is now satisfactorily decided to be mainly the work of Edmund Burke, assisted by his brother Richard, and his friend, William Bourke. An advertisement, by the editor of the quarto edition, now very scarce, places the question beyond doubt. *See* McCulloch's "Lit. of Pol. Economy," p. 88; M. R., XVIII, 537. Its popularity was so great, that it was translated into many languages, as below:

BURKE (W.) Histoire des Colonies Européennes dans l'Amerique septentrionale, en six parties. Chaque partie contient une description de la colonie, de son étendue, de son climat, de ses productions, de son commerce, etc., traduite de l'anglois de M. William Burck [*sic*], par M. E. [Marc Ant. Eidous]. *Paris:*

Merlin. 1767. 2 vols., 12mo, Half-Title, pp. xviij, 384; 2 l., pp. 352. 2 Maps. + *Paris.* 1780. 2 vols., 12mo. M. 9284

[BURKE.] Beknopte en zakelyke beschryving der voornaamste Engelsche volkplantingen in Noord-Amerika, neffens aanmerkingen over den oorsprong en voortgang der tegenwoordige geschillen, en des oorlogs, tusschen Groot-Brittannie en deszelfs kolonisten. *Amsterdam: P. Conradi.* [n. d.?] 2 vols., 8vo. N. 9285

[BURKE.] Beschreibung der Europäischen Kolonien in Amerika nach der sechsten verbesserten Ausgabe aus dem Englischen übersetzt von J. *Leipzig.* 1778. 2 vols., 8vo. 2 Maps.

[BURKE (E.)] Edmund Burke's Jahrbucher der neuern Geschichte der Englischen Pflanzungen in Nord America, seit dem Jahre 1755, bis aus jetzige Zeiten. *Dantzig: Jobst Herrmann Flörke.* 1777. 4 vols., 16mo, Title, 7 l., pp. 396; Title, 11 l., pp. 238; Title, 3 l., pp. 486; Title, 3 l., pp. 588. H. + *Dantzig.* 1781. 4 vols., 12mo. 9287

[BURKE.] Geschichte der Englischen Kolonien in Nord-America von der esten Entdeckung dieser Länder durch Sebastien Cabot bis auf den Frieden 1763. ... Aus dem Englischen. [Vignette.] *Leipzig: Caspar Fritsch.* 1775. 2 vols., 16mo, Title, 7 l., pp. 452; Title, 3 l., pp. 424, 4 l. Map. + *Leipzig.* 1778. 2 vols., 8vo. 9288

[BURKE (E.)] Storia degli stabilimenti europei in America divisa in sei parti ... tradotta in Italiano della seconda edizione inglese ... . [Vignette.] *Venezia: Antonio Graziosi, e Angiolo Pasinello.* M DCC LXIII. 2 vols., 8vo, Title, pp. xvi, 368; 368. 3 Maps. S. 9289

BURKE. A Letter from Edmund Burke, Esq; One of the Representatives in Parliament for the City of Bristol, to John Farr, and John Harris, Esqrs. Sheriffs of that City, On the Affairs of America. *Bristol: Printed by William Pine.* M,DCC,LXXVII. 8vo, pp. 79. BA. + *London: J. Dodsley.* M DCC LXXVII. 8vo, pp. 75. + The Second Edition. *London: J. Dodsley.* MDCCLXXVII. 8vo, pp. 75. + The Third Edition. *London: J. Dodsley.* M.DCC.LXXVII. 8vo, pp, 79. + The Fourth Edition. *London: J. Dodsley.* MDCCLXXVII. 8vo, pp. 79. + *Dublin.* 1777. 8vo, pp. 55. C. 9290

BURKE. An Answer to the letter of Edmund Burke, Esq.

one of the Representatives of the City of Bristol, to the Sheriffs of that City. *London: T. Cadell.* M. DCC. LXXVII. 8vo, Half-Title, Title, pp. 60. + The Second Edition. *London: T. Cadell.* M. DCC. LXXVII. 8vo, 2 l., pp. 60. 9291

Perhaps by Dr. Shebbeare. *See* M. R., LVII. 85. For another "Answer," *see* Abingdon (*Earl of*), Vol. I., No. 65.

BURKE. Letter from Edmund Burke to the Committee of Correspondence for the General Assembly of New York, respecting the effect of the Quebec bill upon the boundary of New York. *New York.* 1848. 8vo, pp. 14. S. 9292

BURKE. A letter from the Rt. Hon. Edmund Burke to a noble Lord. ... The first American edition, with a preface, by Peter Porcupine [Cobbett]. *Philadelphia: Davies.* [1797.] 8vo, pp. 58. + *New York.* 1797. 8vo, pp. 40. P. 9293

BURKE. Observations on a Late Publication, entitled "The Present State of the Nation." *London: Dodsley.* MDCCLXIX. + Fifth Edition. *London: Dodsley.* MDCCLXXXIV. 8vo, 2 l., pp. 155. 9294

BURKE. Speech of Edmund Burke, Esq., on American Taxation, April 19, 1774. *London: J. Dodsley.* MDCCLXXIV. 4to, pp. iv, 58. + *London: J. Dodsley.* MDCCLXXIV. 8vo, pp. 96. S. + The Second Edition. *London: J. Dodsley.* MDCCLXXV. 8vo, pp. 96. H. + The Third Edition. *London: Printed for J. Dodsley.* MDCCLXXV. 8vo, pp. 96. + The Fourth Edition. *London: J. Dodsley.* MDCCLXXVI. 8vo, pp. 96. + *Bristol.* 1774. 12mo. + *New York: Printed by James. Rivington.* MDCCLXXV. 8vo, pp. 63. BA. + *Philadelphia.* 1778. 8vo. 9295

See M. R., LII. 543; LVI. 467, 469.

BURKE. Answer to the Printed Speech of Edmund Burke, Esq. *See* [Shebbeare (John).]

BURKE. A Letter to Edmund Burke, Esq. *See* [Cartwright (George)].

BURKE. Speech of Edmund Burke, Esq; on moving his Resolutions for Conciliation with the Colonies, March 22, 1775. *London: J. Dodsley.* M DCC LXXV. 4to, Title, pp. 65. BA. + The Second Edition. *London: J. Dodsley.* MDCCLXXV. 8vo, Half-Title, Title, pp. 107. H. + Third Edition. *London: J. Dodsley.* MDCCLXXV. 8vo, 2 l., pp. 107. + *Dublin.* 1775. 8vo.

+ *New York: Printed by James Rivington.* MDCCLXXV. 8vo, pp. 71. 9296

Contains the famous sentence: "Whatever England has been growing to by a progressive increase of government, brought in by varieties of people, by succession of civilizing conquest and civilizing settlements, in a series of seventeen hundred years, you shall see as much added to her by America in a single life!"—*See* M. R., LIII. 73.

BURKE. Edmund Burke's Reden: On American Taxation und On Conciliation with America. Zum Schulgebrauch mit einer Einleitung und Anmerkungen versehen von J. C. A. Winkelmann. *Gotha: Opetz.* 1864. 8vo, pp. iv, 203. 9297

BURKE. A Speech of Edmund Burke, Esq. At the Guildhall, in Bristol, Previous to the late Election in that City, upon certain Points relative to his Parliamentary Conduct. *London: J. Dodsley.* M.DCC.LXXX. 8vo, Half-Title, Title, pp. 68. BA. + The Second Edition. *London: J. Dodsley.* M.DCC.LXXX. 8vo, Half-Title, Title, pp. 68. 9298

BURKE. A Short Account of a late Short Administration. *London.* 1766. 8vo. 9299

BURKE. Speech of Edmund Burke ... On presenting to the House of Commons (On the 11th February, 1780) a Plan for the Better Security of the Independence of Parliament, and the Economical Reformation of the Civil and other Establishments. *London: J. Dodsley.* M.DCCC.LXXX. 8vo, pp. 95. BA. + Fourth Edition. 8vo, pp. 95. 9300

See the remarks on the "Secretary of State for the Colonies," and the "Board of Trade and Plantations," pp. 70–80.

BURKE. Speeches of Hon. Edmund Burke, with Memoirs and Historical Introduction. *Dublin.* 1854. Post 8vo. 9301

BURKE. Mr. Edmund Burke's Speeches on his Arrival at Bristol, and at the Conclusion of the Poll. *London.* 1774. 4to, pp. 31. 9302

See M. R., LI. 394.

BURKE. Thoughts on the Causes of the Present Discontents. ... *London: J. Dodsley.* MDCCLXX. 8vo. + The Second Edition. *London: ... J. Dodsley.* MDCCLXX. 8vo, pp. 118. BA. + Fifth Edition. *London.* 1775. 8vo. + Sixth Edition. *London: Dodsley.* MDCCLXXV. 8vo, 2 l., pp. 118. + *Dublin.* 1770. 8vo, pp. 79. 9303

Most of the above pieces by "this great master of eloquence" are reproduced in the various editions of his works, which are too numerous to recount here. We note only

the American editions. *Boston.* 1806–7. 4 vols., 8vo. + *New York: Eastburn, Kirk & Co.* 1813. 3 vols., 8vo. + *Boston.* 1826. 7 vols., 8vo. + Reprinted. [*New York:*] *Harper & Brothers.* 1833. 3 vols., 8vo. + *Boston.* 1839. 9 vols., 8vo. And lastly, as below:

BURKE. The Works of the Right Honorable Edmund Burke.. Revised Edition. [Edited by George Nichols.] *Boston: Little, Brown & Co.* 1866–67. 12 vols., 12mo. 9304

Also, on large paper, of which one hundred copies were printed. The following works may be consulted with some advantage: Correspondence of the Right Hon. Edmund Burke, between the year 1744 and the period of his decease in 1797. Edited by Charles William, Earl Fitzwilliam, and Lieut. Gen. Sir Richard Bourke. *London: R. Bentley.* 1844. 4 vols., 8vo, pp. 518, 492, 537, 554. Portrait after Reynolds. P.—A Defence of the Political and Parliamentary Conduct of the Right Hon. Edmund Burke. *London.* 1794. 8vo, pp. 35. P.—Review of Mr. Burke's Conduct as the Representative of Bristol in Parliament. *London.* 1780. 12mo.—The Beauties of the late Edmund Burke, selected from the Writings, &c. of that Extraordinary Man, alphabetically arranged; ... a Sketch of the Life, ... some Original Anecdotes of Mr. Burke. *London.* 1798. 2 vols., 8vo.

BURKE (E.), *of New Hampshire.* The Protective System considered in connection with the Present Tariff, in a Series of Twelve Essays, originally published in the Washington Union, over the Signature of "Bundelcund." Written by the Hon. Edmund Burke. *Washington.* 1846. 8vo, pp. 48. BA. 9305

Also: Speech ... on the Tariff Bill; ... in the House ... July 8. 1842. *Washington.* 1842. 8vo.—Speech ... in the House ... June 13, 1840, on the Independent Treasury Bill, ... [*Washington.* 1840.] 8vo.

BURKE (E.) The Tobacco Manufacture in the United States. A Report adopted in Convention of the Trade, held at Cooper Institute. New York, December 7th and 8th, 1864. By Edward Burke. *New York: American News Company.* [1864?] 8vo, pp. 33. H. 9306

BURKE (E. P.) Reminiscences of Georgia: by Emily P. Burke. [n. p.: *James M. Fitch.*] MDCCCL. 12mo, pp. viii, 252. 9307

BURKE (F.) Trial of Francis Burke before Baltimore City Court, on an Indictment for Manslaughter by Administering to Benj. M. Hazelip, certain Thomsonian Remedies. *Baltimore.* 1832. 8vo. 9308

[BURKE (John).] The Burden of the South, in Verse, or, Poems on Slavery, Grave, Humorous, Didactic, and Satirical. By Sennoia Rubek. *New York: Everardus Warner.* [n. d.] 8vo, pp. 96. 9309

Sennoia Rubek is the anagram for Joannes Burke.

BURKE. Chivalry, Slavery, and Young America. By Sennoia Rubek. *New York: Frederic A. Brady.* 1866. 8vo, pp. 183. C. 9310

[BURKE.] Stanzas to Queen Victoria, and other Poems By Sennoia Rubek. *New York: Frederic A. Brady.* 1866. 8vo, pp. 208. Woodcut. H. 9311

Contains "The Burden of the South," "Brooks and Sumner," etc.

BURKE (Peter). The Public and Domestic Life of the Rt. Hon. Edmund Burke. *London: Ingram, Cooke & Co.* 1853. 12mo, pp. xvi, 315. 2 Plates. C., P. 9312

BURKE (T. A.) Burke's Weekly for Boys and Girls: an illustrated journal of instruction and entertainment. T. A. Burke, editor. July 6, 1867 to June 27, 1868. Vol. I. *Macon, Ga.: J. W. Burke & Co.* 1868. 4to, 2 l., pp. 416. C.

BURKE (W.) South American Independence: or, the Emancipation of South America, the Glory and Interest of England. By William Burke, Author of the History of the Campaign of 1805, &c. *London: J. Ridgway.* 1807. 8vo, 4 l., pp. 82.

BURKE. Additional Reasons for our immediately emancipating South America: deduced, from the New and Extraordinary Circumstances of the Present Crisis: and containing Valuable Information respecting the Late Important Events, both at Buenos Ayres, and in the Caraccas: as well as with respect to the Present Disposition and Views of the Spanish Americans: being intended as a Supplement to "South American Independence." By William Burke, Author of that Work. *London: J. Ridgway.* 1807. 8vo, pp. 91. + Second Edition, enlarged. *London: J. Ridgway.* 1808. 8vo, pp. xxxvi, 132. H. 9315

BURKE (W.) Memoir of William Burke, a Soldier of the Revolution. *Hartford.* 1837. 12mo, pp. 126. 9316

BURKE (W.) The Mineral Springs of Western Virginia, with remarks on their use. ... By William Burke. *New York: Wiley & Putnam.* 1842. 18mo, pp. 291. Maps and Plates.

BURKE. The Mineral Springs of Western Virginia, with Remarks on their Use, and the Diseases to which they are Applicable. Second Edition. To which are added, a Notice of the Fauquier White Sulphur Springs, and a Chapter on Taverns.

Also a Review of a Pamphlet published by Dr. T. T. Moorman. By Wm. Burke. *New York.* 1846. 12mo, pp. 399. C. + *Richmond.* 1851. P. 9318

BURKE. The Virginia Mineral Springs, with Remarks on their Use, the Diseases to which they are applicable, and in which they are contra-indicated, accompanied by a Map of Routes and Distances. 2d Edition. ... enlarged. By W. Burke, M.D. *Richmond.* 1853. 12mo. 9319

BURKE (W. A.) *See* Boutelle (J. A.), Vol. II., No. 6942.

BURKE (W. S.) Directory of the City of Council Bluffs, and Emigrants' guide to the gold regions of the West. By W. S. Burke. *Council Bluffs.* 1866. 8vo. Map. 9320

BURKHART (Gustav Emil). Kleine Missionsbibliothek, oder Land und Leute, Arbeiter und Arbeiten, Kämpfe und Siege auf dem Gebiete der evangelischen Heidenmission. *Bielefeld: Velhagen und Klasing.* 1857–62. 4 vols., 8vo. 9321

Ier Bd. contains Amerika: 1. Lieg. Die evangelische Mission unter den Eskimo's in Grönland und Labrador. pp. vii, 87. 2. Liefg. Die evangelische Mission unter den Indianern in Nord- und Süd-Amerika. pp. 269. 3. Liefg. Die evangelische Mission unter den Negern in Westindien und Südamerika. pp. vi, 294.

BURKITT (Lemuel) *and* READ (Jesse). Concise History of the Kehukee Baptist Association, from its Rise to the Present Time. *Halifax, N. C.: A. Hodge.* 1803. 16mo, pp. 319. C.

Reprinted as below:

BURKITT *and* READ. A Concise History of the Kehukee Baptist Association, from its Original Rise down to 1803. Wherein are shown its first Constitution, Increase, Numbers, Principles, Form of Government, Decorum, Revolution, Revivals, Ministers, Churches, Confession of Faith, Times and Places when and where Associations have been holden, Queries and their Answers, and all other Useful Articles relative to Church History. By Elders Lemuel Burkitt and Jesse Read, Ministers of the Gospel in Northampton and Halifax Counties, North Carolina. Revised and Improved by Henry L. Burkitt: *Philadelphia: Lippincott, Grambo & Co.* 1850. 16mo, pp. 351.

BURLEIGH (C. C.) Reception of George Thompson in Great Britain. By Charles C. Burleigh. *Boston: J. Knapp.* 1836. 18mo, pp. 238. C. 9324

Also: Slavery and the North. [n. p. n. d.] 12mo, pp. 12.—Speech ... at the Annual Meeting of the Massachusetts A. S. Society, Friday, January 28. 1859. *Bos-*

ton. 1859. 18mo, pp. 32.—Thoughts on the Death Penalty. ... *Philadelphia.* 1845, 12mo. B. & C. + Second Edition, revised. *Philadelphia: Merrihew and Thompson. Printers.* 1847. 12mo, pp. 144. H.

BURLEIGH (J. B.) The American Manual, containing a Brief Outline of the Origin and Progress of Political Power and the Laws of Nations; a Commentary on the Constitution of the United States, and a Lucid Exposition of the Duties and Responsibilities of Voters, Jurors, Magistrates, &c. By Joseph Bartlett Burleigh, A.M. *Philadelphia: Grigg, Elliot & Co.* 1848. 8vo, pp. 287, 27. + *Philadelphia.* 1852. 8vo, pp. 287, 27. C.

Also: Legislative Guide for conducting business in the House of Representatives, the Senate of the United States; a Synopsis of Jefferson's Manual; together with a concise system of Rules of Order, based on the regulations of the United States Congress. ... *Philadelphia.* 1853. 8vo.

BURLEIGH (W. A.) Indian Affairs. Speech of Hon Walter A. Burleigh, of Dakota, in the House of Representatives, July 21, 1868, on our present relations with the Indian Tribes of the country. [*Washington.* 1868.] 8vo, pp. 4. H. 9326

[BURLEIGH.] Indian Massacre in Minnesota. Removal of the Sioux Indians. [Correspondence of Hon. W. A. Burleigh and others. *Washington.* 1866.] 8vo, pp. 14. H. 9327

Also: Management of Indian Affairs. Speech ... June 9, 1866. [*Washington.* 1866.] 8vo, pp. 16. H.—Territory of Wyoming. Speech ... July 23, 1868, On the bill to provide a territorial government for the Territory of Wyoming. [*Washington.* 1868.] 8vo, pp. 3. H.

BURLEIGH (W. H.) Our Country; its Dangers and its Destiny: A Desultory Poem. ... By William Henry Burleigh. *Allegheny.* 1841. 12mo, pp. 43. H. 9328

BURLEIGH. The Republican Pocket Pistol, a Collection of Facts, Opinions and Arguments for Freedom. *New York: H. Dayton.* 1860. 12mo, pp. 36. 9329

BURLEIGH. No Slave-Hunting in the old Bay State. *New York American Anti-Slavery Society.* 1860. 12mo, pp. 23. 9330

BURLING (Edward). Some Remarks and Observations by way of Answer to a small Book called a Lecture Sermon, preached at New Milford, by John Graham. *New York.* 1724. 16mo. W. 9331

BURLING (William). *See* Lay (Benjamin).

Burlingame (A.) Address upon the Life and Character of Washington, delivered by Anson Burlingame, before the Brady and Scott Guards, on the 22d of February, 1843. *Detroit.* 1843. 12mo, pp. 25. s. 9332

Burlingame. An Appeal to Patriots against Fraud and Disunion. Speech of Hon. Anson Burlingame, of Massachusetts. Delivered in the U. S. House of Representatives, March 31, 1858. *Washington, D. C.: Buell & Blanchard, Printers.* 1858. 8vo, pp. 8. H. 9333

Also: Defence of Massachusetts. Speech ... in the ... House ... June 21, 1856. *Cambridge.* 1856. 8vo, pp. 33. + [Another Edition.] 8vo, pp. 7. [n. p. n. d.] + *Boston: John P. Jewett and Company. New York: Sheldon, Blakeman and Company.* 1856. 12mo, pp. 33. Portrait. H., M. + Speech ... delivered in the Senate of Massachusetts, March 3, 1852. [n. p. 1852.] 8vo, pp. 8. H. — Mr. Burlingame's Sentiments. The Constitution guarantees Religious Freedom. Mr. Burlingame against this. (Extracts from an Oration delivered by Anson Burlingame on the Fourth of July, 1854, before the Citizens of Salem.) [n. p. 1854?] Slip. H.

Burlington, *Iowa.* The First Annual Report of the Board of Trade, of the City of Burlington, for the Year 1856. By L. H. Shepard. *Burlington: C. Dunham, Printer.* 1857. 8vo, pp. 20. H. 9334

Business Directory, and Review of the City of Burlington, Iowa. *Burlington.* 1856. 8vo. 9335

Burlington, *Mass.* Annual Report of the School Committee of Burlington, for the School Year 1855–6. *Boston: William White, Printer.* 1856. 8vo. pp. 19. H. 9336

Burlington College, *N. J.* ... Address of the Trustees; Prospectus of the Preparatory School. [Motto.] Second Edition. *Burlington: Edmund Morris, Printer.* MDCCCXLVI. 16mo, pp. 16, Table. Continued. H. + Address of the Trustees; [with General Statement, etc.] *Burlington.* 1848. 12mo. + By-laws and Catalogue of the Burlington Social Library. *Burlington.* [n. d.] 16mo, pp. 8. + Fourth of July, 1850, at Burlington College. ... . *Burlington: Published by the College Classes.* 1850. 8vo, pp. 39. H. + First Fruits. *Burlington: S. C. Atkinson.* 1850. 8vo, pp. 72. (Exercises of Commencement Day, September 26, 1850.) + Register of the College. *Burlington.* [v. d.] 9337

Burlington, *Vt.* ... Address of Hon. T. E. Wales, Mayor, April 1st, 1867, and Annual Reports of the Officers of the City of Burlington, Vt., for the Financial Year, ending February 1,

1868. With other Papers relating to the Affairs of the City. *Burlington.* 1868. 8vo, pp. 106. (City Documents, 1868.) H.

The Charter, Ordinances, and Annual Report of the Officers of committees of the City of Burlington, Vt., for 1866. 8vo.

Jubilee: 1817–1867. Services in Celebration of the Fiftieth Anniversary of the Dedication of the First Congregational Church in Burlington, Vermont, Wednesday, the Ninth of January, 1867. *Burlington.* 1867. 8vo, pp. 53. H. 9340

Report of the Selectmen and other Officers to the Town of Burlington, March 6, 1860. *Burlington.* 1860. 8vo, pp. 69.

Burlington Island Association. National Armory. Memorial of Burlington Island Association. 8vo, pp. 4. 9342

Burmannus (Johann). Plantarum Americanarum Fasciculus Primus — Decimus, Continens Plantas, quas olim Carolus Plumierius Botanicorum Princeps Detexit, Eruitque, Atque in Insulis Antillis ipse depinxit, Has primum in lucem edidit, Concinnis descriptionibus, & Observationibus, Æneisque Tabulis illustravit Joannes Burmannus, M.D. ... *Amstelædami: in Horto Medico, Atque Apud Viduam & Filium S. Schouten. Lugd. Batav.: Apud Gerard. Potvliet. & Theodor. Haak.* M. DCC. LV.–[LX.] Folio, 4 l., pp. 262, (4). BA. 9343

See a note in Rich, I. 115, from Sir J. E. Smith, who characterizes the plates as accurate, but inferior to Plumier's; which, considering these *are* Plumier's, it is difficult to understand.

Burmeister (G.) *See* Buenos Aires, Vol. III., No. 8993.

Burmeister (H.) The Black Man. The Comparative Anatomy and Psychology of the African Negro. By Hermann Burmeister, ... Translated by J. Friedlander, Dr. Phil. of Berlin, and Robert Tomes, M.D., of New York. (Republished from the Evening Post.) *New York: William C. Bryant & Co., Printers.* 1853. 8vo, pp. 23. BA., H., P. 9344

Burmeister. Geologische Bilder zur Geschichte der Erde und ihrer Bewohner. Von Dr. H. Burmeister ... . Zweite vermehrte Auflage. *Leipzig: Otto Wigand.* 1855. 2 vols., 8vo, pp. iv, 366, (1); 2 l., pp. 378. BA. 9345

"Die Obstsorten Brasiliens; Der brasilianische Organisationscharakter," II. 277–378.

Burmeister. Landschaftliche Bilder Brasiliens und Portraits einiger Urvölker; als Atlas zu seiner Reise durch die Provinzen von Rio de Janeiro und Minas Geraës entworfen und herausgegeben. *Berlin: G. Reimer.* 1853. Sq. folio, 1 l., pp. 7. 11 Plates. 9346

Burmeister. Reise durch die la Plata-Staaten mit besonderer Rücksicht auf die physiche Beschaffenheit und den Kulturzustand der Argentinischen Republik. Ausgeführt in den Jahren 1857, 1858, 1859 und 1860. Erster Band. Die südlichen Provinzen ... . || Zweiter Band. Die nordwestlichen Provinzen und die Cordilleren zwischen Catamarca und Copiapó ... . Nebst einer systemischen Uebersicht der beobachteten Rückgratthiere und Karte. *Halle: H. W. Schmidt.* 1861. 2 vols., 8vo, pp. vi, 504; v, 539. 1 Plate and 2 Maps. C. 9347

Burmeister. Reise nach Brasilien, durch die Provinzen von Rio de Janeiro und Minas Geraës. Mit besonderer Rücksicht auf die Naturgeschichte der Gold- und Diamantendistricte. *Berlin: G. Reimer.* 1853. 8vo, pp. viii, 608. Map. 9348

Burmeister. Systematische Uebersicht der Thiere Brasiliens, welche während einer Reise durch die Provinzen von Rio de Janeiro und Minas Geraës gesammelt oder beobachtet wurden. ... *Berlin: G. Reimer.* 1854–56. 3 vols., 8vo, pp. x, 341; x, 526; xiv, 466. 9349

Burmeister. Ueber das Klima der Argentinischen Republik. Nach dreijährigen Beobachtungen während einer Reise durch die La Plata-Staaten Geschildert und mit numerischen Angaben der gefundenen Werthe belegt. *Halle: Schmidt.* 1861. 4to, pp. 110. C. 9350

From the "Abhandl. d. nat. Ges. zu Halle."

Burmeister. Ueber das Klima von Buenos Aires. *Halle: Schmidt.* 1863. 4to, pp. 24. C. 9351

From the "Abhandl. d. naturf. Ges. zu Halle." Also: Beschreibung eines behaarten Gürtelthiers Praopus hirsutus, aus d. National-Museum zu Lima. Mit einer Abbildung. 1861. 4. — Erläuterungen zur Fauna Brasiliens, enthaltend Abbildungen und ausführliche Beschreibungen neuer oder ungenügend bekannter Thierarten. *Berlin: G. Reimer.* 1856. Folio, pp. viii, 115. 22 colored and 10 uncolored Plates. C. — Uebersicht der brasilianischen Mutillen. *Halle: Schmidt.* 1854. 4to, pp. 12. (From the "Abhandl. d. naturforsch. Ges. zu Halle.")

Burmeister (H.) *and* Giebel (C.) Die Versteinerungen von Juntas im Thal des Rio de Copiapó. Nach ihren Lagerungsverhältnissen und physischen Eigenschaften geschildert. *Halle: Schmidt.* 1861. 4to, pp. 34. 2 Lithographs. 9352

Burn (A.) Memoirs of the life of the late Major-General Andrew Burn, of the Royal Marines; collected from his Journals. ... . *London: W. Winchester.* 1815. 2 vols., post 8vo, pp. xxiii, 287; 248, Subscribers, 55. Portrait. 9353

Contains his reflections on the state of the American Indians, travels in the West Indies, etc.

Burn (D.) Colonial Legislation on the Subject of Education; Two Letters published in the Hamilton Gazette, under the Signature of Scotus. By David Burn. *Toronto.* 1841. 8vo, pp. 16. 9354

Burn (J. I.) Case of the Right Hon. Alexander Earl of Stirling and Dovan, respecting his Lordship's title to Nova Scotia, and other Territorial Possessions in North America, containing a Narrative of the Proceedings taken on his Lordship's behalf for the Restitution of his Property, with Observations thereon. By J. I. Burn, Esq. *London: J. Hatchard.* 1833. 8vo, pp. 92. Map. 9355

Burn (J.) Statistics of the Cotton Trade. *London.* 1847. 8vo.

Burn (J. S.) Registrum Ecclesiæ Parochialis. The History of Parish Registers in England, also of the Registers of ... the ... West Indies ... Foreign Countries ... . By John Southerden Burn. *London: Suter.* 1829. 8vo, pp. viii, 246. + Second Edition. ... *London: John Russell Smith.* M.DCCC.LXII. 8vo, pp. vii, (1), 296. BA. 9357

Burnaby (A.) A Sermon ... before the ... House of Commons ... February 21, 1781: Being the Day ... for a General Fast. By Andrew Burnaby, D.D. ... *London: T. Payne & Son.* 1781. 4to. BA. 9358

Burnaby. Travels through the Middle Settlements in North America, in the Years 1759 and 1760: With Observations upon the State of the Colonies. By the Rev. Andrew Burnaby, A.M. ... *London: T. Payne.* MDCCLXXV. 4to, pp. viii, 106, Errata, 1 l. Maps and Plates, Plan of New York. + The Second Edition. *London: T. Payne.* MDCCLXXV. 8vo, pp. xvi, 198, Erratum, 1 l. + *Dublin.* 1775. 12mo. + Edition the Third: revised, corrected, and greatly enlarged, by the Author. *London: T. Payne.* 1798. 4to, pp. xix, 209. Engraving of Passaic Falls, and a Map. BA., H., P. 9359

Valuable as exhibiting a view of the colonies immediately preceding the Revolutionary War. Reprinted in Pinkerton's Voyages, Vol. XIII. *See* M. R., LV. 401, and "Biog. Universelle."

Burnaby. Voyages dans les colonies du milieu de l'Amérique Septentrionale, fait en 1759 et 1760. Avec des observations sur l'état des colonies. Traduit par M. Wild. *Lausanne.* 1778. 8vo. + *A la Haye.* 1778. N. 9360

Burnaby. Reisen durch die Mittlern Kolonien der Engländer in Nord-Amerika. Von M. Andreas Burnaby aus dem Englischen ... [von Ch. Dn. Ebeling]. *Hamburg und Kiel: Carl Ernst Bohn.* 1776. 12mo, Title, 7 l., pp. 192. 9361

Also: A Sermon preached in Greenwich Church, on Thursday, July 29, 1784, the day appointed for a General Thanksgiving ... By the Rev. Andrew Burnaby, D.D. ... *London.* 1784. 4to, pp. 23.

Burnaby (*Sir* W.) Regulations for the better government of His Majesty's subjects in the Bay of Honduras. Presented to them by Sir William Burnaby. *London.* 1809. 8vo, pp. 143.

Burnap (G. Washington). Memoir of Henry Augustus Ingalls. By Rev. George W. Burnap, of Baltimore. ... [Motto.] *New York: the Metropolitan Association.* 1845. 18mo, pp. 224. H. + *Boston: James Munroe and Company.* 1846. 12mo, pp. 80. BA. 9363

Burnap. Origin and Causes of Democracy in America: A Discourse By George W. Burnap. [Vignette.] Delivered in Baltimore, before the Maryland Historical Society, on its Eighth Anniversary Celebration, December 20, 1853. [*Baltimore: John D. Toy, Printer.* 1853.] 8vo, pp. 29. 9364

Also: An Address delivered at the Funeral of Henry Payson, on Sunday, December 28, 1845. ... *Baltimore: printed by John Murphy.* 1846. 8vo, pp. 8. H. — Church and State: or the Privileges and Duties of an American Citizen. A Discourse, ... on Thanksgiving Day, December 12, 1844 ... . *Baltimore: printed by John D. Toy.* 1844. 8vo, pp. 24. H. — Commemorative Discourse, delivered in ... Baltimore, September 17, 1843, on the Occasion of the Decease of the Rev. F. W. P. Greenwood, D.D. ... *Baltimore: Printed by John Murphy.* [1843.] 8vo, pp. 16. H. — The Duties of the Citizen Soldier. A Discourse ... in ... Baltimore ... July 21, 1844, before Maryland Cadets, and their Guests, the Boston City Greys. By George W. Burnap. *Baltimore: printed by John Murphy.* 8vo, pp. 20. BA. — Miscellaneous Writings of George W. Burnap. *Baltimore.* 1845. 12mo. P. — The Philosophical Tendencies of the American Mind. An Address ... Dickinson College, July 7th, 1852 ... . *Baltimore: printed by John D. Toy.* 1852. 8vo, pp. 31. H. — The Voice of the Times; a Sermon in ... Baltimore ... May 14, 1837. By George W. Burnap. ... *Baltimore: John D. Toy, Printer.* 1837. 8vo, pp. 16. BA. — Life of Leonard Calvert. (In Sparks's "Amer. Biog.," 2d Ser., Vol. IX.)

Burnap (Jacob). Discourse at Dunstable, N. H. Sept. 8, 1818, at the Funeral of Rev. Joseph Kidder, A.M., Senior Pastor of the Church in that place; with a History of the Church there, by Rev. E. P. Sperry. *Amherst, N. H.: Richard Boylston.* 1819. 8vo. 9365

Burnap. Fast Sermon at Merrimack, N. H. April 25, 1799. *From Preston's Printing Office: Amherst. July,* 1799. 8vo, pp. 15.

Burnap (U. C.) Bible Servitude. A Sermon, delivered in ... Lowell, on the Day of Annual Thanksgiving, November 30, 1843. By U. C. Burnap ... . *Lowell: A. E. Newton and A. O. Ordway.* 1843. 8vo, pp. 20. H. 9367

Burnay (J.) A Sermon preached ... before ... the ... Senate and House ... of ... New Hampshire. By Jacob Burnay. *Concord.* 1801. 8vo. BM. 9368

Burnel (N. N.) Supplément à l'ouvrage de J. J. Aymé. *Paris, an* VIII [1800]. 8vo. 9369

A refutation of No. 2521, Vol. I.

Burnell (George Pratt). A Letter to the Hon. Henry Clay, of Kentucky, containing a brief Reply to some Statements of Joseph John Gurney, in relation to Jamaica. *New York.* 1840. 8vo. N. 9370

Burnet (Gilbert), *Bp. of Salisbury.* A | Compleat | Collection | of | Papers. | In Twelve Parts: | Relating to the Great Revotions | In England and Scotland, | From the Time of the Seven Bishops | Petitioning K. James II. against the | Dispensing Power, June 8. 1688. to | the Coronation of King William | and Queen Mary, April 11. 1689. | *London: Printed by J. D. for R. Clavel at the Peacock, Henry | Mortlock at the Phenix, and Jonathan Robinson at | the Golden Lion in St. Paul's Church-Yard,* 1689. | 4to.

Burnet. A Sixth Collection of Papers relating to the Present Juncture of Affairs in England. *London: R. Janeway.* 1689. 4to, pp. 34. M. 9372

The sixth collection contains a narrative of the miseries of New England by reason of an arbitrary government erected there. Also the petition and address of John Gibson, aged eighty-seven, and George Willow, aged eighty-six, on behalf of the inhabitants of Cambridge, in New England; and another petition by Increase Mather, and two New England gentlemen.

Burnet (J.) Notes on the Early Settlement of the North-Western Territory. By Jacob Burnet. *Cincinnati: Derby, Bradley & Co.* 1847. 8vo, pp. 501. Portrait. BA. + *New York: D. Appleton & Co.* 1847. [*Ibid.*] 9373

See N. A. R., LXV. Also: Speech ... in the Whig National Convention, giving a brief history of the life of Gen. W. H. Harrison. *Washington.* 1839. 8vo. — The Annual Address, delivered before the Cincinnati Astronomical Society, June 3, 1844, ... together with the Act of Incorporation ... . *Cincinnati.* 1844. 8vo, pp. 46. H.

The Burnet House City Guide Book, and Railroad and Steamboat Directory ... . *Cincinnati.* 1858. 24mo, pp. 28. H.

Burnet (M.) An Election Sermon, preached at Hartford, on the Day of the Anniversary Election, May 12, 1803. By Matthias Burnet, D.D. Pastor in ... Norwalk. *Hartford: printed by Hudson & Goodwin.* 1803. 8vo, pp. 29. BA., C., W. 9375

Burnet. A Sermon, Preached the second Lord's Day after the Death of his ... Wife, Mrs. Ann Burnet. ... By Matthias Burnet, A.M. ... in Norwalk, Connecticut. *New-Haven: Printed by Thomas and Samuel Green.* MDCCXC. 8vo, pp. 24. BA.

[Burnet (William).] An | Essay | on | Scripture-Prophecy, | Wherein it is Endeavoured | To | Explain the Three Periods | Contain'd in the XII Chapter of the | Prophet Daniel. | With some Arguments to make it Probable, | That the First of the Periods did Expire in the Year | 1715. | [Motto.] | *Printed in the Year* MDCCXXIV. | 4to. JCBt. 9377

Probably printed in New York? by Wm. Bradford. *See* Smith's "New Jersey," pp. 417, 418, and Allen, p. 193. The author was the son of Bishop Burnet, and Governor of the Colony of New York. It is introduced here on account of the imprint.

Burnet. A Poem presented to his Excellency W. Burnet, Esq., on his arrival at Boston. [*Boston.* 1728.] 8vo. 9378

Burnett (Alfred). Incidents of the War, Humorous, Pathetic, and Descriptive. *Cincinnati.* 1863. 12mo. C. 9379

Burnett (H. C.) Force Bill. Speech of Hon. Henry C. Burnett, of Kentucky, in the House of Representatives, Feb. 26, 1861. [*Washington.* 1861.] 8vo, pp. 8. H. 9380

Also: Speech ... on the Bill to regulate Suffrage in the City of Washington: in reply to Hon. Humphrey Marshall, ... and Hon. H. Winter Davis, ... House, May 25, 1858. [*Washington: T. McGill, Printer.* 1858.] 8vo, pp. 16. H.

Burnett (H. L.) Reply of the Judge Advocate, H. L. Burnett, to the Pleas of the Counsel for the Accused, to the Jurisdiction of the Military Commission, convened by Major-General Hooker, commanding Northern Department, in the Case of the United States vs. Charles Walsh, Buckner S. Morris, Vincent Marmaduke, R. T. Semmes, Charles Travis Daniel, George E. Cantril, G. St. Leger Grenfell, Benjamin M. Anderson, charged with conspiring to release the Rebel Prisoners

at Camp Douglas, Chicago, Illinois, and to lay waste and destroy that City. *Cincinnati: Moore, Wilstach & Baldwin, Printers.* 1865. 8vo, pp. 44, 2 l. H. 9381

Burnett (P. H.) The American Theory of Government considered with reference to the Present Crisis. By Peter H. Burnett. ... *New York: D. Appleton & Co.; London.* 1861. 8vo, pp. 93. BA. + Second Edition ... enlarged. ... *New York: D. Appleton & Co.* 1863. 8vo, pp. viii, 119. H. 9382

Burnett (*Sir* William). An Account of a Contagious Fever amongst the Danish and American Prisoners of War at Chatham, in the Years 1813, 14. *London.* 1831. 8vo. 9383

Burnett (W. B.) Synopsis of a Report made to the President and Directors of the Long Island Water Works Company, January, 1853. By Ward B. Burnett, Civil Engineer. *Williamsburgh: Printed at the Office of the Independent Press, South Seventh Street.* 1853. 8vo, pp. 24. 9384

Burnett, Drake & Co.'s Bank Note Reporter, and Counterfeit Detector. For January, 1864. *Boston: Thomas Groom & Co.* [186–?] Large 8vo, pp. 33, (3). H. 9385

Burney (J.) A Chronological History of the North-Eastern Voyages of Discovery; and of the Early Eastern Navigation of the Russians. By Captain James Burney, F.R.S. *London: Payne & Foss.* 1819. 8vo, pp. viii, 310. Map. BA., S. 9386

Burney. A Chronological History of the Discoveries in the South Sea or Pacific Ocean. — Part I. Commencing with an Account of the earliest Discovery of that Sea by Europeans, And terminating with the Voyage of Sir Francis Drake, in 1579. Illustrated with Charts. By James Burney, Captain in the Royal Navy. *London: G. and W. Nicol.* 1803–1817, 5 vols., 4to, Title, pp. xii, (viii), 391; v, (xi), 482; (x), 437; xviii, 580; vii, 236. 45 Maps and Plates. BA. 9387

Vol. II. was printed in 1806 (from 1579 to 1620); Vol. III. in 1813 (from 1620 to 1688); Vol. IV. in 1816 (from 1688 to 1723); and Vol. V. (to the year 1764) in 1817. "A masterly digest of the voyages in the South Sea, displaying a rare union of nautical science and literary research." — *Quarterly Review. See also* M. R., XLII. 414; XLIII. 135; LXXXVIII. 196.

Burney. History of the Buccaneers of America. By James Burney, F.R.S. ... *London: Payne and Foss.* 1816. 4to, pp. xii, 326. 3 Maps. 9388

This is Vol. IV. of the preceding work, with a new title-page.

BURNEY. A Memoir on the Geography of the North-Eastern Part of Asia, and on the question whether Asia and America are contiguous, or are separated by the Sea. By Captain James Burney, F.R.S. From the Philosophical Transactions. *London: William Bulmer & Co.* 1818. 4to, Title, pp. 15. 9389

BURNEY. A Memoir of the Voyage of d'Entrecasteaux, in search of La Pérouse. By James Burney, Esq. Of the Royal Navy, and F.R.S. *London: Luke Hansard and Sons.* 1820. 8vo, pp. 21. 9390

BURNHAM (A.) A Discourse addressed to the Congregational Church and Society in Pembroke, N. H., March 5, 1848. By their Pastor, Rev. Abraham Burnham. It being the Fortieth Anniversary of his Ministry. *Concord: Asa McFarland.* 8vo, pp. 20. 9391

BURNHAM (A. A.) Who are the Agitators? Speech of Hon. A. A. Burnham, of Connecticut. Delivered in the U. S. House ... March 7, 1860. [n. p. n. d.] 8vo, pp. 8. H. 9392

BURNHAM (A. W.) Historical Discourse delivered on the Fortieth Anniversary of his Pastorate in Rindge, N. H., November 14, 1861, By A. W. Burnham, D.D. With Addresses, &c. on the same Occasion. *Boston: Crosby and Nichols.* 1862. 8vo, pp. 102. BA. 9393

BURNHAM (George P.) The History of the Hen Fever (a Humorous Record). By G. P. Burnham. *Boston.* 1855. 12mo, pp. 326. C. 9394

BURNHAM (R.) Pious Memorials, or the Power of Religion on the Mind Exemplified in the Experience of many Eminent Persons, with their Lives, by R. Burnham. *Paisley.* 1788. 8vo.

Contains many American biographies, Mr. Hutson, of South Carolina, Governor Hopkins, of Connecticut, Dr. Samuel Mather, Charles Chauncy, etc.

BURNHAM (W.) God's Providence in placing Men In their Respective Stations & Conditions asserted & shewed. A Sermon Preached before the General Assembly of the Colony of Connecticut, at Hartford, May, 10, 1722. The Day for Electing the ... Governour ... By William Burnham ... *New-London: T. Green.* 1722. 16mo, Title, pp. 41. H. 9396

BURNLEY (W. H.) Observations on the Present Condition of the Island of Trinidad, and the Actual State of the Experiment of Negro Emancipation. By William Hardin Burnley. *London: Longman.* 1842. 8vo, pp. 177. C. 9397

BURNLEY. Opinions on Slavery and Emancipation in 1823 ... with additional observations applicable to Hon. E. G. Stanley's plan for the extinction of Slavery. *London.* 1833. 8vo, pp. lv, 44. 9398

BURNLEY. Observations sur la situation actuelle de l'île de la Trinité. Par W. Hardin Burnley. *Paris.* 1842. 9399

BURNS (A.) Boston Slave Riot, and Trial of Anthony Burns. Containing the Report of the Faneuil Hall Meeting; the Murder of Batchelder; Theodore Parker's Lesson for the Day; Speeches of Counsel on both Sides, ... Judge Loring's Decision; and Detailed Account of the Embarkation. *Boston: Fetridge and Company.* 1854. 8vo, pp. 86. BA., C., H. 9400

BURNS. Rendition of Anthony Burns. Murderers, Thieves, and Blacklegs employed by Marshal Freeman! [n. p. n. d.] Broadside. 9401

BURNS (D.) Sermon at the Ordination of Abel Leonard, at Woodstock, by David Burns, of Scituate. *Boston: New England.* 1764. 8vo. 9402

BURNS (J.) Missionary Enterprises in many Lands. By the Rev. Jabez Burns. Second Edition. 32mo, pp. 428. + Third Edition. *London: Knight & Son.* 1854. 9403

BURNS (J.) Notes of a Tour in the United States and Canada in the Summer and Autumn of 1847. By Jabez Burns. *London: Houlston.* 1848, 18mo, pp. 180. S. 9404

BURNS (J. R.) Battle of Williamsburg, with Reminiscences of the Campaign, Hospital Experiences, Debates, etc. By James R. Burns. *New York: The Author.* 1865. 24mo, pp. 119.

BURNS (J. L.) Report of the Committee recommending that a Pension be granted to John L. Burns, of Gettysburg. [*Washington.* 1864.] 8vo, pp. 2. (Sen. Rep. Com., No. 13, 38th Cong., 1st Sess., '64.) 9406

"Mr. Burns, an aged citizen of Gettysburg, was the only person of that place who took up arms, and joined the Federal army in its defence."

BURNS (R.) Poems, Chiefly in the Scottish Dialect. By Robert Burns. *Philadelphia: Printed for, and sold by Peter Stewart and George Hyde.* 1788. 12mo, pp. 304. Portrait. W. + *New York.* 1788. 8vo, pp. 306. 9407

These have no reference to America, but are interesting to the collector, as they *both* claim to be the *first* American edition. The New York edition contains some Scottish poems, selected from Robt. Ferguson. The following are partly historical: Burns Celebration. Celebration of the Hundredth Anniversary of the Birth of Robert Burns, by the Boston Burns Club, January 25th, 1859. *Boston.* 1859. 12mo, pp. 84. — Burns Club of Washington City. Celebration of the Centennial Anniversary of the Birth of Robert Burns. *Washington.* 1859. 8vo. C.

BURNS (*Rev.* Robert), D.D. Report of a Visit to Canada and Nova Scotia. *Edinburgh.* 1844. pp. 50. 9408

BURNS (R. T.) Lecture on the Maine Law. *Kingston.* 1853. 8vo, pp. 11. 9409

Also: Progress and Principle of the Temperance Reformation. *Kingston.* 1857. 12mo, pp. 12. *See* "Maple Leaves."

BURNS (W. Scott). Connexion between Literature and Commerce: in two Essays. Read before the Literary and Historical Society of Toronto. *Toronto.* 1845. 8vo, pp. 16. 9410

BURNSIDE (Ambrose Everett). Speech of General Burnside [made on the Eighth of February, before a Meeting of the United States Christian Commission, in New York. *New York.* 1853.] Slip. H. 9411

BURNSIDE. Report of Col. A. E. Burnside, commanding the First Regiment Rhode Island Volunteers, May 23, 1861. [n. p. n. d.] 8vo, pp. 7. 9412

Also: Proclamation to the Citizens of North Carolina. [n. p. n. d.] Slip. H.

BURNSIDE (M.) Oration, ... delivered before the Officers and Members of Merimack Lodge, Haverhill, ... By M'Gregore Burnside, A.B. ... *Haverhill: printed by Francis Gould.* ... *Jan.* 1807. 8vo, pp. 16. 9413

BURNSIDE (S. M.) Oration delivered at Worcester, on the Thirtieth of April, A.D. 1813, before the Washington Benevolent Society of the County of Worcester, in Commemoration of the First Inauguration of General Washington as President of the United States. By Samuel M. Burnside. ... *Worcester: printed by Isaac Sturtevant.* 1813. 8vo, pp. 20. H. 9414

BURNYEAT (J.) An Epistle from John Burnyeat to Friends in Pennsylvania; to be disperced by them to the neighbouring Provinces, which for convenience and dispatch was thought good to be printed, and so ordered by the Quarterly Meeting, of Philadelphia, the 7th of the 4th month, 1686. *Printed and sold by William Bradford, near Philadelphia.* 1686. 4to, pp. 4. 9415

BURNYEAT. Journal of the Life and Gospel Labours of John Burnyeat. *London: Harvey and Darton.* 1839. 8vo. 9416

This was issued with William Caton's Journal and John Crooker's Life, and forms Vol. VI. of John Barclay's Select Series. Also reprinted in "The Friends' Library," Vol. XI.

BURNYEAT. The Truth Exalted in the Writings of that Eminent and Faithful Servant of Christ John Burnyeat, collected Into this Ensuing Volume as a Memorial to his Faithful Labours in and for the Truth. ... *London: Thomas Northcott.* 1691. Sm. 4to, 4 l., pp. 264. BA. 9417

Contains an account of his travels and labors in various parts of America, and sundry epistles addressed to the Friends in Barbadoes, Maryland, New Jersey, etc. *See* Smith's "Catalogue of Friends' Books," I. 348–9.

BURPEE (E. R.) Report of the Survey of Extension of the European and North American Railway to the American Boundary, and Branch Line to Fredericton. By E. R. Burpee. [Vignette.] *Fredericton: printed by John Graham.* 1865. 8vo, pp. 19, Appendix, i–xiv. 9418

BURR (*Rev.* Aaron). A discourse delivered at New-Ark in New-Jersey, January 1, 1755. Being a Day set apart for solemn Fasting and Prayer, on Account of the late Encroachments of the French, and their Designs against the British Colonies in America. By Aaron Burr, President of the College of New Jersey. [Motto.] *New York: Hugh Gaine.* M,DCCLV. 4to, pp. 41. H. 9419

BURR. ... A Funeral Sermon, Preached At the Interment of ... Jonathan Belcher, Esq; Governor of ... New-Jersey ... By the late Reverend Mr. Aaron Burr ... *New-York:* [n. d.] 4to, pp. v, iv, 22. + *Boston, N. E.: Re-printed and Sold by Edes and Gill.* M,DCC,LVIII. 8vo, pp. iv, iv, 23. BA. 9420

BURR. Sermon at the Ordination of David Bostwick. *New York.* 1745. 8vo. 9421

[BURR.] The Supreme Deity of our Lord Jesus Christ, maintained, in a Letter to the Dedicator of Mr. Emlyn's "Inquiry into the Scripture Account of Jesus Christ," Inscribed to the Reverend the Clergy of all Denominations in New-England. Wherein Mr. Emlyn's Objections are fairly answered, and shewn to have no Validity, by the late Rev. Aaron Burr, President of the College in New-Jersey. [Mottoes.] *Boston, N. E.: J. Draper.* 1757. 8vo, pp. 92. + *Boston: Re-Printed by Edward E. Powars.* MDCCXCI. 8vo, Title, pp. 61. B., BA. 9422

See Webster's "Presbyterian Ch. in America," I. 52.

BURR. The Watchman's Answer to the Question, What of the Night? &c. A Sermon Preached before the Synod of New York, Convened at Newark in New-Jersey, September 30. 1756. By Aaron Burr, A.M. President of the College of New-Jersey. Published by the Desire of the Synod. *New York.* 1756. 8vo, pp. 43. + The Second Edition. [Motto.] *New York: Printed. Boston: Re-printed and sold by S. Kneeland.* 1757. 8vo, pp. 46. BA. + The Third Edition. *Boston: S. Kneeland.* 1757. 8vo, pp. 46. 9423

See "Gentleman's Magazine" for 1855.

BURR (A.) The Private Journal of Aaron Burr, during his Residence of Four Years in Europe; with Selections from his Correspondence. Edited by Matthew L. Davis, Author of "Memoirs of Aaron Burr," &c. ... *New-York: Harper & Brothers.* 1838. 2 vols., 8vo, pp. 451; Title, 9–453. Plate.

Reprinted [on thinner paper]. *New York.* 1856.

BURR. Burr's Conspiracy Exposed, and Gen. Wilkinson Vindicated. *See* [Wilkinson (J.)]

BURR. The Conspiracy of Colonel Aaron Burr: a Historical Romance. *New York.* 1854. 16mo, pp. 311. 9425

BURR. The Examination of Col. Aaron Burr, before the Chief Justice of the United States, upon the Charges of a High Misdemeanor, and of Treason against the United States; together with the Arguments of Counsel and Opinion of the Judge. To which is added An Appendix, containing the opinion of the Supreme Court, delivered by Chief Justice Marshall, in the case of Bollman and Swartwout. *Richmond: S. Grantland.* 1807. 8vo, pp. 46. BA. 9426

BURR. An Examination of the various Charges exhibited against Aaron Burr. *See* [Van Ness (P.)]

BURR. A Letter to Aaron Burr, Vice-President of the United States of America, on the Barbarous Origin, the Criminal Nature and the Baneful Effects of Duels; occasioned by his late fatal interview with the deceased and much lamented General Alexander Hamilton. By Philanthropos. *New York: Printed for the Author.* 1804. 8vo, pp. 32. N. 9427

BURR. Message from the President of the United States [Thomas Jefferson] transmitting Information touching an Illegal Combination of Private Individuals against the Peace and Safety of the Union, Jan. 22, 1807. [*Washington.* 1807.] 8vo, pp. 16. M. 9428

Case of Aaron Burr's conspiracy.

BURR. Message from the President of the United States, [Thomas Jefferson] transmitting a Copy of the Proceedings, and of the Evidence exhibited, on the Arraignment of Aaron Burr and others before the Circuit Court of the United States, held in Virginia, in 1807. *Washington.* 1807. 8vo, pp. 554. (Pub. Doc.) 9429

BURR. Particulars of the late Duel, fought at Hoboken, July 11, between Aaron Burr and Alexander Hamilton, Esqrs. in which the latter unfortunately fell. Containing all the papers relating to the Event; together with the Will of Gen. Hamilton, and the Letters of Bishop Moore, and the Rev. J. M. Mason. *New York: A. Furman.* 1804. 8vo, pp. 32. N. 9430

BURR. A Narrative of the Suppression by Col. Burr, of the History of the Administration of John Adams. *See* [Wood (John)].

BURR. Strictures upon the Narrative by the Suppression, by Col. Burr, of Wood's History of the Administration of John Adams. By a Yeoman. [n. p. n. d.] 8vo, pp. 26. 9431

BURR. [Sale] Catalogue of Revolutionary Relics, from the Collection of Aaron Burr. *New York.* 1852. 8vo, pp. 24.

BURR. The Trial of Colonel Aaron Burr, on an Indictment for Treason, before the Circuit Court of the United States, held in Richmond, (Virginia,) May Term, 1807; including the Arguments and Decisions on all the Motions made during the Examination and Trial, and on the Motion for an Attachment against Gen. Wilkinson. Taken in Short-hand by T. Carpenter. *Washington City: Westcott & Co.* 1807–8. 3 vols., 8vo, Title, pp. 147, 135; 465; 416, Appendix, 1 l. BA., C. 9433

BURR. Reports of the Trial of Col. Aaron Burr, (late Vice President of the United States) for Treason, and for a Misdemeanor, in preparing the means of a Military Expedition against Mexico, a Territory of the King of Spain, with whom the United States were at peace. In the Circuit Court of the United States, Held in the City of Richmond, in the district of Virginia, in the Summer Term of the year 1807. To which is added An Appendix, containing The Arguments and Evidence in Support and Defence of the Motion afterwards made by the Counsel of the United States, to Commit A. Burr, H. Blennerhassett and J. Smith, To be sent for Trial to the State of Kentucky, for Treason or Misdemeanor, Alleged to be committed there. Taken in Short Hand. By David Robertson, Counsellor at Law. In Two Volumes. *Philadelphia: Published by Hopkins and Earle.* 1808. 2 vols., 8vo, Title, 4 l., pp. 596; 539. CH. 9434

Some copies are labelled "Fine Paper;" they are but little better than ordinary copies. Uncut copies sell for about $25.

BURR. The Trial of Aaron Burr for High Treason, ... 1807. Compiled from Authentic Reports made during the Trial. To which is added an Account of the Subsequent Proceedings against Burr, Blennerhassett, and Smith, in the same Court. With Notes ... By J. J. Coombs, ... *Washington: W. H. & O. H. Morrison, Publishers.* 1865. 8vo, pp. lii, 392.

BURR. View of the Political Conduct of Aaron Burr, Esq. *See* [Wood (John)].

BURR (C. C.) The History of the Union, and of the Constitution. Being the Substance of Three Lectures, on the Colonial, Revolutionary, and Constitutional Periods of American History, with an Appendix containing the Constitution of the United States. By C. Chauncey Burr. *New York: Van Evrie, Horton & Co.* 1862. 12mo, pp. 92. + [With] the Virginia and Kentucky Resolutions of '98. ... Third Edition. *New York: Van Evrie, Horton & Co.* 1863. 12mo, pp. 92, 4. 9436

BURR. Notes on the Constitution of the United States, with Expositions of the Most Eminent Statesmen and Jurists, Historical and Explanatory Notes on every Article. By C. Chauncey Burr. *New York: J. F. Feeks.* [1864.] 12mo, pp. 96, Index, viii. BA. 9437

Also: The Nation. *New York.* 1855. Imp. 8vo, pp. 80. — Speech in the Peace Convention, New York, June 3, 1863. pp. 4. (And other speeches.)

BURR (D. H.) The American Atlas. Exhibiting the Post Offices, Post Roads, Rail Roads, Canals, and the Physical and Political Divisions of the United States of North America. ... By David H. Burr ... [n. p. 184–.] 13 Maps. Lithographic Views, 1 l. BA. 9438

The maps are copyrighted in the *District of Columbia*, the lithograph views were printed at *Boston*.

BURR. Guide to Burr's Map of New-York ... for 1834. *New York: J. H. Colton.* 18mo. Map. 9439

BURR (F.) The Field and Garden Vegetables of America; containing Full Descriptions of nearly Eleven Hundred Species and Varieties; with Directions for Propagation, Culture, and Use. By Fearing Burr, Jr. Illustrated. *Boston: Crosby and Nichols.* 1863. 8vo, pp. xv, 674. C. + Second and enlarged Edition. *Boston: J. E. Tilton & Co.* 1866. 8vo, pp. 700. H.

BURR (J.) God's Presence removes the Fear of Death. A Sermon, preached at Barnstable, February 14, 1807, at the Interment of the Rev. Oakes Shaw ... who departed this Life Feb. 11, 1807 ... By Jonathan Burr ... *Boston: printed by Manning and Loring.* 1807. 8vo, pp. 28. H. 9441

BURR (L. S.) A Voice from Sing Sing. *Albany.* 1833. 8vo.

BURR (S. J.) The Life and Times of William Henry Harrison. By S. J. Burr. *New York: L. W. Ransom.* 1840. 18mo, pp. 304. Portrait. H. + Eighth Edition. *New York: L. W. Ransom.* 1840. pp. 300. Portrait. C. 9443

BURR (William). Descriptive and Historical View of Burr's Moving Mirror of the Lakes, the Niagara, St. Lawrence and Saguenay Rivers embracing the Entire Range of Border Scenery, of the United States & Canadian Shores, from Lake Erie to the Atlantic. *New York: printed by George F. Bunce.* 1850. 8vo, pp. 48. H. 9444

BURR SEMINARY, *Manchester, Vt.* Catalogue. 1851. 8vo. Continued 9445

[BURRAGE (Henry Sweetser).] Brown University in the Civil War. A Memorial. ... *Providence.* 1868. Sm. 4to, pp. xii, (1), 380. B. 9446

[BURRIEL (A. M.)] De la Californie. *See* Venegas (M.)

BURRILL (G. R.) An Oration pronounced at the Baptist Meeting-House in Providence ... the Seventh of January, 1800, at the Funeral Ceremony on the Death of Gen. George Washington. By Col. George R. Burrill. *Providence: Printed by John Carter.* [1800.] 8vo, pp. 15. BA. 9447

BURRILL. An Oration delivered ... on the Fourth of July, A.D. 1797, in Commemoration of American Independence. By

George R. Burrill, Esq. ... *Providence: Carter and Wilkinson.* 1797. 8vo, pp. 18. BA. 9448

Also, Oration ... April 11, 1796. *Providence: Bennett Wheeler.* 1796. 8vo, pp. 18. N.

BURRILL (Joseph). Vindication of the Bank of Credit projected in Boston from the Aspersions of Paul Dudley, Esq. [*Boston.*] 1714. 16mo. M. 9449

BURRINGTON (G.) Seasonable Considerations on the Expediency of a War with France, and a Comparison between the British and French Dominions. By George Burrington. *London.* 1743. 8vo. 9450

Relates, in part, to the American colonies.

BURRITT (E.) A Plan of Brotherly Copartnership of the North and South, for the Peaceful Extinction of Slavery. By Elihu Burritt. *New York: Dayton and Burdick.* 1856. 12mo, pp. 48. BA. 9451

BURRITT. Thoughts and Things, at Home and Abroad; By Elihu Burritt, with a Memoir by Mary Howitt. *Boston.* 1854. 12mo, pp. 364. P. 9452

BURRITT. The Year-Book of the Nations, for 1855. 2d Edition. By Elihu Burritt. *London.* 1855. Post 8vo. + For 1856. *New York: D. Appleton & Co.* 1856. 12mo, pp. iv, 50.

BURRITT. The Works of Elihu Burritt: containing 'Sparks from the Anvil,' 'Voice from the Forge,' and 'Peace Papers for the People.' *London: A. W. Bennett.* 1848. C. 9454

Each of these works were also published separately. Also: The Proposition of a Universal Ocean Penny Postage. By Elihu Burritt. [n. p. n. d.] 8vo, pp. 4. — Sparks from the Anvil. *Worcester.* 1846. 16mo. + Illustrated Edition. *London: J. Partridge.* 12mo, pp. viii–150. — Twenty Reasons for Total Abstinence from Slave-Labor Produce. [n. p. n. d.] 8vo, pp. 4. N.

[BURROUGH (E.)] A | Declaration Of the Sad and Great | Persecution and Martyrdom | Of the People of God, called | Quakers, in New-England, | for the Worshipping of God. | Whereof | 22 have been Banished upon pain of Death. | 03 have been Martyred. | 03 have had their Right-Ears cut. | 01 hath been burned in the Hand with the letter H. | 31 Persons have received 650 Stripes. | 01 was beat while his Body was like a jelly. | Several were beat with Pitched Ropes. | Five Appeals made to England, were denied | by the Rulers of Boston. | One thousand forty four pounds worth of Goods hath | been taken from them (being poor

men) for meeting | together in the fear of the Lord, and for keeping the | Commands of Christ. | One now lyeth in Iron-fetters, condemned to dye. | Also, | Some Considerations, presented to the King, which is | in Answer to a Petition and Address, which was presented | unto Him by the General Court at Boston: Subscribed by | J. Endicot, the chief Persecutor there; thinking thereby to | cover themselves from the Blood of the Innocent. [By Edward Burrough] | *London: Printed for Robert Wilson, in Martins Le Grand.* | [1660] | 4to pp. 32. C. 9455

The pamphlet is signed on page 32, "*London*, the 15th of the first *month*, 1660. E. B." Contains the first printed account of the execution of Mary Dyer, and others, of Boston. *See* "Hist. Mag.," II. 119; Sewell's "Hist. of Quakers;" Hazard's Collection, II. 594; Hutchinson Papers, 325–9; Smith's Catalogue, I. 351.

BURROUGHS (C.) Address delivered by Request of the City Government at the Dedication of the New High School House ... Portsmouth, N. H. September IV, MDCCCLVI. By Rev. Charles Burroughs, D.D. ... *Portsmouth: Edward N. Fuller, Printer.* 1856. 8vo, pp. 31. H. 9456

BURROUGHS. A Discourse, on the Preservation of Documents as the Materials of History; delivered ... in Concord, N. H. before the New-Hampshire Historical Society, at the Celebration of their Anniversary, June 14, 1843. By Rev. Charles Burroughs, D.D. ... *Concord: printed by Asa McFarland.* [1843.] 8vo, pp. 29. B., H. 9457

BURROUGHS. A Discourse delivered in the Chapel of the New Alms-House in Portsmouth, N. H., Dec. 15, 1834, on the occasion of its being first opened for Religious Services. By Charles Burroughs, D.D., ... *Portsmouth, N. H.: J. W. Foster.* 1835. 8vo, pp. 108. 9458

BURROUGHS. Memoirs and Select Papers of Horace B. Morse, A.B. of Haverhill, N. H. who was drowned near Portsmouth Harbor, June 22, 1825. By Charles Burroughs. [Motto.] *Portsmouth, N. H.: Printed by Miller and Brewster.* 1829. 12mo, pp. vi, 203. H. 9459

BURROUGHS. An Oration on the Moral Grandeur of George Washington, delivered on the Centennial Anniversary of his Birth Day, February XXII, MDCCCXXXII, at the Request of the Citizens of Portsmouth, N. H. By Charles Burroughs ... . *Portsmouth: Nathaniel March & Co.* 1832. 8vo, pp. 59. H.

Also: Eulogy delivered ... at the Interment of James Hervey Pierrepont, M.D. Sunday, January XXVII, MDCCCXXXIX, by Request of the Medical Faculty. ... . *Ports-*

mouth, N. H.: J. W. Foster. 1839. 8vo, pp. 58. H. + A Funeral Discourse, ... Newburyport ... April XXVIII, MDCCCXLII, at the Interment of the Reverend James Morss, D.D. Rector ... who died ... April XXVI, MDCCCXLII. ... *Portsmouth, N. H.: J. W. Foster.* 1842. 8vo, pp. 29. H. — Memorial of Moody Kent, Esq., a Munificent Benefactor to the New Hampshire Asylum for the Insane. ... *Concord: printed by Cogswell & Sturtevant.* 1866. 8vo, pp. 15. H.

BURROUGHS (C.) Rich | Newes | from | Jamaica: | Of | Great Spoyl made by the English, | upon the Enemy, both | by | Land, & Sea. | Being the Substance Of a | Letter | from | Cornelius Bvrrovhs, | Steward Generall, Dated | from | Point-Cagway. | *London: Printed by M. Simmons.* 1689. | 4to, Title, pp. 4. 9461

BURROUGHS (E.) The Memorable Works of a Son of Thunder and Consolation: Namely, That True Prophet, and Faithful Servant of God, and Sufferer for the Testimony of Jesus, Edward Burroughs, Who Dyed a Prisoner for the Word of God, in the City of London, the 14th of the 12th Moneth, 1662. *Published and Printed for the good and benefit of generations to come, in the Year* 1672. Folio, pp. (52), 806, (8). B. 9462

"To the churches in New-England, Barbadoes, and other Islands, pp. 544–547; To Friends in Barbadoes, Virginia, and New-England, &c., pp. 548–550; Answer to a Petition of the General Court of Boston, presented to the King Feb. Eleaventh, 1660, pp. 756–763."

BURROUGHS (J.) The Rare Jewel of Christian Contentment. ... Eighteen Rules. Added a few Passages from Mr. Bolde's Preparation for Death. By Jeremiah Burroughs. *Boston: Benj. Gray.* 1731. 12mo. B. 9463

BURROUGHS (John). Notes on Walt Whitman as Poet and Person. By John Burroughs. *New York: American News Co.* 1867. 16mo, pp. 108. C. 9464

BURROUGHS (P.) An Oration with some observations, pronounced at the Congregational Meeting House in Tiverton, on the 22d Feb'y, 1800, at the funeral ceremony on the Death of General George Washington. By Peleg Burroughs, V.D.M. [With a Poem.] *Newport: Henry Barber.* 1800. 8vo, pp. 13, 2. 9465

BURROUGHS (Stephen). Memoirs of Stephen Burroughs, [by himself.] Copy Right Secured. *Printed at Hanover, Newhampshire: printed by Benjamin True.* MDCCXCVIII. 8vo, pp. vii, 7–296. BA., H. + *Otsego: E. Phinney.* 1810. 18mo, pp. 100. + Memoirs, with notes and an appendix. *Albany.* 1811. 12mo, pp, 396. C. + Sketch of his Life. *New-York.* 1811. 18mo.

BURROUGHS. Memoirs of the Notorious Stephen Burroughs: containing many Incidents in the Life of this Wonderful Man ... Stereotype Edition ... . *Boston: Charles Gaylord.* 1832. 16mo, pp. 439. + *Boston: Charles Gaylord.* 1832. 18mo, pp. 356, (4). + *Boston.* 1835. 2 vols., 12mo. C., H. 9467

The subject of these memoirs was a notorious swindler.

BURROUGHS (S.) Sermon at Rutland, Mass. on a Haymow. [n. p. n. d.] 12mo, pp. 10. W. 9468

BURROWES (T. H.) Pennsylvania School Architecture. A Manual of Directions and Plans for grading, locating, constructing, heating, ventilating and furnishing Common School Houses. Thomas H. Burrowes, Editor. Published by authority. *Harrisburg: printed by A. Boyd Hamilton.* 1855. 8vo, pp. 276. Plate and Woodcuts. C., H. 9469

BURROWES. State Book of Pennsylvania, Containing an account of the Geography, History, Government, Resources, and Noted Citizens of the State; With a map of the State and of each County. By Thomas H. Burrowes. *Philadelphia: Uriah Hunt & Son.* 1847. 12mo, pp. 314. C. 9470

BURROWS (E. J.) The Great Rebellion of 1861. Twelve Months' History of the United States. Showing what a Republic can Do. Skirmishes and Battles. What the Rebels have done to Destroy the Union. The Lessons of the Year, Etc. Etc. Collected and Arranged by E. J. Burrows. *Philadelphia: C. Sherman and Son.* 1862. 8vo, pp. 60. 9471

The cover title reads: *Published by H. Derousse, Philadelphia.*

BURROWS (*Rev.* George). A discourse delivered in the First Presbyterian Church of Easton, Pa., on the day of the Annual Thanksgiving, Nov. 27, 1851. *Easton, Pa.* 1852. 8vo. 9472

BURROWS (J. L.) American Baptist Register, for 1852. J. Lansing Burrows, Editor. *Philadelphia:* 1853. 8vo, pp. 491, 1 l. H., P. 9473

Contains a list of all the Baptist ministers, and twenty-seven plates.

BURROWS. A Christian Merchant: a memoir of James C. Crane. By J. S. Burrows, D.D. *Charleston, S. C.: Southern Baptist Publication Society.* 1858. 12mo, pp. 90. Portrait. C.

BURROWS. The New Richmond Theatre. A Discourse, delivered ... February 8, 1863, in the First Baptist Church,

Richmond, Va. By J. L. Burrows, D.D. ... *Richmond: Smith, Bailey & Co.* 1863. 8vo, pp. 16. H. 9475

BURROWS. Palliative and Prejudiced Judgments Condemned. A Discourse delivered in the First Baptist Church, Richmond, Va., June 1, 1865, The Day appointed by the President of the United States for Humiliation and Mourning, on Account of the Assassination of President Lincoln, together with an Extract from a Sermon, Preached on Sunday, April 23, 1865, upon the Assassination of President Lincoln. By J. Lansing Burrows, D.D. ... *Richmond, Va.: Office Commercial Bulletin.* 1865. 8vo, pp. 12. 9476

A small edition printed, as it was originally intended for private distribution.

BURROWS (R. L.) Remarks of Hon. R. L. Burrows, and Address by Hon. Noah Davis, on the Occasion of the National Obsequies of President Lincoln, at Albion, N. Y., April 19, 1865. *Rochester, N. Y.: C. D. Tracy & Co., Printers.* 1865. 8vo, pp. 24. 9477

BURROWS (S. E.) Important Trial for Seduction in the Superior Court of New York, before Justice Oakley. Nancy Van Hann *vs.* Silas E. Burrows, 27th and 28th November, 1833. [*New York.* 1833.] 8vo, pp. 20. C. 9478

BURS (William P.) An Address to the Legislature and People of the State of Connecticut, on the Subject of dividing the State into Districts for the Election of Representatives in Congress. By W. Pitt Burs. *New Haven: T. & S. Green.* 1791. 8vo, pp. 37. C. 9479

BURT (A.) The Coronation; or, Hypocrisy Exposed. Also, Sullivan Island: a Satirical Poem, with Notes. By Adam Burt. *Charleston, S. C.* 1822. 12mo, pp. 71. 9480

BURT (F.) Sketches of the Civil and Ecclesiastical History of Durham. By Rev. Federal Burt. *Concord: Asa McFarland.* 1837. 9481

See "New Hampshire Historical Collections," V. 129.

BURT (J.) Earthquakes the Effects of God's Wrath. A Sermon Preached at Bristol, The Lord's Day after a very terrible Earthquake, which was on Tuesday, November 18, 1755. A few minutes after four o'clock in the Morning. By John Burt A.M. Pastor of a Church in Bristol. *Newport.* [n. d.] 4to, pp. 17. M. 9482

BURT. The Law of Christian Rebuke; a Plea for Slave-Holders. A Sermon, delivered at Middletown, Conn., before the Anti-Slavery Convention of Ministers and other Christians, October 18, 1843. By J. Burt ... . *Hartford: N. W. Goodrich & Co.* 1843. 8vo, pp. 20. BA., M. 9483

BURT (J. H.) En Stemme fra St. Croix. *Kjöbenhavn Lose & Delb.* 1852. 8vo. 9484

BURT (N. C.) National Character; a Thanksgiving Discourse, delivered 1855, in the Franklin Street Presbyterian Church. By N. C. Burt, D.D. *Baltimore: John D. Toy.* 1855. 8vo, pp. 28. C. 9485

BURT (Wm. A.) Report on Lake Superior, 1846. *See* Houghton (J.)

BURT (W. A.), *and* HUBBART (Bela). Report on the Geography, Topography, and Geology of the South Shore of Lake Superior for 1845. *Detroit.* 1846. 16mo, pp. 109. 9486

BURT (William L.) [Circular containing proposed amendments to the constitution of the United States, in regard to slavery. Dated Boston, November, 1862.] Folio, 1 page. H.

BURTIS (W. R. M.) Essay. New Brunswick, as a Home for Emigrants; with the Best Means of promoting Immigration, and developing the Resources of the Province. By W. R. M. Burtis. *St. John: printed by Barnes and Company.* 1860. 12mo, pp. 50. 9488

Also: The New Dominion; A Poem. By W. R. M. Burtis. *St. John.* 1867. — Prize Essay on the History of New Brunswick. Read before the St. John's Young Men's Debating Society. 1857.

BURTON (A.) A Journal of the Cruise of the United States Ship Susquehanna during the Years 1860, 1861, 1862 and 1863. By Amos Burton. *New York: E. O. Jenkins.* 1863. 8vo, pp. 177. 9489

BURTON (A.) A Discourse delivered before ... Governor, ... Council, etc., of ... Vermont, ... Oct. 8. being the Day of General Election. By Asa Burton. *Rutland.* 1795. 8vo.

Also: Sermon at the Installation of Daniel Breck, at Hartland, Vt. Nov. 11, 1789. *Windsor, Vt.* 1791. 8vo. — Sermon at the Ordination of Benjamin White. *Kennebunk.* 1811. 8vo. — Sermon before the Phi Beta Kappa at Dartmouth College, Aug. 26, 1800. *Hanover.* 1801. 8vo. — A Sermon preached at the Ordination of the Rev. Caleb J. Tenney, to the Pastoral Care of the First Congregational Church of Christ, in Newport, R. I., Sept. 12, 1804. *Newport: Mercury Office.* [1804.] 8vo, pp. 24. W.

— ... A Sermon preached at the Ordination of the Rev. Timothy Clark, to the Pastoral Care of the Church of Christ in Greenfield, January 1, 1800. ... . *Windsor, Vermont: printed by Alden Spooner.* 1800. 8vo, pp. 24. N. + *Newburyport.* 1806. 8vo, pp. 24.

BURTON (C.) The Waking Dreams of a Foreigner During the five years of his probation written in his leisure hours, for amusement. By C. Burton, Professor of Perspective. *New York: printed for the Author, by C. N. Baldwin.* 1820. 12mo, pp. viii, 56. 9491

BURTON (J.) The Duty and Reward of Propagating Principles of Religion and Virtue exemplified in the History of Abraham. A Sermon preach'd before the Trustees for Establishing the Colony of Georgia, in America. And before the Associates of Dr. Bray for Converting the Negroes in the British Plantations ... At their Anniversary-Meeting ... March 15, 1732. By John Burton. ... *London: Hatchard, Mount and Page.* M.DCC.XXXIII. 4to, pp. 50. H. 9492

BURTON (J. E.) Essay on Comparative Agriculture; or a Brief Examination into the State of Agriculture as it now Exists in Great Britain and Canada. By Rev. J. E. Burton, A.B. *Montreal.* 1828. 12mo, pp. 107. 9493

BURTON (J. H.) The Emigrant's Manual; containing, Australia, New Zealand, America, and South Africa: with a Preliminary Dissertation. By John Hill Burton. *Edinburgh: W. & R. Chambers.* 1851. 12mo. 9494

BURTON. A Narrative of Criminal Trials in Scotland. By John Hill Burton. In Two Volumes. *London: Chapman and Hall.* 1852. 2 vols., post 8vo, pp. iv, 310; 319. C. 9495

Contains an account of the Darien expedition. The "Book-Hunter," written by the same author, contains some notices of libraries in New York, extracted from Dr. Wynne's "Private Libraries of New York."

BURTON (N. J.) A Discourse delivered January 29th, 1865, in Memory of Robert H. Gillette, by Nathaniel J. Burton . ... Hartford, Conn. Published by Request. *Hartford: Press of Wiley, Waterman & Eaton.* 1865. 12mo, pp. 44. H. 9496

BURTON (R. F.) The City of the Saints and across the Rocky Mountains to California. By Richard F. Burton ... . *London: Longman, [etc.]* 1861. 8vo, pp. x, (2), 707. 3 Maps. BA. + Second Edition. *London: Longman.* 1862. 8vo, pp. 707. Map and Plates. C. + *New York: Harper & Brothers,* 1862. 8vo, pp. 574. 9497

BURTON. Explorations of the Highlands of the Brazil; with a Full Account of the Gold and Diamond Mines. Also, Canoeing down 1500 Miles of the Great River São Francisco, from Sabará to the Sea. By Captain Richard F. Burton, F.R.G.S., etc. ... *London: Tinsley Brothers.* 1869. 2 vols., 8vo, pp. xii, 443; viii, 478. Map and Woodcuts. BA., C. 9498

The "Mission to Gelele, King of Dahome," by the same author, includes an account of the "Present State of the Slave Trade, and the Negro's Place in Nature. *London: Tinsley.* 1864." 2 vols., post 8vo.

B[URTON] (R[obert]). The English | Empire | in | America: | Or a Prospect of His Majesties Dominions | in the West-Indies. Namely, | Newfoundland | New-England | New-York | Pennsylvania | New-Jersey | Maryland | Virginia | Carolina | Bermuda's | Barbuda | Anguilla | Montserrat | Dominica | St. Vincent | Antego | Mevis, Or | Nevis | S. Christophers | Barbadoes | Jamaica | With an account of the Discovery, Scituation, | Product, and other Excellencies of these Countries. | To which is prefixed a Relation of the first Discovery | of the New World called America, by the Spaniards. | And of the Remarkable Voyages of several English- | men to divers places therein. | Illustrated with Maps and Pictures. | By R. B. ... . *London: Printed for Nath. Crouch.* ... 1685. 12mo, 2 l., pp. 209. Map, and 2 Plates. + The Second Edition. *London: N. Crouch.* 1692. 12mo. C. + The Third Edition. *London: Printed for N. Crouch.* ... 1698. + The Fourth Edition. *London.* 1704. + The Fifth Edition. *London: Nath. Crouch.* 1711. 18mo, pp. 191. + Sixth Edition. *London: A. Bettsworth.* 1728. 18mo, pp. 192. + The Seventh Edition. *Dublin:* 1729. 12mo. + *Dublin.* 1735. 12mo. + [Another] Seventh Edition. *London.* 1739. 12mo. W. 9499

"A name placed in the title-pages of a number of books by Nath'l Crouch, a bookseller, who is supposed to have written them himself." — WATT.

B[URTON] (R[obert]). The | English Heroe: | or, | Sir Francis Drake Revived. | Being a full Account of the Dangerous Voyages, | Admirable Adventures, Notable Discoveries, | and Magnanimous Atchievements of that | Valiant and Renowned Commander. As, | I. His Voyage in 1572. to Nombre de Dios in | the West-Indies, where they saw a Pile of Bars of Silver | near seventy feet long, ten feet broad, and 12 foot high. | II. His incompassing the whole World in 1577. | which he performed in Two years and Ten months, | gaining a vast quantity of Gold and Silver. | III. His Voyage into America in 1585. and | taking the Towns of St. Jago, St. Domingo, Carthagena, | and St. Augustine. | IV. His last Voyage into those Countreys in | 1595. with the manner of his Death and Burial. | Recommended as an Excellent Example to all | Heroick and Active Spirits in these days to endeavour | to benefit their Prince and Countrey, and Immortalize | their Names by the like worthy Undertakings. | Revised, Corrected, very much Inlarged, reduced into Chap- | ters with Contents, and beautified with Pictures. | By R. B. | Licensed and Entred according to Order, | March 30. 1687. | *London: Printed for Nath. Crouch at the Bell in | the Poultrey near Cheapside.* 1687. | 12mo, 1 l., pp. 206. Portrait of Drake. + Fifteenth Edition. *London: C. Hitch.* 1756. 2 l., pp. 186. + Sixteenth Edition. 3 l. pp. 162. 9500

Other editions: 1695, 1702, 1706, 1710, 1716, 1739, and 1762.

BURTON (Robert). Der Englische Held und Ritter Franciscus Drake in einer Beschreibung von dessen Leben, Thaten, und See Reisen. Aus dem Englischen. *Leipzig.* [1690.] 8vo.

BURTON. Wonderful Prodigies of Judgment and Mercy. By Robert Burton. Eighth Edition. *London.* 1729. 18mo, pp. 189, (3). 9502

Contains a few "Admirable Deliverances from Danger by Sea and Land," in New England, etc. The following contain some references to America: Extraordinary Adventures & Discoveries of several famous Men. 1685. 12mo. — General History of Earthquakes, particularly those lately in ... Jamaica, and Sicily. *J. Hodges: on London Bridge.* 1734. 12mo. — Memorable Accidents and Unheard-of Transactions (contains the Adventures of French-men in the Islands of Antilles; ...) *Printed on London Bridges* 1733. 12mo, Frontispiece. — Miracles of Art and Nature; or, A Brief Description of the several varieties of Birds, Beasts, Fishes, Plants, and Fruits of other Countreys. Together with several other Remarkable Things in the World. ... *London: William Bowtel.* 1678. 18mo, pp. 120.

BURTON (Robert). A True Exposition of the Transactions which led to the Failure of the late Franklin Bank, etc. *New York.* 1831. 8vo. N. 9503

[BURTON (Warren).] The District School as it Was, by One who Went to It. Revised Edition. *New York.* 1838. 8vo. + *Boston: Phillips, Sampson and Company.* 1850. 12mo, pp. 206. BA., C. 9504

BURTON. The District School as it was, Scenery-Showing, and other Writings. *Boston: T. R. Marvin.* 1852. 12mo, pp. 364. C. 9505

BURTON. Helps to Education in the Homes of our Country. By Warren Burton. *Boston: Crosby and Nichols.* 1863. 12mo, pp. viii, 368. C. 9506

BURTON. The Scenery-Shower; with Word Paintings of the Beautiful, the Picturesque, and the Grand in Nature. *Boston.* 1844. 12mo. 9507

[BURTON.] White Slavery: A new Emancipation Cause, presented to the People of The United States. By the author of "The District School as it was." *Worcester: M. D. Phillips. Boston: C. C. Little & Co.* ... 1839. 8vo, pp. xi, 199. BA., C.

BURTON (William E.) Waggaries and Vagaries. A series of sketches, humorous and descriptive. *Philadelphia: Carey & Hart.* 1848. 12mo, 8 l., pp. 192. C. 9509

BURTON. *See* Gentlemen's Magazine.

B[URTT] (J[ohn]). The Young Patriot, and other Poems; By J. B., a Friend of the Aborigines Protection Society. *Manchester: William Irwin.* [1846.] 16mo, 6 sheets. 9510

BURWELL (William B.) Mr. Burwell's Motion [in the House of Representatives of the United States of America, relative to Armaments]. Feb. 8, 1808. *Washington.* 1808. 8vo. C. 9511

BURWELL. Mr. Burwell's Motion for authorizing the President immediately to employ the Public Armed Vessels, for the Purpose of convoying the Merchant Vessels of the United States. January 19, 1810. ... . *Washington.* 1810. 8vo, 2 l. H. 9512

BURWELL (W. M.) Address delivered before the ... University of Virginia, at their Annual Meeting, June 29, 1847. By William M. Burwell, Esq. *Richmond: Printed by Shepherd and Colin.* 1847. 8vo, pp. 27, 7. M. 9513

BURWELL. Memoir Explanatory of the Transunion and Tehuantepec Route between Europe and Asia. Prepared for the Company by William M. Burwell, Esq., of Virginia. *Washington: Printed by Gideon & Co.* 1851. 8vo, pp. 36. Map.

[BURY (Richard).] A Collection of Several Messages and Warnings, to the Inhabitants of the City of Bristol, concerning the sad Calamities and Overthrow to come upon them, except they speedily Repent ... *London.* 1701. 4to, 2 sheets. || A Continuation of the Messages ... . 1705. 4to. + [Both Parts.] Second Edition, with Additions. *London.* 1712. 4to. 9515

Reprinted with the title:

BURY. A Collection of Sundry Messages ... . [First Part,

comprising the Two Former Parts.] *London.* 1712. || [Second Part.] *Bristol.* 1728. 6516

Part II. (*Bristol,* 1728) contains "A Collection of Earth-Quakes, in Foreign Parts," including Boston in New England, Jamaica, and Barbadoes. *See* Smith's "Catalogue of Friends' Books," I. 369–71.

BURY. Bury's Genealogical Account of the Family of Leck or Leake of Bedlington, and of the Charity of John George Leake in New York. [n. p.] *Privately Printed* 1844. Rl. 8vo.

BURY (*Viscount*). *See* Keppel (W. C.)

BUSBEE (Perrin). Reports. *See* North Carolina.

BUSCH (M.) Die Mormonen, ihr Prophet, ihr Staat, und ihr Glaube. Von Dr. Moritz Busch. *Leipzig: Carl B. Lorck.* 1855. 8vo, 1 l., pp. 158. (Conversations- und Reisebibliothek, Band VIII.) C. 9518

BUSCH. De Mormonen. Een overzigt van het ontstaan, de inrigting en geloofsleer dezer sekte. Uit het Hoogduitsch. *Amsterdam: H. W. Mooy.* 1855. 8vo. 9519

BUSCH. Geschichte der Mormonen nebst einer Darstellung ihres Glaubens und ihrer gegenwärtigen socialen und politischen Verhältnisse. 1859. 8vo. 9519*a*

BUSCH. Wanderungen zwischen Hudson und Mississippi, 1851 und 1852. Von Moritz Busch. *Stuttgart: Cotta.* 1854. 2 vols., 8vo, 4 l., pp. 381. (Reisen und Länderbeschreibungen, Lief. 39, 40.) C., P. 9520

BUSCHMANN (J. C. E.) Das Apache als eine athapaskische Sprache erwiesen; in Verbindung mit einer systematischen Worttafel des athapaskischen Sprachstammes, von Joh. Carl Ed. Buschmann. Erste Abtheilung. Aus den Abhandlungen der Königl. Akademie der Wissenschaften zu Berlin 1860. *Berlin: Dümmler.* 1860. 4to, pp. 98. 9521

BUSCHMANN. Der Athapaskische Sprachstamm, dorgestellt von Hrn. Buschmann. Aus den Abhandlungen der Königl. Akademie der Wissenschaften zu Berlin 1855. *Berlin: Dümmler.* 1856. 4to, pp. 171. C. 9522

BUSCHMANN. Grammatik der sonorischen Sprachen, vorzüglich der Tarahumara, Tepeguama, Cora und Cahita, als IX. Abschnitt der Spuren der aztekischen Sprache ausgearbeitet. Erste Abtheilung. Das Lautsystem. Aus den Abhandlungen der Königl. Akademie der Wissenschaften zu Berlin 1863. *Berlin: Dümmler.* 1864. 4to, pp. 85. C. 9523

BUSCHMANN. Die Lautveränderungen aztekischer Wörter in den sonorischen Sprachen und die sonorische Endung AME dargestellt von Joh. Carl Ed. Buschmann. Aus den Abhandlungen der Königl. Akademie der Wissenschaften zu Berlin aus dem Jahre 1856. *Berlin: Dümmler.* 1857. 4to, pp. 118. C.

Kayser gives the number of pages as 25; another authority as 126.

BUSCHMANN. Die Pima-Sprache und die Sprache der Koloschen, dargestellt von Joh. Carl Ed. Buschmann. Aus den Abhandl. d. k. Akad. d. W. zu Berlin aus dem Jahre 1856. *Berlin: Dümmler.* 1857. 4to, pp. 132. C. 9525

BUSCHMANN. Die Sprachen Kizh und Netela von Neu-Californien, dargestellt von Joh. Carl Ed. Buschmann. Aus den Abhandlungen der Königl. Akademie der Wissenschaften zu Berlin 1855. *Berlin: Dümmler.* 1856. 4to, pp. 31. C.

BUSCHMANN. Die Spuren der aztekischen Sprache im nördlichen Mexiko und höheren amerikanischen Norden. Zugleich eine Musterung der Völker und Sprachen des nördlichen Mexiko's und der Westseite Nordamerika's von Guadalaxara an bis zum Eismeer. Von Joh. Carl Ed. Buschmann. (Zweiter Supplement-Band der Abhandlungen der Königl. Akademie der Wissenschaften zu Berlin 1854.) *Berlin.* 1859. 2 vols., 4to. C.

This work consists of two volumes; for the portions taken from it and published as separate treatises will have to be added to it as a second or supplementary volume, according to the author's explanation on pp. 119 and 120. Their separation from the main work has been owing to practical reasons; and they form, as shown by the continuous pagination, essential parts of the work. In fact, without their embodiment into the work, the use of the copious geographical index, which also refers to them, would be made nugatory. These treatises, or chapters, should be added to the second volume in the following order: I. Die Lautveränderung aztekischer Wörter in den sonorischen Sprachen. II. Die Pima Sprache. III. Der Athapaskische Sprachstamm. IV. Die Völker und Sprachen Neumexicos. V. Die Völker und Sprachen des britischen Ostlandes (contained in the October part of 1858, of "Monatsberichte der Berliner Akademie," pp. 465 to 486). VI. Die Sprachen Kizh und Netela von Neu-Californien.

BUSCHMANN. Systematische Worttafel des athapaskischen Sprachstamms, aufgestellt und erläutert von Carl Ed. Buschmann. Dritte Abtheilung des Apache. Aus den Abhandlungen der Königl. Akademie der Wissenschaften zu Berlin 1859. *Berlin: Dümmler.* 1860. 4to, pp. 88. C. 9528

BUSCHMANN. Die Verwandtschafts-verhältnisse der athapaskischen Sprachen dargestellt. Zweite Abtheilung des Apache. Aus den Abhandlungen der Königl. Akademie der Wissenschaften zu Berlin 1862. *Berlin: Dümmler.* 1863. 4to, pp. 60. C. 9529

BUSCHMANN. Die Völker und Sprachen Neu-Mexiko's und der Westseite des britischen Nordamerika's dargestellt von Joh. Carl Ed. Buschmann. Aus den Abhandlungen der Königl. Preuss. Akademie der Wissenschaften zu Berlin 1857. *Berlin: Dümmler.* 1858. 4to, pp. 204. C. 9530

BUSCHMANN. Über die aztekischen Ortsnamen. Von Joh. Karl Ed. Buschmann. Erste Abtheilung. *Berlin: F. Dümmler.* 1853. 4to, pp. 205. C. 9531

From the "Abhl. d. k. Akad. d. W. zu Berlin."

BUSEY (S. C.) Immigration; its Evils and Consequences. By Samuel C. Busey, M.D. *New York:* 1856. 12mo. C.

BUSH (G.) Address delivered at Hope Chapel, New York, May 15th, 1857, during the Celebration of the First Centenary of the Church of the New Jerusalem. By Rev. George Bush. *New York.* 1857. 8vo, pp. 39. H., S. 9533

BUSH (J. S.) Death of President Lincoln, A Sermon, Preached in Grace Church, Orange, N. J., Easter, April 16, 1865. By the Rector James S. Bush, M.A. *Orange, N. J.: E. Gardner, Printer.* 1865. 8vo, pp. 8. 9534

[BUSHE (Gervase Parker).] *See* [Butler (George B.)]

BUSHEL (J.) A true and perfect | Narrative | of | The late dreadful fire which happened | at Bridge-Town, in the Barbadoes, April 18. 1688. | As the same was communicated in two | Letters from Mr. John Bushel, and Mr. Francis Bond, | two Eminent Merchants there, to Mr. Edward Bushel | Citizen and Merchant of London. | Containing the beginning, progress, and event of that | dreadful fire; with the estimation of the | loss accrewing thereby, as it was delivered | to his Majesty, by several Eminent | Merchants concerned in that | Loss. | Licenced According to Order. | *London: Printed by Peter Lillicrap, Living in Clerken- | well Close.* | [1668.] 4to, Title, pp. 6. 9535

BUSHNELL (A.) A Brief Memorial of Rev. Henry Martyn Adams, a Missionary of the A. B. C. F. M. ... . By Rev. Albert Bushnell. ... *Boston: Mass. Sabbath School Society.* [n. d.] 18mo, pp. 69. Plate. H. 9536

BUSHNELL (C. I.) An Arrangement of Tradesmen's Cards, Political Tokens; also, Election Medals, Medallets, etc., Current in the United States of America for the last Sixty years.

Described from the Originals, Chiefly in the Collection of the Author, With Engravings. By Charles I. Bushnell. ... *Printed for the Author: New York.* 1858. 8vo, pp. x, 119. 4 Plates.

Twelve copies printed on large paper, 4to.

BUSHNELL. Crumbs for Antiquarians: Vol. I. Containing Early New York Business Tokens, Memoirs of Samuel Smith, Journal of Solomon Nash, Memoirs of Tarleton Brown, Narrative of Levi Hanford, Journal of R. J. Meigs during the Expedition against Quebec. *New York: Privately Printed.* 1862. 8vo, pp. 17, 41, 65, 65, 80, 57. 12 Plates. Vol. II. *New York: Privately Printed.* 1866. 8vo, 4 l., Narrative of Leggett, pp. 71, Moody, 98, Blatchford, 127, Fletcher, 86. 9538

The above is a general title for a series of tracts, written or edited by Mr. Bushnell. For the titles at length, *see* under the names of the authors. About a hundred copies were printed, and complete sets have become scarce. The portraits, &c., were engraved by Dr. Anderson, when in his eighty-eighth year. Mr. Bushnell's notes on these authors are both copious and minute, and, in some cases, exceed in volume the original text.

BUSHNELL. A | Memoir | of | Eli Bickford, | a | Soldier of the Revolution. | *New York:* | *Privately Printed.* | 1865. | 8vo, pp. 15. Woodcut. 9539

Thirty copies printed.

BUSHNELL. An Historical Account of the First Three Business Tokens issued in the City of New York. By Charles I. Bushnell. *New York: Privately printed.* 1859. 8vo, pp. 23. Plate. + [Second Edition.] *New York: Privately Printed.* 1859. 8vo, pp. 23. Plate. 9540

This second edition forms No. 1 of Bushnell's "Crumbs for Antiquarians," of which fifty copies were printed.

BUSHNELL. A Narrative of the Life and Adventures of Levi Hanford, a Soldier of the Revolution. By Charles I. Bushnell. *New York: Privately Printed.* 1863. 8vo, pp. 80. 2 Plates. 9541

Forms No. 5 of "Bushnell's Crumbs for Antiquarians," Vol. I.

[BUSHNELL (Horace).] California, its Characteristics and Prospects. (From the New Englander for February, 1858.) [n. p. 1858.] 8vo, pp. 42, (1). H. 9542

Reprinted as "Characteristics and Prospects of California: ... *San Francisco.* 1858." 8vo.

BUSHNELL. The Census and Slavery; a Thanksgiving Discourse, delivered in the Chapel at Clifton Springs, N. Y., No-

vember 29, 1860. By Horace Bushnell. *Hartford: Lucius E. Hunt.* 1860. 12mo, pp. 24. H. 9543

BUSHNELL. A Discourse on the Slavery Question. Delivered in the North Church, Hartford ... Jan. 10, 1839. By Horace Bushnell. (Published by Request.) *Hartford: Printed by Case, Tiffany & Co.* 1839. 8vo, pp. 32. 9544

BUSHNELL. The Fathers of New England. An Oration delivered before the New England Society of New York, December 21, 1849, and published at their Request. By Horace Bushnell. *New York: G. P. Putnam.* 1850. 8vo, pp. 44. C.

BUSHNELL. Reverses Needed. A Discourse delivered on the Sunday after the Disaster of Bull Run, in the North Church, Hartford. By Horace Bushnell. *Hartford: L. E. Hunt.* 1861. 8vo, pp. 27. H. 9546

BUSHNELL, Speech for Connecticut. Being an Historical Estimate of the State, delivered before the Legislature and other invited Guests at the Festival of the Normal School in New Britain, June 4, 1851. By Horace Bushnell. ... *Hartford: Boswell and Faxon.* 1851. 8vo, pp. 43. H. 9547

BUSHNELL. Twentieth Anniversary. A Commemorative Discourse delivered in the North Church, of Hartford, May 22, 1853. By the Pastor, Horace Bushnell. *Hartford: Elihu Geer, Printer.* MDCCCLIII. 8vo, pp. 32. H., S. 9548

BUSHNELL. Women's Suffrage; the Reform against Nature. By Horace Bushnell. *New York: Charles Scribner and Company.* 1869. 12mo, pp. 184. BA. 9549

Also: An Address before the Hartford Co. Agricultural Society, Oct. 2, 1846. *Hartford.* 1846. pp. 24. C. Barbarism the first Danger. A Discourse for Home Missions. *New-York.* 1847. 8vo, pp. 32. H. — Common Schools. A Discourse on the Modifications demanded by the Roman Catholics ... on the Day of the late Fast, March 25, 1853. *Hartford: Press of Case, Tiffany and Company.* 1853. 8vo, Title, pp. 24. H. — The Day of Roads. A Discourse, delivered on the Annual Thanksgiving, 1846. ... . *Hartford: Elihu Geer.* MDCCCXLVI. 8vo, pp. 35. H. — ... . Popular Government by Divine Right. [Delivered on the late National Thanksgiving in Hartford, Conn.] *Hartford: L. E. Hunt.* [1864.] 8vo, pp. 16. H. — An Oration delivered before the Society of Phi Beta Kappa, at Cambridge, August 24, 1848. By Horace Bushnell. *Cambridge: George Nichols.* 1848. 8vo, pp. 39. H. + Second Edition. *Cambridge.* 1848. 8vo. + Third Edition. *Cambridge: George Nichols.* 8vo, pp. 39. H., S.

BUSHNELL (W.) Sermon preached at the Funeral of Dea. Elijah F. Woodward, April 26, 1846, in the Church in Newton Centre. By Rev. Wm. Bushnell ... . *Boston: J. Howe, Printer.* 1847. 8vo, pp. 20. H. 9550

BUSHNELL. Sermon preached at the Funeral of Hon. William Jackson, March 2, 1855 ... . By William Bushnell. *Boston: S. Chesm.* 1855. 8vo, pp. 23. BA. 9551

BUSHNELL (W. H.) The Hermit of the Colorado Hills. A Story of the Texan Pampas. By W. H. Bushnell. *New York: S. Tousey.* 1864. 8vo, pp. 46. 9552

BUSHNELL. White Wolf. A Story of the Sante Fe Trail. By William H. Bushnell. *Boston: Elliott, Thomas & Talbot.* [1868.] 12mo, pp. 100. C. 9553

Business and Diversion Inoffensive. *See* [Seccombe (Joseph)].

Business Directory of the Principal Southern Cities, with a Business Register of Northern Firms who either have already or desire to have Business Relations with the Southern Cities. 1866 and 1867. *New York: Dunkley & Woodman.* 1866. 8vo, pp. 453. C. 9554

The title-page is indicative of a political bias.

Business Directory and Gazetteer to the Towns on the Albany and Susquehanna Railroad, and of Coopertown, Delhi, Norwich, Oxford, etc. *Albany: C. Van Benthuysen & Sons, Printers.* 1868–9. 8vo, pp. 220. 9555

Business Register of Manufacturers in the States of Massachusetts, Connecticut, Rhode Island, and New Hampshire, and the Principal Manufacturers in New York, New Jersey, Ohio, Pennsylvania, Maine, and Vermont. *New York: Freeman, Cleary & Co.* 1868–9. 4to, pp. 410. 9556

BUSK (H.) The Navies of the World; their Present State and Future Capabilities. By Hans Busk. ... [Motto.] ... . *London: Routledge, Warnes, and Routledge.* 1859. 16mo, pp. xvi, 312, Appendix, 127. Woodcuts. C., H. 9557

[BUSK (M. M.)] The History of Spain and Portugal. From B.C. 1000 to A.D. 1814. ... *London: Baldwin and Cradock.* MDCCCXXXIII. 8vo, Title, pp. xvi, 364. BA., C. 9558

Includes notices of Brazil, Mexico, etc. Published under the superintendence of the Society for the Diffusion of Useful Knowledge.

[BUSS (F. J.)] Ueber die Verfassungs-Urkunde der Vereinigten Staaten von Nord-Amerika. Historischer Theil, nach Story's Commentarien bearbeitet. *Leipzig: Hinrichs'sche Buchhandlung.* 1838. 8vo. 9559

BUSSIERE (Th. de). Le Pérou et sainte Rose de Lima (sainte Rose de Sainte-Marie). Par le vicomte M. Th. de Bussiere. *Paris: Plon.* 1863. 8vo, pp. 478. 9560

BUSSIÈRE. L'Empire mexicain, histoire des Toltèques, des Chichimèques, des Aztèques et de la conquête espagnole. Par le vicomte Th. de Bussière. *Paris: Plon.* 1863. 8vo, 2 l., pp. 427. 9561

BUSTAMANTE (A. Sanchez de). Geografia del Peru, Bolivia y Chile. *Lima.* 1843. 8vo. 9562

BUSTAMANTE (Anastasio). Manifiesto á la Nacion. *Mexico.* 1830. 4to, pp. 20. 9563

BUSTAMANTE. Manifesto dirige à sus Compatriotas como General en Gefe del ejercito de Operaciones sobre Tamaulipas y demas Departamentos de Oriente y Documentos Justificativos. *Mexico.* 1839. 4to, pp. 29. 9564

Also: Documentos Justificativos. 8vo, pp. 75.

BUSTAMANTE. Reflecsiones sobre el manifesto de D. Anastasio Bustamente dado en 14 de Agosto de 1832. *Mexico.* 1832. 4to, pp. 22. 9565

BUSTAMANTE (C.) El Lazarillo de Ciegos Caminantes desde Buenos-Ayres, hasta Lima con sus Itinerarios segun la mas puntual observacion, con algunas noticias utiles á los Nuevos Comerciantes que tratan en Mulas; y otras Historicas. Sacado de las memorias que hizo Don Alonso Carriò de la Vandera en este dilatado Viage, y Comision que tubo por la Corte para el arreglo de Correos, y Estafetas, Situacion y ajuste de Postas, desde Montevideo. Por Don Calixto Bustamante Carlos Inca, alias Concolorcorvo Natural del Cuzco, que acompañò alreferido Comisionado en dicho Viage, y escribiò sus Extractos. Con Licencia. *En Gijon: en la Imprenta de la Rovada. Año de* 1773. Sm. 8vo, 246 l. H. 9566

"This work bears all the marks of having been printed in Lima. The author was a descendant from the ancient Incas. He accompanied Don Alonso Carrio in a journey from Buenos Ayres to Lima, for the purpose of establishing the posts between those places, in the humble capacity of a servant. This work is a joco-serious account of the expedition." — RICH, I. 194.

BUSTAMANTE (C. M.) La Aparicion de Ntra Señora de Guadalupe de Mexico, comprobada con la refutacion del argumento negativo que presenta D. Juan Bautista Muñoz, fondándos en el testimonio del P.-Fr.-Bernardino Sahagun, ó sea:

historia original de este escritor que altera la publicada en 1829, en el equivocado concepto de ser la única y original de dicho autor. Precediendo una disertacion sobre la Aparicion Guadalupana, y con notas sobre la conquista de Mexico. *Mexico: J. Cumplido.* 1840. 12 l., pp. 247, Table, 2 l. C. 9567

The frontispiece represents Our Lady of Guadeloupe.

BUSTAMANTE. Apuntes para la historia del gobierno del general D. Antonio Lopez de Santa-Anna, desde principios de octubre de 1841 hasta, 6 de diciembre 1844, en que fué depuesto por uniforme voluntad de la nacion. *Mexico: José M. Lara.* 1845. 4to, pp. 111, (1 l.), pp. 460. C. 9568

BUSTAMANTE. Campañas del General D. Felix Maria Calleja, comandante en gefe del ejercito real de operaciones, llamado del centro. *Mexico.* 1828. 8vo. C. 9569

BUSTAMANTE. Cronica Mexicana. Teomóxtli o Libro que contiene todo lo interesante à Usos, Costumbres, ... de los Indios antiquos Tultecas y Mexicanos, redactado da un antiquo Codice di Boturino. *Mexico.* 1821–2. 4to. 12 Maps. 9570

BUSTAMANTE. Cuadro Histórico de la Revolucion de la América Méxicana, comenzada en quince de Septiembre de Mil Ochocientos Diez, por el Ciudadano Miguel Hidalgo y Costilla. Primera [y Secunda] Epoca. Dedicada al Ciudadano General José Maria Morelos. Su Autor, Carlos Maria De Bustamante. *México.* 1823. *Imprenta de la Aguila.* 2 vols., 4to, Title, pp. 360, 7 l.; Title, pp. 420, 6 l. C. 9571

Of this valuable work, a second edition, enlarged, was published in *Mexico*, 1843–47, 6 vols., 8vo.

BUSTAMANTE. El Gabinete mexicano durante el segundo periodo de la administracion del exmo. Señor Presidente D. Anastasio Bustamante, hasta la entrega del mando al exmo. Señor Presidente interino D. Antonio Lopez de Santa-Anna, y continuacion del Cuadro Historico de la Revolucion mexicana. *Mexico: José M. Lara.* 1842. 2 vols., sm. 4to, 3 l., pp. 216, Table, viii; 249, Table, x, pp. 46. C. 9572

BUSTAMANTE. Galeria de antiguos Principes Mejicanos. *Puebla.* 1821. 2 pts., 4to. A. 9573

BUSTAMANTE. Historia de la Compañia de Jesus en Nueva-España. *Mexico.* 1841–2. 3 vols., 8vo. 9574

See Cavo (D. A.), Ternaux (H.), and Tocqueville (A. de).

BUSTAMANTE. Historia del imperador D. Agustin de Iturbide, hasta su muerte y sus consecuencias; y establicimiento de la República popular federal. Su Autor el Lio. D. Carlos Maria Bustamante. *Mexico: imprenta de J. Cumplido.* 1846. Sm. 4to, pp. vii, 293. 9575

This forms a continuation of "Cuadro Historico," No. 9572.

BUSTAMANTE. Horribles crueldades de los conquistadores de México y de los Indios que los auxiliaron. *Mexico.* 1829.

BUSTAMANTE. Los horores de Cortes. *Mexico.* 1821. 4to.

"A virulent pamphlet, in which Bustamante endeavored to show that O'Donoghue (the last Vice-Roy of Mexico) surpassed even Cortes in cruelty." — HARRISSE.

BUSTAMANTE. Mañanas de la Alameda de México. Publícalas para facilitar a las Señoritas el Estudio de la Historia de su pais, Carlos Maria Bustamante. *Mexico: Imprenta de la Testamentaria de Valdés, á cargo de José Maria Gallego.* 1835–6. 2 vols., sm. 4to, 3 l., pp. 325; 2 l., pp. xix, 309. 2 Plates. C.

This work relates entirely to the ancient history of Mexico, before the arrival of the Spaniards at Vera Cruz. It contains two steel engravings, one of whichr epresents a calendar with Mexican inscriptions.

BUSTAMANTE. Manifiesto de la Junta Guadalupana a los Mexicanos, y Disertacion historico-critica sobre la aparicion de Nuestra Señora en Tepeyac: escrita por el lic. D. Carlos Maria de Bustamante. *Mexico.* 1831. 4to, pp. 20, 22. 9579

BUSTAMANTE. Martirologio de algunos de los primeros insurgentes por la libertad é independencia de la America Mexicana, Mexico, 1841. ... Necesidad de la Union de Todos los Mexicanos, etc. *Mexico.* 1826. 9580

BUSTAMANTE. Memoria de la republica di Tlaxcalla, Galeria de los principes mexicanos, por Carlos Maria de Bustamante. *Mexico.* 18—. 9581

BUSTAMANTE. Mexico por dentro y fuera bajo el gobierno de los Vireyes. O sea enfermedades politicas que padece la capital de la N. Espana en casi todos los cuerpos de que se compone, y remedios que se deben aplicar para su curacion. Manuscrito inedito que dá á luz por primer Suplemento al tomo IV. de la Voz de la Pátria Carlos Maria de Bustamante. *Mexico: Alejandro Valdés.* 1831. 4to, pp. 173. 9582

A very important work on the history of the Spanish dominion in Mexico. Continuation of "Cuadro Historico," No. 9572.

BUSTAMANTE. Noticias biograficas y juicio critico de sus obras. *Mexico.* 1849. Sm. 8vo, pp. 56. 9583

BUSTAMANTE. El nuevo Bernal Diaz del Castillo, ó sea historia de la invasion de los Anglo-Americanos en Mexico. *Mexico.* 1847. 2 vols., sm. 4to. 9584

BUSTAMANTE. ... La Politica de los Editores del Tiempo analizada ante la Nacion. *Mexico.* 1846. 9585

The catalogue of the Andrade (Maximilian) collection includes a list of several other works, written or edited by this author, who was a native of the city of Antequera de Oaxaca. His works will furnish the student with a vast amount of instructive documents. *See* Boturini, Vol. II., No. 6835, and Murguia, *infra.*

BUSTAMANTE (Javier Aquiler). Defensa del Breve de Monseñor Clementi. *Mexicò.* 1853. 4to. 9586

BUSTAMANTE. Defensayo politico, literario, teológico dogmático. *Mexico.* 1862. 4to. 9587

BUSTAMANTE. Representacion al supremo Magistrado de la Nacion, manifestando los inconvenientes que presenta la ley de 11 de Abril, sobre derogacion de los antiguos derechos parroquiales. *Mexico.* 1857. 8vo, pp. 24. 9588

BUSTAMANTE (J. L.) Biografia del Gobernador y Capitar General Manuel Guillermo Pinto. Escrita por José Luis Bustamante. *Buenos-Aires,* 1853. 8vo, pp. viii, 44. 9589

BUSTAMANTE. Bosquejo de la Historia civil y politica de Buenos Ayres, desda la batalla Monte-Caseros, por José Luis Bustamante. *Buenos Ayres.* 1856. 8vo, pp. 360. Portraits.

BUSTAMANTE. Ensayo historico de la Defensa de Buenos-Aires, contra la rebelion del Ex-Coronel D. Hilario Lagos, Apoyada y sostenida por el Gobernador de la Provincia de Entre-Rios, Brigadier D. Justo José de Urquiza, Director provisorio de las Provincias Argentinas reunidas en Confederacion. Por José Luis Bustamante. *Buenos Ayres.* 1854. 8vo, pp. xii, 660.

A volume of extreme rarity.

BUSTAMANTE. Los cinco errores capitales de la intervencion anglo-francesa en el Plata. Por José Luis Bustamante. *Montevideo.* 1849. 4to, pp. 384. 9592

BUSTAMANTE. Memorias sobre la Revolucion del xi. de Septiembre de 1852. Por José Luis Bustamante. *Buenos Aires.* 1853. 8vo, pp. 270. 9593

BUSTAMENTE (J. M.) Descripcion de la Serranía de Zacatecas, aumentada con planes etc. por C. de Berches. *Méjico.* 1834. 4to. 9594

"L'auteur dit dans ce livre qu'il avait l'intention de donner des plans, vues etc. avec l'ouvrage, mais qu'il ne pouvait pas les faire exécuter au Mexique et qu'il y a rénoncé."

BUSTAMENTE (P.) Relacion de los meritos de P. Bustamente. *Orizava.* 1844. 8vo. 9595

BUSTEED (G. W.) The Great Railway Enterprise, from "Whitehaven" Harbor, on the Eastern Coast of Nova Scotia, to the Head of the Bay of Fundy; or a Plan to shorten the Passage between Europe and America, and also to give a Continuous Land Route through Nova Scotia, New Brunswick, and all the United States, with the Canadas also included. *Boston: J. E. Farwell and Company, Printers.* 1865. 8vo, pp. 10. H.

BUSTEED. Letters to the Members, comprising the Parliament of Great Britain and Ireland, complaining of the most Atrocious Cruelties exercised towards the Slaves and Free People of Colour in the West Indies. *Brooklyn.* 1858. 8vo. 9597

BUSTEED (R.) Speech of Richard Busteed, delivered at Faneuil Hall, Boston, October 31st, 1862. On the Issues of the War, and the Duty of sustaining the Government. *New York: C. S. Westcott & Co.* 1862. 8vo, pp. 24. H. 9598

BUSTEED. An Oration, delivered at Huntington, L. I., New-York, by Richard Busteed, Esq., on Friday, July 4th, 1862. *New York: C. S. Westcott & Co.* 1862. 8vo, pp. 21. H. 9599

BUSTOS (G.) Españoles en Chili. Par D. Gonzales Bustos. [n. d.] 9600

See Ternaux-Compans, page 82.

BUTE (John), 3d *Earl of. See* Stuart (J.)

[BUTEL-DUMONT (George Marie).] Histoire et commerce des Antilles angloises. Où l'on trouve l'état actuel de leur population & quelques détails sur le Commerce de contrebande des Anglois avec les Espagnols dans le Nouveau Monde. On y a joint l'Histoire des Loix principales qui concernent les

Colonies Angloises établies tant dans les isles, que sur le continent de l'Amérique. [*Paris.*] M.DCC.LVIII. 18mo, pp. x, 284. 2 Maps. C., H. 9601

[BUTEL-DUMONT.] Histoire et commerce des colonies angloises dans l'Amérique septentrionale. Où l'on trouve l'état actuel de leur population, et des détails curieux sur la constitution de leur gouvernement, principalement sur celui de la Nouvelle Angleterre, de la Pensilvanie, de la Caroline, & de la Géorgie. *Londres, et se vend à Paris: Le Breton.* 1755. 12mo, pp. xxiv, 336. B., C. + Nouvelle édition. *La Haye.* M, D, CC, LV. 12mo, pp. xvi, 246. H. 9602

"The Present State of North America, *London*, 1735," is principally translated from this work.

[BUTEL-DUMONT.] Historia del establecimiento y commercio de las colonias Inglesas en la America Septentrional: en que se da noticia del estado actual de su poblacion y algunas relaciones individuales y curiosas, acerca de la constitucion de su gobierno, principalmente de el de la Nueva Inglaterra, de la Pennsylvania, de la Carolina, y de la Georgia. Traducido del Frances. *Madrid.* 1768. Sm. 8vo. 9603

[BUTEL-DUMONT.] Geschichte und Handlung der englischen Colonien im nördlichen Amerika. *Frankfurt a. M.: Andreä.* 1758. 8vo. 9604

[BUTEL-DUMONT.] Conduite des François. *See* Jefferys (T.)

BUTEL-DUMONT. Mémoires historiques sur la Louisiane, Contenant ce qui y est arrivé de plus mémorable depuis l'année 1687. jusqu'à présent; avec l'établissement de la Colonie Françoise dans cette province de l'Amérique Septentrionale sous la direction de la Compagnie des Indes; le climat, la nature & les productions de ce pays; l'origine & la Religion des Sauvages qui l'habitent; leures mœurs & leurs coutumes, &c. Composés sur les Mémoires de M. Dumont, par M. L. L. M. [l'abbé Le Mascrier]. *Paris: Chez Cl. J. B. Bauche.* M.DCC.LIII. 2 vols., 12mo, 2 l., pp. x, 261, 4 Plates; 2 l., pp. 338. 5 Plans. BA., M.

Written by an officer, who served twenty-five years in Louisiana. The first volume is the "Natural History," etc.; the second volume, an "Historical Narrative from the death of La Salle, in 1687 to 1740." *See* Rich, I. 104, 114, 146, and Faribault, 83. For a translation, *see* Benjamin F. French's "Historical Collections of Louisiana," Part v.

BUTIN (J.) A Compendious Treatise, containing a Proposal

to preserve the Noblest of Vegetables, and the most Useful to Mankind, the Wheat, from the Smoth ... By James Butin, Farmer in the Settlement of Casinovia, N. Y. *Amsterdam: Printed by H. Van Munster.* 1803. 8vo, pp. 8. S. 9606

BUTLER (A. P.) Speech of Hon. Andrew P. Butler, of South Carolina, in the Senate, Jan. 24, 1850, Surrender of Fugitive Slaves. *Washington.* 1850. 8vo, pp. 12. S. 9607

Also: Speech ... on the Difficulty of Messrs. Brooks and Sumner, and the causes thereof. ... June 12–13, 1856. *Washington.* 1856. 8vo, pp. 31. H., M.

BUTLER (B. F.), *Attorney-General.* Anniversary Discourse, delivered before the Albany Institute, April 23, 1830. By Benj'n Franklin Butler. ... *Albany: printed by Webster and Skinners.* 1830. 8vo, pp. 88. S. 9608

BUTLER. The Military Profession in the United States and the Means of promoting its Usefulness and Honor; an Address ... [at] West Point, at the Close of the Annual Examination, June 19th, 1839. By Benjamin F. Butler. ... . *New York: Samuel Colman.* M DCCC XXXIX. 8vo, pp. 46. H., N. 9609

BUTLER. Outline of the Constitutional History of New-York; an Anniversary Discourse, ... November 19, 1847. By Benjamin Franklin Butler. [Motto.] *New York: Bartlett & Welford.* 1848. 8vo, Title, pp. 11–75. S., H. 9610

BUTLER. Proceedings and Addresses on the Occasion of the Death of Benjamin F. Butler, of New York. *New York: D. Appleton & Co.* 1859. 8vo, pp. 88. 9611

Also: Mr. Butler's Letters to Harmanus Bleecker, Esq. in reply to Certain Charges concerning his Conduct as Attorney-General of the United States, originally published in the New York Evening Post Of the 20th and 22d Nov. 1841. [*New York?*] *Wm. G. Boggs, printer.* 8vo, pp. 12. — Jeffersonian Democracy Defined and Vindicated, in opposition to its definition by Daniel Webster: in a Speech at Tammany Hall, New York, 24th Sept., 1840. 8vo. N. — Plan for the Organization of a Law Faculty ... in the University of the City of New York ... . *New York:* 1835. 8vo, pp. 40. H., B. & S. — Representative Democracy in the United States: an Address delivered before the Senate of Union College, on the 26th July, 1841. ... *Albany: printed by C. Van Benthuysen.* 1841. 8vo, pp. 43. B., H.

BUTLER (B. F.) Argument of Benjamin F. Butler, in behalf of the Government, in the Cases of Lambdin P. Milligan and others, Petitioners for a Writ of Habeas Corpus, before the Supreme Court of the United States, at Washington, D. C., December Term, 1865. *Lowell: Hildreth & Hunt, Printers.* 1866. 8vo, pp. 86. H. 9612

BUTLER. General Orders from Headquarters Department of the Gulf, issued by Major-General B. F. Butler, From May 1st, 1862, to the present time. *New-Orleans: E. R. Wagner, Printer.* 1862. 8vo, pp. 35. H. 9613

First issued on a series of sheets of note paper.

[BUTLER.] Report of a Speech on the Increase of Bank Capital in Massachusetts and the General Banking Law, delivered in the House ... March 31, 1853. [n. p. 1853.] 8vo, pp. 8.

BUTLER. Speech of Maj.-Gen. Benj. F. Butler, upon the Campaign before Richmond, 1864. Delivered at Lowell, Mass., January 29, 1865. With an Appendix: The Two Attacks on Fort Fisher; Speech on the Treatment of the Negro, delivered at Boston, Mass., February 4, 1865; Speech of Hon. Geo. S. Boutwell, in reply to Charges of Hon. James Brooks, of New York, against Gen. Benj. F. Butler, delivered in the House of Representatives, January 24, 1865. *Boston: Wright & Potter, Printers.* 1865. 8vo, pp. 88. 9615

Also: The Candidature for the Presidency in eight years of Stephen A. Douglas. His selfishness, and the Duplicity in principle of his followers. Speech ... in Lowell, August 10, 1860. *Lowell.* 1860. 8vo, pp. 12. H. — Character and Results of the War. How to Prosecute and how to End it. A Thrilling and Eloquent Speech, ... *New York. April* 2, 1863. 8vo, pp. 28. + *Philadelphia.* 1863. 8vo, pp. 32. H. + *Loyal Publication Society, No.* 7. 8vo, pp. 16. C. + *N. Y. Tribune War Tracts, No.* 2. + *Cincinnati.* 1863. 8vo, pp. 16. — The Currency Question. Gen. Butler's Letter to the Editor of the Boston Daily Advertiser. [n. p. 1867.] 8vo, pp. 4. H. — Genuine and Bogus Democracy. Speech ... at the N. Y. Academy of Music ... April 2, 1863. [n. p. 1863.] 8vo, pp. 8. H. — How we may Relieve ourselves from Taxation. Speech ... delivered in the House ... July 14, 1868. [Motto.] *Washington.* 1868. 8vo, pp. 15. H. — Impeachment of the President. Speech ... delivered in the House of Representatives, February 24, 1868. *Washington.* 1868. 8vo, pp. 8. H. — Lecture delivered at the Brooklyn Academy of Music, ... November 24th, 1866. [n. p. n. d.] 8vo, pp. 20. H. — Letter from General Butler to Hon. Daniel S. Richardson. [Dated Lowell, Feb. 3, 1862.] 8vo, pp. 8. H. — Opening Argument of Mr. Butler, of Massachusetts, one of the Managers on the Impeachment of the President. *Washington.* 1868. 8vo, pp. 38. H. — ... Raising of Money to be used in Impeachment. ... Report. [*Washington.* 1868.] 8vo, pp. 48. (40th Cong., 2d Sess., House, Report No. 75.) H. — Reduction of the Currency. Speech ... in the House ... November 26 and 27, 1867. [*Washington.* 1867.] 8vo, pp. 16. H. — Remarks ... on the Exchange of Prisoners; delivered in the House of Representatives, July 17, 1867. *Washington.* 1867. 8vo, pp. 8. H. — Speech ... Against further delays in the Trial of Impeachment in the Senate sitting on the Trial of Andrew Johnson, President of the United States, Thursday, April 16, 1868 ... [*Washington.* 1868.] 8vo, pp. 7. H. — The Status of the Insurgent States, upon the Cessation of Hostilities. The Rights of the Disloyal --- The Duties of the Loyal States. A Speech ... before the Legislature of Pennsylvania. [n. p. 1866.] 8vo, pp. 12. H. — Speech ... . upon his Bill To Authorize the Issue of a National Currency. ... January, 1869. [*Washington.* 1869.] 8vo, pp. 16. — ... The Steamer Gray Jacket and Cargo, Timothy Meaher, Claimant, *vs.* the United States. ... Appeal from the District Court of the United States for the Eastern District of Louisiana. Brief of Claimant. ["Supreme Court of the United States. December Term, 1866."] *Washington, D. C.* [1866.] 8vo, pp. 56.

BUTLER. Correspondence between Gov. Andrew and Major-Gen. Butler. *Boston: J. S. Dyer.* [1862.] 9616

BUTLER. The Life and Public Services of Major-General Butler, the Hero of New Orleans. ... *Philadelphia: T. B. Peterson & Bros.* [n. d.] 12mo, pp. 15, 108. H. 9617

[BUTLER.] Official Documents relating to a "Chaplain's Campaign (not) with General Butler," but in New York. *Lowell: Charles Hunt, Printer.* 1865. 8vo, pp. 48. H. 9618

An answer to [Hudson (Henry N.)] *See infra.*

[BUTLER.] Ye Exploits of Ye Distinguished Attorney and General B. F. B. (Bombastes Furioso Buncombe). [n. d.] Imp. 8vo. 2 Plates. 9619

A series of "Pen and Ink Sketches."

BUTLER. The American Cyclops, the hero of New Orleans, and spoiler of silver spoons, dubbed LL.D. By Pasquino [*pseudon.*]. *Baltimore: Kelly & Piet.* 1868. Sm. 4to, pp. 27. 12 Plates. C. 9620

BUTLER *and* BINGHAM. Debate in the House of Representatives between Mr. Butler, of Massachusetts, and Mr. Bingham, of Ohio, on the Million Appropriation Bill of the Senate for the relief of the Southern Rebels; and the amendment of Mr. Butler that a like sum be appropriated to the relief of the Widows and Orphans of our Soldiers starved in rebel prisons; or that the rich rebels should be taxed to feed their own poor. [*Washington.* n. d.] 8vo, pp. 12. H. 9621

[BUTLER *and* PEABODY.] The Case of Thomas C. A. Dexter. Military Commission at Mobile. Arguments for the Defendant before the President of the United States [by Genl. B. F. Butler and Hon. C. A. Peabody.] *New York: Wm. C. Bryant & Co., Printers.* 1866. 8vo, pp. 57. H. 9622

[BUTLER (*Hon.* Caleb).] A Collection of Facts and Documents relating to Ecclesiastical Affairs in Groton, Mass. ... *Boston: Stephen Foster, Printer.* 1827. 8vo, pp. 44. C., H. 9623

BUTLER. History of the Town of Groton, including Pepperell and Shirley, from the First Grant of Groton Plantation in 1655, with Appendices containing Family Registers, Town and State Officers, Population, and other Statistics. By Caleb Butler. ... *Boston: T. R. Marvin.* 1848. 8vo, pp. xx, 9–499. Map, and Plates. BA., C. 9624

BUTLER. A Review reviewed in a Letter to David Andrews, Nehemiah Cutter, Samuel Farrer, Arnold Hutchinson, and Vryling Shattuck, Committee of the Church. By Caleb Butler. *Boston: Benjamin H. Greene.* 1850. 8vo, pp. 36. H.

BUTLER. Some Account of Deacon John Butler of Pelham, N. H. and of his descendants. By Caleb Butler of Groton. [1849.] 8vo, pp. 15. 9626

BUTLER (C. Moore). Address Delivered by Rev. Clement M. Butler, at the President's Mansion, on the occasion of the Funeral of Abel P. Upshur, T. W. Gilmer, and Others, who lost their lives by the explosion on board the Princeton, February 28, 1844. *Washington.* 1844. 8vo, pp. 8. C. 9627

BUTLER. Funeral Address on the Death of Abraham Lincoln, delivered in the Church of the Covenant, April 19, 1865, by the Rev. C. M. Butler, D.D. Published by Request. *Philadelphia: Henry B. Ashmead, Printer.* 1865. 8vo, pp. 32. H.

BUTLER. Our Country and our Washington. A Discourse, delivered ... February 22, 1852, the Birthday of Washington, in the Hall of the House of Representatives, by the Rev. C. M. Butler, D.D. ... *Washington: printed by Jno. T. Towers.* 1852. 8vo, pp. 23. C. 9629

BUTLER. Sermon giving an Historical Account of St. John's Church, Georgetown, D. C.; Delivered October 17, 1843, and an Address ... Also a Farewell Sermon, delivered April 7, 1844 ... . By Rev. C. M. Butler. ... *Washington.* 1844. 8vo, pp. 40. 9630

Also: Mission of the Protestant Episcopal Church in Boston. A Farewell Sermon, delivered in Grace Church, February, 21, 1847. ... *Boston: James B. Dow.* 1847. 8vo, pp. 26. H. — Our Union — God's Gift A Discourse delivered in ... Washington, D. C. on Thanksgiving Day, November 28, 1850. ... *Washington: printed by Jno. T. Towers.* 1850. 8vo, pp. 29. H. — The Ritualism of Law in the Protestant Episcopal Church of the United States. By the Rev. C. M. Butler, D.D. *Philadelphia: J. Hamilton.* 1867. 18mo, pp. 180. — "A Wise Man is Strong." A Sermon on the Death of Daniel Webster, ... Washington, D. C., December 7, 1852, ... *Washington: W. M. Morrison & Co.* 1852. 8vo, pp. 32. B., H. *See also* Calhoun (J. C.)

BUTLER (David). Sermon at the Induction of the Rev. Frederick Van Horn into St. John's Church at Balltown, and the Church at Charlton, August 8, 1805. *Troy.* 1805. 8vo, pp. 24. N. 9631

Also: A Discourse delivered at Stillwater, before the members of Montgomery Lodge, August 12, 1806. ... *Troy: printed by Wright, Goodenow & Stockwell.* ... 1806. 8vo, pp. 24. BA.

BUTLER (F. A.) Journal. By Frances Anne Butler. *London: John Murray.* 1835. 2 vols., post 8vo. + Reprinted. *Philadelphia: Carey, Lea & Blanchard.* 1835. 2 vols., 12mo, 3 l., pp. 13–252; 218. C. 9632

Also reprinted as: "Journal of a Residence in America. By Frances Anne Butler. *Paris.* 1835." 8vo. *See* N. A. R., XLI. 109. "This book is what it professes to be — 'my personal journal' — and not a history or a description of men and manners in the United States." — *Preface.* This was satirized in the following piece:

BUTLER. My Conscience! Fanny Thimble Cutler's Journal of a Residence in America. whilst performing a Profitable Theatrical Engagement: Beating the nonsensical Fanny Kemble Journal All Hollow!!! ... *Philadelphia: Published to Purchase for the Authoress A Wedding-Gown, Being about to Honor Pierce Cutler, Esq. with Her Hand in Wedlock.* 1835. 18mo, pp. 36.

BUTLER (F.) A Complete History of the United States of America, embracing the whole period from the Discovery of North America down to the year 1820. By Frederick Butler, A.M. In Three Volumes. *Hartford: Printed for the Author.* 1821. 3 vols., 8vo, pp. 468, Portrait; 459; 459. C. 9634

Some copies have the imprint: *Elizabethtown, N. J.* 1822. "One of the most notable productions of the catch-penny school of literature that hath lately appeared: entirely destitute of any literary pretensions." — N. A. R., XVI. 156.

BUTLER. Memoirs of the Marquis De La Fayette, with his Tour through the United States. By F. Butler. *Wethersfield.* 1825. 12mo. Plates. 9635

BUTLER (*Rev.* F. E.) Our Prospects and Duties. A Sermon on the War, preached at Patterson, N. J., April 28, 1861. *Patterson: Van Deerhaven & Fish.* 1861. 8vo, pp. 12. 9636

[BUTLER (George B.)] The Case of Great-Britain and America, addressed to the King, and both Houses of Parliament. *London: T. Becket and P. A. de Hondt.* M.D.CC.LXIX. 8vo, 2 l., pp. 43. + The Second Edition. [*Ibid.*] C. + The Third Edition. *Dublin: Printed for James Williams.* MDCCLXIX. 8vo, Title, pp. 43. C., G. + *Philadelphia: Re-Printed by W. T. Bradford.* MDCCLXIX. 8vo, Title, 1 l., pp. 16. 9637

In the catalogue of the Bodleian Library, this work is attributed to Gervase Parker Bushe.

BUTLER (G. B.) The Conscript Act. A Series of Articles communicated to the Journal of Commerce, By George B. Butler, Esq. of New York. *Loyal Publication Society, No.* 40. 1863. 8vo, pp. 22. C. 9638

BUTLER. The Currency Question, from Strictures on the Pamphlet of James Gallatin, Esq.: A series of Articles originally published in the Evening Post and Journal of Commerce, by Geo. B. Butler. *New York: Sanford, Harroun & Co., Printers.* 1864. 8vo, pp. 30. 9639

BUTLER (H. E.) God's Way of Leading the Blind. A Discourse Commemorative of the Death of Abraham Lincoln, delivered by Rev. Henry E. Butler, in the Congregational Church, Keeseville, N. Y., April 23, 1865. *Burlington: Free Press Office.* 1865. 8vo, pp. 23. 9640

BUTLER (J.) American Bravery Displayed in the Capture of Fourteen Hundred Vessels of War and Commerce since the Declaration of War by the President. Compiled from the best authorities. By James Butler. *Carlisle: for the Author.* 1816. 12mo, pp. 322, List of Subscribers, 4 l. C. 9641

BUTLER. An Eulogy upon the Character of George Swan. ... By J. Butler. March, 1840. [Motto.] *Oxford, Ohio.* 1840. 8vo, pp. 15. BA. 9642

BUTLER (J. D.) Deficiencies in our History. An Address delivered before the Vermont Historical and Antiquarian Society at Montpelier, October 16, 1846. By James Davie Butler ... . *Montpelier: Eastman & Danforth.* 1846. 8vo, pp. 36. Map.

BUTLER. An Address Delivered in the Representatives Hall, Montpelier, October 20, 1848 [on the Battle of Bennington]. By James Davie Butler, of Wells River, Vt. *Burlington.* 1849. 8vo, pp. 40. 9644

Also: Sermon at Norwich, Vermont, February 22, 1848, during the Obsequies of Truman Ransom, Colonel of the Ninth Regiment. *Hanover.* 1848. 8vo.

BUTLER *and* HOUGHTON (G. F.) Addresses on the Battle of Bennington, and the Life and Services of Col. Seth Warner; Delivered before the Legislature of Vermont, in Montpelier, October 20, 1848. By James Davie Butler, and George Frederick Houghton ... . *Burlington.* 1849. 8vo, pp. 99. C., H., M. 9645

BUTLER (J. G.) God with Us. A National Thanksgiving Discourse, by the Rev. J. Glentworth Butler, ... Philadelphia, November, 1863. *Published by the Union League of the Twenty-fourth Ward, Philadelphia.* [1863.] 8vo, pp. 18. 9646

BUTLER. The Martyr President. Our Grief and Our Duty.

By J. G. Butler. Pastor of St. Paul's Lutheran Church. *Washington, D. C.: McGill & Witherow, Printers.* 1865. 8vo, pp. 14. 9647

BUTLER (J.) A Sermon ... before the ... House of Commons ... December 13, 1776; being the [Fast] Day ... [on account of the Troubles in America.] ... By John Butler, LL.D. Archdeacon of Surrey ... . *London: T. Cadell.* MDCCLXXVII. 4to, pp. 16. BA. 6948

See "Monthly Review," LVI. 78.

BUTLER. A Sermon ... before the ... House of Commons ... On ... February 17, 1758; ... [Fast] Day [for the Rebellion in America]. By John Butler, LL.D. ... *London: J. & R. Tonson.* M DCC LVIII. 4to, pp. 24. BA. 9649

BUTLER. The Political Fugitive; being a Brief Disquisition into the Modern System of British Politics, etc.; written during a Voyage from London to New York. By John Butler. *New York: T. Greenleaf.* 1794. 8vo, pp. 115. B. 9650

Dedicated to General Washington.

BUTLER (J.) A Sermon Preached before the Incorporated Society for the Propagation of the Gospel in Foreign Parts; ... February 16, 1738–9. By Joseph Lord Bishop of Bristol. *London: J. & P. Knapton.* M DCC XXXIX. 8vo, pp. 91, (1). B., S.

BUTLER (M.) An Appeal from the Misrepresentations of James Hall, respecting the History of Kentucky and the West. By Mann Butler. To which is annexed, a Chronology of the principal Events as far as they could be ascertained, in the History of the Western Country of the United States, from the Earliest Spanish and French Explorations to 1806. *Frankfort, Ky.: A. G. Hodges.* 1837. 8vo, pp. 32. C. 9652

BUTLER. A History of the Commonwealth of Kentucky. By Mann Butler, A.M. *Louisville, Ky.: Wilcox, Deckerman & Co.* 1834. 12mo, pp. xi, 396. Portrait of G. R. Clarke. C., H.

BUTLER. A History of the Commonwealth of Kentucky, from its Exploration and Settlement by the Whites, to the Close of the Northwestern Campaign, in 1813; with an Introduction, exhibiting the Settlement of Western Virginia, from the First Passage of the Whites over the Mountains of Virginia, in 1736, to the Treaty of Camp Charlotte, near Chilicothe, Ohio, in 1774. By Mann Butler. Second Edition; revised and enlarged

by the Author. *Cincinnati: J. A. James and Co.* 1836. 12mo, pp. xvi: xiii–lxxii, 551. C., H. 9654

Some copies have a Louisville imprint.

BUTLER. An Oration on National Independence, delivered ... on the Fourth of July, 1837, at Fort Gibson, Mississippi, consisting principally, of a Sketch of the Rise of the State of Mississippi, from the Exploration of De Soto, in 1539, to the present time. By Mann Butler. *Frankfort, Ky.: Albert G. Hodges.* 1837. 8vo, pp. 23. H. 9655

BUTLER (N.) A Lecture on the Constitution of the United States, delivered in the Power Valley, Kentucky. By Noble Butler. *Louisville, Ky.: J. P. Morton.* [1862?] 8vo, pp. 16.

BUTLER (Pierce). Mr. Butler's Statement, originally Prepared in aid of his Professional Counsel, including Letters from Mrs. Butler, now Frances Ann Kemble. [*Philadelphia: privately Printed.* 1845.] 8vo, pp. 188. 9657

Relates to the divorce case. A descriptive list of Pierce Butler's slaves, which were sold in 1860, was published.

BUTLER (P. M.) Extracts from Reports made by P. M. Butler, United States Agent for the Cherokee Indians. [*Fort Gibson?* 1845.] 12mo. 9658

BUTLER (R. R.) Speech of Hon. R. R. Butler ... In the House ... upon the Resolutions introduced by Mr. Bayless, in reference to the Harper's Ferry Insurrection. [n. p. n. d.] 8vo, pp. 7. 9659

BUTLER (Samuel). The Emigrant's Hand-book of Facts concerning Canada, New Zealand ... [etc.] with the Relative Advantages each of the Colonies offers for Emigration. *Glasgow.* 1843. 8vo. BD. 9660

Also: The Emigrant's Complete Guide to Canada. *London.* 1858.

[BUTLER (W. A.)] Barnum's Parnassus; being Confidential Disclosures of the Prize Committee on the Jenny Lind Song. ... *New York: D. Appleton & Company.* 1850. 12mo, pp. 52. + Second Edition. [*Ibid.*] 1850. 9661

BUTLER. Martin Van Buren: Lawyer, Statesman and Man. By William Allen Butler. *New York: D. Appleton & Company.* 1862. 24mo, pp. 47. H. 9662

[BUTLER.] Memorial of Charles H. Marshall. *New York: D. Appleton and Company.* 1867. 8vo, pp. 96. Portrait. H.

[BUTLER.] Nothing to Wear. An Episode of City Life. (From Harper's Weekly.) Illustrated by Hoppin. *New York: Rudd & Carleton.* MDCCCLVII. 16mo, pp. 68. 8 Plates. BA., C.

Also: Two Millions. ... *New York: D. Appleton & Co.* 1858. 12mo, pp. 93.

BUTLER (W. O.), *of Kentucky.* Speech ... on the proposition to restore the Fine to Gen. Jackson, delivered in the House of Representatives, Jan. 11, 1843. [*Washington.* 1843.] 8vo, pp. 16. S. 9664

BUTLER HOSPITAL. *See* Providence, R. I.

BUTRON (Jacinto Miran de). La Azucena de Quito, que brato en el Florido campo de la Iglesia en las Indias occidentales (Vida de la Virgin Mariana de Jesus). *Lima.* 1702. 9665

BUTTERFIELD (C.) United States and Mexican Mail Steamship Line, and Statistics of Mexico. By Carlos Butterfield. *New York.* 1860. 8vo, pp. 109, 159. 9666

BUTTERFIELD. The National Debt and the "Monroe Doctrine:" how to extinguish the one and establish the other. A Practical Plan to secure the Peace and Prosperity of the Spanish-American States, and greatly to augment the Commerce and Wealth of the United States. [*New York.* 1866.] 8vo, pp. 31.

BUTTERFIELD (C. W.) History of Seneca County: containing a Detailed Narrative of the principal Events that have occured since its First Settlement down to the Present Time; a History of the Indians that formerly resided within its Limits; Geographical Descriptions, Early Customs, Biographical Sketches, &c., &c. With an Introduction, containing a Brief History of the State, from the Discovery of the Mississippi River down to the Year 1817, to the whole of which is added an Appendix, containing Tabular Views, &c. By Consul W. Butterfield. *Sandusky: D. Campbell & Sons.* 1848. 12mo, pp. 252. H., B.

BUTTERFIELD (H. Q.) Christian Commission. A Delegate's Story. By Rev. H. Q. Butterfield. [n. p. 1863.] 16mo, pp. 8. H. 9669

BUTTERWORTH. Three Years' Adventures of a Minor in England, Africa, the West Indies, South Carolina and Georgia. By Wm. Butterworth. *Leeds.* [1823.] 8vo. Portrait. P.

BÜTTNER (J. G.) Briefe aus und über Nordamerika oder Beiträge zu einer richtigen Kenntniss der Vereinigten Staaten

und ihrer Bewohner. *Dresden und Leipzig: Arnoldsche Buchhandlung.* 1845. 2 vols., 8vo. + [*Ibid.*] 1847. 2 vols. in 1, 8vo, pp. xiv, 440. 9671

BÜTTNER. Das jedem nach den Vereinigten Staaten von Nordamerika Auswandernden unenthbehrliches Büchlein. Enthaltend: Die Unabhängigkeits-Erklärung, nebst der Rede des John Adams, die Versassung der Vereinigten Staaten, Washington's Abschiedsadresse und das Hauptsächlichste aus den Verfassung der Staaten New-York, Pennsylvanien, Ohio, Illinois, Indiana, Missouri, Michigan, Kentucky, Maryland, Iowa und Wisconsin. *Bayreuth: Buchner.* 1849. 8vo, pp. x, 69. 9672

BÜTTNER. Die hochdeutsche reformirte Kirche in den Vereinigten Staaten von Nord-Amerika, von ihrer Gründung bis auf die neueste Zeit. Nebst 4 Beilagen. Nach authentischen Quellen. *Schleiz: Bockelmann.* 1846. 8vo, pp. 154. 9673

BÜTTNER. Nordamerikanischer Krieger, eine Selbstbiogaphie. *Camenz.* 1828. Portrait. 9674

BÜTTNER. Nordamerikanische Bilder und Zustände. *Hamburg.* 1842. 12mo. + Zweite Auflage. [*Ibid:*] *Geber.* 1843. 12mo. 9675

With the second title: Die Enthaltsamkeits-Vereine in den Nordamerikanischen Freistaaten. Fortsetzung der Baird'schen Geschichte der Mässigkeits-Gesellschaft in den Vereinigten Staaten Nord-Amerika's, bis zum Jahre 1842.

BÜTTNER Warnungen und Rathschläge der deutschen Gesellschaft in New-York an auswanderer, Nebst de Preisen der Inland-Passage. *Hamburg: Tramburgs Erben.* 1845. 8vo.

BÜTTNER. Der Staat Ohio. Eine geograph.- statist.- topographische Beschreibung für Einwanderer und Freunde der Länder- und Völkerkunde. *Leipzig.* 1849. 8vo, pp. viii, 206.

BÜTTNER. Die Vereinigten Staaten von Nord-Amerika. Meine Aufenthalt und meine Reisen in denselben vom Jahre 1834 bis 1841. *Hamburg: Schuberth & Comp.* 1847. 2 vols., 8vo, pp. vi, 440; 450, 1 Table, folio. 9678

BUTTRICK (Tilly), *Jr.* Voyages, Travels and Discoveries of Tilly Buttrick, Jr. *Boston: the Author.* 1831. 12mo, pp. 58. H. 9679

BUTTS (I.) Brief Reasons for Repudiation; applicable to the War Debts of all Countries. By Isaac Butts ... . *Rochester, N. Y.* 1869. 8vo, pp. x, 100. 9680

BUXTON (C.), *M.D.* An Oration Delivered before the Society of Black Friars in the City of New-York, at their Anniversary Festival on Tuesday the 7th of Nov. 1797. By Charles Buxton, M.D. ... *New-York: Friar McLean.* 1798. 8vo, pp. 22, Errata, 1 l. 9681

BUXTON (C.), *M.A.* Slavery and Freedom in the British West Indies. By Charles Buxton, M.A. M.P. ... *London: Longman, Green, Longman, and Roberts.* 1860. 8vo, 2 l., pp. 92. B., C.

BUXTON (C.) Leben des Sir Th. Fowell Buxton nach dem Englischen des Charles Buxton deutsch bearbeitet von Bernh. Brandis. *Hamburg: Agentur des Rauhen Hauses.* 185–. 12mo, pp. viii, 381. (Lebensbilder aus d. Geschichte d. inneren mission, Bd. VIII.) 9684

BUXTON (T. F.) The African Slave Trade. By Thomas Fowell Buxton, Esq. *London: John Murray.* 1839. 8vo, pp. 240. + The Second Edition. [*Ibid.*] + First American, From Second London Edition. With An Appendix. *Philadelphia: Merrihew and Thompson.* 1839. 12mo, pp. 188. 9685

BUXTON. The African Slave Trade and its Remedy. By Thomas Fowell Buxton. *London: John Murray.* 1840. 8vo, pp. viii, 582. Maps. C. 968

The first part is a reprint of No. 9685.

BUXTON. Abridgment of ... "The African Slave Trade an its Remedy." With an Explanatory Preface and an Appendix Second Edition. *London: John Murray.* 1840. 8vo, pp. 71.

BUXTON. Der Afrikanische Sklavenhandel und seine Ab hülfe. Aus dem Englischen ubersetzt von G. Julius. M einer Vorrede: die Niger-expedition und ihre Bestimmung, vo Carl Ritter. *Leipzig: Brockhaus.* 1841. 8vo, 33 sheets. Ma

BUXTON. A Review of "The African Slave Trade, t Thomas Fowell Buxton, Esq." Reprinted from the Lee Mercury. *Birmingham: Printed by B. Hudson.* 1839. 12m 1½ sheets. 96

BUXTON. A Letter to Lord J. Russell ... on certain All gations recently made in the House of Commons, in the Deba on Sir George Strickland's Motion for the Abolition of Neg Apprenticeship. *London.* 1838. 8vo. 96

BUXTON. The Remedy: being a Sequel to the African Slave Trade. *London: John Murray.* 1840. 8vo. 9691

Appended to the second edition of "The African Slave Trade."

BUXTON. Memoirs of Sir Thomas Fowell Buxton, Baronet; with selections from his correspondence. Edited by his son, Charles Buxton, Esq. *London: John Murray.* 1848. 8vo, pp. 510. + Third Edition. *London: John Murray.* 1849. 8vo, pp. 632. + *Philadelphia.* 1849. 8vo. + Fourth Edition. 1851. P. + With an inquiry into the results of Emancipation. New edition. *London, Edinburgh* [*printed.*] 1860. 12mo, pp. 260.

The last is one of a series called "Murray's Railway Reading."

BUXTON. Brief Memoirs of T. F. Buxton and Elizabeth Fry. *London.* 1845. 8vo. BD. 9693

BUXTON. Vie de Buxton précédée et suivie de deux notices sur l'esclavage et sur la colonie de Liberia ... Traduit par Mlle Rilliet de Constant. *Paris: Joel Cherbuliez* [etc.] 1853. 8vo, Title, pp. 340. B. 9694

BUXTON. A Letter to Tho. Fowell Buxton, Esq. on ... his Reported Speech, April 2d, 1835, in the Debate upon Lord John Russell's Resolution. *London.* 1835. 8vo. BD. 9695

BUYS (J. F.) Voorlezingen over de circulatie-banken, meer bijzonder in Frankrijk, Groot-Brittannië en de Vereenigde Staten van Noord-Amerika ... . *Haarlem: A. C. Kruseman.* 1856. 8vo. 9696

By the King. A Proclamation, Declaring the Cessation of Arms, as well by Sea as by Land, agreed upon between His Majesty, the Most Christian King, the King of Spain, the States General of the United Provinces, and the United States of America, and enjoining the Observance thereof. ... *London: Printed by Charles Eyre and William Strahan, Printers to the King's Most Excellent Majesty.* 1783. + *New-York: Re-printed by James Rivington, Printer to the King's Most Excellent Majesty.* 1783. Folio, broadside. P. 9697

This is headed by a woodcut of the royal arms.

By the Queen, a Proclamation, For Settling and Ascertaining the Current Rates of Foreign Coins in Her Majesties Colonies and Plantations in America. [Colophon:] *London: Printed by Charles Bill, and the Executrix of Thomas Newcomb, deceas'd: Printers to the Queens most Excellent Majesty.* 1704. Folio, broadside. 9698

BYAM (G.) Wanderings in some of the Western Republics of America; with Remarks upon the Cutting of the Great Ship Canal through Central America. By George Byam. *London: J. W. Parker.* 1850. Post 8vo, pp. 276. Plates. 9699

BYAM. Wanderungen durch Südamerikanische Republiken. Aus dem Englischen von M. B. Lindau. *Dresden: Kunze.* 1851. 8vo, pp. vi, 275. 9700

Republished with the title:

BYAM. Wanderungen durch Chile und Peru. Von Geo. Byam. Aus dem Englischen von M. B. Lindau. *Dresden: Kuntze.* 1852. 8vo, pp. vi, 275. 3 Lithographic Views. 9701

BYAM. Wild Life in the Interior of Central America. By George Byam ... . *London: John W. Parker.* 1849. 16mo, pp. viii, 253. H. 9702

BYAM. Wildes Leben im Innern von Central-America. Aus dem Englischen von M. B. Lindau. *Dresden: Kunze.* 1850. 8vo, pp. vi, 208. + [*Ibid.*] 1852, 8vo, pp. viii, 208. Lithographic View. 9703

[BYAM (Wm.)] An | Exact Relation | of | The most Execrable, Attempts | of | John Allin, | Committed on the Person of | His Excellency | Francis Lord Willovghby | of Parham, Captain General of the Continent of | Guiana, and of all the Caribby-Islands, | and our Lord Proprietor. | *London:* | *Printed for Richard Lowndes.* 1665. | 4to, 1 l., pp. 12, Licence, 1 l. C. 9704

BYERS (J.) References to the Plan of the Island of Dominica, As surveyed from the Year 1765 to 1773. By John Byers, Chief Surveyor. *London: S. Hooper.* MDCCLXXVII. 8vo, 5 l., pp. 30. 9705

BYERS. References to the Plan of the Island of St. Vincent, As surveyed from the Year 1765 to 1773; by John Byers, Chief Surveyor. *London: S. Hooper.* MDCCLXXVII. 8vo, pp. viii, 8. 9706

BYERS (W. N.) A Hand-Book to the Gold Fields of Nebraska and Kansas: being a Complete Guide to the Gold Regions of the North and South Platte, and Cherry Creek, embracing a Reliable Description of the Country, Climate, Streams, Scenery, etc.; Different Routes from the Mississippi River to the Mines, the Best Camping Places on each Route, and a Reliable Map of the same; and Valuable Information as regards a Complete Outfit for the Journey; containing Narratives of Trips to and from the Gold Regions in the years 1858–59. By William N. Byers, late Government Surveyor, and John H. Kellom Sup't. of Pub. Instruction of Nebraska. *Chicago: D. B. Cooke & Co.* 1859. 12mo, pp. 113. Map. 9707

BYFIELD (N.) An | Account | of the | Late Revolution | in | New-England. | Together with the | Declaration | of the | Gentlemen, Merchants, and Inhabitants of Boston, | and the Country adjacent. April 18. 1689. | Written by Mr Nathanael Byfield, | a Merchant of Bristol in New-England, to his Friends | in London. | Licensed, June 27. 1689. J. Fraser. | *London:* | *Printed for Ric. Chiswell, at the Rose and Crown in* | *St. Paul's Church-Yard.* M DC LXXXIX. | 4to, pp. 20. BA., H. + *Edinburgh: Reprinted in the Year* 1689. 4to, pp. 7. 9708

These editions are now scarce, and sell at from $30 to $35. Reprinted in Force's Tracts, Vol. IV., No. 10, and in the Andros Tracts, published by the Prince Society; and, again, with the following title:

BYFIELD. An Account of The Late Revolution in New-England. By Mr. Nathanael Byfield. *New York: Reprinted for Joseph Sabin.* 1865. 4to, pp. 27. 9709

Edition, 250 copies, of which 50 are on large paper. Forms No. 1 of Sabin's Reprints, quarto series.

BYINGTON (C.) Holisso Anumpa Tosholi: An English and Choctaw Definer; for the Choctaw Academies and Schools. By Cyrus Byington. First Edition, 1500 copies. *New York: J. W. Benedict.* 1852. 24mo, pp. 252. S. 9710

BYLES (M.), *of Boston.* The Glories of the Lord of Hosts, and The Fortitude of the Religious Hero. A Sermon Preached to the ancient and honorable Artillery Company June 2. 1740. Being the Anniversary of their Election of Officers. By Mather Byles, A.M. ... *Boston: Thomas Fleet and Joseph Edwards.* 1740. 8vo, pp. 31. BA. + Third Edition. *Boston: Re-Printed by Thomas and John Fleet.* 1769. 8vo, pp. 26. B., H. 9711

BYLES. On the Death of the Queen. A Poem. Inscribed to His Excellency Governor Belcher. By the Reverend Mr. Byles. *Boston, in New England: Printed by J. Draper, for D. Henchman in Cornhill.* 1738. 4to, pp. 7. M. 971

BYLES. A Poem on the Death of his late Majesty King George, and the Accession of ... George II. [*Boston.* 1727.] 8vo, pp. 5. N. 9713

BYLES. Poems: The Conflagration. The God of Tempest and Earthquake. *Boston.* 12mo. W. 9714

BYLES. Sermon Occasioned by the late Earthquake in New England, Nov. 18, 1755. *Boston.* 1755. 8vo. W. 9715

BYLES. To His Excellency Governor Belcher on the death of his Lady. An Epistle. By the Reverend Mr. Byles. [*Boston.* 1736.] 4to, pp. (2), ii, 6. BM. 9716

BYLES. The Vanity of every Man at his best Estate. A Funeral Sermon On the Honorable William Dummer, Esq. Late Lieut.-Governor and Commander in Chief over the Province of the Massachusetts-Bay in New-England, Who died October 10, 1761. Aged 84 Years. By Mr. Byles. [Motto.] *Boston: printed by Green & Russell.* 1761. 4to, pp. 24, 3. H., M.

Also: The Character of the Perfect and Upright Man ... a Discourse ... *Boston.* 1729. 12mo, pp. 27. M.—A Discourse on the Present Vileness of the Body, and its Future Glorious Change by Christ. To which is added, A Sermon on the Nature and Importance of Conversion. Both occasionally delivered at Dorchester April 23, 1732. *Boston.* 1732. 8vo, pp. 14. + *Boston.* 1771. 8vo, pp. 23.—The Flourish of the Annual Spring. Improved in a Sermon preached at the Thursday Lecture, in Boston, May 3, 1739. Second Edition. *Boston: Reprinted.* 1760. 8vo, pp. 25.—The Glorious Rest of Heaven. A Sermon at the Thursday Lecture in Boston, Jan. 3, 1744–45. *Boston.* 1745. 16mo, pp. 31.—God Glorious in the Scenes of the Winter. A Sermon, Preached at Boston, Dec. 23, 1744. *Boston.* 1744. 16mo, pp. 15.—God the Strength and Portion of His People, ... A Funeral Sermon on the Honourable Mrs. Katherine Dummer, The Lady of his Honour William Dummer, Esq; Late Lieutenant Governor and commander in chief over this Province. Preach'd at Boston, January 9, 1752, the Lord's-Day after her Death and Burial. *Boston: printed by John Draper.* 1752. 8vo, pp. 25.—The Man of God thoroughly furnished to every Good Work. A Sermon preached at the Ordination of the Rev. Mather Byles, to the Pastoral Office in the first church of Christ in New London, Nov. 18, 1757. To which is added the charge given him upon that occasion. By His Father. *New London.* 1758. 4to, pp. 23.—The Nature and Necessity of Conversion. Sermon. *Boston.* 1732. 8vo, pp. 10. + *Boston.* 1769. 8vo.—Sermon before the Execution of a Young Negro Servant for poisoning an infant. *Boston.* 1751. 8vo.—The Visit to Jesus by Night. An Evening Lecture. *Boston.* 1741. 24mo, pp. 24.

BYLES (M.), *of New London.* A Sermon, delivered March 6th, 1760, Being a Day appointed by Order of his Majesty, as a Public Thanksgiving, for the late Signal Successes Granted to the British Arms: By Mather Byles, A.M. ... . [Motto.] *New London: Timothy Green.* MDCCLX. 16mo, pp. 22. H., M.

Also: The Christian Sabbath explained and vindicated. In a Discourse ... delivered Jan. 14, 1759. ... *New London.* 1759. 8vo, pp. 20. M.—A Debate between the Rev. Mr. Byles, late Pastor of the First Church in New London, and the Brethren of that Church. 1768. 16mo.—Sermon delivered at St. John's, New Brunswick, 2 December, 1798, on the late Signal Success granted to his Majesty's Arms, *St. John's.* 1798. 8vo.

BYNUM (A.) An Oration, delivered ... [at] Columbia, S. C. on the Fourth of July, 1828. By Alfred Bynum, Esq. *Columbia: D. & J. M. Faust.* 1828. 8vo, pp. 24. 9719

BYNUM (Jesse A.) Speech of Mr. Bynum on the Motion of Mr. Wagner, to be excused from serving on the Investigating Committee, to examine into the defalcation of S. Swartwout; in the House of Representatives, Jan. 1839. *Washington.* 1839. 8vo. 9720

BYRD (W.) The Westover Manuscripts: containing the History of the Dividing Line betwixt Virginia and North Carolina; a Journey to the Land of Eden, A.D. 1733; And a Progress to the Mines. Written from 1728 to 1736. And now first Published. By William Byrd ... . *Petersburg: Edmund and Julian C. Ruffin.* 1841. Imp. 8vo, pp. iv, 143, (1). C., H.

The *cover* title reads: "Supplement to The Farmers' Register: containing the Westover Manuscripts. *Petersburg.* 1842." Reprinted with the following title:

BYRD. History of the Dividing Line and Other Tracts. From the Papers of William Byrd, of Westover, in Virginia, Esquire. *Richmond, Va.* 1866. pp. xix, 233; 3 l., pp. 276.

Edition, 200 copies, of which 20 are on large paper; *Printed by J. Munsell, Albany.* Includes a "Journey to the land of Eden," and forms Nos. II. and III. of the "Historical Documents from the Old Dominion," of which Lewis's "Williamsburgh Orderly Book" was the first. The introduction and notes are by Thomas H. Wynne, Esq. *See* "Notes and Queries," Vol. IX. 229.

BYRDSALL (F.) The History of the Loco-Foco or Equal Rights Party, its Movements, Conventions and Proceedings, with Short Characteristic Sketches of its Prominent Men. By F. Byrdsall. *New York: Clement and Packard.* 1842. 12mo, pp. 192. H. 9723

BYRE (J.) A Letter to a Friend at Edinburgh from Rotterdam, giving an account of the Scots' Affairs in Darien. By James Byre. [*Edinburgh?*] 1702. 8vo, pp. 171. 9724

BYRNE (B. M.) Letters on the Climate, Soils, and Productions of Florida: by Bernard M. Byrne, M.D., U. S. Army. *Ralston, Pa.: J. D. Mitchell.* [n. d.] 8vo, pp. 15. H. 9725

BYRNE. Proceedings of a Court-Marshal for the Trial of Surgeon B. M. Byrne, held at Fort Moultrie (S. C.), March 24, 1859. *Charleston.* 1859. 8vo. C. 9726

BYRNE (P.) Trial of Patrick Byrne for Mutiny. Before a General Court Martial, Held at Fort Columbus, on the 22d of May, 1813. Sentence — Death. *New York.* 1813. 8vo, pp. 12.

BYRNE (W. S.) Directory of Grass Valley Township for 1865, containing an Historical Sketch of Grass Valley, of Allison Ranch and Forest Springs; also, a Description of the Principal Mines, all the Quartz Mills, Religious and other Organizations, etc. By William S. Byrne. [*San Francisco?*] 1865. 8vo, pp. 114. 9728

Also: Chart of the Colorado River, ... drawn from actual bearings and soundings by Capt. A. D. Byrne, engaged for the past seven years as a pilot and shipmaster in the navigation of that river. *San Francisco.* 1864.

BYRNES (Daniel). A Short Address to the English Colonies in North-America. [*Wilmington, 6th Mo. 20th,* 1775.] Folio, pp. 2. 9729

On a day being set apart for fasting and prayer.

BYRON (John). The Narrative of the Honourable John Byron (Commodore in a Late Expedition round the World) containing an Account of the great Distresses Suffered by Himself and His Companions on the Coast of Patagonia, From the Year 1740, till their Arrival in England, 1746. With a Description of St. Jago de Chili, and the Manners and Customs of the Inhabitants. Also a Relation of the Loss of the Wager Man of War, One of Admiral Anson's Squadron. Written by Himself, And now First Published. *London: S. Baker* ... . MDCCLXVIII. Title, 2 l., pp. viii, 257. Plate. S. + Second Edition. *London: Printed for S. Baker and G. Leigh and T. Davies.* MDCCLXVIII. 8vo, pp. viii, 257. Plate. + *London.* 1782. 18mo, pp. xii, 264. + *London.* 1785. 16mo, pp. x, 193. 9730

Admiral Byron's narrative of the loss of the Wager is one of the most thrilling accounts in the language, and supplied his illustrious descendant with many particulars for the shipwreck in "Don Juan." Other editions were printed. *London.* 1780. 12mo. *Edinburgh.* 1812. 12mo. *London.* 1832. It also included, in Kerr's Collection, Vol. XVII. *See also* Hawkesworth (John), and Ortega (D. C.)

BYRON. Des Commodore Johann Byron Erzählung der grossen Unglücksfälle, die er nebst seiner Gesellschaft, von dem Jahre 1740 an bis zu seiner Ankunft in England 1746 auf der Küste von Patagonien ausgestanden hat, nebst einer Beschreibung von St. Jago in Chili und den Sitten und Gebräuchen der Einwohner dieses Landes. Von ihm selbst beschreiben und aus dem Englischen übersetzt. *Nürnberg.* 1769. 8vo, 14 sheets.

BYRON. A Voyage round the World, in His Majesty's Ship the Dolphin, Commanded by the Honourable Commodore Byron. In which is contained, A faithful Account of the several Places, People, Plants, Animals, &c. seen on the Voyage: And, among other particulars, A minute and exact Description of the Streights of Magellan, and of the Gigantic People called Patagonians. Together with an accurate Account of Seven Islands lately discovered in the South Seas. By an Officer on Board the said Ship. *London: Printed for J. Newbery.* M DCC LXVII. 8vo, 2 l., pp. 186. 3 Plates. H. + The Second Edition. *London: J. Newbery.* M DCC LXVII. 8vo, 2 l., pp. 186. 3 Plates. S. 9732

See M. R., XXXVI. 327; XXXIX. 309. This voyage was satirized in a squib, called "An Account of the Giants lately discovered (in Patagonia), in a Letter to a Friend in the Country. 1766." 12mo.

BYRON. Viage del commandante Byron al rededor del Mundo, hecho ultimamente de orden del Almirantazgo de Inglaterra. En el qual se da noticia de varios payses, de las costumbres de sus habitantes, de las plantas y animales estraños que se crian en ellos; juntamente con una descripcion muy circumstanciada del Estrecho de Magallanes y de cierta Nacion de Gigantes. Llamados Patagones, con una lamina fina que los representa, &c. Traducido del Ingles e ilustrado con notas sobre muchos puntos de geographia, de physica, de botanica, de historia natural, de comercio, &c. y con un nuevo mapa del Estrecho. Por el Dr. D. Casimiro de Ortega. *Madrid.* 1769. 4to, pp. xvi, 245. S. + Segunda edicion, en que se anade el Resumen historico del viage emprendido por Magallanes, y concluido por el Capitan Español Juan Sebastian del Cano. ... *Madrid.* 1769. 4to, pp. xvi, 176, xii, 55. Map. 9733

A translation of the account of Byron's voyage, published by one of the officers of the Dolphin, in 1767. To the second edition (*see* C. de Ortega) was added the following:

BYRON. Voyage autour du monde, fait en 1764 et 1765, sur le vaisseau de guerre anglois Le Dauphin, commandé par le chef d'escadre Byron; dans lequel on trouve ... une description exacte du détroit de Magellan, et des géans appellés Patagons, ainsi que des sept isles nouvellement découvertes dans la mer du Sud. Traduit de l'anglois par M. R*** [Suard]. *Paris: Molini.* 1767. 12mo, pp. lxviij, 335. Plates. 9734

BYRON. Voyage à la mer du Sud, completant la Relation du Voyage d'Anson, avec un extrait du second voyage de Byron autour du monde. Traduit de l'Anglais par A. de Cantwell. *Paris.* 1799. 8vo. 9735

BYRON. John Byrons, obersten Befehlshaber über ein englisches Geschwader, Reise um die Welt, in den Jahren 1764 und 1765, nebst einer genauen Beschreibung der Magellanischen Strasse, der patagonischen Riesen, und der ganz neu entdeckten Inseln, in der Südsee. Mit einem Anhange, worinn eine Beschreibung der patagonischen Küsten. *Frankfurt und Leipzig.* 1769. 8vo. 9736

Kayser gives the imprint, *Stuttgart: Metzler.* 1769. 8vo. 8vo.

BYRON. Erzählung der Unglucksfälle die er auf der Küste von Patagonien ausgestanden hat, nebst einer Beschreibung von St. Jago in Chili. *Nürnberg.* 1769. 8vo. 9737

Kayser gives the imprint, *Stuttgart: Metzler.* 1769.

BYRON. Reizen rondom de weereld, ondernomen op bevel von dan ... Koning von Groot Brittanje, door den Commandeur Byron, Kaptein Wallis, Kaptein Carteret en den Lieutenant Cook. *Rotterdam: R. Arrenberg.* 1775. 4to. 9738

BYRON. Reis rondom den aardkloot gedaan in de jaren 1765 en 1766. Tweede druk. *'s Hage: H. H. van Drecht.* 1783. 8vo. Plates. 9739

BYRON. Schiffbruch und Drangsale. *See* [Haken (J. C. L.)]

Bystander; or A Series of Letters on ... The "Legislative Choice" of Electors in Maryland: In which the Constitutional Right to a Legislative Choice in that State, and the Necessity of adopting it, for the Present Election only, in order to counteract the Artifices of the Anti-federalists in Virginia and other States, and to prevent a President from being elected by the Minority of the Nation ... are ... proved. ... *Baltimore: printed by Yundt and Brown.* M,DCCC. 12mo, pp. 30. BA. 9740

C. (A.) *See* C[aillot] (A[ntoine]).

C. (E.) *See* C[ook] (E[dward]).

C. (F.) La Guerre civile en Amérique et l'esclavage, par F. C. ... *Paris: E. Dentu.* 1861. 8vo, pp. 31. BA. 9741

In favor of secession, but against slavery.

C*** (F.) Histoire des disastres de Saint Domingue, and Soirées bermudiennes, ou entretiens, etc. *See* [Carteaux (F.)]

C. (G.) *See* C[arew] (G[eorge]), and C[artwright] (G[eorge]).

[C. (G.)] Breaking the Line. — Statement of Facts, in the Nature of Memoir, leading to and connected with the great Battle of the 12th of April, 1782, between the Fleet of Great Britain, commanded by the late Lord Rodney, and that of France, under the Compte de Grasse. By an old Naval Officer, who served under Lord Rodney, &c. *Cheltenham.* 1830. 8vo, pp. 52, Appendix, xxx. 9742

C. (G.) A Little Looking-Glass for the Times. Or, A Brief Remembrancer for Pennsylvania, containing some Serious Hints, Affectionately Addressed to People of Every Kind and Station in the Province. With an Appendix by Way of Supplication to Almighty God. By G. C. *Wilmington.* 1764. 12mo, pp. 24. 9743

C. (J.), *Esq.* *See* C[alef] (J[ohn]), and C[otton] (J[ohn]).

C. (J.) Slavery in the South; or What is our Present Duty to the Slaves. *Boston: Prentiss & Deland.* 1862. 8vo, pp. 15.

C. (J. M.) Précis des gémissements des sang mêles dans les colonies françaises. *Paris.* 1829. 8vo. 9745

C. (John). *See* C[lowes] (John), and C[otton] (John).

C. (J. T. de). El comerciante de perlas, novela americana escrita por J. T. de C. *Paris: Rosa et Bouret.* 1869. 18mo, pp. 360. 9746

C. (L.) Relation d'un voyage fait récemment dans les provinces de La Plata, par L. C., ex-agent supérieur du service des

hôpitaux militaires des armées françaises; et description de Buenos-Ayres, de son gouvernement, de son indépendance, et des troupes d'Artigas opposées à l'armée portugaise de Montevideo, etc. etc. *Paris: Delaunay.* 1818. 8vo, pp. 63. H. 9747

See M. R., Second Series, LXXXVIII, 541.

C** (M.) *See* C[hambon] (M.)

C. (le M. de). Mémoire sur l'esclavage et sur la traite des nègres. *London.* 1798. 8vo. BD. 9748

C. (M. B.) Remarks on New-York banking, and the recent disaster or crisis. ... *New-York.* 1858. 8vo, pp. 33. 9749

C. (M. L. G. D.) *See* Grange de Chessieux (De la).

[C. (M. J.)] Ab-sa-ra-ka. *See* [Carrington (*Mrs.* M. J.])

C. (M. T.) Flowers from the Battle-Field, and Other Poems. By M. T. C. *Philadelphia: Hen. B. Ashmead, Printer.* 1864. 18mo, pp. 36. 9750

[C. (M. W.)] Songs of the Free, and Hymns of Christian Freedom ... . *Boston: Isaac Knapp.* MDCCCXXXVI. 12mo, pp. 227. H. 9751

C. (*Marquis* de). *See* [Condorcet (J. A. N. de C., *Marquis* de)].

C. (O.) Letters from the South on Northern and Southern Views respecting Slavery, and the American Tract Society. By O. C. *Boston.* 1857. 8vo, pp. 16. H., M. 9752

C. (P.) A Short and Impartial View of the Manner and Occasion of the Scots Colony's coming away from Darien. In a letter to a person of quality. [n. p.] 1699. 4to. 9753

C. (R.) Lithobolia. *See* C[hamberlaine (R.)]

C. (R.) The Duty of Christians in Respect to War. By R—— C——, of New York. *New York: Published by the American Tract Society.* [n. d.] 8vo, pp. 16. H. 9754

C. (S. T.) The Little Fox; or, The Story of Captain Sir F. L. McClintock's Arctic Expedition. Written for the Young. By S. T. C. *New York: M. W. Dodd.* 186–. Sq. 18mo, pp. 198. 9755

C. (T.) *See* C[hurch] (T[homas]).

C. (V. D.) Examen de l'Esclavage en général et particuliérement de l'Esclavage des nègres dans les Colonies Françaises de l'Amérique. Par V. D. C. *Paris.* 1802. 2 vols., 8vo. 9756

C. (V. W.) Trou-hertighe|onderrichtinge,|Aen alle hooft Participan-|ten, en Lief-hebbers vande Ge-octroyeerde|West-Indische Compagnie.|Nopende|Het open stellen vanden handel op de Cust van|Africa, namentlijck, St. Thomé, Guinea, Angola,|St. Paulo de Loando, mitsgaders de Marignian,|Nieu Nederlant ende West-Indien.|Door een trou Lief-hebber, V. W. C.||[Vignette. n. p.] *Ghedruckt in't laer* 1643.| 4to, 10 l. 9757

Respecting this "Friendly advice to all shareholders and friends of the West Indian Company, concerning the opening of the trade on the coasts of Africa, particularly St. Thomas, Guinea, Angola, St. Paulo de Loando, and at Marignian, the New Netherlands and the West Indies, by a true friend, V. W. C.," *see* Aitzema, II. 892.

C. (W.) *See* C[astell (W.)]

C. (W.) The Dutch Svrvay. Wherein are related and truly discoursed, the chiefest losses and acquirements, which have past betweene the Dutch and Spaniards, in these last foure yeares Warres of the Netherlands, with a comparative ballancing and estimation of that which the Spaniards haue got in the Dutchies of Cleeve and Juliers, with that which they have lost vnto the Dutch and Persians in Brasilia, Lima, and Ormus. Whereunto are annexed the Mansfeldian motiues, directed vnto all Colonels, Lieutenant Colonels, Serjeant Majors, priuate Captaines, inferiour Officers and Souldiers, whose service is engag'd in this present expedition vnder the conduct and command of the most illustrious Prince Ernestvs, Earle of Mansfield. *London: Edw. Aldie, for N. Bvtter.* 1625. 4to, Title, Dedication signed W. C., pp. 3, To the Reader, pp. 2, Text, pp. 36. 9758

C. (W.) A Plaine|Description|of the Barmvdas,|now called Sommer|Islands.|With the manner of their discouerie|Anno 1609. by the shipwrack and admirable deliuerance|of Sir Thomas Gates, and Sir George Sommers, wherein|are truly set forth the commodities and profits of|that Rich, Pleasant, and Healthfull|Cøvntrie.|With|An Addition, or more ample relation of|diuers other remarkeable matters concerning those|Ilands since then experienced, lately sent|from thence by one of the Colonie now|there resident.|Ecclesiastes 3: 11.|God hath made euery thing

beautifull in his time.|*London.*|*Printed by W. Stansby, for W. Welby.*|1613.| 4to, 4 l., pp. 43. N. 9759

Twenty pages of the text are in black letter, the remainder in Roman. The dedication is signed "W. C." [Castell?]. This is the very rare, curious, and interesting voyage which Malone considered as having suggested to Shakespeare his different allusions to these Islands, as the still-vexed Bermoothes in the "Tempest." But Joseph Hunter, in his "New Illustrations of ... Shakespeare, *London*, 1845," 2 vols., 8vo, I. 145–164, maintains that the play was written in 1596, that the scene is laid in Lampedusa, and that the allusion to "the still-vex'd Bermoothes" was derived from Raleigh's "Discoverie of Guiana, 1596." Reprinted in Force's Tracts, Vol. III. Priced, by Thorpe, 1843, £5 5s.

C. (W. B.) *See* C[rafton] (W[illiam] B[ell]).

O Cabalista Electoral ou Collecção alphabetica e resumida de todos os avisos do ministerio do Imperio relativos à mateira eleitoral desde o anno de 1846, acompanhada de notas explicativas dos que se achão revogados ou modificados pela legislação moderna, ou por outros avisos. Por. ... *Rio de Janeiro.* 1868. 8vo, pp. viii, 310. 9760

CABALLERO (D. J. A.) Discurso pronunciado por el Dr. D. José Agustin Caballero, en la Junta general de la Sociedad Patriótica de 11 de Diciembre de 1796. *Imprenta del Gobierno.* 1796. 4to, pp. 16. 9761

CABALLERO (J. de la L.) Informe presentado á Real Junta de Fomento de Agricultura y Comercio de la Isla de Cuba, por Dr José de la Luz Caballero (Pepe de la Luz). *Habana.* 1834. Folio. 9762

CABALLERO (Raimondo Diosdado). Avertimenti amichevoli all'erudito tradottore romano della Geografia di W. Guttrie. [*Napoli.* 1799.] 9763

"A refutation of errors committed by the English geographer in regard to Spain and her colonies." — BACKER. Caballero left several MSS. relating to America. *See* Backer.

CABALLERO. L'Eroismo di Ferdinando Cortese confermato contre le censure nemiche. Per Raimundo Diosdado Caballero. *Roma: Ant^o. Fulgoni.* 1806. 8vo. 9764

CABALLERO Y ONTIVEROS (Felix). Poema á la solemne y magnífica funcion que con motivo de la dignidad que S. M. confirió al serenisimo príncipe de la Paz de general almirante de España é Indias. [*Havana:*] *D. Estevan Boloña.* 1807. 4to, pp. 27. 9765

CABAÑAS Y CRESPO. Exequias que por muerte de D. J. C. Ruiz de Cabañas y Crespo se celebraron en la iglesia catedral de Guadalajara. *Guadalajara.* 1825. Folio, Title, pp. 82. 9766

CABEÇA DE VACA. La relacion que dio Aluar nu-|ñez cabeça de vaca de lo acaescido enlas Indias|enla armada donde yua por gouernador Pã-|philo de narbaez, desde el año de veynte|y siete hasta el año d' treynta y seys|que boluio a Seuilla con tres|de su compañia.:.| [Colophon:] *Fue impresso el presente tra-|tado enla magnifica, noble, y antiquissima çiudad|de Zamora: por los honrrados varones Augu-|stin de paz y Juan Picardo compañeros im|pressores de libros vezinos dela dicha çiu|dad. A costa y espensas del virtuoso va|ron Juan pedro musetti mercader|de libros vezino de Medina del|campo. Acabose en seys dias|del mes de Octubre. Año|del nasçimiento d' nto sal|uador Jesu Cristo de|mil y quinientos y|quarenta y dos|Años.|* [1542.] Sm. 4to, Title, 66 l. L. 9767

This account was translated into Italian by Ramusio, and paraphrased into English by Purchas. Ternaux gave a French version, and Mr. Buckingham Smith a new translation from the original Spanish. The text was printed by Barcia, who availed himself of the opportunity to add a dissertation vindicating Cabeça de Vaca from the aspersions of Honorio Philipono. Respecting the name of this author, the reader may consult Ternaux's reprint, or a quotation in [Harrisse's] "Bib. Am. Vet.," pp. 381–384, where also will be found an interesting account of the book and its author.

CABEÇA DE VACA. La relacion y comentarios del gouerna|dor Aluar nuñez cabeça de vaca, de lo acaescido en las|dos jornadas que hizo a las Indias.|Con priuilegio.|¶ Esta tassada por los señores del consejo en Ochẽta y cinco mrs:| [Colophon:] *Impresso en Valladolid, por Francisco fer-|nandez de Cordoua. Año de mil y quinien-|nientos* [sic] *y cinquenta y cinco años* [1555].| 4to, fol. i–lvj, (2), lvij–clxiiii. H. 9768

The running title of the "relacion" is "Naufragios", etc. After fol. lvj there is a title-page: "Commenta | rios de Alvar Nvnez Cabe | ça de Vaca, adelantado y gouernador dela pro | uincia del Rio dela Plata. | Scriptos por Pero hernandez scriuano y secre | tario de la prouincia. ... | ... | ... ." | Sold, in 1845, for £4 4s. These are translated in Ternaux's "Voyages," filling two volumes, with the following titles:

CABEÇA DE VACA. ... Commentaries d'Alvar Nuñez Cabeça de Vaca ... . *Paris: Arthus Bertrand.* M. DCCC XXXVII. 8vo, 2 l., pp. 507. BA. 9769

CABEÇA DE VACA. ... Relation et naufrages d'Alvar Nuñez Cabeça de Vaca ... . *Paris: Arthus Bertrand.* M. DCCC XXXVII. 8vo, Title, pp. 7, 302. BA. 9770

CABEÇA DE VACA. The Narrative of Alvar Nuñez Cabeça de Vaca. Translated by Buckingham Smith. *Washington.* 1851. Folio, pp. 138. 8 Maps. BA. 9771

One hundred and ten copies printed for private circulation only, by Mr. G. Riggs, of Washington, ten of which are on large paper. A new edition, with additional notes, is now (1869) in press.

CABELL (Edward C.) Hon. E. Carrington Cabell's Letter respecting Florida. [Dated Washington, Aug. 29, 1852. n. p. n. d.] Broadside. H. 9772

CABELL. Speech of Mr. Cabell of Florida, on the Mexican War. Delivered in the House of Representatives, March 4, 1848. [*Washington:*] *Towers, printer.* 8vo, pp. 16. H. 9773

Also: Letter ... on the Subject of the Election of Speaker of the House of Representatives, January 13, 1848. *Washington: printed by John T. Towers.* 1848. 8vo, pp. 8. H. — The Slave Question. Speech ... March 5, 1850, ... [n. p. n. d.] 8vo, pp. 8. — Speech ... on the Subject of the Political Parties of the Country. ... Feb. 3, 1852. [n. p. n. d.] 8vo, pp. 8. H. — Speech ... on the Subject of Fortifying Key West and Tortugas: ... Tuesday, December 21, 1852. *Washington.* 1853. 8vo, pp. 12. H.

CABELL (J. C.) Speech on the Anti-Tariff Resolutions passed at the Session of the Legislature of Virginia, 1828–9. Accompanied by sundry Notes and Documents. By Joseph C. Cabell ... . *Richmond.* 1831. 8vo, pp. 58. B. 9774

CABELL (J. C.) University of Virginia. *See* Jefferson (T.)

CABELL (Julia Mayo). An Odd Volume of Facts, in Prose and Verse. *Richmond, Va.* 1852. 12mo, pp. 276. 9775

CABELL (N. F.) Early History of Agriculture in Virginia. By N. F. Cabell. *Washington.* [n. d.] 8vo, pp. 41. S. 9776

CABELLO (P. M.) Guia politica eclesiastica y militar del Peru, para el ano de 1865, por Pedro M. Cabello. *Lima.* 1865. 12mo, pp. 347. + Guia politica eclesiastica y militar del Peru, para el ano de 1865, por Pedro M. Cabello. De orden suprema. *Lima.* 1865. 16mo, pp. 352. + Para el ano de 1866. *Lima.* 1866. 16mo, pp. 316. 9777

[CABET (Étienne).] Célébration à Nauvoo du septième anniversaire du départ de la première avant-garde icarienne, 3 février 1848. [Signed Cabet.] *Paris: l'auteur.* 1855. 16mo. 9778

CABET. Colonie icarienne aux États-Unis d'Amérique. Sa constitution, ses lois, sa situation matérielle et morale après le premier semestre de 1855. *Paris: rue Baillet.* 1856. 12mo.

[CABET.] Colonie icarienne. Guerre a mort de l'opposition contre le Cit. Cabet, fondateur et Président d'Icaire, et mémorable séance de la nuit du 12 au 13 Mai 1856 de 71, 2 du soir à 6 du matin. *Nauvoo: typographie icarienne.* 1856. 8vo, pp. 72. 9779

CABET. Colonie ou république icarienne dans les États-Unis d'Amérique. Son histoire. Système icarien. Doctrine icarienne. ... Deuxième édition. [Signed Cabet.] *Paris: l'auteur.* 1854. 16mo. + Deuxième édition. 1855. 16mo. 9781

CABET. Colonie icarienne. Situation dans l'Iowa, au 15 octobre 1853. [Signed Cabet.] *Paris: l'auteur.* 1853. 8vo, pp. 409. 9782

CABET. Colony or Republic of Icaria in the United States of America Its History ... . By Mr. Cabet, ... *Nauvoo: Icarian printing office.* 1852. 8vo, pp. (1), 19, (1). H. 9783

CABET. Notre Procès en escroquerie, ou Poursuites dirigées contre les citoyens Cabet et Krolikowski, à l'occasion de la fondation d'Icarie. *Paris: rue J. J. Rousseau.* 1849. 18mo.

CABET. Procès et acquittement du citoyen Cabet, accusé d'escroquerie pour l'émigration icarienne. *Paris: rue Baillet.* 1851. 8vo. 9785

CABET. Progrès de la colonie icarienne établie à Nauvoo (États-Unis d'Amérique). M. Cabet à Julien jeune Icarien disposé à venir en Icarie. *Paris: l'auteur.* 1854. 16mo. 9786

CABET. Voyage en Icarie, roman philosophique et social. 5e édition. *Paris: Mallet et Cie.* 1848. 18mo. 9787

CABET. Voyages et aventures de lord William Carisdall en Icarie. Traduits de l'anglais de Francis Adams, par Th. Dufruit. *Souverain.* 1840. 2 vols., 8vo. 9788

Also: Adresses des Icariens de Nauvoo à citoyen Cabet. Protestacion de quelques dissidents et répons du citoyen Cabet. *Paris: imp. de Malteste.* 1851. 8vo. — A long list of his other writings, some of which may relate to this country, will be found in Chéron's "Cat. gén. de la libr. française au XIXe siècle," II. 500–505.

CABEZA DE BACA. *See* Cabeça de Vaca, No. 9767.

CABEZAS (J.) Historia prodigiosa de la admirable aparicion, y milagros portentoses de la imagen de Maria N. S. de la Soterraña de Nieva, especialissima defensora de truenos, rayos, centellas, y terremotos. *Mexico.* 1748. 4to, 2 l., pp. 68. Engraving. 9789

EL CABILDO DE MICHOACAN. *See* Michoacan.

CABILDO. Relation de la fúnebre ceremonia y exequias de D. Ildef. Nuñez Arzobispo. *Mexico.* 1802. 4to, 44 l. 9790

The Cabinet. *Philadelphia: J. Laval & S. F. Bradford.* [n. d.] 12mo, 5 l., pp. 143. 9791

Portraits and biographies of Andrew Jackson and his Cabinet.

The Cabinet; or, a Collection of Choice Things; comprising the Beauties of American Miscellanies for the Last Thirty Years. By a Citizen of New York. *New York.* 1815. 8vo.

The first article is a description of the Federal procession, on the 23d day of July, 1788, in honor of the adoption of the Constitution by the States.

The Cabinet Conference; or, Tears of Ministry. Present the King — Duke of Richmond — Earl Shelburne — Lord North, Lord G. Germaine. *London: Kearsly.* 1779. 8vo.

Another thing of the "Anticipation" kind. *See* M. R., LXI. p. 466.

The Cabinet of Freedom, under the supervision of the Hon. William Jay, Rev. Professor Bush, of the University of New York, and Gerrit Smith, Esq. *New York.* 1836. 3 vols., 12mo. N. 9794

The Cabinet of Natural History, American Rural Sports, with Fifty-two illustrations. *Philadelphia.* 1832. 2 vols., 4to, pp. viii, 298; viii, 292, and Index. 9795

Originally published in 26 parts. The plates include a portrait of Rembrandt Peale.

Cabinet of Portraits consisting of Distinguished Characters, British & Foreign; accompanied with A brief Memoir of each Person. *London.* 1823. 3 vols., 8vo. 192 Portraits. 9796

Includes some Americans.

The Cabinet, or Works of Darkness, 1824. *See* P (L.)

CABLE (J.) Homes, Vines, and Fig-Trees for All. Speech of Hon. Joseph Cable, of Ohio, in the House of Representatives, March 11, 1852, or the Bill to encourage Agriculture, &c. *Printed at the Globe Office, Washington.* 8vo, pp. 7. H.

Le Cable transatlantique reliant la France et les États-Unis d'Amerique. *Paris: imprimerie Poitevin.* 1867. 8vo, pp. 8. H.

CABOT (George). A Short Account of the Hartford Convention. An attested copy of the Secret Journal of that body. *Boston.* 1823. 8vo. 9799

Title from S. G. Drake's catalogue.

[CABOT (J. E.)] Discovery of America by the Norsemen. [n. p. n. d.] 8vo, pp. 30. H. 9800

[CABOT.] Letter to the Governor of Massachusetts, on Occasion of his Late Proclamation, of August 20, 1861. *Boston: A. K. Loring.* 1861. 8vo, pp. 12. H. 9801

CABOT (M.) The Nature of Religious Fasting Opened. In Two Short Discourses Deliver'd At Thompson in Kellingley, Connecticut Colony. On a Day of Publick Fasting and Prayer. April 18. 1773. By Marston Cabot, V.D.M. ... *Boston: John Eliot.* MDCCXXXIV. 8vo, 2 l., pp. ii, 18. B. 9802

CABOT. The Nature of Religious Thanksgiving Opened. A Sermon Preach'd At Thompson in Kellingley, Connecticut Colony. On a Day of Thanksgiving, November 7. 1734. By Marston Cabot, V.D.M. ... *Boston: S. Kneeland & T. Green.* MDCCXXXV. 8vo, 2 l., pp. 23. B. 9803

Also: A Sermon at Thompson, Con. Oct. 17, 1742. *Boston.* 1743. 12mo. — A Sermon at the Ordination of the Rev. Mr. Aaron Brown, Killingley, Jany 9. 1754. *New London.* 1754. 8vo.

CABOT (S.) Description of the Cartoon of Sebastian Cabot, presenting Indians from Newfoundland to Henry VII. 1843. 4to. Plate. 9804

CABOT. Memoir of Sebastian Cabot. *See* [Biddle (R.)], Vol. II., No. 5248.

See also Ramusio, Vol. II.; Sparks (J.); "Westm. Rev.," XVI. 22; M. R., CXXV. 515; Hakluyt, Vol. III.; "Blackwood's Mag.," LXXXI. 369; N. A. R., XXXIV. 405.

CABOT (S. C.) What have we, as Individuals, to do with Slavery? By Susan C. Cabot. [*New York: American Anti-Slavery Society.* n. d.] 12mo, pp. 7. B. 9805

CABOT INSTITUTE. Constitution and By-Laws of the Cabot Institute, with a Catalogue of the Books contained in the Library. *Springfield: printed by Horace S. Taylor.* 1846. 16mo, pp. 35. 9806

CABRAL (Fredrico Augusto de Vasconcellos A. Pereira). Memoria geologica sobre Os terranos do Carral alto, e Serro de S. Roque, na provincia de S. Pedro do Sul. *Porto Alegre.* 1857. 4to. 9807

CABRAL (P. A.) Historia do Brasil desde o descobrimento por Pedro Alvares Cabral, até á abdicação do imperador D. Pedro I. *Paris: Casimir.* 1839. 2 vols., 8vo. Map. 9808

CABRAL. Don Alvarez, oder die Entdeckung von Brasilien, und Alex. Graf von Bonreval. Zwei historiche Erzählungen für d. jugend. *Neubaldensleben: Eyraud.* 1839. 8vo. 4 Illustrations. 9809

CABRAL (P. G. T. da Viega). *See* Viega Cabral (P. G. T. da).

CABREDO (Rodrigo de). Historia Insignis Miraculi, quod Deus Invocatione S. Ignatii Patriarchæ nostri patravit Limæ Die 8 Novembris Anno 1607 in Religioso quodam ex ordine S. Dominici. *Græcii: Typis Widmanstadii.* 1609. 4to. 9810

Ternaux, No. 319, gives the title differently. Ternaux's title is likely enough to be correct. Perhaps there were two title-pages, if not two editions.

CABRER (J. M.) Reconocimiento del rio Pepiri-Guazu, por D. Jose Maria Cabrer ... extractado de su diario inedito. ... *Buenos-Aires: imprenta del Estado.* 1836. Folio, Title, pp. iv, 3–11. (Angelis. Coleccion, T. IV.) H. 9811

CABRERA (C.) [Recto of the last leaf:] Christophorus Cabrera Burgensis ad lectorem | sacri baptismi ministrū. Gicolon Icastichon. | Si pancz pnosse cupz uenerādi sacerdos: | Vt baptizari quilibet Indus habet: | ... [Errata.] *Imprimiose este Manual de Adultos en la | grā ciudad d' Mexico por mādado d' los | Reuerēdissimos señores obispos d' la nueua | España y a sus expēsas: en casa de Iuā | Cromberger. Año d'l nacimiēto d' nuestro señor | Iesu Christo d' mill y quiniētos y quarēta. | A xiij dias d'l mes d' Deziēbre.* | 9812

This work exists only in fragments. Mr. Harrisse, "Bib. Am. Vet.," pp. 365–376, makes this book the text for an extended dissertation, founded on data furnished by D. J. G. Icazbalceta, on the date of the first book printed in Mexico; and, after quoting from Davila Padilla, Alonso Fernandez, and Gonzales Davila, leaves the impression that this is probably the first book *known* to be printed in the New World, and that the honor of printing it is due to Juan Cromberger. *See* Climacio.

CABRERA (Manuel de). Verdad Aclarada y Disvanecidas Imposturas, con que lo ardiente de una pluma poderosa en esta Nueva España, quiso persuadir, averse acabado el Año de 1675, la Fabrica del real desague de la insigne ciudad de Mexico. [*Mexico.*] 1678. Folio, pp. 123, 2 l. 9813

CABRERA (M.) Maravilla Americana, y conjunto de raras Maravillas, observadas con la direccion de las reglas de el arte de la pintura en la prodigiosa imagen de Nuestra Sra. de Guadalupe de Mexico, por Don Miguel Cabrera, pintor ... .

Mexico: en la imprenta del Colegio de San Ildefonso. 1756. 4to, 8 l., pp. 30. 9814

Also in the "Coleccion" published by Luis Antonio and Cayetano Torres Tuçon. *See* Bartolache's "Manifesto," pp. 22 n., 49–52, 55.

CABRERA (T. M.) Tesoro de la Virtud, escondido en el Tesoro Publico de Opulento Caudel, Sermon Funebre, en Honras del Señor D. Fernando de la Campa, Cos. *Mexico: J. B. de Hogal.* 1743. 4to. 9815

CABRERA BUENO (*Almirante D.* Joseph Gonzalez). Navegacion especulativa, y Practica. *Manila.* 1734. Folio. Plates.

Printed on paper manufactured in the Philippine Islands. "This valuable work on navigation seems totally unknown to bibliographers. It contains directions for coasting South America." — LIBRI.

CABRERA Y QUINTERO (Cayetano de). Escudo de armas de Mexico: celestial proteccion de esta nobilissima ciudad, de la Nueva-España, y de casi todo el Nuevo Mundo, Maria Santissima, en su portentosa imagen del Mexicano Guadalupe, milagrosamente apparecida en el palacio arzobispal el Año de 1531. Y jurada su principal patrona el passado de 1737. En la angustia que ocasionò la Pestilencia, que cebada con mayor rigor en los Indios, mitigò sus ardores al abrigo de tanta sombra: describiala ... D. Cayetano de Cabrera, y Quintero, ... *Mexico: Impresso por la Viuda de D. Joseph Bernardo de Hogal.* 1746. Folio, Engraved Frontispiece, and 17 l., pp. 522, Index, 12 l. H. 9817

See Bartolache's "Manifiesto," pp. 44–47. Priced, £5 5s.; by J. R. Smith, £4 4s.

CABRERA Y QUINTERO. Viva Copia del M. Sagrado Machabeo Joan Hyrcano, el D. J. A. de Vizarron y Eguiaretta. Discurrida en Arco Triumphal, que á sú publica entrada erigiò la Santa Iglesia Metropolitana, por D. Cayetano de Cabrera y Quintero. *Mexico.* 1732. 9818

In prose and verse.

CABRERA (Felix). *See* Rio (Antonio del).

CABRERA DE NAVARES (M.) Memoria sobre el estado actual de las Américas, y medio de pacificarlas. Escrita de órden del Excmo. Sr. D. Ramon Lopez Pelegrin, Secretario de Estado, y del Despacho de la Gobernacion de Ultramar, y presentada á S. M. y á las Córtes extraordinarias por el Ciudadano Miguel Cabrera de Nevares. *Madrid: Imprenta de Don José del Collado.* 1821. 8vo, pp. (6), 71. C., H. + *Habana: Reimpressa en la imprenta Fraternal.* 1822. 8vo. 9819

CACCIA (*Dr.* Antonio). Europa ed America scene della vita dal 1848 al 1850. *Monaco: Franz.* 1850. pp. iv, 500. 9820

The Cacique of Ontario; an Indian Tale. *London: Fielding.* 1786. 4to. 9821

An alteration of Richardson's "The Indians, a Tale." *See* M. R., LXXV. 474.

CADDELL (C. M.) A History of the Missions in Japan and Paraguay. By Cecilia Mary Caddell. *London: Burns.* 1856. 12mo, pp. 250. + *New York: Sadlier & Co.* 1856. 12mo.

CADDELL. Historia de las misiónes, en la Japon y Paraguay. Escrita en inglés, traducida por C. Pedregal. Segunda edicion. *Madrid.* 1857. 8vo. 9823

CADDY (*Lieut.* J. H.) Scenery of the Windward and Leeward Islands. *London.* 1837. Folio. 12 colored Plates. 9824

Cadet Life at West Point. *See* [Strong (G. C.)]

CADET (J. Marc). Observations sur l'Expedition de 1827 pour le Pole Nord. *Paris: Imp. de Balzac.* 1827. 8vo. 9825

CADET. Précis des Voyages entrepris pour se rendre par le Nord dans les Indes; et les lois physiques à consulter pour le succès des navigations ultérieures. *Paris: Beaucé-Rusand.* 1818.

Reprinted with the title: "Direction des glaces déduite des relations de Ross et de Parry. *Paris: Dondey-Dupré; Beauci-Rusand.* 1824." 8vo. Map.

CADIEUX (J. N.) The Franco-Canadian Annexionists of Elmira, N. Y., to Gen. Benjamin F. Butler, on Canado-American Annexation. [n. p. 1866.] Broadside. 9827

Signed by J. N. Cadieux and 5 others as Committee.

CADIEUX. Observations sur un ecrit intitule: Questions sur le gouvernement ecclesiastique du district de Montreal, par un pretre du diocese de Quebec. *Three Rivers.* 1823. 8vo.

CADOGAN (G.) The Spanish Hireling Detected: being a Refutation of the several Calumnies and Falsehoods in a late Pamphlet, Entitul'd "An Impartial Account of the late Expedition against St. Augustine under Gen. Oglethorpe. By George Cadogan, Lieutenant in General Oglethorpe's Regiment. ... *London: J. Roberts.* M DCC XLIII. 8vo, Title, pp. 68. H. 9829

CADOGAN. A Full Reply to Lieut. Cadogan's Spanish Hire-

ling, &c. and Lieut. Mackay's Letter Concerning the Action at Moosa. Wherein The Impartial Account of the late Expedition to St. Augustine [Fla.] is clearly vindicated, by plain Facts and Evidence. ... By the Author of the Impartial Account. *London: J. Huggonson.* M.DCC.XLIII. 12mo, Title, pp. iv–viii, 63. C., H. 9830

The expedition referred to is known as Oglethorpe's. *See* "Gentlemen's Mag."

CADORET (E.) La vie de Christophe Colomb par l'abbé Eug. Cadoret. *Paris: libraire internationale. Bruxelles: Verboeckhoven et Cᵉ. Leipzig: A. La Croix. Livourne.* 186 . 18mo, pp. 416.

El Caduceo, Periódico del estado libre de la Puebla de los Angeles. *Puebla.* 1824. 8vo. Continued to 1826. 9832

CADUSCH (*Marquis de*), BRULLEY (C. A.), *and* PONS (Fr. S. de). Rapport de MM. le marquis de Cadusch, Brulley, et de Pons, nommés commissaires pour l'examen de la déclaration sur interprétation, par M. le gouverneur général de Saint-Domingue. [15 juillet 1790.] *Port-au-Prince: Bourdon.* 1790. 4to, pp. 48 or less. 9833

CADWALLADER (B.) A Letter to Friends of Philadelphia yearly meeting. By Benjamin Cadwallader. *Philadelphia.* 1855. 8vo. P. 9834

CADWALLADER (G.) The Philadelphia Gray's Collection of Official Reports of Brigadier-General George Cadwallader's Services during the Campaign of 1847, in Mexico. *Philadelphia.* 1848. 8vo. P. 9835

[CADWALLADER (John).] A | Reply | to | General Joseph Reed's | Remarks, | on a | Late Publication | in the | Independent Gazetteer, | With some Observations on his | Address | to the | People of Pennsylvania. | *Philadelphia: | Printed and Sold by T. Bradford, in Front-Street, the Fourth | Door below the Coffee-House,* MDCCLXXXIII. | 8vo, pp. 54. BA., P. 9836

By Gen. John Cadwallader, though its real authorship has been attributed to Dr. B. Rush. The original edition of this and Reed's remarks having been suppressed by one or other of the parties concerned, are two of the rarest pieces in Pennsylvania literature, and may be estimated at from twenty to thirty dollars each. The occasion of the dispute was the assertion, by Gen. Cadwallader, that in Dec., 1776, before the battle of Trenton, Gen. Reed was so much depressed by the sad state of American affairs as to meditate withdrawing from the service. This assertion Gen. Reed denies, and Gen. Cadwallader defends, in very heated and bitter language. The dispute was revived on the publication of the ninth volume of Mr. Bancroft's history. *See* Reed (W. B.) Reprinted with the following title:

CADWALLADER. A Reply to Gen. Joseph Reed's Remarks on a late Publication in the Independent Gazetteer: with some Observations on his Address to the People of Pennsylvania. By Gen. John Cadwallader. With the Letters of Gen. George Washington, Gen. Alexander Hamilton, Major David Lenox, Dr. Benjamin Rush, Gen. P. Dickinson, Gen. Henry Laurens and others. *Philadelphia: printed and sold by T. Bradford.* MDCCLXXXIII. *Trenton, Reprinted.* 1846. 12mo, pp. 56. 9837

Also reprinted in H. W. Smith's "Nuts to Crack," pp. 15–54, and with Reed's "Remarks, *Philadelphia,* 1863," 8vo.

CADY (C. W.) *See* Indiana.

CADY (D. R.) Memorial of Lieut. Joseph P. Burrage: a Funeral Sermon, preached December 25, 1863, by Rev. Daniel R. Cady ... . *Boston: Gould and Lincoln.* 1864. 12mo, pp. 48.

Caert-thesoor, inhoudende de tafelen des gantsche werelts Landen, met beschryvingen verlicht. *Middelburg: B. Langenes.* 1598. 2 pts., oblong 4to. + *Amsterdam: C. Claese.* 1599.

The second part contains eleven maps of America. Another edition, *Amsterdam, C. Claese,* 1609, contains two additional maps of America.

CAFFREY (A.) A Sketch of Blockley Poor-House Hospital, about Twelve Years ago. By Andrew Caffrey. [n. p. n. d.] 8vo, pp. 4. 9840

CAHITA. Arte de la Lengua Cahita. *Mexico.* 1737. 12mo.

A dialect of the Indians in the northern part of Mexico. *See* Ludewig.

[CAHOONE (Sarah S.)] A Visit to Grandpa; or a Week at Newport. *New York: J. S. Taylor.* 1840. 12mo, pp. 213. Plate. 9842

Reprinted with the following title:

[CAHOONE.] Sketches of Newport and its Vicinity; with Notices respecting the History, Settlement and Geography of Rhode Island. Illustrated with Engravings. *New York: John S. Taylor & Co.* 1842. 12mo, pp. 213. BA., H. 9843

CAICEDO (J. M. Torres). *See* Torres Caicedo (J. M.)

CAIL *and* DEROSNE (Ch.) De la fabrication du sucre au colonies, et des nouveaux appareils propres à améliorer cette fabrication. *Paris: impr. de Bouchard-Huzard.* 1843. 2 pts., 4to. + Seconde édition, considérablement augmentée. 1844.

CAIL (J. F.) ET Cᴵᴱ. Mesures proposées au gouvernement pour changer la situation de nos colonies des Antilles. [Signé J.-F. Cail et Cie. 3 janvier 1860. *Paris:*] *lith. de Haristéguy.* [n. d.] Folio, pp. 48 or less. 9845

CAILLOT (Antoine). Abrégé des voyages modernes, réduits aux traits les plus curieux ... . *Paris: Ledentu.* 1820. 2 vols., 12mo. 8 Engravings. + 1821. 2 vols., 12mo. + Quatrième édition. 1826. 2 vols., 12mo. 8 Plates. 9846

Intended to form a sequel to "Abrégé de l'histoire générale des voyages, par La Harpe, réduit aux traits les plus intéressants et les plus curieux par Ant. C*** [Caillot]. *Paris: Ledentu.* 1820." 2 vols., 12mo. 8 Plates. + 1820–21. [*Ibid.*] + Troisième édition. [*Ibid.*] 1826. [*Ibid.*] + Quatrième édition. 1834. [*Ibid.*] Perhaps I should mention here his "Nouvelle histoire des naufrages anciens et modernes ... par Ant. C***. *Paris: Corbet aîné.* 1824." 12mo. Plates. + Par Ant. Caillout [*sic*]. Seconde édition. 1834. 12mo. 2 Engravings.

C[AILLOT]. Morceaux choisis des Lettres édifiantes et curieuses, écrites des missions etrangères, par A. C. *Paris.* 1810. + Quatrième édition. *Paris: Brunot-Labbe.* 1826. 2 vols., 12mo. 9847

[CAINES (Clement).] Account of the Commencement and Progress of an Institution for the Relief of Poor and Destitute Children throughout the Island of Saint Christopher. *St. Christopher: printed by Richard Cable.* M.DCCC.III. 8vo, pp. 24, (1).

CAINE (S. C.) History of the Convention of the Leeward Islands, for the purpose of Meliorating the Condition of the Slaves. *St. Christopher.* 1804. 8vo. C. 9849

CAINES (C.) Letters on the Cultivation of the Otaheite Cane; the Manufacture of Sugar and Rum; the Saving of Molasses; the Care and Preservation of Stock; with the Attention and Anxiety which is due to Negroes. To these Topics are added, a few other Particulars analogous to the Subject of the Letters; and also Speech on the Slave Trade, the most important Feature in West Indian Cultivation. By Clement Caines, Esq. *London: Messrs. Robinson.* 1801. 8vo, pp. v, xi–xv, 301. H. 9850

See M. R., XLIII. 39.

CAINES. Reflections on the Embargo, which has been substituted by the United States of America, for Proclamations of War. *St. Christopher.* 1808. 8vo. C., W. 9851

[Caines (George).] An Enquiry into the Law-Merchant of the United States; or, Lex Mercatoria Americana, on Several Heads of Commercial Importance. ... *New-York: Abraham and Arthur Stansbury.* 1802. 8vo, pp. xxxviii, (2), 648, clxvii, (1).

The dedication to President Jefferson is signed Geo. Caines.

Caird (J.) Letter on the Lands of the Illinois Central Railway Company. By James Caird, Esq., M.P. *London.* 1859. 8vo, pp. 15. H. 9853

Caird. Prairie Farming in America. With Notes by the way on Canada and the United States. By James Caird, M.P. ... *London: Longman [etc.]* 1859. Post 8vo, pp. viii, 128. Map. BA. + *New York: D. Appleton & Co.* 1859. 12mo. C. 9854

Cairnes (J. E.) ... The American Revolution; A Lecture delivered before the Dublin Young Mens' Christian Association in Connection with the United Church of England and Ireland, October 30th, 1862. By John Elliott Cairnes, A.M. [Second Edition.] *Dublin: Hodges, Smith & Co.* [1862.] 16mo, Title, pp. 44. B. + Seventh Edition—Revised and Enlarged. [*Ibid.* n. d.] 16mo, Title, pp. 48. B. + *New York: T. J. Crowen.* 1862. 8vo, pp. 15. B. 9855

Cairnes. The Slave Power: its Character, Career, & Probable Designs: being an Attempt to Explain the real Issues Involved in the American Contest. By J. E. Cairnes, M.A. ... *London: Parker, Son and Bourn.* 1862. 8vo, pp, xviii, 304. C., H. + *New York: Carleton.* M DCCC LXII. 8vo, Title, pp. vii–171. BA. + Third Edition. *New York: Follett, Foster & Co.* M DCCC LXIII. 8vo, Title, pp. vii–171. H. 9856

See Mill (J. Stuart).

Cairnes. The Southern Confederacy and the African Slave Trade. The Correspondence between Professor Cairnes, A.M., and George M'Henry, Esq., with an Introduction and Notes by Rev. George B. Wheeler, A.M. *Dublin: McGlashan and Gill.* 1863. 8vo, pp. 61. 9857

Also: Who are the Canters: *London Ladies' Emancipation Society.* 1863. 8vo, pp. 8.—Colonization and Colonial Government: a Lecture ... Dublin ... October the 26th, 1864. ... [n. p. n. d.] 8vo, pp. 54. H.—"The Negro Suffrage." By Professor Cairnes. [n. p. n. d.] 8vo, pp. 12. H.

Cairo, *Illinois.* 1856. [n. p. n. d.] 4to, pp. 20. B. 9858

An Act to Incorporate the Cairo City and Canal Company, in the State of Illinois. *Alton: Printed by L. A. Parks.* 1837. 8vo, pp. 7. 9859

Circular, Engineers Reports and other Documents relating to the Cairo property at the confluence of the Ohio and Mississippi Rivers. Illinois. Trustees, Thomas Taylor [and others]. *Printed for the Trustees [New York].* 1848. 8vo, pp. 44. 2 Maps. 9860

Map of Cairo City Property and Catalogue of Lots comprised in the first plot of the City of Cairo, Illinois. [*New York.* *July,* 1853. 4to. 3 Maps and 27 Plates. 9861

Prospectus of the Cairo City and Canal Company, with the Act of Incorporation, and Documents relating to the City of Cairo. *New York: James Marine, Printer.* 1838. 8vo, pp. 12, 7, 4, 11, 3, 38, 23, 8, 15, 2. Maps, etc. H. 9862

Caius. A Few Remarks on Mr. Hamilton's late Letter, concerning the Public Conduct and Character of the President. By Caius. *Baltimore: Printed by Warner & Hanna.* 1800. 8vo, pp. 24. BA., C., M. 9863

Cajiga (Ramon), *Gobernador.* Memoria que presenta al segundo Congreso de Oaxaca en el primer periodo de sus sesiones ordinarias, el 16 Septiembre de 1861. *Oaxaca.* 1861. Folio, pp. 95, 54 l. 9864

Calado (M.) O | Valeroso | Lvcideno, | e | Trivmpho | da | Liberdade. | Primeira Parte. | Composta | por o P. Mestre Frei Manoel Calado | da Orden de S. Paulo primeiro Ermitão, da Congregação dos | Eremitas da Serra d'Ossa, natural de Villaniçosa. | Dedicada | ao Serenissimo Senhor Dom Theodosio | Principe do Reyno, & Monarchia de Portugal. | *Em Lisboa.* | *Com licença da Sancta Inquisição, Ordinario, & Mesa do Paço.* | *Por Paulo Craesbeeck, Impressor, and livreiro das Ordẽs Militares.* | *Anno do Senhor de* 1648. | 2 l., pp. 356. J.C.B. 9865

Calado. O Valeroso | Lvcideno, | e | Trivmpho | da | Liberdade. | Primeira Parte. | Composta | Pelo Padre Mestre Fr. Manoel Calado, | Da Orden de Sam Paulo primeyro Ermitam, da Congregaçam dos Eremitas | da Serra d'Ossa, natural de Villa-Viçosa; | Dedicada | Ao Excelentissimo Senhor | D. Theodosio. | Principe deste Reyno, e Monarqvia | de Portugal. | *Em Lisboa.* | *Com todas as*

licenças necessarias. | *Na Officina de Domingos Carneiro. An.* 1668. | Folio, Title, pp. 8, 3 l., pp. 356. 9868

Probably the same edition, with a new title, and additional preliminary leaves.

Calageras (João Baptista). Compendio do Historia da edade media, adoptado pela commissão de Instrucçã Publica. *Rio de Janeria: Typ. Moderna de George Bertrand.* 1839. 2 vols., 8vo, pp. xv, 429; 347. 9866

Calamy (E.) An Historical Account of My Own Life, with Some Reflections on the Times I have lived in. (1671–1731.) By Edmund Calamy, D.D. Now first printed. Edited and illustrated with Notes, Historical and Biographical, by John Towill Rutt. In Two Volumes. *London: Henry Colburn and Richard Bentley.* 1829. 2 vols., 8vo, pp. xi, 508; xii, 561. BA., G.

Contains some reference to New England, Darien, etc. See "British Critic," VII. 295.

Calamy. The Noncomformist's Memorial; being an Account of the Lives, Sufferings, and Printed Works, of the Two Thousand Ministers Ejected from the Church of England, chiefly by the Act of Uniformity Aug 24, 1666 [so in Vol. I.; correctly 1662 in II. and III.] Originally written by Edmund Calamy, D.D. Abridged, Corrected, and Methodized, with many additional Anecdotes and several New Lives, by Samuel Palmer. The Second Edition. In Three Volumes. Embellished with Heads of the principal Divines, chiefly from original Pictures. *London: Button & Son.* 1802–03. 3 vols., 8vo, pp. xvi, (2), 434, (1); Title, 479, (1); vi, (2), 528, (23).

The former editions were printed in 1715, 1727, and 1788. Contains lives and lists of works of all the early New England divines. Mr. Allibone quotes a "Life of Increase Mather, 1725," 8vo, by this author.

Calancha (A. de). Coronica | moralizada | del orden de | San Avgvstin en el | Perv, con svcesos | egenplares en esta | monarquia. | ... | ... | ... . | Compvesta por el mvy reverendo | Padre Maestro Fray Antonio de la Calancha ... | ... . | ... | ... | ... . | *Año* 1638. | ... | *En Barcelona: Por Pedro Lacavalleria* ... | ... . | Folio, Engraved and Printed Titles, 13 l., pp. 922, (27). BA., C., H. 9870

The plate of the Martyrdom of Diego Ostez, by De Jode, on page 783, is often deficient. For a continuation, see Torre (B. de). This very curious account of the foundation of churches and religious houses in Peru, by the Augustin Order, has but seldom occurred for sale. Mr. Heber's copy sold for £3 3s.; Puttick's, 1860, for £2; Leclerc's, No. 249, for 126 fr. For a Latin version, see Brulius.

Calancha. Coronica de S. Augustin en el Peru con sucesos exemplares de esto Monarquia. *Lima.* 1653. Folio, Book I.,

7 l., pp. 15, 268; Book II., 1 l., pp. 42; Book V., pp. 92, Table, 2 l. 9871

This second volume of the Chronicle of Calancha was not published. It is a smaller folio than the first, and rarer. Book V. is the *third* in order.

Calancha. Informe al virrey del Peru sobre los castores que se caçan desde Callao haste Chile, manifestando que son los verdaderos, y renta que puede sacar de ellos su majestad por fray A. de la Calancha, de la orden de S. Agostim. *Lima.* 1642.

Title from Ternaux, No. 617.

Calancha. Histoire du Peru, partie principale des Antipodes, ou Nouveau Monde. Et du grand progres de la Foy Chrestienne, en la conversion de ces Peuples Gentiles; par la predication, bons examples, mesme du Martyre des PP. FF. de l'ordre des Hermites du Glorieux Patriarche Saint Augustin, etc. *Toulouse: François Bonde.* 1653. 4to, Engraved Title, 5 l., pp. 481, Table, pp. 8. J.C.B. 9873

At the end, separately paged, is "Le Martyre du Venerable P. Bernardin De Guistang, arrive à Marque ou Barbarie le 18 d'Avril 1606, pp. 26. Title from J. C. Brown's Cat. See Ternaux, No. 730. Brunet, 1468, gives the title differently, and quotes another book by the same author: "De Immaculatæ Virginis Mariæ conceptioni certitudine. *Limæ Inderum.* 1629. 4to.s

Calatayud y Borda (C. G. de). Oracion Funebre que en las solemnes Exequias de la R. M. Maria Antonia de San Joseph, Larrea, Arispe, de los Reyes: Quatro veces Ministra en el Monasterio de Trinitarias Descalzas de esta Ciudad de Lima: Dixo en la Iglesia del Referido Monasterio en XXX. de Octubre de M.DCC.LXXXII. El R. P. Pr. Fr. Cypriano Gerónimo de Calatayud y Borda: del orden de Nra. Sra. de la Merced: Dr. Teólogo, sóstituto que fue de la Cátedra de Prima de Sto Tomas: Regente actual de la de Nona de Teologia en la Real Vniuersidad de S. Marcos: Examinador Sinodal de este Arzobispado, y Rector del Colegio, de S. Pedro Nolasco. Y la dedica a la Señora Condesa de San Isidro. *En Lima: en la Imprenta de los Huérfanos. Año de* M.DCC.LXXXIII. 4to, 58 l., pp. 144. 9874

Amongst the commendatory matter is a "Labyrinthus" composed in the form of a cross, so arranged that the words "Maria Innocens Penitens" may be read in a great variety of ways, commencing from the centre. Sold at Puttick's, 1860, for 10s.

Calcott (Alexander). Treatise on the Deluge. *London.* 1761. 8vo. + Second Edition Enlarged. *London.* 1768. Rl. 8vo, pp. 423. 9875

The time when, and the manner how, America was first peopled, occupies thirty-one pages of the second edition.

Calcott (*Lady*). *See* Graham (Maria).

Caldas (F. J. de). Semenario de la Nueva Granada, Miscelane de Ciencias, Literatura, Artes, é Industria, publicada por una sociedad de patriotas Grandinos, bajo la direccion de Francisco Juan de Caldas. ... Nueva edicion, corrigida, aumentado ... *Paris: Lasserre* 1849. 8vo, pp. 572. Portrait. 9876

Caldcleugh (A.) Travels in South America, during the Years 1819–20–21; containing an Account of the Present State of Brazil, Buenos Ayres, and Chile. By Alexander Caldcleugh, Esq. *London: John Murray.* MDCCCXXV. 2 vols., 8vo, pp. viii, 373; viii, 380. Map, and 10 colored Plates. C. 9877

See "Quarterly Rev.," XXXII. 125–152.

Caldcleugh. Reisen in Süd-Amerika während die Jahren 1819–25; enthaltend eine Schilderung der gegenwärtigen Zustandes von Brasilien, Buenos-Ayres und Chile. *Weimar: Ind.-Comptoir.* 1826. 8vo. (Neue Bibl. d. wichtigsten Reisebschr. Bd. XLI.) 9878

Calderon (Fern.) Obras poeticas. *Mexico.* 1844. Rl. 8vo. 6 Portraits. 9879

Calderon (Francisco). Vida del P. Gaspar de Carvajal de la Comp. de Jesus. 9880

Carvajal was a Mexican Jesuit. The Backers give this title without any imprint.

Calderon (F.) Sermon en las Exequias de doña Leonor Carreto, marquesa de Mancera, virreyus desta neuva España, por Fr. Francisco Calderon. *Mexico.* 1675. 4to. 9881

Title from Ternaux, No. 916.

Calderon (F. G.) Diccionario de la legislacion Peruana, por Francisco Garcia Calderon. Tomo I. A—D. *Lima.* 1860. Folio, pp. viii, 886. + Tomo II. E—Z. Suplemento. *Lima.* 1862. Folio, pp. xxxii, 1260. 9882

Calderon (Ignacio). Relacion de la obediencia, que los Indios de Nayarit dieron al rey de España, en 1721. *Megico.* 1722. 4to. 9883

Calderon (Juan Alonso). Memorial juridico-politico de la S. Iglesia Catedral de la Puebla de los Angeles en la Neuva-España, sobre restituirla las armas reales de Castilla, Leon ... que puso en la capilla mayor de su iglesia, de que ha sido despoiada injustamente. [n. p. n. d.] Folio, 6, 89 l. Plates. BD.

Calderon (L.) Evidence taken at Port of Spain, Island of Trinidad, in the Case of Louisa Calderon, with Letter to Sir Sam. Hood, by Col. Thomas Picton. *London.* 1806. 8vo.

Calderon (P.) Memorial del R. P. M. Pedro Calderon de la comp. de Jesus, procurador de la provincia del nuevo reyno y de Quito, etc. *Colonia: Herman Dehmen.* 1695. Folio.

Relates to the quarrels of the Dominicans with the Jesuits.

Calderon. El Apostel de los Indios. *Mexico.* 1661. 4to.

C[alderon] de la B[arca] (Frances Erskine Inglis). Life in Mexico during a Residence of two Years in that Country. By Mme. C—— De La B——. ... In Two Volumes. *Boston: Charles C. Little and James Brown.* 1843. 2 vols., 12mo, pp. xii, 412; xi, 427. Plates. B., H. 9888

Reprinted with the following title:

Calderon de la Barca. Life in Mexico, during a residence of two Years in that Country. By Madame Calderon de la Barca. With a Preface by W. H. Prescott. *London: Chapman & Hall.* 1843. 8vo, pp. xii, 436. H. + *Belfast: Simms & McIntyre.* 1852. Post 8vo, pp. 234. C. 9889

See N. A. R., LVI. 137. The "Edinburgh Review" remarks: "A more genuine book, in air, as well as in reality, it would be difficult to find."

Calderon de la Barca (Pedro). Aurora en Copacabana.

Relates to the conquest of the new world, see Ternaux, No. 443, p. 82. I cannot ascertain the date of the first publication. The play is in "Las comedias de D. Pedro Calderon de la Barca ... corregidas y dadas á luz por Juan Jorge Keil. ... *Leipsique.* 1827–30." 4 vols., 8vo, Vol. II. pp. 443–476 (B.), and in the edition of the "Comedias de Don Pedro Calderon de la Barca," 4 vols., which belongs to the "Biblioteca de autores españoles ... ordenada é ilustrada por D. Buenaventura Carlos Aribau. *Madrid.* 1846," etc. B.

Calderon de la Varca (D. M.) Reales Aranzeles de los ministros de la real avdiencia, sala del crimen, oficios de govierno, juzgado de bienes de difuntos, tribunal de quentas, real caxa, escrivano de ella ... formados dichos Aranzeles por ... D. Miguel Calderon de la Varca, y D. Balthazar de Tovar, el año de 1699. Y aprobados por su Magestad el año de 1701. impressos de orden verbal del señor Marqués de Casa-Fuerte, virrey, año de 1727. *Mexico: Imprenta real. Reimpressos segunda vez: Por los herederos de la viuda de Miguel de Rivera,* 1727. Folio, pp. 112.

Caldicott (Thomas Ford), *D.D.* Hannah Corcoran; an Authentic Narrative of her ... Abduction from Charlestown. ... *Boston.* 1853. 18mo. 9892

Caldwell (C.) Autobiography of Charles Caldwell, M.D. With a Preface, Notes and Appendix. By Harriot W. Warner. *Philadelphia: Lippincott, Grambo, and Co.* 1855. 8vo, pp. viii, 17–454. B., C. 9893

Caldwell. A Discourse on the First Centennial Celebration of the Birth-Day of Washington, delivered ... [at] Lexington, On the 22nd of February, 1832. By Charles Caldwell, M.D. *Lexington, Kentucky.* 1832. 8vo, pp. 56. C., H. 9894

Caldwell. A Discourse on the Genius and Character of the Rev. Horace Holley, LL.D., Late president of Transylvania University, by Charles Caldwell, M.D. ... With an Appendix, containing Copious Notes, Biographical and Illustrative. *Boston: Hilliard, Gray, Little, and Wilkins.* 1828. 8vo, pp. viii, 294. Portrait and 2 Plates. C., H. 9895

Caldwell. An Elegiac Poem on the Death of General Washington. By Charles Caldwell, A.M., M.D. *Philadelphia: Printed at the office of "The True American."* 1800. 8vo, 2 l., pp. 12. 9896

Caldwell. Memoirs of the Life and Campaigns of the Hon. Nathaniel Greene, Major General in the Army of the United States, and Commander of the Southern Department, in the War of the Revolution. By Charles Caldwell, M.D. ... . *Philadelphia: Robert Desilver.* 1819. 8vo, pp. xxiii, (1), 452, Errata, 3 lines. Portrait and 2 Facsimiles. BA., C., H. 9897

See N. A. R., X. 183.

Caldwell. An Oration Commemorative of the Character and Administration of Washington, delivered before the American Republican Society of Philadelphia, On the 22d day of February, 1810. By Charles Caldwell, M.D. ... *Philadelphia: Bradford and Inskeep.* 1810. 8vo, pp. 37. BA., N. 9898

Caldwell. Reviewer Reviewed; Reply to an Attack on Delaplaine's Repository. *Philadelphia.* 1816. 8vo. B. 9899

Also: An Anniversary Oration on the subject of Quarantines, ... Philadelphia ... January 21, 1807. *Philadelphia.* 1807. 8vo.—An Eulogium on Caspar Wistar, M.D. ... *Philadelphia.* 1818. 8vo. P.—An Eulogium to the Memory of Dr. Samuel Cooper, ... March, 1799. ... *Philadelphia.* 1799.—Eulogium on Mr.

George Lee, ... Feb. 24, 1802. *Philadelphia.* 1802. 8vo.—Essays on Malaria and Temperance. *Lexington.* 1831. 12mo.—Address, on the Advantages and Facilities of establishing a Medical School in the Western States, delivered ... in Lexington, ... 1819. ... *Lexington, K.: printed by Thomas Smith:* 1819. 8vo, pp. 28. BA., H.—Medical & Physical Memoirs, containing, among other subjects, a Particular Enquiry into the Origin and Nature of the Late Pestilential Epidemics of the United States. ... *Philadelphia: Thomas & William Bradford.* 1801. 8vo, 8 l., pp. 348. B.—Medical and Physical Memoirs. ... *Lexington: Printed at the Office of the Kentucky Whig.* 1826. 8vo, 2 l., pp. 224. BA. (Entirely different from the preceding. Memoir II., pp. 77–178, is on Yellow Fever.)—An Oration, ... delivered before the American Republican Society of Philadelphia, On the Fourth of July, 1810. ... *Philadelphia: Bradford and Inskeep.* 1810. 8vo, pp. 34.—An Oration ... before the Washington Benevolent Society of Pennsylvania, on the Fourth Day of July, 1814. ... *Philadelphia: Printed at the Office of the United States Gazette.* 1814. 8vo, pp. 66. H.—An Oration on the Causes of the Difference, in point of Frequency and Force, between the Endemic Diseases of the United States of America and those of the Countries of Europe. *Philadelphia: Bradford.* 1802. 8vo, pp. 46.—Report to the Legislature of Kentucky, on the Medical Department of Transylvania University. *Lexington.* 1836. 8vo, pp. 34.—Thoughts on Popular and Liberal Education, ... delivered September 28th, 1836. ... *Lexington, Ky.: intelligencer print.* 1836. 8vo, pp. 73. H.—Thoughts on the Impolicy of Multiplying Schools of Medicine. + *Lexington.* 1834. 8vo, pp. 35.—Thoughts on the Original Unity of the Human Race, ... *New York.* 1830. + *Philadelphia.* 1831. + Second Edition, with Additions. *Cincinnati.* 1852. 8vo. B., C.—Thoughts on Quarantine and other Sanitary Systems. Boylston Prize Essay, August, 1834. *Boston.* 1834. 8vo, pp. 72. M.—Thoughts on the Spirit of Improvement. Address ... April 1, 1835, ... Nashville University. *Nashville.* 1835. 8vo, pp. 56. M.—A Valedictory Address on some of the Duties and Qualifications of a Physician, ... Transylvania University, ... 17th day of March, 1830. ... [n. p. n. d.] 8vo, pp. 22.

Caldwell (G. A.) Speech of the Hon. Geo. Alfred Caldwell, of Kentucky, on the California and Territorial Question. ... June 7, 1850. *Washington.* 1850. 8vo, pp. 16. 9900

Caldwell (H.) Documents accompanying a Bill for the Relief of Harry Caldwell and Amasa Jackson. *Washington City.* 1809. 8vo, pp. 11. BA. 9901

Caldwell. Defence prepared and intended to be delivered at the Bar of Court of the King's Bench in the City of Quebec, Nov. 1790, in a prosecution for a Libel, at the Instance of Henry Caldwell, Esq. *Quebec.* [n. d.] 8vo. W. 9902

Caldwell. The Invasion of Canada in 1775. By Major Henry Caldwell. *Quebec.* 1865. 8vo. pp. 19. 9903

Written the year following the event.

Caldwell (J.) The Genealogy of Richard Nason. Compiled by J. Caldwell. *Boston.* July 1, 1859. 18mo, pp. 8.

Caldwell (J.) An impartial Trial of the Spirit operating in this Part of the World ... . Sermon Preached at New London-derry, October 14th. 1741. On 1 John, 4. 1. By John Caldwell, A.M. ... *Boston: T. Fleet.* 1742. 8vo, 2 l., pp. 50. BA., H. + *Glasgow.* 1742. 8vo. + *Williamsburg.* 1746. Sm. 4to. C. 9905

The Glasgow edition contains a second anti-Wesley and Whitefield preface.

CALDWELL. The Nature, Folly, and Evil of rash and uncharitable Judging. A Sermon Preachd at the French Meeting-House in Boston, New-England, July the 11th. 1742. By John Caldwell, A.M. ... With ... an Answer to some Observations in the Weekly Journal of June 8th. 1742. on my Sermon upon the Trial of the Spirit, &c. ... *Boston: Tho. Fleet.* 1742. 8vo, pp. 37. B., BA., H. 9906

CALDWELL. The Scripture Characters or Marks of False Prophets or Teachers. A Sermon Preached at the French Meeting-House, in Boston, before the Presbytery of Boston; May 26th. 1742. By John Caldwell, A.M. ... *Boston: Tho. Fleet.* 1742. 8vo, pp. 32. B., BA., H. 9907

Also: Answer to the Appendix of the Second Edition of Mr. McGregorie's Sermon on the Trial of the Spirits, &c. *Boston.* 1743. 12mo. W.

CALDWELL (J. H.) Slavery and Southern Methodism. Two Sermons preached in the Methodist Church in Newman, Georgia. By the Pastor, Rev. John H. Caldwell. *New York: Carleton & Porter.* 1865. 12mo, pp. 80. 9908

CALDWELL (J. W.) Oration at Worcester, July 4, 1803. By John William Caldwell. *Worcester.* [1803.] 4to. W.

CALDWELL (Joseph). A Discourse delivered at the University of North Carolina, at the commencement in July, 1802; concluding with an Address to the Senior Class. *Raleigh.* 1802. 12mo. 9910

CALDWELL (J. Blake). An Oration ... at Barre ... July 4, 1808: by Joseph B. Caldwell, A.M. ... Added ... Fourteen Spirited Resolutions, adopted on the Occasion. ... *Worcester: Isiah Thomas, Jun. July,* 1808. 8vo, pp. 31. B., BA. 9911

CALDWELL (M.) An Address delivered before the Readfield Temperance Society, at their First Anniversary, July 4, 1832. By Merritt Caldwell, Esq., ... *Hallowell: Advocate Office.* 1832. 8vo, pp. 23. H. 9912

Also: An Address ... Annual Commencement of Dickinson College, Carlisle, Pennsylvania, July 16, 1835. *Hallowell: Glazier, Masters & Smith.* 1835. 8vo, pp. 24. H. — Christianity tested by eminent Men; being brief Sketches of Christian Biography. ... *New York.* 1852. 16mo.

CALDWELL (S. B. T.) An Oration ... at Manchester, N. H. before the Republican Citizens of Goffstown, Bedford and Manchester ... [July 4,] 1814. By Samuel B. T. Caldwell. ... *Concord, N. H.: printed by Isaac & W. R. Hill.* 1814. 8vo, pp. 23.

CALDWELL (S. L.) A Discourse at the Completion of the First Century of the Warren Association. By Rev. S. L. Caldwell. *Providence: The Author.* 1868. 8vo, pp. 19. 9914

CALDWELL. A Sermon preached ... in Providence, ... June 9, 1861, before the Second Regiment of Rhode Island Volunteers: by Samuel L. Caldwell. ... . *Providence: Knowles, Anthony & Co., Printers.* 1861. 8vo, pp. 12. 9915

Also: Oration ... Providence, ... July 4, 1861. ... *Providence: Knowles, Anthony & Co., Printers.* 1861. 8vo, pp. 23.

CALDWELL (S. T. J.) The History of a Brigade of South Carolinians, known first as "Gregg's," and subsequently as "McGowan's Brigade." By S. T. J. Caldwell, lately an officer of the First Regiment S. C. V. *Philadelphia: King & Bird.* 1866. 12mo, pp. 247, (1). 9916

[CALDWELL (T.)] A Tour through Part of Virginia, in the Summer of 1808. In a Series of Letters, including an Account of Harper's Ferry, the Natural Bridge, the New Discovery called Weir's Cave, Monticello and the Different Medicinal Springs, Hot and Cold Baths, visited by the Author. *New York: printed for the Author.* 1809. 8vo, pp. 31. + *Belfast.* 1810. 8vo, pp. 63. 9917

CALDWELL MONUMENT. Inauguration Ceremonies: Address by Samuel Miller, November 24, 1845. *Elizabeth-Town.* 1846. 8vo, pp. 24. N. 9918

Caledonia; or, the Pedlar turn'd Merchant. A Tragi-Comedy As it was Acted by His Majesty's Subjects of Scotland, in the King of Spain's Province of Darien. *London, printed.* 1700. 4to, pp. 30. 9919

A satirical poem, almost unknown to American bibliographers. Part of the title is given in the "Biographia Dramatica," where it is supposed to be a dramatic piece. In reality, it consists of 127 four-line stanzas. It is a humorous, though somewhat coarse, satire, in Ned Ward's style, on the Scots settlement at Darien, and Will. Paterson, the projector of it. It was burnt at Edinburgh by order of the Parliament. *See* the "New Retrospective Review," No. 2. Brockett's copy sold for 7s. 6d. Priced, by J. R. Smith, at £2 2s.

The History of Caledonia, or the Scots Colony in Darien in the West Indies, with an Account of the Manners of the Inhabitants and Riches of the Countrey. *London.* 1699. 8vo.

CALEDONIA-COUNTY GRAMMAR SCHOOL, *Vt.* Catalogue of the Officers and Students of the Caledonia-County Grammar School, Peacham, Vt., 1834. *Windsor, Vt.* [1834.] 16mo, pp. 16. M. 9921

Caledonia County Teachers' Institute, Danville, Vt., 1851. Catalogue. *Danville.* 1851. 9922

History, Rise, and Progress of the Caledonia Springs, Canada West ... . *Montreal: printed by James Stark and Co.* 1844. 16mo, Title, pp. 77, (1). BA., H. 9923

The Caledonian Dream. Inscribed to the Rt. Hon. the Earl of Chatham. *London: Fielding and Co.* 1777. 4to. 9924

See M. R., First Series, LVIII. 82.

C[ALEF] (J[ohn]). The | Siege of the Penobscot | by the | Rebels; | containing a | Journal of the Proceedings | of | His Majesty's Forces detached from the 74th and 82nd Re-| giments, consisting of about 700 Rank and File, under | the Command of Brigadier-General Francis M'Lean, | and of | Three of His Majesty's Sloops of War, of 16 Guns | each, under the command of Captain Henry Mowat, | Senior Officer; | when Besieged by | Three Thousand Three Hundred (Rebel) Land Forces, | under the Command of Brigadier-General Solomon Lovell, | and | Seventeen Rebel Ships and Vessels of War, under the Com-| mand of G. Saltonstall, Commodore. | To which is annexed | A Proclamation issued June 15, 1779, by General | M'Lean and Captain Barclay to the Inhabitants; | Also | Brigadier-General Lovell's Proclamation to the Inha-| bitants; and his Letter to Commodore Saltonstall, found | on board the Rebel Ship Hunter; | Together with | the Names, Force, and Commanders, of the Rebel Ships | destroyed in Penobscot Bay and River, August 14 and | 15, 1779. | With | A Chart of the Peninsula of Majabigwaduce, and of | Penobscot River, | To which is subjoined | A Postcript, wherein a short Account of the Country of | Penobscot is given. | By J. C., Esq., a Volunteer. | *London:* | *Printed for G. Kearsley, in Fleet Street, and Ashby and Neele (late Spilsbury's in Russel-Court, Covent-Garden* | M,DCC,LXXXI. | 8vo, Title, pp. 44. 2 Charts. BA., H. 9925

The long title to this rare little volume is, in fact, an abridgment of its contents. The book consists chiefly of a daily journal, in which the events of the siege are recorded with apparent precision, but with a strong English bias. *See* Rich. An indifferent copy of this tract brought $20, at an auction in New York, Dec. 18, 1868.

CALEF (R.) More | Wonders | of the | Invisible World: | Or, The Wonders of the | Invisible World, | Display'd in Five Parts. | Part I. An Account of the Sufferings of Margaret Rule, Written by | the Reverend Mr. C. M. | P. II. Several Letters to the Author, &c. And his Reply relating | to Witchcraft. | P. III. The Differences between the Inhabitants of Salem-Village, and | Mr. Parris, their Minister in New-England. | P. IV. Letters of a Gentleman uninterested, Endeavouring to prove | the received Opinions about Witchcraft to be Orthodox. With short | Essays to their Answers. | P. V. A short Historical Accout [*sic*] of Matters of Fact in that Affair. | To which is added, A Postcript relating to a Book intitled, The | Life of Sir William Phips. | Collected by Robert Calef, Merchant, of Boston in New-England. | Licensed and Entred according to Order. | *London:* | *Printed for Nath. Hiller, at the Princes-Arms, in Leaden-Hall-street,* | *over against St. Mary-Ax, and Joseph Collyer, at the Golden Bible,* | *on London-Bridge.* 1700. | Sm. 4to, 6 l., pp. 156. B., M. 9926

"The author gave great offence by opposing the then popular belief concerning witches. 'In his discussion with Cotton Mather, he is as superior to him in reasoning as he was in good sense and courage.'" — N. A. R., III. 316. Priced, by J. R. Smith, London, 1865, at £4 4s. Woodward's copy sold, in 1869, for $130. *See* Rich, No. 485.

CALEF. More Wonders of the Invisible World: or, The Wonders of the Invisible World displayed in Five Parts. ... To which is added, a Postscript, Relating to a Book entitled, "The Life of Sir William Phips." Collected by Robert Calef, Merchant, of Boston, in New-England. *Re-printed in Salem: Cushing and Carlton.* 1796 12mo, pp. 318. BA., H. + *Re-printed in Salem, by John D. and T. C. Cushing, Jr.: for Cushing and Appleton.* 1823. 12mo, pp. 312. H. + A New Edition. *Boston: T. Bedlington.* 1828. 24mo, pp. 333. BA. 9927

See also Drake's "Witchcraft delusion in New England," v. 2–3, and "Salem Witchcraft" for other reprints; and, for a reply, *see* Gill (Obadiah).

Calendrier américain, avec éphémérides, 1860. *Paris: imp. Bonaventure et Ducessois.* 1859. 18mo, pp. 366. 9928

For other calendars *see* Bolivia, and other names of countries and states.

CALHOUN (G. A.) An Historical Address delivered before the Church of Christ, in North Coventry, Connecticut, at their First Centennial Celebration, October 9, 1845. By George A. Calhoun. *Hartford, Conn.* 1846. 8vo, pp. 44. N. 9929

CALHOUN (Jas. E.) Speech on the Sunday Question, before

the Stockholders of the South Carolina Railroad, in Charleston, February 9, 1853. 8vo. 9930

CALHOUN (J.) Petition of Commander John Calhoun, U. S. Navy, Protesting against the Action of the late Advising Board, and praying for Relief. *Philadelphia: J. B. Chandler.* 1863. 8vo, pp. 12. 9931

CALHOUN (J. C.) A Disquisition on Government, and a Discourse on the Constitution and Government of the United States. By John C. Calhoun. Edited by Richard K. Cralle. Published under the Direction of the General Assembly of the State of South Carolina. *Columbia, S. C.: printed by A. S. Johnston.* 1851. 8vo, pp. vii, 406. C., H. 9932

Forms. Vol. I. of his works. Some copies have the imprint: *New York: D. Appleton & Co.* 1851.

CALHOUN. Speeches ... in Congress, on the Collection of Duties on Imports. *Washington.* 1833. 8vo. 9933

CALHOUN. Speeches of John C. Calhoun. Delivered in the Congress of the United States from 1811 to the Present Time. *New York: Harper & Brothers.* 1843. 8vo. 9934

CALHOUN. Speeches, Reports and other writings, subsequent to his election as Vice President of the United States, including his leading speeches on the late war, delivered in 1811. *New York.* 1844. 8vo, pp. 554. Portrait. 9935

CALHOUN. The Works of John C. Calhoun. [Edited by Richard K. Crallé.] *New-York: D. Appleton & Co.* 1853–M.DCCC.LV. 6 vols., 8vo, pp. viii, 406; viii, 652; viii, 648; viii, 578; viii, 461; vi, (1), 445. H. 9936

Published under the direction of the General Assembly of the State of South Carolina. Each volume has a second title-page: I. — "A Disquisition on Government and A Discourse on the Constitution and Government of the United States. ... Edited by Richard K. Cralle. II., III., IV. — Speeches ... in the House of Representatives, and in the Senate of the United States. Edited ... . V., VI. — Reports and Public Letters ... . Edited ... ." The general titles of Vols. V. and IV. are dated M.DCCC.LV.; the second title, M.DCCC.LVI. Also issued with the date of 1863. Also: ... In Senate ... . February 9, 1835. ... Mr. Calhoun made the following Report ... [on] Executive Patronage ... [n. p. n. d.] 8vo, pp. 29. BA. — Letter in Answer to an Invitation from a Committee appointed by a Convention of Democratic Republican Electors of the City of New York, to deliver an Oration on Sixty-fourth Anniversary of the Independence of the United States. *New York.* 1840. 8vo. N. — Mr. Calhoun's Reply to Col. Benton. [n. p. 1850?] 8vo, pp. 25. H. — Mr. Calhoun's Sentiments, upon the Subject of State Rights, and the Tariff; together with Copies of the Virginia

Resolutions of 1798; of the Kentucky Resolutions of 1799; and of the Decision of the Supreme Court of Pennsylvania, pronounced in 1799, by Chief Justice M'Kean. ... *Boston: printed by Beals and Homer.* 1831. 8vo, pp. 18. BA. — Remarks ... delivered ... January 13, 1834, on the subject of the removal of the deposites from the Bank of the U. States. *Washington.* 1834. 8vo, pp. 16. — Remarks ... March 21, 1834, on Mr. Webster's Bill to continue the Charter of the Bank of the United States. *Washington.* [1834.] 8vo. — Remarks ... May 6, 1834, on the President's Protest. *Washington.* [1834.] 8vo. W. — Remarks ... on the Bill authorizing an Issue of Treasury Notes: ... September 19, 1837. *Washington.* 1837. 8vo, pp. 16. BA. — Remarks ... on the Graduation Bill. ... Tuesday, January 15, 1839. *Washington: printed by Blair and Rives.* 1839. 8vo, pp. 7. H. — ... In Senate ... . February 4, 1836. ... Report ... [on] the attempt to circulate, through the mail, inflammatory appeals, to excite the slaves to insurrection ... . [*Washington.* 1836.] 8vo, pp. 12. (24th Cong. 1st Sess. Senate, 118.) — Speech ... on his Amendment to Separate the Government from the Banks, delivered in the Senate of the United States, October 3, 1837. *Washington.* 1837. 8vo, pp. 12. H. — Speech ... on the Sub-Treasury Bill: delivered in the Senate ... February 15, 1838. *Washington.* 1838. 8vo, pp. 24. H. — Speech ... in reply to Mr. Clay on the Sub-Treasury Bill, ... March 10, 1838. *Washington: Chronicle Office.* 1838. 8vo, pp. 16. — Speech ... In Senate ... February 5, 1840 — On Mr Grundy's report in relation to the Assumption of the Debts of the States by the Federal Government [With Calhoun's reply to Webster, March 3] *Worcester: E. W. Bartlett & Co., Printers.* [n. d.] 8vo, pp. 20. BA. + *Washington.* 1840. 8vo, pp. 14. — Speech of Mr. Calhoun ... [Jan. 12, 1841] on the Prospective Pre-emption Bill. [n. p. n. d.] 8vo. pp. 8. H. — Speech ... in Support of the Veto Power. ... Monday, Feb. 28, 1842. [n. p. n. d.] 8vo, pp. 8. H. — Speech ... on Mr. Clay's Resolutions in relation to the Revenues and Expenditures of the Government: ... March 16, 1842. *Washington: printed at the Globe Office,* 1842. 8vo, pp. 14. H. — Speech ... on the Loan Bill: ... April 12, 1842. *Washington: printed at the Globe Office.* 1842. 8vo, pp. 8. H. — Speech ... August [16], 1842. On the Treaty of Washington. [n. p. n. d.] 8vo, pp. 8. H. — Speech ... on the Resolutions giving notice to Great Britain of the Abrogation of the Convention of Joint Occupancy. ... March 16, 1846. [*Washington:*] *Towers, printer.* [n. d.] 8vo, pp. 16. — Speech ... on the Bill making Appropriation of 10,000,000 dollars to bring the existing war with Mexico to a conclusion. *Washington.* 1847. 8vo. — Speech ... on his Resolutions in reference to the War with Mexico. *Washington.* 1848. 8vo. — Speech ... on the Oregon Bill. ... June 27, 1848. *Towers, printer.* 8vo, pp. 16. H. — Speech ... on the Ten Regiment Bill, 1848. 8vo. — Speech ... on the Slavery Question. ... March 4, 1850. *Buell & Blanchard.* 8vo, pp. 8. H. — Besides these, the following speeches were published, of which I have not been able to find the imprint: Feb. 15, 1833, Against the Force Bill. — Feb. 26, 1833. On his Resolutions and in reply to Mr. Webster. — April 9, 1834. On the Bill to repeal the Force Act. — March 9, 1836. On the Abolition Petitions. — April 12, 1836. On the Bill to prohibit Deputy Postmasters from receiving or transmitting through the Mail certain Papers therein mentioned. — Feb. 1837. On the Reception of Abolition Petitions. — May 28, 1836. On the Public Deposites. — Jan. 2, 1837. On the Bill for the Admission of Michigan. — Jan. 5, 1837. [On the same.] — March 22, 1838. On the Sub-Treasury Bill, in reply to Mr. Webster. — Feb. 22, 1839. On the Bill to prevent the Interference of certain Federal Officers in Elections. — March 13, 1840. On his Resolutions in reference to the Case of the Enterprise. — June 2, 1840. On the Bankrupt Bill. — Jan. 23, 1841. On the Bill to distribute the Proceeds of the Public Lands. — Jan. 30, 1841. In reply to the Speeches of Mr. Webster and Mr. Clay on Mr. Crittenden's Amendment to the Pre-emption Bill. — June 11, 1841. On the Case of M'Leod. — Aug. 24, 1841. On the Distribution Bill. — Jan. 25, 1842. On the Treasury Note Bill. — Aug. 5, 1842. On the Passage of the Tariff Bill. — Feb. 1843. On the Bill for the Occupation of the Oregon Territory.

CALHOUN *and* BUCHANAN. Oregon. The Claim of the United States to Oregon, As Stated in the Letters of The Hon. J. C. Calhoun and the Hon. J. Buchanan, ... To the Right Hon. R. Packenham. ... With an Appendix, containing The Counter Statement of Mr. Packenham to the American Secretaries of State. And a Map, Showing the Boundary Line Proposed by each Party. *London: Wiley and Putnam.* 1846. 8vo, Title, pp. iv, 3–55, Appendix, 16. Map. H. 9943

CALHOUN *and* GROSVENOR (T. P.) Speeches in the House of Representatives of the United States, upon Mr. Webster's Resolutions. 1813. 8vo. H. 9944

CALHOUN *and* WEBSTER (D.) Speeches of Hon. John C. Calhoun, and Hon. Daniel Webster, on the Subject of Slavery. Delivered in the Senate ... March, 1850. *New York: Stringer & Townsend.* 1850. 8vo, pp. 32. BA., H., S. 9945

CALHOUN *and* WEBSTER. Speeches of John C. Calhoun and Daniel Webster, in the Senate of the United States, on the Enforcing Bill. *Boston: Beals, Homer & Co., and Russell, Odiorne & Co.* 1833. 8vo, Title, pp. 89. BA., H. 9946

CALHOUN *and others.* Speeches ... of Messrs. Calhoun, Webster and Poindexter, March 25, 1833, on the Revenue Collection Bill. 8vo. S. 9947

The Calhoun Doctrine, or State Nullification discussed. Originally published in the "Irishman and Southern Democrat." By a Democratic Republican. *Charleston, (S. C.)* 1831. 8vo, pp. 32. H. 9948

The Calhoun Text Book. *New York: M. Y. Beach, Sun Office.* [n. d.] 8vo, pp. 36. 9949

The Death and Funeral Ceremonies of John Caldwell Calhoun, containing the Speeches, Reports, and other Documents ... , the Oration of the Hon. R. B. Rhett, before the Legislature, &c. &c. Published by Order of the Legislature. *Columbia, S. C.: printed by A. S. Johnston.* 1850. 8vo, 2 l., pp. 168. BA. 9950

CALHOUN. A Letter to the Hon. Mr. Calhoun, Chairman of the Committee on a National Currency. *Philadelphia: M. Carey.* 1816. 12mo, pp. 21, 10. 9951

CALHOUN. The Letters of Lowndes, addressed to the Hon. John C. Calhoun. *New-York: D. Appleton & Co.* M DCCCXLIII. 8vo, pp. 100. BA. 9952

CALHOUN. Life and Character of the Hon. John C. Calhoun, with Illustrations: Containing Notices of his Father and Uncles, and their Brave Conduct during our Struggle for Independence, in the American Revolutionary War. *New-York: J. Winchester.* 1843. 8vo, pp. 24. Woodcuts. B., C. 9953

CALHOUN. Life of John C. Calhoun. Presenting a Condensed History of Political Events from 1811 to 1843. Together with a Selection from his Speeches, Reports, and other Writings subsequent to his Election as Vice-President of the United States, including his leading Speech on the late War, delivered in 1811. *New-York: Harper and Brothers.* 1843. 8vo, pp. 76. Portrait. C. 9954

See "National Portrait Gallery," II. 16.

CALHOUN. Measures, not Men. Illustrated by some Remarks on the Public Conduct of John C. Calhoun. By a Citizen of New York. 1823. 8vo, pp. 49. 9955

CALHOUN. Obituary Addresses delivered on the Occasion of the Death of the Hon. John C. Calhoun, ... in the Senate ... April 1, 1850. Printed by order of the Senate ... . *Washington: Jno. T. Towers.* 1850. 8vo, pp. 39. C., H., S. 9956

CALHOUN (John C.) *See* Thomas (J. P.)

CALHOUN (J. S.) Life and Confession of Mary Jane Gordon, who was tried ... for the murder of Mary Jane Anderson. *Augusta, Me.* 1847. 8vo, pp. 32. + *Covington.* 1849. 8vo, pp. 32. H. 9957

CALHOUN (S. H.) An Oration delivered July 4, 1829, before the Faculty and Students of Williams College. By Simon H. Calhoun. *Williamstown: Printed by Ridley Bannister.* 1829. 8vo, pp. 13. H. 9958

CALIFORNIA ACADEMY OF SCIENCES. Memoirs presented to the California Academy of Sciences. Vol. I, Part I, Catalogue of Pacific Coast Mosses. [Leo] Lesquereux. Vol. I, Part II. The Natural System of Volcanic Rocks. [F. Baron] Richthofen. *San Francisco: Towne and Bacon, printers.* 1868. 4to, pp. 38, 94, (1). H. 9959

The President's Annual Address, delivered January 6, 1868, together with the Constitution adopted at that meeting, and List of Officers and Members for 1868. *San Francisco: Edward Bosqui & Co., printers.* 1868. 8vo, pp. 31. H. 9960

Proceedings of the California Academy of Natural Sciences. Vol. I. *San Francisco.* 1861. 8vo. Continued. C. 9961

De los territorios de Californias. *Mexico.* 1827. 8vo. 9962

California and New Mexico. Message from the President of the United States. January 24th, 1850. *Washington.* 1850. 8vo, pp. 967. Maps. 9963

Many other of the messages of the president relate to California.

California and her Gold Regions, compiled from the best sources. *Philadelphia: G. B. Zieber.* 1849. 16mo, pp. 70. C.

California and New York Steamship Company. ... . Prospectus. *San Francisco: Printed by Charles F. Robbins.* 1857. 8vo, pp. 8. H. 9965

California Characters and Mining Scenes and Sketches. ... *San Francisco: Bonestell & Williston.* [n. d.] 8vo, pp. 24. H.

Inside, "By Whittlestick."

California, dess klimat, och Guldminor, jemte räd för utvandrare. ... *Stockholm: E. Bonnier.* 1850. 12mo, pp. 205. Map and Plate. 9967

The California Farmer and Journal of Useful Sciences. ... By Warren & Company. Vol. V. No. 5. *Sacramento.* 1856. 4 l. H. 9968

Map of Sacramento on the cover. *See* Agriculture, *infra.*

California, from its Discovery by the Spaniards to the present time, with a brief description of the Gold Region, its present position, together with a few hints to Gold Hunters, and Guide to those about to visit that Country. By a Traveller [Charles E. Kells?]. *New York.* 1848. 8vo, pp. 32. 9969

California Gold Regions, with a full account of their Mineral Resources; how to get there, and what to take; the expenses; the time and the various routes. With Sketches of California; an account of the Life, Manners, and Customs of the Inhabitants, its history, climate, soil, productions, &c. ... *New-York: F. M. Pratt.* [1849.] 8vo, pp. 48. C. 9970

California Guide Book. *New York.* 1849. *See* Fremont (J. C.)

California Illustrated: Including a description of the Panama and Nicaragua Routes. By a Returned Californian. *New York: William Holdridge.* 1852. 8vo, pp. 224. 9971

California, its Characteristics. *See* [Bushnell (Horace)], Vol. III., No. 9542.

California: its Gold and its Inhabitants. By the Author of "Seven Years on the Slave-Coast of Africa." *London: Thomas Cautley Newby.* 1856. 2 vols., post 8vo, pp. iv, 303; 286.

California; Its Past History, its Present Position, and its Future Prospects. 1850. 8vo. Map. 9973

California; its Situation and Resources, from Authentic Documents; with a few Practical Hints to intending Emigrants. *London.* 1849. 8vo, pp. 32. 9974

California Medical Society. Proceedings of the Convention and of the Medical Society of the State of California, held in Sacramento, March, 1856. *Sacramento, Cal.: James Anthony & Co., Printers.* 1856. 8vo, pp. 36. H. 9975

California Pioneers. Constitution and By-Laws of the Society of California Pioneers, organized August, 1850. Constitution Revised July, 1853. *San Francisco: printed by C. Bartlett.* 1853. 16mo, pp. 12. H. 9976

Also: Seventeenth Anniversary of the corporate Society of California Pioneers. Oration: By William H. Clark, Esq. ... Poem: By Charles Warren Stoddard. *San Francisco.* 1867. 8vo. H.

California Scenery; a Series of [672] Stereoscopic Views of most of the points of Interest. *San Francisco: [Published by Lawrence and Houseworth.* 1866.] 4to. C. 9977

California Sketches, with Recollections of the Gold Mines. 12mo, pp. 57. 9978

California State Almanack and Annual Register for 1855. ... *Sacramento.* 1855. 8vo, pp. 48. BA. 9979

The California State Almanac and Hand-book of Statistics for 1863. Compiled By Henry G. Langley. *San Francisco: H. G. Langley.* 1863. 12mo, pp. 95. Continued. 9980

California Sketches, with recollections of the Gold Mines. *Albany.* 1850. 12mo. BM. 9981

California State Library. Catalogue of the California State Library, Prepared by W. C. Stratton, State Librarian. *Sacramento: Printed by O. M. Clayes, State Printer.* 1866. 8vo, pp. 460, 205. 9982

California State Prison. Report of the Directors of the California State Prison. December 1, 1867. *Sacramento: D. W. Gelwicks, State printer.* 1867. 8vo, pp. 98. H. 9983

California und seine Goldminen. Mittheilungen aus der Geographie und Geschichte dieses Landes und über seine Goldschätze. ... *Kreuznach: Voigtländer.* 1849. 8vo, pp. 32. 9984

The Californian Crusoe; or, The Lost Treasure Found: a Tale of Mormonism. *London: J. H. Parker.* 1854. Fcap, pp. 162. 9985

La Californie, journal des intérêts généraux de l'Océan Pacifique. *Paris: 25 mai, 9 sept.*, 1849. 6 nos., folio. 9986

For a list of 17 other journals relating to California published at this time, *see* Hatin's "Bibliog. de la presse périod française," pp. 507, 508.

Le Californien, journal de l'industrie et du commerce français dans l'Océan Pacifique. Rédactear en chef: Aug. Lacoste, ancien marin. *Paris: 5 août, 7 déc.*, 1849. 3 nos., folio. 9987

The edition said to be 40,000 copies.

La Californie. Récit d'un chercheur d'or. *Cambrai: imp. de Levêque.* [1851.] 8vo, ½ sheet. 9988

Californien, dessen Minen, Ackerbau, Handel und Gewerbe in ihrem gegenwärtigen Zustande, sowie dessen Aussichten für die Zukunft. Dargestellt von einem kürzlich von jener Regionen zurückgekehrten Deutschen Minenarbeiter. *New York.* 1831. 16mo, pp. 32. 9989

Californien. Mit besonderer Berücksichtigung des Gold- und Quecksilber-Distriktes. Mit Ergänzungen nach Duflot de Mofras und Fremont. *Wintherthur: Steiner.* 1849. 8vo, pp. 13. Map. 9990

An Account of California and the Wonderful Gold Regions; with a description of the different routes to California; information about the country, and the ancient and modern discoveries

of Gold; how to test precious metals; Accounts of Gold Hunters ... . Illustrated ... . *Boston: J. H. Hall.* [1849.] 8vo.

Adventures in California and its Gold Fields. *London: Dean & Sons.* 1851. 2 vols., crown 8vo. 9992

Agriculture. Official Report of the California State Agricultural Society's Third Annual Agricultural Fair, Cattle Show and Industrial Exhibition, Annual Meeting, &c., held at San Jose, October 7th, 8th, 9th and 10th, 1856. [*San Francisco.* 1856.] 8vo, pp. 80. Continued. BA. 9993

Also: Transactions of the California State Agricultural Society during the year 1858. Published by resolution of the Senate at the Tenth Session of the Legislature. *Sacramento.* 1859. 8vo, pp. 373. Continued. C., S. — Report of the Board of Agriculture to the California State Agricultural Society, at the Annual Meeting, January 26, 1865. ... *Sacramento: H. S. Crocker & Co., printers.* 1865. 8vo, pp. 24. H. — Transactions of the California State Agricultural Society during the Years 1864 and 1865. [Published together.] *Sacramento: O. M. Clayes, State Printer.* 1866. 8vo, pp. 413, (1), (2). Woodcuts. H.

Almanach californien pour 1851. Guide de l'émigrant, Manuel du Commerçant et de l'Actionnaire, documents complets pour tout le monde sur la Californie. *Paris: Martinon.* [1850.] 16mo, pp. 160. Woodcuts. 9994

Beretning om Californien og dets Guldrigdom. Med et Kart over Californien. *Christiania.* 1849. 16mo, pp. 125. 9995

COLLEGE OF CALIFORNIA. Oration, Poem, and Speeches, delivered at the General Alumni Meeting, held at the College of California, Oakland, Cal. Tuesday, May 31st, 1864. *San Francisco: H. H. Bancroft and Company.* 1864. 8vo, pp. 96.

Also: Oration and Poem, delivered at the Commencement of the College of California, Wednesday, June 7th, 1865. Together with the Annual Report of the Vice President of the College. *San Francisco: Printed by Towne and Bacon.* 1865. 8vo, pp. 30.

Colleccion de los principales trabajos ... para promovere el progreso de la cultura y civilizacion de los territorios de la alta y de la baja California. *Mexico.* 1827. S. 9997

Constitution of the State of California. *San Francisco.* 1849. 8vo, pp. 19. 9998

Description of Oregon and California, embracing an account of the Gold Regions; to which is added an appendix, ... with ... map ... *Philadelphia: Thomas Cowperthwait & Co.* 1849. 18mo, pp. 76. 9999

A Description of the Recently Discovered Petroleum Region in California, with a Report on the Same by Professor Silliman. *New York: Francis & Loutrel, Printers. December,* 1864. 8vo, pp. 23. H. + *New York: J. Ketcham, Printer. December,* 1864. 8vo, pp. 24. H. 10000

Education. First Biennial Report of the Superintendent of Public Instruction of the State of California for the School Years 1864 and 1865. [*Sacramento: O. M. Clayes, State Printer.* 1865.] 8vo, pp. 422, (1). Woodcuts. Continued. 10001

Also: Report of the Superintendent of Public Instruction of the State of California. April 10, 1851. *J. B. Devoe, State Printer.* 8vo, pp. 11. — An Act to establish a System of Common Schools, in the State of California; and other Acts providing for the Revenue of the same, with Explanatory Forms. By John G. Marvin, Superintendent of Public Instruction. *Sacramento.* 1852. 8vo, pp. (vi), 40. H. — First Annual Report of the Superintendent of Public Instruction to the Legislature of the State of California. 1852. *Eugene Cassely, State Printer.* 8vo, pp. 52. Continued. H. — The Law establishing and regulating Common Schools in the State of California, as amended during the Fourth Session of the Legislature, 1853. With Notes and Explanatory Forms. By John G. Marvin, Superintendent of Public Instruction. Second Edition. *San Francisco: George Kerr, State Printer.* 1853. 8vo, pp. (iv), 38. C., H. + *Sacramento: B. B. Redding, State Printer.* 1855. 8vo, pp. 44. H. — Movement for a University in California. A Statement to the Public, by the Trustees of the College of California, and an Appeal, by Dr. Bushnell. *San Francisco: printed at the office of the Pacific Publishing Co.* 1857. 8vo, pp. 23. H. — Proceedings of the California State Teachers' Institute and Educational Convention, in Session in the City of San Francisco, from Monday, May 27th, 1861, to Saturday, June 1st, 1861. *Sacramento: Charles T. Botts, State Printer.* 1861. 8vo. pp. 96. H. — Proceedings of the California State Teachers' Institute, in Session at the City of San Francisco, From Monday, May 4th, to Saturday, May 9th, 1863. *Published by the Department of Public Instruction. Sacramento: Benj. P. Avery, State Printer.* 1863. 8vo, pp. vi, (1), 166. H. — Decimotercio informe anual del superintendente de instruccion pública del estado, por el año de 1863 *Sacramento: O. M. Clayes, impresor del estado.* 1864. 8vo, pp. 221. H. — Report [to the Governor] relative to Establishing a State University ... . *Sacramento: O. M. Clayes, State Printer.* 1864. 8vo, pp. 29. H. (Signed J. D. Whitney, J. F. Houghton, John Swett.) — First Biennial Report of the Trustees of the State Reform School for the Years 1864–65. *Sacramento: O. M. Clayes, State Printer.* 1866. 8vo, pp. 15. H. — Revised School Law, approved March 24, 1866. ... *Sacramento: O. M. Clayes, State printer.* 8vo, pp. 63. H.

The Emigrant's Guide to California, describing its Geography, Agricultural and Commercial Resources; ... with ... Map, and an authentic Sketch of San Francisco; to which is appended, Colonel Mason's Official Dispatches concerning the Gold Districts. By a Traveller recently returned from California. *London.* 1849. 8vo, pp. 78. 10002

Facts for Emigrants to California: A Circular Issued to Workingmen, from The California Labor Exchange. *San Francisco: Fred'k MacCrellish & Co.*, ... 1869. 8vo, pp. 12. 10003

Geographical and Mineralogical Notes to accompany Wyld's Map of the Gold Regions of California. *London: J. Wyld.* 1849. 8vo, pp. 32. 10004

Gids naar California. Bevattende een verslag van de luchtstreek, den bodem en de natuurlijke voortbrengselen van Opper-California. *Amsterdam.* 1849. 8vo. Map. 10005

Geology. Reports on the Geology of the coast, mountains, and part of the Sierra Nevada, by J. B. Trask. 1853, 54. 2 vols., 8vo, pp. 381; 553. (Legislative Documents.) 10006

Geological Survey of California. J. D. Whitney, State Geologist. Geology. Volume I. Report of Progress and Synopsis of the Field-Work, from 1860 to 1864. *Caxton Press of Sherman & Co.: Philadelphia.* 1865. 4to, pp. xxvii, 498. Plates and Woodcuts. H. 10007

The following works are in continuation of this series:

Palæontology. Volume I. Carboniferous and Jurassic Fossils. By F. B. Meek. Triassic and Cretaceous Fossils. By W. M. Gabb. || Volume II. Cretaceous and Tertiary Fossils. By W. M. Gabb. *Caxton Press of Sherman & Co.: Philadelphia.* 1864–69. 4to, pp. xx, 243; xiv, 299. Plates. H. + Palæontology. Volume II. Section I. Part I. Tertiary Invertebrate Fossils. By W. M. Gabb. *Published by Authority of the Legislature of California. February,* 1866. 4to, pp. v, (1), 38. + Mining Statistics. No. 1. Tabular Statement of the Condition of the Auriferous Quartz Mines and Mills in that Part of Mariposa Tuolumne Counties lying between the Merced and Stanislaus Rivers, August–November, 1865. By A. Rémond. *Published by Authority of the Legislature of California. April,* 1866. 4to, pp. 16. H. + Geographical Catalogue of the Mollusca found West of the Rocky Mountains, between Latitudes 33° and 49° North. By J. G. Cooper, M.D. *San Francisco: Towne & Bacon, Printers.* 1867. 4to, pp. 40. H. 10008

An Address on the Propriety of Continuing the State Geological Survey of California delivered before the Legislature at Sacramento, Thursday Evening, January 30th, 1868: [several Reports appended] ... . By J. D. Whitney, State Geologist. *Towne and Bacon.* 1868. 8vo, pp. 23, 14, 15, 14. H. 10009

Also: An Address delivered before the Legislature of California, at Sacramento, Tuesday Evening, March 12th, 1861. By J. D. Whitney. State Geologist. To

which is appended a Copy of the Act authorizing the Survey. *San Francisco: Towne & Bacon ... Printers.* 1861. 8vo, pp. 50. H. — Annual Report of the State Geologist, for the Year 1863. *Sacramento: O. M. Clayes, State Printer.* 1864. 8vo, pp. 7. Continued. H. — Letter of the State Geologist relative to the Progress of the State Geological Survey. *San Francisco: Benj. P. Avery, State Printer.* 1862. 8vo, pp. 7. H. — Letter of the State Geologist relative to the Progress of the State Geological Survey during the Years 1866–7. *Sacramento: D. W. Gelwicks, State Printer.* 1867. 8vo, pp. 15. H. — Report of Committee on Joint Resolutions to Congress for a Geological and Mineralogical Survey of the Mineral Lands in this State. Introduced by Mr. Snyder, March 24, 1852. [n. p.] *Eugene Casserly, State Printer.* 8vo, pp. 14. H.

The Gold Regions of California: a Geographical, Topographical, and Historical View of that Country; with exclusive Authentic Particulars, and coloured Map of the Country. *London.* 1849. 8vo, pp. 88. 10010

Grand Council U. L. A. State of California. San Francisco. April 20th, 1865. Resolutions adopted at a Meeting of the Grand Council U. L. A., and transmitted to the Members of the Grand and Subordinate Councils of the Union League on the Death of Abraham Lincoln. S. H. Parker, Grand President. Alfred Barstow, Grand Secretary. p. 1, 2 l. H. 10011

The Great California Tree. Over 3000 years old. Ninety Feet in Circumference, now Exhibiting at No. 596 Broadway. *New York.* 1854. 8vo, Title and 2d Title, pp. 83. 10012

Guide to the Gold Region of California, with Map, and the latest Information; an Account of the Climate, Soil, and Natural Productions of Upper California; with Authentic Particulars respecting the Gold Region. *London.* 1850. 18mo, pp. 36.

Histoire naturelle et civile de la Californie. *See* [Venegas (M.)]

Journal of the Proceedings of an adjourned meeting of the Second Triennial Convention ... May 1855 ... *San Francisco.* 1855. 8vo, pp. 35. S. 10014

Kalifornien, das Goldland. Mit Berücksichtigung der Auswanderung dorthin. Nach den officiellen Berichten des nordamerikanischen Obersten Mason, und den Privatmittheilungen der HH. Sutter, Marshall, Brannan u. A. Von L. B. *Rorschach: Koch.* 1849. 16mo, pp. 30. 10015

Kalifornien, das Goldland Seine Lage, seine Grösse, sein Klima, sein jetziger Zustand. ... *Leipzig: Weber.* 1849. 4to, pp. 16. 10016

Kaliforniens Gold- und Quecksilber- District. Nach: The California Herald von Fr. Gerstäcker. *Leipzig: Jurany,* 1849. 8vo, pp. 31. Lith. Map. + Zweite Auflage. [*Ibid.*] 8vo. + Dritte Auflage. [*Ibid.*] 8vo. 10017

Last Night of the Session of the Assembly of the California Legislature ... with ... Anecdotes [and] copious Notes, descriptive of the events, persons, and peculiarities to which the different jeux d'esprit allude ... . By an Eye-Witness. *Sacramento: James Anthony & Co.* 1854. 8vo, pp. 42. H. 10018

Land. ... Session of 1856. Report of Select Committee in relation to U. S. Land Commissioners. [n. p. n. d.] *James Allen, State Printer.* 8vo, pp. 11. H. 10019

Also: Report of the Surveyor General of California from November 1st, 1865, to November 1st, 1867. *Sacramento: D. W. Gelwicks, State Printer.* 8vo, pp. 123.

Laws. Annual Report of the Attorney Geiger. [n. p.] *G. K. Fitch & Co., and V. E. Geiger & Co., State Printers.* [1853.] 8vo, pp. 7. H. 10020

Compiled Laws of the State of California; containing all the Acts of the Legislature of a public and general Nature, now in Force, passed at the Sessions of 1850, '51, '52, '53. ... By S. Garfielde and F. A. Snyder, Esqs. *Benicia.* 1853. 8vo, pp. 1071. S. 10021

The General Laws of the State of California, from 1850 to 1864 inclusive; being a Compilation of all Acts of a General Nature now in force, with full References, &c. By Theodore H. Hittell. *San Francisco: H. H. Bancroft & Co.* 2 vols., rl. 8vo, pp. 1186. 10022

The General Railroad Laws of California, the Pacific Railroad Act of Congress, and the By-Laws of the Central Pacific Railroad Company of California. *Sacramento: H. S. Crocker & Co.'s Print.* 1862. 8vo, pp. 104. BA. 10023

Journal of the Senate of the State of California at their First Session. December, 1849. *San José.* 1850. Continued.

Journal of the Proceedings of the House of Assembly of the State of California; at its First Session, December, 1849. *San José.* 1850. 8vo. Continued. 10025

Journals of the Third Session of the Legislature of the State of California. ... Published by Authority. *San Francisco: G. K.*

Fitch & Co., and V. E. Geiger & Co., State Printers. 1852. 8vo, pp. 794. Continued. B. 10026

Ley del fondo piadoso de Californias. *Mejico.* 1833. 8vo.

Report of the Attorney-General for the Years 1866 and 1867. *Sacramento: D. W. Gelwicks, State Printer.* 1867. 8vo, pp. 55. H. 10028

The Statutes of California, passed at the First Session of the Legislature, Dec., 1849. With an Appendix and Index. 4to, pp. 482. *San José.* 1850. 4to. Continued in 8vo. 10029

Also in the Spanish language. *See* Browne (J. R.), Vol. II., No. 8661.

Los Estatutos de California, aprobados a la Terceza Sesion de la Legislatura; comenzada en el Cuinto Dia de Enero 1852, y terminada en el Quarto Dia de Mayo 1852, a las Cuidades de Vallejo y Sacramento. *San Francisco.* 1852. 8vo. 10030

Life in California during a Residence of several Years in that Territory, comprising a Description of the Country and the Missionary Establishments, Incidents, Observations, etc., etc. Illustrated with numerous engravings. By an American. To which is annexed, An Historical Account of the Origin, Customs, and Traditions of the Indians of Alta-California. Translated from the Original Spanish Manuscript. *New York: Wiley and Putnam.* 1846. Post 8vo, pp. xiii, 341. 9 Illustrations.

Life on the Plains; or, Scenes and Adventures in an Overland Journey to California. *New York.* 12mo. Illustrated.

Military. Report of the Adjutant-General of the State of California from November 30th, 1865, to November 1st, 1867. *Sacramento: D. W. Gelwicks, State Printer.* 1867. 8vo, pp. 153. Continued. H. 10033

Report of the Adjutant General, for 1863. *Sacramento.* 1863. 8vo. Continued. 10034

Mysteries of California. Being an accurate Journal of one who has seen the Elephant. *Syracuse, N. Y.*, 1850. 8vo, pp. 52.

Northern California. *See* [Metlar (G. W.)]

Notes on California and the Placers: How to get there and what to do afterwards. By one who has been there. [James Delavan?] *New York: H. Long & Brother.* 1850. 8vo, pp. 128. 2 Plates. C., S. 10036

Noticias de la ... California. 1794. *See* S. (F. L.)

Report of the Committee of Commerce and Navigation, on the Governor's Message in relation to Peruvian Bark "Eliza." [n. p. n. d.] *George Kerr, State Printer.* 8vo, pp. 10. H. 10037

Resolutions and Memorial of the Miners of California, Adopted in State Convention, January 16th and 17th, 1866. *Sacramento: O M Clayes, State Printer.* 1866. 8vo, pp. 18. 10038

Resolutions of the Legislature of California on State Rights and the Rebellion. *House Reps. Misc. Document, No.* 66, *38th Congress*, 1864. 8vo. 10039

Revenue. Biennial Report of the Controller of State for the Seventeenth and Eighteenth Fiscal Years, 1865–6, 1866–7. *Sacramento: D. W. Gelwicks, State Printer.* 1867. 8vo, pp. 173.

Scenes of Wonder and Curiosity in California. Illustrated by 105 well executed Engravings ... *Published by J. M Hutchings & Co., San Francisco.* 1862. 8vo, pp. 267. 10041

A Sketch of the Route to California, and China and Japan, via the Isthmus of Panama. ... *San Francisco: A. Roman & Company.* 1867. 12mo, pp. 104, (4). B. 10042

Statistics. Annual Report of the State Registrar, for the Year 1859. [n. p. n. d.] *Charles T. Botts, State Printer.* 8vo, pp. 25.

The State Register and Year Book of Facts: for ... 1857. Published Annually. *San F an isco: Henry G. Langley and Samuel A. Mathews. Sacramento: James Queen.* 1857. 12mo, pp. viii, 384. H. 10044

The State Register and Year Book of Facts: for ... 1859. Published annually (Second Year of Publication.) *San Francisco: Henry G. Langley and Samuel A. Morison.* 1859. 12mo, pp. 420. BA., C. 10045

The Volcanic Diggings, a Tale of California Law. By a Member of the Bar. *New York.* 1851. 12mo. BM. 10046

CALIGNY (A. de). Essai sur les Colonies Françaises. Par. M. Antenor de Caligny, Lieut. de Vaisseau. *Paris.* 1839. 8vo, pp. 58. 10047

Title from Rich II. 332; not mentioned in the "Bibliographie de la France."

CALL (R. K.) Eulogium upon Gen. Andrew Jackson. Delivered in Tallahassee ... 19th July, by R. K. Call, by Request of the Legislature of Florida. *Tallahassee: Office of the Florida Sentinel.* 1845. 8vo, pp. 21. 10048

CALL. Union.—Slavery.—Secession. Letter from Governor R K. Call, Of Florida, to John S. Littell, Of Germantown, Pennsylvania. *Philadelphia: C Sherman & Son.* 1861. 8vo, pp. 30, (1). H. 10049

Also: An Address to the People of Florida. *Lake Jackson, Fla.*

Call from Death to Life. *See* [Stephenson (M.)]

Call to my Countrymen. *See* [Dodge (M. A.)]

CALLAN (J. F.) The Military Laws of the United States, relating to the Army, Volunteers, Militia, and to Bounty Lands and Pensions, from the Foundation of the Government to the Year 1858. *Baltimore.* 1858. + To 3d March, 1863. ... Prefixed ... a Synopsis of the Military Legislation of Congress during the Revolutionary War. By John F. Callan, Clerk to the Military Committee, United States Senate. *Philadelphia. George W. Childs.* 1863. 8vo, pp. 641. H. 10050

CALLAN. Navy and Marine Corps Laws of the United States, from the Formation of the Government to 1859; to which are prefixed the Constitution of the United States (with an index thereunto), and a Synopsis of the Legislation of Congress respecting Naval Affairs during the Revolutionary War. *New York: D. Van Nostrand.* 1859. 8vo. 10051

CALLAN (J. F.) *and* RUSSELL (A. W.) Laws of the United States relating to the Navy and Marine Corps; from the formation of the government to 1859. *Baltimore.* 1859. 8vo. 10052

CALLANDER (John). Terra Australis Cognita: or Voyages to the Terra Australis, or Southern Hemisphere, during the Sixteenth, Seventeenth and Eighteenth Centuries. Containing an Account of the Manners of the People, and the Productions of the Countries, hitherto found in the Southern Latitudes; the Advantages that may result from further Discoveries on this great Continent, and the Methods of Establishing Colonies there, to the Advantage of Great Britain. With a Preface by the Editor, in which some geographical, nautical, and commercial Questions are discussed. *Edinburgh: Hawes, Clark and Collins.* 1766–'68. 3 vols., 8vo, pp. 516; 3-692; 2 l., pp. 745. Map. C., H. 10053

"The dedication is signed 'John Callander,' who was probably the translator of the work, which was written originally in French, by the President de Brosses, and printed at Paris in 1756. Mr. Callander merely acknowledges that he had 'drawn many helps' from the *French* writer, whom he does not name, and appears inclined to take the principal merit of the work to himself, although the translation is almost literal, and the additions trifling."—RICH. The second and third volumes were published in 1768, and were reissued in 1788, with new title-pages, as a "A Collection of Voyages to the Southern Hemisphere," the *last leaf* of each volume only being reprinted. A list of the contents of these volumes is contained in the "Alphabetical Catalogue of the Library of Congress, 1864," pp. 203. *See* M. R., XXXVI. 284; XXXIX. 66.

CALLAVA (José). Manifiesto sobre las tropellas y bejaciones que cometió el Gobernardo Americano de Panzacola Andres Jackson, contra la persona y representacion del Comisario de la España Coronel Don José Callava nombrado para la entrega de la Florida occidental á los Estados-Unidos de America. Hecho y publicado por el Mismo Callava. *Habana.* 1821. 4to, pp. 70.

CALLAWAY. Charter, By-Laws, &c. of the Callaway Mining and Manufacturing Company. *New York: Van Nordan & King.* 1847. 8vo, pp. 24. Map. H. 10055

CALLICOTT (*Lady*). *See* Graham (Maria).

CALKIN (J. B.) The Geography and History of Nova Scotia. *Halifax.* 1859. 12mo. + Second Edition. 1864. 12mo, pp. 110. 10056

CALLE (Juan Diez de la). Memorial Informatorio | al | Rey Nvestro Señor, | en sv Real y Svpremo Conseio | de las Indias, Camara, y Ivnta | de Gverra. | En Manos del Señor Ivan Baptista | Saenz Nauarrete, Cauallero de la Orden de Alcantara, | de su Consejo, su Secretario en èl, y el de la | Camara, y Iunta. | Contiene | Lo qve sv Majestad Provee en | su Cõsejo, y Iunta, y por las dos Secretarias de la Nueua | España, y Pirù, Eclesiastico, Secular, Salarios, Estipen- | dios y Presidios, su Gente, y Costa, y de que Cajas, y | Hazienda Real se paga: valor de las Encomiendas | de Indios, y otras cosas curiosas, y ne- | cessarias. | Por | Ivan Diez de la Calle. | *Año de* M.DC.XXXXV. | 4to, 12 l., Memorial Informatorio, etc., 32 leaves. 10057

"Rich makes no mention of this volume, which was privately printed for the use of the King and Council. It must not be confounded with the book described in the following number. It is a book of the utmost importance to the historian of Spanish America, being a kind of private official handbook or directory of Mexico, Yucatan, Honduras, Guatemala, Nicaragua, etc. The author was Secretary to the Council of the Indies."

CALLE. Memorial, | y Noticias Sacras, | y Reales del Imperio | de | las Indias Occidentales, | al | mvy Catolico, Piadoso, y | Poder-

oso Señor Rey de las Españas, y Nueuo | Mundo, D. Felipe IV. N. S. | En sv real y svpremo Consejo de | las Indias, Camara, y Ivnta de Gverre: | En Manos | de Iuã Baptista Saenz Nauarrete, Cauallero de la Ordẽ Mi- | litar de Alcantara, de su Consejo, y su Secretario en el, y en | el de la Camara, y Iunta: Confirmador de los priuile- | gios Reales de Castilla. | Comprehende | lo Ecclesiastico, Secular, Politico, y Militar que por su Secretaria | de la Nueua-España se prouee: Presidios, gente, y costas, valor de las | Encomiendas de Indios, y otras cosas, curiosas, neces- | rias, y dignas de saberse. | Escriuiale por el año de 1646. Iuan Diez de la Calle, Oficial | Segundo de la missma Secretaria. | 4to, 12 l., Text, 183 l., Erratas, 1 l., Memorial, pp. 8, Noticias, 5 leaves. J.C.B. 10058

An exceedingly rare volume; the supplemental leaves, "Memorial Breve," pp. 1–8, and "Noticias Importantes," 5 leaves, were subsequently printed, and are frequently wanting. In Stevens' "Nuggets," No. 437, a copy is described, with some variations. The author remarks, in folio 180, that only a few copies had been printed for the use of the King, his Council, and Ministers. It is probably a later issue of the preceding, with additions, alterations, and corrections. Two of the preliminary leaves have been cancelled and reprinted with alterations, viz.: the last leaf of the Epistle Dedicatory and the first leaf of the Indice. Two preliminary leaves are added, making in this impression 14, viz.: "Prosegue el Indice deste Memorial" and "Notas," 2 pages; and Erratas, 1 page, reverse blank; folios 10, 11, 22, 23, 33, and 35 of the text are reprinted, with considerable additions and some omissions. The errata after folio 183 are cancelled, and placed here on the 14th preliminary leaf, reprinted with corrections. Sold, at Puttick's, in 1860, for £5 10s.

CALLE. Memorial, y resvmen breve de Noticias de las Indias Occidentales, la Nveva-España, y el Perv. Al excelentissimo señor Don Gaspar de Bracamonte y Gvzman, conde de Peñaranda ... Presidente del Real y Svpremo (Consejo) de las Indias ... Comprehende las Erecciones de las Audiencias, y Chancillerias Reales, y de los Arçobispados, y Obispados, con lo Eclesiastico, y Secular, que por la Camara, y Junta de Guerra dellas seprouee, Presidios, gente, y costa, valor de las Encomiendas de Indios, armas de las Ciudades, y Iglesias; y otras cosas necessarias, y dignas de saberse para la verdad, y autoridad de la historia. *En Madrid, Por Alonso Victor Pantoja, Año de* 1654. Folio, 52 l. 10059

Concerning this, *see* Leclerc, No. 253, where it is said to be of extreme rarity, and almost unknown. "Alcedo mentions, in the prologue of his manuscript bibliography, a 'Biblioteca Americana,' composed by Juan Diez de la Calle; a few sheets only were printed about the year 1646."—HARRISSE.

CALLEJO (B. M. del). Alegato en favor del presbit. M. Guzman acusado criminalmente por algunos indigenas del mismo pueblo. *Puebla.* 1830. 4to, pp. 25. 10060

CALLENDAR (G.) Nautical Remarks and Observations for the Chart of the Harbour of Boston. Composed from different Surveys, but principally from that taken in 1769, by G. Callendar. *London.* 1775. 4to, pp. 11. 10061

[CALLENDER (James Thomson).] The American Annual Register, or, Historical Memoirs of the United States, for the Year 1796. *Philadelphia: Bioren & Madan. January 19th*, 1797. 8vo, pp. vii, 288. BA. 10062

CALLENDER. The Conduct of Meriwether Jones, in a Series of Letters addressed to the Public, By James T. Callender. *Richmond: Printed by H. Pace.* 1802. 18mo, pp. 120. 10063

[CALLENDER.] The History of the United States for 1796; including a Variety of Intesesting Particulars Relative to the Federal Government previous to that Period. *Philadelphia: Press of Snowden & M'Corkle.* 1797. 8vo, pp. viii, 312. C., H.

Originally published in numbers. Chapters VI. and VII. contain the charges against Alexander Hamilton, which occasioned his celebrated defence, at the expense of his private character. *See* [Hamilton's] Observations, etc.

CALLENDER. Letters to Alexander Hamilton, King of the Feds. Ci-Devant Secretary of the Treasury of the United States of America, Inspector-General of the Standing Armies thereof, Counselor-at-Law, &c., &c., &c. Being intended as a reply to a Scandalous Pamphlet lately published under the sanction, as it is presumed, of Mr. Hamilton, and signed with the signature of Junius Philænus. By Tom Callender, Esq., Citizen of the World. *New York: Printed by Richard Reynolds.* 1802. 8vo, pp. 64. BA. + *New York: Hamilton Club.* 1866. 8vo, 2 l., pp. 89. BA. 10065

This reprint forms No. IV. of the Hamilton Club Series. 40 copies printed in octavo, and 20 in quarto.

[CALLENDER.] The Political Progress of Britain: or, An Impartial History of Abuses in the Government of the British Empire, in Europe, Asia, and America. From the Revolution, in 1688 to the Present Time: the whole tending to prove the Ruinous Consequences of the Popular System of Taxation, War, and Conquest. [Motto.] Part First. Second Edition. *Philadelphia: Wrigley and Berriman.* 1794. 8vo, pp. 80. + Third Edition. *Philadelphia: Richard Folwell.* 1795. 8vo, pp. 120. H. ‖ Part Second. *Philadelphia: Richard Folwell.* 1795. 8vo,

pp. 96. C., H. + [Both parts.] *London: Daniel Isaac Eaton.* 1795. 8vo, pp. 156. H. 10066

Postcript to the third edition signed, James Thomson Callender. *See* M. R., Second Series, XIX. 80.

CALLENDER. The Political Register; or, Proceedings in the Session of Congress, commencing November 3^{d}, 1794, and ending March 3^{d}, 1795. With An Appendix, containing a Selection of Papers laid before Congress during that Period. By James Thomson Callender. Vol. I. *Philadelphia: printed by Thomas Dobson.* M.DCC.XCV. 8vo, pp. viii, 245. BA. 10067

All published. *See* M. R., XXI. 341.

[CALLENDER.] The Prospect before us. ... *Richmond, Virginia: the Author, and M. Jones, S. Pleasants Jun. and J. Lyon.* 1800–M,DCCC,I. 2 vols., 8vo (Vol. II. in 2 pts.), pp. 184; 152, 96. BA., C. 10068

Sold by the author in the jail at Richmond.

CALLENDER. Sedgwick & Co. or A Key to the Six Per Cent Cabinet. By James Thomson Callender. *Philadelphia: the Author.* 1798. 8vo, Title, pp. 88. C., H. 10069

CALLENDER. Sketches of the History of America. By James Thomson Callender. ... *Philadelphia: Press of Snowden & M'-Corkle.* 1798. 8vo, pp. 263. C., H. 10070

CALLENDER. Short History of the Nature and Consequences of Excise Laws. *Philadelphia.* 1795. 8vo. C. 10071

CALLENDER. ... Trial of James Thompson Callender for Sedition ... the 3d day of June, 1800, ... at Richmond ... Virginia. [n. p. n. d.] 8vo, pp. 75, (1). BA. 10072

There was, apparently, no title-page; the caption given above occurs on p. 2, preceded by, "Copy taken from the Virginia Gazette ... 18th July 1800, till the 19th August, 1800 ... corrected by David Robertson ... ."

CALLENDER (John.) The | Advantages of Early Religion. | A | Sermon, | Preached at Newport, | On Rhode Island, | To a Society of Young Men, | On the Lord's Day Evening, | Jan. 3d, 1741–2. | *Newport: Printed by the Widow Franklin, under the Town School-House.* [1742.] 12mo, pp. 37. 10073

CALLENDER. A | Discourse | Occasioned by the | Death | Of the Reverend | Mr. Nathaniel Clap, | Pastor of a Church | At | Newport on Rhode-Island, | On October 30. 1745. | in the 78th Year of his Age. | By John Callender, A.M. | *Newport: Printed by the Widow Franklin,* | *at the Town-School-House*, 1746. | Sm. 8vo, pp. 36. BA. 10074

CALLENDER. An | Historical Discourse | on the | Civil and Religious Affairs | of the Colony of | Rhode-Island | and | Providence Plantations | in New-England | in America. | From the first Settlement 1638, to the End of | first Century. | By John Callender, A.M. | *Boston: | Printed and Sold by S. Kneeland and T. Green | in Queen Street.* MDCCXXXIX. | 8vo, pp. 14, 120, (1). BA., H.

CALLENDER. An Historical Discourse on the Civil and Religious Affairs of the Colony of Rhode-Island. By John Callender, A.M. With a Memoir of the Author; Biographical Notices of some of his Distinguished Contemporaries; and Annotations and Original Documents, illustrative of the History of Rhode-Island and Providence Plantations, from the First Settlement to the End of the First Century. By Romeo Elton ... . *Providence: Knowles, Vose & Company.* 1838. 8vo, pp. 270, (2). H.

Forms the fourth volume of the collections of the Rhode Island Historical Society. This was also issued as a third edition, with the title: "The Early History of Rhode Island. *Boston: Thomas Wells & Co.* 1843." 8vo, pp. 270. Facsimile. *See* N. A. R., XLVII. 253.

CALLENDER. A Sermon preach'd at the Ordination of Mr. Jeremiah Condy, To the pastoral Care of the Baptist Church in Boston, Feb. 14th. 1738, 9. by John Callender. *Boston: Printed by S. Kneeland and T. Green.* MDCCXXXIX. 8vo, pp. (4), 32.

CALLENDER (John), *Esq.* An Oration pronounced July 4, 1797 at ... Boston ... . By John Callender. ... *Boston: Benjamin Edes.* 1797. 8vo, pp. 19. BA., H. 10078

CALLENDER (Tom). *See* Callender (James Thomson).

CALLICOT (T. C.) Speech of Hon. Theophilus Callicot of Kings, against the Personal Liberty Bill. In Assembly, March 14, 1860. *Albany: Comstock & Cassidy, Printers.* 1860. 8vo, pp. 13. H. 10079

Calm Address. 1814. *See* [Carey (M.)]

The Calumet. *New York.* 1860. 8vo, pp. 32. 10080

The Calumet. New Series oft he Harbinger of Peace. *New York.* [1831–'36.] 8vo. [Bi-monthly.] 10081

Calumny Refuted; or a Glance at John Wilbur's Book [against J. J. Gurney, entitled "A Narrative and Exposition"]. ... [By Abigail Barker and others.] *London: printed by John Hasler.* MDCCCXLV. 8vo, 2 l., pp. 108. H. 10082

CALVERT (George). Case of Charles Lord Baltemore, a Minor, with Relation to his Government of Maryland, granted by King Charles I., to Cecil Lord Baltemore, in 1632, which was settled on the Marriage of Lady Charlotte Lee with Benedict Leonard Lord Baltemore. 1689. Single sheet. 10083

See "Indenture of Agreement," Vol. I., 1851.

CALVERT (G. Henry). Arnold and André. An Historical Drama. By George H. Calvert. *Boston: Little, Brown & Co.* 16mo, pp. 95. + New Edition. *Boston.* 1864. 2 vols., 12mo.

CALVERT. Oration, on the Occasion of celebrating the Fortieth Anniversary of the Battle of Lake Erie; delivered on the tenth of September, 1853, in Newport, R. I. By George H. Calvert. *Cambridge: Metcalf & Company.* 1853. 8vo, pp. 40. + Second Edition. *Providence: B. T. Albro, Printer.* 1854. 8vo, pp. 32. H. 10085

CALVET (P. du). *See* Du Calvet (Peter).

CALVETO (Urbanus). *See* Benzoni (H.)

CALVO (Alonso). Carta de Alonso Calvo, de la Compañia de Jesus, en que da noticia á todos los Superiores de las Casas, y Colegios de esta Provincia de Nueva-España de la vida exemplàr, gloriosos trabajos, y dichosa muerte del P. Joseph Maria de Guevara, Professo de la misma Compañia. *Mexico.* 1725. 4to, pp. 42. + *Megico: Hogal.* 1727. 4to. 10086

CALVO (Charles). Annales Historiques de la révolution de l'Amérique latine, accompagnées de documents à l'appui, de l'année 1808 jusqu'à la reconnaissance par les etats européens de l'indépendence de ce vaste continent. *Paris: A. Durand.* 1864–1865. 5 vols., 8vo. 10087

CALVO. Derecho internacional teorico y practico de Europa y America. Por Carlos Calvo ... . *Paris: Amyot; Durand et Pedone Lauriel.* 1869. 2 vols., 8vo, pp. xvi, 525; xvi, 573.

CALVO. Recueil complet des traités, conventions, capitulations, armistices, et autres acts diplomatiques de tous les états de l'Amérique Latin, Compris entre le golfe du Mexique et le cap de Horn, depuis l'année 1493, jusqu'à nos jouis, précédé d'un mémoire sur l'état actuel de l'Amérique, de tableaux statistiques, d'un dictionnaire diplomatique, avec une notice historique sur chaque traité important. Par M. Charles Calvo ... . *Paris: A. Durand.* 1862–69. 11 vols., 8vo. 10089

Also with Spanish titles. Vols. VII.–XI. have the titles:

CALVO. Amérique latine. Recueil historique complet des traités, conventions, capitulations, armistices, questions de limites, et autres actes diplomatiques et politiques de tous les états Compris entre le golfe du Mexique et le cap de Horn, depuis l'année 1493, jusqu'à nos jours. Première période. Limites. Tome septième neuvième. || Limites. Répertoire de manuscrits et de cartes rares et inédites, relatifs aux limites, etc. Tome dixième-onzième *Paris: Durand.* 1865–66. 8vo. 10090

This is followed by:

CALVO. Recueil historique [as before]. Seconde période. Depuis la révolution . . [And with a second title-page:] Annales historiques de la révolution de l'Amerique latine, accompagnées de documents à l'appui. De l'année 1808, jusqu'à la reconnaissance par les états européens de l'indépendence de ce vaste continent. *Paris: Durand.* 1864–67. 5 vols., 8vo. 10091

There is to be a third series, covering "l'époque qui s'est écoulée depuis l'indépendance."

CALVO (C.) Una pagina de derecho internacional, o la America del Sur ante la ciencia del derecho de gentes moderno. Por Carlos Calvo. *Paris: Durand.* 1869. 8vo, pp. xii, 307.

CALVO DE LA TORRE (J. del C.) Commentaria in Legum Indicarum Recopilationem. [*Madrid?*] 1736. 4 vols., folio, pp. 418; 579, (46); 325, (15); 61, (3). H. 10093

"Without titles or preliminaries. From 2 royal orders inserted at pages 46 and 47, of Vol. IV., we learn that the work was composed by D. Juan del Corral Calvo de la Torre, Oidor in the Audiencia of Santiago de Chile; and that in 1732 he was ordered to send the work to Spain to be printed. In 1735 the first and second volumes had been examined and highly approved by the Council of the Indies, and the author was requested to send the 3d and 4th, and to finish the 5th and 6th, which would complete the work, but it appears that death prevented his completing the 4th volume, which only reaches to the 12th title of the 5th book — the index to this volume being headed thus: 'Rerum quæ in hac parte Quarti tomi, (morte auctoris ita relicti) continentur,' &c. Apparently the work was left in this state, and never published. The indexes to each volume are also imperfect. This copy was found in sheets among the papers of D Bernardo Yriarte." — RICH.

CALYO. Description of Calyo's Panorama of the Connecticut River, ... *New York: printed by H. Ludwig & Co.* 1850. 8vo, pp. 30. Woodcut. H. 10094

CALZADO (Bernardo Maria de). El Triunfo de la Moral Christiana: ó los Americanos: tragedia Francessa. *Madrid.* 1788. Sm. 4to. C. 10095

CAMAC (T.) Facts and Arguments respecting the great Utility of an extensive Plan of Inland Navigation in America. By Turner Camac. *Philadelphia.* 1805. 8vo, pp. 61. P.

CAMACHO (R.) Contestacion á las Reflexiones de J. M. Alvirez sobre los decretos episcopales que prohiben el juramento constitucional. Por R Camacho y Jose G. Romero. *Morelia.* 1857. 2 pts., 8vo, pp. 23, 30. 10097

CAMACHO (Sebastian). America libre. Oda. *Mexico.* 1821. 12mo, pp. 12. 10098

CAMACHO. Breve Manifestacion. *Jalapa.* 1832. 4to, pp. 92. 10099

CAMARA (Manoel Arruda da). Discurso sobra a utilidade da instituição de Jardins nas principaes provincias do Brazil. *Rio de Janiero: Na. Imp. Reg* 1840. 8vo. 10100

CAMAGO. Dissertaçao sobra as plantas da Brasil, que podem dar linhos propria para muitas usos da sociedade e supprir a falto de cambana. *Rio de Janeiro.* 1840. 8vo. 10101

CAMARGO (J.) Noticia de la vida religiosa, virtudes y dichosa muerte del P. Joaquim Camargo, de la Compañia de Jesus, Prefecto de la Congregacion del Salvador de Megico. *Mégico.* 1727. 4to. 10102

CAMBEFORT (J. P. A.) Mémoire justificatif de Joseph-Paul-Augustin Cambefort, colonel du régiment du Cap; commun à Anne Louis Tousart, lieutenant-colonel; à tous les officiers, sous officiers et soldats du même régiment, déportés de Saint-Domingue, par ordre des Commissaires civils, délégués par le pouvoir éxécutif aux isles françoises de l'Amérique-sous-le-Vent. *Paris: Des imprimeries des frères Chaignieau.* 1793. 8vo, pp. 58, 120. 10103

CAMBEFORT. Précis de la justification de Joseph-Paul-Augustin Cambefort ... et des autres militaires déporté de Saint-Domingue, rigoureusement démontrée par les seules pièces justificatives déposées au comité colonial de la Convention nationale. [26 janvier 1793. *Paris:*] *imp. de N. H.-Nyon.* 1793. 8vo.

CAMBESSÈDES (Jacques). Cruciferarum, Elatinearum, Caryophyllearum Paranychiearumque Brasiliae Meridionalis Synopsis. *Paris: impr. de Belin.* 1827. 8vo, pp. 8. 10105

CAMBESSÈDES. Portulacearum, Crassulacearum, Ficoidearum Cunonicearumque Brasiliæ Meridionalis Synopsis. *Paris: impr. de Belin.* 1830. 8vo, pp. 4. 10106

See also St. Hilaire (A. de).

CAMBIAGI (F.) La Repubblica Argentina, e il comercio Italo-Platense, per il cav. Cambiagi Francesco console della Repubblica Argentina. *Prato: tip. Giacchetti e Comp.* 1869. 4to, pp. 31.

CAMBRAY (*Dr.*) Réminiscences et Confessions d'un ancien chirurgien de corsaires. Voyage aux Antilles, au continent américain, et croisière dans le golfe du Mexique, pendant les années 1800, 1801 et 1802 et le commencement de 1803. *Cambria: imprimerie Simon.* 1856. 8vo, pp. 304. 10108

[CAMBRELENG (Churchill C.)] An Examination of the new Tariff proposed by the Hon. Henry Baldwin, a Member of Congress. By One of the People. *New-York: Gould and Banks.* 1821. 8vo, Folded Table, Title, pp. 268. BA., C. 10109

"A well-reasoned, conclusive tract." — MCCULLOCH's "Lit. Pol. Econ.," p. 59.

[CAMBRELENG.] Report of the Committee of the House of Representatives of the 8th of Februrary, 1830, on Commerce and Navigation. *New York.* 1830. 8vo. 10110

"A forcible exposition of the mischievous influence of the restrictive system." — MCCULLOCH.

CAMBRELENG. Merchants' Second Edition of Mr. Cambreleng's Report on Commerce and Navigation ... . [Read in the House, Feb. 8.] *New-York. March*, 1830. 8vo, pp. 63.

For a review, *see* [Kennedy (J. P.)]

CAMBRELENG. Report of Mr. Cambreleng on the State of the Treasury and Expenditures of Government. Jan. 24, 1839. [*Washington.* 1839.] 8vo. 10112

CAMBRELENG. Speech of Mr. Cambreleng, of New York, on the Question of Restoring the Deposites to the Bank of the United States. Delivered in the House of Representatives, On the 14th January, 1834. *Washington: printed by Jonathan Elliot.* 1834. 8vo, pp. 24. + *New York.* 1835. 8vo, pp. 16.

Also: Speech ... (In reply to M. McDuffie and Mr. Storrs,) on the Proposition to amend the Constitution ... respecting the Election of President and Vice-President. Delivered in the House ... March 7, 1826. [n. p. n. d.] 16mo, pp. 15. H.

CAMBRELENG. Speech, ... on increasing the Duty on Wool, and the Manufactures thereof. *Washington.* 1827. 8vo. 10114

Also: ... Statement, made by Mr. Cambreleng op [*sic*] the Duties, ad Valorem ... on Woolens ... under the Amendment proposed ... by Mr. Mallary to the Bill No. 132 ... *Washington.* 1828. 8vo, pp. 7. (20th Cong. 1st Sess. House Doc. 143.) *See* [Carey (M.)]

Cambria Iron Company. A Statement of some of the Advantages of the Vicinity of Johnstown, Pa., in the Manufacture of Iron. [Dated New York, 12th Oct., 1852. n. p. n. d.] 8vo, pp. 12. Map. H. 10115

[CAMBRIDGE (John).] A Description of Prince Edward Island. 1805. 8vo. Map. 10116

The Cambridge Almanac and Business Directory for the Year 1847. By George Adams. *Boston: James French.* 16mo, pp. 65. 10117

The Cambridge Directory. Containing a General Directory of Citizens and a Business Directory. Together with An Almanac and City Record for 1848. By J. Ford. *Cambridge (Mass.): ... Chronicle Office.* 1848. 16mo, pp. 112, (20). Continued. B. 10118

Cambridge Ephemeris. An Almanack for the Year 1683. *Cambridge, Mass.* 1685. 16mo. 10119

The Cambridge Platform ... and The Confession of Faith, adopted in 1680. To which is prefixed A Platform of Ecclesiastical Government, by Nathanael Emmons, D.D. *Boston: Congregational Board of Publication.* 1855. 12mo, 2 l., pp. 128. H.

For early editions, *see* Platform.

Address at the Consecration of the Cambridge Cemetery, Nov. 1st, 1854. By John A. Albro, D.D., with Preliminary Remarks by the Mayor, &c. *Cambridge.* 1854. 8vo.

Bulletin of the Museum of Comparative Zoölogy, Cambridge, Massachusetts, U. S. A. *Published April 28th*, 1863. No. 1, pp. 1–16. 10122

City of Cambridge. The Municipal Register, for the Year 1849–50. *Cambridge: Metcalf and Company.* 1852. 16mo, pp. 109. Continued. H. + For the Year 1855. *Cambridge: John Ford, Chronicle Press.* [n. d.] 8vo, pp. 112. 10123

Bridges. Report of a Committee of the Town of Cambridge, relating to the West Boston and Canal Bridges. ... *Cambridgeport: L. Cox, Jr. & Co.* 1843. 8vo, pp. 7. H. 10124

Churches. An Account of the Controversy in the First Parish in Cambridge, 1827–1829. ... *Boston: T. R. Marvin, printer.* 1829. 12mo, pp. 58. BA., H. 10125

Also: Controversy betwen the First Parish in Cambridge and the Rev. Dr. Holmes, their Late Pastor. Published by the Parish Committee. *Cambridge: printed by E. W. Metcalf and Company.* 1829. 8vo, pp. viii, 103. BA., H. — Report on the Connection at Various Times existing between the First Parish in Cambridge and Harvard College. Accepted May 20, 1850. *Cambridge: Metcalf and Company.* 1851. 8vo, pp. 52. H. — Report of the Committee of the First Parish in Cambridge, for the Year 1849–50. [*Cambridge.* 1850.] 8vo, pp. 18. Continued. H. — Some Passages in the History of the First Church, Cambridge, Mass. *Cambridge.* 1842. 12mo.

A Brief History of the First Baptist Church, in Cambridge; with ... List of Members. *Cambridge: printed at the Chronicle Office.* 1860. 12mo, pp. 77. H. 10126

Christ Church, Cambridge. One Hundredth Anniversary Tuesday, Oct. 15th, 1861. *Geo. C. Rand & Avery, Printers, Boston.* + [Another.] *Cambridge.* MDCCCLXI. H. 10127

Commemoration of the Twenty-Fifth Anniversary of the Settlement of John A Albro, D.D., as Pastor of the First Church and Shepard Society, Cambridge, Mass. *Cambridge: printed by Allen and Farnham.* 1860. 8vo, pp. 76. 10128

Circular. [On the subject of repairs on "the Episcopal Church at Cambridge." *Boston.* 1824.] 8vo, pp. 5, (1). H.

Constitution of the Church Union Auxiliary of Christ Church, Cambridge. *Cambridge, Mass.* MDCCCLXIV. 8vo, pp. 16. H.

The Confession of Faith, and the Covenant, of the Evangelical Congregational Church in Cambridge-port. *Boston: T. R. Marvin, printer.* 1828. 12mo, pp. 8. H. 10131

Also: Manual of the First Evangelical Congregational Church in Cambridge-port, ... *Boston: press of T. R. Marvin.* 1857. 12mo, pp. 26. H.

The Confession of Faith of the Second Evangelical Congregational Church in Cambridgeport. [n. p.] 1843. 12mo, pp. 12. 10132

The Declaration of Faith and Covenant of the Second Baptist Church, Cambridge, 1840. *Boston: Press of Jonathan Howe.* 1840. 12mo, pp. 24. H. 10133

Proceedings of a General Assembly at Cambridge, May 30, 1770. [n. p. n. d.] 8vo, pp. 83. 10134

Education. Annual Report of the School Committee of Cambridge, March 15, 1841. *Cambridge Press: Metcalf, Torry, and Ballou.* 1841. 8vo, pp. 15. Continued. H. 10135

Also: An Address to the People of Cambridge from the School Committee, concerning a Recent Case of Corporal Punishment in the Allston Grammar School. *Cambridge: Press of John Wilson and Son.* 1866. 8vo, pp. 24. H. — Report of a Committee, appointed August 4, 1834, to Consider the Subject of a Reorganization of the Public Schools in the Town of Cambridge. *Cambridge Press: Metcalf, Torry, and Ballou.* 8vo, pp. 12. H. — Catalogue of the East Cambridge Female School, instituted at Cambridge, Massachusetts, August, 1837. *Boston: Marden & Co., Printers.* 1839. 16mo, pp. 7. H.

A Classed Catalogue of the Library of the Cambridge High School; with an Alphabetical Index. [Compiled by Ezra Abbot, Jr.] ... *Cambridge: John Bartlett.* 1853. 8vo, pp. xvi, 239. C., H. 10136

Fourth Party in the Field! The Ladies of Cambridge To their Sisters of the Fourth District: ... *Cambridge.* 1850. 1 l., 4to. H. 10137

Funeral Services at Christ Church, Cambridge, 12, M., April 19, 1865. Abraham Lincoln, President of the United States of America, died April 15, 1865. [*Cambridge.* 1865.] 8vo, 2 l.

Government. An Act to establish the City of Cambridge, approved March 17, 1846. [n. p. n. d.] 8vo, pp. 20. H.

Also: ... An Act In addition to an Act to establish the City of Cambridge. [1851.] 8vo, pp. 4. H. — ... An Act in Addition to ... [1853.] 8vo, pp. 7. H.

An Act of the Legislature establishing a Fire Department in Cambridge; Rules and Regulations for the Government of the Department; and a City Ordinance for the Prevention of Fires. *Cambridge: Metcalf and Company.* 1846. 12mo, pp. 21. H.

Address of the Mayor upon the First Organization of the City Government, May 4, 1846. *Cambridge.* 1846. 8vo, pp. 16.

The Mayor's Address at the Organization of the City Government, and Reports of the Committee of Finance and the School Committee. *Cambridge: John Ford, Printer.* 1848. 8vo, pp. 89. + Also for the Year '49. 10142

Annual Report of Receipts and Expenditures. *Cambridge.* 1845. 8vo. 10143

The Charter and Ordinances of the City of Cambridge; with the Municipal Register for 1857. *Cambridge.* 1857. 8vo.

Also: Extracts from the Act authorizing the Town of Cambridge to establish a Board of Health; with the Rules and Regulations of said Board. [*Cambridge.* 1832.]

1 large sheet, printed on one side. H. — An Ordinance prescribing the Duties of City Marshal: also Rules and Regulations for the Government of the Police and Night Watch. *Cambridge: printed by John Ford.* 1853. 12mo, pp. 12. H. — ... . Report relating to the Enclosure of Cambridge Common. [n. p. 1832.] 8vo, pp. 11. H. — Opinion of the Supreme Judicial Court on the Petition of Jeduthan Wellington and Others, in Relation to Cambridge Common. *Boston: Dutton and Wentworth.* 1835. 8vo, pp. 24. H. — Report of the Committee appointed by the Town of Cambridge, to investigate the Affairs of its Almshouse. *Boston: J. E. Hinckley & Co., printers.* 1833. 8vo, pp. 43. H. — Report of the Survey of the Roads in Cambridge. Printed by Vote of the Selectmen. *Cambridge Press: Metcalf, Torry, & Ballou.* 1838. 8vo, pp. 16. H. — Report of the Committee adopted to Consider the Expediency of Consolidating certain Boards of Officers of the Town of Cambridge. *Boston: Jones' power press office.* 1846. 8vo, pp. 8. H. — Rules and Orders of the City Council, and a List of the Officers of the City of Cambridge, for 1846. *Cambridge: printed by Andrew Reid.* 1846. 12mo, pp. 23. H. + The same, with Ordinances of the City of Cambridge. pp. 66. H. — Rules and Orders for the Management of the House of Correction at Cambridge, and the Government of Persons therein. *Freeman Press, Concord, Mass.* [1842.] 8vo, pp. 4. H.

Mount Auburn. Guide through Mount Auburn Cemetery, in Cambridge, Mass. *Boston.* 12mo. Plates. 10145

A Hand-Book for Passengers over the Cambridge Railroad, with a Description of Mount Auburn Cemetery. ... *Boston: William V. Spencer.* 1858. 24mo, pp. 70. Map and Woodcuts. + Guide through Mount Auburn. A Hand-Book for Passengers over the Cambridge Railroad. ... Third Edition. *Boston: Bricher & Russell.* 1859. 24mo, pp. 70. Map and Woodcuts.

Libraries, Lyceums, etc. Catalogue of the Cambridge Circulating Library. September [and] December. [*Cambridge:*] *John Bartlett.* 1858. 12mo, pp. 24, 7. 10147

Also: Constitution and By-Laws of the Cambridgeport Lyceum. Instituted, Dec. 13, 1831. *Boston: printed by Perkins & Marvin.* 1833. pp. 12. — Constitution and By-Laws of the East Cambridge Lyceum, As Revised and Adopted, November, 1837. *Boston: Cassady and March, printers.* 32mo, pp. 8. H. — By-Laws of the Lechmere-Point Library Association. Instituted May 22, 1822. *Cambridge: printed by Hilliard and Metcalf.* 1822. 32mo, pp. 8. H. — Platform and Regulations of the Printers' Literary Union of Cambridge, Mass. (Organized March 29, 1833.) With the Names of the Foundation Members, and Officers for 1853–54. *Cambridge.* M.DCCC.LIII. 8vo, pp. 14, (2). H.

Politics. An Appeal to the Whigs of Cambridge [Mass.] who are in favor of the existing "License Law." [Dated November 10th, 1838. n. p. n. d.] 4to, p. 1. H. 10148

Constitution and By-Laws of the Whig Republican Association of Cambridge. Instituted March 4, 1840. *Cambridge Press: Metcalf, Torry, and Ballou.* M DCCC XL. 16mo, pp. 8.

Also: Constitution of the Cambridge Free Soil Club, formed September, 1848. [n. p. n. d.] 2 l. H.

List of Votes in Cambridge, Nov. 1836. [n. p. n. d.] Continued. H. 10150

List of Persons in the City of Cambridge, against whom a Poll Tax has been assessed. *May* 1, 1868. 4to, pp. 84. H.

Societies. By-Laws of the Savings Institution in the town of Cambridge. *Cambridge: Metcalf and Company.* 1853. 32mo, pp. 16. H. 10152

Also: An Account of the Cambridge Humane Society. [n. p. 1819.] 8vo, pp. 7. H. ("The Society was formed in 1814" ... "It is gratifying ... after an experiment of five years" ... [From the "Account," which will determine the date of publishing.]) — Laws and Members of the Cambridge Humane Society, to which is prefixed an Account of its Origin. *Cambridge Press: Metcalf, Torry, and Ballou.* 1841. 16mo, pp. 14. H. + *Cambridge: Metcalf and Company.* 1853. 16mo, pp. 14. + *Cambridge: John Ford, Chronicle Press.* 1858. 16mo, pp. 16. H. — Report of the Agent to the Trustees of the Cambridge Humane Society. [*Cambridge.* 1854.] 8vo, pp. 12. H.

Regulations of the Friendly Fire Society, instituted at Cambridge, March 17, 1797, as amended to the Present Time, January 29, 1827. *Cambridge: printed by Hilliard, Metcalf, and Co.* 1827. 24mo, pp. 11. + Amended to the Present Time, January 28, 1833. *Cambridge: printed by Charles Folsom.* 1833. 12mo, pp. 11. H. 10153

Also: Report of the Trustees of the Subscription Fund for the Benefit of Cambridge Volunteers. *Cambridge: Press of John Ford.* 1863. 8vo, pp. 10, (4). H. — Report of a Committee of the East Cambridge Union Temperance Society, ... submitted at a Public Meeting, Sunday Evening, January 8, 1843. [*Cambridge?* 1843.] 12mo, pp. 12. H. — [Appeal] To all those Citizens of Cambridge who deal in Intoxicating Liquors. [n. p. n. d.] 8vo, pp. 4. H.

Stolen! From many Citizens in Cambridge, on the 4th instant, the Rest and Quiet of the Holy Sabbath Day. [*Cambridge.* 1862.] 8vo, pp. 4. H. 10154

"Union Railway Company *versus* God's Law."

University in Cambridge. *See* Harvard College.

Water. Cambridge Water Works. Report of the Directors of the Cambridge Water Works to the Stockholders of the Company, February, 1857. ... *Cambridge: John Ford.* 1857. 8vo, pp. 30. H. 10155

Also: The Connection of the City of Cambridge with the Cambridge Water Works, as Shown by the City Records. *Cambridge.* 1857. 8vo, pp. 28. H. — Report of the Board of Engineers concerning Reservoirs. July 1, 1843. *Cambridgeport: Cox, Brown, & Co.* 1843. 8vo, pp. 8. H. Petition of the Directors of the Cambridge Water Works. 8vo, pp. 12, (1). ("Printed for the City Council, by order of the Board of Aldermen, August 23, 1853.")

Cambridge Essays, contributed by Members of the University. 1855. *London: John W. Parker and Son.* [n. d.] 8vo, 4 l., pp. 308. 10156

Contains "The English Language in America. By Charles Astor Bristed, B.A.," pp. 57–78.

CAMDEN (*Lord*). *See* Bernard, VOL. II., No. 4948.

CAMDEN (William). Annales Rervm Anglicarvm, et Hibernicarvm, regnante Elizabetha, ad Annvm Salvtis M. D. LXXXIX. Gvilielmo Camdeno Avthore. || Tomvs Alter Annalivm ... . || *Londini: Impensis Simonis Watersoni.* M. DC. XV.–1627. 2 vols., folio, Portrait, 4 l., pp. 499, 9 l.; 2 l., pp. 286, 5 l. BA. + *Lugduni Batavorum.* 1625. 2 vols., 8vo. BD. + [*Id.*] *Elzev.* 1628. 8vo. + [*Ibid.*] 1639. BD. + *Amst.: Elzev.* 1677. 8vo. + E Codice ... Propria Auctoris Manu correcto [et] ... locupletata ... edidit, cum Præfatione et Notis Tho. Hearnius. [n. p.] 1717. 3 vols., 8vo. BD. 10157

CAMDEN. Annales ... . Translated ... by A. Darcie. *London.* 1625. 4to. + Annales, or, The Historie of ... Elizabeth ... . Translated into English by R. N. Gent. Together with divers Additions of the Authors ... . The third Edition. *London: Benjamin Fisher.* MDCXXXV. Folio, Portrait and Engraved Title, 18 l., pp. 586, (18). BA. + The History of ... Elizabeth ... . The Third Edition, revised ... . *London: Charles Harper, and John Amery.* 1675. Folio. + Tomus alter et idem. [A translation of second volume, by Thomas Browne.] *London.* 1629. 4to. BD. + 1688. Folio. 10158

The first edition of the version by R. R. was: "*London.* 1630." Folio. BD. These Annales relate in part to the first settlement of the American Colonies.

CAMDEN. Annales des choses ... sous le regne d'Elizabeth, ivsques à l'an ... M.D.LXXXIX. Traduit par Paul de Bellegent ... . *London: Field.* 1624. 4to. BM. + [Another translation, to 1603.] *Paris.* 1627. 4to. 10159

CAMDEN, *N. J.* Act of Incorportion of the City of Camden, and the Supplement thereto; together with the Ordinances of City Councils; also Historical Reminiscences of Camden. *Camden, N. J.* 1857. 8vo, pp. 182, xxv. 10160

Chew's Camden City Directory for 1867. *Camden, N. J.: Sinnickson Chew.* 1867. 8vo, pp. 114. 10161

Also: Documents Respecting the Bridge from Camden to the Island. *Philadelphia.* 1821. 8vo. P.

Camden and Amboy Railroad. Accounts and Papers relating to the late ... accident at Burlington, N. J. ... and the correspondence between B. F. Stockton and C. Van Rensselaer, D.D. *Philadelphia.* 1855. 8vo. 10162

Also: Camden and Amboy Railroad, and Delaware and Raritan Canal Companies: Address to the People of New-Jersey. *Trenton.* 1846. 8vo. — Report of the Executive Committee to the Camden and Amboy Railroad on the Accident of 29th August, 1855. *Trenton.* 1855. 8vo. P. *See* Carey (H. C.)

CAMERON (*Major* A.) Proceedings of a General Court Martial on Major Allen Cameron, held in Kingston Barracks, in the Island of Jamaica. *Privately printed.* 1802. 8vo. 10163

[CAMERON (Allan).] The Cultivation of Flax, and preparation of Flax Cotton by the Chevalier Claussen Process. ... [Signed Allan Cameron.] *New-York: printed by John A. Gray.* 1852. H. 10164

Cameron's proposed ... Steamers between Panama and Australia. J. Whitman, Sec. 8vo, pp. 30. 10165

[CAMERON (Hugh).] The Troublesome Trio. [*Washington.* 1867.] 12mo, pp. 11. H. 10166

A defence of Pres. Johnson, in verse.

CAMERON (J. H.) Address of John Hillyard Cameron on his Installation as Chancellor of the University of Trinity College. *Toronto.* 1864. 8vo, pp. 8. 10167

CAMERON (M.) Reminiscences of a Voyage to British Columbia; a lecture delivered before the Young Men's Mutual Improvement Association. By Malcolm Cameron. *Quebec.* 1865. 8vo, pp. 23. 10168

Also: Speech on the International Railway. *Quebec.* 1862. 8vo.

CAMERON (S.) Address of the People's Club of Philadelphia, in favor of General Simon Cameron for the next Presidency of the U. S. *Philadelphia.* 1859. 8vo, pp. 31. 10169

Also: Speech ... on the Reduction of the Tariff of 1842: delivered in the Senate of the United States, July 22, 1846. *Washington: printed by Ritchie & Heiss.* 1846. 8vo, pp. 23. H. — Speeches of Messrs. Cameron and Seward on the Tariff delivered in the Senate of the U. S., June 15, 1860. [n. p. n. d.] 8vo, pp. 8.

CAMERS (J.) *See* Solinus (C. J.)

CAMILLA. ... [*Philadelphia.*] 1778. 4to, pp. 1. P. 10170

Advertisement for sailors for H. B. M. S. Camilla; Philad'a. 24 copies, printed by J. Humphreys; Feb. 1778.

CAMILLUS, *pseudon.* An Enquiry into the Evils of general suffrage and frequent elections in Lower Canada. By Camillus. *Montreal.* 1810. 8vo, pp. 32. S. 10171

CAMILLUS, *pseudon.* The Mississippi Question fairly stated, and the Views and Arguments of those who clamor for War, examined. In Seven Letters. By Camillus. *Philadelphia: printea by William Duane.* 1803. 8vo, pp. 48. BA. 10172

CAMILLUS, *pseudon.* *See* [Hamilton (Alex.)]

CAMM (J.) A Single and Distinct View of the Act, Vulgarly entitled, Three-Penny Act; Containing an Account of its beneficial and wholesome effect in York-Hampton Parish. In which is exhibited A Specimen of Col. Landon Carter's Justice and Charity; as well as of Col. Richard Bland's Salus Populi. By the Reverend John Camm, Rector of York-Hampton. [Mottoes.] *Annapolis: Printed by Jonas Green, for the Author.* 1763. 4to, pp. 55. 10173

There is another tract by this author on the same subject, the title of which I have mislaid. I believe it is entitled "The Colonels Dismounted," in answer to Colonels Bland and Carter, who had roughiy handled Dr. Camm. *See* Wirt's "Life of Patrick Henry."

CAMMANN *and* CAMP. The Charities of New York, Brooklyn and Staten Island. By Henry J. Cammann and Hugh N. Camp. *New York: Hurd and Houghton.* 1868. 8vo, pp. xi, 596, (1). Woodcuts. BA., C. 10174

CAMP (D. N.) The American Year-Book and National Register for 1869. Astronomical, Historical, Political, Financial, Commercial, Agricultural, Educational, and Religious. ... Edited by David N. Camp. Vol. 1. *Hartford: O. D. Case & Company.* 1869. 8vo, pp. 824. BA., C. 10175

CAMP (G. S.) Democracy. By George Sidney Camp. *New-York: Harper & Bros.* 1845. 18mo, pp. 249. C. 10176

CAMP (P.) Poems of the Mohawk Valley. *Utica.* 1859. 18mo. 10177

The Camp and the Field. By one of our Chaplains. *Boston: American Unitarian Association.* 1861. 18mo, pp. 18. 10178

Camp Charlotte. A Tale of 1774. By a Member of the Bar. *Philadelphia.* 1844. 8vo, pp. 39. S. 10179

The Camp Fire Companion: A Choice Collection of Songs

for the Soldier. *Philadelphia: King & Baird.* 1861. 18mo, pp. 72. 10180

The Camp-Fire Songster; a Collection of Popular, Patriotic, National, Pathetic, and Jolly Songs, Suited for the Camp or March. Containing a Number of Songs never before Printed. *New York: Dick & Fitzgerald.* [n. d.] 18mo, pp. 70. B. 10181

The Camp Jester; or, Amusement for the Mess. *Augusta, Ga.: Blackmar & Bro.* 1864. Sm. 12mo, pp. 71. 10182

Camp McDonald, the School of Instruction of the Fourth Brigade of Georgia Volunteers. Organized June 11th, 1861. J. McPherson & Co., Atlanta, Georgia, Agents. *Atlanta, Georgia: Wood, Hanleiter, Rice & Co.* [1861.] 8vo, pp. 29, (3). 10183

Camp Songs; a Collection of National, Patriotic, and Social Songs, for the Volunteers. *Boston: Oliver Ditson & Co.* [n. d.] 16mo, pp. 64. H. 10184

Camp Ward Journal. No. 4. *Kingston. August* 23, 1855.

Contains sketch of Geo. W. Pratt.

Compagne de circumnavigation de la frégate l'Artémise, pendant les années 1837, 1838, 1839 et 1840 sous le commandement de M. Laplace. ... *Paris: Arthus-Bertrand.* 1841, '42, '44. 3 vols., 8vo. Maps and Engravings. 10186

Four volumes were announced, but the fourth, apparently, never was published.

Campaign Document. No. 1. The Democratic Platform. General McClellan's Letter of Acceptance. 8vo, 4 leaves. + No. 2. Speech of Judge Geo. F. Comstock. Delivered at the Brooklyn Academy of Music. 8vo, pp. 12, and others. 10187

A Campaign in New Mexico with Col. Doniphan. With a Map of the Route and a Table of Distances traversed. *Philadelphia: Cary & Hart.* 1847. 12mo, pp. 184. 10188

The Campaign in Mexico. *See* [Scribner (B. F.)]

Campaign in Northern Mexico in 1846–47, by an Officer of the Ohio Volunteers. *New York.* 1853. Map. 10189

The Campaign of 1860. Comprising the Speeches of Abraham Lincoln, William H. Seward, Henry Wilson, Benjamin F.

Wade, Carl Schurz, Charles Sumner, William M. Evarts, &c. *Albany: Weed, Parsons & Company.* 1860. 8vo. 10190

A series of 18 tracts, originally issued under the name of "Evening Journal Tracts. — No. 1," etc. Each tract is paged separately.

Campaign Songs. [1864.] 8vo, pp. 12. 10191

A Campaign Tract for 1864. [n. p. n. d.] pp. 16. 10192

Containing "Extract from A. H. Stephens' Speech in Georgia, Jan., 1861," etc.

Campaigns and Cruises, in Venezuela and New Grenada, and in the Pacific Ocean; From 1817 to 1830: with the Narrative of a March from the River Orinoco to San Buenaventura on the Coast of Chocò; and Sketches of the West Coast of South America from the Gulf of California to the Archipelago of Chilöe. Also, Tales of Venezuela, Illustrative of Revolutionary ... Incidents. ... *London.* 1831. 3 vols., 12mo, pp. xiii, 471; Title, 332; Title, 349. BA. 10193

The Campaigns of the British Army. *See* [Gleig (G. R.)]

Campagnes et croîsades dans les états de Venezuela et de la nouvelle Grénada. *Paris.* 1837. Map. 10194

Campaña contra los Americanos del Norte. Primera parte. Relacion histórica de los 40 dias que mandó en gefe el ejercito dél Norte el General D. Marino Arista. *Mexico.* 1846. 4to, pp. 37, 6 l. Plan. 10195

Campaña del Interior. Documentos relativos a las operaciones contra los sublevados de San Luis en Enero y Febrero de 1857. *Mexico.* 1857. Folio, pp. 20. Plan. 10196

CAMPANELLA (Th.) De Monarchia Hispanica Discursus. [Cum Appendice.] *Amst.: Elzev.* 1640. 8vo. BD. + [*Id.:*] *Jansen.* 1640. 12mo. + *Harderovici.* 1640. 12mo. BM. + *Lugd. Bat.: ap Elzev.* 1641. 16mo. BM. + [*Ibid.*] 1643. + [*Ibid.*] 1646. + Editio nouissima, aucta & emendata ... . *Amsterodami: Apud Ludovicum Elzeuirium.* 1653. Sm. 16mo, 4 l., pp. 376. H. + *Francofurti: V. Schrey.* 1686. 12mo. + [*Ibid.*] 1709. 12mo. 10197

The last two chapters treat of the other hemisphere, and of the New World and navigation.

CAMPANELLA. Discourse touching the Spanish Monarchie. Translated. *London.* 1654. 4to. BD. 10198

Campanella recommends castles and block-houses to be built at the mouths of all rivers and harbors in the New World, "lest the English should break in, and bring in heresy."

CAMPANELLA. Thomas Campanella, an Italian Friar, his Advice to the King of Spain for attaining the Universal Monarchy of the World: translated ... by Ed. Chilmead, with an Admonitorie Preface, by Wm. Prynne ... . *London.* 1659. 4to. BM. 10199

Contains a curious account of the Spanish king's dominions in America, and the treasure he draws from them, etc.

CAMPANELLA. Discursus von der Spanischen Monarchia. *Getruckt im Jahr.* 1623. 4to. 10200

CAMPANELLA. Unhang der Spanischen Monarchi Campanellæ. [n. p.] 1623. 4to. 10201

CAMPANIUS (Th.) Kort Beskrifning | Om | Provincien | Nya Swerige | uti | America, | Som nu förtjden af the Engelske Kallas | Pensylvania. | Aflärde och trowärdige Mäns skriften och berättelser ihopaletad och sammanskrefwen, samt med äthskillige Figurer | utzirad af | Thomas Campanius Holm. | *Stockholm Tryckt uti Kongl. Boktr. hvs Sal. Wantijfs | Antiamed egen bekostnad, af J. H. Werner Ahr* MDCCII. | 4to, Engraved and Printed Title, 9 l., pp. 190, Errata, 1 l, 6 Maps, and Plates. 10202

"The author was never in America. His work is made up from verbal accounts received from his father, and notes left by his grandfather, to which he has added facts obtained from the manuscripts of Peter Lindström, an engineer." — DUPONCEAU. The engraved title reads: "Novæ Sueciæ, seu Pennsylvania in America descriptio." "A very scarce work relating to the establishment of the Swedes in New Sweden, afterwards Pennsylvania." — RICH. ; *See* the "Biog. des Contemporarius" for a notice of this work.

CAMPANIUS. Description | of the | Province of New Sweden. | Now called, by the English, | Pennsylvania, in America. | Compiled | from the Relations and Writings of Persons worthy of credit, | and adorned with Maps and Plates. | By Thomas Campanius Holm. | Translated from the Swedish, | for the Historical Society of Pennsylvania. | With Notes. | By Peter S. Du Ponceau, LL.D. | ... | ... | ... | *Philadelphia:* | *McCarty & Davis.* 1834. | 8vo, pp. vi, v-166. 5 Maps, and Plates. B., C. 10203

Also forms pages 1–168 of the "Hist. Soc. of Pennsylvania," Vol. III., Part I. For "An Extract of a Translation of the History of New Sweed Land in America ...," *see* "New York Hist. Col.," Vol. II. The book is often improperly catalogued under the name of Holm.

CAMPANO (L.) Viajes a las cinco partes del mundo, relaciones, esploraciones y descubrimientos, estractados de las mejores obras de los célebres viajeros y ordenados por Lorenzo Campano. *Paris: Rosa et Bouret.* 18mo, pp. xi, 362. 10204

CAMPBELL (Alex.) The Sequel to Bulkley and Cummins' Voyage to the South Seas; or, Adventures of the Crew of the Wager wrecked on a desolate Island on the South Seas. By A. Campbell. *London.* 1747. 8vo. 10205

Called in soon after it was published, and suppressed, so that few copies are at present to be seen.

CAMPBELL (Alexander), *D.D.* The Sacred Writings of the Apostles and Evangelists. Translated. *Bethany, Va.* 1835. 8vo. 10206

Also: The Millennial Harbinger for 1830. *Bethany.* 1830. 8vo. Continued. — Address on the Amelioration of the Social State. *Louisville.* 1839. 8vo, pp. 31. — Delusions. An Analysis of the Book of Mormon; with Prefatory Remarks by Joshua V. Himes. *Boston.* 1832. 8vo, pp. 16. Campbell was the founder of the sect of Christians known as the "Disciples," and a man of much learning and eloquence.

CAMPBELL (A.) The True American System of Finance, a Lecture delivered before the Mercantile Association of Chicago, Oct. 1st, 1862. By Alexander Campbell. [n. p. n. d.] 8vo, pp. 16. 10207

Mr. Bartlett quotes an edition, 8vo, pp. 8.

CAMPBELL. A Glance at Illinois, her Lands, and their comparative values, her Coal Fields, Railroads and general resources, and advantages. *La Salle, Ill.: Boynton & Co.* 1856. 10208

CAMPBELL (A.) Report on a Direct Route for the Eastern Termination of the Erie Canal ... . By Allan Campbell ... . *Albany.* 1836. 8vo, pp. 36. B. 10209

CAMPBELL (A.) A Voyage round the World, from 1806 to 1812; in which Japan, Kamschatka, the Aleutian Islands, and the Sandwich Islands, were visited. Including a Narrative of the Author's Shipwreck on the Island of Sannack, and his Subsequent Wreck in the Ship's Long Boat. With an Account of the Present State of the Sandwich Islands, and a Vocabulary of their Language. By Archibald Campbell. ... *Edinburgh: Archibald Constable and Company* [etc.] 1816. BA., C. + *New York.* 1817. 12mo. P. + Second American Edition. *New York: Roderick & Ritter.* 1819. 12mo. Map. B. + Fourth American Edition. *Roxbury.* 1825. 12mo. 10210

Campbell was an unfortunate seaman, who, in one of his shipwrecks, had both his feet frozen, which rendered amputation necessary. On his return to England, a charitable Mr. Smith drew up this account from his relations, and had it published for his benefit.

CAMPBELL. Reise um die Welt, 1806–1812. Aus dem Englischen. *Jena.* 1817. 8vo. 10211

Campbell. Reize rondom de wereld, in 1806–1812. *Amsterdam: J. C. van Kesteren.* 1818. 8vo. 10212

Campbell (C.) Genealogy of the Spotswood Family in Scotland and Virginia. By Charles Campbell. *Albany: Joel Munsell.* 1868. 8vo, pp. 44. BA. 10213

Campbell. History of the Colony and Ancient Dominion of Virginia. By Charles Campbell. *Philadelphia: J. B. Lippincott and Co.* 1860. 8vo, Title, pp. xi–765. C., H. 10214

Campbell. Introduction to the History of the Colony and Ancient Dominion of Virginia. By Charles Campbell. ... *Richmond: B. B. Minor.* MDCCCXLVII. Rl. 8vo, pp. 200, (Corrigenda and Index), 4 l. BA., C., H. 10215

Campbell. Some Materials to serve for a Brief Memoir of John Daly Burk, Author of a History of Virginia. With a Sketch of the Life and Character of his Only Child, Judge John Junius Burk. Edited by Charles Campbell. *Albany, N. Y.: Joel Munsell.* 1868. 8vo, pp. 123. BA. 10216

Campbell. *See* "The Bland Papers," Vol. II., No. 5867, and Lewis (A.)

Campbell (G.) The Nature, Extent, and Importance of the Duty of Allegiance: A Sermon, preached at Aberdeen, December 12, 1776, being the Fast Day ... on account of The Rebellion in America. The Second Edition, with Notes ... . By George Campbell, D.D. ... *Aberdeen.* MDCCLXXVIII. 8vo, pp. 74. B. 10217

The M. R., LVI. 315, quotes an edition: "*London: Cadell.* 1777." He considers the Americans a proud, fierce, jealous, stubborn, untractable, suspicious, litigious, chicaning race of pettifoggers.

[Campbell (G. L.)] A Relation or Journal of a late Expedition to the Gates of St. Augustine on Florida under the conduct of Gen. Oglethorpe. *London.* 1744. 8vo. 10218

See British Museum Catalogue.

Campbell (G. W.) Letter of G. W. Campbell to the chairman of the Committee on the Invasion of Washington. January 2, 1815. 8vo. (Cong. Doc.) 10219

Campbell (H. J.) Speech of the Hon. Hugh J. Campbell ... in the Senate of Louisiana ... February 5, 1869, upon the Civil Rights Bill ... . [n. p. n. d.] 8vo, pp. 7. H. 10220

Campbell (J.) An Oration in Commemoration of the Independence of the United States of North-America, Delivered July 4, 1787; At the Reformed Calvinist Church in Philadelphia. By James Campbell, Esquire. To which is proposed, an Introductory Prayer, delivered on the Same Occasion, By the Hon. William Rogers, A.M. Published at the Request of the Pennsylvania Society of the Cincinnati. *Philadelphia: Prichard and Hall.* MDCCLXXXVII. 8vo, pp. 24. P. 10221

Campbell (J.) A British Army, as it was,—is,—and Ought to be; Illustrated by Examples during the Peninsular War; with observations upon India, the United States of America, Canada, the Boundary Line ... By Lieut. Colonel James Campbell. *London.* 1810. 8vo, pp. 337. 10222

Campbell. Speech of Hon. James Campbell, of Philadelphia, Delivered at Scranton, Pennsylvania, on Thursday, September 17, 1863. [n. p. n. d.] 8vo, pp. 8. 10223

Campbell. A Protective Tariff. Necessary Rights of Labor. Speech of Hon. James H. Campbell, of Pennsylvania, delivered in the House of Representatives, April 24, 1860. [n. p. n. d.] 8vo, pp. 8. 10224

Campbell. Tariff, or Rates of Duties ... after the First Day of January, 1838, until December 31st, 1839. ... By James Campbell ... . *New-York: Mahlon Day.* [n. d.] 8vo, pp. 186, (1). H. 10225

Campbell (J.), *died* 1701, *aged* 70. After Souls by Death are separated from their Bodies, they come to Judgment. Asserted in a Sermon Deliver'd At Worcester, November 24th, 1737. Being The Day of the Execution of John Hamilton, alias Hugh Henderson. (With his Confession and Dying Warning.) By John Campbell, M.A. And Pastor of the Church in Oxford, N. E. ... *Boston: S. Kneeland & T. Green.* 1738. 8vo, 2 l., pp. 36. B. 10226

[Campbell (John), *2d Duke of Argyle.*] The Conduct Of His Grace The D-ke of Ar--le, For the Four last Years, review'd. Together with His Grace's Speech, April 15th, 1740. Upon the State of the Nation. *London: Mr. Webb.* 1740. 8vo, pp. 63. B. 10227

Relates in part to Spanish interference with the American trade.

[Campbell.] Speech upon the State of the Nation, April 15, 1740. *Boston.* 1740. 8vo, pp. 19. 10228

[Campbell.] The Second Edition of The Speech of The D-ke of A---le, upon the State of the Nation; April 15. 1740. [Colophon:] *Boston: T. Fleet.* 1740. 8vo, pp. 19. B. 10229

Relates chiefly to Admiral Vernon's capture of Portobello, and to affairs in the West Indies.

[Campbell (John), *LL.D.*] *See* An Account of the Spanish Settlements in America, 1762, Vol. I., No. 102.

Campbell. Biographia Nautica: or, Memoirs of ... illustrious [British] Seamen ... By Dr. J. Campbell and J. Kent, Esq. ... *Dublin.* 1785. 6 vols., 8vo. 10230

[Campbell.] Candid and Impartial Considerations on the Nature of the Sugar Trade; the Comparative Importance of the British and French Islands in the West-Indies: With the Value and Consequence of St. Lucia and Granada, truly stated. illustrated with Copper Plates. *London: R. Baldwin.* MDCCLXIII. 8vo, 2 l., pp. 226. 3 Plates. 10231

See McCulloch's "Lit. Pol. Ec.," 89; R. I. 139. "Upon the whole, we think it a masterly performance."—*Monthly Review.* Watt has a title, "A Description and History of the New Sugar Islands in the West Indies. *London.*" 8vo, by which, probably, the work above is intended.

[Cambell.] A Compleat History of Spanish America: containing a distinct account of the discovery, settlement, trade, and present condition of New Mexico, Florida, New Galicia, Guatimula, Cuba, Hispaniola, Terra Firma, Quito, Lima, La Plata, Chili, Buenos Ayres, &c. With a particular detail of the commerce with Old Spain by the galeons, flota, &c. As also of the contraband trade with the English, Dutch, French, Danes, and Portuguese. Together with an appendix, in which is comprehended an exact description of Paraguay. Collected chiefly from Spanish writers. *London.* 1742. 8vo. C. 10232

The "Concise history" of 1741, No. 10235, with a new title. Two more new titles for the same book were printed in 1747.

Campbell. Histori van het Spansche Ryk in Amerika, etc. *Amsterdam.* 1745–6. Maps and Plates. 10233

Campbell. Beknopte Historie en tegenwoordigen staat van het Spaansche ryk in Amerika. *Amsterdam: B. Mourik.* 1750. 8vo. Plates. 10234

[Campbell.] A Concise History of the Spanish America; containing a succinct Relation of the Discovery and Settlement of its several Colonies: A circumstantial Detail of their respec-

tive Situation, Extent, Commodities, Trade, &c. And a full and clear Account of the Commerce with Old Spain by the Galleons, Flota, &c. As also of the Contraband Trade with the English, Dutch, French, Danes, and Portugueze. Together with an Appendix, in which is comprehended an exact Description of Paraguay. Collected chiefly from Spanish writers. *London: John Stagg.* MDCCXLI. 8vo, pp. viii, 2 l., pp. 336. C., H.

Republished, with new titles, in 1742 and 1747. Also on large paper.

Campbell. Lives of the Admirals and other eminent British seamen, including an accurate Naval History, from the earliest accounts, with passages relating to Discoveries, Plantations, and Commerce. *London.* 1750. 4 vols., 8vo. + *London.* 1779. 4 vols., 8vo. 10236

The first edition was, "*London,* 1742–44." 4 vols., 8vo.

Campbell. Lives of the British Admirals, from the Earliest Periods; with a Continuation down to the Year 1779. Written under the inspection of Dr. Berkenhout. *London.* 1785. 4 vols., 8vo. Maps and Engravings. + Continued by Dr. Berkenhout and H. Yorke. *London.* 1808. 8 vols., rl. 8vo. Portraits. + Continued to the Year 1779, by Dr. Berkenhout. A New Edition, revised, corrected, and brought down to the Present Time, by Henry Readhead Yorke ... . Vol. I.–VI. *London: J. C. Barrington.* 1812–14. || the Historical Part further continued to ... 1780, by ... Yorke ... with The Lives of the most Eminent Naval Commanders, from the Time of Dr. Campbell to the above Period, by William Stevenson, Esq. ... Vol. VII.–VIII. *London: J. Harris.* 1817. 8 vols., 8vo. Portraits. H. + The same. Abridged. *London.* 1841. 12mo. + *London.* 1848. + 5th Edition. *London: Griffin & Co.* 186–. 12mo, pp. 380.

See M. R., LXXXVIII. 318.

Campbell. Leben und Thaten der Admirale und anderer berühmten Britanischen See-Leute. Aus dem Englischen übersetzt. *Göttingen: Luzac.* 1755. 2 pts., 4to, 154 sheets.

Campbell. A Political Survey of Britain: being a Series of Reflections on the Situation, Lands, Inhabitants, Revenues, Colonies, and Commerce of this Island: intended to shew That we have not as yet approached near the Summit of Improvement, but that it will afford Employment to many Generations before they push to their utmost Extent the natural Advantages of Great Britain. By John Campbell, LL.D. *London: the*

Author [etc.] M DCC LXXIV. 2 vols., 4to, 2 l., pp. vi, 726, (24); 2 l., pp. 739, (31). BA., C. + Second Edition. *Dublin.* 1775. 4 vols., 8vo. C. 10239

"The British Colonies and Settlements in America," II. 634–694. A very useful work, displaying wonderful research and labor, though held in little estimation. The index is sometimes wanting. *See* M. R., LI. 14, 110.

[Campbell.] The Spanish Empire in America. Containing, A succinct Relation of the Discovery and Settlement of its several Colonies; a View of their respective Situations, Extent, Commodities, Trade, &c. And A full and clear Account of the Commerce with Old Spain by the Galleons, Flota, &c. Also of the Contraband Trade with the English, Dutch, French, Danes, and Portuguese. With an exact Description of Paraguay. By an English Merchant. *London: M. Cooper.* 1747. 8vo, 6 l., pp. 330. C. 10240

The same work as Nos. 10232 and 10235, with a new title.

[Campbell.] Das spanische Reich in Amerika, oder kurze Beschreibung aller spanischen Pflanzstädte und Besitzungen. *Sorau.* 1763. 4to. 10241

Cambell. A Treatise on the Trade of Great Britain to America. *London.* 1772. 4to. 10242

Campbell. Voyages and Travels, containing all the Circumnavigators, from the Time of Columbus to Lord Anson ... Historical Details of the several Attempts made for the Discovery of the North-east and North-west Passages ... the Russian Discoveries by Land and by Sea; a Distinct Account of the Spanish, Portuguese, British, French, Dutch, and Danish Settlements in America ... . *London.* 1744. 2 vols., folio. 10243

A tract, entitled, "The Regulations lately made Concerning Colonies, and the Taxes imposed upon them Considered. *London.* 1765," 8vo, has been ascribed to Dr. John Campbell. *See* Bancroft, IV. 157.

Campbell (J.) The Complete Soldier's Pocket Companion ... By John Campbell, Late Adjutant in the British 73d. Regiment of Foot. *Philadelphia: Printed by Thomas Dobson* ... M,DCC,XCVIII. 8vo, pp. 52, 9 folded sheets. P. 10244

Campbell (J.), *Esq.* A Letter to Sir Robert Peel, Bart. on ... British Colonial Slavery, by John Campbell, Esq. F.R.S.E. *Edinburgh: William Oliphant, Waugh and Innes, and J. Wardlaw.* MDCCCXXX. 8vo, Title, pp. 64. 10245

Campbell (J.), *D.D.* Memoirs of David Nasmith; his La-

bours and Travels in Great Britain, France, the United States, and Canada. By John Campbell, D.D. *London.* 1844. Post 8vo, pp. 496. Portrait. 10246

Campbell (J.), *Editor.* Services at the Centenary Celebration of Whitefield's Apostolic Labors, held May 21, 1839. *London.* 1839. 12mo. 10247

Campbell (J.), *Bookseller.* Negro-Mania; being an Examination of the falsely-assumed Equality of the Various Races of Men; Demonstrated by the Investigations of Champollion, Wilkinson, Rosellini, Van-Amringe, Gliddon, Young, Morton, Knox, Lawrence, Gen. J. H. Hammond, Murray, Smith, W. Gilmore Simms, English, Conrad, Elder, Prichard, Blumenbach, Cuvier, Brown, Le Vaillant, Carlyle, Cardinal Wiseman, Burckhardt, and Jefferson. Together with a concluding Chapter, presenting a Comparative Statement of the Condition of the Negroes in the West Indies before and since Emancipation. By John Campbell. ... *Philadelphia: Campbell and Power.* 1851. 8vo, pp. 549. C., P. 10248

Campbell (J.) Unionists versus Traitors. The Political Parties of Philadelphia; or the Nominees that ought to be Elected in 1861. By John Campbell, a Douglas Democrat. *Philadelphia.* 1861. 8vo, pp. 24. 10249

Campbell (J. A.) United States and Foreign Postage Directory, containing the Laws, Rules, and Regulations of the Post Office Department. *Philadelphia.* 1865. 16mo. 10250

Campbell (John Douglas Sutherland), *Marquis of Lorne.* A Trip to the Tropics and home through America. By the Marquis of Lorne. *London: Hurst and Blackett.* 1867. 8vo, pp. xii, 355. Plate. BA., C. 10251

Campbell (John H.) Pacific Railroad. Speech of Hon. J. H. Campbell, of Pennsylvania, in the House of Representatives, Tuesday, April 8, 1862 ... . *Washington, D. C.: Scammel & Co., Printers.* ... 1862. 8vo, pp. 8. 10252

Campbell (J. L.) Idaho; Six Months in the New Gold Diggings. The Emigrant's Guide Overland. Itinerary of the Routes, Features of the Country, Journal of Residence, &c. &c. By J. L. Campbell. *Chicago: John R. Walsh.* 1864. 16mo, pp. 62. Map. 10253

Republished with the title:

Campbell. The Great Agricultural & Mineral West: a ... Guide for the Emigrant. ... Third Annual Edition. By J. L. Campbell. *Chicago.* 1866. 8vo, 12 l., pp. 17–74, (15). BA. + Fourth Annual Edition. *Chicago: Western News Co.* 16mo, pp. 98. 10254

Campbell (John N.) Discourse on the Occasion of the Death of James King, Esq. *Albany: J. Munsell.* 1841. 8vo.

Campbell. Rev. John N. Campbell, D.D., late Pastor of the First Presbyterian Church, Albany. Memorial compiled by a Member of the Congregation, and published by order of the Trustees. *Albany: C. Van Benthuysen, Printer.* 1864. 8vo, pp. 70. S. 10256

Campbell (*Rev.* John P.) The Nashville, State of Tennessee, and General Commercial Directory. *Nashville.* 1853. 8vo, pp. 352. 10257

[Campbell.] The Southern Business Directory and Commercial Advertiser ... . *Charleston: Press of Walker & James.* 1854. 8vo, pp. 404, 171, (1). H. 10258

Campbell (J. W.) A History of Virginia, from its Discovery till the year 1781: with Biographical Sketches of all the most distinguished Characters that occur in the Colonial, Revolutionary or Subsequent Period of our History. By J. W. Campbell. *Philadelphia: J. W. Campbell & M. Carey.* [1813.] 12mo, pp. 310. C. 10259

Also: "The Columbian Reader. *Petersburg.* 1814." 12mo.

Campbell (J. Wilson). Biographical Sketches; with other Literary Remains of the Late John W. Campbell, Judge of the United States Court for the District of Ohio. Compiled by his Widow [Eleanor W. Campbell]. *Columbus, Ohio: printed by Scott & Gallagher.* 1838. 8vo, 3 l., pp. 279. Portrait. BA., C., H.

Campbell (L. D.) Americanism. Speech of Hon. Lewis D. Campbell ... at the American Mass Meeting, held in Washington City, February 29th, 1859 ... . [*Washington.* n. d.] 8vo, pp. 8. BA. 10261

Also: Speech on Southern Aggression, Feb. 19, 1850. *Washington.* [n. d.] 8vo.—Kansas and Nebraska—Georgia and Ohio—Free Labor and Slave Labor. Speech ... December 14, 1854. [n. p. n. d.] 8vo, pp. 16. B.—Speech ... March 5, 1852, on Presidential Platforms, Internal Improvements, The Demands of the Mississippi Valley, and the Inland Lakes. [n. p. n. d.] 8vo, pp. 8.—Supremacy of the Constitution and Laws. Speech ... in reply to ... J. R. Giddings, The Senate's Amendments to the Deficiency Bill being under consideration. [*Washington.* 1856.] 8vo, pp. 8. B.

[Campbell (L. J.)] Historical Sketch of Minnesota, to accompany Seavey's edition of Goodrich's History of the United States. [By Loomis Joseph Campbell.] *Boston: Brewer and Tileston.* [n. d.] 8vo, pp. 321–329. B. 10262

Campbell (*Mrs.* M.) Revolutionary Services and Civil Life of General William Hull; Prepared from his Manuscripts, by his Daughter, Mrs. Maria Campbell: together with the History of the Campaign of 1812, and Surrender of the Post of Detroit, by his Grandson, James Freeman Clarke. *New-York: D. Appleton & Co.* M DCCC XLVIII. 8vo, pp. xx, 17–482.

Campbell (P.) Travels in the Interior Inhabited Parts of North America. In the years 1791 and 1792. In which is given an account of the manners and customs of the Indians, and the present war between them and the Fœderal States, the mode of Life and system of farming among the new settlers of both Canadas, New York, New England, New Brunswick, and Nova Scotia; interspersed with anecdotes of people, observations on the soil, natural productions, and political situation of these countries. Illustrated with Copper-Plates. By P. Campbell. *Edinburgh: John Guthrie.* MDCCXCIII. 8vo, pp. x, 387, 2 l. Portrait and 2 Plates. 10264

A curious and entertaining book. "The author set out from the Highlands of Scotland, with the intention to explore the interior inhabited parts of North America, attended with an old faithful servant, a dog and gun, only, as he travelled much in wildernesses and in birch bark canoes, through lakes and rapid streams, where the mind could not at all times be inattentive to safety, he wrote on canoes and on the stumps of trees occasionally, as he went along."—*Preface.*

Campbell (R.) Memorial to the Senate of Georgia relative to the Cherokee-Indians. By Robert Campbell. *Savannah.* 1829. 8vo. 10265

Campbell (R.) Two Lectures on Canada, by Rollo Campbell, of Montreal, delivered at Greenock, 20th and 23d January, 1857. *Greenock.* 1857. 12mo, pp. 47. + *Montreal.* 1857. + *Toronto.* 1857. 12mo, pp. 47. 10266

[Campbell (Thomas).] Annals of Great Britain from the Ascension of George III. to the Peace of Amiens. In Three Volumes. *Edinburgh: Printed for Mundell, etc.* 1807. 3 vols., 8vo, xv, 505; viii, 498; viii, 406. G. 10267

See M. R., LIX. 356.

Campbell. Gertrude of Wyoming; a Pennsylvanian Tale. And other Poems. By Thomas Campbell ... . *London: pub-*

lished for the Author, by Longman ... . 1809. 4to, 2 l., Note, 1 line, pp. 134. BA. + Second Edition. *London.* 1810. 12mo, pp. 131. 10268

CAMPBELL. Gertrude of Wyoming; or, the Pennsylvanian Cottage. With 35 Illustrations by the Brothers Dalziel. *London: S. Low, Son & Co.* 1858. 8vo. 10269

Some copies have the imprint, "*New York: D. Appleton & Co.*" *See* M. R., LIX. 239. Of course it is contained in the numerous editions of his "Poetical Works." A German version, by H. Schmick, is in the "Archiv f. d. Stud. d. neueren Sprachen," XXVI. 163–186.

[CAMPBELL.] History of Our Own Times. *London.* 1845. 2 vols., 12mo. 10270

CAMPBELL (T.) A Poem delivered before the Mechanic Apprentices' Library Association, at their 20th Anniversary, Feb. 22, 1840. By Thomas Campbell, a Member of the Association. [n. p. n. d.] 8vo, 2 l. H. 10271

CAMPBELL (T.) Union and Secession. Speech of Hon. Thompson Campbell, of San Francisco, delivered at Sacramento. July 30th, 1863. ... *Sacramento.* 1863. 8vo, pp. 16. H. 10272

CAMPBELL (William Frederick), *2d Baron Campbell.* Speech of Lord Campbell, in the House of Lords, on the Rights of the Neutral Powers to acknowledge the Southern Confederacy, March 23rd, 1863. *London: James Ridgway.* 1863. 8vo, pp. 28. BA. 10273

CAMPBELL (W. H.) A Funeral Discourse, occasioned by the Death of Rev. Andrew Yates, D.D. By Wm. H. Campbell, D.D. ... delivered before the Classis of Schnectady, in the R. P. Dutch Church ... Nov. 17, 1844. *Albany: printed by Munsell and Tanner.* 1844. 8vo, pp. 34. B. 10274

CAMPBELL (W. W.) Annals of Tryon County; or, The Border Warfare of New-York during the Revolution. By William W. Campbell. ... *New-York: J. & J. Harper.* 1831. 8vo, pp. 191, Appendix, 78. Map and Facsimile. BA. 10275

The second edition has the title:

CAMPBELL. The Border Warfare of New York, during the Revolution; or, The Annals of Tryon County. By William W. Campbell. ... *New York: Baker & Scribner.* 1849. 12mo, pp. 396. Without the Map and Facsimile. BA., H. 10276

Includes a letter to John Brant from Thomas Campbell, in regard to the mention of Brant's father in "Gertrude of Wyoming."

CAMPBELL. Address delivered at the Centennial Celebration at Cherry Valley, Otsego County, New York, July 4, 1840. *New York: Taylor & Clement.* 1840. 12mo, pp. 60. 10277

CAMPBELL. An Historical Sketch of Robin Hood and Captain Kidd, by William W. Campbell. ... *New York: Charles Scribner.* 1853. 12mo, pp. 263. BA., C., P. 10278

CAMPBELL. Lecture on the Life and Military Services of General James Clinton, read before the New-York Historical Society, Feb. 1839. By William W. Campbell. *New-York: printed by William Osborn.* 8vo, pp. 23. B. 10279

CAMPBELL. Life and Writings of De Witt Clinton. *New York: Baker & Scribner.* 1849. 8vo, pp. 417. C. 10280

CAMPBELL. Oration, Feb. 22, 1852, at the Celebration of the Birth-day of G. Washington, by the Order of the United Americans. *New-York.* 1852. 8vo, pp. 18. 10281

CAMPBELL. Speech on the Bill for raising a Regiment of Mounted Riflemen; House of Representatives of the United States, April 8, 1846. *Washington.* 1846. 8vo, pp. 14. 10282

CAMPE (J. H.) Columbus; oder die Entdeckung von Westindien ... . *Paris.* 1784. 16mo. + *Tübingen.* 1798. 3 vols., 12mo. + *Paris.* 1803. 12mo. + Neue Ausgabe, herausgegeben von Junker. *Paris: Th. Barrois fils.* 1825. 12mo. + Nouvelle édition, revue et corrigée par M. Schuster. *Paris: Hingray, Th. Barrois, Baudry.* 1837. 12mo. 10283

CAMPE. Columbus; or, The Discovery of America: as related by a Father to his Children, and designed for the Instruction of Youth. Translated from the German of J. H. Campe. By Elizabeth Helme. *London: Low.* 1799. 12mo. + *Dublin.* 1800. 12mo. + A New Edition, with the Translator's last Corrections and Improvements. *London: C. Cradock and W. Joy.* 1811. 12mo, pp. iv, 271. + *Boston: Munroe and Francis. New-York: Charles S. Francis.* [n. d.] 24mo, pp. 270. Lithograph. B. 10284

CAMPE. Cortez; or, the Conquest of Mexico: as related by a Father to his Children, and designed for the Instruction of Youth, Translated from the German of J. H. Campe. By Elizabeth Helme. *London: Law.* 1799. 12mo. + *Dublin.* 1800. + *Boston: Munroe and Francis, and Charles S. Francis, New York.* [n. d.] 12mo, pp. 255. B. 10285

CAMPE. Histoire de Christophe Colomb, ou la Decouverte de l'Amérique. Traduit par G. Heumann. *Rouen: Mégard.* 1854. 8vo. 10286

CAMPE. Voyages des premiers navigateurs dans le Nouveau Monde, Colomb, Cortès et Pizarre. *Paris: Cordier.* 1802. 6 vols., 8vo. Maps and Plates. + Sixième édition. [*Ibid.*] 1826. 10287

This, according to Quérard, is a translation of his "Columbus."

CAMPE. Voyages et conquêtes de Christophe Colomb, Traduit de l'allemand par E. C. Piton. *Limoges et Paris: Ardant frères.* 1863. 18mo. 10288

CAMPE. Voyages et conquêtes de Ferdinand Cortez, Pizarre, Améric Vespuce, Traduit de l'allemand de Campe par C. C. Piton. *Limoges* [*et*] *Paris: Ardant frères.* 1857. 12mo, pp. 216. Engraving. 10289

CAMPE. Columbus, Cortez, Pizarro, of de ontdekking van Amerika. Naar den 14e druk uit het Hoogduitsch vertaalt. *Amsterdam: ten Brink en de Vries.* 1839. 2 pts., 8vo. 10290

[CAMPE.] Amerikas Opdagelse og Erobring af Columbus, Cortez og Pizarro. Efter det Tydske. *Kjöbenhavn: Iversens Boghandlung.* 1856. 8vo. 7 Colored Plates. 10291

CAMPE. Voyages et conquêtes de Fernand Cortez au Mexique. Traduit de Campe par E. C. Piton. *Limoges et Isle: L. et E. Ardant frères.* 1863. 18mo, pp. 152. Engravings. + [*Id.:*] *E. Ardant et Thibaut.* 1866. 12mo, pp. 120. Illustrations. 10292

CAMPE. Die Entdeckung von Amerika ... *Hamburg.* 1780–81. 3 vols., 8vo. + *Amsterdam: Weduwe J. Doll.* 1782–83. 8vo. 2 Maps. + *Amsterdam.* 1787. 3 vols., 8vo. + *Braunschweig.* 1830. 3 vols., 18mo. + 14. Auflage. *Braunschweig: Schulbuchhandlung.* 1831. 3 vols., 12mo. 3 Maps, and 3 Lithographs. + Fünfzehnte Auflage. *Braunschweig.* 1834. 12mo. Maps and Plates. + [*Ibid.*] 1852. 12mo. + 16. Auflage. *Braunschweig: Schulbuchhandlung.* 1843. 3 vols., 8vo. + 17. Auflage. [*Ibid.*] 1844. 3 vols., 8vo. + 18. rechtmässige Auflage. Mit 1 Titelkupfer und 3 Karten. [*Id.:*] *Vieweg und Sohn.* 3 pts., 8vo, pp. x, 862. + 19. ... Auflage. [*Ibid.*] 3 pts., 8vo, pp. xii, 662. 8vo. 10293

CAMPE. De ontdekking van America, geschikt ter ... Leezing voor kinderen ... . *Amsterdam.* 1782–83. 8vo. + *Amsterdam.* 1783. 3 vols., 8vo. 10294

CAMPE. La Découverte de l'Amerique pour l'instruction and l'amusement des enfans et les jeunes gens. *Hamburgh.* 1782. 3 vols., 12mo. + *Hamburgh.* 1785. + *Hamburgh.* 1792. + *Genève.* 1798. 3 vols., 12mo. 2 Maps. + [Traduit de l'allemande par un anonyme.] Revu et corrigé par P. Blanchard. *Paris: Leprieur.* 1804. 3 vols., 12mo. 31 Engravings, and 2 Maps. + *Paris.* 1808. 3 vols., 12mo. + Quartrième édition. [*Ibid.*] 1817. 3 vols., 12mo. + *Paris.* 1833. 3 vols., 12mo. + *Braunschweig: Schulbuchhandlung.* [n. d.] 3 vols., 12mo. + Troisième édition. [*Ibid.*] 1810. 3 vols., 12mo. + *Berne: Société typographique.* 1799. 3 vols., 12mo. + Traduit ... par Junker. *Leipzig.* 1809. 2 vols., 8vo. + Nouvelle édition. *Stuttgart: Erhard.* 1835. 3 vols., 16mo. + Traduit de l'allemand par F.-C. Gérard. *Paris: Lauglunié et Peltier.* 1843. 12mo. 10295

CAMPE. Histoire et découvertes de l'Amérique, et voyages des premiers navigateurs au Nouveau-Monde. Traduit de l'allemand, et précédés d'une notice biographique sur Campe. Par M. de Larenaudière. *Paris: Denn.* 1826. 2 vols., 12mo. 8 Plates. + Traduit de l'allemand, précédé d'un essai sur la vie et les ouvrages de l'auteur, par Charles Saint-Maurice. *Paris: Lavigne.* 1844. 8vo. Engravings. + Ornée de 120 vignettes gravées sur bois par M. Lacoste aîné, d'après les dessins de M. Bertrand. *Paris: Garnier frères.* 1859. 8vo, pp. xii, 420. + Nouvelle édition. *Paris: Delalain.* 1860. 8vo, pp. xvi, 356. Engraving. + [*Ibid.*] 1861. 2 vols., 12mo, pp. 515. 2 Engravings. + Traduite de l'allemand par E.-C. Piton. *Paris.* [n. d.] 2 vols., 12mo. 10296

"A version of his 'Columbus.'" — QUÉRARD.

CAMPE. The Discovery of America. Ein Lesebuch für Anfänger in dem Englishen Sprache ... . *Oldenburg: Schulze.* 1808. 8vo. 10297

CAMPE. Descubrimiento y conquista de la America, o compendio de la historia general del nuevo mundo, por el autor del nuevo Robinson: traducido del Frances, corregido y mejorado por d. Juan Corradi. *Madrid.* 1803. 3 vols., 18mo. C. 10298

CAMPE. Historia da descuberta e conquista da America,

viagens e conquistas dos primeiros navegantes ao Novo-Mondo, precedida da huma noticia biographica de seu autor, por M. Larenaudière; traduzida em portuguez e accrescentada de notas criticas e historicas, por J.-Ignacio Roquete. *Paris: Aillaud.* 1836. 2 vols., 12mo. Plates. + Historia ... . *Madrid.* 1845. 4to. 10299

CAMPE. Historia del descubrimiento y conquista de America, escrita en aleman, trad. al castellano por F. F. Villabrille ... . *Mejico.* 1854. 8vo. 10300

CAMPE. Crtice iz Kolumbova Zivota, ili odkrice Amerike. Knjiga poucnozabavna od J. H. Kampe'a. Preveo Bozidar Budinjacki. Dio I. *Agram.* 1862. pp. 232. 10301

This is Campe's "Skizzen aus dem Leben des Kolumbus," translated into Croatic by Budinjacki. Part 1. We have not the type to represent some of the Croatic letters.

CAMPE. Die Entdeckung Amerikas. Achter Auflage. Dritter Theil: Pizzaro. *Braunschweig.* 1817. 12mo. 10302

CAMPE. Das Interessanteste aus Joh. Carver's Reisen durch Nordamerika. *Braunschweig.* 1788. + Vierte Auflage. *Braunschweig.* 1820. 12mo. 10303

CAMPE. Pizarro, or the Conquest of Peru: being a continuation of the Discovery of America, for the use of Children and Young Persons. *London: Law & Co.* 1799. + *Birmingham: J. Belcher.* 1800. 12mo, Title, pp. 243. Map. + Translated by Elizabeth Helme. ... New Edition. *London.* 1811. 16mo, pp. 237. Map. + *Boston: Munroe and Francis. New-York: Charles S. Francis.* [n. d.] 24mo, pp. 228. Lithograph. B. + *Limoges, etc.: Ardant, etc.* 1869. 18mo, pp. 71. Engravings.

CAMPE. Recueil de voyages interessants, traduits de l'allemand. *Frankfurt.* 1786–93. 7 vols., 12mo. + Traduits de l'allemand par Breton. *Breslau: W. G. Korn.* 1805. 2 vols., 12mo. 4 Plates and 1 Map. 10305

The "Bibliothèque géographique et instructive des jeunes gens ou recueil des voyages intéressants dans toutes les parties du monde, traduit par M. le Breton. *Paris.* 1802–7." 72 vols., 12mo, includes Carver's and other travels in America.

CAMPE. Reisbeschrijvingen voor de jeugd. Uit het Hoogduitsch. *Zwolle: J. de Vri.* 1786–1804. 5 vols., 8vo.

CAMPE. Nieuwe reisbeschrijvingen. Uit het Hoogduitsch. 1ste deel. *Amsterdam: de Weduwe J. Döll.* 1805. 8vo.

CAMPE. Robinson's Reise um die Welt. Amerika. *Nürnburg.* 1816. 2 vols., 12mo. Plates. 10308

CAMPE. Voyage d'un allemand au lac Onéida dans l'Amérique septentrionale. Traduit de l'allemand, avec des artes, par J.-B.-J. Breton. *Paris: G. Dufour.* 1803. 18mo. 10309

CAMPELLOS (*Fr.* João da Apresentação). Epitome historica da vida do arcebispo da Bahia D. F. Jose Fialho. 1740.

See Silva, V. 295; Varnhagen's "Hist. Brazil," II. 462.

CAMPI (P. M.) Dell' historia | ecclesiastica | di Piacenza | Di Pietro Maria Campi Canonico di quella Catedrale; | parte terza; | ... [10 lines] | E nel fine l'Historia vera circa l'Origine, e Nascita di Cristoforo Colombo | Piacentino Scopritore del nuouo Mondo; | Con vn Registro de' Priuilegi, Bolle, & altre Scritture latine citate in quest' Opera; | e con piv tavole copiosissime. | All' altezza serenissima | di Violante Margherita | di Savoia | Dvchessa di Piacenza, Parma, &c. [Vignette.] *Piacenza | nella stampa dvcale di Giovanni Bazachi.* M DC LXII. | Con licenza de' svperiori. | Folio, 12 l., pp. 388. 10311

This memorial, on the birth and family of Columbus, is nowhere else printed. It is in pp. 221–257. The complete work forms 3 vols., folio.

CAMPILLO. Pastoral que el Ilustr. Señor D. D. Manuel Ignacio Goncalez del Campillo Dignisimo Obispo de la Puebla de los Angeles dirige a sus diocesanos. [Colophon:] *Dada en la ciudad de la Puebla de los Angeles.* 1810. 4to, pp. 16. 10312

CAMPILLO (Gonzalez). *See* [Mendizabal (L. de)].

CAMPILLO. Exequias de D. Manuel Ignacio Gonzalez del Campillo, Obispo de la Puebla de los Angeles, celebradas en los dias 26 y 27 de Noviembre de 1813. Con el elogio funebre que dixo D. Francisco Pablo Vasquez. *Mexico.* 1814. 4to, pp. 17, 34. 10313

CAMPILLO Y COSIO (J. del). Nuevo Sistema de Gobierno Ecónomico para la América: Con los males y daños que le causa el que hoy tiene, de los que participa copiosamente España; y remedios universales para que la primera tenga considerables ventajas, y la segunda mayores intereses: Por el Señor Don Joseph del Campillo y Cosio. *Madrid: imprenta de Benito Cano.* MDCCLXXXIX. 12mo, pp. 32, 297. H. 10314

"This book was written in 1748, but never printed until 1789, probably on account of the unpleasant truths it contains relating to the treatment of the unfortunate Indians." *See* Rich, I. 360.

CAMPO (Est. del). Fausto. Impresiones del gaucho Anastasio el Pollo en la representacion de esta ópera. *Buenos Aires.* 1866. 8vo. Plate. 10315

"Cet ouvrage, en vers, est écrit dans le langage des *Gauchos* paysans de la république Argentine." — LECLERC.

CAMPO (F.) *See* Ocampo (F.)

CAMPO (Josefo). Llanto de las aguas en la muerte del mas caudaloso Rio: Honras debidas, que se hicieron en Queretaro à su Alferez Real el Doctor D. Pedro Bernardino Primo y Jordan. *Megico.* 1759. 4to. 10317

CAMPO (J. de). Romance lastimoso del incendio que succedio en la ciudad de Mexico dia de la Santa-Cruz a las ocho y media de la noche año 1636, compuesto por Juan de Campo. *Mexico.* 1636. 4to, pp. 8. 10318

In verse. *See* Ternaux, No. 569, and Rich, No. 215.

CAMPOAMOR (Ramon de). Colon. Poema. *Valencia.* 1853. 8vo. Map and Portrait of the Author. 10319

CAMPOS (B.) Oracion fúnebre del St. General D. Luis G. de Osollo. *Puebla.* 1858. 4to, 9 leaves. 10320

CAMPOS (Domingo). Relacion que hace de su viaje á Yucatan, y cuenta que dá al publico de su piadosa comision. *Mexico.* 1849. 4to, pp. 40. 10321

CAMPOS (Frederico Carneiro de). Alguns apontamentos estatisticos sobre a primeira secção das Obras publicas do Rio de Janeiro no anno de 1842. *Rio de Janeiro.* 1842. 4to. 10322

CAMPOS (J. G.) Oratio Apologetica, quæ velut supplex libellus Potent. Hispaniarum Regi Philippo V. D. Marchionis de Belzunce, etc. porrigitur à Regia Pontificia Mexicana Academia, ... 15 Nov. 1745. *Mexico.* 1746. 4to. 10323

This imperfect title is from an English catalogue.

CAMPOS (José Paulo Rodrigues de). Ecloga tragico-pastoril na morte do Senhor D. José, principe do Brasil. *Lisboa: na Typ. de Antonio Rodrigues Gallardo.* 1788. 4to, pp. 16. 10324

CAMPOS (Juan de). Relacion de todo lo succedido en Nueva España desde la formacion de la armada real de Barlovento, despacho de flota a cargo del general Juan de Campos hasta el primer aviso del año de 1642. *Mexico.* 1642. Folio. 10325

CAMPOS (Luis Caetano de). Voz da America, etc. *Lisboa.* 1810. 10326

CAMPVILLE (J. A. P.) Histoire d'une jeune créole de la Guadeloupe, ou La constante amie. 1805. 18mo. 10327

CAMUS (A. G.) Mémoire sur la Collection des grands et petits voyages, et sur la Collection des voyages de Melchisedech Thévenot; par A. G. Camus ... . Imprimé par l'ordre et aux frais de l'Institut. *Paris: Baudouin, imprimeur.* 1802. 4to, Half-Title, pp. iij, 401, 2 l. BA., C. 10328

An excellent specimen of bibliographical analysis, and indispensable to the "De Bry" and "Thévenot" collectors.

Can we enter into Treaty with the New Slave Trading Confederacy? [By W. Alexander.] *Leeds: Alice Mann, Printer.* [1861.] 8vo, pp. 8. 10329

CANADA. — Many anonymous books relating to Canada will be found in other parts of this Dictionary. The following arrangement is entirely arbitrary, but seemed desirable, — the various names of Upper and Lower Canada, Haute et Bas-Canada, and the more recent distinctions of the provinces of Ottawa and Quebec, are merged into this one dominion—Canada; still, some books overlooked here may be found under their respective captions. For references to the British Parliamentary documents which relate to Canada, *see* the Catalogue of the Public Library of Boston, art. "Great Britain. Parliament;" *also*, a "Catalogue of the Library of the Parliament of Canada."

CANADA. An Account of the French Settlements in North America: Shewing from the latest Authors, the Towns, Ports, Islands, Lakes, Rivers, &c. Of Canada, Claimed and improved by the French King. By a Gentleman. To which is added ... a more particular ... Account of Quebec ... . By P. Charlevoix. *Boston: Printed and Sold by Rogers and Fowle in Queen-Street next to the Prison.* 1746. 8vo, pp. 26. H., W. 10330

"The Compiler ... has principally improved Mr. Salmon's Present State of French America. But he has ... added sundry Particulars." — *Advertisement By the Printer.* This title is given imperfectly in Vol. I., No. 95.

An Act to enable the members of the United Church of England and Ireland in Canada to meet in Synod; together with the Canons passed by the Synod of the diocese of Toronto, under the Episcopate of John Strachan, D.D., Lord Bishop of the diocese of Toronto, A.D. 1857. ... *Toronto.* 1857. 8vo, pp. 15. 10331

Address of the Constitutional Reform Association to the People of Upper Canada. *Toronto.* 1860. 8vo, pp. 48. H.

Address of ... the Legislative Council to Her Majesty, on

the State of the Province ... Upper Canada. [n. p.] 1838. 8vo, pp. 16. 10333

An Address to the People of Canada, from the Constitutional Committee of Reform and Progress. [*Montreal.* 1847.] 4to, pp. 4. H. 10334

Addresses of the Lords and Commons to the King, on the capture of Canada and Quebec. 1759. Folio, four documents.

These doubtful titles are from an auctioneer's catalogue.

Addresses to His Excellency [George, Earl of Dalhousie] the Governor in Chief, from Different Parts of Lower-Canada, with His Excellency's Answers. [n. p. 1828.] 8vo, pp. 51. H.

Affaire du Canada. Observations sur les Profits prétendus induement faits par la Société de Lemoine des Pius, Martel et Varin. *Paris.* 1763. 10337

See Faribault, No. 869.

Affaires du Pays, depuis 1828 jusqu'a 1834. *Quebec.* 1834. 12mo. 10338

Extracted from the "Gazette de Quebec."

Affairs of the Canadas, in a series of Letters, by a Canadian. *London:* [*privately printed.*] 1837. 8vo. 10339

Agriculture. The Agricultural, Mechanical, and Educational Association of Canada West. [n. p. n. d.] 8vo, pp. 6. 10340

The Canadian Quarterly Agricultural and Industrial Magazine. By Wm. Evans. *Montreal.* 1838. Vol. I., No. 1, May, 1838. 8vo, pp. 72. 10341

The Farmer's Journal, and Transactions of the Lower Canada Board of Agriculture. *Montreal.* 1857. 8vo. Continued.

Also in the French language, edited by M. J. Penault.

Journal and Transactions of the Board of Agriculture, of Upper Canada. Vol. I. *Toronto: published for the Board by Thompson & Co.* 1856. 8vo, pp. viii, 667. Continued. H.

Journal of Agriculture and Proceedings of the Lower Canada Agricultural Society. *Montreal.* 1848. 8vo. Continued. 10344

With the title, etc., also in French, as below:

Journal d'agriculture et procédés de la Société d'Agriculture du Bas-Canada. *Montréal.* 1848. 8vo. Continued. 10345

Journal du Cultivateur, et Procédés du Bureau d'Agriculture du Bas-Canada. *Montreal.* 1853. 4to. 10346

Report of the Commissioners of Agriculture and Arts of the Province of Ontario, for the year 1868. *Toronto.* 1869. Rl. 8vo, pp. v, 214. Supplement, pp. 58. 10347

Also: Agricultural Association for Lower Canada. Prize List for 1858. *Montreal.* 1858. 8vo, pp. 23.—Annual Report of the Minister of Agriculture for 1856. *Toronto.* 1856. Rl. 8vo, pp. 7. Continued.—Monthly Report on the Agriculture of the Province of Canada. 1867. *Halifax.* 1867. 8vo. Continued. H.—Papers and Letters on Agriculture, recommended to the Attention of the Canadian Farmer, by the Agricultural Society in Canada [in English and French]. *Quebec.* 1790. 8vo, pp. 35.—Rapport du Comité Spécial sur le Rapport de la Société d'Agriculture du Bas-Canada, et sur celui de la Société d'Agriculture du Comté de Beauharnois. *Quebec.* 1851. 8vo. S.—Report of the Special Committee on the State of Agriculture in Lower Canada. *Toronto.* 1850. 8vo. Continued.—Report of the Minister of Agriculture [and Statistics] for 1866. *Ottawa: Hunter, Rose & Co.* 1867. 8vo. C.—Société d'agriculture du Bas-Canada. Objet, statuts et réglements. Liste des directeurs, etc. *Montréal.* 1847. 8vo, pp. 16.

Album du Canadien. Choix de morceaux littéraries, historiques, scientifiques et artistiques. *Québec.* 1849. 8vo, pp. 73.

Contains Boucher (P.), "Histoire de la Nouvelle France, 1663."

All Canada in the Hands of the English; or, an Authentick Journal of the Proceedings of the Army under General Amherst, etc., from 10th August to 8th September, 1760, etc. *Boston.* [n. d.] 8vo. N. 10349

Analyse d'un entretien sur la conservation des établissemens du Bas-Canada du loix, des usages, &c. de ses habitans. Par un Canadien ... . *Montreal: imprimé chez James Lane.* 1826. 8vo, pp. 46, "Fautes", 1 slip. B. 10350

Ancient French Archives or Extracts from the Minutes of Council Relating to the Records of Canada While under the Government of France. *Quebec: printed by Samuel Neilson.* M.DCC.XCI. 4to, 49 l. H. 10351

Printed in English and French on opposite pages. The French title is:

Anciennes Archives Françaises; ou, Extrait des Minutes du Conseil qui concernent les Régistres du Canada. 10352

Ansiedelungen in den Urwälden. *See* [Traill (C. P.)]

An Apology for the Church of England in the Canadas. *Kingston.* 1826. 8vo, pp. 22. 10353

Appel au Parlement imperial et aux habitans des colonies

angloises, Dans l'Amérique du Nord, sur les pretentions exorbitants du Gouvernement Exécutif et du Conseil Législatif de la Province du Bas-Canada. Par un Membre de la Chamber d'Assemblee. *Quebec: Imprimé par Flavien Vallerand.* 1824. 8vo, pp. 70. H. 10354

Appendix to the Canada Papers, relating to the Continental Army after its arrival near Boston in 1777–8. [n. p. n. d.] 8vo, pp. lxxxvii. C. 10355

Arrest du Conseil d'Estat du roy du 12 février 1726, qui casse une ordonnance de l'intendant du Canada, et condamne la dame Pascal et le sieur Caillaud, capitaine du vaisseau le Comte de Toulouse, etc. *Paris.* 1726. 4to. Map. 10356

Arrest du Roy concernant le Commerce du Castor en Canada. 1719. 4to. 10357

Relates to the beaver trade. *See* Vol. I., No. 2103.

L'Arrivee|des|ambassadevrs|dv royavme|de|Patagoce|et|de la Novvelle|France.|Ensemble ce qui s'est passé à leur voyage, auec des|remarques curieuses.|Traduit par le Sieur I. R.|*A Paris,*| *Chez la vefue Iean Remy, ruë S. Iacques, à|l'Image S. Remy, prés le College du Plessis.*|M.DC.XLIX.|Avec Permission.| 4to, pp. 8.

"C'est seulement pour son titre et la forme que l'auteur a donnée à ses attaques contre Mazarin, que nous plaçons cette 'Mazarinade' dans notre collection. Son contenu a beaucoup plus d'intérêt pour l'histoire de la France que pour celle de l'Amérique."—TRÖEMEL. Rich has the following: "Arrivée des Ambassadeurs de Patagoce et de la Nouvelle France. *Paris.* 1648. 4to, pp. 4," in his addenda, which may be the same work.

Articles accordés entre les directeurs et associés en la compagnie de la Nouvelle-France, et les députés des habitants dudit pays, agrées et confirmés par le roi [6 mars 1645]. *Paris: S. Cramoisy.* 1645. Folio, pp. 48 or less. 10359

Articles accordés par le roi à la compagnie de la Nouvelle-France [6 août 1628. n. p. n. d.] 4to, pp. 48 or less. 10360

Articles de la Compagnie de Canada. *Paris.* 1627. 8vo.

Au Roi. Raisons qui font voir combien il est important au roi et à son État de défendre ses sujets de la Nouvelle-France, dit Canadas, contre les invasions des Iroquois, et d'étendre sa protection sur ce nouveau monde. [n. p. n. d.] Folio, pp. 48 or less. 10362

Au Roi, sur la Nouvelle-France. [n. p.] 1626. 8vo, pp. 48 or less. 10363

The caption, p. 1., is, "Avis au roi sur les affaires de la Nouvelle-France."

Aux Habitants de la Province du Canada. *** Signé au Nom & par l'Ordre du Congrès: John Hancock, Président. *A Philadelphie: Chez Fleury, Mesplet & Charles Berger. le 24 Janvier,* 1776. Fol. p. 1. P. 10364

Avis du Roi sur les Affaires de la Nouvelle-France en 1620. *Paris.* 1620. 8vo. 10365

Backwoods of Canada. *See* [Traill (C. P.)]

Beschryvinge ende vindinge van het landt Canada ofte Nieuw Vranckrijck, geseydt Missisipi. *Leyden.* 1720. 8vo. 10366

Bibliothèque Canadienne. *See* Vol. II., No. 5206.

Bubbles from Canada. *See* [Haliburton (T. C.)]

Canada. *London: Roake and Varty.* 1838. 8vo. 10367

Canada: A Brief Outline of her Geographical Position, Productions, Climate, Capabilities, Educational and Municipal Institutions, &c. *Toronto.* 1857. 12mo, pp. 24. + Third Edition. *Quebec.* 1861. 8vo, pp. 64. 10368

Published by authority. Also in French, as below:

Le Canada, courte esquisse de sa position géographique, son climat, ses ressources, etc. *Toronto.* 1857. 8vo, pp. 23. 10369

There is also an edition in the German language, 8vo, pp. 26, and in the Norwegian, 8vo, pp. 20.

Canada. A Descriptive Poem, Written at Quebec, 1805. With Satires, Imitations, and Sonnets. [*Quebec.* 1805.] 8vo.

Canada Affairs. *Brighton.* 1836. 8vo, pp. 22. 10371

From the "Brighton Gazette," advocating the cause of the colonists.

Canada and the Western States of America described. *London: Baillière.* 1859. 8vo. 10372

Canada as a Field for Emigration. [*London.* 1853.] 12mo, pp. 16. 10373

Canada at the Universal Exposition. *See* [Taché (J. C.)]

The Canada Baptist Magazine. Vol. I. *Montreal.* 1838. 8vo. Continued. 10374

Canada. Eine Darstellung der natürlichen, socialen und Verkehrsverhaltnisse dieses Landes. Mit besonderer Rücksicht auf die Ansiedelung. *Berlin: Nicolai'sche Verlagshandlung.* 1858. 8vo, 3 l., pp. 108. Map. 10375

Canada. Ein kurzer Abriss von der geographischen Lage, Producten, Klima, Bodenbeschaffenheit, Erziehungs- und Municipalwesen, Fischereien, Eisenbahnen ... Dritte Ausgabe. *Leipzig: Wagner.* 1861. 8vo, pp. vi, 58. Map. 10376

Le Canada in 1868. *Saint-Cloud: imp. Ve Belin.* 1868. 18mo, pp. 36. 10377

Canada Guarantee Company: Act of Incorporation. 1851. 8vo. S. 10378

Canada in the years 1832, 1833, and 1834; Information to Emigrants, by an Ex-Settler. *Dublin.* 1835. 12mo. 10379

Canada; its Systematic Colonization. *London.* 1850. 8vo.

Canada Medical Journal and Monthly record of Surgical Science. *Montreal.* 1865. 8vo. 10381

Canada mit besonderer Rücksicht auf dessen Kolonisation nach den gegenwärtigen Verhältnissen geschildert. *Leipzig.* 1864. 8vo, pp. 46. 10382

Le Canada, mœurs, diverses races, langues, usages, etc. *Limoges: Barbou frères.* 12mo, pp. 192. Engravings. 10383

1st July, 1856. ... The Canada (Monthly) General Railway and, Steam Navigation Guide. [No. 2.] *Toronto: published for the Proprietor by Maclear & Co.* [n. d.] 16mo, pp. 40. H. 10384

Canada, Nova Scotia, New Brunswick, Newfoundland, etc. With the History, Present State, and Prospects of these Colonies in regard to Emigration. *London: Cradock and Co.* 1843. 16mo, pp. 64. Map. (New Lib. of Useful Knowl.) H. 10385

Canada. Petition from Lower Canada, with Explanatory Remarks. *London.* 1836. 8vo, pp. 40. 10386

Le Canada Pittoresque. *See* Bartlett (W. H.), Vol. I., No. 3787.

Canada. State of Political Parties, Economy in the Government, the St. Lawrence as a Great Commercial Highway, Public

Instruction, &c. &c. Translated from the Journal de Quebec. *Toronto: printed by C. Donlevy.* 1851. 8vo, pp. 35. H. 10387

Canada the Land of Hope. *London.* 1857. 8vo. 10388

Canada under successive Administrations. From the Port Folio, for September, 1844. *London.* 1845. BD., C. 10389

The Canadas as they now are; comprehending A View of the Climate, Rivers, Lakes, Canals, Government, Laws, Taxes, Towns, Trade, &c., with a Description of the Soil; derived from the Reports of the Inspectors made to the Judges at Quarter Sessions and from other Authentic Sources, assisted by Local Knowledge. By a late Resident. *London: James Duncan.* 1838. 12mo, pp. xv, 116. Map. BM., C. 10390

Rich describes another edition this same year. *See* Rich, Vol. II., pp. 302, 303.

Candid and Impartial Considerations. *See* [Campbell (J.)], Vol. III., No. 10231.

Case of the Holders of Reconnoissances given in Exchange for Canada Paper. 1772. Folio, 1 l. 10391

Le Clergé Canadien vengé par ses Ennemis; ou Observations sur un ouvrage recént intitulé: "Tableau Statistique et Politique des deux Canada" (d'Isidore Lebrun); par Vinder. *Québec: Neilson & Cowan.* 1834. 12mo. 10392

Catalogues. Alphabetical Catalogue of the Library of Parliament: being an Index of the Classified Catalogue Printed in 1851 and 1858, and to Books added to 1st March, 1862. *Québec: Hunter, Rose & Co.* 1862. 8vo, pp. 313. B., C. + ... Printed in 1857, 1858 and 1864, and to the Books and Pamphlets since added to the Library, up to 1st October, 1867. ... *Ottawa: printed by G. E. Desbarats.* 1867. 8vo, pp. 496. 10393

The title-pages, rules, etc., of all the following catalogues, are also given in French.

Canada. Catalogue of the Library of Parliament: General Library. *Toronto: John Lovell.* 1857. 8vo, 1 l., pp. 1074. B., C.

Canada. Catalogue of the Library of Parliament. Works relating to America. Pamphlets and Manuscripts. Index to Authors and Subjects. *Toronto: John Lovell.* 1858. 8vo, pp. viii, 1075–1895, (1). B., C. 10395

Catalogue of Books relating to the History of America, forming Part of the Library of the Legislative Assembly of Canada.

Quebec. 1845. 8vo, Title, pp. 29. H. + ... Books added ... . *Montreal.* 1846. 8vo, pp. 8. 10396

With a second title-page: "Catalogue d'ouvrages," etc.

Catalogue of Books in the Library of Parliament. ... *Quebec.* 1852. 8vo, pp. 130. BA. 10397

Catalogue of Books in the Library of the Legislative Assembly of Canada. ... *Montreal.* 1846. 8vo, pp. 123. H. + Alphabetical Catalogue. [No title-page.] 8vo, pp. 21. + Supplement ... . (... Books added in ... 1846.) *Montreal.* 1847. 8vo, pp. 24. H. 10398

This library was entirely destroyed by the mob in the spring of 1849.

Supplementary Catalogue of the Library of Parliament. Books added ... since 12th February, 1864. ... *Quebec.* 1865. 8vo, pp. 19. 10399

Titles, rules, etc., also in French. Other catalogues of the Library of the House of Assembly were published: *Quebec.* 1835, *Kingston.* 1842, and *Toronto.* 1850–51, all in octavo.

Census. Abstract of the Census of Canada. 1861. Origins and Religions. ... *Quebec.* 1862. 8vo, pp. 160. H. 10400

Also: "Census and Statistical Returns of Lower Canada, 1831," in French and English, folio.

The Census of the Canadas. 1851–2. Personal Census. Vol. I. ... || ... Agricultural Produce, Mills, Manufactories, Houses, Schools, Public Buildings, Places of Worship, &c. Vol. II. ... *Quebec.* 1853–'55. 2 vols., 8vo, 1 l., pp. xliii, 586; 2 l., pp. 475. C., H. 10401

With the title, etc., in French.

Miscellaneous Statistics of Canada for 1866. Municipal Returns. *Ottawa.* 1867. 8vo. 10402

Recensement des Canadas. *See* No. 10401, *supra.*

Returns of the Census of Upper Canada, for 1850. Folio.

Chansonnier Canadien. *Montréal.* 1825. 8vo, pp. 128.

Collection de mémoires. *See* Quebec.

The Constitution, By-laws, Minutes, Circular Letter, Articles of Faith, and the Covenant, of the Canadian Anti-Slavery Baptist Association. *Windsor.* 1854. 8vo, pp. 8. 10404

Convention for the Liquidation of the Canada Paper Money belonging to the Subjects of Great Britain. 1766. 8vo.

In French and English.

A Correct Account of the Rise and Progress of the Recent Popular Movements in Lower Canada. From the Patriot, Extra, (United States Newspaper,) December 15. 1837. *Bungay.* 1838. 8vo, pp. 12. 10407

Correspondence respecting the Recent Fenian Aggression upon Canada. ... *London.* [1867.] Folio, 3 l., pp. 84. (Parl. Doc.)

Crown Lands. Regulations relative to the Waste Lands of the Crown, Lower Canada. *Printed at the New Printing Office, Quebec.* 1798. 10409

First Report of the Committee of the House of Assembly, on that Part of the Speech of ... the Governor in Chief, which relates to the Settlement of the Crown Lands with the Minutes of Evidence taken ... . *Quebec: printed by J. Neilson.* 1821. 8vo, pp. 128. H. 10410

Report of a Committee appointed by the House of Assembly of Quebec, to enquire into the Settlement of the Crown Lands. *Quebec.* 1824. 8vo, pp. 136. 10411

"This report has no title, and was probably printed solely for the use of the members of the Assembly. It contains much interesting matter relating to the Indians and to the geography of Canada."—RICH. The following titles are from the "Cat. of the Lib. of Parliament:" Seventh Report of the Committee to the House of Assembly on the settlement of the Crown Lands. With the minutes of evidence ... *Quebec.* 1824. 8vo, pp. 295.—Eighth and ninth Report of the same Committee; concerning the claims of the Lorette Indians to the Seigniory of Sillery. *Quebec.* 1824. 8vo, pp. 62.

Report of the Commissioner of Crown Lands, for ... 1856. *Toronto.* 1857. 8vo, pp. 300. + [Second Edition. *Ibid.*] Continued. (Some vols. published at Quebec, and at Ottawa.) H.

Also in French as: "Rapport du Commissaire des terres de la couronne du Canada pour l'année 1856. *Toronto.* 1857." 8vo, pp. 304. Continued. M. There is also an appendix to this report, consisting of maps of Canada.

Report of the Select Committee appointed to enquire into the present System and Management of the Public Lands. ... *Quebec.* 1855. 8vo, pp. 187. H. 10413

Curiae Canadenses, or the Canadian Law Courts; a Poem, by Plinius Secundus [*pseudon.*] *Toronto: H. & W. Rowsell.* 1843. 8vo, 3 l., pp. 126. C. 10414

Diagrams of the Townships in Upper Canada, showing the lots purchased from His Majesty's Government by the Canadian Company. [n. p. n. d.] 2 vols., folio. 10415

Directory. The Canada Directory ... . Brought down to November, 1851. By Robert W. S. Mackay. *Montreal: John Lovell.* 1851. 8vo, Title, pp. xi–692. H. + A Supplement ... brought down to April, 1853, ... with a map. *Montreal.* 1853. 8vo. 10416

The Canada Directory, 1857-58 ... . *Montreal: John Lovell.* [n. d.] 8vo, pp. 1366 [to 1544 advertisements]. 10417

Documents relating to the Resignation of the Canadian Ministry in September, 1854. Speech of ... Inspector General Hincks in the Legislative Assembly ... 8th September — Address to the Electors of South Oxford — Correspondence with Mr. Wilson ... . *Quebec.* 1852. 8vo, pp. 27. H. 10418

Education. Account of the Endowments. 1838. *See* [Stuart (A.)]

Annual Report of the Normal, Model and Common Schools In Upper Canada, for ... 1850: with an Appendix. By the Chief Superintendent of Schools. ... *Toronto: Lovell and Gibson.* 1851. 8vo, pp. 376. Continued. H. 10419

The reports for 1847, '48, and '49, were published in folio.

Copies of Correspondence between the Chief Superintendent of Schools for Upper Canada, and other Persons, on the Subject of Separate Schools (being a Continuation of the Return ... printed ... 1852.) *Toronto.* 1855. 8vo, pp. 256. 10420

Also: Copies of Correspondence between Members of the Government and the Chief Superintendent of Schools on the Subject of the School Law for Upper Canada and Education generally, with Appendices. ... *Toronto.* 1850. Folio, Title, pp. iv, 59. H. — Correspondence between the Roman Catholic Bishop of Toronto and the Chief Superintendent of Schools in Upper Canada. ... Corrected from the Originals. With an Appendix ... . *Toronto: Thomas Hugh Bentley.* 1853. 8vo, pp. 31, (1), (1). H.

The Educational Directory. *See* Hodgins (T.)

General Provisions of the Law, and Rules and Regulations for the establishing and maintaining of Public School Libraries in Upper Canada ... *Toronto.* 1854. 10421

Journal de l'Instruction Publique ... . *Montreal.* 1857. 4to.

Journal of Education for Upper Canada: ... . *Toronto.* 1848. Continued. 10423

Vol. I. was in 8vo, the subsequent volumes in 4to.

Laws relating to Grammar and Common Schools in Upper Canada, together with Forms, General Regulations and Instructions, prepared according to Law, arranged with Notes and References. *Toronto.* 1855. 8vo, pp. 115. 10424

Letter to the Catholic Clergy and the Seigniors of Lower Canada, recommending the Establishment of Schools. *Quebec.* 1810. 8vo. 10425

Notes and Statistics on Public Instruction in Canada. Compiled for the Canada Directory for 1857-58. *Montreal: John Lovell, Printer.* 1857. 8vo, pp. 22. H. 10426

Proceedings at the Ceremony of laying the Corner Stone of the Normal & Model Schools and Education Offices for Upper Canada ... the Second Day of July, 1851, by the ... Earl of Elgin ... with an Introductory Sketch of the System of Public Elementary Instruction in Upper Canada ... . *Toronto.* 1851. 12mo, pp. 29. 3 Woodcuts. H. 10427

Rapport définitif des commissaires chargés de l'enquête sur les affaires de l'Université de King's College, et du Collége du Haut-Canada. ... *Quebec: imprimerie de Louis Perrault.* 1851. 8vo, pp. xvi, (1), 366. H. 10428

Also: Rapport du Commité du Conseil, sur l'objet d'Augmenter les Moiens d'Education. *Quebec.* 1790. 4to, pp. 26. — Rapport du comité spécial de la chambre d'assemblée du Bas-Canada, nommé pour s'enquérir de l'état actuel de l'éducation dans le Bas-Canada. *Quebec.* 1824. 8vo, pp. 240. — Rapport du Superintendant de l'Education pour le Bas-Canada. Pour 1853. *Quebec.* 1854. Continued. — Rapport Spécial sur les Mesures qui ont ete adoptées pour l'Établissement d'une École Normale, ... *Montréal.* 1847. 8vo, pp. 94. S.

Remarks on the State of Education in the Province of Canada: a Reprint from the British American Medical Journal, by L. *Montreal.* 1848. 12mo. S. 10429

Report of a Committee of the Council on promoting the Means of Education. *Quebec.* 1790. 4to, pp. 20. 10430

Report of a special Committee of the House of Assembly appointed to enquire into the State of Education in this Province. ... *Quebec.* 1824. 8vo, pp. 223. H. 10431

Also in French, *see* note to No. 10428.

Report of the Superintendent of Education for Lower Canada, 1849. *Toronto.* 1850. 8vo. Continued. 10432

The same in French.

Report of the Proceedings of the Canada Education and Home

Missionary Society, during the Seventh Year of its Operation. *Montreal: the Society.* 1834. 8vo, pp. 16. H. 10433

Also: Statutes relating to Elementary Education; with Circulars 9 and 12 of the Superintendent of Education for Lower Canada. *Montreal.* 1849. 8vo, pp. 95. — Statutes relating to Elementary Education and for the Establishment of Normal Schools; with Circulars, Instructions and Tables of the Superintendent of Education for Lower Canada. *Quebec.* 1852. 8vo, pp. 87.

Emigration. An Address to Persons who entertain the wish to better themselves by emigrating to Canada. *London.* 1832. 8vo. BM. 10434

Answers to Circular on Immigration, Issued by Bureau of Agriculture and Statistics. March 18th, 1858. *Toronto.* 8vo.

Emigration to Canada. The Province of Ontario: Its Soil, Climate, Resources, Institutions, Free Grant Lands, &c. For the Information of Intending Emigrants. Issued by Authority of the Government of Ontario. With Maps. *Toronto: Hunter, Rose, & Co.* 1869. Rl. 8vo, pp. 39. 10436

Outline of Plan of Emigration to Upper Canada. *London.* [1823?] 8vo, pp. 10, Appendix, xv. 10437

Report of the Chief Emigrant Agent, for ... 1858. ... *Toronto.* 1859. 8vo, pp. 34. H. 10438

Report of the Select Committee of the Legislative Assembly, on the Emigration which takes place annually from Lower Canada to the United States. *Montreal.* 1849. 8vo. 10439

Report of the Select Committee ... [on] the causes of Emigration from Canada to the United States and elsewhere. [*Toronto.* 1857?] 8vo, pp. 144. H. 10440

Also in French, as follows: "Rapport du Comité Spécial nommé pour s'enquérir des causes de l'émigration du Canada aux États-Unis d'Amérique ou ailleurs. *Toronto.* [1857?] Rl. 8vo, pp. 149.

An Enquiry into the Evils of General Suffrage and frequent Elections in Lower Canada. By Camillus. *Montreal.* 1810. 8vo. 10441

Etablissement de la compagnie du Canada sous le titre de Nouvelle-France, par les articles des 29 avril et 7 mai 1627; avec les arrêts et commission des 6 et 18 mai 1628, portant ratification, confirmation et exécution d'iceux. *Paris: Vve Saugrain et P. Prault.* 1725. 4to, pp. 48 or less. 10442

Evidence taken before the Committee of the House of Com-

mons on the Affairs of Lower Canada, in 1834. *London.* 1837. Folio. 10443

Extracts of Letters from Poor Persons who Emigrated last Year to Canada and the United States. *London.* 1831. 8vo.

"These letters from pauper emigrants sent out at the public expense, exhibit a picture drawn by the hand of untaught simplicity, but with the warmth of real feeling, and the force of unsophisticated truth." — *Quarterly Review*, XLVI. 366.

Extracts from the Reports of the Paris Industrial Exhibition of 1855, relating to Canadian Products. *Toronto.* 1857. 8vo, pp. 35. 10445

Also in French: "Extraits du Rapport sur l'Exposition de Paris relativement aux produits du Canada. *Toronto.* 1857." 4to, pp. 26.

A Few Observations on Canada. *London.* 1849. 8vo. C.

A Few Plain Directions for Persons intending to proceed as Settlers to ... Upper Canada. ... Also ... Journal of the Author's Voyage across the Atlantic, In June, 1819. By an English Farmer ... . *London: Baldwin, Cradock, and Joy.* 1820. 12mo, pp. vii, 100. Map. C., H. 10447

A hastily-written, but useful little work.

A Few Words on the Subject of Canada. By a Barrister. *London: Longman.* 1837. 8vo, pp. 52. BD. 10448

Few Words upon Canada, and her Productions in the Great Exhibition. *London.* 1851. 12mo. C., S. 10449

Finance. Estimate of Certain Expenses of the Civil Government of the Province of Canada for the Year 1852. *Quebec.* 1852. 8vo, pp. 11. 10450

First and Second Reports of the Select Committee of the Legislative Assembly, on the Public Income and Expenditures of the Province: Third Session. 3d Parliament. 1850.

Public Accounts for the Province of Canada, for 1857 and 1858. *Toronto.* 1858-59. 2 vols., rl. 8vo. 10452

Rapport. Revenu du Canada et paiements faits à même ce revenu; — Revenu et dépenses du département de la poste; — Achat, loyer et réparations de Spencer Wood, et réparations de certains édifices publics; — Dépenses du recensement; — Cautionnements donnés par les surintendants d'éducation; — Rapport relatif aux cautionnement, etc., donné par le receveur des honoraries, dans le bureau du secrétaire provincial. *Quebec.* 1852.

pp. 75. + Second Report of the Standing Committee on Public Accounts. *Quebec.* 1854. pp. 93. + Third and Fourth Reports of the Standing Committee on Public Accounts. (Decimal currency — Weights and Measures.) *Quebec.* 1855. pp. 80.

Report of Committee appointed by the Legislative Council, and House of Assembly, respecting the Financial Concerns with Lower Canada. 1821. 8vo. 10454

Les forêts interieures du Canada. *See* [Traill (C. P.)]

Le foyer canadien Recueil littéraire et historique. La Littérature Canadienne de 1850 à 1860. *Quebec.* 1863–1864. 2 vols., 8vo, pp. 390; 389. B. 10455

"L'objet de 'La Littérature Canadienne' est de réunir en qulques volumes les plus remarquables de ces travaux épars et de combler ainsi la lacune qui existe dans notre collection de littérature national."

From Canada. An Address and Caution to the Public. [dated from] Montreal 9th October 1789. [*London:*] *J. Stockdale, and J. F. and C. Rivington.* [1789.] 4to, pp. 2. 10456

Signed by Boucherville, and twenty-two other Canadians.

A Gazetteer of Upper Canada, 1813. *See* [Smith, (D. W.)]

Geology. Esquisse géologique du Canada suivie d'un catalogue descriptif de la collection de cartes et coupes géologiques, livres imprimés, roches, fossiles et minéraux économiques envoyée à l'Exposition universelle de 1867. Commission géologique du Canada. *Paris: Bossange.* 1867. 8vo, pp. 72. 10457

Geological Survey of Canada. *See* Billings (E.), Vol. II., No. 5410.

Geological Survey of Canada. Figures and Descriptions of Canadian Organic Remains. Decade I, 10 Plates. || Decade II, Graptolites of the Quebec Group. By James Hall. With 21 Plates. || Decade III, 11 Plates. || Decade IV, 9 Plates. *Montreal.* 1858. 10458

Geological Survey of Canada. Report of Progress For the Years 1853-54-55-56. ... *Toronto.* 1857. 8vo, 2 l., pp. iv, 494. 11 Maps. H. + Report of Progress from its Commencement to 1863. Illustrated by 498 wood cuts in the Text, and accompanied by an Atlas of Maps and Sections. *Montreal: Dawson Brothers.* 1863. 8vo, pp. xxvii, 983. + Report of Progress from Commencement to 1863, with Maps and Sections. *Mont-*

real: Dawson Brothers. 1865. 8vo, pp. 42, 3 l. 10 Maps. + Report of Progress from 1863 to 1866. *Ottawa: G. E. Desbarats.* 1866. 8vo, pp. viii, 321. 10459

Message from His Excellency the Governor General; with Reports on a Geological Survey of the Province of Canada; January 27, 1845. *Montreal.* 1845. 8vo. 10460

This preliminary report is by A. Murray, who is also the author of a "Report of Progress for 1845–46. *Montreal.* 1847."

Government of Canada. *See* Cavendish (*Sir* Henry).

Hints on the Case of Canada for the Consideration of Members of both Houses of Parliament. *London: Murray.* 1838. 8vo. BD. 10461

History and Description of the Canadas. With Accounts of the Civil War ... . *London.* [1838.] 8vo, (pp. 192, all printed of the work.) BD. 10462

Histoire ... Nova Francia, 1613. *See* [Lescarbot].

Histoire Veritable, 1664. *See* [Boucher (P.)], Vol. II., No. 6843.

Historical Memorial. *See* Mémoire historique.

An Impartial Account of the Civil War in the Canadas, with a General Description of the Provinces; comprising 1. History. 2. Resources and Trade. 3. Climate, &c. 4. The People, their Manners, Habits, Customs, Amusement, Songs, &c. 5. Religion, Education, the Press. 6. Population. 7. Information for Emigrants. Biographical Notices of the Principal Canadian Leaders. By a Gentleman, many Years resident in Canada. *London: Saunders.* 1838. 10463

Importance of Canada. *See* [Lee (Charles)].

Information relative to the Canadian Company. 1824. 8vo.

Information respecting the Eastern Townships of Lower Canada, in which the British American Land Company intend to commence Operations for the Sale and Settlement of Lands in the Ensuing Spring. 3d Dec. 1833. *London.* 1833. 8vo, pp. 21. Map. 10465

Indians. First Annual Report of the Society for Converting and Civilizing the Indians and Propagating the Gospel in Upper Canada. *York.* 1832. 8vo. 10466

Report of the Special Commissioners, appointed on the 8th of September, 1856, to investigate Indiana Affairs in Canada. *Toronto.* 1858. 8vo, pp. 293. 10467

Report on the Affairs of the Indians in Canada, laid before the Legislative Assembly 20th March, 1845. [n. p.] 1845. Folio, pp. 44. 10468

Report on the Indians of Upper Canada. By a Sub-Committee of the Aborigines' Protection Society. *London.* 1839. 8vo, pp. 52. 10469

Also: Return to an Address of the Legislative Assembly, for Correspondence regarding the setting apart of a tract of land in the Valley of the River Gatineau for the use of certain Indians. 1850.

Joint Address of the Legislative Council and House of Assembly of Upper Canada to His Majesty. [1821 or 1822.] 8vo, pp. 107. 10470

"This pamphlet appears to have been printed for private distribution only, apparently without a title-page." — RICH.

Journal of the Campaign in Canada. 1760. 10471

Jugement rendu souverainement et en dernier ressort, dans l'affaire du Canada, Par Messieurs les lieutenant général de police, lieutenant particulier et conseillers au Châtelet et Siége presidial de Paris, Commissaires du Roi en cette Partie Du 10 Décembre 1763. *Paris.* MDCCLXIII. 4to, pp. 78. H. 10472

See Faribault, No. 871, and "Ency. Method. Jurisprudence," Vol. II.

Key to Canada. Every Place in Canada and how to get to it; a Key to the Post Offices, Railway and Steamboat Stations, Stages, and Telegraphs, in Canada; with an Hotel Guide, and other Useful Memoranda. Published for W. R. Brown and E. A. Copleston. *Toronto.* 1857. 12mo. 10473

Laws. Abstract of a Bill for uniting the Legislative Councils and Assemblies of the Provinces of Lower and Upper Canada in one Legislature. *London.* 1824. 8vo, pp. 29. 10474

Les Actes et ordonnances revisés du Bas-Canada. ... . *Montreal.* 1845. 8vo, pp. xiii, (1), 728. H. 10475

Arrêts et Réglements du Conseil Supérieur de Quebec, et Ordonances et Jugements des Intendants du Canada. *Quebec.* 1855. 8vo. 10476

Civil Code of Lower Canada. First, Second and Third Reports || Fourth and Fifth Reports || Sixth and Seventh Reports and Supplementary Report. *Quebec.* 1865. 3 vols., folio, pp. 565; 471; 399. H. 10477

In French and English, printed on opposite pages. Also: Analytical Index to the Civil Code of Lower Canada. *Ottawa: printed by G. E. Desbarats.* 1867. 8vo, pp. 100. B. — Table analytique du code civil du Bas-Canada. *Ottawa: G. E. Desbarats.* 1867. 8vo, pp. 98. B.

A Collection of some of the most Useful Acts and Ordinances in force in Lower Canada, relating to Criminal Law and to the Duties of Magistrates. ... *Toronto.* 1858. 8vo, pp. 145, x. H.

Collection of the Acts passed in the Parliament of Great Britain and of other Public Acts relative to Canada. *Quebec.* 1800. 4to. + *Quebec.* 1824. 10479

Collections of the Acts passed in the Parliament of Great Britain, particularly applying to the Province of Upper Canada, and of such ordinances of the late Province of Quebec, as have force of law therein. *York.* 1818. 4to. C. 10480

Collections of Treaties, of Imperial Statutes, and of other Public Acts relative to Canada. 1759-1834. *Quebec.* 1834. 4to. 10481

In English and French.

Complement des Ordonnances et Jugements des Gouverneurs et Intendants et des différents officiers civils et de justice, avec une table alphabétique ... . *Quebec.* 1856. 8vo. 10482

The Consolidated Statutes of Canada. ... *Toronto.* 1859. 8vo, pp. viii, (2), xl, 1377. H. 10483

Consolidated Statutes for Upper Canada. ... *Toronto.* 1859. 8vo, pp. vii, (2), 1228, (1). H. 10484

The Consolidated Statutes for Lower Canada. ... *Quebec.* 1861. 8vo, pp. vii, (2), 1167. C., H. 10485

Also: An Act of the King's Council of State, which orders the Liquidation of the Bills of Exchange, and Money Bills of Canada. [In English and French. n. p. n. d.] 4to, pp. 26. (There are acts, dated June 29, 1764, July 2, 1764, Dec. 29, 1765, and Dec. 31, 1765.) — An Act to alter and amend Certain Provisions of the Act re-uniting the Provinces of Upper and Lower Canada. [n. d.] 8vo, pp. 9. — The Act to Restrain the Sale of Intoxicating Liquors, From Saturday Night till Monday Morning. (For Upper Canada only — Sanctioned 26th March 1859.) With Letter on the subject, by John J. E. Linton, of Stratford, C. W. *Montreal.* 1859. 12mo, pp. 12. — Acts relating to Patents for Useful Inventions in Canada. 12 Vict. Cap. 24; 14–15 Vict. Cap. 79; 16 Vict. Cap. 11. *Toronto.* 1856. 8vo, pp. 36. B. — Acts relating to the Powers, Duties and Protection of Justices of the Peace in Lower Canada, with a Full Synoptical Index. ... *Toronto.* 1858. 8vo, pp. xxvii, 95, (1). B.

Edits, Ordonnances Royaux, déclarations et arrêts du Conseil de l'Etat du Roi, (1540–1758) concernant le Canada. Ordonnances des Intendants et Arrêts du Conseil Supérieur de Québec (1627–1756). *Québec.* 1803–1806. 2 vols., 4to. + Revu et augmenté. *Québec* 1854-55. 2 vols., 8vo. 10486

General Index to the Journals of the Legislative Assembly of Canada; in the 1st, 2nd and 3d Parliaments. 1841-45. By Alfred Todd. ... *Montreal.* 1855. 4to. 10487

Index to the Statutes in Force in Lower Canada, at the End of the session of 1856. Prepared by Order of the Legislative Assembly, by G. W. Wicksteed. *Toronto.* 1857. 8vo. 10488

Index to the Statutes in Force in Upper Canada at the End of the Session, 1854-5, including a classification thereof, a Revision of the Public General Acts, and an Index to the Statutes not in force. ... By G. W. Wicksteed. *Toronto.* 1856. 8vo, pp. vii, 419. + For 1856. *Toronto.* 1857. 8vo, pp. xiv, 506.

Index des statuts en force dans le Bas Canada, a la fin de la session de 1856, Comprenant la Classification de ces Statuts — la Révision des Actes Publics Généraux — et un Index des Statuts qui ne sont pas en force, Préparé par G. W. Wicksteed ... . *Toronto.* 1857. 8vo, pp. xiii, 560. H. 10490

Journal of the House of Assembly of Lower Canada [in French and English]. *Quebec.* M.DCC.XCIII. 4to, pp. 528. H.

Journal of the House of Assembly of Upper Canada. *Toronto.* 1824. Folio. Continued to 1840. C. 10492

Journals of the Legislative Council and Legislative Assembly of the Province of Canada. *Kingston.* 1841. 10493

Continued in folio to 1851, subsequently in 8vo. The Sessional Papers are included in the issues since 1860. *See* "Catalogue of the Library of Congress. 1864," p. 211.

Journal of the Special Council, from April to June 26, 1840. *Quebec.* 1840. 4to. 10494

Lower Canada Reports. Decisions des tribunaux du Bas-Canada. Seigniorial Questions; a Compilation Containing the Seigniorial Act of 1854, the amendment to the Seigniorial Act, of 1854, the Questions submitted by the Attorney General for Lower Canada, the Counter Questions submitted by divers Seigniors ... &c. &c. Editors: MM. [Siméon] Lelievre et [François R.] Angers. Volume A. *Printed, Partly at Quebec by A. Coté, and partly at Montreal, by Duvernay Brothers.* || Volume B. *Printed Partly at Quebec, by Augustin Coté: and Partly at Montreal, at the Office of "La Minerve."* 1856. 8vo, 2 l., pp. 446, (2); 2 l., pp. 14, 19, 60, 70, (1), 133, (1), 59, 116, (1), 95, 9, 7 l. 10495

Lower Canada Municipal & Road Act of 1855, and certain Acts relating thereto ... the Parliamentary Representation Acts ... and the Seigniorial Acts ... . Accompanied by a Map ... exhibiting the Municipal Divisions ... *Quebec.* 1855. 8vo, pp. (1), xx, 211. H. 10496

Provincial Statutes of Lower Canada, enacted from the first Session of the first Provincial Parliament to the first Session of the fourteenth (1792–1831). *Quebec.* 1795–1831. 10 vols., 4to.

The Revised Acts and Ordinances of Lower-Canada. Published by Authority, under the Superintendence of the Commissioners for revising said Acts and Ordinances. *Montreal: printed by S. Derbishire & G. Desbarats.* 1845. 8vo, pp. xiii, (1), 716.

Statutes of the Province of Upper Canada; together with such British Statutes, Ordinances of Quebec, and Proclamations, as relate to the said Province. Revised by James Nickalls, Junior. *Kingston.* 1831. 4to. 10499

Also: Statutes of Upper Canada, passed in the 2d, 3d, and 4th Sessions of the 11th Provincial Parliament, and in the 1st Session of the 12th Provincial Parliament, 1831 to 1835. *York* and *Toronto.* 1832–1836. 4to. — The Statutes of Upper Canada, to the Time of the Union. Revised and published by Authority. Vol. I. Public Acts. || Vol. II. Local and Private Acts. *Toronto.* [1843.] 2 vols., 4to, 2 l., pp. 1096, lxxi; 1019, viii. H.

Statutes of the British Parliament relating to Canada, passed from 1847 to 1853. *Quebec.* 1853. 8vo. 10500

Table of the Provincial Statutes in force or which have been in force in Upper Canada, in their chronological order. With a continuation of the index, to the end of the session of 1856. Prepared by order of the legislative assembly, by G. W. Wicksteed. *Toronto.* 1856. 8vo, pp. 147. + To 1857. *Toronto.* 1857. 8vo, pp. 184. C. 10501

Tables relative to the Acts and Ordinances of Lower-Canada. ... *Kingston.* 1843. 8vo, pp. 175. H. 10502

Also published in French. Also: Proceedings of the Legislative Council of Upper Canada, on the Act to amend the Jury of this Province. 1836. 8vo. — Third Report and Proceedings of the Special Committee of the Legislative Assembly ... on ... the Seigniorial tenure. ... *Quebec: printed by Rollo Campbell.* 1852. 8vo, pp. 129, (1). H. — Réponse a Deux Adresses de l'Assemblée Législative sur les Actes de la Tenure Seigneuriale de 1854. *Toronto.* 1856. 8vo, pp. 30. — Réponse à Deux Adresses de l'Honorable Assemblée Legislative à S. E. l'Gouverneur-Général, 28 Fev., 1856. [*Toronto.*] 1856. 8vo, pp. 30. — Standing Rules and Regulations of the Legislative Assembly of Canada. *Toronto.* 1851. 12mo.

Les 92 résolutions, et débats sur icelles. *Montréal.* 1834. 8vo. 10503

A Letter from a Gentleman to his Friend, in England, Descriptive of the different Settlements in ... Upper Canada. *Philadelphia: printed by W. W. Woodward.* 1795. 12mo, pp. 30. H. + *London: R. Egerton.* 1795. C. 10504

"Gives a very advantageous account of the country, and of the settlers there, subjects to the British government; it also contains some particulars relative to the American Indians." — M. R., xx. 479.

A Letter From an Old Whig in Town, to a Modern Whig in the Country, Upon the late Expedition to Canada. *London: J. Morphew.* [1711.] 4to, pp. 8. 10505

Subscribed X. Z., dated October 23, 1711.

Letter on the Prospect of Peace in Canada, and at Louisberg, and on the Terms of Negociation. 1760. 8vo. 10506

Letter to a Friend in the Country. *See* [Dummer (J.)]

A Letter to a Noble Lord concerning the Late Expedition to Canada, (offering Satisfaction in Three Points. I. Of what Importance the Conquest of that Country would have been to the Crown, and whether it would have answered the Expense of the Great Armament that was made against it. II. Whether the Expedition was well concerted? And, lastly, if the Ill Success of it ought wholly to be charged on New England, as People here are made to believe.) *London: Printed for A. Baldwin.* 1712. 8vo, pp. 26. 10507

See "Bib. Am. Prim.," p. 213.

A Letter to Edward Baines, Esq., M.P., on the Insurrection in Canada. *Leeds.* 1838. 8vo, pp. 16. 10508

Lettre addressée aux Habitans de la Province de Quebec, cidevant le Canada. De la part du congrès général de l'Amérique Septentrionale, tenu à Philadelphie. *Philadelphia.* 1774. 8vo, pp. 18. 10509

Liste Chronologique des Évêques et des Prêtres tant Seculiers que Reguliers, employés au Service de l'Église du Canada, depuis l'Établissement de ce Pays, et aussi la Liste des Évêques des autres Possessions Britanniques de l'Amérique du Nord. Revue au Secrétariat de l'Evéché de Québec. *Québec: T. Cary.* 1834. 8vo, pp. 52. 10510

Letter to Lord Castlereagh on the Province of Upper Canada. *London.* 1809. 8vo. 10511

Manuscript relating to Canada. *See* [Johnstone (*The Chevalier*)].

Mémoire accompagnant la Requête présentée à la Chambre d'Assemblée du Bas-Canada, par le Clergé Catholique du Bas-Canada, contre l'Admission des Notables dans les Assemblées de Fabrique. *Québec: Fréchette & Cie.* 1831. 8vo. 10512

This was answered by a "Friend of the Order." *See* "Question des Fabriques."

Mémoire historique sur la négociation de la France et de l'Angleterre, depuis le 26 mars 1761 jusqu'au 20 septembre de la même année; avec les pièces justificatives. *Paris.* 1761. 8vo.

Translated as,

An Historical Memorial of the Negociation of France and England, from the 26th of March 1761 to the 20th September following; with the Vouchers; translated from the Original French. *London.* 1761. Folio. 10514

Mémoire sur le Canada. *La Rochelle: imp. de L. Bourdin.* [n. d.] Folio, pp. 48 or less. 10515

Advocates free trade between Canada and France.

Memoires et Documents. *See* Montreal.

Mémoires sur le Canada. *See* Quebec.

Memoirs of the Administration of the Government of Lower Canada by the Right Honorable the Earl of Dalhousie, G.C.B.; comprehending a period of Eight Years, viz., from June, 1820, till September, 1828. *Quebec.* 1829. 8vo. 10516

Memoranda of a Settler in Lower Canada. *See* Abbott (J.), Vol. I., No. 29.

Messages from ... the Governor-General, on the ... Re-union of the Provinces of Upper and Lower Canada. *Toronto.* 1839. 8vo, pp. 18. 10517

All the annual messages of the governor-general bear, more or less, on historical subjects.

Militia. An Act to amend, and reduce into one act, the Militia Laws. *Toronto.* 1838. 8vo. 10518

Annual Volunteer and Service Militia List of Canada. *Quebec.* [n. d.] 18mo, pp. 115. 10519

Report of the State of the Militia of the Province. ... *Toronto.* 1857. 8vo, pp. 67. Continued. 10520

Miscellaneous Statistics for 1866. Municipal Returns. Part II. *Ottawa: Hunter, Rose & Co.* 1867. 8vo. C. 10521

Missions. Mission du Canada. Relations inédites de la Nouvelle-France (1672–1679) pour faire suite aux anciennes relations (1615–1672) avec deux cartes géographiques. *Paris: Charles Douniol, éditeur.* 1861. 2 vols., 12mo, pp. xxviii, 356, Map; Title, 384, Map. 10522

French Canadian Missionary Society. First and Second Annual Reports, 1841. *Montreal.* 1841. 8vo, pp. 42. Continued. 10523

Seventh Annual Report of the Canada Mission. *Rochester.* 1844. 8vo, pp. 23. 10524

Minutes of the Upper Canada Baptist Association, 1822. *Niagara.* 1822. 10525

Municipal Returns for Upper and Lower Canada For ... 1864. ... *Quebec.* 1865. 8vo, pp. 27. H. 10526

A Narrative of the Canadian Rebellion; containing a Faithful Account of all the Important Occurrences connected with that Momentous Event, from its Commencement to its Final Suppression. With a Map of both the Canadas. *London: Ackermann.* 1838. 8vo. 10527

A Narrative of the Rebellion in the Canadas. By a Resident Canadian. With Copious Extracts from the Despatches of Sir John Colborne, Sir Francis Head, &c., &c., and other Official Documents. *London: Ackermann.* 1838. 8vo. Map. 10528

Noms, surnoms et qualités des associés en la compagnie de la Nouvelle-France, suivant les jours et dates de leurs signatures. [n. p. n. d.] 4to, pp. 48 or less. 10529

Notes upon Canada. *See* Todd (H. C.)

L'Observateur, ci-devant La Bibliothèque Canadienne. *See* Vol. II., No. 5207.

Observations on the Canada Thistle. 1810. 8vo. 10530

Observations on the "Plan for promoting Colonization in Upper Canada, connected with the Application of Convict Labour to the Construction of Canals." [1824.] 8vo. 10531

Observations on the Proposed Union of the Provinces of Upper and Lower Canada, under One Legislature, by the Agent of the Petitioners for that Measure. *London.* 1824. 8vo.

Observations on the Union of the Canadas and on the Canada Government Bill. *Greenock: privately printed.* 1840. 8vo.

Observations sur le Plan d'Acte de Parlement pour la Religion, & autres Objets qui y sont traités, au Sujet du Canada. [n. p. n. d.] Folio, pp. 24. H. 10534

No title-page. The title above is the caption.

Observations sur la réponse de Mathieu, Lord Aylmer, à la députation du Tattersall et sur le discours du très Honorable E. G. Stanly délivré dans la Chambre des Communes sur les affaires du Canada, le 15 avril 1834. *Montreal.* 1834. 8vo, pp. 40.

The Oil Districts of Canada. *New York: American News Co.* 1865. 16mo, pp. 40. 10536

On the origin and progress of the North West Company of Canada, with a History of the Fur Trade as connected with that Concern, &c. *London: Cox, Son, and Baylis.* 1811. Rl. 8vo, pp. 38. Map. 10537

Parochial and Township Subdivisions of Lower-Canada, in return to the Annexed Addressed of the Legislative Assembly, 1853. *Quebec.* 1853. 8vo, pp. 152. H. 10538

Also in French.

Patents of Canada, from 1824 to 1849. *Toronto.* 1860. 8vo, pp. 566, and 37 l. of Woodcuts. C., H. 10539

Petition of the House of Assembly of Lower Canada, to the King, and the Two Houses of Parliament; adopted in consequence of the Disclosure of the Instructions to the Governor and Commissioners. *London.* 1836. 8vo, pp. 20. 10540

Plain Directions for Settlers in Upper Canada. *London.* 1820. 8vo. BD. 10541

Plain Statement of the Quarrel with Canada; in which is considered who first infringed the Constitution of the Colony. *London.* 1838. 8vo, pp. 20. 10542

Plainte|de la Novvelle France|dite Canada,|A la France sa Germaine.|Pour seruir de Factum en vne cause pandente|au Conseil.|[n. p. 1620?] 8vo, pp. 15. H. 10543

No title-page. The title above is the caption.

Plan for the Systematic Colonization of Canada. By an Officer of Rank. *London: Hatchard.* 1850. 8vo. C., P. 10544

Plan for promoting Colonization in Upper Canada, connected with the Application of Convict Labour to Construction of Canals, etc. 1824. 8vo. 10545

Plans of Various Lakes and Rivers between Lake Huron and the River Ottawa, to accompany the Geological Reports for 1853, 54, 55, 56. *Toronto.* 1857. 4to. 22 Plans. C., S. 10546

Political Account of Lower Canada, 1830. *See* [Laterriere (Pierre de Salles)].

Political Annals of Lower Canada, 1828. *See* [Fleming (M.)]

Political View of Upper Canada. *London.* 1809. 8vo.

Post Office. Annual Report of the Post-master General, for the Year ending 1855. *Toronto.* 1856. 8vo. Continued.

Also in French, as the "Rapport Annual du Maitre-Général des Postes. Année expirée le 31 Mars 1855. *Toronto.* 1855. 8vo.

Present State of the Canadas; containing Practical and Statistical Information respecting the Climate, Soil, ... Trade ... &c. ... *London: Geo. Hebert. Liverpool: Egerton, Smith, and Co.* 1833. 12mo, pp. vi, 198. BA. 10549

Principales requêtes du procurer général en la commission établie dans l'affaire du Canada. [Colophon:] *Paris: Boudet.* [1763.] 4to, 1 l., pp. 51. H. 10550

Prisons. Report of the Board of Inspectors of the Provincial Penitentiary, for 1838. ... [n. p. n. d.] 8vo, pp. 67. H. 10551

Report of the Commissioners appointed to Inquire into the Conduct, Discipline and Management of the Provincial Penitentiary. ... *Montreal.* 1849. Folio. 10552

Rapport Annuel des Inspecteurs du Pénitencier Provincial pour l'Année 1855. *Toronto.* 1856. 8vo, pp. 76. Continued.

Proceedings of the Legislature on the Subject of the Resignation of the Members of the Late Executive Council. 1843. 4to. B. 10554

Proposals for a Subscription to Form Colonies in Canada. [n. p. n. d.] 8vo. 10555

Prospectus of the Canada Landed Credit Company ... . *Toronto.* 1859. 8vo, pp. 24. H. 10556

Public Accounts for the Province of Canada for 1857 and 1858. *Toronto.* 1858-9. 2 vols., 8vo. Continued. C.

Public Documents relating to Lord Aylmer. *See* Vol. I., No. 2519, and add to that title, pp. 126.

Public Works. General report of the Commissioner of Public Works, for 1865-66. *Ottawa: Hunter, Rose & Co.* 1867. 8vo.

Report of the Commissioners of Public Works for the Year ending Dec. 31, 1850. *Toronto.* 1857. Folio. Continued in 8vo. 10559

Railways in Canada. Schedule of the Several Companies incorporated for the Construction of Railways in Canada. *Quebec.* [1853.] 3 sheets, broadside. 10560

Rapport des Commissaires des Travaux Publics pour l'Année 1855. *Toronto.* 1856. 8vo. Continued. 10561

Rapport du comité de la Chambre des Communes sur le Gouvernement Civil du Canada; mis devant la Chambre, le 28 juillet. 1828. 8vo, pp. 13. 10562

Rapport du comité choisi sur le gouvernement civil de Canada. *Quebec: Neilson et Cowan.* 1829. 8vo, 1 l., pp. 388. 10563

Premier et second rapports du comité spécial, nommé pour s'enquérir des causes qui retardent la colonisation des townships des l'Est du Bas-Canada. *Quebec.* 1851. pp. 170. 10564

Rapport sur le pays entre les rivières Saguenay, St. Maurice et St. Laurent. 8vo, pp. 50. 10565

Rapports du comité spécial sur les chemins et autres communications intérieurs. *Quebec.* 1829. 8vo, pp. 144. 10566

Premier et Second Rapports du Comité Spécial nommé pour s'enquérir du fonctionnement de l'acte des municipalités et des chemins du Bas-Canada, de 1855. *Toronto.* 1857. 4to, pp. 247. s. 10567

Rapports et Témoignages du Comité spécial de la Chambre d'Assemblée du Bas-Canada, sur les petitions se plaignant de griefs. *Quebec.* 1829. 10568

Recueil de chansons canadiens et françaises devisé en deux parties. ... *Montreal: John Lovell.* 1859. 24mo, pp. 360. B.

Recent Occurrences in Canada. *Printed from the "Monthly Repository," of February*, 1836. 8vo, pp. 16. 10570

The Rectories of Upper Canada: a Return to an Address of the House of Commons dated 11th March, 1839; with an Appendix of documents relating to the Clergy Reserves, from the Toronto Colonist ... *Toronto.* 1852. 8vo, pp. 54. 10571

Relation de ce qui s'est passé à la Nouvelle France. *See* under the names of the Authors *and* Relation.

Relation des Affaires du Canada, En 1696. Avec des Lettres des Pères de la Compagnie de Jésus depuis 1696 jusqu'en 1702. *Nouvelle-York: De la Presse Cramoisy de Jean-Marie Shea.* MDCCCLXV. 8vo, pp. 73, 26, 18. 10572

100 copies printed from the manuscript in the possession of Mr. Henry C. Murphy. Forms No. XIX. of Shea's "Cramoisy Series."

Relations inédites de la Nouvelle-France (1672–79) pour faire suite aux anciennes relations (1615–72). Publ. par Felix Martin. *Paris.* 1861. 2 vols., 8vo. Maps. 10573

Remarks on the Proceedings as to Canada, in the present Session of Parliament: by one of the Commissioners. 10th April, 1837. *London.* 1837. 8vo, pp. 67. C. 10574

Reponse a une Adresse pour les noms des personnes nommées à des charges depuis le 28 Mars, 1855. *Toronto. Mai*, 1857. 4to, pp. 24. s. 10575

Report from the Select Committee on the Civil Government of Canada; with the evidence ... printed by order of the House of Commons, July, 1828. *London.* Folio. + *Quebec.* 1829. 4to. 10576

Seventh Report from the Select Committee of the House of Assembly on Grievances. [With] Report on the Petition of William Forsyth, late Proprietor of the Niagara Falls Pavilion. W. L. Mackenzie, Chairman. *Toronto: M. Reynolds.* 1835. 8vo, pp. 372, 26. C. 10577

Report of the Select Committee of the Legislative Council of Upper Canada on the State of the Province. [*Toronto.*] 1838. 8vo, 2 l., pp. 91, 60. 10578

Report from the Select Committee of the Legislative Council on the Accusations made against the Members of the Late Administration, together with the Minutes of Evidence, Appendix and Correspondence. ... *Quebec.* 1855. 8vo, pp. 115. H.

Report of a Select Committee of the House of Assembly, on the political state of ... Upper and Lower Canada. ... [*Montreal.*] 1838. 8vo, pp. 65, 16. s. 10580

Report on the Public Departments of Upper Canada in 1839. *Toronto.* 1839. Folio. Continued. 10581

Reports of the Commissioners appointed to inquire into the grievances complained of in Lower Canada. ... *London.* 1837. Folio, pp. 182, 73, 160. Map. (Parl. Doc.) 10582

Report of the Commissioners employed to investigate the Origin, etc. of the Epidemic Cholera of Canada, July 8, 1832. *New York.* 1832. 10583

Report of the Court of Directors of the Canada Company, 28th June, 1827. *London.* 1827. 8vo, pp. 24. 10584

Report of the Royal Commissioners appointed to enquire into the State of Canada. *Quebec.* 1836. 8vo, pp. 87. 10585

Fourth Report of the Society for Propagating the Gospel among the Destitute Settlers and Indians in Lower Canada. 1839 and 1840. *Quebec.* [n. d.] 8vo, pp. 17. H. 10586

Report of the Special Committee on the Magdalen Islands, and the Western Part of this Province, above Lake Huron. ... *Quebec.* 1853. 8vo, pp. 75. Map. H. 10587

Report of the State Trials before a general Court Martial held at Montreal in 1838–9, exhibiting a complete History of the Late Rebellion in Lower Canada. *Montreal.* 1839. 2 vols., 8vo. 10588

Report on the Case of the Canadian Prisoners. With an Introduction on the Writ of Habeas Corpus, by Alfred A. Fry. *London.* 1839. 8vo. 10589

Report on the Exploration of the Country between Lake Superior and the Red River Settlement. Printed by order of the Legislative Assembly. *Toronto: John Lovell, Printer.* 1858. 8vo, pp. 425. 2 Maps. C., H. 10590

The reports are by G. Gladman, H. Y. Hind, and others.

Report on the Progress of Settlement in the Townships of Lower Canada, during ... 1855, by T. Boutillier ... . *Toronto.* 1856. 8vo, pp. 71, (1). H. 10591

First Report on the State of the Representation of the People of Upper Canada in the Legislature of that Province. *York.* 1831. 8vo. 10592

Report on Trade and Commerce. *Quebec.* 1855. 8vo. Continued. 10593

Report ... upon the Provision made by Law for the Support of a Protestant Clergy in the Province. *Toronto.* 1835. 8vo, pp. 86. 10594

First & Second Reports of the Special Committee ... [on] the Causes which retard the Settlement of the Eastern Townships of Lower Canada. ... *Quebec.* 1851. 8vo, pp. 145, (1). H.

The Resources of the Canadas; or Sketches of the Physical and Moral Means, which Great Britain and her Colonial Authorities will successfully employ in securing those Valuable Provinces from Open Invasion and Insidious Aggression on the part of the Government of the United States. By a Querist. *Quebec.* 1813. 8vo, pp. 43. 10596

Responsible Government for Canada; an Enquiry as to the Causes and Consequences of the Late Ministerial Resignations. ... *Montreal: Armour & Ramsay.* [*Etc.*] 1844. 8vo, Title, pp. 23 [25]. H. 10597

Return to an Address for Names of Persons appointed to Office since 28th March, 1855, with Salary and Fees in Each Case. *Toronto.* 1857. 8vo, pp. 24. 10598

Return to an Address on the State of the Colonies. ... *Quebec.* 1853. 8vo, pp. 80. H. 10599

Review of the Proceedings of the Legislature in 1831. *See* [Stuart (A.)]

A Review of the Report made in 1828, by the Canada Committee of the House of Commons. *Montreal Herald Office, Aug.* 1835. 12mo. 10600

Originally published in the "Montreal Herald."

Seigniorial Tenure. Titles and Documents relating to the Seigniorial Tenure, required by an Address of the Legislative Assembly, 1851. *Quebec.* 1852. 8vo, pp. 216. H. 10601

Titles ... [as above] in return to an Address ... . *Quebec.* 1852. 8vo, pp. 490. H. 10602

The matter of these two collections differs.

Edits, Ordinances, Declarations and Decrees relative to the Seigniorial Tenure, ... 1851. *Quebec.* 1852. 8vo, pp. 337.

Le Bill Seigneurial exposé sous son vrai jour. *See* Vol. II., No. 5383.

Also: Correspondence between the French Government and the Governors and Intendants of Canada, relative to the Seigniorial Tenure, ... *Quebec.* 1853. 8vo, pp. 56, (1). H. — Débats dans l'assemblée législative sur la tenure seigneuriale ... *Québec.* 1853. pp. 40.

Les Servantes de Dieu en Canada. Essai sur l'Histoire des Communautés religieuses de femmes de la province. Édition ... préparée pour le Canada. *Montréal.* 1855. 8vo, pp. 159.

See also Courcy (H. D.)

Shall we Keep the Canadas? *London.* 1849. 8vo, pp. 26.

A Short Account of the Rise and Progress of the Recent Popular Movements in Lower Canada. *Bungay.* 1838. 8vo, pp. 12. 10606

Short Topographical Description of Upper Canada. *See* [Smyth (D. W.)]

Six Years in the Bush; or Extracts from a Journal of a Settler in Upper Canada. *London: Simpkin.* 1838. 12mo. BD.

Sketches ... for settling Canada, 1822. *See* [Bannister (J. W.)] Vol. I., No. 3214.

Sketches of Canadian Life. *See* [Darling (W. S.)]

Some Considerations on this Question, Whether the British Government acted wisely in granting to Canada her present Constitution? With an Appendix. *Montreal: J. Brown.* 1810. 8vo, pp. 26. 10608

A Statement of the Satisfactory Results which have attended Emigration to Upper Canada from the Establishment of the Canada Company until the Present Period; comprising Statistical Tables and other Important Information communicated by Respectable Residents in the various Townships of Upper Canada: with a general Map of the Province. Compiled for the Guidance of Emigrants. *London: Smith, Elder & Co.* 1841. 8vo, pp. 60. Map. + Third Edition, with Additional Information to the Present Time. *London.* 1842. 8vo, pp. 114. Map. + Fourth Edition. *London.* 1842. + Fifth Edition, with Additional Information to the Present Time. *London.* 1846. 8vo, pp. 118. s. 10609

Statistical Sketches of Upper Canada, for the Use of Emigrants: by a Backwoodsman. ... *London.* 1832. 12mo. BM. + Third Edition. *London: John Murray.* MDCCCXXXIII. 16mo, pp. viii, 120. B. 10610

Subdivisions du Bas-Canada en paroisses et townships, en réponse à l'adresse ci-jointe de l'Assemblée Législative. *Quebec.* 1853. 8vo, pp. 146. H. 10611

Also in English. *See* No. 10538.

Tableaux du commerce et de la navigation de la province du Canada, pour l'année 1851. ... F. Hincks, Inspecteur-Général. *Quebec.* 1852. 8vo, pp. 508. Continued. H. 10612

Tables of the Trade and Navigation of the Province of Canada, for the Year 1850. *Toronto.* 1851. Continued. C. 10613

Thoughts on the Canada Bill, now depending in Parliament. *London: J. Debrett.* M.DCC.XCI. 8vo, 2 l., pp. 50. C., H.

A | Tour | through | Upper and Lower Canada. | By a Citizen of the United States. | Containing | A View of the present State of Religion, Learn- | ing, Commerce, Agriculture, Colonization, | Customs; and Manners, among the | English, French, and Indian | Settlements. *Printed at Litchfield (according to Act of Congress).* 1799. 12mo, pp. 119. P. 10615

Travels in Lower Canada, with the Author's Recollections of the Morals, Habits, &c. of that Country. *London.* 1820. 8vo. Plates. 10616

Travels through Upper and Lower Canada, with an Accurate Description of Niagara Falls. *New York.* 1821. 2 vols., 8vo.

View of the Political Situation of Canada. *See* [Jackson (J. W.)]

Views of Canada and the Colonists: embracing the Experience of a Residence; Views of the present State, Progress and Prospects of the Colony; with Detailed and Practical Information for intending Emigrants. By a Four-Years' Resident. *Edinburgh.* 1844. Fcap. 8vo, pp. xvi, 266. + *London: Longman.* 1844. s. 10618

A Visit to Canada. *Liverpool.* [n. d.] 8vo. 10619

Voyages de Decouverte au Canada, entre les années 1534 et 1542, par Jacques Quartier, le Sieur de Roberval Jean Alphonse de Xanctoigne, &c. Suivis de la description de Québec et de ses environs en 1608, et de divers extraits relativement au lieu de l'hivernement de Jacques Quartier en 1535–36. (Avec gravures fac-simile.) Réimprimés sur d'anciennes Relations, et publiés sous la direction de la Société Littéraire et Historique de Québec. *Québec: Imprimé chez William Cowan et fils.* 1843. 8vo, pp. iv, 130. 2 Plates. C. 10620

What shall we do with Canada? *London.* 1837. 8vo, pp. 8.

Year-Book and Almanac of British North America. *Montreal.* 1866. 8vo. Continued. 10622

Die Canadenser, oder der Kampf der Freiheit am Niagara und Lorenzo in den Jahren 1837 und 1838. Vom Herausgeber des G. Schobri. *Leipzig: Klein.* 1839. 8vo. 10623

Canadian Almanac, and Repository of Useful Knowledge, for the year 1851. *Toronto: Hugh Scobie.* 1851. 8vo. Continued.

Canadian, British American, and West Indian Magazine. 1839. 8vo, pp. 224. 10625

Contains a "History of Canada to the Treaty of Utrecht, in 1713," "Reviews of Lord Durham's Report," "Letters from Canadian Politicians," "Papers on Emigration," etc.

Canadian Colonization. *London: Hatchard.* 1850. 8vo.

Canadian Controversy. *See* [Elliot (F.)]

Canadian Crisis. *See* O. (M. N.)

Canadian Freeholder. *See* [Maseres (*Baron*)].

The Canadian Guide Book, with a Map of the Province [by E. Staveley]. *Montreal: Armour & Ramsay [etc.]* 1849. 18mo, Title, pp. 153, (1). C., H. 10627

Canadian Handbook and Tourist's Guide; a Description of Canadian Lake and River Scenery and Places of Interest, with the Best Spots for Fishing and Shooting. *Montreal.* 1866. 12mo, pp. 208. 10628

The Canadian Inspector, No. 1, containing a Collection of Facts concerning the Government of Sir George Prevost, in the Canadas. *Montreal: Nahum Mower. July*, 1815. 8vo. 10629

Written in answer to the "Letters of Veritas." *See* Veritas.

The Canadian Journal of Industry, Science, and Art. *Toronto.* 1852–55. 5 vols., folio. + New Series. Vol. I. *Toronto.* MDCCCLVI. 8vo, 2 l., pp. 580. Continued. H. 10630

Originally edited by Henry Youle Hind, M.A.; since 1856, edited by Daniel Wilson, LL.D. Contains many valuable papers on the geology, mineralogy, and natural history of Canada, as well as notices of the construction of some of the public works. Issued in bi-monthly numbers.

Canadian Land Agency for the Investment of Capital on an Original and Approved Plan. [*London.*] 1825. 8vo, pp. 23.

Canadian Life. *See* Christmas (H.)

Canadian Literary Magazine. Vol. I. No. I. April, 1833. *York, U. C.* 1833. 10632

Contains a description of the Falls of Niagara.

Canadian Magazine. Edited by Edward John Barker. Vol. I. *Kingston.* 1846. N. 10633

Canadian Medical Journal. Edited by G. E. Fenwick, M.D., and F. W. Campbell, M.D. 10634

A Canadian Merchant's Letter on the Prospect of British Shipping. 1858. 8vo. 10635

The Canadian Merchant's Magazine and Commercial Review. Vol. I. No. I. April, 1857. *Toronto: William Wier & Co.* 1857. 8vo. Continued. 10636

The Canadian Naturalist and Geologist, and Proceedings of the Natural History Society of Montreal. *Montreal.* 1856. 8vo. Continued. 10637

Commenced in February, 1856, at Ottawa, under the editorial supervision of E. Billings. After the third number it was published at Montreal. It is principally devoted to the diffusion of information upon the geology, zoology, and botany of British North America.

The Canadian Portfolio, Containing a faithful Exposition of the Causes that have produced the Civil War in Canada, together with the various Official Documents, necessary to elucidate and support the history of this disgraceful contest, conducted by John Arthur Roebuck, Esq., and other Friends of Canada. *London.* 1838. 8vo, pp. 193. 10638

Probably discontinued at this point. This work figures under two or three different titles in one of J. R. Smith's catalogues.

Canadian Railways; Great Western Railway of Canada, Buffalo and Lake Huron, and Grand Trunk Railway of Canada, considered in reference to the Proposed Fusion of the Lines. *Glasgow: Maclehose.* 1862. 8vo. 10639

The Canadian Review, and Literary & Historical Journal. No. I. July, 1824. ... *Montreal: H. H. Cunningham.* 1824. 8vo, 2 l., pp. 232. Continued. H. 10640

"Contains three or four valuable articles on the discovery and early history of the provinces, on the aborigines, and the fur trade." — N. A. R., XIX. 457. I have seen no number later than No. V., Sept., 1826.

Canadian Scenery. *See* Bartlett (W. H.), Vol. I., No. 3786.

The Canadian Settler's Guide. Tenth Edition. *London: Stanford.* 1860. Crown 8vo. 10643

The Canadian Tourist. Accompanied by a Map of the British American Provinces, and an Appendix containing Useful Statistical Information. *Montreal: Hew Ramsay. Toronto: A. H. Armour & Co. [etc.]* 1856. 18mo, pp. iv, 211. H. 10644

Le Canadien. *Quebec.* 1806–1808. 2 vols., 4to. 10645

A periodical in the French language, commencing Nov., 1806, and ending 19th Nov., 1808. The following periodicals contain many articles on Canada: "Blackwood's Mag.," "Dublin Univ. Mag.," "Fraser's Mag.," "Quarterly Rev.," "North Amer. Rev.," "Revue des deux Mondes," "Westminster Review," etc.

Le Canadien émigrant, ou pourquoi le Canadien français quitte-il le Bas-Canada? *Québec.* 1851. pp. 46. 10646

Other anonymous works relating to Canada will be found under the first word of the title-page.

CANAJOHARIE. Fourth Annual Report of the Directors of the Central Asylum for the Instruction of the Deaf and Dumb. *Albany.* 1828. 8vo, pp. 30. 10647

Canal interoceanic par l'isthme de Darien, Nouvelle Grenade (Amérique du Sud) Canalisation par le Colonisation. *Paris: France.* 1860. 8vo, pp. 203. 6 Plates. 10648

CANALE (M. G.) Vita e viaggi di Cristoforo Colombo. *Firenze.* 1863. 8vo. 10649

CANALS (T.) Tratado domestico de algunas enfermedades bastante comunes en esta capital, escrito por D. Tomas Canals ... . *Lima: imp. real del Telegrafo peruano.* [1800.] 4to.

CANANDAIGUA ACADEMY. Catalogue, 1858. *Canandaigua.* 1858. 8vo. S. 10651

CANCELADA (*D.* Juan Lopez). Ruina de la Nueva España si se declara el comercio libre con los extrangeros. Exprésanse los motivos. Quaderno segundo, y primero en la materia. *Cadiz: D. Manuel Quintana.* 1811. 4to, pp. 84. 10652

CANCELADA. Conducta del excelentisimo señor D. Jose Iturrigaray durante su gobierno en Nueva-España. Se contesta a la vindicacion que ha publicó D. Facundo Lizarza. Cuaderno y segundo tercero en la materia: Por Don Juan Lopez Cancelado ... . *Cádiz: Imprenta del espanol-mayor-general.* 1812. 4to, 2 l., pp. 135. BA. 10653

CANCELADA. La Verdad Sabida y Buena Fé Guardada Orígen de la Espantosa Revoluccion de Nueva España comenzada, en 15 de Sept. de 1810. *Cádiz.* 1811. 10654

CANCELADA. Vida de J. J. Desalines, gefe de los negros de Santo Domingo; con notas muy circumstanciadas sobre el origen, caracter y atrocidades de los principales gefes de aquellos rebeldes desde el principio de la insurreccion en 1791. Traducida del frances por D. M. G. C. Año de 1805, reimprimese por J. L. Cancelada. *México: Mar. de Zuñigay Ontiveros.* 1806. 4to, 1 l., pp. 106. Portrait. 10655

CANCELLIERI (F.) Dissertazioni epistolari bibliografiche di Francesco Cancellieri sopra Cristoforo Colombo di Cvccaro nel Monferrato discopritore dell' America e Giovanni Gersen ... al ... cavaliere Gianfrancesco Galeani Napione. *Roma: Francesco Bovrliè.* MDCCCIX. 8vo, pp. xi, 415. H. 10656

"Dissertation savante et fort curieuse."—LECLERC. There are also special titles for the two dissertations; the first reads "Notizie storiche e bibliografiche di Christoforo Colombo ... . *Roma* ... ." The dissertation on Columbus ends at p. 282.

Candid and Impartial Considerations on the Preliminary Articles of Peace with France and Spain, and the Provisional Treaty with the United States of America. By a Country Gentleman. *London: J. Robson.* M DCC LXXXIII. 8vo, Title, pp. 53. BA., H.

See M. R., LXVIII. 179.

Candid and Impartial Considerations. *See* [Campbell (John)], Vol. III., No. 10231.

A Candid and Impartial Narrative of the Transactions of the Fleet, under the Command of Lord Howe, from the Arrival of the Toulon Squadron, on the Coast of America, to the Time of his Lordship's Departure for England, with Observations. By an Officer then serving in the Fleet. *London: J. Almon.* 1779. 8vo, pp. 44. + The Second Edition, Revised and Corrected, with a Plan of the Situation of the Fleet, within Sandy-Hook. *London: J. Almon.* [1779.] 8vo, pp. 58. Plan. 10658

Praises Lord Howe and abuses the ministry, particularly Lord Sandwich. *See* M. R., LX. 70.

Candid Animadversions. By Vindex. *See* [Ellison (Patrick)].

A Candid Appeal to the Present Ruling Party of the United States. *Alexandria.* 1816. 8vo. P. 10659

Candid Considerations on Libels. By a Friend to Harmony. *Boston.* 1789. 12mo. W. 10660

A Candid Defence of Administration, against the Ill founded Charges of Opposition. *London: J. Wilkie.* 1781. 8vo.

Partly relates to the American Revolution. *See* M. R., LXVI. 142.

A Candid Examination of the Address of the Ministry of the Council of Censors. *Philadelphia.* 1784. 12mo. 10662

Candid Examination of the Mutual Claims of Great Britain. *See* [Galloway (J.)]

A Candid Examination of the Objections to the Treaty of Amity, Commerce, and Navigation, between the United States and Great Britain, as stated in the Report of the Committee, appointed by the Citizens of the United States, in Charleston, South-Carolina. By a Citizen of South-Carolina. ... *Charleston: Printed by W. P. Young, ... July* 31, 1795. 8vo, pp. 42. + *New-York: Re-printed for James Rivington.* 1795. 8vo, pp. 42. H. + With sundry Resolutions and Proceedings in Cases before the Board of Commissioners for carrying into effect the Sixth Article, &c. *Philadelphia.* 1799. 4to. 10663

Candid Observations. *See* Barbadoes, Vol. I., No. 3262.

Candid Reflections upon the Judgment, lately awarded by the Court of King's Bench, in Westminster-Hall, on what is called the Negro Cause. By a Planter. *London: Lowndes.* 1772, 8vo. 10664

See M. R., XLVII. 152.

Candid Remarks addressed to Christians on the Subject of their having Concern in Lotteries. *Boston.* [n. d.] 8vo. W.

The Candid Retrospect; or, The American War examined, by Whig Principles. *Charlestown printed, New-York re-printed.* MDCCLXXX. Sm. 8vo, pp. 28. BA., C., H. 10666

Candid Thoughts; or, an Enquiry into the Causes of National Discontents and Misfortunes since the Commencement of the Present Reign. *London: W. Nichol.* 1781. 8vo, pp. 73. S.

Candide Anglois ou avantures tragi-comiques d'Amb. Gwinett avant et dans ses voyages aux deux Indes. *Frankfort.* 1771. 2 vols., 12mo. 10668

CANDIDO (Franc. de Paula). Relatorio ácerca da saude publica. *Rio de Janeiro.* 1856. 8vo, pp. 85, 1 l., 9 Tables.

CANDIDO (J.) Rozas e goivos. Poezias de Joao Candido. *Pernambuco.* 1866. 4to, pp. 62. 10670

CANDIDUS, *pseudon.* Plain Truth; Addressed to the Inhabitants of America, Containing, Remarks on a late Pamphlet entitled Common Sense: Wherein are shewn, that the Scheme of Independence is Ruinous, Delusive and Impracticable: That were the Author's Asseverations, respecting the Power of America, as Real as Nugatory; Reconciliation on liberal Principles with Great Britain, would be exalted Policy: And that circumstanced as we are, Permanent Liberty, and True Happiness, can only be obtained by Reconcilliation with that Kingdom. Written by Candidus. ... *Philadelphia: R. Bell.* MDCCLXXVI. 8vo, pp. 74. H. + *London: Reprinted for J. Almon.* M.DCC.LXXVI. 8vo, pp. (4), 47, (1). + *Dublin: Reprinted by M. Mills.* M,DCC,LXXVI. 8vo, 2 l., pp. 44. N. 10671

"It is written with such outrageous zeal, and contains so many scurrilous reflections against the author of 'Common Sense' and the supposed favorers of independency, that we may safely conclude, from its having been printed in Philadelphia, that the congress either do not aim at a separation from this country, or that their government is not of the tyrannical nature which some have chosen to represent it."—M. R., LIV. 502. Dr. Parr says that this tract produced a wonderful effect throughout America and England.

CANDISH (Th.) *See* Cavendish (T.)

[CANDLER (Isaac).] A Summary View of America: comprising a Description of the Face of the Country, and of several of the Principal Cities; and Remarks on the Social, Moral and Political Character of the People: being the Result of Observations and Enquiries during a Journey in the United States. By an Englishman. *London: T. Cadell. Edinburgh: W. Blackwood.* 1824. 8vo, pp. viii, 503. H. 10672

See "Blackwood's Mag.," XVI. 617, and N. A. R., XXI. 453.

CANDLER (J.) Brief Notices of Hayti: with its Condition, Resources, and Prospects. By John Candler. *London: Thomas Ward & Co.; and Charles Gilpin & Co.* 1842. 12mo, pp. viii, 175. B. 10673

CANDLER. Extracts from the Journal of John Candler, whilst travelling in Jamaica. Parts 1 and 2. *London: Harvey and Darton.* 1840–41. 8vo, 6 sheets. P. 10674

CANDLER *and* BURGESS (W.) Narrative of a Recent Visit to Brazil, by John Candler and Wilson Burgess: to present an Address on the Slave Trade and Slavery, issued by the Religious Society of Friends. *London: Edward Marsh.* 1853. 8vo, 5¾ sheets. P. 10675

CANDLER (Maria) *and* ALEXANDER (Catharine). Extracts of Letters lately received from the West Indies, in regard to Education and the Cholera. [n. p. 1851.] Folio. 1 sheet.

[CAÑEDO (E.)] De la revolution au Mexique Mars 1860 [Signed Estanislao Cañedo.] *Nouvelle Orleans: L. Marchand, Imprimeur.* [n. d.] 8vo, pp. 43. H. 10677

CANEDO. La verité sur la révolution actuelle au Mexique. Par Estanislao Canedo. *Paris: impr. Guyon et Scribe.* 1860. 8vo, pp. 47. 10678

CAÑEDO (Juan de Dios). Manifesto á la Nacion Española sobre la Representacion de la Provincias de Ultimar en las proximas Córtes. *Madrid.* 1820. 4to. 10679

CANELAS (Ramon). Apelacion a S. A. la regencia del reyno; y quexas contra excmo. señor D. Juan Ruiz de Apodaco, y otros individuos. [Colophon:] *Habana: Oficina de la Cena.* 1813. 4to, pp. 107, 2 l. 10680

[CANER (H.)] A Candid Examination of Dr. Mayhew's Observations on the Charter and Conduct of the Society for the propagation of the Gospel in foreign parts. Interspers'd with a few brief reflections upon some other of the Doctor's Writings. To which is added, A Letter to a Friend, Containing a short Vindication of the said Society against the Mistakes and Misrepresentations of the Doctor in his Observations on the Conduct of that Society. By one of its Members [Samuel Johnson, D.D.]. ... *Boston, New-England: Thomas and John Fleet, and Green & Russell, and Edes & Gill.* 1763. 8vo, 2 l., pp. 93. H.

CANER. The Great Blessing of Stable Times ... . A Sermon preached ... in Boston, August 11. 1763. Being a Day of Thanksgiving ... on Occasion of the General Peace. By Henry Caner, M.A. ... *Boston: Thomas and John Fleet.* MDCCLXIII. 4to, Title, pp. vi, 24. BA. 10682

CANER. The Piety of Founding Churches for the Worship of God: Being a Discourse ... Preach'd at King's-Chapel in Boston, August 11. 1749. Upon Occasion of laying the First Stone for re-building and enlarging the said Chapel. By Henry Caner ... . *Boston, New-England: J. Draper.* 1749. 8vo, 3 l., pp. 18. H., W. 10683

CANER. True Nature and Method of Christian Preaching examined and stated. Sermon at Newport, R. I. June 12, 1745. *Newport: Printed by the Widow Franklin at the Town School House.* 1745. 12mo, pp. 40. W. 10684

Also: ... Discourse ... May 22d, 1751, Upon the Death of Frederick Prince of Wales &c. By Henry Caner ... . *Boston.* 1751. 8vo, Half-Title, pp. 20. N. — ... A Sermon ... January 1, 1761. Upon ... the Death of ... George the Second. *Boston.* [1761.] pp. 31. — ... A Sermon ... November 21st. 1758. Upon the Death of Charles Apthorp, Esq; *Boston, New-England: Printed by John Draper.* [1758.] 8vo, pp. 24. H. — ... Sermon August 20. 1765. At the Funeral of the Rev. Timothy Cutler, D.D. ... *Boston.* MDCCLXV. 4to, 2 l., pp. iv, 24. M.

CANFIELD (S. B.) The American Crisis; a Discourse delivered on the Day of National Thanksgiving, November 24th, 1864, by Sherman B. Canfield, D.D., ... *Syracuse: Journal Office.* 1865. 8vo, pp. 32. 10685

CANIZARES (Josef). El Pleyto de Hernan Cortez. 10686

A comedy on the conquest of Mexico. *See* Ternaux-Compans, No. 443.

CANNABICH (Johann Günther Friedrich). Hülfsbuch beim Unterrichte in der Geographie für Lehrer ... . *Eisleben: Reich-*

ardt jetzt Hermes in Berlin. 1833–38. 33 pts., 8vo. + Zweiter verbesserte Auflage. [*Ibid.*] 1840. 3 vols., 8vo. 10687

"Dritter Band. Amerika und Australien." Imprint taken from Kayser.—Cannabich's "Lehrbuch der Geographie," "Schulgeographie," etc., of course, treat of America.

CANNE (Abednego). A New Windmill. *Oxford.* 1643.

On page 1, the author refers to his brethren in New England.

Cannelton, Perry County, Ind., at the Intersection of the Eastern Margin of the Illinois Coal Basin, by the Ohio River; its Natural Advantages as a Site for Manufacturing. Published by the American Cannel Coal Company. *Louisville.* 1850. 8vo, pp. 108. BA., H. 10689

CANNER (T.) Scheeps-togt van M. Pringe gedaan in't jaar 1603, van Bristol na't noorder gedeelte van Virginien. Mitsgarders een tweede reys in't selve jaar 1603 naar Virginien gedaan van B. Gilbert. Beschreven door Thomas Canner. Nu aldereerst uyt het Engelsch vertaald. *Leyden.* 1606. 8vo.

Forms Vol. 84 of Van der Aa's "Naaukeurige versameling."

[CANNING (George).] A Letter to the Right Honourable Wills Earl of Hillsborough, on the Connection between Great Britain and her American Colonies. ... *London: T. Becket and J. Almon.* MDCCLXVIII. 8vo, pp. 47. BA. + *Dublin: Elizabeth Lynch.* 1768. 8vo, pp. 40. 10691

CANNING (*Hon.* G.) Speech of the Right Hon. G. Canning on a Resolution Declaratory of Slavery being Contrary to the Constitution. *London.* 1823. 8vo, pp. 38. 10692

CANNING. Speech of the Rt. Hon. George Canning ... on the 16th Day of March, 1824, on ... the "Papers in Explanation of Measures adopted for the Amelioration of the Condition of the Slave Population in the ... West Indies." *London: John Murray.* MDCCCXXIV. 8vo, Title, pp. 44. BA. + To which is added An Order in Council for Improving the Condition of Slaves in Trinidad. ... *London: Lupton Reeve, and Hatchard and Son.* 1834. 8vo, pp. 78. BA., C. 10693

Also: Speech upon a Motion, for the Early Consideration of Measures, &c., touching Slaves. *London.* 1826. 8vo, pp. 16.

[CANNING (Josiah D.)] The Harp and the Plow. By the "Peasant Bard." Sing of New-England, favored land! ... *Greenfield: M. H. Tyler.* 1852. 12mo. pp. 204. H. 10694

CANNING (Josiah W.) Sermon at Williamstown, Mass. Feb. 20, 1830, at the Funeral of Elisha M. Chase. *Williamstown.* 1831. 8vo. W. 10695

CANNON (A.) Case of Passmore Williamson. Report of the Proceedings on the Writ of Habeas Corpus, issued by Hon. John K. Kane ... in the Case of the United States ex rel. John H. Wheeler vs. Passmore Williamson, including the several Opinions delivered; and The Arguments of Counsel, Reported by Arthur Cannon, Esqr., Phonographer. *Philadelphia: Uriah Hunt & Son.* 1856. 8vo, pp. 196. B. 10696

This case caused much excitement at the time. Williamson aided in the escape of some fugitive slaves.

CANNON (John). History of Grant's Campaign for the Capture of Richmond, 1864–1865; with an Outline of the Previous Course of the American Civil War. *London: Longmans.* 1869. Post 8vo, pp. 474. 10697

CANNON (J. S.) Lectures on History and Chronology. By J. S. Cannon, D.D. *New Brunswick.* 1830. 8vo. 10698

CANNON (R.) ... Historical Records of the British Army, comprising the History of every regiment in Her Majesty's Service. By Richard Cannon, Esq., Adjutant General, Office Horse Guards. London. Printed by authority. [*London.* 1834.] etc. 8vo, over 70 vols. C., S. 10699

This is the general engraved title-page, without date. Each volume, after several preliminary pages, has a title for each regiment, and date. The later volumes are not by Cannon. This comprehensive work contains full details of the regiments that served in America during the Revolution, and the War of 1812.

CANNON (W.) Inaugural Address as Governor of Delaware. *Wilmington.* 1863. 8vo. C. 10700

The Cannonade. *See* [Clarke (W. A.)]

CANO Y OLMEDILLA (J. de la C.) Mapa Geografico de America Meridional, dispuesto y gravado por D. Juan de la Cruz Cano y Olmedilla, teniendo presente varios mapas y noticias originales, &c. Año de 1775. *Londres: Faden.* 1799. 6 sheets.

A copy of the map published at Madrid in 1775.

CANO (Juan Sebastian del). *See* Byron (John), No. 9733.

CANOT (*Captain*). *See* Mayer (Brantz).

CANOVAI (S.) Difensa d'Amerigo Vespuccio. *Firenze.* 1796. 12mo, pp. 15. 10702

CANOVAI. Dissertazione sopra il primo viaggio d'Amerigo Vespucci alle Indie Occidentali. *Firenze.* 1809. 8vo. 10703

CANOVAI. Elogio d'Amerigo Vespucci che ha riportato il premio dalla nobile Accademia etrusca di Cortona ... con una dissertazione giustificativa di questo celebre navigatore del P. Stanislas Canovai. ... *Firenze.* 1788. 4to, pp. viii, 80. BA., H. + Seconda edizione. Con Illustrazioni ed Aggiunte. [*Cortona.*] 1789. 8vo. + Terza editione. [n. p.] 1790. 4to. + Quarta edizione. *Firenze: Giovacchino Pagani.* 1798. 8vo, pp. 196, 15. Portrait. H. 10704

See Napione, also, "Biog. des Contemp.," also "Biog. Universelle," and Faribault, No. 105.

CANOVAI. Esame Critico del primo viaggio d'Amerigo Vespucci al Nuovo Mondo. *Firenze.* 1811. 10705

"Ou voit que le P. Canovai eut à cœur ce sujet intéressant jusqu'à la fin de sa vie, puisqu'il publia ce dernier écrit peu de temps avant sa mort," [arrivée le 17e Novembre 1811].—*Biog. Univ.*

CANOVAI. Lettera allo Stampat. Sig. P. Allegrini, a nome dell' autore dell' elogio prem. di Am. Vespucci. *Firenze.* 1789. 8vo. 10706

CANOVAI. Monumenti relativi al giudizo pronunziato dall' Accademia Etrusca di Cortona di un Elogio d'Amerigo Vespucci. *Firenze.* 1787. 8vo. 10707

CANOVAI. Viaggi d'Amerigo Vespucci con la vita, l'elogio e la dissertazione giustificativa di questo celebre navigatore, del Padre Stanislao Canovai ... Opera postuma *Firenze: Giovacchino Pagani.* 1817. 8vo, 2 l., pp. 392. Plate. BA., C., H. + Firenze. 1832. 4 vols., 12mo. 10708

"It is hardly possible to understand how the calumnies against Amerigo, which have so long been taught in every school, could have, for many years, survived this excellent refutation."

CANTABRANA (Emanuele). Guatemalensis Ecclesiae in Optimi sui Parentis Orbitate Lugubris Lamentatio: Sive Oratio habita in Metropolitano Templo Guatemalensi in Funere Illmi D. Francisci Figueredo, ejusdem Ecclesiæ Archipræsulis. *Mexici.* 1766. 4to. 10709

CANTERBURY (*Dean of*). *See* [Lynch (*Dr.*)]

[CANTO (Francisco del).] Arte, y Vocabulario|en la lengua| general del Perv|llamada Quichua, y en la|lengua Española. |El mas copiosa y ele-|gante que hasta agora se ha impresso.| [Vignette.] En los Reyes.|Con Licencia del Excellentissimo Señor Marques de|Montes Claros Virrey del Peru. Por Francisco del Canto.|*Año de* M.DC.XIIII. 16mo, 209 leaves. 10710

A volume of extreme rarity. Ternaux, No. 367, Brunet, No. 1553, and Bartlett "Catalogue of J. C. Brown's Library," all attribute this work to Francisco del Canto, who signs the dedication, and may have been the author, but Troemel regards the work as anonymous. *See* San Thomas. Heber's copy sold for £3 10s. Priced, in Troemel, No. 68, at 25 thalers.

Canto a la Compana del Ejercito Chileno Libertador del Peru en 1838 y principios de 1839. *Santiago.* 1839. 4to, pp. 20.

Canto à Cortés en Ulúa. G. ... de Aguilar. *Mexico: Imprenta de Arizpe.* 1808. 4to, 23 l. 10712

"Poëme en octaves, en l'honneur de Fernand Cortez. L'éditeur de cette pièce (qui en est probablement l'auteur) annonce dans son avertissement qu'un de ses parents, habitant l'Andalousie, a trouvé ce poëme dans les archives de sa famille et qu'il le lui envoie pour qu'il le fasse imprimer à Mexico." — LECLERC.

Canto patriótico al Ciudadano Esclarecido J[osé] A[ntonio] P[aez]. *Carácas.* 1858. 12mo, pp. 24. Portrait. 10713

CANTON, *Mass.* Annual Report of the School Committee of Canton. ... April 7, 1845. [*Dedham.* 1845.] 8vo, pp. 6. Continued. H. 10714

The Taxable Valuation of the Polls and Estates, and Amount of Tax, in the Town of Canton. 1856. *Canton.* 1856. 8vo, pp. 46. M. 10715

Charter and By-Laws of the Canton Run Improvement Company, and a Report of William H. Marshall, Esq., on their Coal Lands ... . *Philadelphia.* 1852. 8vo, pp. 34, (1). 2 Maps. H. 10716

Prospectus of the Canton Company, and some views of the Local Advantages of Baltimore. *Baltimore.* 1829. 8vo, pp. 35.

CANTÙ (Cesare). Vite parallele di Mirabeau e Washington. *Milano: tip. Corona e Caimi.* 1868. 8vo, pp. 314. 10718

Of course Cantù's "Storia universale ... . *Torino: Guiseppe Pomba.* 1838–46." 18 vols., 8vo, with 17 additional vols. on special subjects (BA.), treats more or less of America. The vol. "Biografie," 1845, contains a sketch of Beniamino Franklin, pp. 449–462, and a life of Washington, signed Guizot, 463–522.

CANTWELL (Edward). Benjamin Franklin. *Oxford, N. C.: Published by the Franklin Society.* 1867. 8vo, pp. 31. 10719

CANVANE (P.) Dissertation on the Oleum Palmæ Christi, or Ricinus Americanus, by Peter Canvane, M.D. 8vo. Plate.

CAPACCIO (Giulio Cesare). Oratio in Obitum Philippi II, Hispaniarum Regis Catholici ad Philippum III. *Neapoli.* 1599. 4to. 10721

"Very rare. It contains some mention of America." — LIBRI.

CAPADOSE. Sixteen Years in the West Indies. By Lieut. Col. Capadose. *London: T. C. Newby.* 1845. 2 vols., post 8vo. 10722

"An agreeable pendant to Coleridge's six months." — *N. & M. Gazette.*

CAPE BRETON. Accurate and Authentic Account of the taking of Cape Breton, in the Year 1745. Together with a Computation of the French Fishery in that part of the World; both sent over by Gen. Pepperell, who commanded in that expedition, in a letter to his friend Captain Henry Stafford, &c. From whence will appear the importance of that Island, and the danger we shall be in of losing our superiority at sea, should it now be restored to France. *London: Staples.* 1758. 8vo. 10723

"Probably the same as the 'Accurate Journal,' &c., printed at *Exeter.* 1747." *See* [Pepperell (W.)], and M. R., XIX. 499.

An Accurate Description of Cape Breton. *London.* 1755. 8vo. 10724

See "Gentleman's Magazine" for 1755.

Accurate Journal, 1746. *See* [Pepperell (W.)]

Beschryving van Kaap Breton, waar agter het vredes traktaat in 1713 te Utrecht gesloten. *'s Hage: P. van Os.* 1753. 4to.

Beschryving van de Kaap-Breton, behelzende de importantie en voordeeligheid van dat beruchte Eiland, voor af gaan tydrekenkundige verhaalen der vornaamste ontdekkingen en wingewesten, sedert den eerste ontdekten Columbus, tot het begin der Volkplantingen, door de Engelschen in Nieuw Georgia, en door de Franschen in Noord America gevestigt. *'s Gravenhage.* 1756. 8vo. 2 Maps. 10726

Beschryving van kaap Breton. *Amsterdam: J. Roos.* 8vo.

Beschryving van de importantie en voordeeligheit van kaap Breton. *Deft: R. Boitet.* 1717. 8vo. 10728

The date 1717 is that given by Abkoude; it is a misprint for 1747, if this is a translation of Bollan. *See* Vol. II., Nos. 6214 and 6215.

Description of the Island of Cape Breton; an Account of its Constitution, &c., the Encouragement held out to Emigrants, the Expense of improving Wild Lands, &c. *London.* [n. d.] 8vo, pp. 44. CP. 10729

Genuine Letters and Memoirs. *See* [Pichon (Thos.)]

The Great Importance of Cape-Breton, demonstrated and exemplified by Extracts from the Best Writers French and English who have treated of that Colony. *London.* 1746. 8vo.

The Importance and Advantage of Cape Breton. *See* [Bollan (W.)], Vol. II., No. 6215.

The Importance of Cape Breton consider'd; in a Letter to a Member of Parliament, From an Inhabitant of New-England. *London: R. Dodsley and M. Cooper.* MDCCXLVII. 8vo, Title, pp. 73. H., W. 10731

An entirely different piece from "The Importance and Advantage, etc. 1746," by [Bollan (Wm.)] *See* Vol. II., No. 6215.

Lettres et Memoirs. *See* [Pichon (Thos.)]

Remarks upon a Letter Published in the London Chronicle, or Universal Evening Post, N° 115. Containing an Enquiry into the Causes of the Failure of the late Expedition against Cape Breton. In a Letter to a Member of Parliament. *London: M. Cooper.* M DCC LVII. 8vo, pp. 30. C., H. 10732

Two Letters, concerning some Farther Advantages and Improvements that may seem Necessary to be made on the Taking and Keeping of Cape Breton. *London: Printed in the Year* 1746. Sm. 8vo, pp. 12. J.C.B. 10733

Die Wichtigkeit und Vortheil des Kap-Breton. *See* [Bollan Wm.)], Vol. II., No. 6217.

The Cape Cod Centennial Celebration at Barnstable, Sept. 3, 1839, of the Incorporation of that Town, Sept. 3, 1639. Giving a Full Detail of the Preliminary Proceedings of the Committees, and the Speeches and Toasts at the Dinner. ... *Barnstable: S. B. Phinney.* 1840. 8vo, pp. 92. H. + Second Edition. *Boston.* 1840. 8vo, pp. 71. 10734

Also: Constitution of the Cape Cod Association, with an Account of the Celebration of its First Anniversary, at Boston, November 11, 1851. *Boston.* 1852. 8vo, pp. 80. H. — Programme of the Celebration of the Cape Cod Association at Provincetown ... August 11th, 1852. *Boston.* 1852. 8vo, pp. 7. H. — ... Report of the Commissioners on Cape Cod and East Harbors ... . [*Boston.* 1854.] 8vo, pp. 45. (Mass. Senate Doc., No. 5.) H. — Report on ... Cape Cod Harbor. *Boston.* 1827. 8vo, pp. 28. — Report on the Subject of the Ship Canal Across Cape Cod.

[CAPEL (D.)] Vorstellungen des Norden, oder Bericht von einigen Nordländern und absonderlich von dem so genandten Grünlande aus Schreibern, welche zu unterschiedenen Zeiten gelebet ... zusammen gezogen und endlich zu mehren aus D. Capel P. P. Bibliothec auszgefertiget. *Hamburg: Joh. Nauman und Georg. Wolff.* 1675. 4to, 2 l., pp. 212. J.C.B. 10735

A scarce and curious volume on the possibility of reaching the East Indies by a north passage, on the discoveries of the Dutch in 1594, 1595, 1596, and 1609, on the westward attempts of Captains Winwood and Hudson on the American side, and on the descriptions of Greenland by the Zeni, Captain D. Blefkens, Prince Zichmni (in 1379), H. Megiser, and G. N. Schurtz.

CAPEL (Rudolf). Norden, oder zu Wasser und Lande im Eise und Snee, mit verlust Blutes und Gutes, zu Wege gebrachte, und fleissig beschriebene Erfahrung und Vorstellung des Norden, ... *Hamburg und Stockholm: Johan. Naumann.* 1678. 25 l., pp. 236, Register, 24. Map. J.C.B. 10736

CAPELLAN (Robert Jasper van der). Gedenkschriften van Jonkhr. Alexander van der Capellen, beginnende met den jare 1621 en gaande tot 1632; bij een gezameld en uitgegeven door Jonkhr. R. J. van der Capellen. *Utrecht.* 1777. 2 vols., 8vo.

Relates to Brazil. *See* Netscher, XXIII.

CAPELLINI (Giovanni). Ricordi di un viaggio scientifico nell' America Settentrionale, nel 1863. *Bologna.* 1867. 8vo, pp. xii, 279. Illustrations. 10738

Reviewed by J. G. Kohl in the "Gött. gel. Anz.," 1868.

CAPE MAY. Report of the Joint Committee, to whom was referred that part of the Governor's Message, on the Subject of the Delaware Breakwater at Cape May. February, 1844. *Trenton: Franklin S. Mills.* 1844. 8vo, pp. 11. 10739

CAPEN (J.) A Funeral Sermon occasioned by the Death of Rev. Joseph Green. By Joseph Capen. Preface by Increase Mather. *Boston.* 1717. 8vo, pp. 46. 10740

CAPEN (L.) A Discourse on the Character of Mr. John Hawes, preached ... at S. Boston, February 1, 1829 ... . *Boston: Leonard C. Bowles.* 1832. 8vo, pp. 24. B. 10741

CAPEN. A Farewell Address ... . Second Edition. ... With Documents containing the Reason of his Dismission. *Boston: printed by J. T. Buckingham. October,* 1819. 8vo, pp. 24. BA.

CAPEN. An Exposition of Facts relative to the Administration of the Hawes Charity, at South Boston. By Lemuel Capen, Former Minister of the Hawes Place Society. *Boston: Andrews, Prentiss, & Studley.* 1844. 8vo, pp. 24, (1). 10743

This was answered by the following: The Reply of the Hawes-Place Congregational Society, at South Boston, to a Pamphlet, entitled "An Exposition, &c., by Lemuel Capen." *Boston.* 1844. 8vo, pp. 26. Also: The Memorial of the Proprietors of the New South Meeting-House in Dorchester, to the Ministers of the Boston Association. Together with their Report on the same. [By Lemuel Capen.] *Boston: Watson & Bangs.* 1813. 8vo, pp. 48. B. — Notices of the Late Rev. Peter Whitney, of Quincy, Mass. [n. p. 1843?] 8vo, pp. 6. H. — Tribute of the Affection to John Roulstone, Jr. a Member of the Freshman Class in Harvard University; who died February 20, 1822. Æt. 17. *Boston: printed by John Cotton, Jr.* [n. d.] 12mo, pp. 12. H.

CAPEN (Nahum). Correspondence respecting Postal Improvements and the Removal of the Boston Post Office. [*Boston.* 1858.] 8vo, pp. 3. H. 10744

[CAPEN.] The History of Democracy in the United States of America. ... *Boston.* 1852–53? 8vo. 10745

CAPEN. The Indissoluble Nature of the American Union, considered in connection with the Assumed Right of Secession. A Letter to Hon. Peter Cooper, of New York. By Nahum Capen. *Boston: A. Williams & Company.* 1862. 8vo, pp. 36.

CAPEN. The Massachusetts State Record and Year Book of General Information. [Vol. I.] || .. Edited by Nahum Capen. Volume II–IV. || ... Record, New England Register, and Year Book ... . Volume V. *Boston: James French.* 1847–51. 12mo.

Also: Letter addressed to the Hon. John Davis, concerning the Census of 1849 [1850]. *Washington.* 1849. 8vo, pp. 23. H. — Letter to the Rev. Nathaniel Hall, of Dorchester, Mass., by Nahum Capen, concerning Politics and the Pulpit. *Boston and Cambridge: Jas. Munroe* [illegible]. 1855. 4to, Title, pp. 4. BA., H. — ... Memorial of Nahum Capen ... on the Subject of International Copyright. [*Washington.* 1844.] 8vo, pp. 12. (29th Cong. 1st Sess Reps. Doc. 61.) + *Re-published by Request.* [*Boston?* n. d.] 8vo, Title, pp. 12. H.

CAPERS (G.) Eulogy on the Life and Public Services of the Hon. Henry Clay, delivered at Milton, Florida, On the 16th of August, 1852, by Rev. G. Capers. *Mobile: Dade, Thompson & Co., Printers.* 1852. 8vo, pp. 12. H. 10748

CAPERS (William). Sermon on the Occasion of the Lamented Death of the Rev. Joseph Galluchat. *Charleston.* 1825. 8vo.

CAP-FRANÇAIS. Adresse de la jeunesse de Cap-Français, île Saint-Domingue, à M. le marquis de Condorcet, surnommé le

grand-prêtre Jean, apôtre, député de l'Abyssinie. [Signed Les 4000 J. G. du Cap de la secte d'Emmanuel. 2 janvier 1790. n. p. n. d.] 8vo, pp. 48 or less. 10750

Adresse des capitaines, officiers, officiers-mariners et matelots des bâtiments du commerce mouillés en rade du Cap-Français, aux équipages des vaisseaux *le Fougueux*, *le Borée* et la frégate *l'Uranie*, et autres bâtiments de guerre composant la station des îles sous le vent. [10 mars 1791. n. p. n. d.] 8vo, pp. 48 or less. 10751

Copie d'une lettre d'un capitaine présentement au Cap-Français, venue par le navire *le Cap-Francais*, arrivée à Nantes en trente-huit jours, le 15 novembre 1791; adressée à Paris, à M. W. [*Paris:*] *imp. du Patriote français.* [n. d.] 8vo, pp. 48 or less. 10752

Courrier politique et littéraire du Cap-Français, publié par M. Gatereau. 6 jan.–14 juillet 1791. 2 vols., 8vo. 10753

Le défenseur des colonies, par Nodier, J. C. Royou, Laignel Senancourt, [etc.] 1819–20. 13 nos., 12mo. 10754

At No. 3 takes the title of "Observateur des colonies." — HATIN.

Extrait d'une lettre sur les malheurs de Saint-Domingue en général, et principalement sur l'incendie de la ville du Cap-Français. [Lorient, 22 brumaire an II.] *Paris: au jardin Égalité. An* II. 8vo, pp. 48 or less. + [Another Edition. *Ibid.*]

Les "j'ai vu" d'un habitant du Cap. Nouvelle édition, augmentée par-ci, corrigée par-là, et le tout pour le mieux. [n. p. n. d.] 4to, pp. 48 or less. + [n. p.] 1790. 8vo, pp. 48 or less. 10756

CAPINÉ (Louis de). Aanhangsel Behelzende een Reyze na een Gedeelte van de Spaansche West-Indien, Benevens een Beschrijving van de Expeditie der Franschen op Cartagena ... in den Jaare 1607. [n. p. n. d.] 4to, pp. 47. Map and Plate.

Capital Punishment. Essays from Poulson's [Philadelphia] Daily Advertiser. *Philadelphia.* 1811. 16mo. C. 10758

Capitvlaciones de el Assiento qve con la Magestad de el Rey D. Felipe IV. hizo D. Diego de Vera ... y con el Real Consejo de las Indias, por su Real decreto, para la conquista ó pacificacion, conuersion y poblacion de la prouincia de el Prospero, (alias el Nacandon y de los demas indios de guerra,) que indomitos

auitan los Lacandones, los Taicaes, Tirumpies, Concaches, y otras naciones barbaras, que ocupen cien leguas de tierra, (Norte Sur) de longitud, y ochenta de latitúd, (Leste, Oeste,) en la Nueva-España. *Año* 1639. Folio, 6 l. 10759

"Pièce probablement unique." — ANDRADE.

CAPPE (N.) A Sermon preached December 13th, 1776, being the Day appointed for a Public Fast, on Account of the Troubles in America, to a Congregation of Protestant-Dissenters, in Saint-Saviour-Gate, York, ... By Newcome Cappe. *London: Johnson.* 1777. 8vo. 10760

See M. R., LVI. 75.

CAPPER (G.) Sermon preached after the Funeral of Rev. G. Cooper. *Ipswich.* 1847. 8vo. B. 10761

CAPPER (H.) Emigration Colonies. *London.* 1850. 10762

[CAPPER (Joseph).] Negro's Friend. [n. p. n. d.] 12mo, pp. 12. 10763

CAPRON (E. S.) History of California, from its Discovery to the Present Time; comprising also a Full Description of its Climate, Surface, Soil, Rivers, Towns, Beasts, Birds, Fishes, State of its Society, Agriculture, Commerce, Mines, Mining, &c. with a Journal of the Voyage from New York, via Nicaragua, to San Francisco, and back, via Panama. With a New Map of the Country. By E. S. Capron ... . *Boston: John P. Jewett & Company.* 1854. 12mo, pp. xi, 356. Map. BA., C.

[CAPRON (Eliab W.) *and* BARRON (Henry (D.)] Singular Revelations. Explanation and History of the Mysterious Communion with Spirits, comprehending the Rise and Progress of the Mysterious Noises in Western New York, generally received as Spiritual Communciations. *Auburn, N. Y.* 1850. 8vo, pp. 81. H. + Second Edition, revised and enlarged, with additional proof. *Auburn, N. Y.* 1850. pp. 84. 10765

Also: Modern Spiritualism ... . By E. W. Capron. *Boston.* 1855. 12mo.

CAPSE (Charles François de). Copy of the Letter of The Bishop of Capsa, Coadjutor of Quebec, &c. to The President of the Committee on Education. ... [In English and French. Dated 5th April, 1790. n. p. n. d.] 4to, pp. 10. BA. 10766

In the title the name is Capsa, in the signature, Capse.

Captain Clutterbuck's Champagne. *See* [Scott (Michael)].

The Captives of Abb's Valley. A Legend of Frontier Life. By a Son of Mary Moore. *Philadelphia.* [1854.] 18mo, pp. 169. 10767

CARACAS. *See also* Venezuela.

Actos legislativos vigentes en el Estado de Carabobo, con un apéndice que contiene varios actos del Gobierno Provisorio y del Poder Ejecutivo. *Valencia.* 1865. 4to, pp. 108. 10768

Almanaque para el año de 1867, arreglado al meridiano de Carácas. *Carácas.* 1866. 1 sheet. 10769

Almanaque portátil para el año de 1869 y guia de la Ciudad de Carácas. *Carácas.* 1868. Sm. 8vo, pp. 67. Plan. 10770

Apendice a las Reflexiones Historico Criticas sobre la Insurreccion De Caracas. 8vo, pp. 42. H. 10771

Asignaciones eclesiásticas. El Dean y Cabildo de Carácas sobre las Asignaciones eclesiastica [*sic*] y su cuento. *Carácas.* 1833. 4to, pp. 30, 48. 10772

Boletin de la Sociedad de Ciencias Fisicas y Naturales de Carácas. *Carácas.* 1868. 8vo. Maps, Views, and Meteorological Tables. Continued. 10773

Caja de Ahorros di Carácas. 1846. *Carácas.* 1846. 8vo, pp. xi, 72. 10774

Documentos interesantes relativos à Caracas. [Spanish and English.] *London.* 1812. 8vo. 10775

Estadistica general de la provincia de Caracas en 1855. *Caracas.* 1855. 8vo, pp. viii, 74. 10776

Junta general de la real compañia Guipuzcoana de Caracas del año de 1772. Compendio de sus acuerdos y deliberaciones, como del estado de esta real compania en sus cargas y fondos universales, en 31 de Dec. del proximo año anterior de 1771. *Madrid.* 1773. Sm. 4to, pp. 160. 10777

Memoria de los abonos, cultivo y beneficios que necesitan los diversos valles de la provincia de Carácas para la plantacion de café. Instruccion para el gobierno de las haciendas de Cacoo. *Carácas.* 1833. 4to, pp. 90. 10778

"This treatise is of the greatest rarity." — TRÜBNER.

Memoria que el administrador principal de rentas municipales de la provincia de Caracas, presenta a la H. diputacion provincial en su reunion de 1844. *Caracas: imp. por George Corser.* 1844. 8vo, pp. 22. 2 Tables, folded. H. 10779

Millon de Carácas. Resolucion de la H. diputacion provincial. *Caracas.* 1856. 8vo, pp. 12. 10780

Ordenanzas, resoluciones y acuerdas de la H. Diputacion provincial de Carácas, vigentes el 10 de Diciembre de 1853. *Carácas.* 1854. 8vo, pp. xv, 288, xiii. 10781

Real Compania Guipuzcoana de Caracas. Noticias Historiales practicas de los sucessos y adelantamientos de esta Compañia desde su fundacion año de 1728, hasta el de 1764, por todos los Romos, que comprehende su Negociacion. ... 1765. Sm. 4to. 10782

Recuerdos sobre la Rebelion de Caracas. *Madrid.* 1829. Sm. 4to. 10783

Reflexiones historico-Criticas sobre la Insurreccion de Caracas. Con un apendice. *Cadiz: imprenta de Carreño,* ... 1811. 8vo, pp. 34, 42. H. 10784

Reglamento de la Casa de misericordia establecida ... a virtud de la ordenanza de la H. diputacion provincial de 23 de Noviembre de 1842. *Caracas: impr. por George Corser.* 1845. 8vo, pp. 30. 10785

Reglamento interior y de debates del Ilustre Consejo Municipal del Canton Carácas. *Carácas.* 1859. 8vo, pp. 23. 10786

The Caraguin. A Tale of the Antilles, by the Author of "The Cruise." *London: Macrone.* 1837. 8vo. 10787

CARAMAN (G. J. V. R., *comte de*). Les États-Unis il y a quarante ans. Par Georges Joseph Victor Riquet, comte de Caraman. *Paris: Imprimerie Brière.* 1852–54. 8vo. 10788

Extracted from the "Revue contemporaine."

O Carapuceiro. Perodico sempre Moral, e se per accidens Politico. *Pernambuco.* 1837–42. 4 vols., sm. 4to. 10789

ÇARATE. *See* Zarate.

CARAYON (A.) Bannissement des Jésuites de la Louisiane. Relation et lettres inédites publiés par le P. Auguste Carayon ... . *Paris: L'Écureux.* 1865. 8vo, pp. xi, (1), 136. BA.

CARAYON. Bibliographie historique de la compagnie de Jésus ou catalogue des ouvrages relatifs à l'histoire des Jésuites, depuis leur origine jusqu'à nos jours par le P. Auguste Carayon ... . *Paris: Auguste Durand* [*Etc.*] MDCCCLXIV. 4to, pp. viii, 612.

CARAYON. Première mission des Jésuites au Canada. Lettres et documents inédits publiés par le P. Auguste Carayon. ... *Paris: L'Ecureux.* 1864. 8vo, pp. xvi, 304. BA. 10792

CARBAJAL (B.) Discurso que en la solemne funcion de la bandera del batallon Ligero Guerrero. *Oaxaca.* 1848. 4to, 17 leaves. 10793

CARBAJAL (F. L.) Discurso sobre la legislacion de los antiguos Mexicanos por Francisco Leon Carbajal. *Mexico: J. Abadiano.* 1864. 8vo, pp. 128. 10794

The three following titles are from the [Fischer] catalogue:

CARBAJAL (D. Francisco). Atrocidades cometidas por el malvado Gobierno de Ayutla. *Mexico.* 1858. 4to. 10795

CARBAJAL. Discursos sobre la Propiedad de los Empleos. *Mexico.* 1848. 8vo. 10796

CARBAJAL. Vindicacion de D. Francisco Carbajal. *Mexico.* 1845. 4to. 10797

CARBAJAL ESPINOSA (Fr.) Historia de Mexico desde los primeros tiempos de que hay noticia hasta mediados del siglo XIX. *Mexico.* 1862. 2 vols., 8vo. Plates. 10798

CARBALLIDO Y CABUEÑAS (J. M. de). Oracion Funebre que en sus Exequias del D. Nicolas Carlos Gomez, Obispo de Goathemala, y Guadalaxara. *Mexico.* 1735. 10799

CARBERY (E.) Inducements to the Colored People of the United States to emigrate to British Guiana, Compiled from Statements and Documents furnished by Mr. Edward Carbery, Agent of the "Immigration Society of British Guiana" ... . *Boston.* 1840. 8vo, pp. 24. H. 10800

CARDELL (William S.) Address, on the Subject of an "American Academy of Language and Belles-Lettres." *New York.* 1820. 4to. 18081

CARDEÑA (Patricio G.) Proyecto sobre la fundacion de un Banco Comercial en la Ciudad de Mexico. *Mexico.* 1857. 4to.

CARDENAS (B. de). Colleccion general de documentos, tocantes, a la persecucion, que los regulares de la C^ia^ suscitaron y siguieron tenázmente por medio de sus jueces, conservadores, y ganando algunos ministros seculares desde 1644 hasta 1660 contra D. Bernardino de Cardenas, obispo del Paraguay, expeliendole tres veces de su obispado à uferza de Armas, &c. por evitar que este prelado entrare ni visitare sus misiones del Paraná, Uruguay et Etati. Van añadidos en esta edicion muchos documentos ineditos, &c. *Madrid: Imprenta Real.* 1768–1778. 4 vols., 4to. C. 10803

"A curious collection, containing the following pieces: Vol. I. Prologo que sirve de introduccion, pp. 58; Memorial y Defensorio al Rey N. S. por el credito, &c. del Obispo del Paraguay, respondiendo à las memoriales del P. Julian de Pedraza: Procurador de los religiosos de la Ca., etc., pp. 387. Vol. II. Apendice de monumentos pertenecientes à las controversias de los regulares de la compañia en el Paraguay contra el venerable obispo Fr. B. de Cardenas, pp. 84; Discursos juridicos en defensa de la consagracion de Don. Fr. B. de Cardenas, obispo del Paraguay, etc. Por el Lico. Don Alonso Carillo, pp. 283. Vol. III. Memorial ajustado de D. Josef Antequera, pp. 239; Cartas del Sr. Dr. D. Josef Antequera y Castro Cavallero, &c. y Capitan general que fue del Paraguay escritas al Sr. M. F. Joseph de Palos, obispo taliense y coadiutor de la dicha provincia de Paraguay, pp. 374; Copia del Informe que hizo el Genl. D. Mathias de Angles y Gortari, Corregidor del Potosi, etc., pp. 64. Vol. IV. Coleccion general de documentos tocantes à la tercera época de las conmociones de los regulares de la compañia en él Paraguay.' Contiene el Reyno Jesuitico del Paraguay por siglo y medio negado y oculto, hoy demostrado y descubierto. Su author D. Bernardo Ibañez de Echavarria, pp. 241; Va añadido el diario de la guerra de los Guaranies escrito por el P. Tadeo Henis, pp. 113. A valuable production, containing a great amount of information on the condition of Paraguay under the Jesuits."—RICH.

CARDENAS. Histoire de la persécution de deux Saints Evêques par les jésuites: l'un Dom Bernardin de Cardenas, évêque du Paraguay dans l'Amerique Méridionale; l'autre Dom Philippe Pardo, archévêque de l'église de Manile Métropolitaine des isles Philippines. ... [n. p.] 1691. 12mo, pp. 503, 1 l. C., P., S. 10804

An extremely rare volume, printed in Holland. It is included in the "Collecion," described in the previous number.

CARDENAS. Memorial y defensoria por Don Fr. Bernardino de Cardenas Obispo del Paraguay, con los Religiosos Campani de la Compania de Aguellas Provincias. [1662.] 4to. 10805

CARDENAS. Mémorial | Presenté au Roy d'Espagne, | Pour la deffense de la reputation, de la dignité, | & de la personne de l'Illustrissime | & Reverendissime | Dom Bernardino | de Cardenas | Evesque de Paraguay dans les Indes, &c., &c. [1 line.] | Contre les Religieux de la compagnie | de Jésus. | Et pour répondre aux Memoriaux presentés | à sa dite Majesté, par le P. Julien | De Pedraça Procureur-general | des Jesuites dans les Indes. | Traduit

fidellement sur l'imprimé Espagnols. | [n. p.] M.DC.LXII. | Sm. 12mo, pp. 322. J.C.B. 10806

A beautiful little edition, printed by the Elzevirs, with their device (the sphere) on the title.

CARDENAS. Memorial y Relacion verdadera para el Rey N. S. y su Real Consejo de las Indias de cosas del Reino del Peru, muy importante à su real servicio y consciencia. Por el P. F. Bernardino de Cardenas, Predicador general de la orden de S. Francisco, y Legado del santo Concilio Provincial Argentino. *Madrid: Francisco Martinez.* 1634. 4to, 64 l. J.C.B. 10807

A very rare book, apparently not printed for sale, as it has none of the usual licenses, approbations, etc., customary at the period of its publication. Rich describes a copy, with a manuscript censure by Fray Pedro de Ayala. *See* Rich, No. 204, and Ternaux, No. 550.

CARDENAS (J. de). De los problemas y secretos marauillosos de las Indias. Compuesta por el Doctor Juan de Cardenas Medico. Dirigida al Illustrissimo Señor D. Luiz de Velasco, Virrey desta nueua España. [A coat of arms.] Con Licencia. *En Mexico: En Casa de Pedro Ocharte. Año de* 1591. Sm. 8vo, 7 l., 246 l. 10808

CARDENAS Y CANO (Don Gabriel de). *Anagram. See* Barcia (A. G.), Vol. I., No. 3349.

CARDENAS LEON (Cablos Celedonio Velasquez). Breve práctica del confessionario de Indios, en mexicano y castellano, para instruccion del confessor principiante, habilitacion y examen del penitente. *México: en la imprenta de la Bibliotheca mexicana, junto á las RR. MM. Capuchinas.* 1761. Sm. 8vo, 12 l., pp. 54. 10809

CARDENAS Y RODRIGUEZ (D. Jose M. de). Coleccion de articulos satiricos y de costumbres. *Habana: Imprenta del faro industrial.* 1847. 8vo, pp. x, 257, 2 l. 10810

CARDENAS. La Invasion de Cardenas. Romance historico en que se refieren los sucesos acaecidos a consecuencia de la expedition de piratas que desembarcó en Cardenas el 19 de Mayo de 1850. *Habana.* 1850. 12mo, pp. 47. 19811

CARDENAS. Invasion de la Vuelta-Abajo. Romance historico, por el Autor del Titulado La Invasion de Cardenas. 2^a^. edicion corregida. *Habana: Imprenta del Tiempo.* ... 1851. 8vo, pp. 54. 10812

CARDER (P.) Kort verhaal van Pieter Carder, behelzende een verslag van de ongelukken en rampen, hem 1578. op zijn Reys met François Drake overgekommen. Door den reiziger selfs in't Engels beschreeven, en nu aldereerst vertaald. *Leyden.* 1706. 8vo and Folio. Maps and Plates. BM., J.C.BT. 10813

Forms No. LXI. of Van der Aa's collection of voyages, or part of Vol. XVIII., in 8vo, or Vol. V. of the folio edition.

CARDERA (Valentin). Informe sobre los retratos de Cristobal Colon, su trage y escudo de armas, leida à la Real Academia de la Historia. *Madrid.* 1847. Folio, 14 l. Portrait of Columbus.

From the "Memorias de la Academia de la historia."

CARDIM (F.) Narrativa epistolar de uma viagem e missão jesuitica pela Bahia, Ilheos, Porto-Seguro, Pernambuco, Espirito Sancto, Rio de Janeiro, etc., 1583–1590, indo por visitador o P. Chr. de Gouvea, Escripta em duas cartas ao Padre Provincial em Portugal pelo P. Fernão Cardim. *Lisboa: imp. nacional.* 1847. 8vo, pp. vi, 123. 10815

Published by M. de Varnhagen. "Ce livre est écrit d'un style charmant et donne des détails d'une grâce parfaite."—F. DENIS.

CARDOZO (J. N.). Notes on Political Economy. *Charleston.* 1826. 8vo. C. 10816

CARDOZO. A Plan of Financial Relief ... originally published in the Atlanta Southern Confederacy; By J. N. Cardozo. *Atlanta, Ga.* 1863. 8vo, pp. 37. BA. 10817

CARDOZO. Reminiscences of Charleston. By J. N. Cardozo. *Charleston: Joseph Walker, Agt.* 1866. 12mo, pp. 144.

CARE (H.) English Liberties, or the Free-born Subject's Inheritance, containing Magna Charta, Charta de Foresta, The Statute de Tallagio non Concedendo, The Habeas Corpus Act, and several other Statutes ... . Likewise The Proceedings in Appeals of Murder: Of Ship-Money; Of Tonnage and Poundage. ... Compiled first by Henry Care, and contiued [*sic*], with large Additions, by W. N. of the Middle-Temple, Esq. The Fifth Edition. *Boston, Printed by J. Franklin, for N. Buttolph, B. Eliot, and D. Henchman, and Sold at their Shops,* 1721. 12mo, 6 l., pp. 288. B. + *London: E. & C. Dilly.* 1766. 8vo, 6 l., pp. lxxix, 396. + Sixth Edition. *Providence, R. I.: J. Carter.* 1774. 12mo, pp. (12), 288. B. 10819

Probably Benjamin Franklin worked on the Boston edition, as it was printed during the time he was apprenticed to his brother. Copies of this edition are sometimes found with the imprint, "*Newport: Printed by J. Franklin.* 1721."

CARERI (Gemelli). Giro del Mundo. *Napoli.* 1699–1700. 7 vols., 8vo. 10820

"Humboldt and Clavigero have confirmed his local knowledge of Mexico, and found his book useful and veracious." He first published the famous Mexican map or picture of the migrations of the Aztecs. Included in Churchill's Col., Vol. IV.

CARERI. Voyage autour du Monde, traduit de l'Italien de Gemelli Careri. Par L. M. N. Enrichi d'un grand nombre de Figures. *Paris: Etienne Ganeau.* 1719. 6 vols., 12mo. Maps and Plates. J.C.B. 10821

This translation is by M. Le Noble. These voyages include Mexico, and other parts of America. Reissued, "*Paris.* 1727," 6 vols.

CAREW (Bampfylde Moore). *See* [Goadby (R.)]

C[AREW] (G[eorge]). Fraud and Oppression detected and arraigned, or an Appeal to the Parliament of England, in a Narrative and Deduction of severall Actions at Law, depending in the ordinary Courts of Justice in Holland and Zealand, between diverse Subjects of the King of England, and the Subjects of the States Generall of the Seven United Provinces, with severall remarkable Observations and Animadversions thereupon, by the creditors of Sir William Courten, Sir Paul Pyndar, Sir Edward Lyttleton, and William Courten, Esq. deceased, whereunto are added some necessary Advertisements concerning the Improvement of Navigation and Trade, together with a brief deduction of the Case between George Carew, Esq. Administrator of the Goods of Sir William Courten and Jacob Ryens Bewinthebba, of the West India Company, faithfully digested into a Method by G. C. 1676. Folio. 10822

Relating to the losses of Sir William Courten and Sir Paul Pyndar, under Charles II, in Barbadoes. Evidently privately printed. *See* Courten (W.), and Ternaux, No. 933.

CAREW. Retrospect into the King's Revenue annexed to the Crown under the Survey of his Majesties Court of Exchequer, with various Papers and Petitions relating to the Island of Barbadoes, and other Plantations in the West Indies. By George Carew. 1661. Folio. 10823

Also: Deduction of the Case between George Carew and J. Pergens, of the West Indian Company. 1676. Folio.—Petition of George Carew, Administrator of Sir William Courten, and others. 1675. Folio.

CAREY (A.) Clovernook, or Recollections of our Neighborhood in the West. By Alice Carey. *New-York.* 1852. 12mo, pp. 250. 10824

Reprinted in London. 18mo, pp. 250. 2 Plates.

CAREY (A.) A Full and True Statement of the Examination and Ordination of Mr. Arthur Carey. Taken from the Churchman of July 8, 15, 22, 29, and August 5, 12, 19, and 26. ... *New York: James A. Sparks.* 1843. 8vo, 2 l., slip, pp. 116. B., H. 10825

CAREY (Eustace). Memoir of W. Carey, D.D. ... with an Introductory Essay, by J. Chapin. *Hartford.* 1837. 12mo.

CAREY (Henry C.) American Civil War. *See* [D.]

CAREY. American Labor *versus* British Free Trade. Answers to the Questions: What constitutes Currency? What are the Causes of Unsteadiness of the Currency? And What is the Remedy? By H. C. Carey. ... *Philadelphia: Lea & Blanchard.* 1840. 8vo, Title, pp. 81. B. + *Philadelphia.* 1855. 8vo. C. 10827

For a criticism on this work, *see* McCulloch's "Lit. of Pol. Economy," p. 186.

[CAREY.] Beauties of the Monopoly System in New Jersey. By a Citizen of Burlington. *Philadelphia.* 1848. 8vo. 10828

The following tracts relating to the Camden and Amboy Railroad, were written by Mr. Carey, under the *pseudonym* of "A Citizen of Burlington:" Correspondence between the Commissioners for investigating the Affairs of the Joint Companies, and a Citizen of Burlington. *Philadelphia.* 1850. 8vo, pp. 15. H., P.—An Investigation into the Affairs of the Delaware and Raritan Canal and Camden and Amboy Railroad Companies, in reference to certain Charges ... *Newark.* 1849. 8vo.—Letter to the Senate and House of Assembly of the State of New Jersey. ... *Burlington.* 1851. 8vo.—A Letter to James S. Hulme, Esq., late Commissioner. *Philadelphia.* 1851. 8vo.—Letter to Aaron Robertson, Esq., late Chairman of the Commission for investigating the Affairs of the Joint Companies. ... *Philadelphia.* 1852. 8vo.—Letters to the People of New-Jersey, on the Frauds, Extortions and Oppressions of the Railroad Monopoly ... . *Philadelphia.* 1848. 8vo.—Proceedings of the Late Railroad Commission. ... *Philadelphia: L. R. Bailey, Printer.* 1850. 8vo, pp. 8.—The Railroad Monopoly. *Philadelphia.* 1849. 8vo.—A Review of an Address of the Joint Board of Directors of the Delaware and Raritan Canal and Camden and Amboy Railroad Companies, ... *Philadelphia.* 1848. 8vo, pp. 83. (1). H.—Review of the Report of the Late Commissioners for investigating the Affairs of the Joint Companies ... . *Philadelphia.* 1850. 8vo, pp. 78.

CAREY. Ein Brief an einen Farmer in Ohio. Aus der Monatschrift: „Pflug, Webstuhl und Amboss." [*New York.* 1852.] 8vo, pp. 16. H. 10829

CAREY. Briefe über schriftstellerisches Eigenthum von Henry C. Carey. Nach den amerikanischen Original übersetzt. ... *Berlin: Albert Eichhoff.* 1866. 8vo, pp. 93. H. 10830

[CAREY.] The Harmony of Interests; Agricultural, Manufacturing, and Commercial. [*Philadelphia.* 1849–50.] 3 pts., 8vo. + By Henry C. Carey. *Philadelphia.* 1850. 8vo, pp. 229.

+ [*Ibid.*] *J. S. Skinner.* 1851. 8vo, pp. 235. BA. + *New York: Myron Finch.* 1856. 8vo, pp. 229. + New Edition. *Philadelphia.* 1865. 8vo, pp. ix, 229. P. 10831

CAREY. Letters to the President, on the Foreign and Domestic Policy of the Union, and its Effects, as exhibited in the Condition of the People and the State. By H. C. Carey. *Philadelphia: M. Pollock.* 1858. 8vo, pp. 171. + *Philadelphia: J. B. Lippincott & Co.* 1858. 8vo, pp. iv, 3–171. C., H. 10832

CAREY. The Miscellaneous Works of Henry C. Carey. *Philadelphia: H. C. Baird.* 1868. 8vo, pp. 230, 12, 88, 30, iv, 172, 58, 166, 48, 8, 16, 40, 72, 40, 66, 64, x. 10833

CAREY. The Past, the Present and the Future. By H. C. Carey ... . *Philadelphia: Cary & Hart.* 1848. 8vo, pp. 474.

Like all Carey's works, treats of the questions of political economy as they affect this country.

CAREY. Principles of Political Economy. By H. C. Carey, Esq. *Philadelphia.* 1837, 38. 3 vols., 8vo. 10835

CAREY. Principles of Social Science. *Philadelphia.* 1858–1860. 3 vols., 8vo. C. 10836

CAREY. Principes de la science sociale. Traduits en français par MM. Saint-Germain-Leduc et A. Planche. *Paris: Guillaumin et Cie.* 1861. 3 vols., 8vo. 2 Plates. 10837

CAREY. Socialökonomie. Nach dem amerikanisches Original übersetzt. Mit biographisch-literarischer Skizze ... des Verfassers. ... . *Berlin: Eichhoff.* 1866. 8vo, pp. xli, 490.

CAREY. The Prospect: Agricultural, Manufacturing, Commercial, and Financial: at the Opening of the Year 1851. By Henry C. Carey. *Philadelphia: J. S. Skinner.* 1851. 8vo, pp. 84. BA., H. 10839

CAREY. The Slave Trade, Domestic and Foreign; why it exists and how it may be Extinguished. By H. C. Carey ... . *Philadelphia: A. Hart.* 1853. 12mo, Title, pp. 246. B. + *London.* 1853. 8vo. + Third Edition. *Philadelphia: John A. Martien.* 1859. 12mo, pp. 26. P. 10840

CAREY. Testimonials to Henry C. Carey, Esq. Dinner at the La Pierre House, Philadelphia, April 27, 1859. Receptions in the Counties of Luzerne, Columbia, Montour, and Carbon,

Pennsylvania. *Philadelphia: Collins, Printer.* 1859. 8vo, pp. 79. Portrait. H. 10841

CAREY. The Working of British Free Trade. (Originally Published in the Plough, the Loom, and the Anvil.) By H. C. Carey ... . *New York.* 1852. 8vo, pp. 42. B., C. 10842

Also: Contraction or Expansion? Repudiation or Resumption? Letters to the Hon. Hugh McCulloch, Secretary of the Treasury. By Henry C. Carey. *Philadelphia: H. C. Baird.* 1866. 8vo, pp. 47. — The Credit System in France, Great Britain, and the United States. By Henry C. Carey. *Philadelphia.* 1838. 8vo, Title, pp. 130. BA., C. — The Currency Question. Four Letters to the Hon. Schuyler Colfax. ... By H. C. Carey. *Philadelphia: Collins, printer.* 1865. 8vo, pp. 40. — Essay on the Rate of Wages; with an Examination of the Causes of the Differences in the Condition of the Laboring Population throughout the World. *Philadelphia.* 1835. 8vo. C. — The Farmer's Question. Letters to Schuyler Colfax. *Philadelphia: Collins.* 1865. 8vo, pp. 24. — The French and American Tariffs compared; in a Series of Letters addressed to Mons. Michel Chevalier ... . By Henry C. Carey. *Philadelphia: Collins, Printer.* 1861. 8vo, pp. 29. BA., C., H. — Lettres critiques adressées a M. Michel Chevalier par M. C.-H. Carey ... traduites de l'Anglais . . par Auguste Humbert ... *Paris: A. Lacroix, Verboeckhoven et Ce.* 1864. 8vo, pp. 64. H. — Henry C. Carey on National Matters. *Philadelphia, Nov.* 15, 1859. 4to, 1 p. — Die Hülfsquellen und der Krieg Nordamerika's. Ein Vortrag gehalten in December 1865 vor der statistischen Gesellschaft zu New-York. Nach dem amerikanischen Original übersetzt. Autorisirte Ausgabe. *Berlin: Eichhoff.* 1866. 8vo, pp. 42. — How Protection, Increase of Public and Private Revenues, and National Independence, march Hand in Hand Together. Review of the Report of the Hon. D. A. Wells, Special Commissioner of the Revenue. By H. C. Carey. *Philadelphia.* 1869. 8vo, pp. 64. — How to have Cheap Iron. ... [*Philadelphia.* 1852.] 8vo, pp. 15. C., H. — Letters on International Copyright. By H. C. Carey. *Philadelphia.* 1853. 8vo, pp. 72, (1). BA., H. + Second Edition. *New York: Hurd & Houghton.* 1868. 8vo, pp. 88. — The Iron Question. Letter Fifth. *Philadelphia: Collins.* 1865. 8vo, pp. 18. — Money: a Lecture before the New York Geographical and Statistical Society ... February, 1857. By Henry C. Carey. ... *New York.* 1857. 8vo, pp. 28. BA., C., H. — The North and the South. Reprinted from the New York Tribune. *New York.* 1854. 8vo, pp. 40. C., H., P. — The Paper Question. Letters to the Hon. Schuyler Colfax ... . [Signed, H. C. Carey.] *Philadelphia.* 1865. 8vo, pp. 41. H. — The Railroad Question. [n. p. 1865.] 8vo, pp. 16. H. — Reconstruction: Industrial, Financial, and Political. ... By Henry C. Carey. *Washington: United Press Association.* 1868. 8vo, pp. 79. H. — The Resources of the Union. A Lecture read December, 1865, before the American Geographical and Statistical Society, New York; ... By Henry C. Carey. *Philadelphia: H. C. Baird.* 1866. 8vo, pp. 26. — Present Situation and Prospects of American Railways. *Philadelphia.* 1855. 8vo. — Resumption! How it may profitably be brought about. By Henry C. Carey. *Philadelphia: Collins, Printer.* 1869. 8vo, pp. 16. H. — Review of the Decade, 1857–67. By H. C. Carey. *Philadelphia: Collins, Printer.* 1867. 8vo, pp. 40. H. — Shall we have Peace? Peace Financial, and Peace Political? Letters to the President Elect of the United States: by H. C. Carey. *Philadelphia: Collins, Printer.* 1869. 8vo, pp. 66. B. — The Slave Question. [*Philadelphia.* 1849.] 8vo, pp. 401–411. BA., H. (From "The Plough, the Loom, and the Anvil," with a half-title.) — The Slave Trade, Domestic and Foreign; why it exists, and how it may be extinguished. *Philadelphia.* 1853. 12mo. C. — The True Policy of the South. Remarks on an Article in the Austin (Texas) State Gazette. [n. p. n. d.] 8vo. C. — The Way to outdo England without fighting her. Letters to the Hon. Schuyler Colfax, Speaker of the House of Representatives, on the Paper, the Iron, the Farmer's, the Railroad, and the Currency Questions. By Henry C. Carey ... . *Philadelphia: Henry Carey Baird.* 1865. 8vo, pp. 165.

CAREY *and* LEA (J.) The Geography, History, and Statistics of America and the West Indies, exhibiting a Correct Account of the Discovery, Settlement, and Progress of the various Kingdoms, States, and Provinces of the Western Hemisphere, to the year 1822. With Additions relative to the New States of South America, etc. *London: Sherwood.* 1823. 8vo, pp. 447. 18 Maps, and Plates. + *London.* 1825. 8vo. BD. 10843

"This work appears to be an abstract of the 'Complete Historical Chronological, and Geographical American Atlas,' published at Philadelphia, by Carey and Lea, in the preceding year, in folio." — RICH.

CAREY (Isaac E.) Abraham Lincoln. The Value to the Nation of his Exalted Character. Rev. Mr. Carey's Fast Day Sermon, preached June 1, 1865, in the First Presbyterian Church of Freeport, Ill. [n. p. n. d.] 8vo, pp 8. B. 10844

CAREY. Discourse of Rev. Mr. Carey, on the Death of Abraham Lincoln, Preached on the day of his Funeral, April 19, 1865, in the First Presbyterian Church in Freeport, Illinois. [n. p. n. d.] 8vo, pp. 8. B. 10845

CAREY. The War an Occasion for Thanksgiving. A Discourse for Thanksgiving, preached at Keokuk, Iowa, November 28, 1861. *Keokuk, Iowa.* 1861. 8vo, pp. 22. 10846

Also: The Conflict and the Victory. Two Discourses for the Times. Preached November 6 and 24, 1864, at Freeport, Ill. *Freeport, Ill: Judson & McCluer.* 1864. 8vo, pp. 15. God's Wonderful Doings in behalf of the Nation. A Discourse preached on the National Thanksgiving Day, November 26, 1863, at Freeport, Illinois. *Freeport, Ill.: Judson & McCluer.* 1863. 8vo, pp. 16.

CAREY (J. L.) Slavery and the Wilmot Proviso; with some Suggestions for a Compromise. By John L. Carey. *Baltimore: Joseph N. Lewis.* 1847. 8vo, pp. 64. B., H. 10847

CAREY. Slavery in Maryland briefly considered. By John L. Carey. *Baltimore: John Murphy.* 1845. 12mo, pp. 51, (2).

CAREY (J. P.) Carey's Record of the Great Rebellion. A carefully compiled Chronological History of the War, from the Dawn of the Rebellion to the Dawn of Peace. By James P. Carey. *New York: Dick & Fitzgerald.* [1865.] 8vo, pp. 16.

CAREY (Mathew). An Address to William Tudor, Esq., Author of letters on the Eastern States. Intended to prove the Calumny and Slander of his Remarks on the Olive Branch. *Philadelphia: M. Carey & Son.* 1821. 12mo, pp. xiv, 9–67.

CAREY. Appendix to the Eighth Edition of the Olive Branch

or Faults on Both Sides, Federal and Democrat. *Philadelphia, July* 4, 1817. 8vo. 10851

CAREY. Autobiographical Sketches, in a Series of Letters addressed to a Friend. Vol. 1, containing a view of the Rise and Progress of the American System, &c *Philadelphia.* [1829.] 12mo, pp. xvi, 156. C. 10852

CAREY. Brief View of the System of Internal Improvement of the State of Pennsylvania. ... By M. Carey. Published by Order of the Society for the Promotion of Internal Improvement. *Philadelphia: printed by Lydia R. Bailey.* 1831. 8vo, pp. 36. BA., P. 10853

[CAREY.] A Calm Address to the People of the Eastern States, on the Subject of the Representation of Slaves; the Representation in the Senate; and the Hostility to Commerce ascribed to the Southern States. By the Author of the Olive Branch. ... *Philadelphia: M. Carey. Nov.* 28, 1814. 12mo, 1 l. folded, 1 slip, pp. 47. B., P. + *Boston: reprinted by Rowe and Hooper.* 1814. 12mo, pp. 50. H. 10854

CAREY. Carey's American Atlas: containing twenty Maps and one Chart. *Philadelphia: Engraved for and Published by Mathew Carey.* 1795. Folio. + [With 23 Maps. *Ibid.*] *April,* 1809. 4to. BA. 10855

CAREY. Carey's American Pocket Atlas: containing the [19] following Maps ... . With a Concise Description of each State. *Philadelphia: Mathew Carey.* 1796. 12mo, pp. 118, 13*–16*. + Second Edition, greatly improved and enlarged. *Philadelphia: Mathew Carey.* 1801. 8vo, 4 l., pp. 112. Table folded. + Containing Twenty [23] Maps ... . Fourth Edition ... . [*Ibid.*] 1814. 12mo, pp. iv, 168, 2 l. folded. H. 10856

CAREY. Carey's Minor American Atlas; containing Nineteen Maps ... . With the Main Roads correctly laid down. *Philadelphia: Mathew Carey.* M.DCCC.II. 4to, Title. Maps.

This probably forms the third edition of the "Pocket Atlas."

CAREY. Carey's General Atlas ... *Philadelphia.* 1796. Folded sheets. 45 Maps. + *Philadelphia: Mathew Carey. June,* 9, 1800. Folio. 49 Maps. + *Philadelphia.* 1804. Folio. + Improved and Enlarged. *Philadelphia.* 1814. Folio. 58 Maps. + *Philadelphia.* 1818. 10858

These maps are also included in the American edition of Guthrie's "Geography." Also: Carey's War-Atlas: ... [7 Maps of Portions of Europe, and the West Indies. n. p. n. d.] Folded sheets.

[CAREY.] Common Sense Addresses to the Citizens of the Southern States ... . By a Citizen of Philadelphia. [Signed Hamilton.] *Philadelphia.* 1829. 8vo. + Fourth Edition, enlarged. *Philadelphia. Nov.* 25, 1829. 8vo, pp. 56. BA. 10859

[CAREY.] A Connected View of the whole Internal Navigation of the United States, Natural and Artificial, Present and Prospective. *Philadelphia.* 1826. 8vo. + Corrected and Improved from the edition of 1826, and much Enlarged from Authentic Materials. With ... map, and ... statistical Details. By a Citizen of the United States. *Philadelphia.* 1830. 8vo. 10860

[CAREY.] The Crisis. An Appeal to the Good Sense of the Nation, against the Spirit of Resistance and Dissolution of the Union ... *Philadelphia: printed by William F. Geddes,* ... 1832. 8vo, pp. 28, (4). H. + Third Edition, corrected. [*Ibid.*] *August* 1, 1832. [*Ibid.*] BA., H. 10861

[CAREY.] The Crisis: a Solemn Appeal to the President, the Senate and House of Representatives, ... on the Destructive Tendency of the Present Policy of this Country ... . By a Pennsylvanian. *Philadelphia: H. C. Carey & I. Lea. Nov.* 24, 1823. 8vo, pp. 79. BA., H. + Second Edition. [*Ibid.*] 1823. 8vo. 10862

CAREY. Cursory Reflections on the System of Taxation established in the City of Philadelphia; with a Brief Sketch of its Unequal and Unjust Operation. ... [*Philadelphia:*] *Published by the Author. March* 10, 1806. 8vo, pp. 47. P. 10863

CAREY. Debates and Proceedings of the General Assembly of Pennsylvania, on the Memorials praying a Repeal of Suspension of the Law annulling the Charter of the Bank. Mathew Carey, Editor. *Philadelphia: printed for Carey & Co., Seddon and Pritchard.* M. CC. LXXXVI. 8vo, 2 l., pp. 132. C., H. 10864

CAREY. Desultory Account of the Yellow Fever, in Philadelphia, in October, 1793. By Mathew Carey. *Philadelphia.* 1793. 8vo. 10865

CAREY. Essays on Political Economy, or the most Certain Means of promoting the Wealth, Power, Resources and Happiness of Nations; applied particularly to the United States. By M. Carey ... . *Philadelphia: H. C. Carey & I. Lea.* 1822. 8vo, pp. x, (3), 10–546, (10). B. 10866

[CAREY.] Essays tending to prove the Ruinous Effects of the Policy of the United States on the Three Classes, Farmers, Planters and Merchants. Addressed to Edward Livingston, Esq. ... By a Citizen of Philadelphia. ... . *Philadelphia. December* 11, 1826. 8vo, pp. viii, 34. BA., N. 10867

With the caption, "Hamilton — Eleventh Series, — No. I–VII."

[CAREY.] Examination of a Tract on the Alteration of the Tariff, written by Thomas Cooper, M.D. By a Pennsylvanian. To which is annexed the Tract of Judge Cooper, verbatim. *Philadelphia: Printed for H. C. Carey & I. Lea.* 1824. 8vo, pp. vii, (1), 36, 27. BA. + Second Edition. [*Ibid.*] 8vo. + Third Edition. [*Ibid.*] 24mo, pp. 72. BA. 10868

In the first ed., Judge Cooper's Tract has a title-page and separate paging, pp. 27.

CAREY. Facts and Observations, illustrative of the Past and Present Situation and Future Prospects of the United States; embracing A View of the causes of the late Bankruptcies in Boston. By a Pennsylvanian. Second Edition, greatly improved. *Philadelphia: H. C. Carey & I. Lea.* 1822. 8vo, pp. 54. BA. + Third Edition, improved. ... [*Ibid.*] 1822. 8vo, pp. 54. H. 10869

CAREY. Letters on the Colonization Society; with a view of its probable results, ... By M. Carey. *Philadelphia.* 1832. 8vo. + Second Edition, enlarged and improved. ... *Philadelphia. April* 26, 1832. 8vo, pp. 32. BA. + Third Edition. [*Ibid.*] *May,* 29, 1832. + Fourth Edition. [*Ibid.*] *June* 19, 1832. [*Ibid.*] H. + Fifth Edition. [*Ibid.*] *Sept.* 7, 1832. [*Ibid.*] H. + Seventh Edition. *Philadelphia. April* 15, 1833. [*Ibid.*] H. + Ninth Edition. ... [*Ibid.*] *Sept.* 17, 1834. 8vo, pp. 4, iv, 32. Map and Plate. H. + Thirteenth Edition. *Philadelphia. October* 17, 1838. [*Ibid.*] H. 10870

CAREY. Miscellaneous Essays: containing, among a Variety of other Articles, History of the Yellow Fever which prevailed at Philadelphia in the Year 1793 ... . Reflections on the Subject of Emigration ... . Essays on the Public Charities of Philadelphia ... . A Brief View of the Policy of the Founders of the Colonies ... . By M. Carey ... . *Philadelphia. Nov.* 13, 1830. 8vo, pp. viii, (3), x–472. B. 10871

Other collections of Carey's tracts were bound up and issued as Carey's "Miscellanies."

CAREY. Miscellaneous Trifles in Prose. By Mathew Carey.

Philadelphia: printed for the Author by Lang and Ustick. M.DCC.-XCVI. 24mo, pp. 176. BA., P. 10872

Contains "Funding Bill," Life of General Greene," "Thoughts on the Policy of encouraging Migration," "Theatricus."

CAREY. The New Olive Branch; or, an Attempt to establish an Identity of Interest between Agriculture, Manufactures, and Commerce; and to prove, that a Large Portion of the Manufacturing Industry of the Nation has been sacrificed to Commerce, and that Commerce has suffered by this Policy nearly as much as Manufactures. By M. Carey ... . *Philadelphia: M. Carey & Son.* 1820. 8vo, Title, pp. x, 17–248, 2 l. B., C. + Second Edition. ... [*Ibid.*] 8vo, pp. 130. BA. 10873

CAREY. New Olive Branch: addresssed to the Citizens of South Carolina. *Philadelphia.* 1831. 8vo. + Second Edition. *Philadelphia.* 1831. 8vo. 10874

Relates to the tariff.

CAREY. Nine Letters to Adam Seybert, Representative in Congress for the City of Philadelphia. [On the Bank of the United States.] By M. Carey. ... *Philadelphia: the Author. Dec.* 15, 1810. 8vo, pp. 59. BA. + Second Edition, enlarged. *Philadelphia. Jan.* 7, 1811. 8vo, pp. 80. 10875

CAREY. Observations on Dr. Rush's Enquiry into the Origin of the late Epidemic Fever in Philadelphia: by Mathew Carey. *Philadelphia: from the Press of the Author. December* 14, 1793. 12mo, pp. 23. C., H. 10876

This also forms the seventh of his "Select Pamphlets."

CAREY. The Olive Branch; or Faults on both sides, Federal and Democratic. A Serious Appeal on the necessity of Mutual Forgiveness and Harmony to save our country. By Mathew Carey. *Philadelphia.* 1814. 12mo. + Second Edition, improved and enlarged. *Philadelphia. Jan.* 9, 1815. + Third Edition. *Boston: reprinted by Rowe and Hooper. Feb.,* 1815. 12mo, pp. xxiii, 13–336. H. + Fourth Edition, enlarged. *Philadelphia: the Author. April,* 1815. 2 vols., 12mo, pp. 241; 276. H. + Sixth Edition, enlarged. *Philadelphia: the Author. September,* 1815. 8vo, pp. 454 [455]. B., C. + Seventh Edition. *Philadelphia.* 1815. 8vo, pp. 486. + Seventh Edition. *Middlebury, Vt.: Wm. Slade, Junior.* 1816. 12mo, pp. 468. + Eighth Edition, enlarged. *Philadelphia. July* 4, 1817. 8vo, pp. 452, 56. + Tenth Edition. *Philadelphia.* 1830. 8vo. P.

CAREY. Olive Branch, No. III. Or an Inquiry whether any Arrangement is practicable between the Friends and Opposers of the Protecting System ... . To which is added, an Anticipatory Epitaph on the Constitution, in the Event of a Secession, and its Necessary Result, a Dissolution of the Union. ... By M. Carey. *Philadelphia. March,* 29, 1832. 8vo, pp. xii, 68.

"The Olive Branch," No. IV., pp. 4, is dated April 23, 1832.

CAREY. An Answer to Certain Parts of a Work Published by Mathew Carey, entitled "The Olive Branch; or, Faults on Both Sides." By a Federalist. [*Philadelphia.* 1816.] 12mo, pp. 232. 10879

CAREY. The Plagi-Scurriliad: A Hudibrastic Poem. Dedicated to Colonel Eleazer Oswald. By Mathew Carey. *Philadelphia: Printed & Sold by the Author.* MDCCLXXXVI. 8vo, pp. iv. 27, (3). 10880

CAREY. A Plumb Pudding for the Humane, Chaste, Valiant, and Enlightened Peter Porcupine, By his Obliged Friend, Mathew Carey. ... *Philadelphia: the Author.* [1798.] 8vo, pp. 48, 8. + Second Edition. *Philadelphia.* 1798. 8vo. P. 10881

CAREY. The Porcupiniad; a Hudibrastic Poem. In Four Cantos. Addressed to William Cobbett, by Mathew Carey. Canto I. ... *Philadelphia: ... the Author. March* 2, 1799. 8vo, pp. 52. Plate. BA. + Canto II. & III. ... [*Ibid.*] *April* 15, 1799. 8vo, pp. 44. BA. + Second Edition, Improved. *Philadelphia.* ... *April* 22. M,DCC,XCIX. 8vo, pp. 35. Plate. 10882

CAREY. Select Pamphlets: viz. ... 3. Address to the House of Representatives of the United States [, on Lord Grenville's Treaty. ... *Philadelphia: printed for Mathew Carey.* 1796. 8vo, pp. vi, 8–48.] 4. Features of Mr. Jay's Treaty. [To which is annexed A View of the Commerce of the United States, as it stands at present, and as it is fixed by Mr. Jay's Treaty. [*Ibid.*] 1795. 8vo, pp. 51.] 5. ... [*See* No. 10884.] 6. Dr. Nassy's Account of the same Fever. 7. ... [*See* No. 10884.] 8. Revolution of America — By the Abbe Raynal. *Philadelphia: Mathew Carey.* 1796. 8vo. 10883

Remainder copies collected under a general title.

CAREY. A Short Account of the Malignant Fever, lately Prevalent in Philadelphia: With a Statement of the Proceedings that took place on the Subject in Different Parts of the United States. By Mathew Carey. *Philadelphia.* 1793. 8vo, pp. 103.

C. + Second Edition. *Philadelphia: printed by the Author. November* 23, 1793. 8vo, pp. 103, (1), 4 l. C., H. 10884

This edition also forms the fifth of his "Select Pamphlets."

CAREY. A Short Account of the Malignant Fever lately Prevalent in Philadelphia: with a Statement of the Proceedings that took place on the subject in different parts of the United States. By Mathew Carey. Third Edition, Improved. *Philadelphia: Printed by the Author. November* 30, 1793. 8vo, pp. 112, 4 l., pp. 16. + Fourth Edition, improved. [*Ibid.*] *January* 16, 1794. 8vo, pp. 164. BA., H. + Tenth Edition. *Philadelphia.* 1830. 8vo, pp. 97. 10885

"This pamphlet is rather a historical account of the circumstances attending the visitation of the yellow fever, which proved so fatal in Philadelphia, in the year 1793, and in which Mr. Carey has presented his fellow-citizens with a collection of facts and observations well calculated for the satisfaction of their anxious curiosity." — M. R., XIV. 187.

CAREY. Histoire succincte de la fièvre maligne Qui a régné dernièrement a Philadelphie, suivi D'un Récit des mesures prises dans différentes parties des États Unis, au sujet de cette maladie. Par Mathew Carey. *Philadelphia: Imprimé par Parent pour l'Auteur.* [n. d.] 8vo, pp. 102. BA. + [A Fourth Edition.] *Philadelphia.* [1794.] 8vo. BM. 10886

CAREY. Kort berigt wegens de kwaadaartige koorts, welke onlangs in Philadelphia heerschte; benevens eene opgaaf van het gebeurde omtrent dit onderwerp in verscheidene gedeeltens der Vereenigde Staten van Noord-America. Uit het Engelsch vertaald door N. C. de Fremery. *Haarlem.* 1794. 8vo. 10887

CAREY. Eine kürze Nachricht von dem bösartigen Fieber, welches kürzlich in Philadelphia grassiret. ... [Mit] Nachrichten von der Pest in London [1665] und Marseille [1720] ... . Uebersetzt aus dem Englischen von Carl Erdmann. *Lancaster.* 1794. 8vo. 10888

[CAREY.] A Warning Voice to the Cotton and Tobacco Planters, Farmers, Merchants of the United States, on the Pernicious Consequences to their respective Interests of the Existing Policy of the Country. By a Pennsylvanian. *Philadelphia: H. C. Carey & I. Lea.* 1824. 8vo, pp. xx, 9–76. BA. 10889

Mr. Carey was a voluminous and somewhat vigorous writer on the topics of the day. Many of his tracts were published anonymously. In the list of his works included in the note, the titles have been arranged alphabetically — the anonymous works being preceded by the name in brackets. "Banking," "Political Economy," "The Tariff," "Nullification," etc., are the leading topics.

Address delivered before the Philadelphia Society for promoting Agriculture ... Twentieth of July, 1824. ... *Philadelphia: Joseph R. Skerrett.* 1824. 8vo, pp. 80. BA. — Second Edition. [*Ibid.*] 8vo, Title, pp. 66. H. + Fourth Edition. [*Ibid.*] 24mo, pp. 108. + Fifth Edition, revised ... . *Philadelphia. November* 1827. 8vo, pp. 71. BA. — Address of the Pennsylvania Society for the Promotion of Manufactures and the Mechanic Arts, to the Public. *Philadelphia.* 1827. 8vo. — Address to Congress; being a View of the Ruinous Consequences of a Dependence on Foreign Markets for the Sale of the Great Staples of this Nation, Flour, Cotton, and Tobacco. *Philadelphia.* 1820. 8vo. W. + Second Edition. *Philadelphia: Carey & Lea.* 1820. 8vo. C. — Address to the Farmers of the United States, on the Ruinous consequences to their vital Interests of the Existing Policy of this Country. ... *M. Carey & Son.* 1821. 8vo, pp. 84, (5). BA. + Second Edition. *Philadelphia.* 1821. 8vo. — Address to the Liberal and Humane. *Philadelphia.* 1832. 8vo. — [Carey.] Addresses of the Philadelphia Society for the Promotion of National Industry. ... *Philadelphia: M. Carey and Son.* 1819. 8vo, pp. xvi, 9–280. BA. — [Carey.] ... Addresses to the Citizens of the Southern States: being a Solemn Warning against the Destructive Doctrine of a Separation of the Union, advocated in the Late Message of . George M'Duffie, Governor of South Carolina, as leading inevitably to Civil War ... . Second Edition, improved. ... *Philadelphia: printed by Haswell and Barrington. February* 19, 1835. 8vo, pp. iv, 24. H. — African Colonization. *Philadelphia.* 1829. 8vo. — Annals of Liberality, Generosity, Public Spirit, &c. Third Series, No. III, IV. *Philadelphia.* 1834. 8vo, pp. 4. — An Appeal to Common Sense and Common Justice; ... Intended to prove the extreme injustice as well as the impolicy of the existing tariff. ... *Philadelphia.* 1822. 8vo, pp. 104. + Second Edition, improved. ... *Philadelphia: published by H. C. Carey and I. Lea. March.* 7. 1822. 8vo, pp. (2), 112. H. + Third Edition, improved. ... [*Ibid.*] *April* 2, 1822. 8vo, pp. 112. BA. — Appeal to the Justice and Humanity of the Stockholders of the Chesapeake and Delaware Canal. *Philadelphia.* 1825. 8vo. — Appeal to the Wealthy of the Land, ... on the Character, Conduct, Situation and Prospects of those, whose sole Dependence for Subsistence is on the Labour of their Hands. Second Edition. *Philadelphia.* 1833. 8vo, pp. 36. + Third Edition. *Philadelphia. August* 15, 1833. — ... The Boston Report and Mercantile Memorials. No. I. [Signed Hamilton, dated Feb. 4, 1828. Second Edition, March 14, 1828. n. p. n. d.] 8vo, pp. 4. BA. — Canal Policy. *Philadelphia.* 1824. 8vo. + Second Edition. *Philadelphia.* 1825. 8vo. — [Carey.] Third Edition, March 29, 1827. Colbert, — No. I. [Dated Jan. 22, 1827. n. p. n. d.] 8vo, pp. 4. BA. (I have seen, also: Appendix, No. IV. Colbert, — No. I. Fourth Edition, April 25, 1827. [n. p. n. d.] 8vo, pp. 41–48. — Philadelphia, May 3, 1826. Colbert — Third Series — No. II.–IV. [n. p. n. d.] 8vo, pp. 5–12, 5. II., III., 1st ed., Nov. 1826; 2d ed., May 3, 5, 1827; IV., June 14, 1827.) — Collectanea: Displaying the Rise and Progress of the Tariff System of the United States. ... *Philadelphia.* 1833. 8vo, pp. 25. — Controversy with Fenno. *Philadelphia.* 1806. 8vo. P. — [Carey.] Cursory Views of the Literal and Restrictive Systems of Political Economy; with an Examination of Mr. Huskinson's System of Duties on Imports. By a Citizen of Philadelphia. Second Edition, greatly enlarged and improved. ... *Philadelphia: printed by J. A. R. Skerrett.* 1826. 8vo, pp. 26. BA. + Fourth Edition ... enlarged ... . *Philadelphia: printed by J. R. Skerrett. Dec.* 12, 1826. 8vo, pp. 30. H. (Signed "Hamilton," and called "Twelfth Series.") + Second Edition. *Philadelphia* 1832. 8vo. — [Carey.] A Desultory Examination of the Reply of the Rev. W. V. Harold to a Catholic Layman's Rejoinder. By a Catholic Layman. To which is annexed ... the above Reply verbatim . ... *Philadelphia: H. C. Carey & I. Lea.* 1822. 8vo, pp. 72. BA. + Second Edition. *Philadelphia.* 1822. 8vo. — Desultory Reflections, excited by the Calamitous Fate of John Fullerton. ... Third Edition. *Philadelphia: the Author.* Feb. 10, 1802. 8vo, pp. 24. BA. — Desultory Reflections upon the Ruinous Consequences of a Non-Renewal of the Charter of the Bank of the United States. ... Second Edition. *Philadelphia: the Author.* 1810. 8vo, pp. 23. BA. + Third Edition. ... *Philadelphia: the Author.* 1810. 8vo,

pp. 44. BA., H. — [Carey.] The Dissolution of the Union. A Sober Address to all those who have any Interest in the Welfare, the Power, the Glory, or the Happiness of the United States. ... By a Citizen of Pennsylvania. [Signed Hamilton.] Second Edition. *Philadelphia. September* 1, 1832. 8vo, pp. 36. BA. (*See*, forward, his "Essay.") — Emigration from Ireland and Immigration to the United States. *Philadelphia.* 1828. 8vo. — On Emigration. ... *Philadelphia.* 1814. 8vo. P. — [Carey.] Essay on the Dissolution of the Union threatened by the Nullifiers of South Carolina. ... Second Part. [Signed Hamilton.] Third Edition, improved. *Philadelphia. Oct.* 3, 1832. 8vo, 1 l., pp. 23–36. BA. (*See*, before, his "Dissolution.") — Essays on Banking. ... *Philadelphia.* 1816. 12mo. — Essays on Railroads. Second Edition. *Philadelphia.* 1830. 8vo. — Essays on the Protecting System. ... *Philadelphia.* 1830. 8vo. — Essays on the Public Charities of Philadelphia, intended to vindicate the Benevolent Societies of this City from the Charge of Encouraging Idleness, &c. Fourth Edition, gratuitous. *Philadelphia.* 1829. 8vo. + Fifth Edition. *Philadelphia.* 1830. 8vo. N. — Examination of the Boston Report on Free Trade. *Philadelphia.* 1828. 8vo — [Carey.] Examination of the Charleston (S. C.) Memorial. [Signed Jefferson. Dated Philadelphia, July 17, 23, 25, 28, and Sept. 7, 1827. n. p. n. d.] 8vo, pp. 29. BA. — [Carey.] Examination of the Pretensions of New-England to Commercial Pre-eminence. *Philadelphia.* 1814. 8vo. — Exhibit of the Shocking Oppression and Injustice suffered for sixteen months by John Randall, Contractor for the Eastern Section of the Chesapeake and Delaware Canal. *Philadelphia.* 1825. 8vo. + Third Edition. *Philadelphia.* 1825. 8vo. — Extracts from "Letters on the Colonization Society," with its probable results on the white and colored population of the United States ... . [n. p. n. d.] 8vo, pp. 8. BA. — [Carey.] Extracts from the Crisis ... . By a Pennsylvanian. Second Edition. ... *Philadelphia: H. C. Carey & I. Lea. Dec.* 22, 1823. 8vo, pp. viii, 53–79. BA. — Extracts from the Olive Branch, No. 3, on the Protecting System. In Letters to Hon. W. Drayton and Hon. H. Middleton. [*Philadelphia.* 1832.] 8vo, pp. 68. — Female Wages and Female Oppression. *Philadelphia.* 1835. 8vo, pp. 8. — [Carey.] Fifty-one Substantial Reasons against any Modification whatever of the Existing Tariff: whereby the Consistency and Propriety of the Opposition of the Cotton Planters, the Tobacco Planters, and the Merchants, To the "Infernal Bill," are fully justified. By a Pennsylvanian. ... *Philadelphia: H. C. Carey & I. Lea.* 8vo, pp. 12. BA. (I find an edition mentioned "*Phil.* 1824." pp. xvi, 27.) — [Carey.] Fragment. Addressed to the Sons and Daughters of Humanity, By a Citizen of the World. *Philadelphia: Printed for Mathew Carey.* MDCCXCVI. Sm. 8vo, pp. 8. — [Carey.] Hamilton. New Series. *Philadelphia.* 1824. 8vo. + Fourth Series. *Philadelphia.* 1822. 8vo. — [Carey.] Hamilton. Eleventh Series, — No. I [– VII. *Philadelphia. Aug.* 28–Dec. 5, 1826.] 8vo, pp. 34. — [Carey.] Historical sketch of and remarks upon Congressional Caucuses for President & Vice-President. From the Olive Branch. *Philadelphia: the Author.* 1816. 8vo, pp. 36. H. — Infant Schools. *Philadelphia.* 1830. 8vo. — [Carey.] Internal Improvement. [Dated Philadelphia, Nov. 12, 1829. n. p. n. d.] 8vo, pp. 4. BA., W. — [Carey.] A Last Appeal to the Stockholders of the Chesapeake and Delaware Canal on the Injustice exercised towards Mr. Randall, the Contractor for the Eastern Section. [n. p. 1825.] 8vo, pp. 8. H. + Second Edition. *Philadelphia.* 1825. 8vo. + Third Edition. *Philadelphia.* 1825. 8vo. — A Letter to the Hon. Mr. Calhoun, Chairman of the Committee on a National Currency. ... *Philadelphia.* 1816. 12mo. P. — Letter to the Editor of the New York Daily Sentinel, on Female Wages. March. 1830. 8vo. — Letters on the Condition of the Poor. *Philadelphia.* 1835. 8vo. + Second Edition. *Philadelphia.* 1835. 8vo. — Letters relating to the Chesapeake and Delaware Canal. *Philadelphia.* 1825. 8vo. — Letters to the Bank Directors, on the pernicious consequences of the prevailing System of Banking Operations ... . *Philadelphia.* 1816. 12mo. C. — Letters to Messrs. Abbott Lawrence ... [etc. Signed M. Carey and dated Philadelphia, Nov. 8–17, 1832. n. p. n. d.] 8vo, pp. 16. B. — [Carey.] "Look before you leap." Addresses to the Citizens of the Southern States: being a Solemn Warning against the Destructive Doctrine of a Separation of the Union,

... Second edition, improved. By the author of "The Olive Branch." *Philadelphia: printed by Haswell and Barrington.* ... 1835. 8vo, pp. iv, 24. H. — [Carey.] A Looking Glass for the Nullifiers. [n. p. 1832?] 8vo, pp. 4. BA. — Matter of Fact versus Messrs. Huskinson and Peel. *Philadelphia.* 1828. 8vo. — [Carey.] Memorial of the Citizens of Philadelphia to Congress. *Philadelphia.* 1827. 12mo. — [Carey.] Memorial to Congress of the Pennsylvania Society for the Encouragement of American Manufactures. *Philadelphia.* 1820. 8vo. — [Carey.] Notice of Societies for promoting Manual Labor in Literary Institutions; with Extracts from Report of New-York Society. Third Edition. *Philadelphia.* 1834. 8vo, pp. 12. — On the Tendency of our System of Intercourse with Foreign Nations. *Philadelphia.* 1822. 8vo. — Political Economists, from Jan. 24, to May 1, 1824. Edited by M. Carey, Esq. Vol. I. *Philadelphia.* 1824. 8vo. — [Carey.] Political Economy. [An Examination of the Treasurer's Report. Signed Colbert. Dated Philadelphia, Jan. 2–March 6, 1826. n. p. n. d.] 8vo, pp. 24. BA. — The Prospect before us. *Philadelphia.* 1822. 12mo. + Fourth Edition. *Philadelphia.* 1822. 12mo. — [Carey.] (Third Edition.) Prospects beyond the Rubicon. [Signed Hamilton. *Philadelphia.* 1833.] 8vo, pp. 27. BA. — [Carey.] Second Series. Nos. 1, 2, 6. 1833. (Second Edition, corrected, March 7, 1833. ... No. I. [n. p. n. d.] 8vo, pp. 2.) — [Carey.] Prospects on the Rubicon. Part II. Letters on the prevailing excitement in South Carolina. On the Means employed to produce it. On the Causes that led to the Depreciation of the Great Staple of the State. And on the Misconception of the Effects of the Tariff. Addressed to the Hon. H. Clay. ... By the Author of the Olive Branch. *Philadelphia: Clark and Raser, Printers.* 1832. 8vo, pp. viii, 5–52. + Third Edition. [*Ibid.*] *February* 27. [*Ibid.*] 8vo, pp. viii, 5–52. BA. — [Carey.] Prospects on and beyond the Rubicon. [Signed Hamilton. *Philadelphia: September* 20, 1830.] 8vo, pp. 8. H. — [Carey.] The Protecting System. No. 1–9. [Dated Philadelphia, Oct. 19–Dec. 26, 1829. Signed Hamilton. n. p. n. d.] 8vo, 14 l. BA. — Reflections on the Causes that led to the Formation of the Colonization Society: ... the manumission of Slaves in the Country .. *Philadelphia.* 1832. 8vo. BM. — Reflections on the Consequence of the Refusal of the Banks to receive in Deposite Southern and Western Bank Notes. ... *Philadelphia.* 1815. 8vo. — Reflections on the Present System of Banking in ... Philadelphia. With a Plan to revive Confidence, Trade, and Commerce, and to facilitate the Resumption of Specie Payments. Second Edition corrected. .. *Philadelphia: the Author. Jan.* 30, 1817. 8vo, pp. 31. H. — Reflexions on the proposed Plan for establishing a College in Philadelphia. By M. Carey. *Philadelphia.* 1826. 8vo. — Reflections on the Renewal of the Charter of the Bank of Pennsylvania. Fourth Edition. *Philadelphia.* [About 1828.] 8vo. — Reflections on the Subject of Emigration from Europe, with a View to Settlement in the United States: containing Brief Sketches of the Moral and Political Character of this Country. ... Second Edition. *Philadelphia: H. C. Carey and I. Lea.* 1826. 8vo, pp. 24. BA. + Third Edition. *Philadelphia.* 1826. 8vo. — Rejoinder to the Reply of the Rev. Mr. Harold, to the Address to ... the Catholic Bishop of Pennsylvania, the Catholic Clergy of Philadelphia, and the Congregation of St. Mary's. In which are detailed The inflammatory and violent proceedings of the Rev. Mr. H. in the year 1812 [1821] ... . By a Catholic Layman ... *Philadelphia: H. C. Carey & I. Lea.* 1822. 8vo, pp. 44. S. + Second Edition. *Philadelphia.* [*Ibid.*] 8vo, pp. 44. BA., W. — Report on American Manufactures. *Philadelphia.* 1819. 8vo. — [Carey.] Review of Three Pamphlets lately published by the Rev. W. V. Harold. ... By a Catholic Layman. Second Edition, corrected ... . *Philadelphia: H. C. Carey & I. Lea.* 1822. 8vo, pp. 40. — [Carey.] Signs of the Times. South Carolina Toasts. [Signed. Dated June 13, 1832. n. p. n. d.] 8vo, pp. 16. BA. — Sketches of Contemporaneous History. 8vo. — A Solemn Warning on the Banks of the Rubicon. No. 5. To the Citizens of South Carolina. *Philadelphia. August*, 1820. — (Fourth Edition, March 1, 1833.) ... The Subscribers, the Acting Committee of "The Pennsylvania Society for the Promotion of Internal Improvements in the Commonwealth," ... submit the following essay, on the construction and reparation of roads [New York

Canals, etc.] ... [n. p. n. d.] 8vo, pp. 8. BA. — Strictures on Mr. Cambreleng's Work, entitled "An Examination of the New Tariff," Nos. 1 to 7. *Philadelphia: September* 17, 1821. — Strictures on Mr. Lee's Exposition of Evidence on the Sugar Duty, in behalf of the Committee appointed by the Free Trade Convention. 8vo. — [Carey.] Supplement to the Gazette of the United States. Prospects beyond the Rubicon. A Gratuitous Exhibition of the Great Southern War Horse, yclept Nullification, alias Separation, alias Dissolution of the Union. ... [Signed Hamilton. Dated Philadelphia, Jan. 18, 1833. n. p. n. d.] 8vo, pp. 8. BA. — [Carey.] Thirteen Essays on the Policy of Manufacturing in this Country. From the New York Morning Herald. ... *Philadelphia: printed by Clark & Raser. Jan.* 29, 1830. 8vo, Title, pp. 30. BA. — Thirty Years' Facts against one Reviewer's Opinion, in the Year 1818, &c. 1825. 8vo. — Thoughts on Penitentiaries and Prison Discipline, 1831. — Three Letters to J. M. Garnett, Esq., of Virginia, on the Present Calamitous State of Affairs. *Philadelphia.* 1820. 8vo. — [Carey.] To the citizens of the United States ... . [Signed Hamilton. Suggesting a Memorial to Congress on the Depressed State of the Country. Dated Philadelphia, Oct. 16, 1824. n. p. n. d.] 8vo, pp. 8. BA. — [Carey.] To the Citizens of the United States. Review of the Address of the Free Trade Convention. — No. III. || No. IV. and Last. [Signed Hamilton. n. d. 1831.] 8vo, pp. 17–24. — [Carey.] To Messrs. N. Goddard ... the Committee of the Boston Merchants. [Signed M. C. Dated Philadelphia, Jan. 17, 24, Feb. 18, 23, March 3, 1828. n. p. n. d.] 8vo, pp. 16. (Second Edition of Nos. I–IV., pp. 13, issued Feb. 29, March 14, and 8. BA.) — [Carey.] To the Public. [A Reply to Benjamin Davies. *Philadelphia. Nov.*, 1796.] 8vo, pp. 4. H. — The Tocsin: a Solemn Warning against the Dangerous Doctrine of Nullification; in other Words, Dissolution of the Union. Containing a View of the Doctrines held by Judge Cooper in 1813, contrasted with his Doctrines in 1824, and 1827. A Similar Contrast between those held by Mr. McDuffie and Major (now Governor) Hamilton in 1821, and ... in 1828, 1831, and 1832. Likewise ... between those of Mr. Calhoun at Different Periods. To which is added a Review of the Tariff of 1832. ... Third Edition, corrected. *Philadelphia. November* 23, 1832. 8vo, pp. 16. BA. — Treaty of 1795, between Great Britain and the United States, with Documents and Strictures. *Philadelphia.* 1795. 12mo. — [Carey.] Twenty-One Golden Rules to depress Agriculture, impede the Progress of Manufactures, paralize Commerce, impair National Resourses ... . To which is annexed a Copious Appendix, containing Fifty-one ... Reasons against any Alteration whatever of the Existing Tariff. By a Pennsylvanian. *Philadelphia: H. C. Carey & I. Lea.* 1824. pp. 56. BA. — Universal Emancipation. *Philadelphia.* 1827. 8vo. — View of the Ruinous Consequences of a Dependence on Foreign Markets for the Sale of the Great Staples of this Nation, Flour, Cotton, and Tobacco. ... Read before ... the Board of Managers of the Pennsylvania Society for Promotion of American Manufactures ... . *Philadelphia.* 1820. 8vo, pp. x, 42. BA. — Views on the Liberal and Restrictive Systems. 1826. 8vo.

CAREY (M.), *Jr.* The Democratic Speaker's Hand-book. Compiled by Matthew Carey, jr. [*pseudonym?*] *Cincinnati: Miami print.* 1868. 8vo, pp. 395. 10890

CARIBBEANA. *See* [Keimer (Samuel)], *Editor.*

CARIBBEE ISLANDS. Acts of Assembly passed in the Charibee Leeward Islands, from 1690 to 1730. *London.* 1734. Folio.

Argument at a Court of Grand Sessions, and Oyer and Terminer in one of his Majesty's Carribee Islands. By a Member of the Inner Temple. *Privately printed.* 1765. 4to. 10892

Copy of the petition, in behalf of W. Freeman, Esq., and other owners of several tracts of Land in the Caribbee Islands in America, against Col. Codrington, Governor of the Leeward Islands, &c. *Privately printed.* 1702. 4to. 10893

Letter to the Right Reverend the Lord Bishop of London, from the Inhabitants of His Majesty's Leeward-Caribbee-Islands, containing some Considerations on his Lordship's Two Letters of May 19, 1727 — The first to the Masters and Mistresses of Families in the English Plantations Abroad; the second to the Missionaries there, in which is inserted a short Essay concerning the Conversion of the Negro-Slaves in our Sugar Colonies. 1730. 8vo, 2 l., pp. 103. 10894

Short Account of the Hurricane that passed through the English Leeward Caribee Islands on Saturday, 30th June, 1733, with remarks by an Inhabitant of St. Nevis. 1733. 8vo.

Cariboo, The Newly Discovered Gold Fields of British Columbia fully described. *London: Darton.* 1862. 12mo.

CARILLO Y PEREZ. Lo Maximo en lo Mínimo la Portentosa Imágen de Nuestra Señora de los Remedios, conquistadora y patrona de la imperial ciudad de México, en donde escribia esta historia Don Ignacio Carrillo y Perez. *México.* 1808. 4to, pp. 18, 153. 10897

[CARITAT (H.)] *See* Vol. II., No. 5205.

CARL, *Prinz zu Solms-Braunfels.* Texas. Geschildert in Beziehung auf seine geographischen, socialen und übrigen Verhältnisse mit besonderer Rücksicht auf die deutsche Colonisation. Ein Handbuch für Auswanderer nach Texas. ... *Frankfurt a M.: Sauerländer.* 1846. 8vo. 2 Maps. 10898

Carl, the Young Emigrant; a Memoir of Schools and Schoolmasters. *Philadelphia: Am. S. S. Union.* 1851. 12mo, 1 l., pp. 233. 10899

CARLEILL (J.) A Discourse upon the entended voyage to the hethermoste parts of America written by Captain Carleill for the better inducement to satisfies such merchauntes, as in disburseing their money, do demande forwith a present returne or gaine; albeit their saied particular disbursement are in such slender sommes as are not worth the speaking of. [n. p. 1583.] 4to, 8 l. J.C.B. 10900

A black letter tract, without a separate title-page, date, or place, reproduced from Hakluyt's voyages.

CARLETON (*Sir* D.), *afterwards Lord Dorchester.* Letters from and to Sir Dudley Carleton, Knt. during his Embassy in Holland, from January 161⅝, to December 1620. *London.* MDCCLVII. 4to, pp. lii, (1). [An imperfect (?) copy ends at p. 510.] BA. + With Large Additions to the Historical Preface. *London.* MDCCLXXV. 4to, 2 l., pp. lxix, 510, (25). B., BD. 10901

"Only 20 copies printed and published at the expense of Lord Royston, the second Earl of Hardwick, the author of the Preface. Again, ... *London.* 1775. 4to. 50 copies printed. 1780. 4to. (best edition) with a portrait." — BOHN'S LOWNDES.

CARLETON (G. W.) Our Artist in Cuba. Fifty Drawings on Wood. Leaves from a Sketch-Book of a Traveler During the Winter of 1864–5. By Geo. W. Carleton. *New York: Carleton.* MDCCCLXV. 16mo, pp. viii, 50 l. BA. 10902

CARLETON. Our Artist in Peru. [Fifty Drawings on Wood.] Leaves from the Sketch-Book of a Traveller, during the Winter of 1865–6. By George W. Carleton. *New York: Carleton.* 1866. Sm. 4to, pp. viii, 50. 10903

CARLETON (G.) Proceedings between Sir Guy Carleton, late Gov. of the Province of Quebec, and Peter Livius, Esq., Chief Justice. *London.* 1779. 8vo. 10904

CARLETON (J. H.) The Battle of Buena Vista, with the Operations of the "Army of Occupation" for One Month. By James Henry Carleton, Captain in the First Regiment of Dragoons. *New York: Harper and Brothers.* 1848. 16mo, pp. vii, 238. 2 Maps. BA., C. 10905

Also: Diary of an Excursion to Abó Quarrá and Gran Quivira, in New Mexico, in the "Smithsonian Report" for 1854.

CARLETON (L. C.) The Three Daring Trappers; or, Adventures among the Indians and Beavers. By Latham C. Carleton. *New York: Geo. Munro & Co.* 16mo, pp. 100. 10906

CARLETON (O.) Carleton's Almanac, (Enlarged and Improved) for ... 1794 ... . By Osgood Carleton ... . *Boston: Samuel Hall.* [n. d.] 8vo, pp. (34). B. 10907

CARLETON, *pseudonym. See* [Coffin (Charles Carleton)].

CARLETTI (Francesco). Ragionamenti di Francesco Carletti Fiorentino sopra le Cose da lui vedute ne' suoi Viaggi Si dell' Indie Occidentali, e Orientali Come d' altri Paesi. All' Illustriss. Sig. Marchese Cosimo de Castiglione Gentiluomo della Camera del Serenissimo Granduca di Toscana. *In Firenze nel*

Garbo, Nella Stamperia di Guiseppe Manni 1701. *Per il Carlieri all' Insegna di S. Luigi. Con Licenza de' Superiori.* Sm. 8vo, pp. lxxxviii, (2), 166, 396. H., S. 10908

The first part relates entirely to the West Indies. In the Archivio storico ital. Append., IX. 53–55, is a letter of *Fernando* Carli dated 4 Agosto 1524, relating to the late American discoveries of Juan Verrazani.

CARLI (D.) Il moro trasportato nell' inclita cittá di Venetia, overo Curioso racconto de Costumi, Riti, e Religione de Popoli dell' Africa, America, Asia, & Europa. Rauisati dal ... Padre Dionigio Carli da Piacenza Predicatore Capuccino, et Missionario Apostolico in quelle parti. *Bassano, Antonio Remondinj.* M. DC. LXXXVI. 4to, 8 l., pp. 402, (18); 15–30; 90–106. B.

The first edition is: *Reggio.* 1672. 12mo. Reprinted. *Bologna.* 1674. 8vo. Also: *Bologna.* 1678. Notices of Brazil and Pernambuco on pp. 15–30 of the edition of 1686.

CARLI. Der Nach Venedig überbrachte Mohr, oder Curieuse und warhaffte Erzehlung und Beschreibung aller Curiositäten u. Denckwürdigkeiten welche ihm in seiner etlichjährigen Mission in Africa, America und Europa unter tausendfältigen Leib- u. Lebens-Gefahren aufgestossen. *Augspurg.* 1693. 4to. Plate.

[CARLI.] Delle Lettere Americane. *Cosmopoli.* MDCCLXXX. 2 vols., 16mo, pp. 275, (8); 318, (10). H., P. + Nuova edizione corretta ed ampliata colla 'aggiunta della Parte III. ora per la prima volta impressa. *Cremona.* 1781–83. 3 vols., 8vo. Map. C. 10911

This edition was published by Isidoro Bianchi, dedicated by him to Franklin, and is sometimes erroneously attributed to Bianchi.

CARLI. Lettres américanes, Dans lesquelles on examine l'Origine, l'Etat Civil, Politique, Militaire & Religieux, les Arts, l'Industrie, les Sciences, les Mœurs, les Usages des anciens Habitans de l'Amérique; les grands Epoques de la Nature, l'ancienne Communication des deux Hémisphères, & la dernière Révolution qui a fait disparoître l'Atlantide: pour servir de suite aux Mémoires de D. Ulloa. Par M. le Comte J. R. Carli ... . Avec des Observations & Additions du Traducteur [Jean Bapt. Lefebvre Villebrune]. ... *A Boston, Et se trouve A Paris, Buisson.* M. DCC. LXXXVIII. 2 vols., 8vo, pp. xxii, (1), 520, Map; Title, pp. 4, 536. BA., C. + *Paris.* 1792. 2 vols., 8vo. 10912

"Une troisième partie de ces lettres n'a point été traduite." — *Biog univ.*

CARLI. Les cartas Americanas. Nueva edicion corregida y aumentada con la agregacion de la parte tercera que ahora por

primera vez se da impresa. Traduccion del italiano por Agustin Pomposo Fernandez. *Mexico.* 1821–1822. 3 vols., 4to.

CARLI. Briefe über Amerika, nach der neuesten, verbesserten, und mit dem dritten Theile vermehrten Ausgabe, aus dem Italiänischen des Grafen Carls Carli übersetzt, und mit einigen Anmerkungen versehen von Christian Gottfried Hennig. *Gera: Beckmann.* 1785. 3 vols., sm. 8vo, pp. 468; 502; 368. Map.

The original work is also contained in Tomo XI–XIV, "Della opere del ... Don Gianrinaldo Conte Carli ... . *Milano.* MDCCLXXXIV–XCIX." 19 vols., 8vo. B. "These letters originated in a correspondence of Carli with his cousin, the Marquis Gravisi, in 1777 and 1779. The author describes the manners and customs of the Americans before their country was discovered by the Europeans. Count Carli's object is to confute the assertions of M. de Pauw, in his 'Recherches Philosophiques sur les Américains,' and to show that the Americans were descended from the ancient Atlantides." — RICH, I. 292, 351. *See also* "Biog. Universelle," M. R., LXXIX. 579, and Faribault, p. 22.

CARLI. Della scoperta dell' America del — J. Rin. Conte Carli — in résposta alla lettera di M. Otto intorno a tale argumento, Stampata nel Vol. II. di Transazioni di Società di Filadelfia. *Milano.* 1792. 8vo. 10915

Title from Meusel X. 2, p. 336. This is also perhaps only in Tomo XIX. of his "Opere," pp. 239–317. B.

CARLIER (A.) De l'esclavage dans ses rapports avec l'union américaine par Auguste Carlier ... . *Paris: Michel Lévy frères.* 1862. 8vo, pp. xv, 495. BA., C. 10916

CARLIER. Histoire du peuple américain — États-Unis — et de ses rapports avec les Indiens depuis la fondation des colonies anglaises jusqu'a la révolution de 1776 par Auguste Carlier ... . *Paris: Michel Lévy frères.* 1864. 2 vols., 8vo, 2 l., pp. xxviii, 456, (1); 2 l., pp. 511, (1). BA. 10917

CARLIER. Le mariage aux États-Unis par Auguste Carlier *Paris: L. Hachette et Cie* 1860. 18mo, 2 l., pp. 264. BA., C.

CARLIER. Marriage in the United States. By A. Carlier. Translated from the French by B. J. Jeffries. Third Edition. *Boston: De Vries, Ibarra & Co.* 1867. 16mo, pp. xvi, 179. C.

CARLIER. Mémoire sur L'acclimatement des races en Amerique par M. A. Carlier ... *Paris: imprimé par Hennuyer et Fils* ... 1867. 8vo, pp. 65. H. 10920

CARLILE (R.) The Life of Thomas Paine, written purposely to bind with his Writings. By Richard Carlile. *London: M. A. Carlile.* 1820. 8vo, pp. xxxiv. BA. + Third Edition. *London: R. Carlile.* [1821.] 8vo, pp. 27. 10921

CARLILE (T.) An Address Delivered before Essex Lodge. at Salem, Mass. Dec. 28, 1819. On the Evening of 28th December A.L. 5819. By the Rev. Thomas Carlile, A.M. Published by Request. *Salem: Printed by W. Palfray, Jr.* 1819, 8vo, pp. 13. 10922

CARLISLE (J. S.) Speech of Hon. John S. Carlile, of Virginia, on the Bill to confiscate the Property and free the Slaves of Rebels; delivered in the Senate ... March 11, 1862. *Washington.* 1862. 8vo, pp. 13. H. 10923

Also: Speech ... in the Virginia State Convention, delivered Thursday, March 7, 1861. *Richmond: Whig Office.* 1861. 8vo, pp. 29.

CARLISLE (*Earl of*), *and others.* Letters and other Papers relating to the Proceedings of his Majesty's Commissioners. By the Earl of Carlisle, Sir Henry Clinton, William Eden, Esquire, and George Johnstone, Esquire, Commissioners appointed by his Majesty in Pursuance of an Act of Parliament, to treat, consult, and agree upon the Means of quieting the Disorders now subsisting in certain of the Colonies, Plantations, and Provinces of North America. [*New York: Rivington.* 1778.] 8vo, pp. 58.

CARLISLE. Proposed Appendix to the several Publications relating to the Proceedings of his Majesty's Commissioners. By a Well Wisher to the Prosperity both of Great-Britain and North-America. [*New York: Rivington.* 1778.] 8vo, 10 l.

CARLISLE (*Earl of*). *See* Howard (G. W. F.)

CARLISLE (*Bishop of*). *See* Bradford (Samuel), Vol. II., No. 7254.

CARLISLE (*Bishop of*), 1752. *See* Osbaldiston.

CARLISLE (James M.) Oration at Washington on 4th July, 1855. *Washington.* 1855. 8vo. C. 10926

CARLISLE (*Mr.*) Synopsis of the Argument of Mr. Carlisle in the Prize Cases, before the Supreme Court of the United States, at December Term, 1862. 8vo, pp. 13. 10927

CARLISLE, *Mass.* The Confession of Faith, and Covenant, with the Ecclesiastical Principles and Rules, adopted by the Congregational Church in Carlisle, Mass. May, 1853. *Andover: printed by W. F. Draper and Brother.* 1853. 16mo, pp. 8. H.

CARLISLE, *Pa.* Charter and Ordinances of the borough of

Carlisle, with Incidents of its early History, and a Notice of its Present condition. *Carlisle.* 1841. 8vo, pp. 64. 2 Maps. C.

Also: Regulations, Studies, and System of the Common Schools of Carlisle, Pa. ... *Carlisle: Sanderson & Cornman.* 1839. 8vo, pp. 16. H.

CARLOS (C. B.) *See* Bustamante, No. 9566.

CARLOTA. S. M. La Emperatriz Carlota en Veracruz, Nov. 1865. *Veracruz.* 1865. 8vo. 10930

CARLTON (Robert), *pseudon.* *See* [Hall (B. R.)]

CARLYLE (Alexander). The Justice and Necessity of the War with our American Colonies Examined: a Sermon at Inverness, December 12, 1776.—Fast Day for the American Rebellion. *Edinburgh.* 1777. 8vo, pp. 50. N. 10931

CARLYLE (T.) Critical and Miscellaneous Essays. By Thomas Carlyle ... . *Philadelphia: Carey & Hart.* 1845. 8vo, pp. 568. Portrait. BA. + *London: Chapman & Hall.* 1847. 4 vols., 8vo. + [*Ibid.*] 1857. 4 vols., 8vo. + *Boston: Brown & Taggard.* M DCC LX. 4 vols., 8vo. Portrait. BA. 10932

"Dr. Francia," dictator of Paraguay, (1847) IV. 547–568, (1860) IV. 339–399; from the "Foreign Quar. Rev.," 1843, Vol. XXXI., an article which was reprinted in "Campbell's Foreign Semi-Monthly Mag.," IV. 1–27, and in the "Eclectic Museum," III. 75.

CARLYLE. Ausgewählte Schriften Deutsch von A. Kretzschmar. *Leipzig: O. Wigand.* 1855–56. 6 vols., 8vo.

Vol. IV. contains "Dr. Francia."

CARLYLE. Occasional Discourse on the Nigger Question, communicated by T. Carlyle. 1853. Sm. 8vo. 10934

CARLYLE. Shooting Niagara: and after? By Thomas Carlyle. Reprinted from Macmillan's Magazine for August 1867. With some Additions and Corrections. *London: Chapman and Hall.* 1867. 8vo, pp. 55. BA. 10935

Discusses the "late American War" and "the Nigger Question," pp. 5–8, and Governor Eyre, pp. 13, 14.

CARMANY (J. H.) A Review of the Mining, Agricultural, and Commercial Interests of the Pacific States, for the Year 1866. ... Compiled by John H. Carmany. *San Francisco: H. H. Bancroft and Company.* 1867. 8vo, pp. iv, 3–64. H. 10936

CARMARTHEN (*Marquis of*). *See* Osborne (Thomas), *Marquis of Carmarthen.*

CARMICHAEL (*Mrs.* A. C.) Domestic Manners and Social Condition of the White, Coloured, and Negro Population of the West Indies. By Mrs. Carmichael, Five Years a Resident in St. Vincent and Trinidad. *London: Whittaker, Treacher and Co.* 1833. 2 vols., 8vo, pp. viii, 3–336; Title, 338. BA. 10937

Reprinted in Greenbank's "Periodical Library," II. 488–609, and reissued in London, with the title as below:

CARMICHAEL. Five Years in Trinidad and St. Vincent: a View of the Social Condition of the White, Coloured, and Negro Population of the West Indies. By Mrs. Carmichael. *London: Whittaker & Co.* 1834. 2 vols., post 8vo, pp. viii, 3–336; iv, 338. H. 10938

CARMICHAEL (J.) A Self-Defensive War, Lawful, proved in a Sermon preached at Lancaster, before Captain Ross's Company of Military in the Presbyterian Church, on Sabbath Morning, June 4, 1775. By the Rev. John Carmichael, A.M. Now published at the request of the Author, and corrected by himself from the copy printed at Lancaster: Humbly offered to the Perusal of the Military Associations of the City Liberties and County of Philadelphia. *Philadelphia: Printed for and Sold by John Dean, Bookbinder in Lœtitia Court.* 1775. 8vo, pp. 34. P.

CARMICHAEL (W. M.) The Rise and Progress of St. George's Church, Hempstead, including Short Biographical Sketches of the Missionaries and Rectors of the same. Being a Discourse delivered January 1st, 1841. By the Rev. William M. Carmichael, D.D., Rector. *Flatbush: Charles R. Lincoln.* 1841. 8vo, pp. 55, 5. 10940

CARMICHAEL-SMYTH. *See* Smyth (*Sir* James Carmichael).

CARNAHAN (D. T.) Oration on the Death of Abraham Lincoln ... Delivered before the Citizens of Gettysburg, Pa. June 1, 1865. By Rev. D. T. Carnahan, Pastor of the Presbyterian Church. *Gettysburg: Aughinbaugh & Wible, Printers.* 1865. 8vo, pp. 24. B. 10941

CARNAHAN (James). Discourse, before the ... College of New Jersey, on the Sabbath preceding the Annual Commencement. *Princeton.* 1829. 8vo. 10942

Also: An Address to the Students of the College of New-Jersey, at the Funeral of Gerard Seymour Howe, from Virginia ... March 16th, 1836 ... . *Princeton, N. J.: printed by Robert E. Hornor.* 1836. 8vo, pp. 16. B.

CARNARVON (*Earl of*). *See* Herbert (H. J. G.)

CARNE (J.) Lives of Eminent Missionaries. By John Carne, Esq. *London.* 1833–1835. 2 vols., fcap 8vo, pp. 348; 409; + New Edition. *London: P. Jackson.* 1847. 3 vols., fcap 8vo. + *London: H. Washbourne.* 1852. 3 vols., fcap 8vo.

Includes the lives of John Eliot, Hans Egede, David Zeisberger, Mrs. Judson, and David Brainerd.

CARNE (W.) A | Treatise | on the Lawfulness of Defensive War. | In two parts. | By William Carne. | *Philadelphia: Printed & Sold by B. Franklin & D. Hall,* | *at the New Printing Office, in Market Street.* 1748. 8vo, Title, pp. iii, xxviii, 102. 10944

CARNEIRO (Antonio de Mariz). *See* Mariz Carneiro (A. de).

CARNERO (Juan). Las espinas del Hombre Dios: ó su passion y muerte cantadas en octavas castellanas. *Mégico: Hogal.* 1730. 8vo. 10946

CARNES (J. A.) Slave Trade with Africa. *London: Low & Son.* 1852. 12mo. 10947

Also: Journal of a Voyage from Boston to the West Coast of Africa. *Boston.* 1853. 12mo.

CARNESWORTHE, *pseudonym.* Atlantic City. Its Early and Modern History. By Carnesworth. *Philadelphia: W. C. Harris & Co.* 1868. 16mo, pp. 96. C. 10948

CARNOT (Lazare Hippolyte). De l'esclavage colonial. *Paris: Aux bureaux de la Revue indépendante.* 1845. 8vo, pp. 86.

CARO (Ramon Martinez). Verdadera idea de la primera campaña de Tejas y sucesos ocurridos despuis de la accion de San Jacinto. *Mexico: S. Perez.* 1837. 8vo, pp. vii, 162. C. 10950

CARO DE TORRES (Francisco.) Historia de las Ordenes Militares de Santiago, Calatrava y Alcantara. *Madrid.* 1629. Folio. Engraved Title. 10951

Contains some particulars concerning Cortes.

CARO DE TORRES. Relacion de los servicios qve hizo a Sv Magestad del Rey D. Felipe Segundo y Tercero, Don Alonso de Sotomayor del abito de Santiago ... en los Estados de Flandes, y en los Prouincias de Chile, y Tierrafirme, donde fue captain general, ecc. *Madrid: por la viuda de Corme Delgado.* 1620. 4to, 10 l., Text, 88 leaves. J.C.B. 10952

CAROCHI (Orazio). Arte de la lengva Mexicana con la declaracion de los adverbios dello. Al Illustrisso. y Reuerendisso. Señor Don Juan de Mañozca Arçobispo de Mexico, del Consejo de su Magestad, ecc. Por el Padre Horacio Carochi Rector del Colegio de la Compañia de Jesvs de San Pedro, y San Pablo de Mexico. Año de 1645. *Impresso con licencia En Mexico: Por Juan Ruyz. Año de* 1645. 4to, 6 l., Text, 132 l. 10953

Ludewig quotes the following title: "Grammatica y Vocabulario de la Lengua Otomi. *Mexico.* 1645," 4to, and remarks, "The Otomi is the language of the Indians to the north-west of the Valley of Anahac." The title, probably, is an error. Adelung, in his "Mithridates," III. 92, gives the same title, but following Sotwel, who always translates titles, in Latin. Ternaux also gives the title of this book erroneously, and Brunet copies his error. Thorpe, in one of his catalogues, No. 4755, prices it at £8 8s., and appends a note concerning its rarity, which is incorrect. Quaritch, 1870, marks it £10. The author embarked for Mexico in 1605, and died there in 1666.

CAROCHI. Compendio del Arte de la Lengua Mexicana del P. Horacio Carochi de la Compañia de Jesvs; Dispuesto con brevedad, claridad, y propriedad, por el P. Ignacio de Paredes de la misma Compañia, y morador del Colegio destinado solamente para Indios, de S. Gregorio de la Compañia de Jesvs de Mexico: Y dividido en tres partes: En la primera se trata de todo lo perteneciente à Reglas Arte, con toda su variedad, excepciones, y anomalias; En que nada se podrà desear, que no se halle: En la segunda se enseña la formacion de unos vocablos, de otros. Y assi con sola una voz, que se sepa, se podràn con facilidad derivar otras muchas: En la tercera se ponen los Adverbios màs necessarios de la Lengua. Con todo lo qual qualquiera â poco trabajo, y en breve tiempo podrà con facilidad, propriedad, y expedicion hablar e Idioma. Y el mismo no menos afectuoso, que rendido, y reverente lo dedica, y consagra al Gloriosissimo Patriarcha San Ignacio de Loyola, Autor, y Fundador de la Compañia de Jesus. Con Las Licencias Necessarias, *En Mexico, en la Imprenta de la Bibliotheca Mexicana, en frente de S. Augustin. Año de* 1759. 4to, 11 l., pp. 202. Frontispiece. 10954

This is an abridgment of the previous work, with some additions by Paredes. "Il P. Orazio Carochi, dotto Gesuita milanese, pubblicò alguni eleganti versi degli antichi Messicana nella sua eccelente Gramatica." — *Clavigero,* II. 176. "Tres rare. Vendu 139 fr. Rætzel." — BRUNET. The copperplate frontispiece (often wanting) represents S. Ignacio de Loyola.

CAROLINA. An Account of the Foundation and Establishment of a design now on foot for a Settlement on the Golden Islands to the South of Port Royal, in Carolina. By authority of a Royal Charter. *London.* 1720. 4to, pp. 8. 10955

Relates to the project of Sir Robert Montgomery.

An Account of Carolina, 1682. *See* [Wilson (Samuel)].

An Act for the more effectual Preservation of the Government of the Province of Carolina, by requiring all Persons that shall hereafter be chosen Members of the Commons House of Assembly, and sit in the same, to take the Oaths and subscribe the Declaration appointed by this Act; and to Conform to the Religious Worship in the Province, according to the Church of England, and to receive the Sacrament of the Lord's Supper according to the Rites and Usages of the said Church; Read three times, and ratified in Open Assembly, the 6th day of May, 1704. [n. p. n. d.] 4to. 10956

Allerneueste Beschreibung der Provintz Carolina in West-Indien. Samt einem Reise-Journal von mehr als Tausend Meilen unter allerhand Indianischen Nationen. Auch einer Accuraten Land-Carte und andern Kupfer-Stichen. Aus dem Englischen übersetzet durch M. Vischer. *Hamburg, Gedruckt und verlegt, durch seel. Thomas von Wierings Erben, bey der Börse, im güldnen A, B, C. Anno* 1712. *Sind auch zu Franckfurt und Leipzig, bey Zacharias Herteln zu bekommen.* 8vo, 8 l., pp. 368. Plate and Map. 10957

Another Act for the Establishment of Religious Worship in the Province of Carolina, according to the Church of England; and for the Erecting of Churches for the Publick Worship of God; and also for the maintenance of Ministers, and the building convenient Houses for them. Read three times, and ratified in open Assembly, Novemb. 4. 1704. [n. p. n. d.] 4to.

Bericht von der berühmten Landschaft Carolina, in dem Engelländischen America gelegen. An Tag gegeben von Kocherthalern. Dritter Druck, mit einem Anhang ... nebst einer Land-Charte. *Franckfurt a. M.* 1709. 8vo. 10959

Beschreibung von der unglücklichen Reise derer jüngsthin aus Teutschland nach Carolina und Pensylvanien wallenden Pilgrim, dem Kochenthalerischen Bericht entgegen gesetzt. *Frankfurt und Leipzig: Andreä.* 1711. 8vo. + *Hamburg: Weirng.* 1712. 8vo, 24 sheets, 1 l. 10960

A Brief Description of the Province of Carolina on the Coasts of Florida; And more particularly of a New Plantation begun by the English at Cape Feare, on that River now by them called Charles River, the 29th of May, 1664. Wherein is set forth the Healthfulness of the Air; the Fertility of the Earth and

Waters; and the great Pleasure and Profit will accrue to those that shall go thither to enjoy the same. Also, Directions and Advice to such as shall go thither—whether on their own Accompts, or to serve under another. Together with a most accurate Map of the whole Province. *Printed at London for Robert Horne.* 1666. 4to, pp. 10. BD., J.C.B. 10961

The first printed description of Carolina. Reprinted in Carroll, II. 9–18. *See* Ternaux, No. 840. Priced, 1862, £5 5s., in J. R. Smith's Catalogue.

The Carolina Calendar for 4 Years; beginning 1712 and ending 1716. By John Norris. *London.* 1711. 10962

Carolina described more fully than heretofore, being an impartial Collection from the several Relations of that place, since its first planting by the English, and before under the Denomination of Florida, from Divers Letters from the Irish settled there, and Relations of those who have been there several years, whereunto is added the Charter, with the Fundamental Constitutions of that Province, &c. *Dublin.* 1684. 4to. 10963

"One of the most interesting and rare volumes relating to the Province." Thorpe, in 1844, priced it at £3 13s. 6d.

Carolina Law Journal, by A. Blanding and D. J. M'Cord. Vol. I. *Columbia, (S. C.)* 1821. 8vo. 10964

Carolina Law Repository; containing Biographical Sketches of Eminent Judges, Opinions of American and Foreign Jurists, and Reports of Cases in the Supreme Court of North Carolina. *Raleigh.* 1814–'16. 2 vols., 8vo. 10965

Carolina; Or A Description Of that Country, 1682. *See* A[sh] (T[homas]), Vol. I., No. 2172.

The Carolina Tribute to Calhoun. *See* Thomas (J. P.)

The | Case | of | Protestant Dissenters | in Carolina, | shewing | How a Law to prevent Occasional | Conformity There, has ended in the Total | Subversion of the Constitution in Church and | State. | Recommended to the serious Consideration of all that are true | Friends to our present Establishment. | [Motto.] *London,* | *Printed in the Year* M.DCC.VI. | 4to. S. 10966

Pp. 42, followed by the First Charter and other documents, numbered 1 to 14, making pp. 67. For a list of the contents, *see* Stevens' Nuggets, No. 458.

The Case of the Church of England in Carolina, humbly offered to the Consideration of both Houses of Parliament; with Resolves of the House of Lords. [n. p. n. d.] Folio. 10967

The Copy of an act pass'd in Carolina and sent over to be conform'd by the Lord Granville Palatine, and the Rest of the Lords Proprietors of the said Colony. [n. p. n. d.] 4to. BD.

The First Charter granted by the King to the Proprietors of Carolina, Edward Earl of Clarendon, George Duke of Albemarle, William Lord Craven, John Lord Berkeley, Anthony Lord Ashby, Sir George Cartaret, Sir William Berkeley, and Sir Peter Colleton, being excited with a laudable and pious zeal for the Propagation of the Christian Faith, and the Enlargement of our Empire and Dominion. Witness the King at Westminster the 24th day of March, in the Fifteenth Year of our Reign [1662]. 4to. 10969

The Fundamental Constitutions of Carolina, in Number a Hundred and Twenty, agreed upon by the Palatine and Lords Proprietors, to remain the Sacred and unalterable Form and Rule of Government of Carolina for ever. Dat. the first day of March, 1669. Folio, pp. 25. J.C.B. 10970

The following title, from J. R. Smith's catalogue, seems to describe another edition:

The Fundamental Constitutions of Carolina. [1680.] Folio.

"This is presumed to be a modification of the first edition, drawn up by John Locke. It was printed about 1680–1, as the concluding portion of the 120th article runs thus: 'Witness our hands and seals the 12th day of January, 1680,' which is crossed through with the pen in this copy." — J. R. SMITH.

Grant and Release of One Eighth Part of Carolina, from His Majesty to Lord Cartaret. [n. p. 1744.] 4to, Title, pp. 22. Map. C. 10971

The Humble Address Of the Right Honourable the Lords Spiritual and Temporal, In Parliament Assembled, presented to Her Majesty On Wednesday the Thirteenth Day of March, 1705. Relating to the Province of Carolina, And the Petition therein mentioned. With Her Majesties most gracious Answer thereunto. *London, Printed by Charles Bill, and the Executrix of Thomas Newcomb, deceas'd; Printers to the Queens most Excellent Majesty.* 1705. Folio, 2 leaves. C., H. 10972

Relates to the Church Establishment in South Carolina. *See* Kinnett's "Bib. Am. Prov.," p. 192.

Methods for improving the manufacture of Carolina Indigo, submitted to the consideration of the Carolina Planters. *Bath: printed for the Author.* 1772. 8vo, pp. 8. 10973

A ... New Account of ... Carolina, 1683. *See* [Crafford (John)].

Neue Nachricht alter und neuer Merkwürdigkeiten, enthaltend ein vertrautes Gespräch und sichere Briefe von dem Landschafft Carolina und übrigen Englischen Pflantz-Städten in Amerika. *Zürich.* 1734. 8vo, pp. 80. 10974

Der nunmehro in dem Neuen Welt vergnügt und ohne Heimwehe lebende Schweitzer, oder Beschreibung des gegenwärtigen Zustands der Königlichen Englischen Provinz Carolina. *Bern.* 1734. 8vo, pp. 46. 10975

Olden Times in Carolina. By an Octogenarian Lady of Charleston, S. C. *Charleston.* 1855. 12mo, pp. 202. 10976

Party-Tyranny, 1705. *See* [De Foe (D.)]

Proposals for clearing Land in Carolina. *London.* 1682. 4to.

The Representation and Address of Several Members of this present Assembly, returned for Colleton County, and other Inhabitants of this Province, to the Right Honourable John Grenville, Esq; and to the rest of the true and absolute Lords and Proprietors of the Province of Carolina. Dat. 26. June 1705. [n. p. n. d.] 4to. 10978

Surrender of Seven Eighths of Carolina from Lord Cartaret to His Majesty. [n. p. 1774.] 4to, Title, pp. 22. C. 10979

The Two|Charters|Granted by|King Charles IId.|To the|Proprietors|of|Carolina.|With the First and Last|Fundamental Constitutions|of that|Colony.|*London:|Printed, and are to be Sold by Richard Parker, at the|Vnicorn, under the Piazza, of the Royal Exchange.|* [1705.] 4to, Title, pp. 60, Copy of an Act, pp. viii. BA., C., J.C.B. 10980

The copy of an act is not necessarily included with the work. Its title is: "The Copy of an Act lately pass'd in Carolina and sent over to be confirmed here by the Lord Granville, Palatine, and the rest of the Lords Proprietors of the said Colony; which would be highly prejudicial to Her Majesty's interests, destructive to the colony, discouraging to the trade, and a dangerous precedent to the other plantations: As may appear by the act itself, and some Queries thereupon." The "Two Charters" sold, in 1869, for £1 7s. 6d.

Caroline Almanack, and American Freeman's Chronicle for 1840. *Rochester, N. Y.: Mackenzie's Gazette Office.* 12mo, pp. 124. 10981

Contains particulars of the "Caroline Affairs at Niagara."

Caroline Westerley; or, The Young Traveller from Ohio. Containing the Letters of a Young Lady of Seventeen, written to her Sister. *New York.* 1833. 18mo, pp. 233. 10982

"An intelligent young traveller's account of her journey from Ohio, through Western New York, to Albany."

Carolinians Convinced; or an Examination of the Objections to the British Treaty. *New York.* 1795. 8vo. 10983

Carolvs Quintus diuina fauente Clementia Romanorũ Imperator semper Augustus ac Germanie . Hispaniarũ vtriusq, Sicilie . Gerusalem . Vngarie, Dalmatie, Croacie . Insularũ Balleariũ. Fortunatarũque ac noui Orbis Indiarũ ... [Colophon:] *Datum Bononie sub Anno a Natiuitate d'm Millesimoquingentesimotrigesimo* ... [1530.] L. 10984

One vellum sheet, containing ninety-two printed lines. Concerning these Papal bulls, *see* "Bib. Am. Vet.," No. 152.

CARON (R. E.) Revue de la revue du pamphlet de l'hon. R. E. Caron. *Québec.* 1846. 8vo, pp. 18. 10985

I am unable to find the tract of which this is the Review.

CARPENTER (Davis). Speech of Hon D. Carpenter, of New York, delivered in the House of Representatives, May 10, 1854, on the Nebraska and Kansas Bill. *Washington.* 1854. 8vo. S.

CARPENTER (E. G.) An Address delivered before the Penobscot Association of Teachers, and Friends of Popular Education, at Levant, Dec. 28, 1837. By E. G. Carpenter. ... *Bangor: Published by the Association.* 1838. 8vo, pp. 26. H. 10988

CARPENTER (Francis B.) Six Months at the White House with Abraham Lincoln. The Story of a Picture. By F. B. Carpenter. *New York: Hurd and Houghton.* 1866. 16mo, pp. 359. BA., C. 10989

The twenty-fourth edition, 1867, is entitled, "Inner Life of Abraham Lincoln."

CARPENTER (George W.) Annual Medical Advertiser for 1844. *Philadelphia.* 1844. 8vo, pp. 96. 10990

Mr. Carpenter was a druggist at Philadelphia. This is, probably, a mere advertisement.

CARPENTER. A Brief Description of Phil-Ellena, the Country Seat of George W. Carpenter at Germantown, Philadelphia County, Penn. ... *Philadelphia: printed by Barrington and Haswell.* 1844. 12mo. 10991

CARPENTER (H. Smith). Eulogy on the late William Henry Harrison, President of the United States: ... New York, May 28, 1841, by Hugh S. Carpenter. *New York.* 1841. 8vo, pp. 16. S. 10992

CARPENTER. The Final Triumph of Equity. A Sermon preached in Brooklyn, November 26, 1863. ... *New York: W. A. Townsend.* 1864. 8vo, pp. 28. 10993

CARPENTER. The Relation of Religion to the War: A Sermon ... on Fast-Day, Sept. 26, 1861. By the Rev. Hugh Smith Carpenter. *New York: W. A. Townsend.* 1861. 8vo, pp. 23

CARPENTER (J. S.), *Reporter. See* Chase (D. T.)

CARPENTER (M. H.) Argument of Matt. H. Carpenter in the Supreme Court of the United States, March 3, and 4, 1868, in the matter of Ex Parte Wm. H. McCardle, Appellant. Reported by D. F. Murphy. *Washington: Government Printing Office.* 1868. 8vo, pp. 83. 10995

CARPENTER. The Powers of Congress The Constitutionality of its Acts on Reconstruction Alarming Tendency of the Seymour Democracy. Speech ... at Chicago, Ill., August 12th, 1868. *Washington, D. C.* [1868.] 8vo, pp. 8. 10996

CARPENTER. State of Wisconsin — Supreme-Court. John Druecker vs. Edward Salomon. Immunity of the Executive from civil suit; for acts performed under color of office. Brief for Governor Salomon. Matt. H. Carpenter, Counsel. *Milwaukie: J. H. Yewdale, printer.* [n. d.] 8vo, pp. 28. H. 10997

CARPENTER. War Power Outside the Constitution. Matt. H. Carpenter's Review of Mr. Ryan's Address. *Milwaukie, Wis.: Presses of Starr & Son.* ... 1862. 8vo. pp. 16. H.

CARPENTER (Nathanael). Geography Delineated ... in Two Books, containing the Spærical and Topical parts thereof. *Oxford.* 1625. 2 vols., 4to. 10999

Book II. pp. 115–131, relates to America, and California is mentioned as the fifth continent. The author remarks, that, by a Spanish chart taken by the Hollanders, it has been discovered to be an island, and not part of the continent as supposed.

CARPENTER (P. P.) Lectures on Mollusca; or, "Shell-fish" and their Allies. Prepared for the Smithsonian Institution, by Philip P. Carpenter, BA., PH.D. *Washington.* 1861. 8vo, pp. 140. 11000

CARPENTER. On the Vital Statistics of Montreal. *Montreal.* 1867. 8vo. 11001

CARPENTER. Report on the Present State of our Knowledge with regard to the Mollusca of the West Coast of North America. [Extract.] *London: Taylor & Francis.* 1857. 8vo, 4 l., pp. iv, 159–368. C. 11002

CARPENTER (R. L.) Observations on American Slavery, after a Year's Tour in the United States. By Russell Lant Carpenter, B.A. *London: Edward T. Whitfield.* 1852. 8vo, pp. v, 69. 11003

Also: A Farewell Lecture To the Friends of Temperance, pledged and unpledged, in Halifax ... . *Halifax: T. J. & F. Walker, printers.* 1865. 12mo, pp. 28. H.

[CARPENTER (Stephen Cullen).] Memoirs of the Hon. Thomas Jefferson, Secretary of State, Vice-President, and President of the United States of America; containing a Concise History of those States, from the Acknowledgment of their Independence. With a View of the Rise and Progress of French Influence and French Principles in that Country. ... In Two Volumes. [*New York:*] *Printed for the Purchasers.* 1809. 2 vols., 8vo, pp. iv, 404; 1 l., pp. 434. B., C. 11004

The author criticises very severely the character and administration of Thomas Jefferson.

CARPENTER. Select American Speeches. Forensic and Parliamentary, with prefatory remarks, being a Sequel to Dr. Chapman's Select Speeches. By S. C. Carpenter. *Philadelphia.* 1815. 2 vols., 8vo, pp. 492; 481. 11005

Includes speeches by Patrick Henry, J. Madison, James Wilson, Fisher Ames, Alexander Hamilton, Gouverneur Morris, William Wirt, and others. Also: Report of the Trial of Joshua Nettles and Elizabeth Cannon, for the Murder of John Cannon, On the Night of the 24th October, 1804. By S. C. Carpenter. ... *Office of the Charleston Courier.* 1805. 8vo, pp. 127. BA.

CARPENTER (T.) The American Senator; or A Copious and Impartial Report of the Debates in the Congress of the United States: including all Treaties, Addresses, Proclamations, &c. ... during the Present Session, being the Second of the Fourth Congress. [From December 5, 1796, to March 4, 1797.] By Thomas Carpenter. *Philadelphia: printed by John Page.* 1796–97. 3 vols., 8vo, pp. 352, (4); 366, (4); 2 l., pp. 367–787, (12). B., P. 11006

CARPENTER. *See* Burr (Aaron), and Fries (John).

CARPENTER (W.) The proper Mode of observing a Public Fast; considered and explained. A Sermon preached, December 13, 1776, being the Fast Day on account of the Troubles in America. ... By William Carpenter. *London: Robinson.* 1776. 4to. 11007

CARPENTER (W. H.) The History of Illinois, from its Earliest Settlement to the Present Time. By W. H. Carpenter. *Philadelphia: Lippincott, Grambo & Co.* 1854. 12mo. Portrait of G. R. Clark. 11008

CARPENTER. The History of Massachusetts, from its Earliest Settlement to the Present Time. *Philadelphia: J. B. Lippincott, Grambo & Co.* 1853. 12mo, pp. 330. C. 11009

CARPENTER. History of Tennessee, from its Earliest Settlement to the Present Time. *Philadelphia: Lippincott, Grambo & Co.* 1854. 12mo. 11010

CARPENTER *and* ARTHUR (T. S.) History of Connecticut, from the Earliest Settlement to the Present Time. By W. H. Carpenter and T. S. Arthur. *Philadelphia.* 1854. 12mo.

CARPENTER. History of New Jersey from its Earliest Settlement to the Present Time. Edited by W. H. Carpenter and T. S. Arthur. *Philadelphia: Lippincott, Grambo & Co.* 1853. 24mo, pp. 261. 2 Plates. H. + 1858. 24mo, pp. 261. B.

CARPENTER. History of Ohio, from its Earliest Settlement to the Present Time. *Philadelphia.* 1854. 12mo. 11013

CARPENTER. History of Pennsylvania, from its Earliest Settlement to the Present Time. *Philadelphia.* 1854. 12mo.

CARPENTER. History of Vermont, from its Earliest Settlement to the Present Time. *Philadelphia.* 1853. 12mo.

CARPENTER (W. M.) Sketches from the History of Yellow Fever; showing the Origin: together with the facts and circumstances disproving its domestic Origin, and Demonstrating its Transmissibility. By W. M. Carpenter. *New Orleans: J. B. Steel.* 1844. 8vo, pp. 64. 11016

CARPENTER (W. W.) Travels and Adventures in Mexico, in the course of Journeys of upwards of 2500 miles, performed on foot. Giving an account of the Manners and Customs of

the People, and the Agricultural and Mineral resources of that country. By William W. Carpenter, late of the U. S. Army. *New York: Harper & Brothers.* 1851. 12mo, pp. 300. C., P.

CARPENTIER. Resumé des voyages et explorations dans les rivières de la Guyane. Par le lieutenant de vaisseau Carpentier, capitaine de l'Oyapock. *Paris: imp. Paul Dupont.* 1869. 8vo, pp. 35. 11018

From the "Revue coloniale," Dec., 1856.

CARPIO (M.) Poesias del Sr. Doctor Don Manuel Carpio con su biografia escrita por el Señor Dr. D. José Bernardo Couto. Segunda Edicion. *Mexico.* 1860. 8vo, pp. xxx, 368.

CARPON (C. J. A.) Voyage à Terre-Neuve. Observations et notions curieuses propres à intéresser toutes les personnes qui veulent avoir une idée juste de l'un des plus importants travaux des marins français et étrangers, recueillis pendant plusieurs séjours faits dans ces froides régions. *Caen: Poisson.* 1852. 16 l.

CARR (E. S.) An Inaugural Address delivered ... before the Board of Regents of the University of Wisconsin, Jan. 16, 1856. By Ezra S. Carr. *Madison.* 1856. 8vo, pp. 21. S. 11021

CARR (G. P.) The Contest; A Poem. By George P. Carr. *Chicago: P. L. Hanscom.* 1866. Square 18mo, pp. 115.

CARR (J.) Aura; or the Slave. A Poem. By John Carr. *Philadelphia.* 1788. 12mo. 11023

CARR (J.) Early Times in Middle Tennessee. By John Carr, a Pioneer of the West. *Nashville: E. Carr.* 1857. 16mo. pp. 248. C. 11024

CARR (S.) A Brief Sketch of La Crosse, Wisconsin. By Rev. Spencer Carr. *La Crosse.* 1854. 12mo, pp. 28. M.

CARRABY (S.) Conférence sur Franklin. Par M. S. Carraby. *Paris: imp. Prissette.* 1869. 8vo, pp. 20. 11026

CARRAMELLI (H.) Report of the Committee on the President's Message relating to Hamet Carramalli. *Washington.* 1806. 8vo. W. 11027

CARRANCO (L.) Relacion de la vida y gloriosa muerte del P. Lorenzo Carranco Jesuita missionero de Californias. *Mégico.* 1751. 4to. 11028

CARRANZA (A. J.) Tesis sobre la libre navegacion de los rios, pronunciada y sostenida por A. J. Carranza. *Buenos Aires.* 1856. 8vo, pp. 22. 11029

CARRANZA (D. G.) A Geographical Description of the Coasts, Harbours, and Sea Ports of the Spanish West-Indies; particularly of Porto Bello, Cartagena, and the Island of Cuba. With Observations of the Currents, and the Variations of the Compass in the Bay of Mexico, and the North Sea of America. Translated from A curious and authentic Manuscript, written in Spanish by Domingo Gonzales Carranza, his Catholick Majesty's principal Pilot of the Flota in New Spain, Anno 1718. To which is added, An Appendix, containing Capt. Parker's own Account of his taking the town of Porto Bello, in the Year 1601. With An Index, and a New and Correct Chart of the Whole; as also Plans of the Havannah, Porto-Bello, Cartagena, and La Vera Cruz. *London: Caleb Smith.* M.DCC.XL. 8vo, pp. xi, 136, (8). Map, and 4 Plans. C., H. 11030

CARRANZA (F. X.) Alabanza poetica con motivo de la entrada pública del Exmo Sr. Duque de la Conquista, Virey de la Nueva España. *Mégico: Ribera.* 1740. 4to. 11031

CARRANZA. El Llanto de las Pietras: elogios sepulcrales de la Señora Marquesa de las Torres, Doña Gertrudis de la Peña, Fundadora de la Casa Profesa de la Compañia de Jesus en Mégico. Por F. Xavier Carranza. *Mégico: Sanchez.* 1739. 4to.

Title according to the Backers. Another authority gives it as follows: "Exéquias de la Marquesa de las Torres de Rada. *Mexico.* 1739." 4to. Another has "Torres de Roda."

CARRANZA. La Transmigracion de la Iglesia à Guadalupe. *Mégico: en el Collegio de S. Ildefonso.* 1749. 4to. 11033

"Carranza maintains, in this curious sermon, that St. Peter's chair will be transported to Guadeloupe." — BACKER. Also: Sermon de la Epifania. *Mégico: Ribera.* 1743. 4to.

CARRANZA (J. M.) Discurso sobre el Establecimiento de una Escuela Publica Gratuita de Primeras Letras y Christiana Educacion de los Niños Pobres. *Mexico.* 1788. 4to, 23 l.

CARRARA (U.) Columbus, Carmen Epicum ... Authore Ubertino Carrara, Societat. Jesu. *Romæ: typis Rocchi Bernabò.* MDCCXV. 8vo, pp. 299, 1 l. + *Auguttæ* [sic]: *Sumptibus Mathiæ Wolff.* M. DCCXXX. 8vo, 3 l., pp. 3–330, (29). BA. 11035

This Latin poem, by the Jesuit Carrara, contains a biography of Columbus. "L'invention et la conduite de ce poème héroique en douze chants, sont vraiment poétiques; mais le style l'est beaucoup moins." — BACKER.

CARRASCO Y SAAVEDRA (B.) Synodo diocesana, con la carta pastoral convocatoria para ella y otra en orden à la paga de los Diezmos. Celebrola D. Fray Bernardo Carrasco y Saavedra, Obispo de Santiago de Chile, en la Iglesia Catedral de dicha ciudad. A que se dió principio Domingo 18 de Enero de 1688 y se publicó en 2 de Mayo de dicho año. *Lima.* 1764. Folio, pp. 168. 11036

CARRASCO (E.) Calendario y Guia de Forasteros de la República Peruana pora el año de 1826 por Don Eduardo Carrasco. *Lima: J. Gonzalez.* [1826.] 12mo, pp. 135. 11037

Also for other years; the last of which I have seen a notice is for 1850.

CARRASCO (José Matias). Beschreibung der Provinz Mojos in Süd Amerika. Aus dem Spanischen als Manuscript gedruckten Originale ins Deutsche übersetzt von F. W. Hoffmann. Aus Lüdde's Zeitsch. f. verglich. Erdkunde, III. 1 abgedruckt. *Magdeburg: Baensch.* 1843. 8vo. 11038

CARRASCO Y ENCISCO (Luis). Sermon panegir. del glor. padre Bern. Abad. *Mexico.* 1808. 4to, 33 leaves. 11039

Also: Sermon panegirico de Santjago el mayor, que le hace la congregacion del Reyno de Galicia. *Mexico.* 1809. 4to, 30 leaves. — Sermon moral del Fuego vengador de la Caridad y de la Dureza de las Palabras con que se han de redarguir las impiedades de Napoleon y sus sectarios. Para el Triduo de las Rogaciones que con el fin de impetrar los Triunfos de la Religion y la Patria celebraron ante la Imagen portentosa de Maria Santisima de los Remedios las M. RR. MM. Religiosas Dominicas del Convento de Santa Catalina de Sena de Mexico, en el 15 de Julio de 1810. Y pronuncio el R. P. Ex-Lector Fr. Luis Carrasco y Encisco. *Mexico.* 1810. 4to, 5 l, pp. 64.

CARRÉ (E.) Echantillon de la Doctrine que les Jesuites Enseignent aux Sauvages du Nouveau Monde, pour les convertir, tirée de leurs propres manuscrits, trouvés ces jours passés en Albanie, proche de Nieu Yorke, Examinée Par Ezechiel Carrè cy deuant Ministre de la Rochechalais en France, à present Ministre de l'Eglise Francaise de Boston en la Nouvelle Angleterre. ... *Imprimé a Boston par Samuel Green.* 1693. 4to, Title, 1 l., pp. 3, 2, 11. W. 11040

With a preface by Cotton Mather. An extremely rare tract.

CARREL (N. A.) Œuvres littéraires et économiques d'Armand Carrel recueillis et annotées par M. Charles Romey Précédées d'une notice biographique par M. Émile Littré *Paris: Victor Lecou; Guillaumin et Cie* MDCCCLIV. 18mo, 2 l., pp. 366. B.

Includes "Collaboration de Carrel à la Revue américaine, La mère de Washington," pp. 208–214.

CARRERA (F. la). Arte de la Lengua Yunga de los Valles del Obispado de Trujillo del Peru, con un Confessonario, y todas las Oraciones Christianas traducidas en la Lengua, y otras Cosas. Por D. Fernando de la Carrera cura y vicario de S. Martin de Reque en el corregimiento de Chiclayo. *Lima: Juan de Contreras.* 1644. Sm. 8vo. 11042

Excessively rare, and unknown to the author of the "Mithridates." Lord Kingsborough paid £15 15s. for his copy. The Yunga is the language of the Peruvian Indians of Truxillo, etc., and entirely different from the Quichua. *See* Ludewig, page 206, and Ternaux, No. 631.

CARRERA (L.) Vindicacion documentada, que presenta al juicio del publico y de sus amigos Lorenzo Carrera, Agente de la Convencion Española en Mejico. *Madrid.* 1856. 8vo, pp. 72. 11043

CARRERI. *See* Gemelli Carreri.

CARREY (E.) L'amazone. Les métis de la Savane. Par Émile Carrey. *Paris: Michel-Lévy.* 1857. 18mo, pp. 332.

CARREY. L'Amazone. Les révoltés du Para. *Paris: Michel-Lévy.* 1857. 16mo, pp. 337. C. 11045

CARREY. Émile Carrey. Grandeur et avenir des États-Unis ... *Paris: Dentu.* 1863. 8vo, pp. 48. BA. 11046

CARRIEDO (J. B.) Estudios historicos, y estadisticos del estado Oaxaqueno. *Oaxaca.* 1850. 2 vols., 8vo. 11047

CARRIEDO. Rasgo biografico del presbitero licenciado D. Manuel Sabino Crespo, heroe de la nacion Mejicana, escrito por el ciudadano J. B. Carriedo. *Oaxaca.* 1833. 8vo, pp. 19.

CARRIER (A. H.) The Great Kentucky Statesman, or, the Life and Public Services of Henry Clay. By A. H. Carrier. *Philadelphia.* 1851. 12mo. 11049

CARRIER. Monument to the Memory of Henry Clay. By A. H. Carrier. ... *Philadelphia: Duane Rulison.* ... 1859. 8vo, pp. 516. Portrait. 11050

The Carrier of the Political Index to his Patrons, with the Compliments of the Season [in verse]. *Newburgh.* 1814. 8vo, pp. 14, 1. 11051

The carriers' addresses of sundry newspapers contain incidental references to the topics of the day, but are not of sufficient importance to be included in this Dictionary.

CARRIGLIO (Alonso). Discorsi apologetici, in che si da relatione delle Persecutioni, e trauagli partiti del R. P. D. Fr. Bernardino de Cardenas, Vescouo del Paraguay, nelle Indie Occidentali. Aggiustato il tutto con le scritture presentate nel consiglio dell' Indie, etc. Fra. Gio. di San Diego Vigliaton. [*Madrid.* 1658.] Folio, 5 l., pp. 49, 29, and 15 numbered l.

"This work is almost unknown. The three memoirs of which it consists have been presented to Pope Alexander VII, and were most probably intended for private circulation only." — *Asher.* "Ouvrage Curieux," *Andrade*, p. 163.

CARRILLO (C.) Estudio histórico sobre la raza indigena de Yucatan por D. Crescencio Carrillo ... . *Veracruz: Typografia J. M. Blanco.* 1865. 4to, pp. 26. B. 11053

CARRILLO. Historia de Welinna leyenda Yucateca en dos partes y un apéndice de notas históricas y críticas por D. Crescencio Carrillo, presbítero. Edicion del Repertorio Pintoresco. *Merida: imprenta de Jose Dolores Espinosa.* 1862. 8vo, 1 l., pp. 78. B 11054

CARRILLO (Fernando). Origen y Causa de los Repartimientos de Indios desta Nueva España. *Mexico.* 1633. Folio.

CARRILLO Y PEREZ (Ignacio). Lo maximo en lo minimo; la portentosa imagen de Nuestra Señora de los Remedios, conquistadora y patrona de la imperial ciudad de Mexico. *Mexico: Mariano de Zuñiga y Ontiveros.* 1808. 4to, 10 l., pp. 153, (3), 4 l. Plate. 11056

CARRILLO Y PEREZ. Pensil Americano Florido en el rigor del invierno, la Imágen de Maria Santissima de Guadalupe, aparecida en la corte de la Septentrional América México, en donde escribia esta Historia Don Ignacio Carrillo y Perez ... Año de 1793. *En Mexico.* 1797. Sm. 4to, 12 l., pp. 132. S. 11057

CARRILLO (José). Elogio fúnebre dell Illmo R. D. Nicolás Gomez de Cervantes, en las honras que le hizo como á su Obispo la Stā Iglesia de Guadalaxara. *Megico.* 1736. 4to. 11058

Also: Panegerico de la Sta Monica. *Megico.* 1749. 4to.

CARRINGTON (H. B.) The Hour; the Peril; the Duty. An Address delivered at Columbus, Ohio, April 11th and 17th, 1861, by H. B. Carrington. ... *Columbus, O.: Printed by Harris & Hurd.* 1861. 8vo, pp. 16. H. 11059

[CARRINGTON (J. W.)] The Passage of the Isthmus, or practical hints to persons about to cross the Isthmus of Panama. With a Map. By one who has recently crossed. *New York: Jennings & Harrison.* 1849. 8vo, pp. 14. Map. 11060

[CARRINGTON (*Mrs.* M. J.)] Ab-sa-ra-ka Home of the Crows: being the Experience of an Officer's Wife on the Plains and ... Peril and Pleasure during the Occupation of the New Route to Virginia City, Montana, 1866–7, and the Indian Hostility thereto; with Outlines of the Natural Features and Resources of the Land, Tables of Distances, Maps ... . *Philadelphia: J. B. Lippincott & Co.* 1868. 12mo, pp. 284. 3 Maps.

CARROLL (*Rev.* Andrew). Moral and Religious Sketches and Collections, with Incidents of ten years' Itinerancy in the West. *Cincinnati: the Author.* 1857. 12mo, pp. 302. C. 11062

CARROLL (A. E.) The Great American Battle; or, the Contest between Christianity and Political Romanism. By Anna Ella Carroll. *New York.* 1856. 12mo, pp. 365. 10 Portraits.

CARROLL. A Review of Pierce's Administration; showing its only Popular Measures to have originated with the executive of Millard Fillmore. By Anna Ella Carroll ... *Boston: James French & Company.* 1856. 12mo, pp. 137. C. 11064

CARROLL. The Star of the West; or National Men and National Measures. By Anna Ella Carroll. ... *Boston: James French and Company.* 1856. 12mo, pp. 366. 9 Portraits. H. + Third Edition, Revised. *New York: Miller, Orton & Co.* 1857. 12mo, pp. 461. Portrait. S. 11065

Also: The Relation of the National Government to Revolted Citizens defined. No power in Congress to Emancipate their Slaves or confiscate their property, proved. The Constitution, as it is, the only hope of the Country. *Washington.* 1862. 8vo, pp. 16. — Reply to the Speech of the Hon. J. C. Breckenridge ... in the United States Senate, July 16th, 1861. ... *Washington: Henry Polkinhorn.* 1861. 8vo, pp. 15. H. — The Romish Church opposed to the Liberties of the American People ... *Boston.* 1856. 12mo, pp. 52. — The Union of the States. ... By Anna Carroll. ... *Boston: James French and Company.* 1856. 12mo, pp. 64. H. — The War Powers of the General Government. ... *Washington: printed by Henry Polkinhorn.* 1861. 8vo, pp. 24. H. — Which? Fillmore or Buchanan! ... *Boston: James French and Company.* ... 1856. 12mo, pp. 24. H.

CARROLL (B. R.) Catechism of the United States; History of the Nation, from its earliest Period to the Present Time. By B. R. Carroll. *Charleston, S. C.: McCarter & Co.* 1858. 12mo. 11066

CARROLL. Historical Collections of South Carolina; embracing many Rare and Valuable Pamphlets, and other Documents, relating to the History of that State, from its first Discovery to its Independence, in the Year 1776. Compiled, with various Notes, and an Introduction, by B. R. Carroll. ... *New York: Harper & Brothers.* 1836. 2 vols, 8vo, pp. lxxx, 9–533; 576. BA. 11067

CARROLL (C.) Journal of Charles Carroll of Carrollton, during his Visit to Canada in 1776, as One of the Commissioners from Congress; With a Memoir and Notes by Brantz Mayer ... . Published by the Maryland Historical Society. *Baltimore: printed by John Murphy.* MDCCCXLV. 8vo, pp. 84. BA.

CARROLL (C. H.) Speech of Hon. C. H. Carroll, of New York, on the Mexican War. Delivered in the House of Representatives, February 22, 1847. *Washington.* 1847. 8vo, pp. 7. H. 11069

Also: Speech ... on the Tariff Question. Delivered ... July 1, 1846. [*Washington.*] 8vo, pp. 16. H.

CARROLL (Davis). A Salutatory Address Delivered at a Public Exhibition in Oxford, February 14, 1811. *Sutton, Mass.: Printed by Sewall Goodridge.* 1811. 12mo, pp. 11. 11070

[CARROLL (John).] Address from the Roman Catholics of America to George Washington, President of the United States. *London: Printed by J. P. Coghlan.* 1796. Folio, pp. 8. 11071

Reprinted in facsimile, by Dr. J. G. Shea, with portraits, facsimile of Washington's letter, etc. [*New York.* 1857.] Folio, 2 l., pp. 8.

[CARROLL.] Address to the Roman Catholics of the United States of America. By a Catholic Clergyman. *Annapolis: F. Green.* 1784. M. + *Philadelphia.* 1785. + *Worcester,* [*England*]. 1785. 8vo, pp. 120. + [With the author's name.] *London.* 1785. 8vo. BD. + *London: C. Keating.* 1786. + *New York: ... David Longworth.* 1817. 8vo, pp. 120. 11072

Of the London edition of 1785, Shea says that some additions were made to it, and a note on the suppression of the Jesuits, which had been attacked by Father Arthur O'Leary, was omitted. The pamphlet is in reply to a letter by the Rev. Charles Wharton, of Worcester, England. *See* M. R., LXXII. 395, and H. M., III. 225.

CARROLL. A Discourse on General Washington. Delivered in the Catholic Church of St. Peter, in Baltimore, Feb. 22d, 1800. By the Right Rev. Bishop Carroll. *Baltimore: Printed by Warner & Hanna.* [1800.] 8vo, pp. 24. C. 11073

CARROLL. A Pastoral Letter from the Right Rev. Dr. John Carroll ... Bishop of Baltimore to ... the Congregation of Trinity Church Philadelphia. On the Prostitution of the Rights and the Usurpation of Church Authority by Two Prevaricating Priests and some Misinformed Laicks of the Congregation. *Annapolis.* + *London: printed by J. H. Coghlan.* 1798. 12mo, pp. 20. BD. 11074

CARROLL. Biographical Sketch of the most Rev. John Carroll, First Archbishop of Baltimore; with Select Portions of his Writings. Edited by John Carroll Brent. *Baltimore: John Murphy.* MDCCCXLIII. 12mo, pp. 321. Portrait. 11075

CARROLL. Short Account of Consecrating, etc. *See* [Plowden (C.)]

[CARROLL (J.)] Past and Present, or a description of Persons and Events connected with Canadian Methodism for the last forty years. By a Spectator of the Scenes. *Toronto.* 1860. 12mo, pp. 331. 11076

Also: The Stripling Preacher, or a Sketch of the ... Life of Alexander S. Byrne. *Toronto.* 1852. 12mo, pp. 255. *See* Morgan's "Bib. Canad."

CARROLL (J. H.) A Letter to the Rev. Leonard Bacon, D.D., by J. Halsted Carroll. *New Haven: Printed by Tuttle & Co.* 1866. 12mo, pp. 27. 11077

CARROLL. Memorial of Gerard Hallock: by J. Halsted Carroll. *New Haven: Printed by Tuttle, Morehouse & Taylor.* 1866. 8vo, pp. 79. H. 11078

CARROLL (R. W.) Carroll's Literary Register, May 25, 1865. *Cincinnati.* 1865. 8vo. 11079

CARROLL COLLEGE. Catalogue, 1855. *Waukesha, Wis.* 8vo.

CARRUTHERS (J.) Retrospect of Thirty-six years' Residence in Canada West: Being a Christian Journal and Narrative. *Hamilton.* 1861. 8vo, pp. 253. 11081

CARRUTHERS (J. J.) The War, Its Evils and their Compensations. By the Rev. J. J. Carruthers, D.D. ... *Portland: printed by David Tucker.* 1862. 8vo, pp. 12. H. 11082

CARSON (A.) The History of the Celebrated Mrs. Ann Carson, Widow of the late Unfortunate Lieutenant Richard Smith. With a Circumstantial Account of her Conspiracy against the late Governor of Pennsylvania, Simon Snyder, and of her Sufferings in the several Prisons in that State. Written by Herself. *Philadelphia.* 1822. 12mo. S. 11083

See also Clarke (M.)

CARSON (J. H.) Early Recollections of the Californian Mines, and Description of the Great Tulare Valley. By J. H. Carson. *Stockton.* 1852. 8vo, pp. 64. 11084

CARSON (James). Oration, 12th May, 1802, before the Tammany Society, New York. *New York.* [1802.] 8vo. N.

CARSON (James), *Reporter.* *See* Eberle (F.)

CARSON (J.) A History of the Medical Department of the University of Pennsylvania, from its Foundation in 1765. With Sketches of the Lives of Deceased Professors. By Joseph Carson, M.D., Professor ... &c. *Philadelphia: Lindsay and Blakeston.* 1869. 8vo, pp. xi, 17–227. B. 11086

CARSON. A Memoir of the Life and Character of James B. Rogers, M.D., Professor of Chemistry in the University of Pennsylvania. By Joseph Carson, M.D. ... . *Philadelphia.* 1852. 8vo, pp. 22. H. 11087

Also: Illustrations of Medical Botany. *Philadelphia.* [n. d.] 2 vols., 4to. 100 colored Plates.

CARSON (W.) Reasons for Colonizing the Island of Newfoundland, in a letter to the Inhabitants. By William Carson, M.D. *Greenock.* 1813. 8vo, pp. 26. 11088

See M. R., LXXII. 99.

CARSON. A Letter to the Members of Parliament, on the Address of the Inhabitants of Newfoundland to the Prince Regent. 1813. 8vo. 11089

In Morgan's "Bib. Canad.," the author's name is given as James Carson.

CARSTENSEN (G. J. B.) *and* GILDEMEISTER (C.) New York Crystal Palace. Illustrated Description of the Building. By George Carstensen & Charles Gildemeister, Architects of the Building. With an Oil-color exterior View, and Six large Plates containing Plans, Elevations, Sections, and Details from the working drawings of the Architects. By G. Carstensen and Charles Gildemeister. *New York: Riker, Thorne & Co.* 1854. 4to, pp. 78. 6 Plates. C. 11090

Carta Apologetica. *See* [Yturrizara (Miguel de)].

Carta Athenagorica de la Madre Juana Ynes de la Cruz, Religiosa Profesa de Velo de la ciudad de Mexico. [*Mexico*] *Puebla de los Angeles: D. F. de Leon.* 1690. 4to, 17 leaves. 11091

Carta blanca sobre el negro folleto titulado: Condiciones y semblanzas de los Diputados á Corte por el autor de la "Apología de los Palos." *Habana.* 1821. 8vo. 11092

Carta de un Americano à un Diputado de las Cortes Extraordinarias de España. *Londres.* 1821. 8vo, pp. 50. 11093

Signed "José Isidro Inana y Torre," and addressed to Don A. P. y M.

Carta de un Americano al Español sobre su numero XIX. *London: W. Lewis.* 1811. 8vo, pp. 110. H. 11094

Carta de un amigo á otro que reside en el campo. Describe las fiestas de la Habana en el retorno de Fernando 7º. *Imprenta del Comercio. Octubre de* 1814. 8vo. 11095

Carta Escrita à un Americano sobre la forma de Gobierno que para hacer practicable la Constitucion y las Leyes conviene establecer en Nueva España, atendida su actual situacion. *Madrid: Ibarra.* 1821. Sm. 4to, pp. 12. H. + *San-Sebastian.* 1831. 8vo, pp. 16. 11096

Carta escrita por un regnicola recien llegado á esta capital á un paisana suyo residente en Madrid. *Mexico.* 1789. 4to, pp. 12. 11097

Carta familiar de un Sacerdote, Respuesta a un Colegial amigo suyo, en que le dà cuenta de la admirable Conquista espiritual del vasto Imperio del Gran Thibèt, y la Mission que los Padres Capuchinos tienen alli con sus singulares progressos hasta el presente. *Mexico: en la Imprenta de la Bibliotheca Mexicana.* 1765. 4to, 2 l., pp. 48. Plate. 11098

See on pages 28–29: "Porquè los Capuchinos, teniendo Missiones en la America, no han fundado en ella Conventos?"

Carta que a los Sres. diputados de las Cortes dirige el intendente de exército (D. Rafael Gomez Roubaud), accompañado copia de las representaciones presentadas á S. M. con motivo de haber mandado suspender los efectos de la providencia acordada por S. A. el consejo de regencia, y publicada en la Gazeta de gobierno de 27 de Abril último, número 56. *Cadiz: Imprenta de la junta superior.* 1811. Folio, pp. 79. 11099

"D. Rafael Roubaud était employé à la manufacture des tabacs à la Havana; cette pièce traite longuement de cette marchandise." — LECLERC.

Carta, | qve el P. Francisco | Xavier Rector del Colegio | Maximo de S. Pablo, y al presente Preposito | Provincial de la Provincia del Perù. | Remitio a Los Padres Rectores de | los Colegios, y Casas de la Compañia de Iesvs | de la dicha Provincia. | Dandoles vna breve noticia | de la exemplarissima vida, y dichosa muerte | del Venerable P. Diego de Avendaño. | Año. 1689. | *Con licencia en Lima. Por Ioseph de Contreras.* 4to, 3 l., 63 l.

Carta sobre lo que debe hacer un Principe que tenga Colonias à gran Distancia. *Philadelphia.* 1803. 8vo. C. 11101

CARTAGENA (Juan). La Stā Iglesia de Guatemala, Madre fecundissima de hijos illustrisimos. *Mégico: Ribera.* 1747. 4to.

CARTAGENA. *See* Carthagena.

CARTAGINESE (H.) Giornale Politico, Edicione Terza. *Philadelphia.* 1804. Rl. 8vo. 11103

CARTARI (V.) Le vere e nove imagini de gli Dei delli antichi. Di Vicenzo Cartari. Caveta da' marmi, bronzi, medaglie, gioie ... con esquisito studio da L. Pignoria. Con le allegori e sopra le imagini de C. Malfatti. *Padoua.* 1615. 4to. + *Venetia: Tomasini.* MDCXLVII. 4to, 11 l., 2 folded l., pp. 400. B.A. + *Venetia: Nicolò Pezzana.* M. DC. LXXIV. 4to, 10 l., pp. 368.

Part II. contains: "Imagine de gli dei Indiani Orientali et Occidentali."

Cartas edificantes. *See* Lettres edifiantes. 11105

Cartas sobre la educacion del bello sexo por una Señora Americana, A.M. 1824. 8vo. + *Morelia.* 1855. Sm. 8vo, pp. ix, 124. + *Morelia.* 1858. 11106

CARTEAUX (Félix). Examen politique des colonies modernes, dans le but le plus particulier de savoir si celles de France lui onte été avantageuses ou non. *Bordeaux: P. Beaume.* 1805. 8vo. 11107

C[ARTEAUX]. Histoire des désastres de Saint Domingue. Ouvrage ou l'on expose les causes de ces événemens par F. C*** un de ses précédens colons. *Bordeaux.* 1802. 8vo, pp. 42, 306. 11108

The following is, apparently, an enlarged edition of this work:

C[ARTEAUX]. Soirées bermudiennes, ou entretiens sur les événements qui ont opéré la ruine de la partie française de Saint Domingue. Par F. C***, un de ses précédens colons. *Bordeaux: P. Beaume.* 1802. 8vo. pp. 400. 11109

CARTEAUX. Le Songe de Colomb, en vers, Accompagné de notes historiques, morales et politiques; ... Par Félix Carteaux, Colon réfugié. *Bordeaux.* 1809. 8vo, pp. 143. H. 11110

CARTEAUX (J. F.) Examen politique des Colonies modernes. *Bordeaux: P. Beaume, an* XIII–1805. 8vo, pp. 136. 11111

CARTÉE (Cornelius S.) Elements of Physical and Political Geography. *Boston: Hickling, Swan & Brewer.* 1856. 12mo, pp. 342. C. 11112

[CARTER (*Mrs.* A. A., *wife of* Daniel S.)] Home Ballads: a Book for New Englanders. In Three Parts. By Abby Allin. ... *Boston and Cambridge.* MDCCCLI. 16mo, pp. 238. BA. 11113

CARTER (H.) A Brief Sketch of the Life of Horace Carter, who was executed in Worcester Dec. 7. 1825, for the crime of Rape. ... *Worcester.* 1825. 8vo. W. 11114

CARTER (J.) Oration, delivered at Groton, at the celebration of the nativity of St. John, the Baptist, June 25, A.L. 5821, before St. John's Chapter [and certain lodges]. By James Carter. *Worcester: Manning & Trumbull, Printers.* 1821. 8vo, pp. 20. M., P. 11115

CARTER. Geography of New Hampshire, Historical Sketch of every Town, &c. *Portsmouth.* 1831. 18mo. 11116

CARTER (J. G.) Essays upon Popular Education, containing a Particular Examination of the Schools of Massachusetts, and an Outline of an Institution for the Education of Teachers. By James G. Carter. *Boston: Bowles & Dearborn.* 1826. 8vo, pp. 60. BA. 11117

Remarks upon Mr. Carter's Outline of an Institution for the Education of Teachers. From the U. S. Review. *Boston: Bowles and Dearborn.* 1827. 8vo, pp. 25. BA. — Biographical Sketch of James G. Carter, With his Outline of a Plan of an Institution for the Education of Teachers, ... and his Memorial to the Legislature of Massachusetts, ... Reprinted from Barnard's American Journal of Education, for Sept., 1858. *Hartford, Ct.: F. C. Brownell.* [n. d.] 8vo, pp. 24. Portrait. — Also: Letters to the Hon. William Prescott, LL.D. on the Free Schools of New England, with Remarks upon the Principles of Instruction. By James G. Carter. *Boston: Pub. by Cummings, Hilliard & Co.* 1824. 8vo, pp. 123. C., H. — Also: Address at the Consecration of Plymouth Lodge, Sept. 6, 1826. *Plymouth.* 1826. 8vo, pp. 37. — A Lecture on the Developement of the Intellectual Faculties as the Proper Purpose of Elementary Studies, and on teaching Geography; ... Boston, August 23, 1830, ... *Boston: Hilliard, Gray, Little and Wilkins.* 1830. 8vo, pp. 42. — Letter to the Rev. Nathaniel Thayer, touching his Conduct in connexion with the recent proceedings of the Church in Lancaster under his pastoral care; and upon the Rights, Dignity and Tenure of the Office of Deacon in a Congregational Church. ... *Boston.* 1833. 8vo, pp. 136. H. —

Copy of his Answer to the Vote of the Church of Christ in Lancaster, Mass. 1832. 8vo. — Speech ... delivered in the House of Representatives of Massachusetts, Feb. 2, 1857, ... on the Appropriation of One-half the Surplus Revenue to Common Schools. *Boston.* 1837. 12mo, pp. 30. M. — Proceedings of the Senate and House of Representatives, upon the Petition of George R. M. Withington and Others, ... that James G. Carter be removed from his Office of Justice of the Peace. ... *Boston: George C. Rand & Co., Printers.* 1849. 8vo, pp. 74.

CARTER (J. G.) *and* BROOKS (W. H.) A Geography of Massachusetts; for Families and Schools. ... By James G. Carter and William H. Brooks. With a New Map ... . *Boston: Hilliard, Gray, Little, and Wilkins.* 1830. 18mo, pp. x, 224. Map.

CARTER *and* BROOKS. A Geography of Middlesex County; for Young Children ... . By James G. Carter and William H. Brooks. With a New Map ... . *Cambridge: Hilliard and Brown.* 1830. 18mo, pp. 106. B. 11119

CARTER. (Luther C.) "Propositions with my Imperfect Answers." [Dated] *Hermitage, Flushing, L. I., June* 2, 1862. pp. 14. 11120

This pamphlet has no title. It consists of four Propositions on Government, with the author's Answers, and is submitted to the public, "hoping to receive more perfect ones from the ready writers in our midst." Also: Speech ... in the House of Representatives, January 18, 1860. 8vo, pp. 16. H. — State of the Union. Speech ... in House of Representatives, February 27, 1861. pp. 8.

CARTER (N. H.) An Oration, delivered before the Republicans of Portland ... [July 4, 1815]. By Nathaniel H. Carter. *Portland: printed by F. Douglas.* 1815. 8vo, pp. 19. BA.

CARTER (N. J.), *Reporter.* *See* New York.

CARTER (R.) A Summer Cruise on the Coast of New England. By Robert Carter. *Boston: Crosby and Nichols.* 1864. 12mo, pp. viii, 261. BA., C. 11122

CARTER (T.) French Mission Life; or, Sketches of remarkable Conversions and other Events among French Romanists in the City of Detroit. By the Rev. Thomas Carter. *New York: Carlton & Porter.* 1857. 16mo, pp. 157. C. 11123

CARTER (W.) A Genuine Detail of the Several Engagements, Positions, and Movements of the Royal and American Armies, during the Years 1775 and 1776; with an Accurate Account of the Blockade of Boston, and a Plan of the Works on Bunker's Hill, at the time it was abandoned by his Majesty's Forces on the 17th of March, 1776. In a Series of Letters to

a Friend. By William Carter, Late a Lieutenant of the 40th Regiment of Foot. *London: G. Kearsley.* 1784. 4to, Title, pp. 50. Plan. Errata, 9 lines. BA. 11124

See . R., LXXII. 231.

CARTER (W.) A Memorial of the Congregational Ministers and Churches of the Illinois Association. By Rev. W. Carter. *Quincy, Ill.* 1863. 8vo, pp. 48. 11125

CARTER *and* GLOSSBRENNER. History of York County from its Erection. *York. Penn.* 1834. 12mo. 11126

CARTERET (Philip). Voyage. *See* Hawkesworth (J.), Account, v. 1; Kerr, Coll., v. 12; Fleurieu, C. P. C. de. Découvertes; Henry, D. Hist. Account, v. 3; Montémont, A. Bib. univ., v. 3.

CARTHAGENA. An Account of the Expedition to Carthagena, with Explanatory Notes and Observations. ... *London: M. Cooper.* MDCCXLIII. 8vo, 2 l., pp. 58. H. + The Second Edition. *London: M. Cooper.* MDCCXLIII. 8vo, 2 l., pp. 58. + The Third Edition. *London: M. Cooper.* MDCCXLIII. 8vo, 2 l., pp. 58. + *Dublin.* MDCCXLIII. 8vo. 11128

Also in Smollett's "Compendium of Voy.," Vol v. *See* "Gentleman's Magazine," May, 1743; "Notes & Queries," 3d. S. IV. 310.

An Account of the Taking of Carthagena by the French and Buccaniers, 1740. 11129

An uncertain title from an English sale catalogue.. *See* Pointis.

Acontecimientos de Cartagena con Ad. Barrott, consul frances. *Bogota.* 1833. 11130

Authentic Papers Relating to the Expedition against Carthagena: being the Resolutions of the Councils of War; both of Sea and Land-Officers Respectively, at Sea and on Shore: Also the Resolutions of the General Council of War, composed of both the Sea and Land-Officers, held on Board the Princess Carolina, &c. With Copies of the Letters which passed between Admiral Vernon and General Wentworth; and also between the Governor of Carthagena and the Admiral. *London: L. Raymond.* 1744. 8vo, 2 l., pp. 100. Plate. H. 11131

The second edition has the following title:

Authentic Papers relating to the Expedition against Carthagena. Containing original letters between the Admiral and

General, their Councils of War, &c. Also Letters between the Vice King of Santa Fe, Governor of Carthagena, and the Admiral. Second Edition, to which is prefixed a Preface. *London: L. Raymond.* 1744. 8vo, pp. vi, 100. Plate. J.C.B. 11132

Constitucion del estado de Cartagena de Indias sancionada en 14. de Junio del año de 1812. segundo de su Independencia. *Cartagena de Indias D. Espinosa.* [1812.] 4to, pp. 128, 3 l.

A Journal of the Expedition to Carthagena. *See* [Wentworth (*Gen.*)]

Original Papers Relating to the Expedition to Carthagena. *London: M. Cooper.* MDCCXLIV. 8vo, 2 l., pp. 154. + The Second Edition. *London: M. Cooper.* MDCCLXIV. 8vo, 2 l., pp. 154. C. 11134

Piezas Oficiales relativas a los Acontecimientos de Cartajena. *Bogota.* 1833. 11135

Relation de l'Expédition de Carthagène. *See* [Pointis (J. B. Des Jeans, *sieur de*)].

Remarks on the Canal, or "Dique" of Carthagena, New Granada, and its Navigation by Steam. *New York.* 1855. 8vo, pp. 67. 11136

Viage, y svcesso de los Carauelones, Galeoncetes de la guarda de Cartagena de las Indias, y su costa. Y la grandiosa victoria que han tenido cõtra los Cossarios Piratas en aquel Mar, este año 1621. [Colophon:] *Madrid, por la viuda de Cosme Delgado.* 1621. Folio, 2 leaves. 11137

CARTIER (J.) Brief recit, &|succincte narration, de la nauiga-|tion faicte es ysles de Canada, Ho-|chelage & Saguenay & autres, auec|particulieres meurs, langaige, & ce-|rimonies des habitans d'icelles: fort|delectable à veoir.|Avec priuilege| *On les uend à Paris au second pillier en la grand|salle de Palais, & en la rue neufue Nostredame à|l'enseigne de lescu de frãce, par Ponce Roffet dict|Faucheur, & Anthoine le Clerc frères.*|1545.| Sm. 8vo, 48 leaves. 11138

This original edition is of the greatest rarity. Priced, by Muller, at $125. "Cette édition est de la plus grande rareté; je n'en connais pas d'exemplaire. L'éditeur de celle de Rouen de 1598 annonce qu'il l'a fait traduire de langue étrangère, probablement de l'italien de Ramusio; ce qui prouve que déjà, a cette épocque, cette première édition était introuvable." — TERNAUX, No. 51. It was reprinted with the following title:

CARTIER. Bref récit et succinte narration de la navigation faite en MDXXXV et MDXXXVI par le capitaine Jacques Cartier aux iles de Canada, Hochelaga, Saguenay et autres Réimpression figurée de l'édition originale rarissime de MDXLV avec les variantes des manuscrits de la Bibliothèque Impériale précédée d'une brève et succinte introduction historique par M. D'Avezac. *Paris: Tross.* 1863. 8vo, Title, xvj, (1), 68 l. BA. 11139

This reprint is an elegant volume. Copies were printed on Holland paper, on Whatman's drawing paper, and two on vellum.

CARTIER. Discovrs|dv|voyage|fait par le capit-|aine Iaqves Cartier | Aux Terres-Neufues de Canadas, No-| rembergue, Hochelage, Labrador et|pays adiacens, dite nouuelle France,| auec particulieres|mœurs, langage et|ceremonies des habitans d'icelle. | *A Roven, de l'imprimerie de Raphael Du Petit-Val.* | M.D.XCVIII. | 8vo, pp. 72. 11140

Translated probably from Ramusio, Vol. III. *See* Ternaux, Nos. 51 and 199. Republished by the Quebec Literary and Historical Society. Included in Ternaux's "Archives des Voyages," Vol. I. *See* Faribault, Nos. 111 to 115, Boucher de la Richarderie, "Biogr. universelle," Charlevoix, and Fontette. It was also reprinted with the following title:

CARTIER. Voyage de Jacqves Cartier av Canada en 1534 Nouvelle édition, publiée d'après l'édition de 1598 et d'après Ramusio Par M. H. Michelant avec deux cartes Documents inédits sur Jacques Cartier et le Canada communiqués par M. Alfred Ramé *Paris: Tross.* 1865. 8vo, 2 l., pp. vii, 72, 2 l., pp. 54. 2 Maps. BA. 11141

See Ramusio, Vol. III., and Pinkerton, Vol. XII. Uniform in size and style with the "Brief recit," and a similar number printed. Of the unpublished documents here given, six being all, but two really referring to Cartier, were published by the Quebec Literary and Historical Society in 1862, in Vol. v. of their Transactions, under the care of Faribault, who published another in facsimile.

CARTIER. Relation originale du voyage de Jacques Cartier au Canada en 1534 Documents inédits sur Jacques Cartier et le Canada (nouvelle série) publiés par H. Michelant et A. Ramé Accompagnés de deux portraits de Cartier et de deux vues de son Manoir *Paris: Tross.* 1867. 8vo, Title, 2 l., pp. vii, 76, 54. BA. 11142

CARTIER. Voyages de découverte en Canada entre les années 1534 et 1542; par Jacques Quartier, le Sieur de Roberval, Jean Alphonse de Xanctoigne, ... ré-imprimés sur d'anciennes relations, et publiés sous la direction de la Société littéraire et historique de Québec, avec préface et notes, [par G.

B. Faribault, Ecr.] *Québec: W. Cowan.* 1843. 8vo, pp. 6, 130. 11143

Includes the first, second, and third voyages of Cartier — the third from Hakluyt.

CARTIER. A shorte and briefe narration of the two navigations and discoveries to the north-weast partes called New Fraunce, first translated out of French into Italian by that famous learned man J. B. Ramutius, and now turned into English by John Florio. *London: H. Bynneman.* 1580. 4to, pp. 4, 80. J.C.B. 11144

Cartilla del Federalista. *Mexico.* 1833. Sm. 8vo, pp. 20.

Cartilla para los gefes y los pueblos en America. *Nueva-York.* 1823. 8vo, pp. 36. 11146

The Cartridge Box. Published at the United States Army General Hospital, York, Penn. No. 1, March 1, 1864. 4to.

CARTTER (D. K.) Speech of Hon. David K. Cartter, of Ohio, on the Finality of the Compromise. ... House of Representatives, May 25, 1852. *Washington.* 1852. 8vo, pp. 8. H.

CARTWRIGHT (C.) Faithful Narrative of the Unfortunate Adventures of Charles Cartwright, who, in his Voyage to Jamaica, was Taken by a Spanish Privateer, and carried into St. Sebastian, his Hard Usage there, and Wonderful Escape from thence. *London.* 1741. 8vo. 11149

Title from one of Thomas Thorpe's catalogues.

CARTWRIGHT (G.) A Journal of Transactions and Events, during a Residence of Nearly Sixteen Years on the Coast of Labrador; containing many interesting particulars, both of the Country and its Inhabitants, not hitherto known. Illustrated with proper Charts. By George Cartwright, Esq. In three Volumes. *Newark: Printed and Sold by Allin and Ridge.* 1792. 3 vols., 4to, 2 l., pp. xvi, 287; x, 505; x, 248, 15. Portrait, Plates, and 5 Maps. B., C. 11150

"This Journal is written with care and fidelity; the style of the author is plain and manly; he delivers his sentiments with freedom, and with confidence, asserts only those circumstances which, from his own observations he knows to be facts. The author was a brother of the celebrated Major John Cartwright." Highly commended by Coleridge. There are copies on large paper, rl. 4to. *See* M. R., XIII. 397, and XIV. 43.

C[ARTWRIGHT]. Labrador; a Poetical Epistle. By G. C., Esq. *Doncaster.* 1785. 4to, pp. 24. 11151

[CARTWRIGHT (John).] American Independence the Interest and Glory of Great Britain; or, Arguments to prove, that not only in Taxation, but in Trade, Manufactures, and Government, the Colonies are entitled to an entire Independency on the British Legislature; and that it can only be by a formal Declaration of these Rights, and forming thereupon a friendly League with them, that the true and lasting Welfare of both Countries can be promoted. In a Series of Letters to the Legislature. To which are added copious Notes; containing Reflections on the Boston and Quebec Acts; and a full Justification of the People of Boston, for destroying the British-taxed Tea; submitted to the Judgment, not of those who have none but borrowed Party-opinions, but of the candid and honest. *London: Printed for the Author, by H. S. Woodfall.* M. DCC. LXXIV. 8vo, pp. xvi, iv, 72. 11152

Speaking of this publication, the author's biographer says, "at a time when no Member of Parliament had sufficient decision of mind to propose the Independence of America, Major Cartwright suggested the expediency of an Union between Great Britain and her Colonies under separate Legislatures." *See also* M. R., LVIII, 238. Reprinted with the following title:

[CARTWRIGHT.] American Independence the Interest and Glory of Great Britain; Containing Arguments which prove, that not only in Taxation, but in Trade, Manufactures, and Government, the Colonies are entitled to an entire Independency on the British Legislature; and that it can only be by a formal Declaration of these Rights, and forming thereupon a friendly League with them, that the true and lasting Welfare of both Countries can be promoted. In a Series of Letters to the Legislature. *Philadelphia: Robert Pell.* MDCCLXXVI. 8vo, pp. 127.

See M. R., LVIII. 238. The following year the book was republished with large additions, as below:

CARTWRIGHT. American Independence, the Interest and Glory of Great Britain. A New Edition. To which is added, A copious Appendix, containing two additional Letters to the Legislature; a Letter to Edmund Burke, Esq. controverting his Principles of American Government. And A Postscript, containing new Arguments on the Subject; A Draught of a Bill proposed to be brought into Parliament for restoring Peace and Harmony between Great-Britain and British America, and for perpetuating the same: Together with The essential Materials for a proposed Grand British League and Confederacy, to be entered into by Great-Britain and all the States of British America. The whole of which shews, beyond Denial or Doubt, that

by granting the Colonists an unrestrained civil Freedom and Legislative Independence, we may most effectually secure their future Commercial Dependence upon, and consequently shall best promote the Interest, and support the Glory of Great-Britain. ... *London: J. Wilkie.* M.DCC.LXXV. 8vo, 1 l., pp. xvi, iv, 72, 15, 30, 51, (1). Map. B. 11154

The letter to Burke, referred to on the title, was published with a separate title. *See* No. 11157, *infra.* In this new edition the author gives the names and boundaries of nineteen American States, together with a map of the same. *See* M. R., LVIII. 238.

CARTWRIGHT (J.) Commonwealth in Danger. *London.* 8vo.

"On the American colonies."

CARTWRIGHT. The Legislative Rights of the Commonalty vindicated, Containing proposals for recovering America and saving Great Britain. *London.* 1777. 8vo. + Second Edition. *London.* 1777. 8vo, pp. 249. S. 11156

[CARTWRIGHT.] A Letter to Edmund Burke, Esq; Controverting the Principles of American Government, Laid down in his lately published Speech on American Taxation, Delivered in the Honse of Commons, on the 19th of April, 1774. *London: Printed for the Author, by H. S. Woodfall.* M. DCC. LXXV. 8vo, pp. 30. 11157

Written under the signature of "Constitution," and dedicated to Sir George Saville. Although with a separate title and paging, this tract appears to have been published with the second edition of "American Independence," in one book.

CARTWRIGHT. A Letter to the Earl of Abingdon, discussing a Position relative to a Fundameutal Right of the Constitution, contained in his Lordship's Thoughts on the Letter of Edmund Burke, Esq., to the Sheriffs of Bristol. By John Cartwright. *London: J. Almon.* 1778. 8vo. S. 11158

In defense of the right of the colonists to freedom on trade. *See* M. R., LVIII, 237.

CARTWRIGHT. The Life and Correspondence of Major Cartwright. Edited by his Niece, F. D. Cartwright. ... *London: Henry Colburn.* 1826. 2 vols., 8vo, pp. xv, (1), 413; viii, 433. 3 Portraits, Map, and Plan. B., C., P. 11159

Major Cartwright's early life was passed in America, where he distinguished himself by discoveries in New Foundland. The appendix contains his "remarks on the situation of the Aborigines of Newfoundland," now an extinct race. His liberal opinions made him a correspondent of Jefferson and other of the leading political men of the United States, whose letters are frequent in his life. He died, *circa*, 1828 or 1830. A bronze statue was erected to his memory in Burton Crescent, London. *See* M. R., July, 1826.

CARTWRIGHT (P.) Autobiography of Peter Cartwright, the Backwoods Preacher. Edited by W. P. Strickland. *New York.* 1857. 12mo, pp. 525. c. 11160

CARTWRIGHT. Autobiography of Peter Cartwright, the Backwoods Preacher: the Birth, Fortunes, and General Experiences of the Oldest American Methodist Travelling Preacher. Edited by W. P. Strickland. New Edition. *London: A. Hall.* 1862. Crown 8vo, pp. 240. 11161

CARTWRIGHT. Autobiography of the Backwoods Preacher. Edited by W. P. Strickland. New Edition. *London: Simpkin.* 1858. Post 8vo, pp. 246. + 1862. + 8th Thousand. *London.* 1869. 8vo. 11162

CARTWRIGHT. The Backwoods Preacher: Autobiography of Peter Cartwright. *London: Heylin.* 1859. 12mo, pp. 510.

CARTWRIGHT (R. J.) Remarks on the Militia of Canada. *Kingston: Daily News Office.* 1864. 8vo, pp. 46. 11164

CARTWRIGHT (S. A.) Essays, being Inductions drawn from the Baconian Philosophy proving the Truth of the Bible and the Justice and Benevolence of the Decree dooming Canaan to be Servant of Servants ... by Samuel A. Cartwright, M.D. Of Natchez, Miss. *Vidalia, opposite Natchez.* 1843. 8vo, pp. 68. 11165

CARTWRIGHT (W.) Comedies, Tragi-Comedies, with other Poems, by Mr. William Cartwright, late Student of Christ-Church in Oxford, and Proctor of the University. The Ayres and Songs set by Mr. Henry Lawes, Servant to his late Majesty in his Publick and Private Musick. *London: printed for Humphrey Moseley.* 1651. 8vo, pp. 598. 11166

The "Ordinary" contains some reference to New England. *See* "Hist. Mag.," I. 281.

CARUTHERS (E. W.) Revolutionary Incidents: and Sketches of Character, chiefly in the "Old North State." By Rev. E. W. Caruthers, D.D. *Philadelphia.* 1854. 12mo, pp. 431. Maps. P. 11167

CARUTHERS. Interesting Revolutionary Incidents and Sketches of Character, chiefly in the "Old North State." Second Series. By Rev. E. W. Caruthers, D.D. *Philadelphia.* 1856. 12mo, pp. 448. 11168

CARUTHERS. A Sketch of the Life and Character of the Rev. David Caldwell, D.D., near Sixty Years Pastor of the Churches of Buffalo and Alamance. Including Two of his Sermons; Some Account of the Regulation, Together with the Revolutionary Transactions and Incidents in which he was Concerned; and a very brief notice of the Ecclesiastical and Moral Condition of North-Carolina while in its Colonial State. By the Rev. E. W. Caruthers, A.M. *Greensborough, N. C.: Swain and Sherwood.* 1842. 8vo, pp. 302, Index, 1 l. S. 11169

Contains interesting Revolutionary reminiscences respecting North Carolina.

CARUTHERS (J. E.) God's Hand in the War. A Sermon ... On the National Fast Day, April 30, by the ... Rev. J. E. Caruthers. *Pittsburgh: printed by Ferguson & Co.* 1863. 8vo. pp. 11. 11170

CARUTHERS (R. L.) A Compilation of the Statutes of Tennessee, ... from the Commencement of the Government to the present time. By R. L. Caruthers and A. O. P. Nicholson. *Nashville.* 1836. 8vo, pp. 799, cviii. C. 11171

[CARUTHERS (William), *of Va.*] The Kentuckian in New York; or, the Adventures of Three Southerns. By a Virginian. *New York: Harpers.* 1834. 2 vols., 12mo, pp. 223; 219. C.

Also: The Cavaliers of Virginia, or the Recluse of Jamestown. *New York.* 1835. 2 vols., 12mo.

CARUTHERS The Knight of the Horse Shoe; a Traditionary Tale of the Cocked Hat Gentry in the Old Dominion. *Weptumpka, Ala.* 1845. 8vo, pp. 284. 11173

CARUTHERS (W. A.) A Lecture delivered before the Georgia Historical Society, at the Unitarian church, in Savannah, on Tuesday evening, 14th March, 1843. By William A. Caruthers, M.D. *Savannah.* 1843. 8vo, pp. 36. S. 11174

CARVAJAL (B.) Oratio super præstanda solenni obedientia San'|ctissimo. D. N. Alexandro Papæ VI ex parte Chri'|stianissimorum dominor Fernandi & Helisabe [*sic*] Re|gis & Reginæ Hispaniæ: habita Romæ in consisto|rio publico per R. Patrem dñm Bernardinum Car'|uaial Epm Carthagineñ. die Mercurii. xix. Iunii Sa|lutis Christiane. M.cccc. xciii. Pontificatus eiusdem|D. Alexandri Anno Primo. In qua fuere quattuor ce|lebres Oratores: Nobilissimus dñs Didacus Luppi|de Faro Galleciæ uicerex. R. D. Gundissaluus Fer'|nãdi Heredia Archiepis-

copus Tarraconeñ. Idem. D.|Bernardinus Caruaial Epus Carthagineñ. D. Iohan|nes Methina Episcopus Pacensis.|Vitulus & Leo simul morabuntur: & puer paruu|lus minabit eos. Esayæ. xi. *Romæ.* 1493. Sm. 4to, 8 leaves. 11175

Bernardin de Carvajal, a Spanish Cardinal and statesman, born at Palencia about 1456, died 1523. The author was Spanish Ambassador to the Court of Rome. This very rare volume is curious for its early reference to the discoveries of Columbus. Audiffredi supposes it to be printed by Silber, and quotes a copy in the Vatican. *See* "Bibliotheca Grenvilliana," and [Harrisse] "Bib. Amer. Vet." Priced, 1836, by Thorpe, £3 3s.

CARVAJAL (M.) Cuaderno que contiene las comunicaciones oficiales habidas entre el Exmo. Sr. Gobernador y Comandante general de este Departamento D. Francisco de Paulo Toro, y el comandante de la escuadrilla nacional que estuvo en este puerto, capitan de fregata D. Francisco Reibaud, &c., &c. Publicadas por M. Carvajal, Srio. general. *Merida.* 1836. 8vo, pp. 48.

CARVAJAL Y RIBERA (F. F.) Memorial del Maestro Fr. Fernando de Carvajal y Ribera Arçobispo de St. Domingo. [n. p. n. d.] Folio, pp. 7. J.C.B. 11177

"Probably printed in or about 1699." — J. R. BARTLETT.

CARVALHAES (Rodrigo Pinto Pizarro de Almeida). Noticias biographicas de Francisco Homen de Magalhães Pizarro, do conselho de S. M. commendador de Sancta Marinha de Lisboa, governador e capitão-general nomeado do Maranhão, etc. *Rio de Janeiro: na Imp. Regia.* 1819. 4to, pp. 29. 11178

For other works by this author, *see* Silva, VII. 179–181.

CARVALHO (Hippolyte). Études sur le Bresil au point de vue de l'emigration et du commerce français. *Paris: Garnier frères.* 1858. 8vo. 11179

CARVALHO (S. N.) Incidents of Travel and Adventure in the Far West with Col. Fremont's last Expedition, across the Rocky Mountains: including Three Months' residence in Utah; and a Perilous Trip across the Great American Desert to the Pacific. By S. N. Carvalho, Artist to the Expedition. *New York: Derby and Jackson.* 1860. 12mo, pp. 250; Mormonism, pp. 130. 11180

CARVALLO E MELLO (Sebastião José de), *Marquis de Pombal.* Cartas e outras obras selectas do Marquez de Pombal ... Tomo I. *Lisboa: na Typ. Morandiana.* 1820. 8vo. 11181

The Marquis of Pombal was Secretary of State to Joseph I, of Portugal, and many of his dispatches relate to Brazil. "Four other volumes were successively issued, and

some were reprinted in different years by different printers. It is a very ill arranged collection, and full of errata, but, for want of a better edition, became very rare, and Borel, Borel & Co. published a reprint in two or three volumes." — SILVA, VII. 209–215.

CARVER (H.) A Memorial for a private Charter, asked for by Dr. Hartwell Carver and his associates, to build a Railroad from some point on the Mississippi or Missouri rivers, or from Lake Michigan to the Pacific Ocean. *Washington.* ... 1849. 8vo, pp. 8. H. 11182

One of the first projects of its kind.

CARVER (John), *pseudonym.* *See* [Dodge (N. S.)]

CARVER (Jonathan). The New Universal Traveller. Containing a full and distinct account of all the Empires, Kingdoms, and States, in the known World. *London.* 1779. Folio.

"This compilation the widow of Captain Carver denied to be the work of her husband." — BOHN'S LOWNDES, I. 383.

CARVER. Travels through the Interior Parts of North America, in the Years 1766, 1767, and 1768. By J. Carver, Esq., Captain of a Company of Provincial Troops during the late War with France. Illustrated with Copper Plates. *London: printed for the Author, and sold by J. Walter,* ... M DCC LXXVIII. 8vo, 10 l., pp. xvi, 543, (1). 2 Maps and 4 Plates. + *Dublin: S. Price.* MDCCLXXIX. 8vo, 10 l., pp. 508. Map and 2 Plates. + Second Edition. *London: ... J. Dodsley ...* MDCC.LXXIX. 8vo, pp. (xxii), 543. 2 Maps and 4 Plates. + The Third Edition. To which is added, Some Account of the Author, and a copious Index. *London: C. Dilly; H. Payne; and J. Phillips.* M DCC LXXXI. 8vo, 2 l., pp. 22, 11 l., pp. 543, 21. Portrait and 1 Plate, 3 colored Plates, 2 Maps. BA. 11184

The first edition is printed with a large margin, and is often called, in booksellers' catalogues, large paper. I have seen many copies, but they were all the same size until cut by the binder. To the third and best edition, a biography of the author, and an index, are added by John Coakley Lettsom, M.D., who had become the proprietor of the work, and whose preface is dated March 30, 1781. The new plates include a portrait of Carver, and a colored drawing of the tobacco plant. With the exception of the prefatory matter, however, and the index to this edition, the three are precisely alike. The life and index were printed separately, "for the convenience of the purchasers of the first and second editions; on whom I was unwilling to raise an extraordinary tax for the third edition." — J. C. LETTSOM. Lowndes quotes a large paper copy; but I have not seen one entitled to that appellation. "Carver came to England soon after he returned from his travels, with the intention of publishing his account of them; but when he had already sold the MS. to a bookseller, he was ordered by the government to deliver up all his maps and journals; and it was not until near ten years after, that he obtained permission to publish the work." — M. R., LX. 90.

CARVER. Three Years Travels ... [Without the Account of the Author.] *Philadelphia: Joseph Crukshank, and Robert Bell.* M DCC LXXXIV. 8vo, pp. 217. BA. + *Philadelphia: Joseph Crukshank.* 1789. 12mo, pp. xvi, 282. + [Another Edition.] *Philadelphia.* 1789. 8vo. + *Philadelphia: Printed by Joseph Crukshank.* 1792. 12mo, pp. xvi, 282. + *Printed at Portsmouth, New Hampshire, by Charles Peirce, for David West: Boston.* M,DCC,XCIV. 12mo, pp. xvi, 282. B. + *Philadelphia.* 1795. 8vo. + *Philadelphia: Key & Simpson.* 1796. 8vo, pp. xx, ix, 360, Subscribers, pp. 28. + *Boston: Printed by John Russell, for David West.* 1797. 12mo, pp. xvi, 5–312. BA., H. + *Edinburgh.* 1798. 8vo. + *Charlestown.* 1802. 12mo, pp. 312. P. + *Edinburgh.* 1807. 8vo. + *Edinburgh.* 1808. 8vo. + *Walpole, N. H.: Isaiah Thomas & Co.* 1813. 12mo, pp. 280. + *Walpole, N. H.: Isaiah Thomas.* 1838. 12mo, pp. 280.

"This valuable work lately attracted much attention from its description of parts near to the supposed North-West Passage." — LOWNDES. An admirable work, full of novel information respecting the interior of North America, and its savage inhabitants. Although this work was very favorably received, and went through several editions, its author derived but little benefit from it; and, in 1780, "a putrid fever supervening a long continued dysentery, brought on by want, put an end to the life of a man, who, after rendering, at the expense of fortune and health, and the risk of life, many important services to his country, perished through want, in the first city of the world." — LETTSOM. "Omnia utila aeque ac jucunda, magnem partem nova." — MEUSEL. *See* N. A. R., L. 75, M. R., LXV. 392, and Schoolcraft's "Personal Memoirs, p. 168. The opening of the Wisconsin Territory suggested to an enterprising firm the republication of the work, under the following title:

CARVER. Travels in Wisconsin, from the Third London Edition. *New York: Harper & Brothers.* 1838. 8vo, pp. 376. 5 Plates, 2 Maps, and Portrait. 11186

CARVER. Reisen durch die innern Gegenden von Nord-Amerika in den Jahren 1766, 67 und 68, mit einer Landkarte. Aus dem Englischen. *Hamburg: C. E. Bohn.* 1780. 8vo, pp. xxiv, 456. 11187

CARVER. Voyage dans les parties intérieures de l'Amérique septentrionale, pendant les années 1766, 67 et 68, par Jon. Carver. Traduit sur la troisième édition angloise par M. de C. ... [Chanla, *pseudon.* for Montucla], avec des remarques et quelques additions du traducteur. *Paris: Pissot.* 1784. 8vo, pp. 24, xxviii, 451. Map. 11188

From the third English edition. *See* "Biog. univer.," Volney and Faribault, No. 118, and Campe's "Biblioth. Géog."

CARVER. Aventures chez les sauvages de l'Amérique Septentrionale. 5e édition. *Tours: Mame et Cie.* 1852. 16mo, 2 l., pp. 236. C. 11189

CARVER. Reize door de binnenlanden van Noord-Amerika, door Jonathan Carver schildkn. ... Naar den derden Druk uit het Engelsch vertaald door J. D. Pasteur. Met plaaten. ... *Leyden: A. en J. Honkoop.* 1796. 2 vols., 8vo, 2 l., pp. xxvi, 248; 2 l., pp. 280, (16). 11190

CARVER. A Treatise on the Culture of the Tobacco Plant; with the Manner in which it is usually Cured. Adapted to Northern Climates, and designed for the use of the Landholders of Great-Britain, and Ireland. By Jonathan Carver, Esq. Author of Travels through the Interior Parts of North-America. *Dublin: Luke White.* 1779. 5 l., pp. 52. 11191

CARVER. The Carver Centenary; an account of the Celebration by the Minnesota Historical Society of the One Hundredth Anniversary of the Council and Treaty of Jonathan Carver with the Nandowessies, May 1, 1767. At the "Great Cave." *St. Paul.* 1867. 8vo. C. 11192

CARVER (M.) Mary Carver, Executrix of John Carver, Esq; Jane, Frances, and Ann Thompson, Administratrices of Richard Thompson, Esq; Theobald Taaffe, Esq; and his Wife, Administratrix of Samuel Lowe, Esq; John Cranch and his Wife, and Hannah Turbill, Executrices of George Turbill, Esq; - - - - - Appellants. David Polhill, Esq; and others, on Behalf of themselves and others, Proprietors of Shares in the Gold and Silver Mines in Jamaica. - - - Respondents. The Appellants Case. To be heard at the Bar of the House of Lords, on the Day of 1746. Large folio, pp. 3.

CARVER. Mary Carver, and others, — Appellants. David Polhill, Esq; and others, Respondents. William Wood, - - Appellant. David Polhill, Esq; and others, Respondents. The Case of the Respondents on Both these Appeals. To be Heard at the Bar of the House of Peers the day of 1746. Large folio, pp. 7. 11194

These cases relate to mines in Jamaica.

CARVER (R.) History of Boston. By Robin Carver. *Boston.* 1834. 16mo, pp. 160. 11195

CARVER (W.) A Bone to Gnaw, for Grant Thorburn. By William Carver. *New York.* 1836. 12mo, pp. 24. 11196

CARVER, *Mass.* Report of the School Committee of the Town of Carver, for the Year 1855–56. *Middleboro': Gazette Press.* 1856. 8vo, pp. 7. Also for later years. H. 11197

CARWELL (H. de W.) Insecurity of British Property in Peru; an Appeal to the Representatives of the British Nation. *London.* 1863. 8vo. 11198

CARY (A.) An Address delivered before the Massachusetts Charitable Mechanic Association, October 7th, 1824, ... By Alpheus Cary. *Boston: Monroe and Francis.* .. 1824. 8vo.

CARY (John). Essay on the State of England in relation to its Trade in the East and West Indies, etc. *London.* 1695. 8vo. 11200

CARY (J. L.) Slavery in Maryland briefly considered, with a preliminary Letter by Dr. Richard S. Stewart. By John L. Cary. *Baltimore.* 1845. 8vo, pp. 31. 11201

Also: Slavery and the Wilmot Proviso. *Baltimore.* 1847. 8vo, pp. 64.

CARY (M.) Genealogy of the Families who have settled in the North Parish in Bridgewater, Mass. To which is added a Historical Sketch of North Bridgewater. By Moses Cary. *Boston: Printed by Bannister and Marvin.* 1824. 8vo, pp. 48.

"Contains a very valuable collection of materials; but it is somewhat confused in its arrangement. Judge Mitchell has incorporated most of the facts into his 'History of Bridgewater.'" — WHITMORE.

CARY (R.) Letter To the Members of the Society for propagating the Gospel among the Indians, and others in North America. By Richard Cary, Esq. *Boston: Printed by S. Hall.* [1789]. 4to, pp. 9. H. 11203

CARY (S.) An Address to the Members of the Merrimack Humane Society ... Newburyport, Sept. 2, 1806. By Samuel Cary. ... *Newburyport.* 1806. 8vo, pp. 42, (4). BA + Second Edition. *Newburyport.* 1806. 8vo, pp. 46. 11204

CARY (S.) A Sermon delivered at King's Chapel, Boston, January 1, 1809, being the Sabbath of the Author's Ordination, as one of the Ministers of that Society. By Samuel Cary. *Boston: printed by J. Belcher.* 1809. 8vo, pp. 25, 15. H. 11205

CARY. A Sermon preached at King's Chapel, Boston, September 9, 1813, the Day of the National Fast. By Samuel Cary, one of the Ministers of the Chapel. ... *Boston: Isaiah Thomas, Jun.* 1813. 8vo, pp. 20. BA., H. 11206

CARY. A Sermon preached before the Ancient and Honourable Artillery Company, in Boston, June 6, 1814 ... By Samuel Cary ... *Boston: Thomas Wells.* 1814. 8vo, pp. 26, (1).

CARY. A Tribute of Respect and Friendship to the Memory of the Rev. Samuel Cary, late Junior Minister at the Chapel, Boston. ... [n. p.] *April,* 1816. 12mo, pp. 12. BA. 11208

[CARY (S.) *and* FREEMAN (J.)] Two Sermons, preached at King's Chapel, Boston, Feb. 26, 1815, after the Interment of Madame Susan Bulfinch, Relict of Thomas Bulfinch, M.D. *Boston: printed by Manning & Loring.* [n. d.] 8vo, pp. 40.

CARY (Samuel Fenton), *Editor.* The National Temperance Offering, and Sons and Daughters of Temperance Gift. *New York: R. Vandien.* [1850.] 8vo, pp. 320. 16 Plates. C.

CARY (S. F.) An Address to the People of Ohio, ... prepared by S. F. Cary, H. Canfield, and Thomas Cummings. [n. d.] 8vo, pp. 8. 11211

CARY. Letter to the Volunteers in the Federal Army. By Gen. S. F. Cary. *Published by Samuel W. Hodges: Boston.* [1861.] 12mo, pp. 4. H. 11212

CARY (T.) A Sermon, delivered to the First Religious Society in Newburyport, September 27, 1801: Being the last Lord's-Day of their assembling in the Old Meeting-House. By Thomas Cary, A.M. Senior Pastor. *Newburyport: ... Press of Allen & Stickney.* 1801. 8vo, pp. 28. H. 11213

Also: Sermon delivered July 20, 1796, at the Interment of Rev. Samuel Webster, D.D. *Newburyport.* [n. d.] 8vo, pp. 32. — Sermon delivered at Charlestown, July 23, 1797. *Charlestown.* [1799.] 8vo, pp. 24. — Two Sermons at Newburyport, Mass. *Boston.* 1773. 12mo.

CARY (Thomas), *Jr.* Masonic Oration at Newburyport, June 24, 1801. [*Newburyport.* 1801.] 4to. + Second Edition. [*Newburyport.* 1801.] 4to. H. 11214

CARY (T. Graves). The Dependence of the Fine Arts for Encouragement, in a Republic, on the Security of Property; with an Enquiry into the Causes of Frequent Failure among Men of Business: an Address delivered before the Boston Mercantile Library Association, November 13, 1844. By Thomas G. Cary. *Boston: Charles C. Little & James Brown.* 1845. 8vo, pp. 39. BA. 11215

CARY. Gold from California, ... A Lecture delivered at North Chelsea, Massachusetts. March 25th, 1856. With some reminiscences of the place. By Thomas G. Cary. ... *New York: printed by George W. Wood.* ... 1856. 8vo, pp. 20.

Cary. Letter to a Lady in France on the Supposed Failure of a National Bank, the Supposed Delinquency of the National Government, the Debts of the Several States, and Repudiation; with Answers to Enquiries concerning the Books of Capt. Marryat and Mr. Dickens. By Thomas G. Cary. *Boston: Benjamin H. Greene.* 1843. 8vo, pp. 36. H. + Third Edition. *Boston.* 1844. 8vo, pp. 60. BA. 11217

Cary. Memoir of Thomas Handasyd Perkins: containing Extracts from his Diaries and Letters. With an Appendix. *Boston: Little, Brown and Company.* 1858. 8vo, Title, pp. 304. Portrait. BA. 11218

"In this volume the Memoir prepared for "Hunt's Merchants' Mag." has been extended."

[Cary.] Profits on Manufactures at Lowell. A Letter from the Treasurer of a Corporation to John H. Pendleton, Esq., Virginia. *Boston: Charles C. Little & James Brown.* 1845. 8vo, pp. 23. BA. 11219

Also: An Address delivered before the Mercantile Library Association of Boston, December, 1845. ... [n. p. n. d.] 8vo, pp. 16. H. — Destiny. Progress. Originally published in Hunt's Merchants' Magazine. [Signed T. G. C. n. p. 1848.] 8vo, pp. 4. BA. — An Oration delivered before the Authorities of the City of Boston, ... July 5, 1847. *Boston: J. H. Eastburn, printer.* 1847. 8vo, pp. 38. H. — A Practical View of the Business of Banking. Address before the Mercantile-Library Association, Boston, December, 1845. [*New York.* n. d.] 8vo, pp. 16. — Reply to the Review, by E. H. Derby, Esq., of a Speech concerning the Loan of State Credit for the Hoosac Tunnel, May, 1853. ... *Boston: press of Crocker and Brewster.* 1858. 8vo, pp. 18. BA., H. — Result of Manufactures at Lowell. ... A Letter from the Treasurer of a Corporation to John S. Pendleton, Esq., Virginia. *Boston: Charles C. Little & James Brown.* ... 1845. 8vo, pp. 23. H. — Speech of T. G. Cary on the Use of the Credit of the State for the Hoosac Tunnel, In the Senate of Massachusetts, May 18, 1853. ... To which are added Extracts from a Speech ... containing some Account of the Wealth and Capitalists of Boston ... . *Boston: J. W. Hewes & Co., Printers.* 1853. 8vo, pp. 41, (1). BA.

Cary Improvement Company. Annual Report of the Directors of the Cary Improvement Company, ... *Boston: J. M. Hewes, printer.* ... 1858. 8vo, pp. 11. H. 11220

Casado (D.) Sermon en la profesion religiosa, que hizo la Señora Maria Genara de S. Teresa. *Mexico.* 1806. 4to, 25 l.

Casado. Sermon en la sol funcion, que los naturale y originarios de las montañas de Santander. celebr. *Mexico.* 1809. 4to, 23 l. 11222

Casares (José Hilario). Trial of the Pirates Pepe, Barbato and Couro. Of the Brig Crawford, at Richmond, Va. Also a

Sketch of the Life of the Pirate Tardy. *Boston.* [n. d.] 12mo, pp. 24. H. 11223

Casafuerte (*Marques de*). Meritos que ha justificado y probado el Ldo. D. Antonio de Sossa, Pbro., Colegial presidente del Ille. de Señor de las Reales Audiencias de Mexicô y Guadalaxàra: .. Por el Excmo. Señor Marques de Casâfuerte, Virrey de la Nueva España. *Imprenta de Carlos Habré.* 1724. Folio. 11224

Concerning this work, *see* Bachiller. An early specimen of Cuban typography.

Casaretto (Giovanni). Novae Stirpes Brasilienses. Decades [I–X]. *Genuae.* 1842–45. 8vo, pp. 96. 11225

Continued? Ten decades complete Volume I.

Casarin (Vicente). Dialogo entre Celso y su padre, publicado con objeto de que los Porta-Pliegos de las tres monarquias Europeas aliadas contra la republica mexicana puedan llevarlo á sus respectivos señores. *Mexico.* 1862. 4to, pp. 14. 11226

Casas (Bartholome de las). Breuissima rela|cion de la destruycion de las In-|dias: colegida por el Obispo dõ|fray Bartolome de las Casas, o|Casaus de la orden de Sãcto Do|ming.|o Añõ. 1552.| [Colophon (on the 50th leaf):] *Fue Impressa ... en ... Seuilla|en casa de Sebastian Trugillo ... Año de* M.D.Lij.| 4to, 54 leaves. C. 11227

The last four leaves, an appendix, are entitled:

Casas. Lo que se sigue es un peda-|ço de una carta y relacion que escriuio cierto hombre: ... [No title, place, or date.] 4to, 4 l. 11228

Casas. Entre los re-|medios q dõ fray Bartolome de las casas:|obispo d'la ciudad real de Chiapa: refirio|por mandado del Emperador rey nro se-|ñor: en los ayuntamiẽtos q mãdo hazer su|magestad de perlados y letrados y perso|nas grãdes en Valladolid el año de mill &|quiniẽtos y quarẽta y dos: para reforma-|ciõ de las Indias. El octauo en ordẽ es el|siguiẽte. Dõde se asignã veynte razones:|por las qles prueua no deuerse dar los in-|dios a los Españales en encomiẽda: ni en|feudo: ni en vassallaje: ni d' otra manera al|gũa. Si su majestad como dessea quiere li|brarlos de la tyrania y perdicio q padecẽ|como de la boca delos dragones: y q total-|mẽte no los cõsumã y matẽ y qde vazio to-|do aql orbe d' sus tã infinitos naturales ha|bitadores como estaua y lo vimos poblado| [Colophon:] *Fue impressa ... Seuilla, en las casas de Jacome Crõberger. Año de ... mill & quinientos & cinquenta & dos años* ... 53 leaves. BA., C.

Casas. Este es vn tratado q|el obispo dela cuidad Real de Chiapa dõ|fray Bartholome de las Casas, o Casaus|compuso, por comission del Consejo Real|delas Indias: sobre la materia de los yn-|dios que se han hecho en ellas esclauos El|qual contiene muchas razones y aucto-|ridades juridicas: que pueden apro|uechar a los lectores para deter-|minar muchas y diuersas| questiones dudosas|en materia de re-|stitucion: y de|otras que al|psente los | hõbres | el tiẽpo de agora tratan.| Año 1552.| [Colophon:] ... *Fue impressa .. en . Seuilla, en casa de Sebastian Trugillo .. Año de mil y quienientos cincuẽta y dos.* 4to, 36 l., the last page blank. BA., C. 11230

Casas. Tratado cõpro|batorio del Imperio soberano y|principado vniuersal que los Re|yes de Castilla y Leon tienen so-|bre las indias: compuesto por el|Obispo don fray Bartholome d'|las Casas, o Casaus dela orden d'|Sancto Domingo Año. 1552.| [Colophon:] ... *Fue impressa ... en|en casa d' Sebastiã Trugillo ... . Año.* 1553. 4to, 84 leaves. BA. 11231

Casas. Aqui se cõtienẽ vnos|auisos y reglas para los confessores q | oyeren confessiones delos Españo | les que son, o han sido en cargo a| los Indios delas Indias del|mar Oceano: colegidas por|el obispo de Chiapa don|fray Bartholome d'las|casas, o casaus dela|orden de Sancto|Domingo.| [Colophon:] ... *Fue impressa ... en ... Seuilla, en casa de Sebastian Trugillo ... . Año de mil & quinientos & cin|cuenta y dos.* 4to, 16 leaves. BA., C.

Casas. Aqui se cõtienẽ tre|ynta proposiciones muy juridicas: en|las quales sumaria y succintamente se|tocã muchas cosas pertenecieẽtes al de|recho q la yglesia y los principes chri-|stianos tienen, o puedẽ tener sobre los|infieles de qual quier especie que sean.|Mayormente se assigna el verdadero|y fortissimo fundamento en que se assi|enta y estriba: el titulo y señorio supre-| mo y vniuersal que los Reyes d' Casti|lla y Leon tienen al orbe de las que lla|mamos occidẽtales Indias. Por el ql|son constituydos vniuersales señores y|Emperadores enellas sobre muchos re-|yes. Apuntã se tambien otras cosas cõ|cernientes al hecho acaecido en aql or|be notabilissimas: y dignas d' ser vistas|y sabidas. Colijo las dichas treynta p|posiciones El obispo dõ Fray Bartho-|lome de las Casas, o Casaus: Obispo|q fue d'la ciudad Real de Chiapa: cier|to Reyno de los dela nueua España.|Año. 1552.| [Colophon:] *Impresso en seuilla en casa de sebastiã trugillo.* 4to, 10 l. 11233

Casas. Aqui se contiene|vna disputa, o controuersia: entre el|Obispo dõ fray Bartholome de las|Casas, o Casaus, obispo q fue dela|ciudad Real de Chiapa, que es en-|las Indias, parte dela nueua Espa-|ña: y el doctor Gines de Sepulueda|Coronista del Emperador nuestro se|ñor: sobre q el doctor contendia: q las| conquistas delas Indias contra los|Indios eran licitas: y el obispo por|el cõtrario d'fendio y affirmo auer si|do y fer ĩpossible no serlo: tiranicas,|injustas & iniquas. La qual questiõ|se vẽtilo & disputo en presencia d' mu|chos letrados theologos & juristas |en vna cõgregacion q mando su ma-|gestad juntar el año de mil & qniẽtos|y cincuẽta en la villa de Valladolid.|Año. 1552.| [Colophon:] *Seuilla:|en casa de Sebastian Trugillo impressor de |libros. Frõtero de nuestra señora de Gra|cia. Acabosse a. x. dias del mes de Se-|tiembre. Año de mil & quinien|tos & cincuenta y dos.*| 4to, 62 l., the last blank. 11234

This piece contains the "Argumento" and the "Svmmario," by De Soto, the "Objections," by Sepulveda, and the "Replicas," by Las Casas. "Principia quædam," in the Italian version, is printed after the "Argumento," in its proper place.

Casas. Principia quedã ex quibus|procedendum est in disputatione ad manifestan|dam et defendendam iusticiam Yndorum:|Per Episcopũ. F. Bartholomeũ a Ca-|saus ordinis predicatorũ, collecta.| [Colophon:] *Impressum Hispali in inebo Sebastiani Trugillo.* [n. d.] 4to, 10 leaves. 11235

A complete set of this Spanish series of Las Casas is extremely rare. We believe our list is complete, containing more than De Bure's, in whose time only five parts were known to bibliographers. Richarderie copies De Bure; nor was Llorente, in his notice of the works of Las Casas, better informed, as he only reprints six. Dibdin remarks, "His history is a prodigiously great gun in the bibliographical battery of collectors; especially if the original Spanish work, in seven parts, 1552, 4to, be complete, and in all respects uncounterfeited." A complete set is worth from $100 to $150. The counterfeit edition bears the date of 1552, but is really printed about one hundred years later. Our arrangement is according to subjects, and also nearly chronological. No. 11227, the "Breuissima relacion," was composed in Valencia in 1541–2. No. 11228, "Lo que se sigue," is an appendage added just after No. 11227 was printed, in 1552. No. 11229, "Entre los Remedios," was composed in 1543. No. 11230 "Este es vn tratado," was written in 1543. No. 11231, "Tratado comprobatorio," was written about the same time. No. 11232, known as the "Confessionario," was prepared in America, in 1545 or 1546, and No. 11233, "Treynta propositiones," in Spain, about 1548, as a justification of No. 11232. No 11234 is the "Disputa" of 1550 with Sepulveda, and No. 11235, "Principia quædam," belongs to it, as giving the principles on which the controversy was conducted. Llorente, in 1822, omits Nos. 11231, 11232, and 11235, alluding to the two first, but not aware of their being in print. He gives a translation of the "Quaestio de imperatoriã vel regiã potestate," first printed at Spire in 1571, and two pieces of the author, not before printed. The first translation made, was into Flemish in 1578. The next was Miggrode's translation into French, 1579. The English translation of 1583, by J. P. and M. M. S. comes next. The first Dutch version appeared in 1596, and the earliest German ones in 1597. De Bry, in 1598, published an illustrated Latin version of Nos. 11227, 11228, and 11229, and the "Sumario" of the "Disputa." The first Italian versions appeared in 1626.

Casas. Breve relacion de las Indias Occidentales presentada a Felipe II. Por Fray Bartolomé de las Casas. *Londres: Schulze y Dean.* 1812. 12mo, pp. 140. + *Filadelphia.* 1821. 12mo.

This reimpression of our No. 11227 was produced under the supervision of Dr. de Mier. A few copies only were printed.

[Casas.] Erudita et elegans explicatio quæstionis: utrum reges vel principes jure aliquo, vel titulo, et salva conscientia, cives ac subditos a regia corona alienare et alterius domoni particularis ditione subjicere possint? Cura et studio Wolff. Griestetteri. [*Francofurti ad Mœnum. apud Georg. Coruinum, impensis Hieron. Feyerabend.*] 1571. 4to, 4 l., pp. 67. 11237

First edition of this piece, a translation of which is included by Llorente in the "Œuvres," 1822, p. 50, who ascribes it certainly to the Bishop, though Raynouard, "Journal des Savans," Jan., 1823, doubts its authorship. Las Casas, however, says, towards the close of the "Replicas," in the "Disputa," fol. 55, verso, that he had composed several *tratados*, both in Spanish and Latin, on the title, by which the Spanish sovereigns held the Indies. As the "Tratado comprobatorio" is the only one on this subject, known to be by him, this may well be another; again published as:

[Casas.] Explicatio quaestionis utrum reges ... *Tubingae, ex officina typogr. Eberh. Wilduii.* 1625. Guill. de Montserrat tractatus de successione regum, et præcipue Galliæ, nunc primum in Germania editus, curante Christ. Besddo. *Tubingae, Wildius.* 4to, pp, 47, 55, besides title. + *Jenae.* 1678. 4to. 11238

[Casas.] Las Obras del Obispo Bartholomeo de las Casas. viz. 1. Brevissima Relacion. 2. Treynta proposiciones ... 3. Una disputa ... 4. Un tratado ... 5. Remedios ... 6. Pedaço de una carta ... *Barcelona: Antonio Lacavelleria.* 1646. 4to, 214 numbered leaves. 11239

Some copies have a title dated 1552, without the printer's name, or place; but this edition may be known by the type being Roman, and by the numbered leaves.

Casas. Colleccion de las Obras del Venerable Obispo de Chiapa, Don Bartolomé de las Casas; enriquecida con Obras ineditas, &c. &c.; da todo esto á luz el Dr. Don Juan Antonia Llorente. *Paris: Rosa.* 1822. 2 vols., 8vo. Portrait. C.

A French translation appeared the same year. *See* No. 11276, *infra.* These are not literal translations, but only free versions of the originals. The "Quaestio," however, is a close translation of the edition of 1571.

Casas. El Indio esclavo. Obra compuesta por el Reverendo Obispo de Chiapa D. Fray Bartholomé de las Casas. *Puebla.* 1821. Sm. 8vo, pp. 90. 11241

Casas. Istoria|ò breuissima relatione|Della Distrvttione|dell' Indie Occidentali|di Monsig. Reverendiss.|Don Bartolomeo

dalle Case, ò Casaus, Siuigliano|Vescouo di Chiapa Città Regale nell' Indie.|Conforme al svo vero originale|Spagnuolo, già stampato in Siuiglia.|Con la traduttione in Italiano de Francesco Bersabita.|Dedicata all' Amicitia.|*In Venetia Presso Marco Ginammi.* M.DC.XXVI.|Con Licenza de' Superiori, & Priuilegio.| 4to, 8 l., pp. 154, Libri Stampati and Errori, pp. 2. C. 11242

The real name of the translator is Giacomo Castellani. This first Italian translation of Las Casas' first and most celebrated tract has the original Spanish in parallel columns.

Casas. Istoria|ò breuissima relatione|Della Distrvttione| dell' Indie Occidentali|di Monsig. Reverendiss.|Don Bartolomeo dalle Case, ò Casaus Siuig dell' Ordine|de' Predicatori; & Vescouo di Chiapa|Città Regale nell' Indie.|Conforme al svo vero originale|Spagnuolo, già stampato in Siuiglia.|Tradotta in Italiano dell' Excell. Sig. Giacomo Castellani|già sotto nome di Francesco Bersabita.|Dedicata all' Amicitia.| [Woodcut.] *In Venetia Presso Marco Ginammi.* M DC XXX. Con Licenza de Superiori, & Priuilegio. 4to, 8 l., pp. 150, 1 l. G. 11243

Casas. Istoria,|ò Breuissima Relatione|della Distrvttione| dell' Indie Occidentali|di Monsig. reverendiss.|Don Bartolomeo dalle Case, ò Casaus, Siuigliano dell' Ordine|de' Predicatori; & Vescouo di Chiapa.|Conforme al suo vero Originale Spagnuolo già stampato in Siuiglia.|Tradotta in Italiano dall' Excell. Sig. Giacomo Castellani,|già sotto nome di Francesco Bersabita.|Al Molt' Ill.re, & Ecc.mo Sig.re Sig.r mio Col.mo Il Sig.|Nicolo' Persico.|*In Venetia Presso Marco Ginammi.* M DC XLIII.|Con Licenza de' Superiori, & Priuilegio.| 4to, 4 l., pp. 150, 1 l. C., H.

Casas. La Libertà|Pretesa|Dal supplice Schiauo Indiano|di Monsignor Reverendiss.|D. Bartolomeo dalle Case,|ò Casaus, Siuigliano, dell' Ordine de' Predicatori, & Vescouo|di Chiapa, Città Regale dell' Indie.|Conforme al suo vero Originale Spagnuolo già stampato in Siuiglia.|Tradotto in Italiano per opera di Marco Ginammi.|All' Altezza Serenissima di|Odoardo Farnese |Dvca di Parma, et Piacenza, &c.|*In Venetia, Presso Marco Ginammi.* M DC XXXX.|Con Licenza de' Superiori, & Priuilegio.| 4to, pp. 155, (3). BA., C., H. 11245

Casas. Il svpplice|Schiauo Indiano di Monsig. Reverendiss. |Bartolomeo dalle Case|ò Casaus, Siuigliano, dell' Ordine de' Predicatori, & Vescouo|di Chiapa, Città Regale dell' Indie.| Conforme alsuo vero Orig. inale Spagnuolo giã stampato in Siuiglia.|Tradotto in Italiano per opera di Marco Ginammi. All'

Illustr.mo & Excell.mo Sig.or |il Sig. Henrico de Fois|della valetta Dvca di candalo, &c.|*Venetia, Marco Ginammi,* M DC XXXVI. Con Licenza de' Superiori, & Priuilegio. Sm. 4to, pp. 118, 1 l.

This is a translation of No. 11230, *supra*, with the Spanish version in parallel columns. I find one with the date, "*Venetia.* 1635," in a German bookseller's catalogue, [Brockhaus?] followed by the editions of 1636 and 1657.

Casas. Il svpplice|schiavo Indiano|di Monsig. Reverendiss. |D. Bartolomeo|Dalle Case, ò Casaus, Siuigliano, dell' Ordine| de' Predicatori, & Vescouo di Chiapa,|Città Regale dell' Indie. |Conforme al suo vero Originale Spagnuolo già stampato in Siuiglia.|Tradotto in Italiano per opera di Marco Ginammi.| Al Molto Illustre Sig. Sig. Osseruandiss. il Sig.|Bernardo Moro. |*In Venetia, Per li Ginammi* 1657.|Con licenza de' Superiori, & Priuilegio.| 4to, pp. 96. J.C.B. 11247

Casas. Conqvista|dell' Indie|Occidentali|di Monsignor|Fra Bartolomeo dalle Case,|ò Casaus, Siuigliano, Vescouo di Chiapa. |Tradotta in Italiano per opera di Marco Ginammi.|All' Illmo. & Ecc.mo Sig.re Sig.or & mio Padron Col.mo|Il Sig.or Pietro Sagredo|Procvratore di S. Marco.|*In Venetia,* M DC XXXXV.|*Presso Marco Ginammi.*|Con Licenza de' Superiori, & Priuilego.| 4to, pp. 8, 2 l., pp. xvii, 30–184. J.C.BT. H. 11248

Contains Nos. 11234, and 11235, of which it is the only Italian edition.

Casas. Seer cort Verhael|vande Destructie van d' Indien verga-|dert deur den Bischop don fray Bar-|tholome de las Casas, oft Casaus, van|sinte Dominicus orden. in Bra-|bantsche tale getrouwelick | uyte Spaensche | ouergeset.|Zach. XI.| Voet de beesten des verslagens, welck dict be-|saten slogense doot, ende sy en waren niet droe-|uich ende vercochtense, seggende: Gebenedyt si|de Heere, wy zyn Ryck geworden.|1578.| 4to, 70 l.

This is the first Dutch translation of Nos. 11227, 11228, and 11233. Probably printed at Brussels or Antwerp. *See* Tiele, pp. 319–320.

Casas. Spieghel|der Spaenscher|Tirannije,|Waer inne verhaelt|worden, de moordadige schandelijcke ende|grouwelijcke seyten, die de selue Spaengiarden ghebruyct|hebben in den landen van Indien:|Mitsgaders de beschrijuinghe vander geleghentheyt, zeden, ende|aert vanden seluen landen ende|Lieden.|In Spaenscher talen beschreuen, door den Eerweerdigen|Bisschop Don Fray Bartholome de las Casas, van|S. Dominicus Oorden.| Numero 15.|Schendet dat landt niet, daer ghy inne woonet want wie bloetschuldich is|die schendet dat landt, ende dat landt en can van t'bloet niet versoent|werden dat daer inne vergoten wort,

sonder door dat bloet des gheens|diet vergoten heeft.|...|...|...| [n. p.] 1579.| 4to, 70 leaves. 11250

The same as 1578, with a different title.

Casas. Spieghel der Spaenscher ty-|rannye, in West Indien. Waer inne verhaelt wordt de | moordadige, schandelijcke ende grouwelijcke seyten die, die selve|Spanjaerden ghebruyckt hebben inde selve Landen.|Mitsgaders de beschryvinghe vander ghelegentheyt,|zeden ende aert van de selfde Landenende Volcken. |In Spaenscher Talen beschreuen, door den E. Bischop Don Fray Bartholome|de las Casas, van S. Domicus Oorden.|*t'Amstelredam.|By Nicolaes Biestkens de Jonge. Ende men vintse te| coop by | Cornelis Claesz. Opt Water int Schrijboeck,* 1596. 4to, 43 unnumbered leaves. 11251

The title to this edition contains a map of America from an octavo atlas of Claesz. It is a reprint, word for word, of the previous edition.

Casas. Spieghel der Spaenscher ty-|rannye, in West-Indien. Waer inne verhaelt wordt de moorda-|dighe, schandelijcke, lende grouwejicke feyten, die deselve Spaen-|jaerden ghebruyckt hebben inde selve Landen.|Mitsgaders de beschryvinghe vander ghelegentheyt, zeden|ende aert van de selfde Landen ende Volcken.|In Spaenscher Talen beschreven, door den E. Bisschop Don Fray Bartholome de las Casas, van S. Dominicus Oorden. |*t'Amstelredam,|By Cornelis Claesz. Boeckvercooper woonende opt Water,|int Schrijfboeck. Anno* 1607.| 4to, 43 leaves. 11252

A literal reprint of the previous edition, with the same map in the title-page. The plates to these Dutch versions are from the edition of the De Bry's, being copied from the Warhafftiger vnd gründtlicher Bericht ... . [*Frankfurt.* 1597.]

Casas. Den|Spieghel|Vande Spaensche Tyrannie beeldelijcken af-|gemaelt, leest breederen in-hout door het schrijven van den E. Bisschop|van Chiapa in nieu Spaengien, ghenaemt Don Fray Bartholome de|las Casas, van S. Dominicus Oorden, aen den grootmach-|tigen Coninck van Spaengien Philips de tweede.|*Ghedruckt tot Amstelredam by Cornelis Claesz.* 1609.| 4to, Engraved Title, and 17 Plates, with letterpress description at the foot of each. 11253

The plates are after De Bry, in his edition of 1598, but reversed. This was reissued with the following title:

Casas. Spieghel der Spaenscher ty-|rannye in West-Indien. Waer inne verhaelt wort de moordadige,|sehandeljicke, ende grouwelijcke feyten, die de selve Spaengiaerden|ghebruyckt hebben inde selve Landen.|Mitsgaders de beschryvinghe vander ghelegentheyt, seden|ende aert vande selfde Landen ende Volcken.|In Spaenscher Talen beschreven, door den E. Bisschop Don Fray|Bartholome de las Casas, van S. Dominicus Orden.| [Map of America.] *t'Amstelredam,|By de Weduwe van Cornelis Claesz op't Water,|in't Schrijf-boeck.* 1610.| 4to, 43 leaves.

Same map on the title as in the editions of 1596 and 1607.

Casas. Den Spiegel der Spaensche tierannye-|geschiet in Westindien waerin te|sien is de onmenschelijcke wreede|feyten der Spanjarden met samen|de beschrijvinge der selver lant en| volcken aert en nature| allen Vaderlant lieuende en Vrome Voorstā-|ders ten exempel voorgestelt|In Spans beschreven door den E. bischop|don fray bartholome de las Casas van|S. Dominicus oorden|*Gedruckt tot Amsterdam by David de meyne aende Beurs inde werrelt Caert A°.* 1612.| 4to, 53 l. 11255

Title engraved, copied from the De Bry edition of 1598. Seventeen plates in text, same as the edition of Claesz.

Casas. Den|Spiegel|der Spaensche Tijrannije,|gheschiet in West-Indien.|Waer in te sien is de onmensche-|lycke wreede feyten der Spanjaerdē,|met t' samen de Beschryvinghe|der selver Landē, Volckerē|aert ende natuere.|In 't Spaensch beschreven| Door dē E. Bisschop Don Fraey|Bartholome, de las Casas van |S. Dominicus oorden.|Nu op 't nieuwe met schoone|Kopere Figueren verciert.|*Tot|Amsterdam|Ghedruckt by Ian Evertss. Cloppenburg, op 't Water,|tegen over de Koor-Beurs|iñ vergulden Bijbel.*|1620.| 4to, pp. 104. 11256

The engraved title has a bust of Phil. II., and a full length portrait of Don Juan, of Austria, and the Duke of Alba, and four of the scenes of persecution. Seventeen plates in the text copied from De Bry. It has a second part, being the abridgment of Gysius' "Netherland Disturbances." The first part was printed, without the preface, as

Casas. Eerste deel|Van den|Spiegel|Der|Spaensche Tyrannye,|gheschiet in West-Indien ... [As before]. *tot Amsterdam|Ghedruckt by Jan Evertsz Cloppenburg.* ... 1620.| 4to, pp. 104. 11257

Title printed in the same engraved border as last; preliminary matter different. Reprinted some years later as

Casas. Den|Spiegel|Der|Spaensche Tyranny|gheschiet in West-Indien ... [As before]. *tot Amsterdam|Ghedruckt by Jan Evetsz Cloppenburg.* ... 1620.| 4to, pp. 104. 11258

The engraved date not altered. The word "Finis" in Italic capitals. Ebert, No. 3626, quotes an edition, "*Amsterdam.* 1627," which Tiele had not seen.

Casas. Den Spiegel der|Spaensche tierannije|geschiet in

Westindien ... [As in No. 11255.] *Gedruckt tot Amsterdam by Cornelis|Lodewijcksz vander Plasse, inde Italiaensche Bijbel|Anno* 1620.| 4to, 52 l. 11259

This is a new edition of the impression of 1610, with the same plates. In the dedication, the inscription to the Directors of the W. I. Co. is left out by neglect. The editor complains that Cloppenburg's edition had supplanted his own.

Casas. Den Vermeerderden|Spieghel|der|Spaensche tierannije|geschiet in Westindien waerin te|sien is de onmenschelijcke wreede|feijten der Spanjarden met samen|de beschrijvinge der selver lant en|volcken aert en nature|allen Vaderlant lieuende en vrome voorstā-|ders ten exempel voorgestelt|In Spans beschreven door den E. bischop|don fray bartholome de las Casas van|S. dominicus oorden.|*Gedruckt tot Amsterdam by Cornelis|Lodewijcksz vander Plasse, inde Italiaensche Bijbel.*|[In the border.] *Anno* 1621.| 4to, 52 l., Engraved Title. 11260

Some slight variations from the preceding edition. This edition reappeared with the same date, changed with a pen to 1623 in some copies. A second tome is added, with the date 1625. The "Prologue" has six instead of four lines. "Finis" in Roman capitals.

Casas. Den Vermeerderden|Spiegel [etc.] ... *Anno* 1634.| 4to, 52 leaves. 11261

A reprint of No. 11260; the plates retouched.

Casas. Den|Spiegel|der|Spaense Tyrannye|geschiet in West Indien etc.| [In the second Tome.] *Amsterdam chez Evert Kloppenburg. Anno* 1638. 4to, 52 leaves. 11262

A reprint of No. 11254. The first tome has no date.

Casas. Spiegel der Spaensche|Tirany,|gedaen in|West Indien;|Waer inne men sien kan,|alle de Eylanden,|Provintien, Lantschappen, het|Machtige Ryck van Mexico, en 't Gout|en Silver-rycke Landt van Peru.|'Tsampt|De Coursen, Havenen, Klippen,|Koopmanschappen, etc. soo wel inde Noort als in|de Zuyt zee. Als mede hoe die vande|Spanjaerden eerst geinvadeert syn.|*T'Amsterdam,|By Gillis Ioosten Saeghman,|Boeckdrucker in de Nieuwestraet.*| [1663.] 4to, pp. 96. Engraved Title. 11263

Casas. Den Vermeerderden Spiegel der Spaensche tierannije geschiet in Westindien, [etc.] *Amsterdam: By Gillis Ioosten Saeghman. Anno* 1664. 4to, Engraved Title, pp. 80. 18 Plates in the Text. 11264

The previous editions have seventeen plates in the text. Title as in No 11260, with a new address and date. A preface concerning Columbus, with plate of him breaking the egg, from De Bry, making eighteen plates. To this edition was added, with a separate title and paging, the "Beschryvinghe van West-Indien ... door Benzonius."

Casas. Spiegel der Spaensche Tirany gedaen in West Indien, [etc.] ... *T' Amsterdam, By Gillis Joosten Saeghman, Boeck-drucker in de Nieuwstraat.* 4to, pp. 96. 19 Plates in the Text. 11265

The same as No. 11264, with some alterations, and a title plate of the death of Atabaliba added.

Casas. Spiegel|der Spaense Tyranny in|West-Indien,|Het Magtig Ryk van Mexcico en het Paerel,|Goud en Zilverryk Peru.|*T'Amsterdam,|By Isaac vander Putte, Papier en Boeckverkooper op 't|Water in de Lootsman.*| 4to, pp. 68. 11266

A popular edition, with four woodcuts, and the text of Las Casas and others run into one narrative. Another edition is found with the same imprint, which may be known by the large initial on the third page and the name Columbus with Co- only on the first line, which, in the other, is in full on the line.

Casas. Tyrannies|& Cruautez|des|Espagnols,|perpetrees| e's|Indes Occidentales,|qu'on dit Le Nouueau monde;|Brieuement descrites en langue Castillane par l'Euesque|Don Frere Bartelemy de Las Casas ou|Casaus, Espagnol, de l'ordre de S. Dominique; fide-|lement traduictes par Jaques de Miggrode:| Pour seruir d'exemple & aduertissement|aux XVII Prouinces du païs bas.|Heureux celuy qui deuient sage|En voyant d'autruy le dommage.|*A Anvers,|Chez François de Ravelenghien ioignant le por-|tail Septentrional de l'Eglise nostre Dame.*|M.D.LXXIX.| 12mo, 8 l., pp. 184. J.C.B. 11267

Miggrode, according to Charlevoix, was a Fleming. He says, in his preface, that he had translated one third of the "Relacion" into Flemish, when an edition in that language appeared. He gives Nos. 11227, and 11228, in full, with portions of Nos. 11230, 11233, and 11234.

Casas. Tyrannies|et crvavtez|des Espagnols,|perpetrees|es |Indes Occidentales|qu'on dit le Nouueau monde:|Brieuement descrites en langue Castillane, par l' E-|nesque Don Frere Bartelemy de las|Casas ou Casavs, Espagnol de l'ordre de|sainct Dominique, fidelement traduites par Ia-|qves de Miggrode:| Heureux celuy qui deuient sage|En voyant d' autruy le dommage.|*A Paris, Par Guillaume Iulien, à l'enseigne de l'Amitié,|pres le college de Cambray.* MDLXXXII.|Auec Priuilege du Roy.|12mo, 8 l., pp. 184. J.C.B. 11268

Casas. Histoire|Admirable des|horribles inso-|lences, Crvavtez, & tyrannies exercees|par les Espagnols es|Indes Occiden-|tales.|Briefuement descrite en langue Castillane|par Don F. Barthelemy de Las|Casas, Moine & Euesque Espagnol: fi-| delement traduite par Iaqves de Miggrode. [Motto.] *Paris: Par Gabriel Cartier.* M.D.LXXXII. Sm. 8vo, 8 l., pp. 222. 11269

Tiele says this is a copy of the edition of 1579.

Casas. Le Miroir|De la Tyrannie Espagnole|Perpetree aux Indes|Occidentales.|On verra icy la cruauté plus|que inhumaine, commise par les|Espagnols, assvi la description de|ces terres, peuples, & leur nature.|Mise en lumière par un|Evesque Bartholome de las Casas,|de l'Ordre de S. Dominic.|Nouvellement refaicte, avec les|Figurs en cuyvre.|*tot Amsterdam|Ghedruckt by Ian Evertss.|Cloppenburg, op't Water|tegen over de Koor-Beurs|iñ vergulden Bijbel.*|1620.| 4to, 68 leaves. 11270

With the same engraved border and plates as the Dutch edition of 1620. It forms the second tome of a volume, of which the first is entitled, "Le Miroir|De la|Cruelle, & horrible|Tyrannie Espagnole per-|petree au Pays Bas, par le Tyran |Duc de Albe, & aultres|Commandeurs de par le Roy|Philippe le|deuxiesme.|On a adjoinct la deuxiesme par-|tie de les Tyrannies commises|aux Indes Occidentales par|les Espagnols.|Nouvellement exorné|avec taille douçe en cuyvre.|*tot Amsterdam|Ghedruckt by Ian Evertss.|Cloppenburg, op't Water|tegen over de Koor-Beurs|iñ vergulden Bijbel.*|1620."| 4to 4 l., 87 l. BA., J.C.B. This tome is the second one in the Dutch edition. Ternaux, No. 278, and Brunet, each quote a French version of this publisher, of 1604, which Tiele says is certainly a mistake. The text is a translation from the Dutch, and not the same as the edition of 1579.

Casas. Tyrannies|et|Crvavtez|des|Espagnols,|Commises es Indes|Occidentales, qu'on|dit le Nouueau Monde.|Briefvement descrite en|Espagnol, par Dom Frere Barthelemy de|las Casas de l'Ordre de S. Dominique, &|Euesque de la ville Royalle de Chiappa.|Traduitte fidellement en François par Iacques de Miggrode|sur la Coppie Espagnolle: Imprimée à la ville de Seuille.|*A Roven,|Chez Iacques Cailloüé à la Court du Palais:*| M.DC.XXX.|*Iouxte la Coppie Imprimée à Paris par Guillaume Iulien.* |Avec Privilege dv Roy.| 4to, 11 l., pp. 214. C. 11271

A reprint of Miggrode's translation, with a rubricated title.

Casas. Histoire|des Indies|Occidentales.|Ov l'on reconnoit |la bonté de ces païs, & de leurs|peuples; & les cruautez Tyran| niques des Espagnols.|Décrite premierement en langue Castillane par|Dom Barthelemy de las Casas,|de l'Ordre de S. Dominique, & Euesque|de Chappa; & depuis fidellement|traduite en François.|*A Lyon,|Chez Iean Caffin, & F. Plaignard,|en ruë Merciere, au Nom de Iesvs.*|M.DC.XLII.|Auec Approbation, & Permission.| Sm. 8vo, 4 l., pp. 299. 11272

Graesse quotes an edition, *Paris*, 1635, and says that this is a new translation.

Casas. La decouverte|des|Indes Occidentales,|par|les Espagnols.|Ecrite par Dom Balthazar de Las-|Casas, Evêque de Chiapa.|Dedié à Monseigneur le Comte|de Toulouse.|*A Paris,|Chez Andrè Pralard, ruë Saint|Jacques, à l'Occasion.*|

M.DC.XCVII.|Avec Privilege du Roi.| 12mo, 2 Titles, one of which is Engraved, 4 l., pp. 382, (2). H., J.C.B. 11273

This volume contains a translation of four of the tracts of Las Casas, by the Abbé de Bellegarde, softened in some of the cruel parts, which might have given pain to delicate persons. It appeared again as:

Casas. Relation|des|Voyages|et des|découvertes|Que les Espagnols ont fait dans les|Indes Occidentales;|Ecrite par Dom B. de Las-Casas, Evê-|que de Chiapa.|Avec la Relation curiceuse des Voyages du|Sieur de Montauban, Capitaine des| Filbustiers, en Guinée l'an 1695.|*A Amsterdam,|Chez J. Louis de Lorme Libraire sur le|Rockin, à l'enseigne de la Liberte'.*| M. DC XCVIII.| 12mo, Frontispiece, 5 l., pp. 402. Plate. BA.

Graesse quotes an edition 1692. Trömel calls this a reprint of No 11273, with the addition mentioned in the title.

Casas. La Decouverte des Indes Occidentales par les Espagnols et les moyens dont ils se sont servis pour s'en rendre Maitres. *Paris: Denys Mariette.* 1701. 12mo, 5 l., pp. 382.

Casas. Œuvres de Don Barthélemi de Las Casas, évêque de Chiapa, Défenseur de la liberté des naturels de l'Amérique; précédées de sa vie, et accompagnées de notes historiques, additions, développemens, etc., etc.; avec Portrait; par J.-A. Llorente ... . *Paris: Alexis Emery. Bruxelles: De Mat.* 1822. 2 vols., 8vo, 4 l., pp. cx, 409, (2); 2 l., pp. 503. Portrait BA., S. 11276

Casas. Newe Welt,|Warhafftige Anzeigung|Der Hispanier grewli-|chen, abschewlichen vnd vnmenschlichen Ty-|ranney, von ihnen inn den Indianischen Ländern,|so gegen Nidergang der Sonnen gelegen, vnd die|Newe Welt gennet wird, begangen. |Erstlich|Castilianisch, durch Bischoff Bartholomeum de las Casas oder|Casaus, geborner Hispaniern, Prediger Ordens, beschrieben: Vnd|im Jahr 1552 in der Königlichen Staat Hispalis oder|Sevilia in Spanien gedruckt:|Hernacher in die|Frantzösische Sprach, durch Jacoben von Miggrode, den 17|Provincien desz Niderlands, zur Warnung|und Beyspiel, gebracht;|Jetzt aber erst ins|Hochteutsch, durch einen Liebhaber desz Vatterlands, vmbebenmässiger|vrsachen wissen, vbergesetzt.|*Jm Jahr* 1597.| 4to, 8 l., pp. 158, (12). S. 11277

This translation into German is from the Spanish.

Casas. Warhafftiger vnd gũndtli-|cher Bericht|Der Hispanier grewli-|chen, vnd abschewlichen Ty-|ranney, von jhnen in den West|Indien, so die Neuwe|Welt genennet wirt|began-

gen.|Erstlich, Castilianisch, durch Bi-|schoff Bartholomeum de las Casas|gebornen Hispaniern, Prediger Ordens, beschrie-|ben: Vnd im Jahr 1552. in der Königli-|chen Staat Hispalis oder Sevilia in|Spanien gedruckt:|Jtzt aber erst in Hochteutsch, durch einen Lieb-|haber dess Vatterlands, zur Warnung, vnd|Beyspiel, vbergesezt, vnd mit schönen|Figuren gezieret.|[*Franckfurt.* 1597.] 4to, 7 l., pp. 158, 6 l. 11278

Translated from the French edition, *Anvers.* 1579. Concerning which, *see* "Bibliotheca Grenvilliana," II. 828. A volume of seventeen plates, three of which bear the designer's name, Jodo. a Winghe, accompanies this translation, with the title:

Casas. Kurtze Erklärung|Der Fünembsten Thaten, son durch die Spanier beschehen in etli-|chen Orten der neuwe| |Welt,|So in folgenden Kupfferstücken, schön, zier-|lich vnd künstlich derselben bey jeder Histo-|rien, jetzt ins Teutsch dar gege-|ben werden.|[n. p.] *Anno Christi* M. D. XCIX.| 4to, 1 l., 15 l. 11279

These plates first appeared in the Latin edition of 1598; *see* our No. 11283.

Casas. Warrhaftiger und grundlicher Bericht der Hispanier grewlich und abschewlichen Tyranney Von ihnen in den West Indien die newe Welt genant begangen in Hochteutsch ubergesezt. *Oppenheim: J. Th. de Bry.* 1613. 4to, 22 sheets.

Casas. Umbständige warhafftige|Beschreibung|der|Indianischen Ländern,|so vor diesem von den Spa-|niern eingenommen und|verwüst worden,|Durchgehends mit schönen|kupfferstücken und lebhafften|Figuren auszgezieret,|erst in Lateinischer Sprach auszgeben|durch Bartholomœum de las Casas,|Bischoffen in Hispanien,|Jetzt aber in das Teutsche übersetzt, und an|vielen Orten verbessert, in dieser neu-|und letztern Edition.|*Anno* MDCLXV.| 4to, 2 l., pp. 119. J.C.B. 11281

Mr. J. C. Brown has two copies of this German edition of 1665. *See* his catalogue, Nos. 705 and 706; the one with two, the other with six preliminary leaves. The one with six preliminary leaves has an engraved title, the other a printed one.

Casas. Die Verheerung Westindiens. Beschrieben vom Bischof Bartholomäus de las Casas. Aus dem Spanischen übersetzt von D. W. Andreä. *Berlin: Himburg.* 1790. 8vo, pp. 198. 11282

Other German versions are, according to Beckmann, included in "Curieuse und Historische Reisen, &c. *Leipzig.* 1699." 8vo, pp. 1056. II. "Der curieusen und historischen Reisen, &c. *Ander Haupt Theil*, &c. 1699." 8vo, pp. 968. This second volume, page 626, contains a German translation by August Bobse of No. 11275. All the other pieces in these volumes, preceding and excepting the above, are translated from Claude Jordan's "Voyages historiques de l'Europe, &c. *Paris.* 1692." 8 vols., 12mo. Often reprinted.

Casas. Narratio|regionvm|Indicarvm per|Hispanos qvosdam|deuastatarum verissima: priùs quidem|per Episcopum Barthhlomœum Casaum,|natione Hispanum Hispanicè conscripta,|& anno 1551. Hispali, Hi-|spanicè, Anno verò hoc| 1598. Latinè ex-|cusa,|*Francofvrti,|Sumptibus Theodori de Bry, & Io-|annis Saurii typis.*|*Anno* M.D.XCVIII.| Sm. 4to, Title printed in an engraved border, 3 l., pp. 141. 17 Engraved Plates in Text. P. 11283

Translated from the French edition of 1579. Contains Nos. 11227 and 11228, with the "Argumento" and "Prologo" of the original, and also Nos. 11229 and 11234. This last condensed into ten pages. Iodocus a Winghe designed the plates, each of which, occupying three quarters of a page, bears on its lower left corner the number of the page to which it belongs. Clement "Bibliot. Cur.," VI., gives a full account of this edition. Priced, 1826, Payne and Foss, £4 4s.; Roscoe's copy sold for £11 10s. This edition is much sought for, in consequence of the beauty of the first impressions of the plates.

Casas. Narratio|regionum Indicarum per|Hispanos qvosdam|devastatarum verissima: per Episco-|pum Bartholomœum Casaum, natione Hi-|spanum Hispanicè conscripta, &|Hispali Hispanicè, post alibi|Latinè excusa:|Jam verò denuè Iconibus illustrata edita est.|*Oppenheimii,|Sumptibus Johan-Theod. de Bry,* |*Typis Hieronymi Galleri*|MDCXIV.| 4to, Engraved Title, pp. 138. 17 Plates. P. 11284

Casas. Regionvm|Indicarum per|Hispanos olim devastatarum|accuratissima descriptio, insertis Fi-|guris æneis ad vivum fabrefactis,|Authore|Bartholomæo de las Casas|Episcopo Hispano.|Editio nova Priori longè cor-|rectior. *Heidelbergæ,|Typis Gvilielmi Walteri|Acad. Typogr. A. S.* M DC LXIV.| 4to, 2 Titles, one of which is engraved, 4 l., pp. 112. C., J.C.B. 11285

Clement says the plates are much worn, and that the "Dedication" and "Preface" of De Bry, and the "Disputa" and "Prologo," are omitted.

Casas. The Tears of the Indians:|Being|An Historical and true Account|Of the Cruel|Massacres and Slaughters|of above Twenty Millions|of innocent People;|Committed by the Spaniards|In the Islands of|Hispaniola, Cuba, Jamaica, &c.|As also, in the Continent of|Mexico, Peru, & other Places of the|West-Indies,|To the total destruction of those Countries.|Written in Spanish by Casaus,|an Eye-witness of those things;|And made English by J. P.|*London,|Printed by J. C. for Nath. Brook, at the Angel|in Cornhil.* 1656.| Sm. 8vo, 15 l., pp. 134. H., J.C.B.

Casas. The|Spanish Colonie,|or|Briefe Chronicle of the Acts and|gestes of the Spaniardes in the West In-|dies, called

the newe World, for the|space of xl. yeeres: written in the Ca-|stilian tongue by the reuerend Bi-|shop Bartholomew de las Casas or Casaus, a Friar of the or-|der of S. Dominicke.|And nowe first translated into|English, by M. M. S.|*Imprinted at London for|William Brome.*|1583.| [Colophon:] *Imprinted at London at the three|Cranes in the Vintres by Thomas|Dawson, for William Broome.*|1583. 4to, 8 l., 66 l. C. 11287

Casas. Popery|Truly Display'd in its|Bloody Colours:|Or, a Faithful|Narrative|of the|Horrid and Unexampled Massacres, But-|cheries, and all manner of Cruelties, that Hell and|Malice could invent, committed by the Popish Spanish|Party on the Inhabitants of West-India:|Together|With the Devastations of several Kingdoms in America|by Fire and Sword, for the space of Forty and Two|Years, from the time of its first Discovery by them.|Composed first in Spanish by Bartholomew de las Casas, a Bishop|there, and an Eye-Witness of most of these Barbarous Cruelties;|afterward Translated by him into Latin, then by other hands, into|High-Dutch, Low-Dutch, French, and now Taught to speak|Modern English.|*London, Printed for R. Hewson at the Crown in Cornhil,|near the Stocks-Market.* 1689.| 4to, 4 l., pp. 80. 11288

Casas. An|Account|Of the First|Voyages and Discoveries |Made by the Spaniards in America.|Containing|The most Exact Relation hitherto pub-|lish'd, of their unparallel'd Cruelties|on the Indians, in the destruction of a-|bove Forty Millions of People.|With the Propositions offer'd to the King of Spain,| to prevent the further Ruin of the West-Indies.|By Don Bartholomew de las Casas, Bishop of Chiapa,|who was an Eyewitness of their Cruelties.|Illustrated with Cuts.|To which is added,|The Art of Travelling, shewing how a Man may|dispose his Travels to the best advantage.|*London,|Printed by J. Darby for D. Brown at the Black Swan|and Bible without Temple-Bar, J. Harris at the|Harrow in Little Britain, and Andr. Bell at the |Cross-keys and Bible in Cornhil.* M.DC.XC.IX.| 8vo, 4 l., pp. 248, 40. 3 Plates. H. 11289

Some copies have two folded plates, one with six small scenes, the other sixteen, all from De Bry. Contains our Nos. 11227, 11228, 11233, 11234 abridged, 11230, 11229. All given as in the French edition of 1697, in a free version, and not separated. No. 11229 appears in two versions on pages 114 and 184. Said, in the preface, to be "translated from a new modern French edition," no doubt the one of 1697, *supra*. Mr. Helps closes a fine eulogium in the following language: "His career affords, perhaps, a solitary instance of a man who, being neither a conqueror, a discoveror, nor an inventor, has, by the pure force of benevolence, become so notable a figure that large portions of history cannot be written, or at least cannot be understood, without the narrative of his deeds and efforts being made one of the principal threads upon which the history is strung. ... Take away all he said and did, and preached, and wrote, and preserved (for the early historians of the New World owe the records of many of their most valuable facts to him), and the history of the conquest would lose a considerable portion of its most precious material." *See also* "Retrospective Review," xi. 261-71.

Casas (G.) Libro intitvlado|arte para criar sede, desde que se rebieue vna se|milla hasta sacar otra. Hecho por Gonçalo de|las casas señor dela prouincia y pueblos de Yā|guitan, que es en la mixteca de la nueua|España, vezino de la ciudad de|Mexico. Dirigido a la mvy illvs-|tro Señor Doña Catalina de Galuez mu|ger del muy Illustre Señor Doctor|Antonio Gonçalez del cõsejo|de su Magestad en la au-|diencia Real de|Granada.|Con priuilegio.|*Ympresso en Granada, en casa de Rene Rabut. Ympressor de libros año de|mil y quinientos y ochenta|y vn años.*|[1581.] 12mo, 8 l., Text, 96 l., Table, 4 l. J.C.B. 11290

This excessively rare book, on the production of silk in Yucatan, is not, we believe, noticed by any bibliographer. Reprinted at *Madrid*, 1625, and *Granada*, 1628.

Casas (Lucas de las). Memorial relativo de el hecho en derecho, y justificado gobierno de la Santa Iglesia Cathedral de Guadalaxara en los reintegros que hace el Mayordomo de ella á su fabrica etc. *Mexico.* 1729. Folio, pp. 112. 11291

Casas (L. de las). Elogios fúnebres del excm. señor D. Luis de Las Casas y Aragoni, teniente general de los R[les]. exércitos. Hechos y publicados por la Real sociedad económica de la Havana y por el tribunal del consulado de la misma ciudad. *Havana: Imprenta de la capitana general.* 1802. Folio, 10 leaves. 11292

Casas (M. M. de las). Defensa documentada de la conducta del comandante de La Guaira, Sr. Manuel Maria de las Casas, en la prision del general Miranda y entrega de aquella plaza á los Espagnoles en 1812. *Carácas.* 1843. 8vo, pp. 74. 11293

Casasola (J. M.) Acusacion fiscal en le causa contra J. M. Aviles, R. Negrete y C. Villalpando por el homicidio perpetrado en la persona del diputado D. J. de Dios Cañedo. *Mexico.* 1851. 8vo, pp. 38. 11294

Casasola. Acusacion fiscal que en la tercera sala de la Suprema Corte de Justicia pronuncio el Sr. Fiscal de ella Don Jose Maria Casasola en la causa instruida à varios reos, por el asalto, robos, y asesinados cometidos en la noche del 17 y mañana de 18 de Diciembre de 1856 en las haciendas de Chiconcuac y S. Vicente del Partido de Cuernavaca perteneciente al departamento de Mexico. *Mexico.* 1858. pp. 87, 64. 8 Lithogr. 11295

Casault (L. J.) Souvenir consacré a la memoire venerée de M. L. J. Casault, premier recteur de l'Université-Laval. *Quebec.* 1863. 8vo, pp. 58. 11296

Casaus (R.) Oracion funebre del exmo. señor D. Alonso Nuñez de Haro y Peralta. *Mexico.* 1800. 4to, 26 leaves.

Also: "Oration funebre en las exequias generales. *Mexico.* 1848." 4to, 22 l. Many Sermons by this author are described in Andrade's catalogue.

Cascaliendres (V. A.) Justa Vindicacion por Fr. Veremundo Androminas de Cascaliendres. *Puerto Principe.* 1823. 4to, pp. 30. 11298

Casco Bay. *See* [Colesworthy (D. C.)]

Case (Albert.) Statement of Facts respecting the Supreme Grand Council of Sovereign Grand Inspectors General 33d, Northern Jurisdiction, U. S. A. with a Review of Edward A. Raymond's Address. *Boston: printed by Alfred Mudge & Son.* 1861. 8vo, pp. 21. H. 11299

Case (C.) The President's Special Message. Speech of Hon. Charles Case, of Indiana. Delivered in the U. S House of Representatives, March 11, 1858. [*Washington: Buell & Blanchard. Printers.* 1858.] 8vo, pp. 16. H. 11300

Also: State of the Union Speech ... in the House of Representatives, February 8, 1861. [*Washington.* 1861.] 8vo, pp. 8. H.

Case (George). Our "Constitutional Rights" Vindicated: or an Argument for the Legal Proscription of the Traffic in Alcoholic Beverages. In six Letters to the Hon. F. Hincks. *Toronto.* 1854. 8vo, pp. 22. 11301

Case (T. S.) The Quartermaster's Guide ... . By Col. Theo. S. Case. *Saint Louis: P. M. Pinckard.* 1865. 8vo, pp. 339. B. 11302

[Case (W.)] Poems, occasioned by several circumstances and occurrences in the present grand contest of America for Liberty. *New Haven: Printed by Tho. and Samuel Green.* 1778. 8vo, pp. 41. 11303

No perfect, and but one or two imperfect copies are known. The poems are by the Rev. Wheeler Case, of Dutchess County, N. Y., and were republished with the following title:

Case. Revolutionary Memorials, embracing Poems by the Rev. Wheeler Case, published in 1778, And an Appendix, containing General Burgoyne's Proclamation (in burlesque,) dated

June 23, 1777, A late Authentic Account of the Death of Miss Jane M'Crea—The American Hero, a Sapphic Ode, By Nat. Niles, A M, etc. Edited by the Rev. Stephen Dodd ... *New York: M. W. Dodd.* 1852. 12mo, pp. 69. H. 11304

Case (William). Jubilee Sermon delivered at the request and before the Conference in London, C. W., 6th June, 1855. *Toronto.* 1855. 8vo. 11305

The Case and Claim of the American Loyalists Impartially Stated and Considered. [*London:*] *Printed by Order of their Agents.* [1783.] Sm. 8vo, Title, 1 l., pp. 38. W. 11306

Some copies have the imprint, *London: G. Wilkie.* MDCCLXXXIII. 8vo, Title, 1 l., pp. 38.

Case before the House of Lords relative to the Ship May, alias George, which Sailed from Charlestown in South Carolina, in 1777, and which was previously taken in Privateering by the Rebels. *London printed.* 1779. Folio. C. 11307

One of J. C. Hotten's doubtful titles.

A Case decided in the Supreme Court of the United States, February, 1793, in which was discussed the question "Whether a State be liable to be Sued by a private Citizen of another State?" *Philadelphia: Printed by T. Dobson* ... M.DCC.XCIII. 8vo, Title, 120, (1). BA. + *Boston.* 1793. 8vo, pp. 80. M. 11308

This is the famous case of Chisholm *vs.* the State of Georgia. Chief Justice Jay, in his charge, denied the doctrine of State Sovereignty.

Case of the Episcopal Churches, 1782. *See* [White (Wm.)]

Case of the Free-Labour British Colonies, submitted to the British Legislature and British Nation for an Impartial Re-Hearing. ... *London: James Madden.* 1852. 8vo, pp. xvi, 155. BA.

The Case of Going to War, for the Sake of Procuring, Enlarging, or Securing of Trade, considered in a New Light. Being A Fragment of a greater Work. *London: Printed for R. & J. Dodsley.* 1793. 8vo. pp. 59. W. 11310

Case of Great Britain and America, addressed To the King, 1769. ... The Third Edition. *London, Printed. Boston: Reprinted, and Sold by Edes & Gill, And T. & J. Fleet.* [n. d.] 4to, pp. 15. B. 11311

The title and collation of other editions will be found in No. 9637.

Case of Merchants and Planters trading to, and residing in, Virginia and Maryland. [n. p. n. d.] Folio, pp. 2. 11312

Bartlett places this under 1728. A London bookseller says, [1709].

The Case of our Fellow Creatures. *See* [Benezet (Anthony)]. Vol. II., No. 4669.

The Case of the Agent to the Settlers on the coast of Yucatan, and the late settlers on the Mosquito shore. Stating the whole of his conduct in soliciting compensation for the losses sustained by each of those classes of H. M's injured and distressed subjects.. 18th Nov. 1793. *London: T. Cadell.* 1794. 4to, pp. 320.

Title from Rich, I. 388, who, under the date 1793, reprints it with the remark that the agent's name was White, and, for collation, says pp. 179. There were, in fact, *four* parts, the first being dated 1789,

... Case of the Black Warrior, and other Violations of the Rights of American Citizens by Spanish Authorities. [*Washington.* 1854.] 8vo, pp. 378. (33d Cong. 1st Sess. House, Ex. Doc. 86.) 11314

See also Doc. 76, "Seizure of the Black Warrior."

The Case of the British Northern Colonies. [n. p. About 1750.] Folio, pp. 3. 11315

Case of the Caribbs. *See* [Davidson (George)].

Case of the Importation of Bar-Iron, from our own Colonies of North America. Humbly recommended to the Consideration of the present Parliament, by the Iron Manufacturers of Great Britain. *London: Thomas Tyre.* MDCCLVI. 8vo, pp. 29.

See M. R., XV. 672.

Case of the Seizure of the Southern Envoys. Reprinted, with Additions, from the "Saturday Review." ... *London: James Ridgway.* 1861. 8vo, pp. 26. 11317

The Case of the Sinking Fund. *See* South Sea.

The Case of the Sugar Colonies. *See* [Collins (John)].

The Case of the Trent examined. ... *London: James Ridgway.* 1862. 8vo, pp. 24. B. 11318

Case of the two Vessels, the Defiance bound for Antigua, and the Glasgow bound for New York, when they captured American and Spapish Vessels, but were afterwards recaptured by American Privateers. *Privately printed.* 1787. Folio

This title has J. C. Hotten's usual variations.

Case of the Uncompensated American Loyalists. 1816. 4to.

The Case Stated on Philosophical ground, between Great Britain and her Colonies, &c. *London: Kearsley.* 1778. 8vo, pp. 166. 11321

In Mason's catalogue, No. 252, the date is said to be 1777. "The rhapsody of a vehement advocate for the independency of the colonies, abounding in hard words and unintelligible expressions."—M. R., LVIII. 156.

Caseres y Elorza (Francisco Joseph). Sermon en las Honorificas y sumptuosas Exequias, celebró á la Memoria del Philippo V. el dia 17 de Marzo 1747. *Mexico.* 1748. 4to. 11322

Cases and Queries submitted to every Citizen of the United States and especially the Members of the Administration and of both Houses of Congress as deserving to be impartially considered by them. *New York: E. Sargeant.* 1809. 8vo, pp. 24. BA.

By Egbert Benson. The title, Vol. II., No. 4742, is incomplete.

Cases decided in the District and Circuit Court of the United States for the Pennsylvania District, and also a Case decided in the District Court of Massachusetts, relative to the Employment of British Licences on Board of Vessels of the United States. *Philadelphia: Redwood Fisher.* 1813. 8vo, 2 l., pp. 91. BA.

Cases of Personal Identity. *See* [Munsell (Joel)].

The Cases of some English Ships taken by the Spaniards, wherein is set forth, The unwarrantable manner in which they were seized; the illegal manner of declaring them prizes; and the barbarous treatment the Ships Company met with. Taken from Spanish Documents of unquestionable authority, done in their own courts of Judicature. *London: J. Roberts.* 1731. 8vo, pp. 37. 11325

For many other cases relating to persons and places, *see* under their names.

Casey (C.) Two Years on the Farm of Uncle Sam. With Sketches of his Location, Nephews, and Prospects. By Charles Casey. *London.* 1852. Post 8vo. C. 11326

Casey (Joseph). Speech of Mr. Casey, of Pennsylvania, on the President's Message, communicating the Constitution of California. Delivered in the House ... March 18, 1850. [n. p. n. d.] 8vo, pp. 7. H. 11327

Also: The Tariff. Speech ... Monday, August 12, 1850. On the Protective Policy, and the Iron and Coal Interest of Pennsylvania. [n. p. n. d.] 8vo, pp. 7.

Casey (S.) Infantry Tactics ... . By Brig. Gen. Silas Casey, U. S. Army. Vol. III. Evolutions of a Brigade, and Corps d'Armee. *Columbia: Evans & Cogswell.* 1864. 32mo, pp. 160. Plates. BA. 11328

Casgrain (H. R.) Histoire de la Mère Marie de l'Incarnation, première supérieure des Ursulines de la Nouvelle France, précédée d'une esquisse sur l'histoire religieuse des premiers temps de cette colonie par L'Abbe H. R. Casgrain *Quebec: G. E. Desbarats.* 1864. 8vo, pp. 467. Photographic Portrait, and 2 Engravings. BA. 11329

Some copies on fine paper. *See* "Revue Canad.," and "Hist. Mag."

Casgrain. Légendes canadiennes. *Québec.* 1861. 12mo, pp. 425. 11330

Also reprinted in France. *See* "Jour. de l'Inst. Pub.," and Morgan's "Bib. Canad."

Casgrain. Notice biographique sur le Chevalier Falardeau. Par Eugene de Rives. *Quebec.* 1862. 4to, pp. 96. Portrait.

Casgrain. Un contemporain. A. E. Aubry. Par L'Abbé H. R. Casgrain. *Quebec.* 1865. 18mo, pp. 102. Portrait.

Casgrain. Un contemporain. F. X. Garneau. Par l'Abbé H. R. Casgrain. *Quebec: J. N. Duquet.* 1866. 8vo, pp. 135. Portrait. 11333

Casgrain. Un contemporain. G. B. Faribault. *Quebec.* 1867. 8vo, pp. 123. S. 11334

Cash (Caleb). *See* Philadelphia.

The Casket; or Flowers of Literature, Wit and Sentiment. *Philadelphia: Atkinson.* 1826. 8vo, continued to 1838. 11335

This magazine, known also as "Atkinson's Casket," contains many articles of historic interest, and engravings of localities, etc. Complete sets are scarce.

Caskie (J.) Speech of James Caskie, Esq. ... before the Senate Committee on Banks, ... December 17, 1855. *Richmond.* 1856. 8vo, pp. 16. 11336

Casimir. Gründlicher Bericht des in America zwischen dem Rio Orinoco und Rio de las Amazonas sich erstreckenden Strich Landes welches die Ostindische Compagnie dem Grafen Friedrich Casimir zu Hanau ueberlassen hat. *Franckfurt.* 1669. 4to. 11337

Casler (A.) Trial and Conviction of Abraham Casler for the Murder of his Wife. *Schoharie.* 1817. 8vo. 11338

Caslo (A.) Life of Anthony Caslo; or. a Bonaparte Soldier, Eight years in the armies of France, Spain, England and the United States. *Detroit.* 1856. 8vo, pp. 76. S. 11339

Casmanni (O.) Othonis Casmanni Marinarum Quæstionum Tractatio Philosophica Bipartita, Disceptans Quæstiones parte Priore ad Maris naturam pertinentes interiorem: Posteriore de motu Maris agitatas, præcipue verò de eo qui dicitur Affluxus & Refluxus Marinus. Cum Cæs. Majest. privilegio decennali. *Francofurti. Ex Officina M. Zachariæ Palthenij. Anno* M. D. XCVI. pp. 244. 11340

Title from [Kennett's] "Bib. Am. Prim." Probably bears on the Spanish claims to America.

Casoni. Annali de Genova, de secolo sedicesimo. *Genoa.* 1708. Folio. 11341

Contains some particulars concerning Columbus.

Casos|Notables, Svcedi-|dos en las Costas de la Civdad|de Lima, en las Indias, y como el armada Olandesa procuraua|coger el armadilla neustra, que baxa con la plata de or-|dinario a Cartagena, y se pasò dexandolos|burlados: desde el mes de Iunio deste|año passado de 1624.| [Colophon:] *Con licencia, en Madrid, por Iuan Gonçalez. Año de* 1625.| Folio, 2 l. J.C.B. 11342

In Puttick's catalogue, 1860, the imprint reads: "*Madrid: Bern. de Guzman.*"

Caspipina (Tamoc), *pseudonym.* *See* Duché (Jacob).

Cass (G. W.) New York Central Road. The Buffalo Convention, and the St. Nicholas Compact. [n. p. 1859.] 8vo, pp. 16. 11343

Also: Letter to the "New York Times," in Reply to New York Central Rail Road Company. [n. p. 1859.] 8vo, pp. 6. H.

Cass (L.) A Discourse delivered at the First Meeting of the Historical Society of Michigan, September 18, 1829. ... By Lewis Cass. *Detroit: printed by Geo. L. Whitney.* 1830. 8vo pp. 52. BA., M. 11344

Cass. A Discourse pronounced at the Capitol of the United States ... before the American Historical Society, January 30, 1836, by the Hon. Lewis Cass ... . To which are prefixed its Constitution and the Names of its Officers. *Washington: P. Thompson.* 1836. 8vo, pp. 58. BA., C., H., P. 11345

[Cass.] An Examination of the question now in discussion, between the American and British governments, concerning the Right of Search. By an American. *Baltimore: N. Hickman.* 1842. 12mo, pp. 55. C., S. 11346

[Cass.] Examen de la question aujourd'hui pendante entre le gouvernement des États-Unis et celui de la Grand-Bretagne, concernant le droit de viste; par un américain. [*Paris: H. Fournier.* 1842.] 8vo, pp. 82. C., H. 11347

[Cass.] Inquiries respecting the History, Traditions, Languages, Manners, Customs, Religion, &c., of the Indians living in the United States. *Detroit: Sheldon and Reed.* 1823. 8vo, pp. 64. 11348

See N. A. R., XIV. 34.

Cass. Remarks on the Policy and Practice of the United States and Great Britain in their Treatment of the Indians. *Boston.* 1827. 8vo. C. 11349

Also: Address of Lewis Cass ... before the Association of the Alumni of Hamilton College ... August 25, 1830. ... . *Utica.* 1830. 8vo, pp. 40. B., H.—Address delivered before the N. E. Society of Michigan, Dec. 22, 1848 .. *Detroit.* 1849. 8vo, pp. 47.—Address of Gen. Lewis Cass, delivered before the Kalamazoo County Agricultural Society, ... October 11, 1850. ... *Washington City: Towers.* [n. d.] 8vo, pp. 16. BA., H.—Admission of California. Remarks of Mr. Cass, of Michigan, in reply to the reference to his opinions on the alleged Sovereign Power of Congress over the Territories by Mr. Berrien of Georgia. Delivered in the Senate ... Aug. 12, 1850. [n. p. n. d.] 8vo, pp. 8.—Diplomatic relations with Austria. Speech of Hon. Lewis Cass, ... in the Senate ... January 4, 1850, On Suspending our Diplomatic Relations with Austria. *Washington.* [n. d.] 8vo, pp. 8. B.—[Cass.] France; its King, Court, and Government. By an American. *New York.* 1840. 8vo, pp. 191. N.—Kansas. The Territories. Speech ... delivered in the Senate of the United States, May 12-13, 1856. [*Washington.* 1856.] 8vo, pp. 24.—The Mexican War. Speech ... in the Senate ... February 10, 1847. [*Washington: Blair and Rives.* 1847.] 8vo, pp. 16. H.—The Power of Congress over the Territories. Speech ... March 13 and 14, 1850, on the Compromise Resolutions of Mr. Bell, of Tennessee, ... [n. p. n. d.] 8vo, pp. 15. H.—Remarks ... on the Dissolution of the Union, and the Constitution of California. In the Senate ... February 12 and 20, 1850. [*Washington.* n. d.] 8vo, pp. 8. H., S.—Review of a "Narrative of the Siege of New Orleans. By Captain John H. Cook."—Speech of ... Governor Cass, to the First Legislative Council of the Territory of Michigan. ... June 7, 1824. ... *Detroit: printed by Sheldon and Reed.* 1824. 8vo, pp. 15. BA.—Speech ... on European Interference in American Affairs. ... Senate ... January 26, 1845. *Washington.* 1845. 8vo, pp. 8. H.—Speech ... on the Defences of the Country, ... December 15, 1845. *Washington.* 1845. 8vo, pp. 7. H.—Speech ... on the Oregon Question. ... March 30, 1846. [n. p. n. d.] 8vo, pp. 16. H.—Speech ... in reply to Mr. Benton, of Missouri, with some Additions. ... Senate ... Thursday April 2, 1846. [n. p. n. d.] 8vo, pp. 8. H.—Speech ... on the Bill providing for the Prosecution of the War against Mexico. ... Tuesday, May 12, 1846. *Washington: Blair and Rives.* 1846. 8vo, pp. 8. H.—Speech ... on ... War against Mexico ... May 23, 1846. *Washington.* 1846.

8vo, pp. 8. — Speech on the Wilmot Proviso, ... Senate, March 1, 1847 [*Washington.* 1847.] 8vo. S. — Speech ... on the Bill to protect the Rights of American Settlers in Oregon. ... June 1, 1846. *Washington: Blair and Rives.* 1846. 8vo, pp. 14. H. — Speech, ... War with Mexico, ... Senate ... January 3, 1848. S. — Speech ... on the proposed occupation of Yucatan, ... Senate ... May 10, 1848. *Washington.* 1848. 8vo, pp. 16. — Speech ... on the motion of Mr. Benton for the indefinite postponement of the Compromise Bill, ... Senate ... June 14, 1850. [n. p. n. d.] 8vo, pp. 16. — Speech ... on Non-Intervention. ... Senate ... February 10, 1852. *Washington.* 1852. 8vo, pp. 16. H. — Speech ... on the Clayton-Bulwer Treaty ... Senate ... January 11, 1854. *Washington.* 1854. 8vo, pp. 24. BA. — Speech ... Senate ... May 15, 1854, on the ... Religious Rights of American Citizens residing or travelling in Foreign Countries. *Washington.* 1854. 8vo, pp. 21. — Speech ... on our Relations with Great Britain. ... Senate January 28, 1856. [n. p. n. d.] 8vo, pp. 16. B. — Speech ... Senate ... May 12–13, 1856. [n. p. n. d.] 8vo, pp. 24. — Speech ... on the River and Harbor Appropriation Bills. *Washington.* 1856. pp. 21. S.

CASS. The Cass Platform. ... *Washington.* [1848.] 8vo, pp. 8. BA. 11350

CASS. Biography of General Lewis Cass, including A Voice from a Friend. *New York: J. Winchester.* [1843.] 8vo, pp. 36.

CASS. Facts and Arguments. *See* [Jarvis (R.)]

CASS. In Memoriam. General Lewis Cass. *Detroit.* 1866. Sm. 4to, pp. 220. 11352

CASS. Life and Public Services of Gen. Lewis Cass ... With a Sketch of the Life and Services of Gen. W. O. Butler ... Illustrated ... *Boston: J. B. Hall.* 1848. 8vo, pp. 34. H.

CASS. The Life and Public Services of Lewis Cass, including his pamphlet on the Right of Search. *Detroit.* 1852. 8vo.

CASS. Life of General Lewis Cass: comprising an Account of his Military Services in the North-West during the War with Great Britain, his Diplomatic Career and Civil History. To which is appended, a Sketch of the Public and Private History of Major-General W. O. Butler, of the Volunteer Service of the United States. *Philadelphia: G. B. Zieber & Co.* 1848. 12mo, pp. 210. 2 Portraits. S. 11355

CASS. Life of Lewis Cass, with Letters and Speeches. *Baltimore.* 1848. 12mo. 11356

Perhaps the same as the preceding number.

CASS ... National and Jackson Democratic Association Committee. The Union of the Northern and Southern Democracy upon Cass and Butler. [*Washington.* 1848.] 8vo, pp. 8. BA.

CASS. Outlines of the Life of Cass. *See* [Schoolcraft (H. R.)]

CASS Sketch of the Life and Public Services of Gen. Lewis Cass. [*Washington.* 1848.] 8vo, pp. 8. BA. 11358

CASS Sketches of General Cass and Wm. O. Butler. *New York.* 1848. 8vo. N. 11359

CASS. Cass and Taylor on the Slavery Question. *See* [Bowditch]. Vol. II., No. 7006.

CASSAGNAC (A. De). *See* Granier De Cassagnac.

CASSANI (J.) Glorias del Segundo Siglo de la Compañia de Jesus, dibuxadas en las vidas, y elogias de algunos de sus varones ilustres en virtud, letras, y zelo de las almas, que han florecido desde el año de 1640, primero del segundo siglo, desde la aprobacion de la religion. Escrites por el P. Joseph Cassani, de la misma Compaña. Tomo I. y VII. En el orden de varones ilustres, obra, que empezò el V. P. Juan Eusebio Nieremberg. Dedicase al Venerable Augusto Soberano Sacramento que debaxo de veinte y quatro milagrosamente incorruptas Formas, sa venera en el Colegio de la misma Compaña de Alcalà, y comunmente se nombra las santissimas formas de Alcala. Con Licencia. *En Madrid: Por Manuel Fernandez. Impressor de Libros. Año de* MDCCXXXIV. 3 vols., folio, 17 l., pp. 692; 2 l., pp. 679; 7 l., pp. 727. 11360

This is a continuation of the work of Juan Eusebio Nieremberg, published at Madrid, 1645–1647, in four volumes, folio, entitled "Honor del Gran Patriarcha Incognacio de Loyala," etc. Vols. V. and VI. by Alonzo de Andrade, entitled, "Varones Ilustres en santidad y letras de la Campaña de Jesus," were published in 1566–1667; and the work above mentioned, by Cassani, forms the seventh, eighth, and ninth volumes of the same work. The whole consists of the lives of the members of the Society of the Jesuits, who were celebrated for their piety and learning. The latter writer dedicates his work to "the Sovereign August Venerable Sacrament, which was worshipped in the Jesuits' College at Alcala, under the form of twenty four consecutive wafers, which had been miraculously preserved there, from the year 1595, as white and fresh as when they were first consecrated." Priced, by Thorpe, £4 14s. 6d.

CASSANI. Historia de la provincia de la compañia de Jesus del Nuevo Reyno de Granada en la America, descripcion, y relacion exacta de sus gloriosas missiones en el reyno, llanos, meta, y Rio Orinoco, almas, y terreno, que han conquistado sus missioneros para dios, amento de la Christiandad, y extension de los dominios de su Mag. Catholica, author el Padre Joseph Cassani, Religioso de la misma Compañia ... . *Madrid: Manuel Fernandez.* M. DCC. XLI. Folio, 14 l., pp. 618, 1 l. Map. C., H.

CASSEDAY (B.) History of Louisville, [Ky.] from its Earliest Settlement to the Year 1852. By Benjamin Casseday. *Louisville: Hull and Brother.* 1852. 16mo, pp. 255. Map. C.

CASSEDAY (D. B.) The Hortons; or, American Life at Home. By Davis B. Casseday. *Philadelphia.* 1866. 8vo, pp. 362. 11363

CASSEGRAIN (A.) La Grand-Tronciade ou Itineraire de Québec a la Rivière-du-Loup. Poème badin par Arthur Cassegrain. *Ottawa.* 1866. 12mo, pp. vii, 96. 11364

See Morgan's "Bib. Canad.," p. 67.

CASSELL (Johann Philipp). Dissertatio Philologico-Historica, de Navigationibus Fortuitis in Americam, ante Chr. Columbum factis. *Magdeburgi.* 1742. 4to, 15 leaves. 11365

CASSELL. Observatio historica de Frisonum Navigatione Fortuita in Americam sec. XI. facta. [*Magdeburgi.*] 1741. 4to, 8 leaves. 11366

CASSERLY (E.) The Issue in California. Letter of Eugene Casserly to T. T. Davenport, Esq. ... Nevada County, California: August 27th, 1861. *San Francisco: Charles F. Robins.* 1861. 8vo, pp. 15. H. 11367

CASSES DE XALO (Joachin). Rasgo epico, veridica epiphomena, y aclamacion cierta à favor de España, en el cèlebre Tropheo, que consiguieron en Carthagena Americana las Armas Catholicas contra Inglaterra, governadas por el Virrey de Santa Fe D. Sebastian Eslaba. Sisthema politico, historica descripcion Geographico-Pronostica de Inglaterra y Panegyris Critico-Historico de España Su autor ... D. Joachin Casses de Xalò, ... *Madrid:* MDCCXLI. Sm. 8vo, 20 l., pp. 96. H. 11368

Written in consequence of the repulse of Admiral Vernon at Carthagena. Its author was celebrated, in his time, for the number of works he undertook without finishing any, and for the ridiculous bombast of his style.

La Cassette Verte. *See* [Tickell (R.)]

CASSIN (J.) Illustrations of the Birds of California, Texas and British and Russian America. Intended to contain Descriptions and Figures of all Birds North-American not given by former American Authors, and a General Synopsis of North American Ornithology. By John Cassin ... . *Philadelphia: J. B. Lippincott & Co.* 1856. 8vo, pp. viii, 298. 50 colored Plates. BA., C., H. 11369

CASSIN. United States Exploring Expedition. During the Years 1838, 1839, 1840, 1841, 1842. Under the Command of Charles Wilkes, U. S. N. Mammalogy and Ornithology. By John Cassin ... . With a Folio Atlas. *Philadelphia: J. B. Lippincott & Co.* 1858. 4to, 1 l., pp. viii, 466. Atlas of 53 Plates. BA., C., G., H. 11370

One hundred and fifty copies printed. Forms Vol. VIII. of the "United States Exploring Expedition." *See also* Gilliss (J. M.)

CASSIN (Joseph). Medical Department of the University of Pennsylvania. [n. p.] 1844. 8vo, pp. 36. 11371

CASSINI (Jean Dominique), *Count.* Voyage fait par Ordre du Roi, en 1768, pour eprouver les Montres Marines inventées par M. Le Roy. ... *Paris: Jombert père.* 1770. 4to. Plates. S.

This voyage to Newfoundland was translated in 1778. *See* D'Chappe D'Auteroche.

CASSIUS, *pseudonym.* *See* [Burke (Ædanus)].

CAST (J. F.) Valdivia und Chiloë für deutsche Auswanderer. *Stuttgart: Cast in Commission.* 1849. 8vo, pp. 60. Map.

CASTAING. Memoire sur la Succession de Madame de Castaing, Ouverte au Cap de S. Dominique, Qui est à partager entre des Heritiers, un Donataire, et un Légataire. Et Consultation Du mois de Janvier 1742. Sur les Questions qui suivent, Sçavoir, 1o. Comment on succede aux Propres dans la Coûtumes de Paris. 2o. Ce que c'est que la défaillance d'une ligne, ou ce qu'on appelle dévolution de ligne. 3o. Que les Conquêts de communauté, s'ils passent moyennant soulte aux enfans du premier lit deviennent des Propres naissans, pour le tout dans leur succession. 4o. Que les acquets faits par un Collateral, sont Propres naissans au Collateral qui les recueille. 5o. Que le remploy fait par un mari, des biens de sa femme, n'est parfait que par l'acceptation de la femme, autorisée du mari. 6o. Que les Propres d'un fils décédé, appartiennent à la mere, jusqu'à ce qu'il se presente des héritiers, & lui deviennent Propres. 7o. Qu'une demande en delivrance de legs peut être dirigée valablement contre le mari donataire de part d'enfant, comme contre l'héritier du sang. *A Paris: Chez Pierre Prault.* M.DCC.XLII. 4to, pp. 21.

CASTAN (*Fr.* Felipe), *definidor de la provincia de Lima.* Elogio funebre del Rmo. P. M. fr. Francisco Xavier Vasquez de Sandoval y Romero, dignisimo primer prior general español, y segundo

vitalicio del orden de hermitaños de San Agustin. *Lima: imprenta Real de los Huerfanos.* 1786. 4to, 14 l., pp. 80, 2 l., pp. xxxii. 11375

CASTAÑARES (Manuel). Coleccion de documentos relativos al Departemento de Californias. *Mexico.* 1845. 8vo, pp. 70.

CASTAÑEDA (F. L.) *See* Castanheda (F. L.), No. 11381.

CASTAÑEDA. Alocucion que Pio VI. tuvo en el Consistorio secreto el dia 13. de Noviembre de 1775 sobre la preciosa muerte de Jacinto Castañeda ... *Mexico.* 1776. Folio, pp. 16. 11377

CASTANEDA (Juan Ruiz). Panegirico de Ntrā Srā de Guadalupe, predicado en su Santuario y Real Colegiata. *Megico.* 1766. 4to. 11378

CASTAÑEDA DE NAGERA (P. de). Relation du Voyage de Cibola, Entrepris en 1840, ou l'on traite de toutes les peuplades qui habitent cette contrée, leurs mœurs et coutumes, par Pedro de Castañeda de Nagera (Inédite.) *Paris: A. Bertrand.* M. DCCXXXVIII. 8vo, 2 l., pp. XVI, 392. H. 11379

Forms Vol. IX., First Series of Ternaux's "Voyages et relations."

CASTANEDA Y ESCALADA (José Maria). Oracion que pronunció civica en la alameda de la ciudad federal el ciudadano J. M. C. y E. a 16 de Septiembre de 1834. *Mexico: imprenta de Galvan, á cargo de Mariano Arévalo.* 1834. Sm. 4to, pp. 19.

CASTANHEDA (Ferñao Lopes de). Historia do descobrimento e conquista da India pelos Portuguezes, feyta per Fernaõ Lopez de Castanheda, e approuada pelos senhores deputados da sancta Inquisiçaõ. [Colophon:] *Foy impresso este primeiro liuro da Historia da India em a muyto nobre & leal cidade de Coimbra per Ioão da Barreyra & Ioão Alvarez, empressores del Rey na mesma Universidade. Acabouse aos seys dias de mes de Março. De* M.D.LI. 4to, pp. 267. 11381

A book of extreme rarity, respecting which, *see* the "Bibliotheca Grenvilliana." Figaniere indicates the existence of only *one* copy. *See* Silva, II. 284. It relates principally to the East Indies, but contains some particulars of the Portuguese conquests in the New World, and is included in Dr. Robertson's "Catalogue of Authorities." This first and most important part was reprinted with the following title:

CASTAÑEDA. Historia do descobrimento e conquista de India pelos Portuguezes, feyta per Fernaõ Lopez de Castanheda e approuada pelos senhores deputados da sancta Inquisiçaõ ... [Colo-

phon:] *Foy impresso este primeiro livro de Historia da India en a muyto nobre e leal cidade de Coimbra per Ioaõ da Barreyra e Joao Alvarez, empressores del rey na mesma uniuersidade. Acabouse aos seys dias del mes de Marco de* 1551. 11382

Stevens' "Amer Bibl.," page 55, quotes what he calls a second edition, as below:

CASTANHEDA. Ho primeiro liuro. ... [Colophon:] *Foy impresso este pri-|meiro Livro da Historia da|India em a muyto nobre & leal cidade de Coim-|bra, por Ioão da Barreyra impressor del rey| na mesma vniuersidade. Acabouse aos|vinte dias do mes de Iulho. De*|M. D. LIIII.| Folio, pp. ccji. 11383

Reprinted under the supervision of Prof. F. J. dos Sanctos Marrocas, *Lisboa na Offi. de Simao Thaddeo Ferreira.* 1797. 2 vols., 8vo. The second part has the following title:

CASTANHEDA Histo-|ria do liuro se|gundo do des|cobrimēto & conquista da India pelos|Portugueses.|Feyta per Fernão lopez de|Castanheda.|[Colophon:] ... *Foy impresso este segundo liuro| da historia da India em a muyto nobre & leal cidade de Coymbra|por Ioão de Barreyra, & Ioão aluarez empressores del rey na|mesma vniuersidade. Acabouse aos vinte dias do mes de Ianeyro. De*|M. D. LII.| Folio, 4 l., pp. 239. 11384

This was followed by the "Terceiro livro," 1552, which we have not seen. Parts IV. and V. have the following title:

CASTANHEDA. Os liuros|quarto & quĩto da historia|do descobrimento & cõquista|da India pelos Portu-|gueses.|Com priuilegio Real.|M. D. LIII.| [Colophon:] *Acabouse de empremir a presen|te obra per João|da barreria & Joã aluares em a muyto nobre & sempre|leal cidade de Coimbra. Aos.* XV.|*dias do mes de Outubro.*| *de* M. D. liij. Folio, 4 l., pp. ccx, 1. 11385

The remaining parts we have not seen. They are "Sexto livro," *Coimbra por Joao de Barreira,* 1554, "Seitimo livro por faltar a subscripçao final," 1534, and "Octavo livro," *Coimbra, por Joao Barreira,* 1561, folio. Silva remarks, "Os livros nono e decimo nunca sahiram á luz, apezar de feitos e promittidos. É curioso de vêr o que a este respeito diz o sr. Felner na noticia preliminar ao tomo 1 das Lendas da India de Gaspar Corrêa, actualmente em via de publicaçao por ordem da Acad. R. das Sciencias, V. a pag xiii nota (23)." Brunet pronounces a set of 8 vols., folio, "Ouvrage rare," and, following Barbosa, mentions a Spanish translation of Vol. I., *Anvers,* 1554, 8vo. This is possibly a mistake, as there was a French version with that imprint, but Silva says that a copy of the Spanish is mentioned in the catalogue of the library of F. J. Maria de Brito. The following is the last edition in Portuguese:

CASTAÑEDA. Historia do descobrimento e conquista de India pelos Portuguezes, por Lopez de Castañeda. Nueva edicion. *Lisboa: na Typ. Rollandiana.* 1833. 7 vols., sm. 4to. 11386

CASTANHEDA. Le premier livre de l'histoire de l'Inde, contenant commēt l'Inde a esté decouuerte par le commādement du Roy Emanuel: et la guerre que les capitaines Portugalois ont menee contre Samorin Roy de Calecut: faict par Fernād Lopes de Castagneda: & traduit de Portugués en Frāçois par Nicolas de Grouchy. [*Paris:*] *De l'imprimerie de Michel de Vascosan.* M.D.LIII. Sm. 4to, pp. 346. S. 11387

For an abridged French translation, *see* Osorius.

CASTANHEDA. L'Historie des Indes de Portugal, contenant comment l'Inde a esté découverte, par le commandement du roy Emanuel ... la guerre que les capitaines portugalois ont menée pour la conqueste d'icelles ... *En Anvers, par Iehan Steelsius.* M. D. LIIII. 8vo, 4 l., pp. 221. 11388

CASTANHEDA. Historia|dell' Indie|Orientali,|Scoperte, & conquistate da' Portoghesi, di com-|missione dell' Inuittissimo Re Don|Manuello, di gloriosa memoria.|Nella quale, oltre alle strane vsanze, maniere, riti e costumi di|quelle genti; si uiene anco in notitia di molte Guerre fatte in|quei paesi; & di molte Prouincie, Isole, Città, Castelli, Fiumi,|Monti, Laghi, Mari, Minere di metalli, Perle, Gioie, Ani-|mali, droghe di specierie, & di molte altre cose degne di me-|rauiglia.|Distinta in Libri VII. |Composti dal Sig. Fernando Lopes|di Castagneda.|Et nuouamente di lingua Portoghese in Italiana tradotti|dal Signor' Alfonso Vlloa.|Parte Prima.|[Parte Seconda.] Con le sve Tavole Copiosissime.|Con Privilegio.|[Vignette.] *In Venetia, Appresso Giordano Ziletti.* M D LXXVII.| 2 vols., 4to, 17 l., 518 folioed l., 1 l.; 13 l., 365 folioed l., 1 l. 11389

CASTANHEDA. Warhafftige Historia von erfindung Calecut und anderer Königreich, Landen ... in Indien und dem Indianischen Meer. Auss Frantz. Sprach ins Teutsch gebracht. [n. p.] 1565. 8vo. 11390

This German version is translated from the French.

CASTANHEDA. The first Booke|Of The Histo-|rie of the Discouerie and Con-|quest of the East Indies, enterprised by| Portingales, in their daungerous|Nauigations, in the time of King|Don Iohn, the second of that|name.|VVhich Historie conteineth|much varietie of matter, very profitable|for all Nauigators, and not vnplea-|saunt to the Readers.|Set foorth in the Por-|tingale language, by Hernan|Lopes de Castaneda.|And Now Trans-|lated into English, by|N. L. Gentleman.|*Im-*

printed at London, by|Thomas East.|1582.| 4to, Title, 1 l., 5 l., 164 l. 11391

A most interesting and rare book, respecting which, *see* "Bibliotheca Grenvilliana." The translator was Nicholas Lichefield. Dedicated to Sir Francis Drake.

CASTANIS (C. P.) The Greek Exile, or, Narrative of the Captivity and Escape of Christophorus Plato Castanis, during the Massacre in the Island of Scio by the Turks, with Adventures in Greece and America. Written by Himself. *Philadelphia.* 1851. 12mo. C. 11392

CASTAÑIZA (J. F. de). Relacion del restablecimiento de la Compañia de Jesus en el Reyno de Nueva España, y de la entrega á sus Religiosos del Real Seminario de San Ildefonso de Mexico. Por Juan Francisco Castañiza Gonzalez de Aguero. *Mexico.* 1816. 4to, pp. 47. 11393

Also on large paper.

CASTAÑO (B.) Vida exemplar y muerte dichosa del Ven. P. Bartolomé Castaño, de la Compañia de Jesus de la Nueva-España. *Mégico: Ribera.* 1708. 4to. 11394

The first edition was 1679. Also: Catecismo Breve, por B. Castaño, de la Compañia de Jesus. *Calle de Espiritu Santo.* 1817. Folio, 1 l.

CASTAÑOS (José Maria). Los sucesos de Tepic. *Guadalajara.* 1857. 4to, pp. 31. 11395

CASTELFRANC (Gideon). Sermon at St. Andrew's, 2 Septr., 1763, the Day appointed by his Excellency the Governor, for a General Thanksgiving on Account of the Peace. *Kingston, Jamaica.* 1763. 4to. 11396

C[ASTELL] (W.) Petition of W. C., exhibited to the High Court of Parliament now assembled, for the propagating of the Gospel in America and the West Indies, and for the settling of our Plantations there, which Petition is approved by 70 able English Divines. Also by Master Alexander Henderson, and some worthy ministers of Scotland. *Printed in the yeare* 1641. 4to. J.C.B. 11397

This forms No. 13 of Force's Tracts, Vol. I. The original is priced, in Thorpe's catalogue, 1843, No. 3886, at 7s. 6d.

CASTELL. A Short|Discoverie|Of the Coasts and Continent of|America,|From the Equinoctiall Northward, and|of the adjacent Isles.|By William Castell, Minister of the Gospell at| Courtenhall in Northamptonshire.|Whereunto is prefixed the

Author's Petition to this pre-|sent Parliament, for the propagation of the Gospell|in America, attested by many eminent English|and Scottish Divines.|And a late Ordinance of Parliament for that|purpose, and for the better government of the|English Plantations there.|Together with Sir Benjamin Rudyer's Speech|in Parliament, 21 Jan. concerning America.|*London, Printed in the yeer* 1644.| 4to, 6 l., pp. 48, 54. C. 11398

Reprinted in Vol. II. of the Oxford collection of voyages. A book of much rarity. Roche's copy sold for \$60; Puttick, 1860, £3 7s.

CASTELLAMARE (P.) Versos de Pietro de Castellamare. Primera parte (Traducções) Segunda parte (Originaes) Terceira parte (Humoristicas). *San Luiz do Maranhão.* 1868. 12mo, pp. 156. 11399

CASTELLANOS (Aaron). Simple notice sur le Rio de la Plata. *Dunkerque: impr. de Vanderest.* 1855. 8vo. Map. 11400

CASTELLANOS (J. R.) Manifiesto al público por D. José Rafael Castellanos. *Puerto-Principe, imprenta de Minuese.* 1821.

CASTELLANOS (J. de). Primera Parte,|de las Elegias|de Varones Illvs-|tres de Indias.|Compuestas por Juan de Castellanos Clerigo, Benefi-|ciado de la Ciudad de Tunja en el nueuo|Reyno de Granada.|Con Privilegio.|*En Madrid,|en casa de la viuda de Alonso Gamez Impressor de|su Magestad. Año* 1589.| 4to, 15 l., 11–382 (for 364). S. 11402

Page 319 numbered 337, gaining eighteen pages, with many other errors in pagination. Partly reprinted in the 4th volume of the "Biblioteca de Autores Españoles," 1850. The author of this very rare and interesting work was a clergyman of Tunja, in the province of New Granada. Munoz says, that "he employed the greatest and best part of his life in *singing the various and nmmerous events of the New World, from its discovery.* He commenced by compiling his work in prose, and then reducing it into *verse.* Castellanos is a writer of considerable merit and utility, as respects the events of his own time; those anterior to it he took from authors, particularly Oviedo, from popular traditions, and, from the fertile field of his imagination, as many fables as suited his plan." *See* Munoz, "Hist. del Nuevo Mundo," and Ternaux, No. 179. A second edition, "*Madrid.* 1857," 4to, pp. 567, forms Vol. IV. of the "Bibliotéca de autores españoles." The other two parts were not printed, but are preserved in manuscript in some libraries in Spain.

CASTELLANOS (M.) Defensa hecha por el Licenciado Don Manuel Castellanos ante el Señor Juez del Ramo Criminal Lic. Don Dionisio del Castillo, en el Juicio Verbal sobre Denuncia de un Impreso intitulado; Contestacion de un Español al E. S. Ministro Siliceo. *Mexico.* 1865. Large 8vo, pp. 65. 11403

"With a portrait of Don Man. Castellanos. He was accused of the abuse of the liberty of the press." — TRÜBNER.

CASTELLAR (Thomas del). Triumfo de los martyres de las Indias de la orden de Predicadores. 11404

Printed, according to Antonio, about 1580.

CASTELLI (*l'abbé*). Exposé des motifs et projets d'organisation pour l'amélioration des classes inférieures de la Martinique par l'instruction religieuse; presenté au conseil colonial. *Paris: impr. de Fournier.* 1837 8vo, pp. 16. 11405

CASTELLI. De l'esclavage en général et de l'émancipation des noirs, avec un projet de réorganisation de l'action religieuse considérée comme le premier élément et le plus efficace pour préparer et mêner à bon fin l'œuvre sainte de l'émancipation des esclaves dans les colonies françaises. *Paris: Comon et Cie.* 1844. 8vo. 11406

See the "Moniteur," 8 août 1844.

CASTELLI Précis de la mission qu'a remplie aux Antilles françaises M. Castelli, en sa qualité d'inspecteur de l'enseignement public aux colonies et de préfet apostolique de la Martinique, depuis 1833 jusqu'à 1841. *Paris: imp. Juteau.* 1842. 8vo.

CASTELLI. Mision del Jeneral Castelli á Bogotá. (Termino de la cuestion sobre quejas del gobierno venezolano al gobierno neo-granadino.) *Bogota.* 1856. 4to, pp. 8. 11408

CASTELMAN (Richard). *See* [Chetwood (W. R.)]

CASTELMEHOR (*Conde* de). Relacion do Conde de Castelmehor *Lisboa.* 1642. 4to. 11409

Probably Silva gives more particulars concerning this work; but the peculiar arrangement of that work, under the Christian names of the authors, renders it difficult to find such a work as this.

CASTELNAU (*le Comte* Francis de). Essai sur le système silurien de l'Amérique septentrionale. Par F. de Castelnau. *Strasbourg: Berger-Levrault.* 1843. 4to, pp. 72. 27 Plates.

CASTELNAU. Expédition dans les parties centrales de l'Amérique du Sud, de Rio de Janeiro à Lima et de Lima au Para, executée par ordre du gouvernement français pendant les années 1843 à 1847, sous la direction de Francis de Castelnau. *Paris: P. Bertrand,* 1850, *etc.* 4to and 8vo. 11411

This work received the award of an extra medal from the French Geographical Society. It consists of the following works: Part I. Histoire du voyage. 1850–51. 6 vols., 8vo. Map. — Part 2. Vues et Scènes. 1 vol., 4to. 60 Plates, and Text. — Part 3. Antiquités des Incas et autres peuples anciens. 1 vol., 4to. 60 Plates, and Text — Part 4. Itinéraires et coupes géologiques. 1 vol., folio. 76 Plates, and Text. — Part 5. Géographie. 1 vol., folio. 30 Maps, and Text. — Part 6. Botanique. 2 vols., 4to. 96 Plates, and Text. — Part 7. — Zoologie. 3 vols., 4to. 176 Plates, and Text.

CASTELNAU. Vues et souvenirs de l'Amérique du Nord; par Francis de Castelnau. *Paris: Arthus Bertrand.* 1842. 4to, pp. viij, 165, 1 l. 35 Plates. C. 11412

Plates on India paper, except a few which are colored.

CASTERA (F.), *Translator. See* Mackenzie (A.)

CASTIGLIONI (L.) Viaggio negli Stati Uniti dell' America Settentrionale, fatto negli anni 1785, 1786, e 1787 da Luigi Castiglioni ... . Con alcune Osservazioni sui Vegetabili più utili di quel Paese. *Milano: Nella Stamperia di Guiseppe Marelli.* 1790. 2 vols., 8vo, pp. xii, 403; vi, 402, 5 folded l. 9 Plates, and 5 Maps. BA., C., H. 11413

CASTIGLIONI. ... Reise durch die Vereinigten Staaten von Nord-America in den Jahren 1785, 1786 und 1787. ... Aus dem Italienischen von Magnus Petersen. Erster Theil. Mit Kupfern. *Memmingen: bey Andreas Seigler.* 1793. 8vo, Title, 7 l., pp. 495. Maps and Plates. 11414

CASTILHO (A. F. de). Practicas religiosas de Augusto Frederico de Castilho, doctor nos sagrados canones, etc., precedido de um Elogio historico por Antonio Felician de Castilho. *Rio de Janeiro.* 1866. 8vo, pp. xiv, 122. 11415

CASTILHO (Alexandre Magno de). Almanach de lembranças luso-brasileiro para o anno de 1863, com 473 artigos e 91 gravuras por A. M. de Castilho e A. X. R. Cordeiro. *Lisboa.* 1862. 12mo. 11416

CASTELHO. Poesias d'un Portuguez, offerecidas aos portuguezes seus campatriotas residentes no Brazil. *Rio de Janeiro.* 1826. 11217

CASTILLA (Miguel de). Espejo de Exemplares Obispos Trasumpto Moderno de los Antiguos Prelados de la Primitiva Yglesia Historiado, y Discurrido en la justada Vida y Heroycas Virtudes del Illust. y Rev. Dr. D. Joan Santiago de Leon Garavito, Obispo antes Electo de Puerto-Rico, y despues por mas de dies y ocho años Guadalaxara. *Mexico.* 1698. 4to. 11418

CASTILLERO (A.) Evidence in the Case of the United States, vs. Andres Castillero, introduced by the U. S. District Attorney, to show Fraud and Forgery on the Part of the Claimant. [*San Francisco: Whitten, Towne & Co.* n. d.] 8vo, pp. 35. H.

CASTILLO (Bathasar de). Luz, y Guia de los Ministros Evangelicos, el uno en Idioma Castellano, y el otro en la Mexicana. *Mexico: por Juan Jos. Guillena.* 1694. 4to. 11420

CASTILLO (Bernal Diaz del). *See* DIAZ DEL CASTILLO (Bernal).

CASTILLO (F. del). Defensa juridica del P. Felipe del Castillo, Procurador general de la provincia de la Compañia de Jesus de Lima. 1737. Folio. 11421

CASTILLO (G.) Diccionario historico, biografico y monumental de Yucatan. Desde la conquista hasta el ultimo ano de la dominacion espanola en el pais, por D. Geronimo Castillo. *Merida.* 1866. 8vo, pp. 316. 11422

Tomo I. (Entregas, 1–13), containing letters A to E.

CASTILLO (Juan de). *See* Gonzalez (Roque).

CASTILLO (Juan Joseph de). Tarifa y puntual aprecio, que para el seguro expendio de los medicamentos Galenicos y Chymicos mas usuales en las Oficinas Pharmaceuticas de este Reyno, hà mandado formar. *Lima: Con Liciencia del Govierno. Año de* 1756. 4to, 14 leaves. 11423

CASTILLO (Juan de Torres). Relacion|de los Svcedido en las Provincias de Nexapa, Yz-|tepex, y la Villa Alta. Inqvietvdes|de los Indios svs Natvrales. Castigos en|ellos hechos. Y satisfaction qve se diò à la jvsticia, redvciendo los à la paz, qvietvd, y obediencia devida à tv Magestad,|y à svs Reales Ministros.|Qve execvtò|el Señor Don Ivan Francisco de Monte-|mayor de Cuenca, del Consejo del Rey nuestro Señor, y|su Oydor de la Audiencia y Chancilleria Real de esta Nueua España.|Mediante el zelo, cuydado y desvelo que aplicò à estos negocios.|El Ex.mo Señor Marqves de Leiba, y de Ladrada, Conde de Baños, Virrey, Lu-|gartheniente de su Magestad, Gouernador y Capitan General de|los Reynos de la Nueua España, y Presidente de su Real Chan-|cilleria, que reside en la Ciudad de Mexico: por cuya|mano la dedica, y offrece à la proteccion|de El Ex.mo Señor Conde del|Castrillo, Gentilhombre de la Camara|de su Magestad de sus Consejos de Estado, y Guerra,|y Presidente de Castilla Presidente de Castilla.|El Governador Ivan de Torres|Castillo, Alcalde mayor, y Theniente de Capitan General|de la dicha Prouincia de Nexapa. |[*Mexico.* 1662.] 4to, 4 l, 23 l. J.C.B. 11424

"A privately printed work." — J. R. BARTLETT.

CASTILLO (J. M.) Illustrados y liberales habitantes de Puerto-Principe por José Mariano del Castillo. *Puerto-Principe: imprenta de Minuese.* 1822. 11425

CASTILLO (Luis Maria). Discurso pronunciado el 14 Dic. de 1862, en la capilla de la Universidad de Mérida despues de la distribucion de premios. *Méridá.* 1862. 8vo, pp. 22. 11426

CASTILLO (Fl. M. del). Hermana de los Angeles, por Fl. M. del Castillo. *Mexico.* 1854. 11427

CASTILLO (P. P. del), *Dr.* El 19 de Abril ó en verdadero patriota. Comedia en 2 actos. *Carácas.* 1842. 12mo, pp. 31.

CASTILLO. Teatro de la Legislacion Columbiana y Venezolana vigente. *Valencia.* 1852. 3 vols., 4to, pp. xvi, 592; 549; 412. 11429

"One of the most important juridical publications referring to Venezuela." — TRÜBNER.

CASTINI (Pedro). Constituciones de la Congregacion de la Purisima Conception de Megico. *Megico.* 1648. 8vo. 11430

CASTINI (P. J.) Carta del Padre Alonso Bonifacio, Rector del Colegio de la Compañia de Jesus de Mexico. A cerca de la Muerte, Virtudes, y Ministerios del P. Pedro Jhoan Castini. *Mexico: Viuda de B. Calderon.* 1644. 4to. 11431

CASTILLO Y SAN JUAN (Pedro Antonio). Discurso politico, en que se manifiesta el estado del reyno del Perù, Tierra-Firme, y Chile, y del nuevo de Granada. [n. p. n. d.] Folio. BD.

CASTLE (J.) Centenary Sermon, preached before the Philadelphia Annual Conference of the Methodist Episcopal Church, March 19, 1866. By Joseph Castle, M.D., D.D. *Philadelphia: Bryson & Son, Prs.* 1866. 8vo, pp. 36. 11433

The Castle Builders. *See* Stephens (W.)

CASTLEMAN (A. L.) The Army of the Potomac. Behind the Scenes. A Diary of Unwritten History; from the Organization of the Army, by Gen. George B. McClellan, to the Close of the Campaign in Virginia, about the First Day of January, 1863. By Alfred L. Castleman, Surgeon of the Fifth Regiment of Wisconsin Volunteers ... . *Milwaukee: Strickland & Co.* 1863. 12mo, 3 l., pp. 288. BA., C., H. 11434

CASTLEMAN (*Rev.* T. T.) An Inquiry into the Origin of American Methodism, with selections from the writings of the Rev. John Wesley. [*Richmond, Va.?*] 1843. 11435

CASTLEMAN. A Vindication of the Organization of the Methodist Episcopal Church. Being a Reply to an "Inquiry into the Origin of American Methodism," by T. T. Castleman ... . By a Layman. *Richmond: Christian Advocate Office.* 1843. 8vo, pp. 56. H. 11436

CASTLEMON (H.), *pseudonym.* Frank on the Lower Mississippi. By Harry Castlemon. Illustrated. *Cincinnati: R. W. Carroll & Co.* 1868. 12mo, pp. 236. 3 Plates. C. 11437

Also: Frank before Vicksburg. ... *Cincinnati.* 1868. 16mo, pp. 256. — Frank in the Woods. *Cincinnati.* 1868. 16mo, pp. 256. — Frank on the Prairie. *Cincinnati: R. W. Carroll & Co.* 1868. 16mo, pp. 246.

CASTLEREAGH (*Viscount*). *See* Stewart (R.)

CASTLETON (Thomas). An Address Delivered at the annual exercises of Cayuga Academy, ... Aug. 9, 1843, at Aurora. By Rev. Thomas Castleton. *Aurora, N. Y.* 1843. 8vo, pp. 21.

CASTLETON, *N. Y.* Reply of the Vestry of St. Paul's Church, Castleton, to a Pamphlet entitled the "Case of the Protestant Episcopal Church, at New-Brighton, Staten Island." *New-York: John R. M'Gown, printer.* 1849. 8vo, pp. 28. Map. H. 11439

Castleton Medical College. Announcement of the Autumnal Course of Lectures for 1844, and Catalogue Spring Session, 1844. *Albany.* 1844. 8vo, pp. 14. S. 11440

Also: Thirty-ninth Circular of Castleton Medical College, 1848. *Troy, N. Y.* 1848. 8vo, pp. 16. Continued.

CASTLETON, *Vt. See* Vermont.

CASTORENO (J. de). Sacones de la lealtad clausulas de la finesa en elogio de las Hazañas que en los diez años de Reynado de Chatol. Monarcha Philipo V. ha celebrado la Sta. yglesia cathedr. Metropol. de Mexico. *Mexico.* [1711.] 4to, pp. 21.

CASTRILLON (A.) Oracion funebre panegyrica con que la gratitud de la nobilissima ciudad de San Tiago de Queretaro tintiò la muerte de D. Juan Antonio de Urruta, Arana, Guerrero y Davila. *Mexico: B. de Hogal.* 1744. 4to, pp. 45. Plate.

CASTRIOTTO, *Prince of Albania, pseudonym. See* [Zannowich (S.)]

CASTRO (Agustin). Descripcion del Arco Triunfal, que en la Proclamacion del Sr. Carlos III. erigió el Illmo Sr. D. Manuel Rubio y Salinas, Arzobispo de Mégico. *Mégico.* 1761. 4to.

CASTRO. Elogio del P. Francisco Clavijero, Jesuita Americano. *Ferrara.* 1787. 8vo. 11444

CASTRO. El Nuevo Ulisses: Poema de la Proclamacion de Carlos III. en Valladolid de Michoacan. *Megico.* 1763. 4to.

CASTRO. Vida del P. José Campoi, Jesuita Megicano, por el P. Agustin Castro de la mesma Compañia. *Ferrara.* 1782. 8vo. 11446

CASTRO. Vida de P. Francisco Alegre Jesuita Americano, por el Padre Agustin Castro. 11447

"Printed in Italy." — BACKER. Also: Oratio de Sapientum Laude et Dignitate. *Mexici.* 1751. 4to.

CASTRO (Carlos Bermudez de). Paricer Fiscal, Expression de Previlegios y Meritos de Justicia de la Ven. Tercera Orden de Penitencia de N. P. S. Francisco. Sobre Especial, y Singular Instituto suyo el Exercicio publicado de la Via-Crucis. *Mexico.* 1714. Folio. 11448

CASTRO (C. B. de). Regia parentatio exorans pios manes, seren. Mariae Aloisiae Gabrielae de Emmanuele, et Sabaud. Hispaniar. reginae desid. etc. aeternae memoriae. Funere habito in metropol. ecclesia Mexicea. 4to, 17 and 11 leaves. 11449

CASTRO (Francisco de). La octava maravilla y sin segundo milagro de México perpetrado en las Rosas de Guadalupe y escrito heroicamente en octavas. Por el P. Francisco de Castro. *México: Imprenta de los Herederos de la Viuda de Joseph Miguel de Rivera Calderon.* 1729. 8vo, pp. 90, besides the approbations, etc. 11450

See Bartolache's "Manifiesto," pp. 35–37. "Boturini is wrong in attributing this poem to Father J. Carnero." — BACKER.

CASTRO (Francisco da Silva). Apontamentos para a historia do cholera-morbus no Pará em 1855. ... *Pará: Typ. de Santos & Filhos.* 1853. 11451

CASTRO. Roteiro chorographico (inedito) da viagem que se costuma fazer da cidade de Belem do Grão-Pará para a Villabella de Matto-grosso. ... Mandado imprimir e offerecido ao Instituto Historica Geographica do Brasil, per Francisco do Silva Castro, etc. *Pará: Typ. do Diario.* 1857. 8vo, pp. 36.

CASTRO (H.) Le Texas. *Anvers.* 1845. 8vo. 11453

CASTRO (Ignacio de), *Cura de Chaca en el obispado del Cuzco.* Disertacion sobre la concepcion de Nra. Sra. ... en Carta al D. Juan Domingo Unamunsaga cura de San Pedro de Carabaillo. *En Lima: con las licencias necesarias.* 1782. 8vo, 27 l., pp. 124.

CASTRO. Segunda disertacion ... en repuesta a lo que contra la primera, que publicó sobre la concepcion de N. Señora, opone el P. Juan Prudencio de Osorio del ord. de Predicadores. *Lima.* 1784. 8vo, 12 l., pp. 303. 11455

CASTRO (Joaquim Machado de). Pelo restabelecimento da saude preciosa do sermo sr. D. João principe do Brasil, em Agosto de 1789. Ode saphica. *Lisboa: na Offic. de Simão Thaddeo Ferreira.* 1789. Folio, pp. 3. 11456

CASTRO (*P.* José Constantino Gomes de). Minuta historico-apologetica de conducta do bacharel Manuel Antonio Leitão Bandeira, ouvidor geral, corregedor e provedor da comarca do maranhão pelos annos de 1785 a 1789, etc. [n. p.] 1818. 4to, pp. 47. 11457

CASTRO. Catalogo dos ill.mos e rev.mos Bispos do Maranhão. *Maranhão.* 1827. 11458

Also: Caso do conego José Constantino Gomes de Castro. *London: T. C. Hansard.* 1817. 8vo, pp. 14. For some other works by this author, *see* Silva, IV. 293.

CASTRO (J. de) Tiernos Recuerdos que excitan el Llanto de las Religiosas Descalzas Indias Caziques del Convento de Corpus Christi de Mexico, por la Muerte del Fr. Joseph de Castro, Sermon de las Honras, etc. *Mexico.* 1753. 4to. 11459

CASTRO. Viage de America a Roma, que hizo, y escribió El M. R. P. Fr. Joseph de Castro, Lector de Theologia, Pro Ministro, y Padre de la Santa Provincia de N. P. S. Francisco de Zacatecas. *Impresso en la Europa; y por su original reimpresso en Mexico: por Francisco Rodriguez Lupercio; y ahora nuevamente reimpresso por la Viuda de D. Joseph Bernardo de Hogal, Año de* 1745. 12mo, pp. 156, 2 l. 11460

A poetical narration of a voyage from America to Rome.

CASTRO. Primera regla de Santa Clara de Assis; testamento, y bendicion, que dexò à sus hijas la misma santa etc. Obra posthuma. *Mexico.* 1756. 4to, 11 l., pp. 166, Table, 6 l. 11461

CASTRO (Joseph Agustin de), *Vecino de la Ciudad de Valladolid de Michoacan.* El triunfo del silencio. Cancion heroica, que al glorioso martirio de San Juan Nepomuceno decia. *Mexico.* 1786. 4to, 4 l., pp. 67. 11462

In verse. Also, another poem: "Gratitudes de un Exercitanto á las misericordias de Dios. Canto mistico. *Puebla.* 1793." 4to, 7 l., pp. 102.

CASTRO (Juan de). Historia de las virtudes y propiedades del Tabaco, y de los modos de tomarle para las partes intrinsecas, y de aplicarle a las extrinsecas. *Corduba: Salvador de Cea.* 1620. 8vo. 11463

CASTRO (M. F. de). Estudio sobre las minas de oro de la Isla de Cuba, y muy particularmente sobre la de San Blas de las Meloneras en le Partido de Guaracubuya jurisdiccion de Remedios por Manuel Fernandez de Castro. *Habana.* 1865. 8vo, pp. 104. 11464

CASTRO. Ferro-carril central de la Isla de Cuba. Articulos insertos en el Diario de la Marina, por Manuel Fernandez de Castro. *Habana.* 1862. 8vo, pp. 106. 11465

CASTRO (N. de). Acsiomas Militares ó macsimas de la guerra cuyo comentario es la historia compuestos por D. Nicolas de Castro. *Mexico.* 1840. Sm. 8vo, pp. 64. 11466

CASTRO (*P.* Henrique José de). ... Lusitania triumphante ... . *Lisboa, na Offic. de Antonio Rodriguez Galhardo.* 1790. 8vo, pp. 20. 11467

A dramatic piece on the birth of Don John, Prince of Brazil. *See* Silva, III. 185.

CASTRO (*P.* M. de). Exaltacion de la ... rosa americana jerico, que celebrò a Mexico Fr. de Agura arzobispo de esta ciudad. *Mexico.* 1697. 4to. 11468

CASTRO (Rafael de). La cuestion mexicana ó esposicion de las causas que hacian indispensables la intervencion europea y el restablecimiento de la Monarquia en Mexico. *Mexico.* 1864. 8vo, pp. 88. 11469

CASTRO TAVARES (Jeronymo Villa de). Carta dirigida ao ... D. Romualdo, arcebispo da Bahia, ... *Recife: Typ. Comm de Moura Henriques.* 1853. 8vo, pp. 42. 11470

See Silva, III. 280, for titles of other works on Ecclesiastical Laws, etc.

CASTRUCCI (G. E.) Viaggio da Lima ad algune Tribu barbare del Perù e lungo il fiume delle Amazzoni del sacerdote Giuseppe Emanuele Castrucci da Vernazza Missionario Apostolico. *Geneva.* 1851. 8vo, pp. xvi, 115, 2 l. 9 Plates. C.

CASTRUCCI. Viaji practicado desde el Calles trasto las Misiones de las dos Tribus de Infieles Zaparos i Gevaros, per el P. Fr. Manuel Castrucci de Vernazza de la Ordra de San Francisco de Asis. *Lima.* 1849. 11472

CASWALL (H.) America and the American Church. By the Rev. Henry Caswall, M.A., Rector of Christ Church, Madison, Indiana, &c. Ten Years Resident in the United States. *London: J. G. F. & J. Rivington.* 1839. Post 8vo. Map and Plates. C. + 1849. Post 8vo. Map and Plates. + Second Edition. *London: Mozley.* 1851. 8vo. 11473

CASWALL. The American Church and the American Union. *London: Saunders & Otley.* 1861. 12mo. B. 11474

CASWALL. Californian Crusoe, A Tale of Mormonism. By Rev. H. Caswall. *Oxford: J. H. & J. Parker.* 1853. 12mo.

CASWALL. The City of the Mormons; or, Three Days at Nauvoo, in 1842. By the Rev. Henry Caswall, M.A. ... *London: J. G. F. & J. Rivington.* 1842. 8vo. + Second Edition, revised and enlarged ... . *London: J. G. F. & J. Rivington.* 1843. 16mo, 2 l., pp. 87. B., C. 11476

CASWALL. History of the Mormons, or Latter Day Saints. By Rev. H. Caswall. *London: Rivington.* 1843. 11477

CASWALL. The Prophet of the Nineteenth Century; or, The Rise, Progress, and Present State of the Mormons, or Latter-Day Saints: to which is appended an Analysis of the Book of Mormon. By the Rev. Henry Caswall, M.A. ... *London: J. G. F. & J. Rivington.* 1843. 8vo, pp. xx, 277. 1 Lithograph. BA., C. 11478

CASWALL. The Western World Revisited. By the Rev. Henry Caswall ... . *Oxford and London: John Henry Parker.* M DCCC LIV. Fcap 8vo, pp. xvi, 351. BA., C. 11479

The author was, for fourteen years, in the service of the Church in Canada and the United States.

CASWELL (A.) Meteorological Observations made at Providence, R. I., extending over a Period of Twenty-eight Years and a Half, from December, 1831, to May, 1860. By Alexis Caswell, Professor of Natural Philosophy and Theology, in

Brown University, Providence, Rhode Island. Accepted for Publication, August, 1859. *Washington.* 1860. 4to, pp. viii, 179. H. 11480

Also: Address before the American Association for the Advancement of Science, August, 1859. ... [*Cambridge:*] *Joseph Lovering.* 1859. 8vo, 1 l., pp. 26. H. — A discourse delivered before the Phi Beta Kappa Society of Rhode Island, September 2, 1835. *Boston.* 1836. 8vo, pp. 18.

Catalogue d'un Choix de Livres relatifs à l'Amérique et particulièrement aux Antiquités et à l'Histoire naturelle du Méxique. *Paris.* 1857. 8vo. 11481

"Eine Kleine, aber gut gewählte und geordnete Sammlung von 280 Nrr." — PETZHOLDT.

Catalogue d'une Collection de Livres précieux sur l'Amérique Parus depuis l'an 1508 jusqu'à nos jours en vente chez F. A. Brockhaus a Leipzig. *Leipzig: F. A. Brockhaus.* 1866. 8vo, pp. 71. 11482

See also Trömel (P.)

Catalogue des cartes, plans, etc. qui composent l'hydrographie française. *Paris.* 1847. Rl. 8vo, pp. ix, 220. 11483

Many of these plans are of the American coasts.

Catalogue général des livrés composant les bibliothèques du département de la marine et des colonies. ... *Paris: imprimerie royale.* 1838–43. 5 vols., rl. 8vo. BA. 11484

This elaborate work is quite a "model catalogue." It describes eighteen thousand different works, and shows at one view the contents of three libraries. It is indispensable to the collector of books relating to the French colonies.

Catalogue of a Curious and Valuable Collection of Original Maps and Plans of Military Positions held in the Old French and Revolutionary Wars; with Plans of Different Cities, and Maps of the Country. Most of these are Original Manuscripts, drawn at the Time, by Officers in the English Army. *Boston.* 1862. 8vo, pp. 13. H. 11485

A Catalogue of all Books printed in the United States, with the prices and places where published annexed. *Published by the Booksellers at Boston.* 1804. 12mo. 11486

Catalogue of an extraordinary collection of Original Documents connected with the British Army; its movements and expenses during the struggle that ended in the Independence of the United States of America and other wars consequent thereon; containing also a few Autograph letters, &c., of the leaders of the American Army. For sale by John Gray Bell. *Manchester,* [*Eng.*] 1857. 8vo. 11487

Catalogue of Lands belonging to the American Land Company, to be sold at Public Auction, at the Merchant's Exchange, in the City of New-York, on the Third Wednesday of June ... 1844. ... *New-York, Oct.,* 1843. 8vo, pp. 124. H. 11488

Catalogue of 96,046 Acres of Land belonging to the American Land Company [Arkansas]. *New York.* 1844. 8vo, pp. 28.

Catalogue of Papers Relating to Pennsylvania and Delaware, deposited at the State Paper Office, London. *Philadelphia.* 1850. 8vo. 11490

Catalogue of Postage Stamps, American and Foreign, and U. S. Revenue Stamps. *Cambridge: Sever & Francis.* 1866. 16mo, pp. 78. 11491

A Catalogue of the Damages for which the English demand reparation from the United-Netherlands; as also a list of damages, actions and pretenses for which those of the United-Netherlands demand reparation and satisfaction from the English; together with the Answer of the English. *London.* 1664. Sm. 4to, pp. iv, 75. 11492

Relates to vessels captured on the coast of America, one of which was named "The May Flower."

Catalogus Personarum et Domiciliorum in quibus sub A. R. P. Societatis Jesu, Præposito generali P. Zespedes, J. A. Balthazar Præposito provinciali, Societas Jesu Mexicana pro gloria Dei laborat. *Mexici, ex divi Ildephonsi collegii typogr.* 1751. Oblong sm. 4to. 11493

This list of the Jesuits in Mexico includes over six hundred names, with the places and dates of their birth, and the times of their entry into the Society. Printed for the heads of the order, and, therefore, rare.

Sundry catalogues of books relating to America will be found under the names of the owners of the books, or the editors of the catalogues. Many of the catalogues published by auctioneers in various parts of the world include works relating to America.

CATANEO. Io: Ma|riae Catanaei|Genna.| [Verso of the title:] Data Roma calendis Februarii. M.D.XIIII. [Colophon:] *Impressum Romæ apud Iacobum Mazo-|chium Ro. Acad. bibliopolam.*| 4to, 11 unnumbered leaves, and 1 blank. BM. 11494

"A poem in praise of the city of Genoa. Contains some verses concerning Columbus and his voyages." — HARRISSE.

The Catawissa, Williamsport and Erie Rail Road. [Prospectus.] *New York.* 1853. 8vo. pp. 20. Map. S. 11495

CATCOTT (Alexander). A Treatise on the Deluge, containing Remarks on the Lord Bishop of Clogher's Account of that Event ... . Second edition, considerably enlarged. *London.* 1768. 8vo. 11496

Discusses the time when and how America was first peopled. The first edition was entitled, "Remarks on the second part of the Bp. of Clogher's Vindication ... . *London.* 1756–61." 2 pts., 8vo.

Catechism. A, B, C, des Chrétiens. *Boston.* 1711. 12mo.

Catechism for Free Working Men. By the Son of a Blacksmith. *Cincinnati: Am. Reform Tract Soc.* 1861. pp. 4.

A Catechism setting forth Indisputable Facts for the Consideration of Honest, Thoughtful, and Conservative Men. 1863. 8vo, pp. 8. 11499

Relates to the Connecticut election, April, 1863.

Catechism to be taught orally to those who cannot read; designed for the Instruction of Slaves. *Raleigh.* 1862. 24mo.

Catechisme Algonquin|avec syllabaire et cantiques.| Nūna àiamie kak8edgindisnimasinaigan|ate gaie kekinsamagemagak.| masinaigan gaie gaie aia mie nikamonan|kanactageng.|*Moniang:* |*Taksabikickote endatc John Lovell.*|1865| 16mo, pp. 52.

For other catechisms in Indian dialects, *see* under the name of the language

Catechisme|ou|Abrégé|de la|foi Catholique|publié par ordre de Mgr. l'Archevêque|de Paris pour les fidèles de son diocèse et enseigné dans les missions das R.R.|P.P. Capucins aux isles sous le vent de|l'Amérique|...|*Baltimore ... S. Sower*|... 1796.| 24mo, pp. 113. 11502

Catechismus-Mingnek. *See* Luther (M.)

CATEL (M.) Rapport sur l'épidémie de fièvre jaune qui a éclaté à Saint-Pierre (Martinique) dans les premiers jours du mois d'octobre 1838, et qui continue à régner dans cette ville; par M. Catel ... . Extrait des "Annales maritimes et coloniales," juillet 1840. *Paris: imp. royale.* 1840. 8vo. 11503

CATENACCIIS. *See* Geraldin de Catenacciis.

[CATES (Thomas).] A Svmmarie|and Trve Discovrse|of Sir Francis Drakes|VVest Indian Voyage.|Wherein were taken, the Townes of|Saint Jago, Sancto Domingo, Cartagena &|Saint Augustine.|*Imprinted at London by Richard Field, dwelling|in the*

Blacke-Friars by Ludgate.|1589.| Title, 1 l., Dedication signed Thomas Cates, 1 l., pp. 52. W. 11505

A volume of much rarity. Priced, in the Nuggets, £5 15s. 6d.

CATESBY (M.) Hortus Britanno Americanus; or, a Curious Collection of Trees and Shrubs, the Produce of the British Colonies in North America; Adapted to the Soil and Climate of England. With Observations on their Constitution, Growth, and Culture: and Directions how they are to be collected, packed up, and secured during their passage. Embellished with Copper Plates neatly engraved. By Mark Catesby, F.R.S. *London: John Ryall.* M.DCC.LXIII. Imp. 4to, pp. vi, 41. 17 colored Plates. C. 11506

This work was apparently not published until 1767, when new titles were printed and the present cancelled. "This work was prepared by Catesby, and published after his death." — RICH. The new title reads:

CATESBY. Hortus Europæ Americanus: or, a Collection of 85 Curious Trees and Shrubs, The Produce of North America; adapted to the Climates and Soils of Great Britain, Ireland, and most Parts of Europe, &c. ... . By Mark Catesby ... . *London: J. Millan.* MDCCLXVII. 4to, 2 l., pp. vi., 41. 63 figures on 17 Plates. H. 11507

CATESBY. The Natural History of Carolina, Florida, and the Bahama Islands: Containing the Figures of Birds, Beasts, Fishes, Serpents, Insects and Plants: Particularly the Forest-Trees, Shrubs, and other Plants, not hitherto described, or very incorrectly figured by former Authors. Together with their Descriptions in English and French. To which are added, Observations on the Air, Soil, and Waters ... . By ... Mark Catesby ... Revis'd by Mr. Edwards, of the Royal College of Physicians, London. [With appendix and supplement.] *London: C. Marsh; T. Wilcox; B. Stichall.* 1754. 2 vols., folio, Map, Title, 1 l., pp. vii, 100; 1 l., pp. 100; Appendix, pp. 20, 1 l; Supplement, pp. xliv, 4 l. 220 Plates. H. 11508

This is the title of the second edition. Jefferson remarks: "The drawings are better as to form and attitude than coloring, which is generally too high." The first edition was published in numbers, between 1731 and 1748, with plates etched by the author from his own drawings, and colored under his inspection; and this first edition is to be preferred for the beauty of the plates. "Catesby, after having lived in Virginia, from 1712 to 1719, principally engaged in the study of its natural history, returned to England, when he was induced by Dr. Sherard and others, to undertake another voyage to America, for the express purpose of collecting and describing its natural productions. The fruit of his voyage was this 'Natural History of Carolina.'" "It does great honor to him and his native country, and is perhaps the most

curious and elegant performance of its kind that has anywhere appeared in Europe." — PETER COLLINSON. *See also* Laurens' "Correspondence," p. 187, where it is said to be the best Natural History of this country. The third edition has the following title:

CATESBY. The Natural History of Carolina, Florida, and the Bahama Islands: containing the Figures of Birds, Beasts, Fishes, Serpents, Insects, and Plants: Particularly, those not hitherto described, or incorrectly figured by former Authors, with their Descriptions in English and French. To which is prefixed, A new and Correct Map of the Countries, with Observations on their Natural State, Inhabitants, and Productions. By the late Mark Catesby, F.R.S. Revised by Mr. Edwards ... . To the whole is now added a Linnæan Index of the Animals and Plants. ... *London: Benjamin White.* MDCCLXXI. 2 vols., folio, 2 l., pp. (2), vii, 120, (i), 120 Plates; 2 l., pp. (2), 100, xliv, (6). 100 Plates. BA., C., P. 11509

A very curious vignette follows plate 100 in Vol. II. In some copies the pages xliv are bound with the first volume.

CATESBY. Die naturhist. Beschreibung von Carolina, Florida und den Bahamischen Inseln, worinnen von den vierfüssigen Thieren, den Fischen, Pflanzen, Einwohnern, der Luft, dem Boden, dem Wasser mitgetheilt wird, ... nunmehr aber in das Deutsche übersezet von D. Georg Leonhard Huth. *Nürnberg: Johann Michael Seligman.* [1755.] Folio, 15 sheets. Map.

Georgi gives the date 1756.

CATESBY. Proposals for Printing an Essay towards a Natural History of Florida, Carolina, and the Bahama Islands; containing 12 colored Plates. [n. p. n. d.] Folio. BD. 11511

CATESBY. Abbildung verschiedener Fische Schlangen Insecten, einiger andern Dinge, Pflantzen, so in dem zweiten Theile seines Wercks der natürlichen Historie von Carolina beschrieben sind, mit Abbildung der unsrigen und andern Fische vermehret, und in ihren natürlichen Farben fürgestellet von N. Fr. Eisenbergern und G. Lichtenstegern, Lateinisch und Deutsch. *Nürnberg.* 1750. Folio. Continued, 1755, 1757. 11512

Title from Georgi.

CATESBY. Histoire naturelle de la Caroline, de la Floride et des îles de Bahama, contenant les dessins des oiseaux, des animaux, des poissons, des serpents, etc., qui se trouvent dans ces pays-là. *Londres.* 1751. 2 vols., Folio. 220 colored Plates.

This is merely a French title to the English work.

CATESBY. Histoire naturelle de la Caroline, Floride ... . *Nürnberg.* 1770. Folio. 11514

CATESBY. Piscium, Serpentum, Insectorum, aliorumque nonnullorum Animalium necnon Plantarum quarundam Imagines quas Marcus Catesby, in posteriore Parte splendidi illius Operis quo Carolinæ, Floridæ, et Bahamensium Insularum tradidit Historiam Naturalem, eiusque Appendice, descripsit; additis vero Imaginibus Piscium tam nostratium quam aliarum, Regionum, auxerunt, vivisque Coloribus pictas, ediderunt N. Fridericus Eisenberger et Georgius Lichtensteger. Abbildungen verschiedene Fische ... . Aus dem Englischen ins Dutsche und Lateinische übersetzt [von G. L. Huth]. *Nürnberg.* 1750. Folio. 72 Plates. 11515

Again augmented as

CATESBY. Piscium ... Carolinensium Descriptiones. Aus dem Englischen [von G. W. Panzer]. Lateinisch und Deutsch. *Nürnberg: Knorr.* 1777. Folio. 109 Plates. 11516

CATHCART (C. W.) The late War with Mexico. Speech of Hon. C. W. Cathcart, of Indiana, in the House ... August 3, 1848, On the Bill making Appropriations for the support of the Army. [*Washington.* 1848.] 8vo, pp. 8. H. 11517

Also: Rivers and Harbors. Speech ... in the House ... February 4, 1847, In Favor of Appropriations for Rivers and Harbors. [*Washington: Blair & Rives.* 1847.] 8vo, pp. 7. H. — Speech ... on the Oregon Question. ... in the House ... February 6, 1846. *Washington: Blair & Rives.* 1846. 8vo, pp. 8.

CATHCART (J.) A Letter to the Honourable Edward Vernon, Esq; Vice-Admiral of the Red, &c. from John Cathcart, Director of the Hospital in the late Expedition to the West-Indies, under the Command of the Honourable General Wentworth: concerning some Gross Misrepresentations in a Pamphlet, lately Published, and Intitled, Original Papers relating to the Expedition to the Island of Cuba. *London: M. Cooper.* M.D.CC.XLIV. 8vo, pp. 55. H. 11518

This is a vindication of the Admiral.

CATHÉRINEAU (J.) Le Paramaribo, roman maritime et de mœurs créoles, tiré de la guerre de l'indépendance de l'Amérique du Sud contre l'Espagne. Par J. Cathérineau. *Paris: Ach. Faure.* 1866. 18mo, pp. 358. 11519

CATHERWOOD (F.) Views of Ancient Monvments in Central America, Chiapas, and Yvcatan. By F. Catherwood, Archit [With Descriptive Letter-Press, by J. L. Stephens.] *London.* 1844. Folio, 1 l., pp. 24. Map, and 25 Plates. + *New York:*

Bartlett and Welford. 1844. Folio, 1 l., pp. 24. Map, and 25 Plates. BA. 11520

This was also issued with the plates colored in imitation of the original drawings, and mounted on bristol-board. It exhibits, on a large scale, many of the views in Mr. Stephens' works, with all the detail of ornament, sculpture, etc., of which the small engravings cannot convey an adequate idea. The edition of this beautiful book was limited to three hundred copies. Some with a London, and others with a New York imprint.

Catholic Laity's Directory for 1817. *New York.* 1817. 24mo. Continued. 11521

The title was afterwards changed to, The Laity's Directory to the Church Service for the year 1822. *New York: Creagh.* 1822. 24mo; United States Catholic Almanac. *Baltimore: Myers.* 1833–4. *Baltimore: Lucas.* 1834–1857; American Catholic Almanac. *New York: Dunegan.* 1858–1860; Metropolitan Catholic Almanac. *Baltimore: J. Murphy.* 1864–1870; Catholic Almanac. *New York: Sadlier.* 1864–1870.

Catholic Liturgy; or Forms of Prayer. *Boston: Isaiah Thomas.* 1797. 8vo, pp. 45. 11522

The Catholic Work of the Protestant Episcopal Church in America. ... By a Presbyter. *New York: printed by R. Craighead.* 1855. 8vo, pp. 24. H. 11523

The Catholic World. A Monthly Eclectic Magazine of General Literature and Science. Vol. I. No. I. April, 1865. *New York.* 1865. 8vo. Continued. C., H. 11524

[CATINEAU-LAROCHE (Pierre Marie Sébastien).] De la Guyane Francaise de son Etat physique, de son Agriculture, de son Régime intérieur et du Projét de la peupler avec des Laboureurs Européens: ou Examen d'un écrit de M. le Marquis de Barbe-Marbois sur le même sujet. Suivi de considérations sur le commerce Colonial de la France, et sur l'Administration spéciale de ces Colonies. *Paris: Trouvé; Boiste.* 1822. 8vo, pp. 232.

CATINEAU-LAROCHE. Notice sur la Guiane Française, suivie des motifs qui font desirer que la Colonisation projetée sur la mana soit dirigée par une Association, en concurrence avec le Gouvernement, par M. Catineau-de-la-Roche, &c. *Paris: de l'impr. de Fain.* 1822. 8vo, pp. 20. 11526

CATLETT (H. G.) National Road to California. [n. p. n. d.] 8vo, pp. 8. H. 11527

CATLIN (G.) An Account of an Annual Religious Ceremony Practised by the Mandan Tribe of North American Indians. By George Catlin. *London.* 1865. 4to, pp. 67.

"A very curious and interesting little monograph, of which only fifty copies have been privately printed and distributed in a very select circle. ... Of this bull dance, all

we can say is, that it was an attempt to emblematize the mode of buffalo and human propagation." — TRÜBNER. The notice of this book in Trübner's "Record" elicited from Mr. Catlin a very vigorous note, which concludes, as follows: "The pamphlet you speak of as '*printed privately for a very select circle*,' is a gross and mangled *extract* from my account of the Mandan Religious Ceremony, printed and circulated without my permission or knowledge; of which I have demanded the surrender of every copy printed; and for any reprint or circulation of the same I will prosecute. *September 22nd,* 1865. GEO. CATLIN." It may safely be inferred that this is a rare tract.

CATLIN. Adventures of the Ojibbeway and Ioway Indians in England, France, and Belgium; being Notes of Eight Years' Travels and Residence in Europe with his North American Indian Collection, by Geo. Catlin. ... *London.* 1852. 2 vols., 8vo, pp. 632. Portraits and Plates. + Third Edition. *London: the Author.* 1852. pp. xvi, 636. Woodcuts. H. 11529

This is a reprint of No.1 1533.

CATLIN. Catalogue raisonné de la galerie indienne de Mr Catlin, refermant des portraits, des paysages, des costumes, etc., et des scènes de mœurs et coutumes des Indiens de l'Amérique du Nord. Collection entièrement faite et peinte par Mr Catlin pendant un séjour de 8 ans parmi 48 tribus sauvages. ... [*Paris:*] *Imprimerie Wittersheine.* 1845. 8vo, pp. 47. H. 11530

CATLIN. Catalogue of Catlin's Indian Gallery of Portraits, Landscapes, Manners and Customs, Costumes, &c. ... *New-York.* 1837. 12mo, pp. 36. + *New-York: Piercy & Read.* 1838. 12mo, pp. 36. H. 11531

There is another edition, with the title somewhat different, *New York.* 1838. 12mo, pp. 40.

CATLIN. Catlin's North American Indian Portfolio. Hunting Scenes and Amusements of the Rocky Mountains and Prairies of America. From Drawings and Notes of the Author, made during Eight Years' Travel amongst Forty-eight of the Wildest and most Remote Tribes of Savages in North America. Geo. Catlin. *London.* 1844. Folio, pp. 20. 25 Plates. H., P.

Some copies have the imprint, *New York: James Ackerman.* 1845.

CATLIN. Catlin's Notes of Eight Years' Travels and Residence In Europe, with his North American Indian Collection: with Anecdotes and Incidents of the Travels and Adventures of Three Different Parties of American Indians whom he introduced to the Courts of England, France and Belgium. ... *New York: Burgess, Stringer & Co.* 1848. 2 vols., 8vo, pp. xvi, 296; xii, 336. 24 Illustrations. + Third Edition. *London.* 1848. 2 vols., 8vo. H. 11533

This was reprinted in London, with the title as in No. 11529.

CATLIN. A Descriptive Catalogue of Catlin's Indian Collection, containing Portraits, Landscapes, Costumes, &c., and Representations of the Manners and Customs of the North American Indians. ... *London: the Author* 1848. 8vo, pp. 92.

CATLIN. Fourteen Ioway Indians. Key to their Various Dances, Games, Ceremonies, Songs, Religion, Superstitions, Costumes, Weapons, &c., &c. By Geo. Catlin. *London.* 1844. 16mo, pp. 28. 11535

A second title reads: "Unparalleled Exhibition. The Fourteen Ioway Indians and their Interpreter, just arrived from the Rocky Mountains," etc.

CATLIN. Letters and Notes on the Manners, Customs, and Condition of the North American Indians, by George Catlin. Written during eight years' travel, from 1832 to 1839, amongst the Wildest Tribes of Indians in North America. *New York: Wiley and Putnam.* 1841. 2 vols., rl. 8vo, pp. viii, 264; viii, 266. 312 Plates, and Maps. + Second Edition. [*Ibid.*] 1842. 2 vols., 8vo. H. + Third Edition. [*Ibid.*] 1842. + Fourth Edition. 1843. + Fifth Edition. 1845. + Sixth Edition. 1846. 11536

Some copies form the imprint, "*London: Wiley and Putnam,*" others, *London: Published by the Author* 1841. The plates to this work were afterwards sold to Mr. H. G. Bohn, who issued the work with the following title:

CATLIN. Illustrations of the Manners, Customs, and Condition of the North American Indians: in a Series of Letters and Notes written during Eight Years of Travel and Adventure among the Wildest and most Remarkable Tribes now Existing. With Three Hundred and Sixty Engravings from the Author's Original Paintings. By Geo. Catlin. Seventh Edition. *London: Henry G. Bohn.* MDCCCXLVIII. 2 vols., imp. 8vo, pp. viii, 264; viii, 266. 360 Plates. H. + Eighth Edition. [*Ibid.*] 1857. + Ninth Edition. [*Ibid.*] 1857. + Tenth Edition. [*Ibid.*] 1866. 11537

Mr. Bohn had twelve or more copies colored after the fancy of the artist who did the work, but tolerably well done. Such copies are worth $60 a set. One of the most original, authentic, and popular works on the subject. Humboldt characterizes the author as "one of the most admirable observers of manners who ever lived among the aborigines of America." "These plates, or rather etchings, although merely outlines, are well executed, and appear to be very faithful representations of the objects and scenes described in the book. The author was born at Wyoming about the beginning of the present century ('some thirty or forty years since,' he says, in his first letter.) A considerable part of these letters were published in the New York papers, as early as the years 1832 and 1833. His paintings, from which the plates were taken, and a collection of Indian manufactures, were exhibited for many years in Piccadilly, London." —

RICH. These paintings are now in the gallery of the New York Historical Society. The work received ample notice at the hands of the reviewers. The following may be consulted: "N. Am. Rev.," LIV. 283, "Lit. and Theol. Rev.," II. 96, "Dublin Univ. Mag.," XIX. 371, "Quarterly Rev.," LXV. 384, "Ed. Rev.," LXXIV. 221, "West. Rev" XXXVII. 122, "South. Lit. Mess.," XI. 202, and "N. Y. Rev.," X. 419. A very inferior edition of the work was published at Philadelphia, with the following title:

CATLIN. Letters and Notes [as in No. 11536]. ... With One hundred and fifty illustrations, on steel and wood. *Philadelphia: Willis P. Hazard.* 1857. 2 vols., 8vo, pp. 792.

The plates to this edition are very inferior woodcuts.

CATLIN. Die Indianer Nord Amerika's und die während eines achtjährigen Aufenthalts unter den wildesten ihrer Stämme erlebten Abentheuer und Schicksale, von G. Catlin. Nach der fünften englischen Original-Ausgabe deutsch herausgegeben von Dr. Heinrich Berghaus. *Brüssel und Leipzig.* [1846–]48. 8vo, pp. xii, 382. 20 colored Plates. + Mit 24 vom Verfasser nach der Natur entworfenen Gemälden. Zweite Ausgabe. [*Ibid.*] [1850–]51. 8vo, pp. xii, 382. 11539

CATLIN. Last Rambles amongst the Indians of the Rocky Mountains and the Andes. By George Catlin ... . *London: Sampson Low, Son, and Marston.* 1868. 16mo, pp. x, (1), 361. Woodcuts. BA. 11540

Some copies have the imprint, *New York: D. Appleton and Company.* 1868.

CATLIN. Life amongst the Indians. A Book for Youth. By George Catlin ... . *London: S. Low, Son & Co.* 1861. 16mo, 8 l., pp. xii, 339. + New Edition. *London: Low.* 1867 12mo. 11541

Some copies have the imprint, *New York: D. Appleton & Co.* 1867.

CATLIN. La Vie chez les Indiens; scènes et aventures de voyage parmi les tribus des deux Amériques. Ouvrage écrit pour la jeunesse. Traduit et annoté par F. de Lanoye et illustré de 25 grav. sur bois. *Paris: L. Hachette et Cie.* 1863. 12mo. + Seconde édition. *Paris: L. Hachette et Cie.* 1866. 18mo, pp. 396. 25 Plates. 11542

CATLIN. O-Kee-Pa: a Religious Ceremony; and other Customs of the Mandans. By George Catlin. *London: Trübner & Co.* 1867. Rl. 8vo, pp. vi, (1), 52. 13 Plates. BA. 11543

Some copies have the imprint, *Philadelphia: J. B. Lippincott & Co.* 1867. This publication was occasioned by the work described in No. 11528, *supra.*

CATLIN (George S.) Speech of Mr. Catlin, of Connecticut, on the Right of Members to their Seats in the House of Repre-

sentatives: delivered in the House ... February 10, 1844. *Washington.* 1844. 8vo, pp. 8. H. 11544

CATLIN (Jacob). Masonic Sermon at New Marlborough, Jan. 1, 1796. *Stockbridge, Mass.* 1797. 8vo. W. 11545

Also: A Fast-Day Sermon on the Declaration of War with Great Britain. *Stockbridge.* 1812. W.

CATO, *pseudon.* *See* [Smith (W.)]

CATO, *pseudon.* To the People of the State of New York. 1824. 8vo. S. 11547

CATO. Cato's | Moral | Distichs. | Englished in Couplets. | *Philadelphia:* | *Printed and Sold by B. Franklin.* 1735. | 4to, pp. vi, 25 P. 11548

The translator was the Hon. James Logan, and this is probably the first translation of a classic which was both made and printed in the British colonies. The reader of Franklin's almanicks will recognize some resemblance between "Poor Richard" and "Cato." *See also* Cicero.

El Catolico. Periódico religioso, politico-cristiano, cientifico y literario. *Mexico.* 1846–47. 4 vols., 8vo. 11549

CATSKILL, *N. Y.* Letter to the President of the Town of Catskill, January 10, 1838. *New York.* 1838. N. 11550

Catskill Association, formed for the Purpose of improving the Town of Catskill, in the County of Greene, State of New York, and other Purposes. December 28, 1836. *New York: Mitchell & Turner.* 1837. 12mo, pp. 47. 2 Maps. C. 11551

Guide to Rambles from the Catskill Mountain House. By a Visitor. *Catskill.* 1863. 12mo, pp. 8. 11552

Also: The Rambler! His Guide to, and around the Cauderskill and Haines's Falls. *Catskill: J. Joesbury.* 1864. 18mo, pp. 4.

Scenery of the Catskill Mountains, as described by Irving, Cooper, Bryant, etc. *New York.* 8vo, pp. 39. 11553

CATTANEO *or* CATTANI. Lettere del Padre Gaetano Cattaneo della Compagnia di Gesù al Sign. Giuseppe suo Fratello a Modena. *Venezia: Giambattista Pasquali.* 1743. 4to. 11554

The Backers suggest that this is a part, separately printed, of "Il cristianesimo felice ... descritto da Lod. Ant. Muratori. *Venezia.* 1743." 4to, pp. 134, in which the three letters of Cattani appear, as they also do in the French version of Muratori, *Paris.* MDCC.LIV. 12mo, pp. 283–389, translated by the Jesuit Felix Esprit de Lourmel, and in the English version, *London.* M.DCC.LIX. 12mo, pp. 205–289. They relate to Paraguay.

CATTARAUGUS. Minutes of the Twelfth Anniversary of the Cattaraugus Baptist Association, held with the Church at Richburg, Allegany Co., N. Y., July 7th and 8th, 1847. *Angelica.* 1847. 12mo, pp. 12. S. 11555

CATTELL (Alexander G.) Opinion of Mr. Cattell of New Jersey, on the Impeachment of the President. [n. p. n. d.] 8vo, pp. 13. H. 11556

Also: Speech ... on the Bill to provide Increased Revenue from Imports; delivered in the Senate ... January 22, 1867. *Washington.* 1867. 8vo, pp. 16. H.

CATTERMOLE (W.) The Advantages of Emigration to Canada; being the Substance of Two Lectures delivered at the Town-Hall, Colchester. By William Cattermole. *London.* 1831. BD. 11557

CATTO (W. C.) A Semi-Centenary Discourse, delivered in the First African Presbyterian Church, Philadelphia, on the 4th Sabbath of May, 1857: with a History of the Church from its First Organisation; including a Brief Notice of Rev. John Gloucester, its First Pastor. By the Rev. Wm. C. Catto. Also an Appendix, containing Sketches of all the Coloured Churches in Philadelphia. *Philadelphia: Joseph M. Wilson.* 1857. 8vo, pp. 111. 11558

GAUCHON (Joseph). Etude sur l'Union Projetee des Provinces Britanniques de l'Amerique du Nord. Reproduite du Journal de Quebec. *Quebec.* 1858. 8vo, pp. 36. 11559

CAUCHON. L'Union des provinces de l'Amerique Britanniques du Nord. *Quebec.* 1865. 8vo, pp. 152. 11560

CAUCHON. The Union of the Provinces of British North America. By the Honorable Joseph Cauchon. Member of the Canadian Parliament and Editor-in-Chief of "Le Journal de Quebec." Translated by George Henry Macaulay. *Quebec: printed by Hunter, Rose & Co.* 1865. 8vo, pp. iv, (1), 154. B.

CAUGHEY (*Rev.* J.) A Voice from America. *London.* 1847. 12mo. 11562

CAUGHEY. A Second Voice from America; or, Four Sermons preached by the Rev. J. Caughey, the great American Revivalist. [*Manchester.*] 12mo, pp. 56. 11563

CAUGHEY. [Three] Voices from America. *London: Simpkin.* 1852. 12mo. 11564

CAUGHNAWAGA. Remonstrance of Two of the Directors of the Caughnawaga Bridge Company. ... *Albany: J. Munsell.* 1849. 8vo, pp. 7. S. 11565

CAUGHNAWAGA. Ionteriwaienstakwa | ne | kariwiioston Teisasontha, | Kahnawakeha. | *Tiohtraki,* | *Tehoristorarakon Louiz Perrault.* | 1844. | 16mo, pp. 39. 11566

CAUGHNAWAGA. Kaiatonsera Ionterennaienlaksa | ne teieiasontha | ne taiakoswateten tsi iakoriwiiosson | kahnawake tiakoshon. | Tseatak tuhononwentsiake | ovkweonwe | akoratonsera. | *Twhpaki* | *Tehoristorerakon John Lovell* | 1852. | 12mo, pp. 204. 11567

CAUGHNAWAGA. Ionteriseienstagsa ne Tsialag orisatogentou ogonha. *Paresiis. ononthwke. Tehoristororagon D.-P. Lefebvre.* 1826. 12mo, pp. 72. 11568

CAULFIELD (James). The High Court of Justice; comprising Memoirs of the Principal Persons who sat in Judgment on King Charles the First, and signed his Death Warrant ... Illustrated with their Portraits ... *London.* 1820. Rl. 8vo, pp. 112. 11569

Includes Memoirs of Goffe, Whalley, and Dixwell, who fled to Connecticut.

CAULIN (A.) Historia | coro-graphica | natural y evangelica | dela Nueva Andalucia provincias de | Cumaná, Guayana y Vertientes del Rio Orinoco; | dedicada al rei N.S. | D. Carlos III | Por el M. R. P. Fr. Antonio Caulin, dos vezes Prov.l | de los observantes de Granada | Dada áluz de Orden, y áExpen.s de S. M. [n. p.] *Año de* 1779. Folio, engraved Title, 8 leaves, pp. 482, (13). Map. BA., H. + *Caracas.* 1841. 4to, pp. xvi, 460. BA., C. 11570

The author was several years a missionary in the countries he describes. There are copies of the edition of 1779 on large paper. The work is highly praised by Gillius in his "Saggio."

CAULKINS (F. M.) History of New London, Connecticut. From the First Survey of the Coast in 1612, to 1852. By Frances Manwaring Caulkins. ... *New London: the Author.* 1852. 8vo, pp. 679, (1). Maps and Woodcuts. BA., H. + Second Edition. Continued to 1860. *New London.* 1860. 8vo, pp. 680. C. 11571

CAULKINS. History of Norwich, Connecticut, from its Settlement in 1660, to January, 1845. By Miss F. M. Caulkins. *Norwich: Thomas Robinson.* 1846. 12mo, pp. 359. 6 Plates.

CAULKINS. History of Norwich, Connecticut: from its Possession by the Indians, to the Year 1866. By Frances Manwaring Caulkins. ... [*Hartford:*] *the Author.* 1866. 8vo, pp. xi, 17–704. 16 Portraits. BA., H. 11573

CAULKINS. Memoir of the Rev. William Adams, of Dedham, Mass., and of the Rev. Eliphalet Adams, of New London Conn. *Cambridge: Metcalf and Company.* 1849. 8vo, pp. 5–49.

See "Mass. Hist. Coll.," Vol. I.

CAULKINS (N.) Narrative of Nehemiah Caulkins. An Extract from "American Slavery as It Is." [n. p. n. d.] 12mo, pp. 24. 11575

Causa Jesuitica de Portugal, o Documentos autenticos, Bulas, Leyes reales, Despachos de la Secretaria de Estado y otras piezas originales, que precedieron à la reforma y motivaron despues la expulsion de los Jesuitas de los dominios de Portugal. En que se halla la Republica del Paraguay y Marañon, qui contiene la relacion de la guerra que sustentaron los Jesuitos, contra las tropas Españoles y Portuguesas en el Uraguay y Parana. Traducidas del Latin y Portugues, é illustradas en esta edicion Española. *En Madrid: en la Imprenta Real de la Gazeta.* 1748. 4to, pp. xxviii, 171. 11576

Relates principally to the proceedings of the Jesuits in Paraguay. *See* Rich, I. 167, who gives the date 1768.

Causas para Declarar la Guerra á los Estados-Unidos del Norte y Delitos del Ministro Poinsett, por un Amante de sú Pátria. *Mexico.* 1829. 11577

Cause of, and Cure for Hard Times. A Definition of the Attributes and Qualities Indispensable in Money as a Medium of Commerce. *New York.* 1818. 8vo, pp. 78. 11578

The Causes of the War. [By Col. Charles Anderson.] *New York Loyal Publication Society.* No. 17. 8vo. 11579

Causes and Origin of Slavery in the United States. By an American. *Philadelphia.* 1845. 8vo, pp. 8. P. 11580

The Causes of our late Discontents: Their Consequences and Remedies. In a Letter to the Right Hon. Lord Hawke. *London: T. Hooper.* 1782. 8vo. 11581

See M. R., LXVI, 469.

Causes of the Alienation of the Delaware and Shawanees Indians. *See* [Thomson, (Charles)].

Causes of the Distress of the British West India Colonies; with Remedies suggested. *London.* 1832. 8vo, pp. 39. 11582

The Causes of the Present Crisis. Shown by an Examiner. Originally published in the Daily, Newspapers. [n. p. n. d.] 8vo, pp. 23. H. 11583

The Causes of the Present Distractions in America Explained, 1774. *See* [Bernard (F.)], Vol. II., No. 4920.

Causes of the Progress of Liberal Christianity in New England. *Boston.* 1826. 12mo. + Second Edition. *Boston.* 1827. 12mo, pp. 16. 11584

CAUSTEN (J. H.) Review of the Veto Message of President Pierce of Februrary 17, 1855, on the Bill relating to French Spoliations. [n. p. 1855.] 8vo, pp. 46. C., H. 11585

CAUSTIC (Christopher), *pseudonym.* *See* [Fessenden (T. G.)]

A Caution; or, Reflections on the Present Contest between France and Great Britain. *Philadelphia: Printed by B. F. Bache.* M,DCCXCVIII. 8vo, pp. 14. C., M. 11586

Cautionary Hints to Congress respecting the Sale of the Western Lands belonging to the United States. Second Edition. *Philadelphia.* 1796. 8vo, pp. 13. M. 11587

CAUWET (A.) Les Confédérés. [Vers.] Par Alfred Cauwet. *Paris: imp. Dubuisson et Cie.* 1864. 8vo, pp. 4. 11588

CAUWET. Le négrophile, comédie en un acte et en prose. Par Alfred Cauwet. *Paris: Michel Lévy frères.* 1864. 12mo, pp. 24. 11589

CAVACIO (Alfonso). Monteçuma, Emperador de Mexico; Tragedia. 1709. 12mo. 11590

Title from Pinelo-Barcia, as quoted by Harrisse.

CAVADA (F. F.) Libby Life; Experiences of a Prisoner of War in Richmond, Va., 1863–64, by Lieut.-Colonel F. F. Cavada, U. S. V. *Philadelphia: J. B. Lippincott & Co.* 1864. 12mo, pp. 221. Woodcuts. BA. 11591

Some copies have the imprint, "*Philadelphia: King & Baird.* 1864."

CAVAZZI (G. A.) Istorica | descrizione | de' tre' regni | Congo, Matamba, | et Angola | sitvati nell' | Etiopia inferiore occidentale | e delle | missioni apostoliche | Esercitateui da Religiosi Capuccini, | Accuratamente compilata dal | P. Gio. Antonio Cavazzi da Montecvccolo | Sacerdote Capvccino | il qvale vi fv' prefetto | E nel presente stile ridotta dal | P. Fortvnato Alamandini | da Bologna | Predicatore dell' istesso Ordine. | All' illvstrissimo | Signor Conte | Giacomo Isolani. | *In Bologna* M DC LXXXVII. | *Per Giacomo Monti. Con licenza de' Superiori.* | Folio, 7 l., pp. 933, 1 l. Map and Engravings. 11592

I find in a London catalogue an edition quoted, *Milano.* 1690. Folio. The author was a Capuchin missionary, and his work includes notices of Brazil, and the Jesuit missions. *See* Trömel, No. 396.

CAVE (J.) Poems on Various Subjects, Entertaining, Elegiac and Religious. By Jane Cave. *Winchester: the Author.* 1783. 12mo. Portrait. 11593

Includes poems on the departure of six missionaries to America, the death of Whitfield, etc.

A Caveat against Emigration, 1803. *See* [Smith (W.)]

A Caveat against unreasonable and unscriptural Separations. In a Letter Sent from a Minister to some of his Brethren. *Boston: Printed and Sold opposite to the Prison in Queen Street.* 1748. 8vo, pp. 30. BA. 11594

A Caveat on the Part of Public Credit. *London: J. Almon.* 1778. 11595

A Caveat; or Considerations against the Admission of Missouri, with Slavery, into the Union. *New-Haven: A. H. Maltby & Co.* 8vo, pp. 40. BA. 11596

CAVELIER (Jean). Relation du Voyage Entrepris par feu M. Robert Cavelier, Sieur de la Salle, pour découvrir dans le golfe du Mexique l'embouchure du Fleuve de Missisipy. Par son Frère M. Cavelier, prêtre de St. Sulpice, l'un des compagnons de ce voyage. *À Mante: De la Presse Cramoisy de Jean-marie Shea.* M. DCCC. LVIII. Sm. 8vo pp. 54. BA., C., H. 11597

Forms No. v. of Shea's Cramoisy Series. 100 copies printed. *See* Tonti; also, Joutel. A Translation is included in Shea's "Early Voyages. *Albany.* 1861." 4to, pp. 15–42.

CAVELIER (Z.) An Address to the Citizens of Louisiana, on the Subject of the Recent Election in New Orleans. [Signed by Z. Cavelier and twenty-five others.] *New-Orleans.* 1844. 8vo, pp. 14. H. 11598

[CAVENDER (C. H.)] Catalogue of Works in Refutation of Methodism, From its Origin in 1729, to the Present Time. Of those by Methodist Authors on Lay-Representation, Methodist Episcopacy, etc., etc., and of the Political Pamphlets relating to Wesley's "Calm Address to our American Colonies." Compiled by H. C. Decanver. *Philadelphia.* 1846. 8vo, pp. 54. + Second Edition, Revised by the Author. *New York.* 1868. 8vo, pp. 56. 11599

The author's real name is C. H. Cavender. Decanver is an anagram.

CAVENDISH (H.) The Reefer of '76; or, The Cruise of the Fire-Fly. By Harry Cavendish .... *New York: Beadle.* 18—. 12mo. 11600

Also: The Privateer's Cruise [a Tale of '76. *Ibid.*]

CAVENDISH (H.) Government of Canada. Debates of the House of Commons in the Year 1774, on the Bill for making more effectual Provision for the Government of the Province of Quebec. Drawn up from the Notes of the Right Honorable Sir Henry Cavendish, Bart., Member for Lastwithiel; now first published by J. Wright, Editor of the Parliamentary History, etc. With a Map of Canada, copied from the second edition of Mitchell's Map of North America, referred to in the Debates. *London: Ridgway.* MDCCCXXXIX. 8vo, 6 l., pp. 303. 2 Maps. 11601

These interesting and valuable debates have remained nearly a blank in British history, in consequence of the exclusion of strangers and reporters.

CAVENDISH. Debates of the House of Commons, during the Thirteenth Parliament of Great Britain, commonly called the Unreported Parliament. To which are appended Illustrations of the Parliamentary History of the Reign of George III. Drawn up from the Original Manuscripts by J. Wright. Vol. I. May 10, 1768, to May 3, 1770. *London.* 1841. 8vo. C. 11602

Also: Three parts of Vol. II. May 10, 1768, to March 27, 1771. *London.* 1841. 8vo.

CAVENDISH (Thomas). Advertissement certain contenant les pertes aduenues en l'Armée d'Espagne, vers le Noest, de la coste d'Irlande, en leur voyage intenté depuis les Isles du Nord, par delà l'Escosse enuers Espagne. Et du nombre des hommes et nauires perdus. Auec deux lettres. l'vne d'vn Flamen, Catholique zelé, demeurant à Londres, à vn Seigneur Espagnol, et l'autre de Monsieur Candiche, qui a passé le destroit de Magellan, pour aller aux Indes, et est retourné par le Cap de Bonne-Esperance. [*Paris?*] M.D.LXXXVIII. 8vo, pp. 28, 1 l. 11603

Sold, in 1867, for eighty francs. Contains Cavendish's letter relating to his voyage round the world. *See* Leclerc, No. 25.

CAVENDISH. Copye, | Ouergeset wt de Engel- | sche taele in onse Nederlandtsche | spraecke, Gheschreuen aen Milore Tresorier. | Van Mr. Thomas Candische, Engelsche Edelman, | welcke in September verleden Anno 1588. Met zijne | schepen (de seylen zijnde van Damast) inghecomen is | in Pleymuyt, verhaelende zijn groote rijckdommen die | hy vercreghen heeft: Ende in welcke manie- | ren hy de Werelt om is geseylt, wat plaet- | sen hy versocht heeft. | *Tot Amstelredam by Cornelis Claesz.* | 4to, pp. 4. 11604

The letter, and a brief narrative, appeared first in Hakluyt's vol. of 1589, pp. 808–813, and in extensio in the larger work, Vol. III., 1600, pp. 803–839.

CAVENDISH. Beschryvinge van de obertreffelijcke ende wijdt- | vermaerde Zeevaerdt vanden Edelen Heer ende Meester Thomas Candish, met drie | Schepen uytghevaren den 21. Julij 1586. ende met een Schip wederom ghekeert in Pley- | mouth, den 9 September 1588. Hebbende (door 't cruycen van der Zee) gheseylt 13000. mylen. | Vertellende zyne vreemde wonderlijcke avontueren ende gheschiedenissen: | De ontdeckinge der Landen by hem beseylt. Beschreven door | M. François Prettie van Eye in Suffolck, | die mede inde Voyagie was. | Hier noch by ghevoecht de Voyagie van Sire Françoys Draeck, en Sire Ian Haukens, Ridderen, naer West-Indien, ghepretendeert Panama in te nemen met 6 van des Coningins Majesteyts Schepen, ende 21 an- | dere, by haer hebbende 2500. mannen. Anno 1595. Beschreten door eenen | die daer mede in de Vlote gheweest is. | *t'Amstelredam by Cornelis Claesz. op 't Water, in 't Schrijf-boeck A°* 1598. | Oblong 4to, 2 l., pp. (84). 11605

Small map of the world on title, with track marked on it. Contains Drake's, Harskins', and Cavendish's voyages.

CAVENDISH. Beschryvinge vande overtreffelijcke ende wydt- | vermaerde Zeevaerdt van ... Thomas Candisch, etc. [as before] ... Van nieus gecorrigeert ende verbeetert. | *Tot Amsterdam by Michiel Colijn, Boeckvercooper opt Water aende Oude Brugh,* | *int Huysboeck. Anno* 1617. | Oblong 4to, Title, 1 l, 39 leaves.

Same as No. 11605, with a globe on title; preface omitted.

CAVENDISH. Iournalen | Van drie Voyagien, | Te weten: | 1. Van Mr. Thomas Candish, met drie Sche- | pen door de Magallaensche Straet rondom de Werelt, in den Iare | 1586, 1587, en 1588. hebbende door 't kruycen van der | Zee gheseylt 13000 Mijlen. | 2. Vande Heer Fransoys Draeck, ende Heer Jan | Haukeins, Ridderen, naer West-Indien gepretendeert Panama in | te nemen met ses van des Coningins Majesteyts Schepen,

| ende 21 and're, in den Jare 1593. | Noch een Beschryvinghe vande Zee-vaert der geheeler Werelt | Nassausche Vloot, | 3. Ofte Beschryvinge van de Voyagie om den gantschen Aertkloot, | door de Straet Lemaire, onder 't beleydt van den Admirael Iaques | L'Heremite, in de Jaren 1623, 1624, 1625, en 1626. | Wy hebben hier achter by ghevoeght een Beschrijvinghe vande Rege- | ringhe van Peru, door Pedro de Madriga, gheboren tot Lima, met een kort verhael | van Chili. Als mede een verhael van Capiteyn Pedro Fernandes de Quir, aen | Sijne Majesteyt van Spangien, aengaende de ontdeckinghe van't | onbekent Australia, sijn grooten Rijckdom en vruchtbaerheyt, | ontdeckt by den selben Capiteyn. | *t'Amstelredam* | *By Iacob Pietersz Wachter, Boeck-verkooper op den Dam,* | *inde Wachter, Anno* 1643. | 4to, 2 l., pp. 100. 2 Maps. 11607

Contains Cavendish's voyage, 1586–1588, pp. 1–50; Sir Francis Drake's voyage, pp. 51–67; description of a route round the world, pp. 68–85; description of the coast of Brazil, pp. 86–97; Cavendish's letter, pp. 98–99; and notice of a map, pp. 99–100. Sold at Putticks, in 1860, for £1 3s.

CAVENDISH. Beschryvinge vande overtreffelijcke ende wydt- | vermaerde See-vaert van ... Thomas | Candish etc., [as before] ... *Gedruckt in t' Jaer onses Heeren* 1644. | Oblong 4to, pp. 78.

Forms a piece in Commelin's "Begin ende Voortgang," first edition, Vol. I. A literal reprint of No. 11606, of 1617. A Dutch version is included in Van der Aa's collection, Vol. XX. of the 8vo edition, and Vol. v. of the folio. An English edition is included in Vol. IV. of the new edition of Hakluyt, in Harris' collection of voyages, Vol. I., and Kerr's collection, Vol. X. A Latin version forms Part 8 of Bry's "Grands Voyages." *See* our Vol. III., page 40. Tiele proves that Hakluyt furnished to Van Meteren, then consul in London for the Nethetherlands, the narrative as it is given in the Dutch version of 1598. This translation was made by Van Meteron himself. The full English original account did not appear till two years later. Tiele says that the Latin version in the eight part of De Bry, of 1599, is faulty and incomplete. The sixth part of Hulsius' collection contains an abridged version of Cavendish and Drake's voyages. *See* Tiele, pp. 294–301.

CAVERLY (A. M.) An Historical Sketch of Troy [N. H.], and its Inhabitants, from the First Settlement of the Town, in 1764, to 1855. By A. M. Caverly, M.D. ... *Keene: printed at the N. H. Sentinel Office.* 1859. 12mo, pp. 299. Lithograph and lithographed Portraits. BA., H. 11609

CAVERLY (R. B.) The Merrimac and its Incidents. An Epic Poem by Robert B. Caverly. *Boston: Innes & Niles.* 1866. 12mo, 80 l. 1 steel Engraving, 14 Woodcuts. 11610

CAVERLY. Synopsis of the Court-Martial of Forty Days, by Robert B. Caverly. ... With an Address appended. August, 1858. *Lowell: printed by Samuel N. Merrill.* 1858. 8vo, pp. 24.

CAVERO Y SALAZAR (Don José). Coleccion de las composiciones de eloquencia y Poesia con que la real universidad de San Marcos de Lima celebro el recibimiento de Don Joaquin de la Pezuela y Sanchez. *Lima.* 1816. 4to. Portrait. 11612

CAVO (A.) Los tres siglos de Mexico durante el gobierno español, hasta la entrada del ejército trigarante, obra escrita à Roma por el Padre Andres Cavo de la Compañia de Jesus. Publícala con notas y suplemento, el lic. Carlos Maria de Bustamente .... *Mexico: Luis Abadiano y Valdés.* 1836–38. 4 vols., 4to, Title, pp. iii, 2 l., 281; Title, pp. 158; Title, vii, 419; Title, viii, 281. B. 11613

Important for the history of Mexico. Vol. IV. is very scarce. *See* Bustamente. In the Andrade catalogue the work is quoted, "*Mexico.* 1852," which is probably an error as to date.

CAVO. De Vita Josephi Juliani Parreni, Havanensis ab Andrea Cavo Sacerdote Guadalaxarensi Mexicano. *Roma.* 1792. 4to. Portrait. 11614

Also on large paper.

CAWDREY (D.) The Inconsistencie of the Independent way, With Scripture, and It Self. Manifested in a threefold Discourse, I. Vindiciæ Vindiciarum, with M. Cotton. II. A Review of M. Hookers Survey of Church-Discipline. The first part. III. A Diatribe with the same M. Hooker Concerning Baptism of Infants of Non-confederate parents, Cap 2. Of his third part. By Daniel Cawdrey .... *London: Christopher Meredith.* MDCLI. 4to, 13 l., pp. 219. B. 11615

Each part has a separate title-page. Relates to Church Government in New England.

CAWDREY. Vindiciæ Clavium, or a Vindication of the Keys of the Kingdom of Heaven into the hands of the right owners, being some animadversions upon a Tract by J. C[otton], called "The Keys of the Kingdom of Heaven;" also upon another Tract of his, called "The Way of the Churches of New England," By D. Cawdrey. 1645. 4to. 11616

CAYENNE. Almanach de Cayenne, pour l'année commune 1790, dans lequel on trouve l'heure de la haute mer, matin et soir pour tous les jours de l'année, la force qu' auront les marées des nouvelles et des pleines lunes, et une instruction nautique pour les navigateurs qui veulent atterrir sur les côtes de la Guyane française. *Cayenne: de l'Imprimerie du roi.* [1789.] 8vo.

Bulletin officiel de la Guyane française, pour les année 1827. *A Cayenne: de l'imprimerie du gouvernement.* 1827. Continued.

Lettres écrites de Cayenne, touchant ce qui s'est passé à la descente des François et leur établissement en Amérique. *Paris.* 1653. 11619

Mission de Cayenne et de La Guyane française avec une carte géographique *Paris: Julien, Lanier, Cosnard et Cie.* 1857. 8vo, 2 l., pp. xxi, 544. Map. BA. 11620

Forms Vol. I. of "Voyages et travaux des missionaires de la compagnie de Jésus ... pour servir de complément au Lettres édifiantes."

Narrative of the Deportation to Cayenne of Barthelemy, Pichegru, Willot, Marbois, La Rue, Ramel, &c. *London.* 1799. 8vo. 11621

Neue Reise nach Cayenne. ... Aus den Tagebuche eines französischen Bürgers mit Anmerkungen von M. G. *Leipzig: Reincke und Hinrichs.* 1709. 8vo, pp. viii, (2), 212. H. 11622

Neue Reise nach Cayenne; oder Nachricht von d. französische Guiana. Aus dem Französisch. *Leipzig.* 1802. 8vo. Map. 11623

Rapport des commissaires de la Société royale de médecine, sur le mal rouge de Cayenne ou éléphantiasis. *Paris.* 1785. 8vo. 11624

Tableau de Cayenne, 1798. *See* [Gallard de Terraube].

Tables des actes législatifs publiés dans la Guyane française depuis l'année 1817 jusqu'en décembre 1827, recueillis par ordre de matières, par ordre chronologique et par ordre alphabétique. *Cayenne: imp. du gouvernement.* 1829. 8vo, pp. xj, 352, 106.

Tefereel van Cayenne. *See* [Gallard de Terraube].

Les Veillées de Cayenne; par un déporté. *Paris an* VI. [1798.] 12mo. 11626

A large collection of proclamations, laws, and orders issued at Cayenne, between 1790–1797, in quarto and folio, may be consulted in the New York State Library at Albany. *See also* Guyane.

[CAYET (Pierre Victor).] Chronologie Septenaire | de | L'Histoire de la Paix entre | les Roys de France | et d'Espagne. | Contenant les choses plus memorables adue- | nuës en France, Espagne, Allemagne, Italie, An- | gleterre; Ecosse, Flandres, Hongrie, Pologne, | Suece, Transsiluanie, & autres endroits de l'Eu- | rope:

auec le succez de plusieurs navigations | faictes aux Indes Orientales, Occidentales, & | Septentrionales, depuis le commencement de | l'an 1598. iusques à la fin de l'an 1604. | Divisee en Sept Livres. | Derniere Edition. | *A Paris, Par Iean Richer, ruë S. Iean de Latran à l'Arbre* | *verdoyant: Et en sa boutique au Palais, sur le Perron* | *Royal, vis à vis de la gallerie des Prisonniers.* | M.DC.IX. | 8vo, 5 l., 506 folioed l. 11627

Contains details of voyages to the East and West Indies, more particularly Canada, from 1598 to 1604. The first edition was *Paris.* 1605. This was continued under the title of "Chronologie Neveuaire" to 1612, making four volumes. It is supplemented by the "Mercure Française." Contains the expedition of Du Pont to Canada in 1603, as described by Champlain. "Ouvrage curieux et assez bien écrit."—BRUNET.

CAYETANO DE CABRERA Y QUINTERO. *See* No. 9816.

CAYETANO PORTUGAL (J.) Conducta del reverendo obispo de Michoacan Don J. Cayetano Portugal, con motivo del destierro que impuso el gobierno de aquel estado a varios eclesiasticos desafectos al sistema federal. *México.* 1833. 4to, pp. 43.

CAYETANO PORTUGAL. Honras funebres de Illmo. Sr. D. Juan Cayetano Portugal, dignisimo obispo de Michoacan, verificadas en esta Santa Iglesia Catedral, en los dias 11 y 12 de noviembre del año de 1850. *Mexico.* 1851. Folio, pp. 121.

CAYLEY (A.) Life of Sir Walter Raleigh, Knt. By Arthur Cayley, Jun., Esq. *London.* 1805. 2 vols., 4to. Portrait. + Second Edition. *London: Cadell & Davies.* 1806. 2 vols., 8vo, pp. xv, 435; xi, 457. Portrait. 11630

See M. R., L. 377.

CAYLEY (C.) The Seraphical Young Shepherd. *Boston: J. Thomas.* 1793. 12mo, pp. 179. 11631

CAYLEY (W.) Finances and Trade of Canada at the Beginning of 1855. By W. Cayley, Inspector General of Canada. *London.* 1855. 8vo, pp. 40. 11632

CAYLUS (E.) Politique extérieure des États-Unis, Doctrine de Monroe. Par Ernest Caylus. *Paris: Dentu.* 1865. 8vo, pp. 31. BA. 11633

CAYUGA. Celebration of Cayuga Lake Academy, July 22d, 1857. [n. p. n. d.] 8vo, pp. 22, (2). 11634

Cayuga County Teachers' Institute. Catalogue of the Members during its Session at Auburn, 1843. *Auburn.* 1843. 8vo.

Cayuga Lake, Cayuga Bridge, Taghcanic Falls on the Cayuga. *Albany.* 1860. 24mo, pp. 8. 11636

Minutes of the Cayuga Baptist Association. *Auburn.* 1817. 8vo. 11637

Proceedings of the Cayuga County Convention of Delegates. *Auburn.* 1819. 8vo, pp. 32. 11638

Proceedings of the Board of Supervisors of the County of Cayuga, for 1857. 8vo. Continued. 11639

Cazal (M. A. de). Corografia Brazilica ou relação historico-geografica do Reino do Brazil. Por Manuel Ayres de Cazal. *Rio de Janeiro: na impressão Regia.* 1817. 2 vols., 4to, 5 l., pp. 420, 2 l.; 1 l., pp. 379, 2 l. BD. 11640

Heber's copy sold for £1 15s.; Ternaux's for 48 fr. *See* Leclerc, 304.

Caze (De). Compagnie de colonisation générale à la Guyane française, proposée à l'industrie nationale par M. De Caze (De Provence), homme de lettres. *Paris: Demonville.* 1826. 8vo, pp. xvi, 95. S. 11641

Caze (J. F. A.) Projet de colonisation pour la Guyane française. *Paris: Demonville.* 1827. 8vo. 11642

Cazeau (Fr.) Reclamation à la cour de France d'une dette authentique, reconnue par les Etats-Unis de l'Amérique. Por Fr. Cazeau. 1787. 4to. 11643

Also: Precis de la reclamation du sieur. 1787. 4to

Cazenove (L. de). La guerre et l'humanité aux XIXe siècle par Leonce de Cazenove. *Paris: Arnauld de Vresse.* 1869. 8vo, pp. 412. 11644

Contains a chapter, "La guerre d'Amérique et les hospitaliers."

Cecil (E.) Life of Lafayette. ... For Children. ... By E. Cecil. *Boston: Crosby, Nichols, and Company.* 1860. 16mo, 3 l., pp. 218. 6 colored Lithographs. H. 11645

Cecil. Life of George Washington, Written for Children. By E. Cecil. *Boston.* 1859. 12mo, 2 l., pp. 258. 6 colored Lithographs. 11646

Cecil. Life of Franklin, Written for Children. By E. Cecil. *Boston.* 1859. 16mo. 11647

Cecil, *pseudonym.* Kansas. *See* [Fisher (C. E.)]

Cejudo (J.) En la inauguracion del conservatorio national de déclamacion de Mexico, el director general, Don José Cejudo, a los alumnos de ambos secsos matriculados en la primera época. *Mexico.* 1853. Sm. 8vo, pp. 8. 11648

The Celebrated Speech of a Celebrated Commoner. *See* [Pitt (William)].

Celebrated Trials of all Countries, and Remarkable Cases of Criminal Jurisprudence. Selected by a Member of the Philadelphia Bar. ... *Philadelphia: E. L. Carey and A. Hart.* 1835. 8vo, pp. 4, 2 l., pp. 5–596. H. 11649

Includes "Trial of Captain Kidd," and some other American cases.

Celebrated Trials of all Countries, and Remarkable Cases of Criminal Jurisprudence. Selected by a Member of the Philadelphia Bar. *Philadelphia.* 1843. 8vo. 11650

Contains over eighty-eight trials, among them, "The Samuelston Witches in 1678," "The Salem Witches," "Captain Kidd," etc.

Celebration by the Colored People's Educational Monument Association in Memory of Abraham Lincoln, on the Fourth of July, 1865, on the Presidential Grounds, Washington, D. C. Printed by order of the Board of Directors. L. A. Bell, Recording Secretary. *Washington, D. C.: McGill & Witherow, Printers.* 1865. 8vo, pp. 33. 11651

Celebration of the Battle of King's Mountain, October, 1855, and the Address of the Hon. John S. Preston. Together with the Proceedings of the Meetings and Accompanying Documents. *Yorkville, S. C.: Miller & Melton.* 1855. 8vo, pp. 108. 11652

The Celebration of the Centennial Anniversary of the Introduction of the Art of Printing into New Hampshire, in the city of Portsmouth, Oct. 6, 1856. A Sketch of the Proceeding, the Oration, Decorations, Speeches, Sentiments, Letters, &c., &c. *Portsmouth: Edward N. Fuller.* 1857. 8vo, pp. 60. 11653

Celiar, leyenda americana por Don Alejandro Magariños Cervantes precedida de un discurso preliminar por Don Ventura de la Vega. *Paris: Igno. Boix y C.a. Noviembre de* 1852. 8vo, pp. 120. B. 11654

Cellarius (C.) Notitia Orbis Antiqui, sive Geographia Plenior, Chr. Cellarius collegit, auxit L. J. C. Schwartz. *Lipsiæ.* 1731. 2 vols., 4to. Maps. + *Lipsiæ.* 1773. 2 vols., 4to.

The second volume contains: "Additamentum de novo orbe an cognitus fuerit veteribus."

Cellarius (Franz). Geographische Unterricht über den Weltthiel von Europa; nebst einem Anhange von ... Amerika. *Eichstadt.* 1787. 8vo. 11656

Cellem (R.) Visit of His Royal Highness the Prince of Wales to the British North American Provinces and United States in the Year 1860. Compiled from the Public Journals by Robert Cellem. *Toronto.* 1861. 8vo, pp. 438. 11657

Celliez (*Mlle* Adelaide de). Christophe Colomb, suivi d'une nouvelle américaine. *Paris: Gaume frères.* 1840. 2 vols., 8vo. + Nouvelle édition. *Tournai: Casterman.* 1851. 12mo.

Celliez. Christoph Columbus, oder die Entdeckung von Amerika. Nach dem Französischem der Celliez von Joseph Borscht. *Regensburg: Manz.* 1858. 8vo, pp. 348. Engraving. (Bibl. f. die reifere christl. Jugend, XXI. Bd.) 11659

Celliez. Histoire du Paraguay: Par Mlle Celliez. *Paris: Gaume frères.* 1841. 2 vols., 18mo, 12½ sheets. 11660

The Censor. Numb. I. Saturday, November 23, 1771. [*Boston:*] *E. Russell.* Folio, pp. 4. Continued weekly. BA.

Census. Return of the whole number of Persons within the several Districts of the United States, according to "An Act providing for the Enumeration of the Inhabitants of the United States," passed March 1, one thousand seven hundred and ninty one. *Philadelphia: Printed by Childs and Swaine.* M.DCC.XCI. 8vo, pp. 56. + *London: R. Phillips.* 1793. 8vo, pp. 56. + *Washington.* 1802. 8vo. 11662

Each copy of the Philadelphia edition is signed with the autograph of Thomas Jefferson, at that time Secretary of State. I have not seen the title of the second return. The third is described in the Catalogue of the Library of Congress, thus:

Census of the United States. [Third.] 1810. [*Washington.* 1812?] Oblong folio, 90 l. + *Washington.* [1802?] 8vo.

There is also, "Tabular Statements of the several branches of American Manufactures, exhibiting them by States, Territories and Districts, so far as they are returned in the Reports of the Marshalls, and of the Secretaries of the Territories and their respective Assistants, in the Autumn of the Year 1810, together with similar Returns of Doubtful Goods, Productions of the Soil, and Agricultural Stock, as far as they have been received. *Philadelphia.* 1813." 4to, pp. 50.

Census for 1820, being the Fourth Census. ... *Washington: Printed by Gales and Seaton.* 1821. Folio. 11664

A synopsis of these was printed, *Boston,* 1821. 8vo, pp. 20.

Fifth Census; or Enumeration of the Inhabitants of the United States, 1830. To which is prefixed a Schedule of the whole Number of Persons within the several Districts of the United States; taken according to the acts of 1790, 1800, 1810, 1820. *Washington.* 1832. Folio. 11665

Abstract of the Returns of the Fifth Census of the United States. [*Washington.* 1832.] 8vo, pp. 40. 11666

Compendium of the Enumeration of the Inhabitants and Statistics of the United States, as obtained at the Department of State, from the Returns of the Sixth Census, by Counties and Principal Towns. To which is added an abstract of each preceding Census. Prepared at the Department of State. *Washington.* 1841. Folio, pp. 475. G., P. 11667

See the "Merchants' Magazine" for February, 1845.

A Census of Pensioners for Revolutionary or Military Services; with their Names, Ages, and Places of Residence, as Returned by the Marshals of the Several Judicial Districts under the Acts for taking the Sixth Census. *Washington: Printed by Blair and Rives.* 1841. 4to, pp. 195. 11668

Seventh Census of the United States, 1850. Embracing a Statistical View of each of the States and Territories, arranged by Counties, Towns, etc., under the following divisions: 1. Population by Counties. Classifications of Ages and Color. Aggregates. 2. Population by Sub-divisions of Counties. 3. Nativities of the Population. 4. Births, Marriages, Deaths, Dwellings, and Families. 5. Progress of the Population. 6. Deaf and Dumb, Blind, Insane and Idiotic. 7. Colleges, Academies, Schools, &c. 8. Attending School during Year, as Returned by Families. 9. Adults in the State, who can not read and write. 10. Professions, Occupations, and Trades of the Male Population. 11. Agriculture, Farms and Implements, Stock, Products, Home Manufactures, &c. 12. Newspapers and Periodicals. 13. Libraries other than Private. 14. Churches, Church Property, &c. ... With an Appendix, embracing Notes upon the Tables of each of the States, &c. J. D. B. De Bow. *Washington: Robert Armstrong, Printer.* 1853. 4to, pp. cxxxvi, 1022. 11669

Report of Joseph C. G. Kennedy, Superintendent of the Census, for December 1, 1852. To which is appended, the Report for December 1, 1851. *Washington.* 1853. 8vo. C. 11670

The Seventh Census of the United States of America. *New York.* 1851. 18mo, pp. 56. 116-1

Mortality Statistics of the Seventh Census of the United States, 1850 ... *Washington.* 1855. 8vo. (House of Reps. Ex. Doc. No. 98, 33d Congress, 2d Session.) N. 11672

The census for 1860 is divided into four classes, the titles of which are:

Agriculture of the United States in 1860; Compiled from the Original Returns of the Eighth Census, under the Direction of the Secretary of the Interior, By Joseph C. G. Kennedy, Superintendent of Census. *Washington: Government Printing Office.* 1864. 4to, pp. clxxii, 292. 11673

Population of the United States in 1860; Compiled from the Original Returns of the Eighth Census, under the Direction of the Secretary of the Interior, By Joseph C. G. Kennedy, Superintendent of Census. *Washington: Government Printing Office.* 1864. 4to, pp. cvii, (1), 694. 11674

Manufactures of the United States in 1860; Compiled from the Original Returns of the Eighth Census, under the Direction of the Secretary of the Interior. *Washington: Government Printing Office.* 1865. 4to, pp. ccxvii, 745, (1). 11675

Statistics of the United States, (including Mortality, Property, &c.) in 1860; Compiled from the Original Returns and being the final exhibit of the Eighth Census, under the Direction of the Secretary of the Interior. *Washington: Government Printing Office.* 1866. 4to, pp, lxvi, (1), 584. 11676

Centenera (M. del B.) *See* Barco Centenera, Vol. I., No. 3370. The correct title of No. 3371 is as below:

Centenera. La Argentina, o la conquista del Rio de La Plata, poema histórico por el arcediano D. Martin del Barco Centenera. *Buenos-Aires: imprenta del estado.* 1836. Folio, Title, pp. viii, ii, 312, xxiv, (1). (Angelis. Coleccion, Tomo II.)

The Centennial. 1766–1866. Illustrated. Edited by the Rev. Dr. Curry. *New York: N. Tibbals.* 4to, pp. 16. 11678

Relating to the centenary of Methodism in America.

Centinel (V.) Massachusetts in Agony, or Important Hints to the Inhabitants of the Province; calling aloud for Justice to be done to the Offenders; and avert the impending wrath over the Oppressed. By Vincent Centinel. *Boston.* 1750. pp. 20.

Centenary College. Catalogue of the Officers and Students in Centenary College of Louisiana ... 1851–'52. *Jackson, La.: "Southern Mirror" Office Print. June* 4, 1852. 8vo, pp. 22. H. 11680

Central America. Amerique Centrale. Colonisation du District de Santo Thomas de Guatemala. Collection de renseignements publiés ou recueillis par la Compagnie Belge de Colonisation. *Paris.* 1844. 8vo, 30 sheets. 4 Maps, and 4 Plates.

Centro-Amerika. Nach den gegenwärtigen Zustanden des Landes und Volkes, in Beziehung auf die Verbindung der beiden Oceane, und im Interesse der deutschen Auswanderung bearbeitet von C. F. Reichardt. *Braunschweig.* 1851. 8vo, pp. 254. 3 Maps. 11682

Correspondenee with the United States respecting Central America. Printed by order of Parliament. *London.* 1856–60. Folio, pp. 344. 11683

See also "Quarterly Review," XCIX. 235.

Documents Relative to Central American Affairs and the Enlistment Question. *Washington: Cornelius Wendell, Printer.* 1856. 8vo, pp. 485. Map. H. 11684

Memorias. *See* [Montufau (M.)]

Question anglo-américaine. *See* [Squier (E. G.)]

An article on the ruined cities of Central America is included in "Chamber's Papers for the People." The Messages of the President of the Republic of Central America are published at Guatemala.

Twenty-Seventh Annual Report of ... the Central American Education Society ... . *Philadelphia: Isaac Ashmead, Printer.* 1845. 8vo, pp. 4, 9–35, (1). H. 11685

Central Military Tract Railroad Company. Report, June, 1856. *Chicago.* 8vo. S. 11686

Central Pacific Railroad. Report of the Superintendent of Surveys. On the Preliminary Survey, Cost of Construction, and estimated Revenue of a Branch, of The Central Pacific Railroad, from Marysville, California, to the Columbia River in Oregon; together with a Report on the Wealth and Resources of the State of Oregon. *Salem, Oregon: Statesman Power Press.* 1864. 8vo. 11687

Central Park. *See* New York.

Centre College. The Twelfth Triennial and Thirty-Sixth Annual Catalogue of the Officers and Students of Centre College, at Danville, Kentucky, 1860. *Danville.* 1860. 8vo, pp. 50. H. 11688

Centro-America. *See* Central America.

Century Association. Constitution of "The Century" ... *New York.* 1857. 16mo, pp. 16. 11689

"A body ... located in the city of New York, for the purpose of promoting the advancement of Art and Literature, by establishing and maintaining a library, reading room, and gallery of art," Gulian C. Verplanck, Wm. C. Bryant, etc., being members.

Proceedings of the Century Association in Honor of the Memory of Brig.-Gen. J. S. Wadsworth and Col. Peter A. Porter: with the Eulogies read by Wm. J. Hoppin, and Fred. S. Cozzens. December 3, 1864. *New York: D. Van Nostrand.* M DCCC LXV. 8vo, pp. 88. H. 11690

Twelfth-Night at the Century Club. *See* [Verplanck (G. C.)]

Centz (P. C.) Davis and Lee: a Vindication of the Southern States, Citizens, and Rights. By P. C. Centz. *New York: Van Evrie, Horton & Co.* 1861. 8vo, pp. 80. 11691

Cepeda (Francisco de). Arte de las lenguas Chiapa, Zoque, Celdales, y Cinacanteca. *Mexico.* 1560. 4to. 11692

"Ces diverses langues sont parlées par les Indiens du Mexique."—Ternaux, 85. "Livre tres rare."—Brunet, 1739.

Cepeda (F. de). Relacion | vniversal Legitima, | y verdadera del sitio en qve esta fvndada | la muy noble, insigne, y muy leal Ciudad de Mexico, cabeça de las Provincias de toda | la Nueva España. Lagunas, Rios, y Montes que la ciñen y rodean. Calçadas que las dibiden. Y Aze- | quias que la atrauiesan. Ynundaciones que à padecido desde su Gentilidad. Remedios aplicados. | Desagues propuestos, y emprendidos. Origen y fabrica del de Gueguetoca, y estado en que | oy se halla. Ymposiciones, derramas, y gastos que se an hecho. Forma con que se á auc- | tuado desde el año de 1553. hasta el presente de 1637. | Año de [3 Vignettes] 1637. | De orden, | y mandato del | Excelletissimo | Señor D. Lope | Diez de Armẽ- | dariz, Marques de Cadereita, | del Consejo de | Guerra de su | Magestad, su | Mayordomo, | Virrey, Gouer- | nador y Capitã | General de la | Nueua España, | y Presidente de | la Real Audiẽ- | cia que en esta | Ciudad reside. | Dispuesta, y ordenada por el Licenciado Don Fernando de Cepeda Relator della. Y Don Fernando Alfonso | Carrillo

Escriuano Mayor del Cauildo. | Corregida, ajustada, y concertada con el Licenciado Don Iuan de Albares Serrano del Consejo de su | Majestad Oydor mas antiguo de la dicha Real Audiencia. | *En Mexico, en la Imprenta de Francisco Salbago, Ministro del S. Officio.* | [Colophon:] *En la Emprenta de Francisco Salbago, Mi- | nistro del sancto Officio, en la calle de san Francisco.* M.DC.XXXVII. Folio, 2 l., 31 numbered l., 42 n. l., 28 n. l., 39 n. l. J.C.B., H.

"This very rare book contains an official account of the celebrated Desaque, or canal of Gueguetoca, called, by Humboldt, Huehuetoca, which was constructed to carry off the superabundant waters of the lake of Mexico. Humboldt gives a full account of this stupendous undertaking."—Rich.

Cepeda. ... relacion ... [de] la detencion de la Flota deste Reyno ... . [Signed:] Fernando de Cepeda. [Colophon:] *Mexico: Francisco Salbago.* 1638. Folio, 10 numbered l. H.

Cepeda. Relacion que incluie otra de D. Carlos de Ibarra, al marques de Cadereyta, virrey desta Nueva España, del sucese de su armada año de 1638 con los corsarios y fiestas que se hicieron por la fuga de los ennemigos. *Mexico.* 1658. Folio.

Title from Ternaux-Compans, No. 763.

Cepéva. Resumpta historial de España desde el diluvio hasta el año 1642 [1652]. *Madrid.* 1654. 4to, 182 l. 11696

Contains particulars concerning the discovery of America.

Cerdena (Ant. Machorie de). Arte y Vocabulario de la Lengua Lule y Tonocote. *Madrid.* 1732. 12mo. 11697

An excessively rare book, almost unknown to bibliographers. The author was Procurator-General of the Jesuits in Paraguay. Sold at Puttick's, No. 210, 1854, for £5 12s. 6d.

Cerdeño y Monçon (L.) Manifiesto legal, cosmografico y historico en defensa del derecho del rey y de la sentencia del 20 de febrero dada por los jueces plenipotenciaros de Castilla y Portugal, sobre la situacion de la nueva colonia del Sacramento a la ribera del norte del rio de la Plata, por D. Luis Cerdeño y Monçon. *Madrid.* 1680. Folio. 11698

Title from Ternaux-Compans, No. 956.

Ceremonies ... religieuses. *See* Bernard (J. F.), Vol. II., No. 4931.

Cerero (M. J.) Balanza mercantil de la Isle de Puerto-Rico. 1843. 4to. 11699

Cerfbeer (A. E.) La Guyane, civilisation et barbarie, coutumes et paysages. Par A. E. Cerfbeer. *Paris: Giraud.* 1854. 18mo, 9⅜ sheets. 11700

Cerisier (Antoine Marie). Histoire de la Fondation des Colonies des Anciennes Républiques, adaptée à la Dispute présente de la Grande Bretagne avec des Colonies Américaines traduite de l'Anglais. *Utrecht.* 1778. 12mo. c. 11701

[Cerisier.] Le destin de l'Amerique ou dialogues pittoresques dans lesquels On developpe la cause des evenemens actuels, la politique et les interets des puissances de l'Europe relativement a cette guerre, et les suites qu'elle devroit avoir pour la bonheur de l'humanité, traduit fidelement de l'anglois. ... *London: J. Bew.* [1780?] 8vo, pp. 104. H. 11702

The mistakes in English on the title-page (sha- | re, tot for to, mary for may) show that this was not printed in London. I have seen it quoted with the following imprint: *London: J. Adamson, No. 13, Free Briton Street.* Also, *Londres.* M.DCC.LXXX. 8vo, pp. 115. H. It consists of imaginary dialogues between Lord North, Lord Bute, Mr. Sthevens, etc., and is attributed to M. Cerisier, by Barbier, who says it is "not translated from the English." *See* M. R., LXIII. 142.

Cerqueira e Silva (Ignacio Accioli de). Corografia Paraense, ou descripção fisica, historica, e politica, da provincia do Gram-Para. *Bahia: typografia do Diario.* 1833. 8vo, pp. viii, 347. Table. c. 11703

Cerqueira e Silva. Dissertação historica, ethnographica e politica sobre as tribus aborigines, que habitarun a provincia da Bahia, ao tempo que a Brasil foi descoberto. *Bahia.* 1848. 8vo. 11704

See Revista Trimensal di Inst., etc., XII. 143.

Cerqueira e Silva. Ensaio corographico do impero do Brasil, consagrado a Sua Magestade o imperador, o Sr. D. Pedro II. *Rio de Janeiro.* 1851. 11705

Cerqueira e Silva. Informação, ou descripção topographico e politica do Rio de S. Francisco, escripta em virtude de ordem especial. *Bahia.* 1847. 11706

Cerqueira e Silva. Memorias historicas, e politicas da provincia da Bahai. Por Ignacio Accioli de Cerqueira e Silva. *Bahia: De Précourt et Cie.* 1835. 5 vols., 8vo, pp. viii, 349, Table; viii, 318, 1 l.; pp. 256, 2 l.; pp. 251; 2 l., pp. 219.

Cerqueira e Silva (Jose Antonio de). O Brasil salvo, ou a discordia abysmada. Drama heroico. *Rio de Janeiro.* 1830. 4to. 11708

Cerro y Zamudio (Jose Santiago). *See* Undiano y Gastelu (S.)

Certaine Inducements | To Well Minded | People, | Who are heere straitned in their Estates or otherwise: | or | such as are willing out of Noble and Publique Prin- | ciples, to transport themselves or servants, | or Agents for them into the West- | Indies, for the propagating | the Gospell and in- | crease of Trade. | [*London.* 1644.] 4to, pp. 16. + *New York: reprinted for Joseph Sabin.* 1865. 4to, pp. 24. 11709

The reprint forms No. IV. of Sabin's Reprints. Fifty copies on large paper.

Cerutti (F. E.) Peru and Spain, being a Narrative of the Events preceding and following the Seizure of the Chincha Islands, with an Analysis of the Despatch of Señor Salazar y Mazarredo, Her Catholic Majesty's "Special Commissary" to Peru, and Minister to Bolivia, detailing his Adventurous Voyage homewards. By Captain C. F. Cerruti, Ex-Private Secretary to H. C. M.'s "Special Commissary." *London and Edinburgh: Williams and Norgate.* 1864. 8vo, 2 l., pp. 72. BA. 11710

Cervantes (A. M.) Amor y patria. Drama en cinco actos y en verso original de Alejandro Magarinos Cervantes. *Montevideo.* 1857. 8vo, pp. 132. 11711

Cervantes. Brisas del Plata por Alejandro Magarinos Cervantes. *Montevideo.* 1864. 2 pts., 4to, pp. 256. 11712

Cervantes. Estudios historicos, politicos y sociales sobre el Rio de la Plata, por D. Alejandro Magarinos Cervantes. *Paris.* 1854. 18mo, pp. 414. c. 11713

Cervantes. La iglesia y el estado considerados en sus relaciones religiosas, politicas y civiles por Alejandro Magarinos Cervantes. *Montevideo.* 1856. 8vo, pp. 186. 11714

Cervantes de Salazar. Dialogi di Academio Mexicana: Civitas Mexicus inter. Por Francesca Cervantes de Salazar. *Mexico: Juan Pablos.* 1555. 8vo. 11715

Cervantes (Juan Ortiz de). Memorial por los reinos del Peru. 1621. + 1627. 11716

Titles from Ternaux, Nos. 434, 490.

Cesnola (Louis Palma di). Ten Months in Libby Prison. ... [*New York?* 1865.] 4to, pp. 7. H. 11717

Cespedes (A. G. de). Regimiento de Navigacion | Mando Hazer el Rei Nves | tro Señor | por Orden de sv Conseio | Real de las Indias | a Andres Garcia de Ces | pedes sv Cosmografo Maior | siendo Presidente enel dicho | consejo el conde de Lemos. | [Colophon:] *En Madrid, | En Casa de Iuan de la Cuesta. | Año* M.DCVI. Folio, Engraved Title, 4 l., 184 leaves. Map. J.C.B.

Chapter XXII. relate to the voyages to the West Indies. *See* Brunet, 1756. The second part is entitled, "Hydrographia y theoria de Planetas," and includes a guide to the navigation in the West Indies, and some curions documents relating to the dispute with Portugal about the line of *demarcaion* of the Spanish and Portuguese dominions in America, which was a subject of dispute between the nations for more than two hundred years. Maisonneuve's copy sold, in 1867, for 110 fr.

Cessares. *See* [Burgh (James)], No. 9245.

Cevallos (*Fr.* Fernando). Observaciones sobre reforma eclesiastica. Obra posthuma aumentada. *Reimpreso en Puebla.* 1820. 4to, pp. 167, 2 l. 11719

Cevallos (Pedro Ordoñez de). *See* Ordoñez.

Ch******. *See* [Chabanon (M. P. G. de)].

Ch..... (*M.*), *de Marseille.* *See* [Chambon].

[Chabanon (Michel Paul Guy de).] Plan de constitution pour la colonie de Saint-Domingue, suivi d'une dissertation sur le commerce des colonies, relative à ce plan ... Par M. de Ch****** ... *Paris: imp. de J. B. N. Crapart.* 1791. 8vo.

[Chabanon.] Précis historique sur la révolution d'Irlande, suivi d'inductions relatives à celle qui s'opère à St-Domingue; par M. de Ch******, député suppléant de St-Domingue. 1790.

Chabert (D. de J.) Memoire dans l'Affaire de Canada, pour Daniel de Joncaire Chabert, ci-devant Commandant au petit Fort de Niagara. *Paris.* 1763. 11722

Title from Faribault, No. 863.

Chabert (Joseph Bernard), *Marquis de.* Voyage fait par ordre du Roi en 1750 et 1751, dans l'Amérique Septentrionale, Pour rectifier les Cartes des Côtes de l'Acadie, de l'Isle Royale & de l'Isle de Terre-Neuve; Et pour en fixer les principaux points par des Observations Astronomiques. Par M. de Chabert ... *Paris: De l'Imprimerie Royale.* M.DCC.LIII. 4to, Title, pp. viii, 288, 1 l. folded, 5 l. 1 Plate, 6 Maps, and folded sheet.

Mr. Chabert's work is highly praised by the commission appointed by the French Academy of Science to examine it, and is recommended as a model to future navi-

gators. It is divided into two parts: the first containing an account of the author's voyage from Brest to Louisbourg, and his four expeditions to the neighboring coasts and islands; the second part containing the astronomical observations at large. "It may be important as a scientific work, but can by no means be recommended to those who read for amusement." — Rich, I. 103, 104. The Marquis de Chabert was the author of "Mémoire sur la longitude de Buénos-Ayres," in the "Mém. de l'Acad. des sciences, Savants étrangers," 1750, T. I. *See* "Biog. Univ."

Chabert (X.) Account of the Manners and Customs of the Savage Inhabitants of Brazil, with the Life of the Botocudo Chieftain. *Edinburgh.* 1823. 8vo, pp. 24. 11724

Chabert. Historical Account of the Life and Adventures of the Botocudo Chieftain and Family (from Brazil), exhibited in New Bond Street. *London.* 1822. 8vo. 11725

Chace (B. H.) A Discourse Commemorative of the Life and Services of the late Dr. Dan King. Pronounced in St. Thomas' Church, Greenville, November 14, 1864. By Rev. Benjamin H. Chace. *Providence: Sidney S. Rider and Brother.* 1865. 12mo. 11726

Chace (G. Ide). Mineral Point Mining Company Reports, by Professor George I. Chace and Dr. C. T. Jackson. ... *Boston: Press of Geo. C. Rand & Avery.* 1863. 8vo, pp. 8. B. 11727

Chachereau. Examen rapide du cahier de doléances de la colonie, remis pour instructions à MM. les députés de la partie du nord. Par M. Chachereau ... *Port-au-Prince: Mozard.* 1789. 8vo, pp. 48 or less. 11728

Chadbourne (P. A.) The Influence of History on Individual and National Action. Annual Address before the State Historical Society of Wisconsin, ... January 30th, 1868. By Paul A. Chadbourne, M.D., President of the University of Wisconsin. *Madison: Wis.: Atwood & Rublee.* 1868. 8vo, pp. 22, 1 l. H. 11729

Also: Lecture on Natural History. *New York.* 1860. 12mo.

Chadbourne (S. H.) Catalogue of a Collection of Coins and Medals, the Property of Mr. S. H. Chadbourne, of Boston, comprising many Fine and Rare United States Cents, Colonials and Washington Pieces, and especially Rich in American and Foreign Bronze Medals, to be sold at Auction, on Wednesday, September 25, 1867. ... *Boston: printed at the Herald Job Office.* 1867. 8vo, pp. 28. H. 11730

Chad's Ford, September 11, 1777. 5 o'clock, P.M. .. Published by Order of Congress, Charles Thomson, Secretary. *Philadelphia: Printed by John Dunlap.* Folio, broadside, pp. 1.

This is a letter from R. H. Harrison and Washington to Hancock, announcing the Brandywine defeat.

Chadwick (P.) Remarks on some of the Circumstances and Arguments, produced by the Murder of Mr. Paul Chadwick, at Malta, on the East Side of the Kennebec, On the 7th of September, 1809. [n. p. n. d.] 8vo, pp. 24. BA., H. 11732

Chaffee (C. C.) The Lecompton Constitution; a Measure to Africanize the Territories of the United States. Speech of Hon. Calvin C. Chaffee, of Massachusetts. Delivered in the House of Representatives, February 24th, 1858. *Washington, D. C.: Buell & Blanchard, Printers.* 1858. 8vo, pp. 8. H.

Chaffee (J. B.) *and* Evans (John). Colorado. [n. p. 1865 or 66.] 8vo, pp. 8. H. 11734

Chaffin (W. L.) The President's Death and its Lessons. A Discourse on Sunday Morning, April 23d, 1865, before the Second Unitarian Society of Philadelphia, by its Pastor, William L. Chaffin. Published by Request. *Philadelphia: King & Baird, Printers.* 1865. 8vo, pp. 18. B. 11735

Chagas (*Fr.* Antonio das). Estatutos municipaes da Provincia da Immaculado Conceição do Brasil. *Lisboa: por José Lopez Ferreira.* 1747. Folio. 11736

See Silva's "Bibl.," I. 541.

Chagnon (G.) Précis de diverses ordonnances du conseil spécial et d'actes de la législature pour la ci-devant province du Bas-Canada. Par Godefroy Chagnon. *Montréal.* 1842. 12mo, pp. 108. 11737

Chahita. Arte de la Lengua Chahita. *Mexico.* 1737. 12mo. 11738

The language of the northern part of Mexico. Title from Ludewig.

Chahta. *See* Choctaw.

Chaillé (S. E.) Historical Sketch of the Medical Department of the University of Louisiana: its Professors and Alumni, from 1835 to 1862. *New Orleans: printed at the Bulletin Book and Job Office.* 1861. 8vo, pp. 18. H. 11739

[Chaix (Paul).] Le bassin du Mississipi au seizième siècle. [n. p. n. d.] 8vo, pp. 29–92. H. 11740

Signed Paul Chaix.

Chaix. Histoire de l'Amérique Méridionale au seizième siècle, comprenant les decouvertes et conquêtes des Espagnols et des Portugais dans cette partie du Monde Par Paul Chaix. Primière partie: Pérou. *Genève [et] Paris: Joël Cherbuliez.* 1853. 2 vols., 12mo, pp. xvi, 344; 3 l., pp. 348. 5 Maps.

Chalas (Alexandre). Les Anglais en Amérique, drame en trois actes. *Paris: imp. d'Herhan.* 1833. 8vo, pp. 50. 11742

[Chalesme (*M.* de).] *See* Récit fidéle. *Poitiers.* 1676.

Chalk (Thomas). Some Account of the Gospel Labours of Jonathan Burnyeat, who died A.D. 1709, in the 23d Year of his Age, having been a Minister 11 Years. Second Edition: *London: William and Frederick G. Cash.* 1857. 12mo, 2 sheets.

Chalkley (T.) A Collection of the Works of Thomas Chalkley. In Two Parts. *Philadelphia: Printed by B. Franklin, and D. Hall.* MDCCXLIX. 8vo, pp. xiii, 1 l. pp. 590.

A title to the second part forms pages 327, 328.

Chalkley. A Collection of the Works of Thomas Chalkley. In Two Volumes. The Second Edition. *Philadelphia: Printed and Sold by James Chattin, in Church Alley.* 1754. 2 vols., sm. 8vo, 2 l., pp. viii, 325; iv, 244. S. 11746

Reprinted as:

Chalkley. A Collection of the Works of that Antient, faithful Servant of Jesus Christ, Thomas Chalkley, who Departed this Life in the Island of Tortola, the fourth Day of the Ninth month, 1741. To which is prefix'd, A Journal of his Life, Travels, and Christian experiences, Written by Himself. The Second Edition. *London: Luke Hinde.* 1751. 8vo. 37½ sheets. + Third Edition. *London.* + The Fourth Edition. *London: Luke Hinde.* 1766. 8vo, pp. ix, 580. 11747

Chalkley. Free Thoughts communicated to Free Thinkers, in order to promote thinking on the Name and Works of God; with a Relation of a Remarkable Providence which fell out at Port-Royale, in Jamaica, suitable to the subject: written at Sea. *Barbadoes, printed.* 1735. 8vo, pp 16. + The Second Edition. *Barbadoes, printed.* 1735. 8vo, pp. 16. 11748

The preface and postscript by another hand.

Chalkley. A Journal or Historical Account of the Life, Travels and Christian Experiences of that antient, faithful servant of Jesus Christ, Thomas Chalkley, Who departed this Life in the Island of Tortola, the fourth Day of the Ninth Month, 1741. The Second Edition. *London: Luke Hinde.* 1751. 8vo, pp. ix, 326. + The Third Edition. *London: Luke Hinde.* 1751. 8vo, 21 sheets. + The Fifth Edition. *Philadelphia: James Johnson.* 1790. + *London: James Phillips.* 1798. 8vo, 38¼ sheets. 11749

Thomas Chalkley, a Quaker preacher, came to America in the year 1700, and settled at Philadelphia. He travelled and preached in all the British Colonies from New England to North Carolina. He also visited the West India Islands, and the Bermudas. "Some of the New England priests," he says, "were so bitter against Friends, that, instead of being humbled, under the mighty hand of God upon them in suffering the Indians to destroy them, they express'd their enmity against the poor Quakers. In a sermon preached by one of their priests, he divided it into three heads, viz.: First. That the Judgments of God were upon them, in letting loose the Savage Indians upon them. Secondly. In that he withheld the fruits of the earth from them. Thirdly. That the Quakers prevailed and were suffered to increase so much among them which was worse than the Indians destroying of them." In some copies the edition is not stated. Reprinted with aditions, as below:

Chalkley. The Journal of Thomas Chalkley, to which is annexed, a Collection of his Works. *New York: Samuel Wood. New Bedford: Abraham Shearman, Jun. Philadilphia: Kimber and Conrad.* 1808. 8vo. 34¾ sheets. 11750

Chalkley. A Journal of the Life, Travels, and Christian experiences of Thomas Chalkley. Written by himself. A New Edition, detached from his Works. *London: William Phillips.* 1818. 12mo, 18⅝ sheets. + *London: Harvy and Darton.* 1829. 12mo, 18½ sheets. 11751

Reprinted as Vol. VI. of the Friends' Library, again reprinted as a second edition, 1835, and lastly, *London.* 1851. Fcap 8vo, pp. 386.

Chalkley. Mémoires de Thomas Chalkley, extraits principalement d'un journal de sa vie et de ses voyages. *Paris: impr. de F. Didot.* 1840. 12mo, pp 60. 11752

Chalkley. Youth persuaded to Obedience, Gratitude, and Honour to God, and their Parents. Also, Some Touches upon the Life of Man, from the Cradle to the Grave. Written at Sea by T. C. near the Tropick of Cancer, September, 1730. *Barbadoes: Printed by David Harry, ... Bridge Town.* 1730. 8vo, 3 sheets. + *Newcastle-upon-Tyne: Printed by I. Thompson and Company.* 1754. Large 8vo, pp. 24. 11753

In the year 1706, Thomas Chalkley had printed a book called "A Small Broom," concerning which, *see* Smith's Catalogue of Friends' Books.

Chalkley. Memoirs of Thomas Chalkley; chiefly extracted from a Journal of his Life, Travels, and Christian experiences. [By Luke Howard.] *London: Printed by William and Samuel Graves.* 1817. 12mo, 2⅝ sheets. 11754

No. 23 of a series of tracts. "Chalkley was a Quaker preacher and trader, who spent forty years in different parts of North America and the West Indies, but principally Pennsylvania. He was a man of many virtues." — Rich.

Challen (H.) Publishers' Uniform Trade List Directory, comprising all the Books, Old and New, of upwards of Two Hundred Publishers. By H. Challen. *Philadelphia: H. Challen.* 8vo, pp. 831. 11755

Also: The Uniform Trade List Circular. ... *Philadelphia: Howard Challen.* [1867.] 8vo, Title, pp. 19–323. H.

Challen (J.) Island of the Giant Fairies. By James Challen. *Philadelphia: Howard Challen.* 1868. 12mo, pp. 23. H. 11756

Poem on the Island of Mackinaw.

Challenger (*sloop*). *See* Diary.

Challur (Nicolas). *See* Le Challeux (N.)

Chalmers (G.) Another Account of the Incidents from which the Title and Part of the Story of Shakespeare's Tempest were derived, and the True Era of it ascertained, evincing the Original Connexion of the Royal Family with the Poet's Drama. By George Chalmers ... *London.* 1815. 8vo, pp. viii, 82.

Only forty copies printed, by R. and A. Taylor. An interesting tract, containing notices of Jourdan's "Account of the Tempest off the Island of Bermudas," published in 1610, etc.

[Chalmers.] An Answer from the Electors of Bristol to the Letter of Edmund Burke on the Affairs of America. *London.* 1777. 8vo. BD. 11758

Title from the Bodleian Catalogue; perhaps the same as our No. 9251.

Chalmers. A Collection of Treaties between Great Britain and other Powers. By George Chalmers, Esq. *London: John Stockdale.* M DCC XC. 2 vols., 8vo, pp. xvi, 564; vii, 538. BA.

Including the treaties with the United States. *See* M. R., VI. 39.

Chalmers. An Estimate of the Comparative Strength of Great Britain during the Present and Four Preceding Reigns, and of the Losses of her Trade from every War since the Revolution. By George Chalmers, F.R.S. *London: C. Dilly.* 1782. 4to, pp. 197. + *London.* 1786. 8vo, pp. 250. + *London.* 1794.

8vo. + *London.* 1802. 8vo, pp. 443. + *London.* 1810. 8vo, pp. 443. + *Edinburgh.* 1812. 8vo, pp. 443. 11760

This work shows the advantages to England of the independence of the United States. *See* M. R., LXVIII. 51; *see also* McCulloch's "Lit. Pol. Econ.," 217, who states that the edition of 1802 is the best.

CHALMERS. [An Introduction to the History of the Revolt of the Colonies. *London: Printed by Baker and Galabin.* 1782.] 8vo, pp. 496. 11761

In the sale of Mr. Chalmers' library, Mr. Evans says, that of this most rare work not more than a dozen copies are extant. A manuscript note, by Mr. Tutet, states that after this portion of the book was printed, "the author suppressed it: whether owing to the separation of the Colonies which happened just at the season for publication, viz., December, 1782, or the prior cause in April antecedent, the dismission of a Tory administration, is only known to the author, who is a Scotchman. This was to have made two volumes, the first only was finished, but never published. A few copies only were preserved." *See also* Rich, I. 301, and Stevens' Nuggets, No. 507, where a copy is priced at £5 5s. The entire work, completed from Chalmers' autograph manuscript, was printed in Boston, in 1845, as below. The copy from which it is printed is in the Library of Harvard College.

CHALMERS. An Introduction to the History of the Revolt of the American Colonies; being a Comprehensive View of its Origin, derived from the State Papers contained in the Public Offices of Great Britain. By George Chalmers. *Boston: James Munroe and Company.* 1845. 2 vols., 8vo, pp. (2), xxxiv, 414; Title, xv, 376. C. 11762

[CHALMERS.] The Life of Thomas Pain, the Author of the Rights of Man. With a Defense of his Writings. By Francis Oldys. *London.* 1791. 8vo, pp. 128. 11763

This work is usually attributed to Chalmers; but, in the year 1864, I sold a long letter, written by Chalmers, in which he indignantly denied the statement.

CHALMERS. Opinions | on | interesting Subjects | of | Public Law and Commercial Policy; | arising from American Independence. | § 1. The Question answered — | Whether the Citizens of the United | States are considered by the Law of | England as Aliens; what Privileges | are they entitled to within the King- | dom; what Rights can they claim in | the remaining Colonies of Britain. | § 2. The Regulations for open- | ing the American Trade considered; | Faults found; and Amendments pro- | posed: How the late Pro- | clamations affect the United States discussed: | Objections pointed out; and Altera- | tions suggested. § 2 [for 3]. How far the British West | Indies were injured by the late Pro- | clamations fully investigated; the | Amount of their Wants discovered; | Modes of Supply shewn: And the | Policy of admitting the American Vessels into their Ports amply ar- | gued. | § 3 [for 4].

An Enquiry how far a | Commercial Treaty with the United | States is necessary, or would be ad- | vantageous: What the Laws of | England have already provided on | this Subject; and the fundamental | Laws of the United States compared | with them. | By George Chalmers, | Author of | Political Annals ... | ... | ... | ... . | *London:* | ... *J. Debrett* ... | ... 1784. | 8vo, pp. 195. BA. + A New Edition, corrected. *London: J. Debrett.* 1785. 8vo, Title, pp. 200. C., H. 11764

For the title at length of the new edition, *see* Nuggets, No 508; it is the same as the above, with the typographical errors corrected. "Those who wish to gain solid information on the topics above enumerated, will meet with ample satisfaction in the perusal of this elaborate performance." M. R., LXXI. 385.

CHALMERS. Opinions of Eminent Lawyers on various points of English jurisprudence, chiefly concerning the Colonies, Fisheries and Commerce of Great Britain; Collected and Digested, from the originals in the Board of Trade and other depositories. By George Chalmers, Esq. *London.* 1814. 2 vols., 8vo. + *Burlington: C. Goodrich & Company.* 1858. 8vo, pp. xxviii, 787.

CHALMERS. Political Annals | of the | Present United Colonies, | from their | Settlement | to the | Peace of 1763: | Compiled chiefly from Records, and authorised often by the | Insertion of State Papers. | ... | By George Chalmers, Esq. | Book I. | *London:* | *Printed for the Author and Sold by G. Bowen.* | M. DCC. LXXX. | 4to, pp. (8), 695. H. 11766

The second part was never published. "Chalmers was a strenuous supporter of the right of the mother country to tax the colonies, and, throughout his narrative, every fact which would admit of it was studiously applied to support this principle. ... Valuable for the distinctness of its details, the authenticity of its documents, and the elegant manner in which it is written." So much as relates to Carolina is reprinted in Carroll's Coll., II. 273–345. *See also* "Mass. Hist. Coll.," Vol. XXXIV; M. R., LXII. 464; LXIII. 15; N. A. R., LX., Smyth's Lectures; Rich, I. 282.

[CHALMERS.] Second Thoughts: or, Observations upon Lord Abingdon's Thoughts on the Letter of Edmund Burke, Esq., to the Sheriffs of Bristol. By the Author of the Answer to Mr. Burke's Letter. *London: T. Cadell.* 1777. 8vo, pp. 74. + Second Edition. *London: T. Cadell.* 1777. 8vo, pp. 74.

Chalmers was a native of Scotland, but practised in Maryland as a lawyer for ten years, and, being a staunch loyalist, returned to England at the close of the war. The pamphlet, entitled "Plain Truth," in answer to Paine, has been attributed to Chalmers.

CHALMERS (*Colonel* G.) Proofs and Demonstrations that the Registry of Colonial Negroes is uncalled for; Reports and Resolves of the Bahama Assembly. 1816. Folio. 11768

CHALMERS. Remarks on the late War in St. Domingo, with Observations on the relative situation of Jamaica, and other interesting Subjects. By Colonel Chalmers, late Inspector General of the Colonial Troops in St. Domingo. *London: Rivington.* 1803. 8vo. 11769

Also: Copy of Mr. Chalmers' Letter to the Duke of Portland on the Subject of the Black Troops. 1801. 8vo. Title from Thomas Thorpe's catalogue. *See* M. R., XLI. 97.

CHALMERS (H. J.) To the Good People of South-Carolina. [On Wappoo and Bull Cuts. Signed by Henry J. Chalmers, and Benj. J. Smith. n. p. 1823.] pp. 8. BA. 11770

CHALMERS (J. W.) Speech of Mr. Chalmers of Mississippi, on the Resolutions giving Notice to Great Britain of the Abrogation of the Convention of Joint Occupancy. Delivered ... March 24, 1846. *Washington: printed by John T. Towers.* 1846. 8vo, pp. 15. H. 11771

CHALMERS (L.) An Account of the Weather and Diseases of South-Carolina. By Lionel Chalmers, M.D. Of Charles-town [*sic*], South-Carolina. ... *London: Edward and Charles Dilly.* M DCC LXXVI. 2 vols., 8vo, pp. viii, 222; iv, 224. 2 Tables. BA., C. 11772

Highly praised in the "Monthly Review," LIV. 275.

CHALMERS. Lionel Chalmer's [*sic*] Nachrichten über die Witterung und Krankheiten in Südcarolina. Nebst John Linings Tabelle über die Aus- und Absonderungen des Körpers im dortigen Klima. Aus dem Englischen übersetzt. ... *Stendal: in der Franz- und Grossischen Buchhandlung.* 1796. 2 vols., 8vo, 6 l., pp. 211, (1), 2 l. folded. 11773

CHALMERS (T.) On the Abolition of Colonial Slavery. By Thomas Chalmers, D.D. *Glasgow.* 1826. 8vo, pp. 16.

CHALONER *and* FLEMING. Mahogany Tree, in the West Indies and Central America; with notices of the projected Inter-oceanic Communications of Panama, Nicaragua, and Tehuantepec, in relation to their supply of timber. *Liverpool.* 1851. 8vo.

CHALUSSET (A. de) Curiosités américaines ou Description des animaux, des chasses, des danses, des jeux et des plantes du Canada. Par Abel de Chalusset. *Limoges: Barbou frères.* 1858. 18mo, pp. 106. Engraving. + [*Ibid.*] 1859. 11776

CHALUSSET. Curiosités américaines, ou Description des animaux, des chasses, des danses, des jeux et des plantes du Canada. *Limoges: Barbou frères.* 1858. 12mo. 11777

CHALWILL (W. G.) A Dissertation on the Sources of the Malignant Bilious, or Yellow Fever, and means of preventing it. By William G. Chalwill. *Philadelphia.* 1799. 8vo. P. 11778

CHAMBERLAIN (E. M.) Speech of Hon. E. M. Chamberlain of Indiana, against the Repeal of the Missouri Compromise Act; ... in the House of Representatives, ... March 13, 1854. *Washington: printed by A. O. P. Nicholson.* 1854. 8vo, pp. 23. B.

CHAMBERLAIN (N. H.) The Assassination of President Lincoln. A Sermon preached in St. James' Church, Birmingham, Ct., April 19th, 1865. By Rev. N. H. Chamberlain. *New York: G. W. Carleton.* 1865. 12mo, pp. 22. 11780

CHAMBERLAIN. The Autobiography of a New England Farm-House. ... By N. H. Chamberlain. *New York: Carleton.* MDCCCLXV. 16mo, pp. 365. BA., C., H. 11781

CHAMBERLAIN. Dr. Kane, and Christian Heroism as seen in Arctic Voyaging: a Discourse preached at Canton, Mass., April 16, 1857. By Nathan H. Chamberlain. *Boston: Crosby, Nichols, and Company.* 1857. 8vo, pp. 20. BA., H. 11782

CHAMBERLAIN. A Paper on New-England Architecture, read before the New-England Historic Genealogical Society, September 4, 1858. By Rev. N. H. Chamberlain, of Canton. ... *Boston: Crosby, Nichols, and Company.* 1858. 8vo, pp. 30.

CHAMBERLAIN. The Sacredness of Personality the Shield of Liberty: a Discourse ... April 15, 1858. [Fast Day]. By Rev. N. H. Chamberlain. ... *Boston: Crosby, Nichols, and Company.* 1858. 8vo, pp. 29. BA., H. 11784

Also: The Scholar in the Republic. *New Haven.* 1862. 8vo, pp. 25.

CHAMBERLAIN (William). An Address delivered at Windsor, Vt., on the Fifteenth Anniversary of American Independence. *Windsor, Vt.* 1826. 8vo. BM. 11785

C[HAMBERLAINE] (R[ichard]). Lithobolia: | or, The | Stone-Throwing Devil. | Being | An Exact and True Account (by way of Journal) | of the various Actions of Infernal Spirits, or (Devils Incarnate | Witches, or both; and the great Disturbance and Amaze- | ment they gave to George Waltons Family, at a place

call'd | Great Island, in the Province of New-Hantshire in New- | England, chiefly in Throwing about (by an Invisible hand) | Stones, Bricks, and Brick-bats of all Sizes, with several other | things, as Hammers, Mauls, Iron-Crows, Spits, and other | Domestick Utensils, as came into their Hellish Minds, | and this for the space of a Quarter of a Year. | By R. C. Esq; who was a Sojourner in the same | Family the whole Time, and an Ocular Witness | of these Diabolick Inventions. | The Contents hereof been manifestly known to the Inhabi- | tants of that Province, and persons of other Provinces, | and is upon record in his Majesties Council-Court held | for that Province. | *London,* | *Printed and are to be Sold by E. Whitlock near* | *Stationers-Hall,* 1698. | 4to, 2 l., pp. 16. H. 11786

This rare piece has a poetical address at the beginning. It "details operations very like some modern cases." Reprinted in the "Historical Mag.," Nov., 1861, v. 321–327.

CHAMBERLAYNE (John). Magnæ Britanniæ notitia; or the Present State of Great Britain. 31st Edition. *London.* 1735. 8vo. C., S. 11787

Partly relates to the government of the American Colonies before the Revolution. *See also* "Oratio Dominica."

CHAMBERLAYNE, *Translator.* The Manner of Making of Coffee, Tea, and Chocolate, as it is used in most parts of Europe, Asia, Africa, and America. Translated by J. Chamberlayne. 12mo. C. 11788

CHAMBERLIN (B.) Our Country, and our Duty to it. A Lecture ... before the Mechanics' Institute, Montreal, ... 7th of March, 1854, by B. Chamberlin, ... to which are subjoined some Remarks upon the Progress of Canada. ... . *Montreal: printed by William Salter.* 1854. 8vo, pp. 18. B. 11789

CHAMBERLIN (E. M.) Free Trade: Remarks ... at the Workingmen's Institute, Boston, June 24, 1868, by E. M. Chamberlin. *Boston: A. Williams & Co.* 1868. 8vo, pp. 23.

CHAMBERLIN (J.) Report of Col. James Chamberlin, Pennsylvania State Agent at the South-West. [*Nashville.* 1864.] 8vo, pp. 7. H. 11791

CHAMBERS (A. B.) Proceedings of the St. Louis Chamber of Commerce, in Relation to the Improvement of the Navigation of the Mississippi River, and its principal Tributaries and

the St. Louis Harbor. With a Statement ... by A. B. Chambers, ... *St. Louis: printed by Chambers & Knapp.* 1842. 8vo, pp. 40. H. 11792

CHAMBERS (E. F.) Speech of the Hon. Ezekiel F. Chambers, at the Public Dinner In Cambridge, Md. given him by Citizens of Dorchester County, on The 10th day of August, 1831. [*Baltimore.* n. d.] 8vo, pp. 16. BA. 11793

Also: Speech of Judge Chambers on the Judicial Tenure, in the Maryland Convention, April, 1851. *Baltimore: printed by John Murphy & Co.* 1851. 8vo, pp. 41. H.

CHAMBERS (George). Address of Mr. Chambers, Of the House of Representatives, To the People Of the Counties of Franklin & Adams, composing the 12th Congregational District of Pennsylvania. *Chambersburg: J. Pritts.* 1834. 8vo, pp. 37.

[CHAMBERS.] A Tribute to the Principles, Virtues, Habits and Public Usefulness of the Irish and Scotch Early Settlers of Pennsylvania. By a Descendant. *Chambersburg: printed by M. Kieffer & Co.* 1856. 8vo, pp. 171. H. 11795

CHAMBERS (John), *and* DUANE (W. J.) Settlement of Emigrants from Ireland. [Letter dated Washington City, February 18, 1818.] 8vo, pp. 18. H. 11796

CHAMBERS (J.) Fortieth Anniversary Sermon, May 14, 1865. By Rev. John Chambers, Pastor of the First Independent Church, Broad Street, Philadelphia. (With a History of the First Independent Church, Philadelphia.) *Philadelphia.* 1865. 8vo, pp. 29. 11797

CHAMBERS. Letters, addressed to the Democratic Members of the Legislature of Pennsylvania. *Philadelphia.* 1856. 8vo.

CHAMBERS. Republics Established and Thrones Overturned by the Bible. *Philadelphia.* 1849. 12mo, pp. 202. + *Philadelphia.* [n. d.] 18mo, pp. 36. 11799

Also a Thanksgiving and Fast Sermon in 1862.

CHAMBERS (R.) Hand Book of American Literature, Historical, Biographical and Critical. *Edinburgh: W. & R. Chambers.* [1856.] 12mo, pp. 314. 11800

Some copies have a Philadelphia imprint.

CHAMBERS. History of the English Language and Literature, to which is added, a History of American Contributions to the

English Language and Literature, by Rev. Royal Robbins. *Hartford.* [1837.] 12mo, pp. 329. 11801

The "Book of Days," edited by Robert Chambers, includes many American topics.

CHAMBERS (T). Remarks and Reflections upon the Trial of Colonel Talbot Chambers, before a Court Martial commenced and held at Camp Morgan, in Georgia, on the Fifteenth of March, 1826. By Himself. ... *Washington.* 1827. 8vo, pp. 23

At the end the signature is Talbott Chambers.

CHAMBERS (T. W.) Memoir of the Life and Character of the Late Hon. Theo. Frelinghuysen, LL.D. By Talbot W. Chambers ... . *New York: Harper & Brothers.* 1863. 12mo, pp. 289. Portrait. BA., H., S. 11803

CHAMBERS. The Noon Prayer Meeting of the North Dutch Church, Fulton st., New York. Its origin, character, and progress, with some of its results. By Talbot W. Chambers. ... *Board of Pub. of the Reformed Protestant Dutch Church, New York.* 1858. 12mo. 11804

CHAMBERS (W.) Sketch of the Life of Gen. T. J. Chambers of Texas. By his Nephew, Wm. Chambers, of Liberty Co. *Galveston: printed at the Book and Job Office of the "Galveston News."* 1853. 8vo, pp. 63. H. 11805

CHAMBERS (W.) American Slavery and Colour. By William Chambers. ... *London: W. & R. Chambers.* 1857. 8vo, Title, 1 l., pp. 216. Map. B., H. 11806

CHAMBERS. Things as they are in America by William Chambers. *London and Edinburgh: W. and R. Chambers.* 1854. 8vo, pp. vi, 364. H. 11807

Some copies have the imprint, *Philadelphia: Lippincott, Grambo & Co.* 1854. 8vo, pp. vi, 364. BA.

CHAMBLIT (R.) The Declaration, Dying Warnings and Advice of Rebekah Chamblit, A Young Woman aged near Twenty-seven Years, Executed at Boston, September 27th. 1733. [*Boston: Samuel Kneeland, Printer.*] 8vo, pp. (4). BA.

CHAMBLY. Catalogue of the Officers and Students of St. Peter's College at Chambly. January, A.D. 1831. *Montreal: printed by Ludger Duvernay.* 1831, 12mo, pp. 14. B. 11809

CHAMBOLLE (Adolphe). Les États-Unis. A M. Casimir Delavigne. Par A. Chambolle. *Paris: Brière.* 1825. 8vo, pp. 16. 11810

CHAMBOLLE (François Alexis). Dissertation inaugurale sur la frèure jaune observée aux Antilles pendant les années 1825, 1826 et 1827. Thèse. *Paris: imp. de Didot juene.* 1828. 4to.

[CHAMBON.] Le commerce de l'Amérique par Marseilles, ou Explication des Lettres-Patentes du Roi, portant Reglement pour le Commerce, qui se fait de Marseille aux Isles Françoises de l'Amérique, données au mois de Février 1719. Et Des Lettres-Patentes du Roi, pour la liberté du Commerce à la Côte de Guinée, Données à Paris au mois de Janvier 1716. Avec les reglements que lidt commerce a occasionnés. Par un Citadin. *A. Avignon.* M. DCC. LXIV. 2 vols., 4to, pp. (8), 615, (1); ... . 19 Maps and Plates. 11812

Reprinted with the following title:

CH[AMBON] (M.) Le guide du commerce de l'Amérique, principalement par le port de Marseille. Contenant le detail de la découverte de l'Amerique, et de l'établissement des Européens dans cette partie du monde. Celui des Isles Antilles et de leurs productions. Le recueil des lettres patentes, &c. Ouvrage utile aux negocians qui font ce commerce et aux personnes curieuses de connoitre l'histoire de nos colonies. Par M. Ch..... de Marseille. *Marseilles: Jean Mossy.* 1777. 2 vols., 4to. 19 Maps, and Plates. 11813

Again reprinted with the following title:

C[HAMBON]. Traité général du Commerce de l'Amérique. Contenant l'histoire des découvertes des Européens dans cette Partie du Monde, son étendue, ses productions. La description & le commerce des Côtes de Guinée, de Malaguete, d'Ivoire, d'Or, de la Barre de Juda, des Royaumes d'Andra, Benin, Loanga, Congo, Angola, la Caffrerie, Cap de Bonne-Espérance, &c. Les Mœurs des Negres & des Eslaves; l'état des Marchandises propres à ce commerce; les précautions à prendre dans l'achat des Esclaves, avec les moyens de les conduire en santé en Amérique. Un Traité sur le commerce des Grains du Royaume & de l'Etranger. Et tous les Edits, Déclarations, Lettres Patentes & Réglemens concernant les differentes branches de Commerce. Ouvrage utile aux Négocians, Jurisconsultes, Gens d'affaire, & autres. Orné de figures et cartes géographiques. Par M. C**. Ancien Receveur des Fermes du Roi. ... *Amsterdam: Chez Marc-Michel Rey. Marseille: Jean Mossy.* M. DCC. LXXXIII. 2 vols., 4to, 4 l., pp. 661, (1); 4 l., 618, (1). 12 Plates and 12 Maps. BA. 11814

An important work for the colonial history of America, containing all the French laws, ordinances, etc., for the colonial and slave trade. In Vol. II. is a curious account (with plates) of the "Culture et Usage de Coton," the production of sugar, etc. I have an MS. note by Winthrop Sargent, in which he refers to an edition dated 1787, which is perhaps an error.

· Chambre des Deputés. Documents communiqués à l'appui du projet de loi relatif au traité du 4 Juillet 1831 avec les Etats-Unis. *Paris.* 1835. 2 vols., 4to. 11815

CHAMFORT (Sébastien Roch Nicolas). La jeune indienne, comédie en un acte et en vers ... . Par Mr. de Chamfort. *Paris: N. B. Duchesne.* M. DCC. LXXI. 8vo, pp. 24. BA. + *Paris.* 1774. 8vo. + *Paris.* 1777. 11816

First edition, *Paris.* 1764. 8vo. "La scène est à Charlestown, Colonie Angloise, de l'Amérique Septentrionale." Also in Tome IV. of the "Œuvres complètes de Chamfort ... publiées ... par P. R. Auguis. ... *Paris: Chaumerot jeune.* 1824–25." 5 vols., 8vo, (BA.); in "Répertoire général du Théatre français. *Paris: H. Nicolle.* M. DCCC. XVIII." 18mo, pp. 87–117, (H.); in Tome IV. of his "Œuvres ... publiées par ... [Ginguené] ... . *Paris.* An III" [1795]. 4 vols., 8vo, and probably in the editions of *Paris: Colnet.* 1808. 2 vols., 8vo, and *Paris: Maradan.* 1812. 2 vols., 8vo.

CHAMISSO (Louis Charles A. von). Adelbert von Chamisso's Werke. Vierte Auflage. ... *Berlin: Weidmannsche Buchhandlung.* 1856. 6 vols., 16mo. B. 11817

Vol. I. contains, "Reise um die Welt mit der Romanzoffischen Entdeckungs-Expedition in den Jahren 1815–18," which first appeared as the third volume of O. von Kotzbue's "Entdeckungs-Reise in die Süd-See und nach Bering-Strasse; zur Erforschung einer nördöstliclichen Durchfahrt. ... *Weimar: Hoffmann.* 1821." 3 vols., 4to. B. The previous editions of Chamisso's "Werke" were, *Leipzig: Weidmann.* 1836–40. 6 vols., 12mo. + [*Ibid.*] 1842. 6 vols., 16mo. [*Ibid.*] 1852. 6 vols., 16mo. This third volume has a second title:

CHAMISSO. Bemerkungen und Ansichten auf einer Entdeckungs-Reise ... 1815–1818 ... auf dem Schiffe Rurick unter dem Befehle des Lieutenants ... Otto von Kotzebue ... . *Weimar.* 1821. 4to, Title, pp. 240, 1 l. folded. 13 Plates, 2 Maps.

CHAMPAGNAC (Jean Baptiste Joseph). Le jeune voyageur en Californie; récits instructifs et moraux. *Paris: Lebuby.* 1852. 12mo. 8 colored Vignettes. 11819

Also: Le trésor des voyages. *Paris: Lebuby.* 1842. 12mo. + Nouvelle édition. *Paris: Ducrocq.* 1865. 12mo, pp. 288. 4 Engravings.

CHAMPAGNAC *and* OLIVIER. Le voyageur de la jeunesse dans les cinq parties du monde ... . *Paris: Morizot.* 1850. 8vo. 22 Engravings. 11820

CHAMPAGNAC *and* OLIVIER. Voyage autour du monde, contenant la description géographique et pittoresque des divers pays

... . Par MM. Champagnac et Olivier. *Paris: Morizot.* 1857. 8vo, pp. viii, 645. 22 Engravings. 11821

CHAMPAGNAC *and* OLIVIER. Reis om de wereld. ... Naar het Fransch, door J. Bakker Korff. *Leiden: D. Noothoven van Goor.* 1864–66. 8vo. Colored Plates. 11822

CHAMPAGNY (Jean Baptiste Nompère de), *duc de Cadore.* Letter from M. Champagny, the French Minister to General Armstrong the Minister of the United States at Paris. *Washington.* 1808. 12mo, pp. 7. 11823

CHAMPIGNY. Etat-présent de la Louisiane, avec toutes les particularités de cette Province d'Amérique, Pour servir de Suite à l'Histoire des Etablissemens des Européens dans les Deux Indés [de Raynal]; par le Colonel, Chevalier de Champigny. *La Haye: Frederic Staatman.* MDCCLXXVI. 8vo, pp. 147, (2). BA., H. + *Amsterdam.* 1781. 11824

For a translation, *see* French's "Hist. Coll. of Louisiana," v. 287.

CHAMPIGNY. La Louisaine ensanglantee avec toutes les Particularitees de cette horrible Catastrophe. *Amsterdam.* 1773. 8vo. 11825

CHAMPIGNY. Supplement au Ministere de M. Pitt avec recapitulation exacte de toutes les Demarches de ce sage Politique depuis 1761 jusqu'an 1766. *Paris.* 1766. 8vo. Portrait.

Relates to Pitt's conduct towards America.

CHAMPION (Judah). A Brief View of the Distresses, Hardships and Dangers our Ancestors encountered in Settling New England, etc. In Two Sermons delivered at Litchfield, on the General Fast, April 18, 1770. *Hartford.* 1770. 4to. W.

CHAMPION. Christian and Civil Liberty and Freedom considered and Recommended: | A | Sermon | delivered before the | General Assembly | of the Colony of | Connecticutt | at Hartford | on the day of their | Anniversary Election | May 9th 1776 | By Judah Champion, A.M. | Pastor of the first Church of Christ in Litchfield | ... | *Hartford: | Printed by E. Watson.* 1776. | 12mo, pp. 81. 11828

[CHAMPION (J.)] Reflections on the State of Parties; on the National Debt, and the Necessity and Expediency of the Present War with America. *London: W. Davis.* M,DCC,XLVII [*i. e.* M,DCC,LXXVI]. 8vo, 2 l., pp. 64. 11829

Reprinted with the following title:

CHAMPION. Reflections on the State of Parties; on the National Debt, and the Necessity and Expediency of Suppressing the American Rebellion. By J. Champion. The Second Edition. *London: W. Davis.* M,DCC,XLVI [*i. e.* M,DCC,LXXVI]. 8vo, 2 l., pp. 64. 11830

CHAMPION (R.) Comparative Reflections on the Past and Present Political, Commercial and Civil State of Great Britain: with some Thoughts concerning Emigration. By Richard Champion, Esq. *London: J. Debrett.* 1787. 8vo. S. 11831

See M. R., LXXVII. 313.

[CHAMPION.] Considerations | on the | Present Situation | of | Great Britain | and the | United States | of | North America, | with a View to their future | Commercial Connexions; | particularly designed | To expose the dangerous Tendency of the Arguments | used, and of the Conclusions drawn in a late Pamphlet | published by Lord Sheffield, &c. *London: Printed for John Stockdale.* M DCC LXXIV. 8vo, pp. viii, 3–157. H. 11832

"This writer particularly recommends the cultivation of a close commercial union with the American States, which he considers as still practicable."—M. R., LXX. 233. In the second edition described below, the author adds his name.

CHAMPION. Considerations on the present Situation of Great Britain and the United States of America, with a view to their future Commercial Connexions. Containing remarks upon the Pamphlet published by Lord Sheffield, entitled, "Observations on the Commerce of the American States;" and also on the Act of Navigation, so far as it relates to those States. Interspersed with some Observations upon the State of Canada, Nova Scotia, and the Fisheries; and upon the Connexion of the West Indies with America: Together with various Accounts, necessary to shew the State of the Trade and Shipping of both Countries. The Second Edition, with great Additions. To which is now first added, the Plan of an Act of Parliament for the Establishment and Regulation of our Trade with the American States. Also, a Preface, Containing Remarks upon the Authorities on which Lord Sheffield has formed the principal Part of his Observations. By Richard Champion, Esq., Late Deputy Paymaster General of his Majesty's Forces. *London: John Stockdale.* MDCCLXXXIV. 8vo, pp. xxxiv, 274, 36. PA., C.

CHAMPLAIN (S.) Des Savvages, | ov, | Voyage de Samvel | Champlain, de Brovage, | fait en la France nouuelle, | l'an mil six cens trois: | Contenant | Les mœurs, façon de viuve, mariages

guerres, & habi- | tations des Sauuages de Canadas. | De la descouuerte de plus de quatre cens cinquante | lieuës dans le païs des Sauuages. Quels peuples y ha- | bitent des animaux qui s'y trouuent, des riuieres, | lacs, isles & terres, & quels arbres & fruicts elles produisent. | De la coste d' Arcadie, des terres que l'on y a descouuer- | tes, & de plusieurs mines qui y sont, selon le rapporte | des Sauuages. | *A Paris,* | *Chez Clavde de Monstrœil, tenant sa* | *boutique en la Cour du Palais, au nom de Iesus.* | Avec privilege dv Roy. | Sm 8vo, Dedication and Table, 3 l., Text, 36 l. J.C.B.

The privilege on the reverse of the title is dated *November* 15, 1603:

CHAMPLAIN. Les Voyages | dv Sievr de Champlain | Xaintongeois, Capitaine | ordinaire pour le Roy, | en la marine. | Divisez en Devx Livres. | ou, | Iovrnal tres-fidele des Observa- | tions faites és descouuertures de la Nouuelle France: tant en la descri- | ptiõ des terres, costes, riuieres, ports, haures, leurs hauteurs, & plusieurs | declinaisons de la guide-aymant; qu' eñ la creãce des peuples, leur super- | stition, façon de viure & de guerroyer: enrichi de quantité de figures. | Ensemble deux cartes geografiques: la premiere seruant à la na- | uigation, dressée selon les compas qui nordestent, sur lesquels | les mariniers nauigent: l'autre en son vray Meridien, auec ses | longitudes & latitudes: à laquelle est adiousté le voyage du | destroict qu'ont troué les Anglois, au dessus de Labrador, | depuis le 53e. degré de latitude, iusques au 63e. en l'an 1612. | cerchans vn chemin par le Nord, pour aller à la Chine. | *A Paris,* | *Chez Iean Berjon, rue S. Iean de Beauuais, au Cheual* | *volant, & en sa boutique au Palais, à la gallerie* | *des prisonniers.* | M. DC. XIII. | Avec Privilege dv Roy. | 4to, 10 l. pp. 325, (5), Quatriesme Voyage fait en l'année 1613, pp. 1–52. 8 Maps and 4 Plates, several Plates in the Text. M.

The copies of this edition vary in the maps. Mr. Lenox's copy differs from that in the New York Historical Society. Sometimes in one map there are more references than in the other, and the spelling of the references varies. The large map to this edition is usually in two parts, and is very often wanting or defective.

CHAMPLAIN. Voyages | et descovvertvres | faites en la Novvelle | France, depuis l'année 1615. iusques | à la fin de l'année 1618. | Par le Sieur de Champlain, Cappitaine | ordinaire pour le Roy en la Mer du Ponant. | Où sont descrits les mœurs, coustumes, habits, | façons de guerroyer, chasses, dances, festins, & | enterrements de diuers peuples Sauuages, & de | plusieurs choses remarquables qui luy sont arri- | uées audit païs, auec vne description de la beau- | té, fertilité, & temperature d'iceluy. | *A Paris,* | *Chez Clavde Collet, au Palais, en la* | *gallerie des Prisonniers.* |

M. D. C. XIX. | Auec Priuelege du Roy. | Sm. 8vo, 8 l., including an Engraved and Printed Title, 158 l. 6 Plates, viz.: 2 double folded Plates and 4 printed in the Text. M. 11836

"Première édition de cette relation, fort rare."—BRUNET.

CHAMPLAIN. Voyages et descovvertvres | faites en la Novvelle France, depuis l'année 1615. iusques | à la fin de l'année 1618. | Par le Sieur de Champlain, cappitaine | ordinaire pour le roy en la mer de Ponant. | Où sont descrits les mœurs, coustumes, habits, | façons de guerroyer, chasses, dances, festins, & | enterrements de diuers peuples Sauuages, et de | plusieurs choses remarquables qui luy sont arri- | uées audit païs, auec vne description de la beau- | té, fertilité, et temperature d'iceluy. | *Paris:* | *chez Clavde Collet, au Palais, en la gallerie des Prisonniers.* | MDCXX. | Sm. 8vo, 8 l., 158 l. 6 Plates. 13837

This edition differs from that of 1619 only in the date, on the printed title-page.

CHAMPLAIN. Les | Voyages | du Sr de Cha- | mplain Capita- | ine ordinaire | pour le Roy | en la nouuelle | France es an- | nees. 1615, | et 1618, | dedies au | Roy. | *chez C. Collet, au* | *Pallais a Paris.* | 1619. | Auec preuilege du Roy. | [Printed Title.] Voyages | et Descovvertvres | faites en la Novvelle | France, depuis l'année 1615. iusques | à la fin de l'année 1618. | Par le Sieur de Champlain, Cappitai- | ne ordinaire pour le Roy en la Mer du Ponant. | Où sont descrits les mœurs, coustumes, habits | façons de guerroyer, chasses, dances, festins, & | enterrements de diuers peuples Sauuages, & de | plusieurs choses remarquables qui luy sont arri- | uées au dit païs, auec vne description de la beau- | té, fertilité, & temperature d'iceluy. | Seconde Edition. | *A Paris,* | *Chez Clavde Collet, au Palais, en la* | *gallerie des Prisonniers.* | M.D.C.XXVII. | Avec Privilege dv Roy. | Sm. 8vo, 8 l., 158 l. 2 folded Copperplates, and 4 in the text. H. 11838

The printed title-page, the epistle, and preface, have been reprinted. The engraved title and text are identical with the issue of 1619 and 1620. Priced, by Muller, $15, Nuggets, £4 4s.

CHAMPLAIN. Les | Voyages | de la | Novvelle France | Occidentale, dicte | Canada, | faits par le Sr de Champlain | Xainctongeois, Capitaine pour le Roy en la Marine du | Ponant, & toutes les Descouuertes qu'il a faites en | ce païs depuis l'an 1603. iusques en l'an 1629. | Où se voit comme ce pays a esté premierement descouuert par les François, | sous l'authorité de nos Roys tres-Chrestiens, iusques au regne | de sa Majesté à present regnante Lovis XIII. | Roy de France & de Nauarre. | Auec vn traitté des

qualitez & conditions requises à vn bon & parfaict Nauigateur | pour cognoistre la diuersité des Estimes qui se font en la Nauigation; Les | Marques & enseignements que la prouidence de Dieu à mises dans les Mers | pour redresser les Mariniers en leur routte, sans lesquelles ils tomberoient en | de grands dangers, Et la maniere de bien dresser Cartes marines auec leurs | Ports, Radés, Isles, Sondes, & autre chose necessaire à la Nauigation. | Ensemble vne Carte generalle de la description dudit pays faicte en son Meridien selon | la declinaison de la guide Aymant, & vn Catechisme ou Instruction traduicte | du François au langage des peuples Sauuages de quelque contrée, auec | ce qui s'est passé en ladite Nouuelle France en l'année 1631. | A Monseignevr le Cardinal Dvc De Richeliev. | *A Paris.* | *Chez Clavde Collet au Palais, en la Gallerie des Prisonniers,* | *à l'Estoille d'Or.* | M.DC.XXXII. | Auec Priuilege du Roy. | 4to, pp. 16, 308; Seconde Partie, pp. 310; 1 l. blank; Table, pp. 8; Traité, pp. 54; 1 l. blank; Doctrine Chrestienne, etc., pp. 20; Map, Nouuelle France, 1632, 2 sheets, 35 x 21 inches. BA., C., H., N. 11839

The best edition. Stevens' Nuggets, No. 511, describes a copy which contains the objectionable passage on page 27, which caused the two leaves, Dij and Diij, to be cancelled and reprinted. We usually find that the first paragraph on page 27 ends with the words "telles descouuertes," but in the original issue it reads, "telles descouuertes; ce que n'ont pas les grands hommes d'estat, qui sçauent mieux manier et conduire le gouuernement et l'administration d'vn Royaume, que celle de la nauigation, des expeditions d'outres mer, et des pays loingtains, pour ne l'auoir iamais practique." Mr. Tross has reproduced the two maps in admirable facsimile. These often take the place of the original map. There are at least three variations in the imprint of this edition; one is *A Paris* | *Chez Pierre* | *Le-Mvr, dans la grand Salle* | *du Palais.* | Another is, *Paris: Lovis Sevestre;* they are not alike in other respects. Collet's has a map smaller and entirely different from the others, "faict par le Sieur de Champlain suivant les memoires de P. du Val-en l'Isle du Palais." It has the two leaves 29–30, without the passage supposed to refer to Richelieu, and, what is remarkable, the two cancelled leaves are inserted in another part of the volume. In Sevestre and Le Mvr's imprint the map is "Faict l'an 1632 par le Sieur de Champlain," and is larger than in Collet's.

CHAMPLAIN. [Title as in No. 11839.] *Paris: chez Claude Collet au mont Sainct Hilaire près les Puits.* | M.DC.XL. | Avec Priulege dv Roy. | 11840

This is the same work, with a new title-page only. Mr. Lenox, to whom I am indebted for most of the notes to Champlain, suggests that this edition probably consists of the rejected copies of the edition of 1632, because the volume has the cancelled leaves only, cut through with some sharp instrument. The titles of 1, 2, and 3 (Collet, Le Mvr, and Sevestre) are alike, except in the imprints (1640), the length of the lines and the spelling vary from 1, 2, and 3.

CHAMPLAIN. Voyages de Sieur de Champlain, ou Journal ès découvertes de la Nouvelle France. *Paris: Imprimé aux frais du gouvernement pour procurer du travail aux ouvriers typo-*

graphes. Aôut 1830. 2 vols., 8vo, pp. x, 406; 2 l., pp. 387. BA., C. 11841

Only two hundred and fifty copies printed, to give employment to the journeymen printers, and principally distributed among the public libraries in France by order of the government.

CHAMPLAIN. Narrative of a Voyage to the West Indies and Mexico in the Years 1599–1602, With Maps and Illustrations. By Samuel Champlain. Translated from the Original and Unpublished Manuscript, with a Biographical Notice and Notes by Alice Wilmere, Edited by Norton Shaw. *London: Printed for the Hakluyt Society.* M.DCCC,LVII. 8vo. 3 l., pp. xcix, 48. 10 Plates, and Map. BA., C. 11842

The project of uniting the Atlantic and Pacific Oceans is set forth in this volume.

CHAMPLAIN. Report on the Property of the Champlain Copper Mining Company of Canada East, with the By-Laws of the Company. *Boston: Davis & Farmer, Printers.* 1864. 8vo, pp. 15. Map. H. 11843

Champlain Valley Horticultural Society: Proceedings of Convention. *Burlington, Vt.* 1851. 11844

CHAMPLIN (*Rev.* James). Early Biography, Travels and Adventures: written by Himself. Second Edition. *Columbus, Ohio.* 1842. 12mo. S. 11845

[CHAMPNEY (Julius B.)] History of the Champney Family, containing Biographical Sketches, Letters, Reminiscences, etc. Illustrated. *Chicago: P. L. Hanscom & Co., Printers.* 1867. 8vo, pp. 76. 11846

CHAMPNEYS (B.) An address on the Life and Character of the late Francis R. Shunk. By Benjamin Champneys. *Lancaster: M. D. Holbrook.* 1849. 8vo, pp. 32. 11847

CHAMPNEYS. Oration, before the Literary Societies of Marshall College, Penn., in 1837. By B. Champneys. *Lanaster.* 8vo. 11848

CHAMPNEYS (J.) An Account of the Suffering and Persecution of John Champneys, a Native of South Carolina, inflicted by order of Congress, for his refusal to take up Arms in Defence of the arbitrary proceedings carried on by the Rulers of the said place. Together with his Protest, &c. [n. p.] 1778. 8vo, pp. 20. 11849

A person similarly situated to the Philadelphia Quakers. *See* Pennsylvania, "An Address," etc., 1777.

CHAMPOMIER (P. A.) Statement of the Sugar Crop made in Louisiana, in 1855–56, With an Appendix. By P. A. Champomier. *New Orleans: printed by Cook, Young & Co.* 1856. 18mo, pp. x, (2), 46, (2). Continued. H. 11850

CHANDLER (A.) Address ... at ... the Nineteenth Annual Fair of The American Institute, of the City of New York ... October 23, 1846. By Adoniram Chandler. *New York.* 1846. 8vo, pp. 18. BA. 11851

Also: Oration before the New York Typographical Society, on the Seventeenth Anniversary, July 4, 1816. *New York.* 1816. 8vo. N.

CHANDLER (A.) A Brief Review of a Historical Sermon, delivered at Deerfield, Mass., Sept. 22, 1857, by Rev. Samuel Williard, D.D. by Rev. A. Chandler, D.D. *Greenfield: S. S. Eastman & Company, Printers.* 1859. 8vo, pp. 27. H. 11852

CHANDLER (Amariah). A Discourse delivered July 4, 1833, in ... Greenfield, By A. Chandler. ... *Greenfield: Press of Franklin Freeman.* 1833. 8vo, pp. 25, ii. H. 11853

Also: Sermon at the Installation of Andrew Govan. *Greenfield.* 1839. 8vo.—Thoughts on Speculative Free-masonry. *Danville, Vt.* 1835. 12mo.

CHANDLER (C. F.) Report on Water for Locomotives and Boiler Incrustations: made to the President and Directors of the New York and Central Railroad. By Charles F. Chandler, M.D., ... *New York: printed by John F. Trow & Co.* 1865. 8vo, pp. 35. H. 11854

Contains analysis of waters at different places along the railroad. Also: Dangerous Kerosene. Reports ... to the Metropolitan Board of Health, New York. [*New York.* 1869.] 4to, pp. 8. H.—Report on the Saratoga Seltzer Spring, ... *New York.* 1867. 4to, pp. 4.

CHANDLER (E. M.) Essays, Philanthropic and Moral, by Elizabeth M. Chandler; principally relating to the Abolition of Slavery in America ... . *Philadelphia: Lemuel Howell.* 1835. 12mo, pp. 120. 11855

CHANDLER. The Poetical Works of Elizabeth M. Chandler. With a Memoir of her Life and Character, by Benjamin Lundy ... . *Philadelphia: Lemuel Howell.* 1836. 12mo, pp. 180.

CHANDLER (Henry C.) & Co. Illinois Directory. *See* Illinois.

CHANDLER (I.) New Converts exhorted to cleave to the Lord. Sermon preached July 30, 1740, at a Wednesday-Evening Lecture in Charlestown ... at the Motion and by the Desire of Rev. Mr. Whitefield. By Rev. Isaac Chandler. *Boston.* 1740. 8vo, pp. 43. M. 11857

CHANDLER (J.) An Answer to Mr. Tucker's Letter to Mr. Chandler. Relative ... to ... his Sermon preached at Newbury-Port, June 25, 1727, preparatory to their settling of a Minister. By James Chandler ... . *Boston: printed by Edes & Gill, for Bulkeley Emerson, Of Newbury-Port.* 1767. 8vo, pp. 36. BA.

CHANDLER (J. A.) The Speech ... on the Policy of the State [Virginia] with respect to her Slave Population. ... *Richmond: Thomas W. White, Printer.* 1832. 8vo, pp. 10. B.

CHANDLER (J.) Christians warned of Temptation, and exhorted to Pray ... . Two Sermons, Preach'd at Rowley, West-Parish ... Feb. 10, 1754. By James Chandler ... . *Boston: S. Kneeland.* 1754. 8vo, 2 l., pp. ii, 26. B., BA., M. 11860

CHANDLER. A Serious Address to Part of the Congregational Church in Newbury-Port, which ... attended ... Worship ... in the Court-House. Occasioned By Two Letters published By the Rev. Mr. John Tucker, To make void, in Part, a Sermon preached to Said Church on their solemn Fast, June 25. 1767. It contains also, An Account of the dividing of Said Church and Parish into two Christian Societies. By James Chandler ... . *Boston, N. E.: Printed by Edes & Gill for Bulkeley Emerson, of Newbury-Port.* 1768. 8vo, pp. 38. BA., H.

Also: ... Sermon at the Ordination of Rev. Thomas Lancaster, Scarborough, Nov. 8, 1776. ... *Portsmouth.* 1776. 8vo, pp. 23.

CHANDLER. ... A Sermon preached at Newbury-Port, June 25, 1767. A Fast, sanctified by the Congregational-Church and Society there, under Bereavement of their Pastor. ... By James Chandler, A.M. ... *Boston: Printed by Edes & Gill for Buckley [sic] Emerson, of Newbury-Port.* 1767. 8vo, pp. 30.

CHANDLER (J.) Oration delivered at Monmouth, Me., July 4, 1804. By Joseph Chandler. *Portland.* 1804. 8vo, pp. 15.

CHANDLER (J. R.) Address of the Hon. Joseph R. Chandler, at the Celebration of the Landing of the Pilgrims of Maryland, at the Site of St. Mary's City, May 15, 1855. ... *Baltimore.* 1855. 8vo, pp. 40. 11864

Another edition has the following title:

CHANDLER. An Oration delivered at the fourth Commemoration of the Landing of the Pilgrims of Maryland, Celebrated May 15, 1855, under the Auspices of the Philodemic Society of Georgetown College. By Hon. Joseph R. Chandler, ... To which is prefixed a Notice of the Proceedings at the Celebration. *Philadelphia.* 1855. 8vo, pp. 62. P. 11865

CHANDLER. "The Pilgrims of the Rock." An Oration delivered in the First Congregational Church, before the Society of the Sons of New England, of Philadelphia, at their Second Anniversary, ... 22d December, 1845. By Joseph R. Chandler, .. . *Philadelphia: printed by John C. Clark.* 1846. 8vo, pp. 31.

Also: An Address Delivered on the occasion of placing the Crowning Stone of the Main Building of the Girard College for Orphans, August 29th, 1846. ... *Philadelphia.* 1846. 8vo, pp. 22. — Address, ... Pennsylvania Peace Society, ... 1829. *Philadelphia.* 1829. 8vo. — Address before Marshall College, Sept. 24, 1839. ... *Philadelphia.* 1839. c. — Address before the "Girard Brotherhood" ... *Philadelphia.* 1855. c. — Masonic Discourses. ... *Philadelphia.* 1844. 8vo. — An Oration delivered at the Laying of the Corner Stone of a Monument on Mount Zion In Ephrata, Lancaster County, Pennsylvania, September 11, 1845. ... *Philadelphia.* 1845. 8vo, pp. 32. H. — Public Schools of Washington. Address ... Aug. 1, 1850. [With Historical Sketch by G. J. Abbot.] *Washington.* 1850. 8vo, pp. 23. B. — Sanctity of National Pledges. Speech ... on the Bill to organize Territorial Government in Nebraska. ... House ... April, 1854. [*Washington.* 1854.] 8vo, pp. 7. BA. — Speech ... on the Admission of California ... in the ... March 28, 1850. *Washington.* 1850. 8vo, pp. 15. BA., H. — Speech ... on the Collins line of American Steamers. ... July 6, 1852. ... *Washington: printed by Jno. Towers.* 1852. 8vo, pp. 28. H. — The Temporal Power of the Pope. A Full and Authentic Report of the Brilliant Speech of the Hon. Joseph R. Chandler, of Pennsylvania, in the House of Representatives of the United States. January, 1855. *Philadelphia: published by H. & C. M'Grath.* 1855. 8vo, pp. 32. H. + *Washington.* [n. d.] 8vo, pp. 11.

CHANDLER (L. H.), *of Virginia.* Speech of the Hon. Lucius H. Chandler, of Virginia, in the House of Representatives of the United States, in Defence of his Claim to a Seat in that body. ... [1864.] 8vo, pp. 23. B. 11867

CHANDLER (P. W.) American Criminal Trials. By Peleg W. Chandler. ... *Boston: Charles C. Little and James Brown. London: A. Maxwell.* MDCCCXLI. ‖ Volume II. *Boston: Timothy H. Carter and Company. London: A. Maxwell.* MDCCCXLIV. 2 vols., 12mo, pp. xii, 436; viii, 387. BA., C., H. 11868

Includes an account of the trials of Zenger, Leisler, Major André, Joshua Hett, New York Negro Plot, Boston Massacre, etc. Vol. II. is scarce.

CHANDLER. The Morals of Freedom. An Oration ... Boston, July 4, 1844. By Peleg W. Chandler. *Boston.* 1844. 8vo, pp. 54. BA., H. 11869

Also: Argument in Favor of the Proposed Consolidation of the Western and Worcester Railroad Corporations, before the Committee on Railways and Canals, March

16th, 1864. By Peleg W. Chandler. *Boston: Press of Geo. C. Rand & Avery.* 8vo, pp. 29. H. — The Bankrupt Law of the United States, with an Outline of the System; together with the Rules and Forms in Massachusetts, and References to Recent Decisions. ... *Boston: James H. Weeks.* 1842. 16mo, pp. vi, 102.

CHANDLER (S.) The History of Persecution, in Four Parts, ... IV. Amongst Protestants. By Samuel Chandler. With a Preface, containing Remarks on Dr. Roger's Vindication of the Civil Establishment of Religion. *London.* 1736. 8vo. Plates. + Edited by Chas. Atmore. *Hull.* 1813. 8vo. 11870

"Of persecution in New England" in the edition of 1813, pp. 354-360.

CHANDLER. Sermon preached at Gloucester, Nov. 29, 1759. Anniversary Thanksgiving. *Boston.* [n. d.] 8vo, pp. 30. M.

CHANDLER (S.) A Discourse in Shirley, Feb. 1, 1841, at the Interment of Mr. Stillman S. H. Parker, Who died in St. Mary's, Geo., Jan. 18, 1841. By Seth Chandler ... . *Fitchburg: W. J. Merriam, Printer.* 1841. 8vo, pp. 24. BA., H.

CHANDLER (T. B.) An Appeal to the Public, in Behalf of the Church of England in America. By Thomas Bradbury Chandler, D.D., Rector of St. John's Church, in Elizabeth Town, New Jersey, and Missionary from the Society for the Propagation of the Gospel, &c. ... *New York: Printed by James Parker.* M,DCC,LXVII. 8vo, 2 l., pp. xi, (1), 127. BA., C. + Second Edition, corrected by the Author. ... *New York: Printed; London: Reprinted for John and Francis Rivington.* MDCCLXIX. 8vo, pp. xi, (1), 118. H. 11873

CHANDLER. The Appeal Defended; or, The Proposed American Episcopate Vindicated, ... In Answer to The Objections and Misrepresentations of Dr. Chauncy and Others. By Thomas Bradbury Chandler, D.D. ... *New York: Printed by Hugh Gaine.* 1769. 8vo, 2 l., pp. v, (1), 268. BA., H., P. 11874

CHANDLER. The Appeal farther defended; in Answer to the Farther Misrepresentations of Dr. Chauncy. By Thomas B. Chandler, D.D. ... *New York: Printed by Hugh Gaine.* M,DCC,LXXI. 8vo, pp. vi, (1), 240. BA., C. 11875

This was answered by the following:

CHANDLER. A Letter concerning an American Bishop, &c. to Dr. Bradbury Chandler, Ruler of St. John's Church, in Elizabeth-Town. In Answer to the Appendices Of His Appeal to the Public, &c. *Printed A D.* 1768. 8vo, pp. 19. P.

A number of pieces on the subject of an American Episcopate, are included in the "American Whig." The discussion was somewhat heated. *See* the works of Apthorp, Chauncy (C.), Johnson (S.), Inglis, Mayhew, Secker, and others.

[CHANDLER.] An Appendix to the American edition of the Life of Archibald Secker; containing His Grace's Letter to the Rev. Mr. Macclanechan, on the irregularity of his conduct; with an introductory narrative. *New York: H. Gaine.* 1774.

CHANDLER. A Free Examination of the Critical Commentary on Archbishop Secker's Letter to Mr. Walpole; To which is added, By way of Appendix, A Copy of Bishop Sherlock's Memorial. By Thomas B. Chandler, D.D. *New York: Hugh Gaine.* M.DCC.LXXIV. 8vo, pp. xii, 122, 1 l. 11878

CHANDLER. The Life of Samuel Johnson, D.D., The First President of King's College, in New York, Containing many interesting anecdotes; A General View of the State of Religion and Learning in Connecticut during the former part of the last Century; and an Account of the Institution and Rise of Yale College, Connecticut; and of King's (now Columbia) College, New-York. By Thomas Bradbury Chandler, D.D., ... To which is added an Appendix, containing Many original Letters, never before published, from Bishop Berkeley, Archbishop Secker, Bishop Lowth and others, to Dr. Johnson. *New York: T. & F. Swords.* 1805. 12mo, 4 l., pp. 208. C. + *London.* 1824. 8vo. 11879

CHANDLER. A Sermon preached before the Corporation For the Relief of the Widows and Children of Clergymen, in the Communion of the Church of England in America; At their Anniversary Meeting on October 2d, 1771, at Perth-Amboy. To which is Annexed A brief Abstract of their Proceedings. By Thomas B. Chandler, D.D. ... Sold for the Benefit of the Fund *Burlington: Printed by Isaac Collins.* [n. d.] 8vo, 2 l., pp. 76. P. 11880

Dedicated to Gov. Franklin. The abstract is interesting.

[CHANDLER.] The Strictures on the Friendly Address examined, and a refutation of its principles attempted. Addressed to the People of America. *Printed in the Year* 1775. 8vo, pp. 14. + [Another edition.] *Philadelphia.* 1775. 8vo. P.

[CHANDLER.] What think ye of the Congress Now? Or, an Enquiry, how far the Americans Are bound to abide by, and execute, the Decisions of the late Continental Congress. With a Plan, By Samuel Galloway, Esq; for a Proposed Union between Great-Britain and the Colonies. To which is added, An Alarm to the Legislature of the Province of New-York. Occa-

sioned by the present Political Disturbances. Addressed to the Representatives in General Assembly convened. *New-York: J. Rivington.* 1775. 8vo, pp. 48. + *London: Reprinted for Richardson Urquhart.* 1775. 8vo, Title, pp. 90. W. 11882

"Intended to dissuade the people of New York from concurring with their sister colonies from adhering to the association, etc., of the Congress."—*Monthly Review.* Chandler was born at Woodstock, Conn., graduated at Yale, and ordained in England in 1757. For notice of him, *see* Schroeder's "Memorial of Bishop Hobart. *New York.* 1831." Bishop Lowth speaks very highly of his appeal, etc. He is supposed to have assisted "A. W." (*i. e.* Wilkins) in the letters to Hamilton.

[CHANDLER (T. B.)] Both Sides; or, a Short Chapter of Facts. [n. p. n. d.] 8vo, pp. 4. 11883

A political pamphlet in favor of Martin Van Buren, as opposed to General Zachary Taylor.

CHANDLER (T. P.) Address of Mr. T. P. Chandler, at the Republican Meeting in Brooklyn, Sept. 27, 1860. *Published by order of the Republican State Convention.* 8vo, pp. 4. H. 11884

CHANDLER (W.) A Brief Apology in Behalf of the People in Derision call'd Quakers. Written For the Information of our Sober and Well-Inclined Neighbours in and about the Town of Warminster, in the County of Wilts. By Will. Chandler, Alex. Pyott, Jo. Hodges, And some others. *London Printed, and Re-Printed by Andrew Bradford in Philadelphia.* 1719. 12mo, pp. 104. 11885

Introduced here for the imprint. The first edition is *London: Printed for Thomas Northcott, in George-yard, in Lombard-street.* 1693. Sm. 8vo, 5 sheets.

CHANDLER (W. E.) The Soldier's Right to Vote. Who opposes it? Who favors it? or, the Record of the M'Clellan Copperheads Against allowing the Soldier who Fights, the Right to Vote while Fighting. ... By William E. Chandler, of N. H. *Washington: printed by Lemuel Towers.* 1864. 8vo, pp. 15, (1). H. 11886

Also: Reports of Cases ... in the Supreme Judicial Courts of New-Hampshire. By William E. Chandler, State Reporter. *Concord: published by G. Parker Lyon.* 1861. Vol. XL., 8vo, pp. 618; Vol. XLI., 1861, 8vo, pp. 600. H. (Vol. XL. for years 1859-60; Vol. XLII., 1860-61.)

CHANDLER (Z.) Kansas—Lecompton Constitution. Speech of Hon. Z. Chandler, of Michigan. Delivered in the Senate of the United States, March 12th, 1858. *Washington, D. C.: Buell & Blanchard, Printers.* 1858. 8vo, pp. 16. H. 11887

Also: Conduct of the War. Speech ... in the Senate of the United States .. July 16, 1862. *Washington: Scammel & Co., Printers.* 1862. 8vo, pp. 16. B. — Relations with Great Britain. Speech ... in the ... Senate, April 19, 1869. *Printed at the Congressional Globe Office.* 8vo, pp. 8. H.

CHANDLER *and* NYE (J. W.) Mexico. Speeches of Hon. Z. Chandler, of Michigan, and Hon. James W. Nye, of Nevada, in the U. S. Senate, July 12, 1867, On Maximilian's Decree ordering the Execution of the Liberal Prisoners. [n. p. 1867.] 8vo, pp. 8. H. 11888

CHANDLER. *See* Lichfield and Coventry (*Bishop of*). 1718.

CHANDLESS (W.) A Visit to Salt Lake; being a Journey Across the Plains, and a Residence in the Mormon Settlements at Utah. By William Chandless. *London: Smith, Elder and Co.* 1857. 12mo, pp. xii, 346. Map. C. 11889

Highly commended by the "Critic," "Leader," and "National Review."

Change for the American Notes. *See* Dickens (C.)

The Changery. An Allegoric Memoir of the Boston Exchange Office: or, the Pernicious Progress of Bank Speculation unveiled. By Perspective. *Boston.* 1805. 12mo, pp. 48. H.

CHANGUION (P. J.) Memorie aan den souverainen vorst der Vereenigden Nederlanden [betreffende de overgave van Curaçao aan de Engelschen. n. p. 1814?] 8vo. 11891

CHANGUION. Relaas van het voorgevallen op Curacao, van 22 Dec. 1806 tot 1 Jan. 1807, waarop het in's vijands magt is overgegaan. *'s Hage.* 1808. 8vo, pp. 32. 11892

CHANLER (I.) The Doctrines of Glorious Life unfolded, Defended and Practically Improved, with Appendix containing some Remarks on the Works of Mr. Jas. Foster. By Isaac Chanler, Minister of the Gospel upon Ashley River in South Carolina. *Boston, N. E.: Kneeland and Green.* 1774. 4to.

CHANLER. New Converts exhorted to cleave to the Lord. A Sermon ... Preach'd July 30. 1740. ... in Charlestown ... . With a brief Introduction relating to the Character of ... [Whitefield]. By Isaac Chanler ... . With a Preface by the Reverend Mr. Cooper ... . *Boston: S. Kneeland and T. Green.* 1740. 8vo, pp. (4), iv, (4), 43. B., BA. 11894

CHANLER (J. W.) Down with the Black Flag of Confiscation; up with the Union Jack. Speech of Hon. John W. Chanler, of New York, in the House ... December 10, 1867. ... [*Washington.* 1867.] 8vo, pp. 8. H. 11895

Also: Freedmen's Bureau. Speech ... delivered in the House ... February 3, 1866. *Washington.* 1866. 8vo, pp. 23. H. — This is a White Workingman's Government. Suffrage in the District of Columbia. Speech ... January 12, 1866. 8vo, pp. 14. H.

CHANNING (E. T.) Lectures read to the Seniors in Harvard College, by Edward Tyrrell Channing. *Boston.* 1856. 12mo, pp. xx, 298. H. 11896

Also: "Life of William Ellery." *Boston.* 1836. 12mo. (Forms part of Sparks' "Amer. Biog.," Vol. VI.) — Inaugural Discourse, delivered in the Chapel of the University in Cambridge, December 8, 1819. ... *Cambridge: printed by Hilliard and Metcalf.* 1819. 8vo, pp. 31. H. — An Oration delivered July 4, 1817, at ... Boston ... *Boston.* [1817.] 8vo. pp. 24. BA., W.

CHANNING (G. G.) Early Recollections of Newport, R. I., from the Year 1793 to 1831. By George G. Channing. *Newport, R. I.: A. J. Ward; Charles E. Hammett, Jr.* 1868. 16mo, pp. 284. BA. 11897

CHANNING (H.) ... A Sermon preached at New London, Dec. 20th, 1786, occasioned by the Execution of Hannah Ocuish, a Mulatto girl, aged 12 years and 9 months, for the murder of Eunice Bolles, aged 6 years and 6 months. By Henry Channing, M.A. *New London.* MDCCLXXXVI. 12mo, pp. 31. 11898

CHANNING ... A Sermon ... at New-London, November 27, 1794. Being the day appointed ... For public Thanksgiving In ... Connecticut. By Henry Channing ... . *New-London: printed by Samuel Green.* M,DCCC,XCIV. 8vo, pp. 24. BA.

Also: Sermon at the Funeral of Mrs. Anna Strong, March 22, 1789. *Hartford.* [1789.] 8vo.

CHANNING (W.) A Brief Memoir of Joshua Fisher, M.D. Late President of the Massachusetts Medical Society. From the ... Discourse delivered ... June 5th, 1833. By Walter Channing, D.D., M.M.S. [n. p. n. d.] 8vo, pp. 9. H. 11900

CHANNING. Memoir of the Late Enoch Hall, M.D. ... By Walter Channing, M.D. *Boston: David Clapp, Printer.* 1848. 8vo, pp. 12. Portrait. H. 11901

CHANNING. My own Times, or 'tis Fifty Years since. ... A Lecture ... January, 1845. By Walter Channing, M.D. [n. p. n. d.] 8vo, pp. 34. B. 11902

CHANNING. Sketch of the Life and Character of John D. Fisher, M.D. By Walter Channing, M.D. [Colophon:] *Boston.* 1850. 8vo, pp. 7. H. 11903

CHANNING. Thoughts on the Origin, Nature, Principles and Prospects of the Temperance Reform. By Walter Channing, M.D. From the American Quarterly Observer. *Boston.* 1834. 8vo, pp. 27. BA. 11904

CHANNING. A Topographical Sketch of Nahant, with comparative meteorological tables for July, August, and September, 1820, with some observations on its advantages as a Watering place. By Walter Channing, M.D. [n. p. 1821.] 8vo, pp. 16.

Evidently an article from some magazine, separately printed. Also: An Address on the Prevention of Pauperism. ... *Boston.* 1848. 12mo, pp. 84. H. — Annual Address delivered before the Massachusetts Temperance Society, May 29, 1836. ... With the Annual Report of the Council of the Society, for the same Year. *Boston: printed by John Ford.* 1836. 8vo, pp. 13. H. + Third Edition. 1836. 8vo, pp. 16. + Sixth Edition. 1836. 8vo, pp. 16. H. — Parliamentary Sketches and Water Statistics. Being Another Word addressed to the Citizens of Boston, in support of supplying the City with the Pure Water of Long Pond. ... *Boston: Benjamin H. Greene.* 1845. 8vo, pp. 28. B. — A Plea for Pure Water: Being a Letter to Henry Williams, Esq., by Walter Channing: with an Address "to the Citizens of Boston," by Mr. H. Williams. *Boston: S. N. Dickinson, Printer.* [1844.] 8vo, pp. 39. B. — Thoughts on Peace and War. An Address delivered before the American Peace Society, at its Annual Meeting, May 27, 1844. *Boston.* 1844. 8vo. pp. 38. H.

CHANNING (W. Ellery). An Address on Temperance, by William E. Channing. *Boston: Weeks, Jordan & Company.* 1837. 8vo, pp. 119. H. 11906

Including an appendix, containing a "Report of the Council of the Massachusetts Temperance Society," and a description of the "Fourth Simultaneous Anniversary Meeting at the Odeon, Boston, Feb. 28, 1837."

CHANNING. Channing sa vie et ses œuvres avec une préface de M. Charles De Rémusat. *Paris: Didier et Ce.* 1857. 8vo, Title, pp. xvii, 404. 11907

CHANNING. Discourses, Reviews, and Miscellanies, by William Ellery Channing. *Boston: published by Gray and Bowen.* M DCCC XXX. 8vo, pp. ix, 603, (1). BA., H. + *Boston: Charles Bowen.* 1832. 12mo, pp. viii, 279, (1). BA. 11908

Some copies of the edition of 1830 has the publishers, *Carter and Hendee.*

CHANNING. A Discourse Preached at the Dedication of the Second Congregational Unitarian Church, New York, December 7, 1826. By William Ellery Channing. *New York.* 1826. 8vo, pp. 57, (1). H. + Second Edition. *New York.* 1827. 8vo, pp. 57. + Third Edition. + Fourth Edition. *New York.* 12mo. B., H. 11909

Also: A Review of ... Dr. Channing's Discourse, ... at the Dedication of the Second Congregational Unitarian Church, New York, Dec. 7, 1826. *Boston: Hilliard, Gray, Little, and Wilkins.* 1827. 8vo, pp. 91. H.

CHANNING. Emancipation: by William E. Channing. *Boston: E. P. Peabody.* 1840. 18mo, pp. 111. BA., H. + *New York.* 1841. 18mo, pp. 71. + *London: C. Fox.* 1841. 18mo, pp. 60. BA., H. 11910

CHANNING. A Letter to the Abolitionists, by William E. Channing. With Comments. ... *Boston: printed by Isaac Knapp.* 1837. 16mo, pp. 32. H. 11911

CHANNING. A Letter to the Hon. Henry Clay, on the Annexation of Texas to the United States. By William E. Channing. *Boston: James Munroe and Company.* 1837. 12mo, pp. 72. BA. + (Reprinted from the Fourth Boston Edition.) *Glasgow: James Hedderwick & Son.* 1837. 12mo, pp. 52. B. + Fifth Edition. *Boston.* 1837. 12mo. + Eleventh Edition. [*Ibid.*] 11912

CHANNING. Carta al Honorable Henrique Clay sobre la agregacion de Tejas á los Estados-Unidos. Traducida del ingles. *Megico.* 1837. 4to, pp. 63. 11613

Also: Brief remarks on Dr. Channing's Letter to Henry Clay. By a Texian. *Boston.* 1837. 8vo, pp. 21. — Letters to William Ellery Channing, by Sidney, occasioned by his Letter to Hon. Henry Clay, on the Annexation of Texas. *Charleston, S. C.* 1837. N. — Review of Dr. Channing's Letter to Hon. Henry Clay. By a Citizen of Massachusetts. *Boston: William D. Ticknor.* 1837. 12mo, pp, 24. H., N. — Strictures on Channing's Letter on the Annexation of Texas. *Hoboken.* 1837. (This Hoboken imprint is doubtful.)

CHANNING. Letter of William E. Channing to James G. Birney. *Boston: James Munroe and Company.* 1837. 8vo, pp. 36. BA., H. 11914

On an attempt to suppress the anti-slavery party in Cincinnati by force.

CHANNING. Œuvres sociales de W. E. Channing ... précédées d'un essai sur la vie et les doctrines de Channing ... par M. Edouard Laboulaye. ... *Paris: Comon.* 1854. 12mo, pp. lxv, 512. B. 11915

Includes the "Vie de J. Tuckerman."

CHANNING. Œuvres. De l'esclavage. Précédé d'un préface et d'une étude sur l'esclavage aux États-Unis par M. Édouard Laboulaye. *Paris: Lacroix-Comon.* 1855. 18mo. 11916

CHANNING. Remarks on the Slavery Question, in a Letter to Jonathan Phillips, Esq. By William E. Channing. *Boston: James Munroe & Company.* 1839. 12mo, pp. 91. B., H. + *London.* 1839. 12mo. 11917

Also: Review of the Rev. Dr. Channing's Letter to Jonathan Phillips, Esq. on the Slavery Question. [By James Trecothick Austin.] 1839. 12mo, pp. 77. BA., H. — La esclavitud. Por William Ellery Channing. ... *New York: Juan M. Davis.* 1864. 8vo, pp. 97, 2 l. H.

CHANNING. A Selection from the Works of William E. Channing, D.D. *Boston: American Unitarian Association.* 1855. 12mo, pp. iv, (1), 480. H. 11918

Contains letter on Catholicism to the editor of the "Western Messenger," in which he speaks of the spread of Catholicism in that part of the country.

CHANNING. A Sermon, at the Ordination of the Rev. John Codman ... Second Church ... in Dorchester, Dec. 7, 1808. By William Ellery Channing ... . *Boston: Joshua Belcher, Printer.* 1808. 8vo, pp. 24. H. + [*Ibid.*] 1809. 8vo, pp. 31, (1). BA. 11919

Also the following sermons: A Sermon preached in Boston, April 5, 1810, the Day of the Public Fast ... . *Boston: Press of John Eliot, Jun.* 1810. 8vo, pp. 23. BA., H., W. + Second Edition. *Boston.* 1810. 8vo, pp. 23. + Third Edition. *Boston.* 1810. 8vo B. + *London: J. Hatchard.* 1811. 8vo, pp. iv, 19. BA. — A Sermon preached in Boston, July 23, 1812, the day of the Publick Fast, appointed by the Executive of the Commonwealth of Massachusetts, in Consequence of the Declaration of War against Great Britain ... . *Boston: printed by Greenough and Stebbins.* 1812. 8vo, pp. 20. BA., H. + *Birmingham: C. Wilks.* 1812. 8vo, pp. 16. BA. — A Sermon ... in Boston, August 20, 1812, the Day of Humiliation and Prayer, appointed by the President ... in Consequence of the Declaration of War against Great Britain. By William Ellery Channing ... . *Boston: printed by C. Stebbins.* 1812. 8vo, pp. 15. BA., N., W. — A Sermon, delivered in Boston, September 18, 1814 ... . *Boston: Henry Channing.* 1814. 8vo, pp. 19. BA. — A Sermon delivered at the Ordination of Rev. John Emery Abbot ... North Church ... in Salem; ... April 20, 1815. ... . *Salem: printed by Thomas C. Cushing.* 1815. 8vo, pp. 39. BA., H. — A Sermon ... at the Ordination of the Rev. Jared Sparks ... in Baltimore, May 5, 1819. By William Ellery Channing. *Baltimore.* 1819. 8vo, pp. 63, (8). + *Boston: reprinted by Hews & Goss.* 1819. 8vo, pp. 35, (1). H. + Second Edition. *Baltimore: printed by J. Robinson.* 1819. 8vo, pp. 72. H. (This second edition contains a note on some passages of Scripture used by Trinitarians as proof texts of their doctrine.) + Fourth Edition has the imprint, *Boston: Printed by Wells & Lilly.* 1819. 12mo, pp. 73. + Eleventh Edition. *Boston.* 1824. — Note for the Second Baltimore Edition of the Rev. Mr. Channing's Sermon ... at the Ordination of the Rev. Jared Sparks ... . *Boston: re-printed by Hews & Goss.* 1819. 8vo, pp. 8. BA. — Review of "Letters to W. E. Channing, containing Remarks on his Sermon, ... at Baltimore." ... *Boston.* 1819. 8vo. pp. 20. — A Sermon delivered At the Ordination of the Rev. Ezra Stiles Gannett as Colleague Pastor of the Church ... in Federal Street, Boston, June 30, 1824. By William Ellery Channing ... . *Boston: John B. Russell, Printer.* 1824. 8vo, pp. 47. H. (This edition contains two "Notes," a "Memoir of the Federal Street Church and Society," and nine pages devoted to historical statistics of the "Pastors of the Congregational Churches in Boston.") + Third Edition. *Thomas G. Wells, printer.* 1824. 8vo, pp. 32. H. + Fourth Edition. *Thomas G. Wells, printer.* 1824. 8vo, pp. 32. H. — A Sermon, preached at the Annual Election, May 26, 1830 ... . By William E. Channing. *Boston: Carter and Hendee.* 1830. 8vo, pp. 46. B. + *London: reprinted for the British and Foreign Unitarian Association.* 1830. 12mo, pp. 62. H. — Sermon at the Ordination of Charles F. Barnard and Frederick T. Gray. *Boston.* 1834. 8vo.

CHANNING. Slavery. By William E. Channing. *Boston: James Munroe & Co.* 1835. 12mo, pp. 167. + Second Edition. Revised. [*Ibid.*] 1836. 16mo, 2 l., pp. 183. BA. + Third Edi-

tion. *Boston.* 1836. + Fourth Edition. *Glasgow.* 1836. 12mo. + *Edinburgh: Thomas Clark.* MDCCCXXXVI. 16mo, pp. 112. BA.

This elicited much controversy. The following are some of the pamphlets on the subject: Remarks on "Slavery by William E. Channing." ... First published in the Boston Atlas, in a Series of Numbers. *Boston: J. H. Eastburn, Printer.* 1836. 8vo, pp. 61. H. — Remarks on Dr. Channing's Slavery. By a Citizen of Massachusetts. [James Trecothick Austin.] *Boston: Russell, Shattuck and Co., and John H. Eastburn.* 1835. 8vo, pp. 48. + Second Edition. *Boston.* 1835. 8vo, pp. 48. BA. + Third Edition. *Boston.* 1835. 8vo, pp. 48. — Review of the Remarks on Dr. Channing's Slavery, by a Citizen of Massachusetts. *Boston: James Munroe & Co.* 1836. 8vo, pp. 48. — Reply to the Reviewer of the Remarks on Dr. Channing's Slavery. ... *Boston: John H. Eastburn, Printer.* 1836 8vo, pp. 16. H. (For the "Review," *see* [Simmons (G. F.)]) — Extracts from "Remarks on Dr. Channing's Slavery," with Comments. By an Abolitionist. *Boston.* 1836. 8vo, pp. 55. — A Friend of the South in Answer to Remarks on Dr. Channing's Slavery. *Boston: Otis, Broaders and Company.* 1836. 12mo, pp. 19. BA., H.

CHANNING. The Works of William E. Channing, D.D. First Complete American Edition, with an Introduction. ... *Boston: James Munroe and Company.* 1841. 5 vols., 12mo, pp. xxx, 387; 411; 398; 407; 440. H. 11921

CHANNING. The Works of William Channing, D.D. Seventh Complete Edition, with an Introduction. ... *Boston: James Munroe and Company.* 1847. 6 vols., 12mo. BA. + Tenth Edition. *Boston: George R. Channing.* 1849. 6 vols., 12mo.

Also later editions. Reprinted in London in octavo.

CHANNING. William Ellery Channings Werke. In einer Auswahl aus dem Englischen übersetzt und herausgegeben von F. A. Schulze und Ad. Sydow. *Berlin: H. Schulze.* 1850–52. 12 vols., 16mo. 11923

Vols. 2, 4, 6, 8, and 10, contain the "Sociale Schriften."

Channing Sa vie et ses œuvres avec une préface de M. Charles de Rémusat. *Paris: Didier et Ce.* 1857. 8vo, Title, pp. xvii, (1), pp. 404. B. 11924

Also: An Address, delivered before the Mercantile Library Company, of Philadelphia, May 11, 1851. ... *Philadelphia: J. Crissy, Printer.* 1851. 8vo, pp. 45. BA., H. P., — An Address delivered at Lenox, on the First of August, 1842, the Anniversary of Emancipation, in the British West Indies. ... *Lenox, Mass.: J. G. Stanly.* 1842. 8vo, pp. 38. H. + *London.* 1842. 8vo. BD. — Discourse delivered at the Dedication of Divinity Hall, Cambridge, 1826. ... *Boston: Carter and Hendee.* MDCCCXXX. 8vo, Title, pp. 483–511. H. — A Discourse ... at the Installation of the Rev. Mellish Irving Motte, as Pastor of the South Congregational Society, in Boston. May 21, 1828. ... *Boston: Bowles and Dearborn.* 1828. 12mo, pp. 43. B. + Second Edition. [*Ibid.*] 8vo, pp. 22. H. — A Discourse ... at the Ordination of the Rev. Frederick A. Farley, as Pastor of the Westminister Congregational Society, in Providence, Rhode Island, September 10, 1828 *Boston: Bowles and Dearborn.* 1828 12mo, pp. 28. + Second Edition. [*Ibid.*] 1828. 12mo. + *London: Edward Rain-*

ford. 1829 8vo, pp. 36. — Discourse delivered at the Dedication of the Unitarian Congregational Church in Newport, Rhode Island, July 27, 1836. ... *Boston: S. N. Dickinson.* 8vo, p. 44. H. — A Discourse occasioned by the Death of the Rev. Dr. Follen. ... *Cambridge: Metcalf, Torry, and Ballou.* M DCCC XL 8vo, pp. 23. H. + Second Edition. *Boston: James Munroe and Company.* M DCCC XL. 8vo, pp. 29. BA. — A Discourse on the Life and Character of the Rev. Joseph Tuckerman, D.D. ... *Boston.* 1841. 18mo. — Discourse before the Benevolent Fraternity of Churches — First Anniversary, Boston, April 9, 1835. *Boston.* 1835. 8vo. — The Duty of the Free States; or Remarks suggested by the Case of the Creole. By William E. Channing. *Boston: W. Crosby & Company.* 1842. 12mo, pp. 54. + The Duty of the Free States. Second Part. [*Ibid.*] 1842. 12mo, pp. 93. + Second Edition. [*Ibid.*] + *London: John Green.* 1842. 8vo, pp. 40. — Essays, Literary and Political. *Glasgow.* 1837. 12mo. L'état actuel des lettres dans l'Amérique du Nord. Traduit par Swanton-Belloc. *Paris.* 1838. 8vo. — Letters on the Elevation of the Laboring Portion of the Community. *Boston: William D. Ticknor.* 1840. 12mo, pp. vi, 81, (1). BA., H. + Fifth Edition. *London.* 1840. 8vo. — A Letter to the Rev. Samuel C. Thacher on the Aspersions contained in a Late Number of the Panopolist on the Ministers of Boston and Vicinity. ... *Boston: Wells and Lilly.* 1815. 8vo. B., C., H., P. + Second Edition. *Boston.* 1815. 8vo, pp. 35. BA. + Third Edition. *Boston.* 1815. W. — Letter ... to the Standing Committee of the Proprietors of the Meeting-House in Federal Street, in the Town of Boston, ... May 6, 1840; and the Reply of the Proprietor thereto. ... *Boston: Joseph Dowe.* 1840. 8vo, pp. 16. H. — The Ministry for the Poor, a Discourse delivered ... in Boston, April 9th, 1835. *Boston.* 8vo, pp. 48. B. — [Channing.] Observationns o the Proposition for increasing the Means of Theological Education at the University in Cambridge. *Cambridge.* 1815. 8vo, pp. 22. M., S. — Remarks on the Rev. Dr. Worcester's Letter to Mr. Channing, on the "Review of American Unitarianism" in a Late Panopolist. ... . *Boston: Wells and Lilly.* 1815. 8vo, pp. 39. BA. + Second Edition. *Boston.* 1815. B. — Remarks on the Rev. Dr. Worcester's Second Letter to Mr. Channing. ... . By William E. Channing ... . *Boston: Wells & Lilly.* 1815. 8vo, pp. 48. B. A Tribute to the Memory of the Rev. Noah Worcester, D.D. ... Discourse ... November 12, 1837, ... *Boston: published by Joseph Dowe.* 1837. 8vo, pp. 28. H. + *Boston.* 1837. 12mo, pp. 24. — Tribute of William Ellery Channing to the American Abolitionists, for their Vindication of Freedom of Speech. ... *New York.* 1861. 16mo, pp. 24. H.

CHANNING. Remarks upon the Report of ... the Mayor of Boston, adverse to the Petitions of W. E. Channing, and Others, for a Meeting of the Citizens, to vote upon Licenses to Bar-Rooms and Dram-Shops. *Boston.* 1841. 8vo, pp. 36. BA.

CHANNING. Services in Memory of Rev. William E. Channing, D.D. at the Arlington-Street Church, Boston ... October, 6, 1867. *Boston.* 1867. 8vo, pp. 44. H. 11926

CHANNING (W. E.), *the younger.* Poems by William Ellery Channing. *Boston: Charles C. Little and James Brown.* MDCCCLXIII. 16mo, pp. 151. BA. 11927

CHANNING. Poems by William Ellery Channing. Second Series. *Boston: James Munroe and Company.* M DCCC XLVII. 16mo, pp. vii, 160. BA. 11928

CHANNING. The Woodman, and other Poems. By William Ellery Channing. *Boston: James Munroe and Company.* M DCCC XLIX. 16mo, pp. iv, 92. BA. 11929

These contain various poems illustrating American life or scenery, as "Niagara," "New England," "Wachusett," "Walden," "The Woodman," "Old Sudbury Inn," "Walden Spring," etc.

CHANNING (W. F.) The American Fire-Alarm Telegraph: a Lecture delivered before the Smithsonian Institution, March, 1855. By William F. Channing, M.D. ... *Boston: Redding & Company.* 1855. 8vo, pp. 19. H. 11930

Also: Communication ... respecting a System of Fire Alarms. [*Boston.* 1851.] 8vo, pp. 29. Map. H. — On the Municipal Electric Telegraph; ... . *New Haven: printed by B. L. Hamlen.* 1852. 8vo, pp. 28. H.

CHANNING (W. H.) The Civil War in America: or, the Slaveholders' Conspiracy, an Address by the Rev. William Henry Channing. *Liverpool: W. Vaughan, Printer.* 16mo, pp. 100. H. 11931

CHANNING. Memoir of William Ellery Channing: with Extracts from his Correspondence and Manuscripts. By William Henry Channing. *Boston: William Crosby and H. P. Nichols. London: John Chapman.* 1848. 3 vols., 12mo, pp. xiii, 1 l., pp. 427; vi, 459; vi, 494. 2 Portraits. BA. + Second and Third Editions. *Boston: Crosby & Nichols.* 1848. H. + Sixth Edition. [*Ibid.*] 1854. 3 vols., 12mo. 11932

Also: The Gospel of To-day. A Discourse ... at the Ordination of T. W. Higginson ... in Newburyport, Mass., Sept. 15, 1847. ... *Boston: Wm. Crosby and H. P. Nichols.* 1847 8vo, pp. 63. B., H. — Lessons from the Life of Theodore Parker. A Discourse ... delivered in Liverpool, ... June 10, 1860. *London: Edward T. Whitfield. Liverpool: Henry Young.* 1860. 12mo, pp. 35. B. — A Letter ... to the Unitarian Society of Cincinnati. *Cincinnati: printed by R. P. Brooks.* 1842. 8vo, pp. 23. B., H.

CHANTAL (J. B. J. de). Vies et aventures remarquables des plus célèbres voyageurs modernes. *Paris.* 11933

CHANTAL. Beautés de l'histoire des voyages. *Paris.* 11934

There are various editions of both works of Chantal.

Chanticleer; a Thanksgiving Story of the Peabody Family. Second Edition. *Boston.* 1850. 12mo. 11935

[CHANVALON (Jean Baptiste Thibault de).] Voyage à la Martinique, contenant diverses observations sur la Physique, l'Histoire Naturelle, l'Agriculture, les Mœurs, & les Usages de cette Isle, faites en 1751, & dans les années suivantes. ...

Paris: Cl. J. B. Bauche. M.DCC.LXIII. 4to, 4 l., pp. viii, 46, 192, 40 l. Map. C., H. 11936

"A highly esteemed work, with an account of the Carib race, some of whom yet remained, at that time, in Martinique." "Relation très-estimée." — LECLERC. *See also* M. R., XXIX. 526.

CHAPARRO (Juan Gonzalez), *de la Comp. de Jesus.* Carta en que le dà cuenta del lastimo sucesso del terremoto en la ciudad de Santiago de Chile. *Madrid.* 1648. Folio. 11937

CHAPIN (A. L.) Address and Discourse at the Inauguration of the Rev. Aaron L. Chapin, M.A. as President of Beloit College, July 24, 1850, ... *Milwaukee: J. Hamilton, Printer.* 1850. 8vo, pp. 52. H. 11938

The Address is by A. Kent.

CHAPIN (A. B.) Glastenbury for Two Hundred Years: a Centennial Discourse, May 18th, A.D. 1853. With an Appendix containing Historical and Statistical Papers of Interest. By Rev. Alonzo B. Chapin, D.D. ... *Hartford: Press of Case, Tiffany and Company.* 1853. 8vo, pp. 252. Plan. H. 11939

CHAPIN. History of Christ's Church, West Haven; or, the Early Churchmen of Connecticut. By Rev. A. B. Chapin. *New Haven.* 1839. 8vo. 11940

CHAPIN. A Sermon delivered at Christ's Church, West Haven, the eleventh Sunday after Trinity (August 11,) 1839. The Hundredth Anniversary of laying the Foundation of the Church. By Rev. A. B. Chapin. *New Haven: Hitchcock & Stratford, Printers.* 1839. 8vo, pp. 28. 11941

CHAPIN. Puritanism not Genuine Protestantism. Being a sequel to Puritans and their Principles, by E. Hall. *New York.* 1847. 12mo, pp. 226. 11942

Contains a catalogue of controversial books relating tot he doctrine and discipline of the Episcopal Church in the United States.

CHAPIN. A Sermon, ... at the Ordination of ... Rev. Samuel Whittelsey, ... New Preston, Washington, Conn., Dec. ... 30th, 1807; and ... of Rev. Hosea Beckley, ... Dummerston, Vt., March 2d, 1808. By Calvin Chapin ... . *Hartford.* 1808. 8vo, pp. 24. H. 11943

Also; A Sermon ... 14th January, 1817, at the Funeral of the Rev. Timothy Dwight, D.D. LL.D. President of Yale College ... Who died, Jan. 11th, 1817 ... By Calvin Chapin, D.D. ... . *New-Haven: Maltby Goldsmith & Co.* 1817. 8vo, pp. 35. BA., H. — A Sermon before the "Connecticut Society for Promoting Good Morals," Hartford, May 18, 1814. *Hartford.* 1814. 8vo, pp. 34.

CHAPIN (Edwin Hubbell). The American Idea, and What Grows Out of It. An Oration ... in the New York Crystal Palace July 4, 1854. By E. H. Chapin. ... *Boston: Abel Tompkins.* 1854. 8vo, pp. 18. BA. 11944

CHAPIN. A Discourse ... May 12, 1844, in reference to the Recent Riots in Philadelphia. By E. H. Chapin. *Boston: A. Tompkins.* 1844. 8vo, pp. 16. B. 11945

CHAPIN. The Responsibilities of a Republical Government. A Discourse, preached Fast Day, April 8, 1841. By E. H. Chapin. ... *Boston: A. Tompkins.* 1841. 8vo, pp. 31. H.

CHAPIN. The Relation of the Individual to the Republic. A Sermon delivered ... at the Annual Election, ... January 3, 1844. By E. H. Chapin, ... *Boston: Dutton & Wentworth, Printers.* 1844. 8vo, pp. 36. H. 11947

Also: Humanity in the City. ... *New York: De Witt & Davenport.* [1864.] 12mo, pp. 252. Portrait. H. — Moral Aspects of City Life. ... *New York: Henry Lyon.* 1854. 12mo, pp. 191. H. + New Edition. *New York: H. Lyon.* 1855. 12mo, pp. 192. C. — Occasional Sermon, delivered before the United States General Convention of Universalists, held in Boston, Sept. 17, 1845. ... *Boston: A. Tompkins.* 1845. 8vo, pp. 20. H. — Present Exigencies of the Temperance Cause. An Address delivered at Tremont Temple, Boston, ... November 23, 1845. *Boston.* 1846. 12mo, pp. 21. — ... A Sermon, delivered at the Installation of Rev. Henry Bacon, as Pastor of the First Universalist Society, Providence, R. I. March 17, 1842, ... *Providence: B. Cranston & Co.* 1812. 8vo, pp. 20. H. — True Patriotism. A Discourse delivered on Fast Day, ... *Boston: A. Tompkins.* 1847. 8vo, pp. 19.

CHAPIN (H.) A Poem Delivered at the Celebration of the Two Hundredth Anniversary of the Incorporation of the Town of Mendon, May 15, 1867. By Hon. Henry Chapin, of Worcester. *Milford: G. W. Stacy, Printer.* 1867. 12mo. 11948

CHAPIN (H. B.) Sermon at the Ordination of the Rev. Charles Moulson Browne as Pastor-Colleague with the Rev. Elias Fisher, to the Congregational Church and Society in Lempster, New Hampshire, September 18, 1828. By Horace B. Chapin. *Concord, N. H.* 1828. 8vo, pp. 29. N. 11949

CHAPIN (J. R.) The Historical Picture Gallery; or Scenes and Incidents in American History. ... With 125 Illustrations, by the Author. Vol. v. *Boston: D. Bigelow & Co.* 1856. S.

CHAPIN (O.) The Chapin Genealogy, containing a very Large Proportion of the Descendants of Dea. Samuel Chapin, who settled in Springfield, Mass. in 1642, Collected and Compiled by Orange Chapin. To which is added a "Centennial

Discourse delivered before the First Congregational Society in Chicopee, September 26, 1852, by E. B. Clark, Pastor of the Church, which was organized Sept. 27, 1752." Also, an Address delivered at the opening of the Town Hall in Springfield, March 24, 1828, containing Sketches of the Early History of that Town, and those in that vicinity — with an Appendix — by George Bliss. *Northampton: printed by Metcalf & Company.* 1862. 8vo, pp. viii, 368. H. 11951

CHAPIN. The Chapin Gathering. Proceedings at the Meeting of the Chapin Family in Springfield, Mass., September 17, 1862. *Springfield: printed by Samuel Bowles & Co.* 1862. 8vo, pp. 97. H. 11952

CHAPIN (E.) The Detective's Manual and Officer's Guide. With Official Lists of U. S., State, County, and Canadian Officers: Criminals Liable to Arrest, Summary of Property Stolen, etc., By E. Chapin. Monthly; to be completed in 12 Nos. Vol. 1, No. 1. Aug. 1868. *Springfield, Mass.: The Author.* 1868. 8vo, pp. 86. 11953

CHAPIN (Seth). Sermon at Hanover, Mass. *Boston.* 1819. 8vo. W. 11954

CHAPIN (S.) The Duty of living for the good of Posterity; Sermon at North Yarmouth, Dec. 22, 1820, in Commemoration of the Close of the Second Century from the Forefathers. By Stephen Chapin. *Portland: Thomas Todd & Co.* 1821. 8vo, pp. 48. C. 11955

CHAPIN. ... A Sermon, delivered November 19, 1823, at the Dedication of the Baptist Meeting-House in Winthrop, Me. By Stephen Chapin, D.D. ... *Waterville: printed by William Hastings.* 1823. 8vo, pp. 35. H. 11956

CHAPIN. A Sermon, delivered at the Dedication of the New Meeting-House in Waterville Village, December 6, 1826. By Stephen Chapin. [*Waterville:*] *Wm. Hastings. Printer.* 1826. 8vo, pp. 24. H. 11957

CHAPIN. Two Sermons at Mount Vernon, N. H., November 26th, 1809; also appended: A Brief Sketch of the Life and Character of Rev. John Bruce, Minister of Mt. Vernon. *Amherst, N. H.* 1809. 8vo, pp. 39. 11958

Also: Sermon at the Ordination of A. Merriam, W. Metcalf and E. Johnson, at Royalston, Mass. *Waterville, N. Y.* 1825. 8vo. — On the Duties of an Ambassador of Christ. Two Sermons at Mount Vernon, N. H., Nov. 26, 1809. *Amherst.* 1809. 12mo. — A Series of Letters on the Mode and Subjects of Baptism, addressed to the Christian Public. ... [With] an Account of the ... Author's Trial on those Points. ... Second Edition. With an Appendix, containing Strictures on Mr. Moore's Reply. *Boston.* 1820. 12mo. And other sermons and addresses.

CHAPIN (S. R.) Stray Leaves. By S. R. Chapin. [*Boston.* 1867.] Square 16mo, pp. 78. C. 11959

CHAPIN (W.) The Missionary Gazetteer, and a general History of Missions throughout the World. By Walter Chapin. *Woodstock, Vt.* 1825. 12mo. S. 11960

"Particularly describing Indian localities." — S. G. DRAKE. Also: A Sermon at Woodstock, Vt. Feb. 8, 1818, Sabbath before an Execution. ... *Windsor.* 1818. 8vo.

CHAPIN (William). Complete Reference Gazetteer of the United States. *New-York.* 1839. 8vo. S. 11961

Also: Supplement to the Ninth Annual Report of the Ohio Institution for the Education of the Blind. *Columbus.* 1846. 8vo, pp. 61.

Chapin's City Directory of Ann Arbor, for 1868, with Description and Catalogue of the University of Michigan. *Adrian.* 1868. 8vo, pp. 160, 92. 11962

CHAPLAIN (C. L.) Address of Charles L. Chaplain, Esq. of New Haven, Connecticut, to the General Assembly of Virginia, January 1860. [n. p. n. d.] 8vo, pp. 16. H. 11963

CHAPLAIN (J. F.) A True Fast: A Fast-Day Sermon ... April 30th, 1863, By John F. Chaplain, Pastor ... *Philadelphia.* 1863. 8vo, pp. 14. 11964

A Chaplain's Campaign. *See* [Hudson (Henry N.)]

CHAPLIN (D.) The Dispensations of Divine Providence ... and the Morals of New-England at the Present Day ...; the Duty of Electors ... . A Sermon delivered at Groton Jan. 12, 1815, being the Day of the National Fast. By Daniel Chaplin ... . *Cambridge: printed by Hilliard and Metcalf.* 1815. 8vo, pp. 12. H. 11965

Also: A Discourse delivered before the Charitable Female Society in Groton Oct. 19, 1814. By Daniel Chaplin ... . *Andover Flagg and Gould, Printers.* 1814. 8vo, pp. 15. H., W. — A Sermon, delivered May 26, 1808, in ... Boston, before the Convention of Congregational Ministers, of ... Massachusetts. ... *Boston: printed by Belcher and Armstrong.* 1808. 8vo, pp. 24. H., N., W. — A Sermon delivered in Boston before the Massachusetts Society for promoting Christian Knowledge; ... June 1, 1815. *Boston: printed by Nathaniel Willis.* 1815. 8vo, pp. 32.

CHAPLIN (E.) Civil State compared to Rivers ... . In a Discourse in Sutton, 2d Parish, January 17, 1773. Being the Day preceding the Town Meeting, ... Adjourned to consider and act upon the Letter, &c. From Boston. ... By Ebenezer Chaplin ... . *Boston: John Boyles.* MDCCLXXIII. 12mo, pp. 24.

[CHAPLIN.] A Treatise on Church-Government, ... being, I. A Narrative of the late Troubles and Transactions in the Church in Bolton, in the Massachusetts. II. Some Remarks on Mr. Adams's Sermon, preached there August 26, 1772. With ... Some Remarks on an Account in the Boston Evening-Post, Dec. 28, 1772, of the Dismission of a Minister at Grafton. III. On Councils ... . With an Essay on Ministers negativing the Votes of the Church ... . By a Neighbour. ... *Boston: printed by John Boyles.* MDCCLXXIII. pp. 37, (2). H. 11967

[CHAPLIN.] A Second Treatise on Church-Government ... I. A Continuation of the Narrative of the late Troubles and Transactions in the Church in Bolton: With some Remarks on Mr. Goss's Narrative. II. A Reply to Mr. Adams's Answer to my former Treatise ... . III. Shewing ... the Sole Right People have to call and dismiss their Officers. ... With ... Remarks on a Pamphlet said to be offered to the Churches by the Convention of Ministers. ... [And] The Testimonies of many Persons in Bolton ... in Answer ... to Mr. Goss's Narrative. By a Neighbour. ... *Boston: Printed by John Boyles.* MDCCLXXIII. 8vo, pp. 78. BA. 11968

Also: The Godly Fathers, and a Defence to their People. Sermon delivered April 19, 1772, on the Death of Rev. Nathan Webb. ... *Boston.* 1773. 8vo, pp. 28.

CHAPLIN (J.) Duncan Dunbar; the Record of an Earnest Ministry. A Sketch of the late Pastor of the McDougal St. Baptist Church, New York. By Jeremiah Chaplin. ... *New York: Sheldon and Company.* 1865. 12mo, pp. xi, 311. H.

Also: A Sermon, delivered September 8, 1819, at the ordination of the Rev. Stephen Chapin ... in North-Yarmouth. By Jeremiah Chapin ... . *Portland: Francis Douglas.* 1819. 8vo, pp. 28. BA. — A Sermon preached at North Yarmouth; February 16, 1825, at the Ordination of the Rev. George D. Boardman, as Missionary to the Heathen. ... . *Waterville: printed by W. M. Hastings.* 1825. 8vo, pp. 41.

CHAPLIN (Joseph). The Trader's Best Companion. ... Arithmetical Rules ... applied to Federal Currency ... . By Joseph Chaplin. *Newburyport: Printed by William Barrett. July* 24, 1795. 8vo, pp. 36. BA. 11970

CHAPLIN (W. L.) The Case of William L. Chaplin; ... the Cruel and Oppressive Treatment to which, under Color of Legal Proceedings, he has been subjected, in the District of Columbia and the State of Maryland. *Boston.* 1851. 8vo, pp. xii, 54. Portrait. H. 11971

CHAPMAN (A. W.) Flora of the Southern United States: containing Abridged Descriptions of the Flowering Plants and Ferns of Tennessee, North and South Carolina, Georgia, Alabama, Mississippi, and Florida: arranged according to the Natural System by A. W. Chapman, M.D. The Ferns by Daniel C. Eaton. *New York.* 1860. 8vo, Half-Title, pp. xxviii, 621.

CHAPMAN (C.) Speech of Hon. Charles Chapman ... on the ... Prosecution of Claims against the Government by Members of Congress, etc. ... In the House ... January 11, 1853. *Washington.* 1853. 8vo, pp. 8. BA. 11973

CHAPMAN. Sermon on the Death of Samuel Couch, Esq. on Nov. 24, 1739. By Rev. Daniel Chapman, M.A. *New London.* 1741. 8vo. 11974

CHAPMAN (E.) An Account of the Conduct of the People called Shakers; in the Case of Eunice Chapman and her Children, ... *Albany: printed for the Authoress.* 1817. 12mo, pp. 60.

CHAPMAN. No. 2, being an Additional Account of the ... Shakers ... . Also the Deposition of Mary Dyer ... . *Albany: printed by I. W. Clark.* 1818. 12mo, pp. 82. B., BA. 11976

CHAPMAN (E. J.) A Popular and Practical Exposition of the Minerals and Geology of Canada. By E. J. Chapman, PH.D., Professor in University College, Toronto, late Professor in the London University College. *Toronto.* 1864. 8vo, pp. 236. Woodcuts. 11977

CHAPMAN. A Song of Charity. Canadian Edition. *Toronto.* 1857. 8vo. 11978

See the "Canadian Journal" for January, 1858, page 17.

CHAPMAN (F. W.) The Chapman Family: or the Descendants of Robert Chapman, one of the First Settlers of Say-Brook, Conn. With Genealogical Notes of William Chapman, who settled in New London, Conn.; Edward Chapman, who settled at Windsor, Conn.; John Chapman, of Stonington, Conn.; and Rev. Benjamin Chapman, of Southington, Conn. By Rev. F.

W. Chapman, A.M., a descendant of Robert Chapman of Saybrook. *Hartford: Printed by Case, Tiffany & Co.* M.DCCC.LIV. 8vo, pp. 413, (1). Portraits and Plate. H., P. 11979

CHAPMAN. The Pratt Family; or, The Descendants of Lieut. William Pratt, one of the First Settlers of Hartford and Say-Brook. With Genealogical Notes of John Pratt, of Hartford; Peter Pratt, of Lyme; John Pratt (Taylor), of Say-Brook. By Rev. F. W. Chapman, A.M. *Hartford: Case, Lockwood & Co., Printers.* 1865. 8vo, pp. 421. Portraits and Coats of Arms.

CHAPMAN (G. T.) A Funeral Sermon, ... occasioned by the Death of the Hon. John Chandler Williams, ... By G. T. Chapman, D.D. *Boston: Stimpson and Clapp.* 1831. 8vo, pp. 16. H. 11981

CHAPMAN. A Sermon, occasioned by the Death of the Rev. William Horton, D.D., Rector of St. Paul's Church, Newburyport, Mass., preached ... Nov. 8, 1863, by George T. Chapman, D.D. *Newburyport: William H. Huse & Co., Printers.* 1863. 8vo, pp. 16. H. 11982

CHAPMAN. Sketches of the Alumni of Dartmouth College, from the First Graduation in 1771 to the Present Time, with a Brief History of the Institution. By the Rev. George T. Chapman, D.D. ... *Cambridge: Riverside Press.* 1868. 8vo, pp. 520.

CHAPMAN (G. W.) A Tribute to Kane; and Other Poems. By George W. Chapman. *New York: Rudd & Carleton.* MDCCCLX. 8vo, Title, pp. 5–161. 11984

CHAPMAN (H. S.) Thoughts on the Money and Exchanges of Lower Canada. By Henry S. Chapman. *Montreal.* 1832. 8vo. C. 11985

CHAPMAN (I. A.) A Sketch of the History of Wyoming. By the Late Isaac A. Chapman, Esq. To which is added, an Appendix, containing a Statistical Account of the Valley, and Adjacent Country. By a Gentleman of Wilkesbarre. *Wilkesbarre, Penn.: Sharp D. Lewis.* 1830. 12mo, pp. 209. C., H., P.

CHAPMAN (J.) The Memorial of James Chapman, To the respectable Legislature of the State of New York. ... [n. p. n. d.] 8vo, pp. 8. B. 11987

Dated Albany, 24th March, 1817, and signed James Chapman.

CHAPMAN. Memorial of the Shakers of Watervliet to the Legislature, respecting the Case of James Chapman. *Albany.* 1817. 8vo. 11988

CHAPMAN (J.) Historical Notices of Saint Peter's Church, in the City of Perth-Amboy, New-Jersey. Contained in Two Discourses Delivered in the said Church, June 19th and 26th, 1825, shortly after the erection of a Marble Tablet in the East Wall of the Church, in Memory of the First Benefactors of the same; with some Additions. By James Chapman, Rector. *Elizabeth-Town: printed by Sanderson and Brookfield.* 1830. 8vo, pp. 28. 11989

CHAPMAN (J. G.) Speech of John G. Chapman, of Maryland, on the Revenue System, and the Defence of the Tariff of 1842. ... House of Representatives ... Aug. 1, 1846. [*Washington:*] *J. & G. S. Gideon, printers.* 8vo, pp. 23. H. 11990

Also: Speech ... February 24, 1849, Upon the bill to establish a Territorial Government in California, and upon the power of the Federal Government over slavery in the District of Columbia. [*Washington:*] *Towers, printer.* 8vo, pp. 16. H.

CHAPMAN (J.) An Oration delivered before the Citizens of Boston, ... July 4, 1837. By Jonathan Chapman. ... *Boston.* 1837. 8vo, pp. 24. BA. 11991

Also: Addresses before the Young Men's Temperance Society at Boston. *Boston.* 1832. 8vo. W. — An Oration delivered before the Whigs of Bristol County, at Taunton, July 4, 1839. ... . *Taunton: J. Amsbury, Jr., Printer.* 1839. 8vo, pp. 34. BA.

CHAPMAN (J. G.) The Picture of the Baptism of Pocahontas; painted by order of Congress, ... by J. G. Chapman. *Washington.* 1840. 8vo. C. 11992

Contains an historical address, and extracts relating to the subject of the picture.

CHAPMAN (M. I.) Barbadoes and other Poems. By M. I. Chapman. *London.* 1833. 12mo, pp. 220. 11993

[CHAPMAN (Maria Weston).] Report of the Boston Female Anti-Slavery Society; with a ... Statement of Events Previous and Subsequent to the Annual Meeting of 1835. Second Edition. *Boston: the Society.* 1836. 12mo, pp. 108. BA. 11994

With the half-title: "Wright and Wrong in Boston."

CHAPMAN. Right and Wrong in Massachusetts. By Maria Weston Chapman. *Boston: Dow & Jackson.* 1839. 16mo, pp. 177. + *Boston: Henry L. Devereaux.* 1840. 16mo, pp. 175.

[CHAPMAN.] Songs of the Free, and Hymns of Christian

Freedom. [A Collection.] *Boston: Isaac Knapp.* MDCCCXXXVI. 12mo, pp. 227. BA. 11996

Also: "How can I help to abolish Slavery?" or, Counsels to the newly Converted. ... Anti-Slavery Tracts, No. 14. [n. p. n. d.] 12mo, pp. 12. B. — Pinda: a True Tale. ... *New York: Pub. by Am. Anti-Slavery Society.* 1840. 12mo, pp. 23. H.

CHAPMAN (N.) Select Speeches, Forensic and Parliamentary, with Prefatory Remarks. By N. Chapman, M.D. ... *Philadelphia: J. Hopkins and Earle.* 1808. 5 vols., 8vo, pp. 480; (4), 449; vi, 442; (4), 469; iv, 497. 5 Portraits. BA. 11997

Also: Letter to Hon. Joseph Hopkinson, on the Appointment of Prof. Hare in the University of Pennsylvania. ... *Philadelphia.* 1818. 4to, pp. 6.

CHAPMAN (R.) Speech of Hon. R. Chapman, of Alabama, on the Bill to protect the Rights of American Settlers in Oregon. Delivered in the House ... April 17, 1846. [n. p. n. d.] 8vo, pp. 8. H. 11998

CHAPMAN (Robert H.) Sermon delivered at the Ordination and Installation of Rev. J. Younglove. 1806. 8vo. 11999

CHAPMAN (S.) Hand Book of Wisconsin. By S. Chapman. *Milwaukee.* 1855. + Second Edition, enlarged, ... By S. Chapman. *Milwaukee: S. Chapman.* 1855. 32mo, pp. 117.

CHAPMAN (T. Ellwood). Philadelphia Wholesale Merchants' and Artisans' Business Directory for 1853. To be Continued Annually. *Philadelphia.* [1853.] 18mo, pp. 184. Map.

CHAPMAN (*Rev.* W. R.) Address, Union-Springs Female Seminary. 1852. 8vo. S. 12002

CHAPMAN HALL SCHOOL. Annual Catalogue of the Teachers and Pupils of Chapman Hall School; ... *Boston.* 1847. 12mo, pp. 22, (1). Continued. H. 12002*a*

CHAPPE D'AUTEROCHE (Jean). Voyage en Californie pour l'observation du passage de Vénus sur le disque du soleil, Le 3 Juin 1769; contenant les observations de ce phénomene, et la description historique de la route de l'Auteur à travers le Mexique. Par feu M. Chappe d'Auteroche ... . Rédigé et publié par M. de Cassini fils ... *A Paris: Chez Charles-Antoine Jombert.* M. DCC. LXXII. 4to, Half-Title, Title, pp. 170, (2). Plan and 2 Plates. BA., H. 12003

See Boucher, v. 143–146.

CHAPPE D'AUTEROCHE. A Voyage to California, to observe the Transit of Venus. By Mons. Chappe d'Auteroche. With an Historical Description of the Author's Route through Mexico,

and the Natural History of that Province. Also, a Voyage to Newfoundland and Sallee, to make Experiments on Mr. Le Roy's Time Keepers. By Monsieur De Cassini. *London: Edward and Charles Dilly.* MDCCLXXVIII. 8vo, 4 l., pp. 215. Plan. C., H. 12004

See M. R., LX. 71.

CHAPPELL (E.) Narrative of a Voyage to Hudson's Bay in His Majesty's ship Rosamond, containing some Account of the North-Eastern Coast of America and of the Tribes inhabiting that Remote Region. By Lieut. Edward Chappell, R.N. ... *London: J. Mawman.* 1817. 8vo, 6 l., pp. 279. Map and 9 Plates.

Of little value. *See* Q. R., XVII. 192, and M. R., LXXXVII. 66.

CHAPPELL. Voyage of His Majesty's ship Rosamond to Newfoundland and the Southern Coast of Labrador of which Countries no Account has been published by any British Traveller since the Reign of Queen Elizabeth. By Lieut. Edward Chappell, R.N. ... *London: J. Mawman.* 1818. 8vo, 5 l., pp. xix, 270. Map and 2 Plates. BA., H. 12006

Some copies on large paper.

CHAPPELL. Reise nach Neufoundland und der südlichen Küste von Labrador, nebst Beschreibung der Insel Cuba. Aus dem Englishen. *Jena: Bran.* 1819. 8vo. + *Jena.* 1820.

CHAPPELSMITH (J.) Account of a Tornado near New Harmony, Indiana, April 30, 1852, with a Map of the Track, Diagrams, and Illustrative Sketches, by John Chappelsmith. *Washington.* 1855. 4to, pp. 12. Map and Plate. B. 12008

Included in the publications of the Smithsonian Institute, Vol. VII., Art. II.

CHAPPUS. Histoire abrégée des révolutions du commerce, ou Précis historique et raisonné des changements que le commerce à éprouvés à l'occasion des transmigrations, des conquêtes, des nouvelles découvertes et des révolutions politiques, depuis le commencement du monde jusqu'à nos jours. *Paris.* 1802. 12mo. 12009

CHAPPUZEAU (*Le Sieur*). Histoire des joyaux, et des principales richesses de l'Orient et de l'Occident. *Genève.* 1665. 12mo. + [*Ibid.*] 1669. 12mo. 12010

CHAPPUZEAU. The History of Jewels, and the Principal Riches of the East and West. 1671. 12mo. 12011

I doubt if l'Orient et l'Occident mean East and West *Indies* in these titles copied from an English catalogue of Americana.

A Chapter of American History. Five Years' Progress of the Slave Power; a series of papers first Published in the Boston "Commonwealth," in ... 1851. *Boston.* 1852. 8vo, pp. 84.

A Chapter of American History. Sketches of the Revolutionary War, giving an Account of the Storming of Fort Griswold, on Groton Heights, on the 6th Day of September, 1781. Written by a old Sailor, and now a Citizen of Columbus, February, 1853. ... *Columbus, Ohio: Osgood & Blake, Printers.* 1853. 8vo, pp. 54. 12013

Character of the American Government. *New York: Wiley & Putnam.* 1838. 12014

Characters; Containing an Impartial Review of the Public Conduct and Abilities of the Eminent Personages in the Parliament of Great Britain, Considered as Statesmen, Senators, and Public Speakers. Revised and Corrected by the Author, since the Original Publication in the Gazetteer. *London: J. Bew.* MDCCLXXVII. 8vo, pp. xvi, 153. 12015

"Drawn with tolerable impartiality." — M. R., LVI. 230.

CHARAULT (J. R.) Coup-d'oeil sur Saint-Domingue; observations sur le caractère des nègres et sur la fièvre jaune; moyens de recouvrer cette colonie et de se préserver des maladies qui y règnent. *Paris: Panckoucke.* 1814. 8vo, pp. 44. 12016

[CHARDON (Daniel Marc Antoine).] Essai sur la colonie de Sainte Lucie. Par un ancien Intendant de cette Isle. Suivi de trois Mémoires intéressans, deux concernant les Jésuites, & le troisieme le Général d'Oxat. *Neuchatel.* M. DCC. LXXIX. 8vo, Title, pp. ij, 154. BA. 12017

CHARENCY (Hyacinthe de). Affinité de quelques légendes américaines avec celles de l'ancien monde. *Paris: A. Parent.* 1866. 8vo, pp. 16. 12118

Republished from the "Revue indépendante," 1er mai.

CHARENCY. Compte rendu et analyse de l'histoire des nations civilisées du Mexique et de l'Amérique centrale ... de M. l'abbé Brasseur de Bourbourg. *Paris: Challamel.* 1859. 8vo.

Republished from the "Annales de philos. chrétienne."

CHARENCY. De la parenté le la langue japonaise avec les idiomes tartares et américains. *Paris: Challamel.* 1858. 8vo.

Republished from the "Annales de philos. chrét."

Charency. Eléments de la grammaire Othomi et vocabulaire. *Paris.* 1863. 12021

Only a few copies printed.

Charency. Notice sur un ancien manuscrit mexicain, dit Codex Telleriano-Remensis. *Paris: Challamel.* 1859. 8vo, pp. 7. Colored Plate. 12022

From the "Revue orientale et mexicaine."

Charency (*Le Cte*). Le percement de l'isthme de Panama. *Mortagne: Loncin.* 1859. 8vo, pp. 11. 12023

The Charge Delivered, 1723 and 1736. *See* [Logan (James)].

Charge Given by the Chief Justice of the Province of New-York, to the Grand Jury of the City of New-York. In March Term 1726–7. Printed at the Request of the Said Grand Jury. *New-York: Printed and Sold by John Peter Zenger.* 1727. 4to, pp. 19. P. 12024

Charibbee Islands. Acts of Assembly, passed in the Charibbee Leeward Islands. From 1690 to 1730. *London: Printed by order of the Lords Commissioners of Trade and Plantations by John Baskett.* 1734. Folio, pp. 15, (30), 231. H. 12025

Authentic Papers. *See* Vol. I., No. 2456.

A Short Account of the Hurricane that passed through the English Leeward Charibbee Islands, on Saturday, June 30th, 1733. *London.* 1733. 8vo. 12026

Charlemagne (P.) Royaume d'Hayti. Réfutation D'un Écrit de Charrault, ex-colon, intitule: Coup-d'œil sur St-Domingue. Par M. Philémon Charlemagne, Employé à la Secrétairerie d'État. [Colophon:] *Au Cap-Henry: chez P. Roux.* [n. d.] 8vo, pp. 9. H. 12027

Charles (E.) Edmund Charles & Son's New York Bank Note List. Counterfeit Detector, Wholesale Prices Current and Weekly Journals of Financial News. ... *New York.* ... 1847. H. 12028

The Charles F. Adams Platform, or a Looking Glass for the Worthies of the Buffalo Convention. [n. p. 1848.] 8vo, pp. 8.

Charles II. His Majesty's Propriety, etc., 1665. *See* [Clavell (Rd.)]

Charles River Bridge. Case of the Proprietors of Charles River Bridge against the Proprietors of Warren Bridge, argued and determined in the Supreme Judicial Court of Massachusetts. *Boston.* 1830. 8vo. c. 12030

Opinions of the Judges of the Supreme Court of the United States, in the Case of the Proprietors of Charles River Bridge vs. the Proprietors of Warren Bridge and Others. Delivered at the January Term of the Court, at Washington, 1837. *Boston: Otis, Broaders and Co.* 1857. 8vo, pp. 115. BA. 12031

Also: Account of Some of the Bridges over Charles River, as connected with the Growth of Cambridge. *Cambridge.* 1858. 8vo. — The Proprietors of Charles River Bridge, In Equity vs. the Proprietors of the Warren Bridge. [n. p. n. d.] 4to, pp. 206. H.

Charleston. An Account of the Late Intended Insurrection among a Portion of the Blacks of this City. [Written by James Hamilton, Jun.] Published by the Authority of the Corporation of Charleston. *Charleston: A. E. Miller.* 1822. 8vo, pp. 48. BA. + Second Edition. *Charleston.* 1822. 8vo, pp. 48. + Second Edition. ... *Boston: Joseph W. Ingraham.* 1822. 8vo, pp. 50. BA. + Third Edition. *Charleston.* 1822. 4to, pp. 49.

Charleston College. Catalogue of the Trustees, Faculty and Students, of the Charleston College. *Charleston, S. C.: printed by E. A. Miller.* 1824. 8vo, pp. 8. Continued. H. 12033

Also: Report of the Faculty to the Standing Committee of the Trustees of the College of Charleston, 1831. *Charleston: printed by G. S. Burges.* 1831. 8vo, pp. 19, (1). H. — Report of the Curator of the Museum of Natural History. 1854. 8vo.

Census of the City of Charleston, South Carolina, for the year 1848. Exhibiting the condition, and prospects of the city, illustrated by many statistical details, prepared by J. L. Dawson, M.D., and H. W. DeSaussure, M.D. *Charleston, S. C.* 1849. 8vo, pp. 270. + Census of the City of Charleston for 1861. *Charleston.* 1861. 8vo. BA. 12034

Chamber of Commerce. Charleston, 13th Nov., 1845. ... on the Questions proposed by the Secretary of the Treasury, respecting the Operation of the Tariff ... a Report ... . [n. p. n. d.] 8vo, pp. 24. BA. 12035

The Charleston Almanac for 1868. *Boston: C. C. Roberts, Printer.* 16mo, pp. 32. 12036

Charleston Board of Trade. *Charleston, S. C. July* 2, 1867. 4to, 2 l. H. 12037

Resolution adopted at the meeting of the board, and communication addressed to the general commanding the military district, in relation to recent orders.

The Charleston Book. A Miscellany in Prose and Verse. *Charleston: Samuel Hart, Sen.* 1845. 12mo, pp. viii, 5–404. BA.

The Charleston Directory, and Revenue System. By Jacob Milligan, of the Intelligence Office, September 1790. *Charleston: Printed by T. B. Bowen.* 8vo, Title, pp. 56. Continued.

The Rules and By-Laws of the Charleston Library Society, and the Act of the Legislature of South Carolina incorporating the said Society, with the Royal Confirmation. The Fourth Edition. *Charleston: Printed for the Society by Nathan Childs & Co.* MDCCLXXXV. 4to, pp. 26. + Fifth Edition. *Charleston: printed by W. P. Young.* 1805. Sm. 4to, pp. 23. + *Charleston.* 1840. 8vo. 12040

Also: A Catalogue of Books belonging to the Charleston Library Society. May, 1806. *Charleston.* 1806. 16mo, pp. 79, (1). BA. + *Charleston.* 1811. 12mo, pp. 146. + Supplementary Catalogue. *Charleston, S. C.* 1816. 12mo, pp. 21. H. + Catalogue. *Charleston.* 1826. 8vo, pp. xvi, 375. BA. + 1845. C.

Charleston Medical Journal and Review; Edited and Published by C. Happoldt, Assisted by Drs. Crane and Brewer. *Charleston.* 1854. 8vo. Continued. 12041

Charleston, South Carolina. A Satiric Poem; shewing, that Slavery still exists in a Country, which Boasts, above all others, of Being the Seat of Liberty. By a Westindian [*sic*]. *London: S. Y. Collins.* 1851. 8vo, pp. 12. 12042

City Accounts. *Charleston. August* 31, 1803. 1 l. H. 12043

A Collection of the Ordinances of the City Council of Charleston, from ... October, 1826, to ... March, 1832. To which are added, the Acts of the Legislature of South-Carolina, relating to the Corporation of Charleston, passed in and since December, 1825. ... *Charleston: printed by A. E. Miller.* 1832. 8vo, Title, pp. 90. H. 12044

Comments of the Charleston Mercury on the Cases of Livingston et al., vs. Woodworth et al., and W. J. Bennett vs. J. W. Motte. Decided in the Supreme Court of the United States, ... 1854. *Charleston.* 1854. 8vo, pp. 28, (2). H. 12045

Constitution of the Apprentices' Library Society of Charleston, S. C. Adopted ... March 10th, 1841. *Charleston, S. C.: printed by B. B. Hussey.* 1841. 8vo, pp. 16. H. 12040

Also: The First Exhibition of the Charleston Apprentices' Library Society, for the Ecouragement of Fine Arts, ... *Charleston: printed by B. B. Hussey.* 1842. + Catalogue of the Books. *Charleston, S. C.: B. B. Hussey.* 1840. 12mo, pp. 336. H.

Constitution of the Phœnix Rifles, November, 1861. *Charleston.* 1862. 8vo. 12047

A Digest of the Ordinances of the City of Charleston from 1783 to 1818, to which are annexed Extracts from the Acts of the Legislature which relate to the City of Charleston. *Charleston.* 1818. 8vo. 12048

The Disabilities of Charleston for Complete and Equal Taxation, and the Influence of State Taxation on her Prosperity; also an Examination of the Measure of Mr. James G. Holmes, for the Liquidation of the Debt of the City, ... being Reports of the Committee on Ways and Means, ... April, 1857. ... *Charleston: Walker, Evans & Co., Printers.* 1857. 8vo, pp. 59, (1). H. 12049

Discourses and Proceedings at the Dedication of the Re-modelled Unitarian Church, Charleston, S. C. *Charleston.* 1854. 8vo, pp. 148. 12050

Documents Relative to the Controversy in the First Presbyterian Church of the City of Charleston, (S. C.) which terminated in the Resignation of the Pastor. *Charleston: printed by A. E. Miller.* 1817. 8vo, pp. 42. BA. 12051

Proceedings of the Elliott Society of Natural History of Charleston, South Carolina. Vol. I, Nov. 1853–Dec. 1858. *Charleston.* 1858. 8vo. 12052

Examination of the Charleston Memorial. *Philadelphia.* 1827. 8vo, pp. 29. + No. v. Second Edition. *Philadelphia.* 1827. 8vo. 12053

Relates to the tariff. *See* [Carey (M.)]

The Late contemplated Insurrection in Charleston, S. C.; with the Execution of 36 of the Patriots; the Death of Wm. Irving, the Provoked Husband, and Joe Devaul, for refusing to be a Slave; with the Capture of the American Slaver trading between Washington and New Orleans, and the Capture of the "Amistad." *New York.* 1850. 8vo. 12054

List of the Tax Payers for 1859. *Charleston.* 1860. 8vo.

Memorial and Proceedings of the City Council of Charleston, On the Subject of Securing the City from Fires. *Charleston: printed by James S. Burges.* 1838. 8vo, pp. 24. H. 12056

Memorial of Sundry Masters of American Vessels lying in the Port of Charleston, S. C. ... Washington. 1823. 8vo, pp. 8. (17th Cong. 2d Sess. House Doc.) 12057

The Memorial of the Chamber of Commerce of the Citizens of Charleston, [S. C.] against the Tariff on Woollen Goods, proposed at the 2d Session of the 19th Congress. *Charleston: C. C. Sebring.* 1827. 8vo, pp. 16. H., W. 12058

... Memorial of the Citizens of Charleston, praying the Establishment of an Uniform System of Bankruptcy. ... *Washington.* 1822, 8vo, pp. 7. (17th Cong. 1st Sess. House Doc.) BA.

Minutes of the Convention of Banks, of the City of Charleston, Held on the 3d and 6th of Feb. 1841, to consider the Act of the Legislature, passed at the last Session; with the Opinions of the Solicitors of each Bank. *Charleston, S. C.: printed by A. E. Miller.* 1841. 8vo, pp. 27. H. 12060

Operations of the Commission before Charleston. 8vo, pp. 4.

No. 70 of the United States Sanitary Commission's publications.

Ordinances of the City Council of Charleston ... Collected and Revised by Alexander Edwards. *Charleston: printed by W. P. Young.* MDCCCII. 4to, Title, pp. 234, (2). H. 12062

Pastoral Letter of the Presbytery of Charleston, to the Churches of the Presbyterian Denomination, within their Bounds. *Charleston: printed by Benjamin F. Timothy.* 1799. 8vo, pp. 14.

Port of Charles Town, in South Carolina, Nov. 1, 1736. An Account of sundry Goods imported and of sundry goods the Produce of this Province exported from 1724 to 1735 ... *Charleston.* 1736. Folio, 1 sheet. + Nov. 1, 1736, to Nov. 1, 1737. Folio, 1 sheet. + Nov. 1, 1736, to Nov. 1, 1738. Folio, 1 sheet. 12064

Proceedings at the Semi-Centennial Celebration of the Washington Light Infantry, 22d and 23d February, 1857. ... *Charleston: Walker, Evans & Co., Printers.* 1857. 8vo, pp. 80. BA.

Proceedings at the Annual Meeting of the Stockholders of the Bank of Charleston, S. C. ... July 12th, 1858. *Charleston: printed by A. E. Miller.* 1858. 8vo, pp. 18. H. 12066

Proceedings of the Citizens of Charleston on the Incendiary Machinations, now in Progress Against the Peace and Welfare of the Southern States. ... *Charleston: printed by A. E. Miller.* 1835. 12mo, pp. 12. H. 12067

Proceedings of the Celebration of the 4th July, 1831, at Charleston, S. C. ... *Charleston: Printed by Archibald E. Miller.* 1831. 12mo, pp. 84. H. 12068

The Proceedings of the Citizens & City Council of Charleston, in relation to the Destruction of the Steamboat Horne. ... *Charleston, S. C.: Printed by Thomas J. Eccles.* 1837. 8vo, pp. 39. H. 12069

Proceedings of the Fourth Convention of Merchants and others, held in Charleston, S. C., April 15, 1839, for the Promotion of the Direct Trade. *Charleston: A. E. Miller, Printer.* 1839. 8vo, pp. 64. H. 12070

Proceedings of the Meeting in Charleston, S. C., May 13–15, 1845, on the Religious Instruction of the Negroes, together with the Report of the Committee, and the Address to the Public. ... *Charleston, S. C.: printed by B. Jenkins.* 1845. 8vo, pp. 72.

Proceedings of the State-Rights Celebration at Charleston, S. C., July 1, 1830. *Charleston.* 1830. 12mo, pp. 56. M. 12072

Report of Interments in the City of Charleston, with the Name and Number of each Disease, from 1828 to 1846: ... Prevailing Diseases in each Month, and the Thermometrical Range, &c. from 1834 to 1846. *Charleston: S. C.: printed by Miller & Browne.* 1846. 8vo, pp. 21. H. 12073

Also: Report of the Committee of the City Council of Charleston, upon Interments within the City, and the Memorial from Churches and Citizens. *Charleston, S. C.: Walker, Evans & Co., Printers.* 1859. 8vo, pp. 30. H.

Report of the Board of Commissioners of Free Schools. ... *Charleston.* 1859. 8vo, pp. 31. Plate and Plans. H. 12074

Report of the Investigation by Council of the Charges against General Geddes, relative to his Contract with the Council, upon their widening Berresford's Alley. ... *Charleston: printed by A. E. Miller.* 1824. 8vo, pp. 78. H. 12075

Report on the Free Colored Poor, of the City of Charleston. *Charleston, S. C.: Burges & James.* 1842. 8vo, pp. 12. H.

A Report, relative to the Proceedings for the Relief of the Sick Poor, during the late Epidemic; and on the Subject, ... of the Public Health. ... Presented ... by H. L. Pinckney, Mayor. *Charleston: printed by W. Riley.* 1838. 8vo, pp. 31. H. 12077

Annual Report of the City Registrar, comprising Return of Deaths, ... for the Year 1859; together with Abstracts of the Barometer, Thermometer, Dew-point, Winds and Weather at Charleston, S. C., ... *Charleston, S. C.: Walker, Evans & Co.* [*Printers.*] 1860. 8vo, pp. 8, 1 l. Table. H. 12078

Report of the Committee of the South-Carolina Conference of the Methodist-Episcopal Church, on the Schism in Charleston. *Charleston.* 1835. 8vo, pp. 40. 12079

Report of the Commissioners on the Survey for a Railroad between Charleston and Cincinnati. *Columbia, S. C.* 1836. 8vo, pp. 34. M. 12080

Report on the Harbor of Charleston, S. C., by ... A. D. Bache ... [and others]. Also Report of Capt. A. H. Bowman ... with Estimate for deepening the Bar of Sullivan's Island, or Beach Channel. ... With Report of Commissioners appointed by the State ... . *Charleston.* 1858. 8vo, pp. 62, 10. H. 12081

Rules of the Charleston Chamber of Commerce. *Charlestown: printed by Robert Wells.* MDCCLXXIV. 12mo, pp. 19. H. + *Charleston: Walker, Evans & Co.* 1858. 8vo, pp. 43. H. 12082

Rules for the Government of the Orphan-House, at Charleston, South-Carolina. *Charleston: printed by W. P. Young.* 1806. 12mo, pp. 15. 12083

Rules of the Fellowship Society, established at Charleston, South-Carolina, April IV. A.D. MDCCLXII. Incorporated by an Act of the General Assembly of the said Province ... and finally ratified by our Most Gracious Sovereign, in Council, June XV. A.D. MDCCLXX. The Third Edition. *Charlestown: printed by Robert Wells.* MDCCLXXIV. 8vo, pp. 47. H. + Fifth Edition. *Charleston.* 1804. 4to. W. 12084

Rules of the Incorporated South-Carolina Society, originally established at Charlestown, the First of September, MDCCXXXVI; digested and ratified on the Twenty-first of January, MDCCXCIV. The Sixth Edition. *Charleston: Printed by Markland & M'Iver.* MDCCXCV. 8vo, pp. 62. H. 12085

Rules of the New-England-Society, of Charleston, S. C. Founded Jan. 6, 1819. [With a List of the Officers and Members. *Charleston:*] *printed at the Office of the "Courier."* 1820. 12mo, pp. 12. H. + Revised, 1830. *Charleston.* 1830. 8vo, pp. 25. 12086

Rules of the St. Andrew's Club, at Charles-town, in South Carolina. *London.* 1750. 12mo. P. + Rules of the Saint Andrew's Society of the City of Charleston, S. C. *Charleston.* 1830. 8vo, pp. 46. 12087

A Schedule of the Ordinances of the City Council of Charleston from the year 1783 to May 19th 1813. *Charleston, S. C.: Printed by J. M. Bounethfan.* 1813. 12088

This also contains a "Schedule of the Acts of the Legislature of South Carolina," which relate to the Corporation and City of Charleston, from 13th August, 1783, to the 18th of December, 1812.

The Siege of Charleston, by the British Fleet and Army under the Command of Admiral Arbuthnot and Sir Henry Clinton, which terminated with the Surrender of that place on the 12th of May, 1780. *Albany: J. Munsell.* 1867. Sm. 4to, pp. 224.

Edited by F. B. Hough. Mostly extracts from the newspapers of the period.

Statement of Deaths, with the Diseases and Ages, in the City of Charleston, S. C., October, 1816–October, 1817. [*Charleston.* 1817.] 1 sheet. 12090

Statement of the Comparative Advantages of Charleston, over the Cities South of New-York, which are constructing Rail Roads and Canals to facilitate their Communication with the Country West of the Alleghany Mountains. *Charleston, S. C.: printed by J. S. Burges.* 1833. 8vo, pp. 8. H. 12091

The Strangers' Guide to the City of Charleston. *Charleston, S. C.* 1822. 12mo. 12092

The reports, etc., of the following benevolent societies may be consulted in the Harvard College Library: Charleston Bethel Union, Bible Society, Charleston Infant School Society, Charleston Port Society, Unitarian Book and Tract Society, Female Domestic Missionary Society, Marine Bible Society, Protestant Episcopal Missionary Society, and Reformed Society of Israelites.

Charlestown, *Mass.* An Account of the Conflagration of the Ursuline Convent. ... By a Friend of Religious Toleration. *Boston.* 1834. 12mo, pp. 35. H. 12093

Annual Addresses and Reports read before the Bunker Hill Soldiers' Relief Society April 19th, 1861, & April 20, 1863. ... *Charleston: William H. De Costa ... Advertiser Press.* 1863. 8vo, pp. 26. H. 12094

The Annual Report of the Charlestown Free Schools, ... Together with the Report of the Treasurer of the Board. [*Charlestown:*] *Press of the Bunker-Hill Aurora.* 1841. 8vo, pp. 32. Continued. H. 12095

Also: Catalogue of the High School Library, Charlestown. ... *Boston.* 1851. 16mo, pp. 51. H. — Catalogue of the Teachers and Pupils of the Charlestown High School, 1855. *Boston: printed by John Wilson and Son.* 1855. 16mo, pp. 39. H. — Rules and Orders of the School Committee, and Regulations for the Government of the Public Schools, of the City of Charlestown, Mass. ... *Charlestown: printed by Caleb Rand.* 1848. 12mo, 1 l., pp. 23. H.

Annual Statement of Receipts, Expenditures, &c., of the City of Charlestown, for the Year ending Feb. 28, 1851; together with a list of persons assessed, etc. *Boston.* 1851. 8vo, pp. 79. Continued. B. 12096

The first of which I have seen a notice is for 1843.

An Answer to Six Months in a Convent, exposing its Falsehoods and Manifold Absurdities. By the Lady Superior. With some Preliminary Remarks. *Boston: printed and published by J. H. Eastburn.* 1845. 8vo, pp. xxxvii, 66. H. 12097

For a review, *see* Reed (R. T.)

The Articles of Faith, and Covenant, of the First Church, Charlestown. *Boston.* 1842. 12mo, pp. 19. + *Boston: Press of J. Howe.* 1856. H. 12098

Also: Annual Report of the Charlestown City Mission and Tract Society: presented ... March 25, 1855. *Boston: Press of J. Howe.* 1855. 8vo, pp. 16. H. Continued. — Sixth Semi-Annual Report of the Ministry at Large, with the Report of the Edgeworth Chapel Sunday School, in Charlestown. By Oliver C. Everett. *Boston: William Chadwick, Printer.* 1851. 12mo, pp. 24. H. — Semi-Centennial Celebration of the First Sabbath School Society in Massachusetts, and the First Parish Sabbath School of Charlestown, Oct. 14, 1866. *Boston,* 1867. 12mo. S. — A Summary Declaration of the Faith and Practice of the First Baptist Church in Charlestown. *Boston: printed by C. Crocker.* 1817. 32mo, pp. 8. H.

By-Laws of the Town of Charlestown. Adopted June 20, 1838. ... And Extracts from the Statutes of the Commonwealth. *Boston: J. Howe's ... Press.* 1846. 12mo, pp. 60. H.

By-Laws of the Naval Library and Institute, with a List of Members. *Charlestown, Mass.: published by A. E. Cutter.* 1860. 12mo, pp. 12. H. 12100

Also: Statutes of the Naval Library and Institute, Navy Yard, Charlestown, Mass., adopted Dec. 31, 1866. *Boston: J. C. Farwell and Company, Printers.* 1867. 12mo, pp. 36. H.

By-Laws; with Rules and Regulations for the Government of the Asylum for the Insane in Charlestown and the Hospital in Boston. *Boston.* 1821. 8vo, pp. 24. 12101

Catalogue of the ... Charlestown Female Seminary. ... *Boston: press of Jonathan Howe.* 1834. 8vo, pp. 7. Continued.

Catalogue of the Public Library of the City of Charlestown. *Charlestown: printed by Caleb Rand.* 1862. 8vo, pp. xv, 199, (1). BA., C., H. 12103

Also: Report of the Trustees of the Public Library of the City of Charlestown, November, 1863. ... *Charlestown: printed by William W. Wheildon.* 1864. 8vo, pp. 8

The Charlestown Association for the Reformation of Morals ... I. A Discourse ... By the Rev. Jedidiah Morse, D.D. II. The Constitution ... . III. Rules ... . IV. Extracts from certain Laws of ... Massachusetts ... . *Boston.* 1813. 12mo, pp. 48. BA. 12104

The Charlestown Convent; its Destruction by a Mob, on the Night of August 11, 1834. ... Also, the Trials of the Rioters ... And a Contemporary Appendix. Compiled from Authentic Sources. *Boston: New England News Company.* 1870. 8vo, 1 l., pp. 5–98. 12105

The Charlestown Directory, containing the Names of the Inhabitants for the Year 1834. *Charlestown,* [*Mass.:*] *A. Quimby.* 1834. 18mo, pp. 76. Map. C. + Fletcher's Charlestown Directory. ... *Charlestown: C. P. Emmons.* 1848. 18mo, pp. 148. Continued. BA. 12106

The Charlestown Young Men's Evangelical Union. ... Constitution and By-Laws. *Charlestown.* 1853. 12mo, pp. 13. H.

City of Charlestown. The Inaugural Address of the Mayor delivered April 26th, 1847, upon the First Organization of the City Government of the City of Charlestown. ... *Charlestown.* 1847. 12mo, pp. 26. Continued. H. 12108

City of Charlestown. Documents printed by Order of the City Council, or of one of the Branches thereof during the Municipal Year 1847–8. *Charlestown: Henry S. Warren, Printer.* 1848. 8vo, Title, pp. (2), 26, 83, (1), 14, 8, 7, 14, (1), (1), 15, 7, 36, 63. 12109

Also: Contract. City of Charlestown, with Woodlawn Cemetery. 1858. ... *Charlestown: printed by Caleb Rand & Co.* 1859. 8vo, pp. 15. Map. H.

Documents relating to the Ursuline Convent in Charlestown. *Boston: reprinted by Samuel N. Dickinson.* 1842. 8vo, pp. 32.

History of the High St. Baptist Church in Charlstown, Ms. with the Names of Members. *Boston: Press of J. Howe.* 1853. 12mo, pp. 36. H. 12111

List of Persons assessed a State, Town and County Tax, in the Town of Charlestown, for the Year 1844. ... *Charlestown.* 1845. 8vo, pp. 56. Continued. H. 12112

Municipal Register of the City of Charlestown: containing the Rules & Orders of the City Council, List of City Officers, Charter of the City, Ordinances, &c. ... *Charlestown: printea by Caleb Rand.* 1848. 8vo, pp. 113. Continued. H. 12113

Proceedings of the Town of Charlestown, in the County of Middlesex, and Commonwealth of Massachusetts; in Respectful Testimony of the Distinguished Talents and Pre-eminent Virtues of the late George Washington. [*Charlestown.*] *January,* MDCCC. 8vo, pp. 46, 36, 24. + *London: John Stockdale.* 1800. 8vo, pp. 82. 12114

Contains Morse's "Prayer and Sermon," which was reprinted in London, *see* Morse (J.) The account of the proceedings was written by Josiah Bartlett, Esq.

Report of the Committee, relating to the Destruction of the Ursuline Convent, (at Charlestown, [Mass.]) Aug. 11, 1834. *Boston: J. H. Eastburn, Printer.* 1834. 8vo, pp. 16 H. 12115

Reasons, principally of a public Nature, against a New Bridge from Charlestown to Boston. *Boston.* 1825. 8vo, pp. 32. H.

Also: Report of the Commissioners and Chief Engineer of the Charlestown Water Works. February 28, 1865. *Boston: Little, Brown and Company.* 1865. 8vo, pp. 93. Map. H.

Rules and Regulations of the Charlestown Gas Company. *Charlestown: W. W. Wheildon, Printer.* 1852. 12mo, pp. 8.

Report of a Majority of the Committee appointed by the Town of Charlestown, to consider the Expediency of obtaining a City Charter. *Charlestown: printed by W. W. Wheildon.* 1846. 8vo, pp. 15. H. 12118

Review of the Case of the Free Bridge, between Boston and Charlestown. In which the Expediency and Constitutionality of that Measure are considered; with a Statement of the Legislative Proceedings upon it at the Late January Session. Including the Public Documents. *Boston: Dutton & Wentworth, Printers.* 1827. 8vo, pp. vi, 106. H. 12119

Rules and Orders of the City Council, and a List of the Officers of the City of Charlestown, for 1847. *Charlestown: Henry S. Warren, City Printer.* [n. d.] 12mo, pp. 83. H.

Sacred Performances at the Dedication of the Baptist Meeting-House in Charlestown, May 12, 1801. Consisting of an Introductory Address, by Jedidiah Morse, D.D. A Sermon, adapted to the Occasion, by Samuel Stillman, D.D. and an Address on the Recognition of the Church, by Thomas Baldwin, A.M. *Boston: printed by Manning & Loring.* [n. d.] 8vo, pp. 30, 1 l. BA. 12121

Sketch of the Action on the Heights of Charlestown, 17 June, 1775, between the troops under General Howe, and a large body of American Rebels. Map. 12122

Statement of the Expenses of the Town of Charlestown. Commencing May 1828, and ending April 1829. [*Charlestown:*] *Wheildon and Raymond,* (*Printers*). [n. d.] 8vo, pp. 24. Continued. H. 12123

Statement of the Receipts, Expenditures, &c. of the City of Charlestown, For ... 1849. ... *Boston: J. Howe, Printer,* ... 1849. 8vo, pp. 34. Continued. B. 12124

Third Grand Rally of the Workingmen of Charlestown, Mass., held October 23d, 1840. 8vo, pp. 18. H. 12125

Trial of John R. Buzzell, ... for Arson and Burglary in the Ursuline Convent, at Charlestown. *Boston: published by Russell, Odiorne and Metcalf.* 1834. 8vo, pp. 103. H. 12126

CHARLEVOIX (P. F. X. de). Histoire de l'Isle Espagnole ou de S. Domingue, Ecrite particulierement sur des Memoires Manuscrits du P. Jean-Baptiste le Pers, Jesuite, Missionaire à Saint Domingue, & sur les Pieces Originales, qui se conservent au Dépôt de la Marine. Par le P. Pierre François-Xavier de Charlevoix, de la Compagnie de Jesus. ... *Paris: François Didot.* M. DCC. XXX.–MDCCXXXI. 2 vols., 4to, pp. xxviij, 482, (59), 6 Maps; xiv, 506, (61). 11 Maps. BA. 12127

Some copies have the publisher's name, *Jacques Guerin,* others, *Paris: Prelard. See* Leclerc, No. 320. There are copies on large paper.

CHARLEVOIX. Histoire de S. Domingue. [As before.] *A Amsterdam, Chez François L'Honoré.* MDCCXXXIII. 4 vols., 12mo,

Title, pp. xxiv, 292; Title, xiv, 390; xii, 302; Title, xii, 429, (1). Maps and Plates. BA., H. 12128

The titles to each volume are engraved by Picart. "According to the judgment of Bayle, this is the best of the works of Charlevoix. The worthy father says, however, that if he had listened to the different critics who passed judgment on his work, he should have been in the case of the man in the fable, who, between his two wives, was left without any hair on his head." — RICH, I. 44.

CHARLEVOIX. Histoire du Paraguay. Par le R. P. Pierre François-Xavier de Charlevoix, de la Compagnie de Jesus. ... *Paris: Didot.* M. DCC. LVI. 3 vols., 4to, 5 l., pp. 489, xxxiij, (4); 2 l., pp. 356, clviij, (2); 2 l., pp. 285, cccxv, (2). 3 Maps, and Plans. H. 12129

Contains many original Spanish documents, with a French translation, including "Journal d'un Voiage le long de la Côte de la Mer Magellanique." Mr. Bartlett describes a copy of this edition in which the collation differs.

CHARLEVOIX. Histoire du Paraguay. Par le P. Pierre François-Xavier De Charlevoix, de la Compagnie de Jesus. *Paris: Didot, Giffart, Nyon.* M.DCC.LVII. 6 vols., 12mo, Half-Title, Title, pp. 390, (2), Map; Half-Title, Title, 476, Map; Half-Title, Title, 407, (1), Map; 2 l., pp. 414, (1), Map; 1 l., pp. 461,(2); 2 l., pp. 460, 3 Maps. BA., H. 12130

There are copies with the imprint, *Paris: Chez Desaint.* MDCCLVII. "The most complete and satisfactory work on Paraguay, and the only one in which the vast system of the Jesuits is fully developed, the position of the author affording him peculiar opportunities for its examination." The "Biog. Univ.," however, does not speak well of it. *See* Faribault, 136; M. R., XVI. 558; XXIII. 417, and Backer, VII. 191–2.

CHARLEVOIX. Historia Paraguaiensis Petri Francisci-Xaverii de Charlevoix, ex gallico latina, cum animadversionibus et supplemento. *Venetiis: Fr. Sansoni.* MDCCLXXIX. Folio, 2 l., pp. 608. 12131

This Latin translation was made by P. Dominique Muriel, and contains a number of additional notes.

CHARLEVOIX. Geschichte von Paraguay und dem Missionswerke der Jesuiten in diesem Lande, aus dem Französischen des P. Franz Xavier de Charlevoix von der Gesellschaft Jesu. *Nürnberg, bey Gabr. Nic. Raspe.* 1768. 2 vols., 8vo, Map. + *Wien: Mechitaristen Congreg. B.* 1830. 2 vols., 12mo, 4 l., pp. 332; 370. Map. C. 12132

CHARLEVOIX. The History of Paraguay. Containing, Amongst many other New, Curious, and Interesting Particulars of that Country, a Full and Authentic Account of the Establishments formed there by the Jesuits, from among the Savage Natives, In the very Centre of Barbarism; Establishments allowed

to have realized the Sublime Ideas of Fenelon, Sir Thomas More, and Plato. Written originally in French, by the celebrated Father Charlevoix. ... *London: Lockyer Davis.* MDCCLXIX. 2 vols., 8vo, pp. vii, 463; viii, 415. BA. + *Dublin.* 1769. 2 vols., 8vo, pp. viii, 463; viii, 415. 12133

"An abridgment of Father Charlevoix's large work." — RICH, I. 170. *See* M. R., XLV. 486.

CHARLEVOIX. Histoire du Japon et du Paraguay. Nouvelle édition, revue, corrigée et augmentée jusqu'à nos jours. [Prospectus.] *Paris: Gauthier freres.* 1827. 12mo. 12134

This edition was to be in 14 volumes, with an atlas.

CHARLEVOIX. Histoire et description generale de la Nouvelle France, avec le Journal Historique d'un Voyage fait par ordre du Roi dans l'Amerique Septentrionnale. Par le P. De Charlevoix, de la Compagnie de Jesus. ... *A Paris, chez Pierre-François Giffart, rue Saint Jacques à Sainte Theres.* M.DCC.XLIV. 3 vols., 4to. + *A Paris, Chez Nyon Fils, Libraire, Quai des Augustins, à l'Occasion.* M.DCC.XLIV. 3 vols., 4to. + *A Paris, Chez la Veuve Ganeau, Libraire, rue S. Jacques, près la ruë du Plâtre, aux Armes de Dombes.* M. DCC. XLIV. Avec approbation et privilege du Roi. 3 vols., 4to, Half-Title, Title, pp. (4), viij, lxj, (3), ix–xxvj, 664. 10 Maps, 2 Vignettes. ‖ Vol. II. Half-Title, Title, pp. xv, (1), 582. 8 Maps. Description des plantes principales ... . pp. 56. 44 Plates of Plants. ‖ Vol. III. Journal d'un Voyage fait par ordre du Roi dans l'Amerique Septentrionnale; Addressé a Madame la Duchessse De Lesdiguieres . ... *A Paris: Veuve Ganeau.* M.DCC.XLIV. 4to, Half-Title, Title, pp. xix, xiv, 543. 10 Maps, and Vignette. H. 12135

The arrangement varies in some copies, according to the whim of the binder. I have seen a copy in which Vol. II. has, prefixed to the regular order of the history, two papers, "Plantes de l'Amerique Sept.," pp. 56, and 22 plates (the latter arranged to suit either this or the 12mo edition, described *infra*), and "Projet d'un corps d'histoire du Nouveau Monde," pp. lxi, (iii), followed by the "Table des Sommaires," Tome II., pp. xv, (1), and the continuation of the text of Vol. I., pp. 582; vignette on title, and one in text, 8 maps. Tross describes a copy of Giffart's edition on fine paper. In the Nuggets, No. 518, another edition is described, "*A Paris: Chez Rolin Fils, Libraire. Quai des Augustins* MDCCXLIV." Vol. I., 4 l., pp. xxvi, 644, 10 maps; II. 2 l., pp. lxj, table, 1, permission, 1 l., table, pp. xv, "Fautes," 1, 582, 8 maps, "Description des Plantes Principales de l'Amérique Septentrionnale," 56, 22 plates; III., 19 l., pp. 543, 10 maps. In Mr. Brown's catalogue a copy is described, the collation of which seems to differ from this. Dr. Shea has a copy in which Rolin's name is spelt Ro*ll*in, in Vol. III. It is evident that the arrangement of the preliminary and supplemental matter is often changed by the binder; but our collation of Ganeau's edition describes a *perfect* copy, and any set which does not include the pages lxj (3) in one or other of the volumes, is imperfect. The work was reprinted as follows:

CHARLEVOIX. Histoire et description generale de la Nouvelle France, avec le journal historique d'un Voyage ... dans l'Amérique Septentrionnale. Par le P. De Charlevoix. ... *Paris: Pierre-Francois Giffart.* M DCC XLIV. 6 vols., 12mo, Title, pp. (4), viii, 454; Title, 501; Title, 465; Title, 388; Title, xxviii, 456; Title, 434, (4). 28 Maps. H. 12136

There are the same variations on the imprint in this as in the quarto edition. I have seen the work described with the imprint, "*Paris: Nyon.* MDCCXLIV," "*Paris: Ganeau.* MDCCXLIV," "*Paris: Didot.* MDCCXLIX," and "*Paris: Rolin fils.* MDCCXLIX." They are all the same edition, and, it may be presumed, that the work was a joint-stock speculation, each subscriber having his own name on the title of his own copies. Vols. V. and VI. are entitled, "Journal historique d'un Voyage." The plates to Didot's edition are usually bound up in a separate volume. Dr. J. G. Shea informs us that the index to this edition is very much abridged. "This is is one of the most important works there is relating to Canada. It contains not only what the author saw himself, but he has collected from the best authorities, and with great judgment." — RICH, I. "De toutes des relations de Canada, c'est dans celle-ci, qu'on peut s'instruire le mieux sur les nombreuses peuplades qui y étaient répandues et dont quelques-unes subsistent encore." — BOUCHER. The laborious accuracy with which this work was executed may be estimated by the fact that the maps, dated 1743, are marked with the latest discoveries, in 1742, in the extreme north of America. *See also* Tuckerman's "America and her Commentators," p. 49; N. A. R., XXII. 58; Faribault, pp. 28–39; Murray's "America;" and "Biog. Universelle."

CHARLEVOIX. History and General Description of New France. By the Rev. P. F. X. de Charlevoix, S.J. Translated, with Notes, by John Gilmary Shea. In Six Volumes. *New York: John Gilmary Shea.* 1866–70. 4 vols., 8vo, 2 l., pp. 286, (1); 3 l., pp. 284, (1); 2 l., pp. v, 11–312, (1); 1 l., pp. 308, (1). 9 Portraits, 10 Maps, and 4 Plates. BA., C. 12137

Vols. V. and VI. are in press. Twenty-five copies are printed on large paper, in 4to. This is the first translation into English of Charlevoix's celebrated and important work. Dr. Shea has added notes, corrected references, and improved the bibliography, at the same time retaining, in all its originality, Charlevoix's text.

CHARLEVOIX. Allgemeine Geschichte und Beschreibung von Neu-Frankreich, was die Entdeckungen und groberungen der Franzosen in dem nordlichen America betrifft. *Leipzig: Arkstee & Merkus.* 1756. 4to, 4 l., pp. 648, 20 l. 18 Maps. C.

See "Allgemeine Historie der Reisen," v. 14.

CHARLEVOIX. Journal of a Voyage to North America. Undertaken by Order of the French King. Containing The Geographical Description and Natural History of that Country, particularly Canada. Together with An Account of the Customs, Characters, Religion, Manners and Traditions of the original Inhabitants. In a Series of Letters to the Duchess of Lesdiguieres. Translated from the French of P. de Charlevoix.

... *London: R. and J. Dodsley.* M DCC LXI. 2 vols., 8vo, pp. viii, 382; viii, 380, (22). Map. BA., C., H. 12139

"This translation betrays, by numerous Scotticisms and misrepresentations, the hand of a north Briton, too little acquainted with the French and English languages to read or write either with propriety. — M. R., XXIII. 417.

CHARLEVOIX. Letters to the Dutchess of Lesdiguieres; Giving an Account of a Voyage to Canada, and Travels through that vast Country, and Louisiana, to the Gulf of Mexico. Undertaken By Order of the present King of France, By Father Charlevoix. Being a more full and accurate Description of Canada, and the neighbouring Countries, than has been before published; the Character of every Nation or Tribe in that vast Tract being given; their Religion, Customs, Manners, Traditions, Government, Languages, and Towns; the Trade carried on with them, and at what Places; the Posts or Forts, and Settlements, established by the French; the great Lakes, Water-Falls, and Rivers with the Manner of navigating them; the Mines, Fisheries, Plants, and Animals of these Countries. With Reflections on the Mistakes the French have committed in carrying on their Trade and Settlements; and the most proper method of proceeding pointed out. Including also an Account of the Author's Shipwreck in the Channel of Bahama, and Return in a Boat to the Mississippi, along the Coast of the Gulf of Mexico, with his Voyage from thence to St. Domingo, and back to France. *London: R. Goadby, and R. Baldwin.* 1763. 8vo, pp. xiv, (2), 384. Map. BA., C. 12140

Some copies have the date of 1764. *See* M. R., XXX. 253, and French's "Louisiana," Vol. III.

CHARLEVOIX. La vie de la Mere Marie de l'Incarnation, Institutrice et premiere Supérieure des Ursulines de la Nouvelle France. *Paris: Ant. Claude Briasson.* 1724. 8vo. + *Paris.* 1725. 4to. + *Paris: P. G. Le Mercier.* 1735. 8vo, pp. xxxx, 412, 2 l. Portrait. 12141

In some copies of the edition of 1724, *Louis Ant. Thomelin* appears as the publisher, but the prologue in all is to Briasson. "Sons fils, D. Claude Martin, fit imprimer sa vie à Paris, en 1677. Le P. Charlevoix publia la sienne en 1724, in-8. Une édition de format in-4° parut l'année suivante. L'édition portant la date de 1735 n'est pas citée. Ce doit être certainement la même que celle de 1724, dont on aura changé le titre." — LECLERC.

CHARLEVOIX. Vita della madre Suor Madre dell' incarnazione institutrice, e prima Superiora delle Orsoline della Nuova Francia. Scritta nell' idioma Franzese dal P. F. Saverio di Charlevoix. E transportata nell' Italiano. *Lucca: Sebastiano Domencio Cappuri.* 1727. 12mo, 10 l., pp. 226. J.C.B. 12142

CHARLEVOIX. A | Voyage | to | North-America: | Undertaken by Command of the present | King of France. | Containing | The Geographical Description and Natural History | of | Canada and Louisiana. | With | The Customs, Manners, Trade and Religion | of the Inhabitants; a Description of the Lakes and | Rivers, with their Navigation and Manner of passing | the Great Cataracts. | By Father Charlevoix. | Also, | A Description and Natural History of the Islands in the | West Indies belonging to the different Powers of | Europe. Illustrated with a Number of curious Prints | and Maps not in any other Edition. | In Two Volumes. | *Dublin: | Printed for John Exshaw, and James Potts, in | Dame-Street.* | MDCCLXVI. | 2 vols., 8vo, Title, 1 l., 4 l., pp. 48, 228, Plate, and 3 Maps; Title, 1 l., pp. 335, (1), 10 l., Plate, and 5 Maps. 12143

Charlevoix's account of Quebec is included in an "Account of the French Settlements in North America. By a Gentleman. *Boston.* 1746." 8vo, pp. 26. B.

Charlie, the Drummer Boy. *New York: American Tract Society.* 8vo, pp. 16. 12144

CHARLOTTESVILLE, *N. Y.* Catalogue of the Officers and Students of the New York Conference Seminary. *Albany.* 1851. 8vo. B. 12145

CHARLOTTESVILLE, *Va.* *See* Virginia.

CHARLTON (D.) Narrative of Dimmock Charlton, a British Subject, Taken from the Brig "Peacock," by the U. S. Sloop "Hornet," enslaved while a Prisoner of War, and Retained Forty-five Years in Bondage. [n. p. About 1858.] 8vo, Title, pp. 15. H. 12146

CHARLTON (E. A.) New Hampshire as it Is. In Three Parts. Part I. A Historical Sketch of New Hampshire, from its First Settlement to the Adoption of the Federal Constitution in 1788. Part II. A Gazetteer of New Hampshire; containing a Particular Description of the Several Towns, Cities, Villages, &c.; Remarkable Curiosities, Mineral Localities, Statistical Tables; Also, the Boundary and Area of the State; a General View of the Counties, both Historical and Topographical. Part III. A General View of New Hampshire; containing a Description of its Soil, Productions, Climate; its Geological and Mineralogical Features; the Principal Mountains, Lakes, and Rivers; Education and Religion; Biographical Sketches of Distinguished Men; Literary, Scientific, and Charitable Associations; Banks, Railroads, Newspapers, &c. Together with

the Constitution of the State. Compiled from numerous Authentic Sources, by Edward A. Charlton. *Claremont, N. H.: Tracy & Sandford.* 1855. 12mo. + Third Edition, Revised, with an Appendix. *Claremont, N. H.: Tracy and Company.* 1856. 8vo, pp. 592, (4). B., C., H. 12147

Some copies have the imprint, *Claremont, N. H.: A. Kenney & Company.* 1857. 12mo.

CHARLTON (F.) National Vanity. A Sermon ... on a Day of Public Thanksgiving, ... in Webster, ... November 25, 1852. By Rev. Frederic Charlton ... . *Worcester: printed by Earle & Drew.* 1852. 8vo, pp. 15. H. 12148

CHARLTON (H. M.) Address delivered before ... Oglethorpe University, by H. M. Charlton, Nov. 16, 1842. *Milledgeville.* 12149

CHARLTON (R. M.) The Poetry of Death. A Lecture ... December 21st, 1848. By Robert M. Charlton. *Savannah: Edward J. Purse, Printer.* 1849. 8vo, pp. 19. H. 12150

Also: The Rule of Life; a Lecture, ... January 19, 1853. *Washington: printed by Lemuel Towers.* 1853. 8vo, pp. 20. H.

CHARLTON. Poems by Robert M. *and* Thomas J. Charlton. *Boston.* 1839, 16mo. 12151

CHARLTON (T. U. P.) The Life of Major General James Jackson. By Thomas U. P. Charlton, a Citizen of Savannah. ... Part I. *Augusta, Georgia: printed by Geo: F. Randolph.* 1809. 8vo, pp. ix, 69. BA. 12152

Also: Oration at Savannah, July 3, 1802. By Thomas U. P. Charlton. *Savannah.* 1802. 8vo. — Oration ... in ... Savannah ... July 4, 1805. *Savannah: Printed by James Hely.* 1805. 8vo, Title, pp. 15. BA.

CHARMILLY. *See* Venault de Charmilly.

CHARNAY (D.) Cités et ruines Américaines Mitla, Palenqué, Izamal, Chichen-itza, Uxmal, recueillies et photographiées par M. Désiré Charnay Avec un texte Par M. Viollet-le-Duc, Architecte du gouvernement suivi du voyage et des documents de l'auteur. *Paris: Gide.* 1863. Rl. 8vo, pp. ix, 543. 49 Plates in large folio. C. 12153

The plates are printed in photography, and are of the finest character. It is to be regretted that they not in a more durable form. The text is sold separately at 12 francs. The work, complete, is published at 500 francs, and is certainly entitled to the appellation of *ouvrage magnifique.*

CHARNAY. Le Mexique, souvenirs et impressions de voyage ... Par Désiré Charnay. *Paris: Dentu.* 1863. 18mo, pp. 441.

CHARNOCK (J.) Biographia Navalis: or, Impartial Memoirs of the Lives and Characters of Officers of the Navy of Great Britain, From the Year 1660 ... . By John Charnock, Esq. With Portraits and other Engravings by Bartolozzi, &c. ... *London: R. Faulder.* 1794–97. 5 vols., 8vo. BA. 12155

Later editions are in 6 vols., octavo. The work includes some details of the American Revolution. "The Biographical Memoirs of Lord Viscount Nelson," by John Charnock, contains some account of Nelson's services in the West Indies.

CHAROLAIS. L'indépendence d'Haïti et la France. Par Charolais. *Paris: Dentu.* 1861. 8vo, pp. 32. 12156

CHARPENNE (P.) Mon voyage au Mexique, ou le colon de Guazacoalco. Par Pierre Charpenne. *Paris: Roux.* 1836. 2 vols., 8vo, Title, pp. x, 334; Title, 332. H. 12157

"This book is the relation of the adventures of five or six hundred Frenchmen, who left France in 1831, under the patronage of M. Lainé de Villevêque, to found a colony in Mexico. M. Charpenne is at once the Ulysses and the Homer of this unfortunate epopee, which resulted only in the most miserable deceptions. He set out in the early part of 1831, and returned at the end of the same year, his stomach ruined, his feet and legs swelled, and poorer than before. This book contains interesting details on little known parts of Mexico." — QUÉRARD.

CHARROPPIN (A.) Du libre travail dans les colonies françaises. Par Ad. Charroppin de la Guadeloupe. *Bordeaux: Chaumas-Gayet.* 1848. 8vo. 12158

Charter, Constitution and By-Laws, of the Society for the Development of the Mineral Resources of the United States. Instituted April 1, 1848, and Chartered February 12, 1849. Published by order of the Society. *Philadelphia: T. H. Jones, Printer.* 1849. 12mo, pp. 8. 12159

The Charter Oak. Its History — its Fall. Aug. 21, 1856. *Hartford.* 1856. 12mo, pp. 12. 12160

Proceedings at the Dedication of Charter Oak Hall. By J. Deane Alden. *Hartford.* MDCCCLVI. 8vo, pp. 45. Maps.

Also: Account of the Charter-Oak. 1851. 16mo, pp. 4.

The Charters of the British Colonies in America. *London: J. Almon.* [1774.] 8vo, Title, pp. 142. + *Dublin.* 1776. 8vo, Title, pp. 142. H. 12162

Includes Massachusetts Bay, Connecticut, Rhode Island, Virginia, Pennsylvania, Maryland, and Georgia.

The Charters Of the following Provinces of North America, viz. Virginia, Maryland, Connecticut, Rhode-Island, Pennsyl-

vania, Massachusett's Bay, and Georgia. To which is prefixed, A Faithful Narrative of the Proceedings of the North American Colonies, In Consequence of the late Stamp-Act. *London: W. Owen: J. Almon; and F. Blyth.* M DCC LXVI. 4to, Title, pp. 18, 15, 5, 4, 6, 5, 9, 7. Map. BA., C., H. 12163

The map is dated 1763. "Collected from the 'Daily Gazetteer,' both charters and narrative. There is no doubt of the authenticity of the former, and the latter, being copies of the gazettes, etc., carry their own evidence with them." — M. R.

CHARTON (E.) Voyageurs anciens et modernes, ou Choix des relations de voyages les plus intéressantes et les plus instructives depuis le Ve siècle avant Jésus-Christ jusqu'an XIXe siècle; avec biographies, notes et indications iconographiques, par M. Édouard Charton. *Paris: aux bureaux du Magasin pittoresque.* 1853–56. 4 vols., 8vo. 12164

CHARTON. Los viajeros modernos ... . Por M. Eduardo Charton. Traducida al castellano y arreglada en la parte relative a Cristobal Colon y Hernan Cortes bajo la direccion de Don Mariano Urrabieta. *Paris: El correo de Ultramar.* 1860. 8vo, pp. vii, 421. + *Paris: Lassale y Mélan.* 1861. 8vo, pp. vii, 480. 12165

CHAS (Jean), *and* LEBRUN (M.) Histoire politique et philosophique de la revolution de l'Amérique Septentrionale; par les citoyens J. Chas et Lebrun. *Paris: An* IX [1801]. 8vo, 4 l., pp. viij, 458. BA., C., H. 12166

CHASE (B.) History of Old Chester, from 1719 to 1869. By Benjamin Chase. *Auburn, N. H.: the Author.* 1869. 8vo, pp. xvi, 702. Map, Woodcuts, and 15 Portraits. BA., H.

Old Chester included Raymond, Candia, Hookset, Derryfield, and Auburn.

CHASE (B. C.) An Address delivered at Camden, Maine, September 11, 1855. At the expiration of Half a Century from the Organization of the First Congregational Church in that Town. ... By the Rev. B. C. Chase, Pastor. *Boston.* 1855. 8vo, pp. 28. H., S. 12168

CHASE (C.) A Discourse delivered in ... Claremont, January 4, 1861, being the Day appointed ... for General Fasting and Prayer, on Account of the Distracted State of the Country. By Charlton Chase ... . *Claremont: George G. and Lemuel N. Ide.* 1861. 8vo, pp. 16. H. 12169

CHASE. The Sermon at the Consecration of Jonathan M. Wainwright, ... To the Episcopate ... by Charlton Chase, D.D., Bishop of New-Hampshire. ... *New York: Daniel Dana, Jr.* ... MDCCCLII. 8vo, pp. xv, 2–25. H., S. 12170

Also: A Correspondence between Bishops Chase and McIlvaine. *Detroit.* 1834. 12mo, pp. 32.

CHASE (C. T.) A Manual on School-Houses and Cottages for the People of the South. Prepared by C. Thurston Chase. *Washington: Government Printing Office.* 1868. 8vo, pp. 83, 1 slip. BA. 12171

CHASE (D. T.) Reports of the Trials of David T. Chase and John W. Fellows for an alleged Conspiracy, &c.: and of Jired Bull on an Indictment for Perjury, in the Court of Sessions. Reported by J. S. Carpenter. *New-York.* 1829, 8vo, pp. 48. B. 12172

CHASE (E.) Miscellaneous Selections and Original Pieces, in Prose and Verse. Consisting principally of Pieces of Moral Instruction, Descriptions of Fine Scenery, Delineation of Distinguished Characters, &c. By Elizabeth Chase. *Richmond: Published for the Editor, by R. J. Coale.* 1821. 12mo, pp. 228.

The author was sister to Samuel Chase, of Maryland, one of the signers of the Declaration of Independence.

CHASE (E. B.) Teachings of Patriots and Statesmen, on Slavery. By Ezra B. Chase. *Philadelphia: J. W. Bradley.* 1860. 12mo, pp. 495. Plate. C. 12174

CHASE (F.) Gathered Sketches from the Early History of New Hampshire and Vermont; containing Vivid and Interesting Accounts of a Great Variety of the Adventures of our Forefathers, And of other Incidents of Olden Time. Original and Selected. Edited by Francis Chase, M.A. *Claremont, N. H.: Tracy, Kenney & Co.* 1856. 12mo, pp. 215. Woodcuts. BA., C.

CHASE (G. B.) A Genealogical Memoir of the Chase Family, Chesham, Bucks, England; and of Hampton and Newbury, in New England. *Boston.* 1869. 8vo. 12176

CHASE (G. W.) The History of Haverhill, Massachusetts, from its First Settlement in 1640 to the Year 1860, By George Wingate Chase ... . *Haverhill: published by the Author.* 1861. 8vo, pp. 663, (1), xx. Plates. C., H. 12177

CHASE (H.) The New-Hampshire Probate Directory: containing all the Statute Laws relating to the Courts of Probate and Proceedings therein ... . By Horace Chase. *Concord: published by G. Parker Lyon.* 1854. 12mo, pp. v, 10–342. B.

CHASE (Henry), *and* SANBORN (Charles W.) The North and the South. A Statistical View of the Condition of the Free and Slave States. By Henry Chase, A.M.; and Charles W. Sanborn, M.D. Compiled from Official Documents. *Boston: published by John P. Jewett and Company.* 1856. 12mo, pp. 134. C. 12179

CHASE (H.) Two Years and Four Months in a Lunatic Asylum, From August 20th, 1863, To December 20th, 1865. By Rev. H. Chase. *Saratoga Springs.* 1868. 32mo, pp. 184.

CHASE (I.) Obligations of the Baptised; ... A Sermon Delivered before the Boston Baptist Association, Introductory to their Session at Cambridge, Mass. Sept. 17, A.D. 1828. By Irah Chase ... . *Boston: printed by William R. Collier.* 1828. 8vo, pp. 22. H. 12181

CHASE. A Tribute of Affection to the Memory of Professor Irah Chase. *Boston: privately printed.* 1865. 8vo, pp. 100. H.

Also: ... A Sermon, preached, December 28th, 1825, at the Ordination of Mr. James D. Knowles, as Pastor of the Second Baptist Church in Boston. ... . *Boston: Lincoln & Edmands.* 1826. 8vo, pp. 23. H.

CHASE (L.) National Perils. Oration delivered at Columbia College Commencement, February 20, 1860. By Leslie Chase, Jun. *New York: George F. Nesbitt & Co.* 1861. 8vo, pp. 6.

CHASE (L. B.) History of the Polk Administration. By Lucien B. Chase, a Member of the Twenty-Ninth and Thirtieth Congress. *New York: George P. Putnam.* M.DCCC.L. 8vo, pp. 512. BA., C. 12184

Also: Speech ... on the Tariff. ... June 26, 1846. *Washington.* 1846. 8vo, pp. 23. H.

CHASE (L. G.) A Consideration of some of the Commercial & Manufacturing Wants and Necessities of Saint Louis ... . By L. G. Chase. *Saint Louis: Gray & Crawford.* 1860. 8vo, pp. 71. H. 12185

CHASE (M. M.) Mary M. Chase and her Writings. Henry Fowler, Editor. *Boston: Ticknor and Fields.* MDCCCLV. 8vo, pp. xlvi, 336. B. 12186

CHASE (M.) A Vision which Moses Chase saw in 1849. [With 9 other visions respecting the United States, seen from 1858 to 1861?] 8vo, pp. (4). H. 12187

CHASE (Nahum). [Pedigree of Chase. *Albany: J. Munsell.* 1867.] p. 1. 12188

CHASE (O.) Narrative of the most extraordinary and distressing Shipwreck of the whale-ship Essex, of Nantucket, which was destroyed by a whale in the Pacific Ocean, and an account of the unparalleled sufferings of the crew, &c. By Owen Chase, first mate of said ship. *New York.* 1821. 12mo. 12189

CHASE (Philemon). Bishop Chase's Address delivered before the Convention of the Protestant Episcopal Church, Springfield, Illinois, June 16th, 1845. *Saint Louis: printed by Daniel Davies.* 1845. 8vo, pp. 27. H. 12190

CHASE. Defence of Kenyon College: by the Right Rev. P. Chase, D.D. *Columbus, Ohio: Olmsted & Bailhache, Printers.* 1831. 8vo, pp. 72. H. 12191

CHASE. A Plea for the West. ... *Philadelphia: printed by William Stavely.* 1826. 8vo, pp. 16. H. + *Boston: Samuel H. Parker.* 1827. 8vo, pp. 6, Plan of Kenyon College, Ohio. pp. 7–12, Remarks, 13–15. 12192

CHASE. Reminiscences of Bishop Chase. *Peoria, Ill.: S. H. Davis, Printers.* 1841–42. 4 Nos. in 3 vols., 8vo, pp. 480. H. + *New York.* 1844. 2 vols., 8vo, pp. 480; 400. + Second Edition: ... to A.D. 1847. ... *Boston.* 1848. 2 vols., 8vo, pp. xii, 548; v, 564. Portrait and 4 Engravings. BA., B., C. 12193

CHASE. The Star in the West, or Kenyon College, in 1828. [n. p. n. d.] 8vo, pp. 16. B., W. 12194

Also: Address ... June 7, 1841. — .. Address, at the Convention ... Cincinnati, Ohio, October 16, ... 1850. *Philadelphia: King & Baird, Printers.* [n. d.] 8vo pp. 16. H. — Appeal, ... in behalf of a Protestant Episcopal Theological Seminary for the Diocese of Illinois. [*London: Richard Watts, Printer.* n. d.] 8vo, pp. 8. H. — Defence of himself against the late Conspiracy at Gambier, Ohio. *Steubenville.* [1832.] 8vo, pp. 60. — ... Letters to his Absent Friends. *New York. 12th of July,* 1844. — A Letter on the subject of Bishop Chase's visit to England for the Relief of the Protestant Episcopal Church in Ohio, addressed to the Right Reverend Bishop White. *New York.* 1823. 8vo, pp. 40.

CHASE (P. E.) Catalogue of Tokens, circulated during the Rebellion of 1861. By Pliny E. Chase. [n. p. n. d.] 8vo, pp. 19.

Also: Comparative Statement of Mortality in the Society of Friends and that of the General Population of the City of Philadelphia, from 1800 to 1869. ... [*Philadelphia.*] 1869. 8vo, 2 l. H. — Tidal Rainfall of Philadelphia. Read July 17th and October 2d, 1868. ... [n. p. n. d.] 8vo, pp. 524-537. H.

CHASE (Salmon Portland). Baltimore Democracy and Independent Democracy. Letter to Hon. A. P. Edgerton. [n. p.] 1853. 8vo, pp. 16. M. 12196

CHASE. Reclamation of Fugitives from Service. An Argument for the Defendant, submitted to the Supreme Court of the United States, at the December Term, 1846, in the Case of Wharton Jones *vs.* John Vanzandt. By S. P. Chase. *Cincinnati: R. P. Donogh & Co.* 1847. 8vo, pp. 108. B. 12197

CHASE. A Sketch of the History of Ohio. By Salmon P. Chase. *Cincinnati: Corey and Fairbank.* 1833. 8vo, pp. (2), 40. BA. 12198

Prefixed to the following work; a few copies separately printed.

CHASE. Statutes of Ohio, and of the Northwestern Territory, adopted or enacted from 1788 to 1833, inclusive. Together with the Ordinance of 1787; the Constitutions of Ohio and of the United States; and various Public Instruments and Acts of Congress; illustrated by a Preliminary Sketch of the History of Ohio. *Cincinnati.* 1833–1835. 3 vols., 8vo. 12199

CHASE. U. S. A. "Going Home to Vote." Authentic Speeches of S. P. Chase, Secretary of the Treasury, During his Visit to Ohio, with his Speeches at Indianapolis, and at the Mass Meeting in Baltimore. October, 1863. *Washington: W. H. Moore.* 1863. 8vo, pp. 36. 12200

Also: Loyal Publication Society, No. 37. How the South Rejected Compromise in the Peace Conference of 1861. ... Published from the Notes of a Member. *New York: Wm. C. Bryant & Co.* 1863. 8vo, pp. 11. B., C. — Inaugural Address of Salmon P. Chase, Governor of ... Ohio: delivered before the Senate and House of Representatives January 14, 1856. *Columbus: Statesman Steam Press.* 1856. 8vo, pp. 15. H. — Letter ... to the Loyal National League. Washington, April 9, 1863. [n. p. n. d.] 8vo, pp. 4. — Liberty, or Slavery? Daniel O'Connell on American Slavery. Reply to O'Connell, by Hon. S. P. Chase. [n. p. n. d.] 8vo, pp. 15. — Maintain Plighted Faith. Speech ... February 3, 1854, Against the Repeal of the Missouri Prohibition of Slavery North of 36° 30′. *Washington.* 1854. 8vo, pp. 16. + [Another Edition.] *Washington.* 8vo, pp. 30. — The National Loan; embracing the Appeal in its behalf and the Laws authorizing it, with forms of Bonds, Instructions, etc., connected with the subscription. *Washington: Government Printing Office.* 1861. 8vo, pp. 23. — The Radical Democracy of New York and the Independent Democracy. Letter ... to Hon. B. F. Butler, of New York. Washington, July 15, 1852. [n. p. n. d.] 8vo, pp. 8. B. — Remarks ... on the Bill granting to the State of Ohio the unsold Lands remaining within that State. In the Senate ... April 14, 1852. [n. p. n. d.] 8vo, pp. 8. B. — Remarks ... upon the Pacific Railroad. ... February 17. 1853. [n. p. n. d.] 8vo, pp. 7. B. — Speech ... at Toledo, May 30, 1851. before a Mass Convention of the Democracy of North-Western Ohio. [n. p. n. d.] 8vo, pp. 8. B. — Speech ... on Public Printing, Ohio Politics, &c., Senate of the United States, April 9, 1853. [n. p. n. d.] 8vo, pp. 16. — Speech ... delivered at the

Republican Mass Meeting in Cincinnati, August 21, 1855. ... *Columbus.* 1855. 8vo, pp. 20. B. — Union and Freedom without Compromise. Speech ... in the Senate of the United States, March 26, 1850, on Mr. Clay's Compromise Resolutions. *Washington.* [n. d.] 8vo, pp. (24). — The Address [by A. J. Gordon] and Reply, on the Presentation of a Testimonial to S. P. Chase, by the Colored People of Cincinnati. [With some Account of the Case of Samuel Watson.] *Cincinnati: Henry W. Derby & Co.* 1845. 8vo, Title, pp. 35, (1). BA. And Reports on Finances for 1861, 1862, and 1863, 8vo.

CHASE. The Ferry Boy and the Financier. *See* Trowbridge (J. T.)

CHASE. Mr. Chase's Financial Scheme. Opinion of an Eminent Merchant. (From the N. Y. Evening Post.) [N. Y., 1863.] Slip. 12201

A System of National Finance. Notes Explanatory of Mr. Chase's Plan of National Finance. *Washington: Government Printing Office.* 1861. 8vo, pp. 15. 12202

CHASE (S.) The Answer and Pleas of Samuel Chase, one of the Associate Justices of the Supreme Court of the United States, to the Articles of Impeachment, exhibited against him in the said Court, by the House of Representatives of the United States, In Support of their Impeachment against him, for High Crimes and Misdemeanors ... . Printed by Order of the Senate. *Washington City: printed by William Duane & Son.* 1805. 8vo, pp. 84. BA. + *Newburyport.* 1805. 8vo, pp. 72. + *Salem: Joshua Cushing.* 1805. 8vo, pp. 72. + *Albany: printed by Charles R. and George Webster.* 1805. 8vo, pp. 48. B., C. + *Philadelphia.* 1805. 12203

CHASE. Report of the Trial of the Hon. Samuel Chase, one of the Associate Justices of the Supreme Court of the United States, before the High Court of Impeachment, composed of the Senate of the United States, for Charges exhibited against him by the House of Representatives, ... for High Crimes & Misdemeanors, supposed to have been by him committed; with the necessary Documents and Official Papers, From his Impeachment to final Acquittal. Taken in Short Hand by Charles Evans ... *Baltimore: printed for Samuel Butler and George Keatinge.* 1805. 8vo, 3 l., pp. 12, 268, 68. H. 12204

CHASE. Trial of Samuel Chase, An Associate Justice of the Supreme Court of the United States, Impeached by the House of Representatives, for High Crimes and Misdemeanors, before the Senate of the United States. Taken in Short Hand, by

Samuel H. Smith and Thomas Lloyd. *Washington City: Printed for Samuel H. Smith.* 1805. 2 vols., 8vo, 2 l., pp. 387; 493, viii.

Judge Chase was one of the signers of the Declaration of Indpendence. He was impeached at the instigation of John Randolph, for alleged misdemeanors in the political trials of Fries and Callender.

CHASE. To the Honourable the General Assembly of Maryland, The Memorial of Samuel Chase, Agent of the State, for the Recovery of the Bank Stock. 4to, pp. 18. H. 12206

Signed Samuel Chase. Dated, at the end, Annapolis, Feb. 17, 1786. Also: Exhibits accompanying the Answer and Plea of Samuel Chase. [*Washington.* 1805.] 8vo, pp. 54

CHASE. Replication by the House of Representatives to the Answer of Samuel Chase to the Articles of Impeachment. ... [*Washington.* 1805.] 8vo. 12207

See "Nat. Port. Gallery," IV. 4, and Sanderson's "Biog. of Signers," IX. 187–235.

CHASE (*Rev.* S.) Malignity Exposed; or a Vindication of Bishop Chase against the Malicious Accusations of an Anonymous Pamphlet. ... By the Rev. Samuel Chase. ... *New-York: Stanford and Swords.* 1847. 8vo, pp. 47. B. 12208

Also: Three Letters to Bishop Chase on Present Indebtedness of Kenyon College. ... *Peoria.* 1843. — Remarks upon Recent Publications against Rt. Rev. Philander Chase, D.D. *Steubenville.* 1832. 8vo, pp. 28. — Review of Jubilee College. [n. p. n. d.] 12mo, pp. 32.

CHASE. Columbian Eloquence; being the Speeches of the most celebrated American Orators, as delivered in the Trial of the Hon. Samuel Chase. *Baltimore: S. Butler & S. Cole.* 1806. 3 vols., 18mo, pp. 300; 220; 247. 12209

CHASE (S.) The Angels of the Churches. A Sermon at the Ordination Of ... James Welman, in the Second Parish in Sutton: October the 7th. 1747. ... By Stephen Chase ... . *Boston: J. Draper.* M,DCC,XLVIII. 8vo, pp. 29, (3). BA. 12210

CHASE (T.) An Address on the Character and Example of President Lincoln, delivered before the Athenæum and Everett Societies of Haverford College, By Professor Thomas Chase, on Fifth Day Evening, Seventh Month 6th, 1865. *Philadelphia: Sherman & Co., Printers.* 1865. 8vo, pp. 35. 12211

500 copies printed for distribution on commencement day, July 12th.

CHASE (T.) Sketches of the Life, Character and Times of Paul Jones. By Thomas Chase ... . *Richmond: Chas. H. Wynne, Printer.* 1859. 12mo. pp. 58. H. 12212

CHASE. Oration by Thomas Chase, and Poem by J. G. Whittier, ... before the Alumni Association of the Friend's School at Providence, at ... Newport, 1860. *Philadelphia: Collins, Printer.* 1860. 8vo, pp. 32. H. 12213

CHASE (W.) The American Crisis; or, Trial and Triumph of Democracy. By Warren Chase. *Boston: Bela Marsh.* 1862. 12mo, pp. 82. 12214

[CHASE (Washington).] A Voyage from the United States to South America, performed during the Years 1821, 1822, & 1823. Embracing a Description of the City of Rio Janeiro, in Brazil; of every Port of Importance in Chili; of several in Lower Peru; and of an Eighteen Months Cruise in a Nantucket Whaleship. ... Second Edition. *Newburyport: Herald Press.* 1823. 8vo pp. 80. BA. 12215

The first edition of 500 copies was printed the same year.

CHASE (W. H.) The Secession of the Cotton States; its Status, its Advantages, and its Power. [n. p. n. d.] 16mo, pp. 8. H. 12216

Also: Brief Memoir explanatory of a New Trace of a Front of Fortification in place of the Present Bastion Front. ... *New Orleans.* 1846. 12mo, pp. 11. 3 Plans. H. — Reply ... to the Strictures of "Another who also Knows" upon the Report of the late Board of Visitors at West Point. [*Florida Democrat Print.* 1857.] 8vo, pp. 6.

The Chase of the Rebel Steamer of War Oreto, Commander J. N. Maffitt, C. S. N. into the Bay of Mobile, by the United States Steam Sloop Oneida, Commander Geo. Henry Preble, U. S. N. September 4, 1862. *Cambridge: printed for Private Circulation.* 1862. 8vo, pp. 60. H. + *Cambridge: Allen Farnham, Printers.* 1862. 8vo, pp. 48. H. 12217

CHASLES (P.) Études sur la littérature et les mœurs des Anglo-Américains au XIXe siècle par M. Philarète Chasles ... *Paris: Amyot.* [1851.] 16mo, Half-Title, Title pp. viii, 515.

CHASLES. Anglo-American Literature and Manners, from the French of Philarete Chasles, by Donald MacLeod. *New York.* 1852. 12mo, pp. xii, 312. C. 12219

CHASSANIS (Pierre). Association pour la possession et exploration de 600,000 acres de terre concédées par l'État de New-York, et situées ... sur le Lac Ontario ... *Paris.* 4to. 12220

To the copy in the New York State Library are appended the legal documents, in manuscript, with the autograph of G. Morris, etc.

CHASSEBŒUF DE VOLNEY (Constantine François), *Count.* *See* Volney. 12221

CHASSÉRIAU (Frédéric Victor Charles). Précis de l'abolition de l'esclavage dans les colonies Anglaises. [*Paris: Imprimerie royale.* 1841.] 2 vols., 8vo. 12222

CHASTAIN (E. W.) The Union and the State-Rights Parties. Speech of Hon. E. W. Chastain, of Georgia, on the Position of the Union Party of Georgia. ... in the House of Representatives, March 5, 1852. *Washington.* 1852. 8vo, pp. 7. H. 12223

[CHASTELLUX (Francis Jean)], *Marquis de.* Discours sur les avantages ou les désavantages qui résultent, pour l'Europe, de la découverte de l'Amérique. Objet du Prix proposé par M. l'Abbé Raynal. Par M. P***, Vice-Consul, à E***. ... *Londres: Et se trouve; à Paris: Chez Prault.* 1787. 8vo, pp. 8, 68.

"This discourse is attributed to the Marquis de Chastellux, and is, according to Laharpe, the best of his works; well conceived, tolerably well written, full of luminous conclusions, and of useful truths. He decides the questions in favor of the 'advantages.'" — *Biog. Univ.*

CHASTELLUX. Voyage de Newport a Philadelphie, Albany, etc. *Newport, R. I.: De l'imprimerie Royale de l'Escadre.* 1781. 4to, pp. 188. S. 12225

"The Marquis de Chastellux caused twenty-four copies of this journal to be printed at a press on board one of the ships of the French squadron, at Newport. It consists only of that part which forms the first volume of the edition of Paris of 1785, comprising his travels in the winter of 1780–81, and was printed, he says, to avoid the trouble of making manuscript copies for his friends in Europe." — RICH, I. 300.

CHASTELLUX. Voyage de Mr. Le Chevalier de Chastellux en Amèrique. [n. p.] 1785. 8vo, pp. 228. M. 12226

The vignette on title is a woodcut of a stone slab, with a covered crown in flowers above, and a garden basket reversed below. This appears to be the surreptitious edition of the Marquis de Chastellux's travels, printed at Cassel, which is referred to in the Paris edition of 1786. It consists of extracts taken at random from his manuscript journals, without any connection, which were first published in a periodical journal at Gotha.

CHASTELLUX. Voyages de M. le Marquis de Chastellux dans L'Amerique Septentrionale dans les années 1780, 1781 & 1782. ... *Paris: Prault, imprimeur du roi.* 1786. 2 vols, 8vo, pp. 8, 390, Map; Half-Title, Title, 362, (2), Map, and 3 Plates. BA., C., H. + Seconde édition. *Paris: Prault.* 1788–91. [*Ibid.*] B., BA. 12227

See a favorable notice from the "Crititical Review," in Rich, I.

CHASTELLUX. Voyage en Amérique. *Paris et Bruxelles: B. Le Francq.* 1786. 8vo, pp. 136. + *Leipzig.* 1785. 8vo.

CHASTELLUX. Travels in North America, in the Years 1780, 1781, and 1782. By the Marquis de Chastellux, one of the Forty Members of the French Academy, and Major General in the French Army, serving under the Count de Rochambeau. Translated from the French by an English Gentleman, who resided in America at that Period. With Notes by the Translator. *London: G. G. J. and J. Robinson.* M DCC LXXXVII. 2 vols., 8vo, pp. xv, 462; xii, 432. 2 Maps, and 3 Plates. H. + Second Edition. *London: G. G. J. and J. Robinson,* ... MDCCLXXXVII. 2 vols., 8vo, pp. xv, 462; xii, 432. 2 Maps and 3 Plates. + *Dublin: Colles.* M.DCC.LXXXVII. 2 vols., 8vo, pp. xv, 462; xv, pp. 430. 2 Maps and 3 Plates. B. 12229

CHASTELLUX. [Same title.] Also, A Biographical Sketch of the Author: Letters from Gen. Washington to the Marquis de Chastellux: and Notes and Corrections by the American Editor. *New York: White, Gallaher, & White.* 1827. 8vo, pp. 416. BA. 12230

The translator was J. Kent. "This performance of the Marquis de Chastellux is a heterogeneous and multifarious account of everything that caught the lively traveller's eager eye and minute attention; and, as nothing escaped his active investigation, his work abounds not only with observations which are of importance, but with details of even the most trifling incidents that bad roads, inconvenient inns, and distracted times usually afford. The translator is, in political principles, a violent American, and, as such, he gives to the national reputation of poor old England many a stab, and to that of her troops no quarter." — *Monthly Review.*

CHASTELLUX. Des Ritters von Chastellüx Reisebeobachtungen über America. *Hamburg: bey der Nordischen typographischen litterärischen Gesellschaft.* 1785. Sm. 8vo, pp. viii, 182. + *Hamburg: Chaidron.* 1786. 8vo. 12231

CHASTELLUX. Des Herrn Ritters von Chastellux Reise durch Amerika. Aus dem Französischen. *Frankfurt und Leipzig: bey Stahel.* 1786. 8vo, pp. 113. + *Wien: Schaumburg.* 1786. 8vo. 12232

CHASTELLUX. Critical Examination of. *See* Brissot de Warville, Vol. II., Nos. 8017 and 8019.

CHASTELLUX. Remarks on the Travels of the Marquis de Chastellux in North America. *London: G. and T. Wilkie.* MDCCLXXXVII. 8vo, 2 l., pp. 86. 12233

This writer accuses the Marquis of misrepresentations and exaggerations, and calls his translator an "incendiary, a lurking spy, and an avowed rebel to his country."

CHASTENET-DESTÈRE (G.) La science du cultivateur américain. *Toulouse: Bênichet.* 1801. 12mo. 12234

Also: "Considérations sur l'état présent de la colonie française de Saint-Domingue," in "Le magasin encyclopédique," 6e ann., T. III. The author had been a planter in St. Domingo.

[CHASTENET DE PUYSÉGUR (Antoine Hyacinthe Anne)], *Comte de.* Détail sur la navigation aux côtes de Saint-Domingue et dans ses débouquemens. *Paris.* MDCCLXXXVII. 4to, 2 l., pp. 81.

CHASTENET-PUYSÉGUR. Instructions nautiques sur les côtes et les débouquemens de Saint-Domingue, avec le détail de la position des principaux points qui ont servi de base à la construction des cartes publiées en 1787. Publié pour la première fois, par ordre du Roi, en 1787. *Paris: Imprimerie royale.* 1821. 8vo, pp. 259. 12236

CHATEAUBRIAND (François Auguste), *Vicomte de.* Atala, ou les Amours de deux Sauvages dans le Désert ... . *Paris.* 1801. + Cinquième édition. *Paris: Migneret.* 1801. 18mo, pp. xxiv, 207. B. + *Dresden: Waither.* 1801. 8vo. + *Halle: Waisenhaus Buchhandlung.* 1801. 12mo. + *Paris.* 1803. 12mo. + *Chemnitz: Mauke.* 1805. 12mo. + *Braunschweig und Petersburg: Pluchart.* [n. d.] 18mo. + *Nürnberg und New York: Campe und C.* 1831. 12mo. + Mit grammatikalischen Erläuterungen und Hinweisungen auf den Sprachlehren von Hirzel, Mozin und Sanguin und einer Wörterbuche. Zweite vermehrte Auflage. *Leipzig: Baumgärtner.* 1831. 12mo. + [*Ibid.*] 1833. 12mo. + Édition de Younges. *New York.* 1833. 32mo. + *Stuttgart: Erhard.* 1834. 16mo. + Dritte vermehrte Auflage. [*Ibid.*] 1842. 12mo. + *Amsterdam: de Weduwe Changuion, Hengst.* 18—. 12237

"Atala is an episode of the "Génie du christianisme" (which first appeared about April, 1802, and of which five editions were published within a year). It had such a prodigious success that it was translated into almost all the languages of Europe [I have not found any version in the Scandinavian or Slavonic languages]; yet its style has given occasion to very biting critiques, nearly all of which the author has reprinted in the collected edition of his works." — QUÉRARD.

CHATEAUBRIAND. Atala; avec dessins de Gustave Doré. *Paris: Hachette et Cie.* 1862. Folio, pp. xi, 79. 30 Engravings. 12238

CHATEAUBRIAND. Alala ou les Habitans du Desert, Parodie D'Atala. *Au Grand Village, An* IX [1801]. 24mo. 12239

CHATEAUBRIAND. Atala; or the Love and Constancy of Two Savages in the Desert. Translated from the French of F. A. Chateaubriand, By Caleb Bingham ... . *Boston: Caleb Bingham.* 1802. 12mo, pp. 177. H. + *London.* 1802. 12mo, pp. 129. Plate. + *Boston.* 1814. 12mo. + Atala; or, The Amours of Two Savages in the Desert. Translated from the French of F. A. Chateaubriand ... . *London.* 1813. 16mo, pp. xv, 162. + *London.* 1825. 18mo. + Atala, the Beautiful Indian of the Mississippi ... . *New York.* 1818. 18mo, pp. 133. + Atala. Translated by M. J. Smead and H. P. Lefebvre. *New York.* 1844. 8vo. 12240

CHATEAUBRIAND. Atala. By Chateaubriand. Translated by James Spencer Harry. Illustrated by Gustave Doré. *London: Cassell.* [1867.] Folio, pp. xxii, 86. 30 Plates. 12241

CHATEAUBRIAND. Atala, ó los amores de dos salvages en el desierto. Traducido del frances al castellano, por J. Robinson. *Paris: Th. Barrois.* 1822. 18mo. 12242

Quérard says *Paris.* 1802, ó *Paris: Th. Barrois.* 1822. 18mo. I have met with no other notice of the early edition, but the date is probable. Another translation, anonymous, was published: *Paris: H. Seguin.* 1825 24mo, pp. 192. BA. "Atala. Traduccion libre por D. Francisco Zengotita Vengoa" fills 238 pages of Tomo XV. (*Madrid: Urosa.* 1862. 16mo, pp. 728) of the "Biblioteca universal económica, publicada por los P-P. Escolapios ... ."

CHATEAUBRIAND. Atala, ou os amantes do deserto, par Chateaubriand. Traduzida em portuguez. *Lisboa?* 18–.

This Portuguese version is by Felipe Ferreira de Araujo e Castro.

CHATEAUBRIAND. Atala ou os amores de dous salvagens no o deserto; Pelo Visconde de Chateaubriand. Nova edição revista e emendada. *Em Londres.* 1818. 18mo, pp. 151. H. + *Paris.* 1836. 18mo. 12244

CHATEAUBRIAND. Atala, o gli amori di due selvaggi nel deserto; trasportato in lingua italiana ... da J. F. C. Blanvillain ... . *Parigi: Huguin; Augusto Delalain.* 1801. 18mo, 2 l., pp. viij, 202. B. + *Strasburg: König.* 1802. 8vo. + Traduzione ... di P. L. Costantini. *Berlin.* 1802. 16mo. 12245

CHATEAUBRIAND. Atala. Aus dem Französischen von K. F. Cramer. *Leipzig: Voss.* 1801. 8vo. Plate. + Zweite Auflage. [*Ibid.*] 1805. 8vo. + *Leipzig: Rubach.* 16mo, pp. 118. Engraved Title. 12246

CHATEAUBRIAND. Atala ... . Von Chateaubriand. Aus dem Französischen von J. Günther. *Jena: Mauke.* 1841. 16mo. (Bibl. class. Romane des Auslandes, I. Bd.) + *Leipzig: Schäfer.* 1845. 16mo. 12247

CHATEAUBRIAND. Atala, of de gelieven in de woestigen. Uit het Fransch. *'s Bosch: Sassen Sen.* 1811. 8vo. 12248

"On account of the immense popularity of Chateaubriand, and the great influence which his writings must have had in forming European ideas concerning America, I thought it worth while to take some pains to make out a full list of the editions of his American works." — C. A. C. The following list includes the editions of Atala, with other works: Atala. ... Abencerage Mélanges littéraires. *Paris: G. Roux: Arnauld de Vresse.* 1857. 18mo, pp. 249. — Atala et Chactas ... . *Paris: Le Bailly.* 1860. 18mo, pp. 108. Vignettes. + [*Ibid.* 1866.] [*Ibid.*] — Atala. Réné. *Paris: Le Normant.* 1807. 12mo. (First edition in which these stories were united.) + Douxième et dernière édition. *Paris: Le Normant. Lyon: Ballanche, père et fils.* 1809. 12mo. 6 Engravings. — Œuvres romantiques de M. le vicomte de Châteaubriand ... . *Paris: impr. de F. Didot.* 1831. 5 vols., 32mo. (Contains, among others, Atala and René.) — Atala: Réné: les aventures du dernier Abencerrage. *Paris: Ladvocat.* 1827. 2 vols., 18mo. Plates. + *Paris: Lefèvre: Ladvocat.* 1829. + Et Poésies. *Paris: Lefèvre.* 1830. 8vo. 4 Plates. ("Belle édition." — BRUNET.) + [Sans les Poésies. *Ibid.*] 2 vols., 18mo. + *Paris: Ledentu.* 1830. 18mo. + *Stuttgart: Hoffmann.* 1831. 12mo. + *Paris: Ledentu.* 1834. 18mo. + *Paris: L. Janet.* 1835. 32mo. + *Paris: G. Barba.* 1838. 2 vols., 12mo. — *Paris: F. Didot.* 1844. 12mo. + *London: Colburn.* 1844. 12mo. + *Paris: Michel Lévy frères.* 1869. 18mo, pp. xi, 259. — Atala. René. Les Natchez. *Paris: Hachette et Cie.* 1854. 16mo. + [*Ibid.*] 1863. 16mo, pp. 549. — ... Atala. René. Les aventures du derniere Abencerage. Les Natchez. *Paris: Chaix et Cie.* 1865. 8vo. + *Bernard Béchet.* 1866. 8vo, pp. 356. — Atala, René. Les Abencerrages, suivis du Voyage en Amérique. *Paris.* 1847. 8vo. + *Paris.* 1854. 12mo. + *Paris: G. Harvard.* 1859. 4to, pp. 48. Vignettes. + *Paris: Harvard; Lécrivain et Toubon.* 1860. [*Ibid.*] — Atala. René. ... Abencerages. Les quatre Stuarts. ... *Paris: Bernardin-Béchet.* 1869. 8vo, pp. 355.

CHATEAUBRIAND. Atala y Réné. Nueva edicion, corregida ... . *Blois: Aucher-Éloy.* 1826. + *Paris: Wincop.* 1827. 18mo, + Nueva traduccion. *Perpignan: Alzine.* 1826. 18mo. + *Barcelona.* 1827. 8vo. 2 Engravings. + Sequitada de la Cabana indiana ... por B. de Saint-Pierre. *Paris: Masson y hijo.* 1822. 18mo. 12249

Also the following: Atala. René. [In Spanish.] *Blois: Aucher Eloy.* 1827. 18mo. + *Paris: Pillet.* 1838. 18mo. — La Atala. El René. El Ultimo Abencerrage. ... Traducidos por Don Manuel M. Flamant. *Paris: Rosa et Bouret.* 1862. 18mo, pp. 298. + [*Ibid.*] 1869. 18mo, pp. 321. — Atala. René. [In Portuguese.] *Paris: Pillet.* 1836. 18mo. 2 Plates.

CHATEAUBRIAND. Atala-René. Mit grammatikalischen, geographischen und geschichtlichen Anmerkungen, nebst einem vollständigen Wörterbuche ... . Herausgegeben von L. C. Schnabel. *Leipzig: Volckmar.* 1845. 16mo. + Dritte Auflage. *Berlin: Renger'sche Buchhandlung.* 1844. 8vo, pp. 212.

Also: Atala. René, Le dernier des Abencerrages. Mit einem Wörterbuche versehen. Zum Schulgebrauch. *Quedlinburg: Basse.* 1844. 8vo. — Atala. Die indische Hütte. Von Bernardin de St. Pierre. *Dresden: Bromme.* 1841. 16mo. — Atala und die Abenteuer des Letzten der Abenceragen. Uebersetzt von H. Elsner. *St. Gallen: Scheitlin.* 1843. 8vo. Plate.

CHATEAUBRIAND. Ausgewählte Werke. Uebersetzt von Hermann Kurtz. *Ulm: Stettin'sche Sortiments-Buchhandlung.* 1844–46. 12 pts., 16mo. 12251

The first work is Atala; the second, René. Also: Atala, Réné und der Letzte der Abencerrages. ... aus dem Französischen ubersetzt von Ehrenf. Stroeber. *Paris und Strasburg: Levrault.* 1826. 12mo. — ... Atala. René. ... Les Natchez. *Paris: Chaix et Ce.* 1865. 8vo, pp. 555.

CHATEAUBRIAND. Chateaubriand illustré. *Paris: Marescq.* 1851–52. 7 vols., 4to. 12252

CHATEAUBRIAND. Congrès de Verone. Guerre d'Espagne. Négotiations. Colonies espagnols. *Leipzig et Paris: Brockhaus et Avenarius.* 1838. 2 vols., 8vo. + [*Ibid.*] 2 vols., 12mo.

CHATEAUBRIAND. Der Congress zu Verona. ... Die spanischen Colonien. Aus dem Französischen übersetzt und mit Zusätzen von G. W. ... *Hamburg: Berendsohn.* 1838. 2 vols., 8vo. Portrait. 12254

CHATEAUBRIAND. Études historiques. Voyage en Amérique. ... Nouvelle édition, revue. *Paris: Vermot.* 1860. 18mo, pp. 400. + [*Ibid.*] 8vo, pp. 400. 12255

CHATEAUBRIAND. Memoirs of Chateaubriand. Written by Himself. ... *London: Henry Colburn; also Chapman and Hall.* 1848. 8vo, 4 l., pp. 314, 14 l. BA. 12256

The book ends with Part I of Vol. II. (1836). Vol. I., pp. 226–305, contain the account of his travels in America. Republished with the title, "An Autobiography. *London.* 1849." 2 vols., 8vo. P.

CHATEAUBRIAND. Les Natchez, roman indien. *London.* 1827. 3 vols., 8vo. BD. 12257

The Natchez first appeared in Chateaubriand's "Œuvres complètes," 1826, etc., forming Vols. XIX. and XX. June 21, 1827, "Les Natchez, ou la tribu serpent. mélodrame à grand spectacle tiré de l'ouvrage de M. de Châteaubriand," was represented at the Théâtre de la Gaîté.

CHATEAUBRIAND. Les Natchez. Par M. de Chateaubriand. ... *Paris: Bernardin-Béchet.* 1859. 8vo, pp. 388. + [*Ibid.*] 1867. + *Paris: A. de Vresse.* 1863. 2 vols., 18mo, pp. 508. 2 Engravings. + *Paris: Michel Lévy frères.* 1867. 2 vols., 18mo, pp. 625. 12258

CHATEAUBRIAND. The Natchez; an Indian Tale. By the Viscomte de Chateaubriand. *London: Henry Colburn.* 1827. 3 vols., fcap 8vo, pp. xl, 299; (2), 335; (2), 412. C. 12259

CHATEAUBRIAND. Os Natchez: historia americana pelo viscomte de Chateaubriand; traduzida do francez, com notas, por Caetano Lopez de Moura. *Paris: Aillaud.* 1837. 4 vols., 18mo. Engravings. 12260

CHATEAUBRIAND. Los Natchez, novela americana. *Paris: imp. de Pochard.* 1829. 6 vols., 18mo. + *Paris.* 1830. [*Ibid.*]

Translated, or rather, "refundida en castellano al gusto de la litteratura española," by Mariano José Sicilia. Also: Les Natchez. Zum Schulgebrauch mit einer Wörterbuche versehen von Carl Ludwig. *Quedlinburg: Basse.* 1851. 8vo, pp. 478. The editions of Chateaubriand's collected works are numerous, the latter being somewhat fuller than the earlier ones. In general, the various volumes are sold separately, and some are reissued from time to time, with merely a change of date on the title-page, which greatly increases the number of actual editions of such favorites as Atala, René, Les Natchez. The following list is probably nearly complete: — Œuvres ... de Chateaubriand ... . *Paris: Ladvocat.* M DCCC XXVI–M DCCC XXXI. 28 vols., 8vo. BA., H. (Vols. VI., VII., contain "Voyage en Amérique;" XVI., "Atala, René. Notes et critiques de diverses personnes sur Atala;" XIX., XX., "Les Natchez." One copy was printed on *vellum.*) + Œuvres. *Paris: Lefèvre.* 1829–31. 20 vols., 8vo. + *Paris: Pourrat frères.* 1832. 22 vols., 8vo. + *Lefèvre; Pourrat; Furne; Lebigre.* 1833–38. 20 vols., 18mo. + *Paris: Pourrat frères.* 1834–38. 32 vols., 8vo. Engravings. + *Paris: Lefevre.* 1834. 4 vols., 8vo. Engravings. + *Paris: Delloye.* 1835. 25 vols., 8vo. + *Paris: Lefèvre; Desrez.* 1836–37. 5 vols., 8vo. + *Paris: Ch. Gosselin; Furne.* 1836–37. 25 vols., 8vo. 30 Engravings. + *Paris: Pourrat freres; Dauvin et Fontaine.* 1838. 36 vols., 8vo. 90 Engravings. C. ("Voyage en Amérique," Vol. XII.; "Atala, René," Vol. XVIII.; "Les Natchez," Vol. XXII., XXIII.) + *Paris:* [*Id.?*] 1839. 36 vols., 8vo. + *Paris: Ledentu.* 1838. 6 vols., 8vo. 30 Engravings. + *Paris: F. Didot frères.* 1839–41. 5 vols., 8vo. 30 Vignettes. + [*Ibid.*] 1845–50. 10 vols., 12mo. + *Paris: Penaud.* 1849. 20 vols., 8vo. Engravings. + *Paris: Krabbe.* 1851. 16 vols., 8vo. 6 Engravings. + *Paris: Gabriel Roux.* 1854–55. 30 vols., 12mo. 120 Engravings. + Édition Pourrat frères. Dernière édition revue et augmentée par l'auteur ... . *Paris: Gennequin.* 1857–59. 31 vols., 8vo. + *Paris: Dufour, Mulat et Boulanger.* 1857–59. 20 vols., 8vo. 100 Engravings. + [Edition Pourrat frères.] *Paris: Pick.* 1857–59. 15 vols., 8vo. Vignettes. + *Paris: De Vresse.* 1857–61. 20 vols., 18mo. Engravings. + *Paris: Roux.* 1858– . vols., 18mo. (Perhaps merely a reissue of some volumes of Roux's edition of 1854–55.) + Nouvelle édition, ... précédée d'une étude littéraire sur Chateaubriand, par M. Sainte-Beuve ... *Paris: Garnier freres.* 1859–61. 12 vols., 8vo. + [*Ibid.* n. d.] 12 vols., 8vo. BA. (Vol. III. [1865] contains "Atala, René, Les Natchez;" Vol. VI., "Voyage en Amérique.) + *Paris: Furne et Cie.* 1859–62. 12 vols., 8vo. 31 Engravings. + *Edition Lefèvre Paris: Lécrivain et Toulon.* 20 vols., 18mo. + *Paris: Sarlit.* 1864– . 14 vols., 8vo. 57 Engravings. + *Paris: Parent. Desbarres.* 8vo. (Tom. 8 and 9 published in 1865.)

CHATEAUBRIAND. Œuvres choisies ... comprenant Atala, René ... les Natchez ... les Voyages en Amérique et en Italie ... . *Paris: Poulain.* 18 –60. 8 vols., 8vo. 12262

CHATEAUBRIAND. Sämmtliche Werke. Nach den neuesten Original-Ausgabe übersetzt von L. v. Kronfels ... und Andere. *Freiburg: Wagner.* 1827–32. 53 vols., 8vo. 12263

Some volumes also have independent titles, as "Die Natchez ... übersetzt von Prof. Zell," 6 vols. "Reise in Amerika, übersetzt von K. J. Perleb," 4 vols. "René ... übersetzt von Kreisr. Schnetzler."

CHATEAUBRIAND. Prophéte; Avenir du monde, ... Génie des hommes ... Washington et Bonaparte. ... *Paris: Garnier Frères, Libraires.* 1849. 18mo, pp. 35. B. 12264

CHATEAUBRIAND. René, ou Les effets des passions. *Leipzig: Voss.* 1802. 12mo. + [In German. *Ibid.*] 12265

CHATEAUBRIAND. René, a Tale, translated from the French of F. A. de Chateaubriand. *Boston.* 1815. 12mo. 12266

CHATEAUBRIAND. Vida del jóven René, por Francisco Augusto Chateaubriand. Traducida del frances por el P. Fr. Vicente Martinez Colomer. Segunda edicion. *Valencia.* 1827. 8vo. 12267

CHATEAUBRIAND. Renato, episodo do Genio do Christianismo, e as aventuras de Aristonoo, por Fénélon; traducidos em portuguez por B. L. Vianna. *Paris: Bobée.* 1818. 18mo.

CHATEAUBRIAND. Souvenirs d'Italie, d'Angleterre et de l'Amérique suivis de morceaux inédits de morale et de littérature. *Londres: H. Colburn.* 1815. 2 pts., 8vo. + Seconde édition. *Leipzig: Brockhaus.* 1817. 12mo. + *Braunschweig: Pluchart.* 1817. 8vo. 12269

"The Leipzig edition of 1816 is incomplete: it contains only extracts from the 'Génie du Christianisme' and 'Le Mercure.'" — QUÉRARD.

CHATEAUBRIAND. Recollections of Italy, England, and America, with Essays on various subjects in Morals and Literature. By F. A. de Chateaubriand. *London.* 1815. 8vo. + [*Id.*] 1816. 2 vols., 8vo. + *Philadelphia: M. Carey.* 1816. 8vo.

CHATEAUBRIAND. Erinnerungen aus Italien, England und Amerika. Aus dem Französischen übersetzt von W. A. Lindau. *Dresden.* 1816. 8vo. + *Leipzig.* [n. d.] 8vo. 12271

CHATEAUBRIAND. Œuvres inédites ... . Voyages en Amérique, en France, et en Italie, par M. le vicomte de Chateaubriand ... . *Paris: Ambroise Dupont et Cie.* 1828. 2 vols., 8vo,

Half-Title, Title, pp. xcj, 306; Half-Title, Title, 396. + *Paris: Ledentu.* 1834. 2 vols., 18mo. + *Brux.* 1837. 2 vols., 12mo. + *Paris: Henri, Barba, Molard et Cie.* 1838. 8vo. 12272

Appended to the Voyages are "Description des monuments de l'Ohio, par Caleb Atwater," and "Sur l'origine et l'époque des monuments de l'Ohio, par Malte-Brun," also a letter of Humboldt on the population of America.

CHATEAUBRIAND. Voyages en Amérique ... . Par M. de Chateaubriand. Ornés de gravures. *Paris: Bernardin-Béchet.* 1865. 8vo, pp. 384. + *Paris.* 1866. 32mo, pp. 191. + *Paris. E. Ardant et Thibaut.* 8vo, pp. 219. Engravings. + Troisième édition. *Paris: imp. Bonnet et Ce.* 1867. 32mo, pp. 191. + Nouvelle édition, revue. *Paris: Vermot et Ce.* 1867. 8vo, pp. 228. Engravings. + *Clichy: lib. A. de Vresse.* 1867. 18mo, pp. 247. Engravings. + Nouvelle édition, destinée à la jeunesse. *Limoges: E. Ardant et Thibaut.* 1868. 8vo, pp. 224. + Edition revue par l'abbé G. Guénot. *Limoges: Barbou frères.* 1868. 12mo, pp. 276. Engravings. + [*Ibid.*] 1869. [*Ibid.*] + *Paris.* 1870. 32mo, pp. 191. 12273

Some of these editions contain only the "Voyage en Amérique."

CHATEAUBRIAND. Viage á la América, traducido por el Dr. Moralejo. *Paris: Rosa.* 1836. 3 vols., 18mo. 12274

CHATEAUBRIAND. Voyages et Mélanges littéraires. Par A. F. de Chateaubriand. *Paris: Furne et Ce.* 1864. 8vo, pp. 592.

CHATEAUBRIAND. Travels in America and Italy. By Viscount de Chateaubriand, ... *London: Henry Colburn.* 1828. 2 vols., 8vo, pp. 356; 2 l., pp. 429. C. 12276

CHATEAUNEUF (Agricole Hippolyte la Pierre de). Le Général Lafayette. Mémoires authentiques, Ecrits par A. Châteauneuf. *Paris: Dumont.* 1831. 8vo, Half-Title, Title, pp. (4), 80.

Also: Histoire du général Moreau, surnommé le Grand Capitaine, avec les particularités ... de son retour d'Amérique ... . *Paris: Michaud.* 1814. 8vo.

CHATHAM (James). Speech ... on Commutation of Tonnage Duties. *Harrisburg.* 1862. 8vo. C. 12278

CHATHAM (*Earl of*). *See* Pitt (Wm.)

[CHATHAM, *pseudonym.*] An Address to the Citizens of Connecticut. [Signed Chatham. n. p.] *I. Walter, Printer.* [18—.] 8vo, pp. 24. BA. 12279

CHATHAM, *Mass.* Annual Report of the School Committee of Chatham, for the School Year 1846–7. *Chatham.* 1847. pp. 23. Continued. H. 12280

CHATHAM ACADEMY. Catalogue of the Trustees, Instructors and Students of Chatham Academy, Savannah, Geo. *Savannah: W. T. Williams.* 1833. 8vo, pp. 13. H. 12281

CHATHAM MINING COMPANY. Reports on the Property of the Chatham Mining Company, situated in North Sutton, Canada East. *Boston: Press of Dakin, Davies & Metcalf.* [n. d.] 8vo, pp. 12. Maps. H. 12282

Chattanooga. ... *Cincinnati.* 1858. 12mo. C. + [*Id.*] *Wrightson & Company, Printers.* 1863. 12mo, pp. 400. BA. 12283

An anti-slavery novel.

The Chattel Principle, the Abhorence of Jesus Christ and the Apostles; or no Refuge for American Slavery in the New Testament. *American Anti-Slavery Society.* 1839. 8vo, pp. 71.

CHATTERTON (Aug.) The Buds of Beauty, or Parnassian Sprigs; a collection of Original Poems on Various Subjects. *Baltimore.* 1787. 12mo. 12285

CHAUCHEPRAT (C. F.), *Translator.* *See* Vol. I., No. 1701.

The fourth edition is edited by Ch. Rigault de Genouilly. *Paris: imprimerie Royale.* 1842. 2 vols., 8vo.

CHAUDRON (A. de V.) The First || Second || Third Reader for the use of Primary Schools. Second Edition. Adapted for use in the Public Schools of Mobile. By A. De V. Chaudron. *Mobile, Ala.: W. G. Clark & Co.* 1864. 12mo, pp. 57, 96, 116.

CHAUDRON. Chaudron's Spelling Book, carefully prepared for Family and School use. By A. De V. Chaudron. *Mobile: S. H. Goetzel.* 1865. 12mo, pp. 48. BA. + Fifth Edition. [*Ibid.*] 12287

These Confederate school-books inculcate strong Southern sentiments.

CHAUDRON (S.) Oraison funèbre, du Frére George Washington, Prononcée le premier Janvier 1800, dans la loge française l'Aménité: par Le F.·. Simon Chaudron, Orateur de la Loge. *Philadelphia. Chez John Ormrod.* 1800. 8vo, pp. 35. BA. + *Philadelphie: Thomas and William Bradford.* 1801. 8vo, pp. 35. BA. + *Philadelphia: de l'Imprimiere du F.·., A.·., J.·. Blocquerst.* 1811. 8vo, 2 l., pp. 60. 12288

CHAUDRON. Funeral Oration on Brother Geo. Washington, delivered January 1st, 1800, before the French Lodge. L'Aménité. By brother Simon Chaudron. Translated from the French By Samuel T. Bradford. *Philadelphia: Printed by John Ormrod.* 1800. 8vo, pp. 26. BA., P. 12289

CHAUDRON. Oracion funebre al ciudadano Jorge Washington pronunciada el 1 de Enero de 1800, en una Sociedad francesa en Filadelfia. Traducido del frances al Castellano, por G. J. *Mexico.* 1823. 8vo, pp. 21. 12290

CHAUDRON. Poésies choisies de Jean-Simon Chaudron, suivies de l'oraison funébre de Washington, par le même auteur. *Paris: imp. de Delanchy.* 1841. 8vo. 12291

CHAUFEPIÉ (C. A. de). De servitute in coloniis Americanis tollenda. *Amsterdam.* 1799. 8vo. 12292

CHAUFEPIÉ (J. H.) Historia Febris Flavae Americanae. Specimen inaugurale, quod ... submittit Joan. Henn. Chaufepié, Hamburgensis. *Halae, typis Batheanis.* [n. d.] 8vo, pp. 64.

CHAULMER (C.) Le Novveav-Monde ov l'Ameriqve chrestienne avec le svpplement à l'Abrregé des Annales ecclesiastiqves et politiqves de l'ancien, ov l'histoire des missions, & des autres Affaires de l'Europe, de l'Asie & de l'Afrique.Par Me Charles Chavlmer ... . *Paris: Simon Le Sourd.* M. DC. LIX. 12mo, 7 l., pp. 432, 3 l., pp. 360, (58). BA. 12294

Ternaux remarks: "Hardly true, but the book treats less of America than would be inferred from the title." Priced, by J. R. Smith, in 1863, at £1 11s. 6d.

CHAUMETTE (A.) Catalogue des livres et mss. composant la bibliothèque de feu A. Chaumette des Fossés; dont la vente aura lieu le jeudi 3 novembre 1842 et jours suivants. *Paris.* 1842. 8vo, pp. viij, 190. 12295

Rich in works relating to the languages and history of America.

CHAUMETTE (Pierre Gaspard). Discours prononcé par le Gen. Chaumette, à la Fête célébrée à Paris, en Réjouissance de l'Abolition de l'Esclavage. [*Paris.* 1794.] 8vo, pp. 42. M.

CHAUMONOT (P. J. M.) La Vie du R. P. Pierre Joseph Marie Chaumonot, de la Compagnie de Jesus, Missionnaire dans la Nouvelle France, Ecrite par lui-même par ordre de son Supé-

rieur, l'an 1688. *Nouvelle-York, Isle de Manate: A la Presse Cramoisy de Jean-Marie Shea.* M. DCCC. LVIII. Sm. 4to, pp. 108.

Forms No. VI. of Shea's Cramoisy Series. 100 copies printed, and five on large paper. The original manuscript is in the Hotel Dieu, Quebec.

CHAUMONOT. Suite de la Vie du R. P. Pierre Joseph Marie Chaumonot, De la Compagnie de Jesus, Par un Père de la même Compagnie avec la manière d'oraison du venerable Père, Écrite par lui-même. *Nouvelle York, Isle de Manate: A la Presse Cramoisy de Jean-Marie Shea.* M. DCCC. LVIII. Sm. 4to, pp. 66, (1). B., BA. 12298

Forms No. VII. of Shea's Cramoisy Series. 100 copies printed, and five on large paper. Mr. Shea attributes the authorship of this work to Sebastian Rasles.

CHAUMONT (J. Le R.) An Address delivered at the Meeting at the Agricultural Society of Jefferson County, December 29, 1817. By J. Le Ray de Chaumont ... . *New York: printed by William A. Mercien.* 1818. 8vo, pp. 20. H. 12299

Also other addresses before the same society, in 1820, 1824, 1829, and 1830.

CHAUMONT (L. de). Souvenirs des États-Unis par L. de Chaumont ... *Paris: Jacques Lecoffre et Cie.* 1859. 4to, pp. 16.

CHAUNCEY (C.) An Oration, Delivered before the Society of the Φ B K; at their Anniversary Meeting, in the City of New-Haven. On the Evening preceding Commencement, Anno Domini 1797. By Charles Chauncey, Jun. ... *T. & S. Green: New-Haven.* [n. d.] 8vo, pp. 34. BA. 12301

CHAUNCEY (C.), *of Pa.* Speech of Charles Chauncey in the Convention of Pennsylvania, in 1837, on the Judicial Tenure. *Philadelphia.* 1838. 8vo. 12302

CHAUNCEY (N.) Oration ... before the Washington Association of Philadelphia ... on the Fourth of July, 1815. By Nathaniel Chauncey, Esq. *Philadelphia.* 1815. 8vo, pp. 22.

[CHAUNCY Charles), *President of Harvard College.*] Anti-Synodalia Scripta Americana. Or, A Proposal of the Judgment of the DIssenting [*sic*] Messengers of the Churches of New-England Assembled, by the Appointment of the General Court, March 10. 1662. whereof there were several Sessions afterward. [n. p. 1662.] 4to, pp. 38. 12304

[CHAUNCY.] Examen Confectionis Pacificæ: or, A Friendly Examination of the Pacifick Paper: Chiefly concerning The

Consistency of Absolute Election of Particular Persons with the Universality of Redemption: and The Conditionality of the Covenant of Grace. Wherein also The New Scheme is clearly declared. [Motto.] *London Printed, and are to be Sold by Richard Baldwin, near the Oxford-Arms, in Warwick-Lane.* M DC XCII. 4to, Title, pp. 22. G. 12305

CHAUNCY. God's Mercy Shewed to his People, in giving them a faithfull Ministry and Schools of Learning, for the continual Supplyes thereof. Delivered in a Sermon Preached at Cambridge the Day after the Commencement, by Charles Chauncy, B.D. President of Harvard Colledge in New England. Published with some Additions thereunto, at the Request of Divers Honoured and much Respected Friends, for publick Benefit, as they judged. *Printed by Samuel Green at Cambridge in New England.* 1655. 12mo, pp. 56. 12306

Mr. Corwin's copy sold, in 1856, for $17. It would sell for $50 now.

CHAUNCY. ... The Plain Doctrine of the Justification of a Sinner in the sight of God ... . Explained and Applied in six and twenty Sermons ... . By Charles Chauncy ... . *London: Adoniram Byfield.* 1659. 8vo, 4 l., pp. 306, (8). B. 12307

CHAUNCY. The Retraction of Mr. Cha. Chauncy, formerly Minister of Ware in Harfordshire, wherein is proved the Unlawfulnesse and Danger of Rayling in Altars and Communion Tables. Written with his own hand before his going to New England in the yeer 1637. *London Printed.* 1641. 4to, 4 l., pp. 39. J.C.B.

Chauncy delivered an election sermon in 1656. *See* the appendix to the "Catalogue of the Mass. Hist. Society, 1811."

CHAUNCY (C.) The accursed Thing must be taken away from among a People, if they would reasonably hope to stand before their Enemies. A Sermon Preached at the Thursday-Lecture in Boston, September 3, 1778. ... By Charles Chauncy, D.D., Senior Pastor of the first Church in Boston. *Boston, New England: Printed by Thomas & John Fleet.* 1778. 8vo, pp. 27. BA.

Most of the sermons by this eminent divine, who was pastor of the first church in Boston from 1727 to his death in 1787, contains historical notes and other enlargements not quite appropriate to the pulpit.

[CHAUNCY.] The | Antigionian and Bostonian Beauties; | A | Poem. | Occasion'd by seeing the Assembly, at St. | John's, Antigua, on Thursday the 7th | of July, and afterwards at Boston, in | King-street. | [Motto.] By *W. S.* A.B. | *Boston:* | *Printed and*

Sold by D. Fowle in Queen-street, | [1754.] 8vo, pp. 8, Some Thoughts from Seneca, pp. 8. 12310

CHAUNCY. The Appeal to the Public Answered, In Behalf of the New Episcopal Churches in America; Containing Remarks on what Dr. Thomas Bradbury Chandler has advanced, on the four following Points. The Original and Nature of the Episcopal Office. Reasons for sending Bishops to America. The Plan on which it is proposed to send them. And the Objections against sending them obviated and refuted. Wherein the Reasons for an American Episcopate are shewn to be insufficient, and the Objections against it in full Force. By Charles Chauncy, D.D. And Pastor of the first Church of Christ in Boston. *Boston, N. E.: Printed by Kneeland and Adams. ... for Thomas Leverett*, ... 1768. Sm. 8vo, pp. 205. B., C., H. 12311

CHAUNCY. The Character and Overthrow of Laish ... . A Sermon Preached at the Desire of the ... Artillery-Company ... June 3. 1734. Being the ... Day For their Election of Officers By Charles Chauncy ... . *Boston: D. Henchman.* 1734. 8vo, Title, pp. 19. BA., H. 12312

CHAUNCY. Civil Magistrates must be Just, ruling in the Fear of God. A Sermon: Preached ... May 27. 1747. Being the Anniversary for the Election ... . By Charles Chauncy ... [Appendix from Election Sermons of J. Barnard and N. Appleton.] *Boston.* 1747. 8vo, pp. 69, (2). BA., H. 12313

CHAUNCY. A Compleat View of Episcopacy, As exhibited from the Fathers of the Christian Church, until the Close of the Second Century ... . By Charles Chauncy, D.D. ... *Boston Thomas Leverett.* M,DCC,LXXI. 8vo, pp. 474, (3). BA., C., N., H.

CHAUNCY. A Discourse On "the good News from a far Country." Deliver'd July 24th. A Day of Thanks-giving to Almighty God, throughout the Province of the Massachusetts-Bay in New-England, on Occasion of the Repeal of the Stamp-Act ... . By Charles Chauncy, D.D. ... . *Boston: Thomas Leverett.* MDCCLXVI. 8vo., pp. 32. BA., H. 12315

Reprinted in Thornton's "Pulpit of the American Revolution," pp. 105-146.

[CHAUNCY.] The Late Religious Commotions in | New England Considered. | An | Answer | To | Mr. Jonathan Edwards' | Sermon, | Entitled, | The Distinguishing Marks of a Work | Of the Spirit of God, Applied to that | Uncommon Operation that has

lately | Appeared on the Minds of Many of | The People of this Land, | In a Letter to a Friend, | Together with | A Preface, | Containing an Examination of the Rev. Mr. William | Cooper's Preface to Mr. Edwards's Sermon. | *Boston.* 1743. | 8vo, pp. 20-40. 12316

Title from W. E. Woodward's catalogue. Not in Clark's list of Chauncy's works.

[CHAUNCY.] A Letter from a Gentleman in Boston to Mr. George Wishart, One of the Ministers of Edinburgh, Concerning the State of Religion In New-England. *Edinburgh.* MDCCXLII. 8vo, pp. 24. H. 12317

Not quoted in Clark's catalogue.

CHAUNCY. A Letter To a Friend, Containing, Remarks on certain Passages in a Sermon Preached, by ... John [Ewer] Lord Bishop of Landaff, before the Incorporated Society for the Propagation of the Gospel in Foreign Parts ... February 20. 1767. In which the highest Reproach is undeservedly cast upon the American Colonies. By Charles Chauncy, D.D. ... *Boston: Printed for Thomas Leverett.* MDCCLXVII. 8vo, pp. 56. H. 12318

Reprinted with the following title:

CHAUNCY. A Letter to a Friend, Containing Remarks on certain Passages in a Sermon, preached by ... John [Ewer], Lord Bishop of Landaff, before the ... Society for the Propagation of the Gospel in foreign Parts ... February 20, 1767; in which the highest Reproach is undeservedly cast upon the American Colonies. By Charles Chauncy, M.D. ... With a Supplement, Containing an Answer to the Plea of T. B. Chandler, D.D. of New Jersey, for American Bishops ... . By a Presbyter in Old England [Rev. Caleb Fleming]. *London: S. Bladon.* MDCCLXVIII. 8vo, pp. 79, (1). BA., H. 12319

[CHAUNCY.] A Letter to a Friend; Giving a concise, but just Account, according to the Advices hitherto received, of the Ohio-Defeat; And Pointing out also the many good Ends, this inglorious Event is naturally adapted to promote: Or, shewing wherein it is fitted to advance the Interest of all the American British Colonies. To which is added, some general Account of the New-England Forces, with what they have already done, counter-ballancing the above loss. *Boston: Edes & Gill.* 1755. 4to, pp. 15. C. + *Bristol: re-printed by Edward Ward on the Tolzey.* 1755. 8vo, pp. 30. + *London.* 1755. 8vo, pp. 28.

Signed T. W., Boston, Aug. 25, 1755. This tract has reference to the defeat of the British (Colonial) forces under Col. George Washington in Ohio. The writer

attributes the ill success to the commanding officer. He complains, too, that the southern colonies did not comprehend tne danger to which they were exposed by the union of the French and Indians. The defeat he calls "a terrible evil! New England in general, and Massachusetts province in special, are the chief sources that may be relied on for a supply of effective men to carry into execution any future designs against the French."

[CHAUNCY.] A Letter to a Friend, giving a Concise, but Just representation of the Hardships and Sufferings the Town of Boston is exposed to, and must undergo, in consequence of the late Act of the British Parliament; which, by shutting up its Port, has put a fatal bar in the way of that commercial business on which it depended for its support. Shewing, at the same time, wherein this Edict, however unintended, is powerfully adapted to promote the Interest of all the American Colonies, and, even of Boston itself, in the end. By T. W. A Bostonian. *Boston, N. E.: Greenleaf's Printing Office.* M,DCC,LXXIV. 8vo, pp. 35. 12321

CHAUNCY. A Letter To the Reverend Mr. George Whitefield, Vindicating certain Passages he has excepted against, in a late Book entitled, Seasonable Thoughts on the State of Religion in New-England; and shewing that he has neither sufficiently defended himself, nor retracted his past Misconduct. By Charles Chauncy, D.D. ... *Boston: Printed by Rogers and Fowle for S. Eliot.* 1745. 8vo, pp. 39. BA., H. 12322

See Col. Aspinwall's catalogue, No. 317, for what appears to be another edition.

CHAUNCY. Man's Life considered under the Similitude of a Vapour ... . A Sermon on the Death of ... Mrs. Sarah Byfield ... Who died Decemb. 21st. 1730. ... By Charles Chauncy ... . *Boston: Printed by B. Green.* MDCCXXXI. 8vo, 3 l., pp. 42.

Pages 40-42 comprise "An Appendix. From the Weekly News-Letter, No. 1405. Containing an Account of the Deceased." The first work published by Dr. Chauncy.

CHAUNCY. Marvellous Things done by the right Hand and holy Arm of God in getting him the Victory. A Sermon Preached the 18th of July, 1745. Being a Day set apart for Solemn Thanksgiving to almighty God, For the Reduction of Cape-Breton by his Majesty's New-England Forces, under the Command of the honourable William Pepperrell, Esq; Lieutenant-General and Commander in Chief, and covered by a Squadron of his Majesty's Ships from Great Britain, commanded by Peter Warren, Esq; By Charles Chauncy, D.D. Pastor of a Church in Boston. *Boston: Printed and sold by T. Fleet at the Heart and Crown in Cornhill.* 1745. 8vo, pp. 23. + *Boston: printed. London: Reprinted and Sold by M. Cooper.* 1745. 8vo, pp. 31.

CHAUNCY. Nathanael's Character display'd. A Sermon, Preach'd ... after the Funeral of ... Nathanael Byfield Esq; Late Judge of the Vice-Admiralty ... . Who died ... 6th of June, 1733. ... By Charles Chauncy ... . [n. p.] 1733. 8vo, 2 l., pp. iv, 35. B., BA., H. 12325

The preface is signed Tho. Foxcroft. Pages 32-35 contain "An Account of the deceased. From the Weekly News-Letter, No. 1533. With Amendment."

CHAUNCY. A Reply to Dr. Chandler's 'Appeal defended:' wherein His Mistakes are rectified, his false Arguing refuted, and the Objections against the Planned American Episcopate shewn to remain in full Force, notwithstanding all he has offered to render them invalid. By Charles Chauncy ... . *Boston: Thomas Leverett.* MD,CC,LXX. 8vo, pp. 180, x. BA., C., H.

CHAUNCY. Seasonable Thoughts on the State of Religion in New-England, A Treatise in five Parts. I. Faithfully pointing out the Things of a Bad and Dangerous tendency, in the late, and present, religious Appearance, in the Land. II. Representing, the Obligations which lie upon the Pastors of these Churches in particular, and upon All in general, to use their Endeavours to suppress prevailing Disorders; with the great Danger of a Neglect in so important a Matter. III. Opening, in many Instances, wherein the Discouragers of Irregularities have been injuriously treated. IV. Showing what ought to be corrected, or avoided, in testifying against the evil Things of the present Day. V. Directing our Tho'ts, more positively, to what may be judged the Best Expedients, to promote pure and undefiled Religion in these Times, &c. With a Preface, Giving an Account of the Antinomians, Familists, and Libertines, who infected these churches, above an hundred years ago: Very needful for these Days; the like Spirit and Errors, prevailing now as did then. The whole being intended, and calculated, to serve the Interest of Christ's Kingdom. By Charles Chauncy. D.D. Pastor of the First Church of Christ in Boston. *Boston: Printed by Rogers and Fowle, for Samuel Eliot.* 1743. 8vo, pp. xxx, 18, 424. B.

Against Whitfield and his followers. Contains a list of six hundred subscribers.

[CHAUNCY.] A Second Letter To a Friend, Giving a more particular Narrative of the Defeat of the French Army at Lake-George, by the New-England Troops, than has yet been published, Representing also the vast Importance of this Conquest to the American-British Colonies. To which is added, Such an Account of what the New-England Governments have done, to

carry into Effect their Design against Crown-Point, as will shew the Necessity of their being help'd by Great-Britain, in Point of Money. *Boston, N. E.: Edes and Gill.* M,DCC,LV. 4to, pp. 16.

Signed T. W.

CHAUNCY. A Sermon Delivered at the First Church in Boston, March 13th, 1785: occasioned by the Return of the Society to their House of Worship, after Long Absence ... . By Charles Chauncy. *Boston: Greenleaf.* M,DCC,LXXXV. 8vo, pp. 23. H.

CHAUNCY. Trust in God ... . A Sermon Preached, May 30th. 1770. At the request of ... friends to the Liberties of North-America, who were desirous, notwithstanding the removal of the Massachusetts General-Court (unconstitutionally as they judged) to Cambridge, that God might be acknowledged ... at Boston ... . By Charles Chauncy ... . *Boston: Thomas Leverett.* 1770. 8vo, pp. 38. BA., H., W. 12330

CHAUNCY. The Validity of Presbyterian Ordination asserted and maintained. A Discourse delivered at the Anniversary Dudleian-Lecture at Harvard-College in Cambridge, in New-England, May 12. 1762. By Charles Chauncy ... *Boston: Richard Draper.* 1762. 8vo, pp. 118. B., BA., C. 12331

Also: All nations of the Earth Blessed in Christ ... . A Sermon preached at Boston, at the Ordination of the Rev. Mr. Joseph Bowman, to the Work of the Gospel-Ministry, More especially among the Mohawk-Indians on the Western Borders of New England, August 31, 1762. ... . *Boston: John Draper.* 1762. 8vo, Title, pp. viii, 50. B., BA., W. — The Benevolence of the Deity, fairly and impartially considered. *America: Massachusetts; Boston: Printed by Powars & Willis.* MDCCLXXXIV. 8vo, pp. 293. BA., H., W. — The Blessedness of the Dead who die in the Lord. A Sermon Preached ... after the Funeral of Mrs. Anna Foxcroft ... Who died Oct. 9th 1749, in the 53d Year of her Age. ... *Boston: Rogers and Fowle.* MDCCXLIX. 8vo, pp. 31. BA., H. — "Breaking of Bread," ... . Five Sermons. ... By Charles Chauncy ... . *Boston: Thomas Leverett.* M,DCC,LXXII. 8vo, pp. 170. B., BA., H. — Charity to the distressed Members of Christ ... . A Sermon, Preached the Lord's-Day after the Death of Mr. Edward Gray ... . *Boston: Green & Russell.* 1757. 8vo, pp. 32. B., BA. — Christian Love ... . A Sermon Preached ... in Boston, August 3d. 1773. ... . *Boston: Thomas Leverett,* M,DCC,LXXIII. 8vo, pp. 32. H. — Cornelius's Character. A Sermon Preach'd ... after the Funeral of Mr. Cornelius Thayer, One of the Deacons of the first Church ... Who died, April 10. 1745. Ætat. 60. ... . *Boston: D. Gookin.* 1745. 8vo, pp. 38. BA., H. — The Counsel of Two Confederate Kings to set the son of Tabeal on the Throne, a Sermon Occasion'd by the Present Rebellion in Favour of the Pretender. Preach'd in Boston ... February 6th, 1745, 6. *Boston: D. Gookin.* 1746. 8vo, pp. 43. BA. — A Discourse occasioned by the Death of the Reverend Jonathan Mayhew, D.D. Late Pastor of the West-Church in Boston: who departed this Life ... July 9. 1766, Ætatis 46. ... . *Boston: R. and S. Draper; Edes and Gill; and T. and J. Fleet.* MDCCLXVI. 8vo, pp. 40. B., BA., H. — A Discourse occasioned by the Death of the Reverend Thomas Foxcroft, who departed this life June 18, 1769. *Boston: Thomas Leverett.* MD,CC,LXIX. 8vo, pp. 33 [34], (4). BA. — A Discourse occasioned by the

Death of the Reverend Dr. Joseph Sewall, Late Colleague Pastor of the South-Church ... who departed this Life ... June 27. 1769 ... . *Boston: Kneeland and Adams.* M DCCC LXIX. 8vo, pp. 40. B., BA. (Pages 35-40 contain an "Appendix. From the Boston Evening-Post of July 3d. 1769.") — The Duty of Ministers ... . A Sermon preached at the Ordination of ... Penuel Bowen, a Colleague-Pastor of the New-South-Church ... April 30, 1766. By Charles Chauncy ... . *Boston: Edes and Gill.* 1766. 8vo, pp. 39. BA., H. — Early Piety recommended ... A Sermon Occasioned by the Death of Elisabeth Price. ... . *Boston: B. Gray.* 1732. 8vo, 2 l., pp. iv, 25. BA., H. — The Earth delivered from the Curse. ... . A Sermon Occasioned by the Earth-Quakes in Spain and Portugal, as well as New-England ... Preached at ... Thursday-Lecture, January 22, 1756. ... *Boston: Edes & Gill.* M,DCC,LVI. 8vo, pp. 28. B., H., M. — Earthquakes a Token of the Righteous Anger of God. A Sermon Preached ... the Lord's-Day after the terrible Earthquake ... 18th of November, 1755. ... . *Boston: Edes and Gill.* M,DCC,LV. 8vo, pp. 32. BA., H. — Enthusiasm described and caution'd against. A Sermon Preach'd ... the Lord's Day after ... Commencement, 1742. With a Letter to the Reverend Mr. James Davenport. ... *Boston: S. Eliot and J. Blanchard.* M DCC XLII. 8vo, Title, pp. viii, 27. BA., H., S. — Five Dissertations on the Scripture Account of the Fall, and its Consequences. ... *London.* 1785. 8vo. M. — The Gifts of the Spirit to Ministers ... . A Sermon Preach'd ... Decemb. 17. 1741. ... . *Boston: Rogers & Fowle; Also S. Eliot.* 1742. BA., B., H., W. — The horrid Nature and enormous Guilt of Murder. A Sermon preached ... November 19th. 1734. The Day of the Execution of William Wieer, For the Murder of William Chism. *Boston: Printed by Thomas Fleet.* 1754. 8vo, pp. 24. BA., H. — The Idle-Poor secluded from the Bread of Charity ... A Sermon Preached in Boston, before the Society for encouraging Industry ... Aug. 12. 1752. ... *Boston: Printed by Thomas Fleet.* 1752. 8vo, pp. 26. B., BA., H. — Joy, the Duty of Survivors ... . A .. Discourse On the Death of Mrs. Lucy Waldo ... . *Boston.* 1741. 8vo, pp. (2), 26. B, H. — Ministers cautioned against the Occasions of Contempt. A Sermon preached before ... the ... Annual Convention, In Boston; May 31. 1744. ... . *Boston: Samuel Eliot.* 1744. 8vo, pp. 54 BA., H. — Ministers exhorted ... . A Sermon Preached the 7th of November, At the Installment of the Rev. Mr. Thomas Frink to the Pastoral Care Of the third Church in Plymouth ... . *Boston.* 1744. 8vo, pp. 45. BA., H. — The Mystery hid from Ages and Generations, made manifest by the Gospel Revelation: or, the Salvation of all Men. ... By Charles Chauncy, D.D. *Boston.* [1782.] 8vo, pp. 26. + *London.* 1784. 8vo. — The New Creature Describ'd ... . A Sermon Preach'd at the Boston Thursday-Lecture, June 4. 1741. ... *Boston: J. Edwards and S. Eliot.* 1741. 8vo, pp. 47. BA., H. — *Edinburgh: Reprinted.* 1742. 12mo, pp. 37. — The only Compulsion proper to be made Use of in the Affairs of Conscience and Religion. A Sermon Preach'd ... in Boston, September 2d 1739. ... . *Boston: Printed by J. Draper, for J. Edwards.* MDCCXXXIX. 8vo, 2 l., pp. 26. BA., H. — [Chauncy.] The Opinion of One that has perused the Summer Morning's Conversation, concerning Original Sin, wrote by the Rev. Mr. Peter Clark ... . To which is added, A few remarks on the recommendatory preface by five ... clergymen. In a Letter to a Friend. ... *Boston: Green & Russell.* 1758. 8vo, pp. 28. — The out-pouring of the Holy Ghost. A Sermon ... May 13. 1742. ... . *Boston: D. Henchman and S. Eliot.* 1742. 8vo, pp. 46. BA., H. — Prayer for Help ... . A Sermon occasioned by the death of several worthy Members of the first Church in Boston: Preach'd ... after the funeral of Mr. Jonathan Williams, one of the Deacons ... . *Boston: Printed by J. Fleet* 1737. 8vo. 2 l., pp. 25. B, BA. — A Sermon Preached May 6, 1767. At the Ordination of the Reverend Simeon Howard, ... To the Pastoral Care of the West-Church in Boston. ... *Boston: R. Draper, Edes & Gill, and T. & J. Fleet.* 1767. 8vo, pp. 55. H. — Twelve Sermons On the following seasonable and important Subjects ... . *Boston: Thomas Leverett.* MDCCLXV. 8vo, Title, pp. iv, 344. B., BA. — An Unbridled Tongue ... . A Sermon ... September 10th. 1741. ... . *Boston: Rogers and Fowle.* 1741. 8vo, pp. 30. B., BA. — A Discourse delivered at the Anniversary Dudleian-Lecture at Harvard-College, ...

May 12. 1762. ... . *Boston: Printed by Richard Draper.* 8vo, Title, pp. 5-118. H., W. *See* Mass. Hist. Coll., Vol. x.

CHAUNCY (I.) The Faithful Evangelist ... a Sermon Preach'd at The Ordination of Mr. William Rand, at Sunderland, May 20th. 1724. By Isaac Chauncy ... . *Boston: Daniel Henchman.* 1725. 8vo, Title, pp. 35. B. 12332

CHAUNCY. Neonomianism Unmask'd: or the Ancient Gospel Pleaded, Against the Other, called A New Law or Gospel, In a Theological Debate, occasioned by a Book lately wrote by Mr. Dan. Williams, Entituled, Gospel-Truth Stated and Vindicated: Unwarily Commended and Subscribed by some Divines, Applauded and Defended by the late Athenian Clubb. By Isaac Chavncy, M.A. *London: Printed for J. Harris at the Harrow in the Poultry.* 1692. 4to, 4 l., pp. 40. ‖ Second Part. *London: Printed for D. Barnard.* 1693. 4to, 3 l., pp. 336. ‖ Third Part. 4to, pp. 104. G. 12333

CHAUNCY. A Rejoynder to Mr. Daniel Williams his Reply To the First Part of NeomiAnism UnMaskt, Wherein His Defence is Examined, and his Arguments Answered; whereby he endeavours to prove the Gospel to be a New Law with Sanction: And the contrary is proved. By Isaac Chavncy. M.A. *London: Printed for H. Barnard, at the Bible in the Poultry.* MDCXCIII. 4to, pp. 8. G. 12334

CHAUNCY. A Sermon preached at Hadley upon a Lord's Day, 1731. By Isaac Chauncy, M.A. *Boston: J. Phillips.* 1732. 8vo, pp. 30. C. 12335

Also: A Funeral Sermon on the Death of Rev. John Williams, Pastor of Deerfield, ... *Boston: D. Henchman.* 1729. — The Loss of the Soul, a Lecture Sermon, preached at Hadley, on the 16th day of February, 1732. ... *Boston: J. Phillips.* 1732, pp. 26. — Alexipharmacon, or a fresh Antidote against Neonomian Bane and Poyson to the Protestant Religion. 1700. 8vo. — Christ's Ascension ... A Sermon Preach'd at Horsly-Down, at the Solemn Ordination and setttng a-part of Elders and Deacons, by the Church of Christ, there Assembled. *London.* 1699. 8vo. — The Divine Institution of Congregational Churches, ... *London.* 1697. 12mo. — The Doctrine which is according to Godliness. *London.* 1737. 12mo, pp. 337. — Ecclesiasticum, or a plain and familiar Christian Conference concerning Gospel Churches and Order. 1690. 12mo. — Examen Confectionis Pacificæ, or a Friendly Examination of the Pacifick Paper, chiefly concerning the Consistency of Absolute Election of Particular Persons. 1692. 4to. — A Plea for the Antient Gospel. 1697. 4to. Isaac Chauncy is also the author of many other works bearing on church government, published in Great Britain.

CHAUNCY (N.) The Faithful Ruler Described and Excited: in a Sermon Preach'd before the General Assembly of the Colony of Connecticut, at Hartford, May 9th. 1734. The Day for the

Election of the Honourable the Governour, ... Deputy-Governour, and ... Assistants there. By Nathaniel Chauncy ... . *N. London: Printed and sold by T. Green.* 1734. 16mo, Half-Title, Title, pp. 52. H. 12336

CHAUNCY. The Faithful Servant Rewarded. [A Sermon on the Death of Mr. John Hart.] By Nathanael Chauncy ... *N. London: T. Green.* 1732. 12mo, pp. 39. 12337

CHAUNCY. Honouring God The True Way to Honour. A Sermon Preach'd before the General Assembly of ... Connecticut At Hartford May 14th. 1719. The Day for the Election ... . *New-London: Timothy Green.* 1719. 12mo, Title, pp. 54.

CHAUNCY. A Genealogical Table of the Family of Chauncy's, taken partly from Sir Henry Chauncy's History of Hertfordshire, pages 55-61, and partly from a Genealogical Roll I have in my possession, and other Information. — *N. C., Jan.* 1787. 12339

The heading of a large sheet containing a series of tabular pedigrees relative to the Chauncy family.

CHAUNCY-HALL SCHOOL. Annual Catalogue of the Teachers and Pupils of Chauncy-Hall School, Boston, May, 1846. *Boston.* 1846. 12mo, pp. 24. Continued. 12340

Roll of Former Members of Chauncy-Hall School who served in the Army or Navy of the United States, during the War for the Suppression of the Rebellion. *Boston: Printed by D. Clapp & Son.* 1866. 12mo, Title, pp. 22. H. 12341

Constitution and By-Laws of the Chauncy Society for Mutual Improvement. *Boston: Press of Light and Stearns.* 1836. 12mo, pp. 12. H. 12342

CHAUTARD (L.) Escape from Cayenne. By Leon Chautard. *Salem.* 1857. 8vo, pp. 63. C. 12343

CHAUVEAU (P. J. O.) Charles Guérin, roman de mœurs canadiennes. ... *Montréal: John Lovell, Imprimeur.* 1852. 8vo. + [*Ibid.*] 1853. 8vo H. 12344

CHAUVEAU. Discours prononcé le ... 18 juillet 1855. par l'honorable P. J. O. Chauveau, ... a la cérémonie de la pose de la pierre angulaire du monument dédiée par souscription nationale, a la mémoire des braves tombés sur la Plaine d'Abraham, le 28 avril 1760. ... *Québec: E. R. Fréchette.* 1855. 8vo, pp. 8. H. 12345

Also included in "La littérature canadienne de 1850 à 1860 ... Deuxième édition. *Quebec.* 1863. 8vo," I. 375–387. BA. — Also: Journal de l'Instruction Publique. Rédigé par l'Hon. P. J. O. Chauveau, Surintendant de l'instruction publique du Bas-Canada, etc. *Montreal.* 1857. 4to. Continued.

CHAUVEAU-LAGARDE (N.) Plaidoyer pour les sieurs Bissette, Fabien fils et Volney, condamnés à la marque et aux galères perpétuité par la cour royale de la Martinique. *Paris: Ponthieu.* 1826. 8vo. 12346

CHAUVET-CHAROLAIS (L.) Buénos-Ayres. *Paris: imp. de Simon d'Autreville.* 1851. 8vo. 12347

Extracted from "L'union," 31 déc. 1850.

CHAUVET (Joseph Joachim Victor). Haïti, chant lyrique. *Paris: Delaforest.* 1825. 8vo, pp. 16. 12348

Perhaps his "L'abolition de la traite des noirs ... . *Paris: impr. de F. Didot.* 1823." 4to, pp. 12, deserves mention here. It was also appended to his "Arthur de Bretagne, tragédie ... . *Paris: Barba.* 1824." 8vo, with the insertion of some passages omitted in the first edition by direction of the French Academy, which had granted a prize to the poet.

CHAUVETON (Urbain). *See* Benzoni (G.), Vol. II., No. 4795.

CHAUVIGNY (Magdeline de). *See* Peltrie (*Mme. de*).

CHAVANNES. Patrice, ou Les pionniers de l'Amérique du Nord. Par M. de Chavannes. *Tours: Mame et fils.* 1861. 32mo, pp. 128. Vignette. Also 1868 and 1869. 12349

CHAVANNES DE LA GIRAUDIÈRE (H. de). Voyage en Californie. Par H. de Chavannes de la Giraudière. Nouvelle édition. *Tours: Mame et Ce.* 1857. 18mo, pp. 107. Engraving. + [*Ibid.*] 1858. + Nouvelle édition. [*Ibid.*] 1861. 18mo, pp. 103. Engraving. 12350

CHAVES (Hieronymo de), *Astrologo y Cosmographo.* Chronographia o Reportorio de los tiempos, el mas copioso y preciso que hasta ahora ha salido á luz. *Sevilla: en casa de Alonso Escrivano.* 1572. 4to, 272 l. 12351

"This excessively rare book is one of the handsomest books ever printed in Spain. There is a good woodcut portrait of the author on the title, and many geographical, astronomical, and scientific woodcuts throughout the volume, one of the most interesting of which is a delineation of the New Hemisphere on the reverse of folio 95." *See* Stevens' "Bibl. Hist.," lot No. 2455, for further particulars.

CHAVES (J. F.) Indian Appropriations. Speech of Hon. J. F. Chaves, of New Mexico, in the House of Representatives, March 2, 1867. [n. p. n. d.] 8vo, pp. 4. H. 12352

CHAZELLES (*le comte de*). Emancipation Transformation. Le système anglais. Le système français. Mémoire addressé à la Chambre des députés à l'occasion du project de loi concernant le régime des esclaves dans les colonies. *Paris: imp. de Giraudet.* 1845. 8vo. 12353

CHAZELLES. La question monétaire et la question sociale à Guadeloupe. Par M. le comte de Chazelles. *Paris: imp. de Dubuisson.* 1860. 8vo. 12354

CHAZOTTE (P. S.) Facts and Observations on the Culture of Vines, Olives, Capers, Almonds, &c. in the Southern States, and of Coffee, Cocoa, and Cochineal, in East Florida. By Peter S. Chazotte, &c. *Philadelphia.* 1821. 8vo, pp. 24. H., W.

Title from Rich. The copy we have seen has no title-page, place or date, 8vo, pp. 24.

CHAZOTTE. Historical Sketches of the Revolutions, and the Foreign and Civil Wars in the Island of St. Domingo, with a Narrative of the Entire Massacre of the White Population ... . By Peter S. Chazotte, Esq., an Eye-Witness. *New York: Wm. Applegate.* 1840. 8vo, pp. 71. BA. 12356

CHEADLE (W. B.) *See* Milton (*Viscount*).

Cheap Cotton. *See* [Atkinson (Edward)], Vol. I., No. 2280.

Constitution of the Cheap Postage Association, organized at Boston, March 29th, 1848. [n. p. n. d.] 8vo, pp. 4. H.

The Cheat Unmasked: being a refutation of that Illegitimate Letter said to be wrote by a Clergyman in Town: in a true copy of a letter from that Clergyman to a Friend. *Printed in the year* MDCCLXIV. 12mo, pp. 8. 12358

"They think I would turn Presbyterian again, if they would make me Governor of the Province, or Colonel of the Paxton Boys." Relates to the Lancaster (Penn.) massacre.

The Chebacco Narrative Rescu'd. *See* [Cleaveland (John)], *and* Ipswich, *Mass.*

CHEBUCTO GOLD MINING COMPANY. Report on the Property of the Chebucto Gold Mining Company of Nova Scotia, By John Campbell, Esq., ... With a Sketch of the Gold Region of Nova Scotia, By Benjamin Silliman, Jr. ... . Also a Letter from B. C. Wilson, and the By-Laws of the Company. *Boston: Press of Geo. C. Rand & Avery.* 1864. 8vo, pp. 33. Map. H. 12359

Check List of the Shells of North America. *Smithsonian Institute: Washington.* 1860. 8vo, pp. 44. 12360

[CHECKLEY (John).] Choice Dialogues between a Godly Minister and an Honest Countryman, concerning Election and Predestination. ... [*Boston.* 1720.] 16mo, pp. vii, 47. B.

CHECKLEY. A Defence Of a Book lately re-printed at Boston, entituled A Modest Proof of the Order and Government Settled by Christ and his Apostles in the Church. In a Reply To a Book entituled, Sober Remarks on the Modest Proof, &c. ... *Boston: Printed by T. Fleet.* 1724. 8vo, Half-Title, pp. 73, 14, (1). B., H. 12362

The half-title adds: "With Strictures on J. Dickinson's Defence of Presbyterian Ordination. Also Animadversions upon ... [T. Walter's] Essay upon that Paradox, Infallibility may sometimes mistake. ... [And T. Foxcroft's] The ruling and ordaining Power of Congregational Bishops or Presbyters defended, &c."

CHECKLEY. A Letter to Jonathan Dickinson ["Author of the Remarks." No title-page. 1725.] 8vo, pp. (2), 14. B.

[CHECKLEY.] A Modest Proof of the Order and Government Settled by Christ and his Apostles in the Church. By Shewing I. What Sacred Offices were instituted by them. II. How those Offices were Distinguished. III. That they were to be Perpetual Standing in the Church. And, IV. Who Succeed in them, and rightly Execute them to this Day. *Boston: Reprinted by Tho. Fleet, and are to be Sold by Benjamin Eliot in Boston, Daniel Aurault in Newport, Gabriel Bernon in Providence, Mr. Gallop in Bristol, Mr. Jean in Stratford, and in most other Towns within the Colonies of Connecticut and Rhode-Island.* 1723. 16mo, Title, 1 l., pp. v, 63. B., BA. 12364

CHECKLEY. The Speech of Mr. John Checkley upon his Tryal, at Boston in New-England, for publishing The Short and Easy Method with the Deists: To which was added, A Discourse concerning Episcopacy, in Defence of Christianity, and the Church of England, against the Deists and Dissenters. To which is added the Jury's Verdict; His Plea in Arrest of Judgment; and the Sentence of the Court. *London: J. Wilford.* 1730. 8vo, Title, 1 l., pp. 40. H. 12365

Checkley reprinted and sold in Boston, Leslie's well-known work, entitled "A Short and Easie Method with Deists," first published in London in 1699; to which he prefixed "A Discourse concerning Episcopacy, in Defence of Christianity and the Church of England, against the Deists and Dissenters," and in which he endeavors to show that Dissenters, not being Episcopally ordained, are no ministry. Having used

severe terms towards the Dissenters in New England, he gave great offence, and was, in consequence, prosecuted at the Inferior Court, in 1724, for publishing "a false and scandalous label." Being convicted, he appealed to the Superior Court In his "Plea in arrest of Judgment," he says, in conclusion, "Be that as it will, the Dissenters are affirmed to be no *Ministers*, to be *Scismatics*, and excommunicated by the Canons of the Church of England, which are part of the law of the land; and, therefore, to say the same things of them, I humbly hope shall not be deemed a libel." The court, however, found Checkley guilty, and sentenced him to pay a fine of fifty pounds. This speech is usually found bound up with [Leslie], see *infra*, and is followed by "A Discourse Shewing who is a True Preacher of the Church of Christ," pp. 16, and "A Specimen of a True Dissenting Catechism," 1 l; in the Nuggets, Nos. 536 and 537, they are put down as separate works; and the "Specimen" is reprinted with a long and interesting note. They were all reprinted, "*Windsor, Vt.* 1812," 12mo; and the "Speech" only with an introduction by Rev. E. H. Gillett, D.D., Harlem, N. Y. Privately printed by H. B. Dawson, at Morrisania, N. Y. 1868. 12mo.

CHECKLEY (S.) A Day of Darkness. A Sermon Preach'd ... May 28th. 1755. Being the Anniversary for the Election of His Majesty's Council for said Province. By Samuel Checkley ... . *Boston, N. E.: Printed by John Draper.* MDCCLV. 8vo, pp. 35. B., BA., H., M. 12366

CHECKLEY. The Death of the godly, and especially of faithful gospel Ministers, the greatest loss to survivors. A Sermon Preached September 17th. 1727. ... after the Funeral of the Reverend William Waldron ... . By Samuel Checkley ... . *Boston: Printed for S. Gerrish, S. Kneeland, N. Belknap and B. Love.* 1727. 8vo, 2 l., pp. 21. H. 12367

CHECKLEY. The Duty of a People, to ... Lament the Death of a Good King. A Sermon Preach'd August 20th, 1727. ... after the Death of ... George I. ... . By Samuel Checkley. *Boston: Benj. Gray.* [n. d.] 8vo, 2 l., pp. 23, (4).

CHECKLEY. Little Children Brought to Jesus Christ.|A|Sermon|Preached in Private, May 6th, And|Afterwards in Publick, June 14th,|1741, Upon a Sorrowful Occas-|ion, And Published at the Desire|Of One that Heard it.|By Samuel Checkley ... |*Boston:*|*Rogers and Fowle.*|1741.| 8vo, pp. 24.

Also: Mercy with God for the Chief of Sinners. Sermon Preached March 4th To a Prisoner Under Sentence of Death for Murder. ... . *Boston.* 1733. 12mo, pp. 32. B. — Murder a great and crying Sin. A Sermon Preach'd ... March 4th. 1732–3. To a poor Prisoner Under Sentence of Death ... *Boston: Printed by T. Fleet.* 1733. 8vo, Half-Title, pp. 26. B.

CHECKLEY (S.), *Jr.* The Character and Hope of the Righteous Consider'd, in a Sermon ... after the Funeral of Madam Lydia Hutchinson ... . By Samuel Checkley ... . *Boston: D. Henchman.* 1748. 8vo, 2 l., pp. ii, 22. H. 12370

CHECKLEY. The Duty of God's People when engaged in War. A Sermon ... in Boston, Sept. 21. To Captain Thomas Stoddard, and his Company; On ... their going against the Enemy. By Samuel Checkley ... . *Boston: D. Fowle.* 1755. 8vo, pp. 31. B. 12371

Also: The Christian triumphing over Death through Christ. A Sermon Preached November 10. 1765. in Boston; Upon a mournful Occasion [the death of Mrs. Mary Gallop]. ... *Boston, N. E.: Samuel Webb.* MDCCLXV. 8vo. pp. 45. B. — Sinners minded of a Future Judgment. A Sermon Preached to, and at the Desire of, A Condemned Prisoner, March 18th. 1732--3. Being the Lord's-Day before his Execution. ... . *Boston.* 1733. 12mo, pp. 32. B.

Checkley Family Pedigree. *See* Drake (S. G.)

CHEESMAN (D. W.) An Address on Legal Tenders, ... By Hon. D. W. Cheesman. ... [n. p. n. d.] 8vo, pp. 16. H.

[CHEETHAM (James).] Annals of the Corporation relative to the late Contested Elections. By Lysander. *New York.* 1802. 8vo. C. 12373

[CHEETHAM.] An Antidote to John Wood's Poison. By Warren. *New York: Printed by Southwick and Crooker.* 1802. 8vo, pp. 63. N. 12374

CHEETHAM. A Dissertation concerning Political Equality, and the Corporation of New York. By James Cheetham. *New York: Printed by D. Denniston.* 1800. 8vo, pp. 40 or 50. C., N.

[CHEETHAM.] Letter concerning the Ten Pound Court in the City of New-York. By Mercer. *New York.* 1803. 8vo.

CHEETHAM. A Letter to a Friend on the Conduct of the Adherents to Mr. Burr. By James Cheetham. *New York: Printed by James Cheetham.* 1803. 8vo, pp. 72. C. 12377

CHEETHAM. Letters on our Affairs with Spain. By James Cheetham. *New York.* 1804. 8vo. C. 12378

CHEETHAM. The Life of Thomas Paine, Author of Common Sense ... with a Dedication to George Clinton, &c. By James Cheetham. ... *New-York: Southwick and Pelsue.* 1809. 8vo, pp. 347. BA., C. + *London.* 1817. 12379

[CHEETHAM.] A Narrative of the Suppression by Col. Burr of the History of the Administration of John Adams, Late President of the United States, written by John Wood ... . To which

is added a Biography of Thomas Jefferson ... and of General Hamilton; with strictures on the Conduct of John Adams, and on the Character of General C. C. Pinckney. By a Citizen of New-York. *New-York: Denniston and Cheetham.* 1812. 8vo, pp. 72. BA., N. 12380

CHEETHAM. Nine Letters on the Subject of Aaron Burr's Political Defection, with An Appendix. By James Cheetham. *New York: Denniston & Cheetham.* 1803. 8vo, pp. 139. BA., C.

CHEETHAM. The New Crisis. *New York.* 1810. 8vo, pp. 95. 12382

CHEETHAM. Peace or War? or Thoughts on our Affairs with England. By James Cheetham. *New-York: Mathias Ward.* 1807. 8vo, pp. 44. B., BA., M. 12383

CHEETHAM. Remarks on the "Merchants' Bank," respectfully submitted to the Legislature of the State of New-York. *New York.* 1804. 8vo. C., S. 12384

CHEETHAM. A Reply to Aristides. By James Cheetham, Author of the Narrative ... . *New-York: James Cheetham.* 1804. 8vo, pp. 134. B., BA., C., S. 12385

See "Hist. Mag.," VII. 325.

CHEETHAM. Reply to the Memorial of Thomas Storm, John Hone, and Peter J. Monro. *New York.* 1804. 8vo. 12386

[CHEETHAM.] A View of the Political Conduct of Aaron Burr, Esq. Vice President of the United States. By the Author of the "Narrative." *New-York: Printed by Denniston & Cheetham.* 1802. 8vo, pp. 120. 2. 12387

See also Livingston (M.) and Sampson (W.)

CHEEVER (C. A.) An Address on the Death of Alfred Mason, delivered ... in Portsmouth, by Charles A. Cheever, M.D. [n. p.] MDCCCXXVIII. 8vo, pp. 25. H. 12388

CHEEVER (E.) Ministers are to "testify the Gospel ..." a Sermon Preached October 14, 1772. at the Ordination of The Rev. Jonathan Bascom, ... Over the South Church ... in Eastham. By Edward Cheever ... . *Boston: Edes & Gill.* 1772. 8vo, pp. 36. BA., W. 12389

CHEEVER (E.) Scripture Prophecies Explained. ... By Ezekiel

Cheever ... . *Boston: Green and Russell.* M.DCC.LVII. 8vo, Half-Title, pp. 33. B. 12390

CHEEVER. A short Introduction to the Latin Tongue: For the Use of the Lower Forms in the Latin Schools. Being the Accidence, Abridged and Compiled in that most easy and accurate method, wherein the famous Mr. Ezekiel Cheever taught, and which he found the most advantageous by Seventy Years' experience. *Boston: Printed by Peter Edes.* MDCCLXXXV. 12mo, pp. 79. C. 12391

Perhaps the earliest American Latin grammar.

CHEEVER. [Commendations of] Cheever's Latin Accidence. ... . *Boston.* 1838. 16mo, pp. 15. H. 12392

Contains short memoirs of Ezekiel Cheever.

CHEEVER (E.) Sermons, addressed to the Baptist Church and Society in Deerfield, Mass., &c. By Ezekiel Cheever. *Greenfield.* 1833. 8vo. B. 12393

CHEEVER (George Barrell). *See* Mourt's Journal.

CHEEVER. The American Common-Place Book of Prose; a Collection of Eloquent and Interesting Extracts from the Writings of American Authors. By G. B. Cheever. *Boston.* 1828. 12mo. C. + *Boston: Carter & Hendee.* 1831. 12mo, pp. 468. + *Boston.* 1837. 12mo, pp. 454. + *Philadelphia.* 1839. 12mo. S. + *Cooperstown, N. Y.: H. & E. Phinney.* 1844. 12mo, pp. 468. H. 12394

CHEEVER. The American Common-Place Book of Poetry, with Occasional Notes. By George B. Cheever. *Boston: Carter, Hendee and Babcock. Baltimore: Charles Carter.* 1831. 12mo, pp. 405. H. + *Philadelphia.* 1843. 12mo. 12395

Reprinted as "The Poets of America, with Occasional Notes. *New York.* 1857." 12mo.

CHEEVER. The Curse of God against Political Atheism: with some of the Lessons of the Tragedy at Harper's Ferry. A Discourse delivered in the Church of the Puritans, New York, ... Nov. 6, 1859. By Rev. George B. Cheever, D.D. *Boston: Walker, Wise & Co.* 1859. 8vo, pp. 24. H. 12396

CHEEVER. Deacon Giles' Distillery. *New York.* 1835. Folio, 1 sheet. 12397

This broadsheet gave rise to a famous libel suit, and led to the author's imprisonment. Also: A Defence in Abatement of Judgment for an alleged Libel in the Story en-

titled "Enquire at Amos Giles' Distillery," addressed to the Hon. Chief Justice Shaw. *Salem.* 1836. 12mo. — The True History of Deacon Giles's Distillery; with Mr. Cheever's Defence before the Supreme Judicial Court. *New York.* 1844. 8vo, pp. 48. — The Dream or the True History of Deacon Giles' Distillery, and Deacon Jones' Brewery. Reported for the Benefit of Posterity. ... *New York.* 1848. 8vo, pp. 31. Plates. H.

CHEEVER. The Elements of Natural Greatness, An Address before the New England Society of the City of New York, December 22, 1842. By Rev. George B. Cheever. *New York: John S. Taylor & Co.* 1843. 8vo, pp. 40. C., G. 12398

CHEEVER. The Fire and Hammer of God's Word against the Sin of Slavery. Speech of George B. Cheever, D.D. at the Anniversary of the American Abolition Society, May, 1858. *New York: American Abolition Society.* 1858. 8vo, pp. 16.

There are two editions of this tract.

CHEEVER. God against Slavery; and the Freedom and Duty of the Pulpit to rebuke it, as a Sin against God. By George B. Cheever, D.D. *New York: Joseph H. Ladd.* 1857. 12mo, pp. 272. H. 12400

CHEEVER. God's Hand in America. ... With an Essay [on Patriotism] by Dr. Skinner. *New York.* 1841. 12mo, pp. 168. + Second Edition. *New York* [*printed London*]. 1841. 12mo.

CHEEVER. The Guilt of Slavery and the Crime of Slaveholding, demonstrated from the Hebrew and Greek Scriptures. By Rev. George B. Cheever ... *Boston: J. P. Jewett & Co.* 1860. 12mo, pp. 472. + *New York.* 1860. 12mo, pp. viii, 472. H.

CHEEVER. Reply of the Church of the Puritans to the Protest of their Late Deacons, also to a "Letter" addressed to the Church by sundry Individuals, July 15, 1857, with an Appendix containing certain Documents relating thereto. *New York: Wm. C. Bryant & Co., printers.* 1857. 8vo, pp. 76. 12403

CHEEVER. Rights of the Colored Race to Citizenship and Representation; and the Guilt and Consequences of Legislation against them. A Discourse delivered in ... Washington, D.C., May 29, 1864, by Rev. G. B. Cheever .. *New York: Francis & Loutrel, Printers.* 1864. 8vo, pp. 28. C., H. 12404

CHEEVER. Sketches of American Missionaries. *London: Hamilton.* 1853. 12mo. 12405

Cheever. American Slavery. Demonstrations in favor of Dr. Cheever, in Scotland, Letter of Sympathy from Distinguished Clergymen and other Gentlemen. Speeches at ... Edinburgh and Glasgow ... . And a Statement of Dr. Cheever's Case, by Rev. H. Batchelor. Letter of Dr. Guthrie to the Presbyterian. *New-York: John A. Gray, Printer.* 1860. 24mo, pp. 77. H.

Also: An Address ... before the Society of Inquiry on Missions, in Amherst College, August, 1843. *New-York: John F. Trow & Co., Printers.* 1843. 8vo, pp. 32. H. — Address at a Religious Celebration in Salem, ... July 4, 1833. *Boston.* 1833. 18mo, pp. 60. — Capital Punishment. The Argument of George B. Cheever, in reply to J. L. O'Sullivan, Esq., ... January 27th and February 3d & 17th. *New York: Saxton & Miles.* 1843. 12mo, Title, pp. 108. H. + *New York.* 1846. 12mo. C. — The Commission from God, of the Missionary Enterprise, against the Sin of Slavery ... . An Address ... Boston ... May 27th ... . *Boston: John P. Jewett and Company.* 12mo, pp. 35. + *New York: American Abolition Society.* H. — [Cheever.] Cudworth defended: and Unitarianism delineated. By a Lover of Cudworth and Truth. ... From the Salem Gazette. *Salem.* 1833. 8vo, pp 27. H. (From a series of articles, by different theologians, forming what is called the "Salem Controversy.") — ... A Discourse commemorative of the Virtue and Attainments of the Rev. James Marsh, D.D., .. August 1843. *New York.* 1843. 8vo, pp. 73. — God's Way of Crushing the Rebellion. A Sermon preached at the Church of the Puritans, New York, September 29, 1861. ... *New York.* 1861. 18mo, pp. 20. — The Gospel to be Published and applied against all Sin. A Discourse ... May 28, 1854. *Boston.* 1856. 8vo, pp. 24. — The Hill Difficulty, and some Experiences of Life in the Plains of Ease. With other Miscellanies. *New York.* 1849. 12mo. Portrait. — The Inheritance of Principles ... received from our Pilgrim and Puritan Ancestors, ... A Discourse, preached Dec. 22. 1850 ... . *New York: J. Wiley.* 1851. 8vo, pp. 32. — The Salvation of the Country secured by Immediate Emancipation. A Discourse delivered November 10, 1861. *New-York: John A. Gray, Printer.* 1861, 12mo, pp. 24. H. — The Sin of Slavery, the Guilt of the Church, and the Duty of the Ministry. An Address ... before the Abolition Society at New York. ... 1858. ... *Boston: J. P. Jewett & Company.* 1858. 12mo, pp. 23. H. — Thaddeus Hyatt's Contributions to the Cause of Human Liberty and Constitutional Rights. Sermon ... at New York, Sunday, May 30, 1860. *Boston, Mass.: Thayer & Eldridge.* 1860. 8vo, Title, pp. 18. Portrait. H. — The True Christian Patriot. A Discourse on the Virtues and Public Services of the late Judge Jay, before the American Peace Society. ... *Boston: American Peace Society.* 1860. 8vo, pp. 58. — ... A Discourse preached Dec. 22d, 1850 ... on Occasion of the Anniversary of the Landing of our Pilgrim Fathers. *New York.* 1850. 8vo, pp. 32.

Cheever (H. T.) Autobiography and Memorial of Captain Obadiah Congar. By Rev. Henry T. Cheever. *New York.* 1851. 16mo. 12407

[Cheever.] The Pulpit and the Pew: being the History of a Struggle for Justice between the Two: &c. ... *New York.* 1858. 12mo. 12408

Cheever. The Whale and his Captors, or, the Whaleman's Adventures, and the Whale's Biography, with engravings. By the Rev. Henry T. Cheever. *New York: Harper & Brothers.* 1850. 16mo, pp. 314. C. 12409

Reprinted with the following title:

Cheever. The Whaleman's Adventures in the Southern Ocean, as gathered by the Rev. Henry T. Cheever on the Homeward Cruise of the 'Commodore Preble.' Edited by the Rev. W. Scoresby. *London: Low.* 1850. + Second Edition. *London: Low.* 1855. 12mo, pp. 298. 12410

Also: A Tract for the Times, on the Question, Is it Right to withhold Fellowship from Churches or from Individuals that tolerate or practise Slavery? ... *New York: John A. Gray, Printer.* 1859. 8vo, pp. 23. BA.

Cheever (S.), *b.* 1639, *d.* 1724. God's Sovereign Government Among the Nations ... a Sermon Preached May 28. 1712, being the day for the Election of Her Majesties Council ... . By Samuel Cheever ... . *Boston: Printed by B. Green.* 1712. 8vo, pp. (2), 53. B. 12411

Also: Elijah's Mantle. Boston. 1724.

Cheever (S.) Address, ... New-York Agricultural Society, Albany, Feb. 15, 1856. By Samuel Cheever. *Albany.* 1856. 8vo. S. 12412

Cheever. Malignity Exposed; or a Vindication of Bishop Chase against the Malicious Accusations of an anonymous pamphlet printed in Ann Street, N. Y. *New York.* 1847. 8vo, pp. 47. 12413

Cheever (T.) Two Sermons Preached at Maldon. The First, August 26. 1722. ... The Second on a Particular Fast. June 4th. 1725. By Thomas Cheever ... . *[Boston:] Nicholas Boone.* 1726. 12mo, Title, pp. 94. B. 12414

Cheever (T. P.) Eulogy on Daniel Webster: pronounced before the Chelsea Library Association, December 8, 1852. By Tracy P. Cheever, Esq. ... *Boston: printed by John Bent, at Geo. C. Rand's.* [1852.] 4to, pp. 36. B. 12415

Chelsea Directory ... for 1856 ... . By John Bent. *Chelsea: Geo. C. Rand and Avery, Printers.* 12mo, pp. 102, (2), 40. Continued. H. 12416

City of Chelsea. Mayor's Address and Elective Officers for 1866. Annual Report of the Receipts and Expenditures, Reports of Departments, etc., for 1865. ... *Chelsea.* 1866. 8vo, pp. 87, (1). Continued. H. 12417

Also: Annual Report of the School Committee of Chelsea, Mass. ... March 11, 1844. [n. p. n. d.] 8vo, pp. 8. Continued. H. — First Annual Report of the Chelsea Industrial School. Organized March 1, 1854. *New York: Holman & Gray,*

Printers. 1855. 12mo, pp. 18, (1). H. — Annual Report of the Board of Water Commissioners ... 1869. *Chelsea: printed by Hovey Brothers.* 1870. 8vo, pp. 13. Continued. H. — Report of the Joint Special Committee on Introduction of Water into ... Chelsea. .. Jan. 2. 1868. ... *Chelsea.* 1868. 8vo, pp. 15. H. — The Chelsea Association for the Improvement of Indigent Girls. *New-York: J. R. Winser, Printer.* 1854. 12mo, pp. 8. H. — Catalogue of Lots of the Old Marine Hospital Estate, Chelsea, Mass. To be sold at Auction, on Monday, ... 18th ... May, 1857. ... *Boston.* 1857. 4to, pp. 9. Plan. H.

Chelsea's Roll of Honor. 1864. [n. p. n. d.] 8vo, pp. 25.

List of the inhabitants of Chelsea who enlisted in the army and navy during the Civil War.

Chemist and Meteorological Journal. July 8, 1826. *Amherst, Mass.* 1826. 8vo. Continued. W. 12419

Chemin de la Croix et autres Prieres à l'usage des sauvages des portes d'Albany, Savern, Martin's Falls [Baie d'Hudson]. *Montreal: Imprimerie de Louis Perrault.* 1856. 12mo, pp. 63.

Chemung River. Opinion of the Attorney General of Pennsylvania, in relation to the right of the State of New York to divert the water from the natural bed of the Chemung River. [n. p. n. d.] 8vo, pp. 5. 12421

Chenango. The Boiler Explosion of the Martin Boiler on board the U. S. "Double-Ender" Chenango. ... *New York: Hurd & Houghton.* 1864. 8vo, pp. 141. H. 12422

Thompson's Calendar, or the Chenango Almanac. *Norwich, N. Y.* 1852. 12mo. 12423

Chenango Baptist Association, N. Y.: Minutes, 1833. 8vo. Continued. 12424

Cheney (*Mrs.* Harriet V. Foster). A Peep at the Pilgrims in Sixteen Hundred and Thirty-Six. A Tale of Olden Times. By Mrs. H. V. Cheney. *Boston.* 1850. 12mo, pp. 463. H.

Cheney (J. M.) An Address delivered before the Society of Middlesex Husbandmen and Manufacturers, at Concord, Mass. Oct. 5, 1831. By John M. Cheney. *Concord: Published by Herman Atwill.* 1831. 8vo, pp. 22. H. 12426

Cheney (M.) A Sermon delivered at the Installation of the Rev. Lorenzo D. Johnson, as Pastor of the Roger Williams Baptist Church Society, in Providence, Oct. 25, 1827. By Rev. Martin Cheney. *Providence: H. H. Brown.* 1827. 8vo, pp. 22. 12427

Cheney (T. A.) Historical Sketch of the Chemung Valley. By T. Apoleon Cheney, LL.D. *New York: Watkins.* 1868. 8vo, 6 l., pp. 59. C. 12428

Cheney (T. C.) Reminiscences of Syracuse. By Timothy C. Cheney. Compiled by Parish B. Johnson. From Personal Recollections of the Author first published in the Syracuse Daily Standard. *Syracuse: Summers & Brother.* 1857. 8vo, pp. 32.

Chenu (J. C.) Bibliothèque conchyliologique. *Paris: Franck.* 1845–46. 5 vols., 8vo. 12430

Vol. VIII. (pp. 150, and 34 Plates) contains Th. Say's "Conchyliologie américaine, traduite par Chenu," T. A. Conrad's "Nouvelles coquilles d'eau douce des États-Unis, trad. par C. Chenu," and "Monographie des coquilles bivalves fluviatiles de la rivière Ohio par C. S. Rafinesque." Of course the "Encyclopédie d'histoire naturelle," by this author, includes many particulars of American natural history.

Chepacket. Siege of Chepacket. A Poem. [n. p. n. d.] 8vo, pp. 8. 12431

Cher (H. W. B.), *pseudonym.* Gnaw-Wood; New England Life in a Village. By Henry W. B. Cher. ... *New York.* 1868. 12mo, pp. 22. H. 12432

A parody of "Norwood." *See* Vol. II., No. 4317.

Cherokee. The Acts of the Apostles, translated into the Cherokee Language. Getsinvsidv nunadvnelitolvi taline digaleyvtanvhi. Second Edition. *Park Hill: Mission Press.* 1842. 24mo, pp. 124. BA. 12433

Address of the Cherokee Nation to the People of the United States. 1830. 12mo. P. 12434

Address of the Cherokee Delegation to the President of the United States, March 16, 1837. 8vo. 12435

A Letter from the authorities of the Cherokee Nation to Brigadier General John E. Wool, September 30, 1836. 12436

The Memorial and Petition of the Cherokee Delegates to the Senate and House of Representatives in Congress assembled, February 22d, 1837. 12437

Proceedings of the Cherokee Nation in general Council, assembled at Red Clay, September 28, 1836. 12438

Cherokee Advocate. Vol. I., No. 1, Sept. 26, 1844. *Published [weekly] at Tablequah, Cherokee Nation.* Folio. 12439

Continued to Vol. IX., No. 22, Dec. 28, 1853. The first editor was W. P. Ross. The publication may have continued longer, but No. 22, of Vol. IX., is the last of the copy in the library of Congress. This newspaper, like the "Phœnix," No. 12447, contains many papers in the Cherokee language.

Cherokee Almanack for the Year of our Lord 1840. *Park Hill Mission Press.* 12mo, pp. 24. Continued. C. 12440

Cherokee Alphabet. *Cherokee Baptist Mission Press: H. Upham, Printer.* [1845?] 1 sheet, folio. 12441

Cherokee Hymns Compiled from Several authors. By E. Boudinot and S. A. Worcester. *New Echota.* 1829. 24mo. + [Another.] 1835. + Sixth Edition with the addition of many New Hymns. ... *Park Hill: Mission Press.* 1841. 24mo, pp. 65, (2). BA. + Seventh Edition. *Park Hill: Mission Press.* 1844. 24mo, pp. 69. 12442

Printed in the characters invented by George Guess, an Indian.

Cherokee Indians of North Carolina. Documents: 1. Explanation of their Title to Land; 2. Report of the Commissioner of Indian Affairs; 3. Memorials to Congress, &c. *Washington.* 1846. 8vo. 12443

Cherokee Land Lottery ... A List of the fortunate drawers ... with map of the District, by James F. Smith. *New York.* 1838. 8vo. S. 12444

Cherokee Lands on Walden's Ridge, East Tennessee, for sale by Nicholas Haight, ... Second Edition, with additional Evidences. *New-York: Casper C. Childs, Printer.* 1848. 8vo, pp. 32. Map. H. 12445

Cherokee Messenger. Tsalagi atsinvsidv. 12 Nos., August, 1844, to May, 1846. [Edited by Evan Jones.] *Cherokee Baptist Mission Press.* 1844–46. 8vo, pp. 192. C. 12446

Tsa-la-gi Tsu-le-hi-sa-u-hi, Cherokee Phœnix. Edited by Elias Boudinot. *New Echota: Printed weekly by Isaac H. Harris, for the Cherokee Nation.* Vol. I., No. 1, Feb. 21, 1828, to Vol. V., No. 52, May 31, 1834. Folio. 12447

Perhaps not continued after this date.

Cherokee Primer. Anitsalagi tsunalenvtodi tsu adeloquasdi. *Park Hill: Mission Press.* 1840. 24mo, pp. 24. *Park Hill: Mission Press.* 1846. C. 12448

Communication of the Delegation of the Cherokee Nation to the President of the United States, submitting the Memorial of their National Council, with the Correspondence between John Ross, ... and ... Officers of the Rebellious States. *Washington: Gibson Brothers, Printers.* 1866. 8vo, pp. 48. H. 12449

The Constitution and Laws of the Cherokee Nation: passed at Tah-le-quah Cherokee Nation. *Washington: printed by Gales and Seaton.* 1840. 8vo, pp. 36. B. + *Washington.* 1844. 8vo, pp. 44. + *Tahlequah.* 1845. 12mo. 12450

Constitution of the Cherokee Nation, made and established at a General Convention of Delegates, duly authorized for that purpose, at New Echota, July 26, 1827. *Printed for the Cherokee Nation, at the Office of the Statesman and Patriot, Georgia.* [n. d.] 18mo, pp. 16. 12451

An Enquiry into the Origin of the Cherokees. In a Letter to a Member of Parliament. *Oxford.* 1762. 8vo, pp. 27. 12452

"A mighty learned attempt to prove the Cherokees to be the descendants of Meshek, a son of Japhet." — M. R., XXVIII. 164.

Epistles of John translated into the Cherokee language. Tsani tsuwowelanelvhi. tsunandodi. *Park Hill.* 1840. 24mo, pp. 20. + Second Edition. [*Ibid.*] 1843. BA. + Third Edition. *Park Hill.* 1848. C. 12453

Epistle of Paul, the Apostle, to the Ephesians. Translated into Cherokee by Evan Jones and John B. Jones. Quola atsinosidv etlusi anehi widuwowelanelvhi. *Cherokee Baptist Mission Press.* 1848. 24mo, pp. 24. 12454

Examination of the Cherokee Question. *Washington.* 1832. 8vo. C. 12455

Examination of the Relations between the Cherokees and the Government of the United States. *New York.* 1829. 8vo. S.

A Faithful History of the Cherokee Tribe of Indians, from the period of our first intercourse with them down to the present time; ... with a full exposition of ... their ... division into three parties ... and of the nature and extent of their present claims. (The Commissioner's report.) *Washington.* 1846. 8vo.

The General Epistle of James. Translated into the Cherokee language. Tsimiuwowelanvhi. *Park Hill.* 1847. 24mo, pp. 16. C. 12458

Genesis and Exodus translated into the Cherokee Language. *Park Hill.* 1853. 32mo. 12459

The Gospel according to Matthew. Translated into the Cherokee Language. Third Edition revised. ... *Park Hill: Mission Press.* 1843. 24mo, pp. 120. + Oedvkanohedv maduuwowelanvhi. Fourth Edition. *Park Hill: Mission Press.* 1844. 24mo, pp. 120. C. 12460

The Gospel ... according to John. Translated into the Cherokee language. *Park Hill: Mission Press.* 1838. + Second Edition. ... *Park Hill: Mission Press.* 1841. 24mo, pp. 96. BA. + Third Edition. *Park Hill: Mission Press.* 1847. 24mo, pp. 101. 12461

Holisso Holitopa, Chitokaka Chisus im Anumpeshi Luk, Chani Itatuklo kut Hollssochi tok Mak O. *Utica.* 1831. 12mo. M. 12462

Laws of the Cherokee Nations, adopted by the Council at Various Periods. *Knoxville.* 1826. 8vo, pp. 75, Tables, 10 l.

Letter to the Commissioner of Indian Affairs relative to the Claim of the North Carolina and other Eastern Cherokees to a Participation ... in all The Lands and Moneys of the Cherokee Nation, by Lewis Downing, Principal Chief, H. D. Reese ... [and 4 others]. *Washington.* 1869. 8vo, pp. 16. H. 12564

Letters and Conversations on the Cherokee Mission. *Boston.* 1830. 2 vols., 18mo. 12465

Memorial of a Delegation from the Cherokee Indians. Presented to Congress Jan. 18, 1831. [n. p. n. d.] 8vo, pp. 8.

Another Memorial. *Washington.* 1837. 8vo.

Memorial of the Delegates of the Cherokee Nation to the President of the United States, and Senate and House of Representatives in Congress. *Washington Chronicle Print.* 1866. 12mo, pp. 12. H. 12467

Message of the Principal Chief of the Cherokee Nation. November 1842. [n. p. n. d.] 12mo, pp. 12. H. 12468

Printed in English and Cherokee.

Observations on Two Campaigns against the Cherokee Indians, in 1760 and 1761. *Charlestown.* 1762. 8vo. P. 12469

Productions By Nature and Art of the Cherokee Lands on the Tennessee River, within Ten Miles of the Rail Road connecting with the City of New York. *New-York: Casper C. Childs, Printer.* 1847. 8vo, pp. 15. Map. H. 12470

Reply of the Delegates of the Cherokee Nation to the Pamphlet of the Commissioner of Indian Affairs. *Washington, D. C.* 1866. 8vo, pp. 16. H. 12471

Reply of the Delegates of the Cherokee Nation to the Demands of the Commissioner of Indian Affairs. May 1866. *Washington: Gibson Brothers, Printers.* 1866. 8vo, pp. 14. H.

Reply of the Southern Cherokees to the Memorial of Certain Delegates from the Cherokee Nation, ... with the Message of John Ross, ... and Proceedings of the Council of the "Loyal Cherokees" relative to the Alliance with the so-called Confederate States. To the President, Senate, and House of Representatives. *Washington, D. C.: McGill & Witherow, Printers.* 1866. 8vo, pp. 19. H. 12473

Report from the Secretary of War, in Compliance with a Resolution of the Senate of the 13th of October, 1837, in relation to the Cherokee Treaty of 1835. [*Washington.* 1838.] 8vo, pp. 105. 12474

Select Passages from the Holy Scriptures. [In Cherokee. *Park Hill?* 1844.] 24mo, pp. 24. BA., C. 12475

A Vindication of the Cherokee Claims, addressed to the Town Meeting in Philadelphia, on the 11th of January, 1830. [*Philadelphia.* 1830.] 12476

Western Cherokees, their Claims under Treaties of 1835–46. *Washington.* 1847. 12477

The American Bible Society published a New Testament, with the title in Cherokee characters, in 1860, 12mo, pp. 101. And there is also a "Church Litany of the United Brethren, in the Cherokee Tongue. *New Echota.* 1830."

Cherry. The Missionary; or the Church in the Wilderness. *Philadelphia: American S. S. Union.* 1868. 16mo, pp. 236. 4 Plates. C. 12478

Cherry, Cummings, *and* James. Maps and Reports of the San Juan del Rio Ranche, in Sonora, Mexico; made to the Cincinnati and Sonora Mining Association. *Cincinnati.* 1866. 8vo. C. 12479

The Centennial Celebration at Cherry Valley, Otsego Co. N. Y. July 4th, 1840; the Addresses of W. W. Campbell, and Gov. W. H. Seward, with Letters, Toasts, &c. *New York.* 1840. 8vo, pp. 60. s. 12480

Also: A Catalogue of the Cherry Valley Female Academy. 1854. 8vo, pp. 59.

CHERVIN (N.) De la fièvre jaune qui a régné à la Martinique en 1838 et en 1839. Rapport fait à l'Académie royale de médecine sur un mémoire de M. le docteur Catel ... . Par N. Chervin ... . *Paris: imp. de F. Malteste. Août* 1840. 8vo, 1½ sheets.

CHERVIN. De l'opinion de médicins américains sur la contagion ou la non-contagion de la fièvre jaune, ou réponse aux allégations de MM. les Docteurs Hosack et Townsend de New-York, ... Par N. Chervin, ... *Paris: J. B. Baillière. Londres: même maison.* 1829. 8vo, pp. 192. H. 12482

CHESAPEAK. 12mo, pp. iv, 19. 12483

With a half-title only. It purports to be "A Letter from a reputable Farmer to his friend," and is evidently a Maryland production. Perhaps printed in Philadelphia. It was issued soon after No. 1. of the "Pennsylvania Chronicle."

American Evidences upon the subject of the Capture of the Chesapeake. *London.* 1808. 8vo, pp. (4), 75. 12484

Calm and Dispassionate Enquiry into the Question of the Chesapeake, and Necessity of War. 1807. 8vo. 12485

Letters from the Secretary of State to Mr. Munroe, on the Attack of the Chesapeake, The Correspondence of Mr. Munroe, Mr. Madison and Mr. Rose, on the same subject. *City of Washington.* 1808. 8vo, pp. 88. 12486

Memorial ... to the Honourable Senate and House of Representatives of the United States, January 1, 1809. 8vo. C.

Message from the President of the United States, transmitting Correspondence: 1st. On the Subject of the Attack on the Chesapeake. 2d. On the subject of the Impressments. 3d. On the subjects committed to the joint Negotiations of Messrs. Monroe and Pinckney. March 23, 1808. *Washington.* 1808. 8vo. 12488

Peace without Dishonor, etc. *See* [Lowell (J.)]

Report of the Committee to whom was referred the Corres-

pondence between Mr. Monroe and Mr. Canning, and between Mr. Madison and Mr. Rose, relative to the Attack on the Chesapeake, April 16, 1808. *Washington.* 1808. 12489

Thoughts upon the Conduct of our Administration, in relation both to Great Britain and France, more especially in reference to the late Negotiation, concerning the attack on the Chesapeake. By a Friend to Peace. *Boston.* 1808. 8vo, pp. 28. H. 12490

The Voice of Truth; or, Thoughts on the affair between the Leopard and the Chesapeake. In a Letter from a Gentleman at New-York, to his friend. *New-York.* 1807. 8vo, pp. 55.

"The Chesapeake." The Case of David Collins et al., Prisoners, arrested ... on a charge of Piracy, and the arguments on the Return to the Order of Habeas Corpus ... . *St. John, N. B.: J. & A. McMillan, Publishers.* 1864. 8vo, pp. 62. H.

Papers relating to the Seizure of the United States Steamer "Chesapeake." ... *London: printed by Harrison and Sons.* 1864. Folio, Title, pp. 96. (Parl. Papers, N. America, No. 9.) B.

Chesapeake and Delaware Canal Company. Letters to the Hon. Albert Gallatin, Secretary of the Treasury ... and other papers relative to the Canal, by Joshua Gilpin and B. H. Latrobe. 8vo. C. 12494

A Last Appeal to the Stockholders of the Chesapeake and Delaware Canal. *See* [Carey (M.)]

The Memorials and Petitions of the President and Directors of the Chesapeake and Delaware Canal Company, to the Honourable the Senate and House of Representatives of the United States. *Philadelphia.* 1805–9. 8vo. C. 12495

Observations respecting the Chesapeake and Delaware Canal. December 1, 1805. 8vo. 12496

Petitions to the Legislature of the Commonwealth of Pennsylvania, February 1st, 1805, and January 1st, 1806. 8vo. C.

Regulations to be observed by Vessels navigating the Chesapeake and Delaware Canal, and Bank Creek. [With the Tolls. n. p. 1843.] Folio, pp. 2. H. 12498

Fifth General Report of the ... Chesapeake and Delaware Canal Company. June 7, 1824. [n. p. n. d.] 8vo, pp. 19. 2 Maps. Continued. BA. 12499

Chesapeake and Ohio Canal Company. Report of John J. Abert in reference to the Canal to Connect the Chesapeake and Ohio Canal with the City of Baltimore. *Washington.* 1838. 8vo.

Acts of the States of Virginia, Maryland and Pennsylvania, and of the Congress of the United States, in relation to the Chesapeake and Ohio Canal Company, with the Proceedings of the Convention which led to the Formation of the said Company. Also the Acts of Virginia and Maryland concerning the Potomac Company. *Washington.* 1828. 8vo. 12501

... To ... Congress ... : memorial of ... [*Washington.* 1831.] 8vo, pp. 222. (22d Cong. 1st Sess. House Doc. 18.) 12502

Several other congressional documents relating to this canal are referred to in the Boston Pub. Lit. Catalogue, Upper Hall, p. 819.

Memorial of a Committee of the Chesapeake and Ohio Canal Company to the Legislature of Maryland. [*Annapolis?* 1836.] 8vo. 12503

Proceedings at a General Convention of Delegates held in Washington on the Subject of the Chesapeake and Ohio Canal *Washington. Nov.,* 1823. 8vo. 12504

Proceedings of the Chesapeake and Ohio Canal Convention, held at Washington, on the 6th November, 1823, and re-assembled 6th December, 1826. *Washington.* 1827. 8vo. C. 12505

First Annual Report of the ... Chesapeake and Ohio Canal Company ... 1829. *Washington.* 1829. 8vo. Continued. H.

Report of the general committee of the Stockholders of the Chesapeake and Ohio Canal Company. 1834. 8vo. Continued. 12507

Report of J. J. Abert and J. Kearny, upon an examination of the Chesapeake and Ohio Canal, from Washington City to the "Point of Rocks," made by order of the Secretary of War. *Washington.* 1831. 8vo. 12508

Report of the Probable Revenue of the Chesapeake and Ohio-Canal made to the Baltimore Convention, Dec., 1834. [*Baltimore.* 1834.] 12mo. BM. 12509

Reports and Letters from the Engineers employed on the reserved Location of the Western Section of the Chesapeake and Ohio Canal; with Estimates of the Cut of the same. [*Georgetown?* 1829.] 8vo. 12510

Also: Regulations for navigating the Chesapeake and Ohio Canal ... *Washington* 1831. 8vo. — Rules adopted by the President and Directors of the Chesapeake and Ohio Canal Company, for the Government of the Corps of Engineers. *Washington.* 1828. 8vo.

[CHESBROUGH (E. S.)] Chicago Sewerage. Report of the Results of Examinations made in Relation to Sewerage in several European Cities in the Winter of 1856–7. By the Chief Engineer of the Board of Sewerage Commissioners. *Chicago, Ill.: the Board.* 1858. 8vo, pp. 95. 4 Plates. BA. 12511

[CHESBROUGH.] Report and Plan of Sewerage for the City of Chicago, Illinois, adopted by the Board of Sewerage Commissioners December 31, 1855. *Chicago: printed at the Office of Charles Scott.* 1855. 8vo, pp. 22. BA. 12512

[CHESBROUGH.] Tabular Representation of the Present Condition of Boston, in Relation to Railroad Facilities, Foreign Commerce, Population, Wealth, Manufactures, etc., etc. Also, a Few Statements relative to the Commerce of the Canadas. ... *Boston.* 1851. 8vo, pp. 28. Map. H. 12513

CHESBROUGH (E. S.), *and* DURANT (C. F.) Letters on Hydraulics: a Correspondence between E. S. Chesbrough, of Mass., and C. F. Durant, of N. Jersey, On the Physical Laws that Govern Running Water, applied to a Dam and Mill Privilege on the Housatonic River, at Great Barrington, Mass. *New York: Narine & Co., Printers.* 1849. 8vo, pp. 464, 28. BA.

END OF VOLUME THREE.

A DICTIONARY OF BOOKS

RELATING TO AMERICA.

CHESHIRE, *N. H.* Abstracts of the Reports of the Benevolent Societies and Conference of Churches in Cheshire County, New-Hampshire, for ... 1833. ... *Bellows Falls.* 1833. 8vo, pp. 16.

CATALOGUE of the Officers, Instructors and Students of the Cheshire County Teachers' Institute. Spring Term, 1848, at Walpole. *Keene: printed by H. A. Bill.* 1848. 12mo, pp. 12. 12516

Cheshire Railroad Company. Second Report. ... *Keene, N. H.* 1847. 8vo. 12517

CHESHIRE, *Conn.* Dedication of the Soldiers' Monument at Cheshire, Conn. on the Fourth of July, A.D., 1866. *New York: W. W. Rose.* 1866. 8vo, pp. 48. 12518

A Historical Discourse delivered at St. Peter's Church, Cheshire, July 28th, 1839. *Hartford.* 1839. 8vo, pp. 16.

CHESNEY (C. C.) Military View of Recent Campaigns in Virginia and Maryland. With Maps. *London: Smith & Elder.* 1863. Post 8vo, pp. xii, 230. C. 12520

CHESNEY. Campaigns in Virginia, Maryland, &c. Volume the Second (continuing the History to the End of the Third Year of the War). With Maps. *London: Smith & Elder.* 1865 Post 8vo, pp. viii, 234. 12521

CHESNUT (J.) Relations of States. Speech of the Hon. James Chesnut, Jr. of South Carolina, ... in the Senate of the United States, April 9, 1860, on the Resolutions submitted by the Hon. Jefferson Davis, of Miss. ... *Baltimore: Printed by John Murphy & Co.* 1860. 8vo, pp. 24. H. 12522

CHESSMAN (D.) Memoir of Rev. Thomas Baldwin, D.D. ... who died at Waterville, Me. August 29, 1825. Together with A Funeral Sermon, occasioned by his Death, ... By Rev. Daniel Chessman, ... With an Appendix, containing Letters and Hymns. *Boston: printed by True & Greene.* 1826. 8vo, pp. 72, 12. H. 12523

CHESSMAN (J.) Historical Notices of St. Peter's Church, Perth Amboy, New Jersey. By James Chessman. *Elizabethtown.* 1830. 8vo, pp. 28. 12524

CHESSIEUX (*M. de la* Grange de). *See* Grange de Chessieux.

CHESSMAN (D.) Memoir of Rev. Thomas Baldwin, D.D. Late Pastor of the Second Baptist Church in Boston, who died ... Aug. 25, 1825. By Rev. Daniel Chessman, A.M. ... Second Edition. *Boston: Elder John Peak.* 1841. 24mo, pp. 107.

CHESTATEE. Prospectus of the Chestatee Hydraulic Company, and Report of William P. Blake, ... upon the Gold Placers of a Part of Lumpkin County, Georgia, and the Practicability of working them by the Hydraulic Method, with Water from Chestatee River. *New-York: John F. Trow, Printer.* 1858. 8vo, pp. 39. H. 12526

CHESTER (A. T.) A Funeral Sermon, ... on the Occasion of the Death of Nathaniel Rogers, who died December 24, 1852. By Albert Chester, D.D. ... *Buffalo: C. E. Young, Printer.* 1853. 8vo, pp. 23. H. 12527

Also: A Sermon, occasioned by the Death of Mrs. Abigail Davison. *Saratoga Springs.* 1844. 8vo. — ... A Sermon, preached before the Buffalo Academy of Music, ... April 18, 1852. ... . *Buffalo: Charles E. Young, Printer.* 1852. 8vo, pp. 24. H.

[CHESTER (A.)] Scheeps-togt van Anthony Chester na Virginia, gedaan in het Jaar 1620. Beschreeven door een voornaam Reysiger, die dese Togt met gedaan heelt. *Leyden: Pieter Vander Aa.* 1707. 8vo, pp. 15 and Register. Plate. 12528

Forms part of Vander Aa's collection of voyages, Vol. xxvi, 8vo.

CHESTER (C. A.) Life and Adventures of Charles Anderson Chester, the Notorious Leader of the Philadelphia "Killers," who was murdered Oct. 11th, 1849. *Philadelphia.* 1850. 8vo. pp. 36. Plates. 12529

CHESTER (C. T. *and* J. N.) Catalogue of Telegraph Material, manufactured by Charles T. & J. N. Chester, 104 Centre Street, New-York. With Appendix. [1861.] 8vo, pp. 42. H.

CHESTER (G. J.) Trans-Atlantic Sketches in the West Indies, South America, and the United States. By Greville John Chester ... . *London: Smith, Elder, & Co.* 1869. 8vo.

CHESTER (John). Narrative of the State of Religion within the Presbytery of Albany. *Albany.* 1820. 8vo. B. 12532

CHESTER. A Sermon, in Commemoration of the Landing, of the New-England Pilgrims ... . on the Completion of the Second Century since that Event. *Albany: printed by E. and E. Hosford.* 1820. 8vo, pp. 31, (1). B. 12533

CHESTER. Sermon, before the Albany Moral Society. *Albany.* 1821. 8vo. 12534

Also: Sermon before the Berkshire and Columbian Missionary Society, Canaan, September 21, 1813. *Hudson.* 1813. 8vo, pp. 39.

CHESTER. Obituary Notices of the Rev. John Chester, D.D. Late Pastor of the Second Presbyterian Congregation in the City of Albany. ... *Albany: printed by Packard and Van Benthuysen.* 1829. 8vo, pp. 84. Portrait. B., BA. 12535

CHESTER. Official Documents of the Presbytery of Albany, exhibiting the Trials of Rev. John Chester & Mr. Mark Tucker; together with the whole Case of the Rev. Hooper Cumming. ... *Schenectady: Henry Stevens & Co.* 1818. 8vo, pp. 255. BA.

CHESTER. The Lesson of the Hour. Justice as well as Mercy. A Discourse preached on the Sabbath following the Assassination of the President, in the Capitol Hill Presbyterian Church, Washington, D. C., By the Pastor, Rev. John Chester. *Washington: Chronicle Print.* 1865. 8vo, pp. 16. H. 12537

CHESTER (J. L.) A Genealogical Memoir of the Wentworth Family of England, from its Saxon Origin in the Eleventh Century to the Emigration of one of its Representatives to New

England about the Year 1636. By Joseph Lemuel Chester ... . [*London.* 1867.] 8vo, pp. 121–140. H. 12538

CHESTER. Greenwood Cemetery, and other Poems. By Joseph L. Chester. *New York.* 1843. 12mo. 12539

CHESTER. Notes upon the Ancestry of William Hutchinson and Anna Marbury. From researches recently made in England. By Joseph Lemuel Chester. *Boston: Printed by D. Clapp & Son.* 1866. 4to, pp. 24. 12540

Fifty copies printed.

CHESTER. A Preliminary Investigation of the Alleged Ancestry of George Washington; First President of the United States of America; exposing a Serious Error in the Existing Pedigree. By Joseph Lemuel Chester ... . *Boston: H. W. Dutton & Son, Printers.* 1866. 8vo, pp. 23. H. 12541

Also, with the imprint, *Westminster: Nichols & Sons, printers.* 1866. pp. 15. — John Rogers; the Compiler of the First Authorized English Bible; ... Embracing a Genealogical Account of his Family, Biographical Sketches of some of his Principal Descendants, his Own Writings, etc. etc. ... *London: Longman, Green, Longman, & Roberts.* 1861. 8vo, pp. xii, 452. BA., C.

CHESTER (*Bishop of*). *See* Dawes (*Sir* William), *and* Keene (*Dr.*)

CHESTER (W. F.) An Address delivered before the Mechanic Apprentices' Library Association, ... Thirty-fourth Anniversary, Feb. 22, 1854. By William F. Chester ... . *Boston.* 1854. 8vo, pp. 20. H. 12542

CHESTER Co., *Penn.* Public Meeting. [Address of a Meeting of Anti-Slavery Citizens, Dec. 25, 1835. n. p. n. d.] 8vo, pp. 8. BA. 12543

Report on the Manufactories, Unimproved Mill Seats, &c. *Chester.* 1826. 12mo. 12544

Report on the Progress and Present Condition of the Chester County Cabinet of Natural Science. *Westchester.* 1828. 12mo. + Fourth Report. *Westchester.* 1831. 12mo. 12545

State of the Accounts of Thomas Cheney, Esq., Sub-Lieutenant of Chester County. And of John Hannum, Esq. From March 1777, to March 1780. In which is exhibited the Fines received, the Names of the Persons by whom the same were paid, and the Application of the Money. *Philadelphia: Printed by F. Bailey.* M.DCC.LXXXV. 8vo, pp. 12. P. 12546

The Philadelphia Library contains similar accounts for other years.

To the Representatives of the Freemen of the Counties of Chester, Bucks, and Philadelphia. Now met at the State-House. ... A great Number of your Constituents. *Chester County. May* 9, 1774. Broadside. C., P. 12547

For *May*, read *June*.

CHESTER, *S. C.* Address to the People of Chester District, S. C., assembled to discuss the Question of Nullification, &c.

Chesterfield Travestie; or, School for Modern Manners. *Philadelphia.* 1812. 12mo. 12549

CHESTERTON (G. L.) A Narrative of the Proceedings in Venezuela, in South America, in the Years 1819 and 1820; with General Observations on the Country and People; the Character of the Republican Government, and its Leading Members, &c. also a Description of the Country of Caraccas; of the Force of Gen. Morillo; the State of the Royalists; and the Spirit of the People under their Jurisdiction. By George Laval Chesterton, late Captain and Judge Advocate of the British Legion, raised for the Service of the Republic of Venezuela. *London: John and Arthur Arch.* 1820. 8vo, pp. x, 257. Map.

See M. R., XLIV. 205.

CHESTERTON. Peace, War and Adventure: an Autobiographical Memoir of George Laval Chesterton, formerly of ... Royal Artillery, subsequently a Captain in the Army of Columbia, ... *London.* 1853. 2 vols., 12mo. C., P. + *London: Bickers and Bush.* 186–. 8vo. 12551

CHESSYRE (Henry T. N.) Canada in 1864: A Handbook for Settlers. *London.* 1864. 12mo. 12552

[CHETWOOD (W. R.)] The Voyages and Adventures of Capt. Robert Boyle, in several parts of the World, &c. Intermix'd with The Story of Mrs. Villars, an English Lady with whom he made his surprizing Escape from Barbary: ... To which is added the Voyage, Shipwreck, and Miraculous Preservation of Richard Castleman, gent. With a Description of the City of Philadelphia and the Country of Pennsylvania. *London: J. Watts.* 1726. 8vo, 5 l., pp. 374. Plate. + The Second Edition. *London: J. Watts.* 1727. 8vo, 5 l., pp. 374. Plate. + [Another] Second Edition. 1728. + *London.* 1735. 12mo.

Plate. + *Wolverhampton: Geo. Wilson.* 1744. 16mo, 3 l., pp. 317. C. + *London.* 1762. 12mo. Plate. + *London.* 1777. 12mo. + *Edinburgh.* 1780. 8vo, pp. 264. + *London.* 1787. 12mo. Plate. 12553

Boyle's narrative is probably fictitious, but that of Castleman bears marks of authenticity. The latter's visit to Philadelphia took place in 1710. Boyle's voyages have been often reprinted; but Castleman's relation is only to be found in the early editions. This work has been attributed to Benj. Victor; also to Daniel Defoe.

[CHETWOOD.] Les Voyages et Avantures du Capitaine Robert Boyle; ou l'on trouve l'Histoire de Mademoiselle Villars, avec qui il se sauva de Barbarie; celle d'un Esclave Italien, & celle de Dom Pedro Aquilio, qui fournit des examples dans coups les plus suprenans de la Fortune; avec la Relation du Voyage, du Naufrage & de la Conservation miraculeuse du Sr. Castelman, où l'on voit une description de la Pensylvanie & de Philadelphie sa Capitale. Traduits de l'Anglois. *A Amsterdam: Chez les Wetsteins & Smith.* 1730. 2 vols., 12mo, 4 l., pp. 341; 276, Table, 6 l. 7 Plates. 12554

A French version is also included in Garnier's "Voyages imaginaires."

[CHETWOOD]. Viaggi ed Avventure ... con la Relazione del viaggio, e Salvamento del S. Castelman, in cui si vede una descrizione della Pensilvania e di Filadelfia sua capitale: tradotti dall inglese in italiano. *Venezia.* 1734. 18mo, pp. 447. S.

[CHETWOOD.] Gedenkwaardige Reizen. *Amsterdam: J. Hoffman.* 2 vols., 8vo. Plates. 12556

[CHETWOOD.] Reisen und Begebenheiten; und A. R. Castelmanns Reisen und Nachrichten von Pensylvanien. *Leipzig: Weygand.* 1793. 8vo. 12557

CHEVALIER (Henry É.) Les derniers Iroquois. *Paris: Lécrivain et Toubon.* 1863. 12mo. 12558

CHEVALIER. De laatste Irokezen. Naar de 6e Fransche uitgave. *Amsterdam: Weduwe D. Kunst.* 1865. 8vo, pp. 4, 256. 12559

CHEVALIER. La fille des Indiens rouges. Par H. Emile Chevalier. *Paris: M. Lévy frères.* 1866. 18mo, pp. 363.

CHEVALIER. Les Grand coureurs d'aventures. Jacques Cartier par H. Émile Chevalier *Paris: Lebigre Duquesne.* 1868. 18mo, Title, pp. 314. 12561

CHEVALIER. La Huronne, scènes de la vie canadienne. Par H. Emile Chevalier. *Paris: Poulet-Malassis.* 1861. 18mo, pp. viii, 363. + Sixième édition. *Paris: Toubon.* 1864. 18mo, pp. viii, 363. 12562

CHEVALIER. Het Huronmeisje. Naar de 6e Fransche uitgave. *Amsterdam: Weduwe D. Kunst.* 1865. 2 pts., 8vo, pp. 4, 268; 4, 275. 12563

CHEVALIER. Les Nez percés. Par H. Emile Chevalier. *Paris: Poulet-Malassis.* 1862. 18mo, pp. 324. 12564

CHEVALIER. Peaux rouges et peaux blanches, ou Les Douze apôtres et leur femmes. Par H. E. Chevalier. *Paris: Toubon.* 1864. 12mo, pp. 316. 12565

CHEVALIER. ... Les Pieds noirs. Par H. Emile Chevalier. *Paris: Lith. nouvelle.* 1861. 18mo, pp. 332. Huitième édition. *Paris: Toubon.* 1864. 18mo, pp. 332. 12566

CHEVALIER. De zwart-voeten. Naar het Fransch. *Amsterdam: Weduwe D. Kunst.* 1865. 2 pts., 8vo, pp. 4, 240; 4, 240. 12567

CHEVALIER. Le pirate du Saint-Laurent. Par H. Emile Chevalier. *Paris: Dentu.* 1862. 18mo, pp. 283. 12568

CHEVALIER. Poignet d'Acier, ou les Chippiouais. Par H. Emile Chevalier. *Paris: Lécrivain et Toubon.* 1863. 18mo, pp. 280. 12569

CHEVALIER. La Tête-plate. Par H. Emile Chevalier. *Paris: Poulet-Malassis.* 1862. 18mo, pp. 326. + Troisième édition. [*Ibid.*] 1863. 12570

All the above belong to the series entitled, "Les drames de l'Amérique du Nord."

CHEVALIER. Trente-neuf hommes pour une femme, épisode de la colonisation du Canada. Par H. Émile Chevalier. *Paris: Dentu.* 1862. 18mo, pp. 285. + *Paris: Charlieu frères et Huillery.* 1864. 4to, pp. 64. Illustrated. + [*Ibid.*] 1866. [*Ibid.*]

CHEVALIER. Legends of the Sea. Thirty-Nine Men for One Woman: an Episode of the Colonization of Canada. Translated from the French of H. Émile Chevalier by E. I. Sears, A.M. *New York: J. Bradburn.* 186–. 12mo, pp. xi, 312. C.

CHEVALIER. Adventures by sea and land of the Count De Ganay; or, the devotion and fidelity of a woman. An Episode

in the colonization of Canada. Translated from the French. *New York: J. Bradburn.* 1863. 12mo, 2 l., pp. v, 312.

Also the following, published at Montreal, between 1851 and 1860: La vie à New-York, 6 vols.; Les Mystères de Montréal, 6 vols.; La jolie fille du faubourg Québec; La traite des pelleteries, Le Labrador; Les trappeurs de la baie d'Hudson, 2 vols.; L'île de sable; L'héroine de Chateauguay; Le chasseur noir, 2 vols.; Les déserts de l'Amérique Septentrionale, 2 vols.; Le foyer canadien; and 4 vols. on American geology.

CHEVALIER *and* LABORIEU. Les trois Babylones; Paris, Londres, New York. *Paris: Toubon.* 1863. 2 vols., 18mo.

I do not find that the other volumes have been published yet.

CHEVALIER (H. E.), *and* LABORIEN (Th.) Die drie Babels: Parijs, Londen en New-York. Uit het Fransch, door C. H. Pleijte. *Zalt-Bommel: Joh. Noman & Zoon.* 1864. 8vo, pp. 2, 6, 240; (2), 241-489. 12575

CHEVALIER (H. E.), *and* PHARAOU (F.) Un drama esclavagiste prologue de la sécession américaine suivi de notes sur John Brown, son procès et ses derniers moments par H. Émile Chevalier et F. Pharaon. *Paris: Charlieu et Huillery.* [1864.] 8vo, Title, pp. 60. B. 12576

CHEVALIER *and* PHARAON. Le Nord et le Sud. L'espion noir, épisode de la guerre servile. Par H. Emile Chavalier et F. Pharaon. *Paris: Dentu.* 1863. 18mo, pp. 313. 12577

CHEVALIER ([Jean Damien]). Lettres a M. de Jean ... . I. Sur les Maladies de St. Domingue. II. Sur les Plantes de la même ile. III. Sur le Remora & les Halcyons. Par M. Chevalier, ... ci-devant, Medecin du Roi à St. Domingue. *Paris: Durand.* M. DCC. LII. 8vo, 1 l., pp. (2), 224, (2). H. 12578

CHEVALIER (Jules). Rapports sur les questions coloniales, contenant des études sur l'émancipation dans les Colonies. *Paris: [Imp. Royale].* 1844. 2 vols., folio. 12579

See also Le Chevalier, and Vaillant.

CHEVALIER (M.) De la question de l'intervention dans les travaux publics du gouvernement federal et des gouvernements particuliers d'etats dans l'Amérique du Nord. Par M. Michel Chevalier. *Paris.* 1842. 8vo, pp. 32. 12580

CHEVALIER. L'Expédition du Mexique. Par M. Michel Chevalier ... . *Paris: Dentu.* 1862. 8vo, pp. 94. C. 12581

Reprinted from the "Revue des Deux-Mondes, 1, 15 avril, 1862."

CHEVALIER. France, Mexico, and the Confederate States. By M. M. Chevalier. Translated by Wm. Henry Hurlbut. *New York: C. B. Richardson.* 1863. 8vo, pp. 16. 12582

CHEVALIER. Histoire et description des voies de communication aux États Unis et des travaux d'art qui en dépendent. Par Michel Chevalier. *Paris: Charles Gosselin. Londres: Dulau et Cie.* M. DCCC. XL–XLI. 2 vols., 4to, pp. xiii, (1), 542, (1); 2 l., pp. 582, xv, and atlas of 25 Maps. + Table analytique des matières. *Paris: Capelle.* 1851. 4to. BA. 12583

CHEVALIER. L'isthme de Panama; examen Historique et Geographique des differentes directions suivant lesquelles on pourrait le percer, et des moyens à employer; suivi d'un aperçu sur l'Isthme de Suez. Par Michel Chevalier. *Paris: Ch. Gosselin.* 1844. 8vo, pp. 182. Map. C. 12584

Partly translated in the Journal of the Franklin Institute, 1847. *See* the "Revue des Deux Mondes, 1 juin et 1 sept., 1852." "Composé à l'occasion de la mission confiée par le gouvernement français à M. Garella, ingénieur des mines." — QUÉRARD.

CHEVALIER. Lettres sur l'Amérique du Nord, par Michel Chevalier. Avec une carte des États-Unis d'Amérique. *Paris: Charles Gosselin et Ce.* M DCCC XXXVI. 2 vols., 8vo, 2 l., pp. xv, 470, (2); 2 l., pp. 527, (1). Map. H. + Troisième Edition. *Paris.* 1836. 2 vols., 8vo, 62½ sheets. + Édition spéciale revue, corrigée et augmentée de plusieurs chapitres. ... *Paris: Charles Gosselin et Ce.* M DCCC XXXVII. 2 vols., 8vo, 2 l., pp. xvi, 438; 2 l., pp. 531, (1). BA. + Quatrième Edition. *Paris:* 1837. 2 vols., 8vo. + *Bruxelles.* 1837. 3 vols., 12mo. + *Bruxelles: Société belge de librairie, etc. Haumann, Cattoir et Ce.* M DCCC-XXXVII. 2 vols., 24mo, 2 l., pp. 484; 2 l., pp. 531. Map. BA. + Troisième Edition. *Bruxelles.* 1839. 3 vols., 12mo.

These letters originally appeared in the "Débats." *See* "London Quarterly Review," LVIII. 497.

CHEVALIER. La liberté aux États-Unis par Michel Chevalier. *Paris: Capelle.* 1849. 8vo, pp. 55. B., H. 12586

CHEVALIER. Die Freiheit in den Vereinigten Staaten von Nord-Amerika. *Grimma: Verlags-Comptoir.* 8vo, pp. 81.

CHEVALIER. Le Mexique ancien et moderne par Michel Chevalier ... *Paris: L. Hachette et Cie.* 1863. 18mo, 2 l., pp. 622, (1). BA., H. + Seconde édition. [*Ibid.*] 1864. 18mo.

CHEVALIER. Du Mexique avant et pendant la conquête, par Michel Chevalier. *Paris.* 1845. 8vo. 12589

CHEVALIER. Mexique. Par M. Michel Chevalier. *Strasbourg: Ve Berger. Levrault.* 1864. 8vo, pp. 10. 12590

Reprinted from Block's "Dic. gén. de la politique."

CHEVALIER. Mexico: Before and After the Conquest. By Michael Chevalier. Translated from the French by Fay. Robinson. ... *Philadelphia: Cary and Hart.* 1846. 8vo, pp. 91. C.

CHEVALIER. Mexico, Ancient and Modern. By M. Michael Chevalier ... . Translated, under the Author's Superintendence, by Thomas Alpass ... . *London: J. Maxwell.* 1864. 2 vols., 8vo, pp. xiii, (2), 387; Title, ii, 360. BA., C. 12592

CHEVALIER. Il Messico. *Milano.* 1864. 12mo. 12593

CHEVALIER. On the Probable Fall in the Value of Gold: the Commercial and Social Consequences which may ensue, and the Measures which it invites. By Michel Chevalier ... . Translated from the French, with Preface, by Richard Cobden, Esq. *Manchester: Alexr. Ireland and Co.* [Etc.] 1859. 8vo, pp. xvi, slip, 196. BA. + Third Edition. *Manchester.* 1859. + *New York.* 1859. 8vo. 12594

CHEVALIER. Remarks on the Production of the Precious Metals, and on the Depreciation of Gold. By M. Michael Chevalier. Translated by D. Forbes Campbell, Esq. *London.* 1853. 8vo. 12595

CHEVALIER. Society, Manners and Politics in the United States: being a Series of Letters on North America. By Michael Chevalier. Translated from the Third Paris Edition [by T. G. Bradford]. *Boston: Weeks, Jordan and Company.* 1839. 8vo, pp. iv, 467. BA., C., H. 12596

"Mr. Bradford has executed his task in a very faithful manner. He has translated the work of M. Chevalier into fluent and elegant English." — *N. A. Review*, L. 299. *See* "Hist. Mag.," VII. 337. Also: in the "Revue des Deux Mondes," Lettre sur l'Amérique du Nord; De la présidence du général Jackson et du choix de son successeur, 1836, t. VIII., and many other articles. — In the "Débats," Le Mexique (20 juil., 15 août, 7 sept. 1837); De l'esclavage aux Antilles (27 févr. 1838). — Poëles et calorifères à anthracite en usage aux États-Unis ... . *Paris.* 1840. I also find, in a London catalogue, M. Chevalier on Central America. 1856. 8vo, pp. 8.

CHEVALIER. Studien über die nordamerikanische Verfassung. Nach dem Französichen bearbeitet von M. Engel. *Wien: Beck.* 1849. 8vo, pp. vi, 155. 12597

CHEVALIER (Robert). *See* Beauchêne, Vol. I., No. 4163.

CHEVALLIE (P. J.) Claim of Baumarchais' Heir against The United States, by P. J. Chevallie, her Attorney. January, 1817. *Washington: printed by Jonathan Elliot.* [1817.] 8vo, pp. 42. BA., H. 12598

CHEVES (E. W. F.) Sketches in Prose and Verse. By Mrs. E. W. F. Cheves. *Baltimore.* 1849. 12mo, pp. 264.

CHEVES (Langdon). Occasional Reviews. Nos. 1 and 2. *Charleston.* 1832. 12mo. 12600

CHEVES. Speeches ... in ... Congress on ... Merchants' Bonds, by ... Mr. Cheves, Of South Carolina. and ... Mr. Richardson, Of Massachusetts. *Boston: True and Rowe.* 1813. 8vo, pp. 35. BA. 12601

Also: Speech ... on the Subject of the Navy. *Washington.* 1812. 8vo.

CHEVES. An Oration delivered ... Fourth of July, 1810 ... by Appointment of the Seventy-Six Association ... . By Langdon Cheves ... . *Charleston: printed by E. S. Thomas.* [n. d.] 8vo, pp. 18. BA. 12602

CHEVES. A Reply to the Letter of the Hon. Langdon Cheves. [n. p. 184–.] 8vo, pp. 24. H. 12603

CHEVIGNI (*M.* de). Science des personnes de la cour de l'épée et de robe. Édition augmentée [par de Limiers]. Nouvelle édition augmentée par P. Massuet. *Amsterdam.* 1752–7. 18 vols. Plates. 12604

Contains descriptive accounts of America and the Indies. The first edition was *Paris.* 1706, 3 vols. De Limiers republished it in 3 vols. in 1713. Quérard gives the imprint of the last edition as *Paris.* 1752, 8 vols., 8vo.

CHEVILLARD (André). Les Desseins de Son Excellence le Cardinal de Richelieu, pour l'Amérique; ce qui s'y est passé de plus remarquable depuis l'établissement des Colonies, et un ample traité du naturel, de la religion et des mœurs des Indiens insulaires et de la Terre-Ferme. *Rennes: Durand.* 1659. 4to.

CHEVREAU (Urbain). Histoire du monde. *Paris: Martin & Boudot.* 1686. 2 vols., 4to, 6 l., pp. 702, 84; 628, 92.

The second volume relates, in part, to America.

CHEVREAU. The History of the World, Ecclesiastical and Civil, from the Creation to the Present Time; with Chronological Remarks. Translated into English. *London.* 1703. 5 vols., 8vo. 12607

CHEVREAU. Le Tableau de la Fortune ouvrage enriche de plusieurs Remarques, &c., par M. Chevreau. *Paris.* 1659. 12mo. 12608

CHEVREAU. The Mirror of Fortune; or, the True Characters of Fate and Destiny, wherein is treated of the Growth and Fall of Empires, the Destruction of famous Cities, the Misfortunes of Kings and other great Men, and the ill fate of virtuous and handsome Ladies, &c. *London.* 1676. 8vo. 12609

Chapter VI. treats of the empire or kingdom of Mexico.

[CHEVRIER (*Fr.* Antoine).] L'Acadiade, ou Prouesses anglaises en Acadie, Canada, etc., poëme comi-héroïque en IV chantes, par M. D***. *Cassel.* 1758. Sm. 8vo. 12610

CHEVROLAT (Auguste). Coléoptères du Mexique. *Strasbourg: G. Silberman.* 1833–35. 12mo, pp. vii, 207. + *Paris: Mercklein.* 1834. 12mo. 12611

CHEW (J. H.) God's Judgments Teaching Righteousness. A Sermon delivered on the National Fast Day, January 4, 1861, in St. Matthew's Parish, Prince George's County, Md., by the Rev. John H. Chew, A.M., Rector. *Washington: R. A. Waters, printer.* 1861. 8vo, pp. 13. H. 12612

CHEW (S.) The | Speech | of | Samuel Chew, Esq; | Chief-Justice of the Government of New- | Castle, Kent, and Sussex upon | Delaware: | Delivered from the Bench to the | Grand-Jury of the County of | New-Castle, Nov. 21. 1741; and now pub- | lished at their Request. | *Philadelphia: Printed and sold by B. Franklin.* | MD,CC,XLI. | 8vo, pp. 16. P. 12613

On the lawfulness of defence against an armed enemy.

CHIABRERA (G.) Rime di Gabriello Chiabrera ... . *Milano: Societa' de' Classici Italiani.* 1807–08. 3 vols., 8vo. 12614

Claims Columbus as a Savonese. The poem, which is the 12th of the "Canzoni eroiche," probably appears in his Poemetti. *Fiorenze: Fil. Guinti.* 1598. 4to. + Rime. *Genova: Gius. Pavoni.* 1605–06. 8vo. + *Venezia: Combi.* 1610. 12mo. + Rime per P. Girol. Gentile. *Venezia.* 1605. 2 vols., 12mo. + Poesie. Vol. I.–III. *Firenze: Zanobi.* 1627. Vol. IV. *Ven.: Ciotti.* 1628. 12mo. + Poesie ... accresciute ... . *Roma: Salvioni.* 1718. 3 vols., 8vo. + Opere. *Ven.: Angiolo Geremia.* 1730. 4 vols., 8vo. + Poesie liriche. *Londra* [*Livorno*]. 1781. 5 vols., 12mo. + *Milano.* 1832–33. 2 vols., 32mo. + Rime. *Livorno.* 1841. 2 vols., 32mo.

CHIAPA. Observaciones que hace la Iglesia Catedral del Estado de Chiapa. *Mexico.* 1826. 8vo. 12615

CHIARI (P.) I Privilegi | Della | Ignoranza | Lettere | D'una Americana ad un Letterato | d' Europa | Pubblicate Dall' Ab. Pietro Chiari. | *Venezia* MDCCLXXXIV. *Presso Leonardo e Giammaria Fratelli Bassaglia.* Con pubblica Approvazione, e Privilegio. 8vo, pp. 8, 160. 12616

CHICAGO. Celebration of the Eighty-Sixth Anniversary of the Independence of the United States, in Chicago, July 4th, 1862. ... *Chicago.* MDCCCLXII. 8vo, pp. 31. 12617

Transactions of the Chicago Academy of Sciences. Volume I. Part I. *Chicago: published by the Academy.* 1869. 4to, 6 l., pp. 129. 19 Plates and Map. Continued. B., C. 12618

Also: Constitution, By-Laws, and List of Officers and Members, of the Chicago Academy of Sciences. ... *Chicago: James Barnet, Printer.* 1859. 8vo, pp. 12, 2 l.

The Chicago Almanac and Advertiser, 1855. Compiled by E. H. Hall. *Chicago: Chicago Printing Co.* 1855. 18mo, pp. 82. 12619

The next issue was also called "Hall's Business Directory of Chicago. *Chicago: Hall & Co.*" 16mo, pp. xii, 94.

Chicago; her Commerce and Railroads for 1852. *Chicago.* 1852. pp. 29. 12620

See Railroads, *infra*, and "Hunt's Magazine," XVII. 217; XVIII. 164.

Charter, Constitution and By-Laws, with a List of Officers, etc., of the Chicago Historical Society. ... *Chicago: published by Geo. A. Carnes.* 1854. 8vo, pp. 31. H. 12621

Also: Annual Meeting of the Chicago Historical Society, November 19th, 1868. Addresses by J. Young Scammon, ... and Isaac N. Arnold. ... *Chicago: Church, Goodman, and Donnelley, Printers.* 1868. 8vo, pp. 32. H. — Biennial Report of the Chicago Historical Society, to the Governor of Illinois. *Springfield: Baker & Phillips, Printers.* 1863. 8vo, pp. 14. Continued.

Chicago after Dark; "a Flea in the Ear" of Strangers visiting Chicago, and a Word of Advice to Persons going out after dark. *Chicago: A. C. Anderson.* 1868. 12mo, pp. 95. 12622

Chicago Illustrated. *Chicago: Jevne & Almini.* 1866–67. Oblong 4to. C. 12623

Chicago Land Company. List of Lots in Sheffield's, Wight's, and Ellston's Additions to Chicago, for sale at Auction ... Oct. 16, 1855. 8vo, pp. 64. S. 12624

The Chicago Magazine. The West Illustrated. *Chicago: John Gager & Co. No.* 1, *March*, 1857. Continued. 12625

The Chicago Path-Finder. Established for the Promotion and Extension of Trade in the City of Chicago, [etc.] *Chicago: W. H. B. Smythe & Co.* 1869. 12mo, 1 l., pp. 257, 26 l.

Chicago Record. A Journal devoted to the Church, to Literature, and to the Arts. Vol. 1, April, 1857. *Chicago: J. G. Wilson.* [1862.] 4to. Continued. 12627

Commerce. Annual Review of the Commerce, Manufactures, Public and Private Improvements of Chicago for 1854. *Chicago.* 1855. pp. 72. 12628

Twelfth Annual Review of the Trade and Commerce and of the Condition and Traffic of the Railways centering in the City of Chicago, for ... 1860, With a General Synopsis of the Business of the City, ... *Chicago.* 1861. 8vo, pp. 54. H. 12629

First Annual Statement of the Trade and Commerce of Chicago, ... 1858. Reported to the Chicago Board of Trade by Seth Catlin, Superintendent. *Chicago: S. P. Rounds, Printer.* 1859. 8vo, pp. 55. Continued. H. 12630

Also: Charter, By-Laws and Statement of Property of the Chicago South Branch Dock Co. Chicago, April 1859. *Chicago.* 1859. 8vo, pp. 8. Plan. H.

Chicago Convention, 1847. The Commerce and Navigation of the Valley of the Mississippi, and also that appertaining to the City of St. Louis: Report prepared by Authority of the Delegates from the City of St. Louis ... . *St. Louis.* 8vo. 12631

Memorial to the Congress of the United States of the Executive Committee of the Convention held at Chicago, July 5, 1847. With an Abstract of the Proceedings of the Convention, on the Improvement of Rivers and Harbors. Presented to Congress, June, 1848. *Albany: C. Van Benthuysen, Printer.* 1848. 8vo, pp. 46. H. 12632

Mercantile Record of Chicago. *Chicago.* 1856. 8vo.

Proceedings of the Harbor and River Convention, held at Chicago, July 5, 1847. ... *Chicago: printed by R. L. Wilson.* 1847. 12mo, pp. 79. 12634

Memorial to the President and Congress of the United States, by the National Canal Convention, assembled at Chicago, June 2, 1863. *Chicago.* 1863. 8vo, pp. 24. H. 12635

The Necessity of a Ship-Canal between the East and West. Report of the Proceedings of the Board of Trade, the Mercantile Association, and the Business Men of Chicago, at a meeting held at Metropolitan Hall on the Evening of February 24, 1863. *Chicago: Tribune Company's Book and Job Printing Office,* 51 *Clark Street.* 1863. 8vo, pp. 30. 12636

Report of the Committee on Statistics, for the City of Chicago, submitted to the National Convention, assembled at Chicago, June 2, 1863. *Chicago: Tribune Company's Book and Job Printing Office,* 51 *Clark Street.* 1863. 8vo, pp. 45. 12637

Proceedings of the National Ship-Canal Convention, held at the City of Chicago, June 2 and 3, 1863. *Chicago.* 1863. 8vo, pp. 248. H. 12638

Directory. A Business Advertiser and General Directory of the City of Chicago, for the Year 1845–6, together with a Historical and Statistical Account. ... By J. Wellington Norris. *Chicago: J. Campbell & Co., Publishers.* 1845. 12mo, pp. 156.

Business-Directory and Statistics of the City of Chicago for 1846. By J. W. Norris. *Chicago.* 1846. 12mo, pp. 64. M.

Udall and Hopkins' Chicago City Directory for 1852 and '53. *Chicago.* 1852. 12mo, pp. 294. + Hall and Smith's Chicago City Directory for 1853–54. Second Annual Edition. *Chicago: R. Fergus.* 1853. 12mo, pp. xii, 254. + Hall & Co.'s Chicago City Directory and Business Advertiser, for 1854, 55. Third Annual Edition. 1854, 55. *Chicago: R. Fergus.* + Chicago City Directory Supplement, May, 1856. ... *Chicago: printed by Robert Fergus.* 1856. 8vo, pp. 12, 2 l. H. + D. B. Cooke & Co.'s Directory for 1858 || for 1859. *Chicago: D. B. Cooke & Co.* 1858, 59. + Smith & Du Moulin's ... for the Year ending May 1, 1860. *Chicago: Smith aud Du Moulin.* [1859.] + Halpin & Bailey's Chicago City Directory for the Years 1861, 1862, 1863, and 1864. *Chicago: Halpin & Bailey.* 1861–64. 4 vols., 8vo. + Edwards' Annual Directory to the Inhabitants, etc., in the City of Chicago for 1866. *Chicago: Edwards, Greenough & Deved.* 8vo, pp. 1088. 12641

The directory for 1863–4 was compiled by T. M. Halpin. In 1865–6 there were two. Halpin's and Bailey's. The last we have seen is J. C. W. Bailey's Chicago City Directory for 1866–7. With Business Register, Map, Street Directory, etc. *Chicago.* 1867. 8vo, pp. 1068, 154, lxvii.

Education. Third Annual Report of the Superintendent of Public Schools, for the Year Feb. 1, 1858. *Chicago.* 1858. 8vo, pp. 66. 12642

Twelfth Annual Report of the Board of Education to August, 1866. *Chicago.* 1866. 8vo. Continued. 12643

Rules and Regulations of the Board of Education of the City of Chicago. 1869. *Chicago.* 1869. 8vo, Title, pp. 5–43. H.

Catalogue of the Officers and Students of the Chicago Theological Seminary. *Chicago.* 1859. 8vo. 12645

Catalogue of the Officers and Students of the University of Chicago. 1864. 8vo. Continued. 12646

Exhibition of the Fine Arts. Catalogue of the First Exhibition of Statuary, Paintings, etc. ... in ... 1859. ... *Chicago.* 1859. 8vo, pp. 16. H. 12647

Geschichte, Eisenbahnen und Handel von Chicago. ... *Chicago.* 1854. 8vo, pp. 79. H. 12648

Government. Annual Financial Statement of the City of Chicago, for ... 1854. *Chicago.* 1855. 8vo, pp. 78, (2). H.

Charter of the City of Chicago, with the Various Amendments thereto. Revised, May, 1847. *Chicago, Ill.* 8vo, pp. 32. H. + Charter and Ordinances of the City of Chicago. *Chicago.* 1856. 8vo. B. 12650

City Comptroller's Third Annual Statement of the Receipts and Expenditures of the City of Chicago, for the Financial Year 1859–60. *Chicago.* 1860. 8vo, pp. 15. Continued.

Second Annual Report of the Board of Public Works to the Common Council of the City of Chicago. April 1st, 1863. *Chicago.* 1863. 8vo, pp. 106. Continued. H. 12652

Report, and Plan of Sewerage for the City of Chicago, Illinois, adopted ... December 31, 1855. *Chicago.* 1855. 8vo, pp. 22. Map. H. + Report of Examinations made in 1856–7. *Chicago.* 1858. 8vo, pp. 96. 12653

Fifteenth Semi-Annual Report of the Board of Water Commissioners, to the Common Council of the City of Chicago. January 1st, 1859. *Chicago: William H. Rand, Printer.* 1859. 8vo, pp. 48. Continued. H. 12654

Guide to the City of Chicago; its Public Buildings, Places of Amusement, ... *Chicago: T. Ellwood Zell & Co.* 1868. 18mo, pp. 196. 24 Plates and Map. C. 12655

History of the North-Western Soldiers' Fair, held in Chicago ... 1863 ... *Chicago: Dunlop, Sewell & Spalding, Printers.* 1864. 8vo, pp. 184. B. 12656

First and Second Report of the Chicago Sanitary Commission, 1862. *Chicago: Dunlop & Co.* 1862. 8vo, pp. 30. 12657

Memorial to the Government of the United States from the Citizens of Chicago, setting forth the Advantages of that City as a Site for a National Armory and Foundry. ... 1861. *Chicago: Beach & Barnard.* 1863. 8vo, pp. 22. Map. C., H. 12658

Minutes of the Presbyterian and Congregational Convention, held at Chicago, Illinois, June 17, 1847. *Chicago, Ill.* 1847. 16mo, pp. 41. H. 12659

Narrative of the Massacre at Chicago, August 15, 1812, and of some preceding Events, with plan. *Chicago, Ill.: Printed by Ellis & Fergus.* 1844. 8vo, pp. 34. 12660

Substantially the same as the narrative in Mrs. Kinzie's "Waubun."

Proceedings of the Republican National Convention, Chicago, May 1860. 8vo, pp. 153. S. 12661

Presidential Election, 1868. Proceedings of the National Union Republican Convention held at Chicago, May 20 and 21, 1868. ... *Chicago.* [n. d.] 8vo, pp. 143. B. 12662

Also: The Chicago Copperhead Convention. The Treasonable and Revolutionary Utterances of the Men who composed it. Extracts from all the Notable Speeches Delivered in and out of the National "Democratic" Convention. A Surrender to the Rebels Advocated — A Disgraceful and Pusillanimous Peace Demanded — The Federal Government Shamefully Villified, and not a Word said against the Crime of Treason and Rebellion. *Washington, D. C.* [1864.] 8vo, pp. 16. H. — The Real Chicago Platform, as Expounded by the Democratic Orators at Chicago. [1864] 4to, broadside. — Address of the Cameron and Lincoln Club of the City of Chicago, Ill., to the People of the North West. [n. p. n. d.] 8vo, pp. 8. H. — Constitution of the Bay State Union, Chicago, May 18, 1857. *Chicago: Wm. H. Rand, Printer.* 1857. 12mo, pp. 12. H.

The True Designs of the Chicago Convention, or, the Conspiracy of the Rebels and the Peace Democracy. 8vo, pp. 16.

Railroads. The Rail Roads, History and Commerce of Chicago. *Chicago.* 1854. Rl. 8vo, pp. 67. H. + Second Edition. *Chicago.* 1854. 8vo, pp. 80. H. 12664

Chicago and her Railroads. *Chicago: Democratic Press.* 1854. 8vo, pp. 72. 12665

Also: Chicago and Milwaukie Railroad Co. First Annual Report. *New York: Baker & Godwin, printers.* 1855. 8vo, pp. 8. — Chicago and Rock-Island Railroad Company. Report ... Dec. 22, 1851; with a copy of the charter. *New York.* 1852. 8vo. — Chicago, Burlington and Quincy Railroad Company. Reports, 1856, 57. *Chicago.* 1859. 8vo.

First Annual Report of the Directors of the Chicago, St. Paul & Fond du Lac Rail-Road Company, to the Stockholders, May, 1856. *New York.* 1856. 8vo. Continued. 12666

Also: First Mortgage, convertible bonds. *New York.* 1855.

Documents relating to Land-Grant Extension. *New York.* 1857. 8vo. S. 12667

To the Merchants of Chicago, and Railroad Managers of the Northwest. *Pittsburgh. Ap.* 27, 1859. 8vo, pp. 16. 12668

Relates to the St. Nicholas Compact. Also: Union Pacific Railway, (Eastern Division.) Action of Board of Trade of Chicago, and Extracts from Leading Journals of Illinois, showing the Necessity and Advantages of its Immediate Construction to the Pacific. *Chicago: Rounds & James, Printers.* 1868. 8vo, pp. 20. H. Many other reports respecting railroads connected with Chicago will be found in the library of the Chicago Historical Society.

First Annual Report of the Chicago Charitable Eye and Ear Infirmary. Presented by the Board of Surgeons, for the Year ... 1859. *Chicago: James Barnet, Printer.* 1859. 8vo, pp. 7. Continued. H. 12669

First Annual Report of the Superintendent of the Chicago Reform School ... . *Chicago.* 1856. 8vo, pp. 22. Continued.

Uebersicht der Geschichte und des Handels von Chicago. *Chicago.* 1856. 8vo, pp. 62. 12671

Catalogue of the Library of the Young Men's Association of the City of Chicago. ... *Chicago: Whitmarsh & Fulton, Printers.* 1852. 8vo, pp. 44. H. + Catalogue ... Compiled by John M. Horton, Librarian. *Chicago: Young Men's Assoc.* 1856. 8vo, pp. xxvii, 249, (1). C., H. 12672

Also: Fourteenth Annual Report of the Executive Committee of The Young Men's Association, of Chicago, Illinois, ... 1855, and the Inaugural Address of the President for the ensuing Year. *Chicago: Scott & Fulton, Printers.* 1855. 8vo, pp. 18. Continued. H.

CHICKASAW. Letters on the Chicasaw Mission. By the Author of "Conversations on the Sandwich Islands." *Boston.* 1831. 18mo, pp. 162. 12673

There are Congressional Documents, Nos. 115 and 122, which relate to the Chickasaw Fund, but I do not know the date; probably 1844. *See* N. A. R., July, 1831.

CHICHESTER (*Bishop of*). *See* Hare (F.), Mawson (M.), and Williams (John).

CHICHESTER (*Canon of*). *See* Haley.

CHICHESTER (*Dean of*). *See* Sherlock (T.)

CHICKAMAUGA. Official Report of the Battle of Chickamauga. Published by Order of Congress. *Richmond: R. A. Smith, Public Printer.* 1864. 8vo. 12674

Gen. Bragg commanded, and this report is presumed to be by him. Two hundred copies were printed; it is now very scarce.

CHICKERING (J.) A Statistical View of the Population of Massachusetts, from 1765 to 1840. By Jesse Chickering. *Boston: Charles C. Little and James Brown.* 1846. 8vo, pp. 160.

CHICKERING. Immigration into the United States. By Jesse Chickering. *Boston: Charles C. Little and James Brown.* 1848. 8vo, Title, pp. 94. BA. 12676

Also: City Document — No. 60. Report of the Committee appointed by the City Council; and also a Comparative View of the Population of Boston in 1850, with the Births, Marriages, and Deaths in 1849 and 1850, by Jesse Chickering, M.D. *Boston.* 1851. 8vo, pp. 58. BA.

CHICKERING (J. W.) An Address delivered before the Portland Temperance Society, February 22, 1854. By John W. Chickering, ... *Portland: printed by Brown Thurston.* 1854. 8vo, pp. 16. H. 12677

CHICKERING. The Hillside Church [in Bolton, Mass.]: or Reminiscences of a Country Pastorate. By John W. Chickering ... . *Boston: S. K. Whipple & Company. Portland: Sanborn & Carter.* 1856. 12mo, pp. 280. H. 12678

Also: A Discourse ... at the Funeral of Rev. Joseph Bennett, Woburn, November 22, 1847. ... . *Boston: Damrell & Moore.* 1847. 8vo, pp. 27. H. — ... A Sermon ... at Freyeburg, Me., December 11, 1855, at the Funeral of Rev. Carleton Hurd, D.D. ... *Portland: printed by Brown Thurston.* 1856. 8vo, pp. 23. H. — ... A Sermon ... before the Maine Missionary Society, ... *Portland: William Cushing, Printer.* 1846. 8vo, pp. 53. H.

CHICKERING (J.) A Discourse delivered to the Congregational Society in Woburn, June 28, 1809, at the Dedication of their Meeting-house. By Joseph Chickering, A.M. ... *Charlestown.* 1809. 8vo, pp. 28. BA. 12679

With historical notes.

CHICKERING. A Sermon, preached in Boston, before the

American Society for educating Pious Youth for the Ministry ... Oct. 15, 1817. By Joseph Chickering ... . *Dedham.* 1817. 8vo, pp. 44. BA. 12680

With the "Report," "Donations," etc.

CHICKERING. Chickering and Sons' Piano-Fortes at the Exhibition of 1856. ... *Boston.* 1857. 8vo, pp. 18. H. 12681

CHICO (J.) Discurso pronunciado el dia 19 de Junio de 1864, en que la ciudad de Guanajuato solemnizo la feliz llegada de SS. MM. Maximiliano y Carlota, á la Capital del Imperio. *Guanajuato.* 1864. 8vo, pp. 15. 12682

CHICOPEE. Annual Reports of the ... Town of Chicopee, During the Year ending March 1, 1849. *Chicopee: printed by J. C. Stoever.* 1849. 8vo, pp. 16. H. 12683

By-Laws; ... etc. March 1, 1851. *Springfield.* 1851. pp. 46. Continued. 12684

Catalogue of the Chicopee Falls School Library, ... and the Regulations for its Government. *Springfield: John M. Wood, Printer.* 1848. H. 12685

CHIDLAW (B. W.) A Thanksgiving Sermon, preached before the Thirty-Ninth O. V., U. S. A., at Camp Todd, Macon, Missouri, Nov. 28, 1861, and a Sketch of the Regiment. By Rev. B. W. Chidlaw, Chaplin. *Cincinnati: George Crosby.* 1861. 8vo, pp. 24. 12686

CHIDLEY (Katherine). Justification of the Independent Churches of Christ, in answer to Mr. Edwards his Booke, which he hath written against the Government of Christ's Church, and toleration of Christ's publike Worship. [About 1650.] 4to. 12687

Contains several allusions to John Robinson and the New England church government. From J. R. Smith's catalogue, where the date is conjectured to be 1650; but Joseph Smith does not name the work in his catalogue of "Friends' Books." The author is said to be a Quakeress.

The Chief's Daughter; or, the Settlers in Virginia. *Oxford, [England]: J. H. Parker.* 1859. 12mo, pp. 126. 12688

CHIFFLET (Jean Jacques). Pulvis febrifugus orbis Americani ... ventilatus ratione, experientia, auctoritate. [n. p.] 1653. Sm. 8vo, pp. 45. 12689

Chifflet also published "Recueil des Traittez de Paix, Trêves et Neutralité entre les Couronnes d'Espagne et de France. *Anvers.* 1645," second edition, 12mo; "*Anvers.* 1664," third edition, 12mo, some of which treaties relate to America.

CHIHUAHUA. Ensayo estadistico sobre el Estado de Chihuahua. 1842. Folio, pp. 98. 12690

Estado actual de Chihuahua. *Mexico.* 1839. 4to. 12691

Memoria relativa à los Ramos de la Administracion del Estado de Chihuahua bajo el Gobierno del E. Snr. D. Angel Trias. *Mexico.* 1850. 8vo. 12692

The New York Historical Society possesses a file of the "El Noticioso de Chihuahua," the official paper of the Department of Chihuahua; various dates, between 1835–8.

CHILD (A. B.) A Plea for Farming and Farming Corporations. ... . By A. B. Child ... . *Boston: published by William White & Co.; Kidder, Mo.: Caneday & Huston.* 1862. 12mo, pp. 60. Woodcuts. H. 12693

Also: Whatever is, Is Right. *Boston.* 1861. 12mo, pp. xi, 221.

CHILD (A. P.) Whatcheer, a Story of Olden Times. One of Sister Rhody's Collections of Historical Facts, for the Amusement and Instruction of Young People. Edited by Mrs. Anna P. Child. *Providence: Knowles, Anthony & Co.* 1857. 18mo, pp. ix, 194. 12694

CHILD (D. L.) ... The Despotism of Freedom; a Speech at the First Anniversary of the New England Anti-Slavery Society. By David Lee Child. ... *Boston: Young Men's Anti-Slavery Association.* [1834.] 12mo, pp. 72. BA., H. 12695

[CHILD.] An Enquiry into the Conduct of General Putnam, in Relation to the Battle of Bunker, or Breed's Hill: and Remarks upon Mr. S. Swett's Sketch of that Battle. ... *Boston: printed by Thomas G. Bangs.* 1819. 8vo, pp. 58. C., H., M.

CHILD. Political Extracts from a Leading Adams Paper, The Massachusetts Journal, Edited and Published in Boston By David L. Child, and Recommended To Public Patronage By H. A. S. Dearborn, [and six others. n. p. 1828.] 8vo, pp. 28.

CHILD. Report of the Case of Alleged Contempt, and Breach of the Privileges of the House of Representatives of Massachusetts, ... against David L. Child ... . With Notes ... . *Boston: published by Carter & Hendee.* 1832. 8vo, pp. 151. H., M.

CHILD. Review of a Report to the House of Representatives of the Commonwealth of Massachusetts, on the Case of William Vans. With Observations upon the Dispensing Power of

the Legislature, and upon a Decision of the Supreme Judicial Court, "nullifying" the said Power. By David L. Child ... . *Boston.* 1833. 8vo, pp. iv, 97, 15. C., H. 12699

CHILD. Rights and Duties of the United States relative to Slavery under the Laws of War. No Military Power to return any Slave. "Contraband of War" inapplicable between the United States and their Insurgent Enemies. By David Lee Child. Republished, with notes from "The Liberator." ... *Boston: R. F. Walcutt.* 1861. 12mo, pp. 48. H. 12700

CHILD. The Taking of Naboth's Vineyard, or History of the Texas Conspiracy, and an Examination of the Reasons given by the Hon. J. C. Calhoun, Hon. R. J. Walker, and others, for the Dismemberment and Robbery of the Republic of Mexico. By David Lee Child, ... *New York: S. W. Benedict & Co.* 1845. 8vo, pp. 32. H. 12701

[CHILD.] The Texan Revolution. Republished with Additions from the Northampton (Massachusetts) Gazette, to which is added A Letter from Washington on the annexation of Texas, and the late outrage in California, by Probus. [Republished, with additions, from the Liberator. *Washington.* 1843.] pp. 84. 12702

CHILD. Trial of the Case of the Commonwealth versus David Lee Child, for publishing in the Massachusetts Journal a Libel on the Honorable John Keyes, ... October Term, 1828. Reported by John W. Whitman. *Boston.* 1829. 8vo, pp. 119.

Also: An Address delivered at Watertown March 4th, 1825, at a Dinner in honor of the Inauguration of President John Quincy Adams. ... *Boston: Cummings, Hilliard & Co.* 1825. 12mo, pp. 10. H. — An Appeal ... to the Abolitionists. *Albany.* [1844?] 24mo, pp. 8. B. — The Culture of the Beet, and Manufacture of Beet Sugar ... . *Boston: Weeks, Jordon & Co.* 1840. 12mo, pp. 156. (Contains an account of the manufacture of beet sugar at Northampton, Mass.) — An Oration pronounced before the Republicans of Boston. July 4, 1826. The Fiftieth Anniversary of American Independence. ... *Boston: Josiah B. Clough.* 1826. 8vo, pp. 40. H. — Oration in honor of Universal Emancipation in the British Empire, delivered at South Reading, August First, 1834. ... *Boston: Garrison and Knapp.* 1834. 8vo, pp. 45.

[CHILD (Francis James). Notice of William Thaddeus Harris, Esq. prepared for and published in the ... New England Historical and Genealogical Register, for 1855. *Boston: Samuel G. Drake.* 1855. Sm. 4to, pp. 14. BA. 12704

CHILD (J.) New-Englands | Jonas | Cast up at | London: | Or, | A Relation of the Proceedings of | the Court at Boston in New-England against di- | vers honest and godly persons, for Petition-

ing for Go- | vernment in the Common-wealth, according to the Laws of | England, and for admittance of themselves and children | to the Sacraments in their Churches; and in case | that should not be granted, for leave to | have Ministers and Church-government according to the best | Reformation of En- | gland and Scotland. | Together with a Confutation of some Reports | of a fained Miracle upon the foresaid Petition, being | thrown overboard at Sea; As also a brief Answer to some | passages in a late Book (entituled Hypocrise unmasked) | set out by Mr. Winslowe, concerning the Inde- | pendent Churches holding communion | with the Reformed Churches. | By Major John Child. | *London: Printed for T. R. aud E. M.* 1647. | Sm. 4to, Title, pp. 22. BA., C.

Pages 15 to 22 are erroneously numbered, 9, 8, 9, 12, 13, 12, 13. Reprinted in Force's Tracts, v. 4, "Mass. Hist. Soc. Collections," 2nd Series, v. 4, and again reprinted as below:

CHILD. New-England's Jonas Cast up at London. 1647. By Major John Child. With an Introduction and Notes, by W. T. R. Marvin. *Boston: Wm. Parsons Lunt.* 1869. 4to, Title, pp. lii, 40. B., BA. 12706

[CHILD (*Sir* Josiah).] Britannia Languens; or, a Discourse of Trade. *London: T. Dring.* 1680. 16mo, 4 l., pp. 310, 41.

CHILD. A New | Discourse | of | Trade | Wherein is Recommended several | weighty Points relating to Com- | panies of Merchants. | The Act of Navigation. | Naturalization of Strangers. | And our Woolen Manufactures. | The | Ballance of Trade. | And the Nature of Plantations, and their Consequen- | ces in Relation to the Kingdom, are seriously | Discussed. | Methods for the Employment and Maintenance of | the Poor are Proposed. | The Reduction of Interest of Money to 4*l.* per | Centum, is Recommended. | And some Proposals for erecting a Court of Mer- | chants for determining Controversies, relating to | Maritime Affairs, and for a Law for Transfer- | rance of Bills of Debts, are humbly Offered. | By Sir Josiah Child. | *London: Printed and Sold by T. Sowle, next Door to | the Meeting-House in White-Hart-Court in Gracious- | street, and at the Bible in Leaden-hall-street, near | the Market.* 1698. | 8vo, 24 l., pp. 238. C., P. 12708

This is the title of the third edition. The first edition was published in small 4to, 1668. The second edition, which was very much enlarged, appeared in 1690. Another edition is, "*London.* 1693," 16mo. S. A fourth edition, [1698.] 12mo. "*J. Hodges on London Bridge.*" [n. d.] pp. xlvi, (4), 260, (2). P. Fifth edition, "*Glasgow.* 1751," 12mo, pp. xxix, 184. P. "New edition, *London.* 1774," 12mo. [Another] new edition, "*London: Richardson & Urquhart.* 1775," 16mo, pp. xxxix, 224. C. For an extract from this work, *see* Whitworth (Charles). *See also* McCulloch's "Lit. Pol. Ec.," p. 42, where the work is highly eulogized.

CHILD (L.) Synopsis of Facts and Arguments of Hon. Linus Child, presented to the Joint Standing Committee on Education, in Behalf of the Remonstrants against the Petition ... for an Act to incorporate "The Boston Dental College." May, 5, 1868. *Boston: Wright & Potter, Printers.* 1868. 8vo, pp. 14.

CHILD (Lydia Maria). Anti-Slavery Catechism. By Mrs. Child ... . *Newburyport: Charles Whipple.* 1836. 12mo, pp. 36. + Second Edition. *Newburyport: Charles Whipple.* 1839. 12mo, pp. 36. 12710

CHILD. An Appeal in favor of that Class of Americans called Africans. By Mrs. Child ... . *Boston: Allen & Ticknor.* 1833. 12mo, 3 l., pp. 232. BA. + *New York: John S. Taylor.* 1836. 12mo, pp. 216. C., H. 12711

CHILD. Brief History of the Condition of Women in various Ages and Nations. By L. Maria Child ... . Fifth Edition. *New York: C. S. Francis & Co. Boston: J. H. Francis.* 1845. 2 vols., 1 l., pp. vi, 298; vi, 298. BA., C., P. 12712

Vol. II. treats of "Slave-holding Countries," and "America."

CHILD. Fact and Fiction: a collection of stories. *New York: C. S. Francis & Co.* 1847. 12mo, pp. 282. 12713

[CHILD.] The First Settlers of New-England: or, Conquest of the Pequods, Narragansets and Pokanokets: as related by A Mother to her Children, and designed for the Instruction of Youth. By a Lady of Massachusetts. *Boston: Munroe and Francis* ... [About 1822.] 18mo, pp. 282, (1). Plate. + *Boston.* 1829. 12mo, pp. 282, (1). Plate. C. 12714

CHILD. The Freedman's Book. By L. Maria Child. .:. *Boston: Ticknor & Fields.* 1865. 12mo, Title, pp. vi, 277. BA.

CHILD. Good Wives. By Mrs D. L. Child ... . *Boston: Carter, Hendee & Co.* 1833. 16mo, 1 l., pp. xiv, (1), 316. Plate.

CHILD. [The same.] Biographies of Good Wives. Sixth Edition. *New York: C. S. Francis.* 1855. 12mo, pp. vi, 288.

Includes Lady Arabella [*sic*] Johnson, Mrs. Judson, Baroness Reidesel [*sic*], Mrs. Experience West, Mrs. Winthrop.

[CHILD.] Hobomok, a Tale of Early Times. By an American. ... *Boston: Cummings, Hilliard & Co.* 1824. 12mo, pp. 188. BA., H. 12718

CHILD. Incidents in the Life of a Slave Girl. *See* Brent (Lind), Vol. II., No. 7722.

Reprinted as the "Deeper Wrong, or Incidents, &c. *London: W. Tweedie.* 1863." 12mo, pp. 306.

CHILD. Isaac T. Hopper: a True Life. By L. Maria Child. *Boston: John P. Jewett & Co.* 1853. 12mo. Portrait. C. + Twelfth Thousand. *Boston: John P. Jewett and Company.* 1860. 12mo, pp. xv, (1), 493. Portrait. BA., H. 12719

CHILD. Isak T. Hopper. Lebensgeschichte eines amerikanischen Quäkers und seine Beziehungen zur grossen Sklavenfrage. Aus dem Englischen übersetzt von Gottlob Fink. *Stuttgart: Metzler.* 1854. 8vo, pp. viii, 248. 12720

CHILD. Letters from New York. By L. Maria Child. ... *New York: Charles S. Francis and Co. Boston: James Munroe & Co.* M DCCC XLIII. 12mo, 1 l., pp. ix, 276. H. + *London: R. Bentley.* 1843. Post 8vo. + Second Edition. *New York.* M DCC XLIV. 12mo, pp. 288. || Second Series. *New York: C. S. Francis and Company.* MDCCCXLIV. 12mo, pp. xi, 288. + *New York: C. S. Francis & Co. Boston: J. H. Francis.* 1845. 12mo, pp. 287. BA. + Ninth Edition. [*Id.*] MDCCCXLVIII. + Eleventh Edition. *New York: C. S. Francis & Co.* 1850. 12mo, pp. 287. 12721

[CHILD.] Memoir of Benjamin Lay: Compiled From various Sources. *New-York.* 1842. 24mo, pp. 35. H. 12722

CHILD. The Oasis. Edited by Mrs. Child ... . *Boston: Benjamin C. Bacon.* 1834. 16mo, pp. xvi, 276. 12723

Contains a number of slave stories, by Mrs. Child.

CHILD. The Patriarchal Institution, as described by Members of its own Family. Compiled by L. M. Child. ... *New York.* 1860. 12mo, pp. 55. H. 12724

[CHILD.] The Rebels, or Boston before the Revolution. *Boston: Cummings, Hilliard & Company.* 1825. 12mo, pp. 304. BA. + *Boston.* 1850. 12mo. 12725

CHILD. The Right Way the Safe Way, proved by Emancipation in the British West Indies and elsewhere. By L. Maria Child. ... *New York.* 1860. 12mo, pp. 95. BA. + [Second Edition.] *New York.* 1862. 12mo, pp. 108. H. 12726

CHILD. A Romance of the Republic. By L. Maria Child. *Boston: Ticknor and Fields.* 1867. 12mo, pp. 442. BA., C., H.

Also: Authentic Anecdotes of American Slavery ... . Second Edition, enlarged. *Newburyport: Charles Whipple.* 1838. 12mo, pp. 23. H. — Autumnal Leaves: Tales and Sketches in Prose and Rhyme. ... *New York: C. S. Francis & Co.* 1857. 12mo, pp. 365. BA. — Correspondence between Lydia Maria Child and Gov. Wise and Mrs. Mason, of Virginia. *Boston: American Anti-Slavery Society.* 1860. 12mo, pp. 28. BA. — The Duty of Disobedience to the Fugitive Slave Act. An Appeal to the Legislators of Massachusetts. ... *Boston: American Anti-Slavery Society.* 1860. 12mo, pp. 36. — The Evils of Slavery, and the Cure of Slavery. The first proved by the opinions of Southerners themselves, The last shown by Historical Evidence. ... *Newburyport: Charles Whipple.* 1836. 12mo, pp. 19. + Second Edition. *Newburyport.* 1839. 12mo. — Looking towards Sun Set, from Sources Old and New, Original and Selected. *Boston.* 1865. 12mo, pp. ix, (1), 455. H. — Philothea; A Romance ... *Boston.* 1836. 12mo, pp. 284. — The Progress of Religious Ideas, through Successive Ages. *New York.* 1855. 3 vols., 12mo, pp. 450; 437; 478. — Sketches from Real Life. I. ... II. Home and Politics. *Philadelphia.* 1850.

Childe Harvard; a Romance of Cambridge. By Señor Alguno. ... *Boston: the Author.* 1848. 16mo, pp. 172. BA., H.

By Nathan Ames. Omitted in its proper place.

[CHILDE (Edward Vernon).] Articles from the "London Times" signed A "States'" Man, with others from the "New York Courier and Enquirer," under the same Signature. *Boston: William D. Ticknor & Company.* 1847. 16mo, pp. 95. H.

See also Santarem (*Viscount*).

CHILDE (J.) *See* Child (J.)

The Children of the Frontier. *New York: D. Appleton & Co.* 16mo, pp. 290. 12730

CHILDS (C. G.) Views in Philadelphia and its Vicinity. Engraved from Original Drawings by C. G. Childs. *Philadelphia: C. G. Childs.* 1827–30. Sm. folio, 38 l. 25 Plates.

CHILDS (H.), *of Johnson, R. I.* The Life of Mrs. Hannah Childs, who long in darkness lay, will now be brought to light. *Providence.* [1859.] 8vo, pp. 27. 12732

CHILDS (H. H.) Addresses of H. H. Childs, M.D., and of Rev. J. Todd, D.D. ... At the Dedication of the New College Building of the Berkshire Medical Institution, in Pittsfield, Mass., August 5, 1852. *Pittsfield, Mass.: William D. Axtell, Printer.* 1852. 8vo, pp. 23. BA. 12733

CHILDS. Eulogy on ... John Doane Wells, M.D. ... September, 1830. By Henry H. Childs, M.D. ... . *Pittsfield: printed by Phinehas Allen & Son.* [n. d.] 8vo, pp. 14. BA.

CHILDS (I.) The Vision of Isaac Childs, which he saw in the Year 1757, concerning Pennsylvania, the land of his nativity (never published before this year 1766) To which is annexed, the Explanation. [n. p. n. d.] 12mo. P. 12735

Printed at Philadelphia, probably by W. Mentz. Reprinted with the following title:

CHILDS. The Vision of Isaac Childs, with Explanatory Notes, and a Sketch of his Life. *Philadelphia.* 1840. 12mo. P.

CHILDS (N.) Trial of Nathaniel Childs, Jr., ... on an Indictment charging him with the Embezzlement of Money belonging to the Bank of the State of Missouri. ... *St. Louis: printed by Chambers & Knapp.* 1850. 8vo, pp. 76, 59. H.

[CHILDS (O. W.)] Engineer's Report of the Cost of Constructing the Ship Canal of Nicaragua, ... *New York: Wm. C. Bryant & Co., Printers.* 1852. 8vo, pp. 42. H. 12738

CHILDS. Report of the Survey and Estimates of the ... Inter-Oceanic Ship Canal, from the Harbor of San Juan del Norte, on the Atlantic, to the Harbor of Brito on the Pacific, in the State of Nicaragua ... made for the American, Atlantic and Pacific Ship Canal Co. ... 1850–51, by Orville W. Childs, Chief Engineer. J. D. Fay Principal Assistant. *New York.* 1852. 8vo, pp. ii, 153. 5 Maps. BA. 12739

CHILI. Algunas Observaciones Arregladas a los Principios y a la opinion de los pueblos de Chile. *Valparaiso.* 1841. 4to, pp. 20. 12740

Annales de la Universidad de Chile. Correspondientes al ano de 1843 i al de 1844. *Santiago. Octobre de* 1846. 8vo. Continued. C. 12741

Anuario estadistico de la republica de Chile. Entrega primera. Movimiento de poblacion de la republica de 1848 a 1858. *Santiago de Chile. Agosto de* 1860. 4to, pp. viii, 234. Continued.

Apuntes hidrográficos sobre la costa de Chile, acompañados de algunos planos levantados por los oficiales de la armada de la Republica. *Santiago: imprenta national.* 1866. 8vo, pp. iv, 192. 27 Maps. C. 12743

Boletin de las Leyes y de las Ordenes y Decretos del Gobierno, Feb. 1823. *Santiago de Chile.* 1839. 8vo. Continued. 12744

Boletin de la Sociedad de agricultura. Publicado por la misma Sociedad y destinado al fomento de los intereses agricolas del pais. Vol. I. No. 1–5. *Valparaiso.* 1869. Each number 16 pages.

Bosquejo de la Marcha de la Republica y de la influencia Militar en sus destinos. *Santiago de Chile.* 1841. Sm. 4to, pp. 16. B. 12746

Cartas de un Polaco sobre la Politica de Chile. Num. I. *Santiago de Chile.* 1840. 8vo. 12747

Censo general de la república de Chile, levantado en Abril de 1854. *Santiago de Chile.* 1858. Folio, pp. 10. 42 Tables. C.

Chili and Peru in 1824. Fifth Edition. *Boston.* 1824. 8vo.

Chile and Spain. The whole Question officially stated. ... *New York.* 1865. 8vo, pp. 50. H. 12750

Chili et l'Espagne. *Paris: impr. Guérin.* 1866. 8vo, pp. 54.

Chili, through American Spectacles. *New York: John Bradburn.* [n. d.] 12mo, pp. 158. B. 12752

Código civil de la republica de Chile. Edicion revisada i correjada por D. Manuel Amunategui, en virtud de decreto del supremo gobierno; I Adicionada con el Mensajo al Congreso Nacional, el Reglamento del Rejistro Conservatorio de bienes raices, las leyes sobre Habilitacion de edad i Efecto retroactivo de la lei, i con la carte del Sr. Andres Bello que interpreta el art. 1618. del Código, etc. etc. *Valparaiso.* 1865. 8vo, pp. 516.

Coleccion de historiadores de Chile, y documentos relativos a la historia nacional. *Santiago.* 1861–63. 8vo. 12754

Tomo I. Cartas de Pedro de Valdivia al Emperador Carlos V. — Primer libro de actas del Cabildo de Santiago (1541–1557). *Santiago.* 1861. 8vo, pp. viii, 624. Tomo II. (2 parts). Historia de Gongora Marmolejo (1536–1575). — Documentos. — Historia de Cordoba y Figueroa (1492–1717). *Santiago.* 1862. 8vo, pp. xiv, 316; iv, 330. Tomo III. Cautiverio Feliz, y razon de las guerras dilatadas de Chile, por Don Franzisco Nunez de Pineda y Bascunan. *Santiago.* 1863. 8vo, pp. viii, 560.

Coleccion de tratados celebrados por la republica de Chile con los estados extranjeros. Tomo I. *Santiago: imprenta nacional.* 1857. 8vo. C. 12755

Compendio della storia geografica, naturale, e civile del regno del Chile. *Bologna: Stamperia di S. Tommaso d'Aquino.* MDCCLXXVI. 8vo, pp. vii, (1), 245. Map, and 10 Plates. H. 12756

Meusel attributes this anonymous work to the Abbé Vidaurre, but Molina speaks of it as if by a different author. The American translator of Molina has made large extracts from it, from which it appears to be, though concise, a work of considerable authority. A map of the country, a plan of Santiago, the capital, and other places, all made from accurate observations, add to the value of this work. Translated into German. *See* Kurzgefaste, etc.

Constitucion de la Republica de Chile jurada y promulgada el 25. de Mayo 1833. *Santiago de Chile.* 1833. Folio, pp. 48.

Contestacion a un articulo sobre la republica de Chile publicado en el Mercurio de Nueva-York fecha 12 de Julio de este año; copiado en el Espiritu publico del Jueves 16 de Octubre del mismo. *Mexico.* 1828. 8vo, pp. 24. 12758

Counter Manifest of the Minister of Foreign Relations of Chile, on the Present War between the Republic and Spain. *Washington, D. C.: McGill & Witherow, Printers.* 1866. 8vo, pp. 45. H. 12759

Cuenta jeneral de las entradas i gastos fiscales de la república de Chile en 1864. *Santiago: imprenta nacional.* [1865.] 4to, 5 l., pp. 86, 28, 62, 3 l. C. 12760

Curso de lectura por el método de enseñaza mútua: mandado imprimir por el supremo gobierno de Chile. *Santiago: Imprenta del estado.* 1841. 8vo, pp. 256. C. 12761

Defensa del derecho constitucional que todo Chileno tiene para publicar por la prensa sus ideas y pensamientos sin la menor censura. *Santiago de Chili.* 1839. 4to, pp. 20. 12762

Description Geologique du Chili. pp. 68. 2 Plates. 12763

Defensa de la Viuda e hijos de D. Jose Foribio Larrain en el Pleito que les sigue el S. Senador D. Est. Portales sobre devolucion de la Bacienda de Molina restitucion de los frutos de un Vinculo en dos Anos, dies meses y cinco dias y posesion hereditaria en Viluco Campusano. *Santiago de Chile.* 1838. 4to.

Diario de Documentos del Gobierno, Dec. 1825–Mar. 1826. *Santiago.* 1825–26. Folio. M. 12765

Documentos parlamentarios. Discursos de apertura en los sesiones del congreso i memorias ministeriales. *Santiago: Ferrocarril.* 1858–59. 5 vols., 8vo. C. 12766

Estadística comercial de la república de Chile correspondiente al primer trimestre de 1844. *Valparaiso.* 1844. Folio. Continued. 12767

Estadística comercial de la república de Chile, correspondiente al primer semestre del año de 1857. *Valparaiso. Noviembre de* 1857. 4to, pp. 78. Continued. 12768

Estadistica comercial de la República de Chile, Correspondiente al año de 1866. *Valparaiso.* 1867. 4to, pp. xxvi, 233. + 1868. *Valparaiso.* 1868. 4to, pp. 205. 12769

Estadistica de la republica de Chile Provincia del Maule. *Santiago: imprenta de los tribunales.* 1845. 8vo, pp. viii, 179.

Estudios preparatorios. Datos presentados a la comision nombrada para determinar e indicar al supremo gobierno cuales son los medios que pueden adoptarse, a fin de obtener en grande escala el desarrollo de la industria de la seda en Chile. *Santiago de Chile.* 1865. 8vo, pp. 112. 12771

An Expose of the Existing Dissensions between Chili and the Peru-Bolivian Confederation. By a Peru-Bolivian. *London.* 1837. 8vo, pp. 44. 12772

Exposicion que el Presidente da la Republica Ioaq. Prieto dirije al a Nacion Chilena el Dia 18 Setiembre de 1841, ultimo de su administracion. *Santiago.* 1841. 4to. 12773

Geschichte des Konigreich's Chile. *Hamburgh.* 1782. 8vo. Map. 12774

Instruccion (primera y segunda), que puede tenerse presente en la fundacion da los pueblos, que se forman por mandato de S. M. en el Reyno de Chile, entre los limites del Valle de Copiapò, y la Frontera del Rio Biobio. — Representacion del Reyno de Chile sobre la importancia, y necessidad de reducir à Pueblos sus habitadores, dispersos por las campos: Y de los medios de conseguirlo, sin gasto del Erario, ni gravamen de los particulares. — Representacion del Reyno de Chile sobra la importancia, y necessidad de sujetar, y reducir à Pueblos los Indios Araucanos. [*Madrid?* 1732–40.] Folio, pp. 32, 8 l., 7 l. J.C.B. 12775

El Jeneral de Brigada Ramon Castilla a sus Conciudanos. *Santiago de Chile.* 1836. 4to. 12776

Journal of a Residence in Chili. By a Young American detained in that Country during the Revolutionary Scenes of 1817, 1818, 1819. *Boston.* 1823. 12mo, pp. 237. C. 12777

Lei de presupuestos de los gastos jenerales de la administracion pública de Chile para el año de 1867. *Santiago de Chile.* 1867. Folio, pp. 96. Table. 12778

Manifiesto del Gobierno Protectoral sobre el decreto del Gobierno de Chile de 18 de Deciembre de 1837, en que reusa su ratificacion al tratado di Paz de 17 de Novimbre del mismo ano. *Paz de Ayacucho.* 1838. Sm. 4to. 12779

Memoria presentada al Congreso Nacional en 1841, por el Ministro de Estado en el departamento de hacienda. *Santiago.* 1841. 4to, pp. 16. 12780

Memoria presentada al Congreso Nacional en por el Ministre de Estado en el departamento de Justicia, Culto, e Instruccion publica, en 1841. *Santiago.* 1841. 4to. Continued. 12781

Memoria que el Ministro de Estado en los departamentos de Guerra y Marina presenta al Congreso Nacional ano de 1835. *Santiago de Chile.* 1835. 4to. Continued. 12782

Memoria que el ministro de estado en el departamento de justicia, culto e instruccion publica presenta al congreso nacional de 1856. *Santiago de Chile: imprenta nacional.* 1856. 3 vols., 8vo. Continued. 12783

The tables contain statistics of crime, etc., tried in the various courts of justice in Chili.

Memoria que el ministro de estado en los departamentos de guerra y marina presenta al congreso nacional, 1839. *Santiago: imprenta del estado, etc.* 1839. 4to. Continued. 12784

Memoria que el ministro de estado en el departamento de hacienda presenta al congreso nacional de 1860. *Santiago de Chile: imprenta nacional.* 1860. 8vo. Continued. 12785

Memoria que el Ministro de Estado en el departamento del interior presenta al Congreso Nacional de 1844. *Santiago de Chile.* 1844. 4to. Continned. 12786

Memoria que el ministro estado en el departamento de relaciones exteriores presenta al congreso nacional de 1836. *Santiago de Chile: imprenta nacional.* 1836. 4to. Continued.

Memoria sobre el estado presente de Chile. *Londres.* 1820. 8vo, pp. 29. 12788

Mensaje que hace el Presidente de la Republica de Chile al Congreso Nacional, exponiendo las razones justificativas de la presenta guerra con el Peru. *Santiago de Chile.* 1836. Folio, pp. 25. Continued. 12789

Notes sur le Chili, par un voyageur français. *Paris: A. François.* 1844. 8vo, pp. 43. 12790

Notice statistique sur le Chili et catalogue des minéraux envoyés à l'Exposition universelle de 1867. *Paris.* 1867. 8vo, pp. 83. S. 12791

Noticias del Sur. Despacho y felices succesos de la armada en los reynos del Peru, Tierra Firme y Chile. 1685. Folio.

On the Formal Recognition of Chile and Peru. 1830. 8vo.

Ordenanza de Aduanas de la República de Chile, promulgada por el Supremo Gobierno el 31 de Octubre de 1864. Edicion official. *Santiago.* 1865. 8vo, pp. vi, 159. 12794

Ordenanza para el Réjimen, Disciplina, Subordinacion y Servicio de los Ejércitos de la Republica. *Santiago de Chile.* 1840. 4to. 12795

Papers respecting the War between Chili and Spain. *London.* 1866. Folio. 12796

A Parliamentary paper. There are probably others.

Par Perpetua a los Chilenos. *Valparaiso.* 1840. Sm. 4to, pp. 10. 12797

Pièces principales de la correspondance échangée entre les ministres du Chili et des États-Unis d'Amérique, à Santiago et à Washington, au sujet d'une capture faite par un détachement de l'escadre chilienne dans la vallée de Sitana, territoire péruvien, le 9 mai 1821, [etc.] *Bruxelles: H. Goemaere.* 1861. 8vo, 1 l., pp. 509. C. 12998

Quinto y sexto punto de la Relacion del Desengano de la guerra de Chile, &c. 4to. 12799

Title from J. R. Smith's catalogue.

Rambles in Chili and Life among the Araucanian Indians, in 1836. By "Will the Rover." ... *Thomaston: D. J. Starrett.* 1851. 8vo, 2 l., pp. 9–88. BA. 12800

Reglamento de Aduanas y resguardos del Estado de Chile. *Valparaiso.* 1822. Folio. 12801

Relacion verdadera de las pazes|que capitvlò con el Aravcano rebelado, el|Marques de Baides, Conde de Pedroso, Gouernador, y Capitan Gene-|ral del Reyno de Chile, y Presidente de la Real Audiencia. Sacada de|sus informes, y cartas, y de los Padres de la Compañia de Iesus, que acõ-|pañaron el Real excertio en la jornada que hizo para este efeto|el Año passado de 1641.| [Colophon:] *En Madrid, Por Francisco Maroto, año de* 1642.| Folio, pp. (8). BA. 12802

Repertorio nacional formado por la oficina de estadistica, en conformidad del articulo 12 de la lei de 17 de setiembre de 1847. *Santiago: imprenta del progreso.* 1850. 8vo, 4 l., pp. 184, 36 l. 15 Tab. C. 12803

The Republic of Chili; its Present Position. *London; E. Wilson.* 1867. 12804

Sixteen Years in Chili and Peru, from 1822 to 1839. By the Retired Governor of Juan Fernandez. *London.* 1840. 8vo. 10 Portraits, and Engravings. C. 12805

Tarifa que debe rejir en las Aduanas de republica para el ano de 1845. *Valparaiso.* 1844. Folio. 12806

Teoria de un sistema administrativo y economico por la republica de Chile. *Santiago de Chile.* 1834. 4to. 12807

Three Years in Chili. *New York: Follett, Foster and Company.* 1863. 16mo, pp. viii, 158. C., H. 12808

CHILTON (T.) Mr. Chilton's Letters in Reply to Mr. Wickliffe, on the Expenditures of the last and present Administrations. *Washington City. 22d April,* 1830. 8vo, pp. 8. 12809

Also: A Circular Address ... to his Constituents, Feb. 27, 1837. *Washington.* 1831. 8vo, pp. 20. C.

Chilula: or, the Young Mexican. *Philadelphia: J. P. Skelly & Co.* 1867. 18mo, pp. 233. 12810

CHIMALPOPOCATL (D. F.) *See* Galicia (D. F. C.)

The Chimera: or the French Way of Paying National Debts, laid open. Being an Impartial Account of the Proceedings in France, for raising a Paper Credit, and settling the Mississippi Stock. *London: T. Warner.* 1720. 8vo, pp. 76. J.C.B.

Chimes of Freedom and Union. A Collection of Poems for the Times. *Boston.* 1861. 16mo, pp. 64. 12812

CHINA. Correspondence and Dispatches of the Ministers to China. [1860.] 8vo, pp. 624. (Senate. 36th Congress, 1st Session. Ex. Doc. No. 30.) H. 12813

Also: Message of the President of the United States, Dec. 20, 1858, communicating the Correspondence of Messrs. McLane and Parker, late Commissioners to China; Second Session, Thirty-fifth Congress, Executive Documents. *Washington.* 1859. 8vo. There are also other messages relating to Burlingame's treaty, etc.

CHINN (Thomas W.) Letter to Hon. Thomas Gibbs Morgan, President of the Whig Convention, Second Congressional District, Louisiana, 20th January, 1840. *Washington.* [n. d.] 8vo, pp. 14. 12814

CHINOOK. A Complete Dictionary of the Chinook Jargon; to which is added, Numerous Conversations, thereby enabling any person to speak the Chinook correctly. Third Edition. *Portland, O. T.* 1856. 24mo, pp. 24. 12815

CHIOKVYHIKOY, *pseudon.* Apocalypse de Chiokvyhikoy, chef des Iroquois, sauvages du Nord de l'Amérique. Ecrite par luimême vers l'an de l'Ere Chretienne, 1305, Traduite en François sur l'Original Iroquois. Avec un commentaire pour l'intelligence des endroits les plus difficiles du Texte. Soigneusement revu et corrigé sous les yeux de Congrés général des Colonies Unies. Publié par ordre du Congrés général. *Philadelphie, (La Haye).* 1777. 8vo, pp. 111. 12816

Relates to revolutionary events.

CHIPMAN (C.) Mineral Resources of Northern Mexico, by C. Chipman, ... *New York: Baker & Godwin.* 1868. 8vo, pp. 102. 12817

Also a report to the "Chihuahua and Sinaloa Gold and Silver Mining Association," 12mo, pp. 11.

CHIPMAN (D.) The Life of Hon. Nathaniel Chipman, LL.D., formerly Member of the United States Senate, and Chief Justice of the State of Vermont. With Selections from his Miscellaneous Papers. By his Brother, Daniel Chipman. *Boston: Charles C. Little and James Brown.* 1846. 8vo, pp. xii, 5–402. C., H.

CHIPMAN. The Life of Col. Seth Warner, with an Account of the Controversy between New York and Vermont, from 1763 to 1775. By Daniel Chipman .... *Burlington: C. Goodrich & Company.* 1858. 16mo, pp. 84. H., S. 12819

CHIPMAN. Memoir of Colonel Seth Warner. By Daniel Chipman, LL.D. To which is added, The Life of Colonel Ethan Allen, by Jared Sparks, LL.D. *Middlebury: L. W. Clark.* 1848. 16mo, pp. 226. BA. 12820

CHIPMAN. A Memoir of Thomas Chittenden, the First Governor of Vermont; with a History of the Constitution during his Administration. By Daniel Chipman, LL.D. *Middlebury: Printed for the Author.* 1849. 16mo, pp. 222. H., S.

Also: Speech delivered at Montpelier, Jan. 6, 1836. ... *Middlebury.* 1837, and Reports of Cases in the Supreme Court of Vermont.

CHIPMAN (J.) Seasonable Meditations for the Last Day of the Year. A Sermon Preach'd at the Lecture in Wenham, Dec. 31. 1728. By John Chipman, M.A. ... *Boston: Sam. Gerrish.* M,DCC,XXIX. 8vo, pp. (4), ii, 21. B., S. 12822

CHIPMAN (John Logan). Address, on the State of the Union, before the Detroit Democratic Association, Feb. 19, 1863. *Detroit: Free Press Office.* [1863.] 8vo, pp. 8. 12823

CHIPMAN (N.) Sketches of the Principles of Government; by Nathaniel Chipman, Judge of the Court of the United States, for the District of Vermont. *Rutland: From the Press of J. Lyon, Printed for the Author. June,* M,DCC,XCIII. 12mo, 2 l., pp. 292. BA., C. 12824

Reprinted as: Principles of Government: a Treatise on Free Institutions. Including the Constitution of the United States. By Nathaniel Chipman, LL.D. *Burlington.* 1833. 8vo, pp. viii, 330. H., S.

CHIPMAN (N. P.) Argument by N. P. Chipman in the Trial of Edmund E. Paulding, June, 1866. [1866.] 8vo.

[CHIPMAN, HOSMER, GILMORE, *and* BROWN.] Laws and Information relating to Claims Against the Government of the United States. *Washington, D. C.; McGill & Witherow, Printers.* 1866. 8vo, pp. 32. H. 12826

CHIPMAN (R. M.) The History of Harwinton, Connecticut. By R. Manning Chipman. *Hartford: Williams, Wiley & Turner.* 1860. 8vo, pp. 152. BA. 12827

CHIPMAN. Sketch of the Chipman Family ... by Rev. R. Manning Chipman of Wolcottville, Ct. [*Boston.* 1861.] 8vo, pp. 4. 12828

CHIPMAN (S.) Report of an Examination of Poor-Houses, Jails, &c. in the State of New York, and in the Counties of Berkshire, Massachusetts; Litchfield, Connecticut; and Bennington, Vermont, &c. By Samuel Chipman. *Albany.* 1834. 8vo, pp. 96. + Third Edition. *Albany.* 1835. 8vo, pp. 96. + Fourth Edition. *Albany.* 1836. 8vo, pp. 96. H. 12829

Also: Address, before the Ontario Agricultural Society. ... *Canandaigua.* 1824. 8vo, pp. 10. — The Temperance Lecturer; Being Facts gathered from a personal Examination of all the jails in the State of New-York ... *Albany.* 1845. 8vo, pp. 72.

[CHIPMAN (Ward).] Remarks upon the Disputed Points of Boundary under the Fifth Article of the Treaty of Ghent. Second Edition. *St. John, N. B.* 1839. 8vo, pp. 85, xxvii.

CHIPPEWA. Anamihe-masinahigan. | Jesus ot ijettwawin | gaye| amamihe-nakamunan | tukŏbihikatewan | mih' ejittwawăd | Ketolik-anamihădgek. | Rabekong ŏtenang | Trechette masinhaigmékka-winini entad | *Ibew Pipŏn.* 1839. Kaakko nikit Jesus. 12mo, pp. v, 209. 12831

The Gospel according to St. John. Translated into the Chippeway Tongue by John Jones, and Revised and corrected by Peter Jones, Indian Teachers. *London: Printed for the British and Foreign Bible Society, Instituted* MDCCCIV. 1831. 12mo.

There is also a title in Indian.

Kekitchemanitomenahn Gahbemakjeinnunk Jesus Christ, Oloashke Waww-ecndummahgawin: or, the New Testament in the Chippewa language. *Albany: Packard and Benthuysen.* 1833. 12mo, pp. 484. 12833

This translation is by Dr. Edwin James, assisted by John Tanner. At the end are the Ten Commandments, and a hymn in the Chippewa language.

Okikinoadi-mezinaigan, i. e. Spelling and Reading Book in the Chippeway language; containing Scripture histories of the Old and New Testament, with an addition of a few hymns. *Detroit.* 1852. 12mo, pp. 144. 12834

For a document on the removal of the Chippewas, Ottawas, &c., May 29, 1844, see document No. 519 of Congress for that year.

CHIQUITOS. Erbauliche und angenehme Geschichten derer Chiqvitos, und anderer von denen Patribus der Gesellschafft JEsu in Paraquaria neu-bekehrten Völcker; samt einem ausführlichen Bericht von dem Amazonen-Strom, wie auch einigen Nachrichten von der Landschaft Guiana, in der neuen Welt. Alles aus dem Spanisch-und Französischen in das Teutsche übersetzet, von einem aus erwehnter Gesellschaft. *Wien: Paul Straub.* 1729. 8vo, 8 l., pp. 744, 7 l. C. 12835

CHIRINO (Pedro). Relacion de las Islas Filipinas i de lo que en ellas han trabajado los Padres de la Compañia de Jesus. *Roma, Estevan Paulino,* 1604. 4to. 12836

Mr. Rich, No. 99, remarks, "The early history of the Philippines and Moluccas, from the accounts they furnish of the first voyages through the Straits of Magellan and into the Pacific Ocean, are entitled to a place in an American library."

CHISHOLM (C.) An Essay on the Malignant Pestilential Fever introduced into the West Indian Islands from Boullam, on the Coast of Guinea, As it appeared in 1793 and 1794. By C. Chisholm, M.D. Surgeon to His Majesty's Ordnance in Grenada. ... *London: C. Dilly.* 1795. 8vo, pp. xvi, 279. H. + To which is added, A Description of the American Yellow Fever, which prevailed at Charleston in 1748, In a Letter from Dr. John Lining. *Philadelphia: Thomas Dobson.* 1799. 8vo, pp. xvi, 308. BA. 12837

CHISHOLM. An Essay on the Malignant Pestilential Fever, introduced into the West Indian Islands from Boullam on the Coast of Guinea, as it appeared in 1793, 1794, 1795, and 1796. Interspersed with Observations and Facts, tending to prove that the Epidemic existing at Philadelphia, New-York, &c. was the same Fever introduced by Infection, imported from the West India Islands: ... By C. Chisholm, M.D. ... Second Edition, much enlarged. *London: J. Mawman.* 1801. 2 vols., 8vo, pp. vii, 519; vii, 486. BA., C. 12838

The introduction contains a description of Grenada, with meteorological, mineralogical, and botanical observations. *See* M. R., XIX. 62, and XXXVI. 569.

CHISHOLM. A Letter to John Haygarth, M.D. ... from Colin Chisholm, M.D. ... exhibiting Farther Evidence of the Infectious Nature of the Fatal Distemper in Granada, during 1793, 4, 5, and 6; and in the United States of America, from 1793 to 1805; in order to correct the Pernicious Doctrine ... [of] Dr. Edward Miller, and other American Physicians ... . *London: Joseph Mawman.* 1809. 8vo, 2 l., pp. 272. BA. 12839

CHISHOLM. A Manual of the Climate and Diseases of Tropical Eountries [*sic*] ... . By Colin Chisholm ... . *London: Burgess and Hill.* 1822. 8vo, Title, pp. ii, v, 2, 10 folded l., pp. 232. Plate. BA. 12840

CHISHOLM (C. R.) Chisholm's Hand-Book of Travel, and Tourist's Guide through Canada and the United States. With Fifty Illustrations and Maps. *Montreal: C. R. Chisholm & Bros.* 1866. 32mo, pp. iv, 205. BA. 12841

[CHISHOLME (David).] The Lower Canada Watchman. *Kingston.* [n. d.] 32mo. 12842

CHISHOLME. Observations on the Rights of the British Colonies to Representation in the Imperial Parliament. *Three Rivers, Ca.* 1832. 12mo. 12843

CHISLEY (B. C.) A Short Narrative of Benjamin Crompton Chisley or William Jones ... a Fugitive Slave from Maryland ... . *Manchester* [*Eng.*] 1851. 8vo, pp. 12. 12844

CHISLON. Major Soule. A Memorial of Alfred B. Soule, late Major of the Twenty-Third Regiment, Maine Volunteers. By Chislon. *Salem: Geo. W. Pease & Co.* 1866. 12mo, pp. 199. B. 12845

CHISOLM (J. J.) A Manual of Military Surgery, for the use of Surgeons in the Confederate Army; with an Appendix of the Rules and Regulations of the Confederate Army. By J. Julian Chisolm, M.D. ... *Richmond, Va.: West & Johnston.* 1861. 12mo, pp. xi, 447. B. 12846

Chispa Patriótica. *Puerto-Principe: imprenta de Serrano.* 1821. 8vo. 12847

Observacion crítico-legal que servirá de contestacion á la "Chispa Patriótica." *Puerto-Principe: imprenta de Serrano.* 1821.

CHITTENDEN (L. E.) A Report of the Debates and Proceedings in the Secret Sessions of the Conference Convention, for proposing Amendments to the Constitution of the United States, held at Washington, D. C., in February, A.D. 1861. By L. E. Chittenden, one of the Delegates. *New York: D. Appleton & Company.* 1864. 8vo, pp. 626. B., C. 12849

CHITTENDEN (N. W.) The Influence of Woman upon the Destinies of a People; being an Oration, with Salutatory Addresses, delivered at the Annual Commencement of Columbia College, October 3d, 1837. By Nathaniel W. Chittenden. *New-York.* 1837. 8vo, pp. 22. BA. 12850

CHITTENDEN (T.) Remonstrance of the Council of Vermont against the resolve of Congress, 5 Dec., 1782. By Thomas Chittenden, of Bennington, Vt. *Hartford.* 1783. 12mo.

CHITTY (Joseph). Practical Treatise on the Law of Nations, relative to the Legal Effect of War on the Commerce of Belligerents and Neutrals; and on Orders in Council and Licenses. *Boston.* 1812. 8vo. 12852

CHIVALRY. A Voluntary and Independent Chivalry in the United States, a Desideratum of the Age. *Charleston: A. J. Burke, Printer.* 1852. 8vo, pp. 32. H. 12853

Chivalry, ... and Young America. *See* [Burke], Vol. III., No. 9310.

CHIVERS (Thomas Holly). Nacoochee; or, the Beautiful Star, with Other Poems. *New York.* 1837. 12mo, pp. x, (2), 143. H. 12854

Also: The Lost Pleiad and other Poems. *New York.* 1845. 8vo, pp. 32.—Memoralia; or, Phials of Amber Full of the Tears of Love. *Philadelphia.* 1853. 12mo, pp. 168.—The Sons of Usna. *Philadelphia.* 1858. 8vo, pp. 92.—Virginalia; or Songs of my Summer Nights. *Philadelphia.* 1853. 12mo, pp. 132. And other poems.

[CHIVINGTON (J. M.)] To the People of Colorado. Synopsis of the Sand Creek Investigation. Denver, Colorado, June, 1865. [n. p. n. d.] 8vo, pp. 17. H. 12855

CHOATE (D. L.) Circuit Court of the United States. Massachusetts District, ss. In Admiralty. Daniel L. Choate et al., Libellants, vs Francis B. Crowninshield, Respondent. Record. ... *Boston: Alfred Mudge & Son, Printers.* 1867. 8vo, pp. 87.

CHOATE (J.) Reasons of Dissent from the Judgment of a Council, respecting the Doctrines of Rev. Mr. Bacheller. By Col. John Choate. *Portsmouth.* 1760. 8vo, pp. 17. 12857

CHOATE (R.) A Discourse delivered before the Faculty, Students and Alumni of Dartmouth College, on the day preceding Commencement, July 27, 1853, Commemorative of Daniel Webster. By Rufus Choate ... *Boston and Cambridge: James Munroe and Company.* 1853. 8vo, pp. 100. P., H. + Eighth Thousand. [*Id.*] 8vo, pp. 88. 12858

CHOATE. The Duty of Conservative Whigs in the Present Crisis. A Letter to the Hon. Rufus Choate, by a Conservative Whig. ... *Boston.* 1856. 8vo, pp. 21. BA. 12859

CHOATE. The Works of Rufus Choate with a Memoir of his Life. By Samuel Gilman Brown, Professor in Dartmouth

College. ... *Boston: Little, Brown and Company.* 1862. 2 vols., 8vo, pp. xi, 558; iv, 523. BA., C. 12860

Also: Hon. Rufus Choate on the Presidential Question. "*Boston Courier*" (*Whig*). *August* 14, 1856. 8vo, pp. 8.—Application of Robert Codman and others, for a Railroad between South Dedham and Boston ... Speech ... before a Legislative Committee, Boston, March 26, 1850. ... *Boston.* 1850. 8vo, pp. 40.—Speech ... on the Question of the Removal of the Deposites ... March 28, 1824. *Washington.* 1834. 8vo, pp. 28.— ... Speech ... before the Joint Legislative Committee on Towns, Boston, April 4, 1851. *Boston: George C. Rand & Company.* 1851. 8vo, pp. 42. H.—Speech ... on the Case of Alexander McLeod. Delivered in the Senate ... June 11, 1841. *Washington.* 1841. 8vo, pp. 16. H.—Speech ... on the Power and Duty of Congress to continue the Policy of Protecting American Labour; delivered in the Senate ... March 14, 1842. *Washington.* 1842. 8vo, pp. 36. H.—Speech ... on the Bill to provide Further Remedial Justice in the Courts of the U. States, Delivered in the Senate ... May, 1842. *Washington.* 1842. 8vo, pp. 28. BA.—Speech ... on the Question of annulling the Convention for the Common Occupation of the Territory of Oregon; and in Reply to Mr. Buchanan. Delivered in the Senate ... March 21, 1844. *Washington.* 1844. 8vo, pp. 34. BA.—Speech ... on the Subject of protecting American Labor, by Duties on Imports. ... Senate of the United States, ... April, 1844. *Washington.* 1844. 8vo, pp. 52. H.—Abstract of the Arguments of ... the Petitioners ... for a Railroad from Salem to Malden. ... *Boston.* 1846. 8vo, pp. 60, xv.— ... Speech ... before the Joint Legislative Rail Road Committee, Boston, Feb. 28, 1851. ... *Boston: J. M. Hewes & Co.* 1851. 8vo, pp. 25. H.

CHOCOLATE. The Natural History of Chocolate: being a Distinct and Particular Account of the Cocoa-Tree, its Growth and Culture; and the Preparation, Excellent Properties and Medicinal Virtues of its Fruit. Translated from the Last Edition of the French. By R. Brookes, M.D. Second Edition. *London: J. Roberts.* 1730. 8vo, 8 l., pp. 95. J.C.B. 12861

Also: Opusculum de Qualitate et Natura Chocolatæ; ... *Nurembergæ.* 1644.

CHOCTAW. Acts and Resolutions of the General Council of the Choctaw Nation, from 1852, to 1857, both inclusive; Published by Authority of the General Council. *Fort Smith.* 1858. 8vo. C. 12862

Choctaw; The Acts of the Apostles Translated into the Choctaw Language. [By Rev. Cyrus Byington.] *Boston.* 1839. 12mo, pp. 165. 12863

The Books of Joshua, Judges, and Ruth, translated into the Choctaw Language. *New York: American Bible Society.* 1852. 12mo, pp. 151. 12864

Chahta Holisso, it im Anumpuli; or, the Choctaw Reader. For the use of native schools. *Union: printed for the American Board of Commissioners for Foreign Missions, by John F. Wheeler.* 1836. 12mo, pp. 123. 12865

Chahta Ikhananchi, or the Choctaw Instructor; containing a brief summary of Old Testament History and Biography; with Practical Reflections in the Choctaw Language. By a Missionary. *Utica.* 1831. 12mo. 12866

Chahta vba isht taloa holisso, or Choctaw Hymn-book. *Boston: Crocker and Brewster.* 1830. 12mo, pp. 108. + Second Edition revised and much enlarged. [*Ibid.*] 1833. 18mo. + Third Edition, revised. [*Ibid.*] 1835. 12mo, pp. 72. + Fourth Edition. *New York: S. W. Benedict.* 1851. 18mo, 2 l., pp. 248. C. 12867

Another edition was printed in *Utica.* 1831.

Chahta Na-Holhtina: or Choctaw Arithmetic. *Boston.* 1835. 12mo. 12868

The Choctaw Girl: Written for the American Sunday School Union ... *Philadelphia.* [n. d.] 18mo, pp. 16. 12869

Choctaw Spellingbook, with Prayers and other Matters added. *Boston.* 1835. 12mo. 12870

The Choctaws and their Debts, due Joseph G. Heald and Reuben Wright. *Washington: McGill & Witherow, Printers.* [n. d.] 8vo, pp. 20. H. 12871

The First and Second Books of Samuel, and First Book of Kings, translated into the Choctaw language. Samuel i holisso ummona, atukla itatuklo, micha miko uhleha isht anumpa ummona [etc.] hoke. *New York: American Bible Society.* 1852. 12mo, pp. 256. C. 12872

Gospel according to Matthew, translated into the Choctaw language. Ubanumpa mahlu vt holissocchi tok. [With alphabet.] *Boston: Am. Board For. Miss.* 1842. 16mo, pp. 198. C.

Holisso Holitopa. [Choctaw Bible Stories.] *Utica.* 1831. 12mo. 12874

The New Testament [etc.] translated into the Choctaw Language. Pin chitokaka pi okchalinchi Chisus Klaist in testament himona, [etc.] *New York: American Bible Society.* 1848. 12mo, pp. 818. + [*Ibid.*] 1854. 12mo, pp. 818. 12875

A Spelling-book written in the Chahtah Language, with an English translation. Second Edition, revised. *Cincinnati: Printed by Morgan, Dodge, and Fisher.* 1827. 8vo. 12876

Treaty of Limits between the United States and the Choctaw Nation of Indians. January 30, 1808. 12877

Ulla i Katikisma: or Child's Catechism in Choctaw: being a translation of Dr. Watts Second Catechism for Children. Second Edition. Revised. *Boston: ... Crocker & Brewster.* 1835. 8vo, pp. 16. 12878

Also: "Family Education and Government. 1835;" "On the Sabbath;" and "Triumphant Deaths of Pious Children. In the Choctaw language. *Boston.* 1835." 18mo. Cong. Doc. No. 149, for 1845, relates to the Choctaws.

The Choice. *See* [Church (B.)]

Choice Collection of Papers relating to State Affairs during the late Revolution. Vol. I. *London.* 1703. 8vo. 12879

Includes a Defence of the Scots settlement at Darien, an Enquiry into the causes of the miscarriage of the Scots colony at Darien, etc. Title from J. R. Smith's catalogue.

Choice Dialogues. *See* [Checkley (John)]., Vol., III., No. 12361, and add pp. viii, 46.

Choix des Lettres édifiantes. *See* [Montmignon (J. B.)]

CHON. Essai sur Washington. Par M. Chon. Deuxième partie. *Lille: imp. Danel.* 1863. 8vo, pp. 20. 12880

Reprinted from the "Mém. de la Soc. imp. de Lille."

CHOPIN (J. M.) A la mémoire de Mme Faubert, et aux Haïtiens qui la regrettent. *Paris: impr. de Chaigneau jeune.* 1825. 8vo, pp. 8. 12881

CHOPIN. Ode sur l'indépéndance d'Haïti. *Paris: imp. de Lachevardière.* 1825. 8vo, pp. 4. 12882

CHOQUEHUANCA (J. D.) Ensayo de estadistica completa de los ramos economico politicos de la provincia de Azangaro en el departemento de Puno, de la Republica Peruana, del quinquenio contado desde 1825 hasta 1829 inclusive. Formado por el Ciudadano Josè Domingo Choquehuanca, Diputado que fue de la M. H. J. Departamental de Puno. *Lima: Manuel Carral.* 1833. Folio, 1 l., pp. 72. 12883

CHORIS (L.) Voyage Pittoresque autour du Monde, des Portraits de sauvages d'Amérique, d'Asia, d'Afrique ... leurs armes, leurs habillemens, etc. des paysages et des vues maritimes, plusieurs objets d'histoire naturelle, telle que mammifères et oiseaux, accompagnés de description par M. le Baron Cuvier, et M. A. de Chamisso, et d'observations sur les crânes humains, par M.

le Docteur Gall. Le tout dessiné par M. Louis Choris, peintre; dans le voyage qu'il a fait de 1815, 1816, 1817, et 1818, sur le brick le Rurick, commandé par M. Otto Kotzebue ... . *Paris: L. Choris* [*A. Bertrand*]. 1821–22. Folio. 110 Plates. B., C.

"A general explanation, containing the most memorable facts of the voyage, the description of places, observations on the inhabitants, as well as a map of the route of the Rurick, accompanies this volume; it appeared in 22 livraisons."—QUÉRARD.

CHORIS. Vues et paysages des régions équinoxiales, recueillis dans un voyage autour du Monde, avec une introduction et un texte explicatif. Par Louis Choris. *Paris: l'Auteur; J. Renouard; Treuttel et Würtz; A. Bertrand.* 1826. Sm. folio. 24 Plates. B. 12885

Published at 50 francs, or with the plates colored, 90 francs, and on large paper, 120 francs.

CHORLTON (W.) The American Grape Grower's Guide. ... By William Chorlton. *New York.* 1859. 12mo. 12886

CHORLTON. The Cold Grapery, from Direct American Practice. *New York.* M.DCCC.LIII. 12mo, pp. 95. B., H. 12887

A Chorographical and statistical description of Columbia. *See* [Warden (D. B.)]

CHOTTEAU (L.) Les Américains d'aujourd'hui. I. Le président Andrew Johnson. Par Léon Chotteau. *Paris: Retaux.* 1868. 8vo, pp. 31. 12888

CHOTTEAU. Le président Ulysse Grant et son Vice-Président. 2e édition. *Paris.* 1869. 12889

CHOULES (John Overton). A Sermon upon the Death of the Hon. Daniel Webster, delivered in the North Baptist Church, Newport, R. I., November 21, 1852. By J. O. Choules. *New York: Evans & Brittan.* 1852. 8vo, pp. 24. 12890

Also: Address, delivered at the Opening of the Twenty-First Annual Fair of The American Institute ... . Newport, R. I. *New York.* 1848. 8vo, pp. 13. BA.—An Oration delivered in the German Reformed Church, Red-Hook, New-York, July 4th, 1826. ... *New York.* 1826. 8vo, pp. 15.—The Oration on the Fourteenth Anniversary of the American Institute. ... October, 1841. *New York: printed by J. Van Norden & Co.* 1842. 8vo, pp. 31. *See* Hinton (J. H.)

CHOULES *and* SMITH. The Origin and History of Missions; a Record of the Voyages, Travels, Labours, and Successes of the various Missionaries who have been sent forth by Protestant Societies and Churches to evangelize the Heathen; ... by the Rev. John O. Choules, New Bedford, Mass., and the Rev.

Thomas Smith, late Minister of Trinity Chapel, London. Fourth Edition. *Boston. Oct.,* 1837. 2 vols., 4to, pp. 622; 610. + Sixth Edition. *Boston.* 1842. 2 vols., 4to. + *New York.* 1846. 2 vols., 4to, pp. xxii, 622; xiv, 610. + Ninth Edition. *New York: R. Carter and Brothers.* 1851. 2 vols., 4to, pp. 622; 610. 26 Plates. 12891

CHOVEL (Rafael). Diario de viage de la Comision de Limites que puso el gobierno de la republica, bajo la direccion de Exmo. Sr. general de division Manuel de Mier y Teran. *Mexico: Juan R. Navarro.* 1850. 8vo, pp. 298. 12892

Christ Church Hospital. *See* Philadelphia.

Christ in the Army. A Selection of the Sketches of the work of the United States Sanitary Commission, by various writers. Necessity, Organization, Principles, Sources of Supply. In the Camp, the Hospitals, Field Hospitals, at the Front, on the Battle Field, Prisoners. On the Moral Results of this War. *For the Christian Commission.* 1865. 18mo, pp. 144.

Les chretiens protestants de France à tous leurs frères des États-Unis d' Amérique, salut et paix en Jésus-Christ. [Question de l'esclavage.] *Paris: imper. Mme Smith.* 1857. Sm. folio, pp. 17. 12894

[CHRISTIAN (Charles).] A Brief Treatise on the Police of the City of New York. By a Citizen. *New York.* 1812. 8vo, pp. 32. N., S. 12895

CHRISTIAN. (F.) Letters from Mr. Fletcher Christian, containing a Narrative of the Transactions on Board His Majesty's Ship Bounty, before and after the Mutiny, with his Subsequent Voyages and Travels in South America. *London.* 1796. 8vo. 12896

This curious work is quite at variance with the ordinary account, according to which Christian was killed by the natives soon after the mutiny.

CHRISTIAN (Joseph). Speech of Joseph Christian on the "Oyster Fundum" Bill, delivered in the Senate of Virginia, on Wednesday, February 8th, 1860. *Richmond.* 1860. 8vo, pp. 22.

CHRISTIAN (L. H.) Our Present Position. A Thanksgiving Discourse, delivered in the North Presbyterian Church, Philadelphia, November 27, 1862, by the Pastor, Rev. L. H. Christian, D.D. *Philadelphia: William S. & Alfred Martien.* 1852. 8vo, pp. 46. 12898

[CHRISTIAN (*Capt.*)] All Gentlemen Sailors ... . *Printed by J. Humphreys, Philadelphia: Issued Dec. 25th*, 1777. 4to, p. 1.

Advertisement of Capt. Christian, of H. M. S. Vigilant, for recruits.

Christian Advocate; being a Continuation of the Presbyterian Magazine. Conducted by A. Green, D.D. *Philadelphia.* 1823. 8vo. Continued. 12899*a*

Christian Alliance. Its Constitution ... and Address. *New York.* 1843. 8vo, pp. 16. 12900

The Christian Almanack; Or, New-England Religious Astronomical Diary, For ... 1821. ... *Boston: Lincoln & Edwards.* [n. d.] 12mo, pp. 48. Continued. BA. 12901

The words, "Or, New-England," etc., were omitted after the first number. The numbers for 1821–23 published by the New England Tract Society; the following numbers by the American Tract Society:

Christian Almanac. For Maryland and Virginia, for the Year 1828. *Baltimore.* [n. d.] 12mo, pp. 36. 12902

The Christian Banner. *Fredericksburg, Va. June* 18, 1862. + Vol. I. No. 11. *July* 2, 1862. Folio. 12903

Printed on brown paper.

The Christian Baptist. Published monthly. Edited by A. Campbell. *Buffalo Creek, Brook Co., Va.* 2 vols., 8vo, pp. 300; 288. 12904

The organ of the sect known as the Disciples. *See* Vol. III., No. 10206.

Christian Commission for the Army and Navy of the United States of America. (Address and Circular.) *Philadelphia: Ringwalt & Brown.* 1862. 16mo, pp. 32. H. 12905

The Christian Confession. Of the Faith of the Harmless Christians in the Netherlands, known by the name of Memnonists. *Amsterdam, Printed; and Reprinted, and sold by Andrew Bradford, in Philadelphia, in the year* 1727. Sm. 8vo. 12906

Some of this sect settled in Pennsylvania.

A Christian Conversing. *See* [Mather (C.)]

Christian Directions and Instructions for Negroes. *London.* 1789. 12mo, pp. 156. 12907

The Christian Disciple, published monthly. Vol. I. For 1813. [Edited by Noah Worcester.] ... *Boston.* 1813. 8vo, 2 l., pp. 256. 12908

Vol. VI., 1818; continued as

The Christian Disciple and Theological Review. New Series. *Boston.* 1819–23. 5 vols., 8vo. 12909

Continued as

The Christian Examiner and Theological Review. 1824–28. 5 vols., 8vo. 12910

Continued as

The Christian Examiner and General Review. Vol. VI.–XXXV. ... *Boston.* 1829–43. 12911

In 1844, when it was united with the "Monthly Miscellany," and continued as

The Christian Examiner and Religious Miscellany. Vol. XXXVI.–LXXIX. *Boston.* 1844–65. + Vol. LXXX.–LXXXVII. *New York.* 1866–69. 8vo. 12912

In 1870, merged in "Old and New."

The Christian Doctrine and Society of the Quakers cleared from the Reproach of the late Division of a Few in Some Parts of America. *London.* 1693. 16mo. P. 12913

The Christian Faith | Of the People of God, called in Scorn, | Quakers | In Rhode-Island (who are in Unity with all faithfull Brethren | of the same Profession in all parts of the World) | Vindicated | From the Calumnies of Christian Lodowick, that formerly | was of that Profession, but is lately fallen there-from. | As also from the base Forgeries, and wicked Slanders of | Cotton Mather, called a Minister, at Boston, who hath greatly | commended the said Christian Lodowick, and approved his false | Charges against us, and hath added thereunto many gross, | impudent and vile Calumnies against us and our Brethren, in his | late Address, so called, to some in New-England, the which in | due time may receive a more full answer, to discover his Igno- | rance, Prejudice and Perversion against our Friends in gene- | ral, and G. K. in particular, whom he hath most unworthily | abused. | To which is added, some Testimonies of our Antient | Friends to the true Christ of God; Collected out of their print- | ed Books, for the further Convincing of our Opposers, that it | is (and hath been) our constant and firm Belief to expect Salva- | tion by the Man Christ Jesus that was outwardly crucified without | the Gates of Jerusalem. | *Printed and Sold by William Bradford at Philadelphia in Pennsyl- | vania, in the Year* 1692. | 4to, pp. 3–16. 12914

The Christian History. *See* Prince (T.), *Jr.*

The Christian Indian; or, Times of the First Settlers. ... (The First of a Series of American Tales.) *New York: Collins and Hannay.* 1825. 18mo, pp. 251. BA. 12915

Christian Inquirer — devoted to the support of Free Inquiry, Religious Liberty, and Rational Christianity. New Series. *New York.* 1826. 8vo. 12916

Christian Journal and Literary Register. *New York: T. & J. Swords.* 1817–30. 14 vols., 8vo. N. 12917

The Christian Letter to Presbyterian, Church, & Quaker. *Philadelphia: Printed by Anthony Armbruster.* 1765. 12mo, pp. 12. P. 12918

The Christian Orator; or, a Collection of Speeches delivered before Religious Benevolent Societies. By a Gentleman of Massachusetts. Third Edition. *Charlestown: S. Etheridge.* 1819. 18mo, pp. 298. C. 12919

Christian Rapture. A Poem. *Boston.* 1747. 4to. 12920

The Christian Register, and Moral and Theological Review. Edited by the Rev. Thomas Y. How, D.D. *New York.* 1817. 8vo. 12921

Christian Review. *New York.* 1836. 8vo. Continued.

The Christian Review. Vol. I. Edited by James D. Knowles. *Boston: Gould, Kendall & Lincoln. Utica, N. Y.: Bennett & Bright.* 1836. 8vo, pp. viii, 5–634. Continued to 1863.

Christian Scholar's and Farmer's Magazine: by a number of Gentlemen. *Elizabethtown, N. J.* 1789–90. 2 vols., 8vo.

The Christian Spectator, conducted by an Association of Gentlemen, For the Year 1819. [Monthly.] Volume I. *New Haven: Howe & Spalding.* [n. d.] 8vo, pp. iv, 670. BA.

Continued to 1828. New Series. Vol. II., after which it became "The Quarterly Christian Spectator," and was continued to Vol. X., 1838.

The Christian Year Book: containing a Summary of Christian Work and the Results of Missionary Effort throughout the World. ... *London: Jackson, Walford, and Hodder.* MDCCCLXVII. 16mo, pp. viii, 357. B. 12926

Contains notices of missions in North and South America.

Christiana. December 6. 1771. Christiana-Bridge Land & Cash Lottery, in New Castle County, on Delaware. ... *Wilmington: Printed by James Adams.* [1771.] Folio, broadside. P.

Also: Christiana Bridge, March 23. 1771. The Adventurers in the Second Class of the New-Ark Land and Cash Lottery, &c. 4to, p. 1. P. — Christiana Bridge, July 13. 1771. New-Castle Lottery, Instituted by the Friends of the American China Manufactory, &c. Folio, p. 1. P.

Report of Attorney General Brent, to his Excellency Gov. Lowe, in relation to the Christiana Treason Trials, in the Circuit Court of the United States, held at Philadelphia. *Annapolis: Thomas E. Martin, printer.* 1852. 8vo, pp. 12. 12928

The Christian's New and Complete Family Bible. *Philadelphia: Wm. Woodhouse.* 1790. 12929

Published in numbers. From O'Callaghan's list, who had not seen it. Title from the "Pennsylvania Packet," Nov. 15, 1788, etc.

The Christian's Duty to render to Cæsar, the Things that are Cæsar's, considered; With Regard to the Payment of the present Tax of Sixty Thousand Pounds, granted to the King's Use. In which all the Arguments for the non-payment thereof are examined and refuted. Addressed to the Scrupulous among the People called Quakers. By a Lover of his King and Country. *Philadelphia: Printed in the Year* MDCCLVI. 8vo, pp. over 24.

Christianity, versus Treason and Slavery. Religion rebuking Sedition. *Philadelphia.* [n. d.] 8vo, pp. 16. 12931

CHRISTIE (A. J.) The Emigrant's Assistant, or Remarks on the Agricultural Interests of the Canadas. ... With an Appendix. ... *Montreal.* 1821. 2 vols., 12mo. C. 12932

For the title at length, *see* Morgan's "Bib. Canad.," p. 75.

CHRISTIE (J.) Case of James Christie, Jun., late of the Province of Maryland, Merchant. [Not published. n. p. 1775?] 8vo, pp. 24. 12933

CHRISTIE. State of the Accounts of John Christie, Esq. Collector of Excise, Chester County. From the 26th August, 1783, to 1st October, 1784. *Philadelphia: Printed by John Steele.* M,DCC,LXXXV. 8vo, pp. 6. P. 12934

Also for 1780. 8vo, pp. 5. P.

CHRISTIE (Robert). Brief Review of the Political State of Lower Canada, since the Conquest of the Colony to the Present Day, to which are added, Memoirs of the Administrations of the

Colonial Government of Lower Canada, &c., by Sir Gordon Drummond, and Sir John Coape Sherbrooke. *New York: W. A. Mercein.* 1818. 8vo, pp. 92. 12935

CHRISTIE. A History of the late Province of Lower Canada, Parliamentary and Political, from the Commencement to the close of its existence as a Separate Province. By Robert Christie. In Five Volumes. *Quebec.* 1848–1854. 12mo. [A Sixth Volume.] *Quebec.* 1855. 12mo, pp. 55. C. + [Reissued with new Title-Pages.] *Montreal: R. Worthington.* 1866. 6 vols., 12mo, 2 l., pp. xiv, 360; 2 l., pp. 396; pp. xi, 564; pp. iv, 548; pp. vii, 442; pp. 468. 12936

CHRISTIE. Interesting Public Documents and Official Correspondence, Illustrative of, and Supplemental to the History of Lower Canada. By Robert Christie. *Montreal.* 1855. 12mo.

This is volume IV. of the previous work, with a separate title-page.

CHRISTIE. Memoirs of the Administration of the Colonial Government of Lower Canada, by Sir James Henry Craig and Sir Geo. Prevost. From the Year 1807 until the Year 1815. Comprehending the Military and Naval Operations in the Canadas during the Late War with the United States of America. By Robert Christie. *Quebec.* 1818. 8vo, pp. 150, 9. 12938

"These memoirs are very interesting, and, although intended to please the ruling power, impartially written." — LATERRIÈRE. Reprinted in New York, with the following title:

CHRISTIE. The Military and Naval Operations in the Canadas, during the late War with the United States. Including also, The Political History of Lower Canada during the Administrations of Sir James Henry Craig and Sir George Provost. From the Year 1807 until the Year 1815. By Robert Christie, Esq. *Quebec, printed. New York, re-printed.* 1818. 12mo, pp. 235. P. 12939

[CHRISTIE (William).] A Speech delivered at the Grave of the Revd. Joseph Priestley, LL.D. ... Who died ... February VI. MDCCCIV. ... *Northumberland in Pennsylvania: printed by Andrew Kennedy.* MDCCCIV. 8vo, pp. 28. H. 12940

CHRISTIE (W. C.) Notes on Brazilian Questions. By W. D. Christie ... . *London and Cambridge: Macmillan and Co.* 1865. Crown 8vo, pp. lxxi, 236. BA. 12941

CHRISTMAS (H.) The Emigrant Churchman in Canada, By a Pioneer of the Wilderness. Edited by the Rev. Henry Christ-

mas. *London: Richard Bentley.* 1849. 2 vols., post 8vo, pp. xvi, 372; xi, 326. 4 Plates. C., P. 12942

Reissued with the following title:

CHRISTMAS. Canada in 1849. Pictures of Canadian Life; or, the Emigrant Churchman. By A Pioneer of the Wilderness. Edited by the Rev. H. Christmas, M.D. In Two Volumes. *London: Richard Bentley.* 1850. 2 vols., post 8vo, pp. xvi, 372; xi, 326. 4 Plates. 12943

CHRISTMAS (J. S.) Valedictory Admonitions or a Farewell Letter, addressed to the American Presbyterian Society, of Montreal, L. C. By J. S. Christmas ... . *New-York: printed by E. Conrad.* 1828. 8vo, pp. 36. H. 12944

Christmas, 1863. "A rare Bohemian, full of jests and fancies." Old Play. The Bohemian. Price One Dollar. *Richmond, Va.: G. W. Gary, Printer.* No. 1. pp. 40. 12945

A second number issued tri-weekly, if this succeeds.

Christmas Scenes in New York, and other Stories. Illustrated. *New York.* 1868. 18mo, pp. 62, 64. 12946

CHRISTOPHER (R. L.) The New-York Business-man's Companion. *New York.* 1849. 12mo, pp. 96. 12947

CHRISTOPHILOS, *pseudonym.* Review of Rev. Mr. Cushman's "Calm Review of the Measures employed in the Religious Awakening in Boston, in 1842." By Christophilos. *Boston.* 1846. 8vo, pp. 56. H. 12948

CHRISTOPHORO D' AVALOS (F. A.) Essai sur le commerce et les intérêts de l'Espagne et de ses colonies. *Paris: Brissot-Thivars.* 1819. 8vo. 12949

[CHRISTY (David).] Cotton is King; or, the Culture of Cotton, and its relation to Agriculture, Manufactures, and Commerce; to the Free Colored People, and to those who hold that Slavery in itself is Sinful. By an American. *Cincinnati: Moore, Wilstach & Co.* 1855. 12mo, pp. 210. + Second Edition, revised and enlarged. *New York.* 1856. 12mo. C. 12950

CHRISTY. Letters on Geology ... originally addressed to Dr. John Locke ... giving an Outline of the Geology of the West and the South West ... with an Essay on the Erratic Rocks of North America ... . By David Christy. *Rossville: J. M. Christy, Printer.* 1848. 12mo, pp. 68, 2 l., pp. 11. 6 Plates. B. 12951

CHRISTY. Ethiopia: her Gloom and Glory, as illustrated in the History of the Slave Trade and Slavery, the Rise of the Republic of Liberia, and the Progress of African Missions. By David Christy ... . With an Introduction. By W. P. Strickland ... . *Cincinnati: Rickey, Mallory & Webb.* 1857. 8vo, pp. 255. BA., C. 12952

A Lecture on African Civilization ... and the Relations of American Slavery to African Civilization. ... By David Christy ... . *Cincinnati: printed by J. A. & U. P. James.* 1850. 8vo, pp. 52. H. 12953

CHRISTY. Pulpit Politics; or, Ecclesiastical Legislation on Slavery, in its Disturbing Influences on the American Union. *Cincinnati.* 1862. 8vo, pp. 624. + Fifth Edition. *Cincinnati.* 1863. 8vo. 12954

Also: A Lecture on the Present Relations of Free Labor to Slave Labor. ... *Columbus.* 1853. — Lectures on African Colonization, and kindred subjects. *Columbus: J. H. Riley & Co.* 1853. 12mo.

CHRISTY (Edwin P.) Plantation Melodies. *Philadelphia.* 1851. Nos. I. to V. 12955

Also: Christy's New Songster; Christy's Essence of Old Kentucky. 18mo. — Surrogate's court, county of New York, in the matter of the last will and testament of Edwin P. Christy. *New York: J. W. Bell.* 1864–65. 3 vols., 8vo.

CHRISTY (W.) Proceedings in the Case of the United States versus William Christy, on a Charge of having set on foot A Military Expedition, in New Orleans, against the Territory of Mexico, in November, 1835, containing The Evidence taken on the Examination before Judge Rawle, and other documents connected with the accusation. *New Orleans: Benjamin Levy.* MDCCCXXXVI. 8vo, pp. 55. 12956

Chronica Beschrei- | bung vnd gemeyne anzeyge, Vonn | aller Wellt herkommen, Fürnämen | Lannden, Stande, Eygenschafften, | historien, wesen, manier, sitten, an vnd abgang. Auszden glaubuir | digsten Historiē, On all Glo | se vnd Züsatz, Nach Hi- | storischer Wartheit | beschriben. | *Getruckt zu Franckenfort am Meyn* | *Bei Christian Egenolffen.* | [At the end], M.D.XXXV. *Im Augustmen.* Folio, Title, 5 unnumbered l., Text, CXXXVII l. Woodcut. 12957

Valuable as exhibiting the great geographical discoveries of the fifteenth and sixteenth centuries. On the verso of CIII, the writer treats "Von America dem vierdten Theyl der Welt, Anno M . CCCC XCVII . erfunden." There are also other references to the discoveries of Columbus, Vespucius, Cortes, etc. "We are of impression that the present is a later edition of Henrich Steinhowel's Chronicle, of which the Kloss Catalogue mentions one dated Frankfort, 1531." — HARRISSE. *See* Græsse, II. 140.

Chronica del muy esclavescido. *See* [Nunez (J.)]

Chronica ordinis Sancti Francisci, observantiæ strictioris per Christianum orbem et Americam, Peru, Chinas, Japones, Indos, Chichimecas, etc. diffusæ. *Ingolstadii.* 1625. 4to. 12958

Title from Ternaux-Compans, No. 483. *See also* [Schedel (H.)]

Chronicon, das ist Beschreibung der Occidentalischen und Indianischen Ländern, etc. *Wittenberg: Zacharias Lehmann.* 1606. 4to, pp. 15, 527. J.C.B. 12959

A translation of Benzoni's "Hist. Ind. Occid," by Scherdiger. Forms Part IV., V., and VI., of De Bry's "Grands Voyages."

Chronicles of B***g, the Son of the Great B***g that lived in the Reign of Queen Felicia. By Israel Ben Ader. *Boston.* 1757. 8vo. W. 12960

The Chronicle of Sirrom. *See* [Morris].

The Chronicle of the Kingdom of Cassituides, under the Reign of the House of Lunen. A Fragment. Translated from an ancient Manuscript. *London: J. Wilkie.* 1783. 8vo.

A history of the American war, in the style of Jewish history. *See* M. R., LXVIII. 370.

The Chronicle of the Kings of England. *See* [Dodsley (R).]

Chronicles of Casco Bay. *See* [Colesworthy (D.)]

Chronicles of Cooperstown. *See* [Cooper (J. F.)]

Chronicles of Mount Benedict. A Tale of the Ursuline Convent. ... *Boston.* 1837. 24mo, pp. xv, 191. H. 12962

Chronicles of Pineville. Embracing Sketches of Georgia Scenes, &c. *Philadelphia.* 1850. 12mo. C. 12963

Chronicles of the Fire-Eaters of the Tribe of Mississippi. By Seriah the Scribe. *Brandon.* 1853. 8vo, pp. 38. H. 12964

Chronicles of the Great Rebellion against the United States of America; a Concise [Chronological] Record and Digest of Events, April 23, 1860 — Oct. 31, 1865. *Philadelphia: A. Winch.* 1867. 8vo. pp. 136. 12965

Chronicles of the North American Savages. Vol. I. No. I. May, 1835. [1835.] + No. 2. June, 1835. 8vo. 12966

Chronicles of the Old South Ch.. rch. *See* Boston, Vol. II., No. 6662.

Chronicles of Turkeytown, or the Works of Jeremy Peters. First Series. *Philadelphia.* 1829. 12mo. 12967

Chroniques judiciaires françaises et étrangères. John Brown. Condamnation à mort, par Alphonse Pagès. ... Assassination de la fille du président Geffrard. ... *Paris: Havard.* 1860. 8vo, pp. 47. 12968

Chronological Account of Remarkable Occurrences from the Commencement of the French Revolution to Dec. 1815. Extracted from the Belfast News Letter. *Belfast: Mackay.* 1816. 12mo, pp. xi, 324. 12969

Relates some events of the War of 1812.

Chronological Record of the Remarkable Public Events during the reigns of George III and IV. *London.* 1826. 8vo. 12970

Chronological Tables of History. *See* [Talboys (D. A.)]

Chronologie septenaire. *See* [Cayet (Pierre Victor.)]

Chrysal; or the Adventures of a Guinea. *See* [Johnstone (Charles)].

Chrystal Fount; or, Songs for the Sons and Daughters of Temperance. *New York.* 1854. 18mo. 12971

Chubbuck (Emily.) *See* Judson (Emily).

Chumacero y Carrillo (Juan), *and* Pimentel (D.) Memorial al Papa Urbano VIII., sobre los excessos que se cometen en Roma contra los naturales de estos Reynos de España: trad. de italiano en castellano. 1633. 4to, pp. 232. s. 12972

Chumasero (John C.) Address, ... July 4, 1853. *Le Roy: New York.* 1853. 8vo. s. 12973

Chumillas (J.) Memorial|Jvridico, y Legal,|qve pone|en las Reales Manos de V. Magestad|el|Comissario General de Indias|Fray Julian Chumillas, del Orden de nuestro|Padre San Francisco.|En que representa|la jvsta Razon qve le precisa;|las legales que le assisten, para que en nada se alte-|ren, ni vulneren las prerrogativas de su cargo, ni su|jurisdicion, y que se le reintegere en lo que se pueda|considerar despojado. Y los motivos para que se|mande recoger vn decreto, que à instancia del Pa-|dre General de toda la Familia Fray Marcos Zar-|çosa ha mandado expedir V. Magestad, contra las|Constituciones de la Re-

ligion, y su observancia,|y la creacion, y origen de este Oficio, y el|Real Patronato de V. Magestad.|[1690?] Folio. 12974

Seventy leaves, signed "Lic. D. Balthasar de Azebedo."

Church (A.) A Discourse delivered before the Georgia Historical Society, 12th February, 1845. By Alonzo Church, D.D. *Savannah.* 1845. 8vo, pp. 34, 6. 12975

Church (B.) The History of King Philip's War By Benjamin Church With an Introduction and Notes By Henry Martyn Dexter *Boston: John Kimball Wiggin.* MDCCCLXV. 4to, 1 l., pp. l, 1 l., pp. (3), 205. (Library of N. E. Hist., No. II.)

A reprint of the "Entertaining Passages," only. 250 copies printed in fcap 4to, and 35 on large paper, rl. 4to.

Church. The History the Eastern Expeditions Of 1689, 1690, 1692, 1696, and 1704 against the Indians and French By Benjamin Church With an Introduction and Notes By Henry Martyn Dexter *Boston: J. K. Wiggin and Wm. Parsons Lunt.* MDCCCLXVII. Sm. 4to, pp. xxxii, (1), 203. Map. (Library of N. E. Hist., No. III.) BA., H. 12977

For other and earlier editions, *see* Church (T.)

[Church (B.)], *M.D.* An Address to a Provincial Bashaw. O Shame! where is thy Blush? By a Son of Liberty. Printed in the (Tyrannic Administration of St. Francisco). [*Boston.*] 1769. 4to, pp. 8. + [Reprinted.] *Boston.* 1781. s. 12978

A poem. Governor Barnard is the bashaw. The following is the last stanza:

"Yet trust me B—— not the Heartwrung Tear,
Shall snatch thy Name from obloquy below,
Nor sore Repentance, which absolves thee there,
Shall sooth the Vengeance of a mortal Foe."

[Church.] Elegy on the Death of Rev. Jonathan Mayhew, D.D., July 9, 1766. *Boston.* [1766.] 4to, pp. 15. 12979

[Church.] An Elegy to the Memory of that Pious and Eminent Servant of Jesus Christ the Rev. Mr. George Whitefield. *Boston: Richard Draper.* 1770. 4to, pp. 7. 12980

[Church.] Liberty and Property Vindicated, and the St——pm——n Burnt. By a friend to the Liberty of his Country. [Elizaphan of Parnach, *pseudonym.*] *Boston.* 1766. 8vo, pp. 15. 12981

[Church.] The Monster of Monsters: A true and faithful Narrative of a most remarkable Phænomenon lately seen in this Metropolis; to the great Surprize and Terror of His Majesty's

good Subjects: Humbly Dedicated to all the Virtuosi of New-England. By Thomas Thumb, Esq. [*Boston:*] *Printed in July*, 1754. 12mo, pp. 24. 12982

Thomas, in his "History of Printing in America," Vol. I. 372, has a long account of the arrest of Daniel Fowle on suspicion of being the printer of this obnoxious pamphlet. Fowle himself printed an account of the indignities he suffered in this behalf, entitled, "Total Eclipse of Liberty." Of the work itself, "Tom Thumb," which occasioned all this mischief, not more than three or four copies are known, the general court of Massachusetts Bay having ordered it "to be burnt by the hands of the common hangman, in King Street, Boston."

Church. An Oration delivered March Fifth, 1733, at the Request of the Inhabitants of the Town of Boston; to Commemorate the Bloody Tragedy of the Fifth of March, 1770. By D[r] Benjamin Church. *Boston: Printed and Sold at the New Printing Office.* M,DCC,LXXIII. 4to, pp. 20. + *Boston.* 1773. 4to, pp. 16. + Third Edition. *Boston.* 1733. 4to, pp. 18. + *Boston.* 1785. 8vo, pp. 14. 12983

[Church.] A Poem occasioned by the Death of the Hon. Jonathan Law, Esq., late Governor of Connecticut. 1751. 4to, pp. 8. 12984

[Church.] The Times: a Poem. By an American. [*Boston.* 1765.] 4to, pp. 16. 12985

A satire upon and against the Stamp Act. Also: The Choice: a Poem after the manner of Mr. Pomfret, by a Young Gentleman. *Boston: Edes & Gill.* 1757. 8vo, pp. 15. W. + *Worcester: printed by Isaiah Thomas, Jun. April*, 1802. 8vo, pp. 16. BA. *See* "Massachusetts Historical Society. Collections," 1st Series, Vol. I.

[Church (Edward), *Jr.*] The Dangerous Vice. A Fragment. Addressed to all whom it may concern. By a Gentleman, formerly of Boston. *Columbia, Printed.* MDCCLXXXIX. 4to, pp. 16. 12986

In the catalogue of the Massachusetts Society, another edition is described, without place, 4to, pp. 16. The "Dangerous Vice" was John Adams'.

Church (G. E.) Mexico. Its Revolutions: Are they Evidences of Retrogression or of Progress? A Historical and Political Review, by George E. Church. ... *New York: Baker & Godwin, Printers.* 1866. 8vo, pp. 84. H. 12987

Church (J. H.) The First Settlement of New England. A Sermon delivered in the South Parish in Andover, April 5, 1810; being the Annual Fast in Massachusetts. By John Hubbard Church ... . *Sutton, (Mass.): Sewall Goodridge.* 1810. 12mo, pp. 24. BA., M. 12988

Church. A Sermon, Preached at Concord, ... New-Hampshire, June 3, 1813. Being the Anniversary Election. By John Hubbard Church. *Concord: Printed by George Hough.* 1813. 8vo, 1 l., pp. 41. 12989

Also: The Devoted Servant of Christ. A Sermon delivered at the Funeral of the Rev. Paul Litchfield, of Carlisle ... . *Andover: printed by Flagg and Gould.* 1828. 8vo, pp. 21. H. — Sermon, delivered in Andover, April 5, 1810, Annual Fast, ... *Sutton.* 1810. 8vo. — A Sermon delivered in Boston, May 26, 1829, before The Pastoral Association of Massachusetts. ... . *Boston: Perkins & Marvin.* 1829. 8vo, pp. 24. H.

Church (M. C. C.) The American Republic. Address delivered in Parkersburg, July 4, 1867. *Parkersburg.* 1867. 8vo.

Church (P.) An Address delivered at the Dedication of Mount Hope Cemetery, Rochester, Oct. 2, 1838; and repeated ... before the Rochester Athenæum ... . By the Rev. Pharcellus Church ... . *Rochester: printed by David Hoyt.* 1839. 8vo, pp. 21. Plate. H., S. 12991

Also: ... A Discourse before a Missionary Meeting in Mendon, Monroe Co., N. Y., February 23, 1847. ... . *Boston: John Putnam, Printer.* 1847. 8vo, pp. 12. H. — Mapleton; or new work for the Maine Law. ... *Montreal.* 1853. — Permanency of the Pastoral Relation. A Sermon ... before the Ministerial Conference of the Monroe Baptist Association, at Ogden, July 2, 1845. ... . *Roehester: published by Sage & Brother.* 1845. 8vo, pp. 24. H.

Church (P.) Report of Philip Church and Sylvanus Russell relative to the Angelica and Hamilton Road. *Albany.* 1827. 8vo. 12992

Church (R. S. H.) Two Rebellions. A Few Words to His Excellency the Hon. C. F. Adams, &c., touching his Hereditary Relations to Rebellion, from One who, like Himself, is the Grandson of an American Rebel. *London: Ridgway.* 1865. 8vo. 12993

Church (S.) A Historical Address delivered on the One hundredth Anniversary of the first Town Meeting of the Town of Salisbury, October 20, 1841. By Samuel Church. *New Haven.* 1842. 8vo, pp. 96. M. 12994

Church (Sandford E.) Speech at Batavia, Oct. 13, 1863. pp. 8. B. 12995

This is No. 14 of "Papers from the Society for the Diffusion of Political Knowledge."

C[hurch] (T.) Entertaining Passages|Relating to|Philip's War|which|Began in the Month of June, 1675.|As also of|Expeditions|More lately made|Against the Common Enemy,

and Indian Rebels,|in the Eastern Parts of New-England:|with|Some Account of the Divine Providence|towards|Benj. Church Esqr;|By T. C.|*Boston: Printed by B. Green, in the Year*, 1716.|4to, Title, pp. 2, 120. B., H. 12996

"Having my Minutes by me; my Son has taken the care and pains to Collect from them the Insuing Narrative ... which I have had the perusal of, and find nothing a-miss ... ." — Benjamin Church, *To the Reader* of the "Entertaining Passages." This is one of the rarest books of its class. I have never seen a copy for sale.

Church. The|Entertaining|History|of|King Philip's War,|which began in the Month of June, 1675.|As also of|Expeditions|more lately made|Against the Common Enemy, and Indian|Rebels, in the Eastern Parts of New-England:|With some Account of the Divine|Providence towards|Col. Benjamin Church:|By Thomas Church, Esq., his Son. The Second Edition.|*Boston: Printed* 1716. *Newport, Rhode-Island: Reprinted and Sold|by Solomon Southwick, in Queen-Street*, 1772.|8vo, pp. iv, 198, (1). BA. 12997

The picture of King Philip, first published in this edition, is fictitious; so also is that of Col. Church (*see* Rich, Vol. I. 198), who expresses the opinion that they "are probably among the first specimens of engraving done in New England." The latter is said to have been taken from a picture of Charles Churchill, the poet, with the addition of a powder-horn slung around the neck. This edition is rare.

Church. The History of King Philip's War, Commonly Called The Great Indian War, of 1675 and 1676. Also of the French and Indian Wars at the Eastward, in 1689, 1690, 1692, 1696, and 1704. By Thomas Church, Esq. With Numerous Notes to Explain the Situation of the Places of Battles, the Particular Geography of the Ravaged Country, and the Lives of the Principal Persons Engaged in those Wars. Also, An Appendix, Containing an Account of the treatment of the natives by the early voyagers, the settlement of N. England by the forefathers, the Pequot War, narrative of persons carried into captivity, anecdotes of the Indians, and the most important Indian wars to the time of the Creek War. By Samuel G. Drake. *Boston.* 1825. 12mo. Plates. + Second Edition, with Plates. *Boston: Printed by J. H. A. Frost.* [1827.] 12mo, pp. 360. 3 Plates. + *Boston: Wiat.* 1827. 12mo, pp. 360. + Second Edition, with Plates. ... *Exeter, N. H.: J. & B. Williams.* 1829. 12mo, pp. x, 358. BA. + Second Edition, with Plates. *Boston: Milo, Mower & Co.* 1829. 12mo, pp. viii, 356. Plates. + Third Edition, with Plates. *Boston.* 1825. 12mo, pp. 360. Frontispiece. + *Exeter*, (*N. H.*) 1836. 12mo. C. + [Reprinted,] with Plates. *Exeter, N. H.* 1839. + *Exeter.* 1840. + *Exeter*,

N. H. 1843. 12mo. + [Another Edition.] Revised and Corrected in several places. 1845. + Revised Edition. ... *New York: H. Dayton.* [1845.] 8vo, pp. 360. H. + Revised Edition. ... *Cooperstown: H. & E. Phinney.* 1846. 12mo. + *Hartford: Silas Andrus & Son.* [n. d.] + *Silas Andrus & Son.* 1851. + *Hartford.* 1854. 18mo, pp. 360. 12998

Also printed on large paper, with lines around the page, forming an octavo volume, with coarsely colored woodcuts. The stereotype plates finally passed into the hands of another publisher, and this edition is dated "*New York.* 1859," 8vo; another edition, "*New York.* 1860," 8vo, pp. 360. It was also reprinted in "Knapp's Lib. Amer. Hist.," and finally reissued by a different editor, as in our No. 12976, *supra.*

Church (*Dr.* Wm.) Analysis of the Waters of Bedford Mineral Springs. ... *Bedford, Pa.* 1825. 12999

The Church Almanac for the Year of our Lord 1844. [*New York.* 1843.] 12mo. Continued.

The Church an Engine of the State, a Sermon not preached on the late General Fast, 1778. By a Layman. 1778. 8vo.

Title from J. R. Smith's catalogue.

The Church and the Sword; or a Dialogue between a Minister and a Non-Professor. *Glen's-Falls, N. Y.* 1847. 12mo, pp. 28. 13002

The Church and the Country; being the Action of Ecclesiastical Bodies, on the State of the Country. *Cincinnati.* 1862. 8vo, pp. 20. 13003

Church-Government and Church-Covenant discussed. *See* [Mather (R.)]

Church in Canada; Journal of a Visitation to the Western portion of his Diocese, by the Lord Bishop of Toronto, in the Autumn of 1842. 1844. 18mo, pp. 64. Map. 13004

The Church in Canada, No. 2. — Journal of a Visitation to a part of the Diocese of Quebec, by the Lord Bishop of Montreal, in the Spring of 1843. 1844. 18mo, pp. 80. Map. 13005

Church in the Colonies, No. 3. — Journal of a Visitation in Nova Scotia, Cape Breton, and along the Eastern Shore of New Brunswick, by the Lord Bishop of Nova Scotia, in the Summer and Autumn of 1843. With a Map. 1844. 18mo, pp. 70. Map. 13006

Church in the Colonies, No. 4. — Diocese of Guiana, a Journal of the Bishop's Visitation in 1851. 1852. 12mo, pp. 82.

The Church Record and Protestant Episcopalian, No. 1, April, 1842. 13008

The Church Record. A Weekly Paper, devoted chiefly to the cause of Christianity and Education. [Edited by Francis L. Hawks, D.D.] Volume I. *Flushing: C. R. Lincoln.* 1840–1841. 4to, 2 l., pp. 588. 13009

Contains a great amount of valuable historical matter about the Episcopal Church in the United States, especially in New York.

The Church of England, and in America, compared. *New York.* 1841. 13010

The Church Review and Ecclesiastical Register. *New-Haven, Conn.* 1848. 8vo. Continued. 13011

Subsequently "The American Quarterly Church Review."

The Churches warned to stand fast in the Liberties wherewith Christ has made them free, in an Appeal to the Public, relative to an Act of the General Association of Connecticut at their session in June, 1810, respecting the Eastern Association of the County of Windham. By said Eastern Association. *Norwich.* 1810. 8vo, pp. 25. M., W. 13012

Churchill (C.) Memorials of [Wesleyan] Missionary Life in Nova Scotia. By Charles Churchill. *London: Hamilton, Adams & Co.* 1845. 8vo, pp. 206. 13013

Churchill (George). Address, before the Albany Typographical Society. *Albany.* 1812. 8vo. 13014

[Churchill (John).] A Collection of Voyages and Travels, Some now first Printed from Original Manuscripts. Others Translated out of Foreign Languages, and now first Publish'd in English. To which are Added some Few that have formerly appear'd in English, but do now for their Excellency and Scarceness deserve to be reprinted. In Four Volumes. With a General Preface, giving an Account of the Progress of Navigation, from its first Beginning to the Perfection it is now in ... . Illustrated with a great Number of Useful Maps and Cuts, all engraven on Copper. ... *London: Printed for Awnsham and John Churchill.* MDCCIV. 4 vols., folio. Vol. I. 1 l., Title, c., pp. 813, 6 l.; II. 4 l., pp. 838, 6 l., 42 Plates and 3 Maps; III. 6 l., pp. 901, 8 l., IV; 4 l., pp. 848, 6 l., 9 Plates and 1 Map; V. *London: John Walthoe.* M.DCC.XXXII. 2 Titles, pp. 716, 3 l., 42 Plates and 6 Maps; VI. 3 Titles, pp. iv, 736, 10 l., 4 Plates and 1 Map. H. 13015

Usually called Churchill's collection, as he was the publisher. Two additional volumes making the fifth and sixth, were printed in 1733. All these volumes were reprinted or reissued with the dates of 1744–1747 and 1752. Two more volumes were printed in 1745 by Thomas Osborne, from materials in the library of the Earl of Oxford, whence they are generally known as the "Oxford Collection of Voyages. *London: Thomas Osborne.* MDCCXLVII." 2 l., pp. xii, lxiii, 873, 15 l. Vol. VIII. Title, pp. 932. H. These eight volumes are usually found together. The following are the narratives contained in the six volumes, which relate to America, in Churchill's collection: Vol. I. Brawern and Herckemann's Voyage to Chili in 1642 and 1643, from the Dutch edition of 1649; Capt. John Monck's Voyage in 1619 and 1620, to Hudson's Straits, to discover a passage between Greenland and America, to the West Indies. For the original edition of this work in the Swedish language, *see* Munk (J.) — Vol. II. Nieuhoff's remarkable Voyages and Travels into Brazil, and the best parts of the East Indies. Translated from the Dutch; Capt. John Smith's True Travels and Adventures into Europe, Asia, Africa, and America, from the year 1592 to 1629; Two Journals. The first kept by seven sailors in the Island of St. Maurice in Greenland in 1633 and 1634, who pass'd the winter and died there. The Second, kept by seven other sailors who wintered at Spitzbergen in 1633 and 1634; An Account of Iceland sent to Mons. de la Mothe de Vayer by La Peyrere. From the French; An Account of Greenland, from M. La Peyrere. From the French; James's Strange and Dangerous Voyage for the Discovery of a North-West Passage in 1631 and 1632. First printed in 1633; The Life of Columbus, by his Son, and of his Discovery of the West Indies, by his Son, D. Ferdinand Columbus. — Vol. III. Ovalle's Historical Relation of the Kingdom of Chili. Abriged from the Spanish. First printed at Rome, in 1646; Sir William Monson's Naval Tracts, in six books. Including the discoveries of the Spaniards and Portuguese. Now first published. — Vol. IV. Gemelli Carreri's Voyage round the World. Translated from the Italian. First printed at Naples, 1699; Voyage of Anthony Sepp and Ant. Behme from Spain to Paraguaria. Translated from the Dutch. First printed at Nuremburg in 1697; Techo's History of the Provinces of Paraguay, Rio de la Plata, Parana, Chili, Guaira, and Urvaica. Translated from the Latin; Pelham's Account of the Preservation of Eight men in Greenland, left there in 1630. — Vol. V. Barbot's Description of North and South Guinea and Angola, with a new relation of Guiana, and of the rivers of Amazon and Oronoco, General Observations, and an account of the discovery of America from Herrera's History of the West Indies. With a brief description of the Caribbee Islands of America. — Vol. VI. Colonel Norwood's Voyage to Virginia, made in 1609; Captain Thomas Philips's Voyage to Mountseradoe in Africa, and to Barbadoes and the Island of St. Thomas, in 1693 and 1694; John Gatonbe's Voyage into the North-West Passage undertaken in 1612; The Mosquito Indian and his Golden River, being a familiar description of the Mosquito Kingdom in America. With a relation of their strange customs, etc. Written in 1699; An Account of the Wonderful Preservation of the Ship Terra Nova, of London, homeward bound from Virginia. By C. May.

[Churchill.] A Collection of Voyages and Travels, ... *London: Published by assignment of John Churchill.* MDCCXXXII. 6 vols., folio. 13016

New title-pages only to the preceding work.

Churchill. A Collection of Voyages and Travels, Some Now first printed from Original manuscripts, Others Now first Published in English. In Six Volumes. To which is prefixed, An Introductory Discourse (supposed to be written by the Celebrated Mr. Locke) intitled, The whole History of Navigation, from its Original to this Time. Illustrated with near Three

Hundred Maps and Cuts, curiously Engraved on copper. The Third Edition. *London: Henry Linlot.* MDCCXLIV–VI. 6 vols., folio, pp. lxxii, (4), 668; 2 l., pp. 744; 794; 780; 2 l., pp. 708; 824, Index, 56 l., xxix 305 Plates. BA. 13017

To this edition a copious index is added, and there is some little difference in the arrangement of the articles. The account of books of voyages and travels is also brought down to the present year. Many of the works in this collection have never appeared elsewhere in English. Sir James Macintosh remarks: "The old voyages are always more picturesque and poetical than modern. Churchill and Harris furnish a great abundance of Indian imagery." And Richarderie observes: "This collection is very valuable; its place cannot be supplied by recurring to the original works, as a great part of them are first published in it from the manuscript." In the so-called Mondidier Catalogue, a copy is described as being on the largest paper. It is a work which sells at a price below its real value. In 1825, Wheatley's copy sold for £12 12s.; 1840, Jas. Bohn, mor., £18 18s.; Merly, £12; Reed, £13 6s.; Splidt, £15 5s.; Dr. Heath, £15; Maddison, £20; and Joshua Smith, £22 11s. 6d. It now ranges at from £4 to £6 6s. in booksellers' catalogues.

CHURCHILL. Histoire de la Navigation, son Commencement, son Progrès & ses Découvertes jusqu'à présent. Traduit de l'Anglois. Le Commerce des Indes Occidentales. Avec Un Catalogue des meilleures Cartes Geographiques & des meilleurs Livres de Voyages, & le caractere de leurs Auteurs. ... *Paris: Etienne Ganbau.* MDCCXXII. 2 vols., 12mo, 6 l., pp. 378, 3 l.; 4 l., pp. 316. H. 13018

This work is a translation, with some augmentations, of the introduction to Churchill's collection of voyages. The French editor, in his preface, apologises for the cruelties of the Spaniards to the Indians in this summary way: "It was difficult to use moderation towards beings human only in figure; finally, of these savages were made men, of these animals were made Christians. God is adored where he was not known. The mission truly has not been like that of the first apostles, but the Gospel has been preached and received."

CHURCHILL (J. C.) Niagara Ship-Canal. Speech of Hon. John C. Churchill ... in the House ... January 15, 1869. *Washington.* 1869. 8vo, pp. 8. H. 13019

CHURCHILL (Juvenal). Magazine of Wonders, addressed to the People of New York. *New York.* 1819. 13020

CHURCHILL (S.) A Sermon, occasioned by the Death of Gen. Washington, late President of the United States of America: delivered at Lebanon, in the Town of Canaan, February 22d. 1800. By Silas Churchill, A.M. ... *Albany: Printed by Barber and Southwick.* M,DCCC. 12mo, pp. 31. 13021

CHURCHILL. Sermon on the Restoration of Peace between the United States and Great Britain. ... *Pittsfield.* 1815. 8vo.

CHURCHILL (T. O.) The Life of Lord Viscount Nelson, Duke of Bronté, &c. By T. O. Churchill. Illustrated by Engravings of its most Striking and Memorable Incidents. *London: J. Bentley.* 1808. 4to, pp. viii, 100. 15 Plates. 13023

Contains details of Nelson's services in the West Indies during the Revolutionary War.

Churchill's Guide through the Albany Rural Cemetry. ... *Albany.* 1857. 12mo, pp. 68. S. 13024

CHURCHMAN (J.) An Account of the Gospel Labours and Christian Experiences of a Faithful Minister of Christ, John Churchman, late of Nottingham, in Pennsylvania, deceased; to which is added, — A Short Memorial of the Life and Death of a Fellow Labourer in the Church, our valuable Friend Joseph White, late of Bucks County. *Philadelphia: Printed by Joseph Cruikshank.* 1779. 8vo, pp. 264. + *London: Reprinted by James Phillips.* MDCCLXXX. 8vo, pp. viii, 351. + *London: James Phillips.* M.DCC.LXXXI. 8vo, pp. vii, 351. BA. + *Dublin: Robert Jackson.* 1781. 8vo, pp. 360. + *Philadelphia.* 1818. + *London: Harvey and Darton.* 1829. 12mo, pp. 324. 13025

Reprinted in the Friends' Library.

CHURCHMAN (John). The Magnetic Atlas, or Variation Charts of the whole Terraqueous Globe; comprising a system of the Variation and Dip of the Needle, by which, the observations being truly made, the Longitude may be ascertained. *London: John Sewell.* 1794. 8vo, pp. vii, 80. 3 Plates. + Third Edition. *New York.* 1800. 4to. 13026

Also: Explanation of the Magnetic Atlas, ... *Philadelphia.* MDCCXC. 8vo, pp. 46.

The Churchman's Almanack for 1832. *New York.* 1832. 12mo. 13027

The Churchman's Monthly Magazine; or, Treasury of Divine and Useful Knowledge. By a Committee appointed by the Convocation of the Episcopal Church of Connecticut. Vols. I.–VIII. N. S., Vols. I.–II. *New Haven, N. Y.; Elizabethtown, N. J.* 1804, etc. 8vo. 13028

Churchman's Repository, for the Eastern Diocese. *Newburyport.* 1820. 8vo. 13029

CHURCHWELL (W. M.) Speech of the Hon. Wm. M. Churchwell, of Tennessee, on the Public Lands, and Mr. Johnson's Homestead Bill, for the encouragement of Industry and Agriculture, delivered in the House of Representatives Tuesday, March 30, 1852. [n. p. n. d.] 8vo, pp. 15. 13030

Also: Speech ... on the Nebraska and Kansas Bill ... House of Representatives ... May 19, 1854. *Washington: printed by A. O. P. Nicholson.* 1854. 8vo, pp. 16.

CHURCHWELL (W. M.), *and* CULLOM (William). Letters of an Eye-Witness, Comments and Opinions of the Newspaper Press, upon the late Difficulties [in the U. S. House of Representatives] between Churchwell and Cullom. [n. p. 1854.] 8vo, pp. 16. H. 13031

CHURCHYARD (T.) A Discovrse of the Queenes Maiesties Entertainement in Suffolk and Norfolk (in 1578); with a Description of many Things then presently seene. Deuised by Thos Churchyarde, Gent. With diuers Shewes of his own Inuention sette out at Norwich; and some Rehearsal of her Hignesse Retourne from Progresse. Wherevnto is adioyned a Commendation of Sir Humphrey Gilberts ventrous Iourney. *Imprinted by H. Bynneman.* [About 1788.] 4to. 13032

CHURCHYARD. A | trve discovrse | Historicall of the | svcceeding Governovrs in | the Netherlands, and | the Ciuill warres there begun in the yeare 1565, with the | memorable seruices of our Honourable English Generals, | Captaines and Souldiers, especially vnder Sir Iohn | Norice Knight, there performed from the Yeere | 1577. vntill the Yeere 1589. and afterwards in | Portugale, France, Britaine and Ire- | land, vntill the Yeare | 1598. | Translated and collected | by T. C. Esqvire and Ric. Ro. Ovt | of the Reuerend E. M. of Antwerp. his fifteene bookes | Historiæ Belgicæ; and other collections added: altogether | manifesting all martiall actions meete for euery good | subiect to reade, for defense of Prince | and Couentry. | [Woodcut Vignette.] *at London* | *Imprinted for Matthew Lownes, and are to be Sold at his* | *shop vnder S. Dunston's church in the West.* | 1602. | 4to, 3 l., pp. 3, 2, 1 l., pp. 154. L. 13033

At the end follows a brief discourse of the memorable voyage of Sir John Norice and Sir Francis Drake.

CHURCHYARD. A Prayse and Reporte of Maister Forboishers Voyage to Meta incognita. *London: Andrew Maunsell.* 1578. 16mo. BM. 13034

A volume of extreme rarity.

CHURION (Julian), *Coronel de Ingenieros.* Informe relativo á la esploracion de las dos carreteras que se proyectan entre Valencia y Barquisimeto, pasando por Nirgua y San Cárlos. *Valencia.* 1869. 8vo, pp. 30. 13035

CHWOSTOW *and* DAWYDOW. Reise der russ.-kaiserl. Flotten Officiere Chwostow und Dawydow von Petersburg durch Sibirien nach Amerika in den Jahre 1802, 1803, und 1804. Aus dem Russischen. *Berlin.* 1816. 13036

CHYTRAEUS (N.) Variorum in Europa Itinerum Deliciae seu ex Variis Manuscriptis selectiora tantum Inscriptionum maxime Recentium Monumenta, quibus passim in Italia, ... Anglia ... Templa ... Bibliothecae ... conspicua sunt, collecta et digesta a Nathane Chytraeo. *Herbornae Nassov.* 1594. + Tertia Editio. [*Ibid.*] 1606. 13037

"The importance of this book, for the history of America, has been pointed out in Dr. G. Asher's bibliographical appendix to his 'Hudson the Navigator. *London.* 1860.' 8vo, pp. 261. ... They also contain the date of his first voyage, which was in 1494, not in 1497, as is generally supposed."

CIAPARRO (J. G.) Lettera del P. Giov. Gonzalez Ciaparro della Compagnia di Giesù scritta al P. Alonso d'Ovaglie del Manzano della medesima Compagnia, Procuratore della Vice-Provincia del Cile nell' Indie Occidentali. Ove s'intendono casi stravagantissimi del Terremoto ivi seguito alli 13 di Maggio 1647. *Roma: nella stamperia di Lodovico Grignani.* 1648. 4to, 4 l. 13038

CIBO (S. F.) Cenni storici sugli Stati Uniti d'America per S. Frenfanelli Cibo ... *Foligno: stabil. tip. di. P. Scariglia.* 1865. 16mo, 4 l., pp. 119, xxx, 6 l. folded. BA. 13039

CIBOLA. *See* Castaneda, Relation du Voyage, Vol. III., No. 11379.

CICERO (M. T.) M. T. Cicero's | Cato Major, | or his | Discourse | of | Old-Age: | With Explanatory Notes. | *Philadelphia:* | *Printed & Sold by B. Franklin,* | MDCCXLIV. | Sm. 4to or 12mo, pp. viii, 159. BA., H. 13040

Probably the finest production of Franklin's press, and really a splendid specimen of the art. The title-page is rubricated. The translator was Judge James Logan; and Franklin, in his address, "The Printer to the Reader," calls it, "this first translation of a classic in this Western World," which is not strictly correct. Sandy's translation of Ovid was made in Virginia about ninety years earlier, but printed and published in London; and Franklin himself had printed Cato's "Moral Disticthes," Englished in couplets, in 1739, which translation is attributed to James Logan. *See* our No. 11548. *See also* Epictetus, *infra.* It is, doubtless, the second classic author translated and *printed* in North America, and is eagerly sought after by American collectors. Uncut copies are among the rarest of rare books. I know of but four copies—the two mentioned above, one belonging to Mr. William Menzies, and one to Mr. C. E. Mann, the latter being the copy described in Stevens' Nuggets, No. 551, is on "large and thick paper, and *unique*" — a mistake. It was reprinted in England as

CICERO. Cato Major: or, a Treatise on Old Age, by M. Tullius Cicero, with Explanatory Notes from the Roman History. By the Honourable James Logan, Esq., President of the Council, and Chief Justice of the Province of Philadelphia. Fourth Edition. *Philadelphia, Printed; Glasgow, Re-printed By R. Urie.* M.DCC.LVIII. 12mo, pp. 168, 2 l. 13041

CICERO. M. T. Cicero's Cato Major, or Discourse on Old Age. Addressed to Titus Pomponius Atticus. With Explanatory Notes. By Benj. Franklin LL.D. *Philadelphia: Printed by B. Franklin. London: Re-printed for Fielding and Walker.* MDCCLXXVIII. 8vo, 2 l., pp. 163. Portrait. 13042

In this edition, Dr. Franklin is made to appear as the editor; doubtless a publisher's trick, to increase the sale of the book. *See* M. R., LIX. 467. In the last edition the title is:

CICERO. Cato Major; or, a Discourse on Old Age, addressed to Titus Pomponius Atticus, with Explanatory Notes, by Benjamin Franklin, LL.D. *Philadelphia: W. Duane.* 8vo, pp. 251–357. 13043

This was intended to form part of Duane's edition of Franklin's works, but was omitted.

CICERO, *pseudonym. See* [Galloway (Joseph)].

CIEÇA DE LEON (P. de). Parte Primera | Dela chronica del Peru. Que tracta la demarca- | cion de sus prouincias: la descripcion dellas. Las | fundaciones de las nueuas ciudades. Los ritos y | costumbres de los indios. Y otras cosas estrañas | dignas de ser sabidas. Fecha por Pedro d Cieça | de Leon vezino de Seuilla. | 1553. | Con priuillegio Real. | [Colophon:] *Impressa en Seuilla en casa de Martin* | *de montesdoca. Acabose a quinze de* | *Março de mill y quinientos y* | *cinquenta y tres años.* Folio, 10 l., Text, cxxxiiij l. J.C.B. 13044

"The first part only was printed; the second and third part were seen in MS. in Madrid some time ago, but it is not known what became of them." — RICH. The manuscript of the third part is now in Mr. Lenox's collection. Mr. Prescott bestows much praise on the work, and Mr. C. R. Markham characterizes it as "one of the most remarkable literary productions of the age of Spanish Conquest in America." It is, in fact, the only book which exhibits the "physical aspect of the country as it existed under the elaborate culture of the Incas." — PRESCOTT, II. 328. As long ago as 1835, Mr. Rich priced this at £5 5s.; it would probably sell for five times the price now (1870). In a catalogue of Puttick and Sampson, for 1860, an edition is described as "Anvers en Casa de Juan Steelsio, 1553," which is probably the same as described in our note to No. 13046.

CIEÇA DE LEON. La Chronica | del Perv, nveva- | mente escrita, por | Pedro de Cieça de Leon, | vezino de Se- | uilla. | *En Anvers* | *En casa de Martin Nucio.* | M. D. LIIII. | Con preuilegio Imperial. 12mo, 8 l., Text, 204 leaves. C., J.C.B. 13045

On the reverse of the title is the dedication, "Al Mvy Alto," etc. It is a reprint of the foregoing work.

CIEÇA DE LEON. Parte Primera | De la chro | nica del Peru que tra | ta de la demarcacion de sus prouincias, la descripcion | dellas, las fundaciones de las nueuas ciudades, los | ritos y costumbres de los Indios, y otras co | sas estrañas, dignas de ser sabidas | Hecha por Pedro de Cieça | de Leon, vezino | de Seuilla. | ... | *En Anvers* | *Por Juan Bellero à la enseña del* | *Salmon.* 1554. | 8vo, 8 l., pp. 285, Table, 10 l. Map. J.C.B. 13046

An entirely different edition, though of the same year and place, apparently pirated from the former, as the typographical execution is inferior. The map is only found in Bellero's edition. There is another edition, "En Anvers en casa de Juan Steelsio 1554," collation the same as Bellero's edition, but the map, if found in it, is Bellero's.

CIEÇA DE LEON. La Prima | Parte de la | Cronica del | grandissimo | Regno del | Peru | che parla de la demar- | catione, de le sve Pro- | uintie, la descrittione d'esse, le funda- | tione de le nuoue citta, li ritti | & costumi de l'India- | ni, & altre cose | strane degne | di esser sapute. | Discritta da Pietro de | Cieca di Lione, in Lingua Spagnuola. | Et tradotta pur hora nella nostra lingua Italiana | per Augustino de Cravaliz. | Con Priuilegio del Sommo Pontifice. | Di Carlo Quinto Imperatore. | Del Illustriss. Senato Venitiano. | E d'altri Principi per anni X. | [Colophon:] *In Roma* | *Appresso Valerio, & Luigi Dorici fratelli.* | MDLV. | 8vo, pp. 32, 541. J.C.B. 13047

CIEÇA DE LEON. La prima parte | dell' istorie del Perv; | dove si tratta l'ordine | delle Prouincie, delle Città nuoue in quel Paese | edificate, i riti et costumi de gli Indiani, | con molte cose notabile, & degne, | che uengano à notitia. | Composta da Pietro Cieza | di Leone Cittadino di Siuiglia. | Aggivntovi in dissegno | tvtte le Indie | con la tavola delle | Cose più notabili. | Co'l Priuilegio per anni XX. | *In Venetia, Al Segno del* | *Pozzo. Appresso Andrea* | *Arivabene.* MDLVI. | 8vo, 12 l., 215 l., Colophon, 1 l. 13048

Trömel, No. 19, remarks, concerning this edition, that it is "inconnue aux bibliographes." I find the following title in an English catalogue:

CIEÇA DE LEON. La Prima Parte dell' Istorie del Peru. *Venetia, Andrea Arivabene.* M.D.LVI. La Seconda Parte delle Historie dell Indie. *Venetia, Giordano Ziletti.* M.D.LVII. 2 vols., 8vo. L. 13049

This first part is the same as our No. 13048, except the title La | Prima Parte | etc. The second part is by Gomara. Mr. James Lenox writes: "I have two copies, differing only in the title-page; one has Arivabene's mark (the Woman of Samaria at the Well), and '*In Venetia.* M.D.LVII. | *Appresso Andrea Arivabene, all' Insegna del Pozzo.*' The other, Ziletti's mark of the Star, and '*In Venetia.* M.D.LVII. | *Appresso Giordano Ziletti all' Insegna della Stella.*' | 18 + 324 l."

CIEÇA DE LEON. Cronica | del Gran Regno | del Perv. | Con la descrittione | di tutte le prouincie, e costumi, e riti, | con le nvove citta edificate, | & altre strane & marauigliose notitie. | Parte Prima. | Scritta da Pietro di Cieca | di Leone in Lingua Spagnuola. | Tradotta nella Italiana per Agostino di Cravaliz. | *In Venetia,* | *Per Francesco Lorenzini da Turino.* | M.D.L.X. | 16mo, 11 unnumbered l., Text, 219 numbered l. C., L. 13050

Usually followed by "Historia | della Nuove Indie | Occidentali | Parti-Seconda" | by Gomara. Same imprint as before. 10 and 306 l.

CIEÇA DE LEON. La prima parte dell'istorie del Perv: dove si tratta l'ordine delle Prouincie, delle città nuoue in quel Paese edificate, i riti et costumi de gli Indiani, con molte cose notabile, et degne che uengano à notitia. *Venetia, Lorenzini da Turino.* MDLX. 8vo, 11 l., Text, 219 leaves. 13051

This, doubtless, is the same as No. 13050, with a new title-page. It is also usually followed by the second part, as above.

CIEÇA DE LEON. La prima parte dell' historie del Perv ... . *Venetia: Giordano Ziletti.* MDLX. 8vo, (8), 215, 1 l. BA. La Seconda Parte delle historie dell' Indie ... . *Venetia: Giordan Ziletti.* MDLXV. 8vo, (15), 324 l. BA. La Terza parte delle historie dell' Indie ... . *Venetia: G. Ziletti.* 1556. 3 l., 34 l., 2 of which are blank, 402 l. L. 13052

The second and third parts are by Gomara, and are usually bound up with Cieça. For other editions of these parts, *see* Gomara (F. L.)

CIEÇA DE LEON *and* LOPEZ DE GOMARA (Francisco). Historia, | over Cronica | del Gran Regno | del Perv, | Con la descrittione di tutte le Prouincie, e | costumi, e riti, & con le nuoue Città | edificate, & altre strane e ma- | rauigliose notitie. | Parte Prima. | Scritta da Pietro di Cieca di Leone in lingua | Spagnuola, & Tradotta nella Italiana per | Agostino di Cravaliz. | [Vignette.] *In Venetia per Giouanni Bonadio* 1564. 8 l., 216 leaves. Historia, | delle Nvove Indie | Occidentali, | con tvtti i discoprimenti | & cose notabli, auuenute do- | pò l'acquisto di esse. | Parte Seconda. | Composta da Francesco Lopez | di Gomara in lingua Spagnuola, & Tradotta | nell' Italiana per Agostino di Crauliz. | [Vignette.] *In Venetia per Giouanni Bonadio* 1564. 2 vols., sm. 8vo, 8 l., 312 leaves. 13053

There is a collected edition of the three parts, with the following title:

CIEÇA DE LEON. Cronica | Del | Gran Regno | del Perv, | Con la Descrittione di | tutte le Prouincie, costumi, e riti. | Con le nuove città edificate, | & altre strane & marauigloise notitie. | Parte Prima. | Scritta Da Pietro di Cieca | di Lione in Lingua Spagnuola. | Tradotta nella Italiana por Agostino di Craualiz. | *In Venetia,* | *Appresso Camillo Franceschini.* M.D.LXXVI. | 12mo, pp. 12, (1), Text, pp. 219. Historia | della Nvove | Indie Occidentali, &c. Parte Seconda (Gomara). Same imprint and date. pp. 8 + 306. Historia de | Don Ferdinando | Cortes, Marchese | della Valle | &c. Parte Terza Tradotta nella Italiana por Agostino di Craualiz (Gomara). Same mark, imprint, and date. pp. 8 + 343. L. 13054

CIEÇA DE LEON. Crónica del Peru. *Madrid.* 1852. 13055

Forms Vol. LII. of the "Bib. de Autores Espanoles."

CIEÇA DE LEON. The | Seventeen Years Travels | of | Peter de Cieza, | Through the Mighty Kingdom of | Peru, | and | The large Provinces of | Cartagena and Popayan | in | South America: | From the city of Panama, on the Isthmus, | to the Frontiers of Chili. | Now first Translated from the Spanish, and Illustrated | with a Map, and several Cuts. | *London: Printed in the Year* MDCCIX. 4to, 3 l., pp. 244, 6 l. Map, Plan of Cuzco, and Plates.

Forms also a part of Stevens' "Collection of Voyages." 2 vols., 4to.

CIEÇA DE LEON. The Travels of Pedro Cieza de Leon, A.D. 1532–50, contained in the First Part of his Chrónicle of Peru. Translated and edited, with Notes and an Introduction, by Clements R. Markham ... . *London: printed for the Hakluyt Society.* M.DCCC.LXIV. 8vo, pp. xvi, lvii, (1), 438. Map. BA. 13057

Cifra Felix de las dichas imponderables, qu se promete la Monarchía Hespañola baxo el suspirado Dom D. Fernando VI. ... Justa Literaria certamen Poetico, con que la lealtad, y reconocida gratitud del Real y mas Antiguo Colegio de S. Idelphonso de Mexico, etc. *Salamanca.* 1748. 4to. 13058

CIGANA (A.) Portugal & Brasil para as noites de S. Joao A. Cigana Colleçao completa de sortes, versos, etc. Seconda edição ... aumentada. *Pernambuco: De Lailhacar et Cᵉ. Paris: A. Durand et Pedone-Lauriel,* 1870. 18mo. 13059

CIGLERUS (J.) *See* Ziegler.

CILLEY (J.) Funeral Oration delivered over the Body of the Hon. Jonathan Cilley; with a Full Account of the Duel. *New York.* 1838. 8vo. N. 13060

CILLY (A. Duhant). *See* Duhant-Cilly.

CINCINNATI. An Act incorporating the City of Cincinnati; and a Digest of the Ordinances of said City. *Cincinnati.* 1835. 8vo. M. 13061

Annals of the Cincinnati Historical Society. Published by order of the Society. *Cincinnati: printed by R. Randolph & Co.* 1845. 8vo. 13062

See S. P. Hildreth's "Pioneer History."

Annual Report of the Board of Directors of the New England Society of Cincinnati, 1846. 8vo. 13063

Annual Reports of the City Departments of the City of Cincinnati, for the Year ending February 28, 1867. ... *Cincinnati.* 1867. 8vo, Title, pp. (4), 5–678. Continued. H. 13064

Annual Report of the Cincinnati Chamber of Commerce and Merchants' Exchange, for the ... Year, ending August 31st, 1867. *Cincinnati.* 1867. 8vo, pp. 65, (3). Continued. H.

Annual Review of the Commerce of Cincinnati, for the Commercial Year ending August 31, 1864. Reported to the Chamber of Commerce by William Smith, Superintendent of the Merchants' Exchange. *Cincinnati: Gazette Steam Press.* 1864. 8vo, pp. 64. Continued. 13066

Annual Statement of the Trade and Commerce of Cincinnati, ... for the Year 1848. *Cincinnati.* 1848. 8vo. Continued.

Boyd's Hand-Book of Cincinnati. Being a Complete Guide to the City; its Public Buildings Illustrated; its Railroad, Steamboat, Stage; and Omnibus Lines; its Hotels; its Public Resorts; its Churches; its Parks; briefly, Cincinnati as it is, and the way to find it. By Joseph B. Boyd. Spring, 1869. *Cincinnati: J. B. Boyd.* 1869. 18mo, pp. 135. 25 Plates. 13068

Brief History of the Cincinnati Horticultural Society, with its Transactions for 1858. *Cincinnati.* 1859. 8vo. 13069

Also: Strawberry Report. Read before the Cincinnati Horticultural Society, August, 1847 ... . *Cincinnati: Morgan & Overend, Printers.* 1848. 8vo, pp. 16. H.

The Memorial of the Chamber of Commerce, in the City of Cincinnati to the Congress of the United States, in relation to a National Armòry West of the Alleghenies. *Cincinnati.* 1862. 8vo, pp. 16. H. 13070

To the Congress of the United States. Bridging the Ohio & Mississippi Rivers. Memorial of Cincinnati Chamber of Commerce. ... *Cincinnati.* 1868. 8vo, pp. 36, (1). H. 13071

Reply of the Cincinnati Chamber of Commerce to the Inquiries made ... on the subject of the Improvement of the Falls of the Ohio River. *Cincinnati.* 1853. 8vo. S. 13072

Browne's Cincinnati Almanac for the Year 1809. By Robert Stubbs. *Cincinnati.* [1809.] 8vo. Continued. 13073

Celebration of the Forty-fifth Anniversary of the First Settlement of Cincinnati and the Miami County. December 26, 1833. *Cincinnati.* 1834. 8vo. 13074

Also in the "Western Monthly Magazine, March, 1834."

Charter and Ordinances. *Cincinnati.* 1850. 8vo. B. 13075

The Charter, Rules, and Regulations for the Government of the House of Refuge and its Inmates, and the By-Laws of the Board of Directors. *Cincinnati.* 1850. 8vo, pp. ii, 19. 3 Lithographs. H. + Annual Report of the House of Refuge. *Cincinnati.* 1852. 8vo. Continued. 13076

The Cincinnati Almanac for the Year 1839. *Cincinnati: Glezen & Shepard.* 1839. pp. 88. Map. + For 1840. [*Ibid.*] 12mo. + For 1846, being a complete picture of Cincinnati and its environs, accompanied by a ... Plan of the City ... *Cincinnati.* 1846. 12mo. 13077

Cincinnati at the Close of 1826. 12mo. 13078

The Cincinnati Literary Gazette. *Cincinnati.* 1824. 2 vols., 4to, pp. 416. 13079

Among the contributors are Dr. Caldwell, C. S. Rafinesque, J. C. Percival, and Rembrandt Peale. Perhaps the first literary paper published west of the Alleghany Mountains.

Cincinnati Miscellany. *See* Cist (C.)

Cincinnati Fire Department. Report. *Cincinnati.* 1854. 8vo.

Cincinnati Convention, October 18, 1864, for the organization of a Peace Party, upon State Rights, Jeffersonian, Democratic Principles, and for the promotion of Peace and Independent Nominations for President and Vice-President of the United States. [n. p. n. d.] 8vo, pp. 16. 13081

Constitution and By Laws of the Franklin Typographical Society of Cincinnati, ... *Cincinnati.* 1849. 18mo. 13082

Constitution of the Cincinnati Astronomical Society, together with the Officers and the Names of the Stockholders. *Cincinnati.* 1842. 8vo, pp. 13. H. 13083

Proceedings of the Cincinnati Astronomical Society in Commemoration of Prof. Ormsby M. Mitchel, Late Director of the Cincinnati Observatory. *Cincinnati: Bradley & Webb, Printers.* 1862. 8vo, pp. 9. H. 13084

Directories. The Cincinnati Directory, containing the Names, Profession and Occupation of the Inhabitants of the Town, Alphabetically Arranged; with the Numbers of the Building Occupied by each. Also an Account of its Officers, Population, Institutions and Societies, Public Buildings, Manufactories, &c. With an Interesting Sketch of its Local Situation and Improvements. Illustrated by a Copperplate Engraving exhibiting A View of the City. By a Citizen. *Published by Oliver Farnsworth. October,* 1819. 12mo, pp. 156. C. 13085

The first directory. The next we have seen was for 1825. By Harvey Hall. *Cincinnati.* 1825. 12mo, pp. 137, (2), Plate and Map. The Directory for the year 1829 contains a history of the rise and progress of that city. The directory for 1834 was published by E. Deming; for 1836–'7, by J. H. Woodruff; for 1840, the title was: The Cincinnati, Covington, Newport, and Fulton Directory, for 1840, ... By David Henry Shaffer. *Cincinnati.* [1840.] 8vo. Mr. Charles Cist edited the directory for 1842, and other years; followed by Robinson and Jones' Cincinnati Directory for 1846. First Annual Issue. *Cincinnati.* 1846. 8vo. Since 1853, the title has been: Williams' Cincinnati Directory, City Guide and Business Mirror; or Cincinnati as it Is in 1853. Illustrated. *Cincinnati: C. S. Williams.* 1853. 8vo, pp. 446. Continued. A Classified Business Directory was published in 1844, also The Cincinnati Business Directory for 1844. As also The City Directory, with a Supplement. 1844. 12mo.

Digest of the Principal Ordinances of Cincinnati, passed since 1835. *Cincinnati.* 1838. 8vo, pp. 45. 13086

Education. Annual Report of the Condition of the Common Schools to the City Council of Cincinnati, rendered June 30, 1838, by the Board of Trustees and Visitors, and the Subsequent Proceedings of the Council on the Same. ... *Cincinnati: printed by L'Hommedieu & Co.* 1838. 8vo, pp. 23, (1), viii. Continued.

Cincinnati College. Catalogue, 1836. *Cincinnati.* 1837. 8vo. + Second Edition. *Cincinnati.* 1837. 8vo. Continued.

Also: Board of Education. "University Project." Report of Special Committee. ... Cincinnati, O., June 30, 1869. [n. p. n. d.] 8vo, pp. 82. B., H. — Lane Seminary: Report for 1834. *Cincinnati.* 1834. 8vo. S. — Report of the Superintendent of

Common Schools of the City of Cincinnati on the Organization of Grammar Schools. ... *Cincinnati.* 1854. 8vo, pp. 31. H. — School Laws. Rules and Regulations for the Government of The School Board and the Common Schools of the City of Cincinnati. *Cincinnati Gazette Co. Print.* [n. d.] 8vo, pp. 16. H. — Second Annual Report of the Board of Trustees for the Colored Public Schools of Cincinnati, For the School Year ending June 30, 1856; with Additional Documents, exhibiting the Condition of the Colored Schools. ... *Cincinnati: Jacob Ernst.* 1856. 8vo, pp. 35. H.

The First Annual Report of the Managers of the Association for Aged Indigent Women ... . *Cincinnati.* 1849. 8vo, pp. 14. Continued. H. 13089

Libraries. Annual Report of the Board of Directors of the Young Men's Mercantile Association of Cincinnati for the year 1834. *Cincinnati.* 1835. 8vo. Continued. 13090

Catalogue of Books belonging to the Young Men's Mercantile Association of Cincinnati. *Cincinnati.* 1841. 12mo. + Catalogue of the Young Men's Mercantile Library Association, of Cincinnati. *Cincinnati.* 1846. 8vo, pp. 260. C. + *Cincinnati.* 1855. 8vo, pp. 308. B., C. 13091

Also: Governor Bebb's Anniversary Address before the Young Men's Mercantile Library Association, 1848. *Cincinnati.* 1848.

First and Second Annual Reports of the Board of Directors of the Theological and Religious Library Association of Cincinnati: ... *Cincinnati.* 1865. 8vo, pp. 62. Continued. H. 13092

Also: Constitution and By-Laws of the Theological and Religious Library Association of Cincinnati: with a Statement of its Origin and Organization. May, 1863. *Cincinnati: E. Morgan & Co., Printers.* 1863. 8vo, pp. 20. H.

Public Library of Cincinnati. 1867. Rules, By-Laws, and other Items, with Annual Reports. [n. p. n. d.] 8vo, pp. 23. Continued. H. 13093

Ohio School Library. Catalogue of Books and Papers in the Library and Reading Room. *Cincinnati: C. F. Bradley & Co.* 1856. 8vo, pp. viii, 114. C. 13094

Memorial of the Citizens of Cincinnati to the Congress of the United States, relative to the Navigation of the Ohio and Mississippi Rivers, 1843. *Cincinnati.* 1844. 8vo. C. 13095

Minutes of the Cincinnati Annual Conference of the Methodist Episcopal Church, 1852. *Cincinnati.* 1852. 8vo, pp. 68.

Monthly Bulletin of the Operations of the Cincinnati Branch United States Sanitary Commission. *February,* 1863. 13097

Narrative of the late Riotous Proceedings against the Liberty of the Press, in Cincinnati. With Remarks and Historical Notices, relating to Emancipation. ... *Cincinnati.* 1836. 8vo, pp. 48. BA. 13098

Narrative of the Scenes and Events which occured lately in Cincinnati, entitled, Freedom of Speech Vindicated, Defended, and Maintained. *Cincinnati: Patriarch Kirkland.* 1853. 8vo, pp. 36. B. 13099

Official Proceedings of the National Democratic Convention, held in Cincinnati, June 2–6, 1856. ... *Cincinnati.* 1856. 8vo, pp. 78. BA. 13100

Pastoral Letter of the Second Provincial Council, of Cincinnati, May, 1858. ... *Cincinnati: John P. Walsh.* 1858. 8vo, pp. 32. H. 13101

Petition to Congress from the Tobacco Manufacturers of Cincinnati, Ohio. April 27th, 1866. *Caleb Clark, Printer.* [n. p. n. d.] 8vo, pp. 5. H. 13102

Picture of Cincinnati. The Cincinnati Almanac for 1839, 1840. *Cincinnati.* 1838–39. 12mo. BM. 13103

Proceedings of a Public Meeting of the Citizens of Cincinnati, on the Subject of a Western National Armory. September 30, 1841. *Cincinnati: Republican Office.* 1841. 8vo, pp. 35. BA.

Proceedings of the Cincinnati Colonization Society, at the Annual Meeting, January 14, 1833. ... *Cincinnati: printed by F. S. Benton.* MDCCCXXXIII. 8vo, pp. 17, (1). BA. 13105

Proceedings of the Convention, of the Colored Freemen of Ohio, held in Cincinnati, January 14, 15, 16, 17 and 19. *Cincinnati: printed by Dumas & Lawyer.* 1852. 8vo, pp. 28. BA.

The Queen City. By a Sylvan Pen. *Cincinnati.* 1858. 12mo.

Railroads. Cincinnati and Chicago Railroad. Report ... October, 1854. *Cincinnati.* 8vo. Map. S. 13108

Exhibit of the Affairs of the Cincinnati and Marietta Railroad. *New York.* 1852. 8vo. Map. 13109

The Cincinnati, Wilmington and Zanesville Railroad, and certain County and City Bonds in Ohio, issued in payment of its Stock. *New-York.* 1852. 8vo. S. 13110

Report of the Committee appointed by the Citizens of Cincinnati to inquire into the Causes of the Explosion of the [Steam Boat] Moselle. *Cincinnati.* 1838. 8vo, pp. 76. 13111

Report of the Operations of the Cincinnati Branch of the United States Sanitary Commission, To March 1, 1862. 8vo, pp. 13. 13112

No. 44 of the Publications of the Sanitary Commission.

Report of the Committee of the Contraband's Relief Commission of Cincinnati, Ohio, Proposing a Plan for the Occupation and Government of vacated Territory in the Seceded States. *Cincinnati: Gazette Office.* 1863. 8vo, pp. 16. 13113

Spring Grove Cemetery. Its History and Improvements. With observations on Ancient and Modern Places of Sepulture. *Cincinnati: Robert Clarke & Co.* 1869. 8vo. Plate. 13114

Annual Report to the Lot Holders of the Cemetery of Spring Grove, and the Public. *Cincinnati.* 1849. 8vo. Continued.

Also: Articles of Association of the Cincinnati and Lake Superior Copper and Silver Mining Company, with a few Introductory Remarks. *Cincinnati.* 1847. 8vo, pp. 20. H. — Annual Report of the Managers of the Cincinnati Orphan Asylum: the Twenty-Fourth Anniversary, June 9, 1857. *Cincinnati.* 1857. 8vo, pp. 19. H. — Central Board of Agency for Home Missions. Second Annual Report, presented Oct. 29, 1834. *Cincinnati.* 1834. 8vo, pp. 24.

Society of the Cincinnati.

All the tracts concerning this society were printed for the use of the members, and not for sale; they are, therefore, generally to be classed with rare books.

Cincinnati: with the Bye-Laws and Rules of the New Jersey State Society. *Trenton: Printed by James Oram, for the Society.* 1808. 8vo, 1 l., pp. 120, 1 folded certificate (blank). C. 13116

Circular Letter, addressed to the State Societies of the Cincinnati, by the General Meeting, convened at Philadelphia, May 3, 1784. Together with the Institution, as altered and amended. *Philadelphia: Printed by E. Oswald and D. Humphreys* ... M.DCC.LXXXIV. 8vo, pp. 8. C. 13117

Considerations on the Society, or Order of Cincinnati; lately instituted by the Major-Generals, Brigadier-Generals, and other Officers of the American Army. Proving that it creates a race of Hereditary Patricians or Nobility; and interspersed with Remarks on its consequences to the Freedom and Happiness of the Republic. Addressed to the People of South Carolina, and their

representatives. By Cassius. *Charleston: A. Timothy.* 1783. 8vo, pp. 32. 13118

By Ædanus Burke. This is the first edition, for others, *see* Vol. III, No. 9279. This tract is the basis of Mirabeau's volume. An article on the same subject, by Cassius, is printed in Bailey's "Freeman's Journal, Philadelphia, 1784."

Extract of the proceedings of the New York State Society, of the Cincinnati, convened on the Fourth of July 1786, and continued by adjournments until the 12th of August following. *New-York: printed in the Year of Our Lord* M,DCC,LXXXVI, *and of our Independence the* XI. 8vo, pp. 20. 13119

Contains fuller details of the forms and customs of the society than any other publication.

A Gratulatory Address delivered July 5, 1790, before the Society of the Cincinnati, of the Commonwealth of Massachusetts. *Boston: B. Russell.* 1790. 8vo. 13120

The Institution of the Society of the Cincinnati. Formed by the Officers of the Army of the United States, for the laudable purposes therein mentioned. Published by Order and for the Use of the Members of the State of New-York. *New-York: Printed by Samuel Loudon.* M.DCC.LXXXIV. 8vo, pp. 34. BA.

The Institution of the Society of the Cincinnati. ... Published by Order and for the Use of the Members in the Commonwealth of Massachusetts. *Boston: printed by Manning & Loring.* 1801. 8vo, pp. 23. H. 13122

The Institution of the Society of the Cincinnati. Formed by the Officers of the Army of the United States. Published by Order and for the Use of the Members in the State of Rhode Island. With an engraving. *Boston: printed by Manning & Loring.* 1802. 8vo, pp. 15. H. 13123

The Institution and Proceedings of the Society of the Cincinnati ... May 10, 1783: with the Proceedings of the Massachusetts State Society of the Cincinnati, from its Organization, June 9, 1783, to July 4, 1811. *Boston: printed by Thomas B. Wait and Co.* 1812. 8vo, pp. 112. Plate. BA. 13124

The Institution of the Society of the Cincinnati, formed by the Officers of the American Army of the Revolution, ... at the Cantonment on the Banks of the Hudson River, May, 1783: together with some of the Proceedings of the General Society, and of the New York State Society: also a List of the Officers and Members of the New-York State Society, from its Organi-

zation to the Year 1851. ... *New York: J. M. Elliott, Printer.* 1851. 8vo, pp. 120. 13125

Institution of the Society of the Cincinnati, formed by the Officers of the American Army, at its Cantonment on the Hudson River, May 10, 1783; and establishment of the Society of the Cincinnati of Massachusetts, its Organization, Incorporation, Members original, and admitted, By-laws and Regulations, together with Proceedings of the General and State Societies, Abstracts and Notices. ... *Boston: Press of C. C. P. Moody.* 1859. 8vo, pp. 74. Plate. 13126

The Institution of the Society of the Cincinnati. Together with the Roll of the Orginal, Hereditary, and Honorary Members of the Order, in the State of New Jersey, From 1783 to 1866. *Albany, N. Y.: Printed for the Society, by J. Munsell,* 1866. 8vo, pp. 79. 13127

Observations on "Considerations," etc. *See* Vol. III, No. 9280. 13128

There is also an edition, *Hartford.* 1784. 12mo.

The Original Institution of the General Society of the Cincinnati, as formed by the Officers of the Army of the United States, at the Conclusion of the Revolutionary War, which gave Independence to America, Together with the Rules and By-laws of the State Society of South Carolina, as adopted July 4th, 1848. Published by order, for the Use of the Members of the Society. *Charleston, S. C.: Printed by Walker and Janes.* 1849. 8vo, pp. 40. 13129

Proceedings of the Pennsylvania Society of the Cincinnati. To which is prefixed, the General Institution of the Order, as originally framed, and afterwards altered at the General Meeting, in May, 1784. Published by Direction of that State Society. *Philadelphia: Printed by John Steele.* M,DCC,LXXXV. 8vo, pp. vii, 88. Plate. H. 13130

Proceedings of the General Society of the Cincinnati, with the Original Institution of the Order, To which are annexed the Act of Incorporation by the State of Pennsylvania, The By-Laws of the Pennsylvania Society, and the Testimonial to the Memory of General Washington, as adopted and communicated by the meeting of the General Society. *Philadelphia.* 1801. 8vo, pp. 82. + *Philadelphia: Published by direction of the*

Pennsylvania State Society. 1841. 8vo, pp. 68. + *Philadelphia.* 1847. 8vo, pp. 16, 22. Facsimile. C., M. 13131

There is another edition, [n. p. n. d.] 8vo, pp. 88. Other titles may be found under Society of the Cincinnati.

CINCINNATUS, *pseudonym.* The False Alarm. addressed to the Right Honourable Richard Rigby, Esq. Pay-Master-General of his Majesty's Forces. ... [Signed Cincinnatus.] *London: J. Wilkie.* 1782. 8vo, 2 l., pp. 106, (2). M. 13132

Against the independence of America.

CINCINNATUS, *pseudon.* Freedom's Defence, or a Candid Examination of Mr. Calhoun's Report on the Freedom of the Press, made to the Senate of the United States, Feb. 4, 1836. By Cincinnatus. *Worcester: Door, Howland & Co.* 1836. 8vo, pp. 24. H. 13133

[CINCINNATUS, *pseudon.*] A Letter to the Freeholders And other Inhabitants Of the Massachusetts-Bay, Relating to their approaching Election of Representatives. ... [Signed L. Quincius Cincinnatus.] *Boston: Rogers and Fowle.* [1749?] 8vo, pp. 8. BA. 13134

CINCINNATUS, *pseudon.* A Reply to A. Hamilton's Letter concerning the Public Conduct and Character of J. Adams, President of the United States. By a Federal Republican. *New York.* 1800. 8vo. 13135

Signed Cincinnatus.

Cincinnatus Academy, Cortland Co., N. Y. Catalogue, 1857. *Norwich.* 1856. 8vo. S. 13136

The Cincinnatus; Edited by the Faculty of Farmers' College. *Cincinnati.* 1857. 3 vols., 8vo. 13137

CIPOLLETTI (Tommaso Giacento). Vita del Beato Giovanni Massias, (O. S. B.) Converso della Provincia di S. Giovanni Battista del Perú. *Roma: Salviucci.* 1837. pp. 170. 13138

CIQUARD. J. M. J. Portrait d'un missionnaire apostolique. Par M. Ciquard, Missionaire [*sic*] de Memramkoucq, Province de la Nouvelle Ecosse. *Quebec.* 1810. 12mo, pp. 24. BA.

With especial reference to Canadian missionaries.

CIRCLEVILLE. Facts and Statistics in regard to the Health, Business and Resources of Circleville and Tickaway County. From Reports of Committees appointed ... July 30, 1853, ... from Reports of the Auditor of State, and other Public Documents. *Circleville: Gamaliel Scott, Printer.* 1853. 8vo, pp. 16.

Circular to the Individual Receivers of the Doctrines of the New Jerusalem, westward of the Alleghany Mountains. *Cincinnati.* 1833. 8vo, pp. 32. 13141

Circular Letter. *See* No. 13117, and New York.

Circular Letter from the Congress. *See* Congress.

Circular Letters, containing, an Invitation to the Ministers and Churches of every Christian Denomination in the United States, to unite in Their Endeavours to carry into Execution the "Humble Attempt" of President Edwards, To promote ... Union ... in Extraordinary Prayer, for the Revival of Religion ... . *Concord: printed by Geo. Hough.* 1798. 8vo, pp. 32. BA.

Circular to the Counties requesting Friends to solicit the Interest of the Members of Parliament in support of the Abolition of the Slave Trade, 12 mo, 24. [n. p.] 1790. Folio, 1 l.

Circuli Sphaerae cum V Zonis. [*Tiguri.* 1546.] 8vo, 14 l.

Contains a mappemonde, with America on it.

Circumnavigation of the Globe. *See* "Historical Account," Novara, etc.

A Circumstantial Account of an Attack that happened on the 19th of April, 1775, on his Majesty's Troops by a number of the People of the Province of Massachusetts' Bay. *Printed at Boston, 21st Aprill,* 1775. 13145

A rare broadside. The imprint given is written at the head, and at the back is the following: "Hon^d Sir. If this Copy is not in the London papers, please to let Mr. W. Smith purse it, I was an Eye witnesse of the whole transaction; can vouch the whole for truth." — PUTTICK's *Catalogue.*

CISNEROS (Diego). Sitio, Natvraleza y propriedade dela civdad de Mexico, Aguas y Vientos a que esta sujeta; y Tiempos del Ano, etc. All Ex mo. Senor Diego Fern. de Cordoua Marques de Guadalcazar, Virrey y Cap. gen. de las Prouincias de Nueva Espana, y Presid. de la R. Chancilleria de Mexico. *Mexico: en casa del Bachiller Joan Blanco de Alcaçar.* 1618. 4to, 14 l., Text, 148 l., Table, 10 l. Engraved Frontispiece, Portrait, and Map. 13146

"Extremely scarce. The portrait, and the curious plan of the city of Mexico, are wanting in most of the few copies known." — ASHER. Rich quotes it as "A book of much rarity," and prices it at £6 6s. in 1835.

CISNEROS (Francisco Jimenez de). *See* Ximines de Cisneros.

CISNEROS (J. L. de). Descripcion exacta de la provincias de Venezuela, par D. Joseph Luis de Cisneros. *Impresso en Valencia, año de* 1764. 4to, 3 l., pp. 118. 13147

Leclerc says this is the earliest production of the Venezuelan press, and calls it a "Volume fort rare et presque inconnu."

CISNEROS. Historia de el Principio, y Origen Progressos Venidas à Mexico y Milagros de la Santa Ymagen de Nuestra Señora de los Remedios, extramuros de Mexico. *Mexico: Juan Blanco de Alcaçar.* 1621. 4to. 13148

One of the earliest chronicles of the Sanctuary of "Los Remedios de Mexico." Extremely rare, full of interesting details. Ternaux, No. 435, has the following title, which is, perhaps, the same work:

CISNEROS. Historia de Nuestra Señora de los remedios de Mexico, que llevo Juan Rodriguez de Villa-Fuerte a la conquista, llamada la Conquistadora. *Mexico.* 1621. 13149

CISNEROS (M.) Sermon predicado por el R. P. Fr. Mirano Cisneros, Discreto e hijo del Apostolico Colegio de Pachuca en la funcion solemne, que en accion de gracias al Señor por las Victorias concedias á las armas del Rey contra los Insurgentes, se hizo en la Iglesia Parroquial de dicho real el 25 de febrero del presente año de 1811. *Mexico.* 1811. 4to, pp. 38, or 20 l.

A sermon in celebration of Hidalgo's defeat.

CISNEROS Y QUIXANO (Ignacio Beye). Honras Funerales, que ... al Dr. Francisco Xavier Lazcano, de la Compania de Jesus. *Mexico.* 1763. 4to. 13151

CIST (C.) Cincinnati in 1841: Its Early Annals and Future Prospects. By Charles Cist. *Cincinnati: Printed for the Author.* [1841.] 12mo, pp. 300. Plates. C., H. 13152

CIST. The Cincinnati Miscellany, or Antiquities of the West: and Pioneer History and General and Local Statistics: compiled from the Western General Advertiser, from October 1st, 1844, to April 1st, 1845 ... [Vol. II, to April 1st, 1846.] By Charles Cist. *Cincinnati: Caleb Clark, Printer.* 1845–46. 2 vols., 8vo, pp. 272; 364, iv. + *Cincinnati: Robinson & Jones.* 1846. 2 vols., 8vo. H. 13153

CIST. Sketches and Statistics of Cincinnati in 1851: by Charles Cist. *Cincinnati: Wm. H. Moore & Co.* 1851. 12mo, pp. viii, 356. B., C. 13154

CIST. Sketches and Statistics of Cincinnati in 1859. By Charles Cist. [*Cincinnati.* 1859.] 12mo, pp. iv, 9–368. Plates.

CIST (Lewis J.) Trifles, in Verse; a Collection of Fugitive Poems. *Cincinnati: Robinson & Jones.* 1845. 12mo, pp. 184. Portrait. 13156

Citizen of Nature, in a Series of Letters upon an American Indian in London. *London.* 1824. 12mo. 13157

Citoyen des Etats Unis. *See* [Condorcet].

Citoyen Americain. *See* [Lee (M.)]

Un Citoyen. *See* [Le Febvre de Beauvray], and [Saintard.]

The Citizen Soldiers at North Point and Fort McHenry, September 12 and 13, 1814. Resolves of the Citizens in Town Meeting. Particulars relating to the Battle, Official Correspondence, and Honorable Discharge of the Troops. *Baltimore: N. Hickman.* [n. d.] 12mo, pp. 96. C. 13158

CITRI DE LA GUETTE (S.) *See* Solis (A. de).

City Characters; or, Familiar Scenes in Town ... With ... designs. *Philadelphia.* 1851. 16mo. BM. 13159

City of Refuge. *See* [Mather (C.)]

The City's Heart. By a Daughter of New-York. *New York.* 1866. 13160

Ciudadanos! Papel politico. *Imprenta Tormentaria de Herrera.* 1820. 4to, pp. 6. 13161

The Civil Officer or the whole duty of Sheriffs, Coroners, Constables and Collectors of Taxes. Second Edition. To which is added a Digest of the Principal Decisions in the S. J. Court of Massachusetts, relative to the Powers of said Officers. ... *Boston: published by R. P. and C. Williams.* 1814. 12mo, 6 l., pp. 7–261. B. 13162

Civil Prudence recommended to the Thirteen United Colonies of North America. *Norwich.* 1776. 8vo, pp. 55. 13163

The Civil Service and Jenckes' Bill. [n. p. n. d.] 8vo, pp. 15. H. 13164

Civil War; A Poem, Written the Year 1775. [n. p. n. d.] 4to, pp. 35. J.C.B. 13165

Privately printed. Relates to the Revolutionary War.

The Civil War in America: its Causes and Objects. By Anamnesis, *pseudon.* 13166

Civil War: Its Causes, Its Consequences, Its Crimes, and Its Compromises. Series No. 1. By Henry Ward Beecher and Archbishop Hughes. [An imaginary discussion.] *New York: Reuben Vose.* 1861. 8vo, pp. 37. 13167

Civilization, or the Indian Chief and British Pastor. *London: T. Egerton.* 1818. 12mo, pp. 351, 301, 259. 13168

CIVIS (G. W.) Songs for the great Campaign of 1860. Words and Music. *New York.* 1860. 13169

CIVIS, *pseudon.* Dissertation on the Nature and Effects of Lottery Systems. By Civis. *Portland, [Me.]* 1827. 8vo.

CIVIS, *pseudon.* The following publication, which shews the rancorous disposition of the American Republicans; against his Majesty's Loyal Subjects, is republished, at the ... request of a number of Loyalists. To William Smith ... &c. [Signed Civis; dated State of New-York, 10th July, 1783. n. p. n. d.] 8vo, pp. 8. BA. 13171

CIVIS, *pseudon.* Real Estate and the Betterment Law. ... *Boston: Henry W. Dutton & Son, Printers.* 1866. 8vo, pp. 22.

CIVIS, *pseudon.* Remarks on The Bankrupt Law; To which are added, the Proposed Amendments of Hopkinson and Webster. By Civis. *New-York: Haley & Thomas.* 1819. 8vo, pp. 71.

CIVIS, *pseudon.* Remarks on the Embargo Law. By Civis. *New York.* 1808. 8vo. B. 13174

CIVIS ANGLICUS, *pseudon.* A Voice from the Mother Land, answering Mrs. H. Beecher Stowe's Appeal. By Civis Anglicus. *London: Trübner & Co.* 1862. 8vo, pp. 56. + *London: Trübner & Co.* M.DCCC.LXIII. Title, 1 l., pp. 46. BA., H. 13175

Claar vertooch, 1647. *See* Vol. II., No. 7547.

CLACK (F. H.) An Address ... on the Anniversary of the Birth-Day of Washington, before the Philomathian Society ... of Mount St. Mary's College, Maryland, February 22, 1845. By Franklin Hulse Clack ... . *Washington.* 1845. 8vo, pp. 8.

CLACK (Louise). General Lee and Santa Claus. Mrs. Clack's Christmas Gift to her little Southern Friends. Illus-

trated. *New York: Blelock & Co.* 1866. Sm. 4to, pp. 36. 6 Plates. C. 13177

CLACK. Our Refugee Household. By Mrs. Louise Clack, of Louisiana. *New York: Blelock & Co.* 1866. 12mo, pp. 226.

CLADERA (C.) Investigaciones históricas sobre los principales descubrimientos de los Españoles en el mar Oceano en el siglo XV. y principios del XVI. En respuesta á la Memoria de Mr. Otto Sobre el verdadero Descubridor de América. Por D. Christobal Cladera, dignidad de Tesorero de la Santa Iglesia de Mallorca. *Madrid: Antonio Espinosa.* MDCCXCIV. 8vo or sm. 4to, 6 l., pp. xxxiv, 318. Map, and 5 Portraits. BA., C., P.

Otto's Memoir is translated in Vol. II. of the "Trans. Am. Phil. Soc." It is in the form of letters to Dr. B. Franklin. Priced, large paper, by Quaritch, at £1.

CLAESSE (L.) The | Morning and Evening Prayer, | The | Litany, | Church Catechism, | Family Prayers, | And | Several Chapters of the Old and New-Testament, | Translated into the Mahaque Indian Language, | By Lawrence Claesse, Interpreter to William | Andrews, Missionary to the Indians, from the | Honourable and Reverend the Society for the Propogation | of the Gospel in Foreign Parts. | Ask of me, and I will give thee the Heathen for thine Inheritance | and the Utmost Parts of the Earth for thy Possession, Psalm | 2. 8. | *Printed by William Bradford in New York,* 1715, | 4to, Title in English, 1 l., Title in Mohawk, 1 l., pp. 115 + 21. 13180

Its Indian title reads as follows:

CLAESSE. Ne | Orhoengene neoni Yogaraskhagh | Yondereanayendaghkwa, | Ne | Ene Niyoh Raodeweyena, | Onoghsadogeaghtige Yondadderighwanon- | doentha, | Siyagonnoghsode Enyondereanayendagh- | kwagge, | Yotkade Kapitelhogough ne Karighwadaghkwe- | agh Agayea neoni Ase Testament, neoni Niyadegari- | wagge, ne Kanninggahoga Siniyewenoteagh. | Tehoenwenadenyough Lawrance Claesse, Rowenagaradatsk | William Andrews, Ronwanha-ugh Ongwehoenwighne | Rodirighhoeni Raddiyadanorough neoni Ahoenwadi- | gonuyosthagge Thoderighwawaakhogk ne Wahooni | Agarighhowanha Niyoh Raodeweyena Niyadegogh- | whenjage. | Eghtseraggwas Eghtjeeagh ne ongwehoonwe, neoni ne | siyodoghwhenjooktannighhoegh etho ahadyeandough. | Sm. 4to, 2 Titles, verso of each blank + pp. 1–115 – (verso 115 blank) + The Church Catechism, a Morning Prayer for Masters and Scholars, Evening Prayers, etc., etc., pp. 1–21 13181

This interesting volume is a fine specimen of Bradford's printing; and the impressions having been chiefly distributed among the Indians, and by them destroyed, it has become a book of almost matchless rarity. It is the earliest Book of Common Prayer in any tongue in this country. Mr. Claesse is said to be the translator, but the greater portion of it was prepared, some years previously, by a Mr. Freeman, a Calvinist minister at Schenectady, N. Y. In the "Hist. Mag.," I. 14, it is said to be without date or imprint, which is an error, the copy described being imperfect. Some interesting particulars concerning this work will be found in Humphrey's "Historical Account of the Soc. for Prop. the Gospel," c. XI., Hawkins' "Notes," O'Callaghan's "List of Bibles," etc. Lowndes quotes it at two guineas; it would now command ten times the amount. Mr. T. Bailey Myers, of New York, possesses an uncut copy. Mr. James Lenox and Mr. H. C. Murphy have fine copies.

CLAGGETT (C.) Oration at Litchfield, N. H., July 4, 1803. By Clifton Claggett. *Amherst.* 1803. 8vo. W. 13182

CLAGGETT (N.) A Sermon preached before the Incorporated Society for the Propagation of the Gospel in Foreign Parts; at their anniversary meeting in the Parish-Church of St. Mary-le-Bow, on Friday, February 18, 1736. By Nicholas Lord Bishop of St. Davids. *London: Printed for J. and J. Pemberton, at the Buck, against St. Dunstan's Church, in Fleet Street.* MDCCXXXVII. 4to, pp. 75. J.C.B. 13183

CLAGGETT *and* EVANS (R.) Opinions of the Hon. Clifton Claggett and Richard Evans, Justices of the Superior Court of New Hampshire, on the Act of the Legislature, "establishing a Supreme Judicial Court and Court of Common Pleas." *Concord.* 1813. 8vo. 13184

CLAGGETT (R.). The American Expositor, or Intellectual Definer. Designed for ... Schools. By R. Claggett ... *Boston: Perkins & Marvin.* 1836. Sm. 4to, pp. 200. H. 13185

This is a speller and definer, with sentences relating to American history.

CLAGGETT (T. J.) A Pastoral Letter addressed to the Members of the Protestant Episcopal Church in the Diocese of Maryland. By Thomas John Claggett, D.D. Bishop, and James Kemp, D.D. Suffragan Bishop. *Baltimore: printed by J. Robinson.* 1816. 8vo, pp. 11. H. 13186

CLAGGETT (W.) A Looking-Glass for Elder Clarke and Elder Wightman, And the Church under their Care. Wherein is fairly Represented the very Image of their Transactions. It being a brief but true Relation of the Cause and Prosecution of the Differences between the Baptist Church, under the Pastoral Care of the aforesaid Elders, and John Rhodes, Capt. John Rogers, William Claggett and several others that were Mem-

bers of the aforesaid Church. With some Remarks thereon. By William Claggett. ... *Printed for J. Rhodes, J. Rogers, W. Claggett & Co. And are to be Sold by J. Rhodes, Shop-keeper in Newport, on Rhode-Island, in New-England.* 1721. Sm. 8vo, pp. 26, 230. B. 13187

CLAGGETT (W.) An Address ... before the Portsmouth Anti-Slavery Society, on the Fourth of July, A.D. 1839 ... . By Hon. William Claggett. ... *Portsmouth, N. H.: printed by C. W. Brewster.* 1839. 8vo, pp. 20. BA. 13188

CLAGGETT. An Oration ... at Portsmouth, N. H. on the Fourth Day of July, 1812 ... . By William Claggett, Esq. ... [*Portsmouth:*] *Gazette Office.* [1812.] 8vo, pp. 32. BA. 13189

CLAGGETT. An Essay on the Unity of the Human Family, ... By Hon. William Claggett. ... *Portsmouth: C. W. Brewster & Son, Printers.* 1868. 8vo, pp. 16. H. 13190

CLAIBORNE (J. F. H.) Life and Correspondence of John A. Quitman, Major-General, U. S. A., and Governor of the State of Mississippi. By J. F. H. Claiborne. ... *New York: Harper & Brothers.* 1860. 2 vols., 12mo, pp. 400; 392. Portrait and Plan. BA., C. 13191

CLAIBORNE. Life and Times of Gen. Sam. Dale, the Mississippi Partisan. By J. F. H. Claiborne. Illustrated by John M'Lenan. *New York: Harper & Brothers.* 1860. 12mo, pp. 233. BA., C., S. 13192

The Claim for Fresh Evidence on the Subject of the Slave Trade Considered. *London.* 1807. 8vo, pp. 16. 13193

Claim of the American Loyalists. *See* [Galloway (Joseph)].

Claim of the Colonies, 1765. *See* [Knox (William)].

The Claim for Interest on the Advances of Massachusetts in the War of 1812–15. [n. p. n. d.] 8vo, pp. 3. H. 13194

Claims of American Citizens against the French Republic. Assumed by the United States. By a Citizen of Baltimore. 1822. 8vo, pp. 144. 13195

Claims against the United States, arising under the Sixth article of the Treaty between Great Britain and America; with the Proceedings, Resolutions, &c., of the Board of Commissioners on the Cases before them. *Philadelphia.* 1798, 1799. 4to. C. 13196

Claims of Peace on Cities. *Boston.* [n. d.] 12mo, pp. 4. M.

The Claims of the Church, 1764. *See* [Mayhew (J.)]

[CLAIR ROY.] Notice sur les troubles survenus dans la Province des Para. *Paris.* 1836. 8vo, pp. 8. 13198

CLAIRAC. L'Ingenieur de campagne: or, Field Engineer. Written in French by the Chevalier de Clairac, & translated by Major Lewis Nicola ... *Philadelphia: R. Aitken.* 1776. 8vo, pp. 256. Copperplates. P. 13199

Dedicated "To the Honourable the Delegates of the United States of America, in Congress Assembled 'at this critical time.'"

Clairvoyance; containing Revelations on the Death of Sir John Franklin. *London: H. Baillière.* 1854. 8vo. 13200

[CLAP (Eliza).] Memorial of Mr. James Clap. *Boston: Press of T. R. Marvin & Son.* 1866. 12mo, pp. 32. H. 13201

CLAP (N.) "A Broken Heart Acceptable with God through Christ." A Sermon preached at Newport, March 27, 1715. By Nathanael Clap, A.M., on a Murder committed by Jeremiah Meacham. (The Prisoner being present at the Meeting, and addressed by the Preacher,) with the Dying Words of the Criminal at the Execution at Newport on Rhode Island; April 12, 1715. *Boston.* 1715. 16mo, pp. 54. 13202

CLAP. The Duty of all Christians urged, In a Discourse On I Cor. xv. 58. Delivered in a Congregation at Newport, On Rhode-Island. By Nathanael Clap. ... *Newport; Re printed by the Widow Franklin.* [n. d.] 8vo, pp. 63. BA. 13203

CLAP. The Lord's Voice, Crying to His People ... a Sermon ... Preached 27 d. 3 m. 1715. Occasioned By ... a Man Barbarously Murdering his Wife and her Sister, and then Burning his House, March 22. 1715. Together With some Account about the Poor Man ... . *Boston: Printed by B. Green, Sold at the Booksellers Shops.* 1715. 8vo, Title, pp. 137, (1). B. 13204

Pages 73–137 contain "Some of the Last Words of Several Dying Persons: a Discourse On Luke xxiii. 39,–43. The Last Sermon heard by the Poor Man. Preached April 10. 1715. *Boston.* 1715." Perhaps another edition of No. 13202.

[CLAP.] Zebulon Advised. Serious and Suitable Counsels for them that go to Sea, and for all that mind the good of their Souls. Delivered March 7th, 1735, 6. By a Minister of the Gospel. *Newport: Printed by the Widow Franklin at her Printing House under the Town School.* 1738. 12mo, pp. 6, iv, 52. 13205

CLAP (R.) Memoirs|of|Capt. Roger Clap.|Relating some of God's Remarkable|Providences to Him, in bringing|him into New-England; and some|of the Straits and Afflictions, the|Good People met with here in|their Beginnings.|And|Instructing, Counselling, Directing|and Commanding his Children and|Children's Children, and Household,|to serve the Lord in their Gene-|rations to the latest Posterity.|...|*Boston in New-England:|Printed by B. Green,* 1731.| 8vo, 2 l., pp. 34, 10. H., S.

CLAP. Memoirs|of|Captain Roger Clap,|Relating some of God's remarkable Prov-|idence to him, in bringing him into New|England, and some of the Straits and Af-|flictions the good People met with here, in|their Beginnings,|and|Instructing, Counselling, Directing and Com-|manding his Children, and Children's Children,|and Household, to serve the Lord in their|Generations, to the Latest Posterity.|*Boston, in New England, printed,* 1731. *Reprinted by R. & S. Draper,* 1766.| 8vo, 2 l., pp. 33, 11. 13207

CLAP. Memoirs|of|Capt. Roger Clap.|Relating some of God's remarkable providences|to him, in bringing him into New-Eng-|land; and some of the straits and afflictions,|the good people met with here, in there|beginnings.|And|instructing, counselling, directing, and com-|manding his Children, and children's|children, and hous-|hold, to serve the|Lord in their generations to the latest posterity.| [Motto.]| To which is annexed,|A|Short Account|of the|Author and his Family.|*Boston: Printed at Greenleaf's Printing-|Office, for Samuel Whiting, in Marshal's-|Lane, near the Boston-Stone,* 1774.| 8vo, pp. 48. + With a Preface by T. Prince, and Appendix by James Blake. *Boston: printed for William Tileston Clap.* 1807. 8vo, pp. 39. BA., H. 13208

The edition of 1774 sold for £1 12s., at Puttick's, in 1860. Another edition was published at *Pittsfield.* 1824. 8vo, pp. 36. It is included in "Young's Chronicles," and was last reprinted with the following title:

CLAP. Collections of the Dorchester Antiquarian and Historical Society. Memoirs of Roger Clap. 1630. *Boston: David Clap, Jr.* 1844. 12mo, pp. 62, (2). BA. 13209

[CLAP (Thomas).] A Reply to Col. Clap's Vindication, in Mr. Fleet's Paper of the 28th of April last. [See Boston Evening Post, No. 1287. *Boston.*] *November,* 1760. 16mo, pp. 24.

CLAP. An Answer to an Anonymous Pamphlet, intituled a

Reply to Col. Clap's Vindication. By Col. Thomas Clap. [*Boston.*] 1761. 16mo, pp. 30. M. 13211

CLAP (T.) The Annals or History of Yale-College ... from ... 1700, to ... 1766: With ... the Present State of the College, the Method of Instruction and Government, with the Officers, Benefactors and Graduates. By Thomas Clap ... . *New-Haven: John Hotchkiss and B. Mecom.* M,DCC,LXVI. 8vo, 2 l., pp. 124.

[CLAP.] The Answer of The Friend in The West, to a Letter from A Gentleman in the East, entitled, The present State of the Colony of Connecticut considered. N. B. This Answer happened to fall into the Hands of a Gentleman, who thought it best that it should be communicated to the Publick. *New-Haven: Printed and Sold by James Parker, at the Post-office, near the Hay-Market,* 1755. Sm. 4to, pp. 18. 13213

Attributed to President Clay by President Stiles. *See* the copy in Yale College Library. *See* Gale (B.) for a reply.

CLAP. A Brief History and Vindication of the Doctrines Received and Established in the Churches of New-England, with A Specimen of the New Scheme of Religion beginning to prevail. By Thomas Clap, A.M. President of Yale-College, in New-Haven. *New-Haven: Printed and Sold by James Parker at the Post-Office.* 1755. 8vo, pp. 44. + Second Edition. ... *New-Haven, Printed. Boston: Re-printed: S. Kneeland.* 1757. 8vo, pp. 40. BA., H. 13214

For "Some Remarks on" the above, *see* [Darling (Thomas)]; *see also* Connecticut.

CLAP. [A Catalogue of The most valuable Books in the Library of Yale-College. Disposed under Proper Heads. *New Haven.* 1755.] 8vo, Title, pp. 40, (3). + Title-page wanting. 16mo, pp. (2), 44, (4). H. 13215

CLAP. An Essay on The Nature and Foundation of Moral Virtue and Obligation; being A Short Introduction To the Study of Ethics; For the Use of the Students of Yale-College. By Thomas Clap, M.A. President of Yale-College, in New-Haven. *New-Haven: Printed by B. Mecom.* MDCCLXV. 8vo, Title, pp. ii, 66, (2). BA., B. 13216

CLAP. A Letter from The Reverend Mr. Clap, Rector of Yale-College ... To the Rev. Mr. Edwards of North-Hampton, Expostulating with Him for his Injurious Reflections In his late Letter to a Friend; And shewing That Mr. Edwards in

contradicting the Rector plainly contradicts Himself. *Boston, N. E.: T. Fleet.* 1745. 4to, pp. 11. B., BA., H. 13217

Respecting G. Whitefield.

CLAP. A Letter From the Reverend Mr. Thomas Clap ... To a Friend in Boston ... [on Mr. Edwards's telling him] that Mr. Whitefield said ... that it was his Design to turn the generality of the Ministers in the Country out of their Places, and re-settle them with Ministers from England, Scotland and Ireland. *Boston: T. Fleet.* 1745. 16mo, pp. 8. B., H., M.

CLAP. The Religious Constitution of Colleges, Especially of Yale-College In New-Haven In the Colony of Connecticut. By Thomas Clap, A.M. President of Yale-College. *New-London: Printed and Sold by T. Green.* 1754. Sm. 4to, Title, pp. 20. B., BA., H. 13219

Also: An Introduction to the Study of Philosophy, exhibiting a General View of all the Arts and Sciences for the use of the Pupils. *New London, Con.* [n. d.] 16mo. — A Sermon Preached at the Ordination of the Rev. Ephraim Little, at Colchester, Sept. 20, 1732. ... *Boston.* 1732. 8vo, pp. 30. M.

CLAP (T.), *and others.* Declaration of the Rector and Tutors of Yale College against Rev. Geo. Whitefield, his Principles and designs. *Boston.* 1745. 16mo, pp. 15. B, 13220

CLAPP (A.), *M.D.* A Synopsis, or Systematic Catalogue of the Medicinal Plants of the United States. (Extract.) *Philadelphia Am. Medical Association.* 1852. 8vo, pp. 222. C. 13221

CLAPP (A. H.) God's Purpose in the War. A Sermon preached in ... Providence, R. I., May 12, 1861. By Rev. A. Huntington Clapp. *Providence: Knowles, Anthony & Co., printers.* 1861. 8vo, pp. 15. B., H. 13222

Also: A Discourse delivered (Oct. 16, 1862, at Rockville, Conn.) at the Semi-Centennial of the A. B. C. F. M. Auxiliary. *Hartford: Case, Lockwood & Co., Prs.* 1862. 8vo, pp. 32. — Sermon on the Death of Jos. Warren Fearing, M.D., Preached in Providence. ... *Providence.* 1862. 8vo.

CLAPP (C. B.) Bank Guide. A List of Banks in the New England States and New Jersey, which have surrendered their Charters, ... Compiled and published by Charles B. Clapp, Gardiner, Maine. *Augusta.* 1865. 12mo, pp. 34. H. 13223

CLAPP (D.) A Discourse occasioned by the Death of Rev. James Flint, D.D. Senior Pastor of the East Church in Salem; with an Address delivered on the Day of his Burial, March 7, 1855. By Rev. Dexter Clapp. ... *Salem: published by Henry Whipple & Son.* 1855. 8vo, pp. 26. BA.; H. 13224

CLAPP (O.) An Address to the Stockholders and Friends of the Troy & Greenfield Railroad Company. By Otis Clapp. *Boston: printed by John Wilson and Son.* 1855. 8vo, pp. 11. H.

[CLAPP.] A Letter to the Hon. Abbott Lawrence and the Hon. Robert G. Shaw on the Present Condition and Future Growth of Boston. *Boston: Printed by John Wilson & Son.* 1853. 8vo, pp. 16. + Second Edition. *Boston: Washington Clapp, Printers.* [n. d.] 8vo, pp. 16. H. 13226

Also: Speech of Otis Clapp, of Boston, on the Bill for loaning the Credit of the State to the Amount of Two Millions of Dollars, to the Troy and Greenfield Railroad Corporation, for the Purposes of tunnelling Hoosac Mountain. In the Legislature of Massachusetts, May 8th, 1851. [n. p. n. d.] 8vo, pp. 12. H.

CLAPP (T.) Autobiographical Sketches and Recollections, during a Thirty-five Years' Residence in New-Orleans. By Theodore Clapp. *Boston: Phillips, Sampson & Company.* 1857. 12mo, pp. viii, 419. Steel Portrait. BA., H. 13227

CLAPP. A Discourse delivered in Philadelphia, July 18, 1854, at the Funeral of ... Henry D. Richardson of New Orleans. By the Rev. Theodore Clapp. *Boston: printed by John Wilson & Son.* 1854. 8vo, pp. 18. H. 13228

CLAPP. Slavery, a Sermon delivered in the First Congregational Church in New Orleans, April 15, 1838. By Theodore Clapp. ... *New Orleans: John Gibson, Printer.* 1838. 8vo, pp. 67. H. 13229

Also: A Discourse, First Congregational Church. *New-Orleans, La.* 8vo.

CLAPP. The Report of the Trial of the Rev. Theodore Clapp, before the Mississippi Presbytery, at their Sessions in May and December, 1832. *New Orleans: Hotchkiss & Co.* 1833. 8vo, pp. xiv, 374. C. 13230

CLAPP (W. Warland), *Jr.* A Record of the Boston Stage. By William W. Clapp, Jr. ... . *Boston and Cambridge: James Munroe and Company.* M DCCC LIII. 16mo, pp. xiii, 479. BA.

Also: An Address at the 19th Triennial Festival of the Massachusetts Charitable Mechanic Association, contained in the account of the festival published by the Association, 1863.

CLAPPIER (H.) Détails intimes sur l'état des lieux, des hommes et des choses au Paraguay Le roman et la réalité dans la guerre du Paraguay. Par Hilarion Clappier. *Marseille: imprimerie Clappier.* 1869. 8vo, pp. 47. 13232

Extracted from the "Nouvelliste de Marseille."

Clara y sucinta Exposicion del pequeño Catecismo impreso en el idioma Mexicano siguiendo el orden mismo de sus preguntas y respuetas. ... Por un Sacerdote. ... *Puebla.* 1819. Sm. 8vo, 2 l., pp. 66, 66, 2. 13233

CLARE (M. J.) The Trial of Marie J. Clare. *Albany: J. Munsell.* 1851. 12mo, pp. 70. 13234

CLAREMONT, *N. H.* Dedication of a Soldiers Monument, at Claremont, N. H. October 19, 1869. Proceedings, Speeches, Etc. *Claremont, N. H.: printed by the Claremont Manufacturing Co.* 1869. 8vo, pp. 48. H. 13235

CLARENCE (William Henry), *Duke of.* Substance of the Speech of the Duke of Clarence in the House of Lords on the Slave Trade Limitation Bill, on the 5th of July, 1799. *London.* [1799.] 8vo. C. 13236

CLARET DE FLEURIEUX (Charles Pierre, *Comte de*). *See* Fleurieux.

CLARIGNY (C.) *See* Cucheral-Clarigny.

Clarimonde. A Tale of New Orleans Life, and of the Present War. By a Member of the N. O. Washington Artillery. *Richmond: M. A. Malsby.* 1863. 8vo, pp. 79. BA. 13237

CLARK (A.) List of all the Incorporations in the State of New York except Religious Incorporations. By Aaron Clark, Clerk of the Assembly. *Albany.* 1819. Folio. BM. 13238

CLARK. Manual, compiled ... for the Use of the Assembly ... of the State of New-York. By Aaron Clark ... . *Albany: J. Buel, Printer.* 1816. 12mo, pp. iv, 201. BA. + Second Edition. *New-York.* 1826. 12mo, pp. 211. 13239

CLARK. An Oration. Project for the Civilization of the Indians of North America. Delivered before the P. B. Ph. Society. Schenectady, July 22, 1816 ... . By Aaron Clark. *Albany: printed by Packard & Benthuysen.* 1819. 8vo, pp. 24.

CLARK (A.) Christian Courage. A Sermon for the Times. By Rev. Alexander Clark. *Philadelphia: W. S. Young.* 1862. 18mo, pp. 28. 13241

CLARK. Memorial Sermon. Preached on the National Funeral Day of Abraham Lincoln, Wednesday Noon, April 19,

1865, at Union Chapel, Cincinnati. By Alexander Clark, Pastor. *Cincinnati: Masonic Review Office.* [1865.] 12mo, pp. 16. Portrait. H. 13242

A hymn, set to music, is on the cover.

CLARK. Memory's Tribute to the Life, Character, and Work of the Rev. T. H. Stockton. By Rev. A. Clark. *New York.* 1869. Square 16mo, pp. 55. 13243

CLARK. The Old Log School-House. Furnitured with Incidents of School Life, Notes of Travel, Poetry, Hints to Teachers and Pupils, and Miscellaneous Sketches. By Alexander Clark. New Edition. *Philadelphia: J. W. Doughady.* 1864. 12mo. 13244

CLARK. The Red-Sea Freedmen. *Philadelphia: J. W. Doughady.* 1864. 12mo. 13245

CLARK. The Unavailing Cry: A Sermon for all Times. By Rev. Alexander Clark. *Philadelphia: William S. & Alfred Martien.* 1863. 12mo, pp. 19. 13246

CLARK (Alonzo). The Annual Address delivered before the New-York State Medical Society and Members of the Legislature ... February, 1853, By A. Clark, M.D. ... . *Albany: Charles Van Benthuysen, Printer.* 1853. 8vo, pp. 29. B., BA., H. 13247

[CLARK (A. N.)] Excursion of the Putnam Phalanx to Mount Vernon, Dec. 1860. *Hartford: C. G. Geer.* 1861. 8vo, pp. 40. C. 13248

CLARK (A. S.) Report of the Case Call *vs.* Clark, tried before the Supreme Judicial Court of Maine, containing a Full Statement of the Testimony of more than Fifty Witnesses. By A. S. Clark, M.D. First Edition ... . *Bath: Elisha Clarke, Printer.* 1837. 8vo, pp. 48. H. 13249

CLARK (A. R.) Sermon delivered before the Auxiliary Education Society of Norfolk County ... in Walpole June 13, 1832. By Rev. Ansel R. Clark ... . *Boston: printed by Perkins & Marvin.* 1832. 8vo, pp. 24. B. 13250

CLARK (A. P.) Every Child, Rich or Poor, White or Colored, of School Age, entitled to the Application of an Equal Amount of the Public School Money. Speech of Appleton P. Clark, of the Fifth Ward, Chairman of Committee on Public Schools, in Board of Aldermen, Washington, D. C. November 23, 1868. [n. p. n. d.] 8vo, pp. 8. H. 13251

[CLARK (Benjamin C.)] Geographical Sketch of St. Domingo, Cuba, and Nicaragua, with Remarks on the Past and Present Policy of Great Britain affecting those Countries. By a Traveller. *Boston: Eastburn's Press.* 1850. 8vo, pp. 35. B. 13252

CLARK. A Plea for Hayti, with a Glance at her Relations with France, England, and the United States for the last Sixty Years. By B. C. Clark. *Boston.* 1853. 8vo, pp. 50. + Second Edition. *Boston: Eastburn's Press.* 1853. 8vo, pp. 50. B., H. + Fourth Edition. [*Ibid.*] H. 13253

CLARK. Remarks upon United States Intervention in Hayti, with Comments upon the Correspondence connected with it. By B. C. Clark. *Boston: Eastburn's Press.* 1853. 8vo, pp. 36.

Also: Speech of Hon. B. C. Clark, on the Petition of Levi Baker and Others. In Senate [of Massachusetts], April 21, 1857. [n. p. n. d.] 8vo, pp. 8. BA. — The Recognition of the Republic of Liberia by the Government of the United States. ... [*Boston.* 1862.] 4to, 1 p. H.

CLARK (B. F.) Alarming Developments, connected with our Courts. The Wrong Member of Middlesex Bar convicted of Perjury, and the Means by which it was accomplished exposed! By B. F. Clark ... . *Boston: printed by Bense & Morgan.* 1848. 8vo, pp. 38. H. 13255

CLARK. The Province of Law in Distinction from that of Truth. A Sermon delivered before the Executive and Legislative Departments of the Government of Massachusetts, at the Annuul Election, Wednesday, Jan. 6, 1869. By B. F. Clark. *Boston: Wright & Potter, State Printers.* 1869. 8vo, pp. 55.

Also: Regulation versus Prohibition, or the True Way: B. F. Clark. ... *Lowell: Stone & Huse, Printers.* 1866. 4to, pp. 30. H. — The Perjury Case! Further Developments. Mr. Clark's Replies to the Letters of George F. Farley, and Ashael Huntington, Esq's. *Boston: printed for the Publisher.* 1848. 8vo, pp. 16. H. — Prohibition of the Sale of Intoxicating Liquors impracticable: the Maine Law a Failure: a Stringent License Law the True Policy. ... . *Lowell: printed by Stone & Huse.* 1864. 12mo, pp. 48. H.

[CLARK (Charles).] A Few Words on the Subject of Canada. By a Barrister. ... *London: Longman, Rees, Orme, Brown, Green, & Longman.* 1837. 8vo, pp. 52. H. 13257

CLARK. A Few More Words upon Canada. By Charles Clark, Esq. ... . *London: Longman, Orme, Brown, Green, and Longmans.* 1838. 8vo, pp. 30. H. 13258

CLARK. "Principles that ought naturally to govern the Conduct of Neutrals and Belligerents;" a Paper read before the

Juridical Society, 1 February 1864. By Charles Clark ... . *London: Butterworths.* 1864. 8vo, pp. 42. BA., C. 13259

CLARK. A Summary of Colonial Law; the Practice of the Court of Appeals from the Plantations, and of the Laws and their Administration in all the Colonies; with Charters of Justice, Orders in Council, &c. By Charles Clark, Esq., Barrister at Law. *London.* 1834. C. 13260

See McCulloch's "Literature of Political Economy."

CLARK. The Trent and San Jacinto; being the Substance of a Paper on this Subject, read before the Juridical Society, on the 16th December, 1861. By Charles Clark, Esq. *London: Butterworths.* 1862. 8vo. C. 13261

CLARK (C. R.) A Geography of California for the Use of Schools, by Rev. Charles R. Clark. 13262

Title from Taylor's Bibliography, in a Sacramento newspaper.

CLARK (Christopher). A Shock to Shakerism; or, a Serious Refutation of the Idolatrous Divinity of Ann Lee. *Richmond, (Va.)* 1812. 12mo. C. 13263

[CLARK (Clinton.)] A Concise History of the First Congregational Church in Ridgefield, Connecticut. ... . *Norwalk.* 1843. 18mo, pp. 32. S. 13264

CLARK (D.) Proofs of the Corruption of Gen. James Wilkinson, and of his Connexion with Aaron Burr, with a Full Refutation of his Slanderous Allegations in relation to the Character of the Principal Witness against Him. By Daniel Clark, of the City of New Orleans. ... *William Hall, Jun., & Geo. W. Pierie, Printers: Philadelphia.* 1809. 8vo, Title, pp. 150, 199. BA.

CLARK (D.) Eulogy on the Life and Character of Abraham Lincoln, before the City Government of Manchester, N. H., June 1, 1865. By Daniel Clark. *Manchester, N. H.: Mirror Steam Job Printing Establishment.* 1865. 8vo, pp. 36. B. 13266

Also: Kansas — the Law of Slavery. Speech ... in the Senate ... March 15, 1858. *Washington, D. C.* 1858. 8vo, pp. 23. H. — Slavery Extension and Protection — its Tendencies and Dangers. Speech ... in the Senate ... February 20, 1860. *Washington, D. C.* 1860. 8vo, pp. 15. H. — Speech ... on the Proposed Amendment of the Constitution, forever prohibiting Slavery in the United States ... In the Senate ... March 31, 1864. [*Washington.* 1864.] 8vo, pp. 8. H.

CLARK (D. A.) Independence-Sermon ... July 4, 1814, at

Hanover, N. Jersey. By Daniel A. Clark. *Newark: printed by John Tuttle & Co.* 1814. 8vo, pp. 24. 13267

CLARK. Reminiscences of a Ruined Generation. By Rev. Daniel A. Clark ... *New-York: published by Dayton & Saxton. Boston: Saxton & Pierce.* 1841. 12mo, Half-Title, Title, pp. (2), x–106. B. 13268

CLARK. The Complete Works of the Rev. Daniel Atkinson Clark, edited by J. H. Clark, with a Biographical Sketch ... by G. Shepard. *New York.* 1846. 2 vols., 8vo. 13269

Contains an introduction by W. Patton. Also: Address before the Alexandrian Society of Amherst College. *Amherst.* 1827. — Sermons. By Rev. Daniel A. Clark, ... In Three Volumes. ... *New-York: published by John S. Taylor.* 1836. 3 vols., 12mo, pp. 323, 4 l.; pp. 9–328, 4 l.; pp. 9–324. B. — The Wise Builder, a Sermon ... to the Females of the First Parish in Amherst ... Third Day of May, 1820, when they had assembled to bless their Minister ... with their Good Things. ... *Boston: printed by Ezra Lincoln.* 1820. 8vo, pp. 24. BA.

CLARK (D. W.) An Alarm to Christian Patriots. A Thanksgiving Sermon, delivered November 30th, 1843, ... in Winsted, Conn. By Rev. D. W. Clark ... *Hartford: Press of Elihu Geer.* MDCCCXLIV. 8vo, pp, 23. H. 13270

CLARK. Life and Times of Rev. Elijah Hedding, D.D., late Senior Bishop of the Methodist Episcopal Church ... With an Introduction by Rev. Bishop E. S. Janes. *New-York.* 1855. 8vo. B., C. 13271

Also: Sermons. By Rev. D. W. Clark, D.D., one of the Bishops of the Methodist Episcopal Church. First Series. *Cincinnati: Poe & Hitchcock.* 1867. 12mo, pp. 478. — A series of books, entitled, "Fireside Reading. *Cincinnati.* 1856," edited by D. W. Clark, contain some articles on America.

CLARK (E. L.) Duty of Fasting and Prayer. A Sermon Preached At Winchendon (Mass.) April 3, 1823, the Day of the Annual State Fast. By Eber L. Clark. *Worcester: Printed by William Manning.* 8vo, pp. 15. W. 13272

CLARK (E.) History of the Second Company of the Seventh Regiment (National Guard) N. Y. S. Militia. By Captain Emmons Clark. Vol. I. *New York: James G. Gregory.* 1864. 8vo, pp. 422. B., BA., H. 13273

CLARK (E. B.) A Centennial Discourse, delivered before the First Congregational Society in Chicopee, Sept. 26, 1852. By E. B. Clark, Pastor of the Church, which was Organized September 9, 1752. Published by Request of the Parishioners. *Springfield: George W. Wilson's Steam Power Presses.* 1852. 8vo, pp. 23. H. 13274

Reprinted in G. Chapin's "Chapin Genealogy." H.

CLARK (E. L.) A Record of the Inscriptions on the Tablets and Grave-Stones in the Burial-Grounds of Christ Church, Philadelphia. Compiled and Arranged at the Request of the Vestry. By Edward L. Clark, Church Warden. *Philadelphia: The Author.* 1865. 12mo, pp. xii, 637. 13275

CLARK (E.) Deposition respecting a Letter written by Gen. Elijah Clark to Don Diego Morphy, Spanish Consul at Charleston, S. C. 1798. 8vo, pp. 8. M. 13276

CLARK (F.) The American Captives in Havana, being Ferdinand Clark's Reply to Nicholas P. Twist, Consul at that Place. *Boston: press of Jonathan Howe.* 1841. 8vo, pp. 36.

CLARK (F. G.) Gold in the Fire: Our National Position. A Sermon, preached in ... New-York, on Thanksgiving Day, Nov. 27th, 1862, by the Pastor, Rev. Frederick G. Clark. ... *New-York: John H. Duyckinck, Stationer.* 1862. 8vo, pp. 20.

CLARK. Our National Restoration. A Sermon for the Times. June, 1862. By F. G. Clark. *New York: John A. Gray.* 1862. 8vo, pp. 11. 13279

CLARK. Thankfulness: its Occasions and Responsibilities. A Sermon, preached in ... New-York, on Thanksgiving-Day, Nov. 28, 1861, by the Pastor, Rev. Frederick G. Clark. ... *New-York: Ivison, Phinney & Co.* 1861. 8vo, pp. 27. 13280

Also: The Church and Civil Government. A Sermon ... *New York: John A. Gray, Printer.* 1865. — Labors of Love; or, the Life-Work of Mary M. Maynard. *New York.* 1857. 12mo, pp. 84. — The Stone of Help; or our Five Years' Review. A Discourse delivered ... April 19, 1837. *New York.* 18—. 18mo, pp. 53.

CLARK (Gaylord J.) The Enemies of the Constitution and the Union. Peace or War! Speech delivered before the Democratic Club of Lockport, March 16, 1863. [n. p. n. d.] 8vo, pp. 15. 13281

CLARK (George D.) Proposals for the Formation of a West India Free Labor Company ... *London.* 1833. 8vo, pp. 55. S.

CLARK (George Edward). Seven Years of a Sailor's Life. By G. E. Clark, "Yankee Ned," of Lynn, Massachusetts. *Boston: Adams & Co.* [1867.] 12mo, pp. 358. 9 Plates. C.

CLARK (G. F.) A History of the Town of Norton, Bristol County, Massachusetts, from 1669 to 1859. By George Faber Clark ... . *Boston: Crosby, Nichols, & Company.* 1859. 12mo, pp. xxv, 550. 19 Portraits and Plates. B., BA., C., H. 13284

CLARK (G. H.) The Union. A Sermon ... in ... Savannah, On Fast Day, Nov. 28, 1860, by the Rev. George H. Clark. *Savannah: Geo. N. Nichols, Printer.* 1860. 8vo, pp. 15. BA.

CLARK (George K.) The News. A Poem. *Hartford.* 1856. 8vo. 13286

CLARK (G. R.) Col. George Rogers Clark's Sketch of his Campaign in the Illinois in 1778–9. With an Introduction By Hon. Henry Pirtle, of Louisville and an Appendix containing The Public and Private Instructions to Col. Clark and Major Bowman's Journal of the Taking of Post St Vincents. *Cincinnati: Robert Clarke & Co.* 1869. 8vo, pp. viii, 119. Portrait.

CLARK (G. W.) The Harp of Freedom. ... By Geo. W. Clark. *New-York: Orton & Mulligan. Boston: J. P. Jewett & Co. Rochester: the Author.* 1856. 12mo, pp. 335. Portrait.

CLARK. The Liberty Minstrel. By George W. Clark. *New York.* 1844. 12mo. 13289

[CLARK.] On the Constitution. *Rochester, N. Y. March 20th,* 1860. 8vo, pp. 4. H. 13290

CLARK. Refutation of Mr. Charles O'Connor's Defence of Slavery. Before the Union Meeting in New York. And Before the Court of Appeals in Albany. By Geo. W. Clark. *Rochester, N. Y.: the Author.* 1860. 8vo, pp. 18. H. 13291

CLARK (Hamlet). Letters home from Spain, Algeria, and Brazil. *London: J. Van Voorst.* 1867. 8vo. 13292

CLARK (H.) A Biographical Sketch of Edward Crafts Hopson. Read before the Vermont Historical Society, January 25, 1865. By Henry Clark, of Poultney. 8vo, pp. 6. 13293

CLARK. An Eulogy on the Life and Services of President Lincoln, pronounced before the Citizens of Poultney and Vicinity, April 19th, 1865. By Henry Clark, Esq. *Rutland: Tuttle, Gay & Company.* 1865. 8vo, pp. 20. B. 13294

CLARK. An Historical Address delivered at Hubbardton, Vt., on the Eighty-second Anniversary of the Battle of Hubbardton, July 7, 1859. By Henry Clark, with an Appendix Containing an Account of the Celebration. ... *Rutland: George A. Tuttle & Co.* 1859. 8vo, pp. 16. B. 13295

CLARK (H. C.) History of Chenango County, containing the Divisions of the County, and sketches of the Towns; Indian Tribes and Titles; Gov. Clinton's Purchase of Twenty Townships; Early Inhabitants and Settlements; Also; Land-Patents; Rise and Progress of Agriculture, Manufactures and Trade; Annals of the Chenango Canal; Church History; Eminent Men and Statesmen, Professors, etc., etc. By Hiram C. Clark. *Norwich, N. Y.: Thompson & Pratt.* 1850. 8vo, pp. 120. S.

One hundred copies printed. Made up from the pages of a newspaper.

CLARK (H. Grafton). Outlines of a Plan for a Free City Hospital. By Henry G. Clark, M.D. ... *Boston: printed by Geo. C. Rand & Avery.* 1860. 8vo, pp. 18. 2 Engravings. H.

Also: City Document. No. 14. ... Communication of Dr. Henry G. Clark, late City Physician, transmitting ... [a Report of the Cholera Hospital at Fort Hill, 1854, and other] Documents. [n. p.] 1861. 8vo, pp. 33. BA. — Medical Jurisprudence. The Annual Address before the Massachusetts Medical Society, June 3, 1868. ... *Boston: David Clapp & Son.* 1868. 8vo, pp. 27. H. — Ship-Fever, so called; its History, Nature and Best Treatment. ... *Boston: Ticknor, Reed, and Fields.* MDCCCL. 8vo, Title, 1 l., pp. 48. Plate. BA., H. — Superiority of Sanitary Measures over Quarantines. An Address ... before the Suffolk District Medical Society ... Boston, April 24, 1852. ... *Boston: printed by Thurston, Torry, and Emerson.* MDCCCLII. 8vo, pp. 40. H. *See also* United States Sanitary Commission.

CLARK (H. F.) Speech of Hon. H. F. Clark, upon ... the Admission of Kansas as a State under the Lecompton Constitution. Delivered in the House of Representatives March 24, 1858. [n. p. n. d.] 8vo, pp. 16. H. 13298

CLARK (I.) Clark's Miscellany in Prose and Verse, By Isaac Clark, of Sumner County, Ten. *Nashville, (Ten.): Printed for the Author by T. G. Bradford.* 1812. 18mo, 8 l., pp. 9–120.

This contains Two petitions to Congress, a description of Mero District, Louisiana, Illinois, West Tennessee, and the Mobile Country; a Tour from West Tennessee to Georgia, a Sketch of Arkensaw and Orleans Territory, an account of the Muscle Shoals, and Poems.

CLARK (J. W.) Apology for Anti-Abolitionists. By J. W. Clark. *Philadelphia.* 1842. 13300

CLARK (J.) A Treatise on the Yellow Fever, as it appeared in the Island of Dominica, in the Year 1793, 4, 5, 6: to which are added, Observations on the Bilious Remittent Fever, on the Intermittents, Dysentery, and some other West India Diseases; also, the Chemical Analysis and Medical Properties of the Hot Mineral Waters in the Same Island. By James Clark ... . *London: Murray and S. Highley.* 1797. 8vo, pp. 168. 13301

See M. R., XXII. 468.

CLARK (J.) ... The Sanative Influence of Climate: with an Account of the Best Places of Resort for Invalids in England, the South of Europe, &c. By Sir James Clark ... From the Third London Edition. *Philadelphia: published by A. Waldie.* 1841. 8vo, pp. 96. B. 13302

Contains a description of the West Indies. Also: A Memoir of John Conolly, MD. DCL.; comprising a Sketch of the Treatment of the Insane in Europe and America. By Sir James Clark, Bart. ... *London: Murray.* 1869. (*See* "Athenæum," July 17, 1869, p. 73.)

[CLARK (J. C.)] To the Electors of Chenango County, N. Y. [Signed J. C. Clark. Dated Washington, September, 1841. n. p. n. d.] 8vo, pp. 14. BA. 13303

CLARK (J. H.) The Iron Hearted Regiment: being an Account of the Battles, Marches and Gallant Deeds performed by the 115th Regiment N. Y. Vols. Also a List of the Dead and Wounded; An Account of Hundreds of Brave Men Shot on a Score of hard fought Fields of Strife; a Complete Statement of Harper's Ferry Surrender; Sketches of the Officers; A History of the Flags and those who bore them, together with Touching Incidents, Thrilling Adventures, Amusing Scenes, etc. By Lieut. James H. Clark. *Albany: J. Munsell.* 1865. 12mo, pp. xii, 337. B., BA. 13304

CLARK (J.) Address delivered at the Anniversary Celebration of the Franklin Typographical Society, January 17th, 1826. By Jefferson Clark. ... *Boston: Dutton and Wentworth.* 1826. 8vo, pp. 31, (1). BA., H. 13305

CLARK (Joel W.) Miniature of Dansville Village. Humbly Inscribed to the First Settlers, and their Descendants. By J. W. Clark. *Dansville, N. Y.: Joel W. Clark.* 1844. 12mo, pp. 72. H. 13306

CLARK (J.) Ill | Newes | from | New-England: | or | A Narative of New-Englands | Persecution. | Wherein is declared | That while Old England is becoming new, | New-England is becoming Old. | Also four Proposals to the Honoured Parliament and Councel of State, | touching the way to Propagate the Gospel of Christ (with small | charge and great safety) both in Old England and New. | Also four conclusions touching the faith and order of the Gospel of | Christ out of his last Will and Testament, confirmed and justified. | By John Clark Physician, of Rode Island in America. | *London,* | *Printed by Henry Hills living in Fleet-Yard,*

next door to the Rose | *and Crown, in the year* 1652. | 4to, 10 l., pp. 76. J.C.B. 13307

A rare volume. Reprinted in "Mass. Hist. Coll.," Vol. II., Fourth Series. The Harvard College Library has a copy, in which the title reads as below:

CLARK. Ill Newes | from | NewEngland. | Or a Narrative of New-Englands | Persecution. | Whereunto | Is added Eight severall Arguments to | prove that no servant of Christ hath any Liberty much | less Authority from Christ to prosecute others for | case of Conscience, against those who to | maintain their own interest do invite the Ma- | gistrate, therein to exceed his Commission. | By John C eark Physitian of Rode Island in America. | ... | ... | ... | *London,* | *Printed by Henry Hills, and are to be sold at his house in Fleet-Yard,* | ... | ... . 1652. | 4to, Title, pp. (18), 76. H. 13308

Bartlett's "Bibliog. of R. I." quotes from Prof. Elton's note to (Callender's "Hist. Disc.," p. 210), the title of another tract by Clark, said to have been issued the preceding year, called "A Brief Discourse touching New England, as to the matter in hand, and to that part of it, sci. Rhode Island, where my residence is, together with the occasion of my going out with others from the Mathatusets Bay, and the many providential occurrences that directed us thereto, and pitched us thereon." T.'s abstract fills three pages, and is followed by "A faithful and true relation of the persecution of Obadiah Holmes, John Crandall and John Clark, merely for conscience sake towards God, by the principal members of the church or commonwealth of the Mathatusets in New England, which rules over that part of the world; wherein is shown their discourteous entertainment of strangers, and how that spirit by which they acted, would order the whole world if either brought under them, or should come in unto them. Drawn forth by the aforesaid John Clark, not so much to answer the Importunity of Friends, as to stop the mouths, and slanderous reports of such as are Enemies to the Cross of Christ," etc. Dr. John Clark was the founder of the first Baptist church in Newport, in 1644.

CLARK (J.) Considerations on the Purity of the Principles of William H. Crawford, Esq. deducible from his Conduct in Connexion with Charles Tait, Esq. towards the Author of this Publication. To which is added, Some Remarks upon the Introduction of Africans into this State ... . By John Clark. *Augusta: Georgia Advertiser Office.* 1819. 8vo, pp. 208. BA. + [With a Preface.] *New-York: Charles Wiley.* 1823. 8vo, pp. 78. B. 13309

[CLARK (John).] In Memory of Daniel Webster. ... [*Boston.* 1856.] 8vo, pp. 95, (1). B. 13310

CLARK (*Rev.* John). "Father Clark." *See* Peck (J. M.)

CLARK. Records of the Descendants of Hugh Clark, of Watertown, Mass., 1640–1866. By John Clark, A.B. *Boston: printed for the Author.* 1866. 8vo, pp. 26, 1 l. 15 Lithographic Portraits. BA., H., S. 13311

Also: Genealogy of the Clark Family. [*Cambridge?* 1861?] 4to, pp. 5. H.

CLARK (John), *and others.* The Voice of Jubilee: a Narrative of the Baptist Mission, Jamaica, from its Commencement. With Biographical Notices of its Fathers and Founders. By John Clark, W. Dendy, and J. M. Phillippo. With an Introduction by David J. East. *London: W. Snow.* 1865. Post 8vo, pp. xx–359. 13312

CLARK (J. A.) The Young Disciple; or, A Memoir of Anzonetta R. Peters. By Rev. John A. Clark ... Abridged from the Fifth Edition. *New York: published by the American Tract Society.* [n. d.] 16mo, pp. 230. B. 13313

CLARK (J. C.) Speech of John C. Clark, of New York: on motions pending to refer the President's Message. Delivered in the House of Representatives, Jan. 30, 1839, in Committee of the Whole. *Washington.* 1839. 8vo, pp. 15. S. 13314

CLARK. Speech of John C. Clark on the Bill ... to establish Commercial Relations between the United States and China. *Washington.* 1843. 8vo, pp. 15. 13315

CLARK. The Fate of Blood-thirsty Oppressors, and God's | Tender Care of his Distressed People. | A | Sermon, | preached at Lexington, | April 19, 1776. | To commemorate the Murder, Blood- | shed, and Commencement of Hostilities, be- | tween Great-Britain and America, in that Town, | by a Brigade of Troops of George III, under | Command of Lieutenant-Colonel Smith, | on the Nineteenth of April, 1775. | To which is added, | A Brief Narrative of the principal | Transactions of that Day. | By Jonas Clark ... . | ... . | [Motto, 7 lines.] *Massachusetts-State: Boston:* | *Printed by Powers and Willis.* | M,DCC,LXXVI. | 8vo, pp. 31, 8. B., BA., C. 13316

CLARK. A Sermon preached ... May 30, 1781. Being the First Day of General Election, After the Commencement of the Present Constitution ... . By Jonas Clark ... *Boston: printed by J. Gill and B. Edes and Sons.* 1781. 8vo, Title, pp. (1), 74.

Also: Sermon at Athol, Mass. Nov. 21, 1787, at the Ordination of Joseph Estabrook. *Worcester.* 1788. 8vo. — Sermon at the Ordination of Rev. Wm. Muzzy, Sullivan, N. H. Feb. 7. 1798. *Keene.* 1799. 8vo, pp. 24. — The Use and Excellency of Vocal Music in Public Worship. *Boston.* 1770. The name is also spelled in some title-pages Clarke, which see.

CLARK (Jonathan). Life of General Washington, late President of the United States: together with his Farewell Address, and a short account of the Revolutionary War. By Jona. Clark. ... . *Albany: Packard & Benthuysen.* 1813 18mo, pp. 144. S.

CLARK (J.) An Oration delivered at Rochester [N. H.], on the 4th of July ... 1794. By Joseph Clark. *Dover.* 1794. 8vo, pp. 12. N. 13319

CLARK (J.) The History and Theory of Revolutions. From the Princeton Review for April, 1862. By Rev. Joseph Clark, A.M. Chambersburg, Pa. *Philadelphia: William S. & Alfred Martien.* 1862. 8vo, pp. 35. B., H. 13320

Relates to the Rebellion of the Southern States.

CLARK. (J.) A Sermon on the Death of the Hon. William Paterson, Esq. LL.D. ... New-Brunswick, ... on the Twenty First Day of September. By ... Joseph Clark. ... *New Brunswick: printed by A. Blauvelt.* [n. d.] 8vo, pp. 24. BA. 13321

CLARK (Joseph G.) Lights and Shadows of Sailor Life, as exemplified in fifteen years' Experience, including the more thrilling events of the United States Exploring Expedition, and Reminiscences of an Eventful Life on the "Mountain Wave." *Boston.* 1848. 12mo. 13322

CLARK (J. H.) The Medical Topography of Newark, N. J. By J. Henry Clark, M.D. *New-York: John A. Gray, Printer.* 1861. 8vo, pp. 23. 13323

CLARK (J. S.) God's Remembrance of Bethel. A Discourse preached before the Barnstable Conference. By Joseph S. Clark, D.D. ... Orleans, Dec. 19, 1855. ... *Boston: Press of T. R. Marvin.* 1856. 8vo, pp. 36. B. 13324

CLARK. A Historical Sketch of the Congregational Churches in Massachusetts, from 1620 to 1858. With an Appendix. By Joseph S. Clark ... . *Boston: Congregational Board of Publication.* 1858. 8vo, pp. xii, 344. B., BA. 13325

CLARK. An Historical Sketch of Sturbridge, Mass. from its Settlement to the Present Time. By Joseph S. Clark ... . *Brookfield: E. and L. Merriam, Printers.* 1838. 8vo, pp. 48.

CLARK. Repairing the Breach. A Historical Discourse, preached in Plymouth, Mass., at the Twenty-fifth Anniversary of the Pilgrim Conference of Churches, May 16, 1855. By Joseph S. Clark, D.D. *Boston: Press of T. R. Marvin.* 1855. 8vo, pp. 30. B., W. 13327

CLARK (J. V. H.) Lights and Lines of Indian Character, and Scenes in Pioneer Life. By Joshua V. Clark. *Syracuse: E. H. Babcock & Co.* 1854. 12mo, pp. 375. Portrait. C.

CLARK. Onondaga; or Reminiscences of Earlier and Later Times; being a Series of Historical Sketches relative to Onondaga; with Notes on the Several Towns in the County, and Oswego. By Joshua V. H. Clark, A.M. In Two Volumes ... . *Syracuse: Stoddard and Babcock.* 1849. 2 vols., 8vo, pp. 402; 392, 1 l. Portraits and Maps. BA., C., H. 13329

CLARK. Tradition of Hi-a-wat-ha. Origin of the Narrative of the Onondaga Tradition of Hi-a-wat-ha, and Correspondence relative thereto. By J. V. H. Clark. *Syracuse.* 1856. 8vo.

CLARK (L. G.) Knick-Knacks from an Editor's Table. By L. Gaylord Clark. [Motto.] *New York: D. Appleton and Co.* 1852. 12mo, Title, pp. 335, (1). B. 13331

CLARK. Literary Remains of the Late Willis Gaylord Clark. Including the Ollapodiana Papers ... Edited by Lewis Gaylord Clark. *New York: Burgess, Stringer, & Co.* 1844. 8vo, pp. 480. B. + Fourth Edition. *New York: Stringer and Townsend.* 1851. 8vo, pp. 480. G. 13332

CLARK (L. M.) Letter to the Secretary of the Treasury, August 20, 1862. [n. p. n. d.] 8vo, pp. 14. 13333

CLARK (Lincoln). An Eulogy upon the Life, Character, and Death of Gen. Andrew Jackson, delivered ... before the Societies and Citizens of Tuscaloosa. *Tuscaloosa.* 1845. 8vo. 13334

CLARK (L.) Speech of Lot Clark, on the Internal Improvements of the State of New-York. 1846. 8vo, pp. 12. S.

CLARK (M.) Biographical Sketches of the Fathers of New England ... . By Mary Clark. *Concord: Marsh, Capen and Lyon.* 1836. 16mo, pp. 180. BA., H. 13336

CLARK. A Concise History of Massachusetts, from its First Settlement, and for Fourteen Years the History of all New England. *Boston.* 1837. 24mo. 13337

CLARK (M. P.) Obituary of Mrs. Mary P. Clark, of Northampton, Mass. Second Edition. *Northampton: printed by T. W. Shepard and Co.* 1821. 12mo, pp. 12. H. 13338

CLARK (M. H.) The Maine Law. Speech of Hon. Myron H. Clark, ... on the Bill for the Suppression of Intemperance, in Senate, March 3, 1854. [n. p. n. d.] 8vo, pp. 8. 13339

CLARK (N.) Sermon at the re-opening of the House of Worship of the Congregational Society in Quincy. 1853. By Nelson Clark. 13340

CLARK (N. L.) & Co. History of the Peruvian Syrup. ... *New-York.* [1854.] 12mo, pp. 35. H., S. 13341

CLARK (O.) An Address delivered before the Cadets of Norwich University, at their Annual Commencement. *Hanover.* 1840. 8vo. 13342

CLARK (O.) Funeral Address delivered at the Interment of the Hon. John Nicholas, Jan. 2, 1820. By Orin Clark.

CLARK (O. S.) The One Hundred and Sixteenth Regiment of New York State Volunteers: being a Complete History of its Organization and nearly Three Years' Active Service in the Great Rebellion. By Orton S. Clark, late Captain ... [with] Memorial Sketches, and a Muster Roll of the Regiment, etc. *Buffalo: Matthews & Warren.* 1868. 12mo, pp. 348. Portrait.

CLARK (P.) The Advantages and Obligations arising from Oracles of God committed to the Church and its Ministry ... Sermon Preached before the Ministers Of the Province of the Massachusetts Bay ... at their Annual Convention, in Boston; May 30. 1745. By Peter Clark ... *Boston: D. Gookin.* 1745. 8vo, pp. (4), 56. BA., H. 13345

CLARK. The Captain of the Lord's Host appearing with his Sword drawn. Two Sermons Preach'd at Salem-Village, on the General Fast, Appointed on the Occasion of the War, February 26. 1740, 1. ... By Peter Clark ... . *Boston: S. Kneeland and T. Green.* 1741. 8vo, pp. (4), 55. B., BA., M. 13346

CLARK. Christian Bravery. A Sermon Preached before the ... Artillery Company In Boston, June 7th, 1736. Being the Day of their Election of Officers. ... By Peter Clark ... . *Boston: Printed by S. Kneeland and T. Green for D. Henchman.* 1736. 8vo, Title, pp. 50. BA., H. 13347

CLARK. Religion to be minded under the Greatest Perils of Life. Sermon on Ps. cxix. 109; containing a Word in Season to Soldiers. Preach'd on April 6, 1755, being the Lord's Day, before the Muster of a Number of Soldiers in the North Parish in Danvers. *Boston.* 1755. 8vo, pp. 29. 13348

CLARK. The Rulers highest Dignity, and the People's truest Glory. Sermon Preached in ... the Province of the Massachusetts Bay in New-England, By Peter Clark ... May 30th, 1739. Being the Anniversary for the Election of His Majesty's Council ... . *Boston: Printed by S. Kneeland.* MDCCXXXIX. 8vo, pp. (2), 58. BA., H. 13349

CLARK. The Service of God in the Gospel-Ministry, recommended and encouraged. A Sermon ... at the Ordination of ... William Jenison ... in Salem, May 22. 1728. By Peter Clark ... *Boston: M. Gerrish.* MDCCXXVIII. 8vo, Half-Title, Title, pp. 35. BA., H. 13350

Also: The Banner of Divine Love displayed. Sermon preached at Topsfield, June 29, 1743. By Peter Clark. *Boston.* 1744. 8vo, pp. 47. M. — A Defence of The Divine Right Of Infant Baptism. ... Being In Reply to Dr. John Gill's Book, intitled, The Divine Right of Infant-Baptism examined and disproved. And In Vindication of the late Mr. Jonathan Dickinson's Brief Illustration and Confirmation of the Divine Right of Infant-Baptism. By Peter Clark. *Boston, New England: S. Kneeland.* 1752. Title, pp. vi, 453, (6). BA., H. — A Defence Of the Principles of The "Summer-Morning's Conversation ... Concerning the Doctrine of Original Sin." Against The Exceptions ... of the "Winter Evening's Conversation vindicated" [by S. Webster]. ... By Peter Clark ... . *Boston: Edes and Gill.* 1760. 8vo, pp. 160, (3). BA. — Fair Play! Or, a Needful Word, to temper the Tract, entitled, A Summer Morning's Conversation ... By Rev. Peter Clark ... upon the doctrine of original sin. *Portsmouth, N. H.* 1758. 8vo, pp. 35, 7. W. — Man's Dignity and Duty as a reasonable Creature ... a Sermon ... at the ... Dudleian Lecture, ... May 11. 1763. *Boston: Printed by Richard and Samuel Draper.* 1763. 8vo, pp. 47. BA., H. — Remarks on A late Pamphlet [by C. Chauncy], intitled, "The Opinion of One that has perused the Summer-Morning's Conversation, concerning the Doctrine of Original Sin," &c. *Boston: Edes and Gill.* 1758. 8vo, pp. 43, (1). BA. — Reply to a defence of the Divine right of Infant Baptism, with John Gill's Strictures upon Bostwick, ... *New York.* 1766. — The Scripture-Doctrine of Original Sin, stated and defended. In A Summer-Morning's Conversation between a Minister and a Neighbour. Containing Remarks on a late anonymous Pamphlet, Intitled, "A Winter Evening's Conversation upon the Doctrine of Original Sin," ... . By Peter Clark, A.M. ... *Boston: S. Kneeland.* 1758. 8vo, 2 l., pp. 132, 24. (For an answer to this, *see* [Chauncy (Charles)], Vol. III, note to our No. 12331.) BA., H. — The Scripture-Grounds of the Baptism of Christian Infants, and The Mode of Administration by Affusion or Sprinkling, Briefly Asserted and Defended, In a Letter. Together with a larger Vindication both of the Subject and Mode of Baptism, against Mr. Walton's Exceptions, in a Second Letter. ... By Peter Clark ... . *Boston: J. Edwards & H. Foster.* 1735. 8vo, Title, pp. xxxiv, 136. B., BA. — The Witness of the Spirit in the Hearts of Believers ... a Sermon ... at ... Watertown, Sept. 16. 1743. ... By Peter Clark ... . *Boston: J. Edwards.* 1744. 8vo, pp. 46. BA.

CLARK. The Winter-Evening Conversation Vindicated. *See* [Webster (S.)]

CLARK (Peter), *Nashua.* A Letter to the Hon. James Clark, on the Use of Railroads. [n. p. n. d.] 8vo, pp. 16. H., M.

[CLARK.] A Letter to Thomas Whittemore, Esquire, ...

Upon the Cost of Transportation between Boston and Troy. [n. p. n. d.] 12mo, pp. 12. H. 13352

CLARK (P. H.) The Black Brigade of Cincinnati: being a Report of its Labors and a Muster-Roll of its Members; together with Various Orders, Speeches, etc., relating to it. By Peter H. Clark. *Cincinnati: printed by Joseph D. Boyd.* M.DCCC.LX.IV. 8vo, pp. 30. C., H. 13353

CLARK (P.) On the Rise and signalized Lot of the United Americans. A Sermon, Delivered February 19, M,DCC,XCV, On Occasion of a Thanksgiving throughout the United States, ... in Norton. ... By Pitt Clark ... . *Boston: printed by Samuel Hall.* 1795. 8vo, pp. 30. H. 13354

CLARK. A Sermon ... in Marlborough, at the Ordination of the Rev. Sylvester F. Bucklin, November 2, 1808. By Pitt Clark ... . *Boston.* 1809. 8vo, pp. 34, (1). BA. 13355

CLARK (R. W.) An Address delivered before the American Peace Society at its Annual Meeting, May 26th, 1851. By Rufus W. Clark ... . *Boston: J. P. Jewett & Co.* 1851. 12mo, pp. 38. H. 13356

CLARK. The African Slave-Trade. By the Rev. R. W. Clark. *Boston.* [1860.] 16mo. B., C., S. 13357

CLARK. A Discourse Commemorative of the Heroes of Albany, who have fallen during the Present War, in defense of Our Country, delivered in ... Albany, July 10th, 1864. By Rufus W. Clark, D.D. *Albany: Press of C. Van Benthuysen.* 1864. 8vo, pp. 50. H., S. 13358

CLARK. A Discourse on the Life and Character of Howard Townsend, M.D. ... preached in ... Albany ... Jan. 20th, 1867. By Rev. Rufus W. Clark, D.D. *Albany: S. R. Gray, Publisher.* 1867. 8vo, pp. 18. H. 13359

CLARK. Fifty Arguments in favor of Sustaining and Enforcing the Massachusetts Anti-Liquor Law ... By Rufus W. Clark. *Boston: John P. Jewett & Co. Cleveland, Ohio: Jewett, Proctor & Worthington.* 1853. 12mo, pp. 47. H. 13360

CLARK. The Heroes of Albany. A memorial of the Patriotic Martyrs of the City and County of Albany ... 1861–1865. With Brief Histories of the Albany Regiments. By Rufus W. Clark ... *Albany: S. R. Gray.* 1866. 8vo, pp. 870, 9 l.

CLARK. A Review of the Rev. Moses Stuart's Pamphlet on Slavery, entitled "Conscience and the Constitution." Originally published in the Boston Daily Atlas. *Boston: C. C. P. Moody.* 1850. 12mo, pp. 103. B., H. 13362

CLARK. Romanism in America. By Rev. Rufus W. Clark. *Boston: J. E. Tilton.* 1859. 12mo, pp. 271. 13363

CLARK. The Unity of the American Nationality. A Discourse delivered in ... Albany, November 26th, 1863, the Day of the National Thanksgiving. By Rufus W. Clark, D.D. *Albany: C. Van Benthuysen.* 1863. 8vo, pp. 42. H. 13364

CLARK. War with Mexico. A Sermon preached in the North Church, Portsmouth, N. H. Sept. 7, 1845, by Rufus W. Clark ... . [*Portsmouth.*] *C. W. Brewster, Printer.* 1845. 32mo, pp. 17. H. 13365

Also: Agency of Steam Power in promoting Civilization and Christianity ... . *Portsmouth, N. H.: S. A. Badger.* [n. d.] 12mo, pp. 12. H. — A Discourse Delivered before the Society for the Prevention of Pauperism ... Jan. 8, 1854. ... *Boston: printed by John Wilson and Son.* 1854. 8vo, pp. 23. H. — The Great Evil in New York and Brooklyn. An Address, delivered in the South Congregational Church, Brooklyn, ... June 10th, and repeated ... June 24th, 1850 ... . *New York.* 1860. 8vo, pp. 19. H. — A Memoir of the Rev. J. E. Emerson ... with Extracts from his Writings ... *Boston.* 1852. 8vo. — Popery and the United States, embracing an Account of Papal Operations in our Country, with a View of the Dangers which threaten our Institutions. ... . *Boston: J. V. Bean & Co.* 1847. 12mo, pp. 19. H. — The Question of the Hour: the Bible and School Fund. ... *Boston: Lee and Shepard.* 1870. 16mo, pp. 127. H. — A Sermon preached at the Dedication of the New Congregational Church in Barnstead, N. H., October 29. 1851. ... . *Portsmouth: C. W. Brewster, Printer.* 1851. 8vo, pp. 23. H. — A Sermon preached at the Ordination of Mr. John E. Emerson, ... in Newburyport, ... January 1, 1850, ... *Newburyport: Moses H. Sargent.* 1850. 8vo, pp. 53. H. — The Sources of a Physician's Power. An Address delivered at the Commencement of the Albany Medical College, May 28th, 1863 ... . *Albany.* 1863. 8vo, pp. 30. H.

CLARK (S. A.) The Episcopal Church in the American Colonies. The History of St. John's Church, Elizabeth Town, New Jersey, from the Year 1703 to the Present Time. Compiled from Original Documents, the Manuscript Records and Letters of the Missionaries of the Society for Propagating the Gospel in Foreign Parts, and from other Sources. By Samuel A. Clark. ... *Philadelphia: J. B. Lippincott and Co. New York: Thomas N. Stanford.* 1857. 12mo, pp. 203. Woodcuts. H.

A meritorious performance. There are errors in dates on pages 23, 129, and 130. *See* "Hist. Mag.," I. 378.

[CLARK.] A Pastoral Report of the Rector of the Church of the Advent, Philadelphia. *Philadelphia.* 1855. 16mo, pp. 16.

Also: A Memoir of Rev. Albert W. Duy. *Philadelphia: Am. S. S. Union.* 1847. 18mo. (Also prefixed to Duy's Sermons.)

CLARK (S. W.) Tribute to the Memory of the Rev. Samuel Wallace Clark. *Boston: printed by Damrell & Moore.* 1847. 8vo, pp. 23. B., H. 13368

CLARK (S. D.) The Utility and Glory of God's Immutable Purposes. By Sereno D. Clark. *Boston.* 1857. 12mo. + Second Edition. *Boston: Congregational Board of Publication.* 1860. 16mo, pp. 218. B. 13369

CLARK (S. M.) Trial for Arson ... [Aug. 17, 1820, of] Stephen Merril Clark. [n. p. 1821.] 8vo, pp. 63, (1). BA.

Also: Account of his Short Life and Ignominious Death. *Salem.* 1821. 8vo.

CLARK (Strong). An Address, Investigating Society ... (Lyme, Jefferson County, N. Y.) 18mo, pp. 10. S. 13371

CLARK (S.) *See* Clarke (S.)

CLARK (Thaddeus). A Treatise on the Scarlatina Anginosa, etc. *Norwich, Conn.* 1795. 12mo. S. 13372

CLARK (T.), *of Barbadoes.* A Warning to the Inhabitants of Barbadoes, entitled, The Voice of Truth, uttered forth against the Unreasonableness, Rudenes, and Deboistnes of the Rulers, Teachers and People of the Island of Barbadoes. Through one, who hath suffered by them, for the Testimony of a Good Conscience, and the Word of God, known by the name of Thomas Clark. *London: Printed for Robert Wilson.* 1661. 4to, $1\frac{1}{2}$ sheets.

CLARK (T.) Remarks upon the manner and form of Swearing by touching and kissing the Gospels: in a letter to a friend. ... By the Rev. Mr. Thomas Clark, Minister ... , *Glasgow, printed: Lancaster reprinted by W. Dunlap, in Queen Street, for Mr. Alexander Mure, in Chestnut Street,* 1755. 12mo, pp. 30.

One of the earliest specimens of printing done at Lancaster, Pennsylvania.

CLARK. Observations on the Nature and Cure of Fevers and of Diseases of the West and East Indies, and of America ... . By Thomas Clark ... . *Edinburgh: Bell & Bradfute. London: G. & J. Robinson.* 1801. 8vo, pp. xvi, 256. B. 13375

CLARK. American Chronology from the Discovery of the Western World untill May 3d, 1814. By Thomas Clark. *Philadelphia.* 1814. 18mo, pp. 52. 13376

CLARK. Sketches of the Naval History of the United States; from the Commencement of the Revolutionary War, to the

Present Time, containing Detailed Accounts of all the Interesting Actions of the Public Vessels ... and of Privateers; and an Historical View of the Policy and Acts of the ... Government, relative to the Naval Establishment: likewise ... Documents ... . By Thomas Clark. *Philadelphia: M. Carey.* 1813. 12mo, Title, pp. xiv, 13–177, (1), cxxxix. BA. 13377

In some copies of the first edition the title differs, and is dated 1814. Reprinted as:

CLARK. The Naval History of the United States, from the Commencement of the Revolutionary War to the Present Time. By Thomas Clark. Second Edition. In Two Volumes. *Philadelphia: M. Carey.* 1814. 2 vols., 12mo, 6 l., pp. 13–239, Plate; 2 l., pp. vii–xii, 17–255. Copperplate of the capture of the "Guerriere." B., H. 13378

In this edition the work has been altogether newly modelled.

[CLARK (T. G.)] Be Patient! A Tract for the Times. ... *Philadelphia: American Sunday-School Union.* 8vo, pp. 14.

CLARK (T. M.) An Address delivered in Christ Church, Gardiner, at the Funeral of the Rt. Rev. George Burgess, D.D., First Bishop of Maine, May XXX, MDCCCLXVI. By the Rt. Rev. Thomas M. Clark, D.D. ... *Brunswick: J. Griffin,* [*Printer.*] 1866. 8vo, pp. 21, (1). H. 13380

CLARK. Address in Commemoration of Washington's Birth day, before the First Light Infantry of Providence, Feb. 22, 1861. By T. M. Clark. *Providence: Cooke & Danielson.* 1861. 12mo, pp. 24. 13381

CLARK. Oration ... [at] Providence, on the Eighty-Fourth Anniversary of American Independence, July 4, 1860. By Thomas M. Clark, D.D. *Providence: Knowles, Anthony & Co., City Printers.* 1860. 8vo, pp. 32. B. 13382

CLARK. Relations of the Past to the Present. A Discourse delivered before the Ancient & Honorable Artillery Company on their CCXI Anniversary by Thomas M. Clark ... . Published by request of the Company. *Boston.* 1849. 8vo, pp. 22.

CLARK. State Reform School. A Discourse delivered ... in Hartford, ... May 23, 1852. *Hartford: F. A. Brown.* 1852. 8vo, pp. 16. H. 13384

CLARK. The State of the Country. A Sermon delivered in Grace Church, Providence, November 25, 1860. By Thomas

M. Clark ... *Providence: Cooke, Danielson & Co.* 1860. 8vo, pp. 10. 13385

Also: Annual Address before the Massachusetts Temperance Society, ... May 27, 1838. ... . *Boston: printed by Cassady and March.* 1838. 8vo, pp. 22. B., H. — Christian Culture. A Sermon in behalf of The General Protestant Episcopal S. S. Union, and Church Book Society, ... June 22, 1856. ... *New York.* 1856. 8vo, pp. 20. H. — A Complete Faith. Third Triennial Charge to the Clergy of the Diocese of Rhode Island. ... *Providence: Cooke, Jackson & Co., Printers.* 1864. 8vo, pp. 22. H. — Correspondence between Bishop Clark and Rev. J. P. Hubbard. [n. p. 1868.] 8vo, pp. 4. H. — An Efficient Ministry. A Sermon preached before the Convention of the Protestant Episcopal Church in Pennsylvania, Philadelphia, May 21, 1845. ... *Philadelphia.* 1845. 8vo, pp. 16. — The Lack of Religious Culture fatal to our Public and Social System. Fourth Triennial Charge to the Clergy of the Diocese of Rhode Island ... . *Providence.* 1867. 8vo, pp. 24. H. — Primary Charge to the Clergy of the Diocese of Rhode Island: ... . Printed by order of the Convention. *Providence: G. H. Whitney.* 1855. 8vo, pp. 19. H. — Sermon on the ... Exposition at Fales and Gray's Car Manufactory. *Hartford, Ct.: E. T. Pean & Co.* 8vo, pp. 51. — Semi-Centennial Address before the American Colonization Society. *Washington.* 1867. 8vo, pp. 15.

CLARK (Uriah). The Spiritualist Register ... containing Facts and Statistics of Spiritualism, for 1857. By Mr. & Mrs. U. Clark. *Auburn, N. Y.: U. Clark.* 1857. 18mo, pp. 36. Continued. BA. 13386

[CLARK (W. A.)] The Cannonade. By Anicetus ... . *Boston: A. Williams & Co.* 1861. 12mo, pp. 148. B., H. 13387

"Our country! teeming with the gifts of God,
'Gainst thee we lift stern satire's iron rod."

[CLARK.] Our Modern Athens; or, Who is First? A Poem. By Anicetus ... . *Boston: Redding & Co.* 1860. 12mo, pp. 70. H. 13388

CLARK (W. J.) The National Foundery for the West: where shall it be located? A Letter to the Hon. John Sherman, ... by Rev. William J. Clark, Rector of Christ Church, Portsmouth, Ohio. *Cincinnati: Bradley & Webb, Printers.* 1862. 8vo, pp. 17. H. 13389

CLARK (W.) Trial of Willard Clark for the Murder of Richard W. Wight. *New Haven.* 1855. 8vo, pp. 217.

CLARK (W. R.) A Discourse on the Formation and Progress of the First Methodist Episcopal Church in Lynn; delivered ... November 14, 1858. By William R. Clark. ... *Boston: Press of Geo. C. Rand & Avery.* 1859. 8vo, pp. 37. B. 13391

CLARK. Centennial Anniversary at Athol. 8vo. 13392

CLARKE (A. B.) Travels in Mexico and California ... . By A. B. Clarke. *Boston: Wright & Hasty, Printers.* 1852. 12mo, pp. 138. B. 13393

CLARKE (A. L.) A Discourse delivered at Providence, before the Grand Lodge of ... Masons of ... Rhode Island, June 24. 1794. By Abraham Lynson Clarke, A.M. ... *Providence: Carter & Wilkinson.* 1794. 8vo, pp. 18. W. 13394

CLARKE. A | Discourse, | occasioned by the Death of | General George Washington. | At Mount-Vernon, Dec. 14, 1799. Delivered before the Right Worshipful Master and | Brethren of Mount-Vernon Lodge and | the Congregation of St. John's Church, in | Providence, | on Saturday, the 22d of February A.L. 5800. | By Abraham L. Clark, A.M. | Rector of St. John's Church, Providence. | *Providence: Printed by John Carter.* 1800. | 8vo, pp. 26.

The last page is erroneously numbered 15. It is usually followed by "An Address delivered before Mount Vernon Lodge, On the Anniversary Election of Officers, February 22, 1800. By Amos Mawe Atwell, A.M. *Providence: Printed by Brother John Carter.* 1800." 8vo, pp. 18. Also: The Secrets of Masonry illustrated and explained; in a Discourse Preached at South Kingston, before the Grand Lodge of the State of Rhode Island; ... September 3d, A.L. 5799. *Providence: Bennett Wheeler.* 1799. 8vo.

CLARKE (B.) Speech of Hon Bayard Clarke of New York, on the Senate Kansas Bill, and in Defence of the American Party. ... In the House ... July 24, 1856. *Washington.* 1856. 8vo, pp. 16. H. 13396

CLARKE (C.) ... A Sermon preached at the Funeral of Mrs. Susan Heard, Cleaveland, ... who died at Marshall, Mich. October 1st, 1843. By the Rev. Calvin Clarke, of Kalamazoo. *Cincinnati: printed by Shepard & Co.* 1844. 8vo, pp. 32. B.

CLARKE (C. E.) Speech of Charles E. Clarke, of New York, on the Boundary between Texas & New-Mexico. *Washington.* 1850. 8vo. 13398

Also: Speech ... on the Admission of California. *Washington.* 1850. 8vo.

CLARKE (E.) A Sermon delivered at Middlefield, Mass. March 26, 1845, at the Funeral of Deacon David Mack, by Rev. Edward Clarke ... With an Appendix. ... *Amherst: J. S. & C. Adams, Printers.* 1845. 8vo, pp. 16. H. 13399

CLARKE (E.) A Treatise upon the Laws of Extradition. With the Conventions upon the Subject existing between England and Foreign Nations, and the Cases decided thereon. By Edward Clarke. *London: Stevens & Haynes.* 1867. 12mo, pp. x, 183. C. 13400

CLARKE (F. W.) Views Around Ithaca: Being a Description of the Waterfalls and Ravines Of this Remarkable Locality, by F. W. Clarke ... . *Ithaca, N. Y.: Andrus, McChain & Co., Publishers.* [1869.] 12mo, pp. 155. H. 13401

CLARKE (G.) Voyage of George Clarke, Esq., to America. With Introduction and Notes, By E. B. O'Callaghan. *Albany: J. Munsell.* 1867. 4to, pp. lxxxi, 126. Photograph. BA., C.

CLARKE (H.) History of the Sabbatarians or Seventh Day Baptists in America. Containing their Rise and Progress To the Year 1811, with their Leaders' Name and their Distinguishing Tenets, &c. By Henry Clarke ... . *Utica: Seward & William.* 1811. 12mo, pp. 196, 2 l. + *Utica: the Author.* 1814. 12mo, pp. 196, 2 l. BA. 13403

CLARKE (H. C.) Diary of the War for Separation, A Daily Chronicle of the Principal Events and History of the Present Revolution, to which is added Notes and Descriptions of all the Great Battles, including Walker's Narrative of the Battle of Shiloh. By H. C. Clarke, Vicksburg, Miss. *Vicksburg.* 1862. 8vo, pp. 191. 13404

CLARKE. Diary of the War for Separation ... to the Battle of Shiloh; containing Full and Minute Statements of all the ... Engagements, Lists of Killed and Wounded, Number of Forces engaged, etc. ... with Biographical Sketches of Confederate Generals ... . Edited by H. C. Clarke. *Vicksburg: Clarke's Southern Publishing House.* 1862. 8vo, pp. 56. BA. 13405

Also: Clarke's Confederate Household Almanac, for ... 1863 ... . *Vicksburg, Miss.: H. C. Clarke.* 1863. 8vo, pp. 21 [23]. BA.

CLARKE (H. S.) Speech of Mr. Clarke of North Carolina on the Tariff Bill, Delivered in the House of Representatives, June 30, 1846. [n. p. n. d.] 8vo, pp. 16. H. 13406

CLARKE (I. E.) "Re-union." A Speech delivered at the Decennial Celebration of the Class of 1855, Yale College, New-Haven, Conn., July 26th, 1865, By Col. Isaac Edwards Clarke ... . *New-York: Alfred Cobb, Printer.* 1866. 8vo. pp. 9. H.

Also: Oration at the River House, July 4, 1867. 8vo.

CLARKE (J. A.) A Sermon Preached before the Rhode Island Clerical Convention in Bristol. By Rev. J. A. Clarke. *Providence: Marshall, Brown & Co.* 1834. 8vo, pp. 32. 13408

CLARKE (J. F.) The Annexation of Texas. A Sermon delivered in the Masonic Temple on Fast Day [April 4, 1844]. By James Freeman Clarke ... . *Boston.* 1844. 16mo, pp. 42.

CLARKE. Discourse on the Aspects of the War, delivered in ... Boston, on Fast Day, April 2, 1863. By James Freeman Clarke. ... *Boston: Walker, Wise and Company.* 1863. 8vo, pp. 36. B. 13410

CLARKE. The Duties of Massachusetts. A Sermon ... before the ... Government of Massachusetts, at the Annual Election, Wednesday, Jan. 1, 1868. By James Freeman Clarke. *Boston: Wright & Potter, State Printers.* 1868. 8vo, pp. 46. 13411

CLARKE. A Look at the Life of Theodore Parker: a Discourse concerning Theodore Parker; delivered ... June 3, 1860. By James Freeman Clarke. *Boston: Walker, Wise and Company.* 1860. 8vo, pp. 20. H. 13412

CLARKE. Memorial of the Commemoration by the Church of the Disciples of the Fiftieth Birth-day of their Pastor, James Freeman Clarke, April 4, 1860. *Boston: Prentiss & Deland, Printers.* 1860. 12mo, pp. 47. B. 13413

[CLARKE.] The Pilgrim Fathers; A Poem recited ... on the Festival of the Pilgrims, December 22d, 1842. From the Christian Examiner for May, 1843. *Boston: Thurston & Torry.* 1843. 8vo, pp. 11. B. 13414

CLARKE. Order of Services at Indiana-Place Chapel, on Easter Sunday, April 16, 1865; being the Sunday after the Assassination of Abraham Lincoln. *Boston: Walker, Fuller & Co.* 1865. 12mo, pp. 24. B. 13415

CLARKE. The Rendition of Anthony Burns. Its Causes and Consequences. A Discourse on Christian Politics, delivered in ... Boston ... June 4, 1854. By James Freeman Clarke. ... *Boston: Crosby, Nichols & Co., and Prentiss & Sawyer.* 1854. 8vo, pp. 28. B., BA., M. 13416

[CLARKE.] Secession, Concession, or Self-Possession: Which? *Boston: Walker, Wise and Company.* 1861. 8vo, pp. 48. B., BA., H. 13417

CLARKE. Slavery in the United States. A Sermon delivered in Amory Hall, on Thanksgiving Day, November 24, 1842.

By James Freeman Clarke. ... *Boston: Benjamin H. Greene.* 1843. 12mo, pp. 25. B., BA., H. 13418

Also: The Church, ... as it was, as it is, as it ought to be. A Discourse delivered at the Dedication of the Chapel, built by the Church of the Disciples, March 15, 1848. *Boston.* 1848. 8vo, pp. 36. — The hour which cometh, and now is: Sermons preached in Indiana-Place Chapel, Boston. ... By James Freeman Clarke. *Boston: Walker, Wise and Company.* 16mo, pp. vi, 348. BA. + *Boston: W. V. Spencer.* 1868. 12mo, pp. 6, 364. — Natural and Artificial Methods in Education. A Lecture delivered before the American Institute of Instruction, At Concord, N. H., August 27, 1863 ... . *Boston: Ticknor and Fields.* 1864. 12mo, pp. 29. H — A Poem, delivered before the Phi Beta Kappa Society, Alpha of Massachusetts ... August 27, 1846. ... *Boston: Wm. Crosby and H. P. Nichols.* 1846. 8vo, pp. 24. H. — Present Condition of the Free Colored People of the United States. ... *New-York.* 1859. 18mo, pp. 27. H. — A Sermon preached in Armory Hall, Oct. 9th, 1842, being the Sunday succeeding the Death of William Ellery Channing. ... *Boston: Benjamin H. Greene.* 1842. 12mo, pp. 20. B., BA., H. — A Sermon preached at the Installation of Rev. George F. Simmons, and Rev. Samuel Ripley, ... Waltham, Mass., October 27, 1841. ... *Boston: Benjamin H. Greene.* MDCCCXLI. 8vo, pp. 19. H., M. — A Sermon Preached in the Indiana Place Chapel on Sunday Morning, Nov. 6, 1859. ... *Boston: Walker, Wise & Co.* 1859. 8vo, pp. 14.

CLARKE (J. S.) The Progress of Maritime Discovery, from the Earliest Period to the Close of the Eighteenth Century, forming an Extensive System of Hydrography. By James Stanier Clarke, F.R.S., Domestic Chaplin to The Prince, and Vicar of Preston ... *London: T. Cadell, and W. Davis.* MDCCCIII. 4to, pp. xxxv, ccxxx, 490, 263. Map and Plates. BA., H. 13419

Comes down to the end of the fifteenth century, and is all that was published of the work. The "Edinburgh Review" is rather severe in its criticisms, but allows the author credit for his bibliographical researches. The appendix contains, among other things, Galvano's Discoveries of the World, and Locke's History of Navigation, and Explanatory Catalogue of Voyages from Churchill's collection. *See* M. R., XLV. 403.

CLARKE. The Life of Admiral Lord Nelson, K.B., from his Lordship's Manuscripts. By the Rev. J. Stanier Clarke and John McArthur, Esq. *London: T. Cadell.* 1809–10. 2 vols., 4to, pp. vi, 15, xlv, 375; 511. 16 Plates. B., C. + Another Edition. 3 vols., 8vo. + *London: Fisher, Son & Co.* [n. d.] 8vo, pp. 526. 15 Plates. 13420

The quarto edition contains a fine series of engravings by Golding, Fittler, Landseer, tc. It also contains details of Nelson's services in the West Indies.

CLARKE. Naufragia; or, Historical Memoirs of Shipwrecks, and of the Providential Deliverance of Vessels [1493–1649]. By James Stanier Clarke, F.R.S. ... *London: Mawman.* 1805. 12mo. Map and Plate. 13421

See M. R., LXX. 219. A second volume was published in 1806.

CLARKE (J.) An | Impartial and Authentic | Narrative | of the | Battle | Fought on the 17th of June, 1775, | between | His Britannic Majesty's Troops | and the | American Provincial Army, | on | Bunker's Hill, near Charles Town, in New-England. | With | A True and Faithful Account of the Officers | who were killed and wounded in that memorable | Battle. | To which are added, | Some particular Remarks and Anecdotes which | have not yet transpired. | The whole being collected and written on the Spot. | The Second Edition, | With Extracts from Three Letters lately received from | America; | And all the Promotions in the Army and Marines | since the said Battle. | By John Clarke, | First Lieutenant of Marines. | *London: | Printed for the Author: And Sold by J. Millar, Whitehall; | J. Bew, in Pater-noster Row; and — Sewel, in Cornhill.* | MDCCLXXV. ... | ... | 8vo, Title, pp. 36. S. 13422

This interesting contemporary report is a volume of much rarity. Mr. Rich notices the *first* edition, and describes it as having pp. 36, and as this has no more, it is difficult to understand how the "Extracts from three Letters lately received from America," etc., should have *first* appeared in this second edition. *See* M. R., LIII. 265.

CLARKE (J.) A Discourse ... February 15, 1787. At the Interment of the Rev. Charles Chauncy ... . By John Clarke .... *Boston: printed by James D. Griffith and Edward E. Powars.* M,DCC,LXXXVII. 8vo, pp. 34, (4). BA. 13423

CLARKE. A Sermon delivered at the Church in Brattle-street, January 2, 1784. At the Interment of the Rev. Samuel Cooper, D.D. who Expired, December 29, 1783. By John Clarke ... . *Boston: Printed by John Gill.* M,DCC,LXXXIV. 8vo, pp. 35. BA.

Also: A Discourse ... 19th April, A.D. 1795 ... after the Interment of Nathaniel W. Appleton, M.D. ... *Boston: Samuel Hall.* 1796. 8vo, pp. 22, (1). BA. — A Discourse, delivered before the Humane Society of the Commonwealth of Massachusetts, ... Eleventh of June, 1793. ... . *Boston: printed by Belknap and Hall.* MDCCXCIII. 8vo, pp. 36. B., BA., H. — Letters to a Student [John Pickering] in the University of Cambridge, Massachusetts. By John Clarke ... . *Boston: Printed and sold by Samuel Hall.* 1796. 18mo, pp. 148. B., BA. — The Occasional Discourses preached in Boston. *Boston.* 1804. 12mo. — [Clarke.] Salvation for all Men. Illustrated and Vindicated as a Scripture Doctrine, etc. *Boston.* 1782. 8vo, pp. 26. — A Discourse delivered ... in Boston, 19th April, A.D. 1795, the Lord's-Day after the Interment of Nathaniel W. Appleton, M.D. ... *Boston: Printed by Samuel Hall.* 1796. 8vo, pp. 22, (1). B., BA., H. — [Clarke.] Letter to Dr. Mather, occasioned by his Reflexions upon a Pamphlet entitled Salvation for all Men. *Boston.* 1796. 8vo, pp. 9. H. — Sermon on the Divine Use of Vocal Music. *Boston: N. Bowes.* 1770. — Sermon by the Late Reverend John Clarke, D.D. Minister of the First Church in Boston ... . *Boston: Samuel Hall.* 1799. 8vo, pp. 501, (3). Portrait. BA. Some other pieces by this author are described under Clark (John); he seems to have spelt his name both ways. *See* Mather (R.)

CLARKE (J.) A Treatise on the Mulberry Tree and Silk Worm, and on the Production and Manufacture of Silk. *Philadelphia.* 1839. 12mo. 13425

CLARKE (J.) Memoir of Richard and Joseph Merrick, Missionaries in Jamaica. By John Clarke. *London.* 1850. Fcap 8vo, pp. 104. 13426

CLARKE (John). Address to the People of Pennsylvania, read to the Anti-Masonic Convention, Feb. 25. *Lancaster.* 1830. 8vo. B. 13427

CLARKE (J. H.) Speech of Mr. Clarke, of Rhode Island, on the California Claims. Delivered in the Senate of the United States, April 25, 1848. *Washington.* 1848. 8vo, pp. 15. H.

CLARKE. Speech of the Hon. J. H. Clarke, of Rhode Island. On the Subject of Intervention, Delivered in the Senate of the United States, February 9, 1852. [n. p. n. d.] 8vo, pp. 15.

CLARKE (J.) The Importance of military Skill, Measures for Defence and a Martial Spirit, in a Time of Peace. A Sermon preached To the Ancient and Honourable Artillery Company ... June 6. 1768, Being the Anniversary of their Election of Officers, By Jonas Clarke ... . *Boston, New England: Nicholas Bowes.* MDCCLXVIII. 8vo, pp. 27. BA. 13430

CLARKE. Christ's Mission of the Seventy ... a Sermon ... at the Ordination Of the Reverend Josiah Bridge ... Sudbury, Nov. 4, 1761. *Boston: Edes and Gill.* MDCCLXI. 8vo, pp. 41.

CLARKE (J. S.) Historical Discourse preached in, May 16, 1855. By Joseph S. Clarke, D.D. *Boston.* 1855. 8vo, pp. 30.

CLARKE (L.) Narrative of the Sufferings of Lewis Clarke, during a Captivity of more than Twenty-five Years among the Algerines of Kentucky, one of the so called Christian States of North America. Dictated by Himself. *Boston: David H. Ela, Printer.* 1845. 12mo, pp. 108. Portrait. + *Boston.* 1846. C.

CLARKE (L. *and* M.) Narratives of the Sufferings of Lewis and Milton Clarke, during a captivity of more than twenty years among Slaveholders of Kentucky. *Boston.* 1846. C.

CLARKE (McD.) Afara; or, the Belles of Broadway. By McDonald Clarke. *New York.* 1829. 4 pts., 8vo.

Some other of the works of this eccentric writer bear on local topics; his works are now scarce. The following is a list: "A Cross and a Coronet. *New York.* 1841." 12mo, pp. 46; "Death in Disguise. A Temperance Poem ... *Boston.* 1838." 18mo, pp. 56; "The Elixir of Moonshine; being a Collection of Prose and Poetry, by the Mad Poets. *Gotham.* L.M. 5222." pp. 118; "The Gossip, or a Laugh with the Ladies, a Grin with the Gentlemen, and Burlesque on Byron, a Sentimental Satire; with other Poems. ... *New York.* 1825." 18mo, pp. 226. Portrait; "Poems ... *New York: J. W. Bell.* MDCCCXXXVI." 8vo, pp. 288. Portrait; "A Review of the Eve of Eternity, and other Poems. 1822." 8vo, pp. 24; and "Sketches in Verse —

namely, Dutch Dignity, ... Death of La-Fayette, &c. *New York.* 1826." 18mo, pp. 128. *See* Duyckinck's "Cyclopædia," II. 261–3.

CLARKE (*Mrs.* Mary Nevello, *wife of* Ch. Cowden). World-Noted Women, or Types of Womanly Attributes of all Lands and Ages. By Mrs. Cowden Clark. *New York: D. Appleton & Co.* 1858. Imp. 8vo. 17 Portraits. 13436

Includes Pocohontas.

CLARKE (M.) The Memoirs of the Celebrated and Beautiful Mrs. Anne Carson, Daughter of an Officer in the U. S. Navy and Wife of Another, whose life terminated in the Philadelphia Prison. By Mrs. M. Clarke, Authoress of the Life of Edwin Forrest, etc. *Philadelphia.* 1838. 2 vols., 12mo. 13436*a*

Mrs. Carson was a distinguished member of what she calls "the unsanctified sisterhood that infest our streets."

CLARKE (Matthew St. Clair), *Joint Editor.* *See* Force (Peter), and "American State Papers," Vol. I., No. 1228.

CLARKE. Cases of Contested Elections in Congress, from the Year 1789 to 1834, inclusive. Compiled by M. St. Clair Clarke ... and David A. Hall. Printed by Order of the House of Representatives. *Washington: printed by Gales and Seaton.* 1834. 8vo, pp. 1025. H. 13437

CLARKE. Legislative and Documentary History of the Bank of the United States: including the original Bank of North America. Compiled by M. St. Clair Clarke & D. A. Hall. *Washington: Gales and Seaton.* 1832. 8vo, pp. vi, 832, 799–808.

CLARKE (M. St. C.), *and* FORCE (Peter). Report made to the Hon. John Forsyth, Secretary of State of the United States, on the Subject of the Documentary History of the United States, now publishing under the Act of Congress. *Washington.* 1834. 8vo. 13439

CLARKE (O. L.) Speech of O. L. Clarke against a National Bankrupt Law, in the House of Representatives, Feb. 28, 1863. [n. p. n. d.]. 8vo, pp. 16. 13440

CLARKE (P.) Memorial of Rev. Pitt Clarke, Pastor of the First Congregational Church in Norton, Mass., and of Mary Jones Clarke (his Wife). Printed for Private Distribution. *Cambridge: John Wilson and Son.* 1866. 4to, pp. 94. H., B.

CLARKE (R.) The Prophetic Number of Daniel and John calculated: in order to shew the time when the Day of Judgment for this First Age of the Gospel, is to be expected; and the setting up the Millenial Kingdom of Jehovah and his Christ.

By Richard Clarke, ... Second Edition, with Additions. *South-Carolina, Charles-Town, ... Peter Timothy.* M,DCC,LIX. 8vo, pp. 27. + *Boston: reprinted.* 1759. 13442

The day of judgment was limited to five years from the date of Mr. Clarke's essay. It was answered by the following: "From a Folio Manuscript, in the Archive of a certain aged Gormogon, at present in Province of the Massachusetts Bay, the following Questions and Answers are extracted, &c. In answer to the Pamphlet, call'd The Prophetic Numbers of Daniel and John. *Boston.* 1759." 8vo. W. Also: A Series of Essays, Letters, and Discourses, &c. ... *London.* 1780. 8vo. — Signs of the Times, or a Voice from Babylon. 1773. 8vo. — Voice of Glad Tidings to Jews and Gentiles, 1763, etc.

CLARKE (S.), *Minister of St. Bennets-Fink.* A Geographicall Description of all the Countries in the Known World. As also of the greatest and famousest Cities and Fabricks which have been, or are now remaining ... By Samuel Clarke. *London: Thomas Newberry.* 1657. Folio, pp. 225, Tables, pp. 8.

America is described on pages 169–190.

CLARKE. Geographical Description of all the Countries in the Knowne Worlde; as also of the Chiefest Cittyes, Famousest Structures, Greatest Rivers, Strongest Fountaines, &c. To which is added a True and Faithful Account of the Four Chiefest Plantations of the English in America, to wit: Virginia, New England, Bermudas, Barbados; as also of the Natives of Virginia and New England — their Religion, Customs, Fishing, Huntings, &c. Collected by Samuel Clarke. *London.* 1670–71. Folio. C. 13444

CLARKE. The Life and Death of the Valiant and Renowned Sir Francis Drake. His Voyages and Discoveries in the West Indies and about the World, with his Noble and Heroick Acts. By Samuel Clarke ... *London: Simon Miller.* 1671. Sm. 4to, pp. 71. Portrait of Drake, by Vaughan. J.C.B. 13445

In some copies the title is: "The Life and Death of Sir Francis Drake, with His Voyages into the West-Indies, and about the World; And other of his Valiant Actions. *London.* 1671." 4to, pp. 71. There are other editions in which the titles differ. *See* Drake (F.)

CLARKE. Lives of Sundry Eminent Persons, in this latter Age ... By Samuel Clarke. *London.* 1683. Folio. Portrait by White. 13446

Contains the life, voyage, and settlement in America, of Richard Mather, father of Increase Mather.

CLARKE. A Mirrovr or Looking-Glasse Both for Saints and Sinners ... By ... Examples ... . By Sa. Clarke ... . *London: John Bellamy.* 1646. 8vo, 11 l., pp. 227. B. 13447

Among the examples are, "The wife of Mr. William Dier," and "Mistress Hutchinson," pp. 114–116.

CLARKE. A Mirrour ... . Whereunto are added a Geographical description of all the Countries in the known World, as also the Wonders of God in Nature; and the Rare, Stupendious [*sic*] and Costly Works made by the Art and Industry of Man, As the most famous Cities, Temples, Structures, Statues, Cabinets of Rarities &c. which have been, or are now in the World. *London.* 1657. Folio. + Fourth Edition, much enlarged, with the addition of a True and Faithful Account of the Four chiefest Plantations of the English in America, viz. Virginia, New-England, Bermudas, and Barbados, 1671. *London.* 1671. 2 vols., folio. Frontispieces by R. Gaywood, and Portrait by T. Cross. 13448

CLARKE. A New Description of the World. Or, a Compendious Treatise of the Empires, Kingdoms, States, Provinces, Countries, Islands, Cities and Towns of Europe, Asia, Africa and America: In their Situation, Product, Manufactures and Commodities, Geographical and Historical. With An Account of the natures of the People, in their Habits, Customs, Wars, Religions and Policy, &c. As also, Of the Rarities, Wonders and Curiosities, of Fishes, Beasts, Birds, Rivers, Mountains, Plants, &c. With several remarkable Revolutions, and delightful Histories. By S. Clarke. *London: Henry Rhodes.* 1708. 12mo, 3 l., pp. 218. + *London: Henry Rhodes.* 1712. 12mo, 3 l., pp. 218, 1 l. Plate. C. 13449

CLARKE. A True, and Faithful | Account | of the | Four Chiefest | Plantations | of the | English in America. | To wit, | Of Virginia. | New-England. | Bermvdvs. | Barbados. | With the Temperature of the Air: The nature of the | Soil: The Rivers, Mountains, Beasts, Fowls, Birds, | Fishes, Trees, Plants, Fruits, &c. | As also, | Of the Natives of Virginia, and New-England, their | Religion, Customs, Fishing, Huntings, &c. | Collected | By Samuel Clarke, sometimes Pastor in Saint Bennet-Fink, London. | *London,* | *Printed for Robert Clavel, Thomas Passenger, William Cadman, William* | *Whitwood, Thomas Sawbridge, and William Birch.* 1670. Folio, pp. 85. S. 13450

Also included in No. 13444.

CLARKE (S.) The Character and Reward of the Righteous. A Sermon, occasioned by the Death of John Adams: preached in Princeton, July 16, 1826. By Samuel Clarke ... . *Worcester: William Manning, Printer.* [n. d.] 8vo, pp. 23. BA., H.

CLARKE. A Sermon delivered at the Dedication of the First Congregational Church, Uxbridge, Mass., Jan. 13, 1835. By Samuel Clarke ... *Mendon.* 1835. 8vo, pp. 24. 13452

CLARKE. A Tribute to the Memory of Mrs. Susannah Adams, ... of Uxbridge, who died Oct. 13, 1840 ... and of Miss Sarah W. Capron ... who died Oct. 12, 1840 ... . By their ... Pastor, Samuel Clarke. *Boston: James Munroe and Company.* 1840. 12mo, pp. 18. 13453

CLARKE. Twenty-Fifth Anniversary Sermon preached ... in Uxbridge, January 10, 1858, by ... Samuel Clarke. *Milford: printed by George W. Stacy.* [n. d.] 8vo, pp. 20. H. 13454

Also: Masonic Address at Princeton, Mass. June 24, 1818. *Worcester.* 1818. 8vo. — Masonic Address at Grafton, Mass. June 24, 1819. *Worcester.* 8vo. — Christmas Sermon at Princeton. *Boston.* 1823. 8vo.

CLARKE (S. C.), *and* DEAN (Paul). Addresses delivered at the stated Communication of the Grand Chapter of Mass., June 8, 1830. By the Rev. Samuel Clarke, H.P., and Paul Dean, G.G.K. *Boston: Marsh, Capen & Lyon.* 1830. 8vo, pp. 23. B., H. 13455

CLARKE. Records of some of the Descendants of Thomas Clarke, 1623–1697. Compiled by Samuel C. Clarke. *Boston: printed by David Clapp & Son.* 1869. 8vo, pp. 43. BA. 13456

CLARKE. Records of some of the Descendants of John Fuller, Newton, 1644–98. Compiled ... by Samuel C. Clarke. *Boston: printed by David Clapp & Son.* 1869. 8vo, pp. 16. BA.

CLARKE. Records of some of the Descendants of Richard Hull, New Haven. Compiled by Samuel C. Clarke. *Boston: printed by David Clapp & Son.* 1869. 8vo, pp. 20 B., BA. 13458

CLARKE. Records of the Descendants of William Curtis, Roxbury, 1632. Compiled ... . By Samuel C. Clarke. *Boston: printed by David Clapp & Son.* 1869. 8vo, pp. 29. B., BA. 13459

CLARKE (S. F.) A Centennial Discourse, delivered Sept. 9, 1850, before the First Church and Society in Athol ... . With ... Appendix. By Samuel F. Clarke ... . *Boston: Wm. Crosby & H. P. Nichols.* 1851. 8vo, pp. 95. H., M. 13460

Also: Unitarian Christianity ... . A Sermon preached at the Dedication of the Unitarian Church in Athol, Mass ... December 8, 1847. By Samuel F. Clarke. ... *Boston: Wm. Crosby & H. P. Nichols.* 1848. 8vo, pp. 24. H.

[CLARKE (Sara J.)] Greenwood Leaves, a Collection of Sketches and Letters. By Grace Greenwood. *Boston: Ticknor, Reed & Fields.* 1850. 12mo, pp. 406. 13461

Also: A Forest Tragedy; and other Tales. By Grace Greenwood. *Boston.* 1856. 12mo, pp. 343. — Stories of Many Lands. ... Illustrated. *Boston.* 1867. Square 16mo, pp. viii, 206.

[CLARKE (Sidney).] Remonstrance against the Treaty with the Great and Little Osage Indians. ... *Washington: Gibson Brothers, Printers.* 1868. 12mo, pp. 11. H. 13462

CLARKE. Speech of Hon. Sidney Clarke, of Kansas, in the House of Representatives, March 7, 1868. [*Washington.* n. d.] 8vo, pp. 7. H. 13463

Also: Speech ... on Manhood Suffrage in the District of Columbia; ... January 18, 1866. *Washington.* 1866. 8vo, pp. 8. H.

CLARKE (T.) Sir Copp. A Poem for the Times, in Six Cantos. By Thomas Clarke. *Chicago.* 1866. 12mo, pp. viii, 122. 13464

A sarcastic political effusion, Sir Copp being intended for a Copperhead or Democrat.

CLARKE (T. C.) An Account of the Iron Railway Bridge across the Mississippi River, at Quincy, Illinois. By Thomas Curtis Clarke ... . *New York: D. Van Nostrand.* 1869. 4to, pp. 70, (1). 21 Lithographs. B. 13465

CLARKE (U.) Lectures on City Life and Character. By Uriah Clarke. *Lowell.* 1849. 13466

CLARKE (W.) ... A Discourse preached at the Installation of Rev. Erastus Dickinson, in the First Congregational Church of Colchester, Conn., October 22, 1851. By Rev. Walter Clarke ... . *Hartford: Press of Case, Tiffany and Company.* 1851. 8vo, pp. 31. H. 13467

CLARKE. Half-century Discourse. The First Church in Buffalo. Delivered ... Feb. 2, 1862. By Walter Clarke, D.D. *Buffalo: Theo. Butler.* 1862. 8vo, pp. 92. S. 13468

CLARKE. "The State of the Country." An Oration delivered at Buffalo, July 4th, 1862, by Walter Clarke, D.D. *Buffalo: Breed, Butler & Co.* 1862. 12mo, pp. 20. B. 13469

Also: A Discourse. The American Anti-Slavery Society at War with the Church, ... Canterbury, Conn. June 30, 1844.

[CLARKE (W.)] Observations On the late and present Conduct of the French, with Regard to the Encroachments upon the

British Colonies in North America. Together With Remarks on the Importance of these Colonies to Great-Britain. To which is added, wrote by another Hand; Observations concerning the Increase of Mankind, Peopling of Countries, &c. *Boston: S. Kneeland.* 1755. 4to, 3 l., pp. iv, 47, 15. BA. 13470

The dedication is signed, William Clarke. Reprinted with the following title:

CLARKE. Observations On the late and present Conduct of the French, with Regard to their Encroachments upon the British Colonies in North America. Together With Remarks on the Importance of these Colonies to Great-Britain. By William Clarke, M.D., of Boston, in New England. To which is added, wrote by another hand, Observations concerning the Increase of Mankind, Peopling of Countries, &c. *Boston, Printed ... London: Re-printed for John Clarke.* 1755. 8vo, 5 l., pp. 54. S. 13471

"The author considers that the prior discovery by Sebastian Cabot, in 1497, of the coast of a large portion of the continent of North America, and the subsequent grants by English sovereigns, of Nova Scotia, Connecticut, Massachusetts, and Virginia, with their western limits of the latter three extending to the South Sea, gave the English colonists a full right to the vast region embraced within these limits, and that the French, in all their occupations south of the St. Lawrence and the great lakes, were encroachments. — *Monthly Review,* XIII. 400. For some letters of Clarke, *see* "Mass. Hist. Soc. Coll.," v. 4. The papers added are by Benjamin Franklin. *See* Franklin's Works, II. 311, and Bancroft's "Hist. of the U. S.," IV. 213.

CLARKE (William), *Gov. of Mo.* Brief Notices of the Principal Events in the Public Life of Governor Clarke. [*St. Louis.* 1820.] 8vo, pp. 16. B. 13472

Clarke Institution. First Annual Report of the Clarke Institution for Deaf Mutes, at Northampton, Mass., ... 1867. *Boston: Wright & Potter, Printers.* 1868. 8vo, pp. 19. H. 13473

CLARKSON (M.) An Address to the Citizens of Philadelphia, respecting the Better Government of Youth. By Matthew Clarkson, Esq., Mayor. First Published in the Philadelphia Gazette, of Saturday, June 6, 1795. *Philadelphia: Ormrod & Conrad.* 1795. 8vo, pp. 24. P. + *Washington, Pa.: Reprinted.* 1795. 16mo, pp. 24. M. 13474

CLARKSON (Thomas). Le cri des Africains, contre les Européens leurs oppresseurs: ou Coup-d'œil sur le commerce homicide de la traite des noirs, traduit de l'anglois [par Benj. La Roche]. *Londres.* 1821. 8vo, pp. 56. + *Paris: Cellot.* 1822. 8vo, pp. 64. (Two editions the same year.) 13475

CLARKSON. Cries of Africa. By Thomas Clarkson. 1822. 8vo. 13476

CLARKSON. Histoire du commerce homicide appelé traite des noirs, ou Cri des Africains. ... [traduit] avec des observations préliminaires, par M. Grégoire. *Paris: Marchands de nouveautés.* 1822. 8vo, pp. 88. 13477

CLARKSON. An Essay on the Comparative Efficiency of Regulation or Abolition, as applied to the Slave Trade. Shewing that the Latter only can remove the Evils to be found in that Commerce. By the Rev. T. Clarkson, M.A. *London: printed by James Phillips.* 1789. 8vo, pp. xi, 82. H. + *Philadelphia.* 1804. 12mo. 13478

See M. R., LXXX. 560.

CLARKSON. An Essay on the Impolicy of the African Slave Trade. In Two Parts. By the Rev. T. Clarkson, M.A. To which is added, an Oration Upon the Necessity of establishing, at Paris, a Society to promote the Abolition of the Trade and Slavery of the Negroes. By J. P. Brissot de Warville. [Translated from the French by Charles Crawford.] *Philadelphia: Printed by Francis Bailey.* M,DCC,LXXXVIII. 8vo, pp. iv, 3–159. BA., H. + [*Ibid.*] 8vo, pp. 79, 134. + [*Ibid.*] 8vo, pp. 138. + *Philadelphia.* 1789. 8vo, pp. 155. 13479

The Oration has a title-page of its own. The Essay was reprinted with the following title:

CLARKSON. An Essay on the Impolicy of the African Slave Trade. In Two Parts. By the Rev. T. Clarkson, M.A. The Second Edition. *London: J. Phillips.* MDCCLXXXVIII. 8vo, Title, pp. iv, 3–134. H. 13480

See M. R., LXXXIX. 70.

CLARKSON. Essai sur les désavantages politiques de la traite des nègres, traduit par Gramagnac. *Neufchâtel.* 1789. 2 pts., 8vo. 13481

CLARKSON. Essai sur les désavantages politiques de la traité des Nègres; trad. de l'anglais. *Paris.* 1814. 8vo, pp. 144.

CLARKSON. Dangers du commerce des esclaves africains; traduit de l'anglais. *Paris.* 1814. 8vo. 13483

[CLARKSON.] An Essay on the Slavery and Commerce of the Human Species, particularly the African, translated from a Latin Dissertation, which was honoured with the First Prize in the

University of Cambridge, for the year 1785, with Additions. *London: T. Cadell, and J. Phillips.* M.DCC.LXXXVI. 8vo, pp. xxxi, (1), 256. H. + *Dublin.* M.DCC.LXXXVI. 8vo. C. + *London, printed. Philadelphia, re-printed by Joseph Crukshank.* M DCC LXXXVI. 8vo. BA. + The Second Edition, Revised and considerably enlarged. ... *London: J. Phillips.* MDCCLXXXVIII. 8vo, xxii, 167. + The Third Edition. *Philadelphia: Joseph Crukshank.* M DCC LXXXVII. 8vo, pp. 155. BA., H. + *Philadelphia: Nathaniel Wiley.* 1804. 12mo, pp. 259. BA. 13484

See M. R., LXXVIII. 343.

CLARKSON. De la traite du commerce des nègres; traduit de l'anglais [par Maubert. n. p. Vers 1788.] 8vo. 13485

CLARKSON. The History of the Rise, Progress and Accomplishment of the Abolition of the African Slave-Trade by the British Parliament. By Thomas Clarkson, M.A. ... *London: Longman & Co.* 1808. 2 vols., 8vo, 2 l., pp. 572; Title, 1 l., pp. 592. H. + First American, from the London Edition. *Philadelphia: James P. Parke.* 1808. 2 vols., 12mo, pp. 455; 468. 3 Plates. H. + *New-York: John S. Taylor.* 1836. 3 vols., 12mo, pp. viii, 276; 298; viii, 5–296. Plates. (Cabinet of Freedom.) B., H. + A New Edition, with Prefatory Remarks on the subsequent Abolition of Slavery. *London: John W. Parker.* MDCCCXXXIX. 8vo, pp. viii, 615. Portrait and Plates. + Abridged by Evan Lewis. *Wilmington: Printed by R. Porter.* 1816. 12mo, pp. 348. C., H. + *Augusta.* 1830. 2 vols., 12mo. B. 13486

CLARKSON. De kreet der Africanen tegen hunne Européesche verdrukkers of tafereel van den Slavenhandel. Uit het Eng. vertaald. *Amsterdam.* 1822. 8vo. Plates. 13487

CLARKSON. Résumé du temoinage donné devant un comité de la Chambre des communes de la Grande-Bretagne, touchant la trait des negrès. *Paris: Égron.* 1814. 8vo, pp. 32. 13488

CLARKSON. A Letter to the Clergy of various Denominations, and to the Slave-holding Planters in the Southern Parts of the United States of America. *London: printed by Johnston and Barrett.* 1841. 8vo, pp. 64. BA. + Second Edition. 8vo, pp. 48. 13489

See New-England Anti-Slavery Tract Association, Tract No. 10.

CLARKSON. Letters on the Slave-Trade, and the State of the

Natives in those parts of Africa, which are contiguous to Fort St. Lewis and Goree; with Plates. By T. Clarkson. *London.* 1791. 4to. P. 13490

CLARKSON. Memoirs of the Private and Public Life of William Penn. By Thomas Clarkson, M.A. In Two Volumes. ... *London: Longman, Hurst, Rees, Orme, and Brown.* 1813. 2 vols., 8vo, pp. xii, 520; 2 l., pp. 500. BA. + *Philadelphia.* 1813. 2 vols., 16mo. + *Philadelphia: Bradford and Inskeep; Kimber and Conrad; and Edward Parker.* 1814. 2 vols., 12mo, pp. 403; Title, 390. Portrait and Plate. H. + New Edition, with a Preface, in reply to the Charges against his Character made by Mr. Macaulay in his "History of England," by W. E. Foster. *London and Manchester.* 1849. 12mo, 18 sheets. Maps, Plate, and Portrait. 13491

See "Ed. Rev.," XXI. 444, "Anal. Mag.," II. 442, and M. R., LXXV. 307.

CLARKSON. A Portraiture of Quakerism, as taken from a view of the Moral education, Discipline, Peculiar Customs, Religious Principles, Political and Civil Œconomy, and Character, of the Society. By Thomas Clarkson, M.A. *London: Longman, Hurst, Rees, and Orme.* 1806. 3 vols., 8vo, 83 sheets. + *New York: Samuel Stansbury.* 1806. 3 vols., 8vo, pp. viii, 363; viii, 382; vii, 372. B., C. + Second Edition. *London: Longman,* [*etc.*] 1807. 3 vols., 8vo. + Second American Edition. *Philadelphia.* 1808. 3 vols., 12mo. + Third Edition. *London: Longman,* [*etc.*] 1807. 13492

See M. R., LIII. 152. Reprinted with alterations, entitled:

CLARKSON. A Portraiture of the Christian Profession and Practice of the Society of Friends: embracing a view of the Moral education, &c. of that Religious Society. — "British Friend" Edition, with a Biographical Sketch of the Author. *Glasgow: William and Robert Smeal.* 1847. Imp. 8vo, 19½ sheets. 13493

CLARKSON. The Substance of the Evidence of Sundry Persons on the Slave-Trade, collected in the Course of a Tour made in ... 1788. *London: printed by James Phillips.* MDCCLXXXIX. Folio, pp. vi, 136, (4). B. 13494

[CLARKSON.] A Summary View of the Slave Trade, and of the Probable Consequences of its Abolition. *London.* M.DCC.LXXXVII. 16mo, pp. 16. H. 13495

Clarkson. Strictures on a Life of William Wilberforce by the Rev. W. Wilberforce, and the Rev. S. Wilberforce. By Thomas Clarkson ... . With a Correspondence between Lord Brougham and Mr. Clarkson; also a Supplement, containing Remarks on the Edinburgh Review of Mr. Wilberforce's Life, etc. *London: Longman, Orme, Brown, Green, & Longmans.* 1838. 8vo, pp. xv, 136. BA. + Second Edition. *London.* 1838. 8vo. B., C. 13496

Clarkson. Thoughts on the Necessity of Improving the Condition of the Slaves in the British Colonies, with a view to their Ultimate Emancipation; and on the Practicability, the Safety, and the Advantages of the latter Measure. By T. Clarkson, Esq. *London: Richard Taylor.* 1823. 8vo, pp. iv, 60. + *New York: printed.* 1823. 8vo, pp. 64. BA. 13497

Clarkson. Three Letters, one of which has appeared before to the Planters and Slave Merchants, principally on the Subject of Compensation. By Thomas Clarkson, M.A. ... *London: Phillips and Fardon.* 1807. 8vo. 13498

See M. R., LIII. 337; LVIII. 337.

Clarkson. True State of the Case of the Insurrection at St. Domingo. *Ipswich.* 1792. 8vo. 13499

The following relate to Clarkson: Thomas Clarkson, his Life and Labours, as especially devoted towards the Abolition of Slavery; together with Reminiscences of Sharp and Wilberforce. *London.* 1854. 12mo, pp. 330. — The Present State of the Anti-Slavery Question in Tunis and Algiers, in a Letter addressed to Thomas Clarkson. *London.* 1845. — Reply to the Edinburgh Review on Clarkson's Treatise on the Improvement and Emancipation of Slaves in the British Colonies. 1824. 8vo.

Clarkson (T. S.) A Biographical History of Clermont or Livingston Manor. Before and During the War for Independence, with a Sketch of the first Steam Navigation of Fulton and Livingston. By Thomas Streatfield Clarkson. *Clermont. N. Y.* 1869. Rl. 8vo, pp. 319. 5 Plates. 13500

One hundred and fifty copies privately printed. Some copies lack the plates.

Clary (D.) History of the Churches and Ministers connected with the Presbyterian and Congregational Convention of Wisconsin, and of the Operations of the American Home Missionary Society in the State, for the Past Ten Years; with an Appendix. By Rev. Dexter Clary. *Beloit: printed by B. E. Hale.* 1861. 16mo, pp. 128. H. 13501

Clary (T. F.) Honorable Old Age. A Discourse occa-

sioned by the Centennial Anniversary of Hon. Timothy Farrar, LL.D. Delivered at Hollis, N. H., July 11, 1847. By Timothy Farrar Clary. *Andover.* 1847. 8vo, pp. 28. BA., H., S. 13502

Clason. (A. W.) The American Conflict. By A. W. Clason. *New York: C. B. Richardson.* 1866. 8vo, pp. 46.

[Clason (Isaac Starr).] Horace in New-York. *New York.* 1826. 12mo, pp. 48. S. 13504

Relates to Dr. Mitchell, Halleck, and the Croakers. In 1825, he published the injenious forgeries of Don Juan, cantos XVII. and XVIII.

Classology. *See* [Biglow (William)], Vol II., No. 5343.

Claude d'Abbeville. *See* Abbeville, Vol. I., Nos. 4 and 5.

The following title, from Leclerc's "Bib. Americana," No. 340, appears to be a different edition of the work described in Vol. I., No. 5, of this Dictionary:

Claude d'Abbeville. L'arrivee des Peres Capvcins en l'Inde Nouuelle, appellee Maraguon. Auec la reception que leur ont faict les Sauuages de ce pays, et la conuersion d'iceux á nostre Saincte Foy. Declaree par vne lettre que le R. P. Clavde d'Abbeville predicateur capuçin, enuoyé à Frere Martial pareillement capuçin, et à M. Foullon ses freres. *A Lyon: par Gvichard Pailly.* 1613. 8vo, pp. 16. 13505

"Est resté inconnu à Ternaux et à Brunet. La lettre du P. Claude d'Abbeville occupe les 11 premières pages: elle est datée '*En haste, De Maraguon, au Bresil ce* 20. *iour d'Aoust* 1612.'" — Leclerc.

Claude (William Tell.) Address to the People of Anne Arundell County. (Maryland.) [n. p. About 1861.] 8vo, pp. 7.

Claudet (M.) Hand Book of British Columbia, and Emigrants' Guide. *London.* 1862. 13507

Clausen (Claus Lauridsen). Beretning om de norske Nybyggeres Tilstand i Wisconsin. (In "Fyens Stifts-Avis," 1847, Nr. 266, 67.) 13508

Also a letter dated Visconti, 1846, Novbr. in Block's "Christeligt Folkeblad," I. Nr. 36. Clausen edited "Emigranten, et uafhængigt demokratist Blad. *Immantville, Rock County, Wisconsin.* 1852–53." Folio.

Claussen (*Le Chev.*) The Flax Movement: its National Importance and Advantages, with Directions for the Preparation of Flax-Cotton, and the Cultivation of Flax. By the Chevalier Claussen. With an Appendix by Horace Greeley. *Syracuse: L. W. Hall.* 1851. 8vo, pp. 48. H. + *New York: A. S. Barnes & Co. New York: John Wiley.* 1851. 12mo, pp. 46.

Clausson (L. J.) Liberté, égalité, fraternité. A la Convention nationale. [Signé, Clausson, Thomas Millet, commissaires des colons de Saint-Domingue réfugiées aux Etats-Unis d'Amérique. Maison d'arrêt des Carmes, ce 6 fructidor an II. [n. p. n. d.] 8vo, pp. 48 or less. 13510

Clausson. Précis historique de la révolution de Saint-Domingue; réfutation de certains ouvrages publiés sur les causes de cette révolution; de l'état actuel de cette colonie, et de la necessité d'en recouvrer la possession. *Paris: Pillet aîné.* 1819. 8vo, pp. xii, 155. 13511

Clausson (N. C.) Undersögelse om Amerikas Opdagelse har mere skadet end gavnet det menneskelige Kiön? Af Niels Christian Clausson. ... *Kiöbenhavn: Lauritz Christian Simmelkiær.* 1785. 8vo, 2 l., pp. 160. C., H., J.C.B. 13512

Clausson. *See* Jouon, *and others.*

La Clave. Periódico Político y Noticioso. No. 1. Jun. 1827. *Santiago.* [n. d.] Folio. Continued. M. 13513

[Clavel (Robert).] His | Majesties Propriety | and | Dominion | on the | Brittish Seas | asserted: | Together with a true Account | of the Neatherlanders Insupportable | Insolencies, and Injuries, they have com- | mitted; and the Inestimable Benefits they | have gained in their Fishing on the English Seas: | As also their Prodigious and Horrid Cruelties | in the East and West-Indies and other Places. | To which is added, an Exact Mapp, containing | the Isles of Great Britain, and Ireland, with the se- | veral Coastings, and the Adjacent Parts of our Neighbours: By | an Experienced Hand. | *London, Printed by T. Mabb, for Andrew Kembel,* | *near St. Margarets-Hill in Southwark, and Edward* | *Thomas, at the Adam and Eve in Little Brittain; and Robert* | *Clavel, at the Staggs-Head in Ivy-Lane,* 1665. | 8vo, 8 l., pp. 176. Portrait and Map. B. 13514

Portrait of Charles II, and copperplate map of Great Britain and Ireland.

Claver (P.) Peter Claver: a Sketch of his Life and Labors in behalf of the African Slave. *Boston: Lee & Shepard.* 1861. 16mo, pp. 117. Portrait. 13514

Claver (*Mrs.* Mary), *pseudonym.* *See* Kirkland (*Mrs.* M.)

Clavière (E.) Adresse de la Société der amis des Noirs, à l'Assemblée Nationale; A toutes les Villes de Commerce, à

toutes les Manufactures, aux Colonies ... dans laquelle on approfondit les relations politiques et commercials entre la Métropole et les Colonies, etc. Rédigée par E. Clavière ... . *Paris.* 1791. 4to. C. + Second édition, revue ... . *Desenne; Bailley; Bureau du Patriote François.* 10 *Mai,* 1791. 8vo, pp. 208. H. 13515

Clavière. Commerce of America. *See* Brissot de Warville, Vol. II., No. 8016.

Clavière *and* Brissot. De la France et des États-Unis, ou De l'Importance de la Révolution de l'Amérique pour le bonheur de la France, des Rapports de ce Royaume & des États-Unis, des Avantages reciproques qu'ils peuvent retirer de leurs liaisons de commerce, & enfin de la situation actuelle des Etats-Unis. Par Etienne Claviere; et J. P. Brissot de Warville. *Londres.* 1787. 8vo, pp. xlviij, 344. BA., H. + Nouvelle édition. [n. p. About 1787.] 12mo, pp. xxiii, 448. C. 13516

Clavière *and* Brissot. Considerations on the Relative Situations of France and the United States of America: Shewing the Importance of the American Revolution to the Welfare of France; giving also An Account of their Productions, and the reciprocal Advantages which may be drawn from their Commercial Connexions; and, finally, pointing out the Actual Situation of the United States. Translated from the French of Etienne Claviére and J. P. Brissot de Warville. *London: Robson ana Clarke, T. Longman, and W. Richardson.* 1788. 8vo, Title, pp. xvi, xxxiv, 326. Portrait of Brissot. BA., C., H. 13517

"This translation is faithfully executed, apparently by the authors themselves, or under their immediate inspection; and some explanatory notes are added. The work abounds with political and commercial knowledge, particularly with respect to the interests of France." *See* M. R., LXXX. 77.

Clavigero (F. S.) Storia antica del Messico cavata da' migliori storici spagnuoli, e da' manoscritti, e dalle pitture antiche degl' Indiani: divisa in dieci libri, e corredata di carte geografiche, e di varie figure: e dissertazioni Sulla Terra, sugli Animali, e sugli abitatori del Messico. Opera dell' Abate D. Francisco Saverio Clavigero. ... *In Cesena: Gregorio Biasini.* MDCCLXXX–LXXXI. 4 vols., 4to, pp. vij, (1), 302, 1 l. folded; pp. 276; 260; 331, (1). 20 Plates and 2 Maps. B., H. 13518

"Clavigero was a native of Vera Cruz (born 1731, died at Bologna, 1787), a Jesuit and a thorough antiquarian, who spent thirty years of active research into the archæology and antiquities of Mexico. His book, originally published in Italian, is a mine of precious historical documents, and contains valuable lists of others in the Mendoza,

the Vatican, and the Boturini collections. All the other books that have been elaborated since on the same subject, instead of superseding Clavigero's, have tended rather to magnify its importance." — Stevens. *See also* Prescott's Mexico, I. 52, and M. R., LXXVI. 633.

Clavigero. The History of Mexico. Collected from Spanish and Mexican Historians, from Manuscripts, and Ancient Paintings of the Indians. Illustrated by Charts, and other Copper Plates. To which are added, Critical Dissertations on the Land, the Animals, and Inhabitants of Mexico. By Abbé D. Francesco Saverio Clavigero. Translated from the Original Italian, by Charles Cullen, Esq. In Two Volumes. *London: G. G. J. & J. Robinson.* MDCCLXXXVII. 2 vols., 4to, Title, 1 l., pp. xxxii, 2 l., pp. 476; 2 l., pp. 463. 2 Maps and 25 Plates. H. + The Second Edition. *London: J. Johnson.* 1807. 2 vols., 4to, 18 l., pp. 476; 2 l., pp. 463. Map and 25 Plates. C. + *Richmond.* 1806. 3 vols., 8vo, pp. xxxviii, (1), 378; viii, 444; iv, 435. + *Philadelphia: Thomas Dobson.* 1817. 3 vols., 8vo, pp. xxxviii, (1), 378; viii, 444; iv, 435. 13519

See M. R., LXXVI. 633.

Clavigero. Historia Antigua de Megico: sacada de los mejores historiadores Españoles y de los manuscritos y de las pinturas Antiguas de los Indios; dividida en diez libros; Adornada con Mapas y Estampas, E illustrada con Dissertaciones sobre la tierra, los Animales y los Habitantes de Megico escrita por D. Francisco Saverio Clavigero; y traducida del Italiano por Jose Joaquin de Mora. *Londra.* 1826. 2 vols., 8vo, pp. xxxvi, 882. + *Mexico: Imprenta de Lara.* 1844. 2 vols., 8vo, pp. ix, 285; 319, (1). Maps and Plates. B. 13520

Clavigero. Historia antigua de Mejico. Obra escrita en taliano, traducida por F. P. Vazquez. Con muchas laminas. *Mejico.* 1853. 4to. 13521

Clavigero. Geschichte von Mexico, aus Spanischen und Mexicanischen Geschichtschreibern, Handschriften und Gemälden der Indianer zusammengetragen und durch Karten und Kupferstiche eläutert, nebst einigen kritischen Abhandlungen über die Beschaffenheit des Landes, der Thiere und Einwohner von Mexico. Aus dem Italiänischen durch den Ritter Karl Cullen ins Englische und aus diesem ins Deutsche übersetzt. Mit Kupfern und Karten. *Leipzig: in Schwickertschen Verlage.* 1789–90. 2 vols., 8vo, pp. viii, 638; 610. 2 Maps and 7 Plates. 13522

This translation into German is from the English translation by Cullen. The German editor has added notes.

Clavigero. Historia de la antigua o baja California, Obra posthuma, traducida del italiano por el presbitero D. Nicolas Garcia de San Vicente. *Mejico: Juan R. Navarro.* 1852. 8vo, 7 l., pp. 252, Table, 3 l. B. 13523

Clavigero. Storia della California: Opera Postuma del Nob. Sig. Abate D. Francesco Saverio Clavigero. *Venezia: Modesto Fenzo.* MDCCLXXXIX. 2 vols., 8vo, pp. 276, 1 l.; pp. 212, 1 l. Map. B., C. 13524

I have seen a catalogue which describes what purports to be a large paper copy.

Clawson (I. D.) Speech of Hon. Isaiah D. Clawson, of New Jersey, on National Politics. ... In the House ... July 23, 1856. [*Washington.* 1856.] 8vo, pp. 8. H. 13525

Claxton (C.) Colonial Crisis: First Letter to R. F. Buxton. By Christopher Claxton. *London.* 1831. 8vo, pp. 44. S.

Claxton. Extract of a Letter from Lieut. Christopher Claxton, R. N., to the House of Assembly of Jamaica. *Saint Christopher.* 1831. 8vo. 13527

Claxton. The Logs of the First Voyage made by the Great Western, of Bristol, Lieutenant James Hosken, R. N., Commander. Also, an Appendix. *Bristol.* [n. d.] 8vo. N. 13528

Claxton (R. Bethel). In Memoriam. Captain Charles S. Montgomery. Sermon delivered by the Rev. R. B. Claxton, in St. Luke's Chapel, Rochester, New York. *Rochester.* 1865. 8vo. 13529

Captain Montgomery, commanding the Fifth Regiment of New York Infantry, was killed in action in Hatcher's Run, before Petersburg, Virginia, on the 6th of February, 1865. Also: Sermon on the Death of C. S. Sterling: preached in St. Paul's Church, Cleveland, Ohio, on Sunday Evening, August 14th, 1859. By the Rev. R. B. Claxton, D.D., Rector. *Philadelphia.* 1859. 8vo, pp. 24. — Parish Memories of Forty Years. ... Discourse in St. Luke's Church, Rochester, N. Y. ... . *Rochester, N. Y.: the Parish* 1860. 8vo, pp. 32. B.

Claxton (T.) Sketch of the Life of Timothy Claxton, written by Himself. Together with Miscellaneous Papers. *Boston.* 1839. 12mo. 13530

Clay (Clement C.) Speech on the Bill to admit Kansas. Southern Rights: how menaced by Northern Republicanism. ... United States Senate, March 19, 1858. [n. p.:] *Star Office, Print.* [n. d.] 8vo, pp. 16. H. 13531

Clay (C. M.) Cassius M. Clay's Appeal to All the Followers of Christ in the American Union. [Against Slavery. Dated Lexington, Ky., Dec. 9, 1845. n. p. n. d.] 8vo, pp. 4.

Clay. A Review of the Late Canvass, and R. Wickliffe's Speech on the "Negro Law." By C. M. Clay, September 25, 1840. *Lexington: N. L. Finnell, Printer.* 1840. 8vo, pp. 18.

Clay. Speech ... in the House of Representatives of Kentucky, upon the Bill to repeal the Law of 1832–'3, "prohibiting the Importation of Slaves into this State." ... January, 1841. *Frankfort, Ky.* 1841. 8vo, pp. 16. B. 13534

Clay. To the People of Kentucky. [Signed Cassius M. Clay. Lexington, Ky., January, 1845. n. p. n. d.] 8vo, pp. 8. BA. + *Boston.* 1845. 13535

Clay. The Writings of Cassius Marcellus Clay, including Speeches and Addresses. Edited, with a Preface and Memoir, by Horace Greeley. *New York: Harper & Brothers.* 1848. 8vo, pp. 535, (1). Portrait. BA., C., S. 13536

Also: A Letter from Cassius M. Clay [March 20, 1844] ... with a Review ... By Gerrit Smith. *Utica.* 1844. 12mo, pp. 12. S. — Letter from Cassius M. Clay. Slavery; the Evil — the Remedy. [n. p. n. d.] 8vo, pp. 4. B. — The Pacific Railroad. [Dated New York, April 8, 1863. n. p. n. d.] 4to, 1 p. H. — Speech ... against the Annexation of Texas. ... Dec. 30, 1843. *Lexington.* 1844. 8vo, pp. 22. + *New York: D. Fanshawe.* 1844. 8vo, pp. 24. B., C., H. — Speech ... at the Tremont Temple ... [Nov. 19] after the adjournment of the great Convention on Boston Common ... . [*Boston.* 1844.] Broadside. H. — Speech ... at Lexington, Ky. ... August 1, 1851. [n. p. n. d.] 8vo, pp. 20. H. — Speech ... before the Young Men's Republican Central Union of New York on October 24th, 1856. [n. p. n. d.] 8vo, pp. 19. H. — Speech ... at Frankfort, Ky. ... January 10, 1860. ... [n. p. n. d.] 8vo, pp. 20. B. — Speech ... before the Law Department of the University of Albany, N. Y., February 3, 1863. *New York: Wynkoop, Hallenbeck & Thomas, Printers.* 1863. 8vo, pp. 24. H.

Clay (H.) An Address of Henry Clay to the Public, containing certain Testimony in Refutation of The Charges against him, made by General Andrew Jackson, touching the last Presidential Election. *Washington: Printed by Peter Force.* 1827. 8vo, pp. 61. BA. + *Louisville.* 1828. 8vo, pp. 48. + *Lexington.* 1828. 8vo. + *New Brunswick.* 1828. 8vo, pp. 56.

Clay. A Supplement to the Address of Henry Clay to the Public, ... published in December, 1827. ... in Refutation of the Charges against him ... made by Gen. Andrew Jackson. *Washington.* 1828. 8vo, pp. 22. B. 13538

Clay. The Ashland Text Book. Being a Compendium of Mr. Clay's Speeches on various Public Measures, etc. *Boston.* 1844. 12mo, pp. 72. + Second Edition. *New York.* 1844. 12mo. S. + Fifth Edition. *Boston.* 1844. P. 13539

Clay. The Life and Speeches of Henry Clay ... delivered mainly in the Senate and House ... Between ... 1810 and 1842 ... including his Valedictory in the Senate, and Last Lexington Speech ... revised ... . With ... Notes. *New-York: James B. Swain.* 1842. 8vo. 13540

Clay. The Life and Speeches of Henry Clay. Collected and Arranged by James Swain. *New York.* 1843. 2 vols., 8vo, pp. 531; 579. 13541

Clay. The Life and Speeches of Henry Clay ... . *New-York: Greeley & McElrath.* 1843. 2 vols., 8vo, pp. 307, xxvi; 2 l., pp. 9–597. Portrait, Facsimile, and View. H. 13542

Clay. The Life and Speeches of the Hon. Henry Clay. Compiled and Edited by Daniel Mallory. *New York: Van Amringe & Bixby.* 1843. 2 vols., 8vo. Portrait. + *New York: Robert P. Bixby & Co.* 1843. 2 vols., 8vo, pp. 606; 600. Portrait and 3 Engravings. BA. + Second Edition. *New York.* 1843. 2 vols., 8vo. + Fourth Edition. *New York: Van Amringe and Bixby.* 1844. 2 vols., 8vo, pp. 634; 607. 4 Plates. H. + Fifth Edition. *New York.* 1844. 2 vols., 8vo. Portrait and Engravings. 13543

There is another collection of the life and speeches, *New York: Gates and Stedman.* 1843. 2 vols., 8vo. I have also seen another edition, with the imprint, *Richmond.* 1849, probably a New York edition, with a new title. *See* "N. Am. Rev.," XXXII., and "Dublin Univ. Mag.," XXVII.

Clay. The Private Correspondence of Henry Clay. Edited by Calvin Colton, LL.D. ... *New York: A. S. Barnes & Co.* 1855. 8vo, pp. 642, 2 l. S. + *Boston: Frederick Parker.* 1856. 8vo, pp. 639. 2 Plates. C., H. 13544

Clay. Speech ... in the House ... On the 8th day of January, 1813, on the Bill for raising An Additional Military Force of Twenty Thousand Men, for One Year. *Baltimore: Patriot Press.* [1813.] 8vo, pp. 17. BA., C., S. 13545

Clay. The Speeches of Henry Clay, delivered in the Congress of the United States; To which is prefixed a Biographical Memoir, With an Appendix. *Philadelphia.* 1826. 8vo. Portrait. + *Philadelphia.* 1828. 8vo. C. 13546

Clay. The Speeches of Henry Clay, delivered in the Congress of the United States. To which is added — A Biographical Memoir, with an Appendix containing Speeches at Lexington, and Lewisburgh, and before the Colonization Society at Washington. Together with his address on the Subject of the late Presidental Election. *Cincinnati, Ohio.* 1827. 8vo, pp. 401.

Clay. Speeches of Henry Clay. Collected by Richard Chambers. *Cincinnati: Shepard & Stearns.* 1842. 8vo, pp. 504, 1 l. c. 13548

Clay. The Speeches of Henry Clay. Edited by Calvin Cotton, LL.D. *New York: A. S. Barnes & Co.* 1857. 2 vols., 8vo, pp. 1294. c. 13549

Clay. To the People of the Congressional District composed of the Counties of Fayette, Woodford, and Clarke, in Kentucky. [Signed H. Clay. Washington, 26th March, 1825. n. p. n. d.] 18mo, pp. 33. BA. 13550

Relates to the presidential election. The following is a chronological list of some of Mr. Clay's speeches as published separately: Speech ... on the Direct Tax. March, 1816. *New York.* 1816. 8vo. — Speech ... on the Seminole War. [*Washington.* 1819.] 12mo, pp. 30. w. — Speech in support of an American System for the Protection of American Industry; ... in the House ... 30th and 31st of March, 1824. *Washington City.* 1824. 8vo, pp. 39. H. + [n. p. n. d.] 8vo, pp. 32. H. — Speech ... before the American Colonization Society, ... January 20, 1827. With ... Documents ... . *Washington.* 1827. 8vo, pp. 13, 8. BA., H. — Speech ... at the Dinner at Noble's Inn, near Lexington, July 12, 1827. [n. p. n. d.] 8vo, pp. 14. w. — Speech ... at the Public Dinner, At Fowler's Garden, near Lexington, K'y; on the Sixteenth of May, 1829; ... with Introductory Remarks. By a Citizen of Virginia. *Richmond: printed by Thomas W. White.* 1829. 8vo, pp. 34. H., M. — An Address delivered before the Colonization Society of Kentucky at Frankfort, December 17, 1829. ... *Lexington: Thomas Smith.* 1829. 8vo, pp. 26. — Speech ... at the Mechanics' Collation ... Cincinnati, on the 3d of August, 1830. [n. p. n. d.] 12mo, pp. 24. — Speech ... in defence of the American System, against the British Colonial System: With an Appendix of Documunts referred to in the Speech ... in the Senate ... February 2d, 3d, and 6th, 1832. *Washington: Gales and Seaton.* 1832. 8vo, pp. 43. B., H. — Speech ... in the Senate ... Feb. 25, 1833, in Vindication of ... the Bill ... imposing Duties on Imports. *Washington.* 1833. 8vo, pp. 8. — Speech ... on the subject of the Removal of the Deposites, ... in the Senate ... December 26, 30, 1833. *Washington.* 1834. 8vo, pp. 31. B., H. + [Another Edition.] *Washington.* 1834. 8vo, pp. 48. — Speech ... in the Senate of the United States, April 30, 1834, on the Doctrines, and on the Question of recording the President's Protest against a Resolution of the Senate, which had been prepared by Mr. Clay ... in the Senate ... 30th day of April, 1834. *Washington.* 1834. 8vo. pp. 20. H. — Speech ... on the Specie Circular ... in the Senate ... January 11, 1837. *Washington.* 1837. 8vo, pp. 13. H. — Speech ... on the Bill imposing Additional Duties, as Depositaries, in certain Cases, on Public Officers. ... In Senate ... Sept. 25, 1837. *Boston: Benjamin H. Greene.* 1837. 8vo, pp. 19. B., H. — Speech ... establishing A deliberate design, on the part of the late and present Executive ... to break down the whole Banking System of the United States: ... and in Reply to the Speech of ... J. C. Calhoun ... . February 19, 1838. *Washington.* 1838. 8vo, pp. 16. H., N. — Speech

... on the Sub-Treasury Scheme, delivered in the Senate of the United States, Feby. 19, 1838. *Troy, N. Y.: Tuttle, Belcher & Co.* 1838. 8vo, pp. 48. — Speech ... in the Senate of the United States, on the Subject of Abolition Petitions, February 7, 1839. *Washington.* 1839. 8vo, pp. 16. + *Boston: James Munroe & Company.* 1839. 8vo, pp. 42. H. + *New-Orleans: printed by John Gibson.* 1839. 8vo, d p. 14. H. — Speech ... on the Bill commonly called the Sub-Treasury Bill, ... Delivered Jan. 20, 1840. 8vo, pp. 16. — Speech ... 19th August, 1841, on the Message of President Tyler, returning the Bank Bill, with his Veto. *Washington.* 1841. 8vo, pp. 28. + [n. p. 1841.] 8vo, pp. 16. BA. — Speeches ... In the Senate, ... on the 19th of August, 1841, on the Message of President Tyler, returning the Bank Bill, with his Veto, and in reply to Mr. Rives, defending the Message. [n. p. n. d.] 8vo, pp. 16. H. — Speech ... at Lexington, Ky., Jan. 9, 1842. With the Address of Chief Justice Robertson, also Mr. Clay's Farewell Speech in the Senate of the U. S. *New York.* 1842. 8vo, pp. 18. — Speech ... delivered at the Great Barbecue at Lexington, (Kentucky,) June 9, 1842. *Sing Sing, N. Y.*, 1842. 8vo, pp. 16. B. — Speech at the Lexington Mass Meeting 13th November, 1847, together with the Resolutions adopted on that occasion. *New York.* 1847. 8vo, pp. 14. — Speech ... in reference to Diplomatic Relations with Austria, ... In the Senate ... January 7, 1850. [*Washington.* n. d.] 8vo, pp. 8. H., M. — Remarks ... on introducing his Propositions to compromise, on the Slavery Question. In the Senate ... January 29, 1850. *Washington.* 1850. 8vo, pp. 16. H. — Speech ... on the Report of the Committee of Thirteen. ... In the Senate ... May 13, 1850. [n. p. n. d.] 8vo, pp. 16. H. — Speech of the Hon. Henry Clay, of Kentucky, On Presenting his Compromise Resolutions on the Subject of Slavery. Delivered in the Senate, Feb. 5th & 6th, 1850. ... *New York: Stringer & Townsend.* 1850. 8vo, pp. 32. H. + Revised Edition. *Washington.* [n. d.] 8vo, pp. 32. H. — Speech ... on the Measures of Compromise. ... In the Senate ... July 22, 1850. *Washington.* 1850. 8vo, pp. 31. H.

Clay. The Works of Henry Clay. Edited by Calvin Colton, LL.D. *New York: A. S. Barnes & Co.* 1857. 6 vols., 8vo. + *New York: Barnes & Burr.* 1863. 6 vols., 8vo. + *New York: P. O'Shea.* 1865. 6 vols., 8vo. H. 13551

Some copies have the title, "The Life, Correspondence and Speeches of Henry Clay, edited by Calvin Colton. *New York.* 1857," 6 vols., 8vo, and are thus divided: Vol. I.–III. Life and Times; III. Correspondence, 1843–1851; IV. Correspondence, 1801–1852; V.–VI. Speeches in Congress; and Obituary Sketch. Concerning Mr. Clay, *see* "N. A. Rev.," XXXIII. 350; "Am. Whig Rev.," I. 75; II. 639; VI. 551; "Dem. Rev.," VII. 99; XI. 205; XII. 302; "U. S. Lit. Gaz.," VI. 276; "Dublin Univ. Mag.," XXVII. 325; "Anal. Mag.," XVI.; "Niles' Register," XIV., *et seq.* The following works relate to Mr. Clay:

Clay. Baltimore Patriot Office, August — 1827. Mr. Clay and Gen. Jackson ... complete history of the case ... . [*Baltimore.* 1827.] 8vo, pp. 8. BA. 13552

Clay. The Beauties of The Hon. Henry Clay; to which is added a Biographical and Critical Essay. *New York.* 1830. 12mo. 13553

Clay. Cabinet Eloquence, on the Political House that Clay built. [n. p. n. d.] 8vo, pp. 8. BA. 13554

On Clay's relations to Gen. Jackson.

Clay. The Clay Minstrel, or National Songster; to which is prefixed a Sketch of the Life, Public Services and Character of Henry Clay. By John S. Littell. Second Edition. *New York.* 1844. 24mo, pp. 384. Portrait. S. 13555

Clay. Fifty Reasons why the Hon. Henry Clay should be elected President of the United States. By an Irish Adopted Citizen. *Baltimore: J. Murphy.* 1844. 8vo, pp. 43. 13556

Clay. Henry Clay and the Administration. A Tract for the Times. No. 1. ... By a Friend of the Union. *Philadelphia.* 1850. 8vo, pp. 15. BA. 13557

Clay. Life of Henry Clay, the Statesman and Patriot; containing numerous Anecdotes. *Philadelphia.* 1853. 8vo. c.

Clay. Life and Public Services of Henry Clay. *New York.* 1848. Portrait. 13559

Clay. Mr. Clay's Moral Character. [n. p. n. d.] 8vo, pp. 8. B. 13560

Clay. No. 17. Headlands in the Life of Henry Clay. No. 1, from 1797 to 1827. *Boston.* [n. d.] 8vo, pp. 8. H.

Clay. Obituary Addresses on the Occasion of the Death of the Hon. Henry Clay, a Senator of the United States, from the State of Kentucky, delivered in the Senate and in the House of Representatives of the United States, June 30, 1852, and the Funeral Sermon of the Rev. C. M. Butler, Chaplain of the Senate ... July 1, 1852. ... *Washington.* 1852. 8vo, pp. 135. Portrait. B., BA., H. 13562

Clay. Remarks upon Slavery and the Slave Trade, Addressed to the Hon. Henry Clay. [Signed "A Slave-Holder." *Privately printed at Paris.*] 1839. 8vo, pp. 23. H. 13563

Clay. Report of the Ceremonies on the Fourth of July, 1857, at the Laying of the Corner Stone of a National Monument ... near Lexington, Kentucky, to ... Henry Clay ... with the Oration ... by the Rev. Robert J. Breckinridge ... . [*Cincinnati:*] *Clay Monument Association.* 1857. 8vo, pp. 59. Plate.

Clay. Report of the Committee of Arrangements of the Common Council of the City of New York, of the Obsequies in memory of Hon. Henry Clay. *New York: McSpedon & Baker.* [1852.] 8vo, pp. 362. Portrait and Plates. 13565

Clay. Some Reasons why the Votes of the State of New York ought to be given to Henry Clay for President of the United States, October 7, 1824. [n. p. n. d.] N. 13566

Clay. To the People. The Bargain proved by the testimony of Mr. Clay's Friend's, and from his own Letters. [n. p. n. d.] Rl. 8vo, pp. 16. 13567

Clay (J. B.) Battle Ground. Convention Speech of Hon. James B. Clay. [n. p. n. d.] 8vo, pp. 16. 13568

Clay. Speech of the Hon. James B. Clay, of Kentucky, on the Neutrality Laws; delivered in the House of Representatives, January 13, 1858. *Washington.* 1858. 8vo, pp. 6. 13569

Clay (J. C.) Annals of the Swedes on the Delaware. By the Rev. Jehu Curtis Clay ... . To which is added The Charter of the United Swedish Churches. *Philadelphia: J. C. Pechin.* 1835. 24mo, pp. 180. Portrait. BA. + Second Edition, corrected and enlarged. *Philadelphia: F. Foster.* 1858. 12mo.

Clay (J.), *A.M.* A Discourse Delivered in the First Baptist Meeting-House in Boston, on ... August 19, 1807, by Joseph Clay, A.M. on the Occasion of his Installation. ... *Boston: printed by Manning and Loring.* [1807.] 8vo, pp. 40. H. 13571

Also: Essay delivered in a Competition of the Students of the College of New Jersey for the Annual Medal given by John Dickinson, President of the State of Pennsylvania, by Jos. Clay, Junr., adjudged Victor for the year 1784. *Philadelphia.* 1785. 8vo.

Clay (T. S.) Detail of a Plan for the Moral Improvement of Negroes on Plantations. Read before the Georgia Presbytery. By Thomas S. Clay ... . [n. p. 1833.] 8vo, pp. 23. H.

Clay Lick. An Account of The Celebration of American Independence, at Clay Lick, by the Licking County Pioneers. Together with an Address, by Dr. Coulter, on Early Times in the Clay Lick Settlements. Also, Historical Shetches of the Townships of Licking, Bowling Green, Franklin and Hopewell, &c. By Isaac Smucker. *Newark, Ohio: Clark & Keny, Printers.* 1869. 8vo, pp. 35. 13573

Clayton (A. S.) A compilation of the Laws of the State of Georgia, passed by the Legislature since the political Year 1800, to the year 1810, inclusive; containing all the laws, whether in force or not, ... with a Copious Index to the whole, By Augustin S. Clayton. *Augusta.* 1812. 4to. 13574

Clayton (John). Flora Virginica. *See* Gronovius (J. F.)

Clayton. A Letter from Mr. John Clayton, Rector of Crofton, at Wakefield in Yorkshire, to the Royal Society, May, 12, 1688, giving an Account of several Observables in Virginia, and in his Voyage thither, more particularly concerning the Air. *Washington.* 1844. 8vo, 1 l., pp. 43, (3).

This was originally published in the "Philosophical Trans. of the Royal Society," 1693, Vol. XVII., and is in W. Derham's "Miscellanea Curiosa," Vol. III., and forms No. 12, Vol. III., of Force's Tracts.

Clayton (John Middleton). Speech of Mr. Clayton ... in the Senate ... on the Fourth Day of March, in reply to Mr. Grundy of Tennessee, Mr. Woodbury of New Hampshire, and Others; [on] the Resolution of Mr. Foot, of Connecticut ... [on the Public Lands]. *Washington.* 1830. 8vo, pp. 56. BA.

Also: Speech ... on the Bill for the Apportionment of the Representation in Congress ... in the Senate ... April 25th, 1832. *Washington.* 1832. 8vo, pp. 24. H. — Speech ... in Reply to Mr. Buchanan on National Defence. Feb. 3, 1836. *Washington.* 1836. 8vo, pp. 32. — Speeches ... at the Whig Mass Meeting held in Wilmington on the 15th of June, 1844. *Washington.* 1844. 8vo, pp. 16. H. + *Albany.* [n. d.] 8vo, pp. 15. S. — Speech ... on French Spoliations. In the Senate ... April 23, and 24, 1846. *Washington.* [n. d.] 8vo, pp. 35. H. — Speech ... in Defence of Zachary Taylor ... in the Senate ... July 5, 1848. *Washington.* [n. d.] 8vo, pp. 16. H. — Speech ... in the Senate ... 8th of March, 1853, ... in Vindication of the Central American Treaty concluded with Great Britain on the 19th of April, 1850. *Washington: Printed by Kirkwood & McGill.* 1853. 8vo, pp. 43. H. — Treaty at Washington. Speech ... in the Senate ... January 12 and 16, 1854, in reply to Mr. Cass ... . [*Washington.* n. d.] 8vo. pp. 24. BA., H. — Speech ... on the Bill to organize Territorial Governments in Nebraska and Kansas; discussing the Missouri Compromise and the Doctrine of Non-Intervention. ... In the Senate ... March 1 and 2, 1854. *Washington.* 1854. 8vo, pp. 22. H. — Speech ... on the Veto Message of the President, on the Bill for the Benefit of the Indigent Insane. In the Senate ... June 15, 1854. *Washington.* 1854. 8vo, pp. 22. BA., H. — Speeches ... in Reply to Senator Houston ... and Others, and in Defense of the Naval Board. *Washington.* 1856. 8vo, pp. 22. H. — Speech ... in regard to Captain S. F. Dupont, U. S. N., in the Senate ... March 11, 1856 ... . *Washington.* 1856. 8vo, pp. 14. H. — (Hon. John M. Clayton to James H. Causten.) Washington, March 9, 1855. [On Causten's Service as agent for the French spoliation claimants. n. p. n. d.] 4to, pp. 2. H. — Report on the Removal of the Deposites. 1834. 8vo.

Clayton. Obituary Addresses on the ... Death of Hon. John M. Clayton ... in the Senate and House ... December 3, 1856. *Washington.* 1857. 8vo, pp. 22. BA., H. 13577

Clayton and Bulwer Convention, 19th April, 1850, between the British and American Governments, concerning Central America, with Correspondence. 1856. 8vo. 13578

Title from J. R. Smith's catalogue.

Clayton (T.) Proceedings and Debates in the House of Representatives of ... Delaware, on the Petitions for contesting the Election of David Hall, Esq. To which is added, Proceedings in the Senate, and a Summary of the Debates in that House. By Th. Clayton. *Dover: printed by William Black.* 1802. 8vo, pp. 59. BA. 13579

Clayton (W.) The Latter-day Saints Emigrants' Guide: being a Table of distances showing all the Springs, Creeks, Rivers, Hills, Mountains, camping places and all other notable places, from Council Bluffs, to the Valley of the Great Salt Lake. Also the Latitudes, Longitude and Altitudes of the permanent points on the route. Together with remarks on the nature of the land, timber, grass, &c. The whole route having been measured by a roadometer, and the distance from point to point, in English miles accurately shown. *St. Louis, Mo.: Chambers & Knapp.* 1848. 12mo, pp. 24. 13580

Clayton. Judge Clayton's Review of the Report of the Committee on the President's Message, relating to the United States Bank. *Milledgeville.* 1830. 8vo. 13581

Clear and Certain Truths, relating to the Present Crisis, as well the truly Pious Christians as others. By a Simple Tradesman. *Germantown: printed by C. Sower.* 1747. 8vo. P. 13582

A Clear and Succinct Account of North America. *Dublin.* 1755. 8vo. 13583

Title from J. R. Smith's catalogue.

A Clear Idea of the Genuine and Uncorrupted British Constitution: in an Address to the Inhabitants of the Province of Quebec, from the Forty-nine delegates in the Continental Congress at Philadelphia; Sep. 5th to Oct. 10, 1774 — Extracted from their Votes & Proceedings. [*London:*] *Messrs. Dilly.* 1774. 8vo, pp. 8. 13584

Clearfield. First Annual Report of the Clearfield Coal and Lumber Company. ... *Philadelphia.* 1856. 8vo, pp. 23. Map and Plan. H. 13585

Cleary (N. G.) The Memorial of Nathaniel Greene Cleary, Sheriff of the District of Charleston, to the ... Senate and House ... of South-Carolina. *Charleston: printed by C. C. Sebring.* 1825. 8vo, pp. 35. H. 13586

Cleary (William P.), & Co. Business Directory of the Cities of New York, Philadelphia, Boston, and Baltimore; and a Business Register of the Principal Manufacturers in the Eastern States. 1869. *New York: W. P. Cleary & Co.* 1869. 4to.

Cleaveland (E. L.) A Discourse Occasioned by the Death of Hon. Daniel Webster, preached October 31, and repeated November 14, 1852. By E. L. Cleaveland ... *New Haven: printed by B. L. Hamlin.* 1852. 8vo, pp. 28. H. + Second Edition. *New Haven.* 1852. 8vo, pp. 28. H. + [Another Edition.] *New York.* 1853. 8vo, pp. 40. B. 13588

Cleaveland. Hasting to be Rich. A Sermon, occasioned by the Present Excitement respecting the Gold of California, preached in the Cities of New Haven and Bridgeport, Jan. and Feb. 1849. By E. L. Cleaveland ... . *New Haven: printed by J. H. Benham.* 1849. 8vo, pp. 20. 13589

Also: An Address ... at the Funeral of the Hon. Dennis Kimberly, December 16, 1862. ... *New Haven: Bassett & Barnett.* 1863. 8vo, pp. 22, (2). BA. — Dr. Cleaveland's Statement, in reply to Dr. Dutton's Review of His late Anniversary Sermon, presented in the Third Congregational Church, New Haven, Nov. 28, 1858. *New Haven: Thomas H. Pease.* 1858. 8vo, pp. 16. — A Discourse on the Existing State of Morals in the City of New Haven ... Oct. 13th, 1850. ... *New Haven.* 1850. 8vo, pp. 20. — Love of Country. A Discourse Preached in ... New Haven, on Thanksgiving Day, November 29th, 1860, And Repeated ... Dec. 9th, 1860. ... *New Haven: Thomas H. Pease.* 1860. 8vo, pp. 20. — Our Duty in Regard to the Rebellion. A Fast Day Sermon, preached in ... New Haven, April 3, 1863. ... *New Haven: Thomas H. Pease.* ... 1863. 8vo, pp. 20. B. + *New York: Hall, Clayton & Medole.* 1863. 8vo, pp. 22. — The Patriot's Song of Victory. A Thanksgiving Discourse, for Recent Military Successes, delivered in the Third Congregational Church, New Haven, September 11 ... . *New Haven: Thomas H. Pease.* [1864.] 8vo, pp. 16. H. — Sermon, Twenty-fifth Anniversary of the Author's Ministry ... . *New-Haven.* 1858. 8vo.

Cleaveland. Memorial of Elisha Lord Cleaveland, New Haven. *New Haven.* 1866. 8vo, pp. 70. 13590

Cleaveland (H. W.), *and* Backus (W. and S. D.) The Requirements of American Village Homes Considered and Suggested, with Designs for such Houses of Moderate Cost. By Henry W. Cleaveland, Wm. Backus, and Samuel D. Backus. *New York.* 1855. 8vo, pp. 189. 13591

Cleaveland (John). *See* Cleveland (John).

[Cleaveland (John).] The Chebacco Narrative Rescu'd from the Charge of Falshood and Partiality. In A Reply to the Answer, Printed by Order of the second Church in Ipswich,

And Falshood and Partiality fix'd on said Answer. By a Friend of Truth. *Boston: Kneeland and Green.* 1738 [1748]. 4to, pp. 20. B., BA. 13592

Cleaveland. An Essay, To defend some of the most important Principles in the Protestant Reformed System of Christianity, on which the Churches of Christ in New-England were originally founded ... against ... Jonathan Mayhew, D.D. in his late Thanksgiving Sermons ... . By John Cleaveland ... . *Boston: D. and J. Kneeland.* 1763. 8vo, pp. 108. H., W. 13593

Cleaveland. The Reverend Dr. N. Whitaker's Neighbour is come, and searcheth for him: or, A Brief Defence of The late Council's Result, against the Doctor's Charges In His late Brief History. By John Cleaveland, A.M. A Member of the said Council. ... *Salem: S. Hall.* MDCCLXXXIV. 8vo, pp. 32, 8. BA. 13594

Cleaveland. ... A Sermon Preached at the Ordination of the Rev. John Cleaveland, Jun., to the Pastoral Care of the Church and Congregation in the Town of Stoneham, Oct. 19, 1785. By his Father, John Cleaveland, A.M. *Newbury Port.* [1785.] 8vo, pp. 40. 13595

Cleaveland. A Short and Plain Narrative of the late Work of God's Spirit at Chebacco, in Ipswich, in the Years 1763 and 1764. *Boston, N. E.* MDCCLXVII. 8vo, pp. 89. M.

[Cleaveland.] A Twig of Birch for Billy's Breech; A Letter to Rev. William Hobby. *Boston.* 1745. 4to, pp. 12.

Also: An Attempt to Nip in the Bud, the Unscriptural Doctrine of Universal Salvation, and some other Dangerous Errors connected with it. ... *Salem, N. E.* 1776. 8vo. — Infant-Baptism "from Heaven," and Immersion, as the only Mode of Baptism and a Term of Christian Communion, "of Men:" Or, A Short Dissertation on Baptism, In Two Parts ... . [With] A Short Postscript, containing a few Observations on Mr. Foster's Divine Rite of Immersion. By John Cleaveland ... . *Salem: Printed by Samuel Hall.* 1784. 8vo, pp. 113, 13. C., W. — A Reply to Dr. Mayhew's Letter of Reproof, to Mr. John Cleaveland of Ipswich ... . By John Cleaveland ... . *Boston, N. E.: Printed by W. McAlpine & J. Fleeming.* M,DCC,LXV. 8vo, Title, pp. 96. H., M., W. — Sermon at Stoneham, Mass. Oct. 26, 1794, upon the Dismission of their Minister. *Salem.* 1795. 8vo. W.

Cleaveland (J.) A Sermon delivered at the House of Major Jacob Man, July 7, 1813. Occasioned by the Removal of the Bodies of his Parents and Youngest Son, from their Graves to a Tomb. By John Cleaveland ... . *Providence: printed by H. Mann and Co.* 1813. 12mo, pp. 47. H. 13598

Also: Fast Sermon, [Wrentham, Mass.] Aug. 20, 1812. *Boston.* 1812. 8vo. W.

CLEAVELAND (John). The Banking Sytem of the State of New York, with Notes and References to Adjudged Cases, including also an Account of the New York Clearing House. *New York.* 1857. 13599

CLEAVELAND. The Banking System of the State of New York, with Notes and References to Adjudged Cases; including also the Acts of Congress of June 3, 1864, establishing or providing for a National Banking System. By John Cleaveland. Second Edition. By G. S. Hutchinson. *New York: John S. Voorhies.* 1864. 8vo. c. 13600

CLEAVELAND. Opinion of John Cleaveland as to the Liability, under the Act of April 29, 1863, to State Taxation on Loans to the United States, evidenced or secured by United States Government Stocks, held by New York Banking and Moneyed Corporations. *New York: Hall, Clayton & Medrole.* 1863. 8vo, pp. 65. 13601

CLEAVELAND (J. P.) A Eulogy on William Henry Harrison ... at Ann Arbor, Michigan, April 22, 1841. By Rev. John P. Cleaveland. *Ann Arbor: printed by T. M. Ladd & Co.* 1841. 8vo, pp. 26. H. 13602

Also: Address before the Society of Inquiry, Wabash College, Indiana, July 22, 1845, ... *Cincinnati.* 1845.

CLEAVELAND (M.) An Oration Commemorative of the Life and Death of General George Washington, delivered at Windham (Connecticut,) On the 22d day of February, 1800 ... . By Moses Cleaveland ... . *Windham: printed by John Byrne.* 1800. 8vo, pp. 15. BA. 13603

CLEAVELAND (N.) An Address delivered at Topsfield in Massachusetts, August 28, 1850: the Two Hundredth Anniversary of the Incorporation of the Town. By Nehemiah Cleaveland. ... *New-York: Pudney & Russell, Printers.* 1851. 8vo, pp. 74, (1), xxxix. Portraits. BA., H. 13604

CLEAVELAND. The First Century of Dummer Academy. A Historical Discourse, delivered at Newbury, Byfield Parish, August, 12, 1863. With an Appendix. By Nehemiah Cleaveland. *Boston: Nichols & Noyes.* 1865. 8vo, 2 l., pp. 71, xliii.

CLEAVELAND. Greenwood in 1846. By N. Cleaveland. Illustrated by James Smillie. *New York: R. Martin.* 1846. 4to. Plates. 13606

Issued in parts, the cover title to which is "Greenwood Illustrated, in a Series of Picturesque and Monumental Views from Drawings, by James Smillie. The Literary Department by N. Cleaveland."

CLEAVELAND. Green-Wood: A Directory for Visitors. By N. Cleaveland. *New York.* 1849. 12mo, pp. 471. + *New York.* 1850. 12mo + *New York.* 1852. 12mo, pp. 198. Map and Plate. + *New York.* 1853. 12mo. Plates. + *New York: Pudney & Russell.* 1857. 12mo, pp. vii, 306. Map and Plate.

CLEAVELAND. Greenwood Cemetery: a History of the Institution from 1838 to 1864. By Nehemiah Cleaveland. With Illustrations. *New York: Anderson & Archer.* 1866. Sm. 8vo.

CLEAVELAND. Hints concerning Greenwood; its Monuments and Improvements. *New York.* 1853. 8vo, pp. 44.

Also: An Address, delivered at Newburyport, July 5, 1824, in Commemoration of American Independence. ... *Newburyport: W. & J. Gilman.* 1824. 8vo, pp. 16. BA.—An Address delivered before the New-England Society of Brooklyn, N. Y., December 21, 1849. ... *New York.* 1850. 8vo, pp. 37. N.

CLEAVELAND (P.) An Address before the Brunswick ... Society for the Suppression of Intemperance. By Parker Cleaveland. *Boston.* 1814. 8vo. 13610

CLEAVELAND. An Elementary Treatise on Mineralogy and Geology, for Travellers in the United States of America. Illustrated by six Plates. By Parker Cleaveland. *Boston.* 1816. 8vo, pp. xii, 668. + Second Edition. *Boston: Cummings & Hilliard.* 1822. 2 vols., 8vo, pp. xii, 480; 482–818, 1 l. 5 Plates, and Map. 13611

CLEAVELAND. Smithsonian Contribution to Knowledge. 204. Results of Meteorological Observations ... at Brunswick, Maine, between 1807 and 1859. By Parker Cleaveland ... . *Washington.* 1867. 4to, pp. 53. B. 13612

CLEAVENGER (W. S.) Defence of William S. Cleavenger, Principal of the Locust-street Grammar School, addressed to the Citizens of the Eighth Ward ... *Philadelphia.* 1837. 8vo. s.

CLEAVER, (*Bishop of Chester*). Sermon before the Society for the Propagation of the Gospel. *London.* 1794. 4to. 13614

CLELAND (H.) Memoirs of the Life of William Pitt; with Notices of his Contemporaries, etc. By Henry Cleland. *London.* 1807. 12mo. Portraits. N. 13615

[CLELAND (John).] Tombo-Chiqui; or, The American Savage. A Dramatic Entertainment in Three Acts. *London: S. Hooper.* 1758. 8vo, pp. 55. 13616

Concerning this, *see* Harris' "Mem. of Oglethorp," pp. 376–8.

[CLEMENS (Jeremiah).] Bernard Lile; an Historical Romance, embracing the Periods of the Texas Revolution, and the Mexican War. *Philadelphia: J. B. Lippincott & Co.* 1856. 12mo, 2 l., pp. 9–287. C., H. 13617

CLEMENS. California, Territorial Governments, &c. Speech of Hon. J. Clemens of Alabama, ... May 16 and 20. [n. p. n. d.] 8vo, pp. 8. 13618

CLEMENS. Letter from the Hon. Jere. Clemens. [n. p. 1864.] 16mo, pp. 16. H. 13619

CLEMENS. Tobias Wilson, a Tale of the Great Rebellion. By Hon. Jere. Clemens. First Series. *Philadelphia: J. B. Lippincott & Co.* 1865. 12mo, pp. 179. BA. 13620

The characters and incidents are alleged to be true pictures of the first year of the rebellion. Also: Argument ... in defense of Capt. Schaumburg, indicted for Assault and Battery with intent to kill Edward H. Fuller. 1854.—Mustang Gray: A Romance. *Philadelphia.* 1858. 12mo, pp. 296.—The Rivals: a Tale of the Times of Aaron Burr, and Alexander Hamilton. By Hon. Jere. Clemens ... . *Philadelphia: J. B. Lippincott & Co.* 1860. 12mo, 2 l., pp. 7–286. H.—Speech, ... on L. Kossuth, 1851. 8vo. S.—Speech ... on Non-Intervention ... in the Senate ... February 12, 1852. *Washington.* 1852. 8vo, pp. 8. H.—Speech ... on ... Colonization in North America ... in the Senate ... February 7, 1853. *Washington.* 1853. 8vo, pp. 8. H.

CLEMENS, *and others.* Remarks of Messrs. Clemens, Butler and Jefferson Davis, on the Vermont Resolutions relating to Slavery. Delivered in Senate ... United States, January 10, 1850. *Washington.* 1850. 8vo, pp. 15. B. 13621

CLEMENS (O.) City of Keokuk, in 1856. A View of the City, embracing its Commerce and Manufactures, and containing the Inaugural Address of Mayor Curtis, and Statistical Local Information; also a Sketch of the Black Hawk War, and History of the Half Breed Tract. Historical and Statistical Matter, written by Orion Clemens. *Keokuk: printed by O. Clemens.* 1856. 8vo, pp. 44. B. 13622

[CLEMENS (Samuel).] The Celebrated Jumping Frog of Calaveras County, and other Sketches. By Mark Twain [*pseudonym*]. Edited by John Paul. *New York: C. H. Webb.* 1867. 16mo, pp. 198. C. 13623

CLEMENT VII (*Pope*). Carolvs Quintus diuina fauente Clementia Romanorũ Imperator semper Augustus ac Germanie . Hispaniarũ vtriusq, Sicilie . Gerusalem . Vngarie, Dalmatie,

Croacie . Insularũ Bullarũ . Fortunatarũ*que* . ac noui Orbis Indiarũ ... [Ninety-first line]: Datum Bononie sub Anno a Natiuitate d'm Millesimoquingentesimotrigesimo ... 1 vellum sheet, containing 92 printed lines and a few words in manuscript. L.

Title from Harrisse' "Bib. Am. Vet.," p. 273, which see, for particulars concerning the Bull which enjoins that "you will compel, and, with all zeal, cause the barbarous nations to come to the knowledge of God, the maker and founder of all things, not only by edicts and admonitions, *but also by force and arms, if needful*, in order that their souls may partake of the heavenly kingdom."

CLEMENT X. Bulla Canonizationis S. Rosæ de S. Maria Virgine Limanæ. *Romæ.* 1671. 13625

CLEMENT XIV. [Giovanni Vincenzo Antonio Ganganelli.] Breve sobre la reduccion de asilos en todos los dominios de España y de las Indias, cometida à los ordinarios eclesiásticos, expedido â instancia de S. M. [Carlos IV. *Madrid.*] 1773. 16mo. C. 13626

Extract from "Mercurio historico y politico," *Marzo*, 1773.

CLEMENT XIV. El Llanto de Mexico en los tiernos y lugubreres Recuerdos que à la Aug. Memoria de Clemente XIV. *Mexico.* 1775. 4to. 13627

CLEMENT (C.) Speech of the Hon. Charles Clement on the "Bill for an Act regulating the Disbursement of the Income of the University Fund," delivered in the Senate of Wisconsin. March 27, 1856. ... *Madison, Wis.* 1856. 8vo, pp. 15. H.

CLEMENT (C.) A Woman's Reason why Women should not Vote. By Cora Clement *Boston: J. E. Farwell & Co., Prs.* 1868. 8vo, pp. 16. 13629

CLEMENT (J.) Noble Deeds of American Women: with Biographical Sketches of some of the more Prominent. Edited by J. Clement; with an Introduction by Mrs. L. H. Sigourney. *Buffalo.* 1851. 12mo, pp. 480. + New Edition. *New York.* 1855. 13630

CLEMENT (J.) Discourse Delivered at the Funeral of Hon. William M. Richardson, ... 26th Day of March, A.D., 1838. By Rev. Jonathan Clement ... . *Concord, N. H.: printed by Asa M'Farland.* 1838. 8vo, pp. 16. B., H. 13631

Also: An Address delivered before the New Hampshire Lyceum, ... at their first Annual Meeting ... *Concord.* 1833. 8vo.—Address before the Social Fraternity in Phillips Academy, at Andover, Mass. ... *Andover.* 1828. 8vo. W.

CLEMENTE (C.) Tablas chronologicas, en qve se contienen los svcessos eclesiasticos y seculares de España, Africa, Indias orientales y occidentales, desde su principio, hasta el año 1642. Compuestos por el P. Claudio Clemente. Ilustradas, y añadidas desde el año 1642, hasta el presente de 1689, con las noticias que se hallan entre estas, por Vicente Ioseph Migvel. *Valencia: en la Imprenta de Iayme de Bordazar, año* 1689. Sm. 8vo, 8 l., pp. 275. C. 13632

More than one-fourth of this work relates to America, respecting which it contains much curious matter not to be found elsewhere. Among other things, "Columbus's Prayer," when he first landed in the New World.

CLEMENTIÆ AMATOR, *pseudonym.* A True Description of a Number of Tyrannical Pedagogues, a Poem dedicated to the Sons of H*****d, by Clementiæ Amator. *Printed in the Year* 1769. 4to, pp. 8. 13633

CLEMO (Ebenezer). Canadian Homes; or the Mystery Solved. A Canadian Tale. *Montreal.* 1858. 12mo, pp. 136.

[CLEMO.] The Life and Adventures of Simon Seek; or Canada in all Shapes. By Maple Knot. *Montreal.* 1858. 12mo, pp. 179. 13635

CLENNING (Arthur). *See* [Flint (Timothy)].

CLEPHANE (James O.), *Reporter. See* (Dickenson (E. N.)

CLERC (Lawrent). An Address written by Mr. Clerc, and read ... at a Public Examination of the Pupils in the Connecticut Asylum ... 28th May, 1818. *Hartford: Hudson & Co., Printers.* 8vo, pp. 14. H. 13636

CLERCK (N. de). Tooneel der beroemder hertogen, princen, graven ende krijgshelden van Christenryck binnen dese drij laeste eeuwen ... Hare beeldnissen, afcomsten ... daden, enz. *Amst.* 1617. Folio, 5 l. 13637

Includes a biography, with portraits of Magellan, Athabalipa, Pizarro, Montezuma, Cortès, etc.

CLERCQ. *See* Le Clercq.

The Clergy of America. Anecdotes illustrative of the Character of Ministers of Religion in the United States. *Philadelphia: J. B. Lippincott & Co.* 1869. Crown 8vo, pp. 478.

The Clergy not Recruiting Agents, and the Churches not Recruiting Stations. A Letter to a Member of the Young Men's Christian Association. By Fromelden. *New York.* [About 1862.] 8vo, pp. 12. 13639

Clergyman's Almanac for 1811. *Boston.* [n. d.] 8vo.

There is, also, "The Clergyman's Minor Almanac."

The Clerical Candidates. A Poem. [Motto.] *Washington City, Nov.* 14, 1801. 8vo, pp. 32. 13641

Meeting of the Clerical Association in the Church of the Holy Trinity, Friday, November 9th, 1866. ... *New York: John A. Gray & Green, Printers.* 1867. 8vo, pp. 34. H. 13642

The Clerk's Magazine; containing the most useful and necessary Forms of Writings, and other Instruments calculated for the Use of the Citizen of the United States. *Albany: C. R. & G. Webster.* 1803. 12mo. 13643

Clerkships in Washington. A Letter to Hon. —— Member of Congress. By a Clerk. *Washington: Published by the Author.* 1851. 8vo, pp. 32. H. 13644

CLERVIN (N.) De l'opinion des médecins américains sur la contagion ou la non-contagion de la fievre jaune, ou réponse aux allégations de MM. les docteurs Hosack et Townsend, de New-York ... . *Paris: Baillière.* 1830. 8vo. 13645

Also: De l'identité de nature des fièvres d'origine paludéenne de différents types à l'occasion de deux mémoires de M. le docteur Rufz; sur la fièvre jaune qui a regné à la Martinique de 1838 à 1841 ... . *Paris: Baillière.* 1843. 8vo, pp. 116.—Pétition relative à l'enquête ordonnée par le gouvernement français sur la conduite en Amérique ... . *Paris.* 1833. 8vo. For a list of the numerous other books and articles in which Clervin defended the non-contagiousness of the yellow fever, *see* Quérard, "Lit. franç. contemp.," II. 618, 619.

CLEVELAND (Charles). Custom House Duties. *Salem, Mass.* 1800. 12mo. 13646

CLEVELAND. Farm School. [n. p. n. d.] 12mo, pp. 4.

This is a letter to the children of the Farm School.

CLEVELAND. A Sermon delivered, ... April 25, 1847. At the House of Correction, South Boston; being the Farewell Address of the Chaplain. By Rev. Charles Cleveland. *Boston: Press of Crocker and Brewster.* 1847. 8vo, pp. 16. H. 13648

Also: Sixth Annual Report of Charles Cleveland, City Missionary ... . [*Boston.* n. d.] 8vo, pp. 8. Continued. H.

CLEVELAND. Ninetieth Birthday Gathering of Rev. Charles Cleveland, June 21, 1862. *Boston: Marvin & Sons, Prs.* 1863. 16mo, pp. 64. Portrait. 13649

CLEVELAND (C. D.) Compendium of American Literature; Chronologically arranged, with Biographical Sketches of the Authors. ... By Charles D. Cleveland. *Philadelphia: E. C. & J. Biddle.* 1858. 12mo, pp. xx, 25–740. BA. 13650

CLEVELAND. To General U. S. Grant, President Elect of the United States. [n. p. 1869.] 8vo, pp. 4. H. 13651

CLEVELAND (C. F.) The California Question. Speech of Hon. Chauncy F. Cleveland, of Connecticut, ... April 19, 1860. ... [n. p. n. d.] 8vo, pp. 8. 13652

CLEVELAND. Letters of the Hon. C. F. Cleveland and the Hon. Henry Hubbard, Governors of Connecticut and New Hampshire, to Samuel Ward King, the Charter Governor of Rhode Island, refusing to deliver up Thomas Wilson Dorr, the Constitutional Governor of said State, to the usurping authorities thereof. Also Letters of the Hon. Marcus Morton, [James Buchanan and Martin Van Buren,] to the Suffrage Clam-Bake at Medbury Grove, Seekonk, Mass., August 30, 1842. *Fall River: Thomas Almy.* 1842. 8vo, pp. 17. 13653

Also: Speech of Chauncy F. Cleveland, of Connecticut, on the Homestead Bill, 1852. [n. p. n. d.]

CLEVELAND (*Mrs.* Dorcas C.) Our Book. A Call from Salem's Watch Towers, in behalf of Destitute Churches of the Unitarian Faith. *Salem.* 1844. 12mo. 13654

CLEVELAND (*Mrs.* E. H.) Introductory Lecture ... to the Class of the Female Medical College of Pennsylvania, for the Session of 1858–59. By Mrs. E. H. Cleveland ... . *Philadelphia: Merrihew & Thompson, Printers.* 1858. 8vo, pp. 16. H.

Also: Valedictory Address ... Female Medical College of Pennsylvania ... March 14, 1863, ... *Philadelphia: Crissy & Markley, Printers.* 1863. 8vo, pp. 15, (1). H.—Valedictory Address ... Women's Medical College ... March 14, 1868 ... . *Philadelphia: Jas. B. Rogers, Printer.* 1868. 8vo, pp. 12. H.

CLEVELAND (Edward). The Glory of a House of Worship: A Sermon ... *Stoneham, Mass.* 1840. 13656

CLEVELAND. A Sketch of the Early Settlement and History of Shipton, Canada East; by Rev. Edward Cleveland, A.M. ... *Richmond County, Canada East: C. S. Smith, Printer.* 1858. 12mo, pp. 78. 13657

CLEVELAND (H.) Alexander H. Stephens, in Public and Private, with Letters and Speeches, before, during, and since the War. By Henry Cleveland. *Philadelphia: National Publishing Company.* [1867.] 8vo, pp. 833. Portrait. C. 13658

[CLEVELAND (H. R.)] A Letter to the Hon. Daniel Webster, on the Causes of the Destruction of the Steamer Lexington ... . By A Traveller. *Boston: Charles C. Little and James Brown.* M DCCC XL. 8vo, pp. 46. H. 13659

CLEVELAND. A Selection from the Writings of Henry R. Cleveland. With a Memoir by George S. Hillard. [*Boston:*] *printed for Private Distribution.* MDCCCXLIV. 2 l., pp. li, 384.

Memoir, pp. v–li; American Architecture, pp. 113–156; Correspondence, pp. 334–384. Also: An Address delivered before the Howard Musical Association, at the Annual Meeting ... Aug. 26, 1840. ... *Boston.* MDCCCXL. 8vo, pp. 14. H.

CLEVELAND (J.) Poems. By John Cleveland. With Additions, never before printed. *London: Printed for W. Shears.* 1650. Sm. 8vo, pp. 244. Portrait. 13661

Some of the poems relate to America. Other editions, *London*, 1661, 1662, 1677, and 1687. The edition of 1687 has the following title:

CLEVELAND. The Works of John Cleveland, Containing his Poems, Orations, and Epistles, collected into One Volume, with the Life of the Author. *London.* 1687. Sm. 8vo. Portrait. 13662

CLEVELAND (*Mr.*) Life and Entertaining Adventures of Mr. Cleveland, Natural Son of Oliver Cromwell, giving a particular account of his unhappiness in Love, Marriage, Friendship, &c., and his great sufferings in Europe and America, also, some curious publications of Oliver's History, and Amours, and several remarkable passages in the reign of Charles II., never before made public. *London.* 1734. 4 vols., 12mo. + *London.* 1760. 5 vols., 12mo. 13663

CLEVELAND (Orestes). Views of the Minority of the Committee on Manufactures, presented by Mr. Cleveland ... May 20, 1870. *Washington: Government Printing Office.* 1870. 8vo, pp. 59. H. 13664

CLEVELAND (R. J.) A Narrative of [his own] Voyages and Commercial Enterprises, by Richard J. Cleveland *Cambridge: John Owen.* 1842. 2 vols., 12mo, pp. xvi, 249; viii, 240. H. + Second Edition. [*Ibid.*] + *London.* 1843. + Third Edition. *Boston.* 1850. 12mo. C. 13665

CLEVELAND (W. N.) African Servitude: what is it, and what its Moral Character? A Discourse, by Rev. William Neal Cleveland, Southampton, L. I. *New York: D. Appleton & Company.* 1861. 8vo, pp. 27. 13666

Cleveland (W. S.) The Public Grounds of Chicago. How to give them Character and Expression. *Chicago: Charles D. Lakey.* 1869. 8vo, pp. 20. H. + Second Edition. [*Ibid.*]

Cleveland Almanac and Business Man's Directory, for the Year 1857. *Cleveland, Ohio.* 1857. 24mo. 13668

Cleveland and Mahoning Railroad Company. Annual Report of the Directors and Chief Engineer. *Cleveland.* 1853. 8vo. Continued. 13669

Annual Report of the Cleveland, Columbus and Cincinnati R. R. Co. 1852. 8vo. Continued. 13670

Exhibits of the Condition and Prospects of the Cleveland, Columbus and Cincinnati Railroad. *New York.* 1849. 8vo.

Cleveland Female Seminary. Plan and Proposals ... under the direction of the Rev. E. N. Sawtell, A.M. ... *Boston.* 1850. 8vo. P., S. 13672

Cleveland Library Association. Catalogue. *Cleveland, Ohio.* 1849. 8vo, pp. 60. S. 13673

Cleveland Mining Company. Articles of Association ... Cleveland, O., 1846. 8vo. S. 13674

Cleveland, Past and Present; its Representative Men; comprising Biographical Sketches of Pioneer Settlers and Prominent Citizens, with a History of the City, [etc.] *Cleveland: M. Joblin.* 1869. 8vo, 3 l., pp. 500, 3 l. 81 Portraits. 13675

A Directory of the City of Cleveland for the Years 1837, 38. To which is added an Historical Description of the Place, and the Act incorporating the City. *Cleveland: Sanford & Scott.* 1837. 12mo, pp. 144. 13676

Probably the first directory. The late directories have been prepared by W. H. Boyd.

Cleveland Leader City Directory, 1867–8. With a Business Directory. *Cleveland: Leader Printing Co.* 8vo, pp. 310.

Inauguration of the Perry Statue, at Cleveland, on the Tenth of September, 1860; Including A History of the Battle of Lake Erie by George Bancroft, Addresses and other Proceedings, With A Sketch of William Walcutt, The Sculptor. Published by Direction of the City Council. *Cleveland, O.: Fairbanks, Benedict & Co.* 1861. 8vo, pp. 128. 13678

Twelve copies printed on quarto paper.

Report of the Board of Education. *Cleveland, Ohio.* 1853. &c. S. 13679

Public Schools—City of Cleveland. Report of the Board of Education for ... 1855–6. ... *Cleveland: Harris, Fairbanks & Co.* 1856. 8vo, pp. 89, (1). H. 13680

Sanitary Commission. Report of the Soldiers' Aid Society, of Cleveland, Ohio, and its Auxiliaries to the U. S. Sanitary Commission, at Washington, November 30, 1861. *Cleveland: Fairbanks, Benedict & Co.* 1861. 8vo, pp. 40. 13681

Forms No. 37 of United States Sanitary Publications.

Clever (C. P.) Address to the People of New Mexico, by C. P. Clever, Candidate for Delegate to Congress. ... *Santa Fé, N. M.: Weekly Gazette Office.* 1867. 8vo, pp. 18. H. 13682

Clever. New Mexico: her Resources; her Necessities for Railroad Communication with the Atlantic and Pacific States; her Great Future. By Charles P. Clever ... . *Washington: McGill & Witherow.* 1868. 8vo, pp. 47. 13683

Clibborn (E.) American Prosperity. An Outline of the American Debit or Banking System; to which is added, a Justification of the Veto of the late President, &c. By Edward Clibborn, a late resident in America. *London: Groombridge.* 1837. 8vo. C. 13684

Clifford (J.) The Case and Replication of the legal Representatives of Jeronimy Clifford, a British Subject, and late Merchant and Planter of Surinam, deceased, to the Information of the Directors of the Society of Surinam, presented on the 7th October 1762. *London: C. Say.* 1763. 8vo, pp. 478. Map.

Clifford. The Conduct of the Dutch, relating to their Breach of Treaties with England. Particularly Their Breach of the Articles of Capitulation, for the Surrender of Surinam, in 1667; and their Oppressions committed upon the English Subjects in that Colony, with A full Account of the Case of Jeronimy Clifford, late Merchant and Planter of Surinam, deceased; the unparalleled Injuries and Cruelties inflicted on him and his Estate by the Dutch; and the great Losses he sustained; his Applications for Redress both in England and Holland; the Transactions thereupon between the two States and their respective Ministers; the Parliamentary and other Proceedings upon Mr. Clifford's Case, during the Reigns of King William and

Queen Anne; and the Present State of this Affair. The Whole proving a Series of Facts, authenticated from Papers in the public Offices of State; whereby the Treachery and Injustice of the Dutch, towards the English, are displayed in a very interesting Light. *London: C. Say.* MDCC.LX. 8vo, Title, pp. 220. 13686

The following titles are from J. R. Smith's catalogue:

Clifford. The Case and Proceedings for and against Mr. Jeronimy Clifford, Merchant and Planter of Surinam. *May,* 1715. pp. 55. 13687

Clifford. Another Case of Jeronimy Clifford. *May,* 1714. Folio, pp. 12. 13688

Clifford (J. Henry). Argument on the ... Annexation of Roxbury to Boston, before the Legislative Committee ... February 23, 1865. By John H. Clifford. ... *Boston.* 1867. 8vo, pp. 21. H. 13689

Also: ... Supreme Judicial Court. ... John H. Clifford Esquire, Attorney General, &c. at the Relation of the Associate Reformed Presbyterian Synod of New York, and Others,—Informant, and The Proprietors of the Meeting House in Federal Street ... Defendant. *Boston.* 1850. 4to, pp 32.—Tribute to Edward Everett. [*Boston.* 1865.] 4to, pp. 3. H.

Clifford (Nathan). Speech of Mr. Clifford, of Maine, on the Resolution of Mr. Campbell, of South Carolina, concerning the New Jersey disputed Election. *Washington: Globe Office.* 1840. 8vo, Title, pp. 16. BA. 13690

Clifford. Speech ... on the Apportionment Bill; delivered in the House of Representatives, April 28, 1842. *Washington.* 1842. 8vo. 13691

Clifford (P.) Compendium Geographicum: Or, A more Exact, Plain, and Easie Introduction into all Geography than yet extant, after the latest Discoveries or Alterations. Very Useful, especially for Young Noblemen and Gentlemen, the like not Printed in English. By Peregrine Clifford, Chamberlayne of the Inner Temple, Gent. *London: William Crook.* 1682. 8vo, pp. 140. 13692

Title from "Bib. Am. Prim.," 139.

The Clifford Family; or, a Tale of the Old Dominion. By one of her Daughters. *New York.* 1852. 12mo. C. 13693

Cliffton [(William)]. Poems, chiefly Occasional, by the late Mr. Cliffton. To which are prefixed, Introductory Notices

of the Life, Character and Writings, of the Author, and an Engraved Likeness. ... *New-York: Printed for J. W. Fenno, by C. & R. Waite.* 1800. 18mo, pp. xvii, 119, (1). Portrait. BA.

See "Anal. Mag.," III. 479, and "Duyckinck's Cycl.," I. 605. The remarks on American literature in the introduction are curious.

Cliffton. The Group. *Philadelphia.* 1796. 4to. 13695

A satire in support of Jay's treaty.

Clift (W.) A Thanksgiving Discourse: a Remembrancer of Filial Obligation, delivered at Stonington, Nov. 25th, 1858, by William Clift ... . *Norwich: Manning, Perry & Co.* MDCCCLVIII. 8vo, pp. 15. H. 13696

Clifton (A.) The Trial of Alice Clifton, for the Murder Of her Bastard-Child ... at Philadelphia ... 18th day of April, 1787. [n. p. 1787.] 8vo, pp. 16. BA. 13697

Pages 15 and 16 contain "The Trial of James M'Glochlin for feloniously entering ... ."

Clifton (L. C.) The Crazy Trapper; or, The Prophet of the Senecas. By L. Colfert Clifton. *New York: Geo. Munro & Co.* 1865. 16mo, pp. 100. 13698

Clifton (W.) Philadelphia, November 1, 1777. ... 4to, broadside. P. 13699

Advertisement by Wm. Clifton for woodcutters for the king's troops. One hundred and fifty printed, by J. Humphreys.

Clifton. Description of Clifton, Staten Island, at the Narrows. *New York.* 1838. 8vo, pp. 24. Plate. 13700

Clifton Springs, *N. Y.* The Report of the Addresses and Sermon at the Dedication of the Clifton Springs Water-Cure. Held July 25, 1856. ... *Geneva and Canandaigua: National New Yorker Press.* 1857. 8vo, pp. 16. H., S. 13701

The Climax of Protection and Free Trade capped by Annexation. *Montreal.* [1847?] 12mo, pp. 18. S. 13702

Clinch (J. H.) The Captivity in Babylon, and other Poems. By the Rev. Joseph H. Clinch, A.M. *Boston: James Burns.* 1840. 12mo, 3 l., pp. 115. BA. 13703

Includes "American Antiquities," "Niagara," and "The Kennebec."

Cline (A. J.) Secession Unmasked; or an Appeal from the Madness of Disunion to the Sobriety of the Constitution and

Common Sense. By A. J. Cline. Dedicated to the Citizens of our whole Country, and especially to the Officers and Soldiers in the United States Service. *Washington: Henry Polkinhorn.* 1861. 8vo, pp. 16. B. 13704

Clingan (G.) State of the Accounts of George Clingan, Treasurer of Franklin County, Penn. *Philadelphia.* 1790. 8vo.

Clingman (T. L.) Speech ... on the Political Aspect of the Slave Question. ... In the House ... December 22d, 1847. [*Washington.* 1847.] 8vo, pp. 16. B., BA., H. 13706

Clingman. Letter of T. L. Clingman [to the Editors of the Republic. Dated March 22, 1850. n. p. n. d.] pp. 4.

Also: Address of Thomas L. Clingman on the Political Condition and Prospects of the Country, to the Freemen of the Eighth Congressional District of North Carolina. *Washington.* 1856. 8vo, pp. 16. B.—Speech ... on the Principles of the Whig and Democratic Parties. ... In the House ... March 7, 1844. *Washington.* 1844. 8vo, pp. 24. H.—Speech ... on the Late Presidential Election. ... In the House ... January 6, 1845. [*Washington.* 1845.] 8vo, pp. 16. BA., H.—Speech ... Nebraska and Kansas, April 4, 1854. 8vo, pp. 8.—State Agricultural Society of North Carolina. Annual Address ... October 21, 1858, by Hon. Thos. L. Clingman, of Buncombe. [*Washington.* 1858.] 8vo, pp. 22. H. (The latter part is political and historical.)—Speech ... against the Revolutionary Movement of the Anti-Slavery Party; ... in the Senate ... January 16, 1860 *Washington.* 1860. 8vo, pp 16. H.—Speech ... on the Subject of Congressional Legislation as to the Rights of Property in the Territories. ... in the Senate ... May 7 & 8, 1860. *Washington.* 1860. 8vo, pp. 16. H.—Speech in the Senate ... of Hon. Thos. L. Clingman of North Carolina, on the State of the Union ... February 4, 1861. [*Washington.* 1861.] 8vo, pp. 16. H.

Clinton (C. A.) Oration, Delivered on the 43d Anniversary of American Independence. By Appointment of the Albany Military Association. By C. A. Clinton. *Albany: printed by John O. Cole.* 1819. 8vo, pp. 16. B. 13708

Also: Biographical Sketch of the Clinton Family. *New York.* 1859.

[Clinton (De Witt).] An Account of Abimelech Coody and other Celebrated Writers of New York; In a Letter from a Traveller, to his Friend in South Carolina. [*New York.*] *January,* 1815. 8vo, pp. 16. P. 13709

Abimelech Coody is a *pseudonym* for Gulian C. Verplanck.

Clinton. Account of the Salmo Otsego, or the Otsego Basse. In a Letter ... from De Witt Clinton ... . *New York: printed by C. S. Van Winkle.* 1822. 8vo, pp. 6. Plate. B.

Clinton. An Address delivered before the Holland Lodge, December 24, 1793. By De Witt Clinton, Master of said Lodge, on the Evening of his Installation. *New York.* MDCCXCIV. 8vo, Title, pp. 16. BA. 13711

Two hundred copies printed.

[Clinton.] The Canal Policy of the State of New-York, delivered in a letter to Robert Troup, Esq. By Tacitus. *Albany.* 1821. 8vo. 13712

Clinton. A Discourse, delivered before the American Academy of the Arts. 23d October, 1816. *New-York: T. & W. Mercein.* 1816. 8vo, pp. 30. B., BA., S. 13713

Clinton. Discourse delivered before the New-York Historical Society ... 6th December, 1811. By the Honourable De Witt Clinton ... . *New York: James Eastburn.* 1812. 8vo, pp. 81, (1). BA. 13714

Also included in "New York Hist. Coll.," Vol. II.

Clinton. An Introductory Discourse, delivered before the Literary and Philosophical Society of New-York, on the Fourth of May, 1814,—by De Witt Clinton, LL.D. ... *New-York: David Longworth.* 1815. 8vo, pp. 148. B., BA., P. 13715

With an appendix of notes and illustrations. Also on large paper, 4to.

[Clinton.] Letters on the Natural History and Internal Resources of the State of New-York. By Hibernicus. *New-York: E. Bliss & E. White.* 1822. 12mo, pp. 224. C., H.

Clinton. Letters of Marcus and Phil-Cato. *See* [Davis (M. L.)]

[Clinton.] The Martling-Man; or, Says I to myself—how is this? From the New-York Columbian of March, 1819. *New-York.* 1819. 8vo, pp. 23. A. 13717

Clinton. A Memoir on the Antiquities of the Western Parts of the State of New-York. Read before the Literary and Philosophical Society of New York. By De Witt Clinton ... . *Albany: printed by E. & E. Hosford.* 1820. 8vo, pp. 16. B.

There are two editions of this "Memoir," in the first, which is very rare, the author expresses an opinion that the Spaniards had, at one time, a colony in the country of the Onondagas. In the second issue this opinion is omitted. Later researches seem to indicate that his first opinion was correct.

[Clinton.] Memorial concerning A Canal Navigation, &c. [n. p. n. d.] 8vo, pp. 18. BA. 13719

Clinton. Remarks on the Fishes of the Western Waters of the State of New York. By Hon. De Witt Clinton. *New York.* 1815. 8vo. B., P. 13720

[Clinton.] Remarks on the proposed Canal from Lake Erie to the Hudson River. By Atticus. *New-York: printed by Samuel Wood & Sons.* 1816. 8vo, pp. 14. BA. 13721

Clinton. The Speeches of Governor Clinton, before the Legislature of New-York, between the Years 1817 and 1823. *New-York.* 1823. 8vo, pp. 78. BA. 13722

Clinton. Speeches of the Hon. DeWitt Clinton, Esq. in the Senate of the United States, in 1803, against a War with Spain. *New-York: Re-printed by Pelsue and Goulan.* 1812. 8vo, pp. 44. B., BA. 13723

[Clinton.] A Vindication of Thomas Jefferson; against the Charges contained in a Pamphlet, entitled "Serious Considerations," etc. By Grotius. *New York: Printed by David Denniston.* 1800. 8vo, pp. 47. C. 13724

Also: Address to the Benefactors and Friends of the Free-School Society of New-York ... on the Opening of that Institution ... on the Eleventh of the Twelfth Month ... 1809. *New-York: Collins and Perkins.* 1810. 8vo, pp. 12. BA.—Albany Register—Extra ... January 4, 1820. Speech of His Excellency De Witt Clinton ... to the Legislature ... . [n. p. n. d.] 8vo, pp. 14. BA.—Certain Phenomena of the Great Lakes of America. *New York.* 1817. 4to.—Circular Letter to the Literary and Philosophical Society of New York, on the Subject of a Statistical Account of the State of New York. *New York.* 1815. 8vo. pp. 8.—A Discourse Delivered at Schenectady, July 22, 1823, before the New-York Alpha of the Phi Beta Kappa. ... *Albany: Websters and Skinners.* 1823. 8vo, pp. 47. B., H. + Third Edition. *New York.* 1823. 8vo.—Message ... to the Legislature, in relation to the Improper Interference of the Officers of the General Government in the Local Concerns of the State. ... 12mo.—Message ... To the House of Assembly, January 18th, 1821. [n. p. n. d.] 12mo, pp. 52. (B.A. has a copy, apparently perfect, pp. 45.)—Message ... to the Legislature of the State of New York, January, 1825. *New York.* 1825. 8vo, pp. 26.—Message to the Legislature of the State of New York, Jan. 3, 1826. *Albany.* 1826. 8vo, pp. 17.—The Message ... to the Legislature of the State of New-York ... January 2, 1827. *Albany: printed by John B. Van Steenbergh.* 1827. 8vo, pp. 18. B.—An Oration On Benevolence, delivered before the Society of Black Friars, In ... New York ... 10th November, 1794. ... *New-York.* M,DCC,XCV. Sm. 8vo, pp. 19. BA.—Speech ... in the Senate of the State of New York, Tuesday, January 31, 1809. Introductory to certain Resolutions ... *New York.* 1809. 8vo, pp. 23. BA.—Speech ... to the Legislature of the State of New York, on the Sixth Day of January, 1819. *Albany: Register Office.* 1819. 8vo, pp. 16. BA.—Speech ... delivered to the Legislature of the State of New York, January 4, 1820. *Albany: printed by Jeremiah Tryon.* 1820. 8vo, pp. 24.—Speech ... To the Legislature of the State of New York, At the opening of the Session, 2d January, 1822. [n. p. n. d.] 8vo, pp. 8. B. Concerning Clinton, *see* "N. Am. Rev.," I. 390; XXIX. 496; "Am. Q. Rev.," V. 473, "Christ. Rev.," VI. 507; "Am. Reg.," IV. 156; "Niles's Reg.," XXVIII. 120; "National Portrait Gallery," II. 10. The following works relate to Clinton:

Clinton. Address of the Committee of the City of New-York, acting under the Authority of the General Committee of

Correspondence of the State of New-York, in support of the Nomination of the Hon. De Witt Clinton to the Presidency of the United States at the Ensuing Election. *New-York.* 1812. 8vo. C., P., S. 13725

Clinton. Address of the Democratic Republican Committee of Pittsburgh, [Penn.] &c. for De Witt Clinton, as President. 1812. 8vo. W. 13726

Clinton. The Clinton Monument. MDCCCXLVIII. *New York.* 1848. 8vo, pp. 27. Lithograph. B. 13727

Clinton. The Clinton Monument. Report of the Committee on the Character and Location of the Monument to the Memory of De Witt Clinton. 1848. 8vo. B., N. 13728

Clinton. De Witt Clinton and the Late War. [n. p. n. d.] 8vo, pp. 16. A., B. 13729

Clinton. Letter to the Legislature of South Carolina on the Claims and Qualifications of De Witt Clinton for President of the United States. *Charleston.* 1812. 8vo. C. 13730

Clinton. Letter of Alexander, addressed to De Witt Clinton. *Richmond.* 1811. 8vo. 13731

Clinton. Letters to a Friend at Pittsburgh, on the Character and Conduct of De Witt Clinton. By Milo. *New York.* 1812. 8vo. C. 13732

Clinton. Positive Facts versus Envious Assertions, being an Impartial Review and Refutation of all the Charges preferred against Governor De Witt Clinton. By a Candid Virginian. [n. d.] 1823. 8vo, pp. 87. 13733

Clinton. Presentation of Vases to Governor Clinton by the Pearl Street Merchants of New York; with a Description of them. [n. p.] 1825. 8vo. 13734

Clinton. Public Proceedings on the Removal of De Witt Clinton from the Office of Canal Commissioner. *New York.* 1824. 8vo. 13735

Clinton. Sermon addressed to De Witt Clinton, Mayor of the City of New York. By Amphiaraus. *New York. June,* 1804. 8vo, pp. 13. N. 13736

CLINTON. Tribute to the Memory of De Witt Clinton, Being a Comprehensive Sketch of His Life. By a Citizen of Albany. *Albany.* 1828. 12mo. S. 13737

The catalogue of the N. Y. State Library attributes this to Cuyler Staats.

CLINTON *and* BALDWIN. Letters of Governor Clinton, and of Colonel L. Baldwin ... improved as Evidence Before the Joint Committee of the Legislature of Massachusetts, on the Petition of Samuel Hinkley and Others, for the Extension of the Hampshire and Hampden Canal. February, 1828. *Boston: Dutton & Wentworth.* 1828. 8vo, pp. 22. H., S. 13738

CLINTON (De Witt), *Engineer.* Correspondence on the Importance and Practicability of a Railroad from New York to New Orleans. *New York.* 1830. 8vo, pp. 23. M. 13739

Also: A Report on Neversink River. S.

CLINTON (G.), *Gov. of N. Y.*, 1743–53. A Treaty between ... George Clinton ... Governor of the Province of New-York ... and The Six United Indian Nations, and the other Indian Nations, depending on the Province of New-York. Held at Albany ... August and September, 1746. *New-York: James Parker.* 1746. Folio, pp. 23. BA. 13740

A very rare tract. I have seen but one copy.

CLINTON (G.) Address to the People of the United States who choose Electors. To which is added a Short Sketch of the Biography of Gen. George Clinton, and several Essays. *Washington.* 1808. 12mo, pp. 54. M., P. 13741

CLINTON. Oration, before various Societies in the City of New York, on the Fourth of July, 1798. By George Clinton, Jun. *New York.* [1798.] 8vo. N. 13742

[CLINTON.] Supplement to the Albany Centinel, January 29, 1802. Governor's Speech. [*Albany.* 1802.] 4to, pp. (3).

CLINTON. Revolutionary Relics, or Clinton Correspondence; comprising the celebrated papers found in Andre's boots; private and Confidential Letters from Washington, Hamilton, Lafayette, and others. *New York: Herald Office.* 1842. 8vo, pp. 16.

Reprinted from the "New York Herald."

CLINTON. Clinton's Legacy: The People *vs.* King Caucus. *Washington.* 1808. 8vo. S. 13745

Another edition has the title:

CLINTON. Protest of the Friends of George Clinton against the Doings of King Caucus the First, in 1808. *Washington.* [n. d.] 8vo. 13746

CLINTON. To Federalists, attached to Republican Government, in New York. 8vo. B. 13747

Also: Report of the Committee on the Correspondence between Governor Clinton and Governor Williamson, touching the Arrest of a Ministerial Officer of New York. *Trenton: William L. Pratt.* 1826. 8vo, pp. 18.

CLINTON. Address of George W. Clinton, Esq., delivered before the Young Men's Temperance Society of Buffalo, March, 6th, 1841. *Buffalo: printed by Frechette & Scheffer.* 1841. 8vo, pp. 10. B. 13748

CLINTON. Preliminary List of Plants of Buffalo and its Vicinity. By George W. Clinton, ... *Buffalo: Young, Lockwood & Co., Prs.* 1864. 8vo, pp. 12. 13749

Also: An Address, ... at Canandaigua, June 22, 1830, before the Domestic Horticultural Society ... . *Canandaigua: printed by Morse, Ward and Co.* 1830. 8vo, pp. 23. B.—An Address delivered at the Normal School, July 10, 1836. *Albany.* 1836. 8vo, pp. 16.

CLINTON (H.) A Letter from Lieut. Gen. Sir Henry Clinton, K.B., to the Commissioners of Public Accounts, relative to Some Observations in their Seventh Report, Which may be judged to imply Censure on the late Commanders in Chief of His Majesty's Army in North America. *London: J. Debrett.* M,DCC,LXXXIV. 8vo, pp. 31. C., H. 13750

See "M. Rev.," LXXI. 152.

CLINTON. Narrative of Lieutenant-General Sir Henry Clinton, K.B. relative to his Conduct during part of his Command of the King's Troops in North America; Particularly to that which respects the unfortunate Issue of the Campaign in 1781. With an Appendix, containing Copies and Extracts of those Parts of his Correspondence with Lord George Germain, Earl Cornwallis, Rear Admiral Graves, &c. Which are referred to therein. *London: printed for J. Debrett.* 1783. 8vo, 2 l., pp. 115, Errata, 7 lines. + Second Edition. [*Ibid.*] + Third Edition. [*Ibid.*] + *London, Printed. New York: Re-printed by Sower, Morton and Horner.* M.DCC.LXXXIII. 4to, pp. 39. + Fourth Edition. *London: J. Debrett.* 8vo, 2 l., pp. 112. + Fifth Edition. *London: J. Debrett.* 1783. 8vo, 2 l., pp. 112. BA., H. + Sixth Edition. *London: J. Debrett.* 1783. 8vo. C., M. + Seventh Edition. *London: John Debrett.* 1785. 8vo, 2 l., pp. 87. C. + *Philadelphia: John Campbell.* MDCCLXV. 8vo, 3 l., pp. 115. 13751

Of the Philadelphia edition, there were printed 200 copies in 8vo, 75 in 4to, and 25 in folio. "In this detail Sir Henry Clinton acquits himself of all share in Lord Cornwallis' misfortune; leaving that general to answer for misconceptions of the orders sent him, and for the choice of the post he was reduced to surrender."—*M. Rev.*, LXVIII. 88.

CLINTON. A Narrative of Sir Henry Clinton's Operations with Sir Peter Parker, on the Attack of Sullivan's Island, in South Carolina, in the year 1776; and with Vice-Admiral Arbuthnot, in an Intended Attempt against the French Armament at Rhode Island, in 1780. *New York.* 1780. 8vo, pp. 39. N.

CLINTON. Observations on Mr. Stedman's History of the American War. By Lieutenant-General Sir Henry Clinton, K.B. *London: J. Debrett.* 1794. 4to, Title, pp. ii, 34. H. + *New York: Reprinted.* 1864. 4to, Title, pp. ii, 34. Photographic Portrait. 13753

Of the reprint, 50 copies were privately printed, for presentation only, by F. S. Hoffman.

CLINTON. Observations on some Parts of the Answer of Earl Cornwallis to Sir Henry Clinton's Narrative. By Lieutenant-General Sir Henry Clinton, K.B. To which is added an Appendix; containing Extracts of Letters and other Papers, to which Reference is necessary. *London: J. Debrett.* M.DCC.-LXXXIII. 8vo, 2 l., pp. 35, 113, (1), 1 l., folded. H. + [Reprinted.] *Philadelphia: John Campbell.* MDCCLXVI. 8vo, 4 l., pp. 35, 115, (1), Table. 13754

Of the Philadelphia reprint, 200 copies were printed in 8vo, 75 in 4to, and 25 in folio.

CLINTON. List of the General and Staff Officers serving in North America, under the Command of H. E. Gen. Sir Henry Clinton, K.B. *New York.* 1779. 8vo, pp. 65. M. 13755

CLINTON (H. L.) Speech of Henry L. Clinton, Esq. to the Jury in the Case of Andrew J. Millspaugh against Seth Adams, in the Supreme Court, New York. *New York.* 1865. 8vo.

CLINTON (T. G.) Petition of Thomas George Clinton, Assistant Examiner in the Patent Office preferring Charges Against E. Burke, Commissioner of Patents. ... [*Washington.* 1848.] 8vo, pp. 7. H. 13757

CLINTON CEMETERY, *Clinton, N. Y.* Addresses delivered at the Dedication of the Clinton Cemetery ... with the Rules ... . *Utica: Roberts, Printer.* 1857. 8vo, pp. 46. H. 13758

CLINTON COUNTY. Report of the Clinton County Coal Company of Pennsylvania. *New York.* 1855. 8vo. 13759

Clinton Line Railroad Company. First Annual Report, with the Report of the Chief Engineer. *Hudson, Ohio.* 1854. S.

CLINTON, *Mass.* Catalogue of the Bigelow Association, Clinton, Mass. Incorporated June 19, 1852. ... *Clinton.* 1861. 8vo, pp. xii, 148. B. 13761

Valuation and Taxes of the Town of Clinton, for the Year 1857. *Clinton: Printed at the Courant Office.* 1857. 8vo, pp. 45. H. 13762

Reports of the Selectmen, Overseers of Poor, Treasurer, and Cemetery Committee of the Town of Clinton, for the Year ending March 1, 1856. *Clinton: Courant Office.* 1856. 8vo, pp. 17. H. 13763

CLINTON, *N. Y.* Catalogue of the Officers and Students of Clinton Seminary. *Rome.* 1842. 8vo. B. 13764

CLINTON, *N. Y.* *See* Hamilton College, and New York State.

Clio: The Converted Indian, a Poem; To which is added an Ode on the Incarnation. *Shrewsbury.* [1774.] 4to. 13765

Written on the occasion of an old Indian of Georgia (Tomo Chiehii) being converted by the preaching of George Whitefield.

Clippings from the California Press, in regard to Steam across the Pacific, from March to November. ... *San Francisco: Town & Bacon, Printers.* 8vo, pp. 104. H. 13766

The Clockmaker. *See* [Haliburton (T. C.)]

CLODORÉ (Jean de). Plaintes et Griefs | Presentés | à Monseignevr | de Colbert, | Par Monsieur de Clodoré, Gouverneur de l'Isle | de la Martinique, sur le renvoy fait par le | Roy, de son Placet. | Contre Monsieur de la Barre, Lieutenant general | en l'Amerique. | Le tout renvoyé par sa Majesté à Nosseigneurs les | Mareschaux de France. | [1699.] 4to, Title, pp. 46. 13767

Privately printed, about 1668.

[CLODORÉ.] Relation | de ce qui s'est passé, | dans les Isles & Terre-Ferme de | l'Amérique, pendant la dernière | guerre avec l'Angleterre, & de- | puis en exécution du Traitté de | Bréda. | Avec un Journal | Du dernier Voyage du Sr de la Barre en la | terre-ferme, & Isle de Cayenne, accom- | pagné d'une exacte description du Pays, | mœurs & naturel des Habitans. | Le tout recueilly des Memoires des principaux | Officiers qui ont com-

mandé en ces Pays. | Par I. C. S. D. V. [J. Clodoré, secrétaire de vaisseaux.] Où est joint le Journal d'un nouveau | Voyage fait en Guynée, l'année pre- | sente, qui contient le Traité de Com- | merce, & alliance, fait avec le Roy | d'Ardres, avec l'envoy d'un Ambassa- | deur de ce Prince en France. | ... | *A Paris,* | ... *Gervais Clovzier* ... | ... | ... . | M. DC. LXXI. | ... | 2 vols., 18mo, 30 l., pp. 386; 4 l., pp. 494, 1 l., pp. 495–558. BA., C. 13768

CLOLUS (E.) De la détention preventive et de la mise en liberté provisoire sous caution étude comparée des quatre législations américaine, anglaise, belge et française suivie de la présentation pun nouveau projet de loi par Émile Clolus ... *Paris: Auguste Durand.* 1865. 8vo, Title, pp. xxxvi, 322. B. 13769

[CLOPPER (J.)] Fragments of the History of Bawlfredonia: containing an Account of the Discovery and Settlement, of that Great Southern Continent; and of the Formation and Progress of the Bawlfredonian Commonwealth. By Herman Thwackus. Translated from the Original Bawlfredonian Manuscript, into the French Language, by Monsieur Traducteur, and rendered into English, by a Citizen of America. *Printed for the American Booksellers.* 1819. 8vo, 2 l., pp. 164. BA., C., H. 13770

Copyrighted by Jonas Clopper "as author." A satire on American politics and manners.

CLOPTON (John). Mr. Clopton's Motion, purposing an Amendment to the Constitution of the United States. Feb. 29, 1808. *Washington.* 1808. 8vo. 13771

Also: Address to the Congressional District, composed of Hanover, Henrico, Charleston City, New Kent and City of Richmond. By John Clopton, of New Kent. *Washington. June* 20, 1812. 8vo. S.—Speech ... on the Passage of the Bill to Prohibit the Importation of Certain Goods, Wares and Merchandise, March 21, 1800. 8vo.

CLOQUET (J.) Souvenirs sur la vie privée du général La Fayette par M. Jules Cloquet. *Paris: A. et W. Galignani et Cie.* 1836. 8vo, Title, pp. xvi, 394. Portraits, Woodcuts, and 12 Facsimiles of Writing. BA. 13772

See "Am. Q. Rev.," XX. 102.

CLOQUET. Recollections of the Private Life of General Lafayette. By M. Jules Cloquet, M.D. Embellished with numerous Engravings, as in the Original Paris Edition. *London: Baldwin and Cradock.* 1835. 8vo, pp. xxx, 339. Portrait. + *New York: Leavitt, Lord & Co. Boston: Crocker & Brewster.*

2 vols., 12mo, pp. xvii, 219, (1); 184. Portrait, Woodcuts, and Facsimiles. BA., C. 13773

"Written at the request of Mr. Isaiah Townsend, of Albany, and translated by him and published in the New York 'Evening Star;' afterwards published simultaneously in London, Paris, and New York."

CLOQUET. Rapport sur la Situation de la colonie de Santo-Tomas. *Bruxelles.* 1850. 13774

CLOSE (J.) Discourse at Waterford, before the Orange Lodge No. 43, on the Anniversary Festival of St. John the Baptist, 1800. By John Close. *Lansingburgh.* 1808. 4to. N.

Also: Discourse on Relative and Federal Holiness, etc. *Lansingburgh.* 1808. 12mo, pp. 32. N.

The Close of the Late Rebellion, in Rhode-Island. An Extract from a Letter by a Massachusetts Resident in Providence. *Providence.* 1842. 8vo, pp. 16. 13776

CLOUGH (Samuel). The New-England Almanack, 1703. *Boston.* 1703–6. 16mo. M. + Clough's Farewell Almanac, 1708. With Elegy on the Author. *Boston.* 1708. 16mo.

CLOUGH (S.) An Account of the Christian Denomination in the United States. By Simon Clough. *Boston.* 1827. 8vo. pp. 12. B. 13778

CLOUGH. A Candid Appeal to the Citizens of the United States, proving that the Doctrines advanced and the Measures pursued by the Abolitionists, relative to the Subject of Emancipation, are Inconsistent with The Teachings ... of the Bible ... . By Simon Clough ... . *New-York.* 1834. 8vo, pp. 39.

CLOUGH. A Discourse Delivered at the Opening of the Christian Meeting House in Boston ... December 29, 1825. By Samuel Clough ... . *Boston: printed by Isaac R. Butts and Co.* 1826. 12mo, pp. 36. H., W. 13780

CLOUGH. A Series of Articles and Discourses, Doctrinal, Practical, and Experimental; constituting the Select Works of Simon Clough. *New York: published by the Author.* 1843. 12mo, pp. xii, 340. B. 13781

The Cloven Foot Discovered. *Ephrata.* 13782

Supposed to be written by the Rev. Thomas Barton. Relates to the Lancaster massacre. *See* Watson's "Philadelphia," I. 504.

CLOVER (N.) Debate on Slavery, at Boston, May, 1841, between the Rev. Nath. Clover, of Boston, and the Rev. Jonathan Davis, of Georgia. [n. p. n. d.] 18mo, pp. 120. 13783

CLOWES (*Rev.* J.) Sermon, Public Fast in New Hampshire. *Manchester.* 1809. 8vo. 13784

CLOWES (T.) Sermons preached in St. Peter's Church. Albany, on the several Sundays and Holy-days in the Month of December, 1816. By Timothy Clowes. *Albany.* 1816. 12mo, pp. 288. W. 13785

CLOWES. Answer of St. Peter's Church, in Albany, to the Pamphlet, by Lt. Gov. Taylor and others. [*Albany.*] 1816. 8vo. B. 13786

[CLOWES.] To the Members of the Congregation of St. Peter's Church, in the City of Albany. *Albany.* 1815. 8vo.

Statement of a misunderstanding with the rector, the Rev. Timothy Clowes.

CLOWES (William J.) Hartwood Politician. *Poughkeepsie.* 1853. Nos. 1 and 2 First Series. C. 13788

CLOYNE (George), *Bishop of.* *See* Berkeley (G.), Vol. II.

El Club Jacobino de Francia resucitado en la Capital del Distrito del Sud-oeste del Departamento de Michoacan, ó sean venganzas escandalosas ejercitadas contra los Ciudadanos. *Guadalajara.* 1843. 4to, pp. 16. 13789

Club National (de langue française), fondé à New York, le 16 octobre 1863. Programme et Declaration de principes. [*New York.* 1863.] 8vo, pp. (4). H. 13790

The Club-Room. No. 1–4. February–July 1820. ... *Boston: T. Swan.* [1820.] 8vo, pp. 179. BA., H. 13791

Among the contributors were W. H. Prescott and Edward Everett. Includes "Lake George," and "A Voyage of Discovery," both by Wm. H. Gardiner.

CLUBB (H. S.) The Emigration Guide to Kanzas, Containing Three Maps, and every Information required by Persons desirous of settling in that Territory. By Henry S. Clubb. *New York: Fowlers and Wells.* 13792

CLUBB. Maine Liquor Law; its Origin, History, and Results. Including a Life of Hon. Neal Dow. *New-York.* 1856. 12mo. C. 13793

CLUBB. Results of Prohibition in Connecticut; being Special Returns Received from Every County, as to the Effect of The Maine Liquor Law ... Edited by Henry S. Clubb ... . *New-York: Fowlers and Wells.* 1855. 12mo, 2 l., pp. 99–149. Map and 3 Portraits. H. 13794

CLUBB (S.) A Journal; containing an Account of the Wrongs, Sufferings, and Neglect experienced by Americans in France. By Stephen Clubb, late a Prisoner in that Empire. ... *Printed at Boston.* 1809. 8vo, pp. 60. B., BA. 13795

[CLUNY (Alexander).] The American Traveller; or, Observations on the Present State, Culture and Commerce of the British Colonies in America, And the further Improvements of which they are capable; with An Account of the Exports, Imports and Returns of each Colony respectively,—and of the Numbers of British Ships and Seamen, Merchants, Traders and Manufacturers employed by all collectively: together with The Amount of the Revenue arising to Great-Britain therefrom. In a Series of Letters, written originally to the Right Honourable the Earl of **** **** By an Old and Experienced Trader. *London: E. and C. Dilly, and J. Almon.* MDCCLXIX. 4to, 4 l., pp. 122. Map and Plate. BA., C., H. + [Reprinted. n. p.] 1770. 12mo, pp. 89. 13796

"The author was the first to give accurate intelligence of Hudson's Bay, and to institute an enquiry about a more successful commerce with the Americans. The book is said to have been published under the auspices of Lord Chatham, and both the English and the Americans, at that crisis, were so eager to possess it, that it was bought and read by one party with the same avidity that it was bought and distroyed by the other.—DIBDIN's *Library Companion*, II. 65. *See* "M. Rev.," XLI. 44. It was published in French, with the following title:

[CLUNY.] Le Voyageur américain, ou Observations Sur l'État actuel, la Culture, le Commerce des Colonies Britanniques en Amérique; les Exportations, & Importations respectives entre elles & la Grande-Bretagne, avec un Etat des revenus que cette derniere en retire, &c., Adressées par un Négociant expérimenté en forme de lettres, au très-honorable comte de .... [Chatham] Traduit de l'Anglois, Augmenté d'un précis sur l'Amérique Septentrionale & la République des treize-États-Unis, par M. J^h. [Joseph] M......... [Mandrillon]. *Amsterdam: J. Schuring.* MDCCLXXXII. 8vo, pp. viii, 166, 3 l. folded. Map. H. + *Amsterdam: J. Schuring.* M. DCC. LXXXIII. 8vo, pp. viij, 264. H. 13797

[CLUNY.] The British Merchant. Observations on the present State, Culture, and Commerce of the British Colonies in America, by an Old and Experienced Trader. *London.* 1769. 4to. Map and Plate. 13798

Title from one of Ch. Welford's catalogues, where it is described as a large paper copy. Probably the same as No. 13796.

Cluseret (G.) Mexico, and the Solidarity of Nations. By General G. Cluseret. *New York: Blackwell, Printer.* 1866. 8vo, pp. 109. H. 13799

Also: The American Press. [n. p. n. d.] 4to, pp. (2). H. — The New Nation to the Public. G. Cluseret, Editor. [*New York.* 1864.] 1 l. H.

Clusius (C.) Caroli | Clvsii Atrebatis | aliqvot notæ | in Garciæ | Aromatum Historiam. | Eivsdem | Descriptiones nonnullarum Stirpium, & aliarum | exoticarum rerum, quæ à Generoso viro Fran- | cisco Drake Equite Anglo, & his obseruatæ | sunt, qui eum in longa illa Nauigatione, qua | proximis annis vniuersum orbem circumivit. | comitati sunt: & quorundam peregrinorum | fructuum quos Londini ab amicis accepit. | *Antverpiæ.* | *Ex officina Christophori Plantini,* | M. D. LXXXII. | [Colophon:] *Antverpiae* | *Excvdebat christopho-* | *rvs plantinvs, archi-typographvs, anno* CIƆ. | IƆ. LXXXII. *mense feb.* | 8vo, pp. 44. Plates. 13800

This Botany of Sir Francis Drake's Voyage is now scarce.

[Clusius.] Histoire des Drogues, Espiceries et de certains Médicamens simples, qui naissent és Indes & en l'Amerique, divisée en deux parties, par Antoine Colin. *Lyon.* 1612. + *Lyon.* 1619. 13801

Rich, No. 151, says it is a "Translation from Clusius of Orta, Acosta, Monardes, &c., by Colin." *See also* Ternaux, Nos. 352, 415.

Clusius. Rariorum aliquot Stirpium per Hispanias observatarum Historia, Libris duobus expressa. *Antverpiæ: Christophor. Plantin.* 1576. 12mo, pp. 529. J.C.B. 13802

See also Acosta (C.), Monardes (N.), Costa (A.), and Orta (Garcia ab).

Cluskey (M. W.) Buchanan and Breckinridge: The Democratic Hand-Book recommended by the Democratic National Committee. With the Official Proceedings of the National Democratic Convention held in Cincinnati, June, 1856. By Michael W. Cluskey. *Washington.* 1856. 8vo. C. 13803

Cluskey. The Political Text-Book, or Encyclopedia. Containing everything Necessary for the Reference of the Politicians and Statesmen of the United States. *Washington.* 1857. 8vo. C. + Second Edition. *Philadelphia.* 1858. 8vo. + Twelfth Edition. *Philadelphia.* 1860. + Thirteenth Edition. *Philadelphia: Jas. B. Smith & Co.* 1860. 8vo, pp. 808, (1). 13804

Cluver (Philipp). Introdvctionis in universam Geographiam ... Libri VI. Accessit P. Bertii Breviarium Orbis Terrarum.

Ludg. Batav. 1624. 4to. + *Venetiis.* 1646. + *Amstelodami: apud Elzevirios* 1655. 12mo. + *Oxoniæ.* 1657. 12mo. + *Amstelodami: apud Elzevirios.* 1659. 8vo. + *Brunsvigæ.* 1661. 4to. + *Amsterdam.* 1661. + *Ludg. Bat.* 1661. 4to. + *Amstelodami: Ex Offic. Elzevir. Anno* 1672. 8vo, pp. 388. + *Amstelodami.* 1676. 4to. + *Amst.: Elzevir.* 1677. + *Amstelædami: Apud Janssonio-Waesbergios.* CIƆ IƆC LXXXII. 4to. Maps. BA. + *Amst.* 1686. 12mo. + *Wolfenb.* 1694. 4to. + *Amstelodami.* 1697. 8vo. B., P. + *Londini: Impensis Joannis Nicholsoni.* MDCCXI. 4to, 3 l., pp. 429, 22 l. 36 Maps and 6 Plates. H. + *Trajecti ad Rhenum.* 1717. + *Amstelædami: Apud Joannem Pauli.* MDCCXXIX. 19 l., pp. 688, (63). BA., M. 13805

There is an English translation, *Oxford: Rob. Blagrave.* 1657. 2 l., pp. 341. H. In this translation, America is described on pp. 334–341. In the edition of 1672, the account of America occupies only pp. 139–143. California is still an island. A German version was published, *Nurnberg.* 1678. 12mo.

[Clymer (George).] The Principles of Naval Staff Rank, and its History in the United States Navy, for over Half a Century. By a Surgeon in the U. S. Navy. [n. p.] 1869. 8vo, pp. 240. Plate of facsimile signatures. B., H. 13806

Clymer (H.) Is Emancipation the object of the present War, or is it to sustain the Constitution as it is and restore the Union as it was? Speech of Hon. Hiester Clymer, of Berks County, delivered in the Senate of Pennsylvania, March 11, 1862. [n. p. n. d.] 8vo, pp. 16. 13807

Clymer. Record of Heister Clymer; and Historical Parallel Between him and Major-General John W. Geary. Also, Official Returns of Election on Constitutional Amendments allowing Soldiers the Right to vote. [n. p.] 1866. 8vo, pp. 20. H.

[Coade (G.)] Letter to the Lords Commissioners of Trade and Plantations, wherein the Grand Concern of Trade is asserted and maintained. 1747. 13809

Title from a London catalogue, where it is said to be by George Coade, junr., of Exeter.

Coahuila. Laws and Decrees of the State of Coahuila and Texas, in Spanish and English. To which is added the Constitution of said State; [also,] the Colonization Law of the State of Tamaulipas, [and] Naturalization Law of the General Congress: By Order of the Secretary of State. Translated by J. P. Kimball, M.D. *Houston.* 1839. 8vo. 13810

Coal-Hill, Victoria and Bedford Mines, on the Canadian Frontier. Documents. *London.* 1855. 8vo. S. 13811

Coal: its Producers and Consumers. A Meditation on Coal. *Philadelphia.* [1854.] 8vo. P. 13812

The Coal and Iron Mines of the Union Potomac Company, and of the Union Company, comprising upwards of 56,000 acres of Land situate in Alleghany County, Md., and Hampshire County, Va. With a Map. *Baltimore.* 1840. 8vo. P. 13813

Coale (J.) The Bookes and divers Epistles of that faithful Servant of the Lord, Josiah Coale, collected and published as it was desired by him in the day of his departure out of this Life. *Printed in the year,* 1671. 4to, 43 sheets. 13814

"He travelled by sea through many dangers, and preached the Gospel in many of the Western Islands, and in Maryland and Virginia, from whence he passed through the Wilderness on foot many hundreds of miles to New England," p. 5.

Coale. A Testimony of the Father's Love unto all that Desire After Him, with a few words to England. *London, Printed.* 1661. 4to, Title, 1 l., pp. 22. 13815

Coale. A Visitation of Tender Love (once more) from the Lord unto Charles, 2nd King of England, Scotland, and Ireland. [n. p. 1662.] 4to, 1 sheet. 13816

Contains instances of the persecutions and cruel dealings towards the Quakers of New England. His "Works" include an address "To all People in Jamaica unto whom the Message of Eternal Life is sent," "An Epistle to Friends in New-England," "To the Flock of God Gather'd out of the World in the Province of Maryland," etc.

Coale (W.) A Testimony concerning our dear and well-beloved Friend and Brother in the Truth, William Coale, who departed this Life the 30th of the 8th Moneth, in the Year 1678. *London: Andrew Sowle. Anno* 1682. 8vo, pp. 16.

Coale resided in Maryland.

The Coalition of the Democracy and the Abolitionists in Opposition to the Administration of Gen. Taylor. [n. p. n. d.] pp. 8. BA. 13818

The Coalition [between De Witt Clinton and the Federal Party. n. p. 181–?] pp. 8. BA. 13819

The Coalition: or, An Essay on the present State of Parties. ... *London.* 1783. 8vo, pp. 39. 13820

Coast Survey. Annual Report of the Superintendent of the Coast Survey, showing the Progress of that Work during the year 1849. *Washington.* 1850. 8vo. Continued annually; since 1852, in 4to. 13821

The first law providing for the survey of the coast of the United States was approved February 10, 1807. The survey was commenced under the superintendence of F. R. Hassler in 1816, and stopped by Act of Congress, 14th April, 1818. The papers relating to these operations are included in the "American State Papers," class "Commerce and Navigation," in Senate Document 143, 15th Congress, 1st Session, and in Vol. II., New Series, "Transactions of the American Philosophical Society of Philadelphia." The law of 1807 was renewed in 1832, and the survey was recommenced under Mr. Hassler, whose reports extended to 1843, and are followed by those of A. D. Bache, from 1844 to 1865. The volume for 1866, by J. E. Hillard, was published in 1869. These several reports are contained in the Congressional documents of the respective sessions. *See also* "N. Am. Rev.," XLII. 75; LIV. 446; "Journal of Science," XLIX. 229; Second Series, V. 307; XII. 158; and "Hunt's Magazine," XXI. 266.

The Coast Survey. By One who has examined Public Documents. ... [From the New-York Times. n. p. 1858.] 8vo, pp. 18. 13822

... The Coast Survey: its Cost, Abuses and Power. [n. p. 1858.] 8vo, pp. 15. H. 13823

The Coast Survey. Reply to the Official Defence of its Cost, Abuses and Power. [n. p. 1858.] 8vo, pp. 36. H.

From the "New York Times." Signed B. B.

The Coast Survey. Review of the Operation and Results. *New Haven.* 1858. 8vo. 13825

Extract from Report ... in Relation to Light Houses, Beacons, &c. *Washington.* 1851. 8vo. C. 13826

Coates (B.) Cotton Cultivation in Africa. Suggestions on the Importance of the Cultivation of Cotton in Africa, in reference to the Abolition of Slavery in the United States, through the Organization of the African Colonization Society. By Benjamin Coates. *Philadelphia: C. Sherman & Son.* 1858. 8vo, pp. 52. H. 13827

Coates (B. H.) Annual Discourse, delivered before the Historical Society of Pennsylvania, on the 28th Day of April, 1834, on the Origin of the Indian Population of America. By B. H. Coates, M.D. ... *Philadelphia: M'Carty & Davis.* 1834. 8vo, pp. 63, (1). H. 13828

Also: Biographical Notice of Charles Caldwell, M.D. ... *Philadelphia: Collins, Printer.* 1855. 12mo, pp. 31. — Biographical Sketch of the late Thomas Say ... 1835. 8vo.

Coates (D.) Christianity the Means of Civilization: shown in the Evidence given before a Committee of the House of Commons on Aborigines, by D. Coates, Esq., Rev. John Beecham, and Rev. William Ellis. ... *London: R. B. Seely and W. Burnside.* 1837. Crown 8vo, pp. viii, 360. 13829

Partly relates to the American aborigines.

Coates (K.) [History of the Cherokee Neutral Lands. Signed Kersey Coates: dated Kansas City, May 6, 1869. n. p. n. d.] 8vo, pp. 14. H. 13830

Coates-Kinney. Keeuka, and other Poems. By Coates-Kinney. Private Edition. *Published by the Author.* 1855. 8vo, pp. 61. 13831

Coates (R.) Oration on the Defects in the Present System of Medical Instruction in the United States. ... By Reynell Coates, M.D. ... *Philadelphia: James Kay, Jun. and Brother.* [1835.] 8vo, Title, pp. 32. BA. 13832

Coats (W.) The Geography of Hudson's Bay being the Remarks of Captain W. Coats in many Voyages to that Locality, between the Years 1727 and 1751. With an Appendix, containing Extracts from the Log of Capt. Middleton on his Voyage for the Discovery of the North-West Passage in H. M. S. "Furnace" in 1741–2. Edited by John Barrow Esq. *London: Printed for the Hakluyt Society.* M.DCCC.LII. 8vo, 3 l., pp. x, 147. B., BA., C. 13833

Forms Vol. IX. of the Hakluyt Society's Publications.

Coats. A State of the Accounts of William Coats, Esquire, Lieutenant of Philadelphia County. *Philadelphia: Printed by Robert Aitken,* M DCC LXXXIII. 8vo, pp. 28. P. 13834

Coats. William Coats, Takes this method of acquainting the Public in general, &c. ... *Philadelphia: Printed by Ioan Dunlap, at the Newest-Printing-Office, in Market-Street.* 4to, 1 p.

With rude woodcut of the interior of a grocer's shop at the head. This is the earliest shopkeeper's handbill I have seen. *Circa* Nov. 20, 1773.

Cobarrubias (D.) El diablo en Mexico. Novela de costumbres por Diaz Cobarrubias. *Mexico.* 1858. 13836

[Cobarrubias (Josef de).] Memorias Historicas de la ultima guerra con la Gran Bretaña desde el año 1774 hasta su conclusion. Tomo 1º Estados de America. Año 1774 y 1775. *Madrid.* 1783. 13837

"It does not appear that the continuation was ever published." — Rich, I. 319.

Cobb (A.) God's culture of his Vineyard. A Sermon delivered at Plymouth before the Robinson Congregation, on the 22d December, 1831. By Alvan Cobb. *Taunton.* 1832. 8vo, pp. 24. 13838

Also: Sermon in Attleboro' and Seekonk, December 26, 1832.

Cobb (Charles). American Railway Guide, and Pocket Companion for the United States. *New-York.* 1850. 12mo. S.

Cobb (E.) A Few Observations on some of the Principles of the People called Quakers, in Reply to Asa Rand. By Edward Cobb. *Portland.* 1817. 8vo, pp. 32. 13840

Cobb (H.) A Scriptural Examination of the Institution of Slavery in the United States; with its Objects and Purposes. By Howell Cobb. *Georgia: Printed for the Author.* 1856. 12mo, pp. 173. B. 13841

Cobb. Governor Cobb to Governor Means, on the Boundary between Georgia and South Carolina. *Athens, Ga.* 1852. 8vo, pp. 23. 13842

Also: Analysis of the Statutes of Georgia in General Use; with Forms and Precedents. *New-York.* 1846. 8vo, pp. 719. C. — Compilation of the Penal Code of the State of Georgia, with the forms of bills of indictment necessary in prosecutions under it, and the rules of practice. *Macon.* 1850. 8vo. C. — Speech ... on the Oregon Question; delivered in the House of Representatives, Jan. 8. 1846. *Washington.* 1846. 8vo.

Cobb. The War with Mexico. Speech ... in the House ... February 2, 1848, On the Causes and Conduct of the War ... [n. p. 1848.] 8vo, pp. 8. H. 13843

Cobb (H.) ... Iron Mountain Region. By H. Cobb, Esq. ... *Saint Louis, Mo.: M. Niedner & Co.* 1855. 8vo, pp. 16.

Cobb (J. B.) The Creole; or, Siege of New Orleans, an Historical Romance, founded on the Events of 1814–15. By Joseph B. Cobb. *Philadelphia: A. Hart.* 1850. 8vo, pp. 131.

Cobb. Leisure Labors; or, Miscellanies, Historical, Literary and Political. *New-York.* 1858. 12mo, pp. 408. S. 13846

Cobb (J. H.) A Manual containing Information respecting the Growth of the Mulberry-Tree; with Directions for the Culture of Silk. By Jonathan Holmes Cobb. *Boston.* 1831. 12mo, pp. 68. M. 13847

Cobb (J. B.) Mississippi Scenes, or Sketches of Southern and Western Life and Adventure, humorous, satirical, and descriptive. By Joseph B. Cobb. *Philadelphia.* 1851. C., P. + Second Edition. *Philadelphia.* 1851. 12mo. C. 13848

Cobb (L.) Historical Sketches of the Congregational Church in Marion, Mass. A Sermon, preached Dec. 29, 1861. By L. Cobb, Pastor. *New Bedford: Printed by E. Anthony.* 1862. 8vo, pp. 16. 13849

Cobb (L.) Evil Tendencies of Corporal Punishment as a Means of Moral Discipline in Families and Schools. By Lyman Cobb. *New York.* 1847. 8vo. + *New York.* 1849. 8vo. 13850

[Cobb (Moses Gill).] Report of the Committee on the Coal Lands in the County of Elk, Pennsylvania. *Boston: Alfred Mudge & Son.* 1860. 8vo, pp. 12. Map. H. 13851

Cobb (O.) A Sermon, preached January 18, 1809. At the Ordination of the Rev. Elijah Dexter, ... in Plympton. By Oliver Cobb ... *New-Bedford: Abraham Shearman, Jun., Printer.* 1809. 8vo, pp. 35. H. 13852

Cobb. Two Sermons, preached, the First, on the Evening of June 30. The Second, on the Morning of July 1. 1808. in Sandwich. At a Time of Religious Attention in that Town. By Oliver Cobb, A.M. Pastor of the First Church in Rochester. *Boston: Printed by Belcher and Armstrong.* 1808. 8vo, Title, pp. 20. BA. 13853

Cobb. Two Sermons, preached at Sandwich. The First, February 16, 1813, on a Day of Fasting ... The Second, Feb. 17, 1813, at the Installation of Rev. Jonathan Burr ... By Oliver Cobb ... *Boston: printed & sold by Lincoln & Edwards.* 1813. 8vo, pp. 23. H. 13854

Cobb (Sophia Dickinson). Hillsboro' Farms. *Boston: Lee & Shepard.* 1869. 12mo, pp. 423. C. 13855

Cobb (S.) The Mission and Authority of Christ. A Discourse, delivered at the Dedication of the Universalist Meeting House in Beverly, June 24, 1846. By Sylvanus Cobb. *Boston.* 1846. 8vo, pp. 20. H. 13856

Cobb (S.) Autobiography of the First Forty-one Years of the Life of Sylvanus Cobb, D.D. To which is a added a Memoir, by his Eldest Son, Sylvanus Cobb, Jr. *Boston: Universalist Publishing House.* 1867. 12mo, pp. 552. Portrait. C.

Cobb (S.), *Jr.* The Golden Eagle: or, The Privateer of 1776. A Tale of the Revolution. By Sylvanus Cobb, Jr. *Boston: Elliott, Thomas & Talbot.* 1863. 16mo, pp. 126.

Also: The Yankee Champion; or, The Tory and His League. A Revolutionary Story of Land and Sea. ... *Boston: Elliot, Thomas & Talbot.* 1863. — The Wandering Guerilla, or the Infant Bride of Truxillo: and other semi-historical pieces.

Cobb (T. R. R.) Educational Wants of Georgia. An Address delivered before the Society of the Alumni of Franklin College, at its Annual Meeting. By Thomas R. R. Cobb, Esq. 4th August, 1857. *Athens: Reynolds & Bro.* 1857. 8vo, pp. 23. H. 13859

Cobb. An Enquiry into the Law of Negro Slavery in the United States ... To which is prefixed An Historical Sketch of Slavery. By Thomas R. R. Cobb ... Vol. I. *Philadelphia: T. & J. W. Johnson & Co. Savannah: W. Thorne Williams.* 1858. 8vo, 3 l., pp. ix–ccxxviii, 358. H. 13860

Cobb. An Historical Sketch of Slavery, from the Earliest Periods. By Thomas R. R. Cobb, of Georgia. *Philadelphia: T. & J. W. Johnson & Co. Savannah: W. Thorne Williams.* 1858. 8vo, 2 l., pp. xxiii–cccii. 13861

This is the introduction and two chapters of "The Law of Slavery." Also: Substance of Remarks made in the House of Representatives [of Georgia]. *Atlanta.* 1860. 8vo.

Cobb (Thomas W.) Speech in Congress, Jan. 3, 1821, on the Reduction of Expenditures. [*Washington.*] 12mo. 13862

Cobbe (F. P.) The Red Flag in John Bull's Eyes. By Frances Power Cobbe. Tract No. 1. *London: for the Ladies' London Emancipation Society, by Emily Faithfull.* 1863. 12mo, pp. 24. B., H. 13863

[Cobbe.] Rejoinder to Mrs. Stowe's Reply to the Address of the Women of England. *London: Emily Faithfull.* 1863. 12mo, pp. 11. H. 13864

Cobbet (T.) Civil Magistrates | Power | In matters of Religion Modestly | Debated, Impartially Stated according to the | Bounds and Grounds of Scripture, And Answer | returned to those Objections against the same | which seem to have any weight in them. | Together with | A Brief Answer to a certain Slanderous | Pamphlet called | Ill News from New-England; or, A Narrative | of New-Englands Persecution. | By John Clark of Road-Island, Physician. | By Thomas Cobbet Teacher of the Church at Lynne

|in New-England.|This Treatise concerning the Christian Magistrates Power, and the exerting thereof,|in, and about matters of Religion, written with much zeal and judgement by Mr.| Cobbet of New-England, I doe allow to be printed, as being very profitable for these|times.|Feb. 7th. 1652. Obadiah Sedgwick. |*London, Printed by W. Wilson for Philemon Stephens at the Gilded Lion*|*in Paul's Churchyard.* 1653.| 2 pts., 4to, pp. xii, 108; 52.

COBBET. A Fruitfull and Usefull Discourse touching The Honour due from Children to Parents, and the duty of Parents towards their Children. ... By Thomas Cobbet ... . *London: John Rothwell.* 1656. 8vo, pp. (12), 243. B. 13866

COBBET. A Jvst Vindication of the Covenant and Church-Estate of Children of Church-Members: As also of their Right unto Baptisme. Wherein such things as have been brought by divers to the contrary, especially by Ioh. Spilsbury, A. R. Ch. Blackwood, and H. Den, are Revised and Answered. Hereunto is annexed a Refutation of a certain Pamphlet, styled, The plain and wel-grounded Treatise concerning Baptism. By Thomas Cobbet Teacher of the Church of Lyn in Nevv-England. [Motto.] *London: Printed by R. Cotes for Andrew Crooke.* 1648. 4to, 6 l. pp. 296. J.C.B., S. 13867

COBBET. A | Practical Discourse | of | Prayer. | Wherein is handled,| The Nature, the Duty, the Quali-| fications or Prayer; the several sorts of|Prayer; viz. Ejaculatory, Publick |Private, and Secret Prayer.|With the Necessity of, and In-| gagements unto Prayer.|Together, with sundry Cases of|Conscience about it.|By Thomas Cobbet,| Minister of the Word at Lyn.| [Text, 3 lines.] Imprimatur, Edm. Calamy.| *London, Printed by T. M. for Ralph Smith*|*at the Bible in Cornhil:* 1654.| 8vo, 7 l., pp. 551. B. + *London: Printed by T. M. for Joseph Cranford*|*at the Phœnix in Pauls Church yard.* 1654.| 8vo, 8 l., pp. 551. B. + *London:*|*Printed by R. I. for Thomas Newberry at the three*|*Lions in Cornhill, near the Exchange.* 1657.| 8vo, 8 l., pp. 550. J.C.B. 13868

Reprinted as "Gospel Incense, or a practical Treatise on Prayer. ... From the London Edition of 1657. *Boston.* 1856." 12mo.

COBBETT (J. P.) Causes of the Civil War in the United States. By James Paul Cobbett. *London.* 1861. C. 13869

COBBETT (John M. *and* James P.) *See* Cobbett (W.)

COBBETT (W.) An Address to the Clergy of Massachusetts, written in England, Nov. 13, 1814. By William Cobbett, with a Prefatory Epistle, to Certain Priests, by Jonathan, one of the People called Christians. ... *Boston.* 1815. 12mo, pp. 24. BA.

COBBETT. The American Gardener. By William Cobbett. *London.* 1821. 12mo. + *New York.* 1835. + *Concord, N. H.:* 1842. 13871

[COBBETT.] The American Rush-Light; by the help of which wayward and disaffected Britons may see a complete specimen of the Baseness, Dishonesty, Ingratitude, and Perfidy of Republicans, and of the Profligacy, Injustice, and Tyranny of Republican Governments. By Peter Porcupine. *New York.* 1800. 8vo, pp. 192. 13872

[COBBETT.] The Bloody Buoy; or a Faithful Relation of a multitude of Acts of horrid barbarity, such as the imagination never conceived until the commencement of the French Revolution; with an Instructive Essay, tracing these dreadful effects to their Real Causes. Illustrated with Four Striking Copper-Plates. The Second Edition; With Additional Notes ... . By Peter Porcupine. ... *Philadelphia: Benjamin Davies and William Cobbett.* M DCC XCVI. pp. xii, 15–362. BA., P. 13873

[COBBETT.] The Bloody Buoy; thrown out as a Warning to the Political Pilots of America. ... Third Edition. *Philadelphia: P. M. Davis.* 1823. 12mo, pp. x, 217. Plate. C.

Reissued with the title somewhat altered, the same year; also, *Philadelphia.* 1797. 12mo, pp. 289. The title was also changed to "Annals of Blood: or an authentic relation of the Horrid Barbarity committed by the Authors and Abettors of the French Revolution, By an American. *Cambridge.* 1797," and again as below:

[COBBETT.] A Bone to Gnaw, for the Democrats; or, Observations on A Pamphlet, entitled, "The Political Progress of Britain." *Philadelphia: Thomas Bradford.* 1795. 8vo, pp. viii, 66. H. + Second Edition. *Philadelphia: Thomas Bradford.* 1795. 8vo, pp. v, 66. + Third Edition, Revised. *Philadelphia: Thomas Bradford.* 1795. 8vo, pp. 66. 13875

The pamphlet referred to was written by James T. Callendar.

[COBBETT.] Part II. A Bone to Gnaw, for the Democrats; contain ng, 1st. Observations on a Patriotic Pamphlet . entitled, "Proceedings of the United Irishmen." 2dly. Democratic Principles exemplified by Example. 3dly. Democratic Memories; or an Account of some Recent Feats performed by the Frenchi-

fied Citizens of the United States ... . By Peter Porcupine. ... *Philadelphia: Thomas Bradford.* 1795. 8vo, pp. viii, 66. B.

[COBBETT.] A Bone to Gnaw, for the Democrats, ... By Peter Porcupine, With a Rod for the Backs of the Critics, by Humphrey Hedgehog. *Philadelphia.* 1797. 8vo. 13877

COBBETT. Cobbett's Annual Register. Vol. I. From January to June, 1802. *London: Printed by Cox and Baylis.* 1802. pp. 1462. BA., P. 13878

[COBBETT.] The Democratiad: a Poem, in retaliation for the "Philadelphia Jockey Club." By a Gentleman of Connecticut. *Philadelphia: Thomas Bradford.* 1795. 8vo, pp. 22. + *Philadelphia.* 1796. 8vo. 13879

[COBBETT.] The Democratic Judge: or the Equal Liberty of the Press, as Exhibited, Explained, and Exposed, in the Prosecution of William Cobbett, for a pretended Libel against The King of Spain and his Ambassador, before Thomas M'Kean, Chief Justice of the State of Pennsylvania. By Peter Porcupine. *Philadelphia: W. Cobbett.* 1798. 8vo, pp. 102. BA., C.

Reprinted as "The Republican Judge." *See* No. 13911, *infra.*

[COBBETT.] Detection of a Conspiracy formed by the United Brethren, with the Evident intention of aiding the Tyrants of France in Subverting the Government of the United States of America. By Peter Porcupine. *Philadelphia.* 1799. 8vo.

COBBETT. The Emigrant's Guide; in Ten Letters, addressed to the Taxpayers of England; containing Information of every kind, necessary to Persons, who are about to emigrate; including Several Authentic and most Interesting Letters, from English Emigrants, now in America, to their Relations in England. By William Cobbett. *London: Cobbett.* MDCCCXXIX. 12mo, pp. xx, 153. BA. + [*Ibid.*] 1830. + [*Ibid.*] 1838. C. 13882

[COBBETT.] French Arrogance; or, "The Cat let out of the Bag:" A Poetical Dialogue between the Envoys of America, X. Y. Z. and Lady. *Philadelphia: Published by Peter Porcupine.* 1798. 8vo, pp. 31. 13883

[COBBETT.] The Gros Mosqueton Diplomatique; or Diplomatic Blunderbuss, containing Citizen Adet's Notes to the Secretary of State, as also his Cockade Proclamation. With a Preface by Peter Porcupine. *Philadelphia: William Cobbett.* 1796. 8vo, pp. 72. C. 13884

[COBBETT.] The Guillotina, or a Democratic Dirge, a Poem. By the Author of the "Democratiad." &c. *Philadelphia: Sold at the Political Book-Store, South Front-Street, No. 8.* 1796. 8vo, pp. 14, (1). 13885

[COBBETT.] Kick for a Bite; or Review upon Review, with a Critical Essay on the Works of Mrs. S. Rowson, in a letter to the Editors of the American Monthly Review. By Peter Porcupine. *Philadelphia: Thomas Bradford.* 1795. 8vo, pp. 31. + Second Edition. *Philadelphia: Thomas Bradford.* 1796. 8vo, pp. 31. 13886

COBBETT. Letter from Mr William Cobbett To Mr Huskisson, on the subject of the American Tariff; Intended as a Reply to a Speech of the latter, in the British House of Commons. *London.* 1828. 8vo, pp. 16. + *Philadelphia: John Binns, Printer.* 8vo, pp. 16. 13887

[COBBETT.] A Letter To the Infamous Tom Paine, in Answer to his brutal attack on the Federal Constitution, and on the conduct and character of General Washington, By Peter Porcupine. Second Edition. *Philadelphia: William Cobbett.* 1796. 8vo, pp. 64. + *Philadelphia printed. London reprinted, for David Ogilvy and Son.* 1797. 8vo, pp. 23. BA. 13888

COBBETT. Letters on the Late War between the United States and Great Britain: together with other Miscellaneous Writings, on the same Subject. By William Cobbett, Esq. *New-York: published by J. Belden and Co.* 1815. 8vo, pp. 407.

COBBETT. Letters on the American war, ... to which is added a Glimpse of the American Victories, by Thomas Branagan. *Philadelphia.* 1815. 12mo, pp. viii, 400. 13890

COBBETT. Life of Andrew Jackson, President of the United States of America. By William Cobbett, M.P. ... *London.* 1834. 12mo. Portrait. + *New York: Harper & Brothers.* 1834. 18mo. Portrait. + *New York.* 1834. 8vo, pp. 196. + [n. p.] 1834. 12mo, pp. 206. BA., H. + *New York.* 1837. 18mo.

[COBBETT.] The Life and Adventures of Peter Porcupine, with a Full and Fair Account of All his Authoring Transactions ... . By Peter Porcupine Himself. *Philadelphia: William Cobbett.* M.DCC.XCVI. 12mo, pp. 58. H. + Second Edition. *Philadelphia.* 1796. 8vo, pp. 56. + *Philadelphia.* 1797. 12mo, pp. 58.

A curious account of this work may be found in the "Monthly Review." The following is, perhaps, the same work:

COBBETT. The Life of William Cobbett. Dedicated to his Sons. Second Edition. *London.* 1835. 12mo. + *Philadelphia.* 1835. 12mo, pp. 216. B. + Seventh Edition. *London.* 1835. C. 13893

[COBBETT.] The Life of Thomas Paine, interspersed with Remarks and Reflections, by Peter Porcupine ... *London: printed for J. Wright.* 1797. 8vo, Title, pp. 60. BA. + *Philadelphia: reprinted.* 1797. 12mo, pp. 60. 13894

[COBBETT.] A Little Plain English, addressed to the People of the United States, on the Treaty negotiated with his Britannic Majesty, and on the Conduct of the President relative thereto; in answer to "The Letters of Franklin." With a Supplement, containing an Account of the Turbulent and Factious Proceedings of the Opposers of the Treaty. By Peter Porcupine. *Philadelphia.* 1795. 8vo, 3 l, pp. 8, 111. BA. + *London, reprinted: for F. and C. Rivington.* 1795. 8vo, pp. 110. + Second Edition. *Philadelphia: Thomas Bradford.* 1796. 8vo, pp. 77.

[COBBETT.] A New-Year's Gift to the Democrats; or Observations on A Pamphlet, entitled, "A Vindication of Mr. Randolph's Resignation." By Peter Porcupine. ... *Philadelphia: Thomas Bradford.* 1796. 8vo, pp. 71. B., P., S. + Second Edition. *Philadelphia: T. Bradford.* 1796. 8vo, pp. 71.

[COBBETT.] Observations on the Debates of the American Congress, or the Addresses presented to General Washington, on his resignation: With remarks on the Timidity of the Language held towards France; The Seizures of American Vessels by Great Britain and France; and on the relative situations of those countries with America. By Peter Porcupine, Author of the Bone to knaw for Democrats,—Letter to Tom Paine, &c. &c. To which is prefixed, General Washington's Address to Congress; and the answers of the Senate and House of Representatives. *Philadelphia.* 1797. + *Philadelphia printed: London reprinted, David Ogilvy and Son.* 1797. 8vo, pp. (2), 38.

[COBBETT.] Observations on the Emigration of Dr. Joseph Priestley, and on the Several Addresses delivered to him on his Arrival at New-York. *Philadelphia.* 1794. + [The same], with Additions; containing many curious and interesting facts on the subject, not known here when the first edition was published. Together with A Comprehensive Story of a Far-

mer's Bull. New Edition. *Philadelphia Printed. London: Reprinted for John Stockdale.* 1794. 8vo, pp. 63. + The Third Edition. *Philadelphia: Published by Thomas Bradford.* 1795. 8vo, pp. 88. S. + Fourth Edition. *Philadelphia.* 1796. 8vo. pp. 64. + *London: reprinted for J. Wright.* 1798. 8vo, pp. 73. BA. 13899

"Perhaps a cobbler, with his hammer and awls, is a more valuable acquisition than a dozen philosophi-theologi-political empiricks, with all their boasted apparatus."—COBBETT. *See* "M. Rev.," XXIV. 222. This was answered by:

[COBBETT.] A Twig of Birch for a Butting Calf; or Strictures upon Remarks on the Emigration of Doctor Joseph Priestley, &c., &c. By "A Brother of the Birch." To which is added, An Historical Anecdote Translated from the French. *New York: J. Buel.* M,DCC,XCV. 8vo, pp. 46. P. 14000

[COBBETT.] The Political Censor; or, Monthly Review of the Most Interesting Political Occurrences, relative to the United States of America. [For March, 1796.] By Peter Porcupine. *Philadelphia: Benjamin Davies.* MDCCXCVI. 8vo, pp. 70. BA. + [For May, 1796.] *Philadelphia: Benjamin Davies.* MDCCXCVI. 8vo, Title, pp. 172–239. 14001

[COBBETT.] The Political Censor; or, Monthly Review of Political Occurrences relative to the United States of America. By Peter Porcupine. March, April and May, 1796. The Third Edition. *Philadelphia: William Cobbett.* 1796. 8vo, pp. 70. 14002

[COBBETT.] Porcupine's Political Censor, for September 1796. Containing the Life of Tom Paine, interspersed with Remarks on "A Roaster for Peter Porcupine." "The Blue Shop." "Porcupine, a Print." "History of a Porcupine," etc. *Philadelphia: William Cobbett.* [1796.] 8vo. J.C.B. 14003

[COBBETT.] Porcupine's Political Censor for November, 1796, Containing Observations on the Insolent and Seditious Notes, Communicated to the People of the United States, by the late French Minister Adet. *Philadelphia: ... William Cobbett. Nov.*, 1796. 8vo, pp. 78. 14004

[COBBETT.] Porcupine's Political Censor For December, 1796. Containing Remarks on the Debates in Congress, Particularly on the Timidity of the Language held towards France. Also A Letter to the Infamous Tom Paine, In answer to his Brutal Attack on the Federal Constitution, and on the Conduct

and Character of General Washington. *Philadelphia: Published by William Cobbett.* [1796.] 8vo, pp. 47, 18, 3 l. H. + The Second Edition. [*Ibid.*] pp. 64. B. 14005

Also: A Collection of the Political Censor for 1796. Published by William Cobbett. *Philadelphia.* [n. d.] 8vo, pp. 327.

[COBBETT.] Porcupine's Political Censor for January, 1797. *Philadelphia: William Cobbett.* 8vo, pp. 51. 14006

[COBBETT.] Porcupine's Political Censor, For March, 1797. Containing ... Noah Webster's attack on Porcupine's Answer ... Porcupine's Last Will and Testament ... . *Philadelphia: William Cobbett.* [1797.] 8vo, 2 l., pp. 53–122. H. 14007

[COBBETT.] Porcupine's Political Censor, For April, 1797. Containing Debates in the House of Representatives continued on papers relative to the Treaty with Great Britain. President's Message in reply to request for instructions to Mr. Jay. Porcupine's Remarks on the same. Traitorous advertisement of the bankrupts of Virginia. Loyal address of the Virginians to the King of Great Britain in the year 1769. Lord Grenville's reception of Citizen Gallatin, ... [*Philadelphia.* 1797.] 8vo, pp. 74–134. 14008

A complete series of the "Censor" has never come under my notice.

[COBBETT.] Porcupine's Works; containing various Writings and Selections, exhibiting a Faithful Picture of the United States of America; of their Governments, Laws, Politics, and Resources; of the Characters of their Presidents, Governors, Legislators, Magistrates, and Military Men; and of the Customs, Manners, Morals, Religion, Virtues and Vices of the People: comprising also a Complete Series of Historical Documents and Remarks, from the End of the War, in 1783, to the Election of the President, in March, 1801. By William Cobbett. ... *London: Cobbett and Morgan. May,* 1801. 12 vols., 8vo, pp. 400; 2 l., pp. 472; 2 l., pp. 440; 2 l., pp. 444; 2 l., pp. 432; 2 l., pp. 432; 2 l., pp. 430; 2 l., pp. 480; 2 l., pp. 412; 2 l., pp. 449, 3; 2 l., pp. 434; 2 l., pp. 252, 81.

"Cobbett, in these volumes, has left a picture of the politics and leading politicians of America, which (with caution) must be studied by all who would understand the party questions which agitated America, and the violence with which they were discussed."—KENT.

[COBBETT.] A Prospect from the Congress-Gallery, During the Session, Begun December 7, 1795. Containing the President's Speech, the addresses of both Houses, some of the debates in the Senate, and all the principal debates in the House of Rep-

resentatives; each debate being brought under one head, and so digested and simplified as to give the reader the completest view of the proceedings with the least possible fatigue. With Occasional Remarks. By Peter Porcupine. *Philadelphia: Thomas Bradford.* 1796. 8vo, pp. iv, 63. BA. + [Second Edition.] *Philadelphia:* ... 1796. 8vo, iv, pp. 68. S. 14010

COBBETT. The Pride of Britannia Humbled; or, the Queen of the Ocean Unqueen'd, "By the American Cock Boats," Or, "The Fir built Things, with bits of Striped Bunting at their Mast Heads."—(As the Right Hon. Mr. Canning, in the British parliament, called our American Frigates.) Illustrated and Demonstrated by four letters addressed to Lord Liverpool, on the late American War. By Wm. Cobbett, Esq. Including a number of his most Important Letters, and arguments, in Defence of the American Republic. To which is added, A Glimpse of the American Victories, On Land, on the Lakes, and on the Ocean. With a Persuasive to Political Moderation. Most respectfully addressed to the Persons composing the two great Parties in the United States in general, and to the politicians of Connecticut and Massachusetts, in Particular. *New York: T. Boyle.* 1815. 12mo, pp. 216. Plate. C., P. + A New Edition. *Philadelphia: William Reynolds.* 1815. 12mo, pp. 215, (1). Plate. BA. 14011

This was also issued with a Baltimore imprint. The work was edited by Thomas Branagan. The title to the Philadelphia edition, which was perhaps the first, differs very slightly.

[COBBETT.] Remarks on the Explanation, lately published by Dr. Priestley, respecting the intercepted Letters of his friend and disciple, John H. Stone. To which is added a certificate of Civism for Joseph Priestley, Junr. By Peter Porcupine. *London: John Wright.* 1799. 8vo, pp. 52. 14012

[COBBETT.] The Republican Judge; or the American Liberty of the Press, as exhibited, explained, and exposed in the base and partial prosecution of William Cobbett for a pretended libel against the King of Spain and his Embassador, before the Supreme Court of Pennsylvania. With an Address to the People of England. By Peter Porcupine. *London.* 1798. 8vo, pp. v, 96. + Second Edition. *London.* 1798. 8vo. 14013

The republican judge was Gov. M'Kean; the Spanish Ambassador, the Marquis of Casa Irujo, who married Gov. M'Kean's daughter; and in this and the following piece Cobbett has taken his revenge in spice.

[COBBETT.] The Rush-Light. 15th Feb., 1800. Containing An Introduction to the Rush-Light, etc. Py Peter Porcupine. *New York: William Cobbett.* [n. p. n. d.] 8vo, Title, pp. 208. G. 14015

A complete set consists of six numbers (pp. 309), the last having been issued in London. It is difficult to find a set. It owes its origin to the trial described in No. 14030, *infra*; and our No. 13872, "The American Rush-Light," is an English reprint of the above.

[COBBETT.] The Scare-Crow; being An Infamous Letter sent to Mr. John Oldden, Threatening Destruction to his House, and Violence to the Person of his Tenant, William Cobbett; with Remarks on the same. By Peter Porcupine. *Philadelphia: William Cobbett.* M.DCC.XCVI. 8vo, pp. 23. B. + Second Edition. *Philadelphia.* 1796. 14016

COBBETT. Selections from the Political Works of William Cobbett; being a Complete Abridgment of the 100 Volumes which comprise the Writings of "Porcupine" and the "Weekly Political Register." With Notes, Historical and Explanatory. By John M. Cobbett and James P. Cobbett. *London: published by Ann Cobbett.* [n. d.] 6 vols., 8vo, pp. 544; iv, 507; iv, 523; iv, 527; iv, 507; iv, 812. BA., H. 14017

The great object of the editors has been to preserve all Cobbett's best writings, and to render them easily referred to by a general analytical index. Some copies are entitled, "Selections from Cobbett's Political Works," etc.

[COBBETT.] Tit for Tat; or, A Purge for a Pill: Being an Answer to a Scurrilous Pamphlet, lately published, entitled "A Pill for Porcupine." To which is added, A Poetical Rhapsody on The Times. Describing The Disasters of an Emigrant. ... By Dick Retort. *Philadelphia: Printed for the Author.* [1796.] 8vo, pp. 34, 25. 14018

COBBETT. A Treatise on Cobbett's [*i. e.* Indian] Corn, Containing Instructions for Propagating and Cultivating the Plant, and for Harvesting and Preserving the Crop ... . By William Cobbett. ... *London: William Cobbett.* 1828. 12mo. BA.

[COBBETT.] The Works of Peter Porcupine. Fourth Edition. Revised, Altered, and Corrected by the Author. *Philadelphia: T. Bradford.* 1796. 8vo. C. 14020

COBBETT. A Year's Residence, in the United States of America. Treating of the Face of the Country, the Climate, the Soil, the Products, the Mode of Cultivating the Land, of Labour, of Food, of Raiment; of the Prices of Land, the Expenses of House-keeping, and of the usual manner of Living; of the Manners and Customs of the People; and of the Institutions of the Country, Civil, Political and Religious. In Three Parts. By William Cobbett. *New-York: printed for the Author.* 1818. 12mo, pp. 432. + [Reprinted.] 8vo, pp. 610. + *London: Sherwood, Neely and Jones.* 1818. 8vo, 2 l., pp. 610, including title to each part. + Second Edition. *London.* 1819. 8vo. C. + *London.* 1822. 3 pts., 8vo. + Third Edition. *London.* 1828. Post 8vo, pp. 370. 14021

Part I. was issued separately: "*New York: Clayton & Kingsland.* 1818." 16mo, pp. 134. Also: An Address to the People of England. By William Cobbett. *Philadelphia.* 1812. 8vo. P.—Anti-Galican, or the Lover of his own Country. ... *Philadelphia.* 1797. 8vo, pp. 82.—Cobbett's Weekly Register, for Dec. 13, 1823, contains a Letter to Mr. Wilberforce, on his "Appeal in behalf of Negro Slaves," &c. *London.*—"A History of the American Jacobins, *Philadelphia.* 1796," is added to Playfair's "Jacobinism." Concerning Cobbett, *see* Sir H. Lytton Bulwer's Historical Characters, *London*, 1868, Vol. II. "William Cobbett, a voluminous political writer, was the son of a farmer and publican at Farnham, in Surrey, England. He ran away from his father, enlisted as a soldier, and served for some time in Nova Scotia and New Brunswick. Returning to England, he received his discharge, and came to New York in 1792. In 1796 he settled in Philadelphia, and, establishing 'Peter Porcupine's Gazette,' took a lively interest in the political questions of the day." "He (Cobbett) is a man filled with *odium humani generis.* His malevolence and lying are beyond anything."—JEREMY BENTHAM. "The general characteristics of his style were perspicuity unequalled and inimitable; a homely, muscular vigor, a purity, always simple, and a raciness, often elegant."—*London Times.* The following works relate to Cobbett:

COBBETT. Beauties of Cobbett. Selected from his Works. *London.* [n. d.] C. 14022

COBBETT. The Blue-Shop; or Impartial and Humourous Observations on the Life and Adventures of Peter Porcupine, with the real motives which gave rise to his abuse of our distinguished Patriotic Characters, &c. By James Quicksilver. *Philadelphia: Moreau St. Merey.* 1796. 8vo, pp. 52. P. 14023

COBBETT. Cobbett against Himself. *London.* 1800. pp. 7.

COBBETT. A Congratulatory Epistle to the Redoubtable "Peter Porcupine," on his "Complete Triumph over the Once towering but fallen and despisable faction in the United States." A Poem, By Peter Grievous, Junr. To which is annexed The Vision, A Dialogue between Marat and Peter Porcupine in the Infernal Regions. [Motto.] *Philadelphia: From the free and independent Political & Literary Press of Thomas Bradford.* 1796. 8vo, pp. 44. 14025

COBBETT. The Impostor Detected, or A Review of Some of the Writings of "Peter Porcupine." By Timothy Tickletoby. ... To which is annexed A Refreshment for the Memory of William Cobbet, [*sic*] by Samuel F. Bradford. *Philadelphia: Thomas Bradford.* 1796. 8vo, pp. 51, 23. + Second Edition. *Philadelphia: T. Bradford.* 1796. 8vo, pp. 51, 23. 14026

COBBETT. The Last Confession and Dying Speech of Peter Porcupine; with an Account of his Dissection. *New York.* 1797. 8vo. + Second Edition. *Philadelphia. May* 27, 1797. 8vo, pp. 32 or more. 14027

COBBETT. The Little Innocent Porcupine Hornet's Nest. *United States of America: Printed for the Author.* [n. d.] 8vo.

COBBETT. Ode on the Bones of. *See* [Rodd (Thomas)].

COBBETT. A Pill for Porcupine: Being a Specific for an obstinate itching Which that Hireling has long contracted for Lying and Calumny, containing, A Vindication of the American, French, and Irish Characters, Against his Scurrilities, By A Friend to Political Equality. *Philadelphia: Printed for the Author. September* 1, 1796. 8vo, pp. 83. 14029

COBBETT. A Report of an Action for a Libel, brought by Dr. Benjamin Rush, against William Cobbett, In the Supreme Court of Pennsylvania, December term, 1799, for certain defamatory publications in ... Porcupine's Gazette ... . (Taken in Short Hand by T. Carpenter.) *Philadelphia: Printed by W. W. Woodward.* 1800. 8vo, 35 l. B. 14030

Peter had burnt his fingers by writing against Dr. Rush (who recovered five thousand dollars damages in an action against him for slander), and, in revenge, set up his "Rush-Light" at New York. *See* "The Rush-Light," No. 14015, *supra.* The trial of William Cobbett for libel was also published in New York, in 1810, and again in 1831, pp. 48.

[COBBETT.] A Roaster; or, A Check to the Progress of Political Blasphemy; intended as a Brief Reply to Peter Porcupine, alias Billy Cobler. By Sim Sansculotte. *Philadelphia: Johnson.* 1796. 8vo, pp. 21. N. 14031

[COBBETT.] A Rub from Snub; or a Cursory Analytical Epistle: addressed to Peter Porcupine ... . Containing Glad Tidings for the Democrats, and a Word of Comfort to Mrs. S. Rowson. Wherein the said Porcupine's Moral, Political, Critical and Literary Character is fully illustrated. *Philadelphia: printed for the Purchasers.* 1795. 8vo, pp. 80. BA. 14032

The Cobbler Politics, a Country Dialogue on the Present Times. *Manchester.* [About 1778.] 4to. 14033

Relates to the American war.

COBBS (N. H.) The Doubting Christian encouraged. By the Late ... Nicholas H. Cobbs, D.D. Bishop of ... Alabama. *Uniontown, Ala.* 1864. 8vo, pp. 13. BA. 14034

A Confederate publication. Also: A Farewell Message, and Obituary Notices. *Montgomery.* 1861. BA.

COBDEN (John C.) *See* [Frost (John)].

[COBDEN (Richard).] England, Ireland, and America. By a Manchester Manufacturer. *London.* 1835. 8vo. 14035

[COBDEN.] England and America; a Comparison of the Social and Political State of Both Nations. *London.* 1833. 2 vols., 8vo. 14036

[COBDEN.] A Friendly Voice from England on American Affairs. ... *New York: Wm. C. Bryant & Co., Printers.* 1862. 8vo, pp. 30. H. 14037

Letter of Richard Cobden, and speech of John Bright.

COBDEN. Political Writings of Richard Cobden. *London: Ridgway. New York: D. Appleton & Co.* 1867. 2 vols., 8vo, pp. vii, 496; v, 447, vii. 14038

England, Ireland, and America, 1835, Vol. I.

COBDEN. Speech of Mr. Cobden on the "Foreign Enlistment Act," in the House of Commons, Friday, April 24th, 1863. *London: William Ridgeway.* 1863. 8vo, pp. 25. BA.

COBDEN. Speeches on Questions of Public Policy by Richard Cobden, M.P. Edited by John Bright and James E. Thorold Rodgers ... *London: Macmillan and Co.* 1870. 2 vols., 8vo.

America, Vol. II., pp. 83–119.

COBDEN. The Three Panics: An Historical Episode. By Richard Cobden, Esq., M.P. Fourth Edition. *London: Ward & Co.* 1862. 8vo, Title, 1 l., pp. 152. C., H. 14041

Also: Speeches of Richard Cobden, Esq. on Peace, Financial Reform, Colonial Reform, and other Subjects, delivered during 1849. ... *London.* 1849. 12mo, pp. 260. C.

Cobija. Notice sur le port de Cobija ou Lamar [Bolivia]. *Paris.* 1835. B. 14042

COBLEIGH (N. C.) Iniquity abounding. A Sermon: preached at the Laurel Street Methodist Episcopal Church, on Fast Day, April 10, 1851. By Rev. N. E. Cobleigh. *Worcester: J. Burrill & Co.* 1851. 8vo, Title, pp. 16. BA. 14043

COBURN (D. A.) Historical Discourse, Ware, Mass., commemorative of the formation of the First Church. By Rev. David A. Coburn. *West Brookfield.* 1851. 8vo. S. 14044

COBURN (E. O.) Trial of Edward O. Coburn and Benjamin F. Dalton, for the Manslaughter of Wm. Sumner. *Boston.* [n. d.] 8vo, pp. 58. 14045

COBURN (J.) Resumption and Funding. Speech of Hon. John Coburn, of Indiana, in the House of Representatives, January 7, 1869. *Washington.* 1869. 8vo, pp. 16. H. 14046

COCBURN (J.) *See* Cockburn (J.)

Cocheco Railroad. Reply of the Directors to the "Report of the Directors of the Boston and Maine Railroad, Sept. 8, 1858." *Boston.* 1858. 8vo, pp. 14. M. 14047

COCHEREL. Aperçu sur la constitution de Saint-Domingue, par M. de Cocherel ... . [n. p. 1789 or 1790.] 8vo, pp. 48 or less. 14048

COCHEREL. Copie d'une Lettre écrite à M. le rédacteur de la "Gazette de Paris," le 4 avril 1790. [n. p. n. d.] 8vo, pp. 48 or less. 14049

"Contre le Député Cocherel."

COCHEREL. Dernière Réponse de M. de Cocherel ... à MM. les députés du commerce. *Versailles: Baudouin.* [n. d.] 8vo, pp. 48 or less. 14050

COCHEREL. Motion de M. de Cocherel député de Saint-Domingue, a la Séance du Samedi 29 Aout 1789, soir. *Versailles: Baudouin.* 1789. 8vo, pp. 3. 14051

COCHEREL. Motion de M. de Cocherel, Député de Saint Domingue, a la seance de 29 Aout 1789, au soir. Réponse des Députés des manufactures & du commerce du France aux motions de MM. de Cocherel et de Reynaud. Apperçu sur la Constitution de Saint Domingue par M. de Cocherel. *Port au Prince: Mozard.* 1790. 8vo, pp. 5. 14052

COCHEREL. Observations de M. de Cocherel, Député de Saint Domingue, à l'Assemblée Nationale, sur la demande des Mulatres. *Paris: Clousier.* 1789. 8vo, pp. 12. 14053

COCHEREL. Observations de M. de Cocherel ... sur le Mémoire du Ministre de la marine, renvoyé au comité des douze. [n. p. 1790.] 8vo, pp. 48 or less. 14054

Relates to St. Domingo.

COCHEREL. Projet d'un décret pour les subsistances de l'île de Saint-Domingue, par M. de Cocherel, un de ses députés *Paris: imp. de Clousier.* [n. d.] 8vo, pp. 48 or less. 14055

COCHEREL. Réflexions de M. de Cocherel, Député de Saint-Domingue, sur la Rapport du Comité des Six. *Paris: Clousier.* [1791.] 8vo, pp. 16. 14056

COCHEREL. Réflexiones de M. de Cocherel ... sur le rapport du comité des six. *Paris: Clousier.* [n. d.] 8vo, pp. 48 or less. 14057

Relates to the affairs of St. Domingo.

COCHEREL. Replique de M. Cocherel, député de St-Domingue, aux inculpations du commerce contre M. le marquis Du Chailleau. [n. p. n. d.] 8vo, pp. 48 or less. 14058

COCHEREL. Réponse des Députés des manufactures et du commerce de France, aux Motions de MM. de Cocherel et de Reynaud, Députés de l'Isle de St. Domingue à l'Assemblée Nationale. *Versailles: Ph. D. Pierres.* [1789.] 8vo, pp. 55. + *Paris.* 1790. 8vo, pp. 46. J.C.B. 14059

COCHET (Ignacio). Los Zacatecanos resuscitados. *Megico: Calderon.* 1732. 4to. 14060

COCHIN (Pierre S. A.) Abraham Lincoln. Par Augustin Cochin ... . *Paris: Degorce-Cadot.* 1869. 18mo, pp. 56. + Troisième édition. *Paris:* 1869. 18mo. 14061

COCHIN. L'abolition de l'esclavage. Par Augustin Cochin ... . *Paris: Lecoffre; Guillaumin et Cie.* 1861. 2 vols., 8vo, pp. xxxvii, 1021. 14062

COCHIN. Le régime municipal des capitales, Paris, Londres, Berlin, Vienne, Bruxelles, Genève et New-York. Par Augustin Cochin ... . *Paris.* 1870. 8vo, pp. 40. 14063

Extracted from the "Revue des Deux Mondes, 1 juin 1870."

COCHIN. Resultats de l'abolition de l'esclavage dans les colonies de l'Angleterre et de la France. Par M. Auguste Cochin. ... *Orléans: impr. Colas-Gardin.* 1861. 8vo, pp. 41.

Extracted from the "Compte rendu" of the 'Acad. des Sciences Morales et Politiques."

COCHIN. The Results of Emancipation. By Augustin Cochin ... . Translated by Mary L. Booth ... . *Boston: Walker, Wise, and Company.* 1863. 12mo, pp. xiv, 412. BA. 14065

COCHIN. The Results of Slavery. By Augustin Cochin, Ex-Maire and Municipal Councillor of Paris. Work crowned by the Institute of France. Translated by Mary L. Booth. *Boston: Walker & Co.* 1863. 12mo, pp. x, 413. C. 14066

COCHIN. L'Espagne et l'esclavage dans les iles de Cuba et de Porto-Rico. Par Augustin Cochin ... . *Paris: imprimerie Claye.* 8vo, pp. 29. 14067

From the "Revue des Deux Mondes, 1 mai, 1869."

COCHRAN (J. C.) A Sermon in reference to the Death of the Rt. Rev. John Inglis, D.D., Lord Bishop of Nova Scotia. Preached at Lunenburg. By Rev. James C. Cochran ... *Halifax.* 1850. 8vo, pp. 13. 14068

COCHRAN (Thomas F.) Address ... delivered at McSherrysville, Lower Chanceford Township, York Co., Penn., July 4, 1865. *Lancaster, Pa.: Pearson & Geist.* 1865. 8vo, pp. 24.

COCHRAN (W.) [Fast] Sermon Preached in the Church at Falmouth, Nova Scotia. By William Cochran. *Halifax.* 1793. 8vo. 14070

COCHRANE (Archibald), *Earl of Dundonald.* A Treatise, shewing the Intimate Connection ... between Agriculture and Chemistry. Addressed to ... the Proprietors of West India Estates. By the Earl of Dundonald. ... *London: J. Murray and S. Highley.* 1795. 4to, 4 l., pp. 252. B. 14071

COCHRANE (C. S.) Journal of a Residence and Travels in Colombia, During the Years 1823 and 1824, by Capt. Charles Stuart Cochrane, of the Royal Navy. In Two Volumes. *London: Henry Colburn.* 1825. 2 vols., 8vo, Title, pp. v–xv, (1), 524, (1); viii, 515, (1). Plates. BA., C., H. 14072

"A work of little or no value."—LOWNDES. *See also* "N. Am. Rev.," XXI. 153.

COCHRANE. Reise in Columbia in den jahren 1823 und 1824. Vom Englischen. (Aus dem Ethnographischen archiv abgedruckt). *Iena: Bran.* 1825. 8vo, 1 l., pp. 264. 14073

COCHRANE (C. B.) Address delivered at the Centennial Celebration of the Incorporation of New Boston, New Hampshire, July 4, 1863, by Clark B. Cochrane. *Albany, N. Y.: J. Munsell, Printer.* 1863. 8vo, pp. 44. B. 14074

Also: Speech ... on the Capitol Bill, delivered in the Assembly, March 13, 1866. [n. p. n. d.] 8vo, pp. 13. H.

COCHRANE. Memorial of Clark B. Cochrane. *Albany.* 1867. 8vo. S. 14075

COCHRANE (J.) Speech of Hon. John Cochrane, of New York, on the Union and the Constitution. Delivered in the House of Representatives, December 20, 1859. [n. p. n. d.] 8vo, pp. 8. H. 14076

COCHRANE. Water Boundary. Communication from Hon. John Cochrane, Attorney-General of the State of New York, relative to the Water Boundary between the States of New York and New Jersey. Submitted to the Chamber of Commerce of the State of New York, April 27, 1865, and ordered to be printed for the use of its Members. *New York.* 1865. 8vo, pp. 11. 14077

Also: Speech ... Young Men's Democratic Union Club, April 9, 1856. *New York.* 8vo, pp. 8.—Speech ... on the Homestead Bill, 1859. [n. p. n. d.] 8vo, pp. 16.

COCHRANE (*Lord*). Manifiesto de las Acusaciones que a nombre del General San Martin hicieron sus Legados ante el Gobierno de Chile contra el Vice-Almirante Lord-Cochrane y Vindicacion de este dirigida al Mismo San Martin. *Lima: Imprenta Administrada por J. Antonio Lopez.* 1823. 12mo, 3 l., pp. 68, 1. 14078

COCHRANE. Memorias de Lord Cochrane, conde de Dundonald. *Lima.* 1863. 8vo, pp. xxiv, 336. 14079

COCHRANE (Thomas). O Douttos Cochrane ao respeitavel e sensato poro brasileiro. Breve historia do projecto da estrada de ferro de Pedro II, desde 1838 até à presente epoca. [Colophon: *Rio de Janeiro:*] *Typ. de M. Barreto.* [1855.] 4to, pp. 8. 14080

COCHRANE (T.) Answers to the Queries of the Abolition Society. By Thomas Cochrane, M.D. *Edinburgh.* 1789. 8vo.

COCHRANE (T. L.) The Case of Thomas Lord Cochrane. Containing the History of the Hoax. *New York.* 1814. 12mo, pp. 108. 14082

Cochranism Delineated, or a Description of, and Specifick for, a Religious Hydrophobia in the Counties of York and Cumberland. By a Watchman. *Boston.* 1819. 8vo. W. 14083

Cochut (A.) Chile in 1859: by André Cochut. Translated from the French. [n. p. n. d.] 8vo, pp. 50. 14084

For an article on "Les Finances et les Banques des Etats Unis depuis la Guerre," *see* the "Rev. des Deux Mondes," September, 1862.

Cock (S.) Answer to Lord Sheffield's Pamphlet on the Subject of the Navigation System; proving, that the Act deviating therefrom, which his Lordship censures, was Beneficial to our Trade and Navy, in the last War, and ought to be renewed in the present. By S. Cock. *London: W. J. and J. Richardson.* 1804. 8vo, pp. 74. 14085

Bears on the questions which brought about the War of 1812.

Cockayne (M. S.) History and Adventure of Remarkable Men of all Nations. *London.* 1854. 16mo. c. 14086

Includes some Americans.

[Cockburn (*Sir* A. J. E.)] Charge of the Chief Justice of England to the Grand Jury ... in the Case of the Queen against Nelson and Brand. ... Edited by Frederick Cockburn. ... Second Edition. *London: William Ridgway.* 1867. 8vo.

Cockburn. Nationality; or, the Law Relating to subjects and Aliens, considered with a view to future Legislation. *London: W. Ridgway.* 1869. 8vo, 1 l., pp. 217. c. 14088

Cockburn (G. F.) Report on the Proposed Works, and extension of Lachine Canal, through the city of Montreal. By G. F. Cockburn, esq., Civil Engineer. June, 1854. *Montreal.* 1854. 8vo. 14089

Cockburn. Rapport sur les Cassins, etc. [The same in French.] *Montreal.* 1854. 8vo. 14090

Cockburn (James). The Trial of Lieutenant Colonel Cockburne, Late Governor of the Island of St. Eustatius, for the Loss of the said Island, Before a Court Martial held at the Horse Guards, on Monday, May 12th, 1783, and Nine subsequent Days; Taken In Short Hand, By E. Hodgson, Short Hand Writer at the Old Bailey, and Published by Authority. *London: R. Faulder.* [1783.] 4to, pp. 71. 14091

Cockburn. Dedicated to the Army, and more particularly to the late Garrison of St. Eustatius. An authenticated copy of the proceedings on the Trial of Lieut. Col. Cockburn, (Of the Thirty-fifth Regiment,) for the Loss of the Island of St. Eustatius. *London: J. Debrett.* M.DCC.LXXXIII. 8vo, 2 l., pp. 194, Return, etc., a folded sheet. 14092

The dedication is signed William Rogerson. An English catalogue gives this title, with the addition of, "to which is added an Appendix, containing the Correspondence between Lieut. Rogerson and others, on that important affair."

Cockburn (J.), *of Philadelphia.* A Review of the General and Particular Causes which have produced the late Disorders and Divisions in the Yearly Meeting of Friends, held in Philadelphia: with Introductory Remarks on the State of the Primitive Churches, their Gradual Declension, and Subsequent Advancement in Reformation, to the Rise of the Society of Friends. By James Cockburn. *Philadelphia: John Townsend.* 1829. 8vo, pp. viii, 281, (1). BA. 14093

See Comly's "Miscellany," II. 217.

Cockburn (J.) The Distress and Adventures of John Cockburn, and five other Englishmen, at Porto Cavallo, and Journey from the Gulf of Honduras. 1732. 4to. 14094

Title from J. Bumstead's catalogue.

Cockburn (J.) A|Journey over Land,|from the|Gulf of Honduras|to the|Great South-Sea.|Performed by|John Cockburn, and Five other|Englishmen, viz.|Thomas Rounce, Richard Banister, | John Holland, | Thomas Robinson, and John Ballman;|who were taken by a Spanish Guard-Costa, in the John|and Jane, Edward Burt Master, and set on Shoar at|a Place called Porto-Cavalo, naked and wounded, as|mentioned in several News-Papers of October, 1731.|Containing,|Variety of extraordinary Distresses and Adventures, and some|New and Useful Discoveries of the Inland of those almost un-|known Parts of America: As also, An exact Account of the|Manners, Customs, and Behaviour of the several Indians in-|habiting a Tract of Land of 2400 Miles; particularly of their|Dispositions towards the Spaniards and English.|To which is added, a curious Piece, written in the Reign of King James I.|and never before printed, intitled,|A Brief Discoverye of some Things best worth Noteinge|in the Travells of Nicholas Withington,|a Factor in the East-Indiase.|*London:*|*C. Rivington*, M,DCC,XXXV.| 8vo, pp. viii, 349. Map. B. 14095

"A curious and authentic narrative, and appeared so extraordinary as to be looked upon as little better than a romance."—Lowndes. "In the French title of this work, in the 'Bibliotheque des Voyages,' it is stated to be by Nicholas Withington; and Pinkerton's 'Collection of Voyages,' XVII. 208, re-translates the title, and perpetuates the error. Similar instances are innumerable in the former work, and are all repeated, with additions, in the latter."—Rich, I. 52.

Cockburn. The Unfortunate Englishman; or, a Faithful Narrative of the Distresses and Adventures of John Cockburn, and Five other English Mariners, who were taken by a Spanish Guarda Costa: treated in a most inhuman manner; set on shore on an uninhabited island, naked and wounded and obliged to travel over land from the Gulf of Hondurus to the Great South Sea, being 2400 miles. Containing many new and useful discoveries of the inland of those almost unknown parts of America, and an exact account of the manners and customs of the Indians. Second Edition. *London: Printed for the Booksellers.* 1740. 8vo, pp. 190. 14096

This is the same work as the preceeding; there are also copies of this date, in which the title reads:

Cockburn. A faithful account of the Distresses and Adventures of John Cockburn, Mariner, and Five other Englishmen; who Were taken Prisoners by a Spanish Pyrate; treated in the most Inhuman Manner; set on Shore on an Uninhabited Island Naked and Wounded, and obliged to Travel over Land from the Gulf of Honduras to the Great South-Sea, being 2400 miles. Containing Many New and Useful Discoveries of the Inland of those almost unknown Parts of America; and an Exact Account of the Manners, Customs, and Behaviour of the Several Indians Inhabiting so Vast a Tract of Land. The Second Edition. To which is annexed, The Travels of Mr. Nicholas Whithington, in the East Indies, (&c.) *London.* MDCCXL. 8vo, 4 l., pp. 349, (3). BA. 14097

Cockburn. The Unfortunate Englishmen, or, a Faithful Narrative, of the Distresses and adventures of John Cockburn And five other English Mariners: viz. Thomas Rounce, John Holland, Richard Banister, John Balman and Thomas Robinson, who were Taken by a Spanish Guarda Costa, in the John and Anne, Edward Burt, Master, and set on Shore at a Place call'd Porto Cavallo, naked and wounded. Containing A Journey over Land, from the Gulph of Honduras to the Great South Sea; wherein is some new and very useful Discoveries of the Inland of those almost unknown Parts of America. As also An account of the Manners, Customs, and Behaviour, of the several Indians inhabiting a Tract of Land of 2400 Miles; particularly of their Dispositions towards the Spaniards and English. The Third Edition. *London.* 1773. 12mo, pp. 164. Plate. + The Fourth Edition. *London Printed.* 1779. 12mo. + A New Edition carefully corrected. *London.* 1794. 12mo,

Title, pp. iv, 126. Plate. + [Another Edition.] *Dundee.* 1804. 16mo, pp. 172. + A New Edition. *London: A. Cleugh.* 1810. 12mo, pp. 116. s. + A New Edition. *Edinburgh: Waugh & Innes.* 1831. 16mo, pp. 197. Plate. 14098

Cockburn. Reis-beschryving Door een groot gedeelte van de Spaanse West-Indien, Namentlyk Van de Golf van Honduras door de Land-Engte van Mexico tot aan de Groote Zuydzee; Gedaan door John Cockburn, Een Engelander, in de Jaaren 1730 en 1731, na dat hy van een Spaanse Rover genomen, en met anderen aan een Woest Eiland gezet aus. ... Uit het Engels vertaalt. *Amsterdam: Dirk Swart.* MDCCXL. 8vo, 4 l., pp. 300. H. 14099

Cockburn (*Lt. Col.* R. A.) Picturesque Guide to Quebec and its Environs. *Quebec.* 1831. 12mo, pp. 42. 14100

Cocke (H.) Memorial of Harrison H. Cocke, a Furloughed Captain of the United States Navy. [n. p. 1856.] 8vo, pp. 6.

Cocke (John). Letter to the Hon. John H. Eaton, Dec. 16, 1818. *Knoxville.* 1819. 8vo. W. 14102

Cocke (R. J.) An Address ... William and Mary College, 15th May, 1847, the Anniversary of the Political Independence of Virginia. By Richard Ivanhoe Cocke ... *Richmond: Printed by Shepherd and Colin.* 1847. 8vo, pp. 22. 14103

Cocke (W. A.) The Constitutional History of the United States, from the adoption of the Articles of Confederation, to the close of Jackson's Administration. By William Archer Cocke. *Philadelphia.* 1858. 8vo. C., P. 14104

Cocke (W. M.) Speech of Hon. W. M. Cocke, of Tennessee, on the Bill making Appropriations for Harbors and Rivers. Delivered ... March 17, 1846. *Washington.* 1846. 8vo, pp. 14. H. 14105

Cocke. Speech of Mr. William M. Cocke ... in review of the War, its Costs, and Executive Patronage; delivered in the House of Representatives ... May 18th, 1848. *Washington.* 1848. 8vo, pp. 14. B. 14106

Cockerell (R.) Thoughts on the Education of Youth, By Richd. Cockerell of Newark, Upper Canada. *Printed by G. Tiffany, at Newark.* 1795. 14107

[Cockings (George).] The American War, A Poem; In Six Books. In which the Names of the Officers who have Distinguished themselves, During the War, are Introduced. *London: Printed by W. Richardson.* MDCCLXXXI. 8vo, Title, 1 l., Advt., 1 l., pp. 181. Plan of Bunker's Hill. c. 14108

"A very remarkable specimen of poetry." *See* "M. Rev.," LXV. 469.

Cockings. The Conquest of Canada; or the Siege of Quebec. An Historical Tragedy. Of Five Acts. By George Cockings. *London: Printed for the Author.* MDCCLXVI. 8vo, pp. v, 76. J.C.B. + *Albany.* 1773. 8vo. BM. 14109

A rare and curious production. The following extract will give some idea of the *poetry.* The Lady Abbess at Quebec is comforting her nuns, who dread falling into the hands of the English; she reassures them, and says:

"What the whole Nation is I
Cannot say, but I'm told by a Lady,
Who was at Louisburg taken by them,
That the officers behaved with the greatest
Civility and Politeness to all,
But in a more peculiar manner, to
The Religious Ladies and Orders, of
All sorts; kept the strictest decorum in
The Town, among the Soldiers, and stuck most
Honorably to their Capitulation, &c.
2nd Nun. O! terrible, — if they should take the City —
And we should fall into the hands of those
Rough Englishmen!" &c.

Cockings. War: An Heroic Poem, from the Taking of Minorca by the French to the Reduction of the Havannah, to the Raising the Siege of Quebec by Gen. Murray; with large Amendments and Additions. By George Cockings. The Second Edition. *London: Cooper.* 1762. 12mo, pp. xvi, 190. C. + *Boston.* 1762. 8vo. W. + *Portsmouth, N. H., reprinted.* 1762. Folio, pp. 24. 14110

See "M. Rev.," XXIII. 412. The last edition has the following title:

Cockings. War; an Heroic Poem. From the taking of Minorca by the French, to the reduction of Manilla by the English; in Ten Books; wherein the Names of all the Generals, as well as other Officers, both by Sea and Land, who distinguished themselves during the late War are mentioned with that respect due to their Merit. By George Cockings. *London: J. Wilkie.* [n. d.] 8vo, pp. xvi, 240. 14111

Book I. Relates to the operations of the English in the West Indies, to the taking of Louisburg; II. To the operations of Lord Howe and Admiral Boscawen; III. To the fall of Quebec; V. Gives a recapitulation of England's victories. The remaining books include the operations of the contending nations both in Europe and America. This poem was popular in its day, and passed through four editions. Cockings was also the author of "Stentorian Eloquence and Medical Infallibility," a satire, in verse, on itinerant preachers, published in 1771, and of "Benevolence and Gratitude," a poem, published in 1773. "The American Times. A Satire," has also been attributed to him. *See* our No. 1244, and Duyckinck, I. 432.

The Cockney in America: or the Adventures of Triptolemus Snooks, Esq. Edited by Frank Flip. *New York.* 1848. 12mo, pp. 71. 14112

Cocteau *and* Bibron. Reptiles de l'île de Cuba. *Paris.* 1843. 8vo. Atlas of 31 Colored Plates, folio. 14113

Codazzi (A.) Atlas físico y político de la República de Venezuela, dedicado por su autor, el Coronel de Ingenieros Agustin Codazzi, al congresso constituyente de 1830. *Carácas.* 1840. Folio, pp. 8. 19 Maps. 14114

Scarce; priced at £3 3s., by Trübner, in 1867.

Codazzi. Catecismo de la Geografia de Venezuela. Por Agustin Codazzi. *Paris.* 1841. 18mo, pp. 96. + *Caracás.* 1867. 12mo, pp. 80. 14115

Codazzi. Proyecto de poblar con las razas teutónicas los terrenos altos y hasta ahora incultos de Venezuela. Número extraordinario de "El Liceo Venezolano." *Carácas.* 1842. 8vo, pp. 14. Map. 14116

Codazzi. Resúmen de la geografía de Venezuela. Por Agustin Codazzi. *Paris: Fournier.* 1841. 8vo, pp. 648, and Atlas in folio. c. 14117

"The best geographical work on Venezuela."—Trübner.

[Codding (Milo Defonz).] The Issues of the Hour, Political and Military: being Reminiscences and Conclusions. ... *Rochester, N. Y.: Milo Defonz.* 1863. 12mo, pp. 60. H.

Coddington (D.) Speeches and Addresses of the late Hon. David Coddington, with a Biographical Sketch. *New York: D. Appleton & Co.* 1866. 8vo, pp. xxxii, 177. c. 14119

Coddington (D. S.) Eulogy on President Lincoln. By David S. Coddington. Delivered in the Citadel Square Church, Charleston, S. C., May 6, 1865, at the request of the Officers and Soldiers in the Northern District, Department of the South. *New York: Baker & Godwin, Printers.* 1865. 8vo, pp. 30.

Also: Address, New York, November 1, 1864. 8vo.—The Military and Financial Policy of the National Government. Speech In the Assembly ... January 23, 1862. [n. p. n. d.] 8vo, pp. 5. H.

Coddington (W.) A|Demonstration|of|True Love|unto|You the Rulers of the Colony of the|Massachusets|in|Nevv-England;|Shewing|to you that are now in Authority the unjust|Paths that your Predecessors walked in, and of the|Lord's Dealings with them in his severe Judgments, for|persecuting his Saints and Children.|Which may be a Warning unto you, that you walk not in|the same Steps, lest you come under the same Condemnation.|Written by one who was once in Authority with them; but al-|ways testified against their persecuting Spirit, who am call'd|William Coddington of Road-Island.|[*London:*] *Printed in the Year* 1674.| 4to, pp. 20. 14121

A very interesting and rare tract concerning the persecution of the Quakers by the Puritans of Massachusetts. "The author was one of the first who agreed to form a 'bodie politic' in Rhode Island." *See* Bartlett's "Bib. R. I.," p. 80. Roche's copy sold for $40. Joseph Smith, in his catalogue of "Friends' Books," quotes an edition of 1672, 4to, and calls the edition of 1674 a reprint. I have not met with the edition of 1672.

The Code of 1650, being a Compilation of the earliest Laws and Orders of the General Court of Connecticut. Also, the Constitution or Compact, entered into and adopted by the towns of Windsor, Hartford and Weathersfield, in 1638–9. To which is adeed, some Extracts from the Laws and Judicial Proceedings of New-Haven Colony, commonly called the Blue Laws. *Hartford: Silas Andrus.* 1822. 12mo, pp. 120. + [*Ibid.*] 1825. 12mo, pp. 119, including Plate. + [*Ibid.*] 1830. 12mo, pp. 119. + *Hartford, Ct.: Andrus & Judd.* 1833. 18mo, pp. 119. + [*Ibid.*] 1836. 12mo, pp. 119. + [*Id.:*] *W. Andrus.* 1842. 12mo, pp. 119. + [*Id.* n. d.] 12mo, pp. 120. 14122

See also "Blue Laws," Vol. II., 6010.

Le Code Noir, ou, Édit du Roy, Servant de Règlement Pour Le Gouvernement & l'Administration de Justice et la Police des Isles Françoises de l'Amérique, et pour la discipline et le Commerce des Nègres et Esclaves dans ledit pays. Donné à Versailles au mois de Mars. 1685. *Paris: Veuve Saugrain.* 1718. Sm. 4to, pp. 14. c. 14123

Le Code Noir ou Edit du Roy, Servant de Reglement Pour Le Gouvernement & l'Administration de la Justice, Police, Discipline & le Commerce des Esclaves Negres, dans la Province & la Colonie de la Loüisianne. Donné à Versallles au mois de Mars 1724. ... *A Paris: de l'Imprimerie Royale.* 1727. 4to, pp. 15. 14124

Very important. *See* Gayarre's "Louisiana," p. 368.

Le Code noir, ou Recueil des Réglemens rendus jusqu'a present concernant le Gouvernement, la Discipline et le Commerce des Nègres dans les Colonies Francaises. *Paris.* 1740. 12mo. + *Paris.* 1742. 12mo. + *Paris.* 1743. 12mo. + *Paris.* 1752. 12mo. + *Paris.* 1767. 4to and 12mo. A. 14125

The edition of 1743 has a woodcut of the head of a negro on the title.

Codice diplomatico Colombo-Americano. *See* [Spotorno (G. B.)]

Codigo civil e penal. *See* Bolivia, and other names of countries.

Codigo de comercio de Francia, traducido al castellano, con varias notas relativas á la legislacion y usos de España y América. *Paris.* 1828. 8vo. 14126

Codigo de comercio y de navegacion actualmente en vigor en los Estados de America. *Paris: Rosa et Bouret.* 1859. 8vo, pp. 288. 14127

Código de Policia nacional. *Carácas.* 1854. 8vo, pp. 20.

Codman (J.) A Discourse, delivered before the Roxbury Charitable Society ... Sept. 24, 1817. By the Rev. John Codman ... . *Boston: Munroe & Francis.* 1817. 8vo, pp. 16. H.

Codman. The Importance of Moderation in Civil Rulers. A Sermon delivered before ... the Legislature of Massachusetts at the Annual Election, January 1, 1840. By John Codman ... . *Boston: Dutton & Wentworth.* 1840. 8vo, pp. 32. B., M.

Codman. The Importance of Spiritual Knowledge; A Sermon, delivered before the Society for Propagating the Gospel among the Indians and Others in North America, in ... Boston, November 3, 1825. By John Codman ... *Cambridge: Hilliard & Metcalf.* 1825. 8vo, pp. 44. 14131

Codman. National Sins. A Sermon delivered in Dorchester, May 14, 1841; National Fast on Account of the Death of the President of the United States, By John Codman. *Boston: Samuel N. Dickinson.* 1841. 8vo, pp. 23. 14132

Codman. Oration on the Fiftieth Anniversary of American Independence, July 4, 1826. ... *Boston.* 1826. 8vo, pp. 24. B.

Codman. Review of the Past. A Sermon delivered in Dorchester, Dec. 7, 1845; being the Thirty seventh Anniversary of the Author's Ordination. *Boston: T. R. Marvin.* 1846. 8vo, pp. 27. H. 14134

Codman. Sermons delivered on Various Occasions, with Addresses. By John Codman, D.D. *Boston: Perkins, Marvin & Company.* 1834. 8vo, pp. x, 9–436. 14135

Codman. A Sermon, delivered at the Dedication of the North Congregational Meeting-House, in New Bedford, June 23, 1818. By the Rev. John Codman, A.M., ... *New Bedford: Printed by Benj. Lindsey.* 1818. 8vo, pp. 22. 14136

Codman. The Signs of the Times. A Sermon, delivered before the Pastoral Association of Massachusetts, in ... Boston, May 24, 1838. By John Codman ... . *Boston: D. K. Hitchcock.* 1836. 8vo, pp. 24. H. 14137

Also: An Address ... Interment of Mrs. Harriet Storrs ... July 11, 1834, ... *Boston: Munroe and Francis.* 1834. 8vo, pp. 16. — The Duty of American Christians to send the Gospel to the Heathen. A Sermon ... Hartford, Sept. 14, 1836, ... *Boston: Crocker and Brewster,* 1836. 8vo, pp. 26. H. — A Sermon before the Ancient and Honourable Artillery Company ... June 5, 1820. ... *Boston: E. G. House.* 1820. 8vo, pp. 20. BA. — The Good and Faithful Servant. A Sermon Preached at Milton, Oct. 18, 1836, at the Funeral of the Rev. Samuel Gile ... . *Boston: Perkins and Marvin.* 1836. 8vo, pp. 22. H. — Home Missions. A Sermon ... Boston, May 31, 1826. ... . *Boston: Crocker and Brewster.* 1826. 8vo, pp. 43. H. — Idolatry destroyed, ... A Sermon delivered in ... Boston, ... Jan. 1, 1818. ... *Boston: Lincoln & Edmands.* 1818. 8vo, pp. 28. B. — Ministerial Courtesy. A Sermon ... before the Convention of Congregational Ministers of Massachusetts, in ... Boston, May 26, 1831. ... . *Boston: Pierce and Parker.* 1831. 8vo, pp. 22. H. — Sermon delivered at the Funeral of Gen. Stephen Badlam ... in Dorchester, Aug. 27, 1815. ... *Cambridge: Hilliard and Metcalf.* 1815. 8vo, pp. 15. — Sermon delivered at the Ordination of Rev. Leonard Withington ... in Newbury, Oct. 31, 1816. ... *Newburyport: William B. Allen & Co.* 1817. 8vo, pp. 24. — Sermon on Prayer, Preached at Dorchester, Mass. Dec. 12, and at Dedham, Dec. 17, 1813. ... . *Boston: Samuel T. Armstrong.* 1814. 8vo, pp. 18. — Dr. Codman's Speech in the Board of Overseers of Harvard College, Feb. 3, 1831. [n. p. 1831.] 8vo, pp. 15. B. — Letter to Dr. Codman [on temperance. n. p. n. d.] 4to, pp. 2. *See* Dorchester, Mass.

[Codman (John, Charles R., *and* Francis).] An Exposition of the Pretended Claims of William Vans on the Estate of John Codman. With an Appendix of Original Documents, Correspondence, and other Evidence. *Boston: Samuel N. Dickinson.* 1837. 2 vols., 8vo, pp. viii, 438; viii, 420. H. 14138

[Codman (*Captain* John).] A Letter to the Hon. Charles Sumner of the United States Senate, on the Condition and Requirements of the American Mercantile Marine. [*Washington: G. S. Gideon, Printer.* 1860.] 8vo, pp. 18. B., H. 14139

Codman. Ten Months in Brazil: with Incidents of Voyages and Travels, Descriptions of Scenery and Character, Notices of Commerce and Productions, etc. By John Codman. *Boston: Lee and Shepard.* 1867. 12mo, pp. 208. Woodcut. BA.

Codman. Ten Months in Brazil. Notes on the Paraguayan War. *London: Simpkin.* 1869. 8vo. 14141

Codogna (O.) Nuovo itinerario delle poste per tutto il Mondo. Aggiuntovi il modo di scrivere à tutte le parti. *Venetia.* 1611. Square 16mo. 14142

Contains a brief chapter on America.

Codorniu y Ferreras. Angina exantematica de Mexico, y demas enfermedades endemicas y epidemicas del pais, por el ciudad Manuel Codorniu y Ferreras. *Mexico.* 1825. 12mo, 1 l., pp. xi, 182, 2 l. 14143

"A sanitary work of extreme rarity." — Trübner.

Codrington (*Colonel*). Copy of the Articles Exhibited by Mr. Freeman to the House of Commons against Col. Codrington, and some Observations and Remarks in answer to the same. *London.* 1702. 4to. 14144

Relates to the Leeward Islands.

Codrington. Statements relative to Codrington College. *Barbadoes.* 1829. 8vo. 14145

This and the following title are from a bookseller's catalogue:

Three Reports in reference to the Codrington College and Estate. *Winchester and London.* 1830–31. 14146

Coe (C.) A Valedictory Discourse Delivered at Durham, N. H., April 27, M.DCCC.VI.; By Curtis Coe, A.M. [With Result of Council.] *Portsmouth, N. H.: Printed by William Treadwell.* 1806. 8vo, pp. 32. M. 14147

[Coe (David B.)] Record of the Coe Family, 1596–1865. *New York: John A. Gray.* 1856. 8vo, pp. 14. + [Second Edition.] *New York: John A. Gray.* 1856. 8vo, pp. 16.

Coe (Geo. S.) The Natural Road to Specie Payments. [n. p. n. d.] 8vo, pp. 12. 14149

Coe (J.) A | Sermon | delivered | before the Military Officers, Apollo Lodge | and a large and respectable number | of the Citizens of Troy, | January 12th 1800 | in Consequence of the death of | Lieutenant General George Washington. | By Jonas Coe, A.M. | Minister of the Presbyterian Church, in Troy. | [Published at the Request of the Hearers.] | *Troy: | Printed at the Budget Office, by R. Moffitt & Co.* | 1800. | Sm. 4to, pp. 16. N. 14150

Coe (J.) The True American; containing the Inaugural Addresses ... with the First Annual Addresses and Messages of All the Presidents ... from 1789 to 1839 ... ; also, the Farewell Addresses of Washington and Jackson; an Address to ... Young Men ... and ... Other Matter ... . By Joseph Coe. *Concord, N. H.: I. S. Boyd.* 1840. 12mo, pp. 428, and Contents 1. + *Concord, N. H.* 1841. 2 vols., 12mo, pp. 432; 400.

Coe (Noah). *See* Greenwich, Conn.

Coelho (José Antonio Pereira). Elogio funebre na morte do Sr. D. José, principe do Brasil, pregado na sé de Bragas. *Lisboa na Typ. Nunesiana.* 1789. 4to, pp. 21. 14152

Coello (D. d'A.) Memorias Diarias | de la Gverra del Brasil, | Por discvrso de Nveve | Anos, empeçando desde el | de M. DC. XXX. | Escritas | Por Dvarte de Albvrqverqve Coello, | Marques de Basto, Conde, i Señor de Pernambuco, i de las | Villas de Olinda, San Francisco, Magdalena, Buen-Sucesso, | Villahermosa, i Igaraçù, Gentil-hombre, de la Camara de | su Magestad, i de su Consejo de Estado, en el | de Portugal. | A La Catolica Magestad del Rey | Don Felipe Ovarto | Con Privilegio. | *En Madrid, por Diego Diaz de la Carrera, Impressor del Reyno, Año* 1654. | 4to, Title, 7 l., 287 numbered l. L. 14153

The author took an important part in the war he describes. When the Brazils were united with Portugal, he kept his faith to the King of Spain, and returned to Madrid, where he wrote his account of the war. A Portuguese version was published in the "Jornal de Commercio à Rio de Janeiro." *See* Netscher, xxiii., and Warden, No. 539. Priced, by Asher, at £5 5s.

Coelln (Johann von). *See* Linnæus.

Coello (M.) Carta del Capitan Don | Manuel Coello, Sargento Mayor de la | gente de guerra, que lleuò el Excelentissimo | Señor Conde de Lemos Virrey del Perù, | para la pacificacion de las Prouincias de | Puno, escrita à vn correspondiente | suyo de la Ciudad de | Cadiz. | [Colophon:] *En Cadiz. Por Iuan Lorenço Machado, Impressor* | *de la Ciudad. Año* 1670. | Folio, 4 leaves.

Coetlogon (C. De). A Sermon preached December 13, 1776, being the Fast Day on account of the Trouble in America ... . By C. De Coetlogon. *London: Oliver.* 1776. 8vo.

Coffey (T. J.) "Panoche Grande." Argument of Titian J. Coffey, Esq., against McGarrahan's Claim. [n. p. n. d.] 8vo, pp. 24. H. 14156

[Coffey (W. A.)] Inside Out; or, an Interior View of the New York State Prison. By One who Knows. *New York: printed for the Author.* 1823. 12mo, pp. 251. C. 14157

Coffey (W. S.) Commemorative Discourse Delivered at the Centennial Anniversary of the Erection and the Sixtieth of the Consecration of St. Paul's Church, East Chester ... N. Y., October 24th, 1865. By the Rev. William Samuel Coffey ... . *New York: Perris & Browne.* 1866. 8vo, pp. vi, 1 l., pp. 45.

Coffin (A.), *Jr.* The Death of General Montgomery, or the Storming of Quebec. A Poem. By Alexander Coffin, Jr. *New York.* 1814. 18mo, pp. 69. 14159

Coffin. The Destructive Operation of Foul Air, Tainted Provisions, Bad Water and Personal Filthiness upon Human Constitutions; exemplified in the unparalleled Cruelty of the British to the American Captives at New York during the Revolutionary War, on Board their Prison and Hospital Ships, in a communication to Dr. Mitchill, dated September 4. 1807, Also, A Letter to the Tammany Society, upon the same subject, By Captain Alexander Coffin, Jun. One of the surviving sufferers, with An Introduction by Charles I. Bushnell. *New York: Privately Printed.* 1865. 8vo, pp. 28. Woodcut.

Thirty copies printed.

Coffin (A.) Anniversary Oration delivered before the South Carolina Medical Association, at the Annual Meeting in Charleston ... 31st January, 1853. By Amory Coffin ... . *Charleston, S. C.: Press of Walker and James.* 1853. 8vo, pp. 15. H. 14161

Coffin (C.) History of the Battle of Bunker Hill. By Charles Coffin. *Saco, Me.* 1831. 8vo. W. 14162

Coffin. History of the Battle of Breed's Hill by Major-Generals William Heath, Henry Lee, James Wilkinson and Henry Dearborn. Compiled by Charles Coffin. *Portland: D. C. Colesworthy.* 1835. 8vo, pp. 36. 14163

Coffin. The Lives and Services of Major General John Thomas, Colonel Thomas Knowlton, Colonel Alexander Scammell, Major-General Henry Dearborn. Compiled by Charles Coffin. *New York.* 1845. 12mo, pp. 222. 14164

Coffin. The Life and Services of Major-General John Thomas. Compiled by Charles Coffin. *New York.* 1844. 8vo, pp. 33. 14164

[Coffin (Charles Carleton).] Following the Flag. From August, 1861, to November, 1862, with the Army of the Potomac. By "Carleton." *Boston: Ticknor & Fields.* 1865. 16mo, pp. viii, 336. 14165

Coffin. Four Years of Fighting: ... from the First Battle of Bull Run to the Fall of Richmond. By C. C. Coffin. *Boston: Ticknor & Fields.* 1866. 8vo, pp. xvi, 558. BA. 14166

Coffin. The Great Commercial Prize Addressed to every American who values the Prosperity of his Country. By Charles C. Coffin, a Member of the Boston Press. *Boston: A. Williams & Co.* 1858. 8vo, pp. 23. H. 14167

[Coffin.] My Days and Nights on the Battlefield. A Book for Boys. By "Carleton." *Boston: Ticknor & Fields.* 1864. 16mo, pp. viii, 312. BA. 14168

Coffin. Our New Way Round the World. By C. C. Coffin. *Boston: Fields, Osgood & Co.* 1869. 8vo, pp. xvi, 524.

Coffin. The Seat of Empire. By Charles Carleton Coffin, "Carleton." ... *Boston: Fields, Osgood, & Co.* 1870. 16mo, pp. viii, 232. Map. BA. 14170

Also: Winning his Way. *Boston.* 1866. 18mo.

Coffin (L. C.) The Trapper's Retreat. A Sequel to the Hunter. By Capt. L. C. Carleton. *New York: J. P. Beadle & Co.* 16mo, pp. 103. 14171

Coffin (E.) A Sermon delivered February 22d, 1800, The Day of National Mourning, Recommended By the Government of The United States, For the Death of General George Washington. ... By the Rev. Ebenezer Coffin, A.B., Pastor of a Church in Brunswick. *Printed at Portland: by Rand & Burdick.* 1800. 8vo, pp. 16. 14172

One of the scarcest of Washington Orations. Mr. W. Menzies has the only copy we know.

[Coffin (J. F.)] Journal of a Residence in Chili. By a Young American, detained in that Country, during the Revolutionary Scenes of 1817–18–19. *Boston: Wells and Lilly.* 1823. 12mo, pp. 237. H. 14173

Coffin (J. H.) On the Winds of the Northern Hemisphere. By James H. Coffin. *Washington.* 1853. 4to, pp. 200. 13 Plates. 14174

From Vol. vi. of the "Smithsonian Contributions."

Coffin (J. G.), *M.D.* An Address delivered before the Contributors of the Boston Dispensary, ... Oct. 21, 1813. By John G. Coffin. *Boston: Printed by John Eliot.* 1813. 8vo, pp. 22.

Coffin (J.) An Account of some of the Principal Slave Insurrections, and Others, which have occurred, or been attempted, in the United States and Elsewhere, during the last Two Centuries. ... Collected from Various Sources by Joshua Coffin. *New-York: American Anti-Slavery Society.* 1860. 12mo, pp. 36. H., S. 14176

Coffin (J.) A List of some of the Descendants of Mr. Edward Woodman, Who Settled at Newbury, Mass., A.D. 1635. Compiled by Joshua Coffin. *Printed for Cyrus Woodman (of Mineral Point, Wisconsin), at ... Newburyport, Mass.* 1855. 16mo, pp. 16. H., S. 14177

Coffin. A Sketch of the History of Newbury, Newburyport, and West Newbury, from 1635 to 1845. By Joshua Coffin, A.B., S.H.S. *Boston: Samuel G. Drake.* 1845. 8vo, pp. 416. Portrait. B., C. 14178

Coffin. The Toppans of Toppan's Lane, with their Descendants and Relations. Collected and arranged by Joshua Coffin. *Newburyport: Wm. H. Huse & Co., Prs.* 1863. 8vo, pp. 30. Photograph. 14179

Coffin (N. W.) America, an Ode; and other Poems. By N. W. Coffin. *Boston.* 1843. 12mo. 14180

Coffin. A Few Reasons in favor of the Annexation of a Part of the Town of Dorchester to the City of Boston. *Boston: Wright & Potter.* 1867. 8vo, pp. 12. H. 14181

Coffin (P.) A Sermon, preached before ... the Council, Senate, and House of Representatives of ... Massachusetts. May 29, 1799, being the Day of General Election. By Rev. Paul Coffin ... . *Boston: Young & Minns.* MDCCXCIX. 8vo, pp. 31.

Coffin. The Memoir and Journals of Rev. Paul Coffin, D.D. Edited By Cyrus Woodman, Esq. *Portland.* 1855. 8vo, pp. 181. Portrait. 14183

Also: A Discourse, Delivered at the Ordination of the Rev. Ebenezer Coffin, to the Ministerial Office, in the ... Church at Brunswick, Jan. 1794. ... *Newburyport: Blunt & Robinson.* 1794. 8vo, pp. 28. N. — Sermon preached at the Instalment of the Rev. John Thompson in the Pastoral Office over the First Church of Christ in Berwick, May 7, 1783 ... *Newbury Port.* 1783. 8vo, pp. 40. M.

[Coffin (Robert Barry).] Cakes and Ale at Woodbiney from Twelfth Night to New Year's Day. By Barry Gra; [*pseudon.*] *New York: Hurd & Houghton.* 1868. 12mo, pp. 229.

A novel, delineating some phases of American life. There are others of a like character by this author, as, "Matrimonial Infelicities. *New York.* 1865." 12mo, and "My Married Life at Hillside. *New York.* 1865." 12mo.

Coffin (R. S.) Epistle to Joseph T. Buckingham, Esq. By R. S. Coffin, the "Boston Bard." ... *Boston.* 1826. 8vo, pp. 12.

[Coffin.] The Life of the Boston Bard. Written by Himself. ... *Mount Pleasant, N. Y.: Published by Stephen Marshall.* 1825. 12mo, Title, Half-Title, pp. 203. H. 14186

[Coffin.] Oriental Harp. Poems of the Boston Bard. ... *Providence, R. I.: Smith & Parmenter.* 1826. 8vo, pp. 254. Portrait. H. 14187

Also: The Eleventh Hour; or, Confessions of a Consumptive. *Boston.* 1827. 12mo, pp. 36. — Miscellaneous Poems of the Boston Bard. 1818. 12mo.

Coffin (S. P.) Annual Report of the Agent of the Martha's Vineyard Camp Meeting, Sirson P. Coffin, Esq., made to the Meeting of Preachers and Tent Masters, Aug. 22, 1860. ... *New Bedford: Printed by E. Anthony.* 1860. 8vo, pp. 16.

Coffin (W.) *and* Gardner (A.) Narrative of the Robbery of the Nantucket Bank. Compiled from Original Documents, collected by William Coffin and Albert Gardner, Esq's. *Nantucket.* 1816. 8vo, pp. 69. M. 14189

Coffin (W. F.) 1812: The War, and its Moral: a Canadian Chronicle. By William F. Coffin, Esq. Vol. I. *Montreal.* 1864. 8vo, pp. 296. S. 14190

See Morgan's "Bibliog. Canadensis," p. 79.

Coffin (W. H.) An Essay on the Tariff. By W. H. Coffin, an Inmate of the New York State Lunatic Asylum. *Utica, N. Y.: Printed at the Asylum.* 1847. 8vo, pp. 8. B.

Coffinberry (A.) The Forest Rangers: A Poetic Tale of the Western Wilderness in 1794, connected with and comprising the March and Battle of General Wayne's Army, and abounding with interesting incidents of Fact and Fiction. In Seven Cantos. By Andrew Coffinberry. *Columbus: Wright & Legg.* 1842. 12mo, pp. 220. 14192

Coggeshall (G.) Historical Sketch of Commerce and Navigation from the Birth of our Savior down to the Present Date (1860); with Remarks on their Beneficial Results to Christianity and Civilization. By George Coggeshall ... . *New York.* 1860. 8vo, pp. 526. C. 14193

Coggeshall. History of the American Privateers and Letters-of-Marque, during our War with England in the Years 1812, '13, '14. Interspersed with Several Naval Battles betwen American and British Sloops-of-War. By George Coggeshall. Illustrated. *New York.* 1856. 8vo, pp. liv, 438. C., H. + Second Edition. *New York: published by the Author.* 1856. 8vo, pp. liv, 438. 14194

Coggeshall. Thirty-six Voyages to various Parts of the World, made between the years 1799 and 1841, by George Coggeshall. *New York.* 1858. 8vo. + Third Edition. *New York.* 1858. 8vo, pp. 583. C. 14195

Coggeshall. Voyages to various Parts of the World between 1799–1844; selected from his MS. Journal of Eighty Voyages. By George Coggeshall. *New York: D. Appleton & Co.* 1851. 8vo, pp. 273. + Second Edition. [*Ibid.*] 1853.

Coggeshall. Second Series of Voyages to various Parts of the World, made between the years 1802 and 1841. Selected from his MS. Journal of Eighty Voyages. *New York: D. Appleton & Co.* 1852. 8vo, pp. 335. Portrait. + Second Edition. *New York:* [*Ibid.*] 1853. 8vo, pp. 335. Portraits. 14197

Coggeshall (S. W.) An Anti-Slavery Address. Danielsonville, July 4, 1849. ... *West Killingly: E. B. Carter.* 1849. 12mo, pp. 57. BA. 14198

Also: Introduction of Methodism into Boston, being No. 1 of the "Transactions of the New England Methodist Historical Society."

Coggeshall (W. T.) Lincoln Memorial. The Journeys of Abraham Lincoln: from Springfield to Washington, 1861, as President Elect; and from Washington to Springfield, 1865, as President Martyred; comprising an Account of Public Ceremonies on the Entire Route, and Full Details of Both Journeys. By William T. Coggeshall. *Columbus, O.: Ohio State Journal.* 1865. 12mo, pp. 327. Portrait. C. 14199

Coggeshall. The Newspaper Record, containing a Complete List of Newspapers and Periodicals in the United States,

Canadas, and Great Britain, together with a Sketch of the Origin and Progress of Printing, with some Facts about Newspapers in Europe and America. By W. T. Coggeshall. *Philadelphia.* 1856. 8vo, pp. xiv, 194. C. 14200

COGGESHALL. The Poets and Poetry of the West: with Biographical and Critical Notices. By William T. Coggeshall. *Columbus: Follett, Foster and Company.* 1860. 8vo, pp. vii, 688. C., H. + *New York.* 1864. Rl. 8vo, pp. vii, 688. 14201

COGGESHALL. The Protective Policy in Literature: A Discourse on the Social and Moral Advantages of the Cultivation of Local Literature. By William T. Coggeshall ... . *Columbus, O.: Follett, Foster and Company.* 1859. 8vo, pp. 29. S. 14202

COGGESHALL. The Signs of the Times: comprising a History of the Spirit-Rappers, in Cincinnati and other Places: with Notes on Clairvoyant Revealments, by William T. Coggshall [*sic*]. ... *Cincinnati: the Author.* 1851. 16mo, pp. 144. B.

COGGESHALL. Stories of Frontier Adventure in the South and West. By William T. Coggeshall. *New York: Follett, Foster, and Company.* 1863. 12mo, 4 l., pp. 313. 14204

Also: Historical Sketch of the Ohio State Library. — Index to Ohio Laws, general and local, and to the Resolutions of the General Assembly, from 1845–46 to 1857, inclusive. With an Appendix, containing an Index to the Documents in the Journals of the House and Senate from 1802 to 1836. ... *Columbus.* 1858. 8vo. — The Issue of the November Election. An Address to Young Men: ... Delivered before the Wide-Awakes of Tiffin, Ohio, Oct. 18, 1860. [n. p. 1860.] 8vo, pp. 15. H. — Ohio Prosperity, Social and Material; an Argument against Rebellion, applied to the Duty of Citizens. ... . [n. p. 1863?] 8vo, pp. 8. H.

COGGIN (J.) Sermon at the Dedication of the New Meeting House in Tewksbury, Mass., By Jacob Coggin, A.M. With Historical Appendix. *Chelmsford.* 1824. 8vo. 14205

COGGIN (W. S.) Discourse delivered at Oxford, May 10th, 1863, by Rev. William S. Coggin, on the Twenty-fifth Anniversary of his Settlement. *Augusta.* 1864. 8vo, pp. 81.

COGHLAN (J.) Memoria y plano de las mejoras propuestas para el puerto ejecutados de orden del superior Gobierno por John Coghlan. Traducido del ingles por José P. de Guerrico. *Buenos-Aires.* 1859. 4to, pp. 12. 14207

COGHLAN (Margaret). Memoirs of Mrs. Coghlan, (Daughter of the late Major Moncrieffe,) written by herself, and Dedicated

to the British Nation; being interspersed with Anecdotes of the late American and present French War, with remarks Moral and Political. In Two Volumes. *London: C. and G. Kearsley.* MD.CC.XCIV. 2 vols., 12mo, 3 l., pp. xx, 152; Title, pp. 172. + *London: Printed for the Author, and Dublin, Reprinted by Z. Jackson.* 1794. 12mo, 5 l., pp. x, 171. + *Cork.* 1794. 12mo, 5 l., pp. x, 171. + *New York: Printed by T. & J. Swords, for J. Fellows.* 1795. 12mo, pp. xix, 184. P. 14208

Margaret Coghlan was seduced by Col. Burr, and afterwards led an abandoned life in New York and Europe. *See* Davis' Burr, p. 86. The New York edition contains a preface, which was suppressed, and is frequently deficient, it was lastly reprinted with the following title:

COGHLAN. Memoirs of Mrs. Coghlan, Daughter of the late Major Moncrieffe: written by Herself. With Introduction and Notes. Privately reprinted. *New York: T. H. Morrell.* 1864. 8vo, 4 l., pp. 158. BA. 14209

100 copies printed in 8vo, and 20 copies on large paper, 4to. All the copies of this so-called *private* reprint were sold.

COGOLLUDO (D. L. de). Historia de Yucathan. Compuesta por el M. R. P. Fr. Diego Lopez Cogollvdo, lector jvbilado, y Padre perpetvo de dicha Provincia. ... Sacala à lvz ... Francisco de Ayeta, predicador, Ex-Custodio del Nueuo Mexico ... . *Madrid: Jvan Garcia Infanzon.* 1688. 4to, Title, 13 l., pp. 760, 16 l. C., H., J.C.B. 14210

"Ouvrage rare, et selon M. Ternaux, on y trouve des renseignements precieux sur des pays très peu connus." — BRUNET. This work is justly esteemed as one of the most valuable fountains of information for the student of American history, the author having access to many valuable documents, some of which are given at length. As usual, in the works of the Spanish missionaries, there is no lack of miracles. *See also* Leclerc, No. 350. Sold at Paris, in 1867, for 228 fr.; priced, by Quaritch, in 1870, at £12 12s.

COGOLLUDO. Los Tres Siglos de la Dominacion Española en Yucatan, o sea Historia de esta Provincia. Vol. I. *Campeche.* 1842. Vol. II. *Merida.* 1845. 2 vols., 4to. 14211

Very rare, as nearly the whole edition was destroyed. A third edition was issued, with the following title:

COGOLLUDO. Historia de Yucatan escrita en el siglo XVII por el reverendo padre Fr. Diego Lopez Cogolludo. Tercera edicion. *Merida: imprenta de Manuel Aldana Rivas.* 1867–8. 2 vols., 4to, pp. 615; 663. 14212

COGSWELL (E. C.) History of New Boston, New Hampshire. Compiled and Written by Elliott C. Cogswell, Pastor of

the Presbyterian Church, New Boston, N. H. *Boston: Rand & Avery, Printers.* 1864. 8vo, pp. 470. Map and Illustrations.

Scarce. A small edition only printed for the town.

COGSWELL. Memoir of the Reverend Mr. Samuel Hidden. *Boston.* 1842. 12mo. Portrait. 14214

COGSWELL (Henry C.) Views relative to the Construction of a Railway from Halifax to Quebec, by the British Government; and the most efficient and economical means of promoting the Prosperity of the British North American Colonies; ... *Halifax.* 1852. 8vo, pp. 6. 14215

COGSWELL (James). A Sermon, Preached before the General Assembly Of the Colony of Connecticut, At Hartford, On ... their Anniversary Election, May 9th, 1771. By James Cogswell ... . *New-London.* M,DCC,LXXI. 8vo, pp. 49. M. 14216.

COGSWELL. Sermon at Brooklyn, Pomfret, Conn. April 13. 1757, to the Military Company of Captain Israel Putnam ... *Boston.* 1757. 8vo, pp. 32. 14217

Also: Sermon at Lebanon, Con. March 4, 1776, on the Death of Rev. Solomon Williams. *Norwich.* 1776. 4to, pp. 20. W. — Sermon, delivered at Hampton, July 28th, 1791, at the Interment of the Rev. Samuel Moseley. *Windham.* 1792. 8vo. — The Character ... of Preachers ... . A Sermon ... at Norwich, April 2, 1784. At the Furneal [*sic*], of the Rev. Benjamin Lord, D.D. ... . *Norwich: Printed by John Trumbull.* M,DCC,LXXXV. 8vo, pp. 32. H.

[COGSWELL (Joseph G.)] Alphabetical Index to the Astor Library. *New York.* 1851. 8vo. 14218

This valuable book is a table of the works which Dr. Cogswell intended purchasing for the Astor Library. It contains about 22,000 titles, and will serve as a useful guide in the formation of libraries of reference. Also: Prospectus of a School to be established at Round Hill, Northampton ... by Joseph G. Cogswell and George Bancroft. [*Cambridge: Hilliard and Metcalf.* 1823.] 8vo, pp. 20. H. — Some Account of the School for the Liberal Education of Boys, established at Round Hill, Northampton, Mass., by Joseph G. Cogswell and George Bancroft. *Northampton.* 1826. 8vo. B. — Testimonial Dinner to Joseph Green Cogswell ... by Roundhill Scholars, December 1, 1864. [*Boston.* 1864.] 8vo, pp. 7. Portrait. H.

COGSWELL (N.) An Oration ... before the Republican Citizens of Newburyport, ... Fourth of July, 1808. By Nathaniel Cogswell, Esq. *Newburyport: W. and J. Gilman.* 1808. 8vo, pp. 19. W. 14219

COGSWELL (W.) A Discourse ... Dedham ... Society for the Suppression of Intemperance, at their ... Meeting, Feb. 2. 1818. By William Cogswell, A.M. ... *Dedham: Abel D. Alleyne, Printer.* 1813. 8vo, pp. 16. 14220

COGSWELL. Religious Liberty. A Sermon, preached on the Day of the Annual Fast in Massachusetts, April 3, 1828. By William Cogswell ... . *Boston: Prince and Williams.* 1828. 8vo, pp. 22. H. + Second Edition. *Boston.* 1831. 12mo.

COGSWELL. The New Hampshire Repository; devoted to Education, History, Biography, &c. *Gilmanton, N. H.: A. Prescott.* 1846–7. 2 vols. Portraits. 14222

Contains much valuable historical information about New Hampshire not to be found elsewhere; not often found complete. *See* "New England ... Historical Register."

COGSWELL. Sermon containing a Brief History of the South Church and Parish in Dedham, delivered June 23, 1816. *Dedham.* 1816. 8vo, pp. 23. M. 14223

COGSWELL. Valedictory Discourse preached to the South Church and Parish in Dedham, Dec. 20, 1829. By William Cogswell. *Boston.* 1830. 8vo, pp. 28. W. 14224

Also: The Christian Philanthropist; or, Harbinger of the Millennium. Introductory Essay by J. Matheson, D.D. Second Edition. *Boston.* 1839. 12mo. M. — Masonic Sermon at Walpole, Mass. June 24, 1819. *Dedham.* [n. d.] 8vo. — Sermon before the Auxiliary Education Society of Norfolk County, delivered in Medway, June 14, 1826. *Boston.* 1826. 8vo, pp. 43. — A Sermon ... before the American Education Society of Norfolk County ... June 14, 1826. ... [With the Proceedings.] *Boston: Crocker & Brewster.* 1826. 8vo, pp. 43. H.

COGSWELL (W.), *of N. S.* A Sermon preached before the Nova Scotia Philanthropic Society. *Halifax.* 1840. 8vo, pp. 15.

COHAHUILA. Memorial on the National, Political, and Civil State of the Province of Cohahuila. *Cadiz.* 1812. + [Another Edition.] *London.* 1814. 14226

COHASSET, *Mass.* Articles of Faith and of the Covenant, Second Congregational Church in Cohasset, Nov. 24, 1824. 12mo. 14227

Historical Sketch of Beechwood Church, near Cohasset, (Mass), Jan. 15th, 1867. *Boston.* 1867. 8vo, pp. 20. 14228

Report of the Selectmen on the Financial Affairs of ... Cohasset, for the Year ending Feb. 10, 1865, including the Reports of the Overseers of the Poor and Town Treasurer, with a List of Marriages and Deaths. *Hingham: Blossom & Easterbrook.* 1865. 8vo, pp. 27. H. 14229

COHEN (Bernard). Compendium of Finance; containing an account of the Origin, Progress, and Present State of the Public

Debts, Revenues, Expenditure, National Banks and Currencies of France, ... United States of America, Buenos Ayres, Colombia, and Chili. Also, an Historical Sketch of the National Debt of the British Empire. *London.* 1822. Rl. 8vo. + Second Edition. *London.* 1828. Rl. 8vo. C. 14230

COHEN (M. M.) Notices of Florida and the Campaigns, by M. M. Cohen, (An Officer of the Left Wing.) *Charleston, S. C.: Burgess.* 1836. 12mo, pp. 240. Map, and Portrait of Osceola.

"Sketches of the Seminole War and Sketches during a Campaign. By a Lieutenant of the Left Wing. *Charlestown: Daniel D. Dowling.* 1836." 12mo, pp. 312, has been attributed to this writer; perhaps by mistake.

COHOES, *N. Y.* Laws relating to the Incorporation of Villages and the By-Laws of the Village of Cohoes. *Cohoes: J. H. Masten.* 1855. 8vo, pp. 68. H. 14232

Catalogue of the Cohoes District School Library. *Cohoes, N. Y.* 1857. pp. 29. S. 14233

COIGNET. Instruction Nouvelle des Poincts plus excellentes & necessaires touchant l'Art de naviguer. *Anvers.* 1581. 4to.

This rare work was unknown to Lalande. It contains a map of America, with the opposite coast in the Old World, diagrams and volvelles.

COINDET (L.) Le Mexique considéré au point de vue médico-chirurgical. Par M. le docteur Léon Coindet. *Paris: Rozier.* 1867–69. 3 vols., 8vo, pp. viii, 322; xi, 350; x, 318.

COINS. Report of Gold and Silver Coins, by a Select Committee of the House of Representatives of the United States, February 19, 1834. *Washington.* 1834. 8vo. (House Document 278, 23d Cong., 1st Sess.) N. 14236

COIT (J. C.) Eulogy on the Life, Character and Public Services of the Hon. John C. Calhoun ... before the Citizens of Cheraw ... April 24, 1850. By ... J. C. Coit. ..., *Columbia, S. C.: A. S. Johnston.* 1850. 8vo, pp. 44. H. 14237

Also: A Discourse upon Governments, Divine and Human ... delivered ... April, 1853, ... *Columbia, S. C.: "Banner" Steam-Power Press.* 1853. 8vo, pp. 47. H.

COIT (T. Winthrop). Puritanism: or, a Churchman's Defence against its Aspersions, by an Appeal to its own History. ... By Thomas W. Coit, D.D. ... *New York: D. Appleton & Co. Philadelphia: Geo. S. Appleton.* MDCCCXLV. 12mo, pp. 527, (1). C., H. 14238

See "New England Register," II. 288, and the "Princeton Review," XVIII. 122. Also: An Inaugural Address delivered in the Chapel of Morrison College, Novem-

ber 2, 1835, ... *Lexington, Ky.: Clarke & Co.* 1835. 8vo, pp. 38. H. — "The Sword of the Lord." A discourse delivered in St. Paul's Church, Troy, on the National Fast Day. June 1. ... [n. p. n. d.] 8vo, pp. 14. — Unity of Causes without Uniformity of Results. The Sermon before the Annual Convention of the Protestant Episcopal Church, at Waterbury, Connecticut, June 10th, 1851. ... . *Waterbury: E. B. Cooke & Co.* 1851. 12mo, pp. 24. H.

COKE (Edward Thomas). A Subaltern's Furlough: descriptive of Scenes in various parts of the United States, Upper and Lower Canada, New-Brunswick, and Nova Scotia, during the Summer and Autumn of 1832. By E. T. Coke, Lieutenant of the 45th Regiment. *London: Saunders and Otley.* MDCCCXXXIII. 8vo, pp. xi, 485, (1). Map, and 13 Plates. + *New York: Harpers.* 1833. 2 vols., 12mo, pp. 222; iv, 188. 14239

COKE (H. J.) A Ride over the Rocky Mountains to Oregon and California, with a Glance at some of the Tropical Islands, including the West Indies and the Sandwich Isles. By the Hon. Henry J. Coke. *London: Richard Bentley.* 1852. 8vo, pp. 388, (2). C., H., P. 14240

COKE (R.) England's Improvement. In Two Parts. In the Latter is discoursed, how the Navigation of England may be increased, and the Sovereignty of the British Seas more secured to the Crown of England. By Roger Coke. *London: Henry Brome, &c.* 1675. 4to, pp. 115. 14241

The author's theory was, that the emigration to the colonies was injurious to England. *See* McCulloch's "Lit. Pol. Econ.," p. 40. *See also* his "Treatises, wherein is demonstrated, that the Church and State of England, are in equal Danger with the Trade of it — and from what Causes the Dutch Govern and Manage Trade better than the English."

COKE (T.) Extract from the Journal of the Rev. Dr. Coke from Gravesend to Antigua, in a Letter to Rev. J. Wesley. *London.* 1787. 12mo. W. 14242

Also: "A Continuation. *London.* 1787." 12mo, and a "Further Continuation. *London.* 1787." 12mo.

COKE. Extracts of the Journals of the Rev. Dr. Coke's Three Visits to America. 1790. 12mo. + Extracts of the Journals of the Rev. Dr. Coke's Five Visits to America. *London: Printed by G. Paramore.* 1793. 12mo, pp. 195. H. 14243

"Dr. Coke was an eminent Wesleyan missionary, educated at Oxford. In 1784 he visited America, and made altogether nine visits to the United States." — ALLIBONE.

COKE. A History of the West Indies, containing the Natural, Civil, and Ecclesiastical History of each Island: with an Account of the Missions instituted in those Islands, from the Com-

mencement of their Civilization; but more especially of the Missions which have been established in that Archipelago By the Society Late in Connexion with the Rev John Wesley. By Thomas Coke, LL.D. ... *Liverpool: printed by Nuttall, Fisher and Dixon.* 1808. *London.* 1810 *and* 1811. 3 vols., 8vo, pp. 459; 463; 543. B., C., H., P. 14244

COKE. A Journal of the Rev. Dr. Coke's Visit to Jamaica, and of his Third Tour on the Continent of America. *London: Printed in the Year* M,DCC,LXXXIX. 12mo, Title, pp. 16.

COKE. Journal of Dr. Coke's Third Tour through the West Indies, and Fourth Tour on the Continent of America, in Letters to John Wesley. 3 Parts. *London.* 1791–2. 14246

COKE. [No. III.] A Journal of the Rev. Dr. Coke's Fourth Tour on the Continent of America. *London: G. Paramore.* 1792. 12mo, pp. 23. 14247

COKE. Statements of the Receipts and Disbursements of the Missions to Instruct and Convert the Negroes in the West Indies, by Dr. Coke, 1794. *Sold by G. Whitefield at the Chapel, City Road.* 1793. 12mo, pp. 195. 14248

COKE. The Substance of a Sermon, Preached at Baltimore, in the State of Maryland, before the General Conference of the Methodist Episcopal Church, on the 27th of December, 1784; at the Ordination of the Rev. Francis Asbury, to the Office of a Superintendent. By Thomas Coke, LL.D. Superintendent of the said Church. Published at the Desire of the Conference. *Baltimore: Goddard and Langworthy.* 1785. 8vo. + *London: J. Paramore.* 1785. 12mo, 2 l., pp. 22. + *London: T. Scollich.* 1785. 12mo, pp. 22. C. + *New York: T. Mason and G. Lane.* 1840. 8vo, pp. 15. H. 14249

See [Wesley (Charles)], for strictures on this sermon.

COKE. Substance of a Sermon preached at Baltimore and Philadelphia on the Death of John Wesley by Dr. Coke, 1791. [n. p. n. d.] 12mo. 14250

COKE (Thomas), *and* ASBURY (Francis). Address to the Annual Subscribers for the support of Cokesbury College, with the Rules and Regulations of the College. *New York.* 1787. 12mo. 14251

COKE (Thomas), *and* MOORE (Henry). The Life of the Rev.

John Wesley, A.M.: including an Account of the Great Revival of Religion in Europe and America, of which he was the First and Chief Instrument. By Dr. Coke and Mr. Moore. *London.* 1792. 8vo. C. 14252

See [Colet (J.)], and Whitehead (John).

COKER (D.) Journal of Daniel Cocker, a Descendant of Africa ... on a Voyage for Sherbro in Africa. *Baltimore.* 1820.

COLBERT, *pseudon.* *See* [Carey (M.)], Vol. III.

COLBERT (E.) Chicago. Historical and Statistical Sketch of the Garden City; a Chronicle of its Social, Municipal, Commercial and Manufacturing Progress; from the Beginning until now. Containing also, Names of Early Settlers and the Office Holders. With Full Statistical Tables. By E. Colbert, Commercial Editor Tribune. *Chicago.* 1868. 8vo, pp. 120. 14254

COLBURN (D. P.) Memorial of Dana Pond Colburn. First Principal of the Rhode Island State Normal School. With a Sketch of the Institution. [n. p. n. d.] 8vo, pp. 29. 14255

From Barnard's "American Journal of Education for March, 1862."

COLBURN (S. W.) Sermon at Abington, Mass. at the Funeral of Deacon Josiah Torrey. By Samuel W. Colburn. *Boston.* 1822. 8vo. W. 14256

COLBURN (Z.) A Memoir of Zerah Colburn. Written by Himself, containing his First Discovery of his Remarkable Powers; his Travels in America and Residence in Europe. With his Peculiar Method of Calculation. *Springfield, Mass.* 1833. 12mo, pp. 104. Portrait. C. 14257

Colburn's United Service Magazine, and Naval and Military Journal. Part I. *London: Henry Colburn.* 1829. 8vo. Continued. 14258

Contains many articles on American topics.

COLBY (C.) Hand-book of Illinois, accompanying Morse's New Map of the State. By Charles Colby, A.M. *New York: R. Blanchard.* 1855. 18mo, pp. 36. Map. C. 14259

COLBY. The World in Miniature; with Description of every Nation and Country. Together with a Treatise on Physical Geography. By Charles Colby. The Western Hemisphere. *New Orleans: A. B. Griswold.* MDCCCLVII. Sm. 4to, pp. 239.

Some copies have the title: "The Diamond Atlas; with Descriptions of all Countries, ..." *See* Fisher (R. S.).

Colby (G. J. L.) Address delivered before the Essex Agricultural Society, October, 1862, by George J. L. Colby ... *South Danvers: Charles D. Howard.* 1862. 8vo, pp. 30. H.

Colby (H. G. O.) Anniversary Address before the American Institute of the City of New York, ... October 20, 1842, ... By the Hon. H. G. O. Colby, ... *New York: James Van Norden & Co.* 8vo, pp. 20. B. 14262

Colby (J.) The Life, Experience and Travels of the Rev. John Colby. Written by Himself. Third Edition. *Portland.* 1815. + *Cornish, Me.* 1829. 12mo. + *Newport.* 1831. 12mo. Portrait. + *Lowell: N. Thurston & A. Watson.* 1838. 2 vols., 12mo, 1 l., pp. 248, 64. C. 14263

Colby University. Catalogue of the Officers and Students of Colby University for ... 1866–7, 1867–8. *Waterville: printed for the University.* 1867–68. 8vo. 14264

Colchester, *Conn.* Extracts from the Records of Colchester, with some Transcripts from the Recording of Michael Taintor, of Brainford, Conn. Transcribed by Charles M. Taintor. *Hartford: Case, Lockwood & Co.* 1864. 12mo, pp. 156. 14265

The Cold-Water-Man. By Doctor Springwater, of North America. *Albany.* 1832. 12mo. 14266

[Colden (Cadwallader).] An | Explication | of the | First Causes | of | Action In Matter, | And, | Of the | Cause of Gravitation. | *New-York:* | *Printed By James Parker*, 1745. | Sm. 8vo, pp. vi, 43, (1). 14267

This edition is a volume of the greatest rarity. I have seen but one copy, which belongs to Mr. William Menzies. The dedication to James Alexander, Esq., at New York, is dated, "Coddingham, in the Province of New York, Dec. 10. 1745," and signed Cadwallader Colden. Concerning its rarity, *see* Jefferson's letter to Francis Hopkinson, in 1786. *See also* Sparks' "Franklin," vi. 95, 117, and "M. Rev.," vii. 459; ix. 203; xxi. 397, 500. The first English edition was printed without the author's knowledge or consent. The second English edition was enlarged. Buffon caused it to be translated into French, and there was a German translation published at Hamburg or Leipzig, or both, which I have not seen.

Colden. An Explication of the First Causes of Action in Matter; and of the Cause of Gravitation. By Cadwallader Colden. *New-York: Printed. And London: Reprinted for J. Brindley* ... 1746. 8vo, pp. 75. P. + Second Edition. *London: J. Dodsley.* 1751. 14268

In Bohn's "Lowndes," p. 491, another edition is described as "The Principle of Action in Matter, the Gravitation in Bodies and the Motion of Planets, explained

from those Principles. *London.* 1752." 4to. Its title hardly belongs to our place, seeing that it does *not* relate to America; but the work is eagerly sought after by American collectors, and, at the time of its publication, excited much comment.

Colden. Explication des Premierès Causes de l'Action dans la Matière et de la Gravitation, traduit de l'Anglais [par Dom Castel]. *Bordeaux. Paris: Durand.* 1751. 12mo. 14269

Colden. The | History | of the | Five Indian Nations | Depending on the Province | of | New-York | In America. | By Cadwallader Colden. | *Printed and Sold by William Bradford, in* | *New York*, 1727. | 12mo, Title, 1 l., pp. xviii, 119. 14270

A volume of the greatest rarity, not more than six copies being known in the United States. For some interesting particulars concerning the author, *see* Dr. Shea's introduction to his reprint of this edition. The work was occasioned by a dispute between the government of New York and some merchants, and is mainly a legal argument.

Colden. The History of the Five Indian Nations of the Province of New York. By Cadwallader Colden. Reprinted exactly from Bradford's New York Edition, (1727.) With an Introduction and Notes, by John Gilmary Shea. *New York: T. H. Morrell.* 1866. 8vo, pp. xl, 1 l., pp. xvii, (1), 141. Portrait and Map. 14271

Of this reprint, 100 copies were printed in 8vo, and 25 copies in imp. 8vo. "Notwithstanding the high position of Gov. Colden, the many offices he filled, and the great service he rendered the colony of New York, no biography of him was ever written. Mr. Shea, in his introduction, has now performed this duty, and has done it well."—Bartlett. The following work is, in fact, necessary to complete the first edition:

Colden. Papers | relating to | An Act of the Assembly | of the | Province of New-York; | For Encouragement of the Indian Trade, &c. and | for Prohibiting the Selling of Indian Goods to the French, viz. of Canada | I. A Petition of the Merchants of London to His Majesty, against the said Act. | II. His Majesty's Order in Council, Referring the said | Petition to the Lords Commissioners for Trade & Plantation. | III. Extract of the Minutes of the said Lords, con- | cerning some Allegations of the Merchants before Them. | IV. The Report of the said Lords to His Majesty on the | Merchants Petition, and other Allegations. | V. The Report of the Committe of Council of the | Province of New-York, an Answer to the said Petition. | VI. A Memorial concerning the Furr-Trade of New-York, | by C. Colden, Esq; | With a Map. | Published by Authority. | *Printed and Sold by William Bradford in the City of New-York*, 1724. | Folio, Title, 1 l., pp. about 24. Map. 14272

Mr. H. C. Murphy's imperfect copy of this piece is probably unique. It was reprinted with all the following editions:

Colden. The History of the Five Indian Nations of Canada, which are dependent on the Province of New-York in America, and are the Barrier between the English and French in that Part of the World. With Accounts of their Religion, Manners, Customs, Laws, and Forms of Government; their several Battles and Treaties with the European Nations; particular Relations of their several Wars with the other Indians; and a true Account of the present State of our Trade with them. In which are shewn the great Advantage of their Trade and Alliance to the British Nation, and the Intrigues and Attempts of the French to engage them from us; a Subject nearly concerning all our American Plantations, and highly meriting the Consideration of the British Nation at this Juncture. By the Honourable Cadwallader Colden, Esq; One of his Majesty's Counsel, and Surveyor-General of New York. To which are added, Accounts of the several other Nations of Indians in North America, their Numbers, Strength, &c. and the Treaties which have been lately made with them. A Work highly entertaining to all, and particularly useful to the Persons who have any Trade or Concern in that Part of the World. *London: T. Osborne.* MDCCXLVII. 8vo, pp. 20, 204, 283. BA., C. 14273

Colden dedicated his work to Gov. Burnet, and his dedication explains itself; in this London edition, Burnet gives place to Gen. Oglethorpe, and the dedication becomes nonsense. The English editor also shows an antipathy to Indian names, suppressing them habitually, striking out important passages, and, instead of the speeches which Colden gives at length, substitutes meagre abridgments. In fact, the whole work is so cut up and altered, that the reader of the English edition cannot be sure that he is quoting Colden at all. Still this edition is desirable, as it contains many public documents. The following is the same work, with a new title-page only:

Colden. The History of the Five Indian Nations of Canada, which are the Barrier between the English and French in that Part of the World. With particular Accounts of their Religion, Manners, Customs, Laws, and Government; their several Battles and Treaties with the European Nations; their Wars with the other Indians; and a true Account of the present State of our Trade with them. In which are shewn, the great Advantage of their Trade and Alliance to the British Nation; and the Intrigues and Attempts of the French to engage them from us; a Subject nearly concerning all our American Plantations, and highly meriting the Consideration of the British Nation. By the Honourable Cadwallader Colden, Esq; One of His Majesty's Counsel, and Surveyor-General of New-York. To which are added, Accounts of the several other Nations of Indians in

North-America, their Numbers, Strength, &c. and the Treaties which have been lately made with them. The Second Edition. *London: John Whitson, Lockyer Davis and John Ward.* MDCCL. 8vo, pp. xvi, (4), 283. Map. 14274

Some copies of this issue are without date.

Colden. [Title as above.] In Two Volumes. The Third Edition. *London: Lockyer Davis.* MDCCLV. pp. xii, 2 l., pp. 260; Map, 2 l., pp. 251, 4 l. 14275

[Colden.] The Conduct of Cadwallader Colden, Esquire, Lieutenant Governor of New-York: relating to the Judges' Commissions, Appeals to the King, and the Stamp-Duty. [*New-York:*] *Printed in the Year* MDCCLXVII. 8vo, Half-Title, Title, pp. 66. H. 14276

The assembly of New York made every effort to discover the author, but in vain. *See* Sedgwick's "Livingston," p. 124, and "Anal. Mag.," iv. 307.

Colden (C. D.) The Life of Robert Fulton, by his Friend Cadwallader D. Colden. Read before the Literary and Philosophical Society of New-York: Comprising some Account of the Invention, Progress, and Establishment of Steam-Boats; of Improvements on the Construction and Navigation of Canals, and other objects of Public Utility. With an Appendix. *New York: Kirk & Mercein.* 1817. 8vo, pp. vi, 371, and list of steamboats. Portrait. C. 14277

See "Q. Rev.," xix. 347–57. S. G. Drake describes a copy on large paper.

Colden. An Examination of Cadwallader D. Colden's Book entitled A Life of Robert Fulton. By a Friend of John Fitch, deceased. [n. p.] 1818. 8vo, pp. 38. 14278

Colden. Memoir, Prepared at the Request of a Committee of the Common Council of the City of New York, and Presented to the Mayor of the City, at the Celebration of the Completion of the New York Canals. By Cadwallader D. Colden. ... *Printed by Order of the Corporation of New York, by W. A. Davis.* 1825. 4to, 4 l., pp. 408, 1 l. 6 Portraits and 5 Maps.

Includes portraits of Colden, Philip Hone, S. L. Mitchill, etc., engraved by Durand. The narrative was written by the late W. L. Stone.

Colden. Observations on the Intended Application of the North-American Coal & Mining Company, to the Legislature of ... New-York, February, 1814. [n. p. n. d.] 8vo, pp. 23.

Signed by C. Colden and two others, "in behalf of themselves and their associates."

[Colden.] Review of the Letter addressed by W. A. Duer to C. D. Colden, in answer to Strictures contained in his "Life of Robert Fulton." With Appendix. *New York.* 1818. 8vo, pp. 27. B., C. 14281

Colden. A Vindication by Cadwallader D. Colden, of the Steam Boat Right, granted by the State of New York: In the form of an Answer to the Letter of Mr. Duer, addressed to Mr. Colden. *Albany: Websters and Skinners.* 1818. 12mo, pp. 178. B., C. + *New York: W. A. Mercein.* 1819. 8vo, pp. 96.

Also: A Brief Exposition of the Views of John L. Sullivan, Esq., on his Exclusive Steam Towboat Right. 1822. ... B., S. — Letter ... upon the General Character and Tendency of Freemasonry. *Boston.* [1829.] 8vo, pp. 8. + *New York.* [1829.] 8vo, pp. 15. — Speech ... in the Senate of ... New York, on Repeal of Laws prohibiting Private Banking. *Albany.* 1825. 8vo, pp. 10.

[Cole (A.) & Co.] The New Settlement of Manamuskin, in Cumberland County, N. J. [n. p. 1864.] 4to, pp. (3). H.

Cole (C.) Speech of ... Cornelius Cole ... on Arming the Slaves. Delivered in the House ... February 18, 1864. *Washington.* 1864. 8vo, pp. 15. H. 14284

Also: Speech ... on the Public Debt, delivered in the ... Senate, December 5, 1867. *Washington.* 1867. 8vo, pp. 8. H.

Cole (E.) The Life and Sufferings of Miss Emma Cole, being a Faithful Narrative of her Life, written by herself. Fifth Edition. *Boston: M. Aurelius.* 1844. 12mo, pp. 36. H. 14285

Cole (F. W.) Poems. By Frederick Wing Cole. With a Sketch of his Life and Character. By Rev. S. W. Fisher. *Albany: Van Benthuysen & Co.* 1845. Sm. 4to, 1 l., pp. xxx, 128. 14286

Cole (F. S.) The Suez and Nicaragua Canal Plans Considered. By S. F. Cole. *London: Stanford.* 1851. 8vo.

Cole (G. E.) Letter of ... George E. Cole on the Disaster by Flood at Port Angeles, December 16th, 1863, with his Views on the Location of the Port of Entry for Puget Sound, and a Reply by a Citizen of Washington Territory. [*Washington?* 1864?] 8vo, pp. 8. H. 14288

Cole (J.) The American War, an Ode, being an Impartial Description of the most material Military and Naval Transactions there; from the commencement of Hostilities, to the end of the second Campaign, interspersed occasionally with humour-

ous satyrical Animadversions on the conduct of both Parties, with Explanatory Notes through the whole. To which is added an Appendix, wherein the Author has traced the origin of that People's Revolt, to a cause which he never saw yet adverted to; with the many concurring circumstances which have thus far accelerated the execution of their Plan. By John Cole, late of Plymouth, but now of Beverly in Yorkshire. [Preface dated Sept. 20, 1799. n. p. n. d.] 8vo, pp. 123. C. 14289

Also: A Miscellany of Poems, Odes, and Songs. *Hull.* 1791. 8vo, pp. 112, vi.

Cole (J.) History and Antiquities of Ecton, in the County of Northampton. *Scarborough.* 1825. 8vo. Portrait. + *Philadelphia: H. W. Smith.* 1864. 8vo. 14290

The author was an eccentric bookseller at Scarborough. Contains an account of the Franklin family, the ancestors of the celebrated Benjamin. For three hundred years they had resided on one estate, of thirty acres, carrying on the trade of blacksmiths.

Cole (S. W.) The American Fruit Book; A Book for Every Body, containing Directions for Raising Fruit Trees, Shrubs, and Plants ... . By S. W. Cole ... . *Boston: published by John P. Jewett.* 1849. 16mo, pp. 288. Illustrations.

Also: A Book for every Farmer. ... *Boston: John P. Jewett & Co.* 1847. 12mo, pp. 288. H.

Cole (Thomas). The State of the Newfoundland Fishery, with a Plan Proposed to the Administration The 12th of May, 1761, To exclude the French from that Trade. By Captain T. Cole. [n. p. n. d.] 8vo. 14292

See Williams (Griffith).

Cole (T.) List of Infusorial Objects, found chiefly in the Neighborhood of Salem, Mass. ... By Thomas Cole ... . *Salem: Ives & Pease.* 1853. 8vo, pp. 18. 14293

Coleccion de Cartas y Planos de las Costas de America, construidas en la direccion de trabajos Hidrographicos. *Madrid.* 1801. Large folio. 18 Maps. 14294

Coleccion de documentos. *See* Florida, Guadalaxara, Icazbalceta, Mexico, Navarrete, and Pacheco.

Coleccion de Documentos Oficiales con que el Gobierno instruye al Cuerpo Legislativo de la Provincia del origen y estado de los cuestiones pendientes con la Republica de los E. U. de Norte America, sobre las Islas Malvinas. *Buenos-Aires.* 1832. 4to, 56 l. C. + Apendice á los documentos precedientes. *Buenos Aires.* 1832. 11 l. 14295

Coleccion de las causas mas célebres en lo civil y criminal, del foro frances, ingles, español y mexicano. *Mexico.* 1854–1855. 2 vols., 4to. 14296

Coleccion de las composiciones poeticas inscritas en dos arcos y arojadas al paso de SS. MM. en su solemne entrada á la Capital del Imperio. *Mexico.* 1864. 8vo, pp. 54. 14297

Coleccion de los documentos mas interesantes relativos al prestamo de Medio Millon de Pesos, ofrecido por el venerable clero secular y regular de este Arzobispado. 4to, pp. 16. + Continuacion de los mismos documentos. *Mexico.* 1839. 4to, pp. 7. 14298

Coleccion de los documentos relativos à la navegacion fluviatil del Rio de la Plata, El Amazonas y sus afluentes, publicados en las diversas memorias del Ministerio de Relaciones Exteriores del Imperio del Brasil, traducidos y ofrecidos á la consideracion de las Repúblicas de la América del Sur, que en ella tienen interes. Por un Sur-Americano. *Carácas.* 1857. 8vo, pp. 242. C. 14299

Coleccion de los Tratados de Paz, Alianza, Comercio &c., ajustados por la corona de España con las potencias extrangeras, desde el reynado del Señor Don Felipe Quinto hasta el presente. 1701–1801. *Madrid.* 1796–1801. 3 vols., folio. C. 14300

Coleccion de Obras y Opusculos pertenecientes á la milagrosa Aparicion de la Bellisima Imagen de Nuestra Señora de Guadalupe, que se venera en su santuario extramuros de Mexico. ... *Reimpressa todas juntas ... en Madrid.* 1785. 4to, 9 l., pp. 804, 6 l. C. 14301

Coleccion de tratados celebrados por la Republica Argentina con las naciones estrangeras. *Buenos Aires.* 1863. 4to, pp. 476.

Coleccion de varios documentos interesantes relativas al decreto anteconstitucional. *Leona-Vicario.* 1830. 4to, pp. 45.

Coleccion general de documentos. *See* Vol. III., No. 10803.

Coleccion General de las Provincias hasta aqui tomadas por el gobierno sobre el estrañamiento y ocupacion de temporalidades de los Regulares de la Compañia, que existian en los dominios de S. M. de España Indias, e Islas Filipinas á consequencia del Real Decreto de 27 de Febrero y Pragmática-Sancion de 2 de Abril de este año. Parte Primera. De orden del Consejo, en

el Extraordinario. *En Madrid en la Imprenta Real de la Gazeta. Año de* 1767–69. 3 pts., 4to, 1 l., pp. 157; 1 l., pp. 144; 1 l., pp. 24, 146. 14304

These collections contain the documents relative to the expulsion of the Jesuits from the Spanish dominions, and the confiscation of their property, including the names of the colleges and houses of the order, the application of the confiscated property, &c. A complete series consists of five parts, which are rarely found together. Part v. was published in 1784. Our collation is of parts I. to III. only.

Coleccion Polidiómica Mexicana. *See* Mexico.

Coleman (E.) A Testimony against the Antichristian Practice of making Slaves of Men, wherein it is shewed to be Contrary to the Dispensation of the Law and Time of the Gospel, and very Opposite both to Grace and Nature. By Elihu Coleman. [*Nantucket:*] *Printed in the Year*, 1733. 12mo, pp. 24. + *New Bedford: Abraham Shearman, Jun.* 1825. 12mo, pp. 24. P. 14305

Reprinted in "The Friends' Review, 1851."

Coleman (J.) Life of the Rev. Dr. Jarratt, &c. By Rev. John Coleman. *Baltimore.* 1806. 16mo. 14306

[Coleman (Lyman).] The Coleman Family, Descendants of Thomas Coleman, in Line of the oldest Son. IX Generations. 1598 to 1867, 296 Years. *Philadelphia: J. B. Lippincott & Co.* 1867. 8vo, pp. 24. S. 14307

Coleman. The Nature and Fruits of Political Anti-Masonry practically exhibited. A Concise Statement of Facts and Reasons inducing the Brainard Church in Belchertown to secede from the First Church. *Northampton.* 1835. 8vo, pp. 18.

Also: A Church without a Bishop. ... *Boston: Gould, Kendall & Lincoln.* 1834. 12mo, pp. 432.

Coleman (S.) Memoirs, Journal, and Letters of Seth Coleman, M.D., with a Sermon at his Funeral by the Rev. Nathan Perkins. *New Haven: Flagg & Gray.* 1817. 16mo, pp. 288.

[Coleman (William).] Appeal to the People; being a Review of the late Correspondence and Documents relating to the Rejection of the British Minister, including an Examination of the "Arrangement" of April last. *New-York.* 1810. 8vo, pp. 120. 14310

[Coleman.] A Collection of the Facts and Documents, relative to the Death of Major-General Alexander Hamilton;

with Comments; together with the Various Orations, Sermons, and Eulogies, that have been published or written on his Life and Character. *New York: Printed by Hopkins & Seymour for J. Riley & Co.* 1804. 8vo, Title, pp. (1), 238. C., H. 14311

[Coleman.] An Examination of the President's Reply to the New Haven Remonstrance. *New York: George F. Hopkins.* 1801. 8vo. pp. 69. 14312

[Coleman.] Remarks and Criticisms on the Hon. John Quincy Adams's Letter to Hon. Harrison Gray Otis. *Boston.* 1808. 8vo, pp. 62. 14313

[Coleman.] Report of the Trial of William Coleman for a Libel on Philip I. Arcularius. *New York.* 1807. 8vo. 14314

[Coleman (William).] Appeal to the People of the North. [*Louisville, Ky.: Hanna & Co., Printers.* 1861.] 8vo, pp. 16. H. + Second Edition. *Louisville: Hanna & Co.* 1861. 8vo, pp. 16. 14315

Signed, "A Voice from Kentucky."

Coleman (W. T.) Wm. T. Coleman & Co's Circular and Market Review. No. 15–37. Jan. 19–Dec. 4, 1857. *San Francisco.* 1857. Folio. H. 14316

Coleridge (H.) Lives of Northern Worthies. By Hartley Coleridge. Edited by his Brother. A New Edition, with the Corrections of the Author ... *London: Edward Moxon.* 1852. 3 vols., fcap 8vo. BA., H. 14317

[Coleridge (Henry Nelson).] Six Months in the West Indies, in 1825. *London: John Murray.* MDCCCXXVI. Post 8vo, 2 l., pp. 332. C., H. + Second Edition, with Additions. *London: John Murray.* 1826. Post 8vo. 14318

Vol. III., "Life of Captain James Cook."

Coleridge. Six Months in the West Indies in 1825. By Henry Nelson Coleridge. Third Edition ... . *London: John Murray.* MDCCCXXXII. 16mo, Title, 2 l., pp. 311. H. + Fourth Edition. *London: Thomas Tegg.* 1848. Fcap 8vo.

The author's name first appears in the third edition; the fourth forms part of Murray's "Colonial Library."

[Coleridge.] Zes maanden in de West Indiën, in 1825. Vrij vertaald uit het engelsch door J.G.S. *Dordrecht: Blussé & Van Braam.* 1826. 8vo, pp. lx, 349. 14320

Coleridge (J.) Government a Divine Institution, ... Sermon Preached on December 13, 1776. "The Fast Day appointed by reason of our much-to-be-lamented American War." By Rev. John Coleridge ... . *London: Printed for the Author.* 1777. 4to. S. 14321

Coleridge (Samuel Taylor). Poems ... by S. J. Coleridge ... . *London.* 1796. 12mo. 14322

Frequently reprinted. Some of the verses allude to an intended emigration to America, on the scheme of an abandonment of individual property.

Coleridge (William Hart), *Bishop of Barbadoes.* Charges delivered to the Clergy of the Diocese of Barbadoes and the Leeward Islands. *London.* 1835. 8vo. 14323

Coleridge. Form of Consecration of the British Chapel and Burial Ground, according to the Rites and Ceremonies of the Church of England, by the Right Reverend Father in God, William Hart Coleridge, D.D., Lord Bishop of Barbadoes and the Leeward Islands. *Carácas.* 1834. Folio, pp. 10, 10.

Coles (Abraham). Critique on Scott and Gliddon's Ethnological Works, with some remarks on an Article by W. S. Forwood, M.D., entitled "The Negro — a distinct Species," &c. *Burlington, N. J.* 1857. 8vo. 14325

Bears on the slavery question, as does his "Unity of the Origin of Mankind." *Philadelphia.* 1857.

Coles (B. C.) A Memoir on the Subject of Wheat and Flour of the State of New-York. By Benjamin C. Coles. Read ... Feb. 17, 1820. ... *New-York.* 1820. 8vo, pp. 46.

Coles (E.) History of the Ordinance of 1787. By Edward Coles, formerly Governor of the State of Illinois: ... Read before the Historical Society of Pennsylvania, June 9, 1856. *Press of the Society.* 1856. 8vo, pp. 33. 14327

Coles (G.) Heroines of Methodism; or, Pen and Ink Sketches of the Mothers and Daughters of the Church. By George Coles. *New York.* 1857. 12mo. C. 14328

Coles. Incidents of my Later Years. By Rev. George Coles. *New York: Carlton & Phillips.* 1855. 18mo, pp. 315.

Coles. My First Seven Years in America. By Rev. George Coles. Edited by D. P. Kidder. *New-York.* 1852. 18mo. 14330

Coles (J. A.) [Letters. Trial of Dr. Bronaugh. Letters of Col. J. R. Preston.] *Washington.* 1814. 12mo, pp. 48. S.

Coles (J. F.) The Life and Adventures of Henry Smith, the Celebrated Razor Strop Man ... . To which is added a Choice Selection of Songs, Anecdotes and Witticisms ... . Written and compiled by John F. Coles. *Philadelphia: Smith & Coles.* 1852. 18mo, pp. 96. Woodcuts. H. 14332

Smith was a lecturer on temperance.

Coles (O.) The Memory of Washington. An Address before the Members of St. John's Lodge, ... New Jersey, Feb. 22, 1853. By Oscar Coles. *Newark, N. J.* 1853. 8vo, pp. 24. 14333

Coles (*Capt.*) Captain Coles and the Admiralty: showing, 1st, that the Admiralty has given every Fair Play to Captain Coles; 2ndly, that Ericsson and not Coles is the Author of the Turret System; 3rdly, that the Turret Vessels of Coles are radically Defective; and 4thly, that Ericsson's Monitors have proved themselves, during Two Years' War, to be Shotworthy and Seaworthy, and the Healthiest Vessels in the American Fleet. *London: Longmans.* 1866. 8vo. 14334

Coleson (A.) Miss Coleson's Narrative of her Captivity among the Sioux Indians! An Interesting and Remarkable Account of the Terrible Sufferings and Providential Escape of Miss Ann Coleson, a Victim of the Late Indian Outrages in Minnesota. *Philadelphia: Barclay & Co.* 1864. 8vo, 3 l., pp. 19–70. Woodcuts. BA. 14335

[Colesworthy (D. C.)] Chronicles of Casco Bay. *Boston.* 1814. 12mo. + *Portland: Semborn and Carter.* MDCCCL. 8vo, pp. 56. Plate. 14336

Colet (J. A.) An Impartial Review of the Life and Writings, public and private Character, of the late Rev. John Wesley: in Two Parts. Part I. By John Annesley Colet. *London: Forster.* 1791. 8vo, pp. 46. 14337

See "M. Rev.," v. 218. This and the following are rare tracts:

[Colet.] A Letter to the Rev. T. Coke, LL.D., and Mr. H. Moore, occasioned by their proposals to publish the Life of the Rev. John Wesley, in opposition to that advertised, (under the sanction of the executors,) to be written by John Whitehead, M.D.; also, a letter from the Rev. Dr. Coke to the author, on

the same subject. Together with the whole correspondence, and the circular letters, written on the occasion, and a true and impartial statement of facts hitherto suppressed. To which is added an Appeal and Remonstrance to the people called Methodists. By an old Member of the Society. *London.* 1792. 8vo. 14338

Coleti (G. D.) Dizionario storico-geographico dell' America Meridionale di Giandomenico Coleti della Compagnia di Gesù. Tomo Primo. A — L [Tomo Secondo. M — Z.] *Venezia: Nella Stamperia Coleti.* MDCCLXXI. 2 vols., 4to, pp. 196; 192, (1). Map. C., H. 14339

"The author was many years employed in South America as a missionary; the principal merit of his work consists in being almost entirely the result of personal observation, or of information procured on the spot." — Rich.

Colfavru (J. C.) Du mariage et du contrat de mariage en Angleterre, et aux États-Unis Législation comparée de l'Angleterre, des États-Unis et de la France par J. C. Colfavru ... *Paris: Crosse, Marchal, et Cie.* 1868. 8vo, 2 l., pp. 148. B.

Colfax (R. H.) Evidence against the Vices of the Abolitionists, &c. *New York.* 1833. 14341

Colfax (S.) Fremont's Hundred Days in Missouri. Speech of Schuyler Colfax ... in Reply to Mr. Blair ... delivered in the House ... March 7, 1862. [*Washington.* 1862.] 8vo, pp. 15. H. 14342

Colfax. The "Laws" of Kansas. Speech of Schuyler Colfax, of Indiana, in the House of Representatives, June 21, 1856. [*Washington.* 1856.] 8vo, pp. 16. 14343

Colfax. Life and Principles of Abraham Lincoln. By Hon. Schuyler Colfax. Speech Delivered in the Court House Square, at South Bend, April 24, 1865. *Philadelphia: Jas. B. Rogers, Printer.* 1865. 8vo, pp. 29. B. 14344

This oration was repeated at Chicago the afternoon before Mr. Lincoln's remains arrived there on the route to Springfield, and again at Denver, Colorado, June 1st, the national fast day, and is reissued in a "Life of Lincoln," printed by T. B. Peterson, Philadelphia. Also: Address, ... April 24, 1865. *Philadelphia.* 1865. 8vo. — Free Sugar. Speech ... February 5, 1857. [*Washington.* 1857.] 8vo, pp. 4. H. — Kansas — the Lecompton Constitution. Speech ... in the House ... March 20, 1858. *Washington.* 1858. 8vo, pp. 14, (1). BA. — Speech ... on Confiscation, Delivered in Congress, April 23, 1862. [*Washington.* 1862.] 8vo, pp. 4. — Speech ... on his Resolution Declaring Mr. Long, of Ohio, an Unworthy Member of the House. Delivered ... April 14, 1864. [n. p. n. d.] 8vo, pp. 8. H. — Speeches ... in Reply to Messrs. Dwin and Blair's Attacks on Gen. Fremont, in the House of Representatives, April 21, 1862. 8vo, pp. 8.

Colgan (W. J.) Poems by William James Colgan. *New-York: Leavitt, Trow, & Co.* M DCCC XLIV. 12mo, pp. vi, 112.

"The Birthday of Washington," "On the Death of Channing."

Colhouer (T. H.) Republican Methodism contrasted with Episcopal Methodism; and the policy of the Methodist Church, illustrated and defended. With an Introductory Essay by Rev. W. Reeves. *Philadelphia: Daughaday & Co.* 1868. 16mo, pp. vii, 186. C. 14346

Coligny (A. de). Essai sur les colonies francaises. *Paris.* 1839. 8vo. 14347

Title from a sale catalogue. Not mentioned in the "Bibliog. de la France" for 1839, or the neighboring years.

[Colijn (M.)] Nieuwe | Werelt, | Anders ghenaempt | West-Indien. | *t'Amsterdam,* | *By Michiel Colijn, Boeck-vercooper op 't Water* | *by de Oude Brugh, in 't Huys-Boeck.* | *Anno* 1622. | *Met Privilege.* | 3 pts., folio, 4 l., pp. 111, 17 Maps; pp. 29; 8 l., pp. 85 [98]. 5 Maps. 14348

The three parts of this collection are: 1. Herrera Novis Orbis; 2. Cevallos's Eyghentlijcke Beschryvinge Van West-Indien; 3. Spieghel der Australische Navigatie door ... Jacob le Maire.

Colijn v. Heubeldinck. Oost-Indische ende Vvest-Indische voyagien, | Namelijck | De waerachtighe beschrijvinge vande drie sevlagien, drie Jaren achtermal- | kanderen deur de Hollandtsche ende Zeelandtsche Schepen, by noorden | Noorweghen, ... Met de voyagie van Sir Françoys Draeck, ende Sir P. Haukens naer West-Indien, | ... [16 lines in title.] *Tot Amsterdam, By Michiel Colijn Boeck-Verkoeper op 't water, in't Huysboeck, aen de Kooren-marckt.* 1619. | Oblong 4to, Engraved and Printed Title, 2 l., Dedication, pp. 2, Preface, 1, (1); 10 parts, paged separately. 14349

The dedication varies in different copies, but is signed by Marten Heubeldinck, author of the collection, a bookseller of Groningen, or by Michiel Colijn, the publisher in Amsterdam. It contains the following voyages: G. de Veir, 1617; C. Houtman, 1617; J. Cz. Van Neck, 1619; J. Van Spilbergen, 1617; P. de Maries, 1617; Kandish and Drake, 1617; Raleigh and Keymis, 1617; Bicker and Van Heemskerck, 1617; S. de Weert, 1617; and O. Van Noort, 1618. Colijn published the parts separately, under the above three dates, most of them being printed by J. Lz. Meyn, at Enckhorizen. The titles, at length, of all the parts will be found in Stevens' "Nuggets," No. 629.

[Colijn.] Novvs orbis | Sive | descriptio | Indiae Occi- | dentalis, | Auctore | Antonio de Herrera, | Supremo Castellæ & Indi-

arum authoritate Philippi III. | Hispaniarum Regis Historiographo. | Metaphraste C. Barlæo. | Accesserunt & aliorum Indiæ Occidentalis Descriptiones, & | Navigationis nuperæ Australis Jacobi le Maire Histo- | ria, uti & navigationum omnium per Fretum | Magellanicum succincta narratio. | *Amstelodami,* | *Apud Michaelem Colinivm Bibliopolam, ad* | *insigne Libri Domestici. Anno* M. D. C. XXII. | Cum Privilegio. | [110 fols.] 17 Maps.

For an account of this collection, *see* "Boucher de la Richardiere," VI. 309, and "Trömel," No. 80.

[Colijn (Michel).] Description | des | Indes Occidentales, | Qu'on appelle aujourdhuy | le | Novveav Monde | par | Antoine de Herrera, | Grand Chroniqueur des Indes, & Chroniqueur de Castille: | Translatee d'Espagnol en François. | A la quelle sont adjoustees | Quelques autres Descriptions des mesmes pays, | Avec | La Navigation du vaillant Capitaine de Mer Jaques le Maire, | & de plusieurs autres. | Le contenu de cest œuvre se veoit en la page suyvante. | *A Amsterdam,* | *Chez Michel Colin Libraire, demeurant au Livre* | *Domestique. Anno* M. D. C. XXII. | Avec Privilege. | Folio, 4 l., pp. 254. Portrait and 17 Maps.

See Ternaux, No. 447. This collection was edited by the publisher, Michel Colin. Again, according to Camus, p. 162, "*A Amsterdam, chez Emmanuel Colin de Thovoyon,* and "*à Paris ches Michel Joly.* 1622." Folio.

Colijn. Eyghentlijcke Beschryvinghe | Van | West-Indien: | Hoe die Landen en Provintien ghe- | leghen zijn, op wat maniere datmen die door reysen sal: | Ende wat Rijckdommen van gout en silver elcke | plaetse begriipt: Ghedaen | Van | Pedro Ordonnez, de Cevallos, | Priester. | Die de Landen met groote neersticheyt doorreyst en besichticht heeft. | [Vignette.] *Tot Amsterdam,* | *By Michiel Colijn, Boeckverkooper op't Water, in't Huys-boeck.* | *Anno* 1621. | Folio, pp. 29. 14352

Colijn. Spieghel | der | Avstralische | Navigatie, | Door den | Wijt vermaerden ende cloeck- | moedighen Zee-Heldt, | Iacob le Maire, | President ende Overste over de tvvee Schepen, d'Eendracht | ende Hoorn, uytghevaren den 14. Iunij 1615. | *t'Amsterdam,* | *By Michiel Colijn, Boeck-vercooper op't Water* | *by de Oude Brugh, in't Huys-Boeck.* | *Anno* 1622. | Folio, 8 l., pp. 70, 13 l. 3 Maps and 3 Plates. 14353

This and the two preceding pieces are usually bound together. *See* Trömel, No. 88.

Colima. Ensayo estadistico sobre el territorio de Colima. *México.* 1849. 4to. 14354

Colin (A.) Histoire des Drogues, Espiceries et de certains Médicamens simples, qui naissent és Indes & en l'Amerique, divisée en deux parties, par Antoine Colin. *Lyon.* 1612. + *Lyon: Iean Pillahotte.* 1619. 14355

We have given the title of this under Clusius, where it properly belongs; but, at that time, we had not the collation, which is now added: 3 pts., 8vo, pp. 7, 369, 14; pp. 102, 6; 262, 6. J.C.B. *See* Acosta (C.), [Clusius], No. 13801, Monardes (N.), and Garcia (ab Orto).

Colin (A. F.) Manual do empregado de fazenda. Collecсao dos actos legislativos e executivos, expedidos pelo ministerios da fazenda em 1865. Por Agusto Frederico Colin. Tomo I. *Rio de Janeiro.* 1866. pp. viii, 200. 14356

Published annually. Vol. VI. in 1870.

Colina y Rubio. Segunda Carta Pastoral sobre Jubileo del D. Carlos Maria Colina y Rubio, dignisimo Obispo de Chiapa *Mejico,* 1854. 4to. 14357

Colina (R. de la). Mexico en 1863, por Rafael de la Colina. *Puebla.* 1863. 8vo. Portrait. 14358

Colla (Luigi). Plantae rariores in regionibus Chilensibus a ... Bertero nuper detectae. *Augustæ Taurin.* 1832–36. 4to. 75 Plates. 14359

Collamer (Jacob). Kansas Affairs in the Senate. Minority Report of the Senate Committee on Territories. Made March 12, 1856, by Judge Collamer, of Vermont. [*Washington.* 1856.] 8vo, pp. 15. BA. 14360

Also: In the Senate ... . February 18, 1858. ... Mr. Collamer, from the Committee on Territories, submitted the Following as the Views of the Minority On the Constitution of Kansas, adopted by the Convention which met at Lecompton ... 4th of September, 1857. [*Washington.* 1857.] 8vo, pp. 7. H. — Speech ... on Wool and Woolens. Delivered before the House ... April 29, 1844. [*Washington.* 1844.] 8vo, pp. 16. BA., H. — Speech ... the Constitutional Validity of the Act of Congress requiring the Election of Representatives to be by Districts. *Washington.* 1844. 8vo, pp. 13. — Speech ... on the Annexation of Texas; ... Jan. 23, 1845. *Washington.* [n. d.] 8vo, pp. 16. — Speech ... on the Tariff in June 26, 1846. *Washington.* 1846. 8vo, pp. 16. — Speech ... on Affairs in Kansas. ... In the Senate ... April 3 and 4, 1856. *Washington.* 1856. 8vo, pp. 29. BA. — Speech ... in the House of Representatives, on the Mexican War. *Washington.* 1848. 8vo. — Speech ... on the President's Message, United-States Senate, Dec. 9, 1856. 8vo, pp. 16. — Speech ... on the Acquisition of Cuba; delivered in the Senate ... February 21, 1859. *Washington.* 1859. 8vo, pp. 21. H. — Speech ... on Slavery in the Territories. Delivered in the Senate ... March 8, 1860. [*Washington.* 1860.] 8vo, pp. 24. H. — Speech ... on the Treasury Note Bill, in the Senate, February 12, 1862. 8vo, pp. 15. — On the Reconstruction of the Seceded States. Speech ... made in the Senate ... 6th ... of February, 1865. *Washington* 1865. 8vo, pp. 8. H.

Colleccão de livros ineditos da historia portugueza, publicados por ordem da Academia real das sciencias. *Lisboa.* 1790–1824. 5 vols., folio. 14361

Includes documents relative to Brazil and other Portuguese colonies in America.

Colleçao de Noticias para a historia e geografia das naçoes ultramarinas, que vivem nos dominios portuguezes, ou shes eao visinhas. Publicada pela Academia real dos sciencias. *Lisboa.* 1812–1841. 7 vols., 4to, pp. viii, 178, viii, 118; xvi, 396; 436, 144; x, 274, (6), 120; 312, 6 Tables; 33, (2), 553.

For a list of the contents of this valuable work, *see* Leclerc, No. 357, and Silva, Vol. II., p. 87. Chiefly relates to Brazil, including translations of the voyages of Cadamosto, Pedro de Cintra, Raymond de la Torre, Pedro Alvares Caal, Cartas de Americo Vespucio, and other pieces.

Collecçao de Opusculos reimpressos relativos á historia das navegações, viagens, e conquistas dos Portuguezes. Publicada pela academia real das sciencias. Tomo. I. *Lisboa: Na Typographia de la Academia* ... 1844. Sm. 4to, pp. xii, 139, 4 l. Continued. I

Contents: Vol. I. Relaçam dos trabalhos de Fernando de Souto no descobrimento da Frolida, pp. 148; Vol. II. Cousas de C. da Gama nos reynos do Preste Joao, pp. 96; Vol. III. Maghalhaes de Gandavo, Historia do Brasil, pp. xx, 68. The first volume is a reprint of one of the rarest of books, first printed at Evora, 1557.

Collecçao de vocabulos e frases usados na Provincia de S. Pedro de Rio Grande do Sul no Brazil. *London: N. Trübner & Co.* 1856. 16mo, pp. 32. 14364

Colleccaõ dos Breves Pontificios e Leyes Regias, que foraõ expedidos, e publicadas desde o anno de 1741, sobre a liberdade das Pessoas, Bens e Commercio dos Indios de Brasil; dos excessos que naquelle estado obraram os Regulares da Companhia denominada de Jesu; das Reprezentaçoens que Sua Magestade Fidelissima fez a Santa Séde Apostolica, sobre este materia até a expediçaõ do Breve que ordenon a Reforma dos sobredidos Regulares; dos procedimentos que com elles praticou o Eminentissimo, e Revº. Reformador; dos absurdos em que se precipitaraõ os mesmos Regulares com o estimulo da sobredita Reforma ate o horroroso insulto de 3 de Setembro de 1758; das sentenças que sobre elle se proferiraõ; das Ordens Reaes, que depois da mesme Sentenca se publicaraõ; das Relaçoens que a Filial veneraçañ de el Rey Fidelissimo fez ao Papa de tudo o que havia ordenado sobre o mismo insulto, e suas consequencias; e da participaçam que o mesmo monarca fez ao Eminentissimo, e Revmo. Cardeal Reformador, e mais Prelados

Diocesanos destes Reinos, das ultimas, e finaes Resoluções que havia tomado para expulsar dos seus Reinos, e Dominios o ditos Regulares. *Impressa na Secretaria de Estado por especial Ordem de Sua Magestade.* [*Lisboa.* 1759.] 4to, Nos. i to xxi separately paged, and supplement. A. 14365

Relates principally to the expulsion of the Jesuits from Portugal and the Portuguese possessions. A small edition only was printed, *see* Backer. In J. R. Smith's catalogue, No. 655, an edition is quoted, "*Ulyssipone.* 1755," which is the same work.

Colleccion de los viajes. *See* Navarette, *also* Coleccion.

Collectio in unum corpus librorum, in lucem editorum a nundinis Francofurtensibus anni 1568 usque ad annum 1592. *Francofurti a. M.* 1592. 4to. 14366

This catalogue contains interesting details of books relating to America.

Collectio maxima Conciliorum omnium Hispaniæ et Novi Orbis, epistolarumque decretalium celebriorum, necnon plurium monumentorum veterum ad illam spectantium. Cum notis et dissertationibus illustrata, cura J. S. de Aguirre. Editio altera in sex tomos distributa, et novis additionibus aucta. Auct. Josepho Catalano. *Romæ, Ant. Fulgonii.* 1753–55. 6 vols., folio, pp. xl, 358; xxiv, 495; xii, 475; xii, 476; xii, 530; xvi, 487.

"Collection très-importante, devenue très-rare. Le Vol. vi. contient la relation du premier concile de Lima, suivie des synodes diocésains donnés par D. Toribio. A. 1582 (pp. 27–71). Le concile mexicain, tenu en 1585 suivi des synodes iii.–vi., de Lima (pp. 79–222). La relation du IIe concile de Lima, tenu en 1591, suivie des synodes vii.–viii. de ce diocèse (pp. 395–440). La relation du IIIe concile (1601) de Lima et les synodes ix.–x. de ce diocèse (pp. 477–487. L'ouvrage du cardinal de Aguirre a été imprimé à Rome en 1693–94, 4 vol. in-fol. L'édition de 1753–55, qui en est la seconde, a été publiée par les soins du savant Jos. Catalani. Elle est beaucoup plus complète que la première." — Leclerc, No. 29.

La Collection Géographique crée à la Bibliothèque Royale. *Paris.* 1848. pp. 104. 14368

A Collection of Accurate Hydrographic Plans, on a large scale, of the principal Ports, Bays, Roads, and Harbours, in the West-Indies; namely, those of the Spanish Main and Florida, of the Islands of Jamaica, Hayti, Cuba and Porto-Rico; etc. *London.* 1810. Folio. 21 Maps. 14369

Collection of Acts of Parliament, and Clauses of Acts of Parliament, relative to those Protestant Dissenters, who are usually called by the name of Quakers, from the Year 1688. *London: Luke Hinde.* 1757. 4to. 14370

Contains the acts for encouraging the growth of coffee in his majesty's plantations in America; for the recovery of debts in his majesty's plantations and colonies in America, etc.

Collection of all the Treaties of Peace, Alliance, and Commerce, between Great-Britain and other Powers, from the Revolution of 1688 to the Present Time. *London: J. Almon.* 1772. 2 vols., 8vo. + *London.* 1782. 2 vols., 8vo. 14371

Contents: The Assent for allowing the Subjects of England the Liberty of Importing Negroes into Spanish America, and for obliging them to supply the Spanish West Indies with Blacks; Treaty of Alliance and Commerce between Great Britain and the Cherokee Nation; Spanish Declaration relative to Falkland's Island, etc.

A Collection of all the Treaties of Peace, Alliance and Commerce, between Great Britain and other Powers, from the Treaty signed at Munster, in 1648, to the Treaties signed at Paris in 1783. To which is prefixed A Discourse on the Conduct of the Government of Great Britain in Respect to Neutral Nations; By the Right Hon. Charles Jenkinson. In Three Volumes. *London: J. Debrett.* 1785. 3 vols., 8vo, pp. xlviii, vii, 399; 413; 434. 14372

A Collection of College Words. *See* [Hall (B. H.)]

Collection of Curious Observations. *See* [Lambert (C. F.), *Abbé*].

A Collection of Devotional Tracts, viz. An Extract of the Spirit of Prayer. By W. Law, A.M. A Discourse of Mistakes concerning Religion, &c. By Thomas Hartley, A.M. Christ's Spirit, a Christian Strength. By William Dell. The Stumbling Stone. By William Dell. The Doctrine of Baptism. By William Dell. The Trial of Spirits. By William Dell. The Liberty of Flesh and Spirit distinguished. By J. Rutty. Observations on Enslaving, Importing, and Purchasing of Negroes, &c. The Uncertainty of a Death-bed Repentance. Small 8vo, Title, pp. 47, 168, 43, 55, 64, 16. 14373

This collection consists of six tracts, printed in 1759 and 1760; four by Franklin, at Philadelphia, and two by Christopher Sower, at Germantown, all but two separately paged, and each described in this Dictionary under their author's name.

A Collection of Documents on Spitzbergen & Greenland, comprising a Translation from F. Martens' Voyage to Spitzbergen; a Translation from Isaac de la Peyrère's Histoire du Groenland: and [Edward Pelham's] Gods Power and Providence in the Preservation of Eight Men in Greenland Nine Moneths and Twelve Dayes. Edited by Adam White ... *London: printed for the Hakluyt Society.* M.DCCC.LV. 8vo, 3 l., pp. xvi, 288. Plates and Map. BA. 14374

Collection of Essays on the Subject of Episcopacy which originally appeared in the Albany Centinel, and ascribed princi-

pally to the Rev. Dr. Linn, Rev. Mr. Beasley, and Thomas Y. How, with Notes and Remarks. *New-York.* 1806. 8vo. s.

Collection of Interesting and Important Reports. *See* [Atcheson], Vol. i., No. 2264.

Collection of Interesting, Authentic Papers. *See* Almon (J.), Vol. i., No. 951.

A Collection of Interesting Biography; containing the Life of S. Johnson, LL.D., Mr. Clives, and Captain Cook. *Dublin.* 1792. 12mo. P. 14376

A Collection of Letters on Freemasonry. *See* [Spencer (J. C.)]

A Collection of Memorials concerning divers deceased Ministers and others of the People called Quakers, in Pennsylvania, New-Jersey, and Parts Adjacent, from nearly the First Settlement thereof to the Year 1787. With some of the last Expressions and Exhortations of many of them. *Philadelphia: Printed by Joseph Crukshank, in Market-Street, between Second and Third-Streets.* MDCCLXXXVII. 8vo, pp. vii, 439. + *London: Reprinted for J. Phillips.* MDCCLXXXVIII. 8vo, pp, 3, 408. + *York: Alexander and Son.* 1824. 8vo, pp. 351. 14377

Collection of Modern ... Voyages. *See* [Phillips (*Sir* R.)]

Collection of Original Papers. *See* [Hutchinson (Thos.)]

Collection of Papers containing Declaration of Independence; Treaty of Alliance between France and the United States, 1778; Treaty between France and the United States of America, 16th July, 1782; Treaty between the States General of the United Netherlands and the United States of America, 8th October, 1782; Decree of the Queen of Portugal for a Commercial Intercourse, 13th February, 1783, etc. With General Washington's Circular Letter, June 11, 1783. *New York.* [1784.] 8vo, pp. 96. N. 14378

A Collection of Papers, relative to Half-Pay and Commutation of Half-Pay, granted by Congress to Officers of the Army. Compiled by Permission of His Excellency General Washington, from the Original Papers in his Possession. *Fish-kill: Printed by Samuel Loudon.* M.DCC.LXXXIII. 8vo, pp. 36. + *Boston.* 1783. 4to, pp. 24. N. 14379

A full and most interesting account of the troubles on this subject in the year 1783, including the Newburgh letters, and other important documents. Samuel Loudon, the printer of the first edition, being a warm whig, had removed his press to Fishkill from New York. He seems to have been well thought of by the higher officers of the army.

A Collection of Papers. *See* Burnet (G.), Vol. iii., No. 9372.

The seventh collection contains: "Some queries concerning Liberty of Conscience, Directed to William Pen and Henry Care," pp. 27–33, and "Three Considerations proposed to Mr. William Pen, concerning the Validity and Security of his new Magna Charta for Liberty of Conscience, by a Baptist ... ," pp. 33–36.

Collection of Papers, That have been published at Different Times, relating to the Proceedings of His Majesty's Commissioners, &c. &c. ... to treat ... of quieting the Disorders ... *New-York: Printed by James Rivington, Printer to the King's most Excellent Majesty.* M.DCC.LXXVIII. 8vo, Title, pp. 55, (19). BA. Proposed Appendix ... By a Well-wisher to the Prosperity both of Great Britain and North America. 8vo, pp. 8. BA.

A Collection of Poems. By several Hands. *Boston: Printed and sold by B. Green and Company, at their Printing-House in Newbury-street; and D. Gookin in Cornhil.* 1744. 8vo, pp. 55.

A Collection of Poems. *Worcester.* 1793. 12mo. W. 14382

A Collection of Poems, on Religious and Moral Subjects. Extracted from the most celebrated authors. *Elizabethtown: S. Kollock.* 1797. 16mo, 2 l., pp. 124. 14383

A Collection of Public Acts and Papers, relating to the principles of the armed Neutrality, brought forward in the Years 1780 and 1781. *London.* 1801. 8vo. P. 14384

A Collection of Scarce and Interesting Tracts, written by Persons of Eminence, upon the most Important, Political, and Commercial Subjects during the Years 1763, ... 1770. *London: J. Debrett.* 1770–MDCCLXXXVIII. 4 vols., 8vo. 14385

This is a general title only to a series of tracts relating to the American Revolution, which tracts are, in this Dictionary, described under their respective titles. *See* "M. Rev.," LXXIX. 548.

Collection of Scarce and Valuable Papers. *See* Darien.

Collection of Scarce and valuable Treatises upon Metals, Mines and Minerals. *See* Barba, Vol. i., No. 3254.

A Collection of Several Messages. *See* [Bury (Richard)], Vol. iii., No. 9515.

Collection of Songs, with Music. *New Haven.* 1786. 12mo.

One of the earliest American books of its class.

A Collection of Speeches and Writings on the Commitment of the Lord-Mayor to the Tower, &c. *Re-printed from the London Papers, and sold by John Holt, on Hunter's Quay, Rotton Row, New-York.* MDCCLXXI. 8vo, pp. 48. 14387

A Collection of State-Papers, Relative to the First Acknowledgment of the Sovereignty of the United States of America, And the Reception of their Minister Plenipotentiary, by their High Mightinesses the States General of the United Netherlands. To which is prefixed, the Political Character of John Adams, Ambassador Plenipotentiary from the States of North America, to their High Mightinesses the States General of the United Provinces of the Netherlands. By an American. Likewise, an Essay on Canon and Feudal Law, by John Adams, Esq; *London: John Fielding, John Debrett, and John Sewell.* 1782. 8vo, Half-Title, Title, pp. 100. 14388

See Vol. i., Nos. 228 and 229.

A Collection of State Papers relative to the War against France now carrying on by Great Britain and the several other European powers, containing authentic copies of Treaties, Conventions, Proclamations, Manifestos, Declarations, Memorials, Remonstrances, Official Letters, Parliamentary Papers, London Gazette Accounts of the War, &c. Many of which have never before been published in England. *London: J. Debrett.* 1794. 3 vols., 8vo, pp. iv, 344, 171, 7 l.; pp. 484, 168, 6 l.; pp. iv, 376, 48. J.C.B. 14389

"The object of the editor of this work has been to collect all State Papers illustrative of the sentiments, actions, and views of the European powers, in the present war against France, and also of the United States of America, who, though situated in another quarter of the globe, are, notwithstanding, by language, customs, and connexions, so intimately woven with the European system that their conduct is more important to it than that of many of the European states themselves." — *Introduction.*

A Collection of State Tracts, published on occasion of the late Revolution in 1688, and during the reign of William III; to which is prefixed the History of the Dutch war in 1672. *London.* 1705–07. 3 vols., folio. s. 14390

Vol. iii. includes many of the numerous tracts that were published on the much-vexed question of the Scotch Settlement and Colony at Darien, on the Isthmus of America; *also*, Proceedings in relation to Capt. Kidd's Piracies, etc.

A Collection of Sundry Publications and other Documents, in relation to the Attack made during the Late War upon the Private Armed Brig General Armstrong, of New-York, commanded by S. C. Reid, on the Night of the 26th of September,

1814, by his Britannic Majesty's ships Plantagenet, Rota, and Carnation, at the Island of Fayal. *New York.* 1833. 12mo, pp. 46. 14391

A Collection Of the most Interesting Tracts, Lately published in England and America, On the Subjects of Taxing the American Colonies, and Regulating their Trade. ... *London: Printed for J. Almon.* MDCC.LXVI. 2 vols., 8vo. B. 14392

Each tract has a title-page and separate numbering of pages, and, in this Dictionary, they are described under their respective names. Two or more volumes were afterwards published.

A Collection of the Addresses, Memorials, Petitions, and other Public Papers relating to the Company of Scotland trading to Africa and the Indies, June 1695 to Nov. 1700. *Printed in the Year* 1700. 14393

Relates to Darien.

A Collection of the Constitutions. *See* Constitution.

A Collection of the Speeches, 1796. *See* Vol. i., No. 227.

A Collection of the Statutes. *See* Post Office.

A Collection of Tracts. *See* [Annet (Peter)], Vol. i., No. 1604.

A Collection of Tracts from the Late News Papers, &c. Containing particularly The American Whig, A Whip for the American Whig, With some other Pieces, On the Subject of the Residence of Protestant Bishops in the American Colonies, and in answer to the Writers who opposed it, &c. *New-York: Printed by John Holt, at the Exchange.* 1768. 12mo, pp. 431.

Continued in a second volume, of which the title is:

A Collection of Tracts from the late Newspapers, &c. Containing particularly the American Whig, A Whip for the American Whig, the Centinel, A Kick for the Whipper, the Anatomist, with some other Pieces, On the Subject of the Residence of Protestant Bishops in the American Colonies, and in answer to the Writers who opposed it, &c. &c. Vol. ii. *New York: printed by John Holt, at the Exchange.* M,DCC,LXIX. 12mo, pp. 406, Advt., 1 .. C., P. 14395

These two volumes contain a collection of essays from the "Pennsylvania Journal," Gaines' "New York Gazette," Parker's "New York Gazette," "The Boston Gazette," and the "Connecticut Journal," published between March 14, 1768, and January 23, 1769. They relate to the political questions of the day, and to the dis-

cussion of the question of Protestant bishops in the colonies. By the "Advertisement" on the reverse of the title-page, it appears that a half-sheet of these papers was printed weekly, and served to the patrons of the "New York Thursday's Journal," without additional charge. The "Advertisement" at the end of the second volume calls upon the subscribers to pay up to enable him to "proceed with the third volume." It is a tolerably fair *resumé* of both sides of the question, which was agitated with considerable warmth. The work is very scarce. I know of the sale of one copy only.

Collection of Treaties, of Imperial Statutes, and of other Public Acts relative to Canada. 1759–1834. *Quebec.* 1834. 4to. 14396

In English and French.

A Collection of Treaties, Alliances, and Conventions, relating to the Security, Commerce, and Navigation of the British Dominions, made since ... [1714]. *London.* 1717. 4to. 14397

A Collection of Treaties of Peace and Commerce ... from the Peace of Munster to this Time ... . *London: J. Baker.* 1714. 8vo, 5 l., pp. 354. B. 14398

Treaties No. 16, 24, 26, 31, 39, 94, 99, and 100, relate to America.

A Collection of Treaties of Peace and Commerce, Manifestos, and Public Papers, from the Year 1495 to the end of the Reign of Queen Anne. *London.* 1732. 3 vols., 8vo. 14399

Contains the Assiento Treaty for the importation of Negroes by the South Sea Company. 1713, Right of the Crown of England to Hudson's Bay, &c.

A Collection of Valuable Documents, being Binney's Vindication of Abolitionists — Protest of the American A. S. Society — To the People of the United States, or, to such Americans, as value their Rights — Letter from the Executive Committee of the N. Y. A. S. Society to the Executive Committee of the Ohio State A. S. S. at Cincinnati — Outrage upon Southern Rights. *Boston: Isaac Knapp.* 1836. 12mo, pp. 80. H. 14400

A Collection of Voyages Undertaken by the Dutch East-India Company, for the Improvement of Trade and Navigation. Containing an Account of several Attempts to find out the North-East Passage, and their Discoveries in the East-Indies, and the South Seas. Together with an Historical Introduction, giving an Account of the Rise, Establishment and Progress of that Great Body. Translated into English, and Illustrated with several Charts. *London: W. Freeman.* 1703. 8vo, Title and Introduction, 16 l., pp. 336. 10 Maps. 14401

Includes Pontanus' "Dissertation on a North West Passage," and "An Account of the Five Rotterdam Ships which sailed June the 27, 1598, to the Streight of Magellan."

Collection of Voyages. *See* [Churchill], our No. 13017, Knox (J.), [Osborne (Th.)], Smollett (T.), Stevens (J.), and "Voyages."

Collections with regard to the Case of the American Loyalists. [*London?* About 1783.] Folio, pp. 7. C. 14402

Collections of ... Historical Society. *See* under the respective names of the Societies.

Collection des voyages et des découvertes des Espagnols depuis la fin du 15e siècle. *Paris.* 1828. Portraits. 14403

A College Exercise, delivered December 16, 1765. *London: J. Almon.* 1769. 8vo, pp. 22. 14404

In speaking of the colonies, the writer remarks: "They may one day constitute the greatest empire in the world; when we of this island shall be sunk into ignorance, slavery and barbarity."

College of the Holy Cross. *See* Worcester, *Mass.*

College Point, *N. Y.* Ceremony and Address at Laying Corner Stone, St. Paul's College, at College Point, Queens Co., N. Y. 1836. 14405

College Speeches. *New York: Privately Printed.* 1866. 8vo, pp. 35. 14406

The Collegian. In Six Numbers. *Cambridge: Hilliard and Brown.* MDCCCXXX. 8vo, pp. vi, 290. B. 14407

Published by the students of Harvard College.

The Collegian, i., No. 1–3. [*Cambridge.* 1866.] 4to.

No more was published.

Colleridge (J.) *See* Coleridge (J.), No. 14321.

Colles (C.) Proposal of a Design for the Promotion of the Interests of the United States of America, extending its Advantages to all Ranks and Conditions of Men by Means of Inland Navigable Communication. With a Map of Part of the State of New Jersey, pointing out the Course of an Intended Inland Navigation between New York and Philadelphia, by Christopher Colles. *New-York: Printed for the Author, by Samuel Wood.* 1808. 8vo, pp. 22. Plate. N. 14409

"Colles has the merit of projecting the great Erie Canal, while De Witt Clinton snatched away the prize, and, what is more unfortunate, claimed and obtained the honor which has been wrongfully awarded him." — W. Gowans.

Colles. Proposals for the Speedy Settlement of the Waste and Unappropriated Lands on the Western Frontiers of the State of New-York, and for the Improvement of the Inland Navigation between Albany and Oswego. By Christopher Colles. *New York: Printed by Samuel Loudon.* 1785. 8vo, pp. 14. N. 14410

See O'Reilly's "History of Rochester," p. 183.

Colles. A Survey of the Roads of the United States of America; with a large number of plates. *New York.* 1789. Sm. 4to. 74 Plates. S. 14411

This rare work is referred to in Francis' "Old New York." Also: Description of the Numerical Telegraph, etc. *Brooklyn.* 1812. 12mo, pp. 19. — Syllabus of a Course of Lectures on Natural Experimental Philosophy. By Christopher Colles. ... *Philadelphia: Printed by John Dunlap.* [About Apr. 1773.] P.

Collet (*M.*) L'isle déserte: comédie. *Paris.* 1758. 8vo.

Colley (T.) The Nature and Necessity of a Growth in Grace, under the progressive Operations of the Spirit of Truth, Scripturally demonstrated in a Sermon Preached on Third-day Morning, the 8th of the 5th Month, 1787, at a Youth's Meeting of the People called Quakers, held in Market Street, Philadelphia. By Thomas Colley. Taken in Characters. — The Second Edition. Reprinted. — The Third Edition, corrected. *Philadelphia: Printed by Joseph Crukshank, in Market Street.* 1789. 8vo. W. 14413

Colliber (S.) Columna Rostrata: or, a Critical History of the English Sea-Affairs: Wherein all the Remarkable Actions of the English Nation at Sea are described, and the most considerable Events (especially in the Account of the three Dutch Wars) are proved, either from Original Pieces, or from the Testimonies of the Best Foreign Historians. By Samuel Colliber. *London: R. Robinson.* 1727. 8vo, pp. 312, 4 l. 14414

A large part of this volume relates to affairs in America. It is unnoticed by Rich. Contents: Candish's Adventures in the South Seas: the Discoveries of Seb. Cabot; Drake's Expedition to Cadiz, &c.; Sir Richard Greenvil's Engagement; Account of the English Settlements in Newfoundland; Sir Walter Raleigh's Expedition to Guiana, &c., &c., wherein all the remarkable actions of the English nation at sea are described.

Collier (J. A.) Speech of John A. Collier ... on the United States Bank. *Binghampton.* 1832. 8vo. S. 14415

Collier (J. P.) A Biographical and Critical Account of the Rarest Books in the English Language, alphabetically arranged, which, during the Last Fifty Years, have come under the Obser-

vation of J. Payne Collier, F.S.A. *London: Joseph Lilly.* 1865. 2 vols., 8vo, pp. xii, (1), xlv*, 555; 2 l., pp. 593. BA. + *New York: David G. Francis.* 1866. 4 vols., 12mo, 2 l., pp. xiii, 327; 2 l., pp. 355; 2 l., pp. 371; 2 l., pp. 341. 14416

Hardly deserving of mention here; but there are notes of books relating to America. The note on Smith's "Relation" is erroneous. In the New York edition all the "Addenda and Corrigenda" which are prefixed to the first volume of that edition are placed in their proper positions. The "Index," also, is greatly enlarged. Of the New York edition, five copies were printed on India paper, and fifty copies on large paper.

Collier (R. L.) Moral Heroism; its Essentiality to the Crisis. A Sermon preached in Chicago, Aug. 3, 1862. By Rev. Robert Laird Collier. *Chicago: Tribune Office.* 1862. 8vo, pp. 16. 14417

Collier (R. R.) Correspondence and Remarks on Martial Law and Arrests. *Richmond.* 1863. 8vo. BA. 14418

Collier. The Right Way for Restoring the Late Rebel States to the Federal Union; or, an Argument intended to induce the People and Public Men, in making Elections and filling Offices, State and Federal, to be governed by the Constitution of the United States. Second Edition. By Robert R. Collier, Esq. *Petersburgh: A. F. Crutchfield & Co.* 1865. 8vo, pp. vi, 96. 14419

Also: [Reply] to "Substance of Remarks," by T. S. Gholson. Richmond, Va. 1847; [with] A Notice of T. S. Gholson's last Pamphlet. S.

Collier (W.) ... A Sermon ... in Lyme, Connecticut, at the Ordination of ... George W. Appleton, ... First Baptist Church ... . By William Collier ... . *Boston: printed by Hews & Goss.* 1819. 8vo, pp. 24. 14420

Collier (W. R.) An Essay on the Currency; in which is proposed the Enactment, by Congress of a General Bank Law. By William R. Collier. *Boston.* 1834. 8vo, pp. 16. H., M.

Collier. Remarks on the Protective System; being an Extract from an Address, delivered July 4, 1832. By W. R. Collier. *Andover, Mass.* 1832. 12mo, pp. 12. BA. 14422

Collin (John F.) Speech of the Hon. J. F. Collin, of New York, on the Bill Making Appropriations for Harbors and Rivers. Delivered in the House of Representatives, Thursday, March 12, 1846. *Washington: Blair and Rives.* 1846. 8vo, pp. 8. 14423

Also: Speech ... June 19, 1846. ... on the Bill ... amendatory of the Tariff Law of 1842. [*Washington.* 1846.] 8vo, pp. 8. — Speech ... in Reply to Mr. Albert Smith ... . Delivered in the House ... July 28, 1846. *Washington.* 1846. 8vo, pp. 6. H.

Collin (Nils). Förslag af några Nord-Amerikas Träd, som äro särdeles värde at i Sverige odlas. *Stockholm.* 1823. 8vo, pp. 32. 14424

Republished from the "Kongl. Vet. Ac. Handl. för år 1822."

Collings (Jesse). Outline of the American School System. *London: Simpkin & Co.* 1868. 8vo. 14425

Collings (J.) The Shepherd's Wanderings, discovered in a Re-Vindication of the Great Ordinance of God; Gospel Preachers, and Preaching, in Reply to William Sheppard's book, entitled, The People's Priviledges, &c. By John Collings, Preacher of the Gospel at Norwich, in New England. *London.* 1652. 4to. 14426

Collings. Vindiciæ Ministerii Evangelici; or Vindication of the Great Ordinance of God, By John Collings, Preacher of God's Word in Norwich in New England. *London.* 1651. 4to. 14427

Collingwood (G. L.) A Selection from the Public and Private Correspondence of Vice-Admiral Lord Collingwood; interspersed with Memoirs of his Life. By G. L. Newnham Collingwood. Third Edition. *London: James Ridgway.* M.DCCC.XVIII. 8vo, pp. xvi, 578. Portrait and Plan. BA. + *New York.* 1829. 14428

Relates in part to the Revolutionary War.

Collins (A.) Oration before St. John's Lodge, No. 2d, Middletown. By Alexander Collins. *Middletown.* 1800. 8vo, pp. 21. N. 14429

Collins (C.) A Funeral Discourse on the Death of Joseph J. Stuart ... May 30, 1858, by Rev. Charles Collins ... . *Carlisle, Pa.* 1858. 8vo, pp. 29. H. 14430

Collins (C.) Guide and Directory for Virginia City, Gold Hill, Silver City and American City, for 1864–5. Compiled by Charles Collins. *San Francisco.* 1864. 8vo, pp. 386.

Collins (D.) Narrative of the Shipwreck of the Brig Betsey, of Wiscasset, (Maine,) and Murder of Five of her Crew, by Pirates, on the Coast of Cuba, Dec. 1824. ... By Daniel Collins, One of the only Two Survivors. *Wiscasset: printed by John Dorr.* 1825. 8vo, pp. 52. BA. 14432

Collins (E. K.) Memorial of E. K. Collins & his Asso-

ciates to the Senate and House ... of the United States. [n. p. 1851.] 8vo, pp. 5. H. 14433

Also: The Collins Steamers. A Few Proofs of the Efficiency of these Ships, and Facts as proved by them, from those who know, in Reply to Reports circulated against them, July, 1854. *New-York: J. H. Burnet.* 1854. 8vo, pp. 27. H. — Ocean Mail Service. The Collins Steamers. Letter from E. K. Collins to the Post Office Committees of the Senate and House ... . *Washington.* 1857. 8vo, pp. 10. — The Supremacy of the Seas; or, Facts, Views, &c., relating to the British and American Steamers. *Washington.* 1851. 8vo, pp. 24.

Collins (E.) Memoirs of Elizabeth Collins, of Upper Evesham, New Jersey, a Minister of the Gospel of Christ in the Society of Friends. *Philadelphia.* 1833. 18mo. + *Philadelphia.* 1859. 12mo, pp. 144. H. 14434

Reprinted in Vol. II. of "The Friends' Library." *Philadelphia.* 1847.

Collins. Memories of the Southern States [1859–64.] By Elizabeth Collins. ... [An English Servant Maid]. ... *Taunton: Barnicott, Printer.* 1865. Post 8vo, 3 l., pp. 116. BA., B.

[Collins (Francis).] An Abridged View of the Alien Question Unmasked. By the Editor of the Canadian Freeman. *York. U. C.* 1826. 8vo, pp. 16. 14436

"It was not his habit to write his articles. He put them in type as he composed them." — Charles Lindsay. Quoted in Morgan's "Bib. Canad.," p. 80.

Collins (G. C.) Fifty Reasons why Henry Clay should be elected President of the United States, By George C. Collins. *Baltimore.* 1844. 12mo. 14437

Collins (I.) A List of some of the Benevolent Institutions of ... Philadelphia, and their Legal Titles, together with a Form of Devise and Bequest to them. Compiled by Isaac Collins and John S. Powell ... . *Philadelphia: Henry B. Ashmead.* 1859. 8vo, pp. 36. H. 14438

Collins. Memoir of the late Isaac Collins of Burlington, New Jersey. *Philadelphia.* 1848. 4to. P. 14439

Collins (J.) Salt|and|Fishery,|A Discourse thereof|Insisting on the following Heads.|1. The several ways of making Salt in England, and Foreign|Parts.|2. The Character and Qualities good and bad, of these several|sorts of Salt, English refin'd asserted to be much better than|any Foreign.|3. The Catching and Curing, or Salting of the most Eminent or|Staple sorts of Fish, for long or short keeping.|4. The Salting of Flesh.|5. The Cookery of Fish and Flesh.|6. Extraordinary

Experiments in preserving Butter, Flesh, Fish,|Fowl, Fruit, and Roots, fresh and sweet for long keeping.|7. The Case and Sufferings of the Saltworkers.|8. Proposals for their Relief, and for the Advancement of the|Fishery, the Wollen, Tin, and divers other Manufactures.|By John Collins, Accomptant|to the Royal Fishery Company.|E. Reg. Soc. Philomath.| *London: Printed by A. Godbid, and J. Playford, and are to be Sold by Mr. Robert Horne at the Royal Exchange, Mr. John Kersey, and Mr. Hen-|ry Faithorn, at the Rose in St. Pauls Church-yard, Mr. William Bury, Globe-|maker, at the Globe near Charing-Cross.* 1682.| 4to, 4 l., pp. 164, 2 l. 14440

Pages 93–200 relate to the Newfoundland Fishery, etc.

[Collins (John).] The Case of the Sugar Colonies. *London: Johnson.* 1792. 8vo, pp. 97. 14441

See "M. Rev.," VIII. 215.

Collins (J.) The City and Scenery of Newport, Rhode Island. In a Series of Illustrations, drawn on Stone. By John Collins. *Burlington, N. J.* 1857. Oblong folio. 14442

Collins (J. A.) The Anti-Slavery Picknick; a collection of Speeches, Poems, Dialogues, and Songs for use in Schools and Anti-Slavery Meetings. By J. A. Collins. *Boston: H. W. Williams.* 1842. 18mo, pp. 144. 14443

Collins. Right and Wrong amongst the Abolitionists of the United States. With an Introductory Letter by Harriet Martineau ... And an Appendix. By John A. Collins, Representative of the American Anti-Slavery Society, Glasgow. Second Edition. *Glasgow: Geo. Gallie.* MDCCCXLI. 8vo, pp. 76.

The first edition was published the same year in Glasgow. 8vo, pp. 74.

Collins (L.) Discourse at Funeral of Mrs. Mary Sexton. By Levi Collins ... *Hartford.* 1807. 8vo. 14445

Collins (L.) Historical Sketches of Kentucky: embracing its History, Antiquities; and Natural Curiosities, Geographical, Statistical, and Geological Descriptions; with Anecdotes of Pioneer Life, and more than One Hundred Biographical Sketches of Distinguished Pioneers, Soldiers, Statesmen, Jurists, Lawyers, Divines, etc. Illustrated by Forty Engravings. By Lewis Collins. *Maysville, Ky.: Lewis Collins. Cincinnati: J. A.*

and U. P. James. 1847. 8vo, pp. 560. Map. BA., B. + [*Ibid.*] 1848. [*Ibid.*] 1850. 14446

See "N. Am. Rev.," XXXVI. 1; LXII. 71. There are copies with the imprint, *Philadelphia.* 1847.

Collins (N. G.) Speech of the Rev. N. G. Collins to Regiments in Gen. Dodge's Division, on the Intellectual Condition of the South, compared with the North; with its Bearing upon the Present Rebellion. No. 1. *Chicago: Church & Goodman.* [n. d.] 12mo, pp. 24. + No. 2. pp. 24. 14447

Collins (R.) Essay on the Treatment and Management of Slaves. Written for the Seventh Annual Fair of the Southern Central Agricultural Society. By Robert Collins ... . *Macon, Ga.: printed by Benjamin F. Griffin.* 1852. 8vo, pp. 22. B.

Collins (Ruth). The Friendly Writer and Register of Truth, for the Eleventh Month (stiled by Pagan Rome, January) 1732. *London.* 1732. 8vo. Portrait. 14449

Includes "Tidings of Barbarous Murthers committed in New England;" "Letter from Williamsburgh in the Virginia Country," etc.

Collins (S. H.) The Emigrant's Guide to and Description of the United States of America; including Several authentic and highly important Letters from English Emigrants now in America, to their Friends in England. By S. H. Collins. Fourth Edition. *Hull: J. Noble.* [1830.] 12mo, 3 l., pp. 180. Map. 14450

Collins (S.) Miscellanies. By Stephen Collins. Second Edition. *Philadelphia.* 1845. 8vo. 14451

Collins (T. W.) Review of the Governor's Message. Speech of the Hon. Thad. W. Collins in the House of Assembly of New York, March, 1863. *Albany.* 1863. 8vo, pp. 8.

Collins (William). Speech of Hon. W. Collins ... on the Bill to establish the Territorial Government of Oregon. Delivered in the House ... July 28, 1848. *Washington.* 1848. 8vo, pp. 13. H. 14454

Collins (W. H.) Address to the People of Maryland, [December 20, 1860.] By William H. Collins. *Baltimore: James Young.* 1861. 8vo, pp. 17. + Second Address, [Feb. 23, 1861.] ... *Baltimore: James Young.* 1861. 8vo, pp. 17. + Third Address ... *Baltimore: James Young.* 1861. 8vo, pp. 24. + Second Edition. [*Ibid.*] 1861. 8vo, pp. 24. C. 14455

Collinson (P.) Tribute to the Memory of Peter Collinson. ... *Philadelphia: William H. Mitchell.* 1851. 8vo, pp. 37. Portrait. 14456

Several articles by Collinson on American topics are included in the "Gentleman's Magazine," 1751–56, 63, and 66. *See* [Fothergill (John)].

Collis (Charles H. T.) Case of F. F. Cavada. [*Philadelphia.* 1866.] 8vo, pp. 14. H. 14457

Collot (A. G.) Choix d'anecdotes ou faits mémorables, saillies et bons-mots, tires De la Vie des Hommes Illustres, de l'Histoire de Napoléon, de la Révolution d'Amérique, &c. ... Par A. G. Collot. *Philadelphia: Grigg & Elliot.* 1832. 12mo, pp. 162. H. 14458

Collot (G. H. V.) Précis des Evénémens qui se sont passés à la Guadaloupe pendant l'administration de George Henry Victor Collot, depuis le 20 Mars 1793, jusqu'à 22 Avril, 1794. Presenté à la Convention Nationale. *Philadelphia: Bradford.* 1795. 4to, pp. 50. 14459

Collot. Voyage dans l'Amérique septentrionale, ou description des pays arrosés par le Missisipi, l'Ohio, le Missouri et autres rivières affluentes; observations exactes sur le cours et les sondes de ces rivières; sur les villes, villages hameaux et fermes de cette partie du Nouveau-Monde; suivi de remarques philosophiques, politiques, militaires et commerciales; et d'un projet de ligues frontières et de limites générales. Avec un atlas de 36 cartes, plans, vues et figures. Par feu le Général Collot ... . *Paris: Arthus Bertrand.* 1826. 2 vols., 8vo, Atlas in 4to, Title, pp. iv, viij, 416; Title, pp. 427, 36 l. Maps and Plates. C., H. 14460

"This work was printed both in French and English, but not published, at the time of General Collot's death, which happened in 1805. More than twenty years afterwards, the whole impression came into the hands of M. Bertrand, an eminent publisher in Paris, who reserved one hundred copies of the English and three hundred of the French edition, and made waste paper of the remainder. The translation was made by an English gentleman, under the eyes of the general himself. The journey was undertaken in 1796, at the request of Adet, minister from France to the United States, for the purpose of obtaining 'a minute detail of the political, commercial and military state of the western part of that continent.' An appendix is referred to, but appears to have been printed only in the French edition. It relates to the general's dispute with the Spanish Governor of Louisiana. The maps and plates are beautifully engraved by Tardieu. A few copies were printed on large vellum paper." — Rich. The following is the English title:

Collot. A Journey in North America, containing a Survey of the Countries watered by the Mississippi, Ohio, Mis-

souri, and other Affluing Rivers; with Exact Observations on the Course and Soundings of these Rivers; and on the Towns, Villages, Hamlets, and Farms of that Part of the New World; followed by Philosophical, Political, Military and Commercial Remarks, and by a Projected Line of Frontiers and General Limits. Illustrated by an Atlas of 36 Maps, etc. By Gen. V. Callot. late in the French Service, and Governor of Guadeloupe. *Paris: Arthus Bertrand.* 1826. 2 vols., rl. 4to, pp. 310; 372. Atlas of 36 Maps and Plates. 14461

Collot. Compte rendu de son administration de Saint-Domingue 14462

Collot. Mémoire sur les moyens de soumettre les rebelles de Saint-Domingue 14463

These two imperfect titles are taken from Quérard.

Collyer (I. J. P.) Review of Rev. W. W. Ells' Thanksgiving Sermon, delivered in ... Newburyport, Dec. 29, 1850. By Rev. Isaac J. P. Collyer, ... *Newburyport: Charles Whipple. January,* 1851. 8vo, pp. 20. H. 14464

Collyer (R.) A Man in Earnest: Life of A. H. Conant. By R. Collyer. *Boston: H. B. Fuller.* 1868. 16mo, pp. 230.

Collyer. Some Account of the Chicago Ministry-at-Large, from its Foundation to the Present Time. By Robert Collyer. *Chicago: A. A. Cowdery.* 1860. 8vo, pp. 8. H. 14466

Also: A Letter to a Sick Soldier. ... *Boston.* 12mo, pp. 14. + Sermon, March 9, 1862. B.

Collyer (R. H.) Lights and Shadows of American Life. By Robert H. Collyer ... *Boston: Redding & Co., etc.* [1844?] 8vo, pp. 40. 14467

Colman (B.) A Blameless & Inoffensive Life, a Sermon after the Funeral of David Stoddard. By Benjamin Colman ... . *Boston.* 1723. 8vo, pp. (6), 34. B., W. 14468

Colman. A brief Enquiry Into the Reasons Why the People of God have been wont to bring into their Penitential Confessions, the Sins of their Fathers and Ancestors ... Preached on a Day of Prayer and Fasting, March 22. 1716. By Benjamin Colman. *Boston: Printed by T. Fleet and T. Crump, for Samuel Gerrish.* 1716. 12mo, pp. 32. BA. 14469

See Bancroft's "United States," III. 322.

COLMAN. The Blessing of Zebulun & Issachar. A Sermon ... before the ... General Court ... November 19. 1719. By Benjamin Colman. *Boston: Samuel Gerrish.* 1719. 8vo, 2 l., pp. 30. B., H. 14470

COLMAN. Christ standing for an Ensign of the People. A Sermon preached to the Honourable and Ancient Artillery Company in Boston, June 5. 1738. ... By Benjamin Colman, D.D. ... *Boston: J. Edwards and S. Elliot.* 1738. 8vo, Title, pp. 33.

COLMAN. The Credibility of the Christian Doctrine of the Resurrection. A Sermon Preached (in part) ... July 24th 1729. ... after the Funeral of William Welsteed, Esq; By Benjamin Colman ... *Boston: Printed for Thomas Hancock.* 1729. 8vo, 3 l., pp. 32. BA., H. 14472

COLMAN. David's dying Charge to the Rulers and People of Israel. A Sermon Preached ... May 29th. 1723. Being the Day for the Annual Election of his Majesty's Council. By Benjamin Colman. ... . *Boston: Printed by B. Green.* 1723. 12mo, 5 l., pp. 41. BA. 14473

COLMAN. Death and the Grave without any Order. A Sermon Preached July 7. 1728. Being the Lords-Day after a tragical Duel and most lamented Death. By Benjamin Colman. ... *Boston, in New England: Printed for John Phillips & Thomas Hancock.* 1728. 8vo, 2 l., pp. 19. B., BA., H. 14474

Henry Phillips killed Benjamin Woodbridge.

COLMAN. A Devout and Humble Enquiry Into the Reasons of ... the Death of Good Men. Meditated on the Death of ... the Reverend Mr. Thomas Bridge ... . By Benjamin Colman, A.M. *Boston: Samuel Gerrish, Daniel Henchman, and Benjamin Gray.* 1715. 12mo, pp. 36. 14475

COLMAN. A Devout Contemplation On the Meaning of Divine Providence, in the Early Death Of Pious and Lovely Children. Preached upon the Sudden and Lamented Death of Mrs. Elizabeth Wainwright. Who Departed this Life, April the 8th. 1714. Having just completed the Fourteenth Year of Her Age. By Benjamin Colman, Pastor to a Church in Boston. *Boston: Printed by John Allen, for Joanna Perry, at her Shop on the North-side of the Town-House.* 1714. Sm. 8vo, Title, pp. vi, 28. 14476

COLMAN. A Discourse Had in the College-Hall At Cambridge, March 27. 1722. Before the Baptism of R. Judah Monis. By Benj. Colman, V.D.M. To which are added Three Discourses Written by Mr. Monis himself, The Truth, The Whole Truth, and, Nothing but the Truth. ... [With a Preface by Increase Mather]. *Boston: Printed for Daniel Henchman.* 1722. 4 vols., 8vo, 3 l., pp. 27; (2), iv, vi, 36; 1 l., pp. 40; 1 l., pp. 26. BA. 14477

Each of the four discourses has a title-page and a separate paging. For the others, see Monis (J.)

COLMAN. Dr. Colman's Return in Compliance with Mr. Sergeant's Request. *Boston. August* 22. 1743. 14478

Occupies pages 10–16 of, and is an answer to

COLMAN. A Letter From the Revd Mr. Sergeant Of Stockbridge, to Dr. Colman Of Boston; Containing Mr. Sergeant's Proposal ... for the Education of Indian Children ... . *Boston: Printed by Rogers and Fowle, for D. Henchman.* 1743. 8vo, pp. 16. BA. 14479

COLMAN. Dying in Peace ... . A Sermon ... after the Funeral Of ... Simeon Stoddard ... . By Benjamin Colman ... . *Boston: T. Phillips.* M, DCC, XXX. 8vo, 2 l., pp. 19. H.

COLMAN. The faithful Ministers of Christ mindful of their own Death. A Sermon Preached at the Lecture in Boston; Upon the Death of the Learned and Venerable Solomon Stoddard Late Pastor of the Church of Christ in Northampton: Who departed this Life Febr. 11. 1729. Ætat 86. By Benjamin Colman. ... *Boston, New-England: Printed for D. Henchman in Cornhil, John Phillips and T. Hancock, near the Town Dock.* MDCCXXIX. 8vo, 2 l., pp. 25, (4). BA., H. 14481

COLMAN. Faithful Pastors Angels of the Churches. A Sermon Preached to the Bereaved Flock, March 4. 1739. On the Lord's-Day after the Funeral of the Reverend Mr. Peter Thacher of Boston. ... By Benjamin Colman, D.D. *Boston: Printed by J. Draper for D. Henchman and S. Eliot.* 1739. 8vo, 2 l., pp. 26. BA., H. 14482

COLMAN. The faithful Servant in the Joy of His Lord. A Funeral Sermon On the Death of ... Samuel Holden, Esq; of London: Preached ... in Boston ... Sept. 4. 1740. ... By Benjamin Colman ... . *Boston: D. Henchman.* MDCCXL. 4to, 4 l., pp. 21. BA. 14483

COLMAN. The Fast which God hath chosen. A Sermon Preached at the Lecture in Boston March 21. 1734. Preparatory to an appointed Day of Publick Fasting and Prayer. By Benjamin Colman, D.D. ... *Boston: S. Kneeland & T. Green.* MDCCXXXIV. 8vo, Title, pp. 23. BA., M. 14484

COLMAN. Fidelity to Christ And to the Protestant Succession in the Illustrious House of Hannover. A Sermon, ... after the proclaiming of King George the Second; August 9. 1727. By Benjamin Colman ... . *Boston: Printed by T. Fleet for T. Hancock.* 1727. 8vo, Title, pp. iv, 18. BA., M., W. 14485

COLMAN. The Friend of Christ, and of His People. A Sermon Preached at the Lecture in Boston, April 1. 1731. Before His Excellency the Governour, and the General Court: Upon the News of the Death of the much Honoured Thomas Hollis, Esq; The most generous and noble Patron of Learning and Religion in the Churches of New-England. By his Friend and Correspondent Benjamin Colman ... . *Boston in New-England: Printed by B. Green.* 1731. 8vo, pp. (2), iv, 29. BA. 14486

COLMAN. Government the Pillar of the Earth. A Sermon Preached ... in Boston, Before His Excellency Jonathan Belcher, Esq; Captain General and Commander in Chief, &c., August 13th 1730. By Benjamin Colman. ... *Boston, in New-England: Printed for T. Hancock.* 1730. 8vo, Title, pp. 17, (2). BA., C.

COLMAN. A Holy & Useful Life Recommended from the Happy End of it. A Sermon Preach'd upon the Death of the Honourable and truly Vertuous Isaac Addington Esqr. ... Who departed this Life, March 19. 1714, 15. ... By Benjamin Colman ... *Boston: Printed by B. Green, for Benj. Eliot.* 1715. 12mo, 2 l., pp. 30. BA. 14488

COLMAN. The Holy Walk and Glorious Translation of Blessed Enoch. A Sermon Preached at the Lecture in Boston, Two Days after the Death of the Reverend and Learned Cotton Mather D.D. & F.R.S. who departed this Life Febr. 13. 1728. Ætat. 65. By Benjamin Colman. *Boston: Printed for J. Phillips, & T. Hancock.* 1728. 8vo, Title, pp. 31, (3). BA.

COLMAN. A Holy walk with God. Funeral Sermon Preached upon the Death of The truly Vertuous and Religious Grove Hirst, Esq.; Merchant in Boston New England Who departed

this Life October 28 1717, in the Forty-third Year of his Life. To which is added, An Extract from the Private Writings of Mr. Hirst on Divers Select and Important Heads, shewing his Secret Walk before God in Truth and with a perfect heart. *Boston: B. Green.* 1717. 16mo, Title, pp. viii, (2), 136. B.

COLMAN. The Honour and Happiness of the Vertuous Woman; More especially Considered in the two Relations Of a Wife and Mother. Meditated upon the lamented Death of Mrs. Elizabeth Hirst, the Vertuous Consort of Grove Hirst, Esq; Who departed this Life, July 10. 1716. In the 35 Year of Her Age. By Benjamin Colman, Pastor of a Church of Christ in Boston. N. E. *Boston: Printed by B. Green.* 1716. 12mo, Title, pp. iii, 33. 14491

COLMAN. The Hope of the Righteous in their Death. A Sermon Preached on the Lord's-Day after the Funeral of William Harris Esq. Who departed this Life, September 22. 1721. ... By Benjamin Colman, Pastor of a Church in Boston. *Boston: Printed by S. Kneeland.* MDCCXXI. 8vo, 4 l., pp. 26. BA.

COLMAN. Industry and Diligence in the Work of Religion. A Sermon ... in Boston, After the Funerals of ... The Reverend, Mr. William Brattle, ... And the Reverend, Mr. Ebenezer Pemberton ... . By Benjamin Colman ... . *Boston: Samuel Gerrish, & Daniel Henchman.* 1717. 8vo, Title, pp. iv, 46. B.

COLMAN. It is a fearful thing to fall into the Hands of the Living God. A Sermon Preached to some miserable Pirates July 10. 1726. On the Lord's Day before their Execution. By Benjamin Colman. ... *Boston, N. E.: Printed for John Phillips and Thomas Hancock.* 1726. 8vo, Title, pp. 39. BA. 14494

COLMAN. Jesus weeping over his dead Friend, and with his Friends in their Mourning. A Sermon ... the Lord's Day after the Funeral Of the Reverend Mr. William Cooper, One of the Pastors of the Church in Brattle-Street, Boston. Who died December 13. 1743. Ætat. 50. By Dr. Colman ... . *Boston: J. Edwards.* 1744. 8vo, Title, pp. viii, 45. B., H., W. 14495

COLMAN. The Judgments of Providence in the Hand of Christ: His Voice to us in the Terrible Earthquake. And the Earth devoured by the Curse. In four Sermons. By Benjamin Colman. ... *Boston: J. Phillips, and T. Hancock.* 1727. 8vo, pp. viii, 86. BA. 14496

"The Earth devoured by the Curse" has a separate title-page.

COLMAN. A Letter From the Reverend Dr. Colman of Boston, to the Reverend Mr. Williams of Lebanon, Upon reading the Confession and Retractions of the Reverend Mr. James Davenport. *Boston: Rogers and Fowle. Aug.* 14. 1744. 8vo, pp. 8. B., H., M. 14496

COLMAN. The Lord shall Rejoice in his Works. A Sermon Preach'd at the Lecture in Boston, August 27. 1741. Before His Excellency William Shirley, Esq; Captain-General and Commander in Chief, And in the Audience Of the General Court. By Benjamin Colman, D.D. ... *Boston: Printed by J. Draper.* MDCCXLI. 8vo, pp. 26, Appendix, (2). B., BA., M.

With a congratulatory address of the "Associated Pastors" of Boston to Gov. Shirley, and his reply.

COLMAN. The Master Taken up from the Sons of the Prophets. A Sermon Preached at Cambridge Upon the Sudden Death of the Reverend & Learned John Leverett, President of Harvard College. By Benjamin Colman ... . *Boston.: Samuel Gerrish.* 1724. 8vo, Title, pp. 25. B., BA. 14499

COLMAN. The Merchandise of a People Holiness to the Lord. A Sermon, ... July 1. 1725. ... By Benjamin Colman, D.D. ... *Boston: Printed by J. Draper,* 1736. 8vo, 7 l., pp. 38.

COLMAN. Ministers and People under Special Obligations to Sanctity, Humility & Gratitude; for the Great Grace given Them in the Preached Gospel. A Sermon On a Day of Prayer, Kept by the North Church in Boston ... January 25. 173½. To implore the Divine Direction in their Election of Another Pastor. By Benjamin Colman, D.D. ... *Boston: Printed by S. Kneeland & T. Green, for S. Gerrish.* M,DCC,XXXII. 8vo, Title, pp. 20. B., BA., H. 14501

COLMAN. A | Narrative | of the | Method and Success | of | Inoculating the Small Pox | in New England, | By Mr. Benj. Colman. | With | A Reply | to | The Objections made against it | from Principles of Conscience. | In a Letter from a Minister at Boston. | To which is now prefixed | An Historical Introduction | By Daniel Neal, M.A. | *London:* | *Emanuel Matthews.* M.DCC.XXII. | 8vo, pp. 48. 14502

One of the earliest American books on the subject. The first edition was entitled: "Some Observations." *See* No. 14518.

COLMAN. One chosen of God and called to the Work of the Ministry, willingly offering Himself. A Sermon Preached at the Ordination Of the Reverend Mr. Samuel Cooper, ... May 21. 1746. By Benjamin Colman, D.D. ... *Boston: Printed by Rogers and Fowle for J. Edwards.* MDCCXLVI. 8vo, pp. 33.

COLMAN. Ossa Josephi. Or, The Bones of Joseph. Consider'd in a Sermon, Preached at the Lecture in Boston, After the Funeral Of the very Honourable and Excellent Joseph Dudley, Esq; Late Governour of His Majesty's Provinces of the Massachusetts-Bay, and New-Hampshire, in New-England. *Boston: Printed by B. Green, for Benj. Eliot.* 1720. 12mo, Title, pp. 44, iv, (3). BA., H. 14504

COLMAN. The Peaceful End of a Perfect and Upright Life ... Sermon After the Death of ... Thomas Steel, Esq; ... Who departed this Life January 8th, 1735, 6. ... By Benjamin Colman, D.D. ... *Boston: Printed by S. Kneeland and T. Green.* MDCCXXXVI. 8vo, 2 l., pp. 10. BA. 14505

COLMAN. The Piety and Duty of Rulers To Comfort and Encourage the Ministry of Christ. As it was represented in a Sermon at the Lecture in Boston, before His Excellency and the General Court, June 10th. 1708. By Benjamin Colman, M.A. Pastor of a Church in Boston. ... *Boston in N. E. Printed by B. Green: Sold by Benj. Eliot, at his Shop under the Town-house, at the Head of King Street.* 1708. Sm. 8vo, 2 l., pp. 31.

COLMAN. A Poem on Elijah's Translation, Occasion'd by the Death of the Reverend and Learned Mr. Samuel Willard, Late Pastor to a Church of Christ in Boston, and Vice-President of Harvard Colledge in Cambridge. By Mr. Colman, V.D.M. ... *Boston: Printed for Benjamin Eliot.* 1707. 18mo, Title, pp. 14. BA. 14507

COLMAN. Practical Discourses upon the Parable of the Ten Virgins. Being A serious Call and Admonition to Watchfulness and Diligence in preparing for Death and Judgment. By Benjamin Colman, M.A. Late Preacher at Bath in Somersetshire. *London: Thomas Parkhurst.* 1707. 8vo, 4 l., pp. 423. B., BA.

Also on large paper.

COLMAN. Practical Discourses on the Parable of the Ten Virgins. ... By Benjamin Colman, D.D., Pastor of the Church in Brattle-Street, Boston. The Second Edition. *Boston, N. E.: Rogers and Fowle, and J. Edwards.* MDCCXLVII. 4to, Title, pp. vi, 344 [342]. BA., H. 14509

COLMAN. Prayer to the Lord of the Harvest for the Mission of Labourers into his harvest. A Sermon preached in the Old South Meeting-house in Boston, August 9. 1727. at the Ordination Of The Reverend Ebenezer Pemberton M.A. Pastor of the Presbyterian Church in the City of New-York. By Benjamin Colman. *Boston, N. E.: Printed by Gamaliel Rogers for Daniel Henchman.* 1727. 8vo, Title, pp. 19. BA. 14510

COLMAN. The Prophet's Death Lamented and Improved, in a Sermon Preached Septem. 1. 1723. ... in Boston, on the Lords Day after the Funeral of ... Increase Mather, D.D. ... By Benjamin Colman. ... *Boston: Nath. Belknap.* 1723. 8vo, pp. 37. BA. 14511

COLMAN. The Religious Regards we owe to our Country ... . A Sermon Preached ... May 28. 1718. Being the Day for the Election of His Majesty's Council ... . By Benjamin Colman ... . *Boston: Printed by B. Green.* 1718. 8vo, 4 l., pp. 56. 14512

COLMAN. Reliquiæ Turellæ ... . Two Sermons ... at Medford, April 6. 1735. By Benjamin Colman ... after the Funeral Of His ... Daughter Mrs. Jane Turell. To which are added ... Memoirs of her Life and Death, By her Consort, ... Ebenezer Turell ... . *Boston: Printed by S. Kneeland & T. Green, for J. Edwards and H. Foster.* 1735. 8vo, 6 l., pp. 129. BA.

Prefixed, pp. vi, is "An Epistle To the Reverend Mr. Ebenezer Turrell ... By the Reverend Mr. John Adams."

COLMAN. Righteousness and Compassion the Duty and Character of Pious Rulers. A Sermon Preach'd on a Day of Private Fasting and Prayer In the Council Chamber in Boston December 10th 1736. ... By Benjamin Colman, D.D. ... *Boston: Printed by J. Draper, for D. Henchman.* 1736. 8vo, 3 l., pp. 31.

COLMAN. A Sermon Preach'd at Boston ... the 23d of August. 1716. Being the Day of Publick Thanksgiving, For the Suppression of the late Vile and Traiterous Rebellion in Great Britain. By Benjamin Colman ... . *Boston: Printed by T. Fleet and T. Crump; Sold by Samuel Gerrish.* 1716. 12mo, pp. 28. BA. 14515

COLMAN. A Sermon Preach'd at the Ordination of Mr. William Cooper, In Boston, N. E. May 23. 1716. By Benjamin Colman. With Mr. Coopers Confession of Faith, and his

Answers to the Questions proposed to him upon that Occasion. ☞ N.B. Some Paragraphs omitted in the Preaching, are here inserted in their proper places. *Boston: Printed by B. Green for Samuel Gerrish and Daniel Henchman, and Sold at their Shops near the Town-House.* 1716. 8vo, 2 l., pp. 40, (24). B., BA. 14516

"Mr. Cooper's Confession of Faith" has a separate title-page.

COLMAN. A Sermon for the Reformation of Manners. Being designed as a Suitable Exhortation To Enforce the Reading of the King's Royal Proclamation ... . By Benjamin Colman. ... . *Boston: Printed by T. Fleet and T. Crump.* 1716. 12mo, 2 l., pp. 26. BA. 14517

COLMAN. Some Observations on the New Method Of Receiving the Small-Pox by Ingrafting or Inoculating. By Mr. Colman. Containing also The Reasons, which first induc'd him to, and have since confirm'd him in, his favourable Opinion of it. *Boston: Printed by B. Green, for Samuel Gerrish.* 1721. 8vo, 2 l., pp. 16. BA. 14518

COLMAN. Souls flying to Jesus Christ pleasant and admirable to behold. A Sermon Preach'd at the Opening an Evening-Lecture, in Brattle Street, Boston, ... Oct. 21. 1740. By Dr. Colman. ... *Boston: Printed by G. Rogers and D. Fowle, for J. Edwards and S. Eliot.* 1740. 8vo, pp. 27. BA., H. 14519

Printed in London as

COLMAN. A Sermon preached to a very crowded audience at the opening an Evening Lecture in Brattle Street, Boston, Oct. 21, 1740. By Benjamin Colman ... *London.* 1741. 8vo, pp. 30. 14520

COLMAN. The Vanity of Man as Mortal. A Sermon Preach'd at the Lecture in Boston, September 4. 1746. The Morning before the Funeral Of ... Mrs. Frances Shirley ... . By Benjamin Colman ... . *Boston: Printed by Rogers and Fowle, for D. Henchman.* MDCCXLVI. 8vo, pp. 32. B., BA. 14521

COLMAN. The Wither'd Hand stretched forth at the Command of Christ, and restored. A Sermon Preached at the Lecture in Boston, May 17. 1739. By Benjamin Colman ... . *Boston: J. Edwards.* MDCCXXXIX. 8vo, Title, pp. 19. H. + *Boston: J. Edwards.* MDCCXL. 16mo, Title, 2 l., pp. 19. BA. + Second Edition. [*Ibid.*] MDCCXL. 12mo, Title, pp. 32. BA.

COLMAN. ... Two Sermons ... March 5. 1723 On a Day of Prayer ... . By Benjamin Colman and William Cooper. ... *Boston: J. Edwards.* 1723. 8vo, 2 l., pp. iv, 38, Half-Title, ii, 36. B., H. 14523

COLMAN. The Declaration Of A Number of the associated Pastors of Boston and Charles-Town relating to the Rev. Mr. James Davenport. *Boston: S. Kneeland and T. Green.* 1742. 8vo, pp. 7. B. 14524

COLMAN. On the Death Of the Reverend Benjamin Colman, D.D. Who deceased August 29. 1747. An Eclogue. Attempted by O. E. a Young Student. *Boston: Printed and sold by Rogers and Fowle in Queen Street next to the Prison.* [n. d.] 8vo, pp. 8.

Also: An Argument for, and Persuasive unto the Great and Important Duty of Family Worship ... . *Boston, N. E.: Thomas Hancock.* 1728. 8vo, 2 l., pp. 43. BA. — The Blessing and Honor of Fruitful Mothers. A Sermon ... . at the Baptism of his Daughter ... 1715.—A Brief Dissertation on the Three first Chapters of Genesis. Giving some of the Evident Signatures Of the Inspiration of God in those First Pages of the Holy Oracles. ... . *Boston: Printed by S. Kneeland and T. Green, for J. Edwards and H. Foster.* 1735. 8vo, pp. (2), 59. BA., S., W. — The Case of Satan's fiery Darts in Blasphemous Suggestions and Hellish Annoyances: ... Several Sermons, ... May 1711. and ... 1743. *Boston: Printed by Rogers and Fowle, for J. Edwards.* 1744. 8vo, pp. 95. (pp. 91–95 comprise an "Appendix," containing a letter by a clergyman not named.) BA., B. — The Death of God's Saints Precious in his Sight. A Sermon on the Death of Mrs. Jane Steel, ... January 26, 1722–23. ... 12mo, pp. 20. *Boston.* 1723. — Discourse at a public lecture in Boston, ... with a preface by Mr. Pemberton. *Boston.* 1740. 16mo. — A Dissertation on the Image of God wherein man was created. Genesis. I. 27. ... *Boston: Printea by S. Kneeland and T. Green.* MDCCXXXVI. 8vo, 7 l., pp. 47. BA. — The Doctrine and Law of the Holy Sabbath ... . In Two Sermons, ... October 15. and December 10. 1724. ... *Boston: Thomas Hancock.* 1725. 8vo, 3 l., pp. 43. B., M. — A Discourse of the Pleasure of Religious Worship, in our Publick Assemblies. A Sermon from Psalms CXXII. I. ... *Bosten.* 1717. 16mo. — Divine Compassion Magnified. A Sermon ... 1715. — The Divine Compassions New every Morning. Sermon preached March 4, 1736–37, after a Fire in Union Street. *Boston.* 1737. 8vo, pp. 20. — The Duty of Parents to Pray for their Children, And especially to ask of God for them the Spiritual Blessing. ... [n. p. n. d.] 8vo, 2 l., pp. 36. — The Duty of Young People to give their Hearts to God. Four Sermons. ... *Boston.* [1728.] 12mo. — Early Piety again Inculcated. ... A Sermon ... to a Society of Young Men, July 10. 1720. ... *Boston.* 1720. 8vo, Title, pp. 36. H. — Five Sermons on the Strong Man ... Armed. 1717. — The Glory of God in the Firmament of his Power. A Sermon Preach'd ... October 31st. 1742. ... *Boston: S. Kneeland & T. Green.* 1743. 8vo, 2 l., pp. iv, 22. BA., M. — God deals with us as rational Creatures. A Sermon, February 7. 1722, 3. ... *Boston.* 1723. 8vo, pp. (4), 23. — God is a Great King. A Sermon ... May 13. 1733. ... *Boston: Printed by S. Kneeland & T. Green, for T. Hancock.* MDCCXXXIII. 8vo, 2 l., pp. 20. BA. — A Gospel Ministry The Rich Gift of the Ascended Saviour. A Sermon August 2. 1715. ... *Boston.* 1715. 12mo, pp. (2), 48. — The Government and Improvement of Mirth, according to the Laws of Christianity, in Three Sermons on Civil and Natural Mirth, Carnal and Vicious Mirth, and Spiritual and Holy Joy, designed in particular for the Young Gentlemen of Boston, in New England ... *Boston: B. Green.* 1707. 12mo, pp. x, 170. W. — The great

Duty of Waiting on God in our Straits & Difficulties ... Sermon at Boston, April 17. 1737. ... *Boston: J. Edwards and H. Foster.* 1737. 8vo, 2 l., pp. 23. BA. — The Great God has magnified his Word to the Children of Men. A Sermon Preached at the Lecture in Boston, April 29. 1742. ... *Boston: D. Henchman.* 1742. 8vo, pp. 32. B., BA., W. — Heinous Nature of the Sin of Murder. Boston Lecture, Sept. 24, 1713, before the Execution of David Wallis. ... *Boston.* 1713. 16mo, pp. 34. — A Humble Discourse of the Incomprehensibleness of God. In Four Sermons. 1714. With a Preface by the Reverend Mr. Pemberton. *Boston: Daniel Henchman.* 1715. 8vo, pp. (2), xii, 109. + *Boston: Samuel Gerrish.* 1715. 8vo, pp. (2), xii, 109. + *Northampton.* 1804. 12mo, pp. 142. — Imprecation against the Enemies of God, Lawful and a Duty. ... Sermon at the Lecture in Boston ... . *Boston: Printed by B. Green, for Nicholas Boone.* 1787. 12mo, Title, pp. 26. BA. — It is of the Lord's Mercies that we are not consumed. Sermon at Boston, March 4, 1736–7. ... *Boston.* 1737. 8vo. — Jacob's Vow upon His Leaving his Father's House, ... 2 Sermon Had in Private, Octob. 15. 1722. ... *Boston: Printed by James Franllin* [sic]. 1722. 8vo, Title, pp. 20. BA., H. — Moses a Witness to our Lord and Saviour Jesus Christ. A Discourse had before the Baptism of R. J. Morris, at Cambridge, March 27, 1722. *Boston.* 1722. 8vo, pp. (2), i, (1), 27. — The Nature of Early Piety. ... *Boston.* 1721. — Parents and Grown Children should be together at the Lord's Table. A Sermon before the Sacrament, at the Fryday Lecture in Brattle Street, Boston. *Boston: S. Gerrish.* [1727.] 8vo, Title, pp. 22. BA. — The Rending of the Vail of the Temple at the Crucifixion. ... Sacramental Discourse had at Boston. *Boston.* 1717. 16mo, pp. 22. + Second Edition. *Boston.* 1722. 16mo. — Sermons Preached at the Lecture in Boston, from Luke XI. 21, 22. ... To which is added, A Discourse from Ps. CXXII. I. ... *Boston: S. Gerrish & D. Henchman.* 1717. 16mo. — A Sermon Preached at the Public Lecture in Boston, July 1st, 1725. ... *Boston.* 1736. 8vo, pp. 38. — Some of the Glories of our Lord, exhibited in twenty Sacramental Sermons, preached in Boston in New England. *London: Printed by S. Palmer, for Thomas Hancock, at the Bible and Three Crowns, at Boston, in New England.* 1728. 8vo, pp. 304. (Has a page of errata, printed in Boston, at the end.) — Some of the Honours that Religion Does unto the Fruitful Mothers in Israel. ... Preached Jan. 16. 1714, 15. *Boston.* 1715. 12mo, pp. (4), 22. — A Sermon ... July 22d. 1708: being The Day of the Proclamation Of the Happy Union Of the Two Kingdoms of England and Scotland. By Benjamin ... . *Boston: Benj. Eliot.* 1708. 8vo, pp. (2), 33. H. — The Unspeakable Gift of God; a right Charitable and Bountiful Spirit to the Poor and Needy Members of Jesus Christ. A Sermon. Preached at the publick Lecture in Boston, February 1. 1739. ... *Boston: Printed by J. Draper for H. Foster.* 1739. 8vo, 2 l., pp. 19. BA. — The Warning of God unto Young People. 1716.

COLMAN (George), *the Younger.* Inkle and Yarico: an Opera. *London.* [1787.] 8vo. 14526

Also in Vol. II. of "The Dramatic Works of George Colman the Younger ... . *Paris: Malpeyre.* M DCCC XXII–XXIV." 4 vols., 32mo. BA.

COLMAN (G. W.) Assassination of the President. A Discourse on the Death of Abraham Lincoln, President of the United States. Delivered at Acton, Mass., April 16th, 1865. Repeated in the Baptist Church, West Acton, June 1st, 1865. By the Rev. Geo. W. Colman, Pastor Congregational Church, Acton. *Boston: S. Chism, Printer.* 1865. 8vo, pp. 15.

Two hundred copies printed.

COLMAN (H.) A Discourse delivered before the Ancient and Honorable Artllery [*sic*] Company, in Boston, 1 June, 1818. By Henry Colman. *Boston: Printed by John Eliot.* 1818. 8vo, pp. 24. B., BA. 14528

COLMAN. A Discourse on the Proper Character of Religious Institutions, delivered at the Opening of the Independent Congregational Church, in Barton Square, Salem, Mass., Tuesday, 7 Dec., 1824. By Henry Colman. *Salem: W. & S. B. Ives.* 1825. 8vo, pp. 27, (1). + Second Edition with Notes. *Salem: W. and S. B. Ives.* 1825. 8vo, pp. 48. B. 14529

For a reply, *see* [Cornelius (Elias)].

COLMAN. An Oration delivered in Salem, July 4, 1826, at the Request of the Town, on the Completion of a Half Century since the Declaration of American Independence. By Henry Colman. ... *Salem: Printed by Warwick Palfrey. Jun.*, 1826. 8vo, pp. 28. BA. 14530

COLMAN. Remarks of Henry Colman, in Faneuil Hall, Jan. 25, 1838, on the Annexation of Texas to the United States. [*Boston.* 1838.] 24mo, pp. 12. H. 14531

COLMAN. Terms of Peace. A Sermon at the Dedication of the Church in South Orange, Mass. By Henry Colman. *Greenfield: James P. Fogg and Company.* 1834. 8vo, pp. 27.

COLMAN. A Sermon preached in Hingham and Quincy, 20th, August 1812, the day of the National Fast on Account of the War with Great Britain. By Henry Colman ... . *Boston: printed by Joshua Belcher.* 1812. 8vo, pp. 21. B. 14533

COLMAN. A Sketch of the Character of John Adams, Delivered in ... Salem, 9th July, 1826 ... with Notices of the Character of the late Mrs. Adams. By Henry Colman. ... *Salem: James R. Buffum.* 1826. 8vo, pp. 28. H. 14534

[COLMAN.] A Tribute of Respect and Friendship, to the Memory of the Rev. Samuel Cary ... . [*Boston.*] *April*, 1816. 12mo, pp. 12. H. 14535

Also: Address before the Hampshire, Franklin, and Hampden Agricultural Society; ... Greenfield, Oct. 23, 1833. ... *Greenfield, Mass.: Phelps and Ingersoll.* 1833. 8vo, pp. 28. H. — An Address delivered before the Massachusetts Agricultural Society, ... October 17th, 1821. ... *Boston: Wells and Lilly.* 1822. 8vo, pp. 17. — An Address to the Middlesex Society of Husbandmen and Manufacturers at their Annual Cattle Show. ... . *Boston: Weeks, Jordan, and Company.* 1839. 8vo, pp. 22. H. — Agri-

culture of the United States, an address delivered 14th April, 1841, before the American Institute in New York. ... . *New York, etc.* 1841. 8vo, pp. 30, (2). H. — The Christian Ministry. A Sermon, at the Ordination of ... Linus Hall Shaw ... in Athol, Mass. ... *Greenfield: T. Prince.* 1835. 8vo, pp. 25. H. — A Discourse addressed to the Plymouth and Norfolk Bible Society, at their First Annual Meeting in Hanover, 11 September, 1816. ... *Boston: John Eliot.* 1816. 8vo, pp. 20. H. — Discourse, delivered in Boston, before the Humane Society of Massachusetts, 9 June, 1812. ... *Boston: Printed by John Eliot, Jun.* 1812. 8vo, pp. 32. BA., H. — A Discourse on Pastoral Duty, addressed to the Ministers of the Bay Association, ... Aug. 12, 1822. *Boston: Cummings and Hilliard.* 1822. 8vo, pp. 25. BA. — A Discourse on the Character Proper to a Christian Society, delivered at the Opening of the Second Congregational Church in Lynn, Massachusetts, 30 April, 1823. ... *Cambridge: Hilliard and Metcalf.* 1823. 8vo, pp. 21, (1). H. — First Report on the Agriculture of Massachusetts. By Henry Colman, Commissioner ... . County of Essex. 1837. 8vo, pp. 139. 2 Plates. + Second Report ... . County of Berkshire. 1838. *Boston.* 1839. 8vo, pp. 194. + ... Third Report ... Wheat and Silk. .. *Boston.* 1840. 8vo, pp. 252, 1 l. folded. + Fourth Report ... Counties of Franklin and Middlesex. ... *Boston.* 1841. 8vo, pp. xxix, (1), 528. BA. — The Improvements of Agriculture as an Art and a Profession: An Address ... Rochester, N. Y., ... Oct. 26, 1842. *Rochester: Strong & Dawson, Printers.* 1842. 8vo, pp. 35. BA., H. — Letter to the Farmers of Massachusetts, on ... an Agricultural Survey of the State ... *Boston.* 1837. 8vo, pp. 18. — On Labor, An Address ... October, 1838. *Boston: Otis, Broaders and Company.* 1839. 8vo, pp. 23. — ... Report of the Cultivation of Spring Wheat ... 16 March, 1838. ... . *Boston: Dutton and Wentworth.* 1838. 8vo, pp. 27. H. — Order of Services at the Installation of a Pastor in the Church in Barton Square, Salem, 16th February, 1825. *Salem.* 1825. 12mo, pp. 4. — Report of the Agricultural Meeting held in Boston, Jan. 13, 1840: ... with the Remarks of Daniel Webster and Prof. Silliman. *Salem.* 1840. 8vo, pp. 36, 7. B. — A Sermon preached in Hingham, 17 December, 1817, at the Ordination of ... Daniel Kimball ... as an Evangelist. ... . *Boston: John Eliot.* 1818. 8vo, pp. 32. BA., H. — A Sermon, preached at the Installation of ... Rev. James Flint, in ... Salem. ... *Boston: Thomas B. Wait.* 1821. 8vo, pp. 24. BA., H. — A Sermon at the Dedication of the Independent Congregational Church, in Meadville, Penn., August 20, 1836, ... *Buffalo: Oliver G. Steele.* 1836. 12mo, pp. 27. H. — Sermons on various Subjects. By Henry Colman. *Boston: James W. Burditt.* 1820. 8vo, pp. 367. BA., P. — Sermons on Various Subjects, preached at the Church in Barton Square, Salem, Mass. ... *Boston: Lilly, Wait and Company.* 1833. 12mo, pp. ix, 247. H. (*See also* [Cornelius (Elias)]). — Terms of Peace. A Sermon at the Dedication of the Church in South Orange, Mass. ... Second Edition. *Greenfield: Printed by James P. Fogg.* 1834. 8vo, pp. 27. BA. — The Times. A Discourse delivered in ... Boston ... June 11, 1837. ... *Boston: Jordan & Co.* 1837. 12mo, pp. 28. B.

[COLMAN (John).] The Distressed State of the Town of Boston considered; with a Plan for a Bank. *Boston.* 1720. 16mo, pp. 10. 14536

This was answered by "A Letter from One in the Country to his Friend in Boston, containing some Remarks upon a late Pamphlet, Entituled, The Distressed State of the Town of Boston, &c. *Boston: Printed by J. Franklin for D. Henchman.* 1720." 12mo, Title, pp. 22. B., to which Colman responded in the following tract:

[COLMAN.] The Distressed State Of the Town of Boston Once more Considered. And Methods for Redress humbly proposed. With Remarks on the pretended Country-man's

Answer to the Book, Entituled, The Distressed State of the Town of Boston, &c., With a Schæme for a Bank Laid Down: And Methods for bringing in Silver Money, Proposed. By John Colman. *Boston: Benjamin Gray.* [1720.] 8vo, Title, pp. 22. BA. 14537

This, in its turn, was answered by

[COLMAN.] A Vindication of The Remarks of One in the Country upon The Distressed State of Boston, from some Exceptions made against 'em in a Letter to Mr. Colman. *Boston: Printed by S. Kneeland for D. Henchman.* 1720. 12mo, pp. 20.

COLMAR (Johann). Die Welt in einer Nuss ... . *Nürenberg.* 1730. 8vo. 14539

This "world in a nut-shell," is a sketch of universal history, and relates, in part, to America; it has numerous medallic plates.

COLMEIRO (M.) Derecho constitucional de las repúblicas hispano-americanas. Por Manuel Colmeiro ... *Madrid: A. Calleja.* 1847. 16mo, pp. 387, 1 l. + *Madrid y Santiago.* 1858. 12mo. 14540

COLMENAR (Juan Alvarez de). Annales d'Espagne et de Portugal. Contenant tout ce qui s'est passé de plus important dans ces deux Royaumes ... de même que dans les Indes Orientales et Occidentales ... Avec des cartes géographiques et figures. *Amsterdam.* 1741. 4 vols., 4to, pp. xii, 424; 288; 331; 340, 21 l. 165 Plates. S. 14541

Translated from tbe Spanish by Massuet. Also published, *Amst.* 1741. 8 vols., 12mo, with Plates. BM. I have found no trace of the Spanish original. Georgi gives "*Leide.* 1707. 5 vols., 12mo. Plates. + Augmentées. *Leide.* 1715. 5 vols., 12mo," as the date of the first editions "Delices et Annales de l'Espagne et du Portugal," but I suspect that he is in error, and that only the "Delices" were published in 1707 and 1715.

COLMENERO DE LEDESMA (Antonio). Cvrioso tratado de la natvraleza y calidad del Chocolate, ... Por ... Antonio Colmenero de Ledesma ... . *Madrid: Francisco Martinez.* 1631. 4to, 2 unnumbered, 11 numbered l. BM., H. 14542

"This work treats of the quality of cocoa, and other ingredients in making chocolate: how chocolate is made, and the different modes of using it in the Indies." — RICH, No. 197.

COLMENERO. Chocolata Inda opusculum de qualitate et natura chocolatæ. Autore Antonio Colmenero, M.D. curante Mario Aurelio Severino. *Norimbergæ.* 1644. 16mo. BM.

COLMENERO. Traité ... . Traduit en Français par René Moreau. *Paris.* 1643. 4to. BM. 14544

COLMENERO. Treatise on chocolate. Translated by Capt. James Woodworth. *London.* 1652. 12mo. BM. 14545

COLNETT (J.) A Voyage to the South Atlantic and round Cape Horn into the Pacific Ocean, for the Purpose of extending the Spermaceti Whale Fisheries, and other Objects of Commerce, by ascertaining the Ports, Bays, Harbours, and Anchoring Births, in certain Islands and Coasts in those Seas, at which the Ships of the British Merchants might be refitted. Undertaken and proposed by Captain James Colnett, of the Royal Navy, in the Ship Rattler. *London: the Author* [etc.] 1798. 4to, pp. xviii, 179. Portrait and 9 Charts. H. 14546

See "M. Rev.," XXIX. 27.

COLOGNESI (Ernesto). Dominio temporal del Papa o razones y derechos que tienen los Pontifices Romanos y los catolicos para defender el principado civil de la Santa Sede. *Mexico.* 1860. 8vo, pp. 52. 14547

COLOM (J.) Atlas of Werelts-Water-Deel en desselfs Zee-Custen. Nieulyx vermeerdert door Jacob Colom. *Amsterdam.* 1663. Folio. 23 Maps. 14548

A rare atlas of considerable interest for the early geography of America. The title here given is pasted over the following: "De vyerighe Colom, waer door de Noordsche, Oostersche en Westersche Schipvaert claer verlichtet, ende feylen en misslagen van't voorgaende Licht of Spieghel der See ... verbetert werden. *Amsterdam: Jacob Aertsz Colom.* 1669." It is apparently the same as the following:

COLOM. Nova totius Terrarum Orbis Geographica ac Hydrographica Tabula. *Amstelodami.* [1663.] Folio, Engraved Title, and 23 folded Maps. 14549

"An excessively rare marine atlas, in which are many maps of parts of America. Those of New Netherland and New York Harbor are particularly interesting." — STEVENS.

COLOM. Zee Vaerdt o voor West-Indien Brasilien ... . *Amsterdam.* 1648. 4to. 14550

Perhaps we should mention here his "Spiegel der Zee. *Amsterdam.* 1654." Folio.

COLOMBE (Ch.) *See* Colombo (C.)

COLOMBEL (*Le capitaine*). Rapport sur le Golfo-Dulce, reçu le 25 septembre 1851, de San José, capitate de la république de Costa-Rica, pour servir à la colonisation et à l'explication de la carte de cette partie de la côte du Pacifique. *Paris: Robiquet.* 1851. 8vo, 1¼ sheets. Map. 14551

COLOMBEL (Noël). Compte de l'examen public du Lucée national. *Port-au-Prince.* 1820. 8vo. 14552

COLOMBEL. Examen d'un pamphlet ayant pour titre: Essai sur les causes de la révolution et des guerres civiles d'Haïti ... . *Port-au-Prince.* 1819. 8vo. 14553

[COLOMBEL.] Réflexions sur un prétendu prodige opéré au Port-au-Prince, dans les premiers jour du mois d'août 1820, par le citoy. C. *Port-au-Prince: imp. du gouvernement.* 1820. 4to.

COLOMBIA, *South America.* Actes de la Sesiones de la Camara del Representantes del Congreso Enero, 1826. [*Bogota.*] 1826. 4to, pp. 76. Continued. 14555

Apelacion al Pueblo Colombiano, y a los demas pueblos de América. *Bogota.* 1827. 8vo, pp. 50. S. 14556

Aus Columbien an seine Freunde, von einem hannoverischen Offizier; geschrieben in dem Jahr 1820. *Leipzig: Brockhaus.* 1822. 8vo. 14557

Aviso-Elecciones, Feb. 16, 1826. *Bogota.* 1826. 14558

Breven examen del cuaderno publicado en Popayan con el titulo de "Opinion de un Granadino sobre la division de la dueda columbiana." *Bogota.* 1836. 4to, pp. 18. 14559

Censo de poblacion de la republica de Colombia correspondiente al año de 1825, que presenta el secretario de estado del despacho del interior. [n. p. n. d.] 1 page. H. 14560

Code of Laws of the Republic of Columbia: containing The Constitution and Laws sanctioned by the First General Congress in the Sittings they held from May 6th to Oct. 14th, 1821. Translated from an Official Copy ... . *London: Ridgway.* 1823. 8vo, pp. xiv, 405. C., H. 14561

No more published.

Coleccion de Certamenes presentados por los Colejios y Casas de Educacion de la Republica de Colombia. Año des 1826. *Bogota.* [1826.] 4to, pp. 21. 14562

Coleccion de Decretos expedidos por S. E. el Libertador Presidente de Colombia, desde su entrada en Bogotá por Noviembre de 1826, hasta su partida de Caracas en 5 de Julio de 1827. *Carácas.* 1828. 8vo, pp. 351, iii. 14563

Coleccion de Documentos relativos á la vida pública del Libertador de Colombia y del Perú, Simon Bolivar, para servir á la historia de la independencia del Suramérica. *Carácas.* 21 vols., 4to, I., 1826, pp. cxiv, 262; II., 1826, ii, 316; III., 1826, xxiii, 312; IV., 1826, 330; V., 1826, 335; VI., 1827, 352; VII., 1827, 353; VIII., 1827, 365; IX., 1827, 347; X., 1828, 314; XI., 1828, 320; XII., 1828, 317; XIII., 1828, 373; XIV., 1828, 317; XV., 1828, 342; XVI., 1828, vii, 339; XVII., 1829, 320; XVIII., 1829, 341; XIX., 1829, 386; XX., 1829, 371; XXI., 1829, 356; Apéndice al tomo; XXI., 1833, 248. 14564

"Complete copies of this important work are extremely scarce. 'A publication, such as no other country of South America can boast of, is the Coleccion de Documentos relativos a la vida de Simon Bolivar. *Caracas.* 1826–33. 22 vols., of which only one copy (that in the Library of Darmstadt) is to be found in Germany.' (Gervinus, Geschichte des 19. Jahrhunderts. Vol. III., p. 166.) We may add, that there is another copy belonging to the Bibliothéque de Ste. Geneviéve, of Paris; but these two copies seem to be the only ones which have hitherto reached Europe." — TRÜBNER.

Coleccion de las leyes dadas por el Congreso Constitucional de la Republica de Colombia en las sesiones de los años 1821. *Bogota.* 1822. 27 vols., 8vo. Continued. 14565

Coleccion General de los tratados públicos celebrados por Colombia y Venezuela con varias naciones de Europa y América, desde el tratado de armesticio con el ejercito español hasta el ultimamente concluido con S. M. B. sobre abolicion del trafico de esclavos. ... *Caracas: imprenta de Valentin Espinal.* 1840. 8vo, 2 l., pp. 151. 14566

Columbia; being, etc. *See* [Walker (A.)]

Colombia, comprising its History, Geography, and Topography. *Philadelphia.* 1833. 12mo. Map. 14567

Colombia constituida. Por un Español-Americano, que lo dedica al Libertador Presidente de la Republica; dado a luz por J. de Echeverria. *Paris.* 1822. Sm. 4to, pp. 19. 14568

Columbia in 1826, by an Anglo Columbian. *London.* 1828. 8vo. C. 14569

Included in Vol. XXIX. of the "Pamphleteer."

Colombia ó federacion de sus tres secciones. *Bogota.* [n. d.] 4to, pp. 28. 14570

Another edition is, *Caracas.* [n. d.] 4to, pp. 29.

Columbian State Papers, translated and published from official copies; being the Act of Installation of the Houses of Senate and Representatives; the Message of the Vice-President on the opening of Congress; a Report on the Diplomatic Relations of Colombia, &c. *London: Ridgway.* 1823. 8vo, pp. 48.

El Colombiano. Nos. 1 to 5. *London.* 1810. 8vo, pp. 52.

"A Spanish periodical, published twice a month, devoted to the affairs of South America." — Rich.

Constitucion de la República de Colombia. *Caracás.* 1822. 4to, pp. viii, 40. 14573

"This is the very rare Carácas edition of the first constitution, made by the first General Congress of Columbia in Rosario del Cuenta." — Trübner.

Constitution de la République de Colombia. *Philadelphia.* 1822. 8vo. c., p. + *Paris.* 1822. 8vo. c. 14574

De Constitutie der Republiek Colombia, met bijvoeging van het Decreet van het Congres, betrekkelijk de Aschaffing der Slavernij. Uit het Engelsch vartaald. *Amsterdam.* 1822. 8vo.

Correspondencia entre la republica de Colombia y D. Jose Villa, ministra del Peru. *Bogota.* 8vo. 14576

Correspondencia entre la secretaria de relaciones esteriores de la Republica de Colombia y el Sr. Jose Villa, que vino con el caracter de ministro plenipotenciario de la Republica del Peru. *Bogota.* 1828. Sm. 4to, pp. 167, Table. 14577

Correspondencia general del Libertador Simon Bolivar, enriquecida con la insercion de las manifiestos, mensajes, exposiciones, proclamas, etc., publicados por el heroe Columbiano, desde 1810, hasta 1830. Tomo primero. *New York.* 1865. 8vo, pp. xliii, 616. Portrait and Facsimile. + Tomo segundo. [Vide de Bolivar, second part, from 1820 till his death.] *New York.* 1866. 8vo, pp. 591. Portrait. 14578

Cuerpo de Leyes de la Republica de Colombia. Tom I. Comprende la Constitucion y Leyes sancionadas por el primero Congreso jeneral en las sesiones que celebró desde el 6 de Mayo, hasta el 14 de Octubre de 1821. *Bogota.* 1823. 4to, pp. 200. Continued. B., C. 14579

See "N. Am. Rev.," xxiii. 314.

Cuerpo de leyes de la república de Colombia, que comprende todas las leyes, decretos y resoluciones dictados por sus congresos desde el de 1821 hasta el último de 1827. *Carácas: Valentin Espinal.* 1840. 8vo, pp. xl., 592. B., C. 14580

Diario Oficial. Estados Unidos de Colombia. Ano I., II. (Mayo 1, 1864–30 Diciembre, 1865). *Bogota.* 1864. 14581

Erinneringen uit eene driejarige dienst, bij den allerverniel-endsten en moord-dadigsten oorlog in Columbia; door een Officier bij deszelfs zeemagt. Uit het Engelsch ... *Gorinchem: Jacobus Noorduyn.* MDCCCXXIX. 2 vols., 8vo, pp. xvi, 245; xi, 254. 14582

This is a translation of No. 14618.

Esposicion del secretario de guerra i marina de los Estados Unidos de Colombia, presentada al Congreso nacional de 1866. *Bogotá.* 1866. 4to, pp. 86. 14583

Esposicion de los Sentimientos de los Funcionarios Publicos, hecha para ser presentada al Libertador. *Bogota.* 1826. 4to, pp. 21. M. 14584

Esposicion de los Sentimientos de los Funcionarios Publicos, asi Nacionales como Departamentales y Municipales, presentada al Libertador. *New York: re-imp.* 1827. 8vo, pp. 26. M.

Exposicion que el Secretario de Estado del Despacho del la Guerra hace al Congreso de 1827. *Bogota.* 1827. 4to, pp. 75. Continued. 14586

Exposicion que hace el Secretario de Estado en el Despacho de Hacienda de Columbia al Congreso de 1827. *Bogota.* [1827.] 4to, pp. 59. Continued. 14587

Esposicion que el Secretario de Estado en el Despacho de Marina [Carlos Soublette] hace al Congreso de 1827. *Bogota.* [1827.] 4to, pp. 16. Continued. 14588

Esposicion del Secretario de la Guerra al Congreso, 1824. *Bogota.* 1825. 4to, pp. 15. Continued. M. 14589

Esposicion del Secretario de Marina, pres. al Congreso de 1826. *Bogota.* 1826. 4to, pp. 15. 14590

Esposicion que el Secretario de Estado del Despacho del Interior hiro al Congreso de 1824. *Bogota.* 1824. 4to, pp. 26. Continued. 14591

Esposicion que el Secretario de Estado en el despacho de relaciones esteriores de la republica de Colombia hace al Congreso de 1827. Sobre los negocios de su departamento. *Bogota.* 1827. 4to, Title, pp. 14. M. 14592

Signed José Manuel Restrepo.

Esposicion del Estado de los Departamentos de Maturin, Venezuela, Orinoco, y Zulia. [Sept. 1827.] *Bogota.* 1827. 4to, pp. xxxviii. 14593

Esposicion de Jose R. Revenga, Secretario de Estado, 1826. *Bogota.* 1826. 4to, pp. 8. 14594

Gemaelde von dem Freystaate Columbia. Nach dem Englischen. *Jena: Bran.* 1824. 8vo. 14595

Informe del secretario del tesoro i crédito nacional al congreso de 1865. *Bogotá.* 1865. 4to, pp. 72. 14596

Letters to the Contractors on the Illegality, &c., of the Colombian Loan, With Documents, etc. *London.* 1823. 8vo, pp. 39. 14597

Letters written from Colombia during a Journey from Caracas to Bogotá, and thence to Santa Martha, in 1823. *London: G. Cowie & Co.* 1824. 8vo, pp. viii, 208. Map. C. 14598

Ley y reglamentos organicos de la ensenanza publica en Colombia, acordados en el ano de 1826. *Bogota.* 4to, pp. 24. M.

Manifesto, published by the Government of Colombia, of the Reasons which it has to make War against the Government of Peru; with the Answer given to the Charges, by ... M. L. Vidaurre ... *Boston: Hiram Tupper.* 1828. 8vo, pp. 71.

In Spanish and English.

Manifiesto que hace el Gobierno de Colombia de los Fundamentos que tiene para hacer la Guerra al Gobierno del Peru, Con la Contestacion que da a los cargos el Ciudadano M. L. Vidaurre ... . *Boston: Hiram Tupper.* 8vo, pp. 71. H. 14601

Spanish and English.

Memoria de la Secretario de Estado y Relationes Esteriores leida al Primer Congreso Constitucional, 21 Abril, 1823. *Bogota.* 1823. 4to, pp. 23. B. 14602

Memoria del Secretario de Estado y del Despacho de la Guerra al Primero Congreso Constitucional de Colombia, 1823. *Bogota.* 1823. 4to, pp. 32. 14603

Memoria que el Secretario de Estado y del Despacho de Hacienda presentó al Congreso de Colombia, 1823. *Bogota.* 1823. 4to, pp. 17. 14604

Memoria que el Secretario de Estado y del Despacho del Interior, presentó al Congreso de Colombia. *Bogota.* 1823. 4to, pp. 40. M. 14605

Memoria del Secretario del Estado y del Despacho de Marina al Primero Congreso Constitucional de Colombia, 1823. *Bogota.* 1823. 4to, pp. 8. M. 14606

Memoria del secretario de hacienda i fomento de la union Colombiana dirijida al congreso nacional, 1866. *Bogotá.* 1866. 4to, pp. lii, 137. 14607

Mensaje del Libertador, Presidente de la Republica de Colombia, a la Gran Convencion, 1828. *Bogota.* 1828. 4to, pp. 10. 14608

Mensaje de Vice-Presidente de Colombia [Francisco de Paula Santander], encargado del Gobierno al Congreso de 1824. *Bogota.* 1824. 4to, pp. 16. 14609

Mensaje del Vice-Presidente de Colombia, encargado del Gobierno al Congreso de 1826. *Bogota.* 1826. 4to, pp. 13.

Mensaje del vicepresidente de Colombia encargado del gobierno al Congreso de 1827. [*Bogota.* 1827.] 4to, pp. 15, 5. B. 14611

These are signed, Francisco de Paula Santander.

Mensaje del Libertador Presidente, al Congreso Constituyente de la Republica de Colombia en 1830. *Bogota.* 1830. 4to, pp. 8. 14612

The Modern Traveller: Popular Description of Colombia. *London.* 1825. 18mo. S. 14613

Notes on Colombia. *See* [Bache (R.)], Vol. I., No. 2593.

Noticia sobre la geografia política de Colombia, proporcionada para la primera enseñanza de los niños en este importante ramo de su educacion. *Carácas.* 1830. 12mo, pp. 75, 4. 14614

Oracion fúnebre pronunciada en las solemnes exequias del Excelentisimo Señor Libertador de Colombia, del Perú y de Bolivia, el 21 de febrero del año de 1831 en la iglesia parroquial de la villa de Medellin. *Carácas.* 1832. 4to, pp. 28. 14615

Ordenanzas para el regimen, disciplina, subordinacion y servicio de la Guarda Colombiana. *Bogotá.* 1863. 4to, pp. 192.

The Present State of Colombia; containing an Account of the Principal Events of its Revolutionary War; the Expedition fitted out to assist in its Emancipation; its Constitution; Financial and Commercial Laws; Revenue Expenditure and Public Debt; Agriculture; Mines; Mining and other Associations; with a Map exhibiting its Mountains, Rivers, Departments, and Provinces. By an Officer late in the Colombian Service. *London: John Murray.* MDCCCXXVII. 8vo, pp. iv, 336. Map. H.

"One of the most intelligent and instructive works which has yet been written upon the political affairs of the South American republics." — *Monthly Review.*

Recollections of a Service of Three Years during the War-of-Extermination in the Republics of Venezuela and Colombia. By an Officer of the Colombian Navy. ... *London: Hunt and Clarke.* 1828. 2 vols., 8vo, pp. xx, 251; vii, 277. H. 14618

For a German translation, *see* No. 14582.

Reglamento e instruccion de la infanteria de linea i tiradores, para el servicio de los cuerpos de la guardia Colombiana i la milicia de los estados. *Bogotá.* 1862. 8vo, pp. 260. Plates.

Republic of Columbia: its Geography, Laws, Religion and History. Printed from the Article in the Seventh Edition of the Encyclopædia Britannica. *New York.* 1836. 32mo.

Respuesta del Jeneral Paez a la Carta Confidencial que le dirijio el V. P. de la Republica. *Bogota.* 1826. 4to. M. 14621

State of Colombia, or Reports of the Secretaries of State of the Republic of Colombia, presented to the First Constitutional Congress in the year 1823, the Thirteenth of the Republic. ... Translated from the Official Documents. *London: Treuttel and Würtz.* 1824. 8vo, pp. iv, 199. H., P. 14622

Also in French.

Statement concerning the Colombian Bonds, 11th January, 1823, with the opinions of Counsel on the Contract for the Loan, &c. *London.* 1823. 8vo, pp. 49. 14623

A Statement of Facts connected with the Columbian Loan. ... *London.* 1823. 8vo, pp. 35. 14624

Tratados que la República de Colombia ha celebrado con varias potencias. *Carácas.* 1832. 4to, pp. 149. 14625

Colombini (Francesco Maria). Querétaro triumfante en los Campos del Pueblito. Poema historico sagrado en quatro cantos, de la milagrosa imagen de N. S. del Pueblito. *Mexico.* 1801. 4to, 5 l., pp. 108. Plate. 14626

Colombo: Melodramma Serio in due atti. *Genoa.* [n. d.] 8vo, pp. 75. 14627

Colombo (Cristoforo), *the Discoverer of America; born in Genoa*, 1435, *died in* 1506.

Mr. Harrisse, in his "Notes on Columbus," and his "Bibliotheca Americana Vetustissima," has discussed the bibliography of Columbus and his writings at so much length, and with so much industry, that we shall content ourselves, generally, with a reprint of the titles he has given; submitting them, however, to the revision of those American collectors who are so fortunate as to possess the works described. Mr. R. H. Major's "Bibliography" prefixed to the second edition of the Select Letters of Columbus has also been used. His titles differ slightly from Harrisse's. We need scarcely remark that these letters of Columbus are all of the highest degree of rarity, and will range in value from $250 each to any amount which the competition of any two wealthy collectors would realize.

Colombo. Epistola Christofori Colom: cui *a*etas nostra multū debet: de|Insulis Indi*a*e supra Gangem nuper inuentis. Ad quas perqui-|rendas octauo antea mense auspicijs & *a*ere inuictissimi Fernan-|di Hispaniarum Regis missus fuerat: ad Magnificum dñm Ra|phaelem Sanxis: eiusdem serenissimi Regis Tesaurariū missa:|quam nobilis ac litteratus vir Aliander de Cosco ab Hispano|ideomate in latinum conuertit: tertio kal's Maij. M.cccc.xciij.|Pontificatus Alexandri Sexti Anno Primo.| Sm. 4to. 14628

Four leaves, containing thirty-four lines in a full page, without date or place. This celebrated letter of Columbus is the first printed document relative to America, and appears to have been originally written in Spanish. Mr. S. L. M. Barlow possesses the only known copy in the United States. The only other copies known are in the British Museum [2 copies] and the Royal Library at Munich.

Colombo. De Insulis Inuentis | Epistola Cristoferi Colom (cui etas nostra|multū debet: de Insulis in mari Indico nup*er*| inuētis. Ad quas perquirendas octauo antea|mense: auspicijs et ere Inuictissimi Fernandi| Hispaniarum Regis missus fuerat) ad Mag-|nificum dñm Raphaelez Sanxis: eiusdē sere-|nissimi Regis Thesaurariū missa. quam nobi|lis ac litterat⁹ vir Aliander d' Cosco: ab His-|pano ydeomate in latinū conuertit: tercio kl's | Maij. M.cccc.xciij. Pontificatus Alexandri|Sexti Anno

Primo.| Sm. 8vo, 10 leaves of 27 lines to a full page. 8 Woodcuts. L. 14629

With a portrait of Ferdinand on the recto of the tenth leaf, and coat-of-arms of Granada on the verso. Mr. Lenox possesses the only perfect copy known. Two other copies, both lacking the tenth leaf, are known, one in the British Museum, and one which is said to have been stolen from the Ambrosian Library at Milan. This edition was supposed to have been reprinted in Paris by Pilinski about 1858; but, on examination, the reprint was found to lack the first and last leaves.

Colombo. Epistola Christofori Colom: cui etas nostra multū debet: de|Insulis Indie supra Gangem nuper inuētis. Ad quas perq*ui*ren-|das octauo antea mense auspiciis & ere inuictissemor*um* Fernādi &| Helisabet Hispaniar*um* Regū missus fuerat: ad magnificum dñm|Gabrielem Sanchis eorundē serenissimor*um* Regum Tesaurariū|missa: quā nobilis ac litteratus vir Leander de Cosco ab Hispa|no idiomate in latinum cōuertit tertio kal's Maii. M.cccc.xciii|Pontificatus Alexandri Sexti Anno primo.| Sm. 4to, 4 l., 33 lines to a full page. J.C.B.

Five copies only known, two of them in the United States, and two in the British Museum.

Colombo. Epistola Christofori Colom: cui etas nostra multum debet: de|Insulis Indie supra Gangem nuper inuētis. Ad quas perquiren|das octauo antea mense auspicijs & ere inuictissimorum Fernandi |ac Helisabet Hispaniar*um* Regū missus fuerat: ad Magnificū dñm|Gabrielem Sanches: eorundem serenissimorum Regum Tesau-|rariū missa: Quā generosus ac litteratus vir Leander de Cosco ab|Hispano idiomate in latinū cōuertit: tertio Kaleñ Maij. M.cccc.|xc.iij. Pontificatus Alexandri Sexti Anno Primo.| [Colophon:] *Impressit Rome Eucharius Argenteus Anno dñi.* M.cccc xciij.| 3 unnumbered leaves and 1 blank, 40 lines to a full page. 14631

The only copies in the United States belong to Mr. Lenox and Mr. J. C. Brown. Graesse, II. 73, remarks, that the copy in the Ambrosian Library lacks, in the title, the words "supra Gangem." Mr. Harrisse doubts this.

Colombo. Epistola de insulis de|nouo repertis. *Impressa|parisius in cāpo gaillardi.*|[1493.] 4to, 4 leaves, 39 lines to a full page. 14632

The title in three large black letter lines on the recto of the first of the four leaves, the verso contains the epigram and the woodcut representing the angel appearing to the shepherds, etc. This edition is precisely the same in every respect, and from the same type as No. 14633; it has a subscription at the end, "Christoforus Colom Oceane classis Prefectus," which is omitted in the other. Mr. J. C. Brown, of Providence, possesses the only known copy. *See* [Harrisse], pp. 20, 21.

Colombo. Epistola de insulis noui | ter repertis Impressa parisius In campo gaillardi.| [Vignette. Second leaf begins] Epistola Christofori Co|lom: cui etas n*ost*ra multū debet: de In-

sulis indie supra Gangem|nuper inuentis. Ad quas per quirēdas octauo antea mense au|spicijs & ere inuictissimi Fernandi Hispaniarum Regis missus|fuerat: ad magnificū dñz Raphaelem Sanxis: eiusdē serenissi|mi Regis Tesaurariū missa: quā nobilis ac l*itte*ratus vir Aliāder|de Cosco ab Hispano ideomate in latinū conuertit: tercio kl's|Maij. M.cccc.xciij. Pōtificatus Alexādri. vi. Anno primo:|*Impressa parissius in Campo Gaillardi.*|[1493.] 4 l., 39 lines on a full page. 14633

"The title is on the recto of the first leaf over a woodcut device of the printer, Guiot Marchant, and on the verso is the usual epigram over another woodcut, representing the angel appearing to the shepherds. The title of the letter succeeds on the top of the recto of the second leaf (a ij) and the text, in black letter, fills the next three leaves. Mr. Brown possesses the only known copy in the United States. There is one in the Bodleian Library, at Oxford, another at Göttingen. Five copies have been made in facsimile, by John Harris, Sen., from the copy in the Bodleian Library. These six works represent the various known editions of the Latin translation of the letter addressed by Columbus to Raphael Sanchez on his return in 1493. Mr. Major considers that the order of publication was (our) 14630, 31, 28, 29, 32, 33." Only one of those six editions contains the name of the printer, his place of residence, and the year in which it was printed. It is our No. 14631. Another has the printer's name and residence, but no date (No. 14633); whilst a third (No. 14632) gives only the place. The other three (Nos. 14628, 14629, and 14630) are all *sine anno aut oco.* The text, with the exception of variations in the use of contracted letters, is the same for all. The titles differ. In Nos. 14628, 14629, 14632, and 14633, the name of King Ferdinand only is given; in Nos. 14630, and 14631, that of Queen Isabella is added. In Nos. 14628, 14629, 14632, and 14633, the recipient of the letter is called *Raphael;* in Nos. 14630 and 14631, he is named *Gabriel.* His family name is spelled in Nos. 14628, 14629, 14632, and 14633, *Sanxis;* in No. 14630, *Sanchis;* in No. 14631, *Sanches.* The translator is mentioned as *Aliander* in Nos. 14628, 14629, 14632, and 14633; in Nos. 14630 and 14631, as *Leander;* whilst No. 14631 adds the complimentary adjective of *generosus* where all the others have *nobilis.* No. 14629 is the only one which lacks the words "Indie supra Gangem" in the title. Nos. 14632 and 14633 were certainly printed at Paris, and No. 14631 at Rome, which is said, by Morelli, Gianorini, Bossi, and others, to be also the case with Nos. 14628, 14629, and 14630. There are no positive proofs that the latter are Roman impressions, but the probability is that they were at least published in Italy. The type used in Nos. 14628, 14629, and 14630 differ from each other in size, form, and in the employment of contractions. We suppose, therefore, that they were printed by three different printers. Frank Silber, usually called Eucharius Argenteus or Argyrios, is certainly the printer of No. 14630, Guyot Marchant or Mercator that of Nos. 14632 and 14633. Nos. 14628 and 14631 have the same type, and are, therefore, the work of one printer, who is supposed, from the great similarity found to exist between the latter and the books printed in 1493 by Stephanus Plannck, to be the work of that excellent typographer." Washington Irving, in his life of Columbus, is very eloquent in praise of the language used in this first document ever printed relative to the discovery of America, and he considers it, on the whole, as far more authentic and valuable than the subsequent works of other authors, who, for the most part, wrote of things they never saw, and who recorded as facts circumstances and deeds which were entirely fictitious, and existed only in their own imaginations. All other writers, since the discovery of these precious gems, unite in admiration and the warmest eulogiums of their merit and extraordinary rarity, and some state, "Every word of the letter should be incorporated in all future histories of America." Dr. Robertson, notwithstanding his research, was totally unacquainted with their existence.

COLOMBO. Lettre|de|Christophe Colomb|sur la|découverte du Nouveau-Monde|Publiée d'apres la rarissime version latine| conservée à la Bibliothèque impériale|Traduite en Français|Commentée et enrichie de notes puisées aux sources originales | Par Lucien de Rosny ... . *Paris: Jules Gay.* 1865.| 8vo, pp. 41, (2).

Only 125 copies privately printed, 50 on fine paper, and 1 on vellum. The last leaf contains a list of the principal editions of this celebrated letter. A reprint of our No. 14632.

COLOMBO. La lettera de llisole che ha trouato nouvamente il Re dispagna. [End:] Finita lastoria della iuẽtione del|le nuoue isole dicãnaria ĩdiane trac|te duna pistola dixposano colõbo & | pmesser Giuliano dati tradocta di la | tino ĩ uersi uulgari allaude della ce|lestiale corte & aconsolatione della|christiana religione & apghiera del magnifico caualiere messer Giouã|filippo del ignamine domestico fa|mĩliare dello illustrissimo Re dispa| gna xpianĩssimo a di. XXVI. docto|bre. 14.93. *Florentie.* BM.

The above is the title of the only edition of this curious and valuable poem known before 1847. There are 68 stanzas in *ottava rima.* The whole is reprinted in the introduction to the second edition of Major's "Select letters of Columbus." 4 l., in Roman characters, double columns. The only known copy is in the British Museum. In 1847 the Museum acquired another edition, with the following title:

COLOMBO. Questa e la hystoria della inuentiõe delle diese Isole di Cannaria In|diane extracte duna Epistola di Christofano Colombo & per messer Giu|liano Dati traducta de latino in uersi uulgari a laude e gloria della cele|stiale corte & a consolatione della christiana religiõe & apreghiera del ma|gnifico Caualier miser Giouanfilippo Deligamine domestico familia|re dello Sacratissimo Re di spagna Christianissimo a di. XXV. doctobre.| M.CCCCLXXXXIII.| [End:] Finis. *Joannes dictus Florentinus.* In Gothic characters, double columns. 14636

A complete copy should contain 4 leaves. The copy in the British Museum, the only one hitherto discovered, wants the second and third.

COLOMBO. Primera epistola del admirante Don Cristóbal Colon, dando cuenta de su gran descubrimiento, á D. Gabriel Sanchez, Tesorero de Aragon. Acompaña al texto original castellano el de la traduccion latina de Leandro de Cosco, segun la primera edicion de Roma de 1493, y precede la noticia de una nueva copia del original manuscrito, y de las antiguas ediciones del texto en latin, hecha por el editor D. Genaro H. de Volafan. *Valencia: Garin.* 1858. 4to, pp. x, 25. 14637

"Ce volume a été tiré à 100 exemplares, dont 60 ont été détruits par une inondation au Brésil. Don Pascual de Gayangos a donné un compte-rendu sur cette intéressante publication dans le journal la America, 13 avril 1867. Il n'a pas connu le nom de l'auteur qui s'est caché sous le pseudonymè D. Genaro H. de Volafan, et qui est celui de M. Adolfe de Varnhagen ministre du Brésil."

COLOMBO. Eyn schõn hũbsch lesen von etlichen inszlen|die do in kurtzen zyten funden synd durch dẽ|kũnig von hispania. vnd sagt võ groszen wun|derlichen dingen die in dẽ selbẽ inszlen synd.| [Colophon:] *Getruckt zu straszburg vff gruneck võ meister Bartlomesz | küstler ym iar:* M. CCCC. XCVij. *vff sant Jeronymus tag.*| Sm. 4to, 8 l., the last blank. Thirty lines in a full page.

The woodcut on the title-page is repeated on the last page. "Ebert and Graesse state that this curious German translation of the first Letter of Columbus has been republished in the 'Rheinisch. Archiv.,' Vol. xv, page 17, *sq.*" — HARRISSE. Stevens' "American Bibliographer," page 67, states that it contains "changes and additions." Five copies of this extremely rare tract were made by the elder Mr. Harris with such exactness, that it requires an expert to detect it from the original.

COLOMBO. Señorpor que se que aureis plazer de la grand| victoria que ntro señor me ha dado en mivyaie|vos escriuo esta por la *qua*l sabreys como ẽ xrruj|dias pase alas Indias cõla armada que losillu|strussimos Rey & reynantos señores me dieron |dondeyo falle muy muchas Islas pobladas con gẽte syn|numero. y dellas todas he comado posessiõ por sus altezas|conpregon y vãdera real estẽdida y nõ me fue cõtradicho:| [The above gives the first eight lines of the plaquette; the following the last three:] Esta cartaembio Colon a lescriuano Deracion|delas Islas halladas en las Indias, Contenida|a otra Desus Altezas.| Sm. 4to, without title, colophon, date, or printer's name; 4 leaves, 32 lines to a page. 14639

Title from Harrisse, who describes the copy in the Ambrosian Library. "While still on board his caravel, February 15th, off the island of St. Mary, Columbus wrote two official accounts of his voyage, one of which was addressed to Raphael or Gabriel Sanchez or Sanxis, the Crown Treasurer. No copy, either in print or in manuscript, of the Spanish original, has yet been found, but the discovery made a few years ago, in the Ambrosian Library, of a printed copy of the letter addressed to Luis de Santangel (No. 14640), warrants the belief that not only it may have been printed, but that it is not irretrievably lost. As to the original itself, notwithstanding the diligent searches instituted by Muñoz in Simancas, and Navarrete in the *Lonja* at Seville, where, after the establishment of the General Archives of the Indies, in 1792, all documents relating to the Western World had been transferred, no traces of it have ever been discovered. The Spanish text of the letter to Santangel had been made known through Navarrette, who possessed a transcript from the original, which, in 1818, was still deposited among the archives at Simancas. It was not known then, or even suspected, that this important document had been printed before. This *rarissime plaquette* is printed in a kind of semi-gothic type, of the roughest character, resembling none of the incunabula which we have been able to examine. The fact alone that the text is in the Spanish language authorizes the belief that it was printed in Spain. The text of the Ambrosian plaquette was first published three years ago. It is also in two late American publications. The Marquis D'Adda has lately reproduced the entire letter in facsimile." — HARRISSE, pp. 6, 24, 25, and 27.

COLOMBO. Lettera in lingua Spagnuola diretta da Cristoforo Colombo a Luis de Santangel (15 Febbrajo 14 Marzo 1493)

riprodotta a fac-simile ed illustrata per cura di Gerolamo d'Adda dall' unico esemplare a stampa sinora conosciuto che si conserva nella Bibliotheca Ambrosiana. *Milan: Teodora Laengner.* M.DCCC.LXVI. 4to, pp. xxxii, (8). Facsimile. 14640

A very well-executed facsimile of the letter last mentioned. One hundred and fifty copies printed.

COLOMBO. De Insulis [etc.], 1494. *See* Verardus (C.)

For Columbus' Second Voyage, *see* Syllacio (N.), and Anghiera (P.)

COLOMBO. Columb. de prima Insularum, etc. *Basiliæ*, 1533. *See* Monachus (R.)

COLOMBO. Letter of Columbus to Luis de Santangel, 1493. [*New York.* 1864.] 8vo, Title, Facsimile, 1 p., Description, pp. 12. H. 14641

A facsimile of the Spanish letter of Columbus, published in 1493, from the only known copy in the Ambrosian Library, Milan, with description by James Lenox.

COLOMBO. Copia de la Lettera per Columbo mandata a li Serenissimi Re et Regina di Spagna: de le insule et luoghi per lui trouate. [Verso:] Constantio Bayuera Bressano|Al Magnifico et Clarissimo Francesco|Bragadeno Podesta di Bressa S. [Colophon:] *Stampata in Venetia (a nome de Constantio Bayuera citadano di Bressa), per Simone de Louere. a di 7 di Mazo.* 1505. *cum priuilegio.* Sm. 4to, 8 l., the last blank. 14642

"Prompted by the success of Vasco da Gama's voyage, Columbus, fitting out a new expedition, sailed, taking with him his brother Bartholomew and his own son and future historian, Fernando, May 9th, 1502, from Cadiz, with four small caravels. After a voyage of only twenty-five days, the Admiral reached what is supposed to be the island now called Martinique; discovered, July 30th, the unimportant Island of Bonacca, near the Bay of Honduras; ... The above work is a description of the events of this voyage (which was Columbus' fourth and last), only to July 7th, 1503, and is dated from Jamaica. It was originally written in Spanish. ... We have the authority of Pinelo for the assertion that it was printed; but no such Spanish edition has yet been found. An Italian translation, however, either from that printed original or from a MS., was published in Italy very soon after the return of Columbus; it is the present No. 14642. The latter had long been forgotten when Morelli, the modest, obliging and erudite librarian of the St. Mark Library at Venice, corrected the text of Simon de Lovere's edition, and republished it in 1810 under the title now so frequently quoted of 'Lettera rarissima.'" — HARRISSE. *See* No. 14643, *infra.* An English version of what purports to be Columbus' account of his fourth voyage, is included in "A Miscellaneous Collection: consisting of An Original Letter from the Pen of Columbus, never before published, some Original Poetry, and detached pieces of Prose; interspersed with a few neat Selections. The whole revised and corrected by a Gentleman of the Inner Temple. *London: for the Editor.* 1803." 4to, 5 l., pp. 132, (4). The dedication to this work is signed M. H.

COLOMBO. Lettera rarissima di Cristoforo Colombo riprodotta e illustrata dal Cavaliere Ab. Morelli Bibliotec. Regio in

Venezia. *Bassano nella Stamperia Remondiniana.* M.DCCC.X. 8vo, pp. xvi, (1), 5–66. BA., C., H. 14643

A reprint of the Italian version of the excessively rare letter which Columbus wrote from Jamaica, dated 7 July, 1503, with interesting notes by Morelli.

COLOMBO. Codice diplomatico Colombo-Americano osia Raccolta di Documenti Originali e inediti spettanti a Cristoforo Colombo alla scoperta ed al Governo dell' America Publicato per ordine degl' Ill.mi Decurioni della Città di Genova. *Genova: Ponthenier.* 1823. 4to, pp. lxxx, 348. Plates, etc. BA., H.

This most important and valuable collection was edited by Prof. Spotorno, and consists of an historical memoir of Columbus, by the editor, followed by the letters, notes, privileges, and other writings of the great navigator, comprising every authentic document, with portrait, facsimile, autographs, etc. Translated and published in London, 1823. Respecting this work, *see* the "N. Am. Rev.," XVIII. 415; XXI. 398.

COLOMBO. Raccolta completa degli scritti di Christoforo Colombo, ad illustrare ed documentare la scoperta dell' America, recati in italiano corredati di note e di una introduzione ... da Gio. Battista Torre. [*Lione.*] M DCCC LXIV. 8vo, pp. xii, 9–416. Portrait, Map, and 2 Photographs. BA. 14645

COLOMBO. Lettere Autografe edite ed inedite di Cristoforo Colombo; e fra l'altre quella sulle isole da lui scoperte, tratta da una stampa rarissima. Con un Discurso di Cesare Correnti su Colombo; nove tavole illustrative; ed una avvertenza degli Editori. *Milano: G. Daelli e Comp.* 1863. 12mo, pp. xvi, 142, 1 l. C. 14646

Portrait, plates, and facsimile of the Spanish text of the letter written by Columbus in 1493, now in the Ambrosian Library in Milan.

COLOMBO. Christopher Columbus; his Life, Voyages, and Discovery of the New World. *London.* Woodcuts. 14647

COLOMBO. Columbi Navigatio in Americam. *Roterodami.* 1616. 8vo. 14648

COLOMBO. Columbus and his Times ... . *London Religious Tract Society.* 1842. 18mo, pp. 186. + *Albany: E. H. Pease.* 1844. 18mo, pp. 186. S. 14649

COLOMBO. Columbus — his First Voyage to America, the Conquest of Mexico by Cortes, and the Conquest of Peru by Pizarro. *Philadelphia.* 1795. 8vo. Plates. 14650

COLOMBO. Columbus, or the Discovery of America, as related by a Father to his children. *Dublin.* 1800. 12mo.

COLOMBO. Columbus in Chains, a Prize Poem, Recited in the Theatre, Oxford. *Privately Printed.* 1848. 18mo. 14652

COLOMBO. Cristobal Colon; et descubrimiento de America. Conferencias familiares. *Paris: Rosa et Bouret.* 1870. 18mo, pp. 101. 14653

COLOMBO. Del|Primo Scopritore|del Continente|del Nuovo Mondo|e dei Più Antichi Storici che ne scrissero|Ragionamento |che serve di supplemento alle due lettere su la|scoperta del Nuovo Mondo publicate nel Libro|intitolato della patria di Cristoforo Colombo|Stampato in Firenze nell' Anno MDCCCVIII.| *Firenze:|Presso Molini, Landi e Comp.*|MDCCCIX.| 8vo. 14654

COLOMBO. Christophe Colomb, ou l'Amérique découverte. *See* [Bourgeois (Auguste Anicet)], Vol. II., No. 6896.

COLOMBO. Della Patria di Cristoforo Colombo. *See* [Napione (G. F. Galeani)].

COLOMBO. The First, Second, Third, and Fourth Voyages of Columbus. *Juvenile Repository.* 1800. 3 vols., 16mo.

COLOMBO. The History of the Voyages of Christopher Columbus, in order to discover America and the West Indies. *Glasgow.* MDCCLXI. 12mo. + *London: R. Crowder.* MDCCLXXII. 12mo, pp. 201. + *London: D. Midwinter, M. Cooper, A. Bland, and J. Nicholson.* M,DCC,LXXVII. 12mo, 1 l., pp. 190. H. + *London.* 1783. 12mo. 14656

COLOMBO. Columbus or the New World. A Poem, by Britannicus. *London: Bennett.* 8vo. 14656*a*

COLOMBO. La vera Patria di Cristoforo Colombo, giustificata a favore de Genovesi contro le Eccenzioni di chi pretende non appartenga alla nazione suddetta, e chi si studia provare non esere stato il primo a scoprire il contiente Americano, ma bensi Americo Vespucci. *Roma.* 1814. 8vo. 14657

COLOMBO. ... Memorial ajustado, hecho de orden del real y supremo Consejo de Indias, con citacion y asistencia de las partes, en el pleyto, que en grado de revista se sigue en él por el Señor Don Mariano Colón de Larreategui num. 64 ... sobre la propiedad del Mayorazgo que fundó D. Christoval Colón num. 1, primer descubridor, y Almirante de las Indias, de que proceden dichos Mayorazgos, y Estados, Cargo de Almirante, Titulos de Duque y Marques, y lo de dependiente de ellos ... . [n. p. 1788.] Folio, title, pp. (777). Chart. H. 14658

Every second page only is numbered, so that the last number is 387, and there are 3 pages unnumbered.

COLOMBO. Memorial del hecho, cerca dela hoia dela qve llaman minuta del testamento de don Christoual Colon, primero Almerãte de las Indias, de año de. 97. Que los pretensores del estado de Veragua pretenden que tomò don Francisco de Mendoça Almirante de Aragon marido dela Marquesa de Guadaleste, que es la que ha pretendido y pretende la sucession del dicho Estado. Folio, 25 l. 14659

COLOMBO. Nuove lirichi d'illustri Italiani in lode di Christoforo Colombo. *Genova: Presso G. F. Garbarino.* 1855. 12mo, pp. 71. B. 14660

COLOMBO. Observazione sul ragionamiento del primo scopritore. *See* Napione (G. F. Gal.)

COLOMBO. Osservazioni di un Toscano sopra una falsità inventata da un Lombardo a favore di Cristoforo Colombo. *Firenze.* 1822. 4to. 14661

COLOMBO. Ragionamento nel quale si conferma l'opinione generale intorno alla vita di Cristoforo Colombo. *Genova.* 1812. 4to. 14662

COLOMBO. The Life and Times of Christopher Columbus. Illustrated. *Boston.* 1855. 16mo. 14663

COLOMBO. Life, Voyages, and Discoveries of Christopher Columbus. New Edition. *London: Longman.* 1865. 18mo, pp. viii, 232. 14664

COLOMBO. The Lives of Christopher Columbus, the Discoverer of America, and Americus Vespucius the Florentine. With Engravings. *Boston: Marsh, Capen, Lyon, and Webb.* 1840. 18mo, Title, pp. 278. H. 14665

COLOMBO. Memorials of Columbus; or a Collection of Authentic Documents of that Celebrated Navigator, now first published from the original manuscripts, by order of the Decurions of Genoa; Preceded by a Memoir of his Life and Discoveries. Translated from the Spanish and Italian. *London: Treuttel and Wurtz, Treuttel, Jun., and Richter.* 1823. 8vo, Title, Half-Title, pp. clix, Facsimile, Half-Title, 255. Portrait. B., C. 14666

"The first part of this work is a 'Historical Memoir of Christopher Columbus and his Discoveries, by D. Gio. Batista Spotorno, Professor, &c. Translated from the Italian,' pp. clix. After which follows the 'Letters, Privileges, Notes, and other Writings of Don Christopher Columbus, High Admiral of the Ocean, Viceroy and Governor of the Island and Mainlands,' Index, pp. 253–255, (1). *See* Codice Diplomatico." — *N. Am. Rev.*, XVIII. 415.

COLOMBO. Notes on Columbus. *See* [Harrisse (Henry)].

COLOMBO. Orazione in Lode di Cristoforo Columbo Discopritore del Nuovo Mondo, con Note Storiche ed una Dissertazione intorno la vera Patria di lui. *Milano.* 1825. 8vo. Portrait. 14667

COLOMBO. Personal Narrative of the First Voyage of Columbus to America. From a Manuscript recently discovered in Spain. Translated from the Spanish. [By Samuel Kettell.] *Boston: Thomas B. Wait and Son.* 1827. 8vo, pp. 303. B., H.

COLOMBO. Reflections on the Tomb of Columbus. By a Lady. *London.* 1797. 4to. 14669

COLOMBO. Select Letters of Christopher Columbus, with other Original Documents, relating to his Four Voyages to the New World. Translated and edited by R. H. Major ... . *London: Hakluyt Society.* M.DCCC.XLVII. 8vo, 4 l., pp. xc, (1), 240. BA., P. 14670

"The translated documents are seven in number. Four are letters from the hand of Columbus, describing his four voyages; another, describing the second voyage, is by Dr. Chanca, physician to the fleet; the seventh, an extract from the will of Diego Montez, one of Columbus's officers during the fourth voyage." — *Preface.*

COLOMBO. Select Letters of ... Columbus ... edited by R. H. Major. Second Edition. ... *London: Hakluyt Society.* M.DCCC.LXX. 8vo, 4 l., pp. cxliii, (1), 254. Plate. BA. 14671

COLOMBO. Voyages and Discoveries of Christopher Columbus. Sixth Edition. *London: Parker and Son.* 1857. 18mo.

COLOMBO. Voyage of Columbus, a Poem. *See* [Rogers (Samuel)].

For a translation of the voyages of Columbus, *see* Churchill's "Coll. of Voyages," Vol. I.; Harris, Vols. I. and II.; and Kerr, Vol. III.

COLOMBO (F.) El Iob de la Ley de Gracia,|retratado en la| admirable vida del Siervo de|Dios, Venerable Padre Fray|Pedro Vrraca,|del Real, y Militar Orden|de nuestra Señora de la Merced, Redencion de|Cautiuos, Confessor de las señoras de la |Real familia, en Madrid. | Nacido | al mundo en la Villa de Xadraque,|a la Religion, | En el Conuento de la Ciudad de Quito.|Al cielo,|En el de la Ciudad de Lima en el Perù.|Sacado de lo qve escrivieron el|Ilvstrissimo señor Don Fr. Ioseph Sanchis, M. General de la|Orden. Y el M. R. P. M. Fr. Francisco Mesia, Calificador del|Santo Oficio, y Prouincial de Lima,

su Confessor,|y de otros instrumentos.|Por el Maestro Fray Felipe Colombo,|Coronista General de la Religion.|Dedicado al Excelentissimo Señor|Conde de Medellin, Presidente del Real Consejo|de Indias.|*Con privilegio*|*En la Imprenta Real. Año de* 1674.| 4to, 10 l., 140 l. J.C.B. 14673

COLOMBO (F.) Historie|Del S. D. Fernando Colombo;| Nelle quali s'ha particolare, & vera relatione|della vita, & de' fatti dell' Ammiraglio|D. Christoforo Colombo,|suo padre:|Et dello scoprimento, ch'egli fece dell' Indie|Occidentali, dette Mondo Nvovo,|hora possedute dal Sereniss.|Re Catolico:| Nuouamente di lingua Spagnoula tradotte nell' Italiana|dal S. Alfonso Vlloa.|*Con Privilegio.*|*In Venetia,* MDLXXI.|*Appresso Francesco de' Franceschi Senese.*| 16mo, Title, pp. 36, 496. BA.

First edition; very scarce. "The author was born at Cordova, in 1487, became page to the prince, Don Juan, son and heir to Fernando and Isabella, in 1494. He accompanied his father in his fourth voyage of discovery in 1502, and, after the death of Columbus, made two voyages to the New World. He also accompanied Charles V to Italy, Flanders, Germany, &c.; and, after having travelled over all Europe and a part of Africa and Asia, died at Seville, in 1539, leaving a library of 20,000 volumes, printed and manuscript, to the cathedral of Seville. He was an eye-witness to the facts which he relates in the above volume, particularly the fourth voyage of his father, whose papers and charts he possessed. 'His work is an invaluable document, entitled to great faith, and is the corner-stone of the history of the American continent.'" — *English Catalogue.* "Louis Columbus, a person of debauched character, came to Genoa about 1568, bringing with him the MS. life of the hero, written in Spanish by his son Don Ferdinand, which he left in the hands of the patrician Fornari, from whom it passed to another patrician, Gior. Baptista Marini. The latter, having gone to Venice, procured a translation to be made into Italian by Ulloa." — SPOTORNO. "Œttinger, in his 'Bibl. Biogr.,' mentions, we cannot imagine on what authority, 'Colombo (Fernando), Vida y hechos del almirante D. Christoval Colon, *Madr.* fol., 1530.' The learned bibliographer must mean the wretched translation into Spanish made for Barcia (*Madrid.* 1747. fol.)" On the other hand, according to Barcia, Luis Colon had intrusted the manuscript to one Baltano de Fornari, who, notwithstanding his advanced age, commenced printing the work simultaneously in the original Spanish, in Italian, and Latin, at Venice. If so, some stray sheets of Don Fernando's own version may yet come to light.

COLOMBO. Historie del Sig. Don Fernando Colombo. Nelle quali s'hà particolare, & vera relatione dell Vita, & de' fatti dell' Ammiraglio Don Christoforo Colombo suo Padre. Et dello scoprimento, ch'egli fece dell' Indie Occidẽtali, dette Mondo Nvovo ... . Già tradotte di lingua Spagnuola nell' Italiana [dal Alfonso Ulloa], & hora fatte ristampare. Con aggiunta di Lettere, & Testamento dell' Ammiraglio ... da Cesare Parona. *Milano: Girolamo Bordoni.* [1614.] 8vo, 31 l., pp. 494. J.C.B. + *Venetia, Gio: Pietro Brigonci.* 1676. 12mo, 23 l., pp. 489, Table, pp. 9. J.C.B. + *Venetia: Iseppo Prodocimo.* 1678. 24mo, 24 l., pp. 489,

5 l. + *Venetia: Per il Prodocimo.* 1709. 18mo, 24 l., pp. 494, Table, 6 l. Map. J.C.B. 14675

The original Spanish was never published. The Spanish edition of 17— was a translation from the Italian. The Milano edition contains a dedication by Cæsar Parona, dated Milan, 4 June, 1614, and four verses by the same author. Harrisse quotes an edition, *Milan.* 1672. 8vo, which I have not seen.

COLOMBO. Historie nelle quali s'ha particolare & vera relatione della vita, e de' fatti dell' Ammireglio D. Christoforo Colombo suo padre &c. nuovamente di lingua Spagnuola tradotte nell' Italiana dal S. Alfonso Ulloa. *Venetia.* 1685. 12mo.

"Edition inconnue à Ternaux. Elle manque également dans la nouvelle édition du Manuel de M. Brunet, mais elle est citée dans le Trésor de M. Graesse."—TROSS. A curious kind of chap-book edition. Sold at Puttick's, in 1860, for £1 9s. The work is reprinted in Barcia's "Historiadores primitivos," Vol. I., and a portion of it is translated in Brasseur de Bourbourg's "Relation de Yucatan." Graesse quotes an edition, dated 1675. I have also seen a catalogue giving the date 1728. For an English version of part of the work, *see* Churchill's "Voyages," Vol. II.; Kerr's "Voyages," Vol. III.; and Pinkerton's "Voyages," Vol. XII.

COLOMBO. La vie de Cristofle Colomb, et la decouverte qu'il a faite des Indes Occidentales, vulgairement appellées le Nouveau Monde ... traduite en françois [par C. Cotolendy]. *Paris: Claude Barbin et Ch. Ballard.* 1681. 2 vols., 12mo, 11 l., pp. 262; 11 l., pp. 260. 14677

The epistle, privilege, etc., is repeated in Vol. II.

COLON (C.) *See* Colombo (C.)

[COLON (F. M.)] Geografia General, para el uso de la Juventud de Venezuela. *Caracas.* 1833–37. 4 vols., 8vo, pp. 544; 568; 620; vi, 652, xxviii. 14678

With the exception of the first 120 pages of the first volume, the whole of this work relates to America, and is principally historical. The first volume contains an account of St. Domingo, Cuba, the Arctic Regions, Canada, and the United States. The second contains Mexico, Central America, the Antilles, Brazil, Buenos Ayres, Paraguay, the Cisplatine Republic, Patagonia, and the Islands of the Pacific. The third contains Chili, Peru, Bolivia, Ecuador, and Nueva Granada. The fourth, and most important, is devoted entirely to the History of the Republic of Venezuela. The author promises to give, in a fifth volume, a separate account of each province. The dedication to General Paez is signed Feliciano Montenegro Colon, who says that "the following Lessons of Geography, taken from the best authors, were printed in the Havana in 1826," referring, probably, to the first 120 pages, the rest of the work being probably written by him." The following is probably by the same author:

[COLON.] Compendio de la Historia de Venezuela desde su descubrimiento y conquista hasta que se declaró estado independiente. *Carácas.* 1840. 8vo, pp. xi, 192. 14679

COLON (J. M. E.) Memoria sobre la Conservacion del Puerto de la Habana. *Santiago de Cuba.* 1851. 4to. A. 14680

COLON DE LARREATEGUI (M.) *See* Colombo, No. 14658.

Colonel Berkley and his Friends, containing Sketches of Life South of the Potomac, a Tale. *London.* 1825. 3 vols., post 8vo. 14681

COLONEY (M.) Manomin: a Rhythmical Romance of Minnesota, the Great Rebellion, and the Minnesota Massacres. By Myron Coloney. *St. Louis: Printed for the Author.* 1866. 12mo, pp. 297. 14682

Coloniæ Anglicanæ Illustratæ. *See* [Bollan (W.)], Vol. II.

Colonie icarienne. *See* [Cabet], Vol. III., No. 9780.

Colonial Almanack. *Edinburgh.* 1855. 8vo. Continued.

The Seventh Report of the Colonial Church Society ... . *London.* 1843. 8vo, pp. xii, 60. 14684

Colonial Church Chronicle, 1847. 8vo. Continued.

Report on the Property of the Colonial Gold Company of Nova Scotia. With a General Introduction of the Gold Region of Nova Scotia. By Benjamin Silliman, Jr. ... With Extracts from his Report and from Report of John Campbell ... . Also Extracts from Reports of Gold Commissioner of Nova Scotia. *Boston: Geo. C. Rand & Avery.* 1864. 8vo, pp. 35. Map. H.

Colonial Intelligencer; or, Aborigines' Friend. 1847, 1848. Comprising the Transactions of the Aborigines' Protection Society; interesting intelligence concerning the Aborigines of various climes, and articles upon Colonial Affairs ... . *London.* [1848.] 8vo, 4 l., pp. 256. Continued to Vol. IV. or more.

The Colonial Journal. Vol. I. January to July, 1816. .. *London: Baldwin, Cradock, and Joy.* [1816.] 8vo, Title, pp. ix–xx, (3), 632, Plates. Vol. II. July to December, 1816. 2 Titles, pp. 588, Plates. Vol. III. March to June, 1817. Title, pp. v, (1), iii–viii, 560, Plates. March, 1818. Title, pp. 272, Plate and Map. H. 14688

General Report of the Colonial Land and Emigration Commissioners. *London.* 1840. Folio and 8vo. Continued, after 1842, in 8vo. 14689

Colonial Laws as examined by a Committee of the House of Commons ... 1836, exhibiting some of the Principal Discrepancies between those Laws and the ... Act of Abolition. *London.* 1837. pp. 32. 14690

The Colonial Magazine; Vol. I.; Nov., 1827. *Plattsburgh, N. Y.* 1827. 8vo. S. 14691

The Colonial Magazine and Commercial-Maritime Journal. Edited by Robert Montgomery Martin, Esq. *Fisher, Son & Co: London.* [1840, etc.] 8 vols., 8vo. S. 14492

The Colonial Magazine, or Monthly Miscellany. *Philadelphia.* 1786–92. 10 vols., 8vo. 14693

Colonial Office List for 1862; or, General Register of the Colonial Dependencies of Great Britain. By W. C. Sargeaunt and Arthur N. Birch. *London.* 1862. 8vo. Continued.

The Colonial Policy of Great Britain considered with relation to her North American Provinces and West India Possessions; wherein the Dangerous Tendency of American Competition is developed, and the Necessity of recommencing a Colonial System on a Vigorous and Extensive Scale, exhibited and defended: with Plans for the Promotion of Emigration, and Strictures on the Treaty of Ghent. By a British Traveller. *London: Baldwin, Cradock and Joy.* 1816. 8vo, pp. xxxii, 237. H. + *Philadelphia.* 1816. 12mo. 14695

See "M. Rev.," LXXXII. 329.

Colonial Policy, with Hints upon the Formation of Military Settlements. To which are added, Observations on the Boundary Question, now pending between this Country and the United States. *London.* 1835. 8vo, pp. 49. + Second Edition. *London: James Cochrane & Co.* 1835. 8vo, pp. 40. 14696

Colonial Records *See* Pennsylvania.

Colonial Slavery 1833. 8vo. 14697

Las colonias de Santa Fè. Su origen, progreso y actual situacion. Con observaciones generales sobre la emigracion a la Republica Argentina. Publicados en espanol é inglés. *Rosario de Santa Fè.* 1864. 4to, pp. 170. 14698

Colonies ... *A Paris: de l'imprimerie de Baudouin Imprimeur du Corps Legislatif place du Carrousel No. 662.* [*Circa* 1796.] 8vo, pp. 14. 14699

A well-written work, signed Baco, probably written about this period. Neither Quérard nor Barbier mention the work.

Colonies, Commerce, Agriculture. Aperçu sur les intérêts des Colonies françoises avec la République, autant que les circonstances actuelles permettent de les traiter. *Paris: Baudouin, en X.* 8vo, pp. 31. 14700

See also various reports on the British colonies in the Parliamentary Blue Books. References to the volumes will be found in the Catalogue of the Boston Public Library in the article "Great Britain-Parliament."

Almanach des colonies. Anneé M.DCC.LXXXII. *Paris: de l'imprimerie de d'Houry.* [1781.] 32mo, 8 l., pp. 84. H. 14701

Arrêt du conseil d'état, concernant le commerce étranger dans les isles françoises de l'Amérique. Du 30 août 1784. *Paris: Impr. Royale.* 4to, pp. 10. 14702

Arrêt de conseil d'état, concernant les armemens de commerce pour les isles et colonies françoises. Du 31 octobre 1784. *Paris: Impr. Royale.* 4to, pp. 3. 14703

Arrêt du conseil de'état, qui ordonne que la gratification accordée au commerce, pour la traite des nègres, sera restituée à l'adjudicataire des fermes, avec moitié en sus, par les armateurs qui l'auront reçue, et qui n'auront pas importé des noirs aux Colonies. Du 5 juin 1785. *Paris: Impr. Royale.* 4to, pp. 3.

Arrêt du conseil d'état concernant le commerce interlope des Colonies. Du 23 septembre 1785. *Paris: Impr. Royale.* 1786. 4to, pp. 8. 14705

Arret du Conseil d'état du Roi, concernant l'établissement des Paquebots pour la correspondance avec les Colonies Françoises et les États-Unis de l'Amérique. Du 20 Décembre 1786. [*Paris.* 1786.] 4to, pp. 6. 14706

See also our Vol. I., No. 2104, and note, for other papers on the French Colonies.

Catalogue des produits des colonies françaises envoyees a l'exposition universelle de Londres de 1862. *Paris: Librari Challamel Ainé.* 1862. 8vo, pp. 613–720. 14707

Extrait de la "Revue Maritime et Coloniale" (Avril, 1862).

Les colonies françaises: Essai sur la nature du gouvernement, de la population et du commerce de la Colonie de St. Domingue. *Paris.* 1754. 12mo. 14708

Droit public ou gouvernement des colonies françoises. *Paris.* 1771. 2 vols., 12mo. 14709

Essai sur les colonies françoises. *See* [Saintard (M.)]

Etats des colonies françaises pour 1837. 8vo. 14710

Exposé de la situation actuelle des colonies françaises aux Indes Occidentales. *Bordeaux.* 1822. 8vo, pp. 31. 14711

Exposé générale des résultats du patronage des esclaves dans les colonies françaises. *Paris.* 1844. 4to. 14712

Instruction pour les colonies françoises, contenant un project de Constitution. *Paris.* 1791. 12mo. P. 14713

La Ligne de Démarcation dans l'approvisionnement des isles françaises de l'Amérique, et dans le commerce avec elles. [n. p. n. d.] 4to. C. 14714

Memoire sur le commerce étranger, avec les colonies françaises de l'Amérique. . Présenté à la Chambre d'agriculture du Cap. le 17. Feb. 1784. *Paris: Cuchet.* 1785. 8vo, pp. 51. 14715

Mémoires sur les colonies occidentales de la France. 1814. 8vo. 14716

Ministère de la marine et des colonies. Commission ... pour l'examen des questions relatives à l'esclavage et à la constitution politique des colonies. Procès verbaux. *Paris: imprimerie royale. Juillet* 1840–*Juin* 1842. 3 vols., 4to, Title, pp. 114; Title, 171; Title, 413. + Rapport ... . *Paris: imprimerie royale. Mars* 1843. 4to, pp. xvi, 438. BA. 14717

Notices Statistiques sur les Colonies Françaises, 1837. *See* [Tiby (P. Alex.)]

Notices sur les colonies françaises accompagnées d'un atlas de 14 cartes Et publiées par ordre de S. Exc. le ... Ministre Secrétaire d'État de la Marine et des Colonies. ... *Paris: Challamel aîné.* 1866. 8vo, 3 l., pp. 767, (1). + Atlas ... . [*Ibid.*] 4to, Title, 14 Maps. BA. 14718

Precis pour les grands proprietaires des Colonies Françaises de l'Amérique. [n. p. n. d.] 4to. C. 14719

Renseignements complémentaires à fournir pour la deuxième édition des notices statistiques sur les Colonies Francaises. *Paris.* [n. d.] Folio. 14720

Tableau de Population, de Culture, de Commerce et de Navigation des Colonies Françaises en 1841. *Paris.* 1844. 14721

Tableau Decennal de la commerce avec les Colonies, et les Puissances Etrangeres, publiée par l'Administration des Douanes, 1827 à 1836. *Paris.* 1838. 4to. N. 14722

Tableaux et relevés de population, de cultures, de commerce, de navigation, etc., formant, pour l'année 1839, la suite des tableaux et relevés des notices statistiques sur les colonies françaises. *Paris.* 1842. 8vo. C. 14723

Colonisation dans l'Amérique Centrale du District de Santo Thomas de Guatemala, par la communauté de l'Union, fondé par la compagnie Belge de colonisation. Opinion de la presse Française. *Paris.* 1843. 8vo, pp. 56. 14724

Colonising; or a Plain Investigation of that Subject; with a Legislative, Political and Commercial View of Our Colonies. *London: J. Brotherton.* MDCCLXXIV. 4to, pp. 16. P. 14725

Dated March 14, 1774. *See* "M. Rev.," L. 324.

A Colonist, 1839, *pseudonym.* *See* [Haliburton, (T. C.)]

Colonist, *pseudonym.* The Edinburgh Review and the West Indies; with Observations on the Pamphlets of Messrs. Stephen, Macaulay, &c. and Remarks on the Slave Registry Bill. By Colonist. ... *Glasgow: John Smith and Son.* 1816. 8vo, Half-Title, pp. xv, (1), 360. H. 14726

Colonizacion en el ysmo de Hoazacoalco é Tehuantepec. *Mexico.* 1823. 4to. 14727

Colonizacion y Navigacion del Amazonas. *Lima.* 1853. 4to. 14728

Colonization and Abolition contrasted. *Philadelphia: Herman Hooker.* [1839?] 8vo, pp. 16. H. 14729

Colonization Herald and General Register. Vol. I. 1839. 8vo. Continued. 14730

Colonization Herald and General Register. *Philadelphia.* 1848. Folio. Continued. 14731

Memorial of the Semi-Centennial of the American Colonization Society, celebrated at Washington, January 15, 1867. With Documents concerning Liberia. *Washington.* 1867. 8vo, pp. 190. 14732

Also: Address of the Board of Managers of the American Society for Colonizing the Free People of Color to the Auxiliary Societies, and the people of the United States.

Washington. 1820. 8vo, pp. 32.—Address of the ... Managers ... to the Public. *Washington.* 1822. 8vo.—Address of the Managers ... to the People of the United States, June 19, 1832. *Washington.* 1832. 8vo.—African Colonization, Proceedings of a Meeting of the Friends of African Colonization, held in ... Baltimore, On the 17 October, 1827. [*Baltimore.* 1827.] 8vo, pp. 19. H.—Address to the Clergy of all Denominations, on Colonization [in Africa. *Washington.* 1845?] 8vo, pp. 15. H.—On the British African Colonization Society. To which are added, some Particulars respecting the American Colonization Society; and a Letter from Jeremiah Hubbard addressed to a Friend in England, on the same subject. [*London.* 1834.] 8vo, pp. 32. H.—Constitution, Government and Digest of the Laws of Liberia, as confirmed and established by the Board of Managers of the American Colonization Society, May 23, 1825. *Washington City: printed by Way & Gideon.* 1825. 8vo, pp. 11. H.—Extracts from the North American Review for Jan. 1824, on the subject of Colonization. *Princeton, N. J.* 1824. 8vo.—First Annual Report of the Society for Colonizing the Free People of Color. Jan. 1st, 1818. *Washington.* 1818. 8vo, pp. 49. Continued.—Memorial ... to Congress, Feb. 1820. *Washington.* [n. d.] 8vo.—Proceedings of the Convention of the Friends of African Colonization, held in ... Washington, May 4, 1842. [*Washington.* 1842.] 8vo, pp. 64. H.—Remarks on the American Colonization Society. [From the Christian Examiner.] *Providence* 1833. 12mo, pp. 36.—Report of the Committee of the House of Representatives of the United States on the Memorial of the American Colonization Society. *Washington.* 1818. 8vo. W.—Resolutions and Remonstrances of the People of Colour against Colonizatiou on the Coast of Africa. 1818. [n. p. n. d.] 8vo, pp. 8.—View of the Exertions lately made for Colonizing the Free People of Color in the United States, in Africa, or elsewhere. *Washington.* 1817. 8vo. + [Another Edition.] *Washington.* 1817. 8vo.

The Colonizationist and Journal of Freedom, [April, 1833, to April, 1834, inclusive]. *Boston: G. W. Laight.* 1833–34. 8vo, pp. 384, 1 l. BA., C. 14733

Coloquio de Aristo y de Timandro sobre los principales successos del año de 1741. *Madrid: Se hallarà donde la Gaceta.* 1741. 4to, pp. 35. J.C.B. 14734

A dialogue upon the successes of the Spanish arms in 1741, chiefly relating to operations in the West Indies and Spanish America.

COLORADO. Colorado: its Resources, Parks, and Prospects as a New Field for Emigration; with an Account of the Trenchara and Costilla Estates, in the San Luis Park. *London: Ranken & Co., Privately printed.* 1869. 2 vols., 4to, 1 l., pp. 55; 3 l., pp. 133, 16. 3 Maps. C. 14735

The Colorado of the Pacific. [n. p. 1868.] 8vo, pp. 12.

Additional Catalogue of the Territorial Library of Colorado. *Golden City.* 1867. 12mo. 14737

I have not seen the catalogue proper.

Colorado Veto reviewed. [From the Washington Chronicle. *Denver.* 1866.] 8vo, pp. 7. H. 14738

The Common School Law of the Territory of Colorado, embracing all the Statutes relating to the Subject. ... *Central City,* [*Col.*] 1868. 8vo. 14739

First Annual Message of Governor Cummings to the Legislative Assembly, Territory of Colorado, January, 1866. *Denver: Byers & Daily.* 1866. 12mo, pp. 22. H. + Second ... Message ... Dec. 13, 1866. *Golden City: George West.* MDCCCLXVI. 8vo, pp. 14. H. 14740

Also: Governor's Message, delivered to the Territorial Legislature of Colorado, in Joint Convention ... January 5th, 1866. [*Denver.* 1866.] 8vo, pp. 8. H.

General Laws, Resolutions, Memorials, and Private Acts, passed at the First Session of the Legislature of the Territory of Colorado. *Denver.* 1861. 8vo. C. 14741

General Laws, and Joint Resolutions, Memorials and Private Acts, passed at the Second Session of the Legislative Assembly of the Territory of Colorado. Begun ... 7th ... July, 1862. ... With the Declaration of Independence, the Constitution of the United States, and the Organic Act of the Territory. ... *Denver: Rocky Mountain News Printing Company.* 1862. 8vo, pp. 166, (2). H. + *Denver: Byers & Daily.* 1865. 8vo, pp. 161, (2). Continued. H. 14742

The Geography, Description and Resources of Central and Southern Colorado. Published by the Board of Trade of Southern Colorado. *Pueblo, Colorado.* 1869. 8vo, pp. 32. H.

Gov. Evans' Message, Delivered to the Legislative Assembly of Colorado ... at Denver ... July 17th, 1862. *Denver: News Office.* [1862.] 16mo, pp. 13. H. 14744

See also Evans (*Gov.*)

Journal of the Council of the Legislative Assembly of the Territory of Colorado, 1861. *Denver.* 1862. 8vo. Continued. 14745

Journal of the House of Representatives of the Legislative Assembly of the Territory of Colorado, 1861. *Denver.* 1861. 8vo. Continued. 14746

Leyes Generales aprobados en las sessiones 4ª, 6ª, y 6ª, de la Assemblia Legislativa del Territorio de Colorado junto con la Declaracion de Independencia La Constitucion de los Estados Unidos y les actas organicas del Territorio. *Denver: De Witter.* 1867. 8vo, pp. 207. 14747

The Parks of Colorado. [n. p. 1866.] 8vo, pp. 6. H.

Report of the Proceedings of the Second Annual Exhibition of the Colorado Agricultural Society, held ... on the 9th–12th days of Oct., 1867 ... *Golden City.* 1868. 8vo. S. 17449

To the People of Colorado. *See* [Chivington (J. M.)], No. 12855.

Colored Schools. Will the General Assembly put down Caste Schools? *Providence.* 1857. 8vo, pp. 8. 14750

Also: Reports relating to Colored Schools in Mississippi, Arkansas and Western Tennessee, April, 1865. *Memphis, Tenn.: Freedmen's Press.* 1865. 12mo, pp. 28.

Report and Extracts relating to Colored Schools in the Department of Tennessee and Arkansas, November 30, 1864. *Memphis, Tenn.: Freedmen Press.* 1862. 12mo, pp. 20. 14751

Colored Refugees. Report of a Committee of the Representatives of New York Yearly Meeting of Friends, upon the condition and wants of Colored Refugees. pp. 30. 14752

Also: Second Report of the Committee of the New York Meeting of Friends upon the condition of Colored Refugees, 5th Month 27, 1863. 8vo, pp. 15.

Colored Troops and Military Colonies on Southern Soil. Notes by an Officer of the Ninth Army Corps. *New York.* 1863. 8vo. pp. 16. 14753

The Colors of the United States first raised upon the Capital of the Confederate States, April 3, 1865. *Morrisania, N. Y.* 1865 or 1866. 8vo, pp. 17. 14754

Twenty-seven copies printed for private distribution only.

COLPAERT (E.) Étude sur le Pérou. Des betes à laine des Andes et de leur acclimatation en Europe, de la tonte des alpacas et du trafic des laines par les Indiens. Par M. Émile Colpaert, chargé d'une mission scientifique dans l'Amérique du Sud. *Paris: impr. Martinet.* 1864. 8vo, pp. 60. 14755

Colportage for 1852–53. [n. p. 1852?] 8vo, pp. 32. H.

Colportage in Virginia. Annual Report of Mr. J. Cross, Superintendent. 1852. [*Richmond.* 1852.] 8vo, pp. 16. H.

Also: The American Colporteur System. [n. p. n. d.] 12mo, pp. 28. H. — ... The Colporteur of the American and Foreign Bible Society. New Series, No. 3. April, 1856. Published at the Bible House ... . *New York.* 1856. 8vo. H. — Colporteur Conventions at Richmond and Pittsburgh. Sermon, Letters, and Proceedings. *New York: American Tract Society.* [1852.] 32mo, pp. 79. H. — General View of Colportage as conducted by the American Tract Society in the United States. May, 1845. *New York: Daniel Fanshaw.* [1845.] 8vo, pp. 48. H. — To the Patrons and Friends of the American Tract Society. [On Colportage. *Boston.* 1852.] 8vo, pp. 12. H. — Summary of Colportage, by the American Tract Society, in the Year ending March 1, 1847, with Facts illustrating its Necessity, Method, and Results. *New York: American Tract Society.* MDCCCXLVII. 8vo, pp. 48. H.

COLQUHOUN (J. C.) William Wilberforce; his Friends and his Times. By John Campbell Colquhoun. *London: Longmans, Green, and Co.* 1866. Post 8vo, pp. vii, 448. + Second Edition, with some Additions and Remarks on Reviewers. *London: Longmans.* 1867. Post 8vo, pp. vii, 459. 14758

COLQUITT (Walter T.) Speech of Hon. W. T. Colquitt, of Georgia, on the Oregon Question. Delivered in the Senate ... February 17, 1846. *Washington: Blair and Rives.* 1846. 8vo, pp. 12. H. 14759

COLT (J. Caldwell). An Authentic Life of John C. Colt, now imprisoned for Killing Samuel Adams, in New York, on the Seventeenth of September, 1841. Third Edition. *Boston: S. N. Dickinson.* 1842. 8vo, pp. 70. 14760

COLT. ... Life, Letters and Last Conversation of John Caldwell Colt, who committed Suicide at the New York Prison, Nov. 18, 1842, just before the Time appointed for his Execution, for the Murder of Samuel Adams ... on the 18th Sept., 1841. [*New York.* 1842.] 8vo, pp. 14. Portrait. H. 14761

COLT (N.) The Devil's Hole, with an Account of a visit made to it in 1679, by Robert Cavelier de La Salle. To which is added a Memoir of the Life of La Salle. By Nelson Colt. ... *Lockport: Crandall and Brigham.* 1844. 16mo, pp. 24. H.

[COLT.] Armsmear: the Home, the Arms, and the Armory of Samuel Colt. A Memorial. *New York.* M.DCCC.LXVI. 4to, pp. 399. B. 14763

Also: Proceedings at the Dedication of Charter Oak Hall, belonging to Col. Sam'l Colt, &c. *Hartford.* MDCCCLXI. 8vo, pp. 45.

COLTON (B.) The Danger of Apostasie, shewed in a Sermon preached before the General Assembly of Connecticut at Hartford, May the 12th, 1737. By Benjamin Colton ... . *N. London: T. Green.* 1738. 8vo, Half-Title, Title, pp. 60.

COLTON. Two Sermons Deliver'd at Hartford, in the Colony of Connecticut. ... The first ... of the Change of the Sabbath, from the Seventh, to the First Day ... . The second ... of Baptism. ... By Benjamin Colton, Pastor of a Church at Hartford. ... *N. London: Printed and sold by T. Green.* 1735. 8vo, 2 l., pp. 67. 14765

[COLTON (C.)] The Americans. By an American in London. *London: Frederick Westley and A. H. Davis.* MDCCCXXXIII. 8vo, pp. xii, 389. BA. 14766

A defence of the Americans against Capt. Hall and Mrs. Trollope.

COLTON. Church and State in America. Part II. Review of the Bishop of London's Reply. By C. Colton. *London: Westley and Davis.* 1834. 8vo, pp. 20. 14767

[COLTON.] The Crisis of the Country. By Junius. Second Edition. *New-York.* [n. d.] 8vo, pp. 16. B. 14768

[COLTON.] The Currency. By Junius. *Philadelphia.* 1843. 8vo, pp. 16. M. 14769

[COLTON.] Currency: the Evil and the Remedy. Fourth Edition. [*New York.* 1843.] 8vo, pp. 43. 14770

[COLTON.] Defence of the Whigs. By a Member of the Twenty-Seventh Congress. *New-York: Harper & Brothers.* 1844. 12mo, pp. 152. B. 14771

COLTON. The Genius and Mission of the Protestant Episcopal Church in the United States By Rev. Calvin Colton ... . *New-York: Stanford & Swords.* 1853. 12mo, pp. 306. H.

Reprinted in London as:

COLTON. The Genius and Mission of the Protestant Episcopal Church in the United States of America. By the Rev. Calvin Colton. With a Preface by the Rev. Pierce Conelly. *London.* 1853. 12mo, pp. 300. 14773

COLTON. History and Character of American Revivals of Religion. By the Rev. Calvin Colton, of America. *London: Frederick Westley, and A. H. Davis.* MDCCCXXXII. Post 8vo, pp. xvi, 294. B., BA. + Second Edition. *London:* [*Ibid.*] MDCCCXXXII. 12mo, pp. xvi, 294, (1). + Third Edition. [*Ibid.*]

[COLTON.] The Junius Tracts. No. I. ... Published every Month. The Text ... . By Junius ... *New York: Published by Greeley & McElrath.* 1844. 8vo, pp. 16. B. 14775

Also: No. II. The Currency. pp. 16; No. III. The Tariff. pp. 16; No. IV. Life of Henry Clay. pp. 16; No. V. Political Abolition. pp. 16; No. VI. Democracy. pp 16; No. VII. Labor and Capital. pp. 16; No. VIII. The Public Lands. pp. 16; No. IX. Annexation of Texas. pp. 16; No. X. The Tariff Triumphant. pp. 8.

COLTON. The Last Seven Years of the Life of Henry Clay. By Calvin Colton. *New York: A. S. Barnes & Co.* 1856. 8vo.

COLTON. A Lecture on the Rail Road to the Pacific, delivered August 12, 1850, at the Smithsonian Institute ... *New York.* 1850. 8vo, pp. 16. 14777

COLTON. The Life and Times of Henry Clay. By Calvin Colton ... . *New York: A. S. Barnes & Co.* 1846. 2 vols., 8vo. Portrait and Plates. + Second Edition. *New York.* 1846. 2 vols., 8vo, pp. 504; 504. Portrait. B., C., H. 14778

COLTON. Manual for Emigrants to America. By Calvin Colton ... . *London: F. Westley and A. H. Davis.* 1832. 18mo, Title, pp. vii–x, 203. B. 14779

[COLTON.] Protestant Jesuitism. By a Protestant. ... *New York: Harper & Brothers.* MDCCCXXXVI. 12mo, pp. vii, (2), 13–295. B. 14780

Public Economy for the United States. By Calvin Colton. *New York: A. S. Barnes & Co.* 1848. 8vo, pp. xiv, 536. + Second Edition. *New York.* [*Ibid.*] + Third Edition. + [*Ibid.*] *New York.* 1856. 8vo. C. & P. 14781

See "N. Am. Rev.," LXVIII. 90, and "Am. Whig Rev.," VIII. 142.

COLTON. Thoughts on the Religious State of the Country; with Reasons for preferring Episcopacy. By Rev. Calvin Colton. *New-York: published by Harper & Brothers.* MDCCCXXXVI. 12mo, Title, (2), 12–208. H. + Second Edition. *New-York: Harper & Brothers.* MDCCCXXXVI. 12mo, Title, pp. (1), 11–208. B. + *London: Hudson.* 1837. 12mo. + [*Ibid.*] 1849. 12mo, pp. 188. 14782

The author was formerly a Presbyterian minister.

COLTON. Tour of the American Lakes, and among the Indians of the North-West Territory in 1830: disclosing the Character and Prospects of the Indian Race. By C. Colton. ... *London: Frederick Wesley and A. H. Davis.* MDCCCXXXIII. 2 vols., post 8vo, pp. xxxii, 316; vii, 387. C., H. 14783

COLTON. A Voice from America to England by an American Gentleman. *New York.* 1837. 14784

Also: Abolition a Sedition, and Abolition and Colonization Contrasted. 1838. 8vo. — The Rights of Labor ... . *New York: A. S. Barnes & Co.* MDCCCXLVI. 8vo, pp. 96. B. + [*Ibid.*] MDCCCXLVII. C. + Youthful Pleasure. A Sermon. ... *Philadelphia.* 1834. 8vo, pp. 12.

COLTON (C.) Address delivered at the Inauguration of the Faculty of Bristol College, Bucks County, Pennsylvania, April 2, 1834. By Rev. Chauncey Colton ... *Bristol College Press.* MDCCCXXXIV. 8vo, pp. 43. + Second Edition, with an Appendix, embracing the First Annual Catalogue of Bristol College. *Philadelphia: Key & Biddle.* 1834. 8vo, pp. 55. B. 14785

COLTON (G. Hooker). Tecumseh; or, the West Thirty Years Since. A Poem. By George H. Colton. *New-York: Wiley and Putnam.* 1842. 12mo, Title, pp. vii, 312. + *London: W. Smith.* 1842. Medium 8vo, pp. 80. C., H., P. 14786

Characterized as "American Poetry" in the Publisher's Circular, No. 2084. 1841. *See also* "N. England," I. 53, "Dem. Rev.," XI. 630. Mr. Colton started the "American Review" in 1844.

COLTON (G. W.) Colton's Atlas of the World, illustrating Physical and Political Geography. By George W. Colton. Accompanied by Descriptions Geographical, Statistical, and Historical, by Richard Swainson Fisher, M.D. Volume I. North and South America, etc. *New York: J. H. Colton and Company.* 1856. Large 4to, 64 l. Plate and 62 Maps. BA. 14787

Contains plans of the principal cities of the United States and Canada. This collection of maps was *also* published as "Colton's Atlas of America," for separate sale to those having European atlases of the rest of the world.

COLTON. Colton's Condensed Octavo Atlas of the Union: containing Maps of all the States and Territories of the United States of America. *New York: J. H. Colton.* 1862. 8vo, pp. 7. 25 Maps. 14788

COLTON. Colton's New and Complete Statistical Gazeteer of the United States of America, founded on, and compiled from Official Federal and State Returns. *New York.* 1853. Rl. 8vo. 14789

COLTON. Colton's Journal of Geography and Collateral Sciences. No. I. *New York.* 1867. 8vo. 14790

COLTON (H. E.) Guide Book to the Scenery of Western North Carolina. By Henry E. Colton. *Ashville.* 1860. 8vo, pp. 16. 14791

COLTON. Mountain Scenery. The Scenery of the Mountains of Western North Carolina and Northwestern South Carolina. By Henry E. Colton. *Raleigh, N. C.: W. L. Pomeroy.* 1859. 12mo, pp. 119. Map. C. 14792

COLTON (J. H.) Colton's Travellers' and Tourists' Guide-Book through the United States. Containing the Routes and Distances on the great lines of travel by Railroads, Canals, Stage-Roads, and Steamboats. Together with Descriptions of the Several States, and of the Principle Cities, Towns, and Villages in Each. Accompanied with a Large and Accurate Map. *New York: J. H. Colton.* 1851. 18mo, pp. xiv, 249.

COLTON. Guide to West-Point. *New-York.* 1844. 12mo.

COLTON. Guide to Illinois. By J. H. Colton. *New York.* 1844. 12mo. Map. 14795

COLTON. Traveller and Tourist's Guide-Book through the Western States and Territories. *New-York: J. H. Colton & Co.* 1855. 12mo. + *New York.* [*Id.*] 1856. 12mo, pp. 109. Map. C. 14796

A similar book published at the same time describes the Eastern and Middle States.

COLTON. The Western Tourist, and Emigrant's Guide. *New-York.* 1845. 12mo. + *New York.* 1845, 1850. 18mo, pp. 89. 14797

COLTON (Simeon). [Masonic] Sermon at Amherst, Mass., June 26, 1826. *Amherst.* 1826. 8vo. W. 14798

COLTON (W.) Deck and Port; or, Incidents of a Cruise in the United States Frigate Congress to California. With Sketches of Rio Janeiro, Valparaiso, Lima, Honolulu, and San Francisco. By Rev. Walter Colton, U. S. N. ... *New York: A. S. Barnes & Co.* 1850. 12mo, pp. 408. C. + *London: Partridge.* 1851. 8vo. + *New York: A. S. Barnes & Burr.* 1860. 12mo, pp. 408. Illustrations. H. 14799

COLTON. Three Years in California. By Rev. Walter Colton, U. S. N. Late Alcalde of Monterey ... . *New York: A. S. Barnes & Co.* 1850. 12mo, pp. 456. H. + [*Ibid.*] 1851. + [*Ibid.*] 1852. + [*Ibid.*] 1856. B. + *New York: S. A. Rollo.* 1859. 12mo, pp. 456. 14800

Also: The Bible in the Public Schools. A Reply to the Allegations and Complaints contained in the Letter of Bishop Kenrick to the ... Controllers of Public Schools. *Philadelphia.* 1844. 8vo, pp. 16.

Columbia College. Academic Recreations by the Columbian Peitho-Logian Society of Columbia College. Vol. I. *New York: Eastburn, Kirk & Co.* 1815. 12mo, pp. 288. N. 14801

An Account of the Celebration of the First-Centennial Anniversary of the Incorporation of Columbia College, by the Legislature of New York; with the Oration [by Manton Eastburn, D.D.] and Poem [by William Betts, A.M.] delivered on the Occasion. *New York: G. & C. Corvill & Co.* 1837. 8vo, pp. 62, (1). 14802

An Address to the Citizens of New-York, on the Claims of Columbia College and the New University to their Patronage. *New-York.* 1830. 8vo, pp. 10. H. 14803

Address at the Inauguration of Mr. Charles King as President of Columbia College, New York, on Wednesday, November 28, 1849, in the College Chapel. ... *New York: Snowden.* 1849. 8vo, pp. 53. 14804

The Addresses by the President of Columbia College, at the late Commencement of that Institution, 9th September, 1843, upon delivering Medals to the Students who distinguished themselves at the Last Examination. ... *New-York: J. A. Fraetas.* 1843. 8vo, pp. 8. H. 14805

Addresses of the newly appointed Professors of Columbia College [Charles A. Joy, Francis Lieber, Charles Davies, C. M. Nairne], with an Introductory Address by William Betts, LL.D. February, 1858. *New York: the Trustees.* 1858. 8vo, 4 l., pp. 201. BA., C. 14806

Annual Catalogue of the Officers and Students of Columbia College. 1848–1859. *Published by the Senior Class.* 1860–70. 8vo. 14807

Annual Catalogue of the Officers and Students of the Law School of Columbia College, for ... 1859–60–69. *New York.* 1860–69. 8vo. Continued. H. 14808

Annual Commencement of Columbia College August 7, 1799. *New-York: C. and R. Waite.* [1799.] Broadside. H. 14809

Annual Report of the President of Columbia College, made to the Board of Trustees, June 4, 1866, June 1, 1868. *New oYrk: D. Van Nostrand.* 1866–68. 8vo. Continued. H.

A Brief Vindication of the Proceedings of the Trustees relating to the Columbia College. 14811

By-Laws of the School of Mines of Columbia College, adopted ... April 1st, 1867. *School of Mines.* 1867. 8vo, pp. 7. H.

Catalogue of Columbia College ... embracing the Names of its Trustees, Officers, and Graduates ... from 1752 to 1826 inclusive. *New York.* 8vo. + To 1836. *New York.* 1836. 8vo, pp. 48. + To 1844. *New York.* 1844. 8vo, pp. 69. + To 1864. *New York: D. Van Nostrand.* 1865. 8vo, pp. 112.

Catalogue of the Officers and Students of Columbia College, with the Graduates since 1844. ... *New York.* 1850–1870. 8vo. H. 14814

Catalogue of the Library of the School of Mines of Columbia College. May, 1869. *New York: S. Angell.* 1869. 8vo, pp. 58. 14815

Catalogus Collegii Columbiani Neo-Eboracensis, complectens Nomina eorum, qui aliquo Gradu fuerunt ornati; et eorum, qui in eo Auctoritatem qualemcunque exercuerunt, Nomine Rectorum, seu Moderatorum seu Curatorum; nec non Senatus Academici; ab Origine ad Annum 1814, inclusum. *Novi-Eboraci: typis Petri Van Pelt.* 1815. 8vo, pp. 55. H. 14816

Catalogus eorum exhibens Nomina qui in Collegio Regali Novi-Eboraci Laurea alicujus Gradus donati fuerunt ab anno 1758 ad annum 1774. *New York: H. Gaine.* Broadside.

"The only other known copy of this catalogue is in the Library of Yale College." *See* the Preface to the General Catalogue of 1856.

The Charter of the College of New-York, in America. Published by Order of His Honour the Lieutenant Governor, in Council. *New-York: Printed and Sold by J. Parker and W. Weyman, at the New Printing-Office in Beaver-Street.* MDCCLIV. pp. 13. C. 14818

Royal arms on title. Also: The Additional Charter granted to the Governors of the College of New York, in America. *New York.* 1755. Folio, pp. 4. N.

Charter of King's College, with the Act creating an University within the State of New York, and making Sundry Alterations in the said Charter. *New York: Hugh Gaine.* 1796. 8vo, pp. 47. 14819

The Charter of Columbia College, in the City of New York, as amended ... 23d March, 1810. *New York.* 1810. 8vo, pp. 8. 14820

Columbia College Library. Report of the Librarian to the Library Committee. May 14th, 1862. *New York.* 1862. 8vo, pp. 24. H. 14821

Commencement of Columbia College, of New-York. October, 1850. *New-York: Baker, Godwin & Co.* 1850. 8vo, pp. 14. H. 14822

The Constitution and By-Laws of the Philolexian Society of Columbia College ... . To which are annexed Divisions of the Presidents and Standing Committees upon Questions arising under the Same. Together with a List of Members. *New York.* 1834. 12mo. + *New York.* 1842. 12mo, pp. 32. + *New-York: Henry M. Onderdonk.* MDCCCXLVII. 8vo, pp. 31. H. + *New York.* 1860. 8vo, pp. 46. 14823

Constitution of the Association of the Alumni of Columbia College. *New York: John F. Trow, Printer.* 1859. 8vo, pp. 8. 14824

The Constitution of the Columbian Peithologian Society; with a List of Members. *New York.* 1838. 12mo, pp. 12. + *New York.* 1849. 8vo, pp. 37. + *New York.* 1861. 8vo, pp. 31. 14825

A Draught of Statutes for Columbia College, presented ... September 3, 1810. *New York.* 1810. 8vo, pp. 17. N. 14826

Duty of ... to the Community. *See* [Ruggles (S. B.)]

History of the Controversy in the University of the City of New York, &c. By the Professors of the Faculty of Science and Letters. *New York.* 1838. 8vo. 14827

Inaugural Addresses of Theodore W. Dwight ... and of George P. Marsh ... in Columbia College, New York. *New York: the Trustees.* 1859. 8vo, 2 l., pp. 93. BA. 14828

A Lecture, introductory to a Course of Law Lectures in Columbia College. Delivered February 2, 1824. ... *New York: printed by Clayton and Van Norden.* 1824. 8vo, pp. 23. H.

A Letter to the Trustees. *See* [Wilkins (G. M.)]

The Original Charter of Columbia College, in the City of New-York, October 31st, 1754; with the Acts of the Legislature ... amending the same; or relating to the College [the Statutes, revised and passed by the Board of Trustees, May, 1836; and Catalogue of the Names of the Trustees, Officers, and Graduates of the College; with a List of all the Academical Honours conferred by the Institution, from A.D. 1758, to A.D.

1836, inclusive.] *New York: Columbia College.* M DCCC XXXVI. 8vo, pp. 45. BA. 14830

The Original Charter of Columbia College, ... October 31st, 1754; With the Acts of Legislature altering and amending the same, or relating to the College. *New York: Hall, Clayton & Co.* 1854. 8vo, pp. 34. H. 14831

Proceedings at the Inauguration of Frederick A. P. Barnard ... as President of Columbia College ... October 3, 1864. Published by order of the ... Trustees. 1864. *New York: Hurd and Houghton.* 1865. 8vo, pp. 106. BA., H. 14832

A Remark on the Disputes and Contentions in This Province. By David Marin Ben Jesse, Pastor at Aquenonka. Thou shalt not seethe a kid in his Mother's Milk. Moses. *New-York: Printed by H. Gaine, at the Printing-Office, in Queen-Street, between the Fly and Meal-Markets.* 1755. 4to, pp. 12. B., J. 14833

Relates to the College Trouble in New York.

Report of a Committee of the Trustees of Columbia College, appointed to consider and report on the Subjects of the Removal of the College, a Change in the Collegiate Course, the Establishment of a University System, &c. ... *New York: Hall, Clayton & Co.* 1854. 8vo, pp. 36. H. 14834

Report of a Committee of the Trustees of Columbia College appointed to inquire into the Condition of the Institution, and to consider such Measures as might be judged expedient to increase its Efficiency and Usefulness. ... *New York: pri nted by John W. Amerman.* 1858. 8vo, pp. 67, 35, 56, 103, 99, 6, 83, 6, 11, 24, 40, 27, 166. 14835

Report of a Committee of the Trustees of Columbia College on the Subject of appointing a Teacher of Elocution. *New York: Printed by Order of the Trustees.* MDCCCXL. [Should be MDCCCLX.] 8vo, pp. 6. 14836

Report of the Committee charged with an Inquiry into the State of Columbia College ... Rufus King, Chairman, February 6, 1809. 4to, pp. 14. N. 14837

Report relative to the Course of Instruction and Discipline in Columbia College, presented to the Board of Trustees, February 28, 1810 [Rufus King, Chairman]. *New York.* 1810. 8vo, pp. 24. N. 14838

Report of the Trustees of Columbia College in Reply to the Senate Committee. [*New York.* 1854.] 8vo, pp. 16. H.

School of Mines, Columbia College, 1864–65—1868–69. [*New York.* 1864–6.] 8vo. H. 14840

Semi-Annual Merit Roll of the Under-Graduate Classes in Columbia College, for the First Session of the Year 1864–1865, ... *New York: D. Van Nostrand.* 1865. 8vo, pp. 14, (2). H. 14841

The Statutes of Columbia College in New-York. *New York: Samuel Loudon.* M,DCC,LXXV. 8vo, pp. 18. Plan. H. + *New York.* 1785. 8vo, pp. 18. Plan. + *New York.* 1788. 8vo, pp. 15. C. + *New York.* 1810. 8vo, pp. 17. N. + *New York.* 1811. 8vo, pp. 32. + June 18, 1811. *New York: Printed by T. and J. Swords.* 1811. 16mo, pp. 32. H. + *New York: T. & J. Swords.* 1816. 8vo, pp. 29. + March, 1821. *New York: printed by T. & J. Swords.* 1821. 8vo, pp. 32. H. + Revised ... October, 1827. *New-York: printed by T. and J. Swords.* 1827. 16mo, pp. 32. + *New York: E. B. Clayton.* 1836. 8vo, pp. 40. + *Printed ... by R. Craighead.* 1840. 8vo, pp. 39. + *Printed for Columbia College.* 1848. 8vo, pp. 28. + *New York.* 1851. 8vo, pp. 30. + *New York.* 1853. 8vo, pp. 28. + *New York.* 1856. 8vo, pp. 24. + Statutes of Columbia College and its Associated Schools, to which are added the Permanent Resolutions of the Board of Trustees. *New York.* 1866. 8vo, pp. 92. 14842

These are not reprints, but in all cases except the following, revised statutes: The editions of 1836 and 1840 contain the statutes as revised and passed in May, 1836. The lists of the trustees and faculty differ. The editions of 1851, 1853, and 1856, contain the statutes as revised in 1851, but with different lists of officers. To the editions, from 1811 to 1840, is appended an extract from the second report of a committee appointed to inquire into the state of Columbia College, presented to the trustees Feb. 28, 1810. To the editions from 1836, inclusive, is prefixed a "Historical Sketch of Columbia College." The following were not published by the College, but relate to it: *'Αιέν αριβτευέιν.* ... The Columbiad. Esto perpetua. Published by the Junior Class, April, 1868. *New York: D. Van Nostrand.* 1868. 8vo, pp. 64. Continued.

Statute proposed by the Committee on the Medical Faculty. [n. p. n. d.] 8vo, pp. 8. 14843

A Statute, passed at a Meeting of the Board of Trustees of Columbia College, on the 16th January, 1830. [*New York.* 1830.] 8vo, pp. 4. H. 14844

COLUMBIA, *Conn.* The 150th Anniversary of the Organization of the Congregational Church in Columbia, Conn., Octo-

ber 24th, 1866. Historical Papers, Addresses, with Appendix. *Hartford: printed by Case, Lockwood & Co.* 1867. 8vo, pp. 96.

Prospectus of the Columbia Gold-Mining Co., and Description of its Property in Central City ... Colorado Territory. *Boston: Geo. C. Rand & Avery, Printers.* 1865. 8vo, pp. 23.

Fourth Annual Report of the President and Directors to the Stockholders of the Columbia Oil Company. *Pittsburgh: A. A. Anderson & Sons.* 1866. 8vo, pp. 31. H. 14847

COLUMBIA, *District of.* *See* District of Columbia.

COLUMBIA BRIDGE, *Pa.* A Reply to the Board of Managers, to a Report of a Committee of the Stockholders of the Columbia, Pa., Bridge Company. *Columbia, Pa.: printed by William Greer.* 1820. 12mo, pp. 46. 14848

Also: Opinion of Horace Binney, Esquire, on a Report of a Committee of Stockholders of the Columbia Bridge Company, made on the fourth May, 1820. [n. p. n. d.] 12mo, pp. 12.

COLUMBIA RIVER. Message from the President, communicating the letter of Mr. Provost and other documents relating to an establishment made at the mouth of Columbia River, Jan. 27. *Washington.* 1823. 8vo, pp. 45. 14849

There are numerous papers in the Congressional Documents relating to this river.

Notices of the Harbor at the Mouth of the Columbia River. By the Commander and other Officers of the Exploring Expedition. [n. p. 1846.] 8vo, pp. 22. H. 14850

COLUMBIA SPRINGS, *N. Y.* Descriptive Circular, of the Columbia Springs, Stockport, N. Y. *Hudson: R. Van Antwerp, Printer.* 1855. 12mo. 14851

COLUMBIA, *S. C.* The Report of the Committee of the Convention of the Union and State Rights Party, ... at Columbia, 10th December, 1832. With their Remonstrance and Protest, [*sic.* n. p. n. d.] 8vo, pp. 8. BA. 14852

COLUMBIA. Bank Secrets of the Bank of Columbia. [n. p.] 1801. 4to, pp. 2. C. 14853

A Catalogue of the Officers and Students of the Theological Seminary at Columbia, S. C., March, 1835. *Columbia.* 1835. 8vo, pp. 7. M. 14854

Sack and Destruction of Columbia. *See* [Trezevant (D. H.)]

COLUMBIA, *Tenn.* Annual Catalogue of the Teachers and Pupils of the Columbia Female Institute, Columbia, Tennessee, for the Scholastic Year 1857–8. *Columbia, Tenn.: John E. Hatcher.* 1858. 12mo, pp. 12. H. 14855

The Columbiad: Or, a Poem on the American War, in Thirteen Cantoes. *Philadelphia: Printed by Jacob Johnson & Co.* ... 1795. 12mo, pp. iv, 46. B., H., P., S. 14856

The preface is signed, A New-Jersey Farmer. In heroic verse.

The Columbian Almanac for Town and Country, for 1789. *Wilmington, Del.* 1799. Continued. 14857

The Columbian Almanack and Agricultural Repository for the Year of our Lord 1804. *Dedham, Mass.* 1804. 16mo, pp. 63. 14858

Columbian College, D. C. Annual Circular of the National Medical College (Department of Columbian College,) Washington. For the Session of 1860–61. *Washington: printed by Henry Polkinhorn.* 1860. 12mo, pp. 12. H. 14859

Catalogue of the Columbian College in the District of Columbia; embracing the Names of its Trustees, Officers, and Graduates; together with a List of all Academical Honors conferred, &c. *Washington.* 1839. 8vo. + *Washington.* 1851.

A Catalogue of the Officers and Students of Columbia College, District of Columbia. 1855–56. 1868–69. *Washington.* 1856–69. 8vo. H. 14861

Catalogue of the Enosionian Society, Columbian College, District of Columbia. Instituted ... 1822. *Washington: published by the Society.* 1859. 8vo, pp. 45, 1 l. H. 14862

Columbian Eloquence. *See* Chase (S.), Vol. III., No. 12209.

The Columbian Harmonist, or Songster's Repository: being a Selection of the most approved Sentimental, Patriotic, and other Songs. *New-York: Smith & Forman.* 1814. 24mo, pp. 282 (6). 14863

The Columbian Harp, a Collection of Sacred, Vocal, and Instrumental Music. ... By an American. ... *Northampton, Massachusetts.* 1812. Oblong 4to, pp. 60. H. 14864

Columbian Historical Society. Constitution and By Laws, &c. August, 1833. *Washington.* 1833. 8vo. + *Washington.* 1838. 8vo. 14865

Columbian Institute. Address to the Columbian Institute, on the Question, "What ought to be the Circulating Medium of a Nation?" *Washington.* 1830. 14866

Columbian Lady's and Gentleman's Magazine: Edited by J. Inman. *New York.* 1844. 8vo. S. 14867

The Columbian Library. Vol. I. The Well-Bred Scholar or Practical Essays. ... By W. Milns. *New York.* 1797. 18mo. S. 14868

The Columbian Magazine; or Monthly Miscellany Containing a View of the History, Literature, Manners & Characters of the Year 1787–1789. ... *Philadelphia: T. Seddon, W. Spotswood, C. Cist, and J. Trenchard.* 1786. 8vo. BA. 14869

An extremely rare magazine. It commenced with Nov., 1786, and was continued to the year 1792, forming altogether twelve volumes. It is ornamented with numerous portraits and other engravings, principally by Trenchard, who was one of the proprietors of the work. The others were T. Seddon, Charles Cist, C. Talbot, W. Spotswood, and Mathew Cary. The latter, however, from "the discomfort arising from the discordant views of the different partners, the utter improbability of such a work producing any profit worth the attention of five persons, and other considerations," was induced to withdraw from the concern, and, in January, 1787, commenced, on his own account, "The American Museum." *See* Vol. I., No. 1162.

Columbian Magazine. June, 1798. *Kingston, Jamaica.* 1798. 12mo. 14870

Columbian Magazine. *Hudson, New-York.* 1814. 8vo.

Columbian Magazine ... 1848. Edited by S. M. Chester. *New York: John S. Taylor.* 1848. 8vo. 14872

Columbian Mercury and Canaan Repository of Rural Knowledge: Vol. I. *Canaan, N. Y.* 1794. Folio. S. 14873

The Columbian Muse. | A | Selection | of | American Poetry, | from | various Authors | of | Established Reputation. | *New-York:* | *printed by J. Carey,* | *for Mathew Carey, Philadelphia.* | 1794. 12mo, 2 l., pp. 224. BA. 14874

A garland of poems by the earliest American poets. Morrell's copy sold for $10.

The Columbian Naval Melody; a Collection of Songs and Odes on the late Naval Victories. *Boston.* 1813. 12mo.

Columbian Phœnix and Boston Review, containing Useful Information on Literature, Religion, Morality, Politics and Philosophy. With many Interesting Particulars in History and Biography. Forming a Compendium of the Present State of Society. Vol. I, for 1800. *Boston: Joseph Hawkins.* 1800. 8vo, pp. 451, (1). 2 Plates. BA., C., S. 14876

Edited by J. Hawkins and D. Tillotson. Contains several eulogies, and a number of papers relating to the death of Washington.

The Columbian Preacher; or a Collection of Original Sermons, from Preachers of Eminence in the United States. Embracing the distinguishing Doctrines of Grace. Volume I. *Catskill: published by Nathan Elliot.* 1808. 8vo, pp. 304. H.

Columbian Songster, and Freemason's Companion. *Portsmouth, New Hampshire.* 1798. 14878

Columbian Songster, or Jovial Companion ... Choice Songs ... of which nearly Fifty are American Productions. *New-York: Greenleaf's Press.* 1797. 18mo, pp. 232. S. 14879

Columbian Songster. Being a large collection of Fashionable Songs, for Gentlemen and Ladies. 1799. 16mo. + *Philadelphia.* 1814. pp. 32. 14880

Third Annual Exhibition of the Columbian Society of Artists and the Pennsylvania Academy. 1813. *Philadelphia: Printed by T. and G. Palmer.* 1813. 8vo, pp. 26. BA. 14881

Columbian Star: 1822. *Washington City.* 1826. Folio.

Edited by James D. Knowles, Baron Stow, etc., under the patronage of the General Convention of the Baptist denomination in the United States.

The Constitution of the Columbianum, or American Academy of the Fine Arts. *Philadelphia.* 1795. 14883

The Columbian Telescope and Literary Compiler; being a Miscellaneous Repository of Literary Productions. June 16, 1819, to May 20, 1820. *Alexandria, D. C.: S. H. Davis.* 1819–20. 4to, pp. iv, 204. C. 14884

Columbian Tragedy. *Boston.* 1792. 14885

An ancient handbill, with ballads.

The Columbian Parnassiad. 14886

COLUMBIANA COUNTY. Premiums and Regulations, Rules and Instructions, with the names of Executive and Awarding Committees for the Annual Fair of the Columbiana County Agricultural Society, to be held ... at New Lisbon, O. ... October 13th, 14th and 15th, 1853. *New Lisbon, O.: R. D. Hartshorn, Printer.* 1853. 8vo, pp. 33. H. 14887

Columbia's Freedom, a Series of Poems by a South Carolinean. 12mo. 14888

Columbia's Legacy, 1796. *See* Washington (G.)

Columbia's Naval Triumphs. *New-York: Inskeep & Bradford.* 1813. 18mo, pp. 132. 14889

Pages 67–132 contain historical notes.

COLUMBUS (C.) *See* Colombo (C.)

The Columbus Almanac For ... 1822. By William Lusk. *Washington.* 1821. 12mo. 14890

Columbus. Amerikanische Miscellen. Herausgegeben von C. N. Röding, Phil. Dr. ... *Hamburg: Harold und Hoffman & Campe.* [1825–32]. 16 vols., 8vo. 14891

COLUMBUS, *Ohio.* Catalogue of the Officers and Students of Capital University, Columbus, Ohio. *Columbus: Nevins & Myers.* 1869. 8vo, pp. 19. Frontispiece. H. 14892

City of Columbus, Ohio. City Documents. Reports of the Various Departments; also a Financial Statement of Receipts, Disbursements, &c., for the Municipal Year ending April 9, 1869. ... *Columbus: Nevins & Myers, Printers.* 1869. 8vo, pp. 58. H. 14893

Directory of the City of Columbus for the Year 1848, containing a Brief History of the City, Statistics of Institutions, and the Names, Residence and Business of all Citizens, Inhabitants, &c. By John Siebert. *Columbus: S. Medway, Printer.* 1848. 12mo, 2 l., pp. 264. G. 14894

Perhaps the first Directory. The Directory for 1850–51 was edited by E. Glover and W. Henderson. *Columbus: E. Glover.* 1850. 16mo, pp. 239. C. Continued as the Columbus Directory, City Guide, and Business Mirror, 1856–'7. By C. S. Williams. *Columbus.* 1856. 8vo. C.—Columbus Directory and Classified Business Mirror for 1864. Compiled by C. A. Poland. *Columbus: Rich. Nevins, Printer.* 1864. 8vo, pp. 190.—Williams' Columbus Directory for 1866–7. To which is appended a United States Post Office Directory, corrected up to Date. Compiled by Williams & Co. *Columbus, O.: J. H. Riley & Co.* 8vo, pp. 256.—Williams' Columbus Directory for 1867–8. *Columbus, O.: G. W. Gleason.* 8vo, pp. 246, 72.

A Memorial from the Citizens of Columbus, on the Subject of an Armory and Arsenal, to be established ... at Columbus, Ohio. *Columbus: Richard Nevins.* 1862. 8vo, pp. 22. 14895

New England Society of Columbus, Ohio. Constitution and By-Laws, Dec. 5, 1843. 14896

Columbus, *pseudonym.* The Crisis: An Appeal to the Candid World, on the War Entered into by the United States against Great Britain. By Columbus. [n. d.] 8vo. w. 14897

Columbus, *pseudonym.* The Letters of Columbus, originally published in the Boston Bulletin: to which are added two Letters of Col. Orne to Gen. Duff Green. *Boston: published by Putnam & Hunt.* 1829. 8vo, pp. 24. s. 14898

Columbus, *pseudonym.* Origin and True Causes of the Texas Insurrection, commenced in 1835. By Columbus. *Philadelphia.* 1836. 8vo. 14899

Columella, *pseudonym*, 1806. *See* [Moore (Clement)].

Colver (N.) The Fugitive Slave Bill ... . A Sermon, Preached on Sunday, October 20, 1850; by Rev. Nathaniel Colver ... *Boston: J. M. Hewes & Co.* 1850. 8vo, pp. 24.

Colver. Slavery or Freedom must Die. The Harper's Ferry Tragedy. A symptom of a Disease in the Heart of the Nation; or the power of Slavery to destroy the Liberties of the Nation, from which there is no Escape but in the destruction of Slavery itself. By Nathaniel Colver ... *Cincinnati: Office of Christian Luminary.* 1860. 8vo, pp. 16. 14901

Also: Three Lectures on Odd Fellowship. ... with an Essay on its Practical Influence in regard to Church Discipline. *Boston: William S. Damrell.* 1844. 8vo, pp. 32. H.

Colvill (*Mr.*) Savannah, a Poem in two Cantos to the Memory of the Honourable Colonel John Maitland. By Mr. Colvill. Second Edition. *London: Printed for T. Cadell.* MDCCLXXX. 4to, pp. 20. J.C.B. 14902

Colvin (J. B.) Candid Views of Facts, in a Letter from John B. Colvin to a Federal Friend. *Frederick-Town, Md.* 1804. 12mo. c. 14903

Colvin. Historical Letters, including a Brief but General View of the History of the World. By John B. Colvin, Esq. Second Edition. ... *Georgetown, D. C.: Joseph Milligan.* 1821. 12mo, pp. 290, Subscriber's names, pp. 5. BA. 14904

Colvin. Republican Economy; or Evidences of the Superiority of the present Administration over that of John Adams, &c. By John B. Colvin. *Fredericktown.* [1802.] 8vo, pp. 12. Table. c. 14905

Colvin. Weekly Register. Jan. 15, 1808. *Washington.* 1808. 8vo. c. 14906

Colvocoresses (G. M.) Four Years in the Government Exploring Expedition to ... Brazil, Coast of Patagonia ... . Chili, Peru, &c., commanded by Captain Charles Wilkes. By Lieut. Geo. M. Colvocoresses. *New York.* 1852. 12mo, pp. 372. + Fifth Edition. *New York: J. M. Fairchild & Co.* 1855. 12mo, pp. 371. B., C. 14907

Colwell (S.) The Claims of Labor, and their Precedence to the Claims of Free Trade. By Stephen Colwell. *Philadelphia: C. Sherman & Son.* 1861. 8vo, pp. 52. 14908

[Colwell.] The Five Cotton States and New York; or, Remarks upon the Social and Economical Aspects of the Southern Political Crisis. *January*, 1861. 8vo, pp. 64.

[Colwell.] A Letter to Members of the Legislature of Pennsylvania, on the Removal of Deposits from the Bank of the United States, ... By W. Penn [*pseudonym*]. *Philadelphia.* 1834. 8vo, pp. 45. 14910

[Colwell.] New Themes for the Protestant Clergy: Creeds without Charity, Theology without Humanity, and Protestantism without Christianity. With Notes, by the Editor, on the Literature of Charity, Population, Pauperism, Political Economy, and Protestantism. *Philadelphia.* 1851. 12mo, pp. 398. P. + Second Edition. *Philadelphia.* 1854. 12mo, pp. xxvi–384.

[Colwell.] Politics for American Christians: with an Appendix on the Politics of the New Testament, and some notice of a Review, by a Layman, of "New Themes for the Protestant Clergy." *Philadelphia.* 1852. 8vo, pp. 134. P. 14912

Some copies have the following title:

[Colwell.] Politics for American Christians; a Word upon our Example as a Nation, our Labor, our Trade, Elections, Education, and Congressional Legislation. *Philadelphia.* 1852. 8vo, pp. 134. P. 14913

Colwell. The Position of Christianity in the United States, in its Relations with our Political Institutions, and specially with reference to Religious Instruction in the Public Schools. By Stephen Colwell. *Philadelphia: Lippincott, Grambo & Co.* 1854. 8vo, pp. 175. c. 14914

[Colwell.] The Relative Position in our Industry of Foreign Commerce, Domestic Production, and Internal Trade. By Jonathan B. Wise. *Philadelphia.* 1850. 8vo, pp. 50.

[Colwell.] The South; A Letter from A Friend in the North, with Special Reference to the Effects of Disunion upon Slavery. *Philadelphia: Printed for the Author.* 1856. 8vo, pp. 46. 14916

Colwell. The Ways and Means of Payment: a Full Analysis of the Credit System, with its various Modes of Adjustment. By Stephen Colwell. *Philadelphia: J. B. Lippincott & Co.* 1859. 8vo, pp. xii, 644. B., BA., H. 14917

"Banks of the United States," pp. 444–509, and various incidental comparisons of the financial system of the United States and other countries.

Colyer (V.) Brief Report of the Services Rendered by the Freed People to the United States Army in North Carolina, In the Spring of 1862, after the Battle of Newbern. By Vincent Colyer, Superintendent of the Poor under Major-General Burnside. Illustrated. *New York: Published by Vincent Colyer, 105 Bleecker Street.* 1864. 8vo, pp, 63, (1). 14918

Colyer. Report of Vincent Colyer, Superintendent N. Y. State Soldiers' Depot, in the City of New York. Presented to ... Gov. Fenton, Sept. 21, 1865. *New York: G. A. Whitehorne, Printer.* 1865. 8vo, pp. 56. H. 14919

Colyer. Report of the Christian Mission to the United States Army of Vincent Colyer, ... from April, 1861, to August, 1862, including the Battles of Bull Run, Roanoke Island and Newbern. *New York: George A. Whitehorne, Printer.* [1862.] 8vo, pp. 24. H. 14920

Colyer. Union League Club of New York. Report of Vincent Colyer, on the Reception and Care of the Soldiers returning from the War. Presented September 14th, 1865. [*New York*:] *Club House.* 1865. 8vo, pp. 56. H. 14921

Colyn (M.) *See* Colijn (M.), No. 14351, etc.

[Coman (J. M.)] Report of the President of the Decatur Branch Bank. *Tuscalossa.* 1845. 8vo. 14922

Combat naval de Hampton-Roads (Etat-Unis) 8 et 9 mars 1862. *Paris: Challamel aîné.* 1862. 8vo, pp. 14. 2 Plates.

Reprinted from the "Revue maritime, avr. 1862."

Combe (G.) Notes on the United States of America, during a Phrenological Visit in 1838–9–40. By George Combe. ... *Edinburgh.* 1841. 3 vols., post 8vo. P. + *Philadelphia: Carey & Hart.* 1841. 2 vols., 12mo, pp. xxvi, 13–374; Title, pp. 9–405. B., BA. 14924

See "N. Am. Rev.," LIII. 534, and "Q. Rev.," LXVIII. 281.

Combier (C.) Voyage au golfe de Californie. Grands courants de la mer. ... Description de la Sonora et de ses richesses minérales; de la basse Californie ses volcans, ses produits. La pèche des perles. La chaine des Cordillères, ses forêts. Nuits de la zone torride. Par C. Combier. ... *Paris: A. Bertrand.* 1864. 8vo, pp. xvi, 554. Map of Sonora.

The Combined Petroleum Company. Incorporated under the Laws of the State of New York. ... *New York: B. F. Corlies & Macy.* 1865. 8vo, pp. 15. H. 14926

Combs (L.) Address of General Leslie Combs, delivered before the Public Debt Committee of the Legislature of Texas, January 12, 1854. *Austin: J. W. Hampton.* [1854.] 8vo, pp. 20. H. 14927

Combs. Col. Wm. Dudley's Defeat opposite Fort Meigs, May 5th, 1813. Official Report from Capt. Leslie Combs to General Green Clay. *Printed for William Dodge: Cincinnati.* 1849. 8vo, pp. 13. 14928

Combs. Narrative of the Life of General Leslie Combs; embracing Incidents in the Early History of the Northwestern Territory. *American Whig Printing Office.* 1852. 8vo, pp. 20. + *Washington: J. T. and Lem. Towers.* 1855. 8vo, pp. 24.

Also: A Reply to General Andrew Jackson's Letter, of the 31st October, 1828. Published in the Nashville Republican. By Leslie Combs. [n. p. n. d.] 8vo, pp. 8.

Comella (L. F.) Christoval Colon: comedia en tres actos, por Don Luciano Francisco Comella. *Barcelona: Juan Francisco Piferrer.* [n. d.] 4to, pp. 36. H. 14930

Comer. Annual Catalogue and Circular of Terms of Comer's Commercial College, Boston. ... [*Boston.* 1856.] 8vo, pp. 31, (1). Continued. 14931

Comercio libro vindicado de la nota del ruinoso a la España y á las Americas. *Cadiz: Imprenta del Estado mayor general.* 1811. 4to, pp. 40. 14932

Dated, 8 août, 1811. Signed S. T. O. G., *i. e.*, Satariego–Teran–Obregon G. *See* Leclerc, No. 373.

The Comet. By Walter Wildfire: edited by Joseph T. Buckingham. *Boston.* 1811. 8vo. s. 14933

The Comet. Vol. I. *New York.* 1832. 8vo. 14934

Comettant (O.) En Amérique, en France et ailleurs. Par Oscar Comettant. *Paris: imp. Voisvenel.* 1862. 4to, pp. 136. (Publications du journal le Siècle.) + 1865. [*Ibid.*] + 1868. [*Ibid.*] 14935

Comettant. L'Amérique telle qu'elle est Voyage anecdotique de Marcel Bonneau dans le Nord et le Sud des Etats-Unis excursion au Canada par Oscar Comettant *Paris: Achille Faure.* 18mo, 2 l., pp. 392. + [*Ibid.*] 1864. 18mo, pp. 396. 14936

Comettant. Le naufrage de l'Evening Star et la colère céleste en Amerique. Lettre au Révérend Charles B. Smith, de l'Eglise presbytérienne d'Amérique. Par Oscar Comettant. *Paris: A. Faure.* 1866. 8vo, pp. 32. 14937

Comettant. Le Nouveau-Monde, coutumes, mœurs et scènes de la vie américaine. Par Oscar Comettant. *Paris: impr. Voisvenel.* 1863. 4to, pp. 147. (Publications du journal le Siècle.) + 1864. 4to, pp. 166. (Siècle.) + 1868. 4to, pp. 166. (Siècle.) + 1870. 4to. (Siècle.) 14938

Comettant. Trois ans aux États-Unis. Étude de mœurs et coutumes américaines. Par M. Oscar Commettant. *Paris: Pagnerre.* 1857. 18mo, pp. 368. + Deuxième édition, revue et corrigée. *Paris: Pagnerre.* 1858. 18mo. pp. 396. 14939

Comettant. Voyage pittoresque et anecdotique dans le nord et le sud des Etats-Unis d'Amérique. Par Oscar Comettant. Dessins de MM. Saintin, J. Noel, Lebreton, etc. *Paris: Laplace.* 1865. 8vo, pp. vii, 469. 22 Illustrations. 14940

The following, perhaps, relate to America in part:

Comettant. Les civilisations inconnus. Par Oscar Comettant. *Paris: Pagnerre.* 1863. 18mo, pp. 403. 14941

Comettant. Gustave Lambert au pôle nord. Ce qu'il y va faire. Par Oscar Comettant ... . *Paris: Passart.* 1868. 8vo, pp. 40. + *Paris: Dentu.* 1868. 8vo, pp. 48. Map.

Comfield (A. S.) Alida; or, Miscellaneous Sketches of Incidents during the Late American War, with Poems. By Mrs. Amelia Stratton Comfield. *New York: Angell & Engell.* 1849. 12mo, pp. 240. c. 14943

Comfort (G. F.) Esthetics in Collegiate Education. By George F. Comfort ... . [From the Methodist Quarterly Review, October, 1867. n. p. 1867.] 8vo, pp. 567–593. H.

The Comfortable Chambers. *See* [Mather (Cotton)].

The Comical Adventures of Roderick Random and his Friend Strap, with their Voyage to South America. *Philadelphia: Published by D. Hogan.* 1810. 18mo, pp. 106. 14945

Pages 69–106 consist of the life of the celebrated Commodore Paul Jones.

The Coming Battle, and the Appalling National Convulsions foreshown in Prophecy immediately to occur during the period 1861–67. ... By an Episcopal Minister. *Philadelphia: W. Harbert.* Rl. 8vo, pp. 32. 14946

The Coming Contraband. *See* [Nott (C. G.)]

The Coming of Christ in his Kingdom, and the "gates wide open" to the Future Earth and Heaven. Adventism, Millennarianism, and a gross Materialism exposed and refuted. By a Congregationalist Minister. *New York: N. Tibbals & Co.* [1869.] 2 l., pp. 340, 2 l. c. 14947

The Coming Struggle among the Nations of the Earth; or the Political Events of the next fifteen years ... Author's American Edition. *New York.* 1853. 8vo, pp. 40. s. 14948

Comingo (H. G.) Memorial of Henry G. Comingo, D.D.; containing his Twenty-fifth Anniversary Discourse, Proceedings of the Anniversary Meeting, Two Sermons Nov. 24th, and Funeral Discourse by C. C. Beatty. *Steubenville (O.), Herald.* 1832. 8vo, pp. 62. c. 14949

Comins (L. B.) Assault on Senator Sumner. Speech of Hon. Linus B. Comins, of Massachusetts, ... in the ... House ... July 10, 1856. *Washington.* 1856. 8vo, pp. 16. BA.

Comins. President's Message. Speech of Hon. Linus B. Comins, in Defence of the Financial Institutions of Massachusetts. Delivered in the U. S. House ... January 28, 1858. *Washington: Buell and Blanchard.* 1858. 8vo, pp. 15. H.

Comitatus, *pseudonym.* Reconstruction on "My Policy;" or, its Author at the Confessional. By Zedekiah Comitatus. *Skaggaddahunk: Scantlewood, Timberlake & Co., Printers to the "North River Society."* 1866. 8vo, pp. 29. H. 14952

Annuaire du Comité d'archéologie américaine. Deuxieme édition. *Paris: Maisonneuve et Cie.* 1867. 8vo. 14953

Comitibus (Natalis de). *See* Conti (N.)

Comly (J.) An Epistle, or Salutation in Gospel Love: with a Word of Encouragement to all who believe in the Light, that they may "Walk in the Light," and thereby know an Advancement in the Way of Life and Salvation. To which is added, a Further Address to Friends on the Order and Discipline of our Religious Society. Also, some Views and Remarks intended for the Promotion of the Peace and Harmony of Society, and the Quiet and Solemnity of our Religious Meetings. By John Comly. *Philadelphia: J. Richards.* 1832. 18mo, pp. 36. H.

Comly. Journal of the Life and Religious Labours of John Comly, late of Byberry, Pennsylvania. Published by his Children. *Philadelphia: T. Ellwood Chapman.* 1853. 8vo. P. 14955

Comly (J. *and* I.) Friends' Miscellany: being a collection of Essays and Fragments, Biographical, Religious, Epistolary, Narrative, and Historical; designed for the promotion of piety and virtue, to preserve in remembrance the characters and views of exemplary individuals, and to rescue from oblivion those manuscripts left by them, which may be useful to survivors. Edited by John and Isaac Comly, Byberry. *Philadelphia.* 1831–1839. 12 vols., 12mo. 14956

A second edition of some of the volumes was issued between 1834 and 1845.

[Commelin (Isaac).] Begin ende Voortgang | Vande | Vereenigde Needer- | landtsche | Geoctroyeerde | Oost-Indische | Com-

pagnie. | 't Eerste Deel || 't Tweede Deel. | [*Amsterdam: Jan Jansz.* 1644?] Oblong 4to. 14957

The voyages described are: Vol. I. Candish and Drake; Raleigh and Keymis; De Veer; Houtman; Van Neck and Warwijck; De Weert; Van Noort; Both and Van Caerden; Van Neck (2d voyage); Van der Hagen; Harmansz; Spilbergen and Le Maire. Vol. II. Warwijck and De Weert; Van der Hagen (2d voyage); Matelief; Van Caerden; Verhoeff; Van den Broecke; Van Twist; Spilbergen (1st voyage); L'Hermite; Schram and Van Rechteren. Each part is separately paged, and those which relate to America are fully described under their proper heads in this Dictionary. Tiele, from whom I take the title and contents, had never met with but one copy. *See* his "Navig. néerland," pp. 9–15.

[Commelin.] Begin ende Voortgangh, | van de | Vereenighde Nederlantsche Geoctroyeerde Oost-Indische | Compagnie | Vervatende | De voornaemste Reysen, by de Inwoonderen derselver | Provincien derwaerts gedaen. | Alles | Nevens de beschrijvinghen der Rijcken, Eylanden, Havenen, | Revieren, Stroomen, Rheeden, Winden, Diepten en Ondiepten; Mitsga- | ders Religien, Manieren, Aerdt, Politie ende Regeeringhe der Volcke- | ren; oock meede haerder Speceryen, Drooghen, Geldt ende | andere Koopmanschappen, met veele Discoursen verrijckt: | Nevens eenighe Koopere Platen verciert. | Nut ende dienstigh alle Curieuse, ende andere Zee-varende Liefhebbers. | Met dry Besondere Tafels ofte Registers, in twee Delen verdeelt: | Waer van't eerste begrijpt, | veerthien voyagien, den meeren-deelen voor desen | noyt in't licht geweest. | *Gedruckt in den Jaere.* 1645. | [n. p.] Oblong 4to.

The printed title of Part II. is somewhat abridged. Both parts have also engraved titles. This edition omits Candish and Drake, Raleigh and Keymis, but adds Hagenaer and Caron. This edition contains, for the first time, an introduction by Commelin, which gives a resumé of the Dutch voyages to the Indies till 1631.

Commelin. Begin [as above]. *Gedruckt in den jare* 1646. Oblong 4to, Engraved Title, Title, pp. (22), 71, 112, 56, 31, 56, 20, 51, 31, 27, 62, 88, (10); Engraved Title, Title, pp. 91, 191, 48, 114 [should be 214], 110, 1 l., pp. 112, 118, 79, 94, 217, (17). 224 Maps, and Plates. BA. 14959

Commelin. Begin ... Inwoonderen | der selver Provintien ... Beschrijvingen ... Reeden ... Mitsgaders | Religien ... Politie en Regeeringe der Volckeren; oock | meede ... . *Gedruckt in den Jare* 1646. || Tweede Deel ... Nederlandtsche ... der selver Provintien ... . *Gedruckt in den Jare des Heeren*, 1646. Oblong 4to. 14960

This edition differs from the preceding only in the title.

Commemoration of New Netherland. *See* New York Historical Society.

Commemoration by the Loyal League of Union Citizens. Anniversary Celebration held in Madison Square, New York, April 20, 1863. *New York.* 1863. 8vo. 14961

Commencement, a Poem; 1811. *See* Biglow (W.), Vol. II., No. 5344.

Commentaria in Legum Indicarum recopilationem. *See* Calvo de la Torre (J. del C.), Vol. III., No. 10093.

Commentarius de Republica in America Lusitana, atque Hispana A Jesuitis instituta, belloque ab his cum Hispaniæ, Lusitaniæque exercitibus gesto, Ex iis quæ asservantur in secretioribus conclavibus legatorum, qui cum plena Regum potestate negotia huc pertinentia in America administrabant, aliisque instrumentis certæ auctoritatis concinnatus. E Lusitano in Latinum conversus. [n. p. 1760.] Sm. 8vo, pp. 77. 14962

Comment on a Pamphlet by "A Backsettler," in Defence of the Rights of America. By a Carolinian. *Charlestown.* 1774. 4to. 14963

Comments on the Nebraska Bill, with Views on Slavery in contrast with Freedom. Respectfully Addressed to the Free States, by one acquainted with Southern Institutions. *Albany: J. Munsell.* 1854. 8vo, pp. 58. + Second Edition. [*Ibid.*] 8vo, pp. 53. BA. 14964

Report of the Secretary of the Treasury ... of the Commerce and Navigation of the United States. ... *Washington.* 1849, '50. 2 vols., 8vo. 14965

The report for 1822, forms Sen. Doc. 26, 17th Congress, 2nd Sess., and the subsequent reports are included in "Congressional Documents." A list of many of them is included in the Catalogue of the Public Library, Boston, art. "United States."

Commerce and Navigation of the Upper Mississippi, and also that appertaining to St. Louis. *St. Louis.* 1847. 8vo, pp. 22.

Le commerce de l'Amérique. *See* [Chambon], Vol. III., No. 11812.

Le commerce de la Hollande ou Tableau du Commerce des Hollandois dans les quatre parties du Monde, etc. *Amsterdam: Changuion.* 1765. 3 vols., 12mo. 14966*a*

The author was Joseph Accarias de Serionne, who also wrote "Les intérêts des nations de l'Europe développés relativement au commerce. *Leyde.* 1776. 2 vols., 4to. + *Paris: Desaint.* [*Amsterdam.*] 1767." 2 vols., 4to.

Du Commerce des Colonies, ses principes et ses lois, La Paia est le temps de régler & d'agrandir le Commerce. 1785. 8vo, pp. 63. J.C.B. 14967

Another edition is entitled:

Du Commerce des Colonies, ses Principes et ses Lois, appliquées aux Colonies Françaises de l'Amerique. [n. p.] 1785. 8vo. 14968

The Commercial & Financial Chronicle, Banker's Gazette, Commercial Times, Railway Monitor, and Insurance Journal. A Weekly Newspaper Representing the Industrial and Commercial Interests of the United States. *New York: William B. Dana & Company.* 1865. Folio, pp. iv, 833. Continued. B., C.

The Commercial Conduct of the United States of America considered, and The True Interest thereof, attempted to be shewn by a Citizen of New-York. ... *New-York: printed by S. and J. Loudon.* M,DCC,LXXXVI. 8vo, pp. 21. BA., H. 14970

The Commercial Conduct of the Province of New-York considered, and the True Interest of that Colony attempted to be shewn. In a Letter to The Society of Arts, Agriculture and Œconomy. *Printed for the Benefit of the Society of Arts, Agriculture and Œconomy, of New York.* 1767. 4to, pp. iv, 20.

By a Linen Draper.

Commercial Convention. Proceedings of the Commercial Convention, held in Detroit, July 11th, 12th, 13th and 14th, 1865. ... *Detroit.* 1865. 8vo, pp. 276. H. 14972

British North America at the Detroit Convention. [*Ottawa.* 1865.] 8vo, pp. 15. H. 14973

Commercial Conventions, Direct Trade — A Chance for the South. [n. p. 186–?] 8vo, pp. 26. H. 14974

Commercial Directory; containing, a Topographical Description, Extent and Productions of different Sections of the Union, Statistical Information relative to Manufactures, Commercial and Port Regulations, a List of the Principal Commercial Houses, Tables of Imports and Exports, Foreign and Domestic; Tables of Foreign Coins, Weights and Measures, Tariff of Duties. *Philadelphia: published by J. C. Kayser & Co.* 1823. 4to, pp. viii, 242, (1), 41. H. 14975

Commercial Directory of the Western States and Rivers, for 1867–8. Arranged Alphabetically for each Trade. *St. Louis and Chicago: R. Edwards.* 1867. 4to, pp. xx, 1197, 85, 73.

The Commercial Intercourse of the United States and Great Britain. *New York: Greeley & McElrath.* [1844.] 8vo, pp. 7.

Commercial Intercourse with and in States declared in Insurrection, and the Collection of Abandoned and Captured Property. Embracing the Treasury Department Circulars and Regulations; the Executive Proclamations and License; and the War and Navy Department Orders ... . September 11, 1863. *Washington: Government Printing Office.* 1863. 8vo, Title, pp. 56. BA. 14978

Commercial Navigation Company, Of the State of New York. *New York: Henry Tompkins.* 1868. 8vo, pp. 51. H. 14979

Commercial Reasons for the Non-Abolition of the Slave Trade in the West-India Islands, by a Planter and Merchant, of many Years' Residence in the West Indies. *London: Lane.* 1789. 8vo, pp. 20. 14980

See "M. Rev.," LXXX. 450.

Commercial Regulations of the Foreign Countries with which the United States have Commercial Intercourse, Collected, Digested, and Printed under the direction of the President ... *Washington.* 1819. 8vo, pp. 528. Continued. C. 14981

Commercial Relations of the United States with all Foreign. Nations. Edmund Flagg, Sup't. ... Vol. I.–IV. *Washington.* 1856–'57. 4to. (34th Cong., 1st Sess. Sen. Doc. 107; Exec. Doc. 47.) 14982

Commercial Relations of the United States with Foreign Nations, for the Year ending September 30, 1857. *Washington.* 1858. 4to, pp. 514. (35th Cong., 1st Sess., Sen. Doc. 53.) Continued annually. 14983

Commercial Relations — Letter of the Secretary of State, [Wm. H. Seward] transmitting a Report on the Commercial Relations of the United States with Foreign Countries, for the year ended September 30, 1862. *Washington: Gov. Printing Office.* 1863. pp. xi, 711, 299. 14984

These and subsequent volumes, issued during Lincoln's administration, contain much matter bearing on the rebellion of 1861–65.

Commercial Relations with Foreign Countries, with a Synopsis of the Laws regulating the Foreign and Coasting Trade of the United States. *New York.* 1849. 8vo. 14985

Commercial Reports received at the Foreign Office from her Majesty's Consuls. Presented to both Houses of Parliament in May and June, 1865. *London: Harrison & Sons.* 1865. Rl. 8vo, pp. 306. 14986

The Reports from the United States presenting the Commercial Statistics for 1863–64, are of much interest. Similar reports may be found in the Parliamentary Papers for each session.

Commercial Review. *See* De Bow (J. D. B.)

Commercial Tariffs and Regulations. *See* Macgregor (John).

Commissary-General's Office, Philadelphia, October 6, 1777. ... *Philadelphia: Printed by James Humphreys, junr.* 4to, p. 1.

This rare revolutionary paper orders surrender of liquors, etc.

Commissary General's Office, Philadelphia, Oct. 10. ... *Philadelphia: Printed by James Humphreys, Junr.* [1778.] 4to, p. 1.

An advertisement for purchasing provisions for the king's troops.

Commissioners under the Sixth Article of the Treaty with Great Britain. A Brief Statement of Opinions given in the Board. With Appendix. *Philadelphia.* 1800. 8vo, pp. 71.

Commissioners under the Treaty of Ghent. Message from the President ... [J. Q. Adams] transmitting the Information required by Resolution of the House of Representatives, of the 10th ultimo, relating ... to Indemnities, due under the award of the Emperor of Russia, for Slaves and other Private Property carried away by the British Forces, in Violation of the Treaty of Ghent. ... *Washington.* 1826. 8vo. 14990

Commissions du Roy et de Mons. l'Admiral, au Sieur de Montes, pour l'habitation és terres de Lacadie, Canada et autres endroits en la Nouuelle-France, ensemble les défenses Premierès et Secondes à tous autres, de trafiquer avec les Sauvages des dites terres. *Paris: Philippes Patrisou.* 1605. 12mo, pp. 27. J.C.

Of extreme rarity.

Commission institutée pour l'Examen des Questions relatives à l'Esclavage et à la Constitution politique des Colonies. Procès-Verbaux 1840–43. *Paris.* 1840–43. 4to. A. 14992

Committee Chamber, December 6, 1774. ... Jacob Rush, pro temp. Secretary. 4to, p. 1. P. 14993

Relates to new importations, etc., into Philadelphia.

The Commodities of the Iland called Manati ore Long Isle which is in the Continent of Virginia. *Imprinted by J[oel] M[unsell] for J[ohn] G[ilmary] S[hea], and for sale at the sign of the Two Storks.* [1865.] 8vo, pp. 16. Map. 14994

The Common Almanac. For 1823. *Watertown. N. Y.* Continued. 14995

Common Place Arguments, 1780. *See* [Tickell (R.)]

Common School Assistant: a Monthly Paper, for the Improvement of Common School Education. *Albany. January,* 1836. 2 vols., 4to, pp. 96; 96. B. 14996

Edited by J. Orville Taylor, Albany.

Common School Journal. Edited by Horace Mann. Vol. I. 1st Series. *Boston.* 1839–1848. 10 vols., 8vo. 14997

The second series, by W. B. Fowler, 1849, etc.

Common Sense. *See* [Paine (Thomas)].

Common Sense Addresses. *See* [Carey (M.)], Vol. III., No. 10859.

Common Sense: In nine Conferences, between a British Merchant and a candid Merchant of America, in their private capacities as friends; tracing the several causes of the present contests between the mother country and her American subjects; the fallacy of their prepossessions; and the ingratitude and danger of them; the reciprocal benefits of the national friendship; and the moral obligations of individuals which enforce it: with various anecdotes, and reasons drawn from facts, tending to conciliate all differences, and establish a permanent union for the common happiness and glory of the British empire. *London: J. Dodsley.* M,DCC,LXXV. 4to, pp. x, 117. 14998

"The candid merchant of America, who is here employed to support nine tedious conferences, and to be converted from his opinions, appears to have been a greater booby than even the letter-writer who was brought forward by a reverend Dean." — *Monthly Review,* LII. 261. "Dean Tucker is here probably referred to." — RICH, I. 200.

COMMUCK (T.) Indian Melodies. By Thomas Commuck, A Narraganset Indian, harmonized by T. Hastings. *New York.* 1845. Oblong 8vo. S. 14999

Communicaciones, entre el Señor Carlos Biddle, Coronel de los E. Unidos del Norte, i la sociedad amigos del Paix. *Panama.* 1836. 8vo. 15000

A Communication addressed to "Friends" and all conscientiously scrupulous of bearing Arms, on some important matters at issue in the approaching Election. *Philadelphia: J. W. Allen.* 1823. 8vo, pp. 24. 15001

Communication from the Secretary of War in relation to the System of Internal Improvements carried on by the General Government, &c. *Washington.* 1840. 8vo. C. 15002

Communications between the Collector of Customs, at Liverpool, and Messrs. Klingender & Co., respecting the shipment of Guns on board the "Gibraltar." Folio, pp. 3. 15003

In continuation of papers presented to Parliament in July, 1863.

Communications concerning the Agriculture and Commerce of America: Containing Observations on the Commerce of Spain with her American Colonies in time of War. Written by a Spanish Gentleman in Philadelphia, this present year, 1800. With sundry other papers concerning the Spanish Interests. Edited in London by William Tatham. *London: J. Ridgway.* 1800. 8vo, pp. viii, 120. 15004

Communications from several States on the Resolutions of the Legislature of Virginia respecting the Alien and Sedition Laws; also, Instructions from the General Assembly of Virginia to their Senators in Congress, and the Report of the Committee to whom was committed the Proceedings of sundry of the other States, in answer to the Resolutions of the General Assembly, 21st Dec. 1798. *Richmond: Meriwether Jones.* [1800?] 16mo, pp. 194. 15005

Communications of American Ministers in Relation to the progress of the Treaty of Peace. December 1, 1814. (Cong. Doc.) 15006

Communications on the Next Election for President of the United States, and on the Late Measures of the Federal Administration, ... By a Citizen of New York. [n. p.] *Printed for the Author.* 1808. 8vo, pp. 40. BA. 15007

Communications relative to the Progress of Bible Societies in the United States. *Philadelphia.* 1813. 8vo, pp. 24. 15008

The Communion-Office, or Order for the Administration of the Holy Eucharist or Supper of the Lord. With Private Devotions, Recommended to the Episcopal Congregations in Connecticut, By the Right Reverend Bishop Seabury. *New London: Printed by T. Green.* M,DCC,LXXXVI. 12mo, pp. 23.

The first American edition of these services in English.

COMONFORT (I.) Episodio Historico del Gobierno Dictatorial del Señor D. Ignacio Comonfort en la Republica Mexicana, Años de 1856 y 1857. *Mexico.* 1861. 4to. 15010

COMONFORT. Politica del General Comonfort, durante su gobierno en Mejico. *Nueva-York.* 1858. 8vo, pp. 30. 15011

COMONFORT. La politica del General Comonfort, y la situacion actual de Mexico. [n. p. *Octubre de* 1857.] 4to, pp. 16.

COMONFORT. Politique du général Comonfort pendant son gouvernement au Mexique. [Signé J. Comonfort.] *Paris: imp. d'Aubusson et Kugelmann.* 1858. 8vo, pp. 32. 15013

Several other tracts relating to Comonfort are partially described in Fischer's Catalogue. *London.* 1867.

The Compact with the Charter and Laws of the Colony of New Plymouth, 1836. *See* Brigham (W.), Vol. II., No. 7962.

COMPAEN (K. G.) 't Begin, Midden en Eynde | Der See-Rooveryen, van den Alderfameusten | Zee-Roover, | Klaes G. Compaen, | Van Oostzanen in Kennemer-landt. | Vervattende sijn wonderlijcke, vreemde en Landts | schadelijcke, drijf-tochten. | Waer in verthoont wordt | Hoe hy met weynigh Schepen de Zee onveyligh ghemaeckt, | een ongelooffelijcken Buyt, en groot getal van Schepen van alle | Landen gerooft, en af geloopen heeft. | *t' Amsterdam,* | *By Michiel de Groot, Boeck-verkooper, op den Nieuwen-dijck,* | *tusschen beyde Haerlemmer sluysen.* 1663. | 4to, 3 l., pp. 42. Engravings. 15015

COMPAEN. 't Begin, Midden en Eynde, der | Zee-Rooveryen, | Van den Alderfameusten | Zee-Roover, | Claes G. Campaen; | Van Oost-zanen, in Kennemerlandt. | Vervattende sijn wonderlijcke, vreemde | Landts-schadelijcke, drijf-tochten | Waer in vertoont word | Hoe hy met weynigh Schepen, de Zee onveyligh gemaeckt, een ongeloof- | lijcken Buyt, en groot getal van Schepen, van alle Landen af-geloopen heeft. | *Te Utrecht Gedruckt by Juriaen van Poolsum, Ordinaris Stadts* | *Drucker, wonende*

op de plaets, tegen over t' Stadthuys Anno 1685. 4to, pp. 48. Engravings. 15016

A new edition of the preceding number. There are also editions: *Amsterdam.* 1726. 4to, 3 l., pp. 42; *Amsterdam.* 1732. 4to, 3 l., pp. 42; *Amsterdam.* 1733. 4to, 3 l., pp. 42; and *Amsterdam.* 1762. 4to, 3 l., pp. 42.

[COMPAGNONI (G.)] Storia dell' America, in continuazione del compendio della storia universelle del Sig. Conte di Sigur, opera originale italiana. *Milano: Fusi, Stella e Compagni.* 1820–23. 29 vols., 18mo, Title, pp. 9, 202, (14); 214, (1); 200, (12); 225; 240, (4); 179, (1); 204; 259 (1); 240; 214, (2); 202; 216; 228; 209, (2); 221; 217, (1); 212; 212; 232; 235, (1); 276; 228; 227, (1); 201, (1); 236; 227, (1); 240; 280; 127. 15017

"This is a well-written and original work by the Cav. Giuseppe Compagnoni, intended as a continuation to the Italian translation of Count Segur's Universal History" — *N. A. Rev.,* XXVII. 30. The title of Vol. XXIX. is:

COMPAGNONI. Indice generale della Storia dell' America scritta dal Cav. Giu. Compagnoni in continuazione del compendio della storia universale del Sig. Conte di Segur. ... *Milano.* 1823. B., C., H. 15018

COMPAN (*M. l'Abbé*). Nouvelle Méthode Géographique, Traité de la Sphère, &c. *Paris.* 1771. 2 vols., 8vo. 15019

Compagnie des Indes Occidentales. *See* West Indies.

COMPAÑIA. Real compañia guipuzcoana de Caracas: Noticias historia les practicas de los successos, y adelantamientos de esta Compañia, desde su fundacion año de 1728. hasta el de 1764. por todos los Ramos, que comprehende su Negociacion. ... [*Madrid.*] 1765. 4to, pp. 183. H. 15020

Compania de Almacenes de Santa Catalina. Memoria leida por su presidente en la Junta general de Accionistas celebrada en 23 de Noviembre de 1864. *Habana.* 1864. 8vo, pp. 68.

Compañia Lancasteriana de Mexico. (Añode 1849.) *Mexico.* 1849. 12mo, pp. 12. 15022

The Companion and Weekly Miscellany. By Edward Easy, Esq. Vol. I. *Baltimore.* 1804–5. 4to. 15023

The Companion: being a Selection of the Beauties of the most celebrated authors in the English Language. In Prose and

Verse. *Printed by Nathaniel and Benjamin Heaton for Joseph J. Todd, Providence.* MDCCXCIX. Square 12mo. 15024

Contains, "The Fashionable Songs for 1798," "Adams and Liberty," "The Federal Constitution and Washington for Ever," etc.

Compaño contra los Americanos del Norte, Primera parte. *Mexico.* 1846. 8vo. 15025

Company of Royal Adventurers of England. *See* Vol. I., No. 1650, and the "Several Declarations."

A Comparison between the British Sugar Colonies and New-England, as they relate to the Interest of Great Britain. With Some Observations on the State of the Case of New-England. To which is added A Letter to a Member of Parliament. *London: J. Roberts.* M. DCC. XXXII. 8vo, pp. 43. H., J.C.B. 15026

A Comparison Between the Doctrines taught by the Clergy of the Church of England, And the Doctrines taught by Whitefield, Seagrave, and Others; In which the true Notion of Preaching Christ is stated; the doctrinal Preaching of the Clergy of the Established Church vindicated; and the Methodist proved guilty of not Preaching the Gospel of Christ. To which is added, The Wisdom of fleeing from Persecution, exemplified in the Conduct of the Rev. Mr. Whitefield at Charles-Town in South-Carolina. *London: A. Smith.* 1741. 8vo, 2 l., pp. 28. 15027

A Comparison between the Proposals of the Bank and the South Sea Company. *London.* 1720. 8vo, pp. 19. 15028

A Comparison of the Taxes. *See* New York.

Comparative Calculations, &c., on Internal Improvements; illustrative of the Advantages to be derived from the Improvement of the Lehigh. *Philadelphia.* 1821. 8vo. P. 15029

Comparative Importance of the Commercial Principles of the Late Negotiation between Great Britain and France in 1761, in which the System of that negotiation with regard to our Colonies and Commerce is Considered. The Second Edition. *London: R. & J. Dodsley.* MDCCLXII. 8vo, pp. 108. 15030

Attributed to Mr. Burke.

The Comparative Importance of our acquisitions from France in America, with Remarks on a Pamphlet, intitled, An Examination of the Commercial Principles of the late Negociation in 1761.

London: J. Hinxman. MDCCLXII. 8vo, pp. 59. + Second Edition. *London: J. Hinxman.* MDCCLXXII. 8vo, pp. 59.

See "M. Rev.," XXVII. 507.

Comparative View of the British and American Constitutions, with Observations on the present state of British Politics, and on the probable consequences of introducing into Great Britain the mode of suffrage that exist in the United States. By a Gentleman some time resident in the United States, and author of a "View of the State of parties in America." *Edinburgh.* 1817. 8vo, pp. 51. 15032

See "Edinb. Rev.," XXVIII. 270.

A Comparative View of the Existing Tariff of Duties on goods Imported from Foreign Countries. *Washington: Gales & Seaton.* 1820. 8vo, pp. 7. 15033

A Compassionate Call, 1779. *See* [Hall (D.)]

Compendio de la Historia de los Estados Unidas de America; puesto en Castellano. *Paris.* 1825. 18mo, pp. 422. + *Nueva York: Tompkins y Floyd.* 1825. 18mo, Title, pp. iv, 296. Engraving of the head of Washington. H. 15034

Compendio del confessionario en Idioma Mexicano y Castellano para que los que ignoren el primo puedan á los menos en los casos de necesidad administrar á los indigenas el Sacramento de la Penitencia, por un sacerdote del obispado de Puebla. [*Madrid:*] *Imprenta antigua en el Portal de las Flores.* 1840. 8vo, pp. 43.

Compendio de Indulgencias concedidas á los Ministros, y demas Personas, que se emplean en el servicio del Santo Oficio de la Inquisicion. [n. p. n. d.] Folio, pp. 4. 15036

Published for the tribunal of the inquisition in Mexico, about 1730.

Compendio General de las contribuciones, y gastos que ocasionan todos los Efectos, Frutos, Caudales y demàs, que se trafican entre los Reynos de Castilla, y America. Deducidas del Real proyecto de 5 de Abril del año passado de 1720, despacho de 24 de Julio de 1737 sobre el establecimiento del Almirantazgo General de España, Cedulas, Ordenes, Decretos, y Aranceles, que estàn en practica hasta fines del de 1761 (en que se recopilan las que se comprehendieron en el de 1745,) y deben tenerse presentes, para el mas facil, y pronto despacho. *Impresso en Cadiz en la Real de Marina y Real Audencia de Contratacion de D. Manuel Espinosa de Los Monteros Año de* 1762. 4to, pp. 158, 1 l.

Compendio Historico de la Fundacion y progresso de los clerigos seculares que viven en comun, observando el Instituto de la Congregacion del Oratorio del Glorioso San Phelipe Nevi, en la Ciudad de los Reynos del Peru en las Indias Occidentales. *Sevilla: Juan de Puerta.* 1728. 4to. Unpaged. J.C.B. 15038

Compendio historico del origen y progresos de las sociedades secretas. *Guadalaxara.* 1826. 12mo, pp. 21. 15039

Compendious Account of the British Colonies in North America, with Map of the Theatre of War in North America. *London.* 1776. Folio, 1 l. 15040

Compendious Description of the Thirteen Colonies in British America. *London: Herman, Strong & Co.* MDCCLXXVII. 12mo, pp. 22. J.C.B. 15041

Compendious Exercise for the Garrison and Field Ordnance, as practised in the United States. *New York.* 1812. 12mo.

A Compendious History of the Late War, Containing an Account of all the Important Battles, and many of the smaller Actions between the American and the British Forces, and Indians, in the Years 1811, 1812, 1813, 1814, 1815. *Boston: J. W. Burditt.* 1815. 8vo, pp. 32. B. 15043

Compendium Facultatum, et Indulgentiarum, quæ Religiosis Societatis Jesu, aliis Christi fidelibus, in Indiarum Orientalium, et Occidentalium Provinciis conceduntur, cum Concessio et Prorogatio quarundam facultatum et Indulgentiarum utriusque Indiæ. *Romæ, in collegio ejusdem Societatis,* 1585–7. 8vo.

Title from Thos. Thorpe's catalogue.

Compendium Logicæ Secundum Principia D. Renati Cartesii Plerumque Efformatum, et Catechistice Propositum. *Bostoni in Nov-Anglia Excusum,* 1735. 8vo, 2 l., pp. 60. BA., H. 15045

An early, if not the first book of its class. The compiler was Thomas Brattle.

Compendium of Authentic Voyages, 1750. *See* [Dodsley (J.)]

Compendium of the Enumeration. *See* Census, Vol. III., No. 11667.

The collation should be pp. 375.

A Compendium of the Laws and Government of England and Dominions, Plantations, and Territories thereto belonging. *London.* 1699. 8vo. 15046

"A Description of the English Plantations in America," etc., occupies 42 pages.

A Compilation of the Laws of the United States and of States, in relation to Fugitives from Labor. *Washington: Taylor & Maury.* 1860. 8vo, pp. 32. 15047

Complaint of England. *See* [Lightfoote (William)].

The Complaint of Mexico, and Conspiracy against Liberty. *Boston: J. W. Alden.* 1843. 8vo, pp. 44. BA. 15048

The Complaint: or Britannia lamenting the Loss of her Children. An Elegy inscribed to ... Benjamin Franklin. *London: T. Brewman.* [n. d.] 4to, pp. 7. H. 15049

A Complaint to the —— of —— against a Pamphlet intitled, A Speech intended to have been spoken on the Bill for altering the Charters of the Colony of Massachuset's Bay. *London: Benjamin White.* MDCCLXXV. 8vo, pp. 40. J.C.B. 15050

This author is very angry with the benevolent Bishop of St. Asaph, against whose speech he declaims with much warmth and some invective, without, however, offering any substantial objections to it. *See* "M. Rev.," LII. 84.

A Compleat Collection of Papers. *See* [Burnet (Gilbert)], Vol. III., No. 9371.

A Compleat History of Magic, Sorcery, and Witchcraft. ... *London: E. Curll.* 1715, 16. 2 vols., 12mo, 11 l., pp. 272; 2 l., pp. 235. 15051

Contains the Tryals of several Witches at Salem in New-England. The author was Richard Bolton. Our title under his name is not full.

A Compleat History of Spanish America. *See* [Campbell (J.)], Vol. III., No. 10232.

A Complete and accurate Account of the Very Important Debate in the House of Commons, on Tuesday, July 9, 1782. In which the Cause of Mr. Fox's Resignation, and the great Question of American Independence came under Consideration: Including the several Speeches and Replies of The Right Hon. Mr. Fox, The Right Hon. Isaac Barré, Lord John Cavendish, General Conway, Mr. Burke, Sir William Wake, Mr. Coke. Mr. Frederick Montague, The Hon. Mr. Townsend, Mr. Mar-

tin, Lord Althorpe, Mr. Grenville, Mr. Aubrey, The Hon. William Pitt, Mr. Lee, late Solicitor-General, Mr. Gascoyne, sen. Commodore Johnstone, and Sir Edward Deering. To which are added, the Speeches of the Duke of Richmond and of Lord Shelburne, in the House of Lords, the following Day, on the same subject: With what was thrown out in Reply to Mr. Burke, Lord John Cavendish, and Mr. Fox, afterwards, in the House of Commons. *London.* MDCCLXXXII 8vo, 2 l., pp. 61. H. + Second Edition. *London.* MDCCLXXXII. 8vo, 2 l., pp. 61. + Third Edition. *London: J. Stockdale.* MDCCLXXXII. 8vo, 2 l., pp. 61. + *Philadelphia Arcade.* 1845. 8vo, pp. xi, 64.

"The following debate is universally allowed to be the most important one that ever happened in the House of Commons."—*Preface.*

A Complete Collection of all the Protests of the Peers of Parliament, entered on their Journals since the Year 1774, on the Great Questions of the Cause and Issue of the War between Great Britain and America, &c., to the Present Time. *London: J. Stockdale.* 1782. 8vo, pp. 126. J.C.B. 15053

A Complete Guide to the Gold Mines in Kansas and Nebraska, with a Description of the Shortest and only all Railroad Route to Kansas. ... *Boston: Geo. C. Rand and Avery.* [1859.] 4to, pp. 11. H. 15054

A complete Historical, Chronological, and Geographical American Atlas, being a Guide to the History of North and South America, and the West Indies: exhibiting an accurate Account of the Discovery, Settlement, and Progress of their various Kingdoms, States, Provinces, &c. Together with the Wars, Celebrated Battles, and Remarkable Events, To the Year 1822. According to the plan of Le Sage's Atlas, and intended as a Companion to Lavoisne's Improvement of that celebrated Work. *Philadelphia: H. C. Carey & J. Lea.* 1825. Folio, 53 Maps, etc. + Third Edition corrected and improved. *Philadelphia: H. C. Carey & J. Lea.* 1827. Folio. 53 Maps.

An advertisement prefixed to the work is dated June 21, 1822. It appears to have been first published in 1823. A translation was published in Paris, under the title: "Atlas Géographique." *See* Buchon.

A Complete History of the Late War, or Annual Register, of its Rise, Progress, and Events, in Europe, Asia, Africa, and America. Exhibiting the State of the Belligerent Powers at the Commencement of the War; their Interests and Objects in its Continuance: Interspersed with the Characters of the able and

disinterested Statesmen, to whose Wisdom and Integrity, and of the Heroes, to whose Courage and Conduct, we are indebted for the Naval and Military Success, which is not to be equalled in the Annals of this or any other Nation. With the Additions of a Detail of the Landing of the Forces at Cape Breton, &c. the Progress of the Fleet in their navigating the River St. Lawrence, and a daily Account of the Siege of Quebec, while in the Possession of the French, and afterwards in the Hands of the English; with the different Military Orders that were issued on the Occasion, taken from Capt. John Knox's Historical Journal of the War in America. The Sixth Edition. Illustrated with a Number of Heads, Plans, Maps, and Charts. *Dublin: John Exshaw.* M. DCC. LXXIV. 8vo, 8 l., pp. 572. 10 Portraits, 5 Maps, and a View. BA., P. 15056

A Complete History of the Origin and Progress of the late War, From its Commencement, to the Exchange of the Ratifications of Peace, between Great-Britain, France, and Spain; On the 10th of February, 1763, and to the signing of the Treaty at Hubertsberg, between the King of Prussia, the Empress-Queen, and the Elector of Saxony, On the 15th of the same month. In which, All the Battles, Sieges, Sea-Engagements, and every other Transaction worthy of public Attention, are faithfully recorded; with political and military Observations. In Two Volumes. *London: W. Nicol.* MDCCLXIII. 2 vols., 8vo. + *London: Printed for J. Knox.* MDCCLXIV. 8vo, pp. 771. 15057

A Complete History of the Present War, from its Commencement in 1756. to the end of the Campaign 1760. *London: J. Owen.* 1761. 8vo. 15058

See "M. Rev.," XXIV. 44.

Complete List of the American Navy; ... for October, 1813; and Steel's List of the Navy of Great Britain for July, 1813. *Boston: Russell, Cutler and Co.* 1813. 18mo, pp. 106.

Complete Practical Guide to her Majesty's Civil Service; ... in Great Britain. ... and the Colonies. *London.* 1860. 12mo.

The Complete Trial; or Swaggering John. *Transylvania.* 1765. 8vo. P. 15061

Complot D'Arnold. *See* [Barbé-Marbois], Vol. I., No. 3302.

A Comprehensive History of the Southern Rebellion and the War for the Union. Embodying State Papers, Congressional Proceedings, Remarkable Speeches, etc. [Monthly Ed. No. 2.] *New York: James D. Torrey.* [1861.] Large 8vo. H. 15062

Compromise by a Compensation. A Letter to Hon. L. S. Foster, by a Republican of Connecticut. *H. Benham: New Haven.* 1862. 15063

The Compromises of the Constitution Considered in the Organization of a National Convention. [n. p. 1844.] 8vo, pp. 13. BA. 15064

The Compromise, the Constitution, and the Union. *See* [G. (E.)]

A Compressed View of the Points, 1814. *See* [Atcheson (Nathaniel)], Vol. I., No. 2265.

Comptabilité des Matières appartenant au Département de la Marine des et des Colonies. *Paris.* 1846. Folio. A. 15065

Compte-rendu des Recettes et des Dépenses des Colonies sur les Exercices de 1814 et 1827–1845. *Paris.* 1827–45. 14 vols., 4to. A. 15066

Comptes définitifs, Service colonial, Dépenses de l'Exercice et Situation provisoire 1842–45. *Paris.* 1845–47. 3 vols., 4to.

Comptes généraux présentés par le Ministre de la marine et des Colonies. Exercice 1830. *Paris.* 1832. 4to. Continued.

Los Compuestos de Gualeguaychu. *Buenos-Aires.* 18mo, pp. 14. 15069

COMSTOCK (C.) A History of South Kingston; with a particular description of the Hornet's Nest Company, and the Cats let out of the Bag. By Charles Comstock, LL.D. F.R.S. *Newport: Printed by the Author.* 1806. 12mo, pp. about 32.

A personal satirical narrative, with a woodcut of the "Cat Inspector." The "Hornet's Nest" is the Little Nest Hill.

COMSTOCK (F. G.) A Practical Treatise on the Culture of Silk, adapted to the Soil and Climate of the United States. By F. G. Comstock .... *Hartford: Wm. G. Comstock.* MDCCCXXXVI. 12mo, pp. 108. B. 15071

COMSTOCK (G. F.) Campaign Document, No, 2. Speech of Judge Geo. F. Comstock, delivered at the Brooklyn Academy of Music. [n. p. 1863.] 8vo, pp. 8. 15072

COMSTOCK (J. L.) Elements of Mineralogy. By J. L. Comstock. ... *Boston: S. G. Goodrich.* 1827. 8vo, pp. 338.

COMSTOCK. A History of the Precious Metals ... [and] the Anglo-Mexican Mining Companies, and Speculations concerning the Mineral Wealth of California. By J. L. Comstock. *Hartford.* 1849. 12mo. 15074

COMSTOCK. An Introduction to the Study of Botany in which ... Examples of Nature and Exotic Plants are Explained. ... *Hartford.* 1832. 12mo, pp. 260. 15075

A later edition includes, "Descriptions of the most common Plants in the Middle and Northern States. *New York.* 1854." 12mo, pp. 485. Also: Natural History of Quadrupeds, with Engravings. *New York: Pratt, Woodford & Co.* 1848. 4to, pp. 73.

COMSTOCK (J.) The Tongue of Time and Star of the States ... American Antiquities. Remains of Giants, &c. By Joseph Comstock ... *New York.* 1838. 8vo. 15076

COMSTOCK. A Short History of the Life of Joshua Comstock, together with his Sufferings, Rise, and Conversion to Christianity. Written by Himself. ... *Providence.* 1822. 8vo, pp. 8. B. 15077

COMSTOCK (W.) Life of Samuel Comstock, the Terrible Whaleman; containing an Account of the Mutiny and Massacre of the Ship Globe, of Nantucket; his Subsequent Adventures, and his shot at the Mulgrave Islands; By his Brother, William Comstock. [n. p. n. d.] 12mo, pp. 116. 15078

COMTÆUS. Roberti Comtaei Nortmanni De Origine Gentium Americanarum Dissertatio. *Amstelodami: Typis Nicolai Ravensteinii.* CIↃ IↃCXLIV. 12mo, pp. 41. J.C.B. 15079

Comunicacion circular del ministro de relaciones D. Manuel de la Peña sobre la cuestion de paz ó guerra. *Querétaro.* 1848. pp. 44. 15080

Comunicaciones oficiales entre el Supremo Govierno del Estado de Zacatecas y el Superior eclesiastico de la diocesis de Guadalaxara con motivo de la ley de hacienda en 30 de Enero de 1852. *Guadalaxara.* 1852. 4to, pp. 66. 15081

Comunicaciones relativos á la agregacion del Departamento de Tejas á los Estados-Unidos del Norte, que ha pasado el Supremo Gobierno de la Republica á la Camara de Diputados, e iniciativas que ha hecho con Motivo de la misma agregacion. *Mexico.* 1845. 4to, pp. 30. 15082

Comunicados y documentos a que se refieren, relativos al ruinoso contrato que la administracion provisional del general Santa-Anna, celebró con D. Cayetano Rubio, sobre las Salinas del Peñon Blanco y demas limitrofes del Departamento de San Luis Potosi. *Zacatecas.* 1845. 4to, pp. 27. 15083

COMYN (T.) Apuntes de un Viagero, ó cartas familiares escritas durante la Insurreccion del Reyno de Mégico, en 1811, 12, 13 y 14. Por Tomas de Comyn, Autor del Etado de Filipinas en 1810. Y de la Breve Idea de Marruecos en 1822. *Madrid.* 1843. 8vo. 15084

CONANT (A.) A Sermon delivered at Leominster on leaving the Old Meeting-House, October 12, 1823. By Abel Conant. ... . *Worcester: printed by William Manning.* [n. d.] 8vo, pp. 15. B. 15085

CONANT. A Sermon delivered at Leominster, October 15, 1823, at The Dedication of the New Meeting-House. By Abel Conant ... . *Worcester: printed by William Manning.* [n. d.] 8vo, pp. 20. B. 15086

Also: Address at Leominster, Feb. 26, 1833, on Temperance. *Worcester.* 1833. 8vo.

CONANT (A.) A Poem Sacred to the Memory of Mrs. Abigail Conant, the late Amiable Consort of the Rev. Mr. Silvanus Conant of Middleborough; Who died on January 3d. 1759 in the 28th Year of her Age. ... *New-London [Con.]: printed by Timothy Green.* MDCCLIX. 4to, pp. 7. 15087

CONANT (G.) An Oration pronounced at Franklin on the Fourth of July, 1803. ... By Gaius Conant. *Providence: Nathaniel Heaton, Jun.* M,DCCC,III. 8vo, pp. 12. H. 15088

CONANT (H. S.) The Butterfly Hunters. By Helen S. Conant. With Illustrations. *Boston: Ticknor and Fields.* 1868.

This is a story-book for children, but describing many butterflies peculiar to America.

CONANT (S.) An Anniversary Sermon Preached at Plymouth, Dec. 23, 1776, in grateful Memory of the First Landing of our worthy Ancestors, in that place A.D. 1620. By Sylvanus Conant. *Boston, N. E.* 1777. 8vo. M., W. 15090

CONANT. The Art of War the Gift of God. A Discourse delivered at Middleborough, before three Military Companies, April 6, 1759, being the Day of General Muster in the Massachusetts Provinces for the Canada Expedition. By Sylvanus Conant. *Boston: Edes and Gill.* MDCCLIX. 8vo, pp. 16. M.

CONANT. The Blood of Abel and the Blood of Jesus ... . A Sermon delivered at Taunton, December the First, 1763. Upon the Day of the Execution of Bristol, A Negro Boy, ... for The Murder of Miss Elizabeth McKinstry. By Sylvanus Conant, A.M. ... *Boston: Edes and Gill.* M,DCC,LXIV. 8vo, pp. 36. BA., H. 15092

[CONANT.] A Letter Occasioned by the Death of Mrs. Abigail Conant, Late of Middleborough. *New-London: printed by Timothy Green.* MDCCLIX. 4to, pp. 8. H. 15093

CONANT. Sermon, delivered July 31st, 1768. Being the Lord's-Day after the News of the Death of Daniel Oliver, ... son To the Hon. Peter Oliver ... of Middleborough. ... By Sylvanus Conant ... . *Boston: Printed by Mein and Fleming.* MDCCLXVIII. 8vo, pp. 32. B., W. 15094

See Cotton (John).

CONANT (Thomas Jefferson). Dr. Conant's Letter to the Examiner and Chronicle, December 3, 1868. *Brooklyn, N. Y.* [1868.] 8vo, pp. 27. H. 15095

CONANT (W. C.) Narratives of Remarkable Conversions and Revival Incidents; including ... an Account of ... the Great Awakening of 1857–'58. By William C. Conant. With an Introduction by Henry Ward Beecher. ... *New-York: Derby & Jackson.* 1858. 12mo, 2 l., pp. ix–xx, 444. BA., S. 15096

CONARROE (G. M.) Supreme Court of Pennsylvania, Eastern District. No. 246, of January Term, 1862. The Commonwealth of Pennsylvania, Plaintiff in Error, vs. Joseph Kunzmann, Defendant in Error. Counter Statement and Argument of Defendant in Error. George M. Conarroe, F. Carroll Brewster, for Defendant in Error. *Philadelphia: King & Baird.* [1862.] 8vo, pp. 36. H. 15097

CONART (Louis). La Vie du P. Marcel François Mastrilli de la Compagnie de Jesus. Guery miraculeusement par Sainct François Xavier, et mort depuis au Japon, pour la défense de la Foy, le 17 d'Octobre 1637. Composée en Espagnol, par le P. Eusebe Nieremberg de la mesme Compagnie. Et traduite nouvellement en François par le P. Louys Conart de la mesme Compagnie. *Paris: Mathurin et Jean Henault.* 1646. 12mo, pp. 271. 15098

CONCEIÇAÕ (A. da). Primazia Serafica na Regiam da America, novo descobrimento de Santos, e Veneraveis Religiosos da Ordem Serafica, que ennobrecem o Novo Mundo com suas virtudes, e acçoens. Offrecida ao Senhor Domingos Martins Brito, em a Cidade do Rio de Janeiro primeiro Irmaõ Geral da Confraternidade das Tres Ordens do Serafico Petriarcha S. Francisco, especial da Provincia da Immaculada Conceiçaõ de N. Senhora do Estado do Brasil, Syndico Geral perpetuo da mesma, e Ministro, que foy tres vezes da Veneravel Ordem Terceira da Penitencia. Escrita por Fr. Apollinario da Conceiçaõ, Religioso Leigo Capucho, filho professo da dita Provincia, e natural da Cidade de Lisboa Occidental. *Lisboa Occidental: Na Officina de Antonio de Sousa da Sylva. Com todas as licenças necessarias.* M. D. CC. XXX. III. 4to, 17 l., pp. 366. C. 15099

Pinelo gives the date for this work as 1774, and the size as folio — both erroneous.

CONCEIÇAO (Claudio de). Memoria hist. do ... imperador e rei ... D. João VI. *Lisboa.* 1826. 8vo. 15100

CONCEIÇAO (J. M. da). As exequias de Abrahao Lincoln. Presidente dos Estados da America com um esboço biographico do mesmo afferecido as povo brasileiro por seu patrico José Manœl da Conceiçao. *Rio de Janeiro.* 1865. 8vo, pp. 40. 15101

CONCEIÇAO. Sentença de excommunhão e desautoraçāo fulminada contra o ex-padre José Manoel da Conceiçao, actualmente Ministro da Igreja evangelica e a resposta do mesmo. *Rio de Janeiro.* 1867. 8vo, pp. 32. 15102

Concept Van Reglement op Brasil. *See* Vol. II., No. 7552.

A Concert of Prayer propounded to the Citizens of the United States of America, by an Association of Christian Ministers. *Exeter.* 1787. 8vo, pp. 15. 15103

Concessions and Compromises, 1860. *See* [Fisher (Joshua Francis)].

Concessions to America. *See* [Marryat].

CONCHA (J. de la). Memorias sobre el estado politico, gobierno y administracion de la Isla de Cuba. *Madrid.* 1853. 4to.

Concilia. *See* Lima, Mexico, etc.

Concilia Provincialia, Baltimori habita, ab anno 1829, usque ad annum 1849. *Baltimori: J. Murphy.* 1851. 8vo, pp. 221.

Concilii Plenarii Baltimorensis II., in ecclesia Metropolitana Baltimorensi, a die vii. ad diem xxi. Octobris, A.D. MDCCCLXVI., habiti, et a Sede Apostolica recogniti, Acta et Decreta. Praeside, Illustrissimo ac Reverendissimo Martino Joanne Spalding, Archiepiscopo Baltimorensi, et Delegato Apostolico. Secundis Curis editum. *Baltimore: J. Murphy.* 1868. 8vo, pp. cliv, 346, xxviii, xxvi. C. 15106

Concilium Plenarium Totius Americæ Septentrionalis Fœderatæ. Anno 1852. *Baltimore.* 1852. 8vo, pp. 72. 15107

A Conciliation with America: adapted to the Constitutional Rights of the Colonies and the Supremacy of Great Britain. *London: Hooper and Davis.* MDCCLXXVIII. 8vo, pp. 55. J.C.B.

Conciliation with America, the True Policy of Great Britain. By a Friend to British Manufactures. *London: Printed for John Stockdale.* 1811. 8vo, pp. 31. BA. 15109

CONCILIATOR. Why are we still at War? or the American Question considered ... . By Conciliator. *London: Printed by A. J. Valpy.* 1814. 8vo. BA. 15110

In "The Pamphleteer," IV. 551–575.

Conciliatory Address to the People of Great Britain and of the Colonies on the present important Crisis. *London: J. Wilkie.* MDCCLXXV. 8vo, 2 l., pp. 56. 15111

"This address appears to have been produced by a benevolent desire of promoting the re-establishment of harmony between Great Britain and the colonies on equitable terms." — *M. Rev.*, LII. 265.

The Conciliatory Bills considered. *London: T. Cadell.* M DCC LXXVIII. 8vo, pp. 39. BA. 15112

A defence of the conduct of the administration.

A Concise Account of Voyages, 1782. *See* [Pickersgill (*Lieut.*)]

A Concise and Faithful Narrative of the various steps which led to the Unhappy Division which hath taken place among the Members of the Associate Body in the United States ... . By a Ruling Elder ... . *Philadelphia.* 1789. 8vo, pp. 88. P. 15113

A Concise Answer to the General Inquiry, who, or what are the Shakers. *First Printed at Union Village, Ohio.* 1823. *Reprinted at Enfield, N. H.* 1825. 16mo, pp. 14. H. 15114

A curious poem.

A Concise but Candid Relation of Circumstances previous and Relative to a Duel on Board the King George Transport, Sept. 2, 1777. *New York.* 1777. 12mo. 15115

Title from the Catalogue of H. A. Brady's Library.

A Concise Historical Account of all the British Colonies in North-America, comprehending their Rise, Progress and Modern State; particularly of the Massachusetts-Bay, (The Seat of the present Civil War,) together with the other Provinces of New-England. To which is annexed, An accurate descriptive Table of the Several Countries; Exhibiting, at One View, their respective Boundaries, Dimensions, Longitudes, Latitudes, Divisions, or Counties, Chief Towns, Capes, Harbours, Bays, Rivers, Various Productions, Animals, &c. &c. Interspersed with Particulars relative to the different Soils and Climates, Capital Cities, &c. &c. *London: J. Bew.* 1775. 8vo, pp. iv, 196, and Table of the Counties. + *Dublin: Caleb Jenkin.* 1776. 12mo, pp. 228. Map. C., H., J.C.B. 15116

"A tolerable account of the New England provinces, but that of the other provinces is very brief indeed." — RICH. In the catalogue of the Brunswick library this work is said to be by Paul Wein, with the following note: "So much of the author's name as is given above is written upon the title-page. The remainder was cut off in binding the work."

A Concise History of the Spanish America. *See* [Campbell (J.)], Vol. III., No. 16235.

A Concise History of the United States, from the Discovery of America till 1795. *Philadelphia: Printed by J. McCulloch.* 1797. 12mo. Map. + Second Edition. *Philadelphia: Printed by J. McCulloch.* 1797. 15117

Concise History of the United States, from the Discovery of America till 1813. *Philadelphia.* 1813. 12mo. 15118

A Concise Statement of the Action of Congress in relation to a Navy Yard for Iron Clad Vessels, with Extracts from Reports made on the Subject, and the Comparative Expense of a Navy Yard at League Island and New London. *New London.* 1866. 8vo, pp. 32. H. 15119

A Concise Statement of the Question regarding the Abolition of the Slave Trade. *London: J. Hatchard.* 8vo. 15120

See "M. Rev.," L. 216.

Concise View of ... Religious Denominations. *See* [Branagan], Vol. II., No. 7375.

A Concise View of the Late Proceedings of the Leaders of the Clintonian Party, in New-York and at Albany, for the Suppression of the Merchants' Bank. By a Spectator. *New-York.* 1804. 8vo, pp. 15. H. 15121

CONCIVIS, *pseudonym.* Letters to the People of the United States, published Semi-Monthly, in Six Series, from 15th August to 1st November, 1840. By Concivis. *New York.* 1840. 8vo. N. 15122

CONCLIN (George). ... Conclins' New River Guide, or A Gazetteer of all the Towns on the Western Waters ... . *Cincinnati, O.* 1848. 8vo, pp. 128. + [*Ibid.*:] *H. S. & J. Applegate.* 1850. 8vo, pp. 128. 44 woodcut Maps, and 1 View. BA. + *Cincinnati.* 1852. 8vo, pp. 128. 15123

CONCORD, *Mass.* The Annual Report of the School Committee, of Concord, for the Year 1846. *Concord.* 1846. 8vo. Continued. H. 15124

Annual Reports of the Selectmen and other Officers of the Town of Concord from March 1, 1866, to March 1, 1867, including the Marriages, Births, and Deaths in 1866. Also the Report of the School-Committee. *Concord: Benjamin Tolman.* 1867. 8vo, pp. 26. H. 15125

Catalogue of the Books belonging to the Concord Town Library, January, 1865. *Concord: Benjamin Tolman.* 1865. 16mo, pp. 137. H. 15126

Catalogue of the Teachers and Pupils of the Concord School, 1857–8. *Concord.* 1858. 8vo, pp. 11. Continued. H. 15127

Catalogue of the Trustees, Instructors, and Students, 1838. *Concord, Mass.* 1838. 12mo, pp. 11. Continued. 15128

Catalogue of the Officers and Students, 1840. *Lowell.* 1840. 12mo, pp. 12. Continued. 15129

Concord: a Poem delivered before the Lyceum, Concord, Mass., Jan. 22, 1851. *Boston.* 1851. 12mo. 15130

Concord Directory: containing the names, occupation and residences of the Inhabitants of Concord Village, with other matter of great local interest. *Concord: Charles V. Wheeler.* 1853–4. 18mo, pp. 89. 15131

Contains 1669 names.

Extract from the Proceedings of the Convention at Concord, Mass. W. 15132

Proceedings of the Convention at Concord, July 14, 1779, to carry into effect the Measures recommended by Congress. *Boston.* 1779. 8vo. W. 15133

Regulations of the School Committee of the Town of Concord. Revised and adopted March, 1830. ... *Concord: Herman Atwill.* 1830. 8vo, pp. 8. H. 15134

Reports of the Selectmen and the Overseers of the Poor of Concord, relative to the Expenses of the Town, for the Year 1847–8. *Concord.* 1848–54. 8vo. H. 15135

Reports of the Selectmen, Overseers of the Poor, Superintendent of Public Grounds, and Chief Engineer of the Fire-Department, 1850–51; also the Births, Marriages, and Deaths in 1850. *Concord.* 1851. 8vo, pp. 44. Continued. H. 15136

Result of a Council of Churches at Concord, Mass., June 21, 1743. 16mo. W. 15137

Also: By-Laws of Corinthian Lodge. *Concord, Mass.* 1822. 12mo. + *Concord.* 1859. 12mo. W.

Concord and Boston Oil Company, located in Venango County, Penn. *Boston: Farwell & McGlenen.* 1865. 8vo, pp. 11. H. 15138

CONCORD, *N. H.* Annual Reports of the Schools in the City of Concord, together with the Mayor's Annual Address, and the City Officers for ... 1868. *Concord.* 1868. 8vo, pp. 39. H. 15139

Catalogue of Concord Literary Institution and Teacher's Seminary. For the Year ... 1836. *Concord.* [1836.] 12mo, pp. 11. H. 15140

Concord Directory for 1830. By John Farmer. *Concora [N. H.]* 1830. 12mo, pp. 24. 15141

A Directory ... of Concord Centre Village. By David Watson. *Concord.* 1850. 18mo, pp. 108. Continued. H.

Concord Pocket Almanack for ... 1810, and Register of New-Hampshire ... . *Concord: G. Hough & D. Cooledge.* 12mo, pp. 105, (3). Continued to 1813 at least. BA. 15143

Concord Railroad Corporation. 13th Rep. 1854. *Concord, N. H.* 8vo. 15144

Facilitated Carrying. A Short Statement of the Proceedings at Concord, New Hampshire, on ... the Third Day of June, 1825, on the Subject of Internal Improvements; and some Remarks thereon. *Boston: A. Sampson.* 1825. 8vo, pp. 17. H.

The First Annual Report of the Receipts & Expenditures of the City of Concord for the Fiscal Year ending Feb. 1, 1854; with the other Annual Reports and Papers relating to the Affairs of the City. *Concord, N. H.* 1854. 8vo. Continued. H.

A Municipal Register of the City of Concord, containing the City Charter and Ordinances, the Rules of the City Council, and a List of the City Officers. ... *Concord: Fogg, Hadley & Company.* 1852. 8vo, pp. 159. H. 15147

A Municipal Register, containing the City Charter and Ordinances, [etc.] *Concord: City Council.* 1855. 8vo, pp. 80.

Proceedings of the N. H. Anti-Slavery Convention, held in Concord, on 11th & 12th of November, 1834. *Concord, N. H.: Eastman, Webster & Co., Printers.* 1834. 8vo, pp. 36, (1). BA.

Report of Experiments and Observations on the Concord and Sudbury Rivers, in the Year 1861. By Commissioners Appointed under Chap. 154, Acts of 1861. *Boston: William White, Printer.* 1862. 8vo, pp. 55, clxxiv, 1 l. folded. 2 Maps. BA. 13150

Report of the Bank Commissioners in relation to the Concord Bank. [*Concord.* 1840.] 8vo. pp. 7. H. 15151

Report of the Committee of Citizens appointed to ascertain the Feasibility and Cost of Supplying Water for Fire and other Purposes, to the Compact Part of the City of Concord. *Concord.* 1859. 8vo. pp. 15. H. 15152

Report of the Special Committee, appointed by the Mayor and Aldermen, to ascertain and define the Boundary Lines of the Several School Districts in the City. [n. p. n. d.] 8vo, pp. 25. H. 15153

Reports of the Superintending School Committees of the City of Concord, for the Year ending March, 1860–1861. *Concord: P. B. Cogswell.* 1860–61. 8vo. H. 15154

The Seventeenth Annual Report of the Receipts and Expenditures of the City of Concord, for the Fiscal Year ending

February 1, 1870, together with other Annual Reports and Papers relating to the Affairs of the City. ... *Concord: A. G. Jones.* 1870. 8vo, pp. 116, (2). H. 15155

A Short Statement of the Proceedings at Concord, N. H., 3d June, 1825, on the Subject of Internal Improvements. *Boston.* 1825. 8vo, pp. 17. M. 15156

A Short Summary and Declaration of Faith of the Baptist Church in Concord, to which is added the Church Covenant. ... *Concord: Young & Worth.* 1837. 24mo, pp. 23. H. 15157

Concordia de la Discordia. Sobre un punto grave de Immunidad Ecclesiastica. Al Rey Nro. Señor D. Fernando VI. Rey de las Españas Emperador de las Yndias. *Lima: En la Imprenta de la Calle de Palacio.* 1749. 4to, 12 l., pp. 285.

CONCORDVILLE, *Pa.* Circular of Concordville Seminary, for Young Ladies and Gentlemen, Concordville, Delaware Co., Pa. [n. p. n. d.] 1 sheet. H. 15159

CONDAMINE (C. M. de La). *See* La Condamine (Charles Marie).

CONDE (Francisco). A sus conciudadanos. *Carácas.* 1853. 8vo, pp. 19. 15160

[CONDE (Pedro Garcia).] Ensayo Estadisdico sobre el Estado de Chihuahua. *Chihuahua: Imprenta del Gobierno a cargo de Cayetano Ramos.* 1842. Folio, pp. 98. With folded Tables, A to G. 15161

CONDE Y OQUENDO (Francisco Xavier). Disertacion historica sobre la aparicion de la portentosa Imágen de Maria Sma. de Guadalupe de Mexico. *Mexico.* 1852–53. 2 vols., 8vo.

CONDE Y PINEDA (Fr. Xav.) Oracion moral deprecativa a la milagrosa imagen de Jesus Nazareno en la ciudad de Puebla. *Mexico.* 1809. 4to, 3 l., pp. 47. 15163

The Condensed Anti-Slavery Argument. *See* [Bourne], Vol. II., No. 6918.

A Condensed History of the Independent Roystering Club. [n. p. n. d.] 8vo. 15164

Thirty-two copies only printed, for the cadets at West Point.

CONDER (J.) An Arrangement of Provincial Coins, Tokens, and Medalets, issued in Great Britain, Ireland, and the Colonies within the Last Twenty Years, from the Farthing to the Penny Size. By James Conder. ... *Ipswich.* 1798. 8vo, pp. 330, and Errata. 15165

Includes the coins of Barbadoes and Bermuda. Also published in 4to, and printed on one side only.

CONDER (J.) An Analytical and Comparative View of all Religions now Extant among Mankind, with their Internal Diversities of Creed and Profession. By Josiah Conder. *London.* 1838. 8vo. P. 15166

CONDER. Brazil, and Buenos Ayres. *London.* 1825. 2 vols., 18mo. + *London.* 1831. 2 vols., 18mo. 15167

Forms part of a series, entitled the "Modern Traveller." *See infra.*

CONDER. A Dictionary of Geography, Ancient and Modern; comprising a Succinct Description of all the Countries of the Globe. *London.* 1834. 8vo. C. 15168

CONDER. Mexico and Guatemala. *See* "Modern Traveller."

CONDER. The Modern Traveller. A Description, Geographical, Historical, and Topographical, of the Various Countries of the Globe. Edited by Josiah Conder. *London.* 1824–30. 30 vols., 18mo. Maps and Plates. 15169

CONDER. Wages, or the Whip. An Essay on the Comparative Cost and Productiveness of Free and Slave Labour. By Josiah Conder ... . *London.* 1833. 8vo, pp. 91. 15170

CONDICT (I.) A Funeral Discourse, delivered in the Presbyterian Church of New-Brunswick, on the 31st of December, 1799; the Day set Apart by the Citizens for paying Solemn Honors to the Memory of Gen. George Washington. By the Rev. Ira Condict, A.M. ... [Motto.] *New-Brunswick, New-Jersey: Printed by Abraham Blauvelt.* 1800. 8vo, pp. 23. N.

CONDICT (L.) An Address, delivered by Appointment, at Morristown, New-Jersey, July 4th, 1828. By ... Lewis Condict. *Morristown, (N. J.): Jacob Mann.* 1828. 8vo, pp. 37.

CONDIE (D. F.) Annual Oration ... before the Philadelphia Medical Society ... At the opening of its Session of 1844–5. By D. Francis Condie ... *Philadelphia.* 1845. 8vo, pp. 24. B.

CONDIE. Biographical Notice of Henry Bond, M.D., read before the College of Physicians, of Philadelphia, April 4, 1860. By D. Francis Condie, M.D. *Philadelphia.* 1860. 8vo, pp. 22.

CONDIE. A Memoir of William H. Klapp, M.D., read before the College of Physicians, January 7, 1857, by D. Francis Condie, M.D. *Philadelphia.* 1857. 8vo, pp. 12. 15175

[CONDIE (Thomas).] Biographical Memoirs of the Illustrious Gen. Geo. Washington, late President of the United States of America, &c., &c. Containing, A History of the principal Events of his Life, with Extracts from its Journals, Speeches to Congress, and Public Addresses: — Also — A Sketch of his Private Life. *Philadelphia: Printed by Charless & Ralston.* 1800. 16mo, pp. 243. 15176

[CONDIE.] Biographical Memoirs of General George Washington, containing a History of the Principal Events of his Life, with Extracts from his Journals, Speeches to Congress, and Public Addresses. Third Edition. *Philadelphia: R. Folwell.* 1801. 24mo, pp. 217. C. 15177

[CONDIE.] Biographical Memoirs of the Illustrious Gen. George Washington, late President of the United States of America, &c. Containing a History of the principal events of his life, with extracts from his Journals, Speeches to Congress, and Public Addresses. Also, A Sketch of his Private Life. *Brattleborough: Published by William Fessenden.* 1814. 12mo, pp. 287. 15178

This edition is said to have been edited by the publisher.

CONDIE (T.) *and* FOLWELL (R.) History of the Pestilence, commonly called Yellow Fever, which almost desolated Philadelphia in the Months of August, September and October, 1798. By Thomas Condie & Richard Folwell. *Philadelphia: Press of R. Folwell.* [n. d.] 8vo, pp. 108, xxxii, 33 l. B. 15179

CONDIT (J. B.) An Address delivered before the Library Societies of Dartmouth College, July 28, 1841. By J. B. Condit. *Portland: Newell A. Foster.* 1841. 8vo, pp. 31.

CONDIT. Education at the West; in its Claims on the Church. A Discourse, delivered before the Society for Promoting Collegiate Education at the West, in ... New Haven, Oct. 26, 1848, by J. B. Condit. ... *New York: M. W. Dodd.* 1849. 8vo, pp. 30. B., H. 15181

CONDIT. History of the Second Presbyterian Congregation in Newark, N. J. By J. B. Condit, D.D. *Newark.* 1831. 8vo. S. 15182

CONDIT. The Missionary Enterprise a True Development of the Life of the Church. A Sermon before the American Board of Commissioners for Foreign Missions, at ... Worcester, Mass. October 4, 1864. By Jonathan B. Condit ... . *Boston.* 1864. 8vo, pp. 28. B. 15183

Conditien, de welcke by de Ed. | Groot Mog. Heeren Staten van Hollandt | ende West-Vrieslandt, toegestaen wer- | den aen een yeder, die genegentheydt | mochten hebben om een aensien-elijck | Colonie uyt te setten op een seer bequa- | me ende wel -gelegene plaetse, op de | vaste Kuste van America, die daer toe | vast gesteldt ende aengewesen sal wor- | den. | 4to, pp. 11.

Proposals offered by the States-General to intending emigrants to the American coast, *i. e.*, Guiana.

Conditien, | De welcke by d'Ed. Mog. Heeren Sta- | ten van Hollandt ende West-Vrieslandt, toe-gestaan wer- | den aen een yeder, die genegentheydt mochten hebben, om | een aensienlijcke Colonie uyt te setten op een seer be- | quame ende wel-gelegene Plaetse, op de vaste Kuste van | America, die daer toe vast-gestelt, ende aangewesen | sal worden. | 4to, 4 l. 15185

Proposals offered to emigrants to Guiana, the new colony of Wapoca (Orinoco).

Conditien, Die doore de Heeren Burgomeesteren der Stadt Amsterdam; volgens 't gamaeete Accoort met de West Indische Companie, ... *Amsterdam: E. Nieuwenholt.* 1686. 4to, 4 l.

The Condition of Labor. An Address to the Members of the Labor Reform League of New England. By One of the Members. *Boston.* 1847. 8vo, pp. 32. H. 15187

The Condition of the Free People of Color in the United States. *New York.* 1839. 8vo, pp. 23. 15188

Condition of the Indian Tribes. Report of the Joint Special Committee, appointed under Joint Resolution March 3, 1865. With an Appendix. *Washington: Government Printing Office.* 1867. 8vo, pp. 532. S. 15189

Details the atrocities committed by the whites upon the Indians at Sand Creek — a chapter of horrors.

Condolence; An Elegiac Epistle. *See* Burgoyne (J.), Vol. III., No. 9249.

CONDORCET (Marie Jean Antoine Nicolas Caritat), *Marquis de.* Éloge de M. Franklin lu à la Séance Publique de l'Academie des Sciences. *Paris.* 1791. 8vo. 15190

CONDORCET. Esquisse d'un Tableau Historique des progrès de l'Esprit Humain; suivie de Reflexions sur l'Esclavage des Nègres: Par Condorcet. *A Paris: Chez Masson et Fils.* 1822. 8vo, pp. viii, 440. 15191

[CONDORCET.] Réflexions sur l'Esclavage de Nègres, par Joachim Schwartz. *Paris.* 1788. 8vo. S. + Nouvelle édition. *Neufchatel.* 1788. 8vo, pp. 86. 15192

[CONDORCET.] Sentiments véritables du ministre Swartz sur quelques endroits d'une brochure sur l'esclavage des nègres, qu'on lui a faussement attribuée. *Neufchâtel. Paris: Guillot.* 1789. 8vo. 15193

CONDORCET. Œuvres de Condorcet publiées par A. Condorcet O'Connor ... et M. F. Arago ... . *Paris: Firmin Didot frères.* 1847–49. 12 vols., 8vo. B., BA. 15194

"Eloge de Franklin," III. 372–423; "Réflexions sur l'esclavage des nègres. *Neuchatel.* 1781; "Edition ... corrigée. *Paris.* 1788," VII. 61–141; "De l'influence de la révolution d'Amérique sur l'Europe. ... Par un habitant obscur de l'ancien hémisphère. 1786. Inséré en 1788 dans les Recherches ... sur les États-unis, par Mazzey," VIII. 1–113; "Lettres d'un bourgeois de New-Haven à un citoyen de Virginie, sur l'inutilité de partager le pouvoir législatif entre plusieurs corps. 1787. Inséré en 1788 dans les Recherches ... par Massey," IX. 1–93; "Au Corps électoral contre l'esclavage des noirs," IX. 471–485.

The Condottier; A Poem. — Philadelphia, a Satire. *Philadelphia.* 1821. 18mo, pp. 80. S. 15195

CONDRA (I.) Coleccion de las Antigüedades Mexicanas que ecsisten en el Museo Nacional y dan à luz Isidro Icaza e Isidro Condra. Litografiadas por Federico Waldeck, e impresas por Pedro Robert. *Mexico.* 1827. Folio. 15196

"All I have seen of this work consists of a handsomely ornamented title-page, a sheet of descriptions, and four lithograph drawings of Mexican antiquities." — RICH, Vol. II.

The Conduct of a Noble Commander [the Earl of Loudon] in America, Impartially reviewed. With the genuine Causes of the Discontents at New-York and Halifax. And the true Occasion of the Delays in that important Expedition. Including A regular Account of all the proceedings and Incidents in the Order of Time wherein they happened. *London: R. Baldwin.* MDCCLVIII. 8vo, pp. 45. P. 15197

The design of this pamphlet was to vindicate Lord Loudon from some imputation which was thrown out against him on account of his conduct in America. *See* Tudor's "Otis," ch. IV.

The Conduct of a Rt. Hon. Gentleman. *See* [Pitt (Wm.)]

The Conduct Of The D-ke of Ar--le. *See* [Campbell (John)], Vol. III., No. 10227.

The Conduct of administration, with regard to the Colonies. *London: Williams.* [n. d.] 8vo. 15198

"The whole conduct of the ministry, with respect to the troubles in America, is absolutely condemned by this warm writer, who expresses himself with more zeal than judgment." — *M. Review.*

Conduct of the Administration, 1832. *See* [Everett (A. H.)]

The Conduct of Great Britain respecting Neutrals. *Philadelphia.* 1807. 8vo, pp. 72. 15199

The Conduct of the Allies of the Late Ministry. ... Sixth Edition. *London.* 1712. 8vo. S. 15200

The Conduct of the Dutch, relating to their Breach of Treaties with England. Particularly their Breach of the Articles of Capitulation for the Surrender of Surinam, in 1667; and their Oppressions committed upon the English Subjects in that Colony. With a full Account of the Case of Jeronimy Clifford, Merchant and Planter of Surinam. ... *London: W. Bristow.* M.DCC.LX. 8vo, Title, pp. 220. H. 15201

"Relates entirely to Surinam." — RICH.

The Conduct of the French, With Regard to Nova Scotia. *See* Jeffries (J.), *also*, Nova Scotia.

The Conduct of the Late Administration Examined. With an Appendix, containing Original and Authentic Documents. *London: J. Almon.* MDCCLXVII. 8vo, pp. 160, (2), liv. + *Boston: Reprinted and Sold by Edes and Gill.* 1767. 8vo, pp. 107.

The "Monthly Review" characterizes this as one of the most formidable attacks made on the late administration. The author of a letter to G. G., calls this Mr. G[renville's] celebrated pamphlet on the Stamp Act. It has also been attributed to C. Lloyd, and to C. Jenkinson. Reprinted with the following title:

The Conduct of the late Administration Examined, Relative to the American Stamp-Act. With an Appendix containing Original and Authentic Documents. The Second Edition. *London: J. Almon.* MDCCLXVII. 8vo, pp. 166, (2), liv. BA.

Included in Almon's Tracts, Vol. III. "One of the most formidable attacks that hath as yet been made on the lateadministration, and seems to be the production of some ingenious and well-instructed writer strongly attached to Mr. Grenville. The

American Stamp Act is the grand object of his attention, and he confines himself in this tract to the examination of the conduct of the ministry with regard to it, from the time at which they came into office to that at which it was repealed." — *Monthly Review.*

Conduct of the Late and Present Ministry Compared, &c. *London.* 1742. 8vo, pp. 52. N. 15204

The Conduct of the late Ministry; or Memorial containing a Summary of Facts, with their Vouchers, in answer to the Observations sent by the English Ministry to the Courts of Europe. *London.* 1757. 8vo, pp. 320. J.C.B. 15205

This work is supposed to have been published by the French government, in consequence of a piece sent by direction of H. B. M. to most of the courts of Europe, entitled "Observations on the Memorial of France." Reprinted as "The Mystery Revealed," 1759, which see, *infra.* *See also* "Mémoire contenant," etc., 1756.

The Conduct of the Ministry compared with its Consequences: or an Important View of the Present State of Affairs. *London.* 1733. 8vo. W. 15206

Conduct of the Ministry Impartially Examined. In a Letter to the Merchants of London. *London: S. Bladon.* MDCCLVI. 8vo, pp. 68. + Second Edition. *London: S. Bladon.* MDCCLVI. 8vo, pp. 68. J.C.B. 15207

Relates to the case of some British subjects imprisoned for trading on the Ohio. *See* "M. Rev.," XV. 524.

Conduct of the Ministry Impartially Examined; and the Pamphlet entitled, "Considerations on the present German War" Refuted on its own Principles. *London.* 1760. 8vo, pp. 54. N. 15208

For an answer to this, *see* [Shebbeare (John)].

The Conduct of the Opposition. *See* [Hervey (*Lord* John)].

Conduct of the Paxton-Men, Impartially Represented, The Distresses of the Frontiers, and the Complaints and Sufferings of the People fully stated, etc. With some Remarks upon the Narrative of the Indian-Massacre, lately published. Interspersed with several Interesting Anecdotes, relating to the Military Genius and Warlike Principles of the People called Quakers, etc. In a letter from a Gentleman in one of the Back-Counties, to a Friend in Philadelphia. *Philadelphia: Printed by Andrew Stuart.* M DCC LXIV. 12mo, Half-Title, pp. 34. N., P.

Dated, March 17, 1764. In the Lancaster interest; page 1, of the text, consists of a verbose second title, advertising the book to be "sold by John Creig, shopkeeper in Lancaster." *See* "A Battle," Vol. I., No. 3961. For an answer, *see* Vol. I., No. 1663.

The Conduct of the Present Parliament considered, previous to its Dissolution. *London: Printed for J. Ridgeway.* M.DCC.LXXXIX. 8vo, Title, pp. 75. BA. 15210

The Conduct of Two B——rs [Brothers] Vindicated. *London: M. Cooper.* 1749. 12mo, pp. 37. 15211

The Conduct of the War. Report of the Congressional Committee on the Operations of the Army of the Potomac, Causes of its Inaction and Ill Success. Its Several Campaigns. Why McClellan was Removed. The Battle of Fredericksburgh. Removal of Burnside. *New York: Tribune Association.* 1863. 8vo, pp. 30. 15212

Conducta injurídica del Juzgado de Presas de las Islas de Bahama con respecto al comercio marítimo de la Isla de Cuba y demas neutrales. *Habana: oficina de Arazoza y Soler.* 1814. Folio, pp. 28. 15213

Conductor to attractive places in Boston and Vicinity. *Boston.* [n. d.] 24mo, pp. 84. 15214

Conductor Generalis. Or, The Office, Duty and Authority of Justices of the Peace, High-Sheriffs, Under-Sheriffs, Goalers, Coroners, Constables, Jury-Men, Over seers of the Poor, and also The Office of Clerks of Assize, and of the Peace, &c. Collected out of all the Books hitherto written on those subjects, whether of Common or Statute Law. To which is Added a Collection out of Sir Matthew Hale's, concerning the Descent of Lands. ... *Printed and sold by Andrew Bradford, in Philadelphia,* 1722. 4to, 4 l., pp. 300. C. + Second Edition, with large Additions. *Philadelphia: Printed and sold by B. Franklin and D. Hall, at the New Printing Office, near the Market.* 1749. 8vo, pp. 592. + *New York.* 1749. 8vo, pp. 480. + *Philadelphia.* 1792. 8vo. W. 15215

Conductor Generalis. *See* Parker (James).

Conduite des François, 1755. *See* [Jeffreys (J.)], *also* Nova Scotia.

CONDY (J.) The Godly and Faithful Man characterized: and his decease improved. A Sermon Preach'd at Boston, On the Death of Mr. Benjamin Landon, Merchant: Who deceased January 8, 1747. In the 53d Year of his Age. By Jeremiah Condy, A.M. *Boston: Printed for D. Gookin.* 1747. 8vo, pp. 44. BA. 15216

CONDY. Mercy Exemplified, in the Conduct of a Samaritan, and Recommended to Universal Imitation. A Sermon Preached at Boston, In the Province of the Massachusetts-Bay. By Jeremy Condy, A.M. At Cambridge, in that Province. *Printed.* 1767. [n. p.] 4to, pp. 26. B. + *Salem.* 1769. 4to, pp. 16. *Boston.* 1769. 8vo, pp. 16. 15217

CONDY (T. D.) An Oration, ... before ... the Inhabitants of Charleston, South-Carolina, On the 5th Day of July, 1819; (the 4th being Sunday) ... By Thomas D. Condy. *Charleston: Printed by A. E. Miller.* 1819. 8vo, pp. 21. BA. 15218

CONE (A.) Petrolia: a Brief History of the Pennsylvania Petroleum Region, its Development, Growth, Resources, etc., from 1859 to 1869. By Andrew Cone and Walter R. Johns. Edited by Walter R. Johns. *New York: D. Appleton and Company.* 1870. 8vo, pp. 652. B. 15219

CONE (D. D.) Letters relating to our Agritultural, Manufacturing, and Commercial Interests, and the Action of Congress thereon, by D. D. Cone. Fifth Edition. *Washington: United Press Association.* 1867. 8vo, pp. 36. H. 15220

CONE. Washington Letters to the Vermont Journal, Connecticut Courant, N. Y. Tribune, ... by D. D. Cone, President of the United Press Association. Eighth Edition. *Washington: United Press Association.* 1867. 8vo, pp. 48. H.

[CONE (E. W. *and* S. W.)] Some Account of the Life of Spencer Houghton Cone, A Baptist Preacher in America. *New York: Livermore & Rudd; London: Trübner & Company.* 1856. 8vo, pp. 484. H. 15222

CONEWAGO CANAL. Account of the Conewago Canal, on the River Susquehanna; to which is prefixed, the Act for Incorporating the Company. *Philadelphia.* 1798. 8vo, pp. 18.

CONFEDERATE STATES.

The following list of books and papers issued by the Confederate States is made up principally from the extensive collection belonging to Mr. John F. McCoy, of New York, with additions, chiefly from the Library of the Boston Athenæum. We may add, that all these books are scarce, and command high prices.

Abstract of Drafts of Members of the C. S. House of Representatives, ... April 18th, 1863. [n. p. n. d.] 8vo, pp. 2.
Signed E. C. Elmore, Treasurer C. S.

An Act Imposing Taxes for the Support of Government. Passed March 28, 1863. [n. p. n. d.] 8vo, pp. 56. 15225

An Act to impose Regulations upon the Foreign Commerce of the Confederate States, to provide for the Public Defence. [n. p. n. d.] 8vo, pp. 10. 15226

Act to Provide for the Public Defence, April 11, 1862. *Richmond.* 1862. 8vo. BA. 15227

Act to further provide for the public defence, October 11, 1862. [*Richmond.* 1862.] 8vo, pp. 8. 15228

Acts and Resolutions of the First Session of the Provisional Congress of the Confederate States. *Montgomery, Ala.: Barrett, Wimbish, ...* [1861.] 8vo, pp. 131. + Second Session. *Montgomery, Ala.: Barrett, Wimbish & Co.* 1861. 8vo, pp. 100. + *Montgomery, Ala.: Shorter & Reid, Printers and Binders.* 1861. 8vo, pp. 122. B. + *Richmond: Tyler, Wise, Allegre & Smith,* [*Printers*]. 1861. 8vo, pp. 119. BA. + Third Session, held at Richmond, Va. *Richmond: Tyler, Wise, Allegre & Smith.* 1861. 8vo, pp. 94. BA. + Fourth Session. *Richmond: Tyler, Wise, Allegre and Smith, Printers.* 1862. 8vo, pp. 106, (1), 19. BA., H. 15229

Additional Estimates for the Support of the Government. Richmond, Va., Feb. 11, 1864. 8vo, pp. 14. 15230
Signed Jefferson Davis.

Address of Congress to the People of the Confederate States. [n. p. 1862.] 8vo, pp. 8. BA. 15231
Signed T. J. Semmes, and others.

Address of the Atlanta Register, to the People of the Confederate States. *Atlanta, Ga.* [n. d.] 8vo, pp. 16. 15232

Address to Christians throughout the World. 8vo, pp. 8.

Advertisement of December 31, 1862, inviting Proposals for carrying the Mails of the Confederate States in the States of Florida, Georgia, South Carolina, North Carolina and Virginia, from July 1, 1863, to June 30, 1867. John H. Reagan, Postmaster General. ... [*Richmond.* 1863.] 8vo, pp. 102. BA.

The Aid-de-Camp. *Richmond.* 186–. 12mo. 15235

Army Regulations, adopted for the use of the Army of the

Confederate States, ... Also, Articles of War, for the Government of the Army of the Confederate States of America. *New Orleans: Bloomfield & Steel, Publishers.* 1861. 8vo, pp. 198, (2). 15236

Articles of War, for the Government of the Army of the Confederate States. *Montgomery: Barrett, Wimbish & Co., Printers.* 1851. 12mo, pp. 20. + *Charleston: Evans & Cogswell.* 1861. 8vo, pp. 24. H. 15237

The Second Annual Report of the Bible Society of the Confederate States of America, 1864; with the Constitution of the Society, its List of Patrons, Life Directors, Members, etc. *Augusta, Ga.: Press of Stockton & Co.* 1864. 8vo, pp. 14, (10).

A Bill To be entitled an Act extending the privilege of purchasing clothing at Government cost, ... Richmond, Dec. 21, 1863. 8vo, pp. 2. 15239

A Bill To provide for the safe and expeditious transportation of troops and munitions of war by railroads. 8vo, pp. 8.

The Book of Reference, for Regular and Volunteer Officers and Soldiers of the Confederate States Army; containing the Articles of War ... . *New Orleans: Wm. Bloomfield, Jun., Publisher.* 1861. 8vo, Title, pp. 32. 15241

Brief Review of the Plan and Operations of the Society for the Relief of Maimed Soldiers. [n. p. n. d.] 8vo, pp. 10. BA.

Commercial Relations between the Confederate States and England. A Pamphlet for the Times. *London: Published by J. Moore.* 1861. *Mobile: reprint at the office of the Mobile Daily Register and Advertiser.* 1862. 8vo, pp. 20. 15243

Communication from the Attorney General. Richmond, March 13, 1863. 8vo, pp. 8. 15244
Signed T. H. Watts, Attorney-General.

Communication from the Postmaster General. Richmond, Va., March 6, 1863. 8vo, pp. 6. 15245
Signed John H. Reagan, Postmaster-General.

Communication of the Secretary of the Treasury. Richmond, January 23, 1863. 8vo, pp. 6. 15246
Signed C. G. Memminger, Secretary of the Treasury.

Communication from the Secretary of the Treasury. Treasury Department C. S. A. Richmond, February 4, 1864. 8vo, pp. 2. + May 14th, 1864. [n. p. n. d.] 8vo, pp. 50, (1). + May 20th, 1864. 8vo, pp. 3. BA. 15247
Also: Oct. 3, 1862. 8vo, pp. 2; Feb. 10, 1863. 8vo, 1 l.

Compilation of the Tariff Act of the Confederate States of America, Approved May 21st, 1861, Showing the Rates of Duties Payable on Imported Goods, Wares and Merchandise, From and After September 1st, 1861. Alphabetically Arranged; Also containing Recent Acts of Congress and Circulars of the Treasury Department relative to Commerce, Navigation and the Revenue; Together with the Warehouse System, ... Arranged by P. E. Walden, Deputy Collector, Custom House, Port of New Orleans. *New Orleans: Corson & Armstrong.* 1861. 8vo, pp. vii, 3–282. 15248

The Confederate. By a South Carolinian. *Mobile: S. H. Goetzel & Co.* 1863. 8vo, pp. 103. 15249

The Confederate Confiscation Bill. *New York.* 8vo, pp. 8.
With the instructions of the Confederate States Attorney-General thereon.

The Confederate First Reader; containing selections in Prose and Poetry, as Exercises for Younger Children. ... *Richmond: G. L. Bidgood.* 1864. 16mo, pp. 120. BA., C. + The Confederate Primer. Sixth Edition. [*Ibid.*] 24mo, pp. 32.

Confederate Memorial. [Signed R. W. Gibbs.] 8vo, pp. 4.

Confederate Receipt Book. A Compilation of over One Hundred Receipts, adapted to the Times. *West & Johnston, Richmond.* 1863. 8vo, pp. 28, 1 l. 15253

The Confederate Rhyming Primer. *Richmond, Va.: George L. Bidgood.* 1863. pp. 24. 15254

The Confederate Spelling Book, with Reading Lessons for the Young, adapted to the Use of Schools or for Private Instruction. Fifth Edition. *Richmond: Geo. L. Bidgood.* 1865. 12mo, pp. 162. 15255

The Confederate States Almanac, and Repository of Useful Knowledge, for 1862. *Published by H. C. Clarke, Vicksburg, Miss.* [1862.] 12mo, pp. 80. + Second Edition. [*Ibid.*]

The Confederate States Almanac, and Repository of Useful Knowledge, for the year 1863. ... To which is added a Diary of the War for Separation; a History of the Present Revolution; giving a daily account of all the Battles, Skirmishes, Engagements, List of the Killed and Wounded, &c.; with a Chronicle of Events for the past Year. *H. C. Clarke, Publisher, Augusta, Ga. Vicksburg, Miss.* 15257

Confederate States Almanac for the Year of our Lord 1864 ... the 4th Year of the Independence of the Confederate States of America. ... *Published for the Trade by Burke, Boykin & Co., Macon, Ga. J. McPherson & Co., Atlanta, Ga.* [1864.] 12mo, pp. 20. B. 15258
Some copies have the imprint, *Mobile: S. H. Goetzel.* [1864.]

Confederate States Patent Laws, enacted by the Provisional Congress. *Richmond.* 1862. 8vo, pp. 34, (1). H. 15259

Congress of the Confederate States. Proceedings on the Announcement of the Death of Hon. John Tyler, January 20th, 1862. ... *Richmond.* 1862. 8vo, pp. 54. H. 15260

Congress of the Confederate States. Proceedings on the Announcement of the Death of Col. Francis S. Bartow, of the Army of the Confederate States, ... *Richmond: Enquirer Book and Job Press, Tyler, Wise and Allegre.* 1861. 12mo, 2 l., pp. 25, (1). 15261

Constitution and Canons of the Protestant Episcopal Church, in the Confederate States of America. *Augusta, Ga.* 1863. 8vo, pp. 59. 15262

Constitution of the Confederate States of America. Adopted unanimously by the Confederate States of America, March 11, 1861. *Savannah: John M. Cooper & Company.* 1861. 8vo, pp. 21. BA. 15263

Correspondence between The President and General Joseph E. Johnston, together with that of the Secretary of War and the Adjutant and Inspector General, during the Months of May, June and July, 1863. ... *Richmond: R. M. Smith, Public Printer.* 1864. 8vo, pp. 64. BA. 15264

Correspondence of the Department of State, in Relation to the British Consuls resident in the Confederate States. *Richmond.* 1863. 8vo, pp. 55. H. 15265

A Digest of the Military and Naval Laws of the Confederate States, from the Commencement of the Provisional Congress to the End of the First Congress under the Permanent Constitution. ... Analytically Arranged by Capt. W. W. Lester, ... and Wm. J. Bromwell, ... *Columbia: Evans and Cogswell.* 1864. 8vo, pp. 329, (1). B. 15266

Documents accompanying Report of Secretary of the Treasury. Report of Commissioner of Taxes. [*Richmond. November,* 1863.] 8vo, pp. 45. BA. 15267

Evidence taken before the Committee of the House of Representatives, appointed to enquire into Treatment of Prisoners at Castle Thunder. 8vo, pp. 58, 1 l. 15268

General Directions for Collecting and Drying Medicinal Substances of the Vegetable Kingdom. List and Description of Indigenous Plants, etc.; their Medicinal Properties; Forms of Administration, and Doses. Surgeon General's Office, Richmond, Virginia, March 21, 1862. [n. p. n. d.] 8vo, pp. 22.

General Orders from Adjutant and Inspector-General's Office, Confederate States Army, From January, 1862, to December, 1863, (both inclusive.) In Two Series. Prepared from Files of Head-Quarters, Department of C. S., Ga., and Fla. With Full Indexes. *Columbia: Presses of Evans & Cogswell.* 1864. 8vo, pp. xlvii, 159, lix, 276. BA. 15270

General Orders from the Adjutant and Inspector-General's Office, Confederate States Army, From January 1 to June 30, 1864, inclusive. Prepared from Files of Head-Quarters, Department of South Carolina, Georgia, and Florida. By R. C. Gilchrist ... *Columbia: Evans & Cogswell.* 1864. 8vo, pp. xxxv, 161. H. 15271

General orders from the Adjutant and Inspector-General's Office for 1863. Compiled under authority by R. H. P. Robinson. *Richmond.* 1864. 16mo. 15272

The Import Tariff, and other Revenue Laws. ... *New Orleans: Wm. Bloomfield, Jun., Publisher.* 1861. 16mo, pp. 34.

Inaugural Address of President Davis, delivered at the Capitol. ... February 18, 1861 ... . *Montgomery, Ala.: Shorter & Reid, Printers.* 1861. 8vo, pp. 8. B. 15274

Instructions for Collectors of Taxes, from J. C. Memminger, Secretary of the Treasury. [Dated] *Richmond, May,* 1863. 8vo, pp. 15. 15275

Instructions for the Agents for collecting Subscriptions to the Produce Loan ... . Richmond, January 3rd, 1862. 8vo, pp. 4.
Signed C. G. Memminger, Secretary of the Treasury.

Journal of the proceedings of the General Council of the Protestant Episcopal Church, in the "Confederate States of America," 1862 ... *Augusta.* 1863. 8vo. 15277

Laws of Congress in regard to Taxes, Currency and Conscription, passed February, 1864. Printed by order of the Virginia Senate. *Richmond: James E. Goode, Senate Printer.* 1864. 8vo, pp. 35. 15278

Laws for the Army and Navy of the Confederate States. *Richmond: printed by Ritchie & Dunnavant.* 1861. 8vo, pp. 98. H. 15279

Letter of Secretary of the Navy. Confederate States of America Navy Department, Richmond, April 7th, 1862. [n. p. n. d.] 8vo, pp. 13. BA. 15280

Letter of the Secretary of the Treasury submitting the Report to the Auditor. ... Richmond, Va., Sept. 5, 1862. 15281
Signed C. G. Memminger, Secretary of the Treasury.

A List of Establishments, Discontinuances and Changes in the Name of the Post Offices in the Confederate States, since 1861. [n. p. n. d.] 8vo, pp. 27. BA. 15282

Majority Report of the Committee of Congress to investigate the Management of Castle Thunder. [n. p. n. d.] 8vo, pp. 6.
This includes "Defence of Captain Alexander."

Majority Report of the Committee on Elections. 8vo, pp. 3, (1). 15284

Majority Report of the Committee on Foreign Affairs. 8vo, pp. 3, (1). 15285
Signed H. S. Foote, Chairman.

Majority Report of the Committee on Foreign Affairs. Richmond, Sept. 15, 1862. 8vo, pp. 6, (2). 15286
Signed J. P. Benjamin, Secretary of State.

Memorial of the Railroad Companies on the Exemption Law. January 16, 1864. Broadside. 15287

A Message from the Army of the Valley of Virginia. ... Camp of Smith's Brigade, Feb. 10, 1865. [n. p. n. d.] 8vo, pp. 1. BA. 15288

Message of the President. 8vo, pp. 24. BA. 15289
No title-page. Signed Jefferson Davis. Montgomery, April 29, 1861.

Message of the President, To the Congress of the Confederate States of America. [*Richmond:*] *Ritchie & Dunnavant, Printers.* 8vo, pp. 14. + [Another Edition. *Ibid.*] 8vo, pp. 14. BA.
No title-page. Signed Jefferson Davis. Richmond, July 20, 1861.

Message of the President. [n. p. n. d.] 8vo, pp. (10). BA.
Transmitting a communication from the Secretary of War relative to the suspension of the writ of habeas corpus.

Message of the President, and Report of Albert Pike, Commissioner of the Confederate States to the Indian Nations West of Arkansas, of the Results of his Mission. *Richmond: Enquirer Book and Job Press, Tyler, Wise, Allegre & Smith.* 1861. 8vo, pp. 38. BA. 15292

Message of the President. Richmond, November 18, 1861. [n. p. n. d.] 8vo, pp. 8. 15293
Signed Jefferson Davis.

Message of the President. March 11, 1862. 8vo, pp. 26.
Relates to the fall of Fort Donelson.

Message of the President. April 10, 1862. 8vo, pp. 13.
Transmitting a detailed report of triumph in Hampton Roads.

Message of the President, April 18, 1862. 8vo, pp. 16.
Report of the cruise of the "Nashville." Also: Message ... September 4, 1862, 1 l.; September 12, 1862, pp. 4; September 24, 1862, 1 l.; September 30, 1862, pp. 7; October 2, 1862, pp. 3; October 8, 1862, 1 l.

Message of the President. [n. p. n. d.] 8vo, pp. 16. BA.
Signed Jefferson Davis. Richmond, January 12, 1863.

Message of the President. January 12, 1863. [n. p. n. d.]
Signed Jefferson Davis. Reprinted in England with the following title:

The Second Annual Message of His Excellency the President of the Confederate States to Congress, January 12, 1863. *London: Henry F. Mackintosh.* MDCCCLXIII. 8vo, pp. 38.

President's Message. [n. p. n. d.] 8vo, pp. 29. BA. 15300

Signed Jefferson Davis. Richmond, December 7, 1863.

Message du président Jefferson Davis au sénat et à la chambre des États Confédérés Le 7 Décembre 1863 *Paris: imp. de Dubuisson et Ce.* 1864. 8vo, pp. 46. H. 15301

Other Messages, bearing the following dates, were also issued during the year 1863, all in 8vo: Richmond, January 27, pp. 3; Jan. 30, pp. 16; February 3, pp. 4; Feb. 3, pp. 19; February 4, pp. 6; Feb. 7, 1 l.; February 13, 1 l.; Feb. 16, pp. 8; Feb, 17, pp. 11; Feb. 17, 1 l.; Feb. 19, pp. 15; Feb. 19, pp. 4; Feb. 20, 2 l.; February 20, pp. 3; Feb. 25, 1 l.; Feb. 25, pp. 7; March 5, 2 l.; March 25, pp. 6; April 16, 1 l.; April 18, 1 l.; April 20, pp. 4; April 21, pp. 14; Dec. 11, 1 l.; Dec. 16, pp. 6; Dec. 17, pp. 4; Dec. 21, pp. 3, (1); Dec. 22, pp. 4.

Message of the President. *Richmond, Jan.* 10, 1864. 8vo, pp. 34. 15302

Includes "Communication from the Secretary of War, on the Taxes in kind."

Message of the President. *Richmond, Va. Jan.* 13, 1864. 8vo, pp. 7. 15303

Message of the President. *Richmond, Va. Jan.* 25, 1864. 8vo, pp. 7. H. 15304

Message from the President. *Richmond. February* 5, 1864. 8vo, pp. 14. 15305

President's Message. [n. p. n. d.] 8vo, pp. 5. 15306

Signed Jefferson Davis. May 2, 1864.

President's Message. In relation to the Suspension of the Writ of Habeas Corpus. Richmond, Va., May 20, 1864. [n. p. n. d.] 8vo, pp. 2. BA. 15307

Message of the President. [n. p. n. d.] 8vo, pp. 13. BA.

Signed Jefferson Davis. Richmond, November 7th, 1864.

Message of the President. Richmond, Va., November 11, 1864. [n. p. n. d.] 8vo, pp. 18. Table. BA. 15309

Transmitting communications from the Secretaries of the Treasury and of War, relative to the taxes collected for the year 1863.

Message of the President. Richmond, Va., Dec. 20, 1864. [n. p. n. d.] 8vo, pp. 17. BA. 15310

Transmitting reports made by the heads of the Treasury and War Departments, relative to a bill to impose regulations upon the foreign commerce of the Confederate States, to provide for public "defence." The following messages are dated, Richmond, 1864, all in 8vo: January 7, 1 l.; Jan. 11, 1 l.; January 11, pp. 15, (1); January 12, pp. 7; Jan. 18, pp. 4; February 3, pp. 14; Feb. 5, pp. 3; Feb. 8, pp. 9; Veto Message, February 11, pp. 2; Feb. 12, pp. (1); Feb. 15, pp. 2; May 18, 1 l.; August 20th, 2 l.; Message ... to the Hon. Howell Cobb. [n. p. n. d.] 12mo, 1 l.

Message of the President. Richmond, Va., Jan. 4, 1865. [n. p. n. d.] 8vo, pp. 14. BA. 15311

Transmitting a communication from the Secretary of War, relative to operations of the Army of Tennessee.

Message of the President. Richmond, Va., Feb. 3, 1865. [n. p. n. d.] 8vo, pp. 12. BA. 15312

Transmitting a communication from the Secretary of the Navy, relative to coals of the steamer "Advance."

Message of the President. Richmond. Va., Feb. 3, 1865. [n. p. n. d.] 8vo, pp. 8. BA. 15313

Transmitting a communication from the Secretary of War, relative to the number of persons exempted from military service by reason of being claimed as state officers.

Message of the President. Richmond, Va., Feb. 15, 1865. [n. p, n. d.] 8vo, pp. 9. BA. 15314

Transmitting communications from the Secretary of the Navy and the Postmaster-General, relative to the number of white men between the ages of eighteen and forty-five, and of negroes, whose services are necessary to their respective departments.

Message of the President. Richmond, Va., Feb. 20, 1865. [n. p. n. d.] 8vo, pp. 2. BA. 15315

Transmitting a communication relative to the non-destruction of the cotton in the city of Savannah.

Message of the President. Richmond, Va., Feb. 20, 1865. [n. p. n. d.] 8vo, pp. 2. BA. 15316

Transmitting a communication from the Secretary of War, covering an estimate for an additional appropriation required by the department.

Message of the President. Richmond, Va., March 13, 1865. [n. p. n. d.] 8vo, pp. 3. BA. 15317

Transmitting copies of the correspondence in regard to the proposed conference to adjust terms of peace by means of a military convention.

Message of the President. [n. p. n. d.] 8vo, pp. 3.

Relates to General Johnston's victory at Pittsburgh, Tenn.

Military Laws of the Confederate States, embracing all the Legislation of Congress appertaining to Military Affairs from the First to the Last Session inclusive, with a Copious Index. *Richmond: J. W. Randolph.* 1863. 12mo, pp. 92, xvi. BA.

... Minority Report of the Committee of Ways and Means On the Tax Bill. [n. p. n. d.] 8vo, pp. 4. 15320

Minutes of a Conference of General Officers in Connexion with the Condition of Batteries Wagner and Gregg. *Charleston. Sept.* 24, 1863. 8vo, pp. (1), 82–91, (2). 15321

Objections to Exemption of Old Fire Companies, Considered and Answered. 8vo, pp. 4. 15322

Official Correspondence between the Agents of Exchange, together with Mr. Ould's Report. *Richmond: Sentinel Job Office.* 1864. 8vo, pp. (3), 64–149. B., BA. 15323

Official Report of the Battle of Chickamauga. Published by Order of Congress. *Richmond: R. M. Smith, Printer.* 1864. 8vo, pp. 234. B. 15324

Official Reports of Battles. Published by Order of Congress. *Richmond: Enquirer Press.* 1862. 8vo, pp. 571.

Commences with the "Battle of Seven Pines," and concludes with the "Battle of Chickamauga."

Official Reports of Battles, embracing the Defence of Vicksburg, by Major General Earl Van Dorn, and the Attack upon Baton Rouge, by Major General Breckinridge ... . *Richmond, Va.: Smith, Bailey & Co., Printers.* 1863. 8vo, pp. 170. B.

Official Reports of Battles. ... *Richmond: R. M. Smith, Printer.* 1864. 8vo, pp. 96, (2). 15327

Relates to the skirmish at Olive Branch Creek, operations in North-Western Virginia, and Battle of Fleetwood; with map.

Official Reports of Battles ... *Richmond: R. M. Smith, Printer.* 1864. 8vo, pp. 98. 15328

Relates to Fort McAllister, Fayette Court House, Seven Pines, and Stone River.

Official Reports of Battles. Published by Order of Congress. *Richmond: R. M. Smith, Printer.* 1864. 8vo, pp. 562. B.

Commences with "Evacuation of Pensacola Navy Yard, Forts," etc.

Official Reports of Battles; containing Colonel Wm. J. Jackson's Report of Expedition to Beverly; Major General Price's Report of Evacuation of Little Rock; Major General Stevenson's Report of Battle of Look Out Mountain; and Lieutenant Colonel M. A. Haynes' Report of Engagements at Knoxville, Limestone Creek and Carter's Station ... *Richmond: R. M. Smith, Public Printer.* 1864. 8vo, pp. 72. BA. 15330

Ordnance Instructions for the Navy. Third Edition. *London: Saunders, Otley & Co.* 1864. 8vo, pp. xix, 171, cix. 21 Plates. 15331

The Ordnance Manual for the Use of the United States [*sic*] Army. Second Edition. *Richmond, Va.: West & Johnston.* 1861. 8vo, pp. xx, Errata, 1 l., pp. 475. Numerous Diagrams.

The Ordnance Manual for the Use of the Officers of the Confederate States Army. Prepared under the direction of Col. J. Gorgas, Chief of Ordnance, and approved by the Secretary of War. First Edition. *Charleston: Evans and Cogswell.* 1863. 8vo, pp. 546. Numerous Diagrams. 15333

The Press Association, of the Confederate States of America, ... Printed by Order of the Board of Directors. *Griffin, Georgia: Hill & Swayze's Printing House.* 1863. 8vo, pp. 56. BA.

Proceedings of a Convention of the Commissioners of Appraisement, held in Montgomery, Alabama, Sept., 1864, with Names and Addresses of Officers and Members. *Montgomery.* 1864. 8vo, pp. 16. BA. 15335

Proceedings of the Congress of the Confederate States of America: House of Representatives, 1864, Sec. Congress, Sec. Session. [n. p. n. d.] 4to, pp. 6. H. 15336

Proceedings of the Court of Inquiry, relative to the Fall of New Orleans. Published by Order of Congress. *Richmond: R. M. Smith, Printer.* 1864. 8vo, pp. 206. B. 15337

Private Laws of the Confederate States of America, passed at the First, Second, Third and Fourth Sessions, of the First Congress, and First Session of the Second Congress. *Richmond: R. M. Smith.* 1862–64. Rl. 8vo, pp. 18. 15338

Private Laws of the Confederate States of America, passed at the Second Session of the First Congress; 1862. ... Edited by James M. Matthews ... *Richmond.* 1862. 8vo, pp. (3). + Same, for 1863 and 1864. H. 15339

Provisional and Permanent Constitutions, together with the Acts and Resolutions of the First Session of the Provisional Congress of the Confederate States. 1861. *Montgomery, Ala.: Shorter & Reid, Printers.* 1861. 8vo, pp. 160. BA. 15340

Provisional and Permanent Constitutions of the Confederate States. *Richmond: Tyler, Wise, Allegre ana Smith, Printers.* 1861. 8vo. BA. + [The same], with Acts of 1st Session of the Provisional Congress. *Montgomery.* 1861. 8vo. + *Richmond.* 8vo, pp. 159. 15341

Public Laws of the Confederate States of America, passed at the First Session of the First Congress, 1862; carefully collated with the Originals at Richmond. Edited by James M. Matthews. *Richmond: R. M. Smith.* 1862. Rl. 8vo, pp. v, 1–56, ix. H.

See, below, "Statutes at Large."

Public Laws of the Confederate States of America passed at the Second Session of the First Congress; 1862. ... Edited by James M. Matthews ... *Richmond: R. S. Smith, Printer.* 1862. Rl. 8vo, pp. v, (1), 57–92, ix. 15343

See also "Statutes at Large."

Public Laws passed at the First Session of the Second Congress. *Richmond: R. M. Smith.* 1864. Rl. 8vo, pp. viii, 253–288, xii. 15344

Public Laws of the Confederate States of America, passed at the Third Session of the First Congress; 1863. ... Edited by James M. Matthews ... *Richmond.* 1863. 8vo, Title, pp. v–viii, 93–170, xv. Private Laws. Title, pp. 10–11. H. 15345

Public Laws of the Confederate States of America, passed at the Fourth Session of the First Congress; 1863–4. ... Edited by James M. Matthews ... *Richmond: R. M. Smith, Printer.* 1864. 8vo, pp. 172–252, xxiii. Private Laws of the Confederate States of America ... 1863–4. ... *Richmond.* 1864. pp. 13–15. H. 15346

Register of the Commissioned and Warrant Officers of the Navy of the Confederate States, to January 1, 1863. *Richmond: Macfarlane & Fergusson.* 8vo, 2 l., pp. 38. + [Same], to January 1, 1864. *Richmond: Macfarlane & Fergusson, Printers.* 1864. 8vo, pp. 96. 15347

Regulations for the Army of the Confederate States, 1862. *J. W. Randolph: Richmond, Va.* 1862. 12mo, pp. xxiv, 420. + Second Edition. *Richmond.* 1863. 8vo. C. 15348

Regulations for the Army of the Confederate States, with a Full Index. By Authority of the War Department. ... *Richmond: West & Johnston.* 1864. 8vo, pp. xxx, 432. B., BA., H.

Regulations for the Army of the Confederate States, 1864. Revised and enlarged with a New and Copious Index. Third and only Reliable Edition, in which are corrected over 3,000 Important Errors contained in the Editions published by West & Johnston. ... *Richmond, Va.: J. W. Randolph.* 8vo, pp. xxii, (1), 423, (1). BA. 15350

Regulations for the Commissary's Department of the State of Virginia. *Richmond, Va.: Chas. H. Wynne, Printer.* 1861. 8vo, pp. 38. B. 15351

Regulations for the Government of the Ordnance Department of the Confederate States of America. *Richmond: West & Johnston.* 1862. 12mo, pp. xvi, 122. Table. 15352

Regulations for the Medical Department of the Confederate States Army. *Richmond, Va.: Ritchie & Dunnavant, Printers.* 1861. 8vo, pp. 61. BA. 15353

Regulations for the Medical Department of the C. S. Army. *Richmond.* 1862. 12mo, pp. 58. + *Richmond: Ritchie & Dunnavant, Printers.* 1863. 12mo, pp, 76. H. 15354

Regulations for the Navy, 1862. *Richmond: Macfarlane & Fergusson.* 1862. 16mo, pp. iv, 239. 15355

Regulations for the Subsistence Department. *Richmond: Ritchie & Dunnavant.* 1862. 16mo, pp. 54. 15356

Regulations of the Confederate States School-Ship Patrick Henry. [n. p. n. d.] 8vo, pp. 30. H. 15357

Regulations of the Ordnance Department of the Confederate States, for the use of Troops in the Field. *Richmond: West & Johnston.* 1861. 12mo, pp. 12, folded Table, 1 l. 15358

Report of Brigadier General Echols of the Battle of Droop Mountain ... *Richmond: R. M. Smith.* 1864. 8vo, pp. 16.

Report of Brigadier General R. S. Ripley, of Operations from August 21, to September 10, 1863, with Sub-Reports ... *Richmond: R. M. Smith.* 1864. 8vo, pp. 42. 15360

Report of Brigadier-General Tilghman, on the Bombardment of Fort Henry, February 12th, 1862. [n. p. n. d.] 8vo, pp. 179–193, (1). 15361

Report of Brig. Gen. John S. Williams, of Operations in East Tennessee, from 27th September to 15th October, 1863. .. *Richmond: R. M. Smith, Printer.* 1864. 8vo, pp. 9.

Report of General G. T. Beauregard of the Defence of Charleston ... *Richmond: R. M. Smith, Printer.* 1864. 8vo, pp. 80. 15363

Report of General Robert E. Lee, and Subordinate Reports of the Battle of Chancellorsville; also, Reports of Major General J. E. B. Stuart and Brigadier General Fitz Lee, of Cavalry Engagements at Kelleysville. Also, Report of Brigadier General W. H. F. Lee and Subordinates, of Cavalry Operations of the 14th and 16th of April, 1863. ... *Richmond: R. M. Smith, Printer.* 1864. 8vo, pp. 144, (6). 15364

Report of General Robert E. Lee, of operations at Rappahannock Bridge; also Report of Lieut. Gen. E. R. Smith, of Operations in Lower Louisiana, also Report of Major General Jones, of Engagement at Rogersville, Tennessee ... *Richmond: R. M. Smith, Printer.* 1864. 8vo, pp. 61. 15365

Report of General Joseph E. Johnston, of his Operations in the Department of Mississippi and East Louisiana, together with Lieut. General Pemberton's Report of the Battles of Fort Gibson, Baker's Creek, and the Siege of Vicksburg. ... *Richmond: R. W. Smith, Printer.* 1864. 8vo, pp. 213. 15366

Report of Lieut. General Holmes, of the Battle of Helena; also, Report of Lieutenant General A. P. Hill, of the Battle of Bristoe Station; also, Report of Major General Stevenson, of Expedition into East Tennessee ... *Richmond: R. W. Smith, Printer.* 1864. 8vo, pp. 63, (1). 15367

Report of Major General Hindman, of the Operations in the Trans-Mississippi District ... *Richmond: R. M. Smith, Printer.* 1864. 8vo, pp. 26. 15368

Report of Major General Lorring, of Battle of Baker's Creek, and Subsequent Movements of his Command. ... *Richmond: R. M. Smith.* 1864. 8vo, pp. 29. 15369

Report of Evidence taken before a Joint Special Committee of both Houses of the Confederate Congress, to investigate the Affairs of the Navy Department. P. Kean, Reporter. *Richmond, Va.: Geo. P. Evans & Co., Printers.* [1863.] 8vo, pp. 472. B., BA. 15370

Report of the Attorney-General. *Richmond. Nov.* 18, 1863. 8vo, pp. 15. 15371

Report of the Attorney-General, January 1, 1863. [*Richmond.*] 8vo, pp. 13. + November 18, 1863. 8vo, pp. 15.

Report of the Attorney-General, April 25, 1864. 8vo, pp. 2. + 1st November. 1864. [*Richmond.*] 1864. 8vo, pp. 6.

Report of the Commissioner of Patents. Richmond, January, 1863. [n. p. n. d.] 8vo, pp. 12. + Jan., 1864. 8vo, pp. 15. B. 15374

For the first, *see* Resolution, *infra*.

Report of the Committee on Claims. February 9, 1864. 8vo, pp. 6, (1). 15375

Report of Committee on Claims. In the case of Mary Clark. December 29, 1863. 8vo, pp. 24. 15376

Report of Committee on Deceased Soldiers' Claims. Feb. 10, 1864. 8vo, pp. 8. 15377

Report of the Committee on Federal Relations in regard to the Calling of a Sovereign Convention. *Frederick, Md.: E. S. Riley, Printer.* 1861. 8vo, pp. 22. B. 15378

... Report of the Committee on Finance on the Bill (H. R. 18) to lay Taxes for the Common Defense, and carry on the Government of the Confederate States. [n. p. n. d.] 8vo, pp. 14. BA. 15379

Report of the Committee on Finance ... . January 25th, 1864. 8vo, pp. 12. 15380

... Report of the Minority of the Committee on Finance on the Bill (H. R. 379) to levy additional Taxes for the Year 1865, for the support of the Government. [n. p. n. d.] 8vo, pp. 18.

Report of the Committee on Foreign Relations. November 30, 1864. [*Richmond.* 1864.] 8vo, pp. 9. 15382

Relates to the capture of the Confederate steamer "Florida."

Report of the Committee on the Judiciary, On Senate Bill, No. 150. January 14, 1864. 8vo, pp. 11. 15383

Signed J. Semmes, on behalf of the Committee.

Report of the Committee on Quartermaster and Commissary Departments, February 13, 1864. 8vo, pp. 3. 15384

Report of the Committee on Salt Supply. 8vo, pp. 11.

Report of the Conference Committee on the Exemption Bill. 8vo, 1 l. 15385

Report of the Engagement at Staunton River, June 25th, 1864. [n. p. n. d.] 8vo, pp. 4. 15386

Report of the Postmaster-General to the President, April 29, 1861. [n. p. n. d.] 8vo, pp. 43. + February 28th, 1862. 8vo, pp. 19. BA. 15387

Report of the Postmaster-General, ... December 7, 1863. *Richmond.* 1864. 8vo, pp. 34. + November 7, 1864. 8vo, pp. 21. B. 15388

Report of the Roanoke Island Investigation Committee. *Richmond: Tyler, Wise, Allegre & Smith, [Printers].* 1862. 8vo, pp. 14. B. 15389

Report of the Special Committee, on the Recent Military Disasters at Forts Henry and Donelson, and the Evacuation of Nashville. Hon. H. S. Foote, Chairman, H. C. McLaughlin, Clerk. *Richmond: Tyler, Wise, Allegre and Smith, [Printers].* 1862. 8vo, pp. 178. BA. 15390

Report of Special Committee on Fort Donelson, etc. February 21, 1863. 8vo, pp. (2). 15391

Report of the Second Auditor of the Treasury of the Confederate States to the Honorable Secretary of the Treasury, ... made January 8th, 1862. *Richmond.* 1862. 8vo, pp. 16. H.

Signed W. H. S. Taylor.

Report of the Secretary of the Treasury. *Richmond, January* 10, 1863. 8vo, pp. 78. 15393

Report of the Secretary of the Treasury. ... Richmond, December 7th, 1863. [n. p. n. d.] 8vo, pp. 19. BA. + Same. May 2, 1864. 8vo, pp. 80. B. 15394

Report of the Secretary of the Treasury. *Richmond. Nov.* 7, 1864. 8vo, pp. 17. B. 15395

Report of the Secretary of War, Richmond, 14th Dec., 1861. 8vo, pp. 11. 15396

Signed J. P. Benjamin, Secretary of War.

Report of the Secretary of War. Richmond, January 3, 1863. 8vo, pp. 34. 15397

Signed James A. Seddon, Secretary of War. Includes "Report of the Commissioner of Indian Affairs."

Report of the Secretary of War. Richmond, Nov. 26, 1863. 8vo, pp. 149. 15398

Report of the Secretary of War. *Richmond. April* 28, 1864. 8vo, pp. 29. + Another edition. *Richmond.* 8vo, pp. 37. H.

Signed James A. Seddon.

Report of the Secretary of War. Richmond, Nov. 3, 1864. 8vo, pp. 36. 15400

... Report Of the Select Committee ... [on] that portion of the Message of the President of the Confederate States ... relating to the Action of Congress during the present Session. [n. p. n. d.] 8vo, pp. 8. BA. 15401

Report of the Special Committee to inquire into certain Outrages of the Enemy. 8vo, pp. 3. 15402

Signed W. H. N. Smith, Chairman.

Reports of the Operations of the Army of Northern Virginia, from June, 1862, to and including the Battle at Fredericksburg, December 13, 1862. *Richmond: R. M. Smith.* 1864. 2 vols., 8vo, pp. 626, (1); 602. B., BA. 15403

This is General Robert E. Lee's report.

Resolutions of Congress. January, 1862. 8vo, pp. 17.

Rules and Direction for the Confederate States Patent Office. *Richmond.* 1861. 12mo. 15405

Rules and Regulations for Proceedings in the Confederate States Patent Office. *Richmond: Enquirer Book and Job Press, by Tyler, Wise, Allegre & Smith.* 16mo, pp. 47, ix. BA. 15406

Rules for Conducting Business in the Senate of the Confederate States of America. *Richmond: R. M. Smith, Public Printer.* 1864. 12mo, pp. 18. BA. 15407

Rules for the House of Representatives of the Confederate States. *Richmond: Tyler, Wise, Allegre and Smith.* 1862. 12mo, pp. 18. 15408

Rules of Practice under the Sequestration Act for the District Courts of Confederate States, for the District of Alabama. Adopted, November, 1861. *Mobile: by S. H. Goetzel.* 1861. 8vo, pp. 10. 15409

The Sequestration Act of the Confederate States, ... The Rules of the District Court of the Confederate States for the District of South Carolina, and an Appendix of Forms. *Charleston: printed by J. A. Burke.* 1861. 8vo, pp. 32. 15410

Southern History of the War. Official Reports of Battles, as published by Order of the Confederate Congress at Richmond. *New York: Charles B. Richardson.* 1864. 8vo, pp. 578. B. 15411

Skirmish Drill for Mounted Troops. *Richmond: printed by Ritchie & Dunnavant.* 1861. 12mo, pp. 28. 15412

Special Exemptions from Confederate State Taxes, in Kind. 1864. Broadside. 15413

Special Report. Confederate States of America. Richmond, Va., July 31, 1861. 8vo, pp. 31. 15414

Statement showing the funded debt of the Confederate States on the 1st of January, A.D. 1864. January 25, 1864. 8vo, pp. 4. 15415

Statutes at Large of the Confederate States of America. First Session of the First Congress, 1862. Edited by J. M. Matthews ... *Richmond.* 1862. 8vo, pp. v, 56, ix. 15416

This is the title on cover, but the second title is this: "Public Laws of the Confederate States of America, passed at the First Session of the First Congress; 1862. ... Edited by James M. Matthews. ... *Richmond.* 1862." 8vo, pp. v, 56, ix. Third title: "Private Laws, &c. *Richmond.* 1862." 8vo, pp. 6, (1). H.

The Statutes at Large of the Provisional Government of the Confederate States of America, from the Institution of the Government, February 8, 1861 to its Termination, February 18, 1862 ... Together with the Constitution for the Provisional Government and the Permanent Constitution of the Confederate States, and the Treaties concluded by the Confederate States with Indian Tribes. Edited by J. M. Matthews ... *Richmond: R. M. Smith, Printer.* 1864. 8vo, pp. xv, (1), 411, xlviii. BA. 15417

Supplement Instructions for the Collectors of the War Tax. Confederate States of America, Treasury Department, Richmond, Dec. 26, 1861. [n. p. n. d.] 8vo, pp. 6. BA. 15418

Supplemental Report of the Secretary of War, March 17, 1862. [*Richmond.* 1862.] 8vo, pp. 27. 15419

Signed J. P. Benjamin, Secretary of War.

Tariff of the Confederate States of America approved by Congress, May 21, 1861. To be of force From and After August 31, 1861. *Charleston: steam-power presses of Evans & Cogswell.* 1861. 8vo, pp. 16. 15420

[From "The Sentinel."] To the Congress of the Confederate States. [n. p. n. d.] 8vo, pp. 15. 15421

To the Honorable President of the Congress. Richmond, February 15, 1862. 8vo, pp. 18. 15422

Signed Jefferson Davis.

Treaty with the Cherokees. October 7th, 1861. [n. p. n. d.] 8vo, pp. 26. H. 15423

Uniform and Dress of the Army of the Confederate States. *Richmond.* 1861. Folio. 15424

Uniform and Dress of the Navy of the Confederate States. *Richmond.* 1861. Folio. 15425

Confederation considered on its Merits; being an Examination into the Principle, Capabilities, and Terms of Union, as applicable to Nova Scotia. By a Scotian. *Halifax: R. T. Muir.* 1867. 8vo, pp. 35. BA. 15426

La Confédération argentine à l'Exposition universelle de 1867, a Paris. Notice statistique générale et catalogue. *Paris: Burdet.* 1867. 8vo, pp. 48. 15427

Conférence au profit des victimes du tremblement de terre de l'Amérique méridionale. Par MM. Edouard Laboulaye, Jules Simon, Arthur Mangin et Th. Mannequin. *Paris: imp. Parent.* 1869. 8vo, pp. 48. 15428

A Conference between His Exc. Jonathan Belcher, Esq.; Captain General and Governour in Chief of the Province of His Majesty's Province of Massachuset's Bay, in New-England; and the Chief Sachems of several Indian Tribes, with other Chief Men of said Tribes, at Falmouth, in Casco Bay; in New-England, July 1732. *London: N. Cholmondely.* [1732.] 8vo, pp. 28. 15429

For another edition, *see* Vol. II., No. 4391.

Conference between Secretary Stanton, General Sherman and Freedmen in Savannah. February 12, 1865. *New York.* 1865. 8vo. 15430

A Conference between the Commissaries of Massachusetts-Bay and the Commissaries of New-York; At New Haven in the Colony of Connecticut, 1767. *Boston, New-England: Printed by Richard Draper* ... MDCCLXVII. 4to, pp. 26, (1), 9.

Proceedings of the Conference Convention, Washington, Feb. ruary 4th, 1861. [n. p. n. d.] 8vo, pp. 39. H. 15432

Official Journal of the Conference Convention, held at Washington City, February, 1861. By Crafts J. Wright ... *Washington.* 1861. 8vo, pp. 93. H. 15433

Conference Convention of the Commissioners from the several States, held, at the request of Virginia, at Washington, February, 1861. Report made to the General Assembly of Rhode Island, by the Commissioners on the part of the State. *Providence: Cooke and Danielson.* 1861. 8vo, pp. 9. 15434

A Conference held at the Fort at St. George's in the County of York, on the 4th of August Anno Regni Regis Georgij Secundi ... 1742, between His Excellency William Shirley, Esq; Governor in Chief over the Province of the Massachusetts Bay in New England; and the Chief Sachems & Captains of the Penobscott, Norridgewock, Pigwaket or Amiscogging or Saco, St. John's, Bescommonconty or Ameresscogging and St. Francis Tribes of Indians. August 1742. *Boston: J. Draper.* 4to, Half-Title, pp. 18. 15435

A Conference Held at St. George's in the County of York, on the Twentieth Day of September, Anno Regni Regis Georgii Secundi, Magnæ Britanniæ Franciæ et Hiberniæ, Vicesimo Spetimæ, Annoque Domine, 1753. Between Sir William Pepperell, Baronet, Jacob Wendell, Thomas Hubbard, and John Winslow, Esqrs., and Mr. James Bowdoin. Commissioners appointed by His Excellency William Shirley, Esqr. Captain General and Governour in Chief, in and over His Majesty's Province of the Massachusetts-Bay in New-England, to Treat with the Eastern Indians of the our Part, and the Indians of the Penobscott Tribe of the other Part. *Boston in New-England: Printed by Samuel Kneeland, Printer to the Honourable House of Representatives.* 1753. 4to. pp. 26. W. 15436

Conference of the Governor of Massachusetts Bay with the Sachems of the Eastern Indians, Arrowsick Island, August 9–12th, 1717. *Boston: B. Green.* 1717. Sm. 4to, pp. 13. W.

A Conference on Society and Manners in Massachusetts. A Poem. *Boston.* 1820. 12mo. 15438

Conference on the Occurrences in America. *London.* 1766. 8vo. 15439

Title from a bookseller's catalogue.

Conference held at Deerfield, in the County of Hampshire, in August 1735, by and between his excellency Jonathan Belcher, Captain General and Governor in Chief in and over His Majesty's Province of the Massachusetts Bay in New England, and Duntautoogee, Cuncapot, Marsequunt, Naunaussooghijau, and Weenpauk, Chiefs of the Cagnawaga, Houssatonuoc, Scautacook, and other Indian Tribes. *Boston.* 1735. Sm. 4to. C.

The Converence With the Eastern Indians, at the Ratification of the Peace, held at Falmouth, in Casco-Bay, in July and August, 1726. [*Boston: Benj. Eliot.* 1726?] 4to, pp. 23. C., M. + *Boston.* 1754. 4to. 15441

Conference With the Eastern Indians, at the further Ratification of the Peace, Held at Falmouth, in Casco-Bay, in July 1727. [n. p. 1727?] 4to, pp. 31. M. + *Boston: S. Kneeland.* 1754. 4to, pp. 27 or 31. C., M. 15442

Confession et pénitence de l'Assemblée générale. [n. p.] 17 *juin* 1790. 8vo, pp. 48 or less. 15443

Relates to the affairs of St. Domingo.

Confession générale faite au public par l'auteur du "Mot à l'oreille." [n. p. n. d.] 8vo, pp. 48 or less. 15444

Relates to the affairs of Saint Domingo in 1788 or 1789.

The | Confession of Faith, | Agreed upon by the Assembly of Divines | at Westminister [*sic*], with the Assistance of | Comissioners | from the | Church of Scotland, | as | A Part of the Covenanted Uniformity in Religion be- | twixt the Churches of Christ in the Kingdoms of | Scotland, England, and Ireland, | Approved by the General Assembly 1647. and Ratified | and Established by Act of Parliament 1649, As the | Publick and Avowed Confession of the | Church of Scotland. | With the Scripture Proofs at Large. | *Philadelphia: | Printed and Sold by B. Franklin.* M.DCC.-XLV. | 8vo, Title, pp. 23–164. 15445

Chapter I. commences on page 23. "The Larger Catechism" has a separate title, and the pagination continues to 366. "The Shorter Catechism" (with a separate title) commences on page 369 (or 7), and terminates at 410. The "Directory," with separate title, commences at page 484, and concludes at 521. The "Form of Church Government" (separate title) commences at page 525, and the final termination is at page 551.

A Confession of Faith in the most Necessary Things of Christian Doctrine, Faith and Practice. According to the Testimony of Holy Scriptures. Given forth from the Yearly Meeting at Burlington, the 7th of 7th month, 1692, by the despised Christian People called Quakers. *Printed and Sold by William Bradford in Philadelphia.* 1693. 12mo, pp. 21. 15446

A | Confession | of | Faith | Owned and Consented to by the | Elders and Messengers | Of the Churches | In the Colony of Connecticut in | New-England, | Assembled by Delegation at Say-Brook | September 9th, 1708. | *New-London in N. E. | Printed by Thomas Short,* | 1710. | Sm. 8vo, Title, 1 l., pp. 116. 15447

"The first book printed in Connecticut."—THOMAS. In "Memoirs of Pious Females," published at New Haven in 1833, on page 301, it is said that James Pierpont was the author of the foregoing work. Priced, by J. R. Smith, in 1863, at £7 17s. 6d.

[Same title as above.] *New London: Printed by Timothy Green.* MDCCLX. Sm. 8vo, Title, pp. 118. 15448

A | Confession | of | Faith | Owned and consented unto by the | Elders and Messengers | of the Churches | Assembled at Boston in New-England, | May 12, 1680. | Being the second Session of that | Synod. | *Boston; | Printed by John Foster.* 1680. | 16mo, 2 l., pp. (4), 64, (3). H., S., W. + *Boston: Printed for B. Eliot.* 1725. 12mo, pp. 49. + *Boston: Re-printed for D. Gookin.* 1750. 18mo. + *Boston.* 1846. 12mo. 15449

Another edition is found at the end of J. Wise's works, pp. 225–271. For an Indian version, *see* Rawson (G.)

Confession of Faith, or a Summary of Divinity drawn up by a Young Gentleman in the 23d year of his age. *Boston.* 1704. 12mo. W. 15450

The Confession of Faith, and Covenant, of the South Church in Andover. With a Catalogue. *Andover.* 1848. 12mo, pp. 36. 15451

For other Confessions of Faith, *see* under names of *places*. This title should have appeared under Andover.

Confessionario | para los Cvras | de Indios. | Con la Instrvcion contra svs | Ritos: y Exhortacion para ayudar a bien morir: y sum- | ma de sus Priuilegios: y forma de Impedi- | mentos del Matrimonio. | Compvesto y tradvzido en las | Lenguas Quichua, y Aymara. Por autoridad del Concilio | Prouincial de Lima, del año de 1583. | [Motto and Vignette.] *Impresso con Licencia a dela | Real Audiencia, en la Ciudad de los Reyes, por Antonio | Ricardo*

primero Impressor enestos Rey. | *nos del Piru.* | *Año de* M.D.LXXXV. | *Esta tassado vn Real por cada pliego, en papel.* | 4to, 4 l., 27 l.

Confession of Faith and Covenant of the Old South Church, Boston, with List of Members from its Foundation in 1669. *Boston.* 1855. 12mo, pp. 119. 15453

Confession of Faith of the Evangelical Churches of Bolton, Lancaster, Sterling, and Stow. *Lancaster, Mass.* 1830. 8vo, pp. 16. 15454

The confessions often contain lists of church members.

Confessions, Trials, and Biographical Sketches of the most cold blooded Murderers, who have been executed in this Country from its first settlement down to the present time—compiled entirely from the most authentic sources; Containing also accounts of various other daring outrages ... *Boston: George N. Thompson.* 1840. 12mo, pp. 408. + *Hartford: S. Andrus and Son.* 1844. 12mo, pp. 420. 15455

The Confidential Documents of the United States. *See* United States.

Confidential Message from the President of the United States, including sundry documents from the Departments of State and War, relative to the intercourse of the United States with foreign nations. July 3. 1797. Referred to Mr. Sitgreaves, Mr. Baldwin, Mr. Dana, Mr. Dawson, and Mr. Hindman. Published by order of the House of Representatives. *Philadelphia: printed by W. Ross near Congress-Hall.* 8vo, pp. 8, xxii, 24. 15456

Chiefly relating to the threatened aggressions on the southern territories.

Conflagration. A Poem. *New York: Printed by Hugh Gaine.* M,DCC,LXXX. 8vo, pp. 8. BA. 15457

Written soon after the terrible destruction of a great part of this city by the fire of September 21st, 1776.

Conflict between Despotism and Liberty, or the Right of Trial by Jury abolished in Civil Suits, and sustained by the Courts of the State of New York. *Rochester.* 1860. 15458

Conflit Hispano Chilien. Protestation contre tout la presse française, entre les mains de S. Exc. M. le ministre des affaires étrangères de France à Paris. *Paris: Dentu; Thevelin. Bordeaux: Ferré.* 1865. 8vo, pp. 16. 15459

Le conflit américain. Le Nord et le Sud. *Grenoble: impr. Baratier.* 1862. 8vo, pp. 15. H. 15460

CONGAR. The Autobiography and Memorials of Captain Obadiah Congar, for fifty years Mariner and Shipmaster from the Port of New York. [Edited] By H. T. Cheever. *New York.* 1851. 12mo. 15461

CONGDON (C. T.) Flowers Plucked by a Traveller on the Journey of Life. By Charles T. Congdon. *Boston.* 1840. 12mo, pp. 72. 15462

CONGDON. Tribune Essays. Leading Articles contributed to the New York Tribune from 1857 to 1863. By C. T. Congdon. With an Introduction, by Horace Greeley. *New York: J. S. Redfield.* 1869. 12mo, pp. xxiv, 406. BA., C.

CONGDON. The Warning of War: a Poem ... Dartmouth College, Hanover, N. H., at the Annual Commencement, July 30, 1862. By Charles T. Congdon. *New York: Francis Hart & Co.* 1862. 8vo, pp. 29. 15464

CONGDON (J. B.) An Address, delivered at the Consecration of the Oak Grove Cemetery, in New Bedford, October 6th, 1843. By James B. Congdon. ... With the Regulations of the Selectmen, for ... the Cemetery: and an Appendix. *New Bedford: Printed by Benjamin Lindsey.* 1844. 8vo, pp. 35. H.

[CONGDON.] A Defence of the Currency of Massachusetts, ... By a Practical Banker. *Boston.* 1855. 8vo, pp. 26. + Second Edition. With an Introduction. *Boston.* 1856. 8vo, pp. 28. H. 15466

[CONGDON.] A Letter to His Excellency John Henry Clifford, on the Proposition now before the Legislature, to require the Banks of the Commonwealth to hold in disposit a certain Amount of Specie. By a Practical Banker. *Boston.* 1853. 8vo, pp. 15. H. 15467

[CONGDON.] Letter to the Representatives in the General Court, from the town of New Bedford, in relation to the draft of an Act for a City Charter, now before the Legislature. By a Citizen. *New Bedford: Press of Benj. Lindsey.* 1847. 8vo, pp. 9. 15468

[CONGDON.] New Bedford Money Matters. Speech of

Money Terry, Esq., on the Financial Affairs of New Bedford, delivered at a meeting of the Common Council, September 10th, 1858. *Boston.* 1859. 8vo, pp. 26. 15469

[CONGDON.] Quaker Quiddities; or, Friends in Council. A Colloquy. *Boston.* 1860. 16mo, pp. 48. 15470

CONGDON. Some Remarks on the Banking Policy of Massachusetts, in a letter to his Excellency, George S. Boutwell, Governor of the Commonwealth. By James B. Congdon. *Boston.* 1851. 8vo, pp. 15. 15471

Also: Address at the Laying of the Corner-stone of the Library Edifice, New Bedford, Aug. 28, 1856.—Extract from an Address, by James B. Congdon, a Part of which was delivered by him at the Semi-Centennial Anniversary at the Friends' School, at Providence, August 28th, 1868. [n. p. n. d.] 8vo, pp. 8. H.—[Congdon.] Information relative to the American Lyceum. *New Bedford: Printed by Benj. T. Congdon.* [1828.] 12mo, pp. 12.—[Congdon.] New Bedford, Massachusetts. *New York: printed by Jared W. Bell.* 8vo, pp. 16. H.—The Republican Rally: A Song. Respectfully Inscribed to the New Bedford Wide Awakes. ... *New Bedford: Printed by E. Anthony.* 1860. 12mo, p. 1.—The Teacher's Reunion. Hawthorne Street, February 4th, 1861. [*New Bedford: Printed by E. Anthony.*] 1861. 12mo, pp. 12.

CONGER (A. B.) Memorial of Herman Ten Eyck Foster. Prepared by Hon. A. B. Conger ... *Albany.* 1870. 8vo, pp. 12. H. 15472

CONGER (H. S.) Remarks of Hermon S. Conger, in the House of Representatives, on the Payment of the Galphin Claim. *Washington.* 1850. 8vo, pp. 8. 15473

A Congratulatory Epistle to the Redoubtable "Peter Porcupine," on his "Complete Triumph over the Once towering but fallen and despisable faction in the United States." *See* [Cobbett (W.)], No. 14025.

A Congratulatory Letter, to Mr. G—r. in Philadelphia ... *Printed in the Year* 1766. 12mo, pp. 8. P. 15475

This rare little tract is printed at Philadelphia, with Ambruster's types, and is addressed to the State House Academy in Second Street.

A Congratulatory Letter, 1755. *See* Connecticut.

A Congratulatory Poem, on the late Successes of the British Arms; particularly the triumphant Evacuation of Boston. *London: Baldwin.* 1776. 4to. 15476

"The title-page sufficiently indicates the irony of this Congratulatory Address to the Public."—*M. Rev.*, LX. 237.

Congregational Almanac, 1846. *Boston.* 8vo. 15477

Twenty-fifth Annual Report of the Congregational Board of Publication. With the Constitution, and a List of Life Members and Publication. Presented May 31, 1854. *Boston.* 1854. 12mo, pp. 35, (1). H.

Congregational Churches. *See* Maine, Connecticut, Massachusetts, South Carolina, etc.

The Congregational Quarterly. Volume I. Conducted, under the Sanction of the Congregational Library Association and the American Congregational Union, by Revs. Joseph S. Clarke, D.D., Henry M. Dexter, Alonzo H. Quint, and Isaac P. Longworthy. *Boston. New York.* 1859. 8vo, pp. iv, 426. Woodcuts and 4 Portraits. Still continued. BA. 15479

Congregational Record. *Kansas City, Mo.* 1863. 15480

The Congregational Visiter. ... Edited by the Publishing Committee of the Mass. S. S. Society. Vol. I. 1844. *Boston: Massachusetts Sabbath School Society.* 1844. 8vo, pp. iv, 284. Continued to Vol V., 1848. BA. 15481

The American Congregational Year Book, for the Year 1854. *New York: N. A. Calkins.* 8vo. 15482

First Annual Report of the Directors of the Congregational Library Association. ... May 30, 1854. 8vo, pp. 31. 15483

Official Record of the National Congregational Council, held at Boston, Mass., June 14–24, A.D., 1865. *Boston.* 1865. 8vo, pp. 183. H. 15484

Proceedings of the Triennial Convention of Ministers and Delegates of the Congregational Churches in the Northwest, held ... at Chicago, Oct. 20th, and 21st, 1858: together with the Inaugural Addresses of Profs. Haven and Bartlett. *Chicago.* 1858. 8vo, pp. 98. H. 15485

Congregationalism, as contained in the Scriptures, explained by the Cambridge Platform, and by Approved Authors: Or, the Right and Power of Congregational Churches to choose their Officers, to exercise Discipline, and to remove their Officers from Office, according to the Platform. In a Series of Letters to a Gentleman from his Friend. *Boston.* 1794. 8vo, pp. 86.

Report on Congregationalism, including a Manual of Church Discipline, together with the Cambridge Platform adopted in 1648, and the Confession of Faith adopted in 1680. *Boston:* ... 1846. 12mo, pp. 128. 15486

Congress of Nations. *Boston:* [n. d.] 12mo, pp. 24. H.

Report and Resolves [of the Mass. Senate] in Relation to a Congress of Nations. [*Boston.* 1837.] 8vo, pp. 18. H. 15488

Congress at Panama. Message from the President of the United States, transmitting The Information required by a Resolution of the House of Representatives, of 5th ult. In Relation to the Proposed Congress to be held at Panama, &c., &c. March 17, 1826. *Washington: Printed by Gales & Seaton.* 1826. 8vo, pp. 89. (19th Cong., First Session House of Representatives, Executive Doc. No. 129.) 15489

CONGRESS OF THE UNITED STATES.

Many books and pamphlets which might properly be placed here, will be found under other headings—*i. e.*, the first words of the title, articles excepted. *See also* United States.

Acts of Congress in Respect to Copyrights. [n. p. n. d.] 8vo, pp. 8. H. 15490

The Acts of Congress relating to Loans and the Currency, from 1847 to 1868. With a Synopsis of each Act, etc. *New York: Bankers' Magazine Office.* 1869. 8vo, pp. 77. 15491

Acts Passed at a Congress of the United States of America begun and held at the City of New York on Wednesday the 4th of March in the Year 1789 and of the Independence of the United States, the 13th: Being the Acts Passed at the First Session of the First Congress of the United States, to wit, New Hampshire, Massachusetts, Connecticut, New York, New Jersey, Pennsylvania, Delaware, Maryland, Virginia, South Carolina and Georgia: which eleven States respectively ratified the Constitution of Government for the United States, proposed by the Federal Convention held in Philadelphia on the 17th Sept. 1787. *New York: Hodge, Allen and Campbell.* 1789. 8vo, pp. 185. 15492

"T. Lloyd, whose name is mentioned as one of the publishers, is said, in a manuscript note in the volume, to have been the stenographer, who took down the debates."—RICH, I. 491.

Acts passed at a Congress. ... [Another Edition of No. 15492.] *Philadelphia: Printed by Francis Childs and John Swaine, Printers to the United States.* 1789. Folio, pp. 93, (1). BA. + *Richmond: printed by Augustine Davis, for the General Assembly of Virginia.* [n. d.] Folio. + *New Haven: T. & S. Green.* 1789. Folio. + *Hartford.* 1789. + *Philadelphia.* 1795, and 1796. 15493

Reissued by Childs and Swaine, with the Acts passed at the third session of the Congress of the United States of America, begun and held at the city of Philadelphia, December 6, 1790. Also, treaty with France, dated February 6, 1778; with Netherlands, October 8, 1782. Provisional articles between the United States and Great Britain, dated Paris, November 13, 1782. Treaty with Sweden, dated Paris, April 3, 1783. Original definite treaty of peace between the United States of America and His Britannic Majesty, dated December 3, 1783. A treaty with Prussia, dated July and August, 1785. A treaty with the Emperor of Morocco, dated January, 1787. Convention between His Most Christian Majesty and the United States of America, for the purpose of defining and establishing the functions and privileges of their respective consuls and vice-consuls, dated November 14, 1788. And treaties with various Indian Tribes and Nations. Published by authority. *Philadelphia: Printed by Francis Childs and John Swaine, Printers to the United States.* Folio.

Acts passed at a Congress of the United States, begun and held at ... New-York ... the Fourth of March ... M,DCC,-LXXXIX ... the First Session of the First Congress ... *Hartford: Hudson and Goodwin.* M.DCC.XCI. 8vo, pp. 486, (9). BA.

Notwithstanding the date of publication, this includes acts approved as late as March 2, 1793.

Actes passés à un congrès des États-Unis de l'Amèrique, commencé et tenue dans la ville de New Yorck, le mercredi, quatre mars, en l'année 1789, et la treizième de l'independence des États-Unis. Traduits par Hubert. *Paris.* 1790. 8vo, pp. xi, 280. 15495

Acts passed at the Second Session of the Congress of the United States ... held at ... New-York, ... the Fourth of January ... M,DCC,XC. *Philadelphia: Francis Childs and John Swaine.* 1790. Folio, pp. 284, (30). BA. 15496

Acts passed at the First Session of the Second Congress of the United States of America held in the City of Philadelphia, Oct. 24th, 1791. *Philadelphia.* [1792.] 8vo. 15497

Acts passed at the Second Session of the Second Congress, 5th November, 1792. *Philadelphia.* [n. d.] 8vo. + *Philadelphia.* [1792.] Folio. 15498

Acts passed at the Second Congress of the United States ...

Philadelphia: Francis Childs and John Swaine. [n. d.] 8vo, pp. 289, ii, (24). 15499

Acts Passed at the First [Second and Third] Congress of the United States of America. Published by Authority. *Philadelphia: Francis Childs.* 1795. 3 vols., 8vo, pp. 434, 24 l.; pp. 406, 12 l.; pp. 260, iv, 12 l. 15500

Acts Passed at The First Session of the Fourth Congress of the United States of America: Begun and held at the City of Philadelphia ... on Monday the Seventh of December, one Thousand seven Hundred and Ninety-five, and of the Independence of the United States, the Twentieth. Published By Authority. *Philadelphia: Printed by Francis Childs.* M.DCC.XCVI. 8vo, pp. 137. P. 15501

Acts passed at the First Session of the Fifth Congress of the United States of America at Philadelphia, 15 May, 1797. *Philadelphia.* 1797. 8vo. 15502

Acts passed at the Second Session of the Fifth Congress ... *Philadelphia.* 1798. 8vo. 15503

Acts passed at the Third Session of the Fifth Congress of the United States. *Philadelphia.* 1799. 8vo. + *Providence, R. I.* 1799. 8vo. 15504

Acts passed at the First Session of the Sixth Congress, 1799–1800. [*Philadelphia.* 1800.] 8vo. + Second Session ... Sixth Congress, 1801. [n. p. n. d.] 8vo. + First and Second Sessions ... Sixth Congress, Dec. 2, 1799–March, 1801. *Washington.* 1801. 8vo. + First and Second Sessions ... Seventh Congress, December, 1801–March, 1803. *Washington.* 1803. 8vo. + First and Second Sessions ... Eighth Congress, October, 1803–March, 1805. *Washington.* 1805. 8vo. + First and Second Sessions ... Ninth Congress, December, 1805–March, 1807. *Washington.* 1807. 8vo. + First [and] Second Session ... Tenth Congress, 1807–9. [n. p. n. d.] 8vo. + First ... Third Session ... Eleventh Congress, 1809–11. [n. p. n. d.] 3 vols., 8vo. + First [and] Second Session ... Twelfth Congress, 1811–13. [n. p. n. d.] 2 vols., 8vo. + First ... Second [and] Third Sessions ... Thirtieth Congress, 1813–15. *Washington.* 1815. 3 vols., 8vo. + First Session ... Fourteenth Congress, 1815–16. [n. p. n. d.] 8vo. + Second Session ... Fourteenth Congress, 1817. [n. p. n. d.] 8vo. +

First [and] Second Session ... Fifteenth Congress, 1817–19. [n. p. n. d] 2 vols., 8vo. 15505

It would not be difficult, but it would be almost useless, to continue this list of the acts of the different sessions of each successive Congress; let it suffice to remark that they are continuous, and, with the increased number and importance of the states, have become extremely voluminous. Tolerably complete sets are in the Congressional Library, in the Boston Public Library, and the Libraries of the Boston Athenæum, and of Harvard College, and many of our state libraries contain portions of sets.

Acts of Congress relating to the Direct Tax and the Duty on Furniture and Watches. 1815. 8vo, pp. 56. 15506

The Acts of Congress relating to Loans and Currency, from 1847 to 1868. With a Synopsis of each Act, and Copious details as to the Public Debt of the United States. *New York.* 1868. 8vo, pp. 78. 15507

Address and Recommendations to The States, by The United States in Congress assembled [with sundry papers referred to in the Address]. *Philadelphia: Printed by David C. Claypoole.* M.DCC.LXXXIII. pp. 14, 19, 3, 6, 5, 6, 26. + *Philadelphia, Printed. Hartford: Reprinted by Hudson & Goodwin.* M,DCC,-LXXXVIII. 8vo, pp. 50. + Same, with the Newbugh Letters. *Boston.* 1783. 8vo, pp. 62. + *Trenton: Re-Printed by Isaac Collins.* M.DCC.LXXXIII. 12mo, pp. 36. + *London: J. Stockdale.* 1783. 8vo, pp. 91. 15508

An Address of the Members of the House of Representatives of the Congress of the United States, to their Constituents, on the Subject of the War with Great Britain. *Boston: Press of John Eliot, Jun.* 1812. 8vo, pp. 32. + *New York.* 1812. 8vo, pp. 32. + *Portsmouth: Printed by W. Treadwell.* 1812. 8vo, pp. 34. 15509

For other editions, *see* Vol. I., No. 393.

Address of the Congress to the Inhabitants of the United States of America. ... *Lancaster: printed by John Dunlap.* [*May* 9, 1778.] P. 15510

Address to the Deputies of North America in General Congress. Dated South Carolina, Charlestown, August 10, 1774. 4to, pp. 47.

Signed Freeman. The writer thus closes his address: "The eyes and attention of America, nay, of Europe, are fixed upon the American Congress—O Deputies! I doubt not but that you will act worthy of such an expectation. Calmly deliberate upon, then respectfully and boldly declare the grievances and rights of America. Be wisely cautious what you determine, but let your determination be as fixed as fate."

An Address of the Twelve United Colonies of North Amer-

ica, by their Representatives in Congress, to the People of Ireland. *Philadelphia: printed by W. and T. Bradford.* 1775 12mo, Title, pp. 10. H. 15512

See Vol. I., Nos. 403 and 404.

Address to the Congress of the United States on the Utility and Justice of Restrictions upon Foreign Commerce. *Philadelphia.* 1809. 8vo. 15513

Alleged Corrupt Combination of Members of Congress: Reports submitted by the Select Committee, 1857. [*Washington.* 1857.] 8vo, pp. 279. (H. of R. Doc.) 15514

American State Papers. *See* Vol. I., No. 1228.

An Answer to the Declaration of the American Congress. *See* [Lind (J.)]

Authentic Account of the Proceedings of the Congress. *See* Vol. I., No. 2444.

Cases of Contested Elections in Congress. *See* Clarke (M. St. Clair), No. 13437.

A Circular Letter from the Congress of the United States of America to their Constituents. *Philadelphia: printed by David C. Claypoole. Sept.* 1799. 12mo, pp. 12. H. + *Boston.* 1779. 8vo, pp. 15. 15515

Ministers of the gospel throughout the State of Massachusetts were ordered, by the general assembly, to read this Letter to their respective congregations immediately after Divine service, on the Sabbath after receiving it.

A Clear Idea of the Genuine and Uncorrupted British Constitution: in an Address to the Inhabitants of the Province of Quebec, from the Forty-nine delegates in the Continental Congress at Philadelphia; Sep. 5th to Oct. 10, 1774—Extracted from their Votes & Proceedings. [*London:*] *Messrs. Dilly.* 1774. 8vo, pp. 8. 15516

The Congress Canvassed. *See* [Seabury (Samuel)], and [Wilkins (Isaac)].

Congress of the United States. In Senate, May the 23d, 1794. Ordered, that the message from the President of the United States of this day, with the Communications referred to therein, together with the Communications referred to in the message of the President of the United States of the 21st instant, be printed for the use of the Senate. Attest Samuel A. Otis, Secretary. [n. p. n. d.] 8vo, p. 1. P. 15517

Contested Elections in Congress, from 1834 to 1865, inclusive. Compiled by D. W. Bartlett. *Washington.* 1865. 8vo.

The Debates and Proceedings in the Congress of the United States: with an Appendix, containing Important State Papers and Public Documents, and all the Laws of a Public Nature; with a Copious Index. ... From March 1789 to May 27, 1824, inclusive. Compiled from Authentic Materials, by Joseph Gales, Senior. *Washington: Gales and Seaton.* 1834–1856. 42 vols., 8vo. 15519

Some of the earlier volumes were reprinted, and have, for the half-title, "Annals of the Congress of the United States — First Congress."

Debates in the House of Representatives of the United States, 1st Session of the 4th Congress, upon the Constitutional Powers of the House with respect to Treaties. *Philadelphia.* 1796. 8vo. + *Philadelphia.* 1808. 2 vols. 15520

Debates in the Third Session of the Eleventh Congress; comprising the most interesting Debates in both Houses, in the Session commencing Dec. 1810. [*Washington:*] *Office of the National-Intelligencer.* 1811. 8vo. 15521

The Declaration by the Representatives of the United Colonies in North America, now met in General Congress at Philadelphia, setting forth the Causes and Necessity of their taking up Arms, &c. *Philadelphia; Printed by William and Thomas Bradford.* 1775. 8vo, pp. 13. + *London.* 1775. 8vo.

A Defence of the American Congress in reply to Taxation no Tyranny. By the Author of Regulus. To which are added, General Remarks on the Leading Principles of that Work ... and a Short Chain of Deductions from One Clear Position of Common Sense and Experience. *London: printea for J. Williams.* [n. d.] 8vo, pp. 92. H. 15523

A Digest of the Revenue Laws of the United States. By L. Addington. *Philadelphia.* 1804. 12mo. 15524

Executive Documents, First Session, Seventeenth Congress, 1821–22. *Washington.* 1821–22. 5 vols., 8vo. 15525

These executive documents are published at each session, and sometimes extend to fifteen volumes in one session. With much that is ephemeral, there are to be found many documents of the first importance to the historical student. An extensive series is included in the Library of Congress, and in the Boston Public Library; the latter has published a useful index to their contents. Occasionally a volume is issued in 4to.

Extract, from the Journal of the proceedings, of the honorable the American Continental Congress, held at Philadelphia, September fifth 1774. Being that part of their Address to the Inhabitants of the Province of Quebec, which enumerates, the glorious Rights of Englishmen, and English subjects: Among which are included, the Liberty of the Press. The Committee, to whom the Address to the Inhabitants of Quebec was recommended; reported a draught, which was read, and being debated by Paragraphs and amended, was approved, and is as follows. To the Inhabitants of the Province of Quebec. Friends and Fellow-Subjects, ... [pp. 6; followed by] Additions to Plain Truth; addressed to the Inhabitants of America, ... *Philadelphia: Printed and Sold by R. Bell in Third-Street.* MDCCLXXVI. 8vo, Title, pp. 97–136. 15526

Extracts from the Journals of Congress relative to the Capture and Condemnation of Prizes, and the fitting out Privateers, together with the Rules and Regulations of the Navy, and Instructions to the Commanders of Private Ships of War. *Philadelphia: John Dunlap.* MDCCLXXVI. 12mo, pp. 45. M. 15527

Extracts from the Votes and Proceedings of the American Continental Congress, Held at Philadelphia on the 5th of September 1774. Containing The Bill of Rights, a List of Grievances, Occasional Resolves, the Association, An Address to the People of Great-Britain, and a Memorial to the Inhabitants of the British American Colonies. Published by order of the Congress. *Philadelphia: Printed by William & Thomas Bradford. October 27th,* MDCCLXXIV. 8vo, pp. 36. + *London: Reprinted for J. Almon.* MDCCLXXIV. 8vo, Half-Title, Title, pp. 82. + *Philadelphia, Printed: Boston, Re-printed: And sold by John Boyle in Marlborough-Street, and Mills and Hicks in School-Street, and Cox and Berry in King Street.* 1774.* 8vo, pp. 43. + [Another Edition.] *Boston.* 1744. 12mo, pp. 49. + *London, reprinted.* 1774. 8vo, pp. 59. + *Hartford.* [1774.] 8vo.

"I have another edition, evidently from the same form as the above,* with the words, *and Cox and Berry in King Street*, omitted in the title, the double line at the top of page 3 exchanged for an ornamental head-piece, and the addition of a letter of the Congress 'To the Inhabitants of the Province of Quebec,' extending from pages 44 to 52. 8vo." — STEVENS.

A Few Remarks upon some of the Votes and Resolutions of the Continental Congress, held at Philadelphia in September, and the Provincial Congress, held at Cambridge in November 1774. By a Friend to Peace and good Order. *Printed for the Purchasers in* 1775. 8vo, pp. 20. J.C.B. 15529

Free Thoughts on the Proceedings of Congress. 1774. *See* [Wilkins (I.)], *infra.*

Full Vindication of the Measures of the Congress. *See* [Hamilton (A.)]

General and Public Acts of Congress respecting the Sale and disposition of the Public Lands, with Instructions issued from time to time. *Washington.* 1838. 2 vols., 8vo. 15530

General Index to the Laws of the United States ... from March 4th, 1789, to March 3d, 1827, including all Treaties ... . Arranged to the Edition commenced by Bioren, Duane, and Weightman, in 1815 ... . Compiled, in pursuance of an Order of the House of Representatives ... by Samuel Burch, Chief Clerk in Office of that House. *Washington City: William A. Davis.* 1828. 8vo, pp. 331. BA. 15531

History of Congress; exhibiting a Classification of the Proceedings of the Senate, and the House of Representatives, From March 4, 1789, to March 3, 1793; embracing the First Term of the Administration of General Washington. *Philadelphia: Lea & Blanchard.* 1843. 8vo, pp. 736. (All published.) B.

History of the Extra Session of Congress, convened by proclamation, September 4, and terminated October 4, 1832; with an Abstract of the Currency Debates. *New-York.* 1832. S.

History of the last Session of Congress, which commenced on the Seventh of December, 1801: taken from the National Intelligencer. *Washington: S. H. Smith.* 1802. 8vo, pp. 166.

House Documents, Second Session, Thirteenth Congress, 1814. *Washington.* 1814. 8vo. 15535

These "Documents" are issued at each session of the Congress, and, after the Twenty-ninth Congress, are called "House Miscellaneous Documents." They consist of such papers as are printed for the use of the members, and cover many topics of historical importance.

House List of Private Claims, First to Thirty-first Congress. *See* "Digested Summary," *infra.*

The House of Wisdom in a Bustle. *See* Geoffry Touchstone.

In Congress, Wednesday, April 3, 1776. Instructions to the Commanders of Private Ships or Vessels of War, which shall have Commissions or Letters of Marque and Reprisal, authorising them to make Captures of British Vessels and Cargoes. [n. p. n. d.] Broadside. H. 15537

Independency the Object of the Congress in America. Or an Appeal to Facts. *London: John Francis and Charles Rivington.* MDCCLXXVI. 12mo, Title, pp. 70. 15538

Index to the Executive Communications made to the House of Representatives, from the commencement of the present form of Government until the end of the Fourteenth Congress inclusive; also an Index to all the printed Committee Reports Alphabetically Arranged. *Washington.* 1824. 8vo. 15539

Index to the Executive Communications from 1817–1823, 15th, 16th, and 17th Congress; then, Index for the 18th–21st Congress; and lastly,

Index to the Executive Documents and Reports of Committees of the House of Representatives from the 22d to the 25th Congress, both included, commencing Dec. 1831, and ending March, 1839. *Washington.* 1839. 8vo. 15540

There are also indexes to the executive communications and reports of committees, from 1817–1823, 1823–1831, and 1831–1839, in 3 vols., 8vo.

Journal of the First Congress of the American Colonies, in Opposition to the Tyrannical Acts of the British Parliament, held at New York, October 7th, 1765. *New York: E. Winchester.* 1845. 8vo, pp. 59. 15541

Edited by Lewis Cruger. Relates to the Stamp Act.

Journal of the Proceedings of the Congress Held at Philadelphia, September 5, 1774. *Philadelphia: Printed by William and Thomas Bradford, at the London Coffee-House.* M,DCC,LXXIV. 8vo, pp. 144. H., P., S. 15542

This is the original edition, with the first device of the Confederate States; twelve hands grasping a column based on Magna Charta, and surmounted by the cap of liberty, and the motto, "*Hanc tuemur.*"

Journal of the Proceedings of Congress, held at Philadelphia, May 10, 1775. Published by order of Congress. *New York: H. Gaine.* MDCCLXXV. 8vo, pp. iv, 140. + *Philadelphia: W. and T. Bradford.* M.DCC.LXXV. 8vo, pp. iv, 239. + *London: J. Almon.* 1776. 8vo, pp. 200. 15543

Journal of the Proceedings of the Congress, Held at Philadelphia, September 5th, 1774. Containing, The Bill of Rights; A List of Grievances; Occasional Resolves; The Association; An Address to the People of Great Britain; A Memorial to the Inhabitants of the British American Colonies; and, An Address to the Inhabitants of the Province of Quebec. Published by Order of the Congress. To which is added, (Being now first

printed by Authority) an Authentic Copy of the Petition to the King. *London: E. and C. Dilly.* M.DCC.LXXV. 8vo, Half-Title, pp. 66. + Same. *London: J. Almon.* M.DCC.LXXV. 8vo, Half-Title, pp. 66, Advt., 1 l. 15544

Contains that part of the proceedings of Congress omitted in the "Extracts from the Votes," etc.

Journals of Congress. Containing the Proceedings From Sept. 5. 1774. to Jan. 1, 1776. Published by order of Congress. 13 vols., 8vo. 15545

Vol. I. *Philadelphia: R. Aitken.* M.DCC.LXXVII. 8vo, Title, pp. 310, (12). + *From Folwell's Press. Philadelphia.* 1800. 8vo, pp. 289, (12); Vol. II. From January 1, 1776, to December 31, 1776. *Philadelphia: R. Aitken.* M.DCC.LXXVII. Title, pp. 513, (23). + *York-town: printed by John Dunlap.* 1778. pp. 518, Index. + *From Folwell's Press. Philadelphia.* 1800. 8vo, pp. 480, (22); Vol. III. *Philadelphia: J. Dunlap;* + *New-York: Printed by John Patterson.* 8vo, pp. 603, xii. + *From Folwell's Press. Philadelphia.* 1800. 8vo, pp. 468, (18); Vol. IV. *Philadelphia: David C. Claypoole.* [n. d.] Title, pp. 748, lxxxix, (4). + *From Folwell's Press. Philadelphia.* 1800. pp. 537, (40); Vol. V. *Philadelphia: David C. Claypoole.* M,DCC,LXXXII. 8vo, Title, pp. 464, (1), lxxiv. + *From Folwell's Press. Philadelphia.* 1800. 8vo, pp. 349, (32); Vol. VI. Resolutions, Acts and Orders of Congress For the Year 1780. *Printed by J. Dunlap.* pp. 257, xliii. + Journals, &c., [as before]. *From Folwell's Press. Philadelphia.* 1800. pp. 176, (22); Vol. VII. Journals of Congress, and of the United States in Congress Assembled For the Year 1781. *New York: John Patterson.* M,DCC,LXXXVII. pp. 522. (17), lxxix. + *From Folwell's Press. Philadelphia.* 1800. pp. 396, (37); Vol. VIII. Journal of the United States In Congress Assembled: ... *Philadelphia: David C. Claypoole.* M.DCC.LXXXIII. pp. 489, xxxvi. + *From Folwell's Press. Philadelphia.* 1800. pp. 337, (16); Vol. IX. *Philadelphia: John Dunlap.* pp. 317, xviii. Sometimes followed by "Journal of the Committee of the States." pp. 47. + *From Folwell's Press. Philadelphia.* 1800. 8vo, pp. 227, (39); Vol. X. *Philadelphia: printed by John Dunlap.* M.DCC.LXXXV. pp. 368, xxvi. + *From Folwell's Press. Philadelphia.* 1801. pp. 256, (14); Vol. XI. [n. p.] *Printed by John Dunlap.* [n. d.] pp. 267, xvi. + *From Folwell's Press. Philadelphia.* 1801. 8vo, pp. 193, (10); Vol. XII. *Printed by John Dunlap.* [n. d.] pp. 267, (16). + M,DCC,LXXXVII. pp. 255, (9). + *From Folwell's Press. Philadelphia.* 1801. pp. 169, (5); Vol. XIII. *Printed by John Dunlap.* pp. 170, xcviii, (1), vi. + *From Folwell's Press. Philadelphia.* 1801. 8vo, pp. 182, (5). There are other editions of some of these volumes; they were reprinted with the following title:

Journals of The American Congress: From 1774 to 1788. ... *Washington: Way & Gideon.* 1823. 4 vols., 8vo, Title, pp. 588, xxviii; 639, xxxviii; 740, lviii; 880, 62, (1), lxvii. BA.

Journal of the Proceedings of Congress, Held at Philadelphia, From September 5, 1775 to April 30, 1776. *Philadelphia, Printed: London, Reprinted for J. Almon.* M.DCC.LXXVIII. 8vo.

A Journal of the Proceedings of the Third Session of the Fifth Congress of the United States. *New London, (Conn.)* 1798–9. 8vo. 15548

Journal and Acts of the 1st Session 5th Congress of the

United States of America, held in Philadelphia, May 15, 1797. 8vo. 15549

Journals of Congress, from Saturday, April 24th to Monday, May 3d, 1779. *Philadelphia: printed by David C. Claypoole.* [1779.] 8vo, pp. 16. H. 15550

This was a monthly publication, continued to June, 1779.

Journal of the First Session of the Senate of the United States of America, begun and held at the City of New-York, March 4th, 1789 ... . *New-York: Printed by Thomas Greenleaf.* M,DCC,LXXX,IX. Folio, pp. 172. BA. 15551

Continued to 1795 in folio, afterwards in octavo, as below. Reprinted, *Washington: Gales & Seaton.* 1820. 8vo, pp. 508, liii. BA. Journals of the Senate of the 1st Congress, 2d and 3d Session; 2d Congress, 1st and 2d Session; 3d Congress, 1st and 2d Session, and, perhaps, others were printed at *Philadelphia, by John Fenno.* M.DCC.XC–M.DCC.XCIV. Folio.

Journal of the Senate of the United States of America, being the First Session, of the Fourth Congress, Begun and Held at the City of Philadelphia, December 7th, 1795; and In the Twentieth Year of the Sovereignty of the said United States. *Philadelphia: Printed By John Fenno.* M.DCC.XCV. 8vo, Title, pp. 346, xxi. 15552

Journal of the Executive Proceedings of the Senate of the United States of America, from the Commencement of the First to the Termination of the Nineteenth Congress, from March 4, 1789, to February 23, 1829. Printed by order of the Senate of the United States. *Washington.* 1828. 3 vols., 8vo, pp. 573; 758; 734. 15553

Seven hundred copies published by order of the Senate.

Journal of the House of Representatives of the United States. [1st Congress, 1st Session, March 4, 1789, to Sept. 29, 1789.] *New-York: printed by Francis Childs and John Swayne.* [1789.] Folio, pp. 164, clxxvi. BA., C. 15554

Continued to 1796 in folio, afterwards in octavo. The Journal for the 2d Session was published at *New-York*, of the 3d Session at *Philadelphia.* There is also an octavo edition of some of the earlier volumes, from 1793, 1st Session, 3d Congress.

Journal of the House of Representatives of the United States, from the First Session of the First Congress, (March 4, 1789,) to the close of the Third Session of the Thirteenth Congress, March 2, 1815. *Re-printed by order of the House of Representatives: Washington.* 1826. 9 vols., 8vo. 15555

Journal of the Third Session, Fifth Congress. *New-London.* 1798–9. 15556

Journal, Acts and Proceedings of the Convention, assembled at Philadelphia, Monday, May 14, and dissolved Monday, September 17, 1787, which formed the Constitution of the United States. *Boston.* 1819. 15557

Laws of the United States of America. ... *New-York: Childs and Swaine.* || In Three Volumes. Vol. II–III. Published by authority. *Philadelphia: printed by Richard Folwell.* 1796. || Vol. V. *Washington City: Samuel Harrison Smith.* 1801. || Vol. VI–VIII. *Washington City.* 1803–1807. || Vol. IX–XI. *Washington City: Printed for the Department of State.* 1809–13. 8vo. 15558

Laws, Treaties and other Documents, having Operation and Respect to the Public Lands. Collected and Arranged pursuant to an Act of Congress ... . *Washington City: printed by Joseph Gales, Jun.* [1801.] 8vo, pp. xxvi, 319, 87, 33, (2). BA.

Library of Congress. Catalogue of Books, Maps, and Charts, belonging to the Library of the Two Houses of Congress. April, 1802. *Washington City: printed by William Duane.* [1802.] 8vo, pp. 10. H. 15560

Perhaps the first printed catalogue of the Library of Congress.

Supplemental Catalogue of Books, Maps, and Charts, belonging to the Library of the Two Houses of Congress. October, 1803. *Washington City: printed by James D. Westcott.* [1803.] 8vo, 3 l. H. 15561

Catalogue of the Books, Maps, and Charts, belonging to the Library established in the Capitol at the City of Washington, for the two Houses of Congress. *Washington.* 1812. 8vo.

Report of the Committee to whom was referred the Communication of Patrick Magruder, Clerk of the House of Representatives, relative to the Destruction of the Library, &c. December 12, 1814. ... *Washington: A. & G. Way, Printers.* 1814. 8vo, pp. 12, 4 folded l. (13th Cong., 3d Sess. House Doc. 33.)

Catalogue of the Library of the United States. To which is annexed, a Copious Index, alphabetically arranged. *Washington: Printed by Jonathan Elliot.* 1815. 4to, 4 l., pp. 170, xxxii. BA.

Catalogue of the Library purchased by Congress from Thomas Jefferson, late President of the United States. *Washington.* 1815. 4to. 15565

A Supplement to the Catalogue of the Library of Congress.

Washington City: printed by Daniel Rapine, (Agent). 1820. 4to, pp. 28. H. 15566

A Supplement to the Catalogue of the Library of Congress. *Washington: printed by Peter Force.* 1827. 8vo, pp. 109. BA.

An Additional Supplement to the Catalogue of the Library of Congress. *Washington.* 1828. 8vo. C. 15568

Catalogue of the Library of Congress. December, 1830. *Washington: printed by Duff Green.* 1830. 8vo, pp. 258. BA.

Catalogue of the Library of Congress in December, 1830. A Supplement of the Additions in December, 1831. And an Index to the Names of Authors and Annotators, and to the Publications of Learned Societies, to Encyclopædias, Newspapers, Reviews, Magazines, &c. *Washington.* 1831. 8vo, pp. 362. C. 15570

Library of Congress. December 3, 1832. Additions ... since the publication of the Supplement to the Catalogue, in December, 1831. [*Washington.* 1827.] Sm. folio, pp. 4. BA. 15571

Catalogue of the Library of Congress, in the Capitol of the United States of America, December, 1839. *City of Washington: printed by order of Congress.* 1840. 8vo, pp. 747. H. 15572

Contains a list of the books in the library before the fire which destroyed a portion.

Supplement to the Catalogue of the Library of Congress. December, 1840. [*Washington.* 1840.] 8vo, pp. 28. Continued annually to 1848. BA. 15573

Additions made to the Library of Congress, since the 1st day of December, 1851. *Washington.* 1852. 8vo, pp. 129. Continued annually. 15574

Catalogue of the Library of Congress. Printed by Order of Congress. *Washington.* 1861. 8vo, pp. viii, 1398. BA., C.

Catalogue of the Library of Congress. Chapters XVIII–XXIII. Jurisprudence. *Washington.* 1860. [Second Title:] Catalogue of the Law Department of the Library of Congress. By Charles H. W. Meehan. *Washington.* 1860. 8vo, pp. vii, 325. C., H.

Alphabetical Catalogue of the Library of Congress. Authors. *Washington: Government Printing Office.* 1864. Imp. 8vo, pp. 1236. + Subjects. 1869. 2 vols., imp. 8vo. 15577

Catalogue of the Library of Congress. Chapter I. Ancient

History. Complete to January, 1854. *Washington: stereotyped and printed at the Smithsonian Institution.* 1854. 8vo, pp. 77. BA. + [*Ibid.*] Folio, in double columns, Title, pp. 19, (1). BA. 15578

Published as a specimen of Prof. C. C. Jewett's method of printing catalogues from separate stereotyped titles; apparently the catalogue was prepared by Mr. Jewett.

Catalogue of Additions made to the Library of Congress, from December 1, 1861, to December 1, 1862. *Washington: Government Printing Office.* 1862. 8vo, pp. 151, 33. Continued annually. 15579

Letters to Congress on National Free Schools. 1829. 12mo, pp. 23. 15580

The Petition of the Grand American Continental Congress to the King's Most Excellent Majesty. *Boston.* [1774.] 8vo, pp. 8. C. 15581

The Petition of the grand American Continental Congress to the King's Most Excellent Majesty. *America, Boston: Printed and sold at the Printing office, near Mill Bridge.* [1775.] 15582

The petition sets forth the grievances of the colonies, and then says: "To a Sovereign, who 'glories in the name of Britain,' the bare recital of these acts must, we presume, justify the loyal subjects who fly to the foot of his throne and implore his clemency for protection against them."

Petition of the Continental Congress, to His Majesty; with the Address of the Lord Mayor and Livery of London to the Electors of Great Britain, etc. With Prefatory Address from the New York Committee of Safety. *New York.* 1776. 8vo. 15583

Proceedings and Debates of the United States Senate 1st Session, 30th Congress. By James A. Houston. *Washington.* 1848. 4to. 15584

Proceedings of the 3d Session, 5th Congress: December 3, 1798, to March 3, 1799. *New-London.* 1798–99. 15585

Public and General Statutes passed by the Congress of the United States of America, 1789 to 1827, inclusive, whether expired, repealed, or in force, published under the inspection of Joseph Story. *Boston.* 1828. 3 vols., 8vo. + [The same.] 1828 to 1836. Edited by George Sharswood. *Philadelphia.* 1837. 8vo. + [Same.] 1837 to 1847. Edited by George Sharswood. *Philadelphia.* 1848. 8vo. 15586

Register of Debates in Congress, Comprising the Leading Debates and Incidents of the ... Congress: together with an Appendix, containing Important State Papers and Public Documents ... to which are added the Laws enacted during the Session, with a Copious Index to the Whole. *Washington: Gales & Seaton.* 1825–1835. 14 vols. in 29, 8vo. 15587

Remarks on the Debates in Congress, During the Sessions begun on the 5th of December, 1796. 8vo, pp. 64. C., L., P.

No title-page; apparently printed at Philadelphia. An attack on the members of Congress who opposed the votes of approbation to Gen. Washington; also, a letter to T. Paine in reply to his letter to Washington.

Reponse à la Déclaration du Congrès Américain. Traduite de l'Anglois. *London: T. Cadell.* 1777. 8vo, Title, pp. v, 124, Index, 4. 15589

A translation of the "Answer to the Declaration of the American Congress." "Probably published by authority."—RICH. *See* [Lind (J.)]

The Resolutions of Congress, Of the 18th of April, 1783. Recommending the States to invest Congress with the power to levy An Impost, For the Use of the States; and The Laws of the respective States, Passed in Pursuance of the said Recommendation. Together with Remarks on the Resolutions of Congress, and Laws of the different States, By a Republican. To which is added, An Appendix; containing The Resolutions of Congress, of the 11th of August, recommending the Executive of the State of New-York to convene the Legislature, to take into their Consideration the aforesaid Recommendation; and The Proceedings of the 23d of August, containing the Answer of the Governor of New-York, to the first Recommendation, and the Resolutions of Congress consequent thereon. *New-York: Printed by Carroll & Patterson.* M,DCC,LXXXVII. 8vo, pp. (2), 66. 15590

Resolutions, Acts, and Orders of Congress, 1760. *Philadelphia.* [n. d.] 8vo. 15591

Resolutions, Laws and Ordinances, relating to the Pay, Half Pay, Commutation of Half Pay, Bounty Lands, and other Promises made by Congress, to the Officers and Soldiers of the Revolution, to the Settlement of the Accounts between the United States and the several States, and to the Funding of the Revolutionary Debt. *Washington.* 1838. 8vo, pp. 506. 15592

Report of the Joint Committee on Reconstruction, at the

First Session Thirty-ninth Congress. *Washington.* 1866. 8vo, pp. xxii, (1), 128, (1), 294, (1), 187, (1), 182. B. 15593

The reports of committees of Congress form an important series; but they are too voluminous for us to attempt to give their titles. *See* an extensive list in the Catalogue of the Public Library of Boston. Many of the more important will be found in this Dictionary under the name of the author or subject.

The Rights of Great Britain asserted ... being an Answer to the Declaration, etc. *See* [Germaine (G.)]

Secret Journals of the Acts and Proceedings of Congress, from the First Meeting thereof to the Dissolution of the Confederation, by the Adoption of the Constitution of the United States. Published under the direction of the President of the United States, conformably to Resolution of Congress of March 27, 1818, and April 21, 1820. ... *Boston: Thomas B. Wait.* 1821, 20–21. 4 vols., 8vo, pp. 464; 587; 614; 454. BA.

The Standing Rules and Orders of the House of Representatives, and the Constitution of the United States. *Washington.* 1829–31. 12mo. 15595

State Papers and Publick Documents of the United States. *See* "State Papers."

The Twelve United Colonies, by their Delegates in Congress, to the Inhabitants of Great-Britain. ... *Philadelphia. July* 8, 1775. P. 15596

Without a separate title-page; probably issued in connection with the Declaration, *ante.*

The Two Congresses Cut Up: or a Few Remarks upon some of the Votes and Resolutions of the Continental Congress, held at Philadelphia, in September, and the Provincial Congress, held at Cambridge, in November 1774. By a Friend to Peace and good Order. *Boston, Printed. New York: Reprinted by James Livingston.* [1774.] 8vo, pp. 14. 15597

The writer of this tract was evidently a royalist. He thinks that the opposition made by the colonies to the tax laid upon tea "is inconsistent with our profession of Christianity, with the loyalty we owe to our sovereign, and the reverence and respect that is due to the British Parliament; and, consequently, instead of being a means to obtain a repeal of the acts, will bring on us a heavier condemnation than that of the Port Bill, an act for the alteration of our Constitution."

What think ye of Congress now? 1775. *See* [Chandler (Thomas B.)], Vol. III., No. 11882, and [Cooper (Myles)].

The Whole Proceedings of the American Continental Con-

gress, held at Philadelphia, on the 5th of September, 1774. *New York: Reprinted.* 1775. 8vo. 15598

A Congress of Nations for the peaceful Adjustment of all International Disputes. [*Boston.*] 8vo, pp. 12. 15599

Congressional Addresses. *Washington. July,* 1864. 8vo, pp. 32. 15600

Congressional Banquet in Honor of George Washington and the Principles of Washington, 1852. With Farewell Address. *Washington.* 1852. 8vo, pp. 37. 15601

Congressional and Cabinet Excursion. Programme. [1864.] 8vo, pp. 6. 15602

Congressional Chart, Showing the Commencement and Length of each Session of Congress, Speakers of the House, the Documents, (additional to the Regular Congressional Documents,) elucidating the Legislative History of Congress, and the Events of each Period in Chronological Order. Prepared at the Department of the Interior. [*Washington.* 1861.] 1 sheet. H.

Congressional Directory. *Washington.* 1810. 12mo.

Congressional Directory for the First Session of the Fifteenth Congress of the United States. *Washington City.* 1817. 16mo, pp. 38. H. 15605

Continued in octavo. The last I have seen is:

Congressional Directory for the First Session of the 41st Congress ... . Compiled ... by Ben. Perley Poore ... . Second Edition. *Washington: Government Printing Office.* 1869. 8vo, 1 l., pp. 116. 15606

The Congressional Globe; containing Sketches of the Debates and Proceedings of the Twenty-third Congress. *Washington: Blair and Rives.* 1835. 4to, pp. xvi, 480. B., BA., H.

Continued. December 2, 1833, to the end of the first session of the thirty-sixth Congress, June 19, 1860; with copious indexes. Vols. I. to XX., 1834 to 1849, edited by Blair & Rives. Vols. XXI. to XXXVI., 1850 to 1860, edited by John C. Rives. This series, with the "Debates in Congress," and "Register of Debates," forms a complete official register of the "Proceedings in Congress."

The Congressional Register; or, History of the Proceedings and Debates of the first House of Representatives of the United States of America: namely, New-Hampshire, Massachusetts, Connecticut, New-York, New-Jersey, Pennsylvania, Delaware,

Maryland, Virginia, South-Carolina, and Georgia; Being the Eleven States that have ratified the Constitution of the Government of the United States. Containing an Impartial Account of The most interesting Speeches and Motions, and accurate Copies of remarkable Papers laid before and offered to the House. Taken in Short Hand By Thomas Lloyd. ... *New-York: the Editor.* M,DCC,LXXXIX–M,DCC,XC. 3 vols., 8vo, pp. 614, (1); 449, 185, (2), xiv; 502. BA. 15608

The second paging of Vol. II. has a title-page: Acts passed at a Congress of the United States of America begun and held at ... New-York ... the Fourth of March ... M.DCC.LXXXIX. ... *New-York: Hodge, Allen and Campbell, and T. Lloyd.* M.DCC.LXXXIX.

The Congressional Reporter, containing the Public Documents, and the Debates on all Interesting Questions agitated during the Session, commencing on the First Monday of November, 1812. *Concord, N. H: published by J. & W. R. Hill, at the Patriot Office.* [1812.] 2 pts., 8vo, pp. 56; 262, (2). H.

Congressional Reporter. 22nd Cong., 2nd Sess. *Washington.* 1833. 8vo. C. 15610

The Fifth Anniversary of the Congressional Temperance Society, held in the Hall of the House of Representatives of the United States, on the Evening of the 27th February, 1838. *Washington: Printed by Gales and Seaton.* 1838. 8vo, pp. 22.

Proceedings of the Congressional Total Abstinence Society, at a Meeting held in the Hall of the House of Representatives, Friday, February 25, 1841. *Washington: Printed at the National Intelligencer Office.* 1842. 8vo, pp. 39. BA. 15612

Prospect from the Congress-Gallery. *See* [Cobbett], No. 14005.

CONKLIN (L.) The Fast and the Feast. Discourses preached in the First Congregational Church, East Bloomfield, N. Y. on the Occasions of the National Fast, and Annual Thanksgiving, A.D. 1861. By Rev. Luther Conklin, Pastor. *Rochester: Press of A. Strong & Co.* 1861. 8vo, pp. 23. 15614

CONKLIN (R. H.) Facts and Figures for Fremont and Freedom. *Providence, R. I.* 1856. 8vo, pp. 24. H. 15615

CONKLING (A.) A Discourse Commemorative of the Talents, Virtues and Services of the late Dewitt Clinton, delivered ...

at Schnectady. ... July 22d. 1828. By Alfred Conkling. *Albany.* 1828. 8vo, pp. 51. B. 15616

CONKLING. Opinion of the Hon. Alfred Conkling ... upon the Question of Copyright in Manuscripts, in the Case of Little and Company against Hall, Goulds and Banks, respecting the Fourth Volume of Comstock's Reports. *Albany: Joel Munsell.* 1852. 8vo, pp. 33. B. 15617

CONKLING. A Treatise on the Organization, Jurisdiction and Practice of the Courts of the United States: To which is added an Appendix ... and also a few Practical Forms. By Alfred Conkling. *Albany: published by Wm. & A. Gould.* 1831. 8vo, pp. vi, (1), 537. H. + Second Edition. *Albany.* 1842. 8vo. + *Albany: W. C. Little & Co.* 1848. 8vo, pp. 950. Third Edition. *Albany.* 1856. 8vo. + Fourth Edition, Revised, Corrected, and Enlarged by the Author. *Albany: W. C. Little.* 1864. 8vo, pp. xii, 882. 15618

CONKLING. Powers of the Executive Department of the Government of the United States. By Alfred Conkling. *Albany: Weare C. Little.* 1866. 16mo, pp. 139. 15619

CONKLING. The Young Citizen's Manual; To which is prefixed, an Essay on the Principles of Civil Government. ... By Alfred Conkling. *Albany.* 1836. 16mo. + Second Edition. *New York: W. E. Dean.* 1839. 16mo, pp. 279.

Also: Opinion ... on a Motion in Behalf of the Tenant For a New Trial, in the Case of Martha Bradstreet *vs.* Henry Huntington, delivered at the May Term of the Court in 1834. *Utica: Press of William Williams.* MDCCCXXXIV. 8vo, pp. 40.

CONKLING (C.) Slavery Abolished. Its Relation to the Government. By Rev. C. Conkling. *Oberlin, Ohio: V. A. Shanklin & Co.* 1862. 8vo, pp. 20. 15621

CONKLING (E.) Benton's Policy of selling and developing the Mineral Lands, and the Necessity of Furnishing Access to the Rocky Mountains by the Construction of the Northern and Central Pacific Railroads ... . By Edgar Conkling. *Cincinnati.* 1864. 8vo, pp. 16. H. 15622

[CONKLING.] Exposition of Mackinaw City and its Surroundings. *Cincinnati: Caleb Clark, Printer.* 1865. 12mo, pp. 23. H. 15623

[CONKLING.] Merchants' Magazine Extra. The Pacific Railroad. [n. p. n. d.] 8vo, pp. 14. H. 15624

CONKLING (F. A.) Promotion of Medical Science. [Re-

marks of Mr. F. A. Conkling, on the Bill for the Promotion of Medical Science.] In Assembly, February 28, 1854. *Albany.* 1854. 8vo, pp. 13. H., S. 15625

CONKLING (H.) An Inside View of the Rebellion; and American Citizens' Text-Book ... By Henry Conkling ... . *Cincinnati: Caleb Clark.* 1864. 8vo, pp. 23. H. 15626

CONKLING (M. C.) Memoirs of the Mother and Wife of Washington. By Margaret C. Conkling. *Auburn.* 1850. *Derby & Miller.* 1850. 12mo, pp. 248. + Second Edition, Revised and Enlarged. *Auburn.* 1850. 12mo. + New Edition, Revised and Enlarged. *Auburn: Derby and Miller.* 1853. 12mo, pp. 248. C. + *New York.* 1860. 12mo. Portrait.

CONKLING (R.) Argument of Hon. Roscoe Conkling, June 26, 1866, Before a Special Committee of the House of Representatives, raised to investigate the Administration of the Bureau of the Provost Marshal General, and also the Act of James B. Fry, the Head of the said Bureau, in sending to the House a Letter libelling the Character of One of its Members, and also the Truth of said Letter. [n. p.] 1866. 8vo, pp. 37. H.

CONKLING. Congress and the President. The Political Problem of 1866. Speech of Hon. Roscoe Conkling ... . September 13, 1866. [*Utica.* 1866.] 8vo, pp. 31. H. 15629

CONKLING. Privileges of the House of Representatives. Battle of Ball's Bluff. Speech of Hon. Roscoe Conkling, of New York. Delivered in the House of Representatives, January 6, 1862. *Washington.* 1862. 8vo, pp. 7. H. 15630

Also: The Public Credit. Speech ... In the House of Representatives, February 4, 1862 ... . *Washington.* 1862. 8vo, pp. 8. H.—The Special Committee on Government Contracts—What it has Done. ... In the House ... April 29, 1862. 8vo, pp. 8.—The State of the Union. Speech in the House ... January 30, 1861. 8vo, pp. 8. B., H.—The Supreme Court of the United States. Speech ... . Delivered ... April 16, 1860. [n. d.] 8vo, pp. 8. H.

A Connected View of the Navigation of the U. S., 1826. *See* [Armroyd (George)], Vol. I., Nos. 2012, 2013, and Carey (M.), Vol. III., No. 10860.

CONNECTICUT.

The following list of anonymous books relating to Connecticut is arranged alphabetically, in general, with the following sub-headings: *Agriculture, Almanacs and Registers, Banks, Boundary, Charitable Institutions, Government, Indians, Laws, Prisons,* and *Railroads.*

An Account of the Number of Inhabitants in the Colony of Connecticut. January 1, 1774: together with An Account of

the Number of the Inhabitants, taken January 1, 1756. *Hartford: Printed by Ebenezer Watson.* M,DCC,LXXIV. Folio, 9 l.

An Act for regulating and ordering the Troops that are, or may be raised for the Defence of this Colony. 1775. 8vo, pp. 19. BA. 15632

An Act to incorporate the Trustees of the Missionary Society of Connecticut; an Address ... with a Narrative on the Subject of Missions, and a Statement of the Funds of the Society, for the Year 1802. *Hartford: Printed by Hudson & Goodwin.* 1803. 8vo, pp. 23. BA. 15633

Acts and Laws Of His Majesty's English Colony of Connecticut in New-England, in America: The Charter Granted by His Majesty King Charles II. ... *New-London: Printed and sold by Timothy Green.* 1750. 8vo, 6 l., pp. 268. BA. 15634

Acts and Laws of the State of Connecticut, in America, *New London: Timothy Green.* 1784. Folio, pp. 315. 15635

An Address of the General Association of Connecticut to the Congregational Ministers and Churches of the State, on the Importance of United Endeavours to revive Gospel Discipline. *Litchfield: printed by Hosmer and Goodwin.* 1808. 8vo, pp. 16.

An Address of the General Association of Connecticut to the District Associations on the Subject of a Missionary Society, together with Summaries and Extracts from Late European Publications, on Missions to the Heathen. *Norwich: printed by Thomas Hubbard.* 1797. 8vo, pp. 32. H., M. 15637

Address of the General Committee of the Republicans of Connecticut. 1803. 8vo. 15638

An Address on the Subject of Missions, from the Trustees of the Missionary Society of Connecticut, to the Ministers and People of the State ... . To which is subjoined, a Statement of the Funds of the Society, and a List of Books sent to the New Settlements. *Hartford: Peter B. Gleason and Co., Printers.* 1812. 8vo, pp. 16. H. 15639

An Address to the Citizens of Connecticut. [Signed Chatham. n. p. *I. Walter, Printer.* 18 .] 8vo, pp. 24. BA.

See also [Webster (Noah)].

Address to the Consociated Pastors and Churches. *New York.* 1776. 8vo, pp. 8. M. 15641

Address to General William Tryon, in consequence of his late Expedition into Connecticut. 1779. 12mo. 15642

An Address to the Emigrants from Connecticut, and from New England generally, in the New Settlements in the United States. *Hartford.* 1817. 8vo, pp. 19. 15643

An Address to the Freemen of Connecticut. *Hartford: Printed by Hudson & Goodwin.* 1803. 8vo, pp. 7. BA. 15644

By the Federal legislative caucus, with list of candidates for assistant state senators for the following September election.

Address to the Freemen of Connecticut, May 24, 1806. *Hartford.* 1806. 8vo. 15645

Somewhat similar to the preceding.

An Address to the Inhabitants of the New Settlements in the Northern and Western Parts of the United States. *New-Haven: printed by T. and S. Green.* 12mo, pp. 6. H. 15646

Address to the People of Connecticut. [n. p. n. d.] 8vo, pp. 21. 15647

"For which of you intending to build a tower sitteth not down first and counteth the cost."

Address to the Legislature and People of the State of Connecticut, on the Subject of dividing the State into Districts for the Election of Representatives in Congress. By a Citizen of Connecticut. *New Haven.* 1791. 8vo, pp. 37. W. 15648

Address of the Society for the Encouragement of American Manufactures. Feb. 18, 1817. *Middletown.* 1817. 8vo, pp. 24. W. 15649

Address of the State Convention, Middletown, Jan. 28, 1835, to the Democrats of Connecticut. *New-Haven.* 8vo, pp. 6.

Address to the People of Connecticut on sundry Political Subjects, and particularly on the proposition for a New Constitution. By Jonathan Steadfast. *Hartford.* 1804. 12mo.

Address to the people of Connecticut, adopted at the State Convention held at Middletown, August, 7, 1828, with the proceedings of the Convention. 8vo, pp. 24. 15652

Address to the Public over the Signature of Franklin. [n. p. n. d.] 8vo. W. 15653

The Address of the Episcopal Clergy of Connecticut, to Bishop Seabury; with the Bishop's Answer, and a Sermon ... by J. Leaming, also Bishop Seabury's First Charge to the Clergy of his Diocese; delivered at Middletown, August 4th, 1785. With a List of the Succession of Scot's Bishops from the Revolution in 1688 to the Present Time. *New-Haven: printed by Thomas and Samuel Green.* [1765.] 8vo, pp. 8, 18, more than 10. (Collation taken from an imperfect copy.) H.

Agriculture. First Annual Report of the Secretary of the Connecticut Board of Agriculture. 1866. ... *Hartford.* 1867. 8vo, pp. 243. Continued. 15655

Premium List of the Second Annual Cattle Show and Fair of the Connecticut State Agricultural Society, to be held at Hartford ... Oct. 9th, 10th, 11th, and 12th, 1855. *Hartford: Press of Case, Tiffany, and Company.* M.DCCC.LV. 8vo, pp. 48.

Transactions of the Society for Promoting Agriculture in the State of Connecticut. *New-Haven.* 1802. 4to. 15657

Transactions of the Connecticut State Agricultural Society for the Year 1854, with the Reports of the County Societies for the same year. Published by Order of the Executive Committee. *Hartford.* 1855. 8vo. Continued. H. 15658

See Humphreys (David).

Almanacs and Registers. Annual Register, from 1789 to 1848. 60 vols., 18mo. 15659

The Annual Connecticut Register, and United-States Calendar, for the Year 1823. *New London.* [n. d.] 16mo. 15660

Connecticut Almanack. *Hartford.* 1778, 79. 12mo. S.

Connecticut, Massachusetts, New York and Vermont Almanack. *N. Strong, Litchfield, Conn.* 1795, 98. 12mo. 15662

Connecticut Pocket Almanac, 1803. *Hartford: C. Beers.* 1803. 12mo. 15663

Connecticut, Rhode-Island, Massachusetts, New-Hampshire, Vermont Farmers' Almanac for ... Eighteen Hundred and Three. ... Also, Containing an Affecting Account of the Death Of Miss Polly & Hannah Watts, Who were Taken Prisoners and Murdered by the Indians, on the 5th of April, 1802. By J. Weathermore. *Norwich: Printed for L. Trumbull.* 15664

Connecticut Register and United States Record from 1785 to 1857 inclusive. Astronomical Calculations by N. Daboll, J. Gallup, etc. *New-London* or *Hartford.* 15665

A make-up title.

Connecticut Register. Register of Civil, Judicial, Military, and other officers in Connecticut, and United-States Record, for ... 1827, 28, 29. N° 1, 2, 3. ... *Hartford: Norton & Russell.* 3 vols., 18mo. 15666

Connecticut Register; being a State Calendar of Public Officers and Institutions in Connecticut for 1856. 18mo, pp. 192. Continued. 15667

Green's Almanack and Register, for the State of Connecticut, For ... 1801 ... . *New-London: Samuel Green.* 24mo, pp. 153, (3), 22. Continued till 1846 or later. H. 15668

Watson's Register and Connecticut Almanack, For ... 1776. ... *Hartford: Eben. Watson.* [n. d.] 8vo. H. 15669

Ancient Charters and Papers relating to the History of Connecticut. [Appendix. n. p. n. d.] 8vo. M. 15670

The Answer of The Friend in the West, to a Letter from A Gentleman in the East, entitled, The present State of the Colony of Connecticut considered. *See* Clap (R.), No. 13207.

An Appeal to the Candid, upon the Present State of Religion and Politics in Connecticut. [n. p. n. d.] Sm. 8vo, pp. 16.

As You Were! *See* Vol. I., No. 2161.

Attention! or, New Thoughts on a Serious Subject; being An Enquiry into the Excise Laws of Connecticut. Addressed to the Freemen of the State. By A Private Citizen. *Hartford.* 1789. 8vo, pp. 18. 15672

Annual Report of the State Treasurer to the General Assembly, May Session, 1856. ... *New Haven: Carrington & Hotchkiss, State Printers.* 1856. 8vo, pp. 26. H. 15673

At a General Assembly of the Governor and Company of the English Colony of Connecticut, in New-England in America, holden at Hartford ... on the Second Thursday of May, in the 15th Year of the Reign of ... George the Third ... 1775. An Act for regulating and ordering the Troops that are, or may be raised, for the Defence of this Colony. [n. p. 1775.] 16mo, pp. 19. H. 15674

At a Special Session of the Gederal [*sic*] Assembly of the State of Connecticut, held at Hartford, on the Twenty Third Day of February, A.D. 1809. 8vo, pp. 16. H. 15675

Banks. Abstract from the Statement of the Condition of the Several Banks in Connecticut, March, 1841. *Hartford.* 1841. Sheet. 15676

Report of the Bank Commissioners, [Ebenezer Learned and William L. Storrs.] May Session, 1839. *Hartford.* 1839. 8vo, pp. 22. 15677

Report of the Bank Commissioners to the General Assembly, May Session, 1842. *New Haven.* 1842. 8vo, pp. 46. Continued. H. 15678

Report of the Committee appointed by the Legislature to Visit and Examine the Banks in Connecticut, ... Session 1837. *Hartford: printed by Russell and Jones.* 8vo, pp. 23. H.

Boundary. Articles of Association of the Connecticut Land Company, dated Sept. 5, 1795. *Hartford.* [n. d.] 8vo.

This corporation held and sold the "Western Reserve," in Ohio, to the actual settlers.

The Connecticut Gore Title, stated and considered, showing the Right of the Proprietors, to the Lands lately purchased by them, from the State of Connecticut: lying West of the Delaware River. *Hartford: Printed by Hudson & Goodwin.* 1799. 8vo, pp. 80. BA. 15681

The "Connecticut Gore" was a strip of land along the western part of the south New York State line, and, like the "Connecticut Reserve," was claimed by Connecticut under the old English grants that sever the Atlantic seaboard states clear through to the Pacific Ocean.

An Enquiry concerning the Grant of the Legislature of Connecticut to Andrew Ward and Jeremiah Halsey; and the Rights and Obligations of the Parties under the same. *Hartford.* 1829. 8vo, pp. 26. 15682

Contains a clear and good account of the "Connecticut Gore" and the "Gore Company."

An Examination of the Connecticut Claim to Lands in Pennsylvania. *See* [Smith (William)].

Memorials to the Governor and Legislature of New York, by the Claimants of the Lands purchased of Connecticut, commonly called the Gore, dated Connecticut, March 9, 1801. 8vo. 15683

Papers respecting intrusions by Connecticut Claimants. *Philadelphia: Printed by Hall & Sellers.* 1796. 8vo, pp. 24. 15684

The Susquehannah Title Stated and Examined. *See* Susquehannah.

Report of the Commissioners appointed by the General Assembly of this Colony [Connecticut] to treat with the Proprietaries of Pennsylvania respecting the Boundaries of this Colony and that Province. *Norwich.* 1774. Sm. 4to, pp. 36. 15685

Report of the Commissioners on the Western Boundary Line between Connecticut and New-York, to the General Assembly, May Session, 1857. *Hartford.* 15686

Report of the Commissioners appointed to ascertain the Boundary Line between the States of New-York and Connecticut. *Albany.* 1857. 8vo, pp. 184. 4 Maps. (Leg. Doc., April 10, 1857.) S. 15687

Report of the Committee to whom was referred, on the 26th ultimo, the consideration of the Expediency of Accepting from the State of Connecticut A cession of jurisdiction of the Territory of West Pennsylvania, commonly called the Western Reserve of Connecticut. [March 21, 1800.] 8vo, pp. 31. P.

The Right of the Governor and Company of the Colony of Connecticut, To Claim and Hold the Lands within the Limits of their Charter, Lying West of the Province of New-York, Stated and Considered: In a Letter to J. H. Esquire. To which is added, An Account of the Purchase from the Indians, of Part of those Lands, by the Susquehannah and Delaware Companies, and their Proceedings thereon. *Hartford: Printed by Eben Watson.* 1773. 8vo, pp. 47. B. 15689

Right of Connecticut, with Respect to Eastern Boundary on Connecticut River, as concerns Encroachments under New Hampshire, etc. *New York.* 1773. Folio. 15690

The Rise, Progress, and Effect of the Claim of the Proprietors of the Connecticut Gore, Stated and Considered. *Hartford.* 1802. 8vo. 15691

The State of the Lands said to be once within the Bounds of the Charter of the Colony of Connecticut West of the Province of New York, considered. *New York.* 1770. 8vo, pp. 16.

Charitable Institutions. Report of the Committee of the Connecticut Asylum for the Education and Instruction of Deaf and Dumb Persons, exhibited 1st June, 1817. ... *Hartford: Hudson and Co. Printers.* 1817. 8vo, pp. 15. Continued. BA. 15693

Tenth Annual Report of the Central Asylum: [for the Education of the Deaf and Dumb]. *New York, Central Canajoharie.* 1823. 8vo. 15694

Report of the Commissioners on Idiocy, to the General Assembly of Connecticut, May Session, 1856. ... *New-Haven.* 1856. 8vo, pp. 76, (1). H. 15695

Also: Report of the Medical Visitors of the Connecticut Retreat of the Insane. *Hartford.* 1824. 8vo. — Report of the Medical Visitors of the Connecticut Retreat for the Insane, presented May, 1830. *Hartford.* 1830. 8vo, pp. 22.

First Report of the Board of Trustees of the General State Hospital for the Insane, of the State of Connecticut, Presented to the General Assembly, at its Session in May, 1867. ... *New-Haven: printed by Thomas J. Stafford.* 1867. 8vo, pp. 15. H.

Third Annual Report of the Managers of the Colonization Society of the State of Connecticut. With an Appendix. May, 1830. *New-Haven: Printed by Baldwin and Treadway.* 1830. 8vo, pp. 28. BA. 15697

Also: Report of the President and Directors of the General Hospital Society to the General Assembly. May, 1850. ... *New-Haven: Osborn & Baldwin, Printers.* 1850. 8vo, pp. 8. H.

Report of the Directing Committee of the Connecticut Bible Society; exhibited to the Society, at their Meeting, May 9, 1816. *Hartford: Printed by Hudson & Co.* 1816. 8vo, pp. 19.

Communications from the London Missionary Society to the Missionary Society of Connecticut. *Hartford.* 1803. 8vo, pp. 16. 15699

First Annual Report of the Executive Committee of the Connecticut Temperance Society, May 19, 1830. *Middletown: printed by Wm. D. Starr.* 1830. 8vo, pp. 31. B. 15700

The Code of 1650. *See* No. 14122.

A Congratulatory Letter from a Gentleman in the West. *See* [Hobart (Noah)].

Connecticut Academy of Arts and Sciences. (Proposals for a Statistical History of Connecticut.) *New Haven.* 1800. 24mo, pp. 12. BA. 15701

Connecticut Academy of Arts and Sciences. A Statistical Account of the Towns and Parishes in the State of Connecticut. Vol. I., No. I. *New Haven.* 1811. 8vo, pp. 83.

All that was published. Contains an account of New Haven, by Timothy Dwight.

Memoirs of the Connecticut Academy of Arts and Sciences. Vol. I., Part I. *New-Haven: Printed by Oliver Steele & Co.* 1810. 8vo, pp. vi, (2), 216. + Part II. [*Ibid.*] 1811. 8vo, pp. 217–309, (1). + Part III. [*Ibid.*] 1813. 8vo, Title, pp. 311–412. BA., P. 15703

Transactions of the Connecticut Academy of Arts and Sciences. Vol. I., Part I. *New Haven.* 1868. 8vo. 15704

Address, Constitution, and Subscription Proposal, of the Connecticut Bible Society, presented to the Well Disposed of every Denomination. pp. 14, (1). BA. 15705

The Connecticut Business Directory, giving the Names and Post Office Addresses of Merchants, Manufacturers and Professional Men ... By George Adams ... *Boston.* 1856. 8vo, pp. 100. Continued at least to Vol. II. H. 15706

Connecticut Dissenters' Strong Box. *See* [Leland (John)].

The Connecticut Evangelical Magazine. Volume I. ... From July 1800 to June 1801. ... *Hartford.* [n. d.] 8vo. Continued to June, 1807, Vol. VII. BA. 15707

Connecticut Evangelical Magazine and Religious Intelligencer. ... Vol. I. *Hartford: printed by Lincoln & Gleason.* 1808. 8vo. Continued. BA. 15708

The Connecticut Magazine, or Gentleman's and Lady's Monthly Mirror, of Knowledge and Rational Entertainment. Vol. I. From January to June, 1801. *Bridgeport: L. Black & S. Thompson.* 1801. 8vo. 15709

Continued under the title of

The Charter of Incorporation and By-Laws of the Connecticut Historical Society; together with a List of the Officers, and an Address to the Public. *Hartford.* 1839. 8vo, pp. 11.

See "Am. Quar. Reg.," XII. 284.

Collections of the Connecticut Historical Society. Vol. I. *Hartford: the Society.* 1860. 8vo, 8 l., pp. 332. BA. 15711

A Confession of Faith, 1710. *See* No. 15447.

Articles of Association and Agreement constituting the Connecticut Land Company. Sept. 5. 1795. 15712

The Connecticut War Record. Edited by John M. Morris. *New Haven: Peck, White & Peck.* 1863. 4to. 15713

Commenced in August, 1863, and terminated in August, 1865.

Connecticut Wide Awake Songster. 18mo. 15714

Contributions to the Ecclesiastical History of Connecticut; prepared under the Direction of the General Association, to commemorate the Completion of One Hundred and Fifty Years since its First Annual Assembly. *New Haven: William L. Kingsley.* 1861. 8vo, pp. xiv, (1), 562, (1). B., H. 15715

Count the Cost. An Address to the People of Connecticut on Sundry Political Subjects, and particularly on the Proposition for a New Constitution. By Jonathan Steadfast. ... *Hartford: printed by Hudson & Goodwin.* 1804. 8vo, pp. 21, ii. H.

Education. Address of the Executive Committee of the African Mission School Society. *Hartford.* 1828. 8vo. 15717

Address to the People of Connecticut by the Board of Commissioners of Common Schools; with Second Report of the Joint Select Committee on Common Schools. [*Hartford.*] 1838. 8vo, pp. 7, 24. M. 15718

Annual Report of the Board of Education of the State of Connecticut presented to the General Assembly, May Session, 1870, together with the Annual Report of the Secretary of the Board. *New Haven.* 1870. 8vo, pp. 276. 15719

Considerations suggested by the Establishment of a Second College in Connecticut. *Hartford: B. Gleason & Co., Printers.* 1824. 8vo, pp. 36. 15720

An Examination of the "Remarks" on Considerations suggested by the Establishment of a Second College in Connecticut. *Hartford: printed by Peter B. Gleason & Co.* 1825. 8vo, pp. 26. H. 15721

I have not seen the "Remarks."

First Annual Report of the Board of Commissioners of Common Schools in Connecticut, together with the First Annual Report of the Secretary of the Board. May, 1839. *Hartford: printed by Case, Tiffany and Burnham.* 1839. 8vo, pp. 64. Continued. BA., B. 15722

The Third Annual Report of the Education Society of Connecticut; and of the Female Education Society of New Haven. *New Haven: T. G. Woodward, Printer.* 1818. 8vo, pp. 16.

Annual Report of the Superintendent of Common Schools of Connecticut to the General Assembly. ... [With an Appendix of School Returns, Reports, etc.] *Hartford.* 1846. 8vo, pp. 181, 23. Continued. H. 15724

Board of Commissioners of Common Schools. Legal Provision respecting the Education and Employment of Children in Factories. Education and Labour; or the Influence of Education on the quality and value of labour, and its connection with Insanity and Crime. *Hartford.* 1842. 8vo. 15725

Catalogue of the Episcopal Academy of Connecticut, at Cheshire, from January, 1848, to January 1849. *New Haven.* 1849. 12mo, pp. 11. H. 15726

Catalogue of the Members of the Connecticut Alpha of the ΦΒΚ. 8vo, pp. 16. *New Haven.* 1808. 8vo, pp. 16.

Connecticut Common School Journal, published under the direction of the Board of Commissioners of Common Schools, ... Edited by Henry Barnard, Second Secretary of the Board. *Hartford: Case, Tiffany & Co.* 1838. 3 vols., 4to. C. + New Series, 1854. 8vo. Continued. 15728

Public Acts relating to Common Schools in force in the State of Connecticut, 1843. *Hartford.* 1843. 8vo. 15729

Report of the Joint Standing Committee on Education respecting the Expenses of the Board of Commissioners of Common Schools, May Sessions, 1841. [n. p. 1841.] 8vo, pp. 8. H. 15730

Report of the Joint Standing Committee on Education, relative to Common Schools, May Session, 1842. *New Haven.* 1842. 8vo, pp. 8. 15731

Report of the Trustees of the State Reform School, to the General Assembly, May Session, 1853. ... *Hartford: Alfred E. Burr, Printer.* 1853. 8vo, pp. 16. B., H. 15732

Report of the Doings of the First State Convention of Sabbath School Teachers, held at Hartford, Ct., April 28, 29 and 30, 1857. With Statistics appended. ... *Hartford: Press of Case, Tiffany and Company.* 1857. 8vo, pp. 105, (2). H. 15733

Report of the Trustees of the State Normal School to the General Assembly, May Session, 1853. ... *Hartford: Alfred E. Burr, State Printer.* 1853. 8vo, pp. 104. Continued. 15734

Reports of the Commissioner of the School Fund, May and October, 1818, and May, 1819; Two Reports of the Joint Committee of the General Assembly, May, 1819, and the Proceedings of the Assembly thereon. ... July, 1819. [n. p.] 8vo, pp. 40. H. 15735

An Enquiry concerning the Grant of the Legislature of Connecticut to A. Ward and J. Halsey. *Hartford.* 1829. 8vo.

An Examination of the Connecticut Claims to Land in Pennsylvania. *See* [Smith (W.)]

Facts are Stubborn Things. *See* Hold-Fast (Simon).

Federalism Triumphant in the Steady Habits of Connecticut Alone, or, The Turnpike Road to a Fortune. A Comic Opera or Political Farce In Six Acts, as performed at the Theatres Royal and Aristocratic at Hartford and New Haven October 1801. *Printed in the Year* 1802. 8vo, pp. 40. P. 15737

Festival of the Connecticut Association, at the Revere House, Boston, January 14, 1857. With the Constitution, Officers, and Members of the Association. *Boston: Press of T. R. Marvin.* 1857. 8vo, pp. 52. H. 15738

A General History of Connecticut. *See* [Peters (S.)]

Government. Goodwin's Annual Legislative Statistics, 1850–1865. *New Haven,* [*Conn.*] 1850–65. 2 vols. in 1, 8vo.

Journal of the House of Representatives of the State of Connecticut, May Session, 1838. *Hartford.* 1838. 8vo. Continued. 15740

Journal of the Senate of the State of Connecticut, May Session, 1840. *Hartford.* 1840. 8vo, pp. 94. 15741

Legislative Roll, Rules of the House of Representatives, Joint Rules of Proceedings, &c., May Session, 1841. *Hartford.* 1841. 8vo, pp. 16. 15742

List of Committees of the House of Representatives of Connecticut. [1841?] 8vo, pp. 8. 15743

Message of his Excellency Governor Griswold, to the General Assembly, at their Special Session, August 25, 1812. *New Haven.* 1812. 8vo. 15744

Also: Message of His Excellency William A. Buckingham, Governor of Connecticut, to the Legislature of the State, Special Session, November, 1863. Printed by Order of the Legislature. *Hartford.* 1863. 8vo, pp. 7. — Message of His Excellency William A. Buckingham, Governor of Connecticut to the Legislature of the State, May Session, 1862. ... *New Haven: Babcock & Sizer, State Printers.* 1862. 8vo, pp. 24. H. — Message of Governor Buckingham, accompanying the Report of Col. H. H. Osgood, giving the Number of Drafted Men in the State, to the [Connecticut] General Assembly, December 10th, 1862. ... *New Haven: Babcock & Sizer, State Printers.* 1862. 8vo, pp. 45. H. Several other messages of Governor Buckingham relate to the rebellion.

Private Acts and Resolutions passed by the General Assembly, at the May Session, 1866. *New Haven.* 1866. 8vo. Continued. 15745

Grand List of the State of Connecticut for the First of October, 1854, Prepared by the Comptroller from the Returns of the Several Town Clerks. By Order of the General Assembly. *Hartford: Thomas M. Day, State Printer.* 1855. Oblong 8vo, pp. 21. H. 15746

Heads of Inquiry Relative to the Present State and Condition Of His Majesty's Colony of Connecticut, Signified by His Majesty's Secretary of State, in his Letter of the 5th July, 1773; With the Answers thereto. ... *New-London: printed by T. Green.* M,DCC,LXXV. Folio, pp. 15. BA., H. + [Same.] *Norwich: Reprinted.* 1775. 4to, pp. 16. 15747

The work consists of twenty-one questions, with their answers. Reprinted in "Mass. Hist. Coll.," VII. 231–239; XII. 216–220.

Indians. Governor and Company of Connecticut and Mohegan Indians, by their Guardians. Certified Copy of Book of Proceedings before Commissioners of Review, MDCCLXIII. *London: Printed by W. & J. Richardson.* MDCCLXIX. 4to, pp. xxi, 283. Map. H. 15748

Included in this volume as a part of the testimony in the case, is Major Mason's "Brief History of the Pequot War."

Old John Uncas and the greater part of the Tribe of Mohegan Indians, by Samuel Mason, their Guardian, Appellants. The Governor and Company of his Majesty's Colony of Connecticut in New England in America, and George Richards, and several other persons, intruders on the lands in question. The Appellants Case. To be heard before the Rt. Hon. Lords of the Committee of the Privy Council, in the Council Chamber in the Cockpit 1700. Folio, pp. 24. J.C.B. 15749

Between Old John Uncas, Young John Uncas, and several other Mohegan Indians, on the Behalf of themselves and the Rest of their Tribe, by John Mason and Samuel Mason, Gentlemen, the Trustees for the Guardians of the said Tribe and Appellants, and Governor and Company of the English Colony of Connecticut, in New England in America, and others, Respondents. The Case of the Respondents the Governor and Company of the Colony of Connecticut. [n. p. 1770.] Folio, pp. 35. + The same. The Case of the Respondents the Landholders. [n. p. 1770.] Folio, pp. 15. H. 15750

This is endorsed:

Connecticut. The Moheagan Indians against The Governor and Company of Connecticut, and others. The Case of the Respondents the Governor and Company of the Colony of Connecticut. To be heard before the Right Honourable the Lords of the Privy Council, the Day of 1770. 15751

And is followed by fifteen pages, endorsed:

Connecticut. The Moheagan Indians against The Governor and Company of Connecticut, and others. The Case of the Respondents the Landholders. To be heard before the Right Honourable the Lords of the Privy Council, the Day of 1770. 15752

Journal of the Proceedings of the Convention held in New Haven, May, 1811. *New York.* 1811. 8vo, pp. 36. M.

Laws. The Book of the General Laws For the People within the Jurisdiction of Connecticut; Collected out of the Records of the General Court. Lately Revised, and with some Emendations and Additions Established and Published by the Authority of the General Court of Connecticut holden at Hartford in October, 1672. ... *Cambridge: Printed by Samuel Green.* 1673. Folio, Title, pp. (2), 71, (4). B. 15754

The Laws of Connecticut. An Exact Reprint of the Original Edition Of 1673. With a Prefatory Note by George Brinley. *Hartford: Printed for Private Distribution.* 1865. 8vo, 6 l., pp. 71, (4). BA. 15755

Acts and Laws of his Majesty's Colony of Connecticut in New England. *Boston.* 1702. Folio. P. 15756

Acts and Laws of His Majesties Colony of Connecticut in New England. *New London: Timothy Green.* 1715. C., M.

Acts and Laws of his Majesty's English Colony of Connecticut, in New England, in America. *New Haven: reprinted.* 1769. Folio. W. 15758

Acts and Laws of the Colony and the State of Connecticut, 1752 to 1783. *New London.* 1768–83. Folio. M. 15759

Acts and Laws of the State of Connecticut, in America. *New-London: Printed by Timothy Green.* MDCCLXXXIV. Folio, pp. 8, 6, (2), 311. C., H. + *Hartford: Printed by Elisha Babcock.* MDCCLXXXVI. 8vo, pp. 8, 2, 5, 3, 346, (8). + *Hartford: printed by Hudson and Goodwin.* MDCCXCVI. 8vo, Title, pp. (14), 510. B. + *Hartford.* 1805. 8vo. 15760

The Blue Laws of Connecticut; A Collection of the Earliest Statistics and Judicial Proceedings of that Colony; being An Exhibition of the Rigorous Morals and Legislation of the Puritans. Edited with an Introduction by Samuel M. Smucker, LL.D. *Philadelphia: Duane Rulison.* 1861. 12mo, pp. 235.

For the earlier editions, *see* Vol. II., No. 6010.

The Charter Granted by His Majesty, King Charles II. to The Governour and Company of The English Colony of Connecticut in New-England in America. *New-London: Printed and Sold by Timothy Green.* 1718. Folio. 15762

This precedes the "Acts and Laws."

The General Statutes of the State of Connecticut. To which are prefixed the Declaration of Independence, the Constitution of the United States, and the Constitution of the State of Connecticut. Prepared by Henry Dutton, Loren P. Waldo, and David B. Booth. Published by authority of the General Assembly. *New Haven: J. H. Benham, Printer.* 1866. 8vo, pp. lxi, 892. 15763

The Joint Stock Act of Connecticut, from the Revised Statutes, with Notes and Forms. *New Haven: H. C. Peck.* 16mo, pp. vii, 95. 15764

The Laws of Connecticut. An Exact Reprint of the Original Edition of 1673, with a Prefatory Note by George Brinley. *Hartford: printed for Private Distribution.* 1865. Folio, pp. (4), 76. H. 15765

Laws of Connecticut from 1794 to 1800, including the Charter Granted by Charles II, & Declaration of Independence. *Hartford.* 1800. 8vo. 15766

Letter to the Legislative Authority of Connecticut, in Relation to Debt and Gaols. 1770. 8vo. W. 15767

The Military Laws of the State of Connecticut. ... *New London: S. Green.* 1801. 8vo, pp. 38. H. 15768

Militia Laws of the State of Connecticut. *Hartford.* 1812. 12mo. + Revised and Enacted, May, 1821. *Hartford.* 1821. 8vo. 15769

Public Acts and Laws of the State of Connecticut in America; together with the Charter granted by Charles II, Declaration of Independence, Articles of Confederation and Treaty of Peace, between the United States and Great Britain. September 23, 1783. *Hartford.* 1786. 8vo. 15770

Public and Private Acts of the General Assembly of Connecticut, passed at the May Session, 1848. *New Haven.* 2 vols., 8vo. Continued. 15771

Public Acts, passed by the General Assembly of the State of Connecticut, May Session, 1857. ... *Hartford: Hawley & Faxon, State Printers.* 1857. 8vo, pp. 309. Continued. H.

Public Acts relating to Elections, and the Admission of Electors. Adopted, May, 1842. *New Haven.* 1832. 8vo, pp. 46.

The Public Statute Law of the State of Connecticut respecting Common Schools. ... *Hartford: Printed by J. Holbrook.* 1841. 8vo, pp. 20. H. 15774

The Public Statute Laws of the State of Connecticut. Book I. *Hartford: Printed by Hudson and Goodwin.* 1808. 8vo, 66 l., pp. 696. BA. 15775

Also: Public Statute Laws of the State of Connecticut, as revised and enacted by the General Assembly in May 1821; to which are prefixed the Declaration of Independence, the Constitution of the United States, and the Constitution of Connecticut: Arranged and published under the Authority of the General Assembly. *Hartford: S. G. Goodrich, and Huntington & Hopkins.* 1821. C. + *Hartford: John B. Eldredge, printer.* 1835. 8vo, pp. 640. + *Hartford: John L. Boswell, publisher.* 1839. pp. 717.

Resolves and Private Laws of the State of Connecticut, from the Year 1789 to the Year 1836. Published ... under the Supervision of a special Committee [R. R. Hinman, Elisha Phelps, and Leman Church]. Vol. I., II. ‖ ... from the Year 1836 to the Year 1857. Published ... under the Supervision of a special Committee. [John Hooker, J. Judson Dimock,

Jared B. Foster]. Vol. III., IV. *Hartford. New Haven.* 1837, '57. 8vo. 15776

Resolutions and Private Acts passed by the General Assembly of Connecticut, October Session, 1842. *Hartford.* 1843. 8vo, pp. 20. Continued. 15777

After 1859 the title reads, "Private Acts and Resolutions."

Revised Statutes of Connecticut of 1849; to which are prefixed the Declaration of Independence, &c. Published by Authority of the General Assembly. Henry Dutton, L. P. Waldo and Francis Fellows, Revisers. *Hartford.* 1849. 8vo. 15778

Revision of Swift's Digest of the Laws of Connecticut; also, practice, forms, and precedents. By H. Dutton and N. A. Cowdry. Revised Edition. *New Haven.* 1851–53. 2 vols., 8vo. 15779

Statute Laws of Connecticut, as revised and enacted by the General Assembly in May, 1821; with the acts of three subsequent sessions incorporated. Published by H. Huntington, Jr. *Hartford.* 1824. 8vo. + *New Haven.* 1854. 8vo.

The Statutes of Connecticut. To which are prefixed the Declaration of Independence, etc. Compiled and published by authority of the General Assembly. *New Haven.* 1854. 8vo, pp. 1070. 15781

Liberty and Property vindicated, and the St--pm-n burnt. A Discourse Occasionally made on burning the Effigie of the St--pm-n. In New-London, In the Colony of Connecticut. By a Friend to the Liberty of his Country. Published at the Desire of some of his Hearers, in the Year 1765. 4to, pp. 11. + *Boston, reprinted.* 1765. 8vo, pp. 15. M. 15782

Constitution of the Connecticut Medical Society, with an Abstract of the Journals of theC onvention. *Hartford: P. Canfield, Printer.* 1824. 8vo, pp. 23. B. 15783

Also: Communications of the Medical Society of Connecticut. November 1. *Sidney's Press, New Haven.* 1810. 8vo, pp. 80. B. — Medical Communication, with the Proceedings of the Sixty-Ninth Annual Convention of the Connecticut Medical Society, held at New Haven, May 22d and 23d, 1861. ... *Hartford: Press of Case, Lockwood and Company.* 1861. 8vo, pp. [71]–141, [23]–50. H. — Proceedings at the Annual Convention of the Connecticut Medical Society, May, 1848, together with a List of Members, and the Annual Address. *Hartford: Press of Case, Tiffany and Burnham.* 1848. 8vo, pp. 48. Continued. H. — Proceedings of the President and Fellows of the Connecticut Medical Society, in Convention, May, 1834: and a List of the Members; with "an Act to incorporate the Connecticut Medical Society,"

and "an Act in relation to the Medical Institution of Yale College." *New Haven: Press of Whitmore & Buckingham.* 1834. 8vo, pp. 16. H. + May, 1837: with a List of the Members of the Society. *New Haven: Printed by B. S. Hamlen.* 1837. 8vo, pp. 16. H. — Report of a Committee of the Connecticut Medical Society respecting an Asylum of Inebriates, with the Resolutions of the Society, adopted at their Annual Meeting, May, 1830. *New Haven: printed by Hezekiah Howe.* 1830. 8vo, Title, pp. 9. H.

Military. Annual Report of the Adjutant General of the State of Connecticut, for the Year 1861. *Hartford: J. R. Hawley & Co., State Printers.* 1862. 8vo, pp. 115. BA. + [For 1863.] *New Haven.* 1863. 8vo, pp. 332. + [1864.] *Hartford: J. M. Scofiela & Co.* 1864. 8vo, pp. 356. + [1865.] *New Haven: Harrison, Hotchkiss & Co.* 1865. 8vo, pp. 494. Continued. 15784

Message of Governor Buckingham, accompanying the Report of Col. H. H. Osgood, giving the number of Drafted Men in the State, December 10, 1862. *New Haven: Babcock & Sizer.* 1862. 8vo, pp. 45. 15785

Also: First Annual Report of the Connecticut Soldiers' Relief Association of Washington City, D. C., together with a list of the Officers of the Association for the Years 1862–3 and 1863–4. *Washington.* 1863. 8vo, pp. 17. — Catalogue of the 1st, 2d, 3d, 4th, and 5th Regiments Connecticut Volunteers, 1861. *Hartford: Press of Case, Lockwood & Company.* 1861. 8vo, pp. 117. B. — Catalogue of the 6th, 7th, 8th, 9th, 10th, and 11th Regiments of Infantry. First Light Battery, and First Battalion of Cavalry, Connecticut Volunteers, 1861. *Hartford: Press of Case, Lockwood and Company.* 1862. 8vo, Title, pp. 143, (1). B. — Catalogue of the Twelfth and Thirteenth Regiments Connecticut Volunteers, 1862. *Hartford: Press of Case, Lockwood and Company.* 1862. 8vo, pp. 45. — Catalogue of the 14th, 15th, 16th, 17th, 18th, 19th, 20th, and 21st Regiments, and the Second Light Battery Connecticut Volunteers for three Years; and the 21st, 22d, 24th, 25th, 26th, 27th, and 28th Regiments Connecticut Volunteers for Nine Months. Compiled from Records in the Adjutant-General's Office, 1862. Joseph D. Williams, Adjutant-General. *Hartford: Press of Case, Lockwood and Company.* 1862. 8vo, pp. 327. B. — Catalogue of Connecticut Volunteer Organizations, with Additional Enlistments and Casualties to July 1, 1864. Compiled from Records in the Adjutant-General's Office, and published by Order of the Legislature. Horace J. Morse, Adjutant-General. *Hartford: Press of Case, Lockwood and Company.* 1864. 8vo, pp. iv, 487. H. — Catalogue of Volunteer Organizations (Infantry, Cavalry, and Artillery), in the Service of the United States, 1861–1865, with Additional Enlistments, Casualties, &c., &c., and Brief Summaries, showing the Operations and Service of the Several Regiments and Batteries. Prepared from Records in the Adjutant General's Office. C. M. Ingersoll, Adjutant General. *Hartford: Brown and Gross.* 1869. 8vo, pp. (6), 11–936, (1). H.

Report of the Paymaster General, to Governor, for the year ending March 31, 1864. pp. 20. 15786

Report of Drs. W. H. Coggeswell and W. M. White, State Agents for care of Soldiers. 8vo, pp. 4. 15787

Report of the Quartermaster General to the General Assembly, May Session, 1863. *New Haven.* 1863. 8vo, pp. 56. + May Session, 1864. Printed by Order of the Legislature. *Hartford: J. M. Scofield & Co.* 1864. 8vo, pp. 90, 4 l. + May Session, 1865. *New Haven: Harrison, Hotchkiss & Co.* 1865. 8vo, pp. 65. + May Session, 1866. *New Haven: T. J. Stafford, Printer.* 1866. 8vo, pp. 10. H. 15788

Narrative of the Missions to the New Settlements according to the appointment of the General Association of the State of Connecticut; together with an account of the receipts and expenditures of the money contributed by the people of Connecticut in May 1793, for the support of the Missionaries, according to the act of the General Assembly of the State. *New Haven: Printed by T. & S. Green.* 1794. 8vo, pp. 17. 15789

A Continuation of the Narrative of the Mission to the New Settlements, according to appointment of the General Association of the State of Connecticut; together with an account of the receipts and expenditures of money contributed for the support of the Missionaries, agreeably to the act of the General Assembly of the State. *New Haven: Printed by T. & S. Green.* 1797. 8vo, pp. 15. 15790

The Political Greenhouse for the year 1798, addressed to the Readers of the Connecticut Courant, Jan. 1, 1799. A Poem. *Hartford.* 1799. 12mo, pp. 24. 15791

The Politics of Connecticut; or a Statement of Facts, Addressed to Honest Men of all Parties, Religious and Political, in the State, Particularly to the Mass of Community, A Bold and Hardy Yeomanry, who Compose the Flesh and Muscle the Blood and Bone of the Body Politic. By a Federal Republican. *Hartford.* 1817. 8vo, pp. 36. 15792

The Present State of the Colony of Connecticut considered. *See* [Gale (B.)]

Prisons. Minutes of the Testimony taken before J. Q. Wilson [and others], Committee from the General Assembly to inquire into the Condition of Connecticut State Prison. *Hartford: D. S. Porter, Printer.* 1834. 8vo, Title, pp. 118. H.

Also: Report of the Committee on the Punishment and Reformation of Juvenile Offenders. *New Haven.* 1844. 8vo. — Report of the Committee appointed by the General Assembly, in 1841, on the Connecticut State Prison. *New Haven.* 1842. 8vo, pp. 79. — Report of the Committee ... to inspect the Condition of New-Gate

Prison, May ... 1826. *New-Haven: Printed by J. Barber.* 1826. 8vo, pp. 35. H. — Report of the Directors of the Connecticut State Prison, made to the General Assembly, May, 1835. *Hartford: printed by John Russell.* 1835. 8vo, pp. 48. Continued. H. — Report of the Directors and Warden of the Connecticut State Prison: submitted to the Legislature, May Session, 1828. *New Haven: printed by Hezekiah Howe.* 1828. 8vo, pp. 20. Continued. H. — Report of the Joint Select Committee relative to Capital Punishment, with a Bill and proposed Amendment, May Session, 1842. *New Haven.* 1842. 8vo, pp. 36. — Report of the Joint Standing Committee to whom was referred Several Petitions relative to the employment of Mechanic Labour in Connecticut State Prison. *Hartford.* 1841. 8vo, pp. 8.

Proceedings of the State Convention of National Republican Young Men, at Hartford, [Con.] Oct. 17, 1832. *Hartford.* 8vo. W. 15794

Proceedings of the Anti-masonic State Convention of Connecticut, at Hartford, Feb. 3 and 4, 1830. *Hartford.* 1830. 8vo. W. 15795

Public Documents of the Legislature of Connecticut, May Session, 1862. ... *Hartford.* 1862. 8vo. B. 15796

Contains nineteen different documents, with different pagination. Continued.

The Public Records of the Colony of Connecticut, prior to the Union with New Haven Colony, May, 1665; transcribed and published ... under the Supervision of the Secretary of State, with Occasional Notes, and an Appendix ... by J. Hammond Trumbull ... [Vol. I.] *Hartford.* 1850. 8vo. + From August, 1689, to May, 1706, transcribed and edited ... by Charles J. Hoadly ... *Hartford: Press of Case, Lockwood and Brainard.* 8vo, pp. vi, 574. + From October, 1706, to October, 1716, with the Council Journal from October, 1710, to February, 1717. Transcribed and edited ... by Charles J. Hoadly. *Hartford: Press of Case, Lockwood and Brainard.* 1870. 8vo, pp. v, 612. BA. 15797

Railroads. An Act to aid the Construction of Certain Railroads. *New Haven.* 1838. 8vo. 15798

Connecticut and Passumpsic Rail Road, 1847. *Printed by L. J. McIndoe, Newbury, Vt.* 8vo, pp. 8. Map. B. 15799

First Annual Report of the Directors of the Connecticut and Passumpsic Rivers Rail Road Company, October 6, 1846. *Newbury, Vt.: printed by L. G. McIndoe.* 1856. 12mo, pp. 12. Continued. B. 15800

Also: Report of Committee on Housatanic Railroad Company. ... General Assembly. *Hartford.* 1839. — Report of the Commissioners on the Housatanic Railroad to the General Assembly. *Hartford.* 1843.

Reasons why the British Colonies in America should not be charged with Internal Taxes by Authority of Parliament; humbly offered for consideration in behalf of the Colony of Connecticut. *New Haven.* 1764. 8vo, pp. 39. 15801

Religion. Connecticut Theological Institute, East Windsor, 1840. 8vo. 15802

Acts and Proceedings of the General Association of Connecticut, for the Year 1801. 1801. 8vo, pp. 7. 15803

Address of General Association of Pastors of the Consociated Churches of Colony of Connecticut, to the Consociated Pastors and Churches in said Colony. *New York.* 1776. 8vo. 15804

Also: Address of the General Association of Connecticut to the Congregational Churches ... of the State ... on Gospel Discipline. *Litchfield.* 1808. 8vo, pp. 16. S.

Constitution of the Missionary Society of Connecticut. [*Hartford.* 1800.] 8vo, pp. 27. BA. 15805

Missionary Society of Connecticut. Act of Incorporation. With Address of Trustees, Narrative of Missions, &c., for 1802. *Hartford.* 1803. 8vo, pp. 24. 15806

Narrative of the Missions to the New Settlements, according to the Appointment of the General Association of the State of Connecticut: together with an account of the Receipts and Expenditures of the Money Contributed by the People of Connecticut, in May 1793, For the Support of the Missionaries, according to an Act of the General Assembly of the State. *New-Haven: T. and S. Green.* 1794. 8vo, Title, pp. 16, (1).

Continuation of the Narrative of the Missions to the New Settlements in Connecticut ... *New Haven.* 1794. 8vo, pp. 32.

A Continuation of the Narrative of the Missions to the New Settlements, according to the Appointment of the General Association of the State of Connecticut: together with An Account of the Receipts and Expenditures of the Money Contributed by the People of Connecticut, In May 1794. For the Support of the Missionaries, according to an Act of the General Assembly of the State. *New Haven: T. and S. Green.* 1795. 8vo, pp. 23. 15809

Continuation of the Narrative of the Missions to the New Settlements ... *New Haven.* 1797. 8vo, pp. 15. 15810

Second Address from the Trustees; with Narrative of Missions, &c., to 1800. *Hartford.* 1801. 8vo, pp. 20. 15811

Narrative on the Subject of Missions, and a Statement of the Funds of the Missionary Society of Connecticut, to the Year 1801. *Hartford.* 1802. 8vo, pp. 21. + 1803. *Hartford.* 1804. 8vo, pp. 18. + 1804. *Hartford.* 1804. 8vo, pp. 16. + 1805. *Hartford.* 1806. 8vo, pp. 19. + 1808. *Hartford.* 1809. 8vo, pp. 18. + *Hartford: printed by Lincoln and Gleason.* 1809. 8vo, pp. 18. H. + 1810. *Hartford.* 1811. 8vo, pp. 22. 15812

Also: A Missionary Address from the Trustees ... and a Narrative ... *Hartford.* 1813. pp. 23. — Fifteenth Annual Account of the Missionary Labors directed by the Trustees in 1813. *Hartford.* 1814. 8vo, pp. 28. — Twenty-Fourth Annual Narrative of Missions performed under the Direction of the Trustees of the Missionary Society of Connecticut; principally in 1822. ... *Hartford: printed by Peter B. Gleason & Co.* 1823. 8vo, pp. 18. H. — Twenty Seventh Annual Narrative of Missions performed under the Direction of the Trustees of the Missionary-Society of Connecticut in 1825. ... *Hartford: printed by Peter B. Gleason and Co.* 1826. 8vo, pp. 32. H.

Contributions to the Ecclesiastical History of Connecticut; prepared ... to commemorate the Completion of one hundred and fifty Years since its first Assembly. *New Haven.* 1861. 8vo. 15813

Explanation of the Say-Brook Platform; or, The Principles of the Consociated Churches in Connecticut. *Hartford.* 1765. 4to, pp. 39. M. 15814

Extracts from the Journal of the Annual Convention of the Diocese of Connecticut, held at Middletown; with an Appendix, containing Documents relating to Washington College and the Church Scholarship Society. *Middletown.* 1835. 8vo.

Extract from the Minutes of the General Association of Connecticut. *Hartford.* 1802–10. 8vo. 15816

A Letter to the Clergy of the Colony of Connecticut, from an Aged Layman of said Colony. [*New Haven?*] *Published in the year* 1760. 8vo, pp. 22. W. 15817

Letter to a Clergyman in the Colony of Connecticut from his Friend; in which the true Notion of Orthodoxy is enquired into; &c. *New-Haven.* 1757. 8vo, pp. 24. 15818

Minutes of the Convention of Delegates from the Synod of New-York and Philadelphia, and from the Associations of Connecticut, held annually from 1766 to 1775 inclusive. *Hartford.* 1843. 8vo, pp. 68. S. 15819

Minutes of the General Association of Connecticut at their Meeting in Danbury, June, 1839; with the Report on the State of Religion, &c. *Hartford: E. Gleason, Printer.* 1859. 8vo, pp. 30, (1). Continued. H. 15820

Proceedings of the Connecticut Baptist Convention, ... held at Lebanon, June, 1833. *Hartford: Philemon Canfield, printer.* 1833. 8vo, pp. 36. 15821

Proceedings of the General Association of Connecticut, June, 1812. *Hartford: printed by Peter B. Gleason & Co.* 1812. 8vo, pp. 36. Continued. B. 15822

Proclamation for a General Fast [G. Saltonstall, Governor], 24th August, 1714. 1714. Broadside. M. 15823

Remonstrance of the Baptist Elders at Bristol to the General Assembly [of Connecticut]. *Bristol.* 1803. 8vo. 15824

Report of the Committee on Home Evangelization, presented to the General Association of Connecticut, Convened at Rockville, on the 3d Tuesday in June, 1860. *New Haven.* 1860. 8vo, pp. 96. H. 15825

Politics of Connecticut; or, a Statement of facts addressed to honest men of all parties, religious and political, in the State, particularly to the mass of the community, a bold and hardy Yeomanry who compose the flesh and muscle, the blood and bone of the Body Politic. By a Federal Republican. *Hartford.* 1817. 8vo. 15826

Public Acts relating to Elections, and Admission of Electors; in Force in the State of Connecticut. ... *New Haven: printed by Osborn & Baldwin.* 1842. 8vo, pp. 48. B. 15827

A Register for The State of Connecticut: With an Almanack, For the Year of our Lord, 1785. Calculated for the Meridian of New-London, Lat. 41. 25. North, By Nathan Daboll, Teacher of the Mathematics at the Academic School in Plainfield. *New-London: Printed and Sold by T. Green, near the Court-House.* [1785.] 16mo, pp. 48, Almanack, pp. 12. 15828

The Connecticut Register, for 1804–6; 1811–'15; '17–'18; '19; '20; '21–'22; '24; '25; '25–'27; '31; '33; '35; '38–'39; 1847; '50; '51; '56; '60. *New London and Hartford.* 16mo.

The title-pages are as follows, viz.: 1804–5; Green's Almanack & Register for the State of Connecticut. *Pub. S. Green. New London.* 1806. Register and Al-

manack for the State of Connecticut. *Pub. Cady & Eells. New London.* 1811–12. The Connecticut Register. *Pub. S. Green. New York.* 1814–1820. Connecticut Register & United States Calendar. *New London.* 1822. The Connecticut Register & United States Calendar. *Pub. S. Green. New London.* 1818 and 1824. *Pub. S. Green.* 1825–27. The Annual Connecticut Register & United Slates Calendar. *Pub. S. Green. New London.* 1831. Huntington's State Register. No. 5. *Hartford. H. & F. J. Huntington.* 1833; 35; 36–39. The Connecticut Annual Register & United States Calendar. *Pub. S. Green. New London.* 1847. Connecticut Register, being an Official State Calendar. C. W. Bradley, Jr. *Hartford. Pub. Brown & Parsons.* 1850. Connecticut Register, being a State Calendar for 1850. *Hartford. Pub. Brown & Parsons.* 1851–56; '60. The Connecticut Register, being a State Calendar. *Pub. Brown & Parsons. F. Brown. Brown & Gross. Hartford.*

Report Of the Committee of Defence. To the Hon. General Assembly. *New-Haven: Hudson and Woodward, Printers.* [n. d.] 8vo, pp. 4. H. 15830

Report of the Committee To whom was referred His Excellency's Speech, &c. *New Haven: Hudson & Woodward, Printers.* [n. d.] 8vo, pp. 8. H. 15831

Report of the Committee of the General Assembly at their Special Session, August 25, 1812. On that Part of His Excellency the Governor's Speech which relates to his Correspondence with the Secretary of War, &c. *New-Haven: printed by Walter & Steele.* 1812. 8vo, pp. 14. H. 15832

Report of the Joint Committee, to whom was referred so much of the Governor's Message as relates to The Bank of the United States, the Currency of the Country, ... &c. *New Haven: Jas. F. Babcock, Printer.* 1834. 8vo, pp. 8. BA. 15833

Report of the Committee in Relation to the License Laws. *New Haven.* 1838. 8vo, pp. 8. 15834

Report of the Joint Select Committee, on the Subject of the Public Lands. *Hartford.* 1839. 8vo, pp. 8. 15835

Report of the Joint Committee on Internal Improvements. *New Haven.* 1838. 8vo, pp. 21. 15836

Report on the Joint Standing Committee on the Public Domain; General Assembly, May Session, 1841. [1841.] 8vo, pp. 4. 15837

Report of the Select Joint Committee on the Insane Poor; General Assembly, May Session, 1841. *Hartford.* 1841. 8vo, pp. 14. + May Session. *New Haven.* 1842. 8vo, pp. 7.

Report of the Joint Select Committee, on the Part of the Governor's Message relating to Capital Punishment: together with a Bill in Form for its Abolishment. May Session, 1842. ... *New Haven: printed by Osborn & Baldwin.* 1842. 8vo, pp. 36. H 15839

Report of the Joint Select Committee on the Tariff, May Session, 1842. [1842.] 8vo, pp. 4. 15840

Report of the Joint Select Committee on so much of His Excellency's Message as relates to Resolutions received from the State of Georgia, Alabama, and New Jersey, on the Repudiation of State Debts; General Assembly, May, 1843. *Hartford.* 1843. 8vo, pp. 8. M. 15841

Report of the Comptroller of Public Accounts to the General Assembly, May Session, 1843. *Hartford.* 1843. 8vo, pp. 39. Continued. H. 15842

Report of the Joint Select Committee on so much of the Governor's Message, as relates to Capital Punishment. General Assembly. May, 1850. ... *New Haven: Osborn & Baldwin, Printers.* 1850. 8vo, pp. 35, (1). H. 15843

The Report of a Joint Select Committee of the Joint Legislature of the State of Connecticut, on the Proposed Navy Yard, at New London. ... *New Haven: Babcock & Sizer, Printers.* 1862. 8vo, pp. 16. H. 15844

Report to the Legislature, on the Subject of a Canal by the Ousatonic Valley. *New Haven.* 1822. 8vo. 15845

Report of the Secretary of State relating to the Registration and Returns of Births, Marriages and Deaths, for the Year ending Aug. 7th, 1848. *Hartford.* 1849. 8vo, pp. 26. Continued. H. 15846

A Report on the Geological Survey. *See* Shepard (Charles Upham).

Republican Address To the Free Men of Connecticut. Aug. 30, 1803. 8vo, pp. 16. 15847

Signed Levi Jones, Jun., Clerk.

Resolves and Private Acts of the State of Connecticut, passed May Session, 1838. ... *Hartford: printed by John B. Eldredge.* 1838. 8vo, pp. 84. Continued. H. 15848

Roll of the Senate and House of Representatives, May Session, 1849. ... *Hartford: William H. Burleigh, Printer.* 1849. 8vo, pp. 15. H. 15849

Roll of the State Officers, and Members of the General Assembly of the State of Connecticut; Rules of the Senate, Rules of the House of Representatives, Joint Rules of the Two Houses, and Joint Standing and Joint Select Committees. May, 1856. ... *New Haven: Carrington & Hotchkiss, Printers.* 1856. 8vo, pp. 30, (2). H. 15850

Report of the State Librarian, relating to the Registration of Births, Marriages and Deaths, for the Year ending December 31st, 1854. ... *Hartford: Thomas M. Day, State Printer.* 1855. 8vo, pp. 37. Continued. H. 15851

Rules of the Senate, and Joint Rules of Proceeding of the Senate and House of Representatives of Connecticut. *Hartford.* 1841. 8vo, pp. 9. 15852

Sketch of Connecticut Forty Years since. *See* [Sigourney (L. H.)]

The Security of the Rights of Citizens in the State of Connecticut considered. *Printed at Hartford, By Hudson & Goodwin.* MDCCXCII. 8vo, pp. 102. BA. 15854

Some Reasons that influenced the Governor [of Connecticut] to take and the Councillors to administer the Oath required by the Act of Parliament, commonly called the Stamp-Act. *Hartford: T. Green.* 1766. 15855

Some Seasonable Considerations for the Good People of Connecticut. *New York.* 1694. 15856

Statistics of the Condition and Products of certain Branches of Industry, for the Year ending October 1, 1845. Prepared by Daniel P. Tyler. *Hartford.* 1846. 8vo. 15857

A Statistical Account of the Towns and Parishes in the State of Connecticut. Published by the Connecticut Academy of Arts and Sciences. *New Haven.* 1811. 15858

Vol I., No I, contains "A Statistical Account of the City of New Haven, by T. Dwight."

Steady Habits Vindicated: or a Serious Remonstrance to the People of Connecticut against changing their Government. By a Friend to the Public Welfare. *Hartford: printed by Hudson & Goodwin.* 1805. 8vo, pp. 20. 15859

Their Majesties Colony | of | Connecticut | in New-England | vindicated, | From the Abuses | Of a Pamphlet, Licensed and Printed | at New-York 1694. Intituled, | Some Seasonable Considerations for the | Good People of Connecticut. | Being an Answer Thereunto. | [Texts, 6 lines.] *Boston in New-England.* | *Printed by Bartholomew Green. Anno Dom.* 1694. | 4to, pp. 43.

Reprinted in the "Connecticut Historical Society Collections," Vol. I.

To the General Assembly now in Session at New-Haven. 1800. Folio, pp. 3. 15861

Concerning the purchase of lands.

To the People of Connecticut. "The Extension of Slavery." The Official Acts of Both Parties in Relation to this Question. 8vo, pp. 8. 15862

Transactions of the Society for promoting Agriculture in the State of Connecticut. ... *New Haven: printed by William W. Morse.* 1802. 4to, pp. 21. H. 15863

Words of Patriotism and Wisdom for the Consideration of Freemen of Connecticut. pp. 8. 15864

Relates to the Connecticut Election, April, 1863.

Connecticut River. Excursion on the River Connecticut During a Short Recess. Reported by Amicus Curiæ. [A Poem.] *Boston: Cottons & Barnard.* [1827.] 8vo, pp. 48.

Facts connected with the Application of the Connecticut River Company for Power to Improve the Navigation of the River. [n. p. n. d.] 8vo, pp. 15. W. 15866

Journal of a Convention at Windsor, Vt., Feb. 16, 1825, for the purpose of taking Preliminary Measures to improve the Navigation of Connecticut River. *Windsor.* 8vo. 15867

Journal of the Convention holden at Windsor, Vermont, Sept. 29th and 30th, 1830, for the purpose of taking into consideration subjects connected with the Improvement of the Navigation of Connecticut River. *Windsor, Vt.* 1830. 8vo, pp. 19. 15868

Memorials of the Proprietors of the Upper Locks and Canal on Connecticut River to the General Court [of Massachusetts]. [n. d.] Sheet. M. 15869

Report of the Board of Examiners, appointed by the Connecticut River Steam Boat Company, to inquire into the Causes of the Explosion of the Steam Boat New England, which occurred at Esssex, October 9th, 1833. Published by the Steam Boat Company. *New Haven: printed by Hezekiah Howe & Co.* 1833. 8vo, pp. 24. 15870

Report of the Commissioners concerning the Protection of Fish in the Connecticut River, &c. to the General Assembly, May Session, 1867. ... *Hartford: Case, Lockwood and Company.* 1867. 8vo, pp. 25, (1). Plate. H. 15871

Report of the Connecticut River Company, Jan. 3, 1826. *Hartford.* 8vo. W. 15872

Some Remarks before the Joint Committee on Rivers and Canals, relating to the proposed improvement of Connecticut River and the Extension of the Hampshire and Hampden Canal. *Boston.* 1828. 8vo. W. 15873

Two Reports, made by Committees appointed by the Directors of the Association for Improving the Navigation of Connecticut River above Hartford, etc. *Hartford.* 1825. 8vo.

Connecticutensis. Three Letters to Abraham Bishop containing some Strictures on his Oration, By Connecticutensis. *Hartford.* 1800. 8vo. 15875

Connell (J.) A Letter to the People of the United States, upon the Propriety of establishing an Annual National Jubilee, to commemorate the Adoption of the Constitution of the United States, by John Connell ... . *Wilmington, Del.: printed by Henry Eckel & Co.* 1854. 8vo, pp. 8. H. 15876

Connell (J. M.) Address of the Ohio Soldiers in the Army of the Cumberland to the People of Ohio. (By Col. John M. Connell.) Response of the People of the Northwest Ohio to the Soldiers of Ohio. *Toledo: Pelton & Waggoner, Prs.* 1863. pp. 20. 15877

Connelly (P.) A Letter to the Rt. Rev. Dr. Otey, Bishop of Tennessee, on the Resignation of the Rectorship of Trinity Church, Natchez. By Rev. Pierce Connelly. *Natchez.* 1835. 12mo, pp. 16. M. 15878

[Conner (F.)] The Vindication of Frances Conner, with a Report of her late Case against George W. Matsell, Chief of Police, John W. Latson and James Leonard, combined. With a History of Facts ... *New-York.* 1848. 8vo, pp. 13. H.

Connery (E. D.) American liberty vindicated, and the Right of Foreigners to share its Blessings, defended. An Oration ... By Edward D. Connery. *New York.* 1844. 8vo. 15880

Also: An Oration Delivered on the 2d of October, 1843, before the Washington Prospect Temperance Beneficial Society. 8vo, pp. 8.

Conness (J.) On the Amendment to admit Alabama. Speech of Hon. John Conness ... in the Senate of the United States, June 6, 1868, in Reply to Mr. Doolittle. [*Washington.* 1868.] 8vo, pp. 7. H. 15881

Conness. Speech of Hon. John Conness, delivered at ... San Francisco, on Tuesday evening, October 18, 1864. [n. p. n. d.] 8vo, pp. 7. H. 15882

Conocimiento de los Tiempos Ephemeride del Ano de 1725. ... Al Meridiano ... de Lima, ... con Calendario de las Fiestas y Santos. Por el Doct. D. Pedro de Peralta. [n. p. n. d.] 16mo. Continued. BA. 15883

El conocimiento de los tiempos, ephemeride del Año de 1769 ... Con calendario de las fiestas y Santos ... Va al fin la descripcion de las Provincias del Arzobispado de la Plata. Por el Doct. Don Cosme Bueno ... [n. p. n. d.] 16mo, pages not numbered. Continued. H. 15884

The Conquerors. A Poem, displaying the Glorious Campaigns of 1775, 1776, 1777, &c., &c. *London: H. Satchell.* [1778.] 4to, pp. 72. 15885

See "M. Rev.," LVIII. 237.

Conquerors of the New World. *See* [Helps (Arthur)].

Conquest of Canada. *See* [Warburton (Eliot)].

Conquest of Louisburg. [A Poem.] By John Maylem, Philo Bellum. *Boston.* 1758. 4to, pp. 10. W. 15886

Conquest of Mexico and Peru. By Hernando Cortez and Francisco Pizarro. *London: James Blackwood.* 1860. Fcap 8vo.

See also Mexico.

The Conquest of Santa Fé and the Subjugation of New Mexico, by the Military Forces of the United States; with Documents, embracing the opinions of the Hon. Thomas H. Benton, Gen. Sam. Houston, and others, in reference to Annexation: and a History of Colonel Doniphan's Campaign in Chihauhau. By a Captain of Volunteers. *Philadelphia.* 1847. 8vo, pp. 48. 15888

Conquête du Mexique par Fernand Cortez; suivie de quelques documents officiels sur l'expédition française en 1862; par M ... *Limoges* [*et*] *Paris. F. F. Ardant frères.* 1863. 12mo, pp. 119. Illustrations. 15889

Conqueste van den Indien. *See* Zarate (C.)

Conrad (C. M.) Speech of Hon. C. M. Conrad, of Louisiane, in ... California. ... February 28, 1850. *Washington.* 1850. 8vo, pp. 8. 15890

Conrad (D. H.) A Memoir of the Rev. James Chisholm, A.M., late Rector of St. John's Church, Portsmouth, Pa.; with Memoranda of the Pestilence which raged in that city during the Summer and Autumn of 1855, By David Holmes Conrad. *New-York: Protestant Episcopal Society for the Promotion of Evangelical Knowledge.* 1857. 12mo, pp. 193. Portrait. 15891

Conrad (F. W.) America's Blessings and Obligations. A Discourse delivered in ... Lancaster, Pa., by the Rev. F. W. Conrad, on the day of National Thanksgiving, November 26, 1863. ... *Lancaster: printed by John Baers' Son.* 1863. 8vo, pp. 20. 15892

Conrad. The War for the Unity, and Life of the American Nation. A Thanksgiving Discourse, preached by the Rev. F. W. Conrad, ... May 15, 1864. ... *Chambersburg, Pa.: S. R. Fisher & Company, Printers.* 1864. 8vo, pp. 32. 15893

Conrad (I. A.) The New Diogenes, a Cynical Poem. *Philadelphia.* 1848. 12mo. 15894

Conrad (R. T.) Address delivered before the Historical Society of Pennsylvania, at the Celebration of the 170th Anniversary of the Landing of Penn, on the First Constitution and Government of the State of Pennsylvania. By Robert T. Conrad. [With an Account of the Proceedings at the Dinner, November 8, 1852.] *Philadelphia.* 1853. 8vo. N., P. 15895

Conrad. A Life of Gen. Zachary Taylor; comprising a Narrative of Events connected with his Professional Career, derived from Public Documents and Private Correspondence, by J. Reese Fry, and authentic incidents of his early years, from materials collected by Robert T. Conrad, with an original and accurate portrait and Eleven elegant illustrations Of the Battles of Fort Harrison, Okee-cho-bee, Palo Alto, Resaca de la Palma, Monterey, and Buena Vista, &c., &c., designed by F. O. C. Darley. *Philadelphia: Grigg, Elliott & Co.* 1847. 12mo, pp. 332. 15896

Conrad. Remarks of the Hon. Robert T. Conrad at the Celebration of the Anniversary of American Independence by the Philadelphia Repeal Association, at the Arch street Theatre, July 5, 1841. Published by the Association. *Philadelphia.* 1841. 8vo, pp. 22. 15897

Conrad. The True Aims of American Ambition. An Address Delivered before the Literary Societies of Pennsylvania College. Gettysburg, September 15, 1852. By Robert T. Conrad. *Philadelphia: Crissy & Markley, Printers.* 1852. 8vo, pp. 32. H. 15898

Also: An Address before the Zelosophic Society of the University of Pennsylvania, January 25th, 1842. *Philadelphia.* 1842. 8vo. P. — An Address delivered ... Gerard College, Jan. 2, 1856. *Philadelphia.* 1856. 8vo.

Conrad (Timothy Abbott). Check List of the Invertebrate Fossils of North America, Eocene and Oligocene. By T. A. Conrad. *Washington. May*, 1866. 8vo, pp. iv, 41. 15899

"Smithsonian Miscellaneous Collections," 200.

Conrad. Fossil Shells of California. *See* Blake (W. P.), Vol. II., No. 5802.

Conrad. Fossil Shells of Chile. *See* Gilliss (J. M.)

Conrad. Fossils of the Medial Tertiary of the United States. *Philadelphia.* 1838–40. 2 pts., 8vo. 29 Plates. 15900

Conrad. Fossils of the Miocene Formation of the United States. *Philadelphia: J. Dobson.* 1845. 8vo, 44 l., pp. xvi, 80.

Conrad. Fossils of the Tertiary Formations of the United States. Illustrated by Figures drawn from Nature. By T. A. Conrad. *Philadelphia: J. Dobson.* 1838. 8vo, pp. xvi, 89. 49 Plates. C. 15902

Conrad. Monograph of the Family Unionidæ or Naiades of Lamarck (Fresh Water Bivalve Shells), of North America. Illustrated by Figures Drawn on Stone, and Colored from Nature. By T. A. Conrad. *Philadelphia.* 1836–38. 2 vols., 8vo, pp. 110. 60 Plates. 15903

Conrad. New Fresh-water Shells of the United States, with coloured Illustrations, and a Monograph of the Genus Anculotus of Say; also a Synopsis of the American Naiades. By T. A. Conrad. *Philadelphia: Judah Dobson.* 1834. 12mo, pp. 76. 8 Plates. 15904

Conrad. Notes on American Geology. 1839. 8vo.

Conrad. Nouvelles coquilles d'eau douce des États-Unis, suivis de la monographie du genre anculotus de Say et du tableau synoptique des naiades d'Amérique. De l'Anglais par J. C. Chenu. [Extrait.] *Paris.* 1845. 8vo, 4 l., pp. 36. C. 15905

Conrad. A Synopsis of the Family of Naiades of North America, with Notes, and a Table of some of the Genera and Sub-genera of the Family, according to their geographical distribution, and description of Genera and Sub-genera. By T. A. Conrad. 8vo, pp. 27. 15906

Also: Second Annual Report on the Palæontological Department of the Survey of the State of New York.

Consag (F.) Carta à los Padres Superiores de esta Provincia de Nueva España. Por Fernando Consag, Visitador de las Missiones de Californias. 1748. 4to. 15907

Conscience (A.) André Conscience à la Convention nationale, sur les derniers événements de Saint-Domingue. [Prison de l'Abbaye, 1er thermidor an II. n. p.] *2e année de la république.* 8vo, pp. 69. 15908

The Conscription. Also Speeches of the Hon. W. D. Kelley, of Pennsylvania, in the House of Representatives, on the Conscription; the Way to attain and Secure Peace; and on Arming the Negroes. With a Letter from Secretary Chase. *Philadelphia.* 1863. 8vo, pp. 39, 4. 15909

"The Conscription Act." Will Laboring Men vote for Seymour and invite Civil War, Anarchy, and Ruin? pp. 4. 15910

Relates to the Connecticut Election, April, 1863.

Consecrated Talents; or, the Mission of the Children of the Church ... *New York.* 1852. 15911

Consecration of the Flag, by the Old South Society in Boston. *May* 1, 1861. 8vo, pp. 16. 15912

Le Conseil d'Etat au Peuple et l'Armée de Terre et de Mer de Hayti. [n. d.] 4to, pp. 4. M. 15913

Arrest du Conseil d'Etat du Roy Qui ordonne que les Marchandises qui seront apportées par les Sujets de Sa Majesté de la Coste de Guinée, où des Isles Françoises de l'Amerique, provenant de la vente & du troc des Negres, joüiront de l'exemption de la moitié des Droits d'Entrée dans les Ports du Havre de Grace & de Honfleur, quoique lesdits Ports ne soient pas nommez dans les Lettres Patentes du mois de Janvier 1716 & Arrest du 25. du dit mois. Du 11. Aoust 1716. ... *A Paris, Chez la Veuve Saugrain, à l'entree du Quay de Gèvres, du Côté du Pont au Change, au Paradis.* 4to, pp. 4. 15914

This and the following are in addition to those enumerated in the note to No. 2105, Vol. I.: Arrest du Conseil d'Estat du Roy. Qui Ordonne que, conformément aux Lettres Patentes du mois d'Avril 1717. Toutes les Marchandises du Crû des Isles & Colonies Françoises, même Celles provenantes de la Traite des Noirs, payeront le Droit de Trois pour cent, deû à la Ferme du Domaine d'Occident. *Du* 26 *Mars* 1722. 4to, pp. 4. — Arrest du Conseil d'Estat du Roy qui Ordonne qu'il ne sera plus envoyé de Vagabonds, Gens sans aveû, Fraudeurs & Criminels à la Loüisianne; Que les ordres que Sa Majesté auroit pû donner à ce sujet seront changez, Et la destination desdits Vagabonds faite pour les autres Colonies Françoises. *Du* 9. *May* 1720. *A Paris, De l'Imprimerie Royale.* M.DCCXX. 4to, pp. 4. — Arrest du Conseil d'Estat du Roy, Du quatre Juillet 1722. Portant Reglement Pour la Perception du Droit de Poids ou d'Un pour Cent, sur les Marchandises du Cru des Isles Françoises de l'Amerique, &c. *A Paris, De l'Imprimerie de Georges Jouvenel, Imprimeur des Fermes du Roy, au Bureau General des Aydes.* MDCCXXII. 4to, pp. 8. — Arrest du Conseil d'Estat du Roy, Du premier Decembre 1722. Pour faire passer aux Marchands & Negocians qui font le Commerce aux Isles Françoises, un Dixiéme Sur chaque quantité des Marchandises qui manqueront de celles comprises dans l'Etat de chargement aux Isles, visé par le Commis du Domaine d'Occident, sans que lesdits Negocians puissent encourir les peines portées par la Declaration du 14. Mars 1722. lorsque Sur les Marchandises Comprises dans ledit Etat, il ne manquera qu'un dixiéme de la totalité de chaque nature & qualité desdites Marchandises. ... *De l'Imprimerie de la Veuve & M.-G. Jouvenel, Imprimeurs des Fermes du Roy, au Bureau General des Aydes.* 4to, pp. 4. — Arrest du Conseil d'Estat du Roy, Qui declare en faveur des Habitans de Cayenne & de Saint Domingue, la Declaration du 27. Septembre 1732. Concernant les Cafez provenant des plantations & culture de la Martinique, & autres Isles françoises de l'Amerique y dénommées. Du 20. Septembre 1735. ... *A Paris, de l'Imprimerie Royale.* M.DCCXXXV. 4to, pp. 3. — Arrêt du conseil d'état du Roi, concernant le retour des noirs, mulâtres ou autres gens de couleurs aux Colonies. Du 7 septembre 1777. *Paris: Impr. Royale.* pp. 2 — Arrêt du conseil d'état, qui proroge jusqu'au 1er août 1790, les dispositions de celui du 10 septembre 1786, concernant les primes accordées à l'introduction des noirs de traite françoise aux isles du Vent, à Cayenne et aux Cayes, dans la partie de Sud de Saint-Domingue, ainsi que la liberté provisoire de l'exportation à l'étranger des sucres bruts de l'île de Sainte-Lucie. Du 27 juillet 1789. *Versailles: Impr. Royale.* pp. 3.

Conseil de Liquidation. Doutes et Préventions relativement à la Restitution à faire aux Proprietaires Américains du Navire le New-Jersey. Réponses à ces Doutes. *Paris.* [n. d.] 4to, pp. 46. M. 15915

Also: Motifs qui doivent determiner les Ministres Plénipotentiaires, Français et Américains, etc. *Paris.* [n. d.] 4to, pp. 20. — Nouvelles Questions proposées aux Fondés de Pouvoirs et Défenseurs des Proprietaires du Navire le New-Jersey, etc. Réponses. *Paris.* [n. d.] 4to, pp. 76.

El Consejo de España e Indias à la America Española. *Cadiz.* 1811. 8vo. 15916

El Consejo de la regencia de España y Indias a la America española. *Mexico.* About 1808. Sm. 4to. 15917

Conselhos que dá uno Brasileiro veteranó a todas os seus patricios, que chegarem a este côrte: em que lhes mostra as cousas de que se hão de livrar, para em tudo acerta rem e viverem com honra, etc. *Lisboa na typ. Lacerdina.* 1805. 4to, pp. 16. 15918

A Poem. *See* Silva, II. 96.

Consequences (Not before adverted to) that are likely to result from the late Revolution of the British Empire; with the probable Effects upon the Territorial Possessions, the Commercial Interests, Naval Strength, Manufactures, Population, Resources, Landed Interest, and Public Funds, of Great Britain; and a Comparative Review of the Strength, Resources, and Public Credit, of the late Belligerent Powers, at the Conclusion of the Peace. *London: G. Wilkie.* MDCCLXXXIII. 8vo, pp. 33.

The Consequences of trade, &c. [No title-page. *London?* 17—.] 8vo, pp. 3–35. B. 15920

On the woolen trade and the scheme of Samuel Webber.

El Conservador, Periódico de politica, religion, literatura, teatros y avisos. No. 1. *Mejico.* 1859. Folio. 15921

The Conservative; a Quarterly Publication, April 1, 1860. Reuben Vose, Editor and Proprietor. [*New York.*] 1860. 32mo, pp. 160. 15922

The Considerable Advantages of a South-Sea Trade to our English Nation. Humbly offer'd with other Particulars, to the Consideration of this Present Parliament, partly from the Information of divers French Officios, lately taken by one of Her Majesty's Ships, and who had traded in those Seas. *London: S. Popping.* 1720. 8vo, pp. 16. J.C.B. 15923

Consideraciones sobre peligros de independencia, por un Ingerto. *Habana.* 1821. *See* [Quesada (Rafael de)].

Consideraciones sobre la situacion politica y social de la republica Mexicana, en el año 1847. *Mexico.* 1848. 8vo, pp. 56.

CONSIDÉRANT (Victor). Au Texas. [Communication confidentielle adressée à des amis.] *Paris: imp. de Grimaux.* 1854. 8vo. 2 Maps. 15925

CONSIDÉRANT. Au Texas. 2e éd. contenant 1o. rapport a mes amis; 2o. bases et statuts de la société de colonisation europe-américaine, au Texas; 3o. les bases d'un premier établissement sociétaire. *Bruxelles: société de colonisation.* 1855. 12mo, 2 l., pp. 326. 4 Tables, and Map. 15926

CONSIDÉRANT. European Colonization in Texas; an Address to the American People. By Victor Considerant. *New York: Baker, Godwin & Co.* 1855. 8vo, pp. 38. H. 15927

CONSIDÉRANT. Three Hundred Millions of Dollars saved in Specie by the Meaning of a Word. Letter to Secretary McCulloch from Victor Considerant. [*La Conception, Texas.* 1867.] Large 8vo, pp. 16. H. 15928

Consideratie,|Overgelevert by de Heeren|Bewinthebberen van de Oost-Indische|Compagnie.|Aen de Edele Groot-Mogende Heeren Staten van|Hollant ende West-Vrieslant,|Waeromme het voor de selve Compagnie|onmogelick ende ondienstigh is, om met de West-Indische|Compagnie te treden in handelinge, om beyde onder een Octroy ende Societeyt gebracht te worden. |*In 'sGraven-Hage,*|*By Ian Fransen, Boeckverkooper*, 1644.|4to, 4 l. 15929

Relates to the union of the East and West India Companies.

Consideratien|Ende|Redenen der E, Heeren|Bewind-hebberen, vande Geoctroijeerde West-|Indische Compagnie inde Vergaederinghe vande Ed.|Hoog- Moghende Heren Staten Generael deser Ver-|eenigde Vrye Nederlanden overgelevert, nopen-|de de teghenwoordige deliberatie over den|Treves met den Coning van Hispanjen.|Midtsgaders|Conscientieuse Bedenckingen op dese Vrage,|Ofmen in goeder conscientie mach Treves maecken |met den Coning van Spangjen.|*Ghedruckt te Haerlem, by Adriaen Rooman, Boeckdrucker*|*inde Jacobyne-straet, inde vergulde Parsze.* 1629.| 4to, pp. 32. 15930

Relates to the truce with the King of Spain as it regards the commerce and navigation to America.

Consideratien|Ende|Redenen der E, Heeren|Bewind-hebberen vande Geoctroijeerde West-|Indische Compagnie inde vergaderinge vande Ed. Hoog-|Moghende Heren Staten Generael deser Vereenigde Vrije Ne-|derlan den overgheleverdt, nopende de teghenwoordighe|deliberatie over den Treves met den Ko-|nink van Hispangjen|Midtsgaders|Conscientieuse Bedenkingen op deese Vrage,|Ofmen in goeder Conscientie mach Treves maecken met|den Conink van Spangjen.|Ende eenighe Consideratien op den Treves.|Noch|De Remonstrantie van syn Koninklyke Majest. van Bohe-|men, inde Vergaderinge van de Ed. Hoog. Mogh: Heeren|Staten Generael in-ghegeven.|*Ghedruckt te Haerlem, by Adriaen, Rooman Boeckdrucker*|*inde Jakobijnestraet, inde vergulde Parsze.* 1629.| 4to, pp. 32. 15931

A reprint of the previous title.

... [As above] in goeder Conscientie mach Tceves ... [as above] Vergaderninge ... . *Ghedruckt te Haerlem, by Adriaen Rooman* ... . 1629. 4to, pp. 32. 15932

These two editions are to be distinguished by the two misprints in the second title, "Tceves" and "Vergaderninge", and by numerous differences in the text.

Consideratien|Op de|Cautie|Van|Portugael.| [n. p.] *Gedruct Anno* M.VIC.XLVII.| 4to, pp. 15. 15933

These "Considerations" on the pledge of Portugal relate to Brazil.

Consideratien op de Memorie aan HH. MM. geadresseerd door John Adams ... 19 Apr. 1781. [n. p. 1781.] 8vo.

On the advantages for the Dutch of concluding a treaty of commerce with the United States.

Consideratien tot wederlegginge van de voorstellingen door de Heer Mr. Nicholas Muys van Holy, opgestelt in zyne Memorie, om de Negotie van Oost en West-Indische actien. [n. p. n. d.] 4to, pp. 12. + [Another Edition.] 4to, pp. 20. 15935

Titles from Muller, Nos. 85 and 85a.

Consideration of the Claims and Conduct of the United States. *See* [Bliss (Henry)], Vol. II., No. 5924.

Considerations addressed to all persons of Property in Great Britain, concerning the Present Disposition of the Americans towards this Country. *London: W. Owen.* MDCCLXXVII. 8vo, pp. 17. J.C.B. 15936

This writer states that, as the Americans are united among themselves, "it is imprudent in Britain to persist in the attempt to reduce, because it is impracticable to effect the reduction of that extensive country by force."

Considerations addressed to Professors of Christianity of every Denomination, on the Impropriety of Consuming West India Sugar and Rum, as produced by the oppressive Labour of Slaves. *London: Ritchie and Sammells.* 1792. 8vo. P. 15937

Considerations addressed to the Members of the Yearly Meeting of Friends, of Philadelphia. ... Reprinted from the Philadelphia Edition of 1846. *Boston: printed by S. N. Dickinson & Co.* 1847. 8vo, pp. 86. H. 15938

Considerations against continuing the Great Canal West of the Seneca: addressed to the Members-Elect of the Legislature of the State of New-York: by Peter Ploughshare. ... *Utica.* 1819. 8vo, pp. 29. BA., S. 15939

Considerations Against Laying any New Duty upon Sugar; wherein Is particularly shewn, That a New Imposition will be ruinous to the Sugar Colonies, insufficient for the Purposes intended, and greatly conducive to the Aggrandisement of France. ... *London: J. Roberts.* M DCC XL IV. 8vo, Title, pp. (iv), 30. BA. 15940

Considerations and Documents relating to the Claims of Massachusetts for Expenditures during the Late War. Washington, January, 1818. *Washington: printed by E. De Krafft.* 1818. 12mo, pp. 78. H. 15941

Considerations and Remarks on the Present State of the Trade to Africa; with some Account of the British Settlements in that Country, and the Intrigues of the Natives since the Peace; candidly stated and considered. In a Letter addressed to the People in power more particularly, and the Nation in general. By a Gentleman, who resided upwards of Fifteen Years in that Country. *London: Robinson & Roberts.* MDCCLXXI. 8vo, pp. 88. J.C.B. 15942

Considerations For and Against a South-American Expedition. *London: J. Budd.* 1805. 8vo, pp. 83. 15943

Considerations générales sur les trois classes qui peuplent les Colonies Françaises. *Paris.* 1814. 8vo. 15944

Considedations in Answer to the Pamphlet, containing Mr. Madison's Instructions to Mr. Munroe. *Albany: Printed by E. and E. Hosford.* 1807. 8vo, pp. 26. BA. 15945

Considerations in Favour of the Construction of a Great State Road, from Lake-Erie to the Hudson River. By a Citizen of New York. [Nicholas F. Beck.] *Albany: Websters & Skinners.* 1827. 8vo, pp. 48. 15946

Considerations in Reference to the Establishment of a National School of Mines as a Means of increasing the Product of Gold and Silver Bullion. *Washington.* 1867. 8vo, pp. 17. H.

Considerations offered to Parliament, showing that those Charters relating to the Plantations were taken away upon quite Different Reasons from those in England. *London.* [About] 1690. Folio, pp. 4. 15948

Considerations On Behalf of the Colonists. In a Letter to a Noble Lord. *London: J. Almon.* MDCCLXV. 8vo, Title, pp. 52. + The Second Edition. *London: J. Almon.* M DCC LXV. 8vo, Title, pp. 52. 15949

Signed F. A.

Considerations on an Insolvent Law [for Massachusetts]. *Boston: Bradford and Read.* 1814. 8vo, pp. 44. BA. 15950

Considerations on Both Sides; or, Remarks on the Conduct of Great Britain and Holland at the Present Critical Conjuncture. *London.* 1747. 8vo. 15951

Considerations on certain Political Transactions, 1774. *See* [Leigh (*Sir* Egerton)].

Considerations on Emancipation. 1788. 8vo. 15952

Considerations on Fixing the Supplies, Ways and Means and Taxes for 1781. *London.* 1781. 15953

Considerations on Lowering the Value of Gold Coins, Within the Province Of the Massachusetts Bay. [*Boston:*] *Sold next to the Prison in Queen-Street.* [1761.] 8vo, pp. 27. BA., H., M.

In answer to a project of the Lieutenant Governor, Thomas Hutchinson, published in the Boston "Evening Post," December 14, 1761, and republished in this pamphlet, pp. 3–8. Issued, probably, by D. Fowle.

Considerations on Slavery, and the Expediency of its Abolition. *Burlington.* 1773. 8vo. P. 15955

Considerations on Slavery in the Southern States. *Baltimore.* 1835. 8vo. 15956

Considerations on the Abolition of Slavery, and the Slave Trade, upon Grounds of Natural, Religious, and Political Duty. *Oxford.* 1789. 8vo, pp. 169. 15957

See "M. Rev.," LXXX. 561.

Considerations on the Abolition of the Common Law in the United States. *Philadelphia: William P. Farrand and Co.* 1809. 8vo, pp. 71. BA., P. 15958

Considerations on the alleged necessity of hiring foreign Troops, and the present Method of recruiting the Army: with a Plan for augmenting the Army, and regulating the Militia. *London: Elmsley.* 1778. 4to. 15959

See "M. Rev.," LVIII. 239.

Considerations on the American Inquiry. *London: J. Wilkie.* MDCCLXXIX. 8vo, pp. 56. + The Second Edition. *London: J. Wilkie.* MDCCLXXIX. 8vo, pp. 56. J.C.B. 15960

This tract has reference to the Parliamentary inquiry into the conduct of the army under General Howe. The writer thinks the colonies may be subdued. That not one-fifth of the colonists desire a separation from Great Britain, and that it is disgraceful for any Englishman to propose an acknowledgment of American independence. *See* "M. Rev.," LXI. 230.

Considerations on the American Stamp Act, and on the Conduct of the Minister who planned it. *London: W. Nicoll.* MDCCLXVI. 8vo, pp. 38. B. 15961

The author recommends the repeal of the Stamp Act as the only means to reconcile the colonists to their mother country, and to restore peace, plenty, and cordiality to every part of the British empire. *See* "M. Rev.," XXXIV. 65.

Considerations on the American Trade, Before and Since the Establishment of the South-Sea Company. *London: J. Roberts.* M DCC XXX IX. 8vo, pp. 31. C. + The Second Edition, with Additions. *London.* [*Ibid.*] 8vo, pp. 36. 15962

Written by a Jamaica merchant of some credit and reputation in London. An answer was published by Dr. Houstoun in 1741–2. Houstoun's "Memoirs," (1747), p. 226. It was followed by "Don John Further Displayed; being a Supplement to Considerations on the American Trade. *London: J. Roberts.* MDCCXL." 8vo, pp. 43.

Considerations on the American War. Addressed to the People of England. *London: T. Beckett.* 1776. 8vo, pp. 60.

"The industrious, enterprising, and useful men, who first planted and settled in our American colonies are described by the author as men whose flagitious crimes had rendered them objects of public punishment, or whose turbulent and refractory dispositions made them enemies to every established government." *See* "M. Rev.," LIV. 235.

Considerations on the Approaching Dissolution of Parliament: Addressed to the Elective Body of the People; with some Account of the Existing Parties ... *London: Walter.* 1790. 8vo. S. 15964

Considerations on the approaching Peace. 1762. 8vo. 15965

Partly relating to American possessions.

Considerations on the Attorney-General's propositions for a Bill for the Establishment of Peace with America. By an Old Member of Parliament. ... *London: J. Debrett.* MDCCLXXXII. 8vo, pp. 58. BA. 15966

"The writer is anxious for peace, but considers that it would be a degradation to the country for the offer to come from Parliament." *See* "M. Rev.," LXVI. 385.

Considerations on the Bank of North-America. *Philadelphia: Printed by Hall and Sellers.* 1785. 12mo, pp. 35. P. 15967

In favor of the bank.

Considerations on the Bill Concerning the British Sugar-Colonies in America. *London.* M DCC XXXI. 8vo, pp. 24.

Considerations on the Bill for a General Naturalization, as it may conduce to the improvement of our Manufactures and Traffic, and to the Strengthening or endangering the Constitution, exemplified in the revolutions that have happened in this Kingdom by inviting over Foreigners to settle amongst us. With an Enquiry into the nature of the British Constitution, and the Freedom or Servitude of the lower class of people, in the several changes it has undergone. *London: Printed for W. Owen.* 1748. 8vo, pp. 71. J.C.B. 15969

The question is discussed of permitting foreigners to settle in the colonies. The conclusion arrived at by the writer is, that it is not advantageous, and that "it is more eligible to increase our own people than to invite over strangers, which is to be chiefly done by encouraging matrimony." The subject of holding slaves is also discussed, and arguments for and against it presented.

Considerations on the Bill now depending before the Honorable House of Commons, for Encouraging the Importation of Pig and Bar Iron from America, &c. [n. p. 1736?] Folio, pp. 3. 15970

Considerations on the Bill now depending in Parliament, concerning the British Sugar-Colonies in America. Wherein all the Arguments for the Support of the said Bill are considered. In a Letter to a Member of Parliament. *London: printed for J. Peele.* MDCCXXXI. 8vo, pp. 24. H. 15971

Considerations on the Bill now depending in the House of Lords, relating to the Trade between the Northern Colonies and the Sugar Islands. *London.* 1732. 8vo. C. 15972

Considerations on the British Commerce with Reference Particularly to British India, the United States of America, and the Slave Trade. *London.* 1817. 8vo. 15973

In the "Pamphleteer," XI. 263–275.

Considerations on the Choice of Public Rulers; on the Extent of their Powers; and on the Best Means of securing the Advantages and Reforming the Abuses of Popular Elections. *New York: T. S. Arden.* 1805. 8vo, pp. vi, 156. C., M. 15974

Considerations on the Claims and Conduct of the United States, respecting their North-eastern Boundary, and of the Value of the British Colonies in North America. *London: Hatchard.* 1826. 8vo, pp. 110. Map. 15975

"Reprinted in the British Provinces."—RICH.

Considerations on the Claims of the "Southern Tier of Counties." *Albany.* 1825. 8vo. C. 15976

Considerations on the Commencement of the Civil War in America; Addressed to the People of England, &c. by an American. *London: Printed for J. Williams.* 1775. 8vo, 2 l., pp. 46. BA. 15977

Considerations on the Dependencies of Great Britain. With Obervations on a Pamphlet, intitled The Present State of the Nation. *London: Printed for J. Almon.* MDCCLXIX. 8vo, pp. 92. BA., H. 15978

See "M. Rev.," XL. 253.

Considerations on the Dispute Now depending before The Honourable House of Commons, between the British Southern, and Northern Plantations in America. In a Letter to ——. *London: J. Roberts.* 1731. 8vo, Title, pp. 30. 15979

The dispute here referred to was between the New England and other Colonies, and the British West Indies. It relates to the Sugar Act. *See* "Gent's Mag." for 1731.

Considerations on the Eastern Diocese. By a Presbyter of the Diocese of Massachusetts. *Boston.* 1837. 8vo, pp. 35.

Considerations on the Election of Counsellors humbly offered to the Electors [of Massachusetts. n. p.] 1761. 8vo, pp. 8.

Considerations on the Emancipation of Negroes and the Abolition of the Slave-Trade. *London: J. Johnson.* M.DCC.LXXXVIII. 8vo, Title, pp. 41. C., H. 15982

By a West India planter. *See* "M. Rev.," LXXVIII. 161.

Considerations on the Embargo Laws. *Boston.* 1808. 8vo, pp. 16. M. 15983

Consideration on the Employment of the Press, &c. *Charleston.* 1826. pp. 16. 15984

Considerations on the Establishment of a Uniform System of Bankrupt Laws throughout The United States. *Washington City: Printed by Rapine and Elliot.* 1815. 8vo, pp. 12. BA.

Considerations on the Expediency of a Spanish War. *See* [Wilkes (John)].

Considerations On the Expediency of Admitting Representatives. *See* [Maseres (Francis)].

Considerations|on the|Expediency|of Procuring An Act of Parliament|For the Settlement of the|Province of Quebec.| *London: printed in the Year* M.DCC.LXVI.| 4to, pp. 35. H.

Considerations on the Fatal Consequences of abolishing the Slave Trade, in the Present Situation of Great Britain. *London: J. Debrett.* 1789. 8vo, pp. 36. 15987

See "M. Rev.," LXXXI. 91.

Considerations on the Foundations, Ends and Duties of the Christian Sabbath, and the Late Measures for enforcing its Observance. *Utica.* 1829. 8vo. 15988

Considerations on the Great Western Canal. *See* [Haines (Charles G.)]

Considerations on the Importance of Canada, and the Bay and River of St. Lawrence; and of the American Fisheries Dependant on the Islands of Cape Breton, St. John's, New-Foundland, and the Seas Adjacent. Addressed to the Right Hon. William Pitt. *London: W. Owen.* 1759. 8vo, pp. 23.

Considerations on the Imposition of $4\frac{1}{2}$ per cent. collected on Grenada, and the Southern Charibbee Islands, by Virtue of His Majesty's Letters Patent, Under Pretence of the Prerogative Royal, without Grant of Parliament. *London: J. Almon.* 1774. 8vo, pp. 440. 15990

Considerations on the Impropriety and Inexpediency of Renewing the Missouri Question ... . By a Pennsylvanian. *Philadelphia: M. Carey & Son.* 1820. 8vo, pp. 88. BA. 15991

Considerations on the Indian Trade. Originally published in the Detroit Gazette. *Detroit: Printed by Sheldon and Reed.* 1821. 8vo, pp. 15, 10. 15992

Considerations on the Late Act for Prohibiting all Commercial Intercourse with the Rebellious Colonies: Or, the Weakness of America Exposed. *Edinburgh: Cha. Elliot.* M,DCC,XXIV. 8vo, pp. 19. S. 15993

The object of the writer is to show that the colonies cannot exist if Great Britain enforces the non-intercourse act, and that, "when an effectual stop is put to their export trade, the boasted power and strength of the rebellious colonies must soon be annihilated, and they themselves be rendered sensible of their own folly, weakness, and total inability to subsist for any length of time, as a nation divided from, or in a state of war with Great Britain."—*Page* 7.

Considerations on the Management of the Late Secret Expeditions, and the Conduct of the Court of France. In a Letter to * * *. *London: W. Webb.* MDCCXL. 8vo, Half-Title, Title, pp. 28. J.C.B. 15994

Considerations on the Measures, 1774. *See* [Robinson (M.)]

Considerations on the Mode and Terms of a Treaty of Peace with America. Second Edition. *London: Edward & Charles Dilly.* MDCCLXXVIII. 8vo, pp. 30. + *Philadelphia, Reprinted: Hall and Sellers.* MDCCLXXIX. 8vo, pp. 16. BA., P. + *Hartford: Hudson and Goodwin.* MDCCLXXIX. 8vo, pp. 23. BA., C.

Considerations on the National Debt, and the Net Produce of the Revenue, &c. *London.* 1784. 8vo, pp. 65. 15996

Considerations on the Nature and Extent of the Legislative Authority of the British Parliament. *See* [Wilson (James)].

Considerations on the Necessity of establishing an Agricultural College, and having more of the Children of Wealthy Citizens, educated for the Profession of Farming. *Albany: printed by Websters and Skinners.* 1819. 8vo, pp. 42. H. 15997

Considerations on the Negro Cause, commonly so called. Addressed to the Right Honourable Lord Mansfield. By a West Indian. *London: J. Dodsley.* 1772. 8vo, pp. 46.

The case was that of James Sommersett. The author of these "Considerations," says that he dislikes the term "slavery," preferring the word "property." He shows

his lack of regard for the principles of freedom by maintaining that a man's property, *i. e.*, his slave, is no more entitled to liberty, and remains as much the property of his master when in England as when in a country where slavery is permitted. *See* "M. Rev.," XLIII. 152.

Considerations on the Penal Laws against Roman Catholics in England, and the New Acquired Colonies in America. In a Letter to a Noble Lord. By a Country Gentleman. *London: J. Dodsley.* 1764. 8vo, pp. 70. C. 15999

See "M. Rev.," XXX. 412.

Considerations on the Points, &c. 1766. *See* [Pownall (T.)]

Considerations on the Practicability and Utility of a Central Rail Road from Pottsville to Danville. 1830. 8vo. C. 16000

Considerations on the Present Crisis of Affairs as it respects the West India Colonies, and the Probable Effects of the French Decree for emancipating the Negroes, pointing out a Remedy for preventing the calamitous Consequences in the British Islands. ... *London: J. Johnston.* 1795. 8vo, Half-Title, Title, pp. 76. C., H. 16001

See "M. Rev.," XVII. 453.

Considerations on the Present Decline of the Sugar Trade, and on the Means which are Proposed by the Refiners of London for Re-instating it. *Privately printed.* 1782. 4to. 16002

Considerations on the Present German War. *See* [Mauduit (S.)]

Considerations on the Present Peace, as far as it is relative to the Colonies, and the African Trade. *London: W. Bristow.* MDCCLXIII. 8vo, pp. iv, 68. 16003

Considerations on the Present Situation of Great Britain, 1784. *See* [Champion (Richard)], Vol. III., No. 11833.

Considerations on the Present State of Affairs, 1778. *See* [Dalrymple (A.)]

Considerations on the Present State of ... Sugar Colonies. 1784. *See* [Allen (James)], Vol. I., No. 834.

Considerations On the Present State of the Nation as to Publick Credit, Stocks, the Landed and Trading Interests. With a Proposal for the Speedy Lessening the Publick Debts, and Restoring Credit, in a manner Consistent with Parliamentary Engagements. *London.* 1720. 8vo, pp. 70. 16004

Included in a Catalogue of America.

Considerations on the Propriety and Necessity of annexing the Province of Texas to the United States. By a Revolutionary Officer. *New-York.* 1829. 8vo. C., S. 16005

Considerations on the Proposed Removal of the Seat of Government, addressed to the Citizens of Maryland. By Aristides. *Annapolis: Frederick Green.* 1786. 8vo, pp. 62. J.C.B. 16006

Considerations on the Propriety of imposing Taxes, 1765. *See* [Dulaney (Daniel)].

Considerations on the Provisional Treaty with America. *See* [Kippis (Andrew)].

Considerations on the Relative Situation of France. *See* Clavière *and* Brissot, No. 13517.

Considerations on the ... Sabbath, and the Late Measures for enforcing its Observance. *Utica.* 1829. S. 16007

Considerations on the Slavery Question, addressed to the President of the United States. [n. p. n. d.] 8vo, pp. 15. 16008

Considerations on the Society and Order of Cincinnati. *See* [Burke (Æ.)], Vol. III., No. 9279, and Vol. IV., No. 13118.

Considerations on the Sovereignty, Independence, Trade and Fishery of New Ireland, (formerly known by the Name of Nova Scotia.) 12mo. W. 16009

Considerations on the State of our Northern Colonies, their Interest with Great Britain and Ireland, proved Reciprocal and Inseparable. *London.* 1763. 8vo. 16010

Considerations on the State of the British Fisheries in America, and their Consequence to Great Britain, with Proposals for their Security by the Reduction of Cape Breton, &c. *London.* 1745. Folio, pp. 8. 16011

Considerations on the State of the Sugar Islands and on the Policy of enabling Foreigners to lend Money on Real Securities in those Colonies, in a Letter addresesd to the Right. Hon. Lord North; by a West India Planter. *London: S. Bladon.* MDCCLXXIII. 8vo, pp. 28. H. 16012

Considerations on the Subject of a Communication between the Atlantic and Pacific Oceans, by means of a Ship-Canal across the Isthmus, which connects North and South America

... . By a Citizen of New York, formerly a U. S. Consul at Lima, and for the Ports of Peru. *Georgetown, D. C.* 1836. 8vo, pp. 28. 2 Maps. H. 16013

Considerations on the Subject of Finance. *Philadelphia.* 1781. 8vo. 16014

Considerations on the Times. *London: Printed for J. Almon.* MDCCLXIX. 8vo, 2 l., pp. 40. 16015

Considerations on the Trade, &c. *See* McKerrell (R.), and [Whately (Tho.)]

Considerations on this question, "What should be an Honest Englishman's Endeavour in the Present Controversy between Great Britain and the Colonies. *London: J. Wilkie.* 1775. 8vo. 16016

See "M. Rev.," LII. 175.

Considerations on this Question; whether the British Government acted wisely in granting to Canada her Present Constitution. *Montreal.* 1810. 8vo. 16017

Considerations Preliminary, to the fixing the Supplies, the Ways and Means, and the Taxes, for the Year 1781. Addressed to the Minister and the Public. *London: J. Almon.* 1781. 8vo. 16018

Considerations Relating to the laying any Additional Duty on Sugar From the British Plantations. Wherein is shewn, That such Duty will be injurious to the Commerce and Navigation of this Kingdom, ruinous to our Sugar Colonies, beneficial to those of France, and insufficient for the Purposes intended. *London: M. Cooper.* 1746. 8vo, pp. 38. + The Second Edition. To which is added a Supplement. *London: M. Cooper.* 1746. 8vo, pp. 38. + *London: John Clarke.* 1747. 8vo, pp. 31. 16019

Considerations relative to a Southern Confederacy. *See* [Berguin (H. K.)], Vol. II., No. 4862.

Considerations Relative to the North American Colonies. *See* [Fothergill (John)].

Considerations respecting the Lawfulness of War under the Gospel Dispensation; addressed to the Teachers and Professors of Christianity in the United States of America. *New York:*

Samuel S. & William Wood, Collins & Brother. [1848.] 8vo, pp. 16. 16020

Signed on behalf, and by direction of a meeting of the Representatives of New York Yearly Meeting, the 4th of 1st month, 1848. Richard Carpenter, Clerk.

Considerations sur l'Admission des Navires Neutres aux Colonies Françoises de l'Amérique en tems de guerre ... . 1779. 18mo, pp. 82. S. 16021

Considérations sur l'Amerique Espagnole, ou appel a la Véritié, sur les causes, l'Esprit et le but de La Révolution. Par un Américain ... *Paris: Chez Rodriguez.* 1817. 8vo, pp. (2), iii, 56. 16022

Considerations sur les differends des couronnes de la Grande Bretagnes et de France, touchant l'Acadie et autre parties de l'Amerique Septentrionale. Le tont fondé sur les Memoires des Commissaires des deux puissances, publiés tout nouvellement et redigé en quatre lettres, ecrites par un Français à un Hollandais. *A Franckfort et à la Haye.* 1756. Sm. 8vo, pp. 172. C. 16023

Considerations sur les effets qu'ont produit en Canada, la conservation des établissemens du pays, les mœurs l'éducation, etc. des ses habitans et les consequences qu' entraineroient leur decadence par rapport aux interets de la Grande Bretagne. Par un Canadien, M. P. P. ... *Montreal: James Brown.* 1809. 8vo, Title, pp. ii, 51. BA. 16024

For an answer, *see* Cuthbert (Ross).

Considerations sur l'état actuel de la question relative à l'Independance des Colonies Anglo-Amériquaines, 1782. 16025

Considerations sur l'etat present de l'Amerique du Sud, et sur l'arrivée à Paris de M. Hurtado, Agent de Colombie. *Paris.* 1824. 8vo. 16026

Considérations sur la Guyane française et sur les moyens de donner à cette colonie une impulsion créatrice. *Paris.* 1835. 4to. 16027

Considerations sur une loi passée en Amerique, imposant un droit de dix huit piastres du tonneau sur les navires Français. *Paris.* 1820. 4to, ½ sheet. 16028

Considerations towards a General Plan of Measures for the English Provinces. *New York.* 1756. 8vo. 16029

Considerations upon The Act of Parliament whereby A Duty is laid ... on Molasses, and ... on Sugar of foreign Growth, imported into any of the British Provinces, ... *Boston: Printed by Edes & Gill.* M, DCC, LXIV. 8vo, pp. 28. BA. 16030

Considerations upon the American Enquiry. *See* [Dallas (Robert), *Junr.*]

Considerations upon the French and American War. In a Letter to a Member of Parliament. *London: J. Almon.* MDCCLXXIX. 8vo, pp. 44. B., J.C.B. 16032

Considerations Upon the Present State, &c., 1739. *See* [Littleton (George), *Lord*].

Considerations upon the Question. What should be an Honest Englishman's Endeavour in this Present Controversy between Great Britain and the Colonies? 1780. 16033

Considerations upon the Rights of the Colonists to the Privileges of British Subjects, Introduc'd by a Brief Review of the Rise and Progress of English Liberty, and concluded with some Remarks upon our Present Alarming Situation. *New-York: Printed and Sold by John Holt, at the Exchange.* 1766. 8vo, 2 l., pp. 27. S. 16034

Addressed to T— H— Esq. The pagination of this rare tract is irregular.

Considerations upon the White Herring and Cod Fisheries. *London.* 1789. 8vo. 16035

Considerations which demand the Attention of Farmers, Mechanics, and Friends of the American System. By a Citizen of the State of New-York. *New York: J. Seymour.* 1828. 8vo, pp. 16. G. 16036

Considerations which may tend to. *See* [Young (*Mr.*)]

A Consolation for our Grammer Schooles: Or a faithfull and most comfortable Incouragement, for laying of a sure Foundation of all good Learning in our Schooles, and for prosperous building thereupon. More especially for all those of the inferiour sort, and all ruder Countries and Places: Namely for Ireland, Wales, Virginia, with the Sommer Islands, and for their more speedy attaining of our English Tongue by the same labour, that all may speak one and the same Language, for the perpetual benefit of those our Nations, and of the Churches of

Christ. *London: Printed by Richard Field, &c.* 1622. 4to, pp. 84. 16037

"With an Epistle to the right Honourable and right worshipful the Governour, Councell, and Companie for Virginia, and of the Sommer Islands, that beginning with the Lord, and carefully planting and watering of his sacred Religion, they may find a more happy Growth and Increase, and evermore sound and lasting Joy to their own Souls.—Especially for drawing the poor Natives in Virginia, and all other of the rest of the Rude and Barbarous from Sathan to God.—John Brinsley.—With the Judgment and Approbation of Dr. James Usher and Dr. Daniel Featly, March 16. 1620." *See* "Bib. Amer. Primor.," p. 66.

Consolatory Thoughts on American Independence. *See* [Tod (Thomas)].

Consolidation. An Account of Parties in the United States, from the Convention of 1787 to the Present Period. *Columbia, S. C.: printed by Black & Sweeney.* 1824. 8vo, Title, pp. 17, 4, 4. 16038

Circular of the Consolidated Silver Mining Company, Reese River and Union Districts, Nevada. ... [*Boston.* 1865.] 8vo, pp. 48. H. 16039

A Conspectus or Clear View of the Laws in any way affecting the Titles and Conveyances to Lands in the Eastern Part of the Province [of Maine], which have occasioned Controversies and Disputes, being claimed by virtue of Ancient Grants from the Native Indians. 1753. pp. 4. 16040

Relates to the Plymouth and Pippicot companies.

Conspiracy against the General Freedom of the People. *New York.* 1843. 12mo, pp. 98. 16041

The Conspiracy Trial for the Murder of the President. *See* Lincoln (A.)

The Conspiracy Trials of 1826 and 1827. A Chapter in the Life of Jacob Barker. With an Introduction by R. D. Turner. *Philadelphia: G. W. Childs.* 1864. 12mo, pp. 328. Portrait.

Conspirations trahisons et calomnies devoilées et dénoncées par plus de dix mille Français réfugiés au Continent de l'Amérique. *Paris: Forouge.* 1794. 8vo, pp. 78. J.C.B. 16043

Relates to the revolution in Hayti.

Constable's Pocket-book; or, a Dialogue between an Old Constable and a New. Being a Guide in Serving all Warrants, Observing Orders of Courts, Summoning Town Officers and Town Meetings, Collecting Rates and Assessments, Serving Writs, &c., in their Keeping the Peace, &c. By N. B. Second Edition, corrected. *Boston: Printed, and are to be Sold at the Bible in Cornhill.* 1727. 12mo. 16044

Constable's Miscellany ... . *Edinburgh: Constable & Co.* 1826–34. 78 vols., 12mo. 16045

Voyage of Madame Godin along the River of the Amazons in the year 1770, Vol. XI. 307–334; Roberts' Excursions in Central America, Vol. XVII.; General Register of Politics and Literature in Europe and America for 1827, Vol. XXII; Trueba y Cosio's Life of Cortes, Vol. XLIX.; his Conquest of Peru, Vol. LXII.; Wilson and Bonaparte's American Ornithology, Vol. LXVIII.–LXXI.

CONSTABLE (A.) Speech of Hon. Albert Constable, of Maryland, on the Bill making Appropriation for Harbors and Rivers. Delivered in the House of Representatives ... March 11, 1846. *Washington.* 1846. 8vo, pp. 13. H. 16046

CONSTANCIO (F. S.) Archivio dos conhecimentos uteis, periodico mensal, destinado a promover a agricultura e a industria do Portugal e do Brasil, redigido por Francisco Solano Constancio. *Paris: Aillaud.* 1837. 8vo. 16047

CONSTANCIO. Armazem de conhecimentos uteis nas artes e officios, ou Collecção de receitas, e segredos de utilidade universal, destinado a promovêr a agricultura e a industria de Portugal e do Brasil. *Paris.* 1838. 8vo. + *Paris: Aillaud; Monlon.* 1855. 12mo. 16048

CONSTANCIO Historia do Brasil, desde o seu descobrimento por Pedro Alvarès Cabral, até a abdicação do imperador D. Pedro I. *Paris: Aillaud.* 1838. 2 vols., 8vo. Map. + *Paris: Livrario Portugueza de J. P. Aillaud.* 1839. 2 vols., 8vo, pp. ii, 506; 483. Map. C. 16049

CONSTANCIO. Remonstrances des négociants du Bresil contre les insultes faites au pavillon portugais, et contre la saisie violente de plusieurs de leurs navires par les officiers de la marine anglaise; accompagnées d'autres pièces intéressantes; traduits du portugais et de l'anglais par F. S. Constancio. *Paris: Mme Goullet.* 1814. 8vo. 16050

CONSTANT (L.) Texas. Das Verderben dutscher Auswanderer in Texas unter dem Schutze der Mainzer-Vereins. *Berlin: G. Reimer in Comm.* 1847. 8vo, pp. 32. H. 16051

CONSTANTIA, *pseudonym.* *See* Murray (*Mrs.*)

CONSTANTINE *and* EUGENE. *See* [Kelsall (Charles)].

Constituiçao politica do Imperio do Brasil seguida do acto addicional, da lei da sua interpretaçao e de outras analysada, por um jurisconsulto e novamente annotada, por Jose Carlos Rodriguez. *Rio de Janeiro.* 1863. 8vo, pp. 227. 16052

See also under "Brazil," Vol. II.

Constanzo (Salvador). Ensayos politicas y literarios.

Constituiçao estatutos geraes da Maç: no Imperio do Brasil. *Rio de Janeiro.* 1865. 8vo, pp. 102. 16054

Constitucion de la Republica Federal de Centro-America dada por la Asamblea Nacional Constituyente en 22 de Noviembre de 1824. *Impresa en Guatemala Ano de* 1825. 16mo, 2 l., pp. 49, (7). BA. 16055

Constitucion de la sociedad democratica de los amigos de America. *Nueva York: imprenta de S. Hallet.* 1864. 8vo, pp. 10. 16056

Constitucion del colegio del Espiritu Santo, publicada para satisfaccion de los padres de familia que han honrado al establecimiento. Año de 1848. *Mexico.* 1848. Sm. 8vo, pp. 39.

Constituciones de la Cofradia del glorioso Principe de los Apóstoles San Pedro, erigida el dia 30 de Julio de 1665 en la Santa Iglesia Metropolitana, entónces Catedral, de este Arzobispado de Carácas, confirmadas por el Rey nuestro Señor en Real Cédula de 22 de Junio de 1785. *Carácas.* 1818. 4to, pp. 26. 16058

Constitucion de las provincias unidas en Sud-America, sancionada y mandada publicar por el soberano Congreso general constituyente en 22 de Abril de 1819. *Buenos Ayres.* 1819. 8vo, pp. vi, 71. + [*Reimpreso en Madrid.* 1822.] 16mo, pp. 116. 16059

Constitucion Federal de los Estados-Unidos de America, con dos discursos del General Washington. *Mexico.* 1823. 12mo, pp. 66. 16060

Constituciones de la sagrada religion de la Charidad, de S. Hipolyto martyr, fundada en las Indias occidentales por el P. Bernardino Alvarez. *Mexico: Maria de Ibarra.* 1749. 4to, 11 l., pp. 358. 16061

Constituciones formadas para el gobierno y direccion de la piadosa compañia de cocheros y lacayos. *Mexico.* 1826. 12mo, pp. 26. 16062

Constitutiones Ordinis Fratrum Eremitarum Sancti Augustini. *Mexico.* 1587. 8vo. 16063

Constituciones, que para el mejor Govierno, y Direccion de la real Casa del Señor S. Joseph de Niños expósitos de esta Ciudad de México, formo el Illmo. Sr. Dr. D. Alonso Nuñez de Hara, y Peralta. del consejo de S. Mag. Arzobispo de esta Santa Iglesia Metropolitana. *Mexico: Jos de Jaurequi.* [1774.] Folio, 2 l., pp. 56. 16064

A letter at the end of the volume is dated, *Mexico, 8 de Noviembre de* 1774.

Constitvciones | Synodales del | Arçobispado de los | Reyes en el Perv. | Hechas y ordenadas por el Illustrissimo y Reve | rendissimo Señor Don Bartholome Lobo Guerrero Arçobispo de la dicha Ciu- | dad de los Reyes, del Consejo de su Magestad. | Y pvblicadas en la Synodo Diocesana qve sv | Señoria Illustrissima celebro en la dicha Ciudad en el año del | Señor de 1613. | *En Los Reyes.* [*Lima*]: | *Por Francisco del Canto.* | *Año de* M.DC.XIIII. | Folio, 6 l., Text, 94 l., 6 l. 16065

Constituciones synodales fechas por el illo señor D. Pedro de Valencia, obispo desta ciudad de Nuestra Señora de la Paz. 1620. Folio, pp. 32. 16066

Constitvciones | Synodales | del Arçobispado | de los Reyes en | el Pirv. | Hechas, y ordenadas por el | Illustrissimo, y Reuerendissimo señor Dotor don Fernando | Arias de Vgarte Arçobispo desta ciudad de los Reyes, | del Consejo de su Majestad. | Pvblicadas en la Synodo | Diocesana que su señoria Ilustrissima celebró en la dicha | ciudad el Año del Señor de 1636. | [Arms.] Con Licencia | *Impresso en Lima por Geronymo de contreras, Año de* 1637. | Folio, 2 l., pp. 46. 3 l. 16067

Constitvciones | Synodales | de el Obispado de la | Civdad de Gvamanga, | celebradas en Concilio | diocesano | por el Ilvst.mo y R.o Senor | D. D. Christoval de Cas- | tilla y Zamora. | En el mes de Jvnio de 1672. | [Vignette.] Cñ licencia. *En Lima. Por Geronio de Contreras.* 1677. 4to, 12 l., pp. 1–158, followed by 16 leaves not numbered, Index, 32 l. 16068

A portion of this book is in the Quichuan language.

Constitutiones Synodales, del Obispado de Arequipa hechas

por Don Antonio de Leon, su Obispo, en la Synodo diocessana que celebro año de 1684. *Lima.* 1688. Folio. 16069

Constituciones Synodales establecidas por el Sr. D. Augustin Rodriguez Delgado, Obispo de la ciudad de nuestra Señora de la Paz. Para el govierno ecclesiastico y regimen sacro-politico de su Obispado concluydas en el dia XXIII de Enero MDCCXXXVIII. *Lima: Con Licencia del Real Govierno.* 1739. Folio, pp. vii, 137, with additions irregularly paged. 16070

Constituciones synodales del Arçobispado de los Reyes en el Peru. Hechas y ordenadas por el Ill. y. Rev. S. D. Bartholomé Lobo Guerrero, y publicadas en la Synodo Diocesana del año de 1613. *En los Reyes* [*Lima*]. 1754. Folio. 16071

First printed in 1614. *See* No. 16065. This volume contains also a reprint of the Synod of 1636; and various edicts of the Archbishop of Lima, issued in the same year in which the volume was printed.

Contistvciones [*sic*] y Ordenanças. *See* Lima.

Constitution. *See* Constitutions *and* Zea.

The Constitution a Failure, because radically Defective in its Duty to God, its Duty to its Neighbour, and its Duty to itself. [n. p. 1855.] 8vo, pp. 7. 16072

Constitution and Frame of Government of the Free and Independent State and Commonwealth of New Ireland, &c. *Printed by R. Aitkin, for the Free and Independent State of New Ireland.* 16073

Constitution and Laws, with Sketches of some of the prominent Public Characters, in a Series of Letters from Washington, by a Foreigner in 1817–18. 12mo. 16074

The Constitution and Mr. Motley. *See* [Evans (Rowland E.)]

The Constitution and the Clergy. A Plea for the Freedom of the Church in Missouri. [n. p. n. d.] 8vo, pp. 20. 16075

The Constitution and the Union. Speeches delivered at the American Union Breakfast, given in Paris, May 29, 1861, at the Grand Hotel du Louvre. Reprinted from "Galignani's Messenger" [in French and English]. *Paris: Printed by E. Brière.* 1861. 8vo, pp. 24. 16076

The Constitution expounded, respecting its Bearing on the Subject, of Slavery. In Two Parts. Part First. *New York.* 1850. 8vo, pp. 7. H. 16077

Constitution of a Society for abolishing the Slave Trade; With the Several Acts of the Legislatures of Massachusetts, Connecticut, and Rhode Island for that purpose. *Providence.* 1789. 8vo. W. 16078

The Constitution of the Boston Tontine Association, MDCCXCI. [*Boston.* 1791.] 12mo, pp. 20. 16079

Constitution, &c., of "The Century." Adopted January 13, 1847. *New York.* 1847. 12mo, pp. 8. + Adopted 1857, amended 1859. *New York.* 1862. 18mo. 16080

Constitution of the Company of Scotland trading to Africa and the Indies. *Edinburgh.* 1696. 4to, pp. 3. J.C.B. 16081

Relates to Darien.

Constitution of the Federal Tontine Association. *Philadelphia.* 1792. 8vo, pp. 15. M. 16082

The Constitution of the Female Association of Cincinnati for the Benefit of Africans. *Cincinnati: Morgan, Palmer & Co.* 1817. 12mo, pp. 7. 16083

Constitution of the Republic of Mexico, and of the State of Coahuila and Texas. *New York.* 1832. 8vo. 16084

See also "Mexico," and "Texas."

Constitution of the Roman Catholic Churches of North Carolina, South Carolina and Georgia. *Charleston.* 1826. 12mo. P.

The Constitutions of the several Independent States of America; The Declaration of Independence; The Articles of Confederation between the said States; The Treaties between His Most Christian Majesty and The United States of America. Published by order of Congress. *Philadelphia: F. Bailey.* M. DCC. LXXXI. Sm. 8vo, pp. 226. C., H. 16086

200 copies printed. The first authoritative and original printed text of these important documents. "In Congress, December 29, 1780. Resolved, That a Committee of three be appointed to collect and cause to be published two hundred correct copies of the Declaration of Independence, etc. (as in title above), to be bound together in boards, etc. Extract from the Minutes. Charles Thompson, Secretary."—*Page* 2. "This interesting publication contains a greater portion of unsophisticated wisdom and good sense, than is perhaps to be met with in any other legislative code that was ever yet framed. It is, in short, the book which may be considered as the Magna Charta of the United American States."—*M. Rev.*, LXVIII. 184. It is scarcely necessary to say that this important work has been repeatedly reprinted. We have given below a chronological series of so many as have come under our notice. The titles vary somewhat, but the substance is the same.

The Constitutions [as above]. *Philadelphia printed; London reprinted, with an Advertisement By the Editor, For J. Stockdale, in Piccadilly; and sold by J. Walker.* M DCC LXXXII. 8vo, pp. viii, 168. 16087

This is the first English edition. It was reprinted with additions, as below:

The Constitutions of the several Independent States of America; the Declaration of Independence; and the Articles of Confederation between the said States. To which are now added, the Declaration of Rights; the Non-Importation Agreement; and the Petition of Congress to the King delivered by Mr. Penn. With an Appendix, containing the Treaties between His Most Christian Majesty and the United States of America; the Provisional Treaty with America; and (never before Published) an Authentic Copy of the Treaty concluded between their High Mightinesses the States-General, and the United States of America. The whole arranged, with a Preface and Dedication, By the Rev. William Jackson. Second Edition. *London: Printed for J. Stockdale.* 1783. 8vo, Portrait of Washington, 2 l., pp. xxix, In Congress, 1 l., pp. 472, List of Presidents, 1 l.

The portrait is devoid of any resemblance to the subject. "The American Constitutions differ in many particulars, some partaking more, others less of the nature of a pure democracy; but they are all valuable, because *all favourable* to liberty."—*Preface.*

The Constitutions of the several Independent States of America; The Declaration of Independence; The Articles of Confederation between the said States; The Treaties between His Most Christian Majesty and the United States of America. With an Appendix, containing An Authentic Copy of the Treaty concluded between their High Mightinesses the States-General and the United States of America, and the Provisional Treaty. Published by Order of Congress. *Philadelphia Printed: London, Reprinted, with an Advertisement by J. L. De Lolme, J. Walker, J. Debrett.* MDCCLXXXIII. 8vo, pp. viii, 189, (2). Portrait of Franklin, and Map. 16089

Constitutions of the several Independent States of America, the Declaration of Independence, Treaties, &c. *Dublin.* 1783. 8vo. 16090

With a curious preface, or advertisement. This Irish edition is scarce.

A Collection of the Constitutions of The Thirteen United States of North-America. ... Published by Order of Congress. *Philadelphia, Printed. Glasgow: Re-printed By John Bryce.* M, DCC, LXXXIII. 16mo, Title, pp. 257. C. 16091

The Constitutions of the several independent States of America; ... The Second Edition. *Boston: Norman and Bowen.* M,DCC,LXXXV. 12mo, pp. 181, 29. S. + *New York.* 1786. 12mo. C. 16092

Constitution of the United States of America, Framed by the General Convention at Philadelphia. ... *Philadelphia: Thomas Stephens.* 1795. 8vo, pp. 29. 16093

The Constitution of the United States of America; as proposed by the Convention, held at Philadelphia, September 17, 1787. *Philadelphia: John Oswald.* 1799. 8vo, pp. 27.

The Constitution or Frame of Government of the United States of America as Reported by the Convention of Delegates, begun and held at Philadelphia, May 14–Sep. 17, 1787, with the Resolutions of the Legislature of Massachusetts upon the same. *Boston: Adams and Nourse.* 1787. 8vo, pp. 32. M., W.

The Constitution, as Reported by the Convention of Delegates begun at Philadelphia on the first Monday of May, 1787, and continued to the 17th day of September following. *Boston: Thomas & John Fleet.* [About 1787.] 12mo, pp. 16. C. + *Portsmouth, N. H.* 1787. 12mo, pp. 16. C. + Together with the Articles of Amendment, adopted by the Congress of said States, 1789. *Windsor, Vt.: Alden Spooner.* 1790. Sm. 4to, pp. 23.

The Constitutions of the United States, according to the Latest Amendments. To which are Annexed the Declaration of Independence; and the Federal Constitution, with the Amendments thereto. This edition contains the Constitution of Vermont, not in any former one. *Philadelphia: Caurley, Stewart & Co.* M,DCC,XCI. 12mo, 2 l., pp. 176. 16097

The Constitution of the United States of America, established March 4, 1789, to which is added the Declaration of their reason for separating from this country, made in Congress July 4th, 1776. And a Resolution of Congress Expressive of their High Sense of the Service of Mr. Thomas Paine. *London: D. I. Eaton.* 1794. 8vo, pp. 30. 16098

The Constitutions of the United States, ... This Edition contains the late Constitutions of New-Hampshire, Kentucky and Tennessee, not in any former one. *Philadelphia: W. Woodhouse.* M,DCC,XCVI. 12mo, pp. 250. 16099

The Constitutions of the Sixteen States which compose the Confederated Republic of America, according to the latest

Amendments. To which are prefixed the Declaration of Independence; Articles of Confederation; and the Constitution of the United States, with all the Amendments. *Newburgh: Printed by David Denniston, for Self and H. Craig.* 1800. 12mo, pp. 288. 16100

The Constitutions of the United States, according to the Latest Amendments: To which are prefixed, The Declaration of Independence; and the Federal Constitution, with the amendments. This edition contains the late Constitutions of Vermont, Delaware, Georgia, and Kentucky, with the Regulations for the Government of the Territory north-west of the River Ohio; also, the Amendments to the Constitution of Maryland;—not in any former Edition. *Philadelphia: Printed for Robert Campbell.* 1800. 12mo, pp. xxiv, 5–272. + *Philadelphia.* 1802. 8vo. C. + *Philadelphia.* 1804. 16mo. C. + *Philadelphia: Wm. Duane.* 1806. 8vo, pp. 307. + *Philadelphia.* 1813. 16101

The Constitutions of the United States; According to the Latest Amendments. ... And the Bill of Rights of the State o, Virginia. *Winchester, Va.: Jonathan Foster.* 1811. 8vo, pp. 334, 1 l. C. 16102

The Constitutions of the United States ... *New York.* 1813. 12mo. + *Washington.* 1819. + *New York.* 1820. 16mo, pp. 464. C. 16103

Constitution of the United States ... With the Rules and Orders of the House of Representatives. *Washington.* 1821. 12mo. W. 16104

The Constitution ... the Rules of the Senate, and the House of Representatives: with Jefferson's Manual. ... *Washington.* 1828. 12mo. 16105

Constitution of the United States of America: Rules of the House of Representatives, Joint Rules of the Two Houses and Rules of the Senate, with Jefferson's Manual. ... *Washington: Thomas Allen.* 1837. 8vo, pp. 222. + *Washington.* 1839. 8vo, pp. 78. + *Washington.* 1852. + *Washington.* 1857. 8vo. + *Washington.* 1859. 8vo. + And Barclay's Digest of the Rules of Proceeding in the House. Compiled by J. M. Barclay. *Washington.* 1860–61. 8vo. + *Washington.* 1863. 8vo, pp. 216.

The Constitutions of the United States. ... *Lexington, Ky.* 1823. 12mo. 16107

The Constitution of the United States and Massachusetts. *Boston: H. Crampton.* 1835. 8vo, pp. 43. Portrait of Washington. 16108

The Constitutions of the United States and ... New York. ... *Albany.* 1823. 18mo, pp. 161. + *Boston: H. Crampton.* 1835. 8vo, pp. 32. + *Albany.* 1868. 18mo, pp. 78.

Constitution of the United States of America, the Constitution of the Commonwealth of Pennsylvania and Rules for the Government of the House of Representatives of said Commonwealth. *Harrisburg.* 1842. 8vo. 16110

The Constitution of the United States ...; the Proximate causes of its Adoption and Ratification; the Declaration of Independence; the Prominent Political Acts of George Washington; and other Interesting Matter: with an Alphabetical Analysis of the Constitution, by a Citizen. *Washington: printed by J. and G. S. Gideon.* 1846. 12mo, pp. cxxviii, 225. 16111

The Constitution ... With the Acts of Congress, Relating to Slavery, Embracing, The Constitution, The Fugitive Slave Act of 1793. The Missouri Compromise Act of 1820, The Fugitive Slave Law of 1850. And the Nebraska and Kansas Bill. Carefully Compiled. *Rochester: J. M. Dewey.* [n. d.] 8vo, Title, pp. 43. 16112

The Constitutions of the several States of the Union and United States, including the Declaration of Independence and Articles of Confederation. ... *New York: A. S. Barnes & Co.* 1852. 8vo. + *New-York:* [*Ibid.*] 1854. 8vo. + *New York:* [*Ibid.*] 1858. H. + [*Ibid.*] 1866. 8vo, pp. 602. 16113

Constitution of the United States and Acts of Naturalization. *Rochester, N. Y.* 1855. 16114

Constitution of the United States, and Declaration of Independence. With the last Census. *Boston: J. P. Jewett & Co.* 1855. 16115

Constitution of the United States. *Baltimore.* 1860. 12mo, pp. 34. + *Philadelphia.* 1860. 16mo. + [*Ibid.*] 1861. + *Chicago, Ill.: John R. Walsh.* 1863. 16mo, pp. 64. + *Boston: Taggard & Thompson.* [n. d.] 32mo, pp. 36, 12. + *Boston. T. O. H. P. Burnham.* 1862. 18mo. 16116

The most important of the later editions has the following title:

Constitution of the United States of America with the Amendments thereto: to which are added Jefferson's Manual of Parliamentary Practice and the Standing Rules and Orders for conducting business in the House of Representatives and Senate of the United States. Digest of the Rules of the House of Representatives, U. S. The joint Rules of the Two Houses and of so much of Jefferson's Manual as under the Rules governs the House; of Precedents, of orders and usages of the Houses; together with such portions of the Constitution of the United States, Laws of Congress, and Resolutions of the House as relate to the proceedings of the House, and the Rights and Duties of its Members. Compiled and published by John M. Barclay, Journal Clerk of the House of Representatives. *Washington.* 1865–6. 8vo, pp. 254, 233. c. 16117

Constitutions des Treize États-Unis de l'Amerique. *A Philadelphia; Et se trouve A Paris, chez Ph. D. Pierres.* 1783. 8vo, 2 l., pp. 540. 16118

Printed in France, and the first edition in French, with woodcut of the eagle and stars and stripes on the title. There are copies on large paper, 4to, and on papier velin, de la fabrique de M. Reveillon. The translation is attributed to the Duc de la Rochefoucault. *See* Franklin's Works, by Sparks, IX. 503, 508, 523. It was reissued with a new title, as below:

Constitutions des Treize Etats Unis de l'Amérique; avec la Déclaration de l'Indépendance; les Articles de Confédération; les Traités entre Sa Majesté Très-Chrétienne, les États Généraux des Pays-Bas Unis, le Roi de Suede et les États Unis de l'Amérique. *A Philadelphie et à Paris.* 1783. 8vo, Title, pp. 540. c. 16119

Constitutions des Treize Etats Unis de L'Amerique. *Paris.* 1792. 2 vols., 8vo, Title, 1 l., pp. 324; 317. 16120

This edition contains the Constitution of 1787, and the acts of the first session of Congress, 1789.

Constitution des Etats Unis, suivie de Conseils de Washington au Peuple Americaine. *Paris: Dentu.* 1862. 8vo, pp. 32.

The Constitution of '76. By a Member of the Staunton Convention. [*Printed at Winchester, Va.* n. d.] 8vo, pp. 64.

The Constitution of the United States; also a Document entitled "The Constitution of the Confederate States." Arranged in parallel columns, with the differences indicated, for convenient reference and comparison. *Cincinnati: E. Watkin.* 1862. 8vo, pp. 24. 16123

De Constitutie eenpariglyk geaccordeerd by de Algemeene Conventie gehouden in de stad von Philadelphia, in 't Jaar 1787 ... . Vertaald door Lambertus de Ronde ... . *Albany: Gedrukt by Order van de Federal Committee, Door Charles R. Webster.* 1788. 8vo, pp. 32. B. 16124

Constitutie voor de Vereenigde Staeten van Amerika. Den 17. September. *Dordrecht.* 1787. 8vo. 16125

Die Constitution der Vereinigten Staaten von America, mit ihren Verbesserungen, und die der republik von Pennsylvanien. Nebst der Erklärung der Unabhängigkeit der Vereinigten Staaten und die Abschiedsaddresse von General George Washington. *Reading, (Penn.): C. M'Williams.* [About 1823.] 16mo, pp. 156. C. + *Philadelphia.* 1846. 8vo. 16126

Constitution and Plan of a Society for affording Relief to the Families of Deceased Ministers; with Address to the Clergy. [*Hartford.* n. d.] 8vo, pp. 8. 16127

Constitution of the S. B. Union for the Sake of the Union. 1862. 18mo, pp. 29. 16128

A Constitution of the K. C. G., with Gen. Carrington's Report. 1863. 16129

The Constitutional Advocate. By which from the Evidence of History and of Records, and from the Principles of the British Government, every Reader may form his own Judgment concerning the Justice and Policy of the Present War with America. Addressed to the People at large, and humbly submitted to the Consideration of their Representatives. *London: W. Flexney.* MDCCLXXVI. 8vo, pp. 47. + *London: J. Flexney.* 1778. 8vo, pp. 47. J.C.B. 16130

"Several ancient charters, statutes, and law authorities, are here enlisted in the defence of the colonies, and accompanied with some good arguments and just conclusions."—RICH, I. 239. Sanguine for the colonies, but nothing new on the subject.

A Constitutional Answer. *See* Wesley (John).

Constitutional Considerations on the Power of Parliament to levy Taxes on the North American Colonies. *London.* 1766. 4to. 16131

In this rare pamphlet the author undertakes to prove that the colonies ought not, in sound policy, to be allowed a representation in Parliament, urging, as a reason, their numbers, extent, situation, and advantages of every kind, being such that they only want a government properly regulated to become the masters of Europe.

The Constitutional Duty of the Federal Government to abolish American Slavery: an Expose of the Position of the Abolition Society of New-York City and Vicinity. *New-York: published by the Abolition Soc. of New-York City, etc.* 1855. 16mo, pp. 16.

Constitutional Law: Comprising the Declaration of Independence; the Articles of Confederation; the Constitution of the United States; and the Constitutions of the several States composing the Union, viz. New Hampshire, Massachusetts, Rhode Island, Connecticut, Vermont, New York, New Jersey, Pennsylvania, Delaware, Maryland, Virginia, North Carolina, South Carolina, Georgia, Louisiana, Kentucky, Ohio, Tennessee, Mississippi, Indiana, Illinois, Alabama, Maine. *Washington: Gales and Seaton. Dec.* 1820. 12mo, 2 l., pp. 409. C. + *Philadelphia.* 1823. 24mo. 16133

Constitutional Law. Decisions of the Supreme Court of the United States, relating to Tax on Bank Stock. *New York: J. Smith Homans.* 1863. 8vo, pp. 63. 16134

Constitutional Manual, 1856. *See* [Hazard].

The Constitutional Means For Putting an End to the Disputes between Great-Britain and the American Colonies. *London: Printed for T. Becket and P. A. De Hondt.* M DCC LXIX. 8vo, pp. 33. BA. 16135

Constitutional Queries, humbly addressed to the Admirers of a late Minister. *London.* [n. d.] 8vo. 16136

Partly on American topics.

Constitutional Reform. *Utica.* 1846. 8vo, pp. 7. 16137

A review of A. B. Johnson's "Manual."

Constitutional Reform. *See* [Bigelow (John)], Vol. II., No. 5302.

The Constitutional Right of the Legislature of Great Britain, to Tax the British Colonies in America, impartially Stated. *London: J. Ridley.* M DCC LXVIII. 8vo, pp. iv, 60. 16138

"However impartial this writer may pretend to be, he is an imperious asserter of the right he professes to state so fairly."—*Monthly Review.* The "Letter to the Earl of Hillsborough," 1769, contains an Appendix in answer to this pamphlet. *See* Appendix, No. 1792*a*, I. 239.

The Constitutional Rights of Citizens. [n. p. n. d.] 8vo, pp. 15. J.C.B. 16139

Consists chiefly of extracts from public laws, and from the writings of eminent men as to constitutional rights.

Constitutional Security to the Citizens' Rights of Property: and the Principles of Public Faith. ... [*Boston. January,* 1802.] 8vo, pp. 20. S. 16140

A scarce pamphlet relating to Massachusetts paper-money. Also: Report on the Petitions of Franklin and Wrentham, concerning Bills of Credit of 1780. 1802. 8vo.

The Constitutional Text Book: containing Selections from the Writings of Daniel Webster; the Declaration of Independence; the Constitution of the United States; and Washington's Farewell Address. With Copious Indexes. Liberty and Union, now and forever, one and inseparable. One Country, One Constitution, One Destiny. For the Higher Classes of Educational Institutions, and for Home Reading. *New York and Boston: C. S. Francis and Company.* 1854. 12mo, pp. 503, (1).

Constitutional Union Party. A Calm Appeal to the Friends of American Industry, especially in the States of Pennsylvania and New Jersey. [Constitutional Union Party. *Washington.* 1860.] 8vo, pp. 8. H. 16142

Also: Bell and Everett. Rooms of the National Executive Committee of the Constitutional Union Party, 357 D Street. Washington, D. C., June 12, 1860. [*Washington.* 1860.] 8vo, pp. 16. H.

The Constitutionalist: addressed to Men of All Parties in the United States. By an American. [William Barton, A.M.] *Philadelphia: H. Maxwell.* 1804. 8vo, pp. 49. BA. 16143

The Constitutionalist; or Amendments of the Constitution proposed by the Council of Censors, supported by the Writings and Opinions of James Wilson, LL.D. ... Also by the Writings and Opinions of other Eminent Citizens of the United States. *Montpellier, Vt.: Printed by Walton and Goss.* 1814. 8vo, pp. 36. BA. 16144

CONSTITUTIONALIST, *pseudonym.* Bigotry exposed, or a Calm Discussion of the Abolition Question. *New York.* 1835.

CONSTITUTIONALIST, *pseudonym.* The Alarm Bell. No. 1. By a Constitutionalist. *New York: Baker & Godwin.* 1863. 8vo, pp. 16. 16146

The Constitutionality of Slavery, 1848. *See* [Bowditch], Vol. II., No. 7007.

Constitutionality of Federal Tax upon Business forbidden by State Law. Argument for Government. [n. p. 1866.] 8vo, pp. 15. H. 16147

The Constitutionality of the Embargo Laws, established by Precedent. *Philadelphia: Printed by John Binns.* 1809. 4to, pp. 7. BA., C. 16148

Constituzione della Società Italiana in Nuova York. 1840.

Consular Establishments. Report of the Secretary of State (E. Livingston) in relation to the Consular Establishment of the United States. *Washington.* 1832. 8vo. c. 16150

General Instructions to the Consuls and Commercial Agents of the United States. Prepared under the direction of the Department of State. *Washington.* 1855. 8vo. c. 16151

The Consumers of West India Sugar the Supporters of West India Slavery. [n. p. n. d.] 12mo, pp. 12. BA. 16152

Conta dos Negocios da Repartiçao dada á Asemblea Geral Legislativa per Bento da Silva Lisboa, ministro e secretario d'Estado. *Rio de Janeiro.* 1833. 4to, pp. 39. 16153

The Contest in America. *See* [Mitchell (*Dr.*)]

Contestacion al Impreso del Sr. Conde de Oreilly publicado en Enero último. [*Habana: P. Palmer.* 1812.] 4to, pp. 32.

"Daté et signé à la p. 14. '*Habana y febrero* 18 *de* 1812. El conde de casa Barreto y de St. Crux de Mopox."'—LECLERC, No. 391.

Contestacion á los versos titulados Satira. El Baile en Carácas en 1854. *Carácas.* 1854. 8vo, pp. 10. 16155

Contestacion a un articulo sobre la republica de Chile publicado en el Mercurio de Nueva-York fecha 12 de Julio de este año; copiado en el Espiritu publico del Jueves 16 de Octubre del mismo. *Mexico.* 1828. 8vo, pp. 24. 16156

Contestacion a las observaciones que bajo el nombre de "unos Peruanos," se han publicado en un folleto contra los medidas del Gobierno sobre naturalizacion de extranjeros. *Lima.* 1840. 4to, pp. 37. 16157

Contestacion á la carta publicada por unos accionistas sobre el Banco nacional. *Buenos Aires.* 8vo, pp. 16. 16158

Contestacion, ou la Carta del Indis Patriotæ, con algunas reflexiones sobre el dialogo, entre El Entusiasta Liberal, y Ele Filosophia Rancio, y sobre las notas anonymas con que La Salido reimpreso el manifesto de Dr. Jose Alvarez de Toledo. *Philadelphia.* 1812. 8vo. 16159

Contestacion Rapida al Discurso Opinado que Pronunció un M.·. con Motivo de la Plancha que el G.·. Cons.·. Circuló a las ll.·. simb.·. del rito esc.·. sobre el nuevo Juramento exigido y demas de su contenido. *Habana: Impresso en la oficina del G.·. Or.* 5821. [1821.] 4to, pp. 15. 16160

CONTI (Natale). Universæ historiæ sui Temporis Libri XXX, ab Anno 1545 ad Annum 1581. *Venetia.* 1572. + *Venezia: Zenaro.* 1589. 4to. W. 16161

Contains some notice of Vespucius.

The Continental Key of the Liberties of America. In Three Parts. A Poem. *New York.* 1776. 8vo. 16162

Continental Money. A Review of the Article on Continental Money in Harper's Magazine for March, 1863, signed Antiquarian, March 13th, 1863. [*Privately printed.*] 1863. 8vo, pp. 8. 16163

The Continental Monthly. Devoted to Literature and National Policy. Vol. I. *New York.* 1862. 8vo. Continued.

Continente|Americano,|Argonauta|de las Costas|de|Nueva-España,|y|Tierra-Firme,|Islas, y Baxos|de esta Navegacion,|Longitud,|y Altura de Polo,|de sus Puertos,|y Noticias de estas Habitaciones. [*Cadiz.* 1728.] 12mo, 3 l., pp. 61. J.C.B.

"The author says, in his 'Introduction,' that he entered the Royal service at the age of fourteen, and served by land and sea from 1695 to 1725, during which period he collected, principally from personal observation, the information contained in this work."—RICH.

Continuacion de los documentos oficiales relativos a la celebracion del tratado de Paz entre el Gobierno de la provincia de Buenos Aires, y el General D. Justo José de Urquiza, Gobernador y Capitan-General de la provincia de Entre Rios. *Buenos Aires.* 1853. 8vo, pp. 24. 16166

Continuacion del manifiesto por los oficiales del batallon ligero de Tarragona. *Imprenta de Campe.* 1820. 4to. 16167

Relates to insubordination in Cuba.

Continuation of an Appendix, embracing Historical Sketches of the Town of Alstead, from 1826 to 1836. *Keene, N. H.: B. Cooke.* 1836. 8vo, pp. 12. 16168

A Continuation of Hudibras, in Two Cantos. Written in the Time of the Unhappy Contest between Great Britain and

America in 1777 and 1778. *London: Printed in the Year* MDCCLXXVIII. 12mo, 2 l., pp. 76. J.C.B. 16169

A parody, with comments on the Declaration of Independence.

"Nor shall the muse forget to notice
The names of Adams, Hancock, Otis,
With more for pride of heart to rankle in
As Cushing, Silas Deane and Franklin,
Whose sage descendants we shall see
Shine forth in the next century."—*Canto I.*

A Continuation of the Exercises in Scurrility-Hall. *Philadelphia: Printed in the Year* MDCCLXV. 12mo, pp. 7. P. 16170

Also: A Continuation of the Exercises in Scurrility Hall. With a dialogue between the Professor and Sir John Brute.

Et tu Brute!
He swore they had brought him a Flander's mare.
1 BUR., H. R., 271.

[*Philadelphia:*] *Printed in the Year* MD. CC. LXV. 12mo, pp. 7. P.—A Continuation of the Exercises in Scurrility Hall. Libels, Letters, Circular-Letters, Remonstrances, Manifestos, and the Widow's Mite.—Scurr.—[*Philadelphia:*] *Printed in the Year* MD. CC. LXV. 12mo, pp. 8. P.—A Continuation of the Exercises in Scurrility Hall. Woe to the City, Woe to the People, Woe to the Priest.—Josephus. [*Philadelphia:*] *Printed in the Year* MD, CC, LXV. 12mo, pp. 7. P.—A Continuation of the Exercises in Scurrility Hall. With the Reasons of their Publication. [*Proverb, Philadelphia:*] *Printed in the Year* MD, CC, LXV. 12mo, pp. 7. P.—A Continuation of the Exercises in Scurrility Hall. [*Philadelphia:*] *Printed in the Year* MD, CC, LXV. 12mo, pp. 8. P. For the remainder of this series, *see* "The Substance of Exercises," *and* "A Dialogue."

Continued Corruption, 1768. *See* [Bollan]. Vol. II., No. 6210.

CONTOOCOOK. Catalogue of Contoocook Academy. Contoocook, N. H. ... 1856–7. *Concord.* 1857. 8vo, pp. 15. H:

Report on the Contoocook Valley Plumbago Mine, by Charles T. Jackson, M.D. ... With Assays, Letters and Certificates, from Various Reliable Sources, and By-Laws of the Company. *Boston: Geo. C. Rand & Avery, Printers.* 1864. 8vo, pp. 19.

CONTOSTAVLOS (A.) A Narrative of the Material Facts in Relation to the Building of the Two Greek Frigates. By Alexander Contostavlos. *New York.* 1826. 8vo, Title, pp. 88. BA. + Second Edition. *New York.* 1826. 8vo, pp. 86. 16173

See also Bayard (W.), Duer, and Sedgwick.

Contraband Christmas. With Illustrations by Hoppin. *Boston: E. P. Dutton & Co.* 186–. 16mo, pp. 104. 16174

Contrabands and Vagrants. 12mo, pp. 42. 16175

Contract|d'Association|des Iesvites|au trafique de Canada.| Pour apprendre à Paul de Gimont, l'vn|des donneurs d'aduis pour les Iesvites contre|le Recteur et Vniversité de Paris, et à ses|semblables, pourquoy les Iesvites|sont depuis peu arriuez en | Canada. | M DC. XII.* 8vo. + [*Paris: imprimé par D. Jouast, pour Tross.* 186 .] 4to, pp. 8. + Seconde édition. *Lyon: imprimerie de Louis Perrin.* [1867.] 8vo, pp. 12. 16176

* One copy only of the original edition is known to exist, and of the facsimile reprint twelve copies only were printed, all on vellum.

The Contrast. *Albany.* 1828. 8vo. 16177

The Contrast! Professions and Practice of Republican & Democratic Statesmen contrasted. Published by the Union Republican Congressional Committee. *Washington, D. C.* [n. d.] 8vo, pp. 16. H. 16178

The Contrast. The Whig and Democratic Platforms. 1852. 8vo. 16179

The Contrast, being the Speech of King George III. at the Opening of the Parliament, 1794, and the Speech of President George Washington, at the Opening of the Congress of the United States of America, December 3, 1793. *London: H. D. Symonds.* 1794. 8vo, pp. 24. 16180

Contrast of Great Britain, 1777. *See* [Barron (W.)], Vol. II., No. 3644*a*.

The Contrast; or Plain Reasons why William Henry Harrison should be elected President of the United States, and why Martin Van Buren should Not. By an Old Democrat. *New York.* 1840. pp. 16. 16181

The Contrast of the Two Speeches, one delivered to the Representatives of the United States, Dec. 2, 1817, and the other to the Boroughmongers of Great Britain, Jan. 1818. *London.* 1818. 8vo. 16182

Contrato de asociacion para la Republica de los Estados unidos del Anáhuac. Por un ciudadano del Estado de Xalisco. Segunda ed. revista y corregida. *Guadalaxara.* 1823. Folio, pp. 72. 16183

La contre-guérilla française au Mexique. *Paris: imp. Chaix et Cie.* 1866. 8vo, pp. 15. 16184

Republished from "L'Estafette, *Mexico*, fév. 1866."

CONTRERAS (C. M. de). Relacion|cierta, y verdadera|de lo qve svcedió, y a svcedido|en esta Villa de Gvadalcaçar Provincia|de Tehuantepeque desde los 22. de Março de 1660.|Hasta los quatro de Iulio de 1661. Cerca de *que* los Naturales Indios| destas Prouincias, Tumultados, y amotinados mataron à Don Iuan|de Auellan, su Alcalde mayor, y Theniente de Capitan General; y à|tres Criados suyos, procediendo à otros grauisimos delictos hasta|aclamar Rey de su Naturaleça y las diligencias, aueriguacion,|castigo, y perdon que con ellos se à seguido|Execvtado|Por el Sr. Don Ivan Francisco de Montemayor|de Cuenca del Consejo de su Magestad, y su Oydor de la|Real Audiencia, y Chancilleria desta Nueua España, que| reside en la Ciudad de Mexico.|Escriviala|Don Christoval Manso de Contreras|Regidor de la Ciudad de Antequera Valle de Oaxaca, Alcalde ma-|yor, y Theniente de Capitan General de dicha Villa.|Dedicala debaxo de la|proteccion, y grandeza.| Del Ex.mo Señor Don Iuan de|Leiba, y de la Cerda, de la Lama, Gamboa, y Mendoça,|Marques de Leiba, y de Ladrada, Conde de Baños, Señor de las Cassas|de Arteaga, y la Lama, y de las Villas de Santur Dei Villa Cueba y boço|Vitubia, y Velasco, Preuoste mayor de las Villas de Garnica Ondarruo,| y Vermeo, en el Señorio de Vizcaya, Comendador de la Encomienda|de Alausca, del Orden de Santiago, Virrey Lugartheniente del Rey|nuestro Señor, Gouernador, y Capitan General desta Nueua|España, y Presidente de la Real Audiencia della &c.|*Impresso con licencia en Mexico: por Iuan Ruyz. Año de* 1661.| 4to, 3 l., 37 folioed leaves. J.C.B. 16185

CONTRERAS. Manual de administrar los Sanctos Sacramentos a los Españoles, y naturales, desta nueua España conforme a la reforma de Paulo V. Pont. Max. Ordenado por el Padre Fray Pedro de Contreras Gallardo, Predicador, y Guardian del Conuento de la Concepcion de Nra. Señora de Theoacan, hijo desta sancta Prouincia del sancto Euangelio de Mexico. *Impresso con licencio, y priuilegio. En México: En la Imprenta de Ioan Ruyz. Año de* 1638. 8vo, pp. 8, 147, 4, 1. 16186

This rare and curious "Manual" contains the manner of administering the Sacraments in the Mexican language

CONTRERAS (Francesco Xavier). Ecos del Espiritu Santo en la Congregacion de S. Pedro de la Ciudad de Luis Potosi. *En Megico.* 1757. 4to. 16187

CONTRERAS. Panegirico de Nuestra Señora de Guadalupe de Megico. *Megico.* 1758. 4to. 16189

Contributions to American History, 1858. *Philadelphia: J. B. Lippincott & Co.* 1858. Rl. 8vo, 4 l., pp. 15, 429, List, pp. 7. BA. 16190

Forms Vol. VI. of the "**Memoirs** of the Historical Society of Pennsylvania," and contains articles on the **Society** of the Cincinnati, Whiskey Insurrection, William Penn, Acadian Exiles, and **Major** André.

Controversy between Caius Gracchus and Opimius, in reference to the American Society for Colonizing the Free People of Colour of the United States. *Georgetown.* 1827. 8vo. C.

A Controversy between "Erskine" and "W. M." on the practicability of suppressing Gambling. *Richmond: printed at the Whig Book and Job Office.* 1862. 8vo, pp. 96. BA. 16192

The Controversy between Great-Britain and her Colonies. *See* [Knox (W.)]

The Controversy between Massachusetts and South Carolina. *Boston.* 1845. 8vo, pp. 21. 16193

The Convention, an Excellent New Ballad, to which is added the King of Spain's Protest, and a New Epitaph. *London.* 1739. Folio. 16194

The Convention between the Crowns of Great Britain and Spain, concluded at the Pardo on the 14th of January, 1739, N. S. The King of Great Britain's Full Power. The King of Spain's Full Power. The Two Separate Articles belonging to the Convention. His Britannick Majesty's Ratification of the Convention. His Catholick Majesty's Ratification of the Convention. And their Britannick and Catholick Majesties' several and respective Ratifications of the Two Separate Articles. *London: Samuel Buckley.* 1739. 4to, pp. 28. J.C.B. 16195

Relates to the limits of Florida. In Spanish, French, and English.

Convention between the French Republic and the United States of America. *Washington City: Printed by Samuel Harrison Smith.* 1801. 4to, pp. 12. BA. 16196

Convention entre el Rey Nuestro Señor y el Rey de la Gran Bretaña, transigiendo varios puntos sobre pesca, navegacion y comercio en el Oceano Pacifico y los mares del Sur, firmada en San Lorenzo el Real á 28 de Octubre de 1790, cuyas ratifica-

tiones se cangearon en el mismo real sitio a 22 de Novembre siguente. *Madrid: En la Imprenta Real.* [1790.] 4to, pp. 15.

In French and Spanish.

Convention of Agriculturists and Manufacturers and others, Friendly to the Encouragement and Support of Domestic Industry of the United States, held at Harrisburg, July 30, 1827. 8vo.

Convention of Ministers, 1743. The Testimony and Advice of an Assembly of Pastors of Churches in New-England, July 7. 1743. Occasion'd By the Revival of Religion. Added, Attestations from a Number of their Brethren. *Boston.* [n. d.] 8vo, pp. 51. 16199

Convention of the Friends of Domestic Industry. Address, Reports, and Memorials to Congress. *Baltimore.* 1831. 8vo.

Convention pour l'exécution d'un canal maritime interocéanique sur le territoire de la République de Nicaragua ... *Paris: imprimerie administrative de Paul Dupont.* 1869. Large 8vo, pp. 15. H. 16201

The Convention [of Jan. 14, 1739, between Great Britain and Spain] Vindicated from the Misrepresentations of the Enemies of our Peace. *London: J. Roberts.* 1739. 8vo, pp. 29. B.

Numerous references to trade in American waters.

A Conversation in a Canebrake; or a Talk on Southern Affairs, between a Merchant and a Planter. By a Cotton Planter. *New Orleans: printed at the Daily Delta Book and Job Office.* 1860. 8vo, pp. 11, v. BA. 16203

Conversation, Practical and Philosophical, on the Subject of Currency, having Especial Reference to the Present and Prospective Interests of California. By a Tradesman of San Francisco. ... *San Francisco: A. Roman & Co.* 1865. 8vo, pp. 16.

Conversations on the Mackinaw and Green Bay Indian Missions. In Two Parts. ... *Boston: Massachusetts Sunday School Union.* 1831. 24mo, pp. 128. 16205

Conversations principally on the Aborigines of North America. *Salem: W. & S. B. Ives.* 1828. 24mo, pp. 179. H.

CONVERSE (Francis). Oration, July 4, 1828. *Watertown.* 8vo. 16207

CONVERSE (F.) An Address, delivered before the Members of the Frederick Lyceum, on the 14th March, 1836: by Freeman Converse ... . *Baltimore: printed by Joseph Robinson.* 1836. 18mo, pp. 18. H. 16208

CONVERSE (J. K.) The History of Slavery. A Discourse before the Vermont Colonization Society. ... By J. K. Converse. *Burlington.* 1840. 8vo, pp. 24. 16209

CONVERSE. The Relation of Christianity, and of the several Forms of Christianity, to the Republican Institutions of the United States: a Sermon preached before the Chittenden County Consociation, in Milton, June 24, 1833. By J. K. Converse ... . *Burlington: Edward Smith.* 1833. 8vo, pp. 32. 16210

Also: A Discourse, on the Moral, Legal and Domestic Condition of our Colored Population, preached before the Vermont Colonization Society, at Montpelier, October 17, 1832. By J. K. Converse ... *Burlington: Edward Smith.* 1832. 8vo, pp. 32.

CONVERSE (S.) Report of the Trial of Sherman Converse, at New Haven, 1820, for a Libel on Joshua Stow. 8vo. W.

La Conversion des sauvages qui ont été baptizés en la Nouvelle-France cette année 1610, avec un brief récit du voyage de Poutrincourt. *Paris: Jean Millot.* [1610.] 12mo, pp. 46. J.C.B. 16212

Conversion of an Indian. *See* Harlow (L.)

Convoy, Ter gelegenheid van het beloofd en geweigerd, naar de West-Indiën, 8 dec. 1781. [A Poem. n. p. n. d.] 8vo.

CONWAY (Cornelius). Utah Expedition; With Account of the Mormon Campaign. *Cincinnati.* 1858. 8vo. C 16214

CONWAY [(Henry Seymour)]. The Speech of General Conway, Member of Parliament for Saint Edmondsbury, on moving in the House of Commons, (On the 5th of May, 1780) "That leave be given to bring in a Bill for Quieting the Troubles now Reigning in the British Colonies in America, and for enabling His Majesty to appoint Commissioners, with full Powers to treat, and conclude upon Terms of Conciliation with the said Colonies." *London: T. Cadell.* M,DCC,LXXXI. 8vo, 2 l., pp. 51. B., BA., C. 16215

CONWAY (Martin F.) Letter of Hon. M. F. Conway, to Senator Doolittle ... . In Support of President Johnson's Policy of Reconstruction. *Richmond.* 1865. 24mo, pp. 12. H.

CONWAY. North and South, and Slavery. A Lecture in the Free Trade Hall, Manchester, June 21, 1863. 12mo, pp. 11.

Also: Shall the War be for Union and Freedom, or Union and Slavery? Speech ... in the House of Representatives, Thursday, December 12, 1861. *Washington, D. C.* 1861. 8vo, pp. 14 BA. — The War a Revolutionary Agent. A Speech of Hon. M. F. Conway. ... January 27, 1863. [n. p. 1863.] 8vo, pp. 18. H.

CONWAY (Moncure Daniel). East and West: An Inaugural Discourse, delivered in the First Congregational Church, Cincinnati, O., May 1, 1859. By M. D. Conway ... . *Cincinnati: Truman & Spofford.* 1859. 8vo, pp. 21. 16218

CONWAY. Free-Schools in Virginia; A Plea of Education, Virtue and Thrift, *vs.* Ignorance, Vice and Poverty. ... By Moncure Daniel Conway. *Fredericksburg, Virginia: Recorder Print. Oct.,* 1850. Post 8vo, pp. 36. + *Fredericksburg.* 1850. 12mo, pp. 36. H. 16219

CONWAY. The Old and the New; a Sermon containing the History of the First Unitarian Church in Washington City. Preached ... December 31, 1854, by Moncure D. Conway ... . *Washington: Buell & Blanchard, Printers.* 1855. 8vo, pp. 15. H. 16220

[CONWAY.] The Rejected Stone; or, Insurrection *vs.* Resurrection in America. By a Native of Virginia. *Boston: Walker, Wise and Company.* 1861. 12mo, pp. 132. BA. + Second Edition. *Boston.* 1862. 12mo. + Third Edition. [*Ibid.*] 12mo, pp. 131. BA. 16221

CONWAY. Testimonies Concerning Slavery. By M. D. Conway ... . *London: Chapman and Hall.* MDCCCLXIV. 8vo, pp. viii, 140. BA. + Second Edition. *London: Chapman & Hall.* 8vo, pp. viii, 140. 16222

Also: The Golden Hour. ... *Boston: Ticknor and Fields.* 1862. 12mo, pp. 160. BA. — The One Path: or, The Duties of the North and South, A Discourse ... Washington, D. C., January 26, 1856. ... . *Washington.* [1856.] 8vo, pp. 8. — The Theater: A Discourse ... Cincinnati, O., on June 7, 1857. ... . *Cincinnati: Truman and Spofford.* 1857. 8vo, pp. 29. H. — Thomas Paine: a Celebration. Delivered in ... Cincinnati, Ohio, January 29, 1860. ... . *Cincinnati.* 1860. 8vo, pp. 15. H. — The True ... . A Discourse ... Washington City ... September 16, 1855, in Behalf of the Norfolk and Portsmouth Sufferers. ... . *Washington, D. C: Taylor & Maury.* 1855. 8vo, pp. 20. H. — Virtue vs. Defeat. A Discourse, preached on Nov. 9, 1856, ... in ... Cincinnati, Ohio. ... *Cincinnati, Ohio.* 1856. 8vo, pp. 20.

CONWAY (T. W.) Annual Report of Thos. W. Conway, Superintendent Bureau of Free Labor, Department of the Gulf

to Major General Hurlbut Commanding, for the Year 1864. *New Orleans.* [1865.] 8vo, pp. 16. 16223

Also: Report of the Condition of the Freedmen, of the Department of the Gulf, to Major General N. B. Banks, Commanding, by Chaplain T. W. Conway, U. S. A. Superintendent Bureau of Free Labor. *New Orleans: H. P. Lathrop, Printer.* 1864. 8vo, pp. 11. H. — The Freedmen of Louisiana. Final Report of the Bureau of Free Labor, Department of the Gulf, to Major General E. R. S. Canby, Commanding. By Thomas W. Conway, General Superintendent of Freedmen. *New Orleans.* 1865. 8vo, pp. 38. H.

CONWAY, *Mass.* Celebration of the Hundredth Anniversary of the Incorporation of Conway, Massachusetts ... June 19th, 1867. Including a Historical Address by Rev. Charles B. Rice ... Poem by Harvey Rice ... Oration by William Howland ... . *Northampton.* 1867. 8vo, pp. 137. B. 16224

CONWELL (R. H.) Why and How. Why the Chinese emigrate, and the Means they adopt for the Purpose of reaching America. With Sketches of Travels ... &c. By Russell H. Conwell. *Boston: Lee and Shepard. New York: Lee, Shepard, and Dillingham.* 1871. 12mo, pp. 283. BA., H. 16225

CONYBEARE (W. J.) Essays Ecclesiastical and Social. Reprinted, with Additions, from the Edinburgh Review. By W. J. Conybeare ... . *London: Longmans.* 1855. 8vo, pp. xi, 440.

Mormonism, pp. 280–376, 440.

CONYERS (J. B.) Brief History of the Leading Causes of the Hancock Mob, in the year 1846. By Josiah B. Conyers, M.D., Quincy, Illinois. *Saint Louis: printed for the author by Cathcart & Prescott.* 1846. 12mo, pp. 83, (1). B. 16227

CONYNGHAM (D. P.) The Irish Brigade and its Campaigns, with some Account of the Corcoran Legion and Sketches of the Principal Officers. By Captain D. P. Conyngham. *New York: W. McSorley & Co.* 1867. 12mo, pp. 599. C. 16228

CONYNGHAM. Sherman's March through the South, with Sketches and Incidents of the Campaign. By Captain David P. Conyngham. *New York: Sheldon & Co.* 1865. 12mo, pp. 431. 16229

CONYNGHAM (J. N.) Address delivered by Hon. John N. Conyngham, on the Occasion of Laying of the Corner Stone of the New Court House, Wilkes-Barre, Pa. August 12, 1856. *Wilkes-Barre.* ... 1856. 8vo, pp. 14, Cover, 2 l. 16230

An Account of Abimelech Coody. *See* [Clinton (De Witt)], No. 13709, and [Verplanck (G. C.)]

COOK (A.) Letters of Ann Cook, late Mrs. Beauchamp, to her Friend in Maryland, containing a Short History of her Life. *Washington.* 1826. 12mo, pp. 91. C. 16231

COOK (B. C.) The Tariff. Speech of Hon. Burton C. Cook, of Illinois, in the House ... March 23, 1870. [*Washington.* 1870.] 8vo, pp. 8. H. 16232

COOK (C.) A Brief Account of the African Christian Church, in New-Bedford, being the First of the Christian Denomination in the United States formed by People of Colour. By Charles Cook. *New-Bedford: Benjamin T. Congdon, Printer.* 1834. 8vo, pp. 12. H. 16233

COOK (E.) The|Sot-weed|Factor:|Or, a Voyage to|Maryland.|A|Satyr.|In which is describ'd|The Laws, Government, Courts and|Constitutions of the Country; and also the|Buildings, Feasts, Frolicks, Entertainments|and Drunken Humours of the Inhabitants of|that Part of America.|In Burlesque Verse. |By Eben. Cook, Gent.|*London: Printed and Sold by B. Bragg, at the Raven in Pater-|Noster-Row,* 1708. (*Price 6d.*)| 4to, Title, 1 l., pp. 21. H. 16234

Reprinted with a glossary, as No. II. of Shea's "Reprints of Southern Tracts." [*New York.* 1865], with an introduction by Brantz Mayer of Baltimore. Mr. Mayer says this was reprinted with a poem on "Bacon's Rebellion," by Mr. Green, at Annapolis, Maryland, in 1731. Mr. Green cautiously reminds the reader that it was a description written twenty years before, and "did not agree with the condition of Annapolis at the time of its publication." Sotweed is another name for tobacco. Of the reprint, ten copies were printed on large, and one hundred and twenty-five on small paper.

C[OOK]. Sotweed Redivivus: Or the Planter's Looking-Glass. In Burlesque Verse. Calculated for the Meridian of Maryland. By E. C. Gent. *Annapolis: Printed by William Parks, for the Author.* M.DCC.XXX. 4to, pp. viii, 28. J.C.B.

See "Hist. Mag.," IV. 153.

COOK (F. Joseph). Home-Sketches of Essex County — First number. Ticonderoga: ... By Flavius J. Cook. *Keesville, N. Y.: W. Lansing & Son, Printers.* 1858. 8vo, pp. 140 B., H., S.

COOK (G.) Provision for the Insane Poor of the State of New York. By G. Cook, M.D. *Canandaigua: The Author.* 8vo, pp. 31. 16237

COOK (G. H.) Report upon the Geological Survey of New Jersey, 1863–65. By George H. Cook. *Trenton: State Government.* 1864–66. 8vo, pp. 13, 24, 12. C. 16238

COOK. Geology of New Jersey. By authority of the Legislature. George H. Cook, State Geologist. ... *Newark: Daily Advertiser Office.* 1868. 8vo, pp. xxiv, 899, (1). 8 large Maps folded. BA. 16239

COOK (H.) A Discourse on American Independence; Delivered on the Fourth of July 1811, at Metutchen Meeting House. By the Rev. Mr. [Henry] Cook. *New-Brunswick: David & James Fitz Randolph.* 8vo, pp. 18. 16240

COOK (I.) A Brief Examination of some of the most Prevalent False Doctrines and Ceremonials of the Christian Sects, compared with Apostolic Doctrines. With a Short Account of the Signs and Evidences of his Call to the Work of a Christian Reformation. By Ichabod Cook. *Providence: Knowles & Vose.* 1847. 12mo, pp. 172. C. 16241

COOK (*Capt.* James). A Journal of a Voyage round the World, In His Majesty's Ship Endeavour, In The Years 1768, 1769, 1770, and 1771; Undertaken in Pursuit of Natural Knowledge, at the desire of the Royal Society: containing All the various Occurrences of the Voyage, with Descriptions of several newly discovered Countries in the Southern Hemisphere; and Accounts of their Soil and Productions; and of many Singularities in the Structure, Apparel, Customs, Manners, Police, Manufactures, &c. of their Inhabitants. To which is added, A Concise Vocabulary of the Language of Otaheite. ... *London: T. Becket and P. A. de Hondt.* MDCCLXXI. 8vo, pp. 130. BA. 16242

The first printed account of Captain Cook's voyage. This was not written by Sir Robert Banks, to whom Watt ascribes it, nor by Capt. Cook, nor by Hawkesworth. *See* "M. Rev.," XLV. *See* Kippis's "Cook" (1788), p. 183. An account of this "Voyage" in Henry's "Hist. Ac.," Vols. III. and IV.

COOK. First Voyage. *See* Hawkesworth (John). *See also* Ellis (W.), Forster, Hogg, Kerr, Ledyard, and Wallis.

COOK. Nachricht von den neuesten Endeckungen der Engländer in der Süd-Sea, oder Auszug aus dem Tagebuch des Königl. Schiffs The Endeavour, welches The Endeavour, welches in den Jahren 1768 bis 1771 eine Reise um die Welt Gethan, und auf derselben verschiedene bisher unbekannte

Länder in der südlichen Hemisphäre endeckt hat, nebst einer kurzen Beschreibung dieser Länder, deren vorzüglichen Seltenheiten, Beschaffenheit der Einwohner und einer kleinen Probe von der Sprache, die in jenem Theil der Welt üblich ist. *Berlin.* 1772. 12mo, pp. 248. 16243

Boucher, VI. 249, says 7 vols., 8vo.

COOK. An Authentic Narrative of a Voyage to the Pacific Ocean: Performed by Captain Cook, and Captain Clerke, In his Britannic Majesty's Ships, The Resolution and Discovery, In the Years, 1776, 1777, 1778, 1779, and 1780. Including, A faithful account of all their Discoveries in this Last Voyage, the unfortunate Death of Captain Cook, at the Island of O-why-ee, and the return of the Ships to England under Captain Gore. Also A Large Introduction, Exhibiting, an Account of the several Voyages round the Globe; with an abstract of the principal expeditions to Hudson's Bay, for the Discovery of a North-West-Passage. By an Officer on Board the Discovery. Volume the First [and Volume the Second]. *Philadelphia: Printed and Sold by Robert Bell, in Third-Street. Price two thiras of a Dollar.* M,DC,LXXXIII. 2 vols. in 1, 8vo, Title, pp. 9–229. 16244

COOK. A Voyage towards the South Pole, and Round the World. Performed in His Majesty's Ships Resolution and Adventure, In the years 1772, 1773, 1774, and 1775. Written By James Cook, Commander of the Resolution. In which is included, Captain Furneaux's Narrative of his proceedings in the Adventure during the Separation of the Ships. ... Illustrated with Maps and Charts, and a Variety of Portraits of Persons and Views of places, drawn during the Voyage by Mr. Hodges, and engraved by the most eminent Masters. *London: W. Strahan.* M DCC LXXVII. 2 vols., 4to, pp. xxxvi, 378; 4 l., pp. 396. Portrait, and 63 Plates. + The Second Edition. *London: W. Strahan.* MDCCLXXIII. C. + The Third Edition. *London: W. Strahan, and T. Cadell.* MDCCLXXIX. 2 vols., 4to, pp. xl, 378; 4 l., pp. 396. Portrait, and 63 Maps and Plates. + Fourth Edition. *London: W. Strahan & T. Cadell.* 1784. 2 vols., 4to, pp. xl, 378; 3 l., pp. 396. Map, and 62 Plates.

See "M. Rev.," LVII. 17.

COOK. A Second Voyage round the World, in the years 1772, 1773, 1774, 1775. By James Cook, esq. commander of his Majesty's bark the Resolution. Undertaken by order of

the King, and encouraged by a parliamentary grant of 4000*l.* Drawn up from authentic Papers. *London: J. Almon.* 1776. 4to, 2 l., pp. 102. C. 16246

Also on large paper. "A surreptitious account of Cook's second voyage, abounding in errors, and accounts of occurrences which never took place; many of which are pointed out in the 'Monthly Review,' on the authority of Captain Cook himself." — RICH. *See* "M. Rev.," LV. 270.

COOK. Journal of the Resolution's Voyage in 1772, 1773, 1774, and 1775, on Discovery of the Southern Hemisphere. — Also a Journal of the Adventure's Voyage in 1772, 1773, and 1774. With an Account of the Separation of the two Ships, &c. A chart and other cuts. *London: J. Newbery.* 1776. 8vo. 16247

"Another surreptitious journal." — RICH.

COOK. A Compendious History of Captain Cook's First and Second Voyages; the first performed in the Years 1768, 1769, 1770, and 1771, in the Endeavour; the Second in 1772, 1773, 1774, and 1775, in the Resolution and Adventure. Including an Abridgment of Captain Furneaux's Narrative of his Proceedings during the Separation of the two Ships. *London: G. Kearsley.* 1784. 12mo. 16248

See "M. Rev.," LXXII. 147.

COOK. Voyage dans l'hémisphère australe et autour du monde, fait sur les vaisseaux de roi, l'Aventure et la Résolution, en 1772, 1773, 1774 et 1775. Traduit de l'Anglois [par M. Suard]. *Paris.* 1778. 5 vols., 4to. 65 Plates. 16249

For a German translation, *see* under Forster (J. R.)

COOK. A | voyage | to the | Pacific Ocean. | Undertaken, | by the command of His Majesty, | for making | Discoveries in the Northern Hemisphere. To determine | The Position and Extent of the West Side of North America; | its Distance from Asia; and the Practicability of a | Northern Passage to Europe. | Performed under the Direction of | Captains Cook, Clerke, and Gore, | In his Majesty's Ships the Resolution and Discovery. | In the Years 1776, 1777, 1778, 1779, and 1780. | In three volumes. | Vol. I. and II. written by Captain James Cook; Vol. III. by Captain James King, LL.D. and F.R.S. | Illustrated. | *London: G. Nicol.* MDCCLXXXIV. | 3 vols., 4to, 4 l., pp. xcvi, 421; 6 l., pp. 549; 6 l., pp. 558, (1). Atlas in folio. 81 Plates. + *Dublin.* 1784. 3 vols., 8vo. Map. BA. + Second Edition. *London.* 1785. 3 vols., 4to, and Atlas in folio. 16250

COOK. Voyage to the Pacific. ... Being a copious, comprehensive, and satisfactory Abridgment of the Voyage written by Captain James Cook, ... and Captain James King ... Illustrated with Cuts. *London: John Stockdale.* MDCCLXXXIV. 4 vols., 8vo. H. + *London.* 1785. 4 vols., 8vo. + *New York.* 1796. 4 vols., 8vo. + *Edinburgh.* 1798. 4 vols., 12mo. P. + *London.* 4 vols., 12mo. 16251

See "M. Rev.," LXX. 460.

COOK. Remarks and Conjectures on the Voyage of the Ships Resolution and Discovery, in search of a Northerly Passage from Kampschatka to England after the death of Captain James Cook. *London.* 1780. 8vo. 16252

The Beauties of Captain Cook's Voyages ... . Containing ... the Manners and Customs of the Inhabitants of Nortka Sound ... &c. *London: G. Lister.* [1785.] 12mo, pp. iv, 129. Plate. BA. 16253

A second volume is promised in the publisher's note.

COOK. The Voyages of Captain James Cook Round the World; comprehending a History of the South Sea Islands, &c. &c. ... *London: Jaques and Wright.* 1826. 2 vols., 8vo. 13 Plates. 16254

COOK. A Compendious History of Captain Cook's Last Voyage, performed in the Years 1776, 1777, 1778, 1779, and 1780: in which all the Interesting Transactions are recorded, particularly all those relative to his Unfortunate Death. With a Map of the New Discoveries, and the Track of the Ships. *London: J. Kearsley.* 1784. 12mo. 16255

See "M. Rev.," LXXII. 147.

COOK. Captain Cook's Third and Last Voyage to the Pacific Ocean, in the Years 1776, 1777, 1779 & 1780: together with an Account of his Death. Faithfully abridged from the Quarto Ed. *London: J. Fielding & Co.* 1786. + *Worcester, Mass.: Isaiah Thomas, Jun.* 1795. 18mo, pp. 216. H. 16256

COOK. An Abridgement of Captain Cook's last Voyage. Performed in the Years 1776, 1777, 1778, 1779, and 1780, For making Discoveries in the Northern Hemisphere, by Order of His Majesty. Extracted from the Quarto Edition, in Three Volumes. Containing a Relation of all the interesting Transactions, particularly those relative to the unfortunate Death of Captain Cook; to which is added, extracts from Captain King's

Account of his Life and public Services. The Fifth Edition. Ornamented with several Plates and improved by a copious Index, also a Chart of the Tracts of the Ships. *London: G. Kearsley.* MDCCLXXXVII. 12mo, pp. XXIV, 442, Index, 8 l

COOK. Voyages to the Pacific Ocean, Abridged. *Boston.* 1797. 2 vols., 12mo. W. 16258

COOK. A Voyage to the Pacific Ocean; Undertaken by the Command of His Majesty, for making Discoveries in the Northern Hemisphere, performed under the Directions of Captains Cook, Clerke, and Gore, in the Years 1776, 1777, 1778, 1779, 1780. Compiled from the Various Accounts of that Voyage hitherto published. Embellished with Forty Elegant Engravings. *Philadelphia.* 1818. 2 vols., 8vo, pp. 445; 350.

See "M. Rev.," LXX. 460; LXXI. 283; LXXV. 38; LXXVI. 78.

COOK. Troisième voyage de Cook, ou Journal d'une Expédition faite dans la Mer Pacifique du Sud & du Nord, en 1776, 1777, 1778, 1779 & 1780. Traduit de l'Anglois. Troisième édition. *Versailles: Poinçot. Paris: Belin.* M. DCC. LXXXIII. 8vo, pp. lxiv, 354 [misprint for 454]. H. 16260

COOK. Troisième voyage de Cook, ou voyage à l'Océan pacifique, pour faire des découvertes dans l'hémisphère nord, pour déterminer la position et l'étendue de la côte ouest de l'Amérique septentrionale, sa distance, de l'Asie, et résoudre la question du passage du Nord. Exécuté en 1776, 1777, 1778, 1779 et 1780. Traduit de l'Anglois par M. D*** [M. Demeunier.] *Paris.* 1785. 4 vols., 8vo. 88 Plates. 16261

COOK. Histoire des premier, second et troisieme Voyages, autour du monde, par Cook; mise a la portée du tout le monde, Par Béranger. Avec Figures et une grande Mappe-monde en deux Hémispheres, où sont marquées les Découvertes les plus récentes et les Routes des trois Voyages de Cook, dressée par Henisson. *A Paris, Chez Fr. Dufart, Imprimeur-Libraire.* 1796, *ou An* IVeme. 16262

COOK. Neueste Reisebeschreibungen, oder Jakob Cooks dritte und letzte Reise, welche auf Befehl des Königs von England nach den Südinseln des stillen Meeres und dann weiter nach den nordamerikanischen und asiatischen Küsten, um die Möglichkeit einer nördlichen Durchfahrt nach Europa zu entscheiden, in dem Jahren 1776–1780 unternommen worden.

... *Nürnberg und Leipzig: bey Weigel und Schneider.* 1786. 2 vols., 8vo, pp. 374; 436. Plates and Map. 16263

Vols. VIII. and IX. of the "Bibliothek der neuesten Reisebeschreibungen."

COOK. Reise nach dem Stillen Ocean, auf Befehl des Königs von Grossbrittannien unternommen, Entdeckungen in der nördlichen Halbkugel zu machen, die Lage und Ausdehnung der Westseite von Nordamerika, ihre Entfernung von Asien; und die Möglichkeit einer nördlichen Durchfarth [*sic*] nach Europa zu bestimmen. Unter der Anführung der Kapitaine Cook, Clarke [*sic*] und Gore, in den Schiffen Resolution und Discovery, in den Jahren 1776, 1777, 1778, 1779, 1780. In einigen Auszügen aus dem Englischen übersetzt. Mit einer Reisekarte und Kupfern. *Frankfurt an der Oder: bey Strauss.* 1785. 8vo, pp. 208. 16264

COOK. Leben des Weltumseglers und Entdeckers James Cook, Mitglied der königlichen Societät der Wissenschaften in London, aus authentischen Quellen, nebst Cook's Bildniss. *Frankfurt und Leipzig.* 1781. 8vo, 4¼ sheets. 16265

COOK. Viaje al rededor del mundo, hecho en los años 1768–71, trad. del francés por S. de Alvarado y de la Peña. *Madrid.* 1832. 6 vols., 24mo. 16266

COOK. Entdeckungsreise nach der Südsee 1776–80 unter Cook, Clerke, Gore, und King. *Berlin.* 1781. 8vo. Map and Plate. 16267

A complete set of the best edition of Cook's voyages consists of Hawkesworth's narrative of the first voyage, 3 vols., and our Nos. 16245 and 16250, and, together, 8 vols., 4to, and atlas in folio. Priced, by Thorpe, in 1826, at £15 15s.; 1829, Thorpe, £12 12s.; 1826, J. Bohn, £25, bds., £12; 1840, James Bohn, russia, £14 14s.; 1841, Thorpe, russia, £8 8s.; 1843, James Bohn, mor., £21; 1855, Bernal, £17 15s. The following is the best *collected* modern edition. "So decidedly and correctly authentic, that they may be justly styled the 'classics' of sea voyages." — *United Service Journal.*

COOK. The Voyages of Captain James Cook. Illustrated with Maps and numerous Engravings on Wood. With an Appendix. Giving an Account of the Present Condition of the South Sea Islands, &c. *London: William Smith.* MDCCCXLVI. 2 vols., super-rl. 8vo, pp. xx, 596; xii, 619. 4 Maps. 16268

Reproduced with new title-pages only, by Tallis & Co. Three other editions are: *London.* 1785. 6 vols., 8vo. + *London.* 1790. 6 vols., 8vo. + *London.* 1821. 7 vols., 8vo. B. + *London.* 1809. 7 vols., 12mo. *See also* Hogg (J.)

COOK. Captain Cook's Three Voyages To the Pacific Ocean. ... Faithfully Abridged from the Quarto Edition. Con-

taining A Particular Relation of all The interesting Transactions during the several Voyages. *Boston.* 1792. 2 vols., 12mo, pp. 344; 375. Plates. + *New York: James Rivington.* 1774. 2 vols., 8vo, pp. xvii, 260; (2), 250. Maps and Plates.

The abridged editions are very numerous, and scarcely worth notice. The best is edited by Dr. Kippis. *London.* 1840. + *New York.* 1840.

COOK. Cook's [Voyages, 1768–1780]. New Edition, edited by John Barrows, and Letters of Captn Cook hitherto unpublished, and a facsimile of Log Book. Illustrated by C. A. Doyle. *Edinburgh.* 1860. Square 12mo. 16270

COOK. Life and Voyages of Captain Cook, for the Use of Schools. *Paris.* 1836. 12mo. 16271

COOK. Captain Cook's Voyages around the World for making Discoveries towards the North and South Poles. With an Appendix. *Manchester.* 1811. 8vo, pp. viii, 566, 1 l. 6 Plates. 16272

COOK. Cooks Reise omkring Jordkloden i Aarene 1768–1771, bearbeitit af Campe. ... Oversat. *Kiöbenhavn: Schubothe,* 184–. 8vo, pp. 310. 26273

COOK. Geschichte der Reisen die seit Cook an die Nordwestküste von America unternommen worden sind. Aus dem Englischen von G. Forster. *Berlin: Voss.* 1791, 1792. 3 vols., 4to, and 3 vols., 8vo. 16274

COOK. Reis naar de Zuidpool en Rondom de Weereld. *Rotterdam.* 1778. 4to. Plates. 16275

For accounts of his voyages, *see* Hawkesworth's "Voyages," Vols. II., III.; Kerr's "Collection," Vols. XII., XV., XVI.; Montémont's "Bibliothèque," Vols. V., XI.; Pinkerton's "Collection," Vol. XI.

COOK. Directions for Navigating the West and South-Coast of Newfoundland, with a Chart thereof, and a particular Account of the Bays, Harbours, Rocks, etc. From an actual Survey, taken by order of Commodore Pallisser, Governor of Newfoundland, etc. By James Cook, appointed by the Admiralty to survey the Coast of Newfoundland. *London.* 1766 and 68. 2 pts., 4to, pp. 30. 16276

COOK. The North American Pilot for Newfoundland, Labrador, and the Gulf and River St. Lawrence. By James Cook, Michael Lane, Joseph Gilbert, and others; with plates. *London.* 1784. 2 vols., folio. P. 16277

COOK. The North American Pilot for the two Carolinas and Florida. Drawn from original surveys taken by J. Gascoigne, J. Fisher, J. Blarney and others. Part Second: — The North American Pilot for New England, New York, Pennsylvania, Maryland, and Virginia, the two Carolinas, and Florida. Drawn from original surveys taken by J. Gascoigne, J. Fisher, J. Blarney and others. *Sayer and Bennet.* 1775. 2 vols., folio, 53 sheets. + *London.* 1789. 2 vols. + 1806. 2 vols. 16278

COOK (J.) The Siege of Richmond: a Narrative of the Military Operations of Major-General George B. McClellan during the Months of May and June, 1862. By Joel Cook, Special Correspondent of the Philadelphia Press. *Philadelphia: George W. Childs.* 1862. 12mo, pp. viii, 7–358. BA., C. 16279

COOK (*Rev.* J. T.) Sermon on the Origin of the War, delivered at Genesee, Illinois, July 13, 1862. *Genesee* [*Ill.*] 1862.

COOK (J. E.) Confession of John E. Cook, Brother in Law of Gov. A. P. Willard, of Indiana, and one of the Participants in the Harper's Ferry Invasion. [n. p. n. d.] 8vo, pp. 16. + Second Edition. Published for the benefit of Samuel C. Young, A Non-Slaveholder, who is permanently disabled by a Wound received in Defence of Southern Institutions. [n. p. n. d.] 8vo, pp. 16. 16281

COOK (J. H.) Guide Book and Pocket Map; giving the Early History of St. Louis, etc. By J. H. Cook. *St. Louis: Clayton & Babington.* 1867. 24mo, pp. 44. Map. 16282

COOK (J. P.) Speech of Hon. John P. Cook, of Iowa, on the Nebraska and Kansas Bill. In the House ... May 16, 1854. *Washington.* 1854. 8vo, pp. 16. H. 16283

COOK (*Rev.* J.) The Relations of the Temperance Reform to the Future of Democracy in the United States. An Address, by Joseph Cook ... Boston ... May 23d, 1870. ... *Boston.* 1870. 8vo, pp. 16. H. 16284

Also: Extracts from Remarks made by Rev. Joseph Cook, at the Funeral of Annie J. Lane ... March 8, 1869. *East Abington.* 1869. 32mo, pp. 8. H.

COOK. Remarks on a Passage from The River Balise, in the Bay of Honduras, to Merida; the Capital of the Province of Jucatan, In the Spanish West Indies. By Lieutenant Cook, Ordered by Sir William Burnaby, Rear Admiral of the Red, in Jamaica; With Despatches to the Governor of the Province; Relative to the Logwood Cutters in the Bay of Honduras, In

February and March 1765. *London: C. Parker.* M DCC LXIX. 8vo, 2 l., pp. 34. Map. H. 16285

"Some of Mr. Cook's observations, in his passage through the country, in 1765, though not written with elegance, will be entertaining to readers in general." — *M. Rev.*, XII. 231.

COOK (M. W.) Affectionately Addressed to Robt. J. Walker, [on his Appointment as] Governor of Kansas. By His Sister, Mrs. Martha Walker Cook of New Jersey. [*New York.* 1857?] 8vo, pp. 8. BA. 16286

COOK (M. D.) A Genealogical Address, giving a Brief History of the Parishioners and Founders of the Federal Street Church, from 1745–6 to 1862, with the Names of their Descendants, now Parishioners, delivered May 29, 1862. By Moody D. Cook, of Newburyport. Published for Subscribers. *Newburyport: Wm. H. Huse & Co., Prs.* 1862. 8vo, pp. 35.

COOK (M. P.) A Genealogical Address, giving a Brief History of the Parish and Founders of the Federal St. Church, 1862. Delivered before the Ladies' and Gentlemen's Association, 29th May, 1862. *Newburyport.* 1862. 8vo. 16288

COOK (R. D.) ... Niagara Mineral Spring at Monteagle House, Suspension Bridge, N. Y. *Niagara City.* 1859. 32mo, pp. 16. H. 16289

COOK (R. S.) Masked Batteries, By R. S. Cook. *New York: American Tract Society.* 16290

COOK. Report of a Western Tour [by R. S. Cook, Corresponding Secretary of the American Tract Society. n. p. n. d.] 8vo, pp. 16. H., M. 16291

COOK (S.) A Sermon Preached at Cambridge, on the Ordination of his Honor Thomas Hutchinson, Esq; ... Of the Province of Massachusetts-Bay in New-England, May 30th, 1770. Being the Anniversary for the Election of His Majesty's Council for the said Province. By Samuel Cook, A.M. ... *Boston: Printed by Edes and Gill,* ... MDCCLXX. 8vo, pp. 47. BA. 16292

Also in Thornton's "Pulpit of the American Revolution."

COOK (T. M.), *and* KNOX (T. W.) Public Record: containing the Speeches, Messages, Proclamations, and other Public Utterances of Horatio Seymour, from 1806 to the Present Time. With Appendix. Compiled and Edited by T. M. Cook and T. W. Knox. *New York.* 1868. 8vo, pp. xi, 413. 16293

Cook (W.) The plain Truths of the Gospel ... A Discourse Deliver'd at Hanover, December 1st. 1756. When the Reverend Mr. Samuel Baldwin Was Ordained ... . By William Cook [*sic*] ... . *Boston: Green & Russell.* M.DCC.LVII. 8vo, pp. 27. H. 16294

Cook. The Great Duty of Ministers ... . A Sermon Preach'd in a new Township, Narragansett, No. 2. [Westminster, Mass.] Oct. 20, 1742. When a Church was gathered there, and the Rev. Mr. Elisha Marsh Ordained ... . By William Cooke [*sic*] ... . *Boston: T. Fleet.* M,DCC,XL,II. 12mo.

Cook. A Sermon to a Society of Young People in Sudbury, October 1730. *Boston.* 1731. 8vo, 2 l., pp. 26. B. 16296

Cook (W.) The Eucleia, Works by Rev. William Cook. *Salem.* 1853–1862. 12mo. 16297

This singular collection consists of the following works, all of which were printed, illustrated, and bound by the eccentric author: Chestnut Street, A Poem. 12mo, pp. 40; The Olive Grove Poems. 1853. pp. 25; Sunbeams Through Pagan Clouds. 1853. pp. 16; The Telegraph or Star-Banner Song. pp. 42, (4); The Ploughboy, A Poem. In Three Parts. 1854–5. pp. 108; Fremont, A Poem. *Salem.* 1856. pp. 18; The Neriah. Three Parts. 1858–1860; The Bank. *Salem.* 1862; The Ploughboy's Harrow. In three parts; The Fragments. *Salem.* 1862; The Result. *Salem.* 1863; The Columbia; and Address ... before the Columbian Association, Aug. 22, 1863; Potsandove. *Salem.* 1864; Fireman's Liturgy. *Salem.* 1865; The Eudromia. *Salem.* 1866. These pamphlets were printed by the author, at Salem, are illustrated with woodcuts, also by the author, and are amusing for their absurdity.

Cook (W. A.) Hon. George W. Woodward and the Cubernatorial Contest in Pennsylvania. Review of the Speech in ... Philadelphia, December 13, 1860. A True Exposition of his Principles and Purposes. By William A. Cook. 1863. 8vo, pp. 18. 16298

Cook. Opinions and Practice of the Founders of the Republic, in Relation to Arbitrary Arrests, Imprisonment of Tories, Writ of Habeas Corpus, Seizure of Arms and of Private Papers, Domiciliary Visits, Confiscation of Real and Personal Estate, etc., etc. Or, The Administration of Abraham Lincoln Sustained by the Sages and Heroes of the Revolution. By William A. Cook. *Washington: William H. Moore.* 1864. 8vo, pp. 54. H. 16299

Cook (Z.) An Address, pronounced before the Massachusetts Horticultural Society ... 10th of September, 1830. By Zebedee Cook, Jr. *Boston.* 1830. 8vo, pp. 54. 16300

With an account of the Second Anniversary Festival

Cook Co., *Ill.* ... First Report of the Cook County Schools, by the School Commissioner. *Chicago.* 1862. 8vo, pp. 35. H.

Cooke (C.) A Sermon on the Life and Death of Abraham Lincoln, late President of the United States. Delivered in Smyrna, Delaware. June 1, 1865. By Rev. C. Cooke, D.D. *Philadelphia: Printed by John Richards.* 1865. 12mo, pp. 24.

Cooke (E.) A Voyage to the South Sea, and Round the World, perform'd in the years 1708, 1709, 1710, and 1711, by the Ships Duke and Dutchess of Bristol. Containing a Journal of all memorable Transactions during the said Voyage; the Winds, Currents, and Variation of the Compass; the taking of the Towns of Puna and Guayaquil, and several Prizes, one of which a rich Acapulco Ship. A Description of the American Coasts, from Tierra del Fuego in the South, to California in the North, (from the Coasting-Pilot, a Spanish Manuscript.) Wherein an Account is given of Mr. Alexander Selkirk, his Manner of living and taming some wild beasts during the four Years and four Months he liv'd upon the uninhabited Island of Juan Fernandes. Illustrated with Cuts and Maps. In two Volumes. By Capt. Edward Cooke. *London: Printed by H. M. for B. Lintot.* ... MDCCXII. 2 vols., 8vo, 12 l., pp. 456; (12), xxiv, 328, (8). 18 Maps, and Plate. C. 16303

"Edward Cooke was second captain on board the 'Dutchess,' the ship which accompanied the 'Duke,' both under Woodes Rodgers, on a voyage round the world. Captain Burney says that Cooke's journal and charts are inferior to those published by Woodes Rodgers. Dampier, who projected the expedition, and prevailed upon some able persons at Bristol to venture upon the undertaking, went as pilot in the 'Duke.'" — Rich, I. 20. It is generally supposed that De Foe took his "Robinson Crusoe" from the account here given of Alex. Selkirk, as it was the first book containing it. The Fonthill copy sold for £1, and Constable's for £1 11s. 6d. Cook's voyages is also in Henry's "Historical Account. *London.* 1774," Vol. II.

[Cooke (E.)] Memorial of the Citizens of Sandusky, for the Establishment of a Naval Depot, &c. on Johnson's Island, in Sandusky Bay. [Signed by Eleutheros Cooke and 12 others. n. p. 1865?] 8vo, pp. 8. H. 16304

Cooke (Elisha). Mr. Cook's Just and Seasonable Vindication: Respecting some Affairs transacted in the late General Assembly at Boston, 1720. [*Boston.* 1720.] 12mo, Title, pp. 20. M., W. + The Second Impression, Corrected. [*Boston.* 1720.] 12mo, pp. 19, 3. 16305

Cooke (F.) Proposal for introducing into Jamaica a quantity

of Gold and Silver Specie, sufficient to carry on the internal Commerce of the Country without the Assistance of any Foreign Coin, by the Hon. F. Cooke. *S. Jago de la Vega.* 1773. 16306

Cooke (G. F.) The Life of George Frederick Cooke, Esq. ... Containing an Account of the whole of his Theatrical Career ... to his final dramatic Exit, at Rhode Island, in America. *London: P. Egan.* [n. d.] 8vo, pp. 34. Plate by G. Cruikshank. 16307

Cooke (G. W.) The Former Glory of the African Race. *Norfolk, Va.* 1864. 8vo, pp. 7. H. 16308

Cooke. The History of Party; from the Rise of the Whig and Tory Factions, in the Reign of Charles II., to the passage of the Reform Bill. By George Wingrove ... . *London.* MDCCXXXVI–XXXVII. 3 vols., 8vo, pp. xii, 612; viii, 498; vii, 628, (41). BA., C. 16309

For the American Revolution, *see* the first half of Vol. III.

Cooke (H. B.) Memoirs of my Life Work. The Autobiography of Mrs. Harriet B. Cooke. *New York: Robert Carter & Brothers.* 1858. 12mo, pp. viii, 356. 16310

Cooke (I.) The American Orator, or Elegant Extracts in Prose and Poetry comprehending a Diversity of Oratorical Specimens of the Eloquence of Popular Assemblies ... &c. ... By Increase Cooke. *Hartford.* 1814. 12mo, pp. 408. + *New Haven: John Babcock & Son. Charleston, S. C.: S. & W. R. Babcock.* 1819. 12mo, pp. 408. BA., C. 16311

Cooke (J. W.) A Statement of Facts relating to the Ordination at Grace Church, with the Correspondence on the subject between the Rt. Rev. J. P. K. Henshaw, D.D. and the Rev. James W. Cooke, Rector of St. Michael's Church, Bristol, R. I. *Providence: Charles Burnett, Jr.* 1847. 8vo, pp. 72. H. 16312

For a reply to this pamphlet, *see* Mulchahey.

Cooke (J.) How to Organize a National Bank under Secretary Chase's Bill. Compiled and Presented by Jay Cooke & Co., Bankers. *Philadelphia: Ringwalt & Brown.* 1863. 8vo, pp. 40. + *Philadelphia.* 1863. 8vo, pp. 16. 16313

Also: Questions and Answers, or What the People ought to know about the National Banks. [*Sandusky?* 1867.] 8vo, pp. 11. H. *See also* [Elder (W.)]

Cooke (J. E.) Fairfax; or, the Master of Greenway Court. A Chronicle of the Valley of the Shenandoah. By John Esten Cooke. *New York: Carleton & Co.* 1868. 12mo, pp. 405.

Cooke. Henry St. John, Gentleman. *New York.* 1859. 12mo, pp. 503. 16315

A tale of Virginia life in 1774.

Cooke. Hilt to Hilt; or, Days and Nights in the Shenandoah in the Autumn of 1864. By J. E. Cooke. *New York.* 1869. 12mo, pp. 270. 16316

[Cooke.] Leather Stocking and Silk; or, Hunter John Myers and his Times; a Story of the Valley of Virginia. *New-York.* 1854. 12mo. C. 16317

Cooke. Mohun; or, The Last Days of Lee and his Paladins. Final Memoirs of a Staff Officer serving in Virginia. From the MSS. of Col. Surry of Eagles-nest. *New York: F. J. Huntington & Co.* 1869. 12mo, 6 l., pp. 509. 16318

Cooke. Stonewall Jackson: A Military Biography, with a Portrait and Maps. By John Esten Cooke, formerly of General Stuart's Staff. *New York: D. Appleton and Company.* 1866. Crown 8vo, pp. 470. Portrait, and 6 Maps. BA. 16319

Cooke. Surrey of Eagle's-Nest; or, The Memoirs of a Staff-Officer serving in Virginia. Edited, from the MSS. of Colonel Surrey, By Esten Cooke ... . *New York: Bunce & Huntington.* 1866. 12mo, pp. 484. 4 Woodcuts. BA. + *New York.* 1866. pp. 490. + Fourth Edition. *New York.* 1866. 12mo. 16320

A Confederate war novel. The author served on General Stuart's staff.

[Cooke.] The Virginia Comedians; or, Old Days in the Old Dominion. Edited from the MSS. of C. Effingham, Esq. *New York: D. Appleton & Co.* 1855. 2 vols., 12mo. C. 16321

Afterwards published with the author's name.

Cooke. Wearing of the Gray; being Personal Portraits, Scenes and Adventures of the War. By John Esten Cooke ... . *New York: E. B. Treat & Co.* 1867. 8vo, 11 l., pp. 601.

[Cooke.] The Youth of Jefferson; or, A Chronicle of College Scrapes at Williamsburgh, in Virginia A.D. 1764. *New York: Redfield.* 1854. 12mo, pp. 249. 16323

See Duyckinck's "Cyclopædia," Vol. II. 636. Also: Ellie, or the Human Comedy. (A novel; the scene in Richmond, Va.) — Hammer and Rapier. *New York.* 1870. 12mo, pp. 307. — The Last of the Foresters; or, Humours on the Border; a Story of the Old Virginia Frontier. *New York.* 1856. 12mo, pp. 419.

Cooke (J. H.) A Narrative of Events in the South of France, and of the Attack on New-Orleans, in 1814 and 1815. By Capt. John Henry Cooke. *London.* 1835. 12mo. P.

General Cass wrote a sharp review of this work.

Cooke (M. C.) The Seven Sisters of Sleep. Popular History of the Seven prevailing Narcotics of the World. By M. C. Cooke ... . *London: James Blackwood.* 16mo, pp. xv, 371.

Treats of the discovery of tobacco, coca, the edible earths of America, and the florispondio of Peru.

Cooke (M. F.) Report of the Trial of McLaurin F. Cooke, Sub-Master of the Eliot School, of the City of Boston, for an Assault and Battery upon Thomas J. Wall, a Pupil of that School; with the Arguments of Counsel and the Opinion of the Court reported in Full. Carefully revised and corrected. *Boston: A. M. Lawrence & Co.* [1859.] 8vo, pp. 86. C., H.

Cooke (P.) Address, at laying Corner-Stone of Calvanistic Society, Sept., 1828, in Hardwick, Mass., by Parsons Cooke. *Belchertown.* 1818. 8vo. 16327

Cooke. A Century of Puritanism and a Century of its opposites, with results contrasted to enforce Puritan Principles, and to trace what is peculiar in the People of Lynn, to what is peculiar in their History. By Parsons Cooke, Pastor of the First Church in Lynn. *Boston: S. K. Whipple & Co.* 1855. 12mo, pp. 444. 16328

Cooke. Moral Machinery Simplified. A Discourse, delivered at Andover, Massachusetts, July 4, 1839. By Parsons Cooke, ... *Andover: William Peirce.* 1839. pp. 40. 16329

Cooke. Second Part of Cooke's Centuries, being a Defence and Confirmation of the First, showing that Methodism is not a Branch of the Church of Christ. By Parsons Cooke. *Boston: S. K. Whipple & Company.* 1855. 12mo, pp. 299. 16330

Cooke. The Congregational Register; or Comparative and General Statistics. January, 1847. By Parsons Cooke. *Boston.* [n. d.] 18mo, pp. 113. H. 16331

Cooke. A Discourse ... [in] Lynn, on the ... Death of William Henry Harrison. ... . By Rev. Parsons Cooke. ... *Lynn.* 1841. 8vo, pp. 16. H. 16332

Cooke. A Remonstrance against an Established Religion in Massachusetts. By Parsons Cooke. *Boston: Pierce and Parker.* 1831. 12mo, pp. 24. M. 16333

Cooke. A Sermon ... Dedication of the Meeting-House Belonging to the East Evangelical Church and Society, in Ware, Mass., January 24, 1827. *Amherst.* 1827. 8vo, pp. 22.

Cooke. A Sermon, ... Installation of Rev. Randolph Campbell, as Pastor ... Newburyport, October 12, 1837. By Rev. Parsons Cooke ... . *Newburyport: Hiram Tozer.* 1837. 8vo, pp. 32. 16335

Cooke. Unitarianism an Exclusive System. A Sermon preached on the Annual Fast, April 3, 1828. By Parsons Cooks. *Belchertown.* 1828. 12mo, pp. 12. + Second Edition. *Boston.* [n. d.] 12mo, pp. 12. M. 16336

Cooke. Letter to Parsons Cooke. [In relation to his Fast Sermon.] From the Christian Examiner, July and Aug. 1828. 12mo. W. 16337

Cooke. A Reply to a Letter in the Christian Examiner, addressed to the Rev. Parsons Cooke. *Boston: printed by Peirce and Williams.* 1829. 12mo. pp. 38. H. 16338

Relates, in great measure, to the control of Harvard College by the Unitarians. Also: An Address delivered to the Ware-Village Temperance Society ... July 4, 1829. By Parsons Cooke. ... *Brookfield, Mass.: E. & G. Merriam.* 1829. 12mo, pp. 18. H. — Causes of the Decline of Doctrinal Preaching: A Sermon ... Pastoral Association of Mass. ... May 25, 1841. *Boston.* 1841. 8vo, pp. 24. + Second Edition. *Boston.* 1841. 8vo, pp. 24. M. — The Condition of the Congregational Board of Publication, set forth in a Protest against a Recent Vote of its Executive Committee. ... *Boston: Crocker and Brewster.* 1859. 8vo, pp. 32. H. — An Essay on the Gospel's Relations to the Civil Law. ... Second Edition. *Boston.* 1843. 8vo, pp. 22. H. — Necromancy, or, a Rap for the Rappers. *Boston.* 1857. 12mo.

Cooke (P. St. G.) Scenes and Adventures in the Army; or Romance of Military Life. By P. St. G. Cooke, Lieutenant-Colonel Second Dragoons, U. S. A. *Philadelphia: Lindsay and Blakiston.* 1850. 12mo, pp. 432. C. 16339

Reissued, *Philadelphia,* 1857 and 1859. Includes copious details of Indian warfare.

Cooke. To my Fellow-countrymen of Powhatan; and more generally to my Fellow-citizens of Virginia. *New Orleans.* 1860. 16340

Cooke (P.) Historical Recollections, Discourse delivered at Lebanon, N. H., Nov. 25, 1830, embracing the Leading Events in the Civil and Ecclesiastical History of said Town. Phineas Cooke. *Concord.* 1831. 8vo, pp. 17. 16341

Cooke. Reciprocal Obligations of Religion and Civil Government: A Discourse delivered ... before the Consolidated Constitution of ... New Hampshire, on the day of the Anniversary Election, June 2. ... *Concord.* 1825. 8vo. 16342

Also: A Discourse, delivered at Acworth, ... March 8, 1829. By Phineas Cooke. ... . *Windsor: John C. Allen.* 1829. 8vo, pp. 27. H. — An Oration, delivered at Keene, N. H., before the Washington Benevolent Society, on the 5th Day of July, 1813. *Keene: John Prentiss.* 1813. 8vo, pp. 16. H.

Cooke (R. L.) A Description of Wyer's Cave, Augusta, Va. *Raleigh.* 1856. Map. 32mo. + Second Edition. *Staunton, Va.* 1836. 8vo. 16343

Cooke (Samuel). Divine Sovereignty in the Salvation of Sinners ... . In a Sermon ... before the Eastern Association of Fairfield County ... July 29th. 1741. ... By Samuel Cooke ... . *Boston: J. Edwards.* 1741. 8vo, pp. 40. B., W. 16344

Cooke. Necessarius. The Continuance of an able and Godly Minister very needful to a People. A Sermon preached at the Funeral of the Reverend John Davenport ... Stamford; who died Febr. 5, 1730–1 ... . By the Rev. Samuel Cooke ... . *New-York: Printed by J. P. Zenger.* 1731. 16mo, pp. 62. B., M. 16345

Cooke (S.), *of Cambridge.* The Charge of St. Paul ... a Sermon Preached at the Ordination Of the Reverend Mr. William Symmes ... in Andover, Nov. 1, 1758. By Samuel Cooke ... . *Boston: Green & Russell.* M.DCC.LIX. 8vo, pp. 23.

Cooke. Christ, holding the Stars ... . A Sermon ... at the Ordination Of the Reverend Nathanael Robbins ... in Milton, February 13th, 1750, 1. By Samuel Cooke ... . *Boston: Printed by S. Kneeland.* MDCCLI. 8vo, Title, pp. 20. BA., W. 16347

Cooke. A Sermon ... at Cambridge ... May 30th, 1770. Being the Anniversary for the Election of His Majesty's Council for the said Province. By Samuel Cooke ... . *Boston: Printed by Edes & Gill.* MDCCLXX. 8vo, pp. 47. 16348

Cooke. The solemn Charge given to Ministers ... a Sermon ... at the Ordination Of the Reverend Mr. Cotton Brown, ... in Brooklin. October 26. 1748. By Samuel Cooke ... . *Boston: Printed by Rogers & Fowle.* 1748. 8vo, pp. 31. 16349

Cooke. The violent destroyed: And oppressed delivered. A Sermon, preached at Lexington, April 19, 1777. For a Memorial of the Bloody Tragedy, barbarously acted, by a party of British Troops, in that Town and the Adjacent, April 19, 1775. By Samuel Cooke ... . *Boston: Thomas and Nicholas Bowes.* M,DCC,LXXVII. 8vo, pp. 31. BA., M. 16350

Cooke (S.) The Funeral Sermons, preached ... New-York ... following the Death of Miss Jay on the 13th Nov., and of her Sister, Mrs. Banyer, on the 21st of the same Month. To which is prefixed a short Biographical Memoir. By Rev. Samuel Cooke. *New-York.* 1857. 8vo. S. 16351

Cooke (W.) *See* Cook (W.)

Cooke (W. D.) Revolutionary History of North Carolina, in Three Lectures, by Rev. Francis L. Hawks ... Hon. David L. Swain ... and Hon. Wm. A. Graham: ... . To which is prefixed a Preliminary Sketch of the Battle of the Alamance. Compiled by William D. Cooke, A.M. ... *Raleigh: William D. Cooke. New York: George P. Putnam.* 1853. 12mo, pp. 236. 5 Woodcuts and 1 Facsimile of Writing. BA., C. 16352

Cooke (W. M.) Proceedings and Speeches on the Announcement of the Death of Hon. William M. Cooke, of Memphis, In the House of Representatives of the Confederate States, on the 19th of April, 1863. *Richmond: Smith, Bailey & Co.* 1863. 12mo, pp. 19. 16353

Cool Reply to ... J. Wesley, 1775. *See* S. (T.)

Cool Thoughts, &c. *See* [Franklin (B.)], and [Galloway (Joseph)].

A Coole Conference between the Scottish Commissioners Cleared Reformation, and the Holland Ministers Apologeticall Narration. 1644. 4to, 9 l., pp. 18. 16354

Cooley (B. F.) Exposition of Spirit Manifestation. By Benjamin Franklin Cooley. *Springfield (Mass.)* 1852. 12mo.

[Cooley.] A Summary Exposition of the Social Theory of the ... Perfectionists ... Showing the Relation of the Sexes in the Kingdom of Heaven on Earth ... especially those in the Oneida Association ... . *Worcester.* 1850. 8vo, pp. 23, (1).

Cooley (E.) A Brief Exposition of the Claim of Ebenezer Cooley, of the State of Louisiana, upon the Government of the United States. *Washington.* 1827. 8vo, pp. 23. 16357

Cooley (E. K.) The Southern Trade Directory: a Commercial Register of Prominent New York Houses engaged in the Southern Trade. May, 1859. Published Annually, by E. K. Cooley ... . [*New York.*] 1859. 8vo, pp. 15, (1). H.

Cooley (H. S.) An Appeal in Behalf of Common Schools in Illinois, 1848. S. 16359

Cooley (J.) An Oration delivered at Granville, Massachusetts, in Commemoration of the American Independence, By James Cooley. *Hartford.* 1813. pp. 12. 16360

Cooley (J. E.) Review of the Administration of General Pierce. Anti-Nebraska, Anti-Administration and Anti-Rum Platform. Speech of Hon. James E. Cooley, at a meeting of the Democracy ... Nov. 4th, 1854, at the Village of Patchogue, in Suffolk Co., L. I. *New York: John F. Trow, Printer.* 1854. 8vo, pp. 22. B., H. 16361

Cooley. Speech of the Hon. James E. Cooley, before the Democracy of Syracuse, in Mass Meeting Assembled, on Tuesday Evening, Nov. 1, 1853. *New York: John F. Trow, Printer.* 1853. 8vo, pp. 47. 16362

Also: Mr. Cooley's remarks in the Senate [of N. Y.] ... on the bill ... for the relief of W. W. Niles, for the destruction of his buildings in May, 1847, on Long Island farms, by fire. [n. p. n. d.] 8vo, pp. 29. H. — Parties & Partizans. Speech ... N. Y. Senate, June 2, 1853. 8vo. M. Two fierce poetical satires on Park and Gliddon, bearing the titles of "Humbuggiana," and the "Spawn of Ixion," 1846, are also attributed to Mr. Cooley.

Cooley (J.) A View of Governor Jay's Administration. By Jonathan Cooley. *Goshen: printed by John G. Hunter.* 1801. 8vo. 16363

Cooley (T. M.) A Treatise on the Constitutional Limitations which rest upon the Legislative power of the States of the American Union. By Hon. Thomas M. Cooley of the Supreme Court of Michigan. *Boston: Little, Brown & Co.* 1868. 8vo, pp. xlvii, 720. C. 16364

Cooley (T. M.) A Sermon, ... in Granville, Oct. 24, 1824: on Occasion of the Death of Louisa Maria Cooley Daughter of James Cooley ... . By Timothy Mather Cooley ... . *Springfield: Tannantt & Co.* 1824. 16mo, pp. 15. H.

Cooley. Sketches of the Life and Character of the Rev. Lemuel Haynes, A.M., for many Years Pastor of a Church in Rutland, Vt., and late in Granville, New York. By Timothy Mather Cooley, D.D. ... With some Introductory Remarks by William B. Sprague, D.D. ... *New York: Harper & Brothers.* 1837. 12mo, Title, pp. vii–345. Portrait. BA., S. 16366

Haynes was the son of a negro and a white woman. Also: The Universal Spread of the Gospel, a Sermon, preached at Northampton, before the Hampshire Missionary Society; ... August 25, 1808. ... . *Northampton: William Butler.* 1808. 8vo, pp. 40. H. — A Sermon, Granville, May 1, 1805. *Hartford.* 1805. 8vo.

[Cooley (W. Desborough).] The History of Maritime and Inland Discovery. ... *London: Longman,* [*etc.*] 1830. 3 vols., post 8vo, 2 l., pp. xii, 398; 1 l., pp. xiii, 356; xv, 384. (Lardner's Cab. Cyclop., Vol. 80–82.) BA. 16367

Cooley. Histoire générale des voyages et découvertes maritimes et continentales, depuis le commencement du monde ... traduite de l'anglais, par Ad. Joanne et Old-Nick. *Paris: Paulin.* 1840–41. 3 vols., 12mo. 16368

Coolidge (Austin J.), *and* Mansfield (J. B.) History and Description of New England, General and Local. By A. J. Coolidge and J. B. Mansfield. ... In Two Volumes. Vol. I. Maine, New Hampshire, and Vermont. *Boston: Austin J. Coolidge.* 1859. 8vo, pp. xxvii, 1023, (1). 3 Maps and 81 Woodcuts. BA., C. + *Boston: A. J. Coolidge.* 1864. S.

Coolidge (C.) Report of the Committee on the Memorial of Cornelius Coolidge, 1834. [*Boston.* 1834.] 8vo, pp. 20.

Coolidge. Report of the Committee on the Petition of Cornelius Coolidge; with Remarks by the Petitioner. *Boston.* 1834. 8vo, pp. 26. 16371

Coolidge (G.) Anniversary Poem, delivered before the Mechanic Apprentices' Library Association, ... February 22d, 1844. By George Coolidge ... . *Boston, the Association.* 1844. 8vo, pp. 16. BA., M. 16372

Coolidge. Coolidge's Business Lists of Boston. ... [*Boston:*] *Published by Bradley, Dayton & Co.* [1861.] 4to, pp. 44.

Coolidge (James Ivers Trecothiek). An Address delivered before the Boston Young Men's Christian Union, at the Opening of their Rooms ... May 6, 1853. By Rev. J. I. T. Coolidge. *Boston: Leonard C. Bowles.* 1853. 8vo, pp. 16. B., BA.

Coolidge. A Farewell Discourse, delivered to the Purchase Street Congregation, April 30, 1848, on Occasion of leaving their Old Church. By J. I. T. Coolidge. ... *Boston: Wm. Crosby and H. P. Nichols.* 1848. 8vo, pp. 18. H. 16375

Coolidge. A Farewell Discourse delivered at the Thirteenth Congregational Church, on Occasion of resigning his Charge ... July 4, 1858. By J. I. T. Coolidge. ... *Boston: James Munroe and Company.* 1858. 8vo, pp. 22. H. 16376

Coolidge. The Perfect and Upright Man: a Discourse preached ... June 7, 1857, after the Decease of Isaac Williams, Esq. ... *Boston: John Wilson and Son.* 1857. 8vo, pp. 15. H.

Coolidge. The Power of Christianity. A Discourse preached at the Dedication of the House of the Thirteenth Congregational Church, in Harrison Avenue, Boston, May 3, 1848. By J. I. T. Coolidge. ... *Boston: Wm. Crosby & H. P. Nichols.* 1848. 8vo, pp. 27. H. 16378

Coolidge. A Three Years' Ministry. A Sermon preached February 9, 1845, at the Purchase Street Congregational Church, being the Third Anniversary of his Ordination, by J. I. T. Coolidge. ... *Boston: Samuel N. Dickinson.* 1845. 8vo, pp. 20.

Coolidge (R. H.) Statistical Report on the Sickness and Mortality in the Army of the United States, compiled from the Records of the Surgeon-General's Office, embracing a period of Sixteen Years, from January, 1839, to January, 1855. By Richard H. Coolidge, M.D., Assistant Surgeon, U. S. Army. *Washington.* 1856. 4to, pp. 703. (Senate Ex. Doc., 34th Cong., 1st Sess.) 16380

Coolidge. Statistical Report ... embracing a Period of Five Years from January, 1855, to January, 1860. ... By Richard Coolidge, M.D. *Washington: George W. Bonner.* 1860. 4to, pp. 515. Plate. 16381

Coolidge (*Rev.* S.), *A.M.* A Sermon Preached at ... Castle William, Mareh 26. 1738. Upon the ... Death of ... Caroline, Queen-Consort of ... George the Second ... By Samuel Coollidge ... . *Boston: S. Kneeland & T. Green.* 1738. 8vo, 2 l., pp. 26. H., W. 16382

Coolidge (S.) Major Sidney Coolidge, U. S. A. [n. p. 1863.] 16mo, Title, pp. 14. H. 16383

Coolidge (Valorous P.) Trial of Dr. V. P. Coolidge, for the Murder of Edward Mathews. Before the Supreme Judicial Court at Augusta, March 14, 1848. [*Augusta.* 1848.] 8vo, pp. 64. H. 16384

Cools (*Baron* A. de). Droit et necessité des garanties sociales et politiques réclamées par les colonies françaises, ou Observations sur les rapports des lois organiques coloniales présentées à la Chambre des députés pendant la session de 1831. *Paris: Delaunay.* 1832. 8vo, pp. 80. 16385

Cools. De l'émancipation des esclaves dans les colonies françaises, et spécialement de l'affranchissement des enfants à naître. *Paris: Guiraudet.* 1838. 8vo, pp. 8. 16386

Cools. Lettre à M. le ministre des finances sur son opinion dans la question des sucres. *Paris: imp. de Guiraudet.* 1835. 4to. 16387

Cools. Quelques observations d'un délégué des colonies à MM. les membres de la commission chargée de l'examen de la proposition de M. Passy. *Paris: imp. de Guiraudet.* 1838. 8vo.

Coombe (P.) A Sermon on the Divine Origin of Civil Government, and the Sinfulness of Rebellion. Delivered in the Ebenezer Methodist Episcopal Church, Sabbath, June 30, 1861. By Rev. P. Coombe. Published by Request. *Philadelphia: Barnard & Jones.* 1861. 8vo, pp. 24. 16389

Coombe (Thomas). Edwin: Or the Emigrant. An Ecloque. To which are added Three other Poetical Sketches. By the Rev. Mr. Coombe. *Philadelphia: Printed by John Dunlap, in Market-Street.* D,DCC,LXXV. 4to, pp. 24. P. 16390

Imitates Collins, Gray, and Goldsmith, rather too closely.

Coombe. The Peasant of Auburn; or the Emigrant, etc. By T. Coombe. *Philadelphia:* [n. d.] 8vo, pp. 48. 16391

Coombe. A Sermon, preached before the Congregations of Christ Church and St. Peter's, Philadelphia, On Tuesday, July 20, 1775. Being the day recommended by the Honorable Continental Congress for a General Fast throughout the Twelve United Colonies of North-America. By Thomas Coombe, M.A. Chaplin to the Most Noble the Marquis of Rockingham. Published by Request. *Philadelphia: printed by John Dunlap.* M.DCC.LXXV. 8vo, 2 l., pp. 29. BA., P. + Second Edition.

Philadelphia: Dunlap. MDCCLXXV. 8vo, 2 l., pp. 29. + *Newport.* 1776. 16392

With a dedication to Benjamin Franklin.

Coombe. Two Sermons: Christmas Day, 1773, ... Christ's Church, and St. Peter's. *Philadelphia.* 1774. 12mo, pp. 59.

Coombs (Frederick). The Dawn of the Millenium! Splendid Discovery! A Beautiful plan to give every Man (and Woman also) a Nice House and Lot, and a Nice Little wife or a Husband for all, with nearly One Hundred Pictorial Illustrations or Passages in the Life of the Author, [etc.] *New York: author.* [1869.] 8vo, 1 l., pp. 4, 26 l., pp. 29–143, 27 l. 110 Woodcuts. C. 16394

Coombs (G.) Sketch of the Trial of George Coombs, for the Murder of Maria Henry, alias Maria Coombs, on the 15th of June, 1816. Conducted (on Tuesday, 3d December,) before the Supreme Judicial Court ... . *Boston: T. G. Bangs.* 1816. 8vo, pp. 22. BA. 16395

Coombs (J. J.) Speech at the Union League Reading Room, Washington, D. C., September 1, 1863. 8vo, pp. 16. 16396

Coombs. *See* Burr (Aaron), Vol. III., No. 9435.

Cooney (R.) A Compendious History of the Northern Part of the Province of New Brunswick, and of the District of Gaspe, in Lower Canada. By Robert Cooney. ... *Halifax, N. S.: printed by Joseph Howe.* 1832. 8vo, pp. (7), 288. H. + Second Edition. *Halifax.* 1832. 8vo, pp. (7), 288. 16397

Cooney. The Lord is on our Side. Sermon ... Odelltown, Nov. 9, 1829. Anniversary of the Battle fought at the above place, between the Insurgents and the Loyal Volunteers. *Montreal.* 1840. 16398

Also: The Autobiography of a Wesleyan Methodist Missionary. *Montreal.* 1856. 8vo, pp. 406.

Coope (R.) R. Coope's Letter to the South Sea Proprietors, 1739. 16399

Cooper (C. W.) Prize Essay. Frontenac, Lennox & Addington. ... . By C. W. Cooper ... , *Kingston: James M. Creighton, Printer.* 1866. 8vo, pp. vi, 5–105. H. 16400

Cooper (D. M.) Obituary Discourse on the occasion of the Death of Noah Henry Ferry, Major of the Fifth Michigan

Cavalry, killed at Gettysburg, July 3, 1863. By Rev. David M. Cooper. *New York: J. F. Trow.* 1863. 8vo, pp. 46. Portrait. 16401

Cooper (Edward). *See* Newfoundland.

Cooper (E.) Popular History of America. From the Discovery by Columbus to the Establishment of the Federal Republic of the United States. By Elizabeth Cooper. In Three Periods. *London: Longman & Co.* 1865. Post 8vo, pp. xi, 527. 16402

Cooper (E.) A Funeral Discourse, on the Death of that eminent Man the late Reverend John Dickens. By the Reverend Ezekiel Cooper. *Philadelphia.* 1799. 12mo, pp. 36.

[Cooper (Jacob).] The Loyalty demanded by the Present Crisis. [Republished from the Danville Review.] *Philadelphia: Henry B. Ashmead.* 1864. 8vo, Title, pp. 24. 16404

Cooper (J.) Speech of James Cooper on Nebraska and Kansas. *Washington.* 1854. 8vo, pp. 8. 16405

Cooper. Speech of Hon. J. Cooper, of Pennsylvania, on Non-Intervention. ... In the Senate ... April 28, 1852. *Washington.* 1852. 8vo, pp. 23. H. 16406

Cooper (J.) The Death of President Lincoln; A Memorial Discourse, delivered in the Bureau Baptist Church; West Philadelphia, on Sunday, April 16th, 1865, by the Pastor, Rev. James Cooper. *Washington: James F. Rodgers, Printer.* 1865. 8vo, pp. 24. B. 16407

Cooper (James Fenimore). Adventures in the Woods. From the Leather-Stocking Tales of J. F. Cooper. *London.* 186–. 16408

Cooper. Afloat and Ashore, or the Adventures of Miles Wallingford. By James Fenimore Cooper. *Philadelphia.* 1844. 4 vols., 12mo, pp. 236; 268; 222; 207. + *Paris: Galignani.* 1844. 8vo. + *Paris: Baudry* [etc.] 1844. 8vo. + *London: Bentley.* 1844. 3 vols., post 8vo. + *New York: Stringer and Townsend.* 1852. 2 vols., 12mo, pp. 236; 268. H. + Fourth Thousand. *London: G. Routledge & Co.* 1856. 16mo, Title, pp. 7–300. H. + [*Id.*] 1862. 8vo. + *New York: James G. Gregory.* 1864. 12mo, pp. 502. B. + *New York: Hurd and Houghton.* 1867. 12mo, pp. 502. 16409

Cooper. Sur terre et sur mer, ou Aventures de Miles Vallingford. Traduit ... E. de La Bédollière. *Paris: Gustave Barba.* 1844. 2 vols., 8vo, $44\frac{3}{4}$ sheets. + [*Ibid.*] 1864. 4to, pp. 68. 25 Vignettes. 16410

Cooper. A bord et à terre. Traduit de l'anglais par Defauconpret. *Paris: Furne; Ch. Gosselin.* 1845. 8vo. 2 Engravings and a Frontispiece. 16411

Cooper. The American Democrat; or Hints on the Social and Civic Relations of the United States of America. By J. Fenimore Cooper. *Cooperstown: H. & E. Phinney.* 1838. 12mo, pp. 192. C., H. 16412

See "N. Am. Rev.," July, 1838.

Cooper. Amerikanische Romane, neu aus dem Englischen übertragen. *Stuttgart: S. G. Liesching.* 1840–48. 89 pts., 12mo. + Amerikanische und Seeromane. *Stuttgart: Carl Hoffmann.* 1853, 54. 30 vols., 16mo. 30 Plates. 16413

Cooper. Ausgewählte Romane. ... . *Franckfurt: Sauerländer.* 1839. 10 vols., 8vo. 16414

Cooper. The Battle of Lake Erie, or Answers to Messrs. Burges, Duer, and Mackenzie. By J. Fenimore Cooper. *Cooperstown: H. & E. Phinney.* 1843. pp. 117, (1). H.

Cooper. The Borderers. *London.* 1829. 3 vols., post 8vo. BD. + The Borderers, or The Wept of Wish-ton-Wish: a Tale. By J. F. Cooper. Revised ... with a New Preface, Notes, etc. by the Author. *London: Richard Bentley.* 1837. 16mo. + [*Id.*] 1849. 12mo. + *Paris: Baudry* [etc.] 1835. 8vo, 24 sheets. + *London: Routledge.* 1862. 8vo. 16416

The American edition is entitled "The Wept of Wept-ton-Wish."

[Cooper.] The Bravo; A Tale. *Philadelphia.* 1831. 2 vols., 12mo, pp. 240; 236. B. + *London.* 1831. 3 vols., post 8vo. + *Paris: Baudry* [etc.] 1831. 8vo. + [*Ibid.*] 1836. 8vo. + A New Edition. *Philadelphia.* 1836. 2 vols., 12mo. + *London: Bentley.* 1849. 12mo. + *New York: Stringer & Townsend.* 1852. 2 vols., 12mo, pp. 240; 236. + [*Ibid.*] 1858. + Illustrated by F. O. C. Darley. *New York: W. A. Townsend and Company.* 1859. 12mo. 16417

A political novel. *See* Duyckinck, II. 110.

[Cooper.] Le Bravo ... . Traduit ... par ... [Defauconpret]. *Paris: Ch. Gosselin.* 1831. 4 vols., 12mo, 41 sheets. + Traduction nouvelle avec des ... notes historiques. *Paris: Furne.* 1832. 8vo, $29\frac{3}{4}$ sheets. + *Paris: Gustave Barba.* 1838. 4 vols., 12mo. + Traduction de La Bédollière. *Paris: G. Barba.* 1850. 4to. 16418

[Cooper.] Der Bravo ... . Aus dem Englischen von D. Gottfried Friedenberg. *Berlin: Drencker u. H.* 1832. 3 vols., 8vo. 16419

Cooper. Banditen. *Christianstad: Schmidt & Comp.* 1833. 2 pts., 8vo. 16420

Cooper. Brief Statement of the Pleadings and Argument in the Case of J. Fenimore Cooper versus Horace Greeley and Thomas McElrath, in an action for Libel, tried at ... Saratoga ... December 9, 1842 ... *New York.* 1843. 8vo, pp. 16.

Mr. Cooper was a plantiff in many libel cases. *See* Duyckinck, Vol. II.

Cooper. The Chain-Bearer, or the Little-page Manuscripts. *New York.* 1845. + *London: Bentley.* 1845. 3 vols., post 8vo. + *Paris: Baudry* [etc.] 1846. 8vo. + *Paris: Galignani.* 1846. 8vo. + *New York: Stringer and Townsend.* 1852. 2 vols., 12mo, pp. 212; 228. H. + *London: C. H. Clarke.* 1859. 8vo. + *New York: Hurd and Houghton.* 1865. 12mo. + *New York.* 1856. 12mo, pp. 438. 16422

A continuation of the "Anti-Rent" Satanstoe.

Cooper. Le porte-chaîne. Traduit ... par C. A. Defauconpret. *Paris: Passard.* 1847. 2 vols., 8vo, 41 sheets. + Traduction de La Bédollière. *Paris: Barba.* 1850. 8vo. + [*Ibid.*] 1854. 4to. + [*Ibid.*] 1869. 4to, pp. 80. 16423

Cooper. Christophe Colomb. Traduction de La Bédollière. *Paris: Barba.* 1865. 4to, pp. 84. 16424

A translation of "Mercedes of Castile"?

[Cooper.] The Chronicles of Cooperstown. *Cooperstown: H. & E. Phinney.* 1838. 12mo, pp. 108. C. 16425

Cooper. The Crater, or Vulcan's Peak; a Tale of the Pacific. *New York.* 1847. 2 vols., 12mo, pp. 234; 227. + *New York: Stringer & Townsend.* 1852. 2 vols., 12mo, pp. 234; 227. H. + *New York.* 1856. 12mo, pp. 459. 16426

A Utopian romance, giving the author's idea of government.

COOPER. Le cratère, ou Marc dans son île. Traduit par A. J. B. Defauconpret. *Paris: Furne* [etc.] 1852. 8vo, 23½ sheets. Illustr. + Suite de la traduction de Defauconpret. *Paris: Passard.* 1852. 2 vol., 8vo. 16427

COOPER. Le cratère, ou le Robinson américain. Par J. F. Cooper. Traduction Defauconpret ... corrigée. *Paris: Rigaud.* 1870. 8vo, pp. 352. 16428

COOPER. Das Marcus-Riff oder der Krater. ... Aus dem Englischen des Fenimore Cooper, übersetzt von G. N. Bärman. *Stuttgart: Franckh.* 1848. 2 vols., 4to, pp. 178; 292. (Das belletr. Ausland, 1135.–1143. Bd.) 16429

[COOPER.] The Deerslayer; or the First War-Path. A Tale. By the author of the Last of the Mohicans. *Philadelphia.* 1841. 2 vols. + Second Edition. *London: Bentley.* 1841. 3 vols., post 8vo. + *Paris: Galignani.* 1841. 8vo. + *Paris: Baudry* [etc.] 1841. 8vo. + *Philadelphia.* 1845. 2 vols., 12mo. + Revised Edition. *New-York.* 1850. 12mo. + *London: Richard Bentley.* 1850. 16mo. + *New York: Stringer and Townsend.* 1852. 2 vols., 12mo, pp. 267; 282. H. + *London.* 1855. 12mo. + Illustrated by F. O. C. Darley. *New York: W. A. Townsend* 1859. 12mo. + [*Ibid.*] 1861. 8vo. *London: Routledge.* 1862. 12mo. + *New York: Hurd and Houghton.* 1866. 12mo. 16430

This, in point of order, is the first of the "Leather-Stocking Series."

COOPER. Deerslayer ou le tueur de daims. Traduit ... par A. J. B. Defauconpret. *Paris: Ch. Gosselin.* 1842. 4 vols., 12mo. + *Paris: Furne; Ch. Gosselin.* 1849. 8vo. + Traduction Defauconpret. *Paris: Vermot et Cᵉ.* 1867. 8vo, pp. 439. + [*Ibid.*] 18mo, pp. 439. + [Entitled] Le tueur de daims. Traduit par Marie Guerrier de Haupt. *Paris.* 1867. 2 vols., 32mo.

COOPER. De hertendooder. Een Amerikaansch verhaal. Naar het Engelsch. *Amsterdam: P. N. van Kampen.* 1842. 3 pts., 8vo. + Tweede druk. *Leiden: J. W. van Leeuwen en van den Heuvell en van Santen.* 1869. 2 vols., 8vo, pp. 4, 234; 2, 204. 16432

COOPER. Œil-de-faucon. Traduction de La Bédollière. *Paris: Barba.* 1851. 4to, 8 sheets. + *Paris: Barba.* 1865. 18mo, pp. 308. + [*Ibid.*] 1868. 4to, pp. 64. 25 Vignettes.

COOPER. Eva Effingham, or Home. *London: Bentley.* 1838. 3 vols., post 8vo, pp. 300; 320; 392. + *Paris: Baudry* [etc.] 1839. 8vo. + *London: Routledge.* 1862. 12mo. 16434

This is the title of the English edition of "Home as Found."

COOPER. Eve Effingham. Traduit ... par A. J. B. Defauconpret. *Paris: Gosselin.* 1839. 4 vols., 12mo, 38½ sheets. + *Paris: Furne* [etc.] 1847. 8vo. Illustr. + *Paris: G. Barba.* 1852. 4to. + Traduction de La Bédollière. *Paris: Barba.* 1868. 4to, pp. 64. 25 Vignettes. 16435

COOPER. Eva Effingham, of Schetsen van Amerikaansche zeden. Uit het Engelsch vertaald. *Zutphen: W. J. Thieme.* 1841. 2 pts., 8vo. 16436

[COOPER.] The Headsman; or, the Abbaye des Vignerons. *London.* 1833. 3 vols., 8vo. + *Paris: Baudry.* 1833. 8vo. + A New Edition. *Philadelphia.* 1836. 2 vols., 12mo. + *London: Richard Bentley.* 1842. 16mo. + [*Ibid.*] + *New York: Stringer and Townsend.* 1852. 2 vols., 12mo, pp. 263; 261. H. + [*Ibid.*] 1857. + *New York: W. A. Townsend and Company.* 1860. 18mo. + *London: Routledge.* 1862. 12mo. *New York: Hurd and Houghton.* 1866. 16437

Also political. *See* Duyckinck, II. 110.

COOPER. Böddelen i Bern, Fortælling oversat af T. Levin. *Kiöbenhavn: Liunge.* 1834. 8vo, pp. 488. 16438

A translation of "The Headsman."

COOPER. Le bourreau de Berne. Traduit ... par ... Defauconpret. *Paris: Ch. Gosselin.* 1833. 4 vols., 12mo, 40⅞ sheets. + Traduction nouvelle, avec des éclaircissements et des notes historiques. *Paris: Furne.* 1834. 8vo, 29½ sheets. + Traduction de La Bédollière. *Paris: Barba.* 1851. 4to. + [*Ibid.*] 1865. 8vo, pp. 66. 16439

COOPER. Die Henker ... . Aus dem Englischen von Joh. Sporschil. *Braunschweig: Vieweg und Sohn.* 1834. 3 pts., 16mo. 16440

COOPER. Heathcotes; or, The Wept of Wish-ton-Wish. *London: Hodgson.* 1854. 8vo. 16441

COOPER. The History of the Navy of the United States of America. By James Fenimore Cooper. *Philadelphia: Lea.* 1839. 2 vols., 8vo, pp. 394; 282. Map and Plan. C. +

London: Richard Bentley. 1839. 2 vols., 8vo, pp. xxxv, xii, 456; xii, 558, Note, 1 l. 2 Portraits, and Map. + *Paris.* 1839. 8vo. Portraits and Map. + *Paris: Galignani.* 1839. 2 vols., 8vo. 2 Engravings. + *Paris: Baudry* [etc.] 1839. 8vo. 2 Engravings. + Second Edition, with Corrections. *Philadelphia: Lea and Blanchard.* 1840. 2 vols., 8vo, pp. 438; 417. Plate. + *Philadelphia.* 1841. 8vo, pp. 447. + Third Edition, with Corrections and Additions. *Philadelphia.* 1843. 8vo. + *Cooperstown.* 1846. 2 vols., 8vo. + *New York.* 1851. 8vo. 16442

COOPER. History of the Navy of the United States of America. By J. Fenimore Cooper. Continued to 1853, from the author's Manuscripts and other Authentic Sources. Three volumes in one. *New York: G. P. Putnam & Co.* 1853. 8vo, pp. 276, 248, 100, 1 l. 7 Plates. C. 16443

See "N. Am. Rev.," XLIX.

COOPER. [Same.] Abridged ... . Continued to 1856 ... [by Henry F. Phinney?] With Illustrations. *New York: Stringer & Townsend.* 1856. 12mo, pp. 508. H. 16444

COOPER. Histoire de la marine aux Etats-Unis d'Amérique; traduit de l'Anglais par Paul Jessé. *Paris: Corréard; Dumaine.* 1845–46. 3 vols., 8vo. 16445

COOPER. Geschichte der nordamerikanischen Seemacht und ihrer Kriegsthaten. Aus dem Englischen übersetzt von H. Künzel. *Frankfurt am Main: J. D. Sauerländer.* 1840. 4 vols., 16mo. C. 16446

[COOPER.] Home as Found. ... By the author of Homeward Bound, the Pioneers, &c. *Philadelphia.* 1838. 2 vols., 12mo, pp. 239; 253. + *New York: Stringer and Townsend.* 1852. 2 vols., 12mo, pp. 239; 253. H. 16447

This and the following are satires on newspaper editors. *See* Duyckinck, I. 111.

[COOPER] Homeward Bound; or the Chase. A Tale of the Sea. By the author of the Pilot, the Spy, &c. *Philadelphia.* 1838. 2 vols., 12mo, pp. 276; 288. + *London.* 1838. 3 vols., post 8vo. + A New Edition. *Philadelphia.* 1842. 2 vols., 12mo. + *London: Richard Bentley.* 1842. + [*Ibid.*] 1849. 12mo. + *New York: Stringer and Townsend.* 1852. 2 vols., 12mo, pp. 225; 248. H. + Illustrated by F. O. C. Darley. *New York: W. A. Townsend and Company.* 1860. 12mo, pp. 532. B. + *London: Routledge.* 1862. 8vo.

COOPER. Die Heimkehr, oder die Jagd. ... Uebersetzt von Joh. Sporschil. *Leipzig: Tauchnitz.* 1838. 3 vols., 8vo.

COOPER. Jack Tier, or the Florida Reef. *New York.* 1848. + *London: Hodgson.* 1848. 8vo. + *New York: Stringer and Townsend.* 1852. 2 vols., 12mo, pp. 244; 217. + *New York.* 1856. 12mo, pp. 459. *New York: Hurd and Houghton.* 1866. 12mo. 16450

COOPER. Le lac Ontario ... . Par Fenimore Cooper. Traduit ... par A. J. B. Defauconpret. *Paris: Ch. Gosselin.* 1840. 4 vols., 12mo. + *Paris: Furne; Gosselin.* 1841. 8vo. + *Paris: A. Rigaud.* 1869 18mo, pp. 321. + *Paris: A. Rigaud.* 1869. 8vo, pp. 319. 16451

[COOPER.] The Last of the Mohicans; a Narrative of 1757. *Philadelphia.* 1826. 2 vols., 12mo. + *Paris: Baudry* [etc.] 1835. 8vo, 24½ sheets. + *Philadelphia.* 1836. 2 vols., 12mo. + *London: Bentley.* 1838. 12mo. + *Philadelphia.* 1839. 2 vols., 12mo. + *London: Richara Bentley.* 1849. 16mo. + Revised Edition. *New York.* 1850. 12mo. + *New York: Stringer and Townsend.* 1852. 2 vols., 12mo, pp. 262; 260. H. + Illustrated from Drawings from F. O. C. Darley. *New-York.* 1859. 12mo. 16452

Also as Vol. XXIII. of "Dürr's Collection of Standard American Authors. *Leipzig: A. Dürr.*" 1856. 8vo, pp. viii, 288.

COOPER. Le dernier des Mohicans ... . Traduit ... par M. Defauconpret. *Paris: Ch. Gosselin* [etc.] 1826. 4 vols., 12mo, 41 sheets. + Seconde édition. *Paris.* 1828. 4 vols., 12mo, 37 sheets. + *Paris: Furne.* 1830. 8vo. + *Paris: Gosselin* [etc.] 1838. 4 vols., 12mo. + *Paris: Furne* [etc.] 1846. 8vo. Illustr. + Traduction de La Bédollière. *Paris: Barba.* 1849. 4to. + [*Ibid.*] 1853. 12mo. + *Paris: Vermot.* 1861. 12mo. + [*Ibid.*] 1865. 18mo. + *Limoges et Lisle: Ardant et Thibaut.* 1868. 8vo, pp. 192. + Traduction de La Bédollière. *Paris: Barba.* 1869. 4to, pp. 64. 25 Vignettes. + Traduction nouvelle. *Paris: A. Rigaud.* 1869. 18mo, pp. 340. 16453

COOPER. O Derradeiro Mohicano, historia americana acontecida em 1757, por F. Cooper: traduzida em portuguez por Caetano Lopes de Moura. *Paris.* 1838. 4 vols., 12mo.

COOPER. El ultimo Mohicano, historia americana ... por J. Fenimore Cooper, traducida por J. M. P. *Paris: Lecointe.* 1835. 4 vols., 18mo, 24 sheets. 16455

COOPER. Der Letzte der Mohicans. Eine Erzählung aus dem Jahre 1757. *Braunschweig: Vieweg.* 1826. 3 vols., 8vo. + Aus dem Englischen. *Stuttgart: Brodhag.* 1826. 4 vols., 12mo. 16456

COOPER. De laatste der Mohikanen, of de Engelschen in Amerika. Naar het Engelsch door G. L. van Oosten van Staveren. *Leiden: C. C. van der Hoek.* 1833. 2 pts., 8vo. + Tweede Druk. *Leiden: J. W. van Leeuwen en van der Heuvell en van Santen.* 1868. 8vo, pp. 2, 321. 16457

COOPER. Den sidste Mohicaner. En Fortælling af J. F. Cooper. *Christiania.* 1830–31. 2 vols., 12mo, pp. x, 186; 173. (Bibliothek for Morskabslæsning, B. 1, 2.) 16458

COOPER. Den Siste Mohikanen. *Stockholm: Schreutz.* 1828. 3 pts., 8vo. 16459

COOPER. The Leather-Stocking Tales. By J. Fenimore Cooper. Author's Revised Edition. ... *New-York: G. P. Putnam & Company.* 1853. 5 vols., 12mo. H. 16460

These tales are, I. The Deerslayer. II. The Last of the Mohicans. III. The Pathfinder. IV. The Pioneers. V. The Prairie.

COOPER. Lederstrumpf-Erzählungen. ... Bearbeitet von F. Hoffmann. *Stuttgart: Schmeidt und Spring.* 1845. 8vo.

COOPER. Légendes des treize républiques. Traduit ... par M. Defauconpret. *Paris: Ch. Gosselin; Mame et Delaunay-Vallée.* 1825. 4 vols., 12mo, 48 sheets. 16462

COOPER. Letter of J. Fenimore Cooper to General Lafayette on the Expenditure of the United States of America. *Paris: Baudry.* 1831. 8vo, 3½ sheets. 16463

COOPER. A Letter to His Countrymen. By J. Fenimore Cooper. *New York: J. Wiley.* 1834. Rl. 8vo, pp. 116. C.

Refers to the discussion between the President and Senate of the United States. For a reply, *see* [Cushing (Caleb)].

[COOPER.] Lionel Lincoln; or, the Leaguer of Boston. ... *New-York.* 1823–4. 2 vols., 12mo. + 1825. 2 vols., 12mo. + *Philadelphia.* 1827. + *Philadelphia.* 1831. + *Philadelphia.* 1836. 2 vols., 12mo. + *London.* 1837. 12mo. + *Paris: Baudry* [etc.] 1837. 8vo. + *Philadelphia.* 1838. 2 vols., 12mo, pp. 276; 270. + *London: Bentley.* 1849. 12mo. *New York: Stringer and Townsend.* 1852. 2 vols., 12mo, pp. 276; 273. H.

+ *New York: W. A. Townsend and Co.* 1860. 18mo. + *London: Routledge.* 1862. 8vo. 16465

COOPER. Lionel Lincoln. Traduction de La Bédollière. *Paris: G. Barba.* 1852. 4to. + [*Ibid.*] 1865. 4to, pp. 64.

COOPER. Lionel Lincoln oder die Belagerung von Boston. Uebersetzt von Chr. Fr. Michaelis. *Leipzig: Herbig.* 1825. 3 vols., 8vo. + Aus dem Englischen von *r. Neue Auflage. *Leipzig: Weinbrack.* 1828. 3 vols., 8vo. 1646-

COOPER. Lionel Lincoln, of de belegering van Boston. Naar het Engelsch. *Amsterdam: J. F. Schleijer.* 1838. 2 pts., 8vo. 16468

COOPER. Lionel Lincoln of de belagering van Boston. Naar het Engelsch. 2ᵉ druk. *Leiden: J. W. van Leeuwen en van den Heuvell en van Santen.* 1868. Post 8vo, pp. 2, 317.

COOPER. Lives of Distinguished American Naval Officers. By J. Fenimore Cooper. *Auburn, N. Y.: J. C. Derby.* 1846. 2 vols., 12mo. + *Philadelphia.* 1846. 12mo. + Third Edition. *New York.* 1849. 2 vols. 16470

First appeared in "Graham's Magazine."

COOPER. Lucy Harding. A Second Series of Afloat and Ashore. *London: Bentley.* 1844. 12mo. + [*Ibid.*] 1846. 3 vols., post 8vo, pp. 288; 294; 295. + *Paris: Galignani.* 1844. 8vo. + *Paris: Baudry* [etc.] 1844. 8vo. + [*Ibid.*] 1854. 16mo. B. 16471

Title to the English edition of "Miles Wallingford."

COOPER. Lucie Hardinge. Par Fenimore Cooper. Traduit ... par Defauconpret. *Paris: Furne; Ch. Gosselin.* 1845. 8vo, 2½ sheets. Frontispiece. + Traduction de La Bédollière. ... *Paris: Barba.* 1864. 4to, pp. 64. 25 Vignettes. 16472

COOPER. Lucy Hardinge. Von J. F. Cooper. ... Ins Deutsche übertragen von A. Kretzschmar. *Grimma.* 1847. 3 vols., 8vo, pp. 284; 240; 271. (Europ. Bibliothek, 120.–122. Bd.) 16473

COOPER. Mark's Reef; or The Crater; a Tale of the Pacific. *London: Bentley.* 1847. 3 vols., 8vo. + *London: Routledge.* 1862. 8vo. 16474

COOPER. Miles Wallingford. A Sequel to Afloat and Ashore. *New York.* 1844. + *New York: Stringer and Townsend.* 1852. 2 vols., 12mo, pp. 221; 207. H. + *New York.* 1856. 12mo, pp. 426. + *New York: W. A. Townsend and Company.* 1866. 12mo. + *New York: Hurd and Houghton.* 1867. 12mo. 16475

A German version forms part of the "Echo d. neuester Englischen Tagespresse. *Grimma.* 1845." 8vo.

COOPER. Mercedes of Castile. *London: Bentley.* 1840. 3 vols., 8vo. 16476

COOPER. Mercedes of Castille; or, The Voyage to Cathay. ... *New York: Stringer and Townsend.* 1852. 12mo, pp. (2), ix–260; 232. 16477

Relates to the discovery of America by Columbus. *See also* "Christophe Colomb," No. 16424.

COOPER. Mercedes; or, The Days of Columbus. ... *London: Routledge.* 1869. 8vo. 16478

COOPER. Mercedes of Castile. ... *Paris: Baudry* [etc.] 1840. 8vo. + *Paris: Galignani.* 1841. 8vo. 16479

COOPER. Mercédès de Castile, histoire du temps du Christophe Colomb. Traduit ... par E. de La Bédollière. *Paris: Gustave Barba.* 1841. 4 vols., 12mo, 41¼ sheets. + Traduit ... par A. J. B. Defauconpret, précédé d'une Notice historique sur J. F. Cooper par Charles Romey. *Paris: Ch. Gosselin.* 1841. 4 vols., 12mo, 42⅜ sheets. 16480

[COOPER.] The Monikins; edited by the Author of "The Spy." *Philadelphia: Cary, Lea, & Blanchard.* 1835. 2 vols., 12mo, pp. (2), vii–251; 244. H. + *London: Bentley.* 1835. 3 vols., post 8vo. + *Philadelphia.* 1841. 2 vols., 12mo. + *New York: Stringer and Townsend.* 1852. 2 vols., 12mo, pp. 251; 244. H. + *New York: Hurd and Houghton.* 1865. 8vo, pp. 491. 16481

A political satire.

COOPER. Les monikins. Roman serio-philosophico-politico-bouffon. Par J. Fenimore Cooper. Traduit ... par Benjamin Laroche. *Paris: Charpentier.* 1835. 4 vols., 12mo, 38⅜ sheets. + Traduit ... par A. J. B. Defauconpret. *Paris: Ch. Gosselin.* 1835. 4 vols., 12mo, 39½ sheets. + Traduction de La Bédollière. *Paris: G. Barba.* 1858. 4to, pp. 52. Illustrations. + [*Ibid.*] 1869. 4to, pp. 52. 19 Vignettes. 16482

COOPER. Die Monikins. ... Aus dem Englischen von Geo. Nice. Bärmann. *Zwickau.: Nebr. Schaumann.* 1836. 2 vols., 8vo. 16483

COOPER. Ned Myers; or, a Life before the Mast. Edited by J. F. Cooper. *Philadelphia.* 1843. 12mo, pp. 232. + *London: Bentley.* 1843. 2 vols., 8vo. + *Paris: Baudry* [etc.] 1843. 8vo. + *Paris: Galignani.* 1843. 8vo. + *New York.* 1856. + *London: Ward and Lock.* 1846. 8vo. 16484

"The veritable adventures of an old shipmate." — DUYCKINCK, I. 112.

COOPER. Ned Myers ... . Aus dem Englischen von Ed. Mauch. *Stuttgart: Liesching.* 1845. 16mo. + Edward Myers ... . Deutsch bearbeitet von Erwin von Moosthal. *Stuttgart: Franckh.* 1844. 4 pts., 16mo. 16485

[COOPER.] Notions of the Americans. Picked up by a Travelling Bachelor. *Philadelphia.* 1828. 2 vols., 12mo, pp. 340; 359. P., C. + *London: Henry Colburn.* 1828. 2 vols., 8vo. + A New Edition. *Philadelphia.* 1838. 2 vols., 12mo. + A New Edition. [*Ibid.*] 1840. 2 vols., 12mo. + *New York: Stringer & Townsend.* 1840. 2 vols., 12mo, pp. 340; 359. C.

The "Monthly Review" is severe in its criticism of this work. *See* Duyckinck, I. 110. Translated into French, with the following title:

COOPER. Lettres sur les Mœurs et les Institutions des Etats Unis de l'Amerique septentrionale. Par M. James Fennimore [*sic*] Cooper; traduit de l'Anglais par Mlle. H. Preble. *Paris.* 1828. 4 vols., 12mo. 16487

COOPER. Die Nordamerikaner, geschildert von einem reisenden Junggesellen. Aus dem Englishen. *Stuttgart: Frankh. Brodhag.* 1828. 4 vols., 8vo. 16488

[COOPER.] The Oak Openings, or the Bee-Hunter. *New-York.* 1848. 2 vols., 12mo. + *New York.* 1856. 12mo, pp. 456. + *London: George Routledge and Sons.* 1865. 16mo, pp. vii, 311. 16489

COOPER. Le lac Ontario, ou Le guide. Traduit par Defauconpret. *Paris: Passard.* 1852. 2 vols., 8vo. 16490

COOPER. L'Ontario. Par Fenimore Cooper. Traduction de La Bédollière. ... *Paris: Barba.* 1850. 4to. + [*Ibid.*] 1864. 4to, pp. 68. 25 Vignettes. 16491

Cooper. Pages and Pictures from the Writings of James Fenimore Cooper, with Notes by Susan Fenimore Cooper, Illustrated on Steel and Wood, from Original Drawings. *New York: W. A. Townsend and Company.* 1861. 4to, pp. 400. 40 Plates. 16492

An uncertain number of copies were printed on large paper, with India paper proofs of the plates.

[Cooper.] The Pathfinder; or, the Inland Sea. *Philadelphia: Lea & Blanchard.* 1840. 2 vols., 12mo, pp. 240; 233. + *London: Bentley.* 1840. 3 vols., 8vo. + [*Ibid.*] 12mo. + *Paris: Baudry* [etc.] 1840. 8vo. + *Paris: Galignani.* 1840. 8vo. + *Philadelphia.* 1843. 2 vols., 12mo. + *Philadelphia.* 1845. 12mo. + *London: Bentley.* 1850. 16mo. B. + *New York: Stringer & Townsend.* 1857. 2 vols., 12mo. B. + *New York: W. A. Townsend and Company.* 1860. 12mo. B. + *London: Routledge.* 1862. 8vo. + *New York: James G. Gregory.* 1863. 12mo. 16493

One of the "Leather-Stocking Series." "The Pathfinder" is also published as Part IV. of the "Bibliothek d. neuesten ausländischen Classiker. *Berlin: Liebmann und Comp.* 1841;" and as Vol. XXIX. of "Dürr's Coll. of Standard American Authors. *Leipzig: A. Dürr.*" 1858. 8vo, 4 l., pp. 343.

Cooper. De padvinder, of het meer Ontario. Een verhaal. Naar het Engelsch. *Groningen: W. Zuidema.* 1842. 2 pts., 8vo. 16494

[Cooper.] The Pilot: a Tale of the Sea. *New York.* 1823. 2 vols., 12mo, pp. 276; 293. + *Göttingen: Rosenbusch.* 1826. 3 vols., 12mo. + *Philadelphia.* 1827. 2 vols., 12mo. + Fifth Edition. *Philadelphia: Carey & Lea.* 1833. 2 vols., 12mo., pp. 295; 268. + *Paris: Baudry* [etc.] 1833. 8vo. + *London.* 1835. 12mo. + A New Edition. *Philadelphia.* 1836. 2 vols., 12mo. + Revised and Illustrated, with a new introduction. *New-York.* 1849. 12mo. + *London: Bentley.* 1849. 12mo. + [*Ibid.* n. d.] 16mo. + *New York: W. A. Townsend and Company.* 1859. 12mo. + *London: Routledge.* 1862. 8vo. 16495

Written partly to correct the errors in Sir Walter Scott's "Pirate."

Cooper. Le pilote. Traduit par ... [Defauconpret]. *Paris: Ch. Gosselin* [etc.] 1824. 4 vols., 12mo, 45⅝ sheets. + Seconde édition. 1826. 4 vols., 12mo, 39 sheets. + Traduction nouvelle, par M. Benjamin Laroche. *Paris: Camuzeaux; F. Didot.* 1837. 8vo. + Traduit par Defauconpret. *Paris: Gustave Barba.* 1838. 4 vols., 12mo. + [*Ibid.*] 4to. + Traduction de La Bédollière. *Paris: Barba.* 1868. 4to, pp. 64. 25 Vignettes. 16496

Cooper. De loods. Een verhaal. Naar het Engelsch. *Amsterdam: J. F. Schleijer.* 1835. 2 pts., 8vo. 16497

Cooper. Il pilota; racconto del mare relativo ai tempi della guerra americana. *Milano.* 1831. 2 vols., 12mo. + *Milano.* 1831. 2 vols., 12mo. 16498

Cooper. El piloto ... . Nueva traduccion, con ... notas historicas. *Paris: Rosa.* 1836. 4 vols., 18mo. 16499

Cooper. O piloto, novelle maritima, vertida em portuguez pelo D. Caetano Lopez de Moura. *Paris: Aillaud.* 1838. 4 vols., 18mo. 16500

Cooper. Lotsen. Sjöberättelse. *Stockholm: Lundeqvists förl.* 1831. 8vo. 16501

[Cooper.] The Pioneers; or the Sources of the Susquehanna; a Descriptive Tale. By the Author of "Precaution." ... *New-York: Charles Wiley.* 1823. pp. ix [misprint for xi], 275; 329. P. + Fifth Edition. *Philadelphia: Carey, Lea, and Carey.* 1828. 2 vols., 12mo, pp. 284; 327. H. + *Philadelphia: Carey & Lea.* 1832. 2 vols., 12mo, pp. 284; 327. C. + *Paris: Baudry* [etc.] 1835. 8vo. + A New Edition. *Philadelphia.* 1836. 2 vols., 12mo. + *London: Richard Bentley.* 1849. 16mo. + Illustrated from Drawings by F. O. C. Darley. *New York: W. A. Townsend and Company.* 1859. 12mo, pp. 609. B. + *New York: James G. Gregory.* 1863. 12mo. + *New York: Hurd and Houghton.* 1866. 12mo. + [*Ibid.*] 1868. 12mo. 16502

Cooper. Les Pionniers. Traduit par ... [Defauconpret]. *Paris: Gosselin* [etc.] 1823. 3 vols., 12mo, 35⅝ sheets. + Seconde édition, revue ... . 1825. 4 vols., 12mo, 42⅜ sheets. + *Paris: Furne.* 1830. 8vo. + *Paris: Barba.* 1838. 4 vols., 12mo. + 1849. 12mo. + Traduction de La Bédollière. *Paris: Barba.* 1865. 4to. + Les Pionniers, ou les sources du Susquehanna. *Paris: Vermot.* 1866. 18mo. + Traduit par Marie Guerrier de Haupt. *Paris.* 1867. 2 vols., 32mo. + Ou les sources ... traduit par A. Chaillot. *Avignon: Chaillot. Paris: Sarlit.* 1868. 18mo, pp. 184. + Traduction nouvelle. *Limoges: Ardant et Thibaut.* 1868. 8vo, pp. 221. + Traduit par Marie Guerrier de Haupt. Seconde édition. *Paris.* 1870. 2 vols., 32mo, pp. 384. 16503

Cooper. Die Ansiedler, oder die Quellen des Susquehannah. Aus dem Englishen von *r. *Leipzig: Wienbrack.* 1824. 8vo. + Uebersetzt von L. Hermann. *Leipzig: Klein.* 1824. 3 vols., 8vo. 16504

Cooper. Le sorgenti del Susquehanna ossia i coloni, romanzo storico. *Napoli.* 1864. 4 vols., 16mo. 16505

Cooper. Los plantadores de America, o Los nacimientos del Susquehanna. ... Traducida ... por Don Manuel Bazo. *Paris.* 1827. 4 vols., 18mo. 16506

Cooper. Susquehanna Kallor. *Stockholm: Scheutz.* 1827. 3 pts., 8vo. 16507

Cooper. Colonisterne. Fortælling af Cooper, oversat af A. C. Clausen; udgiven af J. Riise. *Kjöbenhavn.* 1828–29. 2 pts. 16508

A translation of "The Pioneers." Also forms parts 47–52 of Cooper's "Samlede Skrifter, oversat fra Originalsproget. *Kjöbenhavn.* 1834."

Cooper. Havfruen eller Söskummeren, en Fortælling, oversat af F. Schaldemose. *Kiöbenhavn: Liunge.* 1831. 8vo. 16509

[Cooper.] The Prairie; a Tale. *Philadelphia.* 1827. 2 vols., 12mo, pp. 252; 276. + *London.* 1827. 3 vols., 8vo. BD. + 1828. + 1831. + *Philadelphia.* 1836. 2 vols., 12mo. + *London: Richard Bentley.* 1836. 16mo. + [*Ibid.*] 1849. 12mo. + *Paris: Baudry* [etc.] 1837. 8vo. + *London.* 1851. 12mo. + *New York: Stringer and Townsend.* 1858. 12mo. B. + Illustrated from Drawings by F. O. C. Darley. *New York: W. A. Townsend and Company.* 1859. pp. 479. + [*Ibid.*] 1860. 12mo. + *New York: Hurd and Houghton.* 1865. 12mo. 16510

Cooper. La prairie. Traduit par Defauconpret. *Paris: Ch. Gosselin* [etc.] 1827. 4 vols., 12mo, 42⅜ sheets. + Seconde édition. 1828. 4 vols., 12mo. + Traduction nouvelle, par M. Benjamin Laroche. *Paris: F. Didot.* 1837. 8vo. + Traduit par Defauconpret. *Paris: Gustave Barba.* 1838. 4 vols., 12mo. + Traduction nouvelle ... . *Limoges: E. Ardant et Thibaut.* 1868. 8vo, pp. 216. + Traduction de La Bédollière. *Paris: Barba.* 1869. 4to. 16511

Cooper. Die Prairie. ... Aus dem Englischen ... . *Berlin: Duncker und H.* 1827. 3 vols., 8vo. 16512

[Cooper.] Precaution. A Novel. *New York.* 1820. 2 vols., pp. 286; 340. + *London: Richard Bentley.* 1849. 16mo. + [*Ibid.*] 1850. 16mo. + *London: Routledge.* 1862. 8vo. 16513

The first literary production of Cooper. *See* Duyckinck, II. 108.

Cooper. Precaution, ou Le choix de mari. Traduit .. par M. Defauconpret. *Paris: Ch. Gosselin* [etc.] 1825. 4 vols., 12mo, 42$\frac{1}{16}$ sheets. + Seconde édition. 1827. 4 vols., 12mo, 37½ sheets. + *Paris: Gustave Barba.* 1838. 4 vols., 12mo. + Traduction de La Bédollière. *Paris: Barba.* 1850. 4to. 16514

Cooper. Proceedings of the Naval Court Martial in the Case of Alexander Slidell Mackenzie; to which is Annexed, an elaborate Review. By J. F. Cooper. *New-York.* 1844. 8vo, pp. 82. C. 16515

"A severe comment on the course of the commander of the 'Somers.'" — Duyckinck, II. 112.

Cooper. Ravensnest, or The Redskins. *Paris: Baudry* [etc.] 1846. 8vo. + *Paris: Galignani.* 1846. 8vo. 16516

Cooper. Ravensnest, traduit por Defauconpret. *Paris: Furne* [etc.] 1847. 8vo. Plates. 16517

[Cooper.] The Red Rover. A Tale. *Philadelphia.* 1827. + *London.* 1828. 3 vols., 8vo. BD. + New Edition. *Philadelphia.* 1836. + *Paris: Baudry.* 1787. 8vo. + *London: Richard Bentley.* 1848. 16mo. + [*Ibid.*] 1849. 12mo. + *London: Routledge.* 1862. 8vo. 16518

Cooper. Le corsaire rouge ... . Traduit ... Defauconpret. *Paris: Ch. Gosselin* [etc.] 1827. 4 vols., 12mo, 43⅜ sheets. + Avec des ... notes historiques. *Paris: Furne.* 1831. 8vo. + *Paris: Barba.* 1839. 4 vols., 12mo. + *Paris: Vermot.* 1842. 12mo. + *Limoges: Ardant et Thibaut.* 1869. 8vo. 16519

Cooper. Red Rover. Aus dem Englischen von G. Friedenberg. *Berlin: Duncker und H.* 3 vols., 8vo. 1 sheet of music. 16520

Cooper. El Corsario bojo, ... traducida al castellano por D. Blas Maria Araque. *Madrid.* 1854. Folio. 16521

Cooper. Il corsaro rosso. *Milano.* 1858. 2 vols., 16mo. Plates. 16522

Cooper. De Rooder Zeeroover. Naar het Engelsch. *Amsterdam: J. F. Sleijer.* 1836. 3 pts., 8vo. 16523

Cooper. Den Röde Fribytaren. Öfversat af I—m. *Stockholm: Ordens Boktr.* 1830, 31. 3 pts., 12mo. 16524

Cooper. The Red-Skins, or Indians and Injin; being the Conclusion of the Little-page Manuscripts. *New-York: Burgess & Stringer.* 1846. 2 vols., 12mo. + *London.* 1846. 3 vols., 8vo. + *New York.* 1848. 2 vols., pp. 259; 230. + *New York; Stringer & Townsend.* 1852. 12mo. + *New York: W. A. Townsend and Company.* 1860. 12mo. 16525

See also "Satanstoe" and "Chain-Bearer."

Cooper. Fleur des bois, ou Les peaux rouges ... . Traduit ... par E. de La Bédollière. *Paris: Gosselin* [also] *Barba.* 1844. 2 vols., 8vo, 46 sheets. + Fleur-des-bois. Par Fenimore Cooper. Traduction de La Bédollière. ... *Paris: Barba.* 1864. 4to, pp. 64. 25 Vignettes. + [*Ibid.*] 1868. 4to, pp. 64. 25 Vignettes. 16526

Cooper. Le Robinson américain. Par Fenimore Cooper. Traduction de La Bédollière. *Paris: G. Barba.* 1850. 4to. + Traduction revue avec soin pour la jeunesse. Avec illustrations de Bertall. *Limoges et Lisle: Martial Ardant frères.* 1864. 8vo, pp. 228. + Traduction de La Bédollière. *Paris: Barba.* 1865. 4to, pp. 64. Illustrated. + Traduction nouvelle revue avec soin pour la jeunesse. *Limoges: E. Ardant et Thibaut.* 1868. 8vo, pp. 222. 16527

Cooper. Satanstoe, or the Little-page Manuscripts, a Tale of the Colony. *New-York.* 1845. 2 vols., 12mo, pp. 235; 228. + *London: Bentley.* 1845. 3 vols., 8vo. + *New York: Stringer and Townsend.* 1858. 12mo. + *Illustrated by F. O. C. Darley: W. A. Townsend and Company.* 1860. 12mo. *London: Routledge.* 1862. 8vo. 16528

An anti "Anti-Rent" novel.

Cooper. Satanstoe ou La famille Littlepage. *Paris: Baudry.* 1846. 2 vols., 8vo, 45 sheets. + Traduit par Defauconpret. *Paris: Furne: Ch. Gosselin.* 1846. 8vo. Plates. + Traduction de La Bédollière: *Paris: G. Barba.* 1854. 4to. 16529

Cooper. The Sea Lions; or the Lost Sailors. *New York.* 1848? + *London: Bentley.* 1849. 3 vols., 8vo. + *New York.* 1856. 12mo, pp. 432. + *New York: Stringer & Townsend.* 1857. 12mo. + *New York: W. A. Townsend and Company.* 1860. 12mo. + *London: Routledge.* 1862. 12mo. + *New York.* 1864. 12mo. 16530

Cooper. Les lions de mer. ... Traduit par Defauconpret. *Paris: Passard.* 1852. 2 vols., 8vo, 39¼ sheets. + Nouvelle édition. *Paris: Furne, Perrotin et Pagnerre.* 1858. 8vo, pp. 308. + Traduction de La Bédollière. *Paris: Barba.* 1869. 4to. 16531

Cooper. Die Seelöwen. ... Ins Deutsche übertragen von Johannes Hack. *Grimma.* 1850. 3 vols., 8vo, pp. 231; 226; 230. 16532

[Cooper.] The Spy: a tale of the Neutral Ground. *New York.* 1821. 2 vols., 12mo. + *New York.* 1822. 2 vols., 12mo, pp. 265; 275. + Third Edition. *New York.* 1822. 2 vols., 12mo. + *Leipzig: Focke.* 1825. 3 vols., 12mo. + *Philadelphia.* 1827. 2 vols., 12mo. + Seventh Edition. *Philadelphia.* 1829. 2 vols., 12mo, pp. 264; 288. C. + *Paris: Baudry* [etc.] 1835. 8vo. + *Philadelphia: Carey, Lea, & Blanchard.* 1836. 2 vols., 12mo. + Revised Edition. *New-York: Putnam.* 1849. 12mo. + *London: Bentley.* 1849. 12mo. + Illustrated from Drawings by F. O. C. Darley. *New York.* 1859. 8vo, pp. 463. + *London: G. Routledge & Co.* 1862. 8vo. 16533

Cooper. L'Espion roman nouveau, contenant des détails sur la guerre de l'Amérique, et décernant les sites et les mœurs de cette contrée. Traduction libre par ... [Defauconpret]. *Paris:* 1822. 4 vols., 12mo, 34½ sheets. + Seconde édition. *Paris.* 1824. 4 vols., 12mo, 40½ sheets. + Traduit par Defauconpret. *Paris: Barba.* 1840. 4 vols., 12mo. + Traduction de La Bédollière. *Paris: Barba.* 1865. 4to. 16534

Cooper. Der Spion. Roman aus den nordamerikanischen Revolutionskriege. Uebersetzt von L. Herrmann. *Leipzig: E. Klein.* 1824. 2 vols., 8vo. + Der Spion, oder das neutrale Land. ... Aus dem Englischen von *r. *Leipzig: Focke.* 1824. 3 vols., 8vo. + Deutsch herausgegeben von P. Aug. Petri. *Leipzig: Lauffer.* 1826. 3 vols., 8vo. 16535

Cooper. Un episodio della guerra americana ossia la spia. *Napoli.* 1846. 3 vols., 24mo. 16536

Cooper. Spionen. *Stockholm: Scheutz.* 1825, 26. 3 pts., 8vo. 16537

Cooper. Sjötrollet eller Ströfvaren pa Hafvet. *Stockholm: Lundeqvists förl.* 1832. 3 pts., 8vo. 16538

Cooper. Stories of the Prairie, and other Adventures of the Border. Selected from the Works of J. Fenimore Cooper. With Illustrations ... by F. O. C. Darley. *New York: Hurd and Houghton.* 1868. 16mo, pp. 339, 3 l. 3 Plates. C. + Cooper's Stories of the Great Prairies. From the Novels of J. F. Cooper. *London: Sampson, Low, Son & Marston.* 1868. Illustrated. + *New York.* 1869. 8vo. 16539

Cooper. Stories of the Sea; Narratives of Adventure. *London: Low.* 1862. 8vo. 16540

Cooper. Stories of the Woods; or, Adventures of Leather Stocking. *London: Low.* 1862. 8vo. 16541

[Cooper.] The Two Admirals. *London: Bentley.* 1842. 3 vols., 8vo. + *Paris: Baudry* [etc.] 1842. 8vo. + *Paris: Galignani.* 1842. 8vo. + *Philadelphia.* 1843. 2 vols., 12mo. + *London: Bentley.* 1849. 12mo. + *London: Routledge.* 1862. 8vo. 16542

Cooper. Les deux amiraux ... . Par Fenimore Cooper. Traduction de La Bédollière. ... *Paris: Gosselin.* 1842. 4 vols., 12mo, 37½ sheets. + *Paris: Barba.* 1864. 4to, pp. 64. 25 Vignettes. 16543

Cooper. I due ammiragli. Romanzo maritimo. *Napoli.* 1854. 4 vols., 16mo. 16544

[Cooper.] The Water-Witch; or, the Skimmer of the Seas: a Tale. *London.* 1830. 3 vols., 8vo. BD. + *Dresden: Walther.* 1830. 3 vols., 8vo. + *Philadelphia: Carey & Lea.* 1831. 2 vols., 12mo, pp. vi, 256; 251. + *Paris: Baudry* [etc.] 1835. 8vo. + A New Edition. *Philadelphia.* 1838. 2 vols., 12mo. + *London: Bentley.* 1849. 12mo. + *London.* 1850. 12mo. + *London: Routledge.* 1862. 8vo. 16545

Cooper. L'ecumeur de mer, ou la sorcière des eaux ... . Seconde édition. *Paris.* 1831. 4 vols., 12mo, 48 sheets. + Traduction nouvelle, avec des ... notes historiques. *Paris: Furne.* 1831. 8vo, 30¼ sheets. + Traduction de La Bédollière. *Paris: Barba.* 1841. 4 vols., 12mo, 34¼ sheets. + Traduction nouvelle. Édition ... corrigée. *Paris: Vermot et Cie.* 1865. 18mo, pp. 342. + Traduction de La Bédollière. *Paris: Barba.* 1868. 4to, pp. 64. 25 Vignettes. 16546

Cooper. Die Wassernixe ... . Aus dem Englischen von Gottfried Friedenberg. *Berlin: Duncker und H.* 1830. 3 vols., 8vo. 16547

Cooper. Het waterspook, of de Nederlanders in Amerika. Een tafereel iut het begin der 18e eeuw. Naar het Engelsch. *Amsterdam: J. F. Schleijer.* 1837. 2 pts., 8vo. + *Leiden: J. W. van Leeuwen en van den Heuvell & van Santen.* 1867. Post 8vo, pp. 4, 315. 16548

Cooper. The Ways of the Hour. A Tale. *New York.* 1850. 8vo, pp. 512. + *London: Bentley.* 1850. 3 vols., 8vo. 16549

The author's last work; exhibits the evils of trial by jury.

Cooper. Marie, ou Les mœurs du jour. Suite de la traduction de Defauconpret. *Paris: Passard.* 1853. 2 vols., 8vo, 45 sheets. + Les mœurs du jour. Traduit par A. J. B. Defauconpret. *Paris: Furne* [etc.] 1852. 8vo. Illustr. + Traduction de La Bédollière. *Paris: Barba.* 1854. 4to. 16550

[Cooper.] The Wept of Wish-ton-Wish: a Tale. *Philadelphia: Carey, Lea & Carey.* 1829. 2 vols., 12mo, pp. 251; 234. + New Edition. *Philadelphia.* 1836. 2 vols., 12mo. 16551

Dramatized in French's "Mod. Standard Drama," v. 20. The English edition was called "The Borderers." *See* No. 16416.

Cooper. Le puritain d'Amérique, ou La vallée de Wish-ton-Wish. Traduit ... par l'auteur d'Olésia ... . *Paris: Ch. Gosselin.* 1829. 4 vols., 12mo, 38$\frac{1}{16}$ sheets. 16552

Cooper. Les Puritans d'Amérique. Ou la Vallée de Wish-ton-Wish. Traduction De M. Defauconpret. *Paris.* 1830. 8vo. 16553

Cooper. Conanchet eller Grændsebeboerne, oversat af F. Schaldemose. *Kiöbenhavn: Riise.* 1830. 2 pts., 8vo. 16554

Cooper. Conanchet und die Puritaner in Connecticut. Aus dem Englischen von Gottfried Friedenberg. *Berlin: Duncker und H.* 1829. 3 vols., 8vo. 16555

Cooper. Il puritano d'America, o la compianta della valle di Wish-ton-wish. *Milano.* 1835. 3 vols., 16mo. 16556

Cooper. El puritano de America, o El valle de Wish-ton-Wish. Traducido ... por Don J. M. Moralejo. *Paris: Rosa.* 1836. 4 vols., 18mo. 16557

Cooper. Gränsboerna eller Wish-Ton-Wish's Klagan. Öfversat. *Stockholm: Hjerta.* 1836. 2 pts., 12mo. 16558

Cooper. The Works of James Fenimore Cooper. *New York: Stringer and Townsend.* [n. d.] 34 vols., 12mo. + Illustrated from Drawings by F. O. C. Darley. *New York: W. A. Townsend.* 1861, *etc.* 32 vols., 12mo. 16559

The best collected edition; subsequently issued by James G. Gregory, and, afterwards, by Hurd & Houghton. There is another collected edition, *New York: Stringer & Townsend.* [v. d.] 34 vols., 12mo. + "People's Edition." *New York: Hurd and Houghton.* [v. d.] 34 vols., 12mo. Mr. Putnam issued twenty of the most popular works on superior paper, with woodcut vignettes, as "Cooper's Select Works."

Cooper. Œuvres de J. F. Cooper, traduites par A. J. P. Defauconpret. *Paris: Furne et Ce.* 1859–62. 30 vols., 8vo. 90 Engravings. + [Same. *Ibid.*] 30 Engravings. 16560

Cooper. Œuvres complètes. Traduction par Émile de La Bédollière. *Paris: G. Barba.* 1851–54. 6 vols., 4to. Illustrations. 16561

Cooper. Werke. Aus dem Englischen. *Leipzig: Wienbrack.* 1824–25. 12 vols., 8vo. 16562

Cooper. Sämmtliche Werke. Uebersetzt von Mehreren und herausgegeben von Chr. A. Fisher. *Frankfurt am Main: Sauerländer.* 1826–50. 258 pts., 12mo. 16563

Cooper. Gesammelte Romane. *Stuttgart: Liesching.* 1844–49. 85 pts., 16mo. 16564

Cooper. Samlede Skrifter, oversat af Forskjellige. *Kiöbenhavn: Trier.* 1830–47. 124 pts., 16mo, 16565

Cooper. Samlede Romaner, oversat af Güntelberg, Levin og Schaldemose. *Kiöbenhavn: Liunge.* 1831–34. 9 pts., 8vo.

Cooper. Samlede Skrifter. *Kjöbenhavn.* 184–. 16mo.

Cooper. Samlede Skrifter. Oversat af Originalsproget. *Kjöbenhavn: Trier.* 1831–58. 194 pts., 12mo. 16568

Cooper. Uit de wildernis. Amerikaansche verhalen. ... *Leiden: van den Heuvell & van Santen.* 1864. pp. 4, 76, 55, 64. Colored Lithographs. 16569

The stories, which have also separate titles, are "Hertendooder," "De padvinder," "De laatste der Mohikanen."

[Cooper.] Wyandotté; or, the Hutted Knoll. A Tale. *Philadelphia.* 1843. 2 vols., 12mo. + *London.* 1843. 8vo. + *Paris: Baudry* [etc.] 1843. 8vo. + *Paris: Galignani.* 1843. 8vo. + *New York.* 1856. 12mo, pp. 436. 16570

Cooper. Wyandotte. Traduit ... par A. J. B. Defauconpret. *Paris: Furne; Ch. Gosselin.* 1849. 8vo. 16571

Cooper. Wijandotte, of de hutberg. Een roman uit het tijdperk der Amerikaansche omwenteling. Uit het Engelsch vertaald. *Nieuwediep: C. Bakker, Bzn.* 1843. 8vo. Plates.

We have quoted many of these foreign editions of Cooper, not for their importance, but because Europeans have imbibed from them much of their "knowledge (or ignorance) of American topics." For notices of Cooper and his works, *see* "Am. M. Rev.," I. 147; II. 411; "Am. Q. Rev.," XVII. 407; "Am. Whig Rev.," IV. 276; "Ch. Exam.," XII. 78; "Dem. Rev.," X. 409, 513; XV. 1; XXI. 438; XXV. 51; "Eclec. Rev.," XI. 31, 410; "Eclec. Mag.," IX. 57; XI. 430; "Edin. Rev.," LXXI. 128; "Fraser's Mag.," XVI. 233; XIX. 371; "Knickerb. Mag.," XI. 184; "Liv. Age," XXXI. 87; "Month. Rev.," CX. 122; "Museum," XV. 510; XVIII. 561; XXXVII. 449; "Q. Rev.," LVIII. 286; LIX. 85; "N. Am. Rev.," XV. 250; XVIII. 314; XXIII. 150; XXVII. 139; XXXII. 508; XLVI. 5; XLVII. 448; XLIX. 432; LXXI. 121; "N. Y. Rev.," IV. 209; "South. Lit. Mess.," IV. 373, 724; V. 169; VI. 229; "South. Rev.," V. 207; VIII. 382; "U. S. Lit. Gaz.," I. 6, 337; IV. 87; VI. 306; "Westminster Rev.," XVI. 180.

Cooper. Memorial of James Fenimore Cooper *New York G P Putnam* 1852 12mo, pp. 106. Portrait and View. C., H.

Contains Proceedings of various meetings in New York, a Discourse on his life and genius, by W. C. Bryant, speeches by Daniel Webster and others; edited by G. P. Putnam. *See* "National Portrait Gallery," I. 6, and [Cushing (Caleb)].

Cooper (James G.) On the Distribution of the Forests and Trees of North America, with notes on its physical geography. By Dr. J. G. Cooper. Report for 1858. 1859. pp. 246–280. Continuation. Report for 1860. 1861. pp. 439–442. 16574

Cooper. Geographical Catalogue of the Mollusca found west of the Rocky Mountains between Latitudes 33° and 49° north. *San Francisco.* 1867. 4to, pp. 40. 16575

Cooper (James G.) Geological Survey of California. ... Geographical Catalogue of the Mollusca found West of the Rocky Mountains between Latitudes 33° and 49° North. By J. G. Cooper, M.D. *San Francisco: Towne & Bacon, Printers.* 1867. 4to, pp. 40. 16576

Cooper (James G.), *and* Suckley (G.) *See* Pacific Railroad.

[Cooper (James M.)] Government The Partner of The Manufacturer. [Signed James M. Cooper. *Pittsburgh: printed by W. S. Haven.* 1865.] 8vo, pp. 8. H. 16577

Cooper (John). An Oration delivered at Machias, Me., Feb. 11, 1794, at the Celebration of the Birth-Day of President Washington. By John Cooper. *Boston.* 1794. 8vo. W

Cooper (J.) An Historical and Statistical Sketch of Croydon, N. H., from its Incorporation to the year 1832. Containing much Local Information which must be highly interesting to every inhabitant of the Town. By John Cooper. *Concord.* 1852. 8vo, pp. 52. H. 16579

There is a sketch of Croydon, by Lemuel P. Cooper, in "N. Hamp. Hist. Coll.," Vol. VI

Cooper (J. H.) Court of General Sessions. The People vs. John H. Cooper, Kennith Defries and Others, for combination and conspiracy to raise their Wages, &c. *Hudson.* 1836.

Cooper (Mark A.) Speech of Mr. Cooper of Georgia. In the House ... June, 1840 ... On the bill to establish an Independent Treasury. [*Washington.*] 1840. 8vo, pp. 16. BA.

Cooper (*Rev. Mr.*) Cooper's Histories of Greece and Rome, and of South and North America. *Plymouth, Mass.: Joseph Avery.* 1808. 12mo, pp. 294. + Second Edition. *Plymouth, Mass.* 1818. 12mo. 16582

Cooper. The History of North America. Containing, A Review of the Customs and Manners of the Original Inhabitants; The first Settlement of the British Colonies, their Rise and Progress, from The earliest Period to the Time of their becoming United, free and independent States. By the Rev. Mr. Cooper. Embellished with Copper-Plate Cuts. *London: E. Newbery.* [1780?] 12mo, 4 l., pp. 13–184. Frontispiece and Plates. + *London: E. Newbery.* 1789. 12mo, pp. 184. 5 Plates. H. + Second American Edition. *Lansingburgh: Printed by Sylvester Tiffany, for, and sold by Thomas Spencer, at his Book-Store, Albany.* MDCCXCV. 12mo, 4 l., pp. 159. Frontispiece and Plates. + *New Brunswick: printed by A. Blauvelt.* 1802. 32mo, 2 l., pp. 252. H. + With an Appendix. *Lansingburgh.* 1805. + *Hartford.* 1814. 12mo. + *Albany: Samuel Shaw.* 1815. 18mo, pp. xii, 264. + *Albany.* 1818. + *New York.* 1818. 12mo. 16583

Cooper. The History of South America. Containing the Discoveries of Columbus, the Conquest of Mexico and Peru, and the Other Transactions of the Spaniards in the New World. By the Rev. Mr. Cooper. Embellished with Copper-plate Cuts. *London: E. Newbery.* 1780. 6 l., pp. 168. Frontispiece and Plates. + *Bennington: Printed by Anthony Haswell, For Thomas Spencer, Bookseller, Market-Street, Albany.* [1793.] 12mo, 6 l.,

pp. 168. Copperplates. + *London: E. Newbery.* 1789. 18mo, pp. 168. + *Bennington: A. Haswell.* [1793.] 18mo, 5 l., pp. 168. Embellished with 5 Copperplate Cuts. 16584

The plates are by A. Reid, and are early specimens of American art.

[Cooper (Myles).] An Address from the Clergy of New-York and New-Jersey, to the Episcopalians in Virginia; Occasioned by some late Transactions in that Colony relative to an American Episcopate. *New-York: Hugh Gaine.* 1771. 8vo, pp. 58. 16585

[Cooper.] The American Querist: Or, Some Questions Proposed relative to The Present Disputes between Great Britain, and her American Colonies. By a North-American. The Tenth Edition. *New-York: Printed by James Rivington.* 1774. 8vo, 2 l., pp. 31. + *Boston: Re-printed by Mills and Hicks, and Sold at their Printing-Office in School-street.* 1774. 8vo, pp. 32. H. + *London: T. Cadell.* M.DCC.LXXV. 8vo, pp. 55. + [n. p.] *Printed in the Year* 1774. 8vo, 2 l., pp. 31. BA. + Eleventh Edition. pp. 31. 16586

It is stated on the title of the tenth edition, that "this pamphlet, on the 8th day of September last, was, in full conclave of the Sons of Liberty in New York, committed to the flames by the hands of their common executioner; as it contains some queries they cannot, and others they will not answer!"

[Cooper.] A Friendly Address to all Reasonable Americans, on The Subject of our Political Confusions: in which The Necessary Consequences of Violently opposing the King's Troops, and of A General Non-Importation are fairly stated. ... *New York: Printed in the Year* M,DCC,LXXIV. 8vo, pp. 55, (1). + *America: Printed for the Purchasers.* 1774. 8vo, pp. 55. BA. + *London: Richardson and Urquhart.* 1774. 8vo, pp. 56. BA. + *Dublin.* 1775. 8vo. 16587

[Cooper.] The Friendly Address To All Reasonable Americans, On the Subject of Our Political Confusions; Carefully abridged from The Original. *New-York: Printed in the Year* M,DCC,LXXIV. 8vo, pp. 24. P. 16588

Probably printed by James Rivington. This was answered by "The Other Side of the Question; or, a Defence of the Liberties of North-America. In Answer to a late Friendly Address to all Reasonable Americans, on the Subject of our Political Confusions. By a Citizen. *New York: Printed by James Rivington.* MDCC,LXXIV." 8vo, pp. 30. P. Rich says another edition has on the title, *America: printed for the purchasers.* *See* Sparks' "Am. Biog.," XVIII. 68. It was also answered by "Strictures on a Pamphlet, entitled a 'Friendly Address to all reasonable Americans, on the Subject of our Political Confusions.' Addresed to the people of America. *Philadelphia:*

William and Thomas Bradford. MDCCLXXIV." 8vo, pp. 15. + *America; Boston: Re-printed and sold at Greenleaf's Printing Office, opposite the Conduit, near the Market.* M,DCC,LXX,V. 8vo, pp. 20; also in 16mo. W. (A manuscript note appended to a copy of this tract, evidently written at the period of its publication, says, that General Charles Lee is believed to be the author of it.) Also: The General Attacked by a Subaltern; or, the "Strictures on the Friendly Address" Examined and a Refutation of its Principles Attempted. *New York: reprinted.* [1774.] 8vo. — The Strictures on the Friendly Address Examined, *see also* [Chandler (T. B.)], Vol. III., No. 11181.

Cooper. National Humiliation and Repentance recommended, and the Cause of the present Rebellion in America assigned, in a Sermon preached before the University of Oxford ... December 13. 1776 ... the Day ... for a General Fast. By Myles Cooper ... . *Oxford: Clarendon Press; Sold by J. and J. Fletcher, S. Parker, and D. Prince. London: J. F. and C. Rivington; J. Robson; and J. Pridden. Cambridge: J. Woodyer.* M DCC LXX VII. 4to, Title, pp. 24. BA. 16589

"A violent invectivea gainst the Americans." — *M. Rev.*, LVI. 76. Answered by "A letter to the Rev. Dr. Cooper, on the Origin of Civil Government; in Answer to his Sermon, preached before the University of Oxford, on the day appointed for a general fast. *London: J. Almon.*" 8vo, pp. 53. "A poignant antidote to the poison contained in Dr. Cooper's high-flying tory sermon." — *M. Rev.*, LVI. 473.

[Cooper.] What think ye of the Congress Now? or, An Enquiry, how far The Americans are Bound To abide by, and Execute the Decisions of, the late Congress? *New York: Printed by James Rivington.* M,DCC,LXXV. 8vo, pp. 48. 16590

A rare tory tract against the Congress. The following extract is on the title-page: "It is hoped and expected, that this want of Confidence in the Justice and Tenderness of the Mother Country, and this open Resistance to its Authority, can only have found place among the lower and more ignorant of the People. The better and wiser part of these Colonies will know, that Decency and submission may prevail, not only to redress Grievances, but to obtain Grace and Favour; while the outrage of a public violence can expect nothing but Severity and Chastisement." — General Conway. Appended to this tract, with a separate title-page and paging, is the following: "What think ye of the Congress Now? A Plan of a Proposed Union between Great-Britain and the Colonies of New Hampshire, Massachusetts-Bay, Rhode Island, New-York, New-Jersey, Pennsylvania, Maryland, Delaware, North Carolina, South Carolina and Georgia, which was produced by one of the Delegates in Congress from Pennsylvania, as mentioned in the preceding Work." [*New York: James Rivington.* 1775.] 8vo, pp. 4. Reprinted with the following title:

[Cooper.] What think ye of the Congress now? Or, an Enquiry how far the Americans are bound to abide by and execute the Decisions of the Late Continental Congress. With a Plan, by Samuel Galloway, Esq. for a Proposed Union between Great Britain and the Colonies. To which is added, an Alarm to the Legislature of the Province of New York, occasioned by the Present Political Disturbances. Addressed to the Representatives in General Assembly convened. *New York: J. Riv-*

ington. London: reprinted for Richardson & Urquhart. 1775. 8vo, pp. 90. 16591

"Intended to dissuade the people of New York from concurring with their sister colonies in adhering to the association, etc., of the Congress." — *M. Rev.* The author of this tract, quoting from the instructions given to the delegates to the Continental Congress by the colonies, undertakes to show that their desire was to recover their just rights and liberties, civil and religious, and to adopt a plan for the purpose of obtaining a redress of grievances. That the Congress transcended their powers, that the New England Colonies and Pennsylvania had been the cause of the rebellious acts of the Congress, which he characterises as hideous and detestable. He, therefore, calls upon the people of New York to reject these acts, and withdraw from the association. "The first appearance of this Congress," the writer says, "raised our curiosity, but excited no terror. But it was not long before it turned out to be a perfect monster — a mad, blind monster!"

Cooper (Peter). Letter of Peter Cooper on Slave Emancipation. New York, October, 1863. *New York: William C. Bryant & Co.* 1863. 8vo, pp. 8. 16592

Cooper. Letter to Abraham Lincoln, President of the United States, on Slave Emancipation, January, 1862. *Loyal Publication Society, No.* 23. 1863. 8vo, pp. 8. 16593

Cooper. ... The Death of Slavery. Letter to Governor Seymour ... Oct. 1863. *New York: Loyal Publication Society, No.* 28. 1863. 8vo, pp. 7. 16594

Cooper. Reconstruction. Letter from Peter Cooper to President Johnson. [n. p. 1866?] 8vo, pp. 4. H. 16595

Also: Letters of Peter Cooper on the Necessity for a Wise Discriminating Tariff to protect American Labor ... as the only Possible Means to insure a Speedy Return to Specie Payments with a Rapid Payment of the National Debt ... . *New York.* 1866. 8vo, Title, pp. 14. H.

Cooper Union. Charter, Trust Deed, and By-Laws of the Cooper Union For the Advancement of Science and Art: with the Letter of Peter Cooper, accompanying the Trust Deed. *New York: W. C. Bryant & Co., Printers.* 1859. 8vo, pp. 61.

Also: The First Annual Report of the Trustees of the Cooper Union ... . January 1, 1860. *New York.* 1860. 8vo, pp. 39. Continued. H.

Cooper (S.) Sermon Preached to the Ancient and Honourable Artillery Company ... June 3. 1751. Being the Anniversary of their Election of Officers. By Samuel Cooper ... . *Boston: J. Edwards, and D. Gookin.* M,DCC,LI. 8vo, pp. 40.

Cooper. A Sermon ... May 26th. 1756. Being the Anniversary for the Election of His Majesty's Council for the ... Province. By Samuel Cooper ... . *Boston: Printed by Green and Russell.* MDCCLVI. 8vo, pp. 43. BA., H. 16598

[Cooper.] The Crisis. Scire volunt, Secreta Domus atque inde Timeri. [*Boston:*] *Printed in June.* 1754. 8vo, pp. 15.

Reprinted with the following title:

[Cooper.] The Crisis or a Full Defence of the Colonies, in which it is incontestibly proved that the British Constitution has been flagrantly violated in the late Stamp Act, and rendered indisputably Evident, that the Mother Country cannot lay any Arbitrary Tax upon the Americans, without destroying the Essence of her own Liberties. *London: W. Griffin.* MDCCLXVI. 8vo, pp. 30. 16600

A warm defender of the colonists, who asserts, in opposition to some of the advocates of the stamp act, that the colonies are not all *virtually* represented in the British Parliament. *See* Pastor's "Life of Otis," Chap. X., p. 152.

Cooper. A Sermon Preached before His Excellency Thomas Pownall, Esq; Captain-General and Governor in Chief ... Of the Province of Massachusetts-Bay in New-England, October 16th, 1759. Upon Occasion of the Success of His Majesty's Arms in the Reduction of Quebec. By Samuel Cooper ... . *Boston: Green & Russell.* [1759.] 8vo, pp. 53. BA., H. 25

Cooper. A Sermon Upon Occasion of the Death of Our late Sovereign George the Second. Preach'd before His Excellency Francis Bernard, Esq; Captain-General and Governor in Chief, The Honourable His Majesty's Council, and House of Representatives, Of the Province of the Massachusetts-Bay in New-England, January 1. 1761. At the Appointment of the Governor and Council. By Samuel Cooper, A.M. Pastor of a Church in Boston. *Boston: Printed by John Draper.* 1761. 8vo, pp. 40. BL. 16602

Cooper. A Sermon preached before His Excellency John Hancock, Esq; Governour, ... of the Commonwealth of Massachusetts, October 25, 1780. being the Day of the Commencement of the Constitution, and Inauguration of the New Government. By Samuel Cooper, D.D. *Commonwealth of Massachusetts: Printed by T. and J. Fleet and J. Gill.* [1780.] 8vo, 2 l., pp. 55. BA., H. 16603

There is a Dutch translation of this in the "Verzameling van stukken tot de dertien Vereen. Staeten betrekend." Also: A Discourse on the Man of Sin, delivered in the Chapel of Harvard College, in Cambridge, New-England, September 1, 1783: At the Lecture, Founded By the Honorable Paul Dudley, Esq. ... *Boston: Greenleaf's Printing Office.* M,DCC,LXXXIV. 8vo, pp. 68. BA. + The Second Edition, corrected. *Boston: Mills and Hicks.* 1774. 8vo, Title, pp. 5–59. BA. — God's Concern for a Godly Seed: Sermon. 12mo. W. — A Sermon Preached in

Boston ... Before the Society for Encouraging Industry, and Employing the Poor; August 8. 1753. ... . *Boston: D. Henchman.* MDCCLIII. 8vo, 2 l., pp. 38. BA. — A Sermon Preach'd April 9. 1760, at the Ordination Of the Reverend Mr. Joseph Jackson, To the Pastoral Care of the Church in Brooklyn. ... . *New-England: John Draper.* 1760. 8vo, pp. 46. BA. — Dr. Cooper is supposed to be the author of "Two Letters to a Friend on the Present Critical Conjuncture of Affairs in North America, with an Account of the Action at Lake George ... *Boston.* 1755." pp. 54; also of "Hancock's Fifth of March Oration." Dr. Cooper graduated at Harvard College in 1743, and soon exhibited such marks of genius, that, at the age of twenty, he was invited by the church in Brattle Street, Boston, to become their pastor. His reputation increased, and he became one of the most popular preachers in the country, and was a contributor to many of the political journals ofhis day

Cooper (Susan Fenimore). Mount Vernon: A Letter to the Children of America, [sketching the Life of Washington]. *New York: D. Appleton & Co.* 1859. 18mo, 2 l., pp. 70. C.

[Cooper.] Rural Hours, By a Lady. *New-York: George P. Putnam.* 1850. 12mo, pp. 521. + Illustrated Edition. *New-York.* [*Ibid.*] 1851. 8vo. + Sixth Edition. *Philadelphia.* 1854. Sm. 4to. C. 16605

Reprinted in London as "Journal of a Naturalist in the United States of America. *London.* 1856." 2 vols., post 8vo.

Cooper. The Rhyme and Reason of Country Life; a Selection from fields Old and New. *New York.* 1855. 12mo, pp. 426. 16606

Cooper (S. M.) Life in the Forest; or, the Trials and Sufferings of a Pioneer. *Philadelphia: Perry & Erety.* 1854. 16mo, pp. 155. 16607

Cooper (T.) An Account of the Trial of Thomas Cooper, of Northumberland; on a Charge of Libel against the President of the United States; taken in Short Hand, with a Preface, Notes, and Appendix, by Thomas Cooper. *Philadelphia: printed by John Bioren. April* 1800. 8vo, pp. 64. 16608

The trial was for an attack on John Adams. He was found guilty, and sentenced to four months' imprisonment and a fine of $400. *See* Wharton's "State Trial."

Cooper. The Case of Thomas Cooper, M.D., President of the South Carolina College, submitted to the Legislature and People of South Carolina. *Columbia.* 1832. 8vo. 16609

Cooper. Consolidation. An Account of Parties in the United States, from the Convention of 1787, to the Present Period. Second Edition. By Thomas Cooper, M.D. *Columbia, S. C.* 1830. 8vo, pp. 37, Errata, 1 slip. C. 16610

[Cooper.] Extract of a Letter from a Gentleman in America to a Friend in England, on the subject of Emigration. [n. p.

1794.] 8vo, pp. 11. + [Another Edition. n. d.] 8vo, pp. 16. + [Another Edition. 1798.] 8vo, pp. 29. 16611

"Probably printed in London about 1798." — RICH.

COOPER. Letters on the Slave Trade, first published in Wheeler's "Manchester Chronicle;" and since reprinted with Additions and Alterations. By Thomas Cooper. ... *Manchester*. 1787. 8vo, pp. 36. BA. 16612

COOPER. Supplement to Mr. Cooper's Letters on the Slave Trade. *Warrington*. 1788. 8vo. S. 16613

See "M. Rev.," LXXVIII. 65.

COOPER. Political Essays. By Thomas Cooper, Esq., originally inserted in the Northumberland Gazette. With Additions. ... *Northumberland: Andrew Kennedy*. 1799. 8vo, pp. 64. J.C.B. + Second Edition with Corrections and Additions. *Philadelphia: Robert Campbell*. 1800. 8vo, 2 l., pp. 88. B., C.

COOPER Some Information respecting America, collected by Thomas Cooper, late of Manchester. *London: J. Johnson*. MDCCXCIV. 8vo, 4 l., pp. 240, (1). Map. + *Dublin*. 1794. 8vo, pp. 240. + The Second Edition. *London: J. Johnson*. MDCCXCV. 8vo, pp. 240. Map. 16615

COOPER. Renseignemens sur l'Amérique. Rassemblés par Thomas Cooper, ci-devant de Manchester. Traduits de l'Anglois; avec une carte. *Paris: An* III [1795]. 8vo, pp. 292. + *A Hamburg: chez Pierre François Fauche*. 1795. 8vo, pp. 218, 74. 16616

[COOPER.] Strictures addressed to James Madison on The Celebrated Report of William H. Crawford, recommending the Intermarriage of Americans with the Indian Tribes. Ascribed to Judge Cooper, and originally published by John Binns, in the Democratic Press. *Philadelphia: printed by Jesper* [sic] *Harding*. 1824. 8vo, pp. 22. B., BA., P. 16617

COOPER A Tract on the Proposed Alteration in the Tariff. Submitted to the Consideration of the Members from South Carolina in Congress. By Thomas Cooper ... . *New-York*. 1824. 8vo, pp. 19. BA. + *Philadelphia: reprinted by Joseph R. A. Skerrett*. 1824. 8vo, pp. 27. B., BA. 16618

' For a reply to this, *see* Carey (M.), Vol. III., No. 10868.

COOPER. A Treatise on the Law of Libel and the Liberty of the Press; showing the origin, use and abuse of the law of libel; with copious notes and references to authorities in Great Britain and the United States; as applicable to individuals and to Political and Ecclesiastical Bodies and Principles. *New York*. 1830, 8vo, pp. 184. 16619

COOPER. Two Essays: 1. On the Foundation of Civil Government; 2. On the Constitution of the United States. By Thomas Cooper, M.D. ... *Columbia: printed by D. & J. M. Faust*. 1826. 8vo, pp. 71. B. 16620

COOPER. Two Tracts: on the Proposed Alteration of the Tariff; and on Weights and Measures. ... By Thomas Cooper, M.D. *Charleston: A. E. Miller*. 1823. 8vo, pp. 44. 16621

Also: Address of the President of the South-Carolina College to the Graduates, at the Commencement, December 1, 1823. *Columbia*. 1823. 8vo, pp. 10. — Address ... 1830. *Columbia*. 1831. 8vo, pp. 12. — Address ... December, 1831. ... . *Columbia*. 1831. 8vo, pp. 15. H. — The Bankrupt Law of America Compared with the Bankrupt Law of England. *Philadelphia*. 1801. 8vo, pp. 435. — Lectures on the Elements of Political Economy ... *Columbia*. 1826. 8vo, pp. 280. + Second Edition, with Additions. *Columbia, S. C.: Morris & Wilson*. 1829. + *Columbia*. 1831. 8vo. Portrait by Durand. — A Manual of Political Economy ... *Washington*. 1834. 12mo, pp. 109. — The Opinion of Judge Cooper, on the Effect of a Sentence of a Foreign Court of Admiralty. Published ... By Alexander James Dallas. *Philadelphia: P. Byrne*. 1810. 8vo, pp. xiv, 9–39. BA. — Oration delivered on the Fourth of July, 1820. ... *New York*. 1820. — Political Arithmetic ... [n. p. n. d.] 8vo, pp. 40. C. — Statutes at large of South Carolina: ... 1682–1814. *Columbia*. 1836–9. 5 vols., 8vo. — Trial of Dr. Thomas Cooper for Infidelity. *Columbia, S. C.* 1831. 8vo. "The author was a graduate of Oxford. He came to Philadelphia, and became judge of a judicial district in Pennsylvania. Subsequently he was chosen President of Columbia College, South Carolina. He was the author of several works on Jurisprudence, some of which enjoy a high repuattion." — HOFFMAN's *Legal Study*, page 472. *See* "M. Rev.," XVII. 312.

COOPER. Narrative of the Proceedings against Thomas Cooper, Esquire, President Judge of the Eighth Judiciary District of Pennsylvania, on a Charge of Official Misconduct. *Lancaster: Printed by William Hamilton*. 1811. 8vo, pp. 55.

COOPER (*Rev.* T.) Facts Illustrative of the Condition of the Negro Slaves in Jamaica. By the Rev. Thomas Cooper. ... *London*. 1824. 8vo, pp. 64. S. 16623

COOPER. A Letter to Robert Hibbert ... in Reply to his Pamphlet entitled 'Facts verified upon Oath, in contradiction of the Rev. Thos. Cooper, concerning the ... Condition of the Slaves in Jamaica.' To which are added a Letter from Mrs. Cooper ... and ... an Exposure of the Falsehood ... . By Thomas Cooper ... . *London*. 1824. 8vo, pp. 90. 16624

[COOPER.] Negro Slavery in the United States of America and in the Colonies of the West Indies, especially in Jamaica. *London*. 1820. 8vo. C. 16625

COOPER. The Rev. Mr. Cooper and his Calumnies against Jamaica, particularly his late Pamphlet in reply to Facts verified on Oath. By a West-Indian. *Jamaica*. 1825. 8vo, pp. 67.

COOPER (T. J.) Lives of the Departed Heroes and Statesmen of America. *New York*. 1834. 12mo. Woodcuts.

COOPER (W.) The Beatifick Vision ... . A Discourse Upon ... the Death ... of Mr. Moses Abbot, Who departed this Life May 1st 1734. ... By William Cooper ... . *Boston: J. Edwards and H. Foster*. 1734. 8vo, Title, pp. ii, 26, 24.

The last paging contains "An Appendix ... out of his Diary."

COOPER. The Blessedness of the Tried Saint. A Sermon Preach'd ... At the Lecture in Boston, January 19. 1726, 7. By W. Cooper. ... *Boston: Samuel Gerrish*. 1727. 8vo, 2 l., pp. iv, 20. B., BA. 16629

COOPER. Mr. Cooper's Confession of Faith. Together with His Answers To the Questions proposed to him by the Reverend Mr. Colman, Previous to his Ordination. *Boston: Printed by T. Fleet and T. Crump, for Samuel Gerrish and Daniel Henchman*. 1716. 16mo, Title, pp. 24. BA. 16630

Usually found with Colman's Sermon. *See* No. 14516.

COOPER. The Danger of People's loosing the good Impressions made by the late awful Earthquake. A Sermon preach'd a month after it Happened. *Boston*. 1727. 8vo, pp. (2), 23.

COOPER. The Doctrine of Predestination unto Life, Explained and Vindicated: In Four Sermons, preach'd to the Church of Christ, meeting in Brattle-Street, and publish'd at their general Desire: With some additional Passages and Quotations. By William Cooper ... . With a Preface by the Senior Pastors of the Town. ... *Boston: J. Edwards and H. Foster*. MDCCXL. 8vo, Title, pp. 4, 140. BA. + *Boston. Printed. London: Re-printed for E. and C. Dilly*. MDCCLXV. 12mo, pp. iv, 142. + *Boston*. 1804. 16632

COOPER. Man humbled by being compar'd to a Worm. A Sermon Preached March 9th, 1731, 2. The Day after the Funeral of ... William Tailer, Esq; late Lieutenant Governor ... . By William Cooper, A.M. *Boston: B. Green*. 1732. 8vo, 2 l., pp. ii, 25. B., BA., M. 16633

COOPER. One shall be taken and another left. A Sermon Preach'd to the Old South Church ... March 22. 1740 — 1. A Season wherein there was a remarkable Display of the sovereign Grace of God in the Work of Conversion. ... By William Cooper ... . *Boston: D. Henchman*. 1741. 8vo, pp. 23.

[COOPER.] A Reply to The Objections made against taking the Small Pox in the Way of Inoculation from Principles of Conscience. In a Letter to a Friend in the Country. By a Minister in Boston. ... The Third Impression. *Boston: J. Gerrish, and J. Phillips*. 1730. 8vo, 2 l., pp. iv, 14, (2). BA.

Preface signed W. Cooper.

COOPER. A Sermon Preach'd ... May 28. 1740. The Day for the Election of His Majesty's Council ... By William Cooper, A.M. ... *Boston, N. E.: J. Edwards and H. Foster*. MDCCXL. 8vo, 2 l., pp. 48. BA. 16636

COOPER. The Service of God recommended to the Choice of Young People. A Sermon ... on the Death of Mr. John Coney ... . With ... his Life ... . By William Cooper ... . *Boston: J. Gerrish, and J. Phillips*. 1726. 2 l., pp. 35, Title, pp. 86. BA., M. 16637

The "Life" has the title: "An Appendix, Containing a further Account of Mr. Coney, Collected from his private Writings, etc. *Boston*. 1726."

COOPER. The Sin and Danger of quenching the Spirit. Two Sermons Preach'd at Portsmouth ... December 12th and 19th, 1741. A Time in which a remarkable Work of the Spirit of God was going on in that place. By William Cooper ... . *Boston: S. Eliot*. 1741. 8vo, pp. 49. BA. 16638

COOPER. Three Discourses concerning the Reality the Extremity, and the absolute Eternity of Hell Punishments. By William Cooper, A.M. One of the Pastors in Brattle-Street. Published by Desire of many of the Hearers. *Boston: Printed by S. Kneeland and T. Green, for Joseph Edwards, at the Corner Shop on the North-side of the Town-House*. MDCCCXXXII. 12mo, Title, pp. 114. 16639

COOPER. The Work of Ministers represented under the Figure of Sowers. In a Sermon preach'd at Springfield, January 26. 1736. at the Ordination of the Reverend Mr. Robert Breck ... . By William Cooper ... [With Mr. Breck's Confession of Faith.] *Boston: Printed by J. Draper*. 1736. 8vo, 2 l., pp. 26, (2). B., BA., M. 16640

Also: Compendium Evangelicum. Sermon at the Public Lecture, March 1, 1738–39, on the Funeral of Rev. Peter Thacher. *Boston*. 1739. 8vo, pp. 33. M. — Concio Hyemalis. A Winter Sermon. Being a Religious Improvement of the Irresistable Power of God's Cold. Preach'd January 23. 1736, 37. *Boston*. 1737. 8vo, 2 l., pp. 17. B., BA. — Divine Teaching to be sought, that we may be led into Divine Truth. A Sermon Preach'd February 27th. 1731, 2 ... *Boston*. 1732. 12mo, pp. (2), 26. — Early Piety Joyful to Beholders. A Sermon Preached at Rumney-Parish, at the Desire of a Religious Society of Young Men in that place. On Wednesday, Aug., 21. 1728, ... *Boston: T. Hancock*. 1728. 8vo, pp. (4), 30. B., M. — God's Concern for a Godly Seed. Sermon on a Day of Prayer, March 5, 1723. ... *Boston*. 1723. 8vo, pp. 38. M. — How and Why Young People should Cleanse their Way, in Two Sermons. ... Added, another Sermon Preach'd Privately to a Society of Young Men. *Boston*. 1716. 8vo, pp. (2), vi, 46. — Jabez's Character and Prayer. A Sermon To a Society of Young Men, August 21. 1715. ... *Boston*. 1716. 8vo, pp. (2), 24. — Serious Exhortations address'd to Young Men; a Sermon preached May 14. 1732 ... *Boston*. 1732. 8vo, pp. 20. M. — Sermon concerning the Laying the Deaths of others to Heart, occasioned by the Death of John Gore, Nov. 7. 1720. ... Appendix by B. Colman. *Boston*. 1720. 8vo, pp. 32, 6. B. — Sermon on the Occasion of the Funeral of Rev. P. Thacher ... *Boston*. 1739. 8vo. B.

COOPER (William), *and* COLMAN (*Rev.* Benjamin), *D.D.* Two Sermons preached in Boston, March 5, 1723, on a Day of Prayer had by the Church and Congregation usually meeting in Brattle Street. ... *Boston*. 1723. 8vo, pp. 38, 36. 16641

COOPER (W.) Anthem for Thanksgiving Day. By William Cooper. *Boston*. 1792. 4to. W. 16642

COOPER. The Promised Seed. A Sermon Preached to God's Ancient Israel the Jews, at Sion-Chapel, Whitechapel, Aug. 28th, 1796. *Philadelphia*. 1796. 8vo. + *Boston*. 1796. W. + *Concord, N. H. Oct*. 1797. 4to, pp. 32. 16643

COOPER (W.) Notices of Big Bone Lick, including the various Explorations that have been made there, the Animals to which the remains belong, and the quantities that have been found of each. By William Cooper. [n. p. 1830.] 8vo, pp. 20. Map. 16644

COOPER (W. D.) The Oxenbridges of Brede Place, Sussex, and Boston, Massachusetts. By William Durrant Cooper ... . (Reprinted from the Sussex Archæological Collections, Vol. XII.) *London: John Russell Smith*. M.DCCC.LX. 8vo, pp. 20. Woodcut. 16645

COOPER (W. H.) Incidents of Shipwreck; or the Loss of the San Francisco, by Rev. W. H. Cooper, A.B. late Acting Chaplain of the Ship, on a Mission of the P. E. Church to Rio de Janeiro. *Philadelphia: Willis P. Hazard*. 1855. pp. 108. C. 16646

Co-operative Stores, their History, Organization, and Management Based on the Recent German work of Eugene Richter With annotations and amendments rendering the work specially adapted for use in the United States. *New York: Leypoldt & Holt*. 1867. 12mo, 2 l., pp. 131. H. 16647

Cooper's Shop Volunteer Refreshment Saloon, First Annual Report. Philadelphia, May 26, 1862. *Philadelphia: Collins*. 1862. 8vo, pp. 8. + Second ... Philadelphia, May 26, 1863. pp. 8. + Third ... May, 1864. pp. 8. + Fourth ... May 26, 1865. *Philadelphia: Collins*. 1865. 8vo, pp. 16. 16648

Cooperstown Seminary. Circular. 1859. 16649

Cooperstown Classical and Military Academy. Prospectus. [*Cooperstown*.] 1868. 8vo. B. 16650

COOPERSTOWN, *N. Y.* The Chronicles of, &c. *See* [Cooper (J. F.)], No. 16425.

Coose Bay Coal Company ... [Report of William V. Wells and Lorenzo Hubbard on its coal lands.] *San Francisco*. 1855. 8vo, pp. 14. H. 16651

COOTE (C. T.) An Address on the Life and Character of Abraham Howard Quincy ... Fifteenth of November, 1840, by Clement T. Coote ... . *Washington*. 1840. 8vo, pp. 41. H.

COOTE (Richard), 1*st Earl of Bellamont*, *or Bellomont*. An Account of the Proceedings of the earl of Bellamont, governor of New York, and an extraordinary Council, held at that place, May 8, 1698, relative to Colonel Fletcher's giving commissions to Pyrates; with the Earl's Speech to the Assembly. *New York: Printed and Sold by William Bradford, Printer to the King*. 1698. Folio, 1 l. 16653

COOTE. Articles of Agreement | Made the 10th Day of October, in the Year of our Lord 1695. | Between the Right Honourable Richard Earl of Bellomont of the one part, and Robert Levingston Esq; | and | Captain William Kidd, | Of the other part. [Colophon:] *London: J. Richardson*. 1701. | Folio, pp. 2. 16654

[COPE (Gilbert).] The Browns of Nottingham. [1864.] 8vo, pp. 18. B. 16655

COPE A Record of the Cope Family. As established in America, by Oliver Cope, who came from England to Pennsylvania about the Year 1682, with the Residences, Dates of Births, Deaths and Marriages of his Descendants as far as ascertained. By Gilbert Cope. *Philadelphia: King & Baird, Printers*. 1861. pp. xxvii, 10–251. H. 16656

COPE (M.) Some Authentic Extracts, with a Few Deductions and Observations in relation to the State of the Society of Friends ... By Morris Cope. *West-Chester: E. F. James*. 1858. 8vo, pp. 31. H. 16657

COPE (T. P.) Speech of Thomas P. Cope on Banks and Currency, Delivered Dec. 20, 1837. [*Philadelphia*.] 1838. 8vo. 16658

COPELAND (R. M.) Country Life; a Handbook of Agricultural, Horticultural, and Landscape Gardening. By Robert Morris Copeland. Fifth edition, revised. *Boston*. 1866. 8vo, pp. v, 912. BA. 16659

COPELAND. Statement of R. Morris Copeland, Asst. Adjutant-General and Major of Volunteers, discharged from Service August 6, 1862. *Boston: printed by Prentiss and Deland*. 1844. 8vo, pp. 52. BA., H. 16660

COPELAND *and* CLEVELAND. A Few Words on the Central Park, New York. *Boston* 1856. 8vo, pp. 7. H. 16661

COPERNICUS (N.) Nicolai Co | pernici Torinensis | de revolutionibvs orbi | vm cœlestium, Libri VI. | Habes in hoc opere iam recens nato, & ædito | studiose lector, Motus Stellarum, tam fixarum | quam erraticarum, cum ex ueteribus, tum etiam | ex recentibus observationibus restitutos: & no- | uis insuper ac admirabilibus hypothesibus or- | natos. Habes etiam Tabulas expedissimas, ex | quibus eosdem ad quodiis tempus quãm facili | me calculare poteris. Igitur eme, lege, fruere. | ... *Norimbergæ apud Ioh. Petreium*, | *Anno* M. D. XLIII. | Folio, 10 l., Text, 196 numbered leaves. BM. 16662

See in Book 1. cap III. "Quomodo terra cû aqua unum globû perficiat," especially the passage on fol. 2: "Magis id erit clarum, si addantur insulæ," etc. "First and rarest edition of this celebrated work. The author died 24th May, 1543, only a few hours after he had received the first copy of his labors in print." — LIBRI. Copernicus is the Latinized form of Kopernik, or, according to Œttinger, Koppernik.

Copey etlicher brieff | so ausz Hispania kummê | seindt, anzaygent die eygenschafft des, | Newen Lands, so newlich von Kay.

| May. Armadi auffdem newen | Mör gefunden ist worden, durch die Hispanie. | [*S. L.*] M. D. XXXV. | Sm. 4to, 4 l. 16663

"Plaquette de la plus grande rareté, non citée dans Harrisse, 'Bibliotheca Americana Vetustissima.' C'est une courte relation de l'expédition de Pizarro au Pérou." — TROSS.

Copia. | [n. p. n. d.] 4to, 4 l. 16664

"Arrêt des États-Généraux concernant le trafic du sel aves Punto del Rey, daté du 7 juillet 1627." — TRÖMEL.

Copia de Cedula de el Rey dando gracias à los Padres de la Cia de Jesus, à cuyo cargo corren las missiones del Paraguay, y Buenos-Ayres, ecc. — El Rey. Aviendo puesto en mi Real noticia el año de 1726. *Buen Retiro*. 1743. Folio, 18 l. J.C.B.

These letters on the missions of Paraguay are addressed to the viceroys and governors of the Spanish possessions in America. They are dated at Buen Retiro, 1743.

Copia de dos Cartas Escritas de vn Missionero, y del Superior de las Missiones de los Maynas, en el Rio Marañon, jurisdiccion de la Real Audiencia de Quito, avisando al Padre Vice-Provincial de la Compañia de Iesvs, del Nuevo Reyno de Granada, Primera Carta. [1861.] Folio, pp. 4. 16666

Copia | de dos Cartas muy | devotas de los Vene- | rables Padres Guardianes del S. Monte | Sion, en Ierusalen, y del Santo Conuen- | to de Nazaret, embiadas al P. Comissa- | rio de Tierra Santa destas Prouincias | del Perù, residente en esta ciudad de los | Reyes, escritas en los años de 1646. | y el de 1648. | En que dan noticia de particulares cosas | que en los lugares de nuestra Reden- | cion han sucedido, &c. | [Vignette.] Con licencia. | *Impresso in Lima, Por Iorge Lopez de Herrera, año de* 1651. | 4to, 12 l.

Copia de la Real Cedula de su Magestad, expedida para que en la Ciudad de San Christoval de la Habana se forme una Compania a cuyo Cargo este la Conduccion de Tabacos, Azucar, Corambres, y otros Frutos de la Isla de Cuba, con la Direccion, Reglas, Exempciones, y Obligaciones que se expressan. *Madrid*. 1740. 12mo. 16668

Copia delle lettere del prefetto del | la India la nuoua Spagna detta, alla Cesarea Maesta rescritte. | [n. p. 1534.] Sm. 4to, 2 l., Text in Roman characters. 16669

Copia de Reales Ordenes, y cartas del Governador Don Juan de Prado, que se citan en las Defensas, y con estas se presentan los Originales de aquellas. [Dated] *Madrid, April* 28, 1764. Folio, 37 l. J.C.B. 16670

Relates to Havana.

Copia de una lettera venuta da Genova notata a di 25 de Marzo. [n. p. n. d.] 4to, 2 leaves. Woodcut. 16671

"A scarce tract relating to Andrea Doria, printed about 1530, unknown to Brunet."

Copia de unas cartas embiadas del Brasil, por el Padre Nobrega, de la Compañia de Jesus, y otros padres que esten debaxo de su obediēcia ... . Tresladadas de portugues en castellano. Recebidas el año de 1551. [n. p. n. d.] 4to, pp. (27).

Copia | Eines Send-Schreibens auss | der neuen Welt, betreffend | Die Erzehlung einer gefährlichen | Schifffarth, und glücklichen Anländung etlicher | Christlichen Reisegefehrten, welch zu dem En- | de diese Wallfahrt angetretten, den Glau- | ben an JEsum CHristum allda auss- | zubreiten | Tob. XII. 8. | Der Könige und Fürsten Rath und Heimlichkeiten | soll man verschweigen, aber GOttes Werck soll | man herrlich preisen und offenbaren. | *Gedruckt im Jahr* 1695. | 4to, 6 l. c. 16673

This letter recounts the dangerous voyage and happy delivery of certain Christian missionaries who journeyed to America to propagate the knowledge of the true faith. It is dated from German Town, Pennsylvania, August 7, 1694.

Copia van't Octroy | Doer de Hoogh Mog. Heeren | Staten Generael der Vanderael der Vereenighde Nederlanden | gegeven aen Jan Reeps, en syne mede Participan- | ten, om een Colonie op te rechten aen de | Westzyde van Rio de Las Amasones, | tot aen Cabo d'Orange. | Mitsgaders | Een korte beschryvinge vande Landen, Vruchten | Gedierten, ende Visschen, &c. nevens eenige | opgestelde Conditien, om een Compagnie | te maecken, tot voorsettinge van dese | Colonie, ten meesten voordeele van | de gemene Participanten. | *In 'sGraven-Hage,* | *By Jacobus Scheltus, Ordinaris Drucker van de Hoogh* | *Mogende Heeren Staten Generael der Vereenighde* | *Nederlanden. Anno* 1689. *Met Privilegie.* | 4to, pp. 16. J.C.B. 16674

Copiapo Railway Company. Informe relativo a los negocios de la Compañia Ferro-Carril de Copiapó. *Valparaiso.* 1865. 8vo, pp. 30. 16675

Copie de deux | lettres | envoies dela | novvelle France, | Au Pere Procureur des Missions | de la compagnie de Iesvs en ces contrées. | *A Paris* | *chez Sebastien Cramoisy, Imprimeur ordinaire du Roy et Gabriel Cramoisy. rüe S. Iacques aux Ci-* | *cognes.* | M.DC. LVI. *Auec priuilege du Roy.* 18mo, pp. 28. A. 16676

Only one perfect copy known. It was reprinted by Weed and Parsons, Albany, for Mr. James Lenox, in 1855. 12mo, pp. 28. *See* Le Mercier.

Copie Translaet uyt het Portogijs | Waer in verhaelt wort de Vreede dewelcke ghemaeckt is | tusschen de Onderdanen vonden | Koningh van Hispanien, | ende den | Koningh van Portogael, | by die van | Rio Plato | ende die van | Angola. | *Ghedruckt in 's Graven-Hage by Johannes Breeckevelt, ende Michiel Stael, Bouckderkoopers* | *op 't Buyten-Hof* | *teghen-oder de Ghevanghe-Poort* | 1649. | Sm. folio sheet. 16677

Copie | Vande Missive, gheschre- | ven by den Generael Weerdenbvrch, | aende Ho. Mo. Heeren Staten Generael, | noopende de veroveringhe vande Stadt | Olinda de Fernabvco, | met alle sijne Forten ende | stercke Plaetsen. | *In 's Graven-Haghe.* | *By de VVeduwe, ende* | *Erfgenamen van wijlen Hillebrandt* | *Iacobssz van Wouw, Ordinaris Druckers vande Ho: Mo:* | *Heeren Staten Generael, Anno* 1630. | 4to, 4 l. 16678

Copie | Van een Missive gheschreven by een vry Man, in | Brasl, aen seecker zijnen vrient alhier, gevonden onder de verdroncken brie- | ven, uyt het Schip Zeelandia tegen 't Eylant Wicht gestrant, ende de West- | Jndische Compagnie ter hant gekomen. | *Voor Francoys Lieshout, op den Dam,* 1646. | Sm. folio, 6 sheets. 16679

Copie | Van Requesten van de goede gehoorsame Bur- | geren ende Gemeente deser Stede Amstelredamme, | wenschende onse E. E. Heeren Burgemeeste- | ren, 36 Raden, geluck, heyl en salighevd. | Placcaet gevolght op de voorgaende eerste Re- | queste, gepubliceert den eersten April 1628. | Requeste van de dolerende Burgeren aen de E. E. Heeren over het Publiceeren van 't Placcaet. | Requeste van de Predicanten ende Ouderlingen | der gereformeerde ghemeente, aen de Eersame, Wijse, Voorsienige, seer Discrete Heeren, myn | Heeren de Burgemeesteren en ses -en-der-tig- | Raden deser Stede Amsterdam. | Requeste vande West Indische Compaignie | over-gelevert aen sijnen Vorstelijcke Genade, Prince Frederick Hendrick van Nassou- | wen, Prince van Oraignien. | Requeste van de Burgerije ende Nego- | tianten, ofte Koopluiden van Amster- | dam, aen sijne Vorstelicke Genade den Prince van Oraignien. | *Anno* M. D. C. XX VIII. | 4to, pp. 16.

Copie | Vande tween | sententien, | Uytgesproocken vanden Hove Pro- | vinciael van Hollandt eerst, | Ende ten tweeden de | sententie | van | appel | vanden Hoghen Rade van Hollandt, | tegens | Gaspar Dias de Fereira | Geboren tot Lisbon in Portugael. | *Gedruckt nae de originele de Copien vanden selden Hoven.* 1647. | 4to, pp. 8. 16681

'Copies and Extracts of Documents on the subject of British Impressments of American Seamen. *London: Longman.* 1812. 8vo, pp. 61. + *New York.* 1813. 8vo, pp. 64. 16682

Copies and Extracts of several Newspapers printed in New England, in the Months of September, October, and November, 1765, and referred to in the Letters transmitted from Francis Bernard, esq. Governor of the Massachusettes bay, to the Lords Commissioners for Trade and Plantations. [n. p. 1765?] Folio, pp. 5, 108. C. 16683

Copies and Translations of the Royal Charters ... by which the Territories of Nova Scotia and Canada, with the Islands and Seas adjacent, were granted, in 1621, 1625, and 1628, to the Right Hon. Sir William Alexander. [Edited] By T. C. Banks. *London: Ridgway.* 1831. Folio, pp. 3, 62. C. 16684

Copies des Pièces des Aqens du Gouvernement Français etc. *Cap-Henry.* 1814. 8vo, pp. 14. C. 16685

Copies of the Original Grant of Land on the White River, lying in the States of Arkansas and Missouri, made in the year 1793, by the Baron De Carondelet, ... to Captain Don Joseph Valliere. Also, Copies of the Power of Attorney, by the Heirs of ... Valliere, to Creed Taylor, authorizing him to sell and dispose of the same, and a Deed from him as such, to John Wilson, for an Undivided Half thereof. *New York: Jared W. Bell, printer.* 1844. 8vo, pp. 32. H. 16686

Copies of Original Letters recently written by Persons in Paris, to Dr. Priestley in America. Taken on board of a Neutral Vessel ... *London: J. Wright.* 1798. 8vo, pp. 36. BA. + Fourth Edition. *London: Wright.* 1798. 8vo, pp. 36. C.

See "M. Rev.," XXVII. 350, and Cobbett (W.), No. 13899.

Copies of the Proceedings in the several Assemblies, [Massachusetts Bay, Connecticut, Virginia, South Carolina, and North Carolina] in consequence of the Resolutions of Parliament in last Session. [1769.] 4to. 16688

Copies or Extracts of Despatches relative to the Condition of the Sugar Growing Colonies. Part I. British Guiana. *London.* 18—. Rl. 8vo, pp. 643. 16689

[COPITHORNE (R.)] The English Cotejo, or the Cruelties, Depredations, and illicit Trade charg'd upon the English, in a

Spanish libel lately published, compared with the Murders and Robberies of the Spaniards. By a Sufferer. [1730.] 8vo.

COPLAND (P.) Virginia's God be Thanked, | or | a Sermon of | Thanksgiving | for the Happie | successe of the affayres in | Virginia this last | yeare. | Preached by Patrick Copland at | Bow-Church in Cheapside, before the Honorable | Virginia Company, on Thursday, the 18. | of Aprill 1622. And now published by | the Commandement of the said hono- | rable Company. | Hereunto are adjoyned some Epistles, | written first in Latine (and now Englished) in | the East Indies by Peter Pope, an Indian youth, | borne in the bay of Bengala, who was first taught | and converted by the said P. C. ... | *London: William Sheffard and John Bellamie.* | 1622. | 4to, 6 l. H. 16691

A volume of extreme rarity.

COPLAND (S.) Black and White; or, the Jamaica Question. *London: Freeman.* 18—. 8vo, pp. 64. 16692

COPLESTON (E.) Canada: Why we Live in it, and Why we Like it. By Mrs. Edward Copleston. *London: Parker, Son & Bourn.* 1862. Fcap. 8vo, pp. 121. 16693

COPLESTON (Edward), *Bishop of Landaff.* Sermon before the Society for the Promotion of the Gospel in Foreign Parts. *London.* 1828. 8vo. 16694

COPLEY (E.) A History of Slavery, and its Abolition. By Esther Copley. *London.* 1836. 12mo. C., P. + Second Edition, with an Appendix. *London: Houlston & Stoneman.* 1839. 12mo, pp. xi, 648. Portrait. + *London:* [*Ibid.*] 1844. 12mo. A., C., P. + Third Edition. With an Appendix. *London: Henry G. Bohn.* 1852. 12mo, pp. xi, 648. Portrait. H. 16695

COPLEY (J.) Kansas and the Country Beyond, on the Line of the Union Pacific Railway, Eastern Division, from the Missouri to the Pacific Ocean. ... By Josiah Copley. *Philadelphia: J. B. Lippincott & Co.* 1867. 8vo, pp. 86. Map. H. 16696

COPP (J. A.) American Liberty and its Obligations. A Discourse for the Times, delivered in the Broadway Church, Chelsea, Mass., Sabbath, July 2, 1854. By Joseph A. Copp ... *Boston: printed by C. C. P. Moody.* 1854. 8vo, pp. 24. 16697

COPP. The Atlantic Telegraph. A Discourse Preached in Chelsea, 1858. *Boston.* 8vo. 1669[illegible]

COPPEE (H.) The Field Manual of Courts Martial; comprising the exact Forms of Proceeding and the Duties of all persons connected with Military Tribunals in any capacity. To which are added the Modes of Procedure in Courts of Inquiry, Military Commissions, Retiring Boards, Boards of Survey, and Council of Administration. By Captain Henry Coppee. Second Edition, revised and enlarged. *Philadelphia.* 1865. 18mo.

COPPEE. A Gallery of Famous English and American Poets. With an Introductory Essay by Henry Coppee, A.M. *Philadelphia: E. H. Butler & Co.* 1859. Impl. 8vo. Plates. 16700

COPPEE. Grant and his Campaigns: a Military Biography. By Henry Coppee ... . *New York: Charles B. Richardson.* 1866. 8vo, pp. 521. 8 Portraits. B., H. 16701

Reproduced as the

COPPEE. Life and Services of Gen. U. S. Grant. By H. Coppée. With Portrait and Sketch of Colfax. *New York: Richardson & Co.* 1868. 12mo, pp. 566. B. 16702

Also: Obituary Notice of Washington Irving ... Read before the American Philosophical Society, in Philadelphia, September 21st, 1860. 8vo, pp. 16. — Sketch of the Life of Lieut.-Gen. U. S. Grant. ... [From the] United Service Magazine. *New York: C. B. Richardson.* 1864. 8vo, pp. 10. H.

Copper Mines. Report of the United States Revenue Commission in Respect to Copper Mining and Manufacture. [*Washington:*] *Treasury Department.* 1866. 8vo, pp. 32. 16703

Articles of Association of the Copper Rock Mining Company. 1846. 8vo. S. 16704

The Copperhead Catechism. For the Instruction of such Politicians as are of Tender Years. Carefully Compiled by Divers Learned and Designing Men. Authorized and with Admonitions by Fernando the Gothamite, High Priest of the Order of Copperheads. *New York: Sinclair Toucey,* 1864. 12mo, Title, pp. ix–30. B. 16705

Copyrighted and, perhaps, written by Montgomery Wilson.

Copperhead Conspiracy in the North West. An Exposé of the Treasonable Order of the "Sons of Liberty," Vallandigham, Supreme Commander. [*New York: J. A. Gray & Green.* 1864.] 16706

Another edition was printed for the Cong. Committee. 1864. 8vo, pp. 8.

Copperhead Minstrel. A choice collection of Democratic Poems and Songs, for the use of Political Clubs and the Social Circles. *New York: Feeck & Bancker.* 1863. 12mo, pp. 60.

Copperheads vigorously prosecuting Peace. Is it the Peace you want? *New York: A. D. F. Randolph.* 1863. Broadside. 16708

COPPEY (H.) Monsieur de Raousset en Sonore. *Mexico.* 1855. 4to, pp. 48. Map. 16709

COPPIER (G.) Histoire et voyage des Indes Occidentales et de plusieurs autres regions maritimes, & esloignées. Diuisé en deux Liures Par Gvillavme Coppier, lyonnois. *Lyons: Jean Hvgvetan.* 1645. 8vo, 24 l., pp. 182, Table, 9 l. H., 16710

COPPIN (Pasquale). Compendio storico della scoperta di America e dei costumi degli Americani a quel tempo. *Padova.* 1821. 8vo. 16711

COPPINGER (J. B.) The History of the Usury Laws, and a Stricture Thereon, exhibiting its Influence upon Commerce. By John B. Coppinger, A.M. *New-York: Van Norden & King.* 1849. 8vo, pp. 19. 16712

COPPINGER (J.) Manifesto, que hace el Coronel Español Don José Coppinger, demostrando el injusto y violento proceder que se há observado en San Augustin de Florida, despojandole De Orden de la Autoridad gobernante, de los Archivos de su Gobierno y otros papeles, despues de la Entrega de la Provincia á los Estados Unidos de America. *Impresso en Filadelfia, por Juan F. Hurtel, No.* 126, *Calle Segunda, Sur.* 1821. 8vo, pp. 36.

COPPINI (Aquilino). De Hispanicæ Monarchiæ Amplitudine Oratio. *Mediolani.* 1612. 4to. 16714

In this rare tract the author speaks of the Spanish possessions in Peru, Brazil, Mexico, etc.

COPPO DA ISOLA (Peter). Portolano. | [Colophon:] *Stampata in Venetia per Augusti* | *no di Bindoni.* 1528. *Adi.* 14. *de Marzo.* | Very sm. 4to ($2\frac{1}{2}$ by $3\frac{1}{2}$ inches), 24 l. 16715

Preceding the title, there is an oval map of the world filling two pages, upon which appear *Cuba, Iamaiqua, Spagnuolla, môdo nouo,* etc. On the reverse of the title another map. A passage relating to Columbus is reprinted in Harrisse's "Bib. Am. Vet.," pp. 265, 6.

COPWAY (G.) The Life, History, and Travels of Kah-ge-ga-gah-bowh, (George Copway) a Young Indian Chief of the

Ojebwa Nation, a Convert to the Christian Faith, and a Missionary to his People for Twelve Years; with a Sketch of the Present State of the Objebwa [*sic*] Nation, in regard to Christianity and their Future Prospects. Also, an Appeal; with all the Names of the Chiefs now living, who have been Christianized, and the Missionaries now laboring among them. Written by Himself. Second Edition. *Philadelphia: James Harmstead.* 1847. 12mo, pp. 158. Portrait. BA., C., P. + *Albany, N. Y.: Weed & Parsons.* 1847. 8vo, pp. 224. 16716

COPWAY. The Life, Letters and Speeches of Kah-ge-ga-gah-bowh, or, G. Copway, Chief Ojibway Nation ... . *New York: S. W. Benedict.* 1850. 12mo, pp. 224. Portrait. BM., H. + *London.* 1851. 16717

COPWAY. The Ojibway Conquest, a Tale of the Northwest. By Kah-ge-ga-gah-bowh, or, G. Copway, Chief of the Ojibway Nation. *New York: the Author.* 1850. 12mo, pp. 91. Portrait.

COPWAY. Organization of a new Indian Territory, east of the Missouri River. Arguments and Reasons submitted to the ... Congress of the United States. By the Indian Chief Kah-ge-ga-gah-bouh, or Geo. Copway. *New York: S. W. Benedict.* 1850. 8vo, pp. 32. H., C. 16719

COPWAY. Recollections of a Forest Life: or the Life and Travels of Kah-ge-ga-gah-bowh, or George Copway, Chief of the Ojibway Nation. *London: H. Lea.* 1850. 12mo, pp. 256. + *London.* 1854. 12mo, pp. 256. 16720

COPWAY. Running Sketches of Men and Places, in England, France, Germany, Belgium and Scotland. By George Copway (Kah-ge-ga-gah-bowh), Chief of the Ojibway nation, North American Indians. *New York.* 1851. 12mo, pp. 346. P.

COPWAY. The Traditional History and Characterstic Sketches of the Ojibway Nation. By G. Copway, or, Ka-ge-ga-gah-bouh, Chief of the Ojibway Nation. *London: C. Gilpin.* 1850. 8vo, pp. xii, 298. + Illustrated by Darly. *Boston: Benjamin B. Mussey.* 1851. 12mo, pp. xi, 13–266. 2 Plates. H., P. + *Boston: B. B. Mussey & Co.* 1851. 12mo, 2 l., pp. 266. C.

A Copy of a Letter from a Gentleman in Guadaloupe to his Friend in London, (on the value of Canada, Guadaloupe, &c.) *Privately printed.* 1760. 8vo. 16723

A Copy of a Letter from a Gentleman in Virginia, to a Merchant in Philadelphia. [n. p. n. d.] Folio, pp. 2. P.

At Philadelphia, July 22, 1768. Relates to the proceedings against the Stamp Act.

Copy of A Letter from a Post Captain in the Navy of the United States. *Washington: W. Cooper, Jr.* 1830. 8vo, pp. 8.

Copy of a Petition ... relative to the Claim of the Officers of the Artillery Artificers, under the command of the late Colonel Benjamin Flower; ... [for] Half-Pay and Commutation. [n. p. n. d.] 4to, pp. 12. 16726

Signed Alexander Power. Philadelphia, June 10, 1790.

Copy of a Representation of the Board of Trade [to the House of Lords, In pursuance of their Address to His Majesty of June 13. 1733.] relating to the Laws made, Manufactures set up, and Trade carried on, in His Majesty's Plantations in America. Dated Jan. 23. 1733–4. [*London: Printed in the Year* MDCCXLIX.] Folio, pp. 27. 16727

Mr. J. C. Brown has another edition of this with pp. 20.

Copy of an Act lately passed in Carolina, and sent over to be confirmed here by the Lord Granville, Palatine, and the rest of the Proprietors, which would be highly prejudicial to Her Majesty's Interests and destructive to that Colony, as may appear by the Act itself, and some Queries thereupon, (1704.) 4to, pp. 8. 16728

Copy | of Two | Letters, | The first written by a Gentleman | at New-York, to his Friend at Edin- | burgh; the second by a divinity | minister in England to a Gentleman | in Scotland. | Both giving an | Account | of the | Progress and Success of the | Gospel in Foreign Parts. | *Edinburgh: Printed by A. Alison.* MDCCXL. | pp. 8. 16729

Copye, | van een Brief | van den | koningh | van | Portugael, | gheschreven aen | Francisco | de | Souza Coutinho, | Synen Ambassadeur, resideerende | in 's Graven-Hage. | *t'Amsterdam.* | *Ghedruckt by Nicolaes van Ravesteyn,* | *op S. Anthonis Marckt,* 1649 | 4to, pp. 8. 16730

Copye | Van sekere Articulen beraemt | inde vergaderinghe vande Bewindthebberen, ende Gecommitteerde der Hooft-participanten vande West- | Indische Compagnie, binnen Amsterdam. | Streckende | Tot goede verseeckeringe der Participanten, ende ge-| rusticheyt der selfder Bewinthebberen. | Overgelevert ter vergaderinge der Hoogh. Mogh. Heeren | Staten Generael | daer op de andere Cameren verschreven zijn | teghen den 18 May in 'sGravenhage te verschijnen | om | voort te gaen | Dienende, | Om alle Lief-hebbers des Vaderlandts tot het teyckenen op te | wecken ende lustich te maecken, so noch niet gheteyckent en heb- | ben, ende die gheteyckent hebben, tselve te verbeteren, dewijl | het nu onghetwyffelt seer haest ghesloten sal werden. | *Ghedruckt int Iaer ons Heeren* 1623. | 4to, pp. 8. 16731

Copye | vande | Resolutie van de Heeren Burgemee- | sters ende Raden tot Amsterdam. | Op 't stuck vande | West-Indische Com- | pagnie. | Genomen in August. 1649. | 4to, pp. 16. 16732

Copye | vande | Resolutie van de Heeren Burgemeesters ende Raden tot Amsterdam. | Op 't stuck vande | West-Indische | Compagnie. | Genomen in August. 1649. | 4to, pp. 16. W. 16733

Reprinted with the following title:

Copye | vande | Resolutie van de Heeren Burghemee- | sters ende Raden tot Amsterdam | Op 't stuck vande | West-Indische Com- | pagnie. | Genomen in August. 1649. | *Tot Uytrecht,* | *Gedruct by Ian Havick, by de Ganse-Merct,* 1649. | 4to, pp. 20. W.

Copye | Vande | Volmacht van Don Iuan, by der Gratie Godes Coninck van Por- | tugael ende van Algarben etc. Ghesonden ende ghegeven aen | Francisco de Sousa Coutinho sijnen Raet ende Gouverneur ende Capiteijn Generael vande Vlaemsche Eylanden, ende sijnen | Ordinaris Ambassadeur by de Staten Generael vande Veree- | nighde Nederlanden, om met de selve ende de Bewinthebberen | vande Oost- ende West-Indische Compagnie te handelen, ende | vast te stellen een accoort van een Generaele, oft particuliere | Vrede ofte Treves voor een tijt van Iaeren. [1647.] Sm. folio, sheet. 16735

Copye | Van een Missive, waer | inne voorghestelt werdt de | ghelegentheyt van de Oost Indische Com | pagnie, en hoe volghens het Octroy de Par | ticipanten jarelijcks te vorderen hebben ha- | re uytgifte. [1622.] 4to, pp. 16. 16736

Copye | Van eenen Brieff van eenen vrient aen den | anderen geschreven nopende het Redres van de | Oost-Indische | Compaignie. [1622.] 4to, pp. 8. 16737

Copyen. | . [n. p. n. d.] 4to, pp. 16. 16738

An address by the states general concerning the East and West India Company.

Copye | Ofte | Cort ende waerachtigh | verhael van 't gene ghepasseert is soo te | Water als te Lande, sint de komste | ende vertreck van de Spaensche Vloot in | Brasil overgesonden door sijn Genade | Heer Graef Mauritz van Nassau | waer van het principael ghesonden is | aen sijn Hoocheyt den Prince van | Oraengien. | *T' Amsterdam,* | *Door Francoys Lieshout, Boek-verkooper op den Dam in 't* | *Groot Boek. Anno* 1640. | 4to, pp. 16.

The Copyright Law of the United States. ... *New-York: Baker, Godwin & Co.* 1850. 8vo, pp. 12. 16740

Also: An Address to the People of the United States in behalf of the American Copyright Club. *New York.* 1843. 8vo, pp. 20.

Au Coq qui Chante, sur les hommes de couleur libres ... *De l'imprimerie de L. M. Collot.* 1791. Folio, 1 l. P. 16741

A defence of the St. Domingo negroes by Noclauf and Ingitalg.

Coquerel. Réplique des Députés des Manufactures et du Commerce de France à MM. les Députés de S. Domingue, concernant l'approvisionnement de cette Colonie. *Versailles: Ph. D. Pierres.* 1789. 8vo, pp. 20. J.C.B. 16742

The Coquette. *See* [Foster (H. M.)]

Coquimbo. Mémoire sur la terrain tertiaire et les lignes d'Ancien Niveau de l'Ocean du Sud, aux environs de Coquimbo (Chili). pp. 10. Plates. 16743

Coraly et Zamore, ou les Illustres Americains. *Manoa. Et se trouve à Paris chez la Veuve Prault.* 1789. 2 vols., 12mo, pp. 172; 173-335. J.C.B. 16744

A scarce novel, portraying American life in old times.

Coram (R.) Political Inquiries: to which is added, a Plan for the General Establishment of Schools throughout the United States. By Robert Coram, Author of some late Pieces in the Delaware Gazette, under the Signature of Brutus. *Wilmington: printed by Andrews and Brynberg.* M DCC XCI. 8vo, pp. 107, (1).

Corbet (J.) Self-Imployment in Secret. By Rev. John Corbet, late of Colchester. Third Edition. *Boston: R. Pierce.* 1684. 16mo, pp. 44. M. 16746

Corbett (G. O.) Notes on Rupert's America, its History and Resources, enclosed with a Letter to ... [the] Secretary of State for the Colonies, by the Rev. G. O. Corbett, M.D. ... [n. p.] 1868. 8vo, pp. (2), vi, 88, Errata, 1 slip. 16747

Corbett (H. W.) The Currency. Remarks of Hon. Henry W. Corbett, of Oregon, in the Senate of the United States, December 13, 1867. ... *Printed at the Congressional Globe Office.* 8vo, pp. 8. 16748

Corbett. The Funding Bill. Speech of Hon. Henry W. Corbett, of Oregon, delivered in the Senate of the United States, March 11, 1868. *Washington: F. & J. Rives & Geo. A. Bailey, printers.* 1868. 8vo, pp. 8. H. 16749

Corbett (William). Address, Nov. 13, 1814. *Boston.* 1815.

Corbière (Édouard). Elégies brésiliennes, suivies de poésies diverses, et d'une notice sur la traite des noirs. *Paris: Plancher; Brissot-Thivars.* 1823. 8vo. 16751

The first edition was printed at *Rouen.* 1823. 18mo. The same thing was published under the title: Brésiliennes. Séconde édition, augmenté de Poésies nouvelles. *Paris: Ponthieu; Aimé André; Charles Bechet.* 1825. 18mo.

Corbin (W.) A Sermon preached at King's Town in Jamaica, Upon the 7th of June, Being the Anniversary Fast for that Dreadful Earth-Quake which happened there in the year 1692. By William Corbin, T.B. *Printed and Sold by William Bradford, at the Bible in New York.* 1703. 4to, 2 l., pp. 16.

Corbulacho (J. C. A.) Vozes, | Del | Desengaño | Para | La Penitencia, | Por | Juan Carlos De Apello | Corbulacho, | Natural esta Imperial, | Au | gusta, y siempre Leal Ciudad de Mexico. | *Mexico, por Juan Joseph Guillena, Carrascoso,* 1699. | 4to, 2 l., 17 l. + *Mexico.* 1716. 4to. 16753

Also: Accentos morales sobre todos los euangelios de la quaresma, y semana santa *Mexico.* 1710. 4to, 26 l.

Corcoran (D.) Pickings from the Portfolio of the Reporter of the New Orleans "Picayune." *Philadelphia.* 1847. 12mo.

Corcoran (M.) The Captivity of General Corcoran. The only authentic and reliable Narrative of the Trials and Sufferings endured, during his twelve months' Imprisonment in Richmond and Southern Cities, by Brig.-General Michael Corcoran, the Hero of Bull Run. *Philadelphia: Barclay & Co.* [1862.] 8vo, pp. 18-100. S. 16755

Also: State of New York. In the Court Martial to try Col. Michael Corcoran, of the 69th Regiment, 1st Division of New York State Militia, on a Charge of Disobedience of Orders. Charge and Specification. Objection to Specification. Plea in Bar. Defendant's Argument. *New York: Wm. C. Bryant.* 1860. 8vo, pp. 19. H

Corda (August Carl Joseph). Iconum Fungorum hucusque cognitorum Tomus VI. (Ultimus) quem Auctore ipso ex Itinere Texano per Mare Mexicanum Reduce, infelici Sorte abrepto ... edidit Joann. Bapt. Zobel. *Prag: Ehrlich.* 1854. Folio, pp. xix, 91. 16756

The first five volumes were published [*Ibid.*] 1837-42. The title given above implies that Vol. VI. contains American plants, but I have not seen the work.

Cordeiro (C. A.) Codigo Criminal do Imperio do Brasil. Por Dr. Carlos Antonio Cordeiro. *Rio de Janeiro: E. & H. Laemmert.* 1861. 12mo, pp. vi, 245. C. 16757

Cordero (*General* Leon de Febres). Manifiesto en que se vindica á la division restauradora que á las órdenes del Ciudadano Esclarecido abrió la campaña en 1849. [*New York.* 1850.] 4to, pp. 45. 16758

Cordeyro (A.) Historia Insulana das Ilhas a Portugal sugeytas no Oceano Occidental composta pelo padre Antonio Cordeyro ... . *Lisboa: Antonio Pedroso Gairão.* 1717. Folio, Title, pp. (14), 528. H. 16759

Cordley (Cristopher Minta). A Sermon by C. M. Cordley ... . Also, a Biographical Sketch, by Rev. Dr. Blanchard ... . *Lawrence.* 1867. 8vo, pp. 23. H. 16760

Cordner (J.) The American Conflict: An Address spoken before the New England Society of Montreal ... By Rev. John Cordner ... . *Montreal: printed by John Lovell.* 1865. 8vo, pp. 48. H. 16761

Cordner. Canada and the United States. *Montreal.* 1865. 8vo. 16762

Cordner. The Foundations of Nationality. A Discourse ... in the Unitarian Church, Montreal ... after the Great Railway Celebration, November, 1856. By John Cordner. ... *Montreal: Henry Rose.* 1856. 8vo, pp. 28. H. 16763

Cordner. The Vision of the Pilgrim Fathers. An Oration delivered before the New-England Society of Montreal, on 22d December, 1856; with the proceedings at the Dinner. *Montreal: H. Rose.* 1857. 8vo, pp. 54. C. 16764

Also: The Christian Idea of Sacrifice; A Discourse preached at the Dedication of the Church of the Messiah. *Montreal.* 1858. 8vo, pp. 29.

[Córdoba (A. de).] Relacion del ultimo Viage al Estrecho de Magallanes de las Fragata de S. M. Santa Maria de la Cabeza en los años de 1785 y 1786. Extracto de todos los anteriores desde su descubrimiento impresos y MSS. y noticia de los habitantes, suelo, clima y producciones del estrecho. *Madrid.* MDCCLXXXVIII. 4to, 3 l., pp. xvi, 359. 4 Maps, Portrait of Magellan. 16765

In a Paris catalogue (Tross), reference is made to a second voyage in 1783.

Córdoba (J. de). Arte en Lengva Zapoteca, compuesto por el muy reuerendo padre Fray Iuan de Cordoua, de la orden de los Predicadores desta nueua España. *En Mexico. En casa de Pedro Balli. Año de.* 1578. 8vo. 16766

Cordoba (T. R.) El sitio de Puebla, ó apuntes para la historia de Mexico. *Puebla.* 1863. 4to. Map and Plates.

Cordoba. Causa Criminal en Barancayaco, Territorio de Cordoba. *Buenos Ayres.* 1837. 4to. 16768

Cordoba (T. de). Memoria sobre la administracion de Puerto-Rico. Por Pedro Tomas de Cordoba. *Madrid.* 1838. Sm. 4to. 16769

Cordoba Salinas (Diego). Cronica de la religiosisima provincia de los doce Apostles de Perú, de la Orden de N. S. P. Francisco de la regular observancia. *Lima.* 1651. Folio.

Cordova (A. de). Reise nach der Magellansstrasse, nebst einem Berichte über die Sitten und Gebräuche der Einwohner von Patagonien. *Weimar.* 1820. 8vo. C. 16771

An English translation of a part of the work is included in Phillips' "Voyages."

Cordova. A Voyage of Discovery to the Strait of Magellan; with an account of the Manners and Customs of the Inhabitants; and of the Natural Productions of Patagonia. By Admiral Don A. de Cordova. Translated from the Spanish. *Phillips.* 8vo, pp. 104. Portrait and Map. 16772

Phillips' "Collection," Vol II., No. 5.

Cordova (F.) Vida y muerte del siervo de Dios D. Francisco de Cordova y Bocanegra naturel de Mexico. *Mexico.* 1617. 4to. 16773

Cordova (F. M. de). Utilidades de que todos los Indios y Ladinos se vistan y calcen a la Española y medios de conseguirlo sin violencia coaccion ni mandato. Su autor Fray Matias de Cordova, &c. *Nueva Guatemala.* 1798. 4to, pp. 22. 16774

Cordova (J. de). Texas; her Resources and Public Men. A Companion for J. De Cordova's New and Correct Map of the State of Texas. First Edition. *Philadelphia: J. B. Lippincott & Co.* 1858. 12mo, pp. 371. C. 16775

Also: A Lecture on Texas. *Philadelphia.* 1858. 8vo.

Cordova Lasso de la Vega (A. de). Por | D. Antonio de Cordova | Laso de la Vega, Capitan de las Guardas | de el Governador, y Teniente Gene- | ral de la Cavalleria del Reyno | de Chile. | Con | el Señor Fiscal del | Consejo de Indias, y el Promotor Fiscal | de Cobranças de èl. | Sobre, | qve se mande advocar, y rete- | ner en la Real Junta de Guerra de Indias, el conocimien- | to de la causa, tocante à la demasia, y excesso de Sueldos, | que se dize cobrò en aquellos puèstos. | [1690.] Folio, 4 l. 16776

Cordova (P. de). Dotrina xpiana pa | instrucion & informaciõ delos indi- | os: por manera de hystoria. Com- | puesta por el muy reuerendo padre | fray Pedro de Cordoua: de buena | memoria: primero fundador d'la or | den delos Predicadores ẽlas yslas | del mar Oceano: y por otros religio | sos doctos d'la misma ordẽ. La *qual* | doctrina fue vista y examinada y a *pro* | uada por el muy. R. S. el licẽcia | do Tello de Sãdoual Inquisitador en esta nueua España | por su Magestad. La qual fue em- | pressa en Mexico por mandado del | muy. R. S. dõ fray Iuã çumarra- | ga *primer* obispo desta ciudad: del cõ | sejo de su Magestad. &c. y a su costa. | Año de. M. d. xliiij. | Cõ preuilegio de su. S. L. L. M. [Colophon:] *Impressa en la grande y mas leal ciudad de Me-* | *xico: en casa de Iuan Cromberger: que sancta gloria aya a costa del dicho señor obispo.* | ... *Acabose de imprimir. Año de* M. d. xliiij. | 4to, Title, 29 unnumbered leaves. J.C.B. 16777

In a catalogue of the sale of the so-called "Mondidier" collection in London, the following note is appended: "This almost unknown tract, published under the authority and at the expense of the Archbishop of Mexico, contains the date of 1544, both at the beginning and end, and has hitherto been considered the first book printed in the New World. A manuscript note of the late owner says, 'It is unknown to, or at least, unmentioned by all bibliographers I have consulted. Even Ternaux does not seem to be aware of its existence. This is the only copy I ever saw or heard of in Mexico or elsewhere.'" It is scarcely necessary to say that the claim as to priority of printing is a mistake. Señor Icasbalceta, of Mexico, describes three books of an earlier date, and three others dated the same year. Jöcher remarks: "Petrus de Corduba, ein spanischer Dominicaner von Corduba, welches auch sein Geschlechts-Nahme war, gebohren um 1460, studirte zu Salamanca die Rechte, trat aber hernach daselbst in obgedachten Orden, gieng 1510 als Missionarius nach Domingo, wurde Provincial seines Ordens, schrieb *el vocabulario en lengua zapoteca,* und starb den 29 Jun. 1525."

Cordova (R. J. de). The Prince's Visit: A Humorous Description of the Tour of his Royal Highness, the Prince of Wales, through the United States of America, in 1860. By R. J. de Cordova. Illustrated by Stephens, Rosenberg, and J. D. Smillie. *New York: B. Frodsham.* 1861. 8vo. 16778

Also: A Lecture on War, Foreign and Civil, and the Blessings of Union and Peace. Delivered in New York, December 8, 1860. *New York: M. Ellinger.* 8vo, pp. 7.

Cordova y Urrutia. Estadistica, historica, geografica, etc. de los Pueblos que componen las Provincias del Departamento de Lima. *Lima.* 1839. 8vo. 16779

Cordova y Urrutia. Las 3 Epocas del Peru, ó Compendio de su Historia. [*Lima:*] *Imprenta del autor.* 1844. Sm. 4to. 16780

Coreal (F.) Voyages de François Coreal, aux Indes Occidentales, Contenant ce qu'il y a vû de plus remarquable pendant, son séjour depuis 1666, jusqu'en 1697. Traduit de l'Espagnol. Avec vne Relation de la Guiane de Walter Raleigh, & le Voyage de Narborough à la Mer du Sud par le Détroit de Magellan, &c. Traduit de l'Anglois. *Amsterdam: F. Bernard.* MDCCXXII. 3 vols., pp. 332, Table, 1 l., 12 Plates; pp. 302, Table, 1 l., 6 Plates; pp. 278, Table, 1 l., 2 Maps. BA., C. + Nouvelle edition, Revûë, corrigée, & augmentée d'une nouvelle Découverte des Indes Meridionales & des Terres Australes, enrichie de figures. *A Paris: Chez Andres Cailleau.* M DCC XXII. 2 vols., 8vo, Title, pp. 438, 4, 2, Map and Plates; Title, pp. 406, 2. 3 Maps. 16781

Republished with the title:

Coreal. Recueil de Voyages dans l'Amerique Méridionale. *Amsterdam.* 1738. 3 vols., 12mo. Plates. 16782

For the contents and collation, *see* [Bernard], Vol. II., No. 4937a, and correct the date to 1738. The fact that no Spanish edition of these voyages is known, has led to the belief that no such person as Coreal ever lived. In speaking of the work, Mr. Rich says: "There appears to be no reason to doubt of the identity of Francis Coreal, or of the fact of his having visited the different countries he describes.. His relation occupies only one half the work, the other half being made up of a selection from other authors, to which probably the judgment of Marchand, as quoted by Meusel, applies, viz., that the work consisted of fragments taken from several effective voyages by some starving compiler. A certain Rev. Doctor [Dibdin] 'stuck his spurs so hard into the side of his good bibliographical courser,' that he leapt over a good part of the title of this book, as given in Meusel, and makes out Coreal's 'Voyages en les Indes occidentales,' &c., to be a translation of the Flemish journal of Capt. Abel Jansen Tasman!" This Flemish journal is merely one of the before-mentioned relations. *See* Rich, I. 30-31.

Corey (A.) Gazetteer of the County of Washington, N. Y. By Allen Corey. *Schuylerville, N. Y.* 1849-50. 8vo. 16783

Corey (D. H.) Report of the Trial of Daniel H. Corey ... for the Murder of Mrs. M. Noch ... By J. Parker. *Newport, N. H.* 1830. 8vo. BM. 16784

Coriolanus, *pseudonym.* Remarks on the late Infraction of the Treaty at New-Orleans. By Coriolanus. *New York: Printed by Vermilye & Crocker.* 1803. 8vo. 16785

Corley (S.) Right of Suffrage. Speech of Hon. Simeon Corley, of South Carolina, in the House of Representatives, January 28, 1869. *Printed at the Congressional Globe Office.* 8vo, pp. 4. 16786

Corlies (J.) State of New-York, in Chancery. The Joint and several Answer of John Corlies, Barney Corse, Samuel Willets, Robert Hicks, Samuel Hicks, and others, Defendants and Robert J. Walker and Whitehead Hicks, John R. Willis, and others, Complainants. [About 1834.] 8vo, pp. 54.

Relates to the Hicksite controversy.

Corlies (P.) Memorial of Patience Corlies, late of Shrewsbury, N. J. *Philadelphia.* 1841. 12mo. S. 16788

Cormach (W. E.) A Journey Across the Island of Newfoundland, the only one ever performed by a European. *St. John.* 1856. 16789

Cormier. Mémoire sur la situation de Saint-Domingue à l'époque du mois de janvier 1792. [Signed Cormier.] *Paris: imp. de Migneret.* 1792. 8vo. 16790

Cornalia (E.) Illustrazione della mummia Peruviana, esist. nel civico museo di Milano. *Milano.* 1860. Folio. 16791

Corncob (Jonathan), *pseudonym.* *See* Vol. I., No. 479.

Cornejo (J. A. F.) Diario de la primera expedicion al Chaco, emprendida en 1780, por el Coronel D. Juan Adrian Fernandez Cornejo. *Bueuos Aires.* 1837. Folio, pp. 46. 16792

Cornelison (J.) Sermon at Hackensack at the Instalment of J. V. C. Romeyn. By John Cornelison. *New York.* 1800. 8vo. 16793

Cornelius (Elias). The Little Osage Captive, an Authentic Narrative: To which are added some interesting Letters Written by Indians. *York: W. Alexander & Son.* 1824. 18mo, pp. 182. Frontispiece. 16794

Observations of one of the missionaries to the Choctaws, in Arkansaw, in 1817.

Cornelius. Tour in Virginia, Tennessee, etc. By Rev. E. Cornelius. *London.* 1820. 8vo. 16795

Also: God's Ways, not as our Ways. A Sermon, occasioned by the Death of the Rev. Samuel Worcester, D.D. ... *Salem: Henry Whipple.* 1821. 8vo, pp. 56. B., BA. — A Review of the Rev. Mr. Colman's Sermon, delivered at the Opening of the Independent Congregational Church, in Barton Square, Salem. [By Elias Cornelius.] Second Edition. Containing a Reply to Mr. Colman's Notes. *Boston: T. R. Marvin.* 1825. 8vo, pp. 64. H. — A Sermon delivered in Salem, Sept. 25, 1823, at the Ordination of Edmund Frost, as a Missionary to the Heathen, and Aaron W. Warner, Ansel D. Eddy, Nathan W. Fiske, Isaac Oakes, and George Sheldon, Evangelists. *Boston.* 1823. 8vo, pp. 32. M.

Cornell (E.) Speech by Hon. Ezra Cornell, on the Question of a Ship Canal connecting Cayuga Lake with Lake Ontario. *Albany: Weed & Parsons.* 1864. 8vo. pp. 34. 16796

Cornell (W.) "Our Thanksgivings." A Sermon preached at Freehold, N. J., August 6, 1863. By Rev. William Cornell. *Freehold: James S. Yard.* 1863. 8vo, pp. 15. 16797

The Cornell University. First General Announcement. Second Edition, with additions. *Albany: Weed, Parsons and Company, printers.* 1868. 8vo, pp. 27. 16798

Also: Catalogue ... 1868–9 ... *Ithaca, N. Y.* 1869. 8vo, pp. 86. H. — The Cornell University. Account of the ... Inauguration, October 7th, 1868. ... *Ithaca University Press.* MDCCCLXIX. 8vo, pp. 37. *See* Ithaca.

Cornette (P.) Relation d'un voyage de Mexico à Guatémala, ... 1855. Par le P. Cornette, de la compagnie de Jésus. *Le Mans, Paris: Julien, Lanier, Cosnier et Cie.* 1858. 8vo, pp. 24. 16799

Cornford (P. H.) Missionary Reminiscences; or, Jamaica Retraced. By the Rev. P. H. Cornford. *Leeds.* 1856. 12mo, pp. 116. 16800

The Cornhill Monthly and Literary Recorder. July 15 to Nov. 15, 1868. *Boston: D. Lothrop & N. P. Kemp.* 1868. 8vo, pp. 172. c. 16801

Nos. 1–5 of Vol. I. No more published.

Cornillere. De la Martinique, en 1842. Interêts Coloniaux, Souvenirs de Voyages. Par M. le Comte de la Cornillere. *Paris: Gide.* 1843. 8vo, 17 sheets. 16802

[Cornillon (Ch. de).] Odes, suivies d'une lettre sur l'esclavage des nègres dans nos colonies, et d'une autre sur les Anglais. *Paris: Samson.* 1806. 8vo. 16803

Corning (J. L.) Religion and Politics. A Discourse delivered on Thanksgiving Day, November 29, 1860. By James Leonard Corning. *Milwaukie: Strickland & Co.* 1860. 8vo, pp. 23. 16804

Also: A Discourse. Thanksgiving day ... Nov. 18, 1858. 8vo.

Corning (W. H.) Our Epoch: its Significance and History. A Discourse preached at Whitehall, New York, November 29, 1860. By Rev. W. H. Corning. *Whitehall: Chronicle Office.* 1860. 8vo, pp. 17. 16805

Cornish (F. S.), *and* Wright (T. S.) The Colonization Scheme considered in its rejection by the Colored People, in unfitness for Christianizing and Civilizing the Aborigines of Africa, and for putting a stop to the Slave Trade in a Letter to T. Frelinghuysen ... and B. F. Butler ... *Newark: Aaron Guest.* 1840. 8vo, pp. 26. 16806

The Cornplanter Memorial; an Historical Sketch of Gy-ant-wa-chia, and of the Six Nations of Indians. *Harrisburgh, Pa.* 1867. 8vo, pp. 15. Plate. 16807

Cornu (J. François), *and* Grasset-St. Sauveur (J.) Encyclopédie des voyages, contenant l'abregé historique des moeurs usages, habitudes domestiques, religions, etc. Et la collection complette des costumes civils, militaires, religieux, etc., etc. *Bordeaux:* [n. d.] 4to. Plates. 16808

Cornut (Jacques Philippe). Iac. Cornvti | doctoris medici | Parisiensis. | Canadensivm plantarvm, | aliarùmque nondum editarum | historia. | Cui adiectum est ad calcem | enchiridion | botanicvm Parisiense, | Continens Indicem Plantarum, quæ in Pagis, Siluis, Pratis, & | Montosis iuxta Parisios locis nascuntur. | *Parisiis,* | *Venundantur apud Simonem le Moyne.* | M. DC. XXXV. | 4to, 8 l., pp. 238, (2). 68 Plates in the text. A., C., J.C.B.

"Cornut was never in America. Vallot's engravings are well executed. A large number of the plants are described here for the first time." — Trömel.

Cornwall (N. E.) ... An Historical Discourse for the Jubilee of the Society for the Propagation of the Gospel; delivered in ... Fairfield, ... Conn., ... August 16th, 1851. By N. E. Cornwall, A.M., Rector. ... *New Haven: George B. Bassett.* 1851. 8vo, pp. 47. 16810

Cornwallis (C.) An Answer to that Part of the Narrative of Lieutenant-General Sir Henry Clinton, K.B. Which relates to the Conduct of Lieutenant-General Earl Cornwallis, during the Campaign in North-America in the Year 1781. By Earl Cornwallis. *London: J. Debrett.* M.DCC.LXXXIII. 8vo, Title, pp. xvi, (6), 260, Errata, 8 lines. Folded sheet at p. 236. BA. + *Philadelphia: John Campbell.* MDCCCLXVI. 6 l., pp. 260.

Of the Philadelphia edition, twenty copies were printed in folio, seventy-five in 4to, and two hundred and fifty in 8vo. "This answer consists of the chain of correspondence between the two commanders during the campaign referred to, for the purpose of proving that 'the conduct and opinions of the author were not the cause of the catastrophe which terminated the campaign of 1781.'" *See* "M. Rev.," LXVIII. 266.

Cornwallis. Correspondence of Charles, First Marquis Cornwallis. Edited, with Notes by Charles Ross. ... *London: John Murray.* 1859. 3 vols., 8vo. BA. + Second Edition. *London: Murray.* 1859. 3 vols., 8vo, pp. 1860.

Includes much curious and important matter, by various eminent contemporaries, relating to the American War, etc. *See* especially Vol. I. 17–210, 485–518.

Cornwallis. Examination of Lieutenant General The Earl Cornwallis before a Committee of the House of Commons, upon Sir William Howe's Papers. *London: J. Robson.* MDCCLXXIX. 8vo, pp. 60. J.C.B. 16813

Cornwallis. A Reply to Sir Henry Clinton's Narrative. Wherein his Numerous Errors are pointed out, and the Conduct of Lord Cornwallis fully vindicated from all Aspersion: including the whole of the Public and Secret Correspondence between Lord George Germain, Sir Henry Clinton, and his Lordship; as also intercepted Letters from General Washington. ... *London.* MDCCLXXXIII. 8vo, pp. 109. H. + Second Edition. *London.* [*Ibid.*] 16814

Cornwallis. As great a Man as Nelson! Complete in one Number, for 6d. The Life of the most Noble, The Marquis Cornwallis, That Great Friend to his Country! Who has been engaged in the Service of it ever since the year 1776, up to 1805, In the American and Indian War. Who has proved himself a bold and valliant warrior — a Peace Maker — a good Statesman — a Man for the People; a Friend. To which is added the Riddle, Shot from the Camp, with an Explanation. *London.* [n. d.] 12mo, pp. 36. Portrait. 16815

Cornwallis. A Sermon On the Capture of Lord Corn-

wallis. By an African American. Printed in the Month of April 1782. *Philadelphia.* 1782. 16mo, pp. 16. H. 16816

The Philadelphia Library has a broadside, "Philadelphia, October 8, 1777. Notice is hereby given ... . *Printed by Humphreys,*" which relates to the king's seamen, and is signed "J. Watt." By Order of Lieut. General Earl Cornwallis.

Cornwallis (Frederick), *Bishop of Lichfield and Coventry, afterwards Archbp. of Canterbury.* Sermon before the Society for Propagation of the Gospel in Foreign Parts, Feb. 20, 1756. *London.* 1756. 4to, pp. 71. 16817

Cornwallis (James), *Bishop of Lichfield and Coventry, in* 1823 *Earl of Cornwallis.* Sermon before the Society for Propagation of the Gospel in Foreign Parts, Feb. 15, 1788. *London.* 1788. 4to, pp. 81. 16818

Cornwallis (K.) The New El Dorado; or, British Columbia. By Kinahan Cornwallis. With a Map and Illustrations by the Author. *London: Thomas Cantley Newby.* 1858. Post 8vo, pp. xxviii, 405. + Second Edition. [*Ibid.*] 1858. Post 8vo, pp. xxviii, 405. C., G. 16819

Cornwallis. A Panorama of the New World: Travels. By Kinahan Cornwallis. *London: T. C. Newby.* 1859. 2 vols., post 8vo, pp. viii, 430; 390. 16820

Cornwallis. Royalty in the New World; or, The Prince of Wales in America. ... By Kinahan Cornwallis. ... *New York: M. Doolady.* 1860. 12mo. Portrait. B., H. 16821

Cornwell (Francis). A Conference. *See* Cotton (John).

Cornwell (G.) Boston, 25 January, 1769. A Dialogue between Sir George Cornwell, A Gentleman lately arrived from England, with a Design to travel Incog. thro' the Continent of America, and Mr. Flint, An Independent Gentleman, descended from a good Family of the first Settlers of New-England, that is neither Placed nor Pensioned. ... *Printed in London, And Reprinted in Boston.* 1769. 8vo, pp. 14. BA., P. 16822

Cornyn (John K.) Dick Wilson, The Rumseller's Victim; or, Humanity pleading for the "Maine Law." A Temperance Story ... With an Introduction, by T. W. Brown. *Auburn and Buffalo.* 1853. 12mo. + *New York and Auburn: Miller, Orton & Mulligan.* 1855. 12mo, pp. 420. Plate. BM., H.

"Very abusive of some of the leading men of Boston, particularly of those who have held office." — J. R. Bartlett.

Corografia Brazilica. *See* [Cazal (M. A. de)], Vol. III., No. 11640.

Coromina (J.) Carta de la temprana muerte del P. P. Borrote, missionero en el colegio de Guanajuato. *Mexico.* 1763. 12mo, 23 leaves. 16824

Coronado (C. V.) Por | Don Car- | los Vazquez Coronado, ve- | zino de Guatimala. | Con | El Señor Fiscal. | Sobre los treynta y vn mil tostones, | en que se le remato el Officio de Al- | guazil mayor de la Audiēcia de Gua- | timala, para don Antonio Vazquez | Coronado su hijo. | [1632.] Folio, 5 l. 16825

Coronado (Pedro José). Discurso que pronunció el 1º de Setiembre de 1865, en el templo de San Francisco en el acto de la apertura de las Clases de la Universidad Central. *Carácas.* 1865. 8vo, pp. 31. 16826

Corpancho (Manuel Nicolas). Ensayos poéticos, [magallanes, etc.] precedidos de varios juicios escritos en Europa y América. *Paris: Maulde & Renou.* 1854. 8vo, 1 l., pp. 278. Portrait. c. 16827

Corral (Felipe Ruiz). Arte i Vocabulario de la Lengua de Guatemala. 16828

"Printed according to Nic. Antonio and Barcia-Pinelo, and called in the 'Mithridates,' III, 2, p. 10, 'Vocabularium Pocomamum.' L. Léon de Rosny communicates the same title, but designates the language as Kacchiquel." — Ludewig.

Correa (Antonio). Oração funebres do Arcobispo da Bahia D. Fr. Antonio de S. José, recitada no Convento da Graça de Lisboa. *Lisboa: na Regia Off. Typ.* 1779. 4to. 16829

Correa (D.) El Ciudadano Don Diego Correa al Escmo. Sr. Capitan General Gefe Superior Politico &c. &c. &c. Cuarta edicion. — Gratis. *Habana: Impreso por Don Tiburcio Campe en la oficina Liberal.* 1822. 8vo, pp. 13. c. 16830

Correa (E.) Vita venerabilis patris Emmanuelis Correæ e Societate Jesu in Brasilia missionarii. Una cum adjectis animadversionibus historicis. *In Fane S. Martini.* 1789. 8vo.

Correa. Perdida y restauracion de Bahia. 16832

A play. *See* Ternaux, p. 82.

[Corrêa (João de Medeiros).] Breve relação dos ultimos successos da guerra do Brasil, restituição da cidade Mauricia,

fortalezas do Recife de Pernambuco, e mais praças que os hollandezes occuparam n'aquelle, estado. *Lisboa: na Offic. Craesbeeckiana.* 1654. 4to, pp. 30. 16833

[Corrêa.] Panegyrico a André de Albuquerque Ribafria, mestre de campo general na provincia do Alemtejo, com os elogios que á sua morte se fizeram. *Lisboa: por Domingos Carneiro.* 1661. 4to, pp. iv–60. 16834

[Corrêa.] Relação verdadeira de todo o succedido na restauração da Bahia de todos os Sanctos, desde o dia em que partiram as armadas de Sua Magestade, té o em que em a dita cidade foram arvorados seus estandartes etc. *Lisboa: por Pedro Craesbeeck.* 1625. 4to, pp. 16. 16835

Correa (J. N.) El Rey. | Lo qve Por mi mandado se asiē | ta, y concierta con Iuan Nuñez | Correa Portugues, vezino de la ciu | dad de Lisboa, sobre la haberia que | en las ciudades de Seuilla, y Cadiz, y | otras partes, se cobra de todo el oro, y plata, pie- | dras, perlas, y otras cosas que vienen de las | Indias: y de todas las mercaderias que van a ellas, | y a las Islas del mar Oceano, y las q vienēdellas: y so- | bre el apresto y prouision de las armadas, que para | ello se han de poner en orden, y despachar por cuē | ta de la haberia. | [Dated] *Valladolid.* 1603. | Folio, 15 leaves. 16836

Corrêa (Tr. Simão). Sermão no procissão de graças que a muito nobre villa de Villo-real, fez pela restauração da cidade da Bahia: pregado en 15 de Agosto de 1625. *Lisboa: por Geraldo da Vinha.* 1625. 4to. 16837

Correa Junior (A. P.) Da Corte á Fazenda de Santa Fé. Impressões de Viagem. *Rio de Janeiro.* 1870. 8vo, pp. viii, 182. 16838

Correct Copies Of the Two Protests against the Bill To Repeal the American Stamp Act, of Last Session. With Lists of the Speakers and Voters. *Paris:* [i. e. *London*] *J. W.* M.DCC.LXVI. 8vo, pp. 24. BA. 16839

Correct Statement. *See* [Van Ness (W. P.)], and [Wood (John)].

The Corrector or Independent American. *New-York.* 1815. 8vo, pp. 45. + No. II. *New York.* 1816. 8vo, pp. 50. S.

See "Historical Magazine," IV. 120. *See also* Hobart (J.), and Jay (John).

Correia (F. J.) Pensamentos e maximas, por Frederico José Correia. *Maranhao.* 1864. 8vo, pp. 202. 16841

El Correo. Periodico imparcial. *Mexico.* 1851. Folio.

One hundred and thirty-seven numbers published

El Correo, atlántico. Periódico poligloto: comercial, politico y literario. *Mexico.* 1835. Folio. 16843

Sixteen numbers published.

El Correo de Buenos Aires. Historia, Literatura, Artes, Religion, Teatros, Modas, Variedades. *Buenos Aires.* 1864. 4to, each No. pp. 24. 16844

Correo del Domingo (So Publicada todos los domingos). *Buenos Aires.* 1864. Folio, each No. pp. 16. Continued.

A weekly publication of politics, literature, science, and arts, with illustrations.

Correo Mercantil de España y sus Indias, de los meses de Octubre, Noviembre, y Diciembre del año de 1792. ... *Madrid: viuda é hijo de Marin.* [n. d.] 4to, 3 l., pp. 220, (7), 3–17. Continued. 16846

Correspondance de la France avec les Etats-Unis. Extraits de cette correspondance adressés au Sénat, et une copie des actes de la législature de la Caroline du Sud. *Philadelphia.* 1794. 26 leaves. 16847

Correspondançe entre la Legation extraordinaire du Mexique à Washington, et le Ministère des affaires etrangères des Etats-Unis, sur le passage de la Sabine par les troupes commandées par le General Gaines; traduites de l'Espagnol et publiée par le citoyen Mexicain, J. C. C. *Paris: Truchy.* 1837. 8vo, pp. xxxi, 91. Map. 16848

A translation of No. 16854.

Correspondance échangée entre les Ministres du Chili et des États-Unis d'Amérique, à Santiago et á Washington, au sujet d'une capture faite par un détachement de l'Escadre Chilienne dans la Vallée de Sitana, territoire Peruvien. *Bruxelles.* 1861. 8vo. 16849

Correspondence and accompanying Papers between the Secretary of State and the Minister Plenipotentiary of the French, etc. 1794. 8vo. 16850

The Correspondence and Documents relating to the Proposals for Five Millions of Five per cent Stock of the United States. *Philadelphia.* 1822. 8vo, pp. 20. S. 16851

Correspondence between Great Britain and the United States, respecting the Question of Territorial Jurisdiction and Boundary, between the Province of New Brunswick and the State of Maine, and Arrest and Trial of John Baker, by the British Authorities, 1825 to 1829. *London.* 1828. 8vo. 16852

Correspondence between Her Majesty's Government and Messrs. Laird Brothers respecting the Birkenhead Ironclads. *London.* [1864.] 8vo, pp. 60. B. 16853

Correspondence between his Excellency Sir Henry Clinton and Lieutenant-General Earl Cornwallis. [*New York.* 1781.] 8vo, pp. 76, 2 l. + [*London.* 1783.] 16854

Correspondence between Mr. Secretary Canning and The Hon. D. Erskine, As printed and Laid before the House of Lords. *London: Printed for J. Ridgway.* 1810. 8vo, 2 l., pp. 7–74. G. 16855

Correspondence between our Administration and Great Britain and France, with an attempt to show what are the Real Causes of the Failure of the Negotiation. *Boston.* [n. d.] 8vo. pp. 52.

Correspondence between the British Ministry and R. Smith. *Boston.* 1809. 8vo. 16857

Reprinted in London as:

Correspondence between the United States of America and Great Britain. *London: Johnson.* 1809. 8vo, pp. 32. 16858

Correspondence between the Chairman of the Committee of Ways and Means and the Secretary of the Treasury, in regard to the Claims of the Employés of the House. *Washington.* 1857. 8vo, pp. 5. M. 16859

The Correspondence between the Commissioners of the State of South Carolina, to the Government at Washington and the President of the United States; together with the Statement of Messrs. Mills and Keitt. Printed by order of the Convention. *Charleston: Evans & Cogswell, Printers.* ... 1861. 8vo, pp. 26.

Correspondence between the Committee of the Trinitarian

Society and the Committee of the First Society in Castine, on the Subject of a Union of said Societies — With some Remarks by the Latter Committee and an Appendix. *Castine: B. F. Bond.* 1828. 8vo, pp. 24. H. 16861

Correspondence between the English and American Governments upon the Enlistment Question, as presented to the Congress of the United States, Feb. 28, 1856. *London.* 1856. 8vo, pp. 61. 16862

The Correspondence between the Envoys of the American States and Monsieur Talleyrand, on the subject of the Disputes between the two Countries. *London.* 1798. 8vo. M. 16863

Correspondence between the Governments of the United States and Great Britain, relative to the Enlistment of Soldiers by the agents of the latter government, within the Territory of the United States. And the Message ... in compliance with a resolution of the 28th inst. calling for information relative to any proposition submitted to the United States Government by that of Great Britain, to refer the difference between the two Governments as to the construction of the Treaty of July 4, 1850, to Arbitration. *Washington. Feb.* 27, 1856. 8vo, pp. 251. S.

Correspondence between the President and Gen. Jos. E. Johnston, together with that of the Secretary of War and the Adjutant and Inspector General, during the months of May, June and July, 1863. Published by order of Congress. *Richmond: R. M. Smith, Public Printer.* 1864. 8vo, pp. 64. 16865

Correspondence between the Secretary of State and the British Minister, in May, 1794. [*Philadelphia.* 1794.] 8vo, pp. 11. M. 16866

Correspondence between the Secretary of State and the Minister Plenipotentiary of the French Republic, 1793; with Proceedings of the Legislature of South Carolina. [*Philadelphia.* n. d.] 8vo. M. 16867

Correspondence between the Secretary of War and the President of the Baltimore and Ohio Railroad Company. In relation to Additional Routes Between Washington & New York, And Improvements of the Established Railway Line. *Baltimore: John W. Woods, Printer.* 1862. 8vo. 16868

Correspondence between the State Department and the Representative of Her Britannic Majesty's Government, in relation to the capture of British vessels sailing from one port to another, having on board articles Contraband of War, intended for the use of the so-called Confederate States. [*Washington.* 1863.] 8vo, pp. 29. (37th Cong., 3d Sess., Ex. Doc., No. 27, 1863.)

Correspondence between the United States of America and Great Britain. *London.* 1809. 8vo, pp. 32. S. 16870

Relates to the encounter of the "Leopard" and the "Chesapeake." Not printed for sale.

Correspondence between the United States and Great Britain in regard to Recruiting for the British Army within the United States. *Washington.* 1856. 8vo, pp. 66. 16871

Correspondence between Viscount Castlereagh, and Messrs. Foster and Baker. March to August, 1812. Folio, pp. 114.

Correspondence between the War Department and Gen. Lovell, relating to the Defences of New Orleans, Submitted in Response to a Resolution of the House of Representatives of 3d Feb. 1863. *Richmond: R. M. Smith, Public Printer.* 1863. 8vo, pp. 123. 16873

Correspondence concerning the Insults offered to the Flag of the United States. 4to, pp. 23. 16874

Correspondence in relation to the Capture of the British Brigs Detroit and Caledonia, on the night of October 8th, 1812. *Philadelphia.* 1843. 12mo. 16875

Correspondence of the American Revolution; being Letters of Eminent Men to George Washington, from the time of his taking Command of the Army to the end of his Presidency. Edited from the Original Manuscripts By Jared Sparks. *Boston: Little, Brown, and Company.* 1853. 4 vols., 8vo, pp. viii, 549; 4, 554; 4, 560; 4, 555. 16876

Two hundred and fifty copies printed on large paper.

Correspondence of the Department of State, in Relation to the British Consuls resident in the Confederate States. *Richmond.* 1863. 8vo, pp. 55. H. 16877

Correspondence of the French Ministers, Joseph Fauchet and P. A. Adet; with the United States Government, during the years 1794–96. ... [1797?] 8vo. 16878

Correspondence on the Plunder of the Wreck of the Barque "Prince of Wales" and ill-treatment of Officers of H. M. S. "Forte." *London.* 1863. Folio. 16879

A Parliamentary Paper. The wreck occurred off the coast of Brazil.

Correspondence on the Present Relations between Great Britain and the United States of America. *Boston: Little, Brown, and Company.* 1862. Rl. 8vo, pp. 153. S. 16880

Some copies have the imprint, "*Boston: John Wilson & Son, Printers.* 1862." The writers are Edwin W. Field and Charles G. Loring.

Correspondence on the relative Situation of France and the United States of America, 1788. 8vo. 16881

Correspondence on the subjects of Mediation, Arbitration, or other Measures looking to the Termination of the existing Civil War; communicated by the President of the United States, February 12, 1863. *Washington.* 1863. (37th Cong., 3d Sess., Ex. Doc., No. 38.) 16882

Correspondence [between Mr. Secretary Canning and the Hon. David Erskine], relating to America, presented to Parliament in 1810. *London: Printed by A. Strahan, Printers-Street.* 1811. 8vo, 4 l., pp. 5–95, 4. 16883

Correspondence relating to America, presented to Parliament in 1810. *London.* 1811. 8vo. 16884

Correspondence relating to the Boundary between the British Possessions in North America and the United States of America, under the Treaty of 1783. ... *London.* [1838.] 8vo. Map. + Part I. [II.] *London.* [1840.] 8vo. Map. 16885

These are reprints of the "Blue Books." *See* "North American Boundary" for the folio edition.

Correspondence relating to the Civil War in the United States of North America. *London: Harrison and Sons.* [1862.] Folio, pp. 141. + [Same Title. *Ibid.* 1863.] Folio, pp. 53. + Further Correspondence. [*Ibid.*] Folio, pp. 5. 16886

One of the Parliamentary "Blue Books." Also: Correspondence respecting International Maritime Law. Addressed to the contending parties in the United States. *London: Harrison and Sons.* Folio, pp. 37. — Correspondence respecting the Enlistment of British Seamen ... on board the U. S. Ship-of-War "Kearsarge." Folio, pp. 10. (Parl. Papers, N. Am., No. 7, London, 1864.) — Further Correspondence respecting the Enlistment of British Seamen at Queenstown, on board the United States Ship-of-War "Kearsarge." Folio, pp. 7. (Parl. Papers, North America, No. 12, 1864.)

Correspondence Respecting the Removal of British Consuls from the so-styled Confederate States of America. Folio, pp. 39. 16887

Also: Correspondence relating to the Steamers "Nashville" and "Tuscarora," at Southampton. Folio, pp. 30. — Correspondence with Mr. Adams respecting Confederate Agents in England. Folio, pp. 18. (Parl. Papers, N. Am., No. 8, Lond., 1863. — Correspondence respecting Iron-clad vessels building at Birkenhead. Folio, pp. 33. — Correspondence respecting the "Tuscaloosa." Folio, pp. 32. — Correspondence respecting Recruitment in Ireland for the Military Service of the United States. Folio, pp. 14. — Correspondence with Mr. Mason, Commissioner of the so-styled Confederate States of America. (In continuation of Papers presented to Parliament, March, 1863.) Folio, pp. 37. — Correspondence respecting the Enlistment of British Subjects in the United States Army. Folio, pp. 59. — Further Correspondence respecting the Enlistment of British Subjects in the United States Army. Folio, pp. 59. — Correspondence respecting despatch of Letters by private ships to Matamoras. Folio, pp. 2. — Correspondence with Mr. Adams respecting the Enlistment of British Subjects in the Federal Army. Folio, pp. 3. — Correspondence respecting trade with Matamoras. Folio, pp. 5. — Correspondence respecting the seizure of Schooner "Will o' the Wisp," by the United States Ship of War "Montgomery," at Matamoras, June 3, 1862. Folio, pp. 46. — Correspondence respecting the "Alabama." Folio, pp. 48. — Correspondence respecting instructions given to the Naval Officers of the United States, in regard to Neutral Vessels and Mails. Folio, pp. 7. — Correspondence with Mr. Adams respecting Neutral Rights and Duties. Folio, pp. 6 — Correspondence respecting the withdrawal by the Government of the United States, of Mr. Bunch's exequatur as Her Majesty's Consul at Charleston. Folio, pp. 27. — Correspondence respecting the "Alabama." (In continuation of Correspondence presented to Parliament in March, 1863.) Folio, pp. 57. — Correspondence respecting the capture of the "Saxon" by the United States Ship "Vanderbilt." pp. 43.

Correspondence relating to the purchase and fitting out of the Steamship "United States," and the building and fitting out of the Steamship of the Line "General Admiral." *New York: Hall & Clayton.* 1863. 8vo, pp. 8. 16888

Correspondence relative to Emigration, for the Provinces of Canada, New Brunswick, &c. *London.* 1843. Folio. 16889

Correspondence Relative to Neutral Rights between the Government of the United States and the Powers Represented in the Government at Paris, 1856. *Washington.* 1856. 8vo, pp. 18.

Correspondence relative to the American Question. *London.* 1812. 8vo. C. 16891

Correspondence relative to the Discovery of Gold in the Fraser's River District, in British N. America. 1858. Folio.

Correspondence Relative to the Dispute with America, considered in a Series of Letters from a Cosmopolite to a Clergyman. *London.* [1812.] 8vo. M. 16893

In the "Pamphleteer," Vol. II.

Correspondence relative to the Emigration to Hayti, of the Free People of Colour, in the United States. Together with the Instructions to the Agent sent out by President Boyer. *New-York: printed by Mahlon Day.* 1824. 8vo, pp. 32.

... Correspondence Relative to the French Decrees and the Orders in Council, Subsequent to 20th May, 1812. Folio, pp. 35. 16895

Correspondence relative to the Renewal of Treaties between France and the United States. 1793. 4to, pp. 22. 16896

Correspondence respecting British and American claims arising out of the late Civil War in the United States. *London.* 186–. Folio. 16897

Correspondence respecting the "Alabama;" ... and the Temporary Act of Congress passed ... in 1838, to meet the Case of the Rebellion in Canada. [n. p. n. d.] 8vo, pp. 56. H.

Correspondence respecting the Operations of the Commission for tracing the Boundary Line between her Majesty's Possessions in North America and the United States. *London.* 1845. Folio. Map. 16899

Correspondence respecting the Recent Fenian Aggression upon Canada. ... *London.* [1867.] Folio, 3 l., pp. 84. (Parl. Doc.) 16900

Correspondence with British Ministers and Agents in foreign Countries, relative to the Slave Trade. *London.* 1843. 4 vols., folio. + April 1, 1850, to March 31, 1851. *London.* 1851. Folio, pp. 886. 16901

Correspondence with the United States on the Order in Council, 1808. 8vo. 16902

Correspondence with the Governments of Great Britain, France, Spain, Brazil and Netherlands, relative to Insurgent Privateers in Foreign Ports, April 26, 1862. [*Washington.* 1862.] 8vo, pp. 211. (37th Cong., 2d Sess., Ex. Doc., No. 104.) 16903

Correspondencia diplomatica relativa a la cuestion Española. Publicada por orden de S. E. el jefe supremo provisorio para ser presentada al congreso constituyente. *Lima.* 1867. Impl. 8vo, pp. 492. 16904

Correspondencia entre la secretaria de relaciones esteriores de la Republica de Colombia y el Sr. Jose Villa, que vino con el caracter de ministro plenipotenciario de la Republica del Peru. *Bogota.* 1828. Sm. 4to, pp. 167, Table. 16905

Correspondencia habida entre los abogados de la Compañia de Nuevo Almaden y el Gobierno de los Estados Unidos de America sobre la mina de azogue que el Gobierno de Mexico concendió a D. Andres Castillero. *Mexico.* 1860. 8vo, pp. 110.

Correspondencia poetica i patriotica. 1862. 16mo, pp. 15.

Two poems, one "America to Columbia," in English; the other, "Colombia a la América del Norte," in Spanish.

Correspondencia que ha mediado entre el Legacion Extraordinaria de Mexico y el Departamento de Estado de los Estados-Unidos sobre el paso del Sabina por las tropas que mandabo el General Gaines. *Filadelfia.* 1836. 8vo, pp. xxi, 59. + *Mexico.* 1837. 8vo, pp. xxix, 122. + *Paris.* 1837. 8vo, pp. xxxi, 91.

For a French version, *see* our No. 16848.

Correspondencia relativa á las indemnizaciones francesas y á un plan propuesto para el arreglo de todas las acreencias diplomaticás. *Carácas.* 1868. 4to. pp. 72. 16909

Corro (J. del). Forma de el nvevo | beneficio de metales de plata, | por el Capitan de Iuan | del Corro. | [Dated] *Potosi y Junio* 24. | *de* 1676 *años.* | 4to, 4 leaves. 16910

Corriveau (J. B.) Célèbre procès de Jean Baptiste Corriveau, accusé et trouvé coupable du meurtre de Mme. Charlotte Todd, sa belle mère. *Québec.* 1856. 8vo, pp. 32. 16911

Corry (John). The Life of George Washington, late President and Commander in Chief of the Armies of the United States of America; interspersed with Biographical Anecdotes of the Most Eminent Men who effected the American Revolution, Dedicated (by permission) to the Right Honourable the Lord Mayor. By John Corry. *London: J. Kearsley.* 1800. 12mo, pp. 228, (3). B. + *London: J. W. Myers.* 1800. 12mo, pp. viii, 228. + *Dublin: Printed for J. Wogan.* 1801. 12mo, pp. 228, 2 l. Portrait. 16912

The London edition is scarce, but the Dublin edition is much more so. The title of the second London edition reads thus:

Corry. The Life of George Washington, late President

and Commander-in-Chief of the Armies of the United States of America; By John Corry, Author of "A Satirical View of London," &c. A New Edition. [*London:*] *Crosby & Co.* [1802.] 12mo, pp. 57, 2. Portrait of General Washington.

Corry. The | Life | of | George Washington, | late President and Commander-in-Chief | of the Armies of the United States of America. | A New Edition. | By John Corry. [*London:*] *B. Crosby & Co.* 1802. Sm. 8vo, pp. 57, 2. 16914

Reprinted in New York with the following title:

Corry. The Life of George Washington, commander in chief of the Armies, and late President of the United States of America. By John Corry, ... Including the Declaration of Independence, and the Constitution of the United States. First American Edition, from the Second London Edition, with Corrections, Additions and Improvements. ... *New York: J. Low.* 1807. 12mo, pp. 349, 7. C., S. + *New-York: McCarty & White.* 1809. 12mo, pp. 239, 6 l. Portrait by Scoles. + *Poughkeepsie: Printed by Paraclite Potter.* 1812. 18mo, pp. 143. + *Bridgeport: Lambert Lockwood.* 1815. 18mo, pp. 107. + *Boston: Isaiah Thomas, Jun.* 1815. 24mo, pp. 144. Portrait.

Frequently reprinted, with variations in the title, and sometimes alterations of the text. The following have come under our notice:

[Corry.] Biographical Memoirs | of the | Illustrious | General George Washington, | Late President of the United States of | America, | and | Commander in Chief of their Armies, during the | Revolutionary War. | Dedicated to the Youth of America. | Portrait. | *From Sidney's Press. For J. Cooke & Co.: New Haven,* | 1810. | 18mo, pp. 144. Woodcut Portrait. + [*Ibid.*] 1811. 18mo, pp. 144. 16916

[Corry.] Biographical Memoirs | of the | Illustrious | Gen. George Washington, | Late President of the United States of | America, | and | Commander in Chief of their Armies, | during the Revolutionary War. | Dedicated to the Youth of America. | *Barnard, Vt.* | *Published by Joseph Dix.* | 1813. | 24mo, pp. 160.

Corry. The Life of Joseph Priestley, LL.D. ... With Critical Observations on his Works. By John Corry. *Birmingham.* 1804. 8vo, pp. 111. + *Birmingham.* 1804. 12mo, pp. 60. N. 16918

See "M. Rev." XLVI. 88. Dr. Priestley settled in Pennsylvania, and some of his works relate to American topics.

Corry. Description of the District of Maine. Corry and others. 1793. pp. 50. 16919

This imperfect title is from the "N. E. Genealogical Register."

Corry (P.) Discourse ... at the Commemoration of the Landing of the Pilgrims of Maryland, celebrated May 15, 1843 ... . *Gettysburg: printed by H. C. Neinstedt.* MDCCCXLIII. 8vo, pp. 32. H. 16920

Corry (W. M.) Speech on Education, declared at the Inauguration of Rev. T. W. Hall, as President of Miami University. By W. M. Corry. June 28, 1855. *Cincinnati: Moore, Wilstach, Keys & Co.* 1855. 8vo, pp. 32. B. 16921

[Corry.] Vindication of the Rights and Titles, Political and Territorial, of Alexander, Earl of Stirling and Dover, and Lord Proprietor of Canada and Nova Scotia, also The Trial of Lord Stirling. *Washington.* 1853. 2 pts., 8vo. 16922

A note on the fly-leaf of a copy of this volume states that the "Vindication" was written by William M. Corry, Esq., and Ellwood Terry, Esq., of Cincinnati, O. John L. Hayes, Esq., of Washington, wrote the account of the trial, etc. Also: Against the Degradation of the States; An Oration delivered before the Peace Democracy at Canton, Stark County, Ohio, July 4, 1863. *Cincinnati.* M.DCCC.LXIII. 8vo, pp. 32.

The Corsair: A Gazette of Literature, Art, Dramatic Criticism, Fashion and Novelty. Edited by N. P. Willis and T. O. Porter. *New-York.* 1839, 40. 4to. B., S. 16923

Corson (G. N.) Dedicatory Poem ... Dec. 29, 1868, at the Dedication of the Grand Chamber of the Knights of Friendship of Pennsylvania ... . [*Philadelphia.* 1868?] 8vo, pp. (7).

Corson (Robert R.) The Soldiers' Guide in Philadelphia. ... *Philadelphia: Geo. H. Ives, Printer.* 32mo, pp. (8). 16925

Cort Bondigh ende Waerachtigh. *See* Vol. II., No. 7564.

Een cort ende warachtich Verhael van de vermaerde See-strijdt en loffelijke Victorie ... onder 't beleyt van den manhaften Admirael Generael Adriaen Janssen Pater, ende Vice-Admirael Maerten Tyssen, teghen de Spaensche Armade, onder 't beleyt van Don Antonio Doquendo Biscayn, geschiet op de Cust van Brasil ... in desen Jare 1631. *Middelburg: Zach. Roman.* 1631. 4to, pp. 8. 16926

Cort ende waerachtich [1647]. *See* Vol. II., No. 7565.

Cort verhael, 1640. *See* N. (N.)

Corta (M.) Mexique. Discours de M. Corta. *Paris.* 1865. 8vo. 16927

Cortambert (L.) Voyage au pays des osages, Un tour en Sicile. Par Louis Cortambert. *Paris: A. Bertrand.* 1837. 8vo, pp. 96. 16928

Cortambert (L.), *and* Tranaltos (F. de). États-Unis d'Amérique. Histoire de la guerre civile américaine 1860–1865 par L. Cortambert et F. de Tranaltos Avec portraits, cartes et plans ... *Paris: Amyot.* M DCCC LXVII. 2 vols., 8vo, 2 l., pp. 389; 2 l., pp. 350. 2 Maps and 2 Plates, containing 11 Portraits. BA., C. 16929

Cortambert (R.) Richard Cortambert Les illustres voyageuses ... *Paris: E. Maillet.* 1866. 8vo, pp. xiii, 396, (1). Woodcuts. BA. 16930

Includes Mme Godin des Odonais, an American by birth, also La Monja Alferez, Marie Read, pirate, Mistress Trollope, Frederika Bremer, Dona Agostina Libarona, all travellers in America. Also: Description partiailière de l'Asie, de l'Afrique, de l'Amérique et de l'Océanie ... pour le classe de seconde, par E. Cortambert. *Paris: L. Hachette et Ce.* 1858 [1857]. 12mo, pp, 216. + Nouvelle édition. [*Ibid.*] 1859 [1858]. 12mo, pp. 279. — Géographie générale de l'Amérique et de l'Océanie ... pour la classe de quatrieme. *Paris: Hachette et Ce.* 1857. 12mo, pp. 63.

Corte-Real (João Pereira). Discursos sobre la navegacion de las naos de la India de Portugal. [n. p., dated at the end, 1° *de Janeiro* 1622.] 4to, 16 l. 16931

See Silva, IV. 19, No. 1192.

Cortes (A.) Proyecto de pronto pago de la deuda esterior é interior moderna en cinco años. *Mexico.* 1852. 8vo, pp. 97.

Cortes (Hernando). Carta de relaciõ ẽbiada a su . S . majestad del ẽp*era*-|dor n*uestro* señor por el capitã general dela nueua spaña: llamado fernãdo cor|tes. Enla q*ua*l haze relaciõ d'las tierras y prouĩcias sin cuẽto q*ue* hã descubierto|nueuamẽte enel yucatã del año de . xix . a esta p*arte*: y ha sometido ala corona|real de su . S . M . En especial haze relaciõ de vna grãdissima prouĩcia muy|rica llamada Culua: ẽla q*ua*l ay muy grãdes ciudades y de marauillosos edi-|ficios: y de grãdes tratos y riq*ue*zas. Entre las q*ua*les ay una mas marauillosa|y rica q*ue*todas llamada Timixtitã: q*ue* esta por marauillosa arte edificadaso|bre vna grãde laguna. dela q*ua*l ciudad y prouĩcia es rey vn grãdissimo señor|llamado Muteeçuma: dõde le acaeciẽrõ al capitã y alos españoles espãto-|sas cosas de oyr. Cuenta largamẽte del grãdissimo señorio del dicho Muteeçuma y de sus

ritos y cerimonias. y de como se sirue.| [Under cut of Emp. Ch. V. on throne.] [Colophon:] *La presente carta de relacion fue impressa enla muy noble & muy leal ciudad de Se-|uilla: por Jacobo crõberger aleman. A . viij . dias de Nouiẽbre. Año de* M. d. &. xxij.| Sm. folio, Gothic letter, 28 l, 48 lines to a page, Text begins on verso of Title, sigs. a, b, c, in 8, d in 4. J.C.B.

The first Spanish edition of the second letter. According to Dibdin, sold for £26 10s. Leon, 1629, p. 73, had not seen the second and third letters in Spanish. Rich says the Spanish editions of Cortes' letters are of the greatest rarity.

Cortes. Carta de relacion embiada a su|S. majestad del Emperador nuestro señor por el Capitan general|dela nueua España: llamada Fernando cortes. Enla qual faze re-|laciõ delas tierras y prouincias sin cuẽto que hã descubierto nueua-|mẽte enel Yucatã del año de . xix . a esta parte: y ha sometido ala coro|na real de su . S . majestad. En especial faze relacion de vna grãdissi-|ma p*r*ouincia muy rica llamada Culua: enla q*ua*l ay muy grãdes ciuda-|des y de marauillosos edificios: y de grãdes tratos y riquezas. Entre|las q*ua*les ay una mas marauillosa y rica q*ue* todas llamada Temixtitã:|q*ue* esta por marauillosa arte edificada sobre vna grande laguna: dela|q*ua*l ciudad y prouĩcia es rey vn grãdissimo señor llamado Muteeçu-|ma: dõde le acaesciẽrõ al capitã y alos Españoles espãtosas cosas de|oyr. Cuenta largamente del grãdissimo señorio del dicho Muteeçu|ma y de sus ritos y cerimonias: y de como se sirue.| [Under cut of Emp. Ch. V. on throne, with courtiers.] [Colophon:] *La presente carta de relacion fue impressa enla muy noble|& muy leal ciudad de Caragoça: por George Coci Aleman.|A. v. dias de Enero. Año de* M . d . y . xxiij . | Sm. folio, 28 leaves, 48 lines to a full page. J.C.B. 16934

Second Spanish edition of the second letter.

Cortes. Carta tercera de relaciõ: embiada por Fernan|do cortes capitan & justicia mayor del yucatan llamado la nueua españa|del mar oceano: al muy alto y potentissimo cesar & iuictissimo señor dõ|Carlos emperador semper augusto y rey de españa nuestro señor: delas|cosas sucedidas & muy dignas de admiracion enla conquista y recupe-|racion dela muy grande & marauillosa ciudad de Temixtitan: y delas|otras prouincias a ella subjetas que se rebelaron. Enla qual ciudad & di|chas prouincias el dicho capitan y españoles consigieron grandes y se|ñaladas victorias dignas de perpetua memoria. Assi mesmo haze rela-|cion como hã descubierto el mar del Sur: y otras muchas & gra*n*des pro-|uincias muy ricas de minas de oro: y

perlas: y piedras preciosas: & avn|tienen noticia que ay especeria.| [Under same cut as in ed. of 1522.] [Colophon:] *La presente carta de relaciõ fue impressa ẽla muy noble & muy leal ciudad d' seuilla por|Jacobo crõberger alemã: acabose a* . xxx . *dias de março: año d' mill & quiniẽtos &* . xxiij .| Sm. folio, 30 leaves, 48 lines to a page. J.C.B. 16935

First edition of the third letter.

Cortes. La quarta relacion q*ue* Ferna*n*do cortes gouer|nador y capitan general por su majestad enla|nueua España d'l mar oceano embio al muy|alto & muy potentissimo inuictissimo señor|don Carlos emperador semper augusto y|rey de España nuestro señor: enla qual estan|otras cartas o relaciones que los capitanes|Pedro de aluarado & Diego godoy embia|ron al dicho capitan Fernardo [*sic*] cortes.| [Within border and under arms, double-headed eagle, etc.] [Colophon:] *Fue impressa la presente carta de relacion|enla ymperial ciudad de Toledo por Gaspar de auila.|Acabose a veynte dias del mes de Octubre.|Año del nascimiento de nuestro salua-|dor Jesu christo de mil & quinien|tos & veynte y cinco|años .:.|* Sm. folio, 21 leaves, 50 lines to a full page. J.C.B. 16936

First edition of the fourth letter.

Cortes. La quarta relaciõ que Ferna*n*do cortes go|uernador y capita*n* general por sumagestad|enla nueua España delmar oceano ẽbio al|muy alto & muy potentissimo inuictissimo|señor don Carlos emperador semper agusto y rey d'spaña|*nuestro* señor. enla qual estan otras cartas y relaciones que-|los capitanes Pedro de aluarado e Diego godoy embia|ron al dicho capitan Fernardo cortes.| [Within a narrow border, and under large escutcheon, filling half the page.] [Colophon:] *Fue imprenssa la presente carta dere|laciõ delas Indias: enla metropolitana|ciudad de Valencia por Geor|ge costilla Acabose a* xij.|*dias d'l mes de Ju|lio año de*|mil . d . xxvj . *años*.| Sm. folio, 26 leaves, 45 lines to a page. J.C.B. 16937

Second edition of the fourth letter. Mr. J. C. Brown has the only copy known. Gayangos, 1866, p. vii, is certainly wrong in naming this as a *Saragossa* imprint, and the date July 8, 1526. The three letters were first collectively printed by Barcia in his "Historiadores primitivos de las Indias occidentales, &c." Vol. I. (called four letters by Barcia) separately paged, pp. 173. *Madrid.* 1749.

Cortes. Historia|de Nueva-España,|escrita por su esclarecido conquistador|Hernan Cortes,|aumentada|con otros documentos, y notas,|por el ilustrissimo Señor|Don Francisco Antonio|Lorenzana,|Arzobispo de Mexico.| [Engr. Vignette, with

Motto.] |—|Con las Licencias necesarias|*En México en la Imprenta del Superior Gobierno, del Br. D. Joseph Antonio de Hogal|en la Calle del Tiburcio. Año de* 1770.| Folio, 228 l., 35 Engr. Plates, viz.: Title, Engr. Front., 2 l., Ded., 6 l., Err., 1 l., Prol., 2 l., Viage, pp. xvi, Engr. Map fold., Engr. View of Temple, Advertencias and Gobierno, pp. 36, Carta, pp. 37–175, Cordillera, 1 l., 31 Engr. Plates (numbered from 14th as No. 15–32), Carta, pp. 177–328, Engr. copy of Map of 1541 fold., Carta, pp. 329–400, Indice, 9 l. J.C.BT. 16938

Contains the second, third, and fourth Spanish letters of Cortes, being the second collection of them published to that date. This collection led to the appearance of several translations, as will be seen below. The notes by Lorenzana are of value, being chiefly on local questions. "Clavigero, Messico. I. 25, says the explanations of the *Cordillera* or tribute rolls are very inaccurate. These rolls, of which Boturini had a native painted copy, are also copied into Kingsborough's work by Aglio from an outline pen-drawing of them preserved in the Mendoza collection in the Bodleian Library at Oxford." — Prescott, I. 40, note. Lorenzana, in the "Prologo," says he means to reprint the second and third letters, but he adds the fourth also. The "Gobierno Politico," pp. 11–36 is by Vetancourt, apparently from an unpublished manuscript.

Cortes. Historia de Méjico, escrita por su esclarecido conquistador Hernan Cortes: aumentada con otros documentos y notas, por D. Francisco Antonio Lorenzana, Antiguo Arzobispo de Mejico. Revisada y adaptada á la ortografia moderna, por D. Manuel del Mar. *Nueva York: Sres. White, Gallagher y White.* 1828. Large 8vo, Title, Av., 2 l., Notic. Hist., etc., pp. 5–110, blank, 1 l., Prol., pp. vi, Gobierno, pp. 7–42, Cartas, pp. 43–614. Front. and 3 Plates Lithog. 16939

Imperfect reprint of Lorenzana. Icazbalceta's Colleccion, I. xxxv, notes the various omissions, the addition of plates copied from Clavigero, and is out of all patience at the modernized spelling. This edition was gotten up for the Mexican market, with a life of Cortes by R. C. Sands. *See infra.*

Cortes. Carta inedita de Herna*n* Cortes. Primera edicion de sesẽta exemplares, impressa con caracteres goticos del siglo xvj. Publicada segũ el manuscrito original por Joaquin Garcia Icazbalceta. *En Mexico. Año de* M. dccc. lv. Sm. square 8vo, 14 leaves. 16940

Only sixty copies printed. This title is copied from Icazbalceta's Colleccion, 1858, I. xxii, note. The next one of the same letter, is from an original copy, No. 30.

Cortes. Con priuilegio.|—| [Arms of Maximilian.] Esta es vna carta|que el muy ilustre señor Don Hernando Cortes| marques que luego fue del Valle, escruio a la|S. L. L. M. del Emperador: dandole quẽta de lo|que convenia proveer ẽ aquellas partes: y de algunas|cossas en ellas acaescidas. Fecha ẽ la|

gran cibdad de Temistitan Mexico de|la nueua España: a xv. dias del|mes de otubre de M. d. xxiv.|Años.|Agora nueuamẽte impressa por su original.| [In single rule border.] [Colophon:] *En Mexico,|En la Imprenta particular de Joaquin Garcia Icaz-|balceta, y a su costa. Año de* 1865.| [Under a device, in single rule border.] Sm. square 12mo, 14 leaves numbered, Gothic letter, Rubricated Title. J.C.BT. 16941

A beautiful piece of typography. In the "Al Lector," on verso of title, Sen. Icazbalceta says, that after printing a first edition of sixty copies, he had reprinted this letter in his Colleccion, 1858, I. [pp. 470–483], and that he now reprints an edition of seventy copies, of which ten only are offered for sale. This was a secret letter to the Emperor, accompanying Cortes' fourth letter. Gayangos, 1866, pp. 325–339, gives it, with slight variations, from the Muñoz collection of MS., adding that the original is in Simancas. The date is given as Oct. 14 in one copy.

Cortes. Cartas y Relaciones|de|Hernan Cortés|al Emperador Carlos V|colegidas é ilustradas|por|Don Pascual de Gayangos,|&c &c|*Paris Imprenta Central de los Ferro-Carriles|A Chaix y Ca|&c|* 1866.| Rl. 8vo, Title, Introd., etc., pp. li, Text, 576, last blank. J.C.BT. 16942

Gayangos is the author of the "History of the Mohammedan Dynasties of Spain," and the translator, with Vedia, of "Ticknor's History of Spanish Literature." This is the only collection of all the known writings of Cortes, and of papers directly relating to him. The collection consists of thirty pieces, that may be classified as follows: Letters and memorials to the Emperor and Queen, 16; letters and memorials of an official nature, 5; narratives relating to occurrences in Mexico, 5; reports, orders, etc., 4. A small edition only was printed, of which but few were offered for sale.

Cortes. Carta Sexta de Hernando Cortes, escrita al Emperador Carlos V. Publicada ahora por Primera Vez. [Edited by George Folsom.] *New York.* 1848. 8vo. 16943

This must be the *fifth* letter, discovered shortly after Folsom's translation of the first dispatches had been published.

Cortes. Aventuras y conquistas de Hernan Cortes en Méjico. Obra traducida del francés por D. A. Alrich y Elias. Con laminas. *Barcelona.* 1846. Sm. 8vo. 16944

Probably an abridged edition of De Solis, as well as the following:

Cortes. Aventuras y conquistas de Hernan Cortes en Méjico, por una sociedad de literados. V. Segura. *Mexico.* 1853. 18mo, pp. xv, 328, 1 l. 16945

Cortes. Hernan Cortes. Narracion familiar. *Rosa et Bouret. Paris.* 1870. 18mo, pp. 107. 16946

Cortes. Praeclara Ferdina*n*di.|Cortesii de Noua maris Oceani Hy|spania Narratio Sacratissimo. ac Inuictissi-|mo

Carolo Romanorũ Imperatori semper Augusto, Hyspa|niarũ, & ẽ Regi Anno Domini. M. D. XX. transmissa:|In qua continentur Plurima scitu & admiratione|digna Circa egregias earũ puintiarũ Vrbes, In-|colarũ mores, puerorũ Sacrificia, & Religiosas|personas, Potissimũque de Celebri Ciuitate|Temixtitan Variisque illi9 mirabilib9, que|legẽtẽ mirifice delectabũt.|p*er* Doctorẽ|Petrũ saguorgnanũ [*sic*] Foro Iuliensẽ|Reueñ. D. Ioan. de Reuelles|Episco. Viẽnẽsis Sacretariũ|ex Hyspano Idi|omate in lati|nũ versa|Anno Dni. M. D. XXIIII. KL. Martii:|Cum gratia & Priuilegio.| [Within a double border.] [Colophon:] Explicit secunda Ferdinandi Cortesii Narratio per Doc|torem Petrum Sauorgnanum Foro Iuliensem ex Hy-|spano Idiomate in latinum Conuersa. *Im-|pressa in Celebri Ciuitate Norimberga.|Cõuentui Imperali presidente Sere-|nissimo Ferdinando Hyspaniarũ|Infãte, & Archiduce Austriæ|Sac: Ro. Imp: Locũt.|Generali|Anno. Dñi* M. D. XXIIII: *Quar. No. Mar.|Per Fridericum Peypus.|Arthimesius.|* Folio, Roman letter, marginal notes in black letter, 4 l., including Title, Text, fols. numb. i–xlix, and large Cut folded with Plan of City and Gulf of Mexico, Imper. Arms on rev. of Title, Dedication to Clement VII, 1 l., "Auc. ad lect. carmen," 2 l., large Cut of Clement VII on rev. of last, sometimes wanting, printer's Mark at end of Text. 16947

Some copies of the map have five lines of text printed beneath the scale, some have twelve separate numbered leaves more at beginning or end of text, with the tract of Peter Martyr, of Anghiera, first printed 1521, containing: "De Rebus, et Insulis nouiter Repertis|a Sereniss. Carlo Imperatore|Et Variis earum genti-|um moribus.| which appeared again in the next edition. A facsimile of the map appeared in Henry Stevens' "American Bibliographer," No. II., 1854. First edition of the Latin version, by Savorgnanus, of the "Secunda Carta," of great rarity, particularly with map. G.W.R., J.C.B., L. Sold at Puttick's, July, 1868, for £24.

Cortes. Tertia Ferdinandi Cor-|tesii Sac. Caesar. et Cath. Maiesta.|In Nova Maris Oceani Hyspania Gene-|ralis præfecti p*r*eclara Narratio, In qua Celebris Ciuitatis Temix|titan expugnatio, aliarũque Prouintiarũ que defecerant recupe-|ratio continentur, In quarũ expugnatione, recuperationeque Præfe|ctus, una cum Hyspanis Victorias œterna memoria dignas con|sequutus est, preterea In ea Mare del Sur Cortesium detexisse re-|cẽset*ur*, quod nos Australe Indicũ Pelagus putam9, & alias innume|ras Prouintias Aurifodinis, Vnionibus, Variisque Gemmarum|generibus refertas, Et postremo illis innotuisse in eis quoque Aro-|matac ontineri, [*sic*] Per Doctorẽ Petrum Sauorgnanũ Foroiuliensem|Reueñ. in Christo patris dñi Io. de Reuelles Episcopi Viẽnensis|Secretarium Ex Hyspano ydiomate In Latinum Versa. [Within a border.] [Colophon:] *Impressum In Imperiali|Ciui-*

tate Norimberga,|Per Discretum, & proui|dum Virum Fœdericũ|Arthemesium Ciuem|ibidem, Anno Vir-|ginei partus Mil|lesimo quingente|simo vigesimo|quarto.| Folio, Roman, with black letter notes, 4 l., including Title; Text, fols. numb. i–li, Errata, 1 l., Imper. Arms on rev. of Title, Dedication, etc., as before, 3 l., Portrait of Clement VII on rev. of last in some copies. 16948

First Latin edition of the third letter of May 15, 1522. The tract of Peter Martyr is sometimes added, containing twelve folios, numbered, of same impression as before (?), either before or after the letters. The two letters and the "De Insulis" are sometimes found bound together.

Cortes. De insvlis nv|per inventis Ferdinandi Cortesii|ad Carolum V. Rom. Imperatorem Narrationes, cum alio|quodam Petri Martyris ad Clementem VII. Pon-|tificem Maximum consimilis argumenti|libello.|His accesserunt Epistolæ duæ, de felicissimo apud Indos|Euangelij incremento, quas superioribus hisce diebus qui-|dam fratres Mino. ab India in Hispaniam transmiserunt.|Item Epitome de inuentis nuper Indiæ populis idololatris [*sic*]|ad fidem Christi, atque adeo ad Ecclesiam Catholicam conuer-|tendis, Autore R. P. F. Nicolao Herborn, regularis obser-|uantiæ, ordinis Minorum Generali Commissario| Cismontano.|*Venduntur in pingui Gallina.*|Anno M.D.XXXII.| [Large profile medallion of Ch. V. below, repeated at head of two letters, and border, with 25 escutcheons, verso blank.] [Colophon on recto of last leaf:] *Coloniæ ex officina Melchioris Nouesiani, Anno* M.|D.XXXII. Decimo Kalendas mensis Septembris.| [Verso, under printer's device:] *Coloniæ, Impensis honesti ciuis Ar-|noldi BircKman. Anno Domini*|M.D.XXXII. *Mense|Septembri.*| Folio, 82 l., not numb. [4 p. l., with Title, De Insulis, 8 l., Narr. sec., 30 l., Narr. tert., 34 l., Epit., 6 l.], sigs. A, Aa, Bb and L in 4s, A to K and M in 6s. 16949

Contains the "De Insulis" of Martyr, the second and third letters of Cortes, with the two dedications, &c., as in the editions of 1524; also missionary reports, here first published, and reprinted in 1543, in the "Thesoro de virtudes," in Spanish, and all again, in 1555 and 1616, in the "Novus Orbis," in Latin.

Cortes. Noue de le Isole & Terra fer|ma Nouamente trouate|In India pel el Capi|taneo de larmata de la Cesarea| Maiestate.| [Within engr. border.] [On verso of title-page:] Andrea caluo ad Paulo uerrano|& Abramo Tassio,|——————————— *Mediolani, decimo sexto calẽ. Decembris* M.D.XXII.| 4to, 6 l., not numbd., includ. Title, verso of last blank. BM. 16950

Abstract from the second letter.

Cortes. La preclara Narratione di Ferdinan|do Cortese

della Nuoua Hispagna del Mare Oceano, al|Sacratissimo, & Inuictissimo Carlo di Romani Imperatore sem|pre Augusto Re Dhispagna, & cio che siegue, nellãno del Si|gnore. M. D. XX. trasmessa: Nella quale si cõtẽgono mol|te cose degne di scienza, & ammiratione, circa le citta di|egregie di quelle Prouincie costumi dhabitatori, sa-|crifici di Fanciulli, & Religiose persone, Et massi-|mamente della celebre citta Temixtitan, & va-|rie cose marauigliose di quella, e quali dilet-|teranno mirabilmẽte il lettore per il Dot-|tore Pietro Sauorgnano Foroiuliense|Del Riuerendo Messer Giouãni de|Reuelles Vescouo di Vienna Se-|cretario dal iddioma Hispagni|uolo in lingua latina Con-|uersa Nel Anno. M.D.|XXIIII. di Primo Mar|zo: Hora nellestesso| Millesimo di. xvii.|Agosto. Voi|Candidissimi lettori leggerete con dillettatione & piacere|grandissimo la prefata Narratione di Ferdinando Corte|se dalla Facõdia latina al splẽdore della lingua volgare p*er*|Messer Nicolo Liburnio cõ fidelta & diligẽza tradotta al|cõmodo, & sodisfattione de glhonesti & virtuosi ingegni. |Cum gratia & Priuilegio.| [Within an ornamental border.] [Colophon:] *Stampata in Venetia per Bernardino de Viano|de Lexona Vercellese. Ad instantia de Bapti-|sta de Pederzani Brixiani. Anno domi-|ni.* M. D. XXIIII. *Adi.* XX. *Agosto.*| Sm. 4to, 73 l., not numbered, large Plan and Map, folded, often wanting, sigs. in 4s, reverse R iv blank, last has blank recto, device of elephant bearing cross, and castle with shield bearing initials ·Z·B·P· on verso. + [Same in every particular except colophon, which reads:] *Stampata in Venetia per Zuan9 Antonio de Nico-|lini da Sabio. Ad instantia de M. Baptista|de Pederzani Brixiano. Ano D.* [sic.] J.C.BT. 16951

Contains second letter only, translated by Liburnius from the Latin of Savorgnanus as published the same year. An Italian version of the letters appeared in the "Collection of Ramusius," Vol. III., 1556, fols. 225–296 verso, in which the second, third, and fourth letters are given, newly translated from the Spanish, the third and fourth not having been translated before. Ramusius, fol. 225, says, that after diligent research he could not discover the first letter. He also gives the letter of Alvarado and Godoy to Cortes, which were appended to the Spanish edition of the "Cuarta Carta." He then adds the "Relatione di alcune cose della Nuona [*sic*] Spagna, & della gran città di Temestitan Messico. fatta per vno gentil'homo del Signor Ferdinando Cortese," fols. 304 verso to 310, with two cuts. The original Spanish of this is not known. Icazbalceta, Coll. I. 368–398, copies Ramusius, including the plates, and adds a Spanish translation of this curious paper, which he heads "El Conquistador Anónimo." This is followed by the "Narrative of Alvar Nuñez Cabeza de Vaca," fols. 310–330, verso. Next comes a "Relation of Nuño de Guzman," dated from Omitlan, in Mechoucan, July 8th, 1530, fols. 331–339, which is not copied by Icazbalceta, nor does it seem to have been elsewhere published. Another piece not found in any other publication, the "Narrative of Francisco Ulloa," by an officer of the only vessel that returned out of three sent out by Cortes, is next given, fols. 339–354. Prescott's

"Mexico," III. 337, note, refers to this account. Ramusius closes his Mexican documents with reports by Vasquez di Coronado, Fray Marco da Nizza, and Hernando Alarcon. This third volume appeared again in 1565 and 1606. *See* Ramusius. The "Istoria della conquista del Mexico," *Florence*, 1660 and 1699, etc., is from De Solis.

CORTES. Tressacree Imperiale et catholique mageste lui estant en|la cite de Palâce en Castille, eust nouuelles des marches ysles|et terre ferme occeanes, que lon appelle et nôme vulgairemêt]les Indes, pource q vne partie dicelles est a confronte envers lesd. indes.| [Colophon on verso of fol. 16.] Depuis sont venues a sa mageste nouuel-|les de, certaiês ysles trouuez p les espagnolz plaines despecerie et beau-|cop de mines dor, lesqlles nouuelles il receupt en ceste ville de vailladolid|le primier doctobre. xv. cent. xxij. Finis:|*Imprime en Anuers par Michiel de Hoocstraten.*|*Cum gratia et privilegio.*| Sm. 4to, 16 l., Roman letter, except first and last lines (of Title?) which are in Gothic.

This title, copied from a foreign bookseller's list, seems to be the second letter only, and it was not printed before 1523, the first Spanish edition being dated Nov. 8, 1522. It is not in the "Bibl. Am. Vet." of Harrisse, nor does it seem to have been noticed by any bibliographer. The bookseller ascribes to it the date of 1522 or 1523, and thinks that it is composed from the second and third letters of Cortes.

A French translation of the second and third letters, in an abridged form, appears at the close of the "Extrait ov recevil de Isles nouuellement trouuees en la grand mer Oceane," etc., *Paris*, 1532, which is said by Harrisse, "Bibl. Am. Vet.," p. 286, to be a translation of our No. 16952. On leaf 155, begins the "Epitome de les Seconde et Tierce Narrationes de la mar Oceane de Ferdinant Cortese, translatée de latin en francoys." Another French work, entitled "Voyages es conquêtes du capitaine Ferdinand Courtois ès Indes occidentales, traduite de langue espagnole par Guillaume le Breton, Nivernois. *Paris. Abel l'Angelier.* 1588," 8vo, is from Oviedo and Gomara. (Brunet.) The "Histoire de la Conqueste du Mexique ou de la nouvelle Espagne, par Fernando Cortes," 1691 and other dates, is a translation of De Solis. The "Aventures et conquêtes de Cortes au Mexique, par Henri Lebrun, *Tours.* 1843," fourth edition, sm. 8vo, is also probably from De Solis. The account in the "Hist. gen. des voyages. 1754," Vol. XII., is from Herrera, etc.

CORTES. Correspondance de Fernand Cortes avec l'Empereur Charles-Quint, sur la Conquête du Mexique. Traduite par M. le Vicomte de Flavigny, ... *Paris: Cellot et Jombert.* [1778.] 12mo, pp. xxvi, 504, (4). + *Paris.* 1779. 8vo. + *Frankfort: J. J. Kessler.* 1779. 8vo, pp. xvi, 471. Engraved Frontispiece. + *En Suisse: Libraires Associés.* 1779. 8vo, pp. xvi, 471.

See "M. Rev.," LX. 556. A translation abridged from Lorenzana, the letters being called first, second, and third, instead of second, third, and fourth.

CORTES. Translationusz hi|spanischer sprach zũ Frantzõsisch gema|cht, so durch dẽ Vice Rey in Neapole,|fraw Margareten Hertzogiñ iñ Bur|gundi zũ geschriben.| [Over likeness of the Emperor, and within broad border.] Without date or

imprint, *circa* 1522? Sm. 4to, 4 l., not numb., Gothic letter, many Cuts, no water-mark. S.L.M.B. 16954

On verso of title and last leaf, large coat-of-arms, with scroll, inscribed "A. H. 1517, Quy voudra." The conquest of Mexico is alluded to on verso of A iii, as follows: "Nit weit von derselben insel haben|sy erobert ein stat genant Tenustitan, in deren gezalt sind sächtzig tausent härd statten mit ei-|ner güten rinckthmauren ingefaszt." *See* "Bibl. Am. Vet.," and Stevens' "Am. Bibl."

CORTES. Voyages et|conqvestes dv|Capitaine Ferdinand|Courtois, és Indes|Occidentales.|Histoire traduite de langue Espagnole,|par Guillaume le Breton Niuernois.|*A Paris,*|*Chez Abel l' Angelier, au premier|pillier de la grand' Sale du Palais.*|M. D. LXXXVIII.|*Avec privilege dv Roy.*| 8vo, 8 unnumbered, 416 numbered l. H. 16955

Probably a translation from Gomara. *See* Gomara.

CORTES. Ein schöne|Newe zeytung so Kayserlich|Mayestet ausz India yetz|newlich zükommen seind.|Gar hüpsch von den Newen|ynseln, ynd von yrem sytten|gar kurtzweylig züleesen.| [Over double-headed eagle, and in a broad border.] Without date or imprint. Device at end, a pine cone, the mark of Augsburg, where it was probably printed. Supposed to be an imprint of Sigmund Grimm, *circa* 1522. Sm. 4to, 8 l., Gothic letter, 35 lines on a full page, Text beginning on verso of Title, ending on recto of B iii, with device *supra*, verso blank. J.C.B., L. 16956

Contains abridged account of voyages of Columbus and of the "Conquest of Mexico," down to 1522. *See* Mulligan's "Syllacius," *New York*, 1859. "Appendix," by Mr. James Lenox, pp. lvi–lviii, with facsimile of title and device. Also, Harrisse's "Bibl. Am. Vet.," and Stevens' "Am. Bibl.," p. 89.

CORTES. Ferdinandi|Cortesii.|Von dem Newen Hispanien, so im Meer gegem Nidergang, Zwo gantz lustige vnnd|fruchtreiche Historien, an den groszmächtigisten vnüberwindt-|lichisten Herren, Carolvm. v. Römischen|Kaiser &c. Künig in Hispanien &c.|Die erst im M.D.XX. Jar zügeschriben, in wellicher grundt-|lich vnd glaubwirdig erzelt wirdt, der Abendtländern, vnnd|sonderlich der Hochberümpten statt Temixtitan eroberung.|Die andere im 1524. jar, Wie Temixtitan, so abgefallen, wider erobert,|Nachmals andere herrliche Syg, sampt der erfindung des Meers Svr,|So man für das Indianisch Meer achtet.|Darzũ auch von vilen andern Landschafften Indiæ,|So erfunden von dem 1536. bisz auf das 42. Jar.|Wellicher vilfältige frucht, nutz vnd lustparkait, in ainer Sum̃,|auff das kürzest, ainer yetwedern Historien volgendes|Tittel begriffen vnd angezaigt wirdt.|Erstlich in Hispanischer Sprach von Cortesio selbst beschriben, Nachmals|von Doctor Peter Sauorgnan ausz Friaul in Lat-

einische sprach Transferiert,|Entlich aber in Hochteütsche sprach, zũ ehren vnd ausz vnderthänigister|gehorsame, dem Allerdurchleüchtigisten, Groszmächtigisten Fürsten|vñ Herrn, Herrn Ferdinanden, Römischen, zũ Hungern|vnd Böhem &c. Künigen, Infantẽ in Hispanien, Ertzhertzo-|gen zũ Osterreich &c. von Xysto Betuleio vñ Andrea|Diethero von Augspurg, baiden daselbst gemainer Statt Lateinischen Schülmaistern.| *Getruckt inn der Kaiserlichen Reichs Statt Augspurg, durch*| *Philipp Vlhart, in der Kirchgassen, bey S. Vlrich, Anno Domini* M.D.L.|Cum gratia & Priulegio Ro: Regiæ Maiestatis in Decennium. Folio, 108 l., 6 l., inc. Title, 39 l. numb., 1 l. blank, 2 l. unnumb., 60 l. numb. 16957

Contains, according to Harrisse, a translation of the second and third letters from the Latin edition, with extracts from Peter Martyr's fourth decade, from Oviedo, and other extracts relating to the Canary Islands, Venezuela, and American discoveries down to the year 1543.

CORTES. Briefe des Ferdinand Cortes an Kayser Carl den 5ten über die Eroberung von Mexico, nebst einer Einleitung und Anmerkungen. Herausgegeben von J. J. Stapfern. *Heidelberg: bey den Gebrüder Pfähler.* 1779. + 1780. + *Carlsruhe: Braun.* 1779. + *Bern.* 1793. 2 vols., 12mo, Titles, 2 l., pp. 22, lxviii, 253; Title, 1 l, pp. 6, 408. Map and Plate. 16958

Contains second, third, and fourth letters of Cortes, translated from Lorenzana, 1770, or Flavigny. Stapfern was a Swiss.

CORTES. Drei Berichte des General Kapitäns von Neu-Spanien D. Fern. Cortes an Kaiser Karl v. Aus dem Spanischen übersetzt, und mit einem Vorwort und erläuternden Anmerkungen von K. W. Koppe. *Berlin: Th. Enslin.* 1834. 8vo. Map and Plate. 16959

CORTES. Fernando Cortez. Historischer Roman aus der Zeit der ersten Kämpfe zwischen Indianern und Spaniern in Mexiko. Nach den neuesten Quellen ... . *Münster: Aschendorff.* 1869. 2 vols., 8vo, pp. 333; 432. 16960

We place this title here, the work being anonymous.

CORTES. De nieuwe Werelt der Landschappen ende Eylanden, die tot hier toe allen ouden weerelt beschryvers onbekent geweest syn ... . *Antwerpen.* 1563. Folio. 16961

Known as Ablijn's Collection. Contains, according to Harrisse, a Flemish version of Diether's "Savorgnanus."

CORTES. Brieven van Ferdinand Cortes, aan Keizer Karel v. wegens de Verovering van Mexico. ... *Amsterdam: Yntema*

en Tieboel. MDCCLXXX–LXXXI. 2 vols., 8vo, pp. xiv, 178; 2 l., pp. 298, (18). Map and 2 Plates. 16962

A more correct translation than Flavigny's. The letters are properly numbered, second, third, and fourth. An excellent preface and introduction are added, with additional notes, and an appendix, completing the life of Cortes. The Gottfried collection, *Leyden, Van der Aa*, 1706 and 1707, folio and 12mo, has a translation relating to Cortes, from Herrera, entitled, "Roem-Waardige Zee- en Land-togten na Nieuw-Spanje en Mexico."

CORTES. History of the Conquest of Mexico, by Hernan Cortes, to which is added the Voyage of Vasco de Gama. 1759. 12mo. 16963

Probably from De Solis; perhaps a translation from Prévost. *See* "Hist. Gen. des Voyages," XII. 1754.

CORTES. The Despatches of Hernando Cortes, the Conqueror of Mexico, addressed to the Emperor Charles v. Written during the Conquest, and containing a Narrative of its events. Now first translated into English from the original Spanish, with an Introduction and Notes, By George Folsom ... . *New York: Wiley & Putnam; London: Stationers Hall Court.* 1843. 12mo, pp. xii., 431. 16964

First appearance of the three collected dispatches in English, being a translation from Lorenzana, including a portion of his notes. *See* "N. Am. Rev.," LVII. 459. The second letter, translated from Flavigny, by Mr. Alsop, appeared in the "Portfolio," a magazine published in Philadelphia, 1817–18. "The Pleasant Historie of the Conquest of the West India," etc., translated by T.[homas] N.[ichols]. *London.* 1596, is from Gomara. The accounts in Harris, Kerr, Pinkerton, etc., are from Herrera, De Solis, and Bernal Diaz. Some copies were printed on large paper, rl. 8vo.

CORTES. The Fifth Letter of Hernan Cortes to the Emperor Charles V, containing an Account of his Expedition to Honduras. Translated from the Original Spanish by Don Pascual de Gayangos ... . *London: Hakluyt Society.* M.DCCC.LXVIII. 8vo, pp. xvi, 156. 16965

The Spanish text was first printed in the "Documentos Ineditos," 1864, IV. 8–167, and this is the first English translation.

CORTES. The Pleasant Historie of the Conquest of the VVest India. *See* Gomara.

Consult, also, for Cortes, Barcia's "Historiadores Primitivos;" Ternaux's "Recueil," Vol. X.; Navarrete's "Coll. de los Viages &c.," 1825–37, Vol. V.; Nav. Salva and Baranda's "Coll. de Doc. ineditos," 1842–65, Vols. I. and IV.; Vedia's "Historiad. prim. de Indias," 1852–3, Vol. I.; "Archivo Mexicano," 1852–3; Icazbalceta's "Coll. de Doc. para la Hist. de Mexico," 1858–66, Tom. I.; Prescott's "Conq. of Mexico," 1843; and numerous valuable references in Harrisse's "Bib. Am. Vetustiss.," 1866. It is remarkable that De Bry should not have *illustrated* the "Conquest of Mexico," and that Grynæus, in his "Novus Orbis" of 1532, should omit all notice of Cortes.

CORTES (M.) Breve Compendio de la Sphera y de la arte de nauegar, con nuevos instrumentos y reglas, exempliphicado con muy subtiles demonstraciones, ... *Sevilla: Ant. Alvarez.* 1551. Folio, 98 leaves. 16966

A volume of great rarity, frequently reprinted. A map of the New World is on the recto of the sixty-seventh leaf. I have seen an English catalogue in which the work is described [*Cadiz.* 1551], which is, perhaps, an error, though Graesse has it thus also, and Navarrete, in his "Historia de la Nautica," 1816, p. 163, seems to confirm it.

CORTES (M.) The Arte|of Naviga-|tion,|Conteynyng a Compendious description of the Sphere,|with the makyng of certen In-|strumentes and Rules for Na-|vigations: exemplified by|manye Demonstrations.|Wrytten in the Spa-|nish tongue by|Martin Curtes, And Direc-|ted to|the Emperoar|charles the|fyfte.|Translated out of Spanjshe|into Engljshe by Ri-|chard Eden. 1561. [Colophon:] *Imprintea at Lon-|don in Pawles church yarde, by| Richard Jugge, Printer|to the Quenes|Maiestie.*| 4to, 8 l., Text 84 and 2 l., Map of the New World. J.C.BT.

First edition. A very interesting and extremely rare volume, in which are noticed the discovery of Peru, the Straits of Magellan, Brazil, Rio de la Plata, Canary Islands, Indies, etc. It treats also of the signs of approaching storms, which the writer illustrates from St. Matthew, &c. "Dedicated to the Merchant Adventurers for the Discovery of Landes, Territories, Islandes Unknown, by Rich. Eden." Thorpe priced one, in 1842, at £3 13s. 6d. The other editions are, *London: printed by Johan Iugge, Wydowe.* 1584. 4to; *London: Abell Jeffes.* 1589. 4to; *London.* 1596. 4to; 1609, 45, enlarged by John Tapp. The last edition has the following title:

CORTES. The Arte of Navi-|gation.|First written in the Spanish tongue by|that Excellent Mariner and Mathematici-|an of these times, Martine|Cvrtis.|From thence Translated into English by Richard Eden: And|now newly Corrected and inlarged, with many necessa-|rie Tables, Rules, and Instructions, for the more easie attai-|ning to the knowledge of Nauigation:|By John Tapp.|*London: Printed for Iohn Tapp, and are to be sold at his Shoppe at|S. Magnus Corner.* 1609.| 4to, Title, 1 l., pp. 4, 1, 1, 1, 7, 157, 4. 16968

CORTÉS Y LARRÁZ (Pedro), *Archbishop of Guatemala.* Instruccion pastoral sobre el método practico de administrar con fruto el sto. sacramento de la penitencia. Mandándola observar a todos los confessores de su diócesis. La reimprime el dr. frey Joseph Matamóros. *Valencia: B. Monfort.* 1784. Sm. 4to, pp. 203. 16969

CORTES DE ARREDONDO (M. J.) La Voz del Nombre vista en las Obras del Illmo. Sr. Dr. D. Manuel Roxo. Oracion

Panegyrico-funebre por el Sr. Dr. D. Miguel Joseph Cortes de Arredondo. *Mexico.* 1765. 4to, pp. 43. 16970

CORTES Y ZEDEÑO (Geronymo Thomas de Aquino). Arte Vocabulario, y Confessionario en el Idioma Mexicano, como se usa en el Obispado de Guadalaxara. [*Mexico:*] *En la Imprenta del Colegio Real de San Ignacio de la Puebla de los Angeles, Ano de* 1765. 4to. 16971

Extremely rare.

CORTINA (Conde De la). Determinacion fisico-geográfica de la ciudad de Mexico y de su valle, en 1858. *Mexico.* 1858.

CORTINA. Prontuario diplomatico y consular, y resumen de los derechos y deberes de los estrangeros en los paises donde residen, por El Conde de la Cortina. *Mexico.* 1856. 12mo, pp. viii, 172. 16973

CORTINA (José Gomez de la). La calle de Don Juan Manuel. Anecdota historicá del siglo XVII. *Mexico.* 1836. pp. 40.

CORTINA. Biografia de D. José M. Justo Gomez de la Cortina Conte de la Cortina, escrita por una Comision de la Sociedad Mexicana de geografia y estadistica. *Mexico.* 1860. 4to, pp. 19. Portrait. 16975

CORTINA. Apuntes biograficos de la Señora Da. Maria Ana, Comez de la Cortina, Condesa de la Cortina, Formados por D. Bernardo Capca. *Mexico.* 1853. Sm. 8vo, pp. 17. 16976

CORTINES LAXE (J. B.) Regimento das Camaras municipaes ou lei de 1 de Outubro de 1828, Annotada comas leis, decretos, regulamentos e avisos que revogão ou alterao suas disposições e explicão sua doutrina; precedida de uma introducção historica, e sequida de sete appensos, contendo o ultimo uma breve noticia da formaçao dos municipios da provincia do Rio de Janeiro. Por João Baptista Cortines Laxe, Bacharel em direito. *Rio de Janeiro.* 1868. 12mo, pp. xxiv, 290. 16977

The Cortland Academy Jubilee, celebrated at Homer, N. Y. July 7 & 8, 1846. *Syracuse: Stoddard & Babcock.* 1846. 8vo, pp. 95. S. 16978

Also: Catalogue, 1847. *New-York: Homer.* 8vo. Continued. Known also as the Cortlandville Academy.

CORTLAND COUNTY. Proceedings of the Board of Supervisors, of the County of Cortland, 1866. *Cortland.* 1866. 8vo.

CORWIN (E.) Liberty and Loyalty. An Oration, ... July 4, 1863, to the American Residents in Honolulu ... by Rev. E. Corwin ... . *Honolulu: printed by Henry M. Whitney.* 1863. 8vo, pp. 12. H. 16980

CORWIN (E. B.) ... Catalogue of the ... Books, ... &c., of the late Mr. E. B. Corwin, ... relating to America, ... &c. ... sold ... November 10th, 1856, ... [*New York.* 1856.] 8vo, pp. vii, 263. 16981

Prepared by Joseph Sabin. 100 copies printed on large paper.

CORWIN (E. T.) Historical Discourse on the Centennial Anniversary of the Reformed Dutch Church of Millstone. By E. T. Corwin. With Map. *New York: J. J. Reed, Printer.* 1866. 8vo, pp. 113. S. 16982

CORWIN (E. T.) A Manual of the Reformed Protestant Dutch Church in North America. By Edward Tanjore Corwin, Pastor of Paramus. *New York.* 1859. Sm. 4to, pp. 166, (1). S. 16983

CORWIN (M. B.) Speech of Hon. Morris B. Corwin, of Ohio, on ... California ... April 9, 1850. *Washington.* 1850. 8vo, pp. 7. 16984

CORWIN (T.) Speeches of Thomas Corwin, with a Sketch of his Life. Edited by Isaac Strohm. *Dayton, Ohio: Wm. F. Comly & Co.* 1859. 8vo, pp. 518. 16985

Also: Speech ... on the Bill ... to reduce the Revenue ... to the Wants of the Government. ... House ... January 12, 1837. *Washington.* 1837. 8vo, pp. 15. BA., H. — Speech ... in Reply to Gen. Crary's Attack on General Harrison ... House ... February 15, 1840. *Washington.* 1840. 8vo, pp. 16. BA. — Speech ... on the Mexican War ... February 11, 1847. [*Washington.* 1847.] 8vo, pp. 24. — State of the Union. Speech ... House ... Jan. 21, 1861. *Washington.* 1861. 8vo, pp. 16. — Report of the Trade and Commerce of the British North American Colonies with the United States. *Washington.* 1851. 8vo.

CORWINE (A. B.) The Panama Massacre. A Collection of the Principal Evidence and other Documents including the Report of Amos B. Corwine, Esq., U. S. Commissioner ... . *Panama, New Granada.* 1857. Large 8vo, pp. (2), 69. H.

Also: The Argument ... in the Methodist Church Property Case; ... United States Circuit Court for Ohio, ... 1852, ... [n. p. 1852.] 8vo, pp. 52. H.

Cosas de Los Estados Unidos. Par Nazareno. J. Durand, Editor. *New York: Imprenta de "El Porvenir."* 1864. 8vo, pp. 364. Portrait. 16987

Las Cosas del Plata explicadas por sus hombres. Escrito en Buenos Aires por un vecino de esa ciudad. *Parana.* 1858. 8vo, pp. 34. + *Saint Cloud: imp Ve Belin.* 1858. 18mo, pp. 51.

Cosas Notables, Svcedidos en las Costas de la Civdad de Lima, en las Indias, y como el armada Olandesa procuraua coger el armadilla nuestra, que baxa con la plata de ordinario a Cartagena, año passado de 1624. [Colophon:] *Madrid: por Iuan Gonçalez.* 1625. Folio, pp. 4. 16989

Cosas sabidas y cosas por saber ó Federacion colombiana—Tolerancia politica—Universidades é Instruccion elemental—Cuestion holandesa. [By Cecilio Acosta.] *Carácas.* 1856. 8vo, pp. 31. 16990

La Cosecha de trigo de la Republica de Chile en el año de 1867. *Valparaiso.* 1867. 4to, pp. 22. 16991

COSIO (Joseph). Hercules Coronado, que en la Augusta Memoria, a la Real Proclamacion del D. Fernando VI. Rey de las Españas, y Legitimo Emperador de las Indias, le Consagró en Magnificas Fiestas, y Gloriosos aparatos, la Ciudad de Durango, Cabeza del Nuevo Reyno de Vicaya. *Mexico.* 1749. 4to. 1699[illegible]

COSIO. *See* Trueba y Cosio.

Cosmographiæ Introductio. *See* [Waltzeemuller (Martin)].

Cosmopolitan Art Association. Illustrated Catalogue, 1854. 8vo, pp. 32. Continued. 16993

Cosmopolitan Art Journal. A Record of Art, Biography, and General Literature. ... *New York: published by Cosmopolitan Art Association.* 4to. 16994

Cosmopolitan Ideas on the Union. [n. p. n. d.] 8vo, pp. 23.

The Cosmopolite. [Jan. to April, 1866.] *Baltimore: De Leon & Co.* [1867.] 8vo. No more issued. C. 16996

Las Cosquillas. Periodico retozon, impolitico y de malas costumbres. *Mexico.* 1852. Nos. 1–11. + Segunda época. Tomo 1. Nos. 1–30. *Mexico. Enero* 16 *de* 1861—*Mexico.* 27 *Abril*, 1861. Folio. 16997

COSSHAM (H.) The American War: Facts and Fallacies. A Speech ... by Handel Cossham, Esq. at ... Bristol, ... Friday, February 12, 1864. *Bristol: Whereat, Printed by H. J. Mills.* 12mo, pp. 24. + *London: Fred. Pitman.* 1864. + *New York.* 1865. H. 16998

COSSHAM. Friends of America in England. Handel Cossham, Esq. From the Federal American Monthly ... (August, 1865,) ... . *New York: Baker & Godwin, Printers.* 1865. 8vo, pp. 8. H. + *Washington.* 1865. 16999

COSSHAM. Mr. Cossham on America. *Bristol: printed by T. H. Mills.* [n. d.] 12mo, pp. 22, (1). 17000

COSSIO (B. G. de). Sermon panegyrico del gloriosissimo martyr S. Juan Nepomuceno pred. el d. 16. de Mayo en la ciudad de San Luis Potosi. *Mexico.* 1786. 4to, 27 l. 17001

COSTA (Agost. Robello da). Descripçaõ da cidade do Porto. a noticia dos Homens, e das Mulheres illustres. *Porto.* 1789. Plates. 17002

Partly relates to America.

COSTA (Antonio da). Seize années de clinque chirurgicale civile au Brésil ... . *Paris: Labé.* 1855. 8vo. 17003

COSTA (Constantinõ Pereira de). Demonstraçao politica sobre os extinctos direitos do Imperador do Brasil a corao de Portugal. *Lisboa: Imp. Regia.* 1829. 4to, pp. 16. 17004

COSTA (J. A.) *See* Acosta (J.), Vol. I.

COSTA (Joao Severjano Maciel da). Memoria sobre a necessidade de abolir a introducçao dos escravos africanos no Brasil; sobre o modo e condições com que esta aboliçao se deve fazer; e sobre os meios de remediar a falta de braços que alle póde occasionar. *Coimbra: na Imp. da Univ.* 1821. 4to, pp. 90.

COSTA. Analyse e refutaçao do libello accusatorio, que publicou o almirante Barao do Rio da Prata, contra alguns ministros d'Estado em particular, e em geral contra os ministros de 1826, 1827 e 1828; disfarçada com o titulo de "Defeza perante o Conselho de guerra, etc." *Rio de Janeiro: Typ. Imperial de Plancher Seignot.* 1829. 8vo, pp. viii–80. 17006

COSTA (L.) Christoforo Colombo, Libri VIII. Di Lorenza Costa. *Genova.* 1846. 4to. Portrait. P. + Seconda edizione riveduta dall' autore. *Torino.* 1858. 12mo. 17007

A poem on Columbus. Printed on vellum paper.

COSTA (Maria da). Relatorio sobre as medidas mais importantes a tomar-se, obras de maior urgencia, e trabalhos que forao executados pelo hospital maritimo de Santa Isabel no anno de 1855. pp. 30. 32 Plates. 17008

COSTA (S. G. de A.) Codigo commercial do imperio do Brasil annotado ... por Sallustiano Orlando de Aranjo Costa. Segunda ediçao. *Rio de Janeiro.* 1869. 8vo, pp. xvi, 952.

COSTA ALMEIDA (Antonio Lopes da). Roteiro geral des çostas, ilhas e baizos reconhecidos na globo, ... *Lisboa.* 1835. 4to. 17010

Parts VIII.–XI. relate to America.

COSTA E LIMA (Thomàs da Encarnaçao da). Carta pastoral-exhortatorio ao clero e para de Pernambuco, ao tomar posse de cadeira episcopal. *Olinda.* 1774. Folio, pp. 8. 17011

COSTA E SÁ (Manoel José Maria da). Breves annotações á memoria que o exmo. sr. visconde de S. Leopoldo escreveu com o titulo quaes sao os limites naturaes, pacteados e necessarios do imperio do Brazil? *Rio de Janeiro: instituto historico-geographico brazileiro.* 1839. 8vo, 2 l., pp. 159–244. 17012

COSTA PEREIRA (J. S. da). Diccionario Topographico do Imperio do Brasil, por Jose Saturnino da Costa Pereira ... *Rio de Janeiro.* 1834. Oblong 8vo. + [*Ibid.*] 1835. 17013

END OF VOLUME FOUR.

A DICTIONARY OF BOOKS

RELATING TO AMERICA.

OSTA RICA. Coup d'œil sur la République de Costa Rica. *Paris.* 1849. 8vo. Map. 17015

Der Freistaat Costa Rica, in Mittel-Amerika und seine Wichtigkeit für den Welthandel, den Ackerbau und die Kolonisation. Nach dem Französischen des F. M. bearbeitet, mit einem Anhang und 1 Karte versehen von Freiherrn A. v. Bülow. *Berlin: Hempel.* 1850. 8vo, pp. xiv, 88. 17016

Informe del secretario de estado en los departmentos de hacienda, guerra, marina, y caminos, presentado a las camaras legislativas de 1865. *San José: imprenta nacional.* [1866?] Sm. folio. 17017

République de Costa-Rica. Notice statistique et catalogue. Exposition universelle de 1867. *Paris: imp. Ve Bouchard-Huzard.* 1868. 8vo, pp. 18. 17018

[COSTANSO (M.)] Diario Historico de los Viages de mar y tierra hechos al norte de California, de orden del Virrey de Nueva España Marques De Croix y por direccion de D. Jose Galvaz. Executados por la tropa destinada à dicho objeto al mando de Gaspar de Portola, y por los Paquebotes S. Carlos y S. Antonio de orden del Exc. Sr. Virrey. *Mexico: En la imprenta del Gobierno.* 1776. Folio, pp. 56. 17019

Signed D. Miguel Costanso. Printed for private distribution. The following is probably a translation from this rare Spanish original:

COSTANSO. An Historical Journal of the Expeditions by Sea and Land to the North of California: in 1768, 1769, and 1770; when Spanish Establishments were first made at San Diego and Monte Rey. From a Spanish MS., translated by William Revely, Esq. Published by A. Dalrymple. *London: George Bigg.* 1790. 4to, pp. 76. 2 Maps. 17020

According to Rich, this is a translation of a Spanish *manuscript* presented to Dr. Dalrymple by Dr. Robertson. The rarity of the original may have rendered it necessary to cause a transcript to be made; according to the "Monthly Review," the translator has enriched it with notes and two maps.

COSTE (John Francis). Oratio Habita in capitolio Gulielmopolitano In Comitiis Universitatis Virginiæ, Die XII Junii M.DCC.LXXXII. Dùm favente Gallorum Ducum & Militum frequentiâ, Medicæ Cooptationis Laureâ donabatur Christianissimi Regis Exercitûs Archiater, Joannes-Franciscus Coste, Saluberrimarum Medicinæ Facultatum Parisiensis Alumnus, Valentinæ Doctor, Pennsylvaniensis Doctor Honorarius; Regiarum Medicinæ Societatum Londinensis, Edimburg., Paris. Regii Lotharingorum Medicorum Collegii Honorarius; è Regiis Scientiarum, Artium & Litterarum Academiis Nanceianâ, Lugdunensi, Divionensi; ex Humanâ Societate Philadelphiensi; Societatis Philosophicæ Americanæ Socius; Arcis & Militaris Nosocomii Caleti, Navaliumque Regis Exercituum Medicus. . *Lugduni Batavorum.* 1783. 8vo, 3 l., pp. 103. BA. 17021

See "Hist. Mag.," IV. 90; VII. 327.

[COSTELLO (J. M.)] John M. Costello; or, the Beauty of Virtue, exemplified in an American Youth. *Baltimore: J. Murphy & Co.* 1869. 18mo, pp. 204. Portrait. 17022

COSTI (A. M.) Memoir on the Trent Affair. By Ans. Michelo Costi, Publicist of Venice, Italy. *Washington, D. C.: McGill & Witherow.* 1865. 8vo, pp. 23. H. 17023

Costume of America. *Philadelphia: G. S. Appleton.* 1851. 18mo. 17024

Reprinted in *Philadelphia: C. G. Henderson & Co.* 1852. A trifling affair for children.

Cotejo de la Conducta del Rey Felipe V. con la del Rey Britanico antes de la Convencion, año 1739. *Madrid: Antoine Marin.* 1739. 17025

Cotejo de la Conducta de S. M. con de el Rey Britanico, etc. His Catholic Majesty's Conduct compared with that of His Britannick Majesty, as well with regard to what happened before

the convention of the 14th Jan. of this year, 1739, as to what has been done since, until the publication of Reprisals and Declaration of War. Printed by authority at Madrid. *London: T. Cooper.* [1739.] 8vo, pp. 63. 17026

In Spanish and English, and relates principally to affairs in America

[COTES (H.)] An Enquiry into the Conduct of a late Right Honourable Commoner. *London.* 1766. 8vo, pp. 72. S.

By H. Cotes, assisted by R. Grenville The commoner was William Pitt.

COTHEAL (A. J.) A Grammatical Sketch of the Language spoken by the Indians of the Mosquito Shore. [n. p. n. d.] 8vo. 17028

COTHREN (W.) History of Ancient Woodbury, Connecticut, from the First Indian Deed in 1659 to 1854, including the Present Towns of Washington, in Southbury, Bethlem, Roxbury, and Part of Oxford and Middlebury. By William Cothren. ... *Waterbury, Conn.: Bronson Brothers.* 1854. 8vo, pp. xi, 9–833, viii. Portrait and Plates. B. 17029

See Woodbury, Conn.

COTOGNO (Ott). Nuovo itinerario delle poste per tutto il mondo, aggiuntovi il modo di scrivere a tutte le parti. *Milano.* 1616. 16mo. 17030

Includes "Relatione de viaggi per l'Europa, Asia et Africa." Libri's copy sold, in 1847, for thirty francs.

COTTEN (E. R.) Life of the Hon. Edward Macon, of North-Carolina ... his Public Life; his Private Life. By Edward R. Cotten, of N. C. *Baltimore.* 1840. 12mo, pp. 272. S. 17031

COTTER (R.) Sketches of Bermuda, or Somers' Islands. By Richard Cotter, Purser R. N. *London: E. Wilson.* 1828. 8vo, pp. 69. Map and Plates. 17032

COTTEREL (F. F.) Esquisse historique des principaux événemens arrivées à Saint Domingue depuis l'incendie du Cap jusqu' a l'expulsion de Southonax; leurs causes, leurs effects. Situation actuelle de cette colonie et moyens d'y rétablir la tranquillité. A la Chine, on punit le mandarin d'une province qui s'est revoltée, parce que c'est toujours à sa mauvaise conduite qu'on attribue les écarts du peuple. ... J. J. Rosseau. Par Francois Frédéric Cotterel. *A Paris: de l'imprimerie de Christophe Jean Gelé. An* VI. [1798.] 8vo, pp. x, 68. P. 17033

A lively and interesting sketch of the dissensions between the blacks and mulattoes, etc., at St. Domingo. The author was a physician. *See* Quérard.

COTTINEAU (D. L.) Geographical Compilations; being an Accurate Description of all the Kingdoms, Republics, and States of the Known World, arranged in a Catechetical Form. Compiled by D. L. Cottineau. *Baltimore.* 1806. 2 vols., 12mo.

COTTING (Benjamin Eddy). Statistics of Consumption in Roxbury ... . *Boston.* 1854. 8vo, pp. 24. BA. 17035

COTTING (J. R.) Geology of Georgia; being the Result of a Geological and Agricultural Survey of the State, ... in 1836. ... Volume I. *Milledgeville: Park and Rogers.* 1841. 4to pp. 8. B. 17036

[COTTING (Uriah).] The Boston and Roxbury Mill Corporation. [Signed] Uriah Cotting, Boston, Jan. 1818. [n. p. n. d.] 8vo, pp. 20. 17037

COTTON (Alfred Johnson). Cotton's Keepsake. Poems on Various Subjects, By Rev. Judge A. J. Cotton ... [with] Autobiographical Sketch, ... and a Condensed History of the Early [Indiana] Settlements ... . *Cincinnati: Applegate & Co.* 1858. 12mo, pp. 526. Portrait. C., H. 17038

COTTON (Anne) An Account of Our Late Troubles in Virginia. Written in 1676, by Mrs. An Cotton, of Q. Creeke. Published from the Original Manuscript, in the Richmond (Va.) Enquirer, of 12 Sept. 1804. *Washington: Printed by Peter Force.* 1835. 8vo, pp. 11. G. 17039

Forms No. 9, Vol. I., of Peter Force's "Tracts."

[COTTON (E.)] The Peculiar Treasure of the Almighty King Opened, and the Jewels that are made up in it Exposed, at Boston Lecture, July 14, 1726. Whereof one is more particularly exhibited in the character of Mrs. E. Cotton, who was laid up a few days before. *Boston: D. Henchman.* 1726. 8vo.

COTTON (H.) The Typographical Gazetteer, attempted by the Rev. Henry Cotton ... . *Oxford: Clarendon Press.* MDCCCXXV. 8vo, pp. xvi, 219. BA. + Second Edition, corrected and much enlarged. *Oxford: University Press.* MDCCCXXXI. 8vo, pp. xviii, 393. BA. + Second Series. *Oxford: Clarendon Press.* MDCCC.LXVI. 8vo, pp. xvi, 376, (1). BA. 17041

The number of American places cited in the Second Series is very large, and pp. 243–308 are devoted to a monograph on the newspaper press in the United States. The author's "List of Editions of the Bible, and parts thereof, ... *Oxford.* 1821." + "Second Edition *Oxford.* MDCCCLII." 8vo contains some account of American Bibles.

[COTTON (J.)] An Abstract of the Lawes of New England, as they are now Established. *London: F. Coles & W. Ley.* 1641. 4to, pp. 15, 2. 17042

The first printed collection of laws for New England. *See* "Mass. Historical Collections," Vol. VIII, Third Series, "Mr. Gray's Account of the Early Laws of Massachusetts." Reprinted in Force's "Tracts," III.; "Mass. Hist. Soc. Collections," Vol. V., First Series.

COTTON. An | Abstract | of | Laws and Government. | Wherein as in a Mirrour may be seen | the wisdom & perfection of the Government of | Christs Kingdome. | Accomodable to any State or form of | Government in the world, that is not Antichri- | stian or Tyrannicall. | Collected and digested into the ensuing Method, by | that Godly, Grave, and Judicious Divine, Mr. John | Cotton, of Boston in New-England, in his Life-time, | and presented to the generall Court of the Massachusets. | And now published after his death, by | William Aspinwall. | *London,* | *Printed by M. S. for Livewel Chapman, and are to be sold* | *at the Crown in Popes-head Alley,* 1655. | 4to, 3 l., pp. 35, 2. J.C.B., W. 17043

Reprinted in "Mass. Hist. Soc. Colls.," X. 173–187.

COTTON. Answer to Master Roger Williams. Edited by J. L. Dinman. *Providence, R. I.* 1867. 4to, pp. 240. 17044

"Narragansett Club Publications," II. 1–240.

COTTON. The | Bloudy Tenent, | washed, | And made white in the bloud of the | Lambe: being discussed and discharged of | bloud-guiltinesse by just Defence. | Wherein | The great Questions of this present time are | handled, viz. How farre Liberty of Conscience | ought to be given to those that truly feare God? And how farre | restrained to turbulent and pestilent persons, that not one- | ly raze the foundation of Godliness, but disturb the Civill | Peace where they live? Also how farre the Magistrate may pro- | ceed in the duties of the first Table? And that all the Magistrates | ought to study the word and will of God, that they may frame | their Government according to it. | Discussed | As they are alledged from divers Scriptures, out of | the Old and New Testament. Wherein also the practise of | Princes is debated, together with the Judgement of An- | cient and late Writers of most precious esteeme. | Whereunto is added a Reply to Mr. Williams | Answer, to Mr. Cottons Letter. | By John Cotton Batchelor in Divinity, and | Teacher of the Church of Christ at Boston in New-England. | *London,* | *Printed by Matthew*

Symmons for Hannah Allen, at the Crowne | *in Popes-Head-Alley.* 1647. | 4to, Title, pp. 195, 144. BA., C., J.C.B. 17045

A rare volume. Mr. J. A. Rice's copy sold for $62 50 The following is partly made up from Cott

COTTON Wholesome Severity ec nc'led with | Christian Liberty, | or the True Resolution of a present Con- | troversie concerning Liberty of | Conscience. Here you have the Question stated, the middle | way betwixt Popish Tyrannie and Schismatizing | Liberty approved, and also confirmed from | Sc ipture, and the testimon'es of Divines, | yea, of whole Churches | T'e Chief Argument E p 'on | used in The | Bloudy Tenent, The Compassionate Samaritane | M S. to A. S. &c., examined. | Eight Distinctions added for qualifying and | clearing the whole matter. | And in conclusion, a Paraenetick to the five Apo- | logists f r choosing Accommodation rather | than toleration. | Imprimatur. Ia. Crawford. December 16, 1644. | *London: Printed for Christopher Meredith, and are to be sold at the Signe of the Crane in Pauls Churchyard.* 1645. | 4to, pp. 40. J.C.B. 17046

COTTON A Briefe | Expos tion | of the whole Book of | Canticles, o , | Song of Solomon: | Lively describing the Estate of th Church | in all the Ages, thereof, both Jewish | and Christian, to this day. | And modestly point ng at the G o o s- | nesse of the restored Estate of the Church of the | Jewes, and the happy accesse of the Gentiles, in the | approa hing dayes f Reforma tion, when the | Wall of Partition shall be taken away. | A Work very usefull and sea onable o ev y C |s an, b t especially such as endea our and thirs | afte the etling f C urch and S ate a cord ng t | the Rule and Patterne of the Word of God. | By John Cotton. | *London. Philip Nevil.* 1642. | 12mo, pp. 264. B., C. + *London: Charles Green.* 1648 Sm. 8vo, Title, pp. 256 J.C.B 17047

COTTON. A Brief | Exposition | With Practical | Observations | Upon the whole Book of | Canticles, | Never before Printed | By that late Pious and Worthy Di- | vine Mr. John Cotton Pastor of | Boston in New England | Published by Anthony Tuckney D D. Master | f Saint Johns College in Cambridge. | *London: Printed by T. R & E M for Ralph Smith* | ... 1655. | Sm. 8vo, 7 l., pp. 238. J.C.B. 17048

A distinct treatise differing in arrangement, and containing nearly twice as much as the former.

COTTON A Briefe | Expos ion | with | Practicall Observations | upon | The Whole Book | of | Ecclesiastes. | By that late pious and worthy Divine,|Mr. John Cotton,|Pastor of Boston, in New-England |Published,|By Anthony Tuckney, D.D.|...|*London, Printed by T. C. for Ralph Smith* 1654.| 4 l., pp. 277. B, BA C., J.C.B. + The Second Impression, Corrected. *London, printed by W. W. for Ralph Smith* 1657. 8vo, Title, 3 l., pp. 258 [for 260]. B., J.C.B. 17049

COTTON. By the Reverend Old Mr. John Cotton, at Salem, June, 1636. ... a Wo d of Instruction [beginning] with some word of Confession [The Church Covenant a Perpetual Covenant. No title-page.] 8vo pp. 40. BA. 17050

COTTON. A Censure of that Learned and Rever d Man of God, Mr. John Cotton, lately of New-England, upon the way of Mr. Henden, of Benenden, in Kent, a brief and solid Exercitation concerning the coercive power of the Magistrate in matters of Religion, with Mr. Henden's animadversions on Mr. Ilmestone's Epistle, revised and chastized. *London. Printed by J. G. for John Stafford.* 1656. 4to, pp. 56. J.C.B. 17051

COTTON. Certain Queries Tending to Accommodation and Communion of Presbyterian & Congregationall Churches. By John Cotton .. *London.* 1654. 8vo, pp. (2), 22. B 170 2

COTT N. Christ the Fountaine of Life; or Sundry Choyce Sermons on part of the Fift Chapter of the First Epistle of St. John. *London Robert Ibbetson.* 1651. 4to, 3 l., pp. 356.

The orig nal autograph manuscript is in the Library of Bowdoin College.

COTTON. Th |Churche, Resurrection,|or the|Opening of the|Fift and sixt verses of the 20th. Chap.|of the|Revelat on | By that Learned and Reverend,|Iohn Cotton|Teacher to the Church of Boston in|Nevv England, and there corrected|by his own hand.|*London.*|*Printed by R. O. & G. D. for Henry Overton,|and are to be sold at his Shop, in Popes Head-Alley* |1642.| 4to, pp 30. B., BA., J.C.B. 17054

COTTON. A Conference Mr. John Cotton held at Boston With the Elders of New-England .. . With The Difference between the Christian and Antichristian Church. Written by Francis Cornwell ... . *London.* 1646. 8vo, pp. (23), 57, (15), 80. B. 17055

"The Difference" ha a eparate paging and title-page; "A D scription," etc *See* Cornwell (F.) Another edition: *Prin ed for Thomas Banks and are to be sold at his Shop in Black Fryers on the top of Bridwell Staires.* 1646. pp. 14.

COTTON. The|Controversie|Concerning|Liberty of Conscience|in|Matters of Religion,|Truly stated, and distinctly and plainly handled,|By Mr. John Cotton of Boston in New-England,|By way of answer to some Arguments to|the contrary sent unto him.|Wherein you have, against all cavills of|turbulent spirits, clearly manifested, wherein li-|berty of conscience in matters of Religion ought|to be permitted, and in what cases it ought|not, by the said Mr. Cotton.|*London: Printed by Robert Austin, for Thomas Banks, and|are to be sold at Mrs. Breaches Shop in West-|minster-Hall.* 1649 | 4to, pp. 14. J.C.B. 17056

The arguments alluded to in this very rare t act are given entire at the commencement, and are entitled "Scripture and Reasons, written long since by a prisoner in Newgate," etc., being the same tract alluded to by Mr. Williams in "The Bloudy Tenant," as having been written in milk on the paper which formed the stopper to the bottle containing the prisoner s daily supply.

COTTON. A|Coppy|of|a Letter|of Mr. Cotton of|Boston, in New England, sent|in answer of certaine Objections|made against their Discipline|and Orders there, directed|to a Friend.|VVith the Questions propounded to|such as are admitted to the Church-|fellowship, and the Covenant|it Selfe. *Printed in the yeare* 1641. Sm. 4to, pp. 6. J.C.B., H. 17057

COTTON. The Covenant of Gods free Grace ... . By ... Mr. John Cotton, Teacher of the Church at Boston in New-England. Whereunto is added, A Profession of Faith, made by ... Mr. John Davenport, in New-England, at his admission into one of the Churches there. .. *London: Printed for John Hancock.* 1645. 4to, Title, pp. (2), 40. H. 17058

COTTON. The Covenant of Grace, Discovering The Great Work of a Sinner's Reconciliation to God, by John Cotton, Teacher of the Church at Boston, N. E. Whereunto are Added, Certain Queries tending to Accommodadation [*sic*] between the Presbyterian and Congregationall Churches. Also, A Discussion of the Civill Magistrates Power in matters of Religion. By some Elders. *London: J. Allen.* 1655. 8vo, pp. (34), 198, (2), 22, (2), 75, (1). B. 17059

The title-page was printed to cover three pamphlets published the year before: Cotton's "New Covenant," his "Certain Queries," and "The Result of a Synod at Cambridge;" for the latter, *see* Cambridge, *Mass.* "The Epistle Dedicatory" to "Mrs. Catharine Hodson," is signed "W. Retchforde." An address "To the Reader" is signed "Tho: Allen." For other editions, *see* "A Treatise," etc., *infra.*

[COTTON.] A|Description|of the|Spirituall Temple:|or the|Spouse|Prepared for the|Lambe,|The Lord|Jesus.|Written by

Francis Cornwell,|a Minister and Servant of Jesus, the|Christ, for the benefit of poore|distressed consciences, in|City and Countrey,|*London,*|*Printed by John Dawson* 1646.| Sm. 8vo, 4 l., pp. 48. 17060

Though the name of Francis Cornwell appears on the title, he wrote nothing but the "Epistle to the Reader," pp. 5.

COTTON A Discourse about Civil Government. *See* [Davenport (John)].

COTTON. The|Doctrine of the|Church,|To which is committed the Keys of the|Kingdome of Heaven.|Wherein is demonstrated by way of Question and|Answere, what a visible Church is according to the order|of the Gospel: and what Officers, Members, Worship and|Government Christ hath ordained in the New Testament.|By that Reverend and learned Divine. Mr. Jo. Cotton, B.D. and Teacher of the Church at Boston, in New England.|*London: Benjamin Allen.* 1643.| 4to, pp. 13. + The Second Edition, printed according to a more Exact Copy, ... *London: Benj. Allen and Sam: Satterthwaite.* 1644. 4to, Title, pp. 14. + The Third Edition: More exactly corrected. ... . *London: Ben: Allen.* 1644. 4to, Title, pp. 14.

[COTTON.] An Endeavour after the reconcilement of that long debated and much lamented difference between the Presbyterians and Independents, about Church Government, in a Discourse touching the Jews' Synagogue, attributed to John Cotton, of New England. *London.* 1648. 4to. 17062

This title is from one of Thorpe's catalogues, No. 161.

COTTON. An|Exposition|upon|The Thirteenth Chapter|of the|Revelation.|By that Reverend an Eminent ser-|vant of the Lord, Mr. John Cotton, Teacher to|the Church at Boston in New-England.|Taken from his mouth in Short-writing, and some|part of it corrected by Himselfe soon after the Prea-|ching thereof, and all of it since viewed over by a|friend to Him, and to the Truth; wherein some mi-|stakes were amended, but nothing of the sence al-|tered.|*London, Printed by M. S. for Livewel Chapman, at the Crown|in Popes head Alley,* 1655.| 4to, 5 l., pp. 262, (6). B., BA., C. + [Another Edition.] *London, Printed for Tim. Smart, at the Hand and Bible in|The Old Bayly.* 1656.| 4to, 5 l., pp. 262, Table, 3 l. J.C.B. 17063

COTTON. Gods|Mercie|mixed with his|Ivstice, or, his

Peoples|Deli |verance in time of d nger.|Laid open in severall Sermons.|By that learned and judicious Divine, and fa th |full M er of Jesus Christ|John Cotton.|*London: Edward Brewster, and Henry Hood.* 1641.| 4to, 4 l., pp. 135. BA, J C B.

COTTON. Gods|Promise|to his|Plantation.|2 Sam. 7. 10.| Moreover I will appoint a place for my people Israel,|and I will plant them, that they may dwell in a|place of their owne, and move no more.|As it was delivered in a Sermon,|By Iohn Cotton, B D |and Preacher of Gods|word in Boston.| [Motto] *London,|Printed by William Jones for John Bellamy, and|are to be solde at the three Golden Lyons by the|Royall Exchange.* 1630.| 4to, 3 l., pp. 20. C., J.C.B. + *Reprinted at Boston in New-England|by Samuel Green; and are to be sold by John Usher. Anno* |1686. 4to, Title, pp. 20. B., BA., W. 17065

"This sermon was preached by the Rev. author, to Mr. Jno. Winthrop, etc., at Southampton, upon his solemn far well to them in their voyage to New England." There is another edition, which I have not seen.

COTTON The|Grovnds and Ends| f the|Bap sme|of the|Children|of the|Faithfvll |Op ned|In a famil ar Di course by way of a|Dialogue, or Brotherly Conference. By The Learned and Faithfull Minister of Christ, John Cotton, Teacher of the Church of Boston in New-England. *London: printed by R. C. for Andrew Crooke.* 1647.| 4to, Title, pp. (8), 196. B., J.C.B.

An "Epistle to the Reader" is signed "Tho. Goodwin."

COTTON. The|Keyes|Of the Kingdom of|Heaven,|and| Power thereof,|according to the|VVord of God |By|That Learned and Judicious Divine,|Mr. Iohn Cotton, Teacher of the Church|at Boston in New England,|Tending to reconcile some present differences about|Discipline.|Published|By|Tho. Goodwin.|Philip Nye.|*London, Printed by M. Simmons for Henry Overton, and are to be sold at his|Shop entring into Popes-head Alley, out of Lombard-street,* 1644.| 4to, Title, 5 l., pp. 59. 1644.| 4to, Title, 5 l, pp. 59. + The second time Imprinted. [*Ibid.*] J.C.B. 17067

COTTON. The Keyes Of the Kingdom of Heaven and Power thereof, according to the Word of God. By That Learned and Judicious Divine, Mr. Iohn Cotton, ... *Boston: reprinted by Tappan and Dennet.* 1843. 12mo pp. iv, 108. BA. + *Boston: T. K. Whipple & Co.* 1852. 12mo, pp. iv, 108. 17068

COTTON. A Letter of Mr. John Cotton's, Teacher of the Church in Boston, in New England, to Mr. Williams a Preacher there Wherein is shewed, that those ought to be received into the Church who are godly, though they doe not see, nor expressly bewaile all the pollutions in Church fellowship, Ministery, Worship, Government. , *Printed at London, for Benjamin Allen* 1643. Sm. 4to, pp 13. J C.B. 17069

Reprinted by the Hansard Knollys Society, and included in the "Narragansett Club Publications," I 285-332. Sold at Puttick's, in 1860, for £1 2s. 6d

COTTON. A Modest and Cleare|Answer|to|Mr. Ball's Discourse of|set formes of Prayer.|Set forth in a most seasonable time, when|this Kingdome is now in Consultation about|Matters of that Nature, and so many godly|Long after the Resolution on that Point.|Written by the Reverend and Learned John Cotton|B.D. and Teacher of the Church of Christ at|Boston in new England.|*London:|Printed by R. O and G D for Henry Overton|in Popes head-Alley.* 1642.| 4to, 2 l., pp. 49, 1 l. C., J.C.B. 17070

There is another ed t n. *London* [n. d.] 8vo, pp. 90. B

CO TON. Nashauanittue Meninnunk|wutch|Mukkiesog,| Wusse èmumun wutch Sog-kodtunganash|Naneeswe Testamentsash; |wutch|Ukkesitchippooonganoo Ukketeahogkounooh.|Negonáe wussukhùmun ut Englishmánne Unnon-|toowaonganit, nashpe ne ánue, wunnegenùe|Nohtompeantog.|Noh asoowèsit|John Cotton.|Kah yeuyeu qushkinnúmun en Indiane |Unnontoo-|waonganit wutch oonenehikqunàout Indiane|Mukkiesog,|Nashpe|Grindal Rawson.|Wunnaunchemookáe Nohtompeantog ut kenugke|Indianog.| ... | ... | 1 Pet. 2. 2.|*Cambridge:|Printeuoop nashpe Samuel Green, kah|Bartholomew Green.* 1691.| 12mo, pp. 13. BA. 17071

This is "Spiritual Milk for American Babes."

COTTON. The New Covenant, or, ... manner of the giving and receiving of the Covenant of Grace to the Elect. ... The substance of sundry Sermons preached by Mr. Cotton At Boston in New-England ... . *London.* 1654. Sm. 8vo, Title, pp. 198.

COTTON. Of the|Holinesse|of|Church-Members.|By John Cotton, Teacher of|the Church of Christ in|Boston in|New-England.|*London:|Printed by F. N. for Hanna Allen, and are to be sold at|the Crown in Popes-head Alley.* 1650.| 4to, Title, pp. 2, 95. B., W. 17073

COTTON. The|Powring|ovt of the|Seven Vials:|Or an|Exposition, of the|16. Chapter of the Revelation, with|an Application of it to our Times.|Wherein is revealed Gods powring out|the full Vials of his fierce wrath |1. Upon the lowest and basest sort of Catholicks.|2. Their Worship and Religion.|3. Their Priests and Ministers.|4. The House of Austria, and Popes Supremacy.|5. Episcopall Government.|6. Their Euphrates, or the streame of their Supportments.|7. Their grosse Ignorance, and blind Superstitions.|Very fit and necessary for this|Present Age|Preached in sundry Sermons at Boston in New-England:|By the Learned and Reverend Iohn Cotton,|BB. of Divinity, and Teacher to the Church there|*London,|Printed for R. S. and are to be sold at Henry Overtons shop|in Popes-head Alley.* 1642.| 4to, 1 l., pp. 35, 24, 24, 43, 16, 14, 19. + *London: Printed for R. S., and are to be sold at Henry Overton's Shop in Popes Head Alley.* 1645. 4to, 2 l., pp. 156. C., J.C.B. 17074

[COTTON.] The Planter's Plea: or the Grounds of Plantations Examined, and usual objections answered, together with a manifestation of the Causes moving such as have lately undertaken a Plantation in New England, for the satisfaction of those that question the Lawfulnesse of that action. *London: William Jones.* 1630. 4to. 17075

"The agreement in name of printer, date, and subject, induce us to attribute this rare tract to the author of the last (our No. 17065), while the same agreement contributes to substantiate the correctness of its date." Title and note from one of Puttick and Simpson's catalogues.

COTTON. A Practicall Commentary, or an Exposition with Observations, Reasons, and Vses upon the First Epistle Generall of John. By that Pious and Worthy Divine, Mr. John Cotton, Pastor of Boston in New England. *London: Thomas Parkhurst.* M.DC.LVI. Folio, 4 l., pp. 431. J.C.B. + [Second Edition.] *London: Thomas Parkhurst.* M. DC. LVIII. Folio.

COTTON. Reply to Mr. [Roger] Williams, his Examination. *London: Hannah Allen.* 1647. Sm. 4to, pp. 144. M. 17077

With "The Bloudy Tenent," etc. *London,* 1647; but, being separately paged, is sometimes found separately. Reprinted in the "Narragansett Club Publications," v. 2.

COTTON. The|Saints|Support & Comfort,|in|The Time of Distress and Danger,|with divers other Treatises.|Delivered in severall Sermons upon Di-|vers Texts of Scripture.|By that Learned and Judicious|Divine John Cotton, of Boston|in New-

England.|*London,|Printed and are to be sold by Thomas Basset in| St Dunstans Church-yard in Fleet-street.* 1658.| Sm. 4to, Title, pp. 135. H. 17078

COTTON. Sermon preached by the Reverend Mr. John Cotton ... at Salem, 1636; To which is Prefixed, a Retraction of his former Opinion concerning Baptism. *Boston.* 1713 16mo, pp. 40. B. 17079

COTTON. Severall|Qvestions|of|Serious and necessary Consequence,|Propounded by the|Teaching Elders,|Unto M. Iohn Cotton of Boston|in New-England.|With|His respective Answer to each Question.|*London,|Printed for Thomas Banks, and are to bee sold in Black-|Friers on the top of Bride-well Staires, and in West-|minster Hall, at the signe of the Seale.* 1647.| 4to, pp. (2), 10. 17080

COTTON. Singing|of|Psalmes|a Gospel-Ordinance.|Or |a Treatise,|Wherein are handled these foure Particulars.|1. Touching the Duty it selfe.|2. Touching the Matter to be Sing.|3. Touching the Singers.|4 Touching the Manner of Singing.|By John Cotton, Teacher of the|Church at Boston in New-England.|*London,|Printed by M. S. for Hannah Allen, at the Crowne|in Popes-Head-Alley: and John Rothwell at the|Sunne and Fountaine in Pauls-Church-yard.*|1647.| Sm. 4to, Title, 1 l., pp. 72. H. + *London,|Printed for J. R. at the Sunne and Fountaine in Pauls-|Church-yard: and H. A. at the Crowne in Popes-|Head Alley.* 1650.| 4to, Title, pp. 72. J.C.B. 17081

COTTON. Mr. Cotton's Letter lately printed, examined and answered by Roger Williams of Providence in New-England. *London, Imprinted in the Yeere* 1644. 4to, pp. 47 17082

[COTTON.] Some Treasure fetched out of Rubbish; or Three short but seasonable Treatises [found in a heap of scattered papers] concerning the imposition and use of Significant Ceremonies in the Worship of God. *Printed in the year* 1660. 4to.

"Mr. John Cotton, famous in both Englands, was the known author of the first Discourse, and (as its verily believed) of the second also." — *Preface*

COTTON. Spiritual Milk for Babes. ... *London.* 1668. 12mo, pp. (2), 12. 17084

Same, in English and Indian. *See* No. 17071.

COTTON. A|Treatise|of the|Covenant|of|Grace,|As it is dispensed to the Elect Seed,|effectually unto Salvation.|Being| The substance of divers Sermons preached upon|Act. 7. 8. by

that eminently holy and judi-|cious man of God, Mr. John Cotton, Teacher|of the Church at Boston, in N. E.|The second Ed t , by a C py far la ger than the|former; and Corrected also by the Authors own hand.|This Copy was fitted for the Press, by Mr ho |Allen Minister in Norwich.|*London,|Printed by Ja. Cottrel, for John Allen, at the|Rising-Sun in Pauls Church-yard.*|1659.| 16mo, 12 l, pp. 250, (2). B., C. 17085

COTTON. A|Treatise|of the|Covenant|of|Grace,|As it is dispensed to the Elect Seed,|effectually unto|Salvation |Being| The Substance of divers Sermons preached upon|Act. 7. 8. by that eminently holy and judicious|man of God, Mr. John Cotton, Teacher of the|Church at Boston in N. E.|The Third Edition, Corrected, and very much|Enlarged, by the Authors own Hand.|*London,|Printed f Peter Parker, in Popes-head-Alley,|next Cornhill,* 1671.| Sm. 8vo, 8 l., pp. 223. BA., C.

For the first edition, *see* No. 17058.

COTTON. The way of Life |Or,|Gods VVay|and Course,| in bringing the Soule into,|keeping it in, and carrying it on, in| the wayes of life and peace.|Laid downe in foure severall Treatises on foure|Texts of Scripture.|viz. The pouring out of the Spir t, on Zach. 12. 10, 11, &c.|Sins deadly wound, on Acts 2. 37.|The Christians Charge, on Prov. 4. 23.|The life of Faith, on Gal. 2. 19, 20|By that learned and judicious Divine, and faith-|ful Minister of Iesus Christ,|John Cotton.|*London,|Printed by M. F. for L. Fawne, and S Gellibrand, at the Brasen |Serpent in Pauls Church-yard.* 1641.| 4to, 4 l., pp. 481. B.

COTTON. Treatise of Mr. Cotton's, clearing certaine Doubts concerning Predestination, together with an Examination thereof; Written by William Twisse, D.D. Pastor of N wbury, in New England. *London: Printed by J. D. for Andrew Crook.* 1646. 4to, 4 l., pp. 288, 4 l. 17088

COTTON. The Trve Constitvtion of a particular visible Church, proved by Scripture, wherein is briefly Demonstrated by Questions and Answers what Officers, Worship, and Gouernment Christ hath ordained in his Church. *London: Printed for Samuel Scatterthwaite.* 1642. 4to, pp. 13. 17089

COTTON. The|Way of the Churches|of Christ|in New England.|Or,|the VVay of Churches|walking in Brotherly equalitie, or co-|ordination, without Subjection of|one Church to another.|Measured and examined by the|Golden Reed of the

Sanctuary. | Containing a full Declaration of the Church-| way in all Particulars. | By Mr. J. Cotton, Teacher of the | Church at Boston in New-England. | Published according to Order. *London, | Printed by Matthew Simmons in Aldersgatestreet.* | 1645. | 4to, 4 l., pp. 116, (4) BA., C. + *London, | Printed by Matthew Simmons in Aldersgate streete.* | 1645 | 8vo, 4 l., pp 5, 116, 3.

COTTON The Way of Congregational Churches Cleared; In two Treatises In the former, From the Historical Aspersions of Mr Robert Baylie in his Book called, (A Dissuasive from the Errors of the Time.) In the latter, From some Contradictions of Vindiciæ Clavium And from, Some Misconstructions of Learned Mr. Rutherford, in his Book intituled (The due Right of Presbyteries) By Mr. John Cotton, sometimes Preacher at Boston in Lincolnshire, and now Teacher of the Church at Boston in New England. To which is prefixed an Epistle Pacificatory to the Brethren dissenting from this Way, by Nathaniel Holmes Imprimatur, John Bachiler, January 1 1647. *London, Printed by Matthew Simmons, for John Bellamie*, 1648. 4to Title, pp. (9), 104, 44. H. 17091

The following is the title of one of the works referred to above: "Vindiciæ Clavium: or, A Vindication of the Keyes of the Kingdome of Heaven, into the hands of the right Owners. Being some Animadversions upon a Tract of Mr. I. C. ... As also upon another Tract of his, called, The way of the Churches of New-England ... . By an earnest well-wisher to the Truth. *London: Peter Whaley* 1645." Sm. 4to, 2 l., pp (19), 90. H The original edition was a broadside. *See* Hooker (T.)

C[OTTON] (J[ohn]). Poem occasioned by the Death of Jno. Alden, of Doxborough, who died Sept. 12 1687. Written by J. C. *Portsmouth, reprinted.* 1806. N. 17092

COTTON (John), *of Newtown* Funeral Sermon preached after the Death of Mr. Nathanael Cotton, who died July 3, 1729 *Boston.* 1729. 8vo, pp. 34. M. 17093

COTTON. God's awful Determination against a People, that will not obey H's Voice ... . A Sermon Preach'd .. In Boston, Feb 8. 1728. After Repeated Shocks Of the Earthquake. By John Cotton ... . *Boston: Printed by Gamaliel Rogers, for Samuel Gerrish and Thomas Hancock.* 1728. 8vo, 2 l., pp. 42.

The preface is signed "Benjamin Colman."

COTTON. A Holy Fear of God, And His Judgments. ... A Sermon Preach'd at Newtown, November 3. 1727. On a Day

of Fasting ... Occasion'd by the Terrible Earthquake ... . By John Cotton ... . With ... the Impressions made on the Inhabitants of Haverhill, &c. ... *Boston: B. Green, jun. for S. Gerrish.* M.DCC.XXVII. 8vo, pp. (4), xvi, 24, 7. BA. 17095

The impressions is signed "John Brown."

COTTON. The Ministers of Christ should be Speedy and Earnest in speaking to Young People. Four Sermons ... to a Society of Young Men, in Newtown ... . By John Cotton ... . *Boston: John Phillips.* 1729. 12mo, Title, pp. iv, 85. BA.

COTTON. Ministers of the Gospel should speak, not as pleasing Men, But God ... . A Sermon Preach'd at the Ordination of the Rev. Ward Cotton, At Hampton, in New-Hampshire, June 19th. 1734. Where he was Ordain'd a Colleague Pastor with the Rev. Mr. Nathanael Gookin ... . By John Cotton, A.M. Minister of the Gospel in Newtown. *Boston: Printed by B. Green.* 1734. 8vo, Title, 2 l., pp. 23. BA.

COTTON. Two Sermons preach'd at Dorchester, on the Lord's-Day, April 9, 1727. By John Cotton, M.A. Pastor of the Church of Christ in Newtown. Publish'd at the repeated Desire of many that heard them. With a Preface by the Rev. Mr. Danforth, Pastor of the Church in Dorchester. *Boston: Printed by B. Green, jun. for S. Gerrish, at the lower end of Cornhill.* 1727. 12mo, 10 l., pp. 63. J.C.B. 17098

COTTON. Wisdom, Knowledge, and the Fear of God recommended to Rulers and People. A Sermon Preach'd in the Audience of His Honour Spencer Phips, Esq; Lieutenant-Governour and Commander in Chief, The Honourable His Majesty's Council, and House of Representatives Of the Province of the Massachusetts-Bay in New-England, May 30th. 1753, Being the Day for the Election of His Majesty's Council for the Province. By John Cotton, M.A. Pastor of the Church in Newtown. *Boston, N. E.: Printed by John Draper.* 1753. 8vo, Half-Title, Title, pp. 42. B., C., G., W. 17099

Also: Two Sermons at the Lecture in Newtown, April, 29 and May 8, 1741. *Boston.* 1741. 16mo. W.

COTTON (J.), *of Plymouth and Halifax.* The general Practice of the Churches of New-England, relating to Baptism, vindicated: or, some Essays on this Important Question, Whether the Practice of Persons owning or renewing the Covenant, and having Baptism for their Children without coming immediately

into full Communion, be warrantable? ... With some Letters ... . By John Cotton, A.M. of Plymouth. ... *Boston: Ezekiel Russell.* [1772.] 4to, 3 l., pp. 73. BA., W. 17100

COTTON. The General Practice of the Churches of New-England, Relating to Baptism, Further vindicated; Containing an Answer to the Rev. Chandler Robbins's Reply, Relative to this Question ... In Three Parts. By John Cotton ... . *Boston: Joseph Greenleaf.* 1773. 8vo, pp. 154, (1). BA., W.

COTTON. God's Call to His People ... . Two Sermons Preached at Plymouth, June 30. 1757. Being a Day of General Humiliation, Occasioned By the Drought and War By John Cotton (of Plymouth) A.M. ... *Boston. Printed by Benjamin Mecom.* 1757. 8vo, pp. 43. BA. 17102

COTTON. Seasonable Warning to these Churches. A Narrative of the Transactions at Middleborough, In the County of Plymouth, In settling a Minister [Silvanus Conant] in the Room of the Reverend Mr. Peter Thatcher, deceas'd. ... By John Cotton ... . *Boston: S. Kneeland and T. Green.* M,DCC,XLVI. 4to, pp. 38. B., BA. 17103

Also: A Sermon at Attleborough, Mass. upon a particular occasion, Jan. 9. 1746–7. *Boston.* 12mo. W. — The Separation of the Tares and Wheat reserved to the Day of Judgment. A Sermon ... . *Boston.* 1746. 12mo.

COTTON (J.) Vocabulary of the Massachusetts (or Natick) Indian Language. By Josiah Cotton. *Cambridge: Printed by E. W. Metcalf and Company.* 1829. 8vo, pp. 212. BA. 17104

Also included in the "Mass. Hist. Soc. Coll.," Vol. II., Third Series.

COTTON (R.) A Choice Narrative of Count Gondamor's Transactions during his Embassy in England. By ... Sir Robert Cotton ... . *London: John Garfield.* 1659. Portrait + *London: G. Smeeton.* 1820. 4to, pp. 54. B. 17105

Partly relates to Sir W. Raleigh and the Spanish designs in the West Indies. The reprint is one of "Smeeton's Hist. and Biogr. Tracts." A work which we have described as by Robert Clavel, Vol. IV., No. 13514, has been also attributed to Sir R. Cotton.

COTTON (R.) Cain's Lamentations over Abel, in Six Books ... the Third Edition. By Rowland Cotton. *New York: Printed by Wayland and Davis, for the Author.* 1795. 12mo, pp. 239. 17106

Also: An Artillery Election Sermon. 1706, which I have not seen.

[COTTON (Seaborn).] Breif summ of ye chief articles of ye X^n^ Faith — a Catechism. *Camb.* 1863. 8vo, pp. 36. 17107

This title is copied from T. Prince's MS. catalogue of his New England Library. I have met with no other notice of the pamphlet, which has probably perished. Also: An Artillery Election Sermon. 1673. The Rev. Seaborn Cotton was born at sea in 1633 while his parents were on their voyage to New England, and hence his unusual name, which appears Latinized in the "Harvard College Triennial Catalogue" as "Marigena Cotton."

COTTON (W.) Ministers ... . A Sermon Preach'd at the Ordination Of the Reverend Mr. John Brown, Pastor of the Second Church ... in Hingham. By Ward Cotton ... . *Boston: D. Gookin.* 1747. 8vo, pp. 30. BA. 17108

COTTON. The Condition and Prospects of American Cotton Manufactures in 1849–50. 8vo, pp. 29. H. 17109

The Cotton Crisis. *London.* 1857. 8vo. 17110

The Cotton Famine and the Lancashire Operatives. A Poem. By a Factory Girl. *Preston: Dobson.* 1862. 8vo. 17111

Cotton Fields and Cotton Factories. *London.* 1839. 16mo.

Cotton from the Pod to the Factory. *London.* 185–. 12mo.

Cotton is King. *See* [Christy (David)], Vol. IV., No. 12950.

Cotton Manufacture. Boston Memorial to Congress. *Boston.* 1846. 8vo. C. 17114

Cotton Manufacture. Statistics from the Seventh Annual Report of the Boston Board of Trade. *Boston: T. R. Marvin & Son.* 1861. pp. 16. 17115

The Cotton Plant. *New York: Sheldon & Co.* 1864. Sq. 12mo, pp. 16. 17116

The Cotton Question. A portion of the following Letter appeared in the Morning Herald of January 28, 1864. [n. p. n. d.] 8vo, pp. 30. 17117

Cotton Stealing. A Novel. ... *Chicago: John R. Walsh & Co.* 1866. 12mo, pp. 487. BA. 17118

Copyrighted by J. E. Chamberlain, — the author?

The Cotton Supply; a letter to John Cheetham, Esq., President of the Manchester Cotton-Supply Association. By a Fellow of the Royal Geographical Society. *London: Robert Hardwicke.* 1861. 8vo, pp. 40. C. 17119

The Cotton Supply Reporter. No. 1. *Manchester Cotton Supply Association, August,* 1858. 4to, pp. 8. Continued. BA.

The numbers published during the Southern rebellion are, of course, of special interest.

Cotton Trade. Letter from the Secretary of State, transmitting a statement respecting the Tariff Duties ... applicable to American Cotton. June 10, 1856. [n. p. n. d.] 8vo, pp. 21. (H. of R. Doc.) 17121

The Cotton Trade of India. Can India not Supply England with Cotton? *London: Spottiswood.* 1839. 8vo, pp. 19.

Cultivation and Supply of Cotton in South America. Report of Her Majesty's Commissioner. *London: Dalton & Lucy.* 1866. Folio, pp. viii. 17123

Introduction and early Progress of the Cotton Manufacture in the United States. ... *Boston: Little, Brown, and Co.* 1863. 8vo, pp. 108. B., P. 17124

Is Cotton "King?" Sources of Cotton Supply. [n. p. n. d.] 8vo, pp. 4. 17125

Letters from the Secretary of the Treasury, on the Cultivation, Manufacture, and Foreign Trade of Cotton. *Washington.* 1836. 8vo. 17126

New York Convention. Report on the Production and Manufacture of Cotton. *Boston: printed by J. F. & E. Buckingham.* 1832. 8vo, pp. 20. H. 17127

Remarks on the Growth of the Cotton Plant in Alabama. *Boston.* 1850. 17128

Report of a Committee of the Boston Board of Trade upon the Cotton Tax. *Boston.* 1867. 8vo, pp. 16. H. 17129

Report of the Special Committee of the Chamber of Commerce of the State of New York on the Confiscation of Cotton in the Southern States by the Government. *New York.* 1865. 8vo, pp. 12. 17130

Report of the Production and Manufacture of Cotton, [by a Convention of Friends of American Industry]. *Boston: printed by J. T. & E. Buckingham.* 1832. 8vo, pp. 20. B. 17131

Selections from the Testimony taken by the United States Revenue Commission in respect of Cotton as a source of National Revenue. (Appendix to Special Report, No. 3.) [*Washington*], *Treasury Department,* 1866. 8vo, pp. 63. 17132

Table of the Corresponding Prices of Cotton shipped from the United States and sold in London. *Charleston.* 1824. 12mo.

COUCH (P.) A Sermon ... at the Funeral of Rev. Daniel Thomas, Former Pastor of the ... Congregational Church of Abington, by Rev. Paul Couch ... Friday, January 8th, 1847. *Boston: J. E. Farwell & Co., Printers.* 8vo, pp. 16. 17134

COUCH. A Sermon, ... by the Rev. Paul Couch ... of Stonington, Conn. August 6th, 1863, being the Day ... for National Thanksgiving. *New York: Willard, Felt & Co.* 1863. 12mo, pp. 24. H. 17135

[COUES (S. Elliott).] Memoir of Rev. Nathan Parker, D.D. Late Pastor of the South Parish in Portsmouth, N. H. ... *Concord: Marsh, Capen and Lyon.* 1834. 8vo, pp. 28. H. 17136

[COUES.] Remarks on the Bunker-Hill Monument ... . By Elliott. ... *Portsmouth, N. H.: Printed by C. W. Brewster.* 1840. 8vo, pp. 12. H. 17137

COUES. United States Navy. What is its Use? By Samuel E. Coues. *Boston: American Peace Society.* [n. d.] pp. 8. H.

Also: War and Christianity; an Address before the American Peace Society ... May 23, 1842, ... *Boston: American Peace Society.* 1842. 8vo, pp. 26. BA.

COUGHLAN (L.) An Account of the Work of God, in Newfoundland, North-America. In a Series of Letters, To which are prefixed, a few Choice Experiences; Some of which were taken from the Lips of Persons who died triumphantly in the Faith. ... By the Rev. L. Coughlan, Late Missionary ... . *London: W. Gilbert.* 1776. 12mo, Title, pp. 192. C., H.

COULIER (Ph. J.) Tables des principales Positions Géonomiques du Globe. *Paris.* 1828. 8vo, pp. 494. S. 17140

Included in Warden's "Bibl. Am."

COULOMBE (A.) Vie d'Adèle Coulombe, religieuse hospitalière de l'Hôtel-Dieu de Montréal, en Canada. *Tours.* 1863. 12mo, pp. 267. 17141

COULON (Garran). *See* St. Domingo.

COULTER (J.) Adventures in the Pacific; with Observations on the Natural Productions, Manners and Customs of the Natives of the various Islands; together with Remarks on Missionaries, British and other Residents, &c. By John Coulter, M.D. *Dublin.* 1845. Post 8vo, pp. 300. C. 17142

See "Ecl. Rev.," Ser. IV., XXII. 182.

COULTER. Adventures on the Western Coast of South America, and the Interior of California: including a Narrative of Incidents at the Kings Mill Islands, New Ireland, New Britain, New Guinea, and other Islands in the Pacific Ocean; with an Account of the Natural Productions; and the Manners and Customs in Peace and War, of the various Savage Tribes visited. By John Coulter, M.D. ... *London: Longman,* [etc.] 1847. 2 vols., post 8vo, 2 l., pp. vii–xxiv, 288; Title, pp. v–xii, 278. B., C., G., S. 17143

Council Bluffs' Directory, and Emigrant Guide to the West for 1866, containing Valuable Historical, and Topographical Information. *New York.* 1866. S. 17144

Counsel for Emigrants, and Interesting Information from numerous sources, with original Letters from Canada and the United States. *Aberdeen.* 1834. 12mo, pp. 140. Map. + Second Edition. *Aberdeen: John Mathison.* 1835. 12mo, pp. 156. Map. + *London: H. Washburne.* 1839. 12mo. C.

Count the Cost. *See* Connecticut, No. 15716.

Counter-Address to the Public on the late Dismission of a General Officer, [Henry Seymour Conway]. Fourth Edition. *London.* 1764. 8vo. C. 17146

General Conway favored the Americans.

Counter Manifest. *See* Chili, No. 12759.

The Counterpoise, being Thoughts on a Militia and Standing Army. *New York.* 1753. 8vo. 17147

Countries most adapted to Emigration. *London.* 1855. 12mo. 17148

A Country Gentleman's Reasons for voting against Mr. Wilberforce's Motion for a Bill to prohibit the Importation of African Negroes into the Colonies. *London: J. Debrett.* 1791. 8vo, Title, pp. 28. H. + *London.* 1792. C. 17149

The Country Gentleman. A Journal for the Farm, the Garden, and the Fireside. *Albany: L. Tucker & Son.* 1853–65. 4to. 17150

Edited by Luther Tucker, J. J. Thomas, and J. Warren. After December, 1865, the "Country Gentleman" was merged into the "Cultivator and Country Gentleman"

The Countryman's Lamentations on the Subject of a Proper Education of Children, with an Address to the Inhabitants of New-Jersey. *Philadelphia: Printed and Sold by W. Dunlap, for the Author.* M DCC LXII. 8vo, pp. iv, 52. P. 17151

A scarce tract, written in allegorical language.

Coup-d'oeil sur la Grand-Bretagne [et ses colonies]. *Londres.* 1766. 8vo. 17152

Coup-d'œil sur la République de l'Amérique Centrale, et particulièrement sur les États de Nicaragua et Costa Rica. 4to. Map. S. 17153

Coup-d'œil sur La situation des affaires entre la France et les Etats Unis de l'Amerique, 1798. 8vo, pp. 28. BA. 17154

Le Coup de lumière. [n. p.] 1789. 8vo, pp. 48 or less.

Relates to the affairs of St. Domingo

COUPE' DE SAINT-DOUAT (Alexandre). Histoire de l'Etablissement des Français dans l'Amérique du Nord. *Paris.* 1823. 8vo. 17156

La cour de Rome et l'empereur Maximilien. Rapports de la cour de Rome avec le gouvernement mexicain, accompagnés de deux lettres de l'empereur Maximilien et de l'impératrice. *Paris: Amyot.* 1867. 8vo, pp. 157. 17157

COURAZOLLES. Mémoire ou replique à la justification de W. de Lazerne. *Paris.* 1790. 8vo. 17158

Relates to the revolution in Hayti

COURBÉ (Augustin). *See* [Morisot (C. B.)]

COURCELLE-SENEUIL (I. H.) Exámen comparativo de la tarifa i lejislacion aduanera de Chile con las De Francia, Gran Bretaña, i Etados-Unidos. Por I. H. Courcelle Seneuil. *Santiago.* 1856. 8vo, pp. 46. 17159

COURCELLE-SENEUIL (J. G.) Agression de l'Espagne contre le Chili. *Paris: E. Dentu.* 1866. 8vo. 17160

Courcelle-Seneuil Informe sobre el estado de la Hacienda pública en 1º de Octubre de 1861, pasado al Señor Ministro del Ramo por J. G. Courcelle-Seneuil, correjido i anotado segun informes últimamente adquiridos. *Santiago.* 1861. 8vo, pp. 20. Table. 17161

[Courcy (H. de).] *See* De Courcy (H.).

Courier de Boston, affiches, annonces, et avis. ... 23 Avril–15 Octobre, 1789. No. 1–26. [*Boston: Imprimerie de Samuel Hall.* 1789.] 4to, pp. 208. H. 17164

Courier politique et litteraire; annonces et avis divers: or French Evening Post. Externo Robore crescit. *London.* 1777–85. 4to. 17165

"This French journal, which was commenced in the month of May of the present year, had been preceded by the 'Courier de l'Europe,' under which title it was continued from June, 1778. According to Barbier, it was edited by the Irish abbé, Perkins Mac Mahon, Serres de la Tour, and Theveneau de Morande. The eighteenth volume, apparently the last, was published in 1785; and some of the latter volumes contain contributions from the pen of the celebrated Mirabeau. Having been published during the whole course of the American war of independence, one of its principal objects appears to have been that of giving an impartial account of the events which attended it." *See* Rich's "Bibl. Am.," I. 261.

Courmont (Félix de). Des États-Unis, de la guerre du Mexique et de l'île de Cuba. *Paris: Moquet.* 1847. 8vo.

[Cournand (*l'abbé* Antoine de).] Réponse aux Observations d'un habitant des colonies sur le Mémoire en faveur de gens de couleur ou sang mêlé à St. Domingo. *Paris.* 1789. 8vo.

Courrejolles. Mémoire en réplique à la Justification publiée par M. de la Luzerne, sur le cinquième chef d'accusation; par M. Courrejolles, député de S.-Domingue. [n. p. 1790.] 8vo. 171[illegible]

Le "Courrier de la Martinique" à M. Bayle-Mouillard, exprocureur général à la Guadeloupe ... Réponse à La lettre du 24 février 1851, adressé au journal "Le Pays." Extrait du "Courrier de la Martinique." *St-Pierre-Martinique: imp. du Courrier.* [n. d.] 8vo, pp. 48 or less. 17169

Court (J.) Catalogue of the Articles contributed to the Paris Universal Exhibition of 1867, by the Island of Trinidad (West Indies), with an Introductory Sketch of the Colony, its Institutions, Physical Features, Principal Products, etc.; by Dr. J. Court, Special Commissioner. *Paris: Dentu.* 1868. 8vo, pp. 23. 17170

The Court and City Kalendar, for England, Scotland, and America. *London: H. Woodfall* [etc.] MDCCLXVII. 12mo. Continued. 17171

Contains lists of the civil and military establishments, plantation offices, agents, etc., in America. There are calendars for 1755, or earlier.

The Court and City Register, or Gentleman's Complete Annual Kalendar For ... 1772. Containing ... Lists of ... the Army, Navy ... &c. *London: J. Jolliffe.* [etc. n. d.] 12mo, pp. vi, 282. Continued. 17172

The Court of Neptune, and the Curse of Liberty; with other Poems, on Subjects connected with the Late War. *New York: Van Winkle, Wiley & Co.* 1817. 18mo, pp. 106. C. 17173

Court de Gebelin. Monde primitif, analysé et comparé avec le monde moderne, considéré dans l'histoire naturelle de la parole; ou origine du langage et de l'écriture; avec un reponse a une critique anonyme, et des figures en taille-douce. Par M. Court de Gebelin, ... *A Paris: Boudet.* M. DCC. LXXV. 9 vols., 4to. + Considéré dans son génie allégorique et dans les allégories aux quelles conduisit ce génie ... Nouvelle édition. *Paris: L'Auteur* [etc.] M. DCC. LXXXVII. 9 vols., 4to. BA., B., C.

Contains copious details of American languages. "Essai sur les langues d'Amérique," nouv. éd., VIII. 489–560; "Observations sur un monument américain," VIII. 561–568.

Courtauld (G.) Address to those who may be disposed to remove to the United States of America on the advantages of Equitable Associations of capital and labour in the formation of Agricultural Establishments in the interior Country. Including Remarks on Mr. Birbeck's Opinions upon this Subject. By George Courtauld. *London: Hunter.* 1820. 8vo, pp. 40.

See "M. Rev.," XCVII. 200.

Courte de la Blanchardière (*M. l'abbé*). Nouveau| voyage|fait au Pérou.|Par M. l'Abbé Courte|de la Blanchardiere.|Auquel on a joint une Description|des anciennes Mines d'Espagne, traduite de l'Espagnol de Alonso-Carrillo Lazo. *A Paris,|De l'Imprimerie de Delaguette,|*...|M. D. CC. LI.| 12mo, 2 l., pp. 212, (4), 74, (3). Plate. H. 17176

[Courte de la Blanchardière.] A Voyage to Peru; performed by the [Ship] Conde of St. Malo, in the years 1745, 1746, 1747, 1748, and 1749. Written by the Chaplain. To which is added an Appendix, containing the present state of the Spanish

affairs in America in respect to mines, trade and discoveries. *London: R. Griffiths.* 1752. 12mo, pp. xv, 173. 17177

The author's "observations and descriptions are sensible, pertinent, and entertaining. He seems to have little of the priest, and nothing of the bigot about him; yet his sentiments are such as become the good Christian and the gentleman."—*Monthly Review,* IX. 294.

Courte Réponse a Gros Mémoire, 1790. *See* [Bellevue], Vol. II., No. 4545.

Courten (W.) A Brief|Narrative|and Deduction of the several Remark-|able Cases of Sir William Courten, and Sir Paul| Pyndar, Knights; and William Courten late of London|Esquire, Deceased: Their Heirs, Executors, Admi-|nistrators and Assigns, together with their Surviving|Partners and Adventurers with them to the East-In-|dies, China and Japan, and divers other parts of Asia,|Europe, Africa and America: Faithfully represented|to both Houses of Parliament.|Reduced under four Principal Heads, viz.|I. The Discovery and Plantation of Barbadoes.|II. Their Vndertakings, and Expeditions to the East-| India, China and Japan.|III. The Denyal of Justice upon their civil Actions|depending in Holland and Zealand.|IV. Their Loanes and Supplyes for the Service of the|Crown, upon the Collection of Fines and Compositi-|ons out of the Popish Recusants Estates, &c.|Recollected out of the Original Writings and Records,|for publick Satisfaction.|*London: Printed in the Year* 1679.| Folio, 2 l., pp. 12, 115–118. M. 17178

Courten. Case stated between the East India Company of the United Netherlands and the Assigns of W. Courten. *Privately printed.* 1671. Folio. 17179

This celebrated case relates to the Island of Barbadoes.

Courten. Petition of W. Courten and others, 1675.—Lex Talionis; or, the Law of Marque, as regards the Ships, Factories, &c., of Sir W. Courten, and his Partners in the East Indies, China, Japan, &c. 1682. Folio. 17180

There is also an "Address of the Heirs, &c., of Sir W. Courten, 1679," folio. *See also* C[arew] (G[eorge]), Vol. III., No. 10822. Thomas Thorpe, an eminent London bookseller, attributes our No. 9759, in Vol. III., to W. Courten.

Courtenay (E. S.) Eulogy on ... Wm. Crafts ... by E. S. Courtenay. ... *Charleston: Ellis & Neufville.* 1826. 8vo, pp. 15. H. 17181

Courtenay (J.) An Inquiry into the Propriety of Establishing a National Observatory. By James Courtenay ... . *Charleston: printed by W. Riley.* 1827. 8vo, pp. 24. BA. 17182

[Courtenay (Thomas P.)] Observations on the American Treaty, in Eleven Letters. First published in "The Sun," under the signature of Decius. *London: Budd.* 1808. 8vo, pp. vi, 75. 17183

Courtenay. Additional Observations on the American Treaty, with some Remarks on Mr. Baring's Pamphlet; being a Continuation of the Letters of Decius. To which is added an Appendix of State Papers, including the Treaty. By Thomas Peregrine Courtenay, Esq. *London.* 1808. 8vo, pp. viii, 94, lxix. S. 17184

See "M. Rev.," LIV. 214.

Courtney (T. E.) A Guide to Pomerade's Original Panorama of the Mississippi River, from the mouth of the Ohio River to the Falls of St. Anthony. By T. E. Courtney. *New York.* 1849. 8vo, pp. 84. 17185

Courtney (W. S.) The Gold Fields of St. Domingo. By W. S. Courtney. *New York.* 1860. 12mo. 171[illegible]

Courtois (Ferdinand). *See* Cortes (F.), Vol. V.

Courtot (F.) La Vie|du Bien-Heureux Pere|Francois| Solano|Religieux de l'Ordre|de Saint Francois|Patron du Perou, |composée svr les memoires|presentez au S. Siege pour sa Beatification,|Et le recit du Martyre d'onze Religieux du|mesme Ordre, qui souffrirent la mort à Gorkom pour la defense de la Foy, l'an 1572.|Par le R. P. Francois Covrtot|Religieux du mesme Ordre, Docteur en|Theologie de la Faculté de Paris, &c.|*A Paris,|Chez Estienne Michallet,|ruë S. Jacques, à l'Image S. Paul,|proche la Fontaine S. Severin.*|M.DCC.LXXVII.|*Avec Privilege.*| 18mo, pp. xx, 158. 17187

[Courtot.] The Lives of St. Thomas of Villanova ... and of St. Francis Solano, Apostle of Peru, of the Order of St. Francis. *London: Thomas Richardson.* M. D. CCC. XLVII. 12mo, pp. xii, 310. 17188

Some copies have the imprint, *New York: Edward Dunigan.* Courtot is the author of Solano's life only.

Cousin d'Aval (Charles Yves), *called* Cousin d'Avalon. Histoire de Toussaint-Louverture, chef des noirs insurgés de Saint-Domingue ... précédée d'un coup d'œil politique sur cette colonie. *Paris, Pillot, an X*-1802. 12mo, pp. 211. Portrait.

Cousin Frank's Household. *See* [Pearson (L. H.)]

Coussin (J. H. J.) Eugène de Cerceil, ou Les Caraïbes. *Paris: Igonette; Corbet aîné* [etc.] 1824. 3 vols., 12mo.

Coustelin. Contre la reconnaissance de la république haïtienne. *Paris: Le Normant père.* 1825. 8vo. 17191

Coustelin. De l'Europe à l'égard des Nouveaux États du Sud de l'Amérique. *Paris: march. de nouveautés.* 1825. 8vo.

Coustelin. Sur l'Emancipation de Saint-Domingue. *Paris: Le Normant.* 1825. 8vo. 17193

Coute (J. F. de). Enough of War. The Question of Slavery Conclusively and Satisfactorily Solved, as regards Humanity at large, and the Permanent Interests of Present Owners. By Jose Ferrer de Coute. *New York: S. Hallet, Printer.* 1864. 8vo, pp. 312. 17194

Couthouy (J. P.) Descriptions of New Species of Mollusca and Shells; with Remarks on several Polypi, &c., found in Massachusetts Bay. By Joseph P. Couthouy ... . *Charlestown.* 1838. 8vo, Title, pp. 59. Plates. H. 17195

Couthouy. Remarks upon Coral Formation in the Pacific; with Suggestions as to the Causes of their Absence in the same Parallels of Latitude on the Coast of South America. By Joseph P. Couthouy, Extracted from Jour. Bost. Soc. Nat. Hist. for January, 1842. *Boston: Tuttle & Dennett, Printers.* 1842. 8vo, pp. 68. BA., M. 17196

Also: Monograph on the Family Osteodesmacea. [n. p. n. d.] 8vo, pp. 60.—Observations on Recent Icebergs. *New Haven.* 1842. 8vo, pp. 14.

Coutinho (F. de S.) La Proposition faicte à l'Assemblée publié des ... Etats Generaux des Provinces Unies des Païs-Bas, le 16 d'Aougst 1647. Par ... D. Franc. de Sousa Coutinho, Conseiller du Roy de Portugal, Capitaine Général des Isles Tercères, et nommé par sa Maj. Gouverneur de l'Estat du Brésil et son Ambass. ordin. vers les Estats Gen. des Prov. Unies. *La Haye: Jean Breeckvelt.* 1647. 16 l. 17197

Coutinho. Propositie|Ghedaen|Ter Vergaderinge van hare Hoogh Mog: d'Hee-|ren Staten Generael der Vereenigde Neder-|landen, In 's Graven Hage den 16 Au-|gusti, 1647.|Door den Heer|Francisco de Sousa Coutinho,|Raedt van sijn Conickl. Majest. van|Portvgal:|Sijnen Gouverneur ende Capiteyn Ghen-

erael van de|Vlaemsche Eylanden.|Genoemt|Met den selven Tijtel van den Staet van Brasil.|Ende Ambassadeur by Hare Hoogh Moogende.|*Gedruckt Anno* 1647.| 4to, 4 l. 17198

Also: Provisioneel ende particulier Tractaet, gemaeckt, gearresteert ende besloten in 's Graven-Hage den 27. Martij 1645 tusschen de heer Francisco de Sousa Coutinho, Raedt ende Ambassadeur vanden Coninck van Portugael, etc. ende Gouverneur van sijne Majesteyts weghen, als oock Capiteyn Generael vande Insulen van Tercera, ende de Heeren Ghedeputeerden vande Hooch-Mogende Heeren Staten Generael vande Vereenich de Nederlandtsche Provincien, etc. aengaende de Controversie over de Jurisdictie ende Territorie van 't Fort Galle, etc. *'s Graven-Hage.* 1645. 4to, 4 l.

Coutinho (*Fr.* Joaquim Forjaz Pereira). Oração academica gratulatoria pelo restabelecimento da saude do serenissimo Principe do Brasil, nas festas que celebraram os gentis-homens da sua real camara. *Lisboa: na Regia Offic.* 1789. 4to, pp. 15.

Coutinho. Estatuto de recolcimento de N. S. de Gloria de logar de Boa-Vista de Pernambuco. *Lisboa.* 1788. 4to. B.

Coutinho (G.) Copia de la Carta que Gonzalo Coutino escrivio á Su Magestad sobre la Fabrica y sustento de la Armada de Barlovento en las Indias. [n. p. n. d.] Folio. 17201

"Relating to Honduras, the Caribbee Islands, &c., very rare." Title and note from one of C. Welford's catalogues.

Coutinho. *See* Cunha de Azevedo (J. J. da).

Couto (A. C.) Dissertaçao sobre o actual Governo da Republica do Paraguay por Antonio Correa do Couto. *Rio de Janeiro.* 1865. 8vo, pp. 104. 17202

Couto (B.) Defensa del General D. Isidro Reyes, ante la suprema corte de justicia en la causa que se le instruye por haber autorizado como secretario del despacho de guerra y marina, la orden en que se numbró general del ejercito de operaciones al presidente de la Republica. Por el lic. D. Bernardo Couto. *Mexico.* 1845. Sm. 4to, pp. 44. 17203

Couto. Discurso sobre la Constitucion de la Iglesia. Por Don Bernardo Couto. *Mexico.* 1857. Rl. 8vo, pp. 84.

Couto was considered one of the most distinguished Mexican scholars. He died in 1862.

Couto (Jose Ferrer de). *See* Ferrer de Couto.

Couto (J. Vieira). Memoria sobre as salitreiras naturaes de Monte Rodrigo; escrita no anno de 1803. *Rio de Janeiro: Impr. Regia* 1809. pp. 61. 17205

Coutts (W. G.) "The Games," A Nicht wi' Burns, and Other Poems. By W. G. Coutts. *New York: the Author.* 1860. 4to. 17206

Some of the poems are on American topics.

Couture (Louis). Parallèles historiques. Napoléon, Louis XIV, Cromwell, Washington, ou Pourquoi finissent les dynasties, Quand et pourquoi elles naissent. *Paris: Michel Lévy.* 1852. 18mo. 17207

An extract from his "Bonapartisme."

Covarrubias (A. D.) Determinacion de la Posicion geografica de Mexico, por A. Diaz Covarrubias, Ingeniero geógrafo y director de la Comision del valle de México. *Mexico: Tipografía de M. Castro.* [1860.] 8vo, pp. 64. H. 17208

Covarrubias. Informe jeneral presentado a S. E. El Presidente de la Republica sobre los trabajos de la Comision directiva de la Esposicion Nacional de agricultura celebrada en Santiago de Chile en Mayo de 1869. Por su presidente D. Alvaro Covarrubias. *Valparaiso.* 1869. Folio, pp. 636. 17209

Covell (L.) Narrative of a Missionary Tour through the Western Settlements of New York, &c. By Lemuel Covell. *Troy.* 1804. 12mo. W. 17210

For a life of the author, *see* Brown (*Mrs.* D. C.), Vol. II., No. 8464.

The Covenant of Grace not Absolute but Conditional, and the Preachers thereof vindicated from the Unjust Aspersions of Arminianism and Popery. *London.* 1692. 4to. 17211

A curious tract, which refers to the Antinomians of New England.

The Covenanter, devoted to the Principles of the Reformed Presbyterian Church. Edited by James M. Willson. ... *Philadelphia: David Smith.* 1845. No. 1, 8vo, pp. 5–36. H. 17212

From August, 1845, to November, 1846, in all, fifteen numbers.

Coventry (A.) Address to the Agricultural Society of the County of Oneida: delivered at Whitestown, on the 27th Day of Sept. 1818, by Alexander Coventry, Esq. ... *Utica: Printed by William Williams.* 1819. 8vo, pp. 50. BA. 17213

Coventry (C. B.) Extracts from a Lecture on Insanity ... [with an account of the Bloomingdale Asylum. *Utica.* 1842.] 8vo, pp. 8. 17214

Also: Report on Epidemic Cholera. *Utica, N. Y.* 1848. 8vo, pp. 13. + Epidemic Cholera, its History, &c. *Buffalo.* 1849. 12mo. M.

Coventry, *Conn.* *See* Abbot (Abiel), Vol. I., Nos. 16–18.

Coverly (*Sir* Roger de). *See* "A Cure for the Spleen," Vol. V.," and "The Americans Roused," Vol. I., No. 1274.

Covington *and* Newport. Williams' Covington and Newport Directory for 1866–7. To which is appended a United States Post-Office Directory. Compiled by Williams & Co. *Covington, Ky.: Williams & Co.* 8vo, pp. xv, 188, 467–536.

First Annual Report of the Western Baptist Theological Institute, of Covington, Kentucky. May 1, 1843. [By E. Robins.] *Cincinnati: E. Morgan and Company, Printers.* 1843. 8vo, pp. 22. 17216

Covode (J.) Kansas—the Lecompton Constitution. Popular Sovereignty, Theoretical and Practical. Speech of Hon. Jno. Covode, of Pennsylvania. ... March 25, 1858. *Washington, D. C.: Buell & Blanchard, Printers.* 1858. 8vo, pp. 8. H.

Covode. Tariff and the Treasury. Speech of the Hon. John Covode, of Pennsylvania, delivered in the House of Representatives, February 12, 1857. [n. p. n. d.] 8vo, pp. 7.

Covode. Report of the Committee appointed under the Resolutions offered by the Hon. John Covode, March 5, 1860, to investigate and inquire into alleged Corruptions, in the passage of the Law to form the Lecompton Constitution, in the Elections in Pennsylvania, in the Post Office Department, &c. *Washington.* 1860. 8vo, pp. 838, 164. (36th Cong., 1st Sess., House Report 648.) 17219

Covos (J. M.) Manifiesto al publico de José Maria Covos. *Zacatecas.* 1857. Sm. 8vo, pp. 16. 17220

Cowan (E.) The Constitution the True Remedy. Speech of Hon. Edgar Cowan, of Pennsylvania, on the Concurrent Resolution of the Committee of Fifteen. Delivered in the Senate ... March 2, 1866. *Washington, D. C.: L. Towers, Printer.* [n. d.] 8vo, pp. 16. H. 17221

Also: Address before the Literary Society of Washington, Coll., Pa., ... Sept. 24, 1846. 8vo.—The Forfeiture and Confiscation of Rebel Property in the Confederate States. Speech ... in the Senate ... March 4, 1862. *Washington: Scammell & Co.* 1862. 8vo, pp. 16.—National Union Club Documents. Speeches of Hon. Edgar Cowan, of Pennsylvania; [and others]. *Washington, D. C.* 1866. 8vo, pp. 32. H.—Speech ... in the Senate ... June 27, 1864, on Mr. Trumbull's Amendment repealing the Joint Resolution of July 17, 1862, Qualifying the Confiscation Act and Limiting Forfeitures under it to the Life of the Offender. 8vo, pp. 16.

The Coward's Convention. *See* Bristed (C. A.), Vol. II., No. 8041.

Cowdell (T.) The Nova Scotia Minstrel; written while on a Tour from North America to Great Britain and Ireland, Interspersed with Suitable Reflections, and Moral Songs, Adapted to the most Popular Airs. By Thomas Cowdell. *Printed for the Author.* 1811. 12mo. 17222

The author remarks, in his preface, that if any person buys a copy of his book, he will wait upon them at their house with his violincello, and play them a few tunes! Some of the songs are in the Indian dialect.

Cowdell (T. D.) A Poetical Account of the American Campaign of 1812 and 1813. By Thomas D. Cowdell. *Halifax.* 1815. 8vo, pp. 131. 17223

Cowdell. A Poetical Journal of a Tour from British North America to England, Wales & Ireland, interspersed with Reflections Natural, Moral & Political. To which are subjoined, Two Pieces of the Intended Jubilee. By Thomas D. Cowdell. *Dublin: Wilkinson & Courtney.* 1809. 12mo, pp. 76. 17224

Cowden (J.) The African Slave Trade; An Appeal in its Favor, by J. Cowden. *Jackson.* 1859. 8vo. 17225

Title from J. W. Randolph's catalogue, Richmond, Va.

Cowdery (*Dr.*) American Captives in Tripoli; or, Dr. Cowdery's Journal in Miniature, kept during his Late Captivity in Tripoli. ... *Boston: Belcher & Armstrong.* 1806. 12mo, pp. 34. BA. + Second Edition. *Boston.* 1806. 12mo. W. 17226

Cowdin (E. C.) Agriculture — its Dignity and Progress. An Address delivered before the Society of Agriculture and Horticulture of Westchester County, ... September 20, 1866. By Elliot C. Cowdin. *New York: printed by Baker & Godwin.* 1866. 8vo, pp. 20. H. 17227

Cowdin. The Presidential Issue, and its Effects upon the Business and Prosperity of the Country. Speech of the Hon. Elliot C. Cowdin ... before the National Club ... of New York, October 19, 1868. *New York: Printed by Baker & Godwin.* [n. d.] 8vo, pp. 19. H. 17228

Cowdin. The Tax on Cotton. Remarks of Elliot C. Cowdin, before the Chamber of Commerce of the State of New-

York, December 20, 1866. *New York: John W. Amerman, Printer.* [n. d.] 8vo, pp. 14. H. 17229

Also: The Paris Universal Exhibition of 1867. Remarks ... in the Chamber of Commerce of New York ... January 12, 1866. *New York: Baker & Godwin, Printers.* 1866. 8vo, pp. 8. H. — Paris Universal Exhibition of 1867. An Address ... at Albany, Feb'y 12, 1868 ... . *Albany: Chas. Van Benthuysen and Sons.* 1868. 8vo, pp. 56. H.

Cowdin (N. G.) Ellen; or, the Fanatic's Daughter. By Mrs. N. G. Cowdin. *Mobile: S. H. Goetzel & Co.* 186–. 12mo. 17230

Cowdin (Robert). Gen. Cowdin and the First Massachusetts Regiment of Volunteers. *Boston: J. E. Farwell and Company, Printers.* 1864. 8vo, pp. 19. H. 17231

Cowdrey (S.) An Oration delivered before the Tamanny Society or Columbian Order; on their Anniversary, May 12, 1803. By Samuel Cowdrey. *New York.* [1803.] 8vo, pp. 15.

Cowell (B.) A Letter to the Hon. Samuel W. King, late Governor of the State of Rhode Island, May, 1842. By Benjamin Cowell. *Providence: H. H. Brown.* 1842. + Second Edition, with an Appendix. [*Ibid.*] 8vo, pp. 32. 17233

Cowell. An Oration pronounced before the Greene Association, on the Eighth of August, 1814, it being their Anniversary. ... *Providence: Miller, Goddard & Man.* 8vo, pp. 19. BA.

Cowell. Spirit of '76 in Rhode Island: or, Sketches of the Efforts of the Government and People of the War of the Revolution. Together with the Names of those who belonged to Rhode Island Regiments in the Army. With Biographical Notices, Reminiscences, &c., &c. By Benjamin Cowell. *Boston: A. J. Wright, Printer.* 1850. 8vo, pp. 352. BA., C. 17235

Cowell (J.) Thirty Years passed among the Players in England and America ... [by] Joe Cowell, Comedian. Written by himself. ... *London.* 1844. + *New-York: Harper & Brothers.* 1844. 8vo, pp. 103. [*Ibid.*] 1845. 8vo. 17236

Cowell (J.) The Curious and Profitable Gardener; containing, I. The most useful experiments for improving Land by Grains and Seeds. II. Curious Directions for cultivating the choicest Fruits of the East and West Indies at a small expense. III. Extraordinary Remarks concerning the raising of Flowers

from Seed. IV. Particular Observations, and Rules for the management of Dwarf Fruit Trees. To which is added an exact description of the Great American Aloe, etc. By John Cowell, of Hoxton. Adorned with Cuts. *London: Weaver Bickerton.* MDCCXXX. 2 pts., 8vo, 3 l., pp. 126; 67. 17237

Cowell. True Account of the Aloe Americana, or Africana, which is now in blossom in Mr. Cowell's Garden at Hoxton; the like whereof has never been seen in England before. *London.* 1729. 8vo, pp. vi, 44. Copperplate. 17238

Cowell (J. W.) La France et les États Confédérés. Par John Welsford Cowell, agent et représentatif de la Banque d'Angleterre aux États-Unis dans les années 1837, 1838 et 1839. *Paris: Dentu.* 1865. 8vo, pp. 30. 17239

Cowell. Southern Secession. A Letter addressed to Capt. M. T. Maury, Confederate Navy, on his Letter to Admiral Fitzroy. By John Welsford Cowell, Esq. *London: Robert Hardwicke.* MDCCCLXII. 8vo, pp. 99. 17240

Cowen (Esek). Review of the Opinion of Judge Cowen, ... in the Case of Alexander McLeod. By a Citizen of New York. *Washington: printed by Thomas Allen.* 1841. 8vo, pp. 28. H. 17241

Cowen (M. V. B.) The Indiana State Gazetteer and Shippers' Guide, for 1866–7. M. V. B. Cowen, Compiler. *Lafayette, Ind.: Rosser, Spring & Cowen.* 1866. 8vo, pp. xv, 428. S. 17242

Cowie. Considerations on the present Crisis of Affairs as it respects the West India Colonies, ... *London.* 1795. 8vo.

Cowles (Edwin). A Plan for the Gradual Resumption of Specie Payment. ... By E. Cowles ... . *Cleveland, O.* 1868. 8vo, pp. 15. H. 17244

Cowles (H.) A Defence of Ohio Congregationalism and of Oberlin College ... By Rev. Henry Cowles ... . [n. p. n. d.] 8vo, pp. 24. H. 17245

Cowles (S.) Conflict of Races. A Sermon preached in Randolph, New York, Oct. 12, 1862. By Rev. Sylvester Cowles. 8vo, pp. 16. 17246

Cowley (C.) A Hand-Book of Business in Lowell, Mass.; with a History of the City. By Charles Cowley. *Lowell.* 1856. 8vo, pp. 166. 17247

Cowley. Illustrated History of Lowell. Revised Edition. By Charles Cowley. *Boston: Lee & Shepard.* 1868. 12mo, Title, pp. 9–135. Woodcuts. BA. + *Lowell: B. C. Sargeant and Joshua Merrill.* 1868. 17248

Cowley. Memories [*sic*] of the Indians and Pioneers of the region of Lowell. By Charles Cowley. ... *Lowell: Stone & Huse, Printers.* 1862. 8vo, pp. 24, (1). BA. 17249

Cowley (*Captain*). *See* Hacke (W.)

Cowperthwait (J.) An Address at the laying of the Corner-stone of the Holmesburgh Public School. By Joseph Cowperthwait. *Philadelphia.* 1846. 8vo. P. 17250

The Cow Pox Act. With the Order of the Legislature; and a Communication relative to the Subject from the Selectmen of the Town of Milton. ... *Boston: printed by Joshua Belcher.* 1810. 8vo, pp. 16. BA. 17251

Cox (Abraham L.) An Address, delivered on the First Public Exhibition of the Edifice of the New-York Medical College, and the Inauguration of its Faculty, October 16, 1850. By Abm. L. Cox, M.D. ... . *New-York: J. F. Trow, Printer.* M. DCCC. L. 8vo. H. 17252

Cox (C. C.) Oration on the Life, Character and Services of Tristam Thomas, M.D., delivered in Easton, Maryland. By Christopher C. Cox, M.D. *Baltimore.* 1847. 8vo. S. 17253

Cox (E. T.) First Annual Report of the Geological Survey of Indiana, ... 1869. By E. T. Cox. ... *Indianapolis.* 1869. 8vo, pp. 240, (1). Plate and 3 Maps. 17254

Cox (Francis Augustus). The Scriptural Duty of Churches in relation to Slaveholders professing Christianity; By the Rev. F. A. Cox, D.D. ... *London: T. Ward and Co.* 1841. 8vo, pp. 24. 17255

Cox *and* Hoby (J.) The Baptists in America; a Narrative of the Deputation from the Baptist Union in England to the United States and Canada. By the Rev. F. A. Cox ... and the Rev. J. Hoby ... . *London: T. Ward & Co.* 1836. Post 8vo.

pp. x, 516. Illustrations. + Second Edition, Revised, with Additions. *London: [Ibid.]* 1836. Post 8vo. Plates. C. + *New York: Leavitt, Lord & Co.* 1837. 12mo, pp. 476. C.

See "N. Am. Rev.," Oct., 1836, and "Christ. Rev.," I. 455.

Cox (G. F.) Matter for the Times. Three Questions answered. What is Slavery? Were Slave Holders Members of the Apostolic Church? Shall the Church adopt the Apostolic Standard of Disicipline, or make a New One? By Rev. Gershom F. Cox, M.A. *Boston: J. P. Magee.* 1856. 8vo, pp. 40. B. 17257

Cox (J. A.) Reize naar verscheide eilanden op de N. W. kust van Amerika, uitgegeven door G. Mortimer ... . Naar het Engelsch door J. D. Pasteur. *Leyden: A. en J. Honkoop.* 17—.

Title taken from a bookseller's advertisement

Cox (J. D.) Inaugural Address of Jacob D. Cox, Governor of Ohio, delivered before the Senate and House of Representatives, Jan. 8, 1866. *Columbus: Richard Nevins, Printer.* 1866. 8vo, pp. 10. H. 17259

[Cox (James E.)] Exposition of Thomas W. Bartley, the Present Chief Justice of the State of Ohio. Showing him to be the Second Haman that has made his Appearance on this Earth. *Mansfield.* 1857. 8vo, pp. 28. H. 17260

Cox (J.) Rewards and Punishments, or, Satan's Kingdom Aristocratical. To which is subjoined A Voyage to London, and an Acrostic. By John Cox, a Native of Pennsylvania. *Philadelphia, Printed for the Author, at No. 41, Chesnut-street, May,* 1795. 12mo, pp. 20. 17261

Cox (J. R.) First Branch Journal. City Taxation. Remarks of John R. Cox, Chairman Committee on Ways and Means. *Baltimore.* 1865. 8vo, pp. 7. 17262

Cox (L. M.) Speech of Hon. L. M. Cox, of Kentucky, on the Nebraska and Kansas Bill. ... May 9, 1854. *Washington: Congressional Globe Office.* 1854. 8vo, pp. 13. H. 17263

Cox (M. B.) Remains of Melville B. Cox, with a Memoir. *Boston: Light & Horton.* 1835. 16mo, 1 l., pp. 240. Portrait.

Cox (R.) A Letter from Sir Richard Cox, Bart. to Thomas Prior, Esq; Shewing, from Experience, A sure Method to

establish the Linnen-Manufacture, and the Beneficial Effects it will immediately produce. ... *Dublin. London, Re-printed. Boston, N. E.: Re-printed, J. Draper.* 1750. 4to, pp. 36, (2). B.

The preface states that "a Number of Gentlemen are very desirous of establishing the Linnen-Manufacture in this Province," Massachusetts.

Cox (Richard). Farewell Sermon in Zion Church, N. Y., June 12, 1859. *New York.* 8vo. 17266

Cox (R.) Adventures on the Columbia River, including the Narrative of a Residence of Six Years on the Western Side of the Rocky Mountains, among various Tribes of Indians hitherto Unknown: together with a Journey across the American Continent. By Ross Cox. ... *London: Henry Colburn and Richard Bentley.* 1831. 2 vols., 8vo, pp. xxiv, 368; viii, 400. BA. + The Columbia River; or Scenes and Adventures ... . Second Edition. *London.* 1832. 8vo. + *New-York: Harper & Brother.* 1832. 8vo, pp. xv, 25–335. H., C. 17267

See "M. Rev.," II. I, and "Westminster Rev.," XVI. 130.

Cox (S. H.) Consolation in Bereavement. A Discourse occasioned by the Death of the late Rev. Erskine Mason, D.D., Preached ... May 25, 1851; By Rev. Samuel H. Cox, D.D. To which is prefixed the Funeral Address, by Rev. William Adams, D.D. *New York: E. French.* 1851. 8vo, pp. 64.

Cox. Correspondence between the Rev. Samuel H. Cox ... of Brooklyn ... and Frederick Douglass, a Fugitive Slave. *New York: American Anti-Slavery Society.* 1846. 8vo, pp. 16. H., P.

Cox. Missionary Remains: Or Sketches of the Lives of Evarts, Cornelius, and Wisner, With An Introduction. By Samuel H. Cox, D.D. *New York: Taylor & Gould.* 1835. 12mo, pp. iv, 143. 17270

Also: An Address in behalf of the Society for the Promotion of Collegiate and Theological Education at the West. ... Boston, May 30, 1849. ... *New-York: John F. Trow, Printer.* [n. d.] 8vo, pp. 26. — The Dead are the Living ... A Sermon ... October 1, 1843. On Occasion of the Funeral of Mrs. Mary L., the Wife of the Rev. Ward Stafford ... . *New York: John F. Trow & Co., Printers.* 1843. 8vo, pp. 30. H. — Interviews Memorable and Useful, from Diary and Memory Reproduced. ... *New-York.* 1853. 8vo. — Quakerism not Christianity; or, Reasons for renouncing the Doctrine of Friends. In Three Parts. *New York: J. Leavitt.* 1833. 8vo, 1 l., pp. 686. — Sermon preached at the Funeral of Rev. Matthias Bruen, late Pastor of the Blecker Presbyterian Church, New York. *New York.* 1839. 8vo. — Squint at a Co-presbyter, and glance at the Minutes of the High School Synod ... *New York.* 1840 12mo. B.

Cox (S. Sullivan). Eight years in Congress, from 1857–1865. Memoir and Speeches. By Samuel S. Cox. ... *New York: D. Appleton & Company.* 1865. 8vo, pp. viii, 442. Portrait. B.

Also: The Cabinet in Congress. ... Speech ... on the Joint Resolution to admit the Cabinet into the House of Representatives, for ... 1865. *Washington: printed by Lemuel Towers.* 1865. 8vo, pp. 16. — Also: Conciliation and Nationality! Speech ... House of Representatives, January 14, 1861. [*Washington.* 1861.] 8vo, pp. 16. H. — Currency — Funding — Gold and Silver. ... June 7, 1870. ... . *Washington: F. & J. Rives & Geo. A. Bailey.* 1870. 8vo, pp. 16. H. — Emancipation and its results. Is Ohio to be Africanized? Speech ... . June 6, 1862. [*Washington City: L. Towers & Co., printers.* 1862.] 8vo, pp. 16. H. — Eulogy of Hon. Stephen A. Douglass, one of the Regents of the Smithsonian Institute, ... May, 1862. *Washington.* 1862. 8vo, pp. 15. — Laws of National Growth. — Mexican Affairs. Speech ... in the House ... March 19, 1860. [n. p.] 8vo, pp. 15. H. — Meaning of the Elections of 1862. Speech ... December 15, 1862. 8vo, pp. 15. — Miscegenation or Amalgamation; Fate of the Freedmen. Speech ... February 17, 1864. *Washington: Constitution Union Office.* 1864. 8vo, pp. 11. — The Nation's Hope in the Democracy. Historic Lessons for Civil War. Speech on the Bill to Guarantee to certain States, whose Government is usurped or overthrown, a Republican Form of Government. ... May, 1864. 8vo, pp. 16. — Puritanism in Politics. Speech ... before the Democratic Union Association, January 13, 1863. *New York: Van Evrie, Horton & Co.* 1863. 8vo, pp, 14. — The Republic abroad. Speech ... December 17, 1861. [*Washington City: L. Towers & Co., printers.* 1861.] 8vo, pp. 8, H. — Shall the Constitution be repealed? Confiscation or Conciliation? ... Speech ... on the Joint Resolution Explanatory of the Confiscation Act. Delivered in the House of Representatives, January 14, 1864. *Washington: Gibson Bros., printers.* [n. d.] 8vo, pp. 16. — Speech ... in Vindication of Gen. McClellan from the Attacks of Congressional War Critics, Delivered in the House of Representatives, January 31, 1862. [*Washington: Towers & Co., Printers.* 1862.] 8vo, pp. 16 — Speeches on the Tariff and other Economical Questions, delivered in Congress. Extracted from his Forthcoming Volume of "Eight Years in Congress." *New York: D. Appleton & Co.* 1865. 8vo, pp. 31–61. — The Tariff — Its Oppressions, Absurdities, and Spoliations. Speech ... March 28, 1870. ... *Washington: F. & F. Rives & Geo. A. Bailey.* 1870. 8vo, pp. 28. B. — A Buckeye abroad; or, Wanderings in Europe, and in the Orient. *New York: G. P. Putnam,* 1852. 12mo, pp. 444. 9 Plates. (Contains two and a half pages relating to America.) H. The author acquired the *soubriquet* of Sun Set Cox, perhaps because of his initials.

Cox (S. C.) Recollections of the Early Settlement of the Wabash Valley. By Sanford C. Cox. *Lafayette: Courier Printing House.* 1860. 8vo, pp. 160. B., C. 17272

Also: The Evangelist, and other Poems. ... *Cincinnati: the Author.* 1867. 18mo, pp. 134. IC.

[Cox (W.)] Crayon Sketches. By an Amateur. Edited by T. S. Fay. *New York: Harper & Brothers.* 1832. 2 vols., 12mo. 17273

Cox (W. S.) Address delivered before the Sabbath Schools and Citizens of Georgetown, D. C., at their Anniversary Celebration, July 5, 1847. By Walter S. Cox, Esq. *Washington.* 1847. 8vo, pp. 14. M. 17274

Cox (William E.) Viage en las rejiones septentrionales de la Patagonia, 1862–3. *Santiago de Chile: Imprenta nacionale.* 1863. 8vo, pp. viii, 273. Map. 17275

Coxe (A. C.) The Commemoration of the Faithful Departed: being some Account of the Services in the Church of the Advent, Boston, Mass. ... 9th of November, 1852, One Year after the Decease of ... the Rev. William Croswell, D.D., with the Sermon ... by Rev. A. C. Coxe ... . *Boston.* 1852. 8vo, pp. 31. BA. 17276

[Coxe.] Repentance the Acceptable Thanksgiving. A Sermon, preached in ... Hartford ... 1843 ... on the ... Day of Thanksgiving ... . *Hartford: Henry S. Parsons.* 1843. 8vo, pp. 20. H. 17277

Also: "Athanasion," an Ode ... before the Associate Alumni of Washington College, Hartford ... *Hartford.* 1840. 8vo, pp. 32. — Truth and our Times. The Baccalaureate Sermon preached in Calvary Church, June 30, '63. ... *New York: C. Alvord, Printer.* 1863. 8vo, pp. 17. — Unjust Reproaches, in Public Calamity, viewed as part of the Divine Discipline. A Sermon preached in Calvary Church on the Day of National Thanksgiving, Nov. 26, 1863, ... *New York: C. A. Alvord, Printer.* 1863. 8vo, pp. 21.

Coxe (D.) A Collection of Voyages and Travels, in Three Parts. Part I. The dangerous Voyage of Capt. Thomas James, in attempting to discover a North-west Passage to the South-Sea; with an Account of their passing the Winter in an uninhabited Island, &c. This is remarkable for its Integrity and Simplicity. With a Map. Part II. The Sieur Pontis's Voyage to America; Also an Account of the taking Carthagena by the French in 1697. Also an Account of the several Engagements they had with the English in their return to Brest. To which is added, a new and accurate Map. Part III. A Description of the English Province of Carolana; by the Spaniards call'd Florida, and by the French La Louisiane, viz. A Description of the People, Animals, Vegetables, Metals, Minerals, and other rich and valuable Commodities this Province naturally produces. With a Large and Judicious Preface, Proving the Right of the English to that Country; the Manner of the French usurping great Part of it; and the great Danger our Colonies on the Continent will be exposed to, if not timely prevented: With many useful Remarks regarding our Plantations in general. Collected from authentick Journals, Travels, &c. of the English in that Country; the Originals of which are now in the Possession of Dr. Coxe ... . By Daniel Coxe, Esq; To which is added, A Large and Accurate Map of Carolana; and of the River Meschacebe. [*London:*] *Printed for and sold by Oliver Payne, Cornhill.* 1741. 3 pts., 8vo, pp. (6), 142; viii, 86; 27 l., pp. 122. 2 Maps.

This is, in fact, a collection of three separate pieces, with a new general title, the following being the last:

COXE. A Description Of the English Province of Carolana, By the Spainards call'd Florida, And by the French La Louisiane. As Also of the Great and Famous River Meschacebe or Missisipi, The Five vast Navigable Lakes of Fresh Water, and the Parts Adjacent. Together With an Account of the Commodities of the Growth and Production of the said Province. And a Preface containing some Considerations on the Consequences of the French making Settlements there. By Daniel Coxe, Esq: *London: Printed for B. Cowse, at the Rose and Crown in St. Paul's Church-Yard.* MDCCXXII. 8vo, 27 l., pp. 122. Map. BA., H.

"A compilation from various journals to impress the public with the great importance of the region described, and to make them jealous of its occupation by the French. Under the name of Carolana was comprehended the present State of Georgia, the Floridas, Alabama, Mississippi, and Louisiana. The whole of this territory was claimed by Dr. Coxe, the father of the author, as proprietor under the Crown. The author explored great part of it, and lived there fourteen years." *See* "N. Am. Rev.," II. I. The two following numbers are the same work, with new title-pages:

COXE. A Description Of the English Province of Corolana, By the Spainards call'd Florida, And by the French La Louisiane. As also of the Great and Famous River Meschacebe or Missisipi, The Five vast Navigable Lakes of Fresh Water, and the Parts Adjacent. Together With an Account of the Commodities of the Growth and Production of the said Province. And a Preface containing some Considerations on the Consequences of the French making a Settlement there. By Daniel Coxe, Esq; *London: Printed for Edward Symon, against the Royal Exchange in Cornhill.* 1727. 8vo, pp. 56, 122. Map. 17280

COXE. A Description of the English Province of Carolana. By the Spaniards call'd Florida, and by the French, La Louisiane. Viz. I. A Description of the great and famous River Meschabebe or Missisipi. II. A Description of the Countries, People, Rivers, Bays, Harbours and Islands, to the East of the Meschacebe. III. A Description of the Sea Coast, the large Rivers; their Heads and Courses, to the West of the Meschacebe. IV. A Description of the Five great Seas or Lakes of fresh Water. V. A new and curious Discovery of an easy Communication between the River Meschacebe and the South-Sea ... which separates

America from China, by means of several large Rivers and Lakes; with a Description of the said Sea, to the Streights of Uries; as also of a rich and considerable Trade to be carry'd on from thence to Japan, China and Tartary. VI. An Account of the useful Animals, Vegetables, Metals, Minerals, and other rich and valuable Commodities, which this Province naturally produces. VII. An Appendix, containing the original Charter, &c. With a large and curious Preface, demonstrating the Right of the English to that Country, and the unjust Manner of the French usurping of it; their prodigious Increase there, &c. and the inevitable Danger our other Colonies on the Continent will be exposed to, if not timely prevented; interspersed with many useful Hints, in Regard to our Plantations in General. To which is added, a large and accurate Map of Carolana, and of the River Meschacebe. By Daniel Coxe, Esq; [*London:*] *Printed for and sold by Olive Payne, at Horace's Head in Pope's-Head Alley, Cornhill, opposite the Royal Exchange,* 1741. 8vo, 27 l., pp. 122. Map. B., C., H. 17281

This work was also *Reprinted, St. Louis.* 1840, 8vo, pp. vi, 90, and included in French's "Hist. Coll.," II.

COXE (J. R.) An Appeal to the Public, and especially the Medical Public, from the Proceedings of the Trustees of the University of Pennsylvania, vacating the Chair of Materia Medica and Pharmacy. By John Redman Coxe, M.D. *Philadelphia: the Author; sold by J. G. Auner and Desilver, Thomas & Co.* 1835. 8vo, pp. iv, 68. B., H., P. 17282

COXE. The Emporium of Arts & Sciences. ... Conducted by John Redman Coxe, M.D. ... . *Philadelphia: Joseph Delaplaine.* [1812.] 5 vols., 8vo. 17283

Continued to five vols., or more, by Dr. Thomas Cooper.

COXE. The Philadelphia Medical Museum. By John Redman Coxe, M.D. *Philadelphia.* 1805. 6 vols. + New Series. *Philadelphia.* 1811. 8vo. 17284

COXE. A Short Account of the Occurences which led to the removal of Dr. John Redman Coxe from the Chair of Materia Medica & Pharmacy, in the University of Pennsylvania. *Philadelphia.* 1835. 12mo, Title, pp. 12. BA. 17285

Also: Prospectus of the Emporium of Arts and Sciences. *Philadelphia.* 1832. 8vo, pp. vii. M.

COXE (J. R.) Trial of Lieut. J. R. Coxe, of the United States Navy, at Rio Janeiro, March, 1833. *Philadelphia.* 1834. 8vo. C. 17286

COXE [(Margaret)]. Claims of the Country on American Females. By Miss Coxe ... . *Columbus: Isaac N. Whiting.* MDCCCXLII. 2 vols., 12mo, pp. iv, 243, (1); iv, 243. B. 17287

Also: The Duty of American Women to their Country. *New York: Harper & Brothers.* 1845. 12mo, pp. 164.

COXE (R. S.) Address on the Life and Character of Gen. William Henry Harrison ... delivered before the [National] Institution [for the Promotion of Science]. By Richard S. Coxe. June 24, 1841. *Washington: Robert Farnham.* 1841. 8vo, pp. 38. M. 17288

COXE. Brief Examination and Exposition of the Right of Detention, Visit and Search in Time of Peace. Examined on Legal Principles and Authorities. By Richard S. Coxe, LL.D. *Washington: Henry Polkingham, Printer.* 1858. 8vo, pp. 36.

COXE. Claims on Mexico presented before the Board of Commissioners under the late Convention with Mexico. By Richard S. Coxe, Esq., Trustee for the Claimants ... *New York: A. Naum & Co., Printers.* 1844. 8vo, pp. 32. 17590

COXE. Extent and Value of the Possessory Rights of the Hudson's Bay Company in Oregon, South of Forty-Ninth Degree. *Printed by John Lovell, St. Nicholas Street, Montreal.* [1849.] 8vo, Title, pp. 51. 17291

COXE. Review of the Relations between the United States and Mexico, and of the claims of Citizens of the United States against Mexico. *New York.* 1846. 8vo, pp. 120. 17292

Also: Address ... Before the Mechanics and other Citizens of the City of Washington, Friends of Henry Clay, on Monday, July 5, 1830. *Washington: Peter Force.* 1830. 8vo, pp. 15. — Address, delivered ... the Evening before the Annual Commencement of the College of New Jersey, September 24, 1833, ... *Princeton.* 1833. 8vo, pp. 43. B. — Address delivered before the Peithessophian and Philoclean Societies of Rutgers College, July 23, 1844. *New York.* 1844. 8vo. — The Claim of Jonas P. Leavy. [*Washington.* n. d.] 8vo, pp. 11. H.

COXE (T.) An Address to an Assembly of the Friends of American Manufactures. Convened for the Purpose of establishing a Society for the Encouragement of Manufactures and the Useful Arts ... 9th of August 1787, by Tench Coxe ... . *Philadelphia: Printed by R. Aitken & Son.* MDCCLXXXVII. 8vo, pp. 30. B., BA., C. 17293

[COXE.] A Brief Examination of Lord Sheffield's Observations on the Commerce of the United States. In Seven Numbers.

With two Supplementary Notes on American Manufactures. *Philadelphia: from the press of M. Carey.* M.DCC.XCI. pp. vii, 130. + *London: J. Phillips.* MDCCXCII. 8vo, pp. vii, 127.

First printed in the "American Museum." The London edition was edited by Capel Lofft. *See* Holroyd (John)

[COXE.] An Enquiry into the Principles on which a Commercial System for the United States of America should be Founded: to which are added Some Political Observations connected with the subject. Read before the Society for Political Enquiries, convened at the house of his Excellency Benjamin Franklin, Esquire, in Philadelphia, May 11th, 1787. [*Philadelphia:*] *Printed and Sold by Robert Aitken, at Pope's Head in Market Street.* M.DCC.LXXXVII. 8vo, pp. 52. P. 17295

[COXE.] An Essay on the Manufacturing Interest of the United States, &c. &c. By a Member of the Society of Artists and Manufacturers of Philadelphia. With the Memorial of that Society to Congress. *Philadelphia.* 1804. 8vo. P. 17296

[COXE.] An Examination of the Conduct of Great Britain, respecting Neutrals, since the Year 1791. Second Edition. *Boston: printed by Oliver and Munroe.* 1808. 8vo, pp. 72. B.

COXE. An Exposition of Some Facts Relative to the Personal Conduct and Business of the Office of Trench Coxe, Purveyor of Public Supplies. [*Philadelphia.*] *Dec.* 10, 1805. 8vo, pp. 13. BA., C. 17298

COXE. An Important Statement of Facts relative to the Invalidity of the Pretensions of the Connecticut Claimants to Pennsylvania Lands. *Lancaster.* 1801. 8vo, pp. 40. M.

[COXE.] A Memoir, of February, 1817, Upon the subject of Cotton Wool Cultivation, the Cotton Trade, and the Cotton Manufactories of the United States of America. [*Philadelphia.* 1817.] 8vo, pp. 16. BA. 17300

Also: Memoir, of August, 1817, and An Addition to the Memoir of February and August. [*Philadelphia.* 1818.] 8vo.

[COXE.] Observations on the Agriculture, Manufactures and Commerce of the United States. *New York.* 1789. 8vo. C.

COXE. Reflexions on the State of the Union. *Philadelphia.* 1792. 8vo. C. 17302

COXE. Report of the Case of Pennsylvania against Tench Coxe, on a Motion for a Mandamus in the Supreme Court of that State. *Philadelphia.* 1803. 8vo. C. 17303

COXE. A Statement of the Arts and Manufactures of the United States of America, for the year 1810: Digested and Prepared by Tench Coxe, Esquire, of Philadelphia. *Philadelphia, printed by A. Cornman, Junr.* 1814. 4to, 6 l., pp. v–lxiv, 169. 17304

COXE. Thoughts concerning the Bank of North America; with a Plan for Encouraging Agriculture, and increasing the value of Farms in the Midland and Western Counties of Pennsylvania. *Philadelphia.* 1787. 8vo. C. 17305

[COXE.] Thoughts on the Subject of Naval Power in the United States of America; and on Certain Means of Encouraging and Protecting their Commerce and Manufactures. *Philadelphia: Printed in the Year* 1806. 8vo, pp. 34. 17306

COXE. A View of the United States of America, in a Series of Papers, written at various Times between ... 1787 and 1794, By Tench Coxe, of Philadelphia; interspersed with Authentic Documents: the Whole tending to exhibit the Progress and Present State of Civil and Religious Liberty, Population, Agriculture, Exports, Imports, Fisheries, Navigation, Ship-Building, Manufactures, and General Improvement. *Philadelphia: William Hall, and Wrigley & Berriman.* 1794. 8vo, pp. 513. BA., H. + *Philadelphia, Printed* 1794. *London: Re-printed for J. Johnson.* 1795. 8vo, pp. xiv, (2), 512. 3 Tables. + *Dublin: P. Wogan and others.* 1795. 8vo, pp. xv, 439. C. 17307

See "M. Rev.," XX. 192. Also: Oration delivered before the Washington Association of Philadelphia, 22d Feb., 1813. ... *Philadelphia.* 1813.

COXE, MATLACK (T.), MUHLENBERG (F. A.), *and others.* To the Republican Citizens of Pennsylvania. *Lancaster.* 1800. 8vo. C. 17308

COXE (W.) Account of the Russian Discoveries between Asia and America. To which are added, the Conquest of Siberia, and the History of the Transactions and Commerce between Russia and China. By William Coxe ... . *London: T. Cadell.* M DCC LXXX. 4to, pp. xxii, 344, (13). 4 Maps and Plate. BA. + The Second Edition ... Corrected. [*Ibid.*] 4to, pp. xxiii, 344, (11). BA., H. + Third Edition, Revised and Corrected.

London: T. Cadell. MDCCLXXXVII. 8vo, pp. xxviii, 454, 1 l. 3 Maps and Plate. H. + The Fourth Edition, considerably enlarged. *London: Cadell and Davies.* 1803. 8vo, pp. xxiv, 18, 500. 5 Maps and Plate. 17309

"Mr. Coxe's book contains many curious and important facts with respect to the various attempts of the Russians to open a communication with the New World." — ROBERTSON. *See* "M. Rev.," LXIII. I. There are copies on large paper, in 4to. It was translated into French, also into German, as below:

COXE. Nouvelles découvertes des Russes entre l'Asie et l'Amerique, avec L'Histoire de la conquête de la Sibérie & du commerce des Russes & des Chinois. Ouvrage traduit de l'anglois de M. Coxe. *A Neuchatel, De l'Imprimerie de la Société Typographique.* M. DCC. LXXXI. 8vo, pp. xxiv, 320. + [*Paris: Panckoucke.*] 1781. 4to. 17310

COXE. Die neuen Entdeckungen der Russen zwischen Asien und America nebst der Geschichte der Eroberung Sibiriens und des Handels der Russen und Chineser. Aus dem Englischen. *Frankfurt und Leipzig: Johann Georg Fleischer.* 1783. 8vo, pp. xi, 2 l., pp. 409, 4 l. 3 Maps and Plate. 17311

COXE. A Comparative View of the Russian Discoveries with those made by Captains Cook and Clerke; and a Sketch of what remains to be ascertained by future Navigators. By William Coxe, A.M., F.R.S. *London: T. Cadell.* 1787. 4to. 17312

See "M. Rev.," LXIII. I; LXXVIII. 674.

COXE (W.) A View of the Cultivation of Fruit Trees, and the Management of Orchards and Cider; with Accurate Descriptions of the most Estimable Varieties of Native and Foreign Apples, Pears, Peaches, Plums, and Cherries, cultivated in the Middle States of America ... . By William Coxe, Esq. ... *Philadelphia: M. Carey and Son. Nov.* 1, 1817. pp. 253, (15).

COYER (Gabriel François). Discovery of the Island Frivola: or the Frivolous Island. Translated from the French. Now privately handed about in Paris, and said to be agreeable to the English Manuscripts concerning that Island and its Inhabitants. The Second Edition. *London: T. Payne.* MDCCL. 8vo, pp. 40.

A burlesque publication, having reference to Lord Anson's voyage round the world. Another edition is described, *infra.* A Dutch translation also appeared. "It is happily conceived, very ingeniously executed, and has met with universal applause, not only in France, but in almost every country upon the continent where it has followed the book upon which it is founded, and has very justly merited that title which it now bears." — *Translator's Preface.* Lowndes characterizes it as "A satirical romance on the French nation." *See* "M. Rev.," VI. 33.

COYER. A Letter to Doctor Maty, Secretary to the Royal Society; containing an Abstract of the relations of travellers of different nations, concerning the Patagonians; with a more particular account of the several discoveries of the latest French and English navigators, relative to this gigantic race of men; including a full reply to the objections made to their existence. By Abbé Coyer ... . *London: T. Becket and P. A. De Hondt.* MDCCLXVII. 16mo, pp. 136. H. 17315

[COYER.] Lettre au Docteur Maty, sur les géans Patagons. *Bruxelles* [i. e., *Paris*]. 1767. 12mo. 17316

COYER. Ueber die Riesen in Patagonien. Ein Sendschreiben an den Herrn Doctor Maty, Sekretär der Königlichen Societät in London, von dem Herrn Abt Coyer, Mitgliede derselben Gesellschaft. Mit Zusägen der Ubersetzung. *Danzig, Verlegts Daniel Ludwig Wedel.* 1769. 12mo. pp. 144. 17317

COYER. A Supplement to Lord Anson's Voyage round the World. Containing a discovery and description of the Island of Frivola. By the Abbé Coyer. To which is prefixed an introductory Preface by the Translator. *London; A. Millar.* 1752. 4to, pp. ix, 45. + *London: A. Millar and others.* 1752. 8vo, pp. xl, 63. + *Dublin.* 1752. 8vo. + Second Edition. 1752. 8vo. 17318

COYNER (D. H.) The Lost Trappers: A Collection of interesting Scenes and Events in the Rocky Mountains; together with a Short Description of California. Also, some Account of the Fur Trade, especially as carried on about the sources of the Missouri, the Yellow Stone, and on the waters of the Columbia, in the Rocky Mountains. By David H. Coyner. *Cincinnati: J. A. & U. P. James.* 1847. 12mo, pp. 255. + *Cincinnati: E. D. Truman.* 1850. 12mo, pp. 255. + *Cincinnati.* 1859. 12mo. 17319

These trappers were a portion of Lewis and Clark's party.

[COZINE (John).] Dick Twiss: a Poem. Written during the Revolutionary War. 8vo, pp. 8. 17320

COZZENS (F. S.) Acadia; or, a Month with the Blue Noses. By Frederic S. Cozzens ... *New York: Derby & Jackson.* 1859. pp. 329. 2 Lithographs. BA., H. 17321

COZZENS. Col. Peter A. Porter: A Memorial delivered before the Century Club, December, 1864. By Frederic S. Cozzens. *New York: D. Van Nostrand.* 1865. 8vo, pp. 54.

COZZENS. Fitz-Green Halleck: a Memorial. By F. S. Cozzens. *New York: N. Y. Hist. Soc.* 1868. 8vo. Portrait.

COZZENS. Pope's Proclamation. Dated, Washington, July 15, 1862. 8vo, pp. 4. 17324

COZZENS. The Sayings of Dr. Bushwhacker and other Learned Men. By F. S. Cozzens et al. *New York: A. Simpson & Co.* 1867. 16mo, pp. vii, 213. C. 17325

Also: The Sparrowgrass Papers: or, Living in the Country. By Frederic S. Cozzens. ... *New York: Derby & Jackson.* 1856. + [*Ibid.*] 1857. 12mo, pp. 328. BA. — The Stone House on the Susquehanna. — Cozzens' Wine Press; a Vinous, Vivacious Monthly. *New York: J. A. Gray.* 1855–61. 7 vols., 8vo.

COZZENS (I.) A Geological History of Manhattan or New York Island, together with a Map of the Island, and a Suite of Sections, Tables and Columns, for the Study of Geology ... . By Issachar Cozzens, Jr. ... . *New York: W. E. Dean.* 1843. 8vo, pp. 114. 9 Colored Plates. BA. 17326

COZZENS (S. W.) More Laborers needed for the Gospel Harvest. A Sermon, ... before the Auxiliary Education Society of Norfolk County, at their ... Meeting in Wrentham, June 8, 1842. By Samuel W. Cozzens ... . *Boston: Press of T. R. Marvin.* 1842. 8vo, pp. 28. H. 17327

COZZENS. Sermon occasioned by the Death of ... Hon. William Reed, delivered Feb. 26, 1837. By Samuel W. Cozzens ... *Boston: printed by Crocker and Brewster.* 1837. 8vo, pp. 27. 17328

The Cracked Jug, or five Answers to my Neighbour Parley's five Letters, by "Neighbour Smith." Second Edition. *Boston.* 1838. 12mo, pp. 24. B. 17329

CRACRAFT (J. W.) Christian Warfare, Victory and Crown. A Sermon on occasion of the Death of the Rev. Samuel C. Stratton, preached in the Church of the Epiphany. Philadelphia, November 11, 1860. By the Rev. J. W. Cracraft, Rector. *Philadelphia: Ashmead, Printer.* 1860. 8vo, pp. 21.

CRADLEBAUGH (J.) Utah and the Mormons. Speech of Hon. John Cradlebaugh, of Nevada, on the Admission of Utah as a State. Delivered in the House of Representatives, February 7, 1863. *Washington: L. Towers & Co., Printers.* 8vo, pp. 67. H. 17331

CRADOCK (F.) Wealth Discovered; or, an Essay upon a Late Expedient for taking away all Impositions, and Raising a Revenue without Taxes, presented to his Majesty King Charles II. By Francis Cradock of Glastonbury. *London.* 1661. 4to.

In the dedication to the King, is a curious notice of the honor King Henry VII. lost, in refusing the offer of Christopher Columbus.

CRADOCK (T.) A New Version of the Psalms of David. By the Rev. Thomas Cradock, Rector of St. Thomas's, Baltimore county, Maryland. *Annapolis: Jonas Green.* 1756. 8vo, pp. 160. 17333

[CRAFFORD (John)]. A New and Most | Exact Account | Of the Fertile and Famous Colony of | Carolina (On the Continent of America) | whose Latitude is from 36 Deg. of North Latitude, to 29 Deg. | Together with a | Maritine [*sic*] Account of its Rivers, Barrs, Soundings and Harbours; | also of the Natives, their Religion, Traffick and Commodities. | Likewise the Advantages accrewing to all Adventurers by the Cu- | stoms of the Countrey; Being the most Healthful and Fertile | of His Majesties Territories on the said Continent of | America. | As Also an Account of the Islands of Bermudas, the Harbours, Situa- | tion, People, Commodities, &c, belonging to the said Islands; | the whole being a Compendious Account of a Voyage made (by | an Ingenious Person) for a full discovery of the above-said places. | Begun in October 82, and finished this present Year, 1683. | *Dvblin, Printed for Nathan Tarrant at the Kings-Arms in Corn-Market.* 1683. | 4to, pp. 7. 17334

The two last lines read, "Taken by John Crafford, who was Super cargo of the good Ship the James of Erwin, burthen about 50 Tuns."

CRAFTON (William Bell). A Short Sketch of the Evidence delivered before a Committee of the House of Commons for the Abolition of the Slave Trade: to which is added, a Recommendation of the subject to the serious attention of People in General. *Tewkesbury: Dyde and Son.* [n. d.] 8vo, pp. 28. + *London: Printed in the Year* 1792. 12mo, pp. 24. + The Third Edition, with Additions. *London: M. Gurney.* 1792. 12mo, pp. 24.

CRAFTS (F. A.) The Christian Hero, by the Rev. F. A. Crafts, Maine. *New York: American Tract Society.* 17336

CRAFTS (S. C.) ... Memorial of Samuel C. Crafts and Others, Citizens of ... Vermont, praying for Further Protection to Domestic Industry. January 2, 1828. ... *Washington: printed by*

Gales & Seaton. 1828. 8vo, pp. 6. (20th Cong., 1st Sess., House Doc. 31.) H. 17337

CRAFTS (T.) A Sermon ... in Middleborough, at the Annual Fast ... April 5, 1804. By Thomas Crafts ... . *Boston: printed by Manning & Loring. May* 1804. 8vo, pp. 22. BA.

Also: An Oration, pronounced July 4th, 1791, ... Boston, ... By Thomas Crafts, Jun. A.M. ... *Boston: Printed by Benjamin Russell.* MDCCXCI. 8vo, pp. 16. BA., M.

CRAFTS (W.) Address delivered before the New-England Society of South-Carolina ... 22d December, 1820. ... By William Crafts ... . *Charleston: printed by Thomas B. Stephens.* 1820. 8vo, pp. 16. H. 17339

CRAFTS. Address delivered February 28, 1825, before the Palmetto Society of South Carolina, in Commemoration of the Defence of the Palmetto Fort on Sullivan's Island, June 28, 1776. By William Crafts. *Charleston, S. C.* 1825. 8vo, pp. 21. 17340

See "N. Am. Rev.," XXI. 464.

CRAFTS. Oration on the Birth of Washington, delivered in St. Philip's Church, Charleston, (S. C.) on the 22d of February, 1812. By appointment of the Washington Light Infantry ... . By William Crafts, Jun. An Officer in the above Corps. *Charleston: Printed by E. Morford.* 1812. 8vo, pp. 23. 17341

CRAFTS. Eulogium on Keating Lewis Simons, (Late commanding the 29th Regt. of South-Carolina Militia,) Who Died on the 1st of Sept. 1819. ... By William Crafts, Jun. Brigade Major. *Charleston: E. A. Miller, Printer.* 1819. 8vo, pp. 31.

CRAFTS. An Oration on the Influence of moral causes on national character, delivered before the ΦBK Society ... 28 August, 1817. By William Crafts, Jun. *Cambridge: University Press, Hilliard & Metcalf.* 1817. 8vo, pp. 16, BA., H. + *Charleston: re-printed at the Courier Office. January.* 1818. 8vo, pp. 14. 17343

From the "N. Am. Rev."

[CRAFTS.] The Raciad and other Occasional Poems. *Charleston: E. Morford, Wellington & Co.* 1810. 12mo, pp. 32.

CRAFTS. A Selection, in Prose and Poetry, from the Miscellaneous Writings of the late William Crafts. To which is prefixed, A Memoir of his Life. *Charleston: C. C. Sebring and J. S. Burges.* 1828. 8vo, pp. l, (1), 384. BA., H. 17345

[CRAFTS.] Sullivan's Island, the Raciad, and other Poems, reprinted. ... *Charleston: printed by T. B. Stephens.* 1820. 8vo, pp. 100. BA. 17346

Also: An Oration, delivered in ... Charleston, South-Carolina, on the Fourth of July, 1812, ... *Charleston: printed by W. P. Young.* 1812. 4to, 1 l., pp. 26. BA. — Oration, on the occasion of Laying the Corner Stone of The Lunatic Asylum, at Columbia, S. C. July 1822. ... *Charleston: E. A. Miller, Printer.* 1822. 8vo, pp. 24.

CRAFTS (W. Augustus). Forest Hill Cemetery: its Establishment, Progress, Scenery, Monuments, etc. With ten illustrations. ... By William A. Crafts. *Roxbury: Published by John Backup.* 1855. 8vo, pp. iv, (1), 237. 17347

CRAFTS. The Life of Ulysses S. Grant: his Boyhood, Campaigns, and Services, Military and Civil. By William A. Crafts ... . *Boston: S. Walker & Co.* 1868. 12mo, pp. viii, 172. Portrait. BA., H. 17348

CRAFTS. The Southern Rebellion: being a History of the United States from the Commencement of Buchanan's Administration through the War for the Suppression of the Rebellion ... By W. A. Crafts. *Boston: Samuel Walker.* 1862–67. 2 vols., 4to, pp. viii, 652, 2 Maps and 24 Plates; 648, 26 Plates.

The Craftsmen: A Sermon from the Independent Whig, suitable to the peculiar Malignity of the present Day. With a Preface, exposing the Artifices of our Priests and Craftsmen by Philo-Reflector. *New York.* 1753. 12mo, pp. xxvi, 39.

See Sedgwick's "Life of Livingston," p. 89.

The Craftsman Extraordinary. Being Remarks on a Pamphlet, intitled Observations on the Conduct of Great Britain, &c., Published by Caleb D'Anvers, Esq; *London: R. Francklin* M DCC XXIX. 8vo, Title, pp. 28. BA. 17351

Signed W. Raleigh.

CRAGG (S.) George Clinton Next President, and our Republican Institutions Rescued from Destruction: Addressed to the Citizens of the United States: or James Madison Unmasked. By Saunders Cragg ... . *New York: the Author.* 1808. 8vo, pp. 40. B. 17352

CRAGGS (S.), *pseudonym.* A Landscape, sketched in New-Hampshire. By Salisbury Craggs. To which are added, Lines to a Democratic Young Lady, and her Reply. ... *Boston: Charles Callender.* 1821. 8vo, pp. 24. S. 17353

CRAGIN (A. H.) Execution of Laws in Utah. Speech of Hon. Aaron H. Cragin, of New Hampshire, ... in the Senate ... May 18, 1870. *Washington: F. & J. Rives & Geo. A. Bailey.* 1870. 8vo, pp. 23. H. 17354

CRAGIN. Loyal Supremacy. All Rights to All Men! Equality of White Men! Speech of Hon. Aaron H. Cragin in the ... Senate, January 30, 1868, on the Reconstruction Acts. *Published by the Union Republican Congressional Executive Committee.* 8vo, pp. 12. H. 17355

CRAGIN (C. H.) The Genealogy of the Cragin Family, being the descendants of John Cragin of Woburn, Massachusetts, from 1652 to 1858. By Charles H. Cragin. ... *Washington, D. C.: W. H. Moore, Printer.* [1860.] 8vo, pp. 38.

CRAIG (A.) Ourselves; our Principles; our Present Controversy; our Immediate Duties. An Address ... at an Annual Conference of Christian Ministers ... . By Austin Craig ... . *Feltville, N. J.: Printed by David Felt & Co.* 1850. 24mo, pp. 22. B. 17357

CRAIG. The Unity and Faith of the Christian Church. ... Discourse ... at the Dedication of the New Hall, ... New York, ... Sunday, May 6, 1849. By Austin Craig. ... *New-York: printed by David Felt & Co.* 1850. 8vo, pp. 20. H. + [Second Edition.] *New York.* 1850. 8vo, pp. 18, (1). B.

CRAIG (H. K.) A Statement of Col. H. K. Craig ... to Members of Congress; and an Answer by a Citizen. [*Washington.*] 1853. 8vo, pp. 8. H. 17359

CRAIG (I.) The Essence of Slavery. By Ira Craig. *London: Ladies' Emancipation Society.* 1863. 12mo, pp. 8. 17360

[CRAIG (J. N.)] Statement regarding certain Charges against Gen. Jas. W. Ripley. *Washington: H. Polkinhorn, Printer.* [1861.] 8vo, pp. 16. H. 17361

CRAIG (N. B.) Exposure of a Few of the many Misstatements in H. M. Breckenridge's History of the Whiskey Insurrection. By Neville B. Craig. *Pittsburgh: John S. Davidson.* 1859. 18mo, pp. vi, 79, Errata, 3 lines. 17362

CRAIG. The History of Pittsburgh, with a Brief Notice of its Facilities of Communication, and other Advantages for Commercial and Manufacturing Purposes. With Two Maps. By Neville B. Craig, Esq. *Pittsburgh: John H. Mellor.* 1851. 12mo, pp. 312. 2 Maps. BA., H. 17363

CRAIG. Lecture upon the Controversy between Pennsylvania and Virginia, about the Boundary Line, delivered at the University Building, Pittsburgh, December 5, 1843. By Neville B. Craig. *Pittsburgh: Printed by A. Jaynes.* 1843. 8vo, pp. 30.

Reprinted in "The Olden Time," I. 434. See Stobo (R.)

CRAIG. The Olden Time; a Monthly Publication, devoted to the Preservation of Documents and other Authentic Information in relation to the Early Explorations, and the Settlement and the Improvement of the Country around the Head of the Ohio. ... Vol. I. Edited by Neville B. Craig, Esq. *Pittsburgh: Printed by Dumas & Co., Chronicle Buildings; J. W. Cook, Publisher.* 1846. 2 vols., 8vo, pp. viii, 576; iv, 572. Map and Plate. + Vol. II. *Printed by Wright & Charlton, N. E. corner of the Diamond.* 1848. W.M.D. 17365

The name of J. W. Cook is omitted in the second volume. It was first published in monthly numbers, and forms a valuable collection of original documents, now very scarce; the second volume more so than the first. Owing to some pecuniary difficulties of the printers, the sheriff attached their material when the last number of Vol. II. was in the press, and in many copies it is wanting.

CRAIG. Sketch of the Life and Services of Isaac Craig, Major in the Fourth (usually called Proctor's) Regiment of Artillery, during the Revolutionary War. By Neville B. Craig. ... *Pittsburgh: J. S. Davidson.* 1854. 18mo, pp. 70. H.

CRAIG. Washington's First Campaign, Death of Jumonville, and the Taking of Fort Necessity, also Braddock's Defeat, the March of the Unfortunate General Explained by a Civil Engineer; the whole arranged by Neville B. Craig. *Pittsburgh: M. P. Morse.* 1848. 8vo, pp. 32. Map. 17367

This appears also in different parts of "The Olden Time."

CRAIG (R. H.) Regulations for the Sword Exercise of the Cavalry, to which is added The Rules for Drill and the Evolutions of the Light Cavalry. *Baltimore: Robert H. Craig.* 1812. 8vo, pp. 215. B., P. 17368

CRAIG (W.) A Key to our Joy. A Sermon delivered in the Trinitarian Church on Fast Day, April 13, 1865, by Wheelock Craig. ... *New-Bedford, Mass.: E. Anthony & Sons, Printers.* 1865. 8vo, pp. 24. B. 17369

CRAIG. A Sermon on the Fruits of our Bereavement, de-

livered in the Trinitarian Church, Sunday, April 23d, 1865, by Wheelock Craig. ... *New-Bedford, Mass.: E. Anthony & Sons, Printers.* 1865. 8vo, pp. 14. B. 17370

These two sermons are bound together, with separate title-pages, and a cover-title; "Two sermons of April, 1865."

CRAIG. Our Duties at this Crisis. A Sermon ... New Bedford, April 21, 1861, by Wheelock Craig. *New Bedford: Mercury Press.* 1861. 8vo, pp. 19. B. 17371

Also: ... A Sermon preached in the Presbyterian Church, New Bloomfield, Pa., Sept. 7, 1862. ... *Philadelphia: C. Sherman & Son, Printers.* 8vo, pp. 20. — An Address delivered before the New Bedford Port Society, on the Occasion of its Twenty-Seventh Anniversary, February 15th, 1857. ... *New Bedford: Mercury Job Press.* 1857. 8vo, pp. 27. H. — Legislation as an Implement of Moral Reform. A Sermon preached in the Trinitarian Church, New Bedford, Oct. 4, 1857. ... *New Bedford: B. Lindsey, Printer.* 1858. 8vo, pp. 15. BA. + *New Bedford* [*Ibid.*] 1858. 12mo, pp. 15.

CRAIG (W. B.) The Lord a Stronghold in the day of trouble. A Thanksgiving Sermon preached in the Presbyterian Church, New Bloomfield, Penna. Nov. 27, 1862, by Rev. W. B. Craig. *Philadelphia: Sherman & Son.* 1862. 8vo, pp. 21.

CRAIG. Thanksgiving and Praise. A Sermon preached in the Presbyterian Church, Mouth of Juniata, Penna. Aug. 6, 1863, by Rev. W. B. Craig, Pastor. *Philadelphia: Sherman & Son.* 1863. 8vo, pp. 18. 17373

[CRAIK (George Lilly), *and* MAC FARLANE (Charles).] The Pictorial History of England: being a History of the People as well as a History of the Kingdom. ... . *London: Charles Knight and Co.* MDCCCXXXVIII. 8 vols., impl. 8vo. Numerous Woodcuts and 104 Portraits on Steel. + Index ... . By H. C. Hamilton ... . *London: Wm. S. Orr & Co.* 1850. 8vo. BA. 17374

Vol. V. of the English edition covers 1760–1785. Reprinted by *W. & R. Chambers, Edinburgh,* 1857? in 7 vols., and partly reprinted in *New York, Harper & Brothers,* 1846, 4 vols., imp. 8vo. The following work was the joint labor of Craik and Charles Knight: "Pursuit of Knowledge under Difficulties; its Pleasures and Rewards illustrated by Memoirs of Eminent Men. *London: Charles Knight.* 1838." 2 vols., 12mo. + *New York: Harper & Brothers.* 1839. 2 vols., 18mo, pp. (2), ii, vii–ix, 9–287; 275. BA. Includes Dampier, Columbus, Cook, Raleigh, and Benj. West.

CRAIK (J.) Historical Sketches of Christ Church, Louisville, Kentucky. By James Craik, Rector. *Morton & Co., Louisville.* 1863. 12mo, pp. 137. 17375

CRAIK. The Union. National and State Sovereignty alike Essential to American Liberty. A Discourse delivered in ... Frankfort, Ky., December 19, 1859. By The Rev. James Craik, D.D. *Louisville, Ky.: Morton & Griswold, Printers.* 1860. 8vo, pp. 36. B., H. 17376

CRAM (M.) An Address delivered by Hon. Marshal Cram, at the Dedication of the Town House in Bridgeton, January 8, 1852. With an Appendix. *Portland: Brown Thurston, Printer.* 1852. pp. 42. 17377

CRAM (T. J.) Basin of the Mississippi, and its Natural Business Site, at the Confluence of the Ohio and Mississippi Rivers, briefly considered, by T. J. Cram ... . *New York: Narine & Co., Printers.* 1851. 8vo, pp. 10. H. 17378

CRAM. Memoir showing how to bring the Lead, Copper, Silver and Gold of Arizona into the Marts of the World. By Captain T. J. Cram. *Troy, N. Y.* 1859. 8vo, pp. 9. S.

CRAM. Memoir upon the Northern Inter-Oceanic Route of Commercial Transit, between Tide Water of Puget Sound of the Pacific, and Tide Water on the St. Lawrence Gulf of the Atlantic Ocean. ... By General T. J. Cram ... . *Detroit.* [1869.] 8vo, pp. 35. Map. H. 17380

CRAMER (C.) Etwas ueber die Natur-Wunder in Nord-America, zusammengetragen von Charles Cramer. ... *St. Petersburg: Gedruckt bei N. Gretsch.* 1840. 8vo, pp. (3), xiii, 5–86, (3). H. 17381

I have seen a catalogue which describes this as *St. Petersburgh.* 1837. 8vo, pp. 40.

CRAMER (P.) Papillons exotiques des trois parties du monde, l'Asie, l'Afrique et l'Amérique. En flamand et en français. *Amsterdam.* 1779–82. 4 vols., 4to. 400 Colored Plates.

There is a supplement by Stoll, *Amsterdam.* 1787–89. 5 pts., 4to. 42 Colored Plates.

CRAMER. Sammlung und Beschreibung auslandischer Schwetterlinge. *Nuremberg.* [n. d.] A. 17383

A translation of three parts only of the previous work.

[CRAMER (Zadok).] The | Navigator: | or the | Traders useful Guide | in navigating the | Monongahela, Allegheny | Ohio and Mississippi | Rivers; | Containing an ample account | of those much admired Waters | from the Head of the former to the Mouth of

the latter; | A Concise description of their | Towns, Villages, Harbours, Settlements, &c | with Particular Directions | how to navigate them | in all stages of the Water, Pointing out their | Rocks, Ripples, Channel, Islands | Bluffs, Creeks, Rivers &c, | and the distances from place to place. | Illustrated with thirteen accurate Maps of the | Mississippi and one of Pittsburgh. | The fifth edition much improved and enlarged. | To which is added an account of Louisiana: | and a notice of the | Mines, Minerals, Natural Curiosities, &c, | ... | *Pittsburgh.* | *From the press of Zadok Cramer.* | 1806. | 12mo, pp. 94. 17384

The first edition was reprinted with additions as below:

[CRAMER.] The Navigator [etc.] To which is added an Appendix containing an Account of Louisiana, &c., as discovered by the voyage under Captains Lewis and Clarke. Sixth Edition, Improved and Enlarged. *Pittsburgh.* 1808. 12mo. Maps. + Seventh Edition Enlarged — with Maps of the Ohio added and Appendix [as before]. *Pittsburgh, Feby,* 1811. 12mo, pp. 295. 17385

[CRAMER.] The Navigator; Containing directions for Navigating The Monongahela, Alleghany, Ohio, and Mississippi Rivers; With an ample Account of the much admired waters, from the head of the former to the mouth of the latter, and a concise description of their Towns, Villages, Harbors, Settlements, &c. with Maps of the Ohio and Mississippi. To which is added An Appendix, Containing an Account of Louisiana, and of the Missouri and Columbia Rivers, as Discovered by the Voyage under Capts. Lewis and Clarke. Eighth Edition, Improved and Enlarged. *Pittsburgh: Cramer, Spear and Eichbaum.* 1814. 12mo, pp. 360. + Ninth Edition. *Pittsburgh:* [*Ibid.*] 1817. 12mo, pp. 304. + Tenth Edition. *Pittsburgh: Cramer and Spear.* 1818. 12mo, pp. 304. + Eleventh Edition. [*Ibid.*] 1821. 12mo, pp. 283. + Twelfth Edition. [*Ibid.*] 1824. 12mo, pp. 275. W.M.D. 17386

For an amplification of this work, see Cumings (S.) The author's name does not appear on the title. In the tenth and eleventh editions the words "Improved and Enlarged" are left out, otherwise exactly as above; in the twelfth and last edition the words "Monongahela, Alleghany," are left out, as well as the "Improved and Enlarged." On the last page of the seventh, and all subsequent editions, there is a list of articles of merchandise and boats, etc., etc., on the Ohio, "Taken from the Pilots' Books," "By James McCrum." For this list of editions of Cramer, I am indebted to Mr. W. M. Darlington, of Pittsburgh, who is good authority.

CRAMP (John Mocket). Baptist History: from the Foundation of the Christian Church ... . By J. M. Cramp ... . *Phila-*

delphia: American Baptist Publication Society. 1869. 12mo, pp. 598. + *London: Elliot Stock.* 1871. 8vo, pp. xv, 3–491. H.

"Baptists in North America," pp. 403–419, 452–469, of the London edition.

CRAMP. The Centenary of the Baptists in Nova Scotia. A Discourse delivered at Hillsburgh, June 10, 1860. By J. M. Cramp, D.D. ... *Halifax, N. S.: "Christian Messenger" Office.* 1860. 16mo, pp. 30. H. 17388

CRANCH (C. P.) A Poem delivered in ... Quincy, May 25, 1840, the Two Hundredth Anniversary of the Incorporation of the Town. By Christopher Pearse Cranch. ... *Boston: James Munroe and Company.* M DCCC XL. 8vo, pp. 26. B. 17389

Also: Address delivered before The Harvard Musical Association in the Chapel of the University at Cambridge, August 28, 1845 ... *Boston: S. N. Dickinson & Co.* 1845. 8vo, pp. 21. B.

CRANCH (W.) Memoir of the Life, Character, and Writings of John Adams; read March 16, 1827, in ... Washington, at the Request of The Columbian Institute ... By William Cranch. *Washington: S. A. Elliot.* 1827. 8vo, pp. 70, (1).

Also: Laws of the United States relating to Patents, By Hon. Wm. Cranch. *Washington: S. A. Elliot.* 1827. 8vo. c. — The author's "Reports of Cases argued and adjudged in the Supreme Court of the United States 1801–1815. ... *Philadelphia: Carey & Lea.* 1830–1854. 9 vols., 8vo, bears on many topics possessing an historical interest.

CRANDALL (P.) Report of the Arguments of Counsel, in the Case of Prudence Crandall ... before the Supreme Court of Errors ... at Brooklyn, July Term, 1834. By a Member of the Bar. *Boston: Garrison & Knapp.* 1834. 8vo, pp. 34. H.

See May (Samuel J.)

CRANDALL. Report of the Trial of Miss Prudence Crandall. ... August Term, 1833. On an Information charging her with teaching Colored Persons ... *Brooklyn: C. Webber, Printer.* 1833. 4to, pp. 22. H. 17392

CRANDALL (R.) The Trial of Reuben Crandall, M.D., charged with publishing Seditious Libels, by circulating the Publications of the American Anti-Slavery Society. *New York: H. R. Piercy.* 1836. 8vo, pp. 62. 17393

CRANDALL (W. L.) Talks with the People of New York. Reported to the Legislature ... by William Lusk Crandall, April, 1853 ... *Albany.* 1853. 8vo, pp. 248. B., S. 17394

Not published. Advocates a school reform in the State.

CRANE (A. J.) Address delivered at the Request of the Military and Citizens of Richmond, in commemoration of the Life and Services of John Quincy Adams, March 21st 1848. By A. Judson Crane. *Richmond: Macfarlane & Fergusson, Printers.* 1848. Rl. 8vo, pp. 8. 17395

CRANE (C. B.) Sermon on the Occasion of the Death of President Lincoln. Preached in the South Baptist Church, Hartford, Conn., Sunday, April 16, 1865. By Rev. C. B. Crane. *Hartford: Press of Case, Lockwood & Company.* 1865. 8vo, pp. 29. B. 17396

Two editions of five hundred each printed.

CRANE (E.) Abstract of an Address by Edward Crane, Esq., on the Subject of Transportation, at the Green Room, State House, February 13th, 14th, and 18th, 1868. *Boston: Wright & Potter.* 1868. 8vo, pp. 40. H., S. 17397

An argument for the marginal railway for Boston.

CRANE (E.), *and others.* Bytown and Prescott Railway, its Influence on Canada Trade. Report of the Boston Committee, Upon the aid to complete the same. *Boston: C. C. P. Moody, Printer.* pp. 12. H. 17398

CRANE (J. M.) The Past, the Present and the Future of the Pacific. By James M. Crane. *San Francisco, Cal.: printed by Sterett & Co.* 1866. 8vo, pp. 79. H. 17399

CRANE (I. W.) Address delivered before the Jackson Convention of Delegates, from the different Townships of the County of Cumberland assembled at Bridgeton, July 27, 1824. By Isaac Watts Crane ... *Philadelphia.* 1824. 8vo, pp. 13.

Also: A Letter to Andrew Kirkpatrick, Esq. Late Chief Justice of N. Jersey, Containing an Exposition of the Cause between John Den *vs.* Franklin & Sharp. By Isaac Watts Crane ... With some Additional Remarks. By Juridicus. ... *Bridgton, N. J.: Printed by Robert Johnston.* 1825. 8vo, pp. 12. BA.

CRANE (J.) An Oration delivered at Douglass ... July 5th, 1802. ... By John Crane, A.M. *Worcester: Daniel Greenleaf.* 8vo, pp. 23. B., BA., W. 17401

CRANE. A Sermon, preached at Northbridge, November 27, 1800. on the Anniversary Thanksgiving in Massachusetts. By John Crane ... *Worcester (Massachusetts): printed by Daniel Greenleaf.* 1800. 8vo, pp. 21. B. 17402

CRANE (J.) Two Discourses, delivered at Northbridge. The One, February 28th. The Other March 7th, 1802. By John Crane ... *Worcester, Massachusetts: Printed by Daniel Greenleaf.* 1802. 8vo, pp. 24. BA., H. 17403

These sermons are on civil government. Also: Discourse delivered in Franklin, May 17, 1815, ... at the Ordination of the Rev. Calvin Park, ... *Providence: printed by Goddard & Mann.* 1815. 8vo, pp. 28. B. — A Sermon delivered at the Installation of ... Ezekiel Rich, to the Pastoral Care of the Church ... in Troy, N. H., December 24, 1815. ... *Keene.* 1816. 8vo, pp. 28. H. — A Sermon, Delivered July 31, 1816, at the Installation of the Reverend William Preston, to the Pastoral Care of the Pacific Church and Society in Providence. ... *Providence: Miller & Hutchens.* 1816. 8vo, pp. 15. B.

CRANE (J. T.) The Fruitful Bough. The Centenary Sermon preached before the Newark Conference, at Washington, Warren County, N. J., March 23, 1866. By the Rev. J. T. Crane, D.D. *New York: J. W. Oliver & Co., Printers.* 1866. 8vo, pp. 25. 17404

Also: The Annual Sermon before the American Sunday-school Union, Philadelphia, May 2, 1858. *Philadelphia.* 1858. 12mo, pp. 32. M.

CRANE (J.) A Historical Sketch of the Second Congregational Church in Attleborough; delivered at its Centennial Meeting, December 7, 1848. By Jonathan Crane, Pastor, ... *Boston: Damrell & Moore, Printers.* 1844. 8vo, pp. 40. H.

CRANE (S. A.) Address on the Occasion of the Return of the Kentish Guards and Volunteers, July 1, 1842, after the Suppression of the late Rebellion in this State. By the Rev. S. A. Crane. *Providence: B. F. Moore.* 1842. 8vo, pp. 12.

Also: An Anniversary Discourse. *St. Louis.* 1841. 8vo.

CRANE (William). Observations on, and a reply to, a Card (published by Dr. Knolton) addressed to Dr. Crane and others. *Boston.* 1795. 8vo. BM. 17407

CRANEBROOK. Narrarive of Capt. Cranebrook, ... assisting in the Elopement of Miss Baxter from Fayal, and conveying her across the Atlantic, and who suffered Two Years' Imprisonment at St. Salvador in Brazil; with Account of their Shipwreck. *London.* 1820. 8vo. 17408

CRANSTON (R. B.) Proceedings of a General Court Martial, holden in Newport, August 1, 1817, for the Trial of Captain Robert B. Cranston of the Newport Artillery. As officially reported by the Judge Advocate. *Providence: Jones & Wheeler.* 1817. 8vo, pp. 24. N. 17409

CRANTZ *or* CRANZ (D.) Alte und Neue Brüder-Historie oder kurz gefasste Geschichte der evangelischen Brüder-Unität ... Von David Cranz. Zweyte Auflage. ... *Barby.* 1771. Sm. 8vo. B. + *Barby: Christian Friedrich Laux.* 1772. 8vo, 8 l., pp. 868, (55). H. 17410

CRANTZ. The Ancient and Modern History of the Brethren: or, a Succinct Narrative of the Protestant Church of the United Brethren, or, Unitas Fratrum, in the Remoter Ages, and particularly In the present Century: written in German By David Crantz ... Now translated ... with Emendations ... [and] Notes, By Benjamin La Trobe. ... *London: W. and A. Strahan.* MDCCLXXX. 8vo, 8 l., pp. 621, (85). BA., H. 17411

Including Count Zinzendorf's voyages to America, in 1741, Bethlehem, Georgia, New York, etc. *See also* "M. Rev.," March, 1781.

CRANTZ. Fortsetzung von David Cranzens Brüder historie [von J. K. Hegner]. *Barby.* 1791–1804. 3 vols., 8vo. + Vierter Abschnitt. Von Synodo 1789 bis zum Synodo 1801. *Gradau.* 1816. Sm. 8vo, pp. 752. B., H. 17412

CRANTZ. Historie von Grönland enthaltend die Beschreibung des Landes und der Einwohner &c. insbesondere die Geschichte der dortigen Mission der Evangelischen Brüder zu Neu-Herrnhut und Lichtenfels. Von David Cranz. Mit acht Kupfertafeln und einen Register. *Barby: Heinrich Detlef Ebers.* 1765. 2 vols., 8vo, 18 l., pp. 1132, 13 l.; 6 l., pp. 360, 6 l. 2 Maps and 8 Plates. + Zweyte Auflage. ... *Barby: Heinrich Detlef Ebers.* 1770. 2 pts., 8vo, 16 l., pp. 1–512; 1 l., pp. 513–1132, (27). 2 Maps and 6 Plates. H. + *Frankfurt und Leipzig.* 1779. 16mo, 6 l., pp. 402. 2 Maps and 4 Plates. 17413

CRANTZ. Fortsetzung der Historie von Grönland insonderheit der Missions-Geschichte der Evangelischen Brüder zu Neu-Herrnhut und Lichtenfels von 1763. bis 1768. nebst beträchtlichen Zusätzen und Anmerkungen zur natürlichen Geschichte, von David Cranz. *Barby: bey Heinrich Detlef Ebers.* 1770. 8vo, 6 l., pp. 360, (12). H. 17414

CRANTZ. Historie von Groenland behelzende eene nauwkeurige beschrijvinge van 's lands ligging, gesteldheid, en natuurlijke zeldzaamheden; den aart, zeden en gewoonten der inwoonen aan de West-zijde bij de Straate Davis, 's Lands aloude en nieuwe Gescheidenisse, etc. *Haarlem en Amsterdam.* 1767. 3 vols., 8vo. 12 Maps, and Plates. + *Amsterdam: H. de Wit.*

Haarlem: C. H. Bohn. 1767. 3 pts., 4to. + *Amsterdam.* 1779. 3 vols., 8vo. 12 Maps, and Plates. 17415

CRANTZ. Historia om Grönland deruti Landet och desz Inbyggare &c. J synnerhet Evangelista Brödra. Församlingens der warande Mision och desz Förrattningar I Ny-Herrnhut och Lichtenfels beskrifwas. *Stockholm: Johan Georg Lange.* 1769. 2 vols., 12mo, pp. 526; 530–1216, including Index. 17416

CRANTZ. The History of Greenland: containing a Description of the Country, and its Inhabitants: and particularly, A Relation of the Mission, carried on for above these Thirty Years by the Unitas Fratrum, at New Herrnhuth and Lichtenfels, in that Country. By David Crantz. Translated from the High-Dutch, and illustrated with Maps and other Copper-plates. ... *London, Printed for the Brethren's Society for the Furtherance of the Gospel among the Heathen: And sold by J. Dodsley* [etc.] MDCCLXVII. 2 vols., 8vo, 2 l., pp. lix, 405, 2 Maps and 3 Plates; Title, pp. 497, (1). Plate. H. 17417

"As to Greenland, may I not rest satisfied with the exclusive recommendation of the translation by the pious and learned Gambold, from the High Dutch of old Crantz, in 1767." — DIBDIN'S *Lit. Comp.* *See also* "M. Rev.," XXXVI. 231; XCIII, 259. Reprinted with a continuation, with the following title:

CRANTZ. The History of Greenland: Including an Account of the Mission Carried on by the United Brethren in that Country. From the German of David Crantz. With a Continuation to the Present Time; Illustrative Notes; and an Appendix, Containing a Sketch of the Mission of the Brethren in Labrador. *London: Longman.* 1820. 2 vols., 8vo, pp. xi, 359; vi, 323. 7 Maps, and Plates. BA. 17418

In speaking of this work, Dr. Johnson declared that very few books had ever affected him so deeply, and that the man who did not relish the first part was no philosopher, and he who could not enjoy the second, no Christian The following is an abridged continuation:

CRANTZ. Historie von Grönland enthaltend die Beschreibung des Landes und der Einwohner etc., nebst beträchtlichen Zusätzen und Anmerkungen zur natürlichen Geschichte bis auf das Jahr 1779. Mit acht Kupfertafeln und einem Register. *Nürnberg und Leipzig: bey Christoph Weigel und Schneider.* 1782. 8vo, 6 l., pp. 392. 2 Maps and 7 Plates. J.C.B. 17419

Reprinted, in part, in Vol. xx. of the "Bibliothek der neusten Reisebeschr."

CRANTZ. Anmaerkninger over de tre förste Böger af Hr. David Crantzes Historie om Grönland. *Kiöbenhavn: Trykt aj Gerhard Giese Salikath.* 1771. 8vo, 9 l., pp. 388. H. 174

CRAPO (H. H.) Descriptive Catalogue of ... Trees, ... cultivated ... by Henry H. Crapo, ... New Bedford, Mass. *New Bedford, Mass.: Printed by Benj. Lindsey.* 1848. 8vo, pp. 28.

See also New Bedford

CRARY (A. C.) Memorial to Congress from Archibald C. Crary, of Utica, New York, relative to the Rhode Island Brigade. Presented at the 2d Session of the 37th Congress, 1862–63. [n. p. n. d.] Folio, pp. 5. 17422

CRARY (J.) Speech of John Crary in the Senate ... New York, on the Proposition for appointing an Inquisitor in the Case of William Morgan. *New York.* [1828.] 24mo, pp. 18.

Also: Statement to the Anti-Masons of 1828. S.

CRARY (*Mr.*) Speech of Mr. Crary, of Michigan, on the motion to refer the ... President's Annual Message to the Appropriate Committees. In the House ... January, 1839. *Washington: Blair and Rives, Printers.* 1839. 8vo, pp. 8. 17424

CRASHAW (W.) A | Sermon | Preached in | London before the right hono- | rable the Lord Lavvarre, Lord-Gouer- | nour and Captaine Generall of Virginea, | and others of his Maiesties Counsell for that | Kingdome, and the rest of the Aduen- | turers in that Plantation. | At the said Lord Generall his | leave taking of England his Natiue Countrey, | and departure for Virginea, | Febr. 21. 1609. | By W. Crashaw Bachelar of Diuinitie, | and Preacher at the Temple. | Wherein both the lawfulnesse of that Action is | maintained, and the necessity thereof is also demon- | strated, not so much out of the grounds of Policie, | as of Humanity, Equity, and | Christianity. Taken from his mouth, and published by direction. ... *London, | Printed for William Welby, and are to be sold | in Pauls Church-yard at the signe | of the Swan.* 1610. | 4to, 46 leaves. M. 17425

CRASSUS (L.), *pseudonym.* Examination of Mr. Jefferson's Message to Congress, in 1801. By Lucius Crassus. *New York.* 1802. 8vo. 17426

CRAVATH (I. M.) Manual of the Grand Army of the Republic, containing its Principles and Objects, together with Memorial Day in the Department of Michigan, May, 1869, List of Officers, etc. By J. M. Cravath. *Lansing, (Mich.): W. S. George & Co.* 1869. 12mo, pp. viii, 143. C. 17427

CRAVEN (Alfred W.) Report of A. W. Craven, Chief Engineer of the Croton Aqueduct Department ... relative to the Underground Railroad in Broadway, New York. ... *Albany: C. Wendell, Printer.* 1866. 8vo, pp. 11. H. 17428

CRAVEN. Prison Life of Jefferson Davis. Embracing Details and Incidents in his Captivity, Particulars concerning his Health and Habits, together with many Conversations on Topics of Great Public interest. By Bvt. Lieut.-Col. John J. Craven, M.D., Late Surgeon U. S. Vols., and Physician of the Prisoner during his Confinement in Fortress Monroe, from May 25, 1865, up to December 25, 1865. ... *New York: Carleton.* 1866. 8vo, pp. 377. Woodcut. BA. 17429

A few copies are printed on large paper. Also: A Political Letter written to a Citizen of Illinois.

CRAVEN (T. T.) Record of the Testimony taken in the Trial of Commodore T. T. Craven, United States Navy, before a Court-Martial held in Washington, D. C., in November, 1865. *New York.* 1866. 8vo, pp. xii, 176. H. 17430

The preface is signed Alfred W. Craven.

CRAVENS (J. A.) Reconstruction. A Speech of Hon. James A. Cravens, of Ind., ... in the House of Representatives, May 2, 1864. 8vo, pp. 11. H. 17431

Also: Speech ... on the President's Message. ... in the House ... Dec. 8, 1862. [n. p. n. d.] 8vo, pp. 8.

[CRAWFORD (Charles).] The Christian: a Poem; in Four Books, to which is prefixed a Preface in Prose, in defence of Christianity: with an Address to the People of America. *Philadelphia: Joseph Crukshank.* 1783. 12mo, pp. 111. + Second Edition. *Philadelphia.* 1794. 17432

CRAWFORD. An Essay on the Propagation of the Gospel; in which there are numerous Facts and Arguments Adduced to prove that many of the Indians in America Are descended from the Ten Tribes. ... By Charles Crawford, Esq. The Second Edition. *Philadelphia: James Humphreys.* 1801. 12mo, pp. 154, 1 l. BA., C. 17433

CRAWFORD. Observations upon Negro Slavery ... The Author Charles Crawford. *Philadelphia: Joseph Crukshank.* M DCC LXXXIV. 12mo, pp. 24. BA., H. + Second Edition. *Philadelphia.* 1790. 12mo. P. 17434

Another edition is entitled, "Observations upon Slavery. ... By Charles Crawford, Esq. *Tunbridge-Wells: Jasper Sprange.*" [n. d.] 8vo, pp. 42. Also: The Dying

Prostitute; a Poem. *Philadelphia.* 1797. 12mo. — Observations upon the Fall of Anti-Christ and the Concomitant events. ... *Philadelphia: Printed* [1783?] 12mo, pp. 32. — Observations upon the Downfall of the Papal Power, and the consequent events. ... Second Edition. *Philadelphia.* 1788. — Observations upon the Revolution in France. ... *Boston: William Spotswood.* 1793. 8vo, pp. 44. — Poetical Paraphrase of our Savior's Sermon on the Mount. ... *Philadelphia.* 1796. 12mo. — The Progress of Liberty; a Pindaric Ode. ... *Philadelphia.* 1796. 12mo.

CRAWFORD (E.) Sermon: ... History of the Methodist Church in Hartford. By Elijah Crawford. *Hartford.* 1849. 8vo. 17435

[CRAWFORD (G. W.), *and* APPLEWHITE (J.)] Statistical Address to the People of Austin and Washington Counties, on the Subject of Railroads. By a Committee. *Washington.* 1852. 8vo, pp. 8. H. 17436

CRAWFORD (J.) Address delivered at the Grand Convention of the Free Masons of the State of Maryland, held on the 10th May, 1802. By John Crawford, M.D., Grand Master. ... *Baltimore.* 1802. 8vo, pp. 48. 17437

CRAWFORD (J. A.) The Royal Burial. A Sermon, preached, by request, in the Reformed Presbyterian Church, Venice, Ohio, May 31st, 1863, on the occasion of the Death of Daniel McMillan. By J. Agnew Crawford, Chaplain U. S. Army. *Philadelphia.* 1863. 8vo. pp. 24. 17438

CRAWFORD (J.) The Substance of a Sermon delivered at the Funeral of Miss Nabby Frothingham, Feb. 24, 1809. By Joseph Crawford ... *New York.* 1809. 8vo, pp. 36. 17439

CRAWFORD (J. M.) Mosby and his Men: a Record of the Adventures of that Renowned Partisan Ranger, John S. Mosby, (Colonel C. S. A.) Including the Exploits of Smith, Chapman, Richards, Mountjoy, Turner, Russell, Glasscock ... By J. Marshall Crawford of Company B. *New York: G. W. Carleton & Co.* MDCCCLXVII. 12mo, pp. 375. 7 Portraits (Woodcuts). BA. 17440

CRAWFORD (L.) History of the White Mountains, from the First Settlement of Upper Coos and Pequaket. By Lucy, Wife of Ethan Allen Crawford, Esq. *White Hills.* 1846. 18mo, pp. 204. 17441

CRAWFORD (M. J.) Speech of Hon. M. J. Crawford, of Georgia, on the Election of Speaker. Delivered in the House of Representatives, December 15, 1859. [*Washington:*] *Printed by Lemuel Towers.* 8vo, pp. 8. H. 17442

CRAWFORD (W.) Report of William Crawford, Esq., on the Penitentiaries of the United States, addressed to his Majesty's principal Secretary of State for the Home Department. *London.* 1834. Folio. 17443

CRAWFORD (W. H.) Report of the Secretary of the Treasury ... [on] the Condition of the Bank of the United States and its Offices; also Statements in relation to the Situation of the different Chartered Banks ... . *London.* 1820. 8vo, pp. 229–273 of Vol. XVII. of the Pamphleteer. B. 17444

CRAWFORD. Sketches of the Life and Character of William H. Crawford. By Americanus. *Albany.* 1824. 8vo, pp. 38.

CRAWFORD. Strictures addressed to James Madison on the celebrated Report of William H. Crawford; recommending the Intermarriage of Americans with the Indian Tribes, ascribed to Judge Cooper; and originally published by Mr. John Binns, in the Democratic Press. *Philadelphia: Jesper Harding.* 1824. 8vo, pp. 22. 17446

CRAWFORD. Letter to William H. Crawford, Esq. on the Establishment of an Uniform System of Bankruptcy. By a Citizen of Massachusetts. *Boston.* 1821. 8vo. W. 17447

CRAWFORD. Message of the President, transmitting information relative to the reception of Mr. Crawford, Minister to France, by that Court. January 14, 1814. 17448

CRAWFORD (W. N.) Views on the subject of Systematic British Pauper Immigration to Canada. ... By W. N. Crawford. *Montreal.* 1840. 8vo, pp. 28. 17449

The Crayon: a Journal Devoted to the Graphic Arts, and the Literature related to them. ... *New York: Stillman & Durand.* 1855–63. 8 vols., 4to. B. 17450

CRAYON (Geoffrey), *pseudonym.* *See* [Irving (W.)]

Crayon Sketches. *See* Fay (Theodore S).

CREASY (F. S.) The British Empire; Historical, Biographical, and Geographical: with an Introductory Sketch of F. S. Creasy, M.A. *London: R. Griffin & Co.* 1856. Crown 8vo, pp. 700. 17451

Credentiale | Van de Koningin Regente | Van | Portugael | Beneffens | de Propositie | Van haren Extraordinairen Ambassadeur

Ferdi- | nandus Telles de Faro. | Aen haer | Hooghmogende | over gelevert, ende geproponeert den 22 Julij. 1658. | *'t Schiedam voor Philips | by Vaal* 1658. | 4to, pp. 8. 17452

CREE. New Testament, in the Cree Language. *London.* 1859. 12mo. C. 17453

Oo meyo achimoowin St. Mark. The Gospel according to St. Mark; translated into the Language of the Cree Indians, [etc., by Archdeacon Hunter]. *London: British and Foreign Bible Society.* 1855. 12mo, pp. iv, 87. C. 17454

The First Epistle General of John, Translated by Mrs. Hunter into the Language of the Crees. *London.* 1855. 8vo, pp. 13. C. 17455

Portions of the Book of Common Prayer, in the Language of the Cree Indians. [By Archdeacon Hunter.] Transmitted with phonetic Symbols. [By Rev. R. Hunt.] *London: Church Missionary House.* 1856. 8vo, 6 l., pp. 52. C. 17456

CREECY (J. R.) Scenes in the South, and other Miscellaneous Pieces, by the Late Col. James R. Creecy. *Washington: Thomas McGill, Printer.* 1860. 12mo, pp. 294, vi. BA., C.

Some copies have the imprint, *Philadelphia: J. B. Lippincott & Co.* 1860.

CREEK INDIANS. Controversy with the Creek Indians; Report of a Committee of the House of Representatives of the United States, with Resolutions of the State of Georgia. *Washington.* 1827. 8vo. (Cong. Doc.) 17458

Emigrating Indians. Letter from the Secretary of War, transmitting information of the inadequacy of the fund for defraying the Expenses attending the Emigration of the Creek Indians. January 7, 1828. *Washington.* 1828. 17459

Contains six documents illustrating the history of the treatment of the Indians.

The Gospel according to John. Ωρωnvkv hera chanichωyvten, oksumkvlki irkinvkv, H. F. Buckner, [etc.] *Marion, Alabama: Southern Baptist Convention.* 1860. 16mo, pp. 190. C.

"Nakcokv Setempohetv." Introduction to the Shorter Catechism. Translated into the Creek Language, by the Rev. R. M. Loughridge and David Winslett. Second Edition. *Philadelphia.* 1858. 24mo, pp. 34. 17461

An Oration Delivered at a National Council. By a Creek Indian. *Boston.* [1755?] S. 17462

The Speech of a Creek-Indian, against the Immoderate Use of Spirituous Liquors. Delivered In a National Assembly of the Creeks upon the breaking out of the late War. To which are added, I. A Letter from Yariza, an Indian Maid of the Royal Line of the Mohawks, to the principal Ladies of New York. 2. Indian Songs of Peace. 3. An American Fable. Together with Some Remarks upon the Characters and Genius of the Indians, and upon their Customs and Ceremonies at making War and Peace. *London: R. Griffiths.* M.DCC.LIV. 8vo, pp. 68. 17463

CREERY (W. R.) First Annual Address ... before the Public School Teachers' Association, January 25, 1850. By William R. Creery ... . *Baltimore: printed by Sherwood & Co.* 1850. 8vo, pp. 26. H. 17464

CREIGH (A.) History of the Knights Templar of the State of Pennsylvania, from February 14th A.D. 1794, A.O. 676, to Nov. 13th A.D. 1866, A.O. 748, A.O.E.P. 69. ... By Alfred Creigh, LL.D., KT., 33°, ... *Philadelphia: J. B. Lippincott & Co.* 1867. 12mo, pp. 394. C. 17465

CREIGH. Masonry and Anti-Masonry. A History of Masonry as it has existed in Pennsylvania since 1722, in which the True Principles of the Institution are fully developed, and all Misrepresentations corrected; containing the Protests, Speeches, Reports, &c. presented before the Inquisitorial Committee at Harrisburg, Pa. By Alfred Creigh. *Philadelphia.* 1854. 12mo, pp. 322. C. 17466

CREIGH (J. J.) Address, delivered at Paoli Massacre Ground, July 4th, 1867. *West Chester: N. T. Smith, Printer.* 1867. 16mo, pp. 23. H. 17467

CREIGHTON (John Orde). Court Martial. *Washington.* 1818. 8vo, pp. 25. 17468

CREIGHTON (W.) Sermons on the Occasion of the Death of the late Washington Irving, preached in Christ Church, Tarrytown, by the Rev. Wm. Creighton, D.D., Rector, and the Rev. J. Selden Spencer, Assistant Minister. *New York.* 1859. 8vo, pp. 36. 17469

CREMONY (J. C.) Life among the Apaches. By John C. Cremony. *San Francisco: A. Roman & Company.* 1869. 12mo, pp. 322. 17470

The Creole Case and Mr. Webster's Despatch; with the Comments of the N. Y. American. *New York.* 1842. 8vo, pp. 39. BA. 17471

Commissioners of Appeals in Prize Causes. Case of the Creole, of Boston, Capt. Andrew Newell. Respondent's Case. *London.* 1811. Folio, pp. 6. M. 17472

Crescent Almanac. *Crescent, N. Y.* 1853. 12mo. S.

CRESEY (N.) Thanksgiving Sermon, to the Chapel Society, North Yarmouth, December 2, 1824. By Noah Cresey. *Portland.* 1826. 8vo, pp. 17. N. 17474

CRESINUS, *pseudonym.* *See* [Hunt (J.)]

CRESP (Antoine). De la fabrication des sucres aux colonies françaises de l'Amérique. 1803. 8vo. 17475

CRESPEL (E.) Voiages du R. P. E. Emmanuel Crespel dans le Canada, et son naufrage en revenant en France. Mis au Jour par le S^r. Louis Crespel son Frère. *Francfort sur le Meyn.* MD CC XLII. 12mo, 5 l., pp. 158. J.C.B. + *A Francfort sur le Meyn: Henry Louis Broenner.* M D CC LII. Sm. 8vo. H.

See Faribault, No. 177. Reprinted with the following title:

CRESPEL. Voyage au Nouveau-Monde, et Histoire intéressante du naufrage du R. P. Crespel. Avec des notes historiques & geographiques. *A Amsterdam.* M. DCC. LVII. 12mo, pp. x, 140. H., S. 17477

The signatures change with the sheets, thus: A has pp. 16, B, pp. 8, etc.; pp. 231 to 241 are misprinted 131, etc. This work was edited by the author's brother. The scene of the narrative is the northern lakes. *See* "M. Rev.," XIX. 200. Rich gives the imprint, *Paris*, another authority says, *Paris: Lambert*; both are doubtful. *See* Rich, I. 126, 127.

CRESPEL. Des Ehrwürdigen Pater Emanuel Crespels merwürdige Reisen nach Canada, daselbst gehabte Begebenheiten, und erlittener Schifbruch bey seiner Heimreise nach Franckreich; der bewundernswürdigen Vorfälle wegen aus dem Französischen übersezt. *Frankfurt und Leipzig: Georg Peter Monath.* 1751. 12mo, 4 l., pp. 112. H. 17478

CRESPEL. Travels in North America, By Emanuel Crespel, with a Narrative of His Shipwreck, and Extraordinary Hardships and Sufferings on the Island of Anticosti; and an Account of that Island, and of the Shipwreck of his Majesty's Ship Active, and others. *London: Sampson Low.* 1797. 12mo, pp. xxviii, 187.

[CRESPO (Joseph Rafel).] Reflexiones sobre la importante Cuestion, propuesta al Congreso Nacional, acerca de la mejora de gobierno, que la situacion y la justicia reclama en favor de las bastas Provincias Ultra-marinas. *Valencia.* 1821. Sm. 4to.

CRESSE (B. de). Histoire de la Catastrophe de St. Dominique, par B. de Cressé. 1824. 8vo. 17481

CRESSET (E.) Sermon before the Society for Propagation of the Gospel in Foreign Parts, 1763. By the Right Rev. Edward, Bishop of Landaff. *London.* 1753. 4to, pp. 78. M. 17482

CRESSEY (E. H.) Subordination to the Civil Authority the Duty of Christians. A Sermon, preached in ... Lockport, N. Y. ... January 7, 1838. By ... E. H. Cressey ... . *Lockport, N. Y.: printed by R. M. Lyon.* 1838. 8vo, pp. 16. H. 17483

CRESSON (J.) Meditations written during the prevalence of the Yellow fever, in the City of Philadelphia, in the year 1793, which proved fatal to upwards of Four Thousand of its Inhabitants. By Joshua Cresson, — of the People called Quakers and one of the latest Victims of the Disease. *London: W. Phillips.* 1803. 12mo, pp. 36. P. 17484

Edited by William Dillwyn, with prefatory note, dated *London, 8 mo.* 26th, 1803. Republished in the "Irish Friend," II. 77.

CRESSY (B. C.) An Address delivered before the Pelo-Paidensian Society of Washington-County Seminary, Ind. By Rev. B. C. Cressy, A.M. *Salem, Ind.* 1834. 8vo, pp. 22. M.

CRESSY (N.) The Murder of Dr. George Parkman ... a Poem, by Noah Cressy ... . *Portland: Harmon & Williams, Printers.* 1850. 12mo, pp. 40. H. 17486

CRESWELL (J. A. J.) Oration on the Life and Character of Henry Winter Davis, by Hon. John A. J. Creswell. Delivered in the Hall of the House of Representatives, February 22, 1866. *Washington: Government Printing Office.* 1866. 8vo, pp. 43.

CRESWELL (J. A.) Speech of John A. Creswell, on the Proposed Amendment to the Constitution of the United States, in the House of Representatives of the United States, January 5, 1865. [n. p. n. d.] pp. 16. 17488

Creswell Unmasked. [*Baltimore.* 1864.] 8vo, pp. 7.

CRESSWELL (S. G.) A Series of Eight Sketches in Colour: together with a Coloured Map of the Route; By Lieut. S. G. Cresswell, of the Voyages of H. M. S. Investigator, Capt. M'Clure, during the Discovery of the North-west Passage. *London: Day & Son.* 1854. 8 Views. 17490

CRÉTINEAU-JOLY. Histoire religieuse, politique et littéraire de la compagnie de Jésus, composée sur les documents inédits et authentiques. Par Crétineau-Joly. Ouvrage orné de portraits et de fac-simile. *Paris: Paul Mellier.* 1844–46 6 vols., 8vo. BA. + Troisième édition ... augmentée. *Paris.* 1859. 6 vols., 18mo. BA., C. 17491

Contains some particulars concerning the Jesuits in America. *See* Jesuits.

CREUXIUS (P.) *See* Du Creux (P.)

CREUZBAUR (R.) Route from the Gulph of Mexico and the Lower Mississippi Valley to California and the Pacific Ocean. *New York.* 1849. 12mo. A. 17492

CREUZE (M. P.) Lettre de Michel Pascal Creuzé. Membre du Conseil des Anciens, à Jean Philippe Garan, Deputé du Loiret, sur son rapport des troubles de St. Domingue, distribué au Corps legislatif en ventôse an v, dix-huit mois apres la clôture des débats. *Paris. An* v [1797.] 8vo, pp. 66. J.C.B.

[CREVECOUR (J. H. St. J.)] Lettres d'un cultivateur américain, écrites a W. S. Écuyer, Depuis l'année 1770, jusqu'à 1781. Traduites de l'Anglois par ***. ... *Paris: Chez Cuchet, Libraire, rue & hôtel Serpente.* M. DCC. LXXXIV. 2 vols., 8vo, pp. xxiv, iij, (1), 422, (2); 2 l., pp. iv, 400, (2). + *Paris. [Ibid.]* M DCC LXXXV. H. 17494

CREVECŒUR. Lettres d'un cultivateur Américain addressées à W^m. S... on Esqr. depuis l'Année 1770 jusqu' en 1786. Par M. S^t. John Creve Cœur, Traduites de l'Anglois. Keen feelings inspire resistless thoughts. *Paris: Cuchet.* 1787. 3 vols., 8vo, Engraved Title, pp. xxxij, 478, (2), Map and 3 Plates; Engraved Title, pp. 438, (6), 2 Maps; Engraved Title, pp. 592. 2 Maps. BA., H. 17495

This edition is greatly enlarged, the whole of the third volume being added. This translation was made by the author himself. The work is highly recommended in two letters, by way of introduction, from M. de Lacretelle. Boucher de la Richarderie says that the author had been so long unaccustomed to his native language that his translation abounds with Anglicisms, "which, however," he adds, "give greater energy to his expressions."

CREVECŒUR Letters from an American Farmer; Describing Certain Provincial Situations, Manners, and Customs, not generally known; and conveying some Idea of the late and present Interior Circumstances of the British Colonies in North America. Written for the Information of a Friend in England, By J. Hector St. John A Farmer in Pennsylvania. *London: Thomas Davies and Lockyer Davies.* M DCC LXXXII. 8vo, 8 l., pp. 318. 2 Maps. + *Dublin: John Enshaw.* M. DCC. LXXXII. 12mo, 6 l., pp. 256. 2 Maps. + New Edition. ... *London: Thomas Davies.* M, DCC, LXXXIII. 8vo, 7 l., pp. 326. 2 Maps. BA. + *Philadelphia: From the Press of Mathew Carey. March* 4, M, DCC, XCIII. 12mo, pp. 240. + *Philadelphia.* M,DCC,XCVIII. 12mo, pp. 260. 17496

"The author was a native of Normandy, of noble birth, and came to the British colonies at the age of sixteen. Having established himself on a farm near the frontier, he became one of the first victims of the War of Independence, the Indian allies of Great Britain setting fire to and destroying his property. He wrote his letters during the different epochs of the war, in English. Returning to France, he translated them into French." — RICH. His work "is a most pleasing report of the resources and charms of the country when it was far more isolated and exclusively rural than at present. Somewhat like a prose idyl is this record; Hazlitt delighted in its *naive* enthusiasm, and commended it to Charles Lamb, as well as in the 'Quarterly,' as giving an idea how American scenery and manners may be treated with a lively poetic interest. — TUCKERMAN's *America and her Commentators.*

CREVECŒUR. Remarks on the Letters from an American Farmer. ... *London: John Fielding.* MDCCLXXXIII. 8vo, pp. 26.

[CREVECŒUR.] Brieven van eenen Amerikaenschen Landman van Carlisle in Pennsilvanien, geschreven aen eenen zijner vrienden in Engeland. Uit het Engelsch. *Leyden: L. Herdingh.* 1784. 8vo, pp. xvi, 328. J.C.B. 17498

The following seems to be another title for the same work:

[CREVECŒUR.] Brieven, behelzende den Toestand, Zeden, Landbouw, en Gewoonten der Inwoonders van eenige der nu vereenigde dertien Gewesten van Noord Amerika, voor en in den nu geëindigden oorlog. Uit het Engelsch. *Leyden.* 1784. 8vo. 17499

[CREVECŒUR.] Sittliche Schilderungen von Amerika, in Briefen eines Amerikanischen Guthsbesitzers an einen Freund in England. Aus dem Englischen. *Leipzig und Leignitz: David Geigert.* 1784. 12mo, pp. 462. 2 Maps. J.C.B. 17500

[CREVECŒUR.] Voyage dans la Haute Pensylvanie et dans l'Etat de New York, Par un Membre adoptif de la nation Oné-

ida. Traduit et publié par l'auteur des Lettres d'un Cultivateur Américain. *De L'imprimerie de Crapelet. A Paris Maradan An* IX–[1801.] 3 vols., 8vo, pp. xxxii, 427, 4 Plates and Map; xiv, 434, 2 Plates and 2 Maps; xii, 409; Plate and 3 Tables.

There are some copies on large paper, with the plates in folio. Though called a translation, this is believed to be an original work by M. de Crevecœur, whose initials only appear at the end of the dedication to Washington. The author spent nearly a quarter of a century in America, saw Washington, in 1774, come to the first Congress fresh from his farm, witnessed his extraordinary career, and, in 1797, saw him retire to the private life of an agriculturist. His experience, therefore, enables him to give much information and personal gossip not readily found elsewhere. The portrait of Washington in the first volume is an interesting one, "Gravé d'après le Camée peint par Madame Bréhan à Newyork en 1789." There is also a fine portrait of Késkètomah, an Onondagua sachem, and of Koohassen, an Oneida warrior. "This work is distinguished by its valuable details on the aboriginal tribes, and their gradual disappearance. No other writer has so well described the Indian great councils, or assemblies, where they deliberate on their public interests." *See* "M. Rev.," XXXVI. 449.

CREVECŒUR. Reise in Ober-Pensylvanien und in Staate Neu York, von einem adoptirten Mitgliede der Oneida-Nation. Aus dem Französischen übersetzt und mit Anmerkungen begleitet von Dieterich Tiedemann. Mit zwei Kupfern. *Berlin.* 1802. 8vo.

CREVEL. Créance américaine. A M. le president du conseil des ministres. [Signé: Crevel, officier supérieur.] *Paris: imp. de Mévrel.* 1835. 8vo. 17503

CREWDSON (Isaac). Trade to the East Indies. *Manchester: Henry Smith, Printer.* [About 1827.] 4to. 17504

Written in reference to West India slavery.

Le Cri d'un Colon de Saint-Domingue, par un colon mis hors la loi en 1795. *Paris.* 1820. 8vo. S. 17505

CRIDGE (A.) Epitome of Spirit-Intercourse ... . Manifestations in Nova Scotia ... . By Alfred Cridge ... . *Boston: Bela Marsh.* 1854. 8vo, pp. 108. 17506

Crie de Colons contre un ouvrage de M. l'Evêque Grégoire, ou réfutation des inculpations calomnieuses faites aux colons par l'auteur et par les autres philosophes négrophiles. *Paris.* 1810. 8vo. A., P. 17507

CRIME (Admonish), *anagram.* *See* [Richmond (James).]

Crimenes de la Demagogia. El Colegio apostolico de Guadalupe, en Zacatecas. *Guadalajara.* 1859. 4to, pp. 80. 17508

A vigorous invective against the anti-clerical party of Juarez and Ortego.

[Crippen (William G.)] Green Peas, picked from the Patch of Invisible Green, Esq. *Cincinnati: Moore, Wilstack & Co.* [1856.] 12mo, pp. 311. c. 17509

Cripps (J.) A True account of the Dying Words of Ockanickon, an Indian King, spoken to Jahkursoe, his Brother's Son, whom he appointed King after him. By John Cripps of Burlington, N. J. *London: Benjamin Clark.* 1682. 4to, pp. 8. + *Printed in the Year*, 1683. 4to, pp. 6. 17510

Reprinted and inserted in Budd's "Good order established in Pennsylvania and New Jersey, in America," 1685, 4to, pp. 30.

The "Crise" Metcalfe and the Fontaine-Baldwin Cabinet Defended. 1844. 8vo. 17511

Relates to Canadian politics.

Crisfield (J. W.) Speech of Mr. J. W. Crisfield, of Maryland, on ... excluding Slavery from the Territories ... . June 22, 1848. *Washington: printed by John T. Towers.* 1848. 8vo, pp. 16. s. 17512

Crisfield. Speech of Mr. Crisfield; ... on Slavery ... in the District of Columbia. Delivered in the ... House of Representatives, February 17th, 1849. *Washington: printed by John T. Towers.* 1849. 8vo, pp. 16. H. 17513

The Crisis. *See* [Carey (M.)], Vol. iii., No. 10861, [Cooper (S.)], Vol. iv., No. 16599, [Colton (C.)], Vol. iv., No. 14768, [Paine (Thomas)], [Pendleton (Edmund)], and [Scott (T. P.)]

The Crisis. Number 1. To the People of England and America. [*London.* 1774–5.] 8vo, pp. 119. P. 17514

This is the heading of No. 1. No. xv. was published Aug. 29, 1775. Without title-page, place, or printer's name, and the paging is continuous.

The Crisis; In Answer to the False Alarm. *London.* 1770. 8vo. P. 17515

The Crisis. To be continued Weekly during the present Bloody Civil War in America. [*London:*] *Printed and Published for the Authors by T. W. Shaw, Fleet Street, where letters to the publisher will be thankfully received.* 1775–1776. 2 vols., folio, 91 numbers, pp. 574, and Broadside of the Declaration, July 4, 1776. J.C.B. 17516

"A periodical published weekly, commencing January 4, 1775, and continued to June 8th, 1776. The work, which is of great rarity, contains a remarkable collection of papers attacking the ministry and the British government in terms of the greatest

severity. Indeed, one can hardly believe that, in time of war, a publication of such a character would be tolerated. In the opening address to the people of England and America, the publisher says, 'It is in your defence I now unsheath the sword of justice, to oppose the most profligate and abandoned administration that ever shewed the weakness, or abused the confidence of a prince.'—'The altar of despotism is erected in America, and we shall be the next victims to a lawless power.' In taking leave of their readers in the 90th number, the publisher says, 'We now lay down this paper, with grateful thanks to the public, and as liberty and virtue have taken their flight to America, the only asylum for freemen, we are determined to follow, and not longer struggle in vain to animate our dastardly, degenerate countrymen with the noble spirit of their forefathers.'"—J. R. Bartlett. A manuscript note in a copy I have seen, states that, "By order of a vote of the House of Commons, burnt by the common hangman." In one of Welford's catalogues, there are said to be ninety-eight numbers, the last being dated, Oct. 12. 1776. It was reprinted, in part, as below:

The Crisis. Vol. i. Containing xxviii Numbers. *London, Printed; New York, reprinted by John Anderson, at Beekman Slip.* M.DCC.LXXVI. 12mo, pp. 236. 17517

Perhaps more numbers were published. Six or more numbers were also reprinted at *Newport, R. I.* 8vo, pp. 48, and I have seen No. 1. *New London: reprinted.* [n. d.] 8vo, pp. 8.

The Crisis. No. 1. *London.* 1777. 8vo, pp. 12. 17518

The Crisis. *New York: D. Appleton and Company.* 1863. 8vo, pp. 95. 17519

Sympathizes with the South and her institutions. Signed Cae. S.

The Crisis. *New York: W. B. Smith & Co.* 1860. 8vo, pp. 48. 17520

The Crisis. By the Author of Plain Facts, or A Review of the Conduct of the Late Ministers. The Fifth Edition, considerably enlarged. *London: John Joseph Stockdale.* 1808. 8vo, pp. 146. BA. 17521

Pages 102–125 relate to the Right of Search and the Orders in Council.

The Crisis! An Appeal to our Countrymen, on the Subject of Foreign Influence in the United States! Issued under the influence of the General Executive Committee of the American Republican party of the city and county of New-York ... *New-York.* 1844. 8vo, pp. 80. B., S. 17522

The Crisis: being an Enquiry into the Course to be pursued by the Southern States, against the Abolitionists. *Charleston: D. J. Dowling.* 1836. 17523

A Crisis Chapter on Government. *See* [Blanchard (Calvin).] Vol. ii., No. 5817.

"The Crisis." Closing Scenes of the Year 1860. By "Common Sense, Jr." *New York: Ross & Tousey.* 1861.

Crisis del ensayo à la historia de la Florida. *See* [Salazar (Joseph de)].

Crisis Extraordinary. *See* [Paine (T.)]

Crisis in the Affairs of the Domestic and Foreign Missionary Society of the Protestant Episcopal Church, and an Appeal to Episcopalians. *Philadelphia.* 1825. 8vo. pp. 55. M. 17525

The Crisis Met in Reply to the Crisis of the Country. [1840?] 8vo. 17526

See [Colton (C.)], Vol. iv., No. 14768.

The Crisis of Affairs, as it respects the West-India Colonies, and the Probable Effects of the French Decree for Emancipating the Negroes. *London.* 1795. 8vo. 17527

The Crisis of the Colonies Considered. *See* [Williams (J.)]

The Crisis of the Country. By Junius. The Credit System and the no Credit System. *New York & Boston.* [n. d.] 8vo, pp. 16. H. 17528

An electioneering pamphlet in favor of Wm. H. Harrison, by Calvin Colton. *See* [Colton (Calvin)], Vol. iv., No. 14768.

The Crisis of the Dispute with the United States. In Three Letters. With an Explanatory Preface. By a Merchant of the Old School. *London.* 1811. 8vo. + *London.* 1812. 8vo.

The Crisis of the Sugar Colonies; or, an Enquiry into the Objects and Probable Effects of the French Expedition to the West Indies; And their Connection with the Colonial Interests of the British Empire. To which are subjoined, Sketches of a Plan for settling the Vacant Lands of Trinidada. In Four Letters to the Right Hon. Henry Addington ... . *London: J. Hatchard.* 1802. 8vo, pp. vii, 222. BA. 17530

See the "Edinb. Rev.," No. 1., p. 216, and "The Opportunity."

The Crisis: on the Origin and Consequences of our Political Dissensions. To which is annexed, the Late Treaty between the United States and Great Britain. By a Citizen of Vermont. ... *Albany: printed by E. & E. Horsford.* 1815. 8vo, pp. 96.

See "Hist. Mag.," iv. 225.

The Crisis; on the Present State of Affairs *London.* 1761. 8vo, pp. 40. C., P. 17532

Relates to the resignation of William Pitt.

The Crisis; or, A Defence of Administration against the Opposition. *London.* 1785. 8vo, pp. 19, 49. C.P. 17533

The Crisis: or, Essays on the Usurpations of the Federal Government. By Brutus. ... *Charleston: printed by A. E. Miller.* 1827. 8vo, pp. 166. H., S. 17534

The Crisis: or Immediate Concernments of the British Empire. *London: C. Dilly.* 1785. 8vo. 17535

See "M. Rev.," lxxvi. 307.

The Crisis: or Nullification Unmasked. 1832. 8vo. W.

Relates to the tariff.

Crisis No. 1; or Thoughts on Slavery; Occasioned by the Missouri Question. *New Haven.* 1820. 8vo. 17537

The Crisis: Relating to the Celebrated Massachusetts Excise Bill to raise Money to prosecute the French War. *Boston.* 1754. 12mo, pp. 16. 17538

The Crisis. To the People of Connecticut. [*Hartford.* 1819.] 8vo, pp. 14. BA. 17539

Crisostomo (M. de S.) Sermon en la festividad de patrocinio de Señ. San. José. *Mejico.* 1836. 4to, 20 l. 17540

Crisp (S.) Sermons or Declarations, made by Stephen Crisp, one of the Antient Preachers amongst the People called Quakers. ... *Philadelphia: Printed by Joseph Crukshank, in Third-Street, opposite the Work-House.* M DCC LXXIII. 8vo, pp. 60. BA.

This is the last of the tracts which form Benezet's "Potent Enemies of America."

Crisp (T.) The Men of the Age. A Lecture. By Rev. Thomas Crisp. *Halifax.* 1859. 8vo, pp. 25. 17542

Cristobal Colomb. El Descubrimiento de America. *Paris: Rosa et Bouret.* 1866. 8vo. 17543

Criswell (R.) Letters from the South and West. [Before 1852.] 17544

Criswell "Uncle Tom's Cabin" Contrasted with Buckingham Hall, the Planter's Home, or, A Fair View of both sides of the Slavery Question. By Robert Criswell, Esq. ... *New York: D. Fanshaw.* 1852. 12mo, pp. 152. C. 17545

The Criterion: containing Portraits of the Three Candidates, Facts in the Lives of Each, the Platforms of the Three Parties, ... *New-York: J. C. Buttre.* 1856. 8vo, pp. 32. 17546

The Criterion. Literary and Critical Journal. *New York: Charles R. Rode.* 1856. 2 vols., 4to, pp. 414; 174. 17547

Started on an independent basis, ably done, but had to succumb to the *great* publishers.

The Critic. A Weekly Review of Literature, Fine Arts, and the Drama. Edited by W. Leggatt. *New York.* 1828–9. 2 vols., imp. 8vo. 17548

The Critic Criticised, and Worcester vindicated; consisting of a Review ... upon the Comparative Merits of Worcester's and Webster's Quarto Dictionaries. ... *Boston: Swan, Brewer and Tileston.* [n. d.] pp. 72. H. 17549

A Critical Commentary on Archbishop Secker's Letter to the Right Honourable Horatio Walpole, concerning Bishops in America. *Philadelphia: John Dunlap.* M,DCC,LXXI. 8vo, pp. 72. P. 17550

See [Blackburne (F.)], Vol. ii., No. 5689.

Critical Essay concerning Marriage. ... Account of the Marriage Rites and Ceremonies of the Greeks and Romans, and our Saxon Ancestors ... By a Gentleman. *London: Charles Rivington.* M.DCC.XXIV. 8vo, 10 l., pp. 310 (4). 17551

Pages 317–337, Marriage Rites in Chili, America, Canada, etc.

Criticism criticised. Intended as a Supplement to the Law Reporter for January, 1859. ... *Boston: Little, Brown, and Company.* 1859. 8vo, pp. 56. H. 17552

Criticism on the Declaration of Independence, as a Literary Document. By Mon Droit. *New York.* 1846. 8vo, pp. 44.

Crito's Letters to the Electors of the United States, on the Commercial Representations; and the Seat of Government. ... *Philadelphia: printed by Bartram and Reynolds.* 1807. 8vo, pp. 26. BA., P. 17554

Crittenden (J. J.) A Bill To provide for the ascertainment and satisfaction of claims of American citizens for spoilations committed by the French prior to the thirty-first day of July, one thousand eight hundred and one. [*Washington?* n. d.] 4to, pp. 8. H. 17555

Crittenden. The Kansas Conference Bill. Speech of Hon. J. J. Crittenden, of Kentucky. ... April 27, 1858. *Washington, D. C: Buell & Blanchard, Printers.* 1858. 8vo, pp. 8.

Also: Kansas: the Lecompton Constitution. Speech ... March 17, 1858. *Washington.* 1858. 8vo, pp. 16. M.— ... Relation of the States. Speech ... on the Davis Resolutions in the U. S. Senate, May 24, 1860. [n. p. n. d.] 8vo, pp. 8.—Speech ... upon the Resolution of Mr. Ewing, [on] Payment for the Public Lands. ... December 20, 1836. *Washington: printed by Duff Green.* 1836. 8vo, pp. 14. H.—Speech ... on the Oregon Question. ... April 16, 1846. [n. p. n. d.] 8vo, pp. 16. H.—Speech ... on the Admission of the State of Kansas. ... March 17, 1858. [*Washington: printed by Lemuel Towers.* 1858.] 8vo, pp. 16.—Speech ... March 17, 1858. [Corrected by Himself.] *Washington, D. C.: C. W. Fenton.* 1858. 8vo, pp. 16.—Speech ... on his Resolutions. Delivered ... January 7, 1861. [n. p. n. d.] 8vo, pp. 8.—Speech ... on the Abolition of Slavery in the District of Columbia. Delivered in the House ... April 11, 1862. [n. p.] *Towers & Co., Printers.* 8vo, pp. 16.—Speech ... on the Confiscation of Rebel Property. Delivered in the House ... April 23, 1852. [n. p. n. d.] *Towers, Printers.* 8vo, pp. 8. H.

The Croakers. *See* [Drake (J. R.)], *and* [Halleck (F. G.)]

[Crocker (A. B.)] Random Sketches upon Witches, Dreams, Love and Romance. By A Free Thinker. *Albany: J. Munsell.* 185–. 8vo, pp. 16. 17557

A foolish performance by a Presbyterian preacher.

Crocker (Hannah M.) Observations on the Real Rights of Women, with their Appropriate Duties ... . By H. Mather Crocker. ... *Boston: the Author.* 1818. 16mo, pp. viii, 5–92.

Also: A Series of Letters on Free Masonry. By a Lady of Boston. *Boston.* 12mo. 1815. W.

Crocker (H. S.) Railroad Gazetteer for Gratuitous Distribution. ... . *Sacramento: Published Monthly by H. S. Crocker & Co.* 16mo, pp. 127, (1). Map of California. 17559

Crocker (S. L.) Eulogy upon the Character and Services of Abraham Lincoln, Late President of the United States. Delivered by Invitation of the Authorities of the City of Taunton, On the Occasion of the National Fast, June 1, 1865. By Samuel L. Crocker, Jr. *Boston: Printed by John Wilson and Son.* 1865. 8vo, pp. 28. B., H. 17560

[Crocker (U. H.)] Map and Description of Proposed Metropolitan Park for Boston. *Boston: printed by Rand, Avery & Frye.* 1870. 8vo, pp. 12. B. 17561

Crocker. Plan for a Public Park. Letter from Uriel H. Crocker. [*Boston.* 1869 or '70.] 8vo, pp. 8. Map. H.

Crocker (U. H.), *and* Crocker (G. G). Notes on the general statutes of Massachusetts. To which is added a List of Cities and Towns in the States, and of certain State and County Officers. *Boston: Little, Brown & Co.* 1869. 8vo, pp. iv, 609.

Crocker (Z.) The Catastrophe of the Presbyterian Church in 1837. Including a full View of the recent Theological Controversies in New England. By Zebulon Crocker ... . *New Haven: B. & W. Noyes.* 1838. 12mo, pp. xii, 300. B., H., M.

Crockett (D.) An Account of Col. Crockett's Tour to the North and down East, in the Year of our Lord One Thousand Eight Hundred and Thirty-four. His object being to examine the Grand Manufacturing Establishments of the Country; and also to find out the Condition of its Literature and Morals, the extent of its Commerce, and the Practical Operation of "The Experiment." ... Written by Himself. *Philadelphia: E. L. Carey and A. Hart. Baltimore: Carey, Hart, and Co.* 1835. 12mo, pp. 234. Portrait. H. + *New York: Nafis & Cornish.* 1845. 12mo, pp. 234. Portrait. 17565

Crockett. Col. Crockett's Exploits and Adventures in Texas: wherein is contained A full account of his Journey from Tennessee to the Red River and Natchitoches, and thence across Texas to San Antonio; including his many Hair-breadth escapes; Together with a Topographical, Historical and Political View of Texas. Written by himself. The Narrative brought down from the Death of Col. Crockett to the Battle of San Jacinto, by an Eye Witness. Sixth Edition. *Philadelphia: T. K. and P. G. Collins.* 1837. 12mo, pp. viii, 13–216. Portrait. C. + *London.* 1837. 12mo. A. + *Cincinnati: U. P. James.* 1839. 12mo, pp. 216. + *New York.* 1845. 17566

Crockett. The Life of Martin Van Buren, Heir-Apparent to the "Government," and the Appointed Successor of General Andrew Jackson. Containing every Authentic Particular by which his Extraordinary Character has been formed. With a Concise History of the Events that has occasioned his Unparalleled Elevation; together with a Review of his Policy as a Statesman. By David Crockett. *Philadelphia: Robert Wright.* 1835. 12mo, pp. 209. BA. + Tenth Edition. *Philadelphia: Robert Wright.* 1836. 12mo, pp. 209. + Sixteenth Edition. *Philadelphia: Robert Wright.* 1837. 12mo, pp. 209. 17567

Crockett. The Life and Adventures of Col. David Crockett, of West Tennessee. *Cincinnati.* 1833. 12mo.

Crockett. Life and Adventures of Colonel David Crockett. Embracing his Career as Hunter, Soldier and Congressman; with a Full Account of his Texan Exploits and Glorious Death at the Alamo. By the Author of "Life of Boone," "Kit Carson," Etc. *New York: Beadle and Company.* [n. d.] 16mo, pp. 96. H.

Crockett. Life of Col. David Crockett, written by Himself. Comprising his Early Life, Hunting Adventures, Services under General Jackson in the Creek War, Electioneering Speeches, Career in Congress, Triumphal Tour in the Northern States, and Services in the Texan War. To which is added an account of Col. Crockett's glorious Death at the Alamo, while fighting in defense of Texan Independence. By the Editor. *Philadelphia: G. G. Evans.* 1859. 12mo. 17570

Crockett. A Narrative of the Life of David Crockett of the State of Tennessee ... Written by Himself. *Philadelphia: E. L. Carey and A. Hart.* 1834. 12mo, pp. 211. C. + *Boston: Allen & Ticknor.* pp. 211. BA., C. + Sixth Edition. *Philadelphia.* 1834. 12mo, pp. 211. + *London.* 1834. 12mo. A. + Twelfth Edition. *Philadelphia.* 1835. 12mo. + *New York.* 1837. 12mo, pp. 211. + *New York.* 1845. 12mo. C. + *New York: Wm. H. Graham.* 1848. 12mo, pp. 211. 17571

Crockett. Pictorial Life and Adventures of David Crockett, written by himself. Embellished ... from original designs in the finest style of art ... This work will in future times ... be prized almost beyond its weight in gold ... *Philadelphia.* [1852.] 8vo, pp. 193. 17572

Crockett. Sketches and Eccentricities of Col. David Crockett, of West Tennessee. ... New Edition. *New-York: J. & J. Harper.* 1833. 12mo, pp. (3), 24–209. BA., C. + *London.* 1834. 12mo. A. 17573

Crockett. Davy Crockett; or the Nimrod of the West, The Only Cure for the Hard Times. A Poem. By a friend to the Colonel. Canto 1. *New York: Printed for the Author.* 1837. 12mo, pp. iv, 46. 17574

Crockett. Davy Crockett Beaten. A Spur to Youth; being the Life of Paddy O'Flarrity, who from a Shoe-Black has by perseverance and good conduct arrived to be a Member of Congress. 1834. 12mo, pp. 56. 17575

CROCKETT. Davy Crockett's Almanack, 1845. Crockett Almanack, Turner & Fisher. *Philadelphia.* 1849, '54. 12mo.

Several almanacs bear the name of Crockett, the following are among them: Vol. 1. "Go Ahead!" No. 4. Davy Crockett's 18 Almanack, 38 of Wild Sports in the West, Life in the Backwoods, Sketches of Texas, and Rows on the Mississippi. *Nashville, Tennessee: Heirs of Col. Crockett.* 12mo, pp. 44, (2). Woodcuts. H. + Vol. 2, No. 1. ... 1839 ... . *Nashville, Tennessee: Ben Harding.* 12mo, pp. 35, (1). Woodcuts. H. + Improved Edition. 1842. Containing Real Stories. Crockett Almanac ... *Boston: S. N. Dickinson.* [n. d.] 8vo, pp. 35, (1). Woodcuts. H. + ... Fisher's Crockett Almanac. Edited by Ben Harding. 1843. ... *Boston: James Fisher.* [n. d.] 12mo, pp. 36. Woodcuts. H.

CROCKETT (G. F. H.) An Address to the Legislature of Kentucky, on the Abolition of Capital Punishment in the United States, and the Substitution of Exile for Life. By G. F. H. Crockett ... . *Georgetown, Ky.: printed by N. L. Finnell.* 1823. 8vo, pp. 8. 17577

CROCKETT (H. C.) The American in Europe. *London: J. Tallis & Co.* 1850. 4to. Plates. 17578

CROCKETT (S. L.) A Voice from Leverett Street Prison, or the Life, Trial, and Confession of Simeon L. Crockett, who was executed for Arson, March 16, 1836. ... *Boston.* [n. d.] + Third Edition. 12mo, pp. 24. + Sixth Edition. 12mo, pp. 22.

CROCKITT (*Mr.*) Speech of Mr. Crockitt, of Tennessee, on the Bill proposing ... a National Road from Buffalo to New Orleans, Delivered in the House of Representatives of the United States, March, 1830. *Washington.* 1830. 8vo, pp. 8.

CROES (J.) A Discourse delivered at Woodbury, in New Jersey, on the Twenty-Second of February Eighteen Hundred. Before the Citizens of Gloucester County, assembled to pay Funeral Honours to the memory of General George Washington. Agreeably to a recommendation of Congress, as announced by the President, in his Proclamation of the 6th of January last: By John Croes, A.M. Rector of Trinity Church at Swedesborough. Published at the desire of the Committee of arrangement, at whose request it was delivered. *Philadelphia: Printed by John Ormrod,* ... 1800. 8vo, pp. 32. H. 17581

Also: An Address ... at the Commencement of the General Theological Seminary of the Protestant Episcopal Church ... New York, ... Thirtieth Day of June, 1826. ... . *New York: printed by T. and J. Swords.* 1826. 8vo, pp. 15. H. — Charge to the Clergy of the Protestant Episcopal Church in the State of New Jersey, at the Annual Convention, Swedesborough, August 18, 1819: ... *New-Brunswick.* 1819. 8vo,

pp. 16. — The Duty and the Interest of contributing to the Promotion of Religious and Benevolent Institutions. Sermon preached in Philadelphia, 20th May, 1823, at the General Convention of the Protestant Episcopal Church in the United States. ... *New York.* 1823. 8vo, pp. 23. — A Sermon before the General Convention, May 23, 1814. ... *Philadelphia.* 1814. 8vo.

CROES (R. B.) The Anniversary Lecture, pronounced before the Historical Society of the County of Vigo, Indiana, on the 14th of March, 1844, by the Rev. Robert B. Croes ... . *Cincinnati.* 1845. 8vo, pp. 23. BA. 17582

CROESE (Gerard). Historia Quakeriana; sive, de vulgo dictis Quakeris, ab Ortu illorum usque ad recens natum Schisma, Libri iii, [etc.] *Amstelodami, apud Henricum & Viduam Theodori Boom.* 1695. 16mo, 8 l., pp. 582, 1 l. + Editio Secunda. *Amstelodami.* 1696. 16mo, 8 l., pp. 580, 9 l. C. 17583

CROESE. The General History of the Quakers: containing the Lives, Tenents, Sufferings, Tryals, Speeches, and Letters of all the most eminent Quakers, both Men and Women; from the first Rise of that Sect, down to this present Time. Collected from Manuscripts, &c., A Work never attempted before in English. Being written originally in Latin by Gerard Croese. To which is added, a Letter writ by George Keith, and sent by him to the Author of this Book. Containing a Vindication of himself, and Several Remarks on this History. *London, Printed for John Dunton, at the Raven in Jewen-Street.* 1696. 8vo, 19½ sheets. S. 17584

Contains some particulars of the Quakers in Pennsylvania. It was also translated into German, *Berlin: Hen Johann Michael Rüdigern.* 1696. 8vo, 49 sheets.

CROFFUT (W. A.), *and* MORRIS (J. M.) The Military and Civil History of Connecticut during the War of 1861–65, comprising a detailed Account of the Various Regiments and Batteries ... . By W. A. Croffut and John M. Morris. Illustrated. *New York: Ledyard Bill.* 1868. 8vo, pp. 892. C. + Third Edition revised. *New York: L. Bill.* 1869. 8vo, 2 l., pp. 891. 14 Plates. B. 17585

[CROFTON (Walter Cavendish).] Brief Sketch of the Life of Charles Baron Metcalfe to the Period of his resigning the Office of Governor General of the British American Colonies in 1845. By Uncle Ben. *Kingston.* 1846. 8vo, pp. 37. 17586

CROFUTT (G. A.) Great Trans-Continental Railroad Guide, containing a Full and Authentic Description of over Five-Hundred Cities, Towns, Villages, Stations, ... *Chicago: Crofutt & Eaton.* 1870. 16mo. B. 17587

[CROFTON.] Sketches of the Thirteenth Parliament of Upper Canada. By Erienensis. *Toronto.* 1840. 12mo, pp. 32.

CROGHAN (G.) Minutes of Conferences held at Fort-Pitt, in April and May, 1768, under the Direction of George Croghan, Esquire, Deputy Agent for Indian Affairs, with the Chief and Warriors of the Ohio and other Western Indians. [Royal Arms.] *Philadelphia: Printed and Sold by William Goddard, at the New-Printing-Office, in Market-Street.* M,DCC,LXIX. Folio, pp. 22. P. 17589

See appendix to Butler's "Kentucky."

[CROGHAN (*Dr.* John).] Rambles in the Mammoth Cave in 1844. By a Visitor. *Louisville: Morton & Griswold.* 1845. 12mo, pp. 101. 17590

CROIL (J.) Dundas, or a Sketch of Canadian History ... By James Croil. *Montreal: B. Dawson & Son.* 1861. 8vo, pp. 352. B. 17591

Also: Our Country. Past and Present: A Lecture delivered at the time of the Trent Difficulty. 1862.

CROIX (Carlos Francisco de). [Vando sobre Limpieza de las Calles de Mexico. *Mexico:*] *Imprenta del Superior Govierno.* 1769. 4to, pp. 17. 17592

CROIX. *See* La Croix, *and* Sainte Croix.

CROKATT (James), *Editor.* Further Observations intended for improving the Culture and Curing of Indigo, &c. in South Carolina. [*London.* 1747.] 8vo. 17593

[CROKE (*Sir* Alexander).] An Examination of the Rev. Mr. Burke's Letter of Instruction to the Catholic Missionaries of Nova Scotia. By Robert Stanser. *Halifax.* 1804. 17594

Robert Stanser is a *pseudonym.* Also: Remarks on Mr. Schlegel's Works upon the Visitation of Neutral Vessels under Convoy. By Alexander Croke, Esq. LL.D. ... . *London: J. White, and J. Debrett, J. Stockdale, J. Wright.* 1801. 8vo, Title, pp. 157. BA.

[CROKER (J. Wilson).] The Letters on the Subject of the Naval War with America which appeared in the Courier under the Signature of Nereus. *London.* 1813. 8vo. 17595

CROLY (D. G.) Campaign Lives of Seymour and Blair. By D. G. Croly. *New York: Richardson & Co.* 1868. 12mo, pp. 119. Portraits. 17596

CROLY. Seymour and Blair; their Lives and Services. With an Appendix containing the History of Reconstruction. By D. G. Croly. *New York: Richardson & Co.* 1868. 12mo, pp. 275. Portrait. 17597

CROLY (G.) A Memoir of the Political Life of the Right Honourable Edmund Burke; with Extracts from his Writings. ... By George Croly ... . *Edinburgh: William Blackwood & Sons. London: Thomas Cadell.* M.DCCC.XL. 2 vols., post 8vo, pp. xv, 305; vii, 267. BA. 17598

CROME (A. F. W.) Uber die Grösse, Volksmenge, Clima und Fruchtbarkeit des Nordamerikanischen Freystaats von A. F. W. Crome. *Dessau und Leipzig.* 1783. 8vo. pp. viii, 64.

CROMELIEN (R.) Cromelien on the American Rebellion. Tri-Party War of 1861 and 1862. *Washington.* 1862. 8vo, pp. 8. B., H. 17600

CROMPTON (S.) The Life of Christopher Columbus in short words. By Sarah Crompton. *London: Bell & Daldy.* 1860. Sq. 12mo, pp. viii, 85. 17601

CROMPTON, *R. I.* Historical Sketch with the Confession and Covenant of the Warwick and Coventry Baptist Church, Crompton, R. I. *Providence: Knowles, Anthony & Co.* [n. d.] 12mo, pp. 8. 17602

CROMWELL (Henry S.) Poem [on the Death of Abraham Lincoln]. 1865. Broadside. 17603

CROMWELL (O.) The Story of the Embarkation of Cromwell and his Friends for New England. Reprinted from the New England Historical and Genealogical Register. *Boston.* 1866. 8vo. pp. 11. 17604

[CROMWELL (Sidney).] Political Opinion in 1776 and 1863: A Letter to a Victim of Arbitrary Arrests and "American Bastiles." *New York: Anson D. F. Randolph.* 1863. 12mo, pp. 19. 17605

Cronica de la orden de S. Augustin, en las provincias de la Nueva Espana, desde 1533 hasta 1592. *Mexico.* 1624. Folio.

La Cronica. Periódico malicioso, imparcial, verídico, griton, novelero y picante. *Carácas.* 1866. 8vo, pp. 128. 17607

Nos. 1–16, all published.

CRONISE (T. F.) The Natural Wealth of California. Comprising Early History, Geography, Topography, and Scenery; Climate; Agriculture and Commercial Products; Geology, Zoology, and Botany; Mineralogy, Mines, and Mining Processes; Manufactures, Steamship Lines, Railroads, and Commerce; Immigration, Population and Society; Educational Institutions and Literature; together with a Detailed Description of each County ... . By Titus Fey Cronise. *San Francisco: H. Bancroft & Company.* 1868. Rl. 8vo, pp. xvi, 696. 17608

CROOKER (Turner), *and others.* To His Excellency the Governor ... of Massachusetts, and to his Honorable Council. [*Boston.* 1808.] 8vo. H. 17609

A memorial from officers of the militia, of June, 1798.

[CROOKSHANKS (J.)] The Conduct and Treatment of John Crookshanks, Esq. late Commander of His Majesty's Ship the Lark, relating to his Attempt to take the Glorioso, a Spanish Ship of War, in July 1747: containing the Original Orders, Letters, and Papers, that passed in consequence of that affair, between Captain Crookshanks, Admiral Knowles, the Secretaries of the Admiralty, and others. With a Plan, shewing the Positions of the Ships. *London: J. Scott.* 1759. 8vo, pp. vii, 155. C. 17610

An interesting narrative, relating to various parts of North America, containing letters and papers of Admiral Knowles, commander at Cape Breton, Robert Kirke, and others. For an answer, *see* Erskine (R.), Knowles (Admiral), also the following "Letter from a Gentleman in the Country to a Member of Parliament in Town; containing Remarks upon a Book lately published, entitled 'The Conduct and Treatment of John Crookshanks, Esq., late Commander of His Majesty's Ship the Lark.' *London.* 1759." 8vo. C.

CROOKSHANKS. Reply of John Crookshanks, Esq., to a Pamphlet lately set forth by Admiral Knowles, intitled "A Refutation of the Charge brought against Admiral Knowles." *London.* 1759. 8vo. C. 17611

CROOKSHANKS. Minutes of the Proceedings of a Court-Martial held on George Crookshanks, Esq., formerly Captain of His Majesty's Ship the Lark, now first published by R. Kirke. 1772. 8vo. 17612

CROOM (H. B.) A Catalogue of Plants, Native or Naturalized, in the Vicinity of Newbern, North Carolina; with Remarks and Synopsis. By H. B. Croom. *New York.* 1837. 8vo, pp. 52. 17613

CROOM. Oration delivered before Capt. J. H. Byrd's Company of Volunteers, July 4, 1825, at Kingston, N. C. By H. B. Croom, Esq. *Newbern, reprinted* 1826. 8vo, pp. 12. M.

CROOME (W.) The Golden Sands of Mexico. A Moral and Religious Tale: to which is added True Riches ... . By W. Croome. ... *Philadelphia: Lindsay and Blakiston.* 1850. 12mo, pp. 211. A., H. 17615

CROPPER (J.) The Extinction of the American Colonization Society the First Step to the Abolition of American Slavery. By James Cropper. *London: printed by S. Bagster, jun.* 1833. 8vo, pp. 24. B. 17616

CROPPER. The Interests of the Country and the Prosperity of the West India Planters mutually secured by the Immediate Abolition of Slavery; being a Review of the Report of a Select Committee of the House of Commons, on the State of the West India Colonies, ordered to be Printed, April 13, 1832. By James Cropper. *London.* 1832. 8vo. + Second Edition. *London: J. & A. Arch.* 1833. 8vo. 17617

CROPPER. A Letter addressed to the Liverpool Society for Promoting the Abolition of Slavery, on the Injurious Effects of High Prices of Produce, and the Beneficial Effects of Low Prices, on the Condition of Slaves. By James Cropper. *Liverpool.* 1823. 8vo, pp. 32. 17618

CROPPER. Letters Addressed to William Wilberforce, M.P. recommending the Encouragement of the Cultivation of Sugar in ... the East Indies, as the certain and natural means of effecting the Total and General Abolition of the Slave Trade. By James Cropper. *Liverpool.* 1822. 8vo, pp. 64. P. 17619

CROPPER. Relief for West-Indian Distress, shewing the Inefficiency of protecting Duties on East-India Sugar, and pointing out other Modes of certain Relief. By James Cropper. *London: Hatchard & Son.* 1823. 8vo, pp. 36. 17620

CROPPER. Slavery in the West Indies. *Liverpool: James Smith.* [n. d.] 4to. 17621

CROPPER. The Support of Slavery Investigated. By James Cropper. *Liverpool: Printed by George Smith.* 1824. 8vo, pp. 27. 17623

CROPPER. A Vindication of a Loan of £15,000,000 to the West India Planters, shewing that it may not only be lent with Perfect safety, but with Immense Advantage both to the West Indians and to the People of England. By James Cropper. *London: J. and A. Arch.* 1833. 8vo, pp. 16. 17624

CROSBY (A.) A Memorial of the College Life of the Class of 1827, Dartmouth College ... . By Alpheus Crosby ... . *Hanover, N. H.* 1869–70. 8vo, pp. 40. H. 17625

CROSBY. The Present Position of the Seceded States, and the Rights and Duties of the General Government in respect to them. An Address to the Phi Beta Kappa Society of Dartmouth College, July 19, 1865. By Alpheus Crosby. ... *Boston: Geo. C. Rand & Avery.* 1865. 8vo, pp. 16. 17626

Also: A Lecture on the Use and Abuse of Emulation as a Motive to Study: ... at Newburyport, April 9, 1852. ... *Lynn: Butterfield & Kellogg, Printers.* 1852. 8vo, pp. 28. B.

CROSBY (A. B.) Memorial Address, Prof. David S. Conant, M.D. Delivered ... by A. B. Crosby ... . *Burlington.* 1866. 8vo, pp. 30. H. 17627

CROSBY (Charles Coteworth Pinckney). Two Letters to the Rev. Horatio Bardwell. *Worcester.* 1826. W. 17628

Also: History of West Boylston, Mass. [Worcester Magazine and Hist. Journal, Vol. II.]

CROSBY (D.) Sermon, on the Ordination of the Rev. Henry Adams, at Worthington, Mass., 1833. By Daniel Crosby ... *Boston.* 1834. 8vo. 17629

Also: Who Troubles Israel. Thanksgiving Discourse ... *Amherst. Nov.* 29, 1832. 8vo.

CROSBY (E. N.) The Letter of a Republican, Edward N. Crosby, Esq., ... to Prof. F. B. Morse, Feb. 25, 1863, and Prof. Morse's Reply, March 2, 1863. 8vo, pp. 12. (N. Y. Soc. for Diff. of Political Knowledge. Papers, No. 4.)

CROSBY. Our Country versus Party Spirit: being a Rejoinder to the Reply of Prof. Morse. By Edward N. Crosby. *Poughkeepsie: Platt & Schram, Printers.* 1863. 8vo, pp. 14. 17631

CROSBY (F.) Life of Abraham Lincoln, Sixteenth President of the United States: containing his Early History and Political Career, together with the Speeches, Messages, Proclamations,

and other Official Documents illustrative of his Eventful Administration. By Frank Crosby. *Philadelphia: John E. Potter.* 1865. 12mo, pp. 476. 17632

Also in the German language, translated by Carl Theodor Eben. *Philadelphia.* 1865.

CROSBY (Frances Jane). Monterey; and other Poems. By a Pupil at the N. Y. Institution for the Blind. *New York.* 1851. 12mo. 17633

Also: The Blind Girl, and other Poems. *New York.* 1844. 12mo.

CROSBY (F. B.) A Memorial of Lieut. Franklin Butler Crosby, of the Fourth Regiment U. S. Artillery, who was killed at Chancellorsville, Va., 1863. *New York: A. D. F. Randolph.* 32mo, pp. 69. 17634

CROSBY (H.) God's View of Rebellion. A Sermon preached in the Fourth Avenue Presbyterian Church, on the occasion of the National Thanksgiving, Sunday, Sept. 11, 1864, By Howard Crosby, D.D. *New York: E. French.* 1864. 8vo, pp. 16.

CROSBY. Sketch of the Fourth Avenue Presbyterian Church. (Formerly the Bleecker Street Church.) By Howard Crosby, D.D. Pastor of the Church. *New York: E. French.* 1864. 8vo, pp. 16. 17636

CROSBY (Jaazaniah). Dedication with Joy. A Sermon ... at the Dedication of the New Meeting House of the First Congregational Society in Charlestown, N. H., Nov. 8, 1843. By J. Crosby, Pastor. ... *Keene: printed by J. & J. W. Prentiss.* 1843. 8vo, pp. 12. H. 17637

CROSBY. History of Charlestown in New Hampshire, from its First Grant by the Province of Massachusetts in 1735 to the Year 1833. By Jaazaniah Crosby, Pastor of the First Church in said town. *Concord: Marsh, Capen & Lyon.* 1833. 8vo, pp. 41. 17638

CROSBY. A Sermon preached by Jaazaniah Crosby, D.D., March 25, 1860, the Day which completed Fifty Years of his Ministry at Charlestown, N. H. ... *Boston: Crosby, Nichols, and Company.* 1860. 8vo, pp. 15. H. 17639

CROSBY. The Tendency of Religious Obedience to promote National Prosperity. A Sermon, preached at Concord, ... New-Hampshire, June 3, A.D. 1830. Being the Anniversary Election. By Rev. J. Crosby. *Concord: printed by Hill and Barton.* 1830. 8vo, pp. 16. H. 17640

CROSBY (J. L.) The Littlejohn Libel Suit. The Case of De Witt C. Littlejohn against Horace Greeley, tried ... at Pulaski, Sept. 10–13, 1861 ... . Phonographically reported by James L. Crosby. *New York.* 1861. 8vo, pp. 56. B. 17641

CROSBY (J.) A Copy of a Case between Joseph Crosby of Worcester, in the County of Worcester, Sadler, Plaintiff; and Jacob Wyman of Woburn in the County of Middlesex, Trader, Defendant. [No Title-page. 1735.] 4to, pp. 11. B. 17642

CROSBY (Josiah). Remarks of Mr. Crosby of Penobscot ... Feb. 20, 1867, on Resolves for an Amendment of the Constitution ... . [n. p. n. d.] 8vo, pp. 6. H. 17643

CROSBY (N.) Annual Obituary Notices of Eminent Persons Who have Died in the United States. For 1857. By Hon. Nathan Crosby. ... *Boston: Phillips, Sampson and Company.* 1858. 8vo, pp. 432. Portraits. BA. + For 1858. *Boston: John P. Jewitt and Company.* 1859. 8vo, pp. 357. B. 17644

CROSBY (Thomas), *d.* 1702. The Work of a Christian. With another Discourse on Preparation for Sudden Death. *Boston.* 1736. 12mo, Title, pp. 34. B. 17645

CROSBY (U. H.) Crosby Opera House Art Association. Crosby's Opera House and Three Hundred Paintings to be awarded as Premiums to Members. ... *Chicago.* 1866. 8vo, pp. 14. H. 17646

Also: Crosby Opera House Art Association. Descriptive Catalogue of ... Premiums! To be Distributed among Subscribers. [*New York.*] *Russell's print.* 8vo, pp. 36. H.

CROSLAND (N.) Memorable Women: The Story of their Lives. By Mrs. Newton Crosland ... . *Boston: Ticknor and Fields.* M DCCC LIV. 16mo, pp. 360. H. + *London.* 1854. 12mo, pp. 355. C. 17647

Contains lives of Mrs. Mary L. Ware (pp. 181–215), and Margaret Fuller (pp. 275–322).

CROSNIER (L.) Géologie du Pérou. Notice géologique sur les départments de Huancavelica et d'Ayacucho. [*Paris.* 1852.] 8vo, pp. 107. Plate. 17648

CROSS (A.) Sermon ... in West Haverhill, on Thanksgiving Day, November 25, 1841. By Rev. Abijah Cross ... . *Haverhill.* 1842. 8vo, pp. 20. B., H. 17649

CROSS (A.) Defensa de Don Alejandro Cross en primera instancia en una causa de Comisa. *Valparaiso.* 1847. 8vo.

CROSS (A. B.) Battle of Gettysburgh and the Christian Commission. By Andrew B. Cross. *Baltimore: Sherwood & Co.* 8vo, pp. 32. 17651

Also: The War and the Christian Commission. By A. B. Cross. 8vo, pp. 56. — Young Women in Convents, or Priests Prisons to be protected by Law; a Lecture at Maryland Institute, February 24, 1856. *Baltimore.* 1856. 8vo, pp. 48.

CROSS (J. C.) An Address on American Literature ... before the Philomathean Society of Indiana University ... September 25th, 1837. By James Conquest Cross, M.D. *Bloomington.* 1838. 8vo, 3 l., pp. 86. B. 17652

CROSS. Analysis and Refutation of the "Statements of Facts in Relation to the Expulsion of James C. Cross from Transylvania University." Recently published by Dudley, Mitchell and Peter. By James Conquest Cross ... . *Louisville: Prentice and Weissinger.* 1846. 8vo, pp. 39, (2). B. 17653

CROSS. An Oration ... before the Chamberlain Philosophical and Literary Society of Centre College, on the 4th of July, 1836, by James Conquest Cross ... . *Danville, Ky.: J. J. Polk, Printer.* 1836. 8vo, pp. 28. B. 17654

Also: Refutation of the Charges made by Dr. Caldwell, through the Columns of the Louisville Journal, against Professor James C. Cross ... . *Lexington, Ky.* 1838. 8vo, pp. 15. B. — Thoughts on the Policy of establishing a School of Medicine in Louisville ... with a Sketch of the ... Condition and ... Prospects of the Medical Department of Transylvania University. By James Conquest Cross, M.D. ... *Lexington.* 1834. 8vo, pp. 113.

CROSS (J. T. H.) Duncan Adair: or, Captured in Escaping. A Story of one of Morgan's Men. By Mrs. Jane T. H. Cross. *Macon, Ga.: Burke, Boyken & Company.* 1864. 12mo, pp. 51.

CROSS (J.) Annual Report of Colportage in Virginia and North Carolina. March 1, 1857. By Jonathan Cross, Agent and Superintendant. [n. p. 1857.] 8vo, pp. 32. 17656

Also: Annual Report of Colportage of the American Tract Society in Maryland, District of Columbia, and Virginia and North Carolina. ... . March 1, 1858. *Baltimore.* 1858. 8vo, pp. 36. H. — Colportage in Virginia. Annual Report of Mr. J. Cross, Superintendant. 1852. [n. p. n. d.] 8vo, pp. 16. H.

CROSS (Joseph). Camp and Field. Papers from the Portfolio of an Army Chaplain. By the Rev. Jos. Cross, D.D. *Macon, Ga.: Burke, Boykin & Company.* 1864. 12mo, pp. iv, 9–141.

CROSS (J. Warren). An Oration delivered at Barnstable, July 4th, 1832. By Joseph W. Cross ... . *Barnstable: Thompson and Underwood.* [n. d.] 12mo, pp. 23. H. 17658

Also: ... A Sermon preached at the Dedication of a House for ... Worship ... Stow, July 8, 1840. ... . *Lancaster: printed by Marsh, Capen, Lyon, and Webb.* 1840. 12mo, pp. 24. H.

CROSS (L. A. L.) Portraiture and Pencilings of the late Mrs. L. A. L. Cross. By her Husband. *Nashville, Tenn.* 1851. 12mo, pp. 352. 17659

CROSS (*Major*). Journal of the March of a Regiment of Mounted Riflemen to Oregon, 1849, 50. *Washington.* 1851. 8vo. (Cong. Doc.) S. 17660

CROSS (Marcus E.) Prohibitory Law and Its Workings. By Rev. M. E. Cross. ... *Boston: Press of Geo. C. Rand.* 1854. 12mo, pp. 137–161. H. 17661

CROSS (R.), *and others.* A Protestation presented to The Synod, of Philadelphia, June 1. 1741. *Philadelphia: Printed and sold by B. Franklin.* 1741. 8vo, pp. 16. B. 17662

Signed by Robert Cross and nineteen others, who soon after became almost the sole members of the synod, in consequence of the withdrawal of the opposite, the "Brunswick" party.

CROSS (R.) An Oration ... at Newburyport, ... July 4, 1822. By Robert Cross. *Newburyport: W. and J. Gilman.* 8vo, pp. 16. BA., W. 17663

CROSS (T.) Military Laws of the United States; including those relating to the Marine Corps ... Compiled by Colonel Truman Cross. Second Edition. *Washington.* 1838. 8vo.

CROSS. Military Laws of the United States; ... Third Edition. The First and Second Editions were compiled by Colonel Truman Cross, United States Army. This Edition brings the Military Laws through the First Session of the Twenty-Ninth Congress, or to 10th August, 1846. Under the Supervision of Captain A. R. Hetzell, U. S. Army. *Washington.* 1846. 8vo.

[CROSS ——.] An | Answer | To an invidious Pamphlet, intituled, | A Brief State of the Province of | Pensylvania. | Wherein are exposed | The many false Assertions of the Author or | Authors, of the said Pamphlet, with a | View to render the Quakers of Pensylvania | and their Government obnoxious to the | British Parliament and Ministry; | and the | Several Transactions, most grosly misrepre- | sented therein, set in their true light. | *London:* | ... *S. Bladon* ... | MDCCLV. | 8vo, pp. 80. H.

Cross was a counsellor, and for a long time resident in Pennsylvania. "In [Smith's] 'Brief View of the Conduct of Pennsylvania,' published in 1756, this answer is said to be the production of one + [*Cross*], formerly an attorney's clerk, but who was convicted of forgery and sentenced to be hanged, but after some time obtained the favor of transportation, and did us the honor to take up his residence in this province." *See* "M. Rev.," XII. 397.

CROSSMAN (J. W.) A Sermon ... at the Ordination of the Reverend William L. Strong ... Somers, April 3d, 1805. By Joseph W. Crossman ... *Hartford: printed by Hudson and Goodwin.* 1805. 8vo, pp. 31. B. 17667

CROSWELL (A.) An Answer to the Rev. Mr. Garden's Three First Letters to the Rev. Mr. Whitefield. With an Appendix concerning Mr. Garden's Treatment of Mr. Whitefield. By Andrew Crosswell, of Groton, in Connecticut. *Boston: S. Kneeland and T. Green.* 1741. 8vo, pp. (4), 60. B., W.

CROSWELL. Brief Remarks on the Satyrical Drollery at Cambridge, Last Commencement Day; with Special Reference to the Character of Stephen, the Preacher, which raised such Extravagant Mirth. By A. Croswell ... . *Boston: Ezekiel Russell.* M,DCC,LXXI. 4to, pp. 15. BA. 17669

CROSWELL. A Letter to the Reverend Andrew Croswell; occasioned by his Brief Remarks on the Satyrical Drollery Last Commencement Day, with Especial Reference to the Character of Stephen the Preacher, which occasioned such Extravagant Mirth. By Simon, the Tanner. *Boston: Ezekiel Russell.* MDCCLXXI. 8vo, pp. 42, (1). BA. 17670

The letter is dated from Charlestown, Aug. 25, 1771.

CROSWELL. A Defence of a Dialogue Intitled, etc. *See* [Dickinson (J.)]

CROSWELL. Free Justification thro' Christ's Redemption. A Discourse ... at the French Meeting-House in School-Street, October 17. 1764. From Romans III. v. 23, 24. In which The New Gospel ... of Messirs. Bellamy and Cumming ... is weigh'd ... . By A. Croswell ... . *Boston: T. & J. Fleet and Green & Russell.* 1765. 8vo, 2 l., pp. ii, 25. B., M. 17671

This was answered by "Animadversions on Rev. Mr. Croswell's Sermon on Justification, in a Letter to a Friend. *Boston.* 1765." 8vo, pp. 16, and that replied to in "Remarks on an Absurd and Abusive Letter, intitled Animadversions on Mr. Croswell's Sermon. *Boston.* 1765." 8vo, pp. 20. W.

CROSWELL. A Letter From the Rev[d] Mr. Croswell, To the Rev[d] Mr. Turell, In Answer to his Directions to his People. *Boston: Rogers & Fowle.* 1742. 8vo, pp. 16. BA. 17672

This elicited "A Sober Reply to a Mad Answer. In a Letter to Mr. A. Croswell, occasioned by his Letter to Mr. E. Turell. By a Private Brother. *Boston.* 1742." 16mo. B., W. *See* Cummings (A.), and Turell (B.)

CROSWELL. A Narrative of the Founding and Settling the New-gathered Congregational Church In Boston: With the Opposition of the South Church to the Minister, his Defence of himself before the Council, and expostulatory Letter to that Church afterwards. By Andrew Crosswell, A.M. Pastor of said Church. To which is added ... The Defence of that Doctrine of Justifying Faith ... by Messirs Boston, Erskines, &c. ... *Boston: Rogers and Fowle.* MDCCXLIX. 4to. pp. 37, (1). BA.

CROSWELL. Observations on ... a Sermon ... by William Warburton, Lord Bishop of Gloucester, Before the Society for propagating the Gospel in Foreign Parts ... February 21. 1766. wherein Our Colonies are defended against his most injurious aud [*sic*] abusive Reflections. By Andrew Croswell ... . *Boston, New-England: Thomas and John Fleet.* 1768. 8vo, pp. 33. BA.

CROSWELL. A Testimony Against the Prophaness of Some of the publick Disputes, On the last Commencement-Day; With Letters to the Rev[d]. President Of Harvard College ... His Letter of Defence, And Remarks upon it. By A. Croswell. *Boston: D. and J. Kneeland.* 1760. 8vo, pp. 20. BA., M. 17675

Also: The Apostle's Advice to the Jaylor improved: being a Solemn Warning Against the Awful Sin of Soul Murder. In a Discourse ... . *Boston: Rogers and Fowle.* 1744. 8vo, pp. 29. — Comfort in Christ. Sermon at Boston. ... *Boston.* 1767. 8vo, pp. 23. M., W. — A Discourse, from ... [1 Thess. ii. 13] in which is shewn, The Cause and Cure of all religious Melancholly ... an Attempt To overturn the pernicious Doctrine of Justification by Works ... . Notice is also taken, Of the Strange Doctrines which have been preached among us ... . By A. Croswell ... . *Boston: the Author, Russell, and Philip Freeman.* 1784. 8vo, pp 46, (1). BA. — Free Forgiveness of Spiritual Debts. Discourse on Luke vii. 42. ... *Boston.* 1766. 8vo, pp. 26. M. — Heaven Shut against Arminians and Antinomians: Sermon. ... *Boston.* 1747. 16mo. W. — The Heavenly Doctrine of Man's Justification Only by the Obedience of Jesus Christ. In a Sermon ... . *Boston: Green and Russell.* M.DCC.LVIII. 8vo, pp. xiv, 20. BA., M. — A Letter To the Reverend Alexander Cumming; Attempting to shew him, that it is not Blasphemy to say, — No Man can love God, while he looks on Him as a God who will damn him. In which are interspersed Remarks upon Mr. Bellamy's late Performance. ... *Boston: J. Kneeland.* 1762. 8vo, pp. 31. H. — Mr. Crosswell's Reply to a Book lately publish'd, Entitled, A Display of God's special Grace, Attested by ... Dr. Colman, Dr. Sewall, Mr. Prince, Mr. Webb, Mr. Cooper, Mr. Foxcroft, and Mr. Gee. *Boston: Rogers and Fowle.* 1742. 8vo, pp. 23. B., BA. — Mr. Murray Unmask'd. In which, among other Things, is shewn, that his Doctrine of Universal Salvation is inimical to Vertue, and Productive of all Manner of Wickedness, &c. *Boston.* 1775. 12mo, pp. 20. + Second Edition. *Boston.* 1775. 12mo. W. — Reply to the Declaration Of a Number of Ministers in Boston and Charlestown, with Regard to the Rev. James Davenport. With a Conference relating to the Church of England Clergy, &c. *Boston.* 1742. 8vo, pp. 18. B. + Second Edition. *Boston.* 1742. 8vo, pp. 18. M. — A Second Defence of the Old Protestant Doctrine of Justifying Faith. Being a Reply to The Exceptions of Mr. Solomon Williams ... Against a Book, entitled, What is Christ to me, if He is not mine? ... *Boston: Rogers & Fowle.* 1747. 4to, pp. 45. BA., M. — What is Christ to me, if He is not mine? Or, a seasonable Defence of the Old Protestant Doctrine of Justifying Faith. ... *Boston.* 1745. 4to. W.

CROSWELL (C.) State of Wisconsin. Report of Caleb Croswell, one of the Board of Public Works, in Response to A Resolution ... adopted ... February 4th, 1851. *Madison: Robert B. Wentworth, State Printer.* 1851. 8vo, pp. 13. H. 17676

CROSWELL (H.) The Speeches at Full Length of Mr. Van Ness, Mr. Caines, The Attorney-General, Mr. Harrison, and General Hamilton in the Great Cause of the People, against Harry Croswell on an Indictment for a Libel on Thomas Jefferson, President of the United States. *New-York: G. & R. Waite.* 1804. 8vo, pp. 78. B., BA. 17677

Also: The Sham Patriot Unmasked. *Concord.* 1805. 8vo.

CROSWELL. Forty Years in Trinity Parish. A Pastoral Letter ... with a Sermon delivered ... 31st of December, 1854, by the Rev. Harry Croswell, D.D. ... *New Haven: T. J. Stafford, Printer.* 1856. 8vo, pp. 14, 1 l. H. 17678

[CROSWELL.] A Memoir of the late Rev. Wm. Croswell, D.D., Rector of the Church of the Advent, Boston, Massachusetts. By His Father. [n. p. n. d.] 8vo, pp. 528, (1). Portrait. BA. 17679

CROSWELL. A Sermon ... at the Anniversary Election, Hartford, May 14, 1818. By the Rev. Harry Croswell, A.M. ... *Hartford: F. D. Bolles & Co., Printers.* 1818. 8vo, pp. 14.

Also: A Discourse on the Death of William H. Harrison, President of the United States. *New Haven.* 1841. 8vo.

CROSWELL (J.) Sketches of the Life, and Extracts from the Journals and other Writings, of the late Joseph Croswell; who, for more than Forty Years, was an Itinerant Preacher in the New England States; and ... died ... May, 1799 ... . *Boston: Lincoln & Edmands.* 1809. 8vo, pp. 96. BA. 17681

Edited by Jacob Norton.

CROSWELL. A New World planted; or the Adventures of the Forefathers of New-England; who landed in Plymouth, December 22, 1620. An Historical Drama ... . By Joseph Croswell. *Boston.* 1802. 8vo, pp. 45. B. 17682

CROSWELL (W.) A Letter to the Bishop of Massachusetts, occasioned by his late Letter to the Clergy. By William Croswell ... . *Boston: Tuttle & Dennett.* 1845. 12mo, pp. 28. B.

This letter elicited the following: "A Layman's Remarks upon a Letter to the Bishop of Massachusetts, by Rev. Mr. Croswell ... . *Boston: Dutton and Wentworth.* 1845." 12mo, pp. 12. Also: A Review of the Rev. William Croswell's Letter to the Bishop of the Diocese of Massachusetts. By Laicus. *Boston: William A. Hall & Co., Printers.* 1845. 12mo, pp. 27. H.

CROSWELL. A Plain Word concerning the late Circular of the Rt. Rev. Manton Eastburn to the Clergy of Massachusetts. By the Rev. W. Croswell ... *Boston.* 12mo, pp. 12. M. 17684

CROTCHETT (T.), *pseudonym.* An Infallible Scheme for the reduction of Canada, by Timothy Crotchett. *New York.* 1747. 12mo. 17685

CROTHERS (S.) The Gospel of the Typical Servitude. A Sermon preached in Greenfield, Ohio, Jan. 1, 1834. By Rev. Samuel Crothers. *Hamilton.* 1834. 8vo, pp. 22. M. 17686

[CROUCH (Nathaniel).] *See* B[urton] (R[obert]), Vol. III., No. 9500.

Mr. Watt, in his "Bibl. Brit.," remarks, that the name of Burton was placed on many books by Nathaniel Crouch, who is supposed to have written them himself. Possibly our Nos. 5969–71 are translations of Burton instead of Blome. *See* our No. 9500, and add, Fourth Edition. *London: Nath. Crouch.* 1695. 18mo, 2 l., pp. 174. Portrait.

CROW (F.) Vanity and Impiety of Judicial Astrology, whereby Men undertake to Foretell Future Contingencies by the Stars, etc. By Francis Crow of Jamaica. *London: John Dunton.* 1690. 12mo. 17687

Dedicated to the inhabitants of Port Royal, in Jamaica.

CROW (W.) The Banks of the Hudson; A Poem, descriptive of Rural Scenery, Manners and Customs in the United States of America. By William Crow. *Leith.* 1821. 12mo, pp. 108. 17688

Also: The Indian; a Poem, in Six Cantos. *London.* 1806. 18mo.

CROWE (C. C.) Address of Col. C. C. Crow, ... at Selma, Alabama, June 23d, 1869, on the Issues of the Day. ... *Montgomery.* 1869. 8vo, pp. 31. H. 17689

CROWE. Speech of Col. C. C. Crowe, Elector for the State at large, of Alabama, At Huntsville, Alabama, October 15th, 1868. [n. p.] 8vo, pp. 12. H. 17690

[CROWE (Frederick).] The Gospel in Central America; containing a Sketch of the Country, Physical and Geographical — Historical and Political — Moral and Religious: a History of the Baptist Mission in British Honduras and of the Introduction of the Bible into the Spanish American Republic of Guatemala. ... With a Map of the Country. *London: Charles Gilpin.* 1850. Post 8vo, pp. xii, 588. Map. C., H. 17691

CROWE (W.) The Duty of Public Spirit Recommended in a Sermon preach'd before the Honourable Trustees for establishing the Colony of Georgia in America, and the Associates of the late Reverend Dr. Bray; at their meeting, March 20, 1739–40. By William Crowe, D.D. *London: John Clarke.* M.DCC.XL. 4to, pp. 23. S. 17692

CROWELL (J.) Sketches of the Life of J. Crowell, with Extracts from his Journals and other Writings. *Boston.* 1809. 12mo, pp. 96. 17693

CROWELL. Slavery in the District of Columbia. Speech of Mr. Crowell, of Ohio ... . Delivered ... July 26, 1848. [*Washington?*] *J. & G. S. Gideon, Printers.* 8vo, pp. 16. H.

CROWELL (J.) Republics Established, and Thrones Overturned by the Bible. By Rev. John Crowell. *Philadelphia: John T. Lange.* 1849. 12mo, pp. 202. 17695

By an unaccountable mistake we have credited this work to Rev. John Chambers. *See* Vol. III., No. 11799.

CROWELL (J. T.) Speech of Joseph T. Crowell against the Anti-War Resolutions, in the Senate of New Jersey, January 22, 1863. [n. p. n. d.] pp. 9. 17696

CROWELL (R.) History of the Town of Essex, from 1634 to 1700. By Robert Crowell, D.D. ... *Boston: C. C. P. Moody, Printer.* 1853. 12mo, pp. 166, (3). Map and Woodcut. BA.

CROWELL. History of the Town of Essex from 1634 to 1868. By the late Rev. Robert Crowell, D.D. ... With Sketches of Soldiers in the War of the Rebellion. By Hon. David Choate. *Essex: the Town.* 1868. 8vo, pp. 488. BA. 17698

CROWELL. Interment of the Dead ... . A Sermon delivered in Ipswich, Second Parish, July 23, 1818, on the Occasion of reinterring the Coffins which had been robbed of their Contents. By Robert Crowell ... . *Andover: Flagg and Gould.* 1818. 8vo, pp. 46. BA., H. 17699

The preface gives a short history of the circumstances.

CROWELL (R.) A Sketch of the History of the Second Parish in Ipswich. A Discourse ... Jan. 1, 1815. By Robert Crowell, ... *Andover: printed by Flagg and Gould.* 1815. 8vo, pp. 32. BA. 17700

Also: A Sermon, delivered November 19, 1827, at the Interment of the Rev. Joseph Dana ... . *Ipswich: printed by John H. Harris.* 1827. 8vo, pp. 20. H. — A Sermon, delivered at Waltham, July 23, 1841, at the Interment of the Rev. David Jewett, late Pastor of the Congregational Church in Rockport ... . *Boston: Press of T. R. Marvin.* 1842. 8vo, pp. 40. H.

Crowell (S.) The Journal of Seth Crowell, containing an Account of his Travels as a Methodist Preacher, for Twelve Years. *New York.* 1813. 12mo, pp. 108. 17701

Crowell (W.) Six Letters to Rev. Wm. H. Wyckoff, Corresponding Secretary of the American Bible Union, by William Crowell, St. Louis, Missouri. [*St. Louis?*] 1855. 8vo, pp. 38. H. 17702

C[rowley] (T[homas]). Account of a Plan for Civilizing the North American Indians. The Second Impression, with a Postcript, by T. C. [About 1766.] Folio, pp. 4. 17703

[Crowley.] Letters and Dissertations on various subjects, by the Author of the Letter Analysis A. P. on the Disputes between Great Britain and America. *London: Printed for the Author.* M,DCC,LXXXII. 8vo, pp. 130. J.C.B. 17704

There are copies without date. First published in the newspapers under the signature Amor Patriæ. There are evidently two or more editions, as Joseph Smith, and another bookseller describes it *without date*, and Mr. Bartlett describes it as dated 1782 *and* 1783.

Crowley. Letters to the King, from an Old Patriotic Quaker, lately deceased. [Edited by T. Crowley?] *London: Printed by R. Baldwin.* 1778. 8vo, 14 sheets. 17705

The Crowning Crime of Christendom, comprising a few facts relative to Slavery and the Slave Trade at the present moment. *Leeds: A. Pickard, Printer.* [About 1851.] 8vo, pp. 2. 17706

Crowninshield (B.) Address delivered By Benjamin Crowninshield, Jan. 9, 1826. *Salem.* 1826. 8vo. 17707

Crowninshield (G.) Trial of George Crowninshield, J. J. Knapp, Jun. and John Francis Knapp, for the Murder of Capt. Joseph White of Salem ... Sixth of April, 1830. Reported by John W. Whitman ... . *Boston: Beals and Homer, and Francis Ingraham.* 1830. 8vo, pp. 104. H. 17708

Crowninshield (Jacob). Mr. Crowninshield's Motion, 23 Jan., 1805. [*Washington.* 1805.] 8vo. BN. 17709

Crowninshield. Mr. Crowninshield's Motion, Feb. 10, 1806. *Washington.* 1806. 8vo. 17710

Relates to commercial restrictions.

Crowninshield. Mr. Crowninshield's Resolutions [in relation to the British Orders in Council of Nov. 1807, and the Committees] Report [thereon]. *Boston. Dated January* 28, 1809. 8vo, pp. 8. H., W. 17711

Crowninshield (Richard). A Biographical Sketch of the Celebrated Salem Murderer [R. Crowninshield] ... . By a Citizen of Danvers. *Boston.* 1830. 8vo, pp. 24. H. 17712

Crowquill (A.), *pseudon.* *See* [Forrester (Alfred Henry)].

Crowther (J.) A Portraiture of Methodism; or, History of Wesleyan Methodists; including their Rise, Progress, and Present State; the Lives and Characters of divers of their Ministers; the Doctrines they believe and teach; with the Plan of their Discipline, &c. Also, a Defence of Methodism. By Jonathan Crowther. With Documents respecting the Extension of their Religious Purposes by a Late Act of the British Legislature. *New York.* 1813. 12mo. P. 17713

Croy (*le duc* de). Mémoire sur le passage par le Nord, qui contient aussi des réflexions sur les Glaces. Par le Duc de Croy. *Paris: Valade.* M. DCC. LXXXII. 4to, pp. 23. H. 17714

Croy-Solre (*le prince* Em. de). Mémoire sur le passage par le Nord, qui contient aussi des réflexions sur les glaces. *Paris: Valade.* 1785. 4to. 17715

Crozet (*M.*) Nouveau Voyage à la Mer du Sud, commencé sous les ordres de M. Marion. Avec un extrait du voyage de M. de Surville. *Paris.* 1783. 8vo, pp. 290. 7 Plates. A., S.

Crozet (C.) Outline of Virginia Internal Improvements. By Claudius Crozet. *Philadelphia.* 1848. 8vo. 17717

Also: Report on the Cumberland Gap and Price's Turnpike Road. *Richmond.* 1841. 8vo.

Croyer (H. P.) The Nation's Loss. A Discourse upon the Life, Services, and Death of Abraham Lincoln, Late President of the United States. By H. P. Croyer. Delivered at Huntingdon, L. I., April 19th, 1865. *New York: John A. Gray & Green, Printers.* 1865. 8vo, pp. 16. B. 17718

Five hundred copies printed for gratuitous distribution, and one thousand copies on fine tinted paper.

Crozier (O. R. L.) The Fortress of the Rebellion: with a Brief Vindication of the Constitution. By O. R. L. Crozier. *Grand Rapids, Mich.: The Author.* 186–. 12mo, pp. 36.

Cruden (J.) An address to the Loyal Part of the British Empire, and the Friends of Monarchy throughout the Globe.

By John Cruden, Esq.; President of the Assembly of the United Loyalists, and Late Commissioner of Sequestrated Estates in Carolina, &c. *London.* 1785. 8vo, pp. 29. 17720

"The unfortunate Loyalists of the Southern States, who took refuge in Florida, under the promise of protection from the British government, found themselves at the peace in the hands of the Spaniards, by whom they were ordered to quit the country. In this dilemma they empowered Mr. Cruden to negotiate a lottery for their benefit, which gave rise to this address." *See* "M. Rev., July, 1785."

The Cruelty of the Spaniards in Peru, 1658. *See* [Davenant (*Sir* William)].

Cruger (J.) Substance of the Speech of John Cruger on retiring from the Mayoralty of the City of New York, 29 Sept., 1782. 8vo. 17721

[Cruger (Lewis).] Sovereign Rights of the States. ... By Justinian, of South Carolina. ... *Washington: W. H. Moore, Printer.* [n. d.] 8vo, pp. 9. H. 17722

Contains several poems about America. Also: Journal of the First Congress of the American Colonies ... New York, Oct. 7, 1765. *New York.* 1845. 8vo, pp. 59.

Cruickshanks (J.) A Bouquet of Flowers, from the Garden of Paradise ... . By James Cruickshanks, Jr., Meriden, N. H. *New York and London.* 1851. 12mo, pp. 38. + *Hanover: Dartmouth Press.* 1851, 16mo, pp. 32. H. 17723

Cruickshanks. A Sermon Preached in ... Spencer, Mass., on ... the National Fast, August 4th, 1864, by Rev. Jas. Cruickshanks. Subject: — The Nation's Trust in the Present Struggle. *Worcester: Adams & Brown, Printers.* [1864.] 8vo, pp. 20.

The Cruise of the Somers: illustrative of the Despotism of the Quarter-Deck. Third Edition. With an Appendix, containing Three Letters from Hon. W. Sturgis. *New York.* 1844. 12mo. S. 17725

Crummell (A.) A Eulogium on the Life and Character of Thomas Clarkson, delivered in New York, Dec. 1846, by the Rev. Alex. Crummell, an African Clergyman; With an Introduction, by W. T. Blair, Esq. *New York.* 1847. 8vo, pp. 76. + *London.* 1849. 17726

Crummell. The Relations and Duties of Free Colored Men in America to Africa. A Letter to Charles B. Dunbar, M.D., ... of New York ... . By ... Rev. Alex. Crummell ... . *Hartford: Case, Lockwood & Co.* 1861. 8vo, pp. 54. 17727

Crump (W. H.) The World in a Pocket Book, or Universal Popular Statistics ... . An ample Political, Commercial, Agricultural, Manufacturing, Historical, Geographical, Statistical, and General Synopsis of the United States; With the Census of 1840 ... . By W. H. Crump. *Philadelphia: J. Dobson.* 1841. 24mo, pp. 192. + Second Edition. *Philadelphia: Judah Dobson.* 1842. + Third Edition; Greatly Enlarged and Improved; ... *Philadelphia: G. S. Appleton.* 1845. pp. 195. + Eighth Edition. *Philadelphia.* 1858. 8vo. 17628

Cruse (E.) Projector Detected; or, some Strictures on the Plan of Mr. James Rumsey's Steamboat. By Englehart Cruse. *Baltimore: J. Hayes.* 1788. 18mo, pp. 14. C. 17729

Crusius (M.) D. Solomoni | Schvveigkero Sultzensi, qui Con-|stantinopoli in Aula Legati Imp. Rom. Aliquot|annos Ecclesiasta fuit: & in Aegypto, Palæsti-|na, Syria, peregrinatus est:|Gratulatio scripta|A|Martino Crvsio.|Cum Descriptione illius peregrinationis:|& Græcorum | Patriarcharum, aliorumq; qui nunc illis locis viuunt| Christianorum commendationibus, scriptisq;|alijs lectu dignissimis.|*Argentorati*|*Excudebat Nicolaus Vvyriot. Anno*|M.D.LXXXII.| 4to, 18 leaves. 17730

Cruse (M. A.) Cameron Hall: A Story of the Civil War. By Mary A. Cruse, ... *Philadelphia.* 1867. 12mo, pp. 543.

A Southern story of the Rebellion.

Cruz (G. J. de). Uma pagina memoravel de historia do reinado do senhor Dom Pedro II., defensor perpetuo do Brasil por Gervasio José da Cruz. *Rio de Janeiro.* 1865. 4to, pp. vi, 48. 17732

Cruz (J. I. de la). Fama, y obras posthumas del feniz de Mexico, dezima musa, poetisa americana, sor Juana Ines de la Cruz, religiosa professa en el convento de San Geronimo de la Imperial civdad de Mexico. Que saco a luz el doctor D. Ivan Ignacio de Castorena y Vrsua. *Madrid: A. Gonçalez de Reyes.* 1714. 4to, 15 l., pp. 318, 1 l. 17733

This volume is sometimes found lettered as Vol. III. of the "Poemas." There appears to have been an edition, *Madrid,* 1801, sm. 4to. It was reprinted with the following title:

Cruz. Fama, y obras posthumas del fenix de Mexico, dezima musa, poetisa, Americana sor Juana Ines de la Cruz, monja professa en el monasterio del Señor San Geronimo de la

Ciudad de Mexico. Pliegos 47. Con Licencia. *En Madrid: En la Imprenta de Angel Pasquel Rubio. Año de* 1725. 4to, 10 l., pp. 352, iii. 17734

The pagination commences on the antepenultimate page of the "Aprobacion" in advance of the text.

Cruz. Poemas de la unica poetisa americana, musa dezima. Que en varios metros, idiomas y estilos fertiliza varios assumptos. Con elegantes, sutiles, claros, ingeniosos, vtiles versos ... Segunda edicion, corregida, y mejorada por su authora. *Madrid: Garcia Infançon.* 1690. 4to, 7 l., pp. 338, 3 l. + Tercera edicion, corregida y añadid. Sacolos a luz Don Juan Camacho Gayna. *Valencia: Ant. Bordazar.* 1709. *Barcelona: Joseph Llopis.* 1693. *Madrid: A. Gonçalez de Reyes.* 1714. 3 vols., 4to, 7 l., pp. 351, 9 l.; 3 l., pp. 467, 5 l. 17735

Vol. III. consists of the "Fama," described in No. 17734, *supra.*

Cruz (M. de la). Différentes Races de l'Amérique. 1784. Folio. Plates. 17736

Cruz (M.) Relacion de la milagrosa Aparicion de la Santa Imagen de la Virgen de Guadalupe de México, sacada de la historia que compuso el Br. Miguel Sanchez. Por el P. Mateo de la Cruz. *En La Puebla,* 1660. + *Madrid: Pedro Gálvez, Consejero de Indias.* 1662. + Tercera edicion. *México.* 1781. 4to, pp. 25. + 1785. 17737

According to Fr. de Florencia, the best written account of the miracle. *See* Bartolache's "Manifiesto," pp. 14–17. Also: Sermon del Patrocinio de la Virgen Maria, predicado en la Catedral de la Puebla en la primera fiesta que de orden del Rey se celebró á este objeto. *Puebla: Borja.* 1656. 4to. — Elogio de la glorioso Santa Catarina de Sena predicada en ... la Puebla. *Mexico: Rodriguez Lupercio.* 1669. 4to.

Cruz (Rodrigo de la), *Prefecto General de la Compañia Bethleemitica*). Representacion juridica, con el Señor Fiscal del Supremo y Real Consejo de las Indias, sobre el pretenso passo de dos Breves Apostolicos, expedidos por Inocencio XI: El vno, en que se aprueban las Constituciones nueve formadas, y el otro, en que se le nombró por Prefecto General di dicha Compañia. *Madrid: por Diego Martinez Abad.* 1693. Folio, 2 unnumb. l., 49 l., 12 l. 17738

A Cry from the Cotton Field. *Newcastle.* 1850. 12mo, pp. 4. 17739

A Cry from the Four Winds. *Boston: Benjamin Jones.* 1827–28. 8vo. 17740

A Cry from the North ... *Boston: Benjamin Jones.* 1827. 8vo, pp. (4), 72. H. 17741

A Cry from the Wilderness! A Voice from the East. A Reply from the West. Troubles in the North, Exemplifying in the South. By a Cosmopolite. *United States.* 1830. 12mo.

Crystal Fount and Rechabite Recorder. *New York.* 1846?

A weekly paper, edited and published by H. B. Dawson.

The Crystal Hunter, 1827. *See* [Edwards (Charles)].

Crystal Palace. *See* New York.

Cuadro historico y espantoso de la Inquisicion, que se publica en esta capital, para la ilustracion de aquellas personas que han ignorado lo que de era acquel horrible, despota y cruel tribunal. *Puebla: P. de la Rosa.* 1816. Sm. 4to, pp. 16. 17744

The Cub New-lick'd; or, A New Story of an Old Monster. [*Boston.* 1754.] 8vo, pp. 16. M. 17745

Relates to the Excise Law.

Cuba. Actas de las juntas generales que celebro la Real Sociedad economiga de amigos del pais De La Habana, en los dias 14, 15, y 16 de Diciembre de 1829. Ympressa de acuerdo de la misma Sociedad. *Habana.* 1830. pp. 366. 17746

Acuerdos hechos en el Ayuntamiento de la Habana en cumplimiento del Real decreto de 15 de Febrero de 1810 convocando las Américas á las Cortes nacionales. *Habana.* 1810. 4to, pp. 18. 17747

Album Pintoresco de la Isla de Cuba. *Berlin.* [n. d.] Oblong 4to. 17748

A series of plates, badly colored, by May & Co.

Alcabalatorio de la Isla de Cuba. *Imprenta del Gobierno.* 1830. 4to. 17749

Anales de la Junta de Fomento y memorias de la Sociedad patriótica desde 1835–1855. *Habana.* [n. d.] 8vo. 17750

Ayuntamiento constitucional de Nuevitas: acta de 25 de Octubre de 1822. *Puerto-Principe: imprenta de Minuese.* 1823.

Aranceles generales para el cobro de derechos de introduccion y estraccion en todas las aduanas de los puertos habilitados de la siempre fiel isla de Cuba para el año de 1824. Folio, pp. 57, 5

l. + Par el año de 1835. *Habana.* 1835. Folio, pp. iv, 76. + Para el año 1847. *Habana.* 1846. 4to, Title, pp. 76, 4 l.

Apparently an annual publication.

Aviso al pueblo sobre las próximas elecciones de Diputados en Córtes. *Habana: imprenta de Palmer é hijo.* 1820. 4to.

Balanza general del comercio de la isla de Cuba en los años 1836–1838. Formada de órden del Exmo. Señor Conde de Villanueva, consejero de estado honorario, intendente de la ejército y superintendente general delegado de real hacienda de la misma. Por Don Raimundo Pascual Harrich. *Habana.* 1837–39. Folio, pp. 20, 54, 38, 14. 17754

Bando de buen gobierno del Excmo. Sr. D. Manuel Cagigal. *Imprenta del Gobierno.* 4to, pp. 35. 17755

Calendario manual y guia de forasteros de la isla de Cuba, para el año de 1794. ... *Havana: Imprenta de la Capitanía General.* 32mo, pp. (50), 185, (5), 3 folded l. Map. H.

Carta de un americano á un amigo suyo. *Imprenta de Boloña.* 1820. 4to. 17757

La Cartera Cubana. Director Vicente Antonio de Castro. *Habana.* 1838, 1840. 24 pts. in 2 vols., pp. 800; 800.

The Case of Cuba. ... With a Letter from John D. Sherwood, Esq., on the Right of Recognition. *New York: American News Company.* 1869. 8vo, pp. 28. H. 17759

Correspondence between the Treasury Department, &c., in relation to the Cuba Expedition, and William Freret, late Collector. *New Orleans: Alex. Levy & Co.* 1851. 12mo, pp. 46.

Correspondence concerning Alleged Projects of Annexation. *London.* 17761

A Parliamentary document, "Accounts and Papers for 1852–53."

Correspondence on the proposed Tripartite Convention relative to Cuba. *Boston: Little, Brown & Co.* 1853. 8vo, pp. 64.

Message from the President, etc. Dispatch of Lord Russell, letter of E. Everett.

Cuadro Estadistico de la siempré fiel isla de Cuba, corresp. al año de 1846. *Habana.* 1847. 4to. 17763

A work with a similar title was published in 1827.

Cuba and Africa. The Cuban Question considered in relation to the African Race. *Paris.* 1853. 8vo. P. 17764

Cuba and the Cubans. *See* [Kimball (R. B.)]

Cuba; or the Policy of England, Mexico, and Spain, with regard to that Island. By an Englishman. *London: J. Ridgway.* 1830. 8vo, pp. 22. 17765

Cuba poetica. Coleccion escogida de las composiciones en verso de los poetas Cubanos desde Zequeira hasta nuestros dias. Directores José Fornaris; Joaquin Lorenzo Luaces. Director José Socorro de Leon. Segunda edicion. *Habana.* 1861. 4to, pp. 238. 17766

Cuba y su gobierno. Con un apendice de documentos historicos. *Londres.* 1853. 8vo. M. 17767

Constituciones de la Universidad. 1734. Folio. 17768

Descriptive Sketches and Statistics of Cuba. *London.* Folio.

A Parliamentary document in "Accounts and Papers for 1847."

Diccionario Provincial, de Voces Cubanas. *Matanzas.* 1836. 18mo, pp. 275. 17770

Estado actual de la Isla de Cuba, y medios que deben adoptarse para fomentar su prosperidad con utilidad de la madre patria. *Madrid.* 1838. Sm. 4to, pp. 131. 17771

Estado general de la poblacion de la Isla en 1817, dispuesto por el Excmo. Sr. D. José Cienfuegos, y acuerdo para que sirviera de base á las elecciones de 1821. *Imprenta del Gobierno.* 1821. Folio. 17772

Estado militar de la isla de Cuba. *Habana: imprenta del gobierno.* 1849. 18mo, pp. 155. 17773

Examen crítico-legal de la Real Orden de 22 de Setiembre de 1820, sobre el establecimiento de los Jueces de letras provisionales de la Isla de Cuba. *Puerto-Principe: imprenta de D. Miguel Serrano.* 1821. 17774

Examen de la Cuestion de Cuba. *Paris.* 1837. 8vo, pp. 16.

Expediente instruido por el Consulado de la Habana sobre los medios que convenga proponer para sacar la agricultura y comercio de esta isla del apuro en que se hallan. *Habana.* 1808. 4to, pp. 116. 17776

Gan Eden! 1854. *See* [Hurlbut (W. H.)]

Guia de forasteros en la siempre fiel Isla de Cuba para el ano de 1830. *Habana.* 1829. 8vo. c. 17777

There are probably earlier volumes. Continued annually.

Informe de Don Francisco de Arango al Sr. D. Rafael Gomez Roubaud, Superintendente Director General de Tabacos, en la Isla de Cuba sobre los males y remedios que en ella tiene este ramo. Escrito en 1805. *Habana.* 1812. 4to, pp. viii, 96.

Informe fiscal sobre fomento de la poblacion blanca en la isla de Cuba, y emancipacion progressiva de la esclava, [etc.] Presentado a la superintendencia general delegada de real hacienda, en diciembre de 1844. Por el fiscal de la misma [el señor Quiepo]. *Madrid: J. Martin Alegria.* 1845. Sm. folio, 1 l., pp. xviii, 1 l., pp. 195, 328, 1 l. 17779

Informe Presentado a la Real Junta de Fomento de Agricula y Comercio de esta Isla, en Sesion de 11 de Diciembre de 1833. *Habana.* 1834. 4to, pp. iv, 154. 17780

Informe sobre los resultados de las operaciones efectuadas por la Sociedad del Credito industrial en el Ano 1864. *Habana.* 1865. 8vo, pp. 38. 17781

Los Ingenios. Colleccion de vistas de los principales Ingenios de azucar de la Isla de Cuba. Ediccion de lujo. El texto redactado por Justo G. Cantero; las laminas dibujadas del natural y litografiadas por Eduardo Laplante. *Habana.* 1857. Folio, pp. 76. 35 Plates. 17782

Contains a series of colored photographic views of sugar estates in the Island of Cuba; also diagrams and plans of the machinery used, as well as descriptive letterpress, showing the extent of the operations on each estate.

Instruccion general para los capitanes y tenientes de partido, impresa en esta ciudad el año 1786 y reimpresa ahora de órden del Excmo. Sr. Gobernador y Capital General. *Imprenta del Gobierno.* 1829. 4to, pp. 33. 17783

Instruction Nautique de les Passages a l'Isle de Cuba et au Golfe de Mexique, par le Canal de la Providence, et le Grand Baie de Bahama. *Paris.* 1825. 8vo. 17784

Letters from the Havana, during the year 1820; containing an Account of the Present State of the Island of Cuba, and observations on the Slave Trade. *London: Miller.* 1821. Crown 8vo, pp. 135. Map. 17785

List of the Shells of Cuba in the Collection of the British Museum, collected by M. Ramon de la Sagra. Described by Prof. Alcide D'Orbigny, In the "Histoire de l'Ile de Cuba." *London.* 1854. 12mo, pp. (2), 48. H. 17786

Llamamiento de la Isle de Cuba a la Nacion Española Dirigido al Excmo. é Illmo. señor don Baldomero Espartero, Duque da la Victoria, Presidente del Consejo de Ministros, por un Hacendado, en Deciembre de 1854. *Nueva-York: Imprenta de Estevan Haleet.* 8vo, pp. 234, lv. 17787

Manifiesto de los antecedentes que han precidido á la suspension de las functiones del Estado Mayor por órden del Excmo. Sr. Capitan General de la Isla de Cuba. *Imprenta Fraternal.* 1821. 4to, pp. 24. 17788

Manual de la Isla de Cuba. *Habana.* 1852. 12mo. Continued. 17789

Manual del cocinero Cubano, completando tan interesante obra un tratado de dulceria y pasteleria, etc. Edicion ilustrada con laminas. *Habana.* 1856. 8vo, pp. 308. 17790

Materiales relativos a la historia de la isla de Cuba. Recogidos y redactados por una comision especial. [*Habana.* 1828.] 8vo, pp. xvi, 274, 2 l. c. 17791

See Bachiller, who describes two volumes.

Message from the President of the United States on the Subject of Cuba, Jan. 5, 1853. [n. p. n. d.] 8vo, pp. 23.

Notes on Cuba. *See* [Wurdiman (F.)]

Ordenanzas rurales de la Isla de Cuba. *Habana.* 1857. 8vo, pp. 68. 17793

Original Papers relating to the Expedition to the Island of Cuba [under Admiral Vernon.] *London: M. Cooper.* M DCC XLIV. 8vo, pp. 219. 17794

Paseo pintoresco por la Isla de Cuba. Obra artistica y literaria, ou que se pintan y describen los edificios, los monumentos, los campos y las costumbres de este privilegiado suelo, publicada por los empresarios de la litografia del gobierno y capitania general. *Habana.* 1841. Sq. 8vo, pp. 290. 17795

Planos de Bosillo, de la Isla de Cuba, la ciudad de la Habana, y sus barrios estramuras, con la tabla de destancias de unos pueblos a otros. *Habana.* 1842. 18mo. 17796

La question de Cuba. *Paris: Dentu.* 1859. 8vo, pp. 63.

Rambles in Cuba. *New York.* 1870. 12mo, pp. 136.

Real cedula de 21 de Octubre de 1817, sobre aumentar la poblacion blanca de la isla de Cuba. ... *Habana.* 1818. Folio, pp. (1), 12. H. 17799

Real cedula [1796] de ereccion del colegio de Escribanos con título de Real, bajo la proteccion del Concejo de Indias. *Imprenta del Gobierno.* 1819. Folio. 17800

Real resolucion sobre terrenos realengos y valdíos, comunicada por el Ministerio de Hacienda de Indias á la Intendencia de ejército de esta Isla. 1819. Folio. 17801

El Recuerdo, ó coleccion de verdades acerca del estado politico de la isla de Cuba. Por el autor del Habanero. No. 1. 12mo, pp. 4. 17802

Reglamento Interior, formado para la Casa de Educacion de Buenavista. [*Habana.*] 1829. 4to, pp. 12. M. 17803

Reflexiones de un habanero sobre la independencia de esta Isla. Segunda edicion corregida y aumentada. *Habana: Imprenta de Arazoza y Soler.* 1823. 4to, pp. 37. 17804

Reglamento de Milicias de la Isla de Cuba. *Imprenta de D. Blas de los Olivos.* 1777. + *Imprenta del Gobierno.* 1812. 4to. 17805

Reglamento interior de la Cárcel. *Habana: imprenta de D. Pedro Nolasco Palmer.* 1821. 4to. 17806

Reglamento para el Casino de Caibarien, el Progreso. *Habana.* 1865. 8vo. 17807

Reglamento para las milicias de infanteria y caballeria de la Isla de Cuba, aprobado por S. M. en Real Cédula, de 19 de Enero de 1769. *Imprenta de Arazoza y Soler.* 1812. 17808

Reglas para el domicilio de nuevos colonos y sus auxilios. [n. p. n. d.] Folio, pp. (1), 6. H. 17809

Relacion del Gobierno superior y Capitania General de la Isla de Cuba, estendida por el Teniente General Don Miguel Tacon, Marques de la Union de Cuba, al hacer la entrego de dichos mandos à su sucesor el Ecsmo Señor D. Joaquin de Ezpeleta. *Habana.* 1838. 8vo, pp. 36. 17810

A note at the end states that an edition of one thousand copies having been disposed of, another of four thousand copies was printed at the expense of several merchants, to be distributed gratis, "in order to give the greatest possible publicity to this important memoir."

Report of the Committee on Foreign Relations, to whom was referred the Bill "making Appropriations to facilitate the Acquisition of the Island of Cuba, by Negotiation." January 24, 1849. By Mr. Slidell. *Washington.* 1849. 8vo, pp. 25.

Resumen de las Reales órdenes y otras disposiciones para la recaudacion y administracion de la manda-pia forzosa en la Isla de Cuba. *Habana: Imprenta de las viudas de Arazoza y Soler.* pp. 21. 17812

Reunion de todos los actos y estatutos formados para el gobierno de los gremios de mareantes y peseadores que se hallan establecidos en la Isla de Cuba ... *Habana: Oficina de D. José Boloña.* pp. 57, and Appendix. 17813

Revista y Repertorio bimestre de la Isla de Cuba. *Habana.* 1831–32. 3 vols., 8vo, pp. 374; 288; 540. 17814

Ultima advertencia sobre abusos de la Capitanía del puerto. *Habana: Imprenta de D. Pedro Nolasco Palmer.* 1821. 17815

Yankee Travels through the Island of Cuba; or, the Men and Government, the Laws and Customs of Cuba, as seen by American Eyes. By Demoticus Philalethes. *New York.* 1856. 12mo. 17816

Cuba y Porto Rico. Las Antillas Españolas ante las naciones civilizadas. Asamblea popular el 5 de Julio de 1869, en Carácas, en favor del reconocimiento del partido republicano de las Antillas como beligerantes legítimos. *Carácas.* 1869. 4to, pp. 57. 17817

Pages one to thirty were written by S. Terrero Atienza. Concerning Cuba, *see* "Blackwood's Mag.," XL. 322, "Brownson's Q. Rev.," Ser. III. Vol. VIII. 66, "N. Am Rev.," XXIX. 199, "Frazer's Mag.," XLII. 107, "Hunt's Mag.," II. III. VI. VII. IX. XVII. XXI.; *see also* Poole's Index, p. 119, for further references.

Cubbeer Burr; or the Tree of many Trunks: Part 1, British Empire; Part 2, United Kingdom; Part 3, Canada. *Montreal.* 1841. 8vo, pp. 33. 17818

CUBERO (P. S.) Breve relacion, de la peregrinacion qve ha hecho de la mayor parte del Mvndo Don Pedro Cvbero Sebastian, predicador apostolico del Assia, natural del Reyno de Aragon; Con las cosas mas singulares que le han sucedido, y viso, entre tan barbaras Naciones, su religion, ritos, ceremonias, y otras cosas memorables, y curiosas que hà podido inquirir; con el viage por tierra, desde Espana hasta las Indias Orientales. *Madrid: Juan Garcia Infançon.* 1680. 4to, 9 l., pp. 360.

CUBERO. Peregrinacion del Mvndo, dedicada a D. F. Joachin Faxardo, virrey de Napoles. *Napoles: Carlos Porsile.* 1682. 4to, 5 l., pp. 551, 2 l. Portraits of the Vice Roy and the Author.

"Cette édition, la seconde de l'ouvrage, n'est pas citée par Pinelo (il indique une édition de 1664, et un abrégé sous la date de 1700).—LECLERC, No. 411.

CUBERO SEBASTIAN (P.) Peregrinacion|qve ha hecho de la|Mayor Parte del|Mundo|Don Pedro Cvbero Sebastian.|Predicador Apostolico del Assia, natural del Reyno|de Aragon; con las cosas mas singulares que le han|sucedido, y visto, entre tan Barbaras Naciones, su Re-|ligion, Ritos, Ceremonias, y otras cosas memorables, y|curiosas, què ha podido inquirir; con el viage|por tierra, desde España, hasta las Indias|Orientales.|Escrita|por el mismo don Pedro Cvbero|Sebastian.|Dedicado Al SS. Christo de las|Injurias, sita en la Iglesia del Señor San Millan,|anexo de S. Iusto, y pastor desta Coronada Villa|de Madrid.|Segvnda Impression.|*En Zaragoza, Por Pasqual Bueno, Impressor del Reyno|de Aragon. Año de* 1688.| 4to, pp. xvi, 288.

Towards the end of the volume, Cubero describes his experiences of the New World, to which he voyaged from the Philippine Islands. "Cubero est le premier qui ait fait le tour du monde d'Occident en Orient, et en partie par terre, ainsi que l'exécuta depuis Gemelli Carreri. Il ne decrit pas minutieusement sa route; il se contente de donner un aperçu général de ce qu'il a observé. Il depeint avec exactitude les steppes d'Astracan et les déserts de la Perse; il donne beaucoup de détailes sur Manille et sur différents personages, avec lesquelles il s'est trouvé, &c. ... Il écrit avec la simplicité qui convient à un missionaire, mais il est un peu crédule."—*Biog. Univ.* Colonel Stanley's copy sold for £6 6s. A copy sold for £1 5s. at Puttick's, in 1860.

CUBIÈRES (*le marquis* Simon L. P. de). Mémoire sur le cyprès de la Louisiane, par M. de Cubieres. *Versailles.* 1809. 8vo. 2 Plates. 17822

CUBIÈRES. Mémoire sur le genévrier rouge de Virginie, que l'on nomme vulgairement cèdre rouge. *Versailles.* 1805. 8vo.

CUBITT (G.) Columbus; or the Discovery of America. By George Cubitt. *London: John Mason.* 1848. 18mo, pp. 144.

CUBITT. Cortes; or the Discovery and Conquest of Mexico. By George Cubitt. *London: John Mason.* 1848. 18mo, pp. 160. 17825

CUBITT. Pizarro; or the Discovery and Conquest of Peru. By George Cubitt. *London: John Mason.* 1849. 18mo, pp. 160. 17826

Part of a series, entitled "Memorable Men and Memorable Events."

CUCHEVAL-CLARIGNY (Athanase). The Election of Mr. Lincoln. A Narrative of the Contest in 1860 for the Presidency of the United States. By Monsr. C. Clarigny. Translated from the "Révue des Deux Mondes," by Sir Willoughby Jones ... *London: James Ridgway, Trübner and Co.* [1861.] 8vo, pp. 91. H. 17827

[CUCHEVAL-CLARIGNY.] Histoire de la Presse en Angleterre et aux Etats Unis. *Paris: Amyot.* 1857. 18mo, pp. 551. S.

Also a translation of Mrs. Stowe's "Pearl of Orr's Island."

CUCULLU (J. S.) La vérité sur Miramon et les Etats-Unis. *Nouvelle Orleans.* 1860. 4to, pp. 44. 17829

CUDENA (Pedro). Beschreibung des Portugiesischen Amerika vom Cudena. Ein Spanisches Manuscript in der Wolfenbüttelschen Bibliothek, herausgegeben vom Herrn Hofrath Lessing. Mit Anmerkungen und Zusätzen begleitet von Christian Leiste, Rektor der Herzoglichen grosen Schule zu Wolfenbüttel. *Braunschweig, in der Buchhandlung des Fürstl. Waysenhauses.* 1780. 8vo, pp. 160. 17830

"Pedro Cudena, a Spaniard, who resided several years in the Brazils, wrote, in 1634 an account of that country, which had not been published, and a copy having been found in the Wolfenbuttel library, it was printed, with a German translation and notes, by Leiste. It is said to be a curious and interesting work, and, although written so long ago, to contain new information respecting that part of America to which it relates."—*Biog. Univ.*

CUDWORTH (W. Handel). Eulogy on the Life, Character and Public Services of the Late President Lincoln, delivered ... at East Boston, May 8, 1865, by Rev. Warren H. Cudworth ... *Boston: Wright & Potter, Printers.* 1865. 8vo, pp. 27. B.

CUDWORTH. History of the First Regiment (Massachusetts Infantry) from the 25th of May, 1861, to the 25th of May, 1864, including Brief References to The Operations of the Army of the Potomac. By Warren H. Cudworth, Chaplain of the Regiment. ... *Boston: Walker, Fuller and Company.* 1866. 12mo, pp. 528. BA. 17832

CUDWORTH. Massachusetts and Rum. An Address, delivered April 9, 1871. ... By ... Rev. W. H. Cudworth. *Boston: Massachusetts Total Abstinence Society.* 1871. 8vo, pp. 16.

Also: ... Sermon in Memory of Henrietta Lamson, preached March 17, 1867 ... . *East Boston Advocate Press.* 1870. 8vo, pp. 38, (1). BA.

CUDWORTH (W.) A Defence of Mr. Hervey's Dialogues against Mr. Bellamy's Theron, Paulinus and Aspasio. By William Cudworth ... . *Boston: Z. Fowle and S. Draper.* M.DCC.LXII. 8vo, pp. 36. BA., M. 17834

CUELEBROUK (B.) Colonie de Santo-Thomas. Enquête de M. Blondel van Cuelebrouk chargé d'Affaires, commissaire extraordinaire du Gouvernement. *Bruxelles.* 1846. Folio, six folded Plans and Charts. 17835

This colony, in the Bay of Honduras, was settled by the Belgians.

CUELLAR (D. J. T. de). Obras poeticas de D. Jose T. de Cuellar. Edicion del Republicano. *Mexico.* 1856. 12mo, pp. ii, 460. 17836

CUENCA (C. M.) Obras poéticas de Don Claudio Mamerto Cuenca dadas á luz por Heraclio C. Fajardo. *Buenos Aires.* 1861. 3 vols., 4to, pp. xlviii, 276; 344; 336. 17837

CUESTA (F. Felipo Arroyo de La). *See* Arroyo, Vol. I., Nos. 2116–18.

Cuestion agrícola. *Carácas.* 1866. 8vo, pp. 22. 17838

Cuestion promovida por los Agentes de Francia y de la Gran Bretana. *Carácas.* 1858. 8vo, pp. 49. 17839

Relates to the expulsion of General Monágas.

La Cuestion de Tehuantepec. Contiene las notas del Enviado de la Republica Mexicana en Washington, y algunos articulos que sobre esta materia se han publicado. *Nueva-York.* 1852. pp. 71. 17840

See also Olarte (R.)

Cuestion entre la confederacion Argentina y la provincia de Buenos Aires. Negociacion Yancey. Publicacion oficial de los documentos relativos á esta negociacion en los idiomas Castellano y Frances. *Parana.* 1859. 4to, pp. 40. 17841

Cuestion Pegones y Tacamahaca. *Valencia.* 1858. 8vo, pp. 12. 17842

CUEVA (P.) Arte de la Gramática de la Lengua Zapoteca, conforme al que de la Gramática Latina escribio Antonio de Nebrija, por Fr. Pedro Cueva. *Megico.* 1607. 8vo. 17843

CUEVAS (J. de J.) El Imperio. Opusculo sobre la situacion actual por J. de J. Cuevas. *Mexico.* 1864. 4to, pp. 75.

CUEVAS. La Immigracion. *Mexico: imprenta literaria.* 1866. 8vo, pp. 97. 17845

CUEVAS (J. M.) Informe que en Contestacion al que hizo el Sr. licenciado D. José Maria Cuevas ante la Exma. Tercera Sala de la suprema corte de Justicia. *Mexico.* 1852. 8vo.

CUEVAS (L. G.) Porvenir de México, ó Juicio sobre su Estada Político en 1821 y 1851. Por Don Luis Gonzaga Cuevas, Miembro del Senado. *Mexico.* 1851–57. 3 vols., large 8vo, pp. xiv, 560. 17847

In consequence of the death of the author, the publication of this work was discontinued with the third part, and the rest remains in manuscript. Cuevas was a distinguished statesman and historian.

CUEVAS AGUIRRE Y ESPINOSA (F. de). Extracto|de los autos de diligencias,|y reconocimientos de los rios, lagunas,|vertientes, y desagues de la capital|Mexico, y su valle:|de los caminos para su communicacion,|y su comercio:|de los daños que se vieron: remedios, que se adbitraron:|de los puntos en particular decedidos:|de su practica:|y de otros a mayor examen reservados,| para con mejor acierto resolverlos.|Todo por disposicion del excmo. Señor|D. Juan Francisco|de Huemez, y Horcasitas,|[four lines].|Lo escribiò ... |D. Joseph Francisco|de Cuevas, Aguirre, y Espinosa,|[six lines].|...|*Impresso en Mexico por la Viuda de D. Joseph Bernardo de Hogal. Año de* 1748.| Folio, Title, pp. 71. Map. H. 17848

"Title in red and black, within a light border, having a 'Soneto' on the reverse. At page 42 is a map, 14 by 16½ inches, engraved on copper by Antonio Morino, of Mexico. This book is of the utmost topographical and historical importance."—STEVENS. Some copies have the date of 1747.

CUFFEE (P.) Enterprize, Benevolence, and Christian Conduct Exemplified in Paul Cuffee, a Negro Philanthropist. 8vo, pp. 12. 17849

CUFFEE. Memoir of Captain Paul Cuffee, a man of Colour [of New Bedford, Mass.]. *Liverpool: Egerton, Smith and Co.* 1811. 8vo, pp. 12. + [Another Edition.] 1811. 12mo, pp. 24. + *York: W. Alexander.* 1812. 12mo, pp. 36. + *Phila-*

delphia: Kimber and Sharpless. 1816. 8vo, pp. 12. + Compiled from authentic sources, by Wilson Armistead. *London: Edmund Fry.* 1840. 16mo, pp. 64. Portrait. 17850

See "The Monthly Repository of Theology and General Literature" for 1807, II. 221, etc.

CUGNET (F. J.) Extraits Des Edits, Declarations, Ordonnances et Reglemens, de sa Majesté Très Chretienne. Des Reglemens et Jugemens des Gouverneurs Generaux et Intendans concernans la justice; et des Reglemens et Ordonnances de Police rendues par les Intendans, Faisans partie de la legislature en force en la Colonie du Canada, aujourd'hui Province de Québec. Tirés des Regîtres du Conseil Superieur et de ceux d'Intendance. Par François Joseph Cugnet ... . *Québec: Guillaume Brown.* MDCCLXXV. 4to, pp. 106. 17851

The half-title reads, "Extraits des Regîtres du Conseil Superieur et Des Regîtres d'Intendance. *Quebec.* 1775." *See* Maseres (F.) for an answer.

CUGNET. Abstract of the several royal Edicts and Declarations, and Provincial Regulations and Ordinances that were in force in the Province of Quebec, in the time of the French Government, and of the Commissioners of the several Governors General and Intendants of the said Province during the same period, faithfully collected from the Registers of the Superior Council of Quebec. By F. J. Cugnet, Secretary to the Governor and Council of the said Province for the French Language. *London.* 1772. 17852

CUGNET. Traité Abregé des ancienes Loix, Coutumes et usages de la Colonie du Canada, aujourd'huy Province de Québec, tiré de la coutume de la prevôté et vicomté de Paris, à laquelle la dite Colonie était assujétie, en conséquence de l'Edit de l'établissement du Conseil Souverain du mois d'Avril 1663; avec l'explication de chaque titre et de chaque article, puisée dans les meilleurs autheurs qui ont écrit et comenté la dite coutume. Nécessaires à toutes les personnes qui voudront avoir une teinture des dites ancienes loix coutumes et usages, et qui pourra les faciliter dans l'étude qu'ils seront obligés d'en faire, tant comme Juges, que comme Avocats ou Procureurs. Par François Joseph Cugnet ... . *Quebec: Guillaume Brown.* MDCCLXXIV. 4to, pp. 188, 2. H. 17853

CUGNET. Traité de la loi des fiefs. Qui a toujours été suivie en Canada depuis son établissement, tirée de celle contenuë en la Coûtume de la Prevôté et Vicomté de Paris, à

laquelle les Fiefs et Seigneuries de cette Province sont assujettis en vertu de leurs titres primitifs de Concession, et des Edits, Reglemens, Ordonances et Declarations de sa Majesté très Crétienne, rendus en consequence; et des diferens Jugemens d'Intendans rendus à cet égard, en vertu de la Loi des Fiefs, et des dits Edits, Reglemens, Ordonances et Declarations. ... Par François Joseph Cugnet ... . *Quebec: Guillaume Brown.* MDCCLXXV. 4to, 2 l., pp. ix–xiv, 71. H. 17854

CUGNET. Traité de la Police. Qui a toujours été suivie en Canada, aujourd'hui Province de Québec, depuis son établissement jusqu'à la conquête, tiré des diférens réglemens, jugemens, et ordonnances d'Intendans, à qui par leurs commissions, cette partie du gouvernement était totalement atribuée, à l'exclusion de tous autres juges, qui n'en pouvaient connaitre qu' en qualité de leurs subdélégués. Traité qui pourrait être de quelqu' utilité aux Grands Voyers, et aux juges de Police en cette province. Par François Joseph Cugnet ... . *Quebec: Guillaume Brown.* MDCCLXXV. 4to, pp. 25. H. 17855

"I have a copy of each of these three tracts bound up in a volume [now in Harvard College Library], which formerly belonged to Francis Maseres, and, characteristically of him, has Craig's 'Methodus figurarum' bound up with them. I can find no notice of Cugnet, or of these tracts, in any work within my reach. The printer's name was William Brown, and they are probably some of the earliest specimens of the press in Canada." — RICH, I. 228. The following title is from J. R. Smith's catalogue:

[CUGOANO (Quobna Ottobouh).] Thoughts and Sentiments on the Evil of Slavery; by a Native African. *London.* 1791. 8vo, pp. 46. M. 17856

CUGOANO (O.) Thoughts and Sentiments on the Evil and Wicked Traffic of the Slavery and Commerce of the Human Species, by Ottobah Cugoano, a Native of Africa. *London.* 1787. 8vo. 17857

CUGOANO. Réflexions sur la traite et l'esclavage des nègres, traduites de l'anglais, d'Ottobah Cugoano, africain, esclave à La Grenade et libre en Angleterre. *Londres et Paris: Royer.* 1788. 8vo. 17858

CULLEN (C. C.) The American Melodies, in Three Parts, and Miscellaneous Poems, by Cassius C. Cullen. *Trenton, N. J.: Murphy & Bechtel, Printers.* 1864. 12mo, pp. 96. 17859

CULLEN (Edward). Isthmus of Darien Ship Canal: with a Full History of the Scotch Colony of Darien, Several Maps,

Views of the Country, and Original Documents. By Dr. Cullen, F.R.G.S. *London: Effingham Wilson.* 1852. 8vo, Maps and Views. + Second Edition, much enlarged. *London: Effingham Wilson.* 1853. 8vo, 4 l., pp. ii, ix–xii, 204. H., P. 17860

A selection from this work, called "The Darien Indians," was published in 1863.

CULLEN (W.) Eulogium in honor of the late Dr. William Cullen, delivered before the College of Physicians of Philadelphia, July 9, 1790. *Philadelphia.* 1790. 8vo. C. 17861

[CULLIÒN (F. Val. de).] Examen de l'esclavage en générale et particulièrement de l'esclavage des nègres dans les colonies françaises de l'Amérique. Par V. D. C. *Paris: Maradan.* 1802. 2 vols., 8vo. 17862

[CULLIS (Charles).] A Work of Faith. History of the Consumptives' Home, and the First Annual Report, to September 30, 1865 ... . *Boston: W. & E. Howe, Printer.* 1865. 12mo, pp. viii, 104. + Second Annual Report. *Boston.* 1866. 12mo, pp. 83. + Third Annual Report. *Boston.* 1867. 12mo, pp. 88. + Fourth Annual Report. *Boston.* 1868. 12mo, pp, 101.

CULLOM (S. M.) Speech of Hon. Shelby M. Cullom, of Illinois, on Rights of Naturalized American Citizens; ... in the House ... January 8, 1868. *Washington.* 1868. 8vo, pp. 8.

CULLUM (G. W.) Biographical Register of the Officers and Graduates of the U. S. Military Academy of West Point, N. Y., from its Establishment, March 16, 1802 to the Army Re-Organization of 1866–67. By Bvt. Major-General George W. Cullum ... . *New York: D. Van Nostrand.* 1868. 2 vols., 8vo, pp. xvi, 619; 665. BA. 17865

CULLUM. Register of the Officers and Graduates of the U. S. Military Academy, at West Point, N. Y. from March 16, 1802, to January 1, 1850. Compiled by Captain George W. Cullum, Corps of Engineers, U. S. Army. From the Official Records of the War Department, and other Reliable Sources. *New York: J. F. Trow, Printer.* 1850. 12mo, pp. 303. N. 17866

CULLOM (W.) Speech ... of Hon. William Cullom on the Nebraska and Kansas Bill, in the House ... April 11, 1854. *Washington.* 1854. 8vo, pp. 13. BA., M. 17867

CULLUM. Systems of Military Bridges in use by the United States Army [etc.] ... . By Brig.-Gen. George W. Cullum ... . *New York: D. Van Nostrand.* 1863. 8vo, pp. vi, 226. 7 Plates.

Un Cultivateur Américain. *See* [Crevecœur (Hector St. John de)].

The Cultivator, a Monthly Publication designed to improve the Soil and the Mind. Conducted by J. Buel, etc. *Albany: N. Y. State Agricultural Society.* 1837–38. 4 vols., 8vo.

Continued as follows: Vols. V.–VI. 1838–39. *Albany: Packard, Van Benthuysen & Co.* 1838–39. 2 vols., folio. + Vols. VII.–X. The Cultivator, a Consolidation of Buel's Cultivator and Genesee Farmer. W. Gaylor and L. Tucker, editors. *Albany: J. Buel & Co.* 1840–43. Folio. + Second Series. The Cultivator, a Monthly Journal devoted to Agriculture, Horticulture, etc. New Series, 1844–52. *Albany: L. Tucker, Editor.* 1844–52. 9 vols., 8vo. + Third Series. The Cultivator, a Monthly Journal for the Farm and Garden, etc. 1853–65. *Albany: L. Tucker.* 1853–65. 13 vols., 8vo. + The Cultivator and Country Gentleman. Devoted to the Practice and Science of Agriculture and Horticulture, etc. Jan. 1860, to June, 1868. *Albany: L. Tucker & Son.* 1866. 4to. Continued. *See also* "The Country Gentleman." 1853–65.

De Cultuur en behandeling der West-Indische. *See* Ament, Vol. I., No. 1006.

CULVER (C. V.) Letter in Relation to the Failure of Culver, Penn, & Co. [*New York.*] 1866. 8vo, pp. 31. 17870

CULVER (E. D.) "Old Federalism" & "Modern Democracy." Speech of Hon. E. D. Culver, of New York, on the Mexican War. ... Jan. 20, 1847. [*Washington?*] *J. & G. S. Gideon, Printers.* [n. d.] 8vo, pp. 15. H. 17871

Also: Speech ... on the Texas and Oregon Questions. Delivered in the House of Representatives, ... Jan. ... 30th, 1846. [n. p.] *J. & G. S. Gideon, Printers.* [n. d.] 8vo, pp. 16. B.

CULVER (N.) The Vision of Nathan Culver, late of Newtown, N. Y., etc. 17872

ÇUMARRAGA *or* CUMMURRAJO (Juan). *See* Zumarraga (Juan).

CUMBACK (William). Politics of the Country. Speech of Hon. Will. Cumback of Indiana. ... December 17, 1856. *Washington, D. C.: Buell & Blanchard, Printers.* 1867. 8vo, pp. 7. H. 17873

CUMBERLAND (Georg Graaf van) Reysen na West-Indien, anno 1586–88. *Leyden.* 1706. 8vo. Map and Plates.

CUMBERLAND. Verscheyde Voornaame Reysen, na West-Indien (1586–98). 8vo. Plates and Map. 17874

Included in Vander Aa's "Collection," folio and octavo.

[CUMBERLAND (Richard).] The West Indian: a Comedy. As it is Performed at the Theatre Royal in Drury-Lane. ... *London: W. Griffin.* MDCCLXXI. 8vo, Title, pp. (3), 102, (2). + With remarks by Mrs. Inchbald. *Paris: Theoph. Barrois.* 1820. 18mo. 17876

"Andrieux, in the IIId volume of his 'Œuvres,' has given an imitation of this piece, under the title of 'Le jeune créole, comédie en 5 actes et en prose,' and in the 1st vol. of the 'Théâtre anglais,' which forms part of the 'Chefs-d'œuvre des théâtres étrangers,' a translation in prose, under the title of 'L'Américain.'" — QUÉRARD

CUMBERLAND. The Westindian. 17877

This was translated into Danish by N. V. Dorph, and performed at Copenhagen, but apparently not published.

CUMBERLAND. The West Indian, mit Anmerkungen von K. Fr. Chr. Wagner. *Marburg.* 1836. 17878

Also: The Jew: or, the Benevolent Hebrew. A Comedy. As performed, with universal applause, at the Theatre in Boston. By Richard Cumberland. *Boston: Printed for and sold by John West.* 1795. 12mo, pp. 48.

CUMBERLAND AND OXFORD CANAL. Report of the Committee appointed to procure a Survey for the Route of the Contemplated Cumberland and Oxford Canal to which is added The Report of the Engineer ... . *Portland.* 1823. 8vo, pp. 15. BA.

CUMBERLAND ASSOCIATION. Minutes of the Cumberland Association, Paris, Me., Sept. 30 and Oct. 1, 1812. *Portland.* 1812. 8vo, pp. 8. + Held in ... Jay (Maine), Sept. 29 and 30, 1813; together with the Circular and Corresponding Letters. *Hallowell.* 1813. 8vo. 17880

CUMBERLAND BAPTIST ASSOCIATION. A Confession of Faith and Church Covenant, approved by the Cumberland Baptist Association ... September 30, 1818. [n. p. n. d.] 16mo, pp. 8. H. 17881

Cumberland Coal District. New York, 17th July, 1852. 8vo, pp. 8. Plan. C 17882

Cumberland Coal and Iron Company. Report to the Stockholders, July 21, 1852. *New-York.* 1852. 8vo. S. 17883

CUMBERLAND COLLEGE. Laws of Cumberland College, ... Nashville, Tennessee: ... November 5, 1825. *Nashville.* 8vo, 1 l., pp. 32, 1 l. H. 17884

CUMBERLAND, *Md.* Message from the President, transmitting a report of the Secretary of State, containing the proceedings under the act authorizing the making of a road from Cumberland, Md., to the State of Ohio. January 18, 1814.

CUMBERLAND CONFERENCE. Minutes of the Cumberland Conference of Churches, at their Annual Meeting in North Yarmouth ... January 10, 1832. [n. p. n. d.] 12mo, pp. 20, (3). H. 17886

Proceedings of the Commissioners appointed to lay out the Cumberland Road. (Cong. Doc., 1808.) 17887

Also: Report on the Cumberland Road. January 31, 1807. (Cong. Doc., 1807.) — Statement of Appropriations heretofore made for the Cumberland Road. February 2, 1815.

CUMBERLAND, *Pa.* The Constitution of the Cumberland Presbyterian Church, ... together with the Form of Government and Discipline, ... *Pittsburgh: Forrester and Campbell, Printers.* 1839. 18mo, pp. 234, (2). 17888

CUMBERLAND COUNTY. State of the Accounts of the Collectors of Excise of Cumberland County, From the 10th of August 1774, ... until the 20th of January 1783. In which is exhibited, The Amount of the Monies received by them respectively, and accounted for; Also, Lists shewing the names of Persons from whom Excise became due, and was received. ... *Philadelphia: F. Bailey.* M,DCC,LXXXIII. 8vo, pp. 7. P. 17889

CUMING (F.) Sketches of a Tour to the Western Country, through the States of Ohio and Kentucky; A Voyage down the Ohio and Mississippi Rivers, and a Trip through the Mississippi Territory and Part of West Florida. Commenced at Philadelphia in the Winter of 1807, and concluded in 1809. By F. Cuming. With Notes and an Appendix, containing some Interesting Facts, together with A Notice of an Expedition through Louisiana. *Pittsburgh: Cramer, Spear & Richbaum.* 1810. 12mo, pp. 504. H. 17890

CUMINGS (H.) An Eulogy on the late Patriot Washington, addressed to the People of Billerica, January 10, 1800, When they honored Him with Funeral Solemnities. By Henry Cumings. *Amherst: Printed by Samuel Preston. Feb.*, 1800. 8vo, pp. 16. N. 17891

CUMINGS. An Half-century Discourse ... Billerica, Feb. 21, 1813. By ... Henry Cumings, S.T.D. ... *Cambridge: Printed by Hilliard and Metcalf.* 1813. 8vo, pp. 31. BA., H., M.

CUMINGS. The Present Times Perilous. Fast Sermon at Sullivan, April 25, 1799 ... *Castine.* [n. d.] 8vo. W. 17893

CUMINGS. A Sermon, Preached in Billerica, ... 23d of November, 1775. Being the Day appointed ... for a Public Thanksgiving Throughout the Province of Massachusetts-Bay. By Henry Cumings ... . *Worcester, Massachusetts-Bay: Printed by J. Thomas.* [n. d.] 8vo, 1 l., pp. 29. H. 17894

CUMINGS. A Sermon Preach'd at Lexington, On the 19th of April, 1781. Being the Anniversary of the Commencement of Hostilities between Great-Britain and America, which took Place in that Town, on the 19th of April, 1775. By Henry Cumings ... . *Boston: Printed by Benjamin Edes & Son.* M,DCC,-LXXXI. 8vo, pp. 39. BA., M., N. 17895

CUMINGS. A Sermon Preached before his Honor Thomas Cushing, Esq; Lieutenant-Governor ... of Massachusetts, May 28, 1783. Being the Anniversary of General Election. By Henry Cumings, A.M. ... *Boston: Printed by T. & J. Fleet.* 1783. 8vo, pp. 55. B., BA., H. 17896

CUMINGS. A Sermon Preached in Billerica, December 11, 1783. The Day recommended by Congress to All the States ... as a Day of Public Thanksgiving ... . By Henry Cumings. *Boston: Printed by T. and J. Fleet.* 1784. 8vo, pp. 39. H.

CUMINGS. Sermon ... at Billerica, December 15, 1797 ... a Day of ... Thanksgiving. By Henry Cumings ... . *Boston.* 1797. 8vo, pp. 35. BA., H., W. 17898

CUMINGS. A Sermon preached at Billerica, November 29, 1798, being the Day of the Anniversary Thanksgiving throughout ... Massachusetts. By Henry Cumings ... . *Boston: Printed by John & Thomas Fleet.* MDCCXCVIII. 8vo, pp. 31.

CUMINGS. A Sermon, preached at Billerica, April 9th, 1801; being the Day of the Annual Fast. By Henry Cumings, D.D. ... *Amherst, New-Hampshire: from Samuel Preston's Office.* 1801. 8vo, pp. 29. H. 17900

CUMINGS. A Thanksgiving Sermon Preached at Billerica, November 27. 1766. By Henry Cumings, A.M. ... *Boston, N. E.: Printed by Kneeland and Adams for Thomas Leverett.* MDCCLXVII. 8vo, pp. 32. B., BA., H. 17901

Also: A Discourse addressed to the Roxbury Charitable Society, Sept. 21, 1802. ... *Boston: Manning & Loring.* 1802. 8vo, pp. 24. BA. — A Sermon preached at Bolton, at the Ordination of the Rev. Phineas Wright, October 26, 1785. ... *Boston: printed by T. & J. Fleet.* [1785.] 8vo, pp. 43. — A Sermon, preached on the 9th Day of October, 1799, at the Ordination of the Rev. Caleb Bradley ... Falmouth. ... *Portland: E. A. Jenks.* [n. d.] 8vo, pp. 36. B., BA.

CUMINGS (S.) The Western Navigator: containing Charts of the Ohio River, in its Whole Extent, and of the Mississippi River, from the mouth of the Missouri to the Gulf of Mexico, accompanied by Directions for the Navigation of the Ohio and Mississippi, and such information concerning the Towns, &c. on their Banks, as will be most useful to Travellers. By Samuel Cumings. *Philadelphia: E. Littell.* 1822. Vol. I., Folio. 17902

This is the title to the volume of charts. The letter-press has the following title:

CUMINGS. The Western Navigator; containing Directions for the Navigation of the Ohio and Mississippi, and ... Information concerning the Towns, &c. on their Banks ... . Accompanied by Charts of the Ohio River in its whole Extent; and of the Mississippi, from the Mouth of the Missouri ... . By Samuel Cumings. *Philadelphia: E. Littell.* 1822. Vol. II., 8vo, pp. 4, 232, (6). BA. 17903

CUMINGS. Western Pilot; containing Charts of the Ohio River and of the Mississippi, from the Mouth of the Missouri to the Gulf of Mexico; accompanied with Directions for Navigating the same, and a Gazetteer; or Description of the Towns on their Banks, Tributary Streams, etc., also, a Variety of Matter interesting to Travelers, and all concerned in the Navigation of those Rivers. By Samuel Cumings. *Cincinnati.* 1828. 8vo. + *Cincinnati: N. & G. Guilford.* 1829. 8vo, pp. 104. Maps and 2 Plates. H. + *Cincinnati: N. & G. Guilford & Co.* 1834. 8vo, pp. 152. + With a Table of Distances from Town to Town on all the above Rivers. By Samuel Cummngs [*sic*]. Revised and Corrected by Capt. Charles Ross & Geo. Conclin. *Cincinnati: George Conclin.* 1840. 8vo, pp. 144. Maps. + [*Ibid.*] 1841. 8vo, pp. 144. Maps.

The charts, forty-three in number, are engraved on wood, and printed with the book, each occupying a page. The copperplates are a vignette title, views of Pittsburgh and Cincinnati, and a portrait of Gabrielle Menou. Cumings' editions of the "Navigator" and "Pilot," and another work, by Jas. C. Gilleland, were amplifications of Cramer (*see* our No. 17384), without acknowledgment of the main source of their material.

CUMMING (Alexander). Animadversions on the Rev. Mr. Croswell's Late Letter &c. ... . By A. Cumming ... . *Boston: S. Kneeland.* M,DCC,LXIII. 8vo, 2 l., pp. 40. B., BA.

Relates to the Hopkinsian controversy.

CUMMING. A Sermon Preached Feb. 25. 1761. By A. Cumming, A.M. at His Instalment in the Pastoral Charge of the

South Church, in Boston ... . *Boston: Benjamin Mecom.* M,DCC,-LX,I. 8vo, pp. 58. B., BA., M. 17906

CUMMING. An Eclogue Occasioned by the Death of Reverend Alexander Cumming, A.M. On the 20th of August A.D. 1763. Ætat. 37. [By Jeremy Belknap.] ... *Boston: J. Edwards.* MDCCLXIII. 4to, pp. 8. BA. 17907

CUMMING (Hiram). Secret History of the Perfidies, Corruptions, etc., of the Tyler Dynasty. *Washington and New York.* 1845. 8vo. B. 17908

CUMMING (Hooper.) Official Documents of the Presbytery of Albany, exhibiting the Trials of the Rev. John Chester and Mr. Mark Tucker; together with the whole Case ... *Schenectady.* 1818. 8vo, pp. 255. 17909

CUMMING. An Oration, Commemorative of Washington. Delivered Feb. 22, 1821. By Hooper Cumming ... . *Albany: Daniel Steele.* 1821. 8vo, pp. 26. B. 17910

Also: ... Introductory Sermon, delivered in the Presbyterian Church in Vandewater Street in the City of New York. ... *New York.* 1823. 8vo, pp. 27.—Oration, on the Fourth of July, 1810 before various Societies. *New York.* 8vo.—Oration, on the Fourth of July, 1821. *Schenectady.* 8vo. B., S.—An Oration delivered in Newark, N. J., July 4, 1823. ... *Newark: Printed by John Tuttle & Co.* 1823. 8vo, pp. 23.—An Oration Commemorative of American Independence; ... July 6, 1824, ... before the Firemen of the City of New-York. ... *New-York: printed by E. Conrad.* 1824. 8vo, pp. 23.—A Plea for the American Bible Society: Sermon, March 29, 1818, in the Third Presbyterian Church, Albany. *Albany.* 1818. 8vo, pp. 23. N.—A Sermon delivered at Schoharie before the Grand Lodge, at the Installation of Hicks' Lodge, No. 305, July 4, 1818. ... *Schoharie: Printed by D. Van Veghten.* 1818. 8vo, pp. 16.

CUMMING (Kate). Journal in the Confederate Army of Tennessee, from the Battle of Shiloh to the End of the War. *Louisville, Ky.* 1866. 8vo. C. 17911

[CUMMINGS (Alexander).] Address. [n. p. n. d.] 8vo, pp. 31. 17912

On the question, "Does the Constitution establish or protect Slavery?" Delivered at Williamsport, September, 1856.

CUMMINGS. Letter in Reply to the Report of the Van Wyck Committee. Presented to Congress March 6, 1862. 8vo, pp. 8.

CUMMINGS (A.) The Character of a Righteous Ruler. A Sermon upon the death of the Honorable Patrick Gordon, Esq; Lieutenant Governor of the Province of Pennsylvania, &c. Preach'd at Christ's Church in Philadelphia, Aug. 8. 1736. By

Archibald Cummings; M.A. Rector of the said Church, and Commissary to the Bishop of London. Published at the request of several Gentlemen in this City. *Philadelphia: printed and sold by Andrew Bradford.* M,DCC,XXXVI. 8vo, pp. 26. P. 17914

CUMMINGS. An Exhortation to the Clergy of Pennsylvania, at Philadelphia, September the 24th. 1729. By the Reverend Archibald Cummings. *Annapolis: W. Parks.* M,DCC,XXIX. 4to.

CUMMINGS. Faith absolutely necessary, but not sufficient to Salvation without Good Works. In Two Sermons. Preached at Christ Church, Philadelphia, April 20, 1740. By Archibald Cummings, M.A. Publish'd in their own Vindication from the false and rash Reflections of the famous Mr. Whitefield. *Philadelphia: Printed by Andrew and William Bradford.* [1740.] 12mo, pp. xvi, 38. P. 17916

CUMMINGS (A.) A Discourse delivered at Brunswick, (Maine,) April 6, 1820, the Day of the Annual Fast ... . By Asa Cummings, A.B. *Brunswick: Joseph Griffin, Printer.* 1820. 8vo, pp. 36. H. 17917

CUMMINGS. A Memoir of the Rev. Edward Payson, D.D. ... By Asa Cummings ... Second Edition. *Boston: Published by Crocker and Brewster. New York: J. Leavitt.* 1830. pp. viii, 400. Portrait. BA., H. + Third Edition. [*Ibid.*] + [*New York:*] *American Tract Society.* [n. d.] 18mo, pp. 486. Portrait.

Also: A Sermon delivered in Gorham, June 25, 1828, before the Maine Missionary Society ... *Portland.* 1828. 8vo, pp. 40.

CUMMINGS (C. A.) Specifications for a New High School House for ... West Roxbury. Charles A. Cummings and W. T. Sears, Architects. *Boston: Alfred Mudge & Son, Printers.* 1867. 8vo, pp. 16. H. 17919

CUMMINGS (E. E.) Annals of the Baptist Churches in New-Hampshire. A Sermon preached before the New-Hampshire Baptist State Convention, at its Tenth Annual Meeting, held at Deerfield, October 20, 1835. By Ebenezer E. Cummings, Pastor of the Baptist Church, Concord. *Concord, N. H.: Marsh, Capen & Lyon.* 1836. 8vo, pp. 52. C., H. 17920

CUMMINGS (H.) *See* Cumings (H.), No. 17901.

CUMMINGS (Jeremiah W.) The Present State of Religious Controversy in America: An Address ... September 22, 1864.

By Rev. J. W. Cummings .. . *New York: P. O'Shea.* 1864. 8vo, pp. 14. H. 17921

CUMMINGS (P.) A Dictionary of Congregational Usages and Principles ... to which are added ... Notices of the principal Writers ... referred to ... . By Preston Cummings ... . *Boston: S. K. Whipple and Co.* 1852. 12mo, pp. 419. + Stereotype Edition; Revised, Collated, and Enlarged. *Boston: S. K. Whipple.* 1853. 12mo, pp. 432. H. 17922

CUMMINGS (T. S.) Historic Annals of the National Academy of Design New York Drawing Association, etc., with Occasional Dottings by the Way-side, from 1825 to the Present Time. By Thos. S. Cummings, N.A., Professor of the Arts of Design ... . *Philadelphia: George W. Childs.* 1865. 8vo, pp. 364. H., S. 17923

CUMMINS (A. G.) The Christian Church's Duty to the Freedmen. A Sermon preached on Thanksgiving Day, December 7, 1865, in Christ Church, Reading, Pa. By Rev. Alexander G. Cummins, M.A. *Philadelphia: Sherman & Co., Printers.* 1865. 8vo, pp. 30. 17924

CUMMINS (E. H.) History of the late War between the United States and Great Britain, with a Critical Appendix, &c., By E. H. Cummins. *Baltimore.* 1820. 8vo. 17925

CUMMINS. A Summary Geography of Alabama, one of the United States. By Ebenezer H. Cummins. *Philadelphia.* 1819. 12mo. 17926

CUMMINS (G. D.) The African a trust from God to the American. A Sermon delivered on the day of National Humiliation, Fasting and Prayer, in ... Baltimore, January 4, 1861, by the Rev. George D. Cummins, D.D. Rector. *Baltimore: printed by John D. Toy.* 1861. 8vo, pp. 28. H. 17927

CUMMINS. The Christian, in time of National Peril, trembling for the Ark of God. A Sermon delivered on Thanksgiving Day, in ... Baltimore; November 29, 1860, by the Rev. George D. Cummins, D.D. Rector. *Baltimore: John D. Toy.* 1860. 8vo, pp. 24. 17928

CUMMINS. Life of Mrs. Virginia Hale Hoffman. *Philadelphia.* 1859. 16mo. 17929

CUMMINS. The Pestilence—God's Messenger and Teacher. Discourse in behalf of the Sufferers of Norfolk and Portsmouth,

Va. delivered in ... Washington, September 9, 1855. By Rev. George D. Cummins, Rector. *Washington: George S. Gideon. Printer.* 1855. 8vo, pp. 13. 17930

CUMMINS. A Sketch of the Life of the Rev. William M. Jackson, ... Norfolk, Va. By Rev. George D. Cummins. *Washington: Gray & Ballantyne.* 1856. 12mo, pp. 118.

CUMMINS (John). *See* Bulkley (John), Vol. III., No. 9108.

CUMMINS (J. D.) Speech of Hon. J. D. Cummins, of Ohio, on the Oregon Question. Delivered in the House of Representatives, Saturday, February 7, 1846. *Washington: Blair and Rives.* 1846. 8vo, pp. 15. 17932

CUMMINS (J.) An Oration on Public Opinion, delivered before the Philomathæan Society of Mt. St. Mary's College, June 28th, 1854. By John Cummins, D.D. *New York.* MDCCCLIV. 8vo, pp. 19. 17933

CUMMINS (Maria S.) Haunted Hearts. A Tale of New Jersey. New Edition. *London: Sampson, Low, Son, & Marston.* 1868. 18mo, pp. viii, 342. 17934

[CUMMINS (Maria S.)] The Lamplighter. *Boston: John P. Jewett & Company.* 1854. 12mo, pp. 523. + *Leipzig: B. Tauchnitz.* 1854. 16mo, 2 l., pp. 460. (Coll. Brit. Auth., 304.) 17935

The novel is inserted, like those of Cooper, because, by its numerous versions and its popularity abroad, it conveyed ideas of American life and manners to so many foreigners.

[CUMMINS.] Der Lampenwärter. ... Aus dem Englischen. Neue Ausgabe. *Leipzig: Friedlein.* [1856.] 8vo, pp. vii, 304. + Mit 15 Illustrationen [in Holzschnitt] von F. Gilbert und 6 Liedern von J. E. Carpenter, in Musik gesetzt von Glover, Farmer, Hime und Linley. *Leipzig: Weber.* 1854. 2 pts., 8vo, pp. xxiv, xv, 360. + [CUMMINS.] Der Laternenwärter. Aus dem Englischen übersetzt von W. E. Drugulin. *Leipzig: Kollmann.* 1854. 4 vols., 8vo, pp. 192; 176; 272; 272. (Amerikanische Bibliothek, 108–111.) + [CUMMINS.] Der Lampenwärter. Aus dem Amerikanischen von Leop. R. v. Blumencron. *Wien: Ludwig und Zang.* 1855. 4 vols., 12mo, pp. 148; 135; 150; 132. (Roman- und Novellen- Zeitung.) + [CUMMINS.] Der Lampenputzer. Aus dem Englischen übersetzt von Rob. Springer. *Berlin: Vieler und Co.* 1854. 4 vols., 8vo, pp. 272; 258; 228; 248. + Deutsch von Treu-

mund Whelp [Ed. Pelz]. *Leipzig: Voigt und Günther.* 1854. 2 vols., 8vo, 3 l., pp. 293; 2 l., pp. 303. + Zweite Auflage. [*Ibid.*] 1856. [*Ibid.*] + [CUMMINS.] Der Laternenmann. ... Uebersetzt von A. Kretzschmar. *Leipzig: O. Wigand.* 1854. 4 pts., 8vo, pp. 218; 267; 294; 307. 17936

CUMMINS. Il lumajo romango americano prima traduzione dall' inglese. *Firenze.* 1855. 12mo. 17937

CUMMINS. Il lampionajo romanzo. *Torino.* 1854. 12mo.

CUMMINS. Mabel Vaughan. Par Miss Cummins ... . traduit par Mme Henriette Loreau. *Paris: L. Hachette et Cᵉ.* 18mo, pp. 496. 17939

CUMMINS. L'allumeur de réverbères. Par Miss Cummins. ... Traduit par MM. Belin de Launay et Ed. Scheffer. *Paris: L. Hachette et Cᵉ.* 1858. 18mo, pp. 375. 17940

CUMMINS (O.) Hard-Scrabble Calendar. Report of the Trials of Oliver Cummins, Nathaniel G. Metcalf, Gilbert Humes and Arthur Farrier, who were indicted with six others for a Riot, and for aiding in pulling down a Dwelling House, on the 18th October, at Hard-Scrabble. *Providence: Printed for the Purchaser.* 1824. 8vo, pp. 32. 17941

CUMPSTON (E. H.) A Discourse on the Death of W. H. Harrison, late President of the United States, at Eastville, Northampton County, Virginia. By Edward H. Cumpston. *Norfolk.* 1841. 8vo. S. 17942

CUNHA BARBOSA. Oração de acção de graças recitada na Capella Real do Rio de Janeiro, celebrando-se o quinto anniversario da chegada de Sua Alteza Real, etc. *Rio de Janeiro: na Imp. Regia* 1813. 4to, pp. 22. 17943

CUNHA BARBOSA. O Nictorey. Metamorphose do Rio de Janeiro. *Londres.* 1822. 8vo. 17944

Also included in Varnhagen, II. 667–682.

[CUNHA BARBOSA.] Os Garimpeiros. *Rio de Janeiro.* 1837. 8vo. 17945

An heroic comic poem on political topics.

CUNHA BARBOSA. Discurso funebre nas exequias celebradas pela Loja Escoceza União Brasileira, ao Oriente do Rio de Janeiro, no dia 9 de Abril de 1835 pelo seu membro, o cavalleiro Rosa-Cruz Bernardo Lobo de Sousa, primeiro Grão-mestre do

Oriente provincial do Pará, em cuja cidade fóra assassinado em 7 de Janeiro do mesmo anno. *Rio de Janeiro.* 1835. 8vo, pp. 12.

CUNHA DE AZEREDO COUTINHO (J. J. da). Defeza de D. José Joaquim da Cunha de Azeredo Coutinho ... . *Lisboa: João Rodrigues Neves.* M. DCCC. VIII. 4to, pp. vii, 129. H.

CUNHA DE AZEREDO COUTINHO. Discurso sobre o estado actual das minas do Brazil dividido em quatro capitulos. *Lisboa.* 1804. 4to, pp. 66. 17948

CUNHA DE AZEREDO COUTINHO. Ensayo economico sobre o comercio de Portugal e suas colonias ... publicado de ordem da Academia Real das Siencias pelo seu socio Joze Joaquim da Cunha de Azeredo Coutinho. *Lisboa: Academia.* 1794. 4to, 4 l., pp. iii, 153. 17949

CUNHA DE AZEREDO COUTINHO. A political Essay on the Commerce of Portugal and her Colonies, particularly of Brasil in South America. By J. J. da Cunha Azeredo Coutinho Bishop of Fernambuco, and Fellow of the Royal Academy of Sciences of Lisbon. Translated from the Portuguese. *London: G. G. and J. Robinson.* 1801. 8vo, 3 l., pp. v, (4), 198, 1 l.

See Rich, II. 31, and "M. Rev.," XLI. 425.

CUNHA DE AZEREDO COUTINHO. An Essay on the Commerce and Products of the Portuguese Colonies in South America ... . Translated from the Portuguese of J. J. Cunha de Azeredo Coutinho ... . *London.* 1807. 8vo, 3 l., pp. v, (4), 198, 1 l. H. 17951

CUNHA DE AZEREDO COUTINHO. A Gratidão Parnambucana o seu Bemfeitor D. Jose Joaquim da Cunha de Azeredo Coutinho Bispo de Elvas os socios da Academia ... Parnambucana e os alumnos de do Seminario Olindense. *Lisboa.* 1808. 4to. 17952

In prose and verse.

CUNHA DE AZEREDO COUTINHO. Informação dada ao ministro de estado dos negocios da fazenda D. Rodrigo de Sousa Coutinho, por D. José Joaquim da Cunha de Azeredo Coutinho, bispo de Elvas, em outro tempo bispo de Pernambuco, eleito de Miranda, e Bragança, director geral dos estudos de Pernambuco. *Lisboa: João Rodrigues Neves.* M. DCCC. VIII. 4to, pp. 34. 17953

CUNHA DE AZEREDO COUTINHO. Politischer Versuch über den Handel Portugals und seiner Kolonien von Jose Joaquim da

Cunha de Azeredo Coutinho ... . *Hamburg: Benjamin Gotlieb Hoffmann.* 1801. 8vo. pp. viii, 183, (1). H. 17954

CUNHA DE AZEREDO COUTINHO. Respostas dadas por D. José Joaquim da Cunha de Azeredo Coutinho bispo de Elvas, então bispo de Pernambuco, a's propostas feitas por alguns dos parochos d'a quella diocese. *Lisboa: João Rodrigues Neves.* M. DCCC. VIII. 4to, pp. 26. H. 17955

CUNHA MATTOS (R. J. da). Memorias da campanha do senhor D. Pedro d'Alcantara, ex-imperador do Brazil, no reino de Portugal, com algunas noticias anteriores ao dia do seu desembarque; escriptas pelo general Raimundo Jose da Cunha Mattos. *Rio de Janeiro: imp. de Seignot-Plancher et Cᵉ. Paris: Delaunay.* 1833. 2 vols., 8vo. 17956

CUNNABELL. Cunnabell's Nova-Scotia Almanac for 1858. *Halifax.* 1858. 12mo. Continued. S. 17957

CUNNING (F. H.) Address delivered at the laying of the Cap Stone of the Ten Combined Locks at Lockport, June 24, 1825. 1825. 8vo. 17958

CUNNING (John P.) Remarks on the Mineralogical Character of the Seigneury of Rigaud Vandreuil, District of Quebec. *Montreal.* 1847. 17959

CUNNINGHAM (A.) Paul Jones; A Romance. By Allan Cunningham. *Edinburgh.* 1826. 3 vols., 12mo. + *Philadelphia: H. C. Carey & J. Lea.* 1827. 12mo. H. 17960

CUNNINGHAM. Paul Jones, ein Roman, aus dem Englischen von W. A. Lindau. *Dresden.* 1827. 3 vols., 12mo. 17961

CUNNINGHAM (E.) Monument to the Praise of the Lord's Goodness and to the Memory of Eliza Cunningham. *Philadelphia.* 1796. 8vo. P. 17962

CUNNINGHAM (F.) Notes recueillies en visitant les prisons de la Suisse ... Par Francis Cunningham, suivies de la description des prisons de Gand, Philadelphie, Ilchester, and Milbank. Par T. F. Buxton, Esq. *Paris.* 1820. 12mo, pp. 87. P.

CUNNINGHAM (J.) The Quakers from their Origin till the Present Time: an International History. By John Cunningham ... . *Edinburgh: John Menzies & Co.; London: Hamilton, Adams & Co.; Crieff: George M'Culloch.* M.DCCC.LXVIII. 16mo, pp. xv, 335. B. 17964

CUNNINGHAM. The Centennial Birthday of Robert Burns, as Celebrated by the Burns Club of the City of New York, Tuesday, January 25, 1859. By J. Cunningham. *New York.* 1860. 8vo, pp. 136. Plates. 17965

CUNNINGHAM (L.) The Case of the Whigs who Loaned their Money on the Public Faith, Fairly Stated, including a memento for Congress to review their Engagements and to establish the Honour and Honesty of the United States of America. By Letitia Cunningham. *Philadelphia: Printed by Francis Bailey.* MDCCLXXXIII. 12mo, pp. 51. J.C.B., P. 17966

CUNNINGHAM (P.) Hints for Australian Emigrants. With ... Descriptions of ... Modes of irrigating Land in ... South America, &c. By Peter Cunningham, Surgeon ... . *London.* 1841. 8vo, pp. x, 119. 17967

[CUNNINGHAM (P. A.)] Ladies Mount Vernon Association of the Union. An Appeal for the purchase and future Preservation of the Home and Grave of Washington. *Charleston.* 1857. 8vo, pp. 8. S., W. 17968

CUNNINGHAM (Robert). Inaugural Address, Lafayette College. 1838. 8vo. S. 17969

CUNNINGHAM (S.) State of the Accounts of Samuel Cunningham, Esq. late Collector of Excise for Chester County. From August 10, 1782, to Nov. 7, 1783 ... . *Philadelphia: Printed by F. Bailey.* MDCCLXXIV. 8vo, pp. 6. P. 17970

Title misprinted, 1774 for 1784.

CUNNINGHAM (W.) The Cosmographical Glasse, conteinyng the pleasant Principles of Cosmographie, Geographie, Hydrographie, or Nauigation. Compiled by William Cunningham, a Doctor of Physicke. *Londoni: in Officina Joan Daij.* 1559. Folio, Title, etc., pp. 202. Portrait. J.C.B. 17971

In the chapter on America the author totally ignores Columbus. An extended notice of the book is in Oldy's "British Librarian," pp. 26–32. Bradley's copy sold for £7 7s.

[CUNNINGHAM (William).] A Letter to A Great Character [John Adams]. ... [n. p.] *Printed And Published for the Public,* 1811. 8vo, pp. 64 BA. 17972

See Adams (John), Vol. I., and Pickering (Timothy).

CUNNINGHAM (W.) An Eulogy delivered at Lunenburg, on ... the 22d of February 1800. The Day recommended by

Congress to commemorate the ... Services of Gen. George Washington ... . By William Cunningham, Jun. ... *Worcester: Isaiah Thomas, Jr.* 1800. 8vo, pp. 16. BA., H., W. 17973

CUNNINGHAM. An Oration at Fitchburg, July, 4, 1803. At the Request of Federal Republicans. ... By William Cunningham, Jun. ... *Leominster: Printed by Adams & Wilder. August*, 1803. 8vo, pp. 78. BA., W. 17974

CUNNINGHAM (W.) & Co. The Claim and Answer in the Case of William Cunningham & Co. against the United States; under the Sixth Article of the Treaty ... between His Britannic Majesty and the United States ... . *Philadelphia: Printed by John Fenno.* M,DCC,XCVIII. 4to, pp. 10, 72, xix. BA. 17975

CUNNINGHAM. The Reply of William Cunningham, & Co. to the Answer of the United States to their Claim and Memorial. *Philadelphia: printed by James Humphreys.* 1798. 4to, pp. 36. 17976

CUNON (J. C.) Memorial and Petition of J. C. Cunon, in behalf of the Directors of the Missionary Concerns of the Moravians. February 18, 1814. (Cong. Doc.) 17977

CUNY (Phil. M.) Letter to Judge John C. Watrous in reply to the Aspersions Cast upon the Writer ... *Austin, Texas.* 1858. 17978

CUNYNGHAME (A.) A Glimpse of the Great Western Republic. By Lieut. Col. Arthur Cunynghame. *London: Richard Bentley.* 1863. 8vo, 2 l., pp. 337. S. 17979

[CUOQ (*Rev.* A.)] Etudes Philologiques sur quelques langues sauvages de l'Amerique Par N. O. Ancien. missionnaire. *Montreal.* 1860. 8vo, pp. 160. 17980

In this and the following work the author claims for the Algonquins and the Iroquois languages a linguistic position which Renan denied.

[CUOQ.] Jugement erroné de M. Ernest Renan sur les Langues Sauvages. Par N. O. *Montreal.* 1864. 8vo, pp. 23. 17981

A Cure for the Spleen. Or Amusement for a Winter's Evening; Being the Substance of a Conversation on the Times, over a Friendly Tankard and Pipe. Between Sharp, ——— A Country Parson. Bumper, ——— A Country Justice. Fillpot, ——— An Inn-keeper. Graveairs, ——— A Deacon. Trim, ——— A Barber. Brim, ——— A Quaker. Puff, ——— A late Representative. Taken in short Hand, by Sir Roger De Coverly. *America: Printed and sold in the Year* MDCCLXXV. 8vo, Title, pp. 3–32. 17982

The scene of this conversation is laid near Boston, and the book is an amusing exposition of the grievances and politics of the Colonies. On page thirty of this copy are four lines of the text with this manuscript note at the bottom of the page: "From this to the conclusion of the period is omitted in all the vendible impressions, as the printer was a woman and ashamed" [illegible] *See* "Nuggets," No. 795. *See also* Vol. I., No. 1274, for another edition.

CURAÇAO. Beschryving van het eiland Curacao en onderhoorige eilanden. *Amsterdam: J. van Selm.* 1781. 8vo. Plates. 17983

Perhaps the same as [Paddenburg (G. G. van)], Bescbrijving, etc., *infra.*

Curiae Canadenses, or the Canadian Law Courts; a Poem, by Plinius Secundus [*pseudonym*]. *Toronto: H. & W. Rowsell.* 1843. 8vo, 3 l., pp. 126. C. 17984

Curieuse Anmerkingen der bysonderste Oost en Westindische verwondenswaardige Dingen. *Utrecht.* 1686. 4to. Plates. 17985

Curiose Beschreibung der auserlesensten Merkwürdigkeiten, so in den dreyen Welt-Theilen Asia, Africa, und America zu finden: etc. *Augsburg.* 1784. Plates. 17986

Curiositäten der physisch- literarische- artistisch- historischen Vor- und Mitwelt ... . *Weimar.* 1811–23. 10 vols., 8vo. 17987

For articles on America, *see* III. 431–427, Lächerlichkeiten der Methodistischen Religions-Sekten in ... Amerika; 497–510, Paris in Hayti [on the court etiquette, etc., of the negro kingdom]; V. 462–464; VI. 448–550, Der wahre Geburtsort des berühmten Christoforo Colombo; VII. 179–186, Jesuiten-Regiment in Paraguay; VIII. 189–193, Religion und sonderbare Aberglaube der Grönländer; IX. 254–257, Rede des Miss Polly Baker vor dem Gerichtshofe von Konnektikut ... als sie wegen des fünften unehelichen Kindes, das sie geboren, vorgefordert wurde; X. 1–19, Die Schlange als Mythe, Hieroglyphe, Emblem etc. und über die Urbevölkerung von Amerika; 271, Entdeckung einer Urstadt in Süd-Amerika.

Curiositez de la nature. *See* [Biron (Claude)], Vol. II., No. 5582.

Curiosities of Nature and Art in Husbandry and Gardening. *London.* 1707. 8vo. Plates. 17988

Contains a letter of six pages from Mr. Lignon to Mr. Auger, Governor of Guadeloupe and other islands, concerning a new manner of easily propagating all sorts of plants and exotic trees.

Curious and Entertaining Voyages undertaken either for Discovery, Conquest, or the Benefit of Trade; commencing with the Earliest Discoveries promoted by Prince Henry of Portugal, and 58 different Portuguese and Spanish Voyages, exhibiting various Scenes of Cruelties, Hardships, Misfortunes and Discoveries, particularly on Columbus's Conquest of Mexico, &c. with Magellan's Voyage Round the World. *London: Stalker.* 1790. 4to. 17989

A Curious Collection of Travels, 1761. *See* [Newbery (J.)]

A Curious Hieroglyphick Bible; or Select Passages in the Old and New Testaments, represented with Emblematical Figures, for the Amusement of Youth, &c. ... Illustrated with nearly Five Hundred Cuts. The First Worcester Edition. *Printed at Worcester, Mass., by Isaiah Thomas.* 1788. 24mo. 17990

The first work of its kind printed in the United States.

Curious Observations [1751]. *See* Lambert (*l'Abbé*).

The Curious Traveller, being a Choice Collection of very Remarkable Histories, Voyages, Travels, etc., containing an Account of the Spanish Cruelties in the West Indies. 1742. 8vo. Frontispiece and Plates. 17991

Currency, or Money; its Nature and Uses, and the Effects of the Circulation of Bank-notes for Currency; by a Merchant of Boston. *Boston.* 1855. 17992

A Report on the Currency. *New York: John F. Trow.* 1858. 8vo, pp. 31. 17993

Report of the Comptroller of the Currency to the Second Session of the 39th Congress of the United States. December 3, 1866. *Washington.* 1866. 8vo, pp. xv, 189. 17994

CURREY (R. O.) A Sketch of the Geology of Tennessee ... . By Richard O. Currey ... . *Knoxville: Kinsloe & Rice.* 1857. 8vo, pp. x, 128. C., H. 17995

CURREY (S.) Argument for the Heirs at Law in the Halsey Will Case. By Samuel Currey. *Providence: Knowles, Anthony & Co.* 1859. 8vo, pp. 19. 17996

[CURRIE (*Dr.*)] A Letter, Commercial and Political, Addressed to the Rt Honble. William Pitt: in which the Real Interests of Britain, in the Present Crisis, are Considered, and Some Observations are Offered on the General State of Europe. The Second Edition, Corrected and Enlarged. By Jasper Wilson, Esq. [Motto.] *London: Printed for G. G. and I. J. Robinson.* MDCCXCIII. 8vo, 2 l., pp. 72. 17997

Contains many references to the American War

CURRIE (M. G.) Gabriel West and other Poems. By Mrs. Margaret Gill Currie. *Fredericton, N. B.* 1866. 17998

Gabriel West was a Loyalist soldier.

CURRIE (W.) A Treatise on the Lawfulness of Defensive War. In Two Parts. By William Currie. *Philadelphia: Printed and sold by B. Franklin and D. Hall.* M.DCC.XLVIII. 8vo, pp. xviii, 119. C. 17999*a*

See "The Doctrine of Christianity" and Tennent (Gilbert).

CURRIE (W.) An Historical Account of the Climates and Diseases of the United States of America; and of the Remedies and methods of Treatment, which have been found most useful and efficacious, particularly in those Diseases which depend upon Climate and Situation. Collected principally from Personal Observation, and the communications of Physicians of Talents and experience, residing in the several States. By William Currie, Fellow of the College of Physicians of Philadelphia. *Philadelphia: Printed by T. Dobson, at the Stone-House, No. 41, South Second-Street.* M,DCC,XCII. 8vo, Title, pp. 4, 409, v. B. 17999

CURRIE. An Impartial Review of that Part of Dr. Rush's ... Publication entitled "An Account of the Bilious Remitting Yellow Fever, as it appeared in ... Philadelphia, in ... 1793 ... " in which his Opinion is shown to be erroneous; the Importation of the Disease established; and the Wholesomeness of the City Vindicated. By William Currie ... . *Philadelphia: printed by Thomas Dobson.* M. DCC. XCIV. 8vo, pp. 15. H. 18000

CURRIE. Memoirs of the Yellow Fever, which prevailed in Philadelphia, and other parts of the United States, in the summer and autumn of 1798; with a collection of Facts respecting the Origin of the Fever. By William Currie, ... M.P. &c. *Philadelphia.* 1798. P. 18001

CURRIE. A Sketch of the Rise and Progress of the Yellow Fever, and of the Proceedings of the Board of Health, in Philadelphia, In the Year 1799: to which is added A Collection of Facts and Observations respecting the Origin of the Yellow Fever in this Country; and a Review of the Different Modes of treating it. By William Currie ... . *Philadelphia: Budd and Bartram.* 1800. 8vo, pp. 112. BA., H. 18002

CURRIE. A Treatise on the Synochus Icteroides, or Yellow Fever; as it lately appeared in the City of Philadelphia, Exhibiting a Concise View of its Rise, Progress, and Symptoms, together with the Method of Treatment found most Successful; also Remarks on the Nature of the Contagion, and Directions for preventing the Introduction of the same Malady, in Future. By William Currie ... . *Philadelphia: Thomas Dobson.* M,DCC, XCIV. 8vo, pp. viii, 85. BA., G., P. 18003

Also: A Dissertation on the Autumnal Remitting Fever. *Philadelphia.* MDCCLXXX. 16mo. — View of the Diseases most Prevalent in the United States of America. ... *Philadelphia.* 1811. 8vo. M.

CURRIE (W. W.) Memoir of ... James Currie, M.D. of Liverpool. Edited by his Son, William Wallace Currie. *London: Longman.* 1832. 2 vols., 8vo, pp. xv, 524; xii, 508. Portrait. 18004

Relates in part to affairs in Virginia in 1774.

CURRIER (E.) The Political Text Book; containing the Declaration of Independence, Lives of Signers, Constitution of the United States, Inaugurals ... Messages, ... By Edward Currier. *Worcester, Mass.: Warren Blake.* 1842. 8vo, pp. 512. Plate. 18005

CURRY (D.) The Judgments of God, confessed and deprecated. A Sermon ... on the ... National Fast Day, August 3d, 1849. ... By Rev. Daniel Curry ... . *New-York: Oliver & Brother, Printers.* 1849. 8vo, pp. 15. H. 18006

The cholera, the Mexican War, and slavery, are the subjects of this sermon.

CURRY (Jabez Lafayette Monroe). The Constitutional Rights of the States. Speech of J. L. M. Curry, of Alabama, in the House of Representatives, March 14, 1860. [n. p.] *J. McGill, Print.* [n. d.] 8vo, pp. 8. H. 18007

Also: Speech ... on the Bill granting Pensions to the Soldiers of the War of 1812. Delivered ... April 27, 1858. [*Washington?*] *Lemuel Towers, Printer.* 8vo, pp. 8. H. — Speech ... on the Election of Speaker, and the Progress of Anti-Slaveryism. Delivered ... December 10, 1859. *Washington: printed by Lemuel Towers.* 1859. 8vo, pp. 15. H.

CURRY (J. P.) Volunteers' Camp and Field book, containing Information on the Art of War. By John P. Curry. *Richmond: West & Johnson.* 1862. 18mo, pp. 144. C. 18008

CURSON (H.) A Compendium of the Laws and Government, Ecclesiastical, Civil, and Military, of Great Britain, Ireland, and the Plantations in America, &c. *London.* 1716. 12mo. 18009

Also: New Description of the World, ... including America, &c. By H. Curson, Gent. *London.* 1709. Sm. 8vo.

A Cursory Examination of the Respective Pretensions of the Colonizationists and Abolitionists. ... *New-York.* 1837. 8vo, pp. 12. B. 18010

A Cursory Glimpse at the State of the Nation on the Twenty-Second of February, 1814. ... or a Physico-Politico-Theologico, Lucubration upon the Wonderful Properties of Nitro Oxide ... in its Effects upon the Human Mind, and Body ... . *Philadelphia: Moses Thomas.* 1814. 8vo, pp. 22. B. 18011

Cursory Observations relative to the Mounting of Cannon in a new way, and to Naval War. *New York: J. Oswald.* 1785. 8vo, pp. 23. 18012

Cursory Observations. *Also,* Cursory Remarks on Dr. Price's Observations. *See* Price (R.)

Cursory Remarks on Men and Measures in Georgia. *Printed in the Year* MDCCLXXXIV. 8vo, pp. (2), 30. 18013

Cursory Remarks on the Emancipation of Slaves. *Liverpool: J. Nevill & Co.* [1823.] 8vo. 18014

Cursory Remarks on Ramsay. *See* [Tobin].

Cursory Review of the Schuylkill Coal, in reference to its Introduction into New York, and the other Atlantic Cities. *New York.* 1823. 8vo. 18015

Cursory ... Views of the Liberal and Restrictive Systems of Political Economy ... with an Examination of Mr. Huskisson's System of Duties ... . By a Citizen of Philadelphia. ... Second Edition ... enlarged and improved. [By Mathew Carey.] *Philadelphia: printed by J. R. A. Skerrett.* 1826. 8vo. pp. 26. 18016

Cursory Sketch, 1809. *See* [Lee (Henry)]

CURT (*M.* de). Motion de M. de Curt, député de la Guadeloupe, Au nom des Colonies réunies. ... *Paris: Baudouin.* 1789. 8vo, pp. 15. H. 18017

CURTES (Martin). *See* Cortes (Martin), Vol. IV., No. 16967.

CURTHS (C.) Die Eroberung Mexico's durch Hernandez Cortez. Historisches Gemälde fur die Jugend von Carl Curths ... . Zweite Ausgabe. *Berlin: August Rücker.* [1828.] 8vo, 2 l., pp. 277. H. 18018

CURTIN (A. G.) Special Message of Governor A. G. Curtin, Transmitted to the Legislature of Pennsylvania, August 9, 1864. [n. p. n. d.] 8vo, pp. 13. 18019

Governor Curtin delivered several messages and speeches during the rebellion of 1860–65, which belong more properly under Pennsylvania. The following are more personal:

CURTIN. Ceremonies of the Second Inauguration of Andrew G. Curtin, Governor of Pennsylvania, with the proceedings of the Presentation of Audubon's Works by the Loyal Citizens of New Jersey. *Harrisburg: Singerly and Myers.* 1864. 8vo, pp. 22. 18020

CURTIN. A Black Record! Gov. Curtin's Portrait drawn by a Black Republican Editor. Who clothed our Soldiers in shoddy? Who plundered our Brave Volunteers? Voters, read! *Philadelphia: Age Office.* [n. d.] 8vo, pp. 4. 18021

CURTIN. The Political Portrait of Andrew G. Curtin, by One of His Own Party. [n. p. n. d.] 8vo, pp. 23. 18022

CURTIN (D.) Curtin's Directory of Astoria, Babylon, Bath, Carnarsi, etc., Long Island. With a Business Directory, 1868–9. *New York: D. Curtin.* 1869. 12mo, pp. 411. C. 18023

CURTIS (B. R.) An Address ... at the Centennial Celebration of the Birth Day of Washington, at Deerfield, Mass., Feb. 22d, 1832. By Benjamin R. Curtis. ... *Greenfield, Mass.: printed by Phelps and Ingersoll.* 1832. 8vo, pp. 23. H. 18024

CURTIS. Address to the People of Massachusetts. [n. p. n. d.] 8vo, pp. 16. B. 18025

On the coalition of 1851.

[CURTIS.] An Article on the Debts of the States. From the North American Review for January, 1844. *Boston.* 1844. 8vo, pp. 36. B. + *New York.* 1844. 8vo, pp. 48. 18026

CURTIS. Executive Power. By B. R. Curtis. *Cambridge: printed by H. O. Houghton.* 1862. 8vo, pp. 28, (1). H. + *Boston.* 1862. 12mo, pp. 34. + *Boston: Little, Brown & Co.* 1862. 8vo, pp. 31. + *Boston: Little, Brown & Co.* 1862. pp. 29. + *New York: [Office of the World].* pp. 15. 18027

CURTIS. The Power of the Commander-in-Chief to declare Martial Law, and decree Emancipation: as shown from B. R. Curtis. By Libertas. *Boston: A. Williams & Co.* 1862. 8vo, pp. 24. 18028

Also: Argument ... in the Case of Francis O. J. Smith ... *vs.* Hugh Downing and als., ... for an Infringement of the Letters Patent of Samuel F. B. Morse, for the Electro Magnetic Telegraph, June 25 and 26, 1850. *Portland: F. W. Nichols & Co., Printers.* 1850. 8vo, pp. 54. H. + Important Opinion of Hon. B. R. Curtis, on the Constitutionality of the Maine Hawkers' and Pedlers' Law, as applicable to Merchants and Travelling Agents of Other States. *Boston: Rhodes & Markham, Printers.* 1865. 8vo, pp. 10. H. + Opinion ... relating to the Right of the Central Branch Union Pacific Railroad Company To continue and extend its road to the "Main Trunk" ... *Washington, D. C.: Gibson Brothers, Printers.* 1869. 8vo, pp. 8. H.

CURTIS (C. P.) An Oration delivered on the Fourth of July, 1823, in Commemoration of American Independence ... . By Charles Pelham Curtis. ... *Boston: Joseph W. Ingraham.* 1823. 8vo, pp. 34. B., H. + Second Edition. [*Ibid.*] 1823. 8vo, pp. 36. BA., W. 18029

CURTIS. In Memory of Charles Pelham Curtis. *Boston: J. H. Eastburn's Press.* 1864. 8vo, pp. 25. H. 18030

[CURTIS (*Mrs.* D. S.)] The Spirit of Seventy-Six; or, The Coming Woman, a Prophetic Drama, followed by A Change of Base, and Doctor Mondschein. *Boston: Little, Brown & Co.* 1868. 12mo, pp. 141. C. + Ninth Edition. [*Ibid.*] 1869. 12mo, pp. 141. H. 18031

In ridicule of the woman's rights movement.

CURTIS (E.) Catalogue of the Microscopical Section of the United States Army Medical Museum. Prepared under the Direction of the Surgeon General, U. S. Army, By Brevet Major Edward Curtis, Assistant Surgeon, U. S. Army. *Washington: Government Printing Office.* 1867. 4to, pp. 161. 18032

CURTIS (G. T.) ... Address of Hon. George Ticknor Curtis at Philadelphia, Sept. 30, 1864. [*New York.* 1864.] 8vo, pp. 16. B. 18033

CURTIS. An Argument against the Constitutional Validity of the Legal Tender Clause, contained in the Act of Congress of February 25, 1862, authorizing the Issue of Treasury Notes. Delivered in the Supreme Court of ... New York ... November 18, 1862, by George Ticknor Curtis ... . *New York: Wm. C. Bryant & Co.* 1862. 8vo, Title, pp. 29. B., C. 18034

CURTIS. Commentaries on the Jurisdiction, Practice, and Peculiar Jurisprudence of the Courts of the United States. *Philadelphia.* 1854. 8vo. C. 18035

Curtis. The Constitutional Power of Congress over the Territories. An Argument delivered in the Supreme Court of the United States, December 18, 1856, in the Case of Dred Scott ... *vs.* John F. A. Sandford. By George Ticknor Curtis. *Boston: Little, Brown and Company.* 1857. 8vo, pp. 42. H.

Curtis. ... Hon. George Ticknor Curtis, on Constitutional Liberty. [*New York.* 1862.] 8vo, pp. 10. B. 18037

Curtis. History of the Origin, Formation, and Adoption of the Constitution of the United States; with Notices of its Principal Framers. By Geo. Ticknor Curtis. *New York: Harper & Brothers.* 1854–1859. 2 vols., 8vo, pp. xxxvi, 518; xvi, 653.

Reprinted *New York,* 1860, also 1865.

Curtis. The Just Supremacy of Congress over the Territories. By George Ticknor Curtis. ... [An Answer to S. A. Douglas, on Popular Sovereignty.] *Boston.* 1859. 8vo, pp. 44.

Curtis. Life of Daniel Webster. By George Ticknor Curtis ... . *New York: D. Appleton & Co.* 1870. 2 vols., 8vo, pp. xvi, 589, Portrait; vii, 729, Portrait. B. + Fourth Edition. [*Ibid.*] 1870. 2 vols., 8vo, pp. xvi, 592; vii, 729. 3 Portraits and Woodcuts. H. 18040

[Curtis.] The Merits of Thomas W. Dorr, and George Bancroft, as they are politically connected. By a Citizen of Massachusetts. *Boston: Redding's.* 1844. 8vo, pp. 36. + Second Edition [with an Appendix]. *Boston: Redding's.* 1844. 8vo, pp. 41. 18041

[Curtis.] Observations on the Rev. Dr. Gannett's Sermon, entitled "Relation of the North to Slavery." Republished from the ... Boston Courier of June 28th and 30th, and July 6th, 1854. *Boston: Redding and Company.* 1854. 8vo, pp. 29. B.

Curtis. An Oration delivered on the Fourth of July, 1862, before the Municipal Authorities of the City of Boston. By George Ticknor Curtis. *Boston: J. E. Farwell and Company, Printers.* 1862. 8vo, pp. 46. B., H. 18043

Curtis. The Rights of Conscience and of Property; or the True Issue of the Convent Question. By George Ticknor Curtis. *Boston: Charles C. Little and James Brown.* M DCCC XLII. 8vo, pp. 39. B. 18044

Curtis. The Strength of the Constitution. A Discourse delivered at the Lowell Institute, in Boston, 7 February, 1850, as the Conclusion of a Course of Twelve Lectures on the Constitution of the United State. By George Ticknor Curtis. *Boston: Ticknor, Reed, and Fields.* M DCC L. 8vo, pp. 39. B.

Curtis. A Treatise on the Law of Copyright in Books, Dramatic and Musical Compositions, Letters, and other Manuscripts, Engravings and Sculpture, as enacted and administered in England and America; with some notices of the History of Literary Property. By George Ticknor Curtis ... . *London: A. Maxwell and Son. Boston: Charles C. Little and James Brown.* MDCCCXLVII. 8vo, pp. xi, 450, Appendix, 103. 18046

Curtis. A Treatise on the Law of Patents for Useful Inventions in the United States of America, and the Remedies for their Infringement. By George T. Curtis, Esq. *Boston.* 185–. 8vo. + Second Edition, with many Additions. *Boston.* 1854. 8vo. 18047

Curtis. The True Uses of American Revolutionary History. An Oration delivered before the Authorities of the City of Boston, ... Fifth of July, 1841 ... By George Ticknor Curtis. ... *Boston: John H. Eastburn.* 1841. 8vo, pp. 33.

[Curtis.] Letters of Phocion. *See* Massachusetts.

Also: Letter ... to the Whig State Central Committee. *Boston.* 1856. 8vo, pp. 16. B. — A Letter to Senator Fessenden, on the Revision of the Patent Laws. ... *Boston: printed by Alfred Mudge & Son.* 1860. 8vo, pp. 8. H. — The Rights and Duties of Merchant Seamen, according to the General Maritime Law and Statutes of the United States, ... *Boston.* 1841. 8vo. — Speech ... on the Presidential Election; delivered in Faneuil Hall, at a Meeting of the Friends of Mr. Webster, October 6, 1852. ... Reported by John Clarke ... . *Boston: Redding & Company.* 1852. 8vo, pp. 16. B. — The True Condition of American Loyalty. A Speech ... delivered before the Democratic Union Association, March 28, 1863. [n. p. n. d.] 8vo, pp. 11. — Two Letters to the Editor [Chas. T. Congdon] of the New Bedford Mercury. First published in the Boston Courier. ... *Boston: Printed by Alfred Mudge & Son.* 1854. 8vo, pp. 12. B. — Sundry legal reports, etc.

Curtis (G. W.) The Duty of the American Scholar to Politics and the Times. An Oration, delivered on Tuesday, August 5, 1856, before the Literary Societies of Wesleyan University, Middletown, Conn. By George William Curtis. *New York: Dix, Edwards & Co.* 1856. 8vo, pp. 46. 18049

Curtis. A Letter to the Young Men of Maine; in Reply to an Invitation to Address the Meeting at Bangor, Aug. 28th, 1856. [n. p. n. d.] 8vo, pp. 8. B. 18050

On the recent letter of Rufus Choate.

Curtis. Lotus Eating. A Summer Book. *New York.* 1854. 12mo, pp. 206. 18051

Relates the author's summer rambles in America.

[Curtis.] The Potiphar Papers. (Reprint from "Putnam's Monthly.") Illustrated by A. Hoppin. *New York: G. P. Putnam and Company.* 1853. 12mo. + By George William Curtis. *New York: Dix, Edwards & Co.* 1856. 12mo, 5 l., pp. 214. H. 18052

Curtis. Right of Suffrage. Remarks of Hon. George William Curtis ... July 19, 1867. [n. p. n. d.] 8vo, pp. 9. H.

The same speech as that entitled "Equal Rights for Women." Also: An Address Vindicating the Right of Woman to the Elective Franchise. Delivered at the Woman's Rights Convention ... May 15, 1858, ... *New York: S. T. Munson.* 1858. 12mo, pp. 21. H. — Equal Rights for Women. A Speech ... at Albany, July 19, 1867. *New York.* 1867. 12mo, pp. 24. H. *See also* Sedgwick (John), and Vinton (F.)

Curtis (J.) America and the Corn Laws. By John Curtis, of Ohio. *Manchester.* 1842. 8vo. 18054

Curtis (Jonah). *See* Vol. II., No. 6626.

Curtis (J.) A Topographical and Historical Sketch of Epsom, New Hampshire. By Jonathan Curtis, A.M. *Concord.* 1823. 8vo, pp. 17. N. 18055

Also in "Farmer & Moore's Collection," II. 321–329. Also: A Sermon at Dedham, Mass., June 9, 1830, before the Auxiliary Education Society of Norfolk County. *Boston.* 1830. 8vo. W.

Curtis (J.) Brief Remarks on the Hygiene of Massachusetts, particularly of the Cities of Boston and Lowell. By Josiah Curtis, M.D. *Philadelphia.* 1849. 8vo, pp. 70. 18056

Curtis (J.) Memoir of Joseph Curtis. A Model Man. *New York.* 1858. 16mo. 18057

Curtis (L.) Civil Government an Ordinance of God. A Sermon delivered in Colchester, April 21, 1861. By Rev. L. Curtis. *Hartford: O. F. Jackson.* 1861. 8vo, pp. 15. 18058

Curtis (Martin). *See* Cortes (Martin), Vol. IV., No. 16968.

Curtis (Moses A.) Botany; Containing a Catalogue of the Indigenous and Naturalized Plants of the State [of North Carolina]. *Raleigh.* 1867. 8vo. C. 18059

In North Carolina (geological, etc., survey), Part III.

Curtis (N.) Memoir of Nathaniel Curtis, Esq. ... *Boston: David Clapp & Son, Printers.* 1868. 8vo, pp. 14. H. 18060

Curtis (N. M.) The Bride of the Northern Wilds: A Tale. By Newton M. Curtis. *New York.* 1843. 8vo, pp. 64.

Also: The Doom of the Tory's Guide. A Tale ... . *New York.* 1843. 8vo, pp. 96. — The Marksmen of Monmouth ... . *New York.* 1849. 8vo. — The Prairie Guide; or the Rose of the Rio Grande. ... . *New York: Garrett & Co.* [1850?] 8vo, pp. 100. C. — The Scout of the Silver Pond ... . *New York.* 1848. 8vo. — Vidette; a Tale of the Mexican War ... . *Boston.* 184–. 8vo. (Mr. Joel Munsell, the printer of Albany, remarks, "The author was a resident of Charlton, of limited education, a whiskey drinking, tobacco chewing, profane swearing, and squalid specimen of humanity.")

Curtis (S.) Curtis's Pocket Almanack for ... 1800: to which is added, A Register of New-Hampshire. *Exeter: printed by H. Ranlet, for the Compiler.* 1799. 18mo, pp. 108. B.

Continued at least till 1809. The vols. for 1804, and following years, were printed at Amherst.

Curtis (S.) Brief Extracts from the Journal of a Voyage performed by the whale ship M[ercur]y, of New Bedford, Mass., commencing May 25, 1841, and terminating August 1, 1844. By Stephen Curtis, Jr., New Bedford, Mass. *Boston.* 1844. 8vo, pp. 46. 18063

Curtis (S. R.) The Mormon Rebellion and the Bill to raise Volunteers. Speech of Hon. Samuel R. Curtis, of Iowa. Delivered ... March 10, 1858. [n. p. n. d.] 8vo, pp. 16. H.

Curtis (S. R.) Gen'l Samuel Ryan Curtis. In Memoriam. *Keokuk, Ia.* 1866. 8vo. 18065

Curtis (T.) An Address at the Funeral of the Hon. Jacob Axson ... of Charleston, S. C. ... By Thomas Curtis, D.D. ... . *Charleston, S. C.: B. B. Hussey, Printer.* 1843. 12mo, pp. 13. H. 18066

Curtis (T. F.) The Progress of Baptist Principles in the last Four Hundred Years. By Thomas F. Curtis. *Boston.* 1855. 12mo, pp. 422. J.C.B. 18067

Curtis (W. J.) Copy of a Letter addressed by W. J. Curtis, ... to the Governors, &c. of the several British Colonies requesting information as to the mode of obtaining Patents for Inventions in the Colonies; and copies of the answers. *London.* 1857. 18068

Curtiss (D. F.) Western Portraiture, and Emigrant's Guide; A Description of Wisconsin, Illinois, and Iowa; with Remarks on Minnesota, and other Territories. By Daniel S. Curtiss. *New York: J. H. Colton.* 1852. 12mo, pp. 351. H. 18069

Curtius, *pseudonym.* A Defence of the Measures of the Administration of Thomas Jefferson. By Curtius [John Taylor?] Taken from the National Intelligencer. *Washington: Samuel H. Smith.* 1804. 8vo, pp. 136. BA. 18070

Curtius, *pseudonym.* A Vindication of the Treaty of Amity, Commerce and Navigation with Great Britain. By Curtius. *Philadelphia.* 1795. 8vo. 18071

Curtius, *pseudonym.* *See* [Grayson (W. J.)], [Thomson (John)], and [Webster (N.)]

Curwen (A.) A Relation of the Labour, Travail and Sufferings of that Faithful Servant of the Lord, Alice Curwen. Who departed this Life the 7th Day of the 6th Moneth, 1679. and resteth in Peace with the Lord. *Printed in the Year,* 1680. 4to, 9½ sheets. 18073

Includes "An Epistle to Friends in Gravesend in Long-Island. From Newport in Road-Island, the 9th of the 5th moneth. 1676," and other pieces on American topics. *See* Smith's "Catalogue of Quaker Books."

Curwen (M. C.) A Sketch of the History of the City of Dayton. By Maskell C. Curwen. Second Edition. *Dayton: James Odell, Jr.* 1850. 8vo. pp. 64. 18074

Curwen (S.) Journal and Letters of the Late Samuel Curwen, Judge of the Admiralty, etc., an American Refugee in England, from 1775 to 1794, comprising Remarks on the Prominent Men and Measures of that Period. To which are added, Biographical Notices of many American Loyalists and other Eminent Persons. By George Atkinson Ward ... . *New-York: C. S. Francis and Co.* 1842. 8vo, pp. xii, 9–578, (2). Portrait. C., H. 18075

Curwen. Journal and Letters of the late Samuel Curwen, Judge of Admiralty, etc., A Loyalist Refugee in England during the American Revolution; to which are added Biographical Notices of many Loyalists and other Prominent Men of that Period. Second Edition. By George Atkinson Ward, A.M. ... *London: Wiley and Putnam.* 1844. 8vo, pp. iv, xii, 9–601.

Portrait. + Third Edition. ... *New-York: Leavitt, Trow & Co.* 1845. 8vo, Title, pp. iv, xiii, xiii, 672, (1). Portrait. H. + *New York: Wiley and Putnam.* 18076

See "N. Am. Rev.," LVI. 89.

Curwen. The Journal and Letters of Samuel Curwen, an American in England, From 1775 to 1783; with an Appendix of Biographical Sketches. By George Atkinson Ward ... . Fourth Edition. *Boston: Little, Brown & Co.* 1864. 8vo, pp. xxiv, 678. Portrait. H. 18077

See "N. Am. Rev.," LVI. 89, "Christ. Exam.," XXXII. 250, and "South. Lit. Mess.," XII. 48, 422.

Cusack (G.) The|Grand Pyrate:|Or, the|Life and Death|of|Capt. George Cvsack|The great Sea-Robber.|With|An Accompt of all his notorious Robberies both at|Sea and Land.|Together|with his Tryal, Condemnation, and Execvtion.|Taken by an Impartial hand.|Licensed Novemb. 19, 1675. Roger L'Estrange.|*London,|Printed for Jonathan Edwin at the Sign of the Three|Roses in Ludgate-street.* MDCLXXVI.| 4to, pp. 31.

Cusack travelled in New England and Virginia.

Cushing (A.) Historical Letters on the First Charter of Massachusetts Government. By Abel Cushing. *Boston: J. W. Bang, Printer.* 1839. 18mo, Title, pp. 11–204. B., C., S.

Cushing. Speech of the Hon. Abel Cushing, in the Senate of Massachusetts ... 30th and 31st of March, 1837, on Resolves relative to the Action of Congress upon Anti-Slavery Petitions, and the Abolition of Slavery in the District of Columbia; and also upon a Resolve respecting the further Admission of Slave-holding States into the Union. *Boston: printed by Beals and Greene.* 1837. 8vo, pp. 23. H. 18080

Cushing (Caleb), *and others.* A Letter from Two Associations of Ministers, to the Associated Ministers of Boston and Charlestown, relating to the Admission of Whitefield into their Pulpits. With the Advice of a third Association. *Boston.* 1745. 4to, pp. 8. B. 18081

Cushinc (Caleb). Arguments, in Behalf of the United States, with Supplement and Appendix, presented to the Commissioners under the Treaty between Great Britain and the United States, for the Final Settlement of the Claims of the Hudson's Bay and Puget's Sound Agricultural Companies. C. Cushing, Counsel. *Washington: McGill & Witherow, Printers.* 1868. 8vo, pp. 24, 156. H. 18082

Cushing. British and American Joint Commission of the Hudson's Bay and Puget's Sound Agricultural Companies' Claims. In the Matter of the Puget's Sound Agricultural Company. Argument for the United States. [n. p. n. d.] 8vo, pp. 65. H. 18083

Cushing. The Claims of the Citizens of the United States on Denmark examined. *Boston.* 1826. 8vo, pp. 18. + Second Edition. *Cambridge.* 1826. 8vo. W. 18084

First published in the "Boston Monthly Magazine."

[Cushing.] Contract of the Mexican Government for the Survey of the Public Lands in the State of Sonora. *Washington.* 1860. 8vo, pp. 33, (1). H. 18085

Cushing. Eulogy on John Adams and Thomas Jefferson ... in Newburyport, July 15, 1826 ... . By Caleb Cushing. *Cambridge: Hilliard and Metcalf.* 1826. 8vo, pp. 60. B., H.

Cushing. A Eulogy on La Fayette, pronounced at the Request of the Young Men of Dover, September 6, 1834. By Caleb Cushing. *Dover, N. H.: Geo. Wadleigh.* M DCCC XXXIV. 8vo, pp. 27. H. 18087

Cushing. The History and Present State of the Town of Newburyport. By Caleb Cushing. ... *Newburyport: printed by E. W. Allen.* 1826. 12mo, pp. viii, 120. B., H. 18088

Cushing. Letters to ... Edward Everett, ... on the question of the North Eastern Boundary. By Caleb Cushing. [*Boston.* 1837.] Imp. 8vo, pp. 8. H. 18089

Cushing. The Harrison Medal. Letters of Mr. Cushing, of Massachusetts, concerning the Resolution for presenting a Medal and the Thanks of Congress to General William Henry Harrison. ... Washington, March 14, 1840. [n. p. n. d.] 8vo, pp. 8. H. 18090

Cushing. An Oration, on the Material Growth and Territorial Progress of the United States, delivered at Springfield, Mass. on the Fourth of July, 1839. By Caleb Cushing. ... *Springfield: printed by Merriam, Wood & Co.* 1839. 8vo, pp. 32. H. 18091

Cushing. Outlines of the Life and Public Services, Civil and Military, of William Henry Harrison. By Caleb Cushing. *Boston.* 1840. 8vo, pp. 24. + *Boston.* 1840. 18mo, pp. 71. H. + *Washington: published by Thomas Allen.* 1840. 8vo, pp. 21. H. 18092

[Cushing.] A Reply to the Letter of J. Fenimore Cooper. By One of his Countrymen. *Boston.* 1834. 8vo, pp. 76. BA.

Cushing. Tehuantepec Transit Company. [*Washington.* 1866.] 4to, pp. 4. H. 18094

A letter from Caleb Cushing to Charles Knap, President of the Tehuantepec Transit Company.

Cushing. Report ... Territory of Oregon, January 4, 1839. [*Washington.* 1839.] 8vo, pp. 49. 18095

Also: Oration delivered at Newburyport, Mass., ... July 4, 1832. *Newburyport.* 1832. — An Address ... before the American Institute of the City of New York ... October 20th, 1836. ... *New York: printed by James Van Norden.* 1836. 8vo, pp. 20. H. — An Address ... at Lynn, before the Associated Lodges of Salem, Lynn, Marblehead, Danvers, & Beverly ... June 24, A.L. 5826. ... . *Newburyport: printed by E. W. Allen.* 1826. 8vo, pp. 28. H. — Address ... September 26, 1850, before the Essex Agricultural Society ... . *Salem.* 1850. 8vo, pp. 18. B. — Discourse on the Social Influence of Christianity, ... at Providence, R. I. Sept. 1838, ... Phi Beta Kappa Society of Brown University. ... *Andover: printed by Gould and Newman.* 1839. 8vo, pp. 28. H. — Letter on the Trent Affair, addressed to Hon. Fernando Wood. ... — Opinion ... concerning the Judical Authority of the Commissioner or Minister, and of Consuls of the United States, in China and Turkey. *Washington.* 1855. 8vo, pp. 36. B. — An Oration, ... in Newburyport, ... July 4, 1821. ... *Newburyport: printed by E. W. Allen.* 1821. 8vo, pp. 19. H. + Second Edition. *Newburyport.* 1821. 8vo. W. — An Oration ... at the Request of the Washington Light Infantry Company, in Newburyport, July 24, 1822, in Commemoration of the Company's Twenty-second Anniversary. ... *Newburyport: E. W. Allen.* 1822. 8vo, pp. 14. H. — An Oration ... Newburyport, on the Fifty-sixth Anniversary of American Independence. ... *Newburyport: T. B. & E. L. White.* 1832. 8vo, pp. 56. BA. — An Oration ... at Boston before the Colonization Society of Massachusetts, ... July 4, 1833. ... *Boston: G. W. Light & Co.* 1833. 8vo, pp. 24. — An Oration ... before the Literary Societies of Amherst College, August 23, 1836. ... *Boston: Light and Stearns.* 1836. 8vo, pp. 40. B. — Remarks ... on the Neutrality Bill. Delivered in the House of Representatives, March 6 and 9, 1838. *Washington: printed by Gales and Seaton.* 1838. 8vo, pp. 7. — Remarks ... on the Navy Appropriation Bill [May 17, 1842]. *Washington.* 1842. 8vo. — The Right of the National Life Insurance Co. to Establish Agencies in the State of New-York. *Washington, D. C.: McGill & Witherow, Printers.* 1868. 8vo, pp. 20. H. — Speech ... in Faneuil Hall, Boston, October 27, 1857. Also, Speech ... in City Hall, Newburyport, October 31, 1857. By Caleb Cushing. [*Boston.*] 1857. 8vo. pp. 48. B., H. — Speeches ... in the House of Representatives of Massachusetts, on the Subject of The Currency and Public Deposites. ... *Salem: Register Press, W. Palfray, Jr.* 1834. 8vo, pp. 31. B., BA., W. — Speech ... on the Right of Petition, as connected with Petitions for the Abolition of Slavery and the Slave Trade in Dist. of Columbia, ... Jan'y 25, 1836. *Washington.* 1836. 8vo, pp. 15. — Speech ... on the Resolutions of Kentucky and Massachusetts, recommending the Distribution of the Proceeds of the Public Lands among the States. House ... May 23, 1836. *Washington.* 1836. 8vo, pp. 41. BA. — Speech ... on the Bill making Appropriations for the ... Indian Department. ... February 1, 1837. *Washington.* 1837. 8vo, pp. 14. BA. — Speech ... on the Message of the President of the United States, at the Opening of the Twenty-fifth Congress. ... Sept. 25, 1837. *Washington.* 1837. 8vo, pp. 34. H., M. — Speech ... on Executive Powers; ... in the House ... Dec. 19, 1837. [*Washington.* 1837.] 8vo. — Speech ... on the Continuation of the Cumberland Road; ... April 19, 1838. *Washington.* 1838. 8vo, pp. 15. M. — Speech ... on the ... Oregon Territory; ... in the

House ... May 17 and 22, 1838. *Washington.* 1838. 8vo.—Speech ... on the Proposition to Censure Mr. John Quincy Adams, for an alleged Disrespect to the House of Representatives. Feb. 7, 1837. [*Washington.* 1837.] 8vo, pp. 15. H.—Speech ... on the Post Office Bill. Delivered in the House of Representatives, August 25, 1841. *Washington: printed by Gales and Seaton.* 8vo, pp. 10. H.—Speeches of Mr Cushing of Massachusetts, on the Bills for the Admission of Arkansas into the Union. [n. p.] *Morss & Brewster.* 1836. 8vo, pp. 14. H.—Speech on the Treasury Note Bill ... in the House ... Oct. 6, 1837. *Washington.* 1838. 8vo.—Speech ... on the Sub-Treasury Bill. ... House ... May 20 and 21, 1840. [*Washington.* 1840.] 8vo, pp. 23. B., H., M.—Speech in the Case of Alexander McLeod. ... in the House ... June 24 and 25, 1841. *Washington.* 1841. 8vo, pp. 16. H.—Speeches on the Amendment of the Constitution of Massachusetts, imposing disabilities on Naturalized Citizens of the United States. ... [*Boston.*] 1859. 8vo, pp. 19. B.—Statement ... presented to the ... House ... April 18, 1836. In reference to ... "An act to authorize the licensing of vessels ... in the Mackerel Fishery." [n. p. 1836?] 8vo, pp. 8. BA.—Statement ... to the ... House of Representatives, ... in relation to House Bill No. 449, which provides for the Relief of those American Citizens, who, prior to the Convention of 1800, had Claims against the Government of France. *Washington: printed by Gales and Seaton.* 1838. 8vo, pp. 28. H.—Supplement and Appendix to the Arguments in behalf of the United States in the Matter of the Claims of the Hudson's Bay and Puget's Sound Agricultural Companies. C. Cushing, Counsel. [*Washington:*] *M'Gill & Witherow, Printers.* [n. d.] 8vo, pp. 74. H.—Tariff *vs.* Distribution. [A Speech. Washington, 1842.] 8vo

CUSHING (Caleb), *and* SCHLEY (William). Privilege of Senators and Representatives of the United States to pass through the State of Maryland without being subject to Suit there, in going to and returning from Sessions of Congress. *Washington: McGill & Witherow, Printers.* [n. d.] 8vo, pp. 38. H. 18096

CUSHING (C.) A Discourse at the Funeral of Dea. Tyler Batcheller, at North Brookfield, Mass., Oct. 10, 1862. By Rev. Christopher Cushing. *Boston: Wright & Potter, Printers.* 1864. 8vo, pp. 32. 18097

CUSHING. A Discourse at the Funeral of the Rev. Thomas Snell, D.D., of North Brookfield, Mass., by Rev. Christopher Cushing ... . Also a Memorial Tribute by Rev. Lyman Whiting. May 7, 1862. *Boston.* 1862. 8vo, pp. 60. Portrait of Snell. 18098

[CUSHING (C.)] [Half-Title:] Early Settlers of Hingham, New England. [Title:] Extracts from the Minutes of Daniel Cushing of Hingham, with a Photograph of his Manuscript, entitled A List of the Names of such Persons as came out of the Town of Hingham, and Towns adjacent, in the County of Norfolk, in the Kingdom of England, into New England, and settled in Hingham in New England. ... Printed for Private Distribution. *Boston: Press of John Wilson and Son.* 1855. 4to, pp. 6, 2 l., pp. 7–28. H. 18099

[CUSHING (E. L.)] The Dublin Suit. Supreme Judicial Court, for the Counties of Cheshire and Sullivan. In Chancery. [Argument for the Respondents. By E. L. Cushing.] *Keene, N. H.: printed at the Office of S. & G. S. Woodward.* 1859. 8vo, pp. 29. H. 18100

CUSHING (E.) An Appeal ... . By Elmer Cushing ... . Wherein is displayed the singular History of the Author; together with that of the Other Americans, settled in the Province of Lower-Canada. ... *Stanstead: printed by S. H. Dickerson.* 1826. 8vo, pp. 88. H. 18101

CUSHING (Jacob). Christian Ministers commissioned by the Great Head of the Church to preach the Gospel: ... a Sermon Preached November 21, 1792. At the Ordination of Mr. Nathan Underwood, ... in Harwich. ... *Boston: Printed by Thomas and John Fleet.* 1793. 8vo, pp. 34. H. 18102

CUSHING. Discourse ... Death of the Rev. Joseph Jackson, late Pastor of the Church in Brookline ... July 25, 1796. *Boston.* 1797. 8vo. B., S. 18103

CUSHING. Divine judgments upon tyrants: And compassion to the oppressed. A Sermon, preached at Lexington, April 20th, 1778. In Commemoration of the Murderous War and Rapine, inhumanly perpetrated, by two brigades of British troops, in that town and neighbourhood, on the Nineteenth of April, 1775. By Jacob Cushing ... . *Boston: printed by Powars & Willis.* M,DCC,LXXVIII. 8vo, pp. 28. BA., H. 18104

CUSHING. A Sermon at the Ordination of the Reverend Mr. Elijah Brown ... Sherburne, ... November 28, 1770. By Jacob Cushing ... . *Boston: Printed by Thomas and John Fleet.* 1771. 8vo, pp. 30. B., BA., W. 18105

CUSHING. A Sermon Preached at the Ordination of the Reverend Mr. Jacob Biglow ... Sudbury, November 11th, 1772. By Jacob Cushing ... . *Boston: Printed by T. and J. Fleet.* M,DCC,LXXII. 8vo, pp. 29. B., BA., H., M. 18106

CUSHING. A Sermon at the Ordination of the Reverend Mr. Samuel Williams ... Bradford, November 20. 1765. By Jacob Cushing ... . *Boston: Printed by Richard and Samuel Draper.* 1766. 8vo, pp. 39. B., BA., H., M. 18107

CUSHING. A Sermon ... at the Ordination of the Rev. Mr. Benj. Green, ... in Medway, June 25, 1788. By Jacob Cushing ... . *Boston: Printed by Thomas and John Fleet.* MDCCLXXXVIII. 8vo, pp. 42. H. 18108

CUSHING (J. B.) Report respecting the Harbor of Van Buren, on Lake Erie, in the County of Chautauque, and State of N. Y., made July, 1836, by the direction of the Proprietors of the Lands there. By Jesse B. Cushing. *New York.* 1836. 8vo, pp. 8. 2 Maps. B. 18109

CUSHING (J.) Gospel-Ministers to preach Christ to their People ... . A Sermon ... at Marshfield, Sept 5. 1759. When The Reverend Thomas Brown was ordained ... . By John Cushing ... . To which is added The Charge, by the Rev. Mr. Appleton. Also, The Right Hand of Fellowship, By the Rev. Mr. Gay. *Boston: Printed by B. Macomb.* 1759. 8vo, pp. 36, vi, vi. B., BA., M. 18110

CUSHING (J.) A Discourse, delivered at Ashburnham, July 4th, 1796, at the Request of the Militia Officers ... . By John Cushing ... . *Leominster: Printed by Charles Prentiss.* 1796. 8vo, pp. 24. BA. 18111

CUSHING. An Half Century Sermon delivered at Ashburnham, Nov. 3, 1818. By John Cushing, A.M., Pastor of the Congregational Church in said Town. *Worcester: Printed by William Manning.* 1818. 8vo, pp. 24. + Second Edition. *Worcester.* 1819. 8vo. pp. 24. M. 18112

Also: Sermon at the Interment of Wm. Merriam. *Worcester.* 1819. 8vo. W.—Sermon at Ashburnham, March 23, 1817, at the Interment of George Wilker, Jun. *Andover.* 1817. 8vo. W.—Two Sermons at Ashburnham, Mass. July 31, 1790, on the Death of Mrs. Dorothy Wilder. *Worcester.* 8vo. W.

CUSHING (Jonathan P.) *See* Virginia Historical and Philosophical Society, 1833.

CUSHING (Luther Stearns). Manual of Parliamentary Practice: rules of proceeding and debate in deliberative assemblies. *Boston.* 1845. + *Boston.* 1849. + *Boston.* 1851. 16mo. + 29th Thousand. *Boston.* 1859. 24mo. H. 18114

CUSHING. Lex Parliamentaria Americana. Elements of the Law and Practice of Legislative Assemblies in the United States of America. By Luther Stearns Cushing. *Boston: Little, Brown, and Company.* 1856. 8vo, Title, 1 l., pp. vii–xxxvi, 1063. B. + Second Edition. *Boston: Little, Brown & Co.* 1863. 8vo, pp. xxxvi, 1063. H. + 1866. C. 18115

CUSHING. Handbuch der parliamentarischen Praxis ... übersetzt und mit einem Vorworte begleitet von Bernard Rölker. *Hamburg.* 1852. 8vo, pp. xii, 100. H. 18116

CUSHING. Practical Treatise on the Trustee Process, or Foreign Attachment, of Massachusetts and Maine; with an Appendix, containing the Statutes of Massachusetts, Connecticut, Rhode Island, New Hampshire, Vermont, and Maine, on that Subject. *Cambridge.* 1833. 8vo. 18117

CUSHING. Proceedings & Debates in the House of Representatives of Massachusetts during the Four Days previous to the Election of a Speaker, January, 1843. *Boston.* 1843. 8vo, pp. 84. 18118

CUSHING. Reports of Contested Elections, in the House of Representatives of the Commonwealth of Massachusetts; from 1780 to 1834 inclusive ... . By Luther S. Cushing ... . *Boston.* 1834. 8vo, pp. xv, 282. H. 18119

CUSHING (T.) Division of Labor in Schools: being the Substance of an Annual Report read at the Exhibition of Chauncy-Hall School, December 31, 1851. By T. Cushing, Jr. ... *Boston: Bazin and Chandler, Printers.* 1852. 8vo, pp. 15. H. 18120

CUSHING (S. W.) Wild Oats Sowings: or, the Autobiography of an Adventurer. *New-York.* 1857. 12mo. C. 18121

CUSHING (Thomas), *and* LADD (W. H.) Roll of Former Members of Chauncy-Hall School, who served in the Army or Navy of the United States, during the War for the Suppression of the Rebellion. ... *Boston: printed by D. Clapp & Son.* 1866. 12mo, Title, pp. 22. H. 18122

CUSHING (T. C.) Trial of Col. Thomas H. Cushing, before a General Court-Martial ... at Baton-Rouge, on Charges preferred by Brig. Gen. Wade Hampton. Reported by the Late Judge Advocate [W. Lee]. *Philadelphia: Moses Thomas.* 1812. 8vo, pp. 114. B., BA., H., S. 18123

CUSHMAN (A. S.) Address of Major A. S. Cushman ... G. A. R. Delivered at the Annual Meeting of the Department in Boston, January 8, 1868. *Boston: H. J. Hallgreen, Printer.* 1868. 8vo, pp. 16. H. 18124

CUSHMAN (E.) A Sermon, ... before the Legislature of ...

Connecticut, at their Annual Election, at New-Haven, May 3d, 1820. By Elisha Cushman; ... *New-Haven: J. Barber, Printer.* 1820. 8vo, pp. 17. 18125

Also: Christian Fortitude. Sermon at Hartford, Conn. May 30, 1813. ... *Hartford.* 1813. 8vo. W.

CUSHMAN (G. F.) The Israelite without Guile. A Memorial Sermon of ... Nicholas Hamner Cobbs, D.D. ... May 4, 1861, by the Rev. Geo. F. Cushman ... . *Mobile: Farrow & Dennett.* 1861. 8vo, pp. 37. H. 18126

C[USHMAN] (F[rederick] E.) History of the 28th Regt. Massachusetts Vols. From the 15th day of September, 1863, to the Close of the Rebellion. By F. E. C. *Washington, D. C.: Gibson Brothers, Printers.* 1865. 12mo, pp. 38. H. 18127

CUSHMAN (H. W.) A Historical and Biographical Genealogy of the Cushmans; the Descendants of Robert Cushman, the Puritan, From the year 1617 to 1855. ... By Henry Wyles Cushman. *Boston: Little, Brown & Company.* 1855. 8vo, pp. 665, (1). 30 Portraits and 50 Facsimile Autographs. B., C.

Its plan is highly eulogized by Mr. S. G. Drake.

CUSHMAN (Joseph B.) *See* New York.

CUSHMAN (J.) A Discourse ... at Winslow ... April 13, 1815: the Day [for] a General Thanksgiving for the Restoration of Peace ... . By Joshua Cushman ... . *Hallowell: printed by N. Cheever.* 1815. 8vo, pp. 24. BA., W. 18129

CUSHMAN. A Discourse delivered at Winslow, Nov. 29, 1804. *Boston.* 1805. 8vo, pp. 23. BA., H. 18130

Also: An Oration ... at Augusta, (Maine) on the Fourth of July, 1807. ... *Augusta: printed by Peter Edes.* 1807. 8vo, pp. 23. BA., H.—An Oration, ... at Wiscasset, On the Fourth of July, 1808 ... . *Wiscasset: T. Loring, Printer.* 1808. 8vo, pp. 22. H.—An Oration, pronounced at Waterville, July 4, 1814 ... . *Hallowell: printed by N. Cheever.* 1814. 8vo, pp. 23. BA.

CUSHMAN (P.) The Romance of the Great Rebellion; the Mysteries of the Scout Service. A genuine and faithful Narrative of the Thrilling Adventures, Hairbreadth Escapes, and Final Capture and Happy Rescue by the U. S. Forces. By Miss Major Pauline Cushman. *New York: Wyncoop & Hallenbeck.* 1864. 12mo, pp. 32. + *Philadelphia.* 1865. 12mo, pp. 374. Portrait. 18131

[CUSHMAN (Robert).] A | Sermon | preached at | Plimmoth in | Nevv-England | December 9. 1621. | In an Assemblie of his | Maiesties faithfull | Subiects, there | inhabiting. | Wherein is shevved | the danger of selfe-loue, and the | sweetnesse of true Friendship. | Together | with a Preface, | Showing the state of the Country, | and Condition of the Savages. | Rom. 12. 10. | ... | ... | Written in the yeare 1621. | *London* | *Printed by J. D. for John Bellamie,* | *and are to be sold at his shop at the two Grey-* | *hound in Corne-hill, neere the Royall* | *Exchange.* 1622. | 4to, Title, pp. (6), 19.

First edition of the first sermon preached in New England, of the greatest rarity. I can only trace the sale of one copy, sold at Puttick's, in 1860, for £11. It has been frequently reprinted. The following have come under our notice:

[CUSHMAN.] The Sin and Danger of Self-Love described; A Sermon preached at Plimmouth in New England in 1621. *Boston.* 1724. 18mo, pp. (2), vi, 26. C. 18133

[CUSHMAN.] The Sin and Danger of Self-Love Described, in a Sermon Preached at Plymouth, in New-England, 1621. By Robert Cushman. *London, Printed. Plymouth,* [*Massachusetts*]: *Re-Printed by Nathaniel Coverly.* D,DCCLXXXV. 8vo, pp. viii, 30. + *England, Printed,* 1622. *Boston, New England, reprinted,* 1815; *T. C. Bangs, Printer.* 8vo. + *Stockbridge: Printed by Charles Webster.* 1822. 8vo. + *Boston: Rebecca Wiswell.* 1846. 12mo, pp. 32. + *Boston: Charles Ewer. Dec.* 22, 1846. 8vo, pp. 32. + *New York: J. E. D. Comstock.* 1858. 12mo, pp. 44.

CUSHMAN. "A Sermon preached at Plimmoth in New-England, December 9, 1621." By Robert Cushman. Supposed to be the Earliest Printed Sermon delivered in the English Colonies in America. With a Historical and Bibliogrphical Preface [by Charles Deane]. *Boston:* [*J. K. Wiggin.*] 1870. 4to, Title, pp. v–xvi, Original Title, pp. (6), 19. BA. 18135

Contains a lithographic facsimile of the whole of the original edition. Sixty copies printed. It is also included in the Cushman genealogy; in Young's "Chronicles of the Pilgrims," p. 253. *See* "Hist. Mag.," II. 61, 213, 344; III. 299; IV. 57.

CUSHMAN (R. S.) Resolutions and Discourse, Occasioned by the Death of Abraham Lincoln, President of the United States. Who died at Washington City, April 15, 1865. The discourse delivered in the Congregational Church of Manchester, Vermont, Wednesday, April 19, 1865. By the Rev. R. S. Cushman. *Manchester.* 1865. 8vo, pp. 20. 18136

CUSHMAN (R. W.) Bowdoin Square Church Book ... a Brief History of the Formation and Organization of the Church ... Articles of Faith, Covenant, etc. By R. W. Cushman, Pastor. *Boston.* 1843. 16mo, pp. 126, (1). H. 18137

CUSHMAN. Calm Review of the Measures employed in the Religious Awakening in Boston, in 1842. Being a Discourse delivered in Bowdoin Square Church, June 28, 1846. By R. W. Cushman. *Boston: William D. Ticknor & Co.* MDCCCXLVI. 8vo, pp. 28. B. 18138

For a Review, *see* Christophilos, *pseudonym*, Vol. IV., No. 12948.

CUSHMAN. Plymouth Rock ... . A Discourse delivered in Plymouth, at the Cushman Festival, August 15, 1855 ... . By Robert W. Cushman ... . *Boston: J. M. Hewes, Printer.* 1855. 8vo, pp. 31. B., H. 18139

Also: Elements of Success. An Address delivered at ... Columbia College, Washington, D. C. ... *Washington: printed by Robert A. Waters* 1848. 8vo, pp. 29. H.—Requisites of Female Education. A Lecture delivered ... at the Request of the Columbian Teachers' Association ... . [n. p. n. d.] 12mo, pp. 72. H.—Temptations of City Life. Third Edition. *Boston.* 1847. 12mo, pp. 64. B.

Cushman Celebration. *See* [Shurtleff (N. B.)]

Proceedings at the Consecration of the Cushman Monument at Plymouth, Sept. 16, 1858. *Boston.* 1859. 8vo, pp. 96.

CUSHMAN (W. M.) Report on Laying a Railroad upon the Turnpike belonging to the Albany and Schenectady Co. [n. p. n. d.] 8vo. B. 18141

CUSICK (D.) History of the Six Nations. David Cusick's Sketches of the Ancient History of the Six Nations:—comprising—First—a Tale of the Foundation of the Great Island, (now North America,) the Two Infants Born, and the Creation of the Universe. Second—A Real Account of the Early Settlers of North America, and their Dissentions. Third—Origin of the Kingdom of the Five Nations, which was called a Long House: the Wars, Fierce Animals, &c. *Published at Tuscarora Village, June* 10, 1825. 12mo. + Second edition of 7,000 copies. ... with 4 engravings, Tuscarora Village. [*Lewiston, Niagara Co.*] 1828. pp. 36. B. + *Lockport: Turner & McCollum, Printers.* 1848. 8vo, pp. 35. 4 Plates. S. 18142

Scarce and curious. The first edition of this tract is of the greatest rarity. Thirty years ago a well known veteran book-buyer and student made a visit to the Tuscarora Village on purpose to buy it, but did not succeed in finding a copy.

CUSSY (Ferd. de). Phases et causes célèbres du droit maritime des nations. *Leipzig: Brockhaus.* 1856. 2 vols., 8vo, pp. xx, 400; xi, 628. 18143

CUSSY. Réglements consulaires des principaux états maritimes de l'Europe et de l'Amérique; fonctions et attributions des consuls; prérogatives, immunités et caractère public des consuls envoyés. ... *Leipzig: Brockhaus.* 1851. 8vo, pp. 492.

CUST (E.) Annals of the Wars of the Eighteenth Century, compiled From the most Authentic Histories of the Period. By the Hon. Sir Edward Cust ... . *London: Mitchell's Military Library.* 1858–60. 5 vols., 12mo. H. + Third Edition. [*Ibid.*] 1862. C. 18145

CUST. Annals of the Wars of the Nineteenth Century, compiled From the most Authentic Histories of the Period. By the Hon. Sir Edward Cust ... . *London: Murray.* 1862–63. 4 vols., fcap 8vo. C., H. 18146

CUST. Lives of the Warriors who have commanded Fleets and Armies before the Enemy. ... Seventeenth Century. By ... Sir Edward Cust ... . *London: John Murray.* 1862. 2 pts., 8vo, pp. xxxvii, (2), 316, Map; 2 l., pp. 317–640. BA., H.

Includes De Ruyter and Benbow. These two parts form Vol. III. of his "Lives of the Warriors of the Seventeenth Century."

CUST. Reflections on West India Affairs, after a Recent Visit to the Colonies. Addressed to the Consideration of the Colonial Office. By Lieut. Col. the Hon. Sir Edward Cust. *London: Hatchard.* 1839. 8vo, pp. 88. 18148

CUST (R. J.) A Treatise on the West Indian Encumbered Estates Acts ... With an Appendix ... . By Reginald John Cust ... . *London: William Amer.* 1859. 12mo, or 18mo, pp. viii, 191. H. 18149

CUSTINE (Adam Philippe), *Comte de.* Observations sur l'administration et le commerce des colonies françaises, appliquées à celle de Saint-Domingue, avec quelques observations sur l'administration de cette colonie, liées à un commentaire sur le tarif destiné à la protection du commerce national; par le comte de Custine ... . *Paris: Baudouin.* 1790. 8vo, pp. 109. J.C.B.

CUSTIS (G. W. P.) An Address occasioned by the Death of General Lingan, who was murdered by the Mob at Baltimore. Delivered at Georgetown, September 1, 1812, by George Washington Park Custis. *Boston: Bradford & Read.* 1812. 8vo, pp. 16. + *Washington City.* 1812. 8vo, pp. 16. 18151

CUSTIS. An Address, ... on the Importance of encouraging Agricultural and Domestic Manufactures. ... By George W.

P. Custis ... . *Alexandria: Printed by S. Snowden.* 1808. 8vo, pp. 43. BA. 18152

CUSTIS. Letter from G. W. P. Custis ... enclosing sundry resolutions agreed to by the inhabitants of Alexandria ... relative to the recession of ... part of the Territory of the District of Columbia, etc. Dec. 11, 1804. [*Washington.* 1804.] 8vo.

CUSTIS. Oration by Mr. Custis, of Arlington, Delivered before the Washington Society of Alexandria, on the Anniversary of the 22d February, 1820. *Alexandria: printed by Samuel H. Davis.* 1820. 8vo, pp. 19. BA. 18154

CUSTIS. Pocahontas; or the Settlers of Virginia, A National Drama, in Three Acts, Performed at the Walnut Street Theatre, Philadelphia, twelve nights, with great success. Written by George Washington P. Custis, Esq. of Arlington House. *Philadelphia Edition.* 1839. 12mo, pp. 45. 18155

CUSTIS. Recollections and Private Memoirs of Gen. Washington, By His Adopted Son, George Washington Parke Custis, of Arlington. Compiled from Files of the National Intelligencer, Printed at Washington, D. C. *Washington, D. C.: Printed by William H. Moore.* 1859. 8vo, pp. 104, 1 l. C.

CUSTIS. Recollections and Private Memoirs of Washington, by his adopted son, George Washington Parke Custis, with a Memoir of the Author, by his Daughter; and ... Notes by Benson J. Lossing. ... With Illustrations. *New York: Derby & Jackson.* 1860. 8vo, pp. 644. 3 Plates and 2 Facsimiles.

CUTBUSH (E.) An Address delivered before the Columbian Institute for the Promotion of Arts and Sciences ... Washington ... . By Edward Cutbush, M.D. ... *Washington.* 1807. 8vo, pp. 29. BA., P. 18158

Also: A Discourse delivered at the Opening of the Medical Institution of Geneva College ... . February 10, 1835. ... *Geneva: John Greves & Co.* 1835. 8vo, pp. 24.

CUTHBERT (Alfred). Speech ... on Abolition, in Reply to Mr. Webster, United States Senate, January 20, 1836. [n. p. n. d.] 8vo. S. 18159

CUTHBERT (Ross). An Apology for Great Britain, in allusion to a Pamphlet, intituled "Considérations sur les effets qu'ont produits en Canada," &c. *Quebec: J. Neilson.* 1809. 8vo. P. 18160

See our Vol. IV., No. 16024.

CUTLER (B. C.) A Quarter Century Discourse. *New York.* 1860. 12mo, pp. 56. 18161

CUTLER (B. C.) A Sermon preached in Christ Church, Quincy, on completing a century since its formation, on Christmas Day, 1827. By Benjamin C. Cutler, Rector. Published by request of the Society. *Cambridge: Hilliard, Metcalf, and Company.* 1828. 8vo, pp. 28. 18162

Also: ... A Discourse occasioned by the Death of Mrs. Mary Augusta Greene, ... Brooklyn ... June 17, 1849. ... *New York: J. F. Trow, Printer.* 1849. 8vo, pp. 24. H. — A Discourse preached on the Death of Rev. Francis C. Clements. By Rev. Benjamin C. Cutler. Also a Discourse by Rev. Francis C. Clements. *New York.* 1853. 8vo. P. — A Sermon on the Death of the Rev. Benjamin C. C. Parker ... . Delivered in ... Brooklyn ... . *New York: Anson D. F. Randolph.* 1859. 8vo, pp. 24. H.

CUTLER (C.) Our Liberties in Danger. A Sermon preached in Windham, Newhampshire, on the Day of the Annual Thanksgiving ... November 26, 1835. By Calvin Cutler ... . *Concord.* 1835. 8vo, pp. 19. B., M. 18163

CUTLER (C.) War a Necessary Evil. A Sermon delivered in Francestown, N. H., September 19, 1863, at the Funeral of William R. Marden, ... who died at ... Annapolis, Md., September 12, 1863, by Rev. Charles Cutler. ... *Manchester, N. H.: Gage, Moore & Co.* 1863. 8vo, pp. 18. 18164

CUTLER (E.) A Memorial of Lieut. John W. Groat, 15th Mass. Vols., killed at Ball's Bluff, Oct. 21, 1861. By Ebenezer Cutler. 4to. 18165

Privately printed.

CUTLER. The Right of the Sword. A Thanksgiving Discourse, at Worcester, Mass., November 21, 1861. *Worcester: Henry J. Howland.* 1861. 8vo, pp. 24. 18166

CUTLER (E. J.) Liberty and Law. A Poem for the Hour. By Elbridge Jefferson Cutler. *Boston: American Unitarian Association.* 1861. 12mo, pp. 11. H. 18167

CUTLER. War Poems. By Elbridge Jefferson Cutler. *Boston: Little, Brown, and Company.* 1867. Sq. 16mo, pp. 59. H.

[CUTLER (*Mrs.* H. M. Tracy).] Letter from an American Woman to ... Lord Palmerston. [1862.] pp. 4. H. 18169

[CUTLER (Jervase).] A Topographical Description of the State of Ohio, Indiana Territory, and Louisiana, comprehending

the Ohio and Mississippi Rivers and their principal Tributary Streams; The face of the country, soils, waters, national productions, animal, vegetable, and mineral; towns, villages, settlements and improvements. And a concise Account of the Indian Tribes west of the Mississippi. To which is added an Interesting Journal of Mr. Charles Le Raye, While a captive with the Sioux Nation, on the waters of the Missouri river. By a late Officer in the United States Army. *Boston: Charles Williams.* 1812. 12mo, pp. 219. Plates. C. 18170

Contains the earliest engraving of the city of Cincinnati. The author was a son of Rev. Manasseh Cutler, of Ohio. *See* "Gen. Reg.," VII. 299.

CUTLER (Joseph). The Insolvent Laws of Massachusetts. With Notes by Joseph Cutler ... . *Boston: Benjamin B. Muzzey.* 1846. 8vo, pp. xii, 108. B. 18171

CUTLER (M.) A Century Discourse, delivered in Hamilton, ... October 27, 1814. By Manasseh Cutler, LL.D. *Salem: printed by Thomas C. Cushing.* 1815. 8vo, pp. 26. B., BA.

[CUTLER.] The Contract of the Ohio Company with the Honourable Board of Treasury of the United States of America — made by the Rev. Mr. Manasseh Cutler and Major Winthrop Sargent as agents for the directors of said Company at New York. October 27. 1787. [n. p. n. d.] 8vo, pp. 4.

Reprinted in N. Ward's "Brief Sketch of Ohio. *Glasgow.* 1808." + *London.* 1823. 8vo. *See* Ludewig's "Bib. of Am. Local History."

[CUTLER.] An Explanation of the Map which delineates that part of the Federal Lands, comprehended between Pennsylvania West Line, the rivers Ohio and Scioto, and Lake Erie; confirmed to the United States by Sundry tribes of Indians, in the treaties of 1784 and 1786 and now ready for settlement. *Salem: printed by Dabney and Cushing.* MDCCLXXXVII. 8vo, pp. 24. C. 18174

[CUTLER.] An Explanation of the Map which delineates that part of the Federal Lands comprehended between Pennsylvania West Line, the Ohio and Scioto Rivers & Lake Erie. *Salem.* 1787. 8vo, pp. 24. Map. S. 18175

Reprinted in [Nahum Ward's] "Brief Sketch of Ohio," and translated as below:

[CUTLER.] Description du Sol, des Productions, &c. &c. de cette portion des Etats-Unis, située entre la Pensylvanie, les rivières de l'Ohio & du Scioto, & le lac Erie. Traduite

d'une Brochure imprimée à Salem, en Amérique en 1787. *Paris.* 1789. 8vo, pp. 30. C. 18176

CUTLER. A Sermon ... at Hamilton, on the Day of the National Fast, April 25, 1799 ... . By Manasseh Cutler, LL.D. ... *Salem: Joshua Cushing.* 1799. 8vo, pp. 32. BA.

Also: Discourse before the Bible Society of Salem and Vicinity, April 21, 1813, with the Second Report of the Society. *Salem.* 1813. 8vo. W.

CUTLER (P.) Trial of Perley Cutler and Agnes White ... for the Murder of Henry Holten ... July 1816. ... *Boston: printed by Russell, Cutler and Co.* 8vo, pp. 31. H. 18178

CUTLER (P. Y.) Argument of Peter Y. Cutler, Esq., ... in the Matter of extending Albany-street to Broadway through Trinity Church-yard. *New-York: Banks, Gould & Co.* 1854. 8vo, pp. 41. H., S. 18179

CUTLER (R. K.) Address of Hon. R. King Cutler, United States Senator of Louisiana. ... August, 1865. *New Orleans.* 1865. 8vo, pp. 22. H. 18180

CUTLER. The Two Speeches of the Hon. R. King Cutler, on the matter of Mr. Thomas P. May, arraigned at the Bar of the Louisiana State Constitutional Convention for Contempt, July 22 and 23, '64. *New Orleans: Rea's Press.* 1864. 8vo, pp. 21. 18181

Also: Address to the Citizens of Louisiana. Proceedings in Congress. The Louisiana Delegation. The President, Cabinet and Congress. The Louisiana Constitution. Compensation and Negro Suffrage. *New Orleans: Rea's Press.* 1865. 8vo, pp. 22.

CUTLER (R. P.) "How is the strong staff broken, and the beautiful rod." A Sermon preached at ... Portland ... Jan. 30, 1853, by Rev. R. P. Cutler. Occasioned by the Death of Rev. Sylvester Judd. *Portland: H. J. Little & Co.* 1853. 8vo, pp. 26. H. 18182

CUTLER. A Thanksgiving Sermon: delivered in the First Unitarian Church, ... November 23d. 1856, by Rev. R. P. Cutler ... . *San Francisco: Monson, Valentine & Co.* 1856. 8vo, pp. 24. B., H. 18183

Also: Valedictory Oration, at Yale College, July 3, 1839 ... *New Haven.* 1839.

CUTLER (S.) The Origin, Progress and Present Condition of St. Andrews Church, Hanover, Mass. A Sermon delivered in St. Andrews Church, Hanover, on the 22nd Sunday after

Trinity, Novemb. 8, 1846. By Rev. Samuel Cutler. *Boston: Abner Forbes.* 1846. 8vo, pp. 24. W. 18184

CUTLER (T.) The Depth of the Divine Thoughts: and the Regards due to Them. A Sermon Delivered in the Audience of the General Assembly of the Colony of Connecticut, At New Haven Oct. 18. 1719. By Timothy Cutler ... . *New London: Timothy Green.* 1720. Sm. 8vo, 2 l., pp. 38. H. 18185

CUTLER. The Final Peace, Security & Happiness of the Upright. A Sermon at Christ-Church in Boston, Novemb. 28. 1734. On ... the Death of John Nelson ... and of Mrs. Elizabeth Nelson ... . *Boston: Printed by J. Draper.* 1735. 8vo, 3 l., pp. 16. M. 18186

CUTLER. The Firm Union of a People Represented ... A Sermon ... before the General Assembly of the Colony of Connecticut, at Hartford, May 9. 1717. ... By Timothy Cutler ... Pastor of the Church in Stratford. ... *New-London: Timothy Green.* 1717. Sm. 8vo, Title, pp. 65, (1). H. 18187

CUTLER. The good and faithful Servant: and the Joy awarded to him, ... a Sermon, At ... Boston, June 28. Occasioned by the Death Of the Honourable Thomas Graves, Esq; Of Charlestown ... . By Timothy Cutler, D.D. ... *Boston: Printed by Rogers and Fowle.* MD,CCXLVII. 8vo, pp. 21. BA., H.

CUTLER (W. P.) The Duty of Citizens in the Work of Reconstruction. Address ... by Hon. William P. Cutler, at Belpre, Ohio, July 4, 1865. ... *Marietta, Ohio.* 1865. 8vo, pp. 24. H. 18189

CUTLER. Slavery, a Public Enemy, and ought therefore to be destroyed; a Nuisance that must be abated. Speech of W. P. Cutler, of Ohio, in the House of Representatives, April 23, 1862. [n. p. n. d.] pp. 12. 18190

CUTTER (B. C.) Century Sermon on the Founding of Christ Church, Quincy, 25 Dec. 1827. *Cambridge.* 8vo. 18191

CUTTER (B.) A History of the Cutter Family of New England. The Compilation of the late Dr. Benjamin Cutter, of Woburn, Mass. Revised and Enlarged by William Richard Cutter. ... *Boston: David Clapp & Son.* 1871. 8vo, pp. xi, 363, (1). Coat of Arms and 6 Portraits. H. 18192

CUTTER (Charles Ammi). The New Catalogue of Harvard

College Library. (Reprinted from the North American Review for January, 1869.) [*Cambridge.* 1869.] 8vo, pp. (1), 96–129. 18193

This was the continuation of an article in the "N. Am. Rev." for Oct., 1868, on the history and wants of the library, which was not reprinted. Concerning Mr. Cutter's bibliographical researches, *see* the preface to this Dictionary.

CUTTER (C. W.) An Oration ... before the Whigs of Portsmouth, on the Fourth of July ... 1834. By Charles W. Cutter. *Portsmouth, N. H.: James F. Shores.* M DCCC XXXIV. 8vo, pp. 32. H. 18194

CUTTER (E. F.) Eulogy on Abraham Lincoln, Delivered at Rockland, Maine, April 19, 1865. By Rev. Edward F. Cutter. *Boston: D. C. Colesworthy.* 1865. 8vo, pp. 16. B. 18195

CUTTER (G. W.) Buena Vista, and other Poems. By G. W. Cutter. *Cincinnati.* 1848. 12mo. 18196

CUTTER. Poems, National and Patriotic. *Philadelphia.* 1857. 8vo. C. 18197

Also: Poems and Fugitive Pieces. *Cincinnati.* 1857. 8vo. Portrait.

CUTTER (O. P.) Our Battery, or the Journal of Company B, 1st. O. V. A. By O. P. Cutter. *Cleveland.* 1864. 12mo, pp. 152. 18198

CUTTER (W.) The Life of Israel Putnam, Major-General in the Army of the American Revolution. Compiled from the best Authors. By William Cutter. *New York: Geo. F. Cooledge & Bro.* 1847. 12mo, pp. 383. + Second Edition. [*Ibid.*] + Third Edition. [*Ibid.*] 1848. + Fourth Edition. *Boston:* 1854. 12mo. + *New York: Derby & Jackson.* 1858. 12mo, pp. 383. H. 18199

CUTTER. The Life of General Lafayette. ... By William Cutter. *New-York: Geo. F. Cooledge.* 1849. 12mo, pp. 408. + *New York.* 1854. 12mo. 18200

CUTTING (Francis B.) "Hards" and "Softs" ... Speech ... United States House of Representatives, 1854. [n. p. n. d.] 8vo. 18201

CUTTING (H. P.) The Crisis. Slavery or Freedom ... A Discourse ... *Burlington.* 1854. 8vo. B. 18202

CUTTING (J. B.) Argument delivered ... in Richmond, Virginia, in the Case of Carter's Executors ... against Cutting

and Others ... by John Browne Cutting. ... March 30. 1816. To demonstrate that ... no Gaming Security can be rendered Valid by Device. *Fredericksburg.* 1817. Title, pp. iv, 3–34.

CUTTING. Facts and Observations justifying the Claims of John Browne Cutting ... against the United States; in a Letter addressed to the Secretary of State. To which is prefixed, A List of the Names of a part of the Seamen of the United States ... succoured or liberated by him, from Impressment, in London, Anno 1790. [Dated, *Philadelphia, December* 1795. n. p. n. d.] 8vo, pp. 60. BA. 18204

Also: Letter from the Secretary of State accompanying his Report on the Claim of John Browne Cutting. *Philadelphia.* 1799. 12mo. P.

CUTTING (S. S.) Historical Vindications; a Discourse on the Province and Uses of Baptist History, delivered before the Backus Historical Society, at Newton, Mass., June 23, 1857. Repeated before the American Baptist Historical Society, at New York, May 14, 1859. With Appendixes, containing Historical Notes and Confessions of Faith. By Sewall S. Cutting, ... *Boston: Gould & Lincoln.* 1859. 12mo, pp. 224. H. 18205

Also: Sermons and Addresses. *Worcester.* 1837.

CUTTS (H.) Address ... before the Windsor County Agricultural Society ... at Windsor, Vt., October 4th, 1849. By Hon. Hampden Cutts. ... *Woodstock.* 1850. 8vo, pp. 16. H.

CUTTS (J. M.) A Brief Treatise upon Constitutional and Party Questions, and the History of Political Parties, as I received it orally from the late Senator Stephen A. Douglas of Illinois. By J. Madison Cutts, Brevet-Lieutenant-Colonel, U. S. A. *New York.* 1866. 8vo, pp. 221. 18207

CUTTS. The Conquest of California and New Mexico, by the Forces of the United States, in the Years 1846 & 1847. By James Madison Cutts. With Engravings, Plans of Battle, etc. *Philadelphia: Carey & Hart.* 1847. 12mo, pp. 264. C.

CUTTS (M. P. S.) The Life and Times of Hon. William Jarvis, of Weathersfield, Vermont. By his Daughter, Mary Pepperrell Sparhawk Cutts. *New York: Hurd & Houghton.* 1859. 12mo, pp. xii, 451. Portrait. C. 18209

CUVIER (Georges Léopold Chrétien Frédéric). Essay on the Theory of the Earth, by M. Cuvier. With mineralogical notes. ... By Professor Jameson. To which are now added, Observa-

tions on the Geology of North America, illustrated by the description of various organic remains found in that part of the world. By Samuel L. Mitchell. *New York: Kirk & Mercein.* 1818. 8vo, pp. 431. 8 Plates. 18210

Of course the author's "Le regne animal" includes details of American natural history. The best French edition is, *Paris.* 1848–49. 22 vols., imp. 8vo. The best English version is, *London.* 1835. 16 vols., 8vo. P. His "Discours sur les révolutions de la surface du globe. 5e éd. *Paris: G. Dufour & E. D'Ocagne.* 1828." 8vo, 6 l., pp. vi, 400, also relates, in part, to America.

CUYLER (C. C.) ... A Sermon occasioned by the Death of Robert Ralston, Esq. ... Preached ... Philadelphia, August 21, 1836. By Cornelius C. Cuyler, D.D. ... *Philadelphia.* MDCCCXXXVI. 8vo, pp. 30 or 40. 18211

The subject of this discourse was the founder of the Philadelphia Bible Society, the first institution of its kind in this country.

CUYLER. Sermon occasioned by the Death of the Rev. John H. Livingston, D.D. ... Preached ... 16th of Feb. 1825. By Cors. C. Cuyler ... . *Poughkeepsie: printed by P. Potter.* 1825. 8vo, pp. 26. B. 18212

Also: Discourse on the Death of Rev. Gilbert R. Livingston ... *Philadelphia.* 1834. 8vo. — The Signs of the Times: a Series of Discourses. *Philadelphia.* 1839. 12mo, pp. 319.

CUYLER (T. L.) A Discourse for City Missions ... May 28, 1854. By Theodore L. Cuyler. *New-York.* 1854. 8vo.

CUZCO. Relacion del temblor y terremoto que succedio en el Cuzco a 31 de marzo y siguientes dias de abril de 1650, que arruino toda la ciudad y muchos pueblos de la provincia, y de las penitencias publicas que hicieron sus moradores. 1651. Folio. 18214

Title from Ternaux, No. 705.

CUZENT (G.) Épidémie de la Guadeloupe (1865–1866). Par Gilbert Cuzent ... . *Paris: V. Masson et fils.* 1867. 8vo, pp. 148. 2 Plates. 18215

The Cynick. By Growler Gruff, Esquire, aided by a Confederacy of Lettered Dogs. *Philadelphia.* 1812. 18mo, pp. 210. 18216

Made up of theatrical criticisms, some historical poems, odes, etc.

The Cemetery of the Cypress Hills. Second Edition. *New York: George W. Wood, Printer.* 1849. 8vo. + *New York.* 1851. 8vo. 18217

Cypress River Mining Company: Articles of Agreement. *New-York.* 1846. 8vo. S. 18218

CYR (N.) Memoirs of the Rev. C. H. O. Côté, M.D., with a Memoir of Mrs. M. P. Côté, and a History of Grand Ligne Mission, Canada East. By the Rev. N. Cyr. *Philadelphia.* 1853. 18mo, pp. 144. Portrait. 18219

CYSATUS (R.) Warhafftiger Bericht von den New erfundnen Japponischen Inseln vnd Königreichen auch von andern zuvor vnbekandten Indianischen Landen. *Freiburg.* 1586. 8vo.

Contains "Ein Sendtbrieff H. Quiritii Caxa auss d. Collegio auff jener seydt d. Meers in Brasilien gelegen im J. 1575 aussgangen." 37 l.

D***. L' ACADIADE, ou Prouesses angloises en Acadie, Canada, etc, poëme comi-héroique en quatre chants, par M. D***. *Cassel.* 8vo. 18221

This is by de Chevrier, and should have been mentioned under that name.

D***. Poëmes sur des sujets pris de l'histoire de notre temps, publiés par M. *Liége: Compagnie.* 1758–59. 2 vols., 8vo. 18222

This includes "L'Acadiade."

D. (A.) La vierge Iroquoise. Simple récit tiré de l'histoire de l'Église. Seconde édition. *Lille: Lefort.* 1852. 18mo.

D. (A.) La Guerre Civile aux Etats Unis, impuissance du Nord, l'independance du Sud inévitable. Par A. D... revenu tout récemment des Etats-Unis. *Paris: E. Dentu.* 1862. 8vo, pp. 32. BA. 18224

D. (B.) *See* B[audry] (D[es Lozières]), Vol. I., No. 3979.

D** (B**). *See* B[çrquin] D[uvallon], Vol. II.

D. (B.) Federals and Confederates; for what do they Fight? The True Issue of the American Civil War. By B. D. Third Edition. *London.* [n. d.] 12mo, pp. 16. 18225

D. (B. S.) Isla de Cuba, sus males y situacion actual. Londres, 6 mai 1855. *Paris: impr. d'Aubuison.* 1855. 8vo.

D. (C.) Le Champ d'Asile au Texas; ou notice curieuse et interessante sur la formation de cette Colonie jusqu'à sa dissolution, avec des renseignemens propre à eclaircir les faits, et a venger les malheureux Colons des calomnies qu'on leur a prodiguées. Par C. D. *Paris: Tiger.* 1820. 18mo, 3 sheets.

D. (Ch. J.) Considerations sur l'Esclavage aux Antilles Françaises et de son Abolition graduelle, suivies d'un aperçu analytique et critique du Système d'apprentissage et de ses resultats dans les Colonies Anglaises. Par Ch. J. D. *Paris.* 1843. 8vo, pp. 128. 18228

D. (C.) New England's Faction discovered; or a Brief Account of their Persecution of the Church of England; the Beginning and Progress of the War with the Indians ... . [n. p. n. d.] 4to. BDL. 18229

D. (E.) *See* D[yer] (E[lifhalet]).

D. (H.) Biography of Louis Moreau Gottschalk, The American Pianist and Composer. By H. D. *Philadelphia: Deacon & Peterson, Printers.* 1853. pp. 22. 18230

D—l (H.) *See* H[illiard] d['Auberteui]l (M. R.)

D. (H. N.) Fifty Years of a Play-Goer's Journal: or, Annals of the New York Stage, from A.D. 1798 to A.D. 1848. With Biographical Sketches of all the Principal Performers. By H. N. D. *New York: Samuel French.* [n. d.] pp. 96.

D. (I.) *See* Eliot (John), and Winslow (Edward).

D. (J.) *See* D[avenport] (J[ohn]).

D. (J.) Almanac for the Year 1679. *Cambridge.* 1679. 12mo. 18232

D. *or le sieur* D***. Voyage de Marseille. *See* [Durret].

D. (M.) *See* Du Buisson (M.), Vol. III., No. 9080, and [Du Mesnil (Marie)].

D. (M.) Discurso que fizeram duas senhoras portuguezas depois de lerem o papel dos Conselhos que deu um Brasileiro a todos os seus patricios, etc. Dialogo entre Marcina e Delmira. Por M. D. *Lisboa: na dita Typ.* 1805. 4to, pp. 16.

A poem. *See* Silva, II. 96. Written in answer to the following:

D. (M.) Conselhos que dá um brasileiro veterano a todos os seus patricios, que chegarem a esta córte; em que lhes mostra as cousas de que se hão de livrar, para em tudo acertarem e viverem com honra ... . *Lisboa: na Typ. Lacerdina.* 1805. 4to, pp. 16.

Written in octosyllabic metre.

D*** (*M.*) Histoire des naufrages. *See* [Deperthes].

D*** (*M.*) Lettre de M. D*** à M. D*** [De la Popelinière, fermier-général] au sujet de la Noblesse commerçante [de l'abbé Coyer], ou l'on démontre la facilité de remédier à la dépopulation dont on se plaint, tant à l'égard de la France que de nos colonies, et spécialement de la Louisiane, et les moyens

de rendre la commerce du royaume plus florisant que par le passé et supérieure à celle d'Angleterre. Avec quelques observations relatives au Mémoire des Protestants. *Paris.* 1756. 8vo. 18235

D**** (*M.*) *See* D[ouble] (M.)

D. (O.) *See* D[apper] (O.), and [Montanus (A.)]

D. (R.) Sir Francis Drake revived, who is or may be a Pattern to stirre up all Herooicke and Active Spirits of these Times to benefit their Countrey and eternize their Names by like Noble Attempts; being a Summary of Foure Voyages made by Sir F. Drake to the West-Indies. *London.* 1653. 4to.

D. (R.) Strange and Prodigious Religious Customs and Manners of Sundry Nations. *London.* 1683. 18mo, 1 l., pp. 228.

D. (R.) A Visit to the Wild West. *London.* 1843. 8vo.

D. (W.) *See* Douglas (W.), and D[uane] (W[illiam]).

D. (W.) A Second Answer to Mr. John Wesley. Being a Supplement to the Letter of Americanus. In which the Idea of Supreme Power, and the nature of Royal Charters, are briefly considered. By W. D. *London: Wallis and Stonehouse.* 1775. 12mo, pp. 22. + Second Edition. *London.* [*Ibid.*] 18239

The writer charges Mr. Wesley with having betrayed great inconsistency in his reasoning, which he could not have done "had not interest blinded the clearness of his judgment;" and, addressing him, says: "Your grand positions are mere assertions. You have so long been used to govern the consciences of your people, that you think an opinion is enough to silence the complaints of all America." — Page 6.

DAA (Ludvig Kristensen). Har Amerikas Erfaring bevist de Pensylvanske Fængslers Fortrinlighed? Et Brev til Hr. Amtmand Möinichen. *Kristiania.* 1843. 8vo, pp. 103.

Reprinted from "Granskeren," VI.

DABADIE (F.) A travers l'Amérique du Sud. *Paris: F. Sartorius.* 12mo. + Seconde édition. [*Ibid.*] 18241

DABADIE. Récits et types américains, par F. Dabadie. *Paris: F. Sartorius.* 18—. 18mo, pp. 400. 18242

DABLON (C.) Relation de ce qui s'est passé de plus remarquable aux Missions des Pères de la Compagnie de Jésus, en la Nouvelle France les années 1670 et 1671. Envoyée au R. P. Jean Pinelle Provincial de la province de France. Par le R. P.

Claude Dablon, Recteur du College de Quebec, et Superieur des Missions de la Compagnie de Jésus à la Nouvelle France. *A Paris: Martin Cramoisy.* 1672. Sm. 8vo, 8 l., pp. 189, 1 l. Map. 18243

Very rare. Tross, of Paris, sold a copy, in 1870, for 150 francs.

DABLON. Relation de ce qui s'est passé de plus remarquable aux Missions des Pères de la Compagnie de Jésus, en la Nouvelle France les années 1671 et 1672. Envoyée au R. P. Jean Pinelle Provincial de la province de France. Par le R. P. Clude Dablon, Recteur du College du Kuebec, et Superieur des Missions de la Compagnie de Jésus à la Nouvelle France. *A Paris: M. Cramoisy.* 1673. Sm. 8vo, pp. 264. S. 18244

DABLON. Relation de ce qui s'est passé de plus remarquable aux missions des peres de la Compagnie de Jesus en la Nouvelle France les annés 1672 et 1673 Par le R. P. Claude Dablon ... . *Nouvelle York Jean-Marie Shea* M. DCCC. LXI. Sm. 4to, pp. v, 219, (1). H. 18245

Forms No. XIII. of Shea's Cramoisy Series. 100 copies reprinted.

DABLON. Relation de ce qui s'est passé de plus remarquable aux missions des peres de la Compagnie de Jesus en la Nouvelle France les années 1673 à 1679 Par le R. P. Claude Dablon ... . *Nouvelle York: Jean-Marie Shea.* M. DCCC. LX. Sm. 4to, pp. xiii, 290, (1). BA., H. 18246

Forms No. XII. of Shea's Cramoisy Series. 100 copies printed. For an English version of the relation of the voyages, &c., see French's "Hist. Coll.," Vol IV.

[DABLON, ALLOUEZ (P.), *and* MILLET (P.)] Relation de ce qui s'est passé de plus remarquable aux Missions des Pères de la Compagnie de Jesus, en la Nouvelle France les années 1669 et 1670. Envoyée au R. P. Estienne Dechamps, Provincial de la province de France. *A Paris: M. Cramoisy.* 1671. Sm. 8vo.

The second part of this volume is made up of "Relations," by C. Dablon, P. Allouez, and Pierre Millet.

DABNEY (J. B.) An Address ... 23d June 1841, at Washington College ... . By John Blair Dabney ... . *Lexington, Virginia: A. Waddill, Printer.* 1841. 8vo, pp. 30. H. 18248

[DABNEY (Jonathan P.)] Remarks on the Harvard Triennial. [n. p. 1846.] 12mo, pp. 12. H. 18249

"Advertisement," by the author, occupies two pages of the cover.

DABNEY (R.) Poems and Translations. By Richard Dabney. *Richmond, Va.* 1812. 12mo. 18250

DABNEY. Poems, Original and Translated. By Richard Dabney. Second Edition. *Philadelphia: Mathew Carey.* 1815. 18mo, pp. 172. C. 18251

DABNEY (R. L.) The Christian's Best Motive for Patriotism. A Sermon: preached in the College Church, Hampden Sidney, Va. On the 1st of November, 1860, a General Fast-Day, Appointed by the Synod of Virginia, to Pray for Escape from National Convulsions. By Robert L. Dabney, D.D. ... *Richmond: Chas. H. Wynne.* 1860. 8vo, pp. 14. 18252

DABNEY. A Defence of Virginia, (and through her, of the South,) in Recent and Pending Contests against the Sectional Party. By Prof. Robert L. Dabney, D.D., of Virginia, late of the Confederate Army. *New York: E. J. Hale & Son.* 1867. 12mo, pp. 356. BA. 18253

DABNEY. Life of Lieut. Gen. Thomas J. Jackson (Stonewall Jackson). *Edinburgh: Nesbit & Co.* 1864. 2 vols., Post 8vo, pp. vi, 333; xvi, 527. Plate. C. 18254

DABNEY. Life and Campaigns of Lieut. Gen. Thomas J. Jackson (Stonewall Jackson). By Prof. Robert L. Dabney, D.D. Edited by the Rev. W. Chalmers, A.M. *New York: Blelock & Co.* 1866. 8vo, pp. xii, 732. 18255

DACOTA. *See* Dakota.

DA COSTA (J.) Narrative of the Persecution of Hippolytas Joseph da Costa Pereira Futa do de Mendonça, a native of Colonia-do-Sacramento, on the River La Plata; imprisoned and tried in Lisbon, by the Inquisition, for the Pretended Crime of Free-Masonry ... . *London.* 1811. 2 vols., 8vo. 18256

DADDOW (S. H.), *and* BANNAN (B.) Coal, Iron, and Oil; or, The Practical American Miner. A Plain and Popular Work on our Mines and Mineral Resources, and a Text-Book or Guide to their Economical Development. With Numerous Maps and Engravings. Illustrating and explaining the Geology, Origin, and Formation of Coal, Iron, and Oil, their Peculiarities, Character, and General Distribution, and the Economy of Mining, Manufacturing, and using them; ... and Special Descriptions of the Anthracite Fields and Mines of Pennsylvania, and the Bituminous Fields of the United States, the Iron-Districts and Iron Trade of our Country, and the Geology and Distribution of Petroleum, the Statistics, Extent, Production, and Trade in

Coal, Iron, and Oil ... . By Samuel Harries Daddow ... and Benjamin Bannan ... . *Pottsville, Pa.: Benjamin Bannan.* 1866. 8vo, pp. 808. BA. 18257

Daden der Zee-Helden en Ontdeckers van Landen deser eeuwen beginnende met Christoffel Columbus vinder van de Nieuwe Wereldt. *Amsterdam.* 1676. 4to. Plates and Portraits. 18258

DADMUN (J. W.) Union League Melodies. A Collection of Patriotic Hymns and Tunes. Original and Selected, by Rev. J. W. Dadmun. *Boston: B. R. Russell.* 1864. 16mo, pp. 32.

Also: Army and Navy Melodies. By Rev. J. W. Dadmun and Rev. Arthur B. Fuller. *Boston.* 1863. 12mo, pp. 64. — Revival Melodies. *Boston.* 1859. 12mo.

Dagboek van het Britisch Ministerie, sedert het begin der N. Americaansche onlusten tot op den tegenswoordigen tyd. Uit het Engelsch vertaald en met opheldenende Aanmerkingen voorzien. Door William Penn, Secundus. *Amsterdam: Joannes Allart.* MDCCLXXXII. 8vo, pp. 156. 18260

Nijhoff's catalogue attributes this to E. Wolff and A. Deken.

DAGG (J. L.) Grammar of the English Language. Book First. By Dr. J. L. Dagg. *Macon, Ga.: Burke, Boykin & Co.* 1864. BA. 18261

The only interest this possesses, consists in the fact that it was published in the "Confederate" States.

DAGGETT (David). Mr. Daggett's Argument, before the General Assembly of ... Connecticut, October, 1804, in the Case of Certain Justices of the Peace. To which is prefixed, A Brief History of the Proceedings of the Assembly. *New-Haven: printed by Oliver Steele & Co.* [1804.] 8vo, pp. 30.

Also: An Eulogium, Commemorative of the Exalted Virtues of his Excellency Roger Griswold, late Governor of this State, written and delivered at the request of the General Assembly, On the 29th of October, 1812 ... . *New-Haven: Walter & Steele.* 1812. 8vo, pp. 24. BA., M., W. — An Oration on the Death of Mr. William Heyliger, of St. Croix, in the West-Indies, Who died in New York, ... Preached ... On the 21st of November, 1794. ... *New-Haven: T. & S. Green.* 8vo, pp. 10. BA. — An Oration, ... in ... New-Haven, on the Fourth of July, A D. 1787. ... *New-Haven: Printed by T. and S. Green.* 8vo, pp. 24. BA. — Sunbeams may be Extracted from Cucumbers, but the Process is Tedious. An Oration pronounced on the Fourth of July, 1799 ... . *New Haven: Thomas Green.* 1799. 8vo, pp. 28. + Second Edition. [*Ibid.*] 1799. 8vo, pp. 28

DAGGETT (D.) The Life and Character of Hon. David Daggett. *New Haven.* 1851. 8vo, pp. 33. 18263

DAGGETT (H.) A Discourse delivered at East-Hampton (Long-Island), Lord's-Day, July 22, 1798. Occasioned by the Death of the Rev. Samuel Buell, D.D, and Pastor of the Church there. Who departed this Life July 19, 1798. By Herman Daggett, A.M. *New London: Printed by Samuel Green.* 1799. 8vo, pp. 23. M. 18264

Also: Discourse on the Nature and Importance of Church Discipline. ... *New London.* 1797. 8vo, pp. 31.

[DAGGETT (John).] Remarks and Documents concerning the Location of the Boston and Providence Rail-Road through the Burying Ground in East Attleborough ... . By a Freeman of Massachussets. ... *Boston.* 1834. 8vo, pp. 28. H. 18265

DAGGETT. Sketch of the History of Attleborough, from its Settlement to the Present Time. By John Daggett. *Dedham: H. Mann, Printer.* 1834. 8vo, pp. 136. BA., H. 18266

DAGGETT (N.) The Excellency of a good Name: A Sermon delivered in Yale College, occasioned by the death of Job Lane, one of the Tutors, Sept. 16, 1768. By Naphtah Daggett. *New Haven.* [1768.] 18267

DAGGETT. Faithful serving of God in our Generation ... . A Sermon on the Death of the Reverend Thomas Clap, (President of Yale College) ... Jan. 7th, 1767; Delivered Jan. 8th. By ... Naphtah Daggett ... . *New Haven: Printed by B. Mecom.* [n. d.] Sm. 4to, pp. 39. H. 18268

Also: Sermon at the Installation of Nathaniel Snerman, at Mount Carmel, May 18, 1763 ... . *New Haven.* 1763. 8vo. — ... A Sermon preached at Danbury, September 19th, 1770, at the Ordination of the Reverend Ebenezer Baldwin. ... *New Haven.* [1770.] 8vo, pp. 32. M. — The Testimony of Conscience a most solid Foundation for Rejoicing. A Sermon Preached at the Ordination of ... Joseph Howe, ... in Boston, May 19, 1773. ... . *Boston: S Mills.* M,DCC,LXXIII. 8vo, pp. 52.

DAGGETT (O. E.) A Sermon on the Death of Abraham Lincoln, April 15th, 1865, Preached in the First Congregational Church, Canandaigua, N. Y., Sunday Morning, April 16th, 1865, and again, by Request, the following Wednesday Evening, by the Pastor, O. E. Daggett. *Canandaigua, N. Y.: N. J. Milliken, Printer.* 1865. 8vo, pp. 16. 18269

Also: "The Beloved Physician." A Sermon preached in ... Canandaigua, N. Y., at the Funeral of Edson Carr, M.D. ... December 1, 1861. ... *Canandaigua, N. Y.: J. J. Mattison. Printer.* 1861. 8vo, pp. 24. H. — The Cavil of Judas; or False Pretences. A Sermon ... *New Haven: J. H. Benham & Son, Printers.* 1868. 8vo, pp. 15.

DAGGS (R.) Fugitive Slave Case. ... Southern Division of Iowa. Burlington, June Term, 1850. Ruel Daggs, *vs.* Elihu Frazier, *et als.* ... *Burlington: Printed by Morgan & M'Kenny.* 1850. 8vo, pp. 40. H. 18270

DAGNALL (J. M.) Daisy Swain: The Flower of Shenandoah. A Poem founded on the Rebellion. By Dr. John M. Dagnall. *Brooklyn, N. Y.* 1865. 12mo, pp. 167 S. 18271

Also: The Mexican; or, Love and Land. Founded on the Invasion of Maximilian. *New York: American News Company.* 1868. 18mo, pp. 228 Plate.

The Daguerreian Journal; devoted to the Daguerreian and Photogenic Arts: S. D. Humphrey, Editor. *New York.* 1850. Continued to Vol. VII. or more. 18272

Dagverhaal wegens den opstand en het afloopen van ... 't schip Nyenburgh schipper J. Ketel ... over Cabo de Goede Hoop naar Batavia ... 1763 ... Vervattende het geene is voorgevallen ... onder de personagien welke ... van het schip gegaan zijn; als hunne aankomst in de Portugeesche West-Indien etc. ... (en) hetgeene met de muitelingen verder is voorgevallen, etc. *Amsterdam: D. Swaan.* [About 1764.] 3 pts., 4to. 18273

DAHLERUP (Hans Birch). Skizzer fra et kort Besög par vore vestindiske Oer i Sommeren 1841, tilligemed nogle Bemærkninger om Negeremancipation. (In the "Nye Archiv for Sövaesenet," I. 1–62.) 18274

Also: in the same periodical, of which he was editor, "To Besö til Sydamerikas Fastland med Briggen St. Croix i 1826," II. 405–448; and in "Den Berlingske Tidende," 1841, Nr. 215, "General gouverneur von Scholten og Almueskolerne paa St. Croix."

DAHLGREEN (C. G.) Letter to His Excellency Gov. Harris, of Tennessee, on State Rights and Secession, from C. G. Dahlgreen. *Natchez.* 1861. 8vo, pp. 45. 18275

DAHLGREN (J. A.) Boat Armament of the U. S. Navy. Designed by, and executed under the direction of J. A. Dahlgren, Commander U. S. N. *Philadelphia.* 1852. 12mo, pp. 216. + Second Edition. *Philadelphia.* 1856. 12mo. 18276

[DAHLGREN.] List of Vessels of the South Atlantic Blockading Squadron. With their Armament, Rate, Stations, &c. Also, Line Officers Of the Squadron. November, 1864. [n. p. n. d.] 21 leaves. H. 18277

Also: Ordnance Memoranda. Naval Percussion Locks and Primers, ... *Philadelphia: Printed by A. Hart.* 1853. 8vo, pp. 125 Plates. — Ordnance Department. Report to the Navy Department, by Captain Dahlgren, Chief of Bureau. ... . December 1, 1862. *Washington: Government Printing Office.* 1862. 8vo, pp. 16. B., P. — Shells and Shell-Guns. ... *Philadelphia: King & Bain, Printers.* 1856. 8vo, pp. 436. Plates. B.

DAHLONEGA. The Gold Placers of the Vicinity of Dahlonega, Georgia. Report of William P. Blake. ... and of Charles T. Jackson, M.D., ... to the Yahoola River and Creek Hydraulic Hose Mining Company, with a Description of the Hydraulic Process of Mining and an Historical Notice of Gold Mining in Georgia. *Boston.* 1859. 8vo, pp. 45. BA. 18278

DAIGREMONT (J. de Laon, *Sieur*). *See* Laon (J. de).

DAILEY (C. F.) Report upon the Disabled Rhode Island Soldiers; their Names, Condition, and in what Hospital they are. Made to his Excellency Governor Sprague, and Presented to the General Assembly of Rhode Island January Session, 1863. By Mrs. Charlotte F. Dailey, Commissioned by the Governor to visit the Hospitals, etc. *Providence: Alfred Anthon Young.* 1863. 8vo, pp. 24. 18279

DAILEY (J. P.) *See* Lincoln (A.)

The Daily Campaign Record. *Memphis, Tenn.* 4to.

This and the following are records of the war of 1860–65:

The Daily Countersign. A Waif of the St. Louis Sanitary Fair. *St. Louis.* 1864. 4to. 18281

The Daily Public School in the United States. ... *Philadelphia: J. B. Lippincott & Co.* 8vo, pp. 158. BA. 18282

DAINVILLE (D.) Beautés de l'Histoire du Canada, ou Epoques mémorables, traits intéressants, mœurs, usages, coutumes des Habitants du Canada, tant indigènes que Colons, depuis sa découverte jusqu'à ce jour. *Paris: Bossange frères.* 1821. 12mo.

DAKE (O. C.) Nebrask Legends and Poems. *New York.* 1871. 12mo, pp. 165. 18284

DAKOTA. Dakota dowanssi kin. Hymns in the Dakota or Sioux Language. Composed by Mr. J. Renville and Sons, and the Missionaries of the A. B. C. F. M. *Boston: American Board of Foreign Missions.* 1842. 18mo, pp. 71. C. 18285

Dakota Tawaxitku Kin, or The Dakota Friend, published [monthly] by the Dakota Mission. G. H. Pond, editor. *St. Paul, Minnesota.* Vol. I., Nos. 1–12, Nov., 1850, to Oct., 1851, 4to; Vol. II., Nos. 1–8, Jan., 1852, to Aug., 1852, folio.

Suspended at this point, on account of Indian troubles. Contains many articles in the Dakota language, besides specimens of the language in short sentences, with interlinear English translations, etc.

Dakota Tawoonspe [Primer]. 2 pts., square 12mo. 18287

Extracts from Genesis and the Psalms, with the third Chapter of Proverbs and the third Chapter of Daniel, in the Dacota Language. Translated from the French Bible, by Joseph Renville, Sr. Compared with other Translations, by Thomas S. Williamson. *Cincinnati.* 1839. 18mo, pp. 72. 18288

Extracts from the Gospels of Matthew, Luke, and John, from the Acts of the Apostles, and from the First Epistle of John, in the Language of the Dacota or Sioux Indians. Translated from the French, by Joseph Renville, Sr., and written by Th. S. Williamson. *Cincinnati.* 1839. 18mo, pp. 48. 18289

The History of Joseph in the Language of the Dakota, or Sioux Indians. Translated from Genesis, by Samuel W. and Gideon H. Pond. *Cincinnati.* 1839. 18mo, pp. 96. 18290

Jesus ohnihde wicaye cin oranyanpi qon: qa Palos wowapi kage ciqon; nakun, Jan woyake ciqon dena eepi, [etc.] The Acts of the Apostles, and the Epistles of Paul, with the Revelation of John, in the Dakota Language; Translated from the Greek, by Stephen R. Riggs. *Cincinnati: American Bible Society.* 1843. 8vo, pp. 228. C. 18291

Wicoicage wowapi, qa odowan wakan, heberi iapi etanhan kagapi, [etc.] The Book of Genesis, and a Part of the Psalms, in the Dakota language; Translated from the original Hebrew, by the Missionaries of the A. B. C. F. M. and Joseph Renville, Sr. [With] Wootanin waxte Luka qa Jan, owapi qon hena eepi, [etc.] The Gospels of Luke and John, in the Dakota language; Translated by G. H. Pond and Joseph Renville, Sr. *Cincinnati: American Board of Commissioners for Foreign Missions.* 1842–43. 8vo, pp. 296. C. 18292

Wowapi Mitawa Tamakoce Kaga. My own Book, prepared from the Rev. T. H. Gallaudet's "Mother's Primer." *Boston.* 1842. 18293

DAKOTAH TERRITORY. Council and House Journal of the Legislative Assembly of Dakota, First Session, 1862. 2 vols., 8vo. S. 18294

Council and House Journal of the Territory of Dakota, passed at the Fifth Session of the Legislature, 1865–6. *Yankton.* 2 vols., 8vo. S. 18295

General Laws of the Territory of Dakota, passed at the First and Second Sessions of the Legislative Assembly, 1862, 1863. *Yankton.* 1862–3. 2 vols., 8vo. Continued. S. 18296

Sixth Annual Session. First Annual Message of Governor A. J. Faulk, to the Legislative Assembly, of the Territory of Dakota. Delivered, December 1866. *Yankton, Dakota Territory: Geo. W. Kingsbury, Printer.* 1866. 8vo, pp. 13. H. + Third Annual Message of Governor A. J. Faulk, ... *Yankton, Dakota Territory: Geo. W. Kingsbury, Printer.* 1868. 8vo, pp. 14. H. 18297

DALAGER (Lars). Gronlandske Relationer. *Kiobenhaun.* 1752. 4to. 18298

DALCHO (F.) An Historical Account of the Protestant Episcopal Church, in South-Carolina, from the First Settlement of the Province, to The War of the Revolution; with Notices of the Present State of the Church in each Parish: and some Account of the Early Civil History of Carolina, never before published. To which are added; the Laws relating to Religious Worship; the Journals and Rules of the Convention of South Carolina; the Constitution and Canons of the Protestant Episcopal Church, and the Course of Ecclesiastical Studies: with an Index, and List of Subscribers. By Frederick Dalcho, M.D. ... *Charleston: E. Thayer.* 1820. 8vo, pp. vii, (1), 613, (3). BA.

Also: Masonic Oration at Charleston, S. C., Sept. 23, 1801. ... *Charleston.* 8vo. W. — Masonic Oration at Charleston, S. C., March 21, 1803, with an Historical Inquiry. ... *Charleston.* 8vo. W. — Sermon, on St. John's Day, 5817, before the Grand Lodge of Ancient Masons in South Carolina. ... *Charleston.* 8vo. — Sermon in Charleston, S. C., Dec. 27, 1817, before the Grand Lodge S. C. ... *Charleston.* 1817. 8vo.

DALE (J. W.) Northern Hearts embrace Southern Homes. Two Sermons by the Rev. James W. Dale. I. Abolitionism in its Fruits. II. Abolitionism in its Morals; or, Is the Relation of Master and Servant a Sin, per se? [n. p.] 1861. 8vo, pp. 46. B. 18300

DALE (R.) Notes of an Excursion to the Isthmus of Tehuantepec, in the Republic of Mexico. By R. Dale. *London: Effingham & Wilson.* 1851. 8vo, pp. 58. Map and Plate. C.

DALE CEMETERY. The Dale Cemetery, (at Claremont, near Sing-Sing,) its Incorporation, Rules and Regulations, and the Dedication Addresses. *New York: Casper C. Childs, Printer.* 1852. 8vo, pp. 40. H. 18302

DALEY (D.), *and* HALLIGAN (J.) Report of the Trial of Dominic Daley and James Halligan for The Murder of Marcus Lyon ... April 1806. *Northampton: S. & E. Butler.* 8vo, pp. 88. BA., H. 18303

DALL (*Mrs.* C. H.) The College, the Market, and the Court; or, Woman's Relation to Education, Labor and Law. By Caroline H. Dall ... . *Boston: Lee and Shepard.* 1867. 8vo, pp. xxxv, (2), 498, (1). BA. 18304

DALL. "Woman's Right to Labor;" or, Low Wages and Hard Work: In Three Lectures, delivered in Boston, November, 1859. By Caroline H. Dall. ... *Boston: Walker, Wise, and Company.* 1860. 16mo, pp. xv, 184, (1). H. 18305

DALL. Woman's Rights under the Law: In Three Lectures, delivered in Boston, January, 1861, by Caroline H. Dall ... . *Boston: Walker, Wise, and Company.* 1861. 18mo, pp. xix, 164, (1). H. 18306

DALL (C. H. A.) Home Missions. First Annual Report to the Trustees and Friends of the Baltimore Ministry at Large, 1843. By Rev. Charles Henry Appleton Dall. *Baltimore.* 1843. 8vo, pp. 16. 18307

DALL (W. H.) Alaska and its Resources. By William H. Dall ... . *Boston: Lee & Shepard.* 1870. 8vo, pp. 627, (1). Map and Woodcuts. BA. 18308

Some copies have a London imprint.

[DALLAS (Alexander James).] An Exposition of the Causes and Character of the late War with Great Britain. *Philadelphia: Thomas S. Manning.* 1815. 8vo, pp. 82. + *Middleburg, (Vt.): William Slade, Jun. July* 4, 1815. 8vo, pp. 55 or 59. + *Washington City: Roger Chew Weightman.* 1815. 8vo, pp. 72. C. + [*Boston.* 1815.] 8vo, pp. 47. M. + *Concord, N. H.* 1815. 12mo. 18309

Another edition has the following title:

[DALLAS.] Exposition of The Causes and Character of the late War Attributed to the Pen of Mr. Secretary Dallas. [*Boston.* 1815?] 8vo, pp. 47. 18310

It was reprinted in London with the following title:

[DALLAS.] An Exposition of the Causes and Character of the Late War with Great Britain. Published by Authority of the American Government. *London.* 1815. 8vo, pp. 101. + The Eleventh Edition. *London.* 1815. 8vo, pp. 101. BA.

"This document is official; it is all pith, all home blows." — COBBETT.

DALLAS. The Opinion of Judge Cooper on the Effect of a Sentence of a Foreign Court of Admiralty. By Alexander James Dallas. *Philadelphia: P. Byrne.* 1810. 8vo, pp. 79.

DALLAS. Reports of Cases ruled and adjudged in the Courts of Pennsylvania, before and since Revolution: By A. J. Dallas, Esquire. *Philadelphia: Printed, for the Reporter, by T. Bradford.* M,DCC,XC. 4 vols., 8vo, pp. x, 494, xxiv, (1); Vol. II. *Printed at the Aurora Office.* M,DCC,XCVIII. pp. iv, 480, xix; Vol. III. *Printed by J. Ormrod.* 1799. pp. (v), 519, xiii; Vol. IV. *Printed for J. Byrne by Fry and Kammerer.* 1807. pp. (iv), 472, xxxiv, (xi). 18313

Of this very valuable work there is a second edition of Vol. I. *Philadelphia.* 1806. — Vol. IV. Second Edition with Notes & Additions by Benjamin Gerhard. C. — The Third Edition with Notes & Additions by Thomas I. Wharton. *Philadelphia: P. H. Nicklin.* 1830. (Many of the cases have an historic interest.) Also: A Report of the Case of the Commonwealth *vs.* Tench Coxe, Esq. on a motion for a Mandamus in the Supreme Court of Pennsylvania. ... *Philadelphia.* 1803.

DALLAS (Angus). Appeal on the Common School Law, its incongruity and maladministration setting forth the necessity of a Minister of Public Instruction, responsible to Parliament. *Toronto.* 1858. 8vo, pp. 32. 18314

DALLAS (G.) Biographical Memoir of Sir Peter Parker, killed in Action while Storming the American Camp at Bellair, near Baltimore, in 1814. By Sir George Dallas. *London.* 1815. 4to. C. 18315

DALLAS (George Mifflin). Mr. Dallas's Letter on the Mexican Treaty ... . *Philadelphia.* 1849. 12mo, pp. 29. 18316

DALLAS. Eulogy on the Life and Character of the late President James K. Polk, delivered at the Request of a Committee of Democratic Citizens. By George Mifflin Dallas, at the Chinese Museum, on the 16th July, 1849. *Philadelphia.* 1849. 8vo, pp. 28. 18317

DALLAS. Great Speech of the Hon. George Mifflin Dallas, upon the Leading Topics of the Day, delivered at Pittsburgh, Pa., with a Brief Biographical Sketch, &c., &c. *Philadelphia: "Times & Keystone" Office,* 1847. 8vo, pp. 24. 18318

DALLAS. Life and Writings of Alexander James Dallas. By his Son, George Mifflin Dallas. *Philadelphia: J. B. Lippincott & Co.* 1871. 8vo, pp. 487. BA. 18319

DALLAS. Obsequies in honor of Andrew Jackson. Eulogium by George M. Dallas, Vice President of the United States, on the occasion of the Jackson Obsequies at Washington Square, in the City of Philadelphia, 26th June, 1845. *Philadelphia: Mifflin & Perry.* 1845. 8vo, pp. 16. 18320

Also. An Address delivered ... at Princeton, ... Annual Commencement of the College of New-Jersey, September 27, 1831. By George M. Dallas, Esquire. ... *Princeton, N. J.: printed for the Societies, by D'Hart and Connolly.* 1831. 8vo, Half-Title, pp. 26. — Address delivered on Occasion of laying the Corner Stone of the Smithsonian Institution; May 1, 1847. By George M. Dallas, Chancellor of the Institution. *Washington: Printed at the Office of Blair and Rives.* 1847. 8vo, pp. 8. BA. — The Casting Vote of Vice-President Dallas on the Tariff of 1846. *Philadelphia.* 1846. 8vo, pp. 16. — Speech ... in the Senate ... on the Tariff, Feb. 27, 1832. *Philadelphia.* 1832. 8vo. W. — Brief Memoir of George Mifflin Dallas. *Philadelphia.* 1853. — Life of George Mifflin Dallas, Vice President of the United States. *Philadelphia.* 1847. 8vo, pp. 18. — Proceedings of the R. W. Grand Lodge of Pennsylvania, at a quarterly Grand Communication, held at the Masonic Hall, Chesnut St., Philadelphia, March 6, 1865, A.L. 5865, in reference to the Death of P. G. M. Brother, the Hon. George Mifflin Dallas. *Philadelphia: King and Baird.* 1865. 8vo, pp. 37. Allibone's "Dictionary," Vol. I., contains a long list of pieces by Mr. Dallas, some of which do not exist in book form. *See* "National Portrait Gallery," II. 16, and Kneas (H. R.)

[DALLAS (Robert), *Jr.*] Considerations upon the American Enquiry. *London: Printed for J. Wilkie.* M DCC LXXIX. 8vo, Title, pp. 55. BA. + Second Edition. [*Ibid.*] 18321

Relates to the army under the command of General Howe. *See* the "Essay on Modern Martyrs," Vol. III., No. 9261.

DALLAS (R. C.) The History of the Maroons, from their origin to the establishment of their Chief Tribe at Sierra Leone: including the Expedition to Cuba, for the Purpose of procuring Spanish Chasseurs; and the State of the Island of Jamaica for the last Ten Years: with a Succinct History of the Island previous to that Period. By R. C. Dallas, Esq. *London: T. N. Longman and O. Rees.* 1803. 2 vols., 8vo, pp. xii, cxiv, 359; xi, (1), 514, (1). H. 18322

DALLAS (R. C.) Geschichte der Maronen-Neger auf Jamaika. Aus dem Englischen von Ehrmann. Map. 18323

Forms part of Vol. XXII. of "Bibliothek der neueste Reisebeschreibungen. *Weimar.* 1800–14." 50 vols., 8vo.

DALLAS. The King against Picton. Mr. Dallas's Speech for a New Trial, in the Case of Louisa Calderon. *London.* 1808. 8vo. 18324

DALLAS. Journey in the West Indies, in which are interspersed Anecdotes and Characters. By R. C. Dallas. *London.* 1790. 2 vols., 12mo. P. 18325

DALLAS. Letter to Sir William Poulteney, on the Subject of Trade. 4to. 18326

DALLAWAY (James.) Poems to the Memory of C. H., killed in America, ... *Privately printed at the Press of J. Dallaway, at the Fort in Gloucestershire.* 1788. Folio, sheet. 18327

DALLIBA (J.) Improvements in the Military Establishments of the United States. By James Dalliba. *Troy.* 1822. 8vo.

DALLIBA. A Narrative of the Battle of Brownstown, which was fought on the 9th of August, 1812, during the Campaign of the North Western Army under the Command of Brigadier General Hull. By James Dalliba ... . *New York.* 1816. 8vo, pp. 37. S. 18329

DALLO Y ZAVALA (M. R.) El Gali-Hispano Herve de la Fé el Sr. D. Phelippe V. Sermon Funebre, celebró en Mexico dia 28. Febrero del Año de 1747. *Mexico.* 1747. 4to. 18330

DALLOZ. Consultation de MM. Dalloz, Delagrange, Hennequin, Dupin Jeune, et autres Jurisconsultes, pour les anciens Colons de St. Domingue. *Paris: Madame Veuve Agasse.* 1829. 8vo, pp. 64. A. 18331

DALLY (E.) Sur les Races indigènes et sur l'Archéologie du Mexique. *Paris.* 1862. 8vo, pp. 36. 18332

Extrait des Bulletins de la Société d'anthropologie.

DALMAS (A.) Histoire de la révolution de Saint-Domingue, depuis le commencement des troubles, jesqu'à la prise de Jérémie et du Mole S. Nicolas par les Anglais; suivie d'un mémoire sur le rétablissement de cette colonie. Par A. Dalmas. *Paris: Mame frères.* 1814. 2 vols., 8vo, pp. xvj, 352; 2 l., pp. 301, 1 folded l. BA., C., H. 18333

Also: Recherches historiques et médicales sur la fièvre jaune. Nouvelle édition. *Paris: Compère jeune.* 1822. 8vo. (1st ed., 1805.) Dalmas translated Brackenridge's "History of the War of 1812."

DAL RIO (Ercole). *See* Rio (Ercole dal).

[Dalrymple (Alexander).] An Account of the Discoveries made in the South Pacifick Ocean, Previous to 1764. Part i. Containing, i. A Geographical Description of Places. ii. An Examination of the Conduct of the Discoverers in the Tracks they pursued. iii. Investigations of what may be further expected. ... *London.* 1767. 8vo, 2 l., pp. xxxi, 103. 7 folding Plates. H. 18334

In his "Historical Collections," printed in 1770, Mr. Dalrymple states that only a few copies of this work were printed, and that is was not published till some time after, when it was reported that the French had discovered the Southern continent, the great object of all his researches. Rich had a copy, with plates on India paper.

Dalrymple. Catalogue of Authors who have written on Rio de la Plata, Paraguay, and Chaco, collected by A. Dalrymple, 1807. *London: F. Wingrave.* 1807–8. 4to, Title, pp. 22. H. 18335

"'Pinelo-Barcia,' enlarged with few additions, taken chiefly from Muratori's 'Cristianisimo Felice,' and such books as the compiler could find in the British Museum." — Harrisse.

Dalrymple. A Collection of Voyages, Chiefly in The Southern Atlantic Ocean. Published from Original m.s.s. By Alexander Dalrymple. *London: the Author.* 1775. 4to, 2 l., pp. 19, (2), 22, 88, 16, 16, 13. 4 Maps. H. 18336

Contains: i. Dr. Edmund Halley's two voyages in 1698 and 1700; ii. Voyage fait aux terres Australes par M. des Loziers Bouvet en 1738–9; iii. Journal de navigation pour un voyage de la Mer du Sud fait par le S. Ducloz Guyot, en 1753–6; iv. Journal of winds, weather, &c., at Falkland's Island, in 1766–7, by Captain Macbride.

[Dalrymple.] Considerations on the Present State of Affairs between England and America. *London: J. Nourse.* 1778. 8vo, pp. (4), 39. 18337

"Against the American war; sensible, not violent in favor of the colonies, but totally againstallowing their independency." — *Monthly Review*, lviii. 157.

Dalrymple. An Historical Collection of the several Voyages and Discoveries in the South Pacific Ocean. Vol. i. Being chiefly a Literal Translation from the Spanish Writers. || Vol. ii. Containing the Dutch Voyages. || By Alexander Dalrymple, Esq. *London: J. Nourse.* mdcclxx–mdcclxxi. 2 vols., 4to, pp. xxx, (2), (3), 21, (3), 204; 2 l., pp. 24, 2 l., pp. 224, (60).

In this collection of voyages, the compiler has confined himself entirely to the discoveries made between South America and the great island of New Guinea, the narratives being literal translations from the original Spanish authors. A French translation from this version was printed in 8vo, at *Paris*, by *Saillant & Nyon*, 1774.

Dalrymple. Historische Sammlung der Reisen nach der Südsee im 16^{n}, 17^{n} und 18^{n} Jahrhundert. Aus dem Englischen. *Hamburg.* 1786. 8vo. 18339

Dalrymple. An Historical Journal. *See* Costanso (Miguel), No. 17020.

Dalrymple. A Letter from Mr. Dalrymple to Dr. Hawkesworth, occasioned by some groundless and illiberal imputations in his account of the late Voyages to the South. *London: J. Nourse.* md cc lxxiii. 4to, pp. 35, (4). Map? c. 18340

"Mr. Dalrymple, in the record of his voyage to the South, endeavors to prove the existence of a South Polar Continent. Dr. Hawkesworth disputes these assertions, with some reflections on the former, which are answered in this 'Letter.'" *See* Rich, i. 195.

Dalrymple. Plan for promoting the Fur Trade and securing it to this country, by uniting the operations of the East India and Hudson's Bay Company. *London.* 1789. 4to. 18341

Dalrymple. The Spanish Memorial of the 4th June Considered. By A. Dalrymple. *London: George Bigg.* 1790. 8vo, pp. 41. 18342

The cause of complaint against Spain was the seizure by her of an English vessel near Nootka Sound, upon the plea that these were Spanish waters. The captain of another English vessel was put in the stocks by a naval officer of Spain, who further "to insult the British nation, celebrated the Declaration of American Independence, and hoisted the Spanish flag on that of Great Britain." I have seen the following collation, "pp. 21. 2 Maps."

Dalrymple. The Spanish Pretensions Fairly Discussed, by A. Dalrymple. ... *London: Printed by Elmsly* [etc.] 1790. Rl. 8vo, pp. 19. H. 18343

"A discussion of the claims of Spain to the whole of the Magellanic regions, and to the whole of the N. W. coast of America." — *M. Rev.*, ii. 357.

Dalrymple. Voyages dans la mer du sud, par les Espagnols et les Hollandois, ouvrage traduit de l'anglois de M. Dalrymple, par M. de Fréville. *Paris: Saillant et Nyon.* 1774. 8vo, pp. xiv, 502. 3 Maps. J.C.B., S. 18344

Also: Considerations on Buache's Memoir concerning New Britain and the North Coast of New Guinea. *London.* 1790. 4to.

Dalrymple (C.) Extracts from a Military Essay, containing Reflections on the Raising, Arming, Clothing and Discipline of the British Infantry and Cavalry. By Campbell Dalrymple, Esq; Lieut. Colonel to the King's Own Regiment of Dragoons. *Philadelphia: Printed by Humphreys, Bell, and Aitken.* m.dcc.-lxxvi. 8vo, pp. 31. 8 Engravings. P. 18345

[Dalrymple (*Sir* John).] The Address of the People of Great Britain to the Inhabitants of America. *London: T. Cadell.* mdcclxxv. 8vo, Title, pp. 60. 18346

"This address is said to have been written by Sir John Dalrymple, and printed at the public expense, to be distributed in America, where the greatest part of a large impression has been sent, apparently to coöperate with a late conciliatory resolution of the House of Commons." — *Monthly Review.* "By that Sophistical perverter of the Truth, Sir J. Dalrymple." — MS. note on the title of Bernard Romans' copy. *See* Rich, Vol. i.

[Dalrymple.] The Rights of Great Britain Asserted against the Claims of America: being an Answer to the Declaration of the General Congress. *London: T. Cadell.* mdcclxxvi. 8vo, pp. 92. + *Philadelphia: R. Bell.* mdcclxxvi. 8vo, pp. 92. J.C.B. + The Second Edition, with Additions. [*Ibid.*] + The Third Edition, with Additions. *London: T. Cadell.* mdcc-lxxvi. 8vo, pp. 96. + The Fourth Edition, with Additions. [*Ibid.*] + The Fifth Edition, with Additions. [*Ibid.*] + Sixth Edition, with Additions. *Edinburgh.* 1776. 8vo. + Seventh Edition. *London: T. Cadell.* m dcc lxxvii. + The Eighth Edition. To which is now added, a Refutation of Dr. Price's Statement of the National Debt. *London: T. Cadell.* m dcc-lxxvi. 8vo, pp. 123. + The Ninth Edition. To which is now added, a Further Refutation of Dr. Price's State of the National Debt. *London: Printed for T. Cadell.* m dcc lxxvi. 8vo, pp. 131. 18347

"This celebrated performance is said to have been written, printed, and liberally distributed both in Great Britain and America, at the instance and expense of government; but whether this be true or not, the work itself, we are afraid, will answer no other purpose than to exasperate the people of Great Britain against their brethren of America; and, by inflaming misrepresentations and invectives, aggravate the evils of our present civil discord." — *Monthly Review.* Also ascribed to James Macpherson, translator of Ossian. *See also* Rich, Vol. i.

[Dalrymple.] Les droits de la Grande-Bretagne établis contre les prétentions des Américains, Traduite de l'anglais par A. F. J. Fréville. 1776. 18348

Also: Address to, and Expostulation with the Public. ... *London.* 1784. 8vo, pp. 48. — An Attempt to balance the Income and Expenditure of the State: ... *London.* 1783. 8vo, pp. 19. — Memoirs of Great Britain and Ireland, from the Dissolution of the last Parliament of Charles ii., till the Capture of the French and Spanish Fleets at Vigo. *London.* 1771, 1773. 3 vols., 4to. + *Edinburgh.* 1788. 3 vols., 4to. C. + Fourth Edition. *Dublin.* 1773. 8vo. + New Edition. *London: J. Strahan.* 1790. 3 vols., 8vo. — The State of the National Debt, the National Income, and the National Expenditure. With ... Reflections applicable to the present dangerous Crisis. By John Earl of Stair. ... *Edinburgh: John Wood.* m,dcc,lxxvii. 8vo, pp. 21. H. + Fourth Edition. *London.* 1776. Folio. H. — State of the Public Debts, and of the Annual Interest and Benefits paid for them ... *London.* 1783. 8vo, pp. 49. + Second Edition. *London.* 1783. 8vo, pp. 45. — Three Letters from Sir John Dalrymple, Bart, ... to the Right Honourable Lord Viscount Barrington, Late Secretary at War, On his Lordship's official Conduct. *London.* mdcclxxviii. + The Second Edition. To which is Added A Fourth Letter, ... *London: J. P. Coghlan.* mdcclxxix. 12mo, pp. 70. BA. The "Reply to Lieut.-Gen. Burgoyne's Letter" has also been attributed to Dalrymple. *See also* "A Bill," etc., Vol. ii., No. 5378.

Dalton (E. B.) State of New York. Report of Ed. B. Dalton, m.d. Sanitary Superintendent of the Metropolitan Board of Health, 1866. *Albany: Printing House of C. Van Benthuysen & Sons.* 1867. 8vo, pp. 36. H. 18349

Dalton (H. G.) History of British Guiana; comprising a General Description of the Colony; A Narrative of some of the Principal Events from its Discovery to the Present Time; together with an Account of its Climate, Geology, Staple Products, and Natural History. By Henry G. Dalton, m.d. ... *London: Longman, Brown, Green, and Longmans.* 1855. 2 vols., 8vo, pp. xv, 518, slip; vii, 580. Map and 3 Plates. BA.

Also on large paper, royal 8vo.

Dalton (J.) Life and Actions of James Dalton, a noted Street Robber, ... with account of his running away with the ship when he was first transported, and likeways the tricks he played in New York, the Bermudas, Virginia, Carolina, and other parts of America, taken from his own mouth while in Newgate. [*London.* 1730.] 12mo. 18351

Dalton (W.) Travels in the United States of America, and Part of Upper Canada. By William Dalton. *Appleby: W. Dalton.* 1821. 12mo, 3 l., pp. 256. C. 18352

Dalwig (J. C.) Florida als Auswanderung-Kolonie für Deutschland und die Schweitz. *St. Gallen: Scheitlin und Zollikofer.* 1845. 8vo. 18353

Daly (Augustin). A Legend of "Norwood;" or, Village Life in New England. An Original Dramatic Comedy of American Life. Founded on a Novel by the Rev. H. W. Beecher. *New York: Author.* 1867. 8vo, 79 l. C. 18354

Daly (C. P.) Are the Southern Privateersmen Pirates? Letter to the Hon. Ira Harris, ... By Charles P. Daly, ... *New-York: James B. Kerker.* 1862. 8vo, pp. 13. 18355

Daly. Historical Sketch of the Judicial Tribunals of New York, from 1623 to 1846. By Charles P. Daly. *New York.* 1855. 8vo, pp. 68. N. 18356

Daly. Naturalization. ... By Charles P. Daly ... . *New York: John F. Trow, Printer.* 1860. 8vo, pp. 48. H. 1835[illegible]

Daly. The Nature, Extent and History of the Jurisdiction of the Surrogate's Court of the State of New York. Opinion of the Hon. Charles P. Daly, ... in the Matter of Joseph W. Brick, deceased. Printed by Order of the Board of Supervisors. *New York: Bloom & Smith.* 1863. 8vo, pp. 52. BA. 18358

Also: Annual Address ... before the American Geographical and Statistical Society, January 25, 1870. *New York: C. S. Westcott & Co., Printers.* 1870. 8vo, pp. 46. H. — Origin and History of Institutions for the Promotion of the Useful Arts. Discourse ... at the Thirty-fifth Anniversary of the American Institute ... New York ... on the 11th of November, 1863. ... . *Albany.* 1864. 8vo, pp. 35. H. — When was the Drama Introduced in America? An Historical Inquiry, anterior to Dunlap's History of the American Theatre. ... *New York: W. C. Bryant & Co., Printers.* 8vo, pp. 12. S.

Dalzell (J. M.) John Gray, of Mount Vernon; the Last Soldier of the Revolution. Born near Mount Vernon, Va., January 6, 1764; Died at Hiramsburg, Ohio, March 29, 1868. Aged 104 Years. By J. M. Dalzell. *Washington: Gibson Brothers, Printers.* 1868. 8vo, pp. 64. 18359

Damariscotta, *Maine.* Minutes of the Thirteenth Anniversary of the Damariscotta Baptist Association. September 5 and 6, 1855. ... *Portland: Foster & Co.* 1855. pp. 15. H.

Damas (*M.* de). Pièces justificatives sur l'affaire de la Martinique, qui constatent la conduite patriotique de M. de Damas, Gouverneur-Général de cette colonie. 1791. 8vo.

Damaschka (Wilhelm Fr.) Die Entdeckung von Amerika. Christoph Columbus. Neu bearbeitet. Mit Bildern. Herausgegeben von Fr. Ed. Sandtner. *Prag: Sandtner.* 1842. 16mo.

Dambourgès (Francois). Le Colonel Dambourgès. Etude historique Canadienne. *Québec.* 1865. 8vo, pp. 58. 18363

Damon (D.) A Sermon ... before ... the Legislature of Massachusetts, at the Annual Election, January 6, 1841. By David Damon, ... *Boston: Dutton and Wentworth, Printers.* 1841. 8vo, pp. 34. H. 18364

Also: Address at Amesbury, Mass., Aug. 2, 1829, previous to the Organization of the Salisbury and Amesbury Society for the Promotion of Temperance ... . *Boston.* 1829. 8vo, pp. 24. — An Address delivered at the Consecration of the New Cemetery in West Cambridge, Mass., June 14th, 1843. ... . *Somerville: Edmund Tufts.* 1842. 12mo, pp. 12. H. — A Sermon, delivered at Lunenburg, December 2, 1827, by David Damon, at the Close of his Ministry in that Town. *Lancaster.* 1828. 8vo, pp. 22. M. — A Sermon preached at Concord, Massachusetts, May 15, 1823, at the ... Meeting of the "Evangelical Missionary Society in Massachusetts." *Boston.* 1823. 8vo, pp. 10.

Damon (J. W.) The Havana Ice-House Controversy: ... in regard to Transactions between Frederic Tudor and John W. Damon. *Boston.* 1846. 8vo, pp. 270. H. 18365

Damon (N.) Hints for Buncombe. A Sermon delivered ... Billerica, Mass., July 4, 1858. By Norwood Damon. ... *Boston: Crosby, Nichols & Co.* m dccc lviii. 12mo, pp. 21. H.

Damon. The Holy Voice. A Discourse, delivered ... in West Cambridge, Mass. ... May 14, 1841, the Day of the National Fast, appointed in consequence of the Death of William Henry Harrison, President of the United States. By Norwood Damon. *Boston: Charles C. Little and James Brown.* 1841. 8vo, pp. 16. H. 18367

Also: Haying Hayed. A Discourse delivered ... in Sudbury, Mass. July Twenty-six, m.dccc.xl. ... *Boston: Charles C. Little and James Brown.* 1840. 12mo, pp. 12. H. — Remarks on the Importance of Obedience to Law ... . Delivered ... December 30, 1839. ... *Boston: Charles C. Little and James Brown.* 1840. 8vo, pp. 16. H.

Damon (S. C.) History of Holden, Massachusetts, 1667–1841. By Samuel C. Damon. *Worcester.* 1841. 8vo, pp. viii, 155, (1). B., H., P. 18368

Damon. An Historical Address delivered at Holden, Mass., May 4, 1841, the first Centennial Celebration of the Municipal Organization of the Town; with Notes and an Appendix. By Samuel C. Damon. *Worcester.* 1841. 8vo, pp. 155. 18369

Also: Puritan Missions in the Pacific: A Discourse, delivered at Honolulu, (S. I.,) ... June 17, 1866. By Rev. Samuel C. Damon. Second American Edition. *New Haven: printed by Tuttle, Morehouse & Taylor.* 1868. 12mo, pp. 48, (1). H.

Damotte (C.) Solution mexicaine. ... Par C. Damotte. *Tonnerre: impr. Hérisé.* 1864. 8vo, pp. 16. 18370

Damour (A.) Note sur l'Argent jodé du Chili, par M. A. Damour. [n. p. n. d.] 8vo, pp. 22. 18371

Dampier (T.) Sermon before the Incorporated Society for the Propagation of the Gospel in Foreign Parts, February 21, 1806. By Thomas, Lord Bishop of Rochester. *London.* 1806. 8vo, pp. 72. J.C.B., M. 18372

Dampier (W.) A Collection of Voyages. In Four Volumes. Containing i. Captain William Dampier's Voyages round the World: Describing particularly, the Coasts and Islands in the East and West Indies. The South-Sea Coasts of Chili, Peru and Mexico. The Countries of Tonquin, Achin and Malacca.

The Cape of Good Hope, New-Holland, &c. ii. The Voyages of Lionel Wafer; Giving an Account of his being left on the Isthmus of America, amongst the Indians, and of their Treatment of him; with a particular Description of the Country, &c. Also The natural History of those Parts. By a Fellow of the Royal Society. And Davis's Expedition to the Golden Mines. iii. A Voyage round the World: Containing an Account of Capt. Dampier's Expedition into the South-Seas in the Ship St. George. With his Various Adventures and Engagements, &c. together with a Voyage from the West Coast of Mexico to East-India. By W. Funnell, Mate of Capt. Dampier. iv. Capt. Cowley's Voyage round the Globe. v. Capt. Sharp's Journey over the Isthmus of Darien, and Expedition into the South Seas. vi. Capt. Wood's Voyage through the Streights of Magellan. vii. Mr. Roberts's Adventures and Sufferings amongst the Corsairs of the Levant: His Description of the Archipelago Islands, &c. Illustrated with Maps and Draughts: Also several Birds, Fishes, and Plants, not found in this part of the World: Curiously Engraven on Copper-Plates. *London: Printed for James and John Knapton, at the Crown in St. Paul's Churchyard.* Mdccxxix. 4 vols., 8vo, 5 l., pp. vi, 550, Books, 2 l.; 4 l., pp. 184, 132, 112, Index, 38 l.; 8 l., pp. 463, (13); 8 l., pp. 208, 175, (9). Maps and Plates. H. 18373

"This is generally considered the best edition of Dampier's voyages, though it contains much that Dampier not only had no hand in writing, but against which he protested. The truth appears to be that he was at the mercy of his publisher, Knapton, who used Dampier's saleable volumes as mules for carrying off his unsaleable stock. Vols. i. and ii. of this edition are reprints of the earlier editions, page for page, and with the same plates and maps, except that in the first volume, the publisher has suppressed Dampier's Dedication to Charles Mountague, President of the Royal Society, to make room for a second title, 'A New Voyage round the World,' etc. 'The Seventh Edition Corrected,' which here occupies A 2. Vol. iii. is a reprint of Dampier's third volume, described below (No. 18376), but in a broader page, and paged continuously. It has eight preliminary leaves, and the text is paged 1 to 260, including the index. The plates are the same as in the previous editions. Beyond this Dampier had nothing to do with the work. The remaining half of this third volume consists of a reprint of Wafer's voyage, which is here called The Third Edition. It contains title and pp. 263 to 463, followed by 9 pp. of index. The map and the three plates are the same as in the first and second editions, published also by Knapton in 1699 and 1704. Vol. iv. contains Funnell's voyage, exactly as described, *infra*, with a new title, thus working in bodily the remainder of the edition of 1707, against which Dampier protested. To this are added reprints of Cowley's, Sharp's, Wood's, and Roberts' voyages, filling 175 pp. and 6 pp. of index, with 5 maps. In some copies, however, Funnell's voyage is reprinted with the same maps and plates, but in a closer type, it being in 8 p. l., 208 pp. of text, with 8 pp. of index. With these facts in view, it seems to the writer that it is better to have Dampier undefiled, and therefore the best editions of Dampier are his three volumes as originally published. Then let the other works by Funnell, Wafer, Sharp, etc., stand on their own merits, in their own editions, under their own names." — Stevens.

Dampier. A New Voyage round the World. Describing particularly, The Isthmus of America, several Coasts and Islands in the West Indies, the Isles of Cape Verde, the Passage by Terra del Fuego, the South Sea Coasts of Chili, Peru, and Mexico; the Isle of Guam one of the Ladrones, Mindanas, and other Philippine and East India Islands near Cambodia, China, Formosa, Luconia, Celebes, &c. New Holland, Sumatra, Nicobar Isles; the Cape of Good Hope, and Santa Hellena. Their Soils, Rivers, Harbours, Plants, Fruits, Animals, and Inhabitants. Their Customs, Religion, Government, Trade, &c. By William Dampier. Illustrated with Particular Maps and Draughts. *London: James Knapton.* mdcxcvii. 8vo, 4 l., pp. vi, 550, 2 l. 5 Maps. + The Second Edition Corrected. *London:* [*Ibid.*] mdcxcvii. 8vo. + The Third Edition Corrected. *London:* [*Ibid.*] mdcxcviii. 8vo. + The Fourth Edition Corrected. *London:* [*Ibid.*] mdcxcix. 8vo. + The Fifth Edition Corrected. *London:* [*Ibid.*] 1703. 8vo. + The Sixth Edition Corrected. *London:* [*Ibid.*] 1717. 8vo. + The Seventh Edition, Corrected. *London: James and John Knapton.* m dcc-xxix. 8vo, 4 l., pp. vi, 550, Books, 2 l. 18374

The collation of all these editions is the same. In the second, the errata of the first is omitted, because the errors were corrected. The other editions are verbal reprints.

Dampier. Voyages and Descriptions. Vol. ii. In Three Parts, viz. 1. A Supplement of the Voyage round the World, Describing the Countreys of Tonquin, Achin, Malacca, &c. their Product, Inhabitants, Manners, Trade, Policy, &c. 2. Two Voyages to Campeachy; with a Description of the Coasts, Product, Inhabitants, Logwood-Cutting, Trade, &c. of Jucatan, Campeachy, New Spain, &c. 3. A Discourse of Trade-Winds, Breezes, Storms, Seasons of the Year, Tides and Currents of the Torrid Zone throughout the World: With an Account of Natal in Africk, its Product, Negroe's &c. By Captain William Dampier. Illustrated with Particular Maps and Draughts. To which is Added, A General Index to both Volumes. *London: James Knapton.* mdcxcix. 8vo, 4 l., pp. 184, 132, 112, Index, etc., 38 l. + Second Edition. *London:* [*Ibid.*] mdcc. 8vo. + The Third Edition. *London:* [*Ibid.*] mdccv. 8vo. + [Another Edition.] *London: James and John Knapton.* M dcc xxix. 8vo. 18375

These editions are alike, except that the errata is corrected in the second.

Dampier. A Voyage to New Holland, &c. In the Year,

1699. Wherein are described, The Canary-Islands, the Isles of Mayo and St. Jago. The Bay of All Saints, with the Forts and Town of Bahia in Brasil. Cape Salvadore. The Winds on the Brasilian Coast. Abrohlo-Shoals. A Table of all the Variations observ'd in this Voyage. Occurrences near the Cape of Good Hope. The Course to New Holland. Shark's Bay. The Isles and Coast, &c. of New Holland. Their Inhabitants, Manners, Customs, Trade, &c. Their Harbours, Soil, Beasts, Birds, Fish, &c. Trees, Plants, Fruits, &c. Illustrated with several Maps and Draughts; also divers Birds, Fishes, and Plants, not found in this part of the World, Curiously Ingraven on Copper-Plates. Vol. III. By Captain William Dampier. *London: Printed for James Knapton, at the Crown in St. Paul's Church-yard.* 1703. 8vo, 12 l., pp. 162, (9), 8 l., pp. 198, (8). + The Second Edition. *London:* [*Ibid.*] 1709. + The Third Edition. *London: James and John Knapton.* MDCCXXIX. 8vo, 2 l., pp. 463, (13). M. 18376

A second part was added, with the title as below:

DAMPIER. A Continuation of a Voyage to New Holland, &c. In the Year 1699. Wherein is described, the Islands Timor, Rotee and Anabao. A passage between the Islands Timor and Anabao. Copang and Laphao Bays. The Islands Omba, Fetter, Bande, and Bird. A Description of the Coast of New-Guinea. The Islands Pulo Sabuda, Cockle, King William's, Providence, Garret Dennis, Ant. Cave's and St. John's. Also a new Passage between N. Guinea and Nova Britannia. The Islands Ceram, Bonao, Buoro, and several Islands before unknown. The Coast of Java, and Streights of Sunda. Author's arrival at Batavia, Cape of Good Hope, St. Helens, I. Ascension, &c. Their Inhabitants, Customs, Trade, &c. Harbours, Soil, Birds, Fish, &c. Trees, Plants, Fruits, &c. Illustrated with Maps and Draughts: Also divers Birds, Fishes, &c. not found in this part of the World, Ingraven on Eighteen Copper-Plates. By Captain William Dampier. *London: James Knapton.* 1709. 8vo, 8 l., pp. 198, (8). S. 18377

DAMPIER. Capt. Dampier's | Vindication | of his | Voyage | To the South-Seas in the Ship St. George. | With some small Observations for the Present on Mr. | Funnell's Chimerical Relation of the Voyage Round | the World; and Detected in Little, until he shall be | Examined more at Large. | [Colophon:] *London.* | [1707.] 4to, pp. 8, without a separate title. 18378

The date is erroneously printed 2707. "In this vindication, which does not occupy more than a single sheet, Dampier points out several misrepresentations made by Funnell, and accuses him of having pirated from charts and papers with which he had been intrusted, but of which Dampier says, he afterwards rendered a very slender account, pretending that some of them were lost." — BURNEY.

DAMPIER. The Voyages and Adventures of Capt. William Dampier. Wherein are Described the Inhabitants, Manners, Customs, Trade, Harbours, Soil, Animals, Vegetables, &c. of the principal Countries, Islands, &c. of Asia, Africa, and America. *London: Printed in the Year* M,DCC,LXXVII. 2 vols., 8vo, pp. 454; 396. J.C.B. 18379

The editor remarks: "The first edition of Dampier's voyages was published by himself, but not in the same order they were performed, which has a little perplexed the narrative; the language is now partly become obsolete, which renders the perusal more difficult to common readers; and the edition is now also extremely scarce. To remedy these inconveniences, the chronological order wherein the series of events happened is observed in this edition."

DAMPIER. The Voyages and Discoveries of Capt. William Dampier in the South Seas and round the World. Wherein he gives a particular account of the different places he discovered. *London: Printed in the year* MDCCXC. 2 vols., 12mo, pp. 276; 117. J.C.B. 18380

DAMPIER. Nouveau | voyage | autour du monde, | Où l'on décrit en particulier les Isthmes de l'Amerique, | plusieurs Côtes & Isles des Indes Occidentales, les Isles | du Cap Verd, le Passage par la terre del Fuego, | les Côtes Meridionales du Chili, du Perou, & de | Mexique; l'Isle de Guam Mindanao, & les autres Phi- | lippines, les Isles Orientales qui sont prés de Cam- | boye; & del a Chine; Formosa, Luçonie, Colebes, &c. | la Nouvelle Hollande, les Isles de Sumatra & Nicobar, & | de Sainte Helene & le Cap de bonne Esperance. | Où l'on traite des differens Terroirs de tous ces Pais, de | leurs Ports, des Plantes, des Fruits, & des Animaux | qu'on y trouve: de leurs Habitans, de leurs Coûtumes, de | leur Religion, de leur Gouvernement, de leur Negoce, &c. | Par Guillaume Dampier. | Enrichi de Cartes & de figures, | ... | *Amsterdam:* | *Paul Marret.* | M. DC. XCVIII. | 2 vols., 12mo.

A second edition appeared the same year, also in two volumes. The third volume was subsequently issued, with the following title: "Suplement du Voyage autour du Monde, ... Enrichi de Cartes & de Figures en Taille-douce. ... Par Guillaume Dampier. *Amsterdam: Paul Marret.* M DCC XI." 12mo, 27 l., pp. 20, 351. The fourth is entitled: "Voyage de Guillaume Dampier, aux terres Australes. A la Nouvelle Hollande, &c. fait en 1699. Où l'on trouve la Description des Isles Canaries, des Isles de Mayo & de S. Jago; de la Baye de Tous les Saints, des Forts & de la Ville de Bahia dans le Bresil, &c. Avec le Voyage de Lionel Wafer, Où l'on trouve la Description de l'Isthme de Darien dans l'Amerique, &c. Tome IV. Enrichi de Cartes & de Figures. *A Amsterdam.* ... *Paul Marret* ... . M DCC XI." 12mo, pp. 274, 14.

DAMPIER. Nouveau Voyage. [As before.] *Paris.* 1701–'5. 4 vols., 12mo. + *Amsterdam.* 1701. 4 vols., 12mo. + *Amsterdam.* 1705–12. 4 vols., 12mo. + *Amsterdam.* 1711. 4 vols., 12mo. + *Rouen: E. Herault.* 1715. 5 vols., 12mo, 5 l., pp. 408, 12 l.; 1 l., pp. 396, 5 l.; 3 l., pp. 393, 5 l.; pp. 20, 381, 7 l.; 1 l., pp. 363, 12 l. 45 Plates and Maps, and Engraved Title-Pages. + *Amsterdam: Paul Marret.* M.DCC.XVII. 5 vols., 12mo, 7 l., pp. 408, 12 l.; Engraved Title, 7 l., pp. 396, 5 l.; 4 l., pp. 393, 10; 10 l., pp. 309, (15); 2 l., pp. 363, 23, 1 l. Maps and Plates. + *Amsterdam.* 1723. 5 vols., 12mo. 18382

DAMPIER. Nouveau | Voyage | autour | du Monde | Où l'on décrit en particulier l'Istme de l'Ameri- | que, plusieurs Côtes & Isles des Indes Occiden- | tales, les Isles du Cap Verd, le passage par la | Terre del Fuego, les Côtes Meridionales de Chi- | li, du Perou, & du Mexique; l'Isle de Guam, | Mindanao, & des autres Philippines; les Isles | Orientales qui sont prés de Cambodie, de la | Chine, Formosa, Luçon, Celebes, &c. la Nou- | velle Hollande, les Isles de Sumatra, de Nicobar, | de sainte Helene, & le Cap de Bonne Esperance. | Où l'on traite des differens Terroirs de tout ces Païs, de | leur Ports, des Plantes, des Fruits, & des animaux | qu'on y trouve: De leur Habitans, de leurs Coûtu- | mes, de leur Religion, de leur Gouvernement, de leur | Négoce, &c. | Par Guillaume Dampier. | Enrichi de Cartes & Figures. | *A Rouen,* | *Chez Jean-Baptiste Machuel, ruë Etoupee.* | M.DCC.XXIII. | Avec Aprobation & Privilege du Roi. | 5 vols., 12mo. + *Rouen.* 1723. 8vo. 18383

A reprint of the edition of 1715, with the same plates and collation. The following piece sometimes occurs separate, as a treatise, but is included in the five vols.:

DAMPIER. Traité | des | vents | alisez | ou reglez, | des | vents Frais | De Mer & de Terre, | des Tempêtes, | des Saisons de l'Année, des | Marées, & des Courans | De toute la Zone Torride. | Par le S[r]. Dampier, | Capitaine sur Mer. | *A Amsterdam:* | *Paul Marret.* | ... 1701. | Sm. 8vo, pp. 104. 18384

DAMPIER. Nieuwe Reystogt | rondom de | Werreld, | waarin omstandiglyk beschreeven worden | De Land-engte van Amerika, verscheydene Kusten | en Eylanden in Westindie, de eylanden van Kabo Verde, de door- | togt van de Straat Le Maire na de Zuydzee, de kusten van Chili, | Peru, Mexiko; 't eyland Guam een van de Ladrones, 't eyland Min- | danao een van de Filippines; en de Oostindische eylanden ontrent Kam- | bodia, Cina,

Formosa, Lukonia, Celebes, enz. voorts Nieuw | Holland, Sumatra. de eylanden van Nikobar, de Kaap van Goede | Hoop, en 'teyland Sante Helena. | Mitsgaders | Derzelver Landsbouw, Rivieren, Havens, Gewassen, Vruchten, | Gedierten, en Inwooners, beneffens hunne Gewoonten, | Godsdienst, Regeering, Handel, enz. | In 't Engelsch beschreeven door | William Dampier, | en daaruyt vertaald door | W. Sewel. | Met naauwkeurige Landkaarten, en kopere Plaaten vercierd. | *In's Gravenhage,* | *By Abraham de Hondt, Boekverkooper op de* | *Zaal* | *van't Hof, in de Fortuyn.* 1698. | 4to, 2 Titles, 3 l., pp. 395, 11 l. 4 Maps. + Tweede Deel | van | William Dampiers | reystogt | rondom de | Werreld | · *In's Gravenhage.* | *By Abraham de Hondt, Boekverkooper op de Zaal* | *van 't Hof, in de Fortuyn.* 1700. | 2 Titles, 6 l., pp. 284, 4 l. 5 Maps. + Nieuwe reystogt | en | beschryving | van de | land-engte | van | Amerika, | *In 's Gravenhage,* | *By Abraham de Hondt, Boekverkooper op de* | *Zaal van't Hof, in de Fortuyn* 1700. | 4to, pp. 88. Map. 18385

DAMPIER. Nieuwe Reize naar de Zuidzee gedaan onder het beleyt van William Dampier, int Engelsch beschreven door Woodes Rogers, vertaald door A. P. *Amsterdam.* 1715. 4to.

DAMPIER. Nieuwe Reistogt rondom de Wereld, waarin omstandiglyk beschreeven worden de Land-Engte van America, verscheidene Kusten en Eilanden in West-Indiën, de Eilanden van Cabo Verde, de doortogt van de Straat Le Maire na de Zuid-Zee, etc. *Nymegen.* 1771–72. 4 pts., 4to. 43 Maps and Plates. 18387

DAMPIER. Reystogten rondom de Waereldt; Begrypende, in vier beknopte Boekdeelen, een naauwkeurige Beschryving van verscheyde Nieuwe ontdekte Zeën, Kusten en Landen, zo in Amerika, Asia, als Afrika ... . Uyt het Engelsch in 't Nederduyts overgebragt, door W. Sewel. *Amsterdam: J. Ratelband & A. van Damme.* 1717. 4 pts., 4to. C. 18388

Some copies of Part I. are dated 1716.

DAMPIER. Neue Reise um die Welt worinnen umständlich beschrieben wird: Die Erd-Enge oder Isthmus von America, vielerley Kusten und Insuln in West-Indien die Insuln des grünen Vorgebürges die Durchfahrt an dem Lande del Fuego, die Mittagigen Kusten von Chili, Peru, und Mexico: die Insuln Guam, Mindanao, und andere von dem Philippinen; die ostlichen nahe an Cambodia und China gelegenen insonderheit

Formosa, Lusson, Celebes, &c. Neu Holland die Insuln Sumatra, Nicobar, und S. Helena, wie auch das Vorgebürge der guten Hoffnung. *Leipzig: Verlegets Michael Rohrlachs sel. Wittib und Erben.* 1702. 4 vols., 8vo, 6 l., pp. 1004, 35 l.; 6 l., pp. 788, 27 l.; 14 l., pp. 421, 12 l.; 2 l., pp. 480, 50 l., 2 l. 42 Maps and Plates, and Engraved Title-Pages. J.C.B. 18389

DAMPIER. Dampiers Reise um die Welt. Ein Lesebuch für Kinder und junge Leute. *Celle: Kunge und Richter.* 1783. 3 vols., 12mo, pp. 142; 64; 64. J.C.B. 18390

"It is not easy," says Dr. Burney, "to name another voyager and traveller who has given more useful information to the world; to whom the merchant and mariner are so much indebted, or who has communicated his information in a more unembarrassed and intelligible manner. And this he has done in a style perfectly unassuming, equally free from affectation and from the most distant appearance of invention." — *Hist. of Voyages and Dis. in the South Sea,* IV. 486.

DAMRELL (W. S.) Kansas Contested Election. Speech of Hon. W. S. Damrell, of Massachusetts, in the House of Representatives, March 18, 1856. On the Resolution reported from the Committee of Elections, in the Contested Election Case from the Territory of Kansas. [n. p. n. d.] 8vo, pp. 8.

Also: Assault on Mr. Sumner. Speech ... July 12, 1856. *Washington, D. C.* 1856. 8vo, pp. 8. H.

Dan to Beersheba; or, Northern and Southern Friends. *London: Chapman and Hall.* 1864. Post 8vo, pp. iv, 336. C.

DANA (A. G.) In Memoriam. *Cambridge, Mass.* 1863. 12mo. 18393

DANA [(Amasa)]. Speech of Mr. Dana, of New York, on the Post Office Bill: delivered in the House ... February 25, 1845. *Washington.* 1845. 8vo, pp. 6. H. 18394

DANA. Speech of Mr. Dana, of New York, on the Bill making Appropriations for the Military Academy at West Point. Delivered in the House ... March 6, 1844. *Washington.* 1844. 8vo, pp. 6. H. 18395

DANA (C. A.) The United States illustrated; in Views of City and Country. With Descriptive and Historical Articles, edited by Charles A. Dana. *New York: Herrmann J. Meyer.* [n. d.] 4to. 36 Plates. H. 18396

DANA (C. A.), *and* WILSON (J. H.) The Life of Ulysses S. Grant, General of the Armies of the United States. By Charles A. Dana and J. H. Wilson. *Springfield: Gurdon Bill & Co.* 1868. 8vo, pp. xvi, 424, 9. Portrait and 4 Maps. B. 18397

DANA (C. W.) The Great West, or the Garden of the World; Its History, its Wealth; its Natural Advantages, and its Future, also comprising a Complete Guide to Emigrants, with a full description of the different routes Westward. By C. W. Dana. *Boston: Thayer & Eldridge.* 1861. 12mo, pp. 396. Map. 18398

DANA. The Connection between Moral and Intellectual Improvement. Address delivered ... [before] the Φ Β Κ Society, Dartmouth College, Aug. 26, 1817. *Exeter.* 1817. 8vo, pp. 20. 18399

DANA (D.) A Discourse at the Interment of Rev. John Boddily, ... By Daniel Dana. *Newburyport: Allen & Barnard.* M.DCCC.II. 8vo, pp. 22. B. 18400

DANA. A Discourse delivered ... in Newburyport ... Nov. 19, 1844, it being the Fiftieth Anniversary of the Author's Ordination. By Daniel Dana, D.D. ... . *Newburyport: published by John G. Tilton.* 1845. 8vo, pp. 32. BA., H., W. 18401

DANA. A Discourse on the Character and Virtues of General George Washington: delivered on the Twenty-second of February, 1800 ... . By Daniel Dana ... of ... Newburyport. ... *Newburyport: Press of Angier March.* [n. d.] 8vo, pp. 31.

DANA. Sermon, November 26, 1812. The Day of Thanksgiving in Massachusetts ... *Newburyport* 1813. 8vo. B.

DANA. A Sermon preached Dec. 30. 1819, at the Dedication of the House of Worship of the First Church in Dedham. By Daniel Dana, D.D. ... . Second Edition. *Dedham: Printed by H. & W. H. Mann.* [n. d.] 8vo, pp. 16. BA. 18404

DANA. A Sermon delivered at the Annual Election on Wednesday, January 4, 1837, before ... the Legislature of Massachusetts. By Daniel Dana, D.D. ... *Boston: Dutton and Wentworth, Printers.* 1837. 8vo, pp. 44. B., H. 18405

Also: An Address to the Members of the Merrimack Humane Society ... Newburyport, September 7th, 1813. ... *Exeter: printed by Charles Norris & Co.* 1813. 8vo, pp. 20. H. — Address on Sacred Music at Hampton, N. H., 6 Oct. 1813. *Exeter.* 8vo. W. — The Character &c. of the Perfect and Upright. Sermon delivered March 7, 1802, on the Death of Benj. Moody. *Newburyport.* 1802. 8vo, pp. 23. — A Discourse delivered in Newburyport, July 4, 1814, ... *Newburyport: Printed by William B. Allen & Co.* 1814. 8vo, pp. 20. BA. — Discourse before the New Hampshire Colonization Society, June 2, 1825. ... *Concord.* 1825. 8vo. — A Discourse, delivered Nov. 23, 1794. The First Sabbath after his Ordination. ... *Newburyport: John Mycall.* [n. d.] 8vo, pp. 39. H. — The Duty and Reward of loving our Country, and seeking its Prosperity. A Discourse delivered in two parts, at the National Fast, April 25th, 1799. ... *Boston: Printed by Manning and Loring.* 1799. 8vo,

pp. 41. BA. — Evangelical preaching ... A Sermon ... November 2, 1825, at the Ordination of the Rev. William K. Talbot ... in Nottingham-West. By Daniel Dana, D.D. ... of .. Londonderry. *Concord, N. H.: printed by Isaac Hill.* 1826. 8vo, pp. 28. H. — A Farewell Sermon addressed to the First Presbyterian Church and Society in Newburyport, November 19, 1820. ... *Newburyport: printed by W. & J. Gilman.* 1820. 8vo, pp. 20. H. — The Importance of a Purified Literature. An Address delivered at the Anniversary of the Associated Alumni of Dartmouth College, August, 1833. ... *Boston: printed by Perkins & Marvin.* 1834. 8vo, pp. 24. H. — The Importance of Virtue and Piety as Qualifications of Rulers: A Discourse delivered March 31, 1805. ... *Newburyport: Printed by Edmund M. Blunt.* 1805. 8vo, pp. 27. BA. — Memoirs of Eminently Pious Women ... Abridged from the large Work of Dr. Gibbons, London. *Newburyport.* 1803. 12mo. — Ministerial Fidelity. Sermon ... at the Ordination of ... Daniel Fitz ... in Ipswich, June 28, 1826. *Newburyport.* 1826. 8vo, pp. 36. — Ministerial Firmness. A Sermon preached at the Installation of the Rev. John M. C. Bartley, As Pastor ... in Hempstead, N. H., October 12, 1836. ... *Newburyport: Press of Hiram Tozer.* 1836. 8vo, pp. 22. — New Hampshire Election Sermon. *Concord.* 1823. 8vo. W. — Objections against the Gospel Refuted. A Sermon ... March 4, 1829, at the Installation of the Rev. John Brown, D.D. ... Boston. ... *Boston: T. R. Marvin, Printer.* 1829. 8vo, pp. 24. H. — Oration at Newburyport, Mass., July 4, 1814. ... W. — A Remonstrance addressed to the Trustees of Phillips Academy, on the State of the Theological Seminary under their care, Sept., 1849. ... *Boston: Crocker & Brewster.* 1853. 8vo, pp. 24. BA., H. — A Sermon occasioned by the Death of Mr. William Combs, and delivered June 12, 1814. ... *Newburyport: Edward Little & Co.* 1814. 8vo, pp. 27. B., H. — A Sermon delivered before the Gloucester Female Society for Promoting Christian Knowledge, at their Anniversary ... [at Gloucester, Mass.] April 18, 1815. ... . *Newburyport: Printed by W. B. Allen & Co.* 1815. 8vo, pp. 20, (4). BA. — Sermon ... at Newburyport, before the Merrimack Bible Society. ... July 27, 1815. 8vo, pp. 21. B. — A Sermon ... at the Ordination of the Rev. Levi Hartshorn ... in Gloucester, Oct. 18, 1815. ... *Newburyport: printed by William B. Allen & Co.* 1815. 8vo, pp. 24. H. — A Sermon delivered at the Ordination of the Rev. Jacob Weed Eastman ... in Methuen, Dec. 13, 1815. ... of Newburyport. *Newburyport: printed by William B. Allen & Co.* 1815. 8vo, pp. 23. H. — A Sermon Preached in Boston, before the Massachusetts Society for Promoting Christian Knowledge, May 28, 1817. ... . *Andover: Printed by Flagg and Gould.* 1817. 8vo, pp. 59. BA. — A Sermon delivered at the Ordination of the Rev. Hervy Wilber ... in Wendell, Jan. 1, 1817. ... *Newburyport: printed by William Brown Allen & Co.* 1817. 8vo, pp. 23. H. — A Sermon ... at the Installation of the Rev. Henry Blatchford ... in Salem, Jan. 6, 1819. ... *Newburyport: printed by Ephraim W. Allen.* 1819. 8vo, pp. 20. H. — A Sermon preached December 30, 1819, at the ... First Church in Dedham. ... Second Edition. *Dedham: printed by H. & W. H. Mann.* [n. d.] 8vo, pp. 16. H. — Sermon on the Death of Levi Hartshorn. ... *Newburyport.* 1820. 8vo. W. — Sermon at the Ordination of William K. Talbot; ... *Concord, N. H.* 1826. 8vo. — Sermon at the Ordination of Daniel Fitz; ... *Newburyport.* 1826. 8vo. — Sermon at the Installation of John Brown, D.D. ... *Boston.* 1829. 8vo. — Sermon at the Ordination of John C. March ... *Newburyport.* 1832. 8vo. — A Sermon occasioned by the Death of Mrs. Hariot Putnam, ... delivered June 17, 1832. ... *Portsmouth: Printed by Miller & Brewster.* 1832. 8vo, pp. 23. B. — A Sermon in Commemoratiom of William Bartlet, Esquire, an Associate Founder of the Theological Seminary in Andover. Delivered ... April 19, 1841. By Daniel Dana, D.D. ... *Andover: printed by Gould, Newman and Saxton.* 1841. 8vo, pp. 36. BA., H. — Thanksgiving Sermon, Nov. 26, 1812, [at Newburyport, Mass.] *Newburyport: E. W. Allen.* 1812. 8vo, pp. 19. B., P. — Two Sermons, at Newburyport, Mass., March 24, 1799. ... *Newburyport.* 1800. 8vo. W. — Two Sermons ... April 25, 1799: the Day ... for National Humiliation, Fasting and Prayer. By Daniel Dana ... . *Newburyport.* MDCCXCIX. 8vo, pp. 56. H.

DANA (David D.) The Fireman: The Fire Departments of the United States, with a Full Account of all Large Fires ... . By D. D. Dana. Second Edition. *Boston.* 1828. 12mo, pp. 367. 18406

DANA (*Dr.*) A Review of Dr. Dana's Remonstrance, addressed to the Trustees of Phillips Academy, September 1849, on the State of the Theological Seminary under their Care. By a Layman. *Boston: Press of Crocker and Brewster.* 1853. 8vo.

DANA (E.) A Description of the Bounty Lands in the State of Illinois: also, the Principal Roads and Routes through the United States ... . By E. Dana. *Cincinnati: Looker, Reynolds & Co.* 1819. 12mo, pp. 108. C., H. 18407

DANA (E.) Geographical Sketches on the Western Country: designed for Emigrants and Settlers: being the Result of Extensive Researches and Remarks. To which is added, a Summary of all the most Interesting Matters on the Subject, including a Particular Description of the Unsold Public Lands ... . By E. Dana. *Cincinnati: Looker, Reynolds & Co.* 1819. 12mo, pp. 312. BA. 18408

[DANA (Eliza A.)] Gathered Leaves. *Cambridge: Private Edition.* 1864. 12mo, pp. viii, 160. 18409

Includes "Iona: An Indian Tragedy."

DANA (E.) Vindication of the Character of Mrs. Elizabeth Dana. By an Impartial Observer. *Newburyport, Mass.* 1806. 8vo. W. 18410

[DANA (Francis).] Letter of the Justices of the Supreme Judicial Court to His Excellency the Governor, with two Judiciary Bills drawn by them ... June, 1804. ... *Boston: Massachusetts, printed by Young and Minns.* 1804. 8vo, pp. 28. H.

DANA, FREEMAN (T.), *M.D., and* SAMUEL (L.), *M.D.* Outlines of the Mineralogy and Geology of Boston and its Vicinity. With a Geological Map. *Boston.* 1818. 8vo. 18412

DANA (J.) The African Slave Trade. A Discourse, delivered in the City of New Haven, Sept. 9, 1790, before the Connecticut Society for the Promotion of Freedom. By James Dana ... . *New Haven: printed by Thomas and Samuel Green.* M,DCC,XCI. 8vo, pp. 33. BA., P. 18413

DANA. A Century Discourse, Delivered at the Anniversary Meeting Of the Freemen of ... Wallingford, April 9, 1770. By James Dana ... Pastor of the First Church in said Town. *New-Haven: Printed by T. and S. Green.* 8vo, pp. 51. H.

DANA. The Character and Reward of the Good and Faithful Servant. A Sermon occasioned by the ... Death of Charles Whittelsey ... July 2d, 1764 ... . By James Dana ... of ... Wallingford. ... *Boston: Printed by Richard and Samuel Draper.* 1764. 8vo, pp. 30. H. 18415

DANA. A Discourse delivered at Kensington, (Con.) Dec. 1, 1774, on occasion of first Assembling ... in the New Church. By James Dana, D.D. ... . *New Haven: Printed by Thomas & Samuel Green.* M,DCC,LXXV. 8vo, pp. 31. BA. 18416

DANA. A Sermon preached before the General Assembly of the State of Connecticut, at Hartford, on the Day of the Anniversary Election, May 13, 1779. By James Dana, Pastor of the First Church in Wallingford. ... . *Hartford: Printed by Hudson and Goodwin.* M DCC LXXXX. 8vo, pp. 46, (1). W. 18417

DANA. Two Discourses: I. On the Commencement of a New Year. II. On the Completion of the Eighteenth Century; delivered in New Haven; ... Jan. 4th, ... 11th, 1801. By James Dana, D.D. ... *New Haven: William W. Morse.* 1801. 8vo, pp. 68. BA., C. 18418

DANA. The Wisdom of Observing the Footsteps of Providence. A Sermon preached at Weatherfield on the Annual Thanksgiving, November 28, 1805. By James Dana, D.D. *Hartford: Printed by Hudson & Goodwin.* 1805. 8vo, pp. 27.

Also: The Doctrine and Mission of Jesus Christ. A Sermon ... at Installation of Rev. Abiel Holmer ... Cambridge. ... Jany. 25, 1792. *Boston: Printed by Samuel Hall.* MDCCXCII. 8vo, pp. 35.—Discourse at New Haven, Oct. 20, 1790, at the Execution of Joseph Mountain, for Rape. ... *New Haven.* 1790. 8vo, pp. 28.—A Sermon Preached May 14, 1795, ... At the Interment of the Reverend Ezra Stiles, D.D., LL.D., President of Yale-College. ... *Printed at New Haven, by Thomas and Samuel Green.* [1795.] 8vo, pp. 37, (1).—Illustrations on Human Frailty and Vanity. A Discourse Occasioned by the ... Death of John Hall ... Son of Elihu Hall, Esq; Of Wallingford ... 1763. ... *New Haven: Printed by B. Mecom.* 1765. 12mo, pp. 34.—Letter to Scripturista; containing Remarks on this Answer to Paulinus, &c. and Three Questions more, relative to Mr. Dana. *Boston.* 1761. 8vo, pp. 24.—Men's Sins not Chargeable on God, but on themselves. A Discourse delivered at Wallingford, Dec. 22, 1782, on th Tragical Exit of William Beadle, his Wife and four Children. ... By James Dana D.D. ... *New Haven: Printed by T. & S. Green.* 4to, pp. 27.—The Pastoral Care. A Sermon Preached at Suffield, Conn., March 6, 1793, at Ordination of Rev. Ebenezer Gay, jun. ... *New Haven: Printed by T. & S. Green.* MDCCXCIII. 8vo, pp. 32.— ... A

Sermon Preached in the City of New-Haven, July 29, 1787. ... Funeral of the Reverend Chauncey Whittelsey, Pastor of the First Church in that City; ... *New-Haven: Printed by Daniel Bowen.* MDCCLXXXVII. 8vo, pp. 30—A Sermon, Preached April 29, 1789, at his Installation, ... New-Haven. ... *New-Haven: Printed by T. & S. Green.* M, DCC, LXXXIX. 8vo, pp. 43.—Sermon at the Installation of Rev. Abiel Holmes, at Cambridge, Mass. Jan. 25, 1792. ... *Boston.* MDCCXCII. 8vo, pp. 35.—A Sermon, preached, October 1, 1794, at the Ordination of the Rev. Elijah Waterman, to the Pastoral Care of the First Church and Society Windham, Connecticut. ... *Printed by John Byrne, in Windham.* M,DCC,XCIV. 8vo, pp. 25.—Christianity the Wisdom of Good. A Sermon preached October 17, 1798, at the Ordination of the Rev. Daniel Huntington to the Pastoral Care of the First Church and Society in Litchfield, Connecticut. ... *Litchfield: Printed by Thomas Collier.* 1799. 8vo, pp. 30. BA.—A Sermon on the much-lamented death of Mr. Eben'r Grant Marsh, Tutor in Yale College, who died Nov. 16, 1803, in the 27th year of his age. ... By James Dana, D.D. *Hartford: Printed by Hudson & Goodwin.* 1803. 8vo, pp. 24. BA.—Sermon before the Merrimac Humane Society, 4th Sept. 1804. ... *Newburyport.* 8vo.—There is no Reason to be ashamed of the Gospel. A Sermon preached at East Hartford, Dec. 23, 1801, at the Ordination of Rev. Andrew Yates, as Colleague-pastor with the Rev. Eliphalet Williams, D.D. ... *Hartford: Printed by Hudson & Goodwin.* 1802. 8vo. BA.—Two Discourses delivered at Cambridge, May 10, 1767, to the Congregation under the Pastoral Care of the Rev. Mr. Appleton. ... . *Boston: Edes & Gill.* M, DCC, LXVII. 8vo, pp. 70. B., BA.—Two Discourses delivered Oct. 1st, 1780. ... *Newburyport.* 1782. 8vo. W.

DANA (J. D.) Manual of Geology ... with Special Reference to American Geological History ... . By James D. Dana ... . *Philadelphia: Theodore Bliss & Co.* 1863. 8vo, pp. xvi, 798. 18420

DANA. Manual of Mineralogy, With Illustrations. *New Haven.* 1837. 8vo. + Second Edition. *New Haven: Durrie & Peck.* 1849. 16mo, pp. 432. C. 18421

DANA. On the Classification and Geographical Distribution of Crustacea: from the Report on Crustacea of the United States Exploring Expedition, under Capt. Chas. Wilkes, U. S. N., during the years 1838–1842, By James D. Dana, A.M., ... *Philadelphia.* 1853. 4to, pp. 198. 18422

DANA. Synopsis of the Report on Zoophytes of the U. S. Exploring Expedition around the World, under C. Wilkes, U. S. N., Commander, in the Years 1838–1842. By James D. Dana. *New Haven.* [1859.] 8vo, pp. vi, 1 l., pp. 17.

DANA. A System of Mineralogy. Descriptive of Mineralogy, comprising the most Recent Discoveries. By J. D. Dana, ... aided by George Jarvis Brush ... . Fifth Edition, Re-written and Enlarged, and Illustrated. *New York: John Wiley & Son.* 1867. 8vo, pp. xlviii, 827. H. 18424

"Catalogue of American Localities of Minerals," pp. 765–791.

DANA. United States Exploring Expedition. During the Years 1838, 1839, 1840, 1841, 1842. Under the Command of Charles Wilkes, U. S. N. Vol. VII. Zoophytes. By James D. Dana, A.M., Geologist of the Expedition. With a Folio Atlas of Sixty-one Plates. *Philadelphia: Printed by C. Sherman.* 1846. 4to, pp. x, 7–740. 18425

DANA. ... Vol. X. Geology. By James D. Dana, A.M., Geologist to the Expedition. With Folio Atlas of Twenty-one Plates. *Philadelphia: Printed by C. Sherman.* 1849. 4to, pp. xii, 766. 18426

DANA. ... Vol. XIII. Crustacea. By James Dana, A.M. With a Folio Atlas of Ninety-six Plates. Part I. *Philadelphia: Printed by C. Sherman.* 1852. 4to, pp. viii, 685. 18427

Also: Address before the American Association for the Advancement of Science, August, 1855. ... [n. p.] *published by Joseph Lovering.* 1855. 8vo, pp. 36. H.—A Brief Account of the Discoveries and Results of the United States Exploring Expedition. ... *New Haven: printed by B. L. Hamlen.* 1843. H. (From the "American Journal of Science and Arts," XLIV.) An American Geological History. *New Haven.* 1856. 8vo, pp. 45. Map.—On Coral Reefs and Islands ... . *Philadelphia.* 1853. 8vo, pp. 144.—Science and Scientific Schools. An Address before the Alumni of Yale College, ... August, 1856. ... *New Haven: S. Babcock.* 1856. 8vo, pp. 28. H.—8vo, pp. 28.—The Yale University Scheme. The Academic College and the Scientific College at New Haven, in their Relations to the University. ... *New Haven: printed by Tuttle, Morehouse & Taylor.* 1870. 16mo, pp. 8. H.—(For a list of scientific papers by Mr. Dana, *see* Trübner's "Am Bibl. Guide.")

DANA (J. F. *and* S. L.) Outlines of the Mineralogy and Geology of Boston and its Vicinity, with a Geological Map. By J. Freeman Dana, M.D. and Samuel L. Dana, M.D. ... *Boston.* 1818. 8vo, pp. 108. P. 18428

See "Memoirs of the American Academy," etc., Vol. IV.

DANA (J. J.) The Acceptable Fast. A Sermon ... in Cummington, Mass., On the Day of the National Fast, September 26, 1861, By J. Jay Dana ... *Northampton: printed by Metcalf & Company.* 1861. 8vo, pp. 20. H. 18429

DANA. Memoranda of some of the Descendants of Richard Dana. Compiled by Rev. John Jay Dana. ... *Boston: printed by Wm. H. Chandler & Co.* 1865. 8vo, pp. 64. 18430

DANA (J. G.) Report of the Trial of J. O. Beauchamp for the Murder of Col. S. P. Sharp. By J. G. Dana and R. S. Thomas. *Frankfort, Ky.* 1826. 12mo, pp. 153. B. 18431

DANA (J.) A Discourse on the Character and Death of General George Washington ... delivered at Ipswich ... 22d. February, A.D. 1800. By Joseph Dana ... . *Newburyport: printed by Edmund M. Blunt.* 1800. 8vo, pp. 28, (1). H.

DANA. The Duty and Reward of Loving our Country, and seeking its Prosperity. A Discourse delivered in two parts, at the National Fast, April 25, 1799; By Joseph Dana, A.M. *Boston: Printed by Manning & Loring.* 1799. 8vo, pp. 41. BA.

DANA. A Sermon, delivered Feb. 19, 1795, being a day of General Thanksgiving ... . By Joseph Dana, A.M. *Newburyport: Printed by Blunt and March.* 1795. 8vo, pp. 26. BA.

[DANA.] The Question of War with Great Britain examined on Moral and Christian Principles. *Boston.* 1808. 8vo, pp. 14.

Also: Address ... before the ... Lodges of St. John, St. Peter and St. Mark ... in Newburyport ... . *Newburyport: printed by E. W. Allen.* 1807. 8vo, pp. 15. H.—Observations upon Baptism, delivered At Ipswich, South Parish, June 22, 1806. By Joseph Dana, D.D ... With a View of Introductory Circumstances; and Proceedings in the said Church. *Newburyport: E. M. Blunt, Printer.* 1806. 8vo, pp. 24. H.—Sermon ... at Newburyport, December 19, 1794; at the Ordination of Daniel Dana ... *Newburyport.* MDCCXCV. 8vo, pp. 37. H.—A Sermon preached at ... Amesbury, at the Ordination of the Rev. David Smith, ... January, 28, 1795. ... . *Newburyport: Printed by Blunt & March.* [1795.] 8vo, pp. 35. BA.—A Sermon, delivered before An Annual Convention of the Congregational Ministers of Massachusetts. ... . *Boston: Printed by Andrew Newell. May,* 28, [1801.] 8vo, pp. 32. BA.—A Sermon delivered October 7, 1801, at the Ordination of Mr. Samuel Dana, ... Marblehead. ... . *Printed by Thomas C. Cushing, Salem,* 1801. 8vo, pp. 31. BA.—A Sermon delivered before the Merrimac Humane Society, ... September 4, 1804. ... . *Newburyport: Edmund M. Blunt, Printer.* 1804. 8vo, pp. 30. BA.—A Sermon ... at Haverhill, December 21, 1808; at the Ordination of the Rev. Joshua Dodge, ... *Haverhill: Printed by William B. Allen.* 1809. 8vo, pp. 10. B., P.—A Sermon delivered in Boston, before the Massachusetts Society for Promoting Christian Knowledge, Oct. 21, 1812. ... . *Cambridge: Printed by Hilliard and Metcalf.* 1812. 8vo, pp. 28. BA.—Two Discourses, delivered at the South Meeting in Ipswich, Mass. Jan. 14, 1810. By Joseph Dana, D.D. *Newburyport: E. W. Allen.* 1810. 8vo, pp. 37. BA.

DANA (M. M. G.) National Life, its Characteristics and Perils. A Discourse preached Nov. 27, 1862, at Winsted, Ct. By Rev. M. M. G. Dana ... *New York: Sackett & Cobb.* 1862. 8vo, pp. 15. 18436

DANA (M. S. B.) Charles Morton, or the Young Patriot. A Tale of the American Revolution. By Mary S. B. Dana. *New York.* 1843. 18mo, pp. 236. 18437

DANA (R. H.) The Buccaneer, and other Poems. By Richard Henry Dana. *London.* 1844. 24mo, pp. 156. B.

[DANA.] The Idle Man. ... *New York: W. Grattan, Printer.* 1821. 8vo, pp. 55. H. 18439

DANA. An Oration delivered before the Washington Benevolent Society, at Cambridge, [Mass.] July 4, 1814. By Richard H. Dana, Esq. *Cambridge: Printed by Hilliard and Metcalf.* 1814. 8vo, pp. 22. BA. 18440

DANA. Poems and Prose Writings. By Richard H. Dana. *Boston: Russell, Odiorne, and Co.* 1833. 12mo, pp. iii–ix, 1 l., pp. 450. + *New-York.* 1850. 2 vols., 12mo. BA. 18441

Also: A Poem delivered before the Porter Rhetorical Society ... Andover, Sept. 22, 1829. ... *Boston: Perkins & Marvin.* 1829. 8vo, pp. 15. H.

DANA (R. H.), *Junr.* An Address upon the Life and Services of Edward Everett, delivered before the Municipal Authorities and Citizens of Cambridge, February 22, 1865. By Richard H. Dana. *Cambridge: Sever and Francis.* 1865. 8vo, pp. 70. BA. 18442

Fifty copies printed on large paper.

DANA. The Bible in Schools. Argument of Richard H. Dana, Jr., Esq., and Opinion of the Supreme Court of Maine ... . *Boston.* [n. d.] 12mo, pp. 59. H. 18443

DANA. Enemy's Territory and Alien Enemies. What the Supreme Court decided in the Prize Causes. By R. H. Dana, Jr. *Boston: Little, Brown and Company.* 1864. 8vo, pp. 11.

DANA. Remarks of Richard H. Dana, Jr., Esq., before the Committee on Federal Relations, on the proposed Removal of Edward G. Loring, Esq., from the Office of Judge of Probate. March 5, 1855. *Boston: printed by Alfred Mudge & Son.* 1855. 8vo, pp. 28. H. 18445

DANA. Supreme Court of the United States. February, 1863. The Amy Warwick. Brief of R. H. Dana, Jr. For the United States and the Captors. [n. p. n. d.] 8vo, pp. 30.

DANA. To Cuba and Back. A Vacation Voyage. By Richard Henry Dana, Jr. ... *Boston: Ticknor and Fields.* M DCC LIX. 12mo, pp. 288. BA. + *London: Smith and Elder.* 1859. Post 8vo, pp. 268. C. 18447

[DANA.] Two Years before the Mast. A Personal Narrative of Life at Sea. *New York: Harper and Brothers.* 1840. 18mo, pp. 483. (Harper's "Family Library," No. 106.) + [*Ibid.*] 1847. + *London: Edward Moxon.* MDCCCXLI. 8vo, 2 l., pp. 124. BA. 18448

DANA. Two Years before the Mast. A Personal Narrative by Richard Henry Dana, Jr. New Edition, with Subsequent Matter by the Author. ... *Boston: Fields, Osgood & Co.* 1869. 12mo, pp. vii, 470. BA., C. 18449

[DANA.] Twee jaren voor den mast. Lotgevallen op eene zeereis naar de west-kust van Amerika. Uit het Engelsch. *Deventer: M. Ballot.* 1842. 2 vols., 8vo. 18450

Ascribed, in Brinkman's "Alphabetische Naamlyst," to Capt. Marryat. Also: Argument of Richard H. Dana, Jr., Esq., for the Holders of Bonds in the Boston, Hartford and Erie Railroad ... April 14, 1870. *Boston: Wright & Potter.* 1870. 8vo, pp. 67.—An Oration ... before the Washington Benevolent Society at Cambridge, July 4, 1814. ... *Cambridge: printed by Hilliard and Metcalf.* 1814. 8vo, pp. 22. H.—Points and Authorities in support of the Price Charity before the Supreme Judicial Court of Massachusetts ... *Boston: Press of John Wilson and Son.* 1864. 8vo, 2 l., pp. 64. H.—Speech ... at Manchester, N. H. ... February 19, 1861. *Boston: Redding & Co.* 1861. 8vo, pp. 16. H.—Speech ... at a Meeting of Citizens held in Faneuil Hall, June 21, 1865, to consider the subject of Re-organization of the Rebel States. [n. p. n. d.] 8vo, pp. 4. H.—Speech ... At Middleton, in the Fifth District, October 26, 1868. [n. p. n. d.] 8vo, pp. 11. H.—A Tribute to Judge Sprague. Remarks ... at a Dinner given to the Officers of the "Kearsarge," ... . *Boston: Alfred Mudge & Son, Printers.* 1864. 8vo, pp. 16. H.—Usury Laws. Speech ... February 14, 1867, on the Repeal of the Usuary Laws. *Boston: Wright & Potter, Printers.* 1867. 8vo, pp. 30. H.

DANA (S.) An Address on the Importance of a Well Regulated Militia ... at Concord, September, A.D. 1801. By Samuel Dana ... . *Charlestown: printed by Samuel Etheridge.* 1801. 8vo, pp. 14. H. 18451

DANA. A Discourse, on the History of the First Christian Church and Society in Marblehead; delivered to his People Jan. 7, 1816. By Samuel Dana, A.M. ... *Boston: Printed by Samuel T. Armstrong.* 1816. 8vo, pp. 31. BA., M. 18452

DANA. An Oration ... at Groton ... Massachusetts ... Fourth of July, 1807. ... By Samuel Dana. ... *Amherst, N. H.: printed by Joseph Cushing.* 1807. 8vo, pp. 20. H., S.

Also: An Address, ... in Amherst, August 10, 1797; before the ... Grand Lodges of New-Hampshire and Massachusetts; at the Consecration of Benevolent Lodge. ... [n. p.] *Samuel Preston, Printer.* 1797. 8vo, pp. 12. BA., H.—Mr. Dana's Answer to the Report of the Committee of the House of Representatives. [*Boston.* 1808.] 8vo, pp. 12. BA.—Sermon at Danvers at the Interment of the Rev. B. Wadsworth. ... *Salem.* 1825. 8vo, pp. 24. B.—Two Sermons delivered October 11, 1801, the Sabbath following his Ordination, ... of ... Marblehead. *Salem: Printed by Thomas C. Cushing.* 1801. 8vo, pp. 48. BA., H.

DANA (S. W.) Speech of Samuel W. Dana, Representative in Congress, on a Resolution concerning Francis J. Jackson, Minister Plenipotentiary from Great Britain to the United States. [December 19, 1809.] *Washington.* 1810. 8vo, pp. 28. BA.

DANA (S. W.) An Oration, delivered by Stephen W. Dana, at ... Northampton, July 4, 1856. *Boston.* 1856. 8vo, pp. 32. H. 18455

DANA (W. C.) A Sermon delivered in the Central Presbyterian Church, Charleston, S. C., [on Fast Day] Nov. 21, 1860. ... By Rev. W. C. Dana. *Charleston: Evens & Cogswell, [Printers].* 1860. 8vo, pp. (2), 12. BA. 18456

The Dana Hill Public Schools. *See* Cambridge, Vol. III.

DANA. Annual Report of the Superintending School Committee of the Town of Dana, for the year 1862–3. *Barre: printed by Henry Goddard.* 1863. 8vo, pp. 13. H. 18457

DANBURY. The Minutes of the Danbury Baptist Association, held in Danbury, Sep. 1790, with the Sentiments and Plan of the said Association. *Danbury, printed New York, W. Durrell,* 1790–1. + *Stratfield.* 1791. + *New Hartford.* 1792.

DANCER (T.) A Brief History of the Late Expedition against Fort San Juan, so far as it relates to the Diseases of the Troops: together with some Observations on Climate, Infection and Contagion; and several of the Endemical Complaints of the West Indies. By Thomas Dancer ... Physician to the Troops on that Service. *Kingston: D. Douglass & W. Aikman.* MDCCLXXXI. 4to, pp. 63. H. 18459

[DANCER.] Catalogue of Plants ... in the Botanic Garden, Jamaica, MDCCXCII. *St. Jago de la Vega.* [1792?] 4to, 3 l., pp. 16. 18460

Also: The Medical Assistant; or Jamaica Practice of Physic. *Kingston, Jamaica.* MDCCCI. 4to, 6 l., pp. 372, (12). + Second Edition. *St. Jago de la Vega.* 1809. 4to. Portrait.

DANE (J.) A Declaration of Remarkable Providences in the course of my Life. By John Dane of Ipswich, 1682. To which is added a Pedigree of the Dane Family, and a few notes. By [John Dean] a Member of the New England Historic-Genealogical Society. ... *Boston: Samuel G. Drake.* 1854. 8vo, pp. 16. BA. 18461

DANE (N.) A General Abridgment and Digest of American Law, with occasional Notes and Comments. By Nathan Dane, LL.D. ... *Boston.* 1823–29. 9 vols., 8vo. 18462

Dane Baptist Association. Minutes at Medina, Dane County, Wis., 1856. *Madison.* 1856. 8vo. S. 18463

DANDOLO (C. T.) I secoli dei due sommi italiani Dante e Colombo, frammento d'una storia del pensiero ne' tempi moderne. *Milano.* 1852. 2 vols., 12mo. Plates. 18464

DANDOLO. Il settentrione dell' Europa e dell' America nel secolo passato sin 1789, altro frammento d'una storia del pensiero ne' tempi moderni. *Milano.* 1853. 12mo. B. 18465

DANDY (W. G.) American Nationality. A Sermon delivered in Lexington, Kentucky, August 5, 1863. By Rev. W. G. Dandy. [n. p. n. d.] 8vo, pp. 8. 18466

See "Hist. Mag.," I. 153.

DANFORTH (F. T.) Thrilling and Interesting Narrative of the Life, Sufferings, Singular and Surprising Adventures of Fanny Templeton Danforth, who, disguised in the Uniform of a Midshipman, went in search of her Lover, an Officer in the United States Navy, and was taken Prisoner by the pirate ship Demon of the Seas, May 17, 1848, and was rescued by the crew of the United States Man of War Macedonian, led on by her Lover, just as she was to have been burned alive by her captors, the pirates of the Isle of Pines. 1849. 8vo, pp. 36.

DANFORTH (J.) The Blackness of Sins against Light. Or, Men offering Violence To their Knowledge, and Forcibly breaking thorow all the interposing Flames of it, to work Iniquity Considered in its Criminalness, & as no small Aggravation of their vile Transgression. By John Danforth. *Boston in N. E. Printed and Sold by Timothy Green, in Middle-Street.* 1710. 12mo.

DANFORTH. A Sermon, Occasioned by the Late Great Earthquake and the Terrors that attended it. Delivered at a Fast in Dorchester, Mass. 7, 1727. By John Danforth. *Boston: G. Rogers.* 1728. 12mo, (4), 40, 5. B. 18469

With Peter Thacher's "Two Great Bereavements Commemorated." Verses on Peter Thacher and Samuel Danforth.

DANFORTH. The Vile Prophanations of Prosperity by the Degenerate among the People of God. ... [A Fast] Sermon at Boston, March 15, 1703. By John Danforth. *Boston.* 1704. 16mo, pp. (2), 44. B. 18470

The signatures are continuous with S. Williard's "Israel's True Safety." Also: Judgment begun at the House of God: and the Righteous scarcely Saved. ... *Boston.* 1716. 16mo. W.—King Hezekiah's Bitterness and Relief. A Sermon. ... *Boston.* 1710. 16mo.—Kneeling to God, at Parting with Friends: or the Fraternal Intercessory Cry of Faith and Love. [With a Poem, to the Memory of John Eliot.] *Boston.* 1697. 16mo, pp. 72. M. — Massachusetts Election Sermon. 1697. 8vo. — The right Christian Temper, in every condition; endeavoured (as the Lord vouchsafed to assist) to be set forth and recommended. *Boston.* 1702. 16mo. W.

DANFORTH (J. N.) Gleanings and Groupings from a Pastor's Portfolio. By Rev. Joshua N. Danforth. *New York: A. S. Barnes & Co.* 1852. 12mo, pp. 360. 18471

DANFORTH. Memoir of W. C. Walton, late Pastor of the Second Presbyterian Church in Alexandria, D. C. By J. N. Danforth. *Hartford.* 1837. 12mo. S. 18472

DANFORTH (S.) MDCXLVII. An | Almanack | for the Year of our | Lord | 1647 | Calculated for the Longitude of 315 | degr. and Elevation of the Pole Ar- | ctic 42 degr. & 30 min. & may ge- | nerally serve for the most part of | New-England. | By Samuel Danforth of Harvard College | Philomathemat. | *Cambridge* | *Printed by Matthew Day. Are to be sold by Hez. Usher at Boston.* | 1647. | 16mo, pp. 16, including Title. G.B. 18473

Title-page with a type metal border of full moons and half moons. This is the almanac quoted by Savage, Winthrop's "History of N. E.," II. 379 (edition of 1853) It is probably the earliest American almanac extant. It is of special interest in the annals of American printing, as having the imprint of *Mathew Day*, no other book having been discovered in which the name appears. Thomas does not mention him. He was a brother of Stephen Day, the first printer, and probably conducted the press during the imprisonment and disgrace of the latter. (*See* "Mass. Records," 7th Sept., 1643.) Mathew Day was a man of some estate, as appears by his will and inventory ("Gen. Reg.," III. 181), while "Stephen," says Savage, "appears to have been unthrifty." Danforth's almanacs of 1648 and 1649, from the same press, are without the name of printer or bookseller, only *Printed at Cambridge*. The only known copy is in the possession of Mr. George Brinley, of Hartford, Conn.

DANFORTH An Astronomical Description of the late Comet, or Blazing Star, as it appeared in New England in 1664, with a Theological application thereof. By Samuel Danforth. *London.* 1666. 12mo. M. 18474

"Very rare, having been printed in the year of the great fire in London, when probably most of the copies were lost." Title and note from J. R. Smith's catalogue. It was also printed at *Cambridge, N. E.* 1667. 16mo, pp. 22. M.

DANFORTH. A Brief | Recognition | of | New-Englands | Errand | into the | Wilderness; | Made in the Audience of the General Assembly of the | Massachusets Colony, at Boston in N. E. on the | 11th of the third Moneth, 1670. being the | Day of Election | there. | By Samuel Danforth, Pastor of the Church of | Christ in Roxbury in N. E. | *Cambridge:* | *Printed by S. G. and M. F.* 1671. | 4to, 2 l., pp. 23. B., W. 18475

The address to the "Christian Reader," p. 4, is signed Thomas Shepard.

[DANFORTH.] The Cry of Sodom Enqvired into; [Discourse] Upon Occasion of the Condemnation of Benjamin Goad. *Cambridge: Printed by Marmaduke Johnson.* 1674. 4to, pp. (4), 25. B. 18476

An address to the "Christian Reader," p. 2, is signed John Sherman, Urian Oakes, and Thomas Shepard.

DANFORTH. An Exhortation To All: To use Utmost Endeavours to obtain A Visit of the God of Hosts, for the Preservation of Religion, and the Church, upon Earth. In a Sermon Preached ... on May 26. 1714. being the Anniversary Day of the Election of Councillors of the said Province. By Samuel Danforth, Pastor of the Church in Tanton, ... *Boston: Samuel Gerrish.* 1714. 8vo, Title, pp. 38. BA., H. 18477

DANFORTH. Ne Kesukod Uttiyeu Lord Kessehtunkup. The Day which the Lord hath made. Discourse on the Institution and Observation of the Lord's Day. [In Indian and English.] *Boston, reprinted.* 1707. 16mo, pp. 35. M. 18478

DANFORTH. The Woful Effects of Drunkenness, a Sermon when two Indians, Josias and Joseph were executed for Murther, occasioned by the Drunkenness both of the Murthering and the Murthered Parties. *Boston, N. E.: by B. Green.* 1710. 18479

Also: Piety Encouraged; a Discourse to the People of Taunton, etc. ... *Boston.* 1705. 12mo, pp. 25. M.

DANFORTH (T.) A Discourse, before the Humane Society, of the Commonwealth of Massachusetts, Boston, June 14, 1808. By Thomas Danforth. *Boston: Russell & Cutler, Printers.* 1808. 8vo, pp. 39. H. 18480

DANFORTH. An Oration, pronounced July 4, 1804, at the request of the Selectmen of the Town of Boston, in Commemoration of the Anniversary of American Independence. By Dr. Thomas Danforth. ... . *Boston: printed by Russell and Cutler.* 1804. 8vo, pp. 23. W. + Second Edition. 1804. 8vo, pp. 23. H. 18481

DANFORTH (W. R.) An Oration pronounced in the Universalist Chapel, on Thursday, July 4, 1833. By Walter Raleigh Danforth, Esq. *Providence: John Hutchins.* 1833. 8vo, pp. 22. 18482

DANFORTH. An Oration delivered before the Providence Association of Mechanicks and Manufacturers, April 2, 1822, being the Anniversary of the Election of Officers. *Providence: Miller & Hutchins.* 1822. 8vo, pp. 22. 18483

The Dangerous Condition of the Country, the Causes which have led to it, and the Duty of the People. By a Marylander. *Baltimore.* 1867. 8vo, pp. 24. H. 18484

The Dangerous Vice. A Fragment. Addressed to all whom it may concern. By a Gentleman, formerly of Boston. *Columbia, Printed.* MDCCLXXXIX. 4to, pp. 16. 18485

We have given this title twice, under the respective names of [Bourne (Silvanus)], Vol. II., No. 6927, where it is erroneously printed as "The Dangers of Vice," and [Church (Edward), *Jr.*)], Vol. IV., No. 12986. It is most probably by Bourne.

The Dangers of Church Centralization. Some Remarks on the Proposed Changes in the Constitution of the Protestant Episcopal Church in the United States. By a Layman. ... *Detroit, Mich.: printed by Palmer, Fisher & Fleming.* 1856. 8vo, pp. 21. H. 18486

The Dangers of the Country. By the Author of War in Disguise. ... . *London: J. Butterworth.* 1807. 8vo, pp. iv, 227. + The Second Edition. *London: J. Butterworth.* 1807. 8vo, pp. xvi, 163. BA. + *Philadelphia: Samuel L. Bradford.* 1807. 8vo, pp. (iv), 142. 18487

See "M. Rev.," LIII. 302. This tract is usually attributed to Sir John Stephen; but I have seen it ascribed to John Brown, author of "Memoirs of the Northern Courts." *See* "War in Disguise."

Dangers of the Deep; or, Narratives of Shipwrecks and Adventures at Sea. *Edinburgh: T. Nelson & Sons.* 1854. 32mo, pp. 416. 18488

Dangers of the Theatre; Extract from a Printed Account of the Conflagration of Richmond Theatre, in Virginia, which happened 26th of December, 1811. *Woodbridge.* 1812. 12mo.

DANIEL (C.) Études de théologie, de philosophie et d'histoire publiées par Ch. Daniel et J. Gagarin. *Paris.* 1858. 3 vols., 8vo. 18490

Vol. III. contains, on pp. 205–324, "Relation d'un voyage de Mexico à Guatémala dans le cours de l'année 1855."

DANIEL, *pseudonym*. *See* [Garcia (Edward)].

DANIEL (H.) Trial of H. Daniel for the Murder of Clifton R. Thomson. ... *Cincinnati, O.* 1845. 8vo, pp. 36. 18491

[DANIEL (John M.)] The Life of Stonewall Jackson. From Official Papers, Contemporay Narratives, and Personal Ac-

quaintance. By a Virginian. *Richmond.* 1863. 12mo. + From ... the Richmond Edition. *New York: Charles B. Richardson.* 1863. 12mo, pp. 305. Portrait. BA. 18492

Some copies of the New York edition have the imprint, "*London: S. Low* [etc.] 1863."

DANIEL. The Richmond Examiner during the War; or, the Writings of John M. Daniel. With Memoir. By his Brother, F. S. Daniel. *New York: Am. News. Co.* 1869. 8vo, pp. 232.

DANIEL (J. R. J.) Speech of Mr. Daniel, of North Carolina, on the Bill to reduce the Duty on Imports, &c., delivered in the House ... July 1, 1846. *Washington.* 1846. 8vo, pp. 15. H. 18494

DANIEL (Louis). La guerre aux États-Unis Topographie-Mœurs-Histoire-Documents diplomatiques et politiques avec une carte du théatre de la guerre par Louis Daniel *Paris: Jules Vanackere.* 1862. 8vo, 2 l., pp. 156. BA., H. 18495

DANIEL (*Mr.*) Speech of Mr. Daniel, of Kentucky, on the Bill authorizing the President to use Force against South Carolina, delivered in the House ... February 28, 1833. *Washington: printed by Duff Green.* 1833. 8vo, pp. 25. 18496

Also: Speech ... in the House ... on the Judiciary ... 8vo, pp. 8.

DANIELL (W. C.) Observations upon the Autumnal Fevers of Savannah. By W. C. Daniell, M.D. *Savannah: W. T. Williams.* 1826. 8vo, pp. 152. 18497

DANIELS (R.) First Annual Report on the Geological Survey of Wisconsin. By Edward Daniels. *Madison: D. Atwood, Printer.* 1854. 8vo, pp. 83. 18498

DANIELS (T. H.) Particulars of the Life of Thomas H. Daniels. *Boston.* 1819. 18499

DANIELSZ (T.) Vertoog | van de Redenen die den Capitein | Thomas Danielsz. | van het Schip | St. Jago de la Victoria | bewogen hebben, in Jamaica aan- en inteloopen, | en de Proceduuren door de Regeringe van dat | Eiland ontrent hem gehouden: | Mitsgaders een kort verhaal van het gene op zijn geheele reize | is voorgevallen, tot het aanhouden van het Schip toe; | alles bekrachtigd met autentijke bewijzen: | Dienende tot justificatie van de conduites van dito Capitein, | tegens die gene die dezelve hebben getracht de taxeeren, | en met onwaarheid te bekladden. | *Te Rotterdam,* | *Bij Reinier Leers,* | MDCXC. | 4to, 2 l., pp. 73. 18500

Danish Laws; or, the Code of Christian the Fifth. Faithfully translated for the use of the English inhabitants of the Danish Settlements in America. *London.* 1756. 8vo. C.

Danish Missions to the East Indies, South America, &c. *London.* 1718. 12mo. 18502

DANKERS (J.), *and* SLUYTER (P.) Journal of a Voyage to New York and a Tour in several of the American Colonies in 1769–80 by Jaspar Dankers and Peter Sluyter of Wilwerd in Friesland Translated from the Original Manuscript in Dutch for the Long Island Historical Society and Edited by Henry C. Murphy ... *Brooklyn.* 1867. 8vo, 4 l., pp. xlvii, 440. 12 Plates. 18503

"Long Island Hist. Soc. Publications," Vol. I.

DANNETT (H.) Examination of Mr. Harris's Scriptural Researches on the Licitness of the Slave Trade. By the Rev. H. Dannett, of Liverpool. *London.* 1788. 8vo. 18504

DAÑON (P.) Sombra fúnebre, oracion que dixo el R. P. Fray Pedro Dañon, Predicador General jubilado, Ex-Secretario General de las Provincias de la Nueva España, Ex-Guardian de el Convento Grande de San Francisco de Mexico. ... *Mexico.* 1715. 4to, 8 l., Text, 11 leaves. 18505

DANSEREAU (Arthur). Annales Historiques du Collége de L'Assomption depuis sa fondation. — Première livraison. *Montreal.* 1864. 8vo, pp. 44. 18506

DANSON (J. T.) Some Particulars of the Commercial Progress of the Colonial Dependencies of the United Kingdom, ... 1827–46. By J. T. Danson ... . 19th February, 1849. [*London:*] *M. & W. Collis, Printers.* [1849?] 4to, 3 l., pp. 64, (1), 39. H. 18307

DANTI (A.) Osservationi di diverse Historie et d'altri Particolari degni di memoria. *Venetia.* 1573. 4to. 18508

This rare work contains "Osservatione sopra la Navigatione de gli Spagnuoli sotto Christoforo Colombo nell' Indie Occidentali dette el Mondo Nuovo;" "sopra il Mal Francese et donde fu traportato in Italia;" "sopro gl' Indiani dello Mondo Nuevo;" etc.

DANTIER (A.) Elisabeth Seton et les commencements de l'èglise catholique aux États-Unis; Par Mme de Barberey. Seconde édition. Etude historique par M. Alphonse Dantier. *Paris: Douniol.* 1870. 8vo, pp. 58 18509

D'ANVERS (Caleb), *pseudonym*. *See* [Amherst (Nicholas)], Vol. I., No. 1335*a*.

D'ANVERS. Answer to the Considerations occasioned by the Craftsman upon the Excise, so far as relates to the Tobacco Trade. *London.* 1733. 12mo. W. 18510

D'ANVERS. French Counsels Destructive to Great Britain, or Seasonable Advice to Sir R—— W——, in the present Critical Conjuncture. *London.* 1739. 8vo. W. 18511

Partly on West Indian affairs.

DANVERS (J. H.) A Picture of a Republican Magistrate of the New School; being a Full-length Likeness of his Excellency Thomas Jefferson, President of the United States. To which is added a Short Criticism on the Characters and Pretensions of Mr. Madison, Mr. Clinton, and Mr. Pinckney. By John Thierry Danvers, of Virginia. ... . *New York: Printed by E. Sargeant.* 1808. 8vo, pp. 96. BA. 18512

DANVERS, *Mass.* Account of the Centennial Celebration in Danvers, June 16, 1852, together with the Proceedings of the Town in relation to the Donation of George Peabody, Esq., of London. *Printed by Order of the Town.* 1852. 8vo, pp. 208, Errata, 1 slip. 19 Plates. 18513

The second title reads: Centennial Celebration, at Danvers, Mass. June 16, 1852. *Boston: printed by Dutton and Wentworth.* 1852.

Catalogue of the Library of the Peabody Institute, South Danvers, Mass. *Boston: printed by John Wilson and Son.* 1855. 8vo, pp. xix, (1), 102. BA. + Supplement ... . July 1857. [*South Danvers.*] 1857. 8vo, pp. 26. B., BA. 18514

The Danvers Discussion. A Report of the Discussion at Danvers, Mass. on November 6, 1833, between Revs. M. P. Braman, and Thomas Whittemore. [n. p.] 1833. 8vo, pp. 95.

A Memorial to the Legislature of Massachusetts. *Salem.* 1843. 8vo, pp. 15. 18516

Relates to the manner of treatment of an insane female at the Alms House in Danvers.

Proceedings at the Reception and Dinner in Honor of George Peabody, Esq., of London, by the Citizens of the old Town of Danvers, October 9, 1856. ... [With] An Historical Sketch of the Peabody Institute, &c. *Boston: Henry W. Dalton & Son, Printers.* 1856. 8vo, pp. vi, (1), 195. 18 Portraits and Engravings. BA. 18517

Real and Personal Estate, 1852. *Salem.* 1852. 8vo, pp. 56.

Report of the School Committee of the Town of Danvers. [1842–3] ... *Salem: Ives and Pease, Printers.* 1843. 8vo, pp. 24. Continued. H. 18519

South Danvers is now a separate town, called Peabody.

DANVILLE THEOLOGICAL SEMINARY. Addresses delivered at the Inauguration of the Professors in the Danville Theological Seminary, October 13, 1853. ... *Cincinnati: printed by T. Wrightson.* 1854. 8vo, pp. 74. H. 18520

Danville Quarterly Review. Vol. I. 1861. *Danville, Ky.* 8vo. Continued. 18521

Also: An Annual Catalogue of the Theological Seminary at Danville, Ky., 1852. *Louisville.* 1852. 8vo. Continued. — Theological Seminary of the Presbyterian Church at Danville, Ky., 1856. *Louisville.* 1857. 8vo. S.

DANVILLE, *Vt.* Catalogue Caledonia County Teachers' Institute, Danville, Vt., 1851. 18522

DAPPER (Olfert). *See* Montanus (A.)

The translator of the Dutch version of Montanus attributes the authorship to Dapper, "Durch Dr. O. D.," which is an error. Dapper was the collector and publisher of a collection of voyages and descriptions of foreign countries in Dutch, *Amsterdam.* 1670–88. 12 vols., folio, of which there are some sets on large paper. For the American portion, *see* Montanus (A.), and Nieuhoff (J.)

DAPPER (Olfert). Dappervs exoticvs cvriosvs. Das ist des viel-belesenen Hn. Odoardi Dapperi Africa- America- und Asiatische Curiositäten, so in den drey Haupttheilen der Welt verwundert vorkommen, [etc.] Zusammen getragen von M. J. C. Männling. *Franckfurt und Leipzig: M. Rohrlach.* 1717. 12mo, 7 l., pp. 536, 36 l., pp. 184, 18 l., pp. 174, 14 l. Plate.

DAPPER. Exotici curiosi continuatio. Oder des viel-belesenen, Hn. Odoardi Dapperi Americanische Curiositäten so in diesen Haupt Theile der Welt verwundernd vorkommen auffs kürtzeste zusammen getragen von M. J. C. Männling. *Frankfurt und Leipzig, bey Michael Rohrlachs.* 1718. 2 vols., 12mo, pp. 184, 18 l., pp. 172, 15 l.; pp. 246, 13 l., pp. 100, 9 l.

DARBY (J.) Botany of the Southern States; in Two Parts. ... Part II. Description of Southern Plants. Arranged on the Natural System; preceded by a Linnæan and a Dichotomous Analysis. By Prof. John Darby, A.M. *New York.* 1855. 12mo, pp. 612. C., P. 18525

DARBY (Joseph). Letter on the subject of British Colonial Fisheries. [n. p.] 1853. 8vo, pp. 16. 18526

DARBY (W.) The Emigrant's Guide to the Western and Southwestern States and Territories; comprising a Geographical and Statistical Description of the States of Louisiana, Mississippi, Tennessee, Kentucky, and Ohio; — the Territories of Alabama, Missouri, Illinois, and Michigan; and the western parts of Virginia, Pennsylvania, and New York. ... By William Darby, ... *New-York: Kirk & Mercein.* 1818. 8vo, pp. (6), 311. 2 Maps.

See "N. Am. Rev.," VIII. 268.

DARBY. A Geographical Description of the State of Louisiana: presenting a View of the Soil, Climate, Animal, Vegetable, and Mineral Productions; illustrative of its Natural Physiognomy, its Geographical Configuration, and Relative Situation; with an Account of the Character and Manners of the Inhabitants. Being an Accompaniment to the Map of Louisiana. By William Darby. ... . *Philadelphia: Printed for the Author by J. Melish.* 1816. 8vo, 9 l., pp. 270, xvii. Map. C. 18528

DARBY. A Geographical Description of the State of Louisiana, the Southern Part of the State of Mississippi, and Territory of Alabama; Presenting A View of the Soil, Climate, Animal, Vegetable, and Mineral Productions, Illustrative of their Natural Physiognomy, their Geographical Configuration And relative Situation; With an Account of the Character and Manners of the Inhabitants, Together with a Map ... Second Edition, Enlarged and Improved. By William Darby. *New York: James Olmstead.* 1817. 8vo, pp. xi, 356, (4). Map. C. 18529

DARBY. Geographical, Historical, and Statistical Repository; Vol. I. A Geographical View of Pennsylvania. By William Darby. *Philadelphia.* 1824. 8vo. P. 18530

DARBY. Lectures on the Discovery of America, and Colonization of North America by the English. By William Darby. *Baltimore: Pluskitt & Co.* 1828. 12mo, pp. 223. 18531

DARBY. Memoir on the Geography and Natural and Civil History of Florida, attended by a Map of that Country, connected with the Adjacent Places; And An Appendix containing the Treaty of Cession, and other Papers relative to the subject. By William Darby. *Philadelphia; Printed by T. H. Palmer.* 1821. 8vo, 2 l., pp. viii, 5–92. Map. BA., C., P. 18532

"A slight and superficial performance." *See* "N. Am. Rev.," XIII. 99.

DARBY. A Tour from the City of New-York to Detroit, in the Michigan Territory, made between the 2d of May and the 22d of September, 1818. The Tour extends from New-York, by Albany, Schnectady, and Utica, to Sacket's Harbor, and thence through Lake Ontario, to St. Lawrence River, and down that stream to Hamilton Village, Thence along both banks of the St. Lawrence, from Hamilton to the Thousand Islands; thence to Sacket's Harbor by water. [With] Notices of ... the Natural History and Geography ... . By William Darby ... . *New-York: Kirk & Mercein.* 1819. 8vo, pp. 288, lxxiii, (7.) Map. BA. 18533

DARBY. Universal Gazetteer; or, a New Geographical Dictionary; ... By William Darby. *Philadelphia.* 1827. 8vo. + Second Edition, with Additions. *Philadelphia.* 1827. Rl. 8vo, pp. 892. Map. + Third Edition. *Washington.* 1843. 8vo.

DARBY. View of the United States, Historical, Geographical, and Statistical; exhibiting in a Convenient Form, the Natural and Artificial Features of the several States, and Embracing those Leading Branches of History and Statistics best adapted to develop the Present Condition of the North American Union. Illustrated with Maps, &c. By William Darby. *Philadelphia: H. S. Tanner.* 1828. 2 l., pp. 622. 14 Maps. BA., C. 18535

Also: Mnemonika; or the Tablet of Memory; being a Register of Events from the Earliest Period to the Year 1829: comprehending an epitome of Universal History, &c. ... *Baltimore.* 1829. 12mo. P. — Prospectus of Historical and Geographical Tracts on Louisiana. Bv Mr. Wm. Darbv and Louis Bringier. *New York, June* 12, 1815. 8vo, pp. 16

DARBY (W.), *and* DWIGHT (T.), *Jr.* A New Gazetteer of the United States of America ... with the Population of 1830, &c. By William Darby, and Theodore Dwight, Jr. *Hartford: Edward Hopkins.* 1833. 8vo, pp. 630. + United States of America. Second Edition, revised. *Hartford.* 1834. 8vo.

D'ARCY (Uriah Derick). The Black Vampyre; a Legend of St. Domingo. Second Edition. *New York.* 1819. 16mo.

DARDE (Jean). Histoire de ce qui s'est passé en Ethiopie, Malabar, Brasil, et es Indes Orientales. Tirée des lettres escrites és années 1620 jusques en 1624. Addressée au ... Général de la Compagnie de Jésus. Traduit de l'Italien en François par un Père de la mesme Compagnie. *Paris: Sebastien Cramoisy.* 1628. 8vo, pp. 451. 18538

DARDIN (A.) Petition of Amey Dardin, Feb. 3, 1803. *Washington.* 1803. 8vo, pp. 20. 18539

For a stud horse impressed for the United States army.

[DARDIS (George)]. Description of the State Capitol of Tennessee. *Nashville: B. R. M'Kennie & Co., Printers.* 1854. 32mo, pp. 8. H. 18540

DARE (C. P.) Philadelphia, Wilmington and Baltimore Railroad Guide: ... including Historical Sketches, Legends, &c. By Charles P. Dare. *Philadelphia: T. Fitzgibbon.* [1856.] 12mo, pp. 142. 4 Maps. 18541

DARG (J. P.) Exposition of the Proceedings of John P. Darg, Henry W. Merritt, and others, in relation to the Robbery of Mr. Darg, the Elopement of his Alleged Slave, and the Trial of Barny Corse, who was unjustly charged as an Accessory. *New York: Isaac T. Hopper.* 1840. 8vo, pp. 42.

DARGAN (E. S.) Speech of Hon. E. S. Dargan, of Alabama, on the Oregon Question. Delivered in the House ... Thursday, February 5, 1846. *Washington: Blair & Rives.* 1846. 8vo, pp. 6. 18543

DARIEN. Act|for a|Company|Trading to|Africa and the Indies. |June 26. 1695.|*Edinburgh,|Printed by the Heirs and Successors of Andrew Anderson, Printer to His most|Excellent Majesty, Anno Dom.* 1696.| Folio, pp. 7. 18544

An|Act|of the|Parliament|of|Scotland|For Erecting an|East-India Company|in that|Kingdom.|*Edinburgh,|Printed by the Heirs and Successors of Andrew Anderson, Printer to his most|Excellent Majesty,* 1695. *And Re-printed at London, for Sam. Manship at|the Ship in Cornhill, and Hugh Newman at the Grasshopper in the Poultrey.*| [3 *Oct.* 1695.] Folio, Title, pp. 8.

Caledonia; or, the Pedlar turn'd Merchant. *See* Vol. III., No. 9919.

A Catalogue of the several Books and Pamphlets that have been hitherto published (to 1700) concerning the Indian and African Company of Scotland, set down according to order of time, for the Information of the Curious. 18546

Title from an English catalogue.

Constitution of the Company of Scotland trading to Africa and the Indies. *Edinburgh.* 1696. 4to, pp. 3. J.C.B. 18547

The Darien Papers; being a Selection of Original Letters and Official Documents relating to the Establishment of a Colony at Darien by the Company of Scotland Trading to Africa and the Indies, 1695–1700. *Printed at Edinburgh.* MDCCCXLIX. 4to, pp. xxxii, 417. Map and Facsimiles. C. 18548

Edited by J. W. Burton, Esq., and contains a great mass of curious and interesting matter relating to the subject. One hundred copies printed for the Bannatyne Club.

A Defence of the Scots Abdicating Darien. *See* Scott (P.)

A|Defence|of the|Scots Settlement|At Darien.|With|An Answer to the Spanish|Memorial against it.|And|Arguments to prove that it is the|Interest of England to join with the|Scots, and Protect it.|To which is added,|A Description of the|Country,|and a particular Account of|the Scots Colony.|*Edinburgh,* |*Printed in the Year* M.DC.XC.IX.| 8vo, Title, 4 l., pp. 86. + [Another Edition.] *Edinburgh.* 1699. 4to. C. 18549

The dedication is signed Philo-Caledon, who is said to be Ridpath, or Riddpath. There is also another edition of the same date attributed to Mr. Fletcher, of Saltoun, printed in smaller type, 12mo.

The|Defence|of the|Scots Settlement|at|Darien,|Answered, |Paragraph by Paragraph.|By Philo-Britan.|*London, Printed and Sold by the Booksellers of London and Westminster.* 1699.| 8vo, Title, pp. 92. 18550

An Enquiry into the Caledonian Project, with a Defence of England's Procedure (In point of equity) in relation thereunto. In a friendly Letter from London, to a member of the Scots African and Indian Company in Edinburgh, to guard against passion. *London: John Nutt.* 1701. 4to, pp. 54, misprinted 92. C. 18551

An Enquiry into The Causes of the Miscarriage of the Scots Colony at Darien or an Answer to a Libel entituled A Defence of the Scots Abdicating Darien. Submitted to the Consideration of the Good People of England. [n. p.] 1699. 8vo, pp. 84. C. Another Edition. *Glasgow.* 1700. 8vo, pp. 112.

Declared by a royal proclamation to be a "*a false*, scandalous, and traitorous libel."

An Exact List of all the Men, Women, and Boys that Died on|Board the Indian and African Company's Fleet, during their Voyage|from Scotland to America, and since their Landing in Caledonia;|Together with a particular account of their qualities, the several Days|of their Deaths, and their respective Distempers or Accidents of which|they Died.|[Colophon:] *Edinburgh, Printed by George Moseman, in the Year* 1699. Folio, 1 l.

A Full and Exact Account of the Proceedings of the Court of Directors and Council General of the Company of Scotland trading to Africa and the Indies, with relation to the Treaty of Union, now under the Parliament's Consideration. In a Letter to a Person of Quality containing the Author's Apology for Printing the same. [*Edinburgh:*] *Printed in the year* MDCCVI. 4to, pp. 40. C. 18554

A|Full and Exact|Collection|of|All the Considerable Addresses, Memorials,|Petitions, Answers, Proclamations, De-|clarations, Letters and other Publick|Papers, relating to the Company of|Scotland Trading to Africa|and the Indies, since the passing|of the Act of Parliament, by which the said|Company was established in June 1695, till|November 1700.|Together with a short Preface (including|the Act it self) as also a Table of the|whole Contents.|*Printed in the Year* 1700.| 8vo, pp. x, 144, 6. 18555

The|History|of|Caledonia:|or, the|Scots Colony|in|Darien |In the West Indies.|With an Account of the|Manners of the Inhabitants,|and Riches of the Country.|By a Gentleman lately Arriv'd.|*London:|Printed, and Sold by John Nutt, near|Stationers-Hall.* MDCCXCIX.| 8vo, pp. 54. + *Dublin.* 1699. 8vo. 18556

The Humble Representation of the Council of the Company of Scotland trading to the Indies. [n. p.] 1706. Folio, 2 l.

Information concernant l'affaire de Darien. *Paris.* [1680?] 4to, pp. 15. 18558

Relates to the Scotch "Invasion of Darien," and the claims of Spain upon the province.

Just and Modest Vindication. *See* [Hodges (James)].

Letter concerning the Consequence of an Incorporating Union in relation to Trade. 1706. 4to. 18559

Containing some interesting notices of the trade of the Scotch colony of Darien, and other parts of the East and West Indies.

A|Letter|From a Member of the|Parliament of Scotland,| To his Friend at London,|concerning Their Late Act|For Establishing a|Company|Of that Kingdom Tradeing to|Africa and the Indies.|*London,*| ... *John Whitlock* ... |1695.| Folio, Title, pp. 14. 18560

Letter|from the|Commission|of the|General Assembly|of the|Church of Scotland|to the|Honourable Council and Inhabi-

tants|of the Scots Colony of Caledonia|in America.|Dated at Glasgow, July 21. 1699.|*Glasgow,|Printed by Robert Sanders, One of his Majesties Printers.* 1699. 4to, Title, pp. 16.

Memoirs of Darien. *See* [Borland (F.)], Vol. II., No. 6428.

A New Darien Artifice laid open; in a notable instance of Captain Maclean's Name being used (in the Flying Post, February 11 & 13, 17$\frac{00}{01}$.) to vouch for the Caledonia Company, after that gentleman hath been persecuted by them these thirteen months past for vouching against them. Authore Anti-Dariensi. *London: Printed for any Body, and sold by the Booksellers of London and Westminster.* 1701. 4to, pp. 14. J.C.B. 18562

See "Bibl. Am. Prim.," p. 182.

The|Original Papers|and|Letters,|Relating to the|Scots Company,|Trading to|Africa and the Indies:|From the Memorial given in|against their taking Subscripti-|ons at Hamburgh, by Sir Paul|Ricaut, His Majesty's Resident|there, to Their last Address sent|up to His Majesty in December,|1699. Faithfully extracted from the Companies Books.|*Printed Anno* 1700.| 8vo, pp. 56. 18563

A Perfect|List|Of the several Persons Residenters in|Scotland,|Who have Subscribed as|Adventurers in the Joynt-Stock |of the|Company of Scotland|Trading to Africa and the Indies.| Together|With the respective Sums which they have severally Subscribed in the Books|of the said Company, Amounting in the Whole to the Sum of 400000 lib.|Sterling.|*Edinburgh,*| *Printed and Sold by the Heirs and Successors of Andrew Anderson, Printer to the King's|most Excellent Majesty, Anno Dom.* 1696.| Folio, Title and pp. 14 of Names. 18564

Report of the Committee upon the petition of William Paterson, Esq. [1712.] 8vo, Half-Title, pp. 16. J.C.B. 18565

Representation and Petition of the Council General of the Indian and African Company to Parliament. *Edinburgh.* 1700. 8vo, pp. 20. 18566

Representation of the Council and Company of Scotland trading to Africa and the Indies. Dated at Edinburgh, November 7, 1706. Folio, pp. 2. 18567

Scotland's Grievances relating to Darien, &c. Humbly offered to the Consideration of the Parliament. [n. p.] 1700. 8vo, pp. 54. 18568

Scotland's|Present Duty:|or, a|Call|to|The Nobility, Gentry, Ministry, and Com-|monality of this Land, to be duely affected|with, and vigorously to act for, our Com-|mon Concern in Caledonia, as a|Mean to Enlarge Christ's Kingdom, to Be-|nefit our Selves, and do Good to all Pro-|testant Churches. *Printed in the Year* 1700. 4to, pp. 28. 18569

Also on large paper.

Scotland's Right to Caledonia (formerly called Darien) and the Legality of its Settlement, asserted in three several Memorials presented to His Majesty in May, 1699. By the Lord President of the Session and Lord Advocate, on behalf of the Company of Scotland trading to Africa and the Indies. *Printed in the Year* 1700. 8vo, pp. 34. 18570

A short Vindication of Phil. Scot's Defence of the Scots abdicating Darien. Being in Answer to the Challenge of the Author of The Defence of that Settlement, to prove the Spanish Title to Darien, by Inheritance, Marriage, Donation, &c. With a Prefatory Reply to the false and scurrilous Aspersions of the new Author of The Just and Modest Vindication, &c. And some Animadversions on the material Part of it, relating to the Title of Darien. *London, Printed in the Year* 1701. 8vo, pp. 48. 18571

A|Speech|in|Parliament|On the 10th day of January 1701,| by the|Lord Belhaven,|On the Affairs of the Indian and African Com-|pany, and its Colony of Caledonia. *Edinburgh: Printed in the Year* 1701. 8vo, pp. 12. 18572

A State of Mr. Paterson's claim upon the Equivalent with Original Papers and Observations relating thereto. *London: Printed in the Year* 1712. Sm. 4to, pp. viii, 72, 2 l. J.C.B.

A|Supplement|of|Original Papers|and|Letters,|relating to the Scots Company Trading to|Africa and the Indies.|*Anno Dom.* 1700.| 8vo, pp. 16. 18574

A Vindication of the Scots Design for the having established a Colony at Darien. *Printed in the Year* 1699. 18575

See Burney's "Voyages," IV. 359; and pp. 94–100 of the "Monthly Miscellany. 1707." *See also* "Memoirs of North Britain."

DARINEL DE TIREL. La Sphere|des deux mondes, composée en Fran-|çois, par Darinel pasteur des Amadis.|Auec vn Epithalame, que le mesme Autheur ha|faict, sur les nopces &

mariage de Tresillustre,|& Serenissime Prince, Don Philippe Roy|d'Angleterre, &c.|Commenté, glosé, & enrichy de plusieurs fables Poeticques, | Par G. B. D. B. C. C. de C. | N. L. Ovbli. Amys Lecturs, achetez ce liuret,|Si vous aymez Cronicques & Histoires,|Car l'achetant y trouuerez au net,| Bien figurez pays & territoires.|*En Anvers, Chez Ie. Richart.*| *Auec Priuilege.* 1555.| 4to, 4 l., 58 folioed leaves, erroneously numbered 57. 19 Maps. 18576

A poetical volume of some rarity.

DARISTE (A. J.) Conseils aux Européens qui passent dans les pays chauds, et notamment aux Antilles. Par A.-J. Dariste, D.M. *Bordeaux: Lawalle jeune.* 1824. 8vo, pp. 40 or less.

DARISTE. Mémoire sur la non-contagion de la fièvre jaune, Suivi de Conseils aux Européens ... [as above. *Ibid.*] 18578

DARISTE. Recherches practiques sur la fièvre jaune ... . *Paris: Beaucé-Rusand, Gabon et comp.* 1825. 8vo. 18579

Darkness at Noon; or, the Great Solar Eclipse of the 16th of June, 1806, described and represented in every Particular ... . By an Inhabitant of Boston. ... *Boston: D. Carlisle & A. Newell. May,* 1806. 12mo, pp. 34. Plate. B., BA. 18580

This is probably by Andrew Newell.

DARLEY (F. O. C.) The Cooper Vignettes. From Drawings by F. O. C. Darley. *New York: James G. Gregory.* 1862. Folio, pp. 8. 64 Plates, and Letter-Press Descriptions.

These are India proofs before letters. *See* Cooper.

DARLEY. Illustrations of Rip Van Winkle, designed and etched by Felix O. C. Darley, for the Members of the American Art Union. [*New York.*] MDCCCXLVIII. Oblong folio, Illustrated Title, pp. 11. 6 Plates. BA. 18582

DARLEY. Scenes in Indian Life, a Series of Original Designs portraying Events in the Life of an Indian Chief, Drawn and Etched on Stone by F. O. C. Darley, To which is added an Illustration of the Death of the War Eagle, a pseudo-biographical Sketch, with Copious Notes. *Philadelphia.* 1843. 5 pts., oblong 4to. 14 Plates. 18583

Also: A Selection of War Lyrics. With [8] Illustrations on Wood. *New York.* MDCCCLXIV. 4to. — Yankee Doodle, Illustrated. *New York.* [n. d.] 4to.

DARLING (H.) Grief and Duty. A Discourse Delivered in the Fourth Presbyterian Church, Albany, April 19th, 1865, the day of the Funeral Obsequies of President Lincoln. By Henry Darling, D.D. ... *Albany: S. R. Gray.* 1865. 8vo, pp. 24.

Two editions printed. The sermon was repeated at the Military Hospital on the 23d April.

DARLING. Memoir of Otis Allen; with the proceedings of the Albany Bar and of other public bodies, with the Sermon ... by Rev. H. Darling, D.D. *Albany.* 1865. 8vo. S. 18585

DARLING. Slavery and the War. A Historical Essay. By Rev. Henry Darling, D.D. *Philadelphia: J. B. Lippincott & Co.* 1863. 8vo, pp. 48. 18586

[DARLING (Thomas).] Some Remarks on Mr. President Clap's History and Vindication Of the Doctrines, &c. of the New-England Churches. ... *New-Haven: Printed by J. Parker.* 1757. 8vo, pp. 127. W. 18587

DARLING (William A.) The New York [City] Tax-Book. ... 1850. *New York.* 1851. 8vo, pp. 99. 18588

[DARLING.] Report on Internal Revenue Frauds. *Washington.* 1867. 8vo. 18589

DARLING. Speech of Hon. William A. Darling, of New York, on the Loan Bill ... in the House ... March 16, 1866. *Washington.* 1866. 8vo, pp. 6. H. 18590

[DARLING (William Stewart).] Sketches of Canadian Life, Lay and Ecclesiastical. Illustrative of Canada and the Canadian Church. By a Presbyter of the Diocese of Toronto. *London: Bogue.* 1849. 8vo, pp. 310. 18591

[DARLING.] The Emigrants; A Tale [in verse]. *London: [Reprinted from the Brit. Amer. Mag.]* 1863. 8vo, pp. 39.

DARLINGTON (W.) Agricultural Botany; an Enumeration and Description of Useful Plants and Weeds which merit the Notice, or require the Attention of American Agriculturists. By William Darlington, M.D. *Philadelphia.* 1847. 8vo. C., P.

DARLINGTON. American Weeds and Useful Plants: being a Second and Illustrated Edition of Agricultural Botany, an Enumeration and Description of Useful Plants and Weeds, which merit the Notice or require the Attention of American Agriculturists. By William Darlington, M.D. ... Revised, with

Additions, by George Thurber. *New York: A. O. Moore & Company.* 1859. 12mo, pp. xvi, 460. BA. 18594

DARLINGTON. Florula Cestrica: an Essay towards a Catalogue of the Phænogamous Plants, Native and Naturalized, growing in the Vicinity of the Borough of West Chester, in Chester County, Pennsylvania; with brief Notices of their Properties, and Uses, in Medicine, Rural Economy and the Arts. To which is subjoined, An Appendix of the Useful Cultivated Plants of the same District. By William Darling, M.D. *West-Chester, Penn.: Printed for the Author.* 1826. 8vo, pp. xx, 152. + Second Edition. *West Chester: the Author.* 1837. 12mo, pp. xxiii, pp. 640. Map. C. 18595

DARLINGTON. Flora Cestrica: an Herborizing Companion for the Young Botanists of Chester County, State of Pennsylvania. By William Darlington. Third Edition. *Philadelphia.* 1853. 12mo. 18596

DARLINGTON. Memorials of John Bartram and Humphrey Marshall. With Notices of their Botanical Contemporaries. By William Darlington, M.D. ... *Philadelphia: Lindsay & Blackiston.* 1849. 8vo, Title, pp. 585. Woodcuts. BA. + New Edition. *Philadelphia.* 1850. 8vo, pp. 602. 18597

[DARLINGTON.] Perry-Patetic Songs and other Jollification Ditties; collected chiefly from the columns of the American Republican. *West Chester: Printed at the Office of the Republican.* 1824. 24mo, pp. 31. 18598

Suppressed by the author.

DARLINGTON. Reliquiæ Baldwinianæ; Selections from the Correspondence of the Late William Baldwin, M.D., Surgeon in the United States Navy, with Occasional Notes, and a Short Biographical Memoir. Compiled by William Darlington, M.D. ... *Philadelphia: Kimber and Sharpless.* 1843. 12mo, pp. 346, (1). Portrait. B. 18599

DARLINGTON. Sesqui-Centennial Gathering of the Clan Darlington: at the residence of Brinton Darlington, in East Bradford, Chester county, Pennsylvania, on the 20th of August, 1853. Printed by Request of the Tribe. [n. p. n. d.] 8vo, pp. 52. 18600

Also: Address before the Pennsylvania Agricultural Society. ... *Philadelphia.* 1825. 8vo. — Address before the Philadelphia Society for Promoting Agriculture, October 17, 1844. ... — Address before the Chester County Horticultural Society, West Chester, September 11, 1846. ... — A Discourse upon Agriculture ... September 4, 1847. ... [*Philadelphia?*] 1847. 8vo, pp. 16.

DARLINGTON (William M.), *Editor.* *See* Smith (James).

DARNALL (H.) A Just and Impartial Account of the Transactions of the Merchants in London, for the Advancement of the Price of Tobacco, [in 1727] In a Letter from Henry Darnell to the Inhabitants of Maryland. September 18, 1728. *Annapolis: W. Parks.* 1728. 12mo, pp. 53. J.C.B. 18601

DARNELL. A Journal containing an Accurate and Interesting Account of the Hardships, Sufferings, Battles, Defeat, and Captivity of those Heroic Kentucky Volunteers and Regulars, commanded by General Winchester, In the Years 1812–13. Also, Two Narratives, by men that were wounded in the Battles on the River Raisin, and taken Captive by the Indians. By Elias Darnell. *Philadelphia: Lippincott, Grambo, and Co.* 1854. 18mo, pp. 98, (1). 18602

DARNELL (*Rev.* Henry Faulkner), *M.A.* Songs by the Way: a Collection of Original Poems for the Comfort and Encouragement of Christian Pilgrims. *Montreal.* 1862. 8vo, pp. 186.

DARLING. Verses in Memory of the Right Rev. G. J. Mountain, Lord Bishop of Quebec. *St. John's, L. C.* 1863. 8vo, pp. 7. 18604

DARNES (William P.) A Full Report of the Trial of W. P. Darnes on an Indictment [on a Charge of Manslaughter] ... for the Death of Andrew J. Davis, ... on the first of June, 1840. By [T. S. Nelson]. *St. Louis.* 1840. 8vo, pp. 248. + Second Edition. *Boston: Printed by Tuttle, Dennett & Chisholm.* 1841. 8vo, pp. 268. BA.

DARRACH (William). Memoir of George McClellan, M.D. ... By W. Darrach ... . *Philadelphia: J. G. Auner.* 1827. 8vo, pp. 40. H. 18606

DARRAGH (Cornelius). Speech of Mr. C. Darragh, of Pennsylvania, on the Oregon Question, Delivered in the House ... Monday, February 9, 1846. [n. p. n. d.] 8vo, pp. 8. 18607

DARROW (David), MEACHAM (John), *and* YOUNGS (Benjamin Seth). Testimony of Christ's Second Appearing exemplified by the Principles and Practice of the Church of Christ. History of the Progressive Work of God, extending from the Creation of man to the "Harvest." Second Edition, Corrected and Improved. *Albany.* 1810. 12mo, pp. xxx, 620. + Third Edition, Corrected and Improved. *Union Village, O.* 1823. 12mo, pp. xvii, 573. + Fourth Edition. [*Albany:*] *United Society of Shakers.* [1856.] 8vo. 18608

DARTMOOR, *Eng.* The Prisoners' Memoirs or Dartmoor Prison. *See* Andrews (Charles), Vol. I., No. 1484.

DARTMOUTH, *Mass.* Celebration of the Two Hundredth Anniversary of the Incorporation of the town of Dartmouth. *New Bedford.* 1865. 8vo, pp. 129. 18609

Centennial Celebration. Proceedings in connection with the Celebration at New Bedford, September 14th, 1864, of the Two Hundredth Anniversary of the Incorporation of the Town of Dartmouth. ... *New Bedford, Mass.: E. Anthony & Sons, Prs.* 1865. 8vo, pp. 129. BA., S. 18610

Report of the Auditing Committee of the town of Dartmouth, for the year ending March 1, 1863. *New Bedford: Printed by E. Anthony.* 1863. 8vo, pp. 11. Continued. 18611

The Creed and Covenant of Dartmouth Church, with a Sketch of its History and a Catalogue of its Members, to January 4, 1855. *Hanover: Dartmouth Press.* 1855. 18612

DARTMOUTH COLLEGE. Argument for the Plaintiffs in the Dartmouth-College Case. [n. d.] 8vo, pp. 43. M. 18613

Candid Analytical Review of the "Sketches of the History of Dartmouth College." *See* [Parish (Elijah J.)]

Catalogue of the Books in Dartmouth-College Library. [*Hanover?* n. d.] 12mo, pp. 24. M. + Catalogue of the Books in the Social Friend's Library. *Concord.* 1824. 12mo. + Catalogue of Books in the United Fraternity's Library. *Concord.* 1824. 12mo. 18614

Catalogue of the Class of 1812, Dartmouth College. By S. Clarke. *Boston.* 1854. 8vo. Continued. + Catalogue of the Society of Social Friends from 1783 to 1826, Dartmouth College. *Boston.* 1826. pp. 38. 18615

Catalogue of the Officers and Students of Dartmouth University ... 1805. *Walpole, Northamptonshire.* Broadside. Continued in 8vo, usually at *Hanover*, occasionally at *Concord* and *Windsor.* 18616

Catalogus Universitatis Dartmuthensis. 1804. *Leuphanæ: Typis Mosis Davis.* 1804. 8vo, pp. 16. Continued. 18617

The Charter of Dartmouth College, 1769. [n. p. n. d.] 4to, pp. 14. + *Hanover.* 1816. 8vo, pp. 14. M. 18618

Class of Alumni of Dartmouth College in 1811, Minutes of their Meeting in 1849, and Biographical Notices. *Concord.* 1850. 8vo, pp. 35. 18619

Documents relative to Dartmouth College. Published by Order of the Legislature [of N. H.], 1816. [n. p.] 1816. 8vo, pp. 39. 18620

Narrative of the Origin and Progress of the Difficulties in the Vicinity of Dartmouth College. *Hanover.* 1815. 8vo, pp. 68.

Observations on Facts, vindicating the Rights of Dartmouth College and Moors' Charity School to the Grant made by the Legislature of Vermont in June 1785. [*Windsor, Vt.* 1807.] 8vo. 18622

Opinion of the Superior Court of the State of New Hampshire, in the Case of the Trustees of Dartmouth College versus William H. Woodward, Esq., pronounced at Plymouth, in the County of Grafton, at the November Term, 1817. *Concord: Isaac Hill.* 1818. 8vo, pp. 27. 18623

Remarks made by the Pastor in "The Congregational Church and Dartmouth College" on the Sunday (March 9, 1862) after the President's Emancipation Message. 8vo, pp. 3. 18624

Report of the Case of the Trustees of Dartmouth College against Woodward, together with the Constitution, Charter, Laws, &c. *Dartmouth Press.* [n. d.] 18625

See also Vol. I. "Newhampshire Reports," and Farrar (T.)

A Report on a Memorial of the Alumni of Dartmouth, at Boston, to the Trustees, on Scholarships and Prizes. *Boston.* 1858. 8vo, pp. 54. S. 18626

Septenary Catalogue of the Class of 1843 of Dartmouth College. *Manchester, N. H.* 1851. 8vo, pp. 42. 18627

Sketches of the First Graduates of Dartmouth College, from 1771 to 1783. *Concord.* 1823. 18628

Sketches of the Graduates of Dartmouth College from its Foundation in 1769 to the year 1834. *Concord: Jacob B. Moore.* 1832–34. 18629

Sketches of the History of Dartmouth College and Moors' Charity School, with a particular Account of some late Remarkable Proceedings of the Board of Trustees, from the Year 1779 to the Year 1815. [n. p. n. d.] 8vo, pp. 88. 18630

Statutes of Dartmouth University relating to Medical Gradation. Passed August 25, 1812. [n. p. n. d.] 8vo, pp. 8.

True and Concise Narrative of the Origin and Progress of the Church Difficulties in the Vicinity of Dartmouth College. *Hanover, N. H.* 1815. 8vo, pp. 68. 18632

A Vindication of the Official Conduct of the Trustees of Dartmouth College, in Answer to "Sketches of the History of Dartmouth College," and "A Candid Analytical Review of the Sketches," &c. Published by the Trustees. *Concord: George Hough.* 1815. 8vo, pp. 104. BA. 18633

For answers, *see* Dunham (J.), and Freeman (P. R.) John Wheelock was the reputed author of the "Sketches," or at least furnished the materials for that pamphlet.

DARTNELL (G.) A Proposed Plan for a Railroad Clearing House. By George Dartnell. *Buffalo.* 1858. 8vo, pp. 31.

DARTNELL (G. R.) A Brief Narrative of the Shipwreck of the Transport "Premier," near the Mouth of the River St. Lawrence, on the Fourth November, 1843. By George R. Dartnell. *London: Jeremiah How.* 1845. 4to, pp. xv, 37. 6 Plates. 18635

DARTON (T. G.) Statistical Tables of Population, ... Commerce, Shipping, Emigration, &c. 1801 to 1851. Compiled from Parliamentary and other Authentic Documents. By T. G. Darton. *London: Longman.* 1854. 8vo, pp. 36. 18636

D'ARUSMONT (F. W.) Biography, Notes, and Political Letters of Frances Wright D'Arusmont. From the first British Edition. ... *New-York: by John Windt.* 1845. 2 pts., 16mo, pp. 48; 47. H. 18637

D'ARUSMONT. Biography, and Notes of Frances Wright D'Arusmont. [From the Dundee (Scotland) Northern Star.] *Boston: printed by J. P. Mendum.* 1848. 12mo. 18638

D'ARUSMONT. Course of Popular Lectures, Historical and Political, as delivered by Frances Wright Darusmont, in ... the United States, being introductory to a Course on the Nature and Object of America's Political Institutions. Vol. II. *Philadelphia.* 12mo, pp. 90. H. 18639

[D'ARUSMONT.] Views of Society and Manners in America; in a Series of Letters from that Country to a Friend in England During the Years 1818, 1819 and 1820. By an English-Woman. *London: Longman.* 1821. 8vo, pp. x, 523. + *New York: E. Bliss.* 1821. 8vo, pp. xii, 387. 18640

The New York edition has additions and corrections by the author.

D'ARUSMONT. Views, [etc.] By Frances Wright. Second Edition. *London: Longman.* 1822. 8vo, pp. x, 483. 18641

Roughly handled in the "Q. Rev.," XXVII. 71. *See also* "M. Rev.," XCVII. 247.

D'ARUSMONT. Voyage aux États-Unis d'Amérique; ou Observations sur la société, les mœurs, en 1818–20: trad. de l'anglais par J. T. Parisot. *Paris.* 1822. 2 vols., 8vo. 18642

D'ARUSMONT. Tafereelen van Noord Amerika, of Reize door de Vereenigde Staten. Uit het engelsch vertaald. *Amsterdam.* 1822. 2 pts., 8vo. 18643

DARWELL (J.) Political Lamentations, written in the Years 1775 and 1776. To which is annexed a Political Sermon, preached in ... Walsal December 13. 1776, being the Day appointed for a General Fast, on account of Troubles in America. By John Darwell. *London: T. Nichol.* 1777. 4to.

The "Political Lamentations" are lamentable poetry, and the sermon is lamentable prose. *See* "M. Rev.," LVI. 390.

DARWIN (C.) Geological Observations on Coral Reefs, Volcanic Islands, and on South America. Being the Geology of the Voyage of the Beagle, under the Command of Captain Fitzroy, R. N., during the Years 1832 to 1836. By Charles Darwin, M.A., ... Naturalist to the Expedition. With numerous Illustrations and Maps. *London: Smith, Elder & Co.* 1851. 3 pts., 8vo, Title, pp. xii, 214; vii, 175; vii, (1), 279. 3 Maps and 5 Plates. 18645

DARWIN. Geological Observations on South America. Being the Third Part of the Geology of the Voyage of the "Beagle," under the Command of Capt. Fitzroy, R. N. during the Years 1832 to 1836. By C. Darwin, Naturalist to the Expedition. *London.* 1846. 8vo, pp. 286. Map and 5 Plates. P. 18646

The second part does not relate to America.

DARWIN. Journal of Researches into the Natural History and Geology of the Countries visited during the Voyage of H. M. S. Beagle round the World, under the Command of Captain Fitz Roy, R. N. By Charles Darwin. *London: J. Murray.* 1845. Post 8vo, pp. 336. + *New York.* 1846. 2 vols., 12mo. + New Edition. *London: J. Murray.* 1852. Post 8vo. C.

This was first published as the third volume of King, Fitzroy, and Darwin's "Narrative of the Surveying Voyages of ... [the] Adventure and Beagle. *London: Henry Colburn.* 1839." 8vo, pp. xiv, 615. Map. BA. Also forms Nos. 22 and 23 of Murray's "Home and Colonial Library."

DARWIN. The Structure and Distribution of the Coral Reefs; being the first part of the Geology of the voyage of the Beagle during the years 1832 to 1836. By Charles Darwin. *London.* 1842. 8vo. 18648

DARWIN. The Zoology of the Voyage of H. M. S. Beagle, under the Command of Capt. Fitzroy, R. N., during the Years 1832 to 1836. ... Edited and Superintended by Charles Darwin, Esq. M.A. F.R.S. Sec. G.S. Naturalist to the Expedition. *London.* MDCCCXXXIX–XLIII. 5 vols., 4to. BA., C. 18649

Consists of Fossil Mammalia, by Richard Owen, F.R.S., with a Geological Introduction, by Charles Darwin, Esq., etc., pp. 120, 32 plates; Mammalia, by George R. Waterhouse, Esq., pp. 106, 35 plates; Birds, by John Gould, Esq., F.R.S., with a Notice of their Habits and Ranges, by Charles Darwin, Esq., etc., pp. 164, 35 plates; Fish, by the Rev. Leonard Jenyns, M.A., F.R.S., pp. 188, 29 plates; Reptiles, by Thomas Bell, F.R.S., etc., pp. 56, 20 plates.

DARWIN. Naturwissenschaftliche Reisen nach des Inseln den grünen Vorgebirges, Südamerika, dem Feuerlande, den Falkland-Inseln Chiloe-Inseln und Galopagos-Inseln, Otaheiti, Neuholland, Neuseeland on Deutsch und mit Anmerkungen von Er. Dieffenbach. *Braunschweig: Vieweg und Sohn.* 1844. 2 vols., 8vo. Map and Woodcuts. 18650

DASCOMB (A. B.) A Discourse preached by Rev. A. B. Dascomb, to the People at Waitsfield, Vt., in Honor of our late Chief Magistrate, on Sunday, April 23, 1865. Published by Request. *Montpelier: Walton's Steam Printing Establishment.* 1865. 8vo, pp. 23. 18651

DASHIELL (A. H.) An Oration ... before the Hermean Society, February 22, 1811. By Alfred H. Dashiell. [*Philadelphia.* 1811.] 8vo, pp. 15. 18652

Also: Sermon on Life and Character of Rev. Joseph Eastburn. *Philadelphia* 1828.

DASHIELL (G.) The State of Maryland, against the Vestry of St. Peter's Church ... enjoining and prohibiting them from further permitting George Dashiell to occupy the Parsonage House, and to officiate ... in said Church ... . *Baltimore: Joseph Robinson.* 1817. 8vo, pp. 80. H. 18653

DA SILVA. *See* Silva.

DASSIÉ (*Sieur* C. R.) Description generale des costes de l'Amérique, Havres, Isles, Caps, Golfes, Bancs, Ecueils, Basses, Profondeurs, Vents & Courans d'Eau. Des Peuples qui les habitent, du temperamment de l'air, de la qualité des Terres & du Commerce ... . Par Mr Dassié, C.R. *Imprimé à Rouen, & se vend a Paris, Robert J. Baptiste de la Caille* ... . M. DC. LXXVI. 16mo, 9 l., pp. 421. BA. + *Rouen: B. Le Brun.* MDCLXXVII. 12mo, 8 l., pp. 421. S. + *Havre.* 1680. 12mo. 18654

DASSIÉ. Le routier des Indes Orientales et Occidentales: traitant des saisons propres à y faire Voyage: Une description des Anchorages, Profondeurs de plusieurs Havres et Ports de Mer. Avec vingt-six differentes navigations. *Paris, Jean de la Caille.* 1677. 4to, pp. 209, 1 l. 18655

DATI (G.) Questa e la hystoria della inuentiõe delle diese Isole di Cannaria in In|diane extracte duna Epistola di Christofano colombo & per messer Giu|liano Dati traducta de latino in uersi ulgari a laude e gloria della cele|stiale corte & aconsolatione della Christiana religiõe & apreghiera del ma|gnifico Caualier miser Giouanfilippo Delignamine domestico familia|re dello sacratissimo Re di Spagna Christianissimo a di. xxv. doctobre.|M.cccclxxxxiii.| [Colophon:] Joannes dictus Florentinus.|[*Florence.* 1493.] 4to, 4 l. BM. 18656

The only known copy is in the British Museum, and lacks the second and third leaves. "It is not a translation of the first letter of Columbus, but only an ottava rima paraphrase, in sixty-eight stanzas."—[HARRISSE], who gives some extracts from the work.

DATI. Lalettera dellisole che ha trouato nuouamente il Re dispagna.| [Large Woodcut.] [Colophon:] Finita lastoria della iuẽtione del|le nououe isole di canãria ĩdiane trac|te duna pistola dixpofano colõbo & *per* messer Giuliano dati tradocta di la|tino ĩ uersi uulgari allaude della ce|lestiale corte & aconsolatione della|christiana religione & ap*re*ghiera del|magnifico caualiere messer Giouã-|filippo del ignamine domestico fa-|miliare dello illustrissimo Re dispa|gna xpianissimo a di. XXVI. docto-|bre. 14.93.|*Florentie.*| 4to, 4 l. BM. 18657

One copy only known, which is in the British Museum. The woodcut is repeated n the Vespuccius of 1516, and is reproduced in facsimile in the "Bibl. Am. Vet." Harrisse remarks, "There are material differences between this edition and the above. Here, we find a woodcut, the text is in Roman, the spelling is different, and the text, even, presents variations. Yet, according to the colophon, only one day elapsed between the publications of Nos. 18657 and 18658." There is another edition, "cavaliere messer Giovanfilippo de lignamine | domestico famigliare dello illustrissimo | re di Spagna Christianissimo | adi xxvi doctobre 1495 | *Florentie.*" | *See* Harrisse, p. 461.

D'ATIENZA (Giovanni), *and* DIAZ (Pietro). Raggvaglio d' alcuni avisi notabili dell' Indie Orientali y Occidentali. Con l' arrivo delli Signori Ambasciatori Giaponesi alli loro Stati. Cuatro da alcune lettere scritte gli anni 1590 et 1591. *Roma & Bologna: Vittoria Benacci.* 1593. 12mo, pp. 48. J.C.B. 18658

Relates to the missions to Peru and Mexico. Translated into German in the "Fortsetzung der Zeytungen."

Datos oficiales: La Republica Arjentina. — Poblacion; Immigracion; Colonias Agricolas; Concesiones de terrenos; Ferrocarriles, etc. *Paris.* 1867. Rl. 8vo, pp. 16. 18659

DAUBENY (C. Giles Bridle). A Description of Active and Extinct Volcanos ... . By Charles Daubney, M.D., F.R.S. ... . *London: W. Phillips.* 1826. 8vo, pp. xx, 466, 1 l. BA. + Second Edition, Enlarged. *London.* 1848. 8vo, pp. 752.

DAUBENY. Sketch of the Geology of North America. Being the Subtance of a Memoir read before the Ashmolean Society, November 26, 1838. *Oxford.* 1839. 8vo. Map. 1

DAUBENY. Journal of a Tour through the United States, and in Canada, made during the years 1837–38. *Oxford.* 1843. Post 8vo, pp. 231. 18662

Printed for private circulation only.

[D'AUBERTEUIL (Hilliard).] *See* Hilliard d'Auberteuil.

DAUBIGNY. *See* [Baudouin (Jean Marie Théodore)], Vol. I., No. 3978.

D'AUBRÉE (Paul). Colonists and Manufacturers in the West Indies. Translated from the French. *London.* 1844. 8vo.

DAUDET (A.) Le Camp de Jackson, ou le Prix de la Valeur, Vaudeville en un acte, impromptu de circonstance, Par Alexis Daudet. Représenté pour la première fois, le 28 Janvier 1815, sur le Théatre St.-Philippe, á Nlle.-Orléans. *A La Nlle.-Orleans.* M.DCCC.XV. 8vo, pp.32. 18664

The Daughters of the Prairie. *Boston: American Tract Society.* 1865. 16mo, pp. 301. 3 Illustrations. c. 18665

DAUL (A.) Das Buch von der amerikanischen Nähmaschine. Geschichte der Erfindung, Construktion und Fabrikation derselben ... . *Hamburg: Fischer.* 1864. 8vo, pp. viii, 19. 32 Woodcuts in the text, and 1 folded woodcut. 18666

DAUMONT (Alexandre). L'ile de Cuba. Le comte de Villanueva et le général Tacon. Article inséré dans les numéros des 28 septembre, 8, 15 et 20 octobre 1837 du Moniteur industrial par Al. Daumont. Revu et corrigé. Suivi d'extraits de la Revue britannique [janvier 1837] sur le même sujet. *Paris: imp. de Maulde.* 1837. 8vo, pp. 47. B. 18667

DAUNCE (Edward). A briefe Discourse dialoguewise, shewing how false and dangerous their reports are, which affirm, the Spaniards' intended invasion to be, for the re-establishment of the Romish Religion; for her Majestie's succours given to the Netherlanders, and for Sir Francis Drake's Enterprise three yeares past into the West Indies. *London: R. Field.* 1590. 4to. BM. 18668

Title from Lowndes. *See* "Bibl. Grenvilliana." Dedicated to Admiral Lord Howard.

DAUNCEY (John). A Compendious Chronicle of the Kingdom of Portugal. *London.* 1661. 8vo. Frontispiece and Portrait. 18669

Contains notices relating to the West Indies, the discovery of Brazil, etc.

Report of the Stockholders of the Dauphin and Susquehanna Coal Company. *Philadelphia: T. K. and P. G. Collins, Printers.* 1848. 8vo, pp. 16. H. 18670

DAURICO (Maron). Cartas sobre la variacion de nuestro sistema gubernativo. *Mexico.* 1815. 12mo, pp. 133. 18671

D'AUTEROCHE (J. C.) *See* Chappe D'Auteroche, Vol. III., Nos. 12003–4.

DAUXION-LAVAYASSE (J. J.) Reise nach den Inseln Trinidad, Tabago und Margaretha, so wie in verschiedenen Theile von Venezuela. Aus dem Französischen. Mit Noten von C. A. W. von Zimmermann. *Weimar.* 1816. 8vo. Map. (Neue Bibl. d. wichtigsten Reisebeschr., 5.) 18672

DAUXION-LAVAYASSE. Voyage aux Iles de Trinidad, de Tabago, de la Marguerite, et dans diverses parties de Venezuela, dans l'Amerique Méridionale, par J. J. Dauxion Lavaysse. *Paris.* 1813. 2 vols., 8vo, 60 sheets. 2 Maps. 18673

DAUXION-LAVAYASSE. A Statistical, Commercial, and Political Description of Venezuela, Trinidad, Margarita, and Tobago; Containing Various Anecdotes and Observations, illustrative of the past and present state of those interesting Countries; from the French of M. Lavayasse; with an Introduction and Explanatory Notes, By the Editor [E. Blaquière]. *London: G. ana W. B. Whitaker.* 1820. 8vo, pp. xxxii, 480. Map. 18674

DAUXION-LAVAYASSE. A Statistical [as before]. From the French of M. Lavayasse, with a Preface and Explanatory Notes. By Edward Blaquiére, Esq. Second Edition. *London: G. ana W. B. Whitaker.* 1821. 8 l., pp. xviii, 490. Map. 18675

The dedication to General Devereux is omitted in this edition, the preface is abridged, and ten pages of appendix are added. The body of the work is the same. *See* "M. Rev.," XCIII. 483.

DAVALOS. Miscellanea Austral. *London.* 1602. 4to.

DAVATZ (Thomas). Die Behandlung der Kolonisten in der Provinz St. Paulo in Brasilien und deren Erhebung gegen ihre Bedrücker. Ein Noth- und Hilsruf an die Behörden und Menschenfreunde der Länder und Staaten, welchen die Kolonisten gehörten. *Chur: Hitz.* 1858. 8vo, pp. 243. 18677

DAVEGA (I.) The New York City Railroad Directory. By Isaac Davega. *New York: J. M. Bradstreet & Son.* 1864. 32mo, pp. 175. 18678

DAVEIS (C. Stewart.) An Address delivered on the Commemoration at Fryeburg, May 19, 1825, by Charles S. Daveis. *Portland: James Adams, Jr.* 1825. 8vo, pp. 84. BA., C. 1

DAVEIS. An Address delivered at Portland, on the Decease of John Adams and Thomas Jefferson, August 9. 1826, by Charles Stewart Daveis. *Portland: Jas. Adams, Jr.* 1826. 8vo, pp. 55. 18680

DAVEIS. The North-Eastern Boundary of the United States. By Charles S. Daveis. *Boston: Printed by Pierce & Parker.* 1832. 16mo, pp. 100, (2). BA. 18681

DAVEIS. Report of Charles S. Daveis, Esq. Agent appointed by the Executive of the State of Maine To inquire into and report upon certain facts relating to aggressions upon the rights of the State, and of individual citizens thereof, by inhabitants of the province of New-Brunswick. *Portland.* 1828. 8vo, pp. 48.

Also in "Documents rel. to the N. E. Boundary," published by the Mass. legislature. Also: Address delivered before the Alumni of Bowdoin College on the evening before Commencement. September 1, 1835. ... *Portland.* 1835. 8vo, pp. 67.

DAVEISS (J. H.) Sketch of a Bill for an Uniform Militia of the United States, with Reflections on the State of the Nation; addressed to the Secretary of War, by Joseph Hamilton Daveiss. *Frankfort, Ky.: Printed by Henry Gore.* 1810. 8vo, pp. 85.

DAVEISS. A View of the President's Conduct, concerning the Conspiracy of 1806. By J. H. Daveiss ... . *Frankfort, Ky.: From the Press of Joseph M. Street.* 1807. 8vo, pp. 64.

D'AVENANT (C.) Account of the Trade with Great Britain, etc. particularly of the Woollen Manufacturers, By Chas. D'Avenant. *London.* 1736. 18685

[D'AVENANT.] Discourses on the Publick Revenues, and on the Trade of England. ... *London: James Knapton.* 1698. 2 vols., 8vo, 8 l., pp. 279, (1), 62; 4 l., pp. 434. 18686

Relates to Jamaica, New England, etc.

D'AVENANT. The Political and Commercial Works of that celebrated Writer Charles D'Avenant, LL.D. ... . Collected and revised by Sir Charles Whitworth, ... To which is annexed a copious Index. *London: Printed for R. Horsfield.* MDCCLXXI. 5 vols., 8vo, pp. 459; 382; 430; 439; 463, (42). BA 18687

D'Avenant was Inspector-General of Imports and Exports under Queen Anne. His writings had great influence on the colonial and commercial policy of the government for nearly a century. *See* "M. Rev.," XLIV. 494; *also* "Select Dissertations."

D'AVENANT. A Report on the Hon. the Commissioners for putting in Execution the Act, Intituled, an Act for the Taking, Examining and Stating the Publick Accounts of the Kingdom. 2 pts., 8vo, pp. 78; 75. c. 18688

The second part relates to the trade of the West Indies, etc.

[D'AVENANT (*Sir* William).] The Cruelty of the | Spaniards | in | Peru. | Expresst by Instrumentall and | Vocall Musick, and by Art of | Perspective in Scenes, &c. | Represented daily at the

Cockpit | in Drury-Lane, | at Three after noone | punctually. | *London,* | *Printed for Henry Herringman, and are to be sold at his Shop* | *at the Anchor in the Lower walk in the* | *New Exchange.* 1658. | 4to, 2 l., pp. 27. BD. 18689

Oliver Cromwell, who prohibited all theatrical representations, not only allowed the piece to be performed, but even himself actually read and approved it. It was subsequently incorporated in D'Avenant's piece "Playhouse to Let." *See* Works, fol. 1673, p. 103; *also* Genest's "Account of the English Stage."

D'AVENANT. The History of Sir Francis Drake, Exprest by Instrumentall and Vocall Musick, and by Art of Perspective in Scenes, &c., The First Part Represented Daily at the Cockpit, in Drury Lane, at 3 Afternoon punctually. *London.* 1659. 4to. Frontispiece. s. 18690

Also included in his works, *London.* 1673. Folio. B.

DAVENPORT (A. B.) A History and Genealogy of the Davenport Family in England and America, from A.D. 1806 to 1850. ... By A. Benedict Davenport (of the twenty-fourth Generation), ... *New York: S. W. Benedict.* 1851. 12mo, pp. 398. Portrait. 18691

DAVENPORT (B.) A History and New Gazetteer; or, Geographical Dictionary of North America and the West Indies, etc. By Bishop Davenport. *New York.* 1842. 8vo. 18692

DAVENPORT. History of the United States, for the Use ot Schools. ... New Edition. *Philadelphia: Marshall & Co.* 1837. 18mo, pp. 144. + New Edition, revised ... by John J. Anderson ... . *Philadelphia: Uriah Hunt & Son.* 1852. 12mo, pp. 174. H. + [1867.] 16mo, pp. 296. c. 8693

DAVENPORT. A New Gazetteer; or Geographical Dictionary of North America and the West Indies. ... By Bishop Davenport. *Baltimore: George M'Dowell.* 1832. 8vo, pp. 471. Map. B., C. 18694

DAVENPORT. Pocket Gazetteer, or Travellers' Guide through North America and the West Indies. *Trenton.* 1833. 18mo, pp. 408. Woodcuts. + *Baltimore.* 1833. 18mo. 18695

DAVENPORT (D.) The Sexton's Monitor, and Dorchester-Cemetery Memorial ... *Roxbury: Printed by Thomas S. Watts.* 1826. 12mo, pp. 38. + Second Edition. *Boston.* 1838. 12mo, pp. 36. 18696

DAVENPORT (E.) An Oration on the Death of General George Washington, delivered at Stamford, Connecticut, on the 22d day of February, A.D. 1800. By Ebenezer Davenport, Esq. Published by the Committee of Arrangements. *New York.* 1800. 8vo, pp. 15. N. 18697

DAVENPORT (J.) The Declaration of a number of the Associated Pastors of Boston and Charlestown relating to the Rev. James Davenport, and his Conduct. *Boston: Printed by S. Kneeland & T. Green.* 1742. 16mo, pp. 7. BA. 18698

DAVENPORT. A Letter from the Rev. Mr. James Davenport, to Mr. Jonathan Barber, Preacher of the Gospel at Bethesda in Georgia; published with the free consent of Mr. Davenport. [*Philadelphia: W. Bradford.* 1744?] 12mo, pp. 32. P. 18699

DAVENPORT. To the Reverend James Davenport on his Departure from Boston. With a Line to the Scoffers of Religion. [Verses.] Added, A Postscript to Rev. A--d--w C--w-ll [Andrew Crosswell]. By a Female Friend. [Colophon:] *Boston.* 1742. 8vo, pp. 8. B. 18700

DAVENPORT. The Reverend Mr. James Davenport's Confession & Retractations. *Boston: Printed by S. Kneeland and T. Green.* 1744. 8vo, pp. 8. B., W. 18701

Accompanying the "Confession," etc., p. 2, is "A Letter from the Rev. Mr. Solomon Williams of Lebanon to the Rev. Mr. Prince."

DAVENPORT (James). *See* Davenport (M.), No. 18716.

DAVENPORT (James R.) The Lord our Helper; a Sermon in Commemoration of the Sixth Anniversary of the Commencement of the Parish of Grace Church, Albany, ... Feb. 15, 1852. *Albany: J. Munsell.* 1852. 12mo, pp. 22. 18702

DAVENPORT (J.) Another Essay For Investigation of the Truth in Answer to Two Questions Concerning, I. The Subject of Baptism. II. The Consociation of Churches, By John Davenport, of Newhaven. *Cambridge.* 1663. pp. (16), 71.

DAVENPORT. A Defence of the Answer and Arguments of the Synod Met at Boston in the Year 1662. Concerning The Subject of Baptism and Consociation of Churches. Against the Reply made thereto, by the Rev. Mr. John Davenport, Pastor of the Church at New-Haven, in his Treatise Entituled, Another Essay for the Investigation of the Truth, &c. To-

gether with an Answer to the Apologetical Preface Set before that Essay. By some who were Members of the Synod abovementioned. *Cambridge: Printed by S. Green, for Hezekiah Usher.* 1664. 4to, pp. 46, 102. 18704

[DAVENPORT.] A | Discourse | about | Civil Government | in a | New Plantation | Whose Design is | Religion. Written many years since, | By that Reverend and Worthy Minister of the Gospel, | John Cotton B.D. | and now Published by some Undertakers of | a new Plantation, for General Direction | and Information. *Cambridge:* | *Printed by Samuel Green and Marmaduke Johnson.* | MDCLXIII. | 4to, pp. 24. B. 18705

"In the title-page whereof, the name of Mr. Cotton is, by a mistake, put for that of Mr. Davenport." — MATHER'S *Magnalia*, B. 3, p. 56. *See also* Bacon's "Historical Discourse." It is a rare volume. A copy was sold by Royal Gurley, in 1847, for $14.50; was re-sold by Bangs, in 1852, purchased by Mr. Corwin, and sold with his collection, in 1856, for $25, and would now (1871) command at least three times that amount.

DAVENPORT. Gods Call | to | His People | To Turn unto him; | Together with | His Promise to Turn unto them. | Opened and Applied in | II. Sermons | At two Publick Fasting-dayes appointed by Authority. | By Mr. John Davenport B.D. and Pastor to the First | Church of Christ at Boston in New-England. | Published at the desire of sundry Friends. | *Cambridge:* | *Printed by S. G. & M. J. for John Usher of Boston.* | MDCLXIX. | 4to, pp. 27. 18706

J. A. Rice's copy sold, in 1870, for $41.

DAVENPORT. The knowledge of Christ indispensably required of all Men that would be saved; or Demonstrative Proofs from Scripture that Jesus is the Christ, wherein the Types, Prophesies, Genealogies, Miracles, Humiliation, Exhaltation, and the Mediatorial Office of Christ, are opened and applied, in sundry Sermons on Acts ii. 36, by John Davenport, Pastor to the Church of Christ at New-Haven, in New England. 1653. 4to.

DAVENPORT. The Power of | Congregational Churches | Asserted and Vindicated, | In Answer to a | Treatise | of | Mr. J. Paget, | Intituled | The Defence of Church-Government | exercised in Classes and Synods. | By John Davenport, B. of D. | and Pastor to the Church in Newhaven | in New-England. | [Text, 5 lines.] *London,* | *Printed in the Year,* | 1672. | 16mo, Title, 5 l., pp. 21, 2, 179. 18708

The copies in the Boston Public and Harvard College Libraries have the imprint, *London: Printed for Rich. Chiswell, and to be sold by John Usher of Boston in New-England.* 1672. 8vo, Title, pp. (8), 179 [misprint for 163].

DAVENPORT. The | Profession | of the Faith | of that Reverend | and worthy Divine Mr. J. D., some- | time Preacher of Stevens Coleman- | street. London. | Made publiquely before the Congrega- | tion at his Admission into one of the Churches | of God in New-England. | Containing twenty severall heads as it was drawn | from his own Copy. ... . *London:* | *John Handcock* ... | 1641. | Sm. 4to, pp. 8. c. 18709

DAVENPORT The | Saints | Anchor-Hold, | in all | Storms and Tempests. | Preached in Sundry | Sermons, | And Published for the Support | and Comfort of Gods People, in | all Times of Tryal. | By John Davenport, B.D. sometime | Minister of Stephens Coleman-street; | London; and now Pastor of the Church | of Christ in New-Haven, in New-England. | *London: Benjamin Harris.* 1701. | 12mo, 3 l., pp. 156. B. 18710

There are some slight variations in the title of the edition of 1701. Also, a Massachusetts Election Sermon, 1670, the title of which I cannot find, and "An Answer of the Elders of the severall Churches in New-England unto Nine Positions sent over to them," by ministers in England, which is published, with a separate title-page, but a continuous paging (pp. 49–78), in Rich, Mather's "Church Government," *London.* 1643. 4to.

DAVENPORT (J.) Catalogue of the Persons Admitted to the First Church in New Haven, during the Ministry of the Rev. James Pierpont and the Rev. Jas. Noyes, from 1685 to 1757. By Rev. John Davenport. *New Haven.* 1855. 12mo.

DAVENPORT (J.) Chapter in the History of Abolition at Syracuse, Oct. 26, 1839. *Syracuse.* 1839. 8vo. 18712

[DAVENPORT (John J.)] The Wig and the Jimmy; or, a Leaf in the Political History of New York. ... *New York.* 1869. 8vo, pp. 32. H. 18713

DAVENPORT (J. L.) Official Documents relating to a Chaplain's Campaign, (not) with General Butler. By J. L. Davenport. *Lowell.* 1865. 8vo. 18714

DAVENPORT (J. S.) A Letter to the Rt. Rev. Wm. H. Delancey, D.D. from John S. Davenport, Presbyter, showing Cause why Sentence of Deposition should not be pronounced against him. *New York: John Moffet.* 1855. 8vo, pp. 23.

DAVENPORT (M.) A Brief Historical Sketch of the Town of West Boylston ... [Mass.] from its First Settlement to the Present Time. By Matthew Davenport. *Lancaster, Mass.: Printed by Carter, Andrews and Company.* 1831. 8vo, pp. 28. B.

The author's Christian name was subsequently changed to James.

[DAVENPORT (R.)] The Petitions of Rufus Davenport to the Twenty-four States, for the Adoption of the Free-Debt Rules. ... . Also, The Rise and Progress—The usurped Dominion, and the Urged Abolition, of Imprisonment for Debt. Extracted from Gov. Giles' Speech to the Legislature of Virginia. 1829. 8vo, 2 l., pp. 8. BA., H. 18717

[DAVENPORT.] The Right-Aim School Appeal to the Members of the Honorable House of Representatives of ... Massachusetts, for the Years of 1835 and 1836. [n. p.] 1836. 8vo, pp. 32. BA., H. 18718

DAVENPORT (Thomas). Electro-Magnetism. History of Davenport's Invention of the Application of Electro-Magnetism to Machinery; with Remarks on the Same ... by Professor Silliman. ... *New-York: G. & C. Carville & Co., and Geo. F. Hopkins & Son.* 1837. 8vo, pp. 94. H. 18719

The Davenport Brothers, the World renowned Spiritual Mediums: their Biography and Adventures in Europe and America. *Boston: W. White & Co.* [1869.] 12mo, 10 l., pp. 426. C.

DAVENPORT, *Iowa*. Mayor's Message, with accompanying Report of City Treasurer. Submitted to the City Council, of ... Davenport, Iowa, April 8th, 1857. *Davenport.* 1857. 8vo, pp. 13. Continued. H. 18721

Davenport City Directory for 1866. To which is added a Business Directory, etc. Compiled by A. G. Smallfield & L. Bruning. *Davenport: Luse & Griggs.* 8vo, pp. 164. 18722

Root's Davenport City Directory for 1868–9. *Davenport: Luse & Griggs.* 1869. 8vo, pp. 200. Continued. C. 18723

D'AVEZAC. *See* Avezac-Macaya (M. A. P. d'), Vol. I., Nos. 2491–93.

DAVID (Chr. Georg Nath.) Om Redningsanstalterne. (In Borger-Vennen, 1834, Nr. 4–10.) 18724

Also: Demokratiet i Nordamerika, efter Tocquéville. (In the same, 1848, Nr. 30–40.)—Uddrag af Beretningen fra den Komité, som af det franske Deputeretkammer var bleven nedsat for at undersöge de Tracys Forslag angaaende Slaverne i Kolonierne; aflagt ... i Komiteens Navn af M. A. de Tocquéville ... . (In Dansk Ugeskrift, 2den Raekke, IV. Nr. 90, 91.)—Uddrag af Beretningen fra den Commission, som ved Ordonnance af 26de Mai 1840 blev nedsat i Frankrig, for at tage Spörgsmaalene om Negeremancipationen og Coloniernes politiske Forfatning under Overveielse. (In the same, IV. Nr. 102–104, V. 112–114.)—On snarest muligt at ivaerksætte Negerslaveriets fuldkomme Ophör paa de dansk vestindiske Oer. (By himself and four others, Tidende for Forhandl. ved Prov.-St. for Ostisterne, 1844, pp. 999–1006.)—Om Ophævelse inden en vis kort Tid af Slaveriet paa de dansk vestindiske Besiddelser. (By the same, in the same, 1846, pp. 226, 227.)

DVAID (J. C.) Display of the Specific Distinctions. ... also, of all the Members Composing the Synod of the Federal Government at Washington, in the Years 1834, 1835, 1836, ... *Philadelphia: the Author.* 1836. 8vo, pp. 12. 18725

Also: Hierarchy of the American Scientific, Educational and Philosophical Society. No. 1. *Philadelphia.* 1835. 8vo. pp. 16.

DAVIDGE (F. H.) Oration on the Death of Lafayette, delivered July 10th, 1834. By F. H. Davidge. *Baltimore:* [n. d.] 8vo. 18726

[DAVIDSON (George).] The Case of the Caribbs in St. Vincent's. [*London.* 1787.] 12mo, pp. 23. 18727

"Signed 'George Davidson.' Probably privately printed."—STEVENS.

DAVIDSON (G. M.) The Traveller's Guide through the Middle and Northern States, and the Provinces of Canada. By G. M. Davidson. Seventh Edition. *Saratoga Springs.* 1837. 18mo. + Eighth Edition. *Saratoga Springs.* 1840. 18mo. 18728

DAVIDSON (Henry). Ecclesiastical Register. *Portland.* 1830. 8vo. W. 18729

DAVIDSON (H. M.) Fourteen Months in Southern Prisons. By H. M. Davidson, Member Battery A 1st O.V.L.A. *Dubuque: W. E. Tunis & Co.* 1865. 12mo, pp. 393. 18730

DAVIDSON (J.) An Address on Embalming; Delivered on Unrolling a Mummy. By J. Davidson. ... . *London.* 1833. Rl. 8vo. Plates. 18731

Added to this, is an "Account of the Palo de Vaca, the Cow Tree of Caracas, with an Analysis of its Milk and Bark."

DAVIDSON (J. W.) The Living Writers of the South. By James Ward Davidson. *New York: Carleton.* MDCCCLXIX. 12mo, pp. xxii, 17–635. BA., C. 18732

DAVIDSON (J.) Address on The Death of Abraham Lincoln, President of the United States. Delivered before the Lexington Literary Association, New York, April 19, 1865. By John Davidson. *New York: John S. Reed, Printer.* 1865. 8vo, pp. 16. 18733

Also: Oration delivered before the Legislature of N. J., upon "Our Sleeping Heroes," Feb. 22, 1866, ... *Trenton: Printed at the "State Gazette" Office.* 1866. 8vo, pp. 27.

DAVIDSON (L. M.) Poetical Remains of Lucretia Maria Davidson. Collected and arranged by her Mother: with a Biography, by Miss Sedgwick. *Philadelphia: Lea & Blanchard.* 1843. 16mo, pp. 248. B. + New Edition, revised. [*New York.* 1851.] 8vo. P. 18734

Also: Amir Khan, and other Poems, [etc.] with a Biographical Sketch, by Samuel F. B. Morse. *New York: G. & C. & H. Carvill.* 1829. 12mo, 1 l., pp. xxix, 174.

DAVIDSON (M. M.) The Biography and Poetical Remains of Margaret Miller Davidson. By Washington Irving. *Philadelphia: Lea and Blanchard.* 1841. 12mo, pp. 359. BA. + Third Edition. *Philadelphia.* 1842. 12mo. + New Edition, Revised. *New-York.* 1852. 8vo. 18735

Also: Selections from the Writings of Mrs. M. M. Davidson. *Philadelphia.* 1843. 12mo.

DAVIDSON (R.) Geography Epitomized; or a Description of the Terraqueous Globe, attempted in Verse. By Robert Davidson. *Philadelphia.* 1784. 18736

DAVIDSON. Geography Epitomized; or a Tour round the World. *Morris Town.* 1803. 12mo, pp. 60. 18737

DAVIDSON. A Sermon on the Freedom and Happiness of the United States, at Carlisle, October 5, 1794. By Robert Davidson. *Philadelphia.* 1794. 8vo. P., S. 18738

DAVIDSON (R.) An Excursion to the Mammoth Cave and the Barrens of Kentucky. With some Notices of the Early Settlement of the State. By the Rev. R. Davidson. *Philadelphia: Thomas Compertbwaite & Co.* 1840. 24mo, pp. ix, 148.

Some copies have the imprint, *Lexington, Ky.: A. T. Skillman & Son.* 1840.

DAVIDSON. A Historical Sketch of the First Presbyterian Church in the City of New-Brunswick; Read before the Historical Society of New-Jersey, September 8th, 1852, By Robert Davidson, D.D. Pastor of Said Church. ... *New Brunswick, N. J.* MDCCCLII. 8vo, pp. 52. Portrait of Gilbert Tennent. S.

DAVIDSON. History of the Presbyterian Church in the State of Kentucky; with a Preliminary Sketch of the Churches in the Valley of Virginia. By Robert Davidson, D.D. *New York: Robert Carter.* MDCCCXLVII. 8vo, pp. 371. B., C., P., S. 18741

DAVIDSON. The Lessons of the Hour. A Discourse upon President Lincoln, Delivered in the First Presbyterian Church,

Huntington, Long Island, April 19th, 1865, By Rev. Robert Davidson, D.D. Published by Request. *Huntington: Long-Islander, Printer.* [1865.] 8vo, pp. 12. + Second Edition. [*Ibid.*] 8vo, pp. 12. 18742

DAVIDSON. A Nation's Discipline; or, Trials not Judgments. A Discourse ... National Fast Day, September 26, 1861, ... New York, by Rev. Robert Davidson, ... *New York: W. S. Dorr, Printer.* 1861. 8vo, pp. 24. 18743

DAVIDSON. Presbyterianism, its True Place and Value in History. A Discourse delivered before the Presbyterian Historical Society, at the Annual Meeting, May 19, 1853. By Robert Davidson, D.D. *Philadelphia.* 1854. 8vo, pp. 28.

DAVIDSON. A Reply to the Late Manifesto. By R. Davidson. *Lexington.* 1820. 8vo. P. 18745

Also: Plea for Presbyterianism, N. Brunswick, N. J., 1844. 8vo. S.—A Vindication of Colleges and College Endowments. An Inaugural Address delivered in the Chapel of Morrison College, November 2, 1849, ... *Lexington, Ky.* 1841. 8vo, pp. 28.

[DAVIE (John Constanse).] Letters from Buenos Ayres and Chili, with an Original History of the latter Country. By the author of Letters from Paraguay. *London: R. Ackerman.* 1819. 8vo, pp. xi, 323. 6 Colored Plates. C. 18746

DAVIE. Letters from Paraguay; describing the Settlements of Montevideo and Buenos Ayres, the Presidencies of Rioja Minor, Nombre di Dios, St. Mary and St. John, &c. with the Manners, Customs, Religious Ceremonies, &c. of the Inhabitants. Written during a Residence of seventeen Months in that Country. By John Constanse Davie. *London: G. Robinson.* 1805. 8vo, pp. viii, 293. BA., C. 18747

DAVIE (W. R.) Instructions to be observed for the Formation and Movements of the Cavalry. ... By William Richardson Davie, Esquire, Governor, Captain-General and Commander in Chief of the Militia of the State of North-Carolina. *Halifax: Abraham Hodge.* M,DCC,XCIX. 8vo, pp. ix, (2), 180. Plate.

DAVIES (B.) The Bank Torpedo; or, Bank Notes Proved to be a Robbery on the Public. ... . By Benjamin Davies. *New York: Printed by M'Carty & White.* 1810. 12mo, pp. 59. 18749

DAVIES. Some Account of the City of Philadelphia, the Capital of Pennsylvania, and Seat of the Federal Congress; of its Civil and Religious Institutions, Population, Trade and Government; interspersed with Occasional Observations. By Benjamin Davies. *Philadelphia: Printed by Richard Folwell, for the Author.* 1794. 12mo, 2 l., pp. 93, and a folded sheet. BA.

Davies was a bookseller at No. 68 Market Street, Philadelphia. He issued an engraved plan to accompany this volume.

DAVIES (C.) The Metric System explained and adapted to the Systems of Instruction in the United States. By Charles Davies, LL.D. ... . *New York: published by A. S. Barnes & Co.* 1867. 16mo, pp. 20. H. 18751

DAVIES (E.) American Scenes and Christian Slavery: a Recent Tour of Four Thousand Miles in the United States. By Ebenezer Davies. *London: J. Snow.* 1849. Post 8vo, pp. 336. + [Cheap Edition.] *London: J. Freeman.* 1853. Post 8vo. 18752

DAVIES (Henry E.) Opinions delivered by the Judges of the Court of Appeals, on the Constitutionality of the Act of Congress, declaring Treasury Notes a Legal Tender for the Payment of Debts. *Albany: Weed, Parsons, and Company, Printers.* 1863. 8vo, pp. 68. H. 18753

DAVIES. Compilation of the Laws of the State of New-York, relating particularly to the City of New-York: Prepared by H. E. Davies. *New-York.* 18754

DAVIES (John). The History of the Caribby-islands. *See* [Rochefort]. 18755

DAVIES (R.) An account of the Convincement, Exercises, Services, and Travels of that ancient servant of the Lord Richard Davies: with some relation to Ancient Friends, and the spreading of Truth in North Wales, etc. Second Edition. [1st American ed.] *Philadelphia: J. Chattin.* 1752. 16mo, 10 l., pp. 223. C. 18756

DAVIES (S.) The Crisis; or the Uncertain Doom of Kingdoms at particular Times, Consider'd With Reference to Great-Britain and her Colonies in their present Circumstances. A Sermon Preached in Hanover, Virginia, October 28, 1756; a Day appointed by the Synod of New York, to be observed as A General Fast, on account of the present War with France. By

the Reverend Mr. Samuel Davies, A.M. With a Preface By the Reverend Mr. Thomas Gibbons. *London: J. Buckland.* MDCCLVIII. 8vo, pp. viii, 36. 18757

Contains curious particulars relating to the loss of Oswego, Braddock's defeat, etc.

DAVIES. The Curse of Cowardice: a Sermon preached to the Militia of Hanover County, in Virginia, at a General muster, May 8, 1758. With a view to raise a Company for Captain Samuel Meredith. By Samuel Davies, A.M. *London: J. Buckland.* MDCCLVIII. 12mo, pp. 36. P. + *Re-printed by James Parker, in Woodbridge.* 1759. 8vo, pp. 19. BA. + *Boston.* 1759. 12mo, pp. 30. W. 18758

DAVIES. The Duty of Christians to propagate their Religion among Heathens, Earnestly recommended to the Masters of Negroe Slaves in Virginia. A Sermon Preached in Hanover January 8, 1757. By Samuel Davies, A.M. *London: Printed by J. Oliver.* MDCC,LVIII. pp. 46, 1 l. 18759

DAVIES. The Good Soldier. Extracted from a Sermon Preached to a Company of Volunteers, Raised in Virginia, August 17, 1775. *London: Printed in the Year* MDCCLVI. 8vo, pp. 15. 18760

DAVIES. Letters from the Rev. Samuel Davies, and others, shewing the state of Religion in Virginia particularly among the Negroes. Likewise an Extract of a Letter from a Gentleman in London to his Friend in the Country, containing some Observations on the same. *London.* 1757. 12mo, pp. 44. + The Second Edition. *London: R. Pardon.* 1757. 12mo, pp. 44.

DAVIES. Little Children invited to Jesus Christ: A Sermon preached in Hanover County, Virginia, May 8, 1757. ... . *London: Printed by J. Buckland.* M DCC LXIII. 12mo, pp. 36. BA. + With An Account of the late remarkable religious Impressions among the Students in the College of New-Jersey. By Samuel Davies, A.M. The Sixth Edition. *Boston: Printea for Knight Sexton at Hartford.* M DCC LXX. 8vo, pp. 32. BA.

DAVIES. Religion | and | Patriotism | the | Constituents | of a Good | Soldier. | A Sermon preached to Captain Over- | ton's Independant Company of Volunteers, | raised in Hanover County, Virginia, Au- | gust 17, 1755. | By Samuel Davies, A.M., Minister of the | Gospel there. | *Philadelphia:* | *Printed by James Chattin.*

1755. | 4to, pp. 24. + *London: Re-printed for J. Buckland, J. Ward, and T. Field.* 1756. 8vo, pp. (2), 38. H. 18763

Contains the following prophetic note: "As a remarkable instance of this, I may point out to the Public that heroic youth, Col. Washington, whom I cannot but hope Providence has hitherto preserved in so signal a Manner for some important Service to his Country." *See* pages 9 and 12.

DAVIES. A Sermon, Preached before the Reverend Presbytery of New-Castle, October 11, 1752. By S. Davis, V.D.M. In Hanover, Virginia. Published at the Desire of the Presbytery and Congregation. *Philadelphia: Printed by B Franklin, and D. Hall.* M.DCC.LII. 8vo, pp. 38. 18764

DAVIES. A Sermon delivered at Nassau Hall, Jan. 14, 1761, on the death of ... George II. ... By Samuel Davies, A.M. ... . To which is prefixed, A brief account of the Life, Character, and Death, of the Author, By David Bostwick, A.M. ... New-York. *Philadelphia: W. Bradford.* 1761. 8vo, pp. ix, 18. J.C.B. + *Boston: R. Draper.* 1761. 8vo, pp. xii, 20. S. + *Boston.* [n. d.] 8vo, pp. 32. B., BA. 18765

DAVIES. Sermons on the Most Useful and Important Subjects ... . By the Rev. Samuel Davies, A.M. Late President of the College at Princeton in New-Jersey. *London: J. Buckland.* MDCLXVI. 3 vols., 8vo. + The Second Edition. ... To which are prefixed, A Sermon on the Death of Mr Davies, By Samuel Finley, D.D. and Another Discourse on the same Occasion, together with an Elegiac Poem to the Memory of Mr Davies, By Thomas Gibbons, D.D. *London: J. Buckland.* M.DCC.LXVII. 3 vols., 8vo. BA. + The Third Edition. *London: J. Buckland.* M DCC LXXIX. 4 vols., 8vo, pp. cxxviii, 288; viii, 392; vii, 397; xxxii, 367. + *New York.* 1792. 3 vols., 8vo. + Fifth Edition. *London.* 1804–6. 4 vols., 8vo. + Sixth Edition. *Philadelphia.* 1794. 3 vols., 8vo. + Third [American] Edition. *Boston.* 1811. 3 vols., 8vo. + *Baltimore.* 1816. 5 vols., 12mo. + *London: W. Baynes and Son.* 1824. 4 vols., 8vo, pp. xxviii, 461; iv, 475; iv, 448; iv, (3), 472. + Fourth American Edition. *New York: J. & J. Harper.* 1828. 3 vols., 8vo, pp. 420; 416; 372. + With an Essay on the Life and Times of the Author, by Albert Barnes. *New York: R. Carter and Brothers.* 1844. 3 vols., 12mo. + [*Ibid.*] 1849. 18766

DAVIES. Sermons and Tracts, separately Published at Boston, Philadelphia, etc. *Edinburgh.* 1793. 8vo, pp. 483.

DAVIES. The State of Religion among The Protestant Dissenters in Virginia; In a Letter To the Rev. Mr. Joseph Bellamy of Bethlem, in New England; From the Reverend Mr. Samuel Davies, V.D.M., in Hanover County, Virginia. *Boston, N. E.: S. Kneeland.* MDCCLI. 8vo, pp. 44. B. 18768

DAVIES. The Vessels of Mercy, and the Vessels of Wrath, delineated, in a new, uncontroverted, and practical Light. A Sermon First preached in New-Kent, Virginia, August 22, 1756. By Samuel Davies, A.M. *London: J. Buckland.* MDCCLVIII. 8vo, pp. 35. 18769

DAVIES. Virginia's Danger and Remedy. Two Discourses, Occasioned by The severe Droughts in sundry parts of the Country; and the Defeat of General Braddock. By Samuel Davies, A.M. ... *Williamsburg: Printed by William Hunter.* MDCCLVI. 8vo, pp. 16. H. 18770

Also: The Method of Salvation. A Sermon. By Mr. Samuel Davies, of New Jersey. *Reprinted at Providence: John Carter.* 1793. 8vo. pp. 52.—Religion and Public Spirit: Valedictory Address to the Senior Class in Nassau Hall, Sept. 21, 1760. *Portsmouth. N. H.* 1762. 8vo.—A Sermon on Man's Primitive State; and the First Covenant. Delivered before the Reverend Presbytery of New Castle, April 13th, 1748. ... . *Philadelphia.* 1748. 8vo, pp. 42.—Sermon at the Installation of Rev. John Todd to the Presbyterian Congregation of Hanover County in Virginia. *Glasgow.* 1754.—Substance of Sermons ... given in his own words. *New York.* 1851. 12mo, pp. 394.

DAVIES. Memoir of Rev. S. Davies ... *Boston.* 1832. 12mo.

DAVIES (T.) A Biographical Sketch of Rev. Thomas Davies, A.M., Missionary for Propagating the Gospel in Foreign Parts, from 1761 to 1766. *New Haven.* 1843. 12mo, pp. 59.

DAVIES (T.) Miscellaneous and Fugitive Pieces. *London.* 1774. 3 vols., 8vo. 18773

Contains "Life of Sir F. Drake," and a Letter on the American Colonies," etc.

DAVIES (W.) A Trve Relation of the Travailes, and most miserable Captiuitie of William Davies, Barber-Surgeon of London, under the Duke of Florence, wherein is truly set downe the manner of his taking, the long time of his Slaverie and means of his Deliverie, after 8 yeers and 10 moneths Captiuitie in the Gallies, Discouering mayne Mayne Landes, Islandes, Riuers, Cities and townes, of the Christians and Infidels, the Condition of the People and Manner of their Gouernment, and many more strange things. *London: Nich. Bourne.* 1614. 2 vols., 4to.

The author was a native of Hereford, and brother to the poet of that city. Sold in Mr. Jadis's sale for £7 7s. It is reprinted in Vol. I. of the Oxford "Collection of Voyages.". A perfect copy has an extra leaf, "The conclusion of the Booke," etc. It contains a description of the River of the Amazons, and the Island of Morria.

DAVIES (*Col.* William), *and* HARRISON (Robert H.) Report of Commissioners for a settling Cartel for the Exchange of Prisoners. *Philadelphia.* 1779. 8vo, pp. 20. 18775

DAVIESS (S.) Trial of Samuel Daviess, for the Murder of Henry Pendleton Smith, Sept., 1818. *Frankfort, Ky.* 1819. 12mo, pp. 104. 18776

DAVILA (G. G.) Teatro|eclesiastico|de la primitiva iglesia|de las Indias Occidentales,|Vidas de svs arzobispos,|obispos, y cosas memorables|de svs sedes.|Al mvy Alto y mvy Catolico|y por esto mvy poderoso|Señor Rey|Don Filipe Qvarto|de las Españas, y|Nvevo Mvndo.|Dedicasele sv Coronista|Mayor de las Indias, y de los Reynos de las|dos Castillas|el Maestro Gil Gonzalez Davila.| ... |*En Madrid, por Diego Diaz de la Carrera,*|*Año* M. DC. XLIX.| 2 vols., folio, 7 l., pp. 308, 4 l., 16 l., Map; 8 l., 119 leaves. 18777

Includes some valuable vocabularies, and accounts of the first introduction of arts and letters. *See* "Biog. Universelle," and Leclerc, No. 421. Sold, in 1869, for 100 francs. Leclerc's collation differs, Vol. I., 6 l., pp. 308, 4 l.; Vol. II., 7 l., pp. 119.

DAVILA (J. G.) Memorias historicas|de la|congregacion|de el oratorio|de la ciudad de Mexico.|Bosqvejada antes con el nombre de Vnion,|y fundada con auctoridad Ordinaria.|Despues, con la apostolica, erigida, y confirmada|en Congregacion de el Oratorio: Copiada à el exemplar de la que en Roma|fundo el esclarecido Patriarca|San Philipe Neri.|En las quales se da noticia, assi de su fundacion,|come de sue Apostolico ereccion, y confirmacion: Y juntamente de muchas|de las Personas, que en uno, y otro tiempo la han illustrado.|Recogidas, y publicadas|por el P. Julian Gutierrez Davila ... | ... [7 lines]| ... *Mexico:* ... | ... | *Doña Maria de Ribera* ... 1736.| 3 vols., folio, 12 l., pp. 260; 198; 316, 24 l. BA. 18778

DAVILA. Vida y Virtudes de el Siervo de Dios el Ven. Padre D. Domingo Perez de Barcia, Presbytero Secular, Fundador de la Casa, y Voluntario recogimiento de Mugeres, nombrado San Miguèl de Bethlèn, en la Ciudad de Mexico. *Madrid.* 1720. 4to. Portrait. 18779

DAVILA PADILLA (A.) Historia de la fundacion y discurso de la provincia, de Santiago de Mexico, de la Orden de Predicadores por las vidas de sus varones insignes y casos Notables de Nueua España. Por el Maestro Fray Augustin Davila Padilla.

Al Principe de España Don Felipe nuestro Señor. [*Madrid.* 1596.] Folio, 5 l., pp. 815, 12 l. + Edition Segunda. *En Brusselas. En casa de Iuan de Meerbeque.* MDCXXV. Folio, Title, 3 l., pp. 654, 3 l. C. 18780

The first edition is a volume of extreme rarity. *See* Brunet's "Manuel;" also, Leclerc, No. 422, price 135 francs. It was reprinted as:

DAVILA PADILLA. Varia Historia de la Nueva España y Florida. *Valladolid.* 1634. Folio. C. 18781

DAVILA (P.) Carta del Rey|Catholico a Pedra Arias Dauila Gouernador de Cas|tilla del oro, por la qual se conocera si pudo cortar la|cabeça a su yerno el Adelantado Basco Nunez de Bal|boa, o a lomenos sy como lo dize la Historia|Pontifical deuiera otorgalle apelacion.| Folio, pp. 3. 18782

Should have appeared under Andagoya (Pascual de).

DAVILA. Narrative of the Proceedings of Pedrarias Davila in the Provinces of Tierra Firme or Castilla del Oro, and of the Discovery of the South Sea and the Coasts of Peru and Nicaragua. Written by the Adelantado Pascual de Andagoya. Translated and edited, with Notes and an Introduction, by Clements R. Markham. *London: Hakluyt Society.* M.DCCC.LXV. 8vo, 3 l., pp. xxix, (1), 88. Map. BA. 18783

For Dutch versions, *see* Van der Aa's "Collection," Vols. VII. and XI.

DAVILA (Raf.) Taller de Coheteria, dialogos entre un cohetero y un tamborilero. *Mexico.* 1827. 18784

DAVILA. El toro dialogos criticos-jocoserios entre un cohetero y un tamborilero, por R. Davila. *Mexico.* 1830–32. 5 vols., sm. 4to. 18785

DAVILA (Salvador). Oracion funebre de los militares españoles difuntos, dicha en la Iglesia de la Casa Profesa de Megico año 1765. *Megico.* 1766. 4to. 18786

DAVIN (F.) Las Casas, poëme à trois époques, couronné [à Saint-Quentin] ... . *Saint-Quentin: imp. de Cottenest.* 1830. 8vo. 18787

DAVIS (A. L.) Memoir of Rev. Gustavus F. Davis, D.D. By Abigail L. Davis. *Hartford: Canfield and Robins.* 1837. 12mo, pp. 152. 18788

DAVIS (A.) Acts of Congress in relation to the District of Columbia, from July 16th, 1790, to March 4th, 1831, inclusive; and of the Legislatures of Virginia and Maryland, passed

especially in regard to that District, or to persons or property within the same. With preliminary notes of the Proceedings of the Congress, under the Convention, as well as under the Present Constitution, in regard to the Permanent Seat of Government of the United States. By A. Davis. *Washington.* 1831. 8vo.

DAVIS (A J.) Defeats and Victories; their Benefits and Penalties. A Lecture delivered in N. Y., Jan. 11, 1863. By Andrew Jackson Davis. *New York: A. J. Davis & Co.* 1863. 12mo, pp. 24. 18790

DAVIS. Memoranda of Persons, Places, and Events: embracing Authentic Facts, Visions, Impressions, Discoveries in Magnetism, Clairvoyance, Spiritualism; also Quotations from the Opposition. By Andrew Jackson Davis. ... *Boston: W. White & Co.* 1868. 12mo, pp. 488. C. 18791

Also: The Harmonial Man: or, Thoughts for the Age. .. Third Edition. *Boston: Bela Marsh, Publisher.* 1853. 8vo, pp. 129. H. Mr. Davis is the great apostle of his believers, and his numerous works are illustrative of a remarkable delusion; a few bear on national topics.

DAVIS (Ashel). Ancient America: Including the Ruins of Central and other parts of America, the first inhabitants of the Western Continent, etc. By A. Davis. *Buffalo.* 1852. 8vo, 8 l. 18792

DAVIS. Antiquities of America. The First Inhabitants of Central America, and the Discovery of New-England by the Northmen, Five Hundred Years Before Columbus; with Important Additions. A Lecture, delivered in New-York, Washington, Boston, and other Cities; also, in some of the first Literary Institutions in the Union. By A. Davis ... . Ninth Edition. *Boston.* 1842. 8vo, pp. 24. + Tenth Edition, from the Ninth Boston Edition, with important additions. *Buffalo: Steele's Press.* 1842. pp. 24. BA. + Eleventh Edition. *Rochester.* 1843. + *Boston.* 1844. 8vo. C. + Fourteenth Edition, from the Twelfth Boston Edition. *Troy, N. Y.: Press of N. Tuttle.* 1846. 8vo, pp. 20 or 30. + Nineteenth Edition, with Important Additions. *New York: Daniel Odel.* 1847. 8vo, pp. 32. + *Buffalo.* 1848. + Twentieth Edition. *Boston.* 1848. 8vo. + *Buffalo.* 1849. + *Buffalo.* 1852. 8vo, pp. 32.

For earlier editions, *see* "A Lecture," *infra.*

DAVIS. A Lecture on the Discovery of America by the Northmen, Five-hundred years before Columbus, etc. Third Edition. *New York.* 1839. 8vo, pp. 23. + Fourth Edition.

New York. 1840. 8vo, pp. 22. + Fifth Edition, with Improvements. *New York: Bartlett and Company; Boston: Dutton and Wentworth.* 1840. 8vo, pp. 23, (1). BA. + Sixth Edition, with Additions. *New York:* [*Ibid.*] 1840. 8vo, pp. 23, (1). + *Rochester.* 1841. 8vo. + *Troy.* 1845. 8vo. 18794

DAVIS. History of New Amsterdam; or, New York as it was in the days of the Dutch Governors. Together with Papers on Events connected with the American Revolution; and on Philadelphia in the Times of William Penn. By Professor A. Davis. *New York.* 1854. 12mo, pp. 240. 6 Plates.

DAVIS (Alex. S.) A Loud Call to the Citizens of the Nation ... Investigation of the present Temperance Question. *Hanover, Pa.* 1842. 8vo, pp. 104. 18796

Also: Travellers' Legal Guide and Directory. *Rochester.* 1855. 12mo, pp. 84.

DAVIS (A. C.) Frauds of the Indian Office. Argument of A. C. Davis before the Committee of Indian Affairs of the House of Representatives, January 12, 1867. ... *Washington.* 1867. 8vo. 18797

[DAVIS (Charles A.)] The Life and Writings of Major Jack Downing, of Downingville, away down East in the State of Maine; Written by himself. *Boston.* 1834. 12mo. S. 18798

[DAVIS.] Letters of J. Downing, Major, Downingville Militia, Second Brigade, To his old friend Mr. Dwight, of the New York Daily Advertiser. *New York: Harper & Brothers.* 1834. 18mo, pp. 367. Frontispiece of Portraits. + *New York.* 1835. 24mo. 18799

[DAVIS.] Select Letters of Major Jack Downing, Written by Himself. *Philadelphia.* 1834. 12mo. S. 18800

Also: May Day in New York. ... *New York.* 1845. 12mo. For another Jack Downing, *see* [Smith (Seba)].

DAVIS (C. G.) United States *vs.* Charles G. Davis. Report of the Proceedings and the Examination of Charles G. Davis, Esq., on a charge of Aiding and Abetting in the Rescue of a Fugitive Slave. Held in Boston, in February, 1851. *Boston: White and Potter, Printers.* 1851. 8vo, pp. 44. C., H. 18801

DAVIS. Report of the Trial of S. M. Andrews, indicted for the Murder of C. Holmes. ... By C. G. Davis. ... *New York: Hurd & Houghton.* 1869. 8vo, pp. (4), 287, (1). Plate.

DAVIS (C. H.) Astronomical and Meteorological Observations made at the United States Naval Observatory during the Year 1866. Rear-Admiral C. H. D. Davis, Superintendent. *Washington: Government Printing Office.* 1868. 4to, pp. xlviii, 1 l., pp. 472, 1 l. 2 Plates. C. 18803

DAVIS. The Coast Survey of the United States. By Lieut. C. H. Davis, U. S. N. *Cambridge: Metcalf and Company, Printers.* 1849. 8vo, pp. 34. + *Washington.* 1851. 8vo, pp. 28. H. 18804

DAVIS. Letter of the Secretary of the Navy communicating, ... a Report of Rear-Admiral Charles H. Davis, ... in relation to the various proposed lines for Inter-Oceanic Canals and Railroads between the Waters of the Atlantic and Pacific Oceans. *Washington.* 1867. 8vo, pp. 28. 13 Plates. 18805

Contains copious lists of books and maps, relating to inter-oceanic communication through the American isthmuses. Also: Report on Interoceanic Canals and Railroads between the Atlantic and Pacific Oceans. ... *Washington: Government Printing Office.* 1867. 8vo, pp. 37. 14 Maps. BA.

DAVIS. Smithsonian Contributions to Knowledge. The Law of Deposit of the Flood Tide ... . By Charles Henry Davis. ... *Washington City.* 1852. 4to, pp. 13. H. 18806

Different points on the coast of Nova Scotia taken in illustration.

DAVIS. The Testimony of Captain Charles H. Davis, and Wm. P. Parrott ... on the Petition of the City of Charlestown for leave to take Water from Mystic Pond, February, 1860. [n. p. n. d.] 8vo, pp. 4. H. 18807

Also: Address to the Graduating Class of the United States Naval Academy. ... *Cambridge: Metcalf and Company.* 1855. 8vo, pp. 32. H. — Memoir on Boston Harbor. By Charles Henry Davis ... . From the Memoirs of the American Academy of Arts and Sciences, New Series, Vol. V. *Cambridge: Metcalf and Company, Printers.* 1852. 4to, pp. 93–110. H. — A Memoir upon the Geological Action of the Tidal and Other Currents of the Ocean. ... *Cambridge: Metcalf and Company, Printers.* 4to, pp. 115–156. Maps. H. (From the "Memoirs of the American Academy of Arts and Science," New Series, Vol. IV.) — Remarks upon the Establishment of an American Prime Meridian. ... . *Cambridge: Metcalf and Company, Printers.* 1849. 8vo, pp. 40. H. — Report of the Secretary of the Navy, communicating, ... a Report of Lieutenant Charles H. Davis ... . *Cambridge: Metcalf and Company.* 1852. 8vo, pp. 36. H. — Two Memoranda on the Objects and Construction of the American Ephemeris and Nautical Almanac. ... *Cambridge: Welch, Bigelow, and Company, Printers.* 1860. 12mo, 2 l., pp. 12, 7. H. — The United States Coast Survey. ... Senate, 35th Congress, 2d Session. ... [*Washington.*] 1860. 8vo, pp. 32. H. *See* Boston, "Communications."

DAVIS (C. H. S.) History of Wallingford, Conn., from its Settlement in 1670, to the Present Time, including Meriden,

which was one of its Parishes until 1806, and Cheshire, which was Incorporated in 1780. By Charles Henry Stanley Davis, M.D. ... *Meriden, Conn.: the Author.* 1870. 8vo, 4 l., pp. 956. Portraits. B. 18808

DAVIS (D.) An Oration, delivered at Portland, July 4th, 1796. ... By Daniel Davis. ... . *Portland: Printed by Thomas Baker Wait.* 1796. 8vo, pp. 20. BA., W. 18809

DAVIS. Book of the Telegraph, Boston, Daniel Davis, 1851. *Boston.* 1852. 8vo, pp. 44. B., C., S. 18810

DAVIS (D.) A Poem, recited before the Citizens of Edgartown, July 4, 1836 ... . By David Davis. ... *New-Bedford: Printed by Benjamin T. Congdon.* 1836. 8vo, pp. 15. BA. 18811

DAVIS (Edwin Hamilton.) *See* Squier (E. G.)

DAVIS (E.) The Half Century; or, a History of Changes that have taken place, and Events that have Transpired, chiefly in the United States, between 1800 and 1850. With an Introduction by Mark Hopkins, D.D. By Emerson Davis, D.D. *Boston.* 1851. 8vo, pp. xxiii, 444. 18812

DAVIS. A Historical Sketch of Westfield. By Emerson Davis, A.M. Preceptor of Westfield Academy. *Westfield: Joseph Root.* 1826. 8vo, pp. 36. W. 18813

DAVIS, *and others.* Sketches of the Churches and Pastors in Hampden County, Mass.; and also an Address delivered to the Pastors, by Rev. T. M. Cooley, D.D. at Mettineague, September 13, 1853. By a Committee of Pastors [E. Davis, G. A. Oviatt, E. B. Clarke]. *Westfield: S. W. Edson.* 1854. 12mo, pp. 144. BA., S. 18814

DAVIS (E.) Can a Negro hold Office in Georgia? Decided in Supreme Court of Georgia, June Term, 1869. Arguments of Counsel, with the Opinions of the Judges, and the Decision of Court in the Case of Richard W. White ... versus ... Wm. J. Clements ... . Phonographically reported by Eugene Davis. *Atlanta, Ga.* 1869. 8vo, pp. 179. H. 18815

DAVIS (F. C.) Great Western Business Guide; or, the Pittsburgh, Fort Wayne and Chicago Railway, and its Connections. By Franklin Carsley Davis. *Philadelphia: F. C. Davis & Co.* 1861. 18mo, pp. 284. Map. C. 18816

DAVIS (G.) Opinion of Hon. Garrett Davis, of Kentucky, Filed under the order of the Senate sitting as a Court of Impeachment for the Trial of Andrew Johnson, President of the United States. [*Washington.* n. d.] 8vo, pp. 16. H. 18817

DAVIS. The War not for Emancipation or Confiscation. A Speech By Hon. Garrett Davis of Kentucky, delivered in the U. S. Senate, January 23, 1862. *New York: E. D. Barker.* 1862. 12mo, pp. 55–65. B. 18818

Also: Decision of Constitutional Questions. Speech ... January 14, 1868. [*Washington.* n. d.] 8vo, pp. 16. H. — Extract from the Speech of Mr. Garrett Davis, of Kentucky, exhibiting the Expenditures of Mr. Van Buren's Administration, ... delivered in House of Representatives, ... April 5, 1844. *Washington.* [n. d.] 8vo, pp. 8. BA. — The Public Credit. Speech ... on the Bill to strengthen the Public Credit, ... February 27th, 1869. *Washington.* 1869. 8vo, pp. 8. H. — Reconstruction. Speech ... in the Senate ... February 11 and 20, 1868. *Washington: F. & J. Rives & Geo. Bailey, Printers.* 1868. 8vo, pp. 22. H. — Speech ... on the Mexican War and the President's Message in the House ... December 22, 1846. *Washington.* [n. d.] 8vo, pp. 16. M. — Speech, ... in which he gives a Sketch of the Political History of Massachusetts. ... February 16 & 17, 1864. *Washington: L. Towers & Co., Printers.* 1864. 8vo, pp. 39. H. — Speech ... on District of Columbia Suffrage. Delivered in the Senate ... January 16, 1866. [*Washington:*] *Lemuel Towers, Printer.* [n. d.] 8vo, pp. 16. H. — Speech ... on the Civil Rights Bill — Veto Message; ... April 6, 1866. *Washington.* 1866. 8vo, pp. 15. H. — Speech ... on Reconstruction, ... February 16, 1867. *Washington.* 1867. 8vo, pp. 16. H. — Tenure-of-Office-Law. Speech ... March 29, 1869. *Washington: F. & J. Rives & Geo. A. Bailey, Printers.* 1869. 8vo, pp. 8. H.

DAVIS (G.) Sketch of the Debates of the House of Representatives of the Mississippi Territory. By George Davis. *Natchez.* 1808. 12mo. C. 18819

DAVIS (G.) Historical Sketch of Sturbridge and Southbridge, Mass. By George Davis. *West Brookfield: W. S. Cooke & Son.* 1856. 8vo, pp. 233. B. 18820

DAVIS (G. L.) The Day-Star of American Freedom; or the Birth and Early Growth of Toleration, in the Province of Maryland: with a Sketch of the Colonization upon the Chesapeake and its Tributaries, preceding the Removal of the Government from St. Mary's to Annapolis ... . By George Lynn-Lachlan Davis ... . *New York: C. Scribner.* 1855. 12mo, pp. 290.

Also: A Paper upon the Origin of the Japan Expedition, read the 7th of May, 1857, Before the Maryland Historical Society, by Geo. Lynn-Lachlan Davis, of Baltimore. [*Batimore.*] 1860. 8vo, pp. 14.

DAVIS (G. R.) Speech of Hon. George R. Davis, on the Financial Policy of the Democratic and Whig Parties. *Albany.* 1843. 8vo. P. 18822

Also: Annual Address, Rensselaer County Agricultural Society, Sept. 24, 1852. 8vo

[DAVIS (George T.)] An Address to the Republicans of Massachusetts. *Boston.* 1862. 8vo, pp. 8. H. 18823

Also: Speech, ... Jan., 1852, on the Mexican Indemnity Bill. 8vo, pp. 8. S.

DAVIS (G. T. M.) An Authentic Account of the Massacre of Joseph Smith, the Mormon Prophet, and Hyrum Smith, his Brother, together with a Brief History of the Rise and Progress of Mormonism, and all the Circumstances which led to their Death. By George T. M. Davis, of Alton, Ill. *St. Louis.* 1844. 8vo, pp. 47. 18824

DAVIS (H.) A Narrative of the Embarrassment and Decline of Hamilton College. By Henry Davis, President ... [*Clinton, New York?*] 1833. 8vo, pp. iv, vii, 151. C. 18825

DAVIS. A Sermon, delivered on the Day of General Election, at Montpelier, October 12, 1815, before the Honorable Legislature of Vermont. By Henry Davis, D.D. President of Middlebury College. ... *Montpelier, Vt.: printed by Walton & Goss.* 1815. 8vo, pp. 40. 18826

Also: Address, Commencement of Hamilton College. ... 1828. 8vo. S. — A Farewell Address to the Students of Hamilton College. ... *New York.* 1833. 8vo, pp. 20. N. — An Inaugural Oration, ... Feb. 21, 1810. ... Middlebury College. ... *Boston: Farrand, Mallory, and Co.* 1810. 8vo, pp. 36. — Sermon delivered to the Candidates for the Baccalaureate of Middlebury College, Aug. 12, 1810. ... *Middlebury.* 1810. 8vo, pp. 32. M. — A Sermon delivered before the A.B.C.F.M. ... Sept. 18–20, 1816. *Boston.* 1816. 8vo, pp. 36.

DAVIS (Henry Winter). Epistle Congratulatory to the Bishop of the Episcopal Court at Camden. *New York.* 1853. 8vo, pp. 74. 18827

DAVIS. The Southern Rebellion and the Constitutional Powers of the Government for its Suppression. An Address delivered by Hon. Henry Winter Davis, before the Mercantile Library Society of Brooklyn, November 26, 1861. *New York: E. D. Barker.* 1862. 12mo. B. 18828

DAVIS. War of Ormuzd and Ahriman in the Nineteenth Century. By Henry Winter Davis ... . *Baltimore: James S. Waters.* MDCCCLII. 8vo, pp. 45. B. 18829

DAVIS. Speeches and Addresses ... by Henry Winter Davis. ... With a Sketch of his Life, Public Services, and Character, being an Oration by the Hon. J. A. J. Cresswell. ... With Notes, Introductory and Explanatory. *New York: Harper & Brothers.* 1867. 8vo, pp. 596. Portrait. C. 18830

Also: Address of Hon. Henry Winter Davis, delivered at Baltimore ... October 16, 1861 ... . [n. p. 1861?] 8vo, pp. 16. H. — Speech ... before the Electors of the Fourth Congressional District of Maryland. ... *Baltimore. September* 27, 1860. 8vo, pp. 16. — Speech ... on Mr. Corwin's Report. ... in the House ... February 7, 1861. [n. p.] *printed by Lemuel Towers.* [n. d.] 8vo, pp. 16. H. — Speech at ... Philadelphia, September 24, 1863. [n. p. n. d.] 8vo, pp. 29. H. — Speech ... on Confiscation of Rebel Property. Delivered in the House ... January 14, 1864. [*Washington:*] *L. Towers & Co., Printers.* [n. d.] 8vo, pp. 8. H. — Speech ... on the President's Colonization and Compensation Scheme ... in the House ... Feb. 25, 1864. [*Washington:*] *L. Towers & Co.* [n. d.] 8vo, pp. 8. H. — Speech ... on the Expulsion of Mr. Long. *Washington.* 1864. — Speeches ... on his Bill for a Board of Admiralty, in Navy Department. ... in the House ... February 3 and 6, 1865. *Washington: printed by Lemuel Towers.* 1865. 8vo, pp. 46. H. — Speech ... and the Debate on his Amendment to the Miscellaneous Bill, prohibiting the Trial of Citizens by Military Commission; in the House of Representatives, March 2 and 3, 1865. *Washington: Lemuel Towers.* 1865. 8vo, pp. 32.

DAVIS. Portrait of Henry Winter Davis, Esq. by his own hand. His Political Inconsistencies Daguerreotyped in Colors warranted not to Fade, as his Principles have always done, under the corroding touch of Time. [n. p. n. d.] 8vo, pp. 16.

DAVIS. Read and Judge for Yourself. A Review of the Pamphlet of Henry Winter Davis, entitled the Origin, Purposes and Principles of the American Party. [Signed Madison. n. p. n. d.] 8vo, pp. 14. 18832

DAVIS. Review of Hon. Henry Winter Davis and Freesoilism. His Hampden Letter, or Ormuzd and Ahriman in the 19th Century. [n. p. n. d.] 8vo, pp. 12. 18833

DAVIS (I.) The Defence of Isaac Davis, of Dover, Del., on the Charge of using undue Influence over Laws, in devising his Estate. *Dover, Del.: J. B. Wootten.* [1806?] 12mo, pp. 21. C. 18834

DAVIS. An Historical Discourse on the Fiftieth Anniversary of the First Baptist Church in Worcester, Mass., Dec. 19th, 1862. By Isaac Davis. With an Appendix. *Worcester: printed by Henry J. Howland.* 8vo, pp. 52. 18835

DAVIS (J.) Relations of States. Speech of the Hon. Jefferson Davis of Mississippi, Delivered in the Senate of the United States, May 7th, 1860, On the Resolutions submitted by him on 1st of March, 1860. *Baltimore: printed by John Murphy & Co.* 8vo, pp. 15. H. 18836

DAVIS. Speeches of the Hon. Jefferson Davis, of Mississippi, Delivered During the Summer of 1858. *Baltimore: Printed by John Murphy & Co.* 1859. 8vo, pp. 56. 18837

Also: An Address to the People of the Free States by the President of the Southern Confederacy. [Dated] *Richmond. January* 5, 1863. Broadside. — Reply ... To the Speech of Senator Douglas, In the U. S. Senate, May 16 & 17, 1860. [n. p. n. d.] 8vo, pp. 16. — Speech ... on the Oregon Bill, delivered in the Senate of the U. S., July 12, 1848. [n. p. n. d.] 8vo, pp. 20. — Speech ... Senate, Jan. 10, 1850, on Slavery. (*See* Clemens (J.) — Speech ... Senate, Feb. 19, 1849, on the Coast Survey. [n. p. n. d.] 8vo. S. — Speech ... on the Exercise of Civil Power and Authority by Military Officers, United-States Senate, Aug. 5, 1850. [n. p. n. d.] 8vo, pp. 16. M. — Speech ... on the French Spoliation Bill ... in the Senate of the United States Jan. 6 and 10, 1859. *Baltimore.* 1859. 8vo, pp. 16. — Speech ... in the Senate January 10, 1861, upon the Condition of things in South Carolina. *Baltimore.* 1861 8vo. B. *See* "Confederate States," Vol. IV.

DAVIS. Jefferson Davis, and his Complicity in the Assassination of Abraham Lincoln, ... and where the Traitor shall be Tried for Treason. *Philadelphia: Sherman & Co., Printers.* 1866. 8vo, pp. 15. H. 18838

DAVIS. Life of Jefferson Davis, from Authentic Sources. By a South Carolinian. *London: G. W. Bacon & Co.* 12mo, pp. iv, 96. 18839

DAVIS. Life and Imprisonment of Jefferson Davis, together with the Life and Military Career of Stonewall Jackson, from Authentic Sources. *New York.* 1866. 12mo. 3 Portraits.

[DAVIS, *and* BROWN (Joseph E.)] Correspondence between the President and the Governor of Georgia, relative to the ... Conscription Law. *Richmond: Ritchie & Dunnavaut, Printers.* 1862. 16mo, pp. 20. H. 18841

DAVIS (J.) The Seaman's Secrets, Devided into 2 partes, wherein is taught the three kindes of Sayling, Horizontall, Paradoxall, and sayling upon a great Circle. Newly corrected by the author, John Davis of Sandrudge, neere Darthmouth in the Countie of Devon, Gent. *London: by Thomas Dawson.* 1599. 4to. Woodcuts and folded Table. 18842

In the dedication the author speaks of his three several attempts for the discovery of the strait which now bears his name. The preface, dated August, 1594, contains some interesting notices of Cavendish, Diggs, Hariott, Molleneaux, Hawkins, etc. It was frequently reprinted. The eighth edition is dated, *London.* 1657. 4to.

DAVIS. The Worlde's Hydrographical Description; wherein is proued that the Worlde in all his Zones, Clymats and Places, is habitable and inhabited, and the Seas universally navigable, without any naturall Annoyance to hinder the same, Whereby appeares that from England there is a short and speedie passage into the South Seas to China, Molucca, Phillipina, and India, by Northerly Nauigation to the Benefit of Her Majestys State. *London: Printed by Thomas Dawson.* 1595. Sm. 4to, pp. 48.

Of extreme rarity. Has sold for £21. Reprinted in Hakluyt.

DAVIS (J.) Discourse before the Massachusetts Historical Society, Dec. 22, 1813, at their Anniversary Commemoration of the first landing of our Ancestors at Plymouth in 1620. By John Davis, LL.D. *Boston: John Eliot.* 1814. 8vo, pp. 31. C.

Also in the "Mass. Hist. Coll.," Vol. I., Second Series.

DAVIS. An Eulogy, on General George Washington, pronounced at Boston, on Wednesday, February XIX, MDCCC. before the American Academy of Arts and Sciences, by their Appointment, and published at their Request. By John Davis ... . *Boston: Printed by W. Spotswood.* MDCCC. 4to, pp. 24. BA. + *Boston: Reprinted.* 1859. 4to. 18845

Included in "Memoirs of the American Academy," Vol. II., Part 2.

[DAVIS.] The Life Boat. A Poem. By a Member of the Humane Society. [n. p. n. d.] 8vo, pp. 40. H. 18846

Also: An Address ... before the ... Massachusetts Charitable Fire Society, ... May 31, 1799. ... . *Boston: Printed by John Russell.* 1799. 8vo, pp. 24. BA., W. — Address at the Dedication of the Town Hall, in Worcester (Mass.), May 2, 1825. ... *Worcester: Printed by William Manning.* [n. d.] 8vo, pp. 36. B. — Duties on Woollens. Speech ... in the House of Representatives on the Bill for protecting the Woollen Manufactures. [n. d.] 8vo, pp. 8. M. — An Oration ... Worcester, (Mass.) on the Fortieth Anniversary of American Independence. ... *Worcester: Printed by William Manning.* 1816. 8vo, pp. 23. BA., H. — Reply ... To the charge of Mirepresenting Mr. Buchanan's Argument in favor of the Hard Money System, Delivered March 6th, 1840. *Washington.* 1840. pp. 6. — Reply ... to Mr. Buchanan, of Pennsylvania, on the Reduction of Wages, Delivered in the Senate of the United States, January 23rd, 1840. *Washington.* 1840. pp. 12. — Speech ... on the Tariff Bill, March 12, 1828. *Washington: Printed by Gales & Seaton.* 1828. 12mo, pp. 38. B. — Speech .. on the Bill for the More Effectual Collection of Impost Duties. ... May 4, 1830. *Washington: Peter Force, Print.* 1830. 8vo, pp. 28. W. — Speech ... in Congress on the Tariff Bill of 1832. *Boston.* 1833. 8vo. W. — Speech ... upon the Subtreasury Bill, United-States Senate, 28th February and 1st March, 1838. *Washington.* 1838. 8vo, pp. 27. BA. — Speech ... on the Sub-treasury Bill, United-States Senate, Jan. 23, 1840. *Boston: Printed by J. H. Eastburn.* [n. d.] 8vo, pp. 16. BA. — Speech ... upon the Bill "to reduce Duties, and for other Purposes," in which the Modern Doctrines of Free Trade are ... examined. United-States Senate, July, 1846. *Washington: Printed by J. & G. S. Gideon.* 1846. 8vo, pp. 31. BA. — Speech ... on the Compromise Bill, delivered in the Senate ... June 28 and 29, 1850. *Washington.* 1850. 8vo, pp. 16. *See* Morton (Nathaniel.)

[DAVIS (J.)] The American Mariners, or the Atlantic Voyage. A Moral Poem. Prefixed is a vindication of the American Character from the Aspersions of the Quarterly Reviewers. To which are added Naval Annals; or an Impartial Summary of the actions fought during the late War at Sea, and on the Lakes, between the ships of Great Britain and those of the United States of America. Copious Notes and Illustrations. *Salisbury: Brodie & Downing.* [1822.] Sm. 8vo, pp. xii, 384.

[DAVIS.] Captain Smith and Princess Pocahontas. An Indian Tale. *Philadelphia.* 1805. 12mo, pp. 176. 18848

Also included in his "Travels."

[DAVIS.] The First Settlers of Virginia, An Historical Novel, Exhibiting a View of the Rise and Progress of the Colony at James Town, A Picture of Indian Manners, the Countenance of the Country, and its Natural Productions. *New York: I. Riley & Co.* 1805. 12mo, pp. xii, 284. C. + The Second Edition, considerably Enlarged. *New York: I. Riley & Co.* 1806. 12mo, pp. xii, 284. S. 18849

[DAVIS.] The Post-Captain; or, the Wooden Walls Well Manned; Comprehending a View of Naval Society and Manners. *London: printed for Thomas Tegg.* 1806. 18mo, pp. 300. + [*Ibid.*] 1813. 18mo. + [*Ibid.*] 1824. 18mo. 18850

Contains a sketch of American Indians. *See* "M. Rev.," L. 205.

DAVIS. Travels of Four Years and a Half in the United States of America; During 1798, 1799, 1800, 1801, and 1802. Dedicated by Permission to Thomas Jefferson, Esq. President of the United States. By John Davis. ... *London: sold by T. Ostell* [etc.] *R. Edwards, Printer, Bristol.* 1803. 8vo, pp. viii, 454. BA. 18851

Davis came to the United States in search of literary employment, and had much intercourse with Col. Burr, Jefferson, and others, concerning whom he gives many new facts. *See* Rich, II. 13, for a long note; *see also* "Edinb. Rev.," II. 443; and "M. Rev.," XLIV. 387. Reprinted with a few alterations and omissions, with the following title:

DAVIS. Personal Adventures and Travels of Four Years and a Half in the United States of America. By Mr. John Davis. Being Travels in Search of Independence and Settlement. *London: J. Davis.* 1816. Rl. 8vo, pp. 96. P. 18852

"With more sincerity than is usual among travellers, he states that he made his tour on foot, because he could not afford the expense of a horse." — RICH.

DAVIS. A Tribute to the United States. A Poem. *New York.* 1798. 12mo, pp. 8. 18853

See [Berquin-Duvallon], Vol. II., No. 4965.

DAVIS (John C. B.) The Massachusetts Justice: a Treatise upon the Powers and Duties of Justices of the Peace. ... *Worcester.* 1847. 8vo. 18854

DAVIS (J. B.) On Synostotic Crania among Aboriginal Race of Man. *Haarlem and London: Williams & Norgate.* 1863. 4to. 11 Plates. 18855

[DAVIS (J. C.)] An Appeal from the Colored Men of Philadelphia to the President of the United States. ... *Philadelphia. August,* 1862. 16mo, pp. 8. H. 18856

DAVIS (J. L.) The Trooper's Manual: or, Tactics for Light Dragoons and Mounted Riflemen. Compiled, abridged and arranged by J. Lucius Davis, ... Third Edition. *Richmond, Va.: published by A. Morris.* 1862. 12mo, pp. 284, 11. 18857

For the use of the Confederate army.

DAVIS (J.) Some Queries sent to the Rev. G. Whitefield. By Jonathan Davis, in the Year 1740, which remain yet Unanswered. *Philadelphia: Printed by B. Franklin, and D. Hall.* 1749. 8vo. 18858

DAVIS (Josiah G.) The Good Minister. A Discourse preached at Hollis, N. H., Sept. 26, 1869, in commemoration of ... Rev. Pliny B. Day, D.D., who deceased July 6, 1869. By J. G. Davis ... Amherst, N. H. *Concord: printed by McFarland & Jenks.* 1870. 8vo, pp. 32. H. 18859

Also: Historical Discourse, May 6, 1862. ... *Concord.* 1862. 8vo, pp. 76.

DAVIS (J.) Narrative of Joshua Davis, an American Citizen, who was pressed and served on board six ships of the British Navy ... . *Boston: Printed by B. True.* 1811. 12mo, pp. 72.

[DAVIS (L. D.)] Life in the Itinerancy, in its relations to the Circuit and Station, and to the Minister's Home and Family. *New York and Auburn: Miller, Orton & Mulligan.* 1856. 12mo, pp. 335. C. 18861

DAVIS (M. L.) A Brief Account of the Epidemical Fever which lately prevailed in the City of New York. By M. L. Davis. With the Different Proclamations, Reports and Letters of Gov. Jay, Gov. Miffin, the Health Committee of New York, upon the Subject. To which is added an accurate list of the names of those who have died of the disease, from July 29 to Nov. 1. By M. L. Davis. *New York: M. L. Davis.* 1795. 8vo, pp. 66. B., P. 18662

[DAVIS.] Letters of Marcus and Philo-Cato, addressed to De Witt Clinton, esq., Mayor of the City of New-York. A New Edition, containing one letter of Marcus, and several numbers of Philo-Cato, never published before. *New York.* 1810. 8vo, pp. 86. S. 18863

A caustic, and sometimes comical, exposé of the political quarrels arising out of the Burr Union, etc., formed about the year 1806 between the Clintonians and Burrites.

DAVIS. Memoirs of Aaron Burr. With Miscellaneous Selections from his Correspondence. By Matthew L. Davis. ... *New York: Harper & Brothers.* 1836. 2 vols., 8vo, pp. 436; 453. 2 Portraits, and Facsimile. BA. + *New York: Harper & Brothers.* 1837. 2 vols., 8vo, pp. 436; 449. 2 Portraits. + *New York:* [*Ibid.*] 1858. 2 vols., 8vo. 18864

The author's motto is, "I come to bury Cæsar, not to praise him." *See* Burr (A.), Vol. II., No. 9424.

DAVIS. An Oration delivered in St. Paul's Church, on the Fourth of July, 1800, being the Twenty-fourth Anniversary of American Independence. By M. L. Davis. To which is added, An Ode ... by Samuel Low. *New York.* 1800. 8vo, pp. 21.

[DAVIS.] The Plot Discovered, by Marcus. *Poughkeepsie.* 1807. 8vo. B. 18866

DAVIS. Report of the Case between the Rev. Cave Jones, and the Rector and Inhabitants of the City of New-York. ... . By Matthew L. Davis. *New-York: Printed by William A. Davis.* 1813. 8vo, pp. vii, 587, (1). C. 18867

DAVIS. The Speech of Matthew L. Davis, on his Trial for Conspiracy. Taken in Short-Hand, by Nathaniel B. Blunt. *New York.* 1827. 8vo, pp. 31. 18868

DAVIS (N. W.) The Writ of Habeas Corpus. Speech of Nathaniel W. Davis in the House of Assembly of New York, March 5, 1863. [n. p. n. d.] 8vo, pp. 10. 18869

DAVIS (N.) A Narrative of the Life of Rev. Noah Davis, a Colored Man. Written by himself, at the age of Fifty-Four. Printed solely for the Author's Benefit. *Baltimore: Published by John F. Weishampel, Jr.* 1859. 18mo, pp. 86. C. 18870

DAVIS. *See* Burrows (R. L.), Vol. III., No. 9477.

DAVIS (N. S.) History of Medical Education and Institutions in the United States, from the First Settlement of the British Colonies to the year 1850, etc. By N. S. Davis, M.D. *Chicago.* 1841. 8vo. 18871

DAVIS. History of the American Medical Association, from its Organization up to January, 1855. By N. S. Davis, M.D. To which is added Biographical Notices, ... Edited by S. W. Butler, M.D. *Philadelphia: Lippincott, Grambo & Co.* 1855. 8vo, pp. 191. 9 Portraits. B., P. 18872

Also: Address on Free Medical Schools, Introductory to the Session of 1849-50, in Rushton Medical College. ... *Chicago.* 1849. 8vo, pp. 16.

DAVIS (Pardon). Principles of the Government of the United States. *Philadelphia.* 1823. 12mo. C. 18873

DAVIS (P. M.) The Four Principal Battles of the Late War; being a Full Detailed Account of the Battle of Chippeway, Fall and Destruction of the City of Washington, &c. *Harrisburg.* 1832. 8vo, pp. 32. 18874

DAVIS. An Authentic History of the Late War between the United States and Great Britain. With a Full Account of every Battle by Sea and Land; the Defection of General Hull, his Trial and Sentence; the Massacre at the River Raisin; the Destruction of the City of Washington; the Treaty of Peace in 1815. To which will be added, the War with Algiers, and the Treaty of Peace. The Treaties of Peace with the various Tribes of North American Indians and the United States Army Register, and Peace Establishment. By Paris M. Davis, late of the Army. *Ithaca.* 1829. 12mo, pp. 360. + *New-York: Ebenezer F. Baker.* 1836. 12mo, pp. 360. 5 Woodcuts. BA., C. 18875

DAVIS. An Official and Full Detail of the Great Battle of New Orleans, which Closed the late War with Great Britain and her Dependencies. By Paris M. Davis. *New York.* 1836. 12mo. 18876

DAVIS (P. B.) Two Years and Three Months in the New York Lunatic Asylum at Utica. By Phebe B. Davis, formerly of Barnard, ... Vt. *Syracuse.* 1855. 12mo, pp. 87. 18877

DAVIS. Reports on the Laws of New England, by Mrs. Davis, Mrs. Dall, and others. *Boston: Bela Marsh.* 1855. 8vo. 18878

DAVIS (P.) Faithful Narrative of the Wonderful Dealings of God toward Polly Davis, of Newcastle, N. H. *Boston.* 1792.

DAVIS (R. Bingham). Poems by Richard B. Davis; with a Sketch of his Life. ... *New York: T. & J. Swords.* 1807. 12mo, pp. xxxi, 154. C. 18880

DAVIS (Robert). The Currency; What it Is, and what it Should be. *Ottawa.* 1867. 4to, pp. 33. 18881

DAVIS (R. D.) Speech of the Hon. R. D. Davis, of Dutchess, at the Great Democratic Ratification Meeting, at the Capitol, ... Sept. 26, 1848; also Speech of Gen. Shields, at Cleveland. *Albany: J. Munsell.* 1848. 8vo, pp. 8. 18882

DAVIS (S.) Shekomoke; or the Moravians in Dutchess County. By Rev. Sheldon Davis, A.M. *Poughkeepsie.* 1858. 8vo, pp. 29. 18883

DAVIS (S.) An Appeal to the Citizens of Newton, embracing a Brief History of the Town. By S. Davis. [n. p.] 1847. 8vo, pp. 25. Map. BA. 18884

DAVIS. Prayer-Book in the Language of the Six Nations of Indians, containing the Morning and Evening Service, the Litany, Catechism, some of the Collects, and the Prayers and Thanksgivings upon several occasions, in the Book of Common Prayer of the Protestant Episcopal Church, etc. By the Rev. Solomon Davis. *New York: Swords, Stanford & Co.* 1837. 12mo, pp. 168. C. 18885

DAVIS (S.) Notes of a Tour in America, in 1832 and 1833. By Stephen Davis. ... *Edinburgh: Waugh & Innes.* MDCCCXXXIII. 18mo, pp. 150. 18886

DAVIS (T.) A General History of the Sabbatarian Churches: ... with the Seventh-Day Baptist Denomination in the United States. By Mrs. Tamar Davis. *Philadelphia: Lindsay and Blakiston.* 1851. 12mo, pp. 255. 18887

DAVIS (T.) A Biographical Sketch of the Rev. Thomas Davis, Missionary of the Society for Propagating the Gospel in Foreign Parts, in several of the Towns of Litchfield Co., Conn., from the Year 1761 to the Year 1776. By a Minister of the County. *New Haven, Conn.* 1843. 12mo. Portrait. 18888

DAVIS (T.) Rhode Island Politics, and Journalism. A Letter from Thomas Davis, to Hon. Henry B. Anthony ... . *Providence: A. Crawford Greene, Printer.* 1866. 8vo. 18889

DAVIS (T. T.) Daniel Webster. Eulogy on Daniel Webster, delivered in Syracuse, N. Y., Nov. 13, 1852. By Thomas T. Davis. *Syracuse: Hall, Mills & Co.* 1852. 8vo, pp. 24.

DAVIS. A Historical Discourse, delivered March 29, 1839, at Green's Farms. By Thomas T. Davis. *New Haven.* 1839. 8vo, pp. 31. 18891

DAVIS. Speech of Hon. T. T. Davis, of New York, on Military and Post Roads. Delivered in the House of Representatives, March 23, 1864. *Washington: printed by L. Towers.* [n. d.] 8vo, pp. 8. H. 18892

Also: Speech ... on Equality of Rights ... in the House of Representatives, February 28, 1866. *Washington.* 1866. 8vo, pp. 12. H.

DAVIS (T.) An Address to the People called Quakers, concerning the manner in which they treated Timothy Davis, for writing and publishing a Piece on Taxation. *Boston.* 1784. 8vo. w. 18893

Also: Anti-Christian Religion delivered, in a Treatise on the Millenium. ... *Leominster, Mass.* 1807. 12mo. w.

DAVIS (T.) The Privateer System. Speech ... delivered in the House of Representatives, July 23, 1856. [n. d.] 8vo, pp. 16. M. 18894

Also: Speech ... on the Fishing Bounties, delivered in the House of Representatives, Feb. 10, 1857. [n. d.] 8vo, pp. 8. M.

[DAVIS (Wendell).] Barnstable, Massachusetts. A Description of the Eastern Coast of the County of Barnstable, from Cape Code or Race Point ... to Cape Mallebarre, or the sandy point of Chatham, pointing out the spots on which the Trustees of the Humane Society have erected Huts, etc. By a Member of the Humane Society. *Boston.* 1802. 8vo, pp. 88. 18895

From the "Mass. Hist Coll.," VIII. 119-202.

DAVIS (W. B.) Southern Book.—Origin of the Constitution. Incorporation of the General Government by the States, as National Public Agents in Trust, with no Sovereignty ... History of the Puritans. Origin and Cause of Trouble between the North and South ... Legal Mode of Redress ... W. B. Davis. *Wilmington, N. C. Dec.,* 1854. 8vo, pp. 184. S. + Supplement ... *Wilmington, N. C.* 1856. 8vo, pp. 185-298.

[DAVIS (William J.) *See* Dawson (Henry B.)

DAVIS (W. M.) Ship Canal. Speech of Hon. W. M. Davis, In the House ... March 3, 1863. On the Illinois Canal and the right of the West to an unrestricted passage, to market. *Philadelphia: Merrihew & Thompson, Printers.* [n. d.] 8vo, pp. 16. H. 18897

DAVIS. The War: its Cause and Cure. Speech of the Hon. William M. Davis, of Penn., in the House ... March 6, 1862. [*Washington:*] *Scammell & Co., Printers.* 8vo, pp. 8.

DAVIS (W. P.) Funeral Discourse on Wm. Crounse, Killed at Port Hudson. By Rev. W. P. Davis. 1863. 8vo. S.

Also: The Pastor's Farewell: containing a Series of Discourses, delivered in view of a Dissolution of the Pastoral Relation. ... *Albany: J. Munsell.* 1841. 12mo, pp. 225.

DAVIS (W. W. H.) El-Gringo; or, New Mexico and her People. By W. W. H. Davis. *New York: Harper & Brothers.* 1857. 12mo, pp. 432. C., S. 18900

Contains a vocabulary of upwards of sixty words in Nabajo and English.

DAVIS. History of the Battle of the Crooked Billet, fought May 1st, 1778. By W. W. H. Davis, A.M. ... *Printed at the Democrat Office, Doylestown, Pa.* 1860. 8vo, pp. 19, Corrections, 9 lines. 18901

DAVIS. History of the Hart Family, of Warminster, Bucks County, Pennsylvania. To which is added the Genealogy of the Family, from its First Settlement in America. By W. W. H. Davis. Printed Privately. *Doylestown, Pa.: W. W. H. Davis.* 1867. 8vo, pp. 139, 20. Plate. 18902

DAVIS History of the 104th Pennsylvania Regiment, from August 22nd, 1861, to September 30th, 1864. By W. W. H. Davis, late Colonel. *Philadelphia: Jas. B. Rogers, Printer.* 1866. 8vo, pp. 364. 6 Plates. C. 18903

DAVIS. Sketch of the Life and Character of John Lacey, a Brigadier General in the Revolutionary Army. By W. W. H. Davis. [*Doylestown.*] 1868. 8vo, pp. 118, 6. C. 18904

DAVIS. The Spanish Conquest of New Mexico. By W. W. H. Davis. ... *Doylestown, Pa.* 1869. 8vo, pp. 438. Portrait and Map. BA. 18905

Published by subscription. Also: Message to the Legislative Assembly of Mexico, delivered December 3, 1855. By W. W. H. Davis, Acting Governor. 8vo. C.

DAVIS (Woodbury). Argument of Rufus Choate, Henry W. Paine and Francis O. J. Smith, on the [question of his] Removal from the Office of Justice of the Supreme Court of Maine; [with] the Vote of the Legislature thereon, and "Protest" of the Minority. 1856. S. 18906

DAVIS. The Davis Family Record. Edited by Chas. H. S. Davis, M.D. A Monthly Journal devoted to the History and Genealogy of the Davis Family. Vol. I. *Meriden, Conn. Nov.* 1867. No. 1. 8vo, pp. 8. Continued. BA., H. 18907

DAVISON (D.) Progress of Naval Architecture. ... Explanation of the Principles and Advantages of Darius Davison's New American Model ... . By Darius Davison. *New York: Baker, Godwin & Co., Printers.* 1852. 8vo, pp. 46. H. 18908

DAVISON (G. M.) The Fashionable Tour, and Guide to Travellers through the Northern and Middle States, and Canada. By G. M. Davison. *Saratoga.* 1830. 12mo. 18909

DAVISON. The Travellers' Guide through the Middle and Northern States and ... Canada. By G. M. Davison. Eighth Edition. *Saratoga Springs: G. M. Davison.* 1840. 18mo, pp. 395. Map. C. + *Saratoga: [Ibid.]* 1848. 18mo. 18910

DAVITY (P.) Description generale | de | l'Ameriqve | troisiesme partie | dv | Monde. | Avec tovs ses empires, royavmes, | estats et repvbliqves. | Ov sont dedvits et traitez par ordre levrs | Noms, Assiettes, Confins, Mœurs Richesses, Forces, Gouuernement & | Religion; Et la Genealogie des Empereurs, Roys, & Princes | Souuerains, lesquels y ont dominé iusques à present. | Composé premierement par Pierre Davity, Seigneur de Montmartin, Gentil-homme | ordinaire de la Chambre du Roy; Et dans cette | Novvelle Edition, Reuue, Corrigé & augmenté, tant pour les Descriptions | Geographiques, que pour l'Histoire, iusques à nostre temps. | Par Iean Baptiste de Rocoles, Conseiller & Aumosnier du Roy, | & Historiographe de sa Majesté. | *A Troyes, & | a Paris, | Chez Denys Bechet, et Lovis Baillaine.* | M. DC. LX. | Folio, 2 l., pp. 208, 6 l. Map. 18911

"Ce volume fait partie des 'Etats ou Empires du Monde' de Pierre Davity, compilation médiocre, où l'on trouve cependant des passages qui n'avaient pas encore paru en français. La première édition date de 1626, la nôtre est augmentée et précédée de l'éloge de Davity par Jean Baptiste de Rocoles. La carte de P. Bertius, qui se trouve jointe à la partie concernant l'Amérique, porte la date de 1662, ce qui fait présumer que la date de publication sur le livre même est inexacte."—TRÖMEL. There is also an edition, *Paris, Claude Sonnius.* 1637. Folio, 1 l., pp. 189, 6 l. Map.

DAVITY. Le Monde, ou la Description des ses Quatre Parties, avec tous ses Empires, Royaumes, Estats et Républiques. *Paris.* 1637. 5 vols., folio. Map. 18912

This includes our No. 18911, *supra.* *See* Linda (L. de).

DAVITY. Les etats, empires, et principautes du monde, avec l'origine de toutes les religions et de tous les Chevaliers et ordres militaires. Par Pierre Davity. *Rouen.* 1644. 4to. + *Rouen.* 1649. 4to. P. 18913

Pages 238-325 are occupied with a History of the New World.

DAVY (C. W.) Five Years' Residence in the West Indies. By Charles William Davy. *London.* 1852. 2 vols., post 8vo.

Davy Crocket. *See* Crockett (D.), No. 17574.

DAVY (J.) The West Indies, before and since Slave Emancipation, comprising the Windward and Leeward Islands' Military Command; founded on Notes and Observations collected during a Three Years' Residence. By John Davy, M.D. ... . *London: W. & F. G. Cash. Barbados: J. Bowen.* 1854. 8vo, Title, pp. vii, viii, 551, 1 l. BA. 18915

See "Westminster Rev.," VI. 275.

Daw's Doings, or the History of the late war in the Plantations. By Sampson Short-and-fat, author of Quozziana. With wood cuts. *Boston: Wm. White & H. P. Lewis.* 1842. 12mo, pp. 68.

Relates to Rhode Island affairs.

DAWES (E.) A Sermon preached in ... Dighton, at the Funeral of Joseph Emmons Briggs, M.D., May 12, 1867. By Rev. Ebenezer Dawes. ... *Cambridge: Welch, Bigelow & Co.* 1867. 8vo, pp. 34. H. 18917

DAWES (H. L.) The Lecompton Constitution Founded Neither in Law nor the Will of the People. Speech of Hon. Henry C. Dawes, of Massachusetts. Delivered in the U. S. House ... March 8, 1858. [*Washington, D. C.: Buell & Blanchard, Printers.* 1858.] 8vo, pp. 8. H., S. 18918

Also: Defence of the Committee on Government Contracts. Speech ... in House of Representatives, April 25, 1862. 8vo, pp. 15.—Government Contracts. Speech ... in the House ... January 13, 1862. [n. p. n. d.] pp. 8.—The New Dogma of the South—"Slavery a Blessing." Speech ... in the House ... April 12th, 1860. [n. d. n. d.] 8vo, pp. 7. H.—Public Expenditures. Speech ... in reply to Mr. Voorhees, of Indiana, In the House ... May 27, 1862. *Washington, D. C.: Scammell & Co., Printers.* 1862. 8vo, pp. 16. H.

[DAWES (Matthew).] A Letter to Lord Chatham concerning the present War of Great Britain against America, by a Gentleman of the Inner Temple. *London.* 177-. pp. 60. 18919

[DAWES (Rufus).] Nix's Mate: an Historical Romance of America. ... *New-York: Samuel Colman.* 1839. 2 vols., 12mo, 3 l., pp. 13-270; 261. BA. 18920

Also: The Valley of the Nashaway and other Poems. *Boston.* 1830. 12mo, pp. 96.

[DAWES (Thomas).] The Law given at Sinai: a Poem. By a Young Gentleman. *Boston: Thomas & John Fleet.* 1777. 4to, pp. 11. 18921

DAWES. An Oration, Delivered July 4, 1787, at the Request of the Inhabitants of The Town of Boston, in Celebration of The Anniversary of American Independence. By Thomas Dawes, jun. Esq. *Boston: Printed by Samuel Hall.* MDCCLXXXVII. 8vo, pp. 22. H. 18922

DAWES. An Oration, delivered March 5th, 1781, at the Request of the Inhabitants of the Town of Boston, to Commemorate the Bloody Tragedy of the Fifth of March, 1770. By Thomas Dawes, Jr. *Boston.* 1781. 4to, pp. 22. 18923

DAWES (T.) An Address, delivered on Sunday Evening, July 7, 1850, at the Consecration of the River-Side Cemetery, in Fairhaven, Mass. By Thomas Dawes, ... *New Bedford: Printed by Benj. Lindsey.* 1850. 8vo, pp. 31. 18924

Also: An Address to the Massachusetts Peace Society ... December 25, 1817. *Boston: printed by Joseph J. Buckingham.* 1818. 8vo, pp. 32. H.

DAWES (*Sir* W.) A Sermon preached before the Society for the Propagation of the Gospel in Foreign Parts ... at St. Mary le Bow, Feb. 18, 1708-9. By William, Lord Bishop of Chester. *London: Ann Speed.* 1709. 4to, pp. 24. J.C.B. 18925

DAWLEY (T. R.) The Life of Gen. William T. Sherman. By T. R. Dawley. *New York: T. R. Dawley.* 1866. 12mo, pp. 108. 18926

DAWSON (Æneas McDonell). Lines for October. *Ottawa.* 1866. 18927

Partly on the volunteers who fell at Ridgeway.

DAWSON (C. C.) Saratoga: its Mineral Waters, and their Use in preventing and eradicating Disease, and as a Refreshing Beverage. By C. C. Dawson. *New York: [Russell Brothers.]* 1868. 32mo, pp. 64, and cover, which alone has the publisher's name. Map and Woodcuts. C., H. 18928

DAWSON (Eli). A Discourse delivered at Quebec, in the Chappel belonging to the Convent of the Ursulins, September 27th, 1759; Occasioned by the success of our Arms in the reduction of that Capital: at the Request of Brigadier General Monckton, and by order of Vice Admiral Saunders, Commander in Chief. By Rev. Eli Dawson. *London: Griffiths.* MDCCLX. 4to, pp. 14. J.C.B. 18929

Dedicated to the widow of the illustrious General Wolfe.

DAWSON (H. B.) The Assault on Stony Point, by General Anthony Wayne, July 16, 1779. Prepared for the New York Historical Society, and read at its Regular Monthly Meeting, April 1, 1862, with a Map, Fac-similes, and Illustrative Notes.

By Henry B. Dawson. *Morrisania, N. Y.* 1863. Rl. 8vo, pp. viii, 156. 18930

Two hundred and fifty copies printed. Forms Part XI. of Dawson's "Gleanings from the Harvest-field of American History."

DAWSON. Battles of the United States, by Sea and Land: embracing those of the Revolutionary and Indian Wars, the War of 1812, and the Mexican War; with Important Official Documents, ... By Henry B. Dawson, ... Illustrated with ... Engravings. *New York: Johnson, Fry, and Company.* [1858.] 2 vols., 4to, pp. 746; 530. 18931

Published by subscription, in parts. A new edition was announced in 1864, but the publishers took exception to its reissue, and Mr. Dawson changed the title to

DAWSON. Battles of the War of the Revolution. *Morrisania.* 1867. Rl. 8vo, pt. I., pp. 96. 18932

Edition, 100 copies on small, and 25 copies on large paper. As four years have elapsed since Part I. was printed, it seems probable the work will not be completed, which is much to be regretted. It is understood that all the copies were subscribed for, and such was the eagerness at that time for the large paper copies, that large sums were paid for a subscriber's right to the work.

DAWSON. Current Fictions tested by Uncurrent Facts, &c. A Correspondence between John Jay and Henry B. Dawson, and between James A. Hamilton and Henry B. Dawson, concerning the "Fœderalist." *New York: J. M. Bradstreet & Son.* 1864. 8vo, 2 l., pp. 48. 18933

Twenty-five copies printed on large paper, in 4to. *See also* Jay (J.)

DAWSON. The Fœderalist: A Collection of Essays, written in favor of the New Constitution, as agreed upon by the Fœderal Convention, September 17th, 1787. Reprinted from the original Text, with an Historical Introduction and Notes. By Henry B. Dawson. Vol. I. *New York: Charles Scribner.* 1864. pp. cxlii, 615. Portrait. 18934

Some copies were printed in imperial 8vo, with the imprint, *Morrisania.* 1864. The second volume is not yet (1871) published; but the text of the work is complete in this volume. In the late issues the publishers omit "Vol. I."

DAWSON. Gleanings from the Harvest-field of American History. 18935

This is the general title of a series of books projected by Mr. Dawson. We have a prospectus, published in 1865, in which seventeen numbers are said to be ready, or nearly ready for the press. Parts I., IV., V., VI., and XI., are the only numbers issued up to 1871.

DAWSON. The Gazette Series. Vol. I. *Yonkers, N. Y.* 1866. [Second Title.] Papers Concerning the Capture and

Detention of Major André. Collected by Henry B. Dawson. *Yonkers, N. Y.* 1866. 8vo, 4 l., pp. 246. + Vol. II. Papers Concerning the Town and Village of Yonkers, Westchester County. A Fragment by Henry B. Dawson. *Yonkers, N. Y.* 1866. 8vo, 4 l., pp. 293. + Vol. III. Papers Concerning the Boundary between the States of New York and New Jersey, Written by Several Hands. *Yonkers, N. Y.* 1866. 8vo, 4 l., pp. 159. + Vol. IV. Rambles in Westchester County, New York. A Fragment. By Henry B. Dawson. *Yonkers, N. Y.* 1866. 8vo, 4 l., pp. 43. 18936

Twenty-six copies printed, for private circulation only. Made up from the columns of the "Westchester Gazette."

DAWSON. Letter to the Hon. Luther Bradish, on the Declaration of Independence by the Colony of Massachusetts Bay, May 1, 1776, By Henry B. Dawson, with facsimile. *New York Historical Society.* [1862.] 8vo, pp. 12. B. 18937

DAWSON. The Magazine Miscellany. VOL. I. *Morrisania.* 1869. 8vo. 18938

Twenty-five copies only printed. Consists of the "Trial of Joshua Hett Smith," and "Fugitive Pieces" by various hands. Vol. II. has not been published. First printed in the "Historical Magazine."

DAWSON. Major-General Israel Putnam. A Correspondence on this Subject, with the Editor of the "Hartford Daily Post." By "Selah," of that city, and Henry B. Dawson, of White Plains, N. Y. *Morrisania, N. Y.* 1860. Rl. 8vo, pp. 169.

Two hundred and fifty copies privately printed, some of which were destroyed by fire. Forms Part VI. of Dawson's "Gleanings from the Harvest-field of American History." The writers were Henry B. Dawson, A. Griswold, Clifford, and others.

DAWSON. The Park and its Vicinity, in the City of New York. By Henry B. Dawson. *Morrisania, N. Y.* 1867. Rl. 8vo, pp. viii, 95. 18940

Forms Part I. of "Gleanings," etc., and is an amplification of the following:

[DAWSON.] Reminiscences of the Park and its Vicinity. *New York.* 1855. 12mo, pp. 64. 18941

Twenty five copies printed. First appeared in Valentine's "Manual." Pages 58-64 are by William J. Davis.

DAWSON. The Sons of Liberty in New York. A Paper Read Before the New York Historical Society, May 3d, 1859. By Henry B. Dawson. *Printed, as Manuscript, for Private Circulation.* 1859. 8vo, pp. 118. 18942

DAWSON. William Jackson Davis. In Memoriam. *New York.* 1865. 4to, pp. 48. 18943

Seventy copies printed. Also: Reply to an Attack by John Jay, on the Assessors of Bedford, N. Y. 1863. 8vo. S. Mr. Dawson also edited the "Trial of the Officers and Crew of the Privateer Savannah," and is now the editor of the "Historical Magazine." All Mr. Dawson's works display much research, mixed with some acerbity.

[DAWSON (H. B.)] State Sovereignty. A Dialogue. *Frankfort, Ky.* 1862. 18944

DAWSON (J. B.) Address to the Electors of the Second Congressional District of Louisiana, Nov. 23, 1841. By John B. Dawson. [n. p.] 1841. 8vo, pp. 8. 18945

DAWSON (J. L.) Speech ... John L. Dawson, of Pa., on the Bill Granting one quarter Section of the Public Land to Actual Settlers. Delivered in the House ... March 3, 1852. *Washington.* 1852. 8vo, pp. 15. H. 18946

Also: Speech ... on the Homestead Bill. ... in the House ... February 14, 1854. *Washington: printed by Robert Armstrong.* 1854. 8vo, pp. 28. H.—Speech ... on the Homestead Bill ... in the House ... January 9, 1855. *Washington: A. O. P. Nicholson.* 1855. 8vo, pp. 17. H.—Speech ... on the State of the Union ... in the House ... February 24, 1864. *Washington: L. Towers & Co.* 1864. 8vo, pp. 29. —Speech ... on the Reconstruction of the Union. ... in the House ... January 16, 1867. *Washington: printed by Lemuel Towers.* 1867. 8vo, pp. 23. H.

DAWSON (J. L.) Census of Charleston, S. C., 1848. B.

DAWSON (J. W.) Acadian Geology: an Account of the Geological Structure and Mineral Resources of Nova Scotia, and Portions of the Neighbouring Provinces of British America. By John William Dawson ... . *Edinburgh: Oliver and Boyd.* 1855. 12mo, pp. xii, 388. Map. Woodcuts in the text. BA., C. + With a Supplementary Chapter on the Coal Measures, etc. *Montreal.* 1860. 12mo, pp. 458. Woodcuts and Map. 18948

Some copies have an Edinburgh imprint. The "Supplementary Chapter," pp. 60, was issued separately.

DAWSON. Acadian Geology. The Geological Structure, Organic Remains, and Mineral Resources of Nova Scotia, New Brunswick, and Prince Edward Island. Second Edition. Revised and Enlarged. With Map and Illustrations. *London: Macmillan & Co.* 186-. 8vo, pp. xxvii-694. 18949

DAWSON. Airbreathers of the Coal Period; a Descriptive Account of the Remains of Land Animals found in the Coal Formation of Nova Scotia, with Remarks on their Bearing on

Theories of the Formation of Coal, and of the Origin of Species. By J. W. Dawson. ... *Montreal: Dawson Bros.* 1863. 8vo, pp. iv, 81. 6 Plates. 18950

DAWSON. Contributions toward the Improvement of Agriculture in Nova-Scotia. *Pictou, N. S.* 1853. 8vo, pp. 99. + Second Edition ... *Halifax, N. S.* 1856. 8vo, pp. 280.

DAWSON. Geography and Natural History of Nova Scotia. Second Edition. *Pictou.* 1851. 24mo. B. 18952

DAWSON. Hand Book of Geography and Natural History of Nova Scotia. *Pictou.* 1848. + Sixth Edition. 1863. 8vo, pp. 95. 18953

DAWSON. On the Conditions of the deposition of Coal, more especially as illustrated by the Coal Formation of Nova Scotia and New Brunswick. [With] Appendix. Descriptive List of Carboniferous Plants. [*London:*] *Geological Society.* 1866. 8vo, pp. 77. 9 Plates. C. 18954

DAWSON. Reports on Schools of Nova Scotia. *Halifax.* 1850–1–2. 18955

Also: Alpine and Arctic Plants. ... *Montreal.* 1862. 8vo. — Duties of Educated Young Men in British America ... *Montreal.* 1865. — Improvement of Agriculture in Nova Scotia. Second Edition. *Halifax.* 1853. 8vo. B. — Inaugural Discourse of Collegiate Education in British North America ... *Montreal.* 1855. 8vo, pp. 29. — Microscopic Structure of some Canadian Limestones. ... *Montreal* 1863. 8vo. S. — On some points in the History and Prospects of Protestant Education in Lower Canada; A Lecture ... *Montreal.* 1864. 8vo, pp. 20. — On the Newer Pliocene and Post Pliocene Deposits of the Vicinity of Montreal, with Notices of Fossils recently discovered in them. ... *Montreal: printed by John Lovell.* 1858. 8vo, pp. 28. H. Mr. Dawson is the author of many articles in the "Proceedings and Journal of the Geological Society of London," "Canadian Naturalist," "American Journal of Education," and other journals, some of which pieces are separately issued.

DAWSON (M.) A Historical Narrative of the Civil and Military Services of Major-General William H. Harrison, and a Vindication of his Character and Conduct as a Statesman, a Citizen, and a Soldier. With a Detail of his Negotiations and Wars with the Indians, until the final Overthrow of the celebrated Chief Tecumseh, and his Brother the Prophet, the whole written and compiled from Original and Authentic Documents, furnished by many of the most respectable characters in the United States. By Moses Dawson. ... *Cincinnati: M. Dawson.* 1824. 8vo, pp. viii, 464, 5 l. 18956

See "N. Am. Rev.," XXI. 248.

DAWSON. Sketches of the Life of Martin Van Buren, ... *Cincinnati.* 1840. 18mo. 18957

DAWSON (S. J.) Report on the Exploration of the Country between Lake Superior and the Red River Settlement, and between the latter place and the Assiniboine and Saskatchewan. By S. J. Dawson. With Maps and Plans. *Toronto.* 1859. 4to, pp. 45. Maps. C. 18958

DAWSON (T. M.) Semi-Centennial Sermon of the Seventh Presbyterian Church ... New York City ... March 29th, 1868, by ... Rev. T. M. Dawson ... with an ... Address ... by the Rev. T. Ralston Smith, D.D. *New York: Egbert, Bourne & Co., Printers.* 1868. 8vo, pp. 43. H. 18959

DAWSON (W. C.) Speech of Hon. W. C. Dawson, of Georgia, on the Bill Granting Land to the State of Iowa in Aid of Constructing certain Railroads. Delivered in the Senate ... March 1, 1852. *Washington.* 1852. 8vo, pp. 12. 18960

[DAWSON (Wm. McD.)] Memorandum in relation to the Gold Mines of the Chaudiere, in Lower Canada. *New York: C. S. Westcott & Co., Printers.* 1865. 8vo, pp. 16. H. 18961

The Day Breaking, 1647. See [Eliot (John)].

DAY (C. D.) Address, delivered at the Provincial Industrial Exhibition, Montreal ... Oct. 19, 1850, by the Honorable Charles D. Day ... . *Montreal: printed by Rollo Campbell.* 1850. 8vo, pp. 25. H. 18962

DAY (*Mrs.* C. M.) Pioneers of the Eastern Townships; A Work containing Official and Reliable Information respecting the Formation of Settlements; with Incidents in the Early History, and Details of Adventures, Perils, and Deliverances. *Montreal.* 1863. 4to, pp. 171. 18963

DAY (C. W.) Five Years' Residence in the West Indies. By Charles William Day. *London.* 1852. 2 vols., post 8vo, pp. 640. 18964

See "Blackwood's Mag.," LXXXI.

DAY (G. E.) The Dangers of our Country, and the Means of averting them. A Discourse delivered in Marlbourough, Mass., on the Day of the Annual State Fast, April 7, 1842. By George E. Day ... . *Boston: Press of T. Marvin.* 1842. 8vo, pp. 17. H. 18965

[DAY.] A Genealogical Memoir of the Descendants of Robert Day, of Hartford, Conn., who Died in the Year 1648. *New Haven: Printed by William Storer, Jun.* 1840. 8vo, pp. 44.

[DAY.] A Genealogical Register of the Descendants in the Male Line of Robert Day of Hartford, Conn., who Died in the Year 1648. Second Edition. *Northampton: Printed by J. & L. Metcalf.* 1848. 8vo, pp. 129. 18967

DAY (H. H.) Testimonials in favor of the Plan of Horace H. Day, of New York, for the Cheap Transit of Loaded Vessels between Navigable Waters, by means of Ship Canals with Inclined Planes; especially applicable to the Proposed Work around Niagara Falls. *New York: Wm. C. Bryant & Co., Printers.* 1866. 8vo, pp. 20. H. 18968

DAY (J.) The Divine Right of Infant Baptism, Concisely proved from the Holy Scriptures; and Objections answered. A Sermon, delivered by Jeremiah Day, A.M. Pastor of the Church of New-Preston. (Published by Request.) *Litchfield: Printed by Thomas Collier, in the South End of the Court-House.* 1790. 8vo, pp. 43. 18969

Also: The Christian Preacher's Commission: A Sermon ... before the General Association of Connecticut, at Saybrook ... June 22, 1831. *New Haven.* 8vo, pp. 20. — Sermon delivered ... at Bethlehem, Jan. 4, 1774. ... *New Haven.*

DAY (L. M.) Argument of L. Madison Day, before the United States District Court, (Eastern District of Louisiana,) in the Case of the United States vs. The Property of Thomas Griswold & Co. ... 1863. *New Orleans.* 1864. 8vo, Title, pp. 62. 18970

DAY. United States District Court, (Eastern District of Louisiana,) The United States vs. the Property of Thomas Griswold & Co. L. Madison Day ... . [n. p. n. d.] 8vo, pp. 60. + Second Edition. 8vo, 1 l., pp. 62. H. 18971

DAY (M.) The Literary Remains of Martha Day; with Rev. Dr. Fitch's Address at her Funeral; and Sketches of her Character. *New Haven: printed by Hezekiah Howe & Co.* 1834. 12mo, pp. 121. 18972

DAY (M. L.) Incidents in the Life of a Blind Girl. By Mary L. Day. *Printed for the Author.* 1860. 12mo, pp. 206. Portrait. 18973

DAY (Pliny Butts). A Discourse on Victory and its Dangers, delivered in Dublin, N. H., Fast Day, April 13, 1865. By Rev. P. B. Day. *Concord: McFarland & Jencks,* 1865. 8vo, pp. 20. 18974

DAY. A Memorial Discourse on the Character of Abraham Lincoln, President of the United States, delivered at Hollis, N. H., on the Day of the National Fast, June 1, 1865. By P. B. Day. ... *Concord: Printed by McFarland & Jencks.* 1865. 8vo, pp. 20. B., H. 18975

Fifty copies printed.

DAY. A Tribute to the Memory of Lieut. John Howard Worcester, in a Discourse delivered at Hollis, N. H., January 24, 1864. By Rev. P. B. Day. *Nashua: Telegraph Office.* 1864. 8vo, pp. 16. 18976

Also: Duty of Parents in Educating their Children. A Sermon delivered ... January 28, 1855. ... *Nashua, N. H.: printed by Albin Beard.* 1855. 8vo, pp. 18. H. — [Day.] A Pastor's New Year's Address to his Parishioners. [*Manhaster.*] 16mo, pp. 8. H. — A Sermon delivered at the Funeral of Benjamin Franklin Nichols, August 6, 1854. ... *Nashua: Dodge & Noyes, Printers.* 1854. 8vo, pp. 16. H.

DAY (S. P.) Down South; or, An Englishman's Experience at the Seat of the American War. By Samuel Phillips Day. *London: Hurst & Blackett.* 1862. 2 vols., post 8vo, pp. 328; 827. C. 18977

DAY. English America; or Pictures of Canadian Places and People. By Samuel Phillips Day. *London: T. C. Newby.* 1864. 2 vols., post 8vo. 18978

DAY (S.) Historical Collections of the State of Pennsylvania; containing a copious Selection of the most interesting Facts, Traditions, Biographical Sketches, Anecdotes, &c. relating to its History and Antiquities, both general and local: with Topographical Descriptions of every County and all the larger Towns in the State. By Sherman Day. *Philadelphia.* [1843.] 8vo, pp. 708. 165 Engravings. C. 18979

[DAY (Thomas).] The Desolation of America: A Poem. *London: Printed for E. and C. Dilly.* MDCCLXXVII. 4to, pp. 26.

[DAY.] The Desolation of America: A Poem. *London: Printed for G. Kearsly and Richardson & Urquhart.* MDCCLXXVII. 4to, pp. 26. 18981

A different edition from No. 18980, though printed in the same year. See "M. Rev.," LVII. 424.

[DAY.] The Devoted Legions. A Poem. Addressed to Lord George Germaine, and the Commanders of the Forces against America. *London: J. Ridley.* MDCCLXXVI. 4to, pp. 8. J.C.B. + Second Edition. *London: J. Kearsly, and J. Ridley.* M,DCC,LXXVI. 4to, 4 l., pp. 14. + Third Edition. MDCCLXXVI. 4to. 18982

DAY. Four Tracts. Reflections on the present state of England and the Independence of America; upon the Peace, ... Fragment of an original on the Slavery of the Negroes. *London.* 1785. 8vo. 18983

DAY. Fragment of an original Letter on the Slavery of the Negroes. Written in the Year 1775, By Thomas Day, Esq. *London: J. Stockdale.* 1784. 8vo. B. 18984

See "M. Rev.," LXXI. 154.

[DAY.] The Letters of Marius: or Reflections upon the Peace ... the Present Crisis. *London.* 1784. 8vo. S. + Third Edition. *London.* 1784. 8vo. 18985

DAY. Reflections upon the Present State of England, and the Independence of America. By Thomas Day, Esq; Second Edition. *London: J. Stockdale.* 1782. 8vo, pp. 102. P. + The Third Edition: with Additions. [*Ibid.*] 1783. 8vo, pp. (1), 129. + Fourth Edition, with Additions. [*Ibid.*] 1783. 8vo. B. + The Fifth Edition, with Additions. *London.* 1783. 8vo, pp. 129. 18986

Originally commenced in the "London Courant," but left unfinished for private reasons. The author thinks the independence of the American colonies should be acknowledged, and that great advantages will result to England from such measure. See "M. Rev.," LXVII. 321, and Rich, I. 308.

DAY, *and* BICKNELL (John). The Dying Negro, a Poem with a Fragment of a letter on the Slavery of Negroes, written at the request of an American Gentleman. *London.* 1793. 8vo. Plate. 18987

DAY (T.) An Oration on Party Spirit ... 4th of July, 1798. By Thomas Day. *Litchfield: printed by J. Collier.* [n. d.] 8vo, pp. 28. H. 18988

DAY (T.) Digested Index to the Reported Decisions of the Several Courts of Law in the United States. By Thomas Day. *New York.* 1816. 8vo. 18989

DAY. A Concise Historical Account of the Judiciary of Connecticut. *Hartford.* 1817. 8vo, pp. 32. S. 18990

DAY. An Historical Discourse delivered before the Connecticut Historical Society, Twenty-sixth December, 1843. ... By Thomas Day. *Hartford.* 1844. 8vo, pp. 36. N. 18991

Also: Brief Memoirs of the Class of 1797. By Thomas Day and James Murdock *New Haven.* 1848. 8vo.

DAY (T. C.) The Democratic Party as it Was and as it Is! Speech of Hon. Timothy C. Day, of Ohio, in the House of Representatives, April 23, 1856. [n. p. n. d.] 8vo, pp. 8.

[DAY.] The Humbug and the Reality. An Address to the People of the First Congressional District of Ohio. *Washington, D. C.: Buell & Blanchard, Printers.* 1856. 8vo, pp. 8. H.

Another edition has the title: "The Humbug, and the Reality. An Address of the Hon. Timothy C. Day, of Ohio, to his Constituents." [n. p. n. d.] pp. 8.

DAY (W.) Slavery in America shown to be peculiarly Abominable, both as a Political Anomaly and an Outrage on Christianity. By William Day ... . *London: Hamilton, Adams, and Co., and J. Balle.* 1841. 12mo, pp. 84. + Second Edition. [*Ibid.*] 8vo, pp. 94. H. 18994

Day's Bank Note List and Counterfeit Detector. Sept. 8, 1848. *New-York.* 8vo. 18995

The Day-Breaking, 1647. See [Shepard (T.)]

[DAYRELL (John).] A Treatise of the Church, written against them of the Separation, commonly called Brownists. *London: by W. Jones.* 1617. 4to. 18996

Included in a catalogue of Americana, sold by Puttick and Simpson, in 1860, for 18s.

The Days of Old: or the Battle of Hexham. *Boston.* 12mo.

The Days of Sixty-Three. *Philadelphia: Printed for the Sanitary Committee.* 1864. 12mo, pp. 54. 18998

DAYTON (A. O.) Address delivered before the American Whig and Cliosophic Societies of the College of New Jersey. September 24, 1839. By Aaron Ogden Dayton, Esq. *Princeton: printed by Robert E. Hornor.* 1839. 8vo, pp. 50. B.

DAYTON. Eulogy on La Fayette, pronounced before the Society of Cincinnati of the State of New-Jersey, on the 4th of July, 1835, By Aaron Ogden Dayton ... . 1835. 8vo, pp. 44.

DAYTON (J.) Public Speculation Unfolded: in Sixteen Letters, addressed to F. Childs and J. H. Lawrence. By Jonathan Dayton of New Jersey. *New York.* 1800. 8vo. N. 19001

DAYTON (W. C.) Tariff, or the Rates of Duties Payable on Goods, Wares and Merchandise, imported into the United States of America, on and after the Thirtieth of August, 1842, ... Revised and corrected by William C. Dayton ... *New-York: Baker, Crane & Day.* [n. d.] 8vo, pp. 36, xxiv. 19002

DAYTON (William L.) Speech of Mr. Dayton, of New Jersey, on the Subject of Oregon, &c. Delivered in the Senate of the United States, February 23 and 26, 1844. *Washington: printed by Gales and Seaton.* 1844. 8vo, pp. 25. H. 19003

Also: Address delivered before the American Whig and Cliosophic Societies of the College of New Jersey, Sept. 26, 1843 ... *Princeton.* 1843. 8vo, pp. 30. — Speech ... on the Compromise Bill: ... in the Senate ... June 11 and 12, 1850. [n. p. n. d.] 8vo, pp. 16. H., M. — Speech ... on the Territorial Question, ... in the Senate ... March 22, 1850. *Washington: printed by John T. Towers.* 1850. 8vo, pp. 32. — Speech ... on the Mexican War, the Plans and Conduct of the Campaign. Delivered in the Senate of the United States, Jan. 27 and 28, 1847. [n. p.] *J. & G. S. Gideon, Printers.* [n. d.] 8vo, pp. 16. H. — The Territorial Question. ... in Senate ... March 22, 1850. [n. p. n. d.] 8vo, pp. 16. H.

DAYTON. Correspondence of William L. Dayton, U. S. Minister to France, and Mons. Drouyn de l'Huys, on the subject of "Mediation, arbitration, and other measures looking to the Termination of the existing Civil War." 8vo, pp. 16. (37th Cong., 3d Sess., Ex. Doc., No. 38, 1863.) 19004

DAYTON, *Ohio.* Dayton Directory, City Guide, and Business Mirror, 1856–'7. By C. S. Williams. *Dayton, (O.)* 1856. 8vo. C., P. + Business Directory for 1864–65. *Cincinnati: Hawes & Redfield.* 8vo, pp. 113. 19005

Dayton and Cincinnati (Short Line) Railroad. Report. *Cincinnati.* 1853. 8vo. Continued. 19006

First Exhibit ... of the Condition and Prospects of the Dayton and Michigan Railroad Company. *New-York.* 1852. 8vo.

Third Annual Report of the Dayton and Western Railroad Co. *New York: Baker & Godwin.* 1855. 8vo, pp. 12. Continued. 19008

DAZILLE (M.) Observations sur les Maladies des Negres ... . Par M. Dazille ... . *Paris: Didot le Jeune.* M. DCC. LXXVI. 8vo, pp. xvj, 316, (4). H. 19009

DEACON (W. F.) The Author; or Sketches from Life. *St. John, (N. B.)* 1866. 12mo, pp. 64. 19010

[DEACON.] Warreniana: with Notes, Critical and Explanatory, by the Editor of a Quarterly Review. ... *Boston: Ticknor, Reed, and Fields.* M DCCC LI. 16mo, pp. 192. 19011

This clever book of parodies is mentioned here on account of the imitation of Washington Irving.

DEADY (M. P.) Organic and General Laws of Oregon, 1845–'64. By M. P. Deady. *Portland* 1866. 8vo. S.

DE AHNA (C. H.) [Memorial to Congress. Dated Feb. 14. *Washington.* 1863.] 8vo, pp. 11. H. 19013

DE AHNA. Report of the Committee on Military Affairs, on the Petition of Col. Charles H. De Ahna. 8vo, pp. 17. (House of Representatives, Report No. 124, 38th Congress, 1st Session, 1864.) 19014

Dealings with the Dead. See [Sargent (L. M.)]

DEALTRY (W.) Money, its History, Evils and Remedy. By William Dealtry. *Albany.* 1858. 8vo, pp. 36. S. 19015

DEAN (A.) An Attempt to present the Claims of Long Lake [N. Y.] to the Consideration of all those who are in Search of Good Land at a Low Price. By Amos Dean. *Albany.* 1846. 8vo, pp. 35. 19016

DEAN. Eulogy on the Life and Character of the late Judge Jesse Buel. Pronounced before the New-York State Agricultural Society, ... 5th February, 1840. *Albany.* 1840. 8vo, pp. 29. 19017

Also: Address ... before the Young Men's State Association of ... New York, at their ... Meeting, at Geneva, Sept. 2, 1841. *Albany: Joel Munsell.* 1841. 8vo, pp. 31, (3). B. — Address, New York State Agricultural Society. ... *Albany.* 1850. S. — Address delivered before the Albany Institute, April 3, 1833. *Albany.* 1833. 8vo, pp. 22. B. — Introductory Lecture before the Young Men's Association for Mutual Improvement in the City of Albany, Delivered Dec. 17. 1839. ... *Albany: J. Munsell.* 1839. 8vo, pp. 33. — Introductory Lecture, ... before the ... Association, Dec. 7, 1848. *Albany: J. Munsell.* 1848. 8vo, pp. 30. — The True Method of Studying and Teaching History: ... *Albany.* 1857. 8vo. S.

DEAN (Argus). The Ohio River and its Obstructions, with a Plan for its Improvement; and the Mississippi River, its Geological Character, Overflows, &c., together with a Review of Ellet's "Mississippi and Ohio Rivers." *Cincinnati.* 1857. 8vo, pp. 128. 19018

DEAN (C. B.) The Trial of Cyrus B. Dean, for the Murder of Jonathan Ormsby and Asa Marsh, before the Supreme Court of ... Vermont ... . *Burlington: Samuel Mills. Middlebury: Mills and White.* 1808. 8vo, pp. 48. BA., H., W. 19019

DEAN (G.) The Emancipation Proclamation and Arbitrary Arrests. Speech of Gilbert Dean in the House of Assembly of New York, February 12, 1863. *Albany.* 1863. 8vo, pp. 15.

Also: Nebraska and Kansas. Speech ... House ... May 19, 1854. [*Washington.*] 1854. 8vo, pp. 7. H. — Speech ... on the Position of N. York on the Presidency ... . House ... April 23, 1852. *Washington.* 1852. 8vo. H.

DEAN (H. C.) Address of Henry Clay Dean, Delivered ... January 16th A.D. 1862. The Supremacy of the Written Constitutional Law ... . [*Des Moines.*] 8vo, pp. 30. H. 19021

DEAN. Letter upon the Connexion of the Methodist Episcopal Church with Slavery. By Henry Clay Dean. [n. p. n. d.] 8vo, pp. 13. B. 19022

DEAN (J.) An Alphabetical Atlas, or Gazetteer of Vermont; affording a Summary Description of the State, its several Counties, Towns, and Rivers . ... By James Dean, A.M. ... *Montpelier: printed by Samuel Goss for the Author. January,* 1808. 8vo, pp. 43, (1). BA., W. 19023

DEAN (Jaspar). A Narrative of the Sufferings, Preservation, and Deliverance of Capt. John Dean and Company; In the Nottingham-Galley of London, cast away on Boon-Island, near New England, December 11, 1710. *London: Printed by R. Tookey and Sold by S. Popping.* [1711.] Sm. 8vo, Title, pp. iv, 23. H. + *Boston.* 1711. 8vo. 19024

DEAN. Narrative of the Sufferings, Preservation, and Deliverance of Capt. John Dean, of the Nottingham Galley, sailing from Boston, and wrecked on Boon Island, near Massachusetts Bay. *London.* 1722. 8vo, pp. 16. C. 19025

For another account, *see* No. 19029.

DEAN. A Narrative of the Shipwreck of the Nottingham-Galley, &c. Publish'd in 1711. Revis'd, and Reprinted with Additions in 1726, by John Deane, Commander. [*London.*] 8vo, pp. 24. + *Reprinted.* 1727. 8vo, pp. 22. + *London.* 1730. 8vo. 19026

DEAN. A Narrative of the Shipwreck of the Nottingham Galley, &c. First published in 1711. Revis'd and Reprinted with Additions in 1726. Republished in 1730, and now propos'd for the Last Edition during the Author's Lifetime. [*London.*] 1738. 8vo, pp. 2, 28. J.C.B. 19027

DEAN. A Narrative of the Shipwreck of the Nottingham Galley, In her Voyage from England to Boston. With An Account of the Miraculous Escape of the Captain and his Crew on a Rock, called Boone-Island; the Hard-ships they endured there, and their happy Deliverance. By John Deane, then Commander of the said Galley; But for many Years after His Majesty's Consul for the Ports of Flanders, residing at Ostend. The Fifth

Edition. [*London:*] *Printed in the Year* M.DCC.LXII. 8vo, 2 l., pp. 28. J.C.B. + Fifth Edition. [*Boston.*] 1762. 8vo, pp. 28.

DEAN. A True Account of the Voyage of the Nottingham-Galley of London, John Deane Commander, from the River Thames to New-England, Near which place she was cast away on Boon-Island, Dec. 11, 1710. by the Captain's Obstinacy, who endeavour'd to betray her to the French, or run her ashore; with an account of the False-hoods in the Captain's Narrative. And a faithful Relation of the Extremities the Company was reduc'd to for Twenty-four Days on that desolate Rock, where they were forc'd to eat one of their Companions who died, but were at last wonderfully deliver'd. The whole attested upon Oath, by Christopher Langman, Mate; Nicholas Mellen, Boatswain; and George White, Sailor in the said Ship. *London: S. Popping.* 1711. 8vo, Title, 4 l., pp. 36. 19029

DEAN (J. W.) A Brief History of the New-England Historical & Genealogical Register ... by John Ward Dean. [n. p. n. d.] 8vo, pp. 8. 19030

DEAN. A Brief Memoir of Rev. Giles Firmin; one of the Ejected Ministers of 1662. By John Ward Dean ... . *Boston.* 1866. 8vo, pp. 16. S. 19031

DEAN. Henry Kingsbury and his Descendants. By John Ward Dean of Boston. 8vo, pp. 4. 19032

Reprinted from the "N. E. Gen. Register," XIII. 157.

DEAN. A Memoir of the Rev. Nathaniel Ward, A.M., Author of the Simple Cobler of Aggawam in America, with Notices of his Family. By John Ward Dean. *Albany: J. Munsell.* 1868. 8vo, pp. 213. BA. 19033

DEAN. Sketch of the Life of Rev. Michael Wigglesworth, A.M. ... By John Ward Dean, ... To which is appended a Fragment of his Autobiography, some of his Letters, and a Catalogue of his Library. Reprinted from the Register for April, 1863. *Albany: J. Munsell.* 1863. 8vo, pp. 20. B. 19034

One hundred copies printed. Reprinted as

DEAN. Memoir of Rev. Michael Wigglesworth, Author of the Day of Doom. By John Ward Dean. Second Edition [enlarged]. *Albany, N. Y.: J. Munsell.* 1871. 8vo, pp. 160.

Edition fifty copies.

DEAN. The Story of the Embarkation of Cromwell and his Friends for New England. (Reprinted from the New England Historical and Genealogical Register.) *Boston.* 1866. 8vo, pp. 11. 19036

DEAN (P.) A Discourse, delivered at the Annual Election, January 4, 1832. ... By Paul Dean. *Boston: Dutton and Wentworth, Printers.* 1831 [*sic*]. 8vo, pp. 38. BA. 19037

DEAN. A Sermon, preached before the Antient and Honorable Artillery Company, on the 177th Anniversary of their Election of Officers; Boston, June 3, 1816. By Rev. Paul Dean ... Second Edition. *Boston: published by E. G. House.* 1816. 8vo, pp. 22, (1). BA., H. 19038

Also: Masonic Address, Dedham, 1816. *Attleborough.* 1817. — Masonic Address at Walpole, Mass., June 24, 1823. *Boston.* 1823. 8vo. W. — Discourse delivered at Bulfinch Street, on taking leave of the Society ... *Boston.* 1840. 8vo. — Discourse ... before the African Society ... on the Abolition of the Slave Trade by the Government of the United States ... July 14, 1819. By Paul Dean ... . *Boston: Nathaniel Coverly.* 1819. 8vo, pp. 16. BA. — Discourse ... on the Character and Death of the Rev. John Murray ... . Oct. 29, 1815. *Boston.* 1815. 8vo. — Eulogy ... on the Character of ... Thomas Smith Webb. *Boston: E. G. House.* 1819. 8vo, pp. 16. BA. + Second Edition. *Boston.* 1819. 8vo. H. — A Sermon ... at the Installation of the Rev. Hosea Ballou, ... Roxbury, July 26, 1821. ... *Boston.* 1821. 8vo, pp. 24. BA.

DEAN (Samuel). *See* Deane (Samuel).

DEAN (S.) A Plain and Candid Statement of Facts of the Difficulty existing between Mr. B. L. Hamlen and Mrs. Sarah Dean; being an Appeal to the Moral and Religious Community from a defenceless Widow for Justice and Protection. *New Haven.* 1843. 8vo. BM. 19039

DEAN (S.) Eulogy Pronounced in the City Hall, Providence, April 19, 1865, on the Occasion of the Funeral Solemnities of Abraham Lincoln, before his Excellency, James Y. Smith, Governor of the State of Rhode Island; Members of the General Assembly; City Authorities; The Military; Civic Societies, and Others. By Rev. Sidney Dean. *Providence: H. H. Thomas & Co.* 1865. 8vo, pp. 23. B. 19040

DEAN. The War: and the Duty of a Loyal People. A Sermon, ... Providence, R. I., ... July 27, 1862, by the ... Rev. Sidney Dean. *Providence: Pierce & Budlong, Printers.* 1862. 8vo, pp. 16. 19041

Also: Oration ... July 4, 1864 ... 1864. 8vo.

DEAN (S.) A Brief History of the Town of Stoneham, Mass. from its First Settlement to the Present Time: with an Account of the Murder of Jacob Gould, On the Evening of Nov. 25, 1819. By Silas Dean. ... *Boston: Printed at S. R. Hart's.* 1843. 12mo, pp. 36. C., H. 19042

El Dean de la Santa Iglesia Cathedral de Guatemala, expresa los fundamentos, que tuvo, para ordenar, que en la Collecta del Santo Sacrificio de Missa, se pidiesse por toda la Real Audiencia; diciendo Regium Senatum, haviendo fallecido el Señor Presidente de dicha Real Audiencia; y que no se nombrase separadamente en la referida Collecta á el Señor Oidor mas antiguo. [*Guatemala.* About 1640.] Folio, 4 leaves. 19043

DEANE (C.) A Bibliographical Essay on Governor Hutchinson's Historical Publications. By Charles Deane. *Boston: privately printed.* 1857. Sq. 8vo, pp. 39. H. 19044

Fifty copies printed.

[DEANE.] A Brief Memoir of Robert Waterston, a Boston Merchant. By one who knew him many years. A Few Copies for Private Distribution. *Boston.* 1869. 8vo, pp. 11. H.

[DEANE.] Bibliographical Tracts. No. 1. Spurious Reprints of Early Books. *Boston.* 1865. Rl. 8vo, pp. 19. H.

"From the Boston Daily Advertiser of March 24, 1865." This reprint was not made by Mr. Deane. It is a review of "Salem Witchcraft by ... Calef, and Cotton Mather ... with Notes by Samuel P. Fowler." 135 copies printed, 6 copies on India paper.

DEANE. Communication [to the Mass. Hist. Soc. 1866–67], respecting the Seal of the "Council for New England." By Charles Deane. [*Cambridge, Mass.* 1867.] 8vo, pp. 4. C., H.

Thirty copies printed from the "Proceedings of the Massachusetts Hist. Soc."

DEANE. The Forms of issuing Letters-Patent by the Crown of England, with some Remarks on the Massachusetts Charter of the 4th of March, 1628–9. A Paper read before the Massachusetts Historical Society, 21st December, 1869. By Charles Deane. Fifty copies for private distribution, reprinted from the Proceedings. *Cambridge.* 1870. 8vo, pp. 24. 19048

Fifty copies reprinted for private distribution.

DEANE. Memoir of George Livermore. Prepared agreeably to a Resolution of the Massachusetts Historical Society.

By Charles Deane. *Cambridge.: Press of John Wilson and Son.* 1869. 8vo, pp. 60. B., BA., H. 19049

Also on large paper.

DEANE. Remarks on Sebastian Cabot's Mappemonde. From the Proceedings of the American Antiquarian Society, for April, 1867. *Cambridge: Press of John Wilson and Son.* 1867. 8vo, pp. 8. BA., C., H. 19050

Fifty copies printed.

DEANE. Some Notices of Samuel Gorton, one of the First Settlers of Warwick, R. I., during his Residence at Plymouth, Portsmouth, and Providence; chiefly derived from early Manuscripts; with a Brief Introductory Memoir. ... By Charles Deane. *Boston: printed by Coolidge & Wiley.* 1850. 4to, pp. 41. H. 19051

Twenty-five copies reprinted from the "N. E. Hist. and Geneal. Register," for private distribution. Mr. Deane also edited Bradford's "History of Plymouth Plantation," Bradford's "Third Dialogue," the "First Plymouth Patent," Smith's "True Relation," Wingfield's "Discourse of Virginia," Phillis Wheatley's "Letters," Cushman's "Sermon preached at Plymouth, 1621," Wheelwright's "Antimonian Sermon," C. Mather's "Life of T. Dudley," Captain Smith's "Last Will and Testament," the "History of Bacon's and Ingram's Rebellion," and the "Records of the Council for New England," the principal part of these having been first printed in the publications of the Massachusetts Historical Society, or the "Archæologia Americana." Some of these pamphlets might have been entered under Mr. Deane's name, for his notes and discussions are of greater length than the text.

DEANE (E.) Oration [Poetical] pronounced at Tiverton, July 4, 1804. *Dedham.* 1804. 8vo. N. 19052

DEANE. An Oration pronounced at Plympton. Feb. 23, 1809. On the Present Alarming Situation to which the United States are Reduced. By E. Deane, M.D. *Dedham: Printed by H. Mann. February,* 1811. 16mo, pp. 12. H. 19053

DEANE (J.) Iconographs, from the Sandstone of Connecticut River, [With Memoir upon the Fossil Footprints and other Impressions.] By James Deane, M.D. *Boston: Little, Brown and Company.* 1861. 4to, pp. 61. 46 Plates. B., BA. 19054

Also: Illustrations of Fossil Footprints of the Valley of the Connecticut. [*Cambridge, Mass.* 1849.] 4to. 9 Plates.

DEANE (John). *See* Dean (John).

DEANE (S.) The Death of an Aged Servant of God considered and improved. Funeral Discourse delivered at Portland, May 31, 1795, on the Death of Rev. Thomas Smith. By Rev. Samuel Deane. *Portland.* 1795. 8vo, pp. 24. M., W. 19055

DEANE. The New-England Farmer; or Georgical Dictionary: containing a Compendious Account of the Ways and Methods In which the most Important Art of Husbandry, in all its various Branches, is, or may be, practised to the Greatest Advantage in this Country. ... By Samuel Deane, A.M. ... *Worcester, Mass.: Isaiah Thomas.* MDCCXC. 8vo, pp. viii, 335. BA. + *Worcester, Mass.* 1797. 8vo, pp. 332. C. + Third Edition, Corrected, Improved ... and Adapted to the Present State ... of Agriculture. *Boston.* 1822. 8vo. 19056

The first work of the kind published in this country.

DEANE. An Oration, delivered in Portland, July 4th, 1793, in Commemoration of the Independence of the United States of America. By Samuel Deane, D.D. *Portland: Thomas B. Wait.* 1793. 8vo, pp. 14. BA. 19057

DEANE. A Sermon ... February 19th. 1795. being a Day of National Thanksgiving ... . By Samuel Deane ... . *Portland: Thomas B. Wait.* 1795. 8vo, pp. 20. BA. 19058

DEANE. A Sermon preached before ... the Hon. the Council, Senate, and House of Representatives of the Commonwealth of Massachusetts, May 28th, 1794. Being the Day of General Election. By Samuel Deane, D.D. ... *Boston: Printed by Adams and Larkin.* 1794. 8vo, pp. 31, 6. B., BA., H., W., 19059

The appendix contains a list of preachers *See* Barnard (Thomas), and Smith (Thomas).

DEANE (Samuel). Discourse delivered at the Dedication of the Second Congregational Church, Scituate, Oct. 13, 1830. ... *Boston.* 1830. 8vo. pp. 19. M. 19060

DEANE. History of Scituate, Massachusetts, from its First Settlement to 1831. By Samuel Deane. *Boston: James Loring.* 1831. 8vo, 2 l., pp. 406, (2). BA., C. 19061

DEANE. Sermon at Scituate, Mass. May 26, 1817, before the Scituate Auxiliary Society for the Suppression of Intemperance. ... *Boston.* 1817. 8vo, pp. 15. M., W. 19062

One of the rarest town histories. A large portion of the edition was destroyed by fire at the time of publication. *See* "Christian Examiner," XII. 163, and "Am. M Rev.," I. 72. Also: The Populous Village: a Poem, recited before the Philermenian Society of Providence, Sept., 1826. ... *Providence: Miller & Grattan.* 1826. 8vo, pp. 18.

DEANE (Silas). An Address to the Free and Independent Citizens of the United States of North-America. *Hartford: Printed by Hudson & Goodwin.* MDCCLXXXIV. Sm. 8vo, pp. 30.

Charges of fraud and peculation in the management of the public moneys, and of engaging himself in the interest of the enemies of his country, etc., led to this publication.

DEANE. An Address to the United States of North America. To which is added, A Letter to the Hon. Robert Morris, Esq. with Notes and Observations. By Silas Deane, Esq. Late one of the Commissioners Plenipotentiary from the United States, to the Court of Versailles. *London: J. Debrett.* 1784. 8vo, 2 l., pp. 95. BA., P. + *London Printed. New-London: Re-printed and sold By T. Green.* 1784. 8vo, pp. 54. M. 19064

DEANE. Papers in Relation to the Case of Silas Deane. Now first Published from the Original Manuscripts. [Edited by Edward D. Ingraham.] *Philadelphia: printed for the Seventy-Six Society.* 1855. 8vo, 2 l., pp. 17–201, 3, (1). BA., C. 19065

DEANE. Paris Papers; or Mr. Silas Deane's late intercepted Letters, to His Brothers, and other intimate Friends, in America. To which are annexed for Comparison, the Congressional Declaration of Independency in July 1776, and that now inculating [*sic*] among the revolted Provinces, with the never-to-be-forgotten Orders of the Rebel General in August 1776, for preventing a Pacification. *New-York: James Rivington.* [1782.] Sm. 8vo, pp. xii, 141, xxxii, 24 [36]. BA. 19066

See Lee (Arthur).

DEANE. An Echo from the Temple of Wisdom; or an Answer to an Address to Silas Deane, Esq. *Philadelphia.* 1779.

DEANE (W. R.) A Biographical Sketch of Elkanah Watson, Founder of Agricultural Societies in America, and the Projector of Canal Communication in New York State. With a Brief Genealogy of the Watson Family early settled in Plymouth Colony. By Wm. R. Deane ... . *Albany: J. Munsell.* 1864. 8vo, pp. 16. 19068

DEANE. Brief Memoirs of John and Walter Deane, Two of the First Settlers of Taunton, Mass., and of the Early Generations of their Descendants. ... with Incidental Notices of other Deans in England and America. By William Reed Deane. assisted by others. *Boston: Printed by Coolidge & Wiley.* 1849, 8vo, pp. 16. B. 19069

DEANE. A Genealogical Memoir of the Leonard Family; containing a Full Account of the First Three Generations of the Family of James Leonard, who was an Early Settler of

Taunton, Ms.; with Incidental Notices of Later Descendants. ... By Wm. R. Deane ... . *Boston: S. G. Drake.* 1851. 8vo. Portrait of Perez Fobes. 19070

DEARBORN (Henry). An Account of the Battle of Bunker Hill. Written for the Portfolio, at the request of the Editor. By H. Dearborn, Maj.-Gen. U. S. A. Illustrated by a Map, drawn by Henry de Berniere, 10th Royal British Infantry, and corrected by Gen. Dearborn. *Philadelphia.* 1818. 8vo, pp. 16. Map. B., C. 19071

See Putnam (D.) for a reply.

DEARBORN. Sketch of the Life of Major Gen. Henry Dearborn, From 1775, to 1812. *Printed at the Office of the Yankee, Boston.* [18—.] 8vo, pp. 24. H. 19072

DEARBORN (Henry Alexander Scammell). An Address Delivered on the VIII of October MDCCCXXX, the Second Centennial Anniversary of the Settlement of Roxbury. By H. A. S. Dearborn. ... *Roxbury: Charles P. Emmons.* MDCCCXXX. 8vo, pp. 40. BA. 19073

DEARBORN. Defence of Gen. Henry Dearborn, against the Attack of Gen. William Hull. By H. A. S. Dearborn. *Boston: printed by Edgar W. Davis.* 1824. 8vo, pp. 28. H.

DEARBORN. Enquiry into the Conduct of Gen. Putnam in relation to the Battle of Bunker Hill, and Remarks on S. Swett's Sketch of that Battle. *Boston.* 1819. 8vo. B. 19075

DEARBORN. Letters on the Internal Improvements and Commerce of the West. By H. A. S. Dearborn. *Boston.* 1839. 8vo, pp. 120. B., S. 19076

DEARBORN. Sketch of the Life of the Apostle Eliot, prefatory to a Subscription for erecting a Monument to his Memory. By H. A. S. Dearborn. *Roxbury: Norfolk Co. Journal Press.* 1850. 8vo, pp. 32. Plate. 19077

Also: Address before the Berkshire Agricultural Society, at Pittsfield, October 8, 1840 ... *Pittsfield.* 1840. — An Address delivered before the Massachusetts Horticultural Society, on the Celebration of their First Anniversary, September 19, 1829. ... *Boston.* 1829. 8vo. + Second Edition. *Boston.* 1833. 8vo. — Address delivered before the Massachusetts Society for promoting Agriculture, Oct. 14, 1835. *Boston.* 1835. 8vo, pp. 27. — An Oration delivered at Salem on the Fourth of July, 1806, ... *Salem.* 1806. pp. 14. — An Oration ... at Boston, on the Fourth Day of July, 1811, before the ... Bunker-Hill Association. *Boston: Munroe & French.* [1811.] 8vo, pp. 15. BA., M. — Speech ... on the Tariff Bill ... House of Representatives, Jan. 14, 1833. [1833.] Broadside. H. Allibone quotes, "Biography of Commodore Bainbridge," and "Life of his Father," which I have not seen.

Dearborn (N.) Boston Notions; being an Authentic and Concise Account of "that Village" from 1630 to 1847. By Nathaniel Dearborn ... . *Boston: Nathaniel Dearborn*. 1848. 18mo, pp. xx, 7–426, List of [30] Engravings, 1 l. BA., C.

Dearborn. Concise History of, and Guide through Mount Auburn ... . *Boston: Nathaniel Dearborn*. 1843. 18mo, pp. 74, (1). Map. H. + Guide through Mount Auburn ... . By Nathaniel Dearborn ... . *Boston*. 1847. 12mo, pp. 12. H. + Dearborn's Guide Through Mount Auburn ... . Fourth Edition, with Fifty-Four Engravings of the Monuments. *Boston*. 1850. + 1851. 12mo, pp. 44. M. + With Eighty Engravings ... of Monuments ... *Boston*. 1852. 8vo, pp. 48. H. + 1854. 12mo, pp. 53. H. + With Seventy-Six Engravings ... and a Plan of the Cemetery. *Boston*. 1856. 18mo, pp. 53. + Eleventh Edition. *Boston: Nathaniel S. Dearborn*. 1857. 18mo, Title, pp. 55. Map. BA. 19079

Dearborn. A New and Complete Map of the City of Boston. By Nathaniel Dearborn. *Boston*. 1839. 19080

Dearborn. Reminiscences of Boston, and Guide through the City and Environs. *Boston: Nathaniel Dearborn*. [1851.] 18mo, pp. 180. BA. 19081

Dearborn (W.) Portland and Lake Champlain Rail Road. By W. Dearborn. 19082

Dearborn (W. L.) Description of a Railroad Route from St. Louis to San Francisco, in Letters to P. P. F. Degrand, from W. L. Dearborn, Civil Engineer, 1849. With Map and Profile. *Boston*. 1850. 8vo, pp. 16. H., S. 19083

[Deas (Anne Izard).] *See* Izard (R.)

Deaubonneau (*Citoyen*). Un mot sur les Colonies Françaises, et particulièrement sur Saint Domingue par le Citoyen Deaubonneau. *Paris*. 1800. 8vo, pp. 44. 19084

De B***. *See* Brosses (C. De), Vol. II., No. 8588.

De Backer. *See* Backer, Vol I., No. 2619.

Debar (J. H. Diss). Memorial on the Necessity of inviting Foreign Emigration to West Virginia. February, 1864. [*Wheeling*. 1864?] 8vo, pp. 8. H. 19085

Also: Office of the Commissioner of Immigration for West Virginia, St. Clara Colony, Doddridge Co., W. V., Oct. 1st, 1865. [Letter to] ... A. J. Boreman, Governor of West Virginia ... . [Signed J. H. Diss Debar, Commissioner of Immigration. n. p. 1865.] 8vo, pp. 4. H.

Debarquement de la Flotte Française à St. Domingue; faisant suite aux revolutions de cette île. Revolte des negres, etc.: avec un Precis Historique de l'erection de cette île en royaume d'Haiti. *Paris: Tiger*. 1820. 18mo, 2 sheets. 19086

Debate at the Lane Seminary, Cincinnati. Speech of James A. Thorne, of Kentucky, delivered at the Annual Meeting of the American Anti-Slavery Society, May 6, 1834. Letter of the Rev. Dr. Samuel H. Cox, against the American Colonization Society. *Boston: Garrison and Knapp*. 1834. 8vo, pp. 16.

Debate in the House of Commons, on the Abolition of the Slave Trade, 2nd April, 1792. *London*. [n. d.] 8vo, pp. 178.

Debate in the House of Commons, on the Measures of Government, for the Amelioration of the Condition of the Slaves. *London*. 1824. 8vo, pp. 71. 19089

Debate in the Massachusetts Senate, on the Bill to Incorporate the Boston and Halifax Telegraphic Cable Co. March 24 and 26, 1859. Phonographic Report by J. M. W. Yerrinton. *Boston: Henry W. Dutton & Son, Printers*. 1859. pp. 48. H.

The Debate in the House of Lords, 7th March, 1826, on Slavery in the West Indies. *London*. 1826. 8vo, pp. 54.

Debate in the House of Representatives of the United States, on the Seminole War, in January and February, 1819. *Washington*. 1819. 12mo, pp. 591. C., M. 19092

Debate in the Senate on the Protection of Property in the District of Columbia. From Houston's Senate Debates. Thursday, April 20, 1848. [*Washington*. 1848.] 8vo, pp. 16. H.

The Debate on a Motion for the Abolition of the Slave-Trade; in the House of Commons. ... April 18 and 19, 1791. Reported in Detail. *London: W. Woodfall*. 1791. 8vo, pp. 123. B., C., W. 19094

See "M. Rev.," VI. 226.

Debate on a Motion for the Abolition of the Slave-Trade, in the House of Commons, on Monday the Second of April 1792, Reported in Detail. *London: W. Woodfall*. MDCCXCII. 8vo, pp. 178. 19095

Debate on the Resolution providing for the Publication of the

Debates of Congress; in the Senate of the United States, February 24, 1869. *Washington*. 1869. 8vo, pp. 16. H. 19096

Debate on the Resolutions Providing for the Publication of the Debates of Congress; in the Senate and House of Representatives, February and March, 1869. *Washington*. 1869. 8vo, pp. 24. H. 19097

The Debates and Proceedings in the Congress. *See* Congress, Vol. IV., No. 15519.

The Debates at Large between the House of Lords and House of Commons, at the Conference relating to the Word Abdicate, and the Vacancy of the Throne, by the flight of James II. *London*. 1695. 16mo. M. 19098

The revolution of New York, in which James Leisler was unjustly executed, arose from the flight of James II.

Debates in both Houses of Parliament, on the Seventeenth and Twenty-first of February, 1783, on the Articles of Peace. *London*. 1783. 8vo. 19099

Debates in the British House of Commons, May 13, 1789, on the Petitions for the Abolition of the Slave Trade. *Philadelphia*. 1789. 8vo. P. 19100

Debates in the Congress of the United States, on the Bill for Repealing the Law "for the more Convenient Organization of the Courts of the United States;" during the First Session of the Seventh Congress, and a List of the Yeas and Nays on that Interesting Subject. *Albany: printed by Whiting, Leavenworth and Whiting*. 1802. 8vo, pp. 796. 19101

Debates de la Camara de Senadores de Buenos Aires sobre el proyecto que autoriza al Gobernador de la Provincia a convocar e instalar el Congreso nacional. Edicion oficial. *Buenos Aires*. 1862. 4to, pp. 192. 19102

Debates in Council, on the Banks of the Ottawa River, November, 1791. *Philadelphia*. 1792. 8vo. P. 19103

Debates in the Conventions of the various States and of the United States. *See* "United States," and the names of the several States holding such conventions.

Debates in the House of Representatives, of the United States, during the First Session of the Fourth Congress. Part I.

Upon the Constitutional Powers of the House, with respect to Treaties. ‖ Part II. Upon the Subject of the British Treaty. *Philadelphia: printed for Benj. Franklin Bache*. 1796. 2 pts., 8vo, pp. 386; 362. C. + The Second Edition. *Philadelphia: Wm. Duane*. 1808. 8vo. 19104

Debates in the Senate of the United States, on the Judiciary, during the First Session of the Seventh Congress; also the several Motions, Resolutions and Votes taken on that Momentous Subject, and a complete List of the Yeas and Nays as entered on the Journals. *Philadelphia: E. Bronson*. 1802. 8vo, pp. 324. C. 19105

Debates of the House of Commons, 1774. *See* Cavendish, Vol. III., 11601.

Débats entre les accusateurs et les accusés dans l'affaire des colonies ... . *Paris: Imprimerie nationale. An* III [179–]. 9 vols., 8vo, Title, 369; 354; 383; 390; 355; 391; 406; 354; 111 [misprint for 208]. H. 19106

[De Beck (William L.)] Murder will out. The first step in Crime leads to the Gallows. The Horrors of the Queen City. By an Old Citizen. *Cincinnati*. 1867. 8vo, pp. 128.

Reproduced with a long title as

De Beck. The Horrors of the Queen City; being an account of the two Soldiers who were executed at old Fort Washington ... . By Colonel William L. De Beck. *Cincinnati*. 1867. 8vo. 19108

De Bellgraves (H.) The True and Affecting History of Henrietta De Bellgraves, a Woman born only for Calamities; ... giving an Account of her Shipwreck, ... her Rescue by a party of Indians ... . Written by herself, and Addressed to her Daughter Zoa. *New York*. 1828. 12mo, pp. 40. 19109

De Boileau (L.) Recollections of Labrador Life. By Lambert De Boileau. *London: Saunders and Otley*. 1861. Post 8vo, pp. 251. 19110

De Bonelli (L. H.) Travels in Bolivia and Across the Pampas. By L. H. De Bonelli. *London: Hurst and Blackett*. 1854. 2 vols., post 8vo. 19111

Debouchel (V.) Histoire de la Louisiane depuis la première découverte jusqu'en 1840. *Nouvelle-Orléans*. 1841. 12mo, pp. 197. 19112

De Boucherville (C. B.) Programme d'étude pour la formation d'une Banque Agricole Nationale pour le Bas Canada. *St. Hyacinthe*. 1862. pp. 23. 19113

De Boucherville. The system of Credit Foncier, annexed to the Report of the Special Committee appointed by the Legislative Assembly to enquire into the expediency of Establishing it in Lower Canada. [In French and English.] *Quebec*. 1863. 8vo, pp. 177. (Sess. Paper.) 19114

De Bow (James Dunworthy Brownson). Cotton Commerce, and the Southern States, embracing a Series of Papers condensed from the earlier volumes of De Bow's Reviews upon the Cultivation, Commerce, and Manufacture of Cotton. *New Orleans*. 1856. 8vo. 19115

De Bow. Commercial Review of the South and West. ... J. D. B. De Bow, Editor ... . *New-Orleans*. 1846. 8vo. Continued. 19116

The title was changed to "De Bow's Review, of the Southern and Western States. Devoted to Commerce ... &c. ... Edited by J. D. B. De Bow. ... Vol. IX. — New Series, Vol. I. *New-Orleans*. 1850." 8vo; the numbers for March and April, 1862, were published at New Orleans; July and August, 1864, at Columbia, S. C., and the title was then changed to "De Bow's Monthly Review. Agricultural, Commercial Industrial Progress & Resources. New Series. Vol. I. No. I. January, 1866. *New York: J. D. B. De Bow*. 1866," and afterwards to "De Bow's Review, devoted to the Restoration of the Southern States and the Development of the Wealth and Resources of the Country. ... Vol. II. *Nashville* 1866," published at New Orleans since 1867. R. G. Barnwell and E. Q. Bell appear as editors in 1867, after De Bow's death.

De Bow. Encyclopædia of the Trade and Commerce of the United States, more particularly of the Southern and Western States; giving a View of the Commerce, Agriculture, Manufactures, Internal Improvements, Slave and Free Labour, Slavery Institutions, Products, &c. of the South. By J. D. B. De Bow. Second Edition. *New York*. 1854. 2 vols., 8vo. 19117

Another name for the "Industrial Resources," etc., described below:

De Bow. The Industrial Resources, etc., of the Southern and Western States: embracing a View of their Commerce, Agriculture, Manufactures, Internal Improvements; Slave and Free Labor, Slavery Institutions, Products, &c., of the South; Together with Historical and Statistical Sketches of the different States and Cities of the Union ... . By J. D. B. De Bow ... . *New Orleans*. 1852–53. 3 vols., 8vo, pp. vii, 464; iv, 560; iv, 584, x. BA., H. + Third Edition. *New York*. 1854. 1 vol., 8vo. 19118

De Bow. Mortality Statistics of the Seventh Census of the United States, 1850 ... . By J. D. B. De Bow, Superintendent United States Census. *Washington: A. O. P. Nicholson, Printer*. 1855. 8vo, pp. 303, (1). 19119

See also "Census," Vol. III., No. 11669.

[De Bow.] The Political Annals of South Carolina. By a Citizen. ... *Charleston: Burges & James*. 1845. 8vo, pp. 50.

De Bow. Statistical View of the United States, embracing its Territory, Population — White, Free Colored, and Slave — Moral and Social Condition, Industry, Property, and Revenue; the detailed Statistics of Cities, Towns, and Counties; being a Compendium of the Seventh Census; to which are added the Results of every previous Census, beginning with 1790, in Comparative Tables. ... By J. D. B. De Bow. *Washington*. 1854. 8vo, pp. 400. 19121

De Brahm. *See* Vol., I., No. 1147, and Vol. II., Nos 7324–26.

Debret (J. B.) Voyage pittoresque et historique au Brésil depuis 1816 jusqu'en 1831, ou Séjour d'un artiste français au Brésil pendant les quinze premières années de la régénération politique de ce territoire, époque de l'avenement de l'abdication de S M. D. Pedro, premier fondateur de l'empire bresilien. [Prospectus.] *Paris: F. Didot*. 1833. 4to. + *Paris*. 1834–39. 2 vols., folio. 144 Plates, a Portrait, and a Facsimile. 19122

A fine work. There are copies with colored plates.

Debrett (J.) A Collection of Scarce and Interesting Tracts; written by persons of Eminence, upon Political and Commercial Subjects, from 1763 to 1770. *London: J. Debrett*. 1788. 4 vols., 8vo. C. 19123

This is the general title to a series of tracts published by Debrett, all of which are described in this Dictionary in their proper place

Debrett. Collection of all the Treaties of Peace, Alliance, and Commerce, between Great Britain and other Powers, from 1648 to 1784. To which is prefixed, a Discourse on the Conduct of Great Britain in respect to Neutral Nations, by Charles Jenkinson. *London: J. Debrett*. 1785. 3 vols., 8vo. 19124

De Brun (*M.*) Recueil du discours| fait par| Monsieur de Brun| Ambassadeur d'Espagne à Mes-| sieurs les Estats-Generaux, en la| grand assemblée de 28 Mars| 1651. | *Imprimée à*

Anvers chez Jean Hu-| sens, demeurant au Marche, 1651.| 4to, pp. 12. 19125

De Bry (Theodore). *See* Bry (T. de), Vol. III.

The Debtor & Creditor's Vade Mecum. A Commentary on the Insolvent Laws of New-York, with a Digest thereof. To which is prefixed an Address to the Legislature. *New-York: D. Longworth*. 1810. 24mo, pp. xi, 72. H. 19126

The Debtor's Prison. A Tale of a Revolutionary Soldier. *New York*. 1834. 18mo. S. 19127

Deby (P. N. H.) De l'Agriculture en Europe et Amérique, considérée et comparée dans les intérêts de la France et de la Monarchie. ... *Paris: Mme. Huzard*. 1825. 2 vols., 8vo. 3 Plates. S. 19128

Decaisne (J.) *See* Du Petit Thouars.

Decalves (A.), *pseudonym*. New Travels to the West Ward, or unknown parts of America, Being a Tour of almost Fourteen Months: Containing An Account of the Country upwards of Two Thousand Miles West of the Christian parts of North America; with an Account of white Indians, their Manners, Habits, and many other Particulars. By Don Alonso Decalves. Confirmed by three other Persons. *Boston: John W. Folsom*. [n. d.] 16mo, pp. 45. C. 19129

Decalves. Eine ganz neue und sehr merkwürdige Reisebeschreibung, oder, zuverlässige ... Nachrichten von den Westlichen bisjetzt noch unbekannten Theilen von America. ... Von Don Alonso Decalves. *Philadelphia*. 1796. 12mo, pp. 82. H.

De Camp (J.) Reply of Com. John De Camp, to Aspersions upon his Character Contained in an Article Published in the Charleston Mercury, of November 6, 1855, Entitled "Commander Thomas Petigru and the Naval Board." [n. p.] 1856. 8vo, pp. 12. H. 19131

Decanver (H. C.), *anagram*. *See* Cavender (C. H.), Vol. III., No. 11599.

Decatur (S.) Correspondence between the late Commodore Stephen Decatur and Commodore James Barron, which led to the unfortunate meeting of the twenty-second of March. *Boston: printed for Private Distribution*. 1820. 8vo, pp. 22. +

Washington: Gales & Seaton. 1820. 8vo, pp. 26. + *Richmond*. [n. d.] 8vo. + *Charleston*. 1820. 8vo. 19132

Relates to the affair of the "Chesapeake." *See* Niles' "Register," XVIII. 98, and "National Portrait Gallery," III. 6.

Decatur. Proceedings of a Court of Inquiry, Held on the U. S. Frigate Constitution at N. Y., in April 1815, To investigate the Causes of the Loss of the Frigate President, while under the Command of Commodore S. Decatur. *New York*. 1815. 8vo. 19133

Decatur. Sketch of the Naval Exploits of the Late Commodore Decatur. [From the Analectic Magazine, Vol. I., for 1813.] [n. p. 1813.] 8vo, pp. 8. H. 19134

Decatur (*Mrs.* S. W.) Documents relative to the Claims of Mrs. Decatur, with her Earnest Request that the Gentlemen of Congress will take the Trouble to read them. *Georgetown, D. C.: James C. Dunn, Printer*. 1826. 8vo, pp. 62. H.

Decatur. Documents relative to the Claim of Mrs. Decatur against the Government of the United States. *Georgetown*. 1827. 8vo. C. 19136

Decatur. Documents relative to the Claim of Mrs. Decatur, with her earnest request that Congress will do her the favor to read them. *Washington*. 1834. 8vo, pp. 52. 19137

Decatur Bank, *Ala.* Preamble and Resolutions of the Decatur Bank. [*Tuscaloosa?* 1839.] 8vo. BM. 19138

Decaze. Compagnie de colonisation générale à la Guyane française, proposée à l'industrie nationale. *Paris*. 1826. 8vo.

December 30, 1777. All Gentlemen Volunteers, ... 4to, broadside. 19140

Advertisements for recruits to the armed brig "Stanley," belonging to H. B. M. ship "Roebuck." Fifty copies printed, at Philadelphia, by J. Humphreys.

De Charms (R.) De Charms's Tracts for the Times. No. V. An Opinion on the Nature of our National Union, and the Right Way to restore it. No. VII. The War Spirit of the Present Day is Antichrist. *Philadelphia: Printed and Published by the Author*. 1861. 16mo, pp. 26, 12. H. 19141

De Charms. A Discourse on the True Nature of Freedom and Slavery, delivered before the Washington Society of the

New Jerusalem, in view of the One Hundredth and Eighteenth Anniversary of Washington's Birth. By Richard De Charms. *Philadelphia: J. H. Jones.* 1850. 8vo, pp. 63. 19142

De Charms. Some Views of Freedom and Slavery in the Light of the New Jerusalem. By Richard De Charms. *Philadelphia.* 1851. 12mo, pp. 108. 19143

Decision of the King of the Netherlands considered in reference to the United States and the State of Maine. *Portland.* 1831. 8vo. c. 19144

Decision of the Supreme Court of the State of New York, sustaining the Constitutionality of Legal Tender Notes. Delivered at Rochester, April 4, 1863. *Rochester.* 1863. 8vo, pp. 42. 19145

Decisiones de la Real Audencia, y Chancilleria des Domingo Isla vvlgo Española, del Nuevo Orbe Primada, en Defensa de la Jurisdicion y Auctoridad Real, por el Doctor Don Geronymo Chacon Abarca, y Tiedra, etc. *Salamanca.* 1676. Folio.

Decisions de la Audiencia de la Isla Española con una defensa de la jurisdiction real. 1674. 4to. 19147

Title from Ternaux, No. 910.

Decius, *pseudon.* Letters of Decius. *Louisville.* 1805. 8vo.

Decius, *pseudon.* Letters of Decius, in Answer to the Criticism upon the Political Account of Trinidad, and upon the Defence of the Crimes of Governor Picton. *London.* 1808. 8vo.

Decius, *pseudon.* Letters of Decius; or, a few Observations on the Politics of the Present Time. 1790. 8vo, pp. over 121.

Decius, *pseudonym.* *See* [Courtenay (Thomas P.)], Vol. v., No. 17183.

Deck (I.) Report on certain Mineral Lands Visited and Explored by Isaiah Deck, in the Island of Jamaica, May 20, 1854. 8vo. 19151

Decker (A.) Diurnal vnd Historische | Beschreybung der Nassawischen | Flotten So vnder dem Admiral | Jacob l' Heremite umb die | gantze welt gefahren ist, | Im 1623. 1624. 1625. vnd | 1626. Jahr. | Ordentlich in hochteutsch beschrieben | was sich in dieser raiss von tag zu | tag zugetragen vnd merckwürdiges | vorgangen, vnd mit vnderschielichen, | Küpferstücken gezieret | Durch | Adolf Decker von Strasbürg. | *Gedruckt zu Strasburg in verlegung | Eberhard Zelzners* | MDCXXIX. | 4to, 6 l, pp. 68. Maps and Plates. 19152

This is the engraved title, followed by another printed title. Reprinted in the collections of Hulsius and De Bry. Priced at Puttick's, No. 313, £2 11s.; Nyhoff, 30 florins; Stevens, No. 860, £6 6s.

Declaratie door de Gemagtigden der Vereënigde Coloniën van Noord-America, thans in eene algemeene By-eenkomst te Philadelphia vergadert, de Oorzaakén, en de Noodwendigheid van het opvatten der Wapenen, betoogende. [*Paramaribo.* 1775.] 4to, pp. 7. 19153

Declaratie, ofte precijse Verklaringe van de Plenipotentiarisen ende Ambassadeurs van s. Maj. den Cathol. Con. van Spangien, nopens de versochte Treves voor Portugael, ende den Hertogh van Bregance tegenw. Coningh. *Munster.* 1647. **Declaration des Ambass. d'Espaigne. Touchant une Trefve pour Portugal.** *Munster.* 1647. 4to, pp. 8. 19154

Relates to Brazilian affairs.

Declaratie | Van Sijn Koninghlijcke Majesteyt | Van | Portugael | Don Ioan : | Om over al in sijn Rijck gepubliceert te wer- | den besloten tot Lisbona den 7 Februa- | rius Anno 1649. | *Gedruckt na de Copye tot Lissebon,* 1649. | 4to, pp. 8. 19155

Relates to Brazil.

Declaration and Address of the M. Loyal Associated Refugees assembled at Newport, R. I. *New York.* 1779. 8vo.

A Declaration, Against Prophaneness & Immoralities. [Given at Boston the Twenty-fourth Day of March, 1703.] 8vo, pp. 6.

Printed as part of John Danforth's "Vile Prophanations."

The Declaration by the Representatives of the United Colonies in North America, now met in General Congress at Philadelphia, seting forth the Causes and Necessity of their taking up Arms, &c. *Philadelphia: Printed by William and Thomas Bradford.* 1775. 8vo, pp. 13. P. + [*Ibid.*] MDCCLXXV. 8vo, pp. 13. + *Newport, Southwick.* 1775. 8vo, pp. 11. + *Watertown, Mass.* 1775. 8vo, pp. 15. W. 19159

Of the Philadelphia edition, fifty copies in 8vo, and twenty-five in 4to, were privately reprinted in facsimile, by Joel Munsell, for R. W. Roche.

A Declaration by the Representatives of the United Colonies of North-America, now met in General Congress at Philadelphia, seting forth the Causes and Necessity of their taking up Arms. Also an Address from the Twelve United Colonies to the Inhabitants of Great Britain. *Bristol: W. Pine.* 1775. 12mo, pp. 16. J.C.B. 19159*a*

The | Declaration | by the | Representatives | of the | United Colonies of North America, | now met in | General Congress at Philadelphia, | Setting forth the | Causes and Necessity of taking up Arms. | The | Letter of the Twelve United Colonies | by their Delegates in Congress to the Inhabi- | tants of Great Britain, | Their Humble Petition to his Majesty, | and | Their Address to the People of Ireland. | Collected together for the Use of Serious Thinking Men. | By Lovers of Peace. | *London: Printed in the Year,* MDCCLXXV. | 8vo, pp. vi, 3–32. 19160

Similar to the foregoing, but with some additions.

Declaration and Constitution of the American Society of United Irishmen. *Philadelphia: Printed for the Society, August* 8, 1797. 19161

Reprinted in the appendix to [Carpenter's] "Memoirs of Hon. Thos. Jefferson," 1809.

The Declaration. *See* [Colman (B.)], Vol. iv., No. 14524.

A Declaration of the Inhabitants of Barbados, respecting the demolition of the Methodist Chapel. With an Appendix. *Barbados: Printed at the Barbadian Office.* 1826. 8vo. 19162

A Declaration and Remonstrance Of the distressed and bleeding Frontier Inhabitants Of the Province of Pennsylvania, presented by them to the Honourable the Governor and Assembly of the Province, Shewing the Causes of their late Discontent and Uneasiness and the Grievances Under which they have laboured, and which they humbly pray to have redres'd. *Philadelphia: Printed in the Year* M,DCC,LXIV. 8vo, pp. 18. 19163

Signed M. Smith, and J. Gibson *See* "Col Records," ix. 138, and "Penn. Archives," iv.

Declaration and Testimony for the Doctrine and Order of the Church of Christ, and against the Errors of the Present Times. To which is prefixed, a Narrative, concerning the Maintenance of the Reformation-Testimony. By the Associate Presbytery of Pennsylvania. The Second Edition. Printed at Philadelphia in the year 1784. *Edinburgh: Reprinted for A. Brown.* 1786. 12mo, pp. 135. 19164

Declaration Adressée. *See* [d'Estaing].

Declaration du Roy, Concernant les Marchandises des Colonies Françoises. Donnée à Paris le 14. Mars 1722. ... *A Paris: Chez Louis Denis Delatour & Pierre Simon, Imprimeurs.* 1722. 4to, pp. 4. 19165

Declaration du Roy, Concernant les dettes de cargaison des navires des Ports du Royaume aux Colonies françoises de l'Amérique. Donnée au Camp sous Tournay, le 12 Juin, 1745. ... *A Paris: de l'Imprimerie Royale.* 1745. 4to, pp. 4. 19166

Declaration du Roy, Concernant la Regie & perception du Droit de Capitation aux Isles & Terre ferme du Nord de l'Amerique. Donnée à Versailles le 3. Octobre 1730. Avec Une Instruction pour faciliter l'execution de ladite Declaration. Du 4. Octobre 1731. *A Paris: de l'Imprimerie Royale.* M. DCC-XXXI. 4to, pp. 8. 19167

Declaration du Roy, Concernant les Cafez provenant des plantations & Culture de la Martinique & autres Isles Françoises de l'Amerique, y dénommées. Donnée à Fontainebleau le 27. Septembre 1732. ... *A Paris: de l'Imprimerie Royale.* M.DCC-XXXII. 4to, pp. 8. 19168

A Declaration of His Highness. *See* [Milton (John)].

The Declaration of Independence, etc., 1793. *See* [Richards (George)].

Declaration of Independence and Constitution of the United States of America. *New York.* 1804 or 1864. 8vo, pp. 85.

Declaration of Independence and Constitution of the United States. *New York.* 1857. 8vo. 19170

Declaration of Independence, and Constitution of the United States of America, with its Amendments. Census of 1850. *Boston: John P. Jewett & Company.* 1856. pp. 32, (4).

Declaration of Independence. Imp. 8vo, pp. 83. 19172

Printed with red and blue ink.

The Declaration of Independence. Fac-simile of the Original Document, in the Handwriting of Thomas Jefferson. *New York: Trent, Filmer & Co.* 1865. 4to, pp. 7. 19173

The Declaration of Independence, and Constitution of the United States of America, with the Amendments; together with the Constitution of the State of New-York. *New York.* 1812. 8vo, pp. 58. 19174

The Declaration of Independence of the United States of America, 1776, and Washington's Farewell Address to the People of the United States, 1776. *Boston: Published by A. Williams & Co., under the Direction of the City Authorities.* 1862. 4to. 19175

The Declaration of Independence by Congress in 1776, with the Counter Declaration published at New York, 1781. 12mo.

Declaration of Independence and Constitution of the United States of America. *New York: R. Spalding.* 1865. 8vo, pp. 85. 19177

Declaration of Independence, by Citizens of Mecklenburg County, (N. C.), May 20, 1775. *Raleigh, (N. C.)* 1831. 8vo.

Declaration of Principles comprised in the Address and Resolutions of the Native American Convention, held at Philadelphia, July 4, 1845, to the Citizens of the United States. *New York.* 1845. 8vo, pp. 14. 19179

The | Declaration | of the | Reasons and Motives | For the Present | Appearing in Arms | of | Their Majesties | Protestant Subjects | In the Province of | Maryland. | Licens'd, November 28th 1689. J. F. | [Colophon:] *Maryland, Printed by William Nuthead at the City of St. | Maries. | Re-printed in London, and Sold by Randal Tay- | lor, near Stationers Hall,* 1689. | Folio, pp. 8. 19180

The reader will notice that 1689 is *very* early for a Maryland imprint. We are unable to find any account of the Maryland printer.

A Declaration of the Sad Persecution of Quakers in New-England. *See* [Burrough (E.)], Vol. iii., No. 9455.

Declaration of the Society of People (commonly called Shakers) Shewing their Reasons for Refusing to Aid or Abet the Cause of War and Bloodshed. *Albany, N. Y.* 1815. 8vo, pp. 20.

A Declaration of the State, etc., 1620. *See* "Virginia."

Declaration of the True Causes of the Great Troubles presupposed to be Intended Against the Realme of England, wherein the Indifferent Reader shall manifestly Perceave by Whom and by what Means the Realme is brought into these Pretended Perils. [*Surreptitiously printed.* 1592.] 8vo. 19182

Very rare. Contains interesting notices of Sir Humphrey Gilbert, Drake, Cavendish, Hawkins, and other early navigators.

A Declaration of the Yearly Meeting of Friends, held in Philadelphia, respecting the Proceedings of those who have lately separated from the Society: and also, shewing the Contrast between their Doctrines and those held by Friends. *Philadelphia: Printed by Thomas Kite.* 1828 8vo, pp. 32. + [Reprinted.] *New York.* 1828. + 1831. 19183

Declaration of War [against Great Britain, 1812] with the Law concerning Letters of Marque, [etc. n. p. n. d.] 12mo, pp. 23. B. 19184

A Declaration of what God has done for our Souls. By some Baptist People, called Quakers, in New-London County, in Connecticut Colony. March 25, 1760. 12mo, pp. 4. P.

No title-page, but apparently printed in Philadelphia, by W. Bradford.

A Declaration or Manifest of the High and Mighty Lords the States General of the United Netherland Provinces Comprehending a true Relation of their sincere Intention and lawful Proceedings in the Treaty with the Extraordinary Embassadors and the Commissioners of the present Government of England, so as the same hath been held here in the Hague, as also at London. At Amsterdam. Translated out of the Original Copy. 1652. 4to. 19186

Declarations of the Yearly Meetings of Ohio, Indiana, and Baltimore, respecting a publication entitled "A Beacon to the Society of Friends," ... From "The Friend." *London: Edmund Fry and Son.* 1836 8vo, pp. 8 19187

Decoigne, *Illinois.* Articles of Association, and other Documents, relating to the Decoigne City and Canal Company. *Alton.* 1837. 8vo, pp. 11. 19188

De Coin (R. L.) History and Cultivation of Cotton and Tobacco. By Colonel Robert L. De Coin. *London: Chapman & Hall.* 1864. 12mo, pp. vi, 306. Map. BA., C. 19189

De Cordova (J.) Lecture on Texas delivered by Mr. J. De Cordova, ... Also, a paper read by him before the New York Geographical Society, April 15th, 1858. ... *Philadelphia: Printed by Ernest Crozet.* 1858. 12mo, pp. 32. H.

See Cordova (J. de), Vol. iv., No. 16775.

DeCosta (Benjamin Franklin.) The Eighteenth Massachusetts Regiment. A Discourse in Commemoration of Washington's Birthday, delivered in Falls Church, Fairfax Co., Va., ... February 23, 1862. By Rev. B. F. De Costa, ... *Charlestown, Mass.* 1862. 8vo, pp. 15. H. 19191

DeCosta. Footprints of Miles Standish. By the Rev. B. F. DeCosta. *Charlestown: Re-printed from the Church Monthly for Private Distribution.* 12mo, pp. 24. B., H. 19192

DeCosta. Lake George: Its Scenes and Characteristics, with Glimpses of the Olden Times. To which is added some Account of Ticonderoga, with a Description of the Route to the Schroon Lake and the Adirondacks. With an Appendix, containing Notes on Lake Champlain. By B. F. DeCosta. *New York: A. D. F. Randolph.* 1868. 16mo, pp. 181, xiv. Map and Woodcuts. + Third Edition. ... *New York: Anson D. F. Randolph & Company.* 1871. 16mo, pp. 186, xiv. Map and Woodcuts. BA. 19193

DeCosta. A Narrative of Events at Lake George, from the Early Colonial Times to the Close of the Revolution. *New York: The Author.* 1868. Imp. 8vo, pp. 75. 19194

Seventy-five copies printed.

DeCosta. The Northmen in Maine; a Critical Examination of the Views expressed in connection with the Subject, by Dr. J. H. Kohl, in Volume I of the New Series of the Maine Historical Society. To which are added Criticisms on other Portions of the Work, and a Chapter on the Discovery of Massachusetts Bay. By the Rev. B. F. DeCosta ... *Albany: Joel Munsell.* 1870. 8vo, pp. 146. BA. 19195

DeCosta. Notes on the History of Fort George during the Colonial and Revolutionary Periods, With Contemporaneous Documents and an Appendix. By B. F. DeCosta, ... *New York: J. Sabin & Sons.* 1871. 8vo, 2 l., pp. 72. 19196

DeCosta. The Pre-Columbian Discovery of America by the Northmen, illustrated by Translations from the Icelandic Sages, edited with Notes and a General Introduction, by B. F. DeCosta. With a Map of Cape Cod, as it appeared at the beginning of the Seventeenth Century. *Albany: Joel Munsell.* 1868. 8vo, pp. lx, (1), 11–118. Map. BA. 19197

Also: Notes on a Review of "the Pre-Columbian Discovery of America by the Northmen," in the North American Review for July. ... *Charlestown, Mass: Advertiser Press.* 1869. 16mo, pp. 14. H.

DeCosta. Sailing Directions of Henry Hudson, prepared for his use in 1608, from the Old Danish of Ivar Bardsen. With an Introduction and Notes, also a Dissertation on the Discovery of the Hudson River. By the Rev. B F. DeCosta ... *Albany: Joel Munsell.* 1869. 8vo, pp. 102. BA., S. 19198

DeCosta. Scenes in the Isle of Mount Desert. By Rev. B. F DeCosta. Illustrated. *New York: A. D. F. Randolph & Co.* 1869. Sm 4to, pp. 138. 19199

DeCosta. Sketches of the Coast of Maine and Isles of Shoals, with Historical Notes. By B. F. DeCosta. *New York.* 1869. 4to, pp. 231. Photographic Plate. 19200

Twenty four copies printed. Also. Antiquities. To the Editor of the Advertiser. *New York. Dec.* 1, 1869. 4to, slip H.

De Courcy (H.) The Catholic Church in the United States; Pages of its History. By Henry De Courcy . . Translated and Enlarged by John Gilmary Shea .. *New York.* 1856. 12mo, pp. 591. B. + Second Edition, revised. *New York: Edward Dunigan and Brother.* 1857. 12mo, pp. 591 C. 19201

[De Courcy.] Les Servantes de Dieu en Canada, Essaie sur l'historie des communautes religieuses de femmes de la Province. Edition revue, corrigée, augmentée et spécialement préparée pour le Canada. Par C de La Roche-Héron. *Montréal.* 1855. 8vo, pp. 158. 19202

Written for the "Ami de la Religion," and the "Univers."

Courcy (R.) Two Sermons Preached December 13. 1776, being the Fast Day on account of the Troubles in America, By the Rev Rd. de Courcy ... Shrewsbury. ... *London: J Robson* 1776 8vo. C. 10203

Condemns the Americans, but compassionates them as fellow-Christians. *See* "M. Rev." LVI 78

Decouvertes des François. *See* [Fleurieu (*Count* Claret de)].

Decouvertes des Scandinaves en Amérique du dixième au treizième siècle. Fragments de Sages Islandaises, traduits . . par Beauvois. *Paris.* 1859. 8vo 19204

Decow (S.), *and* Hendrickson (J.) A Full Report of the Case of Stacy Decow and Joseph Hendrickson *vs.* Thomas L. Shotwell. Decided at a Special Term of the New Jersey Court of Appeals, held at Trenton, in July and August, 1833: embracing the Decision of the Court of Chancery from which the appeal was made, the arguments of Counsel on each side, and the Final Decision of the Court of Appeals. ... *Philadelphia: P J. Gray.* 1834. 8vo, pp. 720. C. 19205

There is another edition, "With Argument of Samuel L. Southard. *Philadelphia.* 1834." 8vo, pp. 283. *See also* Shotwell (T L.)

De Courtenay (J. M.) The Culture of the Vine and Emigration. Second Edition. *Quebec.* 1853. 8vo, pp. 53.

De Courtenay. The Canadian Vine Grower. *Toronto.* 1866. 19207

Decreto de la Magestad del Rey Catholico Phelipe v. Sobre varias acusaciones dadas en su Real Consejo de Yndias con los Jesuitas del Paraguay. *Napoles.* 1744. 4to, pp. 55. J.C.B.

Decreto di sua Maesta il Re Catolico Filipo v. Sopra varie Accuse portate al Suo Real Consiglio delle Indie contro i Gesuiti del Paraguay. Con la Lettera dell' Illustrissmo D. Frà Guiseppe de Peralta dell' Ordine di S. Domenico Vescovo de Buenosayres. *Napoli: Coll' Aggiunta di due Lettere di Sua Maestà Cattolica al Provinciale delle Compagnia de Gesù nel Paraguay.* 1744. 4to, pp. 66. J.C.B. 19209

Decreto sobre uniformidad de las cuotas de Alcabala en todos los departamentos y reglas para su cobro, acordado en 11 de Julio del Corriente Año. *Mexico.* 1843. 8vo, pp. 24. 19210

Dedham (R. C.) Clergy Reserves Alienation. *London.* 1853. 8vo. 19211

Relates to Canadian land titles.

The Dedham Pulpit; or Sermons by the Pastors of the First Church in Dedham, in the 17th and 18th Centuries; with a Centennial Discourse by the Present Pastor, [Ebenezer Burgess, D.D.] *Boston.* 1840. 8vo, pp. 517. 19212

Comprises twenty-four accurate reprints of historical and other sermons, dating back to 1671.

Dedham, *Mass.* Annual Report of the School Committee for 1839–40. *Dedham.* 1840. 8vo, pp. 8. Continued.

Brief Summary of Christian Doctrine, and Form of Covenant, adopted in the First Church in Dedham. *Dedham.* 1822. 8vo.

Catalogue of the Norfolk Law Library. *Boston.* 1863. 8vo, pp. 44. 19215

The Confession of Faith, and the Covenant, of the South Church in Dedham ... . *Dedham.* 1827. 8vo, pp. 30. M.

With a list of church members from the foundation.

Dedham Pocket Almanac and New-England Calendar, for the Year ... 1812 ... . *Dedham.* [1811.] 12mo, pp. 60. H.

Dedication of the Memorial Hall, in Dedham, September 29, 1868. With an Appendix. *Dedham, Mass.: printed by John Cox, Jr.* 1869. 8vo, pp. 91, (1). H. 19218

A Report of the Selectmen of Dedham, of the Expenses of the Town, for the Year ending March 6, 1837. *Dedham: Printed by Herman Mann.* 1838. 8vo, pp. 16. H. 19219

Report of a Committee of Citizens of Dedham relative to the Advance of Fares upon the Boston and Providence Railroad. *Dedham.* 1856. S. 19220

Statement of the Proceedings in the First Church and Parish in Dedham, Settling a Minister. By a Member of the said Church and Parish. *Cambridge.* 1819. 8vo. W. 19221

Valuation and Tax on the Polls and Estates of the Inhabitants of the Town of Dedham. *Dedham.* 1844. 8vo, pp. 55. M.

Dedication of Antioch College, and Inaugural Address of its President, Hon. Horace Mann; with other Proceedings. Yellow Springs, O. *Sulphur Springs, O.: A. S. Dean.* 1854. 8vo.

The Dedication; or, An Essay on the True Modern Cæsar. By Cid Hamet Benengeli. *Baltimore: Sands & Nelson.* 1831. 8vo, pp. 76. 19224

Relates to Andrew Jackson.

Deduccas ou Manifesto dos factos Que na crise actual suscitao a plena observancia dos diretos Publicos da Nacao Portugueza, etc., 1826. 8vo. 19225

Relates to South America.

Deductie van den representant van syne doorlugtigste Hoogheid en bewindhebberen van de geoctroyeerde Westindische Compagnie ter Præsidiale kamer te Amsterdam, over de saake van Isequibo en Demarari, den 28 July 1767. Folio, pp. 93.

Dedvctie, | Waer by onpartijdelijck over-vvogen ende | bevvesen vvort, vvat het beste voor de | Compagnie van West-Indien zy: | Den Handel te sluyten, | of open te laten. | *In 's Graven-Hage,*

Gedruckt by Isaac Bvrchoorn, Boeck-Drucker op | de west-zijde van't Speuy, inde nieuwe Druckery, over de Bagijne-Straet. | [1638.] 4to, pp. 32. W. 19227

Relates to commerce with Brazil.

Deedes (H.) Sketches of the South and West; or, Ten Months Residence in the United States. By H. Deedes. *London.* 1869. 8vo, pp. vi, 170. 19228

De el Rio (A. M.) Exclamacion y declamacion funeral de el D. Juan J. de Veytia. *Mexico.* 1723. 4to, 58 l. 19229

Deems (C. F.) Annals of Southern Methodism for 1855. *Nashville, Tenn.:* [n. d.] 12mo, pp. 311. + For 1856. Edited by the Rev. Charles F. Deems, D.D. *New York.* 1856. 12mo, pp. 385. S. 19230

Deep River Mining and Transportation Company, N. C. Charter. *Albany.* 1851. 8vo. 19231

The Deeper Wrong: or, Incidents in the Life of a Slave Girl. Written by Herself. Edited by L. Maria Child. *London: W. Tweedie.* 1862. Post 8vo, pp. 306. 19232

See Brent (L.), Vol. II., No. 7722.

Deer Island and the City Institutions. [Reprinted] (From the Daily Evening Traveller). [*Boston.* 18—.] 8vo, pp. 8.

Deerfield, *Mass.* A Brief Sketch of the First Settlement of Deerfield, Mass.: Together with a few of the Events which took place there in Early Times. By one of the Descendants of the First Settlers of the Town. *Greenfield.* 1833. 18mo, pp. 48. Plate. G.B. 19234

Deering (N.) Carrabasset: a Tragedy, in Two Acts. *Portland.* 1830. 18mo, pp. 54. M. 19235

Deering (R.) Louisville, her Commercial, Manufacturing and Social Advantages. Including ... her History ... &c. ... . By Richard Deering. *Louisville, Ky.. Hanna & Co.* 1859. 8vo, pp. 99. Woodcuts. BA. 19236

La Déesse, an Elssler-atic Romance. By the Author of "Straws." *New-York: Carvill & Co.* 1841. 12mo, pp. 44.

Defence of a Book lately reprinted at Boston, 1724. *See* [Checkley (J.)] Vol. III., No. 12362.

Defence of Christian Revelation, as contained in West on the Resurrection, and Lyttleton on St. Paul. *Printed by Private Subscription in order to be dispersed in his Majesty's Colonies and Islands in America.* 1748. 8vo. 19238

The Defence of Injur'd Merit Unmasked; or, The Scurilous Piece of Philander dissected and exposed to Public View. By a Friend to Merit, wherever found. *Printed Anno* M.DCC.LXXI. 8vo, pp. 12. P. 19239

Relates to an election dispute in Accomac County, Virginia.

A Defence of New Jersey in relation to the Camden and Amboy Railroad and its Privileges. *Washington: Gideon & Pearson, Printers.* 1864. 8vo, pp. 13. H. 19240

The Defence of Richmond against the Federal Army, under Gen. McClellan. By a Prussian Officer in the Confederate Service. *New York: George F. Nesbitt & Co.* 1863. 8vo, pp. 16. 19241

A Defence of the American Congress. *See* "Congress," Vol. IV., No. 15523.

Defence of the Answer of the Synod at Boston in 1662. *See* Davenport (J.), Vol. V., No. 18704.

Defence of the Colonies, with remarks on the French district of St. Domingo, by Amicus Mundi. *London.* 1816. 8vo.

A Defence of the Conduct of Barbadoes. *See* Vol. I., No. 3264.

A Defence of the Constitution of England against the Libels that have been Lately Published on it; Particularly in Paine's Pamphlet on the Rights of Man. *London: Printed for R. Baldwin.* M DCC XCI. 8vo, pp. 67. 19243

Contains many references to America.

Defence of the Convention of the Protestant Episcopal Church in the State of Massachusetts, against certain Editorial Statements of the Paper, called "The Banner of the Church." *Boston.* 1832. 8vo. S. 19244

Defence of Country Banks; being a Reply to a Pamphlet entitled An Examination of the Banking System of Massachusetts, in reference to the Renewal of the Bank Charters. *Boston: Stimpson and Clapp.* 1831. 8vo, pp. 42. BA. 19245

A Defence of the Currency of Massachusetts. *See* [Congdon (J. B.)], Vol. IV., No. 15466.

A Defence of the Dutch, against the Imputations of Fraud, Cruelty, and Perfidiousness. ... To which is added, A Supplement relative to the Settlement of Nova Scotia. *London: Printed for R. Spavan in* 1749. 8vo, pp. 35. 19246

Defence of the Exposition of the Middling Interest. *See* [Sullivan (George)].

The Defense of the Great Lakes; its Necessity, and the quickest, cheapest, and best Way to accomplish it. *Ithaca, N. Y.: Andrus & Co.* [1863.] 8vo, pp. 16. 19247

A Defence of the Legislature of Massachusetts, or the Rights of Newengland vindicated. *Boston: Printed at the Repertory Office.* 1804. 8vo, pp. 28. H. + *Northampton.* 1804. 8vo, pp. 24. 19248

A Defence of the "Letter from a Gentleman at Halifax to his Friend in Rhode Island," with Appendix. *Newport.* 1765. 8vo, pp. 31. P. 19249

Defence of the Majority. *See* Lloyd (Charles).

Defence of the Minority. *See* [Townsend (Charles)].

Defence of the National Administration. *See* [Webster (Ezekiel)].

Defence of the New-Jersey Dissent; being a Brief Answer to a Pamphlet recently published by the Family of the late N. Webster. 8vo. S. 19250

A Defence of the Observations on the Assiento Trade, as it has been exercised by the South-Sea Company. I. In Relation to the Controversy. II. In Relation to the Queries published in the Craftsman, and other Aspersions on the Author of the "Observations," as well as on the Island of Jamaica. *London: H. Whitridge.* 1728. 8vo, pp. vi, 66. J.C.B. 19251

A Defence of the Remarks of the Plymouth Company, on the Plan and extracts of Deeds published by the Proprietors (as they term themselves) of the Township of Brunswick, being a reply to their answer to said remarks, lately published, according to their vote of March 28, 1753. *Boston, N. E.* 1753. 4to, pp. 50. J.C.B. 19252

A Defence of the Resolutions and Address of the American Congress, in reply to Taxation no Tyranny. By the Author of Regulus. To which are added, General Remarks on the Leading Principles of that Work, As Published in The London Evening Post of the 2d and 4th of May; and a Short chain of Deductions from one clear Position of Common Sense and Experience. *London: J. Williams.* [1775.] 8vo, pp. 96. BA., H.

"This pamphlet contains many very harsh, and some very just, strictures on the doctrines and tenets advanced by Dr. Johnson, whose pamphlet has been honored with unmerited notice."—*M. Rev.*, LII. 181.

Defence of the Rockingham Party in their late Coalition with ... Lord North. *London.* 1783. 8vo, pp. 53. 19254

A Defence of the Slave Trade, on the Grounds of Humanity, Policy, and Justice. *London: J. Highley.* 1807. 8vo. 19255

See "M. Rev.," LII. 226.

Defence of the Treaty. *See* [Hamilton (Alex.)]

Defence of the Whigs. By a Member of the Twenty-Seventh Congress. *New York: Harper & Brothers.* 1844. 12mo, pp. 152. C. 19256

A Defence of Truth and Character against Ecclesiastical Intolerance. Extracts of some Letters, occasioned by the Proceedings of the Hopkinton Association, and of the New Hampshire General Association. *Concord, N. H.* 1812. 8vo, pp. 24.

Defensa canonica y real por las Provincias de la Compañia de Jesus en la Nueva-España, y Philipinas, en los Autos con el Ven. Dean y Cabildo de la S. Iglesia Metropolitana de Mexico, sobre las censuras impuestas á los Jesuitas por los ecclesiasticos Hacedores de aquel Arzobispado. [*Mexico.*] 1736. Folio, 56 l.

Defensa Canonica y Real por las Provincias de los Jesuitas de la Nueva España y Filipinas sobre las Censuras impuestos por los Jueces di Dieznos de la Iglesia de Megico. *Madrid.* 1738. Folio. 19259

Defensa de los diez y seis cargos hechos por el Señor J. de Valdenebro, Corregidor de la Coruña sobre la causa que se formó por ultrajar, por acriminar bajo el asumido titulo de crimen de Estado à V. de Fronda, Consul General, que frié cerca de las Estados-Unidos de la America, &c. *Pamplona.* 1820. 16mo. 19260

Defensa de la jurisdiccion ordinaria de los Obispos para conocer de los negocios de los Regulares en grado de apelacion de sus Tribunales propios, ó sea respuesta al impreso que dió a luz el P. Provincial de San Diego sosteniendo la incompetencia del Tribunal eclesiastico ordinario para el conocimiento de tales asuntos. *Mexico.* 1841. 4to, 2 l., pp. 105. 19261

Defensa juridica del P. Felipe del Castillo, Procurador General de la provincia de la Compañia de Jesus de Lima. 1737. Folio. 19262

The Defensive League of Freedom [for the Protection of Fugitive Slaves. Circular, with the Constitution of the League. *Boston.* 185–.] 12mo, pp. 12. H. 19263

Defensor, *pseudonym.* The Enemies of the Constitution Discovered, or, An Inquiry into the Origin and Tendency of Popular Violence. Containing a Complete and Circumstantial Account of the Unlawful Proceedings at the City of Utica, October 21st, 1835; the Dispersion of the State Anti-Slavery Convention By the Agitators, the Destruction of a Democratic Press, and of the Causes which led thereto. Together with a Concise Treatise on the Practice of the Court of His Honor Judge Lynch. ... By Defensor. *New-York: Leavitt, Lord, & Co. Utica: G. Tracy.* 1835. 12mo, pp. xii, 9–183. 19264

El Defensor de la integridad nacional. Periodico politico, cientifico, literario é industrial. *Mexico.* 1844. Vol. I. 8vo. Continued. 19265

Defermon. Convention nationale. Rapport sur la Colonie de Saint Domingue fait au nom du comité de salut-public, Dans le séance du 25 messidor, an 3, Par Defermon ... . *Paris: l'imprimerie nationale. Messidor an III.* [1795.] 8vo, pp. 14.

Defermon. Rapport fait, au nom du comité de salut public, sur la Guadeloupe & autres Isles du Vent. Par Defermon, Imprimé par ordre de la Convention nationale. *Paris: de l'imprimerie nationale.* An III. 8vo, pp. 15. H. 19267

Deffaudis (S. E.) Suplemento al Diario del Gobierno de Mégico, Num. 1066, contiene el ultimatum remitido por S. E. el Sr. Baron Deffaudis. *Mégico.* 1838. 19268

Deffaudis. Justa Represalia en desagravio del Honor Na-

cional contra malignidad, inactitud e injusticia con que el Baron Deffaudis ... por J. J. Conseca. *Mégico.* 1838–39. 8vo.

Relates to the first French expedition to Mexico, under the command of Admiral Baudin, in 1838.

Deffaudis. Intervention anglo-française dans le Rio de la Plata. Missions de MM. Deffaudis et Walewski. [Documents destinées aux Chambres.] *Les Batignolles: imp. d' Hennuyer.* 1848. 8vo. 19270

Deffaudis. Questions diplomatiques, et particulièrement des travaux et de l'organisation du ministère des affaires étrangères. *Paris: Goujon et Milon.* 1849. 8vo. 19271

Definition of Parties; or the Political Effects of the Paper System Considered. Philadelphia, April 5th, 1794. *Philadelphia: Printed by Francis Bailey.* M,DCCXCIX. 8vo, pp. 16.

Definitive Treaty between Great Britain and the United States of America, signed at Paris, the 3d day of September 1783 [n p.] MDCCLXXXIII. 8vo, pp. 22. J.C.B., P. 19273

With the device and motto of the American eagle, one of the first instances of its use.

The Definitive Treaty of Christian Universal and Perpetual Peace, Friendship and Union, concluded at Aix-la-Chapelle, Oct. 7–18, 1748. Between ... Great Britain and France, &c. *Boston, reprinted.* 1749. 16mo, pp. 23. 19274

The Definitive Treaty of Peace and Friendship, between His Britannick Majesty, the Most Christian King, and the King of Spain. Concluded at Paris, the 10th Day of February, 1763. To which, The King of Portugal acceded on the same Day. Published by Authority. *London: E. Owen and T. Harrison.* 1763. 4to, pp. 48. 19275

[Defoe (Daniel).] *See* Carolina, Vol. III., No. 10966.

Defoe. Daniel Defoe; his Life, and recently discovered Writings ... 1716 to 1729. By William Lee. ... *London: John Camden Hotten.* 1869. 3 vols., 8vo, pp. lv, 484; xix, (1), 519; xvii, (1), 471. BA. 19276

Defoe's writings fill Vols. II. and III. Some of the essays relate to this country.

[Defoe.] An Essay on the South Sea Trade. With Enquiry into the Grounds and Reasons of the present Dislike and Complaint against the Settlement of a South Sea Company. By the Author of the Review. *London: J. Baker,* [*Sept.* 6] 1711. 8vo, pp. 47. + Second Edition. *London.* 1712 [*Nov.* 29, 1711]. 8vo, pp. 47. 19277

[Defoe.] The Fortunes and Misfortunes of the Famous Moll Flanders, &c., who was born in Newgate, and during a Life of continued Variety, for Threescore Years, beside her Childhood, was Twelve Years a Whore, Five Times a Wife (whereof once to her own Brother,) Twelve Years a Thief, Eight Years a Transported Felon in Virginia, at last grew Rich, liv'd Honest, and died a Penitent. Written from her own Memorandums. *London: W. Chetwood.* 1721. 8vo, pp. xiii, 424. + Second Edition. 23 *July*, 1722. 8vo, 4 l., pp. 366. + Third Edition. 21 *Dec.*, 1722. 8vo, 4 l., pp. 366. + Fourth Edition. 13 *July*, 1723. + Abridged Edition. Reissue of the Third Edition. 2 *Nov.*, 1723. + *Newcastle: Angus.* [1817.] 16mo, pp. 24. + *Edinburgh.* [n. d.] 12mo, pp. 24. 19278

Also in the collected editions of his novels.

[Defoe.] The History And Remarkable Life Of the truly Honourable Colonel Jacque, commonly call'd Colonel Jack, who was born a Gentleman, put Prentice to a Pick Pocket, was Six-and-Twenty Years a Thief, and then Kidnapp'd to Virginia. Came back a Merchant, was Five times married to Four Whores; went into the Wars, behav'd bravely, got Preferment, was made Colonel of a Regiment, came over, and fled with the Chevalier, is still abroad compleating a Life of Wonders, and resolves to dye a General. *London: J. Brotherton,* [etc.] 20 *Dec.*, 1722. 8vo, pp. vii, 399. + Second Edition. [19 *Jan.*] 1723. 8vo, 4 l., pp. 399. + Third Edition. 1724. 8vo, 4 l., pp. 399. + Another Edition. *London.* 1743. 19279

Also in the collected editions of his novels.

[Defoe.] The Judgment of Whole Kingdoms and Nations, Concerning the Rights, Power, and Prerogative of Kings, and the Rights, Privileges and Properties of the People. By Lord Somers. ... *London.* 1710. 8vo, pp. 7 . m. + The Eleventh Edition, Corrected. *Philadelphia: Re-printed, and sold by John Dunlap.* m.dcc.lxxiii. 8vo, pp. viii, 156. + Twelfth Edition. *New York.* 1774. 8vo. + Twelfth Edition. *Boston.* [n. d.] 8vo. w. + Twelfth Edition. *Newport, R. I.* 1774. 8vo.

A liberal constitutional argument about the English Revolution of 1688, reprinted in America to justify the Revolution. Usually attributed to Lord Somers, sometimes to Defoe, but not by his latest biographer, Lee. The first edition, *London.* 1709, was entitled, "Vox Populi; Vox Dei; being True Maxims of Government."

[Defoe.] Life, Adventures and Pyracies of Captain Singleton. *London.* 1720. + Third Edition. *London.* 1754. 12mo. + *London.* 1768, Sm. 8vo, pp. 300. + The Voyages, Travels,

and Surprising Adventures of Captain Robert Singleton. *New York.* 1802. 18mo. 19281

Also in the collected editions of his novels.

[Defoe.] The Life and Strange Surprizing Adventures of Robinson Crusoe, of York, Mariner: Who lived eight and twenty years all alone on an uninhabited Island on the Coast of America, near the mouth of the great River Oroonoque; having been cast on Shore by Shipwreck, wherein all the Men perished but himself. With an Account how he was at last as Strangely deliver'd by Pyrates. Written by Himself. *London: W. Taylor.* [*Apr.* 25] 1719. 8vo, 2 l., pp. 364. Frontispiece. + Second Edition. [*Ibid. May* 12] 1719. [*Ibid.*] + Third Edition. [*Ibid. June* 6] 1719. [*Ibid.*] + Fourth Edition. [*Ibid. Aug.* 8] 1719. [*Ibid.*] + Sixth Edition. 1722. Plates.

[Defoe.] The Farther Adventures of Robinson Crusoe. Being the Second and Last Part of his Life, and of the Strange Surprizing Accounts of his Travels Round three Parts of the Globe. Written by Himself. To which is addded a Map of the World, in which is Delineated the Voyage of Robinson. *London: Printed for W. Taylor.* 20 *Aug.*, 1719. 8vo, pp. 373.

[Defoe.] Serious Reflections during the Life and Surprizing Adventures of Robinson Crusoe. With his Vision of the Angelick World. Written by Himself. *London: Printed for W. Taylor.* 8 l., pp. 270, 84. 19284

First edition, 6 Aug., 1720, 8vo; first and second volume, spuriously abridged, 7th Aug., 1719; fifth edition, 19 Nov., 1720, 1 vol., 8vo; sixth edition, 28th Oct., 1721, 2 vols.; abridged edition, 1 vol., 28 Feb., 1722; another edition, 2 vols., called sixth edition, 5 June, 1722; edition, 2 vols., called seventh edition, 27 Aug., 1726; 12th edition. *London.* 1761. Numerous other editions. Also in Scott's and Bohn's editions of his novels, and Hazlitt's, of his works, and, as a chap-book, entitled "Exploits of Robinson Crusoe." The work is introduced here because the scene is laid in America. It is one of the most charming books in the English language, and has been translated into nearly every European language. The finest English edition is

[Defoe.] The Life and Strange Surprizing Adventures of Robinson Crusoe, of York, Mariner. He being cast on Shore by Shipwreck wherein all the Men perished but himself. With an Account how he was at last as strangely delivered by Pyrates, Written by himself. *London: John Stockdale.* 1790. 2 vols., 8vo. 17 Plates after Stothard's designs. 19285

This edition is printed in three sizes: octavo, royal octavo, and quarto; of this last, only twenty-five copies were printed. Cruikshank illustrated an edition, *London: J. Major.* 1831. 2 vols., fcap 8vo. The best modern editions are:

Defoe.] Robinson Crusoe edited after the Original Editions by J. W. Clark ... . *London and Cambridge: Macmillan and Co.* 1866. 16mo, pp. xii, 607. h. + The Globe Edition. ... Edited after the Original Editions. With a Biographical Introduction by Henry Kingsley ... *London: Macmillan and Co.* 1868. 8vo, pp. xxxi, 607. 19286

Kingsley shows that Crusoe's island was not Juan Fernandez in the Pacific, but an island in the Atlantic in the estuary of the Orinoco. Of the numerous translations, we name only the following on account of the plates:

Defoe. Robinson Crusoé, par Daniel de Foé. Restitution et traduction nouvelle. Illustré de la vie de Daniel de Foe par P. Chasles ... . *Paris. Francisque Borel; Astoin, Biais.* 1835. 2 vols., 8vo. + *Paris. Didier.* 1845. 8vo. 50 Vignettes. + [*Ib'd.*] 12mo. 19287

[Defoe.] Party Tyranny; Or, An Occasional Bill in Miniature, Being an Abridgment of the Shortest Way with the Dissenters as now practised in Carolina. Humbly offered to the Consideration of both Houses of Parliament. *London: Printed in the Year* 1705. Sm. 4to, Title, pp. 30. h. 19288

[Defoe.] Plan of English Commerce, being a complete prospect of the Trade of this Nation, as well Home as Foreign. Second Edition. *London.* 1728. + *London.* 1737. 19289

[Defoe.] A Voyage round the World by a course never sailed before. To which is prefixed the Life of the Author. By William Shiells, Esq. *London: F. Noble.* mdcclxxxvii. 3 vols., 12mo, pp. 284; 288; 257. 19290

A fiction. Is included in the editions of his novels. A map has been published, giving the track of this voyage.

[Defoe.] A New Voyage Round the World, By a Course never Sailed before. Being a Voyage undertaken by some Merchants, who afterwards proposed the setting up of an East India Company in Flanders. Illustrated with Copper Plates. *London: A Bettesworth.* 1725. 8vo, pp. 208, 205. 19291

Defonz (Milo). *See* [Codding (Milo Defonz)], Vol. iv, No. 14118.

De Forest (J. W.) History of the Indians of Connecticut from the Earliest Known Period to 1850. By John W. De Forest. Published with the sanction of the Connecticut Historical Society. .. *Hartford: Wm. Jas. Hamersley.* 1851. 8vo,

pp. xxvi, 509. Map and Woodcuts, by Darley. ba., c. + [*Ibid.*] 1852. 12mo. h + [*Ibid.*] 1853. 19292

Also. Miss Ravenel's Conversion from Secession to Loyalty. ... *New York: Harper & Brothers.* 1867. 12mo, pp. 521. c. — Seacliff, or the Mystery of the Westeroefts. *Boston.* 1859. 12mo, pp. 466.

[De Forest (T. R.)] Olden Time in New-York. By Those who Knew. *New York: Anderson & Smith.* 1833. 12mo, pp. 54. 19293

Deformity of a Hideous Monster, discovered in the Province of Maine. By a Man in the Woods looking after Liberty. [n. p. n. d.] 12mo. w. 19294

Defrees (J. D.) Remarks ... by John D. Defrees, before the Indiana Union Club of Washington, D. C. ... August 1, 1864. [n. p. n. d.] 8vo, pp. 14. h. 19295

Defrees. The War commenced by the Rebels.—Copperheads of the North their Allies. Speech of John D. Defrees, in Washington, D. C. ... August 1, 1864. [n. p. n. d.] 8vo, pp. 14. h. 19296

Degener (E.) The Minority Report, in Favor of extending the Right of Suffrage, with certain Limitations, to all Men without Distinction of Race or Color. Made in the Texas Reconstruction Convention. By E. Degener. February 24, 1866. *Austin: Printed at the Southern Intelligencer Office.* 1866. 8vo, pp. 16. h. 19297

Degioannis (G.) Sull' arresto dei commissari americani del Sud Mason e Slidell a bordo el legno inglese Trent ... lezione ... dall' Avv. Coll. Giovanni Degioannis regio professore ... di diritto internazionale ... 27 dicembre 1861. *Cagliari: Tip di A. Timon.* 1862. 8vo, pp. 126. h. 19298

Degollado. D. Santos Degollado considerado como Gobernador de Jalisco, y como General en Jefe de las fuerzas que sitiaron á Guadalajara. *Guadalajara.* 1859. 4to, pp. 84.

[Degouge (*M.*)] Réponse au Champion Americain, ou colon très-aisé à connoitre. [*Paris: Jan.* 18, 1790.] 8vo, pp. 8. 19300

The Degrading Compromise that the Northern Copperhead Leaders would force upon the Country. *Washington: Printed by the Indiana Union Club.* [186–.] Broadside. (From "Harper's Weekly.") h. 19301

Degrand (P. P. F.) Outline of a Plan for a National Bank. [*Boston.* 1841.] 8vo. b. 19302

Degrand. Proceedings of the Friends of a Rail-Road to San Francisco, at their Public Meeting, held at ... Boston, April 19, 1849, including an Address to the People of the U. States; Shewing that, P. P. F. Degrand's Plan is the only one ... which will secure ... a Railroad to California, ... Fourth Edition. *Boston: Dutton and Wentworth, Printers.* 1849. 8vo, pp. 24. 19303

Degrand. Revenue Laws and Custom-House Regulations, being an Appendix to the Tariff. Compiled by P. P. F. Degrand ... . *Boston.* 1820. 12mo, pp. 88. + Third Edition. [*Boston:*] *P. P. F. Degrand. July* 1, 1824. pp. 196. 19304

Degrand. Tariff of Duties, on Importations into the United States, compiled for P. P. F. Degrand's Boston Weekly Report of Public Sales and of Arrivals, ... and revised & corrected by the Honorable The Secretary of the Treasury. [1820.] 12mo, pp. 64. + Third Edition. [*Boston:*] *P. P. F. Degrand. July* 1, 1824. 12mo, pp. 196. b. + Fourth Edition. *Boston.* 1828. 12mo. 19305

Also: Tariff and Custom House Duties. Being an Appendix to the Tariff of Duties, &c. Compiled by P. P. F. Degrand. *Boston.* 1820. 12mo. w. + Third Edition. 1824. 12mo. w. — An Address ... on the Advantages of Low Fares, and Low Rates of Freight ... *Boston.* 1840. 8vo, pp. 39. s. — To the People of Massachusetts, and to the Friends of Rail-Roads throughout the Union. [*Boston.* 1840.] 8vo, pp. 39. b.

Degray (M.) A Short Inquiry illucidating the Principal Cause that disturbs the Tranquillity of a Republican Government. By Michael Degray. *New York.* 1807. 12mo. n.

De Hart (W. C.) Observations on Military Law and the Constitution and Practice of Courts Martial, with a Summary of the Law of Evidence as applicable to Military Trials, adapted to the Laws, Regulations, and Customs of the Army and Navy of the United States. By William C. De Hart, ... New Edition. *New York.* 1864. 8vo, pp. viii, 433. 19307

De Hass (W.) History of the Early Settlement and Indian Wars of Western Virginia; embracing an Account of the Various Expeditions in the West, previous to 1795. Also, Biographical Sketches of Col. Ebenezer Zane, Major Samuel McColloch, Lewis Wetzel, Genl. Andrew Lewis, Genl. Daniel Brodhead,

Capt. Samuel Brady, Col. Wm. Crawford; and other Distinguished Actors in our Border Wars. By Willis De Hass ... . Illustrated by numerous Engravings [Woodcuts]. *Wheeling: H. Hoblitzell.* 1851. 8vo, pp. 416. ba., h. 19308

Dehay (Louis Timothée). Les colonies et la métropole, le sucre exotique et le sucre indigène, trésor, marine, commerce, agriculture, émancipation commerciale de nos colonies, et abolition de l'esclavage. *Paris: Hortet et Ozanne.* 1839. 8vo. c.

Dehon (Theodore). Constitution of the Protestant Episcopal Society for the Advancement of Christianity in South Carolina. *Charleston.* 1810. 8vo, pp. 11. 19310

Dehon. A Discourse, delivered in Newport, Rhode-Island; Before the Congregation of Trinity Church, The Masonic Society, And the Newport Guards; The Sunday following The Intelligence of the Death of General George Washington. By Theodore Dehon, a.m. *Newport: Printed by Henry Barber.* m,dccc. 4to, pp. (4), 17, (2). 19311

Dehon. A Discourse occasioned by the Death of George Gibbs, delivered in Trinity Church, Newport, Rhode Island, October 23, 1803. By Theodore Dehon, a.m. Rector. *Newport: Ann Barber.* 1803. 8vo, pp. 13. 19312

Dehon. A Discourse delivered in Trinity Church, in Newport, on Thursday, 27 Nov. 1805; an appointed day of Public Thanksgiving and Praise. ... *Newport: Ann Barber.* 1806. 8vo, pp. 14. n. 19313

Dehon. Sermons ... . By the Late Right Rev. Theodore Dehon, d.d. ... Bishop of ... South Carolina. Second American Edition ... . *New York: Thomas N. Stanford.* 1856. 2 vols., 8vo. 19314

There are a consecration, a fast, and a thanksgiving sermon in Vol. ii., and two sermons before the Protestant Episcopal Society for Adv. of Christianity in South Carolina. Also: A Discourse delivered in Providence, September 6, 1804, before the Female Charitable Society, for the Relief of Indigent Widows and Children. ... *Providence: Heaton & Williams.* [1804.] 8vo, pp. 20. m. — A Discourse ... before the General Convention of the Protestant Episcopal Church, ... at Philadelphia, on the 21st of May. 1814. *Philadelphia.* 1814. 8vo, pp. 32. + *Boston.* 1819. 12mo, pp. 36.

Dejean (Aug.) Anichinabek amisinahikaniwa, kicheanameatchik, catonik, Otawak wakanakessi. *Wyastenong: G. L. Whitney.* 1830. 18mo. 19315

A catechism in the Ottawak language.

Dejean (C. F. G.) Essai sur la question coloniale à la Guyane française. *Paris: Le Chevalier.* 1848. 8vo. 19316

Dejean (*Rev.* M.) Anichinabek Amisinaki-Kaniwa. The Indian Book. *Detroit.* 1839. 12mo, pp. 106. 19317

Contains a vocabulary of forty words in French and Ottawa.

Dejean de la Batie. Colonies par M. Dejean de la Batie. Extrait de l'Encyclopédie du xixe Siècle. *Paris.* 1846. 8vo, 12 l. h. 19318

De Kay (J. E.) Anniversary Address on the Progress of the Natural Sciences in the United States: Delivered before the Lyceum of Natural History, of New-York, Feb. 1826. By James E. De Kay. *New-York: G. & C. Carvill.* 1826. 8vo, pp. 78. b., c., p. 19319

De Kay. A Geological Survey of New York. 1838. 8vo, with Atlas in 4to. 19320

[De Kay.] [Not Published.] [A List of the Indian and Dutch Names in Long Island.] 12mo, pp. 12. 19321

Very rare. Privately printed, as a means of procuring additional information

De Kay. Zoology of New York. *See* "New York."

De Kroyft (*Mrs.* S. H.) A Place in thy Memory. ... By S. H. De Kroyft. *New-York: John F. Trow, Printer.* 1850. 12mo, pp. 191. ba. 18322

Also: Letter to President Fillmore's Lady. [*New Orleans Delta.* 1852.] 8vo, pp. 4. l.

De la Beche (H. T.) Notes on the Present Condition of the Negroes in Jamaica. *London.* 1825. 8vo. bd. 19323

Delacoste (J. A.) Corps Législatif. Conseil de Cinq-Cents. Rapport fait par Jean-Aimé Delacoste, sur la résolution du 23 nivôse, relative aux contributions foncière & personelle des colonies occidentales, pour l'an 6. Séance du 26 nivôse an 6. [n. p. n. d.] 8vo, pp. 7. 19324

Delacoste. Catalogue of the Natural Productions and Curiosities which compose the Collections of the Cabinet of Natural History opened for Public Exhibition at No. 38 William Street, New York. *New York.* 1804. 8vo. n. 19325

Delacour (Adolphe). Le Rio de la Plata, Buenos-Ayres, Montevideo. *Paris: Heois.* 1845. 12mo. Portrait. 19326

Extrait de la "Revue indépendante."

Delacroix (Jacques Vincent). Constitutions des principaux états de l'Europe et des États-Unis d'Amérique. Par M. de la Croix ... . *Paris: Buisson.* 1791–1802. 6 vols., 8vo, 2 l., pp. lvj, 539; 2 l., pp. 408; 2 l., pp. xij, 428; 2 l., pp. 387; 2 l., pp. iv, 364; 19327

The first two volumes had a second edition in 1791.

Delacroix. A Review of the Constitutions of the Principal States of Europe, and of the United States of America. Given ... as Lectures by M. Delacroix. Translated from the French ... *London.* 1792. 2 vols., 8vo. 19328

[Delacroix.] Mémoires d'un Américain, Avec une description de la Prusse & de l'Isle de Saint Domingue. Par l'Auteur des Lettres d'Affi à Zurac & de celles d'un Philosophe sensible. *Lausanne & Paris: la V. Regnard & Demonville.* m. dcc. lxxi. 2 pts., 12mo, pp. 240; 191. + *Amsterdam.* 1772. 12mo. ba.

Delafaye-Bréhier (Julie). Les Portugais d'Amérique: souvenirs historiques de la guerre du Brésil en 1635. *Paris: Lehuby.* 1847. Rl. 12mo. 12 Plates. s. 19330

Delafield (E.) Biographical Sketch of J. Kearny Rodgers, m.d., ... by Edward Delafield, m.d. ... . *New York: G. A. C. Beuren, Printer.* 1852. 8vo, pp. 28. h. 19331

Also: Introductory Address to the Students ... of the College of Physicians and Surgeons of the University of the State of New York, Delivered Nov. 7, 1837. *New York.* 1837. 8vo, pp. 44.

Delafield (J.) A Brief Topographical Description of the County of Washington, in the State of Ohio. By J. Delafield, Junr. Manella, O. *New York: Printed by J. M. Elliott.* 1834. 8vo, pp. 39. Folded Plate. 19332

Delafield. An Inquiry into the Origin of the Antiquities of America. By John Delafield, Jr. With an Appendix, containing Notes, and "A View of the Causes of the Superiority of the Men of the Northern over those of the Southern Hemisphere." By James Lakey, m.d. *New-York: J. C. Colt. London: Longman,* [etc.] *Paris: A. & W. Galignani.* 1839. 4to, pp. 142. 10 Plates, and 1 large Plate folded. h. 19333

Some copies have the imprint, *Cincinnati: N. G. Burgess & Co.* The preface is by C. P. MacIlvaine.

Delafield. Journal of the Proceedings of a Convention of Literary and Scientific Gentlemen, held in New-York, October, 1830. *New York.* 1831. 8vo. c. 19334

Also: Mysticism and its Results ... *St. Louis.* 1857. 12mo, pp. 120. c. — Notes for an Address to the Farmers of Ontario County, at their Annual Fair, held at Geneva, September 29, 1853. ... *Canandaigua.* 1854. 8vo, pp. 20. H.

Delafosse de Rouville. Éloge historique du chev. Mauduit-Duplessis, major-général des armées françaises à Saint-Domingue, colonel du régiment du Port-au-Prince ... assassiné au Port-au-Prince le 4 Mars 1791. Suivi d'un essai sur la situation de Saint-Domingue à cette époque. *Senlis: Tremblay. Paris: Volland.* 1818. 8vo. 19335

De la Guard (Theodore), *pseudonym.* *See* [Ward (N.)]

Delahaye (J. C. G.) Corps Législatif. Conseil des Cinq-Cents. Discours de J. C. G. Delahaye, sur l'affaire des Colonies. Séance au 11 prairial an v. 8vo, pp. 26. 19336

Delamardelle (G. P. F.) Éloge funèbre du comte d'Ennery et réforme judiciaire à Saint-Domingue [prononcé ... dans la séance publique du conseil supérieur de Saint-Domingue, le 2 avril 1788, par messire Guillaume-Pierre-François Delamardelle ...]. [n. d.] 4to. 19337

The words within brackets are from the caption.

De l'Amérique, 1771. *See* [Bonneville (C. de)], Vol. II., No. 6327.

De la Mota (J. J.) Panegyrico à la Vida y Martyrio de la Inclita Virgen Catharina. *Mexico.* 1716. 4to, 12 l. 19338

De la Motta (Jacob). Discourse delivered at the Consecration of the Synagogue of the Hebrew Congregation, Mikva Israel, in the City of Savannah, Ga., 21st July, 1820. *Savannah.* 1820. 12mo. 19339

De Lancey (J.) The Charge of the Honourable James De Lancey Esq; Chief Justice of the Province of New-York, to the Gentlemen of the Grand-Jury for the City and County of New-York, on Tuesday the 15th Day of January, Annoq; Domini 1733. Printed at the Request of the Grand-Jury. ... *New-York: Printed and Sold by Wm. Bradford.* 1733. Folio, pp. 6. P. 19340

De Lancey. Some Observations on the Charge by Hon. James De Lancey, Chief Justice of the Province of New York, to the Grand Jury, January 15th, 1733. *New York: J. Peter Zenger.* 1733. Folio, pp. 18. c. 19341

De Lancey. Charge of Chief Justice J. De Lancey to the Grand Jury, 1734. *New-York: Printed by W. Bradford.* [1734.] Folio, pp. 8. s. 19342

De Lancey (W. H.) A Charge to the Clergy of the Diocese of Western New York. Delivered Aug. 21, 1861, ... On the Needs of the Diocese. ... . By William Heathcote De Lancey, D.D., D.C.L., Oxon., Bishop of the Diocese. *New York: Printed by C. A. Alvord.* 1862. 8vo, pp. 48. H. 19343

De Lancey. The Faithful Bishop: his Office, Character and Reward. The Sermon, at the Consecration of the Rt. Rev. Manton Eastburn, D.D. ... of Massachusetts, preached in ... Boston, December 29, 1842, by the Rt. Rev. William H. De Lancey, D.D. ... of Western New York. *Boston.* 1843. 8vo, pp. 64. B. 19344

De Lancey. A Sermon preached at the Centennial Celebration of the Opening of St. Peter's Church, Philadelphia, September 4th, 1861. By William Heathcote De Lancey, D.D., D.C.L. ... . *Philadelphia: King & Baird, Printers.* 1862. 8vo, pp. 78. B. 19345

Also: An Address, delivered before the Trustees, Faculty, and Students of the University of Pennsylvania. ... *Philadelphia.* 1830. P. — Episcopal Address to the ... Convention of ... Western New York, August 17, 1853. *Utica.* 1854. 8vo, pp. 37. — Farewell Letter ... to the Vestry and Congregation of St. Peter's Church, May 2d, 1839. *Philadelphia.* 1839. 8vo. — Ministerial Perils. A Sermon preached at the Opening of the Annual Convention of the Diocese of Pennsylvania, 1830. *Philadelphia.* 1830. 8vo, pp. 22. — An Inaugural Address, delivered before the Trustees, Faculty, and Students of the University of Pennsylvania. ... *Philadelphia: Carey, Lea & Carey.* 1828. 8vo, pp. 31. H., P. — A Pastoral Letter ... on the Regulation of the Convention enjoining Monthly Collections for Church Objects. *Geneva, N. Y.* 1839. 8vo, pp. 15.

[De Lancy (J.)] Letter to the Right Honourable Mr. Pitt ... containing Reasons why no Discrimination or Deduction ought to be made from the Sums found due to the American Loyalists. [Signed] James De Lancy. 1788. 8vo, pp. 11. BA. 19346

[Delaney (Oliver).] Considerations on the Propriety of Imposing Taxes in the British Colonies, For the Purpose of raising a Revenue, by Act of Parliament. *North America:*

Printed by a North-American. New York: Re-printed by John Holt, in the Year 1765. 8vo, pp. 55. + Second Edition. *London.* 1766. 8vo, pp. 81. 19347

Delano (A.) Life on the Plains and among the Diggings; being Scenes and Adventures of an Overland Journey to California; with Particular Incidents of the Routes, Mistakes and Sufferings of the Emigrants, the Indian Tribes, the Present and the Future of the Great West. By A. Delano. *Auburn: Miller, Orton & Mulligan.* 1854 12mo, pp. 384. c. 19348

Delano. A Narrative of Voyages and Travels in the Northern and Southern Hemispheres: comprising three Voyages round the World; together with a Voyage of Survey and Discovery in the Pacific Ocean and Oriental Isles. By Amasa Delano. *Boston: printed by E. G. House.* 1817. 8vo, pp. 598. Map and Portrait. BA. + Second Edition. *Boston: F. G. House.* 1818. P. 19349

Drawn up from the captain's journals, by President Holley. *See* "N. Am. Rev.," v. 244.

Delano (Christopher). A Descriptive Narrative of the Wonderful Petrifaction of a Man into Stone as Perfect as when Alive. *Philadelphia.* 1854. 12mo, pp. 12. H. 19350

Delano (C.) Speech of Hon. Columbus Delano on the Mexican War, House of Representatives of the U. States, Feb. 2, 1847. *Washington.* [n. d.] 8vo, pp. 15. M. 19351

Delano. Speech of Mr. Columbus Delano, of Ohio, against the Bill declaring that "a State of War exists by the Act of the Republic of Mexico." [*Washington.* 1846.] 8vo, pp. 15. H.

Also: Speech ... on the Oregon Question. ... In the House ... February 5, 1846. *Washington.* 1846. 8vo, pp. 15. H.

Delany (M. R.) The Condition, Elevation, Emigration, and Destiny of the Colored People of the United State. Politically Considered, by Martin Robison Delany. *Philadelphia: published by the Author.* 1852. 12mo, pp. 215. c. 19353

Delany. The Origin and Objects of Ancient Freemasonry; its Introduction into the United States, and Legitimacy among Colored Men. ... Delivered ... June 24th, A.D. 1853 — A.L. 5853. By M. R. Delany, ... *Pittsburgh: Printed by W. S. Haven.* 1853. 12mo, pp. 32. H. 19354

Delap (F.) Account of the Trial of Francis Delap, Esq., late Provost Marshal, for a Misdemeanor at a Supreme Court of Judicature held at Kingston, Jamaica. 1755. 8vo. 19355

Delaplain (S.) A Thrilling and Exciting account of the Sufferings and horrible Tortures inflicted on Mortimer Bowers and Miss Sophia Delaplain, by the Spanish Authorities, for a supposed participation with Gen. Lopez in the Invasion of Cuba; together with the Plan of the Campaign of Lopez. ... their isolated condition, on a remote part of the Island, and owing to the impression that their incarceration and treatment would never be made known in the United States, ... By Miss Delaplain. *Charleston, S. C.: E. E. Barclay; U. B. Crossen & Co.* 1852. 8vo, pp. 31. 19356

Delaplaine (Joseph). The Author turned Critic; or The Reviewer Reviewed; being a Reply to a Feeble and Unfounded Attack on Delaplaine's Repository in the Analectic Magazine and Naval Chronicle, for the Month of September in 1816. [*Philadelphia.* 1816.] 8vo, pp. 34, 3 l. 19357

Delaplaine. Delaplaine's Repository of the Lives and Portraits of Distinguished American Characters. *Philadelphia: J. Delaplaine.* 1815. 3 pts, 4to, pp. x, v, 223; 148. 18 Portraits. 16358

See "Analytical Magazine," VIII. 193, 380; X. 483; XIII. 89. Also: Delaplaine's "Prospectus of National Panzographia, for the Reception of the Portraits of Distinguished Americans. *Philadelphia.* 1818." 8vo, pp. 16. s.

Delaporte (*M.*) Le Voyageur François, ou la connoissance de l'Ancien et du Nouveau Monde, Mis au jour par M. l'Abbé Delaporte. *Paris.* 1767–72. 42 vols., 12mo. + Nouvelle edition. *A Paris: L. Cellot.* M. DCC. LXXIII–MDCCXCXV [*sic*]. 42 vols., 12mo. 19359

About six volumes of this work are devoted exclusively to America.

Delaporte. El Viagero Universal o' Noticia del Mundo Antiguo y Nuevo, por Delaporte, trad. en castellano por D. P. E. P. 1795–1801. 43 vols., 8vo. 19360

Delaporte. Reisen eines Franzosen, oder Beschreibung der vornehmsten Reiche in der Welt, nach ihrer ehemaligen und itzigen Beschaffenheit, in Briefen an ein Frauenzimmer abgefasset und herausgegeben von Hrn. Abt Delaporte. *Leipz.: bey Bernh. Christ. Breitkopf und Sohn.* 1774. 12mo. 19361

Delaporte. *See* Fontenay.

Delaroche (P.) The Gospel of Christ preached to the Poor By Peter Delaroche, Missionary. *Lunenburg.* [*Nova Scotia*] *Printed: At the Author's Expence, To be given and not to be Sold.* MDCCLXXIII. 8vo, 5 l., pp. 99. + Reprinted. *Halifax.* 1787. 8vo, pp. 96. 19362

De la Rue (W.) Address on the Presentation of the Gold Medal of the Royal Astronomical Society to Professor G. P. Bond, Director of the Observatory of Harvard College, Cambridge, U. S. By the President, Warren de la Rue, Ph. D., F.R.S., ... *London. February*, 1865. 8vo, pp. 15. H. 19363

De la Rupture des Glaces du Pôle Arctique ou Observations sur les Mers et les Contrées du Pole Arctique. *A Paris.* 1818. 8vo. 19364

De La *and* Del. Names with these prefixes not inserted here will be found under the next letter of the name.

Delatour (A. J.) A Daily Record of the Thermometer for Ten Years, from 1840 to 1850, as kept at Delatour's ... New York. *New York.* 1850. 18mo. s. 19365

Delaval *and* Proissy. Correspondance entre M. le président de l'assemblée coloniale de la partie française de Saint-Domingue [Delaval] et M. le commissaire de Colonies [Proissy] faisant fonctions d'intendant. [23–24 février 1792.] *Le Cap.: imp. royale.* [n. d.] 8vo, pp. 48 or less. 19366

Delavall (J.), *and* Kieth (G.) The | Heresie and Hatred | Which was falsly Charged upon the | Innocent | Justly returned upon the | Guilty. | Giving some brief and impartial Account of the most ma- | terial Passages of a late Dispute in Writing, that hath | passed at Philadelphia betwixt | John Delavall and George Keith, | With some intermixt Remarks and Observations on | the whole. | *Printed and Sold by William Bradford at Philadelphia,* | *Anno Dom.* 1693. | 4to, pp. 22, (1). 19367

Delavan (Edward C.) Letter to Gen. John H. Cocke, or Virginia, Oct. 1, 1856. *Albany.* 1856. 8vo, pp. 7. 19368

Delavan A Report of the Trial of the Cause of John Taylor vs. Edward C. Delavan, Prosecuted for an Alleged Libel; Tried at the Albany Circuit, April, 1840. And Mr. Delavan's Correspondence with the Ex-Committee of the Albany City Temperance Society, &c. ... *Albany: printed by Hoffmann, White & Visscher.* 1840. 16mo, pp. 48. H. 19369

Also: Speech ... at a meeting of the friends of Mr. Fillmore, Ballston, Aug. 9, 1856. 8vo. — Letter to Governor King, of N. Y.: an Appeal for Co-Operation in the

Temperance Reform. By Edward C. Delavan. *Albany.* 1857. 8vo, pp. 24. BA. Mr. Delavan was an early, earnest, and consistent advocate of total abstinence from all alcoholic drinks, and was the author of many tracts on the subject. *See* Taylor (John).

[Delaville (*Abbé*).] État Présent de la Pensylvanie, où l'on trouve le détail de ce qui s'y est passé depuis la défaite du Général Braddock jusqu'à la prise d'Oswego, avec une Carte particulière de cette Colonie MDCCLVI. [n. p. n. d.] 12mo, pp. 128. Map. 19370

The author was the first Commissioner to the Minister of Foreign Affairs. Manuscript note in Mr. J. C. Brown's copy.

Delaville de Mirmont (Alexandre Jean Joseph). Observations sur les maisons centrales de détention, à l'occasion de l'ouvrage de MM. de Beaumont et de Tocqueville, sur les pénitenciers des États-Unis d'Amérique. *Paris: imp. de Crapelet.* 1833. 8vo. 19371

De la Warre (*Lord*). *See* West (Thomas).

Delaware Indians. An Abstract of the Journal of a Mission to the Delaware Indians West of the Ohio, June 19, 1772. 12mo. 19372

A doubtful title, from H. A. Brady's catalogue, No. 1003.

A Collection of Hymns for the Use of the Delaware Christian Indians. *Bethlehem.* 1847. 12mo. 19373

Delaware and Shawanese Indians. *See* [Thompson (Charles)].

The Delaware First Book. By Ira D. Blanchard. [n. p.] 1842. 12mo, pp. 24. 19374

Forty-Six Select Scripture Narratives from the Old Testament. Embellished with Engravings, for the Use of Indian Youth. Translated into Delaware Indian, by J. Luckenbach. *New York: D. Fanshaw, Printer.* 1838. 12mo, pp. xvi, 304.

The History of our Lord and Saviour Jesus Christ; translated into the Delaware Indian Language, as recorded by the Evangelists. By David Zeisberger. *New York.* 1821. 12mo.

Nek Nechenenawachgissitschik Bambilak naga Geschiechauchsitpanna Johanessa elekhangup. Gischitak Elleniechsink, untschi C. F. Denke. *New York: Printed for the American Bible Society.* 1818. 12mo, pp. 21. W. 19377

The three epistles of the Apostle John translated into Delaware Indian, by C. F. Dencke.

Nehiro. Iriniui aiamihe massinahigan, shatshegutsch Mitinekapitsh, Iskuamiskutsh, Netshekatsh, Misht', Assinitsh, Shekutimitsh, Ekuanatsh, Ashuabmushuanitsh, Piakuagamitsh Gaie missi missi Nehiro—Iriniui Astshitsh ka tatjits ka kueiasku aiamihatjits ka utshi. Roman Catholic Prayer Book in the Language of the Delaware-Indians. *Uabistiguiatsh.* 1767. pp. 96. 19378

Delaware. Anno Millesimo Septingentesimo Septuagesimo Sexto. ... 12mo. 19379

Laws of Delaware State for 1776. The only copy I have seen appears never to have had a title-page, and wants all after page 26

Boyd's Delaware State Directory; containing the Names of all Persons in Business on their own Account, also the Census, Manufacturing Statistics, and Names of the Inhabitants of Wilmington City, with a Compendium of much Useful Information. 1859–'60. [*New York: Compiled and published by William H. and Andrew Boyd.*] 1859. 19380

A Calm Appeal to the People of the State of Delaware. *Philadelphia: Printed by Zachariah Poulson, Junr.* [About 1792.] pp. 22. P. 19381

A statement of the Penn's claim to lands, etc., by their agents, Thomas McKean and Edm. Physick.

Catalogue of the Books belonging to the Library of the Delaware College. *Wilmington: Porter & Naff, Printers.* 1843. 12mo, pp. 52. H. 19382

Delaware Farmer's Union Almanac for the Year 1865. *Philadelphia: King & Baird.* 1865. 4to, pp. 36. 19383

Full of patriotic sentiment, and very severe on the copperheads.

The Delaware Register and Farmer's Magazine ... [edited] by William Huffington. *Dover, Delaware: S. Kimmey, Printer.* 1838–39. 2 vols., 8vo, pp. 480, (4); 490, (4). C, H., P.

Directions to Sail into and up Delaware Bay. *Published by the Royal Authorities at Philadelphia:* [*J. Humphreys.*] *Feb. 9th,* 1778. Folio, 1 l. 19385

Draught of a Constitution of Government: published for the Consideration of the Citizens of the Delaware State; pursuant to an Order of the Convention, of the 31st of December, 1791. *Wilmington: Printed by Peter Brynberg and Samuel Andrews.* 1792. 8vo, pp. 24. P. 19386

Health Laws of the State of Delaware. *Wilmington.* 1803. 12mo. 19387

A History of the Delaware Department of the Great Central Fair for the United States Sanitary Commission, at Philadelphia, June, 1864. *Washington: James B. Riggs.* 1864. 8vo, pp. 34.

Inaugural Address of William Cannon, upon taking the Oath of Office as Governor of Delaware, January 20, 1863. *Wilmington: Henry Eckle.* 1863. 8vo, pp. 30. 19389

Also: Illegal Arrests. Special Message of Governor Cannon, March 3, 1863. Also, Governor's Proclamation, March 11, 1863. 8vo, pp. 8. — Special Message of Governor Cannon, January 12, 1864. 8vo, pp. 8. — Special Message of Governor Cannon, July 28, 1864. pp. 11. — Message of Governor Cannon, January 3, 1865. pp. 16.

Journal of the Senate of the State of Delaware, from Jan. 2, 1798, to Jan 25, 1805. *Newcastle.* 1798. Folio. Continued. The latter volumes in 8vo. 19390

Laws of the Government of New Castle, Kent and Sussex, upon Delaware. Published by Order of the Assembly. *Philadelphia: Printed and Sold by B. Franklin and D. Hall, at the New Printing-Office in Market-Street.* M DCC LII. Folio, pp, 363, xvii. C., P. 19391

Laws of the State of Delaware, from the 14th of October 1700, to the 18th of August 1797. *Newcastle.* 1797. 2 vols., 8vo. + From January 2, 1798, to January 25, 1805: Vol. 3; and from January 7, 1806, to February 3, 1813; Vol. 4. *Wilmington.* 1816. + To 1829 inclusive. Revised Edition, published by Authority of the General Assembly, by Willard Hall. *Wilmington.* 1829. 8vo, pp. 760. 19392

Letter to the Delaware Pilots—renewed Instructions from Committee on Tarring and Feathering. Dec. 7, 1773. Folio, 1 l. P. 19393

A List of the Prizes drawn in the Delaware Lottery for the sale of Lands belonging to the Earl of Sterling, September 1, 1774. [*Printed at Philadelphia.*] Folio, pp. 2. P. 19394

Memoir of the Geological Survey of the State. *See* Booth (J. C.), Vol. II., No. 6385.

Minutes of the Grand Committee of the Whole Convention of the Delaware State, which commenced at Dover, on Tuesday, the Twenty-ninth Day of November, in the Year of our

Lord One Thousand Seven Hundred and Ninety-one. For the Purpose of Reviewing, Altering, and Amending the Constitution of this State; or, if they see Occasion, for forming a new One in Stead thereof. *Wilmington: Printed by James Adams.* 1792. Folio, pp. 80. 19395

Minutes of the Convention of the Delaware State, at the Second Session thereof, Which Commenced at Dover, on Tuesday the twenty-ninth day of May, in the Year of our Lord, one thousand seven hundred and ninety-two, for the purpose of reviewing, altering and amending the Constitution of this State, or if they see occasion, for forming a new one instead thereof. *Wilmington: Printed by Brynberg and Andrews.* Folio, pp. 107.

The Managers of the Delaware Lottery for the College of New Jersey, &c. *Philadelphia. March,* 24, 1774. 4to, broadside. P. 19397

Proceedings of the Inaugural Meeting of the Historical Society of Delaware, held at Wilmington, 31st May, 1864, together with the Constitution and By-Laws then Adopted. *Wilmington: James B. Riggs, Printer.* 1864. 8vo. 19398

Prohibitory Liquor Law of Delaware. Opinion of the Supreme Court on its Constitutionality. May 31, 1856. 8vo.

Reflections on the Perils and Difficulties of the Winter Navigation of the Delaware. *Philadelphia.* 1822. 8vo. W. 19400

Report of the Delaware Association for the Moral Improvement and Education of the Colored People of the State. February, 1868. *Wilmington: Press of Jenkins and Atkinson.* 1868. 8vo, pp. 23. H. 19401

To the Delaware Pilots. ... *Philadelphia. Nov.* 27, 1773. Folio, p. 1. P. 19402

From the Committee of Tarring and Feathering, in anticipation of the arrival in Delaware Bay of the sea ship "Polly," Captain Ayres.

To the Delaware Pilots ... *Philadelphia. December* 7, 1773. 4to, p. 1. P. 19403

Renewed instructions concerning the ship "Polly from "The Committee for Tarring and Feathering."

Votes and Proceedings of the House of Assembly of the Delaware State, 1785–86. *Wilmington.* 1786. Folio, pp. 50. Continued. 19404

Ways & Means for the Inhabitants of Delaware, &c. *See* [Rawle (Francis).]

Delaware & Hudson Canal Company, 1827. 8vo. 19405

DELAWARE, *N. J.* Address of the Board of Directors of the Delaware and Raritan Canal and Camden and Amboy Railroad Companies to the People of New Jersey, June, 1848. *Trenton: Printed by Sherman and Harron.* 1848. 8vo, pp. 30.

Delaware and Raritan Canal. [n. p. n. d.] 8vo, pp. 12. Map. 19407

Delaware and Raritan Canal Company. Report. 1831.

Analysis of Memorial of the Delaware & Hudson Canal Co. 1829. 19409

Considerations on the Delaware and Raritan Canal. *Philadelphia.* 1825. 8vo. 19410

Claims of the Delaware and Raritan Canal to a Repeal of a Law of Pennsylvania, passed April 6, 1825. *Philadelphia.* 1826. 8vo. 19411

An Investigation into the Affairs of the Delaware and Raritan Canal and Camden and Amboy Railroad Companies, in reference to certain Charges by "a Citizen of Burlington" [Henry C. Carey]. *Newark.* 1849. 8vo. BM. 19412

Report of the Commissioners of New-Jersey on Connecting the Delaware and Raritan. *Trenton.* 1817. N. 19413

Report of the Canal Commissioners on the Delaware and Raritan Canal. *Trenton.* 1824. 19414

Report of the Committee to whom was referred the subject of the Delaware and Raritan Canal. pp. 32. 19415

Report of the Joint Board of Directors of the Delaware and Raritan Canal, and Camden and Amboy Rail Road Transportation Companies ... January 12, 1848. *Princeton, N. J.: printed by John T. Robinson.* 8vo, pp. 17. H. 19416

Report of the Commissioners appointed to Investigate Charges made against the Directors of the Delaware and Raritan Canal and Camden and Amboy Railroad Companies. *Trenton.* 1850. 8vo. 19417

Address of the Committee of the Delaware and Schuylkill Canal Company to a Committee of the Senate and House of ... Representatives. *Philadelphia.* [1799.] 8vo, pp. 32. H.

DELAWARE COUNTY, *N. Y.* Catalogue of Delaware Academy. *Delhi, N. Y.* 1859. 8vo. 19419

DELAWARE COUNTY, *Pa.* Report of a Committee of the Delaware County Institute of Science, on the Great Rain Storm and Flood, which occurred in that County on the Fifth of August, 1843. With a Map ... *Chester: Printed by Y. S. Walker.* 1844. 8vo, pp. 52. Continued. Map. 19420

The Delawariad; or, a Second Part of the Wilmingtoniad: Being a Touch at the Times. A Dialogue. [Motto.] *Wilmington: J. Wilson.* 1801. 12mo, pp. 22. 19421

DELBAS (A. F.) Assiento qve se|tomô con Antonio Fernandez Delbas, so-|bre la renta y prouision general de esclauos| negros para las Indias, año de mil y seiscien|tos y quinze.| [1615.] Folio, 20 folioed leaves. 19422

DELCHAMPS (J. J.) Love's Ambuscade; the Sergeant's Stratagem a War Drama, in Three Acts. By J. J. Delchamps. *Mobile: A. G. Horn.* 1863. 32mo, Title, pp. 62, (2). BA.

DELCHAMPS. Spiced Slaw for Southern Digestion and other Papers. Written for the Order of W. B. By J. J. Delchamps. With the Constitution of the Order. ... With the Constitution of the Order. ... *Mobile: printed by A. G. Horn.* 1863. 8vo, pp. 62. BA. 19424

W. B. means Working Brothers. Dish No. 3, included in the above, was also published separately, *Mobile.* 1862. 8vo, pp. 16. BA.

DELÉRY (Ch.) Confédérés et fédéraux. Les Yankees fondateurs de l'esclavage aux États-Unis et initiateurs du droit de sécession. Par le Docteur Ch. Deléry. *Paris: Librairie centrale.* 1864. 8vo, pp. 31. 19425

DELESCLUZE (Ch.) De Paris à Cayenne, journal d'un transporté. Par Charles Delescluze. *Paris: Le Chevalier.* 1869. 18mo, pp. 347. 19426

DELESSERT (Benjamin). Les Mines d'or de la Californie. *Paris.* 1849. 8vo. 19427

DELESSERT (Édouard). Les Indiens de la baie d'Hudson;

promenades d'un artiste parmi les Indiens de l'Amérique du nord, depuis le Canada jusqu'à l'île de Vancouver et l'Orégon, à travers le territoire de la compagnie de la baie d'Hudson. Imité de l'anglais. *Paris: Amyot.* 1861. 12mo, pp. vii, 273. 19428

DELESSERT (E.) Voyages dans les deux Océans, Atlantique et Pacifique, 1844 à 1847. Brésil, États-Unis, Cap de Bonne-Espérance, Nouvelle Hollande, Nouvelle Zélande, Taïti, Philippines, Chine, Java, Indies Orientales, Égypte. Par M. Eugène Delessert. *Paris: Frank.* MDCCCXLVIII. Imp. 8vo, 4 l., pp. 326, (2). 15 Engravings, 2 Maps, and Woodcuts. 19429

De L'Etat et du Sort des colonies. *See* [Sainte Croix (M. de)].

DELGADO Y BUENROSTRO (Ant.) Historias varias canonicas moralizadas en sermones. Predicados en las Indias de la Nueva España. *Puebla de Angeles.* 1693. Folio, 12 l., pp. 948, Table, 16 l. 19430

DELHARMS (R.) Discourse on the True Nature of Freedom and Slavery, delivered before the Washington Society of the New Jerusalem, in view of the 118th Anniversary of Washington's Birth. *Philadelphia.* 1850. 8vo, pp. 63. 19431

DELHINOR (E.) Die Entedeckung von Amerika. Ferdinand Cortez oder die Eroberung von Mexico. Nach den besten Quellen bearbeitet von E. Delhinor. *Prag: Sandtner.* 1843. 8vo. 24 Plates. 19432

Deliberation; or, the substance of what may be spoken in the ***** of ***** in the course of this month. Principal speakers L. C.—E. G.—E. S.—E. S.—L. L.—D. D.—D. B.—D. G.—E. S.—E. E.—B——s.—B. P.—B. S* A****. B. L*****, Ghost of Lord S—m—s. *Sold by D. Browne, Strand.* MDCCLXXIX. 8vo, pp. 23. J.C.B. 19433

A debate supposed to have taken place in the House of Lords, on which occasion the ghost of Lord Somers appears, and advises their lordships to "drop all interested and party attachments, and join with unanimity to advance the glory and reputation of their native country."

DELIGNE. L'Intérêt français dans la Plata. [Signé Deligne.] *Paris: imp. de Chaix.* 1851. 8vo. 19434

Extracted from the "Assemblée nationale," 16 fév., 1851.

The Delirium of my Childhood: a Foresight in 1819 of Events witnessed by the same Person in the War of the Rebel-

lion. By an Officer of the U. S. Army. *New York: American News Company.* 1866. 12mo, pp. 24. 19435

De L'Isle *and* Del' Isle (G.) *See* Isle (G. del').

DELITSCH (O.) Westindien und die Südpolar-Länder geographisch und statistisch bearbeitet. *Leipzig: Hinrichs' Verlag.* 1871. 8vo, pp. viii, 310. 19436

Reprinted from Stein's "Handbuch der Geog. u. Statistik."

DELL (W.) Christ's Spirit A Christian's Strength, or A Plain Discovery of the Mighty and Invincible Power, that all Believers receive through the Gift of the Spirit. First held Forth in Two Sermons, or Acts i, viii. and after Published for the Instruction and Use of those that are Spiritual. Anno MDCXLV. By William Dell, Minister of the Gospel of Jesus Christ, at Yelden in the County of Bedford. *Germantown: Printed by Christopher Sower.* 1760. 8vo, Title, 1 l., pp. 75–168.

DELL. The Doctrine of Baptisms, Reduced from its Ancient and Modern Corruptions; And restored to its Primitive Soundness and Integrity: According to the Word of Truth; the Substance of Faith, and the Nature of Christ's Kingdom. By William Dell, Minister of the Gospel of Gonvil and Caius College, in Cambridge. The Fifth Edition. *London, Printed; Philadelphia: Reprinted by B. Franklin and D. Hall.* 1759. 8vo, pp. 43. P. 19438

DELL. The Trial of Spirits both in Teachers and Hearers, wherein is held forth The Clear Discovery and certain Downfall of the Carnal and Antichristian Clergy of these Nations, etc. By William Dell. *London: first printed in the Year* 1666. *Philadelphia: Reprinted by B. Franklin and D. Hall.* MDCCLX. 8vo, pp. 55. 19439

According to Joseph Smith's catalogue, it was first printed in 1653. These are introduced here because printed by Benjamin Franklin.

Della Chiesa Cattolica negli Stati Uniti d'America. Memoria compilata da un Membro della Societa Leopoldina. *Verona.* 835. 8vo. 19440

DELLET (*Mr.*) Remarks of Mr. Dellet, of Alabama, on the Civil and Diplomatic Appropriation Bill, delivered ... in the H. of R., April 25 and 27, 1840. *Washington: Gales and Seaton.* 1840. 8vo, pp. 31. 19441

DELLEVILLE (Philippes). Opinion prononcée dans la séance du 11 prairial an v, sur les troubles et les désastres de Saint Domingue. *Paris: De l'imprimerie nationale. An* v. [1797.] 8vo, pp. 18. J.C.B. 19442

DELLMANN (Fr.) Briefe der nach Amerika ausgewanderten Familie Steines. Für die Verwandten, Freunde und Bekannten der Ausgewanderten ... Briefe aus Bremen, Baltimore, und St. Louis nebst Anhange. *Wesel: Becker.* 1835. 8vo.

DELLON (C.) Relation d'un Voyage fait aux Indes Orientales. 1685. 2 vols., 12mo. 19444

Pages 126–157 give a description of Brazil, where the author stayed on his homeward voyage.

DELLON. Voyages et relation de l'inquisition de Goa augmenté de plusieurs pièces curieuses et l'Histoire des Dieux qu'adorent les gentils des Indes. *Col.* 1709. 2 vols., 8vo. 19445

Pages 154–196, of Vol. II., relate to Brazil; also the following:

DELLON. Reise door Indien met een Tractaat van de bysondere ziekten, welke in d'Oostersche landen vallen. Uit het fransch door W. Calebius. *Utrecht.* 1687. 4to. 19446

DELLON. A Voyage to the East Indies; giving an Account or the Isle of Madagascar and Mascareigne, of Suratte, the Coast of Malabar, of Goa, Gameron, Ormus, and the Coast of Brasil. By Monsieur Dellon, M.D. To which is annexed a Supplement taken out of Monsieur de Rennefort's History ... translated from the French. [By T. Crull.] *London.* 1698. 8vo, pp. 248.

DELMAR (A.) Gold Money and Paper Money. By Alexander Delmar. *New York: Anson D. F. Randolph.* 8vo, pp. 42.

DELMAR. The Great Paper Bubble; or, the Coming Financial Explosion. By Alex. Delmar. ... *New York: Office of the "Metropolitan Record."* 1864. 12mo, pp, 94. 19449

Also: International Almanac for 1866; or, Hand-Book of Geographical [etc.] Statistics, relating to every Country. *New York.* 1866. 8vo, pp. 128.

DELMAR. The Life of George B. McClellan. *New York: T. R. Dawley.* 1864. 12mo, pp. 109. 19450

DELMAR. Statistics of the United States, compiled under the Authority of the Secretary of the Treasury, in compliance with the Request of the Secretary of State, for Transmission to

the U. S. Commissioner General for the "Paris Exposition" of 1867, by Alexander Delmar ... *Washington: Treas. Dept.* 1867. 8vo, pp. 72. 19451

DELMONTE Y TEJADA (A.) Historia de Santo Domingo, desde su desubrimiento hasta nuestros dias, por Antonio Delmonte y Tejada. Tomo I. *Habana.* 1853. 8vo, pp. xxii, 600. 19452

No more published.

[DELMOTTE (Henri Florent).] Voyage pittoresque et industriel dans le Paraguay-roux et la Palingénésie Australe. Par Tridace-Nafé-Théobrôme de Kaout't 'Chouk, gentilhomme breton. *Mons. E. Hoyois-Derely.* [1835.] 8vo, pp. 48. 19453

DEL NINO JESUS (P. A.) Oracion funebre del E. S. Don Augustin de Jturbide. *Puebla.* 1859. 4to, 8 l. 19454

DELORME (E. N.) Les Etats Unis et l'Europe. *See* Nouette-Delorme (E.)

DELPHINE, *pseudonym.* Solon, or the Rebellion of '61. A Domestic and Political Tragedy. By Delphine. *Chicago: S. P. Rounds.* 1862. 8vo, pp. 74. 19455

Del Primo Scopritore del Continente del Nuovo Mondo. *See* [Napione (G. F. G.)]

DEL RIO. *See* Rio (Antonio del).

DELTA, *pseudonym.* Letter from Delta to Senex, containing some Observations and Strictures of a Late Manifesto published in the Newspapers, in a Sinister Form of an Address from a Junto of Members of the Provincial Parliament of Lower Canada to their Constituents, to which is added an Appendix, consisting of the Speech of His Excellency the Governor in Chief on proroguing the Last Session of Provincial Parliament, and the said Manifesto. *Montreal.* 1827. pp. 136. 19456

DELTA, *pseudonym.* *See* [Deane (Charles)], No. 19046.

Delusion; or the Witch of New England. *Boston: Hilliard, Gray, and Company.* 1840. 16mo, pp. iv, 160. H. 19457

The Delusive and Dangerous Principles of the Minority Exposed and Refuted, in a Letter to Lord North. By a Friend to the Public. *London.* 1778. 8vo. 19458

DEMARCHAIS. Voyage en Guinée, Isles voisines, et à Cayenne, fait en 1725, 1726 et 1727. Contenant une description très-exacte et très-étenduë de ces païs, et du commerce qui s'y fait. *Amsterdam.* 1731. 4 vols., 12mo. Maps and Plates.

DEMAREST (D. D.) History and Characteristics of the Reformed Protestant Dutch Church. By David D. Demarest ... Second Edition. *New York: Board of Publication of the Reformed Protestant Dutch Church.* 1856. 12mo, pp. xxviii, 221, Errata, 1 slip. 8 Plates. C. 19460

Also: "The Manly, Independent Thinker," Address by David D. Demarest. 1855. 8vo.

DEMAREST (J.) The Present Duty of American Christians. A Sermon preached in ... Hackensack, N. J., ... July 7th, 1861. By Rev. James Demarest, Jr., Pastor. ... *New-York: John A. Gray, Printer.* 1861. 8vo, pp. 15. 19461

DEMAREST. Thanksgiving Sermon. A Sermon preached ... Hackensack, N. J., on Thanksgiving Morning, Nov. 28, 1861. By Rev. James Demarest, Jr., Pastor. *Hackensack: printed at the Office of the Bergen County Patriot.* 1861. 8vo, pp. 16.

DEMARTRAY (A.), *and* ROUHAND (P.) Coup d'Oeil sur la Republique de l'Amérique Centrale et principalement des Etats de Nicaragua et Costa Rica. Par MM. Demartray et Rouhand. *Paris: Crapelet.* 1832. 4to. Map. 19463

DEMARTRAY *and* ROUHAND. Opusculo sobre la Republica de Contro-America, y particularmente sobre les Estados de Nicaragua y Costa Rica, con un Mapa de ambos estados, publiconte Don Alonzo Demartray y Don Pedro Rouhand. *Paris.* 1833. 8vo, pp. 16. Map. 19464

DEMBY (J. W.) The War in Arkansas, or a Treatise on the Great Rebellion of 1861 ... . By J. W. Demby. *Little Rock, Ark.* 1864. 16mo, pp. 64. H. 19465

DEMERARA. The Demerara & Essequibo Vade-Mecum; containing the Principal Laws and Regulations of the United Colony, and A Variety of Miscellaneous Articles of Local Importance. *Georgetown: A. Stevenson.* 1825. 12mo, pp. xxiv, 311. BA. 19466

Minutes of evidence in the matter of the Demerara and Berbice Manumission Order in Council. [*London.*] 1827. Folio. (Parl. doc.) 19467

Observations on the Demerara Memorial. *London.* 1828. 8vo. 19468

Demerara after Fifteen Years of Freedom. By a Landowner. *London.* 1853. 8vo, pp. 120. 19469

Return respecting the Sanitary Condition of Demerara Barracks, 1862. 19470

Demersay (A.) Étude économique sur le maté ou thé du Paraguay. Par le docteur Alfred Demersay, chargé de missions scientifiques dans l'Amérique du Sud ... . *Paris: Ve Bouchard-Huzard.* 1867. 8vo, pp. 51. 19471

Demersay (L. A.) Études économiques sur l'Amérique méridionale. Du tabac au Paraguay. Culture, consommation et commerce. Avec une Lettre sur l'introduction du tabac en France, par M. Ferdinand Denis. *Paris: Guillaumin.* 1851. 8vo. Plates. 19472

Also on large paper. In this work Denis shows that Thoret, and not Nicot, first introduced tobacco into France.

Demersay. Histoire physique, économique et politique du Paraguay et des établissements des jésuites; accompagnée d'un atlas, de pièces justificatives et d'une bibliographie. Par L. Alfred Demersay ... . *Paris: L. Hachette et Cie.* 1860–1865. 2 vols., 8vo, pp. lxiv, 486; 488. Atlas of 14 colored Plates and 2 Maps. 19473

Demersay. Une Mission géographique dans les archives d'Espagne et de Portugal, 1862–1863. Fragments lus à la Société de géographie dans sa séance générale du 15 avril 1864. Par M. Alfred Demersay ... . *Paris: L. Hachette et Cie.* 1864. 8vo, pp. 45. 19474

Demetz *and* Blouet (A.) Rapports à M. le comte de Montalivet, pair de France, ministre ... de l'intérieur, sur les pénitenciers des États-Unis. Par M. Demetz ... et par M. Abel Blouet ... . *Paris: imprimerie royale.* 1837. Folio, 2 l., pp. 144, 114, (1). 45 Plates. H. + *Paris: imp. royale.* 1839. Folio. 45 Plates. 19475

Démeunier (Jean Nicolas). L'Amérique indépendante, Ou les différentes Constitutions des treize provinces qui se sont érigées en républiques, sous le nom d' États-Unis de l'Amérique. Avec un précis de l'histoire de chaque province, & des remarques sur les Constitutions, la population, les finances & l'état dans

lequel les provinces se trouvent actuellement. Par M. Demeunier ... . *Gand: P. F. de Goesin.* M DCC XC. 3 vols., 8vo, Title, pp. 231, Map; Title, pp. 196; Title, pp. 226, (4). J.C.B.

Démeunier. Essai sur les États-Unis. Par M. Démeunier, Secrètaire ordinaire de Monsieur, Frère du Roi, & Censeur royal. *Paris: Laporte.* M DCC LXXXVI. 4to, Title, pp. 89. BA., C.

"Also in the 'Encyclopédie méthodique.'" — Quérard.

Démeunier. Supplément ou suite aux rémarques de Mr. Démeunier, sur la constitution et les etats de Nouvelle-Yorck et Virginie, Qui ne se trouvnt point dans les tròis volumes de l'Amérique indépendante. *Gand: P. F. de Goesin.* M DCC XCI. 8vo, Title, pp. 120. J.C.B. 19478

Demeur (Adolphe Louis Joseph). L'Expedition belge au Mexique. Appel aux chambres. *Bruxelles, Lacroix, Verbœckhoven et Cie.* 1864. 8vo. 19479

Deming (E.) Address at the First Annual Exhibition of the Philomothean Society of Wabash College. *Crawfordsville, Ind.* 1835. 12mo. 19480

Deming (H. C.) Eulogy on Abraham Lincoln, by Henry Champion Deming, before the General Assembly of Connecticut ... June 8th, 1865. *Hartford: A. N. Clark & Co., State Printers.* 1865. 8vo, pp. 58. H. 19481

Deming. The Life of Ulysses S. Grant. By H. C. Deming. *Hartford: S. S. Scranton & Co.* 1868. 8vo, pp. 533. Portrait. B. 19482

Deming. An Oration upon the Life and Services of Gen. David Wooster, delivered at Danbury, April 27th, 1854, when a Monument was erected to his Memory. ... *Hartford.* 1854. 8vo, pp. 60. S. 19483

Also: Insurgent Relations and Insurgent Animus. A Speech ... on the President's Message, delivered ... January 19, 1866. [*Washington.* 1866.] 8vo, pp. 8. H. — Nothing's been done." Speech ... at the Cooper Institute, New York, September 27th, 1864. [*New York.* 1864.] 8vo, pp. 8. H. — Our Decisive Battle. Speech delivered in the Town Hall, at Suffield, Conn., Fast Day, April 14, 1865. Broadside. — Speech ... on the President's Plan of State Renovation ... February 27th, 1864. *Washington.* 1864. 8vo, pp. 16. H.

Deming (L.) Catalogue of the Principal Officers of Vermont, as connected with its Political History, from 1778 to 1851, with some Biographical Notices, &c. By Leonard Dem-

ing, Middlebury, Vt. ... *Middlebury: the Author.* 1851. 8vo, pp. 119, (1). + Appendix. [Containing Notices of each Town. *Middlebury: Printed by Justice Cobb.* 1852.] 8vo, pp. 121–216.

Demme (Wilhelm Ludwig). Das Buch der Verbrechen. Das interessanteste aus älterer, neuerer und neuester Zeit der Länder dies- und jenseits des Oceans. Ein Volksbuch. + Neue Folge. *Leipzig: Arnold.* 1853, 54. + Zweite Ausgabe, mit Illustrationen. [*Ibid.*] 1854–8. 8vo. 19485

Demmin (A.) Histoire de la céramique en planches phototypiques inaltérables, avec texte explicatif. Par Auguste Demmin. L'Asie, l'Amérique ... par ordre chronologique. ... *Paris: Ve J. Renouard.* 1868. Folio. 19486

Democracy, an Epic Poem. *See* [Livingston (Brockholst)].

Democracy Displayed, or the Democrat's Handbook. *Philadelphia.* 1848. 12mo. 19487

Democracy of Christianity; or, an Analysis of the Bible and its Doctrines in their Relation to the Principle of Democracy. By a Citizen of the United States. *New York.* 1849. 2 vols., 12mo. 19488

Democracy Unveiled. *See* [Fessenden (T. G.)]

An Address to the Democracy of the United States, on the Duty of the Democratic Party, at this Crisis. [n. p. 1860.] 8vo, pp. 26. 19489

Address to the Democracy and the People of the United States, by the National Democratic Executive Committee. Breckenridge and Lane Campaign Documents, No. 15. [*Washington.* 1860.] 8vo, pp. 8. H. 19490

Also: Address to the Democracy and the People of the United States, by the National Democratic Executive Committee. *Washington: McGill & Witherow.* 1860. 8vo, pp. 16. — To the Democracy of the Border State. [n. p. n. d.] 8vo, pp. 3.

To the Democracy of the United States. (Address dated) Washington City, D. C., July 1860. (Signed) Miles Taylor & 2 others, Democratic National Executive Committee. *Baltimore: Printed by Murphy & Co.* [1860.] 8vo, pp. 16. H.

The Democracy; or, the Fundamental Principles of Democracy, as established by the Constitution of the United States. By a Citizen of the United States. *Boston: printed by Wm. M. Kendall.* 1864. 12mo, pp. 12. H. 19492

The Democrat; or Intrigues and Adventures of Jean le Noir, from his Enlistment as a Drummer in General Rochambeau's Army, his Arrival in Boston, &c. *New York.* 1795. 19493

El Demócrata. Periodico politico, literario y comercial. No. 1–103. *Mexico.* 1850. (All published.) 19494

The Democratiad: a Poem, in retaliation for the "Philadelphia Jockey Club." *See* [Cobbett (W.)], Vol. IV., No. 13879.

Democratic Age; Statesmanship, Science, Art, Literature, and Progress. Edited by C. Edwards Lester. Vol. I. *New York.* 1859. 8vo. C. 19495

The Democratic Almanac and Political Compendium for 1868. *New York: Van Evrie, Horton & Co.* 12mo, pp. 82. + 1869. 12mo. 19496

The Democratic and Republican Platforms. [n. p. 1860.] 8vo, pp. 27. 19497

A Democratic Catechism: containing the Self-Evident and Fundamental Principles of Democracy. ... *Providence: B. T. Albro, Printer.* 1846. 12mo, pp. 20. 19498

Democratic Catechism of Negro Equality, July 4th, 1863. 8vo, 1 leaf. 19499

Democratic Convention. Proceedings of the National Democratic Convention, Convened at Charleston, S. C., April 23, 1860. *Washington.* 1860. 8vo, pp. 54. 19500

Democratic Conventions. *See* under the name of the State.

Democratic Documents for the Campaign, and Facts for the People. *Frankfort, Ky.* 1868. 8vo. 19501

Democratic Falsehoods exposed. Facts for the People. *Washington: Gibson Brothers, Printers.* [1868.] 8vo, pp. 4. H.

The Democratic Gospel of Peace, according to St. Tammany. *New York: Published for the Author.* 1863. 12mo, pp. 36.

The Democratic Judge. *See* [Cobbett (W.)], Vol. IV., No. 13880.

Democratic League. Circular. *New York. June,* 1862. 4to, pp. 4. 19504

This circular was the first announcement of the formation and objects of the "Democratic League," which is claimed to be the first of all the "Leagues" formed for sustaining the government against the "Confederate" treason. Signed by C. P. Kirkland, Thomas Ewbank, and others.

Democratic League. ... The Slaveholders' Conspiracy, depicted by Southern Loyalists in its Treason against Democratic Principles, as well as against the National Union; showing a Contest of Slavery and Nobility versus Free Government. [*New York.* 1864.] 8vo, pp. 16. H. 19505

Democratic National Convention at Baltimore, June, 1852. Proceedings. *Washington, D. C.* 1852. 8vo, pp. 44. + [Another Report.] 8vo, pp. 78. S. 19506

Democratic Opinions on Slavery! 1776–1863. [n. p. n. d.] 8vo, pp. 8. H. 19507

Democratic Party. The Record of 1860–1865. I. Secession and Reconstruction. II. Opposition. *Philadelphia.* 8vo, pp. 39. 19508

Democratic Party. Words of Counsel to Men of Business. By a Man of Business. [n. p.] 1856. 8vo, pp. 21. M. 19509

The Democratic Platform. General McClellan's Letter of Acceptance. [n. p. n. d.] 8vo, pp. 7, (1). H. 19510

Democratic Platform. People's Resolutions. A Republican Form of Government: Definition, Manhood Suffrage. *New York: C. S. Westcott & Co.* 1865. 8vo, pp. 15. 19511

Democratic Presidential Campaign Songster, No. 1. McClellan and Pendleton. *New York: J. F. Feeks.* [1864.] 16mo, pp. 72. 19512

Democratic Protests against the Lecompton Fraud. [*Washington.* 1858.] 8vo, pp. 8. H. 19513

The Democratic Reformer. Embodying Documents concerning Governmental Reformation in New York. *Albany.* 1844. 8vo. 19514

The Democratic Review. *See* United States Magazine.

Democratic Statesmen and Generals to the Loyal Sons of the Union. Views of Generals Grant, Sherman, Dix, Wood, Butler, Edward Everett, J. A. Griswold, etc. *Albany: Weed, Parsons & Co.* 1864. 8vo, pp. 14. 19515

The Democratic Text Book being A Compendium of the Principles of the Democratic Party. *Boston: Redding & Co.* 1848. 12mo, pp. 72. 19516

The Democratic Times. Chapter I. A Dishonorable Peace with Rebellion! The Dissolution of the Union. Perpetual War ending in Anarchy or Military Despotism, etc. [n. p. n. d.] 8vo, pp. 4. 19517

Democraticus, *pseudonym.* Jeffersoniad; or, an Echo to the Groans of an Expiring Faction. By Democraticus. [n. p.] 1801. 12mo. 19518

Demond (C.) An Address, delivered before the Society of Alumni of Williams College, at Williamstown, Mass., August 1, 1865. By Charles Demond. *Boston: Press of T. R. Marvin & Son.* 1865. 8vo, pp. 39. H. 19519

[Demontézon.] Mission de Cayenne et de la Guyane Française, avec une carte géographique. *Paris.* 1857. 8vo and 12mo. 19520

The Demoralizing Doctrines and Disloyal Teachings of the Mormon Hierarchy. The Condition of Women in Polygamy. *New York.* 1866. 8vo, pp. 18. H. 19521

The Demos in Council: or 'Bijah in Pandemonium. Being a Sweep of the Lyre In close Imitation of Milton. ... *Boston: Printed by James Cutler. April,* 1799. 8vo, pp. 16. BA., H.

In this piece, 'Bijah is said to signify S. Adams; Honee, Austin; Junius, Jarvis; Tummas, Tho. Edwards; Mozard, Dr. Linnedard (?); Niffey N—, Noyes; Dr. V—, Dr. Vinal; Dr. H—, Dr. Hall; Gov. H—, Gov. Heath (Hancock?).

Demousseaux de Givré (G.) Discours de M. Gaston Demousseaux de Givré sur la constitution des États-Unis, et notamment sur la clause par la quelle elle tolère l'esclavage ... . *Paris: Retaux.* 1868. 8vo, pp. 56. 19523

Dempsey (J. M.) Our Ocean Highway: a Condensed Universal Route Book. *London.* 1870 [1869]. 16mo. B. 19524

Demun (J. J.) Le Sort du Commerce Français, ou Considérations pressantes sur l'importance de l'isle Saint Domingue. Par J. J. Demun. *Paris: Guerbart. An IV.* [1796.] 8vo, pp. 19. J.C.B. 19525

Demund (I. S.) American Liberty. Fourth of July. By Isaac S. Demund. *New York: for the Author.* 1855. 8vo, pp. 16. 19526

Demund. Lamentation on the Death of Abraham Lincoln,

President of the United States. Dy Isaac S. Demund. May 1865. *New York: John A. Gray & Green.* 1865. 8vo, pp. 15.

Also: Liberty Defended. Fourth of July, to the Patriotic Citizens of Pompton Plains. The Oration, by Isaac S. Demund. *New York: John H. Gray.* 1851. 8vo, pp. 20. — Subordination to Government the Salvation of our Country. ... Discourse ... . *Lancaster: Pearsol & Geist, Printers.* 1861. 8vo, pp. 15.

Dénain (A.) Considérations sur les Intérêts Politiques et Commerciaux qui se rattachent à l'Isthme de Panama, et aux différents isthmes de l'Amérique Centrale. Relation directe de ces isthmes avec celui de Suez. *Paris.* 1845. 8vo. C. 19528

Dénain. Ensayo sobre los intereses politicos i commerciales del Istmo del Panama por A. Dénain. ... *Panama: José Maria Bermudez.* 1844. 4to, pp. 56. H. 19529

Denancé (L. V.) Aventures d'une famille allemande émigrée en Amérique. Par L. V. Denance. *Limoges et Lille: Ardant frères.* 1866. 12mo, pp. 190. 19530

Denancé. La Famille de Martel le planteur; épisode de la révolution de Saint-Domingue. *Limoges et Lisle: Ardant frères.* 1865. 12mo, pp. 124. Illustr. + 1867. 19531

Denancé. Les deux chasseurs noirs dans les forêts de l'Amérique. Par L. V. Denancé. *Limoges et Lisle: Martial Ardant frères.* 186–. 12mo, pp. 156. + 1867. 19532

Denancé. Makandal ou le noir marron. Par L. V. Denancé. *Limoges et Lisle: Martial Ardant frères.* 1865. 12mo, pp. 120. + 1867. + 1869. 19533

Denancé. Voyages dans les mers du Sud et dans l'Océanie, ou Aventures du chevalier Dumirail et d'Auguste Martel. *Limoges et Lisle: Martial Ardant frères.* 1865. 12mo, pp. 128. Illustr. + 1867. 19534

Denchausse. Extrait de mes tablettes d'outre-mer, ou Mémoire sur des matériaux pour servir à l'histoire, la statistique et la topographie médicales de la ville de San-Luis-Potosi et ses environs, dans la république Mexicaine ... par le docteur Dencausse. *Toulouse: imp. de A. Labouisse. Rochefort.* 1851. 8vo.

Dencke (C. F.) *See* "Delaware," No. 19377.

Denio (H.), *and* O'Connor (C.) Opinions as to the Constitutionality of transferring Funds of Depositors in Savings Banks to the State ... *New-York.* 1853. 8vo. 19536

Denis (A.) Tammany Hall, and other Miscellaneous Poems, by Alexander Denis. *New York.* 1847. BM. 19537

Denis (Alexandre). L'Oncle d'Amérique; Scènes. *Paris: Douniol.* 1856. 8vo. 19538

Denis (E.) Guyana. Ein Gemälde der Entdeckung und Colonisirung, des jetzigen natürlichen und politischen Zustandes, und der verschiedenen Bewohner dieses Theils von Südamerika, von Ed. Denis. Aus dem Französischen. *Pesth: Hartleben.* 1824. 12mo. (Miniaturgemälde, 37.) 19539

Denis (Jean F.) Les Antilles. Par M. Ferdinand Denis. *Paris: Didot.* 8vo. 28 Plates, and Map. 19540

Denis. Brésil, par M. Ferdinand Denis, Colombie et Guyanes, par M. C. Famin. *Paris: Firmin Didot frères.* M DCCCXXXVII. 8vo, 2 l., pp. 384, 32, 2 l. BA. + *Paris: Didot.* 1846. 8vo, pp. 384, 32. 100 Plates and 2 Maps. 19541

Denis (F.) Brasilien. Deutsch von C. A. Mebold. *Stuttgart.* 1836–38. 8vo. C. 19542

Denis. Geschichte und Beschreibung von Brasilien und Guyana. Aus dem Französischen. Mit 100 Kupfern und 2 Karten. *Stuttgart: Schweizerbarts Verlagshandlung.* 1839. 8vo.

Reprinted from the "Welt. Gemälde-Gallerie."

Denis. Il Brasile di Ferdinando Denis. Colombia e Gujane di C. Famin, traduzione di A. F. Falconetti adorna di centodue incisioni. *Venezia.* 1838. 4to. 19544

Denis. Buénos-Ayres et le Paraguay; histoire, mœurs. usages et coutumes des habitants de cette partie de l'Amérique, Par F. Denis. *Paris: Nepveu.* 1823. 2 vols., 18mo, pp. 211; 199. 18 Plates. 19545

Denis. La Guyane, ou histoire, mœurs, usages et coutumes des habitants de cette partie de l'Amérique, par F. Denis. *Paris.* 1823. 2 vols., 18mo. 16 Plates. 19546

Denis. Histoire géographique du Brésil. *Paris: imp. de Casimir.* 1833. 18mo. + 1835. 18mo. 19547

Denis. Historische Schilderungen interessanter Reiseabentheuer, Volksgebräuche und Naturschönheiten in allen Ländern. ... Aus dem Französischen. *Stuttgart: Scheible.* 1834. 12mo.

Denis. Ismael ben Kaïzar, ou la découverte du Nouveau

Monde. Roman historique. Par Ferdinand Denis. ... *Paris: Charles Gosselin.* M DCCC XXIX. 5 vols., 18mo. + Seconde édition. *Paris.* [*Ibid.*] 19549

"Columbus is the hero of this very curious historical novel. M. Denis has given an exceedingly interesting account of Columbus as a bookseller, in Vol. I., Chap. II."

DENIS. Les navigateurs, ou Choix de voyages anciens et modernes, recueillis par M. F. Denis. *Paris: Louis Janet.* 1833. 18mo. 4 Engravings. 19550

DENIS. Résumé de l'histoire de Buénos-Ayres, du Paraguay et des provinces de la Plata; suivi du Résumé de l'histoire du Chili, avec des notes. *Paris: Lecointe et Durey.* 1827. 18mo, pp. 642. 19551

DENIS. Résumé de l'histoire du Brésil, suivi du Résumé de l'histoire de la Guyane. *Paris: Lecointe et Durey.* 1825. 18mo. + Seconde édition. [*Ibid.*] 1825. 18mo. 19552

DENIS. Résumé de l'histoire littéraire du Portugal, suivi du Résumé de l'histoire littéraire du Brésil. Par Ferdinand Denis. *Paris: Lecointe et Durey.* 1826. 16mo, pp. 642. 19553

DENIS. Robinson Crusoé, par Daniel de Foë. Restitution et traduction nouvelle. Illustré de ... Notices sur le matelot Selkirk et sur Saint-Hyacinth, d'une recherche sur l'île de Juan-Fernandez, et sur les Caraïbes et les Puelches, par F. Denis et d'un dissertation ... . *Paris: Francisque Borel; Astoin; Biais.* 1835. 2 vols., 8vo. 19554

DENIS. Scènes de la nature sous les tropiques, et de leur influence sur la poésie; suivies de Camoëns et Joze India. *Paris: L. Janet.* 1824. 8vo. 19555

DENIS. Une fête brésilienne, célébrée à Rouen en 1550; Suivie d'un fragment du XVIe siècle, roulant sur la théogonie des anciens peuples du Brésil et des poésies en langue tupique de Christovam Valente. Par F. Denis. *Paris: Aillaud.* 1850. 8vo. Plate. 19556

This is an account of a singular dramatic representation, performed before Henry IV. of France, and Mary de Medicis, by 50 Brazilians and 250 Norman sailors; and is in review of "La Deduction du sumptueux ordre, plaisantz spectacles et magnifiques Theatre dresses par les Citoiens de Rouen, etc. *Rouen.* 1551." It is followed by "Documens et Notes Bibliographiques," treating of the ancient language, music (with specimens), and manners of the Brazilians; and works written upon the country and the language, the first discoverers, etc. The Brazilian Theogony, "fragment du XVIe Siècle," and "Poëmas Brasilicos do padre Christovâo Valente," conclude this interesting work.

DENIS (F.), *and* CHAUVIN (V.) De ware Robinson. Naar het Fransch, door S. J. van den Bergh. No. 3. De wilde van Aveyron en de Robinsons van de eilanden Tristan da Cunha en Trinidad. *Leiden: D. Noothoven van Goor.* 1864. 8vo, pp. 50. 6 colored Lithographs. + No. 6. Uit de Braziliaansche bosschen. Margaretha Roberval op het eiland la Demoiselle en andere hoogst belangrijke avonturen te land en ter zee. [*Ibid.*] 1865. 8vo, pp. 82. 10 colored Lithographs. 19557

Denis McArthy; or, A Home in New Brunswick. *London: Macintosh.* 1867. 18mo. 19558

DENISON (A. C.) ... A Sermon ... at the Funeral of Rev. Hervey Talcott, late Pastor of the First Church in Portland, Conn. by Rev. Andrew [Clark] Denison ... . *Middletown: Charles H. Pelton, Printer.* 1866. 8vo, pp. 13, (1). H. 19559

DENISON (C. Wheeler.) The American Village, and other Poems. By Charles W. Denison. ... *Boston: Henry B. Skinner & Co.* 1845. 12mo, pp. 143. H. 19560

DENISON. Illustrated Life, Campaigns and Public Services of Philip H. Sheridan. (Major-General ... .) ... By C. W. Denison. ... *Philadelphia: T. B. Peterson & Brothers.* 1865. 12mo, pp. 17–197. C., H. 19561

DENISON. Winfield [S. Hancock], the Lawyer's Son, and how he became a Major General. *Philadelphia: Ashmead & Evans.* 1865. 12mo, pp. 323. 4 Plates. 19562

Also: The American Village, and other Poems. *Boston.* 1845. — Defence of Rev. Charles W. Denison from the Slanders of the Boston Baptist Bethel Society, and First Baptist Church: showing the interest taken in the affair by "Elder Nathaniel Culver." *Boston.* 1846. 8vo, pp. 61.

DENISON (D.) Irenicon, | or a | Salve | For New-England's Sore. | By Major Daniel Denison. | [*Boston:*] *Printed in the Year.* 1684. | 24mo, 4 l., pp. 177–218. B., H., W. 19563

This was published at the end of W. Hubbard's "Benefit of a Well-Ordered Conversation," with continuous paging, but having its own title-page.

DENISON (F.) Notes on the Baptists and their Principles, in Norwich, Conn., from the Settlement of the Town to 1850. By Rev. Frederick Denison, A.M. *Norwich.* 1857. 12mo, pp. 91.

[DENISON (George T.)] Canada: Is she Prepared for War? or a few Remarks on the State of her Defences. By a Native Canadian. *Toronto.* 1861. 8vo, pp. 24. 19565

DENISON. The Fenian Raid on Fort Erie: with an Account of the Battle of Ridgeway, June, 1866. By Major George T. Denison, Jun., commanding "the Governor-General's Body Guard," Upper Canada. Third Edition, with Map and Plan. *Toronto.* 1866. 8vo, pp. 92. 19566

DENISON. Manual of Outpost Duties, with Instructions for the Defence of Houses, Villages, Bridges, &c., for the Use of the Volunteers. *Toronto.* 1866. 12mo, pp. 61. 19567

DENISON. Modern Cavalry: ... With an Appendix containing Letters from Generals Fitzhugh Lee, Stephen D. Lee, and I. L. Rosser, of the Confederate States' Cavalry, ... *London: T. Bosworth.* 1868. 8vo, pp. xx, 376. 2 Plates and 2 Maps.

DENISON. The National Defences; or Observations on the best Defensive Force for Canada. *Toronto.* 1861. 8vo, pp. 32.

[DENISON.] A Review of the Militia Policy of the present Administration. By Junius, Jr. *Hamilton.* 1863. 8vo, pp. 15.

DENISON (H. M.) Address on the Advantages and Disadvantages to America in being Destitute of a Remote History, delivered before the Associated Alumni of Dickinson College. By Rev. Henry Mandeville Denison, of Virginia, July 13, 1853. *New York: J. H. Watson.* 1853. 8vo, pp. 32. 19571

DENISON (John L.) An Illustrated History of the New World: containing a general History of all the various Nations, States, and Republics of the Western Continent, comprising a Complete History of the United States to the Present Time. *Norwich* [*Conn.*]: *H. Bill.* 1868. 8vo, pp. 868. 33 Plates. C.

DENISON (J.) A Funeral Oration, on the Death of Simeon Bristol, Of New-Haven; A Sophimore in Yale-College: ... Delivered ... July 11, 1782. By Joseph Denison, ... *New-Haven: Printed by T. & S. Green.* M,DCC,LXXXIII. 12mo, pp. 15. 19573

DENISON (Mary A.) Old Hepsy. By Mrs. C. W. Denison. ... *New York: A. B. Burdick.* 1858. 8vo, pp. 459. B., H.

A tale of the South. Also: Florida; or, The Iron Will. A Story ... . *New York and London: Beadle.* [1861.] 16mo.

DENISON UNIVERSITY, *Ohio.* Catalogue of the Officers and Students for 1864, '65. 8vo. Continued. 19575

Denkschrift über die Nothwendigkeit der Beseitigung der Sklaverei in Nordamerika und über die geeignetsten Mittel zu diesem Zweck und eventualiter zur Ausfuhr der Schwarzen. [n. p. 186–.] Folio, pp. xii. H. 19576

Denkschriften der russichen geographischen Gesellschaft zu St. Petersburgh. *Weimar.* 1849. 4 Maps. 19577

This volume contains some very interesting treatises on the geography of Russian North America, illustrated by maps, Indian vocabularies, etc.

DENMAN (*Capt.*) The Slave Trade, the African Squadron, and Mr. Hutt's Committee. By the Hon. Capt. Denman, R. N. *London.* 1850. 8vo, pp. 56. 19578

Also: Practical Remarks on the Slave Trade, and on the Existing Treaties with Portugal. *London.* 1839. 8vo. — West India Interests, African Emigration, and Slave Trade. *London.* 1848. 8vo.

DENMAN (*Lord*). A Letter from Lord Denman to Lord Brougham on the Final Extinction of the Slave Trade. *London.* 1848. 8vo, pp. 78. P. 19579

DENMAN. Uncle Tom's Cabin, Bleak House, Slavery and the Slave Trade: Six Articles. By Lord Denman. Reprinted from "The Standard." With an Article containing Facts connected with Slavery, by Sir George Stephen. *London.* 1852. 12mo, pp. 52. 19580

Printed for private circulation.

DENNE (J.) Want of Universality no Just Objection to the Truth of the Christian Religion. Sermon before the Incorporated Society for the Propagation of the Gospel in Foreign Parts. By John, Archdeacon of Rochester. *London.* 1730. 4to. J.C.B., M. 19581

DENNETT (F.) The Voyages and Travels of Captains Parry, Franklin, Ross, and Mr. Belzoni, forming an Interesting History of the Manners, Customs, and Characters of Various Nations, visited by Enterprising Travellers. Selected by Captain Frederick Dennett. *London: J. Jaques and W. Wright.* 1826. 8vo, 2 l., pp. 682. 8 Plates. 19582

DENNIE (James). Remarks on Judge Thatcher's Sentence in the case of the Commonwealth vs. Dennie, with a Report of the Evidence. *Boston.* 1841. 8vo, pp. 32. 19583

DENNIE. Desultory Reflections on the New Political As-

pects of Public Affairs in the United States of America, since the commencement of the year 1799. *New York.* 1800. 8vo.

DENNIE (Joseph). The Lay Preacher; or Short Sermons for Idler Readers. *Walpole, New Hampshire.* 1796. 12mo, pp. 132. 19585

DENNIE. The Lay Preacher. By Joseph Dennie. Collected and arranged by John E. Hall. *Philadelphia.* 1816. 12mo, pp. 168. 19586

DENNIE. Spirit of the Farmers' Museum, and Lay Preachers' Gazette. J. Dennie, Editor. *Walpole, N. H.* 1801. 12mo.

DENNIS (John). Liberty Asserted. | A | Tragedy. | As it is Acted at the | New Theatre | in | Little Lincoln's Inn-Fields. | Written by Mr. Dennis. | *London: Printed for George Strahan at the Golden Ball, against the* | *Royal Exchange, in Cornhill; and Bernard Lintott at the* | *Middle-Temple-Gate in Fleetstreet.* 1704. | 4to, 7 l., pp. 64. 19588

The scene of this tragedy lies in Agnie, in Canada. The principal characters are Governor Frontenac (French), Governor Beaufort (English), and chiefs of the Iroquois Indians. Southerne, the dramatist, complimented the plot highly, and Betterton, one of the most distinguished actors of his day, took a prominent character in it.

DENNIS. Liberty Asserted. | A | Tragedy. | As it is Acted at the | New Theatre | in | Lincoln's-Inn-Fields. | Written by Mr. Dennis. | *London:* | *Printed for George Strahan at the Golden Ball, against the* | *Royal Exchange, in Cornhill; and Bernard Lintott at the* | *Middle-Temple-Gate in Fleetstreet.* 1704. | 4to, 8 l., pp. 68.

"These two editions are identical as far as page 25, but from thence to the end they differ, the preceeding being in fewer pages and with two or three more lines on a page." — STEVENS.

DENNIS (Jonas). The Character of the King [George III.]; a Sermon preached at Exeter on the 30th November, 1800. 8vo, pp. 14. 19590

DENNIS (R.) Report of the Trial of Richard Dennis the Younger, for the Murder of James Shaw. By S. C. Carpenter. *Charleston.* 1805. 8vo. BM. 19591

DENNIS (W. L.) An Oration delivered before the Authorities and Citizens of Newport, Rhode Island, July 4, 1865. By William L. Dennis. *Philadelphia: E. C. Mackley & Son.* 1865. 8vo, pp. 32. 19592

Relates to the rebellion of 1861–5.

DENNISON (W.), *and others.* The American Union Commission: Speeches of Hon. W. Dennison, Postmaster-General, Rev. J. P. Thompson, D.D., President of the Commission, Col. N. G. Taylor, of East Tennessee, Hon. J. R. Doolittle, U. S. Senate, Gen. J. A. Garfield, M. C., in the Hall of Representatives, Washington, Feb. 12, 1865. *New York: Sandford, Harroun & Co.* 1865. pp. 113. 19593

DENNISTON (Goldsmith). Agricultural Survey of the County of Steuben. By G. Denniston. *Albany.* 1862. 8vo. C. 1

Also: Survey of Orange County. From N. Y. State Agric. Trans. ... *Albany.* 1863. 8vo. S.

DENNY (A.) An Oration delivered at Worcester, Massachusetts, July 4, 1818 ... By Austin Denny. *Worcester. July,* 1818. 8vo. W. 19595

DENNY (E.) Military Journal of Major Ebenezer Denny, An Officer in the Revolutionary and Indian Wars. With an Introductory Memoir. By William H. Denny. *Philadelphia: J. B. Lippincott & Co., for the Historical Society of Pennsylvania.* 1859. Rl. 8vo, pp. 288. Portrait. 19596

Forms part of Vol. VII. of the "Memoirs of the Pa. Hist. Society." *See also* "Hist. Mag.," II. 95, and "Record of the Court at Upland."

DENNY (F. P.) On the Constitution of the Water of the Gulf Stream, compared with that of the Inside Reverse Current. ... By Francis P. Denny. ... . *Cambridge: Welch, Bigelow, & Co., Printers.* 1859. 8vo, pp. 11. H. 19597

Also: Poem ... before the Pickwick Club ... January 9, 1863. ... *Boston.* 1863. 8vo, pp. 8. H. (References to the war.) — Poem delivered before the Pickwick Club, Dorchester, ... January 12, 1866. By Francis P. Denny. [Eulogy of Pres. Lincoln.] *Boston.* 1866. 8vo, pp. 8. H.

DENNY (J.) A Narrative of Facts relative to the Tryal of Joe Denny a Free Coloured Man, for the Murder of John Stroud, a White-Man. At the Grand Sessions in the Island of Barbadoes, held Decembr 13th. 1796. And of a Conditional Pardon granted to the said Joe Denny, by Our Most Gracious Sovereign. *Barbadoes: Printed at the Office of Edw. Archer et Comp.* 1797. 4to 2 l., pp. 45. 19598

DENNY (John F.) An Essay on the Political Grade of the Free Colored Population, under the Constitution of the United States and the Constitution of Pennsylvania. 1836. 8vo.

DENNY (N. P.) Address delivered before the Worcester Agricultural Society, September 25, 1822 ... . By Nathaniel P.

Denny, Esq. ... *Worcester: printed by William Manning.* 8vo, pp. 24. H., W. 19600

DENNY (W. H.) Suc-co-tash. Written on the Occasion of the Centennial Celebration of the Evacuation of Fort Duquesne. By W. H. Denny. *Pittsburgh: W. S. Haven.* 1858. 18mo, pp. 24. 19601

DENNYS (N. B.) An Account of the Cruise of the St. George on the North American and West Indian Stations, during the years 1861–1862. *London.* 1863. 8vo. 19602

DENORES (Jason). Breve trattato del Mondo et delle sue parti semplici et miste. *Venetia.* 1571. 8vo. 19603

Also on large paper. This curious astronomical work was unknown to Lalande. Chapter seventeen contains a description of America.

DE NORMANDIE (J.) Christian Peace. A Discourse delivered on the occasion of the National and State Thanksgiving, November 24, 1864, at Portsmouth, New Hampshire. By Rev. James De Normandie ... . *Portsmouth: C. W. Brewster.* 1864. 8vo, pp. 14. H. 19604

DE NORMANDIE. The Lord reigneth: a Few Words on Sunday Morning, April 16th, 1865, after the Assassination of Abraham Lincoln. By James De Normandie, Minister of the South Parish, Portsmouth, N. H. [n. p. 1865.] 18mo, pp. 8.

DENSLOW (V. B.) Fremont and McClellan, their Political and Military Careers reviewed: ... By Van Buren Denslow. *Yonkers, N. Y.* 1862. 8vo, pp. 32. + Second Edition. *Yonkers, N. Y.* 1862. 8vo. pp. 32. H. 19606

DENSON (A. C.) Westmoreland: or, Secession Ferocity, at the breaking out of the Rebellion; "Southern Barbarism," minute men and citizens firing into the steamer Westmoreland, crowded with men, women and children, at Napoleon, Arkansas, in 1861. By A. C. Denson, of Memphis, Tennessee. *Saint Louis.* 1865. 8vo. 19607

DENSON (J.) A Wonderful and Horrible Thing is committed in the Land by Isaac Hillyard; to which is added the Chronicles of Andrew, containing an Accurate and Brief Account of Gen. Jackson's Victories in the South over the Creeks. Also, his Victories over the British at New Orleans. By Jesse Denson, D.D. *Hamilton, O.* 1822. 8vo. 19608

Title from W. Dodge's catalogue.

DENT (D.) Defence of Capt. Digby Dent, to the Complaint made against him by Rear Admiral Knowles, concerning his behaviour in the Expedition against Saint Jago de Cuba. *London.* 1749. 8vo. 19609

DENT (George). Remarks of Mr. Dent of Charles, in the Maryland State Convention, on the Basis of Representation. [n. p. 18—.] 8vo, pp. 8. H. 19610

DENTON (D.) A | Brief Description | of | New-York: | Formerly Called | New-Netherlands. | With the Places thereunto Adjoyning. | Together with the | Manner of its Scituation, Fertility of the Soyle, | Healthfulness of the Climate, and the | Commodities thence produced. | Also | Some Directions and Advice to such as shall go | thither: An Account of what Commodities they Shall | take with them; The Profit and Pleasure that | may accrew to them thereby. | Likewise | A Brief Relation of the Customs of the | Indians there. | By Daniel Denton. | *London* | *Printed for John Hancock, at the first Shop in Popes-Head Alley in* | *Cornhill at the three Bibles, and William Bradley at the three Bibles* | *in the Minories.* 1670 | 4to, 2 l., pp. 21. J.F.M., S. 19611

The first account of New York printed in English, and very rare. The title-page being printed on paper larger than the rest of the volume, the date is often cut off by the binder. The only copy we have seen with the date not cut off belongs to John F. McCoy, whose copy is uncut, and measures 8 x 6 inches.

DENTON (D.) A Brief Description of New York, formerly called New Netherlands, with the Places Thereunto Adjoining. Likewise a Brief Relation of the Customs of the Indians there. A New Edition, with an Introduction and Copious Historical Notes. By Gabriel Furman. *New York: William Gowans.* 1845. 8vo, pp, 17, 52, 16. 19612

One hundred copies printed in quarto, and five in folio. Forms No. 1 of Gowan's "Bibliotheca." It was also reprinted by the Historical Society of Pennsylvania. Edited by John Pennington. *Philadelphia.* 1845. 8vo, pp. 16.

DENTON (W.) Address delivered on the Anniversary of the Birth-Day of Thomas Paine ... Cincinnati, Ohio, January 29, 1859. By Wm. Denton. *Published by the ... Infidel Society of Cincinnati, O.* 1859. 12mo, pp. 22. H. 19613

DENVER, *Colorado.* Resources of Colorado. By the Board of Trade of Denver City, Colorado. *The "Union" Steam Presses, Brooklyn, N. Y.* 1868. 12mo, pp. 12. H. 19614

DENYS (Nicolas). Description | Geographique | et Historique des costes | de l'Ameriqve | Septentrionale. | Avec l'Histoire naturelle du Païs. | Par Monsieur Denys, Gouverneur Lieutenant | General pour le Roy, & proprietaire de toutes | les Terres & Isles qui sont depuis le Cap de | Campseaux, jusques au Cap des Roziers. | *A Paris,* | *Chez Loüis Billaine, au second* | *pillier de la grand' Salle du Palais,* | *à la Palme & au grand Cesar.* | M.DC.LXXII. | Avec Privilege du Roy. | 2 vols., sm. 8vo, 16 l., pp. 267, Map; pp. 486, 3 l. 19615

Title from Stevens' Nuggets. A copy in Harvard College Library has the imprint, *A Paris,* | *Chez Claude Barbin, au Palais,* | *sur le Perron de la Sainte Chapelle.* | M. DC. LXXII. | Avec Privilege du Roy. | Vol. II. is entitled "Histoire | naturelle Des Peuples, des Animaux des Arbres | & Plantes de l'Amerique | Septentrionale, & de ses | divers Climats. | Avec une Description exacte de la | Pesche des Moluës, tant sur le | Grand-Banc qu'à la Coste; & de | tout ce qui s'y pratique de plus | particulier, &c. | ... [5 lines, as above.] Tome Second. *A Paris,* | [4 lines, as above.] 8vo, pp. 480, 3 l. H. The country over which M. Denys claimed to exercise jurisdiction under the King of France extended from Cape Canso, at the eastern extremity of Nova Scotia to Cape Rosier, at the mouth of Penobscot Bay. "This country the Governor explored and surveyed himself, and hence his book is among the best and most authentic materials we have relating to those provinces." — STEVENS.

DENYS. Geographische en Historische Beschrijving der Kusten von Noord-America, met de Natuurlijke Historie des Landts: Door den Heer Denys ... . *t' Amsterdam: By Jan ten Hoorn.* 1688. Sm. 4to, 4 l., pp. 200, 4 l. H. 19616

Usually found at the end of Hennepin's "Louisiana."

DEODATI (G. L.), *Translator.* *See* Grafigny.

Department of Arms and Trophies, Metropolitan Fair. Catalogue of the Museum of Flags, Trophies and Relics relating to the Revolution, the War of 1812, the Mexican War, and the present Rebellion. *New York: Chas. O. Jones.* 1864. 8vo, pp. 112. 19617

Department of War, December 5th, 1794 ... John Beckley, Clerk. 4to, pp. 2. 19618

Circular from War Office, with resolve of House of Representatives, of Dec. 4, 1794.

[DEPERTHES (Jean Louis Hubert Simon).] Histoire des naufrages; ou Recueil des relations les plus intéressantes des naufrages, hivernements, délaissements, incendies, famines, et autres evénements funestes sur mer, qui ont été publiées depuis le quinzième siècle jusqu à présent. Par M. D.... Avocat. *Paris: Chez Cachet.* M DCC LXXXIX. 3 vols., 12mo, pp. xvi, 368; 407, 3 Tables; 454, 5 Tables. + Nouvelle édition ... augmentée ... par J. B. B. Eyriés. ... *Paris: Ledoux et Tenré.* M. DCCC. XV. 3 vols., 8vo, pp. xviij, 400; Title, pp. 402; Title, pp. 391. BA. 19619

DEPERTHES. Relations d'infortunes sur mer ... . *Reims.* 1781. 3 vols., 8vo. 19620

Reprinted with the title:

[DEPERTHES.] Histoire des Naufrages, ou Recueil Des Relations les plus intéressantes des Naufrages, Hivernements, Délaissements, Incendies, Famines, et autres Événements funestes sur Mer, qui ont été publiées depuis le quinzieme siècle jusqu'à present. Par M. D...., Avocat. *Paris: Maradan Letellier.* 1790. 3 vols., 8vo, pp. xvj, 368; 2 l., pp. 407, (3); 2 l., pp. 454, (6). H. + Nouvelle édition, continuée par Née de la Rochelle. *Paris.* 1795. 5 vols. (of which IV. and V. are the "Continuation"), 8vo. + Nouvelle édition ... augmentée de plusieurs morceaux inédites en français, formant près de moitié de l'ouvrage ... par J. B. B. Eyriès. *Paris: Ledoux et Tenré.* 1816. 3 vols., 12mo. 3 Plates. (Some copies printed in 8vo.) + 1818. 3 vols., 12mo. + *Paris: L. Tenré.* 1821. 3 vols., 12mo. + Nouvelle édition, refondue. *Paris: Dufour et Cᵉ.* 1828. 3 vols., 12mo. 6 Plates. + Nouvelle édition. *Paris: Tenré.* 1832. 3 vols., 12mo. 3 Engravings. + Par Desperthes [*sic*]. *Paris: imp. de Baudouin.* 1841. 2 vols., 12mo. 4 Plates. 19621

"This work was translated into English and published in 1812, without any acknowledgment of the source from which it was derived." — RICH.

[DEPEYSTER (Arent Schuyler).] Miscellanies, By an Officer. Volume I. *Dumfries: O. Munro.* 1813. 4to, pp. 279.

The author of this rare volume seems to have served in the American War, and been in command at Mackinaw, in the Western Territory, in 1799. It contains journals of travels, poetical pieces, etc., all relating to America, and is full of curious particulars. The only copy I have seen belongs to Lyman C. Draper, of Madison, Wis.

DE PEYSTER (F.) An Address delivered before the New York Historical Society, on its Sixtieth Anniversary, Tuesday, November 22, 1864. By Frederic de Peyster, President of the Society. *New York: Published for the Society.* MDCCCLXV. 8vo, 2 l., pp. 76. Portrait of L. Bradish. 19623

Fifty copies printed on large paper.

DE PEYSTER. History of the Tontine Building. Founded 1792, demolished in May, 1855. By Frederick De Peyster, Esq. [*New York:*] *Geo. F. Nesbitt & Co.* 1855. 18mo, pp. 15. Plates. 19624

DE PEYSTER. Memoir of Rip Van Dam. By F. De Peyster. *New York.* 1865. 8vo. 19625

DE PEYSTER. The Moral and Intellectual Influence of Libraries upon Social Progress. An Address before the New York Historical Society, Nov. 21st, 1865. By Frederic De Peyster, President of the Society. *New York: Historical Society.* 1866. 8vo, pp. 96. H. 19626

Fifty copies printed on large paper.

DE PEYSTER (J. W.) Address delivered ... 28th November, 1866, ... Madalin, Township of Red Hook, Dutchess Co., N. Y., by Brevet Maj.-Gen. J. Watts de Peyster (S. N. Y.), upon the Occasion of the Inauguration of a Monument ... to her Defenders ... . *New York.* 1867. 8vo, pp. 122. H. 19627

Two hundred copies privately printed.

DE PEYSTER. Analytical Parallel and Criticism on the Principal Union and Rebel Generals who have held Command-in-Chief of Armies. [n. p. 1865.] 8vo, pp. 8. H. 19628

[DE PEYSTER.] Chancellorsville and its Results. Maj.-Gen. Joseph Hooker in Command of the Army of the Potomac. ... From the Original ... Manuscript of "Anchor," June, 1865. Edited and revised with Additions by Joseph B. Lyman. Fifty copies printed as manuscript for private use ... . *New-York: L. W. Payne, Printer.* [n. d.] 8vo, pp. 20. H. 19629

DE PEYSTER. The Decisive Conflicts of the Late Civil War, or Slaveholders' Rebellion. ... No. 1. The Maryland Campaign of September, 1862. The Battles of the South Mountain and of the Antietam, Sunday, September 14th, to Wednesday, September 17th, 1862. ... By J. Watts De Peyster ... . *New York: Macdonald & Co., Printers.* 1867. 8vo, pp. 76. H. + No. 3. ... The Pennsylvania-Maryland Campaign of June-July, 1863. The Battles of Oak [or Seminary] Ridge and Gettysburg, and before, at, and after Gettysburg, and at Williamsport. June 28th to July 14th, 1863. By J. Watts de Peyster ... . *New York: Macdonald & Co., Printers.* 1867. 8vo, pp. 163. H. 19630

DE PEYSTER. The Dutch at the North Pole, and the Dutch in Maine. A Paper read before the New York Historical Society, 3d March, 1857. By J. Watts de Peyster ... . *New York: the Society.* M DCCC LVII. 8vo, pp. 80, Erratum, 1 slip.

DE PEYSTER. The Eclaireur, devoted to the Army and Militia of the United States. [Edited by Gen. J. W. De Peyster.]

Hyde Park, N. Y. Vol. I., folio; Vol. II., 8vo. *Tivoli, N. Y.* 1853–56. Vol. III., 8vo. M., N. 19632

DE PEYSTER. The History of Carausius, the Dutch Augustus, and Emperor of Britain, ... *Poughkeepsie.* 1858. 8vo, pp. xxvi, 335. 19633

Contains some reference to the settlements in Maine.

DE PEYSTER. Organization of the Militia. Abridged Reports of General De Peyster, dated July 1st, 1852, & June 1st, 1853, made to Gov's. Hunt and Seymour, of New York. [*New York.* 1865.] 4to, pp. 12. (Reprint from "Hist Mag.," Feb., 1865, pp. 12 after p. 72.) H. 19634

DE PEYSTER. Personal and Military History of Philip Kearny, Major-General, United States Volunteers. ... By John Watts De Peyster, *New York: Rice & Gage.* 1869. 8vo, 3 l., pp. 516. 3 Plates and 2 Portraits. C., H. 19635

[DE PEYSTER.] Proofs considered of the Early Settlement of Acadie by the Dutch: being an Appendix to the Dutch in Maine. [n. p. 1858.] 8vo, pp. 19. H. 19636

DE PEYSTER. Secession in Switzerland and in the United States Compared; being the Annual Address, delivered, October 20, 1863, before the Vermont State Historical Society, in the Hall of Representatives, Capitol, Montpelier. By J. Watts De Peyster. *Catskill: Joseph Joesbury.* 1863. 8vo, pp. 72. + 1864. 19637

[DE PEYSTER.] Winter Campaigns the Test of Generalship. *New York: Charles G. Stone.* 1862. 12mo, pp. 24. 19638

Also: Address to the Officers of the New-York State Troops, 19th January, 1858. ... *Tivoli.* [1858.] 8vo, pp 40. M. — Concurrent Resolution New York Legislature, being Special Act authorizing the issue of Commission of Brevet Major-General to Brigadier-General de Peyster. [*Albany.* 1866.] 8vo, pp. 13. H. — Memorials of a Birthday Breakfast, given on the Anniversary of nis One Hundredth Birthday, to Captain Frederic Lahrbush (Labouche), (Ex-Captain H. B. M., 6th Rifles, etc.), by General J. Watts de Peyster, on the same, his 45th Birthday, March 9, 1866. ... New York City. *New York.* 1866. 8vo, pp. 5. H. — Report to ... [the] Governor of ... New York ... on ... the Artillery and Arms best adapted to the State Service ... . *Albany.* [1853.] 8vo, Title, pp. iv, 3–247. (Senate Doc. 74.) H.

The | Deplorable State | of New-England, | By Reason of a Covetous and Treacherous | Governour, | and | Pusillanimous Counsellors | With a Vindication of the Honᵇˡᵉ Mr. Higginson, | Mr. Mason, and several other Gentlemen from the | Scandalous and Wicked Accusation of the Votes, Or- | dered by Them to

be Published in their Boston | News-Letter. | To which is Added, | An Account of the Shameful Miscarriage of | the Late Expedition against Port-Royal. | *London, Printed in the Year* 1708. | 4 l., pp. 39. BA. + [*Boston*], *reprinted.* 1720. 16mo, pp. 36.

"This pamphlet is said to be by the Rev. John Higginson of Salem, then aged 92; but the dedication is signed A. H., probably Alex. Holmes, one of the petitioners. It is written with great warmth, and lays open the disputes which existed between Governor Dudley and some leading characters in New England, who opposed his designs, which were to get rid of the charter, and make the government completely arbitrary." — *North Am. Rev.*, III. 305.

DEPONS (F.) Perspective des rapports politiques et commerciaux de la France dans les deux Indes, sous la dynastie régnante. Par F. J. De Pons. ... . *Paris: Hénée; Nicolle; Treuttel et Würtz.* 1807. 8vo, pp. x, 292, (1). H. 19640

DEPONS. Voyage à la partie orientale de la terre-ferme, dans l'Amérique méridionale, fait pendant les années 1801, 1802, 1803 et 1804: Contenant la Description de la capitainerie générale de Caracas, composée des provinces de Venezula, Maracaibo, Varinas, la Guyane espagnole, Cumana, et de l'île de la Marguerite, et refermant tout ce qui a rapport à découverte, à la conquête, à la topographie, à la législation, au commerce, aux finances, aux habitans et aux productions de ces provinces; avec un aperçu des mœurs et usages des espagnoles, et des Indiens sauvages et civilisés. Par F. Depons, Ex-Agent du Gouvernement Français a Caracas; Avec une carte geographique, et les plans de la ville capitale et des ports principaux. ... *Paris: Colnet, Fain et Compagnie, Debray, Mongie, Et F. Buisson.* 1806. 3 vols., 8vo, Title, pp. 358; Title, pp. 362; Title, pp. 469. 4 Maps. H. 19641

Highly commended by the "Edinburgh Review."

DEPONS. A Voyage to the Eastern part of Terra Firma, or the Spanish Main, in South-America, during the Years 1801, 1802, 1803, and 1804. Containing A description of the Territory under the jurisdiction of the Captain General of Caraccas, composed of the Provinces of Venezuela, Maracaibo, Varinas, Spanish Guiana, Cumana, and the Island of Margaretta; and embracing every thing relative to the Discovery, Conquest, Topography, Legislation, Commerce, Finance, Inhabitants, and Productions of the Provinces, together with a view of the manners and customs of the Spaniards, and the savage as well as civilized Indians. By F. Depons, late Agent of the French Government at Caraccas. ... With a Large Map of the Coun-

try, &c. Translated by an American Gentleman. *New-York: I. Riley & Co.* 1806. 3 vols., 8vo, pp. xxxii, 248, (6); 362, (8); 288, (5). Map. BA. 19642

Partly translated by Washington Irving. Our No. 19644, *infra*, is a different translation.

DEPONS. Travels in South America, during the Years 1801, 1802, 1803, and 1804; containing a Description of the Captain Generalship of Caraccas, and an Account of the Discovery, Conquest, Topography, Legislature, Commerce, Finances, and Natural Productions of the Country; with a View of the Manners and Customs of the Spaniards and Native Indians. By F. Depons, ... Translated from the French. *London: Longman, Hurst, Rees, and Orme.* 1807. 2 vols., 8vo, pp. lii, 503, Map; 6 l., pp. 384. BA., H. 19643

DEPONS. Travels in Parts of South America, during the Years 1801, 1802, 1803, & 1804; containing a Description of the Captain-Generalship of Carraccas, with an Account of the Laws, Commerce, and Natural Productions of that Country; as also a View of the Customs and Manners of the Spaniards and Native Indians. By F. Depons, Agent from the French Government to Carraccas. *London: Richard Phillips.* 1806. pp. 157, (3). 19644

Also included in Phillips' "Voyages." Probably an abridgement.

DEPONS. Reise in dem östlichen Theil von Terrafirme in Süd-Amerika, unternommen in den Jahren 1801–4. Aus dem Französichen von Chr. Weyland. *Berlin: Voss.* 1807. 8vo, pp. viii, 394. Map. + [*Ibid.*] 1808. 8vo. (Magazin von merkwürd. n. Reisebeschr., 29.) 19645

DEPONS. Nachrichten von d. General Hauptmannschaft Caracas, oder der östlichen Theile von Terra-Firma ... in d. Jahre 1801–4. *Weimar.* 1807. 8vo. (Biblioth. d. neuest. Reisebeschr., 34.) 19646

DEPPING. Histoire des découvertes géographiques des Hollandais. *Paris: imp. de F. Didot.* 1828. 8vo. 19647

From the "Bull. univ. des sciences," VIe section, mai 1828.

DEPPING. Rapport sur l'ouvrage intitulé Smithsonian Contributions to Knowledge lu à la séance du 26 mars 1851 de la Société des Antiquaires de France. Par M. Depping. *Paris: de l'imprimerie de Crapelet.* 1852. 18mo, pp. 16. 19648

A notice of Squier and Davis' work on Indian earth-mounds. *Washington.* 1848–51, extracted from the "Annuaire de la soc. des antiq. de France, pour 1852." *See* Navarre.

DEPPING. Die Völker der fremden Welttheile. Ein Charakter und Sittengemälde für die Jugend. Aus dem Francösischen. Mit 6 ill. Steindrucke. *Reutlingen: Macken, jr.* 1836. 12mo.

DEPPING. Depping's Evening Entertainments; comprising Delineations of the Manners and Customs of Various Nations. Second Series. A New Edition, Enlarged and Improved. *Philadelphia: Alexander Towar.* MDCCCXXXIII. 12mo, pp. 288.

DE PRADT. *See* Pradt (De).

DE PUY (H. W.) Ethan Allen and the Green-Mountain Heroes of '76. With a Sketch of the Early History of Vermont. By Henry W. De Puy. ... *Buffalo: Phinney & Co.* 1853. 12mo, pp. 428. Map and 2 Portraits. BA., C., H. + *New York: Phinney, Blakeman & Mason.* 1860. 12mo, pp. 428.

[DE PUY.] Mishaps of an Indian Agent convicted of not plundering the Indians. [*Albany, N. Y.* 1863.] 8vo, pp. 14.

DE QUINCEY (T.) Letters to a Young Man and other Papers. By Thomas De Quincey ... . *Boston: Ticknor, Reed, and Fields.* M DCCC LIV. 16mo, 2 l., pp. 300. BA. 19653

"California and the Gold Mania," pp. 199–244.

DERAGGIS. Adresse au peuple français, libre et souverain, par le citoyen Deraggis, ancien procureur syndic de la commune de Mirebalai, île et côte de Saint-Domingue. [26 pluviôse an II. *Paris:*] *imp. de Pain.* [n. d.] 8vo, pp. 7. 19654

DERBY (Elias Hasket). The Case of Wm. Livingston and ... other Citizens of Lowell, Petitioners for a Cross Rail-Road from Lowell to Andover. ... Argument of E. H. Derby, Esq. ... in reply to Mr. Webster. *Boston: Dutton and Wentworth's Print.* 1845. 8vo, pp. 28. H. 19655

DERBY. Boston: a Commercial Metropolis in 1850. Her Growth, Population, Wealth, and Prospects. ... By E. H. Derby. 1850. 8vo, pp. 16. H. 19656

DERBY. Popular Education in the United States. [*Edinburgh.* 1853.] 8vo, pp. 24. H. 19657

An article from the "Edinburgh Review."

DERBY. The Position and Prospects of the United States with respect to Finance, Currency, and Commerce, With the Financial Policy of Massachusetts. ... E. H. Derby. *Boston: A. Williams & Co.* 1868. 8vo, pp. 32. H. 19658

DERBY. Letter to the Hon. William H. Seward, Secretary of State, in answer to one from him on the Resolution of the Senate as to the relations of the United States with the British Provinces; and the Actual Condition of the Question of the Fisheries, from E. H. Derby, January, 1867. *Washington.* 1867. 8vo, pp. 245.

DERBY. Life of Elias Hasket Derby. [n. p. n. d.] 8vo.

DERBY. The Overland Route to the Pacific. A Report on the Condition, Capacity and Resources of the Union Pacific and Central Pacific Railways. By E. H. Derby, of Boston. October, 1869. *Boston: Lee & Shepard.* 1869. 8vo, pp. 97. H.

[DERBY.] Reality versus Fiction. A Review of a Pamphlet published at Charleston, S. C., entitled, "The Union, Past and Future, how it works and how to save it." Now answered by a Citizen of Boston. ... [Signed E. H. D.] *Boston: Redding & Co.* 1850. 8vo, pp. 15. H. 19662

Also: Argument in behalf of the Eastern Rail-Road Company ... before the Rail-Road Committee ... . *Boston.* 1846. 8vo, pp. 43. H. — ... Argument ... in favor of a State Loan to the Vermont and Massachusetts Railroad Co. ... *Boston.* 1855. 8vo, pp. 17. N. — A Brief Reply to the Report of the Investigating Committee of the Old Colony Railroad Corporation. By the President of the Company. April 12, 1850. [Signed.] *Boston: Damrell & Moore, Printers.* 1850. 8vo, pp. 15. H. — A Brief Review of the Speech of Hon. Thomas G Cary ... against the Loan of the State Credit, for the Hoosac Tunnel ... . *Boston.* 1853. 8vo, pp. 16. H. — [Letter to] Hon. W. P. Fessenden, Secretary of the Treasury. (Dated) Boston, Mass., January 10, 1865. [Proposed tax or duty on Cotton.] (Signed) E. H. Derby. [*Boston.* 1865.] 4to, pp. 3. H. — A Preliminary Report [dated January 1, 1866] on the Treaty of Reciprocity with Great Britain to regulate the Trade between the United States and the British Provinces of North America. Prepared by E. H. Derby, at the request of the Secretary of the Treasury of the United States. *Washington, D. C.* 1866. 8vo, pp. 84. — The Principal Points of the Mystic River Company, in relation to the change of the Line of their Sea-Wall, as presented by their Counsel, E. H. Derby, Esq., April, 1854. [*Boston.* 1854] 8vo, pp. 4. H. — The Troy and Greenfield Railroad. Argument. ... *Boston.* 1856. 8vo, pp. 16. H.

DERBY (*Mrs.* Elias Hasket). National Lincoln Memorial. [Circular addressed] to the Ladies of Massachusetts and other States of the Union: (Signed) Mrs. E. H. Derby, and three others. [*Boston.* 186–.] 4to, 1 page. H. 19663

DERBY (G.) Geographical Distribution of Consumption in Massachusetts. ... George Derby, M.D. [*Boston.* 1867.] 8vo, pp. 17. H. 19664

[DERBY (George H.)] Phœnixiana; or, Sketches and Burlesques. By John Phœnix. ... *New-York.* 1856. 12mo, pp. 274. BA. + *New York.* 1867. 12mo, pp. 274. Portrait.

Also: The Squibob Papers. ... *New York.* MDCCCLXV. 12mo, pp. 247. BA.

DERBY (J. B.) Political Reminiscences, including a Sketch of the Origin and History of the "Statesman Party" of Boston. By John Barton Derby, late Deputy Surveyor of the Customs. *Boston: Printed for the Author, by Homer & Palmer.* 1835. 8vo, pp. 172. 19666

DERBY. A Few Reminiscences of Salem, Mass., embracing Notices of its Eminent Men known to the Author Forty Years ago. By John B. Derby. *Boston.* 1847. 8vo, pp. 15. B., H.

Also: Musings of a Recluse. *Boston.* 1837. 12mo. — Scenes in a Mad-House. ... *Boston: Samuel N. Dickinson.* 1838. 8vo, pp. 24. H. — An Address by ... Derby, and an Oration by Silas P. Holbrook ... Medfield, July 4, 1822. *Dedham.* 8vo. H.

DERBY. Address to the People of the North. *Lexington, Kentucky.* 1856. 8vo, pp. 8. 19668

DERBY (S.) Deed of Lease and Release of Sarah Derby to the Trustees of Derby School, at Hingham, Mass. *Boston.* 1806. 8vo. W. 19669

Derde | Discovrs. | By | Forma van Missive, | Daer in kortelijck ende grondich ver- | toont wort, de nootwendicheyt des Oost ende | West-Indische Navgiatie, oock met goede fondamen- | tale redenen bewesen, dat door gheen ander mid- | del, eenen vasten versekerden vrede en is | te verwachten of te verhopen. | Worden daerom alle ghetrouwe Patriotten des | Vaderlandts, ten voorsten de Regierders, ende volgens | alle vermoghende Inwoonders vermaent, om tot dese, nu nieu- | we gheoctroyeerde West-Indiaensche Compaignie milde- | lijck te contribueren, ten eynde deselve beter succes | tot krenckinghe van de Castiliaensche | Trafijcke ghewinne. | Eerst gheschreven aen eenen seeckeren Vriendt, ende | nu tot dienste van alle ghetrouwe Patriotten | in druck ghebracht, | *By de Liefhebbers der Nederlandtsche vryheyt.* | *Anno* 1622. | 4to, 4 l. W. 19670

Derde | discovrs. | VVaer in | By forme van Missive den geheelen staet van | de Vereenichde Oost-Indische Compagnie vvort ten vollen gere- | monstreert, als ooc vvat de Participanten eñ het gemeene | Landt vanden beginne daer by genoten, tot grooten | afbreuc vande Portegiesche Trafycque. | Ende | Met goede redenen bewesen, dat by soo verre | dese geoctroyeerde West-Indische Navigatie van Godt met | gelijcken succes sal gesegent worden, dat niet alleen de Par- | ticipanten meer vordeels genieten sullen, maer ooc de | vrye Nederlantsche Republicque t'allen tijden so sal gequalificeert wesen int stuc vande Equip- | page ter

Zee, datse voor de Castiliaensche | macht niet meer sal hebben te vresen, | waer op ten lesten eenen verseker- | den vrede sy te verhopen. | VVorden derhalven alle getrouvve vermogende Pa- | triotten des Vaderlants, so noch niet op dese leste Compagnie hebben ge- | teeckent, vriendelicken vermaent, datse tot dese Equippagie, die nu | voorgenomen vvort, mede vvillen na hare gelegenheyt mil- | delick contribueren, also na de betalung vanden eersten | termyn op den lestẽ Decemb. de Compagnie vil- | licht sal gesloten vvorden, om niet meer te | mogen teeckenen. | Hier by een Extract wt een Tegen-vertooch op seecker Discours, | by eenige miscontentierde Participanten vande Oost-Indische | Compagnie wtghegeven. | *Ghedruckt int Iaer ons Heeren* | 1622. | 4to, 12 l. 19671

The author, defending the East India Company, tries to prove that, "as far as it pleases God to bless this chartered West India Company with similar success," the shareholders will enjoy more profit from the West India Company, and, therefore, invites "all true and wealthy patriots who have not yet subscribed to contribute largely to the New Company."

Derecho de las Iglesias. *See* [Betancurt (Luis de)], Vol. II., No. 5064.

DERECOURT (Henry). Colonial and International Postage ... Information on Postal Affairs ... *London.* 1854. 8vo, pp. 62.

D'ERES (C. D. R.) *See* Eres (Charles Dennis Russe D').

DE RHAM (H. C.) The Petition of Henry C. De Rham, to the General Assembly of Rhode Island, to except Paul Daniel Gonsalve Grand d'Hauteville, from the Operation of the Law "to secure the Fulfilment of certain Contracts, and for the Relief of Married Women in certain Cases." Together with the Remonstrance of Ellen S. d'Hauteville, and accompanying Documents. To which is prefixed the Debate upon a Motion to repeal that Law. *Providence: Knowles & Voss, Printers.* 1841. 8vo, pp. 124. H. 19673

[DERHAM (W.)] *See* "Miscellanea Curiosa."

DERKINDEREN (J.) A Narrative of the Sufferings of James Derkinderen, as a Prisoner among the Halifax Indians, 1796. *Philadelphia.* 1796. 8vo, pp. 8. M. 19674

DE ROCHEMONT. Commemorative Gathering. Notes of Proceedings at the Meeting of the De Rochemont Family, at Newington, or Piscatagua, August 23, 1866. ... *Boston: Rockwell and Rollins.* 1866. 12mo, pp. 30. H. 19676

DE ROOS (F. F.) Personal Narrative of Travels in the United States and Canada in 1826 Illustrated by Plates with Remarks on the Present State of the American Navy By Lieut. the Hon. Fred. Fitzgerald De Roos Royal Navy *London William Harrison Ainsworth.* 1827. 8vo, pp. xii, 207. 14 Plates. BA., H. + Second Edition. [*Ibid.*] 8vo. + Third Edition. [*Ibid.*] 8vo. 19677

Derrick and Drill. *See* [Morris] (E.)]

Derrotero de las Islas Antillas, de las Costas de Tierra Firme y de las del seno Mexicano, formado en la direccion de trabajos hidrograficos para inteligencia y uso de las cartas que ha publicado. ... *Madrid: Imprenta Real.* 1810. Sm. 4to, pp. viii, 455. BA. + Segunda edicion, corregida y aumentada con noticias muy recientes y con un Apendice sobre las corrientes del Oceano Atlantico. *Madrid: Imprenta Nacional.* 1820. Sm. 4to, pp. viii, 591, 2 l. + Mandado reimprimir por el Esmo. Sr. Francisco de Paula Santander. *Bogotá. Año de* 1826. 4to, pp. viii, 578. 19678

Derrotero de las islas Antillas, de las costas de Tierra firme y de las del seno mexicano, corregido y aumentado, por Guad. Victoria. *Mexico.* 1825. 8vo. 19679

Derrotero general de las republicas del Peru, Colombia, Buenos-Ayres y Chile, formado circunstanciadamente por Carreras, con el objeto de dar un conocimiento exacto de las comunicaciones para el jiro de diversos intereses, incluyese un plan geografico, etc., etc. *Lima.* 1867. 8vo, pp. 36. Tables. 19680

DESBORDES-VALMORE (*Mme.* Marceline). Les veillées des Antilles. [Nouvelles.] *Paris: Fr. Louis.* 1820. 2 vols., 12mo. 19681

DESALINES *or* DESSALINES. *See* Dubroca.

[DESAUSSURE (Henry William).] Address to the Citizens of South Carolina, on the approaching Election of President and Vice-President. By a Federal Republican. *Charleston.* 1800. 8vo, pp. 34. C. 19682

[DESAUSSURE.] Answer to a Dialogue between a Federalist and a Republican. *Charleston.* [1800.] 8vo, pp. 36. 19683

Also: Oration delivered July 4, 1826, at Columbia, S. C. ... *Columbia, S. C.* 1826. 12mo, pp. 30. — Oration prepared for the American Revolution Society, and the South-Carolina Society of Cincinnati, July 4, 1798. ... *Charleston.* 1798. 8vo, pp. 45.

DESBARATS (George E.), *Jr.* L'Esclavage dans l'Antiquité, et son abolition par le Christianisme. Etude fait devant le Cabinet de Lecture de Montréal. *Quebec.* 1858. 8vo, pp. 19.

DESBARRES. *See* Barres (J. F. W. des), Vol. I.

The following is by the same author:

DESBARRES (J. F. W.) A Statement submitted by Lieutenant Colonel Desbarres for consideration. Respecting his Services from the year 1755, to the Present Time — in the capacity of an Officer and Engineer during the War of 1756. — The Utility of his Surveys and Publications of the Coasts and Harbours of North America, entitled the Atlantic Neptune, and his Proceedings and Conduct as Lieut. Governor and Commander in Chief of His Majesty's Colony of Cape Breton. [n. p. 1795.] Folio, pp. ix, 99. J.C.B. 19685

Apparently a privately printed volume.

DESBOROW (C.) The Humble Address of Charles Desborow, late Captain of his M. S. Ship Mary, under the command of Cap. Norris, in the Expedition to Newfoundland in the year 1697. [n. d.] 1699. 4to. 19686

The following is from a sale catalogue:

DESBOROW. Humble address of the Lords to his Majesty in relation to the Petition of Capt. Charles Desborow, employed in the Expedition to Newfoundland, in the year 1697. [n. p.] 1699. 4to. 19687

DESCAMPS (Ant. Ign.) Llibre de la congregacio y germandat de la sanctissima Verge del Socorro, ab una nova y perpetua capellania de innumerables Misses pena los vias, y difuncta della; en la qual, qui viu pot aggregar al mort, que vulga: fundada en los collegis de la Compañia de Jesus de la ciutat de Sancta Fe del nou regne de Granada. *En Perpinya: J. Boudé.* 1666. Sm. 4to, pp. 473. 19688

"Un des ouvrages les plus rares concernant la Nouvelle-Grenade. Il est écrit en catalan." — TROSS.

[DESCERPZ (François).] Recueil de la diuersité des habits qui sont à présent en usaige tant ès pays d'Europe, Asie, Affrique et Jlles sauuages; le tout fait après le naturel. *Paris: R. Brenton.* 1562. 8vo. 19689

"Petit volume imprimé en lettres cursives, de 3 f. préf. et 61 f. Chaque feuillet, à l'exception du dernier, contient deux fig. en bois, au bas desquelles se trouvent quatre vers français." — TERNAUX, No. 87.

DESCHANEL (Émile). Christophe Colomb. *Paris: Michel Lévy frères.* 1862 [1861]. 18mo, pp. 323. 19690

DE SCHWEINITZ (E.) The Life and Times of David Zeisberger the Western Pioneer and Apostle of the Indians. By Edmund de Schweinitz. *Philadelphia: J. B. Lippincott & Co.* 1871. 8vo, pp. 747. H. 19691

DESCOURTILZ (J. T.) Ornithologie Brésilienne ou histoire des Oiseaux du Brésil, remarquables par leur plumage, leur chant ou leurs habitudes. Par Le Dr. J. T. Descourtilz, ... *Rio de Janiero* [i. e. *London*]: *Editeur, Thomas Reeves.* 1854–6. 19692

Of this fine work four parts, of twelve plates each, only are published. Quarich describes the following: "Oiseaux du Brésil." Rl. Folio. A beautiful series of large colored plates of Brazilian birds, apparently unpublished, without a title.

DESCOURTILZ (Michael Étienne). Flore médicale des Antilles, ou Traité des plantes usuelles des Colonies françaises, anglaises, espagnoles et portugaises; Par M. E. Descourtilz..., ... peinte par J. Th. Descourtilz. ... *Paris: Pichard* [etc.] 1821–29. 8 vols., 8vo. H. 19693

First published in 152 livraisons. The titles of Vol. III.–VIII. read, "Flore pittoresque et médicale des Antilles," as it does in the "Seconde édition" of Vols. I.–III., *Paris: chez l'éditeur.* 1833. 8vo. H.

DESCOURTILZ. Guide sanitaire des voyageurs aux colonies. Conseils hygiéniques en faveur des Européens destinés à passer aux îles, suivis d'une liste de médicaments dont on doit munir la pharmacie domestique à établir sur chaque habitation. Par M. E. Descourtilz ... . *Paris: C. L. F. Panckoucke.* 1816. 8vo.

DESCOURTILZ. Voyages d'un naturaliste, et ses observations Faites sur les trois règnes de la Nature, dans plusieurs ports de mer Français, en Espagne, au continent de l'Amérique septentrionale, à Saint-Yago de Cuba, et à St.-Domingue, où l'Auteur devenu le prisonnier de 40,000 Noirs révoltés, et par suite mis en liberté par une colonne de l'armée française, donne des détails circonstanciés sur l'expédition du général Leclerc ... . Par M. E. Descourtilz ... . *Paris.* 1809. 3 vols., 8vo, 4 l., pp. viii–lxiv, 17–365; Title, pp. 476; Title, pp. 470. 20 Plates. H.

Descripcion Chorographica del terreno, rios, arboles, y animales de las dilatadissimas provincias del gran Chaco, Gualamba, y de los ritos y costumbres de las innumerables naciones barbaras è infieles que le habitan. *Cordoba.* 1733. 4to. A. 19696

Descripcion de la Casa fabricada en Lima, corte del Peru, para que las Señoras ilustres de ella, y las demas mugeres devotas, y las que desean servir á Dios Nuestro Señor, pueden tener en total retiro, y con toda abstraccion y direccion necessaria los exercitos de San Ignacio de Loyola. *Lima: Joseph Padrino.* 1757. 4to, 28 unpaged leaves, pp. 85. J.C.B. 19697

Descripcion de los Costumbres y Usos de todos los pueblos del mundo, en la que se refieren una multitud de anécdotas de los salvages de Africa y de América; de los animales monstruosos, anfíbios, y prodigios. Traducida al Español de la Francés. *Paris.* 1828. 2 vols., 12mo. 19698

Descriptio totius Guineæ tractus Congi, Angolæ, et Monomotapæ, eorumque locorum, quæ e regione C. S. Augustini in Brasilia jacent. Proprietates Oceani; Insularumque ejusdem, S. Thomæ, S. Helenæ, Ascensionis etc. portum, altitudinis, etc. Miræ Narrationes Navigationum Batavorum cum interioris terræ descriptione. *Hagæ Comitis.* 1599. Folio. 19699

Description abrégé des Possessions des Anglois sur le continent de l'Amerique Septentrionale. *Paris.* [1755.] 12mo. Map. 19700

Probably another title for our No. 9602, Vol. III.

Description | de l'Amérique | & des parties d'icelle, comme de la Nouvelle France, | Floride, des Antilles, Iucaya, Cuba, | Jamaica, &c. | Item de l'estendue & distance des lieux, de la fertilité | & abondance du pays, religion & coustu- | mes des habitants, & autres | particularitez. | Avec une Carte Géographique de l'Amérique | Australe, qui doit estre inseree en la | page suivante. | *A Amsterdam,* | *Chez Iean Evertsz Cloppenburch, Marchand libraire, demeu-* | *rant sur le Water à la Bible Dorée. Avec Privilege, pour* 12 *Ans.* 1619. pp. 96. 19701

For other descriptions of places, *see* under the geographical name.

Description de l'Amérique méridionale, d'après Georges Juan Antonio d'Ulloa, de la Condamine et Frazier. + Septième édition. *Tours: Mame et files.* 1865. 12mo, pp. 239. Engraving.

Description de l'Amérique et des Indes Occidentales. Livre de lecture interessant ... . Traduite par G. Mila. *Berlin.* 1813. 4to. 8 Engravings. 19703

Description de l'Amérique en Arabe. *Boulaq.* 1847. 8vo.

Description des isles et terres. *See* [Blome (R.)], Vol. II.

Description des pays mœurs des habitans richesses des provinces les forces le gouvernement la religion et les princes qui ont gouvernés chacun estat. *Paris: N. du Fosse.* 1617. 4to. 19704

Title and note from Nyhoff's catalogue.

Description des terres Magellaniques. *See* [Falkner (Thomas)].

Description du Sol. *See* [Cutler (Manasseh)].

Description Géographique. *See* [Bellin (S.)], Vol. II.

Descripcion Historique d'un monstre symbolique, pris vivant sur les bords du Lac Fagua, pres Santa-Fé, par les soins de Francisco Xaviero de Meunrios, Comte de Barcelonne et Vice-Roi du Nouveau Monde. Envoyée par un négotiant du pays à un Parisien son ami. *Santa Fé et se trouve a Paris: chez le correspondant de l'auteur sous les Portiques du Mystère.* 1784. 8vo, pp. 29. Engraving. J.C.B. 19705

This exceedingly rare and curiously privately printed tract was written by Louis XVIII., when Comte de Province, *see* "Biographie Universalle." It is of a satirical character, though authorities differ as to its subject. The plates of the male and female amphibious monsters are very scarce, and are almost always deficient.

A Description of a Great Sea-Storm, | That happened to some Ships in the Gulph of Florida, in September last; Drawn up by one of the | Company, and sent to his Friend at London. | [Colophon:] Licensed, August the 5th. 1671. Roger L'Estrange. | *London: Printed by Thomas Milbourn, for Dorman Newman, at the King's Armes in the Poultry.* 1671. | Folio. 19706

The concluding lines are:

"Be wise and keep the shoar — then, since you may
Go in by land to your Virginia."

A Description of East Florida. *See* [Stork (W.)]

A Description of Gunæ Island, &c. *Dublin: Printed in the Year* 1708. 12mo, pp. 8. 19707

A facetious tract. On page 5 the author refers to the "Black Americans."

A Description of Kentucky, in North America: To which are prefixed Miscellaneous Observations respecting the United States. [*London:*] *Printed in November,* 1792. 8vo, pp. 124.

Description of Light Houses on the Coast of the United States. *Boston.* 1817. 8vo. W. 19709

A Description of North-America, and the British Settlements in Canada: with An Account of its Cities, Towns, Mountains, Woods, Rivers, Lakes, and of the Native Inhabitants in the Back Settlements. *Falkirk: Printed by T. Johnson.* 1817. 12mo, pp. 24. 19710

A chap-book.

Description of One Hundred Thousand Acres of Oil, Coal, Iron, Salt and Agricultural Land, in the County of Cabell, Western Virginia, with Letters, Reports, Maps and Prospectus. *New York: Clayton & Medole, Printers.* 1864. 8vo, pp. 30, (1). 2 Maps. 19711

Description of Oregon and California, embracing an Account of the Gold Regions, to which is added an Appendix, ... with a Map ... *Philadelphia: Thomas Cowperthwait & Co.* 1849. 18mo, pp. 76. 19712

Description of One Hundred Cities and Large Towns of America. *New York.* 1853. 8vo. Maps. 19713

A Description of the British Possessions in North America, with a Map of the Seat of War in North America. [1813.] 8vo, pp. 26. Plate and Map. N., W. + Second Edition. *Philadelphia:* [*J. Melish.* n. d.] 19714

A Description of the Coast, Tides, and Currents, in Button's Bay, And in the Welcome: Being The North-West Coast of Hudson's Bay, from Churchill River, in 58° 56′ North Latitude, to Wager River or Strait, in 65° 24′ taken from Scrog's, Crow's, Napier's and Smith's Journals, made in the Years 1722, 1737, 1740, 1742, 1743, and 1744. Also, From the Discoveries made in 1742, in the Voyage in the Furnace Bomb, and Discovery Pink, commanded by Captain Middleton and Captain Moor, Shewing from these Journals, a Probability, that there is a Passage from thence to the Western Ocean of America. *Dublin Printed in the Year* M,DCC,XLV. 8vo, pp. 27. J.C.B.

A Description of the Eastern Coast of the County of Barnstable. *See* [Davis (J.)]

A Description of the English and French Territories, in North America: being, An Explanation of a New Map of the Same. Shewing all the Encroachments of the French, with their Forts, and Usurpations on the English Settlements; and the Fortifications of the Latter. Done from the Newest Maps published in

London. And compared with Dr. Mitchell's, F.R.S. and every Omission carefully supplied from it. *Dublin: J. Exshaw.* MDCCLV. 8vo, pp. 28. Plan. J.C.B. 19716

A | Description | of the | Four Parts | of the | World, | viz. | Europe, Asia, Africa, and America. | Giving an Account | Of their Dominions, Religions, | Forms of Government, and Me- | tropolitan Cities. | Also, | How America was First Discovered | by the Europeans, and what Purchases | They have made therein. | Collected from the Writings of the best Historians. | *Edinburgh,* | *Re-printed in the Year,* M.DC.XCV. | 8vo, pp. 23. 19717

Description of the Four Parts of the World, viz., Europe, Asia, Africa, America. About 1770. 12mo. 19718

A scarce chap-book.

A Description of the Golden Islands, With an Account of the Undertaking now on Foot for making a Settlement there: Explaining. 1st. The Nature of that Design in general. 2dly. The Measures already taken. And, 3dly. Those intended to be taken hereafter. *London: J. Morphew.* 1720. 8vo, pp. 45.

"This tract relates to the grant made to Sir Robert Montgomerie referred to in a 'Discourse,' etc., by that gentleman, printed in 1717. He called the district the Margrivate of Azilia. The 'Golden Islands' are within this district, and were called by Sir Robert, St. Symon, Sapella, Santa Catarina, and Ogeche, afterwards changed to Montgomerie. They are described to 'lie within a day's rowing of the English habitations in South Carolina.'" — BARTLETT.

Description of the Great Tree recently felled upon the Sierra Nevada, California, now placed for Public Exhibition, In the spacious Racket Court of the Union Club, No. 596 Broadway, New York. *New York.* 1854. Rl. 8vo, pp. 8. G. 19720

Description of the Great Western Canal, in a Letter from a Traveller. *Saratoga Springs.* 1822. 8vo. 19721

See also Erie Canal.

Description of the Incas of Peru, with their Wives. ... These Elegant Figures are now exhibited at No. 44, North Market Street ... Boston. [*Boston.*] 1827. 12mo, pp. 12. H. 19722

A Description of the Mammoth Cave of Kentucky, the Niagara River and Falls, and the Falls in Summer and Winter; the Prairies, or Life in the West; the Fairmount Water Works and Scenes on the Schuylkill, &c. &c. to illustrate Brewer's Panorama. *Boston: J. M. Hewes & Co.* 1850. 8vo, pp. 24. H.

A Description of the Province of New Albion. And a Direction for Adventurers with small stock to get two for one, and good land freely; And for Gentlemen, and all Servants, Labourers and Artificers to liue plentifully. And a former Description re-printed of the healthiest, pleasantest and richest Plantation of New Albion in North Virginia, proved by thirteen witnesses. Together with a Letter from Master Robert Evelin, that lived there many years, shewing the particularities, and excellency thereof. With a briefe of the charge of victuall and necessaries, to transport and buy stock for each Planter, or Labourer, there to get his Master 50l. per Annum, or more in twelve trades, at 10l. charges onely a man. *London.* 1648. 8vo, pp. 35. 19724

Also included in "Force's Tracts and other Papers," Vol. II.

Description of the Roads in the United States. 1819. 12mo.

A Description of the Windward Passage, and Gulf of Florida, with the Course of the British Trading-Ships to, and from the Island of Jamaica. Also An Account of the Trade-Winds, and of the variable Winds and Currents on the Coasts thereabouts, at different Seasons of the Year. Illustrated with a Chart of the Coast of Florida, and of the Islands of Bahama, Cuba, Hispaniola, Jamaica, and the adjacent smaller Islands, Shoals, Rocks, and other remarkable Things in the Course of the Navigation in the West-Indies. Whereby is demonstrated, The Precariousness of those Voyages to the West-India Merchants, and the Impossibility of their Homeward-Bound Ships keeping clear of the Spanish Guarda Costa's: The Whole very necessary for the Information of such as never were in those Parts of the World. To which are added, Some Proposals for the better securing of the British Trade and Navigation to and from the West-Indies. ... *London: J. Applebee.* 1739. 4to, pp. 23, 5. Chart and Plate. C. 19726

A Description of Three Hundred Animals, with a Particular Account of the Manner of Catching Whales in Greenland. *London.* 1753. 12mo. 19727

With about two hundred very rude plates engraved on copper.

Description Topographique de six cents mille acres de terres dans l'Amérique Septentrionale, mises en vente par Actions, suivant le Plan d'Association ci-joint. Le Bureau de la Com-

pagnie est à Paris, rue de la Jussienne, No. 20. [n. p.] 1792. 4to, pp. 14, 8. J.C.B. 19728

An important tract for the early history of Western New York, describing a plan of colonization projected by a French company.

DESCUBES (Paul). La vérité sur les compagnies californiennes. *Paris: l'auteur.* 1850. 8vo. + Suivie d'une lettre adressée à l'auteur par un actionnaire désillusionné. Réponse à M. Philippart. Les compagnies dévoilées. 1850. 8vo. 19729

Descubrimiento de los terros y riquezas que tiene Dios escondidos en las Indias de su divino cuerpo y sangre. *Barcelona: O. Anglade.* 1608. 2 vols., 8vo. 19730

Title from Ternaux, No. 313.

DESERET. Constitution of the State of Deseret. *New York: S. Booth, Printer.* [186–.] 8vo, pp. 8. H. 19731

DES ESSARTS (A.) La guerre des frères par Alfred des Essarts. A l'Amerique. *Paris: Poulet-Malassis.* 1861. 8vo, pp. 20. H. 19732

DESGEORGE (*Abbé*). Monseigneur Flaget, Evêque de Bardstown et Louisville, sa vie, son Esprit et ses Vertus. *Paris: Lecoffre.* 1855. 8vo, pp. 388. 19733

DESHA (J. B.) Statement of the Trial of Isaac B. Desha, indicted for the Murder of Francis Baker; held at Cynthina, Kentucky, before the Hon. George Shannon. By R. S. Thomas and G. W. Williams. *Lexington.* 1825. 8vo. C., W. 19734

[DESHALLES.] Annales du Conseil Souverain de la Martinique, ou Tableau Historique du Gouvernement de cette Colonie, Depuis son premier etablissement jusqu'à nos jours. &c. &c. [Par Deshalles fils Conseiller au Conseil Souverain de la Martinique.] *A Bergerac, Chez J. B. Puynesge, Imprimeur-Libraire.* M.DCC.-LXXXVI. 2 vols., 4to, pp. xxvi, 554; xviii, 402, 40. 19735

Design and Advantages of the South Sea Trade, with Answers to all the Objections against the Company. [1711?] 19736

Designs (Nos. 1 & 2) for a Marine Hospital on the Western Waters to accommodate 100 Patients. *Washington.* [n. d.] 8vo. 19737

Designs of the Southern Conspirators and their Northern Allies. *Philadelphia.* 186–. 8vo. 19738

DESILVER (R.) Desilver's Annual Almanac. The United States Aimanac. ... With a variety of Public Information, ... *Philadelphia: R. Desilver.* 1825. Continued under various titles.

DESJARDINS (E.) Le Pérou avant la conquête espagnole. *Paris.* 1858. 8vo. B. 19740

DESJARDINS. Rapport sur deux ouvrages de Bibliographie américaine de M. Henri Harrisse ... . Par M. Ernest Desjardins ... . *Paris: imp. Martinet.* 1867. 8vo, pp. 20. 19741

"Extrait de la Bulletin de la Société de Géographie."

DESJARDINS (G.) Bolivar au congrès de Venezuela. Ode. *Paris: Corréard.* 1819. 8vo, pp. 16. 19742

DESLANDES. Discours Sur la grandeur & l'importance de la révolution qui vient de s'opérer dans l'Amérique Septentrionale; Sujet proposé par l'Académie des Jeux Floraux. Par M. le Chevalier Deslandes, Captaine au Régiment de Bretagne ... . *Francfort, et se trouve a Paris: Chez Durand, Musier.* M DCC-LXXXV. 12mo, pp. iv, (3), 6–183. C., H. 19743

DESLANDES. Essay on Maritime Power and Commerce. *London.* 1743. 8vo, pp. 163. 19744

Contains many interesting notices relating to America, particularly the design of Cromwell to become possessor of that country, the expedition of Thomas Gage, etc.

DES LOZIÈRES (Baudry). *See* Baudry des Lozières, Vol. I., Nos. 3979–80.

[DESMAULANTS (J. B.)] Sur Saint-Domingue, et des moyens de le rétablir. Par J. B. D. *Paris: Dentu.* 1814. 8vo.

DE SMET (P.) *See* Smet (P. de).

DES MOINES COUNTY, *Iowa.* Constitution of the Hawk-Eye Pioneer Association, of Des Moines County, Iowa. With a Full Report of the Proceedings of its First Annual Festival ... June 2d, A.D. 1858. *Burlington: Thompson & Sheward, Printers.* 1858. 8vo, pp. 54. H. 19746

Des Moines River Land Grant. History of its Construction by the United States Executive Departments, and by the State of Iowa. Statement. *Des Moines, Iowa: Times Print.* [1861.] 12mo, pp. 12. H. 19747

De[s] Moine[s] Navigation and Railroad Company. Annual Report. 1855. 8vo. Continued. 19748

Des moyens de conserver la santé, etc. *See* [Bertin], Vol. II., No. 5011.

DES MURS (O.) Oiseaux nouvelles ou rares recueillies dans l'Amérique du Sud p. F. de Castelnau. *Paris.* 1855. 4to. 20 Colored Plates. 19749

DESNOYERS (Charles Louis Francois), *and* ALBOISE (Albig). La traite des noirs, drame en cinq actes et à grand spectacle, de MM. Desnoyers et Alboise. [Programme.] *Paris: imp. de Petit.* 1835. 8vo. 19750

DESNOYERS (C. L. F.) Le Tremblement de terre de la Martinique. *See* Lafont (C.), *and* Desnoyers.

The Desolation of America. *See* [Day (Thomas)], No. 18980.

DE SOLIS (A.) *See* Solis (Antiono de).

DESOR (Édouard). Les cascades du Niagara et leur marche rétrograde par E. Desor. ... *Neuchâtel.* 1854. 8vo, pp. 20. Map. H. 19751

DESPARD (G. P.) Hope Deferred not Lost: a Narrative of Missionary Effort in South America in connection with the Patagonian Missionary Society. Edited by the Rev. G. P. Despard. *London.* 1853. 12mo, pp. 470. + Second Edition. *London: Nisbet.* 1864. Fcap, pp, 462. 19752

Despatch from Her Majesty's Minister at Washington, dated Dec. 6th, 1861, inclosing Papers relating to Foreign Affairs laid before the Congress of the United States, at the opening of the Session in 1861. *London.* 1862. 8vo. 19753

DESPERRIÈRES (Poissonnier). Traité des Fièvres de l'Isle de St. Domingue; avec un Mémoire sur les avantages qu'il y aurait à changer la nourriture des gens de mer. *Paris.* 1780. 8vo, pp. 311. S. 19754

Despojo á mano armada, por el Prefecto de Tlaxcala. *Puebla.* 1843. 4to, pp. 32. 19755

This was answered by

Falsedades que contiene el cuaderno titulado: Despojo á mano armada por el Prefecto de Tlaxcala. *Puebla.* 1844. 4to, pp. 32.

Despojo de los bienes eclesiasticos. Apuntes interesantes para la historia de la Iglesia mexicana. [*Mexico.*] 1847. 4to.

DESPORTES (J. B. R. Poupé). *See* Poupé Desportes.

DESPORTES (Félix). Parallèle des constitutions d'Angleterre, des États-Unis et de Genève. 19758

Quérard, from whom this title was taken, gives no imprint.

The Despotism at Richmond. The Confederate Loan in England. The Slave power and its Supporters. (From the London Daily News, March 20.) [*New-York.* 1862.] Broadside. H. 19759

Despotism in America. *See* [Hildreth (R.)]

DESPREZ (A.) Les voyageurs au pole nord; depuis les premières expéditions scandinaves jusqu'à celle de M. Gustave Lambert. Par Adrien Desprez. ... *Paris: Noblet.* 1868. 8vo, pp. 333. Map by Malte-Brun. 19760

DES RIVIÈRES BEAUBIEN (H.) Traité sur les lois civiles du Bas-Canada: Par Henry des Rivières Beaubien. *Montréal.* 1832–33. 3 vols., 8vo. 19761

DES ROTOURS (*Le contre-amiral baron* Noel François Arnot). Exposé des faits par suite desquels M. de Turpin, capitaine de la frégate honoraire, ex-commandant de Marie-Galande, dépendance du Gouvernement de la Guadeloupe, a présenté une requête au Conseil d'État à l'effet d'être autorisé à me poursuivre par abres d'autorité. [Signé.] *Paris: imp. de F. Didot.* 1831. 4to.

Des Rotours had been Governor of Guadeloupe. To the same controversy belong: Lettre adressée à M. le rédacteur en chef de la Gazette des tribunaux. *Paris: imp. de F. Didot.* 1832. 8vo. — Note à MM. les membres du Conseil d'État. [*Ibid.*] 1831. 4to. — Réponse au Mémoire publié contre lui par M. le vicomte de Turpin, capitaine de frégate honoraire, ex-commandant de Marie-Galande ... . *Paris: imp. de Crapelet.* 1830. 8vo.

DESSALLES (Adrien). Histoire générale des Antilles. *Paris: France.* 1846–48. 5 vols., 8vo. 19763

Tome[s] I.–III. form a "première série," embracing the reign of Louis XIV.; IV.–V., a "Deuxième série," reign of Louis XV.

DESSALLES. Notice historique sur la marine française, pour Servir d'Introduction à l'Histoire générale des Antilles. *Paris: France.* 1845. 8vo. 19764

DESSAULLES (L. A.) Discours sur L'Institut Canadien prononcé, par l'Hon. L. A. Dessaulles, Président de l'Institut, à la séance du vingt-trois de décembre, 1862, à l'occasion du dix-huitième anniversaire de sa fondation. *Montreal.* 1863. 4to, pp. 21. 19765

DESSAULLES. La Guerre Américaine son Origine et ses vraies Causes. Lecture Publique faite à l'Institute Canadien le 14 Décembre, 1864. Par L. A. Dessaulles. *Montreal: Typ. du Journal "Le Pays."* 1865. 18mo, pp. 75. BA., H. 19766

DESSAULLES. A Messieurs les électeurs de la Division de Rougemont. *Montreal.* 1858. 8vo, pp. 66. 19767

This is an address to his constituents on the political transactions of the day.

DESSAULLES. Rouge et Noir. *Montreal.* 1848. 19768

This pamphlet was written in vindication of Mr. L. J. Papineau, who, in 1847–8, was violently attacked by the Lafontaine and Nelson party for his conduct at St. Denis during the Rebellion of 1837.

DESSAULLES. Six Lectures sur l'annexion du Canada aux Etats-Unis. *Montreal.* 1851. 4to, pp. 199. S. 19769

Le Destin de l'Amérique. *See* [Cerisier (M.)], Vol. III., No. 11702.

Desultory Facts and Observations, illustrative of the Past and Present Situation and Future Prospects of the United States. *Philadelphia.* 1822. 8vo, pp. 40. 19770

Relates to the Tariff.

Desultory Reflections on the New Political Aspects of Public Affairs in the United States of America, since the Commencement of the Year 1799. *New York: the Author, by C. Waite.* 1800. 2 pts., 8vo, pp. 62; 38. + *Philadelphia, reprinted.* 1800. 8vo, pp. 26. S. 19771

Desultory Remarks on the Question of extending Slavery into Missouri, as enunciated during the First Session of the Sixteenth Congress, by the Representative from Chester County, State of Pennsylvania. ... Extracted from the American Republican Newspaper of 1819–20. [By William Darlington.] *West Chester, Pa.: Lewis Marshall, Printer.* 1856. 8vo, pp. 37. H. 19772

Desultory Sketches and Tales of Barbados. ... *London: Henry Washbourne.* 1840. 16mo, pp. viii, 264. B. 19773

The Detail and Conduct of the American War, under Generals Gage, Howe, Burgoyne, and Vice Admiral Lord Howe. With A very Full and Correct State of the whole of the Evidence, as given before a committee of the House of Commons; and the Celebrated Fugitive Pieces, Which are said to have given Rise to that Important Inquiry. The whole exhibiting A Circumstantial, Connected and Complete History of the Real Causes, Rise, Progress and Present State of the American Rebellion. The Third Edition. *London: Richardson & Urquhart.* M,DCC,LXXX. 8vo, pp. 190. 19774

"Praise is due to the editor of this publication for the care and attention which he has manifested in digesting the very important materials of which it is composed, especially the letters from Boston, New York, &c. This is a much enlarged and improved edition of 'A View of the Evidence,' etc." — *Monthly Review,* LXII. 84. *See also* Rich, I. 285.

A Detail of some Particular Services performed in America during the years 1776, 1777, 1778 and 1779. Compiled from Journals and Original Papers. Supposed to be Chiefly Taken from the Journal kept on board of the Ship Rainbow, commanded by Sir George Collier, While on the American Station during that period; giving a minute account of many important attacks on towns and places, expeditions sent up rivers, skirmishes, negociations, etc., some of which are nowhere else correctly represented, and many others not as minutely described in the histories of that period. Printed for Ithiel Town from a manuscript obtained by him while in London, in the summer of 1830. *New York: Privately printed for Ithiel Town.* 1835. 12mo, ix l., pp. 117. C. 19775

This "Detail" had already appeared in the "Naval Chronicle" twenty years before. The greater part of the edition was consumed by fire.

Détails sur quelques uns des évenemens qui ont eu lieu en Amérique pendant les Années XI. et XII.; publiés par un officier de l'Etat Majeur de l'Armée. *Paris.* 1804. 8vo, pp. 56. A.

Relates to Haiti.

Details der Communication zwischen England, Westindien und America, unterhalten durch die Dampfschiffe der Royal Mail Steam Packet Company in London. ... nebst 1 Charte von Westindien mit den Communications-Linien und Angabe der Entfernung in geographischen Meilen. *Hamburg: Niemeyer.* 1842. 8vo. 19777

Detall de las operacions ocurridas en la defensa de la Capital de la Republica, atacada por el ejercito de los Estados-Unidos del Norte. Año de 1847. *Orizava.* 1847. 4to, pp. 54.

A Detection of the False Reasons and Facts contained in the Five Letters (entitled, Reasons for keeping Guadaloupe at a Peace, preferable to Canada: from a Gentleman in Guadaloupe to his Friend in London.) In which the Advantages of both Conquests are Fairly and Impartially Stated and Compared. By a Member of Parliament. *London: Hope.* 1761. 8vo, pp. 58.

See "M. Rev.," xxiv. 440.

Detection of the Proceedings of the Directors of the Royal African Company from 1672 to 1748. *London.* 1749. 8vo.

A Detection of the State, &c. *See* Vol. I., No. 3265.

De Tivoli (J.) A Guide to the Falls of Niagara, with a ... View, by A. Vaudicault. ... *New York.* 1846. 12mo.

De Tocqueville. *See* Tocqueville.

Detroit, *Mich.* Act of Incorporation, By-Laws and Standing Rules, of the Detroit Young Men's Society, with the Names of Regular and of Honorary Members, and of the Presidents and Vice Presidents of the Society, and a Catalogue of Books in the Library, prepared by the Board of Directors, March, 1842. *Detroit: Morgan Bates, Printer.* 1842. 8vo, pp. 43. H. 19782

Act of Incorporation, By-Laws, Ordinances, Rules and Regulations of the Board of Water Commissioners of the City of Detroit. *Detroit.* 1854. 8vo, pp. 24. + *Detroit.* 1861. 8vo, pp. 32. H. 19783

Annual Review of the Trade and Commerce of Detroit, for the Year 1855. Compiled for the Detroit Advertiser. *Detroit: Advertiser Print.* 1856. 4to, pp. 16. Continued. H. 19784

Catalogue of the Public Library ... . Also the Rules concerning its Use. *Detroit: Advertiser and Tribune.* 1868. 8vo, pp. vii, 149. C. 19785

Detroit City Directory and Advertising Gazetteer of Michigan, 1857–'8. By James Dale Johnston. *Detroit.* 1857. 8vo. Continued annually. C. 19786

Detroit Young Men's Society. Catalogue of the Library, with a Historical Sketch. *Detroit: O. S. Gulley.* 1865. 8vo, pp. 169. C. 19787

Diary of the Siege of Detroit in the War with Pontiac. Also, a Narrative of the Principal Events of the Siege, by Major Robert Rogers; a Plan for Conducting Indian Affairs, by Colonel Bradstreet; and other Authentick Documents never before printed. Edited with Notes, by Franklin B. Hough. *Albany. N. Y: J. Munsell.* M.D.CCC.LX. 4to, pp. xxiii, (1), 288, Index 289–301, Subscribers 302–304. BA. 19788

One hundred copies printed on small paper, and ten copies on large paper. Forms No. IX. of Munsell's Historical Series.

Journal of the Proceedings of the Common Council of the City of Detroit, from March 14, 1854, to April 3, 1855, Inclusive. (With Appendix.) *Detroit: Daily Free Press Print.* 1855. 8vo, pp. 140, 27. H. 19789

Proceedings of the Commercial Convention, held in Detroit, July 11–14, 1865. *Detroit, Convention.* 1865. 8vo, pp. 276.

The Reciprocity Treaty. Report of the Special Committee of the Detroit Board of Trade. [n. p. n. d.] 8vo, pp. 4. H.

Sketches of the City of Detroit, State of Michigan, Past and Present. *Detroit: R. F. Johnstone & Co.* 1855. Imp. 8vo, pp. 64.

Also: Annual Report of the Board of Education of the City of Detroit. By Levi Bishop, Esq., President of the Board. February, 1853. *Detroit: Daily Advertiser Press.* 1853. 8vo, pp. 26. H. Continued.—Annual Report of the Board of Water Commissioners. *Detroit.* 1852. 8vo. Continued.—Annual Report of the Detroit Public Schools. *Detroit.* 1842. 8vo. Continued.—Annual Report of the Detroit Ladies Industrial School Association. *Detroit.* 1858. 8vo. Continued.—Report of the Board of Water Commissioners to the Common Council of the City of Detroit; together with the Reports of the Superintendent and Engineer, and Secretary: to which is appended a Report of Prof. S. H. Douglass, upon the Analysis of Waters. December 31, 1853. *Detroit: Printed by George E. Pomeroy & Co.* 1854. 8vo, pp. 86. H. Continued.—Rules and Regulations of the Board of Education of the City of Detroit. [*Detroit.* 1870.] 8vo, pp. 21. H.—Revised Ordinances of the City of Detroit, 1863. *Detroit.* 1864. 8vo.

Deuber (Franz Xavier Anselm). Deuber's, Dr. u. Prof., Geschichte der Schiffahrt im atlantischen Ozean; zum Beweis, dass Amerika schon lange vor Chr. Colombo, und auch der Compass ... vor Flavio Gioja entdeckt worden sey. Angehängt ist Chr. Colombo's eigener Bericht an Raphael Sanxis ... . *Bamberg: C. F. Kunz in Commission.* 1814. 8vo, pp. viii, 160.

Deuber. Geschiedenis der scheepvaart in den Atlantischen Oceaan; ten bewyze van de bekendheid van Amerika, en van het kompas in de oudste tyden; benevens het eigen berigt van Christoffel Columbus over zyne eerste reize. *Rotterdam.* 1819. 8vo. 19793a

Deutsch-Amerikanische Monatshefte für Politik, Wissenschaft und Literatur ... herausgegeben von Caspar Butz. Erster Bend. *Chicago, Ill.* 1864. 8vo. 19794

Deutsch-Amerikanisches Freiheitsbund. Fliegende Vogel No. 1. ... *St. Louis, Mo.* [186–.] 8vo, pp. 8. H. 19795

Political.

Deutsche Auswanderer-Zeitung. Red.: H. v. Lengerke. [1.] Jahrgang 1852. *Bremen: Heyse.* [1852.] 4to. Semi-weekly.

Die deutsche Bevölkerung der Vereinigten Staaten, ihre Gegenwart und Zukunft. *Cincinnati: Eggers & Co.* 1846. 8vo, pp. 15. 19797

Deutsche Briefe aus den Vereinigten Staaten von Nordamerika. *München: Lentner.* 1861. 3 nos., 8vo. 19798

Contents: I. Die politische Situation, pp. 28; II., III. Sklaverei, Schutzzoll und Heimathsbill, 1, 2, pp. 42.

Der Deutsche in Nordamerika. *See* [Fürstenwächter (M. von)].

Der deutsche Pionier. Monatsschrift für Erinnerungen aus dem deutschen Pionier-Leben in den Vereinigten Staaten. ... I. Jahrgang. Heft 1. März. 1869. *Cincinnati.* 1869. 8vo. Woodcuts. Continued. H. 19799

Die Deutschen in Amerika. *See* [Hollenberg (W. A.)]

[Deutz (J.)] Proeve over de Middelen die tot Bescherming van de Zeevaart en Koophandel en tot verdediging van de binnenen buitenlandsche Bezittingen der Republicq in de Oost-Indien en op 't vaste Land van America zouden kunnen aangewend worden. *Amsterdam.* 1783. 8vo. 19800

Deux-Ponts (W. de). My Campaigns in America: a Journal kept by Count William de Deux-Ponts, 1780–81. Translated from the French Manuscript, With an Introduction and Notes, by Samuel Abbott Green. *Boston: J. K. Wiggin and Wm. Parsons Lunt.* 1868. 8vo, pp. xvi, (1), 176. BA. 19801

Les Deux Expéditions contre le fort Fisher, pris d'assaut le 16 janvier 1865, par l'armée et la marine des États Unis. Explosion des canons Parrott durant la première attaque. Rapport de la commission nommée pour en examiner les causes. *Paris: Corréard.* 1865. 8vo. 19802

Deux soldats américains. Le question des questions. *Paris: Libr. française et etrangère.* 1867. 18mo, pp. 8. 19803

De Veaux (S.) The Falls of Niagara, or Tourist's Guide ... including Notices of the Whirlpool, Islands, &c. and a Complete Guide thro' the Canadas. ... By S. De Veaux. *Buffalo: William B. Hayden.* 1839. 18mo, pp. viii, 17–168, (1). Map and 4 Plates. 19804

De Veaux. The Travellers' Own Book, to Saratoga Springs, Niagara Falls and Canada, containing ... a Complete Guide, for the Valetudinarian and for the Tourist, seeking for Pleasure and Amusement. ... By S. De Veaux. ... *Buffalo.* 1829. 16mo. + *Buffalo: Faxon & Read.* 1841. 18mo. 2 Maps and 4 Plates. BA., C. + Fourth Edition. *Buffalo.* 1843. 16mo. + Fifth Edition. *Buffalo: Faxon & Co.* 1844. 18mo, pp. viii, 251. Map and Plates. + Sixth Edition. [*Ibid.*] pp. viii, 251. Map and Plates. 19805

De Veaux College for Orphan and Destitute Children. Proceedings at the Opening ... at Suspension Bridge, May 20, 1857. Together with the Will of the Founder. *Buffalo.* 1857. 8vo, pp. 34, (4). H., S. 19806

Also: Annual Reports to the Legislature, and an Annual Register.

De Veer (Gerrit). Voyages. *See* Veer (G. de).

Developpement des causes des troubles et désastres des Colonies Françaises, présenté à la Convention Nationale, par les Commissaires de St.-Domingue, sur la demande des comités de Marine & des Colonies, réunis, après en avoir donné communication aux colons residens à Paris, & convoqués, à cet effet, le 11 Juin 1793, l'an. 2e de la République. 8vo, pp. 200. 19807

No title-page, or printer's name. The commissaries signing the report are MM. Page and Bentley.

Devens (C.) (Letter to) Hon. Henry Wilson, U. S. S., Chairman of the Military Committee of the Senate ... . Dated Army of the James. Headquarters, Third Division, Twenty-Fourth A. C. December 16th, 1864. [Signed] Charles Devens. [n. p. 1864.] 4to, pp. 3. H. 19808

[Devens (Samuel Adams)]. Sketches of Martha's Vineyard, and other Reminiscences of Travel at Home, etc. *Boston: ... James Munroe & Co.* 1838. 16mo, pp. viii, 207, (1). C., H., M.

Deverell (R.) Andalusia; or, Notes, tending to show that the Yellow Fever of the West Indies and of Andalusia of Spain, was A Disease well known to the Ancients; and that they assigned a Cause for it, and used effective Means for the Prevention and Cure of it not hitherto attempted in our time. By Robert Deverell, Esq., M. P. January 19, 1805. [*London: privately printed.* 1805.] 4to, pp. 155. 3 Plates. 19810

Devereaux (John C.) Address on the Anniversary of American Independence, Celebrated July 5, 1852, at Jamaica, New York, by the Catholic Temperance Societies of Long Island. *New York.* 1852. 8vo. BM. 19811

Devereux (R.) Poetical Pieces written on several occasions of Unfortunate and Unhappy Facts. ... By Rachel Devereux. *New York: L. Beach.* [1803.] 8vo, pp. 30. 19812

De Verteuil (L. A. A.) Trinidad; its Geography, Resources, Administration, Present Condition, and Prospects. By L. A. A. De Verteuil. *London: Ward & Lock.* 1858. Post 8vo, pp. xii, 508. 19813

Devèze. An Enquiry into and Observations upon the Causes and Effects of the Disease which raged in Philadelphia, from the Month of August till towards the Middle of December 1793. *Philadelphia.* 1794. 8vo. 19814

With a French translation on the opposite pages.

Devèze. Dissertation sur la fièvre jaune qui regna à Philadelphie en 1793, depuis le mois d'août jusque vers le milieu du mois de décembre, Thêse. *Paris: imp. de Mme Huzard. an XII* [1804]. 4to. 19815

The Devil in Dixie. A Tale of the Times. Serio-Comical, Semi-Historical, and Quasi-Diabolical. *New York: American News Company.* 1865. 16mo, pp. 76. 19816

The Devil let Loose; or, a Wonderful Instance of the Goodness of God. In a Letter from a Gentleman in South Carolina, to his friend in Annapolis. *New York.* 1805. 8vo, pp. 24. + *Reprinted by G. Spear, Hanover, N. H.* 1814. 12mo, pp. 24. 19817

The Devil Let Loose, or the Wo occasioned to the Inhabitants of the Earth by his Wrathful Appearance among them. ... Sermon ... April 5, 1799. *Boston.* 1799. 8vo. BA., W. 19818

The Devil's Confessions in his Dying Hour. A Miraculous Revelation of the Nature and Cause of the Present Rebellion, &c. *Du Quoin, Ill.* 1863. 12mo, pp. 12. 19819

Deville (C.) Observations sur le Tremblement de Terre, éprouvé à la Guadaloupe, Fevrier, 1843. Par Ch. Deville. *Basse Terre, Guadaloupe.* 1843. 4to. 19820

De Vinné. The Methodist Episcopal Church and Slavery. A Historical Survey of the Relation of the early Methodists to Slavery. By Daniel de Vinné. ... *New York: Francis Hart.* 1859. 8vo, pp. 95. 19821

Devlin (J. S.) The Marine Corps in Mexico; setting forth its Conduct as Established by Testimony before a General Court Martial, Convened at Brooklyn, N. Y., September, 1852, for the Trial of First Lieut. John S. Devlin, of the U. S. Marine Corps. *Washington: printed by Lemuel Towers.* 1852. 8vo, pp. viii, 62. BA., C., H. 19822

De Voe (T. F.) Abattoirs [in New York and elsewhere]. ... By Thomas F. De Voe. ... . *Albany: Van Benthuysen & Sons' Steam Printing House.* 1866. 8vo, pp. 32. H. 19823

De Voe. The Market-Book containing a Historical Account of the Public Markets in the Cities of New York Boston Philadelphia and Brooklyn With a Brief Description of every Article of Human Food sold therein the Introduction of Cattle in America and Notices of many Remarkable Specimens By Thomas F. De Voe ... . In Two Volumes ... *New York: the Author.* 1862. 8vo, pp. 621. H. + *New York: Hurd and Houghton.* 1867. 8vo, pp. 455. Plate. BA., C. 19824

Devon Mines. Statement concerning the Devon Mines of Lake Superior. *Boston: Press of T. R. Marvin & Son.* 1863. 8vo, pp. 8. H. 19825

Devon (W. A.) War Lyrics. By W. A. Devon, Author of "Red Mark." *New York: S. Tousey.* 1864. 16mo, pp. 64. + Third Edition. + *New York: Devon & Benedict.* 12mo, pp. 64. 19826

Devot (*Mr.*) The Go-Between, or Two-Edged Sword; being an Impartial Address to the Citizens of the United States. By Mr. Devot. *New York.* 1807. pp. 37. 19827

The Devoted Legions, A Poem. *See* [Day (Thomas)], No. 18982.

Devoti (*D.* Felix). Discurso sobre el cementerio general que se ha erigido, extramuros de la ciudad de Lima. *Lima.* 1808. 4to. + *Reimpreso en Habana: por Estevan Boloña.* 1809. 4to, pp. (2), 19. 19828

Devotion (E.) The Civil Ruler, a dignify'd Servant of the Lord, but a dying Man. A Sermon Preached before the General Assembly of the Colony of Connecticut, at Hartford, on the Day of the Anniversary Election, May 10th, 1753. By Ebenezer Devotion, A.M. ... *N. London: Timothy Green.* 1753. 8vo, pp. (2), 59. B., H. 19829

Devotion (J.) The Duty and Interest of a People to sanctify the Lord of Hosts. A Sermon, preached before the General Assembly of the State of Connecticut, at Hartford, on the Day of the Anniversary Election, May 8th, 1777. By John Devotion, A.M. Pastor of the third Church in Saybrook. *Hartford: Printed by Eben. Watson, near the Great Bridge.* M.DCC.LXXVII. 8vo, pp. 39. 19830

This sermon abounds with historical allusions to the various defeats and disasters which attended the army in the winter of '76, '77. Also: A Mourning Piece. Being a discourse ... occasioned by the ... Death ... of ... Mr. Eph. Avery, at Brooklyn, Oct. 22, 1754 ... *Boston: J. Draper.* 1755. 4to.—God the Dwelling Place of the Righteous in all Generations. A Sermon, Preached at the Funeral of Rev. William Hart, July 13. 1784. *Hartford.* 1785. 8vo, pp. 26. N.—The Mutual Obligation upon Ministers, to Speak, and Hear the Word of God. A Sermon delivered at the Ordination of the Reverend Mr. Nathanael Huntington, to the Pastoral Office, Over the Church and Congregation in Ellington in Windsor, On the 15th, of November, 1749, by Ebenezer Devotion, M.A. ... H.—Sermon at the Ordination of Enoch Huntington, at Middletown, Con. Jan. 6, 1762. ... *New Haven.* [n. d.] 4to. W.—A Sermon preached April 8, 1788, at the Interment of Madam Ursula Griswold, Consort of his Excellency Matthew Griswold. ... *New Haven.* [1788.] 8vo, pp. 27.

De Vries, *or* De Vriese. *See* Vries (De).

Devyr (T. A.) Memorial (to Congress on a) Financial System of the Nation. (Signed,) Thomas Ainge Devyr. (Dated) Williamsburgh, New York, 1863. [n. p. 1863.] Broadside.

Devyr. Our National Rights. A Pamphlet for the People. By Thomas A. Devyr. *Williamsburg, L. I.* 1842. 8vo, pp. 50.

Dew (T. R.) An Essay on Slavery. By Thomas R. Dew. *Richmond.* 1849. 8vo, pp. 115. + Second Edition. *Richmond.* 1849. 8vo. B. 19833

Advocates J. C. Calhoun's views.

Dew. The Great Question of the Day. Letter from President Thomas R. Dew, of William and Mary College, Virginia,

to a Representative in Congress from that State; on the Subject of the Financial Policy of the Administration, and the Laws of Credit and Trade. ... *Washington: Thomas Allen.* 1840. 8vo, pp. 16. H. 19834

Dew. Lectures on the Restrictive System; delivered to the senior Political Class of William and Mary College. ... *Richmond.* 1829. 8vo. C. 19835

Dew. Review of the Debate in the Virginia Legislature of 1831–'32. By Thomas R. Dew ... . *Richmond: T. W. White.* 1832. 8vo, pp. 133. C. 19836

On the abolition of slavery; in the Virginia and Kentucky Resolutions of 1798–99, edition of 1832; and in The Pro-Slavery Argument ... . *Charleston.* 1852. Also: An Address on the Influence of the Federative and Republican System of Government upon Literature and the Development of Character, prepared to be delivered before the Historical and Philosophical Society of Virginia at their Annual Meeting in 1836. *Richmond.* 1836. 8vo, pp. 24.—Essay on the Interest of Money, and the Policy of Laws against Usury. ... *Shelbank, Va.* 1834.—Letter to the Representative in Congress from Virginia, on the subject of the Financial Policy of the Administration, and the Laws of Credit and State. ... *Washington.* 1840.

De Warrdenau (D.) The Gift: A Tale of the Washington Soldiers' and Sailors' Orphans' Fair. By D. De Warrdenau. [n. p. n. d.] 8vo, pp. 10. H. 19837

Dewart (Edward Hartley). Selections from Canadian Poets; with occasional Critical and Biographical Notes, and an Introductory Essay on Canadian Poetry. *Montreal.* 1864. 8vo, pp. 304. 19838

[Dewees (J.)] Appeal to the Legislature of the Commonwealth of Pennsylvania. [Signed] Jacob Dewees. Pottsville, January 21, 1863. 8vo, pp. 8. 19839

Dewees. The Great Future of America and Africa; An Essay showing Our Whole Duty to the Black Man, Consistent with Our Own Safety and Glory. By Jacob Dewees, M.D. ... *Philadelphia: Printed By H. Orr.* 1854. 8vo, 2 l., pp. vii–236.

Dewees. Pennsylvania in Self-Defence: An Appeal To the Legislature and the People, upon the Rights of Labor. By Jacob Dewees, M.D. ... *Philadelphia: H. Orr.* 1859. 8vo, pp. 54. C. 19841

Also: To the American Public. [Signed] Jacob Dewees. 8vo, pp. 16.—To the People of Pennsylvania. Signed Jacob Dewees. Pottsville, Sept. 23d, 1862. 8vo, pp. 8.

Dewees (S.) *See* Hannah (J. S.)

DEWEES (W. B.) Letters from an Early Settler of Texas. By W. B. Dewees. Compiled by Cora Cardelle. *Louisville, Ky.: Morton & Griswold.* 1852. 12mo, pp. 312. BA. + *Louisville: Hall & Brothers, Printers.* 1854. 12mo, pp. 312. Map.

D'EWES (J.) Sporting, in Both Hemispheres. By J. D'Ewes. *London: G. Routledge & Co.* 1858. Post 8vo. + [*Ibid.*] 1862. C. 19843

Also issued with the title, "Sporting Adventures in Many Lands."

DEWEY (B.), *et al.* True and Concise Narrative. *See* Dartmouth, No. 18632.

DEWEY (C.) An Appeal to the Friends of Temperance, delivered in Pittsfield, Mass. Oct. 7, 1832. By Rev. C. Dewey. *Pittsfield: Printed by Phinehas Allen & Son.* [1832.] 8vo, pp. 24. H. 19844

[DEWEY (Chester).] Report on the Herbaceous Flowering Plants of Massachusetts, arranged according to the Natural Orders of Lindley, and illustrated chiefly by Popular Descriptions of their Character, Properties, and Uses. ... *Cambridge: Folsom, Wells, and Thurston.* 1840. 8vo, pp. viii, 277. BA.

Forms part of the "Massachusetts Zoological and Botanical Survey."

DEWEY. Introductory Lecture delivered to the Medical Class of the Berkshire Medical Institution; August 5, 1847. By Prof. Dewey. *Pittsfield, Mass.: Charles Montague, Printer.* 1847. 8vo, pp. 32. A. 19846

With historical notes on the medical schools in the United States.

DEWEY. A Sermon, occasioned by the Present Religious Attention in Williams College, Preached May 12th, 1812, at the Desire of the Junior Class ... . By Chester Dewey, A.M. ... *Stockbridge: printed by H. Willard.* 1812. 8vo, pp. 24. H.

DEWEY (Chester), *and others.* A History of the County of Berkshire, Massachusetts. In Two Parts. The First being a General View of the Country; The Second, an Account of the Several Towns. By Gentlemen in the County, Clergymen and Laymen. *Pittsfield: Printed by Samuel W. Bush.* 1829. 12mo, pp. 468. Woodcuts and 2 Maps. BA. 19848

DEWEY (D. M.) History of the Strange Sounds or Rappings heard in Rochester and Western New-York ... *Rochester: D. M. Dewey.* 1850. 12mo, pp. 79. H. 19849

DEWEY (D. P.) A Memorial of Lt. Daniel Perkins Dewey, of the Twenty-fifth Regiment Connecticut Volunteers. *Hartford: Press of Case, Lockwood & Company.* 1863. 12mo, pp. 126. 19850

DEWEY (L. D.) Documents relative to the Dismission of Loring D. Dewey from the Theological Seminary in New-York. 1816. pp. 24. + [n. p. n. d.] 8vo, pp. 43. H. 19851

DEWEY (O.) An Address delivered under the Old Elm Tree in Sheffield, with some Remarks on the Great Political Questions of the Day. By Orville Dewey. *New York.* 1856. 8vo, pp. 26. B. 19852

DEWEY (O.) On American Morals and Manners. By Rev. Orville Dewey, D.D. *Boston: William Crosby.* 1844. 8vo, pp. 34. + *London: J. Chapman.* 1844. 19853

DEWEY. The Claims of Puritanism. A Sermon, preached at the Annual Election, May 31, 1826. ... By Rev. Orville Dewey ... . *Boston: Printed by True & Greene.* 1826. 8vo, pp. 32. B., BA., H. 19854

DEWEY. A Discourse delivered at the Dedication of the Church of the Messiah ... New-York. By the Rev. Orville Dewey ... . *New-York.* 1839. 8vo, pp. 26. H. 19855

DEWEY. A Discourse on Slavery and the Annexation of Texas. By Orville Dewey, ... *New-York: Charles S. Francis & Company.* 1844. 8vo, pp. 18, (1). B., BA., H., N. 19856

[DEWEY?] Letters of an English Traveller to his Friend in England on the Revival of Religion in America. *Boston.* 1828. 18mo, pp. 142. 19857

DEWEY. Moral Views of Commerce, Society and Politics, in Twelve Discourses. By Orville Dewey. *New York: D. Felt & Co.* 1838. 12mo, pp. 300. C., S. + Second Edition. [*Ibid.*] 12mo. 19858

DEWEY. The Old World and the New; or, a Journal of Reflections and Observations made on a Tour in Europe. By the Rev. Orville Dewey. In Two Volumes. *New York: Harper & Brothers.* 1836. 2 vols., 12mo, pp. 262; 330. BA.

DEWEY. On Patriotism. The Condition, Prospects, and Duties of the American People. A Sermon delivered on Fast Day at Church Green, Boston. By the Rev. Orville Dewey ... *Ticknor and Fields.* M DCCC LIX. pp. 39. BA., B., H. 19860

Another edition has the following title: A Sermon, preached on the National Fast Day, at Church Green, Boston. By Rev. Orville Dewey ... . *Boston: Ticknor & Fields.* 1861. 12mo, pp. 22. B.

DEWEY. A Sermon, on occasion of the Late Fire, in the City of New York. ... By the Rev, Orville Dewey ... . *New York: David Felt & Co.* 1836. 12mo, pp. 17, (1). H., N.

DEWEY. Who is right? Rev. Dr. Dewey, or Dr. James M'Cune Smith? Let the Reader judge. Letters from the New-York Tribune. [*New York.* 1844.] Broadside. H. 19862

On the relative prosperity of Free Blacks and Slaves at the South. Also: Works of Orville Dewey, D.D. *New-York.* 1847. 3 vols., 12mo. — An Address delivered before the American Peace Society, Boston, May, 1848. ... *Boston.* 1848. 8vo, pp. 24. B. — Anniversary Address before the American Unitarian Association ... *Boston.* 1848. 12mo. — The Appeal of Religion to Men in Power. A Sermon on Occasion of the Late Calamity at Washington. ... . *New York: C. S. Francis and Company.* 1844. 8vo, pp. 20. H. — ... Discourse ... at the Ordination of the Rev. George Putnam, as Colleague Pastor with Rev. Eliphalet Porter ... over the First Church ... in Roxbury, July 7, 1830. ... *Boston: published by Gray and Bowen.* 1830. 8vo, pp. 32. — A Discourse on Miracles ... . *Cambridge: Folsom, Wells, and Thurston, Printers.* 1836. 8vo, pp. 23. — Discourse on the Character and Writings of Rev. William Ellery Channing, D.D. ... *New York.* 1843. 8vo, pp. 40. — Discourses on various Subjects. *New York: D. Felt & Co.* 1835. 12mo, pp. 299. + *New York.* 1838. 2 vols., 12mo. — Discourses on Human Life. *New York: D. Felt & Co.* 1841. 12mo, pp. 300. — Laws of Human Progress and Modern Reforms. A Lecture ... *New York.* 1852. 8vo. B. — Obedience, A Discourse preached in the City of Washington on Sunday, June 27, 1852 ... *New York.* 1852. 8vo, pp. 18. — An Oration, delivered at Cambridge, before the Society of Phi Beta Kappa, August 26, 1830. ... *Boston.* 1830. 8vo, pp. 32. B. — ... A Sermon delivered at the Installation of the Rev. Edward B. Hall, as Pastor of the First Congregational Society in Providence ... *New Bedford: Benj. Lindsey, Printer.* 1832. 8vo, pp. 36. — A Sermon on the Moral Uses of the Pestilence, denominated Asiatic Cholera. Delivered on Fast-Day, August 9, 1832. ... *New-Bedford: Printed by Benjamin T. Congdon.* 1832. 8vo, pp. 20. B., BA., H. — A Sermon, ... at the Ordination of Joseph Angier, as Pastor of the First Congregational Church in New Bedford, May 20, 1835. ... *New Bedford: Benj. Lindsey, Printer.* 1835. 8vo, pp. 55. — A Sermon, ... on the Moral Importance of Cities, and the Moral Means for their Reformation, particularly on a Ministry for the Poor in Cities, ... *New York: David Felt & Co.* 1836. pp. 23, (1). H. — A Talk with the Camp. *New York: A. D. F. Randolph.* 1863. 32mo, pp. 16.

DEWEY (Sherman). An Account of a Hail Storm which Fell on Part of the Towns of Lebanon, Bozrah and Franklin, on the 15th of July, 1799. Perhaps never Equalled by any other ever Known, not even in Egypt. *Walpole, N. H.* 1799. 12mo, pp. 27.

DEWEY (W.) Remarks of William Dewey in Assembly, March, 1854, on the Bill for the Suppression of Intemperance. 8vo. S. 19864

DEWEY. Suggestions, urging the Construction of a Railroad, from Rome to Watertown and Cape Vincent. *Watertown, N. Y.* 1844. 8vo. S. 19865

DEWHERST (Henry William). The Natural History of the Order Catacea and the Oceanic Inhabitants of the Arctic Regions. By H. W. Dewherst. *London.* 1834. 8vo. BM., C.

DE WINTTON. "Nullus Liber Homo." [n. p. 186–.] 8vo, pp. 7. H. 19867

On granting suffrage to negroes.

DEWIS (J. P.) Guter Rath an Einwanderer in die Vereinigten Staaten von Nord-Amerika. Mit Anmerkungen und einen Anhang versehen und herausgegeben von W. K. Riedler. *Aarau: Christen.* 1834. 12mo. Illustration. 19868

DE WIT (Cornelis). *See* Wit (C. de).

DE WITT (B.) Catalogue of the Minerals in the Cabinet of Benjamin De Witt. *Albany.* 1820. 8vo. B. 19869

DE WITT. On the Necessity of Establishing an Agricultural College. *Albany.* 1819. 8vo. 19870

DE WITT. A Memoir of the Onondaga Salt Springs and Salt Manufactures in the Western part of the State of New York; describing the Situation and Appearance of the Springs, the Nature and Contents of the Waters, and the Process by which the Salt is procured, etc. *Albany.* 1798. 4to, pp. 28.

DE WITT (Francis). Abstract of Returns of Criminal Cases. *See* "Massachusetts."

DE WITT. Industry of Massachusetts. *See* "Massachusetts."

DE WITT (John). Funeral Discourse of J. H. Livingston, D.D. *New-Brunswick.* 1825. S. 19872

See Wit (J. de).

DE WITT (S.) An Atlas of the State of New York, ... by Simeon De Witt, And also the Physical Geography of the State ... By David H. Burr. *New York: David H. Burr.* 1829. Folio, pp. 29. 52 Maps. 19873

DE WITT (S.) Considerations on the Necessity of Establishing an Agricultural College. By Simeon De Witt. *Albany.* 1819. 8vo. 19874

DE WITT (T.) Christ the Resurrection ... A Sermon ... on the ... Death of the Rev. David S. Bogart, ... Aug. 4, 1839 ... *New York.* 1839. 8vo, pp. 22. 19875

DEWITT (T.) A Discourse delivered in the North Reformed Dutch Church, in the City of New York, on the last Sabbath in August, 1856. By Thomas Dewitt, D.D. *New York.* 1857. 8vo, pp. 100, Errata, 3 lines. 9 Plates. 19876

DEWITT. ... A Discourse delivered on the Occasion of the Opening ... the Building Erected by the Consistory of the Reformed Prot. Dutch Church of the City of New-York, on ... Fifth Avenue and Twenty-ninth Street, October 11, 1854. By the Rev. Thomas Dewitt, D.D. With an Appendix. ... *New-York: printed by John A. Gray.* 1854. pp. 47. 19877

Also: A Discourse Commemorative of the Rev. John Knox, D.D. Delivered ... January 24, 1858. *New York.* 1858. 8vo, pp. 86. — The Gospel Harvest and Christian's Duty. Sermon, Oct. 6, 1830. *Boston.* 1831. 8vo. B. — A Sermon preached at the Installation of the Rev. George W. Bethune. ... Philadelphia, ... Sept. 10, 1834. *Philadelphia.* 1834. 8vo, pp. 20.

DE WITT (W. R.) A Discourse on the Life and Character of Francis R. Shunk, Governor of the State of Pennsylvania; delivered at Harrisburg, August 9, 1848. By Rev. William de Witt. [n. p. n. d.] 8vo. 19878

DE WITT. The Memories of the Past; a Sermon, preached by the Rev. William R. De Witt, To his Congregation, Harrisburgh, Pa., on the Seventieth Anniversary of his Birth-Day, and in the Forty-Fourth Year of his Ministry in that Congregation. *New York: John W. Amerman, Printer.* 1862. 8vo, pp. 30. 19879

DE WITT (W. R.), *and* Rev. W. Easton. A Discussion on the Order of the Sons of Temperance. *Philadelphia.* 1847. 12mo. B., S. 19880

De Witt Guard. History of the De Witt Guard, Company A, 50th Regt. National Guard of the State of New York. *Ithaca, N. Y.* 1866. 12mo. S. 19881

D'WOLF (J.) An Address delivered before the Citizens of Bristol, R. I., July 4, 1821. By John D'Wolf. [n. p.] 1821. 8vo, pp. 24. 19882

D'WOLF. A Voyage to the North Pacific, and a Journey through Siberia, more than half a Century ago. By Captain John D'Wolf. *Cambridge: Welch, Bigelow, and Company.* 1861. 8vo, pp. iv, 147. 19883

One hundred copies printed.

DE WOLF (L. E.) Constable's Guide, with the Constitution of Pennsylvania, by L. E. De Wolf. *Towanda.* 1845. 18mo.

DE WOLF (Thaddeus K.), *M.D.* Speech delivered at Huntington, Mass., Oct., 24, 1855. *Springfield.* 1855. 8vo, pp. 32. M. 19885

DEWSBURY (William). A Sermon Preached at Grace Street Church the 6th of the 3d month, 1688. *Providence.* MDCCLXVIII. 8vo, pp. 21. 19886

DEXTER (A.) An Oration on the Importance of Science and Religion, particularly to American Youth. Pronounced at the Commencement of Rhode Island College, Sept. 5, 1798. By Andrew Dexter, Junr. ... *Providence: Carter & Wilkinson.* 1798. 8vo, pp. 8. 19887

[DEXTER (Charles).] In Memoriam [Edmundi Dexter]. *Cambridge.* 1866. 4to, pp. 83. H. 19888

DEXTER (E.) Sermon on the Death of Oliver Cobb. By E. Dexter, Jan. 18, 1809. *New Bedford.* 1809. 8vo. 19889

[DEXTER (Franklin).] A Letter to the Hon. Samuel A. Eliot, ... in Reply to His Apology for voting for the Fugitive Slave Bill. By Hancock. *Boston: Wm. Crosby & H. P. Nichols.* 1851. 8vo, pp. 57. BA. 19890

DEXTER (F.) Oration delivered July 4, 1819, at the request of the Selectmen of the Town of Boston. By the Hon. Franklin Dexter. *Boston.* [1819.] 8vo, pp. 19. B. 19891

[DEXTER (George).] Catalogue of Postage Stamps, American and Foreign, and U. S. Revenue Stamps. *Cambridge.* 1863. 16mo, pp. 78. B. 19892

DEXTER (H. M.) The Church Polity of the Pilgrims the Polity of the New Testament. By Henry M. Dexter. With an Introduction by Hon. R. A. Chapman ... . *Boston: Congregational Publishing Society.* 1870. 8vo, pp. vii, 82. BA. 19893

Fifty copies reprinted from "The Congregationalist."

DEXTER. Congregationalism; What it Is; Whence it Is: How it Works: Why it is better than any other Form of Church Government; and its Consequent Demands. By Henry M. Dexter ... . *Boston: Nichols and Noyes.* 1865. 8vo, pp. xxxii, 306. BA. 19894

[DEXTER.] Memoranda, Historical, Chronological, &c. Prepared ... to aid those whose Interest in Pilgrim Memorials, and History, is freshened by this Jubilee Year ... . [*Printed (but not Published) for the Use of Congregational Ministers.*] 1870. 8vo, pp. 39. BA. 19895

DEXTER. What ought to be done with the Freedmen and with the Rebels? A Sermon ... Boston, ... April 23, 1865. by Henry Martyn Dexter. *Boston: Nichols & Noyes.* 1865. 8vo, pp. 36. H. 19896

See Church (Thos.), and Mourt's "Relation." Also: Discourse at the Dedication of the Franklin Street Church, Manchester, N. H. *Andover.* 1848. 8vo. — A Glance at the Ecclesiastical Councils of New England. By Henry M. Dexter, D.D. *Boston: Wiggin & Lunt.* 1867. 8vo, Title, pp. 68. BA. — Meeting Houses Considered, Historically and Suggestively. *Boston.* 1859. 8vo, pp. 29. B. — The Moral Influence of Manufacturing Towns. A Discourse delivered ... in Manchester, N. H. Dec. 22, 1847 ... . *Andover: printed by William H. Wardwell.* 1848. 8vo, pp. 32. H. — Our National Condition, and its Remedy. A Sermon, June 22, 1866. ... *Boston: John P. Jewett & Co.* 1866. 8vo, pp. 44. B., BA., H. — A Sermon at the Funeral of Rev. W. I. Putnam, D.D. ... *Boston: Pratt Bros.* 1868. 8vo, pp. 24.

[DEXTER (John H.)] Mercantile Honor and Moral Honesty. *Boston.* 1856. 12mo, pp. 20. 19897

DEXTER (S.) A Call from the Dead to the Living. In a Sermon preached on occasion of the ... Death of Mr. Timothy Metcalf, ... By Rev. Samuel Dexter ... . *Boston: J. Eliot.* 1728. 8vo, pp. (4), 34, pp. 219–244 of "The Dedham Pulpit," with separate title-page. B., BA. 19898

DEXTER. Our Father's God, the Hope of Posterity. Some serious Thoughts on the Foundation, Rise and Growth Of the Settlements in New England ... . A Discourse Delivered at Dedham, on the Day of Publick Thanksgiving, Nov. 23. 1738. Upon the Conclusion of the first Century, since a Church of Christ was Gathered in that Place. By Samuel Dexter, V.D.M. *Boston: S. Kneeland and T. Green.* 1738. 8vo, 3 l., pp. 51. H. + The Second Edition. *Boston: Reprinted by Thomas Fleet, jun.* MDCCXCVI. 8vo, Title, pp. ii, 51. B., BA., H. 19899

DEXTER (S.) Mr. Dexter's Address to the Electors of Massachusetts, in favour of his Election. To which is added a Temperate Examination of the said Address. By a Citizen of Massachusetts [John Lowell]. *Boston: Russell, Cutler & Co.* 1814. 8vo, pp. 38. H. 19900

[DEXTER.] Letter to the Grand Master of the Grand Lodge of Massachusetts [Josiah Butler]. *Boston.* [n. d.] 8vo, pp. 4.

[DEXTER.] The Progress of Science. A Poem, delivered at Harvard College ... April 21, 1780. By a Junior Sophister. [n. p.] 1780. 4to, pp. 10. + *New York.* 1790. 8vo. 19902

DEXTER. Review of the Biographical Sketch of the Hon. Samuel Dexter [in the Boston Patriot. *Boston.* 1816.] 12mo, pp. 14. H. 19903

See [Sargent (L. M.)]

DEXTER (T. C. A.) Before the President of the United States. Case of Thomas C. A. Dexter. Arguments for Defence by Gen. Benj. F. Butler, and Hon. Charles A. Peabody. Review and Opinion of Judge Advocate General Holt, prepared for the President. Discharge of Mr. Dexter. *New York: Wm. C. Bryant & Co., Printers.* 1867. 8vo, pp. 80. H. 19904

DEXTER. The Case of Thomas C. A. Dexter, Military Commissioner at Mobile. Arguments for the Defendant before the President of the United States, by Gen. B. F. Butler and Hon. C. A. Peabody. *New York: W. C. Bryant & Co., Printers.* 1866. 8vo, pp. 57. 19905

See Butler, Vol. III., No. 9606, and Peabody; *see also* Holt (*Maj. Gen.*)

DEXTER (T.) Pickle for the Knowing Ones; or, Plain Truths in a Homespun Dress. By Timothy Dexter, Esq. *Salem.* 1802. 12mo. + Second Edition. [n. p.:] *Printed for the Author.* 1805. Sm. 8vo, pp. 36. B., H. + Revised Edition. With a Life of the Author. *Newburyport: Printed by Enoch Hale, Jr.* 1847. 16mo, pp. 24. H. + With an Introductory Preface, by a Distinguished Citizen of "Ould Newberry." Fourth Edition. *Newburyport: Blanchard & Sargent.* 1848. 16mo, pp. 32. H. 19906

DEXTER. A Pickle for the Knowing Ones, or Plain Truths in a Homespun Dress. By the Late Lord Timothy Dexter, with an Introductory Essay on his Life and Genius, and Explanatory Notes. By Peter Quince. *Boston: Otis, Broaders & Co.* 1838. 16mo, pp. 42. H. 19907

DEXTER. Something New, or Memoirs of that truly Eccentric Character, the late Timothy Dexter, Esq.; Together with his last Will and Testament. *Montpelier.* 1808. 8vo. B.

DEXTER *and* ABBOT. Remarks upon the Growth and Culture of the Cotton Plant, more particularly as cultivated in the

State of Alabama. [Signed] Dexter & Abbot. *Boston.* 1850. 8vo, pp. 22. B., H. 19909

Dexter Asylum. Rules and Regulations for the Government of Dexter Asylum, established at a Town Meeting of the Freemen of the Town of Providence, July 26, 1828. *Providence: Smith & Parmenter.* [1828.] 8vo, pp. 14. 19910

First Annual Report of the Board of Attending and Consulting Physicians and Surgeons of Dexter Asylum. *Providence: Smith & Parmenter.* 1829. 8vo, pp. 12. Continued. 19911

DEZA Y ULLOA (C.) Defensa Juridica, y meritos de Justicia de la que assiste a el D. Antonio Deza y Ulloa, Alcalde Mayor, que sué de la Provincia de Zacatlan, en el Pleyto quey oy siguen sus alvaceas con D. Juan de Yramategui, sobre la insubsistencia nullidad de las disposiciones Testamentarias de las S. Doña Clara Deza y Ulloa, etc. *Mexico: J. B. du Hogal.* 1729. Folio. 19912

DÉZOTEUX (*Le Chev.*) L'Administration du Marquis de Pombal, Ministre du Roi de Portugal, Joseph I. *Amsterdam.* 1788. 4 vols., 8vo. S. 19913

Perhaps contains some reference to American matters, as it is included in Warden's "Bibl. Americana."

DEZUELTA (P.) Trial of Pedro Dezuelta on a Charge of Slave Trading, &c. *London.* 1844. Rl. 8vo, pp. 484. 19914

D'HAUTEVILLE (P. D. G.) Report of the D'Hauteville Case: the Commonwealth of Pennsylvania, at the Suggestion of Paul Daniel Gonzalve Grand D'Hauteville, *versus* David Sears, Miriam C. Sears, and Ellen Sears Grand D'Hauteville. Habeas Corpus for the Custody of an Infant Child. *Philadelphia: printed by William S. Martien.* 1840. 8vo, pp. 295. C. 19915

D'HAUTEVILLE. Review of the D'Hauteville Case. *Boston.* 1841. 8vo, pp. 41. 19916

DHORMOYS (Paul). Sous les tropiques; souvenirs de voyage. *Paris: Librairie centrale.* 1865. 12mo. 19917

DHORMOYS. Une visite chez Soulouque, souvenirs d'un voyage dans l'île d'Haïti. Par Paul Dhormoys. *Paris: Librairie nouvelle.* 1859. 18mo. + *Paris: L. Hachette.* 1864. 18mo, pp. 263. 19918

Diagrams of the Floor of the Senate and House of Representatives ... . Also Descriptions of Leutze's Picture ... and Walker's Picture ... . *Washington.* [n. d.] 8vo, pp. (12). H.

The Dial: a Magazine for Literature, Philosophy, and Religion. *Boston.* M DCCC XLI–XLIV. 4 vols., 8vo, pp. vi, 544; vi, 544; iv, 548; iv, 540. BA. 19920

Edited by Miss S. Margaret Fuller; afterwards, Ossoli, R. W. Emerson, and George Ripley. Publishers, Vol. I., *Weeks, Jordan and Company*; II. and III., *E. P. Peabody*; IV. *James Munroe and Co.*

The Dial: A Monthly Magazine for Literature, Philosophy, and Religion. M. D. Conway, Editor. ... *Cincinnati.* 1860. 8vo, pp. 778. 19921

Dialogo entre una señorita y un Indio. [n. p. n. d.] Sm. 8vo, pp. 8. 19922

Dialogo primero y segundo entro un Payo y un Carbonero. *Mexico.* 1810. Sm. 8vo, pp. 16. 19923

Dialogue between A and B, relative to Seizing Goods. *New York.* 1784. 8vo. N. 19924

Dialogue between a Merchant and a Planter. Part II. ... . *Columbia.* 1832. 8vo, pp. 12. BA. 19925

A Dialogue between Andrew Trueman, and Thomas Zealot; About the killing the Indians at Canestogue and Lancaster. *Printed at Ephesus.* 12mo, pp. 7. P. 19926

An extremely rare tract against the Paxton men.

Dialogue between an Episcopalian and a Presbyterian, on the subject of the late Meeting of some Episcopalians at Mechanics' Hall, in the City of New York, 1813. [*New York.* 1813.] 8vo, pp. 8. N. 19927

Dialogue between George III and his Ministers; giving an Account of the late Mob in London, and the Original of the Sect called Shakers. *Worcester.* 1783. 12mo. W. 19928

A Dialogue between the Ghost of General Montgomery and an American Delegate. *See* [Paine (Thomas)].

A Dialogue between the Giant Polypheme and his son Jack Nothing: on occasion of his life being put out by a Stranger: with a Dedication to Sir John Brute. ... *Printed at Constantinople, in the year* 1698. 12mo, pp. 8. P. 19929

Really printed at Philadelphia, and relates to some local squabble.

A Dialogue between a Noble Lord and a poor Woodman. [n. p. n. d.] Broadside, pp. 1. P. 19930

Probably printed in Boston about 1776. A moral poem in doggrel verse.

Dialogue between an Old-fashioned Jackson Democrat and a Copperhead. [n. p. n. d.] 8vo, pp. 4. 19931

Dialogue between a One Thousand-dollar Clerk and a Member of Congress. *Washington.* 1836. 8vo. 19932

Relates to official salaries.

A | Dialogue | between | A Southern Delegate, | and | His Spouse, | on his return from | The Grand Continental Congress. | A Fragment, | inscribed | To the Married Ladies of America. | By their most sincere, | And affectionate friend, | And Servant, | Mary V. V. | *Printed in the Year* M,DCC,LXXIV. 8vo, pp. 14. BA., P. 19933

"This tract, which is in verse, is supposed to have been written by Jefferson." Manuscript note in J. B. Chandler's copy. *See* "M. Rev.," LII. 263.

A Dialogue between Telemachus and Mentor, on the Rights of Conscience and Military Requisitions. *Boston.* 1818. 12mo, pp. 16. H., M. 19934

A Dialogue between two Gentlemen in New York (distinguished by the Names Josiah and Sr. Simon) relating to the publick Affairs of New Jersey. 4to, pp. 7. P. 19935

Probably printed by B. Franklin in 1744.

A Dialogue between Two Great Ladies. *London: M. Cooper.* [n. d.] 8vo. 19936

See "M. Rev.," XXII. 346.

A Dialogue betwixt General Wolfe and the Marquis Montcalm, in the Elysian Fields. *London: Rivington and Fletcher.* [n. d] 8vo. 19937

See "M. Rev., XXI. p. 456.

A Dialogue, containing some Reflections on the Late Declaration and Remonstrance of the Back Inhabitants of Pennsylvania. *Philadelphia.* 1764. 8vo. P. 19938

Dialogue concerning the Slavery of the Africans. *New York.* 1785. 12mo. W. 19939

Dialogue entre deux Députés en présence de quelques collègues et de plusieurs citoyens, à l'issue de la séance du soir de l'Assemblée national, le Samedi 13 Novembre. [n. p. 1790.] 8vo, pp. 48 or less. 19940

"Contre Antoine, député de Sarreguemines [St. Domingo], au sujet du rapport à faire par lui sur la dénonciation du ministre La Luzerne."

"A Dialogue on the actual State of Parliament," and also on ... "Free Parliaments." *London.* 1783. 8vo. 19941

A Dialogue on Peace, an Entertainment, Given by the Senior Class at the Anniversary Commencement, Held at Nassau-Hall, September 28th, 1763. *Philadelphia: Printed by William Bradford.* M,DCC,LXIII. 4to, pp. 27. P. 19942

The odes, etc., were set to music by a resident graduate at Princeton. All in verse.

A Dialogue on the Penitentiary System [of Massachusetts]. *Boston. printed by Sewell Phelps.* 1820. 8vo, pp. 24. BA., M.

Dialogue on the Principles of the Constitution and Legal Liberty, compared with Despotism: applied to the American Question: and the Probable Events of the War; with Observations on some Important Law Authorities. *London: W. Owen.* 1776. 8vo, pp. 92. C. 19944

"This dialogue is judiciously conducted, and exhibits a perspicuous, sober and rational defence of the colonies." — *Monthy Review*, LV. 63.

Dialogue or Conversation between a Planter and some Headmen on a Plantation in British Guiana, joined by the Minister and Schoolmaster. By a Well-wisher to the Labouring Classes and the Colony at large. *Demerara.* 1848. 8vo. 19945

A Dialogue, or, Representation of Matters of Fact. Occasioned by some Mismanagements in an Ecclesiastical Council [in New London on complaints against the Rev. James Hillhouse. n. p.] 1736. 8vo, 2 l., pp. 35. B. 19946

Dialogues in the Shades, between General Wolfe, General Montgomery, David Hume, George Grenville and Charles Townsend. *London: G. Kearsley.* MDCCLXXVII. 12mo, pp. 120. C. 19947

Relates to the Revolution.

Dialogues of the Dead. Second Edition. *London.* 1760. 8vo. 19948

Among the dialogues is one between an English duellist and a North American savage, and another between Fernando Cortes and William Penn. There are several editions.

Diana's Shrines turned into Ready Money. *See* [Mather (S.)]

Diario de las operaciones de la expedicion contre la Plaza de Panzacola concluida por las Armas de S. M. Catolica, baxo las

ordenas del Mariscal de Campo D. Bernardo de Galvez. [n. p. n. d.] 4to, pp. 48. 19949

This tract, without date or place, was apparently printed at Madrid, about 1781.

Diario de los niños. Literatura, entretenimiento e instruccion. *Mejico.* 1839–1840. 3 vols., 4to. Plates. 19950

Diario de todo lo ocurrido en la expugnacion de los fuertes de bocachica y sitio de la ciudad de Cartagena de las Indias, formado de los pliegos remitidos à S. M. por el Virrey de Santa Fè. D. S. de Eslaba. [n. p.] 1743. 4to, pp. 23. 19951

Diario general de todo lo sucedido en España, desde que salieron las dos Armadas de Galeones, y Flota destos Reynos, para los de la America; venida del exercito del enemigo á Madrid, expulsion y huyda del; traydores y traiciones descubiertas; mudada y buelta de los Consejos, reformacion dellos y de los Ministros desleales de todas clases; decretos y hechos de Don Felipe V. y recibimiento que le hizo la villa de Madrid. [n. p. n. d.] 4to, Title, 1 l, pp. 80. 19952

Supposed to be printed at Madrid or Seville, about 1707.

Diario histórico de la Campaña de Apure en 1837. *Carâcas.* 1837. Imp. 8vo, pp. 50. 19953

Diario Historico. *See* [Costanso (Miguel)], No. 17020.

Diario notable de la Marquesa de las Amarillas, virreyna de Mexico, desde el puerto de Cadiz hasta la referida corte, por un criado de su excellencia D. A. J. R. B. F. D. M. *Mexico.* 1757. Sm. 8vo, 35 l. 19954

"Volume de poésies fort rare." — TROSS.

Diario y Derrotero de lo caminado, visto, y obcervado en el discurso de la visita general de Precídios, situados en las Provincias Ynternas de Nueva-España, que de orden de Su Majestad executo D. Pedro de Rivera, haviendo transitado por los Reinos del Nuevo de Toledo, el de la Nueva Galicia, el de la Nueva Vizcaya, el de la Nueva Mexico, el de la Nueva Estramadura, el de las Nuevas Philipinas, el del Nuevo de Leon, las Provincias de Sonora, Ostimuri, Sinaloa y Guasteca. *Impresso en Guathemala.* 1736. Folio, 39 l. 19955

A Diary. Four Months of Prison Life of 1st Maryland Regiment, at Lynchburg and Richmond, by a Sergeant of the 1st Maryland, a Prisoner. *Baltimore: Sherwood & Co.* 1863. 8vo, pp. 24. 19956

The Diary of a Lady of Gettysburg, Pennsylvania, from June 15 to July 15, 1863. [Not published.] 19957

The Diary of a Samaritan. By a Member of the Howard Association of New Orleans. *New York: Harper & Brothers.* 1860. 12mo, pp. 324. 19958

Diary of a Southern Refugee during the War. By a Lady of Virginia. *New York: E. J. Hale & Son.* 1867. 12mo, pp. 360.

Diary of the Great Rebellion. Containing a Complete Summary of each day's Events, from the Inauguration of the Rebellion at Charleston, S. C., December 20, 1860, to the first of January, 1862. ... *Washington: Bixler & Winchester.* 1862. 16mo, pp. 64. 19960

A Diary of the Wreck of H. M. S. Challenger, on the Western Coast of South America, In May 1835; with an Account of the subsequent Encampment of the Officers and Crew, during a period of seven weeks, on the South Coast of Chili. *London: Longman.* 1836. 8vo, 2 l., pp. 160. 4 Maps. C.

DIAS (A. G.) Diccionario da lingua Tupy chamada lingua geral dos indigenas do Brazil, Por Antonio Gonçalves Dias. *Lipsià: F. A. Brockhaus.* 1858. 16mo, pp. viii, 191. C., H.

DIAS. Obras posthumas de A. Gonçalves Dias precedidas de uma noticia da sua vida y obras pelo Dr. Antonio Henriques Leal. *San Luiz do Maranhão.* 1868. 3 vols., 8vo, pp. lxiv, 216; 250; 400. Portrait. 19963

Also: Os Tymbiras. Poema americano. Cantos I.–IV. *Leipzig.* 1857. 8vo.— Cantos. Collecçao de poesias. 3a ediç. Com o retrato do autor. *Leipzig.* 1861. 8vo.

DIAZ DE ARCE (J.) El Proximo Evangelico Exemplificado en la Vida del Ven. Bernardino Alvares, Patriarca de la Orden de la Caridad instituda en sú Hospital General, que fundo en S. Hypolito de Mexico, etc. *Mexico.* 1651. Sm. 4to, 6 l., Text, 6 l., Table, 6 l. 19964

DIAS DE ARCE. Libro de la Vida del proximo evangelico, el vener. Padre Bernardino Alvarez, patriarcha, y fundador de la Sagrada Religion de la Charidad, y S. Hypolito Martyr en esta Nueva España ... Compuesto por D. Juan Dias de Arce, Doctor Theologo Mexicano ... *Reimpressa en Mexico en la Imprenta nueva Antuerpiana de D. Christoval, y D. Phelipe de Zuñiga, y Ontiveros, Calle de la Palma. Año de* 1762. 4to, 5 l., pp. 464, 4 l. Plate. 19965

DIAZ (J. D.) Memoires du General Murillo relatifs aux principaux événements de ses campagnes en Amérique de 1815 à 1821 suivis de deux pieces de Don José Domingo Diaz et de Gen. Don Miguel de la Torre. *Paris: P. Dufart.* 1826.

[DIAZ.] Recuerdos sobre la rebelion de Caracas. *Madrid.* 1829. 4to. 19967

DIAZ (J. F.) Extracto alfabetico de los acuerdos generales e interesantes de la Junta superior directiva de Hacienda, formado de orden del Excmo. Sr. D. Claudio Martinez de Pinillos por Jose Francisco Diaz. Edicion oficial. *Habana.* 1846. 8vo, pp. x, 522. 19968

DIAZ (N. Ant.) Oracion que a glorias del Principe de los Apostoles N. P. S. Pedro, predico en la Iglesia Metropolitana de Lima. *Lima.* 1861. 4to. 19969

DIAZ (P.) De quinquaginta duobus ex Soc. Jesu, dum in Brasiliam navigant, pro catholica fide interfectis, epistolæ duæ Petri Diazii ad Leonem Henricum Provinciæ Lusitaniæ. *Antuerpiæ.* 1605. 8vo. 19970

Title from Carayon's "Bibl. Hist." The following is from Ternaux, No. 291:

DIAZ. Epistolæ duæ de LII Jesuitis interfectis in Brasilia. *Antverpiæ.* 1605. 8vo. 19971

DIAZ (Sosé A.) El Agricultor Venezolano, ó Lecciones de Agricultura práctica nacional. *Carâcas.* 1861–64. 2 pts., 8vo, pp. ix, 316; xiii, 349. 19972

DIAZ CALVILLO (Juan Bautista). Discurso sôbre los males que puede causar la Desunion entre Españoles ultra-marinos y Americanos, aprobado por el ilustre Claustro de esta real y pontificia Universidad en el que se juntó la tarde del 4 de Octubre de 1810. *Mexico.* 1810. 4to, pp. 16. 19973

DIAZ CALVILLO. Sermon que en el Aniversario solemne de gracias a Maria Santisima de los Remedios, celebrado en esta Santa Iglesia catedral el dia 30 de Octobre de 1811 por la Victoria del Monte de las Cruces, predicó el P. Dr. Don Juan Bautista Diaz Calvillo. *Mexico: Arizpe.* 1811. Sm. 4to, pp. 269.

Pages 60 to 269 contain, "Noticias para la Historia de Nuestra Senora de los Remedios desde el Año de 1800, hasta el Corriente de 1812. Ordenabalas el Autor del Sermon antecedente. *Mexico.* 1812." "An extraordinary volume of considerable historical interest. According to this pious author, Our Lady of Mexico, between 1808 and 1812, seems not only to have taken an active interest in the spiritual welfare of

the faithful, but seems to have done her best to thwart the schemes of the rebels and republicans in the various provinces of Mexico. She set her face firmly against the spirit of Mexican independency, and became quite a politician, but always attached to the royal party. The pious political frauds contained in this volume must ever give it a prominent place among the books relating to the history of the Mexican Revolution." — STEVENS.

DIAZ COVARRUBIAS (J.) Gil Gomez el insurgente, o la hija del médico. Novela historica mexicana. *Mexico.* 1858. 12mo.

DIAZ DE HORTEGA. Sermon que el dia 13 de Setiembre, ultimo del Solemne Novenario, celebrado en el Convento de PP. Dieguinos de Nuestra Señora de Guadalupe, por los Comunidades, clero ... de la Ciudad de Valladolid de Michoacan, para implorar el auxilio divino en las necesidades presentes de la Monarquia, predicó El Sr. D. Jose Diaz de Hortega. *Mexico.* 1868. 4to, 2 l., pp. 16. 19976

DIAZ DEL CASTILLO (Antonio). Sermon Funebre en las Honras al Capitan D. Gaspar de Villalpando Centeno. *Mexico.* 1722. 4to. 19977

DIAZ DEL CASTILLO (B). Historia Verdadera de la Conqvista de la Nueva-España. Escrita Por el Capitan Bernal Diaz del Castillo, vno de sus Conquistadores. Sacada a lvz Por el P. M. Fr. Alonso Remon, Predicador, y Coronista General del Orden de Nuestra Señora de la Merced Redempcion de Cautivos. A la Catholica Magestad del Mayor Monarca Don Felipe Qvarto, Rey de las Españas, y Nuevo Mundo, N. Señor. Con Privilegio. *En Madrid: en la Imprenta del Reyno. Año de* 1632. Folio, 6 l., pp. 254, (1), 6 l. C., G., H. 19978

First edition, of much rarity. Lord Rothesay's copy sold for £5 10s. It was reprinted the same year, with the addition of chapter CCXII. [numbered CCXXII.], with the following title:

DIAZ DEL CASTILLO. Historia verdadera de la conquista de la Nueva España por Fernando Cortez, y de la cosas acouncidas desde el año 1518, hasta la en muerte en el año 1547, y despues hasta el 1550; escrita pel el capitan Bernal Diaz del Castillo, uno de sus conquistadores, y sacada a luz per el P. Alonso Remon, coronista del orden de N. S. de la Merced. *Madrid: Emprenta del Reyno.* [1632.] Folio, 10 l., pp. 256. 19979

Priced, in 1870, by Tross, at 45 francs.

DIAZ DEL CASTILLO. Historia Verdadera de la Conquista de la Nueva España. Escrita por el Capitan Bernal Diaz del

Castillo, uno de sus Conquistadores. *En Madrid: en la Imprenta de Don Benito Cano Año de* 1795–1796. 4 vols., 16mo, 4 l., pp. 367; 382, (1); 364, (1); 573. 19980

Diaz del Castillo. Historia verdadera de la conquista de la Nueva España; Escrita por el capitan Bernal Diaz del Castilho. Nueva edicion, corregida. *Paris: Rosa.* 1837. 4 vols., 12mo. + *Mexico.* 1854. 4 vols., 12mo. 19981

Also included in the "Bibl. de Ansores Españoles," Vol. LII.

Diaz del Castillo. The Full and True History of the Conquest of Mexico, by Cortez. ... By Captain Bernal Diaz del Castillo, one of the Conquerors. Translated ... by Arthur Prynne. *Albany: J. Munsell.* [1839.] 8vo. 19982

This was a chap-book, condensed from the well-known work by Diaz, got up by Joel Munsell, to aid in filling a temporary lull in business.

Diaz del Castillo. The Memoirs of the Conquistador Bernal Diaz del Castillo written by himself containing a True and Full Account of the Discovery and Conquest of Mexico and New Spain Translated from the Original Spanish by John Ingram Lockhart, F.R.A.S. ... *London: J. Hatchard and Son.* MDCCCXLIV. 2 vols., 8vo, pp. xvi, 399; viii, 416. BA., C., P.

Diaz del Castillo. The True History of the Conquest of Mexico, By Captain Bernal Diaz del Castillo, One of the Conquerors. Written in the Year 1568. ... . Translated from the Original Spanish, By Maurice Keatinge, Esqr. *London: J. Wright.* 1800. 4to, pp. viii, 514, (1). Plan of Mexico. BA.

Diaz del Castillo. The True History of the Conquest of America. From the Spanish, by M. Keatinge. *Salem, (Mass.): Cushing & Appleton.* 1803. 2 vols., 8vo, pp. viii, 333, Map; iv, 440. + *Re-printed at Salem.* 1803. 2 vols., 8vo, pp. vii, 333; iv, 440, Notes, 1 l. 19985

See Kerr's "Colleetion of Voyages," v. 3, 4.

Diaz del Castillo. Denkwürdigkeiten des Hauptmanns Bernal Diaz del Castillo, oder wahrhafte Geschichte der Entdeckung und Eroberung von Neu-Spanien, von einem der Entdecker und Eröberer selbst geschrieben, aus dem Spanischen ins Deutsche übersetzt und mit dem Leben des Verfassers, mit Anmerkungen und andern Zugaben versehen von Ph. J. von Rehfues. *Bonn: Marcus.* 1838. 4 pts. in 2 vols., 8vo, pp. lxviii, 274; 300; 314; 352. + *Bonn: Marcus.* 1843–44. 4 vols., 8vo. 19986

Diaz del Castillo. Die Entdeckung und Eroberung von Mexiko, nach dessen gleichzeitigen Erzählung bearbeitet von der Uebersetzerin des Vasari. Mit einem Vorwort von Karl Ritter. *Hamburg und Gotha: F. und A. Perthes.* 1848. 2 vols., 8vo, pp. xii, 580. Lithographed Map, folio. 19987

Bernal Diaz was the companion of Cortes in his adventures and battles. *See* an interesting note as to the author and his work in Robertson's "America." Prescott and Ticknor each award Diaz great praise; and a writer in the "Athenæum" characterizes the work as "the most trustworthy of the narrators of this conquest." Lowndes has erroneously placed Gomara under Diaz. "The true history of the conquest of Mexico is, indeed, a delightful work, and the only account of that transaction on which we can rely; yet, because it appeared without any of those scandalous puffs which disgrace our presses, and teach our *literati* how to think, it mouldered on the shelf." — Southey.

Diaz Noriega (José Maria). Funestos recuerdes del libertador de Mexico [Iturbide] Exhumacion y autenticidad de sus restos, conducidos desde Padilla, y depositados actualmente en la iglesia catedral. *Mexico.* 1860. 4to, pp. 22. 19988

Diaz Taño (F.) El Padre Francisco Diaz Taño de la Compañia de Jesus, y Procurador general della, de las prouincias del Paraguay, Tucuman, y Rio de la Plata, dize ... 2 l. 19989

"Demande au roi d'accorder la permission au P. général, d'envoyer 60 religieux de la Compagnie, dans les provinces du Paraguay, Tucuman, et Rio de la Plata. Cette pièce entièrement inconnue a été imprimée en 1632." — Leclerc.

Diaz y Tarado (Jos. Atan.) Sermon panegirico del ss. patriarca S. San Joseph. *Puebla.* 1789. 4to, 16 l. 19990

Dibble (S.) History and General Views of the Sandwich Islands Mission. By Rev. Sheldon Dibble, a Missionary at those Islands for seven Years. *New York.* 1839. 12mo, pp. 268. 19991

Dibble. History of the Sandwich Islands. By Lahainaluna. *Press of the Missionary Seminary.* 1843. pp. viii, 464. Map.

Of great scarcity. The book and engravings appear to be of home manufacture. Also: Refutation of the Charges brought by the Roman Catholics against the American Missionaries at the Sandwich Islands. [By the Rev. Sheldon Dibble?] *Boston.* 1843. 12mo, pp. 24. H.

Diccionario Portuguez e Brasiliano, obra necessaria aos ministros do altar, que emprehenderem a conversaõ de tantos milhares de almas que ainda se achaõ dispersas pelos vastos certões do Brasil, sem o lume da fé, e baptismo. Por ***. Primeira parte. *Lisboa, na officina patriarcal.* 1795. 4to, 2 l., pp. iv, 79. 19993

Diccionario universal de Historia. *See* Alaman, Vol. I., No. 579.

Dicey (E.) Six Months in the Federal States. By Edward Dicey. *London and Cambridge: Macmillan & Co.* 1863. 2 vols., post 8vo, pp. x, 310; 1 l., pp. vi, 326. BA. 19994

The author was the correspondent of "Macmillan's Mag.," and the "Spectator."

Dick (S.) *See* McBride, "Pioneer Biog.," etc.

Dick Shift; a Political Tale. *New York.* 1819. 8vo.

Dick Twist: a Poem. *See* [Cozine (John)], Vol. V., No. 17320.

Dickens (C.) American Notes, for General Circulation. By Charles Dickens. *London: Chapman & Hall.* 1842. 2 vols., 12mo, pp. viii, 308; vii, 306. + *Paris: Galignani.* 1842. 8vo. + *Paris: Baudry; Stassin et Xavier; Amyot; Truchy.* 1842. 8vo. + *New York: Harper & Brothers.* 1842. 8vo, pp. 92. BA. + *Leipzig: B. Tauchnitz.* 1842. 18mo, pp. viii, 310. BA. + New Edition. *London: Chapman & Hall.* MDCCCL. 12mo, pp. xv, 175. + *Philadelphia: T. B. Peterson & Brothers.* 1859. 8vo. + *London: Chapman & Hall.* 1861. 12mo. + *Boston: Ticknor & Fields.* 1867. 8vo, 2 l., pp. 126. + [*New York: Hurd & Houghton.* 1867.] 16mo, 1 l., pp. 335. 19996

In the edition of 1850, Mr. Dickens gives a new preface, in which he assures his American friends that, far from intending to give them offence, he was rather prejudiced in their favor than otherwise. The book elicited much criticism at the time of its publication. *See* Rich, II. 359; "N. Am. Rev.," LVI. 212; "Q. Rev.," LXXI. 502; "Edinb. Rev.," LXXVI. 498; "Blackwood's Mag.," LII. 783; "Fraser's Mag.," XXVI. 617.

Dickens. American Notes and Pictures from Italy. People's Edition. *Chapman & Hall.* Post 8vo, pp. 298. 19997

Dickens. Amerika. Aus dem Englischen von E. A. Moriarty. *Leipzig: Weber.* 1843. 3 pts., 16mo. 8 Engravings. (Sämmtl. Werke, 40–42.) 19998

Dickens. Amerikanische Reisebemerkungen, geschrieben für Jedermann. Von Carl Dickens. (Boz.) Aus dem Englischen. *Stuttgart: Franck'sche Verlagsbuchhandlung.* 1843. 3 vols., 12mo. (Weltpanorama, 1–3.) 19999

Dickens. Amerikanske Antegnelser af Charl. Dickens (Boz). Oversat fra Engelsk ved A. Autenrieth og M. Nissen. Forste Deel. *Christiania.* 1843. 8vo, pp. 119. 20000

Dickens. Charles Dickens aangeboden Snuifje door eene Amerikaansche Dame, in brieven van Londen naar New-York. Uit het Engelsch. *Amsterdam: C. F. Stemler.* 1843. 8vo. Plate.

Dickens. Uitstapje naar Noord-Amerika. Uit het Engelsch. *Amsterdam: C. F. Stemler.* 1842. 8vo. 20002

Dickens. Optegnelser fra Amerika, af Charles Dickens. Oversat af J. R. Dein. *Maribo.* 1852–53. 3 pts. 20003

Dickens. Change for the American Notes: in Letters from London to New-York. By an American Lady. *London: Wiley & Putnam.* 1843. Crown 8vo, pp. 392. + *New York: Harper & Brothers.* 1843. 8vo, pp. iv, (1), 5–88. BA. 20004

See "Q. Rev.," LXXIII. 129.

Dickens. Some Notes on America to be Rewritten: Suggested, with Respect, to Charles Dickens, Esq. *Philadelphia: Sherman & Co., Printers.* 1867. 8vo, pp. 20. 20005

Also: Account of the Dinner given to Charles Dickens in Boston: Feb. 1, 1842. *Boston.* 1842. — Quozziania, or Letters from Great Goslington, Mass., giving an Account of the Quoz Dinner. *Boston.* 1842. — Welcome to Charles Dickens; The Boz Ball, Jan. 26, 1842. 8vo, pp. 8.

Dickens. The Life and Adventures of Martin Chuzzlewit. By Charles Dickens. With Illustrations by Phiz. *London: Chapman & Hall.* 1844. 8vo, pp. 640. [*Ibid.*] 1858. 2 vols., 8vo. + *Paris: Galignani.* 1843–44. 2 vols., 12mo. + *Paris: Baudry; Stassin et Xavier; Amyot.* 1843–44. 2 vols., 12mo. + *New York.* 1844. + *Leipzig: B. Tauchnitz.* 1844. 2 vols., 8vo, Title, pp. 451; 452. + *New-York.* [n. d.] Folio, 2 l., pp. 150. H. + *Boston: Ticknor & Fields.* 1867. 16mo, pp. xii, 480. + [*Ibid.*] 8vo, pp. vii, 522. 20006

Repeatedly reprinted. Martin emigrates to America, and settles in the "Land of Eden."

Dickens. Vie et aventures de Martin Chizzlewit ... Traduit ... par M. Alfred Des Essarts. *Paris: L. Hachette et Cie.* 1858. 2 vols., 12mo. + [*Ibid.*] 1865. pp. viii, 953. 20007

Dickens. Leben und Schicksale des Martin Chuzzlewit. Neu aus dem Englischen von Carl Kolb. *Stuttgart: Hoffmann.* 1855. 2 vols., 8vo, pp. 1218. 20008

Dickens. Leven en lotgevallen van Maarten Chuzzlewit. Naar het Engelsch. *Amsterdam: H. Frijlink.* 1843–44. 3 pts., 8vo. + Uit het Engelsch vertaald door C. M. Mensing. ... *Haarlem: A. C. Kruseman.* 1862. 3 pts., 8vo. Lithog. Plates.

Dickens. Leben und Abentheuer Martin Chuzzlewit's. Aus dem Englischen von E. A. Moriarty. *Leipzig: Weber.* 1843–44. 10 pts., 16mo. 64 steel Engravings. (Sämmtl. Werke, 43–52.) 20010

Dickens. Martin Chuzzlwits Liv og Levnetslob. Oversat. *Odense: Milo.* 1852–53. 6 pts., 12mo. + [Another translation.] *Kjöbenhavn: Jordan.* 1853. 3 pts., 8vo. 20011

Dickens. Optegnelser fra Amerika. Oversat af J. R. Dein. *Maribo: Overs.* 1852–53. 3 pts., 8vo. 20012

[Dickens.] Martin Chuzzlewits Liv og Hændelser af Boz. Oversat fra Engelsk ved Christen Smith. Förste Hefte. *Christiania.* 1843. 8vo, pp. 64. 20013

Dickenson (J.) God's Protecting Providence, Man's surest Help and Defence in the times of the Greatest Difficulty and the most Imminent Danger: Evidenced in the Remarkable Deliverance of divers persons from the Devouring Waves of the Sea, among which they suffered Shipwrack. And, also, from the more Cruelly Devouring Jawes of the inhumane Cannibals of Florida. Faithfully related by one of the persons concerned therein; Jonathan Dickenson. *Philadelphia: Printed by Reinier Jansen.* MDCXCIX. 4to, 3 l., pp. 96. P. 20014

A book of the greatest rarity. I have only seen one perfect copy. Fisher's imperfect copy sold for $87.50. Mr. Rich, in his note to the fifth edition, attributes the work to President Dickinson, *i. e.*, Jonathan Dickinson, who is, doubtless, another person. A Dutch version is included in Van der Aa's Collection. *Leyaen.* 1707. Folio and 8vo. The second edition is equally rare:

Dickenson. [The Same.] *Printed in Philadelphia. Reprinted in London, and Sold by T. Sowle.* 1700. 8vo, 5 l., pp. 89. C. + Third Edition. *Printed at Philadelphia: Reprinted in London and Sold by the Assigns of J. Sowle.* MDCCXX. 8vo, 5 l., pp. 94. + The Second [American] Edition. *Philadelphia: Printed by Benjamin Franklin.* 1735. + Fourth Edition. *Philadelphia.* 1751. 12mo. + The Fourth Edition. *London: Printed and sold by Luke Hinde, at the Bible, in George yard, Lombard street.* 1759. 12mo. + The Fifth Edition. *London: Printed and Sold by Mary Hinde, at No. 2 in George-yard, Lombard-Street.* [1759.] 8vo, 7 l., pp. 126, 2 l. BA. + The Sixth Edition. *London: James Phillips.* MDCCLXXXVII. 12mo, pp. 136. + The Seventh Edition. *London: James Phillips.* MDCCXC. 12mo, pp. 136. + *New-York.* 1803. 12mo. + *Burlington, N. J.* 1811. 12mo. 20015

Dickenson. Jonathan Dickerson's erstaunliche Geschichte von dem Schiffbruche, den einige Personen in dem Meerbusen von Florida erlitten ... . Nebst einem Anhang von William Flemmings Trübsalen, die er nebst seiner Frau erlitten, wie sie beyde bey dem verwichenen Einfall der Indianer in dem grossen Wald (Grät-Grov) bey Canagodschick in Pensylvanien sind gefangen genommen worden. Nach dem Philadelphischen Original. *Frankfurt und Leipzig: Johann Georg Fleischer.* 1774. 8vo, pp. 128. H. 20016

Dickenson. Ongelukkige Schipbreuk en Yslyke Reystogt, van etlyke Engelschen, in den Jaare 1696 van Jamaika in West-Indiën, na Pensylvania t'scheep gegaan, en in de Golf van Florida gestrand, &c. Vertaald door ... W. Sewel. *Te Leyden: By Pieter van der Aa, Boekverkooper.* [n. d.] 8vo, pp. 100, and Index. 3 Engravings and Map. 20017

Dickerson (E. N.) The Navy of the United States. An Exposure of its Condition, and the Causes of its Failure ... by Edward N. Dickerson, of New-York, in the Case of Mattingly vs. the Washington and Alexandria Steamboat Company. ... *New-York: John A. Gray & Green, Printers.* 1864. 8vo, pp. 80. BA., H. 20018

Also: The Steam Navy of the United States; its past, present and future. A Letter to the Hon. Gideon Welles, Secretary of the Navy ... . *New York: J. A. Gray & Green.* 1863. 8vo, pp. 20. C., H.

Dickerson (Mahlon). Observations of Mr. Dickerson, of New Jersey, on the Bill for the Appointment of the Representation in Congress. Made in the Senate of the United States, March 12, 1832. *Washington.* 1832. 8vo, pp. 12. H. 20019

Also: Address delivered at the opening of the Nineteenth Annual Fair of the American Institute ... *New York.* 1846. 8vo. — Speech ... in the Senate ... on the Mission to Panama. March 13, 1826. [n. p. n. d.] 12mo, pp. 15. H. — Speech ... on the Distribution of the Revenue. ... Washington, February 1, 1827. *Washington.* 1827. 8vo, pp. 23. P. — Speech ... on the Reduction of the Tariff, ... January 23, 1832, In the Senate ... . *Washington: Jonathan Elliot.* [n. d.] 8vo, pp. 31. H.

Dickerson (T.) A Lecture on the City of Patterson, its past, present and future, delivered by Th. Dickerson, Esq. ... January 31, 1856. *Patterson: Peoples' Mirror Office.* 1856. 8vo, pp. 26. 20020

Dickeson (M. W.) The American Numismatic Manual of the Currency or Money of the Aborigines, and Colonial, State, and United States Coins. With Historical and Descriptive No-

tices of each Coin or Series. By Montroville Wilson Dickeson, M.D. ... Illustrated by Twenty Plates of Fac-similes. *Philadelphia: J. B. Lippincott & Co.* 1859. 4to, pp. 256. Portrait and 20 Plates. BA. + Second Edition. [*Ibid.*] 1860. 4to, pp. 271. Portrait and 20 Plates. H. + Third Edition. [*Ibid.*] 1865. 4to.

Dickeson (M. W.), *and* Brown (A.) Report on the Cypress Timber of Mississippi and Louisiana. By M. W. Dickeson, and Andrew Brown. *Philadelphia.* 1848. 8vo. P. 20022

Dickey (*Mr.*) Speech of Mr. Dickey of Pennsylvania, on the Tariff Bill. Delivered in the House ... May 4th, 1844. *Washington.* 1844. 8vo, pp. 16. H. 20023

Dickins (A.) An Eulogium on General George Washington, pronounced on the 22d of February, 1800, before the Hermathenian Society of Philadelphia, by Asbury Dickins. [*Philadelphia.* 1800.] 8vo, pp. 29. 20024

Dickins. Oration, delivered in the Capitol in the City of Washington, on the Fourth of July, 1825, by Asbury Dickins. ... . *Washington: Gales and Seaton.* 1825. 8vo, pp. 19. BA.

Dickinson (A.) The City of the Dead; and other Poems. By Andrew Dickinson. *New York: Saxton & Miles.* 1845. 12mo, pp. 108. Plate. 20026

Contains poems on Greenwood Cemetery, Croton Water Works, Fourth of July, etc. Mr. Dickinson is the author of "My First Visit to Europe. ... Fifth Edition. *New York.* 1856."

Dickinson (A. E.) What Answer? [A Story of the War.] By Anna E. Dickinson. *Boston: Ticknor & Fields.* 1868. 12mo, 1 l., pp. 301. C., H. 20027

Dickinson (A.) Appeal to American Youth on Temperance. By Rev. Austin Dickinson. 12mo. S. 20028

Also: Sermon. [In Cherokee.] [With] the Story of David Rouge. [*Cherokee.* About 1845?] 24mo, pp. 24 C. — Memoir of the Rev. Austin Dickinson, A.M. [n. p. n. d.] 8vo, pp. 12. H.

Dickinson (D. S.) Speech of Hon. Daniel S. Dickinson, of New York, ... at the Cooper Institute, New York, July 18, 1860. *Washington City.* 1868. 8vo, pp. 16. 20029

In favor of Breckenridge and Lane.

Dickinson. Speeches, Correspondence, etc., of the late D. S. Dickinson, of New York. Edited, with a Biography, by his Brother, J. R. Dickinson. *New York: G. P. Putnam & Son.* 1867. 2 vols., 8vo, pp. xi, 743; xvi, 719. Portrait. C. 20030

Dickinson. The Union: an Address by the Hon. Daniel S. Dickinson, delivered before the Literary Societies of Amherst College, July 10th, 1861. *New York: James G. Gregory.* 1861. 8vo, pp. 24. H. 20031

Also: Acquisition of Territory: Speech, ... Senate, Jan. 12, 1848. [n. p. n. d.] 8vo, pp. 7. — Address delivered at Hartford on the 17th September, 1861, the Anniversary of the Adoption of the Constitution of the United States, September 17, 1787. ... *Hartford.* 1861. 8vo, pp. 15. — The Duty of Loyal Men. Speech ... at the Union Meeting in New York, October 9, 1862. Seymour Democracy Dissected. 8vo, pp. 15. — An Address ... Law Department of Hamilton College, July 21, 1858. *Utica.* 1858. 8vo. S. — Address at the Exhibition of the Queen's County Agricultural Society, 1843. *Hempstead.* 1844. 8vo. B. — The Governor's Message. Remarks ... In the Senate, January 11, 1840, upon Resolutions to refer the Governor's Message. [*Washington.* n. d.] 8vo, pp. 8. — Great Speech to the Democracy in Mass Meeting Assembled at Wyoming County, Pennsylvania, August 19, 1861, on the Existing Rebellion. 8vo, pp. 8. — Remarks of ... upon Mr. Clemen's Resolutions concerning California. *Washington.* 1850. 8vo. B. — Sectional Agitation. Remarks ... In the Senate ... January 17, 1850, Upon Mr. Clemen's Resolutions calling for the Instructions of the President concerning California; with a Sketch of the Debate on that Day. [*Washington.* n. d.] 8vo, pp. 8. H. — Speech ... on the Annexation of Texas: ... in the Senate ... February 22, 1845. *Washington.* 1845. 8vo, pp. 13. H. — Speech ... on the Oregon Question. ... February 24 & 25, 1846. *Washington: Union Office.* 1846. 8vo, pp. 14. — Speech ... in Reply to Hon. Daniel Webster, on the North-eastern Boundary, the Right of Search, and the Destruction of the Caroline. ... April 9, 1846. [*Washington.* n. d.] 8vo, pp. 16. H. — Speech ... in the Senate on Establishing a Government for California. [n. p. n. d.] 8vo. B. — Speech ... at Tammany Hall Dinner ... 1850. S.

Dickinson. Testimonial of Respect of the Bar of New York to the Memory of Daniel S. Dickinson. *New York.* 1866. 8vo.

Dickinson (J.) A Journal of the Life, Travels, and Labour of Love in the Work of the Ministry, of that Worthy Elder, and Faithful Servant of Jesus Christ, James Dickinson. *London: T. Sowle Raylton and Luke Hinde.* 1745. 8vo. 20033

Reprinted with "The Journal of Thomas Wilson." *London.* 1847. Fcap 8vo, and in "The Friends' Library." *Philadelphia.* 1848.

[Dickinson.] A Salutation of Love to the Seed of God Everywhere. [From on board the Ship, (Providence in the Downs going to America) the 18th 12th month, 1695.] *London: T. Sowle.* 1696. 4to, pp. 4. + *London: Printed, and Reprinted in Dublin by John Ray.* 1710. 12mo. P. 20034

Dickinson visited Barbadoes in 1691, travelled through New Jersey, New York, Virginia, Maryland, etc., went to Antigua, returned to England, and again visited New England in 1714.

Dickinson (James T.) Genealogies of the Lymans of Middlefield, of the Dickinsons of Montreal, and of the Partridges of Hatfield. *Boston: David Clapp & Son, Printers.* 1865. 8vo, pp. 32. 20035

DICKINSON. A Sermon delivered in the Second Congregational Church, Norwich, On the Fourth of July, 1834, at the Request of the Anti-Slavery Society of Norwich & Vicinity. By James T. Dickinson. ... *Norwich: Anti-Slavery Society.* 1834. 8vo, pp. 40. BA., C., M. 20036

[DICKINSON (John)]. An Address to The Committee of Correspondence in Barbados, Occasioned by a late letter from them To Their Agent in London. By a North-American. ... *Philadelphia: William Bradford.* M,DCC,LXVI. 8vo, pp. vi, 18.

[DICKINSON.] A Letter to the North American, On Occasion of his Address to the Committee of Correspondence in Barbados. By a Native of the Island. ... *Barbados: Printed by George Esmand and Camp.* M.DCC.LXVI. 8vo, pp. 47. P. 20038

The Barbadoes letter, which expresses indignation at the Stamp Act, while it terms the opposition of the Northern Colonies rebellious, is printed at length in the preface. *See* Vol. I., No. 3262, and Duyckinck's "Cyclopædia," I. 182.

DICKINSON. Assembly. John Dickinson, (etc.) *** *Philadelphia, October* I. 1772. Broadside, 4to, p. 1. P. 20039

An election circular.

[DICKINSON.] An | Essay | on the Constitutional Power of | Great-Britain | over the Colonies in | America; | with the | Resolves | of the | Committee | for the Province of | Pennsylvania, | and their Instructions | To their Representatives | in Assembly. | *Philadelphia: William and Thomas Bradford.* M,DCC,LXXIV. | 8vo, pp. vii, 127 (1). BA., C., P. 20040

For an English edition, *see* "A New Essay," *infra.* In the "Catalogue of the Philadelphia Library," this work is attributed to William Smith and John Dickinson.

[DICKINSON.] Friends and Countrymen ... [*Philadelphia*, about *Dec.* 5, 1765.] Folio, pp. 2. P. 20041

A denunciation of the Stamp Act.

[DICKINSON.] An Address on the Past, Present and Eventful Relations of the United States to France. *New York.* 1803. 8vo.

[DICKINSON.] The Late Regulations respecting the British Colonies on the Continent of America considered, In a Letter from a Gentleman in Philadelphia to his Friend in London. ... . *Philadelphia: Printed by William Bradford.* M.DCC.LXV. 8vo, pp. 38. + *Philadelphia Printed: London Re-printed for J. Almon.* M.DCC.LXV. 8vo, pp. 62. BA. + *Philadelphia Printed: London; Re-printed for J. Almon.* MDCCLXVI. 8vo, 2 l., pp. 39.

[DICKINSON.] Letters from a Farmer in Pennsylvania, to the Inhabitants of the British Colonies. *Boston: Printed by Mein and Fleeming, and to be sold by John Mein, at the London Book-Store, North-Side of King-Street.* 8vo, pp. 146, (2). + The Second Edition. *Philadelphia: Printed by David Hall, and William Sellers.* MDCCLXVIII. 8vo, pp. 71. + The Third Edition. *Philadelphia: William and Thomas Bradford.* M.DCC.LXIX. 8vo, Title, pp. 104. + *Boston: Edes & Gill.* MDCCLXVIII. 8vo, pp. 146, (2). BA., H. + *London, Re-printed: J. Almon.* M DCCLXVIII. 8vo, 2 l., pp. iii, 118. BA., H. + [*Dublin.*] 1768. 8vo. + *New York: Re-Printed by John Holt.* 1768. 12mo, pp. 118. + *Williamsburgh, (Va.)* 1769. 8vo. C. + *Philadelphia.* 1774. 8vo, pp. 136. C., H. + *London: J. Almon.* MDCCLXXIV. 8vo, pp. 136. C. 20044

The London edition has a preface by the English editor. "A calm yet full enquiry into the right of the British Parliament to tax the American colonies; the unconstitutional nature of which attempt is maintained in a well-connected chain of close and manly reasoning."—*M. Rev.*, XXXIX. 18. "My Lord Hillsborough mentioned the Farmer's Letters to me, said he had read them, that they were well written, and he believed he could guess who was the author, looking in my face at the same time, as if he thought it was me. He censured the doctrines as extremely wild, &c. I have read them as far as No. 8: I know not if any more has been published. I should have thought they had been written by Mr. Delancy, not having heard of the others you point out as joint authors."—*Franklin's Letter to his Son*, "*Memoirs*," III. 306, *March*, 1768.

[DICKINSON.] Lettres d'un fermier de Pensylvanie aux habitans de l'Amérique Septentrionale. Traduites de l'Anglois [par Barbeu Dubourg]. *Amsterdam* [*Paris*]. M. DCC. LXIX. 8vo, pp. xxviij, 258. H., S. 20045

In this translation, it is stated that thirty editions of the original work were printed in six months, in America, and that Dr. Franklin had them reprinted in London.

[DICKINSON.] A New | Essay. | (By the Pennsylvanian Farmer,) | on the Constitutional Power of | Great-Britain | over the Colonies in | America; | with the | Resolves | of the | Committee | for the Province of | Pennsylvania | and their | Instructions | To their Representatives | in Assembly. | *Philadelphia, Printed; London, Re-printed for J. Almon.* 1774. | 8vo, pp. viii, 126, (1).

See "M. Rev.," LI. 390.

[DICKINSON.] Remarks | on the new | Essay | of the | Pennsylvanian Farmer; | and on the | Resolves and Instructions | Prefixed to that Essay; | By the Author of The Right of the British | Legislature vindicated. | ... [9 lines] | *London: Printed for T. Becket.* MDCCLXXV. | 8vo, Title, pp. 62. BA., H. 20047

The writer examines with care the various points of the "New Essay," and believes he has "exposed the futility of every false proposition contained in it," adds, "but I flatter myself I have pulled the veil of deceit from so much of the performance, as will convince every candid reader, that it is a system of obscurity founded upon malevolent misrepresentation and ignorance." *See* "M. Rev."

DICKINSON. The Political Writings of John Dickinson, Esquire, Late President of the State of Delaware, and of the Commonwealth of Pennsylvania. ... *Wilmington: Bonsal and Niles.* 1801. 2 vols., 8vo, pp. xvi, 416; 384, Errata, 1 l., Subscribers, 6 l. Portrait. BA., H. + *Wilmington: Miller Dunott.* 1814. 2 vols., 8vo. 20048

The edition dated 1814 has new title-pages only.

DICKINSON. A | Speech, | Delivered in | The House of Assembly | Of the Province of Pennsylvania, | May 24th, 1764, | By John Dickinson, Esq; | One of the Members for the County of Philadelphia. | On Occasion of a Petition, drawn up by Order, and then | under Consideration, of the House; Praying His Majesty for | a Change of the Government of this Province: | With | A Preface. | *Philadelphia: William Bradford.* MDCCLXIV. | 8vo, pp. xii, 45. C. + Second Edition. *Philadelphia: William Bradford.* MDCCLXIV. 8vo, pp. xii, 30. P. + *Philadelphia, Printed; London, Re-Printed for J. Whiston and B. White.* M.DCC.LXIV. 8vo, pp. xv, 31. BA., C., H. 20049

"Mr. Dickinson reasons like a man of extraordinary good sense, with the knowledge of an able politician, and the pleasing flow of an accomplished orator."—*M. Rev.*, XXXI. 318. The preface to Mr. Dickinson's speech is attributed to Rev. Messrs. Peters, Smith, Allison, and Ewing. *See* W. Franklin's "Humble Attempt at Scurrility, etc. *Philadelphia.* 1765," pp. 13.

DICKINSON. The Maybe; or some observations occasion'd by reading a Speech deliver'd in the House of Assembly, the 24th of May last, by a certain eminent Patriot. ... *Philadelphia: Printed by Anthony Armbruster.* [1764.] 8vo, pp. 7. 20050

DICKINSON. A Reply to a Piece called the Speech of Joseph Galloway, Esq; By John Dickinson. ... *Philadelphia.* MDCCLXIV. 8vo. + *London: J. Whiston and B. White.* M DCC LXV. 8vo, pp. iv, 62, (1). H. 20051

See "Monthly Review," XXXII. 67.

DICKINSON. Letter to John Dickinson. *See* [Macpherson (John)].

For a satire on Dickinson, *see* our No. 5584, Vol. II.

[DICKINSON (John), *and* LEE (Arthur).] The Farmer's and Monitor's Letters to the Inhabitants of the British Colonies. *Williamsburg,* [*Virginia*]. 1769. Sm. 4to, pp. 98. C. 20052

DICKINSON (Jonathan). A Brief Illustration and Confirmation of the Divine Right of Infant Baptism; in a Dialogue between a Minister and one of his Parishioners. *Providence, New England.* 1763. 12mo, pp. 42, v. 20053

DICKINSON. A Call to the Weary & heavy | Laden to come unto Christ for | Rest | A | Sermon | Preached at Connecticut Farms in Elizabeth- | Town Dec. 23. 1739. Published at the desire | of the Hearers | By Jonathan Dickinson, A.M. | Minister of the Gospel at Elizabeth-Town in | New-Jersey. | *New-York: Printed and Sold by | William Bradford.* 1740. | Sm. 8vo, pp. 45.

DICKINSON. A Defence of Presbyterian Ordination. In Answer to a Pamphlet, entituled, A Modest Proof, of the Order and Government settled by Christ, in the Church. By Jonathan Dickinson, M.A., Minister of the Gospel at Elizabeth-Town, New-Jersey. ... *Boston: Printed for Daniel Henchman, and sold at his Shop, over against the Brick Meeting House in Cornhill.* [1724.] 8vo, Half-Title, Title, pp. iii, 44. BA., H., 20055

See Checkley (J.), author of the "Modest Proof," for "Strictures" on the above.

[DICKINSON.] A Defence of the Dialogue Intitled, A Display of God's Special Grace. Against the Exceptions made to it by the Rev. Mr. A. Crosswell. In a Letter to him from the Author of that Book. ... *Boston: S. Eliot.* 1743. 8vo, Title, pp. 46. BA. 20056

Signed Theophilus.

[DICKINSON.] A Display of God's special Grace. In A familiar Dialogue Between A Minister & a Gentleman of his Congregation, About The Work of God, in the Conviction and Conversion of Sinners, so remarkably of late begun and going on in these American Parts. Wherein The Objections against some uncommon Appearances amongst us are distinctly consider'd, Mistakes rectify'd and the Work itself particularly prov'd to be from the Holy Spirit. With An Addition, in a second Conference, relating to sundry Antinomian Principles, beginning to obtain in some Places. To which is prefixed an Attestation, by several Ministers of Boston. *Boston, N. E.: Printed by Rogers and Fowle, for S. Eliot in Cornhill.* 1742. 12mo, Title, pp. vi, 111, (1). BA., H. 20057

Reprinted with the following title: A Display of God's Special Grace, ... By the Rev'd Mr. Jonathan Dickinson, Minister of the Gospel at Elizabeth Town in New-Jersey. *Philadelphia: William Bradford.* 1743. 12mo, pp. x, 74. P.

DICKINSON. Familiar Letters To a Gentleman, upon A Variety of seasonable and important Subjects in Religion. By Jonathan Dickinson, A.M. Minister of the Gospel at Elizabeth-Town, New-Jersey. *Boston: Printed and Sold by Rogers and Fowle in Queen-street; next to the Prison: And by J. Blanchard at the Bible and Crown in Dock-Square.* 1745. 8vo, Title, pp. v, 1, 424. BA. + *Edinburgh.* 1757. 8vo. + *Dundee.* 1772. 12mo. 20058

DICKINSON. Familiar Letters upon a Variety of Religious Subjects. viz. 1. The danger of infidelity. 2. The evidences of Christianity. 3. The history of our Saviour, collected from the prophecies of the Old Testament. 4. The certainty of the facts reported in the gospel. 5. The internal evidences of Christianity. 6. Objections against the internal evidences answered. 7. God's sovereign grace vindicated, &c. 8. A true and false faith distinguished. 9. A legal and evangelical repentance distinguished. 10. The characters in Rom. vii. distinctly illustrated. 11. Moravian and Antinomian justification considered. 12. Imputed righteousness explained and vindicated. 13. The new law of grace examined and disproved. 14. First and secondary justification, a groundless distinction. 15. Justification by works, in James ii. considered. 16. Our obligations to good works distinctly stated. 17. The nature and necessity of our union to Christ. 18. Antinomian pleas for licentiousness considered. 19. Directions for a close and comfortable walk with God. By Jonathan Dickinson, A.M. President of the College of New-Jersey. The Fourth Edition. *Glasgow: John Bryce.* MDCCLXXV. 8vo, pp. viii, 368. + Fourth Edition. *Edinburgh.* 1784. 12mo. + *Newark, N. J.* 1797. 12mo. + *Philadelphia.* 1841. 12mo. 20059

[DICKINSON.] Remarks upon A Discourse intituled An Overture Presented to the Synod of Dissenting Ministers in Philadelphia, in September, 1728 [by J. Thomson]. *New York.* 1729. 8vo, pp. 32. B., M. 20060

DICKINSON. Remarks upon the Postscript to the Defence of a Book lately Reprinted at Boston, entituled, A Modest Proof of the Order, &c. In a Letter of Thanks to the Author. *Boston, N. E.: D. Henchman.* 1724. 8vo, pp. (2), 29. B.

DICKINSON. A Sermon Preached at the opening of the Synod at Philadelphia, September 19, 1722. Wherein is considered the Character of the Man of God, and his Furniture for the Exercise both of Doctrine and Discipline, with the true boundaries of the Churches Power. By Jonathan Dickinson, A.M. Minister of the Gospel at Elizabeth-Town. *Boston: Printed by T. Fleet, for S. Gerrish, at his Shop in Corn-Hill.* 1723. 8vo, Half-Title, Title, pp. 24. B., BA. 20061*a*

DICKINSON. Sermons and Tracts, separately published at Boston, Philadelphia, &c. By Jonathan Dickinson, A.M. ... Now first collected in One Volume, and published in Britain. *Edinburgh: M. Gray.* M.DCC.XCIII. 8vo, 4 l., pp. 483.

Also: The Danger of Schisms and Contentions, with respect to the Ministry and Ordinance of the Gospel, represented in a Sermon ... *New York.* 1739. 12mo.—Discourse on the Divine Appointment of the Gospel Ministry and the Methods of its conveyance through the successive ages of the Church, delivered at the Ordination of Walter Wilmot. *Boston.* 1738. 8vo.—The Nature and Necessity of Regeneration ... Sermon ... preached at Newark, Jan. 19, 1742–3. ... [with] Remarks on a Discourse of Dr. Waterland's ... . *New York.* 1743. 16mo, pp. v, 66.—Observations on that Terrible Disease vulgarly called the Throat Distemper. *Boston.* 1740. 8vo, pp. 12. W. The Reasonableness of Christianity; in Four Sermons. ... . With a Preface by Mr. Foxcroft. *Boston: S. Kneeland and T. Green.* MDCCXXXII. 8vo, Title, pp. xiv, 175. B., BA., C.—The Reasonableness of Nonconformity to the Church of England, in point of Worship. A Second Defence of a Sermon preach'd at Newark, June 2, 1736, Intituled, The Vanity of Human Institutions in the Worship of God, against the Exceptions of Mr. John Beach, in his Appeal to the Unprejudiced. *Boston, New England: printed by Kneeland and Green.* 1738. 12mo, 3 l., pp. 127. BA., W.—Reflections upon Mr. Wetmore's Letter in Defence of Dr. Waterland's Discourse of Regeneration. With a Vindication of the received Doctrine of Regeneration and plain Scripture Evidence, that the Notion of Baptismal Regeneration is of a dangerous and destructive Tendency. ... *Boston, N. E.* M,DCC,XLIV. 8vo, pp. 38. H.—A Second Vindication of God's Sovereign Free Grace. Against John Beach in his God's Sovereignty. With Reflections on Dr. Samuel Johnson's Defence of Aristocles Letter to Authades. Continued [by] Moses Dickinson. *Boston.* MDCCXLVIII. 8vo, pp. 143. B., M.—The True Scripture Doctrine concerning some Important Points of Christian Faith, particularly Eternal Election, Original Sin, Grace in Conversion, Justification by Faith, and the Saints Perseverance. With a Preface by Mr. Foxcroft. *Boston: Printed by D. Fowle, for S. Kneeland and T. Green.* 1741. 8vo, pp. (2), xiii, (1), 253. + *Philadelphia.* 1741. 12mo. + With Sketch of the Life of the Author. By W. Austin. *Elizabeth Town.* 1793. 12mo, pp. 208.—Vanity of Human Institutions in the Worship of God. Sermon at Newark, June 2, 1736. ... *New York.* 1736. 12mo.—A Vindication of God's Sovereign Free Grace. In some Remarks upon Mr. John Beach's Sermon, With some brief Reflections upon H. Carner's Sermon, and on a Pamphlet entitled a Letter from Aristocles to Authades. *Boston.* 1746. 8vo, pp. 80. B. + Second Edition. *Boston.* 1743. 12mo.—The Witness of the Spirit. A Sermon preached at Newark, in New Jersey, May 7th. 1740. *Boston.* 1740. 8vo, pp. 28. + Second Edition. *Boston, N. E.: Printed by S. Kneeland & T. Green.* 1743. 8vo, Title, pp. 32. BA.

[DICKINSON (Moses).] An Answer to a Letter From an

aged Layman, to the Clergy of the Colony of Connecticut. In which the Rights of the consociated Churches are maintained; the consociation that appeared against the Ordination of Mr. Dana at Wallingford vindicated; and the Ministers like minded defended, against the Insinuations, and Reflections contained in that Letter. By an Aged Minister. *New-Haven: Printed by James Parker, and Company, at the Post-Office.* [1767?] 8vo, pp. 30. 20063

Also: An Inquiry into the Consequences both of Calvinistic and Armenian Principles ... *Boston.* 1750. 8vo, pp. 39. S.—Sermon at Ordination of Rev. Elisha Kent, New-Town, Conn., Sept. 27, 1832. *Boston.* 1733. 8vo, pp. 28.—Sermon delivered at the Funeral of Hon. Thomas Fitch, Esq., Governor of Connecticut. *New Haven.* 1774. 8vo, pp. 24.—A Sermon Preached ... on ... the ... Anniversary Election, May 8th, 1755. ... *New-London: Timothy Green.* 1755. 18mo, pp. 58. S.—Letter. *Norwalk, Conn.* 1751. *See* Hobart (N.)

DICKINSON (N.) Observations on the Inflammatory Endemic, incidental to Strangers in the West Indies from Temperate Climates, commonly called the Yellow Fever. ... . By Nodes Dickinson. ... . *London: Callow, Underwood, and Burgess and Hill.* 1819. 8vo, pp. xiv, (1), 216. BA. 20064

DICKINSON (N. S.) Slavery: the Nation's Crime and Danger. A Sermon preached in ... Foxborough, Mass. Sept. 30, 1860. By Rev. S. G. Dickinson. *Boston.* 1860. 8vo, pp. 40. H.

DICKINSON (P.) A Discourse delivered at the Funeral of the Rev. Thomas Fessenden, Senior Pastor of the Church in Walpole, (N. H.) ... . By Pliny Dickinson ... . *Brattleborough, (Vt.): printed by William Fessenden.* 1813. 8vo, pp. 15. H., W.

DICKINSON. A Sermon preached ... before ... the Senate and House ... New Hampshire, June 16 ... being the Anniversary Election. ... By Pliny Dickinson ... *Concord.* 1816. 8vo, pp. 24. 20067

DICKINSON (R.) Speech of Mr. R. Dickinson, of Ohio, on the Power of the General Government to Legislate for the Territories. Delivered in the House ... May 17, 1848. [n. p. n. d.] 8vo, pp. 8. H. 20068

DICKINSON (R. W.) A Sermon, preached ... New York, December 14, 1843, on the day of the Public Thanksgiving ... By Richard W. Dickinson, D.D. *New-York: H. Cogswell.* 1843. 8vo, pp. 30. 20069

Also: The Sincere Preacher; an Introductory Sermon, preached in the Bowery Presbyterian Church, November 13, 1836. ... *New York.* 1836. 8vo, pp. 32. N.

DICKINSON (R.) A Compilation of the Laws of Massachusetts ... . By Rodolphus Dickinson ... . *Boston: Bradford & Read, and A. Lyman & Co., Portland.* 1811. 8vo, 4 l., pp. 279.

DICKINSON. A Description of Deerfield, in Franklin County; intended as an Exhibition of the Plan of a contemplated Gazetteer of Massachusetts Proper. By Rodolphus Dickinson. *Deerfield, Mass.* 1817. 8vo. N. 20071

DICKINSON. A Digest of the Common Law, the Statute Laws of Massachusetts, and of the United States, and the Decisions of the Supreme Judicial Court of Massachusetts, relative to the Powers and Duties of Justices of the Peace. ... . By Rodolphus Dickinson ... . *Deerfield: John Wilson.* 1818. 8vo, pp. viii, 521. BA. 20072

DICKINSON. A Geographical and Statistical View of Massachusetts Proper. By Rodolphus Dickinson, Esq. *Greenfield: Printed by Denio & Phelps.* 1813. 8vo, pp. 80. BA., S. 20073

DICKINSON (S. F.) An Address delivered at Northampton, before the Hampshire, Hampden, and Franklin, Agricultural Society, October, 27, 1831. By Samuel F. Dickinson. ... *Amherst: J. S. & C. Adams, Printers.* 1831. 8vo, pp. 40. BA., H.

DICKINSON. An Oration, In Celebration of American Independence, July 4th, 1797. By Samuel F. Dickinson, A.B. *Northampton, (Massachusetts): William Butler.* M.DCC.XC.VII. 8vo, pp. 23. 20075

DICKINSON (Thomas). A Narrative of the Operations for the Recovery of the Public Stores and Treasure sunk in H. M. S. Thetis, at Cape Frio, on the Coast of Brazil. By Capt. T. Dickinson, R. N. *London.* 1836. 8vo. P. 20076

DICKINSON (T.) Sermon before the Massachusetts Missionary Society in Boston, May 28, 1811. By Timothy Dickinson. *Boston.* 1811. 8vo. W. 20077

DICKINSON COLLEGE. Catalogue of the Belles Lettres Society of Dickinson College, Pa. instituted A.D. 1786. *Philadelphia: T. K. & P. G. Collins.* 1847. 8vo, pp. 31, (1). + 1857. 8vo, pp. 48. Woodcut. H. 20078

Catalogue of the Officers and Students of Dickinson College. *Carlisle.* 1834. 16mo. Continued. C. 20079

Catalogus Senatus Academici, et eorum, qui Munera et Officia Academica gesserunt quique alicujus gradus laurea donati sunt, in Collegio Dickinsoniensi ... . *Carleoli.* M DCCC XL. 8vo, pp. 31. Continued. H. 20080

A Narrative of the Proceedings of the Board of Trustees of Dickinson College, from 1821 to 1830. Setting forth the True History of many Events which have been made the themes of Public Animadversion. Prepared by a Committee appointed by the Board ... . *Carlisle: printed by George Fleming.* 1830. 8vo, pp. 83. H. 20081

Register of the Members of the Union Philosophical Society of Dickinson College, From its establishment, August 31, 1789, to January 1, 1843. *Carlisle, Pa.* MDCCCXLIII. 8vo, pp. 28, (1). H. 20082

Register for 1846–7. *Carlisle, Pa.* S. 20083

Statutes of Dickinson College ... adopted ... April 16, 1830. ... *Carlisle.* 1830. 8vo, pp. 30. H. 20084

Statutes of Dickinson College, Including the Course of Study, Names of the Faculty, &c. *Carlisle.* 1834. 8vo. C. 20085

DICKINSON SEMINARY. Eighth Annual Catalogue of Officers and Students of Dickinson Seminary; 1855–56. *Williamsport, Pa.* 1856. 8vo. Continued. 20086

DICKSON (J. H.) An Address delivered before the Alumni Association of the University of North Carolina, June, 1853. By James H. Dickson, M.D. *Raleigh.* 1853. 8vo, pp. 43. H.

DICKSON. The Fibre Plants of India, Africa, and our Colonies. ... By James H. Dickson. *London: W. Macintosh.* 8vo, pp. xvi, 380, xxx. BA. 20088

DICKSON (John). Remarks of Mr. Dickson, of New York, on the Presentation of Several Petitions for the Abolition of Slavery and the Slave Trade in the District of Columbia. Delivered in the House ... February 2, 1835. *Washington.* 1835. 8vo, pp. 7. H. 20089

DICKSON. Speech of Mr. Dickson, on the Presentation ... of a Memorial of Three Thousand Electors of Ontario County, New York, with certain Resolutions proposed by him, delivered in the House ... May 19, 1834. *Washington: Gales & Seaton.* 1834. 8vo, pp. 28. 20090

DICKSON (M. F.) Scenes on the Shores of the Atlantic. *London.* 1845. 2 vols., post 8vo. C. 20091

[DICKSON (Samuel).] "The Destructive Art of Healing;" or, Facts for Families. ... To which is added, A Word to Women, by Lydia Jane Pierson. ... *New York.* [n. d.] 16mo, pp. 72. H. 20092

DICKSON (Samuel H.) Address before the South-Carolina Society for the Promotion of Temperance, April 6, 1830; By S. Henry Dickson. With Constitution of the Society, and Report of Columbia Temperance Society. *Charleston.* 1830. 8vo, pp. 72. M. 20093

Also: An Address delivered before the Horticultural Society of Charleston, July 11, 1832. *Charleston.* 1832. 8vo, pp. 18. M. — Address ... delivered at the Inauguration of the Public School, Fourth of July, 1856. ... *Charleston, S. C.* 1856. 8vo, pp. 24. H. — Medical Society of South-Carolina. ... . [n. p. n. d.] 8vo, pp. 8. H. — An Oration delivered at New Haven, before the Phi Beta Kappa Society, August 17, 1842. ... *New Haven: printed by B. L. Hamlin.* 1842. 8vo, pp. 47. H. — Speech delivered (in substance) at the Dinner of the New England Society, of Charleston, S. C., on their Anniversary, Dec. 22, 1854. ... *Charleston.* 1855. 8vo, pp. 15. H.

DICKSON (W.) Letters on Slavery, by William Dickson ... . To which are addded, Addresses to the Whites, and to the Free Negroes of Barbadoes; and Accounts of some Negroes eminent for their virtues and abilities. ... *London: J. Phillips,* [etc.] M.DCC.LXXXIX. 8vo, pp. x, 190, (1). BA., H. 20094

See "M. Rev.," LXXX. 357.

DICKSON. Mitigation of Slavery, in Two Parts, Part I, Letters and Papers of the late Hon. Joshua Steele; Part 2, Letters to Thos. Clarkson, Esq. *London.* 1814. 8vo. 20095

DICKSON (W. J.) La guerre d'Amérique. 1860–65. Abolition de l'esclavage par Abraham Lincoln, avec un appendice contenant la biographie de J. Wilkes Booth. Par W. Jonathan Dickson. Troisième édition. *Paris: Rome.* 12mo, pp. 240.

DICKSON (W. H.) The Absolute Equality of all Men before the Law, the only True Basis of Reconstruction. An Address, by William M. Dickson ... with an Appendix, containing John Stuart Mills' Letter on Reconstruction, and the Correspondence therewith connected. *Cincinnati.* 1865. 8vo, pp. 32. H.

DICKSON. . That we may have Peace we must now make War. Address of William M. Dickson at ... Cincinnati, September 23, 1863. *Cincinnati: Robert Clarke & Co.* 1863. 8vo, pp. 31. H. 20098

Also: Review of the Letter of General Cox, of Ohio. ... *Boston.* 1865. 8vo, pp. 4.

DICKSON (W. S.) Sermon on the following Subjects. I. The Advantages of National Repentance. II. The Ruinous Effects of Civil War ... . By William Steel Dickson. *Belfast.* 1782. 12mo. 20099

See "M. Rev.," LXVI. 78. Disapproves and laments the war with America.

DICKSON. Dickson's Narrative of an Attack upon a party of Travellers proceeding from Mexico to the Coast, in which all were destroyed but Himself by Mexican Banditti. 8vo. 20100

Dictamen ... algunas ideas sobre la historia y manera de escribir la de Mexico, especialmente la contemporanea, desde la declaracion de independencia en 1821, hasta nuestros dias. *Mexico.* 1865. 4to, pp. 92, 105. 20101

Contains a "Catalogo de los principales historiadores de Mexico."

Dictamen de la Comision de Credito publico de la Camara de diputados, sobre el arreglo de la deuda inglesa. *Mexico.* 1850. 8vo, pp. lxxv, 130. 20102

In Spanish and English, with appendices.

Dictamen de la comision de hacienda, sobre reforma del arancel provisional de aduanas maritimas. *Mexico.* 1826. pp. 10. 20103

Dictamen de la comision de la cámara de Senadores del Congrese Central, sobre la aprobacion del tratado celebrado por el Gobierno de la Republica con el de los Estados Unidos. *Querétaro.* 1848. 8vo, pp. 24. 20104

Dictamen de la Comision de Negocios eclesiasticòs de la Camara de Diputados, proponiendo se declaren nulas las canongias de ultima provision. *Mexico.* 1833. 4to, pp. 44, 10.

Dictamen de la comision de puntos constitutionales de la cámara de diputados sobre la reforma del titulo 3. de la constitucion federal. *Méjico.* 1831. Sm. 8vo, pp. 19. 20106

Dictamen de la Comision nombrada para proponer medidas conducentes al bien y felicidad de Ambas Americas; y votos adicionales de algunos Señores, Individuos de la Misma. *Madrid.* 1822. Sm. 4to, pp. 12. 20107

Dictamen de la Comision Especial de Convocatoria para un Nuevo Congreso. [*Mexico.* 1823.] 8vo, pp. 22. 20108

Dictamen de las Comisiones Eclesiastica y de Relaciones sobre las Instrucciones que deben darse á Nuesto Enviado á Roma. [*Mexico.* 1826.] Folio, pp. 17. 20109

Dictamen de la primera comision de hacienda de la Camara de Diputados, sobre el acuerdo del senada acerca del arreglo de aduanas maritimas. *Mexico.* 1832. 8vo, pp. 24. + Segunda comision. *Mexico.* 1828. 8vo, pp. 14. 20110

Dictamen de la segunda comision de guerra de la Camara de Senadores, sobre el acuerdo relativo á la coalition de los estados fronterizos para la defensa contra los barbaros. *Mexico.* 1852. 8vo. Map. 20111

Dictamen de las comisiones unidas de Industria y primera de hacienda, sobre las propuestas que se han presentado para la apertura de una comunicacion inter-oceanico por el istmo de Tehuantepec. *Mexico.* 1852. pp. 12. 20112

Dictamen de las comisiones Unidas de Relaciones y Guerra. *Mexico.* 1845. 8vo. 20113

Relates to Texas.

Dictamen de una Comision especial reunida de orden del Poder Ejecutivo de la republica federal de Centro-America en el año de 1825, con objeto de que se informase acerca de la lejitimidad de la agregacion de Chiapas á Mejico. *Guatemala.* 1832. Folio, pp. 30. 20114

Dictamen del Excmo. Consejo de Estado en vista de las reclamaciones del consul de los Estados-Unidos y del agente comercial de Espana, para que los súbditos de sus respectivas naciones no sean comprendidos en el pago de las contribuciones extraordinarias de guerra, etc. etc. *Merida.* 1843. 8vo, pp. 20.

Dictamen del Procurador General sobre La Leva de Tropas en los Estados Unidos por Empleados de la Gran Bretano. *Washington.* 1856. 8vo, pp. 22. 20116

Dictamen sobre etablecimiento de aduanas maritimas y fronterizas. *Mexico.* 1849. 8vo, pp. 46. 20117

Dictamen sobre la langosta, presentado por el Escuela Nacional de Agricultura. *Mexico.* 1856. 4to, pp. 32. Map.

Dictamen sobre Provision de Beneficios Eclesiasticos, y Ejercicio del Patronata. *Mexico.* 1824. 8vo. 20119

Dictamen sobre reformas del arancel general presentado al congreso por sus comisiones de hacienda y comercio unidas. *Mexico.* 1824. 8vo, pp. 36. 20120

Dictionnaire Galibi. *See* Galibi.

DIDIER (Const.) Commentatio Medica de Febre Flava Ameriacana. *Gottingae.* 1800. 4to, pp. 32. 20121

DIELITZ (Theodor). Amerikanische Reisebilder für die Jugend bearbeitet. Mit 8 [lith. und] fein colorirten Bildern von Th. Hosemann. *Berlin: Winckelmann und Sohn.* [1853.] 16mo, 3 l., pp. 335. 20122

DIELITZ. Atlantis. Bilder aus dem Wald- und Prairieleben Amerika's. Für die Jugend bearbeitet. *Berlin: Winckelmann und Söhn.* 1862. 8vo, pp. iv, 316. 8 Lithographs. 20123

DIELITZ. Die neue Welt Erzählungen aus der Geschichte Amerika's. Für die reifere Jugend bearbeitet. Mit 8 [lith. und] colorirten Bildern. *Berlin: Winckelmann.* 1857. 8vo, pp. viii, 351. 10124

Also: Jenseits des Oceans. Neue Land- und Seebilder für die Jugend ... . *Berlin: Winckelmann.* [1857.] 16mo, pp. vi, 338. 8 Liths. — Ost und West. Neue Land- und Seebilder für die Jugend ... . [*Ibid.* 1856.] 8vo, pp. 323. 8 Liths. — Völkergemälde und Landschaftsbilder für die Jugend ... . [*Ibid.*] 1846. 8vo. 8 Liths. + Vierte Auflage. [*Ibid.* 1854.] 16mo, 3 l., pp. 232. 8 Liths.

DIELITZ. De nieuwe wereld. Verhalen uit de geschiedenis van Amerika. ... Naar het Hoogduitsch. *Groningen: J. Oomkens Jz.* 1862. 8vo. 20125

DIEPENBECK (R.) Der Staat Michigan. ... von Rudolph Diepenbeck ... . *Detroit.* 1859. 8vo, pp. 46. H. 20126

DIEPERINK (H. H.) Voorlezing over de Bewaring der Gezondheid in Paramaribo. *Hoorn.* 1825. 8vo, pp. 36.

DIÉREVILLE (*M.*) Relation du voyage du Port Royal de l'Acadie, ou de la Nouvelle-France, dans laquelle on voit un détail des divers mouvemens de la mer dans une traversée de long cours; la description du païs, les occupations des François qui y sont établis, les manières des différentes nations sauvages, leurs superstitions & leurs chasses; avec une dissertation exacte sur le Castor. Par M. Diereville embarqué à la Rochelle dans le navire la Royale-Paix. Ensuite de la relation, on a ajouté le détail d'un combat donné entre les François et les Acadiens, contre les Anglois. *A Rouen: Chez Jean-Baptiste Besongne.* M.DCCVIII. 12mo, 7 l., pp. 236, 1, 7. + *A Amsterdam: Chez Pierre Humbert.* M. DCCX. 12mo, Frontispiece, 9 l., pp. 236, 7.

"M. Diéreville, at the request of M. Begon, wrote the whole of the relation of his voyage in verse, but his friends having represented to him that no credit would be given to it unless it was written in prose, all that they could obtain from him was, that he would intermix some prose with his verses. Some copies have a supplement of eight pages, containing an account of the unsuccessful attack made, in 1707, by the people of New-England on Port Royal." — RICH, I. 16.

DIETRICH (Ew. Chr. Vict.) Abenteuer eines deutschen Auswanderers und seines Sohnes in Nordamerika. Für die liebe Jugend erzählt. *Prag: Leitmeritz und Teplitz.* 1839. 8vo. 4 Illustrations. 20129

DIETRICH (L.) Erlebnisse auf meiner Wanderungen durch Nordamerika und Westindien, von Ludwig Dietrich. Seitenstück zu "Der deutschen Auswanderer Fahrten und Schicksale," von F. Gerstäcker. *Grimma: Verlags-Comptoir.* 1851. 8vo, pp. vi, 147. (Europäische Bibliothek, 416.) 20130

DIETRICHSON (Johannes Vilhelm). Reise blandt de norske Emigranter i de forenede Noramerikanske Fristater. *Stavanger.* 1846. 8vo, pp. 128. 20131

Also: Nogle Ord fra Prædikestolen i Amerika og Norge. *Stavanger.* 1851. 8vo, pp. 86.

DIEZ (M.) Biografia de la actriz Doña Matilde Diez, Perla del teatro español. *Mexico.* 1855. 8vo. Portrait. 20132

DIEZ DE LA CALLE (Juan). Memorial informatoria al Rey en su Real Conseio de las Indias, Camara y Junta de Guerra. Contiene lo que su Magestad provee en su Cõseio y Junta, y por las dos secretarias de la Nueva España y Pirù, Eclesiastico, Secular, Salarios, Estipendios, y Presidios su Gente, y Costa, y de que Cajas, y Hazienda Real se paga: valor de las Encomiendas de Indias, y otras cosas curiosas, y necessarias. [*Madrid.*] 1645. 4to. 20133

"Encore plus rare que l'ouvrage précédent. Presque inconnu. ... Il est de la plus grande importance pour l'histoire du gouvernement espagnol au Nouveau Monde." — ASHER.

DIEZ DE LA CALLE. Memorial, y noticias sacras del Imperio de las Indias occidentales al Rey D. Felipe IV. N. S. Comprehende lo Eclesiastico, Secular, Politico, y Militar: Presidios, Gente, y Costas, valor de las Encomiendas de Indios y otras cosas curiosas, necessarias y dignas saberse. [*Madrid.*] 1646. 4to. 20134

"Extrêmément rare. On voit, page 108 de cet ouvrage, qu'il n'a été tiré qu'à un très-petit nombre d'exemplaires pour être distribué au roi et aux membres du conseil des Indes, ce qui explique sa grande rareté. Il a été composé d'après d'importants documents conservés aux archives du gouvernements espagnol. On n'en connait que très-peu d'exemplaires." — ASHER.

DIEZ DE LA CALLE. Repertorio de los Tiempos. Cinco Tratados, signe la Relacion de las Cosas Memorables sucedidas, assi en este Nueuo Mundo, como en las otras partes del, desde el año de 1520, que se conquisto este Reyno hasta el de 1590. *Mexico.* 1590. 4to. 20135

DIEZ DE SAN MIGUEL (N. A.) La gran Fee del Centurion espanol. Sermon moral. *Lima.* 1695. 4to, 40 l. 20136

DIEZ DE SAN MIGUEL. Oracion panegirica que a Glorias del principe de los Aposteles N. P. S. Pedro, Predico en la Iglesia Metropolitano de Lima. *En Lima.* 1684. 4to. 20137

DIEZ DE SOLANO (José Maria). Manifestacion que hace como Rector de escuelas de este Capital, de la conducta que ha guardado al estinguirse la nacional y pontificia Universidad por Decreto de 14 de Setiembre de 1857. *Mexico.* 1857. 8vo. pp. 22. 20138

Difference between the Royal African Company and the Separate Traders, shewing the Danger of an Exclusive Trade to our American Plantations. 1710. 4to. 20139

DIGBY (*Capt.*) Defence of Captain Digby, Concerning Admiral Knowles's Charge against him for his Behaviour in the Expedition against St. Jago de Cuba. *London.* 1749. 8vo.

Digest of Accounts of Manufacturing Establishments in the United States, and of their Manufactures. Made under direction of the Secretary of State, in pursuance of a Resolution of Congress of 30th March, 1822. *Washington.* 1823. Folio.

Similar digests were made from the census of 1810; also of 1820.

Digest of Opinions of the Judge Advocate General of the Army, Including Opinions given since the Issue of the Digest of 1865. Together with those contained in that edition. War Department. Bureau of Military Justice. *Washington: Government Printing Office.* 1866. 8vo, pp. xi, 252. 20142

Digest of Opinions of the Judge Advocate General of the Army: ... between September, 1862, and July, 1868. Edited by Major W. Winthrop, Judge Advocate U. S. Army. Third Edition. *Washington: Government Printing Office.* 1868. 8vo, pp. xvi, 393. C. 20143

A Digest of Patents, issued by the United States Government, from 1790, to January 1, 1839: published by Act of Congress, under the Superintendence of the Commissioner of Patents, H. L. Ellsworth. To which is added the Present Law relating to Patents. *Washington.* 1840. 8vo, pp. 670. 20144

Digest of the Act to provide a National Currency, approved June 3, 1864, ... to which is Appended a List of National Banks Suspended and in Liquidation, and a List of Stamp Duties. Prepared by A. S. Pratt and Son, National Bank Agents. *Washington, D. C.: McGill & Witherow.* 1870. Sq. 18mo, 1 l., pp. 84. C. 20145

Digest of the Canons for the Government of the Episcopal Church in the United States, ... together with the Constitution. Revised Edition. *Boston: E. P. Dutton & Co.* 1869. 8vo, pp. 122. + *Hartford.* 1869. 8vo, pp. 122. 20146

A Digest of the Commercial Regulations of the Different Foreign Nations, with which the United States have Intercourse ... . February 2, 1824. ... *Washington.* 1824. 8vo, pp. 527. (18th Cong., 1st Sess., Ex. Doc. 130.) BA. 20147

A similar publication, in 1819, was entitled "Commercial Regulations," etc. BA.

Digest of the Decisions of the Courts of the U. S. 1789–1847; with an Appendix of the Rules and Orders of the Circuit Court in Proceedings in Equity, established by the Supreme Court. *New York.* 1855. 2 vols., 8vo, pp. 1637. 20148

A Digest of the existing Commercial Regulations of Foreign Countries with which the United States have Intercourse, as far as they can be ascertained: ... *Washington.* 1833–36. 3 vols., 4to. C. 20149

A Digest of the Statistics of Manufactures, according to the Return of the Seventh Census, 1859. *Washington.* 1859. 8vo, pp. 143. 20150

Digested Index to the Executive Documents and Reports of Committees of the House of Representatives, from the Eighteenth to the Twenty-first Congress, both included. *Washington.* 1832. 8vo. 20151

Digested Summary and Alphabetical List of Private Claims which have been presented to the House of Representatives from the First to the Thirty-first Congress, exhibiting the Action of Congress on each Claim, with References to the Journals, Reports, Bills, &c., elucidating its Progress. Compiled by Order of the House of Representatives. *Washington: printed by Wm. Belt.* 1853. 3 vols., 4to, 2 l., pp. 782; 2 l., pp. 620;

Dignowity (Anthony M.) Reconstruction!! An Appeal to the Patriotic National Republican Members of Congress ... [n. p. n. d.] 8vo, pp. 3. H. 20153

Dike (S. F.) ... A Sermon delivered at the Dedication of the New Jerusalem Temple in Bath, Maine, January 11, 1844. By Samuel F. Dike ... . *Boston.* 1844. 8vo, pp. 63. H. 20154

Dilke (C. W.) Greater Britain: A Record of Travel in English-Speaking Countries during 1866–7. By Charles Wentworth Dilke. *London: Macmillan & Co.* 1868. 2 vols., 8vo, ; 4 l., pp. 428. BA. Maps and Woodcuts. + *Philadelphia: J. B. Lippincott & Co.* 1869. 2 vols., crown 8vo, pp. x, 338; 348. Maps and Illustrations. + [*Ibid.*] 1869. 2 vols., 12mo, 1 l., pp. x, 340; 348. 8 Plates and Map. + *New York: Harper & Brothers.* 1869. 12mo, pp. 561. Maps and Illustrations. + Third Edition. *London: Macmillan.* 1870. Post 8vo, pp. xi, 595. 20155

Dilke (*Mr.*) New York Industrial Exhibition. Special Report of Mr. Dilke. *London: Harrison & Sons.* [n. d.] Rl. 8vo, pp. 108. 20156

Dill. The American Conflict. A Lecture. By the Rev. Dr. Dill. *Belfast, [Ireland]: Whig Office.* 1863. 12mo, pp. 24.

Dill (J. H.) Congregationalism in Western New-York; its Rise, Decline, and Revival; with a Notice of Hotchkin's History of Presbyterianism in this State: An Address before the General Association of New-York, at its Quarter Century Meeting in Rochester, Sept. 21, 1858, by James H. Dill ... . *Rochester: Benton & Andrews, Printers.* 1859. 8vo, pp. 12. H.

Dillard (R. T.) Funeral Oration on the Death of President Giddings; delivered by the Rev. Ryland T. Dillard ... Georgetown, 5th January, 1840. *Louisville.* 1840. 8vo, pp. 16. BA.

Also: Address ... 4th of July, 1844 ... near Chilesburg, Fayette County, Ky *Lexington: Enquirer Office Print.* 1844. 8vo, pp. 12. BA.

Dillaway (Charles Knapp). A History of the Grammar School, or, "The Free School of 1645 in Roxburie." With Biographical Sketches of the Ministers of the First Church, and other Trustees. By C. K. Dillaway ... *Roxbury.* 1860. 12mo, pp. viii, 7–202. BA., H. 20160

Dillaye (S. D.) History of the Pittsburgh Forgery Case. By S. D. Dillaye. *New York.* 1860. 8vo. S. 20161

Dillaye. Letter ... to the Hon. Howell Cobb, Secretary of the Treasury. By Stephen D. Dillaye. Of New York. *New York.* 1858. 8vo, pp. 16. H. + Second Letter. ... *New York. July* 28, 1858. 8vo, pp. 44. H., S. 20162

Dillingham (J. H.) Farewell Address delivered at Haverford College to the Graduating Class of 1869. By Prof. J. H. Dillingham, Superintendent. *Philadelphia.* 1869. 24mo, pp. 31. H. 20163

Dillingham (P.) Report of the Hon. Paul Dillingham, Commissioner of Vermont, on the National Cemetery at Gettysburg, September 28, 1864. pp. 6. 20164

Dillingham (W. H.) Address before the Chester County Horticultural Society, 1847. By Wm. H. Dillingham. *Philadelphia.* 1847. 20165

Dillingham. An Oration delivered before the Society of the Sons of New England of Philadelphia, December 22d, 1847, the Anniversary of the Landing of the Pilgrims, by William H. Dillingham. *Philadelphia: John C. Clark, Printer.* 1847. 8vo, pp. 38. H., P., S. 20166

[Dillingham.] A Tribute to the Memory of Peter Collinson; with some notice of Dr. Darlington's Memorials of John Bartram and Humphrey Marshall. *Philadelphia.* 1851 or 1852.

[Dillon (A.)] Aux Vrais Amis de la Patrie ... *Paris, ce* 11 *juin,* 1791. 8vo, pp. 6. 20168

A *brochure* on the treatment of M. de Dumas, ex-governor of Martinique.

Dillon. Beautés de l'histoire du Mexique, ou époques remarquables, traits intéressants, mœurs, usages, coutumes des indigènes et des conquérans, depuis les tems les plus reculés jusqu'à ce jour. *Paris: Bossange père.* 1822. 12mo. 6 Plates.

Dillon. La Société des Amis des Noirs à Arthur Dillon. *Paris.* 1791. 20170

Dillon (A.) History of a Law Suit in the Republic of Ecuador. By Augustus Dillon. *London: Privately Printed.* 1864. 8vo, pp. 104. 20171

Dillon (J. B.) The History of Indiana, from its Earliest Exploration by Europeans, to the Close of the Territorial Government in 1816. With an Introduction containing Historical Notes of the Discovery and Settlement of the Territory of the United States, North west of the River Ohio. By John B. Dillon. Volume I. *Indianapolis, Ia.: Wm. Sheets & Co.* 1843. 8vo, pp. xii, 456. 20172

This edition was not completed.

Dillon. A History of Indiana, from its Earliest Exploration by Europeans to the Close of the Territorial Government, in 1816; Comprehending a History of the Discovery, ... of the Territory of the U. S. Northwest of the River Ohio, and a General View of the Progress of Public Affairs in Indiana, from 1816 to 1856. By John B. Dillon. *Indianapolis: Bingham & Doughty.* 1859. 8vo, pp. xii, 637. Map, Plate of 5 Portraits, and Woodcuts. BA., C. 20173

Dillon. An Inquiry into the Nature and Use of Political Sovereignty. By John B. Dillon, of Indiana. *Indianapolis.* 1860. 8vo, pp. 30. H. 20174

Dillon (P.) Narrative and Successful Result of a Voyage in the South Seas, performed by order of the Government of British India, to ascertain the actual Fate of La Pérouse's Expedition. By Chevalier Capt. Peter Dillon. *London: Hunt & Co.* 1829. 2 vols., 8vo. C. 20175

Dillon. Voyage aux Iles de la Mer du Sud en 1827 et 1828, et Relation de la découverte du sort de la Pérouse. *Paris.* 1830. 2 vols., 8vo. 20176

Dillon. Reis naar de eilanden der Zuidzee, 1827–28, behelzende het Verslag der ontdekking van het lot van de la Pérouse. Uit het fransch. *Amsterdam.* 1830. 2 vols., 8vo. Plate. 20177

Dillon (R.) Trial of Ensign Robert Dillon of the corps commonly called the Republican Green Riflemen, for Mutiny, and Un-Officerlike Conduct. *New York.* 1839. 8vo, pp. 64.

Dillon (*L'abbé* Roger Henri de). Mémoire sur l'esclavage colonial, la nécessité des colonies et l'abolition de la traite des negrès. *Paris: Blaise.* 1814. 8vo, pp. 44. 20179

Dillwyn (G.) Gathered Fragments: briefly Illustrative of the Life of George Dillwyn, of Burlington, West New Jersey, North America. [Edited by Ann Alexander.] *London: Alfred W. Bennett.* 1858. 8vo, pp. 60. 2 Photographic Engravings.

See Sharp (G.), and "Monthly Repository for 1808," III. 602; IV. 72.

Diluvio Constitucional. *Puerto-Principe: imprenta de D. Miguel Serrano.* 1821. 8vo. 20181

Dilworth (H. W.) The History of the Buccaniers of America: Being an Entertaining Narrative of the Exploits, Cruelties, and Sufferings ... of Noted Commanders. ... By H. W. Dilworth, A.M. *London.* MDCCLIX. 24mo, Title, pp. 140. Copperplates. H. 20182

Dilworth (W. H.) The Conquest of Peru, by Francis Pizarro. Containing an Authentic Detail of the Government, Religion, Laws, etc. Together with the First Adventures, particularly Ferdinand De Soto, for the Discovery of Florida. By W. H. Dilworth ... *London: Wm. Anderson.* 1759. 12mo, pp. 164. J.C.B. 20183

Dilworth. The History of the Conquest of Mexico, by the Celebrated Hernan Cortes. Containing a Faithful and Entertaining Detail of all his Amazing Victories in that Vast Empire. ... To which is added the Voyage of Vasco de Gama. ... By W. H. Dilworth ... *London: Wm. Anderson.* 1759. 12mo, pp. 130. J.C.B. + *Glasgow.* 1785. + *Philadelphia: H. Sweitzer.* 1801. 24mo, pp. 164. C. 20184

Dilworth. The History of the Present War between France and Great Britain, to the end of the year 1759. By W. H. Dilworth. *London.* 1760. 18mo. 20185

Contains a few details of American interest.

Diman (J.) Sermon preached at Salem, January 16, 1772, ... the Day on which Bryan Sheehan was executed, for ... a Rape, on ... Abial Hollowell, the Wife of Benjamin Hollowell, of Marblehead. By James Diman ... . *Salem: printed by Samuel and Ebenezer Hall.* MDCCLXXII. 8vo, pp. 24. BA., M. 20186

Diman (J. L.) A Discourse in commemoration of the Rev. Robinson Potter Dunn, D.D. ... delivered ... in the Chapel of Brown University, October 16th, 1867, by the Rev. J. Lewis Diman ... . *Providence.* 1867. 8vo, pp. 31. H. 20187

Diman. The Nation and the Constitution. An Oration delivered before the City Authorities and Citizens of Providence, July 4, 1866. By J. Lewis Diman. *Providence: Providence Press Company.* 1866. 8vo, pp. 24. 20188

A Dimension proper for an Unit of Measures pointed out, and an Improvement in the Second Pendulum described; which will fit it for making the experiment recommended by The Committee of Congress on Weights and Measures in their Report to that House in last Session: With A Plan for a Reform of our Measures, which shews that they may be extended by a Complete Decimal Scale, formed on the said Unit of Measures. ... By a Citizen of America. *Philadelphia: Printed by Budd and Bartram.* 1796. 8vo, pp. 24. C., P. 20189

Dimmick (L. Fraseur). A Discourse on the Moral Influence of Railroads. By Rev. Luther F. Dimmick. *Boston: Tappan & Dennet.* 1841. 24mo, pp. 125. 20190

Dimmick. Memoir of Mrs. Catherine M. Dimmick ... . *Boston: T. R. Marvin.* 1846. 12mo, pp. 24. BA. 20191

Dimmick. Fortieth Anniversary. A Discourse, commemorative of Forty Years in the Christian Ministry. By L. F. Dimmick ... . *Newburyport: William H. Huse & Co., Printers.* 1860. 8vo, pp. 28. H. 20192

Dimmick. The Position of the American Republic with Reference to the Rest of the World: A Discourse, delivered in the North Church, Newburyport, on the Annual Thanksgiving in the Commonwealth of Massachusetts, November 27th, 1834. By L. F. Dimmick ... . *Newburyport: printed by Morss and Brewster.* 1834. 8vo, pp. 24. BA. 20193

Also: ... Sermon in ... Newburyport, [Mass.] ... April 1, 1824. *Newburyport.* 8vo, pp. 30. W. — The Influence of Truth. A Sermon delivered in Newburyport, March 20, 1827, at the Dedication of the New Brick Church ... . *Newburyport: published by Charles Whipple.* 1827. 8vo, pp. 31. H. — A Sermon preached at the Funeral of Woodbury Dimmick ... . *Concord: printed by Asa McFarland.* 1845. 12mo, pp. 11. H. — Thanksgiving for the Mercies of the Past Year. Sermon, January 2, 1831. *Newburyport.* 1831. 8vo. W. — ... Sermon, occasioned by the Death of Mr. Amos Pettingell ... . *Newburyport: Charles Whipple.* 1832. 8vo, pp. 16. BA.

[Dimmick (Robert A.)] The Little Blue Book: a Register of Federal Officers and Salaries. ... *New York: G. A. Whitehorne, Printer.* 1861. 32mo, pp. xii, 9–122. H. 20194

Dimond (E.) A Christmas Offering. By Mrs. Elizabeth Dimond. *Providence.* 1847. 8vo, pp. 18. 20195

Dimond (William). Foundling of the Forest. *New York.* 1809. 12mo. 20196

Dingley (A.) An Oration, on the Improvement of Medicine: Pronounced ... in the Federal Hall in the City of New York; according to Appointment of the Medical Society of the State of New York: At their Anniversary Meeting, on the 16th January, 1794. By Amasa Dingley, Physician. ... . *New York.* [1794.] 8vo, pp. 39. + Second Edition. *New-York: printed by John Buell.* M,DD,XCV. 8vo, pp. 39. H. 20197

Dingman (J. H.) A Complete List of Booksellers, Stationers, and Newsdealers in the United States and the Canadas. By John H. Dingman. *New York: The Author.* 186–. 8vo, pp. 118. + Addenda ... *New York.* 8vo, pp. 42. 20198

Dingman. Directory of Booksellers, Stationers, Newsdealers and Music Dealers, in the United States and Canada, complete to September 1, 1868. By John H. Dingman. *New York: J. H. Dingman.* 1868. 8vo, pp. 168. C. + Complete to Sept. 1, 1869. *New York: J. H. Dingman.* 1869. 8vo, pp. lx, 317. C. 20199

Dinmore (R.) Select and Fugitive Poetry. With Notes, Biographical and Historical. *Washington City.* 1802. 12mo, pp. 288. 20200

Dinouart, *Chanoine de S. Benoit.* Vie du vénérable Dom Jean de Palafox, évêque d'Angelopolis et ensuite évêque d'Osme. *Cologne; et se trouve a Paris: Chez Nyon.* MDCCLXVII. 8vo, pp. lvj, 576. Portrait of Palafox and 3 Plates. J.C.B. 20201

This work was published under the care of P. Champion, Jesuit, who began a life of Palafox, but the impression was stopped. The Abbé Dinouart in his preface, says that he was happy in being able to procure the entire MSS. of P. Champion indicated in the catalogue of MSS. in the library of the "Maison profuse" at Paris, which enabled him to complete the life of the celebrated bishop.

Dinsmoor (R.) Incidental Poems, accompanied with Letters and a few Select Pieces, mostly original, for their illustration. By Robert Dinsmoor, the Rustic Bard. Together with a Preface and Sketch of the Author's Life. *Haverhill, [Mass.:] A. W. Thayer.* 1828. 12mo, pp. xxiv, 264. C. 20202

See Chapter XVI. of the "Stranger in Lowell," by J. G. Whittier.

Dinsmore (J.) A Golden Wedding, and the Dinsmore Genealogy, from about 1620 to 1865. *Augusta: printed at the Maine Farmer Office.* 1867. 8vo, pp. 24. S. 20203

Dinsmore. American Railroad and Steam Navigation Guide for the United States; January, 1857. *New York.* [n. d.]

Dinwiddie County, *Va.* Memorial of the Society of Friends in Dinwiddie County, Va., to the Legislature on the Subject of War. *New York.* 1812. 8vo. 20205

Diocesan Missions of Pennsylvania. How to pay the Debt of Cities. *Philadelphia: J. S. McCalla, Printer.* 1861. 12mo, pp. 11. H. 20206

The Diocesan Register and New England Calendar, For ... 1812, ... Containing ... Civil, Ecclesiastical, Literary and Military Lists of the States of Massachusetts, Rhode-Island, New Hampshire and Vermont. ... Officers ... of the United States. An Account of the Formation, Constitution and Regulation of the Eastern Diocese. A Sketch of the Life and Character of ... F. Ames. ... Edited by Gentlemen in Dedham, Massachusetts. *Dedham: Printed by H. Mann.* [n. d.] 18mo, pp. 261. BA. 20207

Diodorus Siculus, *pseudonym.* Letter to the Members of the South Carolina Legislature, examining the Claims and Qualifications of De Witt Clinton for the Presidency. By Diodorus Siculus. *Charleston.* 1812. 8vo. 20208

Dionysius, *Periegetes.* Situs orbis Di|onisij Ruffo aui|eno interprete.| [Colophon:] *Vienne | Cuspinianus neuos & verrucas sustulit | Winterburger impressit anno Mdviij.* | 4to, 26 l. BM.

"On the reverse of the title there is an address, containing slight allusions to the Oceanic discoveries. It is Rufus Festus' Latin paraphrase of the hexametrical description of the earth, written in Greek by Dionysius Periegetes, Lybicus or Africanus, toward the latter part of the third century." — Harrisse.

Dionysii|aphride totivs or|bis situ, Antonio Becharia Veronensi inter-|prete, consumatissimum opus. | Joannis præterea| Honteri Coronensis de Cosmographiæ|rudimentis libri duo.| Cœlorum partes, stellas cum flatibus amnes, | Regnaq. cum populis, parue libelle tenes. | *Excudebat Henricus | Petrus Basileae.* | [Colophon:] *Basileae ex aedibus | Henrici Petri. men | se Avgvsto, | anno |* M.D.XXXIIII. | 4to, Title, 3 unnumbered leaves, pp. 99, 2 l. BM. 20210

"There is nothing on America in the 'Dionysius,' not even the slightest allusion contained in the address in the edition of 1518 (No. 20209), but in Honter's work, which commences on page 65, with a separate title, the reader may consult page 91, the chapter: 'Nomina Insvlarvm Oceani et Maris.'" — Harrisse.

Dionysius. Dionysivs Lybicvs Poetae|de Sitv Habitabilis Orbis|a Simone Lemnio Poeta Lavreato|nvper Latinvs factvs.| *Venetiis* M . D . XLIII . | Cum gratia & priuilegio.| [Colophon:] *Venetiis per Bartholomeum cognomento Imperatorem: & | Franciscum eius generum . Anno* M . D . XLIII .| Sm. 4to, Title, 1 l., 39 unnumbered leaves. L. 20211

The title contains a large woodcut, representing two globes, one issuing out of an open eye, the other with the word America.

Diplomacy of the United States. *See* [Lyman (T.)]

A Diplomat on Diplomacy. (Signed California.) 8vo, pp. 8.

Diplomatic and Consular Officers of the United States, together with the Diplomatic and Consular Act of August 18, 1856, and Tariff of Consular Fees. *Washington.* 1857. 8vo. C. + Corrected to July 15, 1865. *Washington.* 1865. 8vo, pp. 67. C. 20213

Diplomatic Correspondence. — Papers relating to Foreign Affairs accompanying the Annual Message of the President to the Second Session Thirty-eighth Congress. *Washington: Government Printing Office.* 1865. 4 vols., 8vo, pp. ix, 896; xx, 814; xx, 596; iv, xvii, 470. + First Session Thirty-ninth Congress. *Washington.* 1866. 4 vols., 8vo, pp. xx, 671; xxxvi, 584; xliii, 850; xxxiv, 717. 20214

Consists entirely of the correspondence. The correspondence during this period is important for the history of the Rebellion.

Diplomatic Correspondence of the American Revolution. *See* Sparks (J.)

The Diplomatic Correspondence of the United States of America, from the Signing of the Definitive Treaty of Peace, 10th September, 1783, to the Adoption of the Constitution, March 4, 1789. Being the Letters of the Presidents of Congress, the Secretary for Foreign Affairs — American Ministers at Foreign Courts, Foreign Ministers near Congress — Reports of Committees of Congress, and Reports of the Secretary for Foreign Affairs on various Letters and Communications; together with Letters from Individuals on Public Affairs. Published under the direction of the Secretary of State, from the original Manuscripts in the Department of State, conformably to an Act of Congress, approved May 5, 1832. *City of Washington: printed by Francis Preston Blair.* 1833–34. 7 vols., 8vo. c. + *Washington: Blair & Rives.* 1837. 3 vols., 8vo, pp. xlviii, 837; xxxiii, 834; xxxix, 819. 20215

"The Diplomatic Policy of Mr. Madison." *See* [Lowell (J.)] *See also* "N. Am. Rev.," XXXIX. 302.

The Diplomatic Year. *See* [Ingersoll ( )].

Diplomatisches Archiv für die Zeit- und Staatengeschichte. *Stuttgart und Tübingen, J. G. Cotta'schen Buchhandlung.* 1821–33. 36 vols., 8vo. H. 20216

With the second title, "Archives diplomatiques pour l'histoire du temps et des états." Bde VII.–XXXVI. have also the title, "Neueste Staats-Akten und Urkunden in monatlichen Heften." This second part contains many documents relating to America, especially South America.

La Diputacion para la junta de gobierno de la casa de Beneficencia ... da cuenta de sus tareas en 1798 por medio del siguiente papal. *Habana.* 1798. 4to, pp. 16. 20217

The report is by D. Pablo Boloxi.

Dirckinck (C.) Gross Britanniens und der Vereinigten Staaten neuere Handelspolitik. Mit Beziehung auf die Grundsätze des Canningschen Ministeriums. Von Constant Dirckinck ... *Copenhagen.* 1829. 8vo, 3 l., pp. 140. H. 20218

Dirckinck-Holmfeld (C.) Danemarks und Nordamerikas Streit. *See* Feddersen (F.)

Directions for making Calcined or Pearl-Ashes, as Practised in Hungary, &c. With a Copper-Plate Drawing of a Calciming Furnace. *Boston: Printed and Sold by John Mein at the London Book-Store, Second Door above the British Coffee-house, North-side King-street.* MDCCLXVI. 8vo, pp. 18. P. 20219

Originally communicated to the New York Society for Promoting Arts and Sciences.

Directions for the Breeding and Management of Silk-Worms. Extracted from the Treatises of the Abbé Boissier de Sauvages, and Pullein. With a Preface, giving some Account of the Rise and Progress of the Scheme for encouraging the Culture of Silk in Pennsylvania, and the adjacent Colonies. *Philadelphia: Printed by Joseph Cruksbank, and Isaac Collins.* M.DCC.LXX. 8vo, pp. xv, 32. P. 20220

See "Am. Q. Rev.," Dec., 1831.

Directions for the Use of the Mineral Water and Cold Bath at Harrowgate, near Philadelphia. *Philadelphia.* 1786. 8vo.

No such place known to an old resident.

Directions to the American Loyalists, in order to enable them to state their Cases, by way of Memorial to the Hon. the Commissioners appointed ... to enquire into the Losses and Services of those Persons who have suffered, in consequence of their Loyalty to his Majesty, and their Attachment to the British Government. By a Loyalist. *London: W. Flexney.* MDCCLXXXIII. 4to, pp. 52. J.C.B. 20222

See "M. Rev.," LXII. 432.

The Directory for the Public Worship of God, Agreed upon by the Assembly of Divines at Westminster, With the Assistance of Commissioners from the Church of Scotland, As A part of the Covenanted Uniformity in Religion betwixt the Churches of Christ in the Kingdoms of Scotland, England and Ireland. With An Act of the General Assembly, and Act of Parliament, both in Anno 1645. Approving and Establishing the said Directory. *Philadelphia: Printed by B. Franklin.* M,DCC,XLV. 8vo, Title, pp. 484–521. C. 20223

Forms part of the "Westminster Catechism," but issued with a separate title.

Dirrhaimer (Ulric). Kirchen-Geschichte ... . In sich begriffend, die Africanischen Länder ... Demnach die Americanische, Perù, Paraquaria, Brasilia, Florida, Canada, Mexico und Marignan. ... *Wien: Verlegts Johann Jacob Wolrab.* 1725. 6 l., pp. 660, 16 l. Plates. 20224

Disbrow (L.) Advertisement of a Proposition for Ward Companies, to supply the City of New York with Rock Water, &c. By Levi Disbrow and J. L. Sullivan. *New York: printed by Clayton & Van Norden.* 1832. 8vo, pp. 16, 1 l. BA. 20225

The Disclosure — No. 1. Documents relating to Violations and Evasions of the Laws during the Commercial Restrictions and Late War with Great Britain: &c. Part First. *Bath: printed for the People. J. G. Torrey, Printer.* 1824. 8vo, pp. 32.

Disclosures relating to the "A. B. C." Affair. From the Essex Register. [n. p. n. d.] 8vo, pp. 8. H. 20227

Discours sur les Américains. *See* [Blanche (*Madame*)], Vol. II., No. 5840.

Discours sur les avantages. *See* [Chastellux (Francis Jean)], Vol. III., No. 12224.

Discours sur l'Esclavage des Nègres, Et sur l'Idée de leur Affranchissement dans les Colonies. Par un Colon de Saint-Domingue. ... *Amsterdam: Hardouin et Gattey.* 1786. 8vo, pp. 126. 20228

Discours sur la nécessité d'établir à Paris une Société pour concourir avec celle de Londres à l'Abolition de la Traite et de l'Esclavage des Nègres; prononcé le 19 Février 1788. 8vo. C.

Discours van Pieter en Pauwels. Op de Handelinghe van de Vreede. 1608. 4to, pp. 4. 20230

"Important for the question of the commerce to Asia and America." — F. Muller.

Discours by Forme van Remonstrantye. *See* [Usselincx].

Constitution and By-Laws of the Discharged Soldiers' Employment Association. ... *Boston: Prentiss & Deland, Printers.* 1863. 16mo, pp. 15. H. 20231

Discipline of the Yearly Meeting of Friends, held in Baltimore, for the Western Shore of Maryland, and the adjacent parts of Pennsylvania and Virginia, in 1821. *Baltimore.* 1821. 12mo.

Discourse intorno, 1829. *See* [Napione].

Discours | Daer in | Kortelijck ende grondigh | werdt vertoont hoeveel de Vereenighde | Nederlanden gheleghen is aen de Oost | ende West Indische Navigatie. | Mitsgaders | 't Profijt dat men van de Oost Indische Com- | pagnie gheduerende den tijt van vierentwintich | jaren herwaerdts daer wt heeft | ghetrocken. | Ende | Met fondamentale redenen werdt bewesen | dat door de geoctroijeerde West Indische Navigatie meer voordeel | voor de Participanten met meerder dienste voor | de Nederlandtsche Provintien grooter schade | ende afbreuck voor den Koninck | van Spaengien zij te | verwachten. | Gheschreven aen een seker Vriendt ende Liefhebber | van de Wel-standt des Vader-landts, en tot ghemeenen | dienst der Inghesetene van dien. | *Tot Arnhem,* | *by Ian Ianss. Boeckverkooper.* | *Anno* 1621. | 4to, pp. 24. 20233

Discours | De la | Paix, | Contre le | Portugais. | [1647.] 4to, pp. 16. 20234

Relates to Brasil.

Discovrs | Op | Verscheyde Voorslaghen | Rakende | d'Oost en VVest-Indi- | sche Trafyken. | Het Eerste Deel. | Waerinne ghehandelt wert van 't Prolon- | geren of vernieuwen van 't Oost- | Indische Octroy. | *Gedruckt int Iaar ons Heeren.* 1645. | 4to, pp. 39. 20235

Relates to the West India Company.

Discovrs | over | Den Nederlandtschen | Vrede-handel. | Ghestelt door een Liefhebber | des Vaderlandts. | *Tot Leeuwaerden,* | *Ghedruckt by Dirck Albertsz. Boeck-vercooper, woonende inde Klockstraet, inden verguldén Bybel,* | *Anno* 1629. | 4to, 16 l. 20236

A discourse on the negotiations for peace with Spain.

A Discourse, Addressed to the Sons of Liberty, at a Solemn Assembly, near Liberty-Tree, in Providence, February 14, 1766. *Providence, in New England: Printed and Sold by Sarah and William Goddard, at the Printing-Office, near the Court-House.* 8vo, pp. 8. P. 20237

Signed Pro Patria.

Discourse at the Thursday Lecture, March 16, 1797. With an Appendix, containing an Account of several daring Attempts to set Fire ro the Town [of Boston]. *Boston.* 1797. 20238

Title from the "Genealogical Register," XX. 147.

A Discourse Concerning the Currencies. *See* [Douglas (Wm.)]

A Discourse ... 1768. By a Son of Liberty. *See* [Downer (Silas)].

A Discourse made on the Burning of the Effigy of the St — pm — n, in New London, in the Colony of Connecticut. *Boston.* 1765. 4to. P. 20239

A Discourse of that which happened in the battell fought between the two Navies of Spaine and Portugall at the Islands of Azores, Anno Dom. 1582. *Imprinted at London by Thomas Purfoote, and are to be sold at his shop over against Saint Sepulchres Church without Newgate.* 1582. 20240

A Discourse on Government and Religion, calculated for the Meridian of the 30th of January. By an Independent. ... *Boston: Reprinted by D. Fowle, and D. Gookin.* 1750. 8vo, Title, pp. ii, 7–56. B., M., W. 20241

A Discourse on the Conduct of the Government of ... Great Britain. *See* [Jenkinson (Charles)].

Discourse of the Duties on Merchandize, More Particularly of that on Sugars, ... in Answer to a Pamphlet, entitled, The Groans of the Plantations, &c. ... *London.* 1695. 4to, 2 l., pp. 32. 20242

Discourse on the English Constitution, extracted from a late Eminent Writer, and Applicable to the Present Times. *London: J. Robinson.* 1776. 8vo, 4 l., pp. 40. 20243

"Given by the editor, Mr. W. S., to T. B. Chandler." — *Manuscript note on Chandler's copy.*

Discourse on the Times. Second Edition. *Norwich.* 1776. 12mo. W. + The Third Edition with an Addition. [n. p.] *printed* *T. Trumbull.* M,DCCCXXII. 24mo, pp. 5–22. H.

Discourse on Trade, more particularly on Sugar and Tobacco, Shewing the True & Natural Means of their Support, and the Unreasonableness of Depending upon the Legislature for their Relief. *London: J. Roberts.* 1733. 8vo, pp. 24. 20245

There are copies on thick paper.

Discourses on Davila. *See* [Adams (J.)], Vol. I., 239.

Discourses on the Publick Revenues. *See* [D'Avenant], No. 18686.

Discoveries of the French in 1768 and 1769. *See* Fluricu (M. L. C. D.)

The Discovery of America, with an Enquiry into the Rise and Progress of the Contest there. *London.* 1776. 8vo. 20246

A Discovery of a Large, Rich and Plentiful Country in the North America, extending above 4000 Leagues. Wherein by a very short passage, lately found out, through the Mer-Bermejo into the South Sea, by which a considerable Trade might be carried on, as well in the northern as the southern parts of America. *London: W. Boreham.* [1720?] 8vo, pp. 22.

Without date; but, being published to raise the credit of the South Sea stock, was probably printed about this time. It is apparently an abstract of Hennepin's discoveries.

A | Discovery | of | Fonseca | In a Voyage to | Surranam. | The Island so long sought for in the | Western Ocean. | Inhabited by Women with the Account of their | Habits, Customs and Religion. | And the Exact Longitude and Latitude of the Place taken from | the Mouth of a Person cast away on the Place in a Hurri-

cane | with the Account of their being Cast away. | *Re-printed at Dublin Anno Domini.* 1682. | 4to, pp. 8. 20248

Discriminating Duties. Memorial of Sundry Merchants of Newburyport, in the District of Massachusetts, to Congress. *Washington.* 1803. 12mo, pp. 8. M. 20249

Discurso en que se Muestra la Obligacion qui su Magestad tiene en Justiĉia, Conciencia y Razon a Cumplir y Mandar Executar la Merced que le rey hiso a Don Francisco Pizarro del titulo de Marques con Veinte Mil Vassallos en la parte doude mas bien le Estieviesse como a Descubridor, Conquistador y Pacificador de los Opulentissimo Reynos del Peru en favor y Gracia de los Successores de su casu y Mayorazgo para qui de tan Grandes hechos no se Obscuresca la Memoria. [n. p. n. d.] Folio. 20250

A most interesting and important work.

Discurso sobre la insurreccion de América, que escribia el Dr. Quixano, secretario que fue del gobierno revolucionario de Quito. *Mexico.* 1814. 4to, 3 l., pp. 18. 20251

Discusion que hubo en las Córtes españolas en el año de 1820 sobre la ley de Aduanas y aranceles generales para ámbas Españas. *Habana: Arazoza y Soler.* 1821. 20252

Discussion of the Greek Question in the House of Representatives of the United States, January, 1824. *Boston.* [1824.] 8vo, pp. 48. M. 20253

Discussion on Finances. From the New York Mercantile Journal of Sept. 23. [n. p. n. d.] 8vo, pp. 7. H. 20254

A Discussion on Slaveholding. Three Letters to a Conservative, by George D. Armstrong, D.D., of Virginia, and Three Conservative Replies, by C. Van Rensselaer, D.D., of New Jersey. I. On the Scriptural Doctrine of Slaveholding. II. Emancipation and the Church. III. On the Historical Argument for Slaveholding. Together with Two Rejoinders, On Slaveholding, Schemes of Emancipation, Colonization, Etc. *Philadelphia: Joseph M. Wilson.* 1858. 8vo. 20255

Discussion Sommaire, 1755. *See* [Mairobert (M. P. de)].

Discussions on the Constitution proposed to the People of Massachusetts by the Convention of 1853. *Boston: Little, Brown, and Company.* 1854. 8vo, 2 l., pp. 306. BA. 20256

Dise figur anzaigt vns das volck vnd insel die gefunden ist durch den christenlichen künig zü Portigal oder von seinen vnderthonen. Die leüt sind also nacket hübsch. braun wolgestalt von leib. ir heübter. | halsz. arm. scham. füsz. frawen vnd mann ain wenig mit federn bedeckt. Auch haben die mann in iren angesichten vnd brust vil edel gestain. Es hat auch nyemantz nichts sunder sind alle ding gemain. | Vnnd die mann habendt weyber welche in gefallen, es sey mütter. schwesster oder freündt. darjnn haben sy kain vnderschayd. Sy streyten auch mit einander. Sy essen auch ainander selbs die erschlagen | werden. vnd hencken das selbig fleisch in den rauch. Sy werden alt hundert vnd füntzig iar. Vnd haben kain ragiment. | [1500?] Folio, 1 l. BM. 20257

The text in German, occupies four lines beneath an old block leaf, nine by thirteen inches square, representing the manners and customs of the natives of the northern and eastern coast of South America, as first found by the Portuguese at the end of the fifteenth or beginning of the sixteenth century. It is without date, but was probably printed at Augsburg, or Nuremberg, between the years 1497 and 1504. It is believed to be unique. A facsimile of this earliest known xylographic leaf respecting America is given in Steven' "American Bibliographer," Part I. At Puttick & Simpson's sale, May 24, 1854, this (lot 27) sold for £3 13s. 6d.

Disertacion que Manifiesta la propriedad que los Eclesiasticos tienen en sús Bienes. *Mexico.* 1834. 4to, pp. 39. 20258

Disertacion sobre la Restitucion de los Bienes Eclesiasticos. *Mégico.* 1838. 4to. 20259

The Disfranchisement of Deserters. The Case of Reilly vs. Huber. *Philadelphia: John Campbell.* [n. d.] 8vo, pp. 45.

Dislère. Note sur la Marine des États-Unis: par P. Dislère. ... Accompagné de Trois Grandes planches. *Paris: Arthus Bertrand.* [1868.] 8vo. BA. 20261

The Disloyal Democracy and the War. Its Record, as made by its Leaders, its Presses, its Legislators, and Party Conventions. [n. p. 1863.] 8vo, pp. 32. H. 20262

Dismal Swamp Canal Company. Annual Report of the President and Directors to the Stockholders of the Dismal Swamp Canal Company, for the ... Year ending Sept. 30th, 1868. *Norfolk, Va.* 1868. 8vo, pp. 15, (1). H. + 1869. 8vo, pp. 14.

An Exhibition of the Dismal Swamp Canal, from its Commencement; its Progress, and the Improvements contemplated by the President, Directors and Company. Submitted to the

Consideration of the Members of the National Legislature. *Norfolk: T. G. Broughton, Printer.* 1825. 8vo, pp. 8. BA.

Disney (D.) The Trial of Daniel Disney, Esq; Captain ... and Town Major of the Garrison of Montreal, ... [for] ... entering Mr. Thomas Walker's House, at Montreal, on the ... 6th Day of December ... 1764, with an intention to murder the said Thomas Walker, ... [and] for feloniously ... cutting off [his] Right Ear, Supposed to be written by Francis Maseras, ... of Quebec. ... *Quebec printed; New-York: re-printed.* M,DCC,-LXVIII. BA., C., P. 20265

See "M. Rev.," XXXIX. 484.

[Disney (D. T.)] Argument in Matter of Application by Randolph Coyle and John Delafield to enter as Public Land Fractional Section Number Eleven, Fractional Township Number Four, of Fractional Range Number One. [n. p.] *Printed by Donelson & Armstrong.* [n. d.] 8vo, pp. 31. H. 20266

Disney. Speech of Hon. David T. Disney, of Ohio, on the Power of Congress over the Territories. Delivered in the House ... March 13, 1850. *Washington.* 1850. 8vo, pp. 14.

[Disney (J.)] Memoir of Thomas Brand-Hollis, Esq., F.R.S. and S.A. *London: Printed by T. Gillet.* MDCCCVIII. 4to, pp. viii, 60. Portrait and 9 Plates. 20268

Preface signed John Disney. The subject of this memoir was a liberal benefactor to Harvard College, and a friend and correspondent of John Adams. *See also* [Blackburne (Francis)].

Disosway (G. P.) The Earliest Churches of New York and its Vicinity. By Gabriel P. Disosway, A.M. ... *New York: James G. Gregory.* M DCCC LXV. 8vo, pp. 416. Woodcuts.

Dispassionate Inquiry into the Reasons. *See* [Lowell (J.)]

Dispassionate Thoughts on the American War: addressed to the Moderate of all Parties. *London: J. Wilkie.* MDCCLXXX. 8vo, pp. 36. BA. 20270

"The advice given by this moderate and judicious writer is, that we should immediately relinquish the American war, as a scheme not only impracticable but impolitic, and turn our whole national strength against the House of Bourbon. He does not seem to be a party man, but, if he leans any way, it is toward administration. — *M. Rev.*, LXII. 166.

A Display of God's Special Grace. In a Familiar Dialogue Between a Minister, a Gentleman of his Congregation about the

Work of God in the ... Conversion of Sinners ... *Boston, N. E.: Printed by Rogers & Fowle.* 1742. 12mo, Title, pp. vi, 111.

With an attestation by Colman, Sewall, Prince, Webb, Cooper, Foxcroft, and Gee.

Disposiciones legales y otros documentos relativos á la prohibicion de impresos por la autoridad eclesiastica, mandados publicar de orden del Supremo Gobierno. *Mexico.* 1850. 4to, pp. 138.

Dispositions concernant le voyage de la colonie suisse dès le port de Rio Janeiro jusqu'à la nouvelle Fribourg. *Rio de Janeiro: Impressao Regio.* 1819. 4to, pp. 17. 20273

In French and Portuguese.

A Disputation concerning Church-Members and their Children, in Answer to xxj Questions: Wherein the State of such Children when Adult, together with their Duty towards the Church, and the Churches Duty toward them, is discussed by an Assembly of Divines meeting at Boston in New-England, June 4th 1657. Now published by a Lover of Truth. *London, Printed for Samuel Tompson.* 1659. Sm. 4to, pp. viii. 31. s.

The Dispute with America, considered in a Series of Letters from a Cosmopolite to a Clergyman ... . *London: Gale and Curtis.* [1812.] 8vo, pp. viii, 220. BA. 20275

See "The Pamphleteer," Vol. II.

Disraeli (B.) Curiosities of Literature. By B. Disraeli. With Curiosities of American Literature. By Rufus W. Griswold. *New York.* 1847. Rl. 8vo. 20276

Frequently reprinted: the last edition, *New York: Leavitt & Allen.* [n. d.]

Diss büchlin, 1509. *See* [Vespucius (A.)]

Dissel (S. van). Curaçao. Herinneringen en schetsen. *Leyden: A. W. Sijthoff.* 1857. 8vo. 20277

The Disseminator of Useful Knowledge. *New Harmony, Indiana.* 1828. 8vo. W. 20278

Les Dissensions des republiques de la Plata et les machinations du Brésil. Ouvrage accompagné d'une carte. *Paris: Dentu.* 1865. 8vo, pp. 93. 20279

Las Disensions de las republicas del Plata y las maquinaciones del Brasil. Traducido del frances. *Paris: Dentu.* 1865. 32mo, pp. 75. + Segunda edicion. *Paris: Dentu.* 8vo, pp. 55. 20280

Dissent and Dissenting Gentleman. *See* [Towgood (Michael)].

A Dissertation on the Manner of acquiring the Character and Privileges of a Citizen of the United States. [n. p.] 1789. 8vo.

A Dissertation on ... the Earl of Abingdon. *See* Vol. II., No. 5008. 20282

Dissertation on the Political Union, 1783. *See* [Webster (P.)]

A Dissertation on the Present Conjuncture; particularly with regard to Trade. By a Merchant of Bristol. *London: John Clarke.* 1739. 8vo, pp. 27. J.C.B. 20283

A Dissertation on the Querulousness of Statesmen. *London.* 1792. 8vo. 20284

On America, the Slave Trade, etc.

A Dissertation on the Rise, Progress, Views, Strength, Interests and Characters of the Two Parties of the Whigs and Tories. *Boston: Joseph Greenleaf.* 1773. 8vo, pp. 71. J.C.B.

Dissertation on the Subject of a Congress of Nations, for the Adjustment of International Disputes without Recourse to Arms. By a Friend of Peace. *New York: Ezra Collier.* 1837. 12mo, pp. 156. 20286

A Dissertation, on the Subject of Procuring the Education of Pious Youths for the Christian Ministry; Addressed to the Religious Public. *Boston: Samuel T. Armstrong.* 1814. 8vo, pp. 40. 20287

Dissertation sur la traite des nègres. *See* [Bellon de Saint-Quentin (J.)], Vol. II., No. 4564.

Dissertation sur les fruits de la découverte de l'Amérique, qui a obtenu en 1785 une mention honorable de l'académie de Lyon; revue et corrigée pour le concours en 1787; par un Citoyen, ancien Syndic de la Chambre de Commerce de Lyon. *Paris.* 1781. 8vo. 20288

Dissertation upon the Constitutional Freedom of the Press in the United States of America. By an Impartial Citizen. ... *Boston: Joseph Nancrede.* 1801. 8vo, pp. 54. BA., W. 20289

Dissertations on Government. *See* [Paine (Thomas)].

Dissertations on the Grand Dispute between Great Britain and America. Signed Amor Patriæ. [*London.* 1774.] + *New York: Privately Printed.* 8vo, pp. 10. 20290

Dissertations sur le Droit Public des Colonies Françoises, Espagnoles, et Angloises, d'après les loix des trois nations comparées entr'elles. *Genève.* 1778. 8vo, pp. 500. S. 20291

The Dissolution of the Union. *See* [Carey (M.)], Vol. III., *note* to No. 10889.

Dissolution of the Union. The Past, the Present, and the Future. From the National Intelligencer. [n. p. 1851.] 8vo, pp. 40. M. 20292

Dissolving Views of Richmond; Three Scenes. *Columbia.* [n. d.] 3 sheets, folio. 20293

Dissuasion to Great-Britain and the Colonies, from the Slave-Trade to Africa, ... Revised and abridged. By James Swan. *Boston: J. Greenleaf ...* . 1773. 8vo, pp. 40. BA. 20294

Distilled Spirits and the Influence of Taxes on American Industry. Letter from the Secretary of the Treasury to the House of Representatives, transmitting a Report of the United States Revenue Commission on Distilled Spirits as a Source of National Revenue and the Influence of the Duplication of Taxes on American Industry. [*Washington.* 1866.] 8vo, pp. 48. C.

Distillers, etc. Appeal to Congress for a Revision of the Internal Revenue Laws concerning Distilled Spirits, embodying Resolves of a National Convention of those Interested in the Manufacture, Refining, and Sale of Spirits, held at Washington ... . *Washington, D. C.: Gibson Brothers, Printers.* 1867. 8vo, pp. 6. H. 20296

District of Columbia. Acts concerning the Territory of Columbia, and the City of Washington. 1791. 8vo. W.

Acts of Maryland and Virginia ceding the District of Columbia to the United States. *Philadelphia.* 1791. 8vo. W. 20298

Acts of Congress in relation to the District of Columbia, from July 16th, 1790, to March 4th, 1831 inclusive; and of the Legislatures of Virginia and Maryland, passed especially in regard to that district. With Notes of the Proceedings of the Congress under the Confederation and the present Constitution, in regard to the permanent Seat of the Government of the United States: By W. A Davis. *Washington City.* 1831. 8vo.

Corographical and Statistical Description of the District of Columbia. *See* [Warden (Daniel B.)]

Code of Laws for the District of Columbia; prepared under the authority of the Act of Congress of the 29th April, 1816, by W. Cranch. *Washington City.* 1819. 8vo. C. 20300

Not adopted.

Compilation of the Laws in force in the District of Columbia, April 1, 1868. *Washington: Government Printing Office.* 1868. 8vo, pp. 494. 20301

Considerations on the Government, 1801. *See* [Woodward (A. B.)]

Enquiries into the Necessity or Expediency of assuming Exclusive Legislation over the District of Columbia. By a Private Citizen. *Washington.* [1801?] 12mo. C. 20302

Essay on the Seat of the Federal Government and the Exclusive Jurisdiction of Congress over a Ten Mile District. By a Citizen of Philadelphia. *Philadelphia.* 1790. 8vo. W.

Florula Columbiensis. List of Plants found in the District of Columbia, arranged according to the Linnæan System. *Washington.* 1819. S., W. 20304

Florula Columbiana: or a List of Plants that have been discovered in the District of Columbia. *Washington.* 1822. 18mo.

General Laws of the Corporation of Washington, passed since the first of June, 1853, and since the publication of Sheahan's Digest. Compiled by the Mayor, 1856. *Washington.* 1856. 8vo. 20306

The Laws, By-Laws, and Organization of the Reform School of the District of Columbia, May, 1870. *Washington: H. Polkinhorn & Co., Printers.* 1870. 8vo, pp. 24. H. 20307

Laws of the United States, for the Government of the Militia of the District of Columbia; and the United States Rules and Articles of War, as now modified; with Explanatory Notes. *Baltimore: John Murphy & Co.* 1861. 8vo, pp. 48. 20308

The Power of Congress over the District of Columbia. Reprinted from the New-York Evening Post, with Additions by the Author. *New-York: John F. Trow.* 1838. 8vo, pp. 57.

Proceedings at the Opening of the Patent Office Fair, under the Auspices of the Ladies' Relief Association, District of Columbia, February 22, 1864. *Washington: Printed for the Fair.* 1864. 8vo, pp. 30. 20310

Proceedings of the Temperance Union, D. C. with the First Annual Report of the Board of Managers. To which is added an Appendix, showing the Origin and Evils of Intemperance in the District of Columbia. *Washington City: printed by Peter Force.* 1835. 8vo, pp. 56. H. 20311

Register of the Militia of the District of Columbia: together with the Militia Laws of the United States ... By Brooke Williams. *Washington.* 1831. 12mo, pp. 44. S. 20312

Resolves in relation to Petitions touching the Subject of Slavery in the District of Columbia. *Boston.* 1837. 8vo.

A System of Civil and Criminal Law, for the District of Columbia, and for the Organization of the Courts therein. *Washington.* 1833. 8vo. P. 20314

Also: Address of the Free Soil Association of the District ot Columbia to the People of the United States. [n. p. n. d.] 8vo, pp. 16.—First Annual Report of the National Freedman's Relief Association of the District of Columbia. *Washington, D. C.: M'Gill & Witherow, Printers.* 1863. 8vo, pp. 8. H. + Fourth Report. 1866. 8vo, pp. 21. + Fifth Report. 1867. 8vo, pp. 16.—Annual Report of the Board of Metropolitan Police of the District of Columbia. 1863. *Washington: J. L. Pearson & Co., Printers.* 1863. 8vo. Continued. H.—Extract from the Report of the Secretary of the Interior relative to the Penitentiary of the District of Columbia. [n. p. n. d.] 8vo, pp. 29. H.—Message from the President of the United States, transmitting the Annual Report of the Inspectors of the Penitentiary in the District of Columbia. January 28, 1834. ... [*Washington.*] 8vo, pp. 13. Continued. H.—The Freaks of Columbia, or the Removal of the Seat of Government, A Farce.—Memorial of the Delegates appointed by various sections of the District of Columbia. Jan. 22, 1805. [*Washington.* 1805.] 8vo.—On the Establishment of a New Bank in the District. *Washington.* 1835. 8vo.—Report on the Expediency of Laying a Direct Tax upon the District of Columbia, and the several Territories. January 23, 1815. (Cong. Doc.)

The District School as it Was. *See* [Burton (Warren)], Vol. III., No. 9504.

El distrito del Petén Itza y su agreg. al esta de Yucatan. *Campeche.* 1829. Sm. 4to. 20315

Disturnell (J.) American and European Railway and Steamship Guide ... through the United States and Canada; ... *New York.* 1851. Continued. C. 20316

Disturnell. Blue Book; or, Register of Officers and Agents, Civil, Military and Naval, in the Service of the United States; Corrected to November, 1862: ... Compiled by J. Disturnell, ... *New York: J. H. Colton.* 1863. 8vo, pp. 262. Continued. 20317

Disturnell. A Description of the City of New York, 1847. *See* [Holley (O. L.)]

Disturnell. Disturnell's Guide through the Middle, Northern, and Eastern States; ... *New York: J. Disturnell. June,* 1847. 18mo, pp. 80. Map. + *July,* 1847. 18mo, pp. 80. C. + *January,* 1848. 18mo, pp. 79. 20318

Disturnell. The Great Lakes, or Inland Seas of America, ... together with the Commerce of the Lakes, and Trips through the Lakes; giving a Description of Cities, Towns, etc. Forming a Complete Guide for the Pleasure Traveller and Emigrant. ... Compiled by J. Disturnell, ... *New York: Charles Scribner.* 1863. 16mo, pp. 192. + [*Ibid.*] 1865. + With a Guide to the Upper Mississippi River. *New York: American News Company.* 1868. Sq. 16mo, pp. 218. 2 Maps and 10 Plates.

Disturnell. Influence of Climate, in a Commercial, Social, Sanitary, and Humanizing Point of View ... . By J. Disturnell ... . Also, a Paper on the Influence of Climate in the Equatorial Regions ... . Accompanied by a Map of the World ... . *New York.* 1860. 4to, pp. 24. + *New York.* 1866. 4to, pp. 32. H. 20320

Disturnell. Influence of Climate in North and South America: showing the varied Climatic Influences operating in the Equatorial, Tropical, Sub-Tropical, Temperate, Cold, and Frigid Regions, extending from the Arctic to the Antarctic Circle, accompanied by an Agricultural and Isothermal Map of North America. Compiled by J. Disturnell, ... *New York: D. Van Nostrand.* 1867. 8vo, pp. 334. Maps and Frontispiece.

Disturnell. Springs, Water Falls, Sea-Bathing Resorts, and Mountain Scenery of the United States and Canada. By John Disturnell. With Embellishments. *New-York.* 1855. 24mo, pp. 227. Maps and Plates. C., S. 20322

Disturnell. Summer Arrangements, ... *New York. July,* 1848. 20323

The printed title to the railroad and steamboat book. Monthly edition.

Disturnell. A Trip through the Lakes of North America; embracing a full Description of the St. Lawrence River, together with all the Principal Places on its Banks, from its Source to its Mouth; Commerce of the Lakes, &c. ... *New York.* 1857. 12mo. C. 20324

Disturnell. United States Register, or, Blue Book for 1866. ... Compiled by J. Disturnell. *New York: Sinclair Tousey.* 1867. 12mo, pp. 100. Continued. 20325

Also: The Blue Book Abridged; or, Abridged Blue Book, or, Biennial Register of Federal Officers and Salaries in all the Civil, Military, and Naval Departments. Corrected to October, 1864. ... *New York: American News Company.* 12mo, pp. 46.—Census of the United States and Territories, and of British America: ... *New York: American News Company.* 1867. 8vo, pp. 64.—The Eastern Tourist, being a Guide through the States of Connecticut, Rhode Island, Massachusetts, Vermont, New Hampshire, and Maine. Also, a Dash into Canada. By J. Disturnell. *New York: J. Disturnell.* 1848. 16mo, pp. 144. Plate. C.—Emigrant's Guide to New Mexico, California, and Oregon: giving the different Routes, with a Map. *New York: J. Disturnell.* 1849. 16mo, pp. 45. C. + *New York.* 1850. 16mo, pp. viii, 80.—Guide between Washington, Baltimore, Philadelphia, New York, and Boston; ... *New York: J. Disturnell.* 1846. 18mo, pp. 80. C. + *June,* 1846. pp. 79. + *September,* 1846. pp. 79. + *January,* 1847. pp. 79.—List of Post-Offices and Postmasters in the United States. ... *New York.* 1870. 4to, pp. 321.—The New-York State Guide; containing an Alphabetical List of Counties, Towns, Cities, Villages, Post Offices, &c., with Census of 1840. *Albany.* 1842. 18mo. S.—The New-York Political Manual; containing the Official Election Returns for 1840–42, and the Census of 1840 ... —The Northern Traveller; containing the Hudson River Guide, and Tour to the Springs, Lake George and Canada, passing through Lake Champlain. *New York.* 1844. 2 Maps.—Post-Office Directory for 1863. Alphabetical List of Post-Offices in the United States, with the Names of Postmasters (except at Suspended Offices). ... Revised ... J. Disturnell, to April 1, 1863. *New York: J. H. Colton.* 1863. Rl. 8vo, pp. xxii, 298. + for 1867. ... *New York: American News Company.* 1867. 4to, pp. xxiv, 320.—Railroad, Steamboat, and Telegraph Book; being a Guide through the Middle, Northern, and Eastern States, and Canada, [etc.] *New York: J. Disturnell.* 1850. 18mo, pp. 108. Map. C. + *New York.* 1855. 18mo, pp. 108. Map. + 1865. *New York.* 1865. Sq. 18mo.—The Traveller's Guide to the Hudson River, Saratoga Springs, Lake George, Falls of Niagara, and Thousand Islands, Montreal, Quebec, and the Saguenay River; also to the Green and White Mountains, and other parts of New England, etc. ... *New York: American News Company.* 1864. 16mo, pp. 324. Map and Illus.—Tourist's Guide to the Upper Mississippi River. ... together with an Account of Cities and Villages and Objects of Interest on the Route, and in the Upper Valley of the Mississippi. ... *New York: American News Company.* 1866. Sq. 16mo, pp. 84.—United States Almanac and National Register for the year 1850. *New York: J. Disturnell.* 1850. 16mo, pp. 100.—Disturnell's United States National Register and Calendar for 1851–1852, containing Authentic Political and Statistical Information relating to the United States, Canada, [etc.] ... *New-York.* 1851–1852. 12mo. Map. Continued. C.—The Western Traveller, embracing the Canal and Railroad Routes from Albany and Troy, to Buffalo and Niagara Falls. ... *New York.* 1844. 12mo. Plate.

Disunion and its Results to the South. A Letter from a Resident of Washington to a Friend in South Carolina. *Washington, D. C.: H. Polkinhorn, Printer.* [n. d.] 8vo, pp. 23. H.

Disunion, and a Mississippi Valley Confederacy. [n. p. n. d.] 8vo, pp. 15. 20327

Ditchfield (*Mr.*) Considerations Touching the New Contract for Tobacco, as the same hath beene propounded by Maister

Ditchfield, and other undertakers. *Printed in the Year* 1625. 4to. 20328

An interesting tract relating entirely to the rights and interests of the Virginian and Sommer Island plantations.

Ditterline (T.) Sketch of the Battles of Gettysburg, July 1st, 2d, and 3d, 1863: with an Account of the Movements of the respective Armies for some Days previous thereto. Compiled from the Personal Observation of Eye Witnesses ... . By T. Ditterline. *New York: C. A. Alvord, Printer.* 1863. 8vo, pp. 24. Map. B., H. 20329

Diuhsawahgwah Gayádoshäh Gówahás. Goyadoh. Sgáóyadih dówänandenyo. Neh Nadigé hjihshohoh dodisdoagoh; was-to'k tadinageh. *Boston: Crocker & Brewster, Printers.* 1836. 12mo, pp. 42, 1 l. Woodcuts. 20330

An elementary reading book in the language of the Seneca Indians, by the Rev. A. Wright.

Diven (A. S.) Speeches of Hon. A. S. Diven, of New-York, on the Appropriation Bill, and the Confiscation of Rebel Property. Delivered in the House ... January 22, & May 12, 1862. *Washington, D. C.: printed by L. Towers & Co.* [n. d.] 8vo, pp. 16. H. 20331

Also: Speech ... on the Kansas Resolutions, Jan. 12, 1858. 8vo, pp. 15.—The Surrender of Mason and Slidell. Speech ... delivered in the House of Representatives, January 7, 1862. pp. 6.

Divers Weighty and Serious Considerations, shewing the Necessity of taking Fort St. Augustine, in Florida, from the Spaniards, and on Fortifying and Preserving it. [n. p. n. d.] 4to, pp. 8. 20332

Diversi avisi particolari dall' Indie di Portogallo riceuuti, dall' anno 1551. sino al 1558. dalli Reuerendi Padri della Compagnia di Giesv ... Tradotti nuouamente dalla lingua Spagnuola nella Italiana. *Venetia: Michele Tramezzino.* 1558. 8vo, 7 l., pp. 286.

Vol. IV. contains letters relating to the American missions.

Diversity, *pseudonym.* Essays on Taxation and Reconstruction. By Diversity. *New York: C. B. Richardson.* 1865. 8vo, pp. 22. 20334

The Diverting History of John Bull. *See* [Paulding (J. K.)]

Divoll (W.) The True American Citizen, by Willard Divoll, to which is appended the Constitution of the United States, with the recent Amendments and Civil Rights Bill. *J. N. Hallock, New York.* 1868. 18mo, pp. 144. 20335

DIX (Dorothy L.) Remarks on Prisons and Prison Discipline in the United States. By D. L. Dix ... *Boston: printed by Munroe and Francis.* 1845. 8vo, pp. 104. + Second Edition, from the First Boston Edition. *Philadelphia: Joseph Kite & Co., Printers.* 1845. 8vo, pp. 108. P., S. 20336

DIX. Memorial to the Legislature of Massachusetts. *Boston: printed by Munroe and Francis.* [n. d.] 8vo, pp. 32. C., H.

Also: Fifth Letter to Convicts in States Prisons and Houses of Correction, or County Penitentiaries. ... Printed but not published, November, 1850. [n. p.] 12mo, pp. 24. H. — Letters to Convicts in Twenty-Six State Prisons, and Ten Houses of Correction or County Penitentiaries. Fifth Thousand. 1848. — Memorial of Miss D. L. Dix, in Relation to the Illinois Penitentiary. February 5, 1847. ... [n. p. n. d.] 8vo, pp. 16. H. — Memorial ... praying a Grant of Land for the Relief and Support of the Indigent Curable and Incurable Insane in the United States. June 27, 1848. ... [n. p. n. d.] 8vo, pp. 32. H., S. — Memorial ... to the Honorable the General Assembly in Behalf of the Insane of Maryland. [n. p. n. d.] 8vo, pp. 19. H. — Memorial soliciting a State Hospital for the Insane, submitted to the Legislature of New Jersey, January 23, 1845. ... Second Edition. *Trenton.* 1845. 8vo, pp. 46. H., N. — Memorial soliciting a State Hospital for the Insane, submitted to the Legislature of Pennsylvania, February 3, 1846. ... *Harrisburg.* 1845. 8vo, pp. 59. N. The same. [Third Edition.] pp. 52. H. — Memorial soliciting an Appropriation for the State Hospital for the Insane, at Lexington; and also urging the Necessity for establishing a New Hospital in the Green River Country. ... *Frankfort, Ky.* 1846. 8vo, pp. 16. H., N. — Memorial soliciting Enlarged and Improved Accommodations for the Insane of the State of Tennessee, by the establishment of a New Hospital. By Miss D. L. Dix. ... *Nashville: B. R. M'Kennie, Printer.* 1847. 8vo, pp. 32. H. — Memorial soliciting a State Hospital for the Protection and Cure of the Insane, submitted to the General Assembly of North Carolina. November, 1848. *Raleigh: Seaton Gales, Printer.* [n. d.] 8vo, pp. 48. H. — Memorial soliciting Adequate Appropriations for the Construction of a State Hospital for the Insane, in the State of Mississippi. February, 1850. ... *Jackson, Miss.* 1850. 8vo, pp. 21. H. — Memorial To the Honorable the Legislature of the State of New-York. [n. p. n. d.] 8vo, pp. 59. H. — A Review of the Present Condition of the State Penitentiary of Kentucky, with Brief Notices and Remarks upon the Jails and Poor-Houses in some of the most Populous Counties. ... *Frankfort.* 1846. 8vo, pp. 40. H. — State of New York. No. 21. In Assembly, January 18, 1844. Annual Report of the Managers of the State Lunatic Asylum. ... [n. p. n. d.] 8vo, pp. 123. H.

DIX (J. A.) Address at the Laying of the Corner-Stone of the Douglas Monument at Chicago, September 6, 1866. By Major-General John A. Dix. *New York: Edward F. Crowen.* 1866. 8vo, pp. 35. 20337

DIX. The City of New York: its Growth, Destinies, and Duties. A Lecture. By John A. Dix. *New York.* 1853. 8vo, pp. 23. 20338

[DIX.] On the Mode of constituting Presidential Electors. Addressed to the People of the State of New-York. *New-York: Johnstone & Van Norden, Printers.* 1823. 8vo, pp. 23. H.

[DIX.] Sketch of the Resources of the City of New York with a View of its Municipal Government, Population, &c., from the foundation of the City to the date of the Latest Statistical Accounts. *New York: G. & C. Carvill.* 1827. 8vo, pp. 104. 20340

DIX. Speeches and Occasional Addresses. By John A Dix. *New York: D. Appleton & Co.* 1865. 2 vols., 8vo, pp. vi, 452; iv, 466. Portraits and Facsimiles. 20341

Also: Address ... before the Alpha Phi Delta and Euglossian Societies of Geneva College, ... 7th of August, 1839. ... *Albany: printed by Packard, Van Benthuysen & Co.* 1839. 8vo, pp. 68. H. — Address ... October 2d, 1851, at the ... Queens County Agricultural Society, at Jamaica, L. I., ... *Hempstead, L. I.* 1852. 8vo, pp. 18. H. — Address ... at the Reception by the Seventh Regiment ... of its Members who have served in the Army and Navy of the United States during the Great Rebellion. ... January 31, 1866. *New York: Francis & Loutrel, Printers.* 1866. 8vo, pp. 17. H. — The American Quarterly Review *vs.* the State of New-York. S. — California Claims. Speech ... in the Senate ... March 29, 1848 ... . [*Washington.* n. d.] 8vo, pp. 8. H. — Communication from Hon. John A. Dix, to the Select Committee of the Senate on the Report of Trinity Church. *New York: John F. Trow, Printer.* 1837. 8vo, pp. 19. N. — Decisions of the Superintendents of Common Schools of the State of New York. ... Selected and Arranged by John A. Dix. *Albany.* 1837. 8vo. — Letter ... to the War Democracy of Wisconsin. ... . *New York.* 1863. 8vo, pp. 14. H. — Letters of Loyal Soldiers. Letter of General Dix, his Opinion of the Chicago Platform. [n. p. n. d.] 8vo, pp. 4. — Opinion [when Adjutant-General] on Two Questions of Alienism. *Albany.* 1833. 8vo. — The Presidency. Letter ... to the Committee of the Mass Meeting in Philadelphia, October 8, 1864. [n. p. n. d.] 8vo, pp. 4. H. — Remarks ... on the Warehouse Bill ... July 9, 1846. 8vo, pp. 23. — Remarks ... on the Propriety of sending a Minister to the Papal States. ... in the Senate ... March 21, 1848. *Washington.* 1848. 8vo, pp. 7. H. — Report [when Secretary of State] in relation to a Geological Survey of the State of New York. *Albany.* 1836. 8vo. — Speech ... on the Tariff. 1830. 8vo. S. — Speech ... on the Oregon Question. ... in the Senate ... February 18 & 19, 1846. *Washington.* 1846. 8vo, pp. 22. — Speech ... on the Bill to Indemnify American Citizens for French Spoliations Prior to 1800. ... in tbe Senate ... April 27, 1846. *Washington.* 1846. 8vo, pp. 16. H. — Speech ... on the Warehouse Bill. ... in the Senate .. June 19, 1846. *Washington.* 1846. 8vo, pp. 23. H. — Speech ... on the Bill to appoint a Lieutenant General. ... in the Senate ... January 14, 1847. 8vo, pp. 7. H. — Speech ... on the Three Million Bill. Delivered in the Senate ... March 1, 1847. *Washington.* 1847. 8vo, pp. 15. B., H., S. — Speech ... on the Bill to Establish a Territorial Government in Oregon. ... in the Senate ... June 26, 1848. *Washington.* 1848. 8vo, pp. 14. H. — Speech ... on the Pilot Laws. ... in the Senate ... June 30, 1848. *Washington.* 1848. 8vo, pp. 8. H. — Speech ... on the Bill to Establish Governments in the Territories. ... in the Senate ... July 26, 1848. *Washington.* 1848. 8vo, pp. 14. H. — Speech ... on the Bill for paying certain claims in California. [*Washington.* 1848.] 8vo. B. — Speech ... in Favor of Reciprocal Trade with Canada ... in the Senate ... January 23, 1849. *Washington.* 1849. 8vo, pp. 14. B., H. — Speech ... in Relation to Territories acquired from Mexico. ... in the Senate ... February 28, 1849. *Washington.* 1849. 8vo, pp. 14. B., H., S. — Speech of Gen. John A. Dix, President of the Mississippi and Missouri Railroad Company, at the Celebration at Iowa City ... on the Completion of the Road to the Latter Point. ... *New York: Wm. C. Bryant & Co., Printers.* 1856. 8vo, pp 19. H. — The War with Mexico. Speech ... in the Senate ... January 26, 1848.

On the Bill reported from the Committee on Military Affairs to raise, for a limited time, an additional Military Force. [*Washington.* n. d.] 8vo, pp. 15. H. — Presentation to Major-Gen. John A. Dix, President of the Metropolitan Fair in aid of United States Sanitary Commission. New York, April 23, 1864. *New York: Francis & Loutrel, Printers.* 1864. 8vo, pp. 10. H.

DIX (J. R.) Amusing and Thrilling Adventures of a California Artist, while Daguerrotyping a Continent ... . Written by John Ross Dix ... . *Boston.* 1854. 12mo, pp. 92. H.

[DIX.] A Hand-book of Newport and Rhode Island. By the author of "Pen and Ink Sketches." *Newport: C. E. Hammett.* 1852. 12mo, pp. xxi, 170. 20343

DIX. Local Loiterings, and Visits in the Vicinity of Boston. By a Looker-on. *Boston: Redding & Co.* 1845. 12mo, pp. 147. H. 20344

DIX. Pulpit Portraits; or, Pen-Pictures of Distinguished American Divines; with Sketches of Congregations and Choirs, and Incidental Notices of Eminent British Preachers. By John R. Dix. *Boston.* 1854. 12mo, pp. 256. 20345

[DIX.] Transatlantic Tracings; or, Sketches of Persons and Scenes in America. *London: W. Tweedie.* 1853. 16mo, pp. 337. 20346

DIX (M.) The Death of President Lincoln. A Sermon preached in Saint Paul's Chapel, New York, on Wednesday, April 19, 1865. By the Rev. Morgan Dix, S.T.D. Rector of Trinity Church. Printed by Order of the Vestry. *Cambridge: Printed at the Riverside Press.* 1865. 8vo, pp. 16. 20347

1000 copies printed.

DIX. Historical Recollections of St. Paul's Chapel, New York. By Rev. Morgan Dix. With an Account of the Services at its Centennial Anniversary. *New York: Huntington & Son.* 1867. 8vo, pp. 64. 20348

DIX. The History of the Past Fifty Years a History of Beneficial Change, Steady Growth, and Valuable Acquisitions. A Sermon ... . *New York.* 1867. 18mo, pp. 20. 20349

Also: Christian Education the Remedy for the Growing Ungodliness of the Times. ... . [n. p. n. d.] 8vo, pp. 16. H. — God's Mercies toward the Nation. A Sermon, preached in ... New York, Thanksgiving Day, 1861. ... . *New York.* 1861. 8vo, pp. 16. H. — The General Convention of 1865. A Sermon preached in ... New York ... October 29th, 1865 ... . *New York.* 1865. 8vo, pp. 15. H. — A Sermon Preached March 13, 1864. By the Rev. Morgan Dix, S.T.D. *New York: D. Appleton & Co.* 8vo, pp. 37. — The Way of God in the Storm. A Sermon preached ... April 21, 1861. *New York: F. J. Huntington.* 1861. 8vo, pp. 15.

DIX (W.) A Salutory Address, on the Social Influence, and Merit of Free Masonry: delivered ... at the Request of the Officers and Members of Washington Lodge in Roxbury, at their Consecration, October 12, A.L. 5796. By Brother William Dix, A.M. *Boston.* 1797. 8vo, pp. 10. H., M. 20350

DIX (William G.) The Deck of the Crescent City. A Poem. By William Giles Dix. ... *Boston and Cambridge.* 1852. 32mo, pp. 46. 20351

DIX. The Deck of the Crescent City; a Picture of American Life. By William Giles Dix. *New York: G. P. Putnam & Co.* 1853. 16mo, pp. 120. B. 20352

DIX. The University of the South. An Address, delivered at Beersheba Springs, Tenn., August 19th and 22nd, 1859, and also ... at ... Nashville, Sept. 8th, 1859. By William Giles Dix. *Nashville, Tenn.: W. T. Berry and Company.* 1859. 8vo, pp. 32. C., H. 20353

Also: The Doom of the Crescent. ... *Boston: Ide and Dutton.* 1853. 16mo, pp. xi, 35. H., M. — The Presidency: a Reply to the Letter of Hon. Rufus Choate to the Whig State Committee of Maine. ... *Boston.* 1856. 12mo, pp. 32. B., H. — The Winter Evening Fireside. *Boston: W. D. Ticknor & Co.* 1847. 12mo, pp. 36. H.

[DIXON (B. Homer).] Brief Memoir of the Family of Shelton, of Connecticut. *Boston: Dutton & Wentworth.* 1857. 8vo, pp. 5.

[DIXON.] Surnames. *Boston: printed by John Wilson & Son.* 1855. 8vo, pp. xviii. 79. H. 20355

[DIXON.] [Revised Edition.] *Boston.* 1857. 8vo, pp. xxxi, 85.

Both editions printed for private distribution only.

DIXON. Surnames. [With supplement.] *Boston, for private distribution.* 1857–58. 8vo, pp. xxxi, 94. H. 20357

DIXON (E. H.) Back-Bone; Photographed from "the Scalpel." By Edward H. Dixon, M.D. *New York: R. M. De Witt.* 1866. 12mo, pp, 306, viii. Portrait. H., C. 20358

DIXON. Scenes in the Practice of a New York Surgeon. By Edward H. Dixon, M.D. With Eight Illustrations by Darley. ... *New York.* [1855.] 12mo, pp. 407. 20359

[DIXON.] The Terrible Mysteries of the Ku-Klux-Klan. A Full Expose of the Forms, Objects, and "Dens" of the Secret Order: with a Complete Description of their Initiation. From the Confession of a Member. By Scalpel, M.D. *New York.* 1868. 8vo, pp. 56. H. 20360

DIXON (G.) Remarks on the Voyage of John Meares, Esq., in a letter to that gentleman by George Dixon, late Commander of the Queen Charlotte in a Voyage round the World. *London: For the Author.* M,DCC,XC. 4to, pp. 37. B., J.C.B. 20361

DIXON. An answer to Mr. George Dixon, late Commander of the Queen Charlotte, in the service of Messrs. Etches and Company. By John Meares, Esq. In which the remarks of Mr. Dixon on the Voyages to the N. W. Coast of America, &c., lately published, are fully considered and refuted. *Walter.* 1791. 4to, pp. 32. 20362

DIXON. Further Remarks on the Voyages of John Meares, Esq.; in which several important facts, misrepresented in the said voyages, relative to Geography and Commerce, are fully substantiated. To which is added, A Letter from Captain Duncan, containing a decisive refutation of several unfounded Assertions of Mr. Meares; and a final reply to his answer. By George Dixon, late Commander of the Queen Charlotte, in a Voyage round the World. *London: J. Stockdale.* 1791. 4to, pp. 80. 20363

See Meares (J.)

DIXON. A|Voyage round the World;|but more particularly [to] the|North-West, Coast of America:|performed in 1785, 1786, 1787 and 1788,|in|the King George and Queen Charlotte,|Captains Portlock and Dixon.|Embellished with Twenty Copper-Plates.|Dedicated, by Permission, to|His Majesty|By Captain Nathaniel Portlock.| *London: J. Stockdale.* |M,DCC,LXXXIX.| 4to, 15 l., pp. 360, 47, xxvii, (2). 22 Plates and Maps. C. + [The Second Edition.] *London: Geo. Goulding.* 1789. 4to, pp. xxix, (2), 360, 47. 22 Maps and Plates. BA.

Also on large and thick paper, with the plates of natural history, colored. *See* "M. Rev.," LXXX. 502. *See also* Foster (J. R), for a German translation, and Portlock (Nathaniel).

DIXON. An Abridgement of Portlock's and Dixon's Voyage Round the World, performed in 1785, 1786, 1787, and 1788. *London: J. Stockdale.* 1789. 8vo, pp. 272. Map and Plate. + [*Ibid.*] 1791. 20365

DIXON. Voyage autour du Monde, et principalement à la Côte nord-ouest de l'Amérique, fait en 1785, 1786, 1787 et 1788. Par les Capitaines Portlock et Dixon. Traduit de l'Anglois, par M. Lebas. *Paris.* 1789. 4to, pp. 499, 46. Map and 21 Plates. + *Paris.* 1789. 2 vols., 8vo. Map and Plates. 20366

DIXON. Reisen nach der nordwestlichen Küste von Amerika von den Kapitainen Meares, Dixon, Portlak u. a. Ein Auszug aus der grösseren Sammlung dieser Reisen für Liebhaber und Lesekabinete. *Nürnberg: E. C. Grattenauer.* 1795. 8vo, pp. 440. C. 20367

DIXON (J.) American Labor: its Necessities and Prospects. Address of the Hon. James Dixon, of Hartford, Conn., delivered before the American Institute ... Oct. 21, 1852. *New-York: printed by Mann & Spear.* 1852. 8vo, pp. 23. H. 20368

Also: The Amistad Claim. Speech ... in the Senate ... January 9, 1860. [*Washington.* n. d.] 8vo, pp. 8. H. — The President Responsible for the Mexican War and its Consequences. Speech ... on the Reference of the President's Message. Delivered in the House ... Jan. 24, 1848. [*Washington.* n. d.] 8vo, pp. 16. H. Speech ... on the Tariff. ... in the House ... June 30th, 1846. [*Washington.* n. d.] 8vo, pp. 16. H. — Speech ... against the Extension of Slave Territory. Delivered in the House ... Feb. 9, 1847. [*Washington.* n. d.] 8vo, pp. 16. H. — Speech, ... January 2, 1858: Texas and Mexico. *Washington.* 1848. pp. 32. — Speech, ... Jan. 24, 1848, on reference of the President's Message. — Speech ... in the Senate ... February 9, 1858. *Washington, D. C.* 1858. 8vo, pp. 15. H. — Speech ... on the ... Naturalization Laws and the Origin of the Native American Party. ... December 30, 1845. *Washington.* 1846. 8vo, pp. 16. BA. — Speech ... on the Thirty Million Bill, for the Acquisition of Cuba. ... Senate ... February 25, 1859. [*Washington.* n. d.] 8vo, pp. 32. H. — Speech ... in the Senate ... June 25, 1862, on his Resolution respecting the Legal Effect of Acts or Ordinances of Secession. *Washington.* 1862. 8vo, pp. 8. H. — Speech ... on the National Finances ... . Senate ... December 17, 1868. *Washington: F. & J. Rives & Geo. A. Bailey, Printers.* 1868. 8vo, pp. 16. H

DIXON (J.) Methodism in America; with the Personal Narrative of the Author, during a Tour through a Part of the United States of America and Canada. By James Dixon, D.D. *London: John Mason.* M DCCC XLIX. Post 8vo, pp. 498. Map.

DIXON. Personal Narrative of a Tour through a Part of the United States and Canada; with Notices of the History and Institution of Methodism in America. By James Dixon, D.D. Second Edition. *New York: Lane & Scott.* 1849. 12mo, pp. 431. Portrait. C. 20370

Altered and abridged by James McClintock.

DIXON (N. F.) Speech of Hon. Nathan F. Dixon, of Westerly, upon the Resolution to Annul the Decree of the Supreme Court, in the Case of Robert H. Ives vs. Charles T. Hazard, et al. *Providence.* 1859. 8vo, pp. 36. BA., H. 20371

DIXON (W.) Petition of William Dixon and James Dixon to the Congress of the United States, praying for Remission of a Forfeiture, &c. *Augusta, Ga.: printed by William J. Bunce.* 1825. 8vo, pp. 22. H. 20372

DIXON (W. H). New America. By William Hepworth. Dixon. With Illustrations from Original Photographs. *London: Hurst and Blackett.* 1867. 2 vols., 8vo, pp. xii, (1), 359; vi, 369. Woodcuts. BA. + *Philadelphia: J. B. Lippincott & Co.* 1867. Cr. 8vo, pp. 495. Woodcuts. BA. + Third Edition. [*Ibid.*] 1867. + *Leipzig: B. Tauchnitz.* 1867. 2 vols., 16mo, pp. 591. (Coll. Brit. Auth., Vol. 797, 798.) + Eighth Edition. *London.* 1869. Post 8vo. 20373

Parts of his "New America" were translated in the "Monatsblätter für innere Zeitgeschichte," 32 Bd. Aug. 1868, etc.

DIXON. La nouvelle Amérique. Par Hepworth Dixon: Traduction de l'anglais avec une préface et la biographie de Hepworth Dixon, par Philarète Chasles ... . *Paris: Libraire internationale.* 1868. 8vo, pp. viii, 430. 20374

DIXON. Robert Blake Admiral and General at Sea. Based on Family and State Papers. By Hepworth Dixon. *London: Chapman and Hall.* MDCCCLII. Post 8vo, pp. xv, 366. Portrait. BA., C. + New Edition. *London: Chapman & Hall.* 1858. 12mo. Portrait. 20375

DIXON. William Penn: An Historical Biography, from New Sources. With an Extra Chapter on the "Macaulay Charges." By William Hepworth Dixon. ... *London: Chapman and Hall.* 1851. 8vo. Portrait. + *Philadelphia: Blanchard and Lea.* 1851. 12mo, pp. xv, 13–353. H. 20376

Reprinted as

DIXON. William Penn. An Historical Biography, founded on Family and State Papers. By Hepworth Dixon. The Second Edition. *London: Chapman & Hall.* 1852. Fcap 8vo. + New Edition, with a New Preface in Reply to the Accusations of Mr. Macaulay. *London: Chapman & Hall.* 1856. 12mo, pp. 420.

DIXON. Spiritual Wives. By W. Hepworth Dixon, ... *London: Hurst and Blackett.* 1868. 2 vols., 8vo, pp. xxi, 331; xiv, 344. BA. + Fourth Edition, with a New Preface. *London: Hurst & Blackett.* 1868. 2 vols., 8vo. Portrait. 20378

Treats of the Mormons, Free Love in America, etc.

DIXWELL (J.) A Report on the State of the Grand Lodge of Massachusetts, and the Lodges under its Jurisdiction, made on the 27th December, A.L. 5823. By John Dixwell, M.D., Grand Master. *Boston: published by Joseph Buckingham.* 1824. 8vo, pp. 15. H. 20379

DIZAC (F.) Excursion aux Indes Occidentales et aux Etats-Unis d'Amérique (1853–1854). Par F. Dizac. Seconde édition. *Tarbes: imp. Larrieu.* 8vo, pp. 183. 20380

DMFY (Dl.) Memoire sur l'Esclavage des Nègres, contenant réponse à divers Ecrits qui ou été publies en leur faveur. Par M. DL. Dmfy. *Paris: Garnery.* 1790. 8vo, pp. 64.

DOAK (J. W.) A Farewell Sermon, Boiling Spring Church, Oct. 18, 1802. By Johnney W. Doak. *Jonesborough, Tenn.* 1803. 12mo. S. 20382

[DOANE (George W.)] An Address to the People of New Jersey, on the Subject of Common Schools. *Burlington.* [n. d.] 8vo, pp. 16. H. 20383

DOANE. America and Great Britain: The Address, at Burlington College, on the Seventy-Second Anniversary of American Independence, July 4, 1848. By G. W. Doane. *Burlington.* 1848. 8vo. S. 20384

[DOANE.] The Argument of the Bishop of New Jersey: in reply to the Paper, read before the Court of Bishops, ... at Burlington, ... 11 October, 1852, by the Bishops of Virginia, Ohio, and Maine; in answer to the Representation from the Diocese of New Jersey, ... *Newark, N. J.* 1852. 8vo, pp. 16.

[DOANE.] A Brief Narrative. [*Burlington.* 1849.] 8vo, pp. 14. H. 20386

Relates to the condition of the Diocese of New Jersey.

DOANE. The Bush that burned with Fire: the Sermon at the Consecration of St. John's Church, Elizabethtown, ... December 31, M DCCC XL; by the Rt. Rev. George Washington Doane, D.D. ... *Burlington: J. L. Powell, Printer.* M DCCC XLI. 8vo, pp. 56. 20387

Very severe on Bancroft's "History of the United States."

DOANE. One World: One Washington. The Oration in the City Hall, Burlington, on Washington's Birthday, 1859; by request of the Lady Managers of the Mount Vernon Association, and Many Citizens of Burlington. *Burlington, N. J.* MDCCCLIX. 8vo, pp. 32. 20388

DOANE. The Sorrow of Lent, for Sin and not for Suffering. A Sermon preached February 22, 1863, at Burlington, N. J. *Philadelphia: J. B. Chandler.* 1863. 8vo, pp. 14. 20389

Relates to the Rebellion.

DOANE. The Young American; his Dangers, his Duties, and his Destinies. An Address at Burlington College, July 4, 1853. *Philadelphia.* 1853. 8vo. B. 20390

DOANE. Life and Writings of Bishop Doane. *New York.* 1860. 4 vols., 8vo. 20391

Also: ... The Address, at the Funeral of the Rev. John David Ogilby, D.D. ... in ... New-York ... 24th March, MDCCCLI ... . *New-York.* M,DCCCLI. 8vo, pp. 28. H. — Address at the Laying of the Corner Stone of Trinity Church, in the Borough of Princeton, N. J., July 4, 1833. ... *Princeton.* 1833. 8vo. W. — An Appeal to Parents for Female Education on Christian Principles; with a Prospectus of St. Mary's Hall, Green Bank, Burlington, New Jersey. ... *Burlington.* M DCCC XXXVII. 8vo, pp. 22. Plate. H. — The Beauty of Holiness: the Sermon at the Convention of Grace Church, Newark, October 5, 1848 ... *Burlington.* 1849. 8vo. — Bishop Doane's Words at the Burial of Mrs. Bradford. ... Privately printed. Advent, MDCCCLIV. [n. p.] 8vo, pp. 15. H. — ... the Bishop's Address to the Members of the Senior Class, at the Closing Exercises of the Summer Term, September 29, 1846; to which is added, the Catalogue and Prospectus, for the Winter Term, 1846–7. [n. p. n. d.] 12mo, pp. 19. H. — A Brief Examination of ... the Rev. Mr. Boardman's ... attempt to cast the Suspicion of Popery on the Protestant Episcopal Church in ... America. ... *Burlington.* 1841. 8vo, pp. 230. — Burlington College; as adapted to the Training of Pastors, and their Work. [n. p. n. d.] 16mo, pp. 11, 1 l. H. — ... The Second Charge to the Clergy of the Diocese of New Jersey, at the Opening of the Annual Convention, in Trinity Church, Newark, May 25, 1836 ... . *Burlington.* M DCCC XXXVI. 8vo, pp. 39, 1 l. H. — ... the Third Charge ... Burlington, May 29, 1839 ... . *Burlington: printed by Powell & George.* M DCCC XXXIX. 8vo, pp. 32. H. — Civil Government a Sacred Trust from God. The Anniversary Oration before the New Jersey State Society ... *Burlington.* 1845. 8vo. — The Convocation of Miletus: Sermon before the Convocation of the Clergy, at Morristown, N. J., July 25, 1834. ... *Burlington.* 1834. 8vo, pp. 30. W. — Correspondence between the Right Rev. George Washington Doane, D.D. ... and the Rev. S. Wilmer ... on the Subject of Associations, &c. to which is annexed an Appendix, with a Protest and Appeal. *Philadelphia: published by J. Whetham.* 1835. 8vo, pp. 62. H. — The Cross and the Church: An Address at Philadelphia at the Laying the Corner Stone of All Soul's Church. ... *Philadelphia.* 1834. 8vo. W. — ... The Discourse Commemorative of the Rev. William Croswell, D.D., preached in the Church of the Advent, Boston, (of which he was Rector) ... . *Boston.* 1852. 8vo, pp. 31. H. — E Pluribus Unum. The Address at Burlington College, on the Seventy-Eighth Anniversary of American Independence, and Eighth Anniversary of the Institution. July 4, 1854. ... *Burlington: Gazette Office.* MDCCCLIV. 8vo, pp. 20. — The Ends and Objects of Burlington College: An Address introductory to a Course of Lectures. Third Edition. *Burlington.* 1848. 8vo. S. — Episcopal Address at the Convention ... May 29, 1833. *Camden.* 1833. 8vo. + May 22, 1834. *Camden.* 1834. 8vo. + May 30, 1838 ... . *Burlington: at the Missionary Press.* M DCCC XXXVIII. 8vo, pp. 36. S. — Epistle to the Bishops of the Episcopal Court at Camden. [n. p.] 1835. B. (On the case of Bishop Doane.) — A Glorious Church; ... the Sermon before the General Convention of the Protestant Episcopal Church in the United States of America. ... October 1, 1856. ... *Philadelphia: printed by King & Baird.* 1856. 8vo, pp. 29. H. — The Glorious Things of the City of God: The First Sermon in St. Mary's Church, Burlington, after a brief Pilgrimage to the Church of England. *Burlington.* 1842. 8vo. B., P., S. — The Goodly Heritage of Jerseymen: The first Annual Address before the New-Jersey Historical Society, at their Meeting, in Trenton, on Thursday, January 15, 1846; By The Right Rev. George Washington Doane, D.D. *Burlington: Printed by Edmund Morris.* 1846. 8vo, pp. 32. + Second Edition. [*Ibid.*] MDCCC.XLVIII. 8vo, pp. 32. — The Gospel in the Church:

the Sermon before the Annual Convention of the Diocese of Massachusetts, in ... Boston, ... June 20, 1832; ... *Boston.* 1832. 8vo. W. + *Burlington, reprinted: Missionary Press.* 1837. 8vo, pp. 20. — The Gospel, in the Church; Triumphant, everywhere: the Jubilee Sermon ... . *Philadelphia: King & Baird, Printers.* MDCCCLI. 8vo, pp. 9, (1). H., S. — A Great Man Fallen, in Israel: the Sermon, the Next after the Death, of Zachary Taylor, President of the United States: ... . *Burlington.* 1850. 8vo, pp. 15, (1). H. — Influence without Intervention. The Duty of our Nation to the World. The Oration at Burlington College, on the Seventy Sixth Anniversary of American Independence, and Sixth of the Foundation of the College. July 5, M.DCCC.LII. ... *Burlington: John Rodgers.* M.DCCC.LII. 8vo, pp. 17. — ... The Introductory Address, at the Opening of the Hall erected by the Burlington Lyceum ... December 18, 1838. ... *Burlington.* M DCCC XXXIX. 8vo, pp. 20. H. — Isaiah's Prospect of the Church; A Sermon at the Consecration of the Right Rev. Christopher Edward Gadsden, Bishop of South Carolina, ... 1840. *Burlington.* 1840. 8vo. — Jesus of Nazareth, ... the Sermon at the Annual Commencement of the General Theological Seminary ... . *Burlington: Edmund Morris, Printer.* M D CCC XLV. 8vo, pp. 18. — A Letter ... to the Clergy and Laity of his Diocese. *Philadelphia.* 1852. 8vo, pp. 12. B. — Looking unto Jesus: a Sermon, ... Burlington, on the Sunday ... after the Decease of the Rev. Benjamin Winslow, ... *Burlington: J. L. Powell, Printer.* M D CCC XXXIX. 8vo, pp. 55. — The Men to make a State; ... an Address, before ... Burlington College; ... July 4, 1849 ... . *Burlington: Samuel C. Atkinson.* M DCCC XLIX. 8vo, pp. 16. — The Missionary Argument. A Sermon preached before the Board of Directors of the Domestic and Foreign Missionary Society ... Philadelphia, May 11, 1830. *Boston.* 1830. 8vo, pp. 24. — The Missionary Spirit: ... Nov. 27, 1831. *Boston.* 1831. 8vo. — The Nation's Grief: a Funeral Address, ... Burlington, ... 13 April, 1841; on Occasion of the Death of William Henry Harrison, late President ... *Burlington: J. L. Powell, Printer.* M DCCC XLI. 8vo, pp. 27. H. — The Office of a Bishop: Sermon at Philadelphia, Jan. 14, 1834, at the Consecration of the Rt. Rev. James Hervey Otey, Bishop of the Diocese of Tennessee. *Philadelphia.* 1834. 8vo, pp. 28. + Second Edition. *New York.* 1834. 8vo. W. — Organizations Dangerous to Free Institutions: The Address at Burlington College, July 4, 1855. *Philadelphia.* 1855. 8vo. S. — Pastoral Address, to the Parishioners of St. Mary's Church, at Burlington, Jan. 31, 1835. 8vo. W. — The Path of the Just. A Sermon in Commemoration of the Right Reverend William White, D.D. ... preached in ... Burlington, N. J. ... July 24, 1836. ... . *Burlington.* MDCCCXXXVI. 8vo, pp. 44. H. — The Protest and Appeal of George Washington Doane ... and his Reply to the False, Calumnious and Malignant Representations of ... on which they ground their Uncanonical, Unchristian and Inhuman Procedure, in Regard to him. *Philadelphia: King & Baird.* 1852. 8vo, pp. 52. H. — The Rector's Christmas Offering for 1835; being a Second Pastoral Address to the Parishioners of St. Mary's Church. *Burlington.* [1835.] 8vo. — The Sacred Sympathy of Sorrow. The Discourse Commemorative of the Rev. W. Croswell ... *Boston.* 1852. 8vo. — ... A Sermon, delivered, by Appointment, at the Opening of the Annual Convention of the Protestant Episcopal Church in ... Massachusetts ... . *Boston.* 1832. 8vo, pp. 40. H. — ... A Sermon ... in Christ's Church, Hartford ... at an Ordination by the Rt. Rev. T. C. Brownell ... . *Hartford.* MDCCCXXXIII. 8vo, pp. 20. H. — A Sermon, delivered ... December, 23, 1832, on the Decease of Gardiner Green, Esq. ... *Boston.* 1833. 8vo, pp. 19. H. — ... The Sermon at the Consecration of St. Mary's Church ... Burlington, December 23, 1834 ... . *Burlington.* MDCCCXXXIV. 8vo, pp. 55. H. — ... The Sermon at the Consecration of the Right Reverend Jackson Kemper, D.D. ... in St. Peter's Church, Philadelphia ... . *Burlington, N. J.* M DCCC XXXV. 8vo, pp. 56. H. — ... A Sermon preached in St. Mark's Church, Orange ... after the Death of the Rector, the Rev. Benjamin Holmes ... . *Burlington.* M DCCC XXXVI. 8vo, pp. 35. H. — ... A Sermon preached in St. Mary's Church, Burlington ... after the Decease of the Rev. Benjamin Davis Winslow, Assistant to the Rector ... . *Burlington.* MDCCCXXXIX. 8vo, pp. 55. H. — ... The Sermon, preached ... at the Consecration of the Parish Church, Leeds ... *Leeds.* 1841.

8vo, pp. 30. H. — ... The Sermon at the Consecration of St. John's Church, Elizabethtown ... . *Burlington: J. L. Powell, Printer.* MDCCCXLI. 8vo, pp. 56. H. — ... The Sermon at the Funeral of the Rev. David Butler, D.D. ... . *Burlington.* MDCCCXLII. 8vo, pp. 35. H. — ... A Sermon, in St. John's Church, Salem, Commemorative of the Late Rector Elect, the Reverend Edward Goldsborough Prescott ... . *Burlington.* MDCCCXLIV. 8vo, pp. 31. H. — ... The Sermon, before the Convention of the Diocese of New Jersey ... . *Burlington: printed by E. Morris.* MDCCCXLVII. 8vo, pp. 14, (1) H. — ... The Sermon at the Consecration of the Chapel of the Holy Innocents, for the Religious Uses of St. Mary's Hall, Burlington, New Jersey ... . *Burlington.* M DCCC XLVIII. 32mo, pp. 23. H. — ... The Sermon, at the Consecration of Grace Church, Newark ... . *Burlington.* MDCCCXLIX. 8vo, pp. 15. H. — The Sermon at the Opening of the Special Convention of the Diocese of New Jersey; ... . *Burlington.* M D CCC LII. 8vo, pp. 8. H. — ... The Sermon at the Institution of the Rev. John Wragg Shackelford, as Rector of the House of Prayer, Newark ... . *Burlington: S. C. Atkinson, Printer.* M DCCC LVI. 8vo, pp. 18. H. — The Shepherd of the Sheep; A Sermon Commemorative of the Rev. E. G. Prescott. ... *Burlington.* 1844. — Systematic Charity upon the Apostolic Model; as illustrated by the Offerings of the Church in the Diocese of New Jersey. ... *Burlington, N. J.* MDCCCXXXV. 12mo, pp. 68. H. — The Voice of the Departed; A Sermon preached ... September 12, 1830; on Occasion of the Death of ... the Reverend John Sylvester John Gardiner, D.D. ... . *Boston.* 1830. 8vo, pp. 27. H. The following relate to Bishop Doane:

DOANE. A Brief Review of Bishop Doane's Sermon, "Rev. Mr. Keith and the Society of Friends." 8vo. P. 20392

DOANE. A Letter to the Bishops of the P. E. Church ... *Philadelphia.* 1855. 8vo. 20393

DOANE. The Record of the Proceedings of the Court of Bishops assembled for the Trial of the Rt. Rev. George Washington Doane, D.D., Bishop of New Jersey, upon a Presentment made by the ... Bishops of Virginia, Ohio, and Maine. *New York.* 1852. 8vo, pp. 136. 20394

DOANE. Review of the Protest and Appeal of Bishop Doane, as aggrieved by Bishops Meade, Burgess and McIlvaine; and Parts of his Reply to the Representations of Messrs. Halstead, Perkins, Coppuck and Gill. By an Ohio Layman. *Cincinnati.* 1852. 8vo, pp. 28. H. 20395

DOANE. Supplement to a Pamphlet, containing the Correspondence between the Right Rev. G. W. Doane, D.D. ... and the Rev. S. Wilmer ... on the Subject of Associations, &c. *Philadelphia: published by J. Whetham.* 1835. 8vo, pp. 14. H.

DOANE. A Vindication of the Four Laymen, who Requested the Three Bishops to present Charges against Bishop Doane. *Trenton.* 1853. 8vo. S. 20397

DOANE (G. C.) 41st Congress, 3d Session. Senate. Ex. Doc. No. 51. ... The report of Lieutenant Gustavus C. Doane

upon the so-called Yellowstone Expedition of 1870. [*Washington.* 1871.] 8vo, pp. 40. BA. 20398

DOANE (R. B.) A Sermon preached in St. John's Church, Providence, April 10, 1865, the Day for the Funeral Obsequies of President Lincoln. By Rev. Richard B. Doane. *Providence: H. H. Thomas & Co.* 1865. 8vo, pp. 15. 20399

DOANE (T.) Report on the Question of Bridging the Missouri River, by Thomas Doane. February, 1868. *Boston.* 1868. 8vo, pp. 11. H. 20400

DOANE (W. C.) The Statesman and the State. In uno, plura; e pluribus unum; The Oration before the Citizens of Burlington, in the City Hall, at their Public Celebration of the Birthday of Washington, February 22d, A.D. 1862, by The Rev. Wm. Croswell Doane, Rector of St. Mary's Parish, February 22, 1862. *Philadelphia: James B. Chandler.* 1862. 8vo, pp. 21. H. 20401

DOBBIN (J. C.) Speech of James C. Dobbin of North Carolina, on the Oregon Question ... in the House, Jan. 15, 1846. [*Washington.* 1846.] 8vo. 20402

[DOBBING (J. C.)] Brief Notice of the Late Commodore Charles Morris. [n. p. n. d.] 8vo, pp. 15. H. 20403

DOBBINS (Peter), *pseudonym.* *See* [Fessenden (William)].

DOBBS (A.) An Account Of the Countries adjoining to Hudson's Bay, in the North-west Part of America: containing A Description of the Lakes and Rivers, the Nature of the Soil and Climates, and their Methods of Commerce, &c. Shewing the Benefit to be made by settling Colonies, and opening a Trade in these Parts; whereby the French will be deprived in a great Measure of their Traffick in Furs, and the Communication between Canada and Mississippi be cut off. With An Abstract of Captain Middleton's Journal, and Observations upon his Behaviour during his Voyage, and since his Return. To which are added, I. A Letter from Bartholomew de Fonte, Vice-Admiral of Peru and Mexico; giving an account of his Voyage from Lima to Peru, to prevent, or seize upon any Ships that should attempt to find a North-west Passage to the South Sea. II. An Abstract of all the Discoveries which have been publish'd of the Islands and Countries in and adjoining to the Great Western Ocean, between America, India, and China, &c. pointing

out the Advantages that may be made, if a short Passage should be found thro' Hudson's Streight to that Ocean. III. The Hudson's Bay Company's Charter. IV. The Standard of Trade in those Parts of America; with an Account of the Exports and Profits made annually by the Hudson's Bay Company. V. Vocabularies of the Languages of several Indian Nations adjoining to Hudson's Bay. The whole intended to shew the great Probability of a North-west Passage, so long desired; and which (if discovered) would be of the highest Advantage to these Kingdoms. By Arthur Dobbs, Esq. *London: J. Robinson.* M DCC XLIV. 4to, Title and Dedication, Title, pp. ii, 211. Map by Joseph La France. BA. 20404

There are copies on large paper. *See* "N. Am. Rev.," II. 9.

DOBBS. An Epistle to the Hon. Arthur Dobbs, Esq., in Europe, From a Clergyman in America. *London: J. Dodsley.* 1752. 8vo. 20405

See "M. Rev.," VI. 236. Mr. J. C. Brown, of Providence, has "An Essay upon the Existence of a North-West Passage," 4to, a manuscript of sixty pages in the handwriting of Captain Dobbs. The author reviews the statements made by all those who had navigated the waters of Hudson's and Baffin's Bays, and says, that "by all the journals I have read, of those who have made any considerable progress in northern discoveries, there seems to be strong reasons to believe there is a passage to the north-west of Hudson's Bay."

DOBBS. Remarks upon Capt. Middleton's Defence: Wherein His Conduct during his late Voyage For discovering a Passage from Hudson's-Bay to the South-Sea is impartially Examin'd; His Neglects and Omissions in that Affair fully Prov'd; The Falsities and Evasions in his Defence Expos'd; The Errors of his Charts laid open, and His Accounts of Currents, Streights, and Rivers, Confuted; Whereby it will appear, with the highest Probability, That there is such a Passage as he went in search of. With An Appendix of Original Papers, and a Map of the In-land and Sea-Coast of North-America in and about Hudson's Bay. By Arthur Dobbs, Esq; *London: Jacob Robinson.* MDCCXLIV. 8vo, 3 l., pp. 171. Map. P. 20406

Also on large paper.

DOBBS. A Reply to Capt. Middleton's Answer To the Remarks on his Vindication of his Conduct, In a late Voyage made by him in the Furnace Sloop, by Orders of the Lords Commissioners of the Admiralty, to find out a Passage from the North-west of Hudson's Bay, to the Western and Southern Ocean of America. Shewing the Art and Evasions he makes use of to

conceal his Mis-conduct and Neglect in prosecuting that Discovery: As Also the false Currents, Tides, Straits, and Rivers he has laid down in his Chart and Journal to conceal the Discovery; with Remarks upon some extraordinary Affidavits he has published in his Favour. To which is added, A Full Answer to a late Pamphlet published by Capt. Middleton, called Forgery Detected. By Arthur Dobbs, Esq; *London: J. Robinson.* MDCCXLV. 8vo, (2), 128. J.C.B. 20407

"Arthur Dobbs had prevailed on the Hudson's Bay Company to send an expedition, under command of Captain Middleton, in 1737, to explore for a new passage, but he did little, and was supposed to have been prevented by the Hudson's Bay Company from making any serious efforts. No account of this voyage was published. Dobbs then sent another expedition, commanded by Middleton, in 1741, in a vessel furnished by the Admiralty. He again returned unsuccessful, and was accused, this time, by Dobbs, of having been bribed by the Hudson's Bay Company. In 1746, Ellis was sent, by private subscription, the Dobbs and California, to repeat the search, which only reached Repulse Bay." — BARROW's *Polar Voyages.* *See* Anderson's "Hist. of Commerce," III. 233, and Middleton (*Capt.*)

DOBBS. Dobbs's Narrative of the unfortunate Voyage and Catastrophe of his Majesty's Ship the Wager, her being cast away on a desolate Island, proceedings of the Crew, &c., in their Boat to Patagonia and through the Straights of Magellan, &c. 1751. 8vo. 20408

Title from Thorpe's catalogue. I have not seen this narrative attributed to Dobbs by any other authority, and incline to the belief that it was a mere conjecture of Mr. Thorpe.

The Dobbs Family in America. By Our Own Correspondent. *London: J. Maxwell.* 1864. Post 8vo, pp. 312. + [*Ibid.*] 1866. Post 8vo, pp. 312. 20409

DOBOURDIEU (J.) The Adventures and Surprizing Deliverances of James Dobourdieu and his Wife, who were taken by Pyrates, and carried to the Uninhabited Part of the Isle of Paradise; also the Adventures of Alexander Vendchurch, whose Ship's Crew rebelled against him, and set him on Shore on an Island in the South Sea, where he liv'd five years, five months, and seven days, and was at last providently releas'd by a Jamaica Ship. 1719. 8vo. 20411

DOBRIZHOFFER (M.) Historia | de | Abiponibus | Equestri, Bellicosaque | Paraquariæ | Natione | locupletata | Copiosis Barbararum Gentium, Urbium, | Fluminum, Ferarum, Amphibiorum, Insectorum, Sfr- | [*sic*] pentium præcipuorum, Piscium, Avium, Arborum, | Plantarum, aliarumque eiusdem Provinciæ, | Proprietatum Observationibus, | Authore | Martino Dobrizhoffer | Presbytero, et per Annos Duo de | Viginti Paraquariæ Missionario. | *Viennæ:*

Typis Josephi Nob. de Kurzbek. | ... | *Anno* 1784. | 3 vols., 8vo, 10 l., pp. 476, (4); 499, (6); 424, (6), 1 l. folded. 7 Plates and 2 Maps. BA. 20412

See "M. Rev.," LXXIV. 498.

DOBRIZHOFFER. Geschichte der Abiponer, einer berittenen und kriegerischen Nation in Paraguay. Bereichert mit einer Menge Beobachtungen über die wilden Volkerschaften, Städte, Flüsze, vierfüszigen Thiere, Amphibien, Insecten und andere Eigenschaften dieser Provinz. Aus dem Lateinischen übersetzt von A. Kreil. *Wien: Jos. Edlen von Kurzbek.* 1783. 3 vols., 8vo, 12 l., pp. 564; 603; Map and Plate; pp. 506. 20413

DOBRIZHOFFER. An Account of the Abipones, an Equestrian People of Paraguay. From the Latin of Martin Dobrizhoffer, Eighteen Years a Missionary in that Country. *London: John Murray.* 1822. 3 vols., 8vo, pp. xii, 435; v, 446; vi, 419. H.

Highly eulogized by Coleridge, Southey, Charles Lamb, Lowndes, and Brunet. It is almost the only work relating to this almost unknown tribe of Indians, and is a memorial of nearly eighteen years of suffering and toil amongst a most savage race. *See* "Q. Rev.," XXVI. 277; Southey's "Brazil," III. 297; Southey's "Tale of Paraguay;" Coleridge's "Table Talk," August 6, 1832.

[DOBSON (John).] Chronological Annals of the War; from its Beginning to the Present Time. In two parts. Part I. Containing from April 2, 1755, to the End of 1760. Part II. — from the Beginning of 1761 to the Signing of the Preliminaries of the Peace. With an Introductory Preface to each part, a Conclusion and a General Index to the Whole. *Oxford: At the Clarendon Press.* MDCCLXIII. 8vo, pp. xv, 327. 20415

Contains full particulars of the French and Indian war in America, as well as the events which took place in Europe.

Doctrina Christiana, 1546 and 1548. *See* [Zummaraga (Juan)].

Doctrina christiana | en lẽgua Española y Mexicana: hecha por | los religios de la orden de *sancto* Domingo . | Agora nueuamẽte corregida y enmẽdada. *Año* 1550 . | ... | [Colophon:] *Acabose de imprimir a | xij . dias del mes de hebrero . Año d' | M . d . l . años | La quel ha sido agora nueuamente corregida y emẽdada.* | Sm. 4to, 9 l., 147 numbered l. C. 20416

Doctrina christiana (en Quichua y Aymara). *Impresso en la ciudad de los Reyes, por Antonio Ricardo, primero, impressor en estos reynos del Piru. Año de* 1584. 4to, 7 l., pp. 84. 20417

"Volume de la plus grande rareté et la première production connue des presses péruviennes." — LECLERC.

Doctrina Christiana: y explicacion de sus Misterios, en nuestro idioma Español, y en lengua Arda. *Madrid: por Domingo Garcia Morrás.* 1658. Sm. 8vo, Title, 13 l. 20418

The Ardas are a barbarous tribe of Indians dwelling between the rivers Napo and Marañon, in the province of Quijos, in Quito. This, as far as we can learn, is not only the sole book published in the Arda language, but only one copy of the work is known. A specimen of this language will be found in Ludewig's "Lit. Ab. Lang.," p. 12.

Doctrina Christiana, y Platices Doctrinales, traducidas en Lengua Opata, por el P. Rector Manuel Aguirre. *Impressas en la Imprenta del Real y mas antiguo Colegio de San Ildefonso de Mexico, año de* 1765. 4to. 20419

For the Christian Indians of Sonora, in the central part of the state.

Doctrina à los Indios, y à las demàs Personas: Conforme a lo que se proveyò en el santo Concilio Provincial de Lima el año passado de 1583. Mandado reimprimir por el Concilio provincial del año de 1773. [*Lima:*] *En la oficina de la calle de San Jacinto.* [1773.] 4to, 10 l., pp. 515. 20420

Doctrina pequeña en Mexicano. Tepiton Teotlatolli. [Colophon:] *Mexico.* 1831. 16mo, pp. 15. 20421

The Doctrine and Formula for the Government and Discipline of the Evangelical Lutheran Church. Published by order of the Hartwick Synod of the Evangelical Lutheran Church in the State of New York. *Troy: N. Tuttle, Printer.* 1832. 18mo, pp. 99. 20422

Doctrine of Christianity. *See* [Smith (John)].

Doctrine of Nullification examined. An Essay, &c. With the Proceedings of the Meeting of the Union and State-Rights Party, Charleston, June 12, 1832. *Charleston.* 1832. 16mo, pp. 24. M. 20423

The Doctrines and Policy of the Republican Party, as given by its Recognized Leaders, Orators, Presses, and Platforms. Breckenridge and Lane Campaign Document, No. 13. *Washington.* 1860. 8vo, pp. 16. H. 20424

Documens communiqués à l'appui du Projet de loi relatif au Traite du 4 Juillet, 1831, par M. le Ministre Secretaire d'Etat au Departement des Affaires Etrangeres. *Paris.* 1835. 2 pts., 4to, pp. 258; 175, etc. 20425

Public documents, not printed for sale.

Documens rélatifs au Commerce des Nouveaux Etats de l'Amérique, communiqués par le Bureau de Commerce et des Colonies aux principales Chambres de Commerce de France. *Paris.* 1826. Sm. 8vo, pp. 100. 20426

Documens sur le commerce extérieur. Etats-Unis. Législation commerciale, nº II. Douanes. Ports mexicains occupés par les Américains.—Régime des douanes. [*Paris: P. Dupont.* 1847.] 8vo, pp. 56. 20427

A Document for the Canvass, containing—The Fugitive Slave Law of 1850. Resolutions of the Baltimore Democratic Convention ... Resolutions of the Baltimore Whig Convention ... The Independent Democratic Platform ... Mr. Pierce's Letter of Acceptance. Gen. Scott's Letter of Acceptance. Mr. Hale's Letter of Acceptance. Record of the Votes of Franklin Pierce, while in Congress, on the Slavery Question. *Washington, D. C.* [n. d.] 8vo, pp. 16. H. 20428

... A Document for the People. Contents. I.—Declaration of Independence, and the Names of the Signers. 2.—Constitution of the United States, and the Amendments. 3.—The Fugitive Slave Law of 1850. 4.—Democratic Platform ... 5.—Whig Platform ... 6.—Independent Democratic Platform ... and 7.—Speech of Honorable Charles Sumner, on his Motion to Repeal the Fugitive Slave Bill. *Washington, D. C.* 1853. 8vo, pp. 16, 30. H. 20429

Documents diplomatiques relatifs à l'annexion aux États-Unis de la partie Espagnole de l'île d'Haïti. *New York.* 1871. 16mo, pp. 180. H. 20430

Documentary History of the American Revolution. *See* Force (Peter).

... Documentary History of the Maine Law ... . *New-York: published by Hall & Brother.* 1855. 8vo, pp. 128. H. 20431

Documentary History of the Public Affairs of the United States, Foreign and Domestic, for the Year 1854. *New York.* 1855. 8vo, pp. vi, 475. 20432

Documentos de la memoria de lo interior. [*Venezuela.*] 1844. pp. 75. Table. 20433

Documentos diplomaticos presentados por el gobierno español al senado. *Mexico: imp. literaria.* 1863. 16mo, pp. 262.

Documentos diplomaticos relativos a la detencion del paquete Argentino "Salto" en las aguas de la República Oriental del Uruguay por el vapor de guerra nacional "Villa del Salto." Publicacion oficial. *Montevideo.* 1863. Rl. 8vo, pp. 124. W.

Documentos en que justifica la ilegalidad de la expropiacion de los haciendas de San Juan de Avilés y San Fernando, Propriedad de D. Juan N. Flores. *Mexico.* 1867. Large 8vo, pp. 37.

Documentos importantes, tocantes á la Representacion que varios electores hicieron al Congreso Constituyente pidiendo se anulen las elecciones verificadas en Toluca. *Mexico.* 1826. 4to, pp. 179, 87. Map. 20437

Documentos interceptados en la Barra de Tampico á los prisioneros Santanistas que cayeron en poder de las tropas de D. Juan José de la Garza, con los que se prueba la alta traicion del bando reaccionario. *Veracruz.* 1858. 4to, pp. 41. 20438

Documentos interessantes para saber el origen de los bienes que tienen en la republica Mexicana los quatro hospicios de Filipinas. 1832. 20439

Documentos justificativos e imparciales que acreditan la conducta que ha observado el Lic. Antonio Maria Vizcaino como Juez de letras del partido do Texcoco de Santa-Anna, desde que lo sirvio interinamente, hasta la fecha que lo desempeño en propiedad, y con cuyo caracter sigue funcionando. *Mexico.* 1854. Sm. 8vo, pp. 51 or 52. 20440

Documentos oficiales relativos a los incidentes ocuridos del 28 de Agosto al 1º de Setiembre ultimos, con motivo de la presencia de las Escuadras de la Confederacion Argentina y de la Provincia de Buenos Aires, en el puerto de Montevideo. Publicacion oficial. *Montevideo.* 1859. Rl. 8vo, pp. 50.

Documentos que justifican el pronunciamiento verificado en esta Capital el 19 del ultimo Noviembre y á los onales se refiere el Gobernador D. Juan Bautista Traconis en su manifiesto de 20 del mismo mes. *San Juan Bautista.* 1846. 8vo. 20442

Documentos relativos á la cuestion de limites y navegacion fluvial entre el Imperio del Brasil y la República de Venezuela. *Carácas.* 1859. 8vo, pp. 165. 20443

Documentos relativos á las ultimas occurrencias de nueva España. *Madrid: por Ibarra, impresor.* 1821. 16mo, pp. 26.

Documentos relativos al expediente sobre establecimiento de las comisiones mercantiles. *Habana: Imprenta Fraternal.* 1822. Folio. 20445

Documentos verdaderos acerca de la Capilla y Santa Cruz nombrada de los Talabarteros. *Mexico.* 1824. 4to, pp. 5.

Documentos y Ordenes del Correo General. *Madrid.* 1662–1777. Folio. 20447

Documents accompanying Report of Secretary. *See* Vol. IV., No. 15267.

Documents accompanying a Message from the President of the United States, with Sundry Statements of Expenditures containing ... a detailed Account of the Expenditure and Application of public Monies in the Quarter Master General's Department ... and in the War Department from the 1st of January 1797 to 31st of December 1801. ... *Washington.* 1803. + Contingencies of the Navy Department ... Part III. *Washington.* 1803. 20449

Documents accompanying the Message of the President of the United States, to the two Houses of Congress, at the Opening of the First Session of the Twelfth Congress. November 6th, 1811. Read, and ordered to be printed. *Washington City: printed by R. C. Weightman.* 1811. pp. 320. 20450

These "Documents" accompany most of the messages of the President, and often contain matter of much historical interest.

Documents accompanying the Report of the Secretary of the Navy, in 1830. *Washington.* 8vo. Continued. 20451

Documents and Facts relating to Military Events during the late War, [1812]. [n. p. n. d.] 8vo, pp. 28. 20452

This is a defence of General J. P. Boyd.

Documents and Facts relative to Military Events during the late War. 1816. 8vo, pp. 24. W. 20453

Documents and Facts showing the Fatal Effects of Interments in Populous Cities. *New York.* 1822. 8vo, pp. 24.

Documents and Official Reports, illustrating the causes which led to the Revolution in the Government of the Seneca Indians in the Year 1848, and to the Recognition of the Representative Republican Constitution, by the Authorities of the United States, and of the State of New York. *Baltimore: Printed by Wm. Wooddy & Son.* 1857. 8vo, pp. 92. 20455

... Documents and other Papers relating to the Boundary Line between the States of Georgia and Florida ... . *Washington: Beverley Tucker, Printer.* 1855. 8vo, pp. xi, 396. (33d Cong., 2d Sess. Senate. Mis. Doc. No. 25.) H 20456

Documents and Proceedings relating to the Formation and Progress of a Board in the City of New York, for the Emigration, Preservation, and Improvement of the Aborigines of America. July 22d, 1829. *New York: Vanderpool & Cole, Printers.* 1829. 8vo, pp. 48. B. 20457

Documents Relating to the Presidential Election in the Year 1801; Containing a Refutation of Two passages in the Writings of Thomas Jefferson, Aspersing the Character of the late James A. Bayard, of Delaware. *Philadelphia.* 1831. 8vo. C. 20458

Documents Demonstrating beyond the possibility of doubt the brutal Violence and Cruelty practiced by the British on Private and Unarmed Citizens, and on helpless American Females; at Hampton, Plattsburgh and Swanton. [n. p. 1813.] 8vo, pp. 24. 20459

Documents Explaining the Failure of the Northern Campaign. *Albany.* 1814. 12mo. 20460

Doubtful title, from an American catalogue.

Documents furnished by the British Government under the Third Article of the Convention of St. Petersburg, 1822; and Bayly's List of Slaves, remaining on Tangier Island, and H. B. M. Ships of War, after the Ratification of the Treaty of Ghent. *Washington: Gales & Seaton.* 1827. 8vo, pp. 112. C. 20461

Documents in Relation to the Claim of the Executor of John J. Bulow, Jr., to be Indemnified for the Loss of Property destroyed by the hostile Seminole Indians. Dec. 21, 1837. [*Washington.*] 1837. 8vo, pp. 12. 20462

Documents, Legislative and Executive. *See* American State Papers, Vol. I., No. 1228.

Documents of the House of Representatives of the United States, of the 1st, 2d and 3d Congress. *New York and Philadelphia.* 1791. Folio. Continued in 8vo. 20463

These and subsequent documents comprise an enormous collection of papers, many of but little interest, and many of much importance to the historical student.

Documents Officiels échangés entre les États-Unis et l'Angleterre au sujet de l'Amérique Centrale. *Paris.* 1856. 8vo.

Documents on the Relations of the United States with Great Britain and France. 1st Session, 10th Congress. *Washington.* 1808. 8vo. 20465

Documents referred to in the President's Speech to both Houses of the Fifth Congress, on the 16th of May, 1797. *Philadelphia.* 1797. 8vo. P. 20466

Documents Published by the Authority of Congress, or by the Legislatures of the several States or Territories. *See* United States, and the names of the States and Territories.

Documents Relating to the Boundary Line and Disputed Territory between Massachusetts and Rhode Island. *Fall River: Henry Pratt.* 1847. 8vo, pp. 64. 20468

Printed by order of the town of Fall River.

Documents relating to the Boundary Line between Maine and New Brunswick. Printed by order of the Legislature of Massachusetts. *Boston.* 1826. 8vo. 20469

Documents relating to the Coal-Hill, Victoria and Bedford Mines. 20470

Situated in the northern part of the State of New York.

Documents relating to the Dominguez Grant of Land in Texas. *New York.* 1831. 12mo, pp. 19. 20471

Documents relating to the Manufactures in the United States, collected and transmitted to the House of Representatives by the Secretary of the Treasury. *Washington.* 1833. 2 vols., 8vo.

Documents relating to the New York Contest, showing the Claims of the Delegation Elected by Congress Districts, (in accordance with Precedent and Usage,) to Seats in the Charleston Convention. New York, March, 1860. *Printed by J. W. Bell.* 1860. Rl. 8vo, pp. 24. 20473

Documents relating to the North Eastern Boundary of the State of Maine. *Boston: Dutton & Wentworth, Printers to the State.* 1828. 8vo, pp. 275. BA., M. 20474

Documents relating to the North-Eastern Boundary. [1838.] 8vo. M. 20475

Documents relating to the Violations and Evasions of the Laws during the Commercial Restrictions and late War with Great Britain. 8vo. 20476

See Hill (M. L.)

Documents relative to Acts of Retaliation upon Prisoners of War by Great Britain and the United States. October 28, 1814. (Cong. Doc.) 20477

Documents relative to Central American Affairs, and the Enlistment Question. Printed by direction of the House of Representatives of the U. States. *Washington: Cornelius Wendell, Printer.* 1856. 8vo, pp. 485. Map. H. 20478

Documents relative to the Negotiations for Peace between the United States and Great Britain. *Philadelphia: T. Melish.* 1814. 12mo, pp. 63. Map. 20479

Documents relative to Savings Banks, Intemperance, and Lotteries. Published by Order of the Society for the Prevention of Pauperism in the City of New York. [*New York:*] *Printed by E. Conrad.* 1819. 8vo, pp. 26. 20480

Documents in Support of the Right of the Inhabitants of the City of New Orleans, to the Alluvion in Front of the Suburb of St. Mary, contested by Jean Gravier. *City of Washington: A. & G. Way, Printers.* 1809. 8vo, pp. 53. BA. 20481

DOCWRA (E. H.) The Devil's Race Course, a Legend of Baltimore. By E. H. Docwra. *Baltimore: H. Taylor.* 1854. 8vo, pp. 31. 20482

DODD (A. C.) The Contrast: or, Strictures on select parts of Doctor Price's "Additional Observations on Civil Liberty, &c." Forming a Concise State of the Present Currency; an Impartial View of the Trade and Government of the Kingdom; the Cause and Consequences of the War with America; and a Sketch of the Debts and Revenues of France. By A. Charles Dodd. *London: Fielding and Walker.* MDCCLXXVII. 8vo, pp. vi, 56. 20483

The "Monthly Review," LVII. 85, calls this tract "a very illiberal and indecent performance."

DODD (B. L.) Genealogies of the Male Descendants of Daniel Dod, of Branford, Conn., a Native of England. 1646 to 1863. By Bethuel L. Dodd, M.D., and John R. Burnet. *Newark, N. J.: The Author.* 1864. 8vo, pp. 221. Plates.

DODD (S.) The East-Haven Register: in Three Parts. Part I. Containing a History of the Town of East-Haven, from its First Settlement in 1644, to the Year 1800. Also, an Account of its Boundaries, Iron-Works and Mills, Division of

Lands, Controversies with New-Haven and Branford, Town Charters, Ecclesiastical Affairs, Schools, Population and Taxes, Losses by War, Natural History and Curiosities, Roads and Public Lands. Part II. Containing an Account of the Names, Marriages, and Births of the Families which have first Settled, or which have Resided in East-Haven, from its Settlement in 1644, to the Year 1800. Part III. Containing an Account of the Deaths in the Families named in the Second Part, from the Year 1647 to the End of the Year 1823. Compiled by Stephen Dodd, Pastor of the Congregational Church in East-Haven. *New-Haven: Published for the Author by A. H. Maltby & Co.* 1824. 12mo, pp. 200. BA. 20485

An extremely rare local history.

DODD. A Family Record of Daniel Dod, who settled with the Colony of Branford, 1644, where he died in 1665: and also of his Descendants in New Jersey. Compiled by Stephen Dodd, ... [n. p.:] *the Author.* 1839. 12mo, pp. 24. BA. 20486

See Case (W.), Vol. III., No. 11304.

An Authentic Narrative of the Loss of the Doddington Indiaman, and of the Surprising Adventures, and Distresses, of those on Board, who Survived the Shipwreck; From the Journal of one of the Surviving Officers. ... *New-York: Printed by James Parker, and Company.* M.DCC.LXII. 12mo, pp. 28.

All books printed by Parker are rare.

DODDRIDGE (J.) Logan, the Last of the Race of Shikellemus, Chief of the Cayuga Nation. A Dramatic Piece. To which is added the Dialogue of the Backwoodsman and the Dandy, first recited at the Buffalo Seminary, July the 4th, 1821. By Dr. Joseph Doddridge, Buffaloe Creek, Brooke County, Va. *Printed for the author, by Solomon Sala.* 1823. 8vo, pp. 47. 20488

A terribly dramatic piece, of much rarity; reprinted with the following title:

DODDRIDGE. Logan, the Last of the Race of Shikellemus. A Dramatic Piece, with the Dialogue of the Backwoodsman and the Dandy. By Dr. Joseph Doddridge. Reprinted from the Virginia Edition of 1823, with Appendix on the Murder of Logan's Family. *Cincinnati.* 1868. Sm. 4to, pp. 76. + *Cincinnati: R. Clarke & Co.* 1868. Sm. 4to, pp. 76. 20489

DODDRIDGE. Notes on the Settlement and Indian Wars of the Western Parts of Virginia and Pennsylvania, from the year

1763 until the year 1783, inclusive. Together with a View, Of the state of society and manners of the first settlers of the Western Country. By the late Rev. Dr. Joseph Doddridge. *Wellsburgh, Va.: Printed at the Office of the Gazette, for the Author.* 1824. 12mo, 5 l., pp. v–316. C. + Second Edition. *Winchester.* 1833. 12mo. 20490

An interesting, authentic work, drawn from original sources; both editions are now scarce. It was reprinted in Kercheval's "Valley of Virginia," pp. 251–410, and in part in Beckley's "Indian Wars."

DODDRIDGE. An Oration delivered before the Masonic Society, of Wellsburgh and its Vicinity, on St. Johns Day. June 24th, 1817. By Dr. Joseph Doddridge. ... *Wellsburgh, Va.: Printed by John Berry.* 1817. 12mo, pp. 21. 20491

Also: A Treatise on the Culture of Bees. *St. Clairsville, O.* 1813. 8vo, pp. 32.

[DODDRIDGE (P.)] Speech of Mr. Doddridge, in the Case of Samuel Houston, Charged with a Contempt and Breach of the Privileges of the House, by assaulting the Hon. William Stanberry ... . Delivered in the House ... May 9, 1832. *Washington.* 1832. 8vo, pp. 32. H., M., W. 20492

DODGE (A. C.) Remarks of Hon. A. C. Dodge, of Iowa, on the Bill to define the Boundaries of the State of Iowa. Delivered in the House ... June 8, 1846. [n. p. n. d.] 8vo, pp. 8. H. 20493

Also: Speech ... on the Oregon Question. Delivered in the House ... February 7, 1846. *Washington: Blair & Rives.* 1846. 8vo, pp. 12.—Speech ... in the Senate ... March 3 and 4, 1852, on the Iowa Land Bill. *Washington.* [n. d.] 8vo, pp. 16. ...—Speech ... [on] Nebraska and Kansas, Feb. 25, 1854. 8vo, pp. 15. S.

DODGE (A. W.) A Prize Essay on Fairs. By Allen W. Dodge, of Hamilton, Mass. *Boston.* 1858. 8vo, pp. 16 H.

DODGE (D. L.) The Mediator's Kingdom not of this World; but Spiritual, Heavenly, and Divine. Illustrated in Remarks upon John, Ch. XVIII. v. 36. By David L. Dodge. *New-York.* 1814. 8vo, pp. 35. 20495

The first peace tract published in America. Also: War Inconsistent with the Religion of Jesus Christ, as it is inhuman, unwise, and criminal. *New York.* 1815. 12mo.

DODGE (G. M.) ... Report of G. M. Dodge, Chief Engineer, to the Board of Directors on a Branch Railroad Line from the Union Pacific Railroad to Idaho, Montana, Oregon, and Puget's Sound. *Washington, D. C.* 1868. 8vo, pp. 13.

Also: Affidavit of G. M. Dodge. [n. p. n. d.] 8vo, pp. 9.

DODGE (H.) Journal of the Expedition of Dragoons, under the command of Col. Henry Dodge, to the Rocky Mountains during the Summer of 1835. *Washington.* 1836. 8vo, pp. 37.

DODGE (J. G.) Appeal on behalf of our Country, Visit to Mount Vernon, and Letter of Senator Bigler. *Louisville.* 1862. 8vo, pp. 23. B. 20498

DODGE (J. R.) Red Men of the Ohio Valley: an Aboriginal History of the period commencing A.D. 1650, and ending at the Treaty of Greenville, A.D. 1795, embracing Notable Facts and Thrilling Incidents, in the Settlement by the whites of the States of Kentucky, Indiana, Ohio and Illinois. By J. R. Dodge. *Springfield, O.: Ruralist Publishing Company.* 1860. 12mo, pp. 435. 20499

DODGE. West Virginia; its Farms and Forests, Mines and Oil Wells; with a Glimpse of its Scenery, a Photograph of its Population, and an Exhibit of its Industrial Statistics. By J. R. Dodge, of the U. S. Department of Agriculture. *Philadelphia: J. B. Lippincott & Co.* 1865. 12mo, pp. 276. 20500

DODGE (J.) A Narrative of the Capture and Treatment of John Dodge, by the English at Detroit. Written by Himself. *Philadelphia.* 1779. 12mo. P. 20501

DODGE (J.) A Sermon delivered in Haverhill, Dec. 22, 1820; being the Second Centesimal Anniversary of the Landing of New-England Fathers at Plymouth. By the Rev. Joshua Dodge, A.M. *Haverhill: Burrill and Hersey.* 1821. 8vo, pp. 28. C. 20502

[DODGE (Mary Abigail).] A Battle of the Books .... Edited by Gail Hamilton. ... *New York: Hurd and Houghton.* 1870. 16mo, 2 l., pp. 288. BA. 20503

An amusing account of her business relations with her former publishers, Ticknor and Fields.

[DODGE.] Call to my Countrywomen. Reprinted from the Atlantic Monthly, of March, 1863. [By Gail Hamilton.] *New York: G. W. Wood.* 1863. 12mo, pp. 12. + [Another Edition.] *New York: A. D. F. Randolph.* 1863. 8vo, pp. 25.

[DODGE.] Country Living and Country Thinking. By Gail Hamilton. *Boston: Ticknor and Fields.* 1862. pp. vi, (1), 461. BA. + [*Ibid.*] 1864. 20505

"Lights among the Shadows of our Civil War" is the subject of the last chapter.

[DODGE.] Gala-Days. By Gail Hamilton. *Boston: Ticknor and Fields.* 1863. 12mo, 3 l., pp. 436. BA., H. 20506

Includes "A Call to my Countrymen," "Side-Glances at Harvard Class-Day," etc. Also under the same *pseudonym*: A New Atmosphere. ... *Boston: Ticknor and Fields.* 1865. 16mo, 2 l., pp. 310. BA. (On the woman question.) — Red-Letter Days in Applethorpe. ... *Boston: Ticknor and Fields.* 1866. 8vo, pp. 141. BA., H. — Skirmishes and Sketches. ... *Boston: Ticknor and Fields.* 1865. 8vo, pp. vi, 447. BA., H. — Stumbling Blocks. ... *Boston: Ticknor and Fields.* 1864. 16mo, 3 l., pp. 435. BA., H. — Summer Rest. ... *Boston: Ticknor and Fields.* 1866. 8vo, 2 l., pp. 356. H. — Tracts for the Times. Courage! ... *New York: Charles B. Richardson, Publisher.* [n. d.] 8vo, pp. 4. H. — Wool-Gathering. ... *Boston: Ticknor & Fields.* 1867. 12mo, pp. 335. BA., C. (Travels in the West and South.) — Woman's Wrongs: a Counter-Irritant. ... *Boston: Ticknor & Fields.* 1868. 16mo, Title, pp. 212. C., H.

DODGE (N.) A Discourse at Lebanon, 4 March, 1805, in Honor of the Election of Thomas Jefferson. By Nehemiah Dodge, of Middletown. *Norwich, Conn.* 1805. 8vo. 20507

[DODGE (N. S.)] Sketches of New England, or Memories of the Country. By John Carver, Esquire, Justice of the Peace and Quorum. *New York: E. French.* 1842. 12mo, pp. 286.

A fiction. *See* "N. Am. Rev.," April, 1842.

DODGE (P.) A Poem delivered at the Commencement of Rhode Island College, September 6, A.D. 1797. ... By Paul Dodge. *Providence: Printed by Carter & Wilkinson.* 1797. 8vo, pp. 8. BA., J.C.B. 20509

[DODGE (Robert).] A Book for every Soldier's Knapsack. Tracts for the War. Secession: The Remedy and Result. *New York: James Miller.* 1861. 18mo, pp. 71. 20510

DODGE. Memorials of Columbus, read to the Maryland Historical Society, by Robert Dodge, 3 April, 1851. *Baltimore.* MDCCCLI. 8vo, pp. 28. H. 20511

Also: Austria and its Polity: a Lecture, delivered at Astoria, N. Y. January 21st, 1853. ... *New York: Wm. C. Bryant & Co., Printers.* 1853. 8vo, pp. 20. H. — Diary, Sketches and Reviews during an European Tour, in the Year 1847. By Robert Dodge. *New York: Printed for his Friends.* 1850. 8vo, 1 l., pp. 304. C.

DODGE (W. C.) Breech-Loaders versus Muzzle-Loaders: or, how to strengthen our Army and crush the Rebellion, with a saving of Life and Treasure. By W. C. Dodge .... *Washington, D. C.: published by W. C. Dodge.* 1865. 8vo, pp. 31, (2).

Also: Memorial to the Hon. Secretary of War, or How to strengthen our Army and crush the Rebellion, with a Saving of Life and Treasure, ... *Washington, D C.: McGill & Witherow, Printers.* 1864. 8vo, pp. 12. H.

DODGE (W. E.) Influence of the War on our National Prosperity. A Lecture, delivered in Baltimore, Md. ... March 13th, 1865, by William E. Dodge, of New York. *New-York: Wm. C. Martin, Printer.* 1865. 8vo, pp. 29. H. + [n. p. n. d.] 8vo, pp. 29. H. 20513

DODGE. Speech of Hon. William E. Dodge, of New York, on Reconstruction; delivered in the House of Representatives, January 21, 1867. *Washington.* 1867. 8vo, pp. 8. H. 20514

Also: Speech ... in the Peace Conference at Washington, 20th February, 1860. [n. p. n. d.] 8vo, pp. 8. H.

DODGE (W. S.) The History of the Old Second Division, Army of the Cumberland, Commanders McCook, Sill, and Johnson. By William Sumner Dodge. *Chicago: Church & Goodman.* 1864. 8vo, pp. 450. Portraits and Map. 20515

DODGE. A Waif of the War; or, the History of the 75th Illinois Infantry, embracing the Entire Campaigns of the Army of the Cumberland. By William Sumner Dodge. *Chicago: Church & Goodman.* 1866. 8vo, pp. 242. 20516

Contains "The Diary of the late George Bubb Doddington. From March 8, 1749, to February 6, 1761. ... A New Edition. By Henry Penruddocke Wyndham. *Salisbury.* 1784. 8vo.

[DODSLEY (Robert).] The Chronicles of the Kings of England, From ... William the Conqueror ... to ... George the Second .... By Nathan Ben Saddi. *London, Printed. Boston, Reprinted: R. Fowle and S. Draper.* 1759. 8vo, pp. 70. H. + *Philadelphia.* 1774. 12mo. P. + *Newport: Printed by the Widow Franklin.* 1774. 12mo, pp. 56. + to ... MDCCXCV. *Worcester: Isaiah Thomas.* MDCCXCV. 12mo, pp. 196. H. 20517

[DODSLEY.] A Compendium Of Authentic and Entertaining Voyages, Digested in a Chronological Series. The whole exhibiting A clear View of the Customs, Manners, Religion, Government, Commerce, and Natural History of most Nations in the Known World. Illustrated and Adorned with a Variety of genuine Charts. Maps, Plans, Heads, &c. curiously engraved. The Second Edition. *London: W. Strahan.* MDCCLXVI. 7 vols., 12mo, 3 l., pp. 286; 288; 285; 299; 342; 339; 1 l., pp. 366. 20518

Contains Columbus, V. de Gama, Alv. de Cabral, Cortez, Pizarro, F. de Soto, Magellan, Drake, Raleigh, Eight Men in Greenland 1630, Seven Sailors in Greenland, Th. James, Wafer, Expedition against Carthagene 1741, Gemelli Carreri, and Woods Rogers.

DODSLEY. Dodsley's Annual Register. *See* Vol. I., No. 1614.

DODSON (C. W.) Life and Adventures of Smith Maythe, the Notorious Robber of the West. By Charles W. Dodson. *Cincinnati.* 1841. 8vo, pp. 48. M. 20519

DOEDES (J. I.) Wanneer zullen onze West Indische slaven vrij worden? *Utrecht.* 1857. 8vo. 20520

DOEHN (R.) Die politischen Parteien in den Vereinigten Staaten von Amerika. *Leipzig.* 1868. 16mo. B. 20521

DOELL. Deutsche Auswanderung nach Chile. [n. p.] 1847.

Does the Country require a National Armory and Foundry west of the Allegany Mountains? If it does, where should they be located? *Pittsburgh: W. S. Haven.* 1862. 8vo, pp. 60.

DOESTICKS, *pseudonym.* *See* [Thompson (Mortimer S.)]

DOGGETT (D. S.) A Nation's Ebenezer. A Discourse ... in Richmond, Virginia ... September 18, 1862: the Day of Public Thanksgiving, appointed by the President of the Confederate States. By Rev. D. S. Doggett, D.D. ... *Richmond.* 1862. 8vo, pp. 18. BA. 20524

DOGGETT. A Sermon on Occasion of the Fast appointed ... by the President of the United States, delivered in the Chapel of Randolph Macon College, by Rev. David S. Doggett. ... *Richmond.* 1841. 8vo, pp. 23. H. 20525

DOGGETT. The War and its Close. A Discourse, delivered in ... Richmond, Va. ... April 8th, 1864, by Rev. D. S. Doggett, D.D. on the Occasion of the National Fast. ... *Richmond.* 1864. 32mo, pp. 20. H. 20526

DOGGETT (John). Guide to New York for 1846. Second Edition. *New York.* 1846. 18mo. 20527

DOGGETT. Doggett's United States Railroad & Ocean Steam Navigation Guide, illustrated with a Map of the United States ... *New York.* 1847. 16mo, pp. 132. Continued. H. 20528

DOGGETT (S.) An Address at the Dedication and Opening of Bristol Academy, Taunton, July 18, 1796. By Rev. Simeon Doggett. *New Bedford: Printed by John Spooner.* 1797.

Also: Discourse preached to the Congregational Society in Norton. *Providence.*

1797. — A Discourse on Education, at the Dedication and Opening of Bristol Academy, on the 18th Day of July, 1796. By Simeon Doggett, Jun. A.M. *New Bedford.* 1797. 8vo, pp. 28. H., N. — A Discourse delivered ... at the Funeral of Richard George, Esquire .... *Boston: True and Green, Printers.* 1827. 32mo, pp. 14. H. — Sermon from Philipp. ii. 12, 13: Dedicated to the Students of Rhode Island College. *Providence.* 1796. 8vo, pp. 24. — An Oration delivered at Taunton, ... on the 4th of July, 1799. By Simeon Doggett, Jun. .... *New Bedford: Printed by John Spooner.* 1799. 8vo, pp. 20. BA. — Two Discourses on Slavery ... *Boston.* 1835. 8vo. B.

DOGGETT (T.) A Sermon, preached on Fast Day, September 26, 1861. By Thomas Doggett .... *Haverhill: E. G. Frothingham, Printer.* 1861. 8vo, pp. 16. H. 20530

DOGGETT (T. P.) Traits requisite in the Character of Modern Reformers. A Sermon, delivered on the Annual Fast, April 5, 1838. By Theophilus P. Doggett .... *Boston: printed by J. R. Butts.* 1838. 8vo, pp. 19. H. 20531

DOHENY (M.) The History of the American Revolution. By Michael Doheny. *Dublin.* 1846. 24mo, pp. 248. + Second Edition. *Dublin.* 1847. 24mo. 20532

DOHENY (M.) The Principle, Progress, Tendency, Obligations and Destiny of Democracy: a Lecture by Michael Doheny. Delivered ... the twenty-second of December, 1852, before the Young Men's Democratic Union Club of New York .... *New-York: published by Dewitt & Davenport.* 1853. 8vo, pp. 26. H. 20533

Doings of the American Commissioners at Paris under the Convention of April 1803. *Philadelphia.* 1807. 8vo. W.

Doings of the Council at their Sitting at Fort George, Nov. 25, 1727, relating to the Abuses in the Court of Chancery: with Appendix Giving Minutes of the Council at Fort George in 1811–12, for erecting a Court of Chancery. Folio. W. 20535

Doings of the Council at their Sitting at Fort George, Dec. 19, 1727. Folio. W. 20536

D[OLE] (A[nna] G[reenleaf]). Writings of Mrs. Dole; with a Sketch of her Character. Second Edition. *Exeter.* 1811. 12mo, pp. 83. N. 20537

DOLE (B.) An Address to the People of Massachusetts, on the Subject of Human Rights. By Benjamin Dole. ... *Boston.* 1838. 12mo, pp. 48. H. 20538

DOLE. An Examination of Mr. Rantoul's Report for Abolishing Capital Punishment in Massachusetts. By Benjamin Dole. *Boston.* MDCCCXXXV. 12mo, pp. 36. H. + *Boston.* 1837. 8vo, pp. 72. 20539

Also: An Address to the People of Massachusetts, on the Subject of the License Law of 1838, and its Repeal. ... *Boston: printed by Kidder & Wright.* 1840. 12mo, pp. 72. H.

DOLE (G. T.) ... A Discourse occasioned by the Death ... of Dr. Joseph Torrey, delivered in Beverly, December 15, 1850. By George T. Dole .... *Salem: printed by Wm. Ives & Geo. W. Pease.* 1851. 8vo, pp. 32. H. 20540

DOLE (I.) Requirements in a Lexicographer of the English Language: a Review of Webster's American Dictionary. By Isaiah Dole, M.A. ... . [n. p. n. d.] 8vo, pp. 161–184. H.

DOLFUS (A.), *et* MONT-SERRAT (E. de). Géologie. Voyages géologique dans les républiques de Guatemala et de Salvador ... . *Paris: imprimerie impériale.* 1868. 4to, pp. 539. 18 Colored Plates. 20542

[DOMAIRON (L.)] Recueil historique et chronologique de faits mémorables pour servir à l'histoire générale de la marine et à celle des découvertes. *Paris.* 1781. 2 vols., 12mo. 20543

DOMAIRON. Le Voyageur Français, ou la Connaissance de l'Ancien et du Nouveau-Monde. *Paris.* 17 vols., 12mo.

Title from Faribault, No. 201.

DOMENECH (E.) Erinnerungen aus Amerika, insbesondere aus Texas. Aus dem Tagebuche von Emanuel Domenech. *Marburg: Elwert.* 1856. 12mo, pp. iv, 95. 20545

DOMENECH. L'Empire au Mexique, et la Candidature d'un prince Bonaparte au trône mexicain, par Emmanuel Domenech, M.A. *Paris.* [n. d.] 8vo. 20546

DOMENECH. L'empire mexicain, par L'Abbé Domenech. *Mexico.* 1866. 8vo. 20547

DOMENECH. Histoire du Mexique. Juarez et Maximilien Correspondances inédites des Présidents, Ministres et Généraux Almonte, Santa-Anna, Gutierrez, Miramon, Marquez, Mejia, Woll, etc. etc. de Juarez, de l'Empereur Maximilien et de l'Impératrice Charlotte. Par Emmanuel Domenech .... Troisième édition. *Bruxelles: A. Lacroix, Verboeckhoven & Cie.* 1868. 2 vols., 8vo, pp. 412, 455. 20548

DOMENECH. Le Journal d'un missionnaire au Texas et au Mexique, (1846–1852.) Par L'Abbé E. Domenech. *Paris: Gaume, frères.* 1857. 8vo. 20549

DOMENECH. Manuscrit pictographique Américain précédé d'une notice sur l'idéographie des Peaux-Rouges. Par l'Abbé Em. Domenech missionaire .... Ouvrage publié sous les auspices de M. le ministre d'état et de la maison de l'empereur. *Paris: Gide.* 1860. 8vo. 20550

This absurd production purports to be a *facsimile* of a manuscript in the "Bibliothèque de l'Arsenal à Paris." It is evidently the drawing-book of some clumsy youth, whose genius was certainly not very bright. It is remarkable that the Emperor Napoleon, and the Ministers of State, and not a few so-called *savans*, should have been beguiled by this publication. It is said to have been suppressed and bo�javascript up, and, consequently, commands a large price. The blunder was exposed by J. Petzholdt, in "Das Buch der Wilden," and by J. P. Meissner in "Wahre Erklärung," etc.

DOMENECH. La vérité sur le livre des sauvages, par l'Abbé Domenech. *Paris: E. Dentu.* 1861. 8vo, pp. 54. 10 Plates.

The author attempts to prove the authenticity of his previous work by reproducing some inscriptions found on the rocks in New Mexico and Sonora. "These pages are directly addressed to the author of the pamphlet of Dresden, [Petzholdt, Buch der Wilden,] to the 'Augsburgsche Zeitung,' to the 'Vossische Zeitung,' to the 'Athenæum,' 'Saturday Review,' 'Notes and Queries,' 'Correspondance Litteraire,' 'Patrie,' 'Indépendance Belge,' and other papers and reviews which have attacked the authenticity of the 'Livre des Sauvages.'" — *From the author's Preface.*

DOMENECH. Le Mexique tel qu'il est, la vérité sur son climat, ses habitants, et son gouvernement. *Paris: Dentu.* 1867. 8vo, 2 l., pp. 350. BA. + Seconde édition. [*Ibid.*]

DOMENECH. Missionary Adventures in Texas and Mexico: a Personal Narrative of Six Years' Sojourn in those Regions. By the Abbé Domenech. Translated from the French under the Author's Superintendence. *London: Longman, Brown, Green, Longman and Roberts.* 1858. 8vo, pp. xv, 366. BA., C., H.

DOMENECH. Seven Years' Residence in the Great Deserts of North America. By the Abbé Em. Domenech .... Illustrated with fifty-eight Woodcuts by A. Joliet, three plates of Indian Music, and a Map, showing the Actual Situation of the Indian Tribes, and the Country Described by the Author. *London: Longman, Green & Co.* 1860. 2 vols., 8vo, pp. xxiv, 445; xii, 465. 59 Plates. BA. 20554

Mostly a compilation from the "Reports of the Surveys for the Pacific Railroad," some of the plates in that work being here reproduced.

DOMENECH. Voyage pittoresque dans les grands déserts du Nouveau Monde. *Paris: Morizot.* 1862. 4to. 20555

DOMENECH. Voyages dans les solitudes américaines: voyage au Minnesota. *Paris: Douniol.* 1858. 18mo. 20556

Domestic Scenes in Greenland and Iceland. *London: Religious Tract Society.* 1841. + Second Edition. *London: J. Van Voorst.* 1851. 18mo, pp. 116. 20557

DOMEYKO (I.) Araucania i sus habitantes. Recuerdos de un viaje hecho en las provincias meridionales de Chile en [1845]. Por Ignacio Domeyko. *Santiago: imprenta chilena.* 1845. 8vo, 5 l., pp. 121. 2 Maps. C. 20558

DOMEYKO. Elementos de Mineralojia o del gonocimiento de las especies minerales en jeneral, i en particular de las de Chile. Por Ignacio Domeyko. Segunda edicion. *Santiago.* 1860. 8vo, pp. xi, 432. 6 Plates. 20559

DOMEYKO. Memoire sur les fossiles secondaires recueillis dans le Chili. *Paris.* 1851. 4to. 8 Plates. 20560

DOMEYKO. Tratado de ensayos, tanto por la via seca como por la via humeda, de toda clase de minerales y postes de cobre, ploms, plata, oro, mercurio, etc. con descripcion de los caracteres de los principales minerales y productos de las artes en America, y en particular en Chile, por Ignacio Domeyko. *Serena: imprenta del colejio.* 1844. 8vo, 3 l., pp. 341, xviii. 2 Plates. + Segunda edicion, aumentada y correjida. *Valparaiso: imprenta del Diario.* 1858. 8vo, pp. viii, 458, xviii. 5 Plates.

El Domingo. Semanario de religion, literatura y variedadas. Noviembre 29, 1863.—Abril 17, 1864. *Mexico.* 1863–64. 4to. 20562

DOMINGO DE LA ANUNCIACION. Doctrina Xtiana breue y cõpendio|sa por via de dialogo entre vn maestro y vn disci-|pulo, sacada en lẽgua castellana y mexicana y|cõpuesta par el muy reuerendo padre fray|domingo de la anunciacion, vicario q*ue*| al presente es de cuyoacan, de|la orden del bien auen|turado padre sct'o|Domingo.|*En Mexico en casa de pedro ocharte.* 1565.| 4to, Title, pp. 83, (1). 20563

For some interesting particulars respecting the only known copp, *see* Leclerc, No. 467. It sold for 1500 francs. It contains four woodcuts, which may be regarded as some of the earliest specimens of Mexican wood engraving.

Domingo de S. Thomas. Gramatica, ó Arte de la Lengua general de los Indios de los Reynos del Peru. Nueuamente compuesto, por el Maestro Fray Domingo de S. Thomas, De la Orden de S. Domingo, Morador en los dichos Reynos. *Impresso en Valladolid, por Francisco Fernandez de Cordoua.* 1560. Sm. 8vo, 7 l., 96 l. 20564

Domingo de S. Thomas. Lexicon, o Vocabulario de la lengua general de Perv, cōpuesta por el Maestro F. Domingo de S. Thomas de la orden de S. Domingo. *Impresso en Valladolid, por Francisco Fernandez de Cordoua, Impressor de la M. R. Con privilegio.* [1560.] Sm. 8vo, 8 l., 179 l. 20565

A volume of extreme rarity. Leclerc's copy, No. 468, sold for 1050 francs. According to Ludewig, it was reprinted as "l'Arte y Vocabulario en la lengua general del Peru. *Imp. par A. Ricardo, à Lima en* 1586." 8vo.

Dominguez (Francisco). Catecismo de la Doctrina Cristiana puesto en el Idioma Totonaco de la Cierra [*sic*] baja de Naolingo, distinto de la Cierra alta de Papautla, cura interno de Xalpan. Por F. Dominguez. *Reimpresso en Puebla* [*Mexico*], *en la Imprenta del Hospital de San Pedro.* 1837. 8vo, pp. 38, 1 l.

Dominguez. Voces a la alma que dá un parroco a sus feligreses. *Mexíco.* 1806. 4to, 34 l. 20567

Dominguez (Francisco Eugenio). Platicas de los principales mysterios de nuestra Sta. Fee, con una breve exortacion al fin del modo con que deben excitarse al dolor de las culpas. Hechas en el Idioma Yucateco, Por orden del Illmo. Sr. Dr. D. F. Ignacio de Padilla. *Mexico: en la Imprenta del Real, y mas Antiguo Colegio de S. Ildefonso.* 1758. 4to, pp. 24. J.C.B. 20568

Dominguez (J. F.) Biena venturanzas del Sant patriarca Séñ. San Joseph. *Mexico.* 1805. 4to, 45 l. 20569

Dominguez (L. L.) Historia Argentina. Por Luis L. Dominguez. *Buenos Aires.* 1861. 8vo, pp. xxiv, 520. + 3a edicion. *Buenos Aires.* 1868. 16mo. B. 20570

Dominguez. History of the Argentine Republic. Vol. I. (1492–1867). Translated from the Spanish by J. W. Williams. *Buenos Aires.* 1865. 4to, pp. viii, 150. 20571

Dominica. Dominica, from an Actual Survey, completed in 1773. *London.* 1775. 20572

For other anonymous books on Dominico not included below, *see* "Hayti," "San Domingo," and "Saint Domingo."

Constitution politica de la republica Dominicana. *Santo Domingo: Imprenta Nacional.* 1854. Sm. 4to, pp. 49. + *Santo Domingo.* 1854. 4to, pp. 32. 20573

The Dominican Republic and the Emperor Soulouque. By 'Britannicus.' *Philadelphia.* 1852. pp. 72. 20574

The Laws of the Colony of Dominica, ... from its earliest establishment to ... 1818. *Roscall: Printed by William P. Stewart.* 1818. 8vo, pp. lxxxviii, 625, xl. 20575

Leyes Dominicanos. Actos legislativos del congreso constitucional y decretos del Presidente de la República Dominicana. *Santo Domingo.* 1846–7. 2 vols., 4to, pp. 212; 124. 20576

Punica Fides! or, A Short Statement of the Facts connected with the recent "Breach" by the Dominican Government of the second article of the Commercial Treaty, exchanged between England and the Dominican Republic in 1850. *St. Domingo.* 1852. Sm. 8vo, pp. 16. 20577

Report of the Committee of the Legislature of Dominica, relative to the Condition, Treatment, &c., of the Negro Population of that island, and Governor of St. Vincent's Letter respecting Insurrection in Demerara. *London.* 1823. 8vo, pp. 43.

La Republica Dominicana y el Emperador Soulouque. *Santo Domingo.* 1851. 8vo, pp. 12. 20579

Dominicans. Haec sunt Acta Capitali Generalis Bononiæ, celebrati in Conuento Sancti Dominici in festo Sanctiss. Pentecostes Anno Domini Milesimo quingentisimo quarto: Die Vigesimo Maij. Sub Reverendissimo Patre Frate Vincentio Justiniano Chiense Sacræ S. Theologie Professore Magistro Generali Ordinis Predicatorū Diffinientibus Reverendis Diffinitoribus: videlicit. *Impressa sunt hæc Acta, Mexici apud Petrum Ocharte, Typographum, Anno Domino,* 1567, *Die quinto decima mensis Aprilis.*

"Of excessive rarity, and probably unique; we have been unable to trace notice of it by any bibliographer, and it appears hitherto to have been unknown. As a specimen of typography and wood engraving in the infancy of printing in the New World, it is of peculiar interest, also for biographical notices of members of the Dominican order then living in Mexico." Title and note from an English catalogue.

Acta Capituli Generalis Romæ in Conventu S. Mariæ super Mineruam celebrati. In Festo S. Pentecostes IX. Junij Anno 1612, sub. Rev. P. Fr. Seraphino Sicco Papiensi. *Mexici: J. Ruyz.* 1613. 20581

Also: Hæc sunt Provisiones pro bono Regimine Provincialum Indiarum Occidentalium Ordinis Fratrum Prædicatorum, etc. *Hispali, excudebat Franciscus de Lira Año,* 1619. — Capituli Provincialis celebrati in Imperiali S. P. N. Dominici Mexicano Conventu, Die xv. Maij, 1773. *Mexico: typis Lic. D. Jos. Juarigi.* 1773. 4to. — Acta Capituli Provincialis celebrati in hoc Imperiali S. Dominici Mexiceo Ceoneobio die 6 Maij, 1809. *Mexico.* 1809. 4to.

Domschcke (Bernhard). Zwanzig Monate in Kriegs-Gefangenschaft: Erinnerungen. *Milwaukee.* 1865. 12mo. C.

Domus (Victor). The Democracy, a Lecture. [n. p. n. d.] 8vo, pp. 70. 20583

Don Diego Rosa; or, He of the Iron Arm. A Chronicle of Louisiana. *New York.* 1838. 8vo. N. 20584

Don Henriquez de Castro, or the Conquest of the Indies, a Spanish Novel. *London.* 1685. 8vo. 20585

Don John Further Display'd: Being a Supplement to Considerations on the American Trade. *London: J. Roberts.* MDCCXL. 8vo, pp. 43. J.C.B. 20586

"Written by a Jamaica merchant of some credit and Reputation in London." — Rich.

Don Quizotes at College; or, A History of the Gallant Adventures lately achieved by the combined Students of Harvard University; interspersed with some Facetious Reasonings. By a Senior. *Boston: Published by Etheridge and Bliss for the Author.* 8vo, pp. 20. BA. 20587

Donaldson (J. L. [Quartermaster's Report of the Department of the Cumberland, for the Year ending June 30, 1865.] 8vo, pp. 12. H. 20588

Donaldson (James). Undoubted Art of Thriveing, shewing that a million sterling money may be raised, for propagating the Trade of the Nation; How the Indian and African Company may propagate their Trade, in New York, Jamaica, and other parts of the West Indies, and how every one, according to his quality, may live comfortably and happy, &c. *Edinburgh.* 1700. 12mo. 20589

Title from one of Thorpes' catalogues, No. 1615.

Donaldson (T.) American Colonial History: an Address made by Thomas Donaldson, Esq., before the Maryland Historical Society, Baltimore, March 29, 1849 ... . *Baltimore.* MDCCCXLIX. 8vo, pp. 28. H. 20590

Donaldson (W.) North America, a descriptive Poem, representing the Voyage to America, a Sketch of that beautiful Country, etc. With Notes. *London: J. Shephard.* 1757. 4to, pp. 19. C. 20591

Dedicated to the Earl of Loudoun.

Donallan (John Whiting). History of the Second Baptist Church, Cambridge, Mass., by John Whiting Donallan. *Lawrence: printed by Geo. S. Merill & Company.* 1866. 8vo, pp. 120. H. 20592

Donck (A. v. d.) Beschryvinge | Van | Nieuvv-Nederlant, | (Ghelijck het tegenwoordigh in Staet is) | Begrijpende de Nature, Aert, gelegentheyt en vrucht- | baerheyt van het selve Lant; mitsgaders de proffijtelijcke en- | de gewenste toevallen, die aldaer tot onderhout der Menschen, (soo | uyt haer selven als van buyten ingebracht) gevonden worden. | Als Mede | De maniere en onghemeyne eygenschappen | vande Wilden ofte Naturellen van den Lande. | Ende | Een bysonder verhael vanden wonderlijcken Aert | ende het Weesen der Bevers, | Daer Noch By Gevoeght Is | Een Discours over de gelegentheyt van Nieuw Nederlandt, | tusschen een Nederlandts Patriot, ende een | Nieuw Nederlander. | Beschreven door | Adriaen vander Donck, | Beyder Rechten Doctoor, die teghenwoor- | digh noch in Nieuw Nederlant is. | *t'Aemsteldam,* | *By Evert Nieuwenhof, Boeck-verkooper, woonende op 't | Ruslandt in't Schrijf-boeck. Anno* 1655. | 4to, 4 l., pp. 100, Register (3).

First edition of this valuable work, of the highest interest for the history of New York, concerning which, *see* Asher, No. 7. The engraved view of "t'Fort Nieuw Amsterdam op de Manhatens," on page 9, is not in the second edition. The recto of the third leaf of this edition is "Inleydinge Van de Autheur;" in the second edition, it is "Aan de leeser." The poem in the first edition is signed G. Verbiest, in the second, E. Nieuwenhoff. "What '*the first folio*' is to an English collector, a *Van der Donck* is to the American. When he has once screwed his courage to the price of a Van der Donck, he seldom flinches at any other rare work that may turn up. This first edition usually commands from £12 to £20 in Europe." — Stevens.

Donck. Beschryvinge | Van | Nieuvv-Nederlant, | (Gelijck het tegenwoordigh in Staet is) | Begrijpende de Nature, Aert, gelegentheyt en vruchtbaerheyt | van het selve Landt; mitsgaders de proffijtelijcke ende gewenste toevallen, die | aldaer tot onderhoudt der Menschen, (soo uyt haer selven als van buyten inge- | bracht) gevonden worden. Als mede de maniere en ongemeyne Eygenschap- | pen vande Wilden ofte Naturellen vanden Lande. Ende een bysonder verhael | vanden wonderlijcken Aert ende het Weesen der Bevers. | Daer noch by-gevoeght is | Een Discours over de gelegentheyt van Nieuw-Nederlandt | tusschen een Ned-

erlandts Patriot, ende een Nieuw Nederlander. | Beschreven door | Adriaen van der Donck, | Beyder Rechten Doctoor, die tegenwoordigh | noch in Nieuw-Nederlandt is. | En hier achter by gevoeght | Het voordeeligh Reglement vande Ed: Hoog. Achtbare | Heeren de Heeren Burgermeesteren deser Stede, | betreffende de saken van Nieuw-Nederlandt. | Den tweeden Druck. | Met een pertinent Kaertje van t' zelve Landt verçiert, | en van veel druck-fouten gesuyvert. | *t'Aemsteldam,* | *By Evert Nieuwenhof, Boeck-verkooper, woonende op | 't Ruslandt, in't Schrijf-boeck, Anno* 1656. | *Met Privilegie voor* 15 *Jaren.* | 4to, 4 l., pp. 100, Register, (4), Conditien, 4 l. Map. 20594

This second edition contains a map, which is not in the first. The map is entitled, "Nova Belgica, sive Nieuw Nederlandt," and is copied from the rare map of N. J. Vischer. *See* Asher's list of the "Maps and Charts of N. Netherland," p. 12. It is usually followed by "Conditien, Die door de Heeren Burgermeesteren der Stadt Amsterdam, volgens't gemaecte accoort met de West-Indische Compagnie, ende de Approbatie van hare Hog. Mog. de Heeren Staten Generael der Vereenighde Nederlanden daer op gevolght, gepresenteert werden aen alle de gene, die als Coloniers na Nieuw-Nederlandt Willen vertrecken ... '*tAmsterdam Met Consent* ... etc. *By Evert Nieuwenhoff* ... 1656." 4to, 4 l. In Puttick and Simpson's catalogue, No. 2202, 1860, a copy is described as the second and best impression of the second edition, containing some variations in the preliminary leaves, which we think is an error. For a translation, *see* "N. Y. Hist. Soc. Coll.," Second Series, Vol. I. After page sixteen, both editions are alike.

[Donck.] Vertoogh | van | Nieu Neder-Land, Weghens de Gheleghentheydt, | Vruchtbaerheydt, en Sobe- | ren Staet deszelfs. | *In's Graven Hage,* | *Ghedruckt by Michiel Stael, Boeckverkooper woonende* | *op 't Buyten Hof, tegen-over de Gevange-Poort.* 1650. | 4to, pp. 49. 20595

A volume of extreme rarity. It was translated as below:

[Donck.] Vertoogh van Nieu Nederland, and Breeden Raedt aende Vereenichde Nederlandsche Provintien. Two rare Tracts printed in 1649–'50. Relating to the Administration of affairs in New Netherland. Translated from the Dutch by Henry C. Murphy. *New York.* 1854. 4to, pp. vii, (1), 190. 20596

125 copies printed. The following is a different translation:

[Donck.] Remonstrance of New-Netherland, and the Occurrences there. Addressed to the High and Mighty Lords States General of the United Netherlands, on the 28th July 1649. With Secretary Van Tienhoven's Answer. Translated from a copy of the original Dutch MS. By E. B. O'Callaghan, M.D. *Albany: Weed, Parsons & Company.* 1856. 4to, 3 l., pp. 65, (1). S. 20597

Forms part of the "Colonial Documents of New York." A few copies only issued with a separate title.

Doniphan (*Col.*) Campaign in New-Mexico. *See* Edwards.

Donkin (R.) Military Collections and Remarks. Published by Major Donkin. *New-York: Printed by H. Gaine, at the Bible and Crown, in Hanover-Square.* M,DCC,LXXVII. 8vo, 16 l., pp. 264. 20598

Published for "the benefit of the children and widows of the valiant soldiers inhumanly and wantonly butchered when peaceably marching to and from Concord the 19th April 1775, by the *rebels,*" — *Introduction.* Contains several anecdotes and remarks relative to the War of Independence.

Donnant (D. F.) Statistical Account of the United States of America. By D. F. Donnant ... . Translated from the French, by W. Playfair: With an Addition on the Trade to America ... . Illustrated by a Divided Circle ... . *London: Greenland and Norris.* 1805. 8vo, pp. 72. Map. C., H., S.

Donnavan (C.) Adventures in Mexico: experienced during a Captivity of Seven Months in the Interior — having been Captured at Camargo, by Canales' Band of Guerrillas, with two other American Citizens — marched to Valladolid, beyond the City of Mexico, and Sold into Slavery; ... By C. Donnavan. *Cincinnati: Robinson & Jones.* 1487 [*sic*]. 8vo. 20600

Donne (J.) A Sermon Vpon the viii Verse of the I. Chapter of the Acts of the Apostles. Preach'd To the Honourable Company of the Virginian Plantation. 30 Nouemb 1622. By John Donne Decone of St Pauls, London. *London: Printed by A. Mat: for Thomas Iones.* 1622. Sm. 4to, 2 l., pp. 49. M.

Donnelly (I.) "Minnesota;" an Address delivered at the Broadway House, New York, March 27, 1857. By Ignatius Donnelly. *New York.* 1857. 8vo, pp. 15. 20602

Also: Freedman's Bureau. Speech ... In the House ... February 1, 1866. *Washington, D. C.: McGill & Witherow, Printers.* 1866. 8vo, pp. 14. H. — Sale of Public Lands. Speech ... in the House ... May 7, 1868. [*Washington.* n. d.] 8vo, pp. 8. H. — Speech ... on the Reconstruction of the Union. ... in the House ... May 2, 1864. [*Washington:*] *W. H. Moore, Printer.* 8vo, pp. 7. H.

Donnelly (T. J.) Trial of James P. Donnelly, for the Murder of Albert S. Moses, on the first of August, 1857, at the "Sea View House," Navisink, New Jersey. *Freehold.* 1857. 8vo. C. 20603

Donoho. ... An Appeal from the Southern States to the Northern, Eastern and Western States, and to the Civilized World. ... by Donoho, Joy & Co., Memphis, Tenn. ... [n. p.] 1870. 8vo, pp. 34, (1). H. 20604

Donop (*Freiherr* Wilhelm Gottlieb Lev.) Das magusanische Europa, oder Phönizier in den Innen-Landen des europaischen Westens. *Meiningen.* 1819–41. 5 pts., 8vo. 20605

"Fünfte Abtheilung und Schluss. Afrika, Amerika und Atlantis."

Donoso (Justo). Instituciones de Derecho Canonico Americano, para el uso de los colegios en las republicas Americanas. Nueva edicion. *Paris.* 1854. 3 vols., 12mo. 20606

Doolittel, *or* Doolittle (Thomas). Earthquakes Explained and Practically Improved: Occasioned By the late Earthquake on Sept. 8. 1692. in England, and beyond Sea. Jamaica's Miseries shew London's Mercies. *London.* 1693. 8vo, pp. (16), 141. B. 20607

Doolittle (B.) An Enquiry into Enthusiasm. Being an Account what it is, the Original, Progress, and Effects of it. By Benjamin Doolittle ... . *Boston: Printed for J. Edwards.* 1743. 12mo, pp. 37. B., BA. 20608

Doolittle (J. R.) Arguments of the Hon. James R. Doolittle ... as of Counsel for the Cherokee Nation to the Senate Committee on Indian Affairs. Washington, D. C., April, 1869. *Washington.* 1869. 8vo, pp. 7. H. 20609

[Doolittle.] Condition of the Indian Tribes. Report of the Joint Special Committee, appointed under Joint Resolution of March 3, 1865. With an Appendix. *Washington.* 1867. 8vo, pp. 10, 532. H. 20610

Doolittle. Record of the Hon. James R. Doolittle in the Twenty-seventh Congresss. [*Washington.* 1862.] 8vo, pp. 7.

Also: The acquisition of Cuba — Colonization of Central America. ... in the ... Senate, February 11, 1859. *Washington, D. C.* [n. d.] 8vo, pp. 8. H. — An Appeal to the Senate to modify its Policy and save from Africanization and Military Despotism the States of the South. Speech ... in the Senate ... January 23, 1868. *Washington: F. & J. Rives & Geo. A. Bailey, Printers.* 1868. 8vo, pp. 15. H. — The Calhoun Resolution: its Basis and its Progress. ... in the ... Senate, December 14, 1859. *Washington, D. C.* 1860. 8vo, pp. 16. H. — Justification of Commodore Paulding's Arrest of Walker and his Command at Punta Arenas. Speech ... Delivered in the United States Senate, January 21st, 1858. [n. p. n. d.] 8vo, pp. 15. H. — Opinion ... on the Impeachment of the President. [n. p. n. d.] 8vo, pp. 5. H. — Railroads in the States. Speech ... in the Senate ... January 22, 1869. *Washington: F. & J. Rives & Geo. A. Bailey, Printers.* 1869. 8vo, pp. 14. H. — Speech ... on Emancipation and Colonization. Delivered in the U. S. Senate, March 19, 1862. [n. p. n. d.] 8vo, pp. 8. — The Rebels, and not the Republican Party, destroyed Slavery. Speech ... delivered in the ... Senate, February 9, 1864. [n. p. n. d.] 8vo, pp. 7. — Speech ... [on] the Lecompton Constitution, March 4, 8, 1858. 8vo, pp. 16. S. — Speech ... on the Bill to Organize the Territory of

Arizuma. ... in the Senate ... December 27, 1860. [n. p. n. d.] 8vo, pp. 16. H. Speech ... on Homesteads for White Men in the Temperate Zone — Homesteads for Black Men in the Tropics — ... delivered in the Senate ... April 11, 1862. *Washington.* 1862. 8vo, pp. 15. H. — Speech ... on the Lincoln-Johnson Policy of Restoration ... in the Senate ... January 17, 1866. *Washington.* 1866. 8vo, pp. 22. H. — ... Speech ... in the Senate ... January 23, 1868. *Washington.* 1868. 8vo, 15. H. — State Rights and the Supreme Court. Speech ... delivered in the United States Senate, February 24, 1860. — Letter to James R. Doolittle on the Public Debt. *New York.* 1866.

Doolittle (M.) Historical Sketch of the Congregational Church in Belchertown, Mass., from its Organization, 114 Years ... and Early History of the Place. By Hon. Mark Doolittle. ... *Northampton, Mass.: Hopkins, Bridgman & Co.* 1852. 12mo, pp. 282. H. 20612

Also: An Address at Northampton, Oct. 11, 1826, to the Society of the Counties of Hampshire, Franklin, and Hampden, for the Promotion of Agriculture and the Mechanic Arts. ... *Northampton.* 1826. 8vo, pp. 24. M.

Doolittle (T.) A Short | Narrative | of Mischief done by the | French and Indian Enemy, | on the | Western Frontiers | of the Province of the | Massachusetts-Bay; | From the Beginning of the French War, | proclaimed by the King of France | March 15th 1743, 4; and by the King | of Great Britain March 29th | 1744, to August 2d 1748. | Drawn up by the Reverend Mr. Doolittle of North- | field in the County of Hampshire; and found among | his Manuscripts after his Death. | And at the Desire of some, is now published, with some small | Additions, to render it more perfect. | *Boston:* | *Printed and Sold by S. Kneeland, in Queen street.* | M.DCCL. | 8vo, Title, pp. 22. P. 20613

Doolittle. Treatise Concerning the Lord's Supper. ... By Thomas Doolittle, M.A. Three Dialogues. The Nineteenth Edition. With Additions. *Boston.* 1700. 12mo, pp. (8), 212, (2). + Twenty-fifth Edition. *Boston.* 1713. 16mo. + The Sixth and Twentieth Edition. *Boston: T. Fleet.* 1727. 18mo, 4 l., pp. 208. 20614

The Doom of Slavery in the Union: Its Safety out of it. ... *Charleston, S. C.: Printed By Evans & Cogswell.* 1860. 8vo, pp. 39, (1). 20615

Doran (J.) New Pictures and Old Panels. By Dr. Doran ... . *London: Richard Bentley.* 1859. 8vo, pp. viii, 376. Portrait. BA. 20616

"The Flowery Legend of Our Lady of Guadalupe," pp. 154–166.

Dorat. Barnewell im Gefängniss und Yariko in der Sklaverei. Aus dem Französischen [von H. W. D. Bräss]. *Braunschweig.* 1766. 8vo. 20617

D'ORBIGNY (A.) *See* Orbigny (A. d').

DORCHESTER, *Mass.* Collections of the Dorchester Antiquarian and Historical Society. *See* Blake (J.), Vol. II., No. 5777, Clap (R.), Vol. IV., No. 13209, and Mather (R.), *infra.*

Dorchester in 1630, 1776, and 1855. An Oration delivered on the Fourth of July, 1855, by Edward Everett. Also an Account of the Proceedings in Dorchester at the Celebration of the Day. *Boston: D. Clapp.* 1855. 8vo, pp. viii, 158.

Epitaphs from the Old Burying Ground in Dorchester. *See* [Woodward].

History of the Town of Dorchester, Massachusetts, By a Committee of the Dorchester Antiquarian and Historical Society. *Boston: Ebenezer Clapp, Jr.* 1859. 8vo, pp. xii, 672.

First published in parts. Mr. E. Clapp is the author of the greater part, and the editor of the whole of the history of Dorchester; Edmund Baker wrote the account of Neponset River, Wm. B. Trask the account of the schools, James M. Robbins, part of the early history, and Mr. Clapp all the rest.

The Memorial of the Proprietors of the New South Meeting-House in Dorchester, to the Ministers of the Boston Association; ... with their Report ... . *Boston: published by Watson & Bangs.* 1813. 8vo, pp. 48. B., BA. 20621

Written by the Rev. L. Capen.

Proceedings of the Second Church and Parish in Dorchester; exhibited in a Collection of Papers. ... *Boston: Printed by Samuel T. Armstrong.* 1812. 8vo, pp. iv, 9–124. + Second Edition. [*Ibid.*] 1812. B., BA., M. 20622

Relative to the difficulties with their pastor, the Rev. John Codman.

Public Expression of Grief for the Death of General George Washington at Dorchester, pp. 6. [Followed by] Everett's Eulogy, pp. 22. Harris' Discourse, pp. 16. The Address of the Late George Washington when President, to the People of the United States, on Declining being Considered a Candidate for the future Suffrages, pp. 30. The Fraternal Tribute of Respect paid to the Masonic Character of Washington in the Union Lodge, in Dorchester, January 7th, A.L. 5800. *Charlestown: Printed by Samuel Etheridge.* M.DCCC. pp. 14, Masonic Dirge, 1 l. 20623

See Everett (C.), and Harris.

Remarks on the Result of an Ecclesiastical Council which met at Dorchester, Nov. 16, 1773. *Boston.* 1774. 8vo. W.

Result of an Ecclesiastical Council at Dorchester, November 16. 1773. *Boston.* 1774. 8vo, pp. 39. 20625

Review of Two Pamphlets which were published on the Subject of the Ecclesiastical Controversy in Dorchester. *Boston: Printed by Samuel T. Armstrong.* 1814. 8vo, pp. 46. BA.

From the "Panopolist." *See* "Proceedings," and "Memorial," *supra.*

The Sexton's Monitor and Dorchester Cemetery Memorial. *Roxbury.* 1826. 12mo, pp. 38. W. 20627

Sundry Votes Passed by the Church of Christ in Dorchester Ann. Dom. 1773. Previous to the Meeting of an Ecclesiastical Council there; the Result of Said Council, &c. ... . *Boston: Printed by Mills and Hicks.* 1774. 8vo, pp. 23. BA., M., N.

Also: First Annual Report of the Executive Committee of the Barnard Freedmen's-Aid Society of Dorchester. [n. p. n. d.] 8vo, pp. 7, 1 l. + Fourth Annual Report. — Annual Report of the Board of Managers of the Industrial School for Girls, in Dorchester, for the Year 1859. *Boston: Prentiss & Sawyer, Printers.* 1860. 12mo, pp. 15. H. + The same for 1860. 12mo, pp. 12. + The same for 1866. 8vo, pp. 15. H. — First Annual Report of the School Committee of the Town of Dorchester. April, 1839. *Boston: printed by D. Clapp, Jr.* 1839. 12mo, pp. 11 Continued after 1843 in 8vo. B. — Annual Report of the Dorchester Temperance Society, December, 1829. *Boston.* 1829. 12mo. Continued. — The Auditor's Second Printed Report of the Receipts and Expenditures of the Town of Dorchester ... from March 21, 1839, to March 21, 1840. ... *Boston: Albert Morgan, Printer.* 1840. 8vo, pp. 23. Continued. H. — By-Laws of the Town of Dorchester, Massachusetts. Adopted by the Town in the Years 1837, 1855, and 1858, and approved by the Court of Common Pleas. ... *Dorchester.* 1858. 8vo, pp. 8. H. — Communication by the Proprietors of the New South Meeting-House, to the Inhabitants of this Town. *Boston.* 1806. 8vo, pp. 7. B. — Constitution of the Dorchester McClellan Club, and List of Officers. [n. p.] 1864. 16mo, pp. 6, 1 l. H. — Dedication of the Soldiers' Monument at Dorchester, September 17, 1867. *Boston: Thomas Groom & Co.* 1868. 8vo, pp. 35, (3). H. — Discovery of some Materials for the Early History of Dorchester. *Boston.* 1851. 8vo. — Exercises at the Consecration of Mount Hope Cemetery in Dorchester and West Roxbury. *Boston.* 1852. — Order of Exercises at the Dedication of the Meeting-house in the First Parish in Dorchester. *Boston.* 1816. 8vo, pp. 4. M. — Prospectus of the Dorchester Mining Company, Portage Lake, Lake Superior. *Boston.* 1863. 8vo, pp. 16. H. — Regulations of the School Committee of the Town of Dorchester, June, 1847. *Boston.* 1847. 12mo, pp. 12. — Regulations of the School Committee of Dorchester. Adopted April, 1854. *Boston: printed by David Clapp.* 1854. 8vo, pp. 14. Continued. H. — Report of a Special Committee on Schools, 1845. [n. p. n. d.] 8vo, pp. 8. — Report of Receipts and Expenditures, 1839–40. *Boston.* 1839. 8vo. Continued. — Rules and Regulations of the Board of Health. *Dorchester.* 1855. 8vo. S. — Selectmen's Report of the Town of Dorchester, for the Year ending March 4, 1850. ... *Boston: C. C. P. Moody, Printer.* 1850. 8vo, pp. 11. H. — The Taxable Valuation of the Polls and Estates of the Town of Dorchester, for the Year 1849. ... *Boston: printed by David Clapp.* 1849. 12mo, pp. 112. Continued. H.

DORE (J.) A Sermon on the Slave Trade. By Rev. James Dore. *London.* 1788. 8vo. + Third Edition. *London.* 1789. 12mo. 20629

DOREMUS (J. C.) Report of the Case of the People of the State of Illinois upon the Relation of John Charles Strickney, vs. John Marshall, President, and Others of the Bank of Illinois, at Shawneetown, at the December Term, 1841, in the Supreme Court of Illinois. *Springfield.* 1842. N. 20630

DORIOL *aîné.* Réflexions sur Saint-Domingue, adressées à S. Exc. le ministre de la marine et des colonies le 18 octobre 1816, qui a daigné les accueillir favorablement. *Bordeaux: Lavigne jeune.* 1817. 8vo, pp. 16. 20631

[DORION (A. A.)] Remonstrance against the proposed Confederation of the British North American Provinces; addressed to the Earl of Carnarvon, Secretary of State for the Colonies, by Members of the Canadian Parliament representing Constituencies in Lower Canada. [Signed by A. A. Dorion and 19 others. n. p. n. d.] 8vo, pp. 10. H. 20632

DORMENON (P.) Reponse à des Calomnies. Par Pierre Dormenon. *Nouvelle Orléans.* 1809. 8vo. C. 20633

DORN (R. C.) Journal of the Court for the Trial of Impeachments in the Case of Robert C. Dorn, a Canal Commissioner of the State of New York. *Albany: Van Benthuysen & Sons.* 1868. 8vo, pp. 1181, 128. C., S. 20634

DORR (B.) The American Vine. A Sermon Preached in Christ's Church, Philadelphia, Friday, January 4, 1861. On Occasion of the National Fast. ... because of the Dangers which threaten the Union. By Benjamin Dorr, D.D. ... *Philadelphia: Collins, Printer.* 1861. 8vo, pp. 32. H. 20635

DORR. A Historical Account of Christ Church, Philadelphia, from its Foundation, A.D. 1605 to A.D. 1841; and of St. Peter's and St. James's, until the Separation of the Churches. By the Rev. Benjamin Dorr, D.D., Rector ... *New York.* 1841. 12mo. + *Philadelphia: Burns & Sieg.* 1859. 12mo, pp. x, 1 l., 430.

DORR. A Memoir of John Fanning Watson, the Annalist of Philadelphia and New York. Prepared by Request of the Historical Society of Pennsylvania, and read ... February 11, 1861. By Benjamin Dorr ... . *Philadelphia: Collins, Printer.* 1861. 8vo, pp. 88. Portrait. 20637

DORR. Memorials of Christ Church, Philadelphia. Two Sermons preached in said Church, April 27 and May 4, 1862. ... *Philadelphia: Collins, Printer.* 1862. 8vo, pp. 64. 20638

Also: The Privileges and Duties of an American Citizen. A Sermon ... Utica ... Dec. 8, 1831, The day of the Annual Thanksgiving in the State of New York. *Utica.* 1831. 8vo, pp. 22. — Sermon preached in Trinity Church, New York, at the Opening of the Convention of the Protestant Episcopal Church, October 7, 1830. ... *New York.* MDCCCXXX. 8vo, pp. 35. H.

[DORR (David F.)] A Colored Man Round the World. By a Quadroon. [n. p.] 1858. 8vo, pp. 192. Plate. C.

DORR (E.) Discourse occasioned by the Death of the Hon. Daniel Edwards, of Hartford, who died at New Haven, September 6, 1765. By Rev. Edward Dorr. *Hartford.* [n. d.] 4to.

DORR. The Duty of Civil Rulers to be Nursing Fathers to the Church of Christ. A Sermon ... At Hartford; on the Day of the Anniversary Election; May 12th, 1765. By Edward Dorr, A.M. *Hartford: Printed by Thomas Green.* [1765.] 8vo, pp. 34. BA. 20641

DORR (H. C.) The Two Donkeys. A Fable for the People. By Herbert C. Dorr. *San Francisco: Valentine & Co.* MDCCCLXIII. 8vo, pp. 16. 20642

DORR (J. A.) Justice to the South! An Address by James A. Dorr, a Member of the New York Bar. October 8, 1856. *New York.* [n. d.] 8vo, pp. 12. H. 20643

DORR (J. A.) Objections to the Act of Congress, commonly called the Fugitive Slave Law, Answered, in a Letter to Hon. Washington Hunt, Governor elect of the State of New York. By James A. Dorr ... . *New York.* 1850. 8vo, pp. 15. H., M.

DORR (T. H.) A Discourse on the Life and Character of Rev. Jason Whitman: delivered ... in Lexington, Feb. 27, 1848. By Theodore H. Dorr ... . *Boston.* 1848. 8vo, pp. 39.

DORR (T. W.) The Case of Thomas W. Dorr, explained. [n. p. 1845.] 8vo, pp. 11. H. 20646

DORR. The Conspiracy to defeat the Liberation of Gov. Dorr; or the Hunkers and Algerines identified, and their policy unveiled; to which is added A Report of the Case *ex parte* Dorr; comprising Motion to Supreme Court of the United States; Petitions of sundry Citizens of Rhode Island; Affida-

vits showing the Treatment of Governor Dorr by the Inspectors of the Prison; Argument of Counsel, and the Decision of the Court. *New York: John Windt.* 1845. 8vo, pp. 47. H.

DORR. The Merits of Thomas W. Dorr. *See* [Curtis]. Vol. v., No. 18041.

DORR. Report of the Trial of Thomas Wilson Dorr, for Treason; including the Testimony at length ... together with the Sentence of the Court, and the Speech of Mr. Dorr before Sentence. From Notes taken at the Trial. *Providence: B. F. Moore, Printer.* 1844. 8vo, pp. 115. H. 20649

Prepared for the press by George Turner and Walter S. Burges, attorneys for the defence.

DORR. Report of the Trial of Thomas Wilson Dorr, for Treason against the State of Rhode Island, containing the Arguments of Counsel, and the Charge of Chief Justice Durfee. By Joseph S. Pitman. *Boston: Tappan & Dennett.* 1844. 8vo, pp. 131. H. 20650

Also: Political Frauds Exposed; or a Narrative of the Proceedings of "The Junto in Providence," concerning the Senatorial Question, from 1833 to 1838. By Aristides. [*Providence.* 1838.] 8vo, pp. 24. (Relates to Dorr.)

[DORR.] Daw's Doings, or the History of the Late War in the Plantations. By Sampson Short-and-Fat ... . *Boston: William White & H. P. Lewis.* 1842. 16mo, pp. 68. H. 20651

DORRANCE (J.) *vs.* FENNER (A.) Report of the Case of John Dorrance against Arthur Fenner, tried at the December Term of the Court of Common Pleas, in the County of Providence, A.D. 1801. To which are added, Proceedings in the Case, Arthur Fenner *vs.* John Dorrance. Carefully Compiled from the Notes taken at the Trial. *Providence: printed by Bennett Wheeler.* 1802. 8vo, pp. iv, 116. H., W. 20652

The Dorriad: or, the Hero of Two Flights. ... [A Poem.] *Boston: Justin Jones.* 1842. 12mo, pp. 12. 20653

DORRIANA. Prospectus of a new and highly interesting work, in two volumes, to be published in "The only Democratic City," as soon as a sufficient number of Subscribers can be obtained to warrant the undertaking. The work will be entitled Dorr-ianna, or a Logical, Historical, Tragical, Magical, Sympathetic, and Democratical account of the late Glorious Revolution in Rhode Island; containing a True and Complete History of all the Say-

ings, Doings, Adventures and Brilliant Achievements of His Excellency, Thomas Wilson Dorr, Governor and Commander-in-Chief of Rhode Island and Providence Plantations. By a Sympathizer. *Providence. June* 17, 1842. 4to, pp. 4. 20654

See "Historical Magazine," II. 290.

DORSEY (A. H.) Woodreve Manor; or, Six Months in Town. A Tale of American Life. By Mrs. Anna Hanson Dorsey. *Philadelphia.* 1852. 12mo, pp. 270. 20655

DORSEY (C.) Speech of Clement Dorsey on the Subject of Retrenchment, in the House ... Jan. 1828. *Washington.* 1828. 12mo. 20656

DORSEY (D. B.) A Review of an "Address," professing to be a Vindication of the Baltimore Annual Conference ... . By Dennis B. Dorsey. To which is added, a Reply to the same "Address," by a Member of the Conference, and an Extract of a Letter from "Vindex." *Baltimore: Matchett, Printer.* 1827. 8vo, pp. 24. 20657

Some reference to America and American people.

DORSEY (J. L.) Address to the Voters of the First Congressional District in Maryland, June, 1831. By John L. Dorsey. [n. p. n. d.] 8vo. W. 20658

DORSEY. Whig Text Book; or, Democracy Unmasked. By John L. Dorsey. *Washington.* 1844. 8vo. C. 20659

DORSEY (S. A.) Recollections of Henry Watkins Allen, Brig.-Gen. Confederate States Army; Ex-Governor of Louisiana. By Sarah A. Dorsey. *New York: M. Doolady.* 1866. 12mo, pp. 420. Portrait. B. 20660

Some copies have the imprint, *New Orleans.* 1866.

DORVILLE. *See* Orville.

DORVO-SOULASTRE. Voyage par terre de Santo-Domingo ... au Cap-Français ... Entrepris ... au mois de germinal an VI, par les ordres du Général de division Hédouville ... . Suivi d'un Rapport sur l'état actuel des mines de la Colonie espagnole; traduit de Don Juan Nieto ... . Par Dorvo-Soulastre ... . *Paris: Chaumerot.* 1809. 8vo, 2 l., pp. 407, (1). Plate. H. 20661

Dos años en Mejico ó memorias criticas sobre los principales sucesos de la republica de los Estados Unidos Mejicanos, desde la invasion de Barradas, hasta la declaracion del Puerto de Tam-

pico contra el gobierno del general del Bustamente. Escritas por un Español. *Valencia: Cabrerizo.* 1838. 12mo, pp. iv, 172. + *Havre: Lemale.* 1838. 12mo, $7\frac{1}{2}$ sheets. *Mexico: [Reimpresa por Jose Uribe.]* 1840. 4to, pp. 69. 20662

The events described occurred between 1829 and 1831.

Dos politicas en candidatura, para el Gobierno de la Republica Argentina. *Paris: Jouby et Roger.* 1868. 8vo, pp. 32.

DOSSIE (R.) Observations on the Pot-Ash brought from America. With respect to its Goodness, Sophistication, &c., Verified by Experimental Examination, together with Instructions for determining the Comparative Value of Any Parcel, by Expedient Methods: To which, is subjoined Processes for making Pot-Ash and Barilla, in North America ... . By R. Dossie. Printed at (the Request of the Soc. for the Encouragement of Arts,) in Consequence of an Application made to them on these Points, by the ... House of Representatives ... of Massachusetts-Bay. *London.* MDCCLXVII. 8vo, 2 l., pp. 41. BA., H.

DOSTIE (A. P.) Freedom *vs.* Slavery. Address of Dr. A. P. Dostie, delivered before the Free State Union Association of New Orleans ... January 2d, 1864. [*New Orleans.* n. d.] 8vo, pp. 8. H. 20665

DOSTIE. The Political Position of Thomas J. Durant, of Louisiana. A Letter from Dr. A. P. Dostie to Hon. Henry L. Dawes, Chairman of the Committee on Elections, of the House of Representatives. *New Orleans: True Delta Office.* 1864. 8vo, pp. 8. 20666

Also: Address ... before the Republican Association of New Orleans, May 9, 1866. [n. p. n. d.] 8vo, pp. 14. H. — A Loyal Voice from Louisiana. Speech ... Jan. 27, 1866. [*New Orleans.* 1866?] 8vo, pp. 4. H.

[DOTY (J. D.)] Wisconsin Territory. [No Title. Colophon:] *Published by C. C. Sholes Madison.* [1838.] 8vo, pp. 16.

Also: Farewell Sermon and Address to the Right Rev. Jacob, Bishop of Quebec, Oct. 24, 1802. 8vo.

DOTY (J.) A Sermon preached at the opening of Christ's Church at Sorel In the Province of Canada, On Sunday the 25th of December 1785: By the Reverend John Doty, a Presbyter of the Church of England; and Missionary from the incorporated Society for the Propagation of the Gospel in Foreign Parts. *Montreal: Printed by Fleury Mesplet.* M.DCC.LXXXVI. 8vo, pp. 14. 20668

DOUAI (Adolf). Land und Leute in der Union. *Berlin: Janke.* 1864. 8vo, pp. xvi, 352. 20669

DOUAI. Personen, Land und Zustände in Nord-Amerika. Rathgeber für Auswanderer. Zweite Auflage. *Berlin: Janke.* 1865. 8vo, pp. xvi, 352. 20670

D[OUBLE] (M.) Abrégé Historique des Troubles de La Martinique. Par M. D*****. *Au Fort Royal, De l'imprimerie de J.-Fs. Bazille, imprimeur de la colonie. Et se trouve dans tous les quartiers de l'isle; chez les directeurs de poste, & dans les autres isles, chez les marchands de nouveautés.* 1791. 8vo, 2 l., pp. 82.

The Double Delusion; or, Faction the Cause of All the Confusion. A Joco-serious Review of our American Embroilment. *London: Printed for E. Johnson.* MDCCLXXVII. 8vo, pp. 23. B., BA., J.C.B. 20672

The writer thus closes his review: "Upon the whole, we may observe, that this unhappy embroilment was as weak as it was wicked, both in the contrivance and conduct of it; and in many respects so ridiculous, absurd and fantastic, as cannot be paralleled in all the annals of history." "Common-place invective." — *Monthly Rev.*, LVI. 309.

DOUBLET DE BOISTHIBAULT. Les Vœux des Hurons et des Abnaquis à Notre Dame de Chartres publiées pour la première fois d'après les manuscrits des archives d'Eure-et-Loir avec les lettres des missionaires-catholiques au Canada, une Introduction et des notes par Doublet de Boisthibault. *Chartres: Noury-Coquard.* M DCCC LVII. 12mo, 2 l., pp. viii, (2), 82. Folded Plate and Map. 20673

One hundred and fifty copies printed, some of which are on Holland paper.

Doubts concerning the Legality of Slavery in any Part of the British Dominions. *London: J. Stockdale.* 1789. 8vo, pp. 14.

See "M. Rev.," LXXXI. 91.

Doubts on the Abolition of the Slave Trade; by an old Member of Parliament. *London: J. Stockdale.* 1790. 8vo, pp. 123.

"The production of a gentleman who has labored at his subject." — *M. Review, Feb.*, 1790.

DOUCET (N. P.) Fundamental Principles of the Laws of Canada, as they existed under the Natives; as they were changed under the French Kings, and under the Domination of England. The Custom of Paris, the Text and a Literal Translation; the Statutes changing the Jurisprudence of Canada, &c. *Montreal.* 1843. 8vo. 20676

DOUGHERTY (D.) The Peril of the Republic the Fault of the People. An Address ... Union College, Schenectady, July 20, 1863. And ... Franklin and Marshall College, Lancaster, Pa., July 20, 1863. By Daniel Dougherty ... *Philadelphia: J. B. Lippincott & Co.* 1863. 8vo, pp. 28. 20677

Also: ... An Address delivered before the Literary Societies of Lafayette College, ... July 26, 1859. *Philadelphia: Ringwalt & Co., Printers.* 1859. 8vo, pp. 20. H.—Oration delivered before the Democracy ... Philadelphia ... July 4, 1856. ... *Philadelphia: William Rice.* 1856. 8vo, pp. 15.

DOUGHERTY (P.) A Chippeway Primer, compiled by the Rev. Peter Dougherty. Printed for the Board of Foreign Missions of the Presbyterian Church. *New York: John Westall.* 1844. 12mo, pp. 84. + Second Edition. [*Ibid.*] 1847. 12mo, pp. 123. C. 20678

DOUGHERTY. Short Reading Lessons in the Ojibway Language, Translated by the Rev. Peter Dougherty. *New York: John Westall and Co.* 1847. 12mo, pp. 95. 20679

DOUGALL (James). The Canadian Fruit Culturist. 1867.

DOUGLAS (A. B. C.) O Tempora! O Mores! A Poem delivered at ... Kimball Union Academy, April 18, 1866. By A. B. Clinton Douglas. *Boston: Wright and Potter, Printers.* 1866. 48mo, pp. 8. H. 20681

DOUGLAS (H.) Considerations on the Value and Importance of the British North American Provinces ... . By Major-General Sir Howard Douglas, Bart. ... *London.* MDCCCXXXI. 8vo, pp. 36. C., H. 20682

See Revans (J.), for a reply. Also: Speech ... on Lord Palmerston's Motion for an Address to the Queen for Copies of Communication referring to the Treaty of Washington. *London.* 1843. 8vo.

DOUGLAS (J.) Facts relative to the Session ... of the Reformed Presbyterian Church, New York, and the Writer James Douglas. *New York.* 1822. 8vo. B. + A Second Statement of Facts ... . *New-York.* 1823. 8vo, pp. 186. 20683

[DOUGLAS (John), *Bishop of Salisbury.*] Letter addressed to Two Great Men, on the Prospect of Peace, and on the Terms necessary to be insisted upon in the Negotiation. Second Edition. *London.* 1760. 8vo. 20684

Written, doubtless, under the direction of his patron, the Earl of Bute. *See* Coxe's "Life of Sir R. Walpole."

DOUGLAS. Sermon preached before the Society for Propagation of the Gospel in Foreign Parts, 1793. By the Rt. Rev. John Douglas, Bishop of Salisbury. *London.* 1793. 4to, pp. 83.

DOUGLAS (J.) Medical Topography of Upper Canada. By John Douglas ... . *London: Burgess and Hill.* 1819. 8vo, 2 l., pp. 126. B., H., S. 20686

DOUGLAS (J.) A Funeral Sermon, occasioned by the Death of Mrs. Ann McClure preached at Chesterville, S. C., January 16th. 1842, by Rev. John Douglas. ... *Charleston, S. C.* 1859. 8vo, pp. 20. H. 20687

DOUGLAS (*Mr.*) An Address on Slavery, Sabbath Protection, and Church Reform. By Mr. Douglas of Cavers. *Edinburgh: A. & C. Black.* 1838? 20688

[DOUGLAS (*Mrs.* R.)] On the Conservative Elements of the American Republic. By a Lady. *Chillicothe.* 1842. 8vo.

DOUGLAS (Stephen A.) Brief Treatise upon Constitutional and Party Questions, and the History of Political Parties, received orally by J. Madison Cutts. *New York.* 1866. 8vo.

DOUGLAS. The Dividing Line between Federal and Local Authority. ... *New York.* 1859. 8vo, pp. 40. B. 20691

From "Harper's Magazine."

DOUGLAS. The Campaign in Illinois. Last Joint Debate. Douglas and Lincoln at Alton, Illinois. *Washington.* 1858. 8vo, pp. 32. H. 20692

DOUGLAS. Observations on Senator Douglas's Views of Popular Sovereignty, as expressed in Harper's Magazine, for September, 1859. *Washington: Thos. McGill.* 1859. 8vo, pp. 16. + Second Edition. [*Ibid.*] 1859. 8vo, pp. 24. 20693

DOUGLAS. Political Debates. *See* Lincoln (A.)

Also: Address ... at the Annual Fair of the New-York State Agricultural Society, held at Rochester, September, 1851. *Albany: C. Van Benthuysen, Printer.* 1851. 8vo, pp. 41. C., H. + *Washington.* 1852. 8vo, pp. 24. H.—Constitution of Kansas. In the Senate ... February 18, 1858. Mr. Douglas, from the Committee on Territories, submitted the following Minority Reports. [n. p. n. d.] 8vo, pp. 24.—Execution of United States Laws. Speeches ... on the Senate ... February 23, 1855, on the Bill ... to protect Officers and other Persons acting under the Authority of the United States. [n. p. n. d.] 8vo, pp. 8.—In the Senate of the United States. ... Mr. Douglas made the following Report. ... [n. p. n. d.] 8vo, pp. 16. H. —Kansas-Lecompton Convention. Speech ... on the President's Message, ... in the Senate ... December 9, 1857. *Washington: printed by Lemuel Towers.* 1857. 8vo, pp. 15. H.—Kansas—Utah—Dred Scott Decision. ... delivered at Springfield, Illinois, June 12, 1857. *Springfield.* 1857. 8vo, pp. 14. H.—Letter ... on the Nebraska and Kansas Territorial Bill. *Washington.* 1854. 8vo, pp. 7.—Letter ... in reply to the Editor of the State Capitol Reporter, Concord, N. H. *Washington: Sentinel Office.* 1854. 8vo, pp. 7.—Letter of Senator Douglas, Vindicating his Character and Position on the Nebraska Bill, against the Assaults contained in the Proceedings in a Public Meeting composed of Twenty-Five Clergymen of Chicago. *Washington. April 6,* 1854. 8vo, pp. 14. B., H.—Non-Intervention—Popular Sovereignty. Speech ... in the Senate ... February 23, 1859, in Reply to Hon. A. G. Brown, of Mississippi ... together with an Appendix ... . *Washington.* 1859. 8vo, pp. 32. H. Non-Interference by Congress with Slavery in the Territories. Speech ... Senate, May 15 and 16, 1860. [*Baltimore.* 1860.] 8vo, pp. 40. + [*Washington.* 1860.] 8vo, pp. 32.—Oration ... on the Inauguration of the Jackson Statue, at the City of Washington, January 8, 1853. *Washington: Printed by Lemuel Towers.* 1853. 8vo, pp. 16.—Popular Sovereignty in the Territories. Judge Douglas in Reply to Judge Black. [n. p. n. d.] 8vo, pp. 24. H.—Popular Sovereignty the Dividing Line between Federal and Local Authority. *New York.* 1859. 8vo, pp. 65. + *New York: Harper & Brothers, Publishers.* 1859. 8vo, pp. 40. H.—Remarks ... on the Memorial of the New England Clergymen; United States Senate, March 14, 1854.—River and Harbor Improvements. Letter ... to Governor Matteson, of Illinois. [n. p. n. d.] 8vo, pp. 8. H.—Speech ... on the Bill to refund the Fine Imposed on General Jackson, at New Orleans. Delivered ... January 7, 1844. *Washington.* 1844. 8vo, pp. 13. H. + *New York: printed by Jared W. Bell.* 1851. 8vo, pp. 8.—Speech ... on the Annexation of Texas ... in the House, ... Jan. 6, 1845. [*Washington.* 1845.] 8vo, pp. 7. H. —Speech ... on the Mexican War. ... In the House ... May 13, 1846. *Washington.* 1846. 8vo, pp. 16. H.—Speech ... on the Territorial Question. Delivered in Senate ... March 13 and 14, 1850. *Washington.* 1850. 8vo, pp. 31. H.—Speech ... in Reply to Mr. Soule, relative to the Public Lands in California. Delivered in the Senate ... June 26th and 28th, 1850. *Washington.* 1850. 8vo, pp. 14. H.—Speech ... on the "Measures of Adjustment," Delivered in ... Chicago, Oct. 23, 1850. *Washington.* [1850.] 8vo, pp. 16. + *Washington: Gideon & Co., Printers.* 1851. 8vo, pp. 32. + *New York: Printed by Jared W. Bell.* 1851. 8vo, pp. 31. —Speech ... on the Munroe Doctrine, Feb. 14, 1853. [n. p. n. d.] 8vo, pp. 16. S.—Speech ... in Reply to Senators Clayton and Butler, on the Clayton-Bulwer Treaty on Central America ... March 10, 17, 1853. pp. 39.—Speech ... on the Nebraska Territory, January 30, 1854. [n. p. n. d.] 8vo, pp. 15. S.—Speech ... on Nebraska and Kansas, March 3, 1854. *Washington.* 1854. 8vo, pp. 30. S.—Speech ... on Kansas Territorial Affairs. ... in the Senate ... March 20, 1856. *Washington: printed at the Union Office.* 1856. 8vo, pp. 29.—Speech ... on the President's Message; Kansas-Lecompton Convention: December 9, 1857. pp. 15. Speech ... against the Admission of Kansas under the Lecompton Constitution. Delivered in the Senate ... March 22, 1858. *Washington.* 1858. 8vo, pp. 29. H.—Speech ... on the Pacific Railroad Bill, April 17, 1858.—Speech ... in the Senate ... February 23, 1859, in reply to Hon. A. G. Brown, of Mississippi, With an Appendix. *Washington: Printed by L. Towers.* 1859. 8vo, pp. 32.—Speeches ... on the occasion of his Public Receptions By the Citizens of New Orleans, Philadelphia and Baltimore. *Washington: Printed by L. Towers.* 1859. 8vo, pp. 16.—State of the Union. Speech ... in the Senate, January 3, 1861. [n. p. n. d.] 8vo, pp. 15. H.

DOUGLAS. The Life of Stephen A. Douglas ... with Selections from his Speeches and Reports. By a Member of the Western Bar. *New York: Derby & Jackson.* 1860. 8vo, pp. 264. + *New York.* 1860. 12mo, pp. 451. C. 29694

DOUGLAS. Life of Stephen A. Douglas, U. S. Senator from Illinois. *Baltimore: John P. Des Forges.* 1860. 12mo, pp. 12.

DOUGLAS. Addresses on the Death of Hon. Stephen A. Douglas. Delivered in the Senate and House of Representatives on Tuesday, July 9, 1861. *Washington.* 1861. pp. 92.

The following relate to Douglas: Biographical Sketch of Stephen A. Douglas. *Washington.* [n. d.] 8vo, pp. 8.—Douglas' Doctrine of Popular Sovereignty in the Territories; its counterpart. By a Missourian. *St. Louis: printed by R. V. Kennedy & Company.* 1860. 8vo, pp. 42. H.—Mr. Douglas and the Doctrine of Coercion; together with Letters from Hon. Herschell V. Johnson ... and Hon. J. K. Paulding. ... [n. p. n. d.] 8vo, pp. 24.—Organization, Constitution and By-Laws of the Douglas Monument Association; together with an Appeal to the Public. *Chicago.* 1862. 8vo, pp. 19. H.—Political Record of Stephen A. Douglas on the Slavery Question. A Tract issued by the Illinois Republican State Central Committee. [n. p. n. d.] 8vo, pp. 16. + Third Edition, Revised and Enlarged. [*Albany.* 1860.] 8vo, pp. 15.—Record of Hon. Stephen A. Douglas on the Tariff. Compiled from the Official Records of Congress, for the Peoples' State Committee of Pennsylvania. 8vo, pp. 7.—Remarks on Popular Sovereignty as Maintained and Denied respectively by Judge Douglas and Attorney-General Black. By a Southern Citizen. *Baltimore: Murphy & Co.* 1859. 8vo, pp. 40.—"See, the Conquering Hero comes." Principles of Stephen A. Douglas illustrated in his Speeches. [n. p. n. d.] 8vo, pp. 16.

[DOUGLAS (Thomas).] The Communications of "Mercator," upon the Contest between the Earl of Selkirk, and the Hudson's Bay Company, on one side, and the North-West Company on the other. Republished from the Montreal Herald. *Montreal.* 1817. 8vo, pp. 100. 20697

[DOUGLAS.] Letter to the Earl of Liverpool from the Earl of Selkirk;—accompanied by a Correspondence with the Colonial Department (in the years 1817, 1818 and 1819,) on the subject of the Red River Settlement in North America. [*London.*] 1819. 8vo, pp. 224. 20698

Printed for private distribution only.

[DOUGLAS.] A Narrative of Occurrences in the Indian Countries of North America, since the Connexion of the Right Hon. the Earl of Selkirk with the Hudson's Bay Company, and his attempt to establish a Colony on the Red River; with a Detailed Account of his Lordship's Military Expedition to, and Subsequent Proceedings at Fort William, in Upper Canada. *London: T. Edgerton* [etc.] 1817. 8vo, pp. xiv, 152, 87. H.

Reprinted at *Montreal,* 1818. 8vo. *See* "M. Rev.," LXXXIV. 443.

[DOUGLAS.] Précis touchant la Colonie du Lord Selkirk, sur la Rivière Rouge; sa destruction en 1815 et 1816, et le massacre du Gouverneur Semple et de son parti. Avec des Observations

sur un ouvrage publié récemment, et intitulé "A Narrative of Occurrences in the Indian Countries," &c. ... De l'ouvrage anglais, publié à Londres en 1817. *Montreal.* 1818. 8vo, pp. viii, 226, lxxxvii. S. 20700

[DOUGLAS.] Report of the Proceedings connected with the Disputes between the Earl of Selkirk and the North-West Company, at the Assizes held at York, in Upper Canada, Oct. 1818. From Minutes taken in the Court. *Montreal.* 1819. 8vo, pp. 404. + *London: McMillan.* 1819. 8vo, pp. 478.

[DOUGLAS.] A Sketch of the British Fur Trade in North America; with Observations relative to the North-West Company of Montreal. By the Earl of Selkirk. Second Edition. *London: James Ridgway.* 1816. 8vo, 3 l., pp. 130. H. 20702

[DOUGLAS.] Statement Respecting The Earl of Selkirk's Settlement of Kildonan, Upon the Red River, In North America; Its Destruction In the Years 1815 and 1816; And the Massacre of Governor Semple and his Party. *London.* [1817.] 8vo, Title, pp. 125, lxxxix. Map. 20703

A note at the beginning is dated January, 1817. It is the work referred to in a postscript to the "Narrative," No. 20699, as having made its appearance in the circle of Lord Selkirk's friends. Rich had a copy with a manuscript note, signed J. Halkett, from which it would appear that he was the author of it. The following is a much enlarged edition of the same:

[DOUGLAS.] Statement respecting The Earl of Selkirk's Settlement upon the Red River in North America; its Destruction in 1815 and 1816; and the Massacre of Governor Semple and his Party. With Observations upon a Recent Publication, Entitled "A Narrative of Occurrences in the Indian Countries," &c. *London: John Murray.* 1817. 8vo, pp. viii, 194, C. Map. H., P. + *New York.* 1818. 8vo. S. 20704

The preface, dated June, 1817, says, "the statement contained in the following sheets was, some time ago, printed, and circulated among Lord Selkirk's personal friends, and some other individuals to whom it was thought proper to communicate the facts which it contained." Also: Observations on the present state of the Highlands of Scotland, with a view of the Causes and Probable Consequences of Emigration. By the Earl of Selkirk. *London: Longman.* 1805. 8vo, pp. vii, 223, lvi. C.—Eight Letters: on the Subject of the Earl of Selkirk's Pamphlet on Highland Emigration; as they lately appeared under the signature of Americus, in one of the Edinburgh Newspapers, with Supplementary Remarks. *London: Longman.* 8vo.

DOUGLAS. *See* Macdonald (John), and Strachan (John).

DOUGLAS (T.) Autobiography of Thomas Douglas, late Judge in Florida. *New York.* 1856. 12mo. Portrait. 20705

100 copies printed for the family.

DOUGLAS. Washington a Free Mason. An Address ... Before ... [the] Ancient Free Masons of ... Florida, At St. Augustine, Florida, ... November 4th, ... By Thomas Douglas, ... *Tallahassee.* 1853. 8vo, pp. 37. H. 20706

DOUGLASS (D. B.) Statement of Facts and Circumstances connected with the Removal of the Author from the Presidency of Kenyon College. By D. B. Douglass. 1844. 8vo, pp. 37.

DOUGLASS. Further Statement of Facts and Circumstances connected with the Removal of the Author from the Presidency of Kenyon College, in Answer to "The Reply of Trustees," etc. By D. B. Douglass, LL.D. *Albany: Erastus H. Pease.* 1845. 8vo, pp. 71. B. 20708

See "Kenyon College."

DOUGLASS (F.) The Anti-Slavery Movement. A Lecture by Frederick Douglass, ... *Rochester: Lee, Mann & Co.* 1855. 8vo, pp. 44. H. 20709

DOUGLASS. The Constitution of the United States: is it Pro-Slavery or Anti-Slavery? By Frederick Douglass. A Speech delivered in Glasgow, March 26, 1860 ... . *Halifax: T. and W. Birtwhistle, Printers.* [n. d.] 16mo, pp. 16. H. 20710

DOUGLASS. Narrative of the Life of Frederick Douglass, An American Slave. Written by Himself. *Boston.* 1845. 12mo, pp. 125. Portrait. + Second Edition. [*Ibid.*] 1846. + Third Edition. 1847. 12mo, pp. 190. H. 20711

The preface is by W. L. Garrison.

DOUGLASS. Vie de Frederick Douglass Esclave Américain, écrite par lui-même ... . *Paris: Pagnerre.* 1848. 16mo, pp. 196. H. 20712

DOUGLASS. Levensverhaal van Frederik Douglass, een' gewezen' slaaf, door hem zelven beschreven. Uit het Engelsch. *Rotterdam: H. A. Kramers.* 1846. 8vo. Portrait. 20713

DOUGLASS. My Bondage and My Freedom. Part I.—Life as a Slave. Part II.—Life as a Freeman. By Frederick Douglass. With an Introduction. By Dr. James M'Cune Smith. ... *New York and Auburn: Miller, Orton & Mulligan.* 1855. + 1856. 12mo, pp. 464. Portrait. H. 20714

DOUGLASS. Sclaverei und Freiheit. Autobiographie von Frederick Douglass. ... *Hamburg.* 1860. 16mo, pp. xiv, 366. H.

DOUGLASS. American Slavery. Report of a Public Meeting held at Finsbury Chapel, Moorfields, to receive Frederick Douglass, the American Slave ... May 22, 1846. ... *London.* 1846. 8vo, pp. 24. H. 20716

Also: Eulogy on the late Hon. William Jay ... delivered on the Invitation of the Colored Citizens of New York, May 12, 1859. *Rochester: A. Strong & Co.* 1859. 8vo, pp. 32. H.—Oration, delivered in ... at Rochester, July 5, 1852. ... *Rochester.* 1852. 8vo, pp. 39.—The Slave's Appeal to Great Britain. ... [n. p. n. d.] No paging. H.—Two Speeches, ... one on West India Emancipation, ... at Canandaigua, Aug. 4th, and the other on the Dred Scott Decision, delivered in New York, on the ... May, 1857. *Rochester, N. Y.: C. P. Deway.* [1857.] 8vo, pp. 46.

DOUGLASS, *and others.* Arguments, Pro and Con, on the call for a National Emigration Convention, to be held in Cleveland, Ohio, August, 1854. By Frederick Douglass, W. J. Watkins, & J. M. Whitfield. With a Short Appendix of the Statistics of Canada West, West Indies, Central and South America, By M. T. Newsom. [n. p. n. d.] 8vo, pp. 34. 20717

DOUGLASS (J. H.) Report on Operations during and after the Battles at Gettysburg, July, 1863. By J. H. Douglass, M.D. *New York.* 1863. 8vo, pp. 29. 20718

Also: Letter from J. H. Douglass, Associate Secretary, giving some idea of the extent of our Operation and Plans to be pursued. December 8, 1862.—Sanitary Commission, No. 57. Reports on the Operations and Relief Agents of the Sanitary Commission, After the Battle of Fredericksburg, December 13, 1862. By J. H. Douglass, M.D., & C. W. Brink, M.D. *New York.* 1863. 8vo, pp. 31.

DOUGLASS (M.) The Personal Narrative of Mrs. Margaret Douglass, imprisoned in Norfolk for the crime of teaching Free Colored Children to Read. *Boston.* 1854. 8vo, pp. 65. B., P.

[DOUGLASS (W.)] The Abuses and Scandal of some late Pamphlets in favour of Inoculation of the Small-pox, as practised in Boston. Letter to A— S—, M.D. & F.R.S. *Boston.* 1722. 8vo, pp. 20. M. 20720

[DOUGLASS.] A Discourse Concerning the Currencies of the British Plantations in America. Especially with Regard to their Paper Money; More Particularly, In Relation to the Province of the Massachusetts-Bay, in New England. *London: T. Cooper.* [1739.] 8vo, pp. 54. + *Boston: ... S. Kneeland & T. Green.* ... 1740. 8vo, pp. 47. + (With a Postscript thereto.) *London: Reprinted.* 1751. 8vo, pp. 40–62. J.C.B. + *London.* 1857. 8vo. BA., C. 20721

"The many schemes," says the author, "at present upon the Anvil in Boston, for emitting enormous quantities of Paper Money, are the occasion of this discourse. ... It

was always my opinion that the Province of the Massachusetts Bay, is by far the most vigorous and promising plant (with proper cultivation) of all the British Plantations." Highly eulogized by McCulloch in his "Literature of Political Economy." For observations on the above, *see* S. (W.)

[DOUGLASS.] A Dissertation concerning Inoculation of the Small-pox. *Boston.* 1730. 8vo, pp. 28. M. 20722

[DOUGLASS.] An Essay, Concerning Silver and Paper Currencies; More especially with Regard to the British Colonies in New England. *Boston: Printed by S. Kneeland and T. Green.* [n. d.] 8vo, Title, pp. 23. BA. 20723

DOUGLASS. The Practical History of A New Epidemic Eruptive Miliary Fever, with an Angina Ulcusculosa, Which Prevailed in Boston, New England, in the Years 1735 and 1736. By William Douglass, M.D. *Boston: Printed by Thomas Fleet.* 1736. 8vo, Title, pp. ii, 18. BA. 20724

Also: A Practical Essay Concerning the Small-pox. *Boston.* 1730. 8vo, pp. 38. These medical treatises are among the earliest on the subject published in the colonies. The following tract bears on this question: A Friendly Debate; or, a Dialogue between Academicus and Sawney, [W. Douglass, M.D.] and Mundungus, two eminent Physicians, about some of their Performances. *Boston.* 1722. 8vo.

[DOUGLASS.] Some Observations on the Scheme projected for emitting 60000*l.* in Bills of a New Tenour, to be redeemed with Silver and Gold. Shewing the Various Operations of these Bills, and their Tendency to hurt the Publick Interest. In a Letter from a Merchant in Boston, to his Friend in the Country. *Boston: Printed by S. Kneeland and T. Green.* MDCCXXXVIII. 8vo, Title, pp. 25. BA. 20725

DOUGLASS. A Summary, Historical and Political, Of the first Planting, progressive Improvements, and present State of the British Settlements in North-America. Containing I. Some general Account of ancient and modern Colonies, the granting and settling of the British Continent and West-India Island Colonies, with some transient Remarks concerning the adjoining French and Spanish Settlements, and other Remarks of various Natures. II. The Hudson's-Bay Company's Lodges, Fur and Skin Trade. III. Newfoundland Harbours and Cod-Fishery. IV. The Province of L'Accadie or Nova-Scotia; with the Vicissitudes of the Property and Jurisdiction thereof, and its present State. V. The several Grants of Sagadahock, Province of Main, Massachusett's-Bay, and New-Plymouth, united by a new Charter in the present Province of Massachusett's-Bay, commonly called New-England. By William Douglass, M.D. Vol. I. ... *Boston, New-England: by Rogers and Fowle.* MD,-CC,XLIX. 8vo, pp. iii, (3), 568. + Vol. II. 1751. 8vo, 2 l., pp. 416. H. 20726

This work was originally printed in numbers, as by W. D., M.D., the first of which appeared in 1747. The first volume was finished in 1749, the second in 1751. The death of the author, in October, 1752, prevented the completion of the work. There are some copies of Vol. II. [With Appendix "to render this work more compleat, from Salmon's Geographical and Historical Grammar," 1751.] *Boston: D. Fowle.* 1753. 8vo, 2 l., pp. 440. C.

DOUGLASS. A Summary, [&c., as before]. *Boston: New-England, Printed: London, re-printed for R. Baldwin.* M.DCC.LV. 2 vols., 8vo, 3 l., pp. iv, 568, Map; 3 l., pp. 416. C. 20727

An exact reprint of the Boston edition of 1749, with the addition of a map. Although at the end of the contents of Vol. I. there is "Place the Map to face the Title of Vol. I.," no copy has yet been found, in its original state, with the map.

DOUGLASS. A Summary, [&c., as before]. *London: R. and J. Dodsley.* MDCCLX. 2 vols., 8vo, 3 l., pp. iv, 568; 3 l., pp. 416, 3 l. Map. 20728

A reprint of the edition of 1745, almost page for page, with a few alterations and corrections. At the heads of each page are placed the parts and sections. The work is authentic and valuable, and should find its place in every American library. Adam Smith characterizes the author as "The honest and downright Dr. Douglass." *See also* Bancroft, IV. 58.

DOUGLASS (William). The Heresy of Secession. Speech delivered at Booneville, Missouri, May 7, 1862. *St. Louis: George Knapp & Co.* 1862. 8vo, pp. 16. 20729

Report of the Trustees of the Douglass Houghton Mining Company, to the Stockholders. *Detroit: printed by Charles Willcox.* 1847. 8vo, pp. 38. H. 20730

DOUIN DE LA MOTTE (*M.*) Mémoire Apologetique, de M. Douin De la Motte, Chevalier, Capitaine d'une Compagnie détacheé de la Marine, Au Cap, Ile St. Domingue: Contenant, Ses Griefs contre Monsieur le Comte d'Estaing, Commandeur des Ordres du Roy très Chretien, et representant sa Personne a St. Domingue, Et Les Raisons qui le forçent a venir chercher un Azile dans les Etats du Roy d'Angleterre. *A Charleston: de l'Imprimerie de Pierre Timothee.* M,DCC,LXV. 4to, pp. 21. P.

A very rare piece. An English translation accompanies the work.

DOUSSEAU (Alphonse). Christophe Colomb. *Le Havre: Lepelletier.* 1870. 8vo, pp. 147. 20732

DOUTRE (Joseph). Le Concours Boucherville. 1851.

DOUTRE. Les Finances de 1812. *Montreal.* 1844. 8vo, pp. 500. 20734

DOUTRE. Les Sauvages des Canada. 1852. 20735

DOUUILY (*Baron*). *See* Gerbier (Balthazar).

DOUVILLE (Jean Baptiste). Trente mois de ma vie, quinze mois avant et quinze mois après mon voyage du Congo, ou ma justification des infamies débitées contre moi; Suivis de détails curieux sur les mœurs et les usages des habitants du Brésil et de Buénos-Ayres, et d'une description de la colonie patagonide. *Paris: l'auteur; Dentu; Delaunay; Treuttel et Wurtz; Paulin; Béchet.* 1833. 8vo. 20736

DOUVILLE. Fin de la monarchie en Amérique. *Paris: Sautelet: Dentu;* [etc.] 1826. 8vo, pp. 72. 20737

DOVE (J.) A Biographical History of the Wesley Family. By John Dove. *London.* 1833. 12mo. 20738

DOVE. A History of the Most Worshipful Grand Lodge of Virginia: its Origin, Progress, and Mode of Development. By John Dove. *[Richmond?] Clemmitt & Fore.* 1855. 12mo, pp. 178. 20739

DOVE. The Virginia Text-Book: containing a History of Masonic Grand Lodges, ... By John Dove. Third Edition. *Richmond: J. E. Goode, Printer.* 186–. 12mo, pp. 380. Portrait. 20740

DOVER, *Del.* Dover, January 1. 1771. Dover Land and Cash Lottery, &c. *[Philadelphia.* 1771.] p. 1. P. 20741

DOVER, *N. H.* Articles of Confession, and Covenant, and other Documents of the First Church in Dover, 1835. *Dover, N. H.* 1835. 12mo, pp. 21. 20742

A Bill of Mortality for the Society of Friends, in Dover, N. H., from 1708 to 1791. Also a General Bill of Mortality for Dover, N. H. (1767–1802.) *[Dover, N. H.:] Printed by James K. Remich.* 1803. 4to, pp. 25. BA., M. 20743

89th Anniversary of the National Independence, July 4, 1865, at Dover, N. H. Full Report of the Celebration ... Oration by Hon. James W. Patterson ... . *Dover, N. H.: B. Barnes, Jr.* 1865. 8vo, pp. 36. H. 20744

The Dover and Great Falls Directory; with the Salmon Falls Directory, Business Directories, etc. By Dean Dudley. *Dover: D. Lothrop & Co.* 1867. 8vo, pp. 115, 32. 20745

Also: Mayor's Address, and Annual Report of the Receipts and Expenditures, Report of Departments, etc., for the Municipal Year 1868. *Dover, N. H.: Libbey & Co., Printers.* 1869. 12mo, pp. 70. H. — Report of the Public Schools in the Town of Dover, for the Year 1865–6. [n. p. n. d.] 8vo, pp. 8. H. — Report of the Receipts and Expenditures of the Town of Dover, for the Year ending Feb. 16th, 1866. [n. p. n. d.] 8vo, pp. 8. H.

DOW (D.) ... A Sermon preached before His Excellency Oliver Wolcott, ... at the General Election, May 4, 1825. By Daniel Dow, ... *Hartford: Charles Babcock, Printer.* 1825. 8vo, pp. 18. 20746

Also: A Discourse delivered in Chepachet, R. I., December 5, 1830. Before the Glocester Temperance Association. ... *Providence: H. H. Brown.* 1831. 12mo, pp. 24. — New Haven Theology, alias Taylorism, alias Neology; in its own Language, with Notes appended. ... *Thompson: printed by George Roberts.* 1834. 8vo, pp. 66.

DOW (J.) Bill of Mortality for Kensington, N. H., Compiled chiefly from the Record of the late Rev. Jeremiah Fogg. By Jabez Dow. *Printed at Dover, N. H.* 1802. pp. 18.

DOW (J. W.) Sermon at Tyringham, [Mass.] July 10, 1831, at the Twentieth Anniversary of his Ordination. By J. Warren Dow. *Lenox.* 1831. W. 20748

DOW (J.) Discourse delivered July 4, 1806, at Belleville. By John Dow. *Newark, N. J.* 1806. 8vo. 20749

DOW (J.) An Historical Address, delivered at Hampton, New Hampshire, on the 25th of December, 1838, In Commemoration of the Settlement of that Town. Two Hundred Years having elapsed since that event. By Joseph Dow, A.M. *Concord: Asa McFarland.* M,DCCC,XXXIX. 8vo, pp. 44. 20750

DOW (Lorenzo). Analectic History touching Nullification, Northern and Southern. The Last Warning. *Washington.* 1834. 8vo. N. 20751

DOW. The Dealings of God, Man, and the Devil; as exemplified in the Life, Experience, and Travels of Lorenzo Dow, in a period of over half a century, together with his Polemic and Miscellaneous Writings. Fourth Edition. *Norwich, (Ct.:) William Faulkner.* 1833. 12mo, pp. 704. C. + To which is added The Vicissitudes of Life, by Peggy Dow. *New York.* 1854. 8vo, pp. 352. + With an Introductory Essay. By the Rev. John Dowling, D.D. *New York.* 1856. 8vo, pp. 613.

DOW. History of Cosmopolite; or, Lorenzo's Journal, containing his Experience and Travels to 1814. *New York: John G. Totten.* 1814. 16mo, pp. 360. Plate. + *Philadelphia.* 1816. 12mo. + Fifth Edition. *Wheeling, Va.: Joshua Martin.* 1848. 8vo, pp. 720. + *Pittsburgh.* 1849. 8vo, pp. 725. + *Cincinnati.* 1851. 8vo, pp. 720. + *Philadelphia: Jas. B. Smith & Co.* 1859. 8vo, pp. 720. H. + *Cincinnati.* 1859. 8vo. C.

DOW. The Life and Travels of Lorenzo Dow, written by himself. *Hartford.* 1804. 12mo. M. 20754

DOW. Perambulations of a Cosmopolite; or, Travels and Labors in Europe and America. [With his other works. Edited] by Orrin Scofield. *Rochester: O. Scofield.* 1842. 8vo, pp. 421. Portrait. C. + *New York.* 1855. 8vo. C. 20755

DOW. The Stranger in Charleston, or the Trial and Confession of Lorenzo Dow, addressed to the United States in general, and South Carolina in particular. *Philadelphia.* 1822. 12mo. P. + Second Edition. *Philadelphia.* 1822. 12mo.

DOW. The Travels and Providential Experience of Lorenzo Dow; written by himself: with an Appendix, containing Credentials, &c. Second Edition. *Liverpool: printed by H. Forshaw.* 1806. 12mo, pp. 240. 20757

The author, a native of Connecticut, was an itinerant Methodist preacher, who, in the exercise of his vocation, travelled through most of the United States. Also: All the Polemical Works of Lorenzo Dow. ... *New York.* 1814. 12mo, pp. 300. — A Chain, with its Concomitants; or, Polemical Reflections. *New York.* 1807. 12mo, pp. 81. B. + *Poughkeepsie.* 1809. 12mo, pp. 81. — [Dow.] A Cry from the Wilderness, &c. By Cosmopolite. *United States.* 1830. 12mo, pp. 70. — [Dow.] A Cry from the Wilderness. A Voice from the East. A Reply from the West. Trouble from the North, Exemplified in the South. Intended as a ... warning to the People of the United States. By Cosmopolite, &c. *United States.* 1837. 32mo, pp. 167. — Extracts from Original Letters, to the Methodist Bishops, mostly from their Preachers and Members, in North America. *Liverpool.* 1806. 8vo. — A Hint to the Public, or Thoughts on the Fulfillment of Prophecy. [n. p. n. d.] 12mo, pp. 22. H. (References to America and American History.) — A Journey from Babylon to Jerusalem ... with an Essay on the Rights of Man. *Lansingburgh.* 1812. 12mo, pp. 149. — [Dow.] Lorenzo's Thoughts on various Religious Opinions. *Newbern, N. C.* 1806. 12mo, pp. 84. — The Opinion of Dow; or, Lorenzo's Thoughts. ... in an Address to the People of New England. *Windham.* 1804. 16mo, pp. 162. — Quintessence of Lorenzo's Works, ... or the Four Volumes of Lorenzo's Journal concentrated in one ... *Philadelphia.* 1815. 8vo, pp. 554. — A Short Account of a Long Travel; with Beauties of Wesley. By Lorenzo Dow. *Philadelphia.* 1823. 8vo, pp. 59. P. — Travels and Labors of Lorenzo Dow in Europe and America, with an account of his Life and Christian Experience, his Chain, Journey from Babylon, Dialogues, and Hints on Prophecy, to which is Added Peggy Dow's Vicissitudes, or the Journey of Life. *Rochester.* 1842. 8vo, pp. 507.

DOW (M.) A Sermon preached in Beverly, August 20, 1812, the Day of the National Fast, on Account of War with Great-Britain; and again at ... Salem, April 8, 1813, the Day of the Annual Fast in Massachusetts. By Moses Dow, A.M. *Salem: printed by Joshua Cushing.* 1813. 8vo, pp. 16. H., M., N.

DOW (P. *or* M.) Vicissitudes in the Wilderness, exemplified in the Journal of Peggy Dow. Fifth Edition. *Norwich, Conn.* 1833. 12mo. 20759

DOW (*Jr.*), *pseudonym.* Short Patent Sermons, by "Dow, Jr.," Originally published in the New York Sunday Mercury. Revised and Corrected. *New York.* 1841. 8vo. 20760

On topics of the day.

DOWDALL (*Commander* P. S.) Narrative of the Loss of the Brig Charles, on her Passage from Liverpool to Newfoundland, and Miraculous Delivery of the Master and two of the Crew in an open boat. *Liverpool.* [1812.] 8vo. 20761

DOWDELL (J. F.) The Kansas Issue. Remarks of Hon. James F. Dowdell, of Alabama, advocating the necessity of additional Guarantees for the Protection of Southern Rights. [n. p. n. d.] 8vo, pp. 7. H. 20762

DOWE (William). Junius — Lord Chatham; a Biography, setting forth the Condition of English Politics preceding and Contemporary with the Revolutionary Junian Period. *York.* 1857. 8vo. C. 20763

DOWLER (B.) Researches upon the Vital Dynamics of Civil Government. By Bennett Dowler, M.D. *New Orleans.* 1849. 8vo, pp. 29. 20764

DOWLER. Tableaux, Geographical, Commercial, Geological, and Sanitary, of New Orleans. By Bennett Dowler, M.D. *New Orleans: Daily Delta Office.* [1853?] 8vo, pp. 40. C. 20765

Also: History of the Gigantic Headed Boy of Georgia. ... *New Orleans.* 1857. 8vo, pp. 8. — A Question of Originality settled ... *New Orleans: printed by Joseph Cohn.* 1846. 8vo, pp. 8. H. (Slight reference to American literature.)

DOWLEY. History and Honorary Roll of the Twelfth Regiment Infantry, N. G. S. N. Y. By Dowley. *New York.* 1870. 12mo, pp. 216. 20766

[DOWNER (Silas).] A Discourse delivered in Providence, in the Colony of Rhode Island, on the 25th day of July, 1768, at

the Dedication of the Tree of Liberty, from the Summer-House in the Tree. By a Son of Liberty. *Providence: John Waterman.* MDCCLXVIII. 8vo, pp. 16. 20767

For an account of this event, *see* the "Providence Gazette," July 30, 1768. Reprinted in J. R. Bartlett's "Catalogue of Mr. J. C. Brown's Library." *See also* Bartlett's "Bibl. of Rhode Island," and Staple's "Annals of Providence," 221.

DOWNES (B.) Brief and Remarkable Narrative of the Life and Extreme Sufferings of Barnabas Downes, particularly in the Brig Arnold, which was cast away near Plymouth 26 Dec. 1778, [when abovt 50 men were frozen to death. *Boston.*] 1786. 12mo. W. 20768

DOWNES (J.) United States Almanack, or complete Ephemeris for 1843. By John Downes. *Philadelphia.* 12mo. Continued to 1845 or later. B. 20769

DOWNEY (Stephen W.) Play of Destiny, as Played by Actors from the Kingdom of the Dead in the Theatre of the Universe. *New Creek, (W. Va.)* 1867. 8vo, pp. 76. 20770

The Downfall of Despotism ... showing ... the Invasion of Britain and the Reign of Liberty in the New World. *London: James Nisbet & Co.* 1853. 8vo, pp. 32. S. 20771

DOWNING (Andrew Jackson). The Architecture of Country Houses; including Designs for Cottages, Farm Houses, and Villas, with Remarks on Interiors, Furniture, and the Best Modes of Warming and Ventilating. ... By J. A. Downing ... . *New York.* 1850. 8vo. + Thirteenth Thousand. *New York: D. Appleton & Co.* M.DCCC.LIV. 8vo, pp. x, (1), 484. 1 Plate and 320 Woodcuts. BA. 20772

DOWNING. Cottage Residences; or, a Series of Designs for Rural Cottages, and Cottage-Villas, adapted to North America. By A. J. Downing. ... . *New-York and London: Wiley and Putnam.* 1842. 8vo, 2 l., pp. 187. Woodcuts. BA. + Second Edition. *New York.* 1844. + Third Edition. *New York and London.* 1847. 8vo. + *New York.* 1852. 8vo, pp. 215.

DOWNING. The Fruits and Fruit Trees of America: or, the Culture, Propagation, and Management, in the Garden and Orchard, of Fruit Trees generally: with Descriptions of all the Finest Varieties of Fruit, Native and Foreign, cultivated in this Country. By A. J. Downing. ... *New York and London: Wiley and Putnam.* 1845. 12mo, pp. xiv, 594. Woodcuts. BA. +

Eleventh Edition, Revised. *New York.* 1849. 12mo, pp. 594. + *New York.* 1850. 8vo. H. + Revised and Corrected by Charles Downing. *New York: John Wiley.* 1857. 12mo, pp. xx, 760. + *New York. [Ibid.]* 1860. + *New York.* 1864. 8vo, pp. xx, 760. + Second Edition, Revised and Enlarged by C. Downing. *New York: J. Wiley & Son.* 1869. 8vo, pp. xxiv, 1098. 20774

Some copies were printed on large paper, with the plates colored.

DOWNING. Rural Essays. By A. J. Downing. Edited, with a Memoir of the Author, by George W. Curtis; and a Letter to his Friends by Frederika Bremer. *New York.* 1853. + *New York: Leavitt and Allen.* 1854. 8vo, pp. lxxi, 557. Woodcuts. BA. + *New York.* 1856. 8vo, pp. 646. 20775

DOWNING. A Treatise on the Theory and Practice of Landscape Gardening, adapted to North America ... . By A. J. Downing. *New-York & London: Wiley and Putnam.* 1841. 8vo, 2 l., pp. 451, (1). BA. + Second Edition, enlarged, revised, and newly illustrated. ... *[Ibid.]* 1844. 8vo, pp. xiv, 9–497. Plate and Woodcuts. BA. + *New York: Saxton & Co.* 1853. 8vo, pp. 532. + 1855. + Sixth Edition, enlarged, revised, and newly illustrated. With a Supplement ... by Henry Winthrop Sargent. *New York: A. O. Moore & Co.* 1859. 8vo, pp. 576. Portrait, Woodcuts, and 6 Plates. BA.

DOWNING (Clement). A Compendious History of the Indian Wars, with the Rise, Progress, Strength and Forces of Angria the Pyrate. Also an Account of John Plantain, a notorious Pirate of Madagascar, &c. *London: T. Cooper.* 1737. Sm. 8vo, pp. iv, 238. C. 20777

DOWNING (Elizabeth [Hedding]). Remains of Rev. Joshua Wells Downing, A.M. ... . With a Brief Memoir. ... Edited by Elijah H. Downing, A.M. *New York: G. Lane & P. P. Sanford.* 1842. 12mo, pp. 329. H. 20778

DOWNING (G.) A | Discourse | Written by | Sir George Downing, | The King of Great Britain's Envoy | Extraordinary to the States of the | Vnited Provinces. | Vindicating his Royal Master from the | Insolencies of a Scandalous Libel, Printed | under the Title of [An Extract out of the | Regicter [*sic*] of the States General of the Vnited | Provinces, upon the Memorial of Sir George | Downing, Envoy, &c.] And delivered by | the Agent De Heyde for such, to several | Publick Ministers. | Whereas no

such Resolution was ever | Communicated to the said Envoy, nor any | Answer returned at all by their Lordships to | the said Memorial. | Whereunto is added a Relation of some | Former and Later Proceedings of the | Hollanders: By a Meaner Hand. | *London, Printed for Dorman Newman, | and John Luttone, at the Kings Arms and | Blew-Anchor in the Poultrey,* 1672. | 12mo, Title, pp. 171. B. 20779

Relates in part to the Dutch West India Company and the New Netherlands, as do all the following:

DOWNING. Twee Memorien van den Heere Downing ... overgegeven aan de Stat.-Gen. ... 3 ende 8 aug. 1661. 4to.

In French and Dutch.

DOWNING. Toestant der swevende verschillen tusschen de Oost- ende West-Indische Compagnien van Engelant, ende van de Vereenighde Nederlanden. [n. p.] 1664. 4to. 20781

DOWNING. Memorie | Vande Heere | Gorge [*sic*] Downing | Extraordinaris Afgesante van Syne Majesteyt | van Groot Britannien, &c. | Overgegeven aen de | Heeren Staten Generael | Der Vereenichde Nederlanden, | den 30. decembre 1664. | [n. p. n. d.] 4to, pp. 11. J.C.BR. 20782

DOWNING. Remarques | succinctes et | Deduction | faites | Par les Deputés des Hauts & Puissants | Seigneurs Estats Generaux | des Provinces Unies des Païs-Bas. | sur le dernier | Memoire | du Sieur George Downing | Envoyé Extraordinaire du Roy de la Grand | Bretagne. | *A la Haye,* | *Au Mois de Feurier* 1665. | 4to, pp. 40. 20783

A work of much interest in relation to the history of New Netherland. This French edition is very rare.

DOWNING. Sommiere | Aenteyckeninge | ende | Deductie | Ingestelt | by de Gedeputeerden vande Hooge Mogende | Heeren Staten Generael | der Vereenighde Nederlanden | Op de lest ingediende | Memorie | van den Heere George Downing, Extra | Ordinaris Envoyé vanden | Coningh | van | Groot Brittannien. | *In's Graven-hage In de maent Februarij* 1665. | 4to, pp. 38, ii. + [Another Edition.] *In's Gravenhage.* CIƆIƆLXV. 4to, pp 29, (iii). + [A Third Edition.] *In's Gravenhage.* 1665. 4to, pp. 24. + [A Fourth Edition. *Ibid.*] 1665. 4to, pp. 29, ii + [A Fifth Edition. *Ibid.*] 1665. 4to, pp. 38, iv. + [A Sixth Edition. *Ibid.*] 1665. 4to, pp. 38, iv. 20784

For the titles at length, *see* Asher, Nos. 346–350.

Downing. Remarques|plus particulieres, ou|Replique|à la|Duplique,|Publiée par le Sieur Downing, envoyé extraordinaire du Roy|de la Grand Bretagne, contre les Remarques, que les Députés des Hauts|& Puissants Seigneurs Estats Generaux des Provinces Unies|ont faites sur le|Memoire|par luy presenté le 30 Decembre 1664.|*A la Haye|chez Hillebrandt de Wouw|Imprimeur ordinaire des Hauts et Puissants|Seigneurs Estats Generaux des Provinces Unies des Païs Bas. l'An* 1666.| 4to, pp. 200.

It was published also in Dutch, with the following title:

Downing. Verdere | Aenteyckeninge | of | Duplyque | op seeckere|Replyque | vanden Heer|George Downing,|Extraordinaris Envoyé vanden Koningh van Groot Brittangien,|jegens de Remarques vande gedeputeerden vande H: Mog: Heeren|Staten generael der vereenigde Nederlanden. Ingestelt op des selfs ingediende|Memori|vanden 30 December 1664.|*Nae de copie | van | Hillebrandt van Wouw, ordinaris Drucker vande Hoog Mog. Heeren Staten|Generael der Vereenighde Nederlanden, Anno* 1666.| 4to, pp. 176, iv. 20786

Asher describes a copy with two indexes, one at the beginning and another at the end of the book. Both the French and the Dutch editions can be considered as originals; for the deduction was written in French, the proofs were originally in Dutch. Priced, by Muller, at $50 and $60.

Downing. A|Reply|of|Sir George Downing|Knight and Baronet,|Envoy Extraordinary from His Majesty|of Great-Britain, &c.|To the|Remarks|of the|Deputies of the Estates-General,|upon his|Memorial|Of Decemder 20, 1644. Old Stile.|*London, Printed Anno Dom.* 1665.| 4to, Title, pp. 104.

A large part of this volume relates to the affairs of New Netherland, now New York. Sir George Downing was one of the earliest graduates of Harvard College, and founder of Downing College, Cambridge. Concerning whom, *see* John Adams' Works, x. 329; Pepey's "Mem.," i. 112, 252, 254; and Palfrey's "Hist. of New England," ii. 430–432.

[Downing (George T.)] To the Friends of Equal Rights in Rhode Island. [n. p. n. d.] 8vo, pp. 8. H. 20788

Downing (*Major* Jack). *See* [Davis (C. A.)], No. 18798, and [Smith (Seba)].

Downing (J. W.) Remains of the Rev. Joshua Wells Downing, with a Brief Memoir. Edited by Elijah Downing. *New York*. 1841. 12mo. 20789

[Downing (L.)] Some Reasons why the Pending Cherokee Treaty should be ratified. ... [Signed by Lewis Downing and five Others.] *Washington*. 1870. 8vo, pp. 20. H. 20790

Downs (S. W.) Biography of the Hon. Solomon W. Downs, of Louisiana. By a Louisianian. *Philadelphia*. 1852. 8vo, pp. 16. H. 20791

Also: Remarks ... on the Bill making a Grant of Public Lands to Iowa to aid in constructing certain Railroads. Delivered in the Senate, March 15, 1852. *Washington*. 1852. 8vo, pp. 8. — Speech ... on the Bill to establish a Territorial Government in Oregon. Delivered in the Senate ... June 3, 1848. *Washington*. 1848 8vo, pp. 8. — Speech ... on the War with Mexico. Delivered in the Senate ... Monday, January 31, 1848: with an Appendix ... *Washington*. 1848. 8vo, pp. 21. H. — Speech ... on the Compromise Resolutions of Mr. Clay. In Senate, February 18 and 19, 1850. 8vo, pp. 24. H. — Speech ... on the Resolution submitted by Mr. Foote, of Mississippi ... . *Washington*. 1852. 8vo, pp. 24. H. In Lanman's "Dict. of Congress," and in the "American Almanac" for 1853, the middle initial is U.

Dowse (T.) The Will of Thomas Dowse, of Cambridgeport. Printed for the Executors. *Cambridge, Massachusetts, U. S. A.* M.DCCC.LVI. 8vo, pp. 7. 20792

Twenty-four copies printed. Mr. Dowse presented his library to the Massachusetts Historical Society.

Dowse. The Dowse Library. Proceedings of the Massa chusetts Historical Society, relating to the Donations from Thomas Dowse; with the Eulogy by Edward Everett. *Boston: Printed for Private Distribution*. 1859. 8vo, pp. v, 80. 3 Plates. 20793

Also: Description of the Dowse Library. 1857. 8vo. — Dowse Institute, Cambridge. Declaration of Trust, June 1, 1858. 1 sheet, folio. M. — Organization of the Dowse Institute. ... *Cambridge*. 1858. 8vo, pp. 9. Portrait.

Dox (H. L.) Christ the Foundation: a Synodical and Dedicatory Discourse, delivered at Gardnersville, Schoharie County, N. Y., June 7th, 1849. *Albany; J. Munsell*. 1849. 8vo, pp. 42. 20794

Dox (P. M.) Restoration of Georgia — The True Condition of the South — Universal Amnesty the Remedy. Speech of Hon. Peter M. Dox, of Alabama, in the House ... June 6, 1870. [n. p. n. d.] 8vo, pp. 8. H. 20795

Doy. The Narrative of John Doy, of Lawrence, Kansas. ... *New York: Thomas Holman, Printed for the Author*. 1860. 12mo, pp. 132. C. 20796

Doyle (J. A.) The American Colonies previous to the Declaration of Independence. By John Andrew Doyle, B.A. *London: Rivingtons*. 1869. 8vo, pp. 228. 20797

The Arnold Prize Essay, read in the theatre at Oxford, June 9, 1869.

Doyle (M.) Hints on Emigration to Upper Canada; especially addressed to the Middle and Lower Classes in Great Britain and Ireland. By Martin Doyle ... . Second Edition, enlarged. *William Curry, Jun., and Co., Dublin*. 1832. 12mo, pp. 92. + *Dublin*. [*Ibid.*] 1834. 20798

Doyle (T.), *pseudonym*. *See* [More (John J.)]

Doyle (W.) Some Account of the British Dominions beyond the Atlantic: containing chiefly What is most interesting and least known with respect to those parts; particularly The important Question about the North-West Passage, Is satisfactorily discussed: with a large Map; in which The said supposed Passage, and all the Arctic Regions, are more fully delineated than ever before. By William Doyle, LL.B. *London: W. Domville*. [1770.] 8vo, 2 l., xvi, 87, (2). Map. J.C.B. 20799

"The author proposes a new scheme of geography, calling South America 'Atlantis;' North America, 'Sebastia,' and classes the British Colonies under the names of 'Neanglia,' 'Jacobea,' and 'Mesia,' or 'Medensia.'" — *M. Rev.*, XLII. 413.

D'Oyley (D.) A Letter, addressed to his Excellency Charles Pinckney, by Daniel D'Oyley. [*Charleston*], *South Carolina*. [1807.] 8vo, pp. 31. BA. 20800

D'Oyley. An Oration delivered in St. Michael's Church ... Charleston, South-Carolina, On the Fourth of July, 1803; in Commemoration of American Independence: By Daniel D'Oyley, ... *Charleston, South Carolina: Printed by T. B. Bowen*. [n. d.] 8vo, Title, pp. 31. BA. 20801

Dozy *and* Molkenboer. Prodromus Florae Bryologicae Surinamensis. Accedit pug. specimina novae florae bryologicae Venezuelanae. *Harlemi*. 1854. 4to. 20802

Drack (F.) *See* Drake (F.)

Dracut. Report of the Selectmen of the Receipts and Expenditures of the Town of Dracut, [Mass.] for the Year ending February 21, 1866. *Lowell, Mass.* 1866. 8vo, pp. 9.

The Draft; or Conscription Reviewed by the People. *Providence: For the author*. 1863. 8vo, pp. 8. S. 20804

All about the Draft. How it will be made. Every Man's exact chance. The Quota for New York State. Exemptions. Physical Disabilities, etc. *New York: Sinclair Tousey*. 1862. 18mo, pp. 16. 20805

Draft|of a|Bill|For declaring the Intentions of the Parliament of|Great-Britain concerning the Exercises of the Right|of imposing Taxes within his Majesty's Colonies,|Provinces and Plantations in North America.| Folio, pp. 4. 20806

Dated at the end, "15th Day of April, 1778," and signed "William Tryon."

Draft of an Act to provide Internal Revenue to support the Government; with Remarks by the Boston Board of Trade. *Washington: H. Polkinhorn*. 1862. 8vo, pp. 45. B. 20807

[Drage (Theodore Swaine).] An Account of a Voyage For the Discovery of a North-West Passage by Hudson's Streights, to the Western and Southern Ocean of America. Performed in the Year 1746 and 1747, in the Ship California, Capt. Francis Smith, Commander. By the Clerk of the California. Adorned with Cuts and Maps. *London: Jonah Warens*. MDCCXLVIII–XLIX. 2 vols., 8vo, 2 l., pp. vii, 237; Title, 326, Index, 9 l. 5 Maps and 4 Plates. C., H. 20808

"A pedantic, disputatious and dogmatical performance." — Barrow's *Arctic Voyages*, 1815, p. 287.

Dragoon Campaigns to the Rocky Mountains, 1836. *See* [Hildreth (James)].

Dragoumis (N.), *Translator*. *See* Washington.

Drainesville. Letter from the Secretary of War, in Answer to a Resolution of the House of Representatives, transmitting Report of the Engagement at Drainesville. 8vo, pp. 22. (H. of Reps., Ex. Doc., No. 59, 37th Cong., 2d. Sess., 1862.)

Drake (B.) The Life and Adventures of Black Hawk: with Sketches of Keokuk, the Sac and Fox Indians, and the late Black Hawk War. By Benjamin Drake. *Cincinnati*. 1838. 12mo, pp. 288. Woodcut Portrait. + *Cincinnati*. 1839. C. + Sixth Edition, Improved. *Cincinnati*. 1841. 12mo. + *Cincinnati*. 1842. 12mo. + *Cincinnati*. 1844. 12mo. + Seventh Edition, Improved. *Cincinnati: George Conclin*. 1850. 12mo, pp. 284. + *Cincinnati: H. S. & J. Applegate & Co.* 1851. 12mo, pp. 288. + *Cincinnati*. 1855. 12mo, pp. 288. + *Cincinnati*. 1858. [*Ibid.*] 12mo. 20810

See "N. Am. Rev.," XLVII. 504.

Drake. Life of Tecumseh and of his Brother the Prophet; with a Historical Sketch of the Shawanoe Indians. By Benjamin Drake ... . *Cincinnati: E. Morgan & Co.* 1841. 12mo, pp.

235. C. + *Cincinnati*. 1850. 12mo, pp. 243. + *Cincinnati: H. S. & J. Applegate & Co.* 1852. + *Cincinnati: H. M. Rulison*. 1855. 12mo, pp. 235. + *Cincinnati and Philadelphia*. 1856. 12mo. + *Cincinnati*. 1858. 12mo, pp. 235. 20811

Drake. Tales and Sketches from the Queen City. By Benjamin Drake ... . *Cincinnati: E. Morgan and Co.* 1838. 12mo, pp. 180. H. 20812

Also: Address before the Sixth Anniversary of the Erodelphian Society of Miami University, Sept. 27, 1831. ... *Cincinnati*. 1831. 8vo. — A Public Oration delivered before the Phi Alpha Theta Society, Cincinnati, July 4, 1826. ... *Cincinnati*. 1826. 12mo, pp. 12.

Drake (B.), *and* Mansfield (E. D.) Cincinnati in 1826. By B. Drake and E. D. Mansfield. ... *Cincinnati: Morgan, Lodge and Fisher. February*, 1827. 8vo, pp. 100. 2 Plates.

For another edition, *see* Bullock (W.), Vol. III., No. 9139.

Drake (C. D.) Address of Charles D. Drake, on the Birthday of Washington. Delivered at the Union Commemoration, in St. Louis, Feb. 22, 1862. [n. p. n. d.] 8vo, pp. 8. H.

Drake. ... Oration of Charles D. Drake, delivered in ... St. Louis, May 11, 1863, on the Anniversary of the Capture of Camp Jackson. To which is subjoined his Reply to the Missouri Republican's Attack upon him, on Account of that Oration. *St. Louis*. 1863. 8vo, pp. 16. H. 20815

Drake. Union and Anti-Slavery Speeches, delivered during the Rebellion. By Charles D. Drake. Published for the Benefit of the Ladies' Union Aid Society of St. Louis, Mo. *Cincinnati: Applegate & Co.* 1864. 12mo, pp. 431. C. 20816

Drake. ... The Veto Power: its Nature and History ... . By Charles D. Drake, of Cincinnati, Ohio. *Washington, D. C.* [1848.] 8vo, pp. 16. H. 20817

Also: Address of the Committee from the State of Missouri to President Lincoln. [n. p. 1863.] 8vo, pp. 12. H. — Address ... to the Radical Union Men of Missouri. [*Washington*. n. d.] 8vo, pp. 4. H. — Betrayal of the Republican Party in Missouri. Speech ... in Reply to Hon. Carl Schurz; delivered in the Senate ... December 16, 1870. *Washington*. 1870. 8vo, pp. 16. H. — Camp Jackson: its History and Significance. Oration ... St. Louis, May 11, 1863. ... *St. Louis*. 1863. 8vo, pp. 16. H. — Censure of the President. Speech ... in the Senate ... December 10, 1867. [*Washington*. n. d.] 8vo, pp. 8. H. — Funeral Oration ... in ... St. Louis, October 29, 1852, on the Occasion of the Obsequies of Daniel Webster, ... *St. Louis: printed by Charles & Hammond*. 1852. 8vo, pp. 34, 1 l. H. — Immediate Emancipation in Missouri. Speech ... delivered in the Missouri State Convention, June 16th, 1863. [n. p. n. d.] 8vo, pp. 12. H. — Letter from the Executive Com-

mittee of the Missouri Delegation to President Lincoln. [*Washington*. 1863.] 8vo, pp. 7. H. — The Missouri State Convention, and its Ordinance of Emancipation. Speech ... in St. Louis, July 9, 1863. [n. p. n. d.] 8vo, pp. 8. H. — Missouri Voters' Oath. Have the People of Missouri the Right to prescribe the Qualifications of Missouri Voters? Argument of Charles D. Drake ... in the Case of Francis D. Blair, Jr., *vs.* Stephen Ridgely and John S. Thomson. ... April 19, 1866. [n. p. n. d.] 8vo, pp. 23. H. — Oration, Oct. 29, 1852, on ... the Obsequies of Daniel Webster. — The Proclamation of Emancipation. Speech ... delivered in ... St. Louis, January 28, 1863. [n. p. n. d.] 8vo, pp. 7. H. — Radicalism Vindicated. Letter ... to Senator Johnson, of Maryland. ... *Washington, D. C.* 1867. 8vo, pp. 12. H. — The Rebellion: its Character, Motive, and Aim. Oration ... at Washington, Mo., ... Fourth of July, 1862. [n. p. n. d.] 8vo, pp. 12. — The Rebellion: its Origin and Life in Slavery. Position and Policy of Missouri. ... Speech Delivered ... In ... St. Louis, April 14, 1862; ... previously spoken, ... at Union, Mo., April 7, 1862. [n. p. 1862.] 8vo, pp. 8. — Slavery's Destruction, the Union's Safety. Speech ... before the Freedom Convention, in Louisville, Kentucky, February 22nd, 1864. [n. p. n. d.] 8vo, pp. 9. H. — Speech ... at the Banquet given in ... Baltimore, on the 20th of July, 1857, to the Excursionists from Ohio and Missouri. *New York: printed by Edward O. Jenkins*. 1857. 8vo, pp. 7. H. — Speech ... delivered in a Union Meeting, at the City of Louisiana, Mo., July 4, 1861. ... *St. Louis*. 1861. 8vo, pp. 16. H. — Speech ... delivered before the National Union Association, at Cincinnati, October 1, 1864. [n. p. n. d.] 8vo, pp. 16. H. — Speech ... at Mercantile Library Hall, September 15, 1868. ... *St. Louis*. 1868. 8vo, pp. 22. H. — Speech ... delivered in St. Louis, November 4th, 1870. ... [n. p. n. d.] 8vo, pp. 7. H. — The War of Slavery upon the Constitution. Address ... on the Anniversary of the Constitution. Delivered in ... St. Louis, Sept. 17, 1862. [n. p. n. d.] 8vo, pp. 7. H. — Which First — the Loyal Negro or the White Rebel? Letter ... to Major Ellis G. Evans, of the Missouri Senate. [*Washington*. n. d.] 8vo, pp. 4. H. — The Wrongs to Missouri's Loyal People. Speech ... before the Mass Convention at Jefferson City, September 1, 1863. [n. p. n. d.] 8vo, pp. 13.

Drake (D.) An Anniversary Discourse, on the State and Prospects of the Western Museum Society: delivered ... in the Chapel of Cincinnati College, June 10th, 1820, on the Opening of the Museum. By Daniel Drake, M.D. *Cincinnati, Ohio*. 1820. 24mo, pp. 36. H. 20818

Drake. Discourse on the History, Character, and Prospects of the West: delivered ... [at] Oxford, Ohio, ... September 23, 1834. By Daniel Drake, M.D. *Cincinnati: Truman and Smith*. 1834. 8vo, pp. 56. BA., S. 20819

Drake. Life of Daniel Boone. By Dr. Drake. 12mo, pp. 230. 20820

Drake. Memoirs. *Cincinnati*. 1856. 12mo, pp. 408.

Drake. Natural and Statistical View, or Picture of Cincinnati and the Miami Country, illustrated by Maps. With an Appendix, containing Observations on the Late Earthquakes, the Aurora Borealis, and South-West Wind. By Daniel Drake. *Cincinnati: Printed by Looker and Wallace*. 1815. 12mo, pp. 251, 2 l. 2 Maps. BA. 20822

Drake. The Northern Lakes a Summer Residence for the Invalids of the South. By Daniel Drake, M.D. ... *Louisville: J. Maxwell, Jr.* 1842. 8vo, pp. 29. BA. 20823

See "M. Rev.," LVII. 108.

Drake. Pioneer Life in Kentucky. A Series of Reminiscential Letters from Daniel Drake, M.D., of Cincinnati, to his Children. Edited, with Notes and a Biographical Sketch, by his Son, Charles D. Drake. *Cincinnati: Robert Clark & Co.* 1870. 8vo, pp. xlvi, 263. H. 20824

Fifty copies on large paper.

Drake. A Systematic Treatise, Etiological, and Practical, on the Principal Diseases of the Interior Valley of North America, as they appear in the Caucasian, African, Indian, and Esquimaux Varieties of its Population. By Daniel Drake, M.D. *Cincinnati: Winthrop B. Smith & Co.* 1850. 8vo, pp. xvi, 878. BA. + Second Series. *Philadelphia: Lippincott, Grambo & Co., Publishers*. 1854. 8vo, pp. xix, 17–985. BA. 20825

Also: An Account of the Epidemic Cholera, as it appeared in Cincinnati. *Cincinnati*. 1832. 8vo, pp. 46. — Discourses ... before the Cincinnati Medical Library Association ... *Cincinnati: Moore & Anderson*. 1852. 12mo, pp. 93. — A Discourse on Intemperance ... March 1st, 1828. ... *Cincinnati*. 1828. 12mo, pp. 26. — Importance of promoting Literary and Social Concert in the Valley of the Mississippi. *Louisville*. 1833. 8vo. — Inaugural Discourse on Medical Education, at the Opening of the Medical College of Ohio, Nov. 11, 1820. *Cincinnati*. 1820. 16mo. B. — An Introductory Lecture at the Opening of the 13th Session of the Medical College of Ohio, Nov. 5th, 1849. *Cincinnati*. [1849.] 8vo. — Means of Promoting the Intellectual Improvement of the Students and Physicians of the Valley of the Mississippi ... Second Edition. *Louisville, Ky.* 1844. 8vo. B. — Oration, on the Intemperance of Cities, &c. *Philadelphia*. 1831. 8vo. — Practical Essays on Medical Education and the Medical Profession in the United States. *Cincinnati*. 1832. 8vo, pp. 104. — A Practical Treatise on the History, Prevention, and Treatment of Epidemic Cholera. ... *Cincinnati*. 1832. 12mo, pp. 180. — Remarks on the Importance of Promoting Literary and Social Concert, in the Valley of the Mississippi, as a means of elavating its character, and perpetuating the Union, delivered in ... Transylvania University, to the Library Convention of Kentucky, November 8, 1833. By Daniel Drake, M D. *Louisville: Herald Office*. 1833. 8vo, pp. 25. — Two Discourses; delivered by appointment, before the Cincinnati Medical Library Association, Jan. 9th and 10th. ... *Cincinnati*. 1852. 12mo. Mr. Allibone quotes "Notices concerning Cincinnati. 1810." 12mo, pp. 64, which we have not seen. *See also* "Western Medical Journal."

Drake (E. C.) A New Universal Collection of Authentic and Entertaining Voyages and Travels, from the Earliest Accounts to the Present Time. Judiciously selected from the best writers in the English, French, Spanish, Dutch, German, Danish, and other Languages, comprehending an account of whatever is curious in the Government, Commerce, Natural History,

Customs, Marriages, Funerals, and other ceremonies of most nations in the known World. Including an account of the most remarkable Discoveries, Conquests, Settlements, Battles, Sea Fights, Hurricanes, Shipwrecks, Sieges, Tortures, Wonderful Escapes, Massacres and Strange Deliverances, both by Sea and Land. Also a Description of the Buildings, Mountains, Rivers, Harbours, Lakes, Islands, Peninsulas, Creeks, &c., of various countries. The whole forming a History of whatever is most worthy of notice in Europe, Asia, Africa, and America. By Edward Cavendish Drake. Illustrated with Maps and beautiful Plates. *London: J. Cooke*. MDCCLXVII. 8vo, pp. 796. 10 Maps. C. + *London: J. Cooke*. MDCCLXX. Folio, pp. 706 (mispaged 506). 46 Maps and Plates. C. + *London*: [*Ibid.*] MDCCLXXI. Folio. S. 20826

Contains Columbus's Four Voyages, and the Voyages of Magellan, Dampier, Woods, Rogers, Anson, Conquest of Mexico by Cortes, Conquest of Peru by Pizarro, Wafer's Voyage to Darien, &c., &c. The plates are by Grignion.

[Drake (*Sir* F.)] The English Hero, 1687. *See* B[urton] (R[obert]), Vol. III., No. 9500.

This is another edition of our No. 9501.

Drake. Der Englische Held und Ritter Franciscus Dracke in einer ausführlichen Beschreibung von dessen Leben, Thaten und See-Reisen darunter besonders die Reise um die Welt sehr merckwürdig. Vormahls von Roberto Brown in Englischer Sprache entworffen; jetzo aber ins Teutsche übersetzet. Welcher ein Anhang beygefüget von dem erstaunens-würdigen Schiffbruch des Ost-Indischen Jagdt-Schiffes der Schelling genannt. *Leipzig: Wolffgang Deer*. 1726. 12mo, pp. 472. Portrait.

Drake. Expeditio Francisci Draki eqvitis angli in Indias Occidentales A. M. D. LXXXV. Quā vrbes, Fanum D. Jacobi, D. Dominici, D. Augustini & Carthagena, captæ fuêre. Additis passim regionum locorúmque omnium tabulis Geographicis quàm accuratissimis. *Leydæ, Apud Fr. Raphelengium*. 1588. 4to, pp. 21. Portrait and 4 folded Maps. J.C.B. 20828

Jadis' copy of this rare piece sold for £14 14s.; Hibbert's for £14; Leclerc's copy, without the maps, sold in Paris, in 1869, for 205 francs. Lowndes says there was a French translation, "*Leyde*, 1588," believing that Ternaux or Boucher de la Richarderie's translation of the above title indicated it.

Drake. The Famous Voyage of Sir Francis Drake, with a Particular Account of his Expedition in the West Indies against the Spaniards, being the first Commander that ever sail'd round the whole Globe. To which is added The Prosperous Voyage of Mr. Thomas Candish round the World; with an Account of the vast Riches he took from the Spaniards, &c. *London.* MDCCXLI. 8vo. + *London: H. Slater.* MDCCLXII. 8vo, 2 l., pp. 53. Map. 20829

DRAKE. A Full | Relation | Of another | Voyage | into the | West Indies, | made by | Sir Thomas Drake; Accompanied with Sir John Hawkins, Sir | Francis Baskerfield, Sir Nicholas Clifford, | and others. | Who set forth from Plimouth on the 28. of | August 1595. | ... *London for Nicholas Bourne* ... | ... 1652. | 4to, pp. (43)–60. H. 20830

Forms part of "Sir Francis Drake Revived," our No. 20840.

DRAKE. The Life And Dangerous Voyages of Sir Francis Drake, With the Surprising of Nombre de Dios, and the manner of his gaining large Quantities of Gold and Silver. And a large Account of that Voyage, wherein he encompassed the whole World. And the Voyage which he made with Francis Knolls and others, with their taking St. Jago, Sancto Domingo, Carthagena and St. Augustin. With the last Voyage in which he Died. *London: Printed by John Willis.* [1708.] 12mo, Title, pp. 162. Portrait. + *London: H. Dean.* [About 1750?] 24mo, pp. 164. Portrait. 20831

Other editions, *London.* 1810. 12mo; *London.* [n. d.]

DRAKE. The Life of the Celebrated Sir Francis Drake, the First Circumnavigator. Reprinted from the Biographia Britannica. Together with the Historical and Genealogical Account of Sir Francis Drake's Family, from Betham's Baronetage: And extracts from Nicholson's History of Cumberland, containing an Account of the Richmond Family of Highhead Castle. [By his descendent, Sir T. Drake.] Not Published. *London: J. Moyes.* 1828. 4to, 5 l., pp. 83. Portrait. 20832

DRAKE. Lives and Voyages of Drake, Cavendish, and Dampier; including an Introductory View of the Earlier Discoveries in the South Seas, and the History of the Buccaneers. *Edinburgh: Oliver and Boyd.* MDCCCXXXI. Post 8vo, pp. 461. 3 Portraits. + *Edinburgh.* [*Ibid.*] 1840. + *New York: Harper and Brothers.* [1831.] 18mo, pp. 332. BA. 20833

DRAKE. Narrationes duæ | admodum memorabiles, | quarum prima | continet diarium ex- | peditionis Francisci Draki | Equitis Angli in Indias Oc- | cidentales susceptæ, | Anno MDLXXXV. |

Altera omnium rerum ab eo- | dem Drako et Norreysio | in Lusitanica irruptione gestarum | fidelem continuationem subjicit. | Emendatiùs quàm antea editæ. | Additis insuper tabulis Geographicis | accuratissimis. | *Noribergæ. Typis Christophori Lochneri, & Jo- | hannis Hofmanni.* | *Anno* MDXC. | 4to, pp. 36. 4 Maps.

DRAKE. Narratio et Continuatio rerum omnium Drako et Norreysio (post felicem ex Occidentalibus Insulis Reditum) in sua Expeditione Portugallensi singulis diebus gestarum. *Francof.* 1590. 4to. 20835

See "Bibliotheca Grenvilliana." Jadis' copy sold for £5.

DRAKE. The Newes of the Exploytes performed and doone by Syr Frauncis Drake: Not onely at Sancto Domingo and Carthagena, but also now at Cales, and vppon the Coast of Spayne. 1587. 4to. 20836

Title from Lowndes, page 668. We have never seen this volume, and infer its rarity.

DRAKE. Relation | Oder Beschreibung der Rheisz | vnd Schiffahrt ausz Engellandt, in die gegen dem | vndergang der Sonne gelegnen | Indien gethan | Durch | Einen Englischen Ritter, | Franciscum Drack genant, | vnd was derselbig vnderwegen mit seinem vnderha- | benden Kriegsvolck allenthalben, sonderlich aber in den Inseln | S. Jacob, S. Dominico, S. Augustin vnd in oder | vmb Carthagena, auch anderstwo dero | orten gesehen vnd auszgericht hat | Sampt hiebey gefüegten, schönen, in Kupffer gestoch- | nen Charten, mit welchen, so wol die gantz Schiffart in gemein, als | auch insonderheit, ein jede für sich selbs eigentlich vnd nach | dem leben gerissen, angedeutet vnd be- | schrieben worden. | *Gedruckt* | *im Jahr nach Christi Geburt,* M.D.LXXXIX. | Folio. 4 Maps. 20837

Priced, by Asher, at £7 10s.

DRAKE. Sir Francis Drake reuiued: calling vpon this dull or effeminate Age to followe his noble Steps for Golde & Siluer, by this memorable Relation of the rare Occurrances (neuer yet declared to the World) in a third Voyage, made by him into the West Indies, in the Yeares 72 & 73, when Nombre de Dios was by him and 52 others only in his Company, surprised. Faithfully taken out of the Reporte of Mr. Christofer Ceely, Ellis Hixon, and others, who were in the same Voyage with him. By Philip Nichols, Preacher. Reviewed also by Sr. Francis Drake himself before his Death, & much holpen and enlarged, by diuers Notes, with his owne Hand here and there

inserted. Set forth by Sr. Francis Drake Baronet (his Nephew) now liuing. *London.* 1626. 4to, Title, Dedication to Charles I., etc., 6 l., pp. 94. J.C.B. + Another Edition. 1628. 4to.

Concerning the edition of 1628, *see* Lowndes, page 668–669. It differs from that of 1626 in having had the advantage of the incorporation of the errata of the latter date under the personal superintendence of the nephew of the great voyager. The last four leaves are larger than the rest of the book. I find the following title in a London bookseller's catalogue; it is probably the edition of 1626 and 1628, with a new title-page only:

DRAKE. Sir Francis Drake Revived, &c., by this memorable relation of the rare occurrences (never yet declared to the world), in a third Voyage made by him into the West Indies, in the years 72 and 73 when Nombre de Dios was by him, and 52 others only in his company. Reviewed by Sir F. Drake himselfe before his death, and much holpen and enlarged by divers notes with his own hand here and there inserted, &c. [n. p. About 1630.] 4to. 20839

DRAKE. Sir Francis Drake Revived. | Who is or may be a Pattern to stirre up all | Heroicke and active Spirits of these | Times, to benefit their Countrey and | eternize their Names by like Noble | Attempts. | Being a Summary and true Relation of foure | severall Voyages made by the said | Sir Francis Drake to the | West-Jndies. | Viz. | His dangerons [*sic*] adventuring for Gold and Silver with | the gaining thereof. And the surprizing of Nombre de dios by | himselfe and two and fifty Men. | His Encompassing the World. | His Voyage made with Christopher Carleill, Martin Frobusher, | Francis Knollis, and others. Their taking the Townes of Saint | Jago, Sancto Domingo Carthagena and Saint Augustine. | His last Voyage (in which he dyed) being accompanied | with Sir John Hawkins, Sir Thomas Baskerfield, Sir Nicholas Clif- | ford, with others. His manner of Buriall. | Collected out of the Notes of the said Sir Francis Drake; | Mastet [*sic*] Philip Nichols, Master Francis Fletcher, Preach- | ers; and the Notes of divers other Gentlemen (who | went in the said Voyages) carefully compared together. | *Printed at London for Nicholas Bourne, dwelling at the* | *South entrance of the royall Exchange,* 1653. | 4to, 3 l., pp. 87, blank l. Portrait. H. 20840

This is followed by three other pieces, viz.: The World Encompassed. 1652. 1 l., pp. 108. A Summarie and True Discourse of Sir Francis Drake's West Indian Voyage. 1652. pp. 41. A Full Relation of another Voyage into the West Indies. 1652. pp. 43–60. The titles of which form our Nos. 20855, 20843, and 20830. For other editions, *see* B[urton] (R.), Vol. III., No. 9500, and add, Fourth Edition. *London: Nath. Couch.* 1695. 18mo, 2 l., pp. 174. Portrait. + *London: Printed at the Bell in the Poultry.* 18mo. + Eighth Edition. [*Ibid.*] 1710. + Ninth Edition. [*Ibid.*] 1716. *See also* Maynarde (Thomas).

DRAKE. A Svmmarie and trve Discovrse of Sir Frances Drakes West Indian Voyage. Wherein were taken, the Townes of Saint Iago, Sancto Domingo, Cartagena, and Saint Augustine. With geographicall Mappes exactly describing each of the Townes with their Scituations, and the Maner of the Armies approching to the Winning of them: diligently made by Baptista Boazio. *London: Roger Ward.* 1589. 4to, pp. 37. 20841

The four maps mentioned on the title were not published with this edition, it being simply the announcement of a translation from the title of the original Latin edition, *Leyden,* 1588. When Field issued the second English edition, he added to some copies the original maps, pasting slips at foot with the English names. But to neither of these editions do the maps rightly belong. The dedication is signed Thomas Cates. The first leaf is blank, except that it has the signature A. It is a volume of great rarity. In the title of some copies the words, "With geographicall Mappes," etc., does not appear. The following is another edition:

DRAKE. A Svmmarie | and Trve Discovrse | of Sir Francis Drakes | VVest Indian Voyage. | Wherein were taken, the Townes of | Saint Jago, Sancto Domingo, Cartagena, & | Saint Augustine. | *Imprinted at London by Richard Field, dwelling* | *in the Blacke-Friars by Ludgate.* | 1589. | 4to, Title, 1 l., Dedication, 1 l., pp. 52. W. 20842

Ternaux and Lowndes each quote "Another edition. *London.* 1596." 4to.

DRAKE. A | Summarie | and | True Discourse | of | Sir Francis Drakes | West Indian Voyage. | Accompanied with Christopher Carleill, | Martin Frobisher, Francis Knollis, with | many other Captains and Gentlemen. | Wherein were taken, the Townes of Saint | Jago, Sancto Domingo, Cartagena and | Saint Augustine. | *Printed at London for Nicholas Bourne* ... | ... 1652. | 4to, Title, pp. 41. H. 20843

Forms part of "Sir Francis Drake Revived," No. 20840.

DRAKE. Le Voyage de Francis Drach à l'Entour du Monde *Paris.* 1613. 8vo, pp. 90. 20844

DRAKE. Le | Voyage | de l'Illvstre | Seignevr et Che- | ualier François Drach, Admiral | d'Angleterre, à l'entour du monde. | Augmentée de la Seconde partie. | A Monsieur de S. Simon, Seigneur & | Baron de Courtomer. | *A Paris,* | *Chez Iean Gesselin, ruē sainct Iacques,* | *à la belle Image: & en sa boutique au Palais* | *en la gallerie des prisonniers.* | M.DC.XXVII. | Auec priuelege du Roy. | 8vo, 3 l., pp. 230, 2 l. J.C.B. 20845

In the "Catalogue of Mr. J. C. Brown's Library," the edition is described as 8vo as well as 12mo. In Ternaux, No. 495, Deuxième édition. The first edition of this translation, No. 20844, *ante,* contained only the first part; the third is our No. 20846, the fourth in 1641. Translated by F. De Lowencourt, Sieur do Vauchelles. We have seen an edition quoted, as "*Paris. Gosselin.* 1626."

DRAKE. Le voyage | cvrievx, | faict avtovr | du Monde, par François | Drach, Admiral d'Angle- | terre. | Augmenté de la Seconde partie. | *A Paris,* | *Chez Antoine Robinot,* ... | M.DC.XXXXI. | 8vo, 4 l., pp. 230. C. 20846

"Nuggets," No. 923, gives the date of this edition 1741.

DRAKE. Voyage curieux fait à l'entour du monde par Francis Drake, admiral d'Angleterre. *Paris.* 1690. 8vo. 20847

DRAKE. The Voyage of Sir F. Drake to America in 1586, edited by Mons. Louis Lacour, from an inedited MS. in French, now in the Bibliotèque Impériale. *Paris.* 1855. 8vo. 20848

DRAKE. Voyages of Sir Francis Drake into the West Indies. *London.* 1623. 8vo. 20849

Title from Lowndes, page 669.

DRAKE. The | Voyages & Travels | Of that Renowned Captain, | Sir Francis Drake, | into the | West-Indies, | and | Round about the World: | Giving a perfect Relation of his strange Adventures, and many wonderful Dis- | coveries, his Fight with the Spaniard, and many barbarous Nations; his | taking St. Jago, St. Domingo, Carthagena, St. Au- | gusta, and many other Places in the Golden Country of America, | and other Parts of the World: His Description of Monsters, and Monstrous Peo- | ple. With many other remarkable Passages not before Extant: Contained in the | History of his Life and Death; both pleasant and profitable to the Reader. | *Printed by C. B. for J. F. and sold by E. Tracy, at the Three Bibles on* | *London-Bridge.* | 4to, pp. 24, beginning on the verso of the Title. [1652?] 20850

DRAKE. The Voyages and Travels of that Renowned Captain Sir Francis Drake into the West Indies and Round the World. *Printed at Stamford, in Lincolnshire.* [n. d.] 4to. 20851

DRAKE. Voyages and Travels of the Renowned Captain Sir Francis Drake into the West Indies, and round the World. *Coventry: J. Turner.* [About 1815.] 16mo, pp. 24. C. 20852

A chap-book.

DRAKE. The World | Encompassed | by | Sir Francis Drake, | Being his next voyage to that to Nombre | de Dios formerly imprinted; | Carefully collected out of the notes of Master | Francis Fletcher Preacher in this im- | ployment, and diuers others his followers in | the same: | Offered now at last to publique view, both for the honour of | the actor, but especially for the stirring

vp of heroick spirits, | to benefit their Countrie and eternize their names | by like noble attempts. | *London, Printed for Nicholas Bovrnes* | *and are to be sold at his shop at the* | *Royall Exchange.* 1628. | 4to, 2 l., pp. 108. Portraits and Map. 20853

DRAKE. The | World | Encompassed | By | Sir Francis Drake. | Being | His next Voyage to that to Nombre de | Dios, formerly imprinted; | Carefully collected out of the Notes of Master | Francis Fletcher, Preacher in this | imployment, and divers others his | followers in the same. | Offered now at last to publike view, both for the honour of | the Actor, but especially for the stirring up of heroick spirits, | to benefit their Country, and eternize their names | by like noble attempts. | *London, Printed by E. P. for Nicholas Bourne, and are to be sold at* | *his Shop at the South Entrance of the* | *Royall Exchange.* 1635. | 4to, 2 l., pp. 90. Portrait and Map. J.C.B. 20854

It is also included in Vol. II. of the "Oxford Collection of Voyages."

DRAKE. The World Encompassed .... *London: Nicholas Bourne.* 1652. 4to, Title, pp. 108. H. 20855

Forms part of "Sir Francis Drake Revived," our No. 20840.

DRAKE. The World Encompassed by Sir Francis Drake, Being his next Voyage to that to Nombre de Dios. Collated with an unpublished Manuscript of Francis Fletcher, Chaplain to the Expedition. With Appendices illustrative of the same Voyage, and Introduction, by W. S. W. Vaux, Esq., M.A. 4 l., pp. xl, 295, 8. *London: Hakluyt Society.* M.DCCC.LIV. Map. 20856

Drake's voyages are included in Hakluyt, Vol. III. A Dutch version is included in Van der Aa's "Collection," Vol. XVIII., in 8vo and folio. *See also* Barrow (J.), Bry (T. de), Part VIII., Burton (R.), Clark (Samuel), Daunce (Ed.), D'Avenant (*Sir* W), Fitzgeffrey, Greeke (Thos.), Hakluyt, Kunstmann (F.), Peele (Geo.), and R[oberts] (H.) *See also* Burney, Cooley, Dalrymple, Dampier (Knapson), La Harpe, Pinkerton, Prevost, &c. The following numbers will be found to give the fullest information about the American voyages: No. 20848, Voyage of 1586. *Paris.* 1835. No. 20856. World Encompassed. *Hakluyt Society.* 1854. No. 20838. Sir Francis Drake Revived. *London.* 1653. *Also* Maynarde's Voyage of 1595. Sir Francis Drake was born about 1544. He made his first voyage, to Africa and the West Indies, with John Hawkins, 1567–8. Second and third voyages to the West Indies, alone, in 1570 and 1571. Fourth, to West Indies in 1572–3. Fifth (called by himself his third), around the world, Dec. 13, 1577, to Sept. 26, 1580. Was knighted, April 4, 1581. Made his sixth voyage, with twenty-five vessels, Sept. 14, 1585, to July 28, 1586. Seventh and last voyage to America, with Richard Hawkins, in twenty-seven vessels, Aug. 28, 1594. Died Jan. 28, 1595, at Porto Bello.

DRAKE (F.) Leben und Seereisen. *Halle.* 1815. 20857

DRAKE (J. H.) Thirty-Two Years of the Life of an Adventurer. ... By John H. Drake, Williamsburgh, L. I. *New York: printed for the Author.* 1847. 18mo. 20858

DRAKE (J. R.) The American Flag: By Joseph Rodman Drake. Illustrated by F. O. C. Darley. *New York.* 1861. 4to, pp. 14. 20859

DRAKE. The Culprit Fay and other Poems. By Joseph Rodman Drake. *New York: George Dearborn.* 1835. 8vo, 3 l., pp. 84. 2 Plates. + *New York.* [*Ibid.*] 1836. 8vo, pp. 90. Portrait. 20860

[DRAKE *and* HALLECK.] Poems by Croaker, Croaker & Co., & Croaker, Jr., as published in the Evening Post. *New York.* 1819. 18mo, pp. 36. 20861

DRAKE *and* HALLECK. The Croakers By Joseph Rodman Drake and Fitz Greene Halleck First complete edition *New York* MDCCCLX Rl. 8vo, 1 l., pp. viii, 191. Portrait. 20862

150 copies printed. Bradford Club Series, No. 2.

DRAKE (M. L.) Lake Superior Railroad. Letter to the Hon. Lewis Cass. By Morgan L. Drake, Esq. *Pontiac, Michigan: W. M. Thompson, Printer.* 1852. 12mo, pp. 12. H. + *Pontiac, Michigan.* 1853. 8vo, pp, 27. S. 20863

DRAKE (*Mrs.*) Trodden Dovvn | Strength, | by the | God of Strength, or, | Mrs. Drake Revived. | Shewing | Her strange and rare Case, great and | many uncouth Afflictions, for tenne | years together: Together, | With the strange and wonderfull manner | how the Lord revealed himselfe unto her, | a few dayes before her death. | Related by her sometime unworthy friend, | Hart On-hi. | ... | *London,* | *Printed by R. Bishop for Stephen Pilkington* ... | 1647. | Sm. 12mo, 3 l., pp. 193. 20864

"The interest to New Englanders of this curious book centres not in the main subject, but in what is incidentally told of one of her spiritual advisers. Mrs. Drake was a half crazed religious enthusiast, whose spiritual health required constant wrestling with Satan and Doctors of Divinity."—STEVENS. Rogers of Dedham, Dod, Culverwell, Forbes, and many other ministers advised Mrs. Drake in her "strange temptations," but none so effectually as "Mr. Hooker, then at Cambridge, now in New-England," who resided some time with her at Esher, where "having acted his part with her," "by God's providence he was married unto her waiting-woman," and shortly after "cal'd to bee Lecturer at Chelmsford in Essex."—*See* pp. 117–129.

DRAKE (R.) Revelations of a Slave Smuggler; being the Autobiography of Capt. Richard Drake, an African trader for

fifty years—from 1807 to 1857; with a Preface by his Executor, Rev. H. Byrd West. *New York: R. M. DeWitt.* 1860. 8vo, pp. 98. 3 folded Plates. 20865

DRAKE (S. Gardner). The Aboriginal Races of North America, comprising Biographical Sketches of Eminent Individuals, and an Historical Account of the Different Tribes, from the First Discovery of the Continent to the Present Period. With a Dissertation of their Origin, Antiquities, Manners, and Customs, Illustrative Narratives and Anecdotes, with a copious Analytical Index. By Samuel G. Drake. Fifteenth Edition. ... Revised, with Valuable Additions, by J. W. O'Neill. *Philadelphia.* 1860. 20866

This is the biography of the Indians, with a new title-page and some additions. The only difference in these editions is in some of the plates; they are all bad enough.

DRAKE. Annals of Witchcraft in New England, and elsewhere in the United States, from their First Settlement. Drawn up from Unpublished and other well Authenticated Records of the Alleged Operations of Witches and their Instigator, the Devil. By Samuel G. Drake. *Boston: W. Elliot Woodward.* MDCCCLXIX. 4to, pp. 306. BA. 20867

No. VIII. of Woodward's "Historical Series." Two hundred and fifty copies printed.

DRAKE. Biography and History of the Indians of North America; comprising a General Account of them and Details in the Lives of all the most distinguished Chiefs and others who have been noted among the various Nations upon the Continent: also a History of their Wars; their Manners and Customs, and the most celebrated Speeches of their Orators, from their first being known to Europeans to the Present Time. Likewise exhibiting an Analysis of the most Distinguished as well as Absurd Authors who have written upon the great question of the first peopling of America. By Samuel G. Drake. Third Edition, with ... Additions ... Corrections and ... Engravings. *Boston: O. L. Perkins.* 1834. 8vo, pp. 518, xxx. 8 Plates. + Fourth Edition. *Boston.* 1835. 8vo. + Fifth Editon, with large Additions and Corrections, and numerous Engravings. *Boston.* 1836. 8vo, pp. 576. + Sixth Edition. ... *Boston.* 1836. 8vo. + Seventh Edition. ... *Boston: Antiquarian Institute.* 1837. 8vo, pp. xiii, 120, 144, 96, 160, 12. + Eighth Edition, with large Additions and Corrections. *Boston.* M.DCCC.XLI. 8vo, pp. xii, 48, 120, 156, 200, 16. + Ninth Edition. ... *Boston.* 1845.

8vo, pp. 748. + Tenth Edition. *Boston.* MDCCCXLIII. 8vo. Eleventh Edition. *Boston: Benjamin Mussey & Co.* M.DCCC.LI. 8vo, pp. 720. 8 Plates. 20868

For the first edition, *see* "Indian Biography," No. 20873, *infra.* On the engraved title-page, this work is called "The Book of the Indians of North America." The eighth edition contains the portraits of Sir William Johnson, Gen. Wayne, Red-Jacket, Pocahontas, etc., omitted in subsequent editions. The eleventh edition was the last published under the eye of the author. Some copies of this edition have the imprint, "*Boston: Sanborn, Carter & Bazin.* 1857." The other editions are *Boston,* 1858, etc., and our No. 20866.

DRAKE. The Book of the Indians. *See* "Biography," etc., No. 20868, *supra.*

DRAKE. A Brief Memoir of Sir Walter Raleigh, prepared for and published In the New England Historical and Genealogical Register for April, 1862, and now Reprinted with Additions, By Samuel G. Drake. *Boston: Printed for the Author for private distribution.* 1862. 4to, pp. 35. Portrait. 20869

Ten copies printed on large paper.

DRAKE. Genealogical and Biographical Account of the Family of Drake in America. With some Notices of the Antiquities connected with the early Times of Persons of the name in England. *Printed at the Private Press of George Coolidge, for Samuel Gardner Drake. August,* 1845. 12mo, pp. (2), 51.

Also in octavo.

DRAKE. An Historical Memoir of the Colony of New Plymouth. By S. G. Drake. Part v. *Boston.* 1867. 8vo, pp. 145.

A continuation of Baylies' "Historical Memoir." *See* Baylies (F.), Vol. I., No 4065.

DRAKE. The History and Antiquities of Boston, the Capital of Massachusetts, and Metropolis of New England, from its Settlement in 1630, to the Year 1770. Also, An Introductory History of the Discovery and Settlement of New England. With Notes, Critical and Illustrative. By Samuel G. Drake, A.M. ... . *Boston: Luther Stevens.* 1856. Rl. 8vo, pp. x, 840. Plates and Woodcuts. BA. + Second Edition. *Boston.* 1857. Rl. 8vo, pp. xii, 816. 20 Plates. 20872

One hundred copies printed on large paper.

DRAKE. Indian Biography, containing the Lives of more than Two Hundred Indian Chiefs: Also such others of that Race as have rendered their names conspicuous in the History of North America, from its first being known to Europeans, to

the Present Period. Giving at large their most Celebrated Speeches, Memorable Sayings, Numerous Anecdotes, and a History of their Wars, Much of which is taken from Manuscripts never before published. By Samuel G. Drake. *Boston: Josiah Drake.* CIↃ.IↃ.CCCXXXII. 12mo, Plate, Half-Title, pp. 348, 1 l. + Second Edition. *Boston.* 1833. 8vo. 20873

Afterwards expanded into the "Book of the Indians." For other editions, *see* No. 20868, *infra.*

DRAKE. Indian Captivities; being a Collection of the most remarkable Narratives of Persons taken Captive by the North American Indians, or Relations of those who by Stratagem and desperate Valor have effected the most surprising Escapes from their cruel hands. To which are added Notes, Historical, Biographical, &c. By Samuel G. Drake. *Boston.* 1839. 12mo, pp. 360. 20874

DRAKE. Indian Captivities; or, Life in the Wigwam. Being True Narratives of Captives who have been carried away by the Indians, from the Frontier Settlements of the United States, from the Earliest Period to the Present Time. By Samuel G. Drake. *Auburn: Derby & Miller.* 1850. 12mo, pp. 360. 3 Plates. + [With Appendix and Index.] *Auburn: Derby & Miller.* 1850. 12mo, pp. 368, 2 l. 3 Plates. + [*Ibid.*] 1851. *Buffalo.* 1853. + *Boston Antiquarian Bookstore.* 1856. 12mo, pp. 360. + *New York and Auburn: Miller, Orton & Mulligan.* 1856. 8vo, pp. 372. 8 Plates. + *New York: C. M. Saxton.* 12mo, pp. 367, 3 l. 20875

DRAKE. Memoir of the Life and Writings of the Rev. Thomas Prince, together with a Pedigree of his Family. By Samuel G. Drake. *Boston: C. C. P. Moody.* 1852. 8vo, pp. 12. Plate. 20876

DRAKE. A Memoir of the Rev. Cotton Mather, D.D. With a Genealogy of the Family of Mather. By Samuel G. Drake. *Boston: C. C. P. Moody.* 1851. 8vo, pp. 16. Plate. 20877

DRAKE. The Old Indian Chronicle; being a Collection of Exceedingly Rare Tracts, Written and Published in the Time of King Philip's War, by Persons residing in the Country. To which are now added Marginal Notes and Chronicles of the Indians. From the Discovery of America to the Present Time. By S. G. Drake. *Boston: Published at Antiquarian Institute.* MDCCCXXXVI.' 2 l., 12mo, pp. 208. C. 20878

Five hundred copies printed. The following is another edition:

DRAKE. The Old Indian Chronicle; being a Collection of Exceeding Rare Tracts, Written and Published in the Time of King Philip's War, by persons residing in the Country. To which are now added an Introduction and Notes. By Samuel G. Drake. *Boston: Samuel A. Drake.* 1867. Sm. 4to, pp. xi, 333. 20879

The tracts here reprinted are described in Rich's catalogue, Nos. 370 to 373, and 378, and are included in this Dictionary, under their proper titles.

DRAKE. A Particular History of the Five Years' French and Indian War in New England and Parts Adjacent, from its Declaration by the King of France, March 15, 1744, to the Treaty with the Eastern Indians, Oct. 16, 1749, sometimes called Governor Shirley's War. With a Memoir of Major-General Shirley, accompanied by his Portrait and other Engravings. By Samuel G. Drake. *Albany: Joel Munsell.* 1870. 4to, pp. 312. BA. 20880

DRAKE. Recovery of some Materials for the Early History of Rochester, General and Particular, ... By Samuel G. Drake. *Boston.* 1851. 8vo, pp. 20. Map and Engravings. BA. 20881

Followed by a catalogue of books for sale.

DRAKE. Result of Some Researches Among the British Archives for Information Relative to the Founders of New England; Made in the Years 1858, 1859 and 1860. Originally Collected for and Published in the New England Historical and Genealogical Register; and now Corrected and Enlarged. By Samuel G. Drake, ... *Boston.* 1860. 4to, pp. 143. Map and 2 Plates. + [Second Edition.] *Boston.* 1862. 4to, pp. xii, 148. + [Third Edition.] *Boston: Press of John Wilson & Son.* 1865. 4to, pp. xxi, 148. Plates. 20882

Seventy-five copies of the third edition were printed on large paper.

DRAKE. Tragedies of the Wilderness; or, True and Authentic Narratives of Captives who have been carried away by the Indians from the Various Frontier Settlements of the United States, from the Earliest to the Present Time. Illustrating the Manners and Customs, Barbarous Rites and Ceremonies, of the North American Indians, and their various Methods of Torture practised upon such as have, from Time to Time, fallen into their hands. By Samuel G. Drake. ... *Boston: Antiquarian Bookstore and Institute.* 1841. 12mo, pp. 360. BA., C., P. 20883

DRAKE. The Witchcraft Delusion in New England: its Rise, Progress, and Termination, as exhibited by Dr. Cotton Mather, in the Wonders of the Invisible World; and by Mr. Robert Calef, in his More Wonders of the Invisible World. With a Preface, Introduction, and Notes, By Samuel G. Drake. ... *Roxbury, Mass.: Printed for W. Elliot Woodward.* MDCCCLXVI. 3 vols., 4to, XCVIII, (4), 247; XXIX, 212; 244. BA. 20884

Forms No. 57 of Woodward's "Historical Series." Copies on large paper, rl. 8vo and rl. quarto. Also: An Address delivered at the Annual Meeting of the New England Historical and Genealogical Society ... January 20th, 1858. ... *Boston. Henry W. Dutton and Son, Printers.* M.DCCC.LVIII. 8vo, pp 20. H. — Catalogue of the Private Library of Samuel G. Drake, of Boston, chiefly relating to the Antiquities, History and Biography of America, and in an especial manner to the Indians, collected and used by him in preparing his Works upon the Aborigines of America. *Boston: S. G. Drake.* 1845. 8vo, pp. 80. (Also many other catalogues.) — The Checkley Family. [*Boston.* 1848.] 8vo, pp. 6. — Notice of William Thaddeus Harris, Esq ... *Boston.* 1855. 4to, pp. 14. H. — Principal Events in the Life of Brant 8vo — [Drake.] A Review of Winthrop's Journal, as edited and published by the Hon. James Savage ... *Boston: Dutton & Wentworth, Printers.* 1854. 8vo, pp. 23. 5 Portraits. H. — Some Memoirs of the Life and Writings of the Rev. Thomas Prince, together with a Pedigree of his Family. ... *Boston.* 1851. 8vo, pp. 12. BA.

DRALSÉ DE GRANDPIERRE. Relation de divers voyages faits dans l'Afrique, dans l'Amérique, et aux Indes Occidentales, &c. Par le Sieur Dralsé de Grandpierre. *Paris.* 1718. 12mo.

DRANE (A.) Trial of Captain A. Drane and others: Proceedings of the Court-Martial at Fort Brown, Texas. *Louisville.* 1847. 8vo. S. 20886

DRANE (R. B.) Historical Notices of St. James' Parish, Wilmington, N. C. By Rev. R. B. Drane. *Philadelphia.* 1843. 12mo. 20887

DRAPEAU (Stanislaus). Appel aux Municipalités du Bas Canada. La Colonisation du Canada envisagée au point de vue National. *Quebec.* 1858. 20888

DRAPEAU. Considérations sur les Classes Ouvrières et la Colonisation. *Quebec.* 1860. 12mo, pp. 24. 20889

DRAPEAU. Coup-d'œil sur les Ressources productives et la Richesse du Canada, suivi d'un "Plan d'Organisation" complet et détaillé, relatif à la Colonisation. Destiné à faire suite aux "Etudes sur la Colonisation." *Quebec.* 1864. 8vo, pp. 36.

DRAPEAU. Etudes sur le developpement de la colonisation du Bas-Canada depuis dix ans (1851–1861.) Constatant les progrès des défrichements, de l'ouverture des chemins, de la colonisa-

tion et du développement de la population Canadienne-Française. *Quebec: Léger-Brousseau.* 1863. 8vo, pp. 600. Map. 20891

DRAPEAU. Le Journal de Québec et le Tombeau de Champlain. *Quebec.* 1867. 8vo. 20892

Also: Observations sur le brochure de MM. les Abbés Laverdière et Casgrain relativement à la découverte du tombeau de Champlain. *Quebec.* 1866. 8vo, pp. 28. — Religion et Patrie! Association de Secours pour venir en aide aux défricheurs du Sol. Projet de Constitution. *Quebec.* 1859. 12mo, pp. 8.

DRAPER (B. H.) The Life of William Penn, to which is added, his Reflections and Maxims, relating to the Conduct of Human Life, By Bourne Hall Draper. *London.* [1835.] Plate.

DRAPER (E. A.) An Address to the British Public, on the Case of Brigadier Picton, late Governor and Captain-General of the Island of Trinidad, with Observations on the Conduct of W. Fullarton, Esq. and the Right Hon. John Sullivan. By Lieutenant-Colonel Edward A. Draper. *London: J. Budd.* 1806. 8vo. 20894

See "M. Rev.," L. 334.

DRAPER (J.) History of Spencer, from its Earliest Settlement to the Year 1841, including a Brief Sketch of Leicester to the Year 1753. By James Draper. ... *Worcester: Spooner and Howland, Printers.* 1841. 8vo, pp. 159. Plan. B., H. + History of Spencer, Massachusetts ... to the Year 1860, ... Second Edition, enlarged and improved. ... *Worcester: printed by Henry J. Howland.* [n. d.] 12mo, pp. 276. BA., H. 20895

DRAPER (J. W.) History of the American Civil War. By John William Draper, M.D., LL.D., Professor of Chemistry and Physiology in the University of New York. Vol. I. Containing the Causes of the War and the Events preparatory to it, up to the Close of President Buchanan's Administration. — Vol. II. Containing the Events from the Inauguration of President Lincoln to the Proclamation of Emancipation of the Slaves. — Vol. III. Containing the Events from the Proclamation of the Emancipation of the Slaves to the End of the War. *New York: Harper & Brothers.* 1867–70. 3 vols., 8vo, pp. 567; 614; 701. B., BA., H. 20896

DRAPER. The Indebtedness of the City of New York to its University. An Address to the Alumni of the University of the City of New York, 28th June, 1853. By Professor J. W. Draper, M.D. *New York.* 1853. 8vo, pp. 30. H. 20897

DRAPER. Thoughts on the Future Civil Policy of America. By John William Draper, M.D., LL.D., ... *New York: Harper & Brothers, Publishers.* 1865. 8vo, pp. 325. B., BA., H. 20898

DRAPER. Gedanken über die zukünftige Politik Amerikas. Aus dem Englischen von A. Bartels. *Leipzig: O. Wigand.* 1865. 8vo, pp. vii, 191. 20899

Also: An Appeal to the People of the State of New York to Legalize the Dissection of the Dead. *New York.* 1853. 8vo. — University of New York, Medical Department. A Valedictory Lecture, delivered by Professor Draper. Session MDCCCXLI–'XLII. *New York: Hopkins & Jennings, Printers.* 1842. 8vo, pp. 14, 1 l. BA. — Address delivered to the American Union Academy of Literature, Science, and Art, at its First Annual Meeting, January 31, 1870, by John William Draper, M.D. ... . *Washington.* 1870. 8vo, pp. 24. H.

DRAPER (L. C.) Madison, the Capital of Wisconsin: its Growth, Progress, Condition, Wants and Capabilities. Compiled by Lyman C. Draper. *Madison: Calkins & Proudfit.* 1857. 8vo, pp. 48. B. 20900

DRAPER. Tenth Annual Report on the Condition and Improvement of the Common Schools and Educational Interests of the State of Wisconsin, In the Year 1858. By Lyman C. Draper, State Superintendent of Public Instruction. [n. p.] *Atwood & Rubley, Printers.* 1858. 8vo, pp. 397. Portrait. + Eleventh for 1859. 8vo, pp. 205. 20901

Mr. Draper is also the editor of the "Collections of the Wisconsin Historical Society," and has in preparation several important historical works, based on valuable documents in his possession.

DRAPER *and* CROFFUT. A Helping Hand for Town and Country: an American Home Book of Practical and Scientific Information concerning House and Lawn; Garden and Orchard; Field, Barn, and Stable; Apiary and Fish-Pond; Workshop and Dairy; and Domestic Economy and Family Health. By Lyman C. Draper and W. A. Croffut. *Cincinnati.* 1870. 8vo, pp. 821. 20902

One of the best works of its class, and includes many historical facts.

DRAPER (S.) Address to the Children on Randall's Island, July 4, 1849. ... By Simeon Draper. *New York.* 1849. 8vo, pp. 16. M. 20903

[DRAPER (*Sir* William).] The Thoughts of a Traveller upon our American Disputes. *London: J. Ridley.* MDCCLXXIV. 8vo, pp. 27. J.C.B. 20904

DRAPER (W. G.) Short Sketch of the History of Kingston. *Kingston* [*Ottawa*]. 1862. 8vo, pp. 28. 20905

DRAPER (W. H.) Correspondance entre l'Hon. W. H. Draper et l'Hon. R. E. Caron; et entre l'Hon. R. E. Caron et les Hons. D. H. La Fontaine et A. N. Morin. *Montréal.* 1846. 8vo, pp. 35. S. 20906

DRAPER. Correspondence between the Hon. W. H. Draper and the Hon. R. E. Caron; and between the Hon. R. E. Caron and the Hons. L. H. La Fontaine and A. N. Morin. *Montréal.* 1846. 8vo, pp. 36. S. 20907

Also: Speech ... in Defence of the Chartered Rights of the University of King's College, delivered at the bar of the Legislative Assembly of Canada, Nov. 24, 1843. *Toronto.* 1843. 8vo, pp. 17.

DRAUDIUS (G.) Bibliotheca Historica. *Lipsiæ.* 1620. 4to.

A chapter, "De Scriptoribus Rerum Americanarum."

Draught of a Bill, for declaring the Intentions of the Parliament of Great-Britain, Concerning the Exercise of the Right Of imposing Taxes within His Majesty's Colonies, Provinces, and Plantations in North America. ... Folio, p. 1. 20909

Published by order of Sir W. Howe, at Philadelphia, 14th April, 1778. Printed by Macdonald and Cameron. Royal arms at head.

A Draught of an Overture for the Government, Worship, & Discipline of the Associate-Reformed Church in North America. *New York: Printed by T. and J. Swords.* 1796. 12mo, pp. 103.

DRAYTON (*Capt.*) Captains Drayton and Sayres, or the Way Americans are treated for aiding the Cause of Liberty at Home. *Philadelphia.* [About 1844.] 8vo. 20911

DRAYTON (D.) Personal Memoir of Daniel Drayton, for Four Years and Four Months a Prisoner (for Charity's Sake) in Washington Jail; including a Narrative of the Voyage and Capture of the Schooner Pearl. *Boston: Bela Marsh.* 1855. 12mo, pp. 122. Portrait. B., BA., H. 20912

DRAYTON (J.) Letters written during a Tour through the Northern and Eastern States of America; By John Drayton. *Charleston, South-Carolina: Printed by Harrison and Bowen.* M,DCC,XCIV. 8vo, pp. iv, 3–138. 3 Plates. C., H. 20913

Mr. Drayton was a district judge, and subsequently Governor of South Carolina. This early production is but little known.

DRAYTON. Memoirs of the American Revolution, from its Commencement to the Year 1776, inclusive; as relating to the State of South-Carolina, and occasionally referring to the States of North-Carolina and Georgia. By John Drayton, LL.D. ... *Charleston; Printed by A. E. Miller.* 1821. 2 vols., 8vo, pp. xxvii, 430; Title, 400. Portrait and 2 Maps. B., BA. 20914

The materials for this work were collected by the author's father.

DRAYTON. A View of South Carolina, as respects her Natural and Civil Concerns. By John Drayton. *Charleston: Printed by W. P. Young.* 1802. 8vo, 2 l., pp. 251. Map and Plates.

A German version, "Beschreibung von Süd-Carolina. Aus dem Englischen," with a map, forms part of Vol. 35 of the "Bibliothek der neuen Reisebeschreibungen. *Weimar.* 1808." 8vo.

DRAYTON (M.) Poems by Michael Drayton, Esquyer, collected into one volume, with sundry pieces inserted, never before Imprinted. *London: Printed for John Smithwicke.* 1619. Folio, pp. 492. Portrait and Frontispiece by W. Hole. 20916

Includes one of the earliest poems on emigration to America. For a list of editions of Drayton, *see* Lowndes, page 671–2.

DRAYTON (W.) An Oration delivered in ... Charleston ... July 4, 1831. By the Hon. William Drayton. To which is annexed, an Account of the Celebration of the 55th Anniversary of American Independence, by the Union and State Rights Party. *Charleston, S. C.* 1831. 8vo, pp. 40. H., S. 20917

Also: Address to the People of the Congressional District of Charleston, ... *Charleston, S. C.: Wm. Estill.* 1832. 8vo, pp. 17. — Speech ... On the Proposition to Amend the Constitution of the United States, Respecting the Election of President and Vice-President. Delivered in the House ... March 7, 8, 1826. 12mo, pp. 24.

DRAYTON (W. H.) A Charge on the Rise of the American Empire, delivered by the Hon. William-Henry Drayton, Esq. Chief Justice of South-Carolina: to the Grand Jury For the District of Charlestown. *Charlestown: Printed by David Bruce.* M DCC LXXVI. 8vo, Title, pp. 25. BA., P., W. 20918

DRAYTON. The Speech of the Hon. William-Henry Drayton, Esquire, Chief Justice of South-Carolina. Delivered on the Twentieth January, 1778. In the General Assembly resolved into The Committee of the Whole; upon the Articles of the Confederation of the United States of America. *Charlestown: Printed by David Bruce.* M DCC LXXVIII. 8vo, pp. 46.

Mr. Drayton was also one of the authors of "The Letters of Freemen to the Deputies of North America." The following is also attributed to him:

[Drayton.] To their Excellencies Richard Viscount Howe, Admiral; and William Howe, Esq; General, of his Britannick Majesty's Forces in America. ... A Carolinian. *Charlestown, South Carolina. Oct.* 22, 1776. 8vo, pp. 8. P. 20920

Drayton; A Story of American Life. *New York.* 1851. 12mo. 20921

Drebing (Gustav L.) Das gemeine Recht (Common Law) der Vereinigten Staaten von Amerika, nebst den Statuten der einzelnen Staaten und dem Bankerott-Gesetze. *New-York: E. Steiger.* 1866–67. 10 pts., 8vo, pp. iv, 684. C. 20922

Dred Scott (Case of). *See* Scott (Dred).

Drees (J. W.) Beitrage zur Mission der Lutherischen Kirchen in der Stadt New-York. Von J. W. Drees, ... *New York: H. Ludwig.* 1863. 16mo, pp. 59. 20923

Dresser (A.) The Narrative of Amos Dresser, with Stone's Letters from Natchez, — an Obituary Notice of the Writer, and Two Letters from Tallahassee, Relating to the Treatment of Slaves. *New York: American Anti-Slavery Society.* 1836. 12mo, pp. 42. M. 20924

Dresser (H. E.) The Battle Record of the American Rebellion by Horace E. Dresser, A.M. *New York: Sinclair Tousey.* [1863.] 8vo, pp. 72. BA. 20925

Also: The Internal Revenue Laws. Act Approved June 30, 1864, as Amended, and the Act Amendatory thereof, Approved March 3, 1865, with Copious Marginal References, a Complete Analytical Index, and Tables of Taxation. *New York: D. Appleton & Co.* 1865. 8vo, pp. 152. + To July 13, 1866. [*Ibid.*] 1866. 8vo, pp. 228. B. — The New Internal Revenue Law, Approved June 30, 1864, with Copious Marginal References, a Complete Analytical Index, and Tables of Taxation. ... *New York: D. Appleton & Co.* 1864. 8vo, pp. iv, 122. B., BA. — The United States Internal Revenue and Tariff Law passed July 13, 1870, together with the Act imposing Taxes on Distilled Spirits and Tobacco, and for other Purposes, approved July 20, 1868 ... *New York: Harper & Brothers.* 1870. 8vo, pp. 99. BA.

Dresserus (M.) Historien vnd Bericht,|Von dem New-licher|Zeit erfundenen Königreich China,|wie es nach vmbsienden, so zu einer rechtmessigen|Beschreibung gehören, darumb|beschaffen.|Item, Von dem auch new erfundenen|Lande Virginia.|Jetzund auffs newe vbersehen, vnd mit einem Zusatz ver-|mehret, Nemlich:|Wie es vmb die Religion in Perser vnd Moh-|ren land,|vnter Priester Johan bewand sey.|In Druck verfertiget, durch|Matthævm Dresservm D.|der Sprachen vnd

Historien Professorn.|*Getruckt zu Leipzig, durch Frantz Schnelboltz.*|*Typis Haeredvm Beyeri.*|*Anno*|M.D.XCVIII.| 4to, 6 l., pp. 297. J.C.B. 20926

The second part is a translation from English into German of Hariot's "Virginia."

Dreuillette (G.) Epistola Rev. P. Gabrielis Dreuillettes, Societatis Jesu Presbyteri, ad Dominum Illustrissimum, Dominum Joannem Wintrop, Scutarium. *Neo-Eboraci in insula Manhattan: Typis Cramoisianis Joannis-Mariæ Shea.* M.DCCC.LXIV. Sm. 8vo, pp. 13. + [*Ibid.*] M. DCCC. LXIX. 8vo, pp. 13. BA.

Forms No. xx. of Shea's "Cramoisy Series."

Dreuillette. Narré du voyage faict pour la Mission des Abnaquiois et des Connaissances tiréz de la Nouvelle Angleterre et dispositions des Magistrats de cette Republique pour le secours contre les Iroquois, ès années 1650 & 1651. Par Le R. Père Gabriel Dreuillette de la Compagnie de Jésus. Imprimé d'après la Copie de l'Original déposé parmi les papiers du Bureau des Biens des Jésuites, à Quebec. [*Albanie: imprimerie de Weed, Parsons & Cie.*] 12mo, 2 l., pp. 33. BA., S. 20928

Privately printed for Mr. James Lenox. For a translation, by J. G. Shea, *see* "New York Hist. Soc. Collections," Second Series, v. 3.

Dreuillette. Recueil de pièces sur la négociation entre la Nouvelle France et la Nouvelle Angleterre ès années 1648 et suivantes. *Nouvelle York: de la Presse Cramoisy de Jean-Marie Shea.* 1866. 12mo, pp. 59. S. 20929

Dreveton (Théodore). Choses coloniales. Guadeloupe. Août 1845. *Paris: Ledoyen.* 1846. 8vo. 20930

Drew (B.) A North Side View of Slavery. — The Refugee; or the Narratives of Fugitive Slaves in Canada, related by Themselves; with an Account of the History and Condition of the Colored Population of Upper Canada. By Benjamin Drew. *Boston: J. P. Jewett & Co.* 1856. 12mo, pp. 387. P., S.

Drew (S.) The Life of the Rev. Thomas Coke, LL.D. including in detail his various Travels and Extraordinary Missionary Exertions, in England, Ireland, America, and the West-Indies: ... By Samuel Drew ... *London.* 1817. 8vo. Portrait. + *New York: J. Soule and T. Mason.* 1818. 8vo, pp. xix, 391. S. + *New York.* 1853. 12mo. B. 20932

Drew (S. S.) The California Battalion Claim. Argument before the Committee of the Legislature of Massachusetts, on

Military Claims, in the Case of Henry H. Wyatt and others, Members of the California Battalion, for State Bounty, March 19, 1866. By S. S. Drew. [n. p. n. d.] 8vo, pp. 14. H.

Drew. The Campaign of 1856. Fremont Songs for the People, Original and Selected ... . Compiled by Thomas Drew ... *Boston: John P. Jewett and Company.* 1856. 32mo, pp. 64.

[Drew.] The John Brown Invasion, an Authentic History of the Harper's Ferry Tragedy .... . *Boston: James Campbell.* 1860. 8vo, pp. 112. B., H. 20935

Also: The Campaign of 1860. Republican Songs for the People, Original and Selected. ... *Boston: published by Thayer and Eldridge.* 1860. 16mo, pp. 64. H.

Drewe (E.) The Case of Edward Drewe, late Major of the Thirty-fifth Regiment of Foot. Published by himself. *Exeter; printed by B. Thorn and Son.* MDCCLXXXII. 8vo, pp. vi, 102. 20936

Contains some particulars of the battle at Bunker's Hill, etc. Major Drewe was tried by court-martial, at Saint Lucia, for repeated neglects of duty.

Drewe. Dedicated to the British Army. Military Sketches. By Edward Drewe, late Major of the 35th Regiment of Foot. *Exeter: B. Thorn and Son.* MDCCLXXXIV. 8vo, pp. (2), 156.

Includes "An Elegiac Epistle, addressed to a Friend, on my leaving Boston in 1775, for the cure of my Wounds, sustained at Bunker's Hill."

[Drewe.] A Letter to a Young Officer, written in the year 1776. By an Officer of the British Army. *New-York: printed by J. Rivington, Printer to the King's most excellent Majesty.* 1778. 4to, pp. 24. S. 20938

Only a few copies printed for the perusal of the author's friends.

Drews (J.) Fasti Societatis Jesu. Res et Personas Memorabiles ejusdem Societatis per Singulos Anni Dies repræsantantes. Operâ et Studio R. P. Joannes Drews. *Hispali.* 1753. 4 vols., Sm. 8vo. 20939

Title from Rich's "Bib. Amer.," Vol. I.

Drexel & Co. Bonds of the United States outstanding October 1st, 1868; with a Compendium of the Acts of Congress under which they were issued. Revised Edition. *Philadelphia.* 1868. 8vo, pp. 36. 20940

Dreyer (J. H.) Concord and Religion; the Principal Sources of Civil Prosperity: a discourse, delivered in the German Reformed Church in ... New York, on the Sunday succeeding the

Thirty-Sixth Anniversary of the Independence of the United States of America. By the Rev. John H. Dreyer ... . Translated from the German. *Printed by E. Conrad.* 1812. 8vo, Title, pp. 14. BA. 20941

Dreyhundert auserlesene Amerikanische Gewächse nach Linneischer Ordnung. *Nürnberg: auf Kosten der Raspischen Buchhandlung.* 1785–1795. 6 parts or 3 vols., 8vo. 300 Colored Plates. 20942

Contains the whole of the plants of Jacquin's "Selectarum Stirpium Americanarum Historia," published in 1780 in folio. Some copies of the first part have the date 1789.

Dreys (Nicolas). Memoria sobre o estado actual da fabricação do assucar no Bresil, e os melhoramentos a introduzir. *Rio de Janeiro: na Imp. de Cremière.* 1842. 8vo, pp. 20.

Dreys. Noticia descriptiva da provincia do Rio-grande de S. Pedro do Sul, contendo além da topographia physica e politica, e de un ensaio de estatistica local, informações sobre o estado actual da população, suas subdivisões, e sobre o caracter e costumes dos habitantes. Com un mappa reduzido do theatro da guerra presente. *Rio de Janeiro: Typ. Imp. e Constit. de J. Villeneuve & C.ª* 1839. 4to, pp. xi–216. 20944

Drezzanio (F.) La mort glorieuse du Père Christophe de Mendoza, de la Compagnie de Jésus, cruellement massacré pour la Foy, au Paraguay, Province du Peru l'an 1636. Ainsi le rapporte le Père Frãçois Drezzanio ... . *Lille: imprimerie de Pierre de Rache.* 1639. 8vo, pp. 8. 20945

Driesen (L.) Leben des Fürsten Johann Moritz von Nassau-Siegen, General-Gouverneur von Niederländisch-Brasilien, etc. *Berlin.* 1849. 8vo. Facsimile. 20946

See also Van Driessen (P.)

Driggs (John F.), *and* Blair (Austin). Speeches of Hons. John F. Driggs and Austin Blair, of Michigan. Delivered in the House ... May 7, 1868. *Washington, D. C.* [1868.] 8vo, pp. 8. H. 20947

Dring (T.) Recollections of the Jersey Prison-Ship; taken, and prepared for Publication, from the Original Manuscript of the late Captain Thomas Dring, of Providence, R. I., One of the Prisoners. By Albert G. Greene. *Providence: H. H. Brown.* 1829. 12mo, pp. 167. Plate of the Prison-Ship. 20948

Greene's copy sold for $21.

Dring. Recollections of the Jersey Prison-Ship: taken and prepared for Publication, from the Original Manuscript of the late Captain Thomas Dring of Providence, R. I., One of the Prisoners. By Alfred G. Greene. Edited by Henry B. Dawson. *Morrisania, N. Y.* 1865. Imp. 8vo, pp. xxii, 201. 2 Plates.

Fifty copies printed on large paper, folio. The plates are [faded] photographs.

[Drinker (John).] Observations on the late Popular Measures. By a Tradesman. *Philadelphia.* 1774. 8vo. P. 20950

Drinkwater (Anne J.) Memoir of Mrs. Deborah H. Porter, Wife of Rev. C. G. Porter, of Bangor. By Anne J. Drinkwater. ... *Portland: Sanborn & Carter.* 1848. 12mo, pp. 269. H. 20951

Drinkwater (D. F.) Letters ... by D. F. Drinkwater, Secretary of the United Press Association. *Washington.* 1867. 8vo, pp. 40. H. 20952

Driscoll (F.) Sketch of the Canadian Ministry. By Frederick Driscoll. *Montreal.* 1866. 12mo, pp. 130. 20953

Driscoll. The Twelve Days' Campaign [in Virginia]. An Impartial Account of the Final Campaign of the Late War. By Frederick Driscoll. *Montreal: Longmore & Co.* 1866. 8vo, pp. 103. Map. C., S. 20954

Also: Remarks on the Defence of the British Provinces.

Drisler (H.) Bible View of Slavery, by John H. Hopkins, D.D., Bishop of ... Vermont, ... Examined by Henry Drisler. *New York: C. S. Westcott & Co.* 8vo, pp. 20. 20955

Also printed as "A Reply to the Bible View of Slavery, By J. H. Hopkins, D.D *New York: C. S. Westcott & Co.* 1863. 8vo, pp. 20.

Droguet (Marc Julien). Propositions sur les préceptes d'hygiène navale à observer sous les tropiques du Cancer, du Capricorne, sous la zône torride, et sur l'acclimatement des Européens à Saint-Domingue et aux Antilles. Thèse. *Paris: imp. de Didot jeune.* 1806. 4to. 20956

Drohojowska (Antoinette Françoise Anne Symon de Latreiche, *comtesse*). L'Esclave. *Paris: Casterman.* 1862. 18mo.

Les Droits. *See* [Dalrymple (*Sir* John)], No. 18348.

Droop (Henry Richmond). On the Political and Social Effects of Different Methods of electing Representatives. By H. R. Droop, Esq. ... . *London: William Maxwell & Son.* 1869. 8vo, pp. 39. H. 20958

Contains references to the United States.

Drouet (H.) Essai sur les Mollusques terrestriales et fluviatiles de la Guyane française. *Paris.* 1859. 8vo. 4 Plates.

Drouet (H.) Sur terre et sur mer. Excursions d'un Naturaliste en France, aux Açores, à la Guyane et à Angola. *Paris: Gide.* 1870. 12mo. 20960

Drouin de Bercy (M.) L'Europe et l'Amérique comparées. Par M. Drouin de Bercy ... . *Paris: Rosa; Londres, Treutell et Würtz; Bruxelles, Lecharlier.* 1818. 2 vols., 8vo, pp. vi, 432; (4), 452. 6 Colored Plates. H. 20961

Drouin de Bercy. Histoire civile et commerciale de la Jamaïque; suivie du Tableau général des possessions anglaises et françaises dans les Deux Mondes, et de Réflexions commerciales et politiques relatives à la France et à l'Angleterre. *Paris: Rosa.* 1818. 8vo, pp. 144. Plate. 20962

Drouin de Bercy. De Saint-Domingue, de ses guerres, de ses revolutions, de ses resources et des moyens à prendre pour y retablir la paix et l'industrie, par M. Drouin de Bercy, Creole, etc. *Paris: Hocquet; Barba.* 1814. 8vo. 20963

Drouyn de Lhuis. Rapport de M. Drouyn de Lhuis, et opinions de M. le contre amiral Romain-Desfossés et de M. Coffinières, sur la question de la Plata. *Paris: imp. de E. Duverger.* 1851. 8vo, pp. 87. 20964

Drown (S. DeWitt). Record and Historical View of Peoria, [Ill.] from the Discovery by the French Jesuit missionaries in the Seventeenth Century to the Present Time. ... To which is added a Business Directory of the City. *Peoria: E. O. Woodcock.* 1850. 12mo, pp. 164. 20965

See also "Peoria."

Drowne (S.) An Oration Delivered at Marietta, April 7, 1789, in Commemoration of the Commencement of the Settlement formed by the Ohio Company. By Solomon Drowne, Esq. M.B. *Printed at Worcester, Mass. By Isaiah Thomas.* 1789. 4to, pp. 17. M., W. 20966

Drowne. An Oration delivered ... in Providence, at the Celebration, February 23, A.D., 1824, in Commemoration of the Birth Day of Washington, ... By Solomon Drowne, M.D. *Providence: Brown & Danforth.* 1824. 8vo, pp. 24. 20967

Also: Annual Address delivered before the Rhode Island Society for the Encouragement of Domestic Industry, October 15, 1823. ... *Providence: Carlile & Brown.* 1826. 8vo, pp. 18. — Funeral Oration in Memory of the Hon. James M. Vernon, Esq., late a Judge in the Western Territory; delivered at Marietta, Ohio, January 13, 1789. ... 8vo. *See* "Historical Magazine," March, 1857; "American Quarterly Register," II. 357; and "New York City, during the American Revolution."

Drowne (T. S.) A Commemorative Discourse on the Completion of the Tower and Spire of the Church of the Holy Trinity, Brooklyn. With Historical Notes. By Rev. T. S. Drowne. *New York: Hurd & Houghton.* 1868. 8vo, pp. 78.

Druid Hill. *See* Vol. I., No. 3037.

A Drum for the Ears of the Drowsy. By an American Lady. *Philadelphia: printed for the author.* 1814. 8vo. P. 20969

Attacks the "imbecile administration" in reference to the war.

Drumm (J. H.) Assassination of Abraham Lincoln, President of the United States: A Sermon, preached on the Morning of Easter Monday, April 16th, 1865, in St. James' Church, Bristol, Pa., By the Rev. John H. Drumm, M.D. *Wm. Bache, Printer: Bristol.* [1865.] 8vo, pp. 21. 20970

Three hundred copies printed; not published.

The Drummer, or New York Clerks and Country Merchant, a Local Play. *Milwaukee.* 1851. 18mo. 20971

The Drummer Boy. A Story of the War. In Verse. By Cousin John. *Boston: Crosby & Nichols.* 1862. 12mo, pp. 48.

Drummond (A. de V. M. de). Prelecções de Diplomacia com referencia e applicação de seus principios a's leis particulares do Brasil ate 1867, pelo Doutor Antonio de Vasconcellos Menezes de Drummond (Natural de Pernambuco). *Pernambuco.* 1867. 8vo, pp. 166. 20973

Drummond (R. B.) President Lincoln and the American War; A Funeral Address, delivered on Sunday, April 30, 1865. By Robert Blackley Drummond, B.A. *London: Trübner & Co.* 1865. 8vo, pp. 12. 20974

Drummond (T.) Musci Americani: or Specimens of the Mosses collected in British North America, and chiefly among the Rocky Mountains during the Second Land Arctic Expedition, under the Command of Captain Franklin. By Thomas Drummond, Assistant Naturalist to the Expedition. *Glasgow.* 1828. 2 vols., 4to. 20975

"Contains 286 specimens of mosses, with printed descriptions. Dr. Hooker informed me that there were not forty copies of this work altogether." — Rich, Vol. II.

[Drummond (R).] Sermon before the Society for Propagation of the Gospel in Foreign Parts. 1754. By Robert, Lord Bishop of Sarum. *London.* 1754. 8vo, pp. 72. M. 20976

Drury (L.) Address before the Bristol Association for the Promotion of Temperance, March 23, 1832. By Luke Drury. *Providence: Weeden & Knowles.* 1832. 8vo, pp. 28. 20977

Also: Report of the Examination of the Rev. Ephraim K. Avery, for the Murder of Sarah Maria Cornell. By Luke Drury. [n. p.] 1833. 8vo, pp. 64.

The Dry Goods Trade, and Cotton, Woollen, Silk, and Linen Manufacture of the United States; a Directory of the Jobbers, Importers, Commission and Retail Dealers; Dry Goods, and Cotton, Woollen, Silk, and Linen Manufacturing Corporations, Firms, etc., in the United States; together with Valuable and Interesting Statistics of the Same. *Boston.* 1869. 4to, pp. 304. 20978

Dryden (J.) The Indian Emperour; or, the Conquest of Mexico by the Spaniards. Being the Sequel of the Indian Queen. By John Dryden, Esq. *London: Printed for H. Herringman.* 1667. + [*Ibid.*] 1668. + Third Edition. [*Ibid.*] 1670. 4to. + [*Ibid.*] 1681. 4to, 4 l., pp. 68, (2). + [*Ibid.*] 1686. 4to, 4 l., pp. 60, 2 l. + [*Ibid.*] 1692. + [*Ibid.*] 1696. + [*Ibid.*] 1700. + [*Ibid.*] 1703. 20979

Also in his "Works." The third edition contains a "Defence of an Essay on Dramatique Society," which was afterwards cancelled, and is now rare.

Dryden. Montésuma, ou Fernand Cortés, tragédie en 5 actes et en prose. Traduit de l'anglais par M. l'abbé D. B. [Dubourg]. *Paris: J. Lesclapart.* 1743. 8vo. S. 20980

Drysdale (Isabel). Scenes in Georgia. Written for the American Sunday School Union. *Philadelphia.* 1850. 18mo.

Duane (James). Decree, on the Admiralty Side of the District Court of New York, etc., in the Case of the Catherine, 28th January, 1794. *New York.* 1794. 8vo, pp. 35. 20982

DUANE (R. B.) A Memorial of Nathan B. Crocker, D.D., Late Rector of Saint John's Church, Providence, R. I. Edited by Richard B. Duane, Rector. *Providence: Sidney S. Rider and Brother.* 1866. 8vo, pp. (1), 103. H. 20983

DUANE. A Sermon preached in ... Providence, on ... April 19, 1865, the Day appointed for the Funeral Obsequies of President Lincoln, by the Rev. Richard B. Duane ... . *Providence.* 1865. 8vo, pp. 15. B., H. 20984

[DUANE (William).] An Examination of the Question, who is the Writer of Two Forged Letters addressed to The President of the United States? Attributed to John Rutledge, Esq. ... [n. p.] 1803. 8vo, pp. 27. BA. 20985

[DUANE.] Experience the Test of Government: In Eighteen Essays. Written during the Years 1805 and 1806. To aid the Investigation of Principles, and Operation of the Existing Constitution and Laws of Pennsylvania. *Philadelphia: printed by William Duane.* 1807. 8vo, pp. 60. 20986

Often found with Duane's Tracts.

[DUANE.] General Assembly's State of the Right of the Colony of New York (with respect to its Eastern Boundary on Connecticut River, so far as concerns the late Encroachments under the Government of New Hampshire) published at their Session, 1773. *Hartford.* 1774. 8vo, pp. 211. 20987

DUANE. A History of the French Revolution, with a free Examination of the Dispute between the French and American Republics. *Philadelphia.* 1798. 4to. 20988

[DUANE] A Letter to George Washington, President of the United States; containing Strictures on his Address of the Seventeenth of September, 1796, notifying his Relinquishment of the Presidential Office. By Jasper Dwight, of Vermont. *Printed at Philadelphia for the Author. Dec.* 1796. 8vo, pp. 48.

One of the most violent invectives against Washington, and far more abusive than the famous letter of Thomas Paine. An example: "Had you obtained Promotion, as you expected for the services [you] rendered after Braddock's Defeat, your sword would have been drawn against your country." This was Duane's first essay in America. *See* [Carpenter's] "Jefferson," II. 130, 412.

DUANE. Mississippi Question. Report of a Debate on the Senate of the United States, On the 23d, 24th, & 25th February, 1803, on Certain Resolutions concerning the Violation of

the Right of Deposit in the Island of New Orleans. By William Duane. *Philadelphia: Printed by W Duane.* 1803. 8vo, Title, pp. 198. BA., G., H. 20990

[DUANE.] Politics for American Farmers; being a Series of Tracts, exhibiting the Blessings of Free Government, as it is administered in the United States, Compared with the boasted Stupendous Fabric of British Monarchy. Originally written for, and published in The Aurora of Philadelphia, in the Beginning of ... 1807. *Washington City: Printed by R. C. Weightman for W. Duane, Philadelphia.* 1807. 8vo, Title, pp. 200. BA.

DUANE. Report of a Debate in the Senate of the United States on a Resolution for Recommending to the Legislatures of the Several States an Amendment to the Third Paragraph of the First Section of the Second Article of the Constitution of the United States, Relative to the Mode of Electing a President and Vice President of the said States. By William Duane. [*Philadelphia:*] *Printed by William Duane.* 1804. 8vo, pp. 158.

[DUANE.] The Two Americas, Great Britain and the Holy Alliance. *Washington.* 1824. 8vo. + Second Edition. [*Ibid.*] 1824. P. 20993

DUANE. A Visit to Colombia, in the Years 1822 & 1823, by Laguayra and Caracas, over the Cordillera to Bogotà, and thence by the Magdalena to Cartagena. By Col. Wm. Duane, of Philadelphia. *Philadelphia: Printed by T. H. Palmer, for the Author.* 1826. 8vo, pp. 632. 2 Plates. BA. 20994

Also: The American Military Library; ... Adapted to the Use of the Militia of the United States ... . By William Duane. ... *Philadelphia: printed for the Author.* 1809. 2 vols., 8vo, Title, pp. ii, iii, 214; Title, v, xvi, 355. BA. — The American Poetical and Prose Miscellany; Original and Selected. By William Duane. *Philadelphia.* 1809. 2 vols., 12mo. P. — The Foul Charges of the Tories against the Editor of the Aurora repelled by Positive Proof and Plain Truth, &c. *Philadelphia.* 1798. 8vo. — A Hand Book for Infantry: containing the First Principles of Military Discipline, founded on Rational Method: intended to explain, in a Familiar and Practical Manner, for the Use of the Military Force of the United States, ... The Fourth Edition. ... . *Philadelphia: printed for the Author.* 1813. 8vo, pp vii, 112. 11 Plates. BA. — The Hand Book for Infantry. The Fifth Edition. *Philadelphia.* 1813. 8vo, pp. (4), 112. H. — A Hand Book for Riflemen; ... conformable to the system established for the United States Military Force, and the Latest Improvements in the Modern Art of War. Second Edition. ... . *Philadelphia: printed for the Author.* 1813. 8vo, pp. vi, 108. 13 Plates. BA. — A Military Dictionary; or Explanation of the several systems of Discipline of different kinds of Troops ... comprising the Pocket Gunner ... *Philadelphia.* 1810. 8vo. — Report on part of the Committee of Privileges, on the form of proceedings in the Case of William Duane. [n. p. 1804.] 8vo. — Return of the whole number of persons within the several Districts of the United States, by W. Duane. *Philadelphia.* 1802. 8vo, pp. 88. —

[Duane.] Sampson against the Philistines, or the Reformation of Lawsuits; and Justice made Cheap, Speedy, and Brought Home to every Man's Door: Agreeable to the Principles of the Ancient Trial by Jury, before the same was Innovated by Judges and Lawyers. Compiled for the Use of the Honest Citizens of the United States. To whom it is Dedicated. [*Philadelphia.* n. d.] 8vo, pp. v, 98, xxiii. BA. + The Second Edition. [Also anonymous.] ... *Philadelphia: printed by B. Graves, for W. Duane.* 1805. 8vo, pp. 96. BA. — The System of Infantry Discipline; according to the Regulation established for the Army of the United States, 19 March, 1818. [*Philadelphia.*] 1814. 8vo, pp. viii, 284. C. — Trial of the Rioters for an Assault on William Duane, 15 May, 1799 — Trial 28 April, 1801. — Catalogue of the Library of the Late Col. William Duane. [*Philadelphia.* 1836.] 8vo, Title, pp. 54. BA. Duane was also the publisher of many pamphlets which he gathered into volumes, and published as Duane's Tracts.

DUANE (W.) Canada and the Continental Congress, delivered before the Historical Society of Pennsylvania, as their Annual Address, On the 31st of January, 1850. By William Duane. *Philadelphia: Edward Gaskill.* 1850. 8vo, pp. 20.

D[UANE] (W[illiam]). Ligan: A Collection of Tales and Essays, by W. D. *Philadelphia: Merrihew & Thompson.* 1857. 12mo, pp. 76. 20996

DUANE (W. J.) Letters, addressed to the People of Pennsylvania respecting the Internal Improvement, of the Commonwealth; by Means of Roads and Canals. By William J. Duane. *Philadelphia: printed by Jane Aitken.* 1811. 8vo, Title, pp. 125. BA. 20997

DUANE. Letter addressed to the People of the United States, in Vindication of his Conduct. By Wm. J. Duane. [*Philadelphia.*] 1834. 8vo, pp. 70. P. 20998

[DUANE.] The Law of Nations, investigated in a Popular Manner. Addressed to the Farmers of the United States. By William John Duane ... . *Philadelphia: Printed by W. Duane.* 1809. 8vo, pp. 103, 3 l. + *Philadelphia.* 1813. BA. 20999

[DUANE.] Mississippi Question fairly Stated, and the Views and Arguments of those who clamor for War examined. [By Camillus.] *Philadelphia.* 1803. 8vo. 21000

[DUANE.] Narrative and Correspondence concerning the Removal of the Deposites, and Occurrences connected therewith. *Philadelphia.* 1838. 8vo, 2 l., pp. 176. BA., H., M., P.

DUANE. Observations on the Importance of Improving the Navigation of the River Schuylkill, for the purpose of connecting it with the Susquehanna. By Wm. J. Duane. *Philadelphia.* 1818. 8vo. P. 21002

Also: Trial of William J. Duane, and others, for an alleged Riot.

DUARTE Y ZENEA (A.) Respuesta que da D. Antonio Duarte y Zenea á la vindicacion del Ldo. D. Gaspar Acosta. *Imprenta del Gobierno.* 1812. 8vo. 21003

DÜBEN (C. von). Resa uti Guiana, Mexico, Californien, China och Ostindien, företagna under åren 1843–58. 1:a häft. *Stockholm.* 1871. 4to, pp. 1–34. 21004

DUBLAR (L. J.) A l'illustre général La Fayette, compagnon d'armes de Washington; départ du général La Fayette, son arrivée en Amérique, son retour dans sa patrie. *Paris: imp. de Pochard.* 1825. 12mo. 21005

In verse.

DUBLIN, *N. H.* The Dublin Suit: decided in the Supreme Judicial Court of New Hampshire, June, 1859. In Chancery. The Attorney-General, at the Relation of Edward F. Abbot and Another, and Edward F. Abbot and Another, *v.* The Town of Dublin, B. F. Bridge and Another ... . *Concord: G. Parker Lyon.* 1860. 8vo, pp. 122. BA. 21006

See also [Cushing (E. L.)], No. 18100.

History of Dublin, 1855. *See* [Leonard (L. W.)]

Also: Report of the Dublin Schools. 1851. *Keene: printed by J. W. Prentiss & Company.* 1851. 8vo, pp. 24. H. — Report of the Superintending School Committee of Dublin, N. H., for the Year ending March 9, A.D. 1852. *Keene: H. Kimball, Printer.* 1852. 8vo, pp. 16. H. — School and Financial Reports, for the Year ending March, 1862, for the Town of Dublin, N. H. Also, a List of the Soldiers from Dublin in the Service of the United States. *Peterborough: printed by K. C. Scott.* 1862. 8vo, pp. 24. Continued. H.

DUBOCCAGE (Marie-Anne). La Columbiade ou la Foi portée au Nouveau Monde. Poëme. Par Madame Duboccage. *Paris: Desaint & Saillant Durand.* M. DCC. LVI. 8vo, pp. viii, 184, (2). Portrait and 10 Plates by Chedel. H. + *Paris: J. F. Bassompierre & Fils.* MDCCLVIII. 8vo, pp. viii, 184. 8 Plates and Portrait of the Author. 21007

An epic poem on the discovery of America. *See* Walpole's "Correspondence," II. 344. The authoress spells her name as above, but the portrait is named Dubocage.

DU BOCCAGE. La Colombiade, poema di Madama Du Boccage tradotto Dal Francese in Milano. ... *Milano: Guiseppe Marelli.* 1771. 8vo, pp. xx, 251, (1). H. 21008

DUBOIS (E.) Le Mexique, ou les Français à Mexique. Par E. Dubois. *Rouen: Mégard et Cie.* 1864. 8vo, pp. 192. Engravings. + [*Ibid.*] 1865. 8vo. 21009

DUBOIS (F. E.) Republique haïtienne. Deux ans et demi de ministère. Par F. E. Dubois. Seconde édition, augmentée. *Paris: imprimerie Bourdier et Cie.* 1867. 8vo, pp. 384. 21010

DUBOIS (Lucien). Le Pôle nord et l'équateur. Études sur les dernières explorations du globe. Le Pole nord. Météorologie. L'Afrique intérieure. *Paris: Douniol.* 1862. 12mo.

DU BOIS (H. A.) Lecture, before the Warren Library Association, upon Kossuth's Doctrine of Non-Intervention, by Henry A. Du Bois. *Warren: printed by J. Dumars.* 1852. 16mo, pp. 36. H. 21012

DU BOIS (T. K.) Tariff: or Rates of Duties payable on goods ... after June 30, 1824. *New York.* 1825. 12mo. S.

DUBOIS (William Ewing). Brief Account of the Collection of Coins belonging to the Mint of the United States, more particularly of the Antique Specimens. *Philadelphia.* 1846. 12mo. Frontispiece. 21014

DU BOIS. Pledges of History. A Brief Account of the Collection of Coins belonging to the Mint of the United States, more particularly of the Antique Specimens. By William E. Dubois ... . *Philadelphia: C. Sherman, Printer.* 1864. 18mo, pp. 138. H. 21015

One hundred and fifty copies privately printed.

DU BOIS. Record of the Family of Louis Du Bois, who emigrated from France to America in 1660. Edition of 150 copies; printed for the use of the family connection only. [*Philadelphia:*] *Press of John C. Clark & Son.* 1860. 8vo, pp. 76.

DU BOIS (W. Ewing *and* Robert Patterson). A Record of the Families of Robert Patterson (the Elder), Emigrant from Ireland to America, 1774; Thomas Ewing, from Ireland, 1718; and Louis Du Bois from France, 1660; connected by the marriage of Uriah Du Bois with Martha Patterson, 1798. Part First, containing the Patterson Lineage. Edition of 150 copies; printed for the use of the Family connection only. [*Philadelphia.*] 1847. 8vo, pp. 103. 21017

DU BOIS. Record of the Family of Thomas Ewing who emigrated from Ireland to America in 1718. Edition of 150 copies; printed for the use of the Family connexion only. *Press of James H. Bryson.* 1858. 8vo, pp. 38. 21018

DU BOIS. Trial of Lucretia Chapman, otherwise called Lucretia Espos y Mina, who was jointly indicted with Lino Amalia Espos y Mina, for the murder of William Chapman, Esq. ... in the Court of Oyer and Terminer, held at Doylestown, for Bucks, December Term, 1831, continued to February Term, 1832. Prepared for Publication by William E. Du Bois ... . *Philadelphia: G. W. Mentz & Son.* 1832. 8vo, Title, pp. 213, 8. C., BA. 21019

The pp. 8 contain "Supplement ... . Trial of Lino Amalia Espos y Mina ... ."

[DUBOIS-FONTANELLE (J. Gaspard).] The Shipwreck and Adventures of Monsieur Pierre Viaud, A Native of Bordeaux, and Captain of a Ship. Translated from the French, by Mrs. Griffith. *London: J. Davies.* 1771. 8vo, pp. 276. 21020

The shipwreck was on the Florida coast.

DU BOSQUE. The History of America; containing the Geographical, Political and Commercial State of the Continent. In which is given a succinct account of the Trade, Customs, and Policy of the French nation, and the foundation they have laid of obtaining the sole dominion in those Colonies. Translated from the French of Mons. Du Bosque. ... *London: James Lowndes.* 1770–71. 2 vols., 8vo, pp. xii, 387; pp. ii, 2 l., pp. 384. 21021

DUBOUCHET (Charles). Dernier mot sur le Guazacoalco. *Paris: imp. d'Auffray.* 1830. 8vo. 21022

DUBOUCHET. Le Guazacoalco, colonie de MM. Laisné de Villévêque et Giordan, ou Les horreurs dévoilées de cette colonie, par Charles Debouchet, échappé au desastre de la première expédition. *Paris: l'auteur.* 1830. 8vo, pp. 28. 21023

DUBOURG (C.) Informe que haze D. Clemente Dubourg, Natural de la Ciudad de Orleans, Vezino de el Puerto de Nantes, en los Reynos de Francia; y residente en esta Ciudad: interessado, en el navio nombrado la Aguila: en el Pleyto, que sigue con Don Gil Lelo de la Rea, en cuyo poder param todos los efectos de dicho navio, sobre que dicho Don Gil entregue a Don Clemente, lo que es suyo, con mas las costas, a Interesses: assi por raçon de la Compañia, como por la revocacion de Poderes. *Mexico.* 1718. 4to, 39 l. 21024

DUBOY (Alexandre). Godefroy et Augustin, ou Deux épisodes de l'histoire de Saint-Domingue, avec une notice sur la découverte de cette île. *Tours: Parnin.* 1847. 12mo. Portrait.

DUBOYS (P. M.) Mémoires pour servir à l'histoire de la révolution de Saint-Domingue, par feu Duboys; publiés d'après les manuscrits autographes de l'auteur par M. P. Lacroix. *Paris: Jébenne.* 1828. 8vo. 21026

This is merely a prospectus, announcing three volumes, which do not appear to have been published.

DUBROCA (Louis). Éloge de Washington par L. Dubroca. *Paris: l'an* VII [1799]. 12mo, pp. 47. C. 21027

DUBROCA. L'Itinéraire des Français dans la Louisiane, contenant l'histoire de cette colonie Française, sa description, le tableau des mœurs des peuples qui l'habitent, l'état de son commerce au moment de sa cession à l'Espagne et le degré de prospérité dont elle est susceptible; d'après les renseignements et les relations les plus authentiques. Par Dubroca. *A Paris.* 1802. 16mo, pp. (1), 104. Map. 21028

DUBROCA. La vie de J. J. Dessalines, chef des noirs révoltés de Saint Domingue, avec des notes très detaillées sur l'origine, le caractère, la vie et les atrocités des principaux chefs des noirs depuis l'insurrection de 1792. Par Dubroca. *Paris.* 1804. 12mo. 21029

DUBROCA. La Vie de Toussaint L'Ouverture, chef des noirs insurgés de Saint Domingue, suivie de notes sur Saint Domingue, &c. Par Dubroca. *Paris: Dubroca, An* X [1802]. 12mo, 2 l., pp. 74. Portrait. 21030

DUBROCA. The Life of Toussaint Louverture, Chief of the French Rebels in St. Domingo. To which are added, Interesting Notes respecting several Persons who have acted distinguished Parts in St. Domingo. By M. Dubroca. Translated from the French. *London: Symonds.* 1802. 8vo. 21031

See "M. Rev.," XXXVIII. 332, and Louverture, Toussaint.

[DUBUC (Jean Baptiste), *and* DUBUISSON (P. M.).] Lettres critiques et Politiques sur les colonies et le commerce des villes maritimes de France, adressées à G. T. Raynal. Par M. ***. *Geneve.* 1785. 8vo. 21032

Du Buc, a native of Martinique, was "chef du bureau des colonies," and published, according to the "Biographie générale," various "Mémoires" relating to the French colonies.

DUBUC-DUFERRET. Projet d'amélioration coloniale. *Paris: imp. de la Ve Porthmann.* 1823. 8vo, pp. 28, including an Appendix. 21033

DUBUCQ (*M.*) Le Pour et le Contre sur un objet de Grande Discorde et d'Importance Majeure. Convient-il à l'Administration de céder part, ou de ne rien céder aux Etrangers dans le Commerce de la Métropole avec ses Colonies? *A Londres* [i. e., *Paris.* 1784?] 4to, pp. 34. 21034

This elicited the following replies: "Observations Sommaires sur Le Pour et le Contre. *Paris.*" [n. d.] 4to; and "Réponse à la brochure, intitulée 'Le Pour et Contre.' *Londres* [*Paris*]. 1785." 4to, pp. 63.

[DUBUCQ.] Réplique à l'auteur du Pour et Contre. *A Londre* [i. e., *Paris*]. 1785. 4to, pp. 84. 21035

The following pieces, by Dubucq, all relate to the French colonies: La Ligne de Démarcation, ou Plan pour l'Approvisionnement des Isles Françaises de l'Amérique. *Paris.* [n. d.] 8vo. C. — Précis pour les grands Propriétaires des Colonies Françaises, contre les divers Ecrits des Négocians des Villes Maritimes. *Paris.* [n. d.] 8vo. C. — Réflexions d'un Vieillard sur l'Admission des Etrangers dans nos Colonies. *Paris.* 1785. 8vo. C. — Réflexions sur le Commerce, la Navigation, et les Colonies. *Paris.* 1787. 4to.

DUBUISSON (M.) Official Report made by the Commanding Officer ... to the Governor-General of Canada, of the War which took place at Detroit, in 1712, between the French and their Allies, and the Ottaganne and Mascoutins Indians. *Detroit.* 1845. 8vo. N. 21036

[DU BUISSON (Paul Ulric).] Abrégé de la révolution de l'Amérique angloise, depuis le commencement de l'année 1774, jusqu'au 1er janvier 1778. *Paris: Cellot et Jombert.* 1778. 12mo, pp. 452, 3 l. 21037

[DU BUISSON.] Nouvelles Considérations sur Saint-Domingue en réponse à celles de M. H. Dl. Par M. D. B ***. *Paris: Cellot et Jombert fils jeune.* 1780. 8vo, pp. 178, 264.

Written in reply to M. Hilliard D'Auberteuil.

DUBUISSON (P.) Mission du P. Dubuisson de la Compagnie de Jesus, dans le nord de la Pennsylvanie; et notice sur l'Eglise de Saint Joseph de Philadelphie. *Rome.* 1836. 8vo. 21039

DUBUQUE, *Iowa.* Dubuque City Directory for 1868–9. With an Accurate History of the City. Compiled by J. M. Wolfe. *Dubuque: Bames & Ryan.* 1868. 8vo, pp. 268. Continued.

History and Manual of the Congregational Church of Dubuque, Iowa. *Dubuque.* 1849. 12mo, pp. 24. 21041

Also: First Annual Report of the Board of Education, together with the Rules and Regulations for the Government of the Public Schools of Dubuque, December 31,

1856. *Dubuque.* 1857. 8vo, pp. 32. + 8vo, pp. 16. H. — Constitution and By-Laws, of the Dubuque Catholic Institute, of the City of Dubuque, Iowa. Instituted March A.D., 1859. *Dubuque.* 1860. 16mo, pp. 15. H. — Plans of the Custom House, Post Office, and Court Rooms. [n. p.] 1856.

DUBUQUE AND PACIFIC RAILROAD. Report given by G. A. Mix ... of the Exploration of the proposed Route. *Dubuque.* 1855. 8vo, pp. 8. 21042

Also: Guide, Gazetteer, and Directory of the Dubuque and Sioux City Railroad. etc. Compiled by A. Bailey. *Dubuque: Bailey & Wolfe.* 8vo, pp. 266.

DUCACHET (H. W.) Biographical Memoir of Samuel Bard, M.D., late President of the College of Physicians and Surgeons of the University of New York, ... By Henry William Ducachet. *New York.* 1821. 8vo, pp. 27. B. 21043

Also: The Substance of Remarks on Episcopal Resignations, and other Points of the Ohio Question; made in the House of Clerical and Lay Deputies of the Protestant Episcopal Church ... New York, October, 1832. ... . *New York: printed by T. G. Broughton.* 1833. 8vo, pp. 42. BA. — Tribute to the Memory of Jacob Dyckman, M.D. A Discourse ... *New York.* 1823. 8vo.

DU CALVET (P.) Appel à la Justice de l'Etat, ou Recueil des Lettres au Roi, au Prince de Galles et aux Ministres: avec une lettre à Messieurs les Canadiens, où sont fidèlement exposés les actes horribles de la violence arbitraire qui a régné dans la Colonie, durant les derniers troubles, & les vrais sentiments du Canada sur le Bill de Quebec, & sur la forme de Gouvernement la plus propre à y faire renaître la paix & le bonheur public. Une lettre au General Haldimand lui-meme. Enfin une dernière lettre a Milord Sidney. Où on lit un précis des nouvelles du 4 & 10 de Mai dernier, sur ce qui s'est passé en Avril dans le Conseil Législatif de Québec, avec les Protêts de six Conseillers, le Lieut. Gouverneur Henri Hamilton à leur tête, contre la nouvelle Inquisition d'Etat établie par le Gouverneur & son parti. Par Pierre Du Calvet, ... *Londres. Juin & Juillet,* 1784. 8vo, pp. (2), xiv, 320, viii. H. 21044

See Faribault, No. 205.

DU CALVET. The Case of Peter Du Calvet, Esq., of Montreal, in the Province of Quebeck, containing, (amongst other things worth notice); An Account of the long and severe Imprisonment he suffered in the said Province by the order of General Haldimand, the present Governor of the same, without the least offence or other lawful cause whatever. To which is prefixed, A dedication of it in the French Language, (Mr. Du Calvet not understanding English) To the King's

Most Excellent Majesty humbly imploring the Protection and Countenance of his Majesty's Royal Justice in his Endeavours to procure some Compensation for the Injuries he has received. *London: Printed in the Year* MDCCLXXXIV. 8vo, pp. xi, 284.

Privately printed. "Du Calvet was a French Protestant, and remained in Canada after the cession of the country to Great Britain in 1783. He was engaged in mercantile business, and was chosen a magistrate for the city of Montreal under the English government. After many quarrels with his colleagues, he was imprisoned for two years and eight months. Upon his release, he went to England in order to obtain justice from the governor." — RICH.

DUCATEL (J. T.) Report. *See* "Maryland."

DUCHASSING (P.), *and* WALPERS (G.) Plantae novae minusve cognitæ: in Isthmo Panamensi et insulis Guadeloupe et S. Thomas collectæ. Decades II. [*Linn.* 1850.] 8vo, pp. 20.

DUCHÉ (J.) The American Vine, a Sermon, Preached in Christ-Church, Philadelphia, Before the Honourable Continental Congress, July 20th, 1775. Being the Day recommended by them for a General Fast throughout the United English Colonies of America. By the Rev[d]. Jacob Duché, M.D. *Philadelphia: Printed by James Humphreys, Junior.* M,DCC,LXXV. 8vo, pp. 34. Plate. BA., N., P. 21047

[DUCHÉ.] Caspipina's Letters; containing Observations on a variety of subjects, Literary, Moral, and Religious. Written by a Gentleman who resided some time in Philadelphia. To which is added, The Life and Character of Wm. Penn, Esq.; Original Proprietor of Pennsylvania. ... *Bath: Reprinted by R. Cruttwell and sold by E. and C. Dilly and J. Phillips.* MDCCLXXVII. 2 vols. in 1, 16mo, pp. x, 188, 3 l.; pp. 236. C. + *Reprinted in Dublin.* 1792. 2 vols., 16mo. S. 21048

The life of William Penn, annexed to this edition of Duché, was written by Edmund Rack, of Bath, and the whole work was edited by him; it includes an entire reprint of "A brief account of the Province of Pennsylvania," published by Penn in 1681, in folio. Duché was "The Assistant Minister Of Christ's Church And St Peter's In Philadelphia In North America," and his signature of "Tamoc Caspipina forms the initial letters of those words. *See* "M. Rev.," LVII. 301; LVIII. 165 and "M. Rev.," New Series, VI. 357. Published in German as:

[DUCHÉ.] Briefe, welche Beobachtungen über verschiedene Gegenstände der Literatur, Religion und Moral enthalten, nebst dem Leben des Herrn Penn. Aus dem Englischen. *Leipzig: Schwickert.* 1778. 8vo. 21049

DUCHÉ. Discourses on various Subjects, By Jacob Duché, M.A. Rector of Christ-Church and St. Peter's, in Philadelphia; and formerly of Clare-Hall, Cambridge. *London: T. Cadell.*

M.DCC.LXXIX. 2 vols., 8vo, pp. xii, (28), 362; 4 l., pp. 450. 2 Plates by Benjamin West. + Second Edition. *London.* 1780. 2 vols., 8vo, pp. xii, 4 l., pp. 362; 4 l., pp. 430. + *Dublin.* 1792. 2 vols., 8vo. + Third Edition. *London.* MDCCXC. 2 vols., 8vo. 21050

There are copies of the second edition on large paper.

DUCHÉ. The Duty of Standing Fast in our Spiritual and Temporal Liberties, a Sermon preached ... July 7th, 1775, Before the First Battalion of the City and Liberties of Philadelphia ... . By the Reverend Jacob Duché, M.A. *Philadelphia: James Humphreys, Junior.* M,DCC,LXXV. 12mo, pp. iv, 25. Portrait. BA., H., P. 21051

DUCHÉ. Human Life a Pilgrimage: or The Christian a Stranger and Sojourner upon Earth: a Sermon, Occasioned by the Death of the Hon. Richard Penn, Esq; One of the Proprietaries of the Province of Pennsylvania: Preached ... in ... Philadelphia, on Sunday, April xxi. 1771. By the Reverend Jacob Duché, M.A. *Philadelphia: Printed by D. Hall, and W. Sellers.* MDCCLXXI. 8vo, pp. iv, 19. BA., P. 21052

DUCHÉ. Letter to Gen. Washington on the Declaration of Independence, by the Congress of America, By Rev. Jacob Duché, Rector of Christ's Church, Philadelphia. *Bath.* 1777. 4to. 21053

DUCHÉ. The Life and Death of the Righteous. A Sermon Preached at Christ Church, Philadelphia, on Sunday, February 13th, 1763, at the Funeral of Mr. Evan Morgan. By Jacob Duché, M.A. One of the Ministers of the United Churches of Christ Church, and St. Peter's, Philadelphia, and Chaplain to the Right Honourable the Earl of Stirling. *Philadelphia: Printed by B. Franklin, and D. Hall.* MDCCLXIII. 8vo, pp. iv, 24. P.

[DUCHÉ.] Observations on a Variety of Subjects, Literary, Moral and Religious; In a Series of Original Letters, Written by a Gentleman of Foreign Extraction, who resided some Time in Philadelphia. Revised by a Friend, to whose 2 Hands the Manuscript was committed for Publication. *Philadelphia: Printed by John Dunlap.* M.DCC.LXXIV. 12mo, pp. x, 241. C., P. + Third Edition. *London: J. Deighton.* M.DCC.XCI. 8vo, pp. xiii, 206. N. 21055

See "Caspipina's Letters," No. 21048. Also: Copy of a Letter from Rev. Jacob Duché to General Washington, October, 8, 1777. Broadside. [One of the spurious letters.] N. *See* (Washington (G.) In one of his letters to his wife, John

Adams gives an interesting account of the scene when Duché made the first prayer in Congress; and, in conclusion, says, "Duché is one of the most ingenious men, and best characters, and greatest orators in the Episcopal order, — yet a zealous friend of liberty and of his country." "Duché's reputation, however, has a less amiable and honorable side; of him it has been written: 'He, whose sublime prayer as Chaplain of the Continental Congress, melted the hearts of his audience every time he bent to repeat it, fell away from his loyalty, and enjoys the sole infamy of having sought to corrupt Washington. While the wretch was praying to Almighty God for the success of the Revolution, his heart was black with treason!'" — TUCKERMAN's *America*, p. 81.

DUCHER (G. J. A. D.) Analyse des Loix Commerciales, avec le Tarif des Droits sur les Batiments & les Marchandises dans les Treize États-Unis de l'Amérique. [*Paris.* 1790.] 8vo, pp. 35. J.C.B. 21056

DUCHER. De la dette publique en France, en Angleterre et dans les États-Unis de l'Amérique. [*Paris.*] 1791. 8vo, pp. 29.

DUCHER. Nouvelle alliance à proposer entre les républiques française et américaine. *Paris.* 1792. 8vo. 21058

DUCHER. Suppression des barrières èntre la France et les colonies. 1792. 8vo. 21059

DUCHESNE. Proposition de former une république suivant le plan du président de Montesquieu, dans les montagnes de Guyane française. Par le citoyen Duchesne. *Blois: imp. de Masson. Nivôse an* X. 8vo. 21060

DUCHESNE. Continuation faite par le citoyen Duchesne à sa "Proposition ... ." *Blois: imp. de Masson. An* X. 8vo.

DU CHILLEAU. Correspondance de M. le Marquis du Chilleau, Gouverneur-Général de Saint Domingue, avec M. le Compte de la Luzerne, Ministre de la Marine, et M. de Marbois Intendant de Saint-Domingue, relativement à l'introduction des farines étrangeres dans cette colonie. Remise à MM. les Députés de Saint-Domingue, d'après la demande de M. le President de l'assemblée Nationale, en date du 16 Septembre 1789. [*Port-au-Prince.* 1789.] 8vo, pp. 36. J.C.B. 21062

DUCHILLEAU. Réponse de M. Duchilleau, ancien gouverneur général de Saint-Domingue, à l'article qui le concerne dans la prétendue justification de M. de La Luzerne ... aussi ancien gouverneur de Saint-Domingue ... . [n. p. n. d.] 4to. 21063

DUCK (S.) Poems on Several Subjects. Written by Stephen Duck ... *Boston.* 1732. 8vo, pp. 27. M. 21064

Not American, except by imprint. It is a little curious, that these poems recited in 1730, should have been reprinted so early. There is another edition, with additions by Mary Collier, a washer-woman. *Cork, Printed. Philadelphia, Reprinted by William Gibbons.* 1793. 12mo, pp. 44.

[DUCLAIRON.] *See* [Maillet Duclairon (Antoine)].

DUCLOS (F.) A Brief Sketch of the Birth, Life & Sufferings, of Capt. Francis Duclos, A Frenchman by Birth. Particularly During the American Revolution, together with a Statement of the Unfriendly and Cruel Treatment he has since received from the British Government in Canada, With some remarks, both in prose and verse, by the reviser of the work, on special and singular occurrances, that transpired from time to time, in and since the Revolution, By consent of the Author. *St. Albans: Printed for the Author By J. Spooner.* 1824. 8vo, pp. 26.

DUCŒUR JOLY (S. J.) Manuel des habitans de Saint Domingue, contenant un précis de l'histoire de cette île depuis sa decouverte; la description topographique et statistique des parties française et espagnole, suivi du premier Vocabulaire Français-Créole et de Conversations Françaises-Créoles. Par S. J. Ducœur Joly. *Paris: Lenoir. An* X. [1802]. 2 vols., 8vo, pp. ccviii, 216, Map and 2 Tables; 406. Illustrations. C. 21066

DUCOUDRAY-HOLSTEIN (*Gen.* H. L. V.) Histoire de Bolivar; continuée jusqu'à sa mort par Alph. Viollet. *Paris.* 1831. 2 vols., 8vo. 21067

DUCOUDRAY-HOLSTEIN. Bolivar's Denkwürdigkeiten, [etc. Aus dem Französischen], deutsch bearbeitet von C. N. Röding. *Hamburg: Hoffmann & Campe.* 1830. 2 vols., 16mo, pp. xii, 324; 196, 1 l. C. 21068

DUCOUDRAY-HOLSTEIN. Memoirs of Simon Bolivar, President Liberator of the Republic of Columbia, and of his Principal Generals, with ... an Introduction. ... By Gen. H. L. V. Ducourdray-Hoistein. *Boston: S. G. Goodrich & Co.* 1830. 8vo, pp. 383. + *London: Henry Colburn and Richard Bentley* 1830. 2 vols., 8vo, pp. xii, 359; iv, 308. Map and Portrait.

DUCPÉTIAUX (Éd.) De l'etat de l'instruction primaire et populaire en Belgique, comparé à celui de l'instruction en Allemagne, ... et aux États-Unis. *Bruxelles: Meline, Cans et Comp.* 1838. 2 vols., 18mo. 21070

DUCPÉTIAUX. Du progrès et de l'état actuel de la réforme pénitentiaire et des institutions préventives aux Etats-Unis, en France, en Suisse, etc. *Paris.* 1838. 3 vols., 18mo. 21071

DUCREUX. Historiæ | Canadensis, | sev | Novæ-Franciæ | Libri Decem, | Ad Annum vsque Christi MDCLVI. | Auctore P. Francisco Crevxio, è Societate Iesv. | [Vignette:] | *Parisiis,* | *Apud Sebastianvm Cramoisy, Et Sebast.* | *Mabre-Cramoisy, Typographos Regis,* | *viâ Iacobæâ, sub Ciconijs.* | M. DC. LXIV. *Cvm Privilegio Regis,* | 4to, 14 l., pp. 810, 3 l. Map and 13 Plates. H., J.C.BT., N., S.

This work was composed from, and contains the substance of, the yearly relations of the Jesuits, which are very rare. Charlevoix rather objects to some of the details. *See* Rich's catalogue, No. 333, and Faribault, No. 178. The large plate, by Huret, of the martyrdom of the missionaries, is often deficient.

DUDEN (Gottfried). Bericht uber eine Reise nach den Westlichen Staaten Nordamerika's und einen mehrjahrigen Aufenthalt am Missouri (in den Jahren 1824, 1825, 1826 und 1827) in Bezug auf Auswanderung und Uebervölkerung, oder; Das Leben im Innern der Vereinigten Staaten, und dessen Bedeutung für die haüslichen und politischen Lage der Europäer ... *Elberfeldt.* 1829. 8vo. + [Auf Kosten der schweizerischen Auswanderungsgesellschaft gedruckt.] *St. Gallen: Scheitlin und Zollikofer.* 1833. 8vo. + Zweite Original-Ausgabe mit dem neuesten Correspondenz-Nachrichten, vielen andern Zusätzen und 1 karte. *Bonn.* 1834. 8vo, pp. 4, 404. 21073

DUDEN. Die Nordamerikanischen Democratie und das von Tocqueville'sche Werk darüber, als Zeichen des Zustandes der theoret. Politik. Nebst einer Aeusserung über Chevalier's nordamerikanischen Briefe insbesondere hinsichtlicht der wahren Ursachen des Bankstreites und der neuesten Unfälle in den Handelsleben. Duden's Selbst-Anklage wegen seines amerikanischen Reiseberichts, zur Warnung vor fernerm leichtsinnigen Auswandern. *Bonn.* 1837. 8vo. 21074

DUDEN. Einige Blätter des Werkes: Europa und Deutschland &c. Für die Besitzer von dessen amerikanischen Reiseberichte besonders abgedruckt. *Bonn.* 1835. 8vo. 21075

DUDEN. Europa und Deutschland von Nordamerika aus betrachtet, oder: Die europäische Entwickelung im 19. Jahrhundert in Bezug auf die Lage der Deutschen, nach einer Prüfung im innern Nordamerika. Von Gottfried Duden. *Bonn.* 1833–35. 2 vols., 8vo. 21076

DUDGEON (T.) A Nine Years' Residence, and a Nine Months' Tour on Foot, in the States of New York and Pennsylvania. By Thomas Dudgeon. *Edinburgh.* 1841. 12mo.

DUDLEY (D.) The Dudley Genealogies and Family Records. ... By Dean Dudley. ... *Boston: the Author.* 1848. 8vo, pp. 144.

DUDLEY. Illustrated Archæological and Genealogical Collections ... Illustrating the History, Genealogy and Archæology of New England. Edited by Dean Dudley. *Boston: L. Prang & Co.* 1861. Folio, 1 leaf. 6 Plates. H. 21079

DUDLEY. Officers of our Union Army and Navy; their Lives, their Portraits. *Boston: L. Prang & Co.* 1862. 18mo, pp. 148. 21080

DUDLEY. Pictures of Life in England and America; Prose and Poetry. By Dean Dudley. *Boston: James French.* 1851. 12mo, pp. 252. BA. 21081

DUDLEY (J.) Shall we save our Country, or the Duty of Prayer for Rulers, as a Means of Self-Preservation. A Sermon, delivered at Quebec Village, Thanksgiving-Day, Nov. 27, 1845. By Rev. John Dudley. *Woodstock, (Vt.): Printed at the Mercury Office.* 1845. 8vo, pp. 12. BA., S., 21082

Also: A Discourse on Means of a Revival. Preached at Quebec, Vt. ... *Windsor: Chronicle Press.* 1849. 8vo, pp. 24. BA.

DUDLEY (J. G.) Cotton — A Paper on the Growth, Trade and Manufacture of Cotton. Prepared at the Request of the New-York Historical Society ... By J. G. Dudley. *New-York: G. P. Putnam & Co.* 1853. 8vo, pp. 96. BA., S. 21083

DUDLEY (J. L.) Discourse Delivered in the South Congregational Church, Middletown, on the Sabbath Morning after the Assassination of President Lincoln. By John L. Dudley, Pastor of the Church. *Middletown: D. Barnes.* 1865. 8vo, pp. 28. B. 21084

The printed cover reads, "Slavery's Last Word." 800 copies printed.

DUDLEY. Discourse on the Death of Gen. Joseph R. F. Mansfield, ... Middletown, ... September 28, 1862. By Rev. John L. Dudley, ... *Middletown, Conn.: D. Barnes.* 1862. 8vo, pp. 31. Portrait. 21085

DUDLEY (Joseph). *See* "New England."

[DUDLEY (Mary).] Scripture Evidence of the Sinfulness of Injustice and Oppression, respectfully submitted to professing Christians, in order to call forth their sympathy and exertions on behalf of the much-injured Africans. *London: Harvey and Darton.* 1828. 12mo, pp. 40. Plate. 21086

[DUDLEY (Paul).] An Essay on the Merchandize of Slaves & Souls of Men, Revel. xviii. 13, with an Application thereof of the Church of Rome. To which is added, An Exercitation on Numb. xxxii. 10, 11, 12. With An Occasional Meditation on 1. Sam. xxiii. 11, 12. By a Gentleman. ... *Boston in N. E.: Printed by B. Green.* MDCCXXXI. 4to, 2 l., pp. iv, 63. BA., C. + *London: J. Downing.* 1732. 8vo, pp. 6, 35, (27 for 35).

"Tho Judg Dudley would not Put his name; yet He was Pleas'd to advise wth me in Correcting it, both before it went to ye Press, & in ye Time of ye Impression." — T. PRINCE.

[DUDLEY.] Objections to the Bank of Credit Lately Projected at Boston. Being a Letter upon that Occasion, to John Burril, Esq; Speaker to the House of Representatives for the Prince of Massachusetts-Bay in New-England. *Boston: printed by T. Fleet.* 1714. Sm. 8vo, pp. 32. W. 21088

This was answered by "A Vindication of the Bank of Credit Projected in Boston from the Aspersions of Paul Dudley, Esqr. in a Letter By him directed to John Burril, Esq. ... [n. p.] *Printed in the Year* 1714." 12mo, Title, pp. 20. BA. *See* [Sewall (S.)]

DUDLEY (R.) Arcano del mare di D. Ruberto Dutleo, Duca di Nortumbria e conte de Warwich. *Fiorenza: Corchini.* 1661. 2 vols., folio. 21089

"Seconde édition, augmentée, d'un ouvrage important dans lequel l'auteur donne ses idées sur la navigation et le développement du commerce maritime. Les cartes, gravées par Lucini, sont bien exécutées; une quarantaine d'elles concernent l'Amérique. On y trouve des cartes très-détaillées du Canada, des États-Unis, du Mexique, de la Guyane, etc." — TROSS *Catalogue.*

[DUDLEY (T.)] Massachusetts, or the First Planters of New England, the End and Manner of their coming thither, and Abode there. In Several Epistles to the Countess of Lincoln. With a Conclusion by John Cotton. [Signed T. D.] *Boston, New England: B. Green & J. Allen, Printers.* 1696. 12mo, pp. 56.

Of great rarity. Reprinted in the "Mass. Hist. Coll.," VIII. 36–47; and "New Hampshire Coll.," Vol. IV.; and with "Explanatory Notes by Dr. John Farmer," in Force's Tracts, Vol. II., No. IV.

DUDLEY (T. H.) Proceedings at the Dinner given by the Bar of New Jersey, to Thomas H. Dudley, Esq., Nov. 25, 1868. *Newark.* 1868. 8vo, pp. 18. H. 21091

DUDLEY (T. P.) Western Reserve Historical Society, Cleveland, O., August, 1870. Historical and Archæological Tracts. Number One. Battle and Massacre at Frenchtown, Michigan, January, 1813. By Rev. Thomas Dudley ... . [n. p. n. d.] 8vo, pp. 4. H. 21092

DUDLEY (*Viscount*). Speech of Viscount Dudley upon a Motion of 19th May, 1826, for the early Consideration of Measures touching Slaves. *London.* 1826. 8vo, pp. 12. 21093

DUDLEY OBSERVATORY. An Address to the Citizens of Albany, and the Donors and Friends of the Dudley Observatory ... . 13th of July, 1858. *Albany: Comstock and Cassidy, Printers.* 1858. 8vo, pp. 32. B., H., S. 21094

See Gould (B. A.)

Annals of the Dudley Observatory. ... *Albany: Weed, Parsons and Company, Printers.* 1866. 8vo, pp. lxvii; Description of Observatory, pp. 126; Appendix, pp. 126. H. 21095

Defence of Dr. Gould by the Scientific Council of the Dudley Observatory. *Albany: Weed, Parsons and Company.* 1858. 8vo, pp. 91. H. 21096

The Dudley Observatory and the Scientific Council. Statement of the Trustees. *Albany: Van Benthuysen, Printer.* 1858. 8vo, pp. 173. B., H. 21097

Inauguration of the Dudley Observatory at Albany, August 28, 1856. *Albany: Charles Van Benthuysen, Printer.* 1856. 8vo, pp. 139. H. + Second Edition [with Chronicle and List of Donors]. *Albany.* 1858. 8vo. 21098

A Letter to the Majority of the Trustees of the Dudley Observatory. [n. p. n. d.] 8vo, pp. 14. H., S. 21099

Who withholds Co-operation? Correspondence between the Officers of the Board of Trustees of the Dudley Observatory and the Directors of the same Institution. *Albany, N. Y.* 1858. 8vo, pp. 93. 21100

Also: Dudley Observatory: Meeting of the Board of Underwriters, &c., Chamber of Commerce, New-York city, 1856. 8vo, pp. 10. — Nebular Hypothesis; or General Theory of the Dudley Observatory in the Abstract. [Signed] Herschel. *Albany.* 1858. 8vo, pp. 12. H., S. — Report of the Astronomer in charge of the Dudley Observatory, for the Year 1863. *Albany: J. Munsell.* 1864. 8vo, pp. 43. H. — Speeches of J. N. Wilder and T. W. Olcott, June, 1858, before the Trustees; with the Resolutions of the Board. *Albany.* 1858. pp. 28.

A Duel and no Duel, or the Skirmish of the West Indian Heroes, a Burlesque Account (in Verse) of the Cause, Rise, and Progress of the Quarrel between Sir C—r O—le and Governor T——ey, and Assault on his Excellency in his own House in Spanish Town, by an Honest Sailor. *London.* 1743. 8vo.

An Essay on Dueling. *New York.* 1830. 8vo, pp. 29.

The Duelist; or a Candid Appeal to the Moral and Religious Portion of our countrymen, who are inclined to support Henry Clay for the Presidency. [n. p. n. d.] 8vo, pp. 8. 21103

DUELL (R. H.) Position of Parties. Speech of Hon. R. H. Duell, of New York, delivered in the ... House ... April 12, 1860. [n. p. 1860.] 8vo, pp. 8. 21104

DUER (J.) A Discourse on the Life, Character, and Public Services of James Kent, late Chancellor of the State of New York. Delivered, ... April 12, 1848. By John Duer. *New York.* MDCCCXLVIII. 8vo, pp. 81. 21105

DUER. An Introductory Lecture on the Evils, Social, Moral, and Political, that flow from our Party Divisions, and the Prevalence of Party Spirit, ... February 2d, 1841. By John Duer, Esq. ... *New York: Baker, Crane & Co.* 1841. 8vo, pp. 27.

DUER. A Vindication of the Public Faith of New-York and Pennsylvania, in reply to the Calumnies of the "Times." By John Duer. *London.* 1840. S. 21107

Also: Speech ... delivered in the Convention of the Protestant Episcopal Church of the Diocese of New York, ... 29th of September, 1843, in Support of the Resolutions offered by Judge Oakley. *New York.* 1843. 8vo, pp. 47. B., N.

DUER (John), *and* SEDGWICK (Robert). An Examination of the Controversy between the Greek Deputies and two Mercantile Houses of New-York, together with a Review of the Publications on the Subject by the Arbitrators, Messrs. Emmet and Ogden and Mr. Wm. Bayard. *New York.* 1826. 8vo, pp. 179. B. 21108

DUER (J. K.) The Nautilus, a Collection of Select Nautical Tales, and Sea Sketches, with a Full Narrative of the Mutiny of the Somers. Edited by John K. Duer ... . *New-York: J. Winchester.* 1843. 4to, pp. 48. H. 21109

DUER [(W.)] Remarks of Mr. Duer of New York, on the Prohibition of Slavery in the newly acquired Territories of the United States. Delivered in the House ... July 29, 1848. *Washington.* 1848. 8vo, pp. 15. B., H. 21110

Also: Speech ... on the Origin of the War with Mexico ... . in the House ... February 14, 1848. *Washington.* 1848. 8vo, pp. 14. H. — The Territorial Question. Speech ... in the House ... April 10, 1850. ... . [n. p. n. d.] 8vo, pp. 8. H. + Speech ... Aug. 6, 1850: Texas and New-Mexico ... [n. p. n. d.] B.

DUER (W. A.) A Course of Lectures on the Constitutional Jurisprudence of the United States, delivered Annually in Columbia College, New York. By William Alexander Duer, LL.D. ... *New-York: Harper & Brothers.* [1843.] 12mo, pp. 419. BA. + Second Edition, Revised, Enlarged, and adapted to Professional as well as General Use. *Boston.* 1856. 12mo. 21111

DUER. Letter, addressed to Cadwallader D. Colden, Esquire. In Answer to the Strictures, contained in his "Life of Robert Fulton" ... . With an Appendix ... . By William Alexander Duer, Esquire. *Albany: E. and E. Hosford.* 1817. 8vo, pp. 127. B., BA., C. 21112

See Colden (C.), Vol. IV., No. 14281, for a "Review."

DUER. The Life of William Alexander, Earl of Stirling, Major General in the Army of the United States, during the Revolution, with Selections from his Correspondence. By his Grandson, William Alexander Duer, LL.D. *New York: Published for the New Jersey Hist. Society, by Wiley & Putnam.* 1847. 8vo, pp. 272. Portrait and Map. H. 21113

Forms Vol. II. of the "Collect. of the New Jersey Historical Society."

DUER. New York as it was during the Latter Part of the Last Century. An Anniversary Address delivered before the St. Nicholas Society of the City of New York, Dec. 1st, 1848. By William Alexander Duer. *New York.* 1849. 8vo, pp. 48.

DUER. Outlines of the Constitutional Jurisprudence of the United States; designed as a Text Book for Lectures, as a Class Book for Academies and Common Schools, and as a Manual for Popular Use. By William Alexander Duer, LL.D. ... *New-York: Collins and Hannay.* 1833. S. 21115

DUER. Reminiscences of an Old Yorker. By the late William A. Duer, LL.D., President of Columbia College, etc. *New York.* 1867. 8vo. C. 21116

Thirty-five copies privately printed for W. L. Andrews, Esq. These articles on Old New York originally appeared in the "American Mail," 1847.

DUER. A Reply to Mr. Colden's Vindication of the Steamboat Monopoly. With an Appendix, containing Copies of the most Important Documents ... . By William Alexander Duer. *Albany: E. & E. Hosford.* 1819. 8vo, pp. 184, xxvii. B., C.

Also: The Duties and Responsibilities of the Rising Generation: an Address ... July 24, 1848, by William Alexander Duer, LL.D. ... *New-York: A. J. Townsend.* 1848. 8vo, pp. 28. — An Eulogy on John Adams and Thomas Jefferson; pronounced

... [at] Albany, at the Public Commemoration of their Deaths, held in that City, on Monday the 31st of July, 1826. ... *Albany.* 1826. 8vo, pp. 20. B., BA. — Letter to C. King, in Answer to his Defence of Bishop Doane. [n. p.] 1852. 8vo.

Duerr's Collection of Standard American Authors. Edited by William E. Drugulin. *Leipzig: A. Dürr.* 1854. 8vo.

Continued. Vol. LXXIV. appeared in 1867

DUFAU (Pierre Armand), DUVERGIER (Jean Baptiste), *and* GAUDET (Joseph). Collection des Constitutions, Chartes, et Lois Fondamentales des Peuples de l'Europe et des deux Amériques; avec des précis offrant l'histoire des libértes et des institutions politiques chez les nations modernes. Par Dufau, Duvergier et Gaudet. *Paris.* 1801. 7 vols., 8vo. B., C. 21119

DUFAU. History of the Political Institutions of the Nations of Europe and America: Translated from the French of Dufau, Duvergier, and Gaudet. By T. E. Evans. *London.* 1824. 8vo. 21120

DUFAY (Jules). L'Amérique histoire des voyages dans cette parte du monde, guerres, mœurs, produits, anecdotes ... . *Paris: Courval et Comp.* 1826. 3 vols., 12mo. 21121

DU FAY. Motion d'ordre faite par Du Fay, deputé de Saint Domingue, sur les moyens de rétablir l'ordre dans les Colonies. *Paris. an* 6 [1798]. 8vo, pp. 8. J.C.B. 21122

DUFET (L.) Recueil général des traités de commerce conclus entre la France et les États suivants: Angleterre, ... Bresil, ... Nicaragua, Salvador, ... *Paris: Didier et Cie.* 1861. 12mo.

DUFEY (P. J. S.) Abrégé de l'histoire des révolutions de l'Amérique Méridionale, depuis les primières découvertes par les Européens, jusqu'à nos jours, [etc.] *Paris: Emler frères.* 1827. 2 vols., 18mo, 2 l., pp. iv, pp. 382; 2 l., pp. 375. C. 21124

DUFEY. Abrégé de l'histoire des révolutions de l'Amérique Septentrionale, depuis les premières découvertes jusqu'au voyage du Général Lafayette, en 1824 et 1825. Par P. J. S. Dufey. *Paris.* 1827. 2 vols., 12mo. 21125

DUFEY. Résumé de l'histoire des révolutions de l'Amérique Méridionale, depuis les premières découvertes par les Européens jusqu'à nos jours. Pérou, Mexique, Brésil, Vénézuéla, Colombie, Chili, Paraguay, Cuba, Porto-Rico ... leurs religions, lois, mœurs, usages, constitutions, actuelles, événements jusqu'à la fin de 1825. *Paris.* 1826. 2 vols., 18mo. 21126

DUFEY. Die Revolution in Südamerika und Mexico, seit die Entdeckung durch die Spanier bis auf die neueste Zeit. Aus dem Französischen von F. A. Rüder. *Ilmenau: Voigt.* 1827. 8vo. 21127

DUFEY. Résumé de l'Histoire des Révolutions de l'Amérique septentrionale, depuis les premières Decouvertes jusqu'au Voyage du Général Lafayette, in 1824 et 1825 ... . Par P. J. S. Dufey ... . *Paris: Achille Jourdan.* 1826. 2 vols., 24mo, pp. iv, 371; 2 l., pp. 452. H. 21128

DUFF (H. J.) Petition of Henry J. Duff and others, for an alteration of the State Constitution, presented to the General Assembly, May, 1846. Report of the Committee on the Petition of Henry J. Duff, and others, by Sylvester G. Sherman, Esq., Chairman of the Committee, made to the House of Representatives of Rhode Island, January, 1847. [*Providence:*] *M. B. Young.* [1847.] 8vo, pp. 4, 16. 21129

DUFF (M. E. G.) A Political Survey. By Mountstuart E. Grant Duff ... . *Edinburgh: Edmonston and Douglas.* 1868. 8vo, pp. xv, 240. 2 Maps, one of South America. BA. 21130

"Northern and Central America," pp. 119-238.

DUFFIELD (D. B.) Bench and Bar, a Post Prandial Rhyme, read at the Bar Supper in Detroit. *Detroit.* 1857. 8vo, pp. 26.

DUFFIELD (G.) A Sermon preached in the Third Presbyterian Church in the City of Philadelphia, On Thursday December 11, 1783. The Day appointed by the United States in Congress assembled, to be observed as a Day of Thanksgiving, for the Restoration of Peace, and Establishment of our Independence, in the Enjoyment of our Rights and Privileges. By George Duffield ... . *Philadelphia Printed; Boston: Re-Printed by T. & J. Fleet.* MDCCLXXXIV. 8vo, pp. 26. BA. 21132

Also: ... A Sermon ... October 30th, 1827, at ... Harrisburg, Tenn., on the ... Ordination of Messrs. Dan'l. McKinley and M'Knight Williamson. ... *Carlisle.* 1827. 8vo, pp. 25. H.

DUFFIELD (G.) The Death of Gen. William Henry Harrison, President of the United States; or the Divine Rebuke, being a Discourse ... by George Duffield ... of Detroit. *Detroit: Dawson & Bates, Printers.* 1841. 8vo, pp. 18. H.

DUFFIELD. Humiliation and Hope: or, the Christian Patriot's Duty in the Present Crisis of our National Affairs A Discourse,

... November 14, 1862, the Day of Fasting, ... appointed by the Synod of Michigan. ... George Duffield, ... *Detroit: printed by O. S. Gulley.* 1862. 8vo, pp. 24. 21134

DUFFIELD. National Union, the Test of American Loyalty, an Historical Discourse, November 24th, 1864, By George Duffield, Jr. ... Adrian, Mich. ... *Detroit.* 1864. 8vo, pp. 31.

DUFFIELD. The Nation's Wail. A Discourse delivered in the First Presbyterian Church of Detroit, on Sabbath, the 16th of April, 1865, the day after receiving the intelligence of the Brutal Murder of President Abraham Lincoln, by a Brutal Assassin. George Duffield, Pastor of the First Presbyterian Church of Detroit. *Detroit: Advertiser and Tribune Print.* 1865. 8vo, pp. 18. B. 21136

DUFFIELD. One Hundred Years Ago: An Historical Discourse. By Rev. Dr. G. Duffield. *Carlisle.* 1858. 8vo. S.

Also: Claims of "Episcopal Bishops," Examined, in a series of Letters. *New-York.* 1842. 12mo. P. — The Divine Organic Law, ordained for the Human Race; or Capital Punishment for Murder authorized by God and sustained by Reason. ... *Detroit: printed by Garrett & Geiger.* 1848. 16mo, pp. 27. H. — Funeral Discourse on Hugh Brady, Brevet Major General of the United States Army ... *Detroit.* 1851. 8vo, pp. 26. — Our Federal Union a Cause for Gratitude to God. A Thanksgiving Discourse, delivered in the First Presbyterian Church of Detroit, November 28th, 1850. ... *Detroit: Harmon, Broadhead & Co., Printers.* 1850. 8vo, pp. 16. BA. — Our National Sins to be repented of, and the Grounds of Hope for the Preservation of our Federal Constitution and Union. A Discourse delivered January 4, 1861. ... *Detroit: Free Press Office.* 1861. 8vo, pp. 40. — A Sermon on American Slavery, its Nature, and the Duties of Christians in relation to it. ... *Detroit: J. S. and S. A. Bagg.* 1840. 8vo, pp. 32. — ... a Sermon ... before the Presbytery of Detroit, October 13, 1842, at the Ordination of Mr. Meigs ... . *Detroit: Morgan Bates, Printer.* 1843. 12mo, pp. 36. H. — Secession: its Cause and Cure. A Thanksgiving Discourse. The Rule of Divine Providence applicable to the present circumstances of our Country, delivered ... in Detroit, Thursday, Nov. 28, 1860. ... *Detroit.* 1861. 8vo, pp. 31. — A Thanksgiving Sermon. The Religious Character of a People the True Element of their Prosperity. ... . Delivered ... Nov. 28, 1839. ... *Detroit: Dawson & Bates, Printers.* 1839. 8vo, pp. 20. H.

DUFFIELD (G.), *Junr.* Courage in a Good Cause: or, The Lawful and Courageous Use of the Sword. A Sermon by George Duffield, Jr., ... Philadelphia. Delivered April 21, 1861. ... [*Philadelphia:*] *T. B. Pugh.* 1861. 8vo, pp. 38. H. 21138

DUFFIELD. The Dark Night, and the Glorious Morning; A Thanksgiving Sermon: December 7th, 1865. By George Duffield, Jr. ... . *Galesburg, Ill.* 1866. 8vo, pp. 31. H.

DUFFIELD. The God of our Fathers. An Historical Sermon, Preached in the Coates' Street Presbyterian Church, Philadel-

phia, on Fast Day, January 4, 1861. By George Duffield, Jr., Pastor. With Copious Notes, and an Appendix. *Philadelphia: T. B. Pugh.* 1861. 8vo, pp. 56. B., H., S. 21140

DUFFIELD. (J. T.) A Discourse at the Opening of the Synod of New Jersey, ... at Elizabeth, N. J., October 16, 1866. By Rev. J. T. Duffield, D.D. With Notes and Appendix. *Philadelphia: J. S. Claxton.* 1867. 12mo, pp. 64.

Also: The Princeton Pulpit, a Collection of Sermons Preached there by Eminent Divines. Edited by J. T. Duffield. *New York: C. Scribner.* 1852. 8vo, pp. 326.

DUFFIN (P. W.), *and* LLOYD (T.) The Trial of P. W. Duffin and Thomas Lloyd a Citizen of the United States for a Supposed Libel. To which is annexed a Letter to Thomas Pinckney, the American Minister, etc. Second Edition. *London.* 1793. 8vo. 21142

DUFIEF (N. G.) The Logic of Facts; or the Conduct of Wm. Rawle, Esq. ... towards N. G. Dufief, arraigned before the Tribunal of Public Opinion: ... . *Philadelphia: Printed for the Author by Abel Dickinson* ... . 1806. 8vo, 2 l., pp. 40, 10.

DUFLOT DE MOFRAS (*M.*) Exploration du territoire de l'Orégon, des Californies et de la Mer Vermeille, exécutée pendant les années 1840, 1841 et 1842, par Duflot de Mofras, ... ouvrage publié par ordre du Roi, ... *A Paris, chez Arthus Bertrand.* 1844. 2 vols., 8vo, pp. xii, (4), 524; 514, 4 Plates. Atlas in folio, 14 Maps and 3 Plates. C. 21144

A very fine work; originally published in parts. Also: L'Orégon. *Paris: Plon.* 1846. 8vo, pp. 44. From the "Revue nouvelle"

DUFOUR (Adolphe Hippolyte). La France; atlas des quatre-vingt-six départements et des colonies françaises, divisés en arrondissements et en cantons, avec un tracé des routes impériales et départementales, des chemins de fer, canaux, rivières et cours d'eaux, etc., avec une notice historique sur chaque département, par Albert Montemont. *Paris: A. Logerot.* [n. d.] Folio.

DUFOUR (Ph. S.) Traité nouv. et curieux du café, du thé et du chocolate. *La Haye.* 1693. 12mo. Plate. 21146

"Le traité du chocolat contient des notices sur l'hist. natur. de l'Amérique."

DU FRESNE DE FRANCHEVILLE (Joseph). Histoire des Finances, ou Histoire de la Compagnie des Indes, avec les Titres de ses Concessions et Privéleges. *Paris.* 1738. 4to, pp. 660. S.

[DU FRESNE DE FRANCHEVILLE.] Relations curieuses de différents pays nouvellement découverts. Par M***. *Paris: Mèrigot.* 1741. 8vo. 21148

DU FRESNOY (L.) Méthode pour étudier la Geographie par Lenglet Du Fresnoy. *Paris.* 1716. 21149

The edition, "augmentée par Barbeau de la Bruyère et Drouet. *Paris.* 1768." 10 vols., 12mo, is considered the best. The list of maps of America is really useful, as a list. No criticisms are given. There is also a list of works on Asia, under different heads.

DU FRESNOY. A New Method of Studying History, Geography, and Chronology, with a Catalogue of the Chief Historians of all Nations, the Best Editions of their Works, and Characters of them. Made English, with Variety of Improvements and Corrections, by Richard Rawlinson, LL.D. *London.* 1730. 2 vols., 8vo. 21150

DUFUR (A. J.) Statistics of the State of Oregon; containing a Description of its Agricultural Development, and Natural and Industrial Resources. Together with the Physical, Geographical, Geological, and Mineral Statistics of the State. Compiled ... by A. J. Dufur ... . *Salem, Oregon: Willamette Farmer Office.* 1869. 8vo, pp. 128. BA., C. 21151

DUGANNE (A. J. H.) Camps and Prisons. Twenty Months in the Department of the Gulf. By A. J. H. Duganne. ... Illustrated. Second Edition. *New York: J. P. Robens, Publisher.* 1865. 12mo, pp. 424. BA. 21152

DUGANNE. The Fighting Quakers: a True Story of the War for our Union. By A. J. H. Duganne. With Letters from the Brothers to their Mother, and a Funeral Sermon by Rev. O. B. Frothingham. By authority of the New York Bureau of Military Records. *New York: J. P. Robens, Printer.* 1866. 12mo, pp. 116. 21153

DUGANNE. A History of Governments; showing the Progress of Civil Society and the Structure of Ancient and Modern States. By Augustine J. H. Duganne. *New York: R. M. de Witt.* 1861. 12mo, 1 l., pp. 303. C. 21154

DUGANNE. Massasoit's Daughter; or, the French Captive. A Romance of Aboriginal New England. By A. J. H. Duganne. *New York: Beadle & Company.* 1864. 12mo, pp. 115. 21155

DUGANNE. The Poetical Works of Augustine J. H. Duganne. *Philadelphia.* 1855. 8vo, pp. 407. 21156

Also: Art's True Mission in America. ... *New York.* 1853. 12mo, pp. 35. B. — Ballads of the War. ... *New York.* 1862. 4to, pp. 36. — The Heroic Succession. An Oration, On the Second Anniversary of the Death of Abraham Lincoln, at Cooper Institute, New York. April 15, 1867. *New York.* 1867. 8vo. S. — Massachusetts, and other Poems. *Boston.* 1843. 24mo, pp. 64. — The Mission of Intellect A Poem. *New York.* MDCCCLIII. 12mo, pp. 33. — The Mysteries of the Three Cities, Boston, New York, and Philadelphia. A True History of Men's Hearts and Habits. *Philadelphia.* 1844. 8vo, pp. 204. — Parnassus in Pillory. A Satire. By Motley Manners, Esq. *New York.* 1851. 12mo, pp. 96. — The Peon Prince: a Tale of Mexico. *New York: Beadle.* 1863. 12mo, pp. 130. — A Sound Literature the Safeguard of our National Institutions. ... *New York.* 1853. 16mo, pp. 9. B., H. — The Tenant Houses; or Embers from Poverty's Hearth. *New York.* 1858. 12mo, pp. 490. — Utterances. ... *New York.* 1865. Rl. 8vo, pp. 36.

DUGDALE (R.) A Letter to the Right Hon. the Lord Colville, ... late Commander in Chief of his Majesty's Squadron in North-America. Wrote By Robert Dugdale, late Commander of his Majesty's armed Schooner, the Magdalen. *London: Printed for the Author.* 1766. 21157

See "M. Rev.," XXXVI, 159.

DUGGAN (G.) Specimens of the Stone, Iron and Wood Bridges, ... of the United States Railroads ... accompanied by ... an Appendix, ... By George Duggan. *New York.* 1850. Folio.

Six or more parts published.

DUGOUJON (*l'Abbé*). Lettres sur l'esclavage dans les colonies françaises. *Paris: Pagnerre.* 1845. 8vo. 21159

DU GRATY (Alfred M.) La Confédération Argentine. *Paris: Guillaumin et Cie.* 1858. 8vo. 10 Plates and 1 Map. + Second Edition. *Bruxelles.* 1865. 8vo, pp. xii, 372. 21160

DU GRATY. La République du Paraguay, par Alfred M. Du Graty. *Leipzig: Gand, Librairie Européenne de C. Muquardt. Londres: Trübner & Comp.* 1862. 8vo. Plate and Maps. BA. + Seconde édition. *Bruxelles.* 1865. 8vo, pp. xxii, 407. Map and Views of Paraguay. 21161

DUGRIVEL (A.) Des bords de la Saône à la baie de San Salvador, ou promenade sentimentale en France et au Brésil. *Paris: Ledoyen.* 1843. 8vo, pp. 394. 21162

DU HAILLY (E.) Compagnes et stations. Une compagne dans l'extrême Orient, les Antilles françaises, Terre-Neuve. Par Ed. Du Hailly. *Paris: L. Hachette et Cie: Challamel aîné.* 18mo, pp. 465. 21163

DUHAUT-CILLY (A.) Voyage autour du Monde, principalement à la Californie et aux Isles Sandwich, pendant les Années 1826, 1827, 1828 et 1829. Par A. Duhaut-Cilly. *Paris: Bertrand.* 1835. 8vo, pp. 428. Plate. 21164

DUHAUT-CILLY. Viaggio intorno al globo, principalmente alla California ed alle isole Sandwich, negli anni 1826–1829, con l'aggiunta delle osservazioni sugli abitanti di quei paesi, di P. E. Botta. *Torino.* 1841. 2 vols., 8vo. Plates. 21165

DUHRING (H.) Remarks on the United States of America, with regard to the Actual State of Europe. By Henry Duhring. *London: W. Simpkin and R. Marshall. Amsterdam: C. G. Sulpke. New York: W. Jackson.* 1833. 12mo, pp. viii, 209.

See "N. Am. Rev.," XL. 457.

DUKE (B. W.) History of Morgan's Cavalry. By Basil W. Drake. *Cincinnati: Miami Printing and Publishing Company.* 1867. 8vo, pp. 578. Portrait. c. 21167

[DUKE (William).] Some Memoirs. *See* Vol. I., Nos. 3278 and 3290.

DUKES (Joseph). The History of Joseph and his Brethren, in the Choctaw Language. Revised by John Pitchlyn. *Utica.* 1831. 16mo. 21168

DUKES (J. H.) An Oration, delivered before the Firemen of Charleston, on the Fourth of July, 1844. By Joseph H. Dukes ... *Charleston.* 1844. 8vo. 21169

DU LAC (F. M. P.) *See* Perrin du Lac (F. M.)

[DULANEY (Daniel).] Considerations on the Propriety of imposing Taxes in the British Colonies, For the Purpose of raising a Revenue, by Act of Parliament ... . *North-America: [Printed by a North American.* MDCCLXV.] 8vo, pp. 47. BA., H. + Second Edition. *Annapolis: Jonas Green.* 1765. 4to, 2 l., pp. 5–55. C., P. + *North-America, Printed; London, Re-printed for J. Almon.* MDCCLXVI. 8vo, 3 l., pp. (6), 81. H., P.

Some copies of this edition read, "By Mr. Dulaney of Maryland." "The author denies the Parliament's right of taxing the Colonists, internally. The zeal of this patriotic North American sometimes carries him rather too far in his reflections on the Mother Country." — *M. Rev.,* XXXIV, 65, 162. "His opinions were thought to have moulded those of Wm. Pitt, by whom they were publicly noticed with great honor.' *See* Bancroft, Chap. XVII.

DULANEY. The Right to the Tonnage, the Duty of Twelve Pence per Hogshead on all exported Tobacco, and the Fines and Forfeitures in the Province of Maryland, stated by Daniel Dulaney, Esq., Secretary to the said Province. *Annapolis.* 1766. Folio. 21171

See "Observations on the Part of the United States."

DULEN (J. W.) Farewell Discourse: preached in St. Stephen's Church, Middlebury, Vt., by Rev. Jacob W. Dulon. *Brooklyn.* 1842. pp. 16. 21172

DULIEN (J.) Mississipi et Indiana; souvenirs d'Amérique. *Bruxelles: Ve Parent et fils.* 1862. 12mo. 21173

DULON (R.) Aus Amerika über Schule, deutsche Schule, amerikanische Schule und deutsch-amerikanische Schule von Rudolph Dulon. *Leipzig und Heidelberg: C. F. Winter.* 1866. 8vo, pp. viii, 440. 21174

DUMAIL (F.) Martinique. Observations sur le régime commerciale de cette colonie. Par M. F. Dumail ... . *Nice: Gunthier et Cie.* 1867. 8vo, pp. 20. 21175

DUMANOIR *or* DU MANOIR (Philippe François Pinel), *and* DENNERY (A. P.) La case de l'oncle Tom; drame en huit actes. *Paris: Lévy frères.* 1853. 12mo. + [*Ibid.*] 1859. 4to.

DUMANOIR *and* DENNERY. De negerhut van Oom Tom. Drama in 8 bedrijven. Uit het Fransch, door Cornelissen en Beems. *'s Gravenhage: A. J. van Tetrode.* 1854. 12mo.

Dumaresq Genealogy. *See* [Perkins (A. T.)]

DUMARTRAY (A.), *and* ROUHAUD (P.) Coup d'œil sur la république de l'Amérique centrale, et particulièrement sur les états de Nicaragua et Costa Rica, accompagné d'une carte de ces deux Etats. Par Alonzo Dumartray et P. Rouhaud. *Paris: J. Andriveau Goujon.* 1832. 4to, pp. 12. Map. 21178

DUMARTRAY. Opusculo sobre la Republica de Centro-America, y particularmente sobre los Estados de Nicaragua y Costa Rica, con un Mapa de ambos estados, publicarle Don Alonzo Dumartray y Don Pedro Rouhaud. *Paris.* 1833. 8vo, 1 sheet. 21179

DUMAS (Alexandre). California ovvero la mania del danaro; racconto romantico. *Firenze.* 1852. 12mo. 21180

DUMAS. Un Gil-Blas en Californie. Par Alexandre Dumas. *Paris: Michel Lévy frères.* 1861. 16mo, Title, pp. 323. BA.

DUMAS. Un Gil Blas in California. *Milano.* 1852. 16mo. Plates. 21181

DUMAS. Le Capitaine Paul par Alexandre Dumas. Nouvelle édition. *Paris: Michel Lévy frères.* 1862. 16mo, pp. (ii), xlviii, 223. BA. 21182

DUMAS. Paul Jones, the Son of the Sea. *New York: Garrett & Co.* [1853.] 8vo, pp. 105. c. 21183

DUMAS. Ein Jahr an den Ufern des Sacramento. Von Alex. Dumas. *Grimma: Verlags-Comptoir.* 1852. 2 vols., 8vo, pp. 155, 131. (Europäische Bibliothek, 748, 749.) 21184

DUMAS. Neueste Schriften. *Wien: Hartleben.* 1853–58. 8vo. 21185

Parts 99–104, 132, 133, contain "Australien. Californien. Mexiko. Reisebilder von Madame Giovanni. Geordnet und herausgegeben von Alex. Dumas. Nach dem französischen Manuscripte von G. F. W. Rödiger." 3 pts., pp. 191, 187, 144.

DUMAS. Schriften. *Leipzig: Kollmann.* 181 –52. 16mo.

505.–506. Bdchn contain "Ein Jahr in Californien." pp. 192.

DUMAS. Ausgewählte Schriften. *Leipzig und Wien: Hartleben.* 1847–52. 8vo. 21187

Lief. 278–280 contain "Reiseerinnerungen aus Californien, oder ein Jahr an den Ufern des San Joaquin und des Sacramento. Nach dem Erzählungen eines Auswanderers. Uebersetzt von Ungewither."

DUMAS (Chas. F. W.), *Translator.* *See* [Smith (W.)]

DUMAS (G.) Voyages et Decouvertes faites par les Russes, sur l'Ocean Oriental, vers le Japan et l'Amérique, avec l'Histoire du Fleuve Amur, &c. *Amsterdam.* 1766. 2 vols., 12mo. Maps. 21188

DUMAS (Mathieu). Rapport fait par M. Dumas, commissaire rapporteur de la commission chargée de présenter à l'Assemblée nationale un plan d'organisation pour Saint-Domingue. [23 avril 1792.] *Le Cap: Dufour de Rians.* [n. d.] 4to, pp. 48 or less. 21189

DUMAS. Traité de la défence et de la conservation des colonies. Par Mathieu Dumas. *Londres et Bruxelles.* 1777. 8vo, pp. viii, 120. c. 21190

DUMAS. Memoirs of his Own Time, including the Revolution, the Empire, and the Restoration. *London.* 1839. 2 vols., 8vo. Portraits. 21191

Count Dumas served in the Revolutionary War under Rochambeau, and gives graphic descriptions of his campaign.

DU MAY (Louis) Le Prudent Voyageur, contenant la Description Politique de tous les Etats du Monde, de l'Asie, de l'Afrique, et de l'Amérique, et particulièrement de l'Europe. *Genève.* 1861. 3 vols., 12mo. 21192

DUMBAR (Gerhard). De Oude en Nieuwe Constitutie der Vereenigde Staaten van Amerika, uit de beste schriften in haare gronden ontvouwd. *Amsterdam: J. A. Crajenschot.* MDCCXCIII–MDCCXCVI. 3 vols., 8vo, pp. xiv, 255: x, 276; xii, 293, 7 l.

Contains an impartial examination of the old constitution, by which he means the thirteen articles of confederation of the 17th November, 1777. This survey is introduced by a concise account of the Revolutionary War, and of the events preceding the adoption of the Constitution. *See* Rich, I. 385, and "M. Rev.," x. 501.

DUMESNIL (Clément). De l'Abolition des droits Féodaux et Seigneuriaux du Canada. *Montréal.* 1849. 21194

DUMESNIL. Réflexions préliminaires des vrais principes politiques. *Montréal.* 1849. 21195

D[UMESNIL] (M[arie.)] L'esclavage, poême, par M. D. *Paris.* 1823. 8vo. 21196

DUMMER (Jeremiah). A Defence of the New-England Charters. By Jer. Dummer. *London: Printed by W. Wilkins, and sold by J. Peele.* MDCCXXI. 8vo, pp. 5, 80. C. + *London: W. Williams. Reprinted at Boston by S. Kneeland.* MDCCXXI. 12mo, pp. 44. B. + *Boston: Re-printed by B. Greene.* 1745. 8vo, pp. (4), 43. + *Boston: New-England: Thomas and John Fleet.* 1765. 8vo, pp. (4), 44. H. + *London: J. Almon.* [1765.] 8vo, pp. 88. 21197

DUMMER. A Discourse on the Holiness of the Sabbath Day; Being a Sermon Preached at Boston, New England, October 29th, 1704. By Jer. Dummer. *Boston.* 1704. 16mo, pp. 54. M. + *Boston: Re-Printed by Edes and Gill.* 1763. 8vo, pp. 8, 31. BA. 21198

[DUMMER.] A Letter to a Friend in the Country, On the late Expedition to Canada: with An Account of Enterprizes, a

Defence of that Design, and the Share the late M—rs had in it. *London: A. Baldwin.* 1712. 8vo, pp. 22. 21199

[DUMMER.] A Letter to a Noble Lord. *See* Vol. III., No. 10507.

DUMMER. Letter dated 10th August, 1729, on the Assembly fixing the Governor's Salary. [No Title.] 4to, pp. 3.

Dummer was also the author of several disquisitions in the Latin language, which are included in the Prince collection in the Boston Public Library. A pamphlet, entitled "Considerations on behalf of the Colonists ... 1765," has been attributed to Dummer, but is more probably by Otis. Dummer was an American scholar of brilliant genius, and possessed of remarkable powers in speaking and writing. He was born in Boston about 1680, and died in England in 1739. He spent a long time abroad, where he was at one time the agent for Massachusetts. Tudor remarks: "In point of style or argument Dummer may vie with any American writer before the Revolution." — *Life of Otis,* Chap. VI. *See also* "M. Rev.," XXXIV. 64.

DUMMER ACADEMY, *Mass.* An Account of Dummer Academy, together with a Statement of the Alterations and Improvements, about to be made, by the Trustees. *Boston.* 1837. 16mo, pp. 12. H. 21201

The Act of Incorporation, By-Laws, Rules, and Regulations of Dummer Academy. *Boston.* 1848. 12mo, pp. 15. W.

Catalogue of the Officers and Students of Dummer Academy. [*Salem.*] 1844. 8vo. 21203

DUMON (M.) Rapport fait au nom de la commission chargée d'examiner le Projet de Loi relatif au traite du 4 juillet. *Paris.* 1831. 4to. 21204

DUMONT (E.) The Address of Col. Ebenezer Dumont Speaker of the House ... delivered on presenting the Address of the Scholars of the Deaf and Dumb Asylum to the Legislature, and also that Address. ... *Indianapolis.* 1851. 8vo, pp. 16.

DUMONT. The U. S. Supreme Court and its Late Adjudications. Speech of Hon. Ebenezer Dumont, of Indiana, in the House ... February 16, 1867. [n. p. n. d.] 8vo, pp. 10.

DUMONT (H.) Article of Faith and Church Covenant of the United Congregational Church, of Newport, R. I., with a Brief Notice of the Origin and History of the Church. Prepared at the request of the Church by the Pastor, Rev. Henry Dumont, A.M. *Newport: James Atkinson.* 1834. 12mo, pp. 46.

This church dates its origin in the year 1640.

[DUMONT (Jean), *Baron von Carlscroon.*] Les Soupirs de L'Europe &c. Or, The Groans of Europe at the Prospect of the Present Posture of Affairs. From the French. [n. p.] MDCCXIII. 8vo, pp. 128, 1 l. B. 21208

Contains numerous references to America.

DUMONT (G. M. Butel). *See* Butel-Dumont, Vol. III.

DUMONT (M.) Mémoires Historiques sur la Louisiane. *See* Vol. III., No. 9605.

DUMONT D'URVILLE (Jules Sébastien César). Rapport sur le Voyage de l'Astrolabe, lu à l'Academie Royale des Sciences, 11 mai 1829. Par M. Dumont D'Urville, capitaine de frégate, etc. *Paris.* 1829. 8vo, 4 sheets. 21209

DUMONT D'URVILLE. Voyage de la Corvette L'Astrolabe Executé par ordre du Roi, pendant les années 1826–1827–1828–1829, sous le commandement de M. J. Dumont d'Urville, capitaine de vaisseau. Publié Par Ordonnance de Sa Majesté. Histoire du Voyage. *Paris: J. Tastu.* 1830. 5 vols., rl. 8vo, pp. (4), cxvi, 528, (1); 632; (4), 790; (4), 716; and Atlas of 243 Plates, in 2 vols., folio. + Zoology. Par MM. Quoy et Gaimard. *Paris; J. Tastu.* 1830. pp. (4), 4, 268, (4), 686; (4), 954, 8 Plates; (4), 390, 198 Plates in folio. + Botanique. Par MM. A. Lesson et A. Richard. *Paris: J. Tastu.* 1832. 8vo, pp. (4), xvi, 376. + Botanique. Par M. A. Richard. *Paris: J. Tastu.* 1834. pp. (6), lvi. 80 Plates in folio. + Faune Entomologique de l'Ocean Pacifique, avec l'illustration des Insectes nouveaux recuellies pendant le voyage. Par le Docteur Boisduval, ... Première Partie. Lépidoptères. ‖ *Paris.* Deuxième Partie. Coléoptères et autres ordres. *Paris: J. Tastu.* 1832–35. 2 vols., rl. 8vo, pp. (4), 267; 716. 12 Plates. + Sciences Naturelles. Rapport fait à l'Institut de France, sur les travaux de MM. Quoy et Gaimard. Par St. Hilaire, Latreille, etc. *Paris.* 1829. 8vo, 3¼ sheets. + Observations Nautiques, Meteorologiques, Hydrographiques et de Physique. *Paris.* 1833. 4to, 18½ sheets. 2 Plates. + Opérations Hydrographiques. *Paris: Didot.* 1833. 4to, 20½ sheets; second part, 22¼ sheets. + Philologie. *Paris.* 1833. 2 vols., rl. 8vo, 23¼ sheets; second part, 19½ sheets. 21210

This splendid work, with all its scientific appendices, forms 13 vols. in 8vo, 1 in 4to, and 5 in folio. There are copies on vellum paper, with India proofs of the plates. Those of natural history are usually colored. Some portions of the work were printed by order of the Minister of Marine, — not for sale.

DUMONT D'URVILLE. Voyage pittoresque autour du monde Resumé général des voyages de découvertes de Magellan, Tasman, Dampier, Anson, Byron, Wallace, Carterel, Bougainville, Cook, Lapérouse, G. Bligh, Vancouver, D'Entrecasteaux, Wilson, Baudin, Flinders, Krusenstern, Porter, Kotzebue, Freycinet, Bellinghausen, Basil Hall, Duperrey, Paulding, Beechey, Dumont d'Urville, Lutke, Dillon, Laplace, B. Morrell, etc. Publié sous la direction de M. Dumont d'Urville ... . *A Paris: chez L. Tenré.* M DCCC XXXIV. 2 vols., 8vo, 2 l., pp. viii, 576; 3 l., pp. 584. Maps and Plates. BA. 21211

DUMONT D'URVILLE. Viaje pintoresco al rededor del mundo, à las dos Americas, Asia y Africa. *Barcelona.* 1841–1842. 3 vols., 4to. 21212

DUMONT D'URVILLE. Viaggio pittoresco intorno al mondo ossia riassunto generale de viaggi e scoperte ... . Illustrato con carte geografiche et vignette ... . *Venezia.* 1841. 4 vols., 4to.

DUMONT D'URVILLE. Malerische Reise um die Welt. Eine geordnete Zusammenstellung des wissenswerthesten von den Entdeckungsreisen eines Magellan, Tasman, Dampier, etc. verfasst von einer Gesellschaft reisender und gelehrter unter der Leitung des Herrn Dumont d'Urville. [Aus dem Französischen] von Dr. A. Diezmann. *Leipzig: Baumgärtner.* 1835. 2 vols., 4to, pp. xii, 338, 4 Maps and 74 Plates; iv, 300, Map and 69 Plates. 21214

DUMONT D'URVILLE. Reize om de wereld, zijnde eene gegelde verzameling van het wetenswaardigste hetwelk de ontdekkingsreizen opleveren, van Magellaan, Tasman, Dampier, Anson, enz. enz. In het Fransch uitgegeven onder opzigt van Dumont d'Urville en in het Hoogduitsch overgebragt, en met eenige aanmerkingen en bijvoegsels vermeerdert door A. Diezmann. Uit het Hoogduitsch vertaald door P. D. Anslijn. *Lsiden: D. Mortier en Zn.* 1838–40. 3 pts., 8vo. 21215

DUMONT D'URVILLE. Voyage au Pole Sud et dans l'Océanie sur les corvettes l'Astrolabe et la Zélée exécuté par ordre du Roi pendant les années 1837–1838–1839–1840 sous le commandement de M. Dumont-d'Urville capitaine de vaisseau pubié sous les auspices du Département de la Marine. Sous la direction superieure de M. Jacquinot, capitaine de vaisseau, commandant de la Zélee. *Paris: Gide.* 1841–7. 21216

This magnificent work consists of the following subjects; it is not yet completed: Histoire du voyage, par Dumont-Durville. *Paris.* 1841–1846. 10 vols., 8vo, 2 vols

Atlas, folio, 192 Plates; Zoologie, par MM. Hombron et Jacquinot. *Paris.* 1846. 5 vols., 8vo, Atlas, folio, 140 Plates; Botanique. La Cryptogamie, par M. Montagne, d'après les collections de MM. Hombron et Jacquinot. La Phanerogamie, par MM. Hombron et Jacquinot. *Paris.* 1845. 2 vols., 8vo, Atlas, folio, 56 Plates; Observations chronometriques et theorie nouvelle de lever sous voile, pai M. Vincendon Dumoulin. *Paris: Gide.* 1844. 8vo, 21½ sheets, 2 Plates; Anthropologie, par Dumoutier. *Paris.* 1846. 8vo, Atlas and 50 Plates, folio; Mineralogie et Geologie, par Grange. *Paris.* 1846. 8vo, Atlas and 13 Plates, folio; Physique, par Vincendon-Dumoulin et Coupvent-Desbois. *Paris.* 1842. 8vo; Hydrographie, par Vincendon-Dumoulin. *Paris.* 1843–1847. 2 vols., 8vo, Atlas, folio, 57 Maps. The following is a cheaper edition of the narrative:

DUMONT D'URVILLE. Relation du voyage au pôle sud et dans l'Océanie, sur les corvettes l'Astrolabe et la Zélée exécuté par ordre du roi pendant les années 1837, 1838, 1839 et 1840, sous le commandement de M. J. Dumont d'Urville, capitaine de vaisseau. *Paris.* 1842. 10 vols., 8vo. 10 Maps. 21217

DUMONT D'URVILLE. Reise nach dem Südpol und nach Ozeanien ... 1837–1840. *Darmstadt.* 1844–48. 4 Maps and 2 Plates. 21218

This forms Vols. IV.–VI. of Sammlung d. vorzügl. neueren Reisebeschreibungen. ... Herausgegeben von Phil. Hedw. Külb. *Darmstadt: Leske.* 1841–48. 8vo.

DUMONT D'URVILLE. Reise nach dem Südpol und Oceanien nebst Reisen auf Neuholland und Tasmanien. Herausgegeben von Friedr. Heinzelmann. *Leipzig: Weichardt.* 1851. 8vo, pp. viii, 545. Plate and Map. (Die Weltkernde, 6.) 21219

DU MONTELLIER. Réponse au Mémoire du Sieur Rossignol Desdunes, ancien maire de Saint-Marc; par le sieur Du Montellier, ancien major du camp de la Saline. *Port-au-Prince: imp. de J.-B. Michel.* [n. d.] 4to, pp. 48 or less. 21220

DUMORTER (E.) La vigne en Amérique. Par E. Dumorter. *Lyon: imp. Pitrat.* 1868. 8vo, pp. 6. 21221

END OF VOLUME FIVE.

A DICTIONARY OF BOOKS

RELATING TO AMERICA.

DU MOULIN (John F.) Essay on Naturalization and Allegiance. *Washington.* 1816. 8vo. W. 21222

DUMOULIN (V.), *and* DEGRAS (C.) Iles Marquises ou Noukahiva. Histoire, Geographie, Mœurs, et Considerations générales d'après les Relations des Navigateurs, et des Documens recueillis sur les lieux. Par MM. Vincendon Dumoulin, et C. Degras. *Paris: Bertrand.* 1841. 8vo, 25½ sheets. 4 Maps. 21223

DUMOULIN. Iles Taïti. Esquisse Historique et Géographique, précédées de consideration générales sur la Colonisation Française dans l'Oceane. Par MM. Vincendon Dumoulin et C. Desgraz. *Paris: Bertrand.* 1844. 2 vols., 8vo, 69¾ sheets. 21224

DUN, BARLOW *and* Co. Mercantile Agency Manual for 1871. A Yearly Publication, containing Information of a Legal, Statistical, and Moral Character of Daily Use to Merchants, Traders and Manufacturers, &c. *New-York: published by Dun, Barlow & Co.* 1871. B. 21225

The first was issued in 1845.

DUNAND (C.) La mort du président Lincoln, poëme, précédé d'une notice historique. Par Charles Dunand ... . *Sens: imp. Duchemin.* 12mo, pp. 23. 21226

DUNANT (J. Henry). L'Esclavage chez les Musulmans, et aux États-Unis d'Amérique. Par J. H. Dunant. *Genève.* 1863. pp. 58. B., C. 21227

DUNBAR (Asa). An Oration: ... June twenty fifth; ... Society of Free and Accepted Masons, ... By our Rev. Brother A. Dunbar. *Worcester: Massachusetts: Printed by Brother Isaiah Thomas.* MDCCLXXXI. A.L. 5781. 8vo, pp. 22. BA. 21228

DUNBAR (E. E.) ... American Pioneering, an Address before the Travellers' Club, by E. E. Dunbar. [n. p.] MDCCCLXIII. 8vo, pp. 45. C., H. 21229

DUNBAR. The Mexican Papers. The Mexican Question. The Great American Question, with Personal Reminiscences. By Edward E. Dunbar. *New York: J. A. H. Hasbrouck.* 1860. Imp. 8vo, pp. 42. H. 21230

DUNBAR. The Mexican Papers, containing the History of the Rise and Decline of Commercial Slavery in America, with reference to the Future of Mexico. By Edward E. Dunbar. *New York.* MDCCCLXI. 8vo, pp. 177–279. H. 21231

DUNBAR. The Romance of the Age; or, The Discovery of Gold in California. By Edward E. Dunbar. *New York: D. Appleton & Co.* 1867. 16mo, pp. 134. 21232

Also: Statement of the Controversy between Louis Tappan and Edward E. Dunbar. *New York.* 1846. 8vo, pp. 86. H.

DUNBAR (E.) A Sermon, delivered at the Ordination of the Rev. James Porter, to the Pastoral Care of the First Church and Society in Pomfret, Connecticut. September 8th, 1814. By Elijah Dunbar ... . *Windham: printed by John Byrne and Son.* 1814. 8vo, pp. 26. BA. 21233

DUNBAR. Sermon preached at the Ordination of Rev. William Richey, Canton, July 1, 1807. By Rev. Elijah Dunbar. Junr. Also an Appendix, giving an Historical Account of Churches in Canton, Sharon, and Stoughton. *Dedham.* 1809. 8vo, pp. 29. M. 21234

DUNBAR (J.) De Primordiis Civitatum Oratio. In qua agitur de bello civili inter M. Britanniam & Colonias nunc flagranti, &c. i. e. An Oration concerning the Origin of States, in which the Author treats of the Civil War between Great Britain and her Colonies. By James Dunbar, Professor of Philosophy in the King's College, Aberdeen. *London: T. Cadell.* 1779. 4to. 21235

See "Monthly Review," July, 1779.

DUNBAR (J.) Case of John Dunbar and William Lem. *Privately Printed.* 1772. Folio. 21236

Mr. Dunbar was a native of Antigua, and a large proprietor of lands.

DUNBAR (John D.) Oration at Pembroke, Mass., July 4, 1805. 21237

DUNBAR (R.) Trial of Reuben Dunbar, for the Murder of Stephen V. Lester and David L. Lester, Eight and Ten Years of Age, in the Town of Waterloo, on Saturday, Sept. 28, 1850. Reported ... by Jacob C. Cuyler. *Albany: P. L. Gilbert.* 1850. 8vo, pp. 75. BA, C. 21238

Another edition in German, *Albany.* 1851. Also: Phrenological Character of Reuben Dunbar, with a Short Treatise on the Causes and Prevention of Crime, by Mrs. Margaret Thompson ... . *Albany: P. L. Gilbert.* 1851. 8vo, pp. 16. BA.

DUNBAR (R. N.) Beauties of Tropical Scenery, Lyrical Sketches, and Love Songs. With Notes. *London: Robert Hardwicke.* 1864. Post 8vo. + [*Ibid.*] 1866. Post 8vo.

DUNBAR. The Cruise; or a Prospect of the West Indian Archipelago. By Robert N. Dunbar. *London.* 1835. 12mo.

DUNBAR (S.) Brotherly Love the Duty and Mark of Christians: a Sermon ... at Medfield, November the 6th, 1748. Being the Lord's-Day next following the Sitting of an Ecclesiastical Council there. By Samuel Dunbar. *Boston, N. E.: Printed by J. Green, for D. Gookin.* 1749. 8vo, pp. 28. BA.

DUNBAR. The Duty of Christ's Ministers to be Spiritual Labourers. A Sermon Preached at Dorchester, April 29th, 1774; a day set apart by the Church and Congregation there, for solemn humiliation and supplication, to seek the Divine direction and blessing, in choice and settlement of a Minister among them. By Samuel Dunbar, M.A. *Boston: Printed by Mills and Hicks.* MDCCLXXV. 8vo, pp. 28. 21242

DUNBAR. The Duty of Ministers, to testify the Gospel of the Grace of God. A Sermon Preached to the First Parish in Braintree, December 13. 1753. Being A Day set a-part by them for solemn Humiliation and Prayer for Divine Direction in their Choice of a Minister. By Samuel Dunbar ... . *Boston: Printed by S. Kneeland.* 1754. 8vo, pp. (4), 23. B., BA., M. 21243

DUNBAR. The Ministers of Christ should be careful, that they do not in their Ministry corrupt the Word of God. A Sermon Preach'd in the First Parish in Scituate, April 20. 1763. At

the Ordination of the Reverend Mr. Ebenezer Grosvenor, to the Pastoral Office. By Samuel Dunbar ... . *Boston: Printed by S. Kneeland.* M,DCC,LXIII. 8vo, pp. (2), 26. BA. 21244

DUNBAR. The Presence of God with his People, their only Safety and Happiness. A Discourse Delivered at Boston, In the presence of His Excellency the Governour, Thomas Pownall, Esq; ... May 28. 1760. The Day for the Election of His Majesty's Council for the Province. ... By Samuel Dunbar, A.M. ... *Boston: Printed by S. Kneeland.* 1760. 8vo, 2 l., pp. 37. B., BA. 21245

DUNBAR. True Faith makes the best Soldiers, A Sermon Preach'd before the ancient and honourable Artillery-Company, On their Anniversary Meeting for the Election of Officers, June 6th 1748. By Samuel Dunbar, A.M. ... Stoughton. *Boston: Printed for D. Henchman in Cornhil.* 1748. 8vo, pp. 38. M.

Also: Righteousness by the Law Subversive of Christianity. A Sermon ... at the Thursday-Lecture, in Boston, N. E., May 9, 1751. By Samuel Dunbar ... . *Boston, N. E.: Printed by S. Kneeland.* 1751. 8vo, pp. 27. B., BA., M. — Sermon delivered at Stoughton, upon the Melancholy occasion of the Premature Deaths of several Young Persons there, February 5, 1748–9. *Boston.* 1749. 8vo. N.

DUNBAR (W.) Discoveries made in Exploring the Missouri, Red River and Washita, by Captains Lewis and Clark, Doctors Sibley and William Dunbar, Esq., with a Statistical Account of the Counties adjacent, with an Appendix. By Mr. Dunbar. *Natchez: printed by Andrus, Marshall & Co.* 1806. 8vo, pp. 174. 21247

DUNBARTON, *N. H.* Record of the Centennial Celebration of the Incorporation of the Town of Dunbarton, Sept. 13, 1865. *Manchester, N. H.: Press of Henry A. Gage.* 1866. Sm. 8vo, pp. 124. B. 21248

DUNCAN (Alexander). The Bank's Bond-Man Answered. Speech of Mr. Duncan on the Bill making Appropriations for Harbors, and a Reply to Mr. Bond of Ohio. ... July 7, 1838. *Washington.* 1838. 8vo, pp. 18. 21249

DUNCAN. Remarks of Mr. Duncan, of Ohio, on the Resolution offered by Mr. Haynes. ... December 18, 1837. *Washington.* 1837. 8vo, pp. 8. 21250

Also: Speech ... [on Defalcation of S. Swartout. *Washington.* 1839.] 8vo. — Speech ... on the Subject of the New Jersey Election, for Members of the Twenty-Sixth Congress. Delivered in the House ... January 9, 1840. *Baltimore.* 1840. 8vo, pp. 24. H. — Speech ... on the Bill to Authorize the Issue of Treasury Notes;

delivered in Committee of the Whole House ... March 26, 1840. *Washington.* 1840. 8vo, pp. 22. H. — Speech ... on the General Appropriation Bill for 1840. Delivered in the House ... April 10, 1840. *Washington.* 1840. 8vo, pp. 22. H. — Speech ... in Committee of the Whole, on the Treasury Note Bill. Delivered in the House of Representatives, January 25, 1841. *Washington: Globe Office.* 1840. 8vo, pp. 23. BA. — Speech ... In the House ... March 6, 1844. On the Bill introduced by him to regulate the Election of Electors for President and Vice President and Members of Congress throughout the United States. [n. p. n. d.] 8vo, pp. 16. — Speech ... on the Oregon Bill, ... Jan. 29, 1845. [*Washington.*] 1845. 8vo. S. — Speech ... in the House ... Feb. 19, in Committee on the Army Appropriation Bill. ... 8vo, pp. 16. — Speech of Mr. Duncan, of Ohio. [n. p. n. d.] 8vo, pp. 16. H.

DUNCAN (A.) The British Trident; or, Register of Naval Actions; including Authentic Accounts of all the most Remarkable Engagements at Sea, ... By Archibald Duncan, Esq. ... . [*London:*] *James Cundee.* 1806. 6 vols., 12mo. 21251

Recounts some of the naval battles of the American Revolution, etc.

DUNCAN. The Mariner's Chronicle; or Authentic and Complete History of Popular Shipwrecks, recording the most Remarkable Disasters which have happened on the Ocean to People of all Nations. *London.* 1805. 6 vols., 12mo, pp. xxix, 334; ii, 360; iii, 365; iv, 386; iv, 394; 414. 50 Plates. + *Philadelphia.* 1806 and 1810. 21252

Some of these popular (?) shipwrecks occurred on the American coasts. The inappropriateness of the title suggested itself to the author, and the titles of volumes II. to VI. omit the word "popular."

DUNCAN (D.) Arctic Regions, Voyages to Davis' Straits, by David Duncan, Master of the Ship Dundee. Sailed from London, 3rd April, 1826, and 25th June, 1827 ... beset by ice more than eight months ... . *London: Printed by E. Billings, For the Author.* 1827. pp. xv, 126. Plate. H. 21253

DUNCAN (F.) Our Garrisons in the West; or, Sketches in British North America. By Francis Duncan, M.A. *London: Chapman & Hall.* 1864. Post 8vo, pp. viii, 319. 21254

DUNCAN [(Garret)]. Speech of Mr. Duncan, of Kentucky, on the Assumption of Power by the Executive delivered in the House ... July 24, 1848. *Washington.* 1848. 8vo, pp. 16. H.

DUNCAN (Greer B.) U. S. Circuit Court. Myra C. Gaines *vs.* City of New Orleans, De la Croix, *et al.* Argument of G. B. Duncan, Esq. *New Orleans.* 1858. 8vo, pp. 62. BA., M.

DUNCAN (H.) Presbyter's Letters on the West India Question. ... By Henry Duncan, D.D. *London.* 1830. 8vo, pp. 139.

DUNCAN (J. H.) Speech of Hon. J. H. Duncan, of Mass., on the California and Territorial Questions. Delivered in the House ... June 7, 1850. *Washington.* 1850. 8vo, pp. 8. H.

DUNCAN (J. M.) Travels through Part of the United States and Canada in 1818 and 1819. By John M. Duncan, A.B. *Glasgow: Printed for Hurst, Robinson & Company, London, &c.* 1823. 2 vols., post 8vo, pp. xvi, 333, (1); xii, 384. 14 Plates. H. + *New York.* 1823. 12mo. 21259

DUNCAN (J. M.) A Discourse, delivered on the Fast Day recommended by the President of the United States. By John M. Duncan, ... of Baltimore. *Baltimore: Cushing & Brother.* 1841. pp. 46. 21260

DUNCAN. A Plea for Ministerial Liberty. A Discourse addressed by appointment to the Directors and Students of the Theological Seminary of the Presbyterian Church at Princeton, on the 17th of May, 1834 (?) *Baltimore.* 1853. 8vo, pp. 57.

DUNCAN. America as I found it. By the Mother of Mary Lundie Duncan. *New York: Robert Carter & Brothers.* 1852. 18mo, pp. 440. 21262

DUNCAN (P.) A Narrative to the Wesleyan Mission to Jamaica, with occasional Remarks on the State of Society in that Colony. By the Rev. Peter Duncan. *London.* 1849. Post 8vo, pp. 412. P. 21263

[DUNCAN (William).] The Gospel in the Far West. Metlahkatlah. Ten Years' Work among the Tsimshean Indians. Third Edition. [*London:*] *Church Missionary House.* 1869. 12mo, pp. 130. Map. 21264

A very interesting narrative of mission work among the Indians on the Pacific coast, between Fraser and Simpson Rivers.

DUNCAN & Co. Floyd's Acceptances. Memorial of Duncan, Sherman & Co. to Congress, January, 1863. 8vo, pp. 8.

Relative to the acceptances of John B. Floyd.

DUNCANSON (A.) The Higher Law: a Sermon for the Times. ... By the Rev. Alexander Duncanson. ... *Plymouth, Massachusetts.* 1853. 8vo, pp. 16. H. 21266

Also: Libertas; or, a Plea in Defence of the Rights of Private Judgment. *Sandusky.* 1855. 8vo, pp. 24. B.

DUNCOMBE (Charles). Duncombe's Free Banking: An Essay on Banking, Currency, Finance, Exchanges, and Political Economy. *Cleveland.* 1841. 18mo. S. 21267

DUNCOMBE (*Dr.* C.) Report upon Education in Upper Canada, to Parliament, 25th February, 1836. *Toronto.* 1836. 21268

DUNDAS (H.) Facts relative to the Conduct of the War in the West Indies; collected from the Speech of the Rt. Hon. Henry Dundas in the House of Commons, April 28, 1796, and from Documents laid before the House on that subject. *London: J. Owen.* 1796. 4to, pp. 205. J.C.B. 21269

DUNDAS. Speech of Henry Dundas in the House of Commons, upon the Bill for the Abolition of the Slave Trade. *London.* 1796. 8vo. C. 21270

DUNDAS (R.) Sketches of Brazil: including New Views of Tropical and European Fever, with Remarks on a Premature Decay of the System incident to Europeans on their Return from Hot Climates. By Robert Dundas, M.D. *London.* 1852. Post 8vo, pp. 450. C. 21271

DUNDEE, *N. J.* ... An Act to Incorporate the Dundee Manufacturing Company. Passed, March 15, 1832. *Paterson, N. J.: Day & Warren.* 1833. 8vo, pp. 8. 21272

DUNDONALD (Thomas Cochrane, *Earl of*). Autobiography of a Seaman. *London.* 1860. 2 vols., 8vo. C. 21273

DUNDONALD. Narrative of Services in the Liberation of Chili, Peru, and Brazil, from Spanish and Portuguese Domination. *London.* 1859. 2 vols., 8vo. C. 21274

A small edition only printed. *See* Vol. III., Nos. 14078–80.

DUNDONALD. Notes on the Mineralogy, Government and Condition of the British West India Islands and North American Maritime Colonies. With a Statistical Chart of Newfoundland, contrasting the French and British Fisheries. By Admiral, the Earl of Dundonald. *London.* 1851. 8vo, pp. 136. P. 21275

D'UNGER (Robert). The Historical Cabinet. The American Continent; its Discovery and Conquest, Description, etc. *Philadelphia: J. J. Fullmer & Co.* 1854. 12mo, pp. 72. Plate.

DUNGLAS (P. M.) Breve Exposicion de la enfermedad del Illmo. Sr. Benavente Arzobispo de Lima. *Lima.* 1839. 4to.

DUNGLISON (R.) A Public Discourse in Commemoration of Peter S. Du Ponceau, LL.D. ... delivered before the (American Philosophical Society) ... on the 25th of October, 1844, By

Robley Dunglison ... . *Philadelphia: printed for the American Philosophical Society, By John C. Clark.* 1844. 8vo, pp. 44. BA.

Also: Address to Medical Graduates of Jefferson Medical College. *Philadelphia.* 1837. Charge to the Graduates of Jefferson Medical College ... March 25, 1847, ... With a List of the Graduates. ... . *Philadelphia.* 1847. 8vo, pp. 20. BA.

DUNHAM (C. L.) ... Speech of Hon. C. L. Dunham, of Indiana, in the House ... April 6, 1852, on the Homestead Bill. [*Washington.* n. d.] 8vo, pp. 8. H. 21279

Also: Speech ... on the Coinage Question, delivered in the House ... February 1, 1853. [n. p. n. d.] 8vo, pp. 8. H.

DUNHAM (J.) Journal of Voyages; containing an Account of the Author's being twice captured by the English and once by Gibbs the Pirate; his Narrow Escape when Chased by an English War Schooner; as well as his being cast away and residing with Indians. To which is added Some account of the Soil, Products, Laws and Customs of Chagres, the Musquitto Shore, and St. Blas, at the Isthmus of Darien. With Illustrations. By Captain Jacob Dunham. *New York: published for the Author.* 1850. 12mo, pp. 243. 21280

DUNHAM (J.) An Answer to the "Vindication of the Official Conduct of the Trustees of Dartmouth College" in confirmation of the "Sketches," with Remarks on the Removal of President Wheelock. By Josiah Dunham. ... *Hanover: Printed by David Watson, Jun. January,* 1816. 8vo, pp. 94, 1. BA.

DUNHAM. A Funeral Oration on George Washington, Late General of the Armies of the United States. Pronounced, at Oxford, Massachusetts, at the request of the Field Officers of the Brigade Stationed at that place, on the 15th Jan., 1800; it being the Day Devoted to the Funeral honors of their departed Chief, pursuant to General Orders from the Secretary of War. By Josiah Dunham, A.M., Capt. 16th U. S. Regiment. *Boston: Manning & Loring.* [1800.] 8vo, pp. 20. BA. 21282

DUNHAM. An Oration, in Commemoration of the Birth of our Illustrious Washington, pronounced at Windsor, February 24, 1812, before the Washington Benevolent Society. By Josiah Dunham. ... *Windsor, Vt.: printed by Thomas M. Pomroy.* 1812. 8vo, pp. 24. BA. 21283

Also: An Oration, ... at Hanover, before the Franklin Lodge of ... Masons; ... Together with some very learned Notes. By Brother Josiah Dunham ... . *Hanover: printed by Dunham & True.* 1797. 8vo, pp. 24. BA. — An Oration for the Fourth of July, 1798 ... at Hanover, Newhampshire ... *Hanover.* [1798.] 8vo. — Oration at Windsor, Vt., Feb. 22, 1814, before the Washington Benevolent Society. *Windsor.* 1814. 8vo. BA. — An Oration. Hanover, N. H. July 5, 1814.

Dunham and True's Almanac, For the Year of our Lord, 1796; Being Bissextile, or Leap Year, and of Independence of the United States the twentieth. Calculated for the Meridian of Hanover, Newhampshire, ... *Hanover: printed by Dunham and True.* [n. d.] 8vo, pp. (22). BA. 21284

DUNHAM (Josiah), *Jr.* Appeal to the Citizens of Boston, to be read before Voting. *Boston.* [n. d.] 12mo, pp. 12. B.

Against Josiah Dunham, Jr.

DUNHAM (S.) An Historical Discourse delivered at West Brookfield, Mass., on Occasion of the One Hundred and Fiftieth Anniversary of the First Church in Brookfield, October 16, 1867. By Samuel Dunham ... . With a Poem and Appendix. *Springfield, Mass.: Samuel Bowles & Company, Printers.* 1867. 8vo, pp. 123. B., H. 21286

[DUNHAM (S. A.)] History of Spain and Portugal. ... *London.* [1832–33]. 5 vols., 16mo. BA., H. 21287

Forms Vols. XXIII.–XXVII. of Lardner's "Cabinet Cyclopædia." Vols. IV. and V. contain some account of the Spanish colonies in America. "A work of singular acuteness and information." — PRESCOTT.

DUNHAM COPPER COMPANY. Reports on the Property of the Copper Mines. *Boston.* [n. d.] 8vo. 21288

Dunigan's American Catholic Almanac for 1858. *New York: Dunigan & Bro.* 1858. 8vo. Continued. 21289

DUNKIN (B. F.) Address, delivered before the Members of the New-England Society, in Charleston, (S. C.) at their Anniversary Meeting December 20th, 1819. By Benjamin Faneuil Dunkin, Esq. ... *Charleston, S. C.* 1820. 16mo, pp. 8. H.

Also: An Oration delivered before the Whig Association and the State Society of Cincinnati; Charleston, S. C., July 4, 1834. ... *Charleston.* 1834. 8vo, pp. 22. M.

DUNKIN (Christopher). Address at the Bar of the Legislative Assembly of Canada, delivered on the 11th and 14th March 1853, on Behalf of Certain Proprietors of Seigniories in Lower Canada, against the Second Reading of the Bill, intituled "An Act to define Seigniorial Rights in Lower Canada, and to facilitate the Redemption thereof." *Quebec: printed at the Canada Gazette Office.* 1853. 8vo, pp. 109. B., BA., S. 21291

Also in French.

DUNKIN. ... Speech delivered in the Legislative Assembly, by Christopher Dunkin, Esq., Member for Brome. During the Debate on the Subject of the Confederation of the British North American Provinces. *Quebec: printed by Hunter, Rose & Co.* 1865. 8vo, pp. 64. H. 21292

Also: Case (in part) of the Seigniors of Lower Canada, submitted to the Judges of the Court of Queen's Bench and of the Superior Court for Lower Canada. *Montreal* 1855. 8vo.

DUNLAP (A.) An Oration, delivered at Salem, on Monday, July 5, 1819, at the Request of the Association of the Essex Reading Room, in Celebration of American Independence. By Andrew Dunlap, Esq. ... . *Salem: Printed by Warwick Palfrey, Jun.* 1819. 8vo, pp. 15. BA. 21293

Also: An Oration, delivered at the Request of the Republicans of Boston, at Faneuil Hall, on the Fourth of July, 1822. ... *Boston: Printed by True and Green.* 1822. 8vo, pp. 24. B., B.A. — An Oration, delivered at the Request of the Washington Society, at the City of Boston, July 4, 1832. *Boston.* 1832. 8vo. — A Speech delivered before the Municipal Court of the City of Boston, in Defence of Abner Kneeland, on an Indictment for Blasphemy. ... *Boston.* 1834. 12mo, pp. 132. H.

DUNLAP (G. W.) Speech of Hon. G. W. Dunlap, of Kentucky, on the Cause of the Rebellion, and the Constitutional Power of Congress to Quell it by emancipating the Slaves. Delivered in the House ... January 31, 1862. [*Washington.*] 8vo, pp. 8. H. 21294

DUNLAP (J.) Sermon, on Board of the Fleet at Whitehall, 1814. By John Dunlap. *Bennington.* 1823. 8vo. 21295

[DUNLAP (William).] André; | A Tragedy, in Five Acts; | as performed by the old American Company, | New-York, March 30, 1798. | To which are added, | Authentic Documents | respecting | Major André; | Consisting of | Letters to Miss Seward, | The Cow Chase, | Proceedings of the Court Martial, &c. | *New-York,* | *Printed by T. and J. Swords,* 1798. | 8vo, pp. 109. P. 21296

See "M. Rev.," XXIX. 336. Roche's copy sold for $18. Reprinted as below:

DUNLAP. André: a Tragedy in five acts: as now performing at the Theatre in New York. To which is added the Cow-Chase: a satirical poem. By Major André: With the proceedings of the Court Martial; and authentic documents concerning him. *London: printed for David Ogilvy and Son.* 1799. 8vo, pp. 11 21297

[DUNLAP.] The Glory of Columbia; her Yeomanry. A Play in Five Acts. The Songs, Duets, and Chorusses, Intended for the Celebration of the Fourth of July, at the New York Theatre. *New York: D. Longworth.* 1803. 12mo, pp. 12.

DUNLAP. The Glory of Columbia her Yeomanry! A Play, in Five Acts. By William Dunlap, Esq. With Songs, Duets, &c. *New York: David Longworth. May,* 1817. 12mo, pp. 56.

DUNLAP. A History of the American Theatre. By William Dunlap ... . *New York: J. & J. Harper.* 1832. 8vo, pp. viii, 420. H. + *London: Richard Bentley.* 1833. 2 vols., 8vo, pp. xii, 412; vi, 387. BA. 21300

Includes "A Catalogue of American Plays and their Authors," at the end. This edition is sometimes found with a new title-page, "History of the American Theatre; and Anecdotes of the Principal Actors. By William Dunlap. ... Two Volumes in One. *London: Richard Bentley.*" To this is usually prefixed a plate by Cruikshank.

DUNLAP. History of the New Netherlands, Province of New York, and State of New York, to the Adoption of the Federal Constitution. By William Dunlap. *New York: printed by Carter & Thorp.* 1839–40. 2 vols., 8vo, pp. 487; 282, ccxlvi, 1 l. Portrait of Peter Stuyvesant, and Maps. BA., H. 21301

DUNLAP. A History of New York, for Schools. By William Dunlap. *New York: Harper & Brothers.* 1837. 18mo, pp. 216, 268. 21302

DUNLAP. History of the Rise and Progress of the Arts of Design in the United States. By William Dunlap ... . *New York: Geo. P. Scott & Co., Printers.* 1834. 2 vols., 8vo, pp. 435; viii, 480. BA., H. 21303

Now scarce, and sells for $20. *See* Vanderlyn (John).

DUNLAP. The Life of Charles Brockden Brown: together with Selections from the Rarest of his Printed Works, from his Original Letters, and from his Manuscripts before unpublished. By William Dunlap. *Philadelphia: James P. Parker.* 1815. 2 vols., 8vo, pp. iv, (9)–396; 472. + *London.* 1822. 8vo. BA.

DUNLAP. Life of William Guthrie. *Exeter, N. H.* 1796. 12mo. W. 21305

DUNLAP. Memoirs of the Life of George Frederick Cooke, Esquire, late of the Theatre Royal, Covent Garden. By William Dunlap. ... Composed principally from Journals and other Authentic Documents, left by Mr. Cooke; and the Per-

sonal Knowledge of the Writer. *New York: published by D. Longworth.* 1813. 2 vols., 18mo, pp. 403; 400. Portrait. BA. + *London.* 1813. 2 vols., 8vo. + Second Edition. *London.* 1815. 2 vols., 8vo, pp. 449; 416. 21306

DUNLAP. A Record, Literary and Political, of Five Months in the Year 1813. By Wm. Dunlap and others. *New York: Printed for the Proprietor, by David Carlisle.* [n. d.] 8vo, pp. 348. 21307

DUNLAP. Thirty Years Ago; or, the Memoirs of a Water Drinker. *New York.* 1836. 2 vols., 12mo, pp. 208; 200.

DUNLAP. Yankee Chronology; or, Huzza for the Constitution! A Musical Interlude, in One Act. To which are added, the Patriotic Songs of the Freedom of the Seas and Yankee Tars. By W. Dunlap, Esq. *New York: D. Longworth.* 1812. 12mo, pp. 16. BA. 21309

Also: Address to the Students of the National Academy of Design, at the Delivery of the Premiums, April 18, 1831. By William Dunlap. *New York.* 1831. 8vo, pp. 20. — A Trip to Niagara; or Travellers in America. A Farce ... . *New York.* 1830. 12mo, pp. 54. B. A list of other pieces by this author will be found at the end of Vol. II. of the English edition of Dunlap's "American Theatre."

DUNLAVY (J.) The Manifesto, or a Declaration of the Doctrine and Practice of the Church of Christ. By John Dunlavy. *Printed at Pleasant Hill, Ky.* MDCCCXVIII. 8vo, pp. viii, 486. + *New-York: Reprinted by E. O. Jenkins.* 1847. 8vo, pp. viii, 486. BA., S. 21310

Also: The Nature and Character of the True Church of Christ proved by Plain Evidences, and showing whereby it may be known and distinguished from all others. Being Extracts from the Writings of John Dunlavy. ... *New York: Printed by George W. Wood.* 1850. 8vo, pp. 93. B., BA.

DUNLEVY (A. H.) History of the Miami Baptist Association; from its Organization in 1797, to a Division in that Body on Missions, etc. in the Year 1836. With Short Sketches of Deceased Pastors of this First Association in Ohio. By A. H. Dunlevy. *Cincinnati: G. S. Blanchard & Co.* 1869. 16mo, 1 l., pp. 193, 1 l. C. 21311

DUNLOP (A.) Notes on the Isthmus of Panama, with Remarks on its Physical Geography and its Prospects in connection with the Gold Regions, Gold Mining and Washing. By Alexander Dunlop. *London.* 1852. 8vo. P. 21312

DUNLOP (*Capt.*) Arguments entered into with the Constitutional Authorities at Vera Cruz, by Captain Dunlop, R. N., and by Captain Alaham, R. N. Presented to the House of Commons by Command of Her Majesty, in pursuance of their Address dated April 19, 1861. *London: printed by Harrison and Sons.* 8vo, Title, pp. 8. BA. 21313

DUNLOP (C.) Brazil as a field for Emigration. Its Geography, Climate, Agricultural Capabilities, and the Facilities afforded for Permanent Settlement. By Charles Dunlop. *London.* 1866. 8vo, pp. 32. 21314

DUNLOP (J.) Private Case before the House of Lords relative to the Affairs of James Dunlop, a large Tobacco Merchant, whose effects were principally in Virginia. *Privately Printed.* 1777. Folio. 21315

DUNLOP (James). Memoir on the Controversy between W. Penn and Lord Baltimore respecting the Boundaries of Pennsylvania and Maryland. Vol. I. *Philadelphia: published by McCarty and Davis.* 1826–40. 8vo. B. 21316

DUNLOP (R. G.) Travels in Central America; being a Journal of nearly Three Years' Residence in the Country; together with a Sketch of the History of the Republic, and an account of its Climate, Productions, Commerce, &c. By Robert Glasgow Dunlop. *London: Longman.* 1847. Post 8vo, pp. 358. Map.

[DUNLOP (William).] Statistical Sketches of Upper Canada, for the Use of Emigrants: By a Backwoodsman. ... *London: John Murray.* MDCCCXXXII. 12mo, 2 l., pp. 120. BA., S. 21318

DUNN (B. S.) Brazil the Home for Southerners; or a Practical Account of what the Author, and others who visited that Country for the same Objects, saw and did while in that Empire. By Rev. Ballard S. Dunn, Rector of St. Philip's Church, New Orleans, and late of the Confederate Army. *New York: C. B. Richardson.* 1866. Crown 8vo, pp. iv, 272. 21319

DUNN (H.) Guatimala, or, the Republic of Central America, 1827–8; being Sketches and Memorandums made during a Twelve-Month's Residence. By Henry Dunn. *New York: G. & C. Carvill.* 1828. 8vo, pp. 318. H. + *London: James Nisbet.* MDCCCXXIX. 8vo, pp. vii, 328. BA., C., H. 21320

DUNN (J.) History of the Oregon Territory and British North-American Fur Trade: with an Account of the Habits and Customs of the Principal Native Tribes on the Northern Continent. By John Dunn, late of the Hudson's Bay Company, Eight Years a Resident in the Country. *London: Edwards and Hughes.* 1844. 8vo, pp. viii, 359. Map. + Second Edition. [*Ibid.*] 1846. 8vo, pp. viii, 359. Map. 21321

Reprinted in Smith's Weekly Volume, Vol. I. *Philadelphia.* 1845. 4to. Also as

DUNN. The Oregon Territory, [as above]. *Philadelphia: G. B. Zieber & Co.* 1845. 18mo, pp. viii, 13–236. BA. 21322

See also "Transactions of the Royal Irish Academy" for an article on the "Native Tribes of North America."

DUNN (J.) A Collection of Curious Observations, &c., 1750. *See* [Lambert (*Abbé*)].

DUNN (J.) A Sermon occasioned by the Burning of the Episcopal Church in the Parish of Grand Manon, N. B. Preached by the Rev. John Dunn, A.B., Rector ... . *New Brunswick.* 1841. 8vo, pp. 15. BA. 21323

DUNN (Nathan). A Peep at China, in Mr. Dunn's Chinese Collection; with ... Notices relating to the Institutions ... of the Chinese, and our Commercial Intercourse with them. By E. C. Wines. *Philadelphia: printed for Nathan Dunn.* 1839. 8vo, pp. 113. BA. 21324

DUNN (T.) A Discourse Delivered in the New Dutch Church, Nassau Street, on Tuesday the 21st of October, 1794, before the New York Society for the Information and Assistance of Persons Emigrating from Foreign Countries. By Thomas Dunn, An Emigrant. *New York: L. Wayland.* 1794. 8vo, 3 l., pp. 28. + *London: Re-Printed by D. J. Eaton.* [1794.] 8vo, pp. 30. BA. 21325

DUNN (T.) ... Sermon Preached in the Prison in Philadelphia, Dec. 12, 1793 ... being the day appointed for ... Thanksgiving for the ceasing of the late Epidemic Fever. By Thomas Dunn. *Philadelphia.* 1793. 8vo. 21326

DUNN (W. M.) Confiscation of the Property of Rebels. Remarks of Hon. W. McKee Dunn, of Indiana. Delivered in the House of Representatives, April 23, 1862. [*Washington:*] *L. Towers & Co., Printers.* 8vo, pp. 8. H. + [n. p. n. d.] 8vo, pp. 8. H. 21327

DUNN. The Republican Party and the Republican Candidate for the Presidency. Speech of Hon. W. McKee Dunn, of Indiana, Delivered in ... Philadelphia, May 26, 1860. *Washington, D. C.: Buell & Blanchard, Printers.* 1860. 8vo, pp. 8.

DUNN. Speech of Mr. Dunn, of Indiana, on the Treasury Note Bill. Delivered in the House ... May 14, 1838. [n. p. n. d.] 8vo, pp. 15. H. 21329

DUNNEL (H. G.) The True Genealogy of the Dunnel and Dwinnel Family of New England. By Henry Gale Dunnell, M.D., of New York City. *New York: Charles B. Richardson.* 1862. Rl. 8vo, pp. 84. B. 21330

DUNNING (H.) Address delivered on the Occasion of the Funeral Solemnities of the late President of the United States, in the First Constitutional Presbyterian Church, April 19, 1865. By Rev. H. Dunning, Pastor. *Baltimore: John W. Woods, Printer.* 1865. 8vo, pp. 12. B. 21331

DUNNING. The Assassination, its Lessons to Young Men, a Discourse delivered in the First Constitutional Presbyterian Church, May 7, 1865, by Rev. H. Dunning, Pastor. Printed by Request. *Baltimore: John W. Woods, Printer.* 1865. 8vo, pp. 12. B. 21332

DUNNING. The Nameless Crime. A Discourse delivered in the First Constitutional Presbyterian Church, April 23d, 1865, Sunday Night, April 23, 1865. By Rev. H. Dunning, Pastor. Printed by Request. *Baltimore: John W. Woods, Printer.* 1865. 8vo, pp. 12. B. 21333

DUNNING (H. N.) Presidential Design of the Slavery Agitation. A Sermon preached January 4, 1861. By Rev. H. N. Dunning. *Gloversville: A. Peirson.* 1861. 12mo, pp. 18.

DUNNING. The Strangeness of God's Ways. A Sermon preached before the Churches of Gloversville, November 24. 1864. *Gloversville: George W. Heaton.* 1865. 8vo, pp. 15.

DUNPHY (T.), *and* CUMMINS (T. J.) Remarkable Trials of all Countries, particularly of the United States, ... with Notes and Speeches of Counsel. Compiled by Thomas Dunphy, of the New York Bar, and Thomas J. Cummins, of the New York Press. *New York: Diossy & Cockcroft.* 1867. 8vo, pp. vi, 464. 21336

Dunscombe (J. W.) Canadian Custom House Guide. *Montreal.* 1844. 8vo. 21337

Also: Provincial Laws of the Customs. *Montreal.* 1844. 8vo.

Dunshee (H. W.) History of the School of the Reformed Protestant Dutch Church, in the City of New-York, from 1633 to the present time. By Henry Webb Dunshee. With an Introduction by Rev. Thomas De Witt, d.d. *New-York: printed by John A. Gray.* 1853. 12mo, pp. 120. 21338

Dunshee. The Knickerbocker's Address to the Stuyvesant Pear Tree. Respectfully dedicated to the Knickerbockers of Manhattan Island. *New York.* 1857. 8vo, pp. 10. 21339

Dunster (H. P.) The Discoveries of Columbus and of the English in America. *London: James Blackwood.* 1860. 12mo.

Dunster (J.) A Sermon ... at the Instalment of the Reverend Mr. Joseph Green, Junr. In the Pastoral Office over the First Church of Christ in Yarmouth; September 15, 1762. By Isaiah Dunster, a.m. ... To which is added the Charge and the Right Hand of Fellowship, on that Occasion. *Boston.* m,dcc,lxiii. 8vo, pp. 24. h. 21341

Dunt (Detlef). Reise nach Texas, nebst Nachrichten von diesem Lande; für Deutsche, welche nach Amerika zu gehen beabsichtigen. *Bremen.* 1834. 8vo. 21342

Dunton (J.) Letters written from New-England, a.d. 1686. By John Dunton. In which are described his Voyages by Sea, his Travels on Land, and the Characters of his Friends and Acquaintances. Now First Published from the Original Manuscript, In the Bodleian Library, Oxford, with Notes and an Appendix, by W. H. Whitmore. *Boston: Published for the Prince Society.* 1867. 4to, pp. xxiv, 340. b., ba. 21343

120 copies printed in fcap 4to, and 20 copies in rl. 4to.

Dunton. The | Life and Errors | of | John Dunton | Late Citizen of London; Written by Himself in Solitvde. With an Idea of a New Life; | Wherein is Shewn | How he'd Think, Speak, and Act, might he | Live over his Days again: | Intermix'd with the | New Discoveries The Author has made In his Travels Abroad, | And in his | Private Conversation at Home. | Together with the Lives and Characters of a Thou- | sand Persons now Living in London, &c. | Digested into Seven Stages with their

Respective Ideas. | ... *London: Printed for S. Malthus.* 1705. | 8vo, 9 l., pp. 463, then pp. 200–251. c. 21344

"This curious work abounds with interesting literary history, anecdotes of Bostonians, &c." — *Blackwood's Mag.*, vi. 26. Lowndes mentions a portrait, but it is evident, from the lines preceding the title-page, "The author's speaking picture," that none was published with this volume. Eighty-four pages are occupied with the account of his visit to New England, his opening a bookstore in Boston; intercourse with the Mathers, John Cotton, Eliot, Hubbard, Indian sachems, and several ladies of Boston, of some of whom he relates very curious particulars. Reprinted with alterations, explanations, and additions, as below:

Dunton. The Life and Errors of John Dunton, ... with the Lives and Characters of more than a Thousand Contemporary Divines, and other persons of Literary Eminence. To which are added Dunton's Conversation in Ireland; Selections from his other Genuine Works; and a faithful Portrait of the Author. [Edited by John Nichols.] *London: J. Nichols, Son, and Bentley.* 1818. 2 vols., 8vo, pp. xxxii, 776. Portrait. ba.

Duodecennium Luctuosum. *See* [Mather (C.)]

Dupaix. *See* Lenoir (A.), Antiquités Mexicaines.

Dupanloup (Félix Antoine Philibert), *Bishop of Orleans.* Lettre ... au clergé sur l'esclavage. *Orléans.* 1862. 8vo, pp. 387–399. h. 21346

Also in Montalembert's "La Victoire du Nord. 1865." 8vo, pp. 43–160.

Du Parc D'Avaugour (*Le Comte*). La France rendue florissante par la Guyane. Par Du Parc d'Avaugour. *Paris.* 1852. 8vo, pp. x, 48. 21347

Contains a list of authors who have written on Guyana.

Du Pasquier (H.) Les Etats-Unis et le Mexique, l'intérêt européen dans l'Amérique du Nord. *Paris: Guillaumin.* 1852. 4to, pp. 88. 21348

Du Perier (M.) Histoire Universelle des Voyages faits par Mer et par Terre dans l'Ancien et dans le Nouveau Monde; pour éclairir la Geographie ancienne & moderne. Par M. Du Perier. *Paris: Chez Pierre Geffart.* mdccvii. 12mo, 6 l., pp. 50, 3 l., pp. 458. 21349

Republished with a new title in 1711; the name of Bellegarde being substituted for that of Du Perier. An English translation appeared in 1708 as below:

[Du Perier.] A Complete Collection of Voyages made into North and South America, in due order as they happen'd, beginning from Christopher Columbus and Americus Vespucius

and descending to this present time. Accurately describing each country, its Natural History and product; the Religion, Customs, Manners, Trade, &c., of the Inhabitants, with whatsoever else is curious and remarkable in any kind. To which is prefixed an Introductory Discourse, showing the great advantage of trading into these parts; with the improvements that have been made by our late Navigators, in order to the effecting speedy Voyages, exactly describing the Coasts, and illustrating both the Ancient and Modern Geography. The whole extracted from the works of considerable Travellers. By M. L'Abbé Bellegarde. Translated from the French version printed at Paris. Adorn'd with cuts. *London: Printed for E. Curll at the Dial and Bible against St. Dunstan's Church.* 1711. 8vo, Frontispiece, Title, 3 l., pp. 364, 4 l. 5 Plates. 21350

The name of Bellegarde in this edition is substituted for that of Du Perier. *See* our Vol. ii., No. 4508, and below:

Du Perier. A General History of all Voyages and Travels Throughout The Old and New World, From the first Ages to this Present Time. Illustrating Both the Ancient and Modern Geography. Containing an Accurate Description of each Country, its Natural History and Products; the Religion, Customs, Manners, Trade, &c., of the Inhabitants and whatsoever is Curious and Remarkable of any Kind. An Account of the Discoveries hitherto made in the most Remote Parts, and the Great Usefulness of such Attempts, for Improving both Natural and Experimental Philosophy; with a Catalogue of all Authors that have ever described any Part of the World. ... By Monsr. Du Perier. Made English from the Paris Edition. Adorn'd with Cuts. *London: Printed for Edmund Curll.* 1708. 8vo, 5 l., pp. 364, 4 l. ba., j.c.b. 21331

With the exception of the introduction the whole of this volume relates to the early voyages of the Spaniards to America. Republished with a new title in 1711. *See* No. 21350, *ante.*

Duperre. Précis de la colonisation de la Mana, à la Guyane Française. *Paris.* 1835. 8vo. 21352

Duperrey (Louis Isidore). Voyage Autour du Monde, exécuté par ordre du Roi, sur le Corvette de Sa Majesté, La Coquille, pendant les années 1822, 1823, 1824, et 1825, sous le ministère et conformément aux instructions de son excellence M. le Marquis de Clermont-Tonnerre, et publié sous les auspices de son excellence M. le Comte de Chabrol, ministre secrétaire d'etat de la marine et des colonies, par M. L.-I. Duperrey, capi-

taine de frégate, commandant de l'expédition. *Paris: Bertrand.* 1826–30. 6 vols., 4to, and Atlas in folio. ·21353

This grand work consists of the following: Historique. Par M. L. I. Duperrey; Zoologie. Par MM. Lesson et Guérin-Méneville. 2 vols., 4to, Atlas, folio. 103 Plates; Reptiles et Poissons. 4to. 45 Plates; Mollusques. 4to. 16 Plates; Zoophytes. 4to. 16 Plates; Botanique, cryptogamie. Par M. Bory de Saint-Vincent. 4to. Atlas and 38 Plates; Hydrographie et physique, par M. L. I. Duperrey. 4to, Atlas, folio. *See also* Lesson (R. P.)

Du Petit-Thouars (A.) Voyage autour du monde sur la frégate la Vénus, pendant les années 1836–1839 publié par ordre du roi, sous les auspices du ministre de la marine, par M. Abel du Petit-Thouars, capitaine de vaisseau, commandeur de la Légion d'honneur. *Paris: Gide.* 1840–55. 10 vols., 8vo, Atlas, 4 vols., folio. c. 21354

This fine work comprises the following divisions: Relation. [Par A. Du Petit-Thouars.] 1840–43. 4 vols., 8vo. Atlas and 70 Plates, folio; Physique. Par U. de Tessan. 1842–44. 5 vols., 8vo; Zoologie. Mammifères, oiseaux, reptiles et poissons. [Par Isidore Geoffroy Saint-Hilaire, F. Prévost et O. Des Murs, Duméril, et A. Valenciennes.] 1855. 8vo, 2 l., pp. 351, iii. 1846. Atlas de zoologie, 3 l. 78 Colored Plates, folio; Botanique. Atlas de botanique. 1846. 3 l. 28 Plates.

Du Petit-Thouars. Voyage autour du monde sur la frégate la Vénus, commandé par Abel Du Petit-Thouars ... . Botanique, par M. J. Decaisne ... . *Paris: Morgand.* 1864. 8vo, pp. 36.

Dupin (André Marie Jean Jacques). Notice la dissertation, sur la nature et l'étendue de la juridiction des cours des États-Unis; discours ... par P. Duponceau ... . *Paris: impr. de Rignoux.* 1825. 8vo, pp. 8. 21356

Republished from the "Revue encyclopédique."

Dupin (*Baron*). The Baron Dupin's Report to the Emperor of the French, upon the Progress in the Arts and Sciences in Massachusetts ... with a Preface and Supplement, by E. H. Derby, addressed to Blake Brothers & Co., of Boston, Massachusetts. *Boston: Wright & Potter, Printers.* 1865. 8vo, pp. 106. h. 21357

Dupin (Charles). Essais sur l'organisation progressive de la marine et des colonies, etc. *Paris.* 1834. 8vo. 21358

Dupin. Mémoire sur la situation des colonies Françaises. Par le Baron C. Dupin. *Paris.* 1844. Folio. p. 21359

Dupin. Les Colonies françaises devant la Chambre de Pairs. *Paris.* 1844. 21360

Du Pin (L. Ellies). Bibliotheque Universelle des Historiens; contenant leurs vies, l'abrégé, la chronologie, la géographie, et la critique de leurs histoires ... Avec des tables chronologiques et géographiques. *Amsterdam.* 1708. 4to, pp. 383. 21361

Du Pin é Almeida (Miguel Calmon). Memoria sobre o establecimento de uma companhia de colonisaçã n'esta provincia. *Bahia.* 1835. 8vo. 21362

Du Pin é Almeida. Memoria sobre os meios de promover a colonisação. *Berlin: Typ. de unger Irmãos.* 1846. 8vo, pp. 64. 21363

Du Pin é Almeida. A missão especial do Visconde de Abrantes de Outubro de 1844 a Outubro de 1846. *Rio de Janeiro: Empreza Typ. Dous de Decembro, de P. Brito.* 1853. 2 vols., 8vo, pp. x–323; x–478. 21364

Du Pin é Almeida. Proposta e relatorio apresentados à Assembléa geral legislativa na primeira sessão da quinta legislatura, pelo Ministro e Secretario d'Estado dos Negocios da Fazenda, visconde de Abrantes. *Rio de Janeiro: Typ. Nacional.* 1843. 8vo, pp. 45. 21365

Duplessis. Duplessis's Memoirs, or a Variety of Adventures in England and America, interspersed with Characters and Reflections, and a Description of some Strolling Players, with whom he travelled. *London.* 1757. 2 vols. 21366

Relates to South Carolina, Georgia, etc.

Duplessis (P.) Aventures mexicaines. Par Paul Duplessis. *Paris: Cadot.* 1860. + 1862. + Troisième édition. *Paris: Cadot.* 1864. 18mo, pp. 328. 21367

Duplessis. Les boucaniers. *Leipzig: Gerhard.* 1856. 16mo, pp. 160, 159, 160, 160, 89 (with Gozlan's "L'homme aux cent femmes," pp. 91–140). + Aus dem Französischen von Adolf Dux. *Presburg: Wigand.* 1854. 5 vols., 12mo, 1 l., pp. 213; 1 l., pp. 179; 189; 192; 186. 21368

Duplessis. Les boucaniers. i.–iv. *Paris: De Potter.* 1853–54. 16 vols., 8vo. 21369

Later editions of the four parts were published by *Cadot.*

Duplessis. Joaquin Dyk aneb dìdectvi aztékûu. Roman amerik'y. ... *Prag: Haase Söhne.* 1857. 3 vols., 8vo, 2 l., pp. vi, 276; 1 l., pp. 206; 1 l., pp. 222. 21370

Duplessis. Juanito le harpiste. Par Paul Duplessis. *Paris: Cadot.* 1864. 18mo, pp. 321. 21371

Duplessis. Les Mormons. Par Paul Duplessis. Première partie. *Paris: Cadot.* 1858. 3 vols., 8vo, pp. 974. + *Paris: Cadot.* 1859. 2 vols., 8vo. + Nouvelle édition. [*Ibid.*] 1859. 5 vols., 12mo. + [*Ibid.*] 1862. 2 vols., 12mo. 21372

Duplessis. Les Mormons, suite du Batteur d'Estrade. *New York.* 1859. 8vo. 21373

Duplessis. Les Peaux-Rouges. Par Paul Duplessis. *Paris: Cadot.* 1864. 18mo, pp. 311. + Seconde édition. [*Ibid.*] 1865. 18mo, pp. 311. 21374

Duplessis. La Sonora. Première série: Le Capitaz Ramirez. Seconde série: Le Gambusino. Paul Duplessis. *Paris: Alex. Cadot.* 1858. 2 vols., 16mo, pp. 626. 21375

Duplessis. Die Sonora. Ein mexikanisches Sittengemälde von Paul Duplessis. Deutsch von Friedrich Thalberg. *Wien: Hartleben.* 185–. 3 vols., 8vo, pp. 175; 191; 200. (Belletristisches Lese-Cabinet, 439.-447. Liefg.) 21376

Du Ponceau (P.) A Brief View of the Constitution of the United States, addressed to the Law Academy of Philadelphia. By Peter Du Ponceau, ll.d. ... *Philadelphia: E. G. Dorsey, Printer.* 1834. 12mo, pp. xxiv, 106. h. 21377

Review of Du Ponceau on the Jurisdiction of the Courts of the United States, etc. By a Retired Barrister. [n. p. n. d.] 8vo. n.

Du Ponceau. Exposé Sommaire de la Constitution des Etats Unis d'Amérique. Par M. Du Ponceau. Traduit de l'Anglais par M. D'Homergue, avec des notes par le traducteur. *Paris.* 1837. 8vo, pp. 84. 21378

Du Ponceau (P. S.) A Discourse on the Early History of Pennsylvania; being an Annual Oration delivered before the American Philosophical Society, ... 6th of June, 1821. By Peter S. Du Ponceau ... . *Philadelphia: Abraham Small.* 1821. 8vo, pp. 38. ba. 21379

Du Ponceau. A Dissertation on the Nature and Extent of the Jurisdiction of the Courts of the United States, ... By Peter S. Du Ponceau ... . To which are added, a Brief Sketch of the National Judiciary Powers exercised in the United States prior to the Adoption of the Present Federal Constitution, by Thomas

Sergeant; ... and the Author's Discourse on Legal Education. ... *Philadelphia: Abraham Small.* 1824. 8vo, pp. xxxiii, 2 l., pp. 254. ba., c. 21380

Du Ponceau. Historical Discourse delivered before the Pennsylvania Historical Society for the Commemoration of the Landing of Wm. Penn, 24 October, 1832, being the One Hundred and Fiftieth Anniversary of that Event. By P. S. Du Ponceau. *Philadelphia: James Kay, Jun.* 1832. 8vo, pp. 32.

See also Penn (W.)

Du Ponceau. Mémoire à l'effet de déterminer le caractère grammaticale des langues de l'Amérique Septentrionale, connues sous les noms de Lenni Lenapé, Mohégan Chippeway, qui a obtenu le prix de linguistique à l'Institut de France fondé par M. de Volney. Par M. Pierre S. Du Ponceau. *Paris.* 1836. 8vo. 21382

Du Ponceau. Mémoire sur le Système grammatical des langues de quelques nations indiennes de l'Amérique du Nord: Ouvrage qui, à la Séance publique annuelle de l'Institut R. de France le 2 Mai 1835, a remporté le prix fondé par M. le Comte de Volney. Par M. P. S. Du Ponceau, ll.d. *Paris: A. Pihan de la Forest.* 1838. 8vo, pp. xvi, 464. 21383

Also: Address at the opening of the Law Academy of Philadelphia ... Feb. 21, 1821. [n. p. n. d.] 8vo. — A Discourse on the Necessity and the Means of making our National Literature independent of that of Great Britain, ... Feb. 15, 1834. ... *Philadelphia.* 1834. 8vo, pp. 37. ba., h. — Eulogium in Commemoration of Hon. William Tilghman, ll.d. ... delivered before the [American Philosophical] Society, ... October 11, 1827. By Peter S. Du Ponceau, Esq. ... *Philadelphia: R. H. Small.* 1827. 8vo, pp. 46. ba. — The History of the Silk Bill, in a Letter from Peter Du Ponceau to D. B. Warden, Esq. ... . *Philadelphia: printed by A. Waldie.* 1837. 8vo, pp. 12. h. — Inaugural Discourse, delivered June 3, 1837, before the Historical Society of Pennsylvania. *Philadelphia.* — Report made to the Historical & Literary Committee of the American Philosophical Society, held at Philadelphia, for promoting Useful Knowledge, By their Corresponding Secretary, stating His Progress in the Investigation committed to Him, of the General Character and Forms of the Languages of the American Indians. Read in Committee, 12th January, 1819. [n. p.] 8vo, pp. 34. ba. (Reprinted as Chap. xv., "Language of the Indians," in James Buchanan's "Sketches of the History of the North American Indians.") — A Review of the Cause of the New Orleans batture; and of the Discussions that have taken place respecting it; containing Answers to the Late Publications of Messrs. Thierry and Derbigny on that Subject. By Peter S. Du Ponceau, Esq. *Philadelphia: printed by Jane Aitken.* 1809. 8vo, pp. (2), 52. h., p.

Du Ponceau (P. S.), *and* Davezac (A.) Case and Opinion of Peter S. Du Ponceau & A. Davezac, Counsellors on the Contested Seat of Hon. David Levy, Delegate from the Territory of Florida to the Congress of the United States. *Alexandria: D. C.* 1842. 8vo, pp. 46. ba. 21384

Du Ponceau *and* Fisher (J. F.) A Memoir of the History of the Celebrated Treaty made by William Penn with the Indians, Under the Elm Tree at Shackamaxon, in the Year 1862. By Peter S. Du Ponceau and J. Francis Fisher. *Philadelphia: McCarty & Davis.* 1836. 8vo, pp. 63. ba., b. 21385

Reprinted in the "Penn. Hist. Coll.," Vol. iii., Pt. ii., 141–203.

Dupont (*Chevalier*). Voyages and Adventures of the Chevalier Dupont, Translated from the French. *London.* 1772. 4 vols., 12mo. 21386

A curious work, mostly relating to America, and from the minute particulars given of the French settlements on the lakes, the Indians, etc., is evidently an authentic narrative.

Dupont (Emilien). Essai sur les Insectes et les Maladies qui affectent le Blé. *Montreal.* 1857. 8vo, pp. 38. m. 21387

Du Pont (S. F.) Report on the National Defences, by Commander S. F. Du Pont, U. S. Navy. *Washington: printed by Gideon & Co.* 1852. 8vo, pp. 28. h. 21388

Du Pont. Du commerce et de la compagnie des Indes. Seconde édition, revue, corrigée, et augmentée de l'histoire du système de Law. *Amsterdam.* 1769. 8vo, pp. 287. 21389

"La première édition de ce traité a été publiée dans les Ephemérides de Citoyen. Tomes 8, 9, et 11 de l'année de 1769." — Baeckmans' *Catalogue.*

[Dupont de Nemours.] Notice sur la Vie et les Écrits de M. Joël Barlow, Ministre Plénipotentiaire des États-Unis d'Amérique auprès de S. M. l'Empereur des Français. [n. p.] 1813. 4to, pp. 31. h. 21390

Duport (S. C.) De la Production des Métaux Precieux au Mexique considérée dans ses rapports, avec la Géologie, la Métallurgie et l'Économie Politique; par St. Clair Duport. *Paris: Chez Firmin Didot.* 1843. 8vo, pp. viii, xiii, 429. 5 Plates in folio. 21391

Duportail (*M.*) *See* Louvet de Couvray.

Du Pouget de Nadaillac. La piazza, histoire mexicaine. Par le vicomte Du Pouget de Nadaillac. *Paris.* 1864. 12mo, pp. 100. 21392

Apparently a novel.

Duprat (L.) Instructions sur le port de Vera-Cruz et ses environs; par L. Duprat, capitaine au L. C. *Bordeaux: impr. de Suwerinck.* [1851.] 8vo, pp. 40. Map. 21393

Du Pratz (*M.*) *See* Le Page du Pratz.

Dupré (L.) An Admonitory Picture and a Solemn Warning: principally addressed to Professing Christians in the Southern States of North America. Being an Introduction ... to the Establishment of a System of Progessive Emancipation. By L. Dupré. ... [n. p.] 1810. 12mo, pp. 44. H. 21394

Dupré. A Rational & Benevolent Plan for averting some of the Calamitous Consequences of Slavery ... . By L. Dupré. ... [n. p.] 1810. 16mo, pp. 32. H. 21395

Du Puis (F. Mathias). Relation de l'establissement d'vne colonie françoise dans la Gardelovpe isle de l'Amériqve, et des moœvrs des Savvages. Dediée à la princesse Marie Leonor de Rohan, abbesse de l'abbaye Royale de Caen. *A Caen: chez Marin Yvon.* 1652. 8vo, 2 l., pp. 248. 21396

"Volume fort rare. Dans l'épître dédicatoire, l'auteur annonce être resté six à sept ans dans la colonie de la Guadeloupe. Son livre a été composé sur des documents communiqués par le P. Raimond Breton, et il ne raconte du reste que des faits qui se sont passés devant ses yeux." Title and note from a German catalogue.

Dupuy (A. E.) The Conspirator. [A Tale.] *New York.* 1850. 21397

Dupuy. The Planter's Daughter: a Tale of Louisiana. By Miss A. E. Dupuy. *New York.* 1857. 12mo, pp. 416. 21398

Du Puynode (Michael Gustave Pastoureau). De l'escavage et des colonies. *Paris: Joubert.* 1847. 8vo. B. 21399

Duquesne (*Marquis*). The Marquis Duquesne Vindicated; in a Letter to a Noble Lord; From the Aspersions cast on his Conduct while Commander of Fort Charles, at Port-Royal in Jamaica, under His Grace the Duke of Portland. Which Aspersions were published in a Letter, said to be wrote by a Gentleman of that Island, and addressed to a Member of Parliament. Dated February, 1725–6 *London: Printed in the Year* M.DCC.-XXVIII. 8vo, pp. 42. C. 21400

Du Quoine Female Seminary. An Argument for securing Christian Education in Southern Illinois, through the Establishment of this Seminary. *New York.* 1856. 21401

Durama de Ochoa (D.) Cuba y la emancipacion de sus esclavos. *Leipzig: Brockhaus.* 1864. 8vo, pp. 65. 21402

Durama de Ochoa. Die Emancipation der Sklaven auf Cuba. Aus dem Spanischen übersetzt von E. Butze. *Leipzig: Brockhaus.* 1864. 8vo, pp. iv, 60. 21403

Durama de Ochoa. Plácido, Dichter und Märtyrer. Eine Biographie. *Hannover: Cruse's Buchhandlung.* 8vo, pp. 22.

Duran (D.) Historia de las Indias de Nueva-España y Islas de Tierra firme, por el Padre Fray Diego Duran. Religioso de la orden de Predicadores (Escritor del Siglo XVI). La publica con un Atlas de Estampas, Notas è Illustraciones, José F. Ramirez. *México.* 1867. 4to, pp. xvi, 535. 21405

The continuation of this work has never been published, in consequence of the departure of M. Ramirez from Mexico. The entire edition of the first volume, with the exception of a small number of copies, distributed privately by the author, as well as the atlas, has been confiscated by the Mexican government.

Duran (Jos. Miguel). Replica Apologetica y Satisfactoria al Defensorio Fr. Juan de Marimon ... dirigido al Concilio Provincial Limense ... con Supplemento. *Lima.* 1773. 4to.

Duran (N.) Litteræ Annvæ Provinciæ Paraquariæ Societatis Iesù Ad admodum R. P. Mvtium Vitellescum eiusdem Societatis Præpositum Generalem. Missæ à R. P. Nicolao Dvran Paraquariæ Præposito Prouinciali; Eius Nomine ac iussu Scriptæ a P. Iacobo Rançonier Belga eiusdem Societatis. *Antverpiæ: Typis Ioannis Meursi. Anno* MDCXXXVI. 18mo, pp. 168. 21407

Duran. Relation des insignes progrez de la religion chrestienne, faits av Paraqvai, province de l'Amérique-Meridionale, & dans les vastes Regions de Guair et d'Vruaig. Nouuellement découuertes par les Pères de la Compagnie de Iésvs, és années 1626. & 1627. Enuoyée au R. P. Mvtio Vitelesci General de la mesme Compagnie, par le R. P. Nicolas Dvran, Prouincial en la Prouince de Paraqui. Et traduite du Latin en François, par un Pere de la mesme Compagnie. *Paris: Sebastien Cramoisy.* M. DC. XXXVIII. 8vo, 10 l., pp. 162, (1). H., P., S. 21408

The translator was Jacques de Machault.

Durand (B.) Report on Standard Weights, Measures and Coins Exchanged between France and the United States. *Paris.* 1853. 8vo. B. 21409

Durand (C.) Letter from the Secretary of State, addressed to Calvin Durand, February 1, 1864. [n. p. n. d.] 8vo, pp. 11.

Relates to the Rebellion.

Durand (J. R.) The Life and Adventures of James R. Durand, during a period of fifteen years, from 1801 to 1816, in which time he was Impressed on board the British Fleet, and held in detestable bondage for more than seven years, ... Written by Myself. *Rochester, N. Y.* 1820. 12mo, pp. 129. 21411

Durand-Molard: Code de la Martinique; par Durand-Molard, continué par Dufresne de St. Cergues. *St. Pierre-Martinique.* 1807–10. 5 vols., 8vo. 21412

Durang (Charles). The Philadelphia Stage from 1749 to 1821. 12mo. 21413

Gives a complete account of André's efforts at scene painting in Philadelphia.

Durant (H. F.) ... The Arguments in the Case of the Eliot School Rebellion, by Henry F. Durant for the Defence, and Sidney Webster for the Prosecution. *Boston.* 1859. 8vo, pp. 16. H. 21414

Also: Defence of the Use of the Bible in the Public Schools. Argument ... in the Eliot School Case. *Boston: Ticknor and Fields.* M. DCCC. LIX. 8vo, pp. 43. H.

Durant (T. J.) Letter of Thomas J. Durant to the Hon. Henry Winter Davis. *New Orleans: printed by H. P. Lathrop.* 1864. 8vo, pp. 30. 21415

Durao (J. de S. R.) Caramurù. Poema Epico do descubrimiento da Bahia, composto por Fr. José de Santa Rita Durão, da orden dos Eremitas de Santo Agostinho, natural da Cata-Preta nas Minas Geraes. *Lisboa: na Regia officina typografica.* MDCCLXXXI. 12mo, 3 l., pp. 307. 21416

The original edition of a poem, very popular in Brazil, and often reprinted. It relates to the shipwreck of a Portuguese vessel near the river Vermelho, in the province of Bahia, and the massacre of most of the passengers and crew by the Indians, with the events that followed. The following is a French translation:

Durao. Caramarù, ou la Découverte de Bahia, romanpoeme brésilien. Par José de Santa Rita Durão. *Paris: E. Renduel.* 1829. 3 vols., 12mo. S. 21417

[Durazzo (J.)] Elogi Storici di Christoforo Colombo e di Andrea D'Oria. *Parma: dalla stamperia Reale.* MDCCLXXXI. 4to, 4 l., pp. 337. Portraits. 21418

"'The Eulogy of Columbus,' published anonymously, with a 'Eulogy of Andrea D'Oria,' but since attributed to the Marquis Ippolito Darazzo, is written with great fullness and elegance, and is particularly valuable for its elucidation of many points of contemporary history bearing on the life of Columbus." — *North Amer. Rev.*, XXI. 425. There are copies on large paper.

Durell (P.) A Particular Account Of the Taking Cape Breton From the French, by Admiral Warren, and Sir William Pepperell, The 17th of June, 1745. With a Description of the Place and Fortifications; the Loss it will be to the French Trade, and the Advantage it will be to Great Britain and Ireland: With the Articles of the Capitulation of Fort Louisbourg. By Philip Durell, Esq. ... To which is added, A Letter from an Officer of Marines to his Friend in London, giving an Account of the Siege of Louisbourg, and a Description of the Town, Harbour, Batteries, Number of Guns, &c. Also The Happy Situation of that Country; and an Account of M. Chambon, Governor of Louisburg, being laid in Irons for surrendering it: In a Letter from a Gentleman in London, to a Merchant in the West of England. *London: Printed for W. Bickerton.* 1745. Folio, pp. 8. BA. 21419

Duret. Trésor de l'histoire des langues de cest univers, contenant les origines, beautez, perfections, decadences, mutations, changements, conuersions et ruines des langues. *Yverdon: de l'imprimerie de la Société Helvetiale Caldoresque.* 1619. 4to.

All after page 947 relates to America.

Durfee (C.) A Centennial Discourse delivered before the South Church and Society, Dedham, Mass. June 26, 1836. By Calvin Durfee, A.M. *Boston: D. K. Hitchcock.* 1836. 8vo, pp. 44. H. 21421

Durfee. Memoir of Rev. Ebenezer Fitch, D.D., First President of Williams College. By Rev. Calvin Durfee ... . *Boston.* 1843. 8vo, pp. 28. H. 21422

Durfee. Williams Biographical Annals. With an Introduction by Rev. S. Irenæus Prime, D.D. By Rev. Calvin Durfee, D.D. ... *Boston: Lee and Shepard, Publishers. New York: Lee, Shepard and Dillingham.* 1871. 8vo, pp. 665. BA., B.

Also: The Character and End of the Righteous. A Sermon occasioned by the Death of Rev. Samuel Gay, delivered in Dedham, Nov. 5, 1848. ... *Boston.* 1848. 8vo, pp. 20. — Commemorative Discourse in Great Barrington, May 13, 1866. B. — Williams College Necrological Annals, 1867–'68. *Pittsfield.* 1868. 8vo, pp. 19.

Durfee (J.) The Complete Works of Hon. Job Durfee, LL.D. ... with a Memoir of the Author. Edited by his Son. *Providence: Gladding and Proud.* 1849. 8vo, pp. xxvi, 523. H.

Durfee. A Discourse delivered before the Rhode-Island Historical Society, ... January 13, 1847. By Hon. Job Durfee ... . *Providence: Charles Burnett, Jr.* 1847. 8vo, pp. 42, 5.

Durfee. Whatcheer! or Roger Williams in Banishment: A Poem. By Job Durfee. *Providence, R. I.* 1832. 12mo.

Durfee. "What Cheer;" or Roger, Williams in Banishment. A Poem. By Job Durfee, Esq. ... With a Recommendatory Preface, by the Rev. John Eustace Giles, Leeds. *Leeds: John Heaton.* 1840. 12mo, pp. 196. H. 21427

It is remarkable that the editor of this English edition should suppose that he could "recommend" himself to Americans, or any other enlightened people, by an aspersion on General Washington. This edition was reprinted, *Providence, R. I.: Cranston & Hammond.* 1840. 12mo, pp. xii, 196. H. Also: Charge ... delivered to the Grand Jury ... at Bristol, Rhode-Island, A.D. 1842. [n. p. n. d.] 8vo, pp. 16. H. — The Influence of Scientific Discovery and Invention on Social and Political Progress. Oration delivered before the Phi Beta Kappa Society of Brown University, of Providence, R. I., on Commencement Day, September 6, 1843. ... *Providence: B. Cranston & Company.* 1843. 8vo, pp. 52. BA. — An Oration before the Municipal Authorities and Citizens of Providence, July 4, 1853. ... *Providence: Knowles, Anthony & Co.* 1853. 8vo, pp. 29.

Durfee (J.) Reminiscences of Col. Joseph Durfee, relating to the Early History of Fall River and of Revolutionary Scenes. [n. p. 1834?] 12mo, pp. 12. H. 21428

Durgin (C.) An Oration, delivered before the Franklin Debating Society, at their Anniversary, January 17, 1831, being the Birth-Day of Franklin. By Clement Durgin. ... *Boston: published by John H. Eastburn.* 1831. 8vo, pp. 23. H. 21429

Durham (A. A.) The Devil's Confession in his Dying Hour. A Miraculous Revelation of the Nature and Cause of the Present Rebellion and War. A Speedy Termination of the War. The Union to be Restored. *De 'Quoin, (Ill.): R. R. Fleming.* 1863. 8vo, pp. 12. 21430

Durham (*Earl of*). *See* Lambton (George F. D'Arcy).

Durham, *N. Y.* Manual for the Communicants of the First Presbyterian Church In Durham, N. Y. Compiled by Order of the Session. March, 1858. *New York: John A. Gray.* 1858. 12mo, pp. 23. P. 21431

[Durivage (Francis Alexander), *and* Burnham (George P.) Stray Subjects, Arrested and Bound Over. Being the fugitive offspring of the "Old 'Un" and the "Young 'Un," that have been "lying round loose," and are now "tied up" for fast keeping. *Philadelphia: Carey & Hart.* 1848. 8vo, pp. 199. 8 Plates. C. 21432

Durkee (C.) Fugitive Slave Law as a "Finality." Speech of C. Durkee in House of Representatives, Aug. 6, 1852. *Washington.* 1852. 8vo. B. 21433

Also: Minority Report on the Reduction of Letter, Periodical, and Pamphlet Postage. [n. p. n. d.] 8vo, pp. 8. H. — Speech of Charles Durkee, of Wisconsin, on the California Question. Made in the House of Representatives, June 10, 1850. 8vo, pp. 15. BA.

Durnford (M.) Family Recollections of Lieut. Genl. E. W. Durnford. By Miss Mary Durnford. Printed for Private Circulation. *Montreal.* 1863. 21434

Durocher (R. Père). Catechism for the Montagnars Indians residing near the River Saguenay. ... *Aimaieu Kukuetshimitun Misinaigan: Kaiakonigants.* 1848. 12mo. S. 21435

Durocher. Missal with Psalms, Hymns, and Gregorian Chants for the Montagnars Indians. ... Aiamie Kushkushkutu Mishinaigan. *Jakonigants.* 1847. 12mo. S. 21436

See Belcourt (George Antoine), Vol. II., Nos. 4406–4408.

Durosoi. *See* Farmian de Rossi.

D[urret]. Voyage de Marseille à Lima et dans les autres lieux des Indes Occidentales. Avec une exacte description de ce qu'il y a de plus remarquable tant pour la géographie, que pour les mœurs les coûtumes, le commerce, le gouvernement, et la religion des peuples, avec des notes et des figures en taille douce. Par le Sieur D****. *Paris: Jean Baptiste Coignard.* 1720. 12mo, pp. xxxv, 282, 244, 1 l. 5 Plates. 21437

"A journey made by the author without leaving his chamber; so that the work contains an infinite number of blunders and contradictions, of which Labat gives a list prefixed to his new 'Voyage aux îles de l'Amérique.'" — Barbier.

Durrie (D. S.) Bibliographia Genealogica Americana; an Alphabetical Index to American Genealogies and Pedigrees, contained in State, County and Town Histories, Printed Genealogies, and Kindred Works. By Daniel S. Durrie ... . *Albany, N. Y.: Joel Munsell.* 1868. 8vo, pp. xii, 5–296. B., BA., C.

A work of much painstaking research, and invaluable to the genealogist.

Durrie. Steele Family. A Genealogical History of John and George Steele, Settlers of Hartford, Conn., 1635–6., and their Descendants. With an Appendix, containing Genealogical Information respecting other families of the Name who settled in Different Parts of the United States. By Daniel Steele Durrie,

... *Albany, N. Y.: Munsell & Rowland.* 1859. Rl. 8vo, pp. x, 145. B., BA. + Enlarged Edition. *Albany, N. Y.: J. Munsell.* 1862. Large 8vo, pp. x, 161. H. 21439

Durrie. A Genealogical History of the Holt Family in the United States: more particularly the Descendants of Nicholas Holt of Newburg and Andover, Mass., 1634–1644, and of William Holt of New Haven, Conn. By Daniel S. Durrie ... . *Albany: J. Munsell.* 1864. 8vo, pp. 367. B., H. 21440

Durroc (*M.*) Life of Toussaint Louverture, The Black Prince. By M. Durroc. *London.* 1802. 18mo. Portrait.

Title from Gowans' catalogue; perhaps incorrect.

Duryea (J. T.) A Call to Humiliation and Reform. A Sermon ... Troy, ... May 19, 1861. By Rev. Joseph T. Duryea, ... *Troy, N. Y.: A. W. Scribner & Co., Printers.* 1861. 8vo, pp. 23. 21442

Duryea. An Oration Commemorative of the Restoration of the Union, with a Tribute to the Alumni and Under-Graduates of the College of New Jersey, who fell in the National Struggle. Delivered Tuesday, June 26th, 1866, at the Bequest of the Trustees of the College, by the Rev. Joseph T. Duryea. *Philadelphia: McCalla & Starely, Printers.* 1866. 8vo, pp. 101. BA.

Also: Civil Liberty. A Sermon preached August 6, 1863. *New York: J. A. Gray.* 1863. 8vo, pp. 19. — Loyalty to our Government. A Divine Command and a Christian Duty. A Sermon preached in Troy, New York, April 28, 1861. ... *Troy: A. W. Scribner & Co.* 1861. 8vo, pp. 28.

Duryee (C.) Duties Payable on Goods, Wares, and Merchandise, imported into the United States ... 1816. ... . Revised and Corrected by C. Duryea, Jun. ... *New-York: Printed by Turner & Day.* 1816. pp. 67. 21444

Dusenbery (B. M.) Monument to the Memory of Genera Andrew Jackson: containing Twenty-Five Eulogies and Sermons delivered on occasion of his Death. To which is added an Appendix, containing General Jackson's Proclamation, his Farewell Address, and a Certified Copy of his Last Will. The whole preceded by a Short Sketch of his Life. Compiled by B. M. Dusenbery. *Philadelphia: Walker & Gillis.* 1846. 12mo, pp. 416. 21445

Some copies have the imprint, *Nashua.* 1846.

Du Simitiere (*M.*) Thirteen Portraits of American Legislators, Patriots, and Soldiers, who distinguished themselves in rendering their Country Independent: viz. 1. General Washington, 2. General Baron de Steuben, 3. Silas Deane, 4. General Reed, 5. Gouverneur Morris, 6. General Gates, 7. John Jay, 8. W. H. Drayton, 9. Henry Laurens, 10. Charles Thompson, 11. S. Huntingdon, 12. J. Dickenson, 13. General Arnold. Drawn from the life by Du Simitiere, Painter and Member of the Philosophical Society in Philadelphia, and engraved by M. B. Reading. *London: W. Richardson.* [1783.] 4to. H. 21446

No letterpress. Issued May 10, 1783. These portraits were reissued. The originals are very rare.

Dussieux (Louis). Le Canada sous la domination française, d'après les archives de la marine et de la guerre. Par L. Dussieux ... . *Paris: Ch. Tanera.* 1855. 8vo, Title, pp. 104. Map. BA., C. + Seconde édition. *Paris: Lecoffre et Cie.* 1862. 12mo. C. 21447

Republished from the "Revue de Paris," 1854–55. *See* "l'Athenæum français," 1856, pp. 500, 501.

Dussillion (Ch. J.) Considérations sur l'esclavage aux Antilles françaises et de son abolition graduelle, suivies d'un aperçu analytique et critique du système d'apprentissage et de ses résultats dans les colonies anglaises. *Paris: Dussillion.* 1842. 8vo.

Dutch (Ebenezer). Discourse at the Dedication of a New Meeting House, Aug. 9, 1791. By E. Dutch. *Newburyport.* 1792. 8vo. B. 21449

Dutch. Discourse delivered at Bradford, January 25, 1795, on occasion of Numerous Deaths in his Parish. By Ebenezer Dutch. *Haverhill.* 1795. 8vo, pp. 31. 21450

Dutch Sailor. An Authentic Relation Of the many Hardships and Sufferings of a Dutch Sailor. *London.* M.DCC.XXVIII. 8vo, pp. 28. 21451

The Dutch Svrvey. *See* Vol. III., No. 9758.

Dutcher (D. L. L.) Historical Discourse on the Rise and Progress of the First Congregational Church, of St. Albans, Vermont, by Dea. L. L. Dutcher. ... *St. Albans: Printed by E. B. Whiting.* 1860. 8vo, pp. 12. 21452

Dutcher (J. W.) Narrative of the Mysterious Cave, Illustrative of the Washingtonian Reform. 1864. 24mo. 21453

Dutcher (S.) Oration, Commemorative of the Birth of Washington, 23d February, 1824. By Salem Dutcher, Jun. *Albany*. 1824. 8vo. B. + *Albany*. 1826. 8vo. B. 21454

Dutchess County, *N. Y.* Report of the Dutchess County & Poughkeepsie Sanitary Fair, held ... in ... Poughkeepsie, from March 15 to March 19, 1864. *Poughkeepsie: printed by Platt & Schram*. 1864. 8vo, pp. 52. H. 21455

Transactions of the Society of Dutchess County for the Promotion of Agriculture, with Select Essays on Rural Economy. *Poughkeepsie: Bowman, Parsons & Potter*. 1807. 2 vols., 8vo, pp. v, 90; 88. C. 21456

Continued to 1809 or later.

The Dutchman's Fireside. *See* [Paulding (J. K.)]

Du Tertre (J. B.) Histoire generale,|des isles|de S. Christophe,|de la Gvadelovpe,|de la Martiniqve,|et avtres|dans l'Ameriqve.|Où l'on verra l'establissement des Colonies Fran-|çoises, dans ces Isles; leurs guerres Ciuiles &|Estrangeres, & tout se qui se passe dans les|voyages & retours des Indes.|Comme aussi plusieurs belles particularitez des Antisles de l'Amerique:|Vne description generale de l'Isle de la Guadeloupe: de tous ces|Mineraux, de ses Pierreries, de ses Riu-'eres, Fontaines &|Estangs: & de toutes ses Plantes.|De plus, la description de tous les Animaux de la Mer, de l'Air, & de a|Terre: & vn Traité fort ample des Mœurs des Sauuages du pays, de l'Estat|de la Colonie Françoise, & des Esclaues, tant Mores, que Sauuages.|Par le R. P. Iean Baptiste dv Tertre, Religieux de l'Ordre des FF. Pres-|cheurs, du Nouitiat du Faux-bourg Sainct Germain de Paris,|Missionaire Apostolique dans l'Amerique.|*A Paris,|Chez Iacqves Langlois, Imprimeur Ordinaire du Roy,|Au Mont de Sainte Geneuiefve, vis à vis la Fontaine.|Et Emmanvel Langlois, dans la Grand' Salle du Palais,|à la Reyne de Paix.*|M. DC. LIV.|Auec Priuilege du Roy, & Approbation des Superieurs.| 4to, 8 l., pp. 481, (11). 3 Maps. BA. 21457

Du Tertre. Histoire Generale des Antilles, habitées par la Français, divisées en deux tomes, et enrichies de cartes et de figures, by R. P. du Tertre, missionaire dans les Antilles. *Paris: Thomas Jolly*. 1667–71. 4 vols., 4to, Engraved Frontispiece, 9 l., pp. 593, (3); 7 l., pp. 539, 13 Plates; 4 l., pp. 317, (8), 1 l.; 2 l., pp. 362, 7 l., 5 Maps. B., C., S. 21458

"The two last volumes of this work (one of the most valuable we possess on the West Indies) were published in 1671, and are extremely scarce; complete sets are difficult to be met with, and bear a high price." — Rich.

Dutertre. Départ du Temple, pour Cayenne, Déportes des 17 et 18 Fructidor, An v. Avec les instructions données au général Dutertre, chargé de les conduire a leur destination. Contenant un precis de la vie civile et militaire de ce général, nommé le 19 fructidor, commandant du Temple. *Paris: Desenne, An* VIII. [1800]. 8vo, pp. 62. J.C.B. 21459

Dudot (S.) France et Brésil. Notice sur dona Francisca, par M. Aubé. *Paris: Guillaumin et Cie*. 1857. 12mo. 2 Maps. + Seconde édition. *Paris: Garnier frères*. 1859. 8vo.

Duties payable on Goods, Wares and Merchandise, imported into the United States of America from June 1792. The Duties of Tonnage, and the Rates of Coins, by which the Duties are to be rèceived and estimated, etc. *Philadelphia: Hall ana Sellers*. MDCCXCII. 8vo, pp. 16. J.C.B. + After the last day of June, 1794. [No imprint.] 8vo, pp. 15. + After the 30th September, 1797, etc. *Boston*. 1799. 8vo. N., W. 21461

Other editions, *New York*. 1803. + *New York*. 1815. 12mo.

Dutroulau. Extrait de la "Revue coloniale" [juin]. De l'endémie dysentérique à Saint-Pierre [Martinique]. Par M. le docteur Dutroulau ... . *Paris: P. Dupont*. 8vo. 21462

Duttenhofer (A.) Bereisung der Vereinigten Staaten von Nordamerika, mit besonderer Hinsicht auf den Erie-Canal. *Stuttgart*. 1835. 8vo. View and Plan. B. 21463

Duttenhofer. Ueber die Emancipation der Neger. Ein Versuch zur Aufstellung humaner Principien in dieser Frage. *Nördlingen: C. H. Beck*. 1855. 8vo, pp. 94. C. 21464

Dutton (A.) The Importance of a Faithful Execution of Law. A Sermon delivered before the Connecticut Society for the Promotion of Good Morals, October 18th, 1815. By Aaron Dutton ... . *New Haven: Hudson & Woodward, Printers*. 1815. 8vo, pp. 22. BA. 21465

Also: ... A Sermon, delivered at the Ordination of the Rev. Thomas Ruggles to the Pastoral Care of the First Church in Derby. August 31, 1809. ... *New Haven: printed by Oliver Steele and Co*. 1809. 8vo, pp. 23. B., BA.

Dutton (A.) A Letter from Mrs. Anne Dutton, to the Reverend Mr. G. Whitefield. *Philadelphia: printed and sold by William Bradford*. [1749.] 12mo, pp. 11. P. 21466

[Dutton (George).] The Present Crisis, or the Currency; a Tract of the Times for every Man who can read: by Bank Crash, Esq. [*Rochester: E. Darrow & Brother*.] *October*, 1857. 8vo, pp. 25. BA. 21467

Dutton (Henry). Writ of Habeas Corpus. Ex parte Merryman. [n. p. n. d.] 8vo. 21468

Reprinted from the "American Law Register."

Dutton (S. W. S.) An Address at the Funeral of Deacon Nathan Beers, on the 14th of February, 1842, by Samuel W. S. Dutton. ... *New Haven: William H. Stanley, Printer*. 1849. 8vo, pp. 23. H. 21469

Dutton. An Address at the Funeral of Hon. Roger Sherman Baldwin, Feb. 23, 1863, by S. W. S. Dutton, Pastor of the North Church in New Haven. *New Haven*. 1863. 8vo, pp. 36.

Dutton. The History of the North Church, New Haven, from its Foundation, in May, 1742, to May, 1842. In Three Sermons. By Samuel W. S. Dutton. *New Haven*. 1842. 8vo, pp. 128. S. 21471

Also: An Address at the Funeral of Hon. Simeon Baldwin, ... *New Haven: A. H. Maltby*. 1851. 8vo, pp. 22. H. — An Address at the Funeral of Eli Ives, M.D., October 10th, 1861, ... *New Haven: printed by Thomas J. Stafford*. 1861. 8vo, pp. 20. H. — Sermon on the Twenty-Fifth Anniversary of his Ministry in North Church, New Haven, July 5, 1863. ... *New Haven*. 1863. 8vo, pp. 20. B.

Dutton (W.) An Oration, pronounced July 4, 1805, At the Request of the Inhabitants of the Town of Boston, in Commemoration of American Independence. By Warren Dutton. [*Boston*:] *A. Newell, Printer*. [1805.] 8vo, pp. 16. BA. 21472

Also: An Address delivered to the Members of the Bar of Suffolk, at their Annual Meeting, in September, 1819. ... *Boston: printed by S. Phelps*. 1819. 8vo, pp. 18. B., BA., H. — The Present State of Literature. A Poem, delivered ... in Yale College, September 10, 1800. ... . *Hartford: printed by Hudson & Goodwin*. 1800. 8vo, pp. 16. BA.

The Duty of Abstaining from the Use of West India Produce, a Speech, delivered at Coach-Maker's-Hall, Jany. 12, 1792. *London*. 1792. 12mo. 21473

The Duty of a Freeman, addressed to the Electors of Great Britain. [n. p. 1780.] 8vo, pp. 7. BA. 21474

The Duty of the Hour. The Great Issue, or the Rebellion against Democracy. ... Published for the Workingmen's Democratic Repulican Association. *New York: Sinclair Tousey*. 1863-4. 4to. 21475

Cover title to "Nine Extras issued by the Iron Platform."

The Duty of the King and Subject, on the Principles of Civil Liberty; Colonists not entitled to Self-government, or to the same Privileges with Britons: being an Answer to Dr. Price's system of Fanatical Liberty. By the Author of the Political Looking-glass. *London: Dixwell*. 1776. 8vo. 21476

The Duty of the Present Generation To Evangelize the World; An Appeal from the Missionaries at the Sandwich Islands to their Friends in the United States. Second Edition. *Buffalo: Charles Faxon*. 1847. 12mo, pp. 75. 21477

Duval (Alfred). Communication in Relation to a Supply of Water for the City of Baltimore from the Gunpowder River. By A. Duval. *Baltimore: J. Lucas*. 1854. 8vo, pp. 30.

Also: [Memorial] to the Honorable Cotton Supply Association, Manchester, England. *Baltimore. February*, 1861. 8vo, pp. 14.

Duval (Jules). Les Colonies et la politique coloniale de la France; avec 2 cartes du Sénégal et de Madagascar, dressées par M. V. A. Malte-Brun. *Paris: A. Bertrand*. 1864. 8vo.

Duval. Histoire de l'émigration européenne, asiatique et africaine au XIXe siècle, ses causes, ses caractères, ses effets par M. Jules Duval ... . *Paris: Guillaumin et Cie*. 1862. 8vo, pp. xvi, 496. BA. 21480

Du Val (M.) A Letter addressed to the Inhabitants of Prince George's County [Md.], on the Court-house Question. By Marcus Du Val. *Baltimore*. 1854. 8vo, pp. 47. M.

Du-Val (P.) La Géographie vniverselle, contenant les descriptions, les cartes, et le blason des principaux païs du monde. (Reuûe, corrigée et augmentée sur les manuscrits de l'auteur, par le R. P. Placide Augustin Deschaussé, géographe du Roy). *Paris: chez Mlle Dv-Dv*. 1688. 2 vols., 12mo, 6 l., Table, 1 l., pp. 612. 63 Maps. 21482

First published in 1682.

[Duval-Sanadon (David).] Aux Colons de Saint-Domingue. *Paris*. 1797. 8vo. 21483

[Duval-Sanadon.] Discours sur l'esclavage des nègres et sur l'idée de leur affranchissement dans les colonies, par un Colon de Saint Domingue. *Amsterdam et Paris, Hardouin et Galtey*. 1786. 8vo. 21484

[Duval-Sanadon.] Tableau de la situation actuelle des colonies, presénté à l'Assemblée nationale. *Paris*. 28 *décembre*, 1789. 8vo, pp. 12. 21485

Duval (*Sieur*). Geographia Universalis; the Present State of the Whole World. 1691. 21486

America occupies pp. 15–91, with 15 maps.

Duvallon (Berquin). Voyage à la Louisiane et sur le Continent de l'Amérique, fait dans les années 1794 à 1798. *Paris*. 1802. 8vo, pp. 381. Map. 21487

Duvallon (Berquin). *See* [Berquin-Duvallon], Vol. II., 4959–4966.

Duvivier (*le général* Franciade Fleurus). Abolition de l'esclavage, civilization du centre de l'Afrique; projet pour y parvenir. *Paris: Dumaine*. 1845. 8vo. 21488

Duvergier de Hauranne (E.) Huit Mois en Amérique, Lettres et Notes de Voyage, 1864–1865. Par Ernest Duvergier de Hauranne. *Paris: Lacroix, Verboeckhoven et Cie*. 1866. 2 vols., 16mo, pp. xi, 439; 503. BA., C. 21489

Duvernois (C.) Histoire de l'Intervention Française au Mexique 1862–1867 Par Clément Duvernois *A. Lacroix Verboeckhoven et Cie*, 1867. 8vo. 21490

See also "Intervention," *infra*.

Duxal (Jules). Les Colonies et la politique coloniale de la France. *Paris: Bertrand*. 1865. 8vo. 21491

Duxbury, *Mass*. Reply of à Committee of the First Parish, in Duxbury, Massachusetts, to the Public Answer of Hon. Gershone B. Weston, to a Statement of said Committee before the Parish, April 5, 1851. ... *Boston*. 1851. M. 21492

See Weston (G.)

The Landing of the French Atlantic Cable, at Duxbury, Mass., July, 1869. *Boston: A. Mudge & Son*. 1869. 8vo, pp. 57. 6 Photo. Plates. B., C. 21493

Report of the Board of School Committee of the Town of Duxbury, for 1858–9. *Boston: William White, Printer*. 1859. 8vo, pp. 25. H. 21494

Duy (A. W.) Sermons by Albert William Duy, with a Biographical Sketch of the Author; by S. A. Clark. *Philadelphia*. 1846. 8vo. 21495

Duyckinck (Evert A.) Fitze-Greene Halleck. From Putnam's Magazine, February, 1868. *New York*. 1868. 4to, pp. 22. Portrait. 21496

Fifty copies privately printed for Mr. W. L. Andrews.

Duyckinck. History of the War for the Union; Civil, Military and Naval, founded on Official and other Authentic Documents. By Evert A. Duyckinck, ... Illustrated with Highly-Finished Steel Engravings, ... By Alonzo Chappel and Thomas Nast. *New York: Johnson, Fry and Company*. 1864–5. 2 vols., 4to, pp. 620; (2), 660; (2), 612. B., H. 21497

Duyckinck. Geschichte des krieges für die Union, politisch und militärisch nach offiziellen und andern authentischen Dokumenten beschrieben. Deutsch bearbeitet von Friedr. Kapp. Mit feinen Stahlstichen von See- und Landschapten und Portraiten berülunter Generale und Seehelden nach Original Gemälden. Von Alonzo Chappel. *New York: Johnson, Fry & Co*. 1853. 4to. 21498

[Duyckinck.] Irvingiana: A Memorial of Washington Irving. *New York: Charles B. Richardson*. 1860. 4to, pp. 64. 3 Portraits and Facsimile. 21499

110 copies printed on large paper.

Duyckinck. Lives and Portraits of the Presidents of the United States, from Washington to Johnson. The Biographies, by Evert A. Duyckinck, and the Portraits, by Alonzo Chappel. *New York: Johnson, Fry & Co*. [1866.] 4to, pp. 208. 17 Portraits. 21500

Duyckinck. A Memorial of Francis L. Hawks, D.D., LL.D. By Evert A. Duyckinck. Read before the New York Historical Society, May 7th, 1867. With an Appendix of Proceedings, Etc., including Catalogue of Books in the Library of the Rev. Dr. Hawks, presented to the New York Historical Society by William Niblo. *New York*. 1871. 8vo, pp. 166. Portrait.

Duyckinck. A Memorial of Henry Theodore Tuckerman, by Evert A. Duyckinck. Read before the New York Historical Society, Jan. 2, 1872. With an Appendix of Proceedings. *New York: Printed for the Society*. 1872. 8vo, pp. 16. Portrait. 21502

[Duyckinck.] Memorial of John Allan. *New York: Printed for the Bradford Club*. 1864. Rl. 8vo, pp. 38. Portrait.

250 copies printed for private distribution.

Duyckinck. National Portrait Gallery of Eminent Americans; including Orators, Statesmen, Naval and Military Heroes, Jurists, Authors, etc., etc. From Original Full Length Paintings by Alonzo Chappel. With Biographical and Historical Narratives, by Evert A. Duyckinck, ... *New York: Johnson, Fry & Company*. [1864–7.] 2 vols., 4to, pp. iv, 470; iv, 470. 21504

Duyckinck. Cyclopædia of American Literature; embracing Personal and Critical Notices of Authors, and Selections from their Writings. From the Earliest Period to the Present Day; with Portraits, Autographs, Photographs, and other Illustrations. By Evert A. Duyckinck and George L. Duyckinck. ... *New York: Charles Scribner*. 1855. 2 vols., imp. 8vo, pp. xv, 676; xiv, 781. BA. + [*Ibid.*] 1856. 2 vols., imp. 8vo, pp. xvi, 676; xiv, 781. 21505

Contains personal and critical notices of authors, and selections from their writings, with 225 woodcut portraits, 425 facsimile autographs, and 75 views of colleges, etc. The editions of a later date (*New York: C. Scribner & Co*. 1866) are on thinner paper, but include the supplement. Some copies of this edition (1866) were printed on large paper, in 5 vols., 4to, including supplement, on India paper.

Duyckinck. Supplement to the Cyclopædia of American Literature, including Obituaries of Authors, Continuations of former Articles, with Notices of earlier and later writers omitted in previous Editions. By E. A. Duyckinck. *New York: Chas. Scribner & Co*. 1866. Rl. 8vo, pp. 164. Portrait. B., C. 21506

This supplement contains sketches of the old Spanish writers on America by Buckingham Smith, and notices of early French writers by John Gilmary Shea. It is included in the later editions of the "Cyclopædia." *See* "Arcturus," and "The Literary World."

Duyckinck (H.) The Rich and Poor Meet Together. A Sermon in behalf of the Mission Work of St. Mark's Chapel, by the Rev. Henry Duyckinck, late minister in charge, with Introductory Remarks at St. Mark's Church in the Bowery, and A Funeral Sermon by the Rev. Edward H. Krans. Preached at St. Mark's Chapel, February 27, 1870. With other Memorial Notices. *New York: Printed for St. Mark's Mission Society*. 1870. 8vo, pp. 48. 21507

Duyn (Nicolaas). Reize rondsom de Vaste Kusten des Aardkloots; beginnende van Nova Zembla, en veroolgens de Noord Kusten van Muscovien, Lapland, Noorwegen, Jutland,— ... Klein Asien, Africa, Asia en wedet tot Nova Zembla en dan rondsom de vaste Kusten van America ... Voorzien met XIX Tafelin, etc. *Te Harlem: Izaak en Johannes Enschedé*. 1740. 2 vols., 8vo. Maps. J.C.B. 21508

Dwarris (F.) Substance of Three Reports of the Commissioners of Inquiry into the Administration of Civil and Criminal Justice in the West Indies: By Sir Fortunatus Dwarris. *London*. 1827. 8vo. S. 21509

Dwarris. The West India Question Plainly Stated, and the Practical Remedy Considered. By Sir Fortunatus Dwarris. *London*. 1828. 8vo, pp. 80. 21510

[Dwerhagen (H. C.)] Ensayo sobre la Topografia de los Rios Plata, Parana, Paraguay, Vermejo y Pilcomayo, para servir de memoria a su Navegacion con un Mapa, calculado con arreglo a las ultimas Observaciones. *Buenos Aires: Impreso en la Imprenta de Hallet y Ca*. 1831. 8vo, pp 16. 21511

Signed "Herman C. Dwerhagen."

Dwight (B. W.) The Higher Christian Education. By Benjamin W. Dwight. *New York: A. S. Barnes & Bros*. 1860. 12mo, pp. xvi, 347. C. 21512

Dwight. The History of the Descendants of Elder John Strong, of Northampton, Mass. By Benjamin W. Dwight, ... *Albany, N. Y.: Joel Munsell*. 1871. 2 vols., 8vo, pp. lix, (2), 1586, (1). 20 Portraits. 21513

Dwight. Reminiscences of the Life and Character of Benjamin Woolsey Dwight, M.D. By his Son. *New York*. 1862. 16mo, pp. 91. 21514

Dwight (E.) A National Currency and Banking System. By Edmund Dwight. *New York*. 1862. 21515

Dwight. A Plan for Military Education of Massachusetts. By Edmund Dwight. *Boston: Little, Brown and Company*. 1862. 8vo, pp. 16. B. 21516

Dwight (E. S.) An Address delivered in Saco, Oct. 12, 1862, on the One Hundredth Anniversary of the Organization of the First Church in Saco, Me. By Rev. Edward S. Dwight. ... *Saco: William Noyes*. 1862. 8vo, pp. 27. 21517

Dwight (H. G. O.) Memoir of Mrs. Elizabeth B. Dwight; including an account of the Plague of 1837. By Harrison Gray Otis Dwight. With a Sketch of the Life of Mrs. Judith S. Grant. *New-York*. 1840. 12mo. B., C. 21518

Dwight (H.) A Farewell Sermon, to the First Utica Presbyterian Society, on the Occasion of the Dismission of their Pastor, who had for some Months, by the Weakness of his Voice, been unable to discharge the Duties of his Office. Delivered the First Sabbath in October, 1817. By Henry Dwight. *Utica: printed by William Williams.* 1817. 8vo, pp. 26. BA.

Dwight (Jasper), *pseudonym*. *See* [Duane (W.)], Vol. v., No. 20989.

Dwight (J. S.) Dwight's Journal of Music, A Paper of Art and Literature. John S. Dwight, Editor. Vol. i. *Boston.* 1853. 4to. Continued to two or more volumes. 21520

Dwight (J.) An Essay to Silence the Outcry that has been made against Regular Singing. A Sermon preached at Framingham. By Rev. Josiah Dwight. *Boston.* 1725. 16mo, pp. 16.

Dwight (N.) The Lives of the Signers of the Declaration of Independence. By N. Dwight, Esq. *New York: Harper & Brothers.* 1839. + [*Ibid.*] 1840. + 1845. + A New Edition. [*Ibid.*] 1851. 12mo. pp. 373. 21522

Dwight. Short but Comprehensive System of the Geography of the World. By Nathaniel Dwight. *Hartford.* 1795. 12mo. + *Philadelphia: printed for Mathew Carey.* 1795. 12mo. B. + *Elizabethtown, N. J.* 1801. 12mo, pp. 128. + First Northampton Edition. *Northampton, Mass. Jan.*, 1805. 12mo. + Fifth Edition. *Northampton.* 1811. 12mo. + Fifth Albany Edition. *Albany.* 1812. 12mo. + Sixth Edition. *New York.* 1813. 12mo, pp. 213. + Albany. 1817. 12mo, pp. 212.

Dwight. Sketches of the Lives of the Signers of the Declaration of Independence, Intended principally for Schools. *New York.* 1830. 12mo. C. 21524

Republished as "Lives," etc., *see* No. 21522, *supra*.

Dwight (S. E.) The Gospel ... a Sermon ... Portland, Nov. 9, 1825, at the Installation of the Rev. Charles Jenkins, by S. Edwards Dwight ... . *Portland: Shirley & Edwards. Printers.* 1826. 8vo, pp. 51. BA. 21525

Dwight. The Life of President Edwards. By S. E. Dwight. *G. & C. & H. Carvill.* 1830. 8vo, pp. 766. Portrait. 21526

Dwight. Select Discourses. By Sereno Edwards Dwight. With a Memoir of his Life, by William T. Dwight. *Boston: Crocker & Brewster.* 1851. 12mo, pp. lxviii, 382. C. 21527

Dwight. Sermon ... at the Funeral of Rev. Joshua Huntington ... Sept 13, 1819. By Sereno Edwards Dwight. *Boston: Samuel T. Armstrong.* 8vo, pp. 44. B. 21528

Dwight (T.) An Oration spoken before the Society of the Cincinnati, of the State of Connecticut, met in Hartford, on the 4th of July, 1792. By Theodore Dwight ... *Hartford: printed by Hudson and Goodwin.* MDCCXCII. 8vo, pp. 18. H., S. 21529

Dwight. An Oration, spoken before "The Connecticut Society, for the Promotion of Freedom and the relief of persons unlawfully holden in bondage." Convened in Hartford, On the 8th day of May, A.D. 1794. By Theodore Dwight, Esquire. *Printed at Hartford, By Hudson and Goodwin.* MDCCXCIV. 8vo, pp. 24. N. 21530

Dwight. An Oration spoken at Hartford, in the State of Connecticut, on the Anniversary of American Independence, July 4th, 1798. By Theodore Dwight. *Hartford: Printed by Hudson and Goodwin.* 1798. 8vo, pp. 31. B. 21531

Dwight. An Oration, delivered at New-Haven on the 7th of July, A.D. 1801, before the Society of the Cincinnati, for ... Connecticut, assembled to celebrate the Anniversary of American Independence. By Theodore Dwight. ... . *Hartford: printed by Hudson and Goodwin.* 1801. 8vo, pp. 43. B. 21532

[Dwight.] Remarks on the Documents accompanying the Late Message of President Madison. (Nov. 29, 1809). To which are appended some Additional Observations. [n. p. n. d.] 8vo, pp. 48. BA. 21533

[Dwight, Alsop (R.), *etc.*] The Echo, with other Poems. [*New York.*] 1807. 8vo, pp. xv, 331, 5 l. BA. 21534

Dwight (T.), *Jr.* The Character of Thomas Jefferson, as exhibited in his own Writings. By Theodore Dwight. *Boston: Weeks: Jordan & Company.* 1839. 12mo, pp. 371. BA. 21535

Dwight. The History of Connecticut from the First Settlement to the Present Time. By Theodore Dwight, Jr. *New York: Harper & Brothers.* [1840.] 12mo, pp. 450. + [*Ibid.*] 1841. 12mo. BA. + [*Ibid.*] 1845. 18mo, pp. 450. + [*Ibid.*] 1859. 18mo. 21536

Dwight. History of the Hartford Convention; with a Review of the Policy of the United States Government, which led to the War of 1812. By Theodore Dwight, Secretary of the Convention. *N. and J. White, New York, and Russell, Odiorne & Co., Boston.* 1833. 8vo, pp. 447. 21537

Dwight. The Northern Traveller; containing the Routes to the Springs, Niagara, Quebec, and the Coal Mines; with the Tour of New England, &c. By Theodore Dwight, Junr. Sixth Edition, with Maps and Landscapes. *New York: J. P. Haven.* 1841. 12mo, pp. 250. 17 Maps. C. 21538

Dwight. Open Convents or Nunneries and Popish Seminaries dangerous to the Morals and Degrading to the Character of a Republican Community. By Theodore Dwight, Junr. *New York.* 1836. 18mo, pp. 176. 21539

[Dwight.] Sketches of Scenery and Manners in the United States. By the Author of the "Northern Traveller." *New York: A. T. Goodrich.* 1829. pp. 188. BA. 21540

Dwight. Summer Tours, or Notes of a Traveller through some of the Middle and Northern States. By Theodore Dwight. Second Edition. *New York.* 1847. 12mo. P., S. 21541

Dwight. Travels in America. By Theodore Dwight ... . *Glasgow: R. Griffin & Co.* MDCCCXLVIII. 12mo, pp. 308.

Also: President Dwight's Decisions of Questions discussed by the Senior Class in Yale College, In 1813 and 1814. From Stenographic Notes, by Theodore Dwight, Jun. *New York: Jonathan Leavitt.* 1833. 18mo, pp. 348. BA. — Family Visitor, and Silk Culturist. ... Theodore Dwight, Jr., and William Allan, Proprietors. *New York: Theo. Foster.* 1839. 4to, pp. 1–152, 190–224. H.

Dwight (T. W.) Argument in the Court of Appeals, of the State of New York, in the Rose Will Case. By Theodore W. Dwight, in behalf of the Rose Beneficent Association. *New York: W. C. Bryant & Co., Printers.* 1868. 8vo, pp. xxxiv, 446. Facsimile. B. 21543

Dwight. Case and Opinion. The Trust on which the Sanitary Commission holds its Funds. By Prof. T. W. Dwight, November, 1864. [n. p. n. p.] 8vo, pp. 26. B. 21544

Dwight. Trial by Impeachment. [*Philadelphia.* 1867.] 8vo, 1 l., pp. 257–283. C., H. 21545

Reprinted from the "American Law Register" for March, 1867. Also: Inaugural Addresses of Theodore W. Dwight and Geo. P. Marsh, in Columbia College, New York. *New York.* 1859. 8vo. B.

Dwight (Timothy). An Address to the Emigrants from Connecticut, and from New England generally, in the New Settlements of the United States. *Hartford.* 1817. 8vo, pp. 19. N. 21546

Dwight. America; A Poem in the Style of Pope's Windsor Forest. 1772. 21547

Title from Allibone's Dictionary. I have never seen the book.

Dwight. The Conquest of Canaan; A Poem, in Eleven Books. By Timothy Dwight. *Hartford: E. Babcock.* M,DCC,-LXXXV. 12mo, 4 l., pp. 304, (2). + *London: J. Johnson.* 1788. 16mo, pp. vii, 363. B., C. 21548

The first epic poem published in America.

Dwight. A Discourse delivered at New-Haven [Conn.], Feb. 22, 1800; on the Character of George Washington, Esq. at the Request of the Citizens; By Timothy Dwight, D.D. President of Yale-College. *New Haven: Printed by Thomas Green and Son.* 1800. 8vo, pp. 55. 21549

Dwight. A Discourse on Some Events of the Last Century, delivered in the Brick Church in New Haven, January 7, 1801. By Timothy Dwight, D.D. ... *New Haven: Printed by Ezra Read.* 1801. 8vo, pp. 56. BA., C. 21550

Dwight. A Discourse, occasioned by the Death of his Excellency Jonathan Trumbull, Esq. Governor of ... Connecticut; and delivered, at the Request of the General Assembly ... . By Timothy Dwight ... . *New Haven: printed by Oliver Steele and Co.* 1809. 8vo, pp. 28. BA. 21551

Dwight. A Discourse, in two Parts, delivered July 23, 1812, on the Public Fast, in the Chapel of Yale College. By Timothy Dwight ... . *New Haven: published by Howe and Deforest.* 1812. 8vo, pp. 54. BA. + *New-York: printed by J. Seymour.* 1812. 8vo, pp. 60. + Second Edition. *Boston: Cummings and Hilliard.* 1813. 8vo, pp. 28–59. BA., H. 21552

Dwight. The Duty of Americans, at the Present Crisis, illustrated in a Discourse, preached on the Fourth of July, 1798; By the Reverend Timothy Dwight, D.D. ... *New Haven: printed by Thomas and Samuel Green.* 1798. 8vo, pp. 32. BA. 21553

Dwight. Greenfield Hill: a Poem, in Seven Parts. ... By Timothy Dwight. *New York: printed by Childs & Swaine.* 1794. 8vo, pp. 183. B., BA. 21554

[Dwight.] Remarks on the Review of Inchiquin's Letters, published in the Quarterly Review; addressed to the Right Honourable George Canning, Esquire. By an Inhabitant of New-England. *Boston: S. T. Armstrong.* 1815. 8vo, pp. 176.

[Dwight.] A Sermon preached at Northampton, on the Twenty-eighth of November, 1781: occasioned by the Capture of the British Army, under the Command of Earl Cornwallis. ... . *Hartford: Printed by Nathaniel Patten.* [1781.] 8vo, pp. 34. BA. 21556

Dwight. A Statistical Account of the Towns and Parishes in the State of Connecticut, Published by the Connecticut Academy of Arts and Sciences. *New-Haven: Walter and Steele.* 1811. 8vo, pp. xi, 83, (1). H. 21557

Dwight. Theology, explained and defended, in a Series of Sermons, by Timothy Dwight, S.T.D. LL.D. Late President of Yale College ... . With a Memoir of the Life of the Author. *Middletown, Conn.: Printed by Clark & Lyman.* 1818–19. 8vo. B. + Second Edition. *New Haven.* 1823. 4 vols., 8vo. + *London: printed for T. and J. Almon.* 1827. + A New Edition. *London: William Baynes.* MDCCXXX. 5 vols., 8vo, pp. 583; 605; 533; 660; 599. + *New York.* 1856–7. 4 vols., 8vo.

Dwight. Travels in New England and New York. By Timothy Dwight, S.T.D., LL.D. ... *New Haven: Timothy Dwight.* 1821–2. 4 vols., 8vo, pp. 524; 527, 534; 527. 3 Maps. BA., C. + *London: William Baynes and Son.* 1823. 4 vols., 8vo, pp. xxxi, (1), 483; xi, 504; xi, 574; xi, 514. BA. 21559

"This work, though the humblest in its pretences, is the most important of Dr. Dwight's writings, and will derive additional value from time, whatever may become of his poetry and of his sermons." — *Quarterly Review*, xxx. 1. *See also* "N. Am. Rev.," xxxix. 208.

[Dwight.] The Triumph of Infidelity, a Poem. *Printed in the World.* 1788. 8vo, pp. 40. + [n. p.] 1788. 12mo, pp. 24. M. + *London: J. Mathews.* 1791. M. 21560

Dedicated to Voltaire, "who taught, by his examples and sentiments extended, that the chief end of man was to slander his God and abuse him forever.

Dwight. The True Means of Establishing Public Happiness. A Sermon delivered on the 7th of July, 1795, before the Connecticut Society of Cincinnati, and Published at their Request. By Timothy Dwight. *New Haven.* 1795. 8vo, pp. 40. N. 21561

Dwight. A Valedictory Address to the Young Gentlemen who commenced Bachelor of Arts at Yale College, July 25 1776. *New Haven.* [1776.] 8vo, pp. 22. 21562

Dwight. Virtuous Rulers a National Blessing. A Sermon, preached at the General Election, May 12th, 1791. By Timothy Dwight, D.D. ... of ... Fairfield. ... *Hartford: printed by Hudson and Goodwin.* M.DCC.XCI. 16mo, pp. 42. H. 21563

Also: The Charitable Blessed. A Sermon preached in ... New Haven, August 8, 1810. ... [*New Haven:*] *Sidney's Press.* 1810. 8vo, pp. 30. BA. — The Dignity ... of the Gospel, ... a Discourse, ... April 8, 1812, at the Ordination of the Rev. Nathaniel W. Taylor, ... New Haven. ... By Timothy Dwight. ... *New York: printed for Howe & Deforest.* 1812. 8vo, pp. 48. BA. — A Discourse ... at the Funeral of the Rev. Elizur Goodrich, D.D. ... Durham, one ... of the Corporation of Yale-College, November 25, 1797. *New Haven.* 1797. 8vo, pp. 39. — Discourse on the National Fast, delivered in Yale-College Chapel, Aug. 20, 1812. *New York.* 1812. 8vo, pp. 61. B., M. — ... a Discourse ... at the Ordination of the Rev. Nathaniel W. Taylor, ... Congregation in New-Haven. ... *New York: printed by J. Seymour.* 1812. 8vo, pp. 48. — A Sermon on Duelling, preached in the Chapel of Yale College, in New Haven, September 9, 1804; and in ... New York, January 21, 1805, ... *Hartford.* 1805. 8vo, pp. 38. + *New York: Printed by Collins, Perkins and Co.* 1805. 8vo. BA. — A Sermon on the Death of Mr. Ebenezer Grant Marsh, ... Yale College, Who died November 16th, 1803, in the 27th Year of his Age; preached ... November 20. ... *Hartford: printed by Hudson & Goodwin.* 1804. 8vo pp. 21. BA. — Sermon preached at the Opening of the Theological Institution in Andover; and at the Ordination of Rev. Eliphalet Pearson, LL.D., September 28th, 1808. ... *Boston: Mallory and Co.* 1808. 8vo, pp. 38. BA., H., W.

Dwight. Incidents in the Life of President Dwight. *New Haven.* 1833. 18mo. 21564

Dwight. Memoir of Timothy Dwight, LL.D. *Glasgow.* 1844. 18mo. 21565

Dwight. Sermons. With a Life of the Author. *New-Haven.* 1828. 2 vols., 8vo, pp. 552; 527. S. 21566

Dwight (W.) Life and Letters of Wilder Dwight, Lieut.-Col. Second Mass. Inf. Vols. [By Mrs. Dwight.] *Boston: Ticknor and Fields.* 1868. 8vo, pp. vii, 349, 1 l. B., BA., C.

Dwight. Proceedings of the Suffolk Bar upon the Occasion of the Death of Wilder Dwight with the Reply of the Court Obiit XIX Septemb. MDCCCLXII. Æt. XXX. *Riverside Press.* [1862.] 8vo, pp. 30. BA. 21568

Dwight (W. T.) The Nationality of a People, Its Vital Element. An Oration, Delivered in the New City Hall, before the City Government, and Citizens of Portland, July 4, 1861. By William T. Dwight, D.D., ... *Portland.* 1861. 8vo, pp. 32.

Dwight. An Oration before the Washington Benevolent Society of Pennsylvania, delivered ... on the 22nd of February, 1827, by William T. Dwight. *Philadelphia: printed by James Maxwell.* 1827. 8vo, pp. 24. BA. 21570

Dwight. Religion, the only Preservative of National Freedom. A Discourse delivered ... on the Day of the Annual Thanksgiving: December 1, 1836. By William T. Dwight. *Portland: Arthur Shirley, Printer.* 1836. 8vo, pp. 16. H.

Also: An Address delivered before the Association of Alumni of Yale College, Aug. 14, 1844. ... *New Haven: Printed by B. L. Hamlin.* 1844. 8vo. B. — A Discourse on the Rightfulness and Expediency of Capital Punishments. *Portland.* 1843. 8vo, pp. 34. H. — The Work and the Workmen. A Discourse in Behalf of the American Home Missionary Society, preached in the City of New York, May 8, 1859. ... *New York.* 1859. 8vo, pp. 31. B.

Dwinell (J. E.) Hope for our Country. A Sermon preached, ... October 19, 1862, by Rev. Israel E. Dwinell. ... *Salem: Printed by Charles W. Swassey.* 1862. 8vo, pp. 19. H. 21572

Dwinelle (J. W.) The Colonial History of San Francisco: being a Synthetic Argument in the District Court of the United States for the Northern District of California, for Four Square Leagues of Land claimed by that City. ... By John W. Dwinelle, Counsellor and Advocate. *San Francisco: Towne & Bacon, Prs.* 1866. 8vo, pp. iv, 102, 115. Map. + Fourth Edition. [*Ibid.*] 1867. 8vo, pp. xlv, 391. 3 Plates and 3 Maps. 21573

Dwyer (C. P.) Memoir of Commodore O. H. Perry, U. S. N., the Liberator of the Lakes, including a Faithful Sketch of the great Battle of Lake Erie, from most Authentic Accounts. By Charles P. Dwyer, Esq. *Cleveland, O.: T. J. Quinlan & Co.* 1860. 8vo, pp. 32. 21574

D*****x (Casimir). Cri des nègres [en vers]. *Paris: impr. de Leblanc.* 1823. 8vo. 21575

Dyckman (J. G.) The American Militia Officer's Manual; ... . By J. G. Dyckman. *New York: N. B. Holmes.* 1824. 12mo. B. + Second Edition. [*Ibid.*] 1825. 12mo. B.

Dyde Supper. Narrative of the celebrated Dyde Supper. By the Editor and Proprietor of the New York Morning Post and Morning Star. *New York.* 1811. 8vo. 21577

Dye (D.) The Life and Public Services of Gen. U. S. Grant. By Deacon Dye. *Philadelphia: The Author.* 1868. 8vo, pp. 82. 21578

Dye (J. S.) The Adder's Den; or, Secrets of the Great Conspiracy to Overthrow Liberty in America; Depravity of Slavery; Two Presidents Secretly Assassinated by Poison. Together with the Dying Struggles of the Great Rebellion. By John Smith Dye. *New York: The Author.* 1864. 8vo, pp. 128.

Dye. History of the Plots and Crimes of the Great Conspiracy to overthrow Liberty in America. ... By John Smith Dye. *New York: The Author.* 1866. 8vo, pp. vi, 364, 2 l. BA., C.

Also: Dye's Bank Note Plate Delineator: A Spurious and Altered Bill Detector, giving Printed Descriptions of the Genuiue Notes of every Denomination of all the Banks doing Business throughout the United States and British North America. ... *New-York.* 1855. Folio, pp. 287.

Dyer (Alexander B.) Proceedings of a Court of Inquiry convened at Washington, D. C., November 9, 1868, by Special Orders ... to examine into the Accusations against Brigadier and Brevet Major General A. B. Dyer, Chief of Ordnance. *Washington.* 1868. 8vo, pp. vii, 257–615. H. + *Washington: Government Printing Office.* 1869. 2 vols., 8vo, pp. v, 531; vii, 617. C. 21581

Dyer (Ch. Geo.) Biographical Sketches of the Lives and Characters of Illustrious and Eminent Men, with their Autographs. Illustrated with 48 Portraits. *London.* 1819. 8vo. + *London.* 1828. Rl. 8vo. 21582

Includes Benjamin Franklin.

Dyer (D.) Discourse Occasioned by the Assassination of Abraham Lincoln, delivered in the Albany Penitentiary, a Military Prison of the U. S. Wednesday, April 19, 1865. By David Dyer. *Albany: Edward Leslie, Printer.* 1865. 8vo, pp. 20.

Six hundred copies printed.

Dyer. A Discourse on the Characteristics of the Puritans, delivered in Dorchester, December 21, 1845. By David Dyer ... . *Boston.* 1846. 8vo, pp. 24. H., M. 21584

Dyer. History of the Albany Penitentiary. By David Dyer, Chaplain. *Albany: J. Munsell.* 1867. 8vo, pp. 273. Portrait and Plate. B. 21585

Dyer. Impressions of Prison Life in Great Britain. Submitted to the Inspectors and Superintendent of the Albany Penitentiary. By David Dyer. *Albany, N. Y.: J. Munsell.* 1868. 8vo, pp. 65. B. 21586

[Dyer (Eliphalet).] Remarks on Dr. Gale's Letter to J. W., Esq. *Printed, Anno* 1769. 8vo, pp. 27. P. 21587

Signed "E. D." The author was a leading Connecticut politician and lawyer. It chiefly relates to the dispute between Connecticut and New York about the settlement in Pennsylvania, under the name of Susquehannah. This was answered by "Observations on a Pamphlet, entitled Remarks on Dr. Gale's Letter to J. W., Esq.; of which the Hon. Eliphalet Dyer is the reputed Author." *Hartford.* [n. d.] 12mo, pp. 40.

Dyer (E. P.) Discourse at the 150th Anniversary of the Incorporation of Abington, Mass., 10 June, 1862. By Porter Dyer. *Boston.* 8vo, pp. 115. 21588

Also: Transactions of the Hingham Agricultural and Horticultural Society from 1858–61. Compiled by E. Porter Dyer. [Also for 1867, 1868.] *Boston.* 8vo. B.

Dyer (G.) Slavery and Famine Punishment for Sedition, by G. Thompson; with some Preliminary Remarks and a Sketch of Thomas Fysche Farmer. By George Dyer. Second Edition. *London.* 1794. 8vo. 21589

Dyer (H.) An Address, delivered in the Chapel of the University, Saturday, May 29, 1847, on the Occasion of the Interment of the Remains of the Late Prof. [Daniel] Stone. By Hernan Dyer, D.D. ... . *Pittsburgh: Geo. Parkin & Co.* 1847. 8vo, pp. 18. 21590

Dyer (J.) A Compendious Narrative, elucidating the Character, Disposition and Conduct of Mary Dyer, from the time of her Marriage in 1799, till she left the Society called Quakers, in 1815. Compiled by her Husband, Joseph Dyer. *Concord, N. H.* 1819. 12mo, pp. 88. + [*Ibid.*] 1824. 12mo. S. + Second Edition. *Pittsfield.* 1826. 8vo, pp. 80. W. 21591

Also included in "Tuke's Biographical Notices," Vol. II., p. 45.

Dyer (J. C.) Notes, on Political Mistakes, addressed to the People of England. *Manchester, Eng.* [n. d.] 8vo, pp. 24.

Relates to the Rebellion of 1861–5.

Dyer (M.) Mary Dyer the Quaker Martyr of New-England, with "Thoughts from Nature." *Published by T. Nelson, London and Edinburgh.* [n. d.] 12mo. 21593

Chiefly from Sewel's "History of Friends." *See* Stephenson (M.)

Dyer. A Brief Statement of the Sufferings of Mary Dyer, occasioned by the ... Shakers. Written by Herself. To which is added, Affidavits and Certificates; also, a Declaration from their own Publication. ... *Boston: published by William S. Spear.* 1818. 8vo, pp. 35. BA. 21594

Dyer. A Portraiture of Shakerism; Exhibiting a General View Of their Character and Conduct, from the First Appearance of Ann Lee in New England, down to the Present Time. And certified by many Respectable Authorities. Drawn up by Mary M. Dyer. ... [*Concord, N. H.:*] *printed for the Author.* 1822. 12mo, pp. 446. 21595

Also: Review of the "Portraiture of Shakerism." *Concord.* 1824. 12mo. — Reply to the foregoing Review. *Concord.* 1824. 12mo. *See* Dyer (Joseph).

Dyer. Remonstrance against her Testimony And application requesting Legislative Interference against the United Society, commonly called Shakers. *Boston.* 1818. 12mo. + *Concord, N. H.: Isaac Hill.* 1818. 12mo. 21596

Dyer. The Rise and Progress of the Serpent from the Garden of Eden, to the Present Day: with a Disclosure of Shakerism, exhibiting a general view of their real character and conduct from the first appearance of Ann Lee. Also, the Life and Sufferings of the Author, who was Mary M. Dyer, but now is Mary Marshall. *Concord, N. H.: printed for the Author.* 1847. 12mo, pp. 268. 21597

Dyer. Shakerism Exposed; being an Account of the Persecution suffered by the Author at the hand of the Shakers of Lebanon and Canterbury. By Mary Dyer. *Concord.* 1855.

Dyer (O.) Oliver Dyer's Phonographic Report of the Proceedings of the National Free Soil Convention at Buffalo, N. Y. August 9th and 10th, 1848. *Buffalo: G. H. Derby & Co.* [1848.] 8vo, pp. 32. H., S. 21599

Dyer (P.) Discourse on the Death of Wm. H. Harrison. By Rev. Palmer Dyer. *Whitehall.* 1841. 21600

Dyer (Sydney). Songs and Ballads. *New York.* 1857. 12mo. 21601

Dyer. Voices of Nature, and Thoughts in Rhyme. *Louisville.* 1849. 12mo. 21602

The author was a Baptist missionary among the Indians.

Dyer (W.) Christ's Famous Titles, and a Believer's Golden Chain handled in Divers Sermons, etc. By William Dyer. *Boston.* 1731. 12mo. + *Newburyport.* 1790. 12mo. 21603

The Dying Legacy. *See* [Mather (Samuel)].

The Dying Negro. *See* [Day (Thos.)], Vol. v., No. 18987.

Dyke (Thomas). Advice to Emigrants. *London.* 1832. 12mo. 21604

Dymond (Jonathan). Dymond on Slavery. [n. p. n. d.] 8vo, pp. 8. BA. 21605

Dymond. An Inquiry into the Accordancy of War with the Principles of Christianity; ... By Jonathan Dymond. ... Notes, by Thomas Smith Grimké ... . Together with an Appendix, containing Extracts from several of his Writings, vindicating or illustrating the Principles of Peace. *Philadelphia: printed by J. Ashmead & Co.* 1834. 12mo, pp. xx, (13)–300. BA. + *Philadelphia.* 1834. 8vo. + *Philadelphia.* 1835. B. 21606

Also: On the Applicability of the Pacific Principles of the New Testament to the Conduct of States: and on the Limitations which those Principles impose on the rights of Self-Defence. ... *Brooklyn.* 1832. 8vo, pp. 19, 4. BA., H.

Dyson (Julia A. P.) Life and Thought: or Cherished Memorials of the Late Julia A. Parker Dyson. Edited by Miss E. Latimer. *Boston: Whittemore, Niles, and Hall.* 1856. 12mo, pp. xiii, 314. BA. 21607

E. (E. B. d'). *See* E[ngel] (S., *le bailli d'*).

E. (J.) *See* E[llis] (Jonathan).

[E. (J. A.)] *See* [Eames (Jane Anthony)], No. 21618.

E. (O.) On the Death of the Reverend Benjamin Colman, D.D. Who Deceased August 29, 1747. An Eclogue. Attempted by O— E— a Young Student... . *Boston: Printed by Rogers and Fowle.* [n. d.] 8vo, pp. 8. BA., M. 21608

E. (P.) *See* E[rondelle] (P.)

E. (P.), *and* A. (J.) Some Miscellany | Observations | On our present Debates respecting | Witchcrafts, in a Dialogue | Between S. & B. | By P. E. and J. A. | *Philadelphia, Printed by William Bradford, for Hezekiah Usher.* | 1692. | 4to, pp. 16. BA. 21609

Attributed to Samuel Willard, and a volume of extreme rarity. It relates to the Salem witchcraft delusion, and was sent to Philadelphia to be printed, for the reason that the Boston printers declined the risk of printing it.

E. (S.) Further Quæries Upon the Present State of the New-English Affairs. [n. p. n. d.] 4to, pp. 18. G., N. 21610

Signed at the end "E. S.," and a tract of the greatest rarity; it relates to Governor Andrus, and was probably printed about 1689.

E. (S.) Further Queries upon the present State of the New-English Affairs. By S. E. 4to. + *New York: Reprinted for Joseph Sabin.* 1865. 4to, 3 l., pp. 18. BA. 21611

Only 250 copies reprinted, of which 50 are on large paper. Forms No. VIII. of Sabin's reprints, quarto series. It was also reprinted by the Prince Society, with the Andrus Tracts.

E. (W.) *See* E[aton] (W.)

Eachard (L.) *See* Echard (E.)

Eacker (G. I.) Observations on the National Character of the Americans: an Oration before the Tammany Society, 12th May, 1798. By George I. Eacker. *New York.* 1798. 8vo.

Eacker. An Oration, delivered at the request of the Officers of the Brigade of the City and County of New York, 4th July, 1801. By George I. Eacker. *New York.* 1801. 8vo, pp. 23.

Eager (S. W.) An Outline History of Orange County, with an Enumeration of the Names of its Towns, Villages, Rivers, Creeks, Lakes, Ponds, Mountains, Hills, and other known Localities, and other Etymologies or Historical Reasons therefor; together with Local Traditions and Short Biographical Sketches of Godly Settlers. By Sam'l W. Eager ... . *Newburgh: S. T. Callahan.* 1846–7. 8vo, Title, pp. 652, 2 l. B., BA., C. 21614

The Eagle and Hawk, a Collection of Patriotic and Humorous Songs and Odes. *Baltimore.* 1812. 12mo. 21615

Eames (J. H.) ... A Sermon on the Character of Joseph Stephens Abbot. By Rev. J. H. Eames, D.D. Preached at ... Concord, N. H., March 26, 1871. *Concord: printed by Butterfield & Hill.* 1871. 8vo, pp. 16. H. 21616

[Eames (*Mrs.* Jane Anthony).] Colonel Jesse A. Gore, U. S. A. Fell at Gaines' Mills, June 27, 1862. ... [*Concord, N. H.* 1870.] 8vo, pp. 28. H. 21617

[Eames.] A Sketch of the Rise and Progress of Grace Church, Providence, compiled by a Layman, for the Providence Journal, 1857. [*Providence.* 1857.] 8vo, pp. 4. H. 21618

Eames (J.) ... Sermon, delivered at Newbury, April 29, 1792. Occasioned by the Decease of the Rev. John Tucker, D.D. ... By Jonathan Eames ... . *Newburyport: printed by John Mycall.* 1792. 8vo, pp. 48. B., BA., H., N. 21619

Eames (T.) An Address delivered at the Opening of Eames and Putnam's English and Classical Hall, Brooklyn, Long Island, March 24th, 1831. By Theodore Eames. ... *New York: Sleight & Robinson, Printers.* 1831. 8vo, pp. 32. H. 21620

Also: An Introductory Lecture, delivered before the Brooklyn Lyceum, November 7, 1833. ... *Brooklyn, L. I.* MDCCCXXXIII. 8vo, pp. 32. H.

[Earhart (T. J.)] In the Supreme Court. ... State of Louisiana versus John Cook and George Logan, Free Men of Color, and a Part of the Crew of the Ship Elizabeth Hamilton, (ex parte.) ... Argument and Brief of Counsel. [n. p. n. d.] 8vo, pp. 51. H. 21621

Earl (J.) An Answer to Richard Harden's Reply to John Earl's Letter. By John Earl. *Newport: Printed.* 1730. 12mo. 3¼ sheets. 21622

Earle (*Rev.* A. B.) Bringing in Sheaves: a Record of Evangelistic Labours in the United States from the Atlantic to the Pacific. *London: Morgan & S.* 1871. 12mo, pp. 154.

Earle (A.) A Narrative of a Nine Months' Residence in New Zealand, in 1827; together with a Journal of a Residence in Tristan d'Acunha. By Augustus Earle. *London.* 1832. 8vo. C. 21624

Title from Rich, Vol. II. The islands of Tristan d'Acunha are in the South Atlantic.

Earle (J.) Sacramental Exercises, or, the Christian's Employment, Before, At, and After the Lord's Supper. Fourth Edition. Added, Hymns, for Sacramental Occasions. *Boston.* 1725. 12mo, pp. (4), 92. B., W. + Fifth Edition. *Boston: reprinted for S. Gerrish.* 1729. 16mo. B. 21625

Earle (J. M.) Report to the Governor ... concerning the Indians of the Commonwealth [Mass.] ... April 6, 1859. By John Milton Earle, Commissioner. *Boston.* 1861. 8vo, pp. 147, lxxxiv. 21626

Earle (O.) Review of the Opinion of the Supreme Judicial Court of Massachusetts, in the case of Oliver Earle and others, in Equity, versus William Wood and others. By the Representatives of the Yearly Meeting of Friends for New England. ... *Boston: Press of T. R. Marvin.* 1855. 8vo, 2½ sheets. B., P.

Earle (P.) History, Description, and Statistics of the Bloomingdale Asylum for the Insane. By Pliny Earle, M.D. *New York: Hovey & King.* 1848. 8vo, pp. 136. Plate. B. 21628

Also: Address, Nov. 24, 1863, by P. Earle. *Utica.* 1867. 8vo. B. — Lessons from the Past. A Poem. *Providence: Knowles, Anthony & Co.* 1861. 8vo, pp. 16. — Poem delivered before the Alumni Association of the New-England Yearly Meeting School, ... at their third Annual Meeting at Newport, 1861. *Providence: Knowles, Anthony & Co., printers.* 1861. 8vo, pp. 16. H. — The Psychopathick Hospital of the Future; June 20, 1867. *Utica.* 1867. 8vo. B. — Ralph Earle and his Descendants. [*Worcester.* 1860.] Broadside. H. — A Visit to Thirteen Asylums for the Insane in Europe; with Notices of similar institutions in Transatlantic Countries and the United States. ... *Philadelphia.* 1841. 8vo.

Earle (T.) Treatise on Rail Roads and Internal Communications. ... With Original Suggestions and Remarks. By Thomas Earle. *Philadelphia.* 1830. 8vo. 21629

Earls (J.) Report of the Trial and Conviction of John Earls, for the Murder of his Wife, Catherine Earls, in the Court of Oyer and Terminer, held at Williamsport, [Pennsylvania,]

for Lycoming County, February Term, 1836. ... Reported ... by W. F. Packer and A. Cummings, Jr. *Williamsport.* 1836. 8vo. C. 21630

Early (J. A.) A Memoir of the Last Year of the War for Independence in the Confederate States of America, containing an Account of the Operations of his Commands in the Years 1864 and 1865. By Lieutenant-General Jubal A. Early, ... *Lynchburg: Charles W. Button.* 1867. 8vo, pp. 145, (1). BA. + *Toronto: Printed by Lovell & Gibson.* 1866. 8vo, pp. 144.

Early History of ... Pennsylvania. *See* "Pennsylvania."

Earnest Address to such of the People called Quakers as are Sincerely Desirous of Supporting and Maintaining the Christian Testimony of their Ancestors. Occasioned by a Piece intituled, "The Testimony of the People called Quakers, given forth by a Meeting of the Representatives of said People in Pennsylvania, &c." *Philadelphia.* 1775. 12mo. P. 21632

Earnshaw (W.) Collection of the Statutes relating to the British Colonies and Plantations in America and the West Indies. 1818. 4to. 21633

Earnshaw. Digest of the Laws relating to the British Provinces and Colonies in America and the West Indies, from Charles II. to 1818. *London.* 1818. 8vo. 21634

Earthquakes. An Account of the Earthquakes which occurred in the United States of North America, on the 16th of December, 1811; the 23d of January and the 7th of February, 1812; with the Inferior Shocks considered as Appendages to the Former, etc. *Philadelphia.* 1812. 12mo, pp. 84. 21635

An Account of the Great Earthquakes in the Western States, particularly on the Mississippi River, Dec. 16–23, 1818. *Newburyport.* 1812. 8vo, pp. 16. W. 21636

Brief and Correct Account of an Earthquake which happened in South America. *Poughkeepsie: G. A. Gardner.* 1820. 8vo.

The Earthquake of Caraccas, a Tale of Venezuela. By the Author of Campaigns and Cruises in Venezuela. 12mo.

The Earthquake of Juan Fernandez, as it occurred in 1835; authenticated by the retired Governor of that Island. To which

is added, a Refutation of several Misstatements in the Nautical Magazine of 1837, and the Public Papers. [*Manchester.*] 1839. 8vo. 21639

See also "Lima," and other names of places.

East (E. H.) Short Review of Leading and Operating Causes of the Distress of the British West India Colonies. By Sir E. H. East. *London.* 1832. 8vo. 21640

The East and the West; Our Doings with our Neighbours. Essays by different Hands. Edited by the Hon. Henry Stanley. *London: Hatchard.* 1865. Post 8vo, pp. v, 271. 21641

East and West India Sugar. *See* [Macaulay (Zachary)].

East Abington, *Mass.* Library Association. Catalogue. *Boston.* 1863. 12mo, pp. 16. B. 21642

East Attleborough. Remarks and Documents concerning the Location of the Boston and Providence Railroad through the Burying-ground in East Attleborough. [By John Daggett.] *Boston.* 1834. 21643

East Boston. Annual Report to the Stockholders of the East Boston Company. May 4, 1857. *Boston.* 1857. 8vo, pp. 11. Continued. H. 21644

See also "Boston."

East Bridgewater. The Selectmen's Report of the Receipts and Expenditures of the Town of East Bridgewater, from April 1, 1850, to March 1, 1851; also, the School Committee's Annual Report, for 1850–51. [n. p.] 1851. 8vo, pp. 16. Continued. H. 21645

Also: Report of the Superintending School Committee of East Bridgewater, for the Year 1849–50. [n. p. n. d.] 8vo, pp. 8. + The same. 1856–7. H.

East Cambridge, *Mass.* People's Union Association. Constitution and By-Laws, 1863, East Cambridge, Mass. *Boston.* 1863. 12mo. B. 21646

East Florida. *See* "Florida."

East Greenwich. Historical Sketch of East Greenwich Seminary; its relation to Public Schools, and Advantages for giving Normal Instruction. [n. p. n. d.] 8vo. 21647

East Hartford. Report of the Committee on the Petition of the Town of East Hartford, &c., against the Hartford-Bridge Company, May Session, 1843. *Hartford.* 1843. 8vo, pp. 7.

East Haven. A Confession of Faith, Covenant, Constitution and Rules of Practice; adopted by the Congregational Church in East Haven. To which is added a Catalogue of the Officers and Members of the Church, from the Year 1755 to December, 1833. *New Haven: printed by Hezekiah Howe & Co.* 1833. 12mo, pp. 24. H. 21649

East Haverhill. Address to the East Haverhill Temperance Society. *Haverhill.* 1830. 21650

East Jersey. *See* "New Jersey."

East Kingston. Auditor's Report of the Receipts and Expenditures of the Town of East Kingston, N. H., commencing March 8, 1854, ending March 7, 1855. Also, the Report of the Superintending School Committee. *Boston: Bazin & Chandler, Printers.* 1855. 16mo, pp. 16. Continued. H. 21651

East Pembroke Seminary: Circular, 1859. *Buffalo, N. Y.* 8vo. 21652

East Saginaw. Holland's East Saginaw City Directory for 1868–9, with a Directory of Saginaw City. *Chicago: Western Pub. Co.* 1868. 8vo, pp. 304. 21653

East Tennessee. Report of the Committee for Relief to East Tennessee, for the State of New York. *New York: J. W. Amerman.* 1865. 8vo, pp. 30. 21654

Report on the Lands of the East Tennessee Mining Company. *Providence.* 1850. 21655

Report to the East Tennessee Relief Association at Knoxville; with Tabular Statements from the General Agent, etc. By Thomas W. Humes ... . To which are appended the Proceedings commemorative of the Death of Edward Everett. *Knoxville.* 1865. 8vo, pp. 50. H. 21656

Eastburn (Benjamin). The Doctrine of Absolute Reprobation, According to the Westminster Confession of Faith, Refuted: And the Universality of the Saving Grace of God asserted. To which is added A Postscript, by Another Hand, wherein those several Texts generally reverted, to vindicate the aforesaid Doctrine of Reprobation, are set in a true Light. *Philadelphia: Printed and Sold by Samuel Hume.* 1723. 16mo, pp. 68. + *Boston.* 1732. 16mo, pp. 46. M., W. 21657

Eastburn (J.) Plan of Public Reading-Rooms, on the Foundation of the late E. Sargeant's. *New York.* 1812. Folio, pp. 4. M. 21658

Also: Plan of Literary Rooms, instituted by Eastburn, Kirk & Co, at the Corner of Wall and Nassau Streets, Newyork [*sic*] ... . *New-York.* 1813. 8vo, pp. 15 BA. — Plan of the Literary Rooms, instituted by James Eastburn & Co., at the Corner of Broadway and Pine-Street, New-York. Second Edition, Corrected and Enlarged ... *New-York: printed by Abraham Paul.* 1817. 8vo, pp. 15, (1). BA. — Prospectus for Printing by Subscription, by James Eastburn & Co., at the Literary Rooms, Corner of Broadway and Pine-Street, New-York, limited Editions of Scarce Books, in the Various Branches of Literature, from the Sixteenth Century down to the Present Time ... . *New-York: printed by Abm. Paul.* 1817. 8vo, pp. 16. BA.

Eastburn (J. W.) Yamoyden, a Tale of the Wars of King Philip: in Six Cantos. By the late Rev. James Wallis Eastburn, A.M. and his Friend [Robert C. Sands]. ... *New-York: James Eastburn.* 1820. 16mo, Frontispiece, Engraved Title, pp. xii, 339, (1). BA. 21659

The introduction and one canto are given in pp. 219–249 of "Specimens of the American Poets ... . *London.* 1822." 12mo.

Eastburn (M.) Sermon, after the Great Fire of 1835, in the Church of the Ascension, New York, December 20, 1835. ... By the Rev. Manton Eastburn. *New York.* 1835. 8vo, pp. 20. N. 21660

Eastburn. A Sermon, delivered on Sunday Morning, June 22, 1851, in Trinity Church, Boston, ... on Occasion of the Celebration, throughout the Diocese of Massachusetts, of the 150th Anniversary of the Incorporation of the Venerable Society for the Propagation of the Gospel in Foreign Parts. By the Right Rev. Manton Eastburn, D.D. ... *Boston: William A. Hall, Printer.* 1851. 8vo, pp. 20. B., BA. 21661

Eastburn. ... A Sermon delivered in Trinity Church, Boston ... October 31, 1852, being the Sunday after the Interment of the Hon. Daniel Webster. By the Right Rev. Manton Eastburn, D.D. ... *Boston.* 1852. 8vo, pp. 20. B., H. 21662

Eastburn. ... A Sermon preached in ... Rochester ... October 18, 1854, at the Consecration of the Rev. Henry Washington Lee, D.D. ... . By the Rt. Rev. Manton Eastburn, D.D. ... . *Rochester: David Hoyt.* 1854. 8vo, pp. 24. H. 21663

Also: Consecration of St. John's Memorial Chapel, Cambridge, November 16, A.D 1869, and Sermon preached on that Occasion by Right Rev. Manton Eastburn ... *Boston: printed by Nathan Sawyer & Son.* 1870. 8vo, pp. 44. H. — Correspondence between the Right Reverend the Bishop of Massachusetts and the Rectors of the Parish of the Advent. Boston, A.D. 1845 to A.D. 1856. Printed, not published

Boston: John Wilson and Son. 1856. 8vo, pp. vi, 1 l., pp. 123. B., BA. — Means of Ministerial Efficiency. The Second Charge to the Clergy of Massachusetts, delivered May 16, 1849. *Boston.* 1849. 8vo, pp. 23. B. — A Sermon, ... Boston ... February 18, 1843: on Occasion of the Interment of the Rt. Rev. Alexander Viets Griswold, D.D. *Boston: James B. Dow, Publisher.* 1843. 8vo, pp. 23. B., BA., H. — ... A Sermon, ... New York ... March 19, 1843 ... on ... the Rev. Gregory Thurston Bedell, M.A., being instituted Rector ... . *New York: Carville and Co.* 1843. 8vo, pp. 23. B., H. — ... A Sermon ... Bristol, Rhode Island, on ... Feb. 28, 1855. At the Funeral of Rev. John Bristed, formerly Rector of said Church. ... *Bristol, R. I.* 1835. 8vo, pp. 22. B. — Signal Work of the Holy Spirit in the United States. Third Charge to the Clergy of Massachusetts, May 4, 1859. *Boston.* 1859. 8vo. — Tributes to the Memory of H. Anthon, D.D., with a Sketch of his Life. *New York.* 1862. 12mo. S.

Eastburn (R.) A Faithful Narrative of the many Dangers and Sufferings, as well as wonderful and surprising Deliverances of Robert Eastburn, during his late Captivity among the Indians: Together with some Remarks upon the Country of Canada, and the Religion and Policy of its Inhabitants, the whole intermixed with devout Reflections. Published at the earnest Request of many Friends, for the Benefit of the Author. With a recommendatory Preface, by the Rev. Gilbert Tennent. *Philadelphia: Printed by Wm. Dunlap.* 1758. 8vo, pp. 45. N. + *Philadelphia: Printed. Boston: Reprinted and Sold by Green & Russell, Opposite the Probate-Office in Queen-Street.* 1758. 8vo, pp. iv, 34. J.C.B., M., P., W. 21664

The author was taken prisoner in March, 1756, near Oswego, by a party of French and Indians, and taken to Canada. After being cruelly treated by both, and carried to various parts of the country as far as Montreal, he made his escape to Quebec, where he received better treatment, and was sent to England. Thence he took ship for Boston, and reached his family in Philadelphia after an absence of twenty months. Both editions are rare, the first especially so. *See* Green (Ashbel), for a reprint.

Easterbrooks (J.) Abraham the Passenger; his Privilege and Duty described. Election Sermon, 1705. By Rev. Joseph Easterbrooks. *Boston.* 1705. 4to, pp. 22. M. 21665

Eastern Indians. *See* Vol. IV., No. 15436–15441.

Eastern Railroad Company. Act of Incorporation and By-Laws of the Eastern Railroad Company, Incorporated April 14, 1836. *Salem: Palfrey and Chapman.* 1836. 12mo, pp. 42.

Also: Annual Report of the Directors of the Eastern Railroad Company, to the Stockholders, for the Year, ending 1843. 8vo. Continued. B. — A Brief Statement relative to the Claim on the Eastern Railroad Company, to pay its Indebtedness to the Commonwealth in Gold. — Report on the Surveys and Definite Location of the Eastern Rail Road. By John M. Fessenden, Civil Engineer. *Boston: Freeman and Bolles, Printers.* 1836. 8vo, pp. 18. BA.

Eastern Yacht Club. Constitution, By-Laws, Sailing Directions, etc., of the Eastern Yacht Club. 1870. *Boston: Nathan Sawyer & Son.* 1870. 18mo, pp. 50. B. 21667

Eastham, *Mass.* A Church of Christ Vindicated. A Short and Plain Relation of some Transactions in the South Church of Eastham, at Eastham. [1723.] 8vo, pp. 56. B., C., W. 21668

Copy of the Result of the Council at Billingsgate, in Eastham, Nov. 8, 1720. With the Narrative of Hannah Doane. *Boston.* [1721.] 16mo, pp. 56. M., W. 21669

The Veracity and Equity of the Members of the Council held at Billingsgate in Eastham, 1720, Asserted and Maintained. *Boston: Tho. Fleet.* 1723. 8vo, pp. 16. B. 21670

Eastlacke (Francis). The Truth of Christ Jesus with the Professors thereof in the Island of Bermudas (commonly called Quakers) cleared from three Ungodly, False charges charged upon them by Samp. Bond, in a Book, entituled The Quakers in Bermuda Tryed, &c. In which book are found many Blasphemies, Slanders, etc. [n. p. n. d.] 4to, pp. 45–92, 38.

Eastman (Charles G.) Poems. *Montpelier.* 1848. 16mo.

Eastman (D.) On the Agencies which affect the Stability of the Union. By Daniel Eastman, of Geneva, Kane Co., Ill. *Chicago.* 1860. 8vo, pp. 32. H. 21673

Eastman (E.) A Statement of Facts, relative to the Petition and Public Hearing before the Legislature, in June, 1818, for the Removal of Ebenezer Eastman from the Office of Major in the Tenth Regiment of New-Hampshire Militia. *Concord: printed by George Hough. July,* 1818. 8vo, pp. 66. BA. 21674

Eastman (F. S.) A History of the State of New York, from the First Discovery of the Country to the Present Time: with a Geographical Account of the Country, and a View of its Original Inhabitants. By F. S. Eastman. ... *New York: E. Bliss.* 1828. 12mo, pp. viii, 279, (1). B., BA., C., S. + A New Edition. *New York: Augustus K. White.* 1833. pp. 455, (1).

Eastman. A History of Vermont ... . With a Geographical Account of the Country, and a View of the Original Inhabitants. For ... Schools. By F. S. Eastman. *Brattleboro': Holbrook and Fessenden.* 1828. 18mo, pp. 110. H. 21676

Eastman (H.) Noyesism Unveiled; a History of the Self-Styled Perfectionists; with a Summary View of their Leading Doctrines. By Rev. H. Eastman ... . *Brattleboro': published by the Author.* 1849. 12mo, pp. 432. BA., S. 21677

Eastman (J. R.) Discussion of the West India Cyclone of Oct. 29 and 30, 1867. Prepared by order of Commodore B. F. Sands, U. S. Navy. By J. R. Eastman ... . *Washington.* 1868. 8vo, pp. 18. Map. B. 21678

Eastman (J. W.) Sermon, at Reading, Mass., before Mount Moriah and Good Samaritan Lodges. ... By Jacob W. Eastman. *Albany.* 1823. 8vo. 21679

Eastman (L. R.) Genealogy of the Eastman Family, for the first four Generations. Compiled by Rev. Lucius Root Eastman, Amherst, Mass., ... *Boston: David Clapp & Son.* 1867. 8vo pp. 11. B. 21080

Eastman (L.) Oration at Lexington, [Mass.] June 24, 1816. By Luke Eastman. *Boston.* 1816. 8vo. W. 21681

Eastman (M. H.) The American Aboriginal Portfolio. By Mrs. Mary H. Eastman. Illustrated with 26 Steel Engravings by S. Eastman Capt. U. S. Army. *Philadelphia: Lippincott, Grambo & Co.* 1853. 4to, pp. 84. 21682

Eastman. Aunt Phillis's Cabin; or, Southern Life as it is. By Mrs. Mary H. Eastman. *Philadelphia: Lippincott, Grambo & Co.* 1852. 12mo, pp. 280. C. 21683

Eastman. Chicora, and other Regions of the Conquerors and the Conquered. By Mrs. Mary H. Eastman. *Philadelphia: Lippincott, Grambo & Co.* 1854. Rl. 8vo, pp. 126. 21 Plates.

Eastman. Dahcotah; or, Life and Legends of the Sioux around Fort Snelling. By Mrs. Mary Eastman, with Preface by Mrs. C. M. Kirkland. Illustrated from Drawings by Captain Eastman. *New York: John Wiley.* 1849. 12mo, pp. xi, (1), 268. 4 Plates. H. 21685

Eastman. Romance of Indian Life; with other Tales. By Mrs. M. H. Eastman. *Philadelphia.* 1852. Rl. 8vo, pp. 310.

[Eastman (Samuel C.)] The White Mountain Guide Book. *Concord: Edson C. Eastman.* 1858. 12mo, 2 l., pp. 152. Woodcuts. H. + Second Edition. [*Ibid.*] 1859. 12mo, pp. 179.

Map. H. + Third Edition. [*Ibid.*] 1863. 16mo, pp. 222. Woodcuts and Maps. BA. + Fourth Edition. [*Ibid.*] 1864. Seventh Edition. [*Ibid.*] 1867. 16mo, pp. 246. Woodcuts and 2 Maps. H. 21687

See Norton's "Literary Letter," New Series, 1860, No. 1, pp. 8–20.

Eastman (T.) Oration on the Death of Thomas Illman. By Thomas Eastman. [n. p. n. d.] 8vo. C. 21688

Eastman. Proceedings of a Division Court-martial, constituted for the Trial of Captain Thomas Eastman, March 14, 1815. With his Defence before the Court, the Division Order of March 27, Disapproving the Judgment of the Court, and an Address to the Public. *Hallowell.* 1815. 8vo. 21689

Eastman (T.) A Sermon, preached in Sharon, Vermont, March 12, 1806, at the Ordination of the Rev. Samuel Bascom. By the Rev. Tilton Eastman, Pastor of the Congregational Church in Randolph, Ver. *Hanover, N. H.: Printed by Moses Davis.* 1806. 8vo, pp. 31. W. 21690

[Eastman (Z.)] ... A Lecture on Slavery the Cause of the Civil War in the United States. Delivered at ... Bristol, June, 1862. ... *Chicago: John R. Walsh.* [n. d.] 16mo, pp. 24. H.

Easton (H.) A Treatise on the Intellectual Character and Civil and Political Condition of the Colored People of the United States, and the Prejudice exercised towards them. By Rev. H. Easton ... *Boston: Isaac Knapp.* 1837. 8vo, pp. 54, (1). B.

Easton (J.) Human Longevity; recording the Name, Age, Place of Residence, and the Year of the Decease of 1712 Persons, who attained a Century and Upwards, from A.D. 66 to 1799; ... By James Easton. *Salisbury.* 1799. 8vo, pp. xxxii, 292, 30 l. C. 21693

Includes notices of some Americans.

Easton (J.) A Narrative of the Causes which led to Philip's Indian War, of 1675 and 1676. By John Easton, of Rhode Island. With other Documents concerning this Event, in the Office of the Secretary of the State of New York. Prepared from the Originals, with an Introduction and Notes. By Franklin B. Hough. *Albany, N. Y.: J. Munsell.* M D CCC LVIII. 4to, pp. xxiii, 207. 21694

Munsell's Historical Series, No. II. One hundred and ten copies printed, ten of which are on large paper. The rarest of this series.

Easton. Objections of Rufus Easton to the Return of John Scott, as a Delegate from the Territory of Missouri, insisting that the said Scott was not, and is not, elected a Delegate from that Territory. [n. p. 1816.] 8vo, pp. 6. BA. 21695

Also: [Circular in Defence of his Conduct, dated St. Louis, November 23d, 1805. n. p.] 8vo, pp. 14. BA.

Easton (W. C.) Eulogium on La Fayette; delivered in ... Washington City, ... 15th September, 1834. By William C. Easton. *Washington: printed by Duff Green.* 1834. 8vo, pp. 18.

Easton, *Mass.* Reports of the Selectmen, Treasurer, and School Committee, of the Town of Easton, for the Year ending March 1, 1863. *Taunton: C. A. Hack, Printer.* 1863. 8vo, pp. 29. H. 21697

Easton, *Pa.* Library Company. Catalogue of the Books. *Phillipsburg: Cooley & Wise.* 1855. 8vo, pp. 99. C. 21698

See also "Indians," "Minutes of Conferences," and "Lafayette College."

Eastwick (E. B.) Venezuela; or, Sketches of Life in a South-American Republic; with The History of the Loan of 1864. By Edward B. Eastwick, C.B. *London: Chapman & Hall.* [1864–5.] 8vo, pp. xi, 418. Map. + Second Edition. [*Ibid.*] 1868. 8vo, pp. xi, 418. Map. BA., C. 21699

Easy Nat: or Boston Bars and Boston Boys. A Tale of Home Trials. By One who knows them ... *Boston: Redding and Company, Publishers.* 1844. 8vo, pp. 48. BA., H. 21700

[Eaton (Amos).] A Geological and Agricultural Survey of Rensselaer County, in the State of New York. To which is annexed, a Geological Profile, extending from Onondagua Salt Springs, across said County, to Williams College in Massachusetts. ... *Albany: printed by E. and E. Hosford.* 1822. 18mo, pp. 70. B., BA., H., M. 21701

[Eaton.] A Geological and Agricultural Survey of the District adjoining the Erie Canal, ... Part I. Containing a Description of the Rock Formations; together with a Geological Profile, extending from the Atlantic to Lake Erie. *Albany: Printed by Packard & Van Benthuysen.* 1824. 18mo, 1 slip, pp. 168. 2 Plates. BA., H. 21702

Eaton. Geological Nomenclature for North America, founded upon Geological Surveys ... *Albany: Packard & Van Benthuysen.* 1828. 8vo, pp. 31. 3 Maps. B., C., H., S. 21703

Also: Geological Prodromus. *Troy.* 1829. 8vo.

Eaton. An Index to the Geology of the Northern States, with a Transverse Section from Catskill Mountain to the Atlantic. Prepared for the Geological Classes at Williams College, Northampton, Belchertown, Leicester and Worcester, Mass. By Amos Eaton ... . *Leicester: printed by H. Brown.* 1818. 8vo, pp. 52. BA. 21704

Eaton. An Index to the Geology of the Northern States, with Transverse Sections, extending from Susquehanna River to the Atlantic, crossing Catskill Mountains. To which is prefixed a Geological Grammar. By Amos Eaton ... . Second Edition, wholly written over anew ... . *Troy, N. Y.: Published by Wm. S. Parker.* 1820. 12mo, pp. 286. Plate. BA. 21705

Eaton. A Manual of Botany for the Northern States. By Amos Eaton. *Albany.* 1817. 12mo. S. 21706

Eaton. A Manual of Botany for the Northern and Middle States. Second Edition, Corrected and Enlarged. *Albany.* 1818. 12mo, pp. 524. + Third Edition, Revised and Corrected. *Albany: printed and published by Websters and Skinners.* 1822. 12mo, pp. 536. BA. + Fourth Edition, Revised and Corrected. *Albany: Websters and Skinners.* 1824. 12mo, pp. 539. H. 21707

Eaton. Manual of Botany for North America: Comprising Generic and Specific Indigenous Plants and Common Exotics growing north of the Gulf of Mexico. Fifth Edition, Revised, Corrected, and much Enlarged. *Albany: Websters and Skinners.* 1829. 12mo, pp. 451, 63, (36). + Sixth Edition. *Albany.* 1833. 12mo. S. + Seventh Edition. *Albany: Oliver Steele.* 1836. 12mo, pp. 672, 125. 21708

Also: Circular to Gentlemen residing in the Vicinity of the Erie Canal. ... *Troy.* 1822–23. 16mo. — Geological Text-Book, prepared for Popular Lectures on North American Geology; with applications to Agriculture and the Arts. ... *Albany.* 1830. 8vo, pp. 63. + Second Edition, with 68 Figures of Organic Remains. *New York.* 8vo, pp. 140. — System of Education proposed for the Improvement of Common Schools. ... *Albany, N. Y.* 1829. 8vo. B. — Zoological Syllabus and Note-Book, for Troy Female Academy. *Troy.* 1822. 12mo. — Text-Book. *Albany.* 1826. 12mo.

Eaton *and* Wright (J.) North American Botany: comprising the Native and Common Cultivated Plants, North of Mexico ... . By Amos Eaton ... [and] John Wright, M.D. ... Eighth Edition ... . *Troy, N. Y.* 1840. 8vo. C., H., S. 21709

Eaton *and* Beck (T. Romeyn). Geological Survey of the County of Albany. Taken under the Direction of the Agricultural Society of the County. B. 21710

[Eaton (*Rev.* Asa).] Historical Account of Christ Church, Boston. A Discourse delivered in said Church, on Sunday, December 28, 1823. By The Rector. *Boston: printed by Joseph W. Ingraham.* 1824. 8vo, pp. 39. Woodcut. B., BA., C., H.

Also: First Semi-Annual Report of ... Eaton, Domestic Missionary in ... Boston ... . *Boston.* 1830. 12mo. H.

Eaton (B. A.) The Minstrel and other Poems, by B. A. Eaton. *Boston: Russell, Odiorne & Company.* 1833. 12mo, pp. 54. 21712

Eaton (C.) Annals of the Town of Warren; with the Early History of St. George's, Broad Bay, and the Neighbouring Settlements on the Waldo Patent. By Cyrus Eaton. *Hallowell: Masters, Smith & Co.* 1851. 12mo, pp. xi, 437. Map. BA., C.

Eaton. History of Thomaston, Rockland, and South Thomaston, Maine, from their First Exploration, A.D. 1605; with Family Genealogies. By Cyrus Eaton ... . *Hallowell: Masters, Smith & Co., Printers.* 1865. 2 vols., 12mo, pp. xii, 468; iv, 472.

Eaton (Dorman Bridgman). Intellect and Education. Oration before the Alumni of the University of Vermont, by D. B. Eaton. August, 1867. [n. p. n. d.] 8vo, pp. 51. H. 21715

Eaton (D. M.) Five Years on the Erie Canal: an Account of some of the most Striking Scenes and Incidents, during Five Years' Labor on the Erie Canal, and other Inland Waters. By Dea. M. Eaton, Missionary of the American Bethel Society. Written by himself. *Utica: Bennett, Backus, & Hawley, Franklin Square.* 1845. 18mo, Title, pp. 10–156. 21716

Eaton (E.) An Almanac. By Edward Eaton, of Philadelphia. *Philadelphia: Printed by William Bradford.* About 1687–8?

Eaton (E. B.) California and the Union. By Edward Byron Eaton, of California. *London: Heardley and Co.* 1863. 12mo, pp. 10. 21718

Eaton. "The Crisis." Its Solution—the Causes—their Removal. A Lecture delivered at Oxford, England, by permission of the Reverend, the Vice-Chancellor, March 14, 1863. By Edward Byron Eaton. *London: Heardley & Co.*, 1863. 8vo, pp. 32. 21719

Eaton (F. B.) History of Candia: (N. H.) once known as Charmingfare; with Notices of some of the Early Families. By

F. B. Eaton. *Manchester, N. H.: James O. Adams, Printer.* 1852. 8vo, pp. 151. Map. BA. 21720

Eaton (G. W.) The Malady and the Remedy. A Sermon, by G. W. Eaton, D.D., LL.D. *New York: Hillman & Lange, Printers.* 1869. 8vo, pp. 22. 21721

Also: An Address Delivered before Adelphian Society of the Hamilton Literary and Theological Institution, on Dec. 23d, 1841. ... *Hamilton.* 1842. pp. 24.—A Discourse Delivered in the Chapel of the Hamilton Literary and Theological Institution, August 10th, 1840. ... *Utica.* 1841. pp. 32.—Claims of Civil and Ecclesiastical History. ... *Utica.* 1841.— ... A Sermon, preached on the Occasion of the Ordination of Geo. W. Lasher, A.M., ... Norwalk, Conn., September 30, 1859. ... *New York: Thomas Holman, Printer.* 1860. 8vo, pp. 29. H.—The True Aim of Life: an Oration, July 24, 1849. *Schenectady.* 1850. 8vo. B.

Eaton (H.) The Early History of Palmyra, New York: A Thanksgiving Sermon, Nov. 26, 1858. By Rev. Horace Eaton. *Rochester.* 1858. 8vo, pp. 26. S. 21722

Eaton. A Treatise on the Intellectual Character, and Civil and Political Condition of the Colored People of the United States ... . By Rev. H. Eaton ... . *Boston: published by Isaac Knapp.* 1837. 8vo, pp. 54, (1). H. 21723

Eaton (H.) An Address delivered before the Associated Alumni Castleton Medical College, at their Annual Meeting, June 18th, 1845. By Horace Eaton, M.D. *Albany.* 1845. pp. 31.

See also "Vermont."

Eaton (H. H.) Plants near Troy, N. Y. 1832. S. 21725

Eaton (I.) Sermon at the Ordination of Rev. John Gano. By Rev. Isaac Eaton. *Philadelphia: Printed by Franklin and Hall.* 1755. 8vo. 21726

Eaton (J.) Memorial of Marvin Wait (1st Lieutenant Eighth Regiment C. V.) Killed at the Battle of Antietam, September 17th, 1862. Written by Jacob Eaton ... . *New Haven: Thomas J. Stafford, printer.* 1863. 8vo, pp. 16. 21727

Eaton (J.) Final Report of Freedmen Schools in the Department of Tennessee and Arkansas, lately under the supervision of Colonel John Eaton, Jr. 1864–5. *Vicksburg, (Miss.): Freedmen Press.* 1865. 8vo, pp. 19. 21728

[Eaton.] Report of the General Superintendent of Freedmen Department of the Tennessee and State of Arkansas for 1864. *Memphis, Tenn.* 1865. 8vo, pp. 98. H. 21729

Eaton (J. H.) Candid Appeal to the American Public, in Reply to Messrs. Ingham, Branch, and Berrien, on the Dissolution of the late Cabinet. By John H. Eaton. *City of Washington: Printed at the Globe Office.* 1831. 8vo, pp. 55. BA., S.

Eaton. The Life of Andrew Jackson, Major General in the Service of the United States: comprising a History of the War in the South, from the Commencement of the Creek Campaign, to the Termination of Hostilities before New Orleans. Commenced by John Reid ... . Completed by John Henry Eaton. *Philadelphia: M. Carey and Son.* 1817. 8vo, pp. 425. BA. + [Second Edition.] *Philadelphia: Samuel F. Bradford.* 1824. 8vo, pp. 468. Portrait. C. + Third Edition. Revised and Corrected by the Author. *Philadelphia: M'Carty & Davis.* 1828. 12mo, pp. 335. 21731

There is no mention of Reid in the titles of the second and third editions.

Eaton. Some Account of General Jackson, drawn up from the Hon. Mr. Eaton's very Circumstantial Narrative, and other Well-Established Information respecting him. By a Gentleman of the Baltimore Bar. ... *Baltimore: Henry Vicary.* 1828. 8vo, pp. 272. 21732

Also: Letter addressed to John Henry Eaton, December 16, 1818. *Knoxville, Tenn.* 1819.

Eaton (J.) Some short Account of the Life and Character of Rev. Joshua Eaton. *Boston.* 1773. 8vo. 21733

Eaton (J.) An Account of the Wonderful Pedestrian, Josiah Eaton, who, in his Seventy-Seventh Year, performed the Extraordinary Feat of Walking One Thousand Miles in One Thousand Successive Hours. ... *New York.* 1846. 8vo, pp. 21.

Eaton (M.) A History of Twenty Years of Dr. G. B. Champlin's Life; or, a Reproof to Heedless Youth. Together with a System of Correspondence, tending to Matrimony. Published by Moses Eaton. *Geneva, N. Y.: Printed for the Editor.* 1822. 12mo, pp. 173. 21735

Eaton (P.) A Discourse delivered at the Dedication of a New House of Worship, at West Boxford, Nov. 22, 1843. By Rev. Peter Eaton, D.D. ... *Andover: printed by Allen, Morrill, and Wardwell.* 1844. 8vo, pp. 24. H. 21736

Eaton. A Sermon, delivered ... on the Anniversary Election, May 26, 1819. By Rev. Peter Eaton, Minister of a Church

in Boxford. *Printed by Russell and Gardner, for Benjamin Russell.* 1819. 8vo, pp. 25. BA. 21737

Also: An Address delivered before the Essex Agricultural Society, at ... Topsfield, Oct. 2, 1822. ... *Salem.* 1823. 8vo, pp. 60. BA., N., W.—Sermon at Boxford, Thanksgiving, November 28, 1799. ... *Haverhill.* 1799. pp. 24. N.—Two Sermons, delivered at Haverhill First Parish, October 19, 1806. ... *Haverhill.* 1806. 8vo, pp. 32. N.—A Sermon, delivered at Topsfield, Mass., June 20, 1815, before the Moral Society of Boxford and Topsfield. ... . *Andover: printed by Flagg and Gould.* 1816. 8vo, pp. 22. BA.—Sermon at the Installation of Humphrey C. Perley, at Beverly, Mass., Dec. 2, 1819. ... *Salem.* [n. d.] 8vo.—A Sermon delivered at the Interment of the Hon. Jacob Abbot, of Brunswick, Maine. *Brunswick: Joseph Griffin, Printer.* 1820. 8vo, pp. 20. BA.—A Sermon delivered in Boxford, April 19, 1829 [on Divisions in the Christian Church]. ... *Haverhill.* 1829. 8vo, pp. 16.

Eaton (R.) A Geography of Pennsylvania for the Use of Schools. By Rebecca Eaton. *Philadelphia.* 1835. 12mo. + Second Edition. *Philadelphia: Edward C. Biddle.* 1837. 12mo.

Eaton (S. J. M.) History of the Presbytery of Erie; with Biographical Sketches of all its Ministers, and Historical Sketches of its Churches. By Rev. Samuel J. W. Eaton. *New York: Hurd & Houghton.* 1868. 12mo, pp. xv, 463. C. 21739

Eaton. Petroleum: a History of the Oil Regions of Venango, County Pa.; its Resources, Mode of Development, and Value, &c. &c. With a Map. By Rev. S. J. M. Eaton. *Philadelphia: J. P. Skelly & Co.* 1866. 12mo, pp. 299. 21740

Eaton (T.) Commemorative Sermon. A Sermon preached in the Church of the Advent, Boston, Mass., April 27, 1858, in Commemoration of the Late Rev. Asa Eaton, D.D. ... . By the Rev. Theodore Eaton, D.D. ... . *Boston: printed by John Wilson and Son.* 1858. 8vo, pp. 26. BA. 21741

Eaton (T.) Review of New York, or Rambles through the City. Original Poems. Moral, Religious, Sarcastic, and Descriptive. By Thomas Eaton. *New York: J. Low.* 1813. 18mo, pp. 144. 21742

E[aton] (W[illiam]). Interesting Detail of the Operations of the American Fleet in the Mediterranean [1804]. Communicated in a Letter from E. W., Esq. To his Friend in the County of Hampshire. *Springfield, Mas.* [sic]: *Bliss & Brewer, Printer.* [1805.] 8vo, pp. 31. BA. 21743

Eaton. The Life of the Late Gen. William Eaton. *See* [Prentiss (Charles)].

Eaton. The Speech of Gen. Wm. Eaton. Delivered in the House of Representatives of Massachusetts, The First Day of March, 1808. On the resolutions to amend the United States relative to the Removal of Judges, otherwise than by Impeachment. *Portland, (Me.:) Printed for the Subscribers.* [n. d.] 8vo.

Also: Letter to the Secretary of the Navy of the United States, dated August 9, 1805. [n. p. n. d.] 12mo. BA.—On the Death of Eaton. A Poem. pp. 4.

Eaton (William). Searsburgh Poetry. *Williamstown, [Mass.]* 1827. 8vo. 21745

Eaton. Sermon at Fitchburg, Jan. 8, 1823, at Close of his Ministry. 8vo, pp. 24. 21746

Eaton (W. W.) The Union, Past, Present, and Future. Speech at Hartford, March 3, 1860. [n. p. n. d.] 8vo. B.

Ebeling (C. D.) Amerikanische Bibliothek. Herausgegeben von C. D. Ebeling. *Leipzig: Weygandische Handlung.* 1777. 9 sheets, 8 l. 21747

Ebeling. Christoph Daniel Ebeling's Erdbeschreibung und Geschichte von Amerika. Die Vereinten Staaten von Nordamerika. *Hamburg: Hoffmann & Campe.* 1793–1816. 7 vols., 8vo. B., C., P. 21748

A continuation of Büsching's "Geography." Contents: Vol. I. Einleitung von Neu England überhaupt. New Hampshire. Massachusetts; II. Rhode Island. Connecticut. New York; III. New York. New Jersey; IV. Pennsylvania; V. Delaware. Maryland; VI. Pennsylvania; VII. Virginia. Ebeling, in collecting the materials for his history of America, formed a large collection of books appertaining to his subject, which are now in the library of Harvard University.

Ebenezer's Dream. ... the Trial of Mrs. Louisa Williams, for an Assault and Battery upon Mr. Ebenezer Albin. *New York.* 1808. 8vo. 21749

Eberle (F.) Trial of Frederick Eberle and Others, at ... Philadelphia, July 1816, ... For illegally conspiring together ... to prevent the introduction of the English Language into the service of St. Michael's and Zion's Churches, belonging to the German Lutheran Congregation, in the City of Philadelphia. Taken in shorthand by James Carson. *Philadelphia.* 1817. 8vo, pp. 240. C. 21750

Eboracus, *pseudonym.* *See* [Broom (W. W.), Vol. II., No. 8375.

Ebony Idol. *New York: D. Appleton & Co.* 1860. 8vo, pp. 283. 21751

Bears on the slavery question.

Eburne (Richard). A Plain Pathway to Plantations: That is a discourse in generall, concerning the Plantations of an English people in other Countries ... With certaine motives for a present Plantation in Newfoundland above the rest. [*London:*] *Printed for John Marriott.* 1684. 4to, 4 l., pp. 120. J.C.B. 21752

A volume of great rarity. *See* Lowndes, page 709.

Eby (P.) Auf nach West Canada! Regierungsbericht über die Zustände Canada's. *Berlin (Canada).* 1854. 8vo. 21753

Eccentric Biography: or Memoirs of Remarkable Characters. *Boston.* 1804. 12mo, pp. 344. + or Sketches of Remarkable Characters ... . *Boston: Samuel Balch, Jr., Printer.* 1825. 12mo, pp. 213, (3). Engraving. BA. 21754

Contains Mather Byles, Timothy Dexter, etc.

The Eccentric Magazine; or Lives and Portraits of Remarkable Characters. *London.* 1812–13. 2 vols., 12mo. 18 Portraits. 21755

Edited by Henry Lemoine and James Caulfield. Contains an account of James Aitken, also Jack the Painter. There are copies on large paper in 4to.

Ecclesine (J. B.) American Underwriters' Manual and Insurance Directory for 1862–3. Compiled by J. B. Ecclesine. *New York: Grierson & Ecclesine.* 1862. 8vo. B. 21756

Ecclesine. A Compendium of the Laws and Decisions relating to Mobs, Riots, Invasion, Civil Commotion, Insurrection, etc., as affecting Fire Insurance Companies in the United States. *New York: Grierson & Ecclesine.* 1863. 8vo, pp. 112.

This publication grew out of the Draft Riots in New York.

Eccleston (T.) Epistle to Friends. *New York.* 1732. 18mo. 21758

Title from E. B. Corwin's catalogue.

Echaiz (J.) Horas perdidas. Poesias Mexicanas por Jesus Echaiz. *Mexico.* 1865. Sm. 4to, pp. vi, 322. 21759

Echard (L.) A most Compleat | Compendium | of | Geography, | General and Special; | Describing all the | Empires, Kingdoms, and Dominions, | in the | Whole World. | Shewing their | Bounds, Situation, Dimensions, Ancient and | Modern Names, History, Government, Religions, | Languages, Commodities, Divisions, Subdivisions, | Cities, Rivers, Mountains, Lakes, with their Arch- | bishopricks, and Universities. | In a more Plain and Easie

Method, more Compendious, | and (perhaps) more Useful than of this bigness. | To which are added, | General Rules for making a large Geography. | Very necessary for the right Understanding of the Tran- | sactions of these Times. | Collected according to the most late Discoveries, and | agreeing with the choicest and newest Maps. | By Lavrence Eachard, | of Christ's-College in Cambridge. | *London: Printed for Thomas Salusbury at the Sign of | the Temple, near Temple-Bar in Fleet-Street.* 1691. | 12mo, 9 l., pp. 168, 17. 2 Maps. + Third Edition. *London.* 1693. 16mo. 21760

Echard. The Gazetteer's, or, Newsman's Interpreter. Being a Geographical Index Of all the Empires, Kingdoms, Islands, Provinces, Peninsulas, [etc.] in Asia, Africa, and America. *London.* 1707. 12mo. W. + Sixth Edition. *London: J. & J. Knapton.* 1732. 16mo, pp. 137, 113 l. BA., C. 21761

Echasseriaux ainé. Rapport au nom de la commission chargée de présenter les lois organiques de la constitution dans les colonies, et les mesures de législation et de politique pour opérer leur rétablissement. [*Paris:*] *l'imprimerie nationale. An* 6. [1798.] 8vo, pp. 46. J.C.B. 21762

[Echavarry (Ibañez de).] Histoire du Paraguay sous les Jésuites, et de la royauté qu'ils y ont exercée pendant un siècle et demi, ouvrage qui peut servir de suite à l'histoire philosophique et politique des établissements et du commerce des Européens dans les deux Indes, orné d'une grande carte du Paraguay, du Chili, etc. *Amsterdam et Leipzig: Arkstée et Merkus.* 1780. 3 vols., 8vo, 3 l., pp. 368, Map; 2 l., pp. 328; 1 l., pp. 426.

A work of some rarity. It is mostly a translation of Vol. IV. of Cardenas' "Coleccion de Documentos." The third volume contains "Journal de la guerre jésuitique." *See* Rich, I. 290, and Leclerc's catalogue.

Echave (B. de). Discursos de la Antiguedad de la Lengua Cantabra Bascongada, compuestos por Balth. de Echave natural de la villa de Cumaya en la Provincia de Guipuzcoa, y vezino de Mexico. *Mexico.* 1607. 4to. 21764

Title inserted for the imprint; from Thorpe's catalogue, where it is priced at £3 3s.

Echave y Assu (D. F.), La Estrella de Lima convertida en Sol sobre svs tres coronas el B. Toribio Alfonso Magrobexo, sv segvndo arzobispo: Celebrado con epitalamios sacros, y solemnes cultos, por su esposa la iglesia metropolitana de Lima ... Descripcion sacro politica de las grandezas de la ciudad de

Lima, y compendio historico eclesiastico de su iglesia. Por D. Francisco Echave y Assu, Corregidor de Lima. *Amberes: Juan Baptista Verdussen.* 1688. 4to, Engraved Title, 10 l., pp. 381.

This rare volume was unknown to Antonio. *See* Leclerc's catalogue for a list of its contents.

Echeagaray (*General*). Apuntaciones para su defensa, escritas por el mismo. *Guanajuato.* 1861. 4to, pp. 62. 21766

Echeagaray (Martin). Declaracion del Quadrante de las Catedrales de Indias. Con nuevas reglas para facilitar sus cuentas. *Megico: Rodriguez Lupercio.* 1682. 4to. 21767

Echegoyen (J.) Confesion pública por D. Juan Echegoyen. [*Habana:*] *Imprenta de Palmer é hijo.* 1821. 4to. 21768

Echenique. El general Echenique, presidente despojado del Peru, en su vindicacion. *New York.* 1855. 8vo, pp. 148.

Echevelar (M. de). Instruccion exacta y util de las derotas y navegaciones, que se executan en todas tiempos en la America Septentrional de unos portos à otros. Por D. Manuel de Echevelar. *Cadiz.* 1753. 4to, 2 l., pp. 36. 21770

See Nodal's "Relacion" for another edition.

Echeverria (D. M.) Contestacion del epílogo de los pasages históricos &c. del P. Dr. D. Manuel Echeverría. *Imprenta del Gobierno.* 1812. 4to. 21771

Echeverria (E.) Dogma socialista de la asociacion mayo precedido de una ojeada retrospectiva sobre el movimiento intelectual en la Plata desde el ano 37. Por Estevan Echeverria *Montevideo.* 1846. 8vo, pp. civ, 88. 21772

Echeverria. Insurreccion del Sud de la provincia de Buenos Aires. En Octubre de 1839. Poema (con notas y documentos) por Estevan Echeverria. *Buenos Aires.* 1854. 8vo, pp. 116.

Echeverria (Juan Nepomuceno de). Cuaderno primero y segundo para comerciantes en oro y plata pasta, corregido y aumentado con mas de 1350 calculos. *Mexico: Imprenta a cargo de Tomas Uribe y Alcalde.* 1830. Folio, pp. 20, 14. 21774

Echeverria (M.) Primera carta del P. D. Manuel Echeverría y Peñalver, en contestacion á la publicada por el caballero D. Nicolás Peñalver y por el Sr. Conde de Sta. María de Loreto su hijo, en fecha 15 de Setiembre último. *Habana: officina de Arazoza y Soler.* 1813. 4to, pp. 17. 21775

Also: Continuacion á la correspondencia entre el uno y el otro; respuesta por el Dr. D. Manuel de Echeverria. *Imprenta del Gobierno.* 1812. — Respuesta á dicho papel por el Dr. Echeverria. *Imprenta del Gobierno.* 1812. *See also* Peñalver (N.)

ECHEVERRIA Y VEITIA (M. F. de). Baluartes de Mexico. Descripcion historico de las cuatro milagrosas imogenes de N. S. que se veneran en la ciudad de Mexico. Obra póstuma, dada á luz por A. M. de San José. *Méjico.* 1820. 4to. 21776

ECHEVERZ (Pedro Ignacio de). Relacion Historica de la Fundacion de este Convento de Nuestra Señora del Pilar, etc. *Mexico.* 1793. 4to. 21777

The Echo. [*New York:*] *Printed at the Porcupine Press, by Pasquin Petronius.* 1807. pp. xv, 331, 5 l. 8 Plates. BA.

The authors were, Alsop, Dwight, Cogswell, Hopkins, and Trumbull.

Echo. A Collection of Songs. *Brookfield, Mass.* [n. d.] 12mo. W. 21779

Echo: or, A Satirical Poem on the Virtuous Ten, and other Celebrated Characters. *Hartford.* 1795. 12mo. W. 21780

The Echo from the Army. What our Soldiers say about the Copperheads. *New York: Printed by Wm. C. Bryant & Co.* 1863. 8vo, pp. 12. + *New York.* 1865. 8vo, pp. 7. 21781

Loyal Publication Society, No. 2.

The Echo, or the Battle of the Shells. A Satirical Parody in Rhyme of the celebrated Letters of Messrs. Guthrie, Bronson & O'Conor, together with the Original Letters. By John Piper, Esq., &c. &c. [n. p. 1854.] 8vo, pp. 44. 21782

Echoes from the Cabinet; comprising the Constitution of the United States; Declaration of Independence; Fugitive Slave Bills of 1793 & 1850; Missouri Compromise; the Kansas and Nebraska Bill of 1854. Also, the Fac-simile Autograph Names of the Signers of the Declaration of Independence. *Boston: Thayer & Eldridge.* 1860. 18mo, pp. 108. 21783

Echoes from the Living Graves. By a Convict in Sing Sing State Prison. With a Sketch of the Author's Life, etc. *New York.* 1869. 16mo, pp. 250. 21783*a*

Echoes from the South; comprising the most important Speeches, Proclamations and Public Acts emanating from the South during the Late War. *New York: E. B. Treat & Co.* [1866.] 12mo, pp. 211. BA., C. 21784

ECHOLS (John). Report of Brigadier General Echols, of the Battle of Droop Mountain, Published by order of Congress. *Richmond: R. M. Smith, Public Printer.* 1864. 8vo, pp. 16.

ECKFELDT (J. R.), *and* DU BOIS (W. E.) American Coins and Coinage, Gold and Silver Coins, Counterfeit Coins and Bullions with Mint Values. By Jacob R. Eckfeldt and William E. Du Bois. *Philadelphia.* 1850. 12mo, pp. 60. + *New York.* 1852. 8vo, pp. 73. Plates. 21786

ECKFELDT *and* DU BOIS. A Manual of Gold and Silver Coins of all Nations, Struck within the Past Century: shewing their History and Legal Basis, and their Actual Weight, Fineness, and Value; chiefly from Original and Recent Assays. By Jacob R. Eckfeldt and William E. Du Bois. Illustrated by Engravings of Coins executed by the Medal-Ruling Machine, and under the Direction of Joseph Saxton, of the U. S. Mint. *Philadelphia.* 1842. 4to, pp. 226. + [*Ibid.*] 1849. BA., C. + [Another Edition.] To which is added, a Supplement to 1850, and Corrections to June, 1851. *Philadelphia.* 1851. 4to. + *Philadelphia: Published at the Assay Office of the Mint.* 1862. 4to, pp. 220. 16 Plates. 21787

ECKFELDT *and* DU BOIS. New Varieties of Gold and Silver Coins, Counterfeit Coins and Bullion, with Mint Values. Second Edition, by Jacob R. Eckfeldt and Wm. E. Du Bois, Assayers U. S. Mint. And a Brief Account of the Collection of Coins belonging to the Mint. Second Edition, Enlarged. By William E. Du Bois. *New York.* 1851. 8vo. BA., C. 21788

ECKLEY (J.) A Discourse before the Society for Propagating the Gospel among the Indians and Others in North America, delivered Nov. 7, 1805. By Joseph Eckley, D.D. Minister of the Old South Church in Boston. *Boston: Printed by E. Lincoln, Water Street.* 1806. 8vo, pp. 36. B., BA. 21789

ECKLEY. A Discourse delivered on the Public Thanksgiving Day, November 29, 1798. By Joseph Eckley, D.D. ... . *Boston: printed by Manning & Loring.* 1798. 8vo, pp. 23. H. + Second Edition. *Boston.* 1798. 8vo. H. 21790

ECKLEY A Sermon, delivered July 1, 1789. At the Installation of the Reverend Israel Evans, ... Concord, New Hampshire. By Josep Eckley, A.M. ... . *Concord: printed by George Hough.* 1789. 16mo, pp. 32. BA., H. 21791

ECKLEY. A Sermon, preached at the request of the Ancient and Honourable Artillery Company, June 4, 1792: being the Anniversary of their Election of Officers. By Joseph Eckley, A.M. ... *Boston: Samuel Hall.* MDCCXCII. 8vo. BA., W.

Also: A Discourse, delivered before the ... Boston Female Asylum, Sept. 24, 1802, being their Second Anniversary. ... *Boston.* [1802.] 8vo, pp. 22. — Sermon delivered at the Installation of the Rev. Horace Holley, ... Hollis Street, Boston. March 8, 1809. ... . *Boston: printed by J. Belcher.* 1809. 8vo, pp. 53. H. — Sketch of the Character of Thomas Dawes, being an Extract from a Funeral Sermon, delivered in January, 1809. *Boston.* 8vo.

The Eclaireur. *See* De Peyster (J. W.), Vol. V., No. 19632.

The Eclipse. [*Boston.*] 1754. 4to, pp. 8. BA., W. 21793

Against the Massachusetts Excise Bill.

Economica. *See* [Blodget (Samuel), *Jun.*], Vol. II., No. 5956.

Economical Causes of Slavery in the United States, and Obstacles to Abolition. By a South Carolinian. *London: Hardwicke.* 1857. 8vo. 21794

Ecsamen de las facultades del Gobierno sobre el destierro de los estrangeros. *Mexico.* 1826. 4to, pp. 47. 21795

ECUADOR. Almanaque para el año de 1863 compuesto por la Academia Nacion... del Ecuador. *Quita: Imprenta del Gobierno.* 1863. 21796

Aun las cuestiones de límites del Ecuador ó sea Pedro Moncayo y su nuevo folleto, sus absurdos y su mala féxe, panfleto escrito ó veces en su estilo, incluyendo curiosos asertos y acompañado de importantes documentos verídicos que por sí solos aclaran todas las cuestiones. *Lima.* 1862. 4to, pp. 58, xviii.

Ecuador und die Ecuador-Land-Compagnie. *Mannheim: Schneider.* 1862. Folio, pp. 36. 2 Maps. 21798

Memoria que presenta el Ministro de Hacienda al Congreso del Ecuador de 1841. *Quito.* 1841. 4to. 21799

Protocolo de las conferencias y notas de las comisiones del Ecuador y Nueva Granada en la cuestion sobre limites de ambos estados. *Guayaquil.* 1832. Folio, pp. xx, 42. 21800

EDDIS (W.) Letters from America, Historical and Descriptive; comprising Occurrences from 1769, to 1777, inclusive. By William Eddis, late Surveyor of the Customs, &c., at Annapolis, in Maryland. ... *London: printed for the Author.* M DCCXCII. 8vo, 25 l., pp. 455. B., BA., C. 21801

Valuable as indicating the state of public feeling anterior to the Revolution. "Mr. Eddis's letters are forty in number. The first contains an account of the country, the government, trade, manners and customs of the inhabitants, followed by others, giving an account of the progress of the war, till his departure from New York. The concluding letters narrate the difficulties and dangers which the author experienced, in consequence of his refusing to take the oath tendered him by the Americans." — *Monthly Review,* VIII. 124.

[EDDOWES (Ralph).] ... A Discourse delivered at the Opening of the Church erected by the First Society of Unitarian Christians in ... Philadelphia, ... 14th February, 1813. *Philadelphia: published by Thomas Dobson.* 1813. 8vo, pp. 39. H.

Also: An Account of the Wheat Moth or Virginia Fly. ... *Philadelphia.* 1805. 8vo. P.

EDDY (A. D.) A Discourse, delivered ... in Canandaigua, N. Y. July 4, 1826. By A. D. Eddy, ... *Canandaigua: printed by Bemis, Morse and Ward.* 8vo, pp. 24. 21803

Also: An Address, delivered before the Pennsylvania Temperance Society, at their Third Anniversary; By the Rev. A. D. Eddy, of Canandaigua, New-York. [*Philadelphia.* 1828.] 8vo, pp. 11. H. — A Discourse ... Eleventh Anniversary of the Society for the Promotion of Collegiate and Theological Education in the West, in Poughkeepsie, N. Y., October 29th, 1854. ... . *New York: J. F. Trow, Printer.* [n. d.] 8vo, pp. 40. H. — The Obligations of the Christian Citizen, with a Review of High Church Principles in relation to Civil and Religious Institutions. *New-York.* 1843. 12mo. B., S. — A Sermon occasioned by the Death of Mrs. Beulah Clarke, ... of Utica, ... Canandaigua, N. Y. February 18, 1827. ... . *New Haven: John P. Haven.* 1827. 8vo, pp. 28.

[EDDY (Caleb).] Historical Sketch of the Middlesex Canal, with Remarks for the Consideration of the Proprietors. By the Agent of the Corporation. *Boston: Samuel N. Dickinson, Printer.* 1843. 8vo, pp. 53. B., H. 21804

EDDY (D. C.) Liberty and Union, Our Country; its Pride and its Peril. A Discourse delivered in Boston, August 11, 1861. By Daniel C. Eddy, D.D. *Boston: James M. Hewes.* 1861. 8vo, pp. 32. B. 21805

EDDY. The Martyr President. A Sermon preached before the Baldwin Place Church, April 16, 1865. By Daniel C. Eddy, D.D. *Boston: Graves and Young.* 1865. 18mo, pp. 23. 21806

EDDY. Roger Williams and the Baptists. An Historical Discourse, delivered ... Dec. 2, 1860. By Daniel C. Eddy ... *Boston: F. Graves.* 1861. 12mo, pp. 146. 21807

EDDY. The Union, the Constitution and the Laws. Secession, a National Crime and Curse: a Discourse, delivered in ... Philadelphia, ... on the National Fast Day, April 30th, 1863. By Daniel C. Eddy. *Philadelphia: American Baptist Publication Society.* 1863. 8vo, pp. 35. B. 21808

Also: Heroines of the Missionary Enterprise; or Sketches of Prominent Female Missionaries. ... *Boston.* 12mo.

EDDY (John) Almanack. 1760. 21809

EDDY (R.) History of the Sixtieth Regiment New York State Volunteers, from the Commencement of its Organization In July, 1861, to its Public Reception at Ogdensburgh as a Veteran Command, January 7th, 1864. By Richard Eddy, Chaplain. *Philadelphia, Pa.: published by the Author.* 1864. 12mo, pp. xii, 360. BA., C. 21810

EDDY. "The Martyr to Liberty." Three Sermons preached in the First University Church, Philadelphia, Sunday, April 16th, Wednesday, April 19th, and Thursday, June 1st. By Richard Eddy. *Philadelphia.* 1865. 8vo, pp. 27. B. 21811

Two copies were printed on *thick* paper.

EDDY. The Necessity for Religion in Politics. A Sermon preached to the United Congregations of Universalists, in Philadelphia, in the Second Church, Thanksgiving Morning, November 26th, 1863. By Rev. Richard Eddy. *Philadelphia: King & Baird.* 1863. 8vo, pp. 20. 21812

EDDY (R. H.) Report on the Introduction of Soft Water into the City of Boston. *Boston.* 1836. 8vo, pp. 40. B., N.

EDDY (S.) Reasons offered by Samuel Eddy, Esquire, for his Opinions, to the First Baptist Church in Providence, from which he was compelled to withdraw, for Heterodoxy. Second Edition. [*Providence: Jones & Wheeler.* 1818. 8vo, pp. 19. BA. + *Baltimore.* 1819. 8vo, pp. 36. + Second Baltimore Edition. *Baltimore.* 1821. 12mo, pp. 23. + *Syracuse.* [n. d.] 8vo, pp. 24. + Fourth Edition. 1826. H. + *Boston.* 1841. 21814

EDDY. A Review of the Reasons offered by S. Eddy, Esq., for his Opinions, to the First Baptist Church in Providence, from which he was compelled to withdraw ... *Providence: Miller & Hutchins.* 1819. 8vo, pp. 12. 21815

EDDY (T.) Account of the State Prison or Penitentiary House in the City of New-York. By Thomas Eddy. *New-York.* 1801. 8vo. 21816

Also: Communication to the Mayor of New York on Prison Discipline. *New York.* 1823. 8vo. — Memoir of the late John Murray, Jun., read before the Governor of the New York Hospital, 9th Month 14th, 1819. ... *New York.* 1819. 8vo, pp. 27, iii. + *New York: William Alexander.* 1819. 8vo, pp. 36. BA.

EDDY (T. M.) Abraham Lincoln. A Memorial Address. By Rev. T. M. Eddy, D.D. Delivered at a Union Meeting, held in the Presbyterian Church, Waukegan, Illinois, April 19, 1865. ... *Chicago: Printed at the Methodist Book Depository.* 1865. 8vo, pp. 24. 21817

EDDY. The Patriotism of Illinois. A Record of the Civil and Military History of the State in the Union, with a History of the Campaigns in which Illinois Soldiers have been conspicuous, Sketches of Distinguished Officers, the Roll of the Illustrious Dead, Movements of the Sanitary and Christian Commissions. By T. M. Eddy, D.D., ... *Chicago: Clarke & Co.* 2 vols., 8vo, pp. 608. 21818

Also: The Elements of Leadership. An Address ... Iowa State University ... June 17, 1863. ... *Chicago: Methodist Book Depository.* 1863. 8vo, pp. 23. B.

[EDDY (Zachariah).] Record of the First Church of Christ in Middleborough, Plymouth Co., Mass., with Notices of other Churches in that Town. *Boston: C. C. P. Moody.* 1852. 8vo, pp. 32. 21819

EDDY. Secession; Shall it be Peace or War? A Fast Day Sermon, delivered in Northampton, April 4, 1861. By Zachariah Eddy. *Northampton: Trumbull & Gere.* 1861. 8vo, pp. 21. 21820

Also: Review of the Berkley Case [Ecclesiastical Council, Mass. 1828]. By Zach. Eddy. 8vo, pp. 28. S.

EDE (Charles R. N.) Warm Hearts in Cold Regions. A Tale of Arctic Life. With Illustrations. *London: T. Nelson & Son.* 1863. Fcap 8vo, pp. 192. 21821

EDELMAN (G. W.) Guide to the Value of California Gold. By George W. Edelman, U. S. Mint. *Philadelphia.* 1850. 8vo.

EDEN (F. M.) Address on the Maritime Rights of Great Britain, by Sir Frederick Morton Eden. *London: Richardson.* 1808. 8vo, pp. 137. + Second Edition. [*Ibid.*] 1808. 8vo, pp. 139. 21823

See "M. Rev.," LVI. 105.

EDEN. Eight Letters on ... the Commerce and Manufactures of Great Britain. By Sir Frederick Morton Eden, Bart. *London: J. Wright.* 1802. 8vo, pp. vi, (2), 132. + Second Edition. [*Ibid.*] 1802. 21824

Refers to the state of St. Domingo, the trade with the conquered islands in the West Indies, trade with the British colonies, etc.

EDEN (J.) The Mt. Holyoke Hand-Book, and Tourist's Guide for Northampton, and its Vicinity. By John Eden. *Northampton, Mass.: Hopkins, Bridgman & Co.* 1851. 18mo, pp. 72. H. 21825

EDEN (Richard). Treaties of the New India, with other Newfoundlandes and Ilandes. *London: E. Sutton.* 1553. 4to.

Black letter. Title from Lowndes. Caldecott's copy sold for £4 14s. 6d. An extremely rare volume; it is a translation from Munster. *See* Vol. I., No. 1561–1563.

EDEN (W.) Four Letters to the Earl of Carlisle from William Eden, Esq., on certain Perversions of Political Reasonings; War between Great Britain and the Combined Powers of France and Spain, etc. *Edinburgh.* MDCCLXXIX. 8vo, pp. 86. J.C.B. + The Second Edition. *London.* MDCCLXXIX. 8vo, 2 l., pp. 163.

He recommends perseverance in the war "till the colonies are reduced." *See* "M. Rev.," LXI. 471.

EDEN. A Fifth Letter to the Earl of Carlisle, from William Eden, Esq., on certain Revene Laws and Regulations connected with the Interests of Commerce; and on Public Œconomy. *London: B. White.* MDCCLXXX. 8vo, pp. 71. J.C.B. 21828

Eden in Virginia, von der Helvetischen Societet Erkaufte, 33. 400 Jucharten Land. *Ao* 1736. 4to. Map. C. 21829

EDER (F. X.) Descriptio provinciæ Moxitarum in regno Peruano, quam e scriptis posthumis Franc. Xav. Eder, e Soc. Jesu annis XV. sacri apud eosdem Curionis digessit, expolivit, et adnotatiunculis illustravit Abb. et Consil. Reg. Mako ... *Budae: typis Universitatis.* 1791. 8vo, pp. xviii, 385. Map, and 7 Plates. C., J.C.B. 21830

EDES (Edward H.) Sermons, with a Sketch of his Life. *Boston: Benj. H. Greene.* 1846. 12mo. B. 21831

EDES (Henry). Sermon at the Ordination of Shearjashub Townsend. July 2, 1817. By H. Edes. *Providence, R. I.* 1817. 8vo. W. 21832

Edes and Gill's North-American Almanack and Massachusetts Register for 1770. *Boston.* 1770. 8vo. Plate by Revere. Continued in 12mo. 21833

These almanacs for the Revolutionary period are rare and interesting.

EDES (R. S.) Discourse delivered at Bolton, Dec. 26, 1844, at the Re-dedication of the Church belonging to the First Parish. By Richard S. Edes ... . *Worcester: printed by Henry J. Howland.* 1845. 8vo, pp. 15. H. 21834

EDES. Discourse preached March 21st, 1844, at the Funeral of the Late Rev. Isaac Allen ... by Richard S. Edes ... . *Worcester: printed by Jonathan L. Estey.* 1844. 8vo, pp. 20. H.

EDGAR (C. H.) The Curse of Canaan rightfully interpreted; and Kindred Topics. Three Lectures delivered in ... Easton, Pa., January and February, 1862. By ... Rev. Cornelius H. Edgar. *New York: Baker & Godwin, Printers.* 1862. 8vo, pp. 48. H. 21836

EDGAR. Earthquakes: Instrumentalities in the Divine Government. A Sermon preached in Easton, Pennsylvania, November 29, 1860. *Easton, (Penn.): Lewis Gordon.* 1860. 8vo, pp. 19. 21837

EDGAR. Josiah and Lincoln, the Great Reformers. A Tribute to the Worth and Work of our Martyr President, delivered in the Reformed Dutch Church, Easton, Pa., On Fast Day, June 1, 1865. By the Pastor, Rev. Cornelius H. Edgar. *Easton, Pa.: Lewis Gordon, Printer.* 1865. 8vo, pp. 12, Cover, 2 leaves. 21838

EDGAR. Three Sermons by Rev. C. H. Edgar, D.D., Occasioned by the Assassination of President Lincoln, Preached in the Reformed Dutch Church, Easton, Pa., April 16th, 19th, and 23d, 1865. *Easton, Pa.: "Free Press" Office.* 1865. 8vo, pp. 20, Cover, 2 l. 21839

Also: Germs of Growth; or Elements and Evidences of National Permanence. A Sermon preached in Easton, Pennsylvania, November 28, 1861. ... *New York: Baker & Godwin, Printers.* 1861. 8vo, pp. 30. — God's Help the Ground of Hope for our

Country. A Sermon preached on the Day of National Thanksgiving, November 24, 1864, at Easton, Pennsylvania. ... *New York: Baker & Godwin, Printers.* 1864. 8vo, pp. 25. — ... A Sermon preached on the Day of Thanksgiving, November 28, 1861, in the Reformed Dutch Church, Easton, Pa. ... *New York: Baker & Godwin, Printers.* 1861. 8vo, pp. 31. H. — ... A Sermon preached on the Day of National Thanksgiving, November 24, 1864, in the Reformed Dutch Church, Easton, Pa., ... *New York: Baker & Godwin, Printers.* 1864. 8vo, pp. 25. H.

EDGAR (J. G.) Footprints of Famous Men, designed as Incitements to Intellectual Industry. By John G. Edgar. *London.* 1856. 12mo, pp. viii, 376. 21840

George Washington is the subject of the first memoir.

EDGAR (Patrick Nisbett). The American Race-Turf Register, Sportsman's Herald, and General Stud-Book: containing the Pedigrees of the most Celebrated Horses, Mares, and Geldings, that have distinguished themselves on the American Turf, &c. *New-York.* 1833. 2 vols., 8vo. C. 21841

EDGE (F. M.) The Alabama and the Kearsarge. An Account of the Naval Engagement in the British Channel, on Sunday, June 19th, 1864, from Information furnished to the Writer by the Wounded and Paroled Prisoners of the Confederate Privateer Alabama, the Officers of the United States Sloop of War, Kearsarge, and Citizens of Cherbourg. By Frederick Milnes Edge. *London.* 1864. 16mo, pp. 48. B., BA. 21842

Reprinted as:

EDGE. An Englishman's View of the Battle between the Alabama and the Kearsarge. ... *New York: Anson D. F. Randolph.* 1864. 8vo, pp. 48. H. 21843

EDGE. The Destruction of the American Carrying Trade, A Letter to Earl Russell, K.G., Her Majesty's Principal Secretary of State for the Foreign Department. By Frederick Milnes Edge. *London: William Ridgway.* 1863. 8vo, pp. 27. B., BA.

EDGE. England's Danger and her Safety. A Letter to Earl Russell, K.G. ... By Frederick Milnes Edge. *London: William Ridgway.* 1864. 8vo, pp. 31. B., C. 21845

EDGE. Major General McClellan and the Campaign on the Yorktown Peninsula. By Frederick Milnes Edge ... late Special Correspondent of the Morning Star with the Armies of the United States. With a Map of the Peninsula, drawn expressly for this Work by James Wyld ... . *London: Trübner & Co.* 1865. 8vo, pp. iv., 203. BA. + *New York: Loyal Pub. Society, No.* 81. 1865. 8vo, pp. 201. B., C. 21846

EDGE. President Lincoln's Successor. By Frederick Milnes Edge. *London: William Ridgway.* 1864. 8vo, pp. 34. BA., H.

Also: Great Britain and the United States. A Letter to the Right Honourable William Ewart Gladstone, M.P. ... . By Frederick Milnes Edge. *London.* 1869. 8vo, pp. 38. H. — Slavery Doomed; or the Contest between Free and Slave Labour in the United States. *London: Smith & Elder.* 1860. Post 8vo. B., BA., C. — Whom do the English Tories Wish Elected to the Présidency ... . *New York: Loyal Pub. Society, No.* 69. 1864. 8vo, pp. 4.

Edge Hill, or the Family of the Fitzroyals. By a Virginian. *Richmond.* 1828. 2 vols., 12mo, pp. iv, 222; 224. 21848

EDGERTON (J. K.) Reconstruction. Speech of Hon. J. K. Edgerton, of Indiana, in the House ... February 20, 1865. 8vo, pp. 16. H. 21849

Also: The Relations of the Federal Government to Slavery. Speech ... at Fort Wayne, Ind., October 30th, 1860. *Fort Wayne.* 1861. 8vo, pp. 64. H.

EDGERTON (S.) Speech of Hon. Sidney Edgerton, of Ohio, on the New Conspiracy; delivered in the House ... May 28, 1862. *Washington.* 1862. 8vo, pp. 15. H. 21850

EDGERTON (W.) A History of the Separation in Indiana Yearly Meeting of Friends; which took place in the Winter of 1842 and 1843, on the Anti-Slavery Question; containing a Brief Account of the Rise, Spread, and Final Adoption by the Society of its Testimony against Slavery; ... By Walter Edgerton ... *Cincinnati: Achilles Pugh, Printer.* 21851

EDGEVILLE (E.) Castine. By Edward Edgeville. Southern Field and Fireside Novellette, No. 2. New Series. *Raleigh: Wm. B. Smith & Co.* 1865. 8vo, pp. (2), 32. BA. 21852

Edifying and Curious Letters of some Missioners, of the Society of Jesus, from Foreign Missions. *Printed in the Year* 1707. 18mo, 7 l., pp. 258, Table, 2 l. 21853

A translation of the famous "Lettres édifiantes et curieuses." One letter relates to South America.

The Edinburgh Review, or Critical Journal: for Oct. 1802 ...... Jan. 1803. ... *Edinburgh.* 1803. 8vo. Continued.

Contains many articles on American topics.

The Edinburgh Review and the West Indies; with Observations on the Pamphlets of Messrs. Stephen, Macaulay, &c. and Remarks on the Slave Registry Bill. By Colonist. ... *Glasgow: John Smith and Son.* 1816. 8vo, Half-Title, pp. xv, (1), 360.

EDINGTON (*Mr.*) Speech of Mr. Edington in the House of Delegates of Virginia on the Tariff. *Steubenville.* 1829. 12mo.

Edit du congrès de Etats-Unis pour les terres dépendantes des Etats, situés au nord-ouest de la Rivière de l'Ohio. *Paris.* 1789. 8vo. 21857

Edit du Roi; portant Création des Princes, Ducs, Comtes, Barons, et Chevaliers du Royaume. *Cap Henry.* 1811. 4to, pp. 5. 21858

Edit du Roy pour l'Establissement de la Compagnie des Indes Occidentalles. *Paris.* 1664. 4to. 21859

Edit du Roy, Qui ordonne une fabrication d'Espices d'Argent, particulières pour les Isles du Vent de l'Amérique. Donné à Versailles du mois de Decembre 1730. ... *A Paris: Chez la Veuve Saugrain & Pierre Prault, Imprimerie des Fermes du Roy, Quay de Gèvres, au Paradis.* 1731. 4to, pp. 4. 21860

EDMANDS (J. C.) Address in Defence of J. Cushing Edmands, Late Colonel 32d Massachusetts Infantry Volunteers, to the General Court Martial ... sitting at Annapolis, Maryland, September, 1865. ... *Washington: printed by R. A. Waters.* 1865. 8vo, pp. 13. H. 21861

EDMANDS (J. W.) Speech of J. Wiley Edmands, of Massachusetts, delivered in the House ... May 20, 1854, on the Nebraska and Kansas Territorial Bill. *Washington, D. C.* 1854. 8vo, pp. 15. H. 21862

EDMERTON (J.) A Frontispiece for a Meeting House. By Jonathan Edmerton of Malden. [n. p. 1812.] 8vo, pp. 12.

EDMESTON (*Lieut.-Col.*) Remarks on his Services in America. [n. p. n. d.] 4to, pp. 2. 21864

EDMONDS (C. R.) The Life and Times of General Washington. By Cyrus R. Edmonds. ... *London: Thomas Tegg and Son.* MDCCCXXXV. 2 vols., fcap 8vo, pp. xvi, 365; x, 365. 4 Plates, and Facsimiles. BA. + Third Edition. *London.* 1839. 2 vols., 18mo. + [*Ibid.*] 1842. 21865

Forms Vols. LIII. and LIV. of the "Family Library."

EDMONDS (F. W.) Defence of Francis W. Edmonds, late Cashier Of the Mechanics' Bank, ... *New York: McSpedon & Baker, Printers.* 1855. 8vo, pp. 55. S. 21866

EDMONDS (J. W.) An Address on the Constitution and Code of Procedure and the Modifications of the Law effected thereby. Delivered on the 7th July, 1848, ... by the Honorable John Worth Edmonds ... . *New York.* 1848. pp. vii, 47. 21867

EDMONDS. Reconstruction of the Union, in a Letter to Hon. E. D. Morgan, U. S. Senator from New York. From Judge Edmonds. *New York: American News Company.* 1867. 8vo, pp. v, 89. 21868

Also: Report of John W. Edmonds, United States Commissioner on the Claims of Creditors of the Potawatamie Indians of the Wabash. *New York: Scatcherd & Adams.* 1836–37. 8vo, pp. 95. C., N., S. — Reports of the United States Commissioner, upon the Disturbance of the Potawatamie Payment, September, 1836. *New York.* 1837. 8vo, pp. 47. C., N.

EDMONDS (S. E. E.) Nurse and Spy in the Union Army — comprising the Adventures and Experiences of a Woman in Hospitals, Camps and Battle-Fields. By S. Emma E. Edmonds. *Hartford: S. Williams & Co.* 1866. 8vo, pp. 84. Illustrated.

EDMUNDS (E.) A Sermon delivered at the Dedication of the Christian Church ... Boston, September 29, 1853, by Edward Edmunds ... . *Boston: printed by Beals, Greene & Co.* 1853. 16mo, pp. 32. H. 21870

EDMUNDS (G. F.) Enforcement of Fourteenth Amendment. Speech of Hon. George F. Edmunds, of Vermont, in the Senate ... April 14, 1871. [n. p. n. d.] 8vo, pp. 24. H. 21871

Also: Impeachment of the President. Opinion of Mr. Edmunds, of Vermont, in the Senate ... May 11, 1868. [n. p. n. d.] 8vo, pp. 16. H. — Speech ... on ... pledging the Faith of the United States to the Payment of the Public Debt in Coin ... December 4 and 5, 1867. *Washington.* 1867. 8vo, pp. 20. H.

EDMUNDS (L.) A Short Sketch of the Life of our dear Friend, John Horn: with some of his Expressions towards his close. By Lucy Edmunds. Also, Considerations on the African Slave Trade and The use of West India Produce. First published by him in his last illness. *London: George Cooke.* 1806. 12mo, pp. 36. 21872

EDMUNDSON (W.) A Journal of the Life, Travels, Sufferings, and a Labour of Love In the Work of the Ministry, of that Worthy Elder, and Faithful Servant of Jesus Christ, William Edmundson, Who Departed this Life, the 31st of the 6th Month, 1712. *London.* 1713. 4to. + *Dublin: Printed by Samuel Fairbrother.* 1715. 4to, 52½ sheets. + *London: Assigns of J. Soule.* 1715. 8vo, Title, pp. lvi, 340. BA. + [Reprinted, and

called] Second Edition. *London: Mary Hinde.* 1774. 8vo, pp. lxxiv, 371. + [Reprinted, and called] Third Edition. *Dublin: Christopher Bentham.* 1820. 8vo. + *London: Harvey and Darton.* 1829. Rl. 12mo, 16½ sheets. 21873

Reprinted in Vol. II. of "The Friends' Library," edited by Wm. and Thos. Evans, *Philadelphia.* 1838, and in Vol. IV. of "The Friends' Library," edited by Wm. Allen, *Lindfield.* 1833. Reprinted and abridged, second edition, *Lindfield.* 1837. Edmundson was a distinguished preacher of the Society of Friends, and made three voyages to America previous to the year 1700. In 1671, "he had movings of the spirit" to come to America, and sailed in company with George Fox. He visited the West Indies, Virginia, Maryland, New Jersey, New York, and New England.

EDSALL (B. B.) The First Sussex Centenary, containing the Addresses of Benj. B. Edsall, Esq., and Rev. T. F. Tuttle. With Notes, Appendix, &c. *Newark: A. L. Dennis & Brother, Printers.* 1853. 8vo, pp. 102, Errata, 12 lines. 21874

EDSALL (J.) Incidents in the Life of John Edsall. [Edited by J. D. P.] *Catskill: the Author.* 1831. 16mo, pp. 156. C.

EDSON (T.) An Address delivered at the Opening of the Colburn Grammar School, in Lowell, December 13, 1848. By Rev. Theodore Edson, D.D. *Lowell.* 1849. 12mo, pp. 37. H.

EDSON. The Commemoration of the Fortieth Anniversary of the Consecration of St. Anne's Church, Lowell, March 19, 1865. The Sermon by the Rev. Theodore Edson, D.D. ... . *Lowell: Thomas J. James, Printer.* 1865. 8vo, pp. 27. B., H.

EDSON. Memoir of Warren Colburn, written for the American Journal of Education. By Theodore Edson, D.D. *Boston: Brown, Taggard & Chase.* MDCCCLVI. Sm. 8vo, pp. 27. B., BA.

Also: Address to the Congregation of St. Anne's Church at Lowell, ... 1829. 8vo. — Lecture in St. Anne's Church, Nov. 24. *Lowell.* 1844. 8vo. — A Sermon, .. St. Anne's Church, Lowell, ... March 18, 1855, in Commemoration of the Thirtieth Anniversary of the Consecration of said Church. ... Also, a Notice of the Commemoration. *Lowell.* 1855. 8vo, pp. 24. H. — ... A Sermon preached at the Convention of the Protestant Episcopal Church of the Eastern Diocese, September 26, 1827. ... . *Boston.* 1827. 12mo, pp. 21. H. — ... A Sermon ... April 27, 1858, in Commemoration of the Late Rev. Asa Easton, D.D. ... . *Boston: printed by John Wilson and Son.* 1858. 8vo, pp. 26. BA., H.

EDUCATION. An Act to Appropriate the Income of the United States Deposite Fund to the Purposes of Education and the Diffusion of Knowledge. *Albany.* 1838. 8vo. 21879

American Education Society. ... Report, 1816. *Andover, Mass.* 1816. 8vo. Continued. 21880

Second Annual Report of the General Agent of the Board of National Popular Education, with the Constitution of the Board. *Cleveland.* 1840. pp. 50. Continued. 21881

An Education of the XVIIth Century. "A Model for the Maintaining of Students of Choice Abilities at the University." *London.* 1648. 8vo, pp. 8. + *Boston, reprinted.* [n. d.] 21882

Sur l'Éducation Nationale dans les États-Unis d'Amérique. Seconde édition. *Paris.* 1812. 8vo, pp. 159. S. 21883

Report of the Commissioner of Education, with Circulars and Documents accompanying the same; submitted to the Senate and House of Representatives, June 2, 1868. *Washington: Government Printing Office.* 1868. 8vo, pp. lx, 856. Continued. B., C. 21884

The Education of Teachers in the South: Embracing a Letter from Prof. Edw'd S. Joynes to Geo. P. Tayloe, Esq., And a Plan for the Foundation of A Normal School In Hollins' Institute, Virginia; To which is added A Catalogue of the Institute, for the Sessions of 1863–4. *Lynchburg, Virginia.* 1864. 8vo, pp. 32. 21885

Also: National Department of Education. Official Circulars, ... 1867. 8vo. Continued. — The System of Public Education adopted by the Town of Boston. [n. p. 17—.] 8vo. BA. — Technical Instruction. Special Report of the Commissioner of Education. House of Representatives, January 19th, 1870. *Washington.* 1870. Rl. 8vo, pp. 784.

EDWARD (D. B.) The History of Texas; or, the Emigrant's, Farmer's and Politician's Guide to the Character, Climate, Soil and Productions of that Country: geographically arranged from Personal Observation and Experience. By David B. Edward. ... *Cincinnati: J. A. James & Co.* 1836. 12mo, pp. 336. Map. H., C. 21886

EDWARD (W. N.) Memoir of Nathaniel Macon. By W. Edward. *Raleigh.* 1862. 8vo. BA. 21887

EDWARDS (B. B.) Address delivered on the Day of the National Fast, May 14, 1841, ... Andover. By B. B. Edwards, ... *Andover: William Peirce.* 1841. 8vo, pp. 30. 21888

Relates to the death of W. H. Harrison.

EDWARDS. Address delivered at Southampton, Mass., at the Centennial Celebration of the Incorporation of the Town, July 23, 1841. By Bela Bates Edwards, D.D. *Andover.* 1841. 8vo, pp. 54. 21889

EDWARDS. Biography of Self-Taught Men. By Bela Bates Edwards. *Boston.* 1832. 12mo. + [Continued by S. G. B.] *Boston.* 1846–7. + With an Introductory Essay. *Boston: Tilton & Co.* 1859. 16mo, pp. 642. 21890

EDWARDS. The Missionary Gazetteer; comprising a Geographical and Statistical Account of the Various Stations of the American and Foreign Protestant Missionary Societies of all Denominations, with their Progress in Evangelization and Civilization. By B. B. Edwards. *Boston: William Hyde & Co.* 1832. 12mo, pp. 431. 21891

[EDWARDS.] Sketch of the Life and Character of Rev. Elias Cornelius. *Boston.* 1832. 8vo. W. + Second Edition. 1834. 12mo. 21892

Also: Discourse delivered August 18, 1847, at the Ordination of Mr. Daniel T. Fisk, as Pastor of the Congregational Church, Belleville, Newburg, Mass. ... . *Andover.* 1848. 8vo, pp. 20. H. — The Writings of Prof. Bela Bates Edwards. With a Memoir by the Rev. E. A. Park. *Boston.* 1853. 12mo.

[EDWARDS (Bryan).] An Account of the Proceedings of the Governor and Assembly of Jamaica in regard to the Maroon Negroes; published by Order of the Assembly. To which is prefixed, An Introductory Account, containing Observations on the Disposition, Character, Manners, and Habits of Life of the Maroons, and a Detail of the Origin, Progress, and Termination of the Late War between those People and the White Inhabitants. *London: J. Stockdale.* 1796. 8vo, pp. 200. Plate. P.

See "M. Rev.," XXI. 414.

EDWARDS. An Historical Survey of the French Colony in the Island of St. Domingo: comprehending a Short Account of its Ancient Government, Political State, Population, Productions, and Exports: A Narrative of the Calamities which have desolated the Country ever since the Year 1789; with some Reflections on their Causes and probable Consequences; and a Detail of the Military Transactions of the British Army in that Island to the end of 1794. By Bryan Edwards, Esq. ... *London: John Stockdale.* 1797. 4to, 3 l., pp. xxiii, (1), 247. Map. B., BA.

"Very full and minute on almost every topic connected with this island." — STEVENSON. *See also* "M. Rev.," XXIII. 77, 176. It is incorporated with the second edition of the author's history of the West Indies, and was reprinted with the following title:

EDWARDS. An Historical Survey of the Island of Saint Domingo, together with an Account of the Maroon Negroes in the

Island of Jamaica; and a History of the War in the West Indies, In 1793 and 1794; by Bryan Edwards, Esq. Also, a Tour through the several Islands of Barbadoes, St. Vincent, Antigua, Tobago, and Granada, in the Years 1791 and 1792. By Sir William Young, Bart. Illustrated with Copper Plates. *London: John Stockdale.* 1801. 4to, pp. xix, (1), 443. BA.

Called in the contents, but not in the title, Vol. III. (of his "History of the West Indies").

EDWARDS. Histoire de l'île Saint-Domingue, 1789 à 1794. Par Bryan Edwards. Traduite pour la premier fois de l'anglais, par J. B. J. Breton. *Paris.* 1802. 8vo, pp. 209. Map. S. + *Paris.* 1812. 8vo. 21896

EDWARDS. Geschiedkundige beschouwing van St. Domingo, door Bryan Edwards. Uit het Engelsch. *Haarlem: A. Loosjes, Pz.* MDCCCII. 8vo, 3 l., pp. xxiv, 288, 1 l., 12 l. folded. BA.

EDWARDS. Geschichte des Revolutionskriegs in Sanct Domingo. Aus dem Englischen. *Leipzig: im Verlage der Dykischen Buchhandlung.* 1798. 2 vols., 8vo, pp. iii, 220, Map; 272.

EDWARDS. Storia dell' Isola di S. Domingo ricavata dalla storia civile e del commercio delle Antille del Sig. Bryan Edwards E continuata sino agli ultimi avvenimenti, che minutamente reppresentano quanto è succeduto in quella importante Colonia pendente la rivoluzione. Tradotta dall' Inglese da J. B. Breton ... e trasportata dal Francese in Italiano da Giammichele Briolo. *Torino. Anno* XI. 8vo, pp. xv, 208. 21899

EDWARDS. The History of the Island of St. Domingo. Abridged from the History of Bryan Edwards, Esq., and Continued to the Present Time. *Edinburgh: T. Brown.* 1802. 16mo, 2 l., pp. 164. 21900

EDWARDS. The History, Civil and Commercial, of the British Colonies in the West Indies: ... By Bryan Edwards, Esq., of the Island of Jamaica. *London: John Stockdale.* MDCCXCIII. 2 vols., 4to, pp. xxxvi, 494; 502. 16 Plates and Maps. + *Dublin: Luke White.* M.DCC.XCIII. 2 vols., 8vo, pp. xxiv, 491, Map; x, 474, (6), 5 Tables folded. + Second Edition. *London: J. Stockdale.* MDCCXCIV–1801. 3 vols., 4to, pp. liv, 494; 520; 2 l., pp. xix, 443. 16 Maps and Plates. + Third Edition, with Considerable Additions. *London: John Stockdale.* 1801. 3 vols., 8vo, pp. xxiv, xxiii, 576; viii, 617; 2 l., pp.

xxxii, 477. 22 Maps and Plates. + Fourth Edition. *Philadelphia: James Humphreys.* 1805–6. 4 vols., pp. xxxix, 398; 406; 352; xxiv, 403, (4), Atlas of Map in 4to. + Fourth Edition, with Considerable Additions. Illustrated with Plates. *London: John Stockdale.* 1807. 3 vols., 8vo, pp. xlviii, 576; viii, 616; xxx, 477. Portrait, Maps, etc. BA. + With a Continuation to the Present Time. [By Sir William Young.] Fifth Edition. *London: G. and W. B. Whitaker.* 1819. 5 vols., 8vo, Atlas in 4to. 21901

The second edition is the same as the first. The third volume consists of our No. 21894, with an appendix, "Hortus Œstensis," by Broughton. There are copies on large paper. The plates are by Bartolozzi. The fourth American edition is from the second English edition. Some copies of this edition read: "Illustrated by an Atlas, and Embellished with a Portrait of the Author, To which is added a General Description of the Bahama Islands, By Daniel M'Kinnen, Esq. *Philadelphia.* 1806." It is also issued with the following imprints: *Baltimore: Coale & Thomas.* 1810. 4 vols., 8vo. + *Philadelphia: Levis & Weaver.* 1810. + *Charleston: E. Morford, Willington, & Co.* 1810. "The most complete edition appears to be that of 1819, in 5 vols., 8vo." — RICH. Vols IV. and V. are now first published. "Obtain, by all means, the history of those islands, by Bryan Edwards, the '*facile princeps*' of writers in his department." — DIBDIN. For a *critique*, *see* Preston (W.) *See also* "M. Rev.," XIV. 158, 293; XVII. 192; XXXVIII. 89.

EDWARDS. Histoire civile et commerciale des Indes Occidentales depuis leur découverte; suivie d'un tableau histor. et polit. de l'île de St. Domingue. Traduite de l'Anglaise 2e édit. corrigée. *Paris: Dentu.* 1804. 8vo. Map. 21902

EDWARDS. Burgerlijke en handelkundige geschiedenis van de Engelsche volkplantingen in de West-Indiën, door B. Edwards. *Haarlem.* 1794–1799. 6 vols., 8vo. 21903

EDWARDS. An Abridgment of Mr. Edwards' Civil and Commercial History of the British West Indies. *London: J. Parsons.* 1794. 2 vols., 8vo, pp. vii, 334, Map; vii, 335–665.

This abridgment was made by Taylor the Platonist. In the prefatory advertisement to this work, after complimenting the author, who is "ranked among the first historians of the day," the publisher adds, that "the avarice of his bookseller has placed this valuable fund of knowledge and entertainment in the reach only of the opulent;" *avarice*, also, most probably produced this abridgment. The following differs:

EDWARDS. The History Civil and Commercial, of the British Colonies in the West Indies. To which is added, an Historical Survey of the French Colony in the Island of St. Domingo. Abridged from The History written by Bryan Edwards Esq. Illustrated with a Map. *London: J. Crosby.* 1798. pp. xvi, 373. 21905

EDWARDS. Poems Written Chiefly in the West-Indies. By Bryan Edwards. *Kingston, Jamaica: A. Aikman.* 1792. 8vo, pp. 67. J.C.B. + 1796. 4to. 21906

EDWARDS. Poyais. An Account of the British Settlements on the Musquito Shore. By Bryan Edwards. *London.* 1823. 8vo. 21907

[EDWARDS.] Proceedings of the Honourable House of Assembly relative to the Maroons; including the Correspondence between Earl Balcarres and Major General Walpole during the Maroon Rebellion. *St. Jago de la Vega.* 1796. 4to, pp. 57.

See our No. 21893 for an enlarged edition.

EDWARDS. Refutation. *See* Venault de Charmilly, etc.

EDWARDS. A Speech delivered at a Free Conference between the Honourable the Council and Assembly of Jamaica, Held the 19th November, 1789. On the Subject of Mr. Wilberforce's Propositions in the House of Commons concerning the Slave-Trade. By Bryan Edwards, Esq. Member of the Assembly of the Said Island. *Kingston, Jamaica: Alexander Aikman.* MDCCLXXXIX. 8vo, pp. 82, xvi. BA., C. *London: Re-printed for J. Debrett.* M.DCC.XC. 8vo, pp. 59, xiii. H. 21909

See "M. Rev.," II. 349.

EDWARDS. Thoughts on the late Proceedings of Government, respecting the Trade of the West India Islands with the United States of America. *London: T. Cadell.* MDCCLXXXIV. 8vo, pp, vi, 55. + The Second Edition, Corrected and Enlarged. To which is now first added a Postscript, addressed To the Right Honorable Lord Sheffield. By Bryan Edwards, Esq. *London: T. Cadell.* M.DCCLXXXIV. 8vo, pp. iv, 91. BA., J.C.B. + *Boston, Reprinted.* 1784. 8vo, pp. 32. M. 21910

"A remonstrance against the ill policy and tendency of restricting the commerce of the West India Islands with North America to British ships." — *M. Rev.*," LXX. 231.

EDWARDS (C.) In Memory of Carlton Edwards. *Albany: Printed for Private Distribution.* 1863. 12mo, pp. iv, 272.

[EDWARDS (Charles).] The Crystal Hunter — A New-York Magazine. *New-York.* 1827. 8vo. 21912

Edited by Charles Edward Ellis, Esq. He changed his name to Charles Edwards, for the purpose of inheriting some property.

EDWARDS. Feathers from my own Wings. By Charles Edwards. *New York.* MDCCCXXXII. 8vo, pp. 200. Plate.

EDWARDS. Pleasantries about Courts and Lawyers of the State of New York. By Charles Edwards. *New York: Richardson & Co.* 1867. 8vo. Portrait. 21914

Also: In the Matter of Thomas Kaine, an Alleged Fugitive from Justice. Argument. [By] Charles Edwards, of Counsel for the Claimant, the British Government. *New York: E. Barnes & Co.* 1852. 8vo, pp. 16. — The Juryman's Guide for the State of New York ... *New York.* 1831. 8vo, pp. 293. — A Practical Treatise on the Stamp Act of July 1, 1862, and Amendatory Statutes to March 3, 1863. ... Second Edition. *New York: Voorhies.* 1864. 8vo, pp. xxvii, 398. B.

EDWARDS (C. L.) An Oration delivered 4th July, 1827, before the Cincinnati and Revolution Societies. By Charles Lee Edwards, M.D. *Charleston.* 1827. 8vo, pp. 21. 21915

EDWARDS (C. L.) The Dacotah Queen; or, Pat Mulloney's Pilgrimage. A Romance of the Indian Country. By C. L. Edwards. *New York: Beadle & Co.* 1865. 8vo, pp. 44.

EDWARDS (C. M.) The Itinerant; or, the Rainbow Side. By Mrs. C. M. Edwards. *New York: Carlton & Porter.* 1856. 18mo, pp. 299. 5 Plates. C. 21917

A portraiture of a Methodist preacher's life.

EDWARDS (D.) Sermon on the Death of Geo. Whitefield, Nov. 11, 1770. By the Rev. D. Edwards. *London: G. Keith.* 1770. 21918

EDWARDS (E.) The Life of Sir Walter Ralegh. Based on Contemporary Documents Preserved in the Rolls House, the Privy Council Office, Hatfield House, the British Museum, and other Manuscript Repositories, British and Foreign. Together with his Letters; now first Collected. By Edward Edwards. ... [n. p.] *Macmillan & Co.* 1868. 2 vols., 8vo, pp. lvi, 723; lxxxv, (11), 530. Portrait, Facsimile, and 3 Pedigrees. 21919

Also: Free Town Libraries, their Formation, Management, and History; in Britain ... and America. ... *London: Trübner & Co.* 8vo, pp. xvi, 371, 262. B., C. — Memoirs of Libraries; together with a Practical Handbook of Library Economy. ... *London: Trübner & Co.* (A few copies were printed on large and thick paper.) — Notes on the Public Libraries of the United States of America, by E. Edwards. [n. p. n. d.] B.

EDWARDS (F. S.) Doniphan's Campaign. A Campaign in New Mexico with Colonel Doniphan. By Frank S. Edwards, a Volunteer. With a Map ... *Philadelphia: Carey and Hart.*

1847. 12mo, pp. 184. H. + [*Ibid.*] 1848. 12mo, pp. 184. BA., C. + [*Ibid.*] 1849. 12mo, pp. 184. 21920

Includes some account of the Apache and Mexican Indians.

EDWARDS (G.) The Adventures of Mr. George Edwards, a Creole. *London.* 1751. 12mo. 21921

A doubtful title from an English catalogue.

EDWARDS (H. L.) Discourse Commemorative of Our Illustrious Martyr, delivered in Congregational Church, South Abingdon, Fast Day, June 1, 1865. By Rev. Henry L. Edwards. *Boston: Wright & Potter, Printers.* 1865. 8vo, pp. 16. B.

EDWARDS (J.) Account of the Trial of John Edwards, of the City of New York; who was Prosecuted for "Collecting, or promoting an assembly of persons, under the pretence of public worship in a public street, on Sunday, June 16, 1822," with a short account of his Life, an Address to the Mayor and Corporation, and advice to the Police, Magistrates, &c. Written by John Edwards, Except the Trial, which was taken down in short hand. *New York: Printed for the Author.* 1822. 8vo, pp. 76. 21923

Also: An Address to all Play-Actors, Play-Hunters, Legislators, Governors, Magistrates, Clergy ... and the World at large. *New York.* 1812. 8vo. — Rules and Regulations of the Christian Society called the Church of Christ, in the City of New York. *New York.* 1809. 8vo, pp. 16. N. — Serious Thoughts on the subject of taking the Lives of our Fellow Creatures, by way of Punishment for any Crime whatever. New York, 17th of 12th month, 1812. The Seventh Edition. [n. p. n. d.] 8vo.

EDWARDS (J. E.) The Confederate Soldier; being a Memorial Sketch of George N. and Bushrod W. Harris, Privates in the Confederate Army. By Rev. J. E. Edwards, D.D. *New York: Blelock & Co.* 1868. 12mo, pp. vi, 139. B. 21924

EDWARDS (J. N.) Shelby and his Men; or the War in the West. By John N. Edwards. *Cincinnati: Miami Pub. Co.* 1867. 8vo, pp. 551. Plate and Map. C. 21925

EDWARDS (J. P.) Uncle Tom's Companions. By J. P. Edwards. Third Edition. *London.* 1853. 12mo. 21926

EDWARDS (J.), *Senr.* An Account of the Life Of the late Reverend Mr. David Brainerd, Minister of the Gospel, Missionary to the Indians, from the Honourable Society in Scotland, for the Propagation of Christian Knowledge, and Pastor of a Church of

Christian Indians in New Jersey. Who died at Northampton in New England, October 9th, 1747. in the 30th Year of his Age: Chiefly taken from his own Diary, and other private Writings, written for his own Use. By Jonathan Edwards, A.M. Minister of the Gospel at Northampton. *Boston, N. E.: D. Henchman.* 1749. 8vo, pp. 1, Subscribers, 9 l., pp. 316, Books, 1 l. BA., C. + To which is Annexed, I. Mr. Brainerd's Journal while among the Indians. II. Mr. Pemberton's Sermon at his Ordination. With an Appendix on Indian Affairs. *Edinburgh: Printed by John Gray.* 1765. 8vo, pp. xi, 504. + To which are added Extracts from Mr. Brainerd's Journal, comprising the most material things in that Publication. *Worcester: L. Winant?* M DC XCIII. 8vo, pp. 346. + Second Edition. *Worcester.* MDCCXCIII. 8vo, pp. 346. 21927

Reprinted as

EDWARDS. An Account of the Life of Mr. David Brainerd, Missionary from the Society for Propagating Christian Knowledge. Pastor of a Church of Christian Indians in New Jersey. Published by Jonathan Edwards, A.M. With Mr. Brainerd's Public Journal, To which is added Mr. Beatty's Mission to the Westward of the Allegany Mountains. *Edinburgh: T. Maccliesh and Co.* 1798. 8vo, pp. 560, 50. 21928

Mr. Beatty's Journal is sometimes found separately. The following are abridgments: Life of David Brainerd, Missionary to the Indians, with an Abridgment of his Diary and Journal, from President Edwards, by John Styles. 1808. 12mo. — Life of David Brainerd. Chiefly extracted from his Diary. ... *New York.* [n. d.] 16mo, pp. 360. — An Account of the Life of the Rev. David Brainerd. *Newark, N. J.* 1811. 12mo. — Life and Journal of David Brainerd Edwards. *Edinburgh.* 12mo. It is also included in the "Evangelical Family Library," Vol. VII. It was translated into Dutch as

EDWARDS. Historiesch verhaal van het leven en den doodt van den Eerw. Heer D. Brainerd, bedienaar des Evangeliums bij de Indianen te Nieuw-Jersey. Getrokken uit zijn eigen dagregister enz. door Jon. Edwards. Uit het Engels vertaalt door J. Ros. Met voorberigt v. G. v. Schuylenborgh. *Utrecht: J. J. v. Poolsum.* 1756. 8vo, pp. 546. 29129

EDWARDS. A Careful and Strict Enquiry into the Modern prevailing Notions of that freedom of Will, which is supposed to be essential to Moral Agency, Vertue and Vice ... By Jonathan Edwards, A.M. Pastor of the Church in Stockbridge. ... *Boston: Printed and sold by F. Kneeland.* MDCCLIV. 8vo, Title, pp. vi, 2 l., pp. 274, 1 l. + *London.* 1762. H. + Third

Edition. *London.* 1768. + The Fourth Edition. *Wilmington.* 1790. 8vo. + *London.* 1790. 8vo. 21930

An Essay on the Fall of Angels and Men; with Remarks on Dr. Edwards' Notion of the Freedom of the Will, ... *Middletown, Conn.: Reprinted by Moses H. Woodward.* 1796. 8vo. BA. — Examination of the late Rev. President Edwards' "Enquiry on Freedom of Will." In Three Parts. With Appendix. [By Dr. Dana.] *Boston.* 1770. 8vo, pp. 140. BA. — Preservative against the Doctrine of Fate; Occasioned by reading Mr. Jonathan Edwards against Free Will, &c. *Boston: J. Fowle.* 8vo, pp. 31. W. — Remarks on Dr. Edwards' Notion of the Freedom of the Will and System of Universality. *Wilmington.* 1796.

EDWARDS. The Church's Marriage: ... A Sermon at the Instalment of Samuel Buel at East Hampton on Long-Island, September 19. 1746. By Jonathan Edwards. *Boston.* 1746. 8vo, pp. 43. B., M. 21931

EDWARDS. Copies of the Two Letters Cited by the Rev. Mr. Clap, concerning what he has reported, as from Mr. Edwards, concerning the Rev. Mr. Whitefield. With some Reflections on the Affair. By Jonathan Edwards, A.M. ... . *Boston: S. Kneeland and T. Green.* 1745. 16mo, pp. 16. B. 21932

EDWARDS. Discourses on Various Important Subjects, Nearly concerning the great Affair of the Soul's Eternal Salvation. ... Delivered at Northampton, chiefly at the Time of the late pouring out of the Spirit of God. By Jonathan Edwards, A.M. ... *Boston: S. Kneeland and T. Green.* MDCCXXXVIII. 8vo, Title, pp. vi, 286. 21933

EDWARDS. The Distinguishing Mark of a Work of the Spirit of God. Applied to that uncommon Operation that has lately appeared on the Minds of many of the People of this Land: With a particular Consideration of the Extraordinary Circumstances with which this Work is attended. A Discourse delivered at New-Haven, September 10th, 1741, being the Day after the Commencement; and now published at the Earnest Desire of many Ministers and other Gentlemen that heard it; with great Enlargement. By Jonathan Edwards, A.M., Pastor of the Church of Christ at Northampton. With a Preface by the Rev. Mr. Cooper, of Boston. ... *Boston: Kneeland & Green.* 1741. 8vo, pp. xviii, 110. + *Boston: Printed. Philadelphia: Re-printed and sold by Benjamin Franklin, in Market Street.* 1742. 8vo, pp. xvi, 84. BA., M. + *London: S. Mason.* 1742. 12mo, pp. 76. C. + To which is Prefixed an Epistle to the Scots Reader by the Rev. Mr. John Willison, Minister of the Gospel at Dundee. *Edinburgh: T. Lumisden.* MDCCXLII. 8vo, pp. 80.

EDWARDS. The Distinguishing Marks of a Work of the Spirit of God. Extracted from Mr. Edwards, Minister of Northampton, in New-England. By John Wesley, M.A. *London: W. Strahan.* M DCC XLIV. 12mo, pp. 48. + The Second Edition. *London: Henry Cocks.* MDCCLV. 12mo, pp. 48. M.

The late Religious Commotions in New England Considered. An Answer to his Sermon, Entitled "The Distinguishing Marks of the Work of the Spirit of God, &c., in a Letter to a Friend, With an Examination of the Preface to this Sermon, by the Rev. William Cooper. By a Lover of Truth. *Boston.* 1743. 12mo. W.

EDWARDS. A Divine and Supernatural Light, Immediately imparted to the Soul by the Spirit of God, Shown to be both a Scriptural, and Rational Doctrine; in a Sermon preached at Northampton. ... By Jonathan Edwards, A.M. ... *Boston: Printed by Kneeland and Green.* M,DCC,XXXIV. 8vo, pp. (4), 31, (1). B., BA. + *Boston.* [n. d.] 8vo, pp. 24. 21936

EDWARDS. Edwards on Revivals: containing a Faithful Narrative of the Surprising Work of God in the Conversion of many Hundred Souls in Northampton, Massachusetts, A.D. 1735. Also, Thoughts on the Revival of Religion in New England, 1742, ... By Jonathan Edwards, A.M., ... With ... Preface by Rev. John Angel James. And ... Revised, with Notes ... by Rev. William Patton, D.D., New York, U.S., N.A. *London: John Snow.* 1839. Rl. 8vo, pp. 116. 21937

EDWARDS An Expostulatory Letter from the Rev. Mr. Edwards of Northampton to the Rev. Mr. Clap, Rector of Yale College in New-Haven ... . *Boston: Printed and Sold by Kneeland and Green.* 1745. 12mo, pp. 16. BA., W. 21938

EDWARDS. A Faithful Narrative of the Surprising Work of God in the Conversion of many Hundred Souls in Northampton, and the Neighbouring Towns and Villages of the County of Hampshire, in the Province of the Massachusetts-Bay, in New England. In a Letter to the Reverend Dr. Benjamin Colman of Boston. Written by the Revd. Mr. Edwards, Minister of Northampton, Nov. 6. 1736. Published with a Large Preface by the Revs. Dr. Watts and Dr. Guyse, of London. ... *London: John Oswald.* M.DCC.XXXVII. 12mo, pp. xvi, 132. + The Second Edition. *London: John Oswald.* M.DCC.XXXVIII. 12mo, pp. xvi, 126. + *Edinburgh: Thomas Lumisden and John Robertson.* M.DCCXXXVIII. 8vo, xii l., pp. 93. + [The Same.] A Shorter [preface] added by Some of the Ministers of Boston. With an Attestation from Some of the Ministers of

Hampshire. The Third Edition. *Boston: Printed & Sold by S. Kneeland.* 1738. 8vo, pp. (2), viii, v, (1), 79. B., BA., S. + *London.* 1744. 12mo. + *London: W. Brittan.* [1800.] 12mo, pp. xii, 147. + Re-published with a Recommendatory Advertisement, By the Rev. J. Fawcett, A.M. and the Rev. W. Steadman. *Halifax.* 1808. 12mo, pp. xviii, 117. + *London: C. Whittingham.* 12mo, pp. xii, 87. + *Boston.* 1831. 12mo, pp. 140. + With Thoughts on the Revival in New England, in 1740. *Worcester, Mass.* 1832. 12mo. W. 21939

The preface to the third edition is by Joseph Sewall and others. The following is a Dutch translation of Watts' edition:

EDWARDS. Nadere geloofwaardige Berichten van het heerlyke werk Godts, geopenbaart in de bekeeringe van veele duysenden van zielen in Nieuw-Engelandt. Uit het Eng. vertaalt de Is. Le Long. *Leeuwarden: R. J. Noordbeek.* 1750. 8vo.

EDWARDS. A Farewel-Sermon Preached at the First Precinct in Northampton, after the People's Publick Rejection of their Minister, and renouncing their Relation to Him as Pastor of the Church there, June 22, 1750. Occasioned by Difference of Sentiments, concerning the requisite Qualifications of Church Members in compleat Standing. By Jonathan Edwards, A.M. ... *Boston.* 1750. Sm. 8vo, Title, pp. vii, (1), 36. BA., C. + *Hartford.* 1750. 8vo. + *Boston: S. Kneeland.* 1751. 8vo, pp. 36.

EDWARDS. The Great Christian Doctrine of Original Sin Defended: Evidences of its Truth Produced, and Arguments to the Contrary Answered. ... *Boston: S. Kneeland.* 1758. 8vo, Title, pp. xviii, 386, Subscribers, 3½ leaves. BA. + *Dublin: Printed for Robert Johnston.* MDCCLXVIII. pp. xxiv, 447. B., H. + *Wilmington.* MDCCLXXI. 12mo. + Fourth Edition. *London: Reprinted.* 1789. 8vo. 21942

EDWARDS. The Great Concern of a Watchman for Souls, ... In a Sermon Preached at the Ordination of the Reverend Mr. Jonathan Judd, ... in the New Precinct at Northampton, June 8. 1743. By Jonathan Edwards, M.A. *Boston: Printed by Green.* MDCCXLIII. 8vo, pp. 50. BA. 21943

EDWARDS. God Glorified in the Work of Redemption, By the Greatness of Man's Dependance. ... A Sermon Preached on the Publick Lecture in Boston, July 8. 1731. ... By Jonathan Edwards, A.M. ... *Boston: Printed by S. Kneeland and T. Green.* 8vo, Title, pp. ii, 25. BA. 21944

The address "To the Reader," pp. ii, is signed "T. Prince, W. Cooper."

Edwards. An Humble Attempt To Promote ... Visible Union Of God's People in Extraordinary Prayer For the Revival of Religion. ... By Jonathan Edwards, A.M. ... *Boston: D. Henchman.* 1747. 8vo, pp. (10), 188. B., BA., C., W. 21945

After "The Contents" is a second title-page, much more full. "The Preface" is signed "Joseph Sewall, Thomas Prince, John Webb, Thomas Foxcroft, Joshua Gee."

Edwards. An Humble Inquiry Into the Rules of the Word of God, Concerning the Qualifications requisite to a Complete Standing and Full Communion in the Visible Christian Church. By Jonathan Edwards, A.M. With an Appendix by Mr. [Thomas] Foxcroft. ... *Boston: S. Kneeland.* 1749. Sm. 4to, Title, pp. v, (1), 136, 16. B., BA., C. 21946

Two prefaces, pp. vii, the second of which is signed "Thomas Prince, John Webb, Thomas Foxcroft, M. Byles. For an answer, *see* Williams (S.)

Edwards. The Justice of God in the Damnation of Sinners: a Discourse delivered at Northampton at the time of the late Wonderful Revival there. *Boston.* 1773. 8vo. S. + *London.* 1774. 8vo. + Revised by Coetlogon. *London: Reprinted.* 1788. 8vo. + To which is added a Farewell Sermon ... June 22, 1750. *Northampton.* [1800?] 18mo. S. 21947

Edwards. The Life and Character of the late Reverend Mr. Jonathan Edwards, President of the College of New-Jersey, Together with a Number of his Sermons on Various Important Subjects. *Boston: S. Kneeland.* M,DCC,LXV. 8vo, 5 l., pp. 97, 279, 4 l. 21948

A general title to "The Life" and "Sermons." Reprinted in *Glasgow.* 1785. 8vo; *Edinburgh: Alexander Jardine.* 1799. 12mo; *Northampton: Andrew Wright.* 1804. 8vo.

Edwards. Life and Journal of the Rev. David Brainerd, Missionary to the Indians. By Jonathan Edwards, A.M. *Edinburgh: Published by H. L. Baynes.* MDCCCXXVI. 12mo, pp. xii, 426. G. 21949

Edwards. The Life of the Late reverend, learned and pious Mr. Jonathan Edwards, Some Time Minister of the Gospel at Northampton, in New-England, and then Missionary to the Indians at Stockbridge, and after that President of New-Jersey College. Who departed this Life at Princeton, March 22. 1758. in the 55th. Year of his Age. *Boston: Printed and Sold by S. Kneeland, opposite the Probate Office, in Queen Street.* M,DCC,-LXV. 8vo, 4 l., pp. 97. 21950

Edwards. The Life of the Rev. David Brainerd, Missionary to the Indians, from the Honorable Society in Scotland for Propagating Christian Knowledge; who died at Northampton in New England, October 9, 1747, in the 30th year of his Age. By Joseph Edwards, A.M. A New Edition, carefully Revised and Corrected. *London.* 1818. 8vo. 21951

Edwards. Het leeven van den weleerwaarden en zeer Geleerden Heer Jonathan Edwards, in dezelfs leeven President van het Collegie van New-Jersey; met uittrekzels uit zijne bijzondere schriften en dagboek. Uit het Engelsch vertaald door Engelbert Nooteboom. *Utrecht: Willem van Yzer Worst.* 1791. 8vo, pp. xvi, 222. J.C.B. 21952

Edwards. Memoir of the Rev. David Brainerd: Missionary to the Indians on the Borders of New York, New Jersey, and Pennsylvania. Chiefly taken from his own Diary; by Rev. Jonathan Edwards, of Northampton. Including his Journal, now for the first time Incorporated with the rest of his Diary, in a Regular Chronological Series, by Sereno Edwards Dwight. *New-Haven: S. Converse.* 1822. 8vo, pp. 507. B., C. 21953

Edwards. Misrepresentations Corrected, and Truth Vindicated. In a Reply to the Rev. Solomon Williams's Book, entitled, The True State of the Question, concerning the Qualifications necessary to Lawful Communion in the Christian Sacraments. *Boston: S. Kneeland.* 1752. 8vo, pp. (2), iv, 173, (4). Plate. BA., W., 21954

Edwards. Narrative of the Surprising Work of God in the Conversion of Many Hundred Souls in Northampton and the Neighbouring Towns and Villages of New Hampshire in New England, in a Letter to Dr. Colman of Boston. *Bristol: Felix Farley.* 1749. B. 21955

Edwards. A Narrative of the late Work of Work At and Near Northampton in New-England. Extracted from M. Edward's Letter to Dr. Colman. By John Wesley, M.A. Late Fellow of Lincoln College, Oxon. The Second Edition. *London: Henry Cock.* MDCCLV. 12mo, pp. 48. + [Another Edition.] With Character of David Brainerd. *Huddersfield.* 1791. 12mo. + Third Edition. *London.* 1798. 12mo. + *Halifax.* 1808. + *London: C. Whittingham.* [n. d.] 12mo, pp. xii, 87. + Revised from the Edition of 1738. *Boston.* 1831. 12mo. B.

Edwards. A Narrative of many Surprising Conversions in Northampton and Vicinity, written in 1736; together with some Thoughts of the Revival in New England in 1740, and an Account of the Conversion of the Author. *Worcester.* 1832. 12mo, pp. 382. Portrait. 21957

Edwards. ... A Sermon preached at Northampton ... June 26, 1748. On the Death of the Honourable John Stoddard, Esq. ... By Jonathan Edwards, A.M. ... . *Boston: printed by Rogers and Fowle.* 1748. 16mo, pp. 29. H. 21958

Edwards. Sinners in the Hands of an Angry God. A Sermon preached at Enfield, July 8, 1741, at a Time of great Awakenings: ... By Jonathan Edwards, A.M. ... *Boston: S. Kneeland and T. Green.* 1741. 8vo, pp. (2), 25. BA. + *Edinburgh: Reprinted.* 1745. Sm. 8vo. + Fourth Edition. *Charlestown.* 1802. 8vo, pp. 20. 21959

Reprinted as "Sinners in the hands of an Angry God. A Sermon, by the Venerated President Edwards, re-written, so as to retain his Thoughts in a Modern Style. By Daniel A. Clark. *Amherst: Carter & Adams.* 1826." 8vo, pp. 20. BA.

Edwards. Hatak Yoshuba Uhleha hut Chihowa Anukhobela ya Ibbak Toyuka. Sinners in the Hands of an Angry God. A Sermon by the Rev. President Edwards. *Park Hill: John Candy and John F. Wheeler.* 1845. 8vo, pp. 28. BA. 21960

Edwards. Some Thoughts Concerning the present Revival of Religion in New-England, and the way in which it ought to be acknowledged and promoted, Humbly offered to the Publick, in a Treatise on that Subject. In Five Parts. ... By Jonathan Edwards, A.M. Pastor of the Church of Christ, at Northampton. *Boston: S. Kneeland and T. Green.* MDCCXLVII. 16mo, pp. (2), iv, 378. B., C. + *Edinburgh: T. Lumisden.* MDCCXLIII. 12mo, pp. iv, 221. + *Boston.* 1768. 8vo. + *New York.* 1768. 8vo. B. + *Edinburgh.* 1772. 8vo. + *London.* 1774. 8vo. + *Boston: B. Larkin.* 1784. 8vo, pp. 406. BA. + With Life, &c. *Elizabethtown (N. J.): Shepard Kollock.* 1787. 8vo, pp. 499. C. + *Edinburgh: W. Laing.* 1789. Title, pp. 472. H. + *Lexington, Ky.* 1803. 12mo. + *Worcester.* 1808. 8vo. + *Philadelphia.* 1821. 8vo. B. 21961

Edwards. A Strong Rod Broken and Withered. A Sermon Preached at Northampton, on the Lord's-Day, June 26. 1748. On the Death of the Honourable John Stoddard, Esq., ... who died at Boston, June 19. 1748. ... By Jonathan Edwards, A.M. *Boston: Printed by Rogers and Fowle.* 1748. 8vo, pp. 29. BA.

Edwards. Thoughts Concerning the Present Revival of Religion in New-England. By Jonathan Edwards, A.M. Pastor of the Church of Christ at Northampton. Abridg'd by John Wesley, A.M. Fellow of Lincoln-College, Oxford. *London: W. Strahan, and sold by T. Tyre.* MDCCXLV. 12mo, pp. 124. H. + *London: J. Mason.* 1845. 12mo. + Abridged by W. Gordon. *London.* 1762. 12mo. 21963

Edwards. Thoughts on the Revival of Religion in New England, 1740. To which is prefixed a Narrative of the Surprising Work of God in Northampton, Mass., 1735. By Jonathan Edwards, A.M. ... . *Published by the American Tract Society. New York.* [n. d.] 12mo, pp. 446. H. 21964

Edwards. True Saints, when absent from the Body, are present with the Lord. A Sermon Preached on the Day of the Funeral of the Reverend David Brainerd, Missionary to the Indians, ... who died at Northampton in New-England, Oct. 9, 1747. ... By Jonathan Edwards, A.M. ... With Account of his Life, Character, &c. *Boston: Rogers and Fowle.* 1747. 8vo, pp. 40. B., BA. H., S., W. 21965

Edwards. Twenty Sermons, on Various Subjects. By the late Reverend Mr. Jonathan Edwards ... [From the Edinburgh Edition.] *Carlisle: Printed by George Kline.* 1803. 12mo, pp. viii, (1), 426, (2). 21966

Edwards. The Works of President Edwards, ... First American Edition. *Worcester: Isaiah Thomas, Jun.* 1808. 8 vols., 8vo. BA. + *London.* 1817. 8 vols., rl. 8vo. + *New York.* 1830. 10 vols., 8vo. + *New York: Leavitt, Trow & Co.* MDCCCXLIV. 2 vols., rl. 8vo. H. + *London: Hamilton.* 1847. 10 vols., rl. 8vo. 21967

See Dr. Robinson's notice in the "Bibliotheca Sacra." Also: An Account of the Conduct of the Council which dismissed the Rev. Mr. Edwards. [n. p. n. d.] 4to, pp. 8. M., W. — Doctrine of Original Sin Defended. *Worcester.* [n. d.] 8vo. W. + *Boston, N. E.: by S. Kneeland.* 1758. + *Hartford.* 1780. 8vo. — A History of the Work of Redemption, containing the Outlines of a Body Divinity, etc. *Boston.* 1782. 8vo + *New York: R. Hodge.* 1786. 8vo, pp. 402. + *Worcester.* 1792. + *New York.* 1793. 8vo. + Second Edition. *Edinburgh: Printed for and by Alexander Jardine and Edmund Whitehead.* 1799. 8vo, pp. xii, 432. BA., H. (Frequently reprinted.) — Jesus Christ Gloriously Exalted above all Evil, in the Work of Redemption: A Sermon at Northampton, in 1738. ... *Providence, R. I.* 1824. 8vo. — Remarks on Important Theological Controversies. By the Late Reverend Dr. Jonathan Edwards, President of the College of New Jersey. *Edinburgh: Printed for J. Galbraith, and Arch. Constable.* MDCCXCVI. 8vo, Title, 1 l., pp. 480. BA. — The Resort and Remedy of those that are bereaved by the Death of an Eminent Minister. Sermon preached at Hatfield, Sept. 2, 1741, at Interment of Mr. William Williams.

... *Boston.* 1741. 8vo, pp. 22. M., N., W. — Result of a Council of Nine Churches Met at Northamption, June 22, 1750. With a Protest against the same, By a Member of said Council. [n. d.] 8vo. W. — Sermon at the Ordination of the Rev. Job Strong, Portsmouth, June 28, 1749. *Boston.* 1750. 8vo, pp. 28. — A Treatise Concerning Religious Affections, In Three Parts. *Boston: Printed for S. Kneeland & T. Green.* 1746. 8vo, pp. (2), vi, 343, (9). B. — The True Excellency of a Minister of the Gospel. A Sermon at Pelham, Aug. 30. 1744. Being the Day of the Ordination of Robert Abercrombie. ... *Boston.* 1744. 8vo, pp. 22. B., W. — True Grace distinguished from the Experience of Devils: in a Sermon before the Synod of New York, New-Ark, N. J., September 28, 1752. ... *New York.* 1753. 8vo, pp. 42. + *Elizabethtown.* 1791. 8vo. — Two Dissertations: 1. Concerning the End for which God Created the World. 2. The Nature of True Virtue. ... *Boston: S. Kneeland.* M,DCC,LXV. 8vo, pp. (2), iii, (3), 191. B., BA. + *Philadelphia.* 1791. 12mo.

Edwards (J.), *Junr.* The Injustice and Impolicy of the Slave Trade, and of the Slavery of the Africans: Illustrated in a Sermon Preached before the Connecticut Society for the Promotion of Freedom, and for the Relief of Persons unlawfully holden in Bondage, at their Annual Meeting in New-Haven, September 15, 1791. By Jonathan Edwards, D.D. Pastor of a Church in New-Haven. [n. p.] *Printed by Thomas and Samuel Green.* M,DCC,XCI. 8vo, pp. (2), 37. + With a Sketch of the Evidence for the Abolition of the Slave-trade before the House of Commons. *Providence.* 1792. 8vo, pp. 60. + Second Edition. *Boston: Wells and Lilly.* 1822. 8vo, pp. 40. BA. + Third Edition. *New Haven: Anti-Slavery Society.* 1832. 8vo, pp. 40. H. + [*Ibid.*] 1833. 8vo, pp. 32. H. + Fourth Edition. *Newburyport: Charles Whipple.* 1834. 12mo, pp. 24. 21968

Edwards. The Necessity of Atonement and the Consistency between that, and Free Grace, in Forgiveness; Illustrated in Three Sermons, Preached before his Excellency the Governor, and a large number of both Houses of the Legislature of the State of Connecticut, during their Sessions at New Haven, (in Connecticut,) in October, A.D. MDCCLXXXV. By Jonathan Edwards, D.D. Pastor of a Church in New-Haven. ... *New-Haven: Printed by Meigs, Bowen and Dana.* MDCCLXXXV. 8vo, pp. 63, (1). BA. 21969

Edwards. ... A Sermon, Preached before his Excellency Samuel Huntington, Esq., LL.D., Governor, ... of the State of Connecticut, Convened at Hartford, on the Day of the Anniversary Election, May 8th, 1794. By Jonathan Edwards, D.D. ... *Hartford: Printed by Hudson and Goodwin.* MDCCXCIV. 8vo, pp. 46. BA. 21970

Edwards. Observations on the Language of the Muhhekaneew Indians; in which The extent of that Language in

North-America is shewn; its Genius is grammatically traced; some of its peculiarities, and some instances of Analogy between that and the Hebrew are pointed out. Communicated to the Connecticut Society of Arts and Sciences, and published at the Request of the Society. By Jonathan Edwards, D.D. ... *New Haven: Printed by Josiah Meigs.* M,DCC,LXXXVIII. 8vo, pp. 17. B., BA. + *London: Reprinted by W. Justins.* M,DCC,LXXXVIII. 8vo, pp. 16. 21971

Ludewig quotes an edition, *New York.* 1801. 8vo, pp. 16, which I have not seen; he also quotes an edition, *Philadelphia.* 1789, which is probably the reprint contained in Vol. v. of the "American Museum. *Philadelphia.* 1789;" it is also appended to Samson Occom's "Sermon," and was edited and republished as

Edwards. Observations on the Language of the Muhhekaneew Indians. By Jonathan Edwards. A New Edition, with Notes by John Pickering. *Boston: Little and Brown.* 1843. 8vo. 21972

Also forms pp. 81–160 of "Mass. Hist. Coll.," Second Series, Vol. x.

Edwards. A Sermon delivered at the Funeral of the Honorable Roger Sherman, Esq., Senator of the United States of America, who deceased the 23 of July, 1793. By Jonathan Edwards, D.D. *New Haven: Printed by Abel Morse.* M,DCC,XCIII. 8vo, pp. 24. BA., W. 21973

Edwards. Works of Jonathan Edwards, with an Essay on his Genius and Writings, by Henry Rogers; and a Memoir by S. E. Dwight, Revised and Corrected by Edward Hickman. *London: H. G. Bohn.* 1839. 2 vols., rl. 8vo. + New Edition. Rogers. *London: W. Tegg.* 1860. 21974

Edwards. The Works of Jonathan Edwards the Younger. With a Memoir of his Life and Character, by T. Edwards. ... *Andover.* 1842, 2 vols., 8vo. + *Boston.* 1850. 2 vols., 8vo.

Also: The Salvation of all Men strictly Examined: and the Endless Punishment of those who die Impenitent, Argued and Defended against the Objections and Reasonings of the late Rev. Doct. Chauncy, of Boston, In his Book entitled "The Salvation of All Men." ... *New Haven: Printed by A. Morse.* M,DCC,XC. 8vo, pp. vi, 331, (3). BA., H. + *Boston.* 1824. 12mo. — A Sermon delivered at the Ordination of Mr. Timothy Dwight, in Greenfield, Nov. 5, 1783. ... *New Haven.* [1783.] 8vo, pp. 27. — Sermon at the Ordination of William Brown to the Church in Glastenbury. ... *New Haven.* 1792. 8vo, pp. 33. — Sermon Preached at Hamden, July 11th, 1792, at the Ordination of the Rev. Dan. Bradley, to the Pastoral Charge of the First Church in White's Town, in the State of New York. ... *New Haven.* 1792. 8vo. N.

Edwards (J.) Discourse on the National Thanksgiving, April 13, 1815. By Jonathan Edwards, A.M. *Dedham.* 1815. 8vo.

Edwards. Sermon at Franklin, Dec. 31, 1820, the last Lord's Day in the Second Century, since our Forefathers first settled in Plymouth. ... *Dedham.* 1821. 8vo. 21977

Also: Discourse at the Funeral of Rev. David Sanford, at Medway, April 7, 1810. ... *Boston.* 1810. 8vo. — Discourse at Attleborough, [Mass.] Jan. 21, 1811, at the Funeral of Mrs. Esther, wife of Rev. John Wilder. ... *Providence.* 1811. 8vo. — Discourse on the Death of Oliver Shepherd, of Wrentham. ... *Dedham.* 1815. 8vo. — Discourse at the Installation of Rev. Thomas Williams, at Foxborough, [Mass.] Nov. 6, 1816. ... *Dedham.* 1816. 8vo — Discourse at Dorchester, [Mass.] June 11, 1817. Second Edition. *Providence.* 1825. 8vo. — The Giver more blessed than the Receiver. Discourse addressed to the Congregation in Franklin. ... *Boston.* 1809. 8vo. — Sermon at the Ordination of Zolva Whitmore, at North Guilford, [Con.] Sept. 5, 1821. ... *New Haven.* 1822. 8vo. — Sermon at Attleborough, Sept. 29, 1824, at the Installation of Rev. Thomas Williams. ... *Providence.* 1824. 8vo. — Sermon at the Installation of Rev. Calvin Park, at Stoughton, [Mass.] Dec. 13, 1826. ... *Boston.* 1827. 8vo. — Thanksgiving Discourse, Nov. 25, 1813. 8vo.

Edwards (J.), *of Woburn.* "One Lawgiver." A Sermon preached on Fast Day, 1854. By Rev. Jonathan Edwards. *Woburn.* 1854. 8vo, pp. 12. 21978

Also: Sermon, Two Hundred and Twenty-Fifth Anniversary of the First Church at Dedham, Nov. 8, 1863. 1863. 8vo, pp. 16.

Edwards (J.) Letter to the Friends of Temperance in Massachusetts. By Justin Edwards, Corresponding Secretary of the American Temperance Society. Second Edition. *Boston.* 1836. 8vo, pp. 36. B. + Third Edition, Enlarged. *Boston: Seth Bliss.* 1836. 8vo, pp. 36, Cover, 4. B., BA. 21979

Also: An Address delivered at the First Anniversary of the Porter Rhetorical Society, in the Theological Seminary, Andover, September 21, 1824. ... *Andover: printed by Flagg and Gould.* 1825. 8vo, pp. 19. B., BA. — Address, Laying the Corner Stone of the West Meeting-House in Andover. *Andover.* 1826. 8vo. S. — ... A Sermon, ... June 12, 1822, at the Installation of the Rev. Thaddeus Pomeroy, as Pastor ... Gorham, Me. ... *Portland.* 1822. 8vo. BA. + Second Edition, Enlarged. 1825. 8vo, pp. 16. + Third Edition, Enlarged. *Andover: prined by Flagg and Gould.* 1836. B. — A Sermon, ... Fourth Anniversary of the Auxiliary Education Society, of the Young Men of Boston, February 12, 1823. ... *Andover: Printed by Flagg & Gould.* 1823. 8vo, pp. 28. BA. — A Sermon delivered at the Installation of Rev. Frederick Freeman ... in Plymouth, Mass. Nov. 3, 1824. ... *Andover: printed by Flagg and Gould.* 1825. 8vo, pp. 31. H. — ... A Sermon, ... before the Penitent Females Refuge Society, ... Dec. 18, 1825. ... *Boston: Printed by T. R. Marvin.* 1826. 8vo, pp. 27, (1). BA. — A Sermon ... Installation of Rev. Jacob Scales, at Hemicker, N. H., January 17, 1827. And at the Ordination of the Rev. Daniel Crosby, at Conway, Mass. January 31, 1827. ... *Andover: printed by Flagg and Gould.* 1827. 8vo, pp. 21. H. — The Temperance Manual. *American Society: New-York.* 18mo and 12mo. + *Boston.* [n. d.] 18mo. B.

Edwards (M.) Life and Adventures of Monroe Edwards, the Accomplished Forger and Swindler. *New York: H. Long & Brother.* 1848. 8vo, pp. 152. Woodcut Portrait. BA.

Also: Life of Monroe Edwards, By a Texan. *Boston.* 1842. 8vo.

Edwards (M.) Materials towards a History of the Baptists in Pennsylvania, both British and German, distinguished into Firstday Baptists, Keithian Baptists, Seventhday Baptists, Tucker Baptists, Mennonist Baptists. By Morgan Edwards, A.M. ... *Philadelphia: Joseph Crukshank & Isaac Collins.* MDCCLXX. 12mo, pp. 132. Plate. 21981

The author states, in a prefatory advertisement, his intention to publish twelve volumes, only two of which appeared. He "fears these volumes will be deemed a heap of dry rubbish, without a sufficient number of anecdotes to give them a relish;" this, he adds, "is owing to the peace which the Baptists have ever enjoyed in Pennsylvania." The second volume is entitled: "Materials towards a History of the Baptists in Jersey. Vol. II. *Philadelphia: Thomas Dobson.* MDCCXCII. 16mo, pp. 155. So much as relates to Rhode Island is included in the "Collections of the Rhode Island Historical Society," Vol. VI.

Edwards. A New-Year's-Gift. Being a Sermon delivered at Philadelphia, on January 1, 1770; and published for rectifying some Wrong Reports, and preventing others of the like sort; but chiefly for the sake of giving it another chance of doing good to them who heard it. By Morgan Edwards, A.M. Fellow of Rhode-Island College, and Minister of the Baptist Church in Philadelphia. *Philadelphia: printed by Joseph Crukshank.* [n. d.] 8vo, pp. 14. P. 21982

Edwards. Two Academical Exercises on Subjects Bearing the Following Titles; Millennium, Last-Novelties. Published By Morgan Edwards, A.M. ... *Philadelphia: Printed by Dobson and Lang.* MDCCLXXXVIII. 8vo, pp. 36. 21983

Also: A Sermon Preached in the College of Philadelphia, at the Ordination of the Rev. Samuel Jones, with a Narrative of the Ordination ... *Philadelphia.* 1763. 8vo.

Edwards (N. W.) History of Illinois, 1775–1833, and Life and Times of N. Edwards. *Springfield (Ill.)* 1870. 8vo. BA.

Edwards (N.) Speech of Ninian Edwards in Congress, on an Appropriation of the Public Lands to the purposes of Education. *Washington.* 1822. 8vo. S. 21985

Edwards (Pierrepont). Practical Guide for British Shipmasters, to United States Ports. *London: Longmans.* 1866. 12mo. pp. viii, 323. 21986

Edwards (R.), *and* Hopewell (M.) Edwards's Great West and her Commercial Metropolis, embracing A General View of the West, and a Complete History of St. Louis, from the landing of Ligueste, in 1764, to the present time; with Portraits and Biographies of some of the Old Settlers, and many of the most

Prominent Business Men, by Richard Edwards and M. Hopewell, M.D. Splendidly Illustrated. *St. Louis: Office of "Edwards's Monthly."* 1860. 8vo, pp. 604. 66 Portraits and 55 Plates.

EDWARDS (R.) Map of Virginia; also its Constitution ... By Richard Edwards. *Richmond.* 1856. 8vo. B. 21988

EDWARDS. Memoir of Nicholas Tillinghast, First Principal of the State Normal School at Bridgewater, Mass. By Richard Edwards ... . *Boston: James Robinson & Co.* 1857. 8vo, pp. 23. Portrait. H. 21989

EDWARDS. Statistical Gazetteer of the States of Virginia and North Carolina. By Richard Edwards. *Richmond.* 1856. 8vo.

EDWARDS (Thomas). Antapologia; Or, a Full Answer to the Apologeticall Narration of Mr. Goodwin, Mr. Nye, Mr. Sympson, Mr. Burroughs, Mr. Bridge, Members of the Assembly of Divines, etc. *London: Printed by G. M. for John Bellamie.* 1644. 4to, 5 l., pp. 307. 21991

At page forty-nine is a reference to Roger Williams.

EDWARDS. A | Letter | to | Mr. Tho. Edwards | The Dedication of the Letter | To our much suspected friend, Mr. T. Edwards, Scavenger Generall, | throughout Great-Britaine, New-England, and the united Pro- | vinces, chiefly Amsterdam, and Munster, and indeed by vertue of | some faire pretences, Intermedler in all the States of Christendome, | principally there where any thing of the Spirit of Christ in the Saints | appeares, trenching upon the Honour, dignity, and preferment of the | Old man. The Grand Reformer, (alias Reducer) of the free born | Sons of God, into the chaines of their old Babilonish captivity, under | the pretence of a Jus Divinum. | At his dwelling in Club Court, between the Pope and the Prelate, a | little on this side the Fagot in Smithfield, (or if in his monethly Pil-grimage) in the Suburbs of Canterbury, at the knowne house of Mi- | stris Gangrena Triplex, where Conscience and he (but for a time | we hope) shook hands and bad each other farewell. Where he was | lately discovered by many eye-witnesses: and where you may be sure | at any time to meet with him. | Published by Authority. | *London, Printed for Tho. Veere, and are to be sold at his shop | at the upper-end of the Old Bayley, near New-gate.* 1647. | 4to, Title, pp. 10. 21992

EDWARDS (T.) Report of a Judgment in the High Court of Admiralty by Sir Wm. Scott, in the Case of the Snipe, and other American Vessels. *London.* 1812. 8vo. C. 21993

EDWARDS (Thomas M.) Treasury Note Bill. Speech ... delivered in the House of Representatives, Feb. 6, 1862. [n. p. n. d.] 8vo, pp. 8. 21994

EDWARDS (T.) ... A Sermon ... Preach'd ... at Hartford, on the day of Election There, On May 11th. 1732. By Timothy Edwards, N. A. ... *N. London: T. Green.* 1732. 12mo, pp. (2), 63. H. 21995

EDWARDS (T.) ... A Discourse in ... Rochester, N. Y., on the Sabbath after the Death of William Henry Harrison, President of the United States, April 11, 1841. By Tryon Edwards. *Rochester: printed by Thomas H. Hyatt.* 1841. 8vo, pp. 16. H.

EDWARDS. ... A Discourse delivered in the First Presbyterian Church in Rochester, N. Y., on the Day of Annual Thanksgiving, December 15, 1836. By Tryon Edwards ... . *Rochester.* 1837. 8vo, pp. 39. BA., H. 21997

See "N. Am. Rev.," XLIV. 558–60.

EDWARDS (W. H.) The Butterflies of North America. With Colored Drawings and Descriptions. By W. H. Edwards. Parts I.–IV. *Philadelphia: Entomol. Society.* 1868. 4to, pp. 16, 10, 15, 18. 21998

EDWARDS. A Voyage up the River Amazon, including a Residence at Para. By William H. Edwards. *New York: D. Appleton & Co.* 1847. 12mo, pp. 256. + *London: John Murray.* 1847. *Post* 8vo. + *London.* 1848. + New Edition. *London.* 1855. Post 8vo. + *[Ibid.]* 1861. Post 8vo. 21999

EDWARDSVILLE, *Ill.* Minutes of the Twelfth Annual Meeting of the Edwardsville Baptist Association, at Hillsborough, Ill., May, 1840. *Louisville.* 1841. 8vo, pp. 8. M. 22000

Edwin and Angelina. *See* [Smith (E. H.)].

EELKING (M. von). Die Deutschen Hülfstruppen im Nordamerikanischen Befreiungskriege, 1776 bis 1783. Von Max von Eelking ... . *Hannover.* 1863. 2 vols., 8vo, pp. xii, 271. BA.

EELKING. Leben und Wirken des Herzoglich Braunschweig'schen General-Lieutenants Friedrich Adolph Riedesel Freiherrn zu Eisenbach. Nebst vielen Original-correspondenzen und historischen Aktenstücken aus dem siebenjährigen Kriege, dem nordamerikanischen Freiheits-Kampfe und dem französischen Revolutions-Kriege. Von Max von Eelking. *Leipzig.* 1856. 3 vols., 8vo, pp. xvi, 288; x, 450; iv, 400. Map and Portrait.

EELKING. Memoirs and Letters, and Journals of Major-General Riedesel, during his Residence in America. Translated from the Original German of Max von Eelking, by William L. Stone. ... *Albany: J. Munsell.* 1868. 2 vols., 8vo, pp. viii, 306, (1); 284. Portrait and Woodcut. BA. 22003

Fifty copies on large paper.

EELLS (E.) ... Sermon, preached before the General Assembly of the Colony of Connecticut, on the Day of the Anniversary Election, May 14th, 1767. By Edward Eells, M.A. ... in Middletown. ... *Hartford: Printed by Thomas Green.* [1767.] Sm. 8vo, pp. 12. H. 22004

EELLS (N.) The Evangelical Bishop. A Sermon preached at Stonington, June 14, 1733, at the Ordination of Rev. Nathaniel Eells [jun.]; ... By Nathanael Eells. ... *New London.* 1734. 16mo, pp. 72. 22005

EELLS. Religion is the Life of God's People: a Sermon Preach'd at Boston, In the Presence of His Excellency William Shirley, Esq; ... And the Honourable His Majesty's Council ... May 25th. 1743, ... By Nathanael Eells, V.D.M. ... *Boston: Printed by S. Kneeland and T. Green.* 1743. Title, pp. (1), 43.

EELLS. ... A Sermon preached in the Audience of the General Assembly of the Colony of Connecticut, on the Day of their Anniversary Election in Hartford, May 12th, 1748. By Nathaniel Eells, M.A. ... . *N. London.* 1748. 32mo, pp. (1), 51.

Also: A Letter to the Second Church and Congregation in Scituate, ... Shewing some Reasons why he doth not invite the Rev. Mr. George Whitfield into his Pulpit. To which is added, a Postscript, containing an Answer to the Reasons given by a Number of Ministers conven'd at Taunton ... . *Boston: D. Gookin.* 1745. 16mo, pp. 14. B., M. — The Ministers of God's Word must Approve themselves unto God. A Sermon, at Plymouth, July, 29th. 1724. when Nathanael Leonard Was Ordained. ... *Boston.* 1725. Sm. 8vo, pp. (2), ii, 27. B. — The Ministers of the Gospel, as Ambassadors for Christ. A Sermon at Taunton, Feb. 21. 1728, 9. At the Ordination of Thomas Clap. ... *Boston.* 1729. 8vo, pp. (4), ii, 47. B., W.

EELLS (S.) Oration delivered before the Biennial Convention of the Alpha Delti Society at New Haven, Conn., August 15, 1839, on the Law and Means of Social Improvement. By Samuel Eells. *Cincinnati.* 1839. 8vo. 22008

EELLS (W. W.) A Discourse occasioned by the Death of Hon. Daniel Webster, preached in Newburyport, Sunday, October 31, 1852. By Rev. W. W. Eells. ... . *Newburyport: Moses H. Sargent, Publisher.* 1852. 8vo, pp. 18. H. 22009

Also: Gratitude for Individual and National Blessings. A Discourse, ... Thanksgiving Day, Nov. 28, 1850. ... *Newburyport: Moses Sargent.* 1850. 8vo, pp. 24. B., BA., H. — How and Why we give Thanks. A Thanksgiving Sermon preached in Pittsburgh, Nov. 26, 1865. ... *Pittsburgh: W. S. Haven.* 1864. 8vo, pp. 20.

Een reeder en handelaar op de West-Indien, aan zijne medereeders en handelaars. *Amsterdam.* [1798.] 8vo, pp. 16.

Eenige Aanmerkingen op het libel: Het waare daglicht v. h. Pol. Systema van Amsterdam, mitsgaders op zekere: Rechtsgeleerde Memorie. [1781.] 8vo, pp. 32. 22011

Some remarks on the pamphlet: "The True Light of the Polit. Syst. of Amsterdam," and on a certain "Juridical Memorial." Relative to privateering during the American Revolution.

De eer der regeering van Amsterdam verdedigd tegen den laster van het Engelsch Ministerie ... in eene Contra-Memorie tegen de "Rechtsgeleerde Memorie" en het "Politiek Vertoog." *Amsterdam.* 1781. 8vo. 22012

This piece on "The honour of the Magistrate of Amsterdam defended against the calumny of the English Ministry" is by N. Bondt. *See also* "Rechtsgeleerde Memorie."

Eerezang voor het Fransche volk by gelegenheid dat het den slavenhandel afgeschaft heeft. In Holland 1794. 8vo, pp. 36.

A poem on the abolition of the slave trade.

Een Vertoogh. *See* Guyane.

Eerste Maandags | Relaes, | van | Den Af-en-optocht van sijn | Ceurvorstelijcke Doorluchtigheyt van | Brandenburg langs en omtrent den Rijn, | in den Jare 1672. | Uytgegeven den 4 December 1673. | *Voor den Autheur gedruckt.* | 4to, pp. 12. 22014

A kind of weekly journal, extending to nine numbers, eighty-four pages in all, and contains interesting particulars of the war between France and Holland, and particularly as to the dispersion of the Spaniards and the English throughout the American continent.

The Effect of Secession. *See* [Lord (Daniel)].

Effects of the Stage. *See* [Haliburton (William)].

EFFINGHAM (C.) *See* [Cooke (J. E.)], Vol. IV., No. 16321.

EGAN (C.) Law of Extradition; comprising the Treaties now in force between England and France, and England and America, for the mutual surrender, in certain cases, of persons Fugitive from Justice, with the recent Enactments and Decisions thereto. By Charles Egan. *London.* 1846. 8vo. C.

[EGAR (John H.)] The Christian Patriot. A Sermon delivered in Grace Church, Galena, in May, 1861. By the Rector. *Quincy, [Ill.]: Whig Press.* 1863. 8vo, pp. 12. 22016

EGAR. The Martyr-President. A Sermon Preached in the Church of St. Paul, Leavenworth, on the First Sunday after Easter, and again by request on the National Fast-Day, June 1st, 1865. By the Rev. John H. Egar, B.D. Rector. *Leavenworth: Bulletin Office.* 1865. 8vo, pp. 16. B. 22017

EGEDE. De gamle Grönlands nye perlustration, eller en kort beskrivelse om de gamle Nordske coloniers begyndelse og undergang, etc. forst Anno 1724 forfattet af H. Egede, og nu Anno 1729 efterseet ... af een der paa nog en tiid har vaeret i Grönland. *Kjöbenhaven: H. Chr. Paulli.* 1729. Sm. 8vo, Title, pp. 58. 22018

"This seems to be the first essay of Egede's celebrated work on Greenland, which was first published in 1741. Both are very similar in the division, etc., but the latter is, of course, much more ample. This work of 1729 is very rare; I have found it nowhere mentioned." — MULLER.

EGEDE. Des alten Grönlands neue perlustration, oder eine kurtze Beschreibung derer alten Nordischen Colonien Anfang und Untergang in Grönland, wobey desselben Situation, Beschaffenheit der Gewächsen, Thieren, Vögeln und Fischen, Lufft und Temperament, des Himmels Constitution, der jetzigen Einwohner Verhalten Wohnungen Sprache Gestalt Ansehen, Kleider-Tracht Nahrung Gebräuche Handthierung Spevsen Handlung Sprach Ehestands-Ceremonien und Kinder-Zucht; nebst ihrer Religion oder Superstition und anderer so wohl in ihren Zusammen Künfften, als auch zu Hausz gebräuchlichen Sitten. ... *Frankfurt: bey Stock Erben und Schilling.* A.D. 1730. 12mo, pp. 47. 22019

EGEDE (H.) Kort Beretning om den Grönlanska Missions Beskaffenhed. [Signed Hans Egede, and dated *Kiöbenhavn. d. 8. May.* 1737.] 8 l., not numbered. J.C.BT. 22020

EGEDE. Omstændelig og udförlig Relation Angaaende den Grönlandske Missions Begyndelse og Fortsættelse, Samt Hvad ellers mere der ved Landets Recognoscering, dets Beskaffenhed, og Indbyggernes Væsen og Leve-Maade vedkommende, er befunden; Af Hans Egede ... . *Kiöbenhavn: Joh. Christ. Groth.* 1738. 4to, 10 l., pp. 408. H. 22021

EGEDE. Det gamle Grönlands Nye Perlustration, Eller Natural-Historie, Og Beskrivelse over det gamle Grönlands Situation, Luft, Temperament og Beskaffenhed; De gamle Norske Coloniers Begyndelse og Undergang der Samme-Steds, de itzige Indbyggeres Oprindelse, Væsen, Leve-Maade og Handtæringer, samt Hvad ellers Landet Yder og giver af sig, saasom Dyer, Fiske og Fugle &c. med hosföyet nyt Land-Caart og andre Kaaber-Stykker over Landets Naturalier og Indbyggernis Handtæringer, Forfattet af Hans Egede ... . *Kjöbenhavn: Trykt hos Johan Christoph Groth.* 1741. 4to, 6 l., pp. 131, (1). Map and 11 Plates. C., H., J.C.BT. 22022

EGEDE. Ausführliche und wahrhafte Nachricht vom Anfange und Fortgange der Gronländischen Mission, wobey die Beschaffenheit des Landes sowohl, als auch die Gebräuche und Lebens-Arten der Einwohner beschrieben werden, getreulich angemerckt und aufgezeichnet von Hans Egede ... . *Hamburg: Christian Wilhelm Brandt.* 1740. 4to, pp. (16), 288. H. 22023

The "Biog. gén." gives the title of this as "Tagebush einer Groenländischen Mission," and adds that La Harpe's "Hist. des voyages," v. XVIII., gives a full abstract of it.

EGEDE. Des alten Grönlands Neue Perlustration, oder Naturell-Historie Und Beschreibung Der Situation, Beschaffenheit, Lufft und des Temperaments dieses Landes; Wie auch vom Anfange und Untergange, derer alten Norwegischen Colonien daselbst; vom Ursprunge, der Sitten, Lebensart und den Gebräuchen derer jetzigen Einwohner, und was dieses Land an Thieren, Fischen, Vögeln ec. heget und mittheilet; deme beygefüget Eine neue Land-Charte und andere in kupfer gestochene Figuren und Abbildungen der Naturalien und Handthierungen derer dasigen Einwohner; Verfasset und beschrieben von Hans Egede ... . Aus den Dänischen ins Teutsche übersetzt. *Copenhagen: gedruckt bey Johann Christoph Grothen.* 1742. 4to, Title, pp. (12), 144. Map and 11 Plates. H., M. 22024

EGEDE. Herrn Hans Egede, Missionärs und Bischofes in Grönland, Beschreibung und Natur-Geschichte von Grönland, übersetzt von D. Joh. Ge. Krünitz. Mit Kupfern. *Berlin: verlegts August Mylius.* 1763. 8vo, pp. xii, 237. Map and 10 Plates. C., H. 22025

EGEDE. Beschryving | van Oud-Groenland, | Of eigentlyk van de zoogenaamde | Straat Davis: Behelzende | Deszelfs Natuurlyke Historie, Standsgelegenheid, Gedaante, | Grenscheidingen,

Veld-Gewassen, Dieren, Vogelen, Vischen, enz. | Mitsgaders | Den Oirsprong en Voortgang der Aeloude | Noorweegsche Volkplantingen | in dat Gewest; | Benevens | Den Aart, Inherst, Woningen, Levenswyze Kleding, Spraak, | Bygelovigheid, Diek'tkunst, | Uitspanningen en Tydverdryven der | Hedendaagsche Inboorlingen. | Eerst in de Deensche Taal beschreven door | Mr. Hans Egede, | van den jare 1721 tot 1736 Missionaris ... | En nu in 't Nederduitsch overgebragt. | Met | Een Nieuw Kaart van dat Landschap en | Aardige Printverbeeldingen verciert. | *Te Delft | By Reiner Boitet*, 1746. | 4to, 12 l., pp. 192. Map and 9 Plates.

EGEDE. Description et histoire naturelle du Groenland. Par Mr. Eggede. Missionnaire & Evêque du Grönland. Traduite en François par Mr. D. R. D. P. *A Copenhague et à Genève: Chez les Frères C. & A. Philibert.* MDCCLXIII. 8vo, Title, pp. xxviii, (4), 171. Map and 10 Plates. 22027

The translator was M. des Roches de Parthenay.

EGEDE. A Description of Greenland. Shewing the Natural History, Situation, Boundaries and Face of the Country: the Nature of the Soil; the Rise and Progress of the old Norwegian Colonies; the Ancient and Modern Inhabitants; their Genius and way of Life, and Produce of the Soil; their Plants, Beasts, and Fishes. By Hans Egede. With a Map of Greenland, and several Copperplates. Translated from the Danish. *London: C. Hitch.* 1745. 8vo, pp. xvi, 2 l., pp. 220. Map and 7 Plates.

The first chapter in this volume gives an account of the discovery and settlement of Greenland in the ninth century by Eric the Red, and of the voyages that followed; also of the establishment of Christianity there. There are some copies on large paper.

EGEDE. A Description of Greenland. By Hans Egede, who was a Missionary in that Country for Twenty-five Years. A New Edition. With an Historical Introduction and a Life of the Author. ... *London: T. and J. Allman.* 1818. 8vo, pp. cxviii, 225. Map. BA. 22029

The copies we have seen read "Second Edition" before "*London*," in addition to the words "New Edition."

EGEDE. Fragmenten uit een dagboek, gehouden in Groenland, in de jaren 1770–1778. Uit het Deenseh in het Hoogduitsch vertaald door G. Fries. *Groningen.* 1818. 8vo. Map.

EGEDE. The History of Hans Egede and the Moravian Missionaries. From the London Edition, ... *Boston: S. S. Soc.* 1845. 32mo. H. 22031

Hans Egede was born in Denmark, Jan. 31, 1686. Was pastor at Vogen and Frontheim, went as missionary to Greenland in 1721. The mission was ordered to be abandoned in 1731, but he remained there with ten seamen, and the mission was assisted again. He returned home in 1736, his son Paul becoming his successor, and died in 1758.

EGEDE (Paul). Dictionarium Grœnlandico-Danico-Latinum, complectens primitiva cum suis derivatis quibus interjectæ sunt voces primariæ e Kirendo Angokkutorum adornatum. *Hafniæ: Typ. Orphanotr. Reg. Gottfr. F. Kisel.* 1750. 8vo, pp. xvi, 312.

EGEDE. Elementa fidei christianae lingua Grönlandica. *Havn.* 1742. 8vo. 22033

Title from Græsse.

EGEDE. Efterretninger om Grönland, uddragne af en Journal holden fra 1721 til 1788 af Paul Egede. *Kiöbenhavn: trykt af Hans Christopher Schröder.* [n. d.] 8vo, 6 l., pp. 284. Portrait, 3 Plates, and 1 Map. C., H. 22034

EGEDE. Continuation af Relationerne Betreffende Den Grönlanske Missions Tilstand Og Beskaffenhed, Forfattet I Form af en Journal fra Anno 1734 til 1740. af Colonien Christians-Haab udi Disco Bugt. Ved Paul Egede. *Kiöbenhavn: Johann Christoph. Groth.* [1741?] 4to, 4 l., pp. 184. 2 Maps. J.C.BT.

EGEDE (N.) Tredie Continuation Af Relationerne Betreffende Den Grönlanske Missions Tilstand Og Beskaffenhed, Fortsattet i Form af en Journal Fra Anno. 1730 til 1743. Holden af Niels Egede. Med hosföyed Designation Over den Grönlandske Ungdoms Forfremmelse i christelig Kundskab, saavel Döbtes som U-döbte Catechumenorum, ved Colonierne Christians-Haab og Got-Haab ... . Disligeste ... Prosopographia Kulalitæ, Incolæ Grœnlandiæ, epico Latina ab Olao Lange, Hvilket ... indholder ... et Compendium af heele Landets Merkvædigheder. *Kiöbenhavn: Johann Christoph. Groth.* [1744?] 4to, 2 l., pp. 144. J.C.BT., H. 22036

With note, by Hans Egede, at end, dated *Kiobenhavn*, 1744, followed by a Latin poem, translated from the Danish of Johannis Egede, by Olao Lange, entitled "Prosopographia Kulalitæ," etc., 11 l., not numbered.

EGEDE. Evangelium Okausek tussarnersok Gub Niarnanik Innungortomik, okansianiglo, Usornartuleniglo, tokomello umannello. Killaliarmello, Innuin annauniartlugit, aggerromartomiglo, tokorsut tomasa umartitsartortlugit. Koralit okausiet attuattlugo aglekpaka Paul Egede. *Kiobenhavnme.* 1744. 8vo.

The Gospels translated by Paul Egede.

EGEDE. Grammatica Grönlandica Danico-Latina, edita à Paulo Egede. *Havniæ: Sumptibus & typis Orphanotrophii Regii Excudit Gottman.: Frid. Kisel. An.* 1760. 12mo, 8 l., pp. 236.

EGEDE. Reisbeskrivelse til Oester Groenland opdagelse, 1786–87. *Kjobenhavn.* 1789. 8vo. 3 Maps. 22039

EGEDE. Nachrichten von Grönland. Aus einem Tagebuche geführt von 1721 bis 1788. Aus dem Danischen. Mit Kupfern. *Kopenhagen: Bey Christian Gottlob Proft.* 1790. 8vo, pp. 333. Portrait, 2 Plates, and a Map. 22040

EGEDE. Testamente Nutak, eller det nye Testamente, oversat i det Grönlandske Sprog, med Forklaringer, Paralleler, og udförlige Summarier, af Paul Egede. *Kiöbenhavn: Trykt paa Missionens Bekostning, af Gerhard Giese Salikath.* 1766. 8vo, 11 l., pp. 1000, 4 l. 22041

First Edition of the New Testament in Greenlandish, with explanations, etc., by Paul Egede. *See also* Saabsye (Hans Egede).

[EGENTER (Franz Joseph).] Amerika ohne Schminke. Eine Quellensammlung zur Darstellung des amerikanischen Lebens in der Wirklichkeit. *Zürich: Beyel.* 1857. 8vo, pp. xvi, 1–452.

Published under the *pseudonym* of Bened. Dalei.

EGERTON (F.) Causa célebre contra los asesinos de Don Florencio Egerton y Doña Ines Edwards. ... Danla a luz los Editores del Observador judicial. *Mexico.* 1844. 16mo, pp. 40.

EGERTON. Egerton's Views in Mexico; being a Series of Twelve Large Colored Plates, executed by himself, from his Original Drawings. *London.* 1841. Folio. 22044

Title from Rich's "Bibl. Am.," Vol. II. Published at £12 12s.

EGERTON (H.) A Sermon before the Society for the Propagation of the Gospel in Foreign Parts, on the 21st of February, 1728. By the Rt. Rev. Henry, Bishop of Hereford. *London.* 1729. 8vo, pp. 64, (3). B. + 4to, pp. 26. M. 22045

EGERTON (J.) Sermon before the Society for the Propagation of the Gospel in Foreign Parts, 1763. By the Rt. Rev. John, Bishop of Bangor. *London.* 1763. 8vo, pp. 114. M. 22046

EGERTON (J. K.) The Relations of the Federal Government to Slavery. Speech of the Hon. Joseph K. Egerton, of Indiana, delivered at Fort Wayne, Indiana, October 30, 1860. *Fort Wayne: Dawson.* 1861. 8vo, pp. 64. 22047

Also: [Egerton.] Letter of a Citizen of Indiana to the Hon. John J. Crittenden, on the Anti-Slavery Policy of President Lincoln, and the Duty of the National Democracy, March 21, 1862. 8vo, pp. 8.—Confiscation. Speech ... delivered in the House of Representatives, January 28, 1864. pp. 8.—Speech ... delivered in the House of Representatives, June 15, 1864. 8vo, pp. 8.—Speech ... at Ligonier, July 20, 1864, before the Democratic Cong. Convention of the Tenth District of Indiana. Broadside.—Reconstruction. Speech ... in the House of Representatives, February 20, 1865. pp. 16.

EGGERLING (H. W. E.) Beschreibung der Vereinigten Staaten von Nord Amerika nach ihren politischen, religiösen, bürgerlichen und gesellschaftlichen Verbindungen, mit besonderer Berücksichtigung deutscher Ansiedelungen daselbst. Den deutschen Auswanderern gewidmet von H. W. E. Eggerling. Zweite durchaus vehmehrte und verbesserte Auflage. *Mannheim: Verlag von Tobias Löffler.* 1833. 12mo, pp. 344. C. 22048

EGGERS (H. P.) Ueber die wahre Lage des alten Ostgrönlands. *Kiel.* 1794. 8vo. 22049

EGGLESTON (C. M.) A Funeral Discourse, preached in Memory of Capt. Ayres C. Barker, 120th Regiment N. Y. S. V., killed at the Battle of Gettysburg, July 2, 1863. By Rev. C. M. Eggleston, Greenville, July 26, 1863. *Coxsackie, (N. Y.): F. O. Dedrick.* 1863. 8vo, pp. 19. 22050

EGGLESTON (N. H.) In Memoriam. A Discourse preached Nov. 1st, 1868, on the Occasion of the Erection of Tablets in the Old Church at Stockbridge, Mass., in Memory of its Former Pastors, John Sergeant, Jonathan Edwards, Stephen West, and David D. Field. By Rev. N. H. Eggleston. *New York: Baker & Godwin.* 1869. 8vo, pp. 35. B. 22051

EGGLESTON. Religion in Politics. A Discourse ... in Madison, Wis., by Nathaniel H. Eggleston ... *Madison, Wis.: Atwood & Ruble.* 1851. 8vo, pp. 31. H., M. 22052

Also: Reasons for Thanksgiving. A Discourse to the Congregational Church and Society, in Stockbridge, Mass., on the Day of Annual Thanksgiving, November 21, 1861. ... *Pittsfield, Mass.: Henry Chickering, Printer.* 1861. 8vo, pp. 21. H.

EGLESTON (Thomas). Catalogue of Minerals, with their Formulas, etc. Prepared for the Smithsonian Institution. By T. Eggleston. *Washington. June,* 1863. 8vo, pp. xiii, 42.

"Smithsonian Miscellaneous Collections," 156.

[EGLESTON.] A Geological and Agricultural Survey of 100 Miles West of Omaha. By [Professor Thos. Egleston, for] the American Bureau of Mines. *New York.* 1866. 8vo, pp. 44.

EGLESTON. Tables of Weights, Measures, Coins, etc., of the United States and England, with their Equivalents in the French Decimal System. Arranged by T. Egleston, ... *New York.* 16mo, pp. ix, 60. 22055

EGLOFFSTEIN (F. W. von). Contributions to the Geology and the Physical Geography of Mexico, including a Geological and Topographical Map, with Profiles, Of some of the Principal Mining Districts; together with a Graphic Description of an Ascent of the Volcano Popocatepetl. Edited by Baron F. W. von Egloffstein. *New York: D. Appleton & Co.* 1864. Rl. 8vo, pp. 40. Maps and Plates. BA. 22056

EGMONT (John), *Earl of.* *See* Percival (John).

EGRON (P.) The Level of Europe and North America, or the Observer's Guide. By Peter Egron, LL.D. *Philadelphia.* 1798. 4to. 22057

A periodical work composed on a plan as novel as instructive, by Messrs. Egron, Tangui, and a Society of Literati, and American and European commercial gentlemen. In English and French.

EGUIA (J. J. de). Memoria sobre la Utilidad é Influjo de la Mineria en el Reino; necesidad de su fomento, y arbitrios de verificarlo. Por Don José Joaquin de Eguia. *Mexico.* 1819. Sm. 4to. C. 22058

"A highly important work upon the regulations of the mines and development of the precious metals in the various provinces of Mexico."—STEVENS.

EGUIA Y MORO (J. P.) Publicas Demonstraciones de Celebridad y Jubilo que este Real Tribunal del Proto Medicato de Nueva España. *México: por D. Felipe de Zúniga, y Ontiveros.* [n. d.] 4to. 22059

EGUIARA Y EGUREN. Bibliotheca Mexicana sive eruditorum Historia virorum, qui in America Boreali nati, vel alibi geniti, in ipsam Domicilio aut Studijs asciti, quavis linguâ scripto aliquid tradiderunt: Eorum præsertim qui pro Fide Catholicâ and Pietate ampliandâ forendâque, egregiè factis and quibusvis Scriptis floruere editis aut ineditis. Ferdinando VI. Hispaniarum Regi Catholico Nuncupata. Authore D. Joanne Josepho de Eguiara et Eguren. Mexicano, electo Episcopo Jucatanênsi, etc. etc. Tomus primus exhibens Litteras A B C. *Mexici: Ex novâ Typographiâ in Ædibus Authoris editioni ejusdem Bibliothecae destinatâ. Anno Domini* 1755. Folio, Title, Half-Title, Dedication, 4 l., Approba-

tion, etc., 2 l., De Bibliothecâ Eguiaræ, 72 unnumbered leaves, Text, pp. 544. 22060

The only volume published of this rare and valuable work. It contains the most authentic notes on the literature and literary men of Mexico, and became the basis of Beristain's celebrated "Bibl. Hisp. Amer.," which appeared sixty years later. Eguiara was one of the most talented members of the Academy of Mexico. "It is unfortunate that no more of this important work was published. It is probable that not many copies were printed of this volume, as it is not often met with."—RICH, I. 115. The remainder of the manuscript was said to be preserved in the Library of the Cathedral of Mexico. Leclerc's collation seems to differ from ours. "Ouvrage curieux, mais don't il n'a paru que le premier volume."—BRUNET.

EGUIARA Y EGUREN. Maria Santissima Pintandose Milagrosamente en bellissima imagen de Guadalupe de Mexico, saluda a la Nueva España, y se constituye su Patrona. Panegyrico, que en su Santa Iglesia Metropolitana, el dia diez de Noviembre de 1756, predicó el Doctor D. Juan Joseph de Eguiara y Eguren. Sacalo a luz la muy noble leal imperial Ciudad de Mexico. *Con licencia en la Imprenta de la Bibliotheca Mexicana. Año de* 1757. 4to, 6 l., pp. 32. 22061

EGUIARA Y EGUREN. El monstruo de Santidad S. Bernardo panegirico. *Mexico.* 1741. 4to, 26 l. 22062

EGUIARA Y EGUREN. La nada contrapuesta en les balanzas de Dios à el aparente cargado peso de los hombres. Assumpto moral que en la Metropolitana de Mexico, en oposicion à la Canongia Magistral, discurriò, y dixo El doctor Don Juan Joseph de Eguíara y Eguren. *Mexico.* 1724. 4to, 18 l. + *Mexico.* 1727. 4to, 6 l., pp. 23. 22063

EGUIARA Y EGUREN. Prelectio exponens vigessimam sextam distinctionem libri tertii sententiarum magistri; in Alma Metropolitana Mexicca Ecclesia, pro Magistralis Canonicatus examine die 23 Augusti Anno Domini 1725, habita, a Doct. D. Joanne Josepho de Eguiara y Eguren. *Mexico.* 1725. 4to, pp. 30.

See Beristain's "Bibl. Hisp. Amer.," I. p. 452.

EGUIARA Y EGUREN. [Begins:] Selectas Dissertationes Mexicanas meas ad Scholasticam spectantes Theologiam, publicam daturus in lucem, etc. Folio, 16 l. 22065

A fragment of a work of Eguiara, probably the preface of "Selectae Dissertationes Mexicanae," in which he gives an interesting account of all the celebrated men, attached, for two centuries, to the Academy of Music. The paper is, therefore, a valuable contribution to the literary history of Mexico.

EGUIARA Y EGUREN. Vida del venerable padre don Pedro de Arellano y Sossa, sacerdote y primer preposita de la Congre-

gacion del Oratorio de Mexico. *Mexico.* 1735. 4to, pp. 368, Table, 16 l. 22066

Also: Intenecio Primogenitorum Ægypti. *Mexici: J. B. de Hogal.* 1729. 8vo.—La Muger Edificativa Panegyrico Funebre en Honras de la M. Aug. Nich. Maria, Abbadesa tercera vez que fue, del Convento de San Phelipe de Jesus y Pobres Capuchinas de Mexico. *Mexico.* 1755. 4to.—Prælectio Theologica. *Mexici: apud M. de Rivera.* 1747. 4to.

EGUILAZ (L. de). La espada de San Fernando. Novela historico-caballeresca original. *Mexico.* 1854. 8vo. 22067

EGUILAZ (P.) Relacion de la mision apostolica de los moxos en la Provincia del Peru, de la Compañia de Jesus, que remite su Provincial P. Diego de Eguilaz à N. M. P. Thryso Gonçalez, Preposito General de la misma Compañia, año de 1696. [n. p. n. d.] 4to. 22068

"Sans autre indication."—CARAYON.

EHREHART (C. J.) A Discourse delivered in St. Peter's Evan. Lutheran Church, Middletown, Pa., on Thanksgiving Day, November 27, 1862. By Rev. Charles J. Ehrehart, A.M. *Lancaster, Pa.: E. H. Thomas & Son, Printers.* 1862. 8vo, pp. 23. 22069

Relates to the Rebellion.

EHRENBERG (Chr. Gottfr.) Verbreitung und Einfluss des mikroskopischen Lebens in Süd und Nord-Amerika. Ein Vortrag. ... *Berlin.* 1843. Folio. 4 Colored Engravings. 22070

EHRENBERG (H.) Fahrten u. Schicksale eines Deutschen in Texas. Von H. Ehrenberg. *Leipzig.* 1845. 8vo. 22071

EHRENBERG. Der Freiheitskampf in Texas im Jahre 1836. *Leipzig.* 1844. 22072

Also: Texas und seine Revolution. *Leipzig.* 1843. 8vo. *See also* Berquin-Duvallon.

EHRENKREUTZ (*Baron* V.) Vollständige Beschreibung des Staates von Texas in historischer, politischen, geographischer und geselliger Hinsicht. ... *Coblenz: Reiff.* 1846. 16mo. Map.

EHRMANN (T. F.) Geschichte der merkwurdigsten Reisen, welche seit dem zwölften Jahrhunderte zu Wasser und zu Lande unternommen worden sind. Von Theophil. Friedrich Ehrmann. *Frankfurt: Hermann.* 1791. 8vo, pp. 408. 22074

[EIBERGEN (Rutg.)] Svvymel-Klacht | Des Spaenschen Conincks | Philippi Qvarti, | Over het eerste verlies | Van sign Silver-

Vlote: | Waer mede dese Landen, door Gods hulpe, verrijckt heeft | Den Moedighen en Manhaften Zee Ridder, en Generael | Pieter Pietersen Heyn, | Anno | PhILIppVs CLaeCht VVeL bang, en berst VVeL haest VVt spIIt, | Maer VVat Ist? aL Vergheess hII bLIIft zIIn zIIn VLote qVVIIt. | *T'Amstelredam,* | *Voor Willem Iansz Stam, Boeckvercooper inde Warmoes* | *straet, inde Hoochduytsche Bybel.* M.DC.XXIX. | 4to, pp. 16. 22075

Relates to the capture of the Silver Fleet by P. Heyn.

EICHTHAL (G. d'). Études sur l'histoire primitive des races océaniennes et américaines. Par Gustave d' Eichthal. *Paris: Dondey-Dupré.* [1845.] 8vo, pp. 172, 1 l. C. 22076

From the "Mémoires de la Société Ethnologique."

EICHTHAL. Etudes sur les origines bouddhiques de la civilisation américaine. *Paris.* 1865. 8vo, 1 l., pp. 86. Plate. C.

From the "Revue Archéologique."

Eigentliche Beschreibung des Lands Guiana welches gelegan an d. vesten meergrentzenden Landschschafft America. Samt zweyen von einem der Hundert Oberhäubtern dieser neuangehenden Coloney abgef. Schreiben an zween seiner guten und wolbek. Freunden hiesiger Stadt Bärn worin ein kurtz verfasster bericht von ob angedeutem Lande enthalten mit fr. Einladung hiesiger Nation Leuthen zur Besatzung dieses orts. *Bärn.* 1677. 4to. Map. 22078

Eigentliche Beschreibung des an dem grossen Flusse Missisippi in Nord-America gelegenen herrlichen Landes Louisiana. *Leipzig.* 1720. 8vo. 22079

Eight Letters on the Subject of the Earl of Selkirk's Pamphlet on Highland Emigration. *Edinburgh.* 1806. 8vo, pp. 59.

Eight Practical Treatises on the Cultivation of the Sugar Cane, written in consequence of the Earl of Elgin's Offer of a Prize of £100, in 1842. *Jamaica.* 1843. 8vo. 22081

Eight Years' Residence in British Guiana, 1840–48, with Anecdotes and Incidents Illustrating the Social Condition of its Inhabitants, and State and Prospects of the Sugar Colonies. *London: Longman & Co.* 1850. 8vo. 22082

Eighteen Hundred and Sixty Association. *See* South Alone and Porter (W. D.)

EIGHTS (J.) Outlines of the Geological Structure of the Lake Superior Mineral Region, belonging to the New York and Lake Superior Mining Company. *Albany.* 1846. 8vo. B. 22083

EIGHTS. Reminiscences of the City of Albany, with an Engraving, showing a view of the City from the opposite side of the Hudson River. *Albany.* 1836. 12mo, pp. 18. 22084

Also: A Report on the Geological, Mineralogical and other resources of the Hiatt Tract of Land ... County of Surry, N. C. ... *Greensborough, N. C.* 1855. 8vo.—Worth Tract, Surry County, N. C. 1855. 8vo.

Eighty Years' Progress of the United States; showing the various Channels of Industry and Education through which the People of the United States have arisen from a British Colony to their present National Importance. With a Large Amount of Statistical Information. Subjects, and Authors: Progress in Agriculture, by Charles L. Flint; Cultivation of Cotton, by C. F. McCoy; Commerce, Manufactures, and Trade, by Thomas P. Kettell; Social and Domestic Life, by Frederick B. Perkins; Arts of Design, by T. Addison Richards; Education, by Henry Barnard; Mining Industry, Free Trade, &c., by James T. Hodge; Steam Engine, by J. C. Merriam. *New York.* 1861. 2 vols., 8vo. C. + *Worcester.* 1861. 2 vols., 8vo. + *New York: L. Stebbins.* 1864. 8vo. B. 22085

Ein auszug ettlicher sendbrieff dem aller durchleüchtigisten groszmechtigisten Fürsten und Herren Herren Carl Römischen und Hyspanischen König, etc. Unseren gnedigen hern durch ire verordent Hauptleut, von wegen einer newgefunden Inseln, der selben gelegenheit und inwoner sitten und gewonheiten inhaltend vor kurtzuerschinen tagen zugesandt. *Nürmberg: Fryderich Peypus.* 1520. 4to, 7 l. 22086

"Contains a relation of the expeditions of Francisco (Hernandez) de Cordova, Grijalva, and Cortes to Yucatan. There is a large woodcut on the title-page, representing the landing of an armed ship, with armed men on shore opposing."—J. R. BARTLETT.

Einfache Worte an einfache Leute von einem Einfachen Mannen. *Philadelphia.* 1863. 8vo, pp. 16. 22087

EINHORN (D.) The Rev. Dr. M. J. Raphall's Bible View of Slavery Reviewed by the Rev. D. Einhorn, D.D. Translated from the February Number of the "Sinai" ... . *New York: Thalmessinger, Cahn & Benedicks.* 1861. 12mo, pp. 22. H.

EINHORN. Trauer-Rede gehalten am 19ten April, 1865, als am tage der Beisetzung des am 15. April entschlummerten Abra-

ham Lincoln, Präsidenten der Vereinigten Staaten im Tempel der Keneseth Israel Gemeinde zu Philadelphia. Von Dr. David Einhorn. *Philadelphia: Druck von Stein und Jones.* 8vo, pp. 8.

Also: Sermon, Delivered on Thanksgiving Day, November 26th, 1863, ... The Proceeds are for the Sanitary Commission. *Philadelphia: Stein & Jones.* 1863. 12mo, pp. 13. B., H.—War with Amalek! A Sermon delivered on Sabbath, P. Lachor, 5624. March 19, 1864, in the Temple of the Congregation Keneseth Israel, Philadelphia, ... *Philadelphia: Stein & Jones.* 1864. 8vo, pp. 12.

EISENACH. *See* Vol. II., No. 4953.

EISENBERGER (N. F.) Piscium serpentum insectorum aliorumque nonnullorum animalium necnon plantarum imagines quas Marcus Catesby in posteriore parte splendidi illius operis quo Carolinæ, Floridæ, et Bahamensium insularum tradidit historiam naturalem, eiusque appendice descripsit. Ediderunt N. F. Eisenberger et G. Lichtensteger. *Norimbergæ.* 1750. Folio. 64 Colored Plates. 22090

The plates in this work are copied from the first sixty-four of the second volume of Catesby's "Carolina." According to Brunet, the work should contain 109 plates.

EKINS (C.) Naval Battles, from 1744 to the Peace in 1814, critically Reviewed and Illustrated. By Rear-Admiral Charles Ekins. *London.* 1824. 8vo. Plates. C., M. 22091

ELA (J. H.) Radical Common Sense—the President and Congress. Speech of Hon. Jacob H. Ela, of New Hampshire, In the House of Representatives, December 17, 1867. [*Washington.* 1867.] 8vo, pp. 7. H. 22092

Also: The True Policy. Speech ... January 21, 1870. *Manchester, N. H.: John B. Clarke.* 1870. 8vo, pp. 15. H.

ELCOCK (E.) Animadversions on a Book called a Plea for Non-Scribers. By Ephraim Elcock. 1651. 4to. 22093

Title from Thorpe's catalogue, who includes it under Americana.

ELDER (W.) Biography of Elisha Kent Kane. By William Elder. *Philadelphia: Childs and Peterson.* 1858. 8vo, Engraved Title, pp. 416. Portrait and 4 Woodcuts. BA., C. 22094

ELDER. Debt and Resources of the United States, and the effect of Secession upon the Trade and Industry of the Loyal States. By Dr. William Elder. *Philadelphia: Ringwalt & Brown.* 1863. 8vo, pp. 32. B., H. 22095

In German, with the following title: Schulden und Hülfequellen der Vereinigten Staaten und die Wirkung der Rebellion auf den Handel und die Industrie der Loyalen Staaten; nebst Anhang. ... *Philadelphia: King und Baird.* 8vo, pp. 32.

ELDER. The Genius of Ecclesiastical Freedom; Comprising the Declaration of Divine Order, made by the First Convention of the New Church in Union County, Indiana. Also, an Exposition of the Order of Divine Order, referred to in the Article of the Declaration. *Cincinnati.* 1843. 12mo, pp. 360. C.

[ELDER.] How our National Debt can be paid. The Wealth, Resources, and Power of the People ... . Issued by Jay Cooke ... . *Philadelphia.* 1865. 8vo, pp. 16. H. 22097

Prepared by Dr. William Elder. Also: The American Farmer's Markets at Home and Abroad; with a Supplement, showing how Protection, under the present Tariff, is distributed between Agriculture and Manufactures. ... *Philadelphia: Ringwalt & Brown.* 1870. 8vo, pp. 10. H. — The Cottage Garden of America, ... *Philadelphia: Moss & Brother.* 1849. 12mo, pp. 233. — Emancipation; its Condition and Policy. A Lecture ... *Philadelphia: McLaughlin Brothers.* 1856. 8vo, pp. 16. — How the Western States can become the Imperial Power in the Union. ... *Philadelphia: Ringwalt & Brown.* 1865. 8vo, pp. 23. — The Western States: their Pursuits and Policy. ... *Philadelphia: Ringwalt & Brown.* 1865. 8vo, pp. 23. H.

ELDERHORST (W.) Analyses of the Hydrant and Well Waters of the City of Troy, presented to the Board of Health for the Year ending March 1st, 1858, by Prof. Wm. Elderhorst. ... *Troy, N. Y.: George Abbott.* 1858. 8vo, pp. 32. H. 22098

ELDERKIN (J.) The Turf and the Trotting Horse of America, by J. Elderkin. *Philadelphia: Porter & Coates.* 1871. 8vo.

ELDRIDGE (A.) A Sermon preached ... in ... Detroit. On Thanksgiving Day, November 29, 1860, by Azariah Eldridge ... . *Detroit: Barns, French & Way, Printers.* 1860. 8vo, pp. 21. H. 22100

Also: The Character and Claims of Seamen. An Address. ... New Bedford Port Society, February 10, 1850. ... *New Bedford: Chas. & Augustus Taber.* 1850. 8vo, pp. 24. — A Sermon, in behalf of the American Education Society, ... May 23, 1853. ... *Boston.* 1853. 8vo, pp. 16. B.

ELDRIDGE (C. A.) The Constitution against Confiscation and outside Reconstruction. Speech of Hon. Charles A. Eldridge, of Wisconsin, delivered in the House of Representatives, December 10, 1867. *Washington.* 1867. 8vo. B., H. 22101

Also: Against the Right of the Federal Government to determine the Qualification of Electors in the States. Speech ... January 27, 1869. [*Washington.* 1869.] 8vo, pp. 8. H. — Has the Revolt destroyed the Union. Speech delivered ... Jan. 25, 1866. [*Washington.* 1866.] 8vo, pp. 8. — Naturalization and Immigration. Speech ... June 9, 1870. [*Washington.* 1870.] 8vo, pp. 8. H. — Reconstruction. Speech ... January 18, 1867. [*Washington.* 1867.] 8vo, pp. 7. H. — Speech ... March 28, 1868, against the Bill making a Constitution for Alabama, and enforcing upon her People Negro Government. [*Washington.* 1868.] 8vo, pp. 8. H.

ELDRIDGE (E.) Memoirs of Eleanor Eldridge. *Providence: B. T. Albro.* 1838–1841. 2 vols., 18mo, pp. 128; 128. Portrait. + 1842. 22102

The subject of this memoir was born in Warwick in 1785, and was the granddaughter of a Narraganset Indian squaw and an African chief.

ELDRIDGE (J.) A Sermon ... at the Funeral of Martin Rockwell, of Colebrook, December 11, 1851. By Rev. Joseph Eldridge. With an Appendix and a Genealogy of the Rockwell Family. ... *New Haven: Printed by L. Hamlin.* 1852. 8vo, pp. 27. 22103

ELDRIDGE. Does the Bible sanction Slavery? A Discourse delivered at Norfolk, Connecticut, February 24, 1861. ... *Litchfield Enquirer Office.* 1861. pp. 28. 22104

Also: A Discourse delivered in Norfolk, Conn., at the Funeral of Benjamin Welch, M.D., December 21, 1849. ... *New York: printed by Edward O. Jenkins.* 1850. 8vo, pp. 16. H. — Reform and Reformers. A Sermon delivered at Norfolk, Conn., Nov. 30, 1843. *New Haven.* 1844. 8vo. BM.

The Election, a Poem. *Kingston, Jamaica.* 1788. 8vo.

The Election. *New York.* 1822. 8vo. 22106

The Election of a President of the United States, considered. Addressed to the People. By a Citizen. *Boston: True & Greene.* 1823. 8vo, pp. 27. B. 22107

Election of President of the United States. To Citizens of the United States, and particularly to those not born therein. By a Republican. [n. d.] 1800. 8vo. 22108

The Election. Humbly Inscrib'd to the Saturday Night's Club, in Lodge Alley. A Copperplate Engraving, being a Caricature of the Election-ground, followed by a Doggrel Poem. *Philadelphia.* [About *Oct.* 1765.] Folio, p. 1. P. 22109

Electioneering Address. *See* "Massachusetts."

Elegiac Epistles on the Calamities of Love and War, Including a genuine Description of the Tragical Engagement between his Majesty's Ships the Serapis and Countess of Scarborough, and the Enemy's Squadron under the Command of Paul Jones, on the Twenty-third of September, 1779. *London: Printed for the Authors, and sold by Pridden.* 1780. 8vo. 22110

See "M. Rev.," LXII. 493.

An Elegy Occasioned by the Rejection of Mr. Wilberforce's Motion for the Abolition of the American Slave Trade. *London: Hughes and Walsh.* MDCCXCI. 4to, 2 l., pp. 10. 22111

See "M. Rev.," v. 104.

An Elegy on the Times. First printed at Boston, September 20th, A.D. 1774. *New Haven: Re-printed by Thomas and Samuel Green.* 1775. 8vo, pp. 15. B., BA., N. 22112

Elementa Philosophica, 1752. *See* [Johnson (Samuel)].

Éléments de la grammaire Othomi. *See* Othomi.

Elements of Discord in Secessia. The Vulgarity of Treason. Extracts from Rebel Organs. *Loyal Publication Society, No.* 15. 1863. 8vo, pp. 16. 22113

ELESPURU (J. B.) Ligero extracto de las causas que impelieron a la Tercera Division a ponerse en disposicion de hacer uso de las Armas. *Lima.* 1831. 8vo. 22114

[ELEUTHERIUS, *pseudon.*] The Scripture-Bishop Vindicated. A Defence of the Dialogue between Prælaticus and Eleutherius, Upon the Scripture-Bishop, or the Divine Right of Presbyterian Ordination and Government: Against The Exceptions of a Pamphlet, Intitled, The Scripture-Bishop Examin'd. By Eleutherius, V.D.M. In a Letter to a Friend. ... *Boston, New-England: Printed by S. Kneeland & T. Green, for D. Henchman in Cornhill.* 1733. 2 vols., 8vo, Half-Title, Title, pp. 126; Title, 158. BA. 22115

This is by Jonathan Dickinson. For a reply, *see* [Foxcroft (Thomas)].

ELGIN. Condition and Prospects of Canada in 1854. As displayed in the Despatches of the ... Earl of Elgin and Kincardine, Governor General of Canada, to her Majesty's Principal Secretary of State for the Colonies. *Quebec.* 1855. 8vo, pp. 83, 2 l. folded. B., H. 22116

ELGIN. Etat et Avenir du Canada en 1854, tel que retracé dans les dépêches du ... comte d'Elgin et Kincardine, gouverneur général du Canada, au principal secrétaire d'état de Sa Majesté pour les colonies. *Québec.* 1855. 8vo, pp. 86, 2 l. folded. H. 22117

ELHUYAR (Don Fausto). Memoria sobre el influjo de la

mineria en la agricultura, industria, poblacion y civilizacion de Nueva-España, en sus diferentes épocas, con varias disertaciones relativas á punto de economia política pública conexos con el propio ramo. *Madrid.* 1825. 8vo. 22118

ELHUYAR. Indagaciones Sobre la Amonedacion en Nueva España presentadas al Real Tribunal general de Mejico, Por Su Derictor Don Fausto de Elhuyar. *Madrid.* 1818. 4to.

ELI (Alfred). Sermon at Ware Factory Village on Constituting a Church there, April 12th, 1826. *Brookfield.* 8vo.

Elijah's Mantle. *See* [Mather (Cotton)].

ELIOT. *See also* Elliot.

ELIOT (A.) Christ's Promise to the Penitent Thief. A Sermon Preached the Lord's-Day before the Execution of Levi Ames, Who suffered Death for Burglary, Oct. 21, 1773. Æt. 22. By Andrew Eliot, D.D. Pastor of a Church in Boston. N.B. This Discourse was preached at the desire of the Prisoner, who was present when it was delivered. *Boston: Printed and Sold by John Boyle, next Door to the Three-Doves in Marlborough-Street.* 1773. 8vo, pp. 36. BA., H. 22121

ELIOT. An Evil and Adulterous Generation. A Sermon Preached on the Public Fast, April 19. 1753. By Andrew Eliot, M.A. Pastor of a Church in Boston. *Boston: Printed by S. Kneeland, for J. Winter, over against the King's Arms in Union-Street.* 1753. 8vo, pp. 26. BA., M., W. 22122

Gives some curious notices of the money spent for liquor "in this poor Province."

ELIOT. The Faithful Steward. A Sermon Delivered By Andrew Eliot, M.A. At his Ordination to the Pastoral Charge Of the New North Church in Boston, in Conjunction with the Rev. Mr. Webb. On April 14. 1742. *Boston: Printed by Tho. Fleet, for Samuel Eliot in Cornhill.* 1742. 8vo, Title, pp. 35. B.

ELIOT. A Sermon Preached before his Excellency Francis Bernard, Esq; Governor, The Honorable His Majesty's Council, and the Honorable House of Representatives, Of the Province of the Massachusetts-Bay in New-England, May 29th 1765. Being the Anniversary for the Election of His Majesty's Council for the Province. By Andrew Eliot, A.M. Pastor of a Church in Boston. *Boston: Printed by Green and Russell, Printers to the honorable House of Representatives.* MDCCLXV. 8vo, pp. 59. BA.

ELIOT. A Sermon Preached October 25th. 1759. Being a Day of Public Thanksgiving Appointed by Authority, For the Success Of the British Arms this Year; Especially In the Reduction of Quebec, The Capital of Canada. By Andrew Eliot, M.A. Pastor of the New-North Church in Boston. *Boston: Printed by Daniel and John Kneeland, for J. Winter in Union-street, opposite to the Kings Arms.* M,DCC,LIX. 8vo, pp. 53. BA.

ELIOT. A Sermon Preached at the Ordination of the Reverend Mr. Joseph Willard, to the Pastoral care of the First Church in Beverly, in conjunction with the Reverend Mr. Joseph Champney, November XXV. MDCCLXXII. By Andrew Eliot, D.D. Pastor of a Church in Boston. To which are annexed, The Charge, By the Rev. Dr. Appleton, and the Right Hand of Fellowship, By the Rev. Mr. Holt. Published at the Desire of the Church and Congregation in Beverley. *Boston, New-England: Printed by Thomas and John Fleet.* 1773. 8vo, pp. 47. W. 22126

ELIOT. A Sermon preached at the Ordination of Andrew Eliot, A.M. To the Pastoral care of the First Church in Fairfield: June 22, 1774. By his Father, Andrew Eliot, D.D. Pastor of a Church in Boston. *Boston: Printed by John Boyle in Marlborough-Street.* MDCCLXXIV. 8vo, pp. 46. BA., G., H. 22127

ELIOT. A Sermon preached at the Ordination of the Reverend John Eliot, A.M. To the Pastoral Care of the New-North Church in Boston: November 3, 1779. By his Brother Andrew Eliot, A.M. Pastor of the First Church in Fairfield. *Boston: Printed by John Boyle.* MDCCLXXX. 8vo, pp. 35. BA. 22128

ELIOT. Twenty Sermons ... . By Andrew Eliot, D.D. ... . *Boston: John Boyle.* MDCCLXXIV. 8vo. B., BA. 22129

Also: A Burning and Shining Light extinguished. A Sermon Preached The Lord's-Day after the Funeral Of the late Reverend Mr. John Webb, Pastor of the New-North Church in Boston; Who died April 16. 1750. Æt. 63. By Andrew Eliot, A.M. Pastor of the same Church. *Boston: Printed by Daniel Fowle, Joshua Winter in Union Street opposite the King's Arms.* [1750.] 8vo, pp. 42, 1 l. B., BA., M., W. — A Discourse on Natural Religion ... May 8. 1771. At the Lecture Founded By the Hon. Paul Dudley, Esq; ... *Boston: Printed by Daniel Kneeland.* M,DCC,LXXI. 8vo, pp. xlv, (2). BA. — An inordinate Love of the World inconsistent with the Love of God. A Sermon Preached at the Thursday Lecture in Boston, August 2. 1744. ... *Boston: Printed by Rogers and Fowle.* 1744. 8vo, pp. 31. B., BA., H. — A Sermon Preached at the Ordination Of the Reverend Mr. Joseph Roberts, To the Pastoral Care of a Church In Leicester. October 23d. 1754. *Boston: J. Winter.* [1754.] 8vo, pp. (2), 41. BA., H. — A Sermon Preached September 17. 1766. At the Ordination Of the Reverend Mr. Ebenezer Thayer, To the Pastoral Care of the First Church in Hampton. ... *Boston: Thomas Leverett.* 1766. 8vo, pp. (2), 35. B., BA., H. *See also* "Mass. Hist. Coll.," Vol. X., First Series; Vol. II., Second Series; and Vol. IV., Fourth Series.

ELIOT (A.), *Junr.* A Sermon, Preached on the Day of the General Election, at Hartford, in the State of Connecticut, May 5th, 1819. By Andrew Eliot, ... New Milford. *Hartford.* 1819. 8vo, pp. 20. 22130

ELIOT (C. W.) Addresses at the Inauguration of Charles William Eliot as President of Harvard College, Tuesday, October 19, 1869. *Cambridge.* 1869. 8vo, pp. 65. B. 22131

[ELIOT (Ephraim)]. Historical Notices of the New North Religious Society, in the Town of Boston; With Anecdotes of the Reverend Andrew and John Eliot. *Boston: Printed by Phelps and Farnham.* 1822. 8vo, pp. 51. BA. 22132

ELIOT (James). Fayette in Prison. *Worcester, Mass.* 1802. 8vo. 22133

ELIOT (J.) An Essay on the Invention or Art of making very good Iron, from black Sea Sand. By Jared Eliot, M.A. of Killingworth. *New York: Printed and Sold by John Holt, at the New-Printing Office near Burling's Slip.* 1762. 12mo, pp. 34.

ELIOT. An Essay upon Field Husbandry in New England. *New London, New York, and New Haven.* 1748–59. Parts I. to VI., 12mo. 22135

ELIOT Essays upon Field-Husbandry in New-England. ... By Jared Eliot, M.A. ... *Boston: Edes & Gill.* 1760. 8vo, Title, pp. (4), 166. BA., H. 22136

A Continuation of the Essays upon Field-Husbandry, ... *N. London: Printed and Sold by T. Green.* 1749. + [*Ibid.*] 1751. 8vo, pp. (2), 52. + Fourth Part. *New York.* 1753. H.

ELIOT. Give Cæsar his Due, or the Obligation that Subjects are under to their Civil Rulers, as was showed in a Sermon Preached before the General Assembly of the Colony of Connecticut, at Hartford, May the 11th, 1738, the Day for the Election of the Honourable, the Governour, the Deputy-Governour and the Worshipful Assistants. *N. London: T. Green.* 1738. Sm. 8vo, pp. (2), 44. B. 22137

ELIOT. God's Marvellous Kindness Illustrated. Thanksgiving Sermon, July 25, 1745, on the Capture of Louisburg. *New London.* 1745. 16mo, pp. 26. M. 22138

ELIOT. Six Essays upon Field-Husbandry in New England, in the year 1747. New Edition, with an Appendix by another hand. *New York.* 1761. 12mo. C. 22139

ELIOT. The Two Witnesses; or, Religion Supported by Reason and Divine Revelation, Being the Substance of a Lecture-Sermon, Preach'd at the North Society in Lyme, October 29, 1735, Before the Association of the County of New-London; and Published at their Desire. By Jared Eliot, A.M. Pastor of the Church at Killingworth. *N. London: T. Green.* 1736. 12mo, 2 l., pp. 79. B. 22140

Also: The Blessedness of those who die in the Lord. Discourse on Death of Rev. William Worthington. ... *New Haven.* 1757. 8vo, pp. 15. — On Field-Husbandry. ... *New York.* 1753. 12mo.

ELIOT (J.), *born* 1604, *died* 1690. A Brief | Answer | to a small book written by | John Norcot, | against | Infant Baptism. | This Answer is written by John | Eliot, for the sake of some of the | Flock of Jesus Christ, who | are ready to be staggered | in point of Infant Baptism | by reading his book. | *Boston: Printed by John Foster*, 1679. | 8vo, pp. 27. 22141

"Of great rarity, possibly unique." — W. E. WOODWARD's *Catalogue.* Cotton Mather refers to it, but Francis, who wrote a life of Eliot, never saw it.

ELIOT. A Brief | Narrative | of the | Progress of the Gospel amongst | the Indians in New-England, in | the Year 1670. | Given in | By the Reverend John Elliot, | Minister of the Gospel there, | In a Letter by him directed to | the Right-Worshipfull the Com- | missioners under his Majesties | Great-Seal for Propagation of the | Gospel amongst the poor Blind Na- | tives in those United Colonies. | *London,* | *Printed for John Allen, formerly living in Little-Britain at | the Rising-Sun, and now in Wentworth street near Bell- | Lane,* 1671. | 4to, pp. 11. J.C.B. 22142

A volume of the greatest rarity. It was reprinted as

ELIOT. A Brief Narrative of the Progress of the Gospel among the Indians of New England. 1670. By Rev. John Eliot. With Introductory Notes. By W. T. R. Marvin. *Boston: John K. Wiggin & Wm. Parsons Lunt.* 1868. Sm. 4to, pp. 36. BA. 22143

One hundred and seventy copies printed, twenty of which are on large paper.

ELIOT. The Christian Commonwealth: or The Civil Policy of The Rising Kingdom of Jesus Christ. Written before the Interruption of the Government, by Mr. John Eliot, Teacher of the Church of Christ at Roxbury in New-England and now published (after his consent given) by a Servor of the season. *London: Printed for Livewell Chapman, at the Crown, in Popes-Head-Alley.* [1659.] 4to, 11 l., pp. 35. J.C.B. 22144

The original edition is almost unique. It is reprinted in "Mass. Hist. Coll.," Vol. IX., Third Series. "On the 18th of March, 1660, the Governor and Council of Massachusetts passed a formal judgment of condemnation against this book, as they found it 'ful of seditious principles and notions.' It was most rigorously suppressed, and Eliot was forced by the General Court, in the following May, to hand in a humiliating written recantation, which was posted in the public places of all the chief towns of the Colony." *See* Francis' "Life of Eliot." Sold, at Puttick's, in 1854, for £5 12s.

ELIOT. Communion of Churches: | or, | The Divine Management of Gospel Churches | by the Ordinance of | Councils, | Constituted in Order according to the | Scriptures. | As Also, | The Way of bringing all Christian | Parishes to be particular Reforming | Congregational Churches: | Humbly Proposed, | As a Way which hath so much Light from the | Scriptures of Truth, as that it may lawfully be | Submitted unto by all; and may, by the blessing | of the Lord, be a Means of Uniting those two | Holy and Eminent Parties, | The Presbyterians and Congregationals. | As Also | To Prepare for the hoped-for Resurrection of the | Churches; and to Propose a way to bring all | Christian Nations unto an Unity of the | Faith and Order of the Gospel. | Written by John Eliot, Teacher of | Roxbury in N. E. | Psal. 1. 10. That ye may try the things that are excellent. | 1 John 4. 1. Try the Spirits. | *Cambridge: Printed by Marmaduke Johnson.* 1665. | 16mo, Title, pp. 38. 22145

The verso of the title reads: Although a few Copies of this small Script are | Printed; yet it is not published, onely [*sic*] committed | privately to some Godly and Able hands, to be Viewed, | Corrected, Amended, or Rejected, as it shall be found to | hold weight in the Sanctuary Ballance [*sic*] or not. ... The procuring of half so many copies written and | corrected, would be more difficult and chargeable, then [*sic*] | the Printing of these few ... | John Eliot. | Beyond any doubt this is the first privately printed American book. Martin, in his "Catalogue of Books Privately Printed," notices but seven titles during the entire century in which this interesting little volume was printed. The only copy we know was sold by us to William Menzies, of New York; it is uncut, and has manuscript alterations by a contemporary hand — probably by Eliot himself.

[ELIOT.] The | Day-Breaking | if not | The Sun-Rising | of the | Gospell | With the | Indians in New-England. | ... | *London,* | *Printed by Rich. Cotes, for Fulk Clifton, and are to bee | sold at his shop under Saint Margaretts Church on | New-fish-street-Hill,* 1647. | 4to, Title, 1 l., pp. 25. 22146

This forms No. II. of the series of tracts published by the Corporation. It was reprinted as

[ELIOT.] The Day Breaking if not the Sun Rising of the Gospel with the Indians in New England. ... *New York: reprinted for Joseph Sabin.* 1865. 4to, pp. 32. B. 22147

Edition, 250 copies, of which 50 are on large paper. Forms No. IX. of Sabin's reprints, quarto series.

ELIOT. The Dying Speeches of several Indians. [n. p. n. d.] 18mo, pp. 12. G.B. 22148

Reprinted, the preface excepted, in "The Sabbath at Home," [June, 1868, pp. 333 *et seq.*] It is also reprinted, with the preface, in the Prince Society's edition of "Dunton's Letters." The date of 1665, which has been assigned to it, is doubtless incorrect, as on page 25 following, Eliot speaks of John Speen and Anthony as living in 1670, whose "Dying Speeches" are given in the tract named.

[ELIOT.] A further Accompt | of the Progresse of the | Gospel | amongst the Indians | in New-England, | and | Of the means used effectually to advance the same. | Set forth | In certaine Letters sent from thence declaring a | purpose of Printing the Scriptures in the | Indian Tongue into which they are already | Translated. | With which Letters are likewise sent an Epi- | tome of some Exhortations delivered by the In- | dians at a Fast, as Testimonies of their obedi- | ence to the Gospell. | As also some helps directing to the Indians how to | improve naturall reason unto the knowledge | of the true God. | *London, Printed by M. Simmons for the Corpo- | ration of New-England*, 1659. | 4to, 5 l., pp. (1), 35, (1). 22149

This forms No. IX. of the series of tracts issued by the Corporation. It is a tract of much rarity. Pages 22 to 35 consist of "Some Helps for the Indians ... By Abraham Pierson. *London: M. Simmons.* 1659," having a separate title-page, it is occasionally found by itself; it forms, however, a part of this tract. It ends abruptly: "The reason why there is so short an imperfect specimen given of it ('Some Helps') is because the ships came away from N. E. before any more of the copy was wrought off from the presse." It was reprinted, omitting Abraham Pierson, with the following title:

ELIOT. A Further Manifestation of the Progress of the Gospel among the Indians in New England. *New York: Reprinted for Joseph Sabin.* 1865. 4to, 6 l., pp. 19, (2). 22150

Edition, 250 copies, of which 50 are on large paper. Forms No. VI. of Sabin's reprints, quarto series.

ELIOT. A further Account of the progress | of the | Gospel | Amongst the Indians | In New-England: being | A Relation of the Confessions made | by several Indians (in the pre- | sence of the Elders and Mem- | bers of several Churches) in or- | der to their admission into | Church-fellowship. | Sent over to the Corporation for Propagating the Gospel of | Jesus Christ amongst the Indians in New-England at Lon- | don, by Mr. John Elliot one of the Laborers in the Word | amongst them. | *London*, | *Printed by John Macock.* 1660. | 4to, 5 l., pp. 76. J.C.B. 22151

ELIOT. The | Glorious Progress | of the | Gospel | amongst the Indians in New England. Manifested | By three Letters, under the

Hand of that fa- | mous Instrument of the Lord | Mr. John Eliot, And another from Mr. Thomas Mayhew jun; both Preachers of | the Word, as well to the English as Indians in New England. Wherein | The riches of Gods Grace in the effectual calling of | many of them is cleared up: As also a manifestation of the hungring | desires of many People in sundry parts of that Country after the | more full Revelation of the Gospel of Jesus Christ, to the | exceeding Consolation of every Christian Reader. | Together, With an Appendix to the foregoing Letters, hol- | ding forth Conjectures, Observations and Applications. | By I. D. Minister of the Gospell. | Published by Edward Winslow ... *London. Printed for Hannah Allen in Popes-head-Alley.* 1649. | 4to, 4 l., pp. 28.

Reprinted in the "Mass. Hist. Coll.," Vol. IV., Third Series, pp. 68–98. The fourth of the series published by the Corporation; it is dedicated to the "Parliament of England And the Councell of State."

ELIOT. The Harmony of the Gospels, | in the Holy | History | of the | Humiliation and Sufferings | of | Jesus Christ, | From His | Incarnation | to His | Death and Burial. | Published by John Eliot, Teacher | of the Church in Roxbury. | ... | *Boston*; | *Printed by John Foster, in the Year* 1678. | 4to, pp. (4), 131. B., M. 22153

The first press in Boston was established by John Foster, who printed his first book in 1676.

ELIOT. The | Holy Bible: | containing the | Old Testament | and the New. Translated into the | Indian Language, | and | Ordered to be Printed by the Commissioners of the Vnited Colonies in New-England, | At the Charge, and with the Consent of the | Corporation in England | For the Propagation of the Gospel amongst the Indians | in New-England. | *Cambridge: Printed by Samuel Green and Marmaduke Johnson.* | MDCLXIII. | Sm. 4to.

Collation: Title, 1 l.; Dedication to King Charles II, 2 l.; List of Books, 1 l.; Text, A to MMMMM in 4s; usually followed by the New Testament, as described, *infra.* Some copies have the Indian title, which reads: Mamvsse | Wunneetupanatamwe | Up-Biblum God | naneeswe | Nukkone Testament | kah wonk | Wusku Testament. | Ne quoshkinnumuk nashpe Wuttinneumoh Christ | noh asoowesit | John Eliot. | *Cambridge: Printeenoop nashpe Samuel Green kah Marmaduke Johnson.* 1663.]

ELIOT. The New | Testament | of our | Lord and Saviour | Jesus Christ: | Translated into the | Indian Language, 4 | and | ordered to be printed by the Commissioners of the United Colonies, in New-England, | At the Charge, and with the Consent of the | Corporation in England | For the Propagation of the Gospel amongst the Indians | in New England. | *Cambridge:* | *Printed by Samuel Green and Marmaduke Johnson.* | M D CLXI. | 4to. 22155

The Indian title to the New Testament reads: Wusku | Wuttestamentum | Nul-Lordum | Jesus Christ | Nuppoquohwussuaeneumun. | [Stars.] *Cambridge* | *Printed by Samuel Green and Marmaduke Johnson.* MDCLXI. | Collation: 1 l. blank; Title, 1 l.; Epistle Dedicatory; Text, A² to verso of L⁴, then Aa to Xx in 4s, making 4 l. and pp. 126. The "stars," whose place is indicated above, form a diamond-shaped ornament, composed of thirty-two printer's flowers, which is wanting in some issues. In some copies of the New Testament, in Luke, the heading at the top of the page, which has Chapter XXI, reads "10;" and for Chapter XXIV, the numeral is "15." These errors are corrected in some copies; but, in correcting it apparently, the last letter in the catch-word on page L³ was pushed into the margin, and it stands thus, "waabe h." This is said to occur in all copies where the headings have been corrected. These last two peculiarities are, accordingly, not confined to the second issue with the English title-page, as O'Callaghan (p. 9) affirms. There are other variations, partly caused by the binder, and the curious collector is referred to Dr. E. B. O'Callaghan's list, page nine, for a description of them. Following the New Testament are the Psalms in Indian metre, translated by Eliot, from the Bay Psalm-Book, without a separate title-page, but with a heading as follows: "VVame Ketoohomae uketoohomaongash David." Sometimes A to N², and two pages containing a short Indian catechism, in all 50 l. The description by Dr. O'Callaghan inferentially conveys the idea that each copy of Eliot's Bible should have the title-page both in Indian *and* English. I have never met with a copy in that condition, and incline to believe that the title-pages were used indiscriminately by the binder. It is usual to find the work with an English title-page to the Old Testament, and an Indian title-page to the New Testament, *or* vice versa. It is probable that all the copies sent to England had the title to the Old Testament in English. Notwithstanding the fact that not less than fifteen hundred copies were printed, this has become an extremely rare book; many copies are known, but they are mostly in public libraries, and, when offered for sale, its price is not less than about a thousand dollars. E. B. Corwin's copy was bought by J. C. Brown, in 1835, for two hundred dollars; and John A. Rice's copy sold, in 1870, for one thousand and fifty dollars; and copies in England have sold for two hundred and fifty pounds during the year 1871. Among the many points of interest which this book possesses, not the least is the fact that it is the language of a nation no longer in existence, and is almost the only monument of the race; another, that it is *the first Bible published in this country.* The very sight of it caused Cotton Mather to exclaim: "*Behold, ye Americans, the greatest honor that ever you were partakers of! This is the only Bible that ever was printed in all America, from the very foundation of the world.*" The names of the books are retained as in the English versions, and such words as were unknown to the Indians are retained with an Indian termination, such as cherub-*imlah*, etc. The longest word is (Mark, I., 40): "Wutteppsittukqussunnoowehtunkquoh," signifying "kneeling down to him." It is certainly a very great typographica curiosity; and, it is said, that there are not now more than two persons living whc can read the language in which it is written. Mather, in his "Magnalia," mentions that Eliot wrote the whole of this great work with one pen. Thomas, in hi "History of Printing," supposes, if this was so, it must have been a metal pen, an not a goose quill. That, however, by no means follows. The Corporation for Prop agating the Gospel among the Indians seems to have felt great interest in the publica tion of this Bible. In 1660, they engaged Marmaduke Johnson, and sent him t America to assist in printing that Bible, and, in a letter dated "Cooper's Hall i London, April 28. 1660," and directed to the Commissioners of the United Colonie: they write: "Wee have out of our desire to further a worke of soe greate consernmen agreed with an able printer for three yeares upon the tearmes and conditions enclosec Wee desire you at the earnest request of Mr. Johnson, the printer, and for his incou ragement in this undertaking of printing the Bible in the Indian language, his nam may be mentioned with others as a printer and person that hath been instrumenta therein; for whose diet, lodging and washing wee desire you to take care of." T commissioners, in their answer, say: "The printers doubt not but to print a shee

every weeke, and compute the whole to amount to a hundred and fifty sheets," which the collation shows to be nearly the fact. Thomas' "History of Printing" says that twenty copies only of the dedication to King Charles were printed; but O'Callaghan doubts the correctness of this statement. It appears, from a "Postscript" to Eliot's "further Accompt ... *London.* 1659," that "Genesis, Matthew, and a few Psalmes in Meeter" had already been "printed in their own Language," but there are no known copies of any or either of these books.

ELIOT. Mamvsse | Wunneetupanatamwe | Up-Biblum God | Naneeswe | Nukkone Testament | kah wonk | Wusku | Testament. | Ne quoshkinnumuk nashpe Wuttinneumoh Christ | noh asoowesit | John Eliot. | Nahohtôeu outchetôt Printeuoomuk. | *Cambridge:* | *Printenoop nashpe Samuel Green.* MDCLXXXV. | BA., N.

Collation: Title, 1 l.; Text, A to Ppppp in 4s; then "VVvskv," etc., 1680, as below; in all, 607 l.; Old Testament, 425 l. Mr. Eliot also had the superintendence of this edition; and, in his letter to the Hon. Robert Boyle, President of the Corporation, he acknowledges the reception of nine hundred pounds sterling, in three payments, for carrying it through the press. Eliot, however, had to give part of his salary towards printing the work. For the English title, *see* O'Callaghan's list. The New Testament has a separate title-page, as follows:

ELIOT. VVvskv | Wuttestamentamentum | Nul-Lordumum | Jesus Christ | Nuppoquohwussuaeneumunx. | *Cambridge,* | *Printed for the Right Honourable* | *Corporation in London, for the* | *propagation* [sic] *of the Gospel among the In-* | *dians in New England.* 1680. | Sm. 4to. 22157

Collation: Title, 1 l.; Text, A1 to Kk² in 4s; the Psalms in Metre, Kh³ to Yy⁴; Catechism, 1 l.; in all, 182 l. After the New Testament follow the Psalms in Indian metre, as in the first edition, without separate title-page, but with the following heading: "Wame Ketoohomae uketoohomaongash David." When this edition occurs for sale, it usually has the Indian title. A writer in the "Mass. Hist. Coll.," VIII. 12–33, states that Eliot's "Indian Grammar" is printed in some editions of the Indian Bible. Such instances must be considered exceptional; I have never seen it. O'Callaghan's "List" includes a copious list of errata. The copy in the Public Library at Boston has a dedication to the Honorable Robert Boyle, and the first word in the title is spelt "Mamvs's." The dedication has been printed in facsimile by George Livermore, Esq., of Boston; it is also reprinted in O'Callaghan's list. Eliot was aided in this edition by Josiah Cotton, son of Rev. John Cotton, of Plymouth, who was well acquainted with the Indian language.

ELIOT. The Indian Grammar begun: or, An Essay to bring the Indian Language into Rules, for the help of such as desire to Learn the same, for the furtherance of the Gospel among them. By John Eliot. ... *Cambridge: Printed by Marmaduke Johnson.* 1666. 4to, pp. 66. BA. 22158

A volume of extreme rarity; but few copies are known. It is not quoted by either Lowndes or Brunet as having occurred for sale. Mr. Bartlett has reprinted the dedication in the "Cat. of the Library of J. C. Brown." Reprinted as below:

ELIOT. A Grammar of the Massachusetts Indian Language. By John Eliot. A New Edition: With Notes and Observa-

tions, by Peter S. Du Ponceau, LL.D., and an Introduction and Supplementary Observations, by John Pickering. ... *Boston: Printed by Phelps and Farnham.* 1822. 8vo, pp. 22. BA., H.

Also forms "Collections of the Mass. Hist. Soc.," Vol. IX., Second Series.

ELIOT. Indian Dialogues, for their Instruction in that great service of Christ, in calling home their countrymen to the knowledge of God and of themselves, and of Jesus Christ. By John Eliot. *Cambridge.* 1671. 8vo. 22160

ELIOT. Indiane Primer Asuh negonneyeuuk. Ne nashpe Mukkiesog Woh tauog wunnamuhkuttee ogketamunnate Indiane Unnontoowaonk. Kah Meninnunk wutch Mukkiesog. *Mushauwomuk.* 1720. 12mo, pp 86, 165. 22161

Second title-page: The Indian Primer. And Milk for Babes [by J. Cotton]. *Boston.* 1820. 12mo. "Mr B Green says composd by Mr. Eliot, & Prind at Camb, abt 1684." — T. PRINCE's note on the first edition, which we have not seen.

ELIOT. A Late and Further | Manifestation | of the | Progress of the Gospel | amongst the | Indians | in | New-England, | Declaring their constant Love and Zeal to | the Truth: With a readinesse to give | Accompt of their Faith and Hope; as of | their Desires in Church Commu- | nion to be Partakers of | the Ordinances of | Christ. | Being a Narrative of the Examinations of the Indians, about | their Knowledge in Religion, by their Elders of the Churches. | Related by Mr. John Eliot, Published by the Corporation, established by | Act of Parliament, for Propagating the Gospel there. | [Motto.] *London: Printed by M. S.* 1655. | 4to, 4 l., pp. 23. C., H., W. 22162

This, like all of Eliot's tracts, is very rare in the original edition. Forms No. IX. in the Propagation Series, and was reprinted in the "Mass. Hist. Soc. Coll.," Vol. IV., Third Series.

E[LIOT]. The Logic Primer. Some Logical Notions to initiate the Indians in the Knowledge of the Rule of Reason, ... especially for the Instruction of such as are Teachers among them. Composed by J. E. for the Use of the Praying Indians. [n. p.] 1672. 16mo. BM. 22163

[ELIOT.] Wame Ketoohomae uketoohomaongash David. *Cambridge.* 1661. 4to. W. + *Cambridge.* 1680. 8vo. M.

Poetical translation of the Psalms into the Indian language of Massachusetts. Some copies of the Psalms were issued separately, and passed through several editions. Marvin refers to one dated, *Cambridge.* 1664. 8vo, pp. 50.

ELIOT. Sampwutteahae | Quinnuppekompauaenin. | Wahuwômook oggussemesuog Sampwutteahâe | Wunnamptamwaenuog, | Mache wussukhúmun ut English-Mane Unnontoowaonk nashpe | Né muttáe-wunnegenúe Wuttinneumoh Christ | Noh asoowesit | Thomas Shephard | Quinnuppenúmun en Indiane Unnontoowaonganit nashpe Ne Quttianatamwe wuttinneumoh Christ | Noh assoowesit | John Eliot. | Kah nawhutche ut aiyeuongash oggussemese ontcheteanun | Nashpe | Grindal Rawson. | [Eight lines.] *Cambridge.* | *Printed by Samuel Green, in the Year*, 1689. | 16mo, Title, 1 l., pp. 161. BA. 22165

Eliot also translated Baxter's "Call," *see* our No. 4012, and Bayly's "Practice of Piety," *see* our No. 4076, into the Natick dialect. *See also* Shepard (T.), Sibellius (Mc), "Strength out of Weakness," and Thorowgood (T.) John Eliot, the celebrated missionary among the Indians, was nearly sixty years pastor of the church at Roxbury, in Massachusetts. He is usually called "The Apostle of the Indians." He made every exertion to promote the welfare of the Indian tribes — he stimulated many clergymen to engage in the missionary work; and, although he mourned over the stupidity of many, who preferred darkness to light, yet he lived to see twenty-four of the copper-colored aborigines fellow-preachers of the Gospel. He possessed an influence over the Indians which no other missionary could obtain, and was their shield in 1675, during Philip's war, when some of the people of Massachusetts, actuated by the most infuriate spirit, intended to have destroyed them. He suffered every abuse for his friendship to them; but nothing could quench the divine charity which glowed in his heart. He died, May 20, 1690, aged about eighty-six years, saying his labors were poor and small, and exhorting those who surrounded his bed to pray. Concerning Eliot, *see* "Mass. Hist. Coll.," First Series, Vols. I., II., VIII., X.; Second Series, Vol. X.; and Third Series, Vol. IV. Also his life by Francis.

ELIOT *and* MAYHEW. Tears of Repentence: | Or, A further | Narrative of the Progress of the Gospel | Amongst the | Indians | in | New-England: | Setting forth, not only their present state and condition, but sundry Confessions of sin | by diverse of the said Indians, wrought upon | by the saving Power of the Gospel; Together | with the manifestation of their Faith and Hope | in Jesus Christ, and the Work of Grace upon | their Hearts. | Related by Mr. Eliot and Mr. Mayhew, two Faithful Laborers | in that Work of the Lord. | Published by the Corporation for propagating the Gospel there, for the | Satisfaction and Comfort of such as wish well thereunto. | [Motto.] *London: Printed by Peter Cole in Leaden-Hall, and are to be Sold at* | *his Shop, at the Sign of the Printing-Press in Cornhill,* | *near the Royal Exchange.* 1653. | 4to, 18 l., pp. 47. C., H., S. 22166

Reprinted in the "Mass. Hist. Soc. Coll.," Vol. IV., Third Series.

ELIOT. The Life of John Eliot, the Apostle of the Indians, including Notices of the Principal Attempts to Propagate Christianity during the Seventeenth Century. *Edinburgh.* MDCCCXXVIII. 18mo, pp. 300. + *Philadelphia.* + *New York.* 1841.

ELIOT. Sketch of the Life. *See* [Dearborn (H. A. S.)], Vol. V., No. 19077.

Also: Authentic Memoirs of John Eliot. *American Tract Society.* 12mo.

ELIOT (J.) A Biographical Dictionary, containing a Brief Account of the First Settlers, and other Eminent Characters among the Magistrates, Ministers, Literary and Worthy Men in New-England. By John Eliot, D.D. Corresponding Secretary of the Massachusetts Historical Society. *Boston.* 1809. 8vo, pp. viii, 511, (1). BA. 22168

ELIOT. A Sermon, delivered before the Members of the New North Religious Society, Boston, May 2, 1804, upon the Completion of their House of Worship. By John Eliot, ... *Boston.* 1804. 8vo, pp. 31. B., H. 22169

The Old North Meeting-House was torn down and burnt for fuel by the British in 1776. Also: Catalogue of the Library of the Late Rev. John Eliot, D.D. *Boston.* 1813. Title, pp. 29. BA. — A Dudleian Lecture ... May 8, 1771. *Boston: Nicholas Bowes.* 1771. 8vo. — A Sermon, ... Boston, Before the Society of ... Free and Accepted Masons, June 24, 1782. ... *Boston: Printed by Brother N. Willis.* MDCCLXXXII. 8vo, pp. 18. BA. — A Sermon, delivered on the Day of Annual Thanksgiving, November 20, 1794. ... *Boston: Printed by Samuel Hall.* MDCCXCIV. 8vo, pp. 26. B., BA., H. — A Sermon, preached in Milton, November 1, 1797, at the Ordination of the Rev. Mr. Joseph M'Kean. ... *Boston.* 1797. 8vo, pp. 54. H. — A Sermon, on ... Attending Public Worship, ... *Boston: Printed by John Russell.* 8vo, pp. 36. BA., H. — A Sermon, ... at the Ordination of the Rev Henry Edes, A.M. July 17, A.D. 1805. ... *Providence: J. Carter.* 1805. 8vo, pp. 40. B., BA. *See* "Mass. Hist. Col.," Vols. VII., IX., and X., First Series; and Vols. I. and V., Second Series.

ELIOT (R. R.) Two Sermons Preached at Watertown [Mass.], Sept. 22, 1816. By Richard B. Eliot, A.M. ... *Concord: Printed by Joseph T. Peters.* 1816. 8vo, pp. 47. BA. 22170

Also: A Discourse delivered at Dedham, at the Consecration of Constellation Lodge, Oct. 19, 1803. ... *Boston.* 1803. 8vo, pp. 18. M., P.

ELIOT (S.) The Functions of a City. An Oration before the City Authorities of Boston, on the Fourth of July, 1868. By Samuel Eliot, LL.D. *Boston: Alfred Mudge & Son, City Printers.* 1868. 8vo, pp. 31. B. 22171

ELIOT. Manual of United States History, from 1492 to 1550. By Samuel Eliot. *Boston.* 1856. 12mo, pp. xvi, 484. C. + *Boston: Hickling, Swan and Brewer.* 1859. 12mo, pp. xvi, 483.

Also: An Address ... Trinity College, Hartford, on his Inauguration as President, ... April 8, 1861, By Samuel Eliot. *Hartford: Press of Case, Lockwood & Company.* 1861. 8vo, pp. 22. BA. — Address before the American Social Science Association ... Nov. 19, 1867. *Boston: Wright & Potter, Printers.* 1867. 8vo, pp. 14. B.

[ELIOT (Samuel Atkins).] A Letter to the President of Harvard College. By a Member of the Corporation. *Boston: Charles C. Little and James Brown.* 1849. 8vo, pp. 53. H. 22173

ELIOT. A Sketch of the History of Harvard College. And of its Present State. By Samuel A. Eliot. *Boston: Charles C. Little and James Brown.* 1848. 12mo, pp. xiii, (1), 190. Plate.

Also: [Eliot.] Remarks on the Constitution of the Society for the Promotion of Theological Education in Harvard University. With a Circular Address. ... . *Boston.* 1825. 8vo, Title, pp. 8. H. — Address before the Boston Academy of Music, on the Opening of the Odeon, Aug. 5, 1835. ... *Boston.* 1835. 8vo, pp. 17. B., N. — An Article on the Charities of Boston. From the North American Review for July, 1860. *Boston: Crosby, Nichols, Lee and Company.* 1860. 8vo, pp. 20. H. — A Complete System of Education. A Lecture. ... January 19, 1853. By Samuel A. Eliot. *Boston: Eastburn's Press.* 1853. 8vo, pp. 19. B., BA., H. *See* Hancock.

ELIOT (T. D.) Address of Thomas D. Eliot, to his Constituents of the First Congressional District of Massachusetts. [*Washington.* 1861.] 8vo, pp. 8. H. 22175

Also: An Address before the New Bedford Port Society, ... April 29, 1855. *New Bedford: Printed by Benj. Lindsey.* 1855. 8vo, pp. 29. H. — Anniversary Address, delivered before the American Institute of the City of New York, ... October 17, 1845, ... *New York.* 1845. 8vo, pp. 19. — Continuation of Freedmen's Bureau. Speech ... March 11, 1868. [*Washington.* 1868.] 8vo, pp. 8. H. — Independence of Hayti. Speech ... June 3, 1862, on the Bill to authorize the Appointment of Diplomatic Representatives to the Republics of Hayti and Liberia. [*Washington.* 1862.] 8vo, pp. 8. H. — Nebraska and Kansas. Speech ... May 10, 1854. [*Washington.* 1854.] 8vo, pp. 7. BA. — Objects of the War. Speech ... December 12, 1861. [*Washington.* 1861.] 8vo, pp. 8. H. — Speech ... on the ... River and Harbor Bill; ... April 30, 1866. *Washington.* 1866. 8vo, pp. 15. H. — Speech ... Feb. 10, 1864, on the Bill for the Establishment of a Bureau of Freedmen's Affairs. [*Washington.* 1864.] 8vo, pp. 16. H. — The Territorial Slave Policy; The Republican Party; what the North has to do with Slavery. Speech ... April 25, 1860. [*Washington.* 1860.] 8vo, pp. 8. H.

ELIOT (W. G.) Discourse preached at the Dedication of the First Congregational Church; St. Louis, Mo. October 29th, 1837, by Wm. G[reenleaf] Eliot, Jr. [n. p.] *printed by Chambers, Harris & Knapp.* 1837. 16mo, pp. 11. H. 22176

ELIOT. Loyalty and Religion. A Discourse for the Times, delivered in ... St. Louis, August 18th, 1861, by Rev. W. G. Eliot, D.D. ... . *St. Louis: printed by George Knapp & Co.* 1861. 8vo, pp. 12. H. 22177

[ELIOT.] Western Sanitary Commission, St. Louis, Mo. ... *Cambridge: Welch, Bigelow and Company.* 1864. 8vo, pp. 16.

Also: Address delivered before the Franklin Society of St. Louis, on ... its First Anniversary, January 7th, 1836. ... *St. Louis: Charless & Paschall.* [1836.] 8vo, pp. 27. H. — A Discourse delivered before the Members of the "Old Guard," of St.

Louis, by their Chaplain, ... *St. Louis: R. P. Studley and Co., Printers.* MDCCCLXII. 8vo, pp. 21. H. — Emancipation in Missouri. A Discourse delivered in ... St. Louis, July 5, 1863, ... *St. Louis: M'Kee & Fishback.* 1863. 8vo, pp. 7 B., H. — Religious and Moral Wants of the West. *Boston.* 1837. 12mo, pp. 20. B. — Statement relating to the Endowment of Washington University, St. Louis, Mo. ... *Boston.* 1864 8vo, pp. 38. B., H. — Washington's Birth-Day. Patriotism. 8vo, pp. 4.

[ELIOT (W. H.)] Description of the Tremont House, with Architectural Illustrations [by Isaiah Rogers]. *Boston.* 1830. 4to. 22178*a*

ELIOT (W. H.), *Jr.* Genealogy of the Eliot Family. Originally Compiled by William H. Eliot, Jr. Revised and Enlarged by William S. Porter, ... *New Haven, Conn.: George B. Bassett & Co.* 1854. 8vo, pp. 154. B., S. 22179

ELIOT, *Maine.* A Short Genealogical Account of a few of the Families of the Early Settlers in Eliot [including the Fogg Family, the Hill Family] and a branch of the Moody Family, from the time they Emigrated to this Country to the year 1850. *Saco: A. A. Hanscom.* 1851. 22180

ELISEO (*Padre*). Aviendo Represen-|tado el Conde de Monterey a su ma-|jestad los agrauios y molestias, que los Indios|de la Nueua España recibian, por orden de los|juezes que los repartian, para seruicios persona-|les, se le mandō que no se repartiessen, pero que|se diesse ordē como se alquilassen, y no estuuiessen ociosos: con la qual los de buen zelo queda-|ron contentos y satisfechos. Y porque los inte-|ressados resistian, el Padre Eliseo (Carmelita|Descalço) Confessor del Conde, escriuio vn pa-|pel, persuadiendole a executar punctualmente|la orden de su Magestad, que es del tenor si-|guiente.| [1643]. Folio, 8 l.

ELISHA (P.) N. J. Patent Right Oppression Exposed. By Patrick Elisha. *Philadelphia.* 1813. 12mo. W. 22182

Elixir Magnum: The Philosopher's Stone Found Out. Being a certain Method to Extract Silver and Gold out of the Earth in Great Plenty. By Way of Address to the Legislative Powers of all the British Colonies in North-America. *Philadelphia: Printed and Sold by James Chattin, at the Newest-Printing-Office, the south side of the Jersey Market.* 1757. 8vo, pp. 29. P.

This desirable object was to be effected by legislative encouragement of provincial industry.

Eliza. The Chippeway Indian. [*New York:*] *American Tract Society.* [n. d.] 8vo, pp. 8. 22184

Eliza Woodson: A Story of American Life. *New York.* 1866. 12mo. 22185

Elizabeth in her Holy Retirement; an Essay to prepare a Pious Woman for her Lying-in. *Boston: N. Boone.* 1710. 12mo. 22186

Introduced here as an early imprint, perhaps by Mather?

ELIZABETH (*Queen*). The Life and Glorious Reign of Queen Elizabeth. Likewise, An Account of Sir Francis Drake's Voyage round the World. Also, An Account of the Destruction of the great Fleet, call'd the Spanish Armada. *London.* 1708. 8vo, pp. 16. 22187

Elizabethæ Angliæ Reginæ Edictum adversus omnes Catholicos sui Regni, cum Andreæ Philopatri Responsione. *Lugduni.* 1593. 8vo. 22188

The "Response" is by Robert Parsons, the Jesuit. This curious volume contains historical notices of Sir F. Drake and his voyages; Sir Richard Grenville, the discoverer of Virginia; Sir W. Raleigh; and many other illustrious persons of Queen Elizabeth's reign.

ELIZABETHTOWN, *N. J.* Address of the Presbytery of Elizabethtown, on the Claims of the Gospel Ministry to an adequate Support. *Elizabethtown.* 1838. 8vo. 22189

Elizabeth (N. J.) Directory for 1865. By J. H. Lant & Co. *New York: Chapin, Bromell, Scott & O'Keefe.* 12mo, pp. 108, xii. Continued. 22190

Boyd's Directory of Elizabeth, Rahway, and Plainfield, with a Business Directory of Union County, 1868–69. *Elizabeth: A. & W. H. Boyd.* 1868. 12mo, pp. 348. 22191

Letter from a Gentleman at Elizabeth Town to his Friend in New York. *Philadelphia.* 1764. 8vo, pp. 8. 22192

Parish Statistics of Christ Church, Elizabeth, N. J., and Third Annual Address of the Rector. 8vo, pp. 24. 22193

ELIZABETH ISLANDS. Description of the Elizabeth Islands in Buzzard's Bay. *New York.* 1836. 8vo, pp. 8. Map.

ELIZAGA (L.) Ensayos políticos. Coleccion de articulos escritos y publicados en diversos periódicos, durante la usurpacion de Maximiliano, por Lorenzo Elizaga. *Mexico.* 1867. 4to, pp. v, 464. Portrait. 22195

ELKING (H.) A View of the Greenland Trade and Whale-Fishery. With the National and Private Advantages thereof. *London: J. Roberts.* MDCCXXII. 8vo, pp. 68. + *London, reprinted.* 1859. 8vo. C. 22196

ELKINS (H.) Fifteen Years in the Senior Order of Shakers a Narration of Facts, concerning that Singular People. By Hervey Elkins. ... *Dartmouth, N. H.* 1852. 8vo, pp. 136. + *Dartmouth Press, Hanover.* 1853. 8vo, pp. 136. B., BA. 22197

ELKING (W.) Eleven Years amongst the Shakers at Enfield. By William Elking. *Hanover: Dartmouth Press.* 1853.

Elkswatawa; or, the Prophet of the West. *See* [French (*Mr.*)]

Ella Cameron, or the Maid, Wife & Widow of a Day. An Extraordinary Revelation of the Deceit and Treachery Practised at the National Capital and in New York City at the time of the Plotting of the great Southern Rebellion. By an Ex-Member of Congress. *Philadelphia: Barclay & Co.* [n. d.] 8vo. pp. 42.

Ella V——, or, the July Tour. *See* [Taylor (F.)]

ELLEGOOD (J.) Sermon on the Death of Miss Dorwin, 23rd April, 1854. By Rev. Jacob Ellegood. *Montreal.* 1854. 8vo.

ELLERY (A. R.) An Oration, delivered July 4th, A.D. 1796, in the Baptist Meeting-House, in Newport; In Commemoration of the Twentieth Anniversary of American Independence. By Abraham Redwood Ellery. ... *Warren, Rhode Island: Printed by Nathaniel Phillips.* M,DCC,XCVI. 8vo, pp. 24. BA., H. 22201

[ELLERY (C.)] A Defence against Calumny; or, Haman, in the Shape of Christopher Ellery, Esq. hung upon his own Gallows. Being the Substance of certain Publications, ... etc., refuting the Accusations against John Rutledge. ... *Printed for the Purchasers.* 1803. 8vo, pp. 64. BA. 22202

ELLET (C.) The Army of the Potomac, and its Mismanagement. Respectfully addressed to Congress. By Charles Ellet, Jr., Civil Engineer. *Washington: L. Towers & Co.*, 1861. + 8vo, pp. 19. H. + *New York: Ross & Tousey.* 1862. 8vo, pp. 19. B., H. 22203

ELLET. Contributions to Physical Geography of the United States. Part I. On the Physical Geography of the Mississippi Valley, with Suggestions as to the Improvement of the Ohio and other Rivers. By Chas. Ellet, Jr. pp. 64. 22204

See "Smithsonian Contributions," Vol. II.

ELLET. An Essay on the Laws of Trade, in reference to the Works of Internal Improvement in the United States. By Charles Ellet, Jr. ... *Richmond: Printed by P. D. Bernard.* 1839. 8vo, pp. 284. Plate. B., BA., C. 22205

ELLET. Military Incapacity, and what it costs the Country. By Chas. Ellet, Junr. ... *New York: Ross and Tousey.* 1862. 8vo, pp. 15. H. 22206

ELLET. The Mississippi and Ohio Rivers: containing Plans for the Protection of the Delta from Inundation; and Investigations of the Practicability and Cost of improving the Navigation of the Ohio and Other Rivers by Means of Reservoirs. With an Appendix, on the Bars at the Mouths of the Mississippi. By Charles Ellet, Jr., Civil Engineer. *Philadelphia: Lippincott, Grambo & Co.* 1853. 8vo, pp. 367. Plates. BA., C. 22207

ELLET. Report on the Improvement of the Khanawa, and incidentally of the Ohio River, by Means of Artificial Lakes. By Charles Ellet, Jun., Civil Engineer. *Philadelphia: Collins, Printer.* 1858. Rl. 8vo, pp. 113. 2 Maps. H. 22208

[ELLET.] The Wheeling Bridge. [*Philadelphia.* 1852.] 8vo, pp. 6. H. 22209

Also: Coast and Harbour Defences, or the Substitution of Steam Battering-Rams for Ships of War. ... *Philadelphia: John C. Clark.* 1855. 8vo, pp. 17. H. — The Mountain Top Track. A Description of the Railroad across the Blue Ridge at Rock Fish Gap, ... Virginia. ... *Philadelphia: T. K. and P. G. Collins.* 1856. pp. 23. B. — Remarks touching the Wheeling Bridge Suit. ... *Philadelphia: John C. Clark.* 1852. 8vo, pp. 24. H. — Report and Plan for a Wire Suspension Bridge, proposed to be constructed across the Mississippi River at Saint Louis.. By Charles Ellet, Jr. ... *Philadelphia: William Starely & Co. Printers.* 1840. 8vo, pp. 58, (1). 2 Plates. Report on a Railway Suspension Bridge across the Connecticut river at Middletown. *Philadelphia.* 1848. 8vo. — Report on the Tariff of Toll for the Virginia Central Railroad. ... [*Washington.* 1838.] 8vo, pp. 38. — Report on the Wheeling and Belmont Suspension Bridge, to the City Council of Wheeling. ... *Philadelphia: John C. Clark.* 1847. 8vo, pp. 43. 2 Plates. — Report on a Suspension Bridge across the Potomac, for Rail Road and Common Travel ... . *Philadelphia: John C. Clark.* 1852. 8vo, pp. 36. Map. H. — Report ... made to the Watering Committee on the 16th December, 1858. *Richmond: H. K. Ellyson.* 1859. 8vo, pp. 23. H. — Report on the Enlargement of the Water Works, of the City of Richmond. *Richmond: H. K. Ellyson.* 1859. 8vo, pp. 19. H.

ELLET (Elizabeth Fries Lummis). Domestic History of the American Revolution. By Mrs. Ellet. *New York: Charles Scribner.* 1850. 12mo, pp. 308. + [*Ibid.*] 1851. 22210

ELLET. Pioneer Women of the West. By Mrs. Elizabeth F. Ellet. *New York.* 1852. 12mo, pp. 434. C. + *New York.* 12mo. 22211

ELLET. The Queens of American Society. By Mrs. E. F. Ellet. *New York: C. Scribner & Co.* 1867. Cr. 8vo, pp. 464. 13 Portraits. C. 22212

ELLET. Summer Rambles in the West. By Mrs. Ellet. *New York: J. C. Riker.* MDCCCLIII. 12mo, pp. 268. C., P.

ELLET. The Women of the American Revolution. ... In Two [Three] Volumes, Second Edition. *New York: Baker & Scribner.* 1848–50. 3 vols., 12mo, pp. 348; 312; 396. Plates. BA. + Third Edition. [*Ibid.*] 1849. 3 vols., 12mo, pp. 348; 312; 396. Plates. + [*Ibid.*] 1849–50. H. 22214

Also: Evenings at Woodlawn. *New York: Baker & Scribner.* 1849. 12mo, pp. 348. — Rambles about the Country. ... *New York: Harper & Brothers.* 1847. 18mo, pp. 257. — Women Artists in all Ages and Countries. *New York.* 1859. 12mo. + *London.* 1859. 12mo. S.

ELLET *and* MACK (*Mrs.* R. E.) The Court Circles of the Republic; or, the Beauties and Celebrities of the Nation; illustrating Life and Society under eighteen Presidents; describing the Social Features of the Successive Administrations from Washington to Grant, [etc.] Illustrated with Original Portraits. By Mrs. E. F. Ellet. With Sketches by Mrs. R. E. Mack. *Hartford, Conn.: J. A. Stoddard & Co.* 1869. 8vo, 1 l., pp. 586. 15 Plates. B. 22215

ELLICOTT (A.) The Journal of Andrew Ellicott, late Commissioner on behalf of the United States during part of the Year 1796, the Years 1797, 1798, and 1799, and part of the Year 1800: For Determining the Boundary between the United States and the Possessions of his Catholic Majesty in America, containing occasional Remarks on the Situation, Soil, Rivers, Natural Productions, and Diseases of the Different Countries on the Ohio, Mississippi, and Gulph of Mexico: ... . *Philadelphia: Thomas Dobson.* 1803. 4to, pp. vii, 299, 151. 6 Maps. BA.

ELLICOTT. The Journal [as above]. Comprehending the Ohio, the Mississippi from the Mouth of the Ohio to the Gulf of Mexico, the Whole of West Florida, and Part of East Flo-

rida. To which is added An Appendix, Containing all the Astronomical Observations made Use of for determining the Boundary, with many Others, made in Different Parts of the Country for settling the Geographical Positions of some Important Places, with Maps of the Boundary on a large scale; likewise a great number of Thermometrical Observations, made at Different Times, and Places. *Philadelphia: Printed by William Fry.* 1814. 4to, pp. vii, 299, 151. 6 Maps. B. 22217

One of the earliest books by an American author, which describes the vast regions traversed by the commission, and is indeed the pioneer account of regions then desert, and now teeming with life, activity and civilization.

[ELLICOTT.] Observations on the River Potomack, the Country Adjacent, and the City of Washington. *New York.* 1794. 8vo, pp. 30. H. 22218

ELLICOTT. Several Methods by which Meridional Lines may be found with ease and accuracy: recommended to the Attention of the Surveyor in the United States. By Andrew Ellicott, A.M. *Philadelphia: Printed by Thomas Dobson.* 1798. 8vo, pp. 32. 2 Plates. 22219

ELLICOTT (T.) Bank of Maryland Conspiracy, as developed in the Report to the Creditors. By Thomas Ellicott, Trustee of said Bank. *Philadelphia.* 1839. 8vo, pp. xiv, 134. S. 22220

ELLINGTON (E.) Christ's Promise to be present where two or three meet together in His Name: Considered in a Sermon, preach'd the 25th March, 1771, the Anniversary of Laying the Foundation of the Orphan-House Academy in Georgia, Before his Excellency James Wright, Esquire, Captain-General and Governor-in-Chief, and a great number of the Principal Inhabitants of the said Province, at the Opening of the New Chapel lately erected there. By Edward Ellington, late Chaplain at the said House. With an Appendix, giving a Short Account of the Proceedings on that Occasion. *Savannah: printed by James Johnston.* 8vo, pp. 39. P. 22221

ELLINGTON. The Reproach of Christ, the Christian's Treasure. A Sermon occasioned by the Death of the Rev. George Whitefield, M.A., who Departed this life on Sunday, September 30th, 1770, at Newbury-Port near Boston. Preached at Christ Church, Savannah, in Georgia, on Sunday, Nov. 17, 1770. *London: E. & C. Dilly.* MDCCLXXI. 8vo, pp. 31. J.C.B. 22222

ELLINGTON (G.) *pseudonym.* The Women of New York; or, the Under-World of the great city. Illustrating the life of Women of Fashion, Actresses, etc. By George Ellington. *New York: the New York Book Company.* 1869. 8vo, pp. 650. 23 Plates. C. 22223

ELLINGTON (J. W.) Sermon at the Ordination of Rev. C. Frost, Feb. 20, 1822. By John W. Ellingwood. *Bath.* 1822. 8vo. B. 22224

Also: Sermon at the Ordination of Rev. Isaac Weston, June 10, 1818. ... *Portland.* 1818. 8vo.

[ELLINGWOOD (N. D.)] A Reply to a Pamphlet, written by George Wotherspoon, relative to a Resolution passed by the Standing Committee, denying the Application of Christ Church, New Brighton, to be admitted into Union. *New York: Israel Sackett.* 1850. 8vo, pp. 32. H. 22225

ELLIOT (C. S.) Songs of Yale: a New Collection. By C. S. Elliot. *New Haven: Charles C. Chatfield & Co.* 1870. 16mo. B. 22226

ELLIOT (Daniel Girard). The Birds of North America. By D. G. Elliot, F.L.S. F.Z.S. *New York: Published by the Author.* 1866–69. 15 pts., folio. 75 Plates. B. 22227

This fine work describes the birds which are not included in the works of Audubon or Wilson. Two hundred copies only printed, most of which were sold to subscribers.

ELLIOT. A Monograph of the Pittidæ. By Daniel Girard Elliot, F.Z.S. *New York: D. Appleton & Co.* 1861–63. Folio, pp. 102. 32 Colored Plates. B. 22228

Two hundred copies printed.

ELLIOT. A Monograph of the Tetraoninæ, or Family of the Grouse. By Daniel Girard Elliot, F.Z.S. *New York: The Author.* 1864–5. Folio. 30 Plates. B., C. 22229

ELLIOT (J.) The Poetical and Miscellaneous Works of James Elliot, Citizen of Guilford, Vermont, and late A Non-Commissioned Officer in the Legion of the United States. In Four Books, ... *Greenfield, Mass.: Printed for the Author.* M,DC,XCVIII. 12mo, pp. 271, (5). BA. 22230

Very rare. Only 300 copies printed. Contains a journal of his three years' services, from 1793 to 1796, and much other information.

ELLIOT (J.) American Diplomatic Code: Embracing a Collection of Treaties and Conventions between the United States

and Foreign Powers, from 1778 to 1834; with an Abstract of Important Judicial Decisions on Points connected with our Foreign Relations; also a Concise Diplomatic Manual, containing a Summary of the Law of Nations, and other Diplomatic Writings on Questions of International Law. *Washington: Jonathan Elliot, Junior.* 1834. 2 vols., 8vo, pp. 62, 566; 27, 17–703. C. 22231

ELLIOT. The Debates, Resolutions, and other Proceedings in Convention, on the Adoption of the Federal Constitution as recommended by the General Convention at Philadelphia, on the 17th Sept., 1787, with the Yeas and Nays on the Decision of the Main Question and Supplement. Collected and Revised from Contemporary Publications. By Jonathan Elliot. *Washington.* 1827–30. 4 vols., 8vo. 22232

Vol. IV. is entitled, "Journal and Debates of the Federal Convention, Held at Philadelphia, from May 14, to September 17, 1787. with the Constitution of the United States, ... *Washington.* 1830." 8vo.

ELLIOT. The Debates in the Several State Conventions, on the Adoption of the Federal Constitution, as recommended by the General Convention at Philadelphia, in 1787. Together with the Journal of the Federal Convention, Luther Martin's Letter, Yates's Minutes, Congressional Opinions, Virginia and Kentucky Resolutions of '98–'99, and other Illustrations of the Constitution. In Four Volumes. Second Edition, with Considerable Additions. Collected and Revised from Contemporary Publications, By Jonathan Elliot. Published under the Sanction of Congress. *Washington: Printed for the Editor.* 1836. 4 vols., 8vo, pp. xvi, 508; xi, (1), 556; xi, (1), 663; xii, 639. + *Philadelphia: J. B. Lippincott & Co.* 1861. 5 vols., 8vo. B., BA., H. + [*Ibid.*] 1866. 5 vols., 8vo. 22233

Vol. V. is entitled, "Debates on the Adoption of the Federal Constitution, in the Convention held at Philadelphia, in 1787; with a Diary of the Debates of the Congress of the Confederation; as Reported By James Madison, a Member, and Deputy from Virginia. Revised and Newly Arranged By Jonathan Elliot. ... . *Philadelphia: J. B. Lippincott & Co.* 1861."

ELLIOT. Diplomatic Code of the United States of America; embracing a Collection of Treaties and Conventions between the United States and Foreign Powers, from the year 1778 to 1827. With an Index to Cases decided in the Courts of the United States, upon points connected with their Foreign Relations. *Washington.* 1827. 8vo, pp. 668. 22234

ELLIOT. The Funding System of the United States and of Great Britain, with some Tabular Facts of other Nations touching the same Subject. Prepared by Jonathan Elliot. ... *Washington: Blair & Rives.* 1845. 8vo, pp. xxiv, 1299. 22235

28th Cong., 1st Sess., Exec. Doc.

ELLIOT. Historical Sketches of the Ten Miles Square forming the District of Columbia; with a Picture of Washington, describing Objects of General Interest or Curiosity at the Metropolis of the Union; ... By Jonathan Elliot. *Washington: J. Elliot.* 1830. pp. 554. Plate. C., H. 22236

ELLIOT. The Virginia and Kentucky Resolutions of 1798 and 1799. With Jefferson's Original Draught thereof; also, Madison's Report, Calhoun's Address, Resolutions of the Several States in relation to State Rights. With other Documents in Support of the Jeffersonian Doctrines of '98. ... Published by Jonathan Elliot. *Washington.* MDCCCXXXII. 8vo, pp. 82. BA.

ELLIOT. Elliot's Washington Pocket Almanac, for 1824. *Washington: Printed and Published by S. A. Eliot.* 18mo, pp. 61. Continued. BA. 22238

Also: Supplement to the United States Register for 1829, with the new appointments. *Washington.* 18mo.

[ELLIOT (Nathan).] The Columbian Preacher. Vol. I. *Catskill.* 1808. 8vo, pp. 304. 22239

ELLIOT (R.) Grace and Truth ... A Funeral Discourse Preached on the Death of the Rev. Mr. George Whitefield, A.B. (who died at Newberry, near Boston in New-England). By Rev. R. Elliot. *London.* 1770. 8vo, pp. 46. C. 22240

ELLIOT (S.) Address at New Fane, Vt. June 11, 1812, before the Washington Benevolent Society. By Samuel Elliot. *Brattleborough.* [n. d.] 8vo. W. 22241

ELLIOT. An Humble Tribute to my Country; or, Practical Essays, Political, Legal, Moral, and Miscellaneous; including a Brief Account of the Life, Sufferings, and Memorable Visit of General Lafayette ... *Boston.* 1842. 18mo. 22242

ELLIOT. Oration, pronounced at Brattleborough, Vermont, before the Washington Benevolent Societies, ... July 6, 1813, in Commemoration of ... American Independence. *Brattleborough, Vt.* 1813. 8vo. 22243

Also: A Voice from the Green Mountains, on the Subject of Masonry & Antimasonry, ... *Brattleboro': George W. Nichols.* 1834. 8vo, pp. 32. B., H

ELLIOT (S. H.) The Attractions of New Haven, Connecticut; A Guide to the City. ... By S. H. Elliot, ... *New York: N. Tibbals & Co.* 1869. 18mo, pp. 143. Map. 22244

Also: "New England's Chattels," etc.

ELLIOT (Seth). American Museum, and Repository of Arts and Sciences, as connected with the Domestic Manufactures and National Industry. Also a list of all the Patents granted by the United States up to the end of the year 1821. With a List of all the Books that have been deposited in the Department of State, for securing their Copy right according to Law. ... *Washington: Printed by Seth Elliot.* 1822. 8vo, pp. 60, 72, xxiv, xix. 4 Plates. 22245

[ELLIOT (T. F.)] The Canadian Controversy, its Origin, Nature, and Merits. *London: Longman.* 8vo, pp. 84. + Second Edition. [*Ibid.*] 1838. 8vo. BD. 22246

ELLIOT (W.) Patentee's Manual; containing a List of Patents granted by the United States, from 1790 to 1830; and the Laws of Congress relating to Patents, &c. By William Elliot. *Washington.* 1830. 8vo. C. 22247

[ELLIOT.] Washington Guide; containing an Account of the District of Columbia, the City of Washington, &c., &c. *Washington.* 1823. 18mo. + *Washington.* 1830. 18mo. 22248

ELLIOT. The Washington Guide; ... By William Elliot. *Washington City: Franck Taylor.* 1837. 18mo, pp. xii, 320. Map and Plates. 22249

ELLIOT (Wm.), *Jr.* Address delivered before the Columbian Society, at Marblehead, on the Sixth Anniversary, January 8, 1830. By William Elliot, Jr. Esq. ... *Boston: True and Greene, Printers.* 1830. pp. 16. BA. 22250

ELLIOT. Elliot's Panama, Nicaragua, and Tehuantepec, or Considerations upon the Question of Communication between the Atlantic and Pacific Oceans. *London.* 1819. Plates.

Title from an English catalogue.

ELLIOTT (A. B.) Northwestern Manual and Traveler's Directory. By A. B. Elliott. *Troy, N. Y.* 1858. 18mo, pp. 56.

ELLIOTT (B.) An Oration, delivered in ... Charleston, South-Carolina; On ... The Fourth of July, 1817, In Commemoration of American Independence; ... By Benjamin Elliott,

Esq. A Member of the '76 Association. *Charleston: Printed by W. P. Young.* 1817. 8vo, pp. 23. BA. 22253

See also "South Carolina Historical Society."

ELLIOTT (C.) The Bible and Slavery. By Charles Elliott. *Cincinnati.* 1857. 12mo. C. 22254

ELLIOTT. History of the Great Secession from the Methodist Episcopal Church, in the year 1845, eventuating in the organization of the New Church, entitled the "Methodist Episcopal Church South." By the Rev. Dr. Elliott. *Cincinnati.* 1855. Rl. 8vo, pp. 1144. C. 22255

ELLIOTT. The Life of the Rev. Robert B. Roberts, One of the Pastors of the Methodist Episcopal Church. By Rev. Charles Elliott, D.D. *Cincinnati: J. F. Wright.* 1844. 12mo. + *New York.* 1853. 12mo. B. 22256

ELLIOTT. Sinfulness of American Slavery; proved from its Evil Sources; its Injustice; its Wrongs; its Contrariety to many Scriptural Commands, Prohibitions and Principles, and to the Christian Spirit; and from its Evil Effects; together with Observations on Emancipation, and the Duties of American Citizens in Regard to Slavery. By Rev. Charles Elliott, D.D. ... Edited by Rev. B. F. Tefft, D.D. *Cincinnati: L. Swormstedt & Power.* 1850. 2 vols., 12mo, pp. 357; 378. C., H. 22257

ELLIOTT (C. W.) Mysteries; or Glimpses of the Supernatural, containing Accounts of the Salem Witchcraft — the Cock-lane Ghost — the Rochester Rappings — the Stratford Mysteries — Oracles — Astrology — Dreams — Demons — Ghosts — Spectres, &c. By Charles Wyllys Elliott. *New York: Harper & Brothers.* 1852. 12mo, pp. 273. C., H., P. 22258

ELLIOTT. Heroes are Historic Men. St. Domingo; its Revolutions and its Hero, Toussaint Louverture. A Historical Discourse ... February 26, 1855. By C. W. Elliott. ... *New York: J. A. Dix.* 1855. 12mo, pp. 83. BA., H. 22259

ELLIOTT. The New England History, from the Discovery of the Continent by the Northmen, A.D. 986, to the Period when the Colonies declared their Independence, A.D. 1776. By Charles W. Elliott ... *New-York: Charles Scribner.* 1857. 2 vols., 8vo, pp. 479; 492. 2 Plates. B., BA. C. 22260

Also: Cottages and Cottage Life, ... with some Sketches of Life in this Country ... *Cincinnati: H. W. Derby & Co.* 1848. 8vo, pp. 226.

ELLIOTT (D.) Life of the Rev. Elisha Macurdy. By the Rev. David Elliott. *Alleghany.* 1840. 12mo. S. 22261

Also: An Introductory Address, ... Western Theological Seminary, December 5th, 1842. ... *Pittsburgh: Luke Loomis.* 1842. 8vo, pp. 23. BA. — Introductory Address delivered at the Inauguration of James Clark, as President of Washington College, Penn., Sept. 24, 1850.

ELLIOTT (E. B.) International Statistical Congress at Berlin. V. Session, from the 6th to the 12th September, 1863. On the Military Statistics of the United States of America, by E. B. Elliott, ... *Berlin; Printed by R. V. Decker.* 1863. 3 l., pp. 44, 3 Engraved Tables. BA. 22262

Also: Expeditions of the United States Government at Different Periods, 1821–'67 (46 years), Prepared for the Special Commissioners of the Revenue by E. B. Elliott. ... [*Washington, D. C.* 1868?] 8vo, pp. 4. H. — Sanitary Commission, No. 46. Preliminary Report on the Mortality and Sickness of the Volunteer Forces of the United States Government, during the Present War. ... *New York: Wm. C. Bryant & Co., Printers.* 1862. 8vo, pp. 28. 10 Diagrams. C. — Statistical Classification of the Occupations of the Population of the United States, ... for the Year 1860. ... *Washington.* 1867. 8vo, pp. 22. H. — Suggestions for the Establishment of an International Coinage on a Decimal and Metric Basis in Germany. ... [*Washington, D. C.* 1869.] 8vo, pp. 14. H.

ELLIOTT (E. N.) Cotton is King, and Pro-Slavery Arguments; comprising the Writings of Hammond, Harper, Christy, Stringfellow, Hodge, Bledsoe, and Cartwright, on this Important Subject. By E. N. Elliott, LL.D. ... With an Essay on Slavery in the Light of International Law, by the Editor. ... *Augusta, Ga.: Pritchard, Abbott & Loomis.* 1860. Rl. 8vo, pp. xv, 908. 2 Portraits. 22263

ELLIOTT (Franklin Reuben). Fruit Book; or, The American Fruit-Grower's Guide, in Orchard and Garden. ... *New-York: C. M. Saxton.* 1854. 12mo, pp. 503. C. 22264

ELLIOTT. Popular Deciduous and Evergreen Trees and Shrubs, for Planting in Parks, Gardens, Cemeteries, etc. By F. R. Elliott. *New York: F. W. Woodward.* 1868. 8vo, pp. 125.

ELLIOTT. Western Fruit Book; or, American Fruit-Grower's Guide for the Orchard and Fruit-Garden. Fourth Edition, Revised, Enlarged, and Improved. *New-York.* 1859. 12mo. C.

ELLIOTT (J. H.) Our Present Position and Duties: An Address before the Beaufort Volunteer Artillery. *Beaufort, S. C.* 1844. 8vo. B. 22267

Also: ... A Sermon preached in St. Michael's Church, Charleston, S. C., on the Day of Public Prayer ... November 21st, 1860. ... *Charleston: Printed by A. E. Miller.* 1860. 8vo, pp. 11. H.

ELLIOTT (J. T.) Right of Suffrage. Speech of James T. Elliott, of Arkansas, ... delivered in the House of Representatives, February 2, 1869. *Washington.* 1869. 8vo, pp. 7. H.

ELLIOTT (Jehi). A Discourse delivered on the Sabbath after the Commencement of the Year 1802. ... *Middletown.* 1802. 8vo, pp. 35, 3. 22269

ELLIOTT (J. D.) Speech of Com. Jesse Duncan Elliott, U. S. N., delivered in Hagerstown, Md., On 14th November, 1843. *Philadelphia: G. B. Zieber & Co.* 1844. 8vo, pp. (4), 55, 82. 3 Woodcuts. BA. 22270

A defence of his conduct in the Battle of Lake Erie.

ELLIOTT. A Biographical Notice of Com. Jesse D. Elliott. *See* [Jarvis (Russell)].

Also: Correspondence in relation to the Capture of the British Brigs Detroit and Caledonia, on the Night of October 8, 1812. ... *Philadelphia.* 1843. 8vo, pp. 29. Plate. BA., C. — Documents in Relation to the Differences which subsisted between the Late Commodore O. H. Perry and Captain J. D. Elliott. *Washington.* 1821. 8vo, pp. 37, (1). BA. + *Boston.* 1834. 8vo, pp. 36. BA. — A Review of a Pamphlet purporting to be Documents in Relation to the Differences which subsisted between the late Commodore Oliver H. Perry and Capt. Jesse D. Elliott. By a Citizen of Massachusetts. ... *Boston: H. B. & J. Brewster.* 1834. 8vo, pp. 55. BA.

ELLIOTT (J.) A Discourse delivered on Saturday, February 22, 1800, the day recommended by the Congress of the United States to Lament the Death and Pronounce Eulogies on the Memory of General George Washington, By John Elliott, Pastor of a Church in Guilford [Conn.], Published by Request. *Hartford.* 1800. 8vo, pp. 23. 22271

ELLIOTT. The Gracious Presence of God, ... A Sermon Preached before ... the Governor ... of Connecticut, ... at Hartford, on the Anniversary Election, May 10th, 1810. By John Elliot, A.M. ... *Hartford: Printed by Hudson and Goodwin.* 1810. 8vo, pp. 52. BA. 22272

Also: A Sermon, ... in New-Haven, at the Ordination of the Rev. Eleazer Thompson Fitch, November 5, 1817. ... *Hartford: George Goodwin & Sons, Printers.* 1818. 8vo, pp. 26. BA.

ELLIOTT (S.) A Humble Tribute to my Country; or, Practical Essays, Political, Legal, Moral, etc. By Samuel Elliott. *Boston.* 1842. 8vo. N. 22273

ELLIOTT. Oration, ... at West-Springfield [Mass.], July Fourth, Eighteen Hundred and Three. By Samuel Elliott, Esq. ... *Bennington, Vt.: Printed by A. Haswell & Co.* 1803. 8vo, pp. 24. BA. 22274

[ELLIOTT (Samuel M.)] The Highland Brigade. [*New York.* 1861.] 8vo, pp. 29. 22275

ELLIOTT (S.) A Sketch of the Botany of South Carolina and Georgia. By Stephen Elliott, LL.D. *Charleston, S. C.: J. R. Schenck.* 1821–24. 2 vols., 8vo, 2 l., pp. 606, vi; viii, 743. 12 Plates. 22276

Originally published in thirteen numbers; No. 1 dated *Charleston.* 1816. Some copies have the imprint, *Philadelphia.* 1821. Also: An Address to the Literary and Philosophical Society of South Carolina; ... Charleston, ... The 10th August, 1814. .. *Charleston: W. P. Young.* 1814. 4to, pp. 20. BA., C., H. — An Address, ... Opening of the Medical College, in Charleston, (S. C.) ... *Charleston: Printed by A. E. Miller.* 1826. 8vo, pp. 23. BA. — Address ... Medical College, in Charleston, S. C., 13 Nov. 1826. *Charleston: Printed by A. E. Miller.* 1826. 8vo, pp. 23. B. — Address ... Savannah Medical College, 7 Nov., 1853. ... *Savannah: Printed by George N. Nichols.* 1853. 8vo, pp. 16. B.

ELLIOTT (S.), *Jr.* God's Presence with the Confederate States. A Sermon preached in Christ's Church, Savannah, on Thursday, The 13th June, [1861]. Being the Day appointed ... By the President of the Confederate States, as a Day of Solemn Humiliation, Fasting and Prayer. By the Rt. Rev. Stephen Elliott, Rector of Christ Church. ... *Savannah: W. Thorne Williams.* 1861. 8vo, pp. 21. BA. 22277

ELLIOTT. A High Civilization the Moral Duty of Georgians. A Discourse delivered before the Georgia Historical Society ... 12th February, 1844. By the Rev. Stephen Elliott, Jr. *Savannah.* 1844. 8vo, pp. 21. A., H. 22278

ELLIOTT. Our Cause in Harmony with the Purposes of God in Christ Jesus. A Sermon Preached in Christ Church, Savannah, on Thursday, September 18th, being the Day set forth by the President of the Confederate States, as a Day of Prayer and Thanksgiving, for our Manifold Victories, and especially for the Fields of Manassas and Richmond, Ky. By the Rt. Rev. Stephen Elliott, D.D. ... *Savannah: Power Press of John M. Cooper & Co.* 1862. 8vo, pp. 23. BA. 22279

ELLIOTT. A Reply to a Resolution of the Georgia Historical Society, read before the Society at its Anniversary Meeting, February 12th, 1866, by Rt. Rev. Stephen Elliott, President, ... *Savannah, Ga.: Purse and Son, Printers.* 1866. 8vo, pp. 13.

The "Resolution" was "The best method of increasing and extending the usefulness of the Society."

ELLIOTT. ... A Sermon preached in ... Savannah ... February 28th, 1862, being the Day of ... Fasting ... appointed by the President of the Confederate States. By the Rev. Stephen Elliott, D.D. ... . *Savannah.* 1862. 8vo, pp. 18. H. 22281

ELLIOTT. "The Silver Trumpets of the Sanctuary." A Sermon preached to the Pulaski Guards in Christ Church, Savannah, on the Second Sunday after Trinity. Being the Sunday before their Departure to join the Army in Virginia. By the Rt. Rev. Stephen Elliott, D.D., Rector of Chfist Church. ... *Savannah: John M. Cooper & Company.* 1861. 8vo. BA. 22282

ELLIOTT. Sermons by the Right Reverend Stephen Elliott, D.D., late Bishop of Georgia. With a Memoir, by Thomas M. Hanckel, Esq. *New York.* 1867. 8vo, pp. xxxv, 594. 22283

Also: Address ... to the ... Convention of the Protestant Episcopal Church, in the Diocese of Georgia. *Savannah: Press of John M. Cooper & Company.* 1861. 8vo, pp. 19. B., H. — Address at the Funeral of N. H. Cobbs ... Jan. 13th, 1861. *Montgomery.* 1861. 8vo, pp. 40. B. — Address at the Burial of L. Polk. ... *Columbia.* 1864. — ... A Sermon preached in ... Savannah, ... September 15, 1864, ... the day of Fasting, Humiliation, and Prayer, appointed by the Governor of the State of Georgia. ... *Macon, Ga.: Burke, Boykin & Company* 1864. 8vo, pp. 13. BA. — ... Two Sermons preached in ... Savannah ... in Connection with the Awful Catastrophe on Board the Princeton. ... *Savannah: W. T. Williams.* 1844. 8vo, pp. 24. H.

ELLIOTT. In Memoriam. [Proceedings in the Legislature of South Carolina on the Death of Gen. Stephen Elliott, and Addrsss of W. H. Trescott.] *Columbia.* 1866. Rl. 8vo.

ELLIOTT (T. E.) An Oration, delivered in St. Philip's Church, Charleston, South-Carolina, on the Fourth of July, 1821; before the '76 Association. By Thomas Odingsell Elliott, a Member of the '76 Association. ... *Charleston: Printed by A. E. Miller.* 1821. 8vo, pp. 36. BA. 22285

ELLIOTT (W.) Carolina Sports, by Land and Water; including Incidents of Devil-Fishing, &c. By the Hon. Wm. Elliott, Of Beaufort, S. C. *Charleston: Burges & James.* 1846. 12mo, pp. 172. C., H. + *New York: Trehern & Williamson.* 1850. 12mo, pp. 172. 22286

ELLIOTT. Carolina Sports by Land and Water; including incidents of Devil-Fishing, Wild-Cat, Deer and Bear Hunting, etc. By the Hon. Wm. Elliott, of South Carolina. With Six Illustrations. *New York: Derby & Jackson.* 1859. 12mo, pp. 292. 6 Plates. C. + *London: Richard Bentley.* 1867. 12mo, pp. 292. BA. 22287

Also: Address to the People of St. Helena Parish [S. C.] ... *Charleston, S. C.* 1832. 8vo, pp. 15. B., M.

Proceedings of the Elliott Society of Natural History, of Charleston, South-Carolina, November 1st, 1853. [*Charleston, S. C.* 1853?] 8vo. Continued to 1858 or longer. H. 22288

ELLIS (A.) Sermon before the Society for Propagation of the Gospel in Foreign Parts, Feb. 23, 1759. By Anthony, Bishop of St. David's. *London.* 1759. 4to, pp. 99. M. 22289

ELLIS (C.) Speech ... upon a Motion on 19th May, 1826, for the Early Consideration of Measures touching Slaves. *London.* 1826. 8vo, pp. 18. 22290

ELLIS (C. Mayo). The History of Roxbury Town. By Charles M. Ellis. *Boston: Samuel G. Drake.* 1847. 8vo, pp. 146. B., BA., C., H. 22291

ELLIS. The Memorial Address on Abraham Lincoln, Delivered at the Hall of the Mechanics' Institute, Saint John, N. B. June 1, 1865, at the Invitation of the Citizens. By Chas. M. Ellis, Esq., of Boston, Mass. *St. John, N. B.: Jared A. McMillan.* 1865. 12mo, pp. 31. H. 22292

[ELLIS.] The Power of the Commander-in-Chief to declare Martial Law, and decree Emancipation, as shown from B. R. Curtis, Esq. ... *Boston: A. Williams & Co.* 1862. 8vo, pp. 24.

Also: Argument, for Opening the Reading Room of the Public Library of the City of Boston on Sunday Afternoons. ... *Boston: Williams & Co.* 1867. 8vo, pp. 40. BA., H. — Hints for Relief, by a General Law to Protect and Promote Amicable Arrangements ... betwixt Debtor and Creditor. ... *Boston: Crosby, Nichols and Company.* 1857. 12mo, pp. 60. B., BA., H., S.

ELLIS (C.) Speech of Chesselden Ellis, of New York, on the Annexation of Texas: delivered in the House ... January 25, 1845. *Washington.* 1845. 8vo, pp. 13. 22294

ELLIS (D.) Thrilling Adventures of Daniel Ellis, the Great Union Guide of East Tennessee ... during the Great Southern Rebellion. Written by Himself. Containing a short Biography of the Author. ... With Illustrations. *New York: Harper & Brothers.* 1867. 8vo, pp. 430. B., BA. 22295

ELLIS (E. S.) The Life of Pontiac the Conspirator, Chief of the Ottawas. Together with a Full Account of the Celebrated Siege of Detroit. By Edward S. Ellis. ... *Beadle and Company, London.* [1861.] 12mo, pp. 102. 22296

ELLIS. The Life of Tecumseh, the Shawnee Chief, including Biographical Notices of Black Hawk, Corn Planter, Little

Turtle, Taohe (the brave), Captain Logan, Keokuk, and other distinguished Shawnee Chiefs. By Edward S. Ellis. *New York: Beadle and Company.* pp. 98. 22297

Also: Beadle's Dime Tales, Traditions, and Romance of Border and Revolutionary Times. Edward S. Ellis, Editor. *New York: Beadle & Co.* 1863. 4 vols., 12mo, pp. 64; 64; 64; 80. — The Fugitives: or, the Quaker Scout of Wyoming. A Tale of the Massacre of 1778. ... . *New York: Beadle and Company.* [1865.] 12mo, pp. 100. H. — Indian Jim. A Tale of the Minnesota Massacre. ... *New York: Beadle & Co.* 1864. 16mo, pp. 100. H. — The Prairie Trail: A Tale of the East and the West. ... *New York: Irwin & Co.* 1863. 18mo, pp. 98. — The Haunted Wood; a Legend of the Mohawk in 1778. *New York: Chapman & Co.* 1864. 12mo, pp. 120. — The Hunter's Escape: A Tale of the Northwest in 1862. *New York: Beadle & Co.* 1864. 16mo, pp. 7–100. — The Rangers of the Mohawk. A Tale of Cherry Valley. ... *New York: Beadle & Co.* 1864. 16mo, pp. 96. — The Rival Scouts; or, The Forest Garrison. A Story of the Siege and Fall of Fort Presq'Isle. ... *New York: Beadle & Co.* 1865. 16mo, pp. 100. — La Captive des Mohawks. Édition illustrée de 17 grav. *Paris: Dentu.* 1865. 12mo. — L'Espion indien. Édition illustrée. *Paris: Dentu.* 1865. 12mo.

ELLIS (F.) Civil Government an Ordinance of God; A Sermon delivered at Concord, before ... the Governor, ... Council, and ... Legislature of ... New Hampshire, June 8, 1826. By Ferdinand Ellis. *Concord.* 1826. 8vo, pp. 26. N. 22298

ELLIS. A Discourse, adapted to the Present Situation of our National Concerns, preached at Marblehead, Massachusetts, July 23 [Fast Day], 1812. *Salem.* 1812. 8vo, pp. 20.

ELLIS [(G. A.)] New Britain. A Narrative of a Journey, by Mr. Ellis, to a Country so called by its Inhabitants, discovered in the Vast Plain of the Missouri; in North America, and Inhabited by A People of British Origin, who Live under an Equitable System of Society, Productive of Peculiar Independence and Happiness, Also, Some Account of their Constitution, Laws, Institutions, Customs and Philosophical Opinions: together with A Brief Sketch of their History from the Time of their Departure from Great Britain. *London: W. Simpkin and R. Marshall.* 1820. 8vo, pp. vii, (1), 336. 22299

"A work of fiction, descriptive of an Utopian state of Society." — RICH.

ELLIS (G. Edward). I. The Aims and Purposes of the Founders of Massachusetts. II. Their Treatment of Intruders and Dissentients. Two Lectures ... delivered before the Lowell Institute, on Jan. 8 and 12, 1869. By George E. Ellis. *Boston: John Wilson and Son.* 1869. 8vo, pp. 100. H. 22300

ELLIS. A Commemorative Discourse delivered in the New South Church, Church Green, Boston, on Sunday, December

25, 1864, on the Fiftieth Anniversary of its Dedication. By George E. Ellis. *Boston: Henry W. Dutton and Son.* 1865. 8vo, pp. 42, (3). B., H. 22301

ELLIS. A Discourse delivered at the Dedication of the First Meeting-House of the First Church and Society in Somerville, Mass., On Wednesday, September 3, 1845. By George E. Ellis. ... *Boston: James Munroe and Company.* 1845. 8vo, pp. 24. B., BA., H. 22302

ELLIS. A Discourse delivered in Harvard Church, Charlestown, On Sunday, March 12, 1865, on the Twenty-fifth Anniversary of his Ordination. By George E. Ellis. With an Historical Note. *Charlestown: Abram E. Cutter.* 1865. 8vo, pp. 43. 22303

ELLIS. A Half-Century of the Unitarian Controversy, with particular reference to its Origin, its Course, and its Prominent Subjects among the Congregationalists of Massachusetts. With an Appendix. By George E. Ellis. *Boston: Crosby, Nichols, and Company.* 1857. 8vo, pp. xxiv, 511. BA., C., H. 22304

ELLIS. Memoir of Jared Sparks, LL.D. By George E. Ellis. ... *Cambridge: John Wilson & Son, Printers.* 1869. 8vo, pp. 102. 2 Plates. H. 22305

Separately printed from the "Proceedings of the Massachusetts Historical Society." Also, fifty copies on large paper.

ELLIS. Memoir of Luther V Bell, M.D., LL.D. Prepared by Vote of the Massachusetts Historical Society. By George E. Ellis. ... *Boston: Wilson and Son.* 1863. Rl. 8vo, pp. 75. Portrait. H. 22306

A few copies printed for the members of the Society.

ELLIS. An Oration delivered at Charlestown, Massachusetts, on the 17th of June, 1841, in Commemoration of the Battle of Bunker Hill. By George E. Ellis. *Boston: William Crosby and Co.* 1841. 8vo, pp. 72. B., BA., C., H. 22307

See Fellows' "Veil Removed," pp. 155–164.

ELLIS. "The Preservation of the States United." A Discourse delivered in Harvard Church, Charlestown, on Thanksgiving Day, Nov. 29, 1860. By George E. Ellis. *Charlestown: Abram E. Cutter.* 1860. 8vo, pp. 29. B., BA. 22308

[ELLIS.] Sketches of Bunker Hill Battle and Monument: with Illustrative Documents. *Charlestown: C. P. Emmons.* 1843. 12mo, pp. 172. H. + Second Edition. [*Ibid.*] + Third Edition. [*Ibid.*] 12mo, pp. 172. Map and Plate. B. + Fourth Edition. [*Ibid.*] 1844. 18mo, pp. 172. 22309

Attributed to George E. Ellis, in the "N. E. Gen. Register," XXI. 156. Also: Address delivered at the Consecration of the Woodlawn Cemetery in Chelsea and Malden, July 2, 1851. ... *Boston: Printed by John Wilson & Son.* 1851. 8vo, pp. 32. B., BA., H. — Address before the Middlesex County Agricultural Society at Concord, Oct. 4, 1854. [n. p. n. d.] 8vo. B. — "Commemoration of Washington." A Discourse, Feb. 22, 1857, ... Charlestown, ... February 22, 1857. ... *Charlestown: Abram E. Cutter.* 1857. 8vo, pp. 30. B., BA. — A Discourse ... before the Ancient and Honorable Artillery Company, June 1, 1846, being the CCVIIIth Anniversary. ... *Boston: Eastburn's Press.* 1846. 8vo, pp. 31. B., BA., H. — ... A Discourse preached at the Unitarian Convention at Baltimore, October 27, 1852, ... *Boston: Crosby, Nichols, and Company.* 1853. 12mo, pp. 31. H. — ... A Discourse delivered in Harvard Church, Charlestown, on Thanksgiving Day, Nov. 29, 1860. ... *Charlestown: Abram E. Cutter.* 1860. 8vo, pp. 29. H. — A Discourse, delivered in Harvard Church, Charlestown, June 13, 1869, at the Close of the Ministry, ... *Charlestown.* 1869. 8vo, pp. 37. H. — Inaugural Address, delivered in ... Harvard College ... July 14, 1857. ... *Boston.* 1857. 8vo, pp. 48. B., H. — A Lecture on Temperance, delivered in ... Charlestown. ... *Boston: Temperance Standard Press.* 1846. 8vo, pp. 22. BA., H. — The Nation's Ballot and its Decision: a Discourse, delivered ... Cambridgeport and in Charlestown, Sunday, November 23, 1864. Being the Sunday following the Presidential Election. ... *Boston: William V. Spencer.* 1864. 8vo, pp. 18. B., H. — "The Organ and Church Music." Two Discourses, delivered in Harvard Church, Charlestown, Sept. 26, 1852. *Boston.* 1852. 8vo. — Our Good Land, and its Good Institutions: a Discourse delivered in ... Charlestown, on Thanksgiving Day, November 30, 1854. ... *Boston.* 1854. 8vo, pp. 26. B., H. — The Preacher and the Pastor. Two Discourses delivered in Harvard Church, Charlestown, Sunday, March 15, 1840, on the Commencement of his Ministry, ... *Boston: William Crosby & Co.* 1840. 8vo, pp. 47. B., H. — Remarks ... at the Funeral of the Hon. Benjamin Thompson, M.C. September 27, 1852. ... *Charlestown: Printed by William W. Whildon.* 1852. 8vo, pp. 16. BA., H. — ... A Sermon, preached in the Meeting-House of the Harvard Church and Society in Charlestown ... October 9, 1842, ... On, ... the Death of Rev. William Ellery Channing, D.D. ... *Boston: William Crosby & Co.* 1842. 8vo, pp. 24. BA. — ... A Sermon ... at the Installation of Rev. H. Alger ... in Marlborough, Mass., January 22, 1845. ... *Boston: James Munroe & Co.* 1845. 8vo, pp. 38. B. — ... A Sermon Preached at the Installation of Rev. Rufus Ellis ... in Boston, May 4, 1853. ... *Boston: Printed by John Wilson & Son.* 1853. 8vo, pp. 55. B., H. — A Sermon ... March 26, 1854, ... after the Interment of the Rev. Alexander Young, D.D. Late Pastor of the New South Church. ... *Boston: Crosby, Nichols, and Company.* 1854. 8vo, pp. 40. B., BA., H. — ... A Sermon ... Installation of the Rev. Horatio Stebbins ... in Portland, Me. January 31, 1855. ... *Portland: published by George R. Davis.* 1855. 8vo, pp. 64. B., H. — ... A Sermon ... at the Dedication of the First Unitarian Church in Marietta, Ohio, On Thursday, June 4, 1857. ... With an Appendix. *Boston: Crosby, Nichols, and Company.* 1857. pp. 43, (1). H. — ... A Sermon ... before the Convention of the Congregational Ministers of Massachusetts, on ... May 27, 1858 ... Boston. ... *Boston: Crosby, Nichols, and Company.* 1858. 8vo, pp. 38. B., H. — ... A Sermon ... Charlestown, December 9, 1860; ... after the Interment of Mrs. Eliza Bradford. ... [n. p. n. d.] 8vo, pp. 18. B., H. — ... A Sermon ... Charlestown, September 20, 1863; ... after the Interment of Mr. Thomas Marshall. ... [n. p. n. d.] 8vo, pp. 22. B., H. *See* Sparks' "Amer. Biogr."

ELLIS (George W.) A Poem on the Awful Catastrophy on board the United States Steam Frigate Princeton. *Boston.* 1844. 16mo. 22310

ELLIS (H.) Considerations on the Great Advantages which would arise of the North-West Passage, and a clear Account of the most practical Method of attempting that Discovery. *London.* 1750. 22311

Title from Lowndes' "Manual."

ELLIS. A Voyage to Hudson's-Bay, by the Dobbs Galley and California, In the Years 1746 and 1747, For Discovering a North West Passage; with An accurate Survey of the Coast, and a short Natural History of the Country. Together with A fair View of the Facts and Arguments from which the future finding of such a Passage is rendered probable. By Henry Ellis, Gent. Agent for the Proprietors in the said Expedition. To which is prefixed, An Historical Account of the Attempts hitherto made for the finding a Passage that Way to the East-Indies. Illustrated with proper Cuts, and a new and correct Chart of Hudson's-Bay, with the Countries adjacent. *London: H. Whitridge.* M.DCC.XLVIII. 8vo, pp. xxviii, 336. Map and Plates. J.C.B., C., H. + Second Edition. [*Ibid.*] MDCCXLIX. 8vo. Map. + *Dublin: Geo. and Alex. Ewing.* 1749. 8vo, pp. xvi, 162. Map. 22312

"A valuable performance, containing many curious and sensible observations." — LOWNDES. There are copies of the edition of 1748 on large paper. Included in Mavor's collection, Vol. I.

ELLIS. Voyage à la Baye de Hudson, fait en 1746 & 1747, par les Navires le Dobbs-Galley & la California pour la découverte d'un passage au Nord-Ouëst. Avec une déscription exacte de la Côte; un abrégé de l'histoire naturelle du Pays, un exposé net des Faits & des Argumens, qui servent à prouver la probabilité de trouver dans la suite ce Passage. Par Mr Henri Ellis. Agent des Propriétaires cette Expédition. Précédé d'un detail historique des tentatives qui ont été faites jusqu'ici pour trouver par cette route un Passage aux Indes-Orientales: Enrichi de Figures en taille douce, & d'une carte nouvelle & exacte de la Baye de Hudson, & des Pays adjacents. Traduit de l'Anglais [par Sellius], & augmenté de quelques Remarques. *Paris: chez Baillard fils.* MDCCXLIX. 2 vols., 12mo, pp. (2), lvi, 182, 2 l., Map; pp. 319, 7 Plates. J.C.B., H. + *Leide: De Sainte et Saillant.* MDCCL. 8vo, pp. xxviii, 413, 3 l. 9 Plates and Map.

Some copies have the imprint, *Paris: Sébastien Jorri.* 1749; others, *Leide: De l'Imp. d'Elie Luzac, Fils.* MDCCL. *See* "Biog., Univ.," and Faribault, No. 220.

ELLIS. Reise nach Hudsons Meerbusen, welehe von zweyen Englischen Schiffen, der Dobbs Galley und California, in den Jahren 1746 und 1747, wegen Entdeckung einer nord-westlichen Durchfahrt in die Süd-See verrichtet worden, nebst einer richtigen Abzeichnung der Küste, und einer kurzen Naturgeschichte des Landes. Beschreibung der Einwohner, auch einer wahren Vorstellung der Umstände und Gründe, welche die künftige Erfindung einer solchen Durchfahrt wahrscheinlich machen: beschrieben von Heinrich Ellis ... . *Göttingen: Abram Vandenhoeck.* 1750. 8vo, 11 l., pp. 364, 5 l. Maps and Plates. H.

ELLIS. Reize naar de Baai van Hudson, ter ontdekkinge van eenen Noord-Wester Doortogt, gedaan in de Jaaren 1746 en 1747 met de Schepen de Dobbs-Galley en de California. Met eene naauwkeurige beschryving der kust, eene korte natuurlyke historie van het Land, en een klaar vertoog der bewysstukken en redenen, dewelke dienen om de waarschynlykheid aan te toonen dat zulk een Doortogt in 't vervolg zal gevonden worden. Uit het Engelsch vertaald. *Leiden: ter Druk van Elias Luzac, Jun.* MDCCL. 8vo, pp. xxxii, 440. Map and 9 Plates. 22315

ELLIS (H. W. R.) Chronologie der geschiedenis van Suriname (1500–1853.) *Paramaribo.* 1853. 8vo. 22361

ELLIS (J.) A Narrative of the Rise, Progress & Issue of the Late Law Suits, relative to Property held and devoted to Pious Uses, in the First Precinct in Rehoboth: containing the Substance of the Records which shew for whose Use and Benefit the Property was originally intended: together with some Observations on certain Constitutional Principles, which respect the Support of public Worship, and the equal Protection and Establishment of all regular Denominations of Christians. By James Ellis, A.M. ... *Warren, (Rhode Island): Printed by Nathaniel Phillips.* M.DCC.XCV. 12mo, pp. 76. BA., H. 22316*a*

Mr. Northrop, a Baptist elder of Narragansett, and the Rev. Isaac Backus, were involved in the controversy to which the above pamphlet refers.

ELLIS (J.) An Historical Account of Coffee. With an Engraving and Botanical Description of the Tree. To which are added Sundry Papers relative to its Culture and Use, as an Article of Diet and of Commerce. Published by John Ellis, F.R.S. Agent for the Island of Dominica. *London: Edward and Charles Dilly.* MDCCLXXIV. 4to, pp. iv, 71. Plate. 22317

ELLIS (*Mr.*) *See* Ellis (G. A.)

[ELLIS (John).] The South Sea Dream, a Poem in Hudibrastic Verse. *London.* 1720. 22318

ELLIS (J.) Directions for bringing over Seeds and Plants from the East Indies and other Distant Countries in a State of Vegetation, together with a Catalogue of such Foreign Plants as are worthy of being encouraged in our American Colonies for the Purposes of Medicine, Agriculture, and Commerce. By John Ellis. *London.* 1770. 4to, pp. 41. Plates. 22319

Also: Some additional Observation on the Method of preserving Seeds, from foreign Parts, for the Benefit of our American Colonies, With an Account of the Garden at St. Vincent, under the Care of Dr. George Young. ... *London: Bowyer & Co.* 1773. 4to.

ELLIS (J. B.) The Sights and Secrets of the National Capital; a work descriptive of Washington City in all its various phases. By John B. Ellis, M.D. *New York: U. S. Publishing Co.* 1869. 8vo, pp. 512. 18 Plates. C. 22320

ELLIS (J. F.) Musical Almanac for 1868. And Washington City General Advertiser. By John F. Ellis. *Washington: J. F. Ellis.* [1868.] 8vo, pp. 168. C. 22321

E[LLIS] (J[onathan]). The Justice of the Present War against the French. Sermon preached to the Soldiers, Sept. 22, 1755. With a Sermon from Gal. ii. 19. By J. E. *Newport.* [n. d.] 4to, pp. 24. 22322

ELLIS (J.) An Eulogical Poem on Gen. George Washington, pronounced at Topsham, Me., Feb. 22, 1800. By Jonathan Ellis. *Portland.* [1800.] 8vo, pp. 24. M., N. 22323

Also: Oration at Topsham, Me., July 4, 1806. *Portland.* 1806. 8vo. W.

ELLIS (J. V.) ... New Brunswick, as a Home for Emigrants; with the Best Means of Promoting Immigration, and developing the Resources of the Province. ... *St. John, N. B.* 1860. 16mo, pp. 60. H. 22324

ELLIS (R.) The Last Sermon Preached in First Church, Chauncy Street, May 10, 1868; being the Lord's Day previous to the Removal of the Congregation ... By Rufus Ellis, ... With an Appendix. ... *Boston: Press of John Wilson and Son.* 1868. 8vo, pp. 32. Plate. H. 22325

ELLIS. A Sermon occasioned by the Death of William Hickling Prescott, preached ... Feb. 6, 1859. By Rufus Ellis. ... *Boston: Crosby, Nichols, and Company.* 1859. 8vo. B., H.

ELLIS. ... A Sermon preached at the Dedication of the Fifth House of Worship of First Church, Dec. 10, 1868. ... A Sermon preached in First Church ... Dec. ... . Address at the Laying of the Corner Stone. With an Appendix. ... *Cambridge.* 1869. 8vo, pp. 42. H. 22327

Also: The Blessedness of Giving; a Discourse preached in the Old South Church before the Howard Benevolent Society, December 11, 1853 ... . *Boston: printed by John Wilson & Son.* 1854. 8vo, pp. 23. H. — The Claims of New England Society upon the Young Student, An Address delivered before the Social Union of Williston Seminary, East Hampton, Mass. ... *Northampton.* 1845. 8vo, pp. 16. H. — ... A Discourse on the Life and Character of Hon. Joseph Lyman, delivered on the 19th of December, 1847. ... . *Northampton: Printed by J. & L. Metcalf.* 1848. 8vo, pp. 16. H. — ... A Discourse preached before the Benevolent Fraternity of Churches, April 22, 1855, ... *Boston: John Wilson & Son.* 1855. 8vo, pp. 22. B., BA., H. — ... A Sermon in Memory of the Late Samuel Bradlee, delivered in the Church of the Redeemer, August 11, 1867, ... [n. p. n] 8vo, pp. 20. H. — Memoir of the Hon. Samuel Howe, with other Notices. ... . ston. 1850. 18mo, pp. 72. B. — The Life, Services, and Character of Edward Everett: a Sermon preached ... Jan. 22, 1865. By R. Ellis. With an Appendix, containing the Action of the First Church on the Occasion of the Death of Mr. Everett, and the Address of the Pastor, at the Public Journal, Thursday, 19th Jan. *Boston: Press of John Wilson & Son.* 1865. 8vo, pp. 32. B., H.

ELLIS (S.) History of the Order of the Sons of Temperance, from its Organization, ... 1842, to ... 1848; also Account of its Formation and Introduction into the several States of the Union. By Samuel Ellis. *Boston.* 1840. 8vo. + Revised Edition. *Boston: Stacy, Richardson & Co.* 1848. 12mo, pp. 238.

ELLIS (T.) Kort Beright van Mr. Ellis, een der Kapiteynen van d' Heer Richard Hawkins, aangaande sijn Reys door de Straat van Magellanes in 't Jaar 1593. Behelzende een naauwkeurige beschrijving die van Straat, en eenige plaatsen opde Kusten van Peru. Mitsgaders Engelse Reysen na de Bermudas of Summer-Eylanden, etc. *Te Leyden: By Pieter Vander Aa.* 1706. 8vo, pp. 26, 2 l. Map. 22329

Forms part of Vander Aa's collection of voyages.

ELLIS. True Report of Martin Frobisher's his last and Third Voyage. *London: Dawson.* 1578. 4to. 22330

Title from Lowndes, page 733. I have never seen the book, and infer its rarity.

ELLIS (T. T.) Leaves from the Diary of an Army Surgeon; or, Incidents of Field, Camp, and Hospital Life. By Thomas T. Ellis, M.D., late Post-Surgeon at New York, and Acting Medical Director at White House, Va. ... *New York: John Bradburn.* 1863. 12mo, pp. pp. 312. BA., H. 22331

ELLIS (V.) Brief View of the Enterprise proposed by Mr. V. Ellis to Navigate the Orinoco and Apure Rivers with Steam boats. [*London.* 1848.] 8vo. Maps. 22332

ELLIS (W.) An Authentic Narrative of a Voyage performed by Captain Cook and Captain Clerke, in his Majesty's Ships Resolution and Discovery, During the Years 1776, 1777, 1778, 1779, and 1780; in search of a North-West Passage Between the Continents of Asia and America. Including A faithful Account of all their Discoveries, and the unfortunate Death of Captain Cook. Illustrated with A Chart and a Variety of Cuts. By W. Ellis, Assistant Surgeon to both vessels. *London: G. Robinson.* MDCCLXXXII. 2 vols., 8vo, 6 l., pp. 358, (1); 4 l., pp. 347. 22 Plates and 1 Map. C., H. + The Second Edition. *London.* [*Ibid.*] MDCCLXXXIII. 2 vols., 8vo, 6 l., pp. 358, (1); 4 l., pp. 347. 22 Plates and 1 Map. + The Third Edition. *London.* [*Ibid.*] MDCCLXXXIV. 2 vols., 8vo. 22333

See "M. Rev.," LXVII. 67; LXX. 474; and LXXI. 48.

ELLIS. Zuverlässige Nachricht von der dritten und letzten Reise des Kap. Cook und Clerke in den Königlichen Schiffen, die Resolution und Discovery, in den Jahren von 1776 bis 1780, besonders in der Absicht, eine nordwestliche Durchfarth [*sic*] zwischen Asien und Amerika ausfindig zu machen. Von W. Ellis, Unterwundarzt auf beyden Schiffen. Aus dem Englischen übersetzt, nebst einer Charte. *Frankfurt und Leipzig, auf Kosten der Verlags kasse.* 1783. 8vo, pp. 324. Map. 22334

ELLIS (W.) The American Mission in the Sandwich Islands: A Vindication and an Appeal, in relation to the Proceedings of the Reformed Catholic Mission at Honolulu. ... By William Ellis. *London.* 1866. 8vo. B., H. 22335

ELLIS (W. H. C.) Oration, delivered by William H. C. Ellis, Esq., at Accomack Court House, Virginia, on the Fourth of July, 1851. *Baltimore: Printed by James Lucas.* 1851. 8vo, pp. 12. 22336

[ELLISON (Patrick).] Candid Animadversions respecting A Petition to the Late General Assembly Of Maryland, In behalf of the Episcopal Ministers in the same. By Vindex. *Baltimore: Hayes.* M.DCC.LXXXIII. 12mo, pp. iv, 19. 22337

ELLISON (T.) A Hand-Book of the Cotton Trade: or, a Glance at the Past History, Present Condition, and Future Prospects of the Cotton Commerce of the World. By Thomas Ellison. ... *London: Longman, Brown, Green, etc.* MDCCCLVIII. 8vo, pp. xxi, 1 l., pp. 191. Map and 6 Tables. B., BA., C., H.

ELLISTON. Slavery and Secession in America, Historical and Economical. By Thomas Elliston, F.S.S., etc. ... With Map and Appendices. *London: Sampson, Low, Son & Co.* 1861. 12mo, pp. (1), xvi, 371. Map. BA. + Second Edition, Enlarged, With a Reply to ... James Spence, ... and Remarks on the Productions of other Writers. *London:* [*Ibid.*] 1862. 12mo, pp. xxxv, 371. C. 22339

ELLITHORPE (A. C.) The Chicago Tribune as a Libeller of Men, a Defamer of Women, and a Menacer of Courts and Juries. *Chicago.* 1864. 8vo, pp. 15. B. 22340

ELLMAKER (E. E.) The Revelation of Rights. By E. E. Ellmaker. *Columbus, Ohio.* 1841. 12mo. S. 22341

ELLSON (W.) Address to the People of Chester District, S. C., on Nullification. By William Ellson. *Charleston.* 1832. 8vo. W. 22342

ELLSWORTH (E. E.) The Zouave Drill. Being a Complete Manual of Arms for the Use of the Rifled Musket, with either the Percussion Cap, or Maynard Primer. Containing also the Complete Manual of the Sword and Sabre. By Col. E. E. Ellsworth. ... With a Biography of his Life. *Philadelphia: T. B. Peterson and Brothers.* 1862. 12mo, pp. 62. H. 22343

Colonel Ellsworth, killed at Alexandria, Va., was one of the earliest victims of the Civil War. *See* "The Patriot's Offering."

ELLSWORTH (H.) A Digest of Patents, issued by the United States, from 1790 to January 1, 1839: Published by Act of Congress, under the Superintendence of the Commissioner of Patents, Henry L. Ellsworth. To which is added, the Present Law relating to Patents. *Washington: Peter Force.* 1840 [to] 1841. 8vo, pp. 670. + *Washington.* 1842. 8vo, pp. xix, 670, 1 l.

[ELLSWORTH.] Information to Persons having Business to transact at the Patent Office. *Washington.* [n. d.] 8vo, pp. 16.

See Illinois in 1837. Also: Sketches of an Address delivered before the Hartford County Agricultural Society, on the 24th March, 1818. ... *Hartford.* 1818. 8vo, pp. 23. N.

ELLSWORTH (H. W.) Valley of the Upper Wabash, Indiana, with Hints on its Agricultural Advantages; Plan of a Dwelling,

Estimates of Cultivation, and Notices of Labor-Saving Machines. By Henry William Ellsworth. *New York: Pratt, Robinson, ana Co.* 1838. 12mo, pp. xii, 175. Map and Plates. B., BA., C.

Also: Improvements in Agriculture, &c., in the United States ... 1843. 8vo.

ELLSWORTH (W. W.) Speech from his Excellency, William W. Ellsworth, Governor of Connecticut, to the Legislature of the State. May Session, 1841. ... *Hartford: Courant Office Press.* 1841. pp. 16. BA. 22347

ELLSWORTH Speech ... on the Removal of the Deposites. March 27th, 1834. *Washington.* 1834. 8vo. 22348

ELLSWORTH (W. W.) Copy-Right Manual; designed for Men of Business, Authors, Scholars, and Members of the Legal Profession. By William W. Ellsworth. *Boston.* 1852. 8vo.

ELLWOOD (T.) An|Epistle|to|Friends|Briefly|Commemorating the Gracious Dealings of the|Lord with them; and warning them to|beware of that Spirit of|Contention and Division| Which hath appeared of late in|George Keith,|And some few others that join with him, who|have made a Breach and Separation from|Friends in some Parts of America.|By Thomas Ellwood.|*London, Printed by T. Sowle at the Crooked-Billet in Holy-|well-lane, Shoreditch, and near the Meeting-House in|White-Hart-Court in Grace-Church-Street.* 1694.| Sm. 8vo, pp. 73. 22350

Some copies read, "*Printed and Sold by T. Sowle.*"

ELLWOOD. A Further|Discovery|Of that Spirit of|Contention & Division|Which hath appeared of late in|George Keith, &c.|Being a Reply to Two Late Printed|Pieces of his, the one Entituled, A Loving|Epistle, &c. the other, A Seasonable Informa-|tion, &c. Wherein his Cavils are Answered, his|Falsehood is laid open, and the Guilt and|Blame of the Breach and Separation in Ame-|rica; and of the Reproach he hath brought| upon Truth and Friends, by his late Printed|Books, are fixed faster on him.|VVritten by way of Epistle, and recommended as a further|VVarning to all Friends.|By Thomas Ellwood.|*London, Printed by T. Sowle at the Crooked-Billet in Holy-|well-lane, Shoreditch, and near the Meeting-House in|White-hart-Court, in Grace-Church-street.* 1694.| 8vo, pp. 128. 22351

ELLWOOD. The History of the Life of Thomas Ellwood, or, An Account of his Birth, Education, &c. with Divers Observations on his Life and Manners when a Youth: and how he came to be convinced of the Truth; with his many Sufferings and Ser-

vices for the same. Also several other Remarkable Passages and Occurrences. Written by his own hand. To which is added, a Supplement. By J[oseph] W[yeth]. *London: Assigns of J. Sowle.* 1714. 8vo, 34 sheets. + The Second Edition. [*Ibid.*] 1714. 8vo. + The Third Edition. *London: Luke Hinde.* 1765. 8vo, 30 sheets. + [Another Edition.] *Philadelphia.* 1775. 12mo. + The Fourth Edition. *London: James Phillips.* 1791. 12mo, pp. 425. + The Fifth Edition: with An Appendix, comprising a Supplementary Memoir of his Life and Writings. *York: W. Alexander and Son.* 1825. 12mo, 15½ sheets. + Reprinted [with alterations]. *London: Hunt and Clarke.* 1827. 18mo. + Sixth Edition. *Manchester: John Harrison and Son.* 1855. 8vo, 20 sheets. Plate. 22352

Also reprinted in "The Friends' Library," edited by William Allen. *Linfield.* 1836. 16mo; and "The Friends' Library," edited by Wm. and Thos. Evans. *Philadelphia.* 1843.

ELLWOOD. Truth Prevailing and Detecting Error. *Printed in the Year* 1676. 22353

Ellwood was secretary to John Milton, and to him we are indebted for the suggestion which induced Milton to write his second great poem. His autobiography is of the most remarkable and instructive character. See "Retrospective Review."

ELMENDORF (J. J.) Loyalty. A Voice from the Sanctuary concerning the Civil War. By Rev. J. J. Elmendorf. *New York: H. B. Durand.* 1863. 8vo, pp. 16. 22354

ELMENDORF (L.) Facts and Observations on the Merits of the Memorial of the President and Directors of the first Great South-Western Turn-Pike Road Company, for Relief. *Albany.* 1829. pp. 15. 22355

ELMER (J.) An Eulogium, On the Character of Gen. George Washington, Late President of the United States: Delivered At Bridge-Town, Cumberland County, New-Jersey, January 30th, 1800. By Jonathan Elmer, M.D.—S.T.P.A. *Trenton: Printed By G. Craft.* MDCCC. 8vo, pp. 25. 22356

We know of only one copy, which belongs to Mr. W. Menzies.

ELMER (L. Q. C.) Genealogy and Biography of the Elmer Family. By Lucius Q. C. Elmer. *Bridgeton, N. J.* 1860. 8vo, pp. 64. 22357

Also: Speech of Mr. Elmer, of New Jersey, on the Rhode Island Controversy. Delivered in the House of Representatives, February 28, 1845. *Washington: Printed at the Globe Office.* 1845. 8vo, pp. 8.

ELMES (J.) Thomas Clarkson; A Monograph. Being a Contribution towards the History of the Abolition of the Slave-Trade and Slavery. By James Elmes. *London: Blackader & Co.* 1854. Fcap 8vo, pp. xxxi, 320. 22358

ELMIRA, *N. Y.* Boyd's Elmira Directory; ... a Business Directory of Chemung County, and an Appendix ... . 1860. *Elmira: Hall Brothers.* 1860. pp. 173. Map. Continued.

Catalogue of the Elmira Female College, Chemung County, N. Y. 1855. 8vo. Continued. S. 22360

Also: Addresses on the Inauguration of the first President. 8vo.

ELMIRA, *N. Y.* *See also* Galatian (A. B.)

ELMORE (F. H.) The Anti-Slavery Examiner, No. 8. Correspondence between the Hon. F. H. Elmore and Jas. G. Birney. *New York: American Anti-Slavery Soc.* 1838. 8vo, pp. 68.

ELMWOOD (Elnathan), *pseudonym.* *See* [Greene (Asa)].

Elogi Storici di Christoforo Colombo. *See* [Durazzo (J.)], No. 21418.

Elogios funebres con que la Santa Iglesia catedral de Guadalaxara ha celebrado la buena Memoria de su prelado el Illmo. y Rmo. Señor Mtro. D. F. Antonio Alcalde. Se ponen al fin algunos Monumentos de los que se han tenido presentes para formarlos. *Guadalaxara.* 1793. 4to, pp. xxviii, 49. 22362

For other funeral elegies, *see* under the name of the author or subject.

ELORRIAGA. Idea sucincta del proceso seguido al C. Fr. Elorriaga por los ultimos acontecimientos occuridos durante su gobierno en el estado de Durango. *Zacatecas.* 1831. 4to, pp. 24.

ELSEMORE (M.) An Impartial Account of the Life of the Rev. John N. Maffitt, with a Narrative of the Difficulties Attending His First Marriage. And ... of his Late Marriage ... . By Moses Elsemore ... . *New York: John F. Feeks.* 1848. 8vo, pp. 31, (1). Portraits. S. 22364

Also: Reflections on the State of Society in the South-West.

ELORZA Y RADA (F. de). Nobiliario de el valle de la Valdorba, illustrada con el Escudos de Armas de sus Palacios y casas Nobles. Por Francisco de Elorza y Rada. Con el extracto de la conquista de el Ytza en la Nueva España: Por el Conde de Lizarraga Vengoa, natural del Valle. *Pamplona: Por Francisco Antonio de Neqra. Año de* 1714. 4to, 18 l., pp. 380, 6 l. J.C.B.

ELSNER (Chrysostom H.) Befreiungskampf der nord-amerikanischen Staaten. Mit Lebensbeschreibungen der vier berühmtesten Männer desselben: Washington, Franklin, Lafayette, und Kosciuszko. Nach den besten Quellen historisch-biographisch bearbeitet von Heinrich Elsner. ... *Stuttgart: J. Scheible.* 1835. 8vo, pp. (1), 768. 9 Plates. BA., C. S. 22366

ELTON (J. F.) With the French in Mexico. By J. F. Elton, ... *London: Chapman & Hall.* 1867. 8vo, pp. x, 206. 2 Maps and Plate. BA., C. + *Philadelphia: J. B. Lippincott & Co.* 1867. 8vo, pp. xii, 206. B. 22367

ELTON (Richard), *and others.* Discipline. The Compleat Souldier; or, Expert Artilleryman. Compiled from Elton, Bariff, &c. *Boston.* 1701. 16mo, pp. 96. M. 22368

One of the earliest books on the subject printed in the American Colonies.

ELTON (R.) Life of Roger Williams, the Earliest Legislator and True Champion for a full and Absolute Liberty of Conscience. By Romeo Elton, D.D., F.R.P.S., Fellow of the Royal Society of Northern Antiquaries, etc. etc. *London: Albert Cockshaw.* [1852.] 16mo, pp. viii, 173. + *London: A. Hall.* 1853. 16mo, pp. viii, 173. + *Providence: Geo. H. Whitney.* 1853. 16mo, pp. viii, 173. BA., C., H. 22369

Taken from Elton's introduction to Callendar's "Rhode Island."

ELVIUS (P.) De navigatione in Indiam per Septentrionem tentata. *Upsaliæ.* 1704. 8vo, pp. 40. 22370

ELWES (R.) Sketcher's Tour round the World. By Robert Elwes. Second Edition. *Hurst and Blackett.* Rl. 8vo. 21 Plates. 22371

Some of the sketches are in America.

ELWES. W.S.W. A Voyage in that Direction to the West Indies. By Robert Elwes. With Illustrations. *London: Kerby & Son.* 1866. 8vo, pp–v, 135. 22372

ELWORTH (T). Sketch of Incidents and Adventures in the Life of Thomas Elworth, the American Pedestrian. Written by himself. *Boston: Brainard & Co.* 1844. 18mo, pp. 60. B.

ELWYN (A. L.) Glossary of supposed Americanisms. *Philadelphia: J. B. Lippincott & Co.* 1859. 12mo, pp. 122. S.

Collected by Alfred L. Elwyn, M.D.

[ELWYN (Thomas).] Letter to a Federalist, in Reply to some of the Popular Objections to the Motives and Tendency of the Measures of the Present Administration, February, 1805. [*Portsmouth.* 1805.] 8vo, pp. 31. C., N. 22375

ELY (A.) A Sermon delivered at Monson, Mass., the Second Centennial Anniversary of the Landing of the Fathers of New England at Plymouth. By Rev. Alfred Ely. *Hartford.* 1821. 8vo, pp. 27. 22376

ELY. A Sermon on Occasion of Constituting a Church at Ware Factory Village, April 12, 1826. By Alfred Ely. *Brookfield.* 1826. 8vo, pp. 23. 22377

Also: Sermon at the Ordination of J. H. Fairchild ... *Hartford.* 1816. 8vo.— ... A Sermon in Brooklyn, Conn., April 14, 1824. At the Ordination of the Rev. Ambrose Edson, ... *Hartford: Printed by Goodwin & Co.* 1824. 8vo, pp. 24. BA.—A Sermon delivered February 23, 1827, at the Interment of the Rev. Henry H. F. Sweet ... . *Belchertown, Mass.* 1827. 8vo, pp. 23. H.—Sermon, the Sabbath preceding the Ordination of S. C. Bartlett, July 30, 1843. By A. Ely. *West Brookfield.* 1843. 8vo, pp. 25.

ELY (A.) ... Journal of Alfred Ely, A Prisoner of War in Richmond. Edited by Charles Lanman. *New York: D. Appleton & Co.* M.DCCC.LXII. 12mo, pp. 359. Portrait. BA., C., H.

Also: Confiscation of Property and Emancipation of the Slaves of Rebels. Speech ... May 26, 1862. *Washington, D. C.* 1862. 8vo, pp. 16. H.—Enlargement of Canal Locks of New York for National Defence. Speech ... June 30, 1862. *Washington, D. C.: Scammell & Co., Printers.* 1862. 8vo, pp. 13. H.—The Reciprocity Treaty. Speech ... June 15, 1860. [*Washington, D. C.* 1860.] 8vo, pp. 8. H.

ELY (A. B.) American Liberty, its Sources,—its Dangers, and the Means of its Preservation: an Oration, delivered ... in New-York, before the Order of United Americans, on the 22d of February, A.D. 1850, being the 118th Anniversary of the Birthday of Washington, By Bro. Alfred B. Ely., Esq. ... *New York: B's Seaman & Dunham, Printers.* 1850. pp. 34. H., S.

ELY. A Eulogy on the Life and Character of Zachary Taylor, late President ... before the Citizens of Newton, Mass. August 13th, 1850: ... By Alfred B. Ely. *Boston: J. E. Farwell & Co.* 1850. 8vo, pp. 43. BA. 22380

ELY. The State of the Country; an Article published in the Boston Recorder, with Additions, etc. By A. B. Ely. *Boston: Alfred Mudge & Son, Printers.* 1861. 16mo, pp. 28. H. 22381

ELY (*Bishop of*), *see* [Greene (Thomas)], *and* [Moore (John)].

ELY (E. S.) The Duty of Christian Freemen to Elect Christian Rulers: A Discourse Delivered on the Fourth of July, 1827, in the Seventh Presbyterian Church, in Philadelphia: By Ezra Stiles Ely, D.D. ... With an Appendix, ... *Philadelphia: William F. Geddes.* 1828. 8vo, pp. 32. B., BA., C., P. 22382

ELY. The Journal of the stated Preacher to the Hospital and Almshouse in the City of New York, for the Year of our Lord 1811. *New York: Whiting & Watson.* 1812. 12mo, pp. 300.

[ELY.] The Second Journal of the Stated Preacher to the Hospital and Almshouse, in the City of New-York, For a part of the year of our Lord 1813. With an Appendix. ... *Philadelphia: M. Carey.* 1815. 12mo, pp. 255. 22384

Reprinted as "Visits of Mercy. *London.* 1815." 12mo. + *Philadelphia.* 1829. 2 vols., 12mo. Also: A History of Ecclesiastical Proceedings, relative to the Third Presbyterian Church in Philadelphia, the Rev. Ezra Stiles Ely, and several of the Judicatories of the Church with which they are connected. *Philadelphia. May,* 1814. 12mo, pp. over 164. C.—Interpretation of the Rev. E. S. Ely's Dream, and Remarks on his Theology, &c. *Philadelphia.* 1825. 8vo. P.—Sermon on the First Sabbath after his Ordination. *Hartford: Lincoln and Gleason.* 1806. 8vo, pp. 15. B.—Sermon for the Rich to Buy. *New York.* 1810.

ELY (I. M.) An Oration delivered February 22d, 1813, ... before the Washington Benevolent Society, of the City of New-York. By Isaac M. Ely. ... *New York: Hardcastle & Van Pelt.* 1813. 8vo, pp. 28. B. 22385

ELY (J.) A Plan to render our Militia Formidable, shewing that the most effectual way to preserve Peace in the United States will be to let Military Knowledge form a part of the Education of Boys. Together with a Short Address to People who are Scrupulous about Bearing Arms in Defence of their Country. By John Ely. *Philadelphia: the Author.* 1800. 8vo, pp. 22. P. 22386

ELY (R.) Sermon at Ripton, [Con.] Oct. 27, 1773, at the Ordination of David Ely. By Richard Ely, A.M. *New Haven.* 1774. 8vo. W. 22387

[ELY (Samuel).] The Deformity of a Hideous Monster discovered in the Province of Maine. *Boston.* [n. d.] 8vo, pp. 12.

ELY (Smith), *Jr.* Mr. Ely's Report on the Sanitary Condition of the City of New York. *Albany.* 1859. 8vo. B. 22389

ELY (S. W.) Union.—Secession. The Case plainly Stated. Order or Anarchy; "That's the Question." *Cincinnati. July* 29, 1861. 8vo, pp. 8. B. 22390

ELY (Z.) The Death of Moses the Servant of the Lord. A Sermon Preached at the Funeral Solemnity Of His Excellency Jonathan Trumbull, Esq., LL.D. Late Governor of the State of Connecticut, August 19. 1785. By Zebulon Ely, A.M. Pastor of the First Church of Christ in Lebanon. ... *Hartford: Printed by Elisha Babcock.* M,DCC,LXXXVI. 8vo, pp. 28. BA. 22391

ELY. The Peaceful End of the Perfect Man. A Discourse, Delivered in Lebanon, at the Funeral of His Excellency Jonathan Trumbull, Governor of the State of Connecticut. ... By Zebulon Ely, A.M. ... *Hartford: Printed by Hudson & Goodwin.* [1809.] pp. 16, 11. BA. 22392

The second paging consists of a sketch of the family of Trumbull.

ELY. The Wisdom and Duty of Magistrates. A Sermon, preached at the General Election, May 10th, 1804. By Zebulon Ely, A.M. ... *Hartford: Printed by Hudson & Goodwin.* 1804. 8vo, pp. 35. BA. 22393

Also: Discourse in Lebanon, October 14, 1810, on the Death of Solomon Williams, of New York. ... *Hartford.* 1811. 8vo, pp. 11.— ... A Discourse occasioned by the Death of the Honourable William Williams, Esq. of Lebanon, Connecticut. ... *Hartford: Hudson and Goodwin.* 1812. 8vo, pp. 15.—Sermon on the Death of Mr. Jonathan Leech. *Norwich.* 1790. W.—Sermon at ... the Funeral of Bethiah, wife of Capt. William Huntington, at Lebanon, [Conn.] *Norwich: John Trumbull.* 1799. 8vo, pp. 16. B.—Sermon Delivered at the Ordination of the Rev. Shubael Bartlett. *Hartford: Hudson & Goodwin. Feb.* 15, 1804. 8vo, pp. 23. B.— ... A Sermon, ... Ordination of the Rev. Ezra Stiles Ely, to ... the ... Church in West-Chester, in Colchester, October 1, 1806. *Hartford: Printed by Lincoln & Gleason.* 1806. 8vo, pp. 22. H.

ELZEARIO (S.) Compendio de las vidas de los gloriossimos Santos Elzeario y sus esposa Delfina. *Mexico: Uribe.* 1837. 12mo, pp. 32. 22394

De Emancipatie der W. I. slaven, beschouwd door eenen belangloozen kolonist. *Amsterdam.* 1858. 8vo. 22395

Emancipatie door centralisatie. Schets van een ontwerp tot behoud van Suriname. Met planteekeningen. *'s Hage.* 1847. 8vo. 22396

Emancipation. By a South Carolinian. *New-York.* 1843. pp. 20. 22397

Emancipation des serfs en Russie. Examen du projet financier de MM. Frænkel et Homberg, banquiers; suivi du Résumé d'un autre projet relatif au même sujet. *Bruxelles: C. Muquardt* 1850. 8vo. 22398

Emancipation; A Poem; with Notes, Caricature Designs, &c., ... *London.* 1823. 8vo. pp. 78. 22399

Emancipation in Disguise, or the True Crisis of the Colonies. To which are added, Considerations upon Measures proposed for their Temporary Relief and Observations upon Colonial Monopoly. Shewing, The different Effects of its Enforcement and Relaxation, exposing the Advantages derived by America from Louisiana; and lastly, Suggestions for a Permanent Plan to supply our Colonies with Provisions and our Navy with certain Naval Stores independent of Foreign Supplies. *London: J. Ridgway.* 1807. 8vo, pp. 220. BA. 22400

The Emancipation Problem in Maryland. [n. p. n. d.] 8vo, pp. 4. 22401

Emancipation of the Negro Slaves in the West India Colonies considered, its Impolicy and Injustice; in answer to Mr. Wilberforce's Appeal. No. 1. *London.* 1824. 8vo, pp. 44.

Report of the Select Committee on Emancipation and Colonization, with an Appendix. *Washington: Government Printing Office.* 1862. 8vo, pp. 83. 22403

The Emancipator. *New York.* 1838. Folio. 22404

EMANUEL, *King of Portugal.* Abtruck ains lateinischen sandtbrieues an bapstliche heiligkeit, von künigklicher wurde zu Portegall, dis iars ausgangen, von d'erobertẽ stadt Malacha, etc. [Colophon:] *Getruckt zu Augspurg durch Erhart Oeglin.* [1513.] Square 12mo. 22405

This does not relate to America, but is often included in catalogues of books on America, because it settles the important question of the approximate date of printing of the "Copia der Newen Zeytung auss Presillg Landt," discovered by Humboldt, "Examen Critique," note B., Vol. v., pp. 239–258, and by Vernhagen and Ternaux Compans, as to the priority of Magellan's discoveries. This tract is by the same printer, in the same type, and with the identical woodcut arms of Portugal on the title. Oeglin succeeded Otman, who printed the "Vesputius" in 1504, and is not known to have printed anything after 1516. Thus we may fairly conclude that the "Presillg Landt" was printed by Oeglin about 1513, and hence Humboldt was wrong in dating it from internal evidences between 1525 and 1540. This tract is also curious in showing the fact that a tract printed in Rome in 1513 could be transmitted to Augsburg, translated and reprinted in twenty-six days.

[EMANUEL.] Of the newe lãdes and of ye people|founde by the messengers of the Kyn|ge of portygale named Emanuel.|Or the .x. dyuers nacyons crystened.|Of pope Johñ and his landes and of the costely keyes and wonders molo|dyes that in that

lande is.| [Colophon:] *Emprented by me Johñ of Desborowe:|* [n. p. n. d.] 4to, 24 l. BM. 22406

"The first book in the English language containing a notice of America (called *Armenica*)." *See* Harrisse's "Bibl. Am. Vet.," p. 197–199.

[EMANUEL *or* EMMANUEL.] Copia de vna littera del Re de Portagallo mãdata|al Re de Castrella del viaggio & successo de India.|*Impresso in Roma per maestro Joanni de Besicken.|nel anno* M.ccccc. *a di.* xxiij. *de Octobre.*| 4to, 4 l. 22407

Harrisse quotes a passage, which he says "shows that had Christopher Columbus never existed, America would have been discovered nevertheless, 22d April 1500."

[EMANUEL.] Copia di una lettera del Re di Portogullo mandata al Re de Castella del viaggio e successo dell' India. *Impresso in Milano per Pietro Martire de' Mantegazzi e fratelli, detti Cassani: ad instanzia di Gio. Giacomo e fratelli de Legnano,* M. ccccc. v, *adi* XVII. *del mese di decembre.* 4to. 22408

The Embargo, or Sketches of the Times. A Satire, by a Youth of Thirteen. *Boston.* 1808. 12mo. 22409

This is the first edition of Mr. W. C. Bryant's verses. *See* Vol. III., No. 8815.

Embargo Acts, 1808. With Supplement and Circulars, and an Appendix, etc. *New York.* 1808. 8vo, pp. 23. N. 22410

Embargo and Non-Importation Laws, with their various Supplements. *Philadelphia.* 1808. 12mo. 22411

The Embargo Laws; with the Message from the President, upon which they were founded; with Appendix [and] the Non-Intercourse Laws. *Boston.* 1809. B., M. 22412

Laws Relative to the Embargo. 1807. 8vo. C. + *Boston.* 1808. 12mo. W. 22413

EMBURY (E. C.) American Wild Flowers in their Native Haunts. By Emma C. Embury. *New York: D. Appleton & Company.* MDCCCXLV. 4to, pp. 256. 20 Plates. 22414

The Emerald, or Miscellany of Literature: Containing Sketches of the Manners, Principles and Amusements of the Age. ... *Boston: Belcher and Armstrong.* 1806–1808. 3 vols., 8vo. B. 22415

EMERESSIO (O.) L'Ammiraglio dell' Indie. Poema. Di Ormildo Emeressio Pastor Arcade. *In Venezia,* MDCCLIX. *Appresso Francesco Pitteri.*. 4to, pp. xv, 236. Plates. BA., J.C.B.

Emeressio Ormildò is a *pseudonym* for Querini Alvise.

EMERICK (A. G.) Songs for the People; comprising National, Patriotic, ... and Naval Songs. Edited by Albert G. Emerick. ... . *Philadelphia.* 1848. 8vo. + *Boston.* [1852.] H. 22417

EMERSON (A. L.) An Oration delivered at Portland, July 5, 1824, on the Celebration of the 48th Anniversary of American Independence ... . By A. L. Emerson. *Portland.* 1824. 8vo, pp. 14. H. 22418

EMERSON (B.) The Causes and Effects of War; A Sermon [on Fast Day], August 20, 1812 ... . By Brown Emerson ... . *Salem: printed by Joshua Cumming.* 1812. 8vo, pp. 16. B.A.

EMERSON. ... A Sermon, preached in Salem, July 23, 1812, a Day of Fasting, ... in Massachusetts, occasioned by the Declaration of War against Great Britain. By Brown Emerson ... . *Salem: printed by Joshua Cushing.* 1812. 8vo, pp. 24.

EMERSON. The Pastor's Jubilee. A Discourse delivered in the South Church, Salem, Mass., April 24, 1855, by Brown Emerson, D.D. on the Fiftieth Anniversary of his Ordination. With an Appendix. ... *Boston: printed for John B. Chisholm.* 1855. 8vo, pp. 96. B., BA., H., M. 22421

Also: ... A Sermon ... Salem, December 25, 1814, ... Interment of the Rev. Daniel Hopkins, D.D. ... . *Salem printed by Thomas C. Cushing.* 1815. 16mo, pp. 28. B., H. — A Sermon, South Church, Salem, on the Thirty-Eighth Anniversary of his Ordination. ... *Salem.* 1843. 8vo, pp. 31. B.

EMERSON (C. N.) Hand-Book of the Internal Revenue, for Popular Use. Edited by Charles N. Emerson. *Springfield, (Mass.): S. Bowles & Co.* 1868. 12mo, pp. 86. H. 22422

EMERSON. Emerson's Internal Revenue Guide, 1867, containing the Law of June 30, 1863, as amended March 3, 1865, July 13, 1866, and March 2, 1867. ... By C. N. Emerson. *Springfield, Mass.* 1867. 8vo, pp. 401. B. 22423

EMERSON. ... New Internal Revenue Guide, etc. ... With the Act passed July, 1868. ... By C. N. Emerson. *Springfield, Mass.: S. Bowles & Co.* 8vo, pp. 88, 86. H. 22424

[EMERSON.] Suggestions of Amendments to the Excise Tax Laws, recommended by a Convention of United States Assessors, holden at Cleveland, Ohio, December 16, 17 and 18, 1863, and Extracts from Proceedings of said Convention. *Boston.* 1864. 8vo, pp. 20. H. 22425

EMERSON (E.), *and* BOYCE (J.) Series of Letters between Enoch Emerson and Joseph Boyce, relative to the Excommunication of said Emerson and others, from the Congregational Church in Rochester, &c. *Windsor, Vt.* 1815. 8vo. W.

EMERSON (E.) Sermon at the Ordination of Kiah Bailey ... . By Ezekiel Emerson. *Pownalborough.* 1798. 8vo. 22427

EMERSON (G. B.) Education in Massachusetts: Early Legislation and History. A Lecture of a Course by Members of the Massachusetts Historical Society, Delivered ... Feb. 16, 1869. By George B. Emerson. *Boston: John Wilson & Son.* 1869. 8vo, pp. 36. BA., H. 22428

[EMERSON (George B.)] A Report on the Trees and Shrubs growing naturally in the Forests of Massachusetts. Published agreeably to an Order of the Legislature, by the Commissioners of the Zoological and Botanical Survey of the State. *Boston: Dutton and Wentworth.* 1846. 8vo, pp. xv, 547, 1 l. 17 Plates. C. + *Boston: [Ibid.]* 1850. 8vo. BA., H. 22429

Also: Address, Delivered at the Opening of the Boston Mechanics' Institute, February 7, 1827. ... *Boston: Hilliard, Gray, Little, and Wilkins.* 1827. 8vo, pp. 24. M. — The Advancement of the Common School. Address delivered Aug. 23, 1843, before the Normal School at Bridgewater. *Boston.* 1842. 8vo, pp. 16. — History and Design of the American Institute of Instruction. ... *Boston.* 1849. 12mo, pp. 12. B., H. — Moral Education. A Lecture, delivered on the Sixteenth of August, [1842], at New Bedford, ... before the American Institute ... *Boston: Wm. B. Fowle.* 1842. 8vo, pp. 16. B., H. + *Boston: Wm. D. Ticknor.* 1842. 12mo, pp. 35. H. — Observations on a Pamphlet, entitled "Remarks on the Seventh Annual Report of the Hon. Horace Mann," ... [n. p. n. d.] 8vo, pp. 16. B., H.

EMERSON (Gouverneur). An Address Delivered at Laurel Hill Cemetery, on the Completion of a Monument erected to the Memory of Thomas Godfrey, June 1st, 1843. By G. Emerson, M.D. *Philadelphia: Young, Printer.* 1843. 8vo, Title, pp. (2), 22. BA., P., S. 22430

EMERSON. Memoirs of Dr. Samuel Powell Griffiths. *Philadelphia.* 1827. 8vo, pp. 24. W. 22431

Published also in "The North American and Surgical Journal."

EMERSON. Medical Statistics, consisting of Estimates relating to the Population of Philadelphia, with its changes as influenced by the Deaths and Births, during ten years, viz. from 1821 to 1830, inclusive. By Gouverneur Emerson, M.D. *Philadelphia: Joseph R. A. Kenett.* 1831. 8vo, pp. 32. H. 22432

Also: Address before the Delaware Horticultural Society. ... *Philadelphia.* 1851. 8vo. P. — Address before the Agricultural Society of Chester County, Pa., September 17, 1853. — Cotton in the Middle States; with Directions for its Easy Culture. ... *Philadelphia: H. L. Butler.* 1862. 8vo, pp. 12. B.

EMERSON (J.) ... A Sermon, ... Northampton, before the Hampshire Missionary Society, ... August 31, 1809. By the Rev. John Emerson, A.M. ... . *Northampton: William Butler.* 1809. 8vo, pp. 42. BA. 22433

Also: Discourse at the Ordination of Joel Barker, at Granville, [Mass.] June 21, 1797. ... *Springfield.* 1797. 12mo. W. — ... Sermon ... at Amherst, May 2, 1804. At the Ordination of the Rev. Thomas H. Wood, A.M. ... . *Northampton, (Mass.): William Butler.* 1804. 8vo, pp. 20. B., BA.

EMERSON (J.) Advice of a Father to a Son, engaging in the Work of the Ministry: A Sermon Preach'd at the Ordination of the Reverend Mr. Joseph Emerson, ... over the Second Church of Christ in Groton ... Feb. 25th, 1746, 7. By His Father [Joseph Emerson] ... . *Boston: S. Kneeland and T. Green.* 1747. 8vo, pp. (2), 19. BA., M., W. 22435

EMERSON. Early Piety Encouraged. A Discourse occasion'd by the Death of a Young Woman of Malden, of the Throat-Distemper, Sept. 6, 1738. *Boston.* 1738. 8vo, pp. (2), viii, 30. 22436

EMERSON. Mr. Emerson's Exhortation to his People With Respect to Variety of Ministers. *Boston: S. Kneeland.* 1742. 8vo, pp. 18. B., BA., H., W. 22437

See Wigglesworth (E.)

EMERSON. Heart-Purity Encourag'd and Press'd Together With the Duty of the Clean in Heart in a Sermon Preach'd at Malden. Decemb. 4th 1726. By Joseph Emerson, M.A. *Boston: John Phillips.* 1727. 12mo, pp. (2), 63. B. 22438

EMERSON. The Important Duty Of a Timely Seeking of God Urged in a Sermon. The Substance of which was delivered on the Lord's-Day April 11th 1725. And now at the repeated Desires of Many of the Hearers Published. By Joseph Emerson, A.M. With a Preface by the Reverend Dr. Cotton Mather. *Boston: S. Kneeland.* 1727. 12mo, pp. (2), vii, 54.

EMERSON. Meat out of the Eater, and Sweetness out of the Strong. A Sermon Preach'd at Malden, September 28th. 1735. By Joseph Emerson, A.M. ... *Boston: S. Kneeland and T. Green for D. Henchman.* 8vo, Title, pp. (iv), 23. BA. 22440

EMERSON. An Offering of Memorial. Or The Penitent, calling the Sins of his Youth to Remembrance, ... A Discourse

from Psalm xxv. 7. By Joseph Emerson ... . *Boston: Printed for John Phillips.* 1732. 8vo, pp. (2), 19. BA. 22441

EMERSON. Wisdom is Justified of all her Children. A Sermon in Boston, August 26. 1742. *Boston.* 1742. 8vo, pp. 26, (3). 22442

EMERSON. A Word to those that are afflicted very much A Sermon in Malden, October 20th 1738. On the repeated Deaths of Children in said Town, by the Throat Distemper. *Boston.* 1738. 8vo, pp. (4), 26. 22443

EMERSON (J.), *of Pepperell.* An Extract from a late Sermon on the Death of the Reverend Mr. Joseph Emerson, Pastor of the First Church in Malden [Mass.]. Who died ... July 13th, 1767, ... By Joseph Emerson, A.M. Pastor of the Church at Pepperrell. ... *Boston: Edes & Gill.* MDCCLXVII. 12mo, pp. 21.

EMERSON. The Fear of God an Antidote against the Fear of Man. Sermon to Capt. Thomas Lawrence and his Company, Pepperrell, May 7, 1758. By Joseph Emerson. *Boston.* 1758. 8vo, pp. 27. 22445

EMERSON. A Thanksgiving-Sermon Preach'd at Pepperrell, July 24th. 1766. A Day set apart by public Authority As a Day of Thanksgiving On the Account of the Repeal of the Stamp-Act. By Joseph Emerson, A.M. Pastor of the Church there. ... *Boston: Edes and Gill.* M.DCC.LXVI. 8vo, pp. 37. BA., H.

EMERSON. A Thanksgiving Sermon, at Pepperrell, January 3d 1760. [On] the Removal of Sickness, and the Return of many Soldiers from the Army. *Boston.* 1760. 8vo, pp. (4), 25.

EMERSON (J.) Discourse at the Dedication of the Seminary Hall in Saugus, Jan. 15, 1822. ... By Joseph Emerson ... . *Boston.* 1822. 8vo, pp. 40. H., W. 22448

EMERSON. Letter to the Members of the Genesee Consociation, New York. *Boston.* 1829. 8vo, pp. 23. + Fourth Edition. *Boston: Beals & Homer.* 1829. 8vo, pp. 15. B., H.

Relates to his expulsion from the church for being a Mason. Also: A Reply of the Genesee Consociation to the Letter of Rev. Joseph Emerson. *Rochester, N. Y.: Edwin Scranton.* 1829. 8vo, pp. 43. B. + *Hartford.* 1829. 8vo. B. — Letter to a Class of Young Ladies upon the Study of the History of the United States. ... *Boston.* 1828. 12mo. — The Poetic Reader. *Wethersfield, Conn.* 1832. 8vo. —

Prospectus of Joseph Emerson's Female Seminary at Wethersfield, Conn. 1826. 12mo. — Questions and Supplement to Goodrich's History of the United States. ... *Boston: Richardson, Lord and Holbrook.* 1830. H. + *Boston: Carter, Hendee & Co.* 1834. Imp. 24mo, pp. 34. + A New Edition, Revised. *Claremont: N. H.* 1839. + Third Edition. *Boston.* 1845. 12mo. + *Boston.* 1846. 12mo. — ... A Sermon, delivered before the Massachusetts Missionary Society, ... Boston, May 25, 1818. ... *Boston: Samuel T. Armstrong.* 1813. 8vo, pp. 22. BA.

EMERSON (*Mrs.* M. Farley). Woman in America: her Character and Position as indicated by Newspaper Editorials, and sustained by American Social Life. *Cincinnati.* 1857. 12mo.

EMERSON (R.) Life of Rev. Joseph Emerson, ... by Rev. Ralph Emerson ... . *Boston: Crocker & Brewster.* 1834. 12mo. pp. 454. B., H. 22451

Also: Sermon, ... Roxbury Charitable Society. *Boston.* 1800. — Farewell Discourse. *Hartford.* 1829. 8vo.

EMERSON (R.) Mining Laws of Spain and Mexico, and Statutes of California, relating to Joint Stock Companies. Compiled and Translated by Ralph Emerson. *San Francisco: A. Gensoul.* 1864. 16mo, pp. 55. 22452

EMERSON (Ralph Waldo). An Address delivered in ... Concord, Massachusetts, on 1st August, 1844, on the Anniversary of the Emancipation of the Negroes in the British West Indies. By R. W. Emerson. ... *Boston: James Munroe and Company.* 1844. 8vo, pp. 34. B., BA., H. + *London.* 1844. 12mo, pp. 32. B. 22453

EMERSON. The Complete Works of Ralph W. Emerson, comprising his Essays, Lectures, Poems and Orations. *London: Bell and Daldy.* 1866. 2 vols., 8vo. B. 22454

EMERSON. Essays. *Boston: J. Munroe & Co.* 1841. 16mo, 2 l., pp. 303. + New Edition. *[Ibid.]* 16mo, pp. vi, 333. H. + Second Series. *Boston: Benton.* 1841. 16mo. + First and Second Series. *Boston: Ticknor & Fields.* 1866. 32mo, pp. v, 315. 22455

Frequently reprinted at Boston and in Great Britain.

EMERSON. An Historical Discourse, delivered before the Citizens of Concord, September 12th, 1835. On the Second Centennial Aniversary of the Incorporation of the Town. By Ralph Waldo Emerson. ... *Concord: G. F. Bemis.* [1835.] 8vo, pp. 52. B. 22456

Reprinted in the "Am. Historical Magazine," Vol. I. *See* "N. Am. Rev.," XL. 448, and XLIII. 455–467.

EMERSON. Orations, Lectures, and Addresses. By Ralph Waldo Emerson. *London: George Slater.* 1849. 18mo, pp. ix, 7–202. 22457

EMERSON. Poems. By Ralph Waldo Emerson. *Boston: James Munroe and Company.* 1847. 16mo, pp. 251. + *Boston: Ticknor and Fields.* 1865. 16mo, pp. 254. 22458

EMERSON. Prose Works. New and Revised Edition. *Boston: Fields, Osgood & Co.* 1870. 2 vols., 12mo, pp. iv, 566, Portrait; iv, 491. C. 22459

EMERSON. Representative Men. Seven Lectures. By R. W. Emerson. *Boston: Phillips, Sampson, and Company.* 1850. 12mo, pp. 285. BA, H. 22460

Also: An Address ... Before the Senior Class in Divinity College, Cambridge, Sunday Evening, 15 July, 1838, ... *Boston: James Munroe and Company.* 1838. 8vo, pp. 31. BA., H. — The Method of Nature. An Oration, Delivered before the Society of the Adelphi, in Waterville College, in Maine, August 11, 1841. ... *Boston: Samuel G. Simpkins.* 1841. 8vo, pp. 30. — Nature; Addresses and Lectures. ... *Boston.* 1836. + *Boston: Phillips, Sampson & Co.* 1850. pp. vi, 383. — An Oration, delivered before the Literary Societies of Dartmouth College, July 24, 1838. ... *Boston: Charles C. Little and James Brown.* 1838. 8vo, pp. 30. B., BA., M. — Oration delivered before the Phi Beta Kappa Society, Cambridge, Aug. 31, 1837. *Boston.* 1837. 8vo, pp. 26. H. + Second Edition. *Boston: James Munroe & Co.* 1838. 8vo, pp. 32.

EMERSON (R.) A Sermon, delivered at S. Reading, November 23, 1820. ... a Day of Public Thanksgiving throughout the Commonwealth. By Reuben Emerson, A.M. ... . *Boston: printed by True and Weston.* 1820. 8vo, pp. 15. H. 22461

Also: A Sermon ... delivered June, 1825, at the Installation of Rev. Noah Emerson ... Baldwin, Me. ... *Portland.* 1827. 8vo, pp. 16. H.

EMERSON (S.) Oration at Kennebunk, Fourth of July, 1798. By Samuel Emerson. *Portland.* 1798. 8vo, pp. 23. 22462

EMERSON. An Oration, ... in Kennebunk, Maine, on the Fourth of July, 1811. By Dr. Samuel Emerson. *Kennebunk, Maine: Printed by J. K. Remich.* 1811. 8vo, pp. 9. BA.

Also: An Oration on Music, ... at Portland, May 28th, 1800. ... *Portland: Press of E. A. Jenks.* 1800. 8vo, pp. 20. BA., H., W. — An Oration, On Medicine, Delivered at Berwick, ... Before the Medical Society of the County of York. ... *Portland: E. A. Jenks.* 1801. 8vo, pp. 24. — Oration before Saco Lodge, at the Celebration of the Anniversary of St. John Baptist. ... *Saco, Me.* 1806. 8vo, pp. 14. N.

EMERSON (W.) An Historical Sketch of the First Church in Boston, from its Formation to the Present Period. To which are added Two Sermons, one on leaving the Old, and the other on entering the New House of Worship. By the Late Rev. William Emerson, A.M. ... *Boston: Munroe & Francis.* 1812. 8vo, pp. 256. B., G. 22464

EMERSON. ... A Sermon, preached at the Request of the Ancient and Honourable Artillery Company, in Boston, June 3, 1799; the Anniversary of their Election of Officers. By William Emerson. *Boston: printed by Manning & Loring.* 1799. 8vo, pp. 23. BA., H. 22465

Also: A Discourse, ... Anniversary of the Massachusetts Humane Society, June 9, 1807. ... *Boston: Munroe & Francis.* 1807. 8vo, pp. 39. B., BA., H. — A Discourse, Delivered before the Roxbury Charitable Society, ... September 15, 1800. ... *Boston: Samuel Hall.* 1800. 8vo, pp. 23. BA., N. — A Discourse delivered in Harvard, July 4, 1794, at the Request of the Military Officers in that Place ... to commemorate the Anniversary of the American Independence. ... *Boston: Joseph Belknap.* MDCCXCIV. 8vo, pp. 18. — A Discourse, ... before ... the Boston Female Asylum, September 20th, 1805. ... *Boston: Russell and Cutler.* 1805. 8vo, pp. 30. — An Oration ... July 5, 1802, ... Boston, in Commemoration of the Anniversary of American Independence. ... *Boston: Manning & Loring.* [1802.] 8vo, pp. 23, (1). BA., H. — A Sermon ... at the Ordination of the Rev. Robinson Smiley ... in Springfield ... Vermont, September 23, 1801. ... [n. p.] *printed by Nahum Mower.* 1801. 8vo, pp. 24. H. — A Sermon on the Decease of the Rev. Peter Thatcher, D.D. ... Dec. 31, 1802, ... *Boston: printed by Young and Minns.* 1803. 8vo, pp. 40. H. + Second Edition. *Boston.* 1803. 8vo. BA., H., W. — A Sermon, delivered March 2, 1803, at the Ordination of the Rev. Thomas Beede ... in Wilton. ... *Amherst, N. H.: printed by Joseph Cushing.* 1803. 8vo, pp. 32. H. — A Sermon ... in ... Boson, ... after the Interment of Madam Elizabeth Bowdoin ... . *Boston: printed by David Carlisle.* 1803. 8vo, pp. 20. BA., H. — A Sermon, ... after the Calamitous Death of Mr. Charles Austin ... . *Boston:* [n. d.] 8vo, pp. 21. + Second Edition. *Boston: Belcher and Armstrong.* [1806.] 8vo, pp. 22. BA., H. — A Sermon, Preached at the Ordination of the Rev. Samuel Clark, ... Burlington, April 19, 1810. ... *Burington, Vt.: Samuel Mills.* 1810. 8vo, pp. 31. BA., H.

EMERSON (W. D.) Occasional Thoughts, in Verse. By W. D. Emerson. *Springfield.* 1856. 8vo, pp. 101. 22466

Emerson's Magazine and Putnam's Monthly. Volume v. July to December, 1857. ... *New-York: J. M. Emerson & Co.* 1857. 8vo, pp. iv, 764. BA. 22467

See "Putnam's Monthly," and "United States Magazine," Vol. v.

EMERY (J.) A Discourse delivered in North Church, Weymouth, Mass., Jan. 5, 1851. By Joshua Emery. *Boston.* 1851. 8vo, pp. 18. 22468

Contains an historical sketch of the town.

EMERY. Sermon at Weymouth ... on the Twenty-fifth Anniversary of the Installation of J. Emery. *Boston: Alfred Mudge & Son.* 1863. 8vo, pp. 93. B. 22469

EMERY (L.) Les nègres de la Louisiane, scènes américaines. Par Louis Emery. *Paris: Lefort.* 1864. 8vo, pp. 156. Engravings. + Troisième édition. [*Ibid.*] 1870. + [*Ibid.*]

EMERY (M.) Oration, Saco, Mass., July 4, 1839. By Moses Emery. 22471

EMERY (S. H.) The Ministry of Taunton, with Incidental Notices of other Professions. By Samuel Hopkins Emery. ... With an Introductory Notice by Hon. Francis Baylies. ... *Boston: John P. Jewett & Co.* 1853. 2 vols., 12mo, pp. (2), 394; viii, 360. Portraits. B., BA., H. 22472

EMIGRANTS. Address to Emigrants, 1817. *See* Vol. IV., No. 15643.

The Emigrant. *See* [Thomas (F. W.)]

The Emigrant: a Contrast. By an Old Etonian. [*Bath.*] 1853. 12mo, pp. 86. 22473

Organization, Objects, and Plan of Operations of the Emigrant Aid Company; also, a Description of Kansas. ... Second Edition. ... . *Boston: Alfred Mudge & Son.* 1854. 8vo, pp. 24. B., BA., H. + Third Edition. *Boston.* 1854. 8vo, pp. 24, 4.

The Emigrant Churchman. *See* Vol. IV., No. 12942.

The Emigrant Farmer: a View of the Advantages of ... Texas, the Central Maritime Portion of the United States of America; ... with Remarks on other fields of Emigration. By a Practical Farmer. *London.* [n. d.] 8vo, pp. 24. 22475

The Emigrant to North America, from Memoranda of a Settler in Canada, being a Compendium of Useful Practical Hints to Emigrants. With an account of Every Day's Doing upon a Farm for a Year. By an Emigrant Farmer of Twenty-Five Years' Experience. *Edinburgh.* 1843. 18mo, pp. 128. + [*Ibid.*] 1844. 18mo. 22476

The Emigrants; A Tale. *See* [Darling], Vol. v., No. 18592.

The Emigrant's and Traveller's Guide to the West, with a View of the Mississippi Valley. *Philadelphia.* 1832. 12mo. Map. 22477

The Emigrant's Friend, by a Southerner. ... for the Purpose of Emigrating to South Carolina ... . *New York.* 1865. 18mo, pp. 23. H. 22478

The Emigrant's Guide, or a Picture of America, exhibiting a View of the United States divested of Democratic Colouring; taken from the Original, now in the Possession of James Madison, and his 21 Governments; also a Sketch of the British Provinces, delineating their native Beauties and superior Attractions: By an Old Scene Painter. *London.* 1816. 8vo, pp. 77.

The Emigrant's Guide, or Pocket Geography of the Western States and Territories, containing a Description of the Several Cities, Towns, Rivers, Antiquities, Population, Manufactures, Prices of Land, Soil, Productions, and Exports ... . *Cincinnati: Phillips & Speir.* 1818. 12mo, pp. 266. B., S. 22480

Emigrant's Guide through the Western States, and the Territory of Michigan, 1832. 22481

The Emigrant's Guide to the State of Michigan. *New York.* 1849. 8vo, pp. 47. A. 22482

In German and English.

Emigrant's Guide. Comprising Advice and Instruction in every Stage of the Voyage to America ... . Also Information which the Emigrants need on their Arrival, etc. *London: Wiley & Putnam.* 1845. 12mo. B. 22483

The Emigrant's Guide to Australia and Canada. *London: G. B. Whittaker & Co.* 1844. 18mo. 22484

The Emigrant's Guide to the United States: Who should and Who should not Emigrate. *London: W. J. Adams.* 1850. 12mo, pp. 100. 22485

Emigrant's Hand-Book; or, a Directory and Guide for Persons Emigrating ' the United States ... especially to those designing to settle in the Great Western Valley; and also, a Concise Description of the States of Ohio, Indiana, Illinois, Michigan, Wisconsin, Missouri, and Iowa, and the Western Territories ... . *New York: J. H. Colton.* 1848. 18mo, pp. 136.

Emigrant's Hand Book to the United States. *London: Smith & Elder.* 1848. 18mo. 22487

Emigrants' Letters from Canada and South Australia. Collected in the Parish of Banham, Norfolk. By the Rev. Scott F. Surtees, Rector. *London.* 1852. 8vo. 22488

Emigrants' Letters; being Recent Communications from Settlers in the British Colonies. *London.* 1850. 12mo, pp. 138. Map.

Emigration of the Emancipated Negroes to British Guiana. [n. p. 1862.] Folio, pp. 7. H. 22490

Emigration Circular: or Complete Hand Book and Guide to the United States; being England and America Contrasted. *London: printed by J. W. Last.* [1849.] Post 8vo, pp. 32.

Emigration Considered; or, a general Description of the Leading Countries most adapted to Emigration. *London.* 1853. 12mo. pp. 82. 22492

Emigration, Emigrants, and Know-Nothings. By a Foreigner. *Philadelphia.* 1854. 12mo. P. 22493

Emigration from Ireland into the United States. 1828. 8vo.

Emigration (North American Colonies). ... Copies of Extracts of Despatches relative to North American Colonies. ... [*London.*] 1861. Folio, pp. 32. BA. 22495

A Parliamentary paper. There are many others on emigration.

Emigration to America, candidly Considered. In a Series of Letters from a Gentleman, resident there, to his Friend in England. [*London:*] *Thomas Clio Rickman.* 1798. 8vo, pp. viii, 62, 1 l. P. 22496

Emigration to Canada. *See* Vol. III., No. 10436.

Emigration to Canada. Canada: a Brief Outline of her Geographical Position, Productions, Climate, Capabilities, Educational and Municipal Institutions, Fisheries, Railroads, &c., &c., &c. Third Edition. Published by Authority. *Quebec: printed by John Lovell.* 1861. 8vo, pp. 64, (2). 22497

Emigration to the United States of North America. Indiana as a Home for Emigrants. Prepared and Published under the Direction and by Authority of Oliver P. Morton, Governor of Indiana. [n. p. n. d.] 8vo. 22498

Emigrating Indians. *See* Vol. v., No. 17459.

Emigration Commission. General Report of the Emigration Commissioners. 1840. Presented to both Houses of Parliament ... *London.* 1840. 8vo. 22499

Emigration: Letters from Sussex Emigrants, who sailed from Portsmouth in April, 1832 ... for Upper Canada: Extracts from Various Writers on Emigration to Canada ... Capt. Hale's In-

structions to Emigrants: and a Gazetteer on the Places named in the Letters. *London: Longman and Co.* MDCCCXXXIII. 8vo, pp. x, (2), 103, (4). BA. 22500

Emigration. Practical Advice to Emigrants on all points connected with their Comfort and Economy, from making Choice of a Ship to Settling and Cropping a Farm. *London.* 1834. 8vo, pp. 120. C. 22501

"Relates entirely to emigration to Canada. A second edition with some additions was printed with the same date." — RICH, Vol. II.

Letters on Emigration. By a Gentleman, lately returned from America. *London: Printed for C. and G. Kearsley.* MDCCXCIV. 8vo, Title, pp. 76. BA. 22502

Report from the Select Committee on Emigration from the United Kingdom. *London.* 1826. Folio. Continued. 22503

Report of the Commissioners for Emigration, addressed to Viscount Goderich, and the Reply. 1832. Rl. 8vo, pp. 30.

Report of the Special Committee of the Union League Club on Emigration, May 12, 1864. *New York: Club House.* 1864. 8vo, pp. 19. B. 22505

Report on Emigration by a Select Committee of the Chamber of Commerce of the State of New York, January 5, 1865. With Appendix, containing Documents and Tabular Statements referred to in the Report. Revised Edition. *New York: Printed by J. W. Amerman.* 1865. 8vo, pp. 32. 22506

Report of the Select Committee of the Senate of the United States on the Sickness and Mortality on Board Emigrant Ships. August 2, 1854. *Washington: Beverley Tucker, State Printer.* 1854. 8vo. 22507

Thoughts on Emigration, Education, &c., in a Letter Addressed to Lord John Russell; by a Citizen. *Montreal.* 1847. pp. 38. 22508

Thoughts on Emigration in a Letter from a Gentleman in Philadelphia to his Friend in England. *London.* 1794. 8vo.

Les Emigrés Français dans la Louisiane, 1800–1804. *Paris.* 1853. 16mo. C. 22510

EMILIO. As Almofadas sem franjas ou a salvaçao do Brasil. *Pernambuco.* 1866. 18mo, pp. 16. 22511

EMILY ST. PIERRE. Papers respecting the "Emily St. Pierre," of Liverpool. *London.* 1862. Folio, pp. 17. BA. 22512

A Parliamentary document.

Eminent Women of the Age. Being Narratives of the Lives and Deeds of the Most Prominent Women of the Present Generation. *Hartford: S. M. Betts.* 1868. 8vo, pp. 628. Portraits. 22513

EMLEN (S.) Extracts from the Diary of the late Samuel Emlen, M.D., Physician to the Pennsylvania Hospital, with a Short Memoir of his Life, by Dr. Meigs. *London: Harvey and Darton.* 1830. 12mo, pp. 24. 22514

Emma Corbett, or the Miseries of Civil War, founded on some recent circumstances which happened in America. *London: Baldwin.* 1780. 12mo. 22515

I have another title, in which the name is Cobbett, and the work is said to be in three vols., 12mo. I have not seen the work.

EMMET (T. A.) At a Meeting of the Subscribers to the Emmet Monument, ... the 26th of March, 1833, ... it was Resolved, That the Accompts of William James Macneven, Treasurer, be now Audited, and that the Same, together with his Report, be published. *New York: Printed For the Subscribers.* 1833. 8vo, pp. 24. 22516

Relates to the monument in St. Paul's Church Yard.

EMMONS (C. P.) Sketches of Bunker Hill Battle and Monument; with Illustrative Documents. By Charles P. Emmons. *Charlestown.* 1844. Map. 12mo. 22517

EMMONS (E.) Agriculture of New York. *See* "New York."

EMMONS. American Geology, containing a Statement of the Principles of the Science, with full Illustrations of the Characteristic American Fossils ... with an Atlas and a Geological Map of the United States. By Ebenezer Emmons. *Albany: Gray, Sprague & Co.* 1854. Part I, 8vo, pp. 194, (1). + Vol. I. *Albany: Sprague & Co.* 1855. 8vo, pp. 445. BA. + Part 6. *Albany.* 1857. 8vo, pp. x, 152. 22518

EMMONS. Geology. *See* "New York," and "North Carolina."

Also: Address before the Albany Medical College ... . *Albany.* 1845. 8vo. B. — The Empire Spring, its Composition and Medical Uses, together with a Notice of the Mineral Waters of Saratoga, and those of other Parts of New-York. ... *Albany:*

Printed by C. Van Benthuysen. 1849. 18mo. S. — Manual of Mineralogy and Geology ... *Albany.* 1826. 12mo. S. + Second Edition. *Albany.* 1832. 12mo. C., H. — Manual of Geology. Second Edition. *New York.* 1860. 8vo. C. — Saratoga Empire Spring; its Composition and Medical Uses ... . *New York.* [1859?] 24mo, pp. 8. + [1861.] 32mo. H. — Strictures ... upon certain Parts of the Report of the Select Committee appointed to investigate matters connected with the Publication of the State Work on Natural History. *Albany: J. Munsell.* [1850.] 8vo, pp. 15. — The Taconic System; based on Observations in New-York, Massachusetts, Maine, Vermont and Rhode-Island. *Albany.* 1844. 4to.

EMMONS (G. F.) The Navy of the United States, from the Commencement, 1775 to 1853; with a Brief History of each Vessel's Service and Fate, as appears upon Record. To which is added a List of Private Armed Vessels, fitted out under the American Flag, Previous and Subsequent to the Revolutionary War; with their Services and Fate. ... Compiled by Lieut. George F. Emmons, U. S. N., ... under the Authority of the Navy Department. *Washington: Gideon & Co.* MDCCCLIII. 4to, 3 l., pp. 208, (1). BA., C., H. 22519

EMMONS (H.) A Sermon: preached in the Unitarian Church, Vernon, N. Y., May 27, 1844, at the Funeral of Abraham Van Eps. By Henry Emmons ... . *Utica: John F. Kittle, Printer.* [n. d.] 8vo, pp. 15. H. 22520

Also: Sermon on the Death of Charles M. Jenkins, delivered in the Unitarian Church, Vernon, N. Y. ... With a Biographical Sketch by A. J. Upson. Albany. 1857. 8vo, pp. 57. S.

EMMONS (Henry) The Way to Fortune; or the mode of sumptuously providing for a large and expensive family, elucidated by Experiments and facts, proved by the practice of an eminent Portuguese Consul, in the City of New York. *New York: Printed for the Author.* 1809. 8vo, pp. 32. 22521

By Henry Emmons, the surviving partner of Martail Laforge & Co., a creditor to the amount of over ten thousand dollars of Joaquim Montiero, late Portuguese consul.

EMMONS (N.) The Dignity of Man, A Discourse addressed to the Congregation in Franklin, upon the Occasion of their receiving from Dr. Franklin, the Mark of his Respect in a Rich Donation of Books, appropriated to the Use of a Parish-Library. By Nathaniel Emmons ... . *Providence, R. I.* [1787.] 8vo. + *New York: J. Buel.* 1798. 24mo, pp. 43. H., W. 22522

See Sparks' "Franklin," Vol. x.

EMMONS. A Sermon, Preached before ... the Council, Senate, and House of Representatives, of ... Massachusetts, May 30, 1798, being the Day of General Election. By Nathaniel Em-

mons, A.M. ... *Boston: Printed for the State.* 1798. 8vo, pp. 31. B., BA., H. 22523

EMMONS. A Sermon on the Death of Gen. George Washington, preached February 22, 1800. By Nathaniel Emmons, D.D. Pastor of the Church in Franklin. *Printed at Wrentham, Massachusetts, by Nathaniel and Benjamin Heaton.* 1800. 8vo, pp. 26. H. 22524

EMMONS A Sermon, Delivered Dec. 31, 1820. The last Lord's Day in the Second Century since our Forefathers first settled in Plymouth. By Nathaniel Emmons, D.D. ... *Dedham: H. & W. H. Mann.* 1821. 8vo, pp. 24, (4). B., BA., H. 22525

"The Pilgrim's Song," pp. 4.

Also: Discourse at the Ordination of Walter Harris, at Dunbarton, R. I., Aug. 26, 1789. ... *Providence.* [1789.] B., W. — Discourse Nov. 3, 1790, at the Particular Request of a number of Respectable Men in Franklin, [Mass.] who were forming a Society for the Reformation of Morals. ... *Providence.* [n. d.] 8vo. — A Discourse, ... September 3d, MDCCXCII, ... Franklin. ... *Worcester: Leonard Worcester.* MDCCXCIII. 8vo, pp. 25. + Second Edition. *New York.* 1798. H. — A Discourse, ... September 2d, MDCCXCIII, ... Franklin. ... *Worcester: Leonard Worcester.* MDCCXCIII. 8vo. — A Discourse, ... at the Ordination of the Rev. Eli Smith, to the ... Church in Hollis, November 27, MDCCXCIII. ... *Worcester: Leonard Worcester.* MDCCXCIV. 8vo, pp. 25. Discourse, delivered August 10, 1795, at the Funeral of the Reverend Elisha Fish ... . *Wrentham: printed by N. Heaton, Jun.* M,DCC,XCVI. 8vo, pp. 25. H. — Discourse at Wardsborough, Vt. Nov. 4, 1795, at the Ordination of James Tufts. *Brattleborough.* 1797. 12mo. B., W. — A Discourse, Delivered May 9, 1798. Being the Day of Fasting and Prayer throughout the United States. ... . *Wrentham (Mass.): Nathaniel and Benjamin Heaton.* M,DCC,XCVIII. 8vo, pp. 28. BA. + *Newburyport: reprinted by Angier March.* [n. d.] 8vo, pp. 24. H. — Discourse, Delivered on the National Fast, at Franklin, April 25, 1799. *Wrentham (Mass.): Nathaniel & Benjamin Heaton.* M,DCC,XCIX. 8vo, pp. 31. B., BA., H. — A Discourse, delivered at the Funeral of Mrs. Bathsheba Sanford ... November 17, 1800. ... *Wrentham: printed by Nathaniel Heaton, Jun.* 1801. 8vo, pp. 22. H. — A Discourse, delivered at the Funeral of Mr. Samuel Rockwood ... . *Wrentham: printed by Nathaniel Heaton, Jun.* 1801. 8vo, pp. 22. H. — A Discourse, delivered on the Annual Fast in Massachusetts, April 9, 1801. ... *Salem: Reprinted by Joshua Cushing.* 1802. 8vo, pp. 38. + Second Edition. *New York.* 1801. 8vo, pp. 37. B. + *Hartford: Reprinted.* 1801. 8vo. — A Discourse delivered on the Day of the Annual Fast in Massachusetts, April 8, 1802. *Wrentham, (Mass.): Nathaniel Heaton, Jun.* 8vo, pp. 35. BA. — A Discourse delivered, July 5, 1802. In commemoration of American Independence. ... . *Wrentham: printed by Nathaniel Heaton, Jr.* 1802. 8vo, pp. 24. + Second Edition. [*Ibid.*] H. — Discourse, on the day of the Annual Fast, in Massachusetts, April 7, 1803. *Wrentham, Mass.* 1803. 8vo. — Discourse ... on the Annual Thanksgiving in Massachusetts, November 29, 1804. ... *Providence: printed by Heaton and Williams.* [n. d.] 8vo, pp. 32. — A Discourse, occasioned by the Death of Doctor Abijah Everett ... . *Dedham: printed by H. Mann.* 1805. 8vo, pp. 18. H. — Discourse at the Ordination of the Rev. Stephen Chapin, ... Hillsborough, June 19, 1805. ... *Amherst.* 1805. 8vo, pp. 30. B., M., N. — A Discourse, ... April 11, 1806, at a Publick Meeting ... of Singers, ... Providence, 1806. ... *Providence: printed at D. Heaton's Office, by David Hawkins, jun.* 1806. 8vo, pp. 31. BA., H. — Discourse at Attleborough, [Mass.] July 19, 1808, at the Funeral of Esther, daughter of Rev. John Wilder. ... *Providence.* 1808. 8vo, pp. 23. — A Discourse, Delivered to the Congregation in Franklin. ... *Boston.* 1809. pp. 24. — A Discourse, ... Delivered at the Funeral of the Rev. David Sanford, A.M. who died April 7, 1810, ætatis 73. ... *Boston: Farrand, Mallory & Co.* 8vo, pp. 23. BA., H., M., W. — A Discourse delivered January 22, 1811, in Attleborough, at the Funeral of Mrs. Esther Wilder ... . *Providence: printed by D. Heaton.* 1811. 8vo, pp. 24. H. — A Discourse, Delivered, October 13, 1813, before the Mendon Association. ... *Boston: Samuel T. Armstrong.* 1814. 8vo, pp. 40. BA. — A Discourse, delivered November 25, 1813, on the Day of the Annual Thanksgiving. ... . *Dedham.* 1813. 8vo, pp. 20. H. + *Newburyport: Wm. B. Allen & Co.* 1814. 8vo, pp. 16. B., H. — A Discourse, ... on the National Thanksgiving, April 13, 1815. ... *Dedham: Gazette Office.* 1815. 8vo, pp. 19. B., BA., W. — A Discourse, delivered at the Funeral of the Rev. Timothy Dickinson ... . *Dedham: Gazette Office.* 1813. 8vo, pp. 20. BA., H. — A Discourse, delivered November 20, 1814, occasioned by the Death of Mr. Oliver Shepherd ... . *Dedham.* 1815. 8vo, pp. 28. — A Discourse, delivered at the Funeral of the Rev. John Cleaveland, A.M. ... . *Dedham: Gazette Office.* 1815. 8vo, pp. 22. — A Discourse, occasioned by the Death of Capt. Amos Hawes ... . *Dedham: printed by H. Mann.* 1815. 8vo, pp. 20. H. — A Discourse ... at the Installation of the Rev. Thomas Williams, at Foxborough, [Mass.] Nov. 6, 1816. ... *Dedham: printed by H. & W. H. Mann.* 1816. 8vo, pp. 24. H., W. — A Discourse, addressed to the Norfolk Auxiliary Society for the Education of Pious Youth for the Gospel Ministry, at Dorchester, June 11, 1817. ... *Dedham.* 1817. 8vo, pp. 39. H. + [Second Edition.] *Providence: Barnum Field & Co.* 1825. 8vo, pp. 23. BA., H. — A Discourse, delivered the next Lord's Day after the Interment of Deacon Peter Whiting ... . *Providence: printed by Heaton & Williams.* [n. d.] 8vo, pp. 24. H. — An Extract from a Discourse, delivered August 10, 1785, at the Funeral of the late Rev. Elisha Fish, Pastor of the Church in Appleton ... . *New York.* 1797. 8vo, pp. 24. — The Giver more Blessed than the Receiver. A Discourse, Addressed to the Congregation in Franklin. ... *Boston: Lincoln & Edmands.* 1809. 8vo, pp. 24. B., BA., M., W. + Second Edition. *Exeter: Printed for Josiah Richardson.* 1823. 8vo, pp. 20. B., BA., H. — ... A Sermon ... at the Installation of the Rev. Caleb Alexander, to the ... Church in Mendon, April 12, 1786. *New York.* 1786. 12mo. + *Providence.* [n. d.] — ... Sermon ... at the Installation of the Rev. David Avery to the ... Church in Wrentham, May 25, 1786. *Providence.* [1786.] 8vo. B., W. — A Sermon delivered at the Ordination of the Rev. John Robinson to the Pastoral Care of the Church in Northborough, January 14, 1789. ... *Providence.* 8vo. — Sermon at Oxford, [Mass.] April 13, 1791, at the Ordination of Elias Dudley. ... *Providence, R. I.* 8vo. — Sermon at Rochester, [Mass.] Oct. 10, 1793, at the Ordination of Calvin Chaddock. *New Bedford.* 1794. 8vo. — Sermon at the Ordination of John Smith, January 4, 1797, at Salem, N. H. *Concord.* 1797. 8vo. — ... A Sermon, ... at Franklin, on the Day of Annual Thanksgiving, December 15th, MDCCXCVI. ... . *Worcester: printed by Leonard Worcester.* MDCCXCVII. 8vo, pp. 23. B., H., W. — A Sermon, ... Massachusetts Missionary Society, ... Boston, May 27, 1800. *Charlestown: Samuel Etheridge.* 1800. 8vo, pp. 44. B., BA., H., M., N. — A Sermon, preached on the Annual Thanksgiving in Massachusetts, November 27, 1800. ... . *Wrentham: printed by Nathaniel Heaton, Jun.* 1801. 8vo, pp. 30. H. — A Sermon, preached at the Funeral of Mr. Daniel Thurston ... . *Wrentham: printed by Nathaniel Heaton, Jun.* 1803. 8vo, pp. 24. H. — Sermon at the Ordination of Joseph Emerson, in Beverly, [Mass.] Sept. 21, 1803. *Salem.* [n. d.] 8vo. B., W. — ... A Sermon, Preached before the Convention of the Congregational Ministers in Boston, May 31, 1804. ... . *Boston: Manning & Loring.* 1808. 8vo, pp. 24. H., W. — A Sermon Preached at the Ordination of the Rev. Edwards Whipple, ... in Charlton, January 25, 1804. ... *Brookfield.* 1804. 8vo, pp. 24. + Second Edition. *New York: George Norman.* 1809. 8vo, pp. 24. — Sermon at the Installation of Rev. Thomas Williams, at Attleborough, Mass., Sept. 20, 1804. *Providence.* [n. d.] 8vo. W. — Sermon ... July 13, 1805, At the Funeral of Mrs. Lydia Fisk, ... at Wrentham, ... *Dedham: printed by*

H. Mann. 1805. 8vo, pp. 18. H. — A Sermon, delivered the next Sabbath after the Interment of the Hon. Jabez Fisher, Esq. ... . *Providence: printed by David Heaton.* 1807. 8vo, pp. 24. H. — Sermon before the Massachusetts Humane Society. *Boston.* 1807. 8vo. W. — Sermon at the Ordination of Gaius Conant, at Paxton, [Mass.] Feb. 17, 1808. ... *Brookfield.* 1808. 8vo. — A Sermon, preached at the Installation of the Rev. Holland Weeks ... in Abington, on the Ninth of August, 1815. ... *Boston: printed by Nathaniel Willis.* 1815. 8vo, pp. 20. H. — Sermon at the Installation of Thomas Williams, at Foxboro', Mass., ... *Dedham.* 1816. 8vo. — Sermon at the Ordination of Zolva Whitmore, at North Guilford, [Con.] Sept. 5, 1821. *New Haven.* 1822. 8vo. — Sermon at Attleborough, Sept. 29, 1824, at the Installation of Rev. Thomas Williams. ... *Providence.* 1824. 8vo. — A Sermon Preached Dec. 13, 1826, at the Installation of the Rev. Calvin Park, D.D. ... Stoughton. ... *Boston: T. R. Marvin.* 1827. 8vo, pp. 22. B., BA., H., W.

EMMONS. The Works of Nathaniel Emmons. With a Memoir of his Life. Edited by Jacob Ide, D.D. *Boston: Crocker & Brewster.* 1842–45. 7 vols., 8vo. + *Boston: Congregational Board of Publication.* 1842. 12mo. + [*Ibid.*] 1860–61. + [*Ibid.*] 1861–63. BA., C. 22526

EMMONS (R.) The Battle of Bunker Hill, or the Temple of Liberty; an Historical Poem in Four Cantos, Respectfully Dedicated to the Friends of Rational Liberty throughout the World. By the late Richard Emmons, M.D. *New York: Published Fourth of July,* 1839. 12mo, pp. 144. Portrait. + Second Edition. *New York: Sackett & Sargent.* 1839. 12mo, pp. 144. C. + [Another] Second Edition. *Boston.* 1841. 12mo, pp. 144. Plate. + Sixth Edition. *Boston.* 1842. 8vo, pp. 144. Portrait. + [Another] Sixth Edition. *Boston.* 1856. 12mo, pp. 144. Plate. + Tenth Edition. *Boston, June 17th,* 1859. 8vo. + [Another] Tenth Edition. *Boston.* 1862. 12mo, pp. 144. Plate. + [*Ibid.*] 1865. C. + Eleventh Edition. *Boston.* 1867. B.

EMMONS. Defence of Baltimore, and Death of General Ross. By Richard Emmons, M.D. *Washington: William Emmons.* 1831. 16mo, pp. 48, 16 l. C. 22528

EMMONS. The Fredoniad; or, Independence Preserved. An Epick Poem on the Late War of 1812. By Richard Emmons, M.D. *Boston: William Emmons.* 1827. 4 vols., 12mo, pp. 333; 338; 295; 293. B., BA. + Second Edition. *Philadelphia.* 1830. 4 vols., 12mo, pp. xii, 357; iv, 371; v, 326; iv, 350. + Third Edition. *Philadelphia: William Emmons.* 1832. H. 22529

EMMONS. Tecumseh, or the Battle of the Thames. A National Drama, in Five Acts. By Dr. Emmons. *New York: Elton and Harrison.* 1836. 12mo, pp. 36. B. 22530

EMMONS (W.) An Address in Commemoration of Lexington Battle, delivered April 19, 1826. ... By William Emmons. *Boston: Printed for the Author.* 1826. 8vo, pp. 16. BA. 22531

Another edition is entitled: Emmons's Oration on Lexington Battle, delivered April 19, 1827. [n. p. n. d.] 8vo, pp. 7.

EMMONS. Authentic Biography of Richard W. Johnson, of Kentucky. *Boston: Proprietor.* 1832. 16mo, pp. 92. C. 22532

EMMONS. Biography of Martin Van Buren, Vice President of the United States. ... . By William Emmons. *Washington: printed by Jacob Gideon, Jr.* 1835. 16mo, pp. vi, 296. H. + Second Edition. [*Ibid.*] 1835. 18mo, pp. vi, 196. 22533

Also: Address on Imprisoning the Unfortunate Debtor. *Boston.* 1824. 8vo, pp. 14. — An Address in Commemoration of the Boston Massacre, of March 5th, 1770. ... March 5th, 1825. *Boston.* [n. d.] 8vo, pp. 14. BA. — An Address Commemorative of the Battle of Bunker Hill, June 17, 1775. ... *Boston.* 1834. 8vo. H. — An Oration, Commemorative of American Independence. Pronounced at Hallowell, July Fourth, 1809. ... *Augusta: Peter Edes.* 1809. 8vo, pp. 20. BA. — An Oration on Bunker Hill Battle, delivered ... in Charlestown, 18th of July, 1827. Together with a Caucus Speech, delivered in Faneuil Hall, May 9th ... . *Boston.* 1827. 8vo. H. — An Oration and Poem, delivered July 4, 1826, being the Fiftieth Anniversary of American Independence. ... *Boston: the Author.* 1826. 8vo, pp. 16. + Second Edition. *Boston.* 1826. 8vo, pp. 16 — Oration Commemorative of the Surrender of Lieut. Gen'l. Earl Cornwallis at Yorktown on the 19th of October, 1781, ... *Washington.* 1828. 8vo, pp. 19. — Oration ... at the Washington Garden, Boston, July 4, 1829. ... *Boston.* 1829. 8vo, pp. 16. — An Oration, Commemorative of the Declaration of Independence, delivered Fourth of July, 1834, ... on Boston Common, ... *Boston: Published for the Author.* 8vo, pp. 16. BA., H. — An Oration on the Death of Mr. Levi Hoppin, ... of ... Brown University, March 27, A.D. 1805. *Providence: J. Carter.* [1805.] 8vo, pp. 12.

EMORY (J.) Defence of "Our Fathers," and of the original Organization of the Methodist Episcopal Church, against the Rev. Alexander M'Caine, and others. With Historical and Critical Notices of Early American Methodism. By John Emory. *New-York.* 1827. 8vo. B., C., S. 22534

EMORY (J.) Discourse, Weymouth, Jan. 5, 1851. By Joshua Emory, Jr. *Boston.* 1851. 8vo, pp. 18. 22535

EMORY (W. H.) Notes of a Military Reconnoissance, from Fort Leavenworth, in Missouri, to San Diego, in California, including part of the Arkansas, Del Norte, and Gila Rivers. By Lieut. Col. W. H. Emory. Made in 1846–7, with the Advanced Guard of the "Army of the West." ... *Washington: Wendell and Van Benthuysen, Printers.* 1848. pp. 614. 69 Plates, Illustrations, and 2 Maps. BA. 22536

Contents: 1. Report of J. W. Abert, of his Examination of New-Mexico in 1846, 47. 2. Report of Lieut. Col. P. St. George Cooke, of his March from Santa Fe, New-Mexico, to San Diego, California. 3. Journal of Capt. A. R. Johnston. An abridged edition was published, *New York.* 1848. 8vo, pp. 230? *See also* "Pacific R. R. Surveys," Vol. II.

EMORY. Notes on the Mexican and U. S. Boundary Line, Maps. *Cincinnati.* 1851. 8vo. 22537

EMORY. Report of the United States and Mexican Boundary Survey, made under the Direction of the Secretary of the Interior. By William H. Emory. *Washington: A. O. P. Nicholson, Printer.* 1857. 2 vols., 4to. BA. 22538

The title of this work, like many other of the government documents, conveys a very inadequate idea of its contents, which are partly as follows: Vol. I. Part I. General Account, General Description of the Country, Lower Rio Bravo, &c. Astronomical and Geodetic Work, Meteorology. Lithograph, 74 steel plates, 24 woodcuts, pp. xvi, 258. Part 2. Geological Reports, by Dr. C. C. Parry, Arthur Schott, Jas. Hall, and T. A. Conrad. 26 woodcuts, 21 steel plates, pp. xiii, 174. Vol. II. Part I. Botany of the Boundary, by John Torrey, 61 plates, pp. 270. Cactaneæ of the Boundary, by George Engelmann, 75 plates, pp. 78. Part 2. Zoology of the Boundary — Mammals of the Boundary, by Spencer F. Baird, 27 plates, pp. 62. Birds of the Boundary, by Spencer F. Baird, 25 colored plates, pp. 33. Reptiles, by S. F. Baird, 41 plates, pp. 35. Icthyology, by Charles Giraud, 41 plates, pp. 85.

Emory College, Oxford, Ga. Catalogue, 1857. *Atlanta.* 1858. 8vo. S. 22539

EMOTT (J.) Speech of the Hon. James Emott, in the House of Representatives ... February 6, 1811, in Relation to the Non-Intercourse. [*Washington.* 1811.] 8vo, pp. 37. B., BA., C., H.

EMOTT. Speech ... 12th January, 1813, on the Bill in Addition to the Act Entitled, "An Act to Raise an Additional Military Force," ... . *New York: Printed by J. Seymour.* 1813. 8vo, pp. 40. + *Utica.* 1813. 8vo. + *Alexandria.* [n. d.] 8vo, pp. 40. + *Boston: Russell & Cutter.* 1813. 8vo, pp. 35. H.

Also: Speech ... in Relation to the Refusal of further Communication from F. J. Jackson. [*Washington.* 1809.] 8vo.

L'Empereur du Mexique. *Paris: Dentu.* 1864. 8vo, pp. 32.

Empire Almanac: G. R. Perkins. *Rochester, N. Y.* 1847. 12mo. S. 22543

"The Empire of Christ is Peace." *New York.* 1862. pp. 12.

Empire of Reason; an Allegory addressed to the Dialectic Society at the United States Military Academy. *Newburgh.* .829. 12mo. B. 22545

Emporium of Arts and Sciences. *See* Vol. v., No. 17283.

Los Empresarios, de fabricas nacionales de Hilados y Tegidos de algodon, solicitan del Supremo Gobierno se serva presentar el Congreso General una Iniciativa, paro que se permita, por tiempo limitado, la importacion de algodones en vama, en los terminos y por los fundamentos que esponen. *Mexico.* 1840. 8vo, pp. 11. 22546

O emprestino brasileiro contrahido em Londres em 1863. *Paris: Ve Aillaud, Guillard et Ce.* 1864. 8vo, pp. 67. 22547

EMPSON (C.) Narratives of South America; Illustrating Manners, Customs, and Scenery. Containing numerous facts in Four Years' Residence in Tropical Regions. By Charles Empson. *London: Edwards.* 1836. 8vo, pp. 322. C., P., S.

Twelve colored facsimiles of drawings, from sketches made at the various localities to illustrate the narratives, were published at the same time, and a few copies of the work were printed in small folio, with these plates inserted. Also: Antiquarian Miscellany. Observations and Correspondence relative to various ornaments of Gold, Idols, Sculptured Stones, Coins, etc. [from South America, etc.] in the possession of C. Empson, Esq. *Privately Printed.* 1838. 4to.

Encarnacion Prisoners. *Louisville.* 1848. 8vo. 22549

ENCINAS (Diego de), *Editor.* Provisiones | cedvlas, capitvlos de | ordenanças, instrucciones, y cartas, libradas y des- | pachadas en diferentes tiempos por sus Magestades de | los señores Reyes Catolicos don Fernando y doña Ysabel, y Emperador | don Carlos de gloriosa memoria, y doña Iuana su madre, y catolico Rey don | Felipe, con acuerdo de los señores Presidentes, y de su Consejo Real de las In | dias, que en sus tiempos ha auido tocantes al buen gouierno de las Indias, y | administracion de la justicia en ellas. Sacado todo ello de los libros del | dicho Consejo por su mandado, para que se sepa, entienda, y se tenga no- | ticia de lo que cerca dello esta' proueydo despues que se | descubrieron las Indias | hasta agora. | *En Madrid,* | *En la Imprenta Real.* | M.D.XCVI. | 4 vols., folio, 14 l., pp. 462; 14 l., pp. 382; 13 l., pp. 482; 10 l., pp. 415. J.C.B. 22550

"Suppressed by the Council of the Indies, as Encinas had prepared them without having been previously authorized." — HARRISSE. Veitia Linage speaks highly of the editor, and says that it was rare in his day (1672).

ENCISO (M. F. de). Suma de geographia *que* | trata de todas las partidas & prouin- | cias del mundo: en especial de las indi- | as. & trata largamēte del arte del mare | ar: Juntamēte con la

esphera en romāce: con el regimiēto del Sol & del norte: nue | uamente hecha. | Con preuilegio real. | [Colophon:] *Fue impressa enla nobilissima & muy leal ciudad de Seuilla por Ja- | cobo crōberger alemā en el año dᵉ la encarnacion de nuestro señor. | de mil & quinientos & diez & nueue.* | [1519.] Folio, Title, 1 l., 75 unnumbered l. L. 22551

"Apparently the first book printed in Spanish relating to America; — unknown to Robertson. Enciso having gained a considerable sum in St. Domingo by practicing law, was induced by Ojeda to join him in an exhibition of discovery and conquest to the continent of America. After suffering great hardships and hairbreadth escapes, which are related by Herrera, he returned to Spain, and published this work for the instruction of Charles v. The account of America is principally from his own observations." — RICH. "We must add that Martin Fernandez de Enciso first came to the New World with Rodrigo de Bastidas, was Alguazil Mayor of the Golden Castil, and the owner of the vessel as well as the planner of the expedition in which Vasco Nuñez de Balboa acquired so much fame. A great hydrographer and explorer, his work is invaluable for the early geographical history of this continent." — HARRISSE. "Livre curieux, parce qu'il est le premier traité de Géographie imprimé en Espagne où l'on trouve des details sur l'Amérique." — BRUNET.

ENCISO. Suma de geographiā *que* | trata de todas las partidas & prouinci | as del mundo: en especial delas indias. | & trata largamente del arte del marear | juntamente con la esfera en romance: conel regimiēto del sol y del norte: ago | ranueuamente emendada de algunos | defectos *que* tenia enla impressiō passada. | [Colophon:] *Fue impressa en la nobilissi | ma & muy leal cibdad de Seuilla por Juā crom- | berger: en el año de la encarnacion de nuestro señor Jesu christo de mil & quini- | entos. & . xxx.* | [1530.] Folio, Title, 1 l., 57 numbered l. L. 22552

ENCISO. Suma de geographia *que* trata de todas | las partidas y prouincias del mundo: en | especial de las indias. y trata largamēte | del arte del marear jūtamente cō la es | pera en romāce: con el regimiento | del sol y del norte: agora nueua | mente enmendada de algu- | nos defectos que tenia | en la impression passada. | M. D. xlvj. | [Colophon:] *fue impressa enla muy noble & muy leal ciudad de Seuilla en | casa de Andres de burgos: en el año de la encarnacion de nuestro señor Je- | su Christo de mil & quinientos & quarenta & seys años.* | Folio, Title, 1 l., 70 numbered l., the last 10 wrongly numbered. J.C.B., L. 22553

Mr. Rich says this is an exact reprint of the edition of 1519. Sold at Puttick's, in 1869, for £4 12s.

Encroachments of the Slave Power upon the Rights of the North. [n. p. n. d.] 12mo. B. 22554

Encyclopædia; or, a Dictionary of the Arts and Sciences and Miscellaneous Literature ... The First American Edition ...

Greatly Improved. *Philadelphia.* M.DCC.XCVIII. 18 vols., 4to, pp. xiv, 807; 799; 806; 793; 807; 794; 797; 799; 800; 788; 814; 799; 799; 797; 799, 4; 799; 827; 945, (3). 542 Plates. 22555

In 1813, the same publisher issued a supplement, in 3 vols., 4to, and afterwards a second supplement, in 2 vols. Includes copious articles on American topics, taken mainly from Dr. Gleig's British edition.

Encyclopædia Americana. A Popular Dictionary of Arts, Sciences, Literature, History, Politics and Biography, brought down to the Present Time; including a Copious Collection of Original Articles in American Biography; on the Basis of ... the German Conversations-Lexicon. Edited by Francis Lieber, assisted by E. Wigglesworth. *Philadelphia: Carey, Lea & Carey.* 1829–33. 13 vols., 8vo. BA., H. 22556

The titles of Vol. v.–xiv. read, "assisted by E. Wigglesworth and T. G. Bradford." Vol. xiii. contains supplementary articles, and there is a "Supplementary Volume." ... Vol. xiv. Edited by Henry Vethake. *Philadelphia.* 1847. Frequently reprinted, — the later editions at Boston. Mr. R. Walsh wrote the American biography; Mr. Bradford the American geography; and Mr. Ingersoll trade and manufactures.

The End of the Irrepressible Conflict. By a Merchant of Philadelphia. ... *Philadelphia: King & Baird, Printers.* 1860. 8vo, pp. 47. B., H. 22557

ENDHOVEN (Jan Van). Denkwürdige und ausführliche Erzehlung Der glücklichen und Siegreichen See Reise: welche H. Lieutenant-Admiral de Ruyter Im Iahr 1664. und 1665. nach Guinea und West-Indien ... verrichtet. [n. p. 1665.] 4to, 6 unpaged l. J.C.B. 22558

ENDICOTT (C. M.) Account of Leslie's Retreat at the North Bridge, in Salem, on Sunday, Feb'y 26, 1775. By Charles M. Endicott. ... *Salem: Wm. Ives and Geo. W. Pease.* 1856. 8vo, pp. 47. B., BA., H. 22559

ENDICOTT. A Genealogy of the Peabody Family, as Compiled by the late C. M. Endicott, of Salem. Revised, Corrected and Enlarged by W. S. Peabody, of Boston. With a Partial Record of the Rhode Island Branch by B. Frank Pabodie. *Boston: David Clapp & Son.* 1867. 8vo, pp. 60. B. 22560

ENDICOTT. Memoir of John Endicott, First Governor of the Colony of Massachusetts Bay. Being also a Succinct Account of the Rise and Progress of the Colony, from 1628 to 1665. *Salem: Printed at the Observer Office.* MDCCCXLVII. 4to, pp. 16. Portrait. H. 22561

Also: History of the Salem and Danvers Aqueduct. ... *Salem.* 1860. 8vo, pp. 16. — Narrative of the Piracy and Plunder of the Ship Friendship, of Salem, on the West Coast of Sumatra, In February, 1831; And the Massacre of Part of her Crew; Also, her recapture out of the Hands of the Malay Pirates. ... *Salem.* 1859. 4to, pp. 20.

ENDLICHER (S.), *and* MARTIUS (C. F. P.) Flora Brasiliensis sive enumeratio plantarum in Brasilia hactenus delectarum, quas cura Musei Caes: Reg: Palat: Vindobonensis suis aliorumque botanicorum studiis descriptas et methodo naturali digestas sub auspiciis Ferdinandi I. Austriæ Imperatoris et Ludovici I. Bavariæ Regis. ediderunt Stephanus Endlicher et Carolus Frid. Phil. de Martius. *Vindibonae apud Frid. Beck.* 1840–54. 10 pts., folio. 22562

A great but unfinished book. 124 rare plates of plants, and 32 of scenery.

Endowment, as it was acted by upwards of Twelve Thousand, in Secret, in the Nauvoo Temple. *New York.* 1848. 8vo, pp. 24. 22563

ENDURAN (L.) France et Mexique, histoire de l'expédition des Français au Mexique. Par L. Enduran. *Limoges et Lisle: E. Ardent et Thibaut.* 1866. 12mo, pp. 191. Engr. 22564

ENESEE, *pseudonym.* The History of Dungeon Rock. Completed Sept. 17th, 1856. By Enesee [N. E. C.] *Boston.* 1856. 16mo, pp. 75. H. 22565

ENFIELD (E.) Indian Corn; Its Value, Culture, and Uses. By Edward Enfield. *New York: D. Appleton & Co.* 1866. 12mo, pp. 308. BA. 22566

ENGEL (S.) Anmerkungen über den Theil von Cap. Cooks Reise-relation, so die Meerenge zwischen Asia und Amerika ansiehet; in einem Brief ... durch Herrn. S. Engel. 1780. 12mo, Title, pp. 30. H. 22567

[ENGEL.] Essai sur cette question; quand et comment l'Amérique a-t-elle été peuplée d'hommes et d'animaux? Par E. B. d'E. *Amsterdam: Marc Michel Rey.* MDCCLXVII. 4to, pp. xi, (5), 610. BA., H. + 5 vols., 12mo, pp. (4), xxii, (vi), 454; (4), 384; (4), 388; (8), 359; (8), 228. B., C., N., S. 22568

The author declares the theories of Grotius, De Laet, Hornius, and other writers on the origin of the Americans untenable — that America was peopled (before the Deluge) by a race superior to the present — that the Deluge did not extend to America, and that the principal theories of the Deluge are erroneous, particularly that of Whiston. He gives his own theories on all these points, as well as upon many others of equally high interest, not excluding the origin of the negro. *See also* "M. Rev.," XXXVI. 531; XXXVI. 535; and Faribault, No. 222.

Engel. Extraits raisonnés des voyages faits dans les parties septentrionales de l'Asie et de l'Amérique, ou nouvelles preuves de la possibilité d'un passage aux Indes par le Nord; démontrées par Mr. Engel, avec deux grandes cartes géographiques. *A Lausanne: Jules Henri Potts.* M.D.CC.LXXIX. 4to, pp. xxiv, 268. 2 Maps. 22569

Engel. Geographische und Kritische Nachrichten und Anmerkungen über die Lage der nördlichen Gegenden von Asien und Amerika, nach den allerneusten Reise-beschreibungen; welchen noch ein Versuch über einen Weg durch Norden nach Indien, und über die Errichtung eines sehr ausgebreiteten und einträglichen Handels in die Südsee beygefüget ist; nebst zwo neuen nach diesem Systeme entworfenen Karten. Aus dem Französischen übersetzt. *Mietau: Hasenpoth. Leipzig: bey Jacob Friedrich Hinz.* 1772. 4to, pp. (2), xvi, 368. 2 Maps. C.

The translation is by the author himself, and is augmented.

[Engel.] Mémoires et Observations Géographiques et Critiques sur la situation des pays septentrionaux de l'Asie et de l'Amérique, d'après les relations les plus recentes. Auxquelles on a joint un Essai sur la route aux Indes par le Nord, & sur un Commerce très vaste & très riche à établir dans la mer du sud. Avec deux nouvelles cartes, dressés conformément à ce systême. Par Mr. ***. *Lausanne: Antoine Chapins.* MDCCLXV. 4to, pp. xxii, 268, 8. 2 Maps. H. 22571

See "Biog. Univ.," and Faribault, No. 221.

[Engel.] Mémoire sur la Navigation dans la mer du Nord depuis le 63e degré de latitude vers le pôle, & depuis le 10 au 100e degré de longitude. Avec une nouvelle carte sur cette étendue. Par M. le B. E. *Berne: F. S. Fetscherin.* 1779. 4to, pp. 28. Map. J.C.B. 22572

Engel. Herrn Samuel Engels, Raths der Republik Bern ... Geographische und Kritische Nachrichten und Anmerkungen über die Lage der nördlichen Gegenden von Asien und Amerika, nach den allerneuesten Reisebeschreibungen; welchen noch ein Versuch über einen Weg durch Norden nach Indien, und über die Errichtung eines sehr ausgebreiteten und einträglichen Handels in der Südsee, beygefüget ist; nebst zwo neuen nach diesem System entworfenen Karten. Aus dem Französischen übersetzet, von dem Hrn. Verfasser selbst sorgfältig und genau durchgesehn, verbessert und mit vielen Zusätzen bereichert, die sich in dem Originale nicht befinden. *Mietau: Hasenpoth. Leipzig: bey Jacob Friedrich Hinz.* 1772. 4to, pp. (2), xvi, 368. 2 Maps. H. 22573

Engel. Herrn Samuel Engels Neuer Versuch über die Lage der nördlichen Gegenden von Asia und Amerika, und dem Versuch eines Wegs durch die Nordsee nach Indien; nebst denen Schriften so Hr. Daines Barrington in London zu Behauptung eben dieses herausgegeben ... . *Basil: Carl August Serini.* 1777. 4to, 2 l., pp. 304, (1). 3 Maps. J.C.B., H.

Engel. Remarques sur la partie de la Relation du voyage du Capitaine Cook, qui concerne le Détroit entre l'Asie et Amérique, dans une lettre addressée à M. D***. Traduite de l'Allemand, pouvant servir de suite au Mémoire du meme auteur de 1779. *Geneve: J. Emanuel Didier.* 1781. 4to, pp. 26. Map. J.C.B. 22575

Engel. Remarks sur la partie de la relation du voyage du Capitaine Cook, qui concerne le Détroit entre l'Asie et l'Amérique, par M. Le Bailly Engel, etc. *Berne: F. Samuel Fetscherin.* 1781. 4to, pp. 26. Map. J.C.B. 22576

Engelands Dwaasheid in den tegenwoordigen oorlog van het begin der onlusten met America tot op de oorlogs-verklaring aan Holland. [1781.] 8vo, pp. 23. 22577

England's folly in the present war from the beginning of the troubles with America till the declaration of war with Holland.

Engelhardt (N.) Narrative of the Expedition to the Polar Sea, in the Years 1820–23; commanded by Lieut., now Admiral F. Wrangell, of the Russian Navy. *New York.* 1845. 12mo.

Engell-Günther (Julia). Weihnachtsabende in Brasilien. Deutsch-brasilianisches Leben und Treiben. ... *Berlin: J. Springer.* 1862. 8vo, pp. 338. 4 Illustrations. 22579

Engelmann (George), *M.D.* Cactaceæ of the [U. S. and Mexican] Boundary. [*Washington.* 1859.] 4to, pp. 78. 76 Plates. S. 22580

Forms part of W. H. Emory's "Report on the United States and Mexican Boundary Survey," Vol. II. *See also* "Illinois," and "Pacific Railroad." Also: Synopsis of the Cactaceæ of the Territory of the United States and Adjacent Regions. *Cambridge.* 1856.—Systematic Arrangement of the Species of the Genus Cusenta, with Critical Remarks on Old Species and Descriptions of New ones [*St. Louis.* 1819.] 8vo.

Engels (L.) Nordamerika — Ohio. Reise nach Nordamerika. Beobachtungen und Erfahrungen in Ohio 1848 und 1849. ... *Elberfeld: Bädeker.* 1850. 8vo, pp. iv, 108. 22581

Den Engelschen Duyvel ontdeckt in twaalf artykelen van Cromwells geloof. 1652. 4to, pp. 36. 22582

Defence of the party of De Witt against the accusation of having abandoned Brazil to the Portuguese, etc.

Engelsche Syllogismen of Verzameling van alle de bewyzen der beste schryveren over den tegenwoordigen toestand. *Arnhem.* [1779.] 8vo, pp. 15. 22583

These "English Syllogisms" on the present state of affairs relate to the American Revolution.

Enghuysen (J. O. v.) Nieuwe volmaeckte Beschryvinghe der vervaerlyker Strate Magellani, waer in van myl tot myl, van baye tot baye de streckingen beschreven werden. [Colophon:] *T'Amsterdam: by Zacharias Heyns, Ghedrùckt by Herman de Buck.* [About 1580.] Sm. oblong 4to. 22584

"Volume de la plus grande rareté. 2 ff. prél. sign. *a.*—8 ff. pour les sign *b* et *c* et 2 ff. pour la sign. *d.* L'auteur, Jan Outghersz van Enghuysen, dit dans la préface que le détroit de Magellan était peu connu, malgré les relations de François Draeck Thomas Candish." Title and note from Asher's catalogue.

Engineer's Opinion of the Marine Railway around the Falls of Niagara. *New York.* 1865. 8vo, pp. 13–34. Map. H.

Engineer's Report of the Cost of Constructing the Ship Canal of Nicaragua, as estimated at New York Prices. *New York: W. C. Bryant & Co., Printers.* 1852. pp. 44. 22586

England (*Rt. Rev.* John), *Bishop of Charleston.* Letters of the Late Bishop England to the Hon. John Forsyth, on the Subject of Domestic Slavery: to which are prefixed copies, in Latin and English, of the Pope's Apostolic Letter concerning the African Slave Trade, with some introductory Remarks, etc., [by W. G. Read]. *Baltimore: John Murphy.* 1844. 8vo, pp. 156. B., C., H. 22587

England. The Works of the Right Rev. John England, First Bishop of Charleston ... Arranged under the Advice and Direction of ... the Right Rev. Ignatius Aloysius Reynolds. ... *Baltimore: John Murphy & Co.* 1849. 5 vols., 8vo, pp. vi, (1), 505; 519; 520; 503; 516, 2 l. Portrait. BA., C., H. 22588

Also: Address ... Franklin College, Athens, Ga., ... August 5th, 1840. ... *Athens.* 1840. 8vo, pp. 33. H.—Oration ... Anniversary of the Literary and Philosophical Society of South Carolina ... the 9th of May, 1832 ... . *Baltimore: J. Myers.* 1832. 8vo, pp. 48. BA.—The Substance of a Discourse preached in the Hall of the House of Representatives of the Congress of the United States, in the City of Washington. On Sunday, January 8, 1826. ... *Baltimore: Published by F. Lucas, Jun'r.* 1826. 8vo, pp. 52. BA., M. + Second Edition. [*Ibid.*] 1826. 8vo, pp. 50.—Substance of a Discourse, Delivered in ... Charleston, S. C. ... on giving the Habit of the Ursuline Order, to a Young Lady, May 19, 1835; ... An Abstract of the History of the Order. ... *Charleston: Dan. J. Dowling.* 1835. 8vo, pp. 68, (1).

England and America. *See* [Hodge (C.)], *and* [Wakefield (E. G.)]

England and France, or the Contrast taken from an American Publication, lately printed at Philadelphia. *London.* [1810.] 12mo. 22589

England Enslaved by her own Slave Colonies. 1826. 22590

England, Her Colonies and her Enemies. *London.* 1840. 8vo, pp. 51. 22591

England, Ireland, and America. *See* [Cobden (Richard)], Vol. IV., No. 14035.

England, the Civilizer; her History developed in its Principles; with Reference to the Civilizational History of Modern Europe [and America], ... By a Woman. *London: Simpkin, Marshall & Co.* 1848. 12mo, pp. vii, 470. H. 22592

England's Defiance. An Irregular Ode. *London: T. Payne.* 4to. 22593

Neither verse, prose, rhyme, or measure. *See* "M. Rev.," LXI. 313.

England's Sympathy with America's Inability to Build her own Ships. [*Washington?* 1869?] 8vo, pp. 3. H. 22594

England's Triumph, or Spanish Cowardice Exposed; being a Complete History of the many Signal Victories gained by the British. *London.* 1739. 12mo. 22595

England's Triumph over the Spaniards, containing the Hardy Atchievements of Sir Henry Morgan in the West-Indies; Account of Porto Bello being taken by Admiral Vernon. Description of Carthagena, Havanna, and the Island of Cuba, &c. [n. p. n. d.] 8vo. 22596

England's Western, or America's Eastern Shore? Old Ireland a New State? with their very Complexities discussed, by an Almost Obsolete Loyalist. *Dublin.* 1851. 8vo. 22597

Der Englandischen Pflanzstädte in Nord-America Geschichte und Handlung nebst einer zuverlässigen Nachricht von der gegenwärtigen Anzahl der dasigen Einwohner, und einer umständlichen Beschreibung der Landesverfassung, absonderlich von Neu-England, Pensylvanien, Carolina und Georgien betrifft. Aus dem französischen übersetzt. *Stuttgart: Johann Benedict Metzlers.* 1755. 12mo, 7 l., pp. 216. J.C.B. 22598

An Address to the People of England, being the Protest of a Private Person against every Suspension of Law that is liable to injure or endanger Personal Security. *London: Printed in the Year* MDCCLXXVIII. 8vo, pp. 76. 22599

Very little on the subject of the war, but enough to show that the writer is bitterly opposed to it.

Engleheart (G. D.) Journal of the Visit of H. R. H. the Prince of Wales to America, in 1860. Privately printed. *London.* 1861. 22600

Engles (W. M.) The Patriot's Plea for Domestic Missions. A Sermon ... at Columbia, Pa., October 31st, 1833 ... . *Philadelphia.* 1833. 8vo, pp. 24. H. 22601

Engles. Records of the Presbyterian Church in the United States of America. By W. M. Engles. *Philadelphia.* 1841. Rl. 8vo. C. 22602

English (H.) A general Guide to the Companies formed for Working Foreign Mines, with their Prospectuses, Amount of Capital, Number of Shares, Names of Directors, &c. By Henry English, Stock and Exchange Broker. *London: Boosey.* 1825. 8vo, pp. 107. 22603

English (Thomas C.) Zephaniah Doolittle. A Poem. Second Edition. *Philadelphia.* 1838. 22604

English (T. D.) The Mormons; or, Life at Salt Lake City. A Drama, in Three Acts. *New York.* [1858.] 8vo, pp. 43. H. 22605

English. 1844; or, The Power of the "S. F." A Tale: Developing the Secret Action of Parties during the Presidential Campaign of 1844. By Thomas Dunn English. *New York: Burgess, Stringer & Co.* 1847. 12mo, pp. 300. 22606

English (William H.) Speech of W. H. English, of Indiana, ... in the House ... on the Nebraska and Kansas Bill, May 9, 1854. [n. p. n. d.] 8vo, pp. 11. S. 22607

English. Speech ... on the Smithsonian Institution, in the House of Representatives, February 27, 1855. [*Washington.* 1855.] 8vo, pp. 7. H., M. 22608

The English and American Intelligencer, Published Weekly for Gardissal & Tolhausen, February, 1855, No. 1. Folio.

English and Dakota Vocabulary: By a Member of the Dakota Mission. ... *New York.* 1852. 8vo, pp. 120. S. 22610

Published by the American Board of Commissioners for Foreign Missions.

The English Cotejo; or the Cruelties, Depredations and Illicit Trade charg'd upon the English in a Spanish Libel lately published compared with the Murders, Robberies, Barbarities, and Clandestine Trade proved upon the Spaniards. By a Sufferer. *London: J. Mechell.* [About 1731.] 8vo, pp. 30. J.C.B.

An English Freeholder's Address to his Countrymen. *London: J. Robinson.* 1780. Sm. 4to, pp. 18. 22612

On the war with America. *See* "M. Rev.," LXIII. 551.

The English Green Box of the R—t H—e E—d L—d Churllow, given by the Celebrated Mrs. Harvey to Roger O'Sickle, Valet de Chambre to — ——, Esq., M.P. *London.* 1779. 22613

The English in America. *See* [Haliburton (T. C.)]

English Neutrality. Is the Alabama a British Pirate? *New York: Anson D. F. Randolph.* 1863. 8vo, pp. 32. + *Philadelphia.* 1863. 8vo. 22614

The English Party's Excursion to Paris, in Easter Week 1859. To which is added A Trip to America, etc., etc., etc. *London: Longman.* MDCCCL. Post 8vo, 3 l., pp. 557. 22615

The English Pilot. The Fourth Book; containing Charts of the North Part of America, or Hudson's Bay, &c., Newfoundland, the Islands of Jamaica, Barbadoes, Bermuda, Hispaniola, &c., &c.; a General Chart of the West Indies, a new Map of Carolina, and Maps of Virginia, Maryland, Pennsylvania, New Jersey, New-York, with Parts of New-England. *London.* 1689. Folio. C. 22616

The Fourth Part of the General English Pilot. Describing the Sea-Coasts, Capes, Head-Lands, Bays, Roads, Rivers, Harbours, Ports, with the Exact Appearances and Representations of the most Principal Marks, Lands, &c. Together with the Soundings, Sands, Shoals, Rocks and Dangers on the East Coast of America; from Greenland to the River Amazones, viz. Baffin's Bay, Hudson's Bay, New Brittanie, New-found-Land, Canada and New-France, New-Scotland, New-England, New-York, New-Jersey, Virginia and Mary-Land; Carolina, Florida, Cuba, Hispaniola and Bahama Islands; Mexico, Campechia, Yucatan, Honduras, Guatimala, Darien, Carthagena, Venezuela, the Leeward and Caribbee-Islands, Guiana and Surinam. ... *London: Printed for Rich. Mount, and Tho. Page.* MDCCVII. Folio, pp. 58. 22 Maps, and Woodcuts. BA.

The English Pilot. The Fourth Book. Describing The West-India Navigation, from Hudson's-Bay to the River Amazones. Particularly Delineating The Sea-Coasts, Capes, Head-Lands, Rivers, Bays, Roads, Havens, Harbours, Straits, Rocks, Sands, Shoals, Banks, Depths of Water and Anchorage, with all the Islands therein, as Jamaica, Cuba, Hispaniola, Barbadoes, Antigua, Bermuda, Porto-Rico, and the rest of the Caribbee and Bahama Islands. Also, A New Description of Newfoundland, New-England, New-York, East and West New-Jersey, Dellawar-Bay, Virginia, Maryland, and Carolina, etc. ... *London: Printed for William Mount and Thomas Page.* M,DCC,XLII. Folio, Title, pp. 16. 16 Maps. BA. + *London: Printed for W. & J. Mount.* M,DCC,LVIII. Folio, pp. 66. Maps and Woodcuts. BA. + *London: Mount & Page.* M,DCC,LXX. Folio. + *London: Mount & Davidson.* M,DCC,XCIV. Folio, pp. 66. 22 Maps. H.

The English Pilot, the Fourth Book. Describing The West-India Navigation, from Hudson's-Bay to the River Amazones. Particularly Delineating The Sea-Coasts, Capes, Head-Lands, Rivers, Bays, Roads, Harbours, etc. with all the Islands therein: Also a New Description of Newfound-Land, New-England, New-York, E. and W. New-Jerzey, Dellawar-Bay, Virginia, Maryland and Carolina. *Dublin: Boulter Grierson.* 1767. Folio. 27 Maps and 230 Woodcuts. 22619

The maps, which have a clear, rough, old-fashioned appearance, are nearly all engraved expressly for this edition, and differ materially from the London editions of the work, containing generally more minute particulars.

The English Practice: a Statement, showing some of the Evils and Absurdities of the Practice of the English Common Law, as adopted in several of the United States, and particularly in the State of New York. ... By a Lover of Improvement. *New York.* 1822. 8vo, pp. 71. H. 22620

The English West Indies, with the Manners and Customs of the Free Inhabitants, including their Civil and Criminal Laws, with the Treatment and Condition of the Negroes, and an Account of the Laws in Cultivation. *London.* 1801. 12mo.

The Englishman. Or Letters found in the State of Tennessee, supposed to be the Production of an Englishman, travelling through the United States as a Spy. *Rogersville, Tenn. Nov.,* 1813. Sm. 8vo, pp. 80. 22622

The Englishman directed. *See* [Wetmore (James)].

The Englishman Deceived; a Political Piece; wherein Some very Important Secrets of State are briefly recited, And offered to the Consideration of the Publick. ... *London.* 1768. 8vo. + *London, Printed. New York, Reprinted by John Holt.* 1768. 8vo, pp. 40. *Reprinted, Salem.* 1768. 8vo, pp. 38. 22623

An Englishman's Answer, | to the | Address, | from the Delegates, | to the | People of Great-Britain, | in | A Letter | To | The Several Colonies, | which were | Represented | in the late | Continental Congress. | *New-York: Printed by James Rivington.* M,DCC,-LXXV. | 8vo, pp. (2), 26. BA., J.C.B. 22624

Perhaps by Dr. Linde.

Englishman's Duty, 1853. *See* [Wicksteed (Charles)].

An Englishman's Sketch-Book; or, Letters from New York. *New York: G. & C. Carvill.* 1828. 12mo, 1 l., pp. 195. C.

The Englishwoman in America. *See* [Bird (J.)], Vol. II., No. 5545, *also* [Maury (S. M.)]

Enlistment and Central-American Questions. Correspondence between the Governments of the United States and Great Britain; with Documents. Communicated to the United States Senate, 28th February, 1856. *Washington.* [n. d.] 8vo, pp. 32.

Ennemoser (J.) The History of Magic. By Joseph Ennemoser. Translated from the German by William Howitt. *London: H. G. Bohn.* MDCCCLIV. 2 vols., post 8vo, pp. viii, xvi, 471; viii, 518. BA., H. 22627

Includes notices of the Salem witchcraft.

Ennery. Eloge Funèbre du Comte d'Ennery et Réforme Judiciare à St. Domingue. *Au Port-au-Prince, del Imprimerie de Mozard.* 1789. 4to. 22628

Ennis (J.) A Memoir of Thomas B. Wilson, M.D. By Rev. Jacob Ennis. *Philadelphia.* 1865. 8vo. s. 22629

The Enormity of the Slave Trade; and the Duty of seeking the Moral and Spiritual Elevation of the Colored Race. Speeches of Wilberforce, and other Documents and Records. *New York. Am. Tract Society.* 1861. 22630

Enquiries into the Necessity of assuming Exclusive Legislation over the District of Columbia. *Washington.* 8vo. c.

An Enquiry into the Caledonian Project. *See* "Darien," Vol. v., No. 18551.

An Enquiry into the Causes of our Ill Success in the present War. *London: Griffiths.* [n. d.] 8vo. 22632

"A clear and succinct account of our conduct with regard to America." — *M. Rev.*, xviii. 559.

An Enquiry into the Causes. *See* Vol. v., No. 18552.

An Enquiry into the Causes of the Alienation of the Delaware Indians. *See* [Thompson (Charles)].

An Enquiry into the Causes of the Present Commercial Embarrassments in the United States. With a Plan of Reform of the Circulating Medium. In Two Letters ... By an Anti-Bullionist. [n. p. n. d.] 8vo, pp. 44, (1). BA. 22633

An Enquiry into the Chymical Character and Properties of that species of Coal lately discovered at Rhode Island; together with Observations on the Useful Application of it to the Arts and Manufactures of the Eastern States. *Boston: Snelling & Simons.* 1808. 12mo, pp. 21. M. 22634

An Enquiry into the Condition and Prospects of the African Race in the United States, and the means of bettering their Prospects. By an American. *Philadelphia.* 1839. 12mo, pp. 214.

Enquiry into the Conduct. *See* [Pitt (William)].

An Enquiry into the Conduct of our Domestick Affairs, From the Year 1721, to the Present Time. In which the Case of our National Debts, the Sinking Fund, and all extraordinary Grants of Money are particularly consider'd. Being a Sequel to Politicks on both Sides. *London: Printed by H. Haines.* 1734. 8vo, pp. 68. BA. + The Third Edition Corrected. *London: H. Haines.* 8vo. 22636

Relates in part to the South Sea scheme.

An Enquiry into the Conduct of the President of the United States in his Execution of the Powers vested in him by Act of Congress of May, 1810; with Reflections upon the Invasion of Florida, &c. *Boston.* 1811. 8vo. 22637

Enquiry into the Conduct of the two B******* [Brothers], and their Prosecution of the War, till the Signing the Preliminaries. Third Edition. *London.* 1749. 12mo. 22638

An Enquiry into the Constitutional Authority of the Supreme Federal Court, over the several States, in their Political Capacity. Being an Answer to Observations upon the Government of the United States of America: By James Sullivan, Esq. ... By a Citizen of South Carolina. *Charleston, S. C.: W. P. Young.* M.DCC.XCII. 8vo, pp. 49. BA. 22639

An Enquiry into the Effects. *See* [Ramsay (James)].

An Enquiry into the Law-Merchant of the United States. *See* [Caines (George)], Vol. iii., No. 9852.

An Enquiry into the Merits of the Supposed Preliminaries of Peace, signed the 3rd Instant. *London.* 1762. 8vo. 22640

Principally on the American Colonies.

An Enquiry into the Methods that are said to be now proposed in England, to retrieve the Sugar Trade. By the Author of The Detection of the State and Situation of the Present Sugar Planters of Barbadoes and the Leeward Islands. *London: J. Wilford.* 1733. 8vo, pp. 31. c. 22641

See "A Detection," etc., Vol. i., No. 3265.

An Enquiry into the Moral and Religious Character of the American Government. *New York.* 1838. 8vo, pp. 208.

An Enquiry into the Nature and Causes of the present Disputes between the British Colonies in America, and their Mother Country; and their Reciprocal Claims and their just Rights Impartially Examined and Fairly Stated. *London: J. Wilkie.* 1768. 8vo. 22643

See "M. Rev.," xxxix. 495.

Inquiry into the Nature and Necessity of a Paper Currency. *Philadelphia: Printed by B. Franklin.* 1749? 8vo. 22644

An Enquiry into the Origin of the Cherokees. *See* Vol. iii., No. 12452.

An Enquiry into the Origin, Progress, and Present State of Slavery. With a Plan for the Gradual, Reasonable, and Secure Emancipation of Slaves. By a Member of the Society of Universal Good Will.... *London: J. Murray.* 1789. 8vo, pp. 43.

See "M. Rev.," lxxxi. 40.

An Enquiry into the Past. *See* [Walsh (R.)]

An Enquiry into the present System of Medical Education in the State of New York: By an Observer. *Albany.* 1830. 8vo.

An Enquiry into the Principles and Tendency of certain Public Measures. *Philadelphia: Thomas Dobson.* M DCC XCIV. 8vo, pp. iv, 92. BA., H., N. 22647

An Enquiry into the Principles. *See* Coxe (T.), Vol. v., No. 17295.

Enquiry into the Question of the Chesapeake. *See* [Lowell (John)].

Enquiry into the Reasons. *See* [Hoadley (B.)]

An Enquiry into the Right to Change the Ecclesiastical Constitution of the Congregational Churches of Massachusetts. *Boston.* 1816. 8vo, pp. 79. 22648

An Enquiry into the State of the Bills of Credit of the Province of the Massachusetts-Bay in New England; in a Letter from a Gentleman in Boston to a Merchant in London. [*London:*] *Printed in the Year* 1743. 8vo, pp. 52. H. 22649

Enquiry into the Validity. *See* [Kewley (John)].

An Enquiry Respecting The Capture of Washington by the British, on the 24th August, 1814. With an Examination of the Report of the Committee of Investigation Appointed by Congress. By Spectator. *Washington. Feb.*, 1816. 16mo, pp. 32.

Remarks on a Pamphlet, "An Enquiry respecting the Capture of Washington by the British, 24 Aug. 1814. By 'Spectator.' *Baltimore.* 1816."

An Enquiry whether the Absolute Independence of America is not to be preferred to her Partial Dependence, as most agreeable to the Real Interests of Great Britain. Addressed to the People of Great Britain, by One of Themselves. *London: J. Bew.* [1782.] 8vo, pp. 36. J.C.B. 22651

"The author, after many sensible observations, candid arguments, and just conclusions from the principles and premises which he lays down, determines this great question in the affirmative. — *M. Rev.*, lxvii. 305.

An Enquiry whether The Act of Congress, "In addition to the Act, entitled an Act, for the Punishment of Certain Crimes against the United States," generally called the Sedition Bill, is Unconstitutional or Not. *Richmond: Printed by S. Pleasants, Jun. Nov.* 1798. 12mo, pp. 15. 22652

Enquiry whether the Guilt, etc. *See* [Roebuck (John)].

Enriquez (J. F.) Documentos verificativos de los servicios, conducta moral y politica del Coronel Don José Frances Enriquez, Mayor General del Exercito del Sur. *Puebla de los Angeles.* 1816. Folio, 2 l., pp. 141. 22653

Enriquez (Pedro). De las Batallas en el Ocean Contra el Mulato y Pie de Palo, piratas. 1641. Folio. 22654

Title from Ternaux-Compans, No. 609.

Enrollment Laws of the United States, for calling out the National Forces. Approved March 3, 1864, and amended February 24, 1864. Official and Complete. *New York: J. W. Fortune.* 1864. 18mo, pp. 48. 22655

Ens (G.) Indiæ | Occidentalis | Historia: | in qva Prima Regionum istarum detectio, situs, | incolarum mores, aliaque eò | pertinentia, breuiter | explicantur. | Ex variis Avtoribvs | collecta, | Opera & Studio | Gasparis Ens L. | *Coloniæ, Apud Gulielm. Lutzenkirchen.* | *Anno* MDCXII. | 8vo, Engraved Title, 3 l., pp. 370 for 371. J.C.B., H. 22656

Pagination very irregular. This is an abridgment of the Petit Voyage of De Bry, and is generally attached to that collection.

Ens. West- vnnd Ost Indischer | Lustgart: | Das ist, | Eygentliche Erzehlung, | Wann vnd von wem die Newe Welt erfunden, | besägelt, vnd eingenommen worden, vnd was sich Denck- | würdiges daebey zugetragen. | Neben Beschreibung aller deren Landschafften, | Inseln, Völcker, Thieren, Früchten, Gewächsen, so | beydes in West- vnd Ost Indien zu finden. | Wie auch Verfassung der fürnembsten Schiffahrten so | nicht allein dahin, sonderen auch vmb die gantze Welt von den Spa- | nieren, Engelländeren, Holländeren, etc. verrichtet | worden. | Auss glaubwürdigen Schrifften zusamen gezogen. | ... | *Gedruckt zu Cöllen,* | *Bey Wilhelm Lützenkirchen.* | *Anno* MDCXVIII. | 4to, 4 l., pp. 436, 236.

Gaspar Ens was one of the editors employed by the De Bry's in their collection of voyages, 1590–1634, and was well read in the history and bibliography of the New World. This volume is a summary of the most interesting sources of American history.

Ensayo cronologico. *See* [Barcia (A. G.)], Vol. i., No. 3349.

Ensayo de estadistica completa de la provincia de Azangaro en el departamento de Puno de la republica Peruana desde 1825. hasta 1829. *Lima.* 1833. Folio. 22658

Ensayo de una Alocucion Patriotica pronunciado en die 28 Sept. de 1853. *Mexico.* 1853. 8vo. 22659

Ensayo Politica, 1823. *See* [Rocafuerte (Vincente)].

Ensayo sobre la conducta del General Bolivar. *Santiago de Chile.* 1826. + *Lima.* 1827. Sm. 4to, pp. 30. 22660

A reprint of Nos. 11, 13, and 14, of "Dueude de Buenos Ayres."

Ensayo sobre la topografia, 1831. *See* [Dwerhagen (H. C.)], No. 21511.

Ensay sobre las Libertades de la Iglesia Española en Ambos Mundos. *Londres.* 1826. 8vo. 22661

Partly relates to America.

Ensign, Bridgman & Fanning's Lake and River Guide; being a Traveller's Companion to the Cities, Towns, and Villages on the Western Waters of the United States; together with ... Thrilling Scenes in Border Warfare. ... *New York: Ensign, Bridgman & Fanning.* 1858. 18mo, pp. 143. Maps. 22662

Ensl. *See* Ens (G.), No. 22656 and 22657.

Enslin (T. C. F.) Bibliotheca Historico-Geographica oder Verzeichniss aller brauchbaren, in älterer und neuerer Zeit, besonders aber vom Jahre 1750 bis zur Mitte des Jahres 1824 in Deutschland erschienenen Bücher über Geschichte, Geographie und deren Hülfwissenschaften ... Herausgegeben von Theodor Christian Friedrich Enslin. ... *Berlin u. Landsberg a. d. W.* 1825. 8vo, 1 l., pp. 299. 22663

The Entertainer. Remarks upon Men, Manners, Religion, and Policy. 1718. 12mo. 22664

"Letter from a Mother to her Son, going to Virginia," page 223.

An Entertaining Account of all the Countries of the Known World ... Adorn'd with Cuts. *London: R. Goadby.* MDCCLII. 8vo, pp. 266, (8). + The Second Edition. *London: R. Goadby.* MDCCLII. 8vo, pp. 490, (8). 22665

The Entertaining and Marvellous Repository: containing Biography, Manners, and Customs, Tales, Adventures, Essays, Poetry, etc. *Boston: Baker & Alexander.* 1827. 3 vols., 16mo.

Entertainment for a Winter's Evening. *See* [Green (Jos.)]

Entick (J.) The General History of the Late War: Containing its Rise, Progress, and Event, in Europe, Asia, Africa, and America. And Exhibiting The State of the Belligerent Powers at the Commencement of the War: their Interests and Objects in its Continuation; and Remarks on the Measures, which led Great Britain to Victory and Conquest. Interspersed with the Characters of the able and disinterested Statesmen, to whose Wisdom and Integrity, and of the Heroes, to whose Courage and Conduct, we are indebted for that Naval and Military Success, which is not to be equalled in the Annals of this, or of any other Nation. And with Accurate Descriptions of the Seat of War, the Nature and Importance of our Conquests, and of the most remarkable Battles by Sea and Land. Illustrated with A Variety of Heads, Plans, Maps, and Charts, Designed and Engraved by the best Artists. By the Rev. John Entick, M.A. And other Gentlemen. *London: Printed for Edward Dilly.* M.DCC.LXIII. 5 vols., 8vo, (4), pp. 495; 464; 480; 480; 469, (27). 36 Portraits and 9 Maps. + *London: Edward and Charles Dilly.* M.DCC.LXVI. 5 vols., 8vo. BA., H. + The Third Edition, Corrected. [*Ibid.*] M.DCC.LXXV. 5 vols., 8vo. + Fourth Edition. *London.* 1779. 5 vols., 8vo. 22667

A reissue, with new titles only, *London: Edward and Charles Dilly.* M.DCC.LXIV. Also issued as Second Edition. [*Ibid.*] MDCCLXV. The "Third Edition, Corrected," was frequently served up; we have met with copies dated *London.* MDCCLXXII, MDCCLXXV, and called a Fourth Edition, *London.* MDCCLXXIX, and *London.* MDCCLXXXIV. The collation of all the editions is the same. "Containing many interesting particulars relative to the Catabaw, Cherokee, Chickesaw, Delaware, and other tribes of Indians. ... The greater part relates to the war in America." — Rich. It is a worthless book, and is only sought for by the *illustrator* for the portraits — bad enough. It contains portraits of Generals Wolfe, Monckton, Lord Howe, and others.

Entick. An Historical and Geographical Description of the British Empire; ... Originally Compiled by the late Rev. John Entick, and Improved by James Webster, Esq. *London.* 1770. 4 vols. P. 22668

Entick. A New Naval History; ... By John Entick. *London.* M.DCC.LVII. Folio, 2 l., pp. lxii, 887, (10). 6 Plates. P.

See "M. Rev.," xviii, 563.

Entick. The Present State of the British Empire and Description of its Colonies, Islands, Conquests, Military and Commercial Establishments, in all Parts of the Globe. *London.* 1774. 4 vols., 8vo. + *London.* 1775. 4 vols., 8vo. 22670

Entrecasteaux (Joseph Antoine Bruni d'). Voyage de d'Entrecasteaux, envoyé a la recherche de La Pérouse. ... Rédigé par M. de Rossel ... *Paris: De l'Imprimerie impériale.* 1808. 2 vols., 4to, 2 l., lvi, 704; 2 l., viii, 692. 40 Plates. BA., C.

Also in Montémont's "Bibliothèque," v. 15.

Entrecasteaux. Atlas du Voyage. Rédigé par C. F. Beautemps-Beaupré. *Paris.* 1807. Folio. 22672

Entrétiens de Guillaume de Nassau, Prince d'Orange, et du Général Montgomery, sur la révolution ancienne des Pays Bas, & les affaires actuelles d'Amérique. *A Londres. Et se trouve à Paris, chez Dessain.* MDCCLXXVI. 12mo, pp. xii, 104. J.C.B.

Entrétiens des Voyageurs sur la Mer, avec des Figures en Taille-douce. *La Haye.* 1740. 4 vols., 12mo. 22674

Entz (J. F.) Cotton Tables; exhibiting, at a glance, the cost of Cotton, with all charges, at Liverpool or Havre, from New-Orleans, Mobile, Charleston, and New-York, at all prices, rates of Freight, and Exchange. *New York.* 1853. 12mo. C.

Entz. Exchange and Cotton Trade between England and the United States. ... By J. F. Entz. *New York: Published by E. B. Clayton.* M DCCC XL. 8vo, pp. 62, (1). C., H. 22676

Enumeration of the Inhabitants. *See* "Census," Vol. iii., No. 11667.

The Envoy, from Free Hearts to the Free. ... *Pawtucket, R. I.* 1840. 12mo, pp. 112. H. 22677

Eolopoesis. *See* [Bigelow (Jacob)], Vol. ii., No. 5294.

Epaminondas: originally published in Numbers, in the New York Gazette. *New York: John Lang.* 1801. 8vo. pp. 17.

On the merits of Jefferson and Burr.

Epaminondas, *pseudonym.* The Address of Epaminondas to the Citizens of the State of New-York. *Albany: Jeremiah Tryon.* 1819. 8vo, pp. 27. BA. 22679

Epaminondas, *pseudonym.* Answer to a Clandestine Address to the Electors of the State of New-York, signed by Robert Troup and others. By Epaminondas. [n. p. n. d.] 8vo, pp. 16.

Epaminondas, *pseudonym.* *See* [Woodward (A. B.)]

Ephrata. Pencillings about Ephrata. By a Visitor. *Philadelphia: J. B. Chandler.* 1856. 8vo, pp. 24. + *Philadelphia.* 1860. 22681

Epictetus, His Morals Done from the Original Greek, and the Words taken from his own Mouth. By Arrian. The Second Edition. *Philadelphia: printed by S. Keimer, in Second Street.* MDCCXXIX. 8vo, pp. 32. 22682

This is the earliest translation of a classic printed in the Colonies, and is a volume of great rarity. A writer in the "Historical Magazine," ii. 212, believes it to be an American translation.

Epidemic Cholera. Circular No. 5. War Department, Surgeon-General's Office, Washington, May 4, 1867. Report on Epidemic Cholera, in the Army of the United States during the year 1866. *Washington.* 1867. 4to, pp. xviii, 66. 22683

Epidemic Cholera and Yellow Fever. Circular No. 1. ... June 10, 1868. Report on Epidemic Cholera and Yellow Fever in the Army of the United States during the year 1867. *Washington.* 1868. 4to, pp. xxxix, 156. 22684

An Epilogue to the late Peace, addressed to the Right Honourable the Earl N——. *London: R. Baldwin.* 1783. 8vo.

See "M. Rev.," lxx. 72.

Episcopal Magazine. 1820 and 1821. *Philadelphia.* 1820-21. 8vo. 22686

Episcopal Education Society. Annual Report of the Managers, 1828. *Philadelphia.* 1828. 8vo. B. 22687

Episcopal Missionary Association for the West. Constitution. &c. *Philadelphia.* 1853. 12mo. 22688

Also: Annual Report of the Board of Managers for 1854-55. *Philadelphia.* 1855. 8vo. *See also* Protestant Episcopal Church.

Episodio de la Revolucion de Marzo de 1858. *Carâcas.* 1858. 8vo, pp. 14. 22689

An Epistle from a Young Lady to an Ensign in the Guards, on his being ordered to America. *London: Sewel.* 1779. 4to.

"The poetry is too good ... for the frivolous subject." — *M. Rev.*, lxi. 76.

An | Epistle | from | Edward, | An | American Prisoner in England, | to | Harriet, | In America. | *London: Fielding and Walker.* | M DCC LXXIX. | 4to, pp. (2), 9. 22691

Poor Edward laments, but not in *poor* verse, the hardships of his confinement, his absence from the fair object of his tenderest affections, and his being withheld from lending his arm to the assistance of his country. *See* "M. Rev.," LX. 231.

An Epistle from our Yearly Meeting at Burlington, for the Jerseys and Pennsylvania, &c. Held by Adjournment, from the 19th to the 23d day of the 7th Month, 1724. To the Quarterly and Monthly-Meetings of Friends, belonging to the said Yearly Meeting. — Signed by Thomas Lightfoot, David Lloyd, Isaac Norris. *Philadelphia: Printed by Andrew Bradford.* 1724. Folio, pp. 4. 22692

An Epistle From our Yearly-Meeting, Held at Philadelphia, for Pennsylvania and New-Jersey, by Adjournments, from the 24th Day of the 9th Month, to the 1st of the 10th Month, inclusive, 1774. [*Philadelphia.* 1744.] Folio, 1 sheet. 22693

For other epistles of Friends, *see* under the names of *States.*

Epistle from Timoleon. *See* [Bollan (W.)], No. 6211.

An Epistle from Yarico to Inkle. [*See* Story (Isaac).]

An Epistle General to them who are of the Royal Priesthood and Chosen Generation given forth from the Movings of the Power and Spirit of Truth, and now made Public to be sent Abroad among the Saints scattered in Old and New England, Germany, Holland, Barbadoes, and Virginia. 1660. 4to.

An Epistle of Caution and Advice concerning the Buying and Keeping of Slaves. *Philadelphia: Printed and Sold by James Chattin, In Church-Alley.* 1754. 12mo, pp. 8. 22695

Signed by John Evans and others.

An Epistle of Tender Caution and Counsel from the Monthly Meetings of Friends of Philadelphia, addressed To the Members of our Religious Society in the said City, 26th, 27th, and 29th of 8th Month, 1788. *Philadelphia.* 1788. 8vo. + *Leeds.* 1791. 8vo. 22696

Epistle of Yarico to Inkle. A Poem. *Glasgow.* 1750. 8vo.

Founded on the Barbadoes story. *See also* [Jerningham (Edward)], *and* Yarico to Inkle.

An Epistle to a Member of the General Court of Massachusetts, for 1809. A Poem. [n. p. n. d.] 8vo, pp. 32. BA., W.

Epistle to the Christian Indians, giving them a Short Account of what the English desire them to Know and to Do. *Boston.* 1700. 12mo, pp. 14. 22698

An Epistle to the General Convention [of the Protestant Episcopal Church in the U. S.] By a Country Bard. ... October, 1847. [n. p. 1841.] 12mo, pp. 23. H. 22699

An Epistle to Zenas. *Boston: Peter Edes.* [1795.] 8vo, pp. 15, (2). BA., H., S. 22700

A political and poetical satire.

Epistola dos Inglezes residentes no Imperio do Brazil. *Rio de Janeiro.* 1841. 22701

Portuguese and English.

Epistola Ill. D. Archiepiscopi Baltimorensis, continens Statuta Synodi Diocesanæ in eadem Civitate Anno 1791, celebratæ. *Mexico.* 1828. 22702

Epistolæ ad Pium Sixtum pro causa Beatificationis Ant. Margil a Jesu Missionarii Apostolici Ord. Min. S. Francisci de Observantia Trium Collegiorum de Propaganda Fide in America Septentrionale, ejusdem Missionibus Præfecti in Indiis Occidentalibus. *Romæ.* 1792. 4to. 22703

Containing forty-six letters on the progress of Christianity in Mexico, Guatemala, etc.

Epistolæ Indicæ, de stvpendis et præclaris Rebus, quas diuina Bonitas in India, et variis Insulis, per Societatem Nominis Jesv operari dignata est, in tam copiosa gentium ad fidem conuersione. [In lucem missæ per Jo. Rut. Berg.] *Lovanii: apud Rutgerum Velpium.* 1566. 18mo, 12 l., pp. 496. B., C. + Secunda Editio. [*Ibid.*] S. 22704

This volume contains much curious matter relating to the early history of the Indians.

Epistolary Lament, supposed to have been written by a surviving Hunker soon after the N. H. Election, and addressed to his old friend in Washington. With Explanatory Notes. *Concord.* 1855. 16mo. 22705

Epitaph, &c. 8vo, pp. 4. P. 22706

Mock epistles (the one adorned with a skull and cross-bones, the other with a coffin) on Alex. Wedderburne and Thomas Hutchinson, struck off, on the occasion of their being hanged in effigy, at Philadelphia, May 3d, 1774.

Epitaphs and Elegies. *New York: Samuel Wood & Son.* 1816. 12mo, pp. 76. 22707

EPPES (John W.). Speech of Mr. Eppes, delivered in the House of Representatives ... on the Proposition for Raising Fifty-Thousand Volunteers, Dec. 30, 1808. [n. p. n. d.] 8vo, pp. 8. BA. 22708

Also: Speech, Feb. 9, 1811, Concerning Commercial Intercourse. [n. p. n. d.] 8vo.

EPPING (J. P. M.) The Civil War and Negro Slavery in the United States of America. *Gottenburg.* 1862. 8vo. C.

EPPING, *N. Y.* Selectmen's Report of the Receipts and Expenditures ... for the Years 1860–61. [*Epping.* 1860–61.] 8vo and 12mo. H. 22710

EPPLER (Christoph Friedrich). Das Leben des Indianermissionars David Brainerd. ... *Zürich: Hancke.* 1851. 8vo, pp viii, 256. 22711

Equality and the New Constitution. [*Boston?* 1854?] pp. 4.

Equality of all Men before the Law Claimed and Defended; in Speeches by Hon. William D. Kelly, Wendell Phillips, and Frederick Douglass, and Letters from Elizur Wright and Wm. Heighton. *Boston.* 1865. 8vo, pp. 44. 22713

EQUIANO (O.) The Interesting Narrative of the Life of Olaudah Equiano, or Gustavus Vassa, Written by Himself. *London: Printed for the Author; and Sold by Johnson & Co.* 1789. 2 vols., 12mo. + *New York.* 1791. 18mo. + Sixth Edition. *London.* 1793. 18mo, pp. xxxvi, 360. + [*Ibid.*] 1794. + *Boston.* 1837. 18mo, pp. 294. 22714

Includes his adventures in the West Indies, etc. *See* "M. Rev.," LXXX, 551.

EQUILUZ (D. de). Relacion de la mision apostolica de los Moxos en la Provincia del Peru, de la Compañia de Jesus, que remite su Provincial P. Diego de Equiluz à N. R. M. P. Thoyso Gonçalez Preposito General de la misma Compañia. [n. p]. *Año de* 1696. 4to. 22715

The Equity ... of Administration. *See* [Erskine (John)].

ERASMUS, *pseudonym.* The Plea of Reason, Religion and Humanity against War. By Erasmus. *New York.* 1813. 8vo, pp. 48. 22716

ERAZU (Joseph, de Burunda). Elogio funebre del ilustrisimo señor doct. Gregorio Francisco de Campos, obispo de Nuestra

Sra. de la paz en el Perù. Pronunciado en las solemnes exequias que por su gratitud, y reconocimiento le hizo en su propia Iglesia, el dia 13 ne Enero de 1790. *Lima: Imprenta de los niños expositos.* 1792. 4to, 38 l., pp. 61, 1 l. 22717

Erbauliche und angenehme. *See* Vol. IV., No. 12835.

ERCILLA Y ZUÑIGA (A. de). La Araucana de Don Alonso de Ercilla y Guñiga. *Madrid.* 1569. + *Madrid: Sancha.* 1776. 2 vols., 8vo. 22718

First edition containing the first part only.

ERCILLA Y ZUÑIGA. La Araucana. ... *Salamanca: Domingo de Portonarijs.* 1574. 8vo. 22719

The verso of the eleventh leaf contains a portrait of the author.

ERCILLA Y ZUÑIGA. Primo y Segunda Parte de la Araucana. *Madrid: Pierres Cosin.* 1578. 4to, 7 l., 195 l., 169 l., 3 l.

First edition with the second part.

ERCILLA Y ZUÑIGA. Primera y segvnda parte de la Aravcana, de don Alonso de Ercilla y Çuñigã ... . *En Anvers: En casa de Pedro Bellero.* 1586. 2 pts., 16mo, 5 l., pp. 334, 4 l.; 1 l., pp. 335–615, 2 l. 22721

ERCILLA Y ZUÑIGA. Primera, Segunda y Tercera partes de la Araucana, etc. *Madrid: Pedro Madrigal.* 1590. 12mo, 30 l., pp. 436, 12 l. + *Barcelona: Hubert Gotart.* 1594. 12mo, 16 l., 33 l. + *Anvers: Pedro Bellero.* 1597. 12mo, 12 l., pp. 329.

ERCILLA Y ZUÑIGA. La Aravcana, Primera, Segunda, y Tercera Parte. De Don Alonso de Ercilla y Zuñica ... . Año 1733. Con Privilegio. *En Madrid: Por Francisco Martinez Abad.* Folio, 8 l., pp. 186, 9 l. 22723

ERCILLA Y ZUÑIGA. Primera parte de la Araucana. *Madrid.* 1610. 8vo. 22724

ERCILLA Y ZUÑIGA. La Araucana. ... Dirigida al Rey Don Felipe Nuestro Señor. Su autor Don Alonzo de Ercilla y Zuñiga. ... *En Madrid: por D. Antonio de Sancha. Año* MDCCLXXVI. 2 vols., 8vo, pp. lvi, 298, Portrait, Map and Woodcut; 2 l., pp. 413, Map and Plate. BA., H. 22725

"The best edition is *Madrid.* 1776." — TICKNOR's *Span. Lit.*, II. 464.

ERCILLA Y ZUÑIGA. La Araucana. *Barcelona.* 1827. 2 vols., 18mo. C. + *Paris: Cormon et Blanc.* 1824. 4 vols., 18mo, 23½ sheets. + *Paris.* 1840. 8vo. + *Madrid.* 1852. Imp. 8vo.

ERCILLA Y ZUÑIGA. L'Araucana; traduit pour la première fois, et abrégé du texte espagnol, par G. de Merlhiac. *Paris.* 1824. 8vo. + Traduit par M. Lavallée. *Paris.* 1824. 4 vols., 12mo. 22727

ERCILLA Y ZUÑIGA. Historiale beschrijvinghe der goudtrycke landen in Chili ende Arauco, ende andere provincien in Chili ghelegen, mitsgaders d'oorloghen die d'inwoonders aldaer ghehadt hebben teghens de Spagniaerden ... overgheset wt de spaensche in de nederl. tale, door I. J. Byl. *Rotterdam: J. v. Waesberghe.* 1619. 4to, 2 l., pp. 60, (3). 22728

ERCILLA Y ZUÑIGA. An Appendix to the Civil and Political History of Chili, consisting of a Sketch of the Araucana of Alonzo de Ercilla, with Copious Translations from that Poem by Wm. Hayley and Rev. H. Boyd. *New York.* 1808. 8vo.

The noblest heroic poem in Spain. Voltaire ranks the author with Virgil, Tasso, and Camoens. It is a real historical record of the endeavors of the Spaniards to subjugate a nation whose independence they were forced to recognize in 1773. "Ercilla wrote in the spirit in which he fought; and his principal work is as military as any portion of his adventurous life. Its subject is the very expedition against Arauco which occupied eight or nine years of his youth; and he has simply called it 'La Araucana.'" — TICKNOR, II. 461.

Die Ereignisse in Amerika in ihrer Rückwirkung auf Deutschland. *Berlin: Ferdinand Schneider.* 1861. 8vo, pp. 80. H.

ERES (C. D. R. d'). Memoirs of Charles Denis Rusoe d'Eres, a Native of Canada, Who was with the Scanyawtauragahroote Indians eleven years, with a particular account of his Sufferings, &c. during his Tarry with them, and his Safe Return to his Family Connections in Canada; to which is added An Appendix, containing A brief account of their Persons, Dress, Manners, Reckoning Time, Mode of Government, &c. Feasts, Dances, Hunting, Weapons of War, &c. Making Peace, Diversions, Courtship, Marriage, Religious Tenets, Mode of Worship, Diseases, Method of Cure, Burying their Dead, Character of the Scanyawtauragahroote Indians, Particular Description of the Quadrupeds, Birds, Fishes, Reptiles and Insects, which are to be met with in ... the Vicinity of Scanyawtauragahroote Island. ... *Exeter: Henry Ranlet.* 1800. 12mo, pp. 176. BA., C., H., W.

These memoirs begin with the attack of Montgomery on Quebec. It is a very rare book, but probably a fiction. The Scanyawtauragahroote tribe is unknown, except to this writer.

ERICSSON (J.) Brief Explanation of some Philosophical and other Instruments, placed in the United States Division of the Industrial Exhibition of all Nations, Hyde Park, London. By J. Ericsson, ... *E. Dunn, Agent, United States Office, Industrial Exhibition, Hyde Park.* MDCCCLI. 8vo, pp. 26. 7 Plates.

ERIE COUNTY, *N. Y.* Board of Supervisors. Correspondence relative to ... establishing a Workhouse ... *Buffalo.* 1846. pp. 26. S. + Proceedings, Oct. 6, 1852. *Buffalo.* 1852. 8vo. Continued. S. 22733

Erie County Penitentiary. Report. *Buffalo.* 1849. 8vo. Continued. 22734

Proceedings of the Union Anti-Lecompton Mass Meeting of the Citizens of Erie County, N. Y. Opposed to the Policy of the National Administration, Held at St. James Hall, Buffalo, Thursday, May 27th, 1858. *Buffalo: Commercial Advertiser Steam Press.* 1858. 8vo, pp. 22. H. 22735

ERIE, *Penn.* Erie Directory for 1867–68. *Erie, Pa.: Lynn & Co.* 8vo, pp. 214. 22736

Erie Cemetery. ... By-Laws, Rules and Regulations, Certificate of Ownership, and Act of Incorporation. *Erie, Pa.* 1851. 8vo, pp. 15. H. 22737

Also: First Report of the Managers ... with the Act of Incorporation; its Rules ... . *Erie, Pa.* 1852. 8vo, pp. 46. H.

War of the Gauges; or Railroading at Erie, Comprising an Official and Authentic Version of the Railroad Troubles at Erie and Harbor Creek. *Cleveland.* 1854. 8vo, pp. 61. 22738

ERIE CANAL. *See also* New York State. *Canals.*

Acts of the Legislature respecting Navigable Communications between the Great Western and Northern Lakes and the Hudson River. *Albany.* 1819. 8vo. 22739

The Advantages of the Proposed Canal from Lake Erie to Hudson's River fully Illustrated, in a Correspondence between the Hon. Gouverneur Morris and Robert Fulton, Esq. [n. p.] 1814. 8vo, pp. 13. M., N. 22740

Appeal to the Representatives of the People, in relation to the proposed Enlargement of the Erie Canal. [n. p. n. d.] S.

Considerations in Favor of the Erie Canal: published by the New York Corresponding Association for the Promotion of Internal Improvements. *Brooklyn.* 1818. 8vo. 22742

Considerations, etc. *See* Vol. IV., Nos. 15939, 15946.

Examination of the Line of the Great Erie Canal from Schoharie Creek to the Hudson River, and contrasting it with a more direct Line. 1822. 8vo. 22743

Facts and Observations in Relation to the Origin and Completion of the Erie Canal. *New York.* 1825. 8vo, pp. 36. N. + Second Edition. *Providence: F. Y. Carlile and H. H. Brown.* 1827. 8vo, pp. 32. BA. 22744

Laws of the State of New York, in relation to the Erie and Champlain Canals; together with the Annual Report of the Canal Commissioners and other Documents requisite for a Complete Official History of those Works. Also, Correct Maps ... *Albany: Published by authority of the State, E. and E. Hosford, Printers.* 1825. 2 vols., rl. 8vo, pp. 615; 666. 22745

Memorial of the Citizens of Buffalo to the Legislature relative to the Termination of the Erie Canal. *Buffalo.* 1821. 8vo.

Memorials of the Citizens of the State of New York, in favor of a Canal Navigation between the Great Western Lakes and the Tide Waters of the Hudson. *New York.* 1816. 8vo, pp. 18. N. 22747

Observations on Canal Navigation. [n. p. About 1811.] 8vo, pp. 15. 22748

Relates to the Erie Canal.

The Official Reports of the Canal Commissioners of the State of New York, and the Acts of the Legislature respecting Navigable Communications between the Great Western and Northern Lakes, and the Atlantic Ocean. With Maps. *New York.* 1817. 8vo. P. 22749

Origin of the Erie Canal ... *Rome.* 1870. 8vo. S. 22750

Proceedings of the Convention, upon the subject of an immediate Enlargement of the Erie Canal; held ... in Rochester, ... January, 1837. *Buffalo: Charles Faxon, Printer.* 1837. 8vo, pp. 28. 22751

Proceedings of the Meetings of the Citizens of Rochester, Buffalo and Palmyra, with reference to the Improvement of the Erie Canal. 22752

Remarks on the Importance. *See* [Williamson (Hugh)].

Remarks on the Proposed Canal. *See* [Clinton (De Witt)], Vol. IV., No. 13721.

Remonstrance of the Inhabitants of Schenectady against the Change of Route of the Erie Canal. By Schenectady. *Schenectady.* 1836. 8vo. S. 22753

The Report of a Committee appointed to Explore the Western Waters in the State of New York, for the purpose of prosecuting the Inland Lock Navigation. *Albany.* 1792. 12mo, pp. 24.

Report of the Commissioners appointed by ... the Senate and Assembly ... of the 13th and 15th of March, 1810, to explore the Route of an Inland Navigation from Hudson's River to Lake Ontario and Lake Erie. *New-York: Printed for Prior and Dunning.* 1811. 8vo, pp. 38. BA. 22755

Signed by Gouv. Morris, S. Van Rensselaer, W. North, De Witt Clinton, etc.

Report of the Commissioners for the Improving of Inland Navigation in the State of New York, April 8, 1811. [n. p. n. d.] 8vo, pp. 40. B. 22756

Report of the Commissioners for Internal Improvement. *Albany.* 8vo. B. 22757

Report of the Joint Committee of the Legislature, on the Subject of the Canals from Lake Erie to the Hudson River, and from Lake Champlain to the same. March 19, 1817. [*Albany.* 1817.] 8vo, pp. 24. S. 22758

Report of the Commissioners on the Canals from Lake Erie to the Hudson River, and from Lake Champlain to the same. *Albany.* 1817. 8vo. 22759

Report of the Canal Commissioners on the Erie and Champlain Canals. *Albany.* 1818. 8vo. 22760

Report of the Canal Commissioners on a Navigable Communication between the Great Western and Northern Lakes and the Atlantic Ocean. *Albany.* 1820. 8vo. S. 22761

Report of a Committee appointed for the purpose of ascertaining the most eligible Route for a Canal from Seneca Lake to the Erie Canal. *Geneva.* 1822. 8vo. 22762

Report of the Committee of the Common Council of the City of Troy, and adopted by them, remonstrating against the Direct Route for the Eastern Termination of the Erie Canal, and an Answer to the Report of Allan Campbell, Civil Engineer, made by the Authority and under the Direction of the Common Council of the City of Albany. *Troy: Printed by Kemble & Hooper.* 1836. 8vo, pp. 36. 22763

Report of the Committee on Internal Improvements relative to the Enlargement of the Erie Canal. [n. p.] 1838. 8vo, pp. 8. B. 22764

Report on ... Supply of Water from Lake Erie for the Western Division of the Enlarged Erie Canal. *Rochester.* 1854. 8vo. S. 22765

Review of the Pamphlet of "Oswego," against the intended Enlargement of the Erie Canal. By Equal Rights. *Buffalo: Printed by Day, Stagg & Cadwallader.* 1836. 8vo, pp. 21.

A Serious Appeal to the Wisdom and Patriotism of the Legislature of the State of New York: on the Subject of a Canal Communication between the Great Western Lakes and the Tide Waters of the Hudson. By a Friend to his Country. [n. p.] *Printed for the Author.* 1816. 8vo, pp. 37. BA., H., N. 22767

The Erie War. [n. p. 1868.] 8vo, pp. 16. H. 22768

For other works, *see* "New York and Erie Railroad."

Erinneringen in Columbia. *See* Vol. IV., No. 14582.

ERLER (Christ. August). Meine Auswanderung nach Polen und Nordamerika. *Zwickau.* 1839. 8vo. 22769

ERMAN (A.) Reise um die Erde durch Nord-Asien und die beiden Oceane in den Jahren 1828, 1829 und 1830. *Berlin.* 1833–1848. 5 vols, 8vo; Atlas, folio. C. 22770

Erman has also published in the "Archiv für wissenschaftliche Kenntniss von Russland. *Berlin.* 1849." 8vo, several vocabularies, etc., on the Indians in Russian America. *See* Ludewig's "Lit. of Am. Ab. Lang."

ERMAN. Travels in Siberia; including Excursions Northwards, down the Obi to the Polar Circle, and Southwards, to the Chinese frontier. By Adolph Erman. Translated from the

German, by William Desborough Cooley. ... *London: Longman & Co.* 1848. 2 vols., 8vo, pp. xi, 495; ix, 536. Map. C., H. + *Philadelphia.* 1850. 2 vols., 12mo. 22771

ERMATINGER (E.) The Hudson's Bay Territories; a Series of Letters on this Important Question. By Edward Ermatinger. *Toronto.* 1858. pp. 32. 22772

ERMATINGER. Life of Colonel Talbot, and the Rise and Progress of the Talbot Settlement; with Sketches of the Public Characters and Career of some of the most conspicuous men in Upper Canada, who were either friends or acquaintances of the subject of these Memoirs. *St. Thomas.* 1859. 8vo, pp. 230.

The Ermine in the Ring: a History of the Wood Lease Case. *New York: G. P. Putnam & Son.* 186–. 8vo, pp. 32. B.

ERNI (H.) Coal, Oil, and Petroleum: their Origin, History, Geology, and Chemistry; with a View of their Importance in their Bearing upon National Industry. By Henri Erni, A.M., M.D. *Philadelphia: H. C. Baird.* 1865. 12mo, pp. 196.

ERNST (A.) Amadeo Bonpland. Apuntes biográficos ficos leidos en la session de 22 de Noviembre de 1869 de la Sociedad de Ciencias fisicas y naturales de Carácas. *Carácas.* 1869. 8vo, pp. 17. 22776

ERNST. Rede gehalten am Abend der Vorfeier des Humboldt-Festes, 13, September, 1869, in der Ruine von Sabana Grande. *Carácas.* 1869. 8vo, pp. 9. 22777

The first German publication printed in Carácas.

ERNST. Republik Chili. Erlebnisse und Betrachtungen daselbst. *Berlin: Scherl.* 8vo, 2 l., pp. 121. 4 Woodcuts.

For an article on the flora of Venezuela, *see* "El Porvenir Parte Literaria."

ERNST (John Frederick). Oration, ... Grand Royal Arch Chapter for the State of New York, in 5800. 1801. 4to, pp. 13.

ERNST. A Sermon Delivered before the Civil and Military Officers, the Members of Franklin and St. Paul's Lodges, and a large and respectable number of Citizens of Montgomery County, and others, in the Church at Fort Plain, on January 28th, 1800, in Consequence of the Death of Lieutenant General George Washington. By John Frederick Ernst, Gospel Minister at Cooperstown. *Cooperstown.* MDCCC. 4to, pp. 20. 22780

Also: Poem at the Dedication of Mason Hall, Hudson, N. Y. *Hudson.* 1797. 12mo. W.

ERNST (F.) Bemerkungen auf einer Reise durch d. Innere der Vereinigten Staaten von Nord-America im Jahre 1819. Nebst e. Uebersetzung de Constitution d. Illinois-Staats. *Hildesheim: Gerstenberg.* 1820. 8vo. Plate. 22781

ERNST V BIBRA (*Dr.* Frhr.) *See* Bibra, Vol. I., No. 5216.

Ernstige Beschouwing. *See* [Theroft (E. J.)]

Eroberer und Sclaven der neuen Welt. Geschichte der Einführung der Sclaverei in Amerika. *Dresden: Kuntze.* 1853. 2 vols., 8vo, pp. vii, 244; 2 l., pp. 275. 22782

This forms Vols. VI.–VII. of "Jenseits des Oceans."

Die Eroberung von Mexico und Peru der zwey grösten reiche in Amerika, durch die spanische Waffen ... . Aus dem Französischen übersetzt. *Frankfurth und Leipzig: Tobias Göbhardt.* 1770. 12mo, 4 l., pp. 157. H. 22783

ERONDELLE (P.) Nova Francia. *See* [Lescarbot].

ERRETT (I.) The Claims of Civil Government. Sermon, April 30, 1863, at Detroit, Michigan. By Isaac Errett. *Detroit.* 1863. 8vo. B. 22784

Errata; Or, the Art of Printing incorrectly: Plainly set forth by a variety of Examples taken from a Latin Grammar, lately printed by Andrew Stewart, for the Use of the College and Academy of this City. ... The Second Edition. *Philadelphia.* M.DCC.LXIII. 12mo, pp. xii, 23. P. 22785

In Franklin's type. Contains nine pages of the errata, copied from the "Grammar." It was answered by the following: "The Ass in the Lyon's Skin; Luckily discover'd by his Braying. *Philadelphia: Printed and Sold by Andrew Stewart.* 1763. (Price 2 Pennies.)" 12mo, pp. 8.

El Error confundidado y la Verdad demonstrada. [Colophon:] *Méjico: En la oficina de Alejandro Valdes.* 1820. 4to, pp. 40.

A defence of the Spanish rule over Mexico.

Errors of the British Minister in the Negociations with the Court of Spain. *London.* 1790. 8vo. 22787

On the affair of Nootka Sound.

ERSKINE (E.) Two Discourses. God in the Pestilence, or Cholera, a Visitation from God; and the Blessed Dead. By Rev. Ebenezer Erskine. *Columbia. October,* 1849. 22788

ERSKINE (David Stewart). The Earl of Buchan's Address to the Americans at Edinburgh, on Washington's Birth-Day, February 22d. 1811. [*Edinburgh.* 1811.] 8vo, pp. 32. BA. 22789

[ERSKINE (John).] The Equity and Wisdom of Administration, in Measures That have unhappily occasioned The American Revolt, Tried by the Sacred Oracles. *Edinburgh: Printed in the Year* MDCCLXXVI. 12mo, pp. 19. BA., M. 22790

The author thinks that "if more gentle measures had been taken with the people of Boston, much blood and treasure might have been saved, and harmony restored between the mother country and the colonies." — Page 7. *See* "M. Rev.," LVI. 401.

[ERSKINE.] Reflections on the Rise, Progress, and Probable Consequences, of the Present Contentions with the Colonies. By a Freeholder. ... *Edinburgh: Printed in the Year* MDCCLXXVI. 12mo, pp. iv, 53. BA., J.C.B. 22791

The writer thinks "the pamphlets setting forth the claims of the North Americans, have influenced the resentment of the mother country." He has therefore brought together evidence "from the writings of the colonists, ... what concessions might have been procured from them by gentle measures." *See* "M. Rev.," LVI. 401.

[ERSKINE.] Shall I go to War with my American Brethren? A Discourse from Judges the xxth and 28th. Addressed to all concerned in determining that Important Question. *London; G. Kearsley.* MDCCLXIX. 8vo, pp. (2), 42, (1). H. 22792

See "M. Rev.," XL. 173.

ERSKINE. [As above.] First Published at London, 1769. To which are now added, a Preface and Appendix. By John Erskine, D.D. One of the Ministers of Edinburgh. *Edinburgh.* 1776. 12mo. 22793

Also: Prayer for those in Civil and Military Offices recommended. Sermon preached before the Election of Magistrates of Edinburgh, Oct. 5, 1779. ... *Edinburgh.* 1797. 8vo, pp. 32.

ERSKINE (R.) Gospel Sonnets, or Spiritual Songs. By Ralph Erskine. Fifth Edition. *Philadelphia: Re-printed and Sold by Benjamin Franklin, in Market-street.* 1740. 8vo, pp. xvi, 270.

Introduced here because of the imprint. There are also editions, *Worcester, Mass.* 1798. 12mo; *Lansingburgh.* 1806.

ERSKINE. A Letter to Geo. Whitefield. By Ralph Erskine. *Philadelphia: Printed and Sold by B. Franklin.* 1741. 8vo, pp. 14.

ERSKINE (R.) Facts and Accusations set forth in a Late Pamphlet, entitled "The Conduct and Treatment of John

Crookshanks, Esq.," proved to be False and Groundless, by Captain Robert Erskine. *London.* 1759. 8vo. C. 22796

ERSKINE (*Mr.*) Letter from Mr. Erskine, the British Minister, to the Secretary of State, on the Subject of the British Orders in Council of the Eleventh of November, 1807. Accompanying a message from the president ... . *City of Washington: A. & G. Way, Printers.* 1808. 8vo, pp. 7. 22797

ERSKINE (Thomas). Speech of Lord Erskine against the Legality of the Orders in Council. March 8, 1808. *London.* 1808. 8vo. P. 22798

ERSKINE, *pseudonym.* Controversy between "Erskine" and "W. M." on the Practicability of Suppressing Gambling. *Richmond.* 1862. 8vo, pp. 96. BA. 22799

ERSKINE COLLEGE. Catalogue of Erskine College, Due West, Abbeville District, S. C. 1849. *Charleston.* 1849. 8vo. S.

ERVENDBERG (L. C.) Neueste Nachrichten aus Texas. *Frankfurt a. M.: Sauerländer.* 1847. 8vo, pp. 16. 22801

ERWIN (*Mr.*) Speech of Mr. Erwin on a Monument to Washington. *Washington.* [n. d.] 12mo. P. 22802

ERWIN COUNTY, *N. Y.* Statistics [of the proposed County], 1856. 8vo, pp. 13. S. 22803

Erzählungen und Beschreibungen aus Amerika. *Berlin.* 1846. 2 vols., 8vo. 22804

Erzählungen und Bilder aus Amerika. *Erfurt: Bartholomäus.* 1852. 8vo, pp. 98. 8 Colored Engravings. 22805

Erzählungen von den Sitten und Schiksalen der Negersklaven. Eine rührende Lektür für Menschen guter Art. *Bern: In der Hallerschern Buchhandlung.* 1789. 12mo, pp. xxiv, 288. J.C.B.

ESBARRA (Joaquim José de Sancta Anna). A gloria dos brasileiros, e o triumpho immortal dos europeus, representado nos ill.mos e ex.mos Governadores que são, e têem sido da America, Africa e Asia etc. *Lisboa: na Offic. de Francisco Borges de Sousa.* 1789. 4to, pp. 16. 22807

ESBARRA. As saudades de Lisboa no coração brasileiro, ou suspiros magoados do pastor Lidoro na despedida que faz de Lysia famosa. *Lisboa: na mesma Imp.* 1791. 4to, pp. 16.

ESBARRA. Saudosa cantilena que repetiram os pastores Limbrano, Anodino e Lizardo na Arcadia brasileira, etc. *Lisboa: na Offic. de Francisco Borges de Sousa.* 1789. 4to, pp. 14.

Esboço biograph. e necrolog. de Conselheiro José Bonifacio de Andrada e Silva. *Rio de Janeiro.* 1838. 8vo. 22810

Escala Espiritual para llegar al Cielo, Tradocido de Latin en Castellano por el Venerable Padre Fr. Juan de la Madalena, Regioso Dominico. [*Mexico: Juan Pablos.* Circa 1535.]

This "Spiritual Ladder" was the first book printed in Mexico; but there is no known copy in existence. Señor Icazbalceta has communicated to Mr. Harrisse a learned and interesting dissertation concerning this and other Mexican imprints, which will be found in the "Bibl. Am. Vet.," pp. 365–376. This book should have been described under Climacio (Juan), and our reference from No. 9812, should now read, "*See* Escala Espiritual." The real name of the translator was Juan Estrada. He is supposed to have been a native of Mexico, and to have died in 1579, says Antonio ("Biblioth. Hisp. Nova, I. 686"). Fernandez gives the date 1535 to this work; Davila says 1532.

ESCALADA (M.) Dictamen del fiscal general del estado sobre la suplica que ha hecho D. Mariano Escalada. *Buenos Aires.* 1834. 4to, pp. 24. 22812

ESCALANTE (Bernard de). A Discourse of the Navigation which the Portugales doe make to the Realmes and Provinces of the East Partes of the Worlde; Translated by Iohn Frampton. *London.* 1576. 4to. BM. 22813

ESCALANTE (F. M.) Poesias de D. Feliz M. Escalante. Edicion del Republicano. *Mexico.* 1856. 12mo, pp. ii, 372. Portrait. 22814

ESCALANTE (Francisco de la Estela). Illustrium Autorum Collectanea ad usum Studiosæ Juventutis facta. Per Congregationem B. Marie Virginis Annunctiate, autoritate Apostolica institutam in Latinitatis Rhetoriceq; Gymnasijs Collegii Mexicani Societatis Jesu ... . *Mexico: H. Martinez.* 1604. 22815

ESCALANTE FONTANEDA (Hernando de). *See* Soto, *also* Ternaux.

ESCALANTE (Thomas). Sermon funebre en las exequias de los militares difuntos españoles. *Mégico: Carrascoso.* 1694. 4to.

ESCALANTE. Vida del Venerable Padre Bartholome Castaño, de la Compañia de Jesus, que dio a los superiores de las Casas, y Colegios desta Provincia de Nueva-España ... . *Mégico: Ribera.* 1708. 4to. 22817

The first edition was 1679.

ESCALERA (E.), *and* LLANA (M.) Historia y descripcion de Méjico. Por Evaristo Escalera y Manuel Gonzales Llanm. *Madrid.* 1864. 8vo. + *Buenos Aires: Medina hermanos.* 1864. 8vo, 5 l., pp. 336, 1 l. 22818

ESCALONA (Gaspar de), *and* AGUERO. Gazophilatium Perubicum. 1. Administrandum. 2. Calculandum. 3. Conservandum. ... editum a Don Gasp. de Scalona Aguero, Argentino Peruano. *Matriti.* 1647. Folio. 22819

The second part is in Spanish, and is entitled "Gazofilacio Real de Peru."

ESCALONA *and* AGUERO. Gazophilacium Regium Perubicum. Opus sane Pulcrum, a Plerisque petitum, & ab omnibus, in universum, desideratum non sine magno labore, & experientia digestum, providèque, & accuratè illustratum. In quo Omnes Materiæ spectantes ad Administrationem calculationem, & conservationem jurium regalium Regni Peruani latissimé discutiuntur, & plena manu pertractantur. Editum a D. Gaspare Escalona Aguero ... . *Matriti: Ex Typographia Blasii Roman.* M.DCC.LXXV. Folio, 6 l., pp. 268 [168], 349. BA., H. 22820

There are copies on large paper. It is a compendium of what was necessary to be known to the officers of the Crown, on going to South America. Priced at Asher's, in 1858, at 130 francs; Salva had a copy for £1 6s.

ESCANDON (J. de), *and* RUSDORFER (B.) Geschichte von Paraguay. Aus Spanischen Handschriften übersetzt nebst dem Criminal Procesz wider die Jesuiten in Spanien. Von Juan de Escandon und Bernard Rusdorfer, der Gesellschaft Jesu Mitglieder. *Frankfurt und Leipzig.* 1769. 12mo, 4 l., pp. 72.

The Escaped Nun; or, Disclosures of Convent Life, and the Confessions of a Sister of Charity. *New York: Dewitt & Davenport.* 1855. 12mo, pp. 344. 22822

ESCARBOT (M.) *See* Lescarbot (M.)

ESCHASSÉRIAUX (*aîné*). Corps Législatif. Conseil des Cinq-Cents. Rapport fait par Eschassériaux aîné, relatif à la contribution foncière des Colonies Occidentales pour l'an 6. Séance du 21 Nivose an 6. ... *Paris: de l'Imprimerie Nationale Nivôse an* 6. [1798.] 8vo, pp. 6. 22823

Also: Opinion sur les moyens de rétablir les Colonies. Séance du 16 Prairial, an V. *De l'imprimerie nationale.* [1797.] 8vo, pp. 18. J.C.B. — Rapport fait au nom de la commission des Colonies sur la division constitutionelle du territoire françois dans les deux Indes. Séance du 29 Ventose, an V. *Paris: De l'imprimerie nationale.* [1797.] 8vo, pp. 23. J.C.B.

ESCHRICHT (D. F.) On the Greenland Eight-Whale: On the Species of Orca inhabiting the Northern Seas. Edited by Wm. H. Fowler. *London: Pub. for Ray Society by Robert Hardwicke.* 1866. 8vo, pp. 188. B. 22824

Also included with W. H. Hower's "Cetacea," 1866.

ESCHWEGE (L. W.) Brasilien, die Neue Welt in topographischer, geognostischer, bergmännischer, naturhistorischer, politischer und statistischer Hinsicht, während eines elfjährigen Aufenthaltes, von 1810 bis 1821, mit Hinweisung auf die neueren Begebenheiten beobachtet. Von L. W. von Eschwege. *Braunschweig: Vieweg.* 1830. 2 vols., 8vo. 2 Plates. 22825

Martius gives the date, *Braunschweig,* 1824.

ESCHWEGE (W. von). Geognostisches Gemälde von Brasilien und wahrscheinliches Muttergestein der Diamanten. Von L. W. v. Eschwege. *Weimar: Ind.-Comptoir.* 1822. 8vo. Map.

ESCHWEGE. Nachrichten aus Portugal und dessen Colonien mineralog. und bergmänn. Inhalts, herausgegeben von J. C. L. Zincken. *Braunschweig: Meyer.* 1820. 8vo. Plate. 22827

ESCHWEGE (W. C. von). Journal von Brasilien oder vermischte Nachrichten aus Brasilien auf wissenschaftlichen Reisen gesammelt. *Weimar: Ind.-Comptoir.* 1818. 8vo, pp. 304. Maps and Plates. (Neue Biblioth. d. wicht. Reisebeschr., 14. u. 15. Bd.) 22828

Includes Indian vocabularies.

ESCHWEGE (W. L. v.) Beiträge zur Gebirgskunde Brasiliens von W. L. von Eschwege: mit 4 petrographisch-geognostischen Karten und Profildurchschnitten. *Berlin: Reimer.* 1832. 8vo. Map. 22829

ESCHWEGE. Pluto Brasiliensis. Eine Reihe von Abhandlungen über Brasiliens Gold- Diamanten- und andere mineralogischen Reichthum, über die Geschichte seiner Entdeckung, über das Vorkommen seiner Lagerstätten, des Betriebs der Ausbeute und die darauf bezüglichen Gesetzgebung ... von W. L. von Eschwege. *Berlin: Reimer.* 1833. 8vo. 8 Maps and Engr., and 2 Tables. 22830

The best work of its date on the gold and diamond mines of Brazil.

ESCLAVAGE. Avis des Conseils spéciaux et coloniaux sur l'Abolition de l'Esclavage. *Paris.* 1843. 4to. 22831

L'Esclavage dans les États Confédérés ; par un Missionnaire. *Paris.* 1865. 8vo. BA. 22832

See also "Slavery."

Escobar (D.) Diligencias practicadas para averiguar un hecho criminal que se dice cometido en la persona del jeneral Desiderio Escobar. *Carácas.* 1869. 4to, pp. 54. 22833

Escobar (D. A. de). Sermon epidictico que en las Honras, que de orden de N. R. M. P. F. Fernando Alonso Gonzalez, etc. hizo el dia 22 de Septiembre de este año de 1732, el Convento Grande de N. P. S. Francisco de esta Ciudad de Mexico al Cappn. M. Miguel Velasquez Lorea, Alguacil Mayor del Santo Tribunal de la Inquisicion etc. predicó el R. B. Diego Antonio de Escobar. *Mexico: J. B. de Hogal.* [1732.] 4to. 19 l., pp. 27. 22834

[Escobar (Manoel de).] Restauraçaõ de Portugal prodigiosa. Por Gregorio de Almarez. *Lisboa: Antonio Alvarez.* 1643. 4to. Portrait. 22835

"Jose Agostinho de Macedo says that the name in the title-page is fictitious, and that this book was written by the Jesuit, Manoel de Escobar." — *Manuscript Note by* R. Southey. *See also* Backer's "Bibl. des écriv," iii. 293. Contains some reference to the Portuguese possessions in America.

Escobar (M. de). Verdad reflexa, platica doctrinal sobre los varios sucessos que intervinieron en la Ciudad de San Luis Potosi desde el dia 10 de Mayo de 1767, hasta el dia 6 de Octubre del mismo año, en que se ejecutaron los ultimos suplicios de los Tumultuarios. Dijola en su plaza mayor el R. P. fr. Manuel de Escobar. *Mexico.* 1768. 4to, 27 l., pp. 57. 22836

Escobar. Voces de Triton Sonoro, queda desde S. Inglesia de Valadolid de Mechoagan la incorrupta, y viva Sangre del Illmo D. Juan Joseph de Escalona y Calatayud, Obispo en la Provincia de Venezuela, &c. [que fue, de esta Diocesis despues de aver estado por siete años sepultada.] *Mexico.* 1746. 4to.

Neither the author nor his work were known to Antonio. Besides entering into a particular description of these remains and their miraculous preservation, this strange work contains much curious matter relative to the various modes of embalming, etc.

Escobeda (P.) Corona funebre de Pedro Escobedo, ó sea coleccion completa de todas las producciones literarias, publicadas con motivo de su muerte. [*Mexico.* 1844.] 8vo. 22838

Escoiquiz (J. de). Mexico Conquestada. Poema Heroyco. Por Don Juan de Escoiquiz, Canonigo de Zaragoza ... . Dedi-

cado al Rey Nuestro Señor. *Madrid: En la Imprenta Real, por Pedro Julian Pereyra.* 1798. 3 vols., 12mo, Engraved Frontispiece, pp. xxii, 342; 386; 345. H. 22839

This epic is in twenty-six books, and about twenty-five thousand lines, beginning with the demand of Cortés to be received in person by Montezuma, and ending with the fall of Mexico. *See* Ticknor's "Hist. of Spanish Lit.," iii. 306.

Escontria (Joseph Gomez de). Oracion Funebre, que en las Honras anniversarias de los Militares difuntos de la Monarchia Española, celebrados en la Iglesia Cathedral de Mexico, el dia 23 de Nov. 1770. *Mexico.* [1770.] 22840

Escorzo y Escalante (P.) Razon de la Sentencia deffinitiva, que diò, y pronunciò D. Pedro de Escorzo, y Escalante. Con Parecer de su Assessor, etc. *Mexico.* 1714. 22841

Escosura (P. de la). La conjuracion de Méjico, ó los hijos de Hernan Cortes. Novela historico, original. *Madrid.* 1850–1851. 5 vols., 8vo. Plates. 22842

Escudero (J. A. de). Memorias con documentos justificativos, que pueden servir para la historia del Congreso Constituyente Mexicano del año de 1847. *Mexico.* 1848. 4to, pp. 98.

Escudero. Noticias Estadisticas del Estado de Chihuahua. Por J. A. de Escudero. *Mexico.* 1834. 8vo. + Reimpresas de orden del Supremo Gobierno. *Mexico: Juan Ojeda.* 1834. 8vo, pp. 256. B., C. 22844

Also: Noticia estadisticas de Sonora y Sinaloa. *Mexico.* 1849. 4to. — Noticias estadisticas del estado de Durango. *Mexico.* 1849. 4to, pp. v, 72. — Noticias estadisticas de Sonora y Sinaloa. *Mexico.* 1849. 4to, pp. 148. — Noticias Historicas y Estadisticas de Nueva-México. 1849. *Mexico.* 1849. Map.

Eskimo. Die Abentheuerinnen im Lande der Esquimaux oder die Geständnisse einer Erbin. Aus dem Englischen. *Leipzig: bey Johann Ambrosius Barth.* 1793. 3 vols., 18mo, pp. 204; 218; 206. J.C.B. 22845

Ajokœrsoirsun Atuagekseit Nalegbingne Grõndlandme. Ritual over Kirke-Forretningerne ved den Danske Mission paa Grönland. *Kiöbenhavn: H. Ch. Schröder.* 1783. 8vo. 22846

A ritual in Danish and Greenlandish, for the use of the Danish mission.

Ajokaersutit illuartut Gudimik pekkorsèjniglo innungnut. *Kiöbenhavnime: C. F. Skabartimit.* 1818. 16mo, pp. 158. C.

The knowledge of the righteous God.

Atuagagdliutit. Nalinginarnik Tusarumi. Nasaassunik Univkat. *Godthaab.* 1861. 4to. Colored Plates. 22848

An Eskimo periodical, Nos. 1 to 4.

A Brief Account of the Mission. *See* Vol. ii., No. 7846.

Eskimaux and English Vocabulary. *See* [Washington (John)].

Evangelia quatuor. A Paul Egede. *Kiobenhavn.* 1744. 4to.

The four Gospels in the Greenland language.

Evangelium S. Johannis, or the Gospel of St. John in the Language of the Esquimaux. *London.* 1810. 8vo. 22850

Printed to facilitate the labors of a mission establishment on the coast of Labrador, under the superintendence of the Rev. Mr. Kohlmeister, who resided among the Esquimaux for eighteen years. Also: Nene Karighwiyoston, etc. The Gospel according to St. John, in Esquimaux and English. *London.* [1820.] 8vo.

Exodus, Deuteronomy, Job, Ezra, Nehemiah, Esther, Ruth. Translated into Eskimo by Peter Kragh. *Kiobenhaven.* 1832.

Genesis. Testamentitokamit Mosesim aglegèj siurdleet. Pellesiúnermit Ottomit Fabriciusimit. *Kiöbenhavnime: C. F. Skubartimit.* 1822. 16mo, pp. 202. C. 22852

Also: The Book of Genesis, Translated into the Esquimaux Language by the Missionaries of the United Brethren. *London.* 1834. 12mo.

The Gospels according to St. Matthew, St. Luke, St. Mark and St. John. Translated into the Language of the Esquimaux Indians, on the Coast of Labrador; By the Missionaries of the Unitus Fratrum, or United Brethren, residing at Nain, Okkak, and Hopedale. *London: printed for the Use of the Mission, by McDowall.* 1813. 12mo, Title, 1 l., pp. v, 416. S. 22853

Also: Gospels and Epistles in the Greenland Language. *Copenhagen.* 1848. 16mo, pp. 744.

Greenlandish Folklore. Popular Tales and Legends: Collected and Edited by Natives of Greenland. The Original Eskimo Text, with Danish Translation. *Godthaab, Greenland.* 1859–1861. 3 vols., 8vo. 22854

"Woodcuts and lithographs designed and engraved by natives. Remarkable as conveying the traditions of the first descent of the Norseman on the shores of Greenland in the eighth century." Title and note abridged from an English auctioneer's catalogue.

Hymn-Book in the Language of the Esquimaux of the Labrador Coast. *London.* 1809. 8vo. 22855

Indreniis Specimen de Esquimaux, gente Americana. *Aboæ, Finland.* 1756. 8vo, pp. 24. 22856

Rare. The last page is a vocabulary.

Imgerutit attorekset illagēktunnut Labradoremētunnut. *Læbaume.* [About 1840.] 12mo, pp. xii, 340. 22857

Moravian Hymn-Book in the Esquimaux language. Another edition is entitled, "Tuksiantit Attuagæsit Illageennut innuit Nunænnetunnut. *Barbime.* 1785."

An Interesting Account of those Extraordinary People the Esquimaux Indians, &c. *Sheffield.* [n. d.] 12mo, pp. 36.

Ivngerutit Tuksiutidlo, kaladlinnut opertunnut attuægeksæt. *Kiöbenhavnime: C. F. Skubartimit.* 1801. 12mo. 22859

A Hymn and Prayer-Book in the Greenland language, translated by Otto Fabricius.

Kaladlit Assilialiait [or some Engravings Designed and Engraved on Wood by Eskimos of Greenland.] *Godthaab, Greenland.* 1860. 24 Plates in 4to, representing 30 subjects. 22860

These interesting engravings are the result of some experiments made between the years 1858–1860, to determine whether among the Eskimos there existed taste or genius for this branch of the arts. They were all engraved, and, with the exception of Nos. 1 to 8, designed by five or six natives, without any other assistance than the furnishing of the wood and of the most necessary instruments. The greater part of these engravings are the work of an Eskimo named Aron, who has received no more than the common education of his countrymen.

Naleganta Jesusil Kristusim Annaurcirsinta sullirsei, okantsinnik Tussarnersunnik, Aglegniartut sissamaet Pissitansimaput Attantsimut. *Barbine.* 1804. 12mo, pp. 280. 22861

The history of the passion of Jesus Christ, in the Greenland language.

Nelegapta Jesuib Kristusib. 1810. 12mo. 22862

Harmony of the Gospels in Eskimo.

Notice sur les mœurs et coutûmes des Indiens Esquimaux de la baie de Baffins, au pôle arctique, suivie d'un vocabulaire esquimau-français. *Tours: Mame.* 1826. 12mo, pp. 24.

Okalluktuaet Opernartut tersãuko Bibelimit Testamentitokamidlo Testamentitâmidlo Ottob Fabriciusib. *Kiöbenhavnime.* 1820. 22864

Biblical tales from the Old Testament.

The Old Testament, Translated into Greenlandish. *Copenhagen.* 1822–1836. 3 vols., 12mo, pp. 2170. 22865

Pok kalalek avalangnek, nunalikame nunakatiminut okaluktuartok. Angakordlo polasimik napitsivlune agssor. — tuissok agdlagkat pisorkat navssarissat nongmiut ilanit. *Godhaab.* 1857.

Pok, a Greenlander, who has travelled, and who, after his return, tells his adventures to his friends at home; and Angekok, who meets (Pok) the priest, and disputes with him (a dialogue); from old manuscripts found with the Greenlanders at Godhaab. The production of native Esquimaux. Though printed as lately as 1857, the book is (out of Greenland, at least) one of the rarest that can be found. Scarcely more than three or four copies have reached Denmark.

Schediasma hocce etymologico-philologicum prodromum Americano Gronlandicum in patronis appropriatum insinuat Twarns Abel. *Havniæ.* 1783. 4to. 22867

Testamentitokamit. Davidim Jungerutej okàuzeenut Nielsimit Wolfimit. *Kiöbenhavnime: C. F. Schubartimit.* 1824. 16mo, pp. 238. C. 22868

The Psalms of David, translated by Niels Wolf. Also: The Book of Psalms translated into the Esquimaux-Language, by the Missionaries of the United Brethren. *London.* 1834. 12mo.

Testamentitokamit Salomonis Ajokaersutéj Erkáïrseksaet okàuzeenut. N. G. Wolfimit. *Kjöbenhavnime.* 1828. 22869

The Old Testament. The Proverbs of Solomon, translated by N. G. Wolf.

Testamentitokamit profetib Esaisim Aglegèj okauzeenut N. G. W[olfimit]. *Kjöbenhavnime: C. F. Skubartimit.* 1825. 16mo, pp. 200. + [Another Edition.] 1837. 12mo. 22870

The Minor Prophets. Translated into Eskimo. By Peter Kragh. *Copenhagen.* 1829. 8vo. 22871

Nalegapta Jesusib Kristusib, piulijipta pinniarningit; okautsiñik tussarnertuñik, aglangniartut sittamæt, kattisimavut attautsimut. *Londonneme, W. Mc. Dowallib.* 1810. 12mo, 9 l., pp. 366.

Printed for the Brethren's Society for the furtherance of the Gospel among the heathen; for the use of the Christian Esquimaux in the Brethren's settlements, Nain, Okkak, and Hopedale, on the coast of Labrador.

Testament nutak. *Kiöbenhavnime: C. F. Skubartimit.* 1799. 16mo, pp. 1072. 22873

New Testament, translated by Otto Fabricius.

Testamente Nutak kaladlin okauzennut nuktersimarsok, narkiutingoaenniglo sukuiarsimarsok. *Kiöbenhavnime.* 1827.

Testamentetak tamedsa nalegapta piulijipta Jesusib Kristuisb Apostelingitalo pinniarnigit Okausingillo. Printed for The British and Foreign Bible Society, for the Use of the Christian Esqui-

maux in the Mission-Settlements of the United Brethren on the Coast of Labrador. *London: W. McDowall, Printer.* 1840. 12mo, 2 l., pp. 637. 22875

Also: New Testament. Translated into the Greenland Language, by the Missionaries of the Unitas Fratrum, or United Brethren. Printed for the Use of the Mission. *London.* 1822. 8vo.

Wadijahun Wunssada-goanti Wappussidagvanti Baddid Jesus Christus, etc. *Philadelphia.* 1799. 8vo. 22876

Eslava (S. de). Diario de todo lo occurrido en la expugnacion de los Fuertes de Bocachica, y sitio de la ciudad de Cartagena de las Indias; formado de los pliegos remetidos à su Majestad por el Virrey de Santa Fé, Don Sebastian de Eslava con Pedro de Mur su Ayudante Genl. De orden de Su Majestad. [*Madrid.*] *Año* 1741. 4to, pp. 23. 22877

Esmangart (C.) Des Colonies françaises et en particulier de l'ile de Saint-Domingue. Par Charles Esmangart. ... . *Paris: H. Agasse. An x.* [1801.] 8vo, Title, pp. 74. H. 22878

Esmangart. La vérité sur les affaires d' Haïti. Par M. Esmangart. Publié par le Comité des Anciens Propriétaires de St.-Domingue. *Paris: imp. de Carpentier-Méricourt.* 1833. 8vo, 8 sheets. C. 22879

Esménard (J.) La navigation, poëme en 6 chants. *Paris.* 1805. 2 vols., 8vo. + Seconde édition. 1806. 8vo. 22880

The second "chant" relates the discovery of America by Columbus.

Espada y Landa (F. J. D. de). Carta pastoral que el Illmo. Sr. D. Francisco Joseph Diaz de Espada y Landa, del Consejo de S. M. y Obispo de la Habana dirige á sus Diocesanos ... Segunda edicion. *Habana.* 1811. 4to, pp. 31. 22881

Espada y Landa (J. J. D. de). Circular del Excmo. é Ilustrísmo Señor D. Juan José Diaz de Espada y Landa, Obispo de la Habana ... . sobre la esplicacion de la Constitucion política de la monarquía española. *Habana: D. José Boloña.* M.DCCCXX. 4to, pp. 16. 22882

Españo y Méjico en el asunto de la convencion española. *Madrid.* 1855. 4to, pp. 92. 22883

El Espanol. *London.* 1812? 22884

This is the title of a monthly periodical on the affairs of South America, started in London about this time, and supposed to be edited by J. M. Blanco White. *See* Rich, ii. 59.

Esparza (M. de). Exposicion á la Seccion des Gran Jurando de la Camara de Senadores, con motivo de la acusacion por la órden relativa á la libre exportacion de los dos Millones y medio de pesos para los acreedores de bonos mexicanos en Londres. *Mexico.* 1852. 4to, pp. 26, 2 l. 22885

Esparza. Informe a consecuencia de la vista que practico en los partidos de Villanueva y Juchipila. *Zacatecas.* 1830. 4to, 2 l., pp. 63. 22886

El Espejo de mi Tierra. *Lima.* 1840. 8vo. 22887

Espejo Juridico Informe que hace la parte de la Santa Iglesia de Durango, Obispado del Reyno de la Nueva Vizcaya, en el Pleto que sigue con las Santas Iglesias Cathedrales de Valladolid y Guadalaxara. *Mexico: J. B. de Hogal.* 1738. Folio.

Espinosa (A. V.) Confesionario general con los tratos y contratos de las Indias. Por Antonio Vazquez de Espinosa. 1624. 12mo.

Title from Ternaux, No. 469.

Espinosa (C.) Las provincias de Sonora y Sinaloa, por C. Espinosa. *Mexico.* 1823. 8vo. 22890

Espinosa. La herencia Española de los Americanos, por e coronel Espinosa. *Lima.* 1852. 12mo, pp. 352. 22891

Espinosa. Prontuario de ordenanza para el ejercito, aprobado por el gobierno y redactado por el coronel Espinosa. Cuerta edicion, mas correcta que las anteriores. *Lima.* 1866. 8vo, pp. ii, 186. + Cuinta edicion. *Lima.* 1869. 8vo, pp. 224.

Espinosa (F. C.) Historia de Mexico desde los primeros tiempos de que hay noticia hasta mediados del siglo xix., por D. Francisco Carbajal Espinosa. *Mexico.* 1863. 2 vols., 8vo, pp. 685; 704. 80 Lithographic Plates. 22893

Espinosa de los Monteros (Ignacio). Oracion continua Funebre en Honras de Fr. Jos. Anfosso, Mayoral, Commissario General de esta Provincia de el Espiritu Santo de Nueva España, y Philipinas. *Mexico.* 1756. 4to. 22894

Espinosa (Isidro Felix de). El Cherubin Custodio de el Arbol de la Santa Cruz de Queretaro. Vida del V. Siervo de Dios Antonio de los Angeles, Bustamente. *Mexico.* 1731. 4to.

Espinosa. Chronica Apostolica, y Seraphica de Todos los Colegios de Propaganda Fide de Esta Nueva-España, de Misioneros Franciscanos Observantes: Erigidos con Autoridad

Pontificia, y Regia, para la reformacion de los Fieles, y Conversion de los Gentiles. Consagrada a la Milagrosa Cruz de Piedra, que como titular se venera en su primer Colegio de Propaganda Fide de la muy Ilustre Ciudad de San-Tiago de Queretaro, sita en el Arzobispado de Mexico. Escrita por el R. P. Fr. Isidro Felis de Ispinosa, ... Parte Primera. *Con Licencia en Mexico: Por la Viuda de D. Joseph Bernardo de Hogal. Impressora del Real, y Apostolico Tribunal de la Santa Cruzada en todo este Regno. Año de* 1746. 2 vols., folio, 50 l., pp. 590, 12 l.; ... + Crónica seráfica y apostólica del Colegio de Propaganda Fide de la Santa Cruz de Querétaro en la Nueva Espana ... . Escrita por Juan Domingo Arricivita. Segunda parte. *Mexico: F. de Zuniga y Ontiveros.* 1792. Folio, pp. 605, 1, 4 l. H. 22896

A rare and important work, containing much information relative to the early missions and the Indian tribes in New Mexico, Texas, and other parts of North Mexico, and also in those of Guatemala, Honduras, Chiapas, and other portions of the old viceroyalty of New Spain. Its rarity, when complete, is owing to the long time which elapsed between the publication of the first and of the second volume. The author was a Franciscan missionary of high standing in Mexico, being the President to the New Hospice of St. Ferdinando. Quaritch prices a copy at sixteen guineas.

Espinosa. Compendio de la Vida Mirabillosa del gloriosissimo Padre S. Francisco de Assis, Patriarcha, y Fundador primero del Orden de los Menores: Deducido de la Chronica Seraphica, y entresacado de lo que escribiò el Il. Sr. D. F. Damian Cornejo, Por Fray I. de Espinosa, Indigno Frayle Menor. *Mexico: por Joseph Bernardo de Hogal.* 1735. 4to, 9 l., pp. 770, 18 l.

Espinosa. El Peregrino in Septentrional Atlante delineado en la exemplarissima vida del ven. Padre Fr. Antonio Margil de Jesus Prefecto de las Missiones de propaganda Fide, en todos las Indias Occidentales y aclamado de la piedad por nuevo Apostol de Guatemala. Por Isidro Felix de Espinosa, Ex Guardian de Colegio de la Santa Cruz de Queretaro. *Valencia.* 1742. 4to, 20 l., pp. 456, (4). Portrait of Margil. + Nuevas impresas del peregrino americano septentrional Atlante. *Mexico.* 1747. 4to, 12 l., pp. 46. 22898

Relates many extraordinary conversions to Christianity among the Indians.

Espinosa (J. D.) Calendario para el año de 1867, tercero despues del bisiestro, arreglado al meridiano de Merida de Yucatan, por José Dolores Espinosa. *Merida.* 1866. 12mo, pp. 64.

Also: 1868. *Merida.* 1867. 12mo, pp. iv, 64.

Espinosa (J. M.) Batalla de Santa Ines, ó rasgo histórico sobre la campaña de occidente en 1859. *Carácas.* 1866. 4to, pp. 29.

ESPINOSA (J.) Diccionario para el pueblo: republicano democratico, moral, politico y filosofico. Por Juan Espinosa, antiguo soldado del ejercito de los Andes. *Lima.* 1855. 8vo, pp. xii, 852. 22901

An expression of democratic and advanced ideas in the form of a dictionary, including many curious articles.

ESPINOSA. La herencia española de los Americanos. Seis cartas criticas a Isabel segunda. Seguidas de otros escritos de interes público. Por Juan Espinosa. *Lima, El Correo.* 1852. 18mo, pp. 11, 359, 1 l. C. 22902

ESPINOSA (Pedro). Defensa de algunos puntos de la doctrina catolica, o sea contestacion a las "Nuevas observaciones sobre el opusculo del Señor Espinosa contra el Retrato de la Virgen." *Guadalajara.* 1851. 4to, pp. 124. 22903

ESPINOSA. Informe que el D. Pedro Espinosa, como Individuo de la Comision del Ven. Cabildo Eclesiastico de Guadalajara, Presentó del Congreso del Estado de Jalisco, etc. *Mexico.* 1831. 22904

The author was Bishop of Guadalajara, and has published several pastoral letters.

ESPINOSA Y TELLO (J.) Memorias sobre las observaciones astronomicas, hechas por los navegantes Españoles en distintos lugares del globo; las quales han servido para la formacion de las cartas de marear publicadas por la direccion de trabajos Hidrograficos de Madrid: ordenadas por Don Josef Espinosa y Tello, &c. *Madrid.* 1809. 2 vols., 4to. 22905

An account of the voyages of Malaspina, and other Spanish expeditions to explore the coasts of America, the Phillipines, etc.

L'Espion Américain in Europe; ou, Lettres Illinoises, qui renferment quantité d'anecdotes amusantes et instructives suivies d'un poëme intitulé la Religion Raisonnable. Par Mr. de V***. *London: aux dépens de la companie.* 1766. 12mo, pp. 32. 22906

L'Espion des Sauvages en Angleterre. *Londres: aux dépens de la Compagnie.* 1764. 8vo. 22907

Relating to America.

Espiritu de los mejores Diarios que se publican en Europa y America. [*Buenos Ayres.*] 1840. 8vo. 22908

Relates to the Argentine Confederation.

Esposicion de la conducta. *See* [Poinsett (J. R.)]

Esposicion de los sentimientos. *See* Vol. II., No. 6135.

Esposicion de los servicios prestados por el Coronel de ejercito D. Juan Dominguez. *Mexico.* 1839. 4to, pp. 23. 22909

Esposicion que elevan al Congreso de la Union varios propietarios, pidiendo la insubsistencia de la llamada ley agraria, que se publicó en el Estado de Aguascalientas el 17 de Agosto ultimo. *Mexico.* 1861. 4to, pp. 85. 22910

Esposicion de los Motivos qui ha tenedo el Presidente de Chile para desaprobar el tratado de Paz celebrado in Paucarpata en 17 de Novembre de 1837 y renovar las hostilidades interrumpidas por el. *Santiago.* 1838. Folio. 22911

Esposicion que hace en Jeneral Blanco al supremo Gobierno sobre su conducta en la Campana del Peru. *Santiago de Chile.* 1838. Folio, pp. 16. 22912

Exposicion del Provincial de la Compañia de Jesus, sobre el derecho que su religion tiene al edificio que actualmente ocupa, y á los bienes del antiguo Colegio de San Gregorio de que esta en posesion a consecuencia de su restablecimiento en esta Capital. *Mexico.* 1855. 4to, pp. 48. 22913

Esposicion dirigida al supremo gobierno por los comisionados que firmaron el tratado de paz con los Estados-Unidos. *Querétaro.* 1848. pp. 27. 22914

Esposicion que por las exenciones de la provincia Cármen hace el N. R. Padre Provincial de la misma, ante los delegados apostolicos a quienes compete su defensa. *Mexico.* 1851. 8vo, pp. 90. 21915

ESPRONCEDA (José de). Obras Poescas. *Valparaiso.* 1844. 2 vols., 8vo. 22916

ESPY (J. P.) The Philosophy of Storms. By John Pollard Espy, A.M. *Boston.* 1841. 8vo. 22917

Also: First Report on Meteorology, to the Surgeon-General of the United States Army ... with Charts, Illustrating the Weather of 1843. [*Washington.* 1843.] Folio, pp. 4. + Second Report on Meteorology, to the Secretary of the Navy, [and] Third Report on Meteorology, with Directions for Mariners, etc. [*Washington: Public Printer.* 1851.] Oblong folio, pp. 65. 101 Maps and 11 Tables. + Message from the President, ... communicating, ... the Fourth Meteorological Report of Prof. James P. Espy. ... *Washington: A. O. P. Nicholson.* 1857. 4to, pp. 240. 70 Plates.

ESPY (J.) Memorandums of a Tour made by Josiah Espy in the States of Ohio and Kentucky, and Indiana Territory, in 1805. *Cincinnati: Robert Clarke & Co.* 1870. 8vo, pp. viii, 28, (1).

Forms one of the "Ohio Valley Historical Series."

ESQUEMELING (John). *See* Exquemelin (Olivier Alexandre).

ESQUERRA (Mathias). Exequias de la Reyna Doña Mariana de Austria, celebradas en la Metropolitana de Megico; descripcion del tumulo, sus epigramas, epitafios e inscripciones latinos y castellanos. *Megico.* 1697. 4to. 22919

ESQUERRA (M. de). Sermon en la festividad del patrocinio de San Joseph. *Mexico.* [1715.] 4to, 4 l. 22920

ESQUIBEL Y VARGAS (Agustin Francisco). El Fenix de el amor, aparicion magna, ilustrada en la milagrosa Efigie de Christo en la espiracion de la Cruz. Tradicion historia del Christo de la Piedad, con cuyo titulo se venera en su Santuario y Parrochial de dicho, Pueblo del Obispado de Michoacan. *Mexico: Imprenta de la Bibliotheca Mexicana.* 1764. 4to, 14 l., pp. 113, (3). 22921

ESQUIMAUX. *See* Eskimo, *and* Greenland.

Esquisse de la Revolution, 1817. *See* [Palacio (M.)]

Esquisse Intéressante du Tableau fidele des causes qui ont occasioné les révolutions actuelles de l'Amérique septentrionale, ornée d'anecdotes historiques & politiques sur la nuissance de la République des treize Provinces-Unies de l'Amérique, contre le Roi d'Angleterre, avec la démonstration des objets intéressants qui regardent chaque état des Provinces-Unis telle qu'elle se trouve fixée par le traité fait à Versailles entre les Puissances belligérantes & ses alliés, le 20 Janvier 1783. *Philadelphie.* M.DCC.LXXXIII. 8vo, pp. 124. H. 22922

Esquisses Americaines, ou Tablettes d'un Voyageur aux Etats Unis d'Amérique. Par Ad. d'A. *Paris: Chez Ebrard.* 1841. 18mo, pp. 178. 22923

ESQUIVÉL Y VARGAS (Ildefonso de). Elogio Funebre en las Exêquias de Melchor de Noriega. *Mexico.* 1794. 4to.

ESQUIVEL (J. M.) Sermon eucharistico por la felicidad que locro la ciudad de Durango en la epidemia de viruelas, etc. *Mexico.* 1799. 4to, 14 l. 22925

Essai Historique sur la Surinam. *See* [Nassy (De la C.)]

Essai sur l'Administration des Colonies Françoises, et particuliérement d'une Partie de celles de Saint-Domingue. Avec deux

Cartes & deux Tableaux géographiques & politiques. ... *Antonina: et se trouve à Paris, chez Monory.* 1788. 8vo, pp. viii, 112. 2 Maps, and Tables. 22926

Essai sur cette question. *See* [Engel (S. B. de)], No. 22568.

Essai sur la Population des Colonies à Sucre. *La Haye.* 1781. 8vo. 22927

Essai sur les Colonies Françoises, 1754. *See* [Saintard (M.)]

Essai sur les Intérets, 1754. *See* [O'Heguerty].

Essay by a Friend to the Constitution. [n. p. n. d.] 8vo.

Relates to the Constitution of the United States.

An Essay, by Several Ministers of the Gospel, for the Satisfaction of their Pious and Conscientious Brethren, as to Sundry Questions and Cases of Conscience concerning the Singing of Psalms. *Boston.* 1723. 12mo. W. 22929

An Essay Concerning Silver. *See* [Douglass (W.)], Vol. v., No. 20723.

An Essay concerning Slavery, and the Danger Jamaica Is expos'd to from the Too great Number of Slaves, and the Too little Care that is taken to manage Them. And a Proposal to prevent the further Importation of Negroes into that Island. *London: Charles Corbett.* [1745?] 8vo, 6 l., pp. 67. 22930

An Essay for Discharging the Debts of the Nation by Equivalents in a Letter to the Earl of Sutherland. And the South Sea Scheme considered in a Letter to the Rt. Hon. Robert Walpole. *London: J. Noon.* 1720. 8vo, pp. vii, 98. J.C.B. 22931

An Essay In Defence of Slave Holding as Existing in the Southern States of our Union. By a Citizen of New York. *New York.* 1837. 12mo, pp. 32. 22932

An Essay in Vindication of the Continental Colonies of America, from a Censure of Mr Adam Smith, in his Theory of Moral Sentiments. With some Reflections on Slavery in general. By an American. *London: Printed for the Author.* MDCCLXIV. 8vo, pp. 46. BA., H. + [Another Edition.] *London: T. Becket.* MDCCLXIV. 8vo, pp. 46. 22933

Smith said, "That fortune never more cruelly exerted her empire over mankind than when she subjected those nations of heroes (the negroes) to the refuse of the jails of Europe" [*i. e.*, the Americans].

Essay on American Slavery, with some Remarks upon a Letter recently addressed to the President of the United States, on Slavery, by an "American Citizen." By a Citizen of Boston. *Boston.* 1855. 8vo, pp. 29. H. 22934

Essay on Canals and Inland Navigation; and the Reports of Engineers to the Welland Canal Company. *Queenstown, U. C.* 1824. 8vo. 22935

An Essay on Commonwealth. *New York.* 1822. 8vo, pp. 64. + *Philadelphia: Printed for the Commonwealth Association.* 1824. 12mo. P. 22936

Relates to the Owenite colony, at Harmony, Ohio.

An Essay on Credit, in which the Doctrine of Banks is considered, and some Remarks are made on the present state of the Bank of North-America. By a Citizen of Philadelphia. *Philadelphia: Printed by Eleazer Oswald.* M,DCC,LXXXVI. 8vo, pp. 42.

In favor of the bank.

An Essay on Currency and Banking. Being an Attempt to shew their True Nature, and to explain the Difficulties that have occurred in discussing them. With an Application to the Currency of this Country. *Philadelphia.* 1832. 8vo. W.

An Essay on Duelling. *New York.* 1830. 8vo, pp. 29.

An Essay on Flogging in the Navy; containing Strictures upon existing Naval Laws, and suggesting Substitutes for the Discipline of the Lash. *New-York: Pudney & Russell, Printers.* 1849. 8vo, pp. 56, 23. S. 22940

An Essay on Free Trade. *See* [Webster (P.)]

An Essay on Hereditary Titles, and University Degrees, ... By a New-England Farmer. *Boston: Caleb Bingham.* 1798. 8vo, pp. 40. BA., W. 22941

Essay on Import Duties and Prohibitions. *Philadelphia.* 1821.

Essay on Civil and Religious Liberty. *London.* 1777. 12mo.

Essay on Modern Martyrs. *See* Burgoyne (J.), No. 9261.

An Essay on Money, as a Medium of Commerce; with Remarks on Paper Money. *Philadelphia.* 1786. P. 22944

An Essay on Naturalization and Allegiance. *Washington City: Printed by Daniel Rapine.* 1816. 8vo, pp. 127, xiv. C.

An Essay on Plantership, &c. By an Old Planter. *Antigua.* 1750. P. 22946

Essay on Political Society. ... *Whitehall: Printed by William Young, Philadelphia.* 1800. 8vo, pp. 234. BA., P. 22947

Essay on Slavery. *Philadelphia.* 1790. 8vo. W. 22948

An Essay on Sugar, ... with Remarks on a Method lately published of procuring a Fermentation in the West Indies. *London.* M DCC LII. 8vo, pp. (iv), 33. 22949

Essay on the Abolition, not only of the African Slave Trade, but of Slavery in the British West Indies. *London: T. Becket.* 1792. 22950

An Essay on the African Slave Trade. *London.* 1790. 8vo, + *Philadelphia: Daniel Humphreys* M.DCC.XC. 8vo. BA.

See "M. Rev.," XI. 223.

An Essay On the Agitations of the Sea, and some other Remarkables Attending the Earthquakes of the Year M,DCC,L,V. To which are added, Some Thoughts on the Causes of Earthquakes, Written in the Year 1756. *Boston: Printed by B. Mecom.* 1761. 8vo, pp. 40. H., M. 22952

Essay on the Antiquities of Great Britain. *See* [Malcolm (D.)]

An Essay on the Climate of the United States: or, an Inquiry into the Causes of the Difference in Climate between the Eastern Side of the Continent of North America and Europe. With Practical Remarks on the Influence of Climate on Agriculture ... *Philadelphia: Hopkins & Earle.* 1809. 8vo, pp. 42. BA. + Second Edition. *Philadelphia: E. L. Carey & A. Hart.* 1833. 8vo, pp. 44. H. 22953

An Essay on the Constitutional Power. *See* [Dickinson John)], Vol. v., No. 20040.

Essay on the Courses pursued by Great Britain, in the Affairs of her Colonies, and in the great importance of our Settlements in America. *London.* 1755. 8vo. 22954

Title from an English sale catalogue

Essay on the Dissolution of the Union. *See* [Carey (M.)], Vol. III., No. 10889, *note.*

Essay on the Earthquake of 1755. *Boston.* 1761. 8vo. B.

Essay on the Effects of Slavery on the Moral Character, &c. of a Nation, read before the Connecticut Society for the Promotion of Freedom to Bondmen. *Printed at Hartford.* 1793. 8vo, pp. 66. 22956

An Essay on the Establishment of a Chancery Jurisdiction in Massachusetts. ... *Boston: Farrand, Mallory & Co.* [n. d.] 8vo, pp. 90. BA. 22957

An Essay on the Intellectual, Moral and Religious Instruction of the Youth of this State, ... by Means of Common Schools. ... *Troy.* 1834. 8vo pp. 43. H., S. 22958

An Essay on the Interests of Britain in regard to America; or, An Outline of the Terms on which Peace may be restored to the Two Countries. *London: J. Sewell.* MDCCLXXX. 8vo, pp. 23.

"After expatiating, with good sense, on the impolicy of our continuing the war in North America, the author proceeds to enumerate the terms on which a happy union between the two countries might be effected; and which, he says, he is well assured would be received by America." — *M. Rev.*, LXII. 492.

Essay on the late Institution of the American Society for Colonizing the Free People of Color of the United States. *Washington: Printed by Davis and Force.* 1820. 8vo, pp. 84.

An Essay on the Legality of Impressing Seamen. *London: T. Cadell.* MDCCLXXVII. 8vo, pp. (2), 126. 22961

Essay on the Liberty of the Press. *See* [Hay (G.)]

Essay on the Management of the present War with Spain, as far as it has been hitherto Conducted on the part of Great Britain. By an Impartial Hand. *London.* 1740. 8vo. 22962

An Essay, on the Manufacture of Straw Bonnets, containing an Historical Account of the Introduction of the Manufacture, its effects upon the Employments, Dress, Food ... of the Inhabitants of the Several Towns in which it has been carried on ... . *Providence: Barnum, Field & Co.* 1825. 12mo, pp. 676. H.

An Essay on the Manufacturing Interest of the United States; with Remarks on some Passages contained in the Report of the Committee of Commerce on Manufactures. By a Member of the Society of Arts and Manufacturers of Philadelphia. To which is annexed, The Memoirs of that Society to Congress. *Philadelphia: Bartholomew Graves.* 1804. 8vo, pp. 32, xvii.

An Essay on ... Merchandize. *See* [Dudley (Paul)], Vol. v., No. 21087.

Essay on the Means of Maintaining the Commercial and Naval Interests of the United States. [n. p. n. d.] 8vo. W. 22965

An Essay on the ... West Indian Diseases. *See* West Indies.

An Essay on ... Colonies, 1775. *See* [Mirabeau.]

An Essay on ... Nova Scotia. *See* Nova Scotia.

Essay on the Principal Branches of Trade of New England. *London.* 1715. 8vo. 22966

Essay on the Right of Conquest. *Florence, privately printed.* 1783. 8vo. 22967

Title from an English catalogue of Americana.

An Essay on the Rights and Duties. *See* [Everett (D.)]

An Essay on the Seat of the Federal Government. *See* Vol. v., No. 20303.

Essay on the Slave Trade. *London: J. Nicol.* 1788. 22968

See "M. Rev.," LXXVIII. 430.

Essay on ... Slavery. *See* [Clarkson (T.)], Vol. IV., No. 13484.

An Essay on the South Sea Trade; with an Enquiry into the grounds of the present dislike and complaint against the Settlement of a South-Sea Company. By the Author of the Review. *London: John Baker.* 1712. 8vo, pp. 47. J.C.B. + Second Edition. [*Ibid.*] 22969

Rich ascribes this to Robert Allen; it is more probably by Daniel Defoe. *See our* Nos. 862 and 863.

An Essay on the Trade of the Northern Colonies of Great Britain in North America. Printed at Philadelphia. *London: Reprinted for T. Becket and P. A. De Hondt.* MDCCLXIV. 8vo, 2 l., pp. 38. BA., C. 22970

"The subject of this essay is treated in a masterly and judicious manner, by one who appears to be perfectly well acquainted with it." — *M. Rev.*, XXX. 464.

An Essay on the Use and Advantages of the Fine Arts; Commencement, New Haven, Sept. 12, 1770. *New Haven.* [1770.] 8vo, pp. 16. M. 22971

Essay on the Warehousing System and Government Credits of the United States. *Philadelphia.* 1828. 8vo, pp. 57. P.

An | Essay | on | Trade and Commerce ; | Containing | Observations on Taxes, | As they are supposed to affect | The Price of Labour in our Manufactories ; Together with Some interesting | Reflections on the Importance | of our | Trade to America, | To which is added the | Out-lines, or Sketch of a Scheme | For the | Maintenance and Employment | of | the Poor | ... | *London :* | *S. Hooper.* MDCCLXX. | 8vo, pp. xiv, 302. 22973

An Essay upon Government, adopted by the Americans. Wherein, The Lawfulness of Revolutions, are Demonstrated ... *Philadelphia.* MDCCLXXV. 8vo, pp. 125. BA. 22974

An Essay upon that Paradox. *See* [Walter (T.)]

An Essay upon the Constitutional Rights as to Slave Property, Republished from the "Southern Literary Messenger." *Richmond. Thos. W. White.* 1840. 8vo, pp. 20. 22975

An Essay upon the Government of The English Plantations on The Continent of America ; Together with some Remarks upon the Discourse on the Plantation Trade, Written by the Author of the Essay on Ways and Means, and Published in the Second Part of His Discourses, on the Publick Revenues and on the Trade of England. By an American. *London : Printed for Richard Parker.* 1701. 8vo, 16 l., pp. 86, (2). BA., H.

Essay upon the King's Friends, with an Account of some Discoveries made in Italy and found in a Virgil concerning the Tories, to Dr. S——l J——n. *London.* 1776. 8vo. 22977

Included in J. R. Smith's catalogue of "Americana."

Essays against the Repeal of the Bankrupt Law. Louisville Journal. *Louisville.* [n. d.] 8vo, pp. 8. M. 22978

Essays and Observations Physical and Literary, published by a Society in Edinburgh. *Edinburgh.* 1754. 2 vols., 8vo. Plates.

Contains papers on the "Natural History of America," etc., by Dr. J. Lining and Dr. Alex. Garden, of Charleston, etc.

Essays Commercial and Political, on the Real and Relative Interests of Imperial and Dependent States, Particularly those of Great Britain and her Dependencies : Displaying the Probable Causes of, and a Mode of Compromising the present Disputes

Between this Country and her American Colonies. To which is added an Appendix, on the Means of Emancipating Slaves, Without Loss to their Proprietors. *Newcastle : T. Saint, for the Author. London : J. Johnson.* MDCCLXXVII. 8vo, pp. viii, (1), 147, (1), 1 l., folded after p. 6. BA., H. 22980

"In favor of the independence of New England, and would make the most of the Southern colonies ; but rather than lose the whole, proposes that they should be divided with some of the maritime States of Europe." — *M. Rev.*, LVI. 149.

Essays designed to elucidate the Science of Political Economy, while serving to explain and defend the Policy of Protection to Home Industry. ... *Boston.* 1870. 12mo. S. 22981

Essays on Husbandry. *See* [Harte (Walter)].

Essays on Political Organization, selected from among those submitted in Competition for the Prizes offered by the Union League of Philadelphia. *Philadelphia : Collins, Printer.* 1868. 8vo, pp. 106. H. 22982

Perhaps by W. E. Barber.

Essays on Political Society. *Philadelphia.* 1800. 8vo. B.

Essays on the Origin of Pauperism and Crime. *Boston.* 1841. 16mo. B. 22984

Essays on the Origin of the Federal Government ; tending to show that it emanates not from the People collectively, but from the People of the Respective States, acting as Confederate Sovereignties. Selected from a Series of Essays, published at various times in The Charleston Mercury. *Charleston : printed by A. S. Miller.* 1830. 8vo, pp. 28. 22985

Essays on the Present Crisis. *See* [Evarts (J.)]

Essays on the Principles of Political Economy. 1805. 12mo.

Essays on the Protecting System. Three of the Addresses of the Philadelphia Society for the Promotion of National Industry. Published in Philadelphia, in the year 1819. ... Extract from a Message of Governor Wolcott, of Connecticut. *Philadelphia : Mifflin & Parry.* 1830. 8vo, pp. 72. 22987

Essays on ... Jacksonism. *See* [McKenney (T. L.)]

Essays on National Policy. *See* [Tucker (George)].

Essays tending. *See* [Carey (M.)], Vol. III., No. 10867.

Essays upon the Making of Salt-Petre and Gun-Powder. Published by order of the Committee of Safety of the Colony of New York. *New-York : Samuel Loudon.* M DCC LXXVI. 8vo, pp. 39. 22988

Thirteen Essays on the Policy of Manufacturing in this Country ; from the New York Morning Herald. *Philadelphia.* 1830. 8vo, pp. 30. 22989

The Essential Rights and Liberties of Protestants. A Seasonable Plea for the Liberty of Conscience and Right of Private Judgment in Matters of Religion, without any Controul from Human Authority. Being a Letter from a Gentleman in Massachusetts to his Friend in Connecticut, &c. *Boston.* 1744. 4to, pp. 66. N., W. 22990

ESSEQUEBO. Brieven over het bestuur der colonien Essequebo en Demerary, gewisseld tusschen Aristodemus en Sincerus met bijlagen en eene voorreden van den Nederl. uitgever. *Amsterdam.* 1785-88. 12 pts., 8vo. 22991

Letters on the government of the colonies Essequebo and Demerara.

Deductie van den representant ... van de West-Ind. Comp. over de saake van Isequebo en Demerari. 1767. Folio, pp. 72.

Memorie van Remarques van Bewinthebb. der Gen. Geoctroy. West-Indische Compagnie ter Kamer Zeeland van 3 Febr. 1773, betreffende het graven van een canaal van communicatie tusschen Essequebo en Demerary. 1773. Folio, pp. 137. 22993

Missive van de Hoofd participanten der Geoctroyeerde West-indische Compagnie ter Kamer Zeeland aan Haar Hoog Mogende 26 Nov. 1765, concernerende de gerezene geschillen over de Colonie van Essequibo en onderhorige Rivieren, op den 3 Dec. daaraanvolgende door Gecommitteer de Hoofd participanten aan Heeren Gedeputeerde uit Haar Hoog Mog. Vergadering over gegeven. *Middleburg.* 1765. Folio, pp. 29. 22994

Plan van Accomodement, waar door de Vaart en Handel op Essequebo en Demerary voor alte Ingezeetenen van den Staat het geheele Jaar door, Vry en Open zoude worden gesteld. [n. p. 1775.] 8vo, pp. 18. + Nieuw Plan. [n. p. 1784.] 8vo, pp. 11. J.C.B. 22995

Reglement, contineerende restrictien en bepaalingen, onder welken de Vaart en Handel op de Colonie van Essequibo en Demarary, voor alle de Commercieerende Ingezeetenen van den

Staat, met den 1 January van het aanstaande jaar 1771 zal worden opengestelt, by Zyne Hoogheid, uit kragte del Delatie vande Heeren Staaten Generael der vereenigde Nederlanden gearresteert. *'sGravenshage.* 1771. Folio, pp. 5. J.C.B. 22996

Regulations for the Administration of Justice and manner of Proceedings in the Rivers Essequebo and Demerary. *Demerary.* 1811. 4to. 22997

In English and Dutch.

Resolutie van Haar Hoog Mogende de Heeren Staten Generaal der Vereenigde Nederlanden, de dato 16 January 1772. Contineerende nadere Poincten omtrent den Vaart en Handel op de Colonie van Essequebo en Demerary. *Amsterdam.* [n. d.] 4to, pp. 7. 22998

ESSEX, *brig.* Case of the Brig Essex, of Salem ; Jos. Orne, Master. *London.* 1803. Folio, pp. 26. M. 22999

ESSEX COMPANY, *Lawrence, Mass.* Report presented to the Stockholders of the Essex Company, May 25, 1852. *Boston.* 1852. 8vo, pp. 14. M., S. 23000

ESSEX CO., *Mass.* The Essex County Directory for the Year ... 1866. *Boston : Briggs & Co.* 1866. 8vo, pp. 224, 152. Continued. C. 23001

Contributions to the Ecclesiastical History of Essex County, Mass. ... *Boston : Congregational Board of Publication.* 1865. 8vo, pp. xi, 396. BA. 23002

Declaration of the County of Essex ... Massachusetts, by its Delegates, assembled in Convention at Ipswich, ... the 21st of July, 1812. *Salem.* 1812. 8vo, pp. 16. H., N. 23003

Premiums offered by the Essex Agricultural Society, December 7, 1819. *Salem : T. C. Cushing.* 8vo, pp. 7. Continued.

Transactions of the Essex Agricultural Society [with the Annual Addresses], 1818. *Salem, Massachusetts.* 1818. 8vo. Continued. BA., H. 23005

Essex Almanack For the Year ... 1773 ... Calculated for the Meridian of Salem, in New England. ... By Philo Freeman. *Salem. S. & E. Hall.* 12mo. Continued. 23006

Perhaps there are some of earlier date.

Resolutions. At a Meeting of Delegates from the Several Towns in the County of Essex, at Topsfield, ... October 6th, 1808. ... *Newburyport : E. W. Allen.* [1808.] 8vo, pp. 14, (1).

The Result of Convention at Ipswich. *See* [Parsons (Theophilus)].

Rules and Orders for the Houses of Correction in the County of Essex. *Salem.* 1857. 12mo. B. 23008

Rules and Regulations of the Bar in the County of Essex ... . *Salem : Printed by Thomas C. Cushing.* 1808. 8vo, pp. 16. BA.

Journal of the Essex-County Natural History Society. *Salem : Wm. Ives & Co.* 1836. 8vo, pp. 135, (1). Continued. H.

Essex Historical Society. Petition for Incorporation ; with the Constitution. *Salem.* 1821. 8vo, pp. 8. 23011

ESSEX INSTITUTE. Act of Incorporation, Constitution and By-Laws of the Essex Institute, Incorporated February, 1848. With a Catalogue of the Officers and Members. *Salem : Wm. Ives and Geo. W. Reed.* 1855. 8vo, pp. 24. BA., H., M. 23012

Bulletin of the Essex Institute. ... Jan. 1869. *Salem : Essex Institute Press.* 1869. 8vo. Continued. B., H. 23013

Historical Collections of the Essex Institute, Volume I. *Salem : for the Institute by Henry Whipple & Son.* 1859. 4to, Title, pp. (2), 206. Continued. H. + Second Series, Part 1, 2. *Salem : Essex Institute Press.* 1868-69. 8vo. BA., H. 23014

A Historical Notice of the Essex Institute ; with the Act of Incorporation, Constitution and By-Laws, and Lists of the Officers and Members. *Salem : Printed by the Institute.* 1866. 8vo, pp. 44. H. 23015

Proceedings of the Essex Institute. Vol. I., 1848 to 1856. *Salem.* 1856. 8vo. Continued. BA., H. 23016

Also : Report of Committee on the First Church of the Pilgrims, June 19, 1865. 8vo, pp. 8.

ESSEX CO., *N. Y.* Proceedings of the Board of Supervisors of the County of Essex, for 1866. *Keeseville.* 1866. 8vo. Continued. S. 23017

Minutes of the Essex Baptist Association. *New York.* 1815. 8vo. Continued. S. 23018

Essex Junto, or Quixotic Guardian : a Comedy. By a Citizen of Massachusetts. *Salem.* 1802. 12mo. W. 23019

See also Hancock, *pseudonym.*

The Essex Junto and the British Spy ; or, Treason Detected. *Printed at Salem.* 1812. 8vo, pp. 36. B., M. 23020

Documents from John Henry.

Essex Street Church and Society. *See* Boston, Vol. II., No. 6641.

ESTABROOK (H.) The Blameless Bishop. Sermon at Ordination of Rev. Joseph Fowler, East Haddam, May 15, 1751. By Rev. Hobart Estabrook. *New London.* 1752. 8vo, pp. 36.

ESTABROOK. The Praying Warrior. Sermon preach'd at Millington, in East Haddam, May 30, 1758, at the desire of Major Joseph Spencer and the other Officers and Company under him, before the Expedition against Canada. By Hobart Estabrook. *New Haven.* 1758. 8vo, pp. 23. M. 23022

ESTABROOK (J.) Abraham the Passenger his Privilege and Duty ... Election-Sermon ... May 30. 1705. By Joseph Easterbrooks ... . *Boston : Bartholomew Green.* 1705. 4to, pp. (2), 22. B., W. 23023

ESTABROOK (J.) ... A Discourse, delivered Feb. 22, 1819, at the Interment of the Rev. Joseph Lee, A.M. ... . By Joseph Estabrook, A.M. ... . *Worcester : printed by William Manning.* 1819. 8vo, pp. 19. H. 23024

Also : Popular Education. An Address delivered at the Annual Commencement of East Tennessee College, September 12, 1838 ... . *Knoxville.* 1858. 8vo, pp. 18.

ESTABROOK (Samuel). A Sermon Shewing that the Peace and Quietness Of a People Is a main part of the Work of Civil Rulers. Deliver'd at Hartford May the 8th. 1718. the Day for the Election. *New-London.* 1718. 8vo, Title, pp. 26. B.

[ESTABROOKS (Henry L.)] Adrift in Dixie ; or, A Yankee Officer among the Rebels. With an Introduction by Edmund Kirke. *New York : Geo. W. Carleton.* 1866. 12mo, pp. 224.

ESTACIO DO AMARAL (M.) Tratado, Das | Batalhas, e Svcessos do | Galeão Sanctiago com os Olandeses na Ilha de | Sancta Elena. E da Não Chagas com os Yngleses | antre as Ilhas dos Açores : Ambas Capitainas da | carreira da India. E da causa, & desastres, por- | qve em vinte annos se perderão trinta & | oito naos della : com ontras | cousas curiosas. | Escripto por Melchior Estacio do Amaral. | Dirigido ao Excellentissimo Principe Dom | Theodosio Duque de Bragança | *Impresso em Lisboa : Com licença d*

Sancta Inqui- | sição : Por Antonio Aluarez. Anno 1604. | 4to, pp. (2), 66 l. Map. 23027

Reprinted in Gomes de Britos' "Historia," Vol. II. 1736.

Estado de Occidente. *Mexico.* 1828. 12mo. 23028

Estado General de las Misiones que tiene à su cargo la religion seráfica en las dos Americas é islas Filipinas segun consta de los documentos mas modernos y seguros que se han remitido à este oficio de la comisaria general de Indias. *Madrid.* 1788. Folio, pp. 28. 23029

Estado de colectura y tesoreria a que hace referencia el mensaje del gobierno del estado en la parta de haciende de 1856. *Buenos Aires.* 1856. 4to, pp. 18. 23030

[ESTAING (Charles Hector, *Count* d').] Apperçu hazardé sur l'exportation dans les colonies. Dédié a feu M. Franklin. *Paris : De l'imprimerie de L. Potier de Lille.* 1790. 8vo, pp. 64. H.

ESTAING. Déclaration adressée au nom du roi à tous les anciens François de l'Amérique Septentrionale. *À bord du vaisseau Languedoc, en rade de Boston, F. P. Demauge.* 1778. Folio, 1 l.

ESTAING. Extrait du Journal d'un Officier de la Marine de l'Escadre de M. Le Comte D'Estaing. [*Paris?*] 1782. 8vo, pp. (2), 158. Portrait. N., S. + [Another Edition.] 1782. 8vo, pp. 126. J.C.B., H. 23033

[ESTAING.] Journal d'un Officier de l'Armée Navale en Amérique, en 1781 & 1782. *Amsterdam.* M,DCC,LXXXIII. 8vo, pp. (2), 72. 23034

All these pamphlets by Estaing are of great rarity.

ESTANCELIN (L.) Recherches sur les voyages et découvertes des navigateurs normands en Afrique, dans les Indes orientales et en Amérique, suivies d'observations sur la marine, le commerce et les établissements coloniaux des Français. 1832. Par L. Estancelin. *Paris : Delaunay et A. Pinard.* 1832. 8vo, pp. xii, 361, (2). 23035

Contains an account of "the supposed expedition of Cousin of Dieppe to Brazil in 1488." — HARRISSE'S *Bibl. Am. Vet.*, p. 173.

L'Estat de l'Eglise avec le discorse des Temps, depuis les Apos tres sous Neron jusques à present ; sous Charles V, contenant en bref les Histories tant anciennes que nouvelles, celles specialement qui concernent l'Empire et le Siege Romaine, entre autres l'Affaires des Indies Occidentales. 1556. 8vo. 23036

Estat | present | de l'Eglise | et de la | Colonie Francoise | dans la Nouvelle | France, | Par M. l'Eveque de Quebec. | *A Paris,* | *Chez Robert Pepee,* ... | M.DC.LXXXVIII. 8vo, pp. (2), 268. 23037

Les Estats Empires. *See* Davity, Vol. V. No. 18913.

Estatutos de la Sociedad anónima denominada Banco Industrial. *Habana.* 1865. 8vo, pp. 20. 23038

Estatutos y Ordenaciones segun las Bulas que nuestro S. Padre Inocencio XI. expedió para los Colegios de Misioneros. ... para el Colegio de Propaganda Fide de nuestro Seráfico Padre de San Francisco de Pachuca en la Nueva España. *Madrid.* 1791. 4to. 23039

For other "Estatutos," *see* under the name of the *place* or the institution.

ESTAUGH (J.) A Call to the Unfaithful Professors of Truth. Written by John Estaugh in his life-time ; and now published for General Service. To which is added divers Epistles of the same Author. *Philadelphia : printed by B. Franklin.* M,DCC,XLIV. 12mo, pp. xviii, 119. P. 23040

The author was a New Jersey Quaker preacher. It was reprinted as below :

ESTAUGH. A Call to the Unfaithful Professors of Truth. Written by John Estaugh, who departed this life in the Island of Tortola in America ; to which is added Divers Epistles of the same author. *London : T. Sowle Raylton and Luke Hinde.* 1745. 8vo, pp. xvi, 63. + *Dublin : Printed by Isaac Jackson.* 1845. 12mo, pp. 104. + *London.* 1753. 8vo. 23041

ESTCOURT (J. H.) Rebellion and Recognition. Slavery, Sovereignty, Secession, and Recognition considered. By J. H. Estcourt. [*Manchester, England.*] 1863. 8vo, pp. 28. H.

ESTE (D. K.) Discourse on the Life and Public Services of the late Jacob Burnet, delivered ... By D. K. Este, ... 21st of June, 1853. *Cincinnati.* 1853. 8vo, pp. 25. 23043

ESTEE (C. F.) The Excise Tax Law. Approved July 1, 1862 ; and all the Amendments ... . *New York : Fitch, Estee & Co.* 1863. 8vo, pp. 355. BA. 23044

ESTES (Benjamin H.) Essay on the Necessity of Correcting the Errors which have crept into the Washingtonian Temperance Movement. *New York.* 1846. 8vo. 23045

ESTES (M.) A Defence of Negro Slavery, as it exists in the United States. By Matthew Estes. ... . *Montgomery.* 1846. 24mo, pp. 260. BA. 23046

ESTEVA (G. A.) Légère réfutation d'un Mexicain aux injustes affirmations et nombreuses inexactitudes des Lettres sur Mexique, publiées dans la Patrie des 2, 3, 4 et 5 août; par Gonzalo A. Esteva. *Paris: Ballitout, Questroy et Ce.* 1865. 8vo, pp. 15.

ESTEVA (J. I.) Exposicion sú Ministro de Hacienda. *Mexico.* 1840–51. 23048

ESTEVA. Guia de hacienda de la republica Mexicana. Parte legislativa. *Mexico.* 1825–28. 4 vols., 24mo. 23049

ESTEVA (J. Y.) Rasgo analitico. *Mexico.* 1827. 4to, pp. 100. 23050

ESTEYNEFFER (H. J. de). Florilegio Medicinal de todas las Enfermedades, sacado de varios y clasicos Authores, y de los 'atta de Medicos, en particular para las Provincias Remotas ... . Por Hermano Juan de Esteyneffer, de la Compañia de Jesus. *Amsterdam.* 1712. 4to, pp. 515 and Index. 23051

A complete treatise on medicine, divided into three books. The first and the second deal with diseases, and the third is a "Catalogo de los Medicamentos, y el modo de componerlos." It relates some curious particulars concerning the diseases among the Indians. The work is extremely rare. Trübner quotes an edition, "*Mexico.* 1713," which date is rather doubtful.

Esther Institute. Catalogue for the First, Second and Third Years, ending June 29, 1855. *Columbus (Ohio).* 1855. 8vo.

ESTIMANVILLE (R. d'). Cursory View of the Local, Social, Moral, and Political State of the Colony of Lower Canada. By the Chevalier R. d'Estimanville. *Quebec.* 1829. 8vo. N.

ESTLACKE (Francis). A Bermudas Preacher proved a Persecutor. Being a Just Tryal of Sampson Bond's Book, entituled, "A Publick Tryal of the Quakers, &c." Fraught with Fallacies, False Doctrine, Slanders, Railings, Aspersions, Perversions, and other abuses, herein Detected, Disproved, and Wiped off. ... by ... Eye and Ear Witnesses in the Dispute at Bermudas; ... *London: Printed by John Bringhurst.* 1683. 4to, 17 sheets.

William Wilkinson, R.R., and John Tysoe, wrote part of this book.

ESTLIN (J. B.) A Brief Notice of American Slavery, and the Abolition Movement. By J. B. Estlin ... . *Bristol: H. C. Evans.* MDCCXLVI [1846]. 24mo, pp. 40. + Second Edition, Revised. *London: William Tweedie.* [1853.] pp. 54. B., BA.

ESTLIN. Reply to a Circular issued by the Glasgow Associaion for the Abolition of Slavery recommending a Discontinuance of British Support to the Boston Anti-Slavery Bazaar. ... *Paris.* 1850. 8vo, pp. 8. H. 23056

ESTRADA (A. F.) Constitucion para la Nacion Española; presentada à la Junta Suprema Guvernativa de España è Indias, en Noviémbre de 1810. Por Don Alvaro Florez Estrada. *Birmingham.* 1810. 8vo. C. 23057

ESTRADA. Exámen Imparcial de les Dissensiones de la America con la España de los Medios de su Reconciliacion, y de la Prosperidad de todas las Naciones. Por Don Alvaro Florez Estrada, Procurador General des Principado de Asturias. *London.* 1812. 4to, pp. (2), 283, (2). + Segunda impresion corregida, y aumentada. *Cadiz: D. M. Ximenez Carreño.* 1812. 4to, 1 l., pp. 283, 1 l. H. 23058

ESTRADA. An Impartial Examiation of the Dispute between Spain and her American Colonies. By Alvaro Florez Estrada. Translated from the Original, by W. Burdon. *London: Sherwood, Neely & Jones.* 1812. 8vo, pp. viii, 199. C., H. 23059

ESTRADA (Francisco). Carta imparcial sobre el Fuero del Clero. *Mexico.* 1812. 4to, pp. 23. 23060

ESTRADA (F. L.) Defensa de D. Francisco Lazo Estrada, Redactor del Boletin de la Democracia, contra la acusacion que le hizo D. Ignacio Trigueros, Gobernador del Distrito federal, pronunciado ante el Jurado de sentencia que se reunió en Mexico el dia 20 de Julio del presente año. *Toluca.* 1847. 8vo, pp. 32.

ESTRADA (J.) Brevis Relatio Missionum Soc. Jesu in America Septentrionali, in quibus tum excolendis, tum extendendis insudat Provincia Mexicana ejusdem Societatis; et Exhibitio status, quem earum Missionum res hoc tempore tenent, in quarum subsidium hoc labente anno 1691, Rex noster Catholicus Carolus II facultatem concessit transferendi eo sexaginta viros apostolicos Provinciis tum sibi, tum Imperatori subditis selectos. Proposita R. R. Patribus Societatis Jesu in Europæ Provinciis degentibus per R. P. Joannem de Estrada pro Provincia Mexicana Romæ Procuratorem. 12mo. 23062

"Cinelli, II, 264, suppose cette relation imprimée à anvers." — CARAYON, 191.

ESTRADA (J. M. G. de). Le Mexique et Maximilien, par Guitterez de Estrada. Portraits. *Paris.* 1862. 23063

ESTRADA. Lettre adresée à Mons. le Redacteurr du Courrie des deux Mondes. *Paris.* 1841. 8vo. 23064

ESTRADA (J. M.) El Catolicismo y la democracia. Refutacion á la América en Peligro del Senor D. Francisco Bilbao. Por José Manuel Estrada. *Buenos Aires.* 1862. 8vo, pp. 126.

ESTRADA (J. E.) Elogio de Nostra Senora de Guadalupe. *Megico.* 1766. 4to. 23066

ESTRADA. Ensayo histórico sobre la revolucion de los comuneros del Paraguay, en el siglo XVIII., seguido de un apendice sobra la decadencio del Paraguay y la guerra de 1865. Por José Manuel Estrada. *Buenos-Aires.* 1865. 8vo, pp. x, 366.

ESTRADA. El génesis de Nuestrá Raza. Refutacion de una leccion del Dr. Gustavo Minelli sòbre la misma materia, por José Manuel Estrada. *Buenos Aires.* 1862. 4to, pp. 82.

ESTRADA (J. M. de). Sermon de la Santa Casa de Loreto, que en la solemnidad annual, con que la celébra el Noble Cuerpo de Abogados de esta Corte Guadalaxara, nuevo Reyno de Galicia dixo el P. M. Jph. Manuel de Estrada. *Mexico.* 1766. 4to, 6 l.

ESTRADA (P. de). Relacion|Svmaria|del Auto parti-|cvlar de Fee, qve el|Tribvnal del Santo Officio de la|Inquisicion de los Reynos, y Prouincias de la Nueua España, celebrò en la muy noble, y muy leal Ciudad de Mexico a los|diez y seis dias del mes de Abril, del año mil y seis-|cientos y quarenta y seis.| Siendo Inqvisideres Apostolicos en el, los|muy Illustres Señores Doctores Domingo Velez de Assas, y Argos, Don|Francisco de Estrada y, Escouedo, Don Iuan Saenz de Mañozca, y|Licenciado Don Bernabe de la Higuera, y Amarilla, y|Fiscal el Señor Don Antonio de|Gauiola.|Escribela|El Doctor Don Pedro de Estrada, y Escovedo,|Racionero de la Santa Iglesia Cathedral de Mexico, Abogado de|presos, y del Real Fisco del mesmo Tribunal.|Ofrecela|Al Illvstrissimo, y Reverendissimo Señor,|Don Iuan de Mañozca Arçobispo de Mexico del Consejo de su Majes-|tad en el de la Santa, y General Inquisicion, y Visitador General|de Tribunal del Santo Officio de esta Nueua|España.| *Impresso en Mexico, Por Francisco Robledo, Impressor del Se-|creto del Santo Officio, Año de* 1646.| Title, 1 l., 26 folioed l. 23070

ESTRADA (S. de). Copia augmentada de la Carta de edificacion del V. P. Sebastian de Estrada, professo de la Compañia de

Jesus: que dirige a su provincia de Nueva-España el P. Provincial Matheo Ansaldo. [Colophon:] *Esto, y las antecedentes cartas, impressas en Mexico. Año de* 1743. 4to, pp. 59. 23071

ESTRADA Y LECLER (M. D.) Articulos de Costumbres, etc. [Obras, tomo I, all published.] *Campeche.* 1853. 8vo.

ESTRUP (H. F. J.) Nogle Bemærkninger angaaende Grönlands Oysterbygde. *Kjöbenhavn.* 1824. 8vo. 23073

Estudios economico-politicos. *Mexico.* 1857. 8vo. 23074

ESTVÀN (B.) War Pictures from the South. By B. Estvàn, Colonel of Cavalry in the Confederate Army. With Illustrations. *London: Routledge.* 1863. 2 vols., post 8vo, pp. xiii, 1 l., 310; x, 320. Map and 10 Plates. BA., C. + *New York: D. Appleton & Co.* 1863. 12mo, pp. viii, 352. BA., H. 23075

ESTVÀN. Kreigsbilder aus Amerika. *Leipzig: F. A. Brockhaus.* 1864. 2 vols., 8vo, pp. xxviii, 435. 23076

ESTWICK (S.) Considerations on the Negroe Cause, commonly so called. Addressed to the Right Hon. Lord Mansfield. By Samuel Eastwick, Agent for Barbados. *London.* 1773. 8vo. + Second Edition. [*Ibid.*] 8vo. + Third Edition. *London: J. Dodsley.* 1788. 23077

See "M. Rev.," LXXVIII. 161.

[ESTWICK.] Considerations on the Present Decline of the Sugar Trade; and on the means which are proposed by the Refiners of London for Reinstating it. [*London:*] *Printed in the Year* MDCCLXXXII. 4to, pp. 58. 23078

ESTWICK. A Letter To the Reverend Josiah Tucker, D.D., Dean of Glocester, In Answer to His Humble Address and Earnest Appeal, &c. With a Postscript, in which The present War against America Is Shewn to be The Effect, Not of the Causes assigned by Him and Others, but of a fixed Plan of Administration, Founded in System: The Landed opposed to the Commercial Interest of the State, Being as the Means in order to The End. By Samuel Estwick, LL.D. ... *London: J. Almon.* M.DCC.LXXVI. 8vo, pp. 125. BA. 23079

"The author is a warm and zealous advocate for the Americans." — *M. Review,* LX. 477.

Etablissement de la compagnie du Canada. *See* Vol. III., No. 10442.

Etat Actuel de la Nouvelle-Ecosse. *See* [Hollingsworth (S.)]

De l'Etat et du sort des colonies. *See* [St. Croix (M. de)].

Etat du Personnel de la Marine et des Colonies, 1839. *Paris.* 1839. 4to. 23080

Etat général de la Marine et des Colonies pour les année 1827. *Paris.* 1827. 4to. Continued. 23081

Etat Physique, etc. *See* Almanach Américain, Vol. I., No. 941.

L'Etat present de la Grande-Bretagne sous le Regne de George I ou l'on trouve un Etat de l'Irlande une description des Etats que le Grand-Bretagne possede en Amérique en Afrique et dans la Mediterranée. *Amsterdam.* 1723. 3 vols., 8vo.

Etat Present de la Pensylvanie. *See* [Delaville (*Abbé*)], Vol. V., No. 19370. *See also* [Smith (W.)]

Les États Confédérés d'Amérique, visités en 1863. Mémoire addressé A. S. M. Napoleón III. *Paris: E. Dentu.* 8vo, pp. 160. Map. 23083

Etats indiquant le movement du commerce et de la marine ... 1850. [n. p. n. d.] Folio, pp. 17. 23084

États-Unis de l'Amérique. Pièces officielles, Messages, Instructions, Dépêches, &c. Relatives à la Negociation qui a eu Lieu en 1797 & 1798, sur les différens élevés entre le gouvernement des États-Unis de l'Amérique et le Directoire Exécutif de France. Traduites de l'Anglois. Par M. Peltier. *London: T. Baylis.* 1798. 8vo, pp. 70. 23085

Etats Unis et l'Angleterre. *See* [Lee (William)].

Les États-Unis en 1866. *Gèneve: Libraire J. Cherbuliez.* 1866. 8vo, pp. 22. B., C. 23086

[ETCHES (John).] An Authentic Statement of all the Facts relative to Nootka Sound; its Discovery, History, Settlement, Trade, and the probable Advantages to be derived from it; in an Address to the King. [Signed Argonaut.] *London: J. Debrett.* 1790. 8vo, Title, pp. 26. H. 23087

See Rich I. 364, *and* "M. Rev.," xi. 458.

[ETCHES.] A Continuation of An Authentic Statement, &c. With Observations on a Libel which has been tracted to a Foreign Ambassador. In a Second Letter, By Argonaut. *London: Fores.* 1790. 8vo, pp. 34. 23088

The libel was an article in the newspapers, supposed to be written by the Spanish minister, containing reflections on one of the proprietors of the Nootka Sound commerce. *See* "M. Rev.," XI. 48.

Ethel Somers, or the Fate of the Union, By a Southerner. *Augusta.* 1857. 12mo. 23089

ETHERIDGE (E.) Speech of Emerson Etheridge, of Tennessee, on The Revival of the African Slave Trade, and the President's Message, delivered ... Feb. 21, 1857. *Washington.* 1857. 8vo, pp. 16. BA. 23090

Also: State of the Union. A Speech ... delivered in the House of Representatives, Jan. 23, 1861. [n. p. n. d.] pp. 15.

Ethices Elementa; or The First Principles of Moral Philosophy. By Aristocles. *Boston.* 1746. 8vo, pp. 70. 23091

Perhaps the first treatise of its kind published in the English colonies.

The Ethics of American Slavery; being a Vindication of the Word of God and a Pure Christianity in all Ages, from Complicity with Involuntary Servitude. *New York: Ross & Tousey.* 1861. 12mo, pp. 146. 23092

ETIENNE, VARIN, *and* DESVERGERS. Arwed, ou les représailles, épisode de la guerre d'Amérique, drame en deux actes, mêlé de couplets; de MM. Etienne, Varin et Desvergers ... . *Paris: Bezou.* 1830. 8vo, pp. 56. 23093

Etliche|Zu dieser Zeit nicht unnûtze|Fragen|Über einige| Schrift-Stellen,|Welche|Von den Liebhabern der lautern Wahrheit|Deutlich erörtert zu werden gewûnschet hat|Ein|Wahrheit-forschender in America, im jahr 1742:|So deutlich und einfältig erörtert als es ihm môglich gewesen ist; und|in folgender klaren und bequemen Form herausgegeben|Von einem| Knecht Jesu Christi.|*Philadelphia: Gedruckt und zu haben bey B. Franklin.*| [n. d.] 4to, pp. 14. 23094

ÉTOURNEAU (*M.*) Le Général Washington et Madame la Générale Washington Biographies. Par M. Étourneau. Ornées Portraits historiques gravés sur acier. *Paris: Bestel et cie et Grassart.* 1860. 8vo, 4 l., pp. 96. 23095

ÉTOURNEAU. Les Mormons. Par Préface par Pierre Vinçard. *Paris: Bestel.* 1856. 18mo, 2 l., pp. xi, 282. Portrait of Joseph Smith. C. 23096

ÉTOURNEAU. De Paris au nouveau monde et du nouveau à Paris; narration d'un voyage de dix ans. *Paris: Bestel.* 1857–1859. 3 vols., 12mo. 23097

Études de théologie, de philosophie et d'histoire publiées par Ch. Daniel et J. Gagarin. *Paris.* 1858. 3 vols., 8vo. 23098

Pages 205–324 of Vol. III. contain a "Relation d'un voyage de Mexico à Guatémala dans le cours de l'année 1855."

ETZEL (Anton von). Grönland geographisch und statistisch beschrieben. Aus danischen Quellschriften. *Stuttgart: J. G. Cotta.* 1860. 8vo, pp. xiv, 655. C. 23099

ETZLER (J. A.) Die Auswanderung nach der Tropenwelt. *Ulm: Müller.* 1847. 16mo, pp. 51. 23100

Eugenia Marshall, or Early Scenes in Cumberland. *New York.* 1823. 32mo. 23101

Eugénie, ou la vierge du Canada. *Limoges: Barbou frères.* 1864. 12mo, pp. 76. Engr. 23102

EULALY. Antwoordt,|op sekeren Brief|Evlaly.|Vervatende de redenen waerom datmen|met den Vyandt in geen Conferentie| behoort te treden.|Door wien, ende met wat ordre de selve| voor den dagh gebracht ende versocht is.|Ende eyntlijck dat den Treves in alle manie-|ren schadelijck voor 't Landt is etc.| *Gedruckt in 't Iaer* M.DC.XXIX.| 4to, 8 l. 23103

Answer to a certain letter of Eulalius, containing the reasons why it was not advisable to enter into transactions with the enemy.

EULALY. Antwoordt,|op sekeren Brief|Evlaly.|Vervatende de redenen waerom datmen|met den Vyandt in gheen Conferentie|behoort te treden.|Door Wien, ende met wat ordre de selve|voor den dagh gebracht ende versocht is.|Ende eyntlijck dat den Treves in aller manieren|schadelijek voor 't Landt is, etc.|*Gedruckt in 't Iaer* M.DC.XXIX.| 4to, 8 l. 23104

Title precisely the same as No. 23103, except "aller," and the division of the lines; the next is a reprint of No. 23104.

EULALY. Antwoordt|Op sekeren Brieff|Evlalii.|Vervatende de redenen, waerom datmen|met den Vyandt in gheene Conferentie van|Treves en behoort te treden.|Als mede door wien,

ende met wat Ordre de sel-|ve voor den dach ghebracht, ende versocht is.|Ende eyndtlijck, dat den Treves in aller ma-|nieren| schadelijck is voor dese Landen, etc.| [Vignette.] *Ghedruckt in 't Iaer* M.DC.XXIX.| 4to, 8 l. 23105

Eulogies and Orations on Washington. *See* Washington (G.)

Eulogies delivered in the Senate and House of Representatives of the United States, on the Life and Character of Hon. John C. Calhoun, of South Carolina, Hon. Henry Clay, of Kentucky, and Hon. Daniel Webster, of Massachusetts. Compiled from Official Documents. *Washington.* 1856. 8vo. Portraits. 23106

EUMENES, *pseudonym.* *See* [Griffiths (William)].

EUPHRASEN (Bengt And.) Reise nach der schwedisch Westindischen Insel St. Bartholemi, und den Inseln St. Eustache und St. Christoph; oder Beschreibung der Sitten, Lebensart der Einwohner, Lage, Beschaffenheit und natürlichen Produkte dieser Inseln. Aus dem Schwedischen von Joh. Georg Lud. Blumhof. *Göttingen: Johann Christian Dieterich.* 1798. 12mo, pp. 308.

Europe and America in 1839. *London: Privately Printed.* 1839. 8vo. 23108

EUROPEAN AND NORTH AMERICAN RAILWAY. Plan for Shortening the Time of Passage between New-York and London ... Convention at Portland, Maine, and the Charter of the European and North American Railway ... . *Portland: Harmon & Williams.* 1850. 8vo, pp. 155, (1), 13, (1). BA., S. 23109

Documents in Relation to the European and North American Railway Company. *Portland.* 1851. Sm. 8vo. Maps.

European Delineation of American Character, as contained in a Letter from a Foreign Traveller in New-York to his Friend in London. *New York: J. Gray and Co.* 1820. 8vo, pp. 16.

The European Magazine, and London Review. ... By the Philological Society of London. *London: John Fielding.* [1782–1825.] 8vo. 23112

This valuable periodical occupied the same position with regard to literature and belles lettres, that the "Gentleman's Magazine" did for antiquarian and historical studies. The plates are numerous, and comprise Dusimitier's portraits of distinguished American characters, views, maps, etc.; it was continued to 1825, and forms eighty-nine volumes.

The European Traveller in America, contained in Three Letters to his Friend in London. *Hartford: Hudson & Goodwin.* M.DCC.LXXXV. 8vo, pp. 40. BA., J.C.B. 23113

In a copy I sold in 1859, several of these letters had the autograph signature of Jo. Young, but in Mr. Brown's catalogue they are ascribed to the Rev. Mr. Brockway, of Lebanon, in Connecticut.

EUSEBIUS. Evsebii | Cæsariẽsis Episcopi Chronicon: quod | Hieronymus presbyter diuino eius in- | genio Latinũ facere curauit, & us*que* in Va | lentem Cæsarẽ Romano adiecit eloquio. | Ad qum & Prosper & Matthæus Palmerius, & Matthias Palmerius demum | & Ioannes Multiuallis complura qu*ae* ad hæc us*que* | tempora sub | secuta | sũt | adiecere. | Henricvs | Stephan⁹. | [Colophon:] In alma Parisiorum Academia ... Millesimo quingen- | tesimo duodecimo. | Idibus ve- | ro Iu | nij. | 4to, Title, 1 l., 19 unnumbered l., leaves numbered 1–175. 23114

On leaf 172, in the continuation of the "Chronicle of Eusebius," will be found a curious account of seven Brazilians, who arrived at Rouen in 1509. Priced by Tross at 120 francs.

EUSEBIUS INERMATUS, *pseudonym.* *See* [Foxcroft (T.)]

EUSTACE (J. S.) Le Citoyen des États-Unis d'Amérique. Jean-Skey Eustace Général ... à ses Frères d'Armes. *Paris: De l'Imprimerie du Cercle Social.* 1793. 8vo, pp. 31. BA. 23115

EUSTACE. Exile of Major-General Eustace, a Citizen of The United States of America (of the State of Georgia), from the Kingdom of Great-Britain, by order of His Grace the Duke of Portland. *London: J. Parsons.* 1797. 8vo, pp. (2), xv, 48.

See "M. Rev.," XXIV. 348.

[EUSTACE.] Letters on the Crimes of George III., addressed to Citizen Denis, by an American Officer in the Service of France. *Paris: H. J. Jansen et Comp.* [1794.] 2 pts., 8vo, pp. 80; 135. B. 23117

[EUSTACE.] Lettres ... sur les Crimes du Roi George III. ... par un Officier Américain ... *Paris: De l'Imprimerie des Sans-Cullottes.* [1794.] 2 pts., 8vo, pp. xi, 80; 135. BA. 23118

EUSTACE. Official and Private Correspondence of Major General J. S. Eustace, ... Colonel and Adjutant-General in the Service of Georgia during the American War: and Maréchal-de-Camp in the Armies of the Republic of France. ... *Paris: Allard and Son.* MDCCXCVI. 8vo, pp. vi, 151. H. 23119

Also in French.

EUSTACE (T.) Adventures and Providential Deliverances of Thomas Eustace, who was Shipwrecked off Long Island, near New York, 18th January, 1809. *London.* 1820. 8vo. Portrait and Plate. 23120

EUSTIS (William). Mr. Eustis' Motion, Jan. 22, 1805. [*Washington.* 1805.] 8vo. 23121

Relates to the navy yards of the United States.

EUSTIS (W.) The Assassination Plot in New-York in 1776. A letter of Dr. William Eustis ... with Notes. By the Rev. Edmund F. Slafter, A.M. ... . *Boston: printed by David Clapp & Son.* 1869. 8vo, pp. 6. H. 23122

EUTAW. The Battle of the Eutaw Springs. A Drama in Five Acts. *Printed at* [*Charleston.* About 1790.] 8vo, pp. 52.

Eutaxia; or, the Presbyterian Liturgies. Historical Sketches, by a Minister of the Presbyterian Church. *New York: M. W. Dodd.* 1855. 12mo, pp. 260. 23124

Evangeliarium epistolarium, 1860. *See* [Sahagan (B.)]

El Evangelio de S. Lucas, del latin al Mexicano, ò mejor Nahuatl. *Impresso por Samuel Bagster, en Londres.* 1833. 8vo, pp. 139. 23125

Evangelical Almanac. *Albany.* 1823. 12mo. 23126

Evangelical Consociation. *See* Rhode Island.

Constitution of the Theological Seminary of the General Synod of the Evangelical Lutheran Church in the United States, etc. *Philadelphia.* 1826. 8vo. 23127

Also: Constitution of the Parent Education Society. *Gettysburg, Pa.* 1835. 12mo.

The Evangelical Lutheran Intelligencer, published under the Auspices of the Synod of Maryland and Virginia. Edited by D. F. Schaeffer. *Frederick.* 1828. 8vo. 23128

Formula for the Government and Discipline of the Evangelical Lutheran Church in Maryland and Virginia. *Hagerstown.* 1823. 8vo. 23129

Also in German. *See also* New York, Philadelphia, etc.

Rules and Regulations for the Government of the Evangelical Lutheran Ebenezer Church. *Albany.* 1851. 12mo. 23130

Evangelical Missionary Society. *See* Massachusetts.

The Evangelical Record and Western Review. Vol. I. 1812.

Evangelical Review: Edited by W. M. Reynolds, etc. *Gettysburg, Pa.* 1849. Continued. H. 23132

C. P. Krauth, W. M. Reynolds, and M. L. Stoever, editors of the later volumes.

The Evangelical Guardian and Review. By an Association of Clergymen in New-York. ... *New York: Published by Eastburn & Co.* 1817. 8vo, pp. 576. 23133

Two or more volumes published.

Evangelical Union Anti-Slavery Society. Address to the Churches of Jesus Christ, with the Constitution, April, 1839. *New York.* 1839. 8vo, pp. 51. M., S. 23134

[EVANS (A. E.)] Catalogue of ... Portraits, comprising ... persons connected with the History and Literature of ... The British Colonies, and the United States of America, accompanied by Concise Biographical Notices. *London: A. E. Evans & Son.* [1853.] 2 vols., 8vo, pp. 431; 393. 23135

[EVANS (A. J.)] Macaria; or, Altars of Sacrifice. By the Author of "Beulah." ... Second Edition. *Richmond: West & Johnston.* 1864. 8vo, pp. 183. BA., H. + *New York: John Bradburn.* [1865.] 12mo, pp. 469. + *New York: Carleton.* 1868. 12mo, pp. 469. 23136

EVANS (A.) Africa. A Poem. By Ann Evans. *Andover.* 1826. 23137

Relates to slavery.

[EVANS (Caleb).] A Letter to the Rev. Mr. John Wesley, Occasioned by his Calm Address to the American Colonies. *London: Printed for Edward and Charles Dilly.* M.DCC.LXXV. 12mo, pp. 24. + New Edition. *Bristol.* 1775. 23138

Signed "Americanus: Bristol, Oct. 2. 1775." "Wrote," says Wesley, "by two Anabaptist ministers, assisted by a gentleman and a tradesman of the Church of England." A clever piece, in favor of America. Reproduced as

EVANS. A Letter to the Rev. Mr. John Wesley, Occasioned by his Calm Address to the American Colonies. By Caleb Evans, M.A. A New Edition, To which are prefixed Some Observations on the Rev. Mr. Wesley's late Reply. *London: Edward & Charles Dilly.* MDCCLXXV. 12mo, pp. viii, 24.

"The publication of this pamphlet occasioned a greater surprise than can easily be described among all ranks of people. The surprise could not, I think, have been greater, had Lord North published a libel upon himself, and without taking the least

notice of so strange a revolution in his ideas, had reprobated his own proceedings with respect to America, and warmly pleaded in favor of the Americans." — EVANS' *Reply to Mr. Fletcher's Vindication,* page 4. *See also* Wesley (J.), *and* "M. Rev.," LIII. 350

EVANS. Political Sophistry Detected, or Brief Remarks on the Rev. Mr. Fletcher's late Tract entitled "American Patriotism." In a Letter to a Friend. By Caleb Evans, A.M. *Bristol: W. Pine.* 1776. 12mo, pp. 36. C. 23140

Rich says, *London: Dilly.* 1776. Perhaps there is another edition.

EVANS. A Reply to the Rev. Mr. Fletcher's Vindication of Mr. Wesley's Calm Address to our American Colonies. By Caleb Evans, M.A. *Bristol: W. Pine.* [1775.] 12mo, pp. 103.

"Mr. Evans is a lively and sensible advocate for the freedom of the colonies, a spirited controvertist, and a zealous asserter of those liberal and noble principles to which we are indebted for the glorious revolution." — *M. Rev.*, LIV. 326.

EVANS (C.) Biographical Notice of Joseph Hartshorne. By Charles Evans. Oct. 7, 1851. *Philadelphia.* 1852. 8vo. B.

Also: Account of the Asylum for the Relief of Persons deprived of Reason, near Frankford. ... *Philadelphia.* 1830. 8vo. B. — Considerations addressed to the Members of the Yearly Meeting of Friends, of Philadelphia. ... *Philadelphia.* 1846. 8vo. + *Boston: Printed by S. N. Dickinson & Co.* 1847. 8vo.

EVANS (C.), *Reporter.* *See* Chase (S.), Vol. III., No. 12204.

EVANS (D). Letter to Rev. Doc. Jones, containing some Remarks on the Circular Letter of the Philadelphia Baptist Association of 1791. [n. p. n. d.] 12mo. W. 23143

[EVANS (De Lacy).] Facts relating to the Capture of Washington, in Reply to some Statements contained in the Memoirs of Admiral Sir George Cockburn, G.C.B. By the Officer serving as Quarter-Master General with the Forces Engaged. *London: H. Colburn.* 1829. 8vo, pp. 20. 23144

Signed "D. L. Evans, Lieut. Col. D. Quarter-Master General with the force engaged."

EVANS (D. M.) The History of the Commercial Crisis 1857–58, and the Stock-Exchange Panic of 1859. By D. Morier Evans. *London: R. Groombridge.* 8vo, pp. 200.

EVANS (Elwood). Puget Sound: its Past, Present and Future. An Address delivered ... at Port Townsend, Washington Territory, January 5th, 1869. *Olympia, Wash. Ter.* 1869. 8vo, pp. 16. H. 23146

Also: Oration ... Portland, Oregon. July 4th, 1865. [*Portland.* 1865.] 8vo, pp. 16. H.

EVANS (E.) Essay on State Rights. (The first of a Series.) The Object of which is to define and illustrate the Spirit of our Institutions and of Liberty, and to renovate our Political Elements. By Estwick Evans, of the North. Second Edition. *Washington. January,* 1844. 8vo, pp. 40. 23147

EVANS (E.) A Pedestrious Tour, of Four Thousand Miles, through the Western States and Territories, during the Winter and Spring of 1818, Interspersed with Brief Reflections upon a Great Variety of Topics: ... . By Estwick Evans. ... *Concord, N. H.: Joseph C. Spear.* 1819. 12mo, pp. 256. Portrait of the author with his dogs. B., BA., C., H. 23148

EVANS. Estwick Evans for the Presidency. To the People of the United States. [*Washington. April,* 1864.] pp. 4. H.

Also: An Address at Portsmouth, July 4th, being the 48th Anniversary of American Independence, upon the occasion of erecting a Liberty-Pole. ... *Portsmouth.* 1824. 18mo, pp. 29. — Letter to the President of the United States [advocating the Immediate Abolition of Slavery]. Dated, *Washington, October,* 1862. 8vo, pp. 8. H. — A National Patriotic Poem, ... *Washington City: Gray & Ballantyne.* 1854. 8vo, pp. 34. H. + Second Edition. *Washington City.* 1854.

EVANS (F. A.) The Emigrant's Directory and Guide to obtain Lands and effect a Settlement in the Canadas. By Francis A. Evans, Esq. Late Agent for the Eastern Townships to the Legislature of Lower Canada. *William Curry, Jun. and Co. Dublin.* 1833. 18mo, pp. vi, iv, (2), 180. 23150

EVANS (F. W.) Autobiography of a Shaker, and Revelation of the Apocalypse. With an Appendix. By Frederick White Evans. *Mt. Lebanon,* (*Col. co. N. Y.*) *author.* 1869. 8vo, pp. 162. C. 23151

EVANS. Shakers. Compendium of the Origin, History, Principles, Rules and Regulations, Government, and Doctrines of the United Society of Believers in Christ's Second Appearing. With Biographies of Ann Lee, William Lee, James Whittaker, J. Hocknell, J. Meacham, and Lucy Wright. By F. W. Evans, *New York: D. Appleton and Company.* 1859. 18mo, pp. 189.

Also: Celibacy from the Shaker Stand-Point. ... *New York: Davis & Kent.* 1866. Sm. 12mo, pp. 12. B. — A Short Treatise on the Second Appearing of Christ. *Boston.* 1853. 12mo, pp. 24. — Tests of Divine Inspiration, ... True and False Revelation ... . *New Lebanon: Published by the United Society called Shakers.* 1853. 12mo, pp. 127.

EVANS. Speech of George Evans, of Maine, in Support of the Protective System. ... June 11, 1832. *Washington: Gales and Seaton.* 1832. 8vo, pp. 30. BA. 23153

Also: Speech in relation to the Failure of making Appropriations for Fortifications, ... delivered ... January 28, 1836. *Washington: Gales and Seaton.* 1836. 8vo, pp. 24. B., BA., M. — Speech ... on the Bill making Appropriations for the Naval Service, ... March 15, 1836. *Washington: Gales and Seaton.* 1836. 8vo, pp. 20. BA. — Speech ... upon ... the Northeastern Boundary. ... February 7 and 8, 1838. ... . *Washington: Gales and Seaton.* 1838. 8vo, pp. 36. B., S. — Speech ... upon the Resolutions of Mr. Clay, relating to the Revenues and Expenditure of the Government ... delivered in the Senate ... *Washington.* 1842. 8vo, pp. 44. B., S. — Speech ... upon the Resolutions of Mr. Clay ... and the Necessity of Augmented Duties upon Imports ... *Washington.* 1842. 8vo, pp. 44. — Speech ... on the Bill to authorize an Issue of Treasury Notes. ... Jan. 19, 1841. *Washington.* 1841. 8vo, pp. 28. B., H., M. — Speech on the ... Oregon Question ... in the Senate ... March 9 and 10, 1846. *Washington: Printed at the Intelligencer Office.* 1846. 8vo, pp. 36. BA., M. — The Tariff of 1842 Vindicated. Speech ... in Reply to Mr. McDuffie, United States Senate, Jan. 22 and 23, 1844. *Washington.* 1844. 8vo, pp. 40.

EVANS (*Gov.*) Reply of Governor Evans, of the Territory of Calorado. To that Part referring to him, of the Report of "the Committee on the Conduct of the War," headed "Massacre of Cheyenne Indians." [*Denver.* 1865.] 8vo, pp. 16, 5, (1). H.

An attempted exculpation of the Chivington massacre.

EVANS (H. B.) Jamaica a Source of National Wealth and Honour. By H. B. Evans. *London: E. Wilson.* 1853 *or* 5. 8vo.

EVANS. Our West Indian Colonies. *London: E. Wilson.* 1855. 8vo. 23156

EVANS (H. D.) An Essay on the Episcopate of the Protestant Episcopal Church in the United States of America. By Hugh Davey Evans, LL.D. ... . *Philadelphia: H. Hooker.* 1855. 8vo, pp. 196 *or* 250. 23157

EVANS (H. S.) A Map and a Guide to all the Emigration Colonies of Great Britain and America. By H. Smith Evans. *London: Letts.* 1855. 12mo. 23158

EVANS (I.) A Discourse, delivered, on the 18th Day of December, 1777, the Day of Public Thanksgiving, appointed by the Honourable Continental Congress. By the Reverend Israel Evans, A.M. ... *Lancaster: Francis Bailey.* M,DCC,LXXVIII. 12mo, pp. 24. H. 23159

EVANS. A Discourse, delivered at Easton, on the 17th of October, 1779, to the Officers and Soldiers of the Western Army, after their Return from an Expedition against the Five Nations of Hostile Indians. By the Reverend Israel Evans, A.M., Chaplain to General Poor's Brigade. *Philadelphia: Thomas Bradford.* M.DCC.LXXIX. 8vo, pp. 40. + *Lancaster.* 1779. 12mo.

EVANS. A Discourse Delivered Near York in Virginia, on the Memorable Occasion of the Surrender of the British Army to the Allied Forces of America and France, before The Brigade of New York Troops and the Division of American Light-Infantry, under the Command of the Marquis de la Fayette. | By Israel Evans, A.M. Chaplain to the Troops of New-Hampshire. *Philadelphia: Printed by Francis Bailey.* M.DCC.LXXXII. 8vo, pp. 45, (1). J.C.B. 23161

EVANS. A Discourse delivered in New-York before a Brigade of Continental Troops, and a Number of Citizens, assembled in St. George's Chapel, On the 11th December, 1783. The Day set apart by the Recommendation of The United States in Congress, As a Day of public Thanksgiving for the Blessings of Independence, Liberty and Peace. By the Rev[d]. Israel Evans, Chaplain in the American Army. *New York: John Holt.* [1783.] 8vo, pp. 23. 23162

EVANS. An Oration, delivered at Hackinsack, On the Tenth of September, 1780. At the Interment of the Honorable Brigadier General Enoch Poor, General of the New-Hampshire Brigade. By the Reverend Israel Evans, A.M., and Chaplain to the said Brigade. ... *Newbury-Port: John Mycall.* MDCCLXXXI. 4to, pp. 36. BA., H., W. 23163

EVANS. National Ingratitude Lamented: Being the Substance of a Sermon ... In Charles-Town in South-Carolina, September 14th, 1744, A Day of Publick Fast. By I. Evans. ... *Charles-Town: Peter Timothy.* 1745. 8vo, pp. 31. BA., H. 23164

EVANS. A Sermon delivered at Concord, before the ... General Court of ... New Hampshire, at the Annual Election. *Concord.* 1791. 8vo, pp. 35. M., W. 23165

EVANS (J.) The Speller and Interpreter, in Indian and English, for the Use of the Mission Schools, and such as may desire to obtain a Knowledge of the Ojibway Tongue. By James Evans ... . *New-York: D. Fanshaw.* 1831. 12mo, pp. 195.

EVANS (J.) A Sketch of the Denominations into which the Christian World is Divided; ... By John Evans, A.M. ... . *London: J. Sammells.* MDCCXCVI. 12mo, pp. xviii, (2), 160. + First Boston Edition. *Boston.* 1807. 12mo. BA. + *Worcester: Isaiah Thomas, Jr.* 1807. 12mo. + First American Edition. *Boston: John Eliot, Jun.* 1811. 12mo, pp. iv, 195. BA.

+ With an Account of a New Indian Sect, &c., of the Shakers, Jerkers and Barkers in the United States. *London.* 1821. 12mo. Portraits. + *Amherst.* 1832. 12mo. 23167

EVANS (J.) A Narrative of the Proceedings of the Religious Society of the People called Quakers, in Philadelphia, Against John Evans. To which is added: A Report of the Evidence delivered on the Trial of the Case of John Evans, versus Ellis Yarnall and others: With an Appendix. Compiled under the Direction of John Evans. ... *Thomas Dobson: Philadelphia.* 1811. 8vo, pp. vii, 238. BA., C., P. 23168

EVANS (J. J.) South-Carolina and Massachusetts: Speech of J. J. Evans in the Senate, June 23, 1856. *Washington.* 1856. 8vo. B. 23169

EVANS (J.) Memoirs of the Life and Writings of the Rev. William Richards, LL.D. who Died at Lynn, September 13, 1819, in the Sixty-ninth year of his Age. With some Account of the Rev. Roger Williams, Founder of the State of Rhode Island, as well as First Assertor of complete Religious Liberty in the United States of America. By John Evans, A.M. *Chiswick: Charles Whittingham.* 1819. 12mo, pp. xxxii, 396. Portrait. 23170

Mr. Richards bequeathed his library to the Brown University.

EVANS (J. D.) A Chart of Geology, designed specially to illustrate the Geology of Canada. *Toronto.* 1866. 23171

EVANS (J.) A Thanksgiving Sermon, delivered in the Evangelical Lutheran Church, Hagerstown, Md., August 6, 1863. By Rev. J. Evans. *Gettysburg: Neiustedt.* 1864. 8vo, pp. 30.

EVANS (J.) A Journal of the Life, Travels, and Religious Labors of William Savery, late of Philadelphia, a Minister of the Gospel of Christ, in the Society of Friends, Compiled from his Original Memoranda. By Jonathan Evans. *Philadelphia.* 1837. + *London.* 1844. pp. vii, 316. 23173

Savery and Heckewelder were government agents on the Ohio.

EVANS (L. D.) Speech of Hon. Lemuel D. Evans, of Texas, on the Foreign Policy of the United States. ... 24th of July, 1856. *Washington, D. C. Sep.,* 1856. 8vo, pp. 32. 23174

Speech ... On the Condition of Texas, and the Formation of New States. Delivered in the Constitutional Convention of Texas, on the 6th of January, 1869. [n. p. 1869.] 8vo, pp. 30. H.

EVANS (L.) Geographical, Historical, | Political, Philosophical and Mechanical | Essays. | The First, Containing | an | Analysis | Of a General Map of the | Middle British Colonies | in | America ; | And of the Country of the Confederate Indians : | A Description of the Face of the Country ; | The Boundaries of the Confederates ; | and the | Maritime and Inland Navigations of the several Rivers | and Lakes contained therein. | By Lewis Evans. | The Second Edition. | *Philadelphia : | Printed by B. Franklin, and D. Hall.* MDCCLV. | 4to, pp. iv, 32. Map $27\frac{1}{2}+20\frac{1}{2}$ inches, sometimes colored. BA., H. + Second Edition. [*Ibid.*] 23175

Some copies have after the date, "*And sold by R. and J. Dodsley, in Pall-Mall, London.* There are copies on large paper. Wight's copy sold for forty dollars in 1863. The memoir was written by Governor Pownall. The book was published at quarter of a piece of eight. The map is a reduced but improved copy of a former publication by the same author, but many copies do not possess it. Some copies are colored ; it is made up in part from actual surveys, and in part from reliable American authorities, and is a very desirable addition. *See* "M. Rev.," XIV. 28.

EVANS. Geographical, Historical, | Political, Philosophical and Mechanical | Essays. | Number II. containing | a | Letter, | Representing the Impropriety of sending Forces to Virginia : | The Importance of taking Frontenac ; | And that the Preservation of Oswego was owing to | General Shirley's proceeding thither. | Containing Objections to those parts of Evan's General Map and Analysis, | which relate to the French Title to the Country, on the North-West | Side of St. Laurence River, between Fort Frontenac and Montreal, &c. | Published in the New-York Mercury, N° 178. Jan. 5, 1756. | With an | Answer | To so much thereof as concerns the Public : and the several Articles set in a just Light : | By Lewis Evans. | *Philadelphia : Printed for the Author, and Sold by him in Arch Street ; And at New-York by G. Noel.* MDCCLVI. 4to, pp. 42, (1). + *London : | Printed for R. and J. Dodsley in Pall-Mall.* | MDCCLVI. | 4to, pp. 35. 23176

Displays solidity of argument and honesty of intention. *See* "M. Rev.," XV. 312. Concerning Evans, *see* Sparks' "Franklin," IV. 326.

EVANS (*Mr.*) Address to the People of Virginia on the Alien and Sedition Law. By Mr. Evans. *Richmond.* 1788. 23177

[EVANS (Nathaniel).] Ode on the late Glorious Successes of his Majesty's Arms, and Present Greatness of the English Nation. *Philadelphia : W. Dunlap.* 1762. 4to, pp. 14.

EVANS. Poems on Several Occasions, with some other Compositions ; By Nathaniel Evans, A.M. Late Missionary ... for Gloucester County in New Jersey ; ... *Philadelphia : Printed*

by John Dunlap. M.DCC.LXXII. 8vo, pp. xxviii, 160, A Discourse, pp. 24, Corrections, 1 l. BA., H. 23179

The *Laura* who composed some of these poems was the famous Mrs. Elizabeth Ferguson (Miss Graeme). The list of 989 subscribers includes Gov. Franklin, of New Jersey ; Gov. Eden, of Maryland ; Hugh Gaine, Joseph Galloway, D. Duché, Gen. Wayne, Wm. Paca, Isaac Hunt, Oliver Goldsmith, etc. The biographical sketch was edited by the Rev. Wm. Smith.

[EVANS (Oliver).] Exposition of Part of the Patent Law, By a Native Born Citizen of the United States. To which is added, Reflections on the Patent Law. 1816. [n. p. n. d.] 8vo, pp. 70. 23180

EVANS. Oliver Evans to his Counsel, who are engaged in Defence of his Patent Rights, for the Improvements he has invented : containing a Short Account of Two out of Eighty of his Inventions, their Rise and Progress in despite of all Opposition and Difficulties ; and Two of his Patents, with Explanations. [n. p. n. d.] 8vo, pp. 55, (1). BA., P., S. 23181

EVANS. The Young Mill-Wright & Miller's Guide ... . *Philadelphia.* 1795. 8vo, 4 l., pp. 160, 178, 90, 10, (9, 2).

Introduced here as one of the earliest books of its class. It was frequently reprinted till 1848. Also : Report of the Committee of the House of Representatives of Congress on the Petition of Oliver Evans. *Washington.* 1807. 8vo.

EVANS (R.) An Oration delivered at Portsmouth, N. H., 4th July, 1805. By Richard Evans. *Portsmouth, N. H.* 1805. 8vo, pp. 20. M. 23183

EVANS (R. E.) The Commonwealth of Pennsylvania At the relation of Rowland E. Evans vs. The Philadelphia Club. Return of Defendants to Writ of Alternative Mandamus. [n. p. n. d.] 8vo, pp. 18. 23184

[EVANS.] The Constitution and Mr. Motley. *Philadelphia.* 1862. 8vo. 23185

[EVANS (T.)] A Series of Letters addressed to Thomas Jefferson, Esq., President of the United States, concerning his Official Conduct and Principles. With Appendix. By Tacitus. *Philadelphia.* 1802. 8vo. B., M. 13186

EVANS (T. C.) Evans' Advertising Hand-Book, containing a List of the Most Desirable Advertising Mediums in the United States, including the Leading Religious, Agricultural and Literary Publications, together with Valuable Suggestions to Advertisers. *Boston : T. C. Evans.* 1871. pp. (71). B., H. 23187

EVANS (T.) A Concise Account of the Religious Society of Friends, commonly called Quakers ; embracing a Sketch of their Christian Doctrines and Practices. By Thomas Evans. *Philadelphia.* 1856. 8vo, pp. 136. H. 23188

EVANS. An Exposition of the Faith of the Religious Society of Friends, commonly called Quakers, in the Fundamental Doctrines of the Christian Religion : principally selected from their Early Writings. By Thomas Evans. *Philadelphia : Kimber & Sharpless.* 1828. 8vo, pp. 360. + Second Edition, with Alterations and Additions. [*Ibid.*] 1828. 12mo. + Third Edition, to which is Prefixed, "A Brief Account of the Rise of the Society." *Philadelphia.* 1848. 8vo, $22\frac{1}{2}$ sheets. + *York : William Alexander and Son.* 1829. 12mo, 15 sheets. + *Philadelphia.* 1849. 23189

EVANS. Letters and Observations relating to the Controversy respecting the Doctrines of Elias Hicks, &c. 1824. 8vo, $4\frac{1}{2}$ sheets.

See also Friends' Library.

EVANS (T. W.) La Commission Sanitaire des États-Unis son origine, son organisation et ses résultats avec une notice sur les Hopitaux Militaires aux États-Unis ... Par Thomas W. Evans ... *Paris : E. Dentu.* 1865. pp. 178. 5 Plates. [*Ibid.*] 1866. + [*Ibid.*] 1867. BA., C., H. 23191

EVANS. Lettres ... sur le Gouvernement des Etats-Unis. ... Par le Dr. Thomas W. Evans. *Paris : E. Dentu.* 1866. 8vo, pp. 73. BA., H. 23192

EVANS (W. F.) Autobiography of a Shaker, etc. By Rev. Warren F. Evans. *Mount Lebanon, N. Y. : the Author.* 8vo, pp. 73. BA., H. pp. 23193

EVANS (William B.), *and* HONOUR (John H.) Questions and Answers, Explanatory of the Government of the Methodist Episcopal and Methodist Protestant Churches, containing also the Causes which produced the Separation of the Latter from the Former, and Dr. Bascom's Declaration of Rights. *Baltimore : Revised and Published by the Book Committee of the Methodist Protestant Church.* 1859. 16mo, pp. 54. 23194

EVANS (W. J.) The Sugar Planter's Manual : being a Treatise on the Art of obtaining Sugar from the Sugar Cane. By W. J. Evans, M.D. *London : Longman & Co.* 1847. 8vo. C. + [*Ibid.*] 1848. S., H. + *Philadelphia : Lea and Blanchard.* 1848. 8vo, pp. 264. Plate. BA., C. 23195

EVANS. A Clerical Treatise on the Endemic Fevers of the West Indies ... by W. J. Evans, Esq. ... . *London : John Churchill.* MDCCCXXXVII. 8vo, pp. viii, 309. B., BA.

EVANSVILLE, *Indiana.* William's Evansville Directory for 1866. With a United States Post-Office Directory. Fourth Issue. Compiled by Williams & Co. *Evansville : S. G. Dobell.* 8vo, pp. 268, 109. Continued. 23197

First Annual Report of the Evansville Board of Trade, together with Historical, Geographical ... Sketches of Evansville and its Surroundings, January, 1858. *Evansville.* 1858. 8vo, pp. 34. B., H. + Annual Report for 1867, with an Historical Sketch of the City. Illustr. *Evansville : Journal Pr.* 1868. 8vo, pp. 108. 23198

Evansville, Indianapolis, and Cleveland Straight-Line Railroad Company. Annual Report of the Directors, May 10, 1855. *Indianapolis.* 1855. 8vo, pp. 23. 23199

[EVARTS (Jeremiah).] Essays on the Present Crisis in the Condition of the American Indians ; First Published in the National Intelligencer, under the Signature of William Penn. *Boston : Perkins & Marvin.* 1829. 8vo, pp. 112. B., H. + *Philadelphia : Thomas Kite.* 1830. 8vo, pp. 116. B. 23200

EVARTS. An Oration, delivered in Charlestown (Mass.), on the Fourth of July, 1812, in Commemoration of American Independence. By Jeremiah Evarts. 8vo, pp. 32. B., BA., H.

EVARTS (W. M.) Heritage of the Pilgrims. An Oration before the New England Society of the City of New York. ... the Two Hundred and Thirty-Fourth Anniversary of the Landing at Plymouth. ... *New York.* 1853. 8vo, pp. 44. B.

EVARTS. The Issues of the Day. Speech of William M. Evarts, of New York City, at Auburn, Tuesday, Oct. 16, 1860. [*Albany.* 1860.] 8vo, pp. 13. 23203

EVARTS. Speeches in the Republican Campaign of 1856. [*New York.* 1856.] 8vo, pp. 35. H. 23204

EVARTS, *and* FINCH (F. M.) An Oration, by William Maxwell Evarts, and a Poem, by Francis Miles Finch, delivered before the Linonian Society of Yale College, at its Centennial Anniversary, with an Account of the Celebration. *New Haven :* 1853. 8vo, pp. 91. B., H. 23205

EVE (Paul F.) Whisky and Tobacco, their Effects upon Soldiers and others. *Nashville, Tenn.* 1866. 8vo. 23206

EVELIN (R.) *See* [Plantaganet (B.)]

EVELINO (G. J.) Especulacion Astrologica, y Physica de la Naturaleza de los Cometas. *Mexico : por la Viuda de B. Calderon.* 1862. 4to. 23207

EVELYN (J.) Navigation and Commerce : their Original and Progress, containing a Succinct Account of Traffic in general, its Benefits, of Discoveries from the Original of Navigation to this day. By John Evelyn. *London.* 1674. 12mo. + *London.* 1859. 8vo. C. 23208

Contains notices of Columbus, Drake, Raleigh, and other early navigators. Included in his "Miscellaneous Writings," edited by William Upcott. *London.* 1825. 4to. C.

Evening Post, Extra. *See* [Ruggles (S. B.)]

Evening Service of Roshashanah, and Kippur. Or The Beginning of the Year, and The Day of Atonement. *New-York : Printed by W. Weyman, in Broad-Street.* MDCCLXI. 8vo. P.

A Jewish ritual, and the only book we have seen with this imprint.

EVENS (J.) A New Mode of Government ... in the Form of Bills : which Bills are to be presented to the Township, and by the Voice of the People, passed up to the Seat of Government ... . Fourth Edition. ... By Joseph Evans. *Warren County, Ohio : Printed for the Author.* 1847. 8vo, pp. 32. BA. 23210

EVENS. A New Mode of Petitioning, Instructing our Representatives, or Voting for Propositions to become Law. Revised and Improved, from the Original Essays of 1816 and 1831. By Joseph Evens. *Warren County, Ohio : Printed for the Publisher.* 1843. 8vo, pp. 30. BA. 23211

The Eventful Day in the Rhode-Island Rebellion, a Poem. By a Looker-On. *Providence : H. H. Brown.* 1842. 12mo, pp. 12. 23212

The Eventful History of the Mutiny and Piratical Seizure of H. M. S. Bounty ; its Cause and Consequences. ... *London : John Murray.* MDCCCXXXI. P. + Third Edition. *London : John Murray.* MDCCCXXXIX. Fcap 8vo, pp. xi, 356. 6 Plates. 23213

Events in Indian History, beginning with an Account of the Origin of the American Indians and Early Settlements in North America, and embracing Concise Biographies of the Principal

Chiefs and Head-Sachems of the different Indian Tribes, with Narratives and Captivities. ... With an Appendix, and Containing an Indian Vocabulary. *Lancaster.* 1841. 8vo, pp. 633. + *Philadelphia.* 1842. 8vo. + *Lancaster.* 1843. 8vo. 23214

Scissors and paste. The title promises eight *fine* [wretched is the proper word] lithographs. The editions are all alike, but there are variations in the title.

ÉVERARD (C.) La Femme chez les Mormons. Relation écrite par l'épouse d'un Mormon, revenue récemment de l'Utah ; traduit de l'anglais par Charles Éverard. Illustrations par Ed. Coppin. *Paris : Marescq.* 1856. 4to. 23215

EVERARD (Giles), *and others.* Panacea ; or the Universal Medicine, being a Discovery of the Wonderful Vertues of Tobacco taken in a Pipe, with its Operation and Use, both in Physick and Chyrurgery. *London : S. Miller.* 1659. 18mo, 8 l., pp. 79, 55. Portrait. S. 23216

"Dedicated to the American Planters. It contains the different Virtues of the *Male* and *Female* Tobacco, and the efficacy of them in curing the Dropsie, Colick, Liver, Spleen, Flux, and many other complaints."

EVERARD (J.) Some Gospel Treasures, or the Holiest of all Unvailing ; discovering yet more the Riches of Grace and Glory to the Vessels of Mercy, unto whom it is given to know the Mysteries of that Kingdom, and the Excellency of Spirit, Power, Truth, above Letters, Forms, Shadows. In several Sermons, preached at Kensington and elsewhere, by John Everard, D.D. *London, printed in the Year* 1653, *And now reprinted in Germantown, by Christopher Sower.* 1757. 2 pts., 4to, xi, 268 ; 280.

EVERARTUS (Ægidius). De Herba Panacea, quam alii tabacum, alli petum aut nicotianum vocant, brevis commentariolus ; quo admirandæ ac prorsus divinæ hujus Peruanæ stirpis facultates et usus explicantur. *Antverpæ.* 1587. 12mo. + *Ultrajecti.* 1644. S. 23218

EVEREST (C. W.) The Poets of Connecticut ; with Biographical Sketches. ... Edited by Rev. Charles W. Everest. *Hartford : Tiffany and Burnham.* 1843. 8vo, Title, pp. 468. B., BA. + Fifth Edition. *New York.* 1847. 8vo. C. + Sixth Edition. *New York : S. A. Rollo.* 1860. 8vo, pp. 468.

EVEREST (R.) A Journey through the United States and Part of Canada. By the Rev. Robert Everest, M.A. *London : John Chapman.* MDCCCLV. 8vo, pp. xi, 178. B., S. 23220

EVEREST. Proportions of Foreigners to Natives, and of Foreign and Native Convicts, in several States of Europe and America. [n. p. n. d.] 8vo, pp. 7. B. 23221

EVERETT (A. H.) An Address delivered at Charlestown, ... 17th of June, 1836, ... in Commemoration of the Battle of Bunker Hill. By Alexander H. Everett. *Boston : Beals & Greene.* 1836. 8vo, pp. 71, (1). B., BA., C., M. 23222

EVERETT. An Address delivered at Salem, on the Eighth of January, 1836, ... in Commemoration of the Victory of New Orleans. By Alexander H. Everett. *Boston : Beals & Greene.* 1836. 8vo, pp. 61. B., BA., C., M. 23223

[EVERETT.] America : or A General Survey of the Political Situation of the Several Powers of the Western Continent, with Conjectures on their Future Prospects. ... By a Citizen of the United States, Author of "Europe," &c. *Philadelphia : H. C. Carey & J. Lea.* 1827. 8vo, 2 l., pp. 9–364. BA., H. + *London : John Murray.* 1828. 8vo, pp. 356. C. 23224

"We have not seen any political composition from the pen of an American, that can at all be compared with this." — *M. Rev.*

[EVERETT.] América : o Examen general. de la situacion política de las differentes potencias del Continente Occidental, con conjeturas sobre su suerte futura. [Motto.] Por un ciudadano de los Estados Unidos. ... . Traducido del Ingles. [Por San-Martin.] *Northampton, Mass. : Simeon Butler.* 1828. 8vo, pp. (3), 296. BA., C., H. 23225

[EVERETT.] Amerika, oder allgemeiner Ueberblick der politischen Lage der verschiedenen Staaten des westlichen Festlandes. nebst Vermuthungen über deren künftiges Schicksal. Ubersetzt und mit Anmerkungen versehen. *Hamburg.* 1828. 2 vols., 8vo, pp. viii, 270 ; 3 l., pp. 207, 1 l. C. 23226

[EVERETT.] The Conduct of the Administration. *Boston.* 1832. 8vo, pp. 86. 23227

EVERETT. Critical and Miscellaneous Essays. To which are added a few Poems. By Alexander H. Everett. 1st and 2d Series. *Boston : James Munroe & Company.* 1845–46. 2 vols., 12mo, pp. iv, 563 ; 2 l., 475. BA., H. 23228

EVERETT. A Defence of the Character and Principles of Mr. Jefferson, being an Address delivered at Weymouth, ... On the 4th of July, 1836. ... By Alexander H. Everett. *Boston : Beals and Greene.* 1836. 8vo, pp. 76. BA., C. H. 23229

[EVERETT.] Europe : or a General Survey of the Present Situation of the Principal Powers ; with Conjectures on their Future Prospects. By a Citizen of the United States. *Boston : Cummings and Hilliard.* 1822. 8vo, pp. (2), 451. B., BA., C. + Second Edition. *London.* 1823. H. + Second Edition. Containing a Brief Examination of MM. Say and Sismondi on the same Subject. *Boston.* 1826. 8vo, pp. xxii, x, 125.

EVERETT. A Few Notes on Certain Passages respecting the Law of Nations, contained in an Article in the North American Review, upon the Work entitled "Europe." ... By the Author of that Work. *Boston : O. Everett.* 1823. 8vo, pp. 32. B., BA.

EVERETT. A Letter on the Texas Question. By Alexander H. Everett. [n. p. n. d.] 8vo, pp. 23. 23232

From the "Democratic Review."

EVERETT. New Ideas on Population : with Remarks on the Theories of Malthus and Godwin. By Alexander H. Everett ... . *Boston : Oliver Everett.* 1823. 8vo. B., BA., H. + Second Edition. *Boston.* 1826. 8vo. 23233

[EVERETT.] Nouvelles Idées sur la Population, avec des Remarques sur les Théories de Godwin, Malthus, Say, Sismondi, &c. ; traduites de l'Anglais, par J. C. Ferry. *Paris.* 1826. 8vo.

[EVERETT.] Remarks on the Censures of the Government of the United States, contained in the Ninth Chapter of a Book, entitled, "Europe." ... By a Citizen of the United States. *Boston : Wells and Lilly.* 1822. 8vo, pp. 20. B., BA. 23235

[EVERETT.] Remarks on the Governor's [Strong's] Speech. By an American. ... *Boston : Patriot Office.* 1814. 8vo, pp. 76.

[EVERETT.] Refutation á una atroz calumnia, ... por Mr. Alejandro H. Everett ... . *Buenos Aires : Impresa en la imprenta de la Independencia.* 1829. 8vo, 2 l., pp. 12, 2 l. BA., C. 23237

Also : An Address delivered before the Massachusetts Charitable Fire Society ; ... May 28, 1813 ... *Boston : Charles Callender.* 1813. 8vo, pp. 23. B., H., M. — An Address delivered before the Massachusetts Horticultural Society, at their Fifth Annual Festival, September 18, 1833 ... *Boston : J. T. Buckingham.* M DCCC XXXIII. 8vo, pp. 62. BA. — An Address ... on the Present State of Polite Learning in England and America, ... Brunswick, Me., September 3, 1834, ... *Boston : Charles Bowen.* MDCCC XXXIV. 8vo, pp. 55. B. — Address delivered before the Peithesophian Society of Rutger's College. 1838. — An Address to the Philermenian Society of Brown University, on the Moral Character of the Literature of the last and present Century. Delivered at Providence, R. I., September 4, 1837. *Providence.* 1837. 8vo, pp. 54. H. — Address : delivered at Jefferson College, ... La., June 30, 1841, on Assuming the

Functions of President of that Institution. ... *New-Orleans.* 1841. 8vo, pp. 36. — British Opinions on the Protective System, being a Reply to ... Several Recent British Publications. Reprinted ... from ... the North American Review for January, 1830. *Boston: Nathan Hale.* 1830. 8vo, pp. 83. B., BA. — Character of Gen. Jackson and Mr. Van Buren. By Alexander H. Everett, in 1832; also Notions of Anti-Masonry. By the same Author, in 1833. [n. p.] 1836. 8vo, pp. 8. BA. — An Oration delivered at the Request of the City Government, before the Citizens of Boston, on the 5th of July, 1830. ... *Boston: John H. Eastburn.* 1830. 8vo, pp. 47. B., BA., H. — An Oration ... Holliston, Mass. ... Fourth of July, 1839 ... *Boston.* 1839. 8vo, pp. 48. — Report of the Committee on Education, on so much of the Governor's Message as relates to the School Fund. *Boston.* 1835. 8vo, pp. 31 BA., H. — Poems. ... *Boston.* 1845. 12mo, pp. 105. S. — Strictures on Nullification. From the North American Review. *Boston: Stimpson and Clapp.* 1832. 8vo, pp. 73, (1). BA.

EVERETT (C. C.) Eulogy on Abraham Lincoln, Late President of the United States, delivered before the Citizens of Bangor, on the day of the National Fast, June 1st, 1865. By Charles Carroll Everett. *Bangor: Printed by Samuel S. Smith.* 1865. 8vo, pp. 30. B., H. 23238

EVERETT. Sermon preached Dec. 17, 1865, the Sunday preceding the Anniversary of the Landing of the Pilgrims, by Charles C. Everett ... . *Bangor: B. A. Burr.* 1865. 8vo, pp. 10. B., H. 23239

EVERETT. A Sermon in Commemoration of the Death of Abraham Lincoln, Late President of the United States, Preached In the Independent Congregational Church of Bangor, on Easter Sunday, April 16, 1865. By Charles Carroll Everett, Pastor of the Society. *Bangor: Benj. A. Burr.* 1865. 8vo, pp. 25.

EVERETT (David). Common Sense in Dishabille; or, The Farmer's Monitor ... [with] a Perpetual Calendar, or Economical Almanack. *Worcester: Isaiah Thomas.* 1799. 12mo. C.

[EVERETT.] An Essay on the Rights and Duties of Nations, relative to Fugitives from Justice; considered with reference to the Affair of the Chesapeake. By an American. *Boston: David Carlisle.* 1807. 8vo, pp. 62. BA., H., N., W. 23242

For "An Appendix," *see* Vol. I., No. 1793.

EVERETT. A Report of the Case of Belchertown Election, with the Documents, and Minutes of the Arguments in the Case. By David Everett. ... *Boston.* 1811. 8vo, pp. 48.

Also: Daranzel; or, the Persian Patriot, an Original Drama, in Five Acts, as performed at the Theatre in Boston. By David Everett. Corrected and Improved by a Literary Friend. *Boston: John Russell.* 1800. 8vo, pp. 66, (2). BA., H. — An

Oration, in Vindication of Free Masonry ... Delivered at Washington, N. H. at the Installation of Mount-Vernon Lodge, September 28, A.L. 5803. ... *Amherst, N. H.: Joseph Cushing.* 1804. 8vo, pp. 32. BA. — An Oration, pronounced at Amherst, New Hampshire, July 4, 1804. ... *Amherst: Joseph Cushing.* 1804. 8vo, pp. 26. BA., M., W. *See* White (Wm. C.)

EVERETT (E.) An Address Delivered at Charlestown, August 1, 1826, in Commemoration of John Adams and Thomas Jefferson. By Edward Everett. *Boston: William L. Lewis.* 1826. 8vo, pp. 36. B., BA., M. 23244

EVERETT. An Address delivered at Bloody Brook, in South Deerfield, September 30, 1835, in Commemoration of the fall of the "Flower of Essex," at that spot, in King Philip's War, September 18, (o. s.) 1675. By Edward Everett. *Boston: Russell, Shattuck, & Williams.* 1835. 8vo, pp. 44. B., BA., H.

EVERETT. An Address, delivered at Lexington, on the 19th (20th), April, 1835. By Edward Everett. *Charlestown: William W. Wheildon.* 1835. 8vo, pp. 66. B., BA., H. + Second Edition. *Charlestown: William W. Wheildon.* 1835. 8vo, pp. 36. B., BA 23246

EVERETT. American Poets. A Poem. [*Cambridge: Hilliard & Metcalf.*] 1812. 8vo, pp. 11. 23247

EVERETT. The Claims of Citizens of the United States of America on the Government of Naples, Holland, and France. By Edward Everett. *Cambridge: Hilliard and Metcalf.* 1826. 8vo, pp. 152. B., BA., H., W. 23248

EVERETT. The Discovery and Coloni zation of America, and Immigration to the United States. A Lecture delivered before the New York Historical Society ... 1st of June, 1853. By Edward Everett. *Boston: Little, Brown, and Company.* 1853. 8vo, pp. 32. B., BA., H., M. 23249

EVERETT. Dorchester in 1630, 1776, and 1855. *See* Dorchester, Vol. V., No. 20619.

EVERETT. Eulogy on Lafayette, delivered ... at ... Boston, September 6, 1834. By Edward Everett. *Boston: Nathan Hale; and Allen and Ticknor.* 1834. 8vo, pp. 104. B., BA., H. + Second Edition. *Boston.* 1834. B. 23250

EVERETT. A Eulogy on the Life and Character of John Quincy Adams, delivered at ... Faneuil Hall, April 15, 1848. ... By Edward Everett. *Boston: Dutton and Wentworth, State Printers.* 1848. 8vo, pp. 71. B., BA. + Second Edition. *Boston.* 1848. 8vo, pp. 71. 23251

EVERETT. Eulogy on Thomas Dowse, of Cambridgeport, Pronounced before the Massachusetts Historical Society, 9th December, 1858. By Edward Everett. With the Introductory Address by Robert C. Winthrop, President of the Society; and an Appendix. *Boston: John Wilson and Son.* M.DCCC.LIX. 8vo, pp. 82. Portraits and View. B., BA., C., H. 23252

A few copies privately printed. Also included in the "Proceedings of the Mass. Hist. Soc.," Vol. I.

EVERETT. The Great Issues before the Country. An Oration. By Edward Everett. Delivered at the New York Academy of Music, on the 4th of July, 1861. *New York: G. Q. Colton.* 1861. 8vo, pp. 52. + *New York: James G. Gregory.* 1861. 16mo, pp. 48. B. 23253

Also in "Pulpit and Rostrum," Nos. 21 and 22.

EVERETT. Letter to the Comte de Sartiges, Dec. 1, 1852. Letter to Lord John Russell, Sept. 17, 1853, by E. Everett, being the Correspondence on the Proposed Tripartite Convention relative to Cuba. *Boston: Little, Brown & Co.* 1853. 8vo, pp. 64. B. 23254

EVERETT. The Life of George Washington. By Edward Everett. *New York: Sheldon and Company.* 1860. 12mo, pp. 348. Portraits. BA., C., H. 23255

100 copies printed on large paper. First published in the "Encyclopædia Britannica."

EVERETT. The Life of John Stark. By Edward Everett. *London: Richard James Kennett.* 1834. 12mo. 23256

One of the volumes of Sparks' "Lib. of Am. Biog.," with a separate title-page.

EVERETT. A Memoir of Mr. John Lowell, Jun., delivered as the Introduction to the Lectures on his Foundation, ... 31st December, 1839. ... By Edward Everett. *Boston: Charles C. Little and James Brown.* M.DCCC.XL. 8vo, pp. 74. B., BA., H.

EVERETT. The Monroe Doctrine. By Edward Everett. Letter of John Quincy Adams. *New York: W. C. Bryant & Co.* 1863. 8vo, pp. 17. + [Another Edition.] *Loyal Publication Society, No.* 34. 1863. 8vo, pp. 11. H. 23258

From the "New York Ledger."

EVERETT. The Mount Vernon Papers. By Edward Everett. *New York: D. Appleton and Company.* M.DCCC.LX. 12mo, pp. xxi, 490, (2). BA., C., H. 23259

Originally contributed to the "New York Ledger."

EVERETT. An Oration pronounced at Cambridge, before the Society of Phi Beta Kappa. August 27, 1824. ... *Boston: Oliver Everett.* 1824. 8vo, pp. 67. B. + *New York: printed by J. W. Palmer & Co.* 1824. 8vo, pp. 40. B., BA. + Fourth Edition. *Boston: Cummings, Hilliard & Co.* 1825. 8vo, pp. 67. B., H. + [*Ibid.*] 8vo, pp. 67. M. 23260

Delivered in presence of General Lafayette.

EVERETT. An Oration Delivered at Plymouth, December 22d, 1824. By Edward Everett. *Boston: Cummings, Hilliard & Co.* 1825. 8vo, pp. 73. B., BA., H. 23261

EVERETT. An Oration delivered at Concord, April the Nineteenth, 1825. By Edward Everett. *Boston Cummings, Hilliard and Company.* 1825. 8vo, 2 l., pp. 59. B., BA., P. 23262

With notes respecting the fight at Concord in 1775.

EVERETT. An Oration delivered on the Battlefield of Gettysburg, (November 19, 1863,) at the Consecration of the Cemetery prepared for the Interment of the Remains of those who Fell in the Battles of July 1st, 2d, and 3d, 1863. By Edward Everett. To which is added interesting Reports of the Dedicatory Ceremonies; Descriptions of the Battlefield; Incidents and Details of the Battles, &c. *New York: Baker & Godwin.* 1863. 8vo, pp. 48. H. 23263

EVERETT. Oration at the Consecration of the National Cemetery, Gettysburg, Nov. 19, 1863. *Boston.* 1863. 8vo. C.

EVERETT. Orations and Speeches, on Various Occasions. By Edward Everett. *Boston: American Stationers' Company.* 1836. 8vo, pp. 637. BA., C. + Second Edition. *Boston; Charles C. Little and James Brown.* 1850. 2 vols., rl. 8vo, pp. xii, 669, (1); xxi, 633. Portrait. BA. + Vol. III. *Boston: Little, Brown, and Company.* 1859. 8vo, pp. xv, 647. Analytical Index of the 3 vols., pp. 649–847. BA. + Vol. IV. [*Ibid.*] 1868. 8vo, pp. xiv, 759, Index, 761–788. BA. 23265

Three hundred copies printed on large paper. For a list of the contents, *see* "Cat. of Public Libr., Boston," p. 267. A seventh edition of 3 vols. was published in 1865.

EVERETT. The Questions of the Day. An Address Delivered in the Academy of Music, in New-York, on the Fourth of July, 1861. By Edward Everett. *New York: Geo. P. Putnam.* 1861. 8vo, pp. 46. B., C., H. + *New York.* 1861. 12mo. B.

EVERETT. Remarks of Mr. Everett [and others] in the Senate on the Memorial of 3,000 Clergymen, Remonstrating against the Passage of the Nebraska Bill. *Washington.* 1856. 8vo.

EVERETT. ... History of America. ... Report ... [on] the expediency of adopting measures to procure from the different public offices, in England, copies of papers ... . [*Washington.* 1827.] 8vo, pp. 16. (19th Cong., 2d Sess., House of Reps., Rep. No. 91.) 23268

EVERETT. A Sermon, preached at the Dedication of the First Congregational Church in New-York, Jan. 20, 1821. By Edward Everett. ... *New-York: Printed by C. S. Van Winkle.* 1821. 8vo, pp. 22. B. + Second Edition. *Boston: Cummings and Hilliard.* 1821. 8vo, pp. 23. B., BA., H. 23269

EVERETT. Speech of Mr. Everett, of Massachusetts, on the Bill for Removing the Indians from the East to the West Side of the Mississippi, delivered ... 19th of May, 1830. *Boston.* 1830. 8vo, pp. 46. P., S., W. + *Washington: Gales and Seaton.* 1830. 8vo, pp. 28. BA. 23270

EVERETT. Success of our Republic. An Oration delivered in Boston, July 4, 1860. *New York.* 1860. 12mo. 23271

"Pulpit and Rostrum," No. 14.

Also: Account of the Fund for the Relief of East Tennessee; with a Complete List of the Contributors. ... . *Boston: Little, Brown and Company.* 1864. 12mo, pp. 99. — An Address at the Funeral of Rev. John Lovejoy Abbot, Pastor of the First Church of Christ in Boston. ... . *Boston.* 1814. 8vo, pp. 20. B., BA., H., M. — Address of the Committee appointed at a Public Meeting held in Boston, December 19, 1823, for the Relief of the Greeks. ... [*Boston.* 1823.] 8vo, pp. 18. BA., H. — An Address Delivered at the Erection of a Monument to John Harvard, September 26, 1828. ... *Boston: Published by Nathan Hale.* 1828. 8vo, pp. 24. Plate. B., BA., H., W. — An Address delivered on the 28th of June, 1830, the Anniversary of the Arrival of Gov. Winthrop at Charlestown. ... *Charlestown: published by William W. Wheildon.* 1830. 8vo, pp. 51. H. — Address delivered before the American Institute of the City of New York, at their Fourth Annual Fair, October 14, 1831. ... *New York: Van Norden and Mason.* M DCCC XXXI. 8vo, pp. 50. B., BA., H., N. — An Address delivered as the Introduction to the Franklin Lectures, in Boston, November 14, 1831. ... *Boston: Published by Gray and Bowen.* 1832. B., BA., N. — An Address Delivered before the Phi Beta Kappa Society in Yale College, New Haven, August 20, 1833. *New Haven: Hezekiah, Howe & Co.* 1833. 8vo, pp. 35. BA., H., M., W. — Address ... at the Opening of the New Medical College, ... November 6, 1846, ... *Boston: William D. Ticknor & Company.* MDCCCXLVI. 8vo, pp. 36. 2 Plates. B., BA. — An Address delivered before the Citizens of Worcester, on the Fourth of July, 1833. *Boston: Joseph T. Buckingham.* 1833. 8vo, pp. 40. BA., W. — An Address delivered before the Literary Societies of Amherst College, August 25, 1835. ... *Boston: Russell, Shattuck, & Williams.* 1835. 8vo, pp. 35. B., BA. — An Address to the Two Branches of the Legislature [of Massachusetts], on the Organization of the Government, Jan. 6, 1836. 8vo, pp. 33. + 1838. 8vo, pp. 27. + 1839. 8vo,

pp. 24. — An Address delivered before the Adelphic Union Society of Williams College, on Commencement Day, August 16, 1837. ... *Boston: Dutton and Wentworth.* 1837. 8vo, pp. 36. B., BA., H., M. — An Address delivered before the Massachusetts Charitable Mechanic Association, 20th September, 1837. ... *Boston: Dutton and Wentworth.* 1837. 8vo, pp. 22. B., BA., M. — An Address, delivered before the Mercantile Library Association, ... Boston, Septemb-r 13, 1838. ... *Boston: William D. Ticknor.* 1838. 8vo, pp. 40. B., BA., H. — Address of ... at the Anniversary of the American Colonization Society ... January 18, 1853. [n. p. n. d.] 8vo, pp. 12. B., BA., H., M. — An Address delivered before the New York Historical Society, by the Hon. Edward Everett. With an Introduction, by the Hon. Joseph R. Ingersoll. *New York.* 1853. 8vo, pp. 44. B. — Academical Education. An Address delivered at St. Louis, 22d April, 1857, at the Inauguration of Washington University of the State of Missouri. *Boston.* 1857. 8vo. — Address delivered before the New York State Agricultural Society, ... at Buffalo, ... October 9, 1857. *Albany.* 1857. 8vo, pp. 56. H., M. — Address [4 July, 1861] by Edward Everett, embracing an Historical Sketch, etc., Revised with Additions by the Author, prepared for this Work: including a Letter by Geo. Ticknor Curtis. *New York: G. P. Putnam.* 1861. 8vo, pp. 46. — An Address delivered before the Union Agricultural Society of Adams, Rodman and Loraine, Jefferson County, New York, September 12, 1861. *Cambridge: H. O. Houghton.* 1861. 8vo, pp. 23. — The Address of Mr. Everett and the Poem of Dr. O. W. Holmes, at the Dinner given to H. J. H. Monseigneur the Prince Napoleon, September 25th, 1861. *Cambridge: privately printed.* 1861. 8vo, pp. 20. BA., H. — An Address delivered at the Inauguration of the Union Club, April 9, 1869. ... *Boston: Little, Brown & Co.* 1863. + [*Ibid.*] 1863. 12mo, pp. 64. — Address ... Boston Union Club, ... April 9, 1863. *Liverpool: Daily Post Office.* 1863. 8vo, pp. 32. — Address delivered before the United States Naval Academy. ... 1863. — Address delivered at the Consecration of the Soldiers' Cemetery, at Gettysburg, Nov. 19, 1863 ... *Boston.* 1863. 8vo. B. — Address delivered in Faneuil Hall, October 19, 1863. The Duty of Supporting the Government in the present Crisis of Affairs. [*Boston.* 1864.] 8vo, pp. 16. B., H. — Defence of Power's Statue of Webster; being the Remarks made on the 8th of June, 1859, at a meeting of the General Committee of One Hundred on the Webster Memorial. *Boston.* 1859. 8vo, pp. 20. H. — Eulogy, at the Dedication of the Statue of Daniel Webster, at Boston, Sept. 17, 1859. *Boston.* 8vo. — French Spoliations Prior to 1800. Report of E. Everett, Feb. 16, 1829. 8vo. — Importance of Practical Education and Useful Knowledge; being a Selection from the Orations and Discourses of Edward Everett, President of Harvard University. *New York.* 12mo. — A Lecture on the Working Men's Party, first delivered October Sixth, before the Charlestown Lyceum ... *Boston: Gray and Bowen.* 1830. 8vo, pp. 27. (*See* Boston Society.) — A Letter to John Lowell, Esq. In Reply to a Publication entitled Remarks on a Pamphlet, printed by the Professors and Tutors of Harvard University, touching their Right to the Exclusive Government of that Seminary. *Boston: Oliver Everett.* 1824. 8vo, pp. (2), 102. B., BA., H. — An Oration Delivered at Cambridge on the Fiftieth Anniversary of the Declaration of the Independence of the United States of America. *Boston: Cummings, Hilliard & Co.* 1826. 8vo, pp. (4), 51. B., BA., N. + Second Edition. *Boston: Cummings, Hilliard and Company.* 1826. 8vo, pp. 51. B. — An Oration delivered before the Citizens of Charlestown, on the Fifty-Second Anniversary of the Declaration of the Independence of the United States of America. ... *Charlestown: N. E.: Wheildon and Raymond.* 1828. 8vo, pp. 43. B., BA., H., W. — Oration delivered on the Fourth Day of July, 1835, before the Citizens of Beverley ... . *Boston: Russell, Odiorne & Co.* 1835. 8vo, pp. 48. BA. — An Oration delivered at Charlestown, on the Seventy-Fifth Anniversary of the Battle of Bunker Hill, June 17, 1850. ... *Boston: Redding and Company.* 1850. 8vo, pp. 77, (3). B., H., M. — Oration delivered on the Dedication of Webster's Statue, in Boston, Sept. 17, 1859. *New York.* 1859. 12mo. B., C. — Oration delivered before the City Authorities of Boston, on the Fourth of July, 1860, ... Together with the Speeches ... at the Celebration of the Eighty-Fourth

Anniversary of American Independence. *Boston: Geo. C. Rand & Avery, Printers.* 1860. 8vo, pp. 48. B., BA., H. — An Oration ... delivered in the New York Academy of Music, July 4, 1861. *New York: James G. Gregory.* 1861. 8vo, pp. 48. — Remarks of Mr. Everett on the Bill for the Relief of Revolutionary Officers, in the House ... April 25, 1826. *Cambridge.* 1826. 8vo, pp. 18. — Remarks, March 20, 1837, before Boston Mercantile Library Association ... 8vo. B. — Remarks on the Public Lands, and on the Right of the State to Nullify an Act of Congress. *Boston: Gray und Bowen.* 1830. 8vo, pp. 86. — Remarks ... in the House of Representatives, May 17, 1832, on the Appropriation Apportionment Bill ... . *Washington.* [n. d.] 8vo, pp. 9. BA., W. — Remarks ... on the French Question in the House ... 7th of February and 2d of March, 1835. With the Reports of the Majority and Minority of the Committee on Foreign Affairs, on the same Subject. *Boston: Nathan Yale.* 1835. 8vo, pp. 31. — Remarks at a Hearing before the Joint Committee of Education, February 4, 1848, in aid of the Memorial of the Colleges. *Cambridge.* 1848. 8vo, pp. 32. H. — Remarks at the Plymouth Festival, on the First of August, 1853, in Commemoration of the Embarkation of the Pilgrims. ... *Boston.* 1853. 8vo, pp. 18. H. — Speech ... on the Proposition to Amend the Constitution of the United States Respecting the Election of President and Vice President. Delivered in the House ... March 9, 1826. 12mo, pp. 43. BA., H. + *Boston.* 1826. 8vo, pp. 38. — Speech ... on the Subject of Retrenchment, ... in the House ... Feb. 1, 1828. *Washington: Gales & Seaton.* 1828. 8vo, pp. 31. BA., H., M. — Speech ... on the Proposal of Mr. McDuffie to Repeal the Laws of 1828 and 1824, Imposing Duties on Imports; ... 7th and 8th May, 1828. *Washington.* 1830. 12mo, pp. 34. — Speech ... in the House ... 14th and 21st of February, 1831, On the Execution of the Laws and Treaties in Favor of the Indian Tribes. [*Washington.* 1831.] 8vo, pp. 23. BA. — Speech ... on the Proposed Adjustment of the Tariff. Delivered in the House of Representatives, ... 25th June, 1832. *Washington: Gales & Seaton.* 1832. 8vo, pp. 38. BA. — Speech in Support of the Memorial of Harvard, Williams, and Amherst Colleges, delivered before the Joint Committee on Education, in ... Boston, on the 7th of February, 1849. ... *Cambridge: Metcalf and Company.* 1849. 8vo, pp. 28. H. — Speech ... on the Central American Treaty. ... in the ... Senate, ... March 21, 1853. *Washington.* 1853. 8vo, pp. 13. B., BA., H., M. — Speech ... in the Senate, ... Feb. 8, 1854, on the Nebraska and Kansas Territorial Bill. *Washington.* 1854. 8vo, pp. 14. BA., H., M. — Speech at the Dinner given in honor of George Peabody, Esq., of London, by the Citizens of the Old Town of Danvers [Ms.], Oct. 9, 1856. *Boston.* 1857. 8vo. — Speech ... at the Boston Union Meeting, Dec. 8, 1858, and [Remarks] of T. H. Seymour and S. Eliot at the Hartford Union Meeting, Dec. 14, 1859. [n. p.] 1860. 8vo. B. — Speech ... on American Institutions in Reply to the Discussion in the British House of Lords, in the City Hall, Boston, July 4, 1860. *Boston.* 1860. 8vo. — Speech, Aug. 27, 1862. (*See* Andrew (J. A.), Vol. I., No. 1469.) — Stability and Progress. Remarks made on the Fourth of July, 1853, in Fanueil Hall. ... *Boston.* 1853. 8vo, pp. 11. B., M. — Substance of the Remarks of ... at the Temperance Meetings in Concord and Salem, on the 11th and 14th June, 1833. [*Boston.* 1833.] 12mo, pp. 12. BA. — Tribute to the Memory of Washington Irving. *New York.* 1860. 12mo. C.

EVERETT. Addresses at the Inauguration of the Hon. Edward Everett, LL.D., as President of the University at Cambridge, Thursday, April 30, 1846. *Boston: Charles C. Little and James Brown.* 1846. 8vo, pp. 66. 23272

EVERETT. A Memorial of Edward Everett, from the City of Boston. *Boston: A. Williams & Co.* 1865. Rl. 8vo, pp. 315.

Edited by Nathaniel Hall. Another edition, in 4to, bears the imprint: *Boston: Printed by order of the City Council.* MDCCCLXV. 4to, pp. 315; portraits; 100 copies only printed.

EVERETT. Proceedings of the American Antiquarian Society, ... in Reference to the Death of ... Edward Everett. *Boston: J. E. Farwell and Company.* 1865. 8vo, pp. 29. B. 23274

EVERETT. Proceedings of the Thursday-Evening Club, on the Occasion of the Death of Hon. Edward Everett. *Boston: Wilson & Sons, Printers.* 1865. 8vo, pp. 20. BA. 23275

EVERETT. Services at the Everett School, in Boston, on the Death of Edward Everett. *Boston.* 1865. 8vo, pp. 23. H.

EVERETT. Tribute of the Massachusetts Historical Society To the Memory of Edward Everett, January 30, 1865. *Boston.* 1865. 8vo, pp. 90. Portrait. B., BA. 23277

EVERETT. Tribute to the Memory of ... Edward Everett, by the New-England Historic-Genealogical Society ... January 17 and February 1, 1865. *Boston: the New-England Historic-Genealogical Society.* MDCCCLXV. 8vo, pp. 97. B. 23278

Portrait and views of Mr. Everett's library and birth-place; 75 copies on large paper.

EVERETT (E. F.) Genealogy of the Everett Family. By Edward F. Everett, of Charlestown, Mass. Reprinted from the New England Historical and Genealogical Register, for July, 1860. *Boston: Henry W. Dutton & Son, Printers.* 1860. 8vo, pp. 7. B., H. 23279

EVERETT (Erastus). Poem at the Celebration of the One Hundredth Anniversary of the Incorporation of the Town of Princeton, Mass., Oct. 20, 1859. [Also] the Address of C. T. Russell. *Worcester.* 1860. 8vo. B. 23280

EVERETT (George). Encouragement for Seamen and Mariners. *London.* 1605. 2 pts., 4to, pp. 24. N. 23281

EVERETT (Horace). Speech of Mr. H. Everett, of Vermont, on the Case of Alexander McLeod. Delivered in the House ... September 3, 1841. *Washington.* 1841. 8vo, pp. 24. H.

Also: Address to the Whigs of Vermont ... July, 1848. *Windsor.* 1848. 8vo. B., H. — Report on Indian Affairs. *Washington.* 1834. 8vo. Map. — Speech in the House of Representatives ... on the Indian Annuity Bill, ... June 3, 1836 *Washington National Intelligencer Office.* 1836. 8vo, pp. 23. BA., H.

EVERETT (J.) Speech of James Everett on Non-Intercourse, 1811. *Washington.* 1825. 8vo.

Everett (John). An Oration ... on the Prospects of the Young Men of America. Delivered ... to the Senior Class, July 14, 1818. ... *Boston: Wells and Lilly.* 1818. 8vo, pp. 19.

Also: An Oration, delivered ... July 5, 1824. ... *Boston: Oliver Everett.* 1824. 8vo, pp. 28. BA., H., W.

Everett (M.) A Sermon ... at the Ordination of the Reverend Oliver Everett, ... Boston: January 2, 1782. By Moses Everett, A.M. ... *Boston, N. E.: Nathaniel Coverley and Robert Hodge.* 1782. 8vo, pp. 24. BA., H., M. 23284

Also: Sermon preached Lord's-day Eve, Feb. 1, 1778, to Two Religious Societies of Young Men in Dorchester, Mass. *Boston.* 1779. 8vo, pp. 27.

Everett (O.) An Eulogy, on General George Washington, Who died on the 14th of Dec. 1799. Pronounced at Dorchester, Feb. 22, 1800. It being the Day Recommended by Congress, for the National Lamentation of his Death. By Oliver Everett, Esq. ... Published at the request of the Town. *Charleston: Printed by Samuel Etheridge.* M.DCCC. 8vo, pp. 22. H. 23285

Forms part of the "Proceedings at Dorchester, on the Death of Washington."

Everett (Oliver Capen). Address delivered at the Opening and Dedication of the Winchester Home for Aged Indigent Women ... Charlestown ... 1866. ... Oct. 3, With an Appendix. *Boston.* 1866. 8vo, pp. 27. H. 23286

Also: Report of the Ministry at large in Charlestown, 1852. *Charlestown.* 1853, etc. B.

Everett (W.) An Oration before the City Authorities of Boston, on Fourth of July, 1870. By William Everett. *Boston: Alfred Mudge & Son.* 1870. 8vo, pp. 39. B. 23287

Also: Changing Base; or, What Edward Rice Learnt at School. ... *Boston: Lee and Shepard.* 1868. 16mo, pp. 282. BA., H.

The Evergreen. A Repository of Religious, Literary and Entertaining Knowledge for Families. *New York.* 1850. Rl. 8vo. Continued. 23288

Gives a short history, with views, of a number of the Protestant Episcopal Churches of the city of New York.

The Evergreen. An Offering for all Seasons, edited by J. Salkeld. *New York.* 1850. 8vo, pp. 380. 23289

The Evergreen, or Church Offering for all Seasons; a Repository of Religious, Literary, and Entertaining Knowledge. *New-Haven.* 1844–51. 8 vols., 8vo. 23290

The Evergreen, or Monthly Church Magazine. ... Edited by William H. Onderdonk. *New-York.* 1843. 8vo. 23291

Continued to ten or more volumes.

Evergreen Cemetery, *Brighton.* Order of Services at the Evergreen Cemetery, Brighton ... August 1, 1850. *Boston.* 1850. 12mo, pp. 4. H. 23292

Evergreens, *N. Y.* Rules and Regulations of the Cemetery of the Evergreens, ... *New York.* 1854. 8vo, pp. 64, (8).

Everhard (*Sir* R.) A Brief Account, 1743. *See* [Stephens (Thomas)].

Evershaw (M.) Five Years in Pennsylvania. By Mary Evershaw. *London.* 1840. 12mo, pp. 227. 23294

Everts (H.) History of the Ninth Regiment of Volunteers of New Jersey Infantry. By Herman Everts. *Newark.* 1865. 8vo. 23295

Everts (M. K.) Christian Womanhood. Life of Mrs. M. K. Everts. With Introduction. *Chicago.* 1868. 12mo, pp. vii, 363. Portrait. 23296

Every-body's Almanac and Diary, for 1851. Containing a List of Government Officers, Commerce and Resources of the Union, Exports, &c. 1851. 12mo. 23297

The Every-Day Book; containing Biographical Sketches; Personal Adventures; Incidents of Travel; ... [n. p. n. d.] 16mo, pp. 324. 23298

Every Man his own Doctor: Or, the Poor Planter's Physician. Prescribing Plain and Easy Means for Persons to Cure themselves of all or most of the Distempers, incident to this Climate, and with very little Charge, the Medicines being chiefly of the Growth and Production of this Country. ... The Fourth Edition. *Philadelphia: Reprinted and Sold by B. Franklin.* M,DCC,-XXXVI. 12mo, pp. 56. P. 23299

Every Man his own Fattener. To which is added, the Art of Fly Catching and Taking Snuff. *New York.* 1809. 8vo, pp. 26. 23300

A curious satire.

Evidence before the Committee of Council relative to the Slave Trade, &c. *London.* 1790. 4to. P. 23301

See also Slavery.

The Evidence Delivered on the Petition presented by the West India Planters and Merchants to the Hon. House of Commons, as it was Introduc'd at the Bar and Summ'd up by Mr. Glover. [*London.* 1775.] 8vo, pp. 95. J.C.B. 23302

Without date or place. The petition is dated Feb. 2, 1775.

Evidence of the Common and Statute Laws of the Realm; Usage, Records, History, with the Greatest and Best Authorities, down to the 3d of George the 3d, in proof of the Rights of Britons throughout the British Empire. Addressed to the People. *London: John Williams.* MDCCXXV. 8vo, pp. 91. 23303

The writer shows that Englishmen emigrating to America and elsewhere, and forming governments, carry with them and should enjoy the same rights that freeholders enjoy within the realm; whence it necessarily follows that in conformity with their constitution, they must "give up the lately-assumed mode of American Taxation, and repeal all the acts they complain of as grievances." *See* "M. Rev.," LIII. 511.

Evidence taken before the Committee of the House of Representatives, appointed to Inquire into the Treatment of Prisoners at Castle Thunder. ... [n. p.] 1863. 8vo, pp. 58. B. 23304

With Capt. Alexander's defence to the committee.

Evidence upon Oath, touching the Condition and Treatment of the Negro Population of the British West India Colonies. Part I. Island of Jamaica. *London.* 1833. 8vo. 23305

The Evident Advantages to Great Britain and its Allies from the Approaching War, especially in Matters of Trade. To which is added two Curious Plans, one of the Port and Bay of Havana, the other of Porto Bello. *London: J. Roberts.* 1727. 8vo, pp. (4), 44. 2 Plans. B., J.C.B. + *Northampton.* 1737. 8vo, pp. 35. 23306

The Evident Approach of a War, and Something of the Necessity of it in Order to Establish Peace, and Preserve Trade, ... *London.* 1727. 23307

The Evil Effects of a High Tariff upon the General Prosperity of the Country, and incidentally upon the Payment of our National Debt. By a Merchant. *Boston: Lee and Shepard.* 1867. 8vo, pp. 28. B. 23308

Evils of the Revolutionary War. *Boston.* 1846. 12mo, pp. 14. + *Brandon, Vt.* 1847. 12mo, pp. 16. 23309

Evreux (*Le P.* Yves d'). *See* Yves d'Evreux.

Ewart (D.) A Scriptural View of the Moral Relations of American Slavery. 1849. By David Ewart, of Columbia, S. C. Revised and Amended in 1859. *Charleston, (S. C.): Walker, Evans & Co.* 1859. 8vo, pp. 12. B., H. 23310

[Ewbank (Henry).] Influence of Democracy. 23311

Ewbank (T.) Inorganic Forces Ordained to Supersede Human Slavery. By Thomas Ewbank, ... *New York: William Everdell & Sons.* 1860. 8vo, pp. 32. H. 23312

Ewbank. Life in Brazil; or, a Journal of a Visit to the Land of the Cocoa and the Palm. With an Appendix, containing Illustrations of Ancient and South American Arts, in recently discovered Implements and Products of Domestic Industry, and Works in Stone, Pottery, Gold, Silver, Bronze, &c. By Thomas Ewbank. *New York: Harper & Brothers.* 1856. 8vo, pp. 469.

Ewell (J.) The Medical Companion; ... treating of the Diseases of the United States; ... A Dispensatory, etc. By James Ewell, M.D. *Philadelphia: J. A. Geer.* 1848. 8vo, pp. 692. Plate. 23314

[Ewer (Charles).] A Genealogy of the Family of Anthony Stoddard, of Boston. ... *Boston: Printed by Coolidge & Wiley.* 1849. 8vo, pp. 23. H. 23315

Ewer (F. C.) Discourse on the National Crisis, ... by the Rev. F. C. Ewer, At ... New-York, ... (May 5,) and repeated, ... (May 12,) 1861. *New-York: Geo. F. Nesbitt & Co.* 1861. 8vo, pp. 19. H. 23316

Ewer. A Protest against Political Preaching; being A Rector's reply to sundry Requests and Demands for a Political Sermon: preached in Christ Church, ... N. Y. By Rev. F. C. Ewer, On the ... Sixteenth Sunday after Trinity, 1864; and Repeated by Request ... *New York: American News Company.* 1864. 8vo, pp. 23. B. + *New York: Francis Hart & Company.* 1864. 8vo, pp. 23. BA., H. 23317

Also: Logical Impossibility of any Compromise between the Church and the Sects. A Sermon. ... *New York.* 1869. 12mo, pp. 36. — Public Health of the City of New York: ... Remarks ... before the Sanitary Association, November 21, 1861. With Appendix. *New York.* 1861. 8vo, pp. 33. H. — Oration ... On the Relationship between Masonry and Christianity, delivered at the Centennial Celebration of St. John's Lodge ... Bridgeport, Conn., Oct. 12, 1862; together with an Account of the ... Celebration, ... *New York.* 1862. 8vo, pp. 46. B., H. — A Sermon, Memorial of the Rev. Henry William Duchalet, M.D. ... Late Rector of St. Stephen's Church, Philadelphia; ... *Philadelphia.* 1866. 8vo, pp. 44. H.

Ewer (J.) A Sermon Preached before the Incorporated Society for the Propagation of the Gospel in Foreign Parts; At their Anniversary Meeting in the Parish Church of St. Mary-le-Bow, On February 20, 1767. By the Right Reverend Father in God, John Lord Bishop of Landaff. *London: E. Owen.* MDCCLXVII. 8vo, pp. 26. + *London: Printed. New-York: Re-printed and Sold by James Parker.* MDCCLXVIII. 8vo, pp. 18. 23318

The bishop gave great offense to the American colonists by the pictures he drew of them as "infidels and barbarians." *See* Chauncy (C.), Vol. III., Nos. 1238–19, *and* Livingstone (W.)

[Ewer.] A Vindication of The Bishop of Landaff's Sermon from The gross Misrepresentations and Abusive Reflections, contained In Mr. William Livingston's Letter To his Lordship: With Some Additional Observations On certain Passages in Dr. Chauncey's Remarks, &c. By a Lover of Truth and Decency. ... *New-York: Printed by J. Holt.* M,DCC,LXVIII. 8vo, pp. viii, 82. BA., C. 23319

Ewing (A.) An Oration delivered on the Occasion of the Inauguration of the Bust erected to the Memory of Gen. Andrew Jackson, In the City of Memphis, January 8, 1859. By Hon. Andrew Ewing ... . *Nashville: E. G. Eastman & Co., Printers.* 1859. 8vo, pp. 26. H. 23320

Also: Speech ... on the Admission of California. Delivered in the House of Representatives, April 18, 1850. *Washington: Printed by John T. Towers.* 1850. 8vo, pp. 15. — Speech ... on the Texas and New Mexico Question. Delivered ... August 16, 1850. *Washington.* 1850. 8vo, pp. 8.

Ewing (C.), *and* Drake (G. R.) Opinions on the Case of Hendrickson *vs.* Shotwell. Chancery of New Jersey, 1832. [n. p. n. d.] 8vo, pp. 90. B. 23321

Ewing (E. H.) Oration on the Life and Services of Daniel Webster. By Edward H. Ewing. *Nashville.* 1852. 8vo. S.

Ewing (G.) A Memoir of Barbara Ewing; by her Husband, Greville Ewing. *Philadelphia.* 1830. 12mo 23323

Ewing (J.) The Columbian Alphabet. Being an Attempt to New Model the English Alphabet ... . By James Ewing. *Trenton: Mathias Day.* M,DCC,XCVIII. 1798. 12mo, pp. 24.

Ewing. Treatise on the Office and Duty of a Justice of the Peace, Sheriff, Constable, and Executors, Administrators and

Guardians. By James Ewing. *Trenton.* 1805. 8vo. S. + Third Edition, with the New Constitution [of New-Jersey]. *New-York.* 1845. S. 23325

Ewing (J. H.) Speech of Hon. J. H. Ewing, ... on the ... Reduction of the Tariff. Delivered in the House ... June, 25, 1846. *Washington.* 1846. 8vo, pp. 8. H. 23326

Ewing (J.) Fidelity in the Gospel Ministry; a Sermon preached at the Ordination of the Rev Ashbald Green, in Philadelphia, May 15, 1787. By John Ewing, Provost of the University of Pennsylvania. *Philadelphia.* 1787. 8vo. 23327

Also: Sermon on the Death of George Bryan ... *Philadelphia.* 1791. 8vo.

Ewing (M. C.) Description of the Water Power at the Great Falls of the Potomac. By M. C. Ewing. 1845. 8vo. Map. N. 23328

Ewing (Presley). Tonnage Duties. Speech ... in the House of Representatives, Jan. 13, 1854, on the Motion to refer the President's Message. [n. p. n. d.] 8vo, pp. 7. M. 23329

Also: Nebraska and Kansas. Speech ... in the House of Representatives, February 20, 1854. [*Washington.* 1854.] 8vo. H. + Speech ... on the Homestead Bill. + Non-Intervention. ... April 24, 1852.

Ewing (Stephen S.) Report of the President of the Branch of the Bank of the State of Alabama, at Huntsville. Nov. 3, 1841. *Tuscaloosa.* 1841. 8vo. + *Tuscaloosa.* 1846. 8vo.

Ewing (T.) Letter ... to his Excellency Benj. Stanton ... in Answer to his Charges against our Generals who fought the Battle of Shiloh, on the 6th April, 1862. By Hon. Thomas Ewing. *Columbus (Ohio):* 1862. 8vo, pp. 24. C., H. 23331

Also: Letter ... to the Finance Committee, on the Public Debt and Currency. *Washington, D. C.* 1869. 8vo, pp. 17. — Speech ... on the Removal of the Deposites; delivered in the Senate ... Jan. 1834. *Washington.* 1834. 8vo, pp. 32. M. — Speech ... On Introducing the Bill to settle and determine the Northern Boundary Line of ... Ohio; delivered in the Senate ... Dec. 21, 1835. *Washington.* 1835. 8vo. — Speech ... on the Bill to appropriate the Proceeds of the Sales of the Public Lands, ... in the Senate ... on the 15th and 16th of March. *Washington.* 1836. 8vo, pp. 24. BA. — Speech ... on Mr. Bradbury's Resolutions relative to Removals from Office [by Gen. Taylor]; in Senate, Jan 7, 1851. *Washington.* [1851.] 8vo, pp. 15. BA., H. — Speech ... at Chilicothe, Ohio, before a Republican Meeting, Sept. 29th, 1860. *Cincinnati.* 1860. 8vo, pp. 24. H.

Ewing. Record of the Family of Thos. Ewing, who Emigrated from Ireland to America in 1718. Edition of 150 copies printed for the use of the Family Connexions only. *Press of James H. Bryson.* 1858. 8vo, pp. 38. Folded Chart. 23332

Ewing (William). Remarks ... delivered in the Tennessee House of Representatives ... December 5th, 1859, on the Second Reading of the Bill ... for the Expulsion of Free Persons of Color from this State. ... [*Nashville.* 1859.] 8vo, pp. 12.

Exact Copies of Advertisements of Persons Wanted to claim Property of Deceased Relatives and Friends, in ... America, that have appeared in the London, Provincial, Colonial, and Foreign Newspapers, within the Past Seventy Years. *London.* 1847. 12mo. 23334

An Exact List. *See* Vol. v., No. 18553.

An Exact List of Parliament. Added, The Trustees for Georgia, and the Places of their Abode. *London.* 1734. 12mo, 36 l. B. 23335

The Exact Time when the Whole American Debt will be entirely paid off. [n. p. 1869.] 8vo, pp. (3). H. 23336

Exaltacion magnifica de la Betlemitica Rosa de la mejor Americana Jerico, y accion gratulatoria por su plausible Plantacion dichosa; ... que celebro en esta Nobilissima Ciudad de Mexico, el Venerable Dean, y Cabildo de esta S. Iglesia Metropolitana. *Mexico: por Doña Maria de Benavides.* 1697. 4to, 12 l., 84 l. 23337

Examen Canonico-Legal de la Libertad Religiosa de las Provincias de la Descalcèz de estos Reynos de España, y de las de San Diego de Mexico, y San Gregorio de Philipinas, para el manejo de sus negocios en esta Corte, segun el arbitrio de los Prelados de ellas. [*Mexico.* n. d.] Folio. 23338

Exámen comparativo de la monarquía y de la república por un Thaboriano. *Lima.* 1867. 8vo, pp. 144. 23339

Examen Confectionis Pacificæ. *See* [Chauncey], Vol. III.

Examen de las Penitenciarias de los Estados Unidos. *New York.* 1853. Rl. 8vo. 23340

Examen de l'esclavage. *See* [Cullión (F. Val. de)], Vol. v.

Examen des questions de juridiction qui se sont elevées entre les gouvernements Anglais et Americain dans l'affaire de La Creole. *Paris.* [n. d.] 8vo, pp. 32. B. 23341

Examen des Recherches, 1771. *See* [Pernetty (A. J.)]

Examen du Gouvernement. *See* [Livingston (W.)]

Examen historique, 1774. *See* [Sanchez (M.)].

Examen Imperiale, 1818. *See* [Montlezun (M.)]

Exámen Sucincto | sobre los antiguos limites | de la Acadia, | y sobre los estipulaciones del | Trabado de Utrecht, | relations à ellos. | [n. p. n. d.] 8vo, pp. 52. Map. 23342

Spanish and French, in parallel columns. Probably published at Madrid about 1751. The following is an answer: "Carta de Monsieur *** a Monsieur *** en repuesta à la de Monsieur *** que se publicò en la Gaceta de Utrecht de 8 de Septiembre de 1755. Con algunas observaciones sobre un Escrito intitulado Examen succinto sobre los antiguos limites de la Acadia. *Año* 1756." 12mo, pp. 26. J.C.B.

Examen du Sentiment d'un pretendu Patriote. 1740. 4to.

An answer to "Sentiment d'un Patriote Hollandois."

Examen | vande | Valsche Resolutie van de Heeren Bur- | gemeesters ende Raden tot Amsterdam. | Op 't stuck vande | West-Indische | Compagnie. | *Tot Amsterdam,* | *By Abraham de Bruyn by de Regeliers-poort* 1649. | 4to, pp. 36. 23344

An Examination and Explanation. *See* South Sea.

Examination by Chemical Analysis and otherwise, of substances emptied into the Public Waters of the State, from Gas and other Manufactories, Sewerage and other Sources, to ascertain if any injury results therefrom to any of the Fisheries in said public waters, in the vicinity of the City of Providence, 1860. *Providence: A. Crawford Greene.* 1861. 8vo, pp. 31. 23345

An Examination into the Conduct of the Present Administration, from the Year 1774 to the Year 1778. And a Plan of Accommodation with America. By a Member of Parliament. *London: J. Almon.* M.DCCLXXVIII. 8vo, pp. (2), 69. + The Second Edition, with Corrections. *London: J. Almon.* MDCCLXXIX. 8vo, pp. (2), 69. BA. 23346

"This writer proposes that the whole force of Great Britain should be employed against France. France being subdued, the Americans, he concludes, will naturally propose such terms of union as could be accepted, without derogating from the national dignity or interest." — *M. Rev.*, LIX. 470.

Examination into the Leading Principles, 1787. *See* [Webster (Noah)].

An Examination into the Principles, Conduct, and Designs, of the Minister. ... *London.* 1783. 8vo, pp. 62. 23347

Relates to Earl Shelburne and the Treaty of Peace.

An Examination into the Prospective Effects of the National Banks upon the Public Welfare. New York, December 1, 1863. By a Bank Director. *New York: Hall, Clayton & Medole.* 1863. 8vo, pp. 23. 23348

Examination into the Rights of the Indian Nations to their respective Countries; and a Vindication of the Grant from the Six Nations, to the Proprietors of Indiana. With Documents. *Philadelphia.* 1781. 8vo. P. 23349

An Examination of a Pamphlet, entitled "His Catholic Majesty's Manifesto, &c. With Reasons for not Paying the £95,000." *London: T. Gardner.* 1739. 8vo, pp. 59. J.C.B.

Examination of Charges against the American Missionaries at the Sandwich Islands, as alleged in the Voyage of the Ship Blonde and in the London Quarterly Review. *Cambridge.* 1827. 8vo. 23351

Privately printed.

An Examination of Some of the Provisions of the Act to create a Fund for the Benefit of the Creditors of certain Monied Corporations, and for Other Purposes. By a Stockholder. *New York.* 1829. pp. 40. 23352

An Examination of the alleged Expediency of the American Intercourse Bill; respectfully inscribed to R. Curling, Esq., and other Gentlemen who compose the Committee of Ship Owners. *London: Asperne.* 1806. 8vo. 23353

"This writer is astonished that any British bosom should entertain a wish below that of chastising the insolence and avenging the calumnies they so long have suffered. He inveighs bitterly against the violent spirit cherished in America towards England, but he deems it by no means improper in the subjects of H. M. to foster the highest possible resentment against the Americans." — *M. Rev.*

An Examination of the British Doctrine. *See* [Madison (James)].

An Examination of the Commercial Principles of the late Negotiation between Great Britain and France In MDCCLXI, in which The System of that Negotiation with Regard to our Colonies and Commerce is considered. *R. and J. Dodsley.* MDCCLXI. 8vo, Title, pp. 108. + The Second Edition. [*Ibid.*] MDCCLXII. 8vo, Title, pp. iv, 108. 23354

"Relates to the West Indies." — *M. Rev.*," XXVII. 362. Attributed to Edward Burke. *See our* No. 15031, Vol. IV., p. 326.

Examination of the Conduct. *See* [Madison (J.)]

An Examination of the Conduct of the Executive of the United States, towards the French Republic; likewise an Analysis of the Explanatory Article of the British Treaty in a Series of Letters. By a Citizen of Pennsylvania. ... *Philadelphia: Francis and Robert Bailey.* M,DCC,XCVII. 8vo, pp. vi, 72. BA. 23355

An Examination of the Constitution for [*sic*] the United States of America. By an American Citizen. With a Speech of James Wilson, Esq., on the same Subject. *Philadelphia: Z. Poulson.* 1788. 8vo, pp. 33. P. 23356

Examination of the Controversy between Georgia and the Creeks. First Published in the New York Review, August, 1825. *New York: Printed by Clayton & Van Norden.* 1825. 8vo, pp. 30, Cover, 2 l. 23357

Examination of the Evidence before Select Committee to enquire into the Present Condition and Prosperity of Sugar and Coffee Planting in the East and West Indian Possessions and the Mauritius. *London.* 1848. M. 23358

An Examination of the Grounds or Causes which are said to Induce the Court of Boston in New England to make that order or Law of Banishment upon pain of Death against the Quakers. [n. p.] 1660. W. 23359

An Examination of the late Proceedings. *See* [Hamilton (A.)]

Examination of the Legality of the General Orders which confer assimilated Rank on Officers of the Civil Branch of the United States Navy. By a Surgeon. *Philadelphia.* 1848. 8vo.

Examination of the Memorial of the Owners and Underwriters of the American Ship the New Jersey. *Philadelphia.* 1806. 8vo. C. 23361

Examination of the ... Tariff. *See* [Cambreleng (C.)], Vol. III., No. 10109.

Examination of the Opinion contained in the Report of the Onondaga Commissioners, [on the Military Grants] of the 17th Feb. 1800, to his Excellency the Governor; and by him transmitted to the Hon. the Legislature, with a view to its Refutation. By a Western Citizen. *Albany.* 1800. 8vo, pp. 24. 23362

An Examination of the Report of a Committee of the Citizens of Boston and its Vicinity, opposed to a Further Increase of Duties on Importation. By a Pennsylvanian. *Philadelphia: J. Maxwell.* 1828. 8vo, pp. 119. BA., H., W. 23363

Examination of the Power of the President to Remove from Office during the Recess of the Senate. *New York: Wynkoop, Hallenbeck & Thomas, Printers.* 1861. 8vo, pp. 23. 23364

Perhaps by James A. Hamilton.

The Examination of the President's Message, 1801. *See* [Hamilton (A.)]

An Examination of the President's Reply to the New Haven Remonstrance; With an Appendix containing The President's Inaugural Speech, the Remonstrance and Reply; together with a List of Removals from Office and New Appointments, made since the Fourth of March, 1801. *New York: George F. Hopkins.* 1801. 8vo, pp. 69. + *New Haven.* 1801. 8vo. H.

By William Coleman.

Examination of the Pretensions of New England to Commercial Pre-eminence. To which is added a View of the Causes of the Suspension of Cash Payments at the Banks. *Philadelphia.* 1814. 12mo. 23366

An Examination of the Principles, and an Enquiry into the Conduct, of the Two B*****rs. In regard to the Establishment of their Power, and their Prosecution of the War; till the Signing of the Preliminaries. In a Letter to a Member of Parliament. *London: A. Price.* MD.CC.XLIX. 8vo, pp. 79. + Third Edition. *London: A. Price.* MDCCXLIX. 8vo, pp. 79. C.

Examination of the Principles, &c. *See* [Lloyd (Charles)], *and* [Perceval (John), *Earl of Egremont*].

Examination of the Principles of Peace and War. *Philadelphia.* 1821. 12mo. 23368

An Examination of the Question now in Discussion between the American and British Governments, concerning the Right of Search: by an American. *Paris.* [1842?] S. 23369

Privately printed. It was answered by "Reply to 'American's Examination' of the 'Right of Search,' with Observations on some of the Questions at Issue between Great Britain and the United States. *London.* 1842." 8vo.

Examination of the Reasons why the present System of Auctions ought to be Abolished, as set forth by the Committee of New York Merchants opposed to the Auction System. *Boston.* 1828. 8vo. 23370

Examination of the Relations between the Cherokees. *See* Vol. III., No. 12456.

An Examination of the "Remarks." *See* Connecticut, Vol. IV., No. 15721.

An Examination of the Right of Secession. By a Friend to States Rights. *Louisville.* 1861. 8vo. 23371

An Examination of the Rights of the Colonies, upon Principles of Law. By a Gentleman at the Bar. *London: R. Dymott, and J. Almon.* MDCCLXVI. 8vo, pp. 42. B., BA., H. 23372

Opposes the stand taken by the colonies.

Examination of the Treaty, etc. *See* [Hamilton (A.)]

The Examiner and Journal of Political Economy; devoted to the Advancement of the Cause of State Rights and Free Trade. *Philadelphia.* 1834. 8vo. 23373

The Examiner; containing Political Essays on the most Important Events of the Time; Public Laws and Official Documents. Barent Gardiner, Esq., Ex-Editor. Rl. 8vo, pp. 76. *New York.* 1812–15. C. 23374

Continued to five or more volumes.

The Examiner examin'd, 1726. *See* [Brown (John)], Vol. II., No. 8505.

The Examiner Examined. A Letter from a Gentleman in Connecticut, to his Friend in London. In Answer to a Letter from a Gentlemam in London to his Friend in America: Intitled, The Claim of the Colonies to an Exemption from Internal Taxes imposed by Authority of Parliament, examined. *New London: Timothy Green.* MDCCLXVI. 8vo, pp. 24. BA., N., P.

The Examiner, or New-York Recorder and Baptist Register. June 28, 1855. *New York.* 1855. S. 23376

The Exchange. A Home and Colonial Review of Commerce, Manufactures, and General Politics. *London: Sampson, Low & Co.* 1862–3. 2 vols., 8vo. 23377

Exchange Alley; or, the Stock Jobber turn'd Gentleman; with the Humours of our Modern Projectors. A Tragi-Comical Farce. Humbly inscribed to the Gentlemen daily attending at Jonathan's Coffee House. *London: Printed for T. Bickerton.* 1720. 8vo, pp. 40. J.C.B. 23378

Relates to the South Sea and Mississippi Bubbles.

Excise Tax Law. An Act to Provide Internal Revenue to Support the Government, to pay Interest on the Public Debt, and for other Purposes. Passed June 30, 1864. *New York: John S. Voorhies.* 1864. 12mo, pp. 112. 23379

Excise Tax Laws. Suggestions of Amendments recommended by a Convention of United States Assessors, holden at Cleveland, Ohio, December 16, 17 and 18, 1863. *Boston: George C. Rand & Avery.* 1864. 8vo, pp. 20. 23380

See also "A Short History," "A Short Letter," and "Some Observations."

Excursion dans l'Amérique du Sud; esquisses et souvenirs. *Paris: Renard.* 1828. 8vo, 13½ sheets. 23381

Excursion made by the Executive and Legislatures of the States of Kentucky and Tennessee, to the State of Ohio, Jan. 1860; containing Letters, Speeches, Toasts, &c. &c. *Cincinnati.* 1860. 8vo, pp. 139. 23382

An Excursion of the Dog Cart, a Poem. By an Imprisoned Debtor. *New York: William Benkers, Junior.* 1822. 12mo.

Excursion of the Putnam Phalanx to Boston, Charlestown, and Providence, ... 1859. *Hartford, Conn.: Published by the Phalanx.* 1859. 8vo, pp. 107. Plate. 23384

See also [Clark (A. N.)], Vol. IV., No. 13248.

Excursion on the River Connecticut. *See* Vol. IV., No. 15865.

An Excursion through the United States. *See* [Blaney (*Capt.*)], Vol. II., No. 5872.

An Excursion to the Springs, Niagara, Quebec, and through the New England States; interspersed with Geographical and Historical Sketches. Third Edition, Enlarged and Improved. *Saratoga Springs.* 1828. 18mo. 23385

Excursions to Murray Bay, River du Loup, Kakouna, and the Far Famed River Saguenay. *Quebec.* 1856. 16mo, pp. 25. Map. 23386

Executive Documents and Reports. *See* Congress, Vol. IV.

An Exercise, containing a Dialogue and Ode on the Accession of his present Gracious Majesty, George III. Performed at the Public Commencement in the College of Philadelphia, May 18th, 1762. *Philadelphia: Printed by W. Dunlap.* MDCCLXII. 4to, pp. 8. P. 23387

An Exercise, containing a Dialogue and Ode on Peace. Performed at the Public Commencement in the College of Philadelphia, May 17th, 1763. *Philadelphia: Printed by Andrew Stewart.* M,DCC,LXIII. 8vo, pp. 8. P. 23388

Dialogue by Mr. Nat. Evans; Ode by Dr. Paul Jackson, of Chester.

An Exercise, containing a Dialogue and two Odes, Performed at the Public Commencement in the College of Philadelphia. November 17, 1767. *Philadelphia: Printed by William Goddard,* 4to, pp. 8. P. 23389

Exercise for Garrison and Field Ordnance, together with Manœuvres of Horse Artillery, as Altered from the Manual of Gen. Kosciusko, and adapted to the Service of the U. S. By an Officer of the U. S. Artillerists. In Two Parts. *New York: Printed by Pelsue & Gould.* 1812. 16mo, pp. 128. B. 23390

Exercises at the Consecration of the Flag of the Union. *See* Vol. II., No. 6664.

EXETER (*Bishop of*). *See* Ross (John).

EXETER, *N. H.* The Result of a Council of Ten Churches, Convened at Exeter, January 31, 1743. *Boston.* 1744. 8vo, pp. 16. B., N. 23391

Result of an Ecclesiastical Council at Exeter, N. H., August 31, 1842. *Boston.* 1842. 8vo. 23392

Review of the Result of an Ecclesiastical Council, Convened at Exeter, N. H., August 31, 1842. *Exeter.* 1842. 8vo.

Rules of the Library Society of Exeter, N. H. 12mo. W.

Catalogue of the Officers and Students of Phillips Exeter Academy. *Exeter.* 1838. 12mo, pp. 59. M. + *Exeter.* 1839. 12mo, pp. 12. M. 23395

An Exhibit of the Losses Sustained at the Office of Discount and Deposit Baltimore, under the Administration of James A. Buchanan, President, ... Compiled by the President and Directors ... . To which is Appended a Report of the Conspiracy Cases, Tried at Hartford County Court in Maryland. *Baltimore: printed by Thomas Murphy.* 1823. 8vo, pp. xix, 278, 116, (2). C. 23396

An Exhibit, showing the Success of Cotton Factories at Augusta, Georgia; and Vicinity. *Augusta, Ga.* 1871. 8vo, pp. 42. H. 23397

Exhibition of Industry, New-York, 1853. Official Catalogue of the Pictures Contributed. ... First Edition. *New York.* 1853. 12mo. S. 23398

See also New York.

Exhibition of 1853. Association for the Exhibition of the Industry of All Nations. Official Awards of Juries. *New York, Association.* 1853. 8vo, pp. 98. S. 23399

An Exhibition of the Unjust and Oppressive Operation of the Present Tariff System. By a Committee of the Free Trade Convention. *Philadelphia.* 1832. 8vo. P. 23400

An Exhibition of Wolves in Sheep's Clothing; or Hypocrisy Unmasked. By a Jeffersonian Republican. *Albany.* 1836. 8vo, pp. 16. S. 23401

Exhortacion a los habitantes del Nuevo Mundo. *Campeche.* 1808. 4to, pp. 10. 23402

EXILES (A. F. P. d'). *See* Prévost d'Exiles.

Exiles in Virginia. *See* [Gilpin (W.)]

The Exiles Lay, Valedictory to the Land of his Birth, and Salutatory to that of his Adoption, and other Poems. *Boston: Jas. French & Co.* 1855. 18mo, pp. 122. 23403

The Expediency of Securing our American Colonies by Settling the Country adjoining the River Mississippi, and the Country upon the Ohio, Considered. *Edinburgh.* MDCCLXIII. 12mo, pp. 68. 23404

Expediente instruido en el Ministerio de Relaciones Esteriores del Gobierno Constitucional, sobre medios de avenimiento para la pacificacion del pais y termina de la guerra civil. *Veracruz.* 1860. Folio, 8 l.; Continuacion, 9 l. 23405

Expediente instruido. *See* Cuba, Vol. V., No. 17776.

Expediente seguido en junta extraordinaria de tribunales, para facilitar arbitrios con que auxiliar á la real hacienda, en las urgentes necesidades del dia. *Lima: B. Bernardino Ruiz.* 1815. Folio, pp. 55. 23406

EXPERIENCE, *pseudonym.* A Treatise on the Cotton Trade; in Twelve Letters. Addressed to the Levant Company, West India Planters, and Merchants. By Experience. *London: Abraham.* 1790. 12mo, pp. 63. 23407

See "M. Rev.," IV., 109.

Experience of a Confederate States Prisoner; being an Ephemeris regularly kept by an Officer of the Confederate States Army. *Richmond: West & Johnston.* 1862. 8vo, pp. 64. B.

Experience preferable to Theory. An Answer to Dr. Price's Observations on the Nature of Civil Liberty, and the Justice and Policy of the War with America. ... *London: T. Payne.* MDCCLXXVI. 8vo, pp. (2), 102. BA., H. 23409

Perhaps by Gov. Thomas Hutchinson. One of the best and most decent answers to Dr. Price.

Experience the Test of Government. *See* [Duane (W.)], Vol. V., No. 20986.

EXPILLY (Charles). Le Brésil tel qu' il est. *Paris.* 1862. 16mo. B. + Seconde Edition. *Paris.* 1863. 16mo. C. 23410

EXPILLY. Les Femmes et les Mœurs du Brésil. Troisième Edition. *Paris.* 1864. 16mo. C. 23411

EXPILLY. La verité sur le conflit entre le Brésil, Buenos-Ayres, Montevideo et le Paraguay. *Paris: Dentu.* 1865.

An Explanation and History of the Book of Common Prayer. To which are added the Articles of Religion, as Established by ... the Protestant Episcopal Church of the United States. *Philadelphia.* 1834. 18mo, pp. 144. 23413

An Explanation of Say-Brook Platform; or, The Principles of the Consociated Churches in Connecticut: Collected from their Plan of Union. By One that humbly desires the Order, Peace, and Purity of these Churches. *Hartford: Thomas Green.* 1765. 4to, pp. 39. M. 23414

An Explanation of the Case Relating to the Capture of St. Eustatius; in which is included the several Commissions, appointing the Agents to manage the Business of the Capture, Pointing out The most effectual Methods to the Captors to obtain Relief, and to secure to them what there is remaining of the captured Property. *London: J. Stockdale.* M DCC LXXXIII. 8vo, pp. 17, (3). 23415

See "M. Rev.," LXXV. 152.

An Explanation of the Conduct of the French Government in their Late Negociations with the American Commissioners. *London: Ridgway.* 1798. 8vo. 23416

See "M. Rev.," XVI. 343.

An Explanation of the First, Second, and Third Heats of the European Race, ... *London.* 1740. 8vo. Plate. 23417

Contains some references to American affairs.

An Explanation of the Map. *See* [Cutler (Manasseh)], Vol. v., No. 18174.

An Explanation of the Prospective-Plan of the Battle of Lake George, Sept. 8, 1755. [n. p. n. d.] 4to. 23418

An Explanation of the Views of the Situation and different Attacks of his Majesty's Ships and Squadrons at the Siege of Havannah, with Names of the Commanders, &c. *London.* 1762. Folio. 23419

An Explanation of the Views of the Society for Employing the Female Poor, with the Constitution and By-Laws, and the Arrangement of the School. *Boston.* 1826. 8vo, pp. 12.

Explanations of Manual Exercise, with some General Field Directions. *Halifax, N. S.* 1759. 4to. W. 23421

Explanatory Article, signed at Philadelphia, May 4th, 1795. To be added to the Treaty of Amity, Commerce, &c., between His Britannic Majesty and the United States of America, Nov. 19, 1794. *London: Johnston.* 1796. 4to, pp. 5. 23422

Explanatory Remarks on the Assembly's Resolves, published in the Pennsylvania Gazette, No. 1840. [*Printed at Philadelphia about April* 12. 1764.] Folio, pp. 2. P. 23423

Explicacion clara y sucinta de los principales misterios de nuestra Santa Fé, oracion dominical, mandamientos y sacramentos en el idioma mexicano y en el castellano. Compuesto por un cura del Obispado de Puebla. *Puebla: imprenta del Hospital de S. Pedro.* 1835. Sm. 8vo, pp. 265, 1 l. 23424

Explicacion de la Bula de la Santa Cruzada, que para la Mayor commodidad de los Reverendos Parrocos, y utilidad de todos los Fieles, manda dar a luz el Ill. Sr. Comissario General de la misma Santa Cruzada. *Toledo.* 1758. 8vo. 23425

"On the utility, facility, and necessity of this Holy Bull, *see* page 13 and following. This Bull was sold for half a dollar, mostly in Mexico. Without it priests are said to have refused to give absolution."—STEVENS.

Exposé de la situacion actuelle des colonies françaises. *See* Vol. IV., No. 14711.

Exposé des Droits des Colonies Britanniques pour justifier le projet de leur Independence. *Amsterdam: chez Marc-Michel Rey.* MDCCLXXVI. 8vo, pp. (4), 43, 74. 23426

Written by a foreigner residing in England, who it appears had already published an "Essai sur la veritable Liberté civile, adressé au peuple d'Angleterre."

Exposé des Faits qui ont Accompagnés l'Agression des Français contre l'île de Taïti, et l'injuste establissement de la domination Française dans cette île. Par les Directeurs de la Société des Missions de Londres. Traduit de l'Anglois. *Paris.* 1843. 8vo, 5½ sheets. 23427

Exposé des Motifs de la conduite du Roi Trés-Cretien relativement à l'Angleterre. Accompagnie d'un pareil exposé de ceux qui ont déterminé le Roi d'Espagne, dans le parti qu'il a pris à l'égard de la même Puissance. Publie par l'ordre de sa Majesté Catholique, à Madrid, de l'imprimerie royale de la Gazette, 1779. Traduit de l'Espagnol. *Paris: de l'imprimerie Royale.* 1779. 4to, pp. 40. J.C.B. 23428

A translation of the "Manifiesto de los Motivos," etc. *Madrid.* 1779. Also printed in French at *Madrid.* 1779, and at *London.* 1780.

Exposés des Motifs, Rapports, et Débats des Chambres Législatives concernant les Lois des 18 et 19 Juillet 1845, relatives au Régime des Esclaves, à l'introduction de cultivateurs Européens et à la formation d'établissements agricoles dans les Colonies Françaises. *Paris.* 1845. 8vo. C. 23429

Exposé générale des résultats. *See* Vol. IV., No. 14712.

An Exposé of Facts concerning Recent Transactions relating to the Corps of Cadets of the United States Military Academy. *Newburgh, (N. Y.): U. C. Lewis.* 1819. 8vo, pp. vii, 68. C.

An Exposé of the Secret Order of Know Nothings. The most Ludicrous and Startling "Yankee Notion" ever conceived. *New York.* 1854 [*or* 1856]. 8vo, pp. 32. 23431

Exposé upon Dissensions. *See* Vol. IV., No. 12772.

Exposicion con que la comision nombrada para la reforma del arancel, de las aduanas maritimas y fronterizas, dió cuenta al gobierno supremo del plan que signió en el cumplimento de su encargo. *Mexico.* 1845. 8vo, pp. 96. 23432

Exposicion de las conferencias con el comisionado de los Estados-Unidos. *Queretaro.* 1847. 8vo. 23433

Exposicion de una persona residente en la Republica Mexicana, sobre la guerra que actualmente sostiene con los Estados-Unidos del Norte. *Mexico.* 1847. 4to, pp. 16. 23434

Exposicion del Ex-Ministro de Relationes, ... *Queretaro.* 1847. 8vo. 23435

Relates to Texas.

Exposicion presentada à las Cortes por los Diputados de Ultramar en la Session de 25 de Junio de 1821, sobre el estado actual de las Provincias de que son Representantes, etc. *Madrid.* 1821. Sm. 4to, pp. 17. 23436

Exposicion que a la legislatura nacional presenta el ministro de hacienda en 1866. *Carácas.* 1866. 4to, pp. xl, 186, 12.

Exposicion que el Congreso Nacional presenta el Ministro de fomento en 1869. *Carácas.* 1869. 8vo, pp. xxv, 134. 12 Tables. 23438

Exposicion que dirijen al Congreso Nacional y al publico algunos proprietarios de fundos Colindantes con las riberas del mar en El puerto de Valparaiso Manifestando su derecho a los terrenos abandonados por el mar en Ese puerto. *Santiago de Chile.* 1844. Folio. 23439

Exposicion que dirije a la legislatura nacional en 1865, el ministro de la interior y justicia. *Carácas.* 1865. 4to, pp. 48, 64. 23440

Exposicion que ha dirigido al augusto Congreso Nacional el Ayuntamiento de la Ciudad de Santiago de Leon de Carácas, representante de la municipalidad de la provincia de su nombre, que lo es tambien del departamento de Venezuela, sobre el origen que tuvo la desgraciada transformacion politica de aquella provincia y de otras sus adyacentes. *Cádiz.* 1813. 4to, pp. 39.

Rare and important for the history of the war of independence.

Exposicion que hace al Publico la Junta de Señoras encargada de la direccion de la casa de niños expositos en esta Capital. *Mexico.* 1838. 4to, pp. 20. Table. 23442

Exposicion que presenta á este sensato público D. J. I. Echegoyen en la cuestion que sobre pureza en el manejo de sus intereses le sostiene el Excmo. Sr. D. Francisco de Arango y Parreño va á hacer cuatro años con detrimento de las respectivas opiniones y mengua del carácter noble y franco de los contendientes. [*Habana:*] *Imprenta de D. Antonio Pereira.* 1812. 4to, pp. 19.

Exposicion que los Conservadores de los Provincias dirigen al Sr. General Almonte a sus correligionarios y proprietarios de la capital sobre los bases de la futura organisacion politica del Pais. *Mexico.* 1863. 8vo, pp. 20. 23444

Exposicion que dirige al congreso de Venezuela en 1841 el Secretario de guerra y marina [Franc. Hernaiz]. *Caracas: Valentin Espinal.* 1841. 8vo, 1 l., pp. 52. 23445

Exposiciones de la Suprema Corte de Justicia y de los jueces de letras de esta Capital, sobre el estado en que se halla la administracion de justicia en lo criminal, y las verdaderas causas de atraso que se advierte en la aprehension y castigo de algunos delincuentes. *Mexico.* 1836. 4to, pp. 34. 23446

Exposition and Protest, Reported by the Special Committee of the House of Representatives [of South Carolina], on The Tariff; Read and Ordered to be Printed Dec. 19th, 1828. [By John C. Calhoun.] *Columbia, S. C.* 1829. 8vo, pp. 43. M.

Exposition of a Pamphlet, entitled Papers relative to the Rupture with Spain. *London.* 1762. 8vo. 23448

An Exposition of Facts and Arguments in Support of a Memorial to the Legislature of Massachusetts, by Citizens of Boston and Vicinity, in favor of a Bank of Ten Millions. *Boston.* 8vo, pp. 90. (Senate Doc., No. 30.) H. 23449

An Exposition of some of the Evils arising from the Auction System. [*New York.* 1822?] 8vo, pp. 16. S. 23450

An Exposition of the Advantages of a Railroad between New York and Albany, on the Interior Route, January, 1847. *New-York: George F. Nesbitt.* 1847. 8vo, pp. 31. 23451

An Exposition of the African Slave Trade, from the year 1840 to 1850, inclusive, prepared from Official Documents, and Published by Direction of the Representatives of the Religious Society of Friends, in Pennsylvania, New Jersey, and Delaware. *Philadelphia: J. Rakestraw.* 1851. 8vo, pp. 160. 23452

An Exposition of the Causes. *See* [Dallas (A. J.)], Vol. v., No. 18309.

Exposition of the Causes and Consequences. *See* [Urquhart (David)].

Exposition of the Federal Constitution, contained in the Report of the Committee of the Virginia House of Delegates, to whom were committed the proceedings of other States, in Answer to the Resolutions of the General Assembly of 21st Dec., 1798—commonly called Madison's Report—together with a series of papers under the signature of "Hampden," being a Critique on the Supreme Court of the United States, in the case of the Bank Law. *Richmond: Printed by Tom Ritchie.* 1819. 8vo. 23453

An Exposition of the Government of the Methodist Episcopal Conference, with Reflections on the Nature and Tendency of its System. Also A Serious Address to the Methodist Community of New England. By an Anti-Episcopal Methodist. *Boston.* 1830. pp. 16. 23454

Exposition of the Houmas Land Claim, and of the ... Missouri Land Bill, ... 1858. ... *Washington.* 1859. 8vo, pp. 30.

An Exposition of the late General Election in New-York. By a Citizen of Pennsylvania. *Philadelphia.* 1826. 8vo, pp. 24. BA. 23456

Ex-Post-Facto Laws. An Explanation of the Meaning of the Prohibitory Terms used in the Constitution of the United States. ... *Boston.* [n. d.] 8vo, pp. 7. M. 23457

See also Bibb (George M.)

An Exposition of the Memorial of Sundry Presbyters of the Protestant Episcopal Church; presented to the House of Bishops, during the General Convention of said Church, 1853. By One of the Memorialists. *New York: Stanford & Swords.* 1834. 8vo, pp. (2), 84, (1). 23458

Exposition of the Motives. *See* [Gibbon (Ed.)]

Exposition of the Objects and Plans of the American Union for the Relief and Improvement of the Colored Race. ... *Boston: Light & Horton.* 1835. 8vo, pp. 23. H. 23459

Exposition of the Peculiarities, Difficulties, and Tendencies of the Oberlin Perfectionism. *Cleveland.* 1841. 8vo. 23460

Exposition of the Penitentiary System of Punishment, but more particularly adapted to that of Virginia, &c. *Richmond.* 1821. 8vo. 23461

An Exposition of the Principles and Regulations of the Shakers. *Albany.* 1830. 12mo. P. 23462

An Exposition of the System pursued by the Baptist Missionaries in Jamaica, by Missionaries and Catechists of the London Missionary Society. *London.* 1842. 8vo, pp. 32. M. 23463

An Exposition of the Treatment of Slaves in the Southern States, Particularly in the States of Maryland, Virginia, North Carolina, South Carolina, and Georgia: Together with a System of Reformation Recommended, by Jarvis Brewster. *New Brunswick: D. & J. Fitz Randolph.* 1815. 8vo, pp. 34. 23464

An Exposition of the Unconstitutionality of the Law of the State of New-York, Compelling the Observance of a Religious Sabbath Day. *New-York.* 1826. S. 23465

Exposition universelle de 1867. Catalogue des produits des colonies françaises, précédé d'une notice statistique. *Paris: Challamel ainé.* 1867. 8vo, pp. (2), cxlvii, (2), 155, Table.

Also in German.

An Exposition of the Weakness. *See* [Fenton (Charles)].

EXPOSITOR, *pseudonym.* A Letter to the Citizens of Charleston, embracing Strictures, &c. &c. By Expositor. *Charleston, (S. C.) April,* 1818. 8vo, pp. 10. H. 23467

An Exposure. *See* [Harison (William H.)]

EXQUEMELIN (Alexandre Olivier). De | Americaensche | Zee-Roovers. | Behelsende een pertinente en waerachtige Beschrijving van alle de | voornaemste Roveryen, en onmenschlijcke wreedheden, | die de Engelse en Franse Rovers, tegens de Spanjaerden | in America, gepleeght hebben. | Verdeelt in drie deelen: | Het Eerste Deel verhandelt hoe de Fransen op Hispanjola gekomen zijn, de | aerdt van't Landt, Inwoonders, en hun manier van leven aldaer. | Het Tweede Deel, de opkomst van de Rovers, hun regel en leven onder mal- | kander, nevens verscheyde Roveryen aen de Spanjaerden gepleeght. | Het Derde't verbranden van de Stadt Panama, door d'Engelsche en Franse | Rovers gedaen, nevens het geen de Schrijver op sijn Reys voorgevallen is. | Hier achter is bygevoeght, | Een korte verhandeling van de Macht en Rijkdommen, die de Koninck van | Spanje, Karel de Tweede, in America heeft, nevens des selfs | Inkomsten en Regering aldaer. | Als mede

een kort begrijp van alle de voornaemste Plaetsen in het selve Gewest, | onder Christen Potentaten behoorende. | Beschreven door A. O. Exquemelin. | Die self alle dese Roveryen, door noodt, bygewoont heeft. | Met schoone Figuren, Kaerten, en Conterfeytsels, alle na't leven geteeckent, versien. | *t'Amsterdam,* | *By Jan ten Hoorn, Boeckverkoper, over't Oude* | *Heeren Logement. Anno* 1678. | 4to, 2 Titles, 1 of which is Engraved, 2 l., pp. 186. 4 Portraits, 6 Copperplates, and 2 Maps. J.C.BT. 23468

First edition, of extreme rarity. Perhaps no book in any language was ever the parent of so many imitations, and the source of so many fictions as this, the original of the buccaneers of America. Mr. F. Muller, of Amsterdam, whose learned researches on the subject of Dutch books relating to America, entitle his opinions to great respect, remarks: "This is the rare original edition of a book, the importance of which is, I believe, plain to every one who knows only one-tenth of the novels, imaginary voyages, books for youths, and for other people, comedies, and tragedies which have been taken from it by almost every European nation; so that to collect all that literature might be the task for a man's life. There is certainly no other book of that time which experienced a popularity similiar to that of the 'Buccaniers of America,' which was, in the ten years following its publication, translated into most of the European languages; and there is a fact most curious in the literary history of all times, that the original was certainly unknown to all translators but one. They were all inclined to take the Spanish edition for the original; nay, even the learned editors of Mr. Grenville's catalogue seem doubtful whether the Dutch edition existed in print, or in MS. only. I leave it to amateurs more learned than myself to decide whether this is owing to the fact of so few people studying the Dutch language, or to the scarcity of the book, and shall only add that it is not mentioned by Rich or by Ternaux, which both contain the Spanish, English and French translations, while Ternaux notices a large number of Dutch books of minor importance. As to myself, *I never saw more than two copies before,* which were sold to American amateurs." In a recent catalogue, Mr. Muller describes a copy, "on large thick paper. Extremely rare." The first account of the buccaneers is to be found in G. Klaes Compaen's "Zee-Roover. *Amsterdam.* 1663." *See our* Nos. 15015–16, Vol. IV.

[EXQUEMELIN.] Histoire | der | Boecaniers, | of vrybuyters | van | America. | Van haar eerste Beginzelen tot deze tegenwoordige tyd toe. | Met Figuuren. | *t'Amsterdam, by Nicolaas ten Hoorn, Boekverkooper, over* | *'t Oude Heeren Logement,* 1700. | 4to, Engraved and Printed Titles, 2 l., pp. 219, 136, Register, 3 l. 7 Plates.

This is a new and very much altered edition of No. 23468. The second part is a translation of the voyages of Sharp and others. The plates are also new.

[EXQUEMELIN.] Americanische Seeräuber. Beschreibung der grössesten durch die Französische und Englische Meer-Beuter, wider die Spanier in America verübten Raubery Grausamkeit ... . Durch A. O. *Nürnberg.* 1679. 12mo. Maps, Portraits, and Plates. 23470

This is evidently a German translation of Exquemelin.

EXQUEMELIN. Piratas | de la | America, | Y luz à la defensa de las costas de | Indias Occidentales. | Dedicado | a | Don Bernardino Antonio | De Pardiñas Villar-de Francos, | Cavallero del Orden de S. Tiago [*sic*], Secretario del Exmo. Sr. | Duque de Medina-Cœli, en el empleo de Primer | Ministro de su Magestad Catholica. | Por el zelo y cuydado de | Don Antonio Freyre, | Natural de la Inclyta Ciudad de la Coruña en el Reyno de | Galicia, y Vezino de la Herculeä de Cadiz. | Traducido de la lengua Flamenca en Española, por el | Dor. Alonso de Buena-Maison, | Español, Medico Practico en la Amplissima y Magnifica | Ciudad de Amsterdam. | *Impresso en Colonia Agrippina en Casa de* | *Lorenzo Struickman, Año de* 1681. | 4to, 19 l., Engraved Arms on reverse of Title, p. xvi, 328, 2 l. 4 Portraits, 2 Plates, and 1 Map, with Vignette Engraving in the Text, p. 20. J.C.BT. 23471

First edition in Spanish, translated from the Dutch, and the plates copied from it. The English version is a translation of this Spanish edition. Some original verses precede the Spanish text, describing American localities, among which mention is made of Labrador, Terra-Nova, Norumbega, etc.

EXQUEMELIN. Piratas | de la | America. | Y Luz à la defensa de las Costas | de Indias Occidentales | Dedicado | Al muy Noble Señor Don | Francisco Lopez Suazo. | Traducido | De la lengua Flamenca en Española, por | el Dor. de Buena-Maison Medico | Practico en la opulentissima | Ciudad de Amsterdam. | Segundo Impression. | *En Colonia Agrippina,* | *En casa de Lorenço Struik-* | *Man Año de* 1682. | 12mo, 24 l., pp. 490, 8. 23472

EXQUEMELIN. Piratas | de la | America. | Y Luz à la defensa de las Costas | de Indias Occidentales | Dedicado | Al muy Noble Señor Don | Ricardo de Whyte, | Cavellero del Orden Militar | de Calatrava &ca. | Traducido | De la lengua Flamenca en Española, | por el Dor. de Bonne-Maison. | Impression Segunda. | *En Colonia Agrippina,* | *En casa de Lorenco Struik-* | *Man, Año de* 1682. | 12mo, 28 l., pp. 490, 8. 23473

Thornbury, in his preface to an account of the buccaneers, describes a Spanish edition dated 1684; but the many errors in his list lead me to question this.

EXQUEMELIN. Piratas | de la America, | y luz à la defensa | de las costas | de Indias occidentales, | En que se tratan las cosas notables de los viages, | descripcion de las Islas Española, Tortuga, Jamay- | ca, de sus frutos y producciones, politica de sus | habitantes, guerras y encuentros entre Españoles y | Franceses, origen de los Piratas, y su modo de vi- | vir, la toma y incendio de la Ciudad de Panama, | invasion de varias Plazas de la America por los roba- | dores Franceses, Lolonois y Morgan. | Traducida del flamenco en Español|por el Doctor de Buena-Maison. Dala á luz esta tercera edicion|D. M. G. R. ... *Madrid: Ramon Ruiz.* MDCCXCIII.| 4to, pp. xxiv, 228, 2 l. c. 23474

EXQUEMELIN. Histoire|des|avanturiers|qui se sont signalez dans les Indes,|contenant|ce qu'ils ont fait de plus remarq-|uable depuis vingt années.|Avec|La Vie, les Mœurs, les Coûtumes des Habitans de|Saint Do-|mingue & de la Tortuë, & une Description|exacte de ces lieux:|Où l'on voit|L'établissement d'une Chambre des Comptes dans les|Indes, & un Etat, tiré de cette Chambre, des Offices|tant Ecclesiastiques que Seculieres, où le Roy d'Es-|pagne pourvoit, les Revenus qu'il tire de l'Ameri-|que, & ce que les plus grands Princes de l'Europe y|possedent.|Le tout enrichi de Cartes Geographiques & de Figures|en Taille-douce.|Par Alexandre Olivier Oexmelin.|*A Paris,|Chez Jacques le Febvre, au dernier pillier|de la Grand Salle, vis-à-vis les Requestes du Palais.*|M.DC.LXXXVI.| 2 vols., 12mo, Engraved and Printed Titles, 15 l., pp. 342, Table, 12 l., 2 Maps and 3 Plates; 3 l., pp. 384, 11 l., Table, 1 l, Advertisement, 1 l., 1 Map and 1 Plate.

First French edition, of extreme rarity, translated from the Spanish. The author's name is rather singularly changed. The translation was made by M. de Frontignières. In 1689 the Journal of Raveneau de Lussan first appeared, and was republished in 1692, and is afterwards generally added to the work. Editions of Oexmelin, with this addition, appeared in 3 vols., 12mo, in 1699. We have seen De Lussan's Journal above, with the date of 1705.

EXQUEMELIN. Histoire|des|avanturiers|qui se sont signalezs dans les Indes,|contenant|ce qu'ils ont fait de plus remarquable|depuis vingt années.|Avec|La Vie, les Mœurs, les Coûtumes des Habitans de Saint Do-|mingue & de la Tortuë, & une Description exacte de ces|lieux:|Où l'on voit|L'établissement d'une Chambre des Comptes dans les Indes,|& un Etat, tiré de cette Chambre, des Offices tant Eccle-|siastiques que Seculiers, où le Roy d'Espagne pourvoit,|les Revenus qu'il tire de l'Amerique, & ce que les plus grands|Princes de l'Europe y possedent.|Le tout enrichi de Cartes Geographiques & de Figures|en Taille-douce.|Par Alexandre Olivier Oexmelin.|*A Paris,|Chez Jacques le Febvre, au dernier pillier de la|Grand Salle vis-à-vis les Requestes du Palais.*|M.DC.LXXXVIII.| 2 vols., 12mo, 12 l., pp. 448 [for 248], Table, (16), 2 Maps; 3 l., pp. 285, Table, (16), 1 Map.

EXQUEMELIN. Histoire des Aventuriers Flibustiers, qui se sont signalés dans les Indes; contenant ce qu'ils y ont fait de remarquable, avec la vie, les mœurs les coûtumes des boucaniers, & des habitans de St. Domingue, & de la Tortue; une description

exacte de ces lieux, & un état des offices, tant ecclesiastiques que séculiers, & ce que les grands princes de l'Europe y possedent. Par Alexandre Olivier Oexmelin. Nouvelle edition, corrigée & augmentée de l'histoire des pirates Anglois, depuis leur établissement dans l'Isle de Providence jusqu' à présent. *Trevoux: Par la Compagnie.* M,DCC,XLIV. 4 vols., 12mo, pp. (12), 394, (2); 428; 347; lx, 355, (4). 7 Plates, and Map.

Vol. III. is Raveneau de Lussan; Vol. IV., Johnson's "Pirates," first published in French in 1726.

EXQUEMELIN. Histoire des Avanturiers Flibustiers, ... par A. O. Oexmelin. Nouvelle edition. *Lyon.* MDCCLXXIV. 4 vols., 12mo, pp. (12), 394, (2); 428; 348; lx, 356, (2). 2 Plates. + Nouvelle Edition, Corrigée & augmentée de l'Histoire des Pirates Anglois, depuis leur établissement dans l'Isle de la Providence jusqu'à present. *A Trevoux: Par la Compagnie.* M,DCC,-LXXV. 4 vols., 12mo, 6 l., pp. 394, 1 l.; pp. 428; 347; lx, 355, 2 l. 7 Plates, and Maps. B., C., S. 23478

The same as the Trevoux edition of 1744. "Mr. Eyries, in the 'Biographie Universelle,' says that the French translation, first printed in 1686, was published from the MSS. of the author by Frontignières; who, he says, printed the work as if translated from the English, which no doubt was the case; but Mr. Eyries appears to have been ignorant of the existence of any other edition, in any language."—RICH.

EXQUEMELIN. Bucaniers|of|America:|Or, a true|Account|of the|Most remarkable Assaults|Committed of late years upon the Coasts of|The West Indies,|By the Bucaniers of Jamaica and Tortuga,|Both English and French.|Wherein are contained more especially,|The Unparallel'd Exploits of Sir Henry Morgan, our En-|glish Jamaican Hero, who sack'd Puerto Velo, burnt Panama, &c.|Written originally in Dutch, by John Esquemeling, one of the|Bucaniers, who was present at those Tragedies; and thence|translated into Spanish, by Alonso de Bonne-maison, Doctor of|Physick, and Practitioner at Amsterdam.|Now faithfully rendred into English.|*London:|Printed for William Crooke, at the Green Dragon, with-|out Temple-bar.* 1684.| 4to. C.

As there is some difficulty in recognizing the editions of this work, except *de viso*, we give the following minute collation: Title, 1 l., "To the Reader," 5 l., Part I., pp. 115; Part II., pp. 151; Part III., pp. 124, Table, 6 l. Sometimes followed by Ringrose, and called Vol. II., Title, 1 l., "To the Reader," 7 l., Text, pp. 212, "Table," pp. 15, "Catalogue," pp. 7; Plates at pp. 95 and 102 of Part I., at pp. 1, 38, 60, 80, and 134 of Part II., at pp. 31 and 54 of Part III., and at p. 98 of Part IV., map at p. 212, and several maps with the text. This Part IV. consists of Sharp's voyage, and is perhaps more properly part of the second edition. Its title is, "Bucaniers|of|America,|The Second Volume|Containing|The Dangerous Voyage and|Bold Attempts of Captain Bartholomew|Sharp, & Others; performed upon the|Coasts of the South

Sea for the space of two years, &c.|From the Original Journal of the said Voyage.|Written|By Mr. Basil Ringrose,|Gent. Who was all along present at those Transactions.|*London,|Printed for William Cooke, &c.* 1685."| In a Catalogue issued by Puttick and Stevens, a copy of the work is described as large paper. All the copies we have seen have an unusually large margin, but we have not met with a large paper copy. The following is from the "London Gazette" of June 8, 1685, and probably refers to this first edition: "Westminster, June 1. There have been lately Printed and Published two Books, one by Will. Crook, the other by Tho. Malthus, both Intitled *The History of the Bucaniers*; both which Books contained many False, Scandalous and Malicious Reflections on the Life and Actions of Sir Henry Morgan of Jamaica Kt. The said Sir Henry Morgan hath by Judgment had 'n the King's-Bench-Court, recovered against the said Libel £20 Damages. And on the humble Solicitation and Request of William Crook, hath been pleased to withdraw his Action against the said Crook, and accept of his Submission and Acknowledgement in Print." —STEVENS.

EXQUEMELIN. The|History|of the|Bucaniers:|Being an|Impartial Relation|of all the battels, sieges, and other most|Eminent Assaults committed for several|years upon the Coasts of the|VVest-Indies|by the pirates of|Jamaica and Tortuga.|Both English, & other Nations.|More especially the Unparallel'd At-|chievements of Sir H. M.|Made English from the Dutch copy: Written by|J. Esquemeling, one of the Bucaniers, very much Cor-|rected, from the Errours of the Original, by the Rela-|tions of some English Gentlemen, that then resided|in those parts.| ... |*London, Printed for Tho. Malthus at the Sun in|the Poultrey.* 1684.| 12 l., pp. 192. C. 23480

This is apparently an abridgment of the foregoing. It is a small volume of great rarity.

EXQUEMELIN. Bucaniers|of|America:|Or, a True|Account|of the Most Remarkable Assaults|Committed of late Years upon the Coasts of|The West-Indies,|By the Bucaniers of Jamaica and Tortuga,|Both English and French.|Wherein are contained more especially,|The unparallel'd Exploits of Sir Henry Morgan, our English|Jamaica Hero, who sack'd Puerto Velo, burnt Panama, &c.|Written originally in Dutch by John Esquemeling, one of the Bucaniers,|who was present at those Tragedies, and Translated into Spanish by|Alonso de Bonne-maison, M.D. &c.|The Second Edition, Corrected and Inlarged with two|Additional Relations, viz. the one of Captain Cook, and the other of|Captain Sharp.|Now faithfully rendred into English.|*London:|Printed for William Crooke, at the Green Dra-|gon without Temple-bar.* 1684.| 4to. 23481

Collation: Part I., 6 l., pp. 47 [really 55, as pp. 46 and 47 should read 54, 55; pp. 42 and 45 *bis* should read 50, 51]; Part II., pp. 80; Part III., pp. 84, Table, 6 l. The Second Volume, Part IV., 8 l., pp. 212, Table, pp. 17. 4 Plates and 3 Maps, besides Cuts and Engravings in Text. This edition, in regard to its paper, type, etc., is much inferior to the edition described in No. 23479, *supra*. The title to the second volume is the same as that given in the note above. *See also* Ringrose (B.)

EXQUEMELIN. The|History|of the|Bucaniers of America;|Or, A True|Account|of|The Most Remarkable Assaults,|Committed (of Late Years) upon the Coasts of|The West-Indies,|by the|Bucaniers of Jamaica and Tortuga,|English, Dutch, Portuguese, &c.|Written by John Esquemeling, and Basil Ringrose, Two of the Bu-|caniers, who were present at those Tragedies.|In this Second Edition is Added the Dangerous Voyages|and Bold Attempts of Capt. Cook, and Capt. Sharp|in the South-|Sea: With a Description of the Cities of Panama, Hispaniola,|Tortuga, &c A New Map of the South-Sea, and Sea-Coasts of A-|merica: Together, With the Effigies of the Bucaniers, Curiously|done in Nineteen Copper-Plates. In IV. Parts Compleat.|*London, Printed for William Whitwood; and Sold by Anthony|Feltham, in Westminster-Hall,* 1695.| 4to. J.C.BT.

Collation same as for 1684, omitting 1 leaf for title of second volume, the two being joined and bound as one. Rich says that this is the second edition of 1684 (our No. 23479), with new title-page, and that the fourth part is exactly the same as the original edition of 1685.

EXQUEMELIN. The History of the Bucaniers of America; from their First Original down to this Time; Written in Several Languages; and now collected into one Volume. Containing I. The Exploits and Adventures of Le Grand, Lolonois, Roche Brasiliano, Bat the Portuguese, Sir Henry Morgan, &c. Written in Dutch by Jo. Esquemeling one of the Bucaniers, and thence Translated into Spanish. II. The Dangerous Voyage and Bold Attempts of Capt. Barth. Sharp, Watlin, Sawkins, Coxon, and others, in the South Sea. Written by Basil Ringrose, Gent. who was a Companion therein, and examin'd with the Original Journal. III. A Journal of a Voyage into the South Sea by the Freebooters of America from 1684, to 1689. Written in French by the Sieur Raveneau de Lussan: never before in English. IV. A Relation of a Voyage of the Sieur de Montaubon, Capt. of Freebooters in Guinea in the Year 1695, &c. The whole newly Translated into English, and Illustrated with 25 Copper Plates. *London: Printed for Tho. Newborough at the Golden Ball in St. Paul's Church Yard, John Nicholson at the King's Arms in Little Brittain, and Benj. Tooke at the Middle Temple Gate, Fleet-street.* 1699. 8vo, pp. (4), 180, Map; Part IV., or Vol. II., pp. 180, Maps in the Text. 23483

EXQUEMELIN. The History of the Bucaniers of America. [Title as in No. 23483.] The Second Edition, Corrected. *London: Printed for Tho. Newborough.* 1704. 8vo, pp. (4), 204; 180. 23484

This *second* second edition has a second title to Parts III. and IV., as follows: "A|Journal|of a|Voyage|Made into the|South Sea, by the|Bucaniers or Freebooters|of|America;|From the Year 1684, to 1689.|Written by the Sieur Raveneau de Lussan.|To which is added,|The Voyage of the|Sieur de Montauban,|Captain of the Freebooters on the|Coast of Guinea, in the Year 1695.|The Second Edition Corrected. *London: Printed for Tho. Newborough* ...|1704.| 8vo.

EXQUEMELIN. The History of the Bucaniers: etc. [Title as in No. 23483.] The Third Edition. *London: Printed for Tho. Newborough.* 1704. 8vo. 23485

Collation the same as in the edition of 1699. Rich says: "The third edition of this 'History of the Bucaniers' is somewhat different from the former: 'for whereas the style before was loose and uncouth in divers parts thereof, the same is now rectified and made more correct throughout the whole body of it.'"—*Preface.* It has the Journals of Lussan and Montauban.

[EXQUEMELIN.] The History of the Buccaniers of America. Containing I. The Exploits and Adventures of Le Grand, Lolonois, Roche Brasiliano, Bat the Portuguese, Sir Henry Morgan, etc. II. The Dangerous Voyage, and Bold Attempts of Capt. Sharp, Watlin, Sawkins, Coxon, and others in the South-Sea. III. A Journal of a Voyage into the South-Sea by the Freebooters of America, from 1684 to 1689. IV. A Relation of a Voyage of the Sieur de Montauban, Captain of the Freebooters in Guinea in the Year 1695. Exhibiting a particular Account and Description of Porto Bello, Chagre, Cuba, Havanna, and most of the Spanish Possessions on the Coasts of the West Indies, and also all along the Coasts of the South-Sea; with the manner in which they have been invaded, attempted, or taken by these Adventurers. The Whole written in several Languages by Persons present at the Transactions. Translated into English, and Illustrated with Copper-Plates. In Two Volumes. The Fourth Edition. *London: Published for D. Midwinter, etc.* MDCCXLI. 2 vols., 12mo, 4 l., pp. 354, 4 Plates; Plate, Title, pp. 406, Index, 11 l. C., S. 23486

This is said to be a different translation from the preceding editions; the portraits and plates also differ. This was abridged, and called "The Fourth Edition ... by H. W. Dilworth, A.M. *London: William Anderson.* MDCCLIX." 16mo.

EXQUEMELIN. The History of the Buccaneers. [Title as in No. 23486.] The Fifth Edition. *Dublin: Printed by S. Powell for Edward Exshaw.* MDCCXLI. 2 vols., 12mo. J.C.B. 23487

EXQUEMELIN. The History of the Bucaniers of America: Being an Entertaining Narrative of the Exploits, Cruelties and Sufferings of the following noted Commanders, viz. Joseph Esquemeling, Pierre le Grand, Lolonois, Roche Brasiliano, Bat the

Portuguese, Capt. Sharp, Capt. Watling, Capt. Cook, &c. &c. Together with a curious Description of the Manners, Customs, Dress, and Ceremonies of the Indians inhabiting near Cape Gracias a Dios. Published for the Improvement and Entertainment of the British Youth of both Sexes. *Glasgow: James Knox.* MDCCLXII. 12mo, Title, pp. 132. C. 23488

Reprinted, *Glasgow.* 1773. 12n

EXQUEMELIN. The History of the Bucaniers of America. Containing, I. The Exploits and Adventures of Le Grand, Lolonois, Roche Brasiliano, Bat the Portuguese, Sir H. Morgan, &c. II. The dangerous Voyage and bold Attempts of Capt. Sharp, Watlin, Sawkins, Coxon, and others in the South Sea. III. A Journal of a Voyage into the South Sea by the Freebooters of America, from 1684 to 1689. IV. A Relation of a Voyage of the Sieur De Montauban, Captain of the Free-booters, in Guinea, in the Year 1695. Exhibiting A particular Account and Description of Porto Bello, Chagre, and Panama, Cuba, Havanna, and most of the Spanish Possessions on the Coasts of the West-Indies, and also along the Coasts of the South Sea; with the Manner in which they have been invaded, attempted, or taken by these Adventurers. The Whole written in several Languages by Persons present at the Transactions. In Two Volumes. The Fifth Edition. *London: T. Evans and Richardson and Urquhart.* M.DCC.LXXI. 2 vols., 12mo, 2 l., pp. 318; (2), 360, (12). BA., C. + [Another] Fifth Edition. *London: T. Evans.* MDCCLXXIV. 2 vols., 12mo, 2 l., pp. 318; Title, 360, 1 l.

This *second* fifth edition is that of 1771, with another date. After this date the book assumed so many different titles and sizes, that it is difficult to enumerate the whole of them. We have met with the following:

[EXQUEMELIN.] History of the Buccaneers of America. *London.* 1800. 18mo. 23490

[EXQUEMELIN.] The History of the Bucaniers of America. *London: J. Walker.* 1810. 18mo, pp. (4), xxiii, 660. C. 23491

EXQUEMELIN. History of the Buccaneers of America. *Dublin.* 1821. 2 vols., 8vo. 23492

[EXQUEMELIN.] The History of the Bucaniers of America. The First American, from the last London Edition. *New-York: William Beastall.* 1826. 3 vols., 18mo. + [Reprinted.] *New York.* 1836. + *New York.* 1840. 18mo. 23493

[EXQUEMELIN.] The History of the Buccaniers of America, containing detailed Accounts of those bold and daring Freebooters, chiefly along the Spanish Main, in the West Indies, and in the Great South Sea, succeeding the Civil Wars in England. *Boston.* 1853. 8vo, pp. 484. B. + New Edition. *Boston: Sanborn, Carter, & Bazin.* 1856. 8vo, pp. 484. 23494

For an extended notice of this work, and a partial reprint, *see* Burney's "Chronological History of Voyages," Vol. III. *See also* the "Retrospective Review," Vol. III., pp. 27–51, and the Preface to Thornbury. I am indebted to Mr. J. C. Brevoort, and Mr. Edward W. West, of New York, for some information concerning this author.

EX-SETTLER. Canada in the Years 1832, 1833, and 1834. Containing Important Information and Instructions to Persons Intending to Emigrate thither in 1835. By an Ex-Settler, who resided chiefly "in the Bush" for the last two years. *Dublin: Philip Dixon Hardy: Richard Groombridge.* MDCCCXXXV. 18mo.

Extincta servitute apud Insulas Occidentales, quænam commoda vel incommoda possint exinde oriri? [18—.] 8vo.

A few copies privately printed.

The Extinction of Slavery a National Necessity, before the Present Conflict can be ended. [n. p. n. d.] 8vo, pp. 8. H.

Extra Official State Papers. *See* [Knox (W.)]

Extract en Copye. *See* Gerbier (B.)

Extract from a Protest against the Nomination of Candidates for President and Vice-President of the United States. *Washington.* 1808. P. 23498

An Extract from a Reply to the Observations of Lieut. Gen. Sir William Howe, on a Pamphlet entitled Letters to a Nobleman. *London: J. Paramore.* 1781. 12mo, pp. 108. 23499

Extract from an Address in the Virginia Gazette, of March 19, 1767. 12mo, pp. 4. P. 23500

An early anti-slavery document.

Extract from an Unpublished Manuscript on Shaker History ... giving an Accurate Description of their Songs, Dances ... *Boston: E. H. Allen.* 1850. 12mo, pp. 48. H. 23501

Extract from the Executive Record, comprehending the Messages of the President in relation to the Nominations of Albert Gallatin, John Q. Adams and James A. Bayard, as Envoys to Negotiate a Treaty of Peace with Great Britain. *Washington.* 1813. 8vo. 23502

Extract, from the Journal. *See* Congress, Vol. IV., No. 15526.

Extract from the Minutes of Council, Containing His Majesty's late Regulations relating to the Waste Lands of the Crown, with His Excellency, the Governor General's order of reference respecting the same, to a Committee of the whole Council, of the Province of Lower-Canada, the said Committee's Report thereon, and his Excellency's Speech in reply. *Quebec: Printed at the New Printing-Office, Palace Street.* 1798. Title, pp. iv, 45. Extract of the Minutes of Council, of the 20th of September, 1798. On the Waste Lands of the Crown, Being a Continuation, of the Extract, of the 11th of June last. *Quebec: Printed at the New Printing-Office, Palace Street.* 1798. 8vo, Title, pp. 47–133, (1). 23503

Extract from the Political State of Great Britain, for the Month of December, 1730. [*Boston, reprinted.* 1731.] 8vo, pp. 16.

Contains an account of the controversy in Massachusetts respecting the governor's salary.

Extract of a Despatch from her Majesty's Minister at Washington, dated December 6, 1861, enclosing Papers relating to Foreign Affairs, laid before the Congress of the United States, at the Opening of the Session in 1861. *London.* 8vo, pp. 367.

Extract of a Letter. *See* [Cooper], Vol. IV., No. 16611, *and* [Sharpe (Granville)].

Extract of a Letter from a Gentleman in Maryland ... Originally Printed in America. Fourth Edition. *London.* 1806. 8vo. N. 23506

Extract of a Letter from the House of Representatives of the Massachusetts-Bay, to their Agent Dennys De Berdt, Esq; with some Remarks. *London: J. and W. Oliver.* MDCCLXX. 8vo, pp. 28. M. 23507

Extract of an Act of the General Assembly of New York for raising a Supply of £100,000 for the Expedition against Canada. *New York.* 1759. 8vo, pp. 19. 23508

Extract|Uyt d'Articulen van het|Tractaet van Bestant ende ophoudinge van alle Acten|van vyantschap, als oock van Traffijcq ende Commercie, mitsgaders van|Secours, ghemaeckt, gearresteert, ende besloten in 's Graven-Haghe den|twaelfden Junij 1641. tusschen de Heer Tristao de Mendoça Furtado|Ambassadeur ende Raedt van den Doorluchtichsten Grootmachtighen|

Don Ian de vierde van die naem van Portugael, Algarves, ende ten weder-|zijden vande Zee in Africa Koningh xc. ter eenre, ende de Heeren Com-|missarisen vande Hoogh Mo: Heeren Staten Generael, ter andere zijde:|Ende dit alles by provisie raeckende de respective Plaetsen ende Zeen gele-|gen in Europa ende elders buyten de Limiten vande Octroyen hier bevo-|rens respectivelijck verleent aen die van d'Oost ende West-Indische|Compagnie respective | *In 's Graven-Hage*, | *Byde Weduwe, ende Erfgenamen van wijlen Hillebrandt Iacobssz van*| *Wouw, Ordinaris Druckers vande Ho: Mo: Heeren Staten*| *Generael, Anno* 1641. *Met Privilegie.*| 4to, 4 l. 23509

Extract from the treaty concerning the places not within the limits of the privileges of the East and West India Company.

Extract. *See* Brazil, Vol. II., Nos. 7577–9.

Extract uit de Dag-Registers van het Noord-Amerikaansche Congres, Betrekkelyk tot het neemen en verbeurdverklaaren van Scheeps-Pryzen en het uitrusten van Kaapers; benevens de Ordonnantiën en Schikkingen der Zee-Vloot, en de Instructiën voor de Bevelhebbers der Particuliere Oorlogschepen. *Philadelphia.* 1777. 8vo, pp. 48. 23510

Extract concerning the capturing of ships and fitting out of privateers.

Extract|Uyt een Brief gheschreven|In | Maurits-Stadt | De|Pernambuco,|In Brasil, den thienden Meert|Anno sestien-hondert negen-en-veertich.|*In 't Jaer ons Heeren Anno* 1649.| 4to, pp. 8. 23511

Extract vnd Augsszug. | Der Grossen vñ | wunderbarlichen Schiff-|farth, Buelij Cataloni, eines Abbten, dess heyligen Orden A. Benedicti. Wel-|cher Anno 1423 mit Almirante Chri-|stophoro Columbo in Indiam Ameri-|cam, oder, Newe Welt, ober das Attlan-|dische Meer, vnd Oceanum alldort die vn-|glaubigen wilde Völcker, vnd Blutdursti|ge hungerige Menschen-fresser zu dem|Christlichen Catholischē Glau-|ben zu bekehren ge-| schiffet. | *Gedruckt zu Lintz, bey Johann Blancken*, 1624.| Folio. 23512

Extract uyt de Missive. *See* Brazil, Vol. II., No. 7578.

Extract|Uyttet Register der|Resolutien|vande Hoogh Mogh. Heeren. Staten | Generael | Der Vereenighde | Nederlanden| *Tot Alckmaer*| *By Jan Claesz, Boeck-vercooper, woonode*| *op Uliscevort (?)*, 1647.| 4to, pp. 8. 23513

Extract|Dan seeckeren Brief ghe-|schreven uyt Loando St. Paulo, in Angola, van|weghen de groote Victorie die de onse| verkregen hebben tegen de Portugesen|onder 't beleydt van onsen Di-| recteur Ouman: mitsgaders | de assistentie van de Ko-| ninginne Linga ae.ı|onse gedaen.| *In 's Graven-Hage*| *By Ludolph Breeckevelt, Boeck-Drucker*,| *woonende in de Pooten in de Vinder vande Druckery.*| *Anno* M. DC. XLVIII.| 4to, pp. 8. 23514

Extracto Alfabetico de los Acuerdos generales e interestes de la junta superior Directiva de Hacienda. *Habana.* 1846. 8vo.

Extracto historial del expediente que pende en el consejo real, y supremo de las Indias, a instancia de la ciudad de Manila, y demàs de las islas Philipinas, sobre la forma en que se ha de hacer, y continuar el comercio, y contractacion de los texidos de China en Nueva-España, ecc. Formado, y ajustado de orden del Rey, y acuerdo del mismo consejo, y a costa de su Magestad, por un Ministro de la Tabla, sobre los Papeles, y Documentos entregados por la secretaria de Nueva-España, y otras memorias particulares, ecc. *Madrid: Juan de Ariztia.* 1736. Folio, 14 ., 324 numbered l. 23516

Contains many important documents concerning the commercial history of the Philippine Islands and the Spanish colonies generally.

Extracts and Collections of Acts, Laws and Orders "of the several Governments of the late Colonies of New Plymouth, Massachusetts-Bay, and of this Province [*i. e.* Massachusetts], relating to Grants and Conveyances." [n. p. n. d.] 4to, pp. 4.

Without title-page or heading; probably refers to the Kennebeck purchases, as it purports to concern "the titles to a great part of the lands in the eastern parts of this province."

Extracts and Remarks on the Subject of Punishment and Reformation of Criminals. *Philadelphia.* 1790. 8vo. 23518

Extracts from a Pamphlet, entitled the Friend of Peace, with Six Letters from Omar to the President. *Stockport, Eng.* 1817.

Extracts from a Review of the Parliamentary and Forensic Eloquence of the United States. *Washington City.* 1834. 8vo, pp. 31. 23520

Extracts from a Work called "Breeden Raedt, aan de Vereenighde Nederlandsche Provintien," printed in Antwerp, 1649: Translated from the Original Dutch, by Mr. [F. W. Cowan]. *Amsterdam: F. M. Muller.* 1850. 12mo, pp. 14. 23521

One hundred copies printed, of which six are on large paper. Partly included in Muller's catalogue, page 38–46.

Extracts from Colony Laws, relating to Land Titles. [n. p. n. d.] 4to, pp. 4. M. 23522

Extracts from Letters of Teachers and Superintendents of the New-England Educational Commission for Freedmen. Fourth Series. January 1, 1864. *Boston: David Clapp, Printer.* 1864. 8vo, pp. 15. 23523

Extracts from Papers. *See* West Indies.

Extracts from the Crisis. *See* [Carey (M.)], Vol. III., No. 10889, *note.*

Extracts from the Debates in the House of Commons, on the Present State of Colonial Slavery. [By William Narsh, Peckham.] *London.* 1828. 12mo, pp. 16. 23524

Extracts from the Editorial Columns of the "New Orleans Picayune." *New-York: James Clarke.* 1861. 8vo, pp. 23.

Extracts from Evidence before the House of Commons, 1790–91, respecting the Slave Trade. *London.* [n. d.] 23525

Also: Abstract of the same. *London.* 1791. 8vo.

Extract from the Journals of Congress, relative to the Capture and Condemnation of Prizes, and the Fitting out Privateers; Together with the Rules and Regulations of the Navy, and Instructions to the Commanders of Private Ships of War. *Philadelphia: Printed by John Dunlap.* M,DCC,LXXVI. 12mo, pp. 45. P.

Extracts from the Report of his Majesty's Commissioners for inquiring into the Administration and Practical Operation of the Poor Laws. London. 1834. Dedicated to the Gentlemen of the Senate and House of Representatives of Massachusetts. *Boston.* 1835. 12mo, pp. 83. 23527

Extracts from the Minutes of the Convention assembled at East Windsor to consider the Expediency of establishing a Theological Institute connected with a System of Manual Labor. *Hartford.* 1833. 8vo. 23528

Extracts of Letters received by the Educational Commission, Boston, from Teachers at Port Royal and its Vicinity. 4to, pp. 4. + Second Series. 4to, pp. 4. + Third Series. June 17, 1863. 4to, pp. 4. 23529

Extracts from the Proceedings of the American Continental Congress, Held at Philadelphia, on the 10th day of May, 1775. Containing an Address to the People of Ireland, an Address to the Assembly of Jamaica, a Letter to the Lord Mayor of London, and the opinion of Congress on the boasted Conciliatory Plan, offered by the Administration in Parliament, February 20, 1775. *Providence: John Carter.* [1775.] 8vo, pp. 22. 23530

Extracts from the Proceedings of the Convention at Concord and Boston, containing the Regulation of the Prices of Merchandize, Provisions, &c. *Boston.* 1779. 8vo. W. 23531

Extracts from the Proceedings of the Court of the Vice-Admiralty in Charles-Town, South-Carolina; In the Cause, George Roupell, Esq; v. the Ship Ann and Goods. With a few Explanatory Remarks. To which is subjoined, some General Observations on American Custom-House Officers and Courts of Vice-Admiralty. ... *America, Printed, Anno Domini* M,DCC,LXVIII. 4to, pp. iv, 20. P. 23532

Believed to be by Col. Henry Laurens, or one of his friends. Laurens was part owner of the ship "Ann." A second edition was advertised in 1769. For an answer, *see* Leigh (Egerton).

Extracts from the Records of the late Provincial Congress, Held at Cambridge in the Months of October, November and December, A.D. 1774. Also Extracts from the Minutes of the Proceedings of the Congress, Held at Cambridge, February A.D. 1775. Published by their Order. *Boston: Printed by Edes and Gill, in Queen-Street.* M,DCC,LXXV. 8vo, pp. 24. 23533

Extracts from the Report of the International Committee on Weights, Measures, and Coins, with a notice of the use of the Metric System in the United States, and its Relations to other Systems of Weights and Measures. Paris Universal Exposition. 1867. Reports of the United States Commissioners. *Washington.* 1870. 8vo, pp. 48. 23534

Extracts from the Reports. *See* Vol. III., No. 10445.

Extracts from the Several Treaties subsisting between Great Britain and other Kingdoms and States, of such Articles, &c., as relate to the Duty and Conduct of H. M. Ships-of-War. *London.* 4to. + Second Edition. *London.* 1747. 4to. + Third Edition. *London.* 1758. 4to. + Another Edition. *London.* 1792. 4to. 23535

Extracts from the Votes. *See* Vol. IV., No. 15528.

In addition to the editions thus described, there are at least four others, viz.: *New-London: Printed by Timothy Green.* M,DCC,LXXIV. 4to, pp. 7–. + *Newport, R. I.* 1774. 8vo, pp. 59. + *New York: James Rivington.* 1774. 8vo, pp. 36. + *Williamsburgh, (Va.)* 1774. 8vo. C. *See* Rich, I., 205–6. The "Address to the Inhabitants of Quebec" is also included in several editions.

Extracts from the Votes and Proceedings of the American Continental Congress, Held At Philadelphia, 10th May 1775. Published by Order of Congress. *New York: Printed and Sold by John Anderson, at Beekman's-Slip*, M,DCC,LXXV. 8vo, 2 l., pp. 192. 23536

Extracts in Prose and Verse, by a Lady of Maryland. Together with a Collection of Original Poetry, never before Published; by Citizens of Maryland. *Annapolis: F. Green.* 1808. 2 vols., 12mo, pp. 364, (8); 359, (12). B., C. 23537

Extracts of Letters. *See* Vol. III., No. 10444.

Extracts of some Letters occasioned by the Proceedings of the Hopkinton Association and of the New Hampshire General Association. *Concord.* 1812. 12mo, pp. 24. W. 23538

Extracts of Several Treatises wrote by the Prince of Conti, with the Sentiments of the Fathers, and some of the Decrees of the Councils, concerning Stage Plays; Recommended to the Perusal and Serious Consideration of the Professors of Christianity in the City of Philadelphia. *Philadelphia: Printed by William Bradford.* MDCCLIV. 8vo, pp. 47. P. 23539

Extrait d'une Lettre, sur les malheurs de Saint-Domingue en général, et principalement sur l'incendie de la ville du Cap Français. *A Paris: Au jardin égalité pavillon No.* 1, 2 *et* 3. *An* II *de la Republique Française.* 8vo, pp. 26. 23540

Extrait du Catalogue de la Bibliothèque d'un Amateur Ouvrages sur l'Amérique. [n. p. n. d.] 12mo, 2 l., pp. 153. 23541

A catalogue of M. Hector Bossange's "Bibliothèque."

Extrait ou recueil des isles nouvelles trouvée en la grande mer Océane du temps du roy d'Espaigne Fernand et Elizabeth sa femme. Item trois navigations dont la première est de Cuba, la second de la mer Océane, in tierce de la prinse de Temistitan. *Paris.* 1552. 4to. 23542

Extraordinary Gazette, Despatches from Admiral Squib, giving Detailed Account of a great Naval Victory obtained over the

Combined Fleets of France and America, in the Serpentine Sea. *London: J. Low.* 1814. 8vo. 23543

A rare poetical political squib.

The Extraordinary Prosperity of Great Britain, and the General Depression in the United States. By a Pennsylvanian. [By M. Carey?] 1823. 8vo, pp. 78. 23544

An Eye-Opener! *See* [Blanchard (C.)], Vol. II., No. 5818.

The Eyes Opened, or Carolinians Convinced by an Honourable and Eloquent Representative in the Congress of the United States, in the following well received and Candid Examination of the Objections to his Excellency Gov. Jay's late Treaty with Great Britain; and which has been ratified by President Washington. *New York: Reprinted for James Rivington.* 1795. 8vo, pp. 43, (10). 23545

This is merely another title for our No. 10663 in Vol. III. It has been attributed to William Smith.

EYMA (X.) Aventuriers et corsaires; par Xavier Eyma. *Paris: Michel Lévy.* 1861. 18mo, pp. 386. 23546

EYMA. Le Canal maritime du Darien. Etat de la question; par Xavier Eyma, ... *Paris: Schiller aîné.* 1861. 8vo, pp. 24.

EYMA. La chasse à l'esclave; par Xavier Eyma. *Paris: Brunet.* 1866. 18mo, pp. 281. 23548

EYMA. Les Deux Amériques. Histoires, mœurs et voyages. Par Xavier Eyma. *Paris: Giraud.* 1853. 18mo, 10½ sheets.

EYMA. Eccentricités Américaines. *Paris: Hetzel.* 1860. 16mo. 23550

EYMA. Les Femmes du Nouveau Monde. Par Xavier Eyma. *Paris: Giraud.* 1853. 18mo, 11½ sheets. + Nouvelle édition. *Paris.* 1854. 12mo. + *Paris: Lévy frères.* 1860. 18mo, pp. 305. + [*Ibid.*] 1861. 4to. 23551

EYMA. Les peaux rouges, scènes de la vie des Indiens. Par Xavier Eyma. *Paris: Michel Lévy frères.* 1860. 18mo, pp. 319.

EYMA. Les Peaux noires. Scènes de la vie des esclaves; par Xavier Eyma. *Paris: Michel Lévy.* 1857. 18mo, pp. viii, 312. 23553

EYMA. La Republique Americaine: ses institutions, ses hommes. *Paris: Michel Lévy frères.* 1861. 2 vols., 8vo, pp. 770. + *Bruxelles: Lacroix Verboeckhoven et Cie.* 1861. 12mo.

EYMA. Le Roi des tropiques. Par Xavier Eyma. *Paris: Lévy frères.* 1860. 18mo, pp. 299. 23555

EYMA. Scenes de mœurs et de Voyages dans le Nouveau-Monde. Par Xavier Eyma. *Paris: Poulet-Malassis.* 1862. 18mo, pp. 396. 23556

EYMA. Les trente-quatre étoiles de l'Union Américaine, Histoire des états et des territoires. Par Xavier Eyma. *Paris: Michel Lévy frères, Libraries-Éditeurs.* 1861. 2 vols., 8vo, pp. xxxviii, 312; 356. BA. + *Paris.* 1862. 8vo. + *Bruxelles: Lacroix Verboeckhoven et Cie.* 1862. 2 vols., 8vo. 23557

EYMA. La Vie dans le Nouveau-Monde. Par Xavier Eyma. *Paris: Poulet-Malassis.* 1862. 18mo, pp. 359. 23558

EYNARD (Charles). Le chevalier Guisan, sa vie et ses travaux à la Guyane. *Paris.* 1844. 12mo. 23559

EYQUEM DU MARTINEAU (M.) Le|Pilote|de l'onde vive,| ou|le secret du Flux|et Reflux de la Mer;|Contenant xxj Mouvemens;|et du Point Fixe.|D'un Voyage abregé des Indies, & de la|Quadrature du Cercle, composez sur|les Principes de la Nature; nouvelle-|ment découverts, & mis en lumiere.|Par Mathvrin Eyqvem,| Sr, dv Martineav, | Bourdelois.|Philosophie Naturelle.| *A Paris, Chez Jean Dhoury, sur le Quay le des Augustins*, | *à l'Image Saint Jean.*| *Et chez l'Autheur, ruë neuve Saint Mederic, l'Enseigne*| *de la Ville de Calais.*| M.DC.LXXVIII.|Avec Privilege dv Roy.| 8vo, pp. (16), 221. 23560

EYRE (Edward John). Report of the Case of the Queen *v.* Eyre, on his Prosecution, in the Court of Queen's Bench, for high Crimes and Misdemeanors alleged to have been committed by him in his office as Governor of Jamaica; containing the Evidence, [taken from the Depositions], the Indictment, and the Charge of Mr. Justice Blackburn. By W. F. Finlason. *London: Chapman & Hall.* 1868. 8vo, pp. xl, 111. C. 23561

See also Finlason (W. F.)

EYRE. Jamaica. Papers laid before the Royal Commission of Enquiry by Governor Eyre. *London.* 1866. Folio. 23562

EYRE (J.) The Christian Spectator; being a Journey from England to Ohio; Two Years in that State. Travels in America. By John Eyre. *Albany: Printed by J. Munsell.* 1838. 12mo, pp. 72. B., C. 23563

EYRE. The European Stranger in America. By John Eyre. *New York.* 1839. 12mo, pp. 84. B., C. 23564

EYRE. The Life of Gregory Lopez, a Hermit in America. *New York.* 1841. 12mo. 23565

EYRE. Travels: comprising a Journey from England to Ohio, Two Years in that State, Travels in America, etc., to which are added the Foreigner's Protracted Journey, Letters, etc. By John Eyre. Fifth Thousand. *New York: Sold at Riker's.* 1852. 12mo, pp. 359. 23566

EYRIES *and* DEPERTHES. Histoire des naufrages: ou Recueil les plus interessantes Naufrages, Delaissemens, Incendies, et autres Evenemens Funestes arrives depuis le XVe siecle jusqu'à nos jours. *Paris.* 1815. 3 vols., 8vo. Plates. + Nouvelle édition. *Paris.* 1871. 23567

See "Nouvelles Annales.

EYRON (P.) Le niveau de l'Europe et de l'Amérique, Septentrionalle; ou le guide de l'observateur; par Pierre Eyron, éditeur et Cie. *Philadelphia: Guilliaume W. Woodward.* 1795. pp. 147. 23568

EYTH (M.) Wanderbuch eines Ingenieurs. *Heidelberg.* 1871. 2 vols. 23569

Vol. II., "Amerika."

EYTON. A History of the Oyster, and the Oyster Fisheries. *London.* 8vo. 23570

EYZAGUIRRE (José Ignacio Victor). Los intereses católicos en América. *Paris: G. Hermanos.* 1859. 2 vols., 8vo, 2 l., pp. vii, 524; 2 l., pp. 475. 23571

EYZAGUIRRE (J. J.) Historia eclesiastica, politica y literaria de Chile. *Valparaiso.* 1850. 2 vols., 8vo. 23572

EYZAGUIRRE. Histoire ecclésiastique, politique et littéraire du Chili, par M. l'abbé Eyzaguirre, doyen de la faculté de Théologie de l'Université Nationale, et vice-président de la chambre des députés du Chili; traduite par L. Poillon. *Valparaiso.* 1850. 3 vols., 8vo. + *Lille: Lefort.* 1855. 3 vols., 8vo.

EZETA (L. G. de). Defensa de F. Santillan procedado por el asalto y herida conmuerte del Dr. D. M. Beistegui. *Mexico.* 1852. 8vo, pp. 78. 23574

EZETA. Promptuario para los Alcaldes de cuartel y Gefes de manzana del distrito federal, y para los Alcaldes constitucionales de los estados de la republica. *Mexico.* 1850. 8vo. 23575

EZGUERRA (Mathias de). Exequias de la reyna de Maria de Austria en Mexico. 1697. 4to. 23576

NOTE. — Since printing the titles of the various editions of Exquemelin, we have received from Mr. E. W. West the following corrections and additions:

No. 23471, Brunet quotes this in 12mo.

Nos. 23475–8, are translated from the English; Brunet quotes an Edition, *Paris: Ganeau.* 1726.

No. 23479, for £20, *read* £200.

" 23480 is a 12mo, and should have a Portrait.

" 23484, for *second*, read *third.*

" 23485, the note from Rich applies with equal truth to Nos. 23483 and 23484.

" 23494, the reference to the "Retrospective Review" should *read* pp. 327–351.

Les américains coureurs des bois; par F... *Limoges, Paris: F. F. Ardent.* 1863. 32mo, pp. 63. (Biblioth. chrét de l'adolescence.)

F. (F.) Journael, | Ofte | Dagh-Register, | Over de Reyse, | Gedaen door de Heer Luytenant Admirael | M. A. de Ruyter. | In de West-Indies. | Door A. F. | *t'Amsterdam,* | *Gedruckt by Samuël Imbrechts, Boeckverkooper in de Raem-steeg,* | *in de Hoop, Anno* 1665. 4to, 4 l. 23578

"Copie d'une lettre de Jan van Eyndhoven sur l'expédition de Ruyter, commençant le 1er octobre 1664 et se terminant en août 1665, et à laquelle Eyndhoven prit part. Ce petit écrit est extrêmement rare; aucun bibliographe n'en fait mention." — TRÖMEL.

F*** (A.) Précis Historique sur la Révolution Des Provinces unies de l'Amérique du Sud ... . Par A. F***. *Paris.* 1819. 8vo, pp. 166. H. 23579

F. (D. B. P.) Carta de un Havanero, A D. P. E. P. Autor, o sea recopilador de la obra el Viagero Universal, sobre la Carta 156 puesta en el Quaderno 34 con que principia el Tomo 12. Por D. B. P. F. *Madrid.* 1797. 12mo, pp. 16. J.C.B. 23580

F. (G.) *See* F[ox] (G[eorge]).

F——n (G——n). L'Héroine du Texas; ou, voyage de Madame *** aux États-Unis et au Mexique. Par Mr. G——n F——n. *Paris: Plancher.* 1819. 8vo, pp. 118. Plate. C.

F. (J.) A Letter to Rev. Thomas Foxcroft. By J. F. *Boston: S. Kneeland.* 1745. 23582

F. (J.) A Letter to the Rev. Mr. William Hobby. By J. F. [n. p.] 1745. 4to, pp. (2), 9. B., W. 23583

Relates to George Whitfield.

F. (J.) Remarks on the Rev. Mr. Cooper's Objections to the Rev. Mr. Ashley's Sermon. [By J. F. ... *Boston.* 1742.] 4to, pp. 8. BA., M., W. + Third Edition. *Boston.* 1742. 4to.

F. (J.) Remarks on the Rev. Mr. Joshua Gee's Letter to the Rev. Mr. Nathanael Eells. By J. F. [n. p. n. d.] 4to, pp. 8. 23585

F. (J.) Remarks, 1793. *See* F[reeman] (J[ames]).

F. (R.) The Present State of Carolina, with Advice to the Settlers. By R. F. 1682. 4to. 23586

"Unknown to all the American bibliographers." — J. R. SMITH's *Catalogue for* 1862, where it is priced at £7 17s. 6d.

F. (W. C.) *See* F[owler] (W. C.)

F. (R. A.) Promtuario de la constitucion de la monarquia Española, con varios decretos de las Cortes generales y extraordinarias, y discusion de las mismas al asunto; para aclarar las dudas que puedan ocurrir en las Juntas electorales de parroquias, de partido y de provincia, y de ayuntamientos por el redactor poblano R. A. F., etc. *Reimpreso en Mejico.* 1820. 12mo, pp. 80, 4. 23587

FABENS (J. W.) Facts about Santo Domingo, Applicable to the present Crisis. An Address delivered before the American Geographical and Statistical Society at New York, April 3, 1862. By Joseph Warren Fabens. Illustrated by the only Complete Map of Santo Domingo and Hayti that has yet appeared. *New York: George P. Putnam.* 1862. 8vo, pp. 32. B. 23588

FABENS. Resources of Santo Domingo ... . By Joseph Warren Fabens ... . *Washington.* 1869. 8vo, pp. 22. Map. H. + *New York: Major & Knapp.* MDCCLXXI. 8vo, pp. 30. Map.

FABENS. A Story of Life on the Isthmus. By Joseph W. Fabens. *New York: George P. Putnam & Co.* MDCCCLIII. 12mo, pp. 215. C. 23590

FABER (C. W.), *and* BIERWIRTH (L.) Petition and Papers of Conrad W. Faber & Leopold Bierwirth, in Relation to the War Steamer United States. [n. p. n. d.] *Gideon & Co.* 8vo, pp. 69. BA., H. 23596

FABER (U.) *See* Bry (T. de), Vol. III., page 40.

FABIAN Y FUERO. Coleccion de Providencias Diocesanas del Obispado de la Puebla de los Angeles, hechas y Ordenadas por D. Francisco Fabian y Fuero, Obispo de dicha Ciudad y Obispado, del Consejo de su Maj. ... [*Puebla:*] *Imprenta del Real Seminario Palafoxiana de la expresada Ciudad.* 1770. 2 vols.

A compilation of rules and orders for the conduct of civil and religious life, based upon the third Provincial Council of Mexico, in 1585. It also relates to questions concerning the treatment of the Indians, the use of their language, etc. It was reprinted as below:

FABIAN Y FUERO. Coleccion de providencias diocesanas dadas por D. Francisco Fabian y Fuero, obispo que fue de la Puebla de los Angeles, y actual arzobispo de Valencia. *Valencia: Benito Monfort.* 1792–93. 2 vols., folio, 2 l., pp. xx, 610; vi, 591.

Also: Carta pastoral de D. Francisco Fabyan y Fuero, Obispo de la Puebla de los Angeles. [n. p.] 1767. 4to, pp. 58. — Carta Pastoral. 1779. 4to. — Oracion en alabanza del angelico doctor Santo Thomas de Aquino, en la sol. funcion del quarto Concilio Megicano. *Puebla.* 1771. 4to, pp. (2), 59.

FABIUS, *pseudonym.* Common Sense. By "Fabius." Nos. 1, 2, and 3. *Nasuville, Tenn.* 1862? 8vo. 23594

FABIUS, *pseudonym.* The Letters of Fabius, in 1788, on the Federal Constitution; and in 1797 on the present situation of Public Affairs. *Wilmington, (Del.): W. C. Smyth.* 1797. 8vo, pp. iv, 202. 23595

FABRE (H.) Confédération indépendence annexion Conférence faite à l'Institut Canadien de Québec, le 15 Mars 1871, Par M. Hector Fabre. *Québec.* 1871. 8vo, pp. 33. H. 23596

FABRE. Ecrivains Canadiens. — N. Bourassa. *Montreal.* 1866. 8vo. 23597

FABRE. Esquisse biographique sur Chevalier de Lorimier. *Montréal.* 1856. 8vo, pp. 15. 23598

FABRI (J. I.) 1628. *See* Hernandez (F.)

FABRICIUS (Jo. A.) Salutaris lux Evangelii toto orbi exoriens. *Hamburgi.* 1741. 4to. 23599

Pages 754–785 contain an account of the progagation of Christianity in the New World.

FABRICIUS (J. F.) Notizen über die Einführung und erste Ausbreitung der Buchdruckerkunst in Amerika. ... *Hamburg.* 1841. 12mo. 23600

FABRICIUS (Otto). Bibelingoak merdlâinnut imaloneet. *Kiöbenhavinme: C. F. Skubart.* 1822. 16mo, pp. 68. 23601

Bible teachings for children in Greenland.

FABRICIUS. Favna Groenlandica, sistematice sistens Animalia Groenlandiae Occidentalis hactenus indagata ... maxima ... parte secundum proprias observationes Othonis Fabricii ... . *Hafniae et Lipsiae: impensis Joannis Gottlob Rothe.* MDCCLXXX. 8vo, pp. xvi, 452. Plate. B., H. 23602

FABRICIUS. Forsög til en forbedret Grönlandsk Grammatica ved Otho Fabricius. Andet Oplag. *Kiöbenhavn: C. Friderich Schubart.* 1791. 8vo, pp. viii, 322, 4 Tables. + *Kiöbenhavn: Schubart.* 1801. 12mo, pp. 388, 4 Tables. 23603

FABRICIUS. Den Grönlandske Ordbog, forbedret og forôget udgivet ved Otho Fabricius. *Kiöbenhavn: C. Frid. Schubart.* 1804. Sm. 8vo, pp. viii, 795. 23604

This Greenlandish and Danish dictionary is very rare.

FABRICIUS, *pseudonym.* *See* [Galloway (Joseph)].

FABRONII (H.) Geographica Historica: Newe summarische Welt-Historia. Mit Beyfügung der Landtafeln und Contrafeten aller Nationen und Völcker Trachten, auch Erzelung der newen wunderlichen Reisen vnd Schiffahrten, so heutiges Tages ... in die newen Welten zu geschehen pflegen. Mit vielen Kostümbildern. *Schmalkalden.* 1627. 2 vols., 4to. 23605

Vol. II. relates to America.

FABRY (J. A.) Compendiosa Demostracion de los Crecidos adelantamientos que pudiera lograr la Real hacienda de Su Magestad mediante la rebaja evel precio de Azogue, que se consume para el laborio de las Minas de este Reyno, ó del aumento tan considerable, que se avia de experimentar en el producto annual de sus Reales Rentas, en beneficio no menos grande, que universal de esta Mineria, de ambos Comercios, y por consiguiente de todo el comun de la Republica. Con una previa impugnacion a las Reflexiones del Contador D. Joseph de Villa-Señor y Sanchez, sobre el mismo assumpto. Añadese un breve modo de reducir, ligar, y alear el Oro, y Plata à la ley de 22. quilates, ô de 11. dineros, de averiguar el valor de cada una de estos mentales, y los respectivos derechos, que deben pagar â S. M. en pasta, ó en especies de moneda, de qualesquiera cantidades propuestas, y leyes averiguables por el ensaye, segun la division de sus respectivos Dinerales, muy comodo para el usso de las Reales Casas de moneda, y Caxas de quintos, de los Mineros, Plateros, y de todos los que comercion en estos metales. Por Don Joseph Antonio Fabry, Guarda de Vista en las Fundiciones de S. M. en esta su Real Casa de Moneda, y Apoderado General para los negocios, y pretensiones de Mineria de todos los principales Reales de Minas de este Reyno. Quien la consagra à la R. M. de nuestro Catholico Monarcha el Señor Don Philippo v. (que Dios guarde) Rey de España, y de las Indias. *Impressa en Mexico con Licencia del Superior Gobierno Por la Viuda de D. Joseph Bernardo de Hogal. Año de* 1743. 4to, 39 l., pp. 178. 23606

Relates to the mines and mining of the Rio de la Plata.

Fabula politica. Los animales en cortes. *Puebla.* 1820. Sm. 8vo, 3 l. 23607

Facsimile of the Illustrated Artic News, published on board H. M. S. Resolute, in Search for Sir John Franklin, Lieut. S. Osborne, and G. F. McDougall, Editors. *London: Ackerman & Co.* 1852. Folio, 2 l., pp. 57. 23608

A curious and amusing production, lithographed with plates.

Facsimile des Autographes des Gouverneurs et Administrateurs du Canada, suivi d'un tableau chronologique de tous ceux qui ont occupé ces emplois distingués, leurs désignations et leurs titres, depuis la colonisation de la Province, pris de "l'Album des Souvenirs Canadiens," du Lieut. Col. Jacques Viger, Premier Maire de la Cité du Montréal, etc. Troisième Edition. *Montréal.* 1857. 8vo? 23609

Facsimile. *See* Jefferson (T.), *and* Washington (G.)

Faction Detected, by the Evidence of Facts. Containing An Impartial View of Parties at Home, and Affairs Abroad. *London.* 1742. 8vo. + Second Edition. *London.* 1743. 8vo, pp. 175. + Third Edition. *London.* 1743. 8vo, pp. 175. + The Fourth Edition. *London: J. Roberts.* M.DCC.XLIII. 8vo, pp. 175. + Fifth Edition. *London.* 1743. 8vo, pp. 175. 23610

Partly on American affairs, and attributed to John Percival, Earl of Egmont, also to William Pulteny.

Factory Tracts. No. I. Factory Life as it is. By an Operative. [*Lowell.* 1845.] 8vo, pp. 8. B. 23611

Facts about Cuba. Published under the authority of the New York Cuban Junta. *New York: Sun Job Printing Office.* 1870. 8vo, pp. 31. 23612

Facts addressed to Landholders. *See* [Tooke (John Horne)].

Facts and Arguments, 1805. *See* [Blodget (William)], Vol. II.

Facts and Arguments in Favour of adopting Railways in preference to Canals, in Pennsylvania, &c. *Philadelphia.* 1825. 8vo. + Fourth Edition. *Philadelphia.* 1825. 8vo, pp. 68.

Facts are Stubborn Things. *See* Hold-Fast (Simon).

Facts as to the Metropolitan Excise Law. [*New York.* n. d.] 8vo, pp. 14. H. 23614

Facts and Authorities on the Suspension of the Privilege of the Writ of Habeas Corpus. [n. p. n. d.] 8vo, pp. 20.

Facts and Calculations respecting the Population and Territory of the United States of America. [n. p. n. d.] 4to, pp. 8.

Facts and Circumstances relative to the Sufferings and Losses of the Merchants residing in Great Britain, who carried on Trade with the United States of America, previous to the Late War. *London.* 1789. 8vo, pp. 26. 23617

Facts Concerning the Freedmen. Their Capacity and their Destiny, Corrected and Published by the Emancipation League. *Boston.* 1863. 8vo, pp. 12. H. 23618

Facts and Considerations for the Democracy of the Empire State. *New-York.* 1852. 8vo, pp. 16. S. 23619

Facts and Documents, relating to the State of the Controversy, between America and Great Britain, and the Dispositions of the Two Cabinets to make Peace. Collected for the use of the American People. By A Friend of Truth and of Honourable Peace. *Boston: True & Rowe.* 1813. 8vo, pp. 31. H., N., W.

Facts and Documents. *See* Fitchburg, Harvard, Jamaica, Rehoboth, Staten Island, and other headings.

Facts Explaining the Nature of the Slavery of the Blacks, followed by Details of the Colony of Sierra Léone. Published by a Committee named by the Religious Society of Friends to assist in the complete Abolition of the Slavery of the Blacks. [n. p. n. d.] 23621

Facts for the Consideration of Ship Builders, Seamen, Merchants, etc. *New York.* 1828. 8vo. 23622

Facts for the Laboring Man: By a Laboring Man. ... "Narragansett" (Herald of the Times). *Newport, R. I.: James Atkinson.* 1840. 8vo, pp. 102. BA., S. 23623

Facts for the People. No. X. Address, of the National Anti-Slavery Convention. [*New York.* 1841.] 8vo, pp. 7. BA.

Facts for the People. *See* [Frieze (Jacob)].

Facts for the People, G. Bailey, Editor. Published Monthly. *Washington, D. C.* 1855–56. 8vo, pp. 192. S. 23625

Facts for the People. The Abolition Leaders convicted out of their own Mouths of Disunion-Abolitionism, of Insurrectionary Doctrines, a Design to change the Government, Override the Constitution and form a Central Despotism of Falsehood, Corruption and Treason. [n. p. n. d.] 8vo, pp. 8. 23626

Facts for the Present Crisis, containing, I. A Letter of Hon. Wiley P. Harris, to Col. J. F. H. Claiborne. II. Portions of the ... Address of the ... Democratic Committee of Virginia, on the Know-Nothing Issues. III. ... The Democratic Platform of 1852. IV. ... Alien and Sedition Laws ... Virginia Resolutions of '98 and '99. ... *New Orleans.* 1855. 8vo, pp. 50.

Facts for the Times. Dissolution of the American Union Question. *Boston: Redding & Co.* 1850. 8vo, pp. 28. 23628

Facts illustrative of the Character of the Anthracite, or Lehigh Coal, found in the Great Mines of Mauch Chunk ... *Boston: printed by T. R. Marvin.* 1825. 12mo, pp. 22. H. + *Philadelphia.* 1827. 12mo, pp. 20. 23629

Facts Important to be Known by the Manufacturers, Mechanics and all other Classes of the Community. ... *New York.* 1831. 8vo, pp. 39. BA. 23630

Facts Involved in the Rhode Island Controversy, with Some Views upon the Rights of Both Parties. *Boston: B. B. Mussey.* 1842. 8vo, pp. 43. BA., S. 23631

Facts, Principles and Progress, October, 1863. *Philadelphia: C. Sherman & Son, for the League.* 1863. 12mo, pp. 36. 23632

Facts relating to the Capture of Washington. *See* [Evans (de Lacy)], No. 21344.

Facts relative to the Campaign on the Niagara, in 1814. *Boston: Printed at the Patriot Office.* 1815. 8vo, pp. 47, (4), 1 l. folded. BA. 23634

Facts relative to the Canadian Indians, published by direction of The Aborigines' Committee of the Meeting for Sufferings. *London: Harvey and Darton.* 1839. Cr. 8vo, pp. 24. M.

Forms No. 4 of tracts relative to the Aborigines.

Facts Relative to the Present State of the British Cotton Colonies, and to the Connection of their Interests with those of the Mother Country. *Edinburgh.* 1871. 8vo, pp. 62. 23635

Facts respecting Slavery. [n. p. n. d.] 16mo, pp. 8. BA.

Facts respecting the Captured Property, and reasons in support of a Bill for vesting in Commissioners, all the Effects and Property Captured at St. Eustatia. *London.* 1781. Folio, pp. 3.

Facts and Statements concerning the Cleveland and St. Louis Railroad ... by Lebanon, Indiana, to Paris, Illinois ... *Cleveland. Aug.*, 1854. 8vo. S. 23638

Facts and Law in the case of the Ship Harvey Birch. Burned [by the Rebel Cruiser Nashville], November 19, 1861, off Ireland. *New York: John W. Amerman.* 1862. 8vo, pp. 25.

Facts and Observations Illustrative of the Past and Present Situation and Future Prospects of the United States. With a Sketch of the Restrictive Systems. Third Edition. *Philadelphia.* 1822. 8vo, pp. 54. W. 23640

Facts and Observations. *See* Erie, *and* Philadelphia.

Facts and Observations relative to the Participation of American Citizens in the African Slave Trade. Published by ... Friends in Pennsylvania, New-Jersey, &c. *Philadelphia.* 1841. 8vo, pp. 36. S. 23641

Facts versus Lord Durham. *See* [Lambden].

Facts without Fiction. 1854. 23642

A concise account of slavery in the West Indian colonies, 1790–1846.

[FADEN (W.)] The North American Atlas, selected From the most Authentic Maps, Charts, Plans, &c. Hitherto Published. *London: William Faden.* MDCCLXXVII. Folio. BA. 23643

Consists of 26 folio maps, etc., of the British colonies in North America and Florida, etc. Faden also published a series of plans of the battles of the Revolutionary War, which are sometimes bound up with this atlas.

FAEHTZ (E. F. M.) The National Memorial Day: a Record of Ceremonies over the Graves of the Union Soldiers, May 29 and 30, 1869. *Washington: Head-Quarters Grand Army of the Republic.* 1870. 8vo, pp. 1064. Portrait. 23644

FAES (José Estevan). Memoria sobre un sistema de defensa para las costas y fronteras de la republica [de Chile]. *Santiago de Chile.* 1844. 4to, 1 l., pp. 14. 23645

FAGE (R.) Cosmography | Or, | A Description | of the | Whole World, | Represented (by a more exact and | certain Discovery) in the Excellencies | of its Situation, Commodities, | Inhabitants, and History: | Of | Their Particular and Distinct | Governments, Religions, Arms, | and Degrees of Honour used | amongst Them. | Enlarged with very many and rare Additions. | Very delightful to be read in so small a volum. | By Robert Fage Esquire. | *London, Printed by S. Griffin for John Overton at | the White-Horse in Little Brittain, next door | to Little St. Bartholomews-Gate.* 1667. | 8vo, 3 l., pp. 166. S. 23646

Mostly relates to America, especially from page 112 to 166; other editions, 1658 and 1663.

FAGES (E.) Noticias estadisticas sobre el departamento de Tuspan. *Puebla.* 1855. 4to. Map. 23647

FAHEY (J.) The Political History of Canada; A Lecture. By James Fahey, Jr. *Dundas.* 1867. 8vo. 23648

[FAHNESTOCK (George Wolff).] A Centennial Memorial of Christian and Anna Maria Wolff, March Twenty-Fifth, 1863. With Brief Records of their Children and Relatives. *Philadelphia: Helfenstein.* 1863. Folio, pp. 113. 2 Plates. 23649

One hundred copies privately printed.

[FAILLON (*l'Abbé*).] L'Heroine chrétienne du Canada, ou Vie de Mlle Le Ber. *Paris: Ve Poussielgue-Rusand.* 1853. 8vo. + *Villemarie.* 1860. 8vo, pp. 404. 23650

[FAILLON.] Histoire de la Colonie Française en Canada. *Villemarie [Montreal].* 1865. 3 vols., 4to, pp. xiii, (2), xxiii, 551; xxiv, 568; (2), xxiii, 548. 2 Maps. BA. 23651

A very important historical work, to be completed in five volumes.

[FAILLON.] Vie de M. Olier, fondateur du séminaire de Saint-Sulpice, accompagnée de Notices sur un grand nombre de personnages contemporains. [*Le Mans, Richelet:*] *Poussielgue-Rusand.* 1841. 2 vols., 8vo. + Édition abrégée. [*Ibid.*] 12mo. Portrait. 23652

[FAILLON.] Vie de Mme d'Youville, fondatrice des sœurs de la Charité de Villemarie, dans l'île de Montréal, en Canada. *Paris: Ve Poussielgue-Rusand.* 1853. 8vo. 23653

[FAILLON.] Vie de Mlle Mance et histoire de l'Hôtel-Dieu de Villemarie, d'île de Montréal, en Canada. *Paris.* 1854. 2 vols., 8vo. 23654

[FAILLON.] Vie de la sœur Bourgeoys, fondatrice de la congrégation de Notre-Dame de Villemarie en Canada; suivi de l'Histoire de cet institut jusqu'à ce jour, et précédée d'une introduction. *Paris.* 1853. 2 vols., 8vo. 23655

The first title reads: "Mémoires particuliers pour servir à l'histoire de l'Eglise dans l'Amérique du Nord."

FAIR (G. Y.) Report of the President of the Montgomery Branch Bank. ... *Tuscaloosa.* 1845. 8vo. BM. 23656

A fair Account. *See* Vol. II., No. 6735.

Fair Harvard: a Story of American College Life. *New York: G. P. Putnam & Son.* 1869. 12mo, pp. vi, 309. C. 23657

FAIR PLAY, *pseudonym.* The True State of the American Question; reply to Mr. Thurlow Weed. By Fair Play. *London.* 1862. 8vo. 23658

A Fair Representation, 1756. *See* Nova Scotia.

FAIRBAIRN (H.) A Defence of William Penn, from the Charges contained in the History of England, by the Right Hon. Thomas Babington Macaulay. By Henry Fairbairn. *Philadelphia.* 1849. 8vo, pp. 38. S. 23659

FAIRBAIRN. Letter to Lord William Bentinck, on the Superior Advantages of a Steam Passage to the East Indies by the Gulf of Mexico and the Pacific Ocean, as compared with the Proposed Route by the Red and Mediterranean Seas. By Henry Fairbairn. *London.* 1837. 8vo. C. 23660

FAIRBAIRN (R. B.) A Sermon in the Chapel of St. Stephen's College. By Robert B. Fairbairn. *Albany.* 1863. 8vo.

FAIRBANK (D.) A Sermon delivered at Plymouth, New-hampshire, on Fast Day, April 12, 1810. By Drury Fairbank. *Hanover.* 1810. 8vo. 23662

FAIRBANKS (Cassie). The Lone House; A Poem, partly founded on Fact. *Halifax.* 1859. 8vo. 23663

FAIRBANKS (C.) The American Conflict as seen from a European Point of View. ... By Charles Fairbanks. *Boston: Press of Geo. C. Rand & Avery.* 1863. 8vo, pp. 44. H. 23664

[FAIRBANKS (Charles R).] Reports and Papers relating to a Canal, intended to connect the Harbour of Halifax with the Basin of Mines; Remarks on its Nature and Importance, and a Plan and Section. Also the Report of a Survey for Canals between St. Peter's Bay and the Bras d'Or Lake, in Cape Breton; and the Bay of Fundy and Bay of Verte. 1826. 8vo, pp. 58. 2 Maps. 23665

FAIRBANKS (E.) Executive Address of ... Fairbanks, Governor of the State of Vermont. Extra Session, April 23, 1861. ... *Montpelier: E. P. Walton.* 1861. 8vo, pp. 8. B. 23666

FAIRBANKS. The Valedictory Address of Erastus Fairbanks, Governor of the State of Vermont, to the General Assembly, at their Annual Session; October, 1861. *Montpelier: Freeman Printing Establishment.* 1861. 8vo, pp. 24. B. 23667

FAIRBANKS (G. R.) The Early History of Florida. An Introductory Lecture, delivered by George F. Fairbanks, Esq., before the Florida Historical Society, April 15th, 1857. With an Appendix, containing the Constitution, Organization, and List of Members of the Society. *St. Augustine, Fla.: the Society.* 1857. 8vo, pp. 31, (1). B., C. 23668

FAIRBANKS. History of Florida from its Discovery by Ponce de Leon, in 1512, to the Close of the Florida War, in 1842. By George R. Fairbanks. *Philadelphia: J. B. Lippincott & Co. Jacksonville, Fla.: Columbus Drew.* 1871. 8vo, pp. 350. BA.

FAIRBANKS. The History and Antiquities of the City of St. Augustine, Florida, founded A.D. 1565. Comprising some of the most Interesting Portions of the Early History of Florida. By George R. Fairbanks ... . *New York: Charles B. Norton.* 1858. 8vo, pp. 8, 2 l., pp. 9–200. Plates. B., C., H. 23670

FAIRBANKS (G.) An Oration, 14 July 1821, at the Request of the Republicans of the Town of Boston ... By Gerry Fairbanks. *Boston: American Statesman Office.* 1821. 8vo, pp. 22.

FAIRBANKS (J.) Report of the Trial of Jason Fairbanks, on an Indictment for the Murder of Miss Elizabeth Fales. At the Supreme Court ... Dedham, ... August, 1801. Second Edition. *Boston.* 1801. 8vo, pp. 87. BA. + Third Edition. *Boston.* 1801. 8vo, pp. 87. + Fourth Edition. *Boston: Russell and Cutler.* 1801. 8vo. B. 23672

FAIRBANKS. The Solemn Declaration of the Late Unfortunate Jason Fairbanks ... To which is added Some Account of his Life and Character. ... Collected and Published by Ebenezer Fairbanks, Jun. ... *Dedham: Minerva Press of H. Mann.* 1802. 8vo, pp. 55. B., BA., W. 23673

Also: A Deed of Horror! Trial of Jason Fairbanks ... for the Murder of Elizabeth Fales, his Sweetheart!!! Correctly taken down by a Gentleman on the Spot. *Salem: W. Carlton.* 16mo, pp. 8. H.

FAIRBANKS (J.) An Address Delivered before the Massachusetts Christian Charitable Mechanic Association, Dec. 17, 1812; being the Anniversary for the Choice of Officers, and the Second Triennial Celebration of their Public Festival. By John Fairbanks ... . *Boston.* 1812. 8vo, pp. 51 23674

FAIRBURN (J.) *See* Vol. III., No. 8999

FAIRCHILD (A. G.) Memoir of Mrs. Louisa A. Lowne, By the Rev. Ashbel G. Fairchild. Second Edition. *Philadelphia: William S. Martien.* 1837. 18mo, pp. 221. Portrait. 23675

FAIRCHILD (J. H.) Educational Arrangements and College Life at Oberlin. Inaugural Address of President J. H. Fairchild ... August 22, 1866. *New York.* 1866. 8vo, pp. 21.

FAIRCHILD. The Joint Education of the Sexes: A Report ... Ohio Teachers' Association. *Oberlin.* 1852. 18mo, pp. 46.

FAIRCHILD. Oberlin: its Origin, Progress and Results. An Address ... August 22, 1860. By Prof. J. H. Fairchild. *Oberlin: Shankland and Harmon.* 1860. 8vo, pp. 70. BA. 23678

FAIRCHILD. Woman's Right to the Ballot. By James H. Fairchild, President of Oberlin College. *Oberlin: G. H. Fairchild.* 1870. 12mo, pp. 67. H. 23679

Also: Oberlin Evangelist. Extras, 1856: Progress of the College, by J. H. Fairchild. — A Sketch of the Anti-Slavery History of Oberlin, by J. H. Fairchild. 4to.

FAIRCHILD (Joy H.) Farewell Address to the Payson Church, South Boston, ... November 22, 1857. By Rev. J. H. Fairchild. ... *Boston: the Author.* 1858. 12mo, pp. 63. Portrait.

FAIRCHILD. Iniquity Unfolded. An Account of the Treatment of Mr. Fairchild by the Deacons in South Boston, and others. Written by Himself. Third Edition. *Exeter, N. H.: Published for the Author.* 1844. 8vo, pp. 84. BA. 23681

FAIRCHILD. Remarkable Incidents in the Life of Rev. J. H. Fairchild ... . Compiled and Published by Himself. ... *Boston: For the Author.* 1855. 12mo, pp. xi, 460. Portrait. B., C. + Third Edition. *Boston.* 1856. 12mo, pp. xi, 449. Portrait.

FAIRCHILD. The Truth Revealed. Statement & Review of the whole case of the Reverend Joy H. Fairchild, ... Compiled from Original Documents, by a Member of the Suffolk Bar. With an Appendix ... . *Boston: Wright's Steam Press.* 1845. 8vo, pp. 104. BA., S. 23683

FAIRCHILD. Trial of Rev. Joy Hamlet Fairchild, on the Charge of Adultery with Miss Rhoda Davidson. *Boston.* 1845. 8vo, pp. 32. 23684

Also: Correspondence between Rev. Nehemiah Adams, and Rev. J. H. Fairchild, with Notes and Comments by a Committee of the Payson Church. *Boston: Dutton and Wentworth.* 1846. 8vo, pp. 48. B. — New Doctrine of Clerical Privilege, An Address, Jan. 26 and 27, 1852. *Boston.* 1852. 12mo. — The South Boston Unitarian Ordination. ... *Boston.* 1841. 8vo, pp. 64.

FAIRCHILD (L.) *See* Wisconsin.

FAIRCLOUGH (J. W.) An Address delivered before the Hibernian Society of Alexandria, D. C., on St. Patrick's Day, 17th March, 1825. By Rev. Joseph W. Fairclough. *Alexandria: H. Pittman.* 1825. 16mo, pp. 16. C. 23685

FAIRFAX (F.) Memorial of Ferdinando Fairfax, against the Extension of the Patents granted to Robert Fulton, for Improvements in Propelling Vessels by Steam. By Ferdinando Fairfax. *Washington: Edward De Krafft.* 1816. 8vo, pp. 8. BA., C., M.

FAIRFAX. Oration delivered in Charlestown, in Virginia, on the 4th July, 1805. By Ferdinando Fairfax. *Washington.* 1808. Sm. 8vo. C., N., P. 23687

FAIRFAX (L.) The Elopement: A Tale of the Confederate States of America. *London: Freeman.* 1863. 8vo, pp. 180.

FAIRFAX, *Va.* Catalogue of the Officers and Students of the Protestant Episcopal Theological Seminary, Fairfax Co., Va. 1832. 8vo. Continued. 23689

The Fairfax Correspondence. Memoir of the Reign of Charles the First. Edited by George W. Johnson, Esq. ... *London: Richard Bentley.* 1848. Memorials of the Civil War: Comprising the Correspondence of the Fairfax Family with the most

Distinguished Personages engaged in that Memorable Contest. Now first Published from the Original Manuscripts. Edited by Robert Bell, ... Forming the concluding volumes of the Fairfax Correspondence. ... *London: Richard Bentley.* 1849. 4 vols., 8vo, pp. cxl, 405; xi, 427, 4 Plates; xxii, 1 l., pp. 403; xv, 427, 4 Plates. B., BA. 23690

The descendants of these families settled in Fairfax County, Virginia.

FAIRFIELD (E. B.) Liberty and Slavery. Oration: by Edmund B. Fairfield ... July 4th, 1856. *Hinsdale, Mich.* [1856.] 8vo, pp. 15. H. 23691

Also: Slavery in the Territories. Speech ... in the Senate of Michigan ... January 24, 1857. *Detroit: Henry Barns, Printer.* 1857. 8vo, pp. 8. H. — True National Greatness. An Oration, delivered at ... Hinsdale, Mich., July 4th, 1853. ... *Buffalo: D. D. Waite, Printer.* 8vo, pp. 27. H.

FAIRFIELD (J.) The Autobiography of Jane Fairfield, embracing a few Select Poems by Sumner Lincoln Fairfield. *Boston: Bazin & Ellsworth.* 1860. 12mo, pp. viii, 328. Portrait.

FAIRFIELD. The Life of Sumner Lincoln Fairfield, Esq. ... By Jane Fairfield. *New York: the Author.* 1847. 12mo, pp. 132. B., BA. + [*Ibid.*] 1847. pp. 62. C. 23693

FAIRFIELD (J.) Speech of John Fairfield, in the House ... on the North-Eastern Boundary Question. *Washington.* 1838. 8vo. 23694

FAIRFIELD (Sumner Lincoln). Poems and Prose Writings. In Two Volumes. Vol. I. [Poems.] *Philadelphia.* 1841. 8vo, pp. 400. C. 23695

No more published. Also: The Last Night of Pompeii; a Poem: and Lays and Legends. *New York: Elliott & Palmer.* 1832. 8vo, pp. 309. — Lays of Melpomene. *Portland: Todd & Smith.* 1824. 12mo, pp. 122.

FAIRFIELD COUNTY, *Conn.* Intemperance. An Address, to the Churches and Congregations of the Western District of Fairfield County. *New-Haven: Printed by Eli Hudson.* 1813. 8vo, pp. 31. S. + *Hartford: Printed by Peter B. Gleason & Co. Nov.* 1813. 8vo, pp. 31. H. + *Schenectady.* 1814. 8vo. B.

Vindication of the Proceedings of the Eastern Association in Fairfield County. 1794. 8vo. 23697

FAIRFIELD WEST, *Conn.* Appeal of the Association of Fairfield West to the Associated Ministers connected with the General Association of Connecticut. *New York.* 1852. 8vo. BM.

FAIRFIELD, *N. Y.* Circular and Catalogue of the Faculty and Students of the College of Physicians and Surgeons of the Western District of the State of New York, in Fairfield, Herkimer County. *Albany.* 1829. 8vo. Continued. 23699

[FAIRFLAY (Francis).] *See* Vol. III., No. 10390.

FAIRHAVEN, (Ontario Bay,) The Terminus of the Lake Ontario, Auburn and New York Railroad. *New York: Edward O. Jenkins.* 1858. 8vo, pp. 28, 1 l. 2 Plates and 2 Maps.

FAIRHAVEN, *Mass.* An Act concerning the Schools, together with the Report of the School Committee of Fairhaven, for the year 1839–40. *New Bedford: Press of Benjamin Lindsey.* [1840.] 8vo, pp. 16. 23701

By-Laws of Fairhaven. Approved June Term, 1838. *New Bedford: Printed by Benjamin Lindsey.* 1838. 12mo, pp. 11.

Extracts from the State Laws, with the Regulations of the Public Schools, in ... Fairhaven, ... 1846. ... *New Bedford.* 1846. 8vo. 23703

Report of the School Committee of the Town of Fairhaven, 1845–46. *New Bedford.* 1846. 8vo, pp. 18. Table. Continued. 23704

Report of the School Committee of the Town of Fairhaven, for the year 1847–48. *Boston: Printed by N. S. Dearborn.* 1848. 8vo, pp. 19. Continued. 23705

Report of the Selectmen of Fairhaven, on the Financial Concerns of the Town, for the year ending April 1, 1843. [*New Bedford.* 1843.] 12mo, pp. 4. Continued. 23706

Statutes in Relation to the Public Schools, and the Report of the School Committee of Fairhaven, 1843–44. *New Bedford: M. Tilden's Press.* 1844. 8vo, pp. 45. 23707

FAIRHOLT (F. W.) Tobacco: its History and Associations: including an Account of the Plant and its Manufacture; with its Modes of Use in all Ages and Countries. By F. W. Fairholt, F.S.A. ... *London: Chapman and Hall.* 1859. Post 8vo, pp. vii, 332. 1 Plate and 100 Woodcuts. H. 23708

FAIRMAN (W. Blennerhasset). A Series of Letters with Editorial Remarks on the Existing Differences between England and

America. Inscribed to the Earl of Darnley. By Captain Fairman, Aid-de-Camp and Military Secretary to the late Governor and Commander-in-Chief of Curaçoa, and its Dependencies, &c. &c. &c. *London: A. J. Valpy.* 1813. 8vo, pp. xi, 68.

See "M. Rev.," LXXII. 55.

FAIRMOUNT PARK. *See* Philadelphia.

FAIRS. Of Sturbridge, Bury, and the most famous Fairs in Europe and America; with Anecdotes and Considerations upon the Origin, Progress and Decline of all [Fairs] in this Kingdom. *Cambridge.* [175–.] 8vo, pp. 39. 23710

FAIRSERVICE (J.), *pseudonym.* Plain Dealing: or, The Proud Man fairly dealt with. ... By James Fairservice. A Volunteer in the late intended Expedition to Canada, and in the Fight at Minas. ... *Boston.* 1750. 8vo, pp. 21. BA., H., M., W. 23711

A Faithful Account of the whole of the Transactions relating to the late Affair of Honour between J. Temple and W. Whately, Esqrs., containing a particular History of that Unhappy Quarrel. Likewise the whole of their Letters that passed on the Occasion, with those signed Antenor, An Enemy to the Villains of Every Denomination, &c. &c. *London: R. Snagg.* 1774. 8vo, pp. 38.

Mr. Temple was accused of having surreptitiously obtained the letters of Governor Hutchinson, and Lieutenant-Governor Oliver, from Mr. Whately, which produced the duel to which this pamphlet relates. The letters in question were procured by Dr. Franklin.

Faithful History ... Cherokee Indians. *See* No. 12457.

Faithful Narrative. *See* Edwards (J.), No. 21939.

A Faithful Narrative. *See* Salem, Mass.

Faits explicatifs de la nature de la Traite des Noirs suivis de détails sur la Colonie des de Sierra Léone. Publié par un Comité nommé par La Societé Religieuse des Amis pour concourir à l'Abolition Complette de la traite des noirs. *Londres.* 1824. 8vo, pp. 43. 23713

FAJARDO (H. C.) Arenas del Uruguay por Heraclio C. Fajardo. *Buenos Ayres.* 1862. 4to, pp. 340. 23714

FAJARDO. La cruz de Azabache. Por Heraclio C. Fajardo. *Buenos-Aires.* 1860. 8vo, pp. 112. 23715

FAJARDO. El azote literario por el demócratia. Folleto crítico-burlesco de las Arenas del Uruguay. Por Heraclio C. Fajardo. *Montevideo.* 8vo, pp. 60. 23716

FALBE (C. F.) Vases Antiques du Perou. *Copenhagen.* 1843. 8vo. 2 Plates. 23717

Probably from the "Transactions of the Royal Society of Northern Antiquarians."

FALCK (N.) Prolegómenos del Derecho, o Enciclopedia Juridica. *México.* 1852. 8vo. C. 23718

FALCKNER (D.) *See* Thomas (G.)

FALCKNER (J.) Grondlycke Onderricht | van | Sekere Voorname Hoofd-Stricken, der | Waren, Lontern, Saligmakenden, Christelycken Leere, | Gegrondet op den Grondt van de Apostelen en Propheten, daer | Jesus Christus | de Hoeck-Steen. | I S. | Angewesen in eenvoudige, dog stigtlycke | Vragen en Antwoorden, | Door | Justus Falckner, Saxo- | Germanos, Minister der Christelycken | Protestantsen Genaemten Lutherschen | Gemeente te N. York en Albanien, | &c. | ... | ... | *Gedrucht te Nieuw-York by W. Bradfordt.* | 1708. | 8vo; 4 l., pp. 126, (2). 23719

Introduced here on account of the imprint. It is a work of extreme rarity, and we have only seen one copy sold, which brought over fifty dollars.

FALCONAR (M. *and* H.) Poems on Slavery: by Maria Falconar, aged 17, and Harriet Falconar, aged 14. *London: Johnson.* 1788. 8vo. 23720

See "M. Rev.," LXXIX. 554.

FALCONBRIDGE (A.) An Account of the Slave Trade on the Coast of Africa. By Alexander Falconbridge, Late Surgeon in the African Trade. *London: J. Phillips.* MDCCLXXXVIII. 8vo, pp. 55. BA. + Second Edition. *London: James Phillips.* 1788. 12mo, pp. 72. N. 23721

See "M. Rev.," LXXVIII. 343.

FALCONBRIDGE, *pseudon.* Dan Marble: a Biographical Sketch of that Famous and Diverting Humorist, with Reminiscences, Comicalities, Anecdotes, &c., By Falconbridge. *New-York.* 1851. 12mo. C. 23722

FALCONER (R.) The Voyages, Dangerous Adventures And imminent Escapes of Captain Richard Falconer: Containing The Laws, Customs, and Manners of the Indians in America; his Shipwrecks; his Marrying an Indian Wife; his narrow Escape from the Island of Dominico, &c. Intermix'd with The

Voyages and Adventures of Thomas Randal, of Cork, Pilot; with his Shipwreck in the Baltick, being the only Man that escap'd: His being taken by the Indians of Virginia, &c. Written by Himself, now alive. *London: W. Chetwood.* 1720. 8vo, pp. (4), 72, 136, 179. Engraved Frontispiece. C., H. + Second Edition. *London.* 1724. + Third Edition. *London.* 1734. 12mo. + Fourth Edition. *London: J. Marshall.* 1734. 16mo, 3 l., pp. 216, 3 l. Plate. C. + Fifth Edition. To which is added, A Great Deliverance at Sea, by W. Johnson, D.D. Chaplain to his Majesty. *London.* 1764. 12mo, pp. 226, vi, 36. + The Sixth Edition, Corrected. *London: George Keith.* 1769. 12mo, pp. (6), 276, (5). Frontispiece. 23723

The edition of 1734 was reprinted in 1838. There is another chap-book edition, *Manchester: J. Imison.* 1785. 12mo.

FALCONER (T.) Expedition to Santa Fé. An Account of its Journey from Texas through Mexico, with particulars of its Capture. By Thomas Falconer, of Lincoln's Inn. *New Orleans.* 1842. 8vo. BM. 23724

FALCONER. Mr. Falconer's Reply to Mr. Greenhow's Answer; with Mr. Greenhow's Rejoinder. [*Washington.*] 1845. 8vo. C., N. 23725

FALCONER. On the Discovery of the Mississippi, and on the Southwestern, Oregon, and Northwestern Boundary of the United States, etc. With a Translation from the Original MS. of Memoirs, &c. relating to the Discovery of the Mississippi by Robert Cavalier de la Salle, and the Chevalier de Tonty. By Thomas Falconer. *London: S. Clarke.* 1844. 12mo, pp. v, 96, 99. C. 23726

[FALCONER.] I. On the Nomination of Agents formerly appointed to act in England for the Colonies of North America. II. A Brief Statement of the Dispute between Sir C. Metcalf and the House of Assembly of the Province of Canada. 1844. Privately printed. *London: printed by Reynell and Weight.* 12mo, pp. 21. H. 23727

FALCONER. The Oregon Question; or, a Statement of the British Claims to the Oregon Territory, in Opposition to the Pretensions of the Government of the United States of America. With a Chronological Table, and a Map of the Territory. By Thomas Falconer, Esq. ... *London: Samuel Clarke.* 1845. 8vo, pp. 46, 1 l. Map. C. + Second Edition. ... . With the Postscript and Second Postscript, etc., in Reply to Mr. Green-

how. *London: Samuel Clarke.* 1845. 8vo, pp. 50, 4. B. + *New York: William Taylor.* 1845. 8vo, pp. 40. BA. 23728

FALES (W. R.) Memoir of William R. Fales, the Portsmouth Cripple. [Being an Autobiography, with Memoranda and Letters, and a Brief Introduction, Edited by S. H. L.] *Philadelphia: Lindsay & Blakiston.* 1851. 12mo, pp. 151. 23729

FALKENSTEIN (Chr. K.) Thaddäus Kosciuszko. Dargestellt von Karl Falkenstein. *Leipzig: Brockhaus.* 1827. 8vo. P.

FALKENSTEIN. Thadée Kosciusko, dans sa vie politique et intime, par M. Charles Falkenstein. Traduit de l'Allemand et accompagné de notes, par M. Charles Forster. *Paris.* 1839. 8vo, 19½ sheets. Lithograph. C., P. 23731

FALKLAND (L.) Review of the Southern Review on Mr. Foote's Resolution. By Lucius Falkland. *Baltimore.* 1830. 8vo.

FALKLAND ISLANDS. Correspondence Relative to the Falkland Islands. 1843. Folio, pp. 89. Chart and Plans. 23733

Also: Papers relating to the Falkland Islands. Presented to Parliament by Her Majesty's Command. *London.* 1841. Folio. *See also* [Johnson (S.)], *and* Papers.

FALKNER (T.) A Description of Patagonia, and the Adjoining Parts of South America: containing an Account of the Soil, Produce, Animals, Vales, Mountains, Rivers, Lakes, &c., of those Countries; the Religion, Government, Policy, Customs, Dress, Arms, and Language of the Indian Inhabitants; and some Particulars relating to Falkland's Islands. By Thomas Falkner, Who resided near Forty Years in those Parts ... *Hereford: printed by C. Pugh. London: T. Lewis.* M.DCC.LXXIV. 4to, 2 l., pp. iv, 144. 2 Maps. BA., H. 23734

"The book is, to this day, the only authentic account we have of the Indians of the Pampas."—SIR W. PARISH. "A judicious author."—*Biog. Univ.* Also highly commended by Dr. Pritchard. *See also* "M. Rev.," LI. 409. It is to Falkner that the world is indebted for some of the stories about the great stature of the natives of Patagonia. He asserts that such was their height, that, when in a sitting posture, they were almost as tall as the commodore of the ship. Navigators who preceded Falkner had made similar statements; but recent visitors, who have seen many of the natives, state that they are no taller than Europeans.

FALKNER. Of the Patagonians. Formed from the relation of Father Falkner, a Jesuit, who had resided among them thirty-eight years; and from the different Voyagers who had met with this tall race. *Darlington.* 1775 (?) 4to. 23735

Printed at the private press of George Allan, Esq., for his friend Thomas Pennant.

FALKNER. Beschreibung von Patagonien und den angrenzenden Theilen von Südamerika aus dem Englischen. *Gotha: Carl Wilhelm Ettinger.* 1775. 8vo, pp. 181. Map. 23736

The translator was Schack Herrmann Ewald.

[FALKNER.] Description des Terres Magellaniques et des Pays adjacens. Traduit de l'Anglois par M. B** [Marc Théod. Bourrit]. *A Geneve: Chez François Dufart. Et à Paris: Hotel Landier, No. 5. Rue Haute-Feuille, au coin de celle Poupée.* M.DCC.-LXXVII. 2 pts., 18mo, pp. 163; 135. C. + *Lausanne: J. P. Heubach.* 1787. 2 pts., 18mo, pp. 163; 135. 23737

This French translation contains some additions. These two editions are exactly alike, except the title-page. Reprinted in 1788.

FALKNER. Descripcion de Patagonia y de las partes adyacentes de la America meridional. Escrita en Ingles por Tomas Falkner. *Buenos-Aires: Imprenta del estado.* 1835. 4to, pp. vii, 64. 23738

Forms part of Vol. I. of Angelis' "Coleccion de Obras y Documentos."

FALKNERN (D.) Curieuse Nachricht von Pensylvanie. ... Von Daniel Falknern ... *Frankfurt und Leipzig.* 1702. 12mo, pp. iv, 58. 23739

See Thomas (Gabriel).

FALL (Robert). Observations on the Report of the Commissioners of the House of Commons ... of the British Fishery. *London.* 1786. 8vo, pp. 103. S. 23740

Fall of British Tyranny, 1776. *See* [Leacock (John)].

The Fall of Fort Sumpter; or Love and War in 1860–61. By the Private Secretary to ——, etc. *New York: H. A. Brady.* 1867. 8vo, pp. 167. 23741

Fall River. An Authentic Narrative. *See* [Williams (*Mrs.* R. C.)]

FALL RIVER, *Mass.* Address of Hon. Nathaniel B. Borden, Mayor, at the last Regular Meeting of the Board of Aldermen, April, 1858. *Fall River.* 1858. 8vo, pp. 18. M. 23742

Catalogue of the Fall River Athenæum Library, with an Appendix ... . *Fall River: Hammond and Earl.* 1838. 12mo, pp. 56. BA. + With Rules and By-Laws. *Boston: Damrell & Moore.* 1855. 16mo. pp. 36. C. 23743

Catalogue of the Public Library of the City of Fall River. Established 1861. *Fall River: Almy & Milne's Steam Press.* 1861. 8vo, pp. 100. B. 23744

Also: Annual Report of the Trustees of the Public Library, of the City of Fall River, 1861. *Fall River.* 1861. 8vo. Continued. B.

City Charter and Ordinances, Rules and Orders of City Council, and City Governments, from 1854 to 1866, of the City of Fall River. *Fall River.* 1866. 8vo. B. 23745

The Fall River Directory ... the Names of the Citizens, a Business Directory ... with an Almanac for 1853. By George Adams ... . *Fall River: R. & J. Adams.* 1853. 18mo, pp. 156. Continued. BA. 23746

Fall River; an Historical Sketch of her Industry, Progress and Improvement, Compiled from Authentic and Official Sources. *Fall River, Mass.: W. W. Armstrong.* 1870. Sq. 16mo, pp. 144. Plate. 23747

The Municipal Register, containing the City Charter, with Rules and Orders of the City Council; also, the Ordinances and a List of the Officers of the City of Fall River, for 1854. *Fall River: Almy & Milne's Steam Printing Office.* 1854. 12mo, pp. 73, (3). 23748

Petition from the Inhabitants of Fall River, by their Committee, to the Legislature of Massachusetts, relative to the South Boundary of Fall River, March 6, 1847. *House Doc. of Mass., No.* 93. *March,* 1847. 8vo, pp. 21. 23749

Report of the School Committee for 1844–5. 8vo. Continued.

Statement of Facts in Defence of the Congregational Church, Fall River, against certain Charges of Unchristian Conduct of A. Bronson. *Providence.* 1835. 8vo. 23751

Fallacies of Freemen, and Foes of Liberty. A Reply to "The American War, the Whole Question Explained." *Manchester: Union and Emancipation Society.* 1863. 8vo, pp. 36.

Fallacy Detected, by the Evidence of Facts; or Considerations on ... a Compulsory Reduction of the Interest of the Public Debt ... [*Philadelphia:*] *Printed* 1790. 8vo, pp. 44. S. 23753

Fallacy of Free-Trade Doctrine. *Brooklyn.* 1864. 23754

The Fallen Brave. *See* Shea (J. G.)

FALLEY SEMINARY, *Fulton, N. Y.* Catalogue, 1849. Continued. S. 23755

Falls of Niagara. *See* Niagara.

FALMOUTH, *Mass.* *See* Vol. IV., Nos. 15429, 15441, and 15442; *also* Indians.

The False Accusers Accused, or the Undeceived Englishman, In a Letter to the pretended Patriots ... By a Member of the House of Commons. *London.* 1741. 8vo, pp. 54. 23756

The False Alarm. *See* [Johnson (S.)]

The False Alarm, Addressed to the Right Honourable Richard Rigby, Esq. Paymaster-General of his Majesty's Forces. *London: J. P. Coghlan.* MDCCLXXXII. 8vo, 2 l., pp. 106, (2).

Signed "Cincinnatus." Our title, No. 13132, Vol. IV., differs in the *imprint* only. Relates to the alarm in England on the reverses of the British arms in America, which the writer calls "the late accident arising from the fickle fortune of war."

The False Alarm: or, the Americans Mistaken. *London: T. Ridley.* 1775. 8vo, pp. 22. 23758

Addressed to Lord North, and signed "Americanus." The writer undertakes to show the necessity and utility of the conduct of the British Government towards the Colonists. *See* "M. Rev.," LIII. 79.

Falsehood and Forgery Detected and Exposed, or the Conduct of Thomas Jefferson, James Madison, James Munroe, Albert Gallatin, Levi Lincoln, John Gailliard, William H. Crawford, Samuel McClay, General Sl. Smith, Andrew Gregg, and other Distinguished Democrats, in relation to the Right of Suffrage in Mississippi, Vindicated against the Slanders and Misrepresentations of John Binns, Stephen Simpson, and John Norvel. *Philadelphia: Peoples' Advocate Office.* 1823. 8vo, pp. 16. 23759

Falses on all Sides. Sundrey Errors, Maxims, and Corruptions of Men and Sects of this Present Age. *Newport, R. I.: Sold by James Franklin and E. Maregreas.* 1728. 12mo. 23760

A Familiar Conversational History of the Evangelical Churches of New-York. *New-York: R. Carter.* 1838. 16mo, pp. 222. Plate. C. 23761

Familiar Letters. *See* [Sullivan (William)].

The Family Christian Almanac for the United States, Calculated for Boston, New York, Baltimore and Charleston, for 1846. *New York.* 1846. 18mo. Continued. 23762

The Family Magazine or General Abstract of Useful Knowledge. *New York: Redfield.* 1834–40. 4to. S. 23763

Eight or more volumes published.

Family Register. *Albany: J. Munsell.* 1859. 12mo, pp. 4.

Traces one branch of the lineage of Simeon Crandall, of Washington County, R. I., and of Aaron Ott.

Family Register; with a Collection of Marriage Rites and Ceremonies, and Funeral Observances, with an Abstract of the Laws of the various States respecting the Ceremony of Marriage. *Columbus, O.* 1851. 8vo. C. 23765

Family Tablet, Containing a Selection of Original Poetry. *Boston.* 1796. 12mo. BM. 23766

FAMIN (C.) Chili, Paraguay, Uruguay, Buenos-Ayres par M. César Famin ... Patagone, Terre-du-Feu et Archipel des Malouines, par Frédéric Lacroix. Iles Diverses des Trois Océans et Regions Circompolaires, par M. le Commandeur Bory de Saint-Vincent ... et par M. Frédéric Lacroix. *Paris: Firmin Didot frères.* M DCCC XL. 8vo, pp. (4), 328. 88 Plates. BA.

Forms Vol. XXV. of "l'Univers."

FAMIN. Chile. Aus dem Französischen. *Stuttgart: Schweizerbart's Buchhandlung.* [183–?] 24 Plates. 23768

FAMIN. Gemälde von Columbien und Guyana. *Frankfurt: Schmerber.* 1837. 8vo. 8 Engravings. 23769

FAMIN. Geschichte und Beschreibung von Columbien und Guyana. Aus dem Französischen. *Stuttgart: Schweizerbart's Buchhandlung.* [183–?] 8vo. 8 Engravings. 23770

FAMIN. Der vereinigten Provinzen des Rio de la Plata (Buenos Ayres), Paraguay und Uruguay. Aus dem Französischen. *Stuttgart: Schweizerbart's Buchhandlung.* [183–?] 16 Engravings. 23771

FAMIN. Colombie et Guyanes. *See* Denis (F.), No. 19541.

Famous Boys; and How they became Great Men. *London: J. Hogg & Sons.* 1860. 16mo. + *New York.* 1861. 16mo.

Includes Franklin, and other Americans.

El Fanal, del imperio mexicano, ó miscelanea politica, extractada y redactada de las mejores fuentes por el autor del Pacto social. *Mexico.* 1822. 2 vols., 4to. 23773

Fanaticism, And its Results: or, Facts Versus Fancies. By a Southerner. *Baltimore: Printed By Joseph Robinson.* 1860. 8vo, pp. 36. 23774

Fancourt (C. St. J.) The History of Yucatan from its Discovery to the Close of the Seventeenth Century. By Charles St. John Fancourt, Esq., recently H. M. Superintendent of the British Settlements in the Bay of Honduras. *London: John Murray.* 1854. 8vo, pp. 340. Map. B., BA. 23775

Fanelli (Antonio Maria). Due relazioni del regno del Cile, ne' viaggi fatti per mare e per terra nella missione allo stesso regno. *Venetia: Gir. Albrizzi.* 1710. 8vo. 23776

The Faneuil Hall Address. To the People of the United States ... . [On the Reorganization of the South. *Boston.* 1865.] 8vo, pp. 6. H. 23777

See also under Boston, Vol. II.

Fanning (D.) The Narrative of Colonel David Fanning (A Tory in the Revolutionary War with Great Britain): giving an Account of his Adventures in North Carolina From 1775 to 1783, as Written by Himself. With an Introduction and Explanatory Notes. *Richmond, Va. Printed for private distribution only,* 1861. *In the First Year of the Independence of the Confederate States of America.* 4to, pp. xxv, 92. B. 23778

Fifty copies printed on thin writing paper, and ten on thicker paper.

Fanning. [Title as in No. 23778.] *New York: Reprinted for Joseph Sabin.* 1865. 8vo, pp. xxvi, 86. 23779

Fifty copies printed on large paper. Forms No. 1 of Sabin's reprints, Second Series. The original manuscript belongs to Mr. Charles Deane, of Cambridge, Mass., who lent it to a friend, who re-lent it to a gentleman in the South, where it was copied, edited, and printed. The notes are by Governor Swaine, of North Carolina, and Thomas H. Wynne, of Richmond.

Fanning (E.) Voyages Round the World; with selected Sketches of Voyages to the South Seas, North and South Pacific Oceans, China, etc., performed under the Command and Agency of the Author. Also, Information relating to Important Late Discoveries, between 1792 and 1832, Together with the Report of the Commander of the First American Exploring Expedition, patronized by the United States Government, in the Brigs Seraph and Annawan, to the Southern Hemisphere. By Edmund Fanning. *New York: Collins & Hanna.* M DCCC XXXIII. 8vo, pp. 499. 5 Plates. B., BA., P. + *London.* 1834. 8vo. 23780

A French version is included in Montémont's "Biblioth. univ.," v. 21.

Fanning. Voyages to the South Seas, Indian and Pacific Oceans, ... North-West Coast, Feejee Islands, ... with an Account of the New Discoveries made in the Southern Hemisphere, Between the Years 1830–1837. Also, the Origin, Authorization, and Progress of the first American National South Sea Exploring Expedition With ... Notes ... By Edmund Fanning, ... Second Edition. *New-York: William H. Vermilye.* 1838. 12mo, pp. 324. + Fourth Edition. [*Ibid.*] 12mo, pp. 324. Plate. BA. + Fifth Edition. [*Ibid.*] 23781

Also: Memorial ... praying that a National Discovery and Exploring Expedition be sent out to the South Seas. [n. p.] 1833. 8vo, pp. 15. B.

Fanning (N.) Memoir of the Life of Captain Nathaniel Fanning, an American Naval Officer, who served during Part of the American Revolution under ... Commodore John Paul Jones ... . *New-York.* 1808. 12mo, pp. 270. BA. 23782

Another edition is entitled:

[Fanning.] A Narrative of the Adventures of an American Navy Officer, who served during part of the American Revolution under Paul Jones. *New York.* 1806. 12mo, pp. 270. H.

Edmund Fanning, in the introduction to his "Voyages Round the World," says his eldest brother "Nathaniel was a midshipman in the navy, and private secretary to the celebrated Captain John Paul Jones, at the time of the bloody engagement between his ship, the Good Man Richard, and H. B. M. ship of war the Serapis." He was afterward in command at the U. S. N. station, Charleston, S. C.

Fanning (T.) A Discourse, delivered in Boston, July 17, 1836. By T. Fanning ... . *Boston: Benjamin H. Greene.* 1836. 8vo, pp. 28. BA. 23784

Fanning (T. W.) The Hairbreadth Escapes and Humorous Adventures of a Volunteer in the Cavalry Service. By Thomas W. Fanning. *Cincinnati: P. C. Browne.* 1865. 8vo, pp. 200.

Fanning's Illustrated Gazetteer of the United States, giving the Location, Physical Aspect, Mountains, Rivers, Lakes, Climate, Productive and Manufacturing Resources, Commerce, Government, Education, General History, etc. of the States, Territories, Counties, Cities, Towns, and Post-Offices in the American Union, with the Population and other Statistics from the Census of 1850. Illustrated with Seals and ... Maps ... *New-York: Phelps, Fanning & Co.* 1853. Rl. 8vo, pp. 400.

Fanny. 1820. *See* [Halleck (F. G.)]

Fanny Hunter's Western Adventures. What Fanny Hunter Saw and Heard in Kansas and Missouri. Illustrated. *Philadelphia.: J. E. Potter & Co.* 1863. 12mo. 23787

Case of the Fanny, a Vessel sent from Greenock to Virginia, where she loaded in the Rappahanock and York Rivers with Tobacco. *Privately printed.* 1796. Folio. 23788

Title twisted to suit the sale, by J. C. Hotten.

Le Fantasque. Journal rédigé par un flâneur [N. Aubin]. *Québec.* 1837–45. 8vo. 23789

Six or more volumes published.

Fanny Fern, *pseudonym. See* [Parton (*Mrs.* S.)]

Far Off. *See* [Mortimer (*Mrs.* J.)]

Far West; or, a Tour beyond the Mountains; embracing Outlines of Western Life and Scenery; Sketches of the Prairies, Rivers, Ancient Mounds, Early Settlements of the French, &c. *New-York: Harper & Bros.* 1838. 2 vols., 18mo, pp. 263; 241.

The Far West, a Sketch of the Illinois and other States in the Valley of the Mississippi, &c. *Bolton-le-Moors.* 1842. 12mo.

The Far West. *See* [Flagg (E.)]

Faran (J. J.) Speech of Mr. James J. Faron, of Ohio, on the Bill to Protect ... American Settlers in Oregon. Delivered in the House ... April 14, 1846. [*Washington.* 1846.] 8vo, pp. 16. H. 23792

The Farcical Tragedy; A History of Striking Events in the "Model Republic." By one of its Loyal Citizens. A Book for the Times. *Cincinnati: A. Moore, Printer.* 1864. 8vo, pp. 29. H. 23793

Farcy (C.) Etudes politiques. De l'aristocratie anglaise, la démocratie americaine, et de la libéralité des institutions françaises, par Charles Farcy. *Paris.* 1843. 8vo. P. 23794

Farcy. Discours sur les antiquités americaines, mexicaines, &c., par M. Charles Farcy. *Paris.* 1833. 4to. 23795

Farcy assisted in the compilation of Lenoir's "Antiquités Mexicanes. This title is from a sale catalogue, and this is perhaps a part of Lenoir.

Farfan (A.) Obras de Medicina. Por Fray Agostin Farfan. *Mexico: en casa de Antonio Ricardo.* 1579. 4to. Woodcut Portrait. 23796

Father Farfan was one of the first who exercised the science of medicine in America.

Farfan. Tratado Breve de Medicina y de todas las Enfermedades. Por Fray Augostin Farfan, Doctor y Religioso en la Nueva España. *Mexico.* 1592. Sm. 4to. + *Mexico.* 1610.

This rare work is dedicated to Don Luis de Velasco, the viceroy. Woodcut of Saint Augustin on the title. The initials throughout the text are woodcuts.

Fargo (F. F.) A ... History of the Assassination of James King of Wm. ... and the Execution of J. P. Casey and C. Cora by the Vigilance Committee. *San Francisco, Cal.* 8vo, pp. 24. S. 23798

Fargues (H.) Les chutes de Magara, d'après les observations les plus récentes. Par H. Fargues. *Paris: Grassart. Tonneins: Fargues. Alais: Bonnefon.* 1870. 8vo, pp. 35. Maps and Engravings. 23799

Fargues. George Washington, le fondateur de la république des États-Unis. La vie, son caractère par H. Fargues. *Tonneins: M. Fargues. Alais: M. Bonnefon.* 1872. 12mo, pp. 83. Engr. 28000

Faria y Sousa (Man. de). Asia Portugueza. *Lisboa: A. Craesbeck.* 1674. 3 vols., folio. 28001

With numerous curious portraits and views. Though not exactly treating of America this valuable work contains many notices of the Spanish and Portuguese colonies in America, the voyages of F. de Magallanes, etc.

Faria y Sousa. The Portugues Asia: | Or, the | History | of the | Discovery and Conquest | of India | by the | Portugues; | Containing | All their Discoveries from the Coast of | Africk, to the farthest Parts of China and | Japan; all their Battels by Sea and Land, | Sieges and other Memorable Actions; a | Description of those Countries, and many | Particulars of the Religion, Government | and Customs of the Natives, &c. | In Three Tomes. | Written in Spanish by Manuel de Faria y Sousa, | of the Order of Christ. | Translated into English by Cap. John Stevens. | *London, Printed for C. Brome, at the Sign of | the Gun, at the West-End of St. Paul's.* 1695. | 3 vols., 8vo, 16 l., pp. 448; 12 l., pp. 526; 11 l., pp. 440. 28002

Also "Comentarios à la Lusiada de Camoes. *Madrid.* 1639." Folio. The fifty-fifth canto is cited by Navarette as concerning Magellan.

Faria y Sousa. Epitome de las Historias Portvguesas. *Madrid.* 1628. 2 vols., 4to. + *Lisboa.* 1673. 2 vols., 4to. + Publicado por Foppens. 1730. Folio. 28003

Faria y Sousa (T.) Breve historia dos felizes acontecimentos politicos no Rio de Janeiro em os dias 6 e 7 de Abril de 1831, remontada á epocha da viagem do ex-Imperador á provincia de Minas-geraes. *Rio de Janeiro.* 1831. 8vo. 23804

Farias (Ignacio). Sermon Funebre en Memoria del F. Mathias de Escobar y Llamas, Dignissimo Prior Provincial de esta Provincia de San Nicolas Toletino de Michoacán, etc. *Mexico.* 1749. 4to. 23805

Faribault (G. B.) Catalogue d'ouvrages sur l'histoire de l'Amérique, et en particulier sur celle du Canada, de la Louisiane, de l'Acadie, et autres lieux, Ci-devant connus sous le nom de Nouvelle-France; avec des notes bibliographiques, critiques, et littéraires. En Trois Partes. Rédigé par G. B. Faribault, Avocat. *Quebec: W. Cowan.* 1837. 8vo, pp. (4), 207. B., BA.

Part I. contains the authors, arranged alphabetically. Part II., annonymous works arranged chronologically. Part III., a catalogue of maps, charts, and plans. The number of works described is 969, and to many of them are added descriptive notes. It is now very scarce. "The list abounds in errors of all kinds, many of which can be traced to Boucher de la Richarderie." — Harrisse.

Farine (Ch.) Benjamin Franklin, docteur en droit ... . D'après les documents authentiques recueillis dans ses œuvres posthumes et ses papiers de famille. *Tours: R. Pornin.* 1846. 12mo, pp. (2), 284. Portrait and Plate. H. 23807

Farinholt (B. F.) Report of the Engagement at Staunton River, June 25th, 1864. [*Richmond.* 1864.] 8vo, pp. 4. BA.

Farist Community. Prospectus of the Farist Community. ... *Chicago.* 32mo, pp. 16. H. 23809

Farley (C. A.) "The Crisis and Its Lessons." An Address before an Encampment of the Grand Army of the Republic at Walnut Fork, Jones Co., Iowa, November 29, 1866 ... by Rev. Charles A. Farley. *Dubuque.* 1866. 8vo, pp. 20. H.

Also: The Moral Aspect of California; A Thanksgiving Sermon, ... San Francisco, California, Sunday, December 1, 1850. ... *New-York: Henry Spear.* [n. d.] 8vo, pp. 16. B. — A Sermon preached in ... Montreal, on Wednesday, 6th February, 1833. Being a Day appointed for Public Thanksgiving ... . *Montreal.* 1833. 8vo, pp. 14. BA.

Farley (F. A.) Death of the President of the United States. A Sermon delivered at Providence, R. I., April 11, 1841. By ... Frederick A. Farley. *Boston.* 1841. 8vo, pp. 12. H.

Farley (F.) A Discourse delivered at the Dedication of Westminster Church in Providence, R. I., March 5, 1829. By Frederick A. Farley ... . *Boston: Leonard C. Bowles.* 1829. 8vo, pp. 31. H. 23812

Farley. A Discourse on the Life and Character of John Quincy Adams, preached ... March 5, 1848, by ... Frederick A. Farley, ... *Brooklyn: Lees & Foulkes.* 1848. 8vo, pp. 31.

Also: Christian Consolation for Bereaved Parents. A Sermon, preached ... [at] Brooklyn, N. Y., ... Aug. 8, 1841. *Brooklyn.* 1841. 8vo, pp. 16. H. — Dangers of a Business Life. A Sermon preached at the Church of the Saviour, Brooklyn, 19th Sept., 1847. *New York.* 1847. 8vo. — A Sermon, preached at the Ordination of the Rev. George W. Briggs ... September 24, 1834. ... . *Fall River: Samuel L. Thaxter.* 1835. 8vo, pp. 22. BA. — A Sermon Preached at the Second Unitarian Church, Brooklyn. ... *Brooklyn.* 1841. pp. 16. — A Sermon, ... Brooklyn, L. I. May 14, 1843, ... after the Interment of Mr. Henry Leeds. ... Printed not Published. *New York.* 1843. 8vo. — ... A Sermon preached at the Consecration of the Polanen Chapel, Bridgeport, Ct., ... October 4, 1849. ... . *New York: Henry Spear.* 1849. 12mo, Title, pp. 16. B. — Military Glory. A Sermon Preached at ... Brooklyn, N. Y. ... July 16, 1848. *New York.* 1848. 18mo, pp. 15. B. — A Tribute to the Memory of Seth Low, Esq. A Sermon ... in ... Brooklyn, N. Y. ... June 26, 1853. *New York.* 1853. 8vo, pp. 24. B., BA.

Farley (H). Operatives' Reply to Hon. Jere. Clemens, being a Sketch of Factory Life and Factory Enterprise, and a Brief History of Manufacturing by Machinery. By Harriet Farley. ... *Lowell: S. J. Varney.* 1850. 8vo, pp. 24. BA. 23814

See Lowell Offering.

Farley (S.) An Oration, pronounced at Hanover, N. H. July 4, 1804 ... . By Stephen Farley ... . *Hanover: Moses Davis.* 1804. 8vo, pp. 16. BA. 23815

Also: Sermon on the Death of the Hon Caleb Ellis, delivered at Claremont, N. H., May 13, 1816. ... [n. p. n. d.] N. — A Sermon on the Death of the Rev. Abijah Wines ... Amesbury, Mass. ... . With a Memoir. ... *Amesbury: John Caldwell.* 1834. pp. 23. B.

Farmer (C. M.) The Fairy of the Stream, and other Poems. By C. M. Farmer. *Richmond, Va.* 1847. 12mo, pp. 167. B.

Includes "Legends of Virginia."

Farmer (D. D.) Trial of Daniel Davis Farmer, for the Murder of the Widow Anna Ayer, at Goffstown, on the 4th of April, A.D. 1821. ... Reported by A. Rogers and H. B. Chase. *Concord: Hill and Moore.* 1821. 8vo, pp. 72. W. + *Amherst, N. H.* 1822. 8vo, pp. 32–72. B. 23817

Farmer (J.) Annals of the Town of Concord, N. H., from its First Settlement in 1726; with Biographical Sketches and a

Memoir of the Penacook Indians. By John Farmer. *Concord: J. B. Moore.* 1824. 8vo, pp. 112. 23818

First appeared in the "New Hampshire Coll.," I. 153–218.

[Farmer.] A Catechism of the History of New Hampshire, From its First Settlement to the Present Period; for the Use of Schools and Families. *Concord.* 1829. 12mo. + Second Edition. *Concord: Hoag & Atwood.* 1830. 12mo, pp. 108.

Farmer. An Ecclesiastical Register of New Hampshire, containing a Succinct Account of the different Religious Denominations, their Origin and Progress, and Present Numbers. With a Catalogue of the Ministers of the several Churches, from 1636 to 1822, the Date of their Settlement, Removal or Death, and the Number of Communicants in 1821. By John Farmer. *Concord: Hill & Moore.* 1821. 12mo, pp. 36. 23820

Farmer. The Emigrants' Guide; or, Pocket Gazetteer of the Surveyed Part of Michigan. By John Farmer. *Albany.* 1830. 24mo. + Second Edition. *Albany.* 1831. 24mo.

Farmer. A Family Register of the Descendants of Edward Farmer, in the Line of the Youngest Branch of his Family. *Concord: Printed by George Hough for John Farmer.* 1813. 12mo, pp. 12. 23822

Farmer. A Genealogical Memoir of the Family by the name of Farmer, who settled at Billerica, Mass. *Hingham: Farmer and Brown, Printers.* 1828. 12mo, pp. 20. H. 23823

Reprinted in the "N. E. Hist. and Gen. Reg.," Vol. I., with some changes.

Farmer. A Genealogical Register of the First Settlers of New-England; containing an Alphabetical List of the Governours, Deputy-Governours, Assistants or Counsellors, and Ministers of the Gospel In the several Colonies, from 1620 to 1692; Representatives of the General Court of Massachusetts, from 1634 to 1692; Graduates of Harvard College to 1662; Members of the Ancient and Honourable Artillery Company to 1662; with many other of the early inhabitants of New-England and Long-Island, N. Y., from 1620 to the year 1675; to which are added various Genealogical and Biographical Notes, collected from Ancient Records, Manuscripts, and Printed Works. By John Farmer ... . *Lancaster, Mass.: Carter, Andrews & Co.* 1829. 8vo, pp. 351, (1). Portrait. B., BA., H. 23824

"The corner-stone of New England genealogy." — Whitmore.

Farmer. An Historical Memoir of Billerica, in Massachusetts. Containing Notices of the Principal Events in the Civil and Ecclesiastical Affairs of the Town, from its First Settlement to 1816. By John Farmer. ... *Amherst: R. Boylston.* 1816. 8vo, pp. 36. B., BA., H. 23825

Also included in "Coll. of Mass. Hist. Soc.," Vol. II., Second Series.

Farmer. Historical Sketch of Amherst, N. H., from the First Settlement to the Present Time. By John Farmer. *Amherst.* 1816. 8vo. 23826

Farmer. An Historical Sketch of Amherst, in the County of Hillsborough, in New-Hampshire, from the First Settlement to the Present Period. By John Farmer. *Amherst: printed by Richard Boylston.* 1820. 8vo, pp. 35. B., BA., H., N. 23827

Farmer. Historical Sketch of Amherst, in the County of Hillsborough, N. H., from its First Settlement to the Year 1837. By John Farmer ... Second Edition, Enlarged. *Concord: N. H.: McFarland.* 1837. 12mo, pp. 52. 23828

The first sketch appeared in the "Mass. Hist. Coll.," Vol. II., Second Series, pp. 247–255; also in "N. H. Coll.," v. 79–128. *See* "N. A. Rev.," XLVI. 536–38.

Farmer. A List of the Graduates, and those who have received Degrees, at all of the New England Colleges, From their foundation ... . By John Farmer ... . *Boston: printed by Perkins, Marvin, & Co.* 1835. 8vo, 1 l., pp. 159. H. 23829

Farmer. A List of the Graduates, and those who have received Degrees at the several Colleges in the States of New York and New Jersey, from the foundation of each to 1834. ... By John Farmer, Esq. ... . *Boston: Perkins & Marvin.* 1838. 8vo, pp. 69, (1). B., BA. 23830

Farmer. A List of the Pastors, Deacons and Members of the First Congregational Church in Concord, N. H., from Nov. 18, 1730 to Nov. 18, 1830. *Concord.* 1830. 8vo. W. 23831

Farmer. List of Literary Publications, by New Hampshire Writers, Edited by John Farmer. *Concord: Jacob B. Moore.* 1829. 8vo. 23832

Farmer. Memorials of the Graduates at Harvard University, in Cambridge, Massachusetts, commencing with the First Class, 1642. By John Farmer. *Concord, N. H.* 1833. 8vo, pp. 48.

Farmer. Michigan and Ouisconsin Territories. By John Farmer. *New York.* 1830. 8vo. C. 23834

FARMER. The New Military Guide ... . Compiled for the Use of the Militia. By John Farmer. *Concord: Hill and Moore.* 1822. 12mo, pp. 144, (1). B., W. 23835

FARMER. Sketches of the Graduates of Dartmouth College, from its foundation in 1769 to the year 1834. *Concord: Jacob B. Moore.* 1832-34. 23836

See "Quarterly Register and Journal of Education," Vol. IV. *See also* "Mass. Hist. Soc. Coll.," Vol. X., Second Series, *and* New Hampshire.

FARMER *and* MOORE (J. B.) Collections, Topographical, Historical and Biographical, relating principally to New-Hampshire. Edited by J. Farmer and J. B. Moore. Vol. I. ... *Concord: Hill & Moore.* 1822. 8vo. + [Reprinted.] *Concord: H. E. and J. W. Moore.* 1831. 8vo, pp. 296. H. 23837

Continued as

FARMER *and* MOORE. Collections, Historical, and Miscellaneous: and Monthly Literary Journal. Edited by J. Farmer and J. B. Moore. *Concord: J. B. Moore.* 1823-24. Vol. II., 8vo, pp. (2), 387, 103; Vol. III., pp. (4), 388, (10), 88. H. 23838

FARMER *and* MOORE. A Gazetteer of the State of New-Hampshire. By John Farmer and Jacob B. Moore. Embellished with an Accurate Map of the State, and several other Engravings: by Abel Bowen. *Concord: Jacob B. Moore.* 1823. 12mo, pp. 276. Map. B., BA., H. 23839

[FARMER (*Major*).] Proceedings of a General Court Martial, held at Pensacola, in West Florida, March 16-April 20. 1769. *London: Johnston.* 1770. 23840

See "M. Rev.," XLIV. 77.

FARMER (M.) Report of a Trial: Miles Farmer, *versus* Dr. David Humphreys Storer, ... relative to the Transactions between Miss Eliza Dolph and George Washington Adams, Esq. ... . *Boston.* 1831. 8vo, pp. 44. BA., C. 23841

The Farmer and Gardener, by I. I. Hitchcock, 1835. *Baltimore.* 4to. 23842

The Farmer and Mechanic: Devoted to Agriculture, Mechanics, Manufactures, Science and Arts; Edited by W. H. Starr and J. M. Stearns. New Series. *New York.* 1847-50. 4to, 4 vols. or more. S. 23843

The Farmer Refuted. *See* [Hamilton (Alexander)].

The Farmer's Almanack, for 1793. By Robert B. Thomas. *Boston.* 1793. 8vo. Still continued. 23844

Many farmers' almanacs adapted to various latitudes are purposely omitted.

The Farmer's and Monitor's Letters. *See* Vol. V., No. 20052.

Farmers' and Planters' Friend. Nos. I.-VII. 1821. 23845

Farmer's Calendar, or New York and Vermont Almanack: A. Beers. *Troy.* 1805. Imp. 12mo. Continued. 23846

Farmer's Calendar, or Utica Almanack for the Western District of New York for ... 1808. *Utica.* 12mo. Continued.

From 1828 called "Williams' Calendar."

Farmer's Calendar, or Northern Almanac. *Pulaski, N. Y.* 1845. 12mo. 23848

Farmer's Calendar. *Baltimore.* 1855. 23849

Farmer's Diary, or Catskill Almanack. 1824. 12mo. S.

Farmer's Hand Book; being a Full and Complete Guide for the Farmer and Emigrant. *Cincinnati: Applegate & Co.* 1855. 12mo, pp. 492. 23851

The Farmer's Journal. *See* Vol. III., No. 10342.

A Farmer's Letters to the People. *Philadelphia: Robert Johnson.* 1802. 12mo, pp. 95. BA., W. 23852

Farmer's Library and Monthly Journal of Agriculture. *New-York.* 1846-48. 3 vols., 8vo. S. 23853

Farmers', Mechanics' and Servants' Magazine. Published for the Benefit of the Widows' and Orphans' Societies of the City of New York. Vol. I. *New York: Whiting & Watson.* 1812. 18mo. 23854

Farmer's, Mechanic's, Manufacturer's, and Sportsman's Magazine: by George Houston. *New-York.* 1827. 8vo. S. 23855

Farmer's Monthly Visitor ... . By Isaac Hill. Vol. I, for 1839. *Concord, N. H.: William P. Foster for the Editor.* [n. d.] 4to, Title, pp. 190. Continued to Vol. VI. or later. B., BA.

The Farmer's Register; a Monthly Publication devoted to the Improvement of the Practice and Support of the Interests of Agriculture. Ed. Ruffin, Editor. *Petersburg, Va.* 1833. 8vo. Continued to 10 vols. or more. 23857

The Farmer's Useful and Entertaining Companion; or, New-Hampshire, Massachusetts, and Vermont Almanack, for the Year of our Lord 1795 ... . *Exeter: Stearns & Winslow.* [1795.] 12mo, 12 l. B. 23858

FARMIAN DE ROSOI, *known as* DUROSOI. Azor ou les Péruviens, tragédie en 5 actes [et en vers]. *Genève* [*Paris*]: *Lesclapart.* 1770. 8vo. 23859

FARMINGTON, *Conn.* Sketches of. *See* [Richards (S.)]

FARNHAM (Benjamin). Dissertations on the Prophecies. *East Windsor.* 1800. 12mo. 23860

FARNHAM (E. W.) California, In-Doors and Out; or, How we Farm, Mine, and Live generally in the Golden State. By Eliza W. Farnham. *New York: Dix, Edwards & Co.* 1856. 12mo, pp. xiv, (1), 508. B. 23861

FARNHAM. Life in Prairie Land. By Eliza W. Farnham. ... *New York: Harper & Brothers.* 1846. 12mo, pp. 408. BA. + [*Ibid.*] 1852. 23862

Also: Woman and her Era. *New York.* 1864. 2 vols., 12mo.

FARNHAM (L.) A Discourse delivered in West Newbury, Mass., Thanksgiving, Nov. 25, 1852. By Luther Farnham. *Boston.* 1853. 8vo, pp. 28. 23863

FARNHAM. A Glance at Private Libraries. By Luther Farnham. *Boston.* 1855. 8vo, pp. 79. N. 23864

The principal collections noticed are those of Webster, Ticknor, Livermore, Hosmer, Lawrence, Prescott, Everett, Choate, Crowninshield, Sparks, Parker, and Adams, six or seven of which are now (1873) dispersed. It is "full of blunders."

FARNHAM (Thomas J.) The Early Days of California; Embracing what I Saw and Heard there, with Scenes in the Pacific. By Col. T. J. Farnham. *Philadelphia: J. E. Potter.* 1860. 12mo, pp. vi, 314. 10 Plates. + [*Ibid.*] 1862. 23865

FARNHAM. History of Oregon Territory, it being a Demonstration of the Title of the United States of America to the same. ... By Thomas J. Farnham, Esq. ... *New-York: J. Winchester.* [1844.] 8vo, pp. 80. Map. + Second Edition. [*Ibid.*] 1845. 8vo, pp. 83. 23866

FARNHAM. Life and Adventures in California, and Scenes in the Pacific Ocean. By Thomas J. Farnham, ... *New York: Wm. H. Graham.* 1846. 8vo, pp. 416. B. + [*Ibid.*] 1847.

FARNHAM. Life, Adventures, and Travels in California. To which are added, the Conquest of California, Travels in Oregon, and History of the Gold Regions. *New-York.* 1849. 8vo, pp. 468. + [*Ibid.*] 1850. 8vo. + [*Ibid.*] 1853. 8vo, pp. 514.

FARNHAM. Pictorial Edition!! Life, Adventures, and Travels in California. By T. J. Farnham. To which are added Conquest of California and Travels in Oregon. *New York: Sheldon.* 1855. 8vo, pp. 468. 23869

FARNHAM. Mexico: its Geography — its People — and its Institutions: ... By Thomas J. Farnham, ... *New-York: H. Long & Brother.* [1846.] 8vo, pp. 64. B. + [Another Edition.] 8vo, pp. 80. H. 23870

FARNHAM. Travels in the Californias, and Scenes in the Pacific Ocean. By Thomas J. Farnham ... . *New York: Saxton & Miles.* 1844. 8vo, pp. 416. B. 23871

Afterwards reissued with the title as in our No. 23867.

FARNHAM. Travels in the Great Western Prairies, the Anahuac and Rocky Mountains, and in the Oregon Territory. By Thomas J. Farnham. *Ploughkeepsie* [sic]: *Killey and Lossing, Printers. New York and London: Wiley & Putnam.* 1843. 12mo, pp. 197. + *New York: Greeley & McElrath.* 1843. 8vo, pp. 112. C. + *London: Richard Bentley.* 2 vols., post 8vo, pp. xxiii, 297; viii, 315. 23872

FARNSWORTH (J. F.) Georgia again! Speech of Mr. Farnsworth of Illinois, in the House of Representatives, March 4 and 5, 1870. [*Washington.* 1870.] 8vo, pp. 8. H. 23873

Also: National Military Asylums. Speech ... March 3, 1871. *Washington.* 1871. 8vo, pp. 14. H. — Reconstruction. Speech ... January 15, 1868. [*Washington.* 1868.] 8vo, pp. 8. H. — Speech ... on the Constitutional Amendment ... on Reconstruction; ... May 10, 1866. *Washington.* 1866. 8vo, pp. 7. H.

FARNSWORTH (J. H.), *and* DUNN (L. A.) A Review of the Fifth Annual Report of the Northern Educational Union. By J. H. Farnsworth and L. A. Dunn. *Montpelier.* 1858. 8vo, pp. 32. H. 23874

FARO (F. T. de). *See* Telles de Faro (Fernando).

El Farol. Periodico semanario de la Puebla de los Angeles, en el imperio mejicano. No. 1-41. [*Domingo.*] 1821-22. 4to.

"Nous ignorons s'il a été publié davantage de ce journal intéressant pour l'histoire du Mexique." — ANDRADE.

FARQUHAR (J.) The Claims of God to Recognition in the Assassination of President Lincoln. A Sermon Preached on the Day of National Humiliation and Prayer, in the Chanceford Presbyterian Church, Lower Chanceford, York Co., Pa., and in the Protestant Methodist Episcopal Church, ... By the Rev. John Farquhar, Pastor of the Former Church. *Lancaster, Pa.: Pearsol & Geist, Printers.* 1865. 8vo, pp. 23. 23876

FARQUHAR (R. T.) Suggestions, ... on the Abolition of the Slave Trade, for Supplying the West India Colonies with Labourers. By R. T. Farquhar. *London.* 1807. 8vo, pp. 66.

FARR (J.) The Death of the Righteous, and the Birth of the Saviour. Two Sermons, delivered in ... Boxborough, March 27, 1836; ... after the Interment of Dea. Oliver Mead ... . By Jonathan Farr ... . *Boston.* 1836. 12mo, pp. 24. H. 23878

FARRAGUT (D. G.), *and* BAILEY (Theodorus). History set right. Attack on New Orleans and its Defences, by the Fleet under Admiral Farragut, April 24, 1862. *New York.* 1869. 8vo, pp. 14. H. 23879

Farragut Testimonial. *New York.* 1865. 23880

FARRAR (C. C. S.) The War, its Causes and Consequences. By C. C. S. Farrar, of Bolivar County, Miss. *Blelock & Co.: Cairo, Ills.; Memphis, Tenn.; Paducah, Ky.* 1864. 12mo, pp. 260. B. 23881

FARRAR (J.) America. A Poem. By John Farrar, of Queen's College, Oxford. *London: the Author.* 1780. 4to, pp. 24.

"Mr. Farrar prophecies that the Americans will be compelled to return to their allegiance." — *M. Rev.*, LXIV. 152.

FARRAR (Eliza Rotch). Recollections of Seventy Years. By Mrs. John Farrar. ... . *Boston: Ticknor & Fields.* 1866. 16mo, pp. viii, 331. B., BA., H. 23883

FARRAR (N.) Dissolution of the Union, and its inevitable Results. *Louisville.* 1850. 8vo. C. 23884

FARRAR (T.) Manual of the Constitution of the United States. By Timothy Farrar. ... *Boston: Little, Brown, & Company.* 1867. 8vo, pp. xii, 532. B., BA., H. 23885

[FARRAR.] Memoir of the Farrar Family. By a Member of the N. E. Hist. Gen. Society. *Boston: Printed for Private Distribution.* 1853. 8vo, pp. 45. 23886

FARRAR (T.) Report of the Case of the Trustees of Dartmouth College against William H. Woodward. Argued and determined in the Superior Court ... New-Hampshire, November 1817. And on Error in the Supreme Court of the United States, February 1819. By Timothy Farrar ... . *Portsmouth: John W. Foster.* [1819.] 8vo, pp. (4), 406. BA., H. 23887

FARRAR (T.) State Rights. By Hon. T. Farrar, Mt. Bowdoin, Mass. [From the "New Englander" for October, 1862.]

Also: Adequacy of the Constitution; from the "New Englander," Jan., 1862.

FARRELL (N. E.) Colorado, the Rocky Mountain Gem, as it is in 1868. ... By N. E. Farrell. *Chicago: Western News Co.* 1868. 16mo, pp. 72. Map. 23889

[FARREN (*Mrs.*)] Boston Common: Tale of our own Times. By a Lady. ... Second Edition. *Boston: E. O. Libby and Company.* 1858. 12mo, pp. 556. H. 23890

Copyrighted in 1856.

FARRENT (J.) Newport Goal, Oct. 4. 1773. To the Public. *Newport.* [1773.] 1 leaf. 23891

An address on the illegality of his confinement.

FARRINGTON (E. F.) A Full and Complete Description of the Covington and Cincinnati Suspension Bridge ... By E. F. Farrington. *Cincinnati.* 1867. 16mo, pp. 17. H. 23892

FARROW (H. P.) The Status of Georgia. Letter to Hon. John B. Dickey ... By Henry P. Farrow, ... Attorney General of Georgia. *Washington.* 1869. 8vo, pp. 8. H. 23893

Also: Argument ... in Support of his Claim to a Seat in the Senate from the State of Georgia. ... January 11, 1871. *Washington.* [1871.] 8vo, pp. 33. H.

A Farther Account | of the | Great Divisions | among the | Quakers | In Pensilvania, &c. | As appears by Another of their Books lately come | over from thence, Intituled, | Some Reasons and Causes of the late Separation | That hath come to pass at Philadelphia, betwixt us, | called by some the Separate Meeting; and others that | Meet apart from us. | More particularly Opened, to Vindicate and clear us | and our Testimony in that respect, viz., That the Separation lieth | at their Door, and They (and not We, are justly chargeable | with it.) With | An Apology for the present Publication of these Things. | *London, Printed for J. Dunton, at the Raven, in the Poultrey,* 1693. | 4to, pp. 23.

A Farther Appeal to the unprejudiced Judgment of Mankind, in behalf of the Indians. In two parts. Containing, I. Animadversions upon some late Arguments of a Rt. Rev. Prelate of the Church of England, in reference to our sending Missionaries to convert the Indians. II. Thoughts upon the proper means and measures of converting the Indians to true Christianity. To which are added Considerations relative to the subject of the foregoing proposals, etc. *London: A. Millar.* 1766. 8vo, pp. 79. J.C.B. 23895

Farther Considerations On the present State of Affairs, at Home and Abroad, As affected by the Late Convention; with an Appendix; containing A true State of the South-Sea Company's Affairs in 1718. *London: T. Cooper.* M DCC XXXIX. 8vo, pp. (4), 60. 23896

Farther Considerations, [etc.] With a Postscript containing some Reflections upon the particular situation of our Merchants. Second Edition. *London: T. Cooper.* 1739. 8vo, pp. 59.

The text of this and the preceding tract is the same. The postscript is different.

A Farther Defence of Col. William Lovetruth Bluster, in a Letter to Major Joseph Antick. Done into Verse by Aminadab Sledgehammer. *New Orleans.* 1826. 8vo, pp. 17. M. 23898

A Farther Examination and Explanation of the South-Sea Company's Scheme. Shewing, That it is not the Interest of the South-Sea Company to offer the Annuitants such Terms as may induce them to come in; and that the Proposal of the Bank is more likely to be accepted by the Annuitants, and the Publick not disappointed. *London: Printed and Sold by J. Roberts.* 1720. 8vo, pp. 39. + Third Edition. [*Ibid.*] 1720. 8vo. 23899

FARWELL (J. H. *and* T. F.) Exhibition Intelligencer, devoted to the Fifth Exhibition of the Massachusetts Charitable Mechanic Association. *Boston.* 1847. 8vo. B. 23900

FARWELL (W. B.). Letter ... from W. B. Farwell in ... Reply to the Report ... on Public Expenditures of the House of Representatives of the Thirty-Ninth Congress. [*New York.* 1867?] 8vo, pp. 15. H. 23901

[FARWELL (William), *and others.*] Letter to the Evangelical Congregational Church in Cambridgeport, under the Pastoral Care of Rev. Wm. A. Stearns. *Boston: Isaac Knapp.* 1837. 16mo, pp. 15, (1). BA. 23902

Fashion's Analysis. *See* [Blauvelt (—.)], Vol. II., No. 5887.

The Fashionable Tour. A Guide to Travellers visiting the Middle and Northern States and the Province of Canada. Fourth Edition. *Saratoga Springs.* 1830. 18mo, pp. 434. 8 Plates.

For a translation of this, *see* "Tournée à la Mode," etc., 1829.

FAST (E. G.) Catalogue of Antiquities and Curiosities collected in ... Alaska, by Edward G. Fast ... . *Leavitt, Strebeigh & Co.:* [*New York.* 1869.] 8vo, pp. 32. H. 23904

Fast Sermon Preached at —— Feb. the 10th, 1799. By the Reverend —— —— shewing the Tyranny and Oppression of the British King and Parliament Respecting the American Colonies. Inscribed to the Congress. [n. p. n. d.] 8vo, pp. 20.

The title is ironical. The author is very severe upon the Americans.

Fast in the Ice; or, Adventures in the Polar Regions. *New York: D. Appleton & Co.* 1865. 16mo, pp. 176. 23906

Fast Day Sermons: or the Pulpit on the State of the Country. *New York: Rudd & Carleton.* M DCCC LXI. 12mo, pp. 336. BA.

Fate, or the Prophecy, a Tragedy. Printed for Private Circulation. *New York.* 1856. 12mo, pp. 74, (2). 23908

Father Abraham's Almanack. By Abraham Weatherwise, for 1759. *Philadelphia: W. Dunlap.* 23909

Continued to 1803 or later.

Father Abraham. *See* [Franklin (Benj.)]

Father Hutchins Revived. Almanack. *New York.* 1791. 12mo. 23910

Father Tammany's Almanack. *Philadelphia.* 1790-1823. 12mo. 23911

The Father; or, American Shandy-ism. A Comedy, as performed at the New-York Theatre, by the Old American Company. Written in the Year 1788. ... *New-York: Hodge, Allen & Company.* M,DCC,LXXXIX. pp. 56, (4), 2 l. BA. 23912

FATIO (L. C. F.) Appeal to the People of the United States against J. K. Paulding. 23913

Fatti accaduti nel Messico in seguito dell' intervento francese. *Roma.* 1863. 4to, pp. 23. 23914

Fauchat (*M.*) Observations sur les Ouvrages de M. de Pradt, intitulés des Colonies et de la Révolution ... et des trois derniers mois de l'Amérique méridionale. Par M. Fauchat. *Paris: Gide.* M.DCCC.XVII. 8vo, Title, pp. 89. H. 23915

See "M. Rev.," LXXXIV. 173.

Fauche (P. F.) Réflexions sur la cession de la Guadeloupe à la couronne de Suède. Par Pierre François Fauche. *Londres: J. C. de Boffe.* 1813. 12mo, pp. 20. 23916

Faucher (J. S.) The American Railway and Steam Navigation Guide for the United States, Canada, etc. J. S. Faucher, Editor. *New York: Edwards & Faucher.* [1866.] 12mo.

Fauchet (*Abbé*). Éloge civique de Benjamin Franklin, Prononcé, le 21 Juillet 1790, dans la rotonde, au nom de la com mune de Paris. Par M. l'Abbé Fauchet, En présence de M. M. les Députés de l'Assemblée Nationale ... . *Paris.* M.DCC.XC. 8vo, pp. (2), 50. H., N. 23918

Also: Éloge de M. Franklin, lu à la séance publique de l'Académie des Sciences, la 13 Nov. 1790. *Paris.* 1791. 8vo.

Fauchet (J.) Coup d'œil sur l'état actuel de nos rapports politiques avec les États-Unis de l'Amérique Septentrionale; par Joseph Fauchet, Ex-ministre de la République à Philadelphie. *Paris: Pougin; Laran An.* V.–1797. 8vo, pp. 42. H. 23919

For an answer to this, *see* "l'Independance absolue," etc. Also: French Original Letters, from Joseph Fauchet and P. A. Adet, to the Executive of the United States. *Philadelphia.* 1794. 8vo. P.

Fauchet. Letter to the Secretary of State of the United States, with Decrees of the National Assembly of France, establishing a New System of Weights and Measures. *Philadelphia.* 1795. 8vo. 23920

Also: A translation of citizen Fauchet's "Political Dispatch. *Philadelphia.* 1795." 8vo, pp. 10.

Fauchet. A Sketch of the Present State of our Political Relations with the United States of North-America. By Joseph Fauchet, Ex-Minister of the French Republic at Philadelphia. Translated by the Editor of the "Aurora" [William J. Duane]. *Philadelphia: Benj. Franklin Bache.* M,DCC,XCVII. 8vo, pp. 31.

Faucon (*Mlle.* Emma). Le petit Trappeur ou trois ans chez les Oricaras, tribu indienne de l'Amérique du Nord. *Paris: Th. Lefèvre.* 1867. 12mo. 23922

Fauconpret (A. J. B.) Voyage vers le Pôle Arctique dans la Baie de Baffin, redigé sur la Relation du Capitaine Ross, etc. *Paris.* 1819. 8vo. 23923

Faugeres (M. V.) Belisarius. A Tragedy. By Margaretta V. Faugeres. *New York: T. & J. Swords.* 1795. 8vo, pp. 53.

Mrs. Faugeres was the daughter of Ann Eliza Bleecker, and edited the poem of her mother in 1793.

Faulkner (Charles James). Address on the Land Policy of the United States. *Washington.* 1857. 8vo. 23925

Faulkner. Report of Hon. C. J. Faulkner, of Virginia, on behalf of the Minority of the Select Committee, vindicating the conduct of the President and Secretary of War in the Sale of the Fort Snelling Reservation. *Washington.* 1858. 8vo, pp. 36.

Also: Speech ... on the Basis Question, delivered in the Virginia Reform Convention ... March 26th and 27th, 1851. *Richmond, Va.* 1851. 4to. H.—Speech ... on the Kansas and Nebraska Bill, House of Representatives, United States, April 10, 1854.—Speech ... on the Compromise, the Presidency, Political Parties. Delivered in the House of Representatives, August 2, 1852. 8vo, pp. 15.—Speech ... in the House of Delegates of Virginia on the Policy of the State with respect to her Slave Population. *Richmond.* 1832. 8vo, pp. 22. B., BA.—To the Conservative People of Virginia. Faulkner on Slavery. Read. Written by a well-known Democrat. *Winchester, Virginia.* 1858. 8vo, pp. 8.

Faulkner (T. C.) Faulkner's History of the Revolution in the Southern States ... . *New York.* 1861. 8vo, pp. 94, (1), 8.

Faults on all Sides. The Care of Religion considered: ... presented to the Inhabitants (especially) ... of Rhode Island. *Newport.* 1728. 8vo. BM. 23928

Fauque (*Mlle.*) La dernière Guerre des Bêtes, Fable pour servir à l'Histoire du 18e siècle. *Londres.* 1758. 12mo.

"Cette allégorie traite des démêlés de la France et de l'Angleterre, au sujet de l'Acadie, lesquels ont occasioné la dernière guerre. Elle ne donne pas une idée favorable des Français."—M. De Fontette.

Fauquier Co., *Va.* Address of the Central Committee of Fauquier, to the People of that County, on the Army Bill. *Washington.* 1840. 8vo. BA. + Second Address [etc.] *Washington.* 1840. 8vo, pp. xi, 34, 11. 23930

The last paging of the second contains the "First Address."

Faussell (B.) Address to the Christian Negroes in Virginia, 1756, &c. 8vo. 23931

Title from an English auction sale catalogue.

Fauvel Gouraud (J. B. G.) L'Hercule et la Favorite, ou la capture de l'Alexandre de Bordeaux, et des Pirates Bordelais, effectuée à New-port, Rhode-Island, Etats-Unis de l'Amérique du Nord, le 21 Mai, 1838. Par J. B. G. Fauvel Gouraud, de la Martinique, Vice-Consul a Newport: suivi d'un Aperçu sur les Mœurs les Institutions Americaines, les grands bateaux à vapeur, les chemins de fer, &c. *Paris: Auteur.* 1840. 2 vols., 8vo. Portrait and Vignette. 23932

Faux (U.) Memorable Days in America: being a Journal of a Tour to The United States, principally undertaken to ascertain, by Positive Evidence, the Condition and Probable Prospects of British Emigrants; including Accounts of Mr. Birbeck's Settlement in the Illinois . ... *London: W. Simpkin and R. Marshall.* 1823. 8vo, pp. xvi, 488. Plate. BA. 23933

This gave rise to a most abusive article on the United States in the "Quarterly Rev.," XXIX. 338, to which Ed. Everett replied in the "N. Am. Rev.," XIX. 92. *See also* "Blackwood's Mag.," Vols. XIV. and XVI., and "South. Lit. Mess.," Vol. I.

Favard (*M.*) De l'Abolition de l'Esclavage dans les Colonies Françaises. Par Favard, Délégué de la Guyane Franç. *Paris.* [n. d.] 8vo. 23934

Favolius (Hugo). Theatri Orbis Terrarum Enchiridion, et minoribus Tabulis per Phil. Gallæum exaratum, et carmine heroico, ex variis geographis et poëtis collecto illustratum. *Antverpiæ: excudebat Philippo Gallæo Chr. Plantinus.* 1585. 4to, 4 l., pp. 170, 1 l. Plate. 23935

Contains maps of America. For a description of this curious poetical work, *see* the "Annales Plantiniennes."

Faxon (W.) Genealogical Register of the Descendants of Richard Faxon, from his Settlement in this Country to August, 1843. Hartford. Compiled by William Faxon. 1843. 18mo, pp. 24. 23936

Faxton (T. S.) Address before the New York State Agricultural Society. By Theodore S. Faxton. *Albany.* 1857. 8vo.

Fay (*Rev.* Cyrus H.) An Address on "The Changes of a Century," delivered before the Members of Norwich University, Aug. 21, 1839. *Newport, N. H.* 1839. 8vo, pp. 31. 23938

Fay (F. B.) Speech of the Hon. Francis B. Fay, on the License Bill. April 7, 1868. *Boston: Wright & Potter, Printers.* 1868. 8vo, pp. 14. 23939

Fay (H. A.) Collection of the Official Accounts, in Detail, of all the Battles fought by Sea and Land, between the Navy and Army of the United States, and the Navy and Army of Great Britain, During the Years 1812, 13, 14, & 15. By H. A. Fay, late Captain in the Corps of U. S. Artillerists. *New York: printed by Conrad.* 1817. 8vo, pp. 295. B., BA., C. 23940

Fay (Joseph). *See* Allen (Ethan), Vol. I., No. 806.

Fay (L.) Advertisement. ... *Philadelphia. Nov.* 1770. P.

In doggerel verse, by Louis Fay, perruquier, etc.

Fay (R. S.) An Oration. Delivered before the Citizens of Boston on the Fifty-Eighth Anniversity of American Independence. By Richard S. Fay. ... *Boston: J. H. Eastburn.* 1834. 8vo, pp. 31. B., N. 23942

[Fay (R. S.)] Remarks on a Protective Tariff and the Principles of Free Trade ... . *Boston.* 1842. 8vo, pp. 40. H.

[Fay (Samuel).] The Carpet Manufacture. A Statement of Facts addressed to the United-States Revenue Commission. *Cambridge.* 1866. 8vo, pp. 9. 23944

Signed by Samuel Fay, and others.

Fay (S. P. P.) An Oration, delivered ... at Concord, July 4th, 1801. By Samuel P. P. Fay. ... *Cambridge: William Hilliard.* 1801. 8vo, pp. 20. BA. 23945

[Fay (Theodore S.)] Crayon Sketches. By an Amateur. *New York.* 1833. 2 vols., 12mo. 23946

Fay. Hoboken: A Romance of New-York. By Theodore S. Fay. *New-York: Harper & Brothers.* 1843. 2 vols., 12mo, pp. 235; 216. C. 23947

Fay "Die Sklavenmacht. Blicke in die Geschichte der Vereinigten Staaten von Amerika zur Erklärung der Rebellion 1860–65." Von Theodor S. Fay ... . *Berlin.* 1865. 8vo, pp. 158, (1). BA., H. 24948

Fay. Statement ... *Privately Printed.* 1844. 8vo, pp. 78.

Concerning a law suit with Harper & Brothers. Also: Sydney Clifton; or, Vicissitudes in Both Hemispheres; a Tale of the Nineteenth Century. *New York.* 1839. 12mo. C. His story of "Norman Leslie," is founded on the mysterious murder of Miss Sands in New York. *See* New York.

Fay (W. F.) A Sermon ... July 17, 1812, in Monson, at the Funeral of Mrs. Nancy Ely ... . *Hartford: Peter B. Gleason & Co.* 1812. 8vo, pp. 17. BA. 23950

Fay (W.) ... Two Sermons, delivered at Harvard, January 30, 1814, being the first Sabbath after his Installation. By Warren Fay, A.M. ... . *Boston: Rowe and Hooper.* 8vo, pp. 23.

Also: A Sermon ... February 28, 1821, at the Installation of ... Calvin Hitchcock ... in Randolph, Mass. ... . *Boston.* 1821. 8vo, pp. 32. BA., H.—A Sermon, ... April 24, 1822, at the Ordination of the Rev. Nathanael Cogswell, ... *Boston: Crocker & Brewster.* 1822. 8vo, pp. 36. B.— ... A Sermon ... March 8, 1826, at the Installation of ... Isaac R. Barbour ... in Ipswich, N. H. ... *Boston: Crocker & Brewster.* 1826. 8vo, pp. 36. B., H.— ... A Sermon, ... Springfield, May 10, 1826, at the Ordination of the Rev. Rufus Anderson, ... *Boston: Crocker & Brewster.* 1826. 8vo, pp. 40. B., BA.—A Sermon ... at the Funeral of the Rev. Benjamin B. Wisner. ... *Boston.* 1835. 8vo, pp. 31. B., BA., H.

Fayette (Gilbert-Motier de la). *See* Lafayette.

Fayette in Prison; or Misfortunes of the Great: A Modern Tragedy. By a Gentleman of Massachusetts. *Worcester, Mass.: Printed for the Author.* 1802. 8vo, pp. 23. 23952

Fayette Co, *Ill.* Proceedings of the Citizens of Fayette County, Illinois, in relation to the National Road. 1831. 8vo.

Fayette Co., *Pa.* State of the Accounts of Samuel Adams, Esquire, Collector of Excise, for the County of Fayette; From the 26th of September, 1783, to the 28th of February, 1785. *Philadelphia: Printed by Robert Aitken.* M.DCC.LXXXVI. 8vo, pp. 3. P. 23954

The Fearful Issue to be decided in November next. [n. p. 1856.] 8vo, pp. 24. BA., H. 23955

Fearon (H. B.) Sketches of America. A Narrative of a Journey of Five Thousand Miles through the Eastern and Western States of America; contained in Eight Reports addressed to the Thirty-nine English Families by whom the Author was deputed, in June 1817, to ascertain whether any, and what Part of the United States would be Suitable for their Residence. With Remarks on Mr. Birkbeck's "Notes" and "Letters." By Henry Bradshaw Fearon. *London: Longman, Hurst, Rees, Orme, and Brown.* 1818. 8vo, pp. vii, (1), 462. B., BA., H. + Second Edition. *London: Longman & Co.* 1819. 8vo, Title, pp. v–xi, 454. + Third Edition. *London: Longman & Co.* 1819. 8vo, pp. xiii, 454. 23956

See "M. Rev.," LXXXVII. 392; *also* "Edinb. Rev."

Fearon. Skizzen von Amerika entworfer auf einer Reise durch die Vereinigten Staaten in den Jahren 1817 und 1818. *Jena: Braun.* 1819. 8vo. 23957

Featherston (W. S.) Speech of Hon. W. S. Featherston, of Miss., on Slavery in the Territories; Delivered in the House ... June 26, 1848. [*Washington:*] *J. & G. S. Gideon, Printers.* [1848.] 8vo, pp. 8. H. 23958

Featherstonhaugh (G. W.) A Canoe Voyage up the Minnay Sotor; with an Account of the Lead and Copper Deposits in Wisconsin; of the Gold Region in the Cherokee Country; and Sketches of Popular Manners, &c., &c., &c. By G. W. Featherstonhaugh, F.R.S. F.G.S. *London: Richard Bentley.* 1847. 2 vols., 8vo, pp. xiv, 416, Map and Plates; viii, 351.

Featherstonhaugh. Excursion through the Slave States, from Washington on the Potomac to the Frontier of Mexico; with Sketches of Popular Manners and Geological Notices. By G. W. Featherstonhaugh, F.R.S., ... *London: John Murray.* 1844. 2 vols., 8vo, pp. 792. Maps and Plates. B., BA. + *New York: Harper & Brothers.* 1844. 8vo, pp. 168. 23960

Highly commended by the "New Monthly Mag." *See* Rich, Vol. II., No. 17.

Featherstonhaugh. Geological Report of an Examination made in 1834, of the Elevated Country between the Missouri and Red Rivers. By G. W. Featherstonhaugh, U. S. Geologist. Published by order of the House of Representatives. *Washington: Printed by Gales and Seaton.* 1835. 8vo, pp. 97. Map. (23d Cong., 2d Sess., Ex. Doc. 151.) B., BA., C. 23961

Featherstonhaugh. Observations upon the Treaty of Washington, signed 9th August, 1842. By George William Featherstonhaugh, with the Treaty annexed, together with a Map to Illustrate the Boundary Line. *London.* 1843. 8vo, pp. 119. C., S. 23962

Also: Supplement to the Same. *London.* 1843. Rl. 8vo. *See* "Q. Review," LXXI. 560.

Featherstonhaugh. Report of a Geological Reconnoissance made in 1835, from the seat of Government, by the way of Green Bay and Wisconsin Territory, to the Coteau de Prairie, an Elevated Bridge dividing the Missouri from the St. Peter's River. By G. W. Featherstonhaugh ... . *Washington: printed by Gales and Seaton.* 1836. 8vo, pp. 168. Map and Diagrams. (24th Cong., 1st Sess., Sen. Doc. 333.) B., BA., C.

Featherstonhaugh. ... Gesta Anglo-Americana scilicit et Progymnasmata Novæ Franciæ Pelasgicæ. Liber Singularis. ... 8vo, 6 l., pp. 144, Lithographed. 23964

Also: Agricultural Address. *Schenectady.* 1822.—Monthly American Journal of Geology and Natural Science.

Featly (J.) Sermon preached to Sir Thomas Warner and his Companions, bound to the West Indies. By John Featly. *London.* 1629. 4to. W. 23965

The author was subsequently the first preacher at St. Christopher's.

Features of Mr. Jay's Treaty. To which is annexed A View of the Commerce of the United States as it Stands at Present, and as it is fixed by Mr. Jay's Treaty. *Philadelphia: M. Carey.* 1795. 8vo, pp. 51. C., N. 23966

Febles (M. de J.) Noticia de las Leyes y Ordenes de Policia que rigen a los profesores del arte de curar. Dispuesta por Manual de Jesus Febles ... *Mexico.* 1830–31. 4to, pp. vi, 108, 18, 20, 27, 10, (8). Portrait. 23967

Febrés (A.) Arte de la lengua general del reyno de Chile, con un dialogo Chileno-Hispano muy curioso: a que se añade la doctrina Christiana, esto es, Rezo, Catecismo, Coplas, Confessionario, y Platicas, lo mas en Lengua Chilena y Castellana: y por fin un Vocabulario Hispano-Chileno, y un Calepino Chileno-Hispano mas copioso. Compuesto por el P. Andres Febres Misionero de la Compañia de Jesus ... . *Lima: en la Calle de la Incarnacion.* 1765. 8vo, pp. 682. 23968

Mr. J. C. Brown's copy has the imprint, *En Madrid en la calle de la Encarnacion. Año de* 1765. 8vo, 14 l., pp. 682. Sold at Puttick's, in 1860, for £17; priced, Thorp, £4 4s.; J. R. Smith, £2 12s. 6d.; Quaritch, £3 3s. Reprinted in the following:

Febrés. Diccionario Hispano Chileno. Compuesto por el R. P. Misionero Andres Febres. De la C. de J. Enriquecido de voces i mejorado por el R. P. Misionero Fr. Antonio Hernandez i Caldaza de la órden de la Regular Observancia de N. P. S. Francisco. Edicion hecha para el servicio de las Misiones por órden del Supremo Gobierno i bajo la inspeccion del R. P. Misionero Fr. Miguel Anjel Astraldi. *Santiago: Imprenta del Progreso.* 1846. pp. (2), ii, 108. BA. 23969

Febrés. Diccionario Chileno-Hispano, compuesto por el R. P. Misionero Andres Febres. Enriquecido de Voces, i mejorado por el R. P. Mis. Fr. Antonio Hernandez i Calzada. Edicion hecha para el servicio de las Misoines por orden del Supremo

Gobierno i bajo la inspeccion del R. P. Misenero Fr. Miguel Anjel Astraldi. *Santiago: imprenta de los Tribunales.* 1846. 8vo, pp. iv, 87. 23970

This and the preceding number are usually found together.

Febrés. Grammatica de la Lengua-Chilena, escrita por el Reverendo Padre Misionero Andres Febres, de la C. de J. Adicionada i correjido por el R. P. Fr. Antonio Hernandez Calzada, de la Orden de la Regular Observancia de N. P. San Francisco. Edicion hecha para el servicio de las Misiones por Orden del Supremo Gobierno i bajo la inspeccion del R. P Misionero Fr. Miguel Anjel Astraldi. *Santjago: imprenta de los Tribunales.* 1846. 8vo, pp. v, 225, Apendice, 227–292, Breve Diccionario, 29, Indice, ii. BA. 23971

Some copies on large paper, in rl. 8vo. Extracts from this work are given by Gallatin in the "Archæologia Americana."

Feddersen (F.) Dänemarks und Nordamerikas Streit über den Sundzoll. Frei nach dem Dänischen des Kammerhern Fr. Feddersen von Carl Dirckinck-Holmfeld. *Kopenhagen.* 1856. 8vo, pp. 55. 23972

The Federal American Monthly. *New York.* 1864–5. 2 vols., 8vo. 23973

The Federal Catechism Metamorphosed: or, the Natural Spirit of Federalism Exposed, from the Works of their Federal Holiness. ... *Grafton, N. H.* 1804. 8vo. BA., C., N. 23974

The Federal Constitution for the United States of America, &c. [Colophon.] *Richmond: Printed by Augustine Davis.* [1787.] 4to, pp. 11. 23975

The Federal Orrery. 1800. 8vo. 23976

The Federal or New Ready Reckoner, and Trader's Useful Assistant; in Buying and Selling all sorts of Commodities, ... adapted to the Federal Money. The First Edition. *Chestnut Hill: Samuel Sower.* M,DCC,XCIII. 12mo, 62 l. BA. 23977

Published at the same time in German. These are the only two books I have seen with this imprint. Chestnut Hill is now a part of Philadelphia.

The Federal Ready Reckoner. ... *Worcester: Leonard Worcester.* MDCCXCV. 12mo, pp. 139, (1). 23978

Federalism Triumphant. *See* Vol. IV., No. 15737.

Federalism Turned Inside Out. *See* [Niles (H.)]

Federalist, *pseudonym.* *See* No. 10879; *also* [Hamilton (A.)]

The | Federalist : | A Collection | of | Essays, | written in Favour | of the | New Constitution, | as agreed upon by the Fœderal Convention, | September 17, 1787. | *New-York : J. and A. M'Lean.* M,DCC,LXXXVIII. | 2 vols., 12mo, pp. vi, 227; vi, 384. BA., C.

First edition in a collected form. Mr. Madison's papers were much changed in the subsequent editions. Nos. 2, 3, 4, 5, and 64 were written by Mr. Jay; Nos. 10, 14, 17, 18, 19, 21, 37 to 58, 62 and 63, were written by Mr. Madison; the remainder by Gen. Hamilton. There are copies of this edition on large and *thick* paper. Lowndes, in noticing this work, says it was "a periodical paper, in which John Williams, *alias* Anthony Pasquin, was concerned," which is a remarkable blunder. John Williams, under the *pseudonym* of Anthony Pasquin, wrote a poem called the "Hamiltoniad," which may have led Lowndes into the mistake; but Richard Grant White, in a note to Burton's "Book Hunter," undertakes to put the matter right, and credits James Munroe with a share of the authorship, which, for an American, is a still more remarkable blunder.

The | Federalist : | A Collection of | Essays, | written in favour of the | New Constitution, | as agreed upon by the | Federal Convention, | September 17, 1787. | ... | *New-York : | Printed and Sold by John Tiebout, | No. 358 Pearl-Street,* | 1799. | 2 vols., 12mo, pp. vi, 227; vi, 384. C. 23980

This is our No. 23979, with a new title only. According to Mr. H. B. Dawson, it is very rare, as he was unable to find it.

The Federalist, on the New Constitution. By Publius. Written in 1788. ... To which is added Pacificus, on the Proclamation of Neutrality. Written in 1793. Likewise, The Federal Constitution, with all the Amendments. Revised and Corrected. ... *New York : George F. Hopkins.* 1802. 2 vols., 8vo, pp. viii, 317, (1); v, 351. C., H. 23981

This edition was probably edited by William Coleman, and was the last issued during Hamilton's life, and the text is much altered. *See* Dawson's introduction, page lxx–lxxii.

The Federalist, on the New Constitution; written in 1788, by Mr. Hamilton, Mr. Jay, and Mr. Madison. To which is added Pacificus, on the Proclamation of Neutrality; written in 1793, by Mr. Hamilton. A New Edition, with the Names and Portraits of the several writers. *New York : Williams & Whiting.* 1810. 2 vols., 8vo, pp. iv, 368; iv, 368. 3 Portraits. 23982

This is, in fact, Vols. II. and III. of Hamilton's works, as edited by John Wells.

The Federalist, on the New Constitution; written in 1788, by Mr. Hamilton, Mr. Jay, and Mr. Madison. A New Edition, with the Names and Portraits of the several writers. *Philadelphia : Benjamin Warner.* 1817. 8vo, pp. 477. 3 Portraits.

The portraits are from the same plates as the New York edition of 1810, and the name of the printer omitted.

The Federalist. [Title as in No. 23983.] *Philadelphia : Benjamin Warner.* 1818. 8vo, pp. 504. 3 Portraits. 23984

The same as the edition of 1817, with the addition of an appendix.

The Federalist, on the New Constitution, written in the Year 1788, by Mr. Hamilton, Mr. Madison, and Mr. Jay, with an Appendix, containing the Letters of Pacificus and Helvidius, on the Proclamation of Neutrality of 1793; Also, the Original Articles of Confederation, and the Constitution of the United States, with the Amendments made thereto. A New Edition. The Numbers Written by Mr. Madison corrected by Himself. *City of Washington : Jacob Gideon, Jun.* 1818. 8vo, pp. 671.

Reissued in 1821, with a new title-page only. Mr. Dawson doubts the existence of an Hallowell edition of 1827, which has been cited. Mr. Homes, of the New York State Library, supposes that the real date is 1837, in which supposition I agree.

The Federalist, on the New Constitution, written in the Year 1788, by Alexander Hamilton, James Madison and John Jay, with an Appendix ... A New Edition ... *Washington : Thompson & Homans.* 1831. 8vo, pp. vii, 3–420. C. 23986

Mostly a reprint of the edition of 1818, with an elaborate index.

The Federalist ... [Title and text as in No. 23985.] *Hallowell, (Me.) : Glazier & Co.* 1826. 8vo, pp. 582. H. 23987

In one of Mr. Gowans' catalogues, an edition is described, *Philadelphia,* 1826, 8vo, pp. 582, which is probably an error as to the place.

The Federalist, on the New Constitution, written in the Year 1788, by Mr. Hamilton, Mr. Madison, and Mr. Jay. With an Appendix, containing the Letters of Pacificus and Helvidius on the Proclamation of Neutrality of 1793. ... A New Edition. ... *Hallowell : Glazier, Masters and Smith.* 1837. 8vo, pp. 500. C. + [*Ibid.*] 1842. 8vo, pp. 484. 23988

Mr. Dawson refers to a prospectus of an edition, 1845; and I have a slip from an auctioneer's catalogue, No. 200 or thereabouts, *circa* 1850, *Washington.* 1845. 8vo. The British Museum Catalogue cites an edition, 2 parts, *Philadelphia.* 1847–1845.

The Federalist ... [with] the Letter of Washington, as President of the Convention, to the President of Congress; the Act of Congress in relation to the Election of President ... Sixth Edition, with ... Index ... *Philadelphia : R. Wilson Desilver.* 1847. 8vo, pp. (2), v, 392, Pacificus, etc, 102. BM. 23989

The "Letter of Pacificus" has the imprint, *Washington : J. and G. S. Gideon.* 1845, which will account for the quotation in the British Museum Catalogue, and leads to the inference that this 1847 edition is a reissue of the apparently unknown edition of 1845. There is an edition cited in Mr. Bartlett's List, *Washington : J. & G. S. Gideon.* 1847. 8vo

The Federalist, on the New Constitution, written in 1788, by Mr. Hamilton, Mr. Madison and Mr. Jay. With an Appendix, containing the Letters of Pacificus and Helvidius on the Proclamation of Neutrality of 1793; also, the Original Articles of Confederation, and the Constitution of the United States. New Edition. *Hallowell : Masters, Smith & Co.* 1852. 8vo, pp. 496. + [*Ibid.*] 1857. 8vo, pp. 496. 23990

The Fœderalist : A Collection of Essays, written in Favor of the New Constitution, as agreed upon by the Fœderal Convention, September 17, 1787. Reprinted from the Original Text, with an Historical Introduction and Notes. By Henry B. Dawson. In Two Volumes. *New York : Charles Scribner & Co.* 1854. 8vo, pp. cxlii, 1 l. blank, pp. 615. Portrait of Hamilton.

Vol. II. is not yet (1873) published; but the entire text is included in this volume. In the later issues all mention of Vol. I. is omitted. 250 copies printed on large paper, with the imprint, *Morrisiana, N. Y.* 1864; also six copies on extra thick paper. The introduction includes a careful, elaborate and rather redundant bibliography. This Mr. Dawson calls the twenty-first edition in book form, and "the result of a careful examination of the work, in its various forms, editions and versions, and of a long-continued and anxious study of the important subject on which it treats;" but the text is a reprint of the first issue.

The Federalist. A Commentary on the Constitution of the United States. A Collection of Essays, by Alexander Hamilton, Jay and Madison. Also the Continentalist, and other Papers, by Hamilton. Edited by John C. Hamilton. ... *Philadelphia : J. B. Lippincott.* 1864. 8vo, pp. clxv, 659, vi. BA. 23992

One hundred copies were printed on large paper, in imperial 8vo, and divided into two volumes, with the imprint, *Philadelphia.* 1865.

Le Fédéraliste, | ou | Collection de quelques Écrits en faveur de | la Constitution proposée aux États-Unis | de l'Amérique, par la Convention convoquée | en 1787; | Publiés dans les États-Unis de l'Amérique par | MM. Hamilton, Madisson et Gay, | Citoyens de l'État de New-York. | *Paris : Buisson.* 1792. | 2 vols., 8vo, pp. lij, 366; 2 l., pp. 511. H. 23993

The translator was M. Trudaine de la Sablière, who added an introduction and many notes. Mr. Dawson says it was reproduced without the introduction — *Paris : Buisson.* 1792, — and in 1795 it was reissued with the same title, except that Gay is corrected to Jay. *Paris : Buisson.* An 3e la République. 2 vols., 8vo, pp. (4), xxij–lij, 366; (4), 506. It is probable that all three are the same edition, in fact — the introduction, for some reason, having been omitted in the second issue of 1792, and in this of 1795.

The Federalist : containing some Strictures upon a Pamphlet, entitled, "The Pretensions of Thomas Jefferson to the Presidency, examined, and the Charges against John Adams, refuted."

Which Pamphlet was first published in the Gazette of the United States, in a Series of Essays, under the Signature of "Phocion." *Philadelphia : Mathew Carey. November* 1796. 8vo, pp. 48. BA., H., P. + Part the Second. [*Ibid.*] 8vo, pp. 27. 23994

FEDERALIST, *pseudonym.* A Letter to General Hamilton, occasioned by his Letter to President Adams. By a Federalist. [n. p. n. d.] 12mo, pp. 8. 23995

Signed "Aristides."

O Federalista, publicado em inglez por Hamilton, Madisson e Jay, cidadãos de Nova-York, e traduzido em portuguez por ... *Rio de Janeiro : Typ. Imperial e Const. de J. Villeneuve & Ca.* 1840. 3 vols., 8vo, pp. 244; 285; 246. 23996

FEDERMANN (N.) Indianische historia. Ein schöne kurtzweilige Historia Niclaus Federmanns des Jüngern von Ulm erster Raise so er von Hispania und Andolosia ausz in Indias des Occeanischen Mörs gethan hat, und was ihm allda ist begegnet bisz auff sein Widerkunfft inn Hispaniam. Auffs kurtzest beschriben, gantz lustig zu lesen. [Colophon :] *Gedruckt zu Hagenaw bij Sigmund Bund.* MDLVII. 4to, 63 l. 23997

Title from the reprint in the "Bibliotek des Litterarischen Vereins, in Stuttgart, [Vol.] XLVII, [56] *Stuttgart, gedruckt auf kosten des Litterarischen Vereins.* 1859." 8vo, pp. (4), 209. Translated by Henri Ternaux-Compans, *Paris,* 1837, 8vo, forming the first volume of his "Voyages, Relations et Mémoires originaux pour servir à l'histoire de la découverte de l'Amérique. *Paris.*" 20 vols., 8vo. This is the narrative of his first trip only, from 1529–32. The original work is quite rare. Federmann commanded part of the German troops sent by the Welser's of Augsburg to Venezuela. The narrative was published by Jean Kiefhaber, his brother-in-law. An extract from it is in Kunziger's work, "Der Antheil der Deutchen an der Entdeckung von Süd-america, &c. *Stuttgart.* 1857." Consult, also, "Simon, Noticias de Tierra-Firme. *Cuenca.* 1626," Oviedo y Baños, "Hist. de Venezuela," etc. See about the Welser's enterprise in Venezuela, "K. von Klöden in Berlin Zeitß. für Allgem. Erdkunde," Vol. V. *See also* Ternaux, No. 80.

FEDERMANN. Belle et agréable Narration du premier Voyage de Nicolas Federmann le Jeune, d'Ulm, aux Indes de la Mer Océane, et de tout ce qui lui est arrivé dans ce pays jusqu'à son retour en Espagne, écrite brièvement et divertissante à lire. *Paris : Arthus Bertrand.* M.DCCCXXXVII. 8vo, pp. 227. B., BA.

Forms Vol. I. of Ternaux-Compans' "Recueil."

FEDERMANN und H. Staden, Reisen in Süd-America, 1529–55. Herausgegeben von Dr. Karl Klüpfel. *Stuttgart.* 1859. 8vo, pp. 4, 209, Federmann, 1–86. B. 23999

Reprint of the extremely rare editions, *Hagenaw,* 1557, and *Frankfort,* 1556. Published by the German Society of Bibliophiles, for the members only. *See* No. 23997.

FÉDIX (P. A.) L'Orégon et les côtes de l'Océan pacifique du Nord, aperçu géographique, statistique et politique. *Paris : Amyot.* 1846. 8vo, pp. 258. Map. 24000

FÉDON (B.) Réclamations de M. Bury Fédon contre un ... intitulé : Campagnes de Français a St. Domingue, et réfutation des reproches faits au Capitaine General Rochambeau. [Par Lattre.] *Paris : Brasseur.* 1805. 8vo, pp. 32. 24001

FEDRIC (F.) Slave Life in Virginia and Kentucky; or, Fifty Years of Slavery in the Southern States of America. By Francis Fedric. With a Preface by the Rev. Charles Lee. *London : Wertheim.* 1863. 12mo, pp. 120. C. 24002

FEE (J. G.) An Anti-Slavery Manual, Being An Examination, in the Light of the Bible, and of Facts, into the Moral and Social Wrongs of American Slavery, with A Remedy for the Evil. By John G. Fee. *Maysville, Ky.* 1848. 12mo, pp. xi, 230. + Second Edition. *New York.* 1851. 12mo, pp. 178. S. 24003

FEE. Non-Fellowship with Slaveholders the Duty of Christians. *New York.* 1855. 12mo, pp. 68. S. 24004

FEE. The Sinfulness of Slaveholding. Shown by Appeals to Reason and Scripture. By John G. Fee. *New York : John A. Gray.* 1851. 12mo, pp. 36. 24005

FELCH (Alpheus). Speech of Mr. Felch, of Michigan, on ceding the Public Land to the States in which they are situated. ... in the Senate ... January 13, 1851. *Washington.* 1851. 8vo, pp. 20. BA., H. 24006

Also : An Address to the Graduating Class of the Law Department, of the University of Michigan, ... March 27, 1861. *Ann Arbor.* 1861. 8vo, pp. 21. H. — Speech ... February 3 and 4, 1852, on ... granting Land to the State of Iowa in Aid of ... Railroads. *Washington.* 1852. 8vo, pp. 16. BA., H. — Speech ... on the French Spoliation Bill, ... April 12 and 14, 1852. *Washington.* 1852. 8vo, pp. 21.

FELCH (C.) An Address ... Lynn, June 24, 1821, ... at which time ... the Lodge laid the the Corner-Stone of a Masonic Hall. By Rev. Cheever Felch, A.M. *Boston.* [1821.] 8vo, pp. 20. B., H., M. 24007

FELDNER (W. Chr. G. von). Reisen durch mehrere Provinzen Brasiliens. Aus seinem nachgelassenen Papieren. *Liegnitz : Leonparat.* 1828. 2 pts., 8vo. 24008

FELICE (G. de). Émancipation immédiate et complète des Esclaves — Appel aux Abolitionistes. *Paris : Delay.* 1846. 8vo.

FELIU (Ramon Olaguer). El uso de la lengua vulgar en el estudio de las ciencias, para defenderse en la real Universidad de San Marcos, en acto que dedica a D. J. F. Abascal y Sousa, Virey del Perú, ecc. D. Manuel Saenz de Texada, á nombre del real convictorio de San Carlos. *Lima.* 1806. 8vo, 7 l., pp. 494. 24010

FELL (F. S.) An Oration, Commemorative of American Independence, ... Savannah, (Geo.) on the Fifth of July, 1813. By Lieut. Frederick S. Fell ... . *Savannah.* 1813. 8vo, pp. 16.

FELL (Lydia). A Testimony and Warning given forth in the Love of Truth, and is for the Governour, Magistrates, and People inhabiting on the Island of Barbadoes; which is a call to turn to the Lord. [n. p. 1676.] 4to, pp. 8. 24012

[FELLECHNER.] Bericht über die im höchsten Auftrage des Prinzen Karl von Preussen und des Fürsten von Schönburg-Waldenburg bewirkte Untersuchung einiger Theile des Mosquito Landes, erstattet von der dazu ernannten Commission [Fellechner, Regierungsrath, Dr. Müller, Kreisphysikus, Hesse, Kaufmann]. *Berlin : A. Duncker.* 1845. 8vo, pp. iv, 274, 1. 2 Maps and 3 Plates. C. 24013

FELLENBERG ACADEMY, *Mass.* Catalogue of the Fellenberg Academy. *Greenfield, Mass.* 1834. 8vo. W. 24014

First and Second Annual Reports of the Fellenberg Academy. *Greenfield : Phelps and Ingersoll.* 1834. 8vo, pp. 15. BA., W.

Fellenberg; or, An Appeal to the Friends of Education on Behalf of Lafayette College. ... Edited by the Rev. John Breckenridge. *Easton : Printed by J. P. Ulrich.* 1835. 8vo, pp. 24.

Emmanuel von Fellenberg established a model school at Hofwyl, near Berne, Switzerland, which, for forty years, was considered the best in Europe. It included an agricultural and a high school.

FELLER (Francois Xavier). Observations sur l'Histoire de las révolution de l'Amérique (par l'abbé Raynal). 24017

Republished from his "Journal hist. et lit.," 1 Nov. 1781. In the No. for 15 Déc., he says, "The first edition of the Observations having been exhausted in a few days, a new edition has just been issued." — BACKER.

FELLKAMPFF (J. L.) Over den toestand der arbeiders en over de handwerks-genootschappen in Engeland en Noord-Amerika. [Uit het Engelsch vertaald] door H. J. G. Mijnssen. *Amsterdam : C. L. Brinkman.* 1871. 8vo, pp. 6, 74. 24018

FELLOWES (W. F.) Narrative of the Loss of His Majesty's Packet, the Lady Hobart, on an Island of Ice in the Atlantic Ocean, 28th of June, 1803. By William Dorset Fellowes. *London.* 1803. 8vo. + Fifth Edition. [*libd.*] 24019

FELLOWS (J.) The Bromsgrove Elegy, in Blank Verse, on the Death of the Rev. George Whitefield, at Newbury in New England, Sep. 30, 1770. By John Fellows. *London.* 1771 8vo.

FELLOWS. An Exposition of the Mysteries; or Religious Dogmas and Customs of the Ancient Egyptians, Pythagoreans, and Druids; ... By John Fellows. *New York.* 1835. 8vo, pp. xvi, 403. 24021

Chapter VIII. relates to the horrors of the American Revolution.

FELLOWS (J.) The Veil Removed; or Reflections on David Humphreys' Essay on the Life of Israel Putnam. Also, Notices of Oliver W. B. Peabody's Life of the same, S. Swett's Sketch of Bunker Hill Battle, etc. etc. By John Fellows. ... *New York : James D. Lockwood.* 1843. 12mo, pp. 231. B., BA. 24022

FELNER (R. J. de L.) Collecçao de Monumentos Ineditos para a Historia das Conquistas dos Portuguezes, em Africa, Asia e America, Publicada da Ordem da Classe de Sciencias Moraes e Politicas e Bellas Lettres da Academia Real das Sciencias de Lisboa e sobre a Direcçao de R. J. de Lima Felner; 1a Serie, Historia da Asia. *Lisboa.* 1858–62. 3 vols., 4to. 24023

A Felon's Account of Fourteen Years' Transportation in Virginia in America. *Aldermary Church Yard.* [n. d.] 8vo.

FELSENHART (J.) Les colonies Anglaises de 1574 à 1660, d'après les State Papers, et Episode de l'émigration Belge en Virginie, par J. Falsenhart ... . *Gand : L. Hebbelynck.* 1868. 8vo, pp. viii, 94. B. 24025

FELSENTHAL (B.) Jüdisches Schulwesen in Amerika. *Chicago.* 1866. 8vo. 24026

FELT (G. H.) Proceedings of a Court of Inquiry, convened by Special Order, No. 85. Headquarters, Department of Washington, at the request of Lieut. George H. Felt ... *New York : Willard Felt & Co.* 1863. 8vo, pp. 64. 24027

FELT (J. B) The Annals of Salem, from its first Settlement. By Joseph B. Felt. ... *Salem : W. & S. B. Ives.* 1827. 8vo, pp. 611. B., BA., H. 24028

First published in numbers; now scarce.

FELT. Annals of Salem. By Joseph B. Felt. Second Edition. *Salem : W. & S. B. Ives.* 1845. 2 vols., 12mo, pp vi, 5–535; 662. 24029

"An accurate and useful work, the fruit of much original research." — BANCROFT, I. 348.

FELT. The Customs of New England. By Joseph B. Felt. ... *Boston : T. R. Marvin.* 1853. 8vo, Title, pp. 208. B., BA.

FELT. The Ecclesiastical History of New England; comprising not only Religious, but also Moral and other Relations. By Joseph B. Felt. ... *Boston : the Congregational Library Association,* 1855–62. 2 vols., 8vo, pp. 670; 4, 664. B., BA. 24031

FELT. An Historical Account of Massachusetts Currency. By Joseph B. Felt. ... *Boston : Perkins & Marvin.* 1839. 8vo, pp. 259. B., BA., P. 24032

See "N. Am. Rev.," I. 526.

FELT. History of Ipswich, Essex, and Hamilton. By Joseph B. Felt. ... *Cambridge : Charles Folsom.* 1834. 8vo, pp. xv, (1), 304. Portrait of John Rogers. B., BA., N. 24033

FELT. A Memoir, or Defence of Hugh Peters. By J. B. Felt. ... *Boston : C. C. P. Moody.* 1851. 8vo, pp. 67. Portrait. B., M. 24034

FELT. Memoir of the Rev. Francis Higginson. By Joseph B. Felt. *Boston.* 1852. 8vo, pp. 23. 24035

FELT. Memorials of William Smith Shaw. By Joseph B. Felt. ... *Boston : S. K. Whipple.* 1852. 12mo, pp. 346. BA.

FELT. Who was the First Governor of Massachusetts? By Joseph B. Felt. ... *Boston : Press of T. R. Marvin.* 1853. 8vo, pp. 17. B. 24037

The occasion of this question is a note on pp. 200–203 of Savage's edition of "Winthrop's Journal." Vol. II. Also : An Address before the Alumni of Atkinson Academy, N. H., August 25, 1859. ... *Boston : Wm. S. Damrell & Frank C. Moore.* 1859. 8vo, pp. 52. BA. — Did the First Church of Salem originally have a Confession of Faith distinct from their Covenant? ... *Boston : Press of Edward L. Balch.* 1856. 8vo, pp. 28. B., N. — Notice of Roger Conant. ... *Boston.* 1848. 8vo. — Selections from the New England Fathers. No. 1. John Norton. *Boston.* 1851. 8vo. BM. *See* "American Statistical Association, Collections," Vol. I.

FELTMAN (W.) The Journal of Lieut. William Feltman of the First Pennsylvania Regiment, 1781–82. Including the March into Virginia, and the Siege of Yorktown. *Philadelphia : Henry Cary Baird.* 1853. 8vo, pp. 48. 24038

Felton (A. C.) *See* New Hampshire Festival.

Felton (C. C.) An Address ... Dedication of the New Building of Bristol Academy in Taunton, August 25, 1852, By C. C. Felton, ... With an Appendix, containing an Historical Sketch of the Academy, an Account of the Festival, and a List of the Trustees and Preceptors. *Cambridge: Metcalf and Company, Printers.* 1852. 8vo, pp. 54. B., BA., M. 24039

Felton. A Memorial of the Rev. John Snelling Popkin, D.D. Late Eliot Professor of Greek Literature in Harvard University. Edited by Cornelius C. Fenton ... . *Cambridge: John Bartlett.* 1852. 12mo, pp. lxxxviii, 392. Portrait. B., BA.

Also: Address at the Inauguration of Cornelius Conway Felton, LL.D., as President of Harvard College, and at the Festival of the Alumni, Thursday, July 19, 1860. ... *Cambridge: Sevir and Francis.* 1860. 8vo, pp. 149. B., BA. — An Address ... August 15, 1828, at ... the Livingston County High School ... Geneseo, N. Y. ... *Cambridge.* 1828. 8vo, pp. 24. H. — An Address pronounced on the Anniversary of the Concord Lyceum, November 4, 1829. ... *Cambridge: Hilliard and Brown.* 1829. 8vo, pp. 39. BA. — A Discourse pronounced at the Inauguration of the Author as Eliot, Professor of Greek Literature in Harvard University, August 26, 1834. ... *Cambridge: James Munroe and Company.* 1834. 8vo, pp. 27. B., BA. — Memoir of Cornelius Conway Felton. Republished from Barnard's American Journal of Education, for March, 1861. [n. p. n. d.] 8vo, pp. 265–296. Portrait. H.

Felton (F. E.) The Purification and Reconstruction of the American Union. An Oration delivered at Vallejo, July iv 1867. By Franklin Eliot Felton. ... *San Francisco: Edward Bosqui & Company.* MDCCCLXVII. 8vo, pp. 22. B. 24041

Felton (J. B.) The Horse-Shoe: A Poem. Spoken before the Phi Beta Kappa Society in Cambridge, July 19, 1849. By John Brooks Felton. *Cambridge.* 1849. 12mo. B., S. 24042

Also: Oration, Fourth Anniversary of the College of California. ... *San Francisco.* 1858. 8vo.

Felton (J. H.) The Decimal System: an Argument for American Consistency in the Extension of the Decimal Scale to Weights and Measures, in Harmony with the National Currency. By John H. Felton. ... *New York: Wiley & Halsted.* 1858. 12mo, pp. (1), 189. B. 24043

Felton (*Mrs.*) Life in America, a Narrative of Two Years' City and Country Residence in the United States. By Mrs. Felton. *Hull.* 1838. 12mo. Map. + [Another Edition.] 1843. 12mo. 24044

Felton (Samuel Morse). Impolicy of Building another Rail Road between Washington and New York. *Philadelphia.* MDCCCLXIV. 8vo, pp. 24. B., H. 24045

Felton. Letter of the President of the Philadelphia, Wilmington & Baltimore Railroad Company to the Secretary of War, in Reference to Improved Facilities of Transportation between New York and Washington ... with ... Documents ... showing the Nature of the Services rendered the Government by the aforesaid Railroad at the Breaking out of the Rebellion. *Washington.* 1862. 8vo, pp. 40. H. 24046

Feltus (H.) Address upon the Ceremony of Dedicating the New Masonic Hall, in the City of New York, the 30th of October, 1827, etc. By Henry Feltus. *New York.* 1827. 8vo.

Feltus (H. J.) Lines Occasioned by the Death of the Rev. Dr. Henry J. Feltus, with Notes, Biographical and Explanatory, By a Friend. *New York.* 1829. 8vo, pp. 80. 24048

Female Life among the Mormons. *See* [Ward (Maria)].

Female Medical Education Society, and the New-England Female Medical College: 1st Report. *Boston.* 1850. 8vo. Continued. 24049

Female Missionary Society of the Western District. The First Annual Report of the Trustees. ... *Utica, N. Y.* 1817. 8vo. Continued. 24050

Female Review. 1797. *See* [Sampson (D.)]

Fendall (P. R.) Argument of Philip R. Fendall, ... on the Trial of George A. Gardiner ... March ... 1853, for False Swearing. ... *Washington: Robert Armstrong, Printer.* 1853. 8vo.

[Fendall.] Remarks on the Address of ... John Quincy Adams, delivered at Washington, July 4, 1821. *Baltimore.* 1821. 8vo, pp. 15. + *New York: printed by G. L. Birch.* 1822. 8vo, pp. 30. + *Alexandria.* 1822. 8vo. P. 24052

Fenderich (Charles). Portfolio of Living American Statesmen. Drawn and Lithographed by C. Fenderich. *Washington: C. Fenderich.* [1837.] Folio, 1 l. 70 Lith. Plates. C. 24053

Fenelon (F. de Salignac de la Mothe). The Archbishop of Cambray's Dissertation on Pure Love. ... . *London: Printed, and Re-printed by C. Sowr, at Germantown.* 1750. 8vo, pp. xlvii, 120.

Included here on account of the imprint. Many of Sower's books were used for cartridges in the Battle of Germantown.

Fenelon, *pseudonym.* Catholicism Compatible with Republican Government. By Fenelon. *New York.* 1844. 8vo. S.

[Fenety (George E.)] The Lady and the Dressmaker; or a Peep at Fashionable Folly. A Story founded on circumstances that occurred some time since in this city. By a "Bluenose." *St. John.* 1842. 8vo, pp. 24. 24056

[Fenety.] Political Notes and Observations, or a glance at the leading Measures that have been discussed in the Assembly of New Brunswick, under the Administrations of Sir W. M. G. Colebrooke, Sir E. W. Head, Hon. J. H. T. Manners-Sutton, and Hon. A. H. Gordon. *St. John.* 1867. 24057

The Fenian Brotherhood. *New York.* 1856. 12mo, pp. 91.

Fenian Brotherhood of America. Official Report of the Investigating Committee of the Management of the Officials at the Fenian Head-quarters (Moffatt Mansion), Union Square, New York. With a History of the "Campo Bello" Fizzle. *New York: T. W. Timpson.* 1867. 8vo, pp, 102. 24059

Seventh National Congress, F. B. Proceedings of the Senate and House of Representatives of the Fenian Brotherhood, in Joint Convention at Philadelphia, Pa., November ... 1868. *New York: D. W. Lee, Printer.* 1868. 8vo, pp. 55. H. 24060

Proceedings of the First National Convention of the Fenian Brotherhood, held in Chicago, Illinois, November, 1863. ... *Philadelphia: James Gibbons, Printer.* 1863. 8vo, pp. 59. H.

El Fenix, Periódico noticioso, politico literario y mercantil. *Campeche.* 1850. 24062

Fenn. Fenn's Compendium of the English and Foreign Funds, ... Debts, and Revenues of all Nations; ... Ninth Edition ... . *London: Effingham Wilson.* 1867. 12mo, pp. xx, 584. + Eleventh Edition ... . 1872. 12mo, pp. xx, 662. 24063

Fenneherg (F. F. von). Transatlantische Studien. *Stuttgart.* 1861. 8vo. 24064

Fennell (J.) An Apology for the Life of James Fennell. Written by Himself. ... *Philadelphia: Moses Thomas.* 1814. 8vo pp. 510. Portrait. B., BA., S. 24065

Fennell. Description of the Principles and Plan of Proposed Establishments of Salt Works, for the Purpose of Supplying the

United States with Home-made Salt. By James Fennell. *Philadelphia.* 1798. 8vo. 24066

Fenner (E. D.) History of the Epidemic Yellow Fever, at New Orleans, La. in 1853. By E. D. Fenner, M.D., ... *New York: Hall, Clayton & Co.* 1854. 8vo, pp. 84. B., C. 24067

Fenner. Southern Medical Reports ... on the Medical Topography, Meteorology, and Prevalent Diseases, in the following States: Louisiana, Alabama, Mississippi, North-Carolina, South-Carolina, Georgia, Florida, Arkansas, Tennessee, Texas. To be published Annually. ... . *New-Orleans: B. M. Norman.* 1849–50. 2 vols., 8vo, pp. 472, Maps; pp. iv, 498. B., S.

Fenner (J.) A Letter to James Fenner, Esq. By a Republican. [n. p. n. d.] 8vo, pp. 8. 24069

Fenner. Letters to James Fenner, Esq., in 1811 and 1831. [Signed Another Republican.] *Providence.* [n. d.] 8vo, pp. 16.

Fenner (Robert), *and others.* Report of the Commissioners appointed to Examine the Branch of the Bank of the State of Alabama at Decatur. *Tuscaloosa.* 1841. 8vo. 24071

Fenning (D.) The Ready Reckoner: or Trader's most useful Assistant. By Daniel Fenning. *London: Printed. Germantown: Reprinted by Chris. Sower.* 1774. 12mo. 24072

Fenno (John). Plan for Establishing a General Marine Society throughout the United States and Systems of Regulations therein; written at Sea, in the Year 1794: now Printed by the Author. *Philadelphia: John Fenno.* 1798. pp. 32. 24073

[Fenno (J. W.)] Desultory Reflections on the Political Aspects of Public Affairs in the United States of America. Part II. ... *New York: The Author, and J. W. Fenno.* 1800. pp. (2), 38. B., BA. 24074

Fenno (Jenny). Original Compositions, in Prose and Verse. On Subjects Moral and Religious. By Miss J. Fenno, of Boston (?). *Wrentham (Mass.): Printed by Nathaniel Heaton, Jr.* 1803. 12mo, pp. 216. 24075

Fenocchio (Antonio). Christoforo Colombo: discorso. *Savona: Tip. Sambolino.* 1871. 8vo, pp. 20. 24076

Fenton (R. E.) A Sketch of the Life of Reuben E. Fenton, ... Governor of the State of New York. Illustrated. *New York: Geo. F. Nesbitt & Co. Printers.* 1861. Sm. 4to, pp. 28. 24077

Fenton. Speech of Hon. R. E. Fenton, of New York, on Democratic Tests, and the Nebraska Bill, delivered ... Feb. 15, 1854. *Washington.* 1854. Rl. 8vo, pp. 8. S. 24078

Also: Position of Parties, and Abuses of Power. Speech ... February 16, 1860. *Washington, D. C.: Buell & Blanchard, Printers.* 1860. 8vo, pp. 8. H. — Revolutionary Claims. Speech ... May 18, 1860. *Washington, D. C.* 1860. 8vo, pp. 8.

Fenwich (*P.*) Korte Beschrijving van de zendelingschap van Pater Fenwich, Bisschop van Cincinnati, in Ohio. *Antwerp.* 1824. 8vo, pp. 8. 24079

This short description of the mission of the Bishop of Cincinnati is almost *unique.*

Fenwick (B. J.) A Sermon, delivered in the Roman Catholic Church, New-York, February 25, 1810; for the Benefit of the City Dispensary. By the Rev. Benedict J. Fenwick, New-York. *New-York: Williams and Whiting.* 1810. 8vo, pp. 22.

Fenwick (John). [No title; begins]: Friends, These are to satisfie you, ... that we shall no doubt find, but that New Cesarea or New Jersey, which is the place which I did purchase: together with the Government thereof, is a healthy, pleasant, and plentiful Country: ... and the character given thereof, by John Ogilby in his America, which I herewith send. ... . dated this 8th of the 1st month, 1675. Folio, 1 leaf. 24081

Fenwick. A Testimony against John Fenwick, concerning his Proceeding about New-Cesaria, or New-Jersey, in the Province of America: Also John Fenwick's Letter of Condemnation sent to Friends; upon their Testifying against his Proceedings. Folio, 1 leaf. 24082

Fenwick. The True State of the Case between John Fenwick, Esq., and John Eldridge & Edmund Warner, concerning Mr. Fenwick's Ten Parts of his Land in West-New-Jersey, in America. *London: Printed in the Year* 1677. *Reprinted for John Hart, Philadelphia.* MDCCLXV. 12mo, pp. 8. 24083

Ferdinandina die Mexicanische Insul. *München.* 1652. 4to.

The scene of this curious and rare play is chiefly in Cuba. *See* Vespucci.

Fereira (G. D. de). Copie vande twee Sententien cytgesproocken vandem Hove Provinciael van Hollandt eerst [18 Mei] ende ten tweeden de Sententie van Appel vanden Hoghen Rade

van Hollandt [31 Julij] tegens Gaspar Dias de Fereira. Gebooren tot Lisbon in Portugael. *Gedr. nae de orig. Copien van dens Hoven.* 1647. 4to, pp. 8. 24085

"Fereira, who had formerly lived in Brazil, took advantage of his acquaintance with Brazilian affairs to injure the West India Company. His correspondence with the King of Portugal was discovered, and he was banished." — Tiele.

Fereira. Epistola|Gasparis Dias|Fereira|In carcere, unde erupit, scripta|Die 17 August. [n. p.] 1649.| 4to, pp. 8.

Relates to Brazilian and Dutch affairs. *See also* our Vol. IV., No. 16681.

[Fergus (Henry).] The History of the Western World. ... The United States. *London: Longman.* 1830. 2 vols., post 8vo, pp. x, 343; xxvii, 328. BA., H. 24087

Forms part of Dr. Lardner's "Cabinet Cyclopedia."

Ferguson (A.) Biographical Sketch|or|Memoir|of|Lieutenant-Colonel|Patrick Ferguson: |originally intended for the| British Encyclopedia.|By Adam Ferguson, LL.D.| ... *Edinburgh:| Printed by John Moir.* 1817.| 8vo, pp. 36. Portrait. 24088

Patrick Ferguson was killed at the battle of King's Mountain, S. C., Oct., 7, 1780.

[Ferguson (*Dr.*)] Remarks on a Pamphlet lately published by Dr. Price, intitled, Observations on the Nature of Civil Liberty, the Principles of Government, and the Justice and Policy of the War with America, &c. In a Letter from a Gentleman in the Country to a Member of Parliament. *London: T. Cadell.* MDCCLXXVI. 8vo, Title, pp. 61. 24089

"Written with less invective, and more decency, candor, and moderation, than have lately appeared in the productions on that side of the American dispute." — *M. Rev.,* LIV. 333. The following is probably another edition of this work:

[Ferguson.] Remarks on Dr. Price's Observations on the Nature of Civil Liberty, &c. *London: G. Kearsley.* MDCCLXXVI. 8vo, 2 l., pp. 76. 24090

Ferguson (James). Annual Address delivered before the Albany Institute, April, 1838 ... . *Albany: Alfred Southwick.* 1838. 8vo, 1 l., pp. 34. H. 24091

Ferguson (J. B.) Address and Correspondence, delivered December 30, 1855, in the "Christian Church," Nashville, Tennessee ... . *Nashville.* 1856. 8vo, pp. 16. B., H. 24092

Ferguson. Address on the History, Authority and Influence of Slavery. *Nashville, Tenn.* 1850. 8vo. B. 24093

Ferguson. History of the Relation of the Pastor to the "Christian Church" of Nashville: being a Discourse delivered upon the Proposal of the Dissentient Members to return to the House and Society they had Voluntarily left. Delivered Sabbath, August 19, 1855. By Rev. J. B. Ferguson. ... *Nashville: M'Kennie & Brown, Printers.* 1855. 8vo, pp. 24. H., S. 24094

Ferguson. Nationality versus Sectionalism. An Estimate of the Political Crisis, ... with an Appeal to the People on the Duties and Dangers of the Hour. ... *Washington.* 1866. 8vo, pp. 15. H. 24095

Also: ... A Record of Communications from the Spirit-Sphere, ... *Nashville.* 1854. 8vo. B. — Relation of Pastor and People; Statement of Relief on Unitarianism and Spiritualism. ... *Nashville.* 1854. 8vo, pp. xxiii. H.

Ferguson (J.) Letters addressed to Rev. Moses Thacher; together with the Result of an Ecclesiastical Council Convened at North Wrentham, Dec. 14, 1830. By John Ferguson. ... *Boston: Peirce & Parker.* 1831. 8vo, pp. 32. 24096

Ferguson. Memoir of the Life and Character of Rev. Samuel Hopkins, D.D., formerly Pastor of the First Church in Newport, Rhode Island; with an Appendix; By John Ferguson, ... *Boston: Leonard W. Kimball.* 1830. 18mo, pp. viii, 196.

Also: Sermon on the Death of Ebenezer Daggett, Jr. ... *Dedham.* 1832. 8vo.

Ferguson (R.) The Penalties of Greatness. *London: Ward & Co.* MDCCCLVII. 12mo, pp. xii, 459. 24098

Contents: Chap. VIII., Discovery of the New World; XII., The Pilgrim Fathers.

Ferguson (T.) A Complete History of the Present Civil War between Great Britain and the United Colonies of North America; in which its Origin and Progress are truly traced; and its Operations to the Close of the Campaign in 1778 are Faithfully Related. By Dr. T. Ferguson, Interspersed with Important Papers and Documents on both sides. *London: J. Hayes.* 1779. 8vo, pp. 358. 24099

Ferguson (W.) America by River and Rail; or, Notes by the Way on the New World and its People. By William Ferguson, F.L.S. *London: James Nesbit.* MDCCCLVI. 8vo, pp. viii, 511. 2 Plates. 24100

Ferguson (W. F.) Letter to Lord Stanley, on the Dearth of Cotton. *London.* 1863. 8vo, pp. 40. B. 24101

Fergusson (A.) Practical Notes made during a Tour in Canada, and a Portion of the United States, in MDCCCXXXI. By Adam Fergusson, of Woodhull, Advocate. ... *William Blackwood, Edinburgh.* MDCCCXXXIII. Post 8vo, pp. xv, 379. Map. + The Second Edition, to which are now added Notes made during a Second Visit to Canada in MDCCCXXXIII. [*Ibid.*] MDCCCXXXIV. Post 8vo, pp. 426. Map. 24102

Also: On the Agricultural State of Canada and Part of the United States of America. ... *Leith.* 1832. 8vo.

Fergusson (David). ... Letter of the Secretary of War, Communicating ... a Copy of the Report of Major D. Fergusson on the Country, its Resources, and the Route between Tucson and Lobos Bay. ... [*Washington.* 1863.] 8vo, pp. 22. Map. H.

Fergusson (J.) Rude Stone Monuments in all Countries; their Age and Uses. By James Fergusson, ... *London: John Murray.* 1872. 8vo, pp. xix, 559. BA. 24104

Chapter XIV.: North America, Central America.

Feria (P.) Aqui comienza una doctrina xpiana, que tanto de las Cosas *que* todo fiel xpiano es obligado a creer y obrar para a salvar: ... [Colophon:] A gloria y alabança nro Redēptor Jesu Christo y de su benedetissima Madre nra Señora y de nro glorioso y sanctissimo padre Sancto Domingo, y pa utilidad y provedo de las aias [*sic*] aquise acaba la declaracio breue y cōpēdiosa de la Doctrina Christiana en leñgua Española y capoteca sentēcia por sentēcia: Copuesta por el muy R. P. Fray Pedro de Feria, prior provĩcial de los Frayles Predicadores de Sancto Domingo iñsta Nueva Espana. ... *Impressa Mexico: en Casa de Pedro Ocharte.* 1567. Sm. 4to, pp. vii, 116. 24105

Ludewig quotes a "Vocabulario de la Lengua Zapoteca," by Bishop Pedro Feria, and adds, "Feria was born 1524, went to Mexico, joined the Dominicans, became a missionary amongst the Zapotecas, and, after filling many posts of dignity in the church, was made Bishop of Chiapas, in 1575. Died about the year 1586. He wrote, besides, 'Confessionario en la Lengua Zapoteca,' and 'Doctrina Christiana en la misma Lengua.'"

Ferland (J. B. A.) Biographical Narrative of Joseph Octave Plessis Bishop of Quebec. Translated by T. B. Trench from the Original by l'Abbé Ferland ... *Quebec G. & G. E. Desbarats* 1864. 8vo, pp. xiv, 177. Portrait. H. 24106

Ferland. Cours d'histoire du Canada. Par M. l'Abbé J. B. A. Ferland. Premiere [et] Seconde Partie 1534–1759. *Quebec: Augustin Coté.* 1861–7. 2 vols., 8vo, pp. xi, 522; 620. 24107

Ferland. Notes sur les Régistres de Notre Dame de Quebec. *Québec.* 1854. 8vo, pp. 75. + Deuxième Edition. *Quebec.* 1863. 8vo, pp. 100. B., BA. 24108

Ferland. Notes sur les plantes recueillies en 1858, par M. l'Abbé Ferland, sur les côtes de Labrador. 8vo. 24109

Ferland. Observations sur un ouvrage intitulé: Histoire du Canada, etc., par M. l'Abbé Brasseur de Bourbourg. ... *Québec.* 1853. 8vo, pp. 79. + Deuxième Edition. *Paris: Douniol.* 1854. 8vo. 24110

Ferlus (L. D.) Nouvelle Notice sur les Indiens arrivés à Paris, le 13 Aout 1827: Observations curieuses sur les Mœurs et les coûtumes de leur tribu guerrière. Par L. D. Ferlus. Deuxième édition. *Paris: Imp. de Guvot.* 1827. 8vo, pp. 16.

Fermin (P.) Description générale, historique, géographique, et physique de la colonie de Surinam, Contenant Ce qu'il y a de plus Curieux de plus Remarquable, touchant sa Situation, ses Rivières, ses Fortresses: son Gouvernement & sa Police; avec les mœurs & les usages des Habitants Naturels du païs & des Européens qui y sont établis; ainsi que des Eclaircissements sur l'œconomie générale des Esclaves Negres, sur les plantations & leurs Produits, les Arbres Fruitiers, les Plantes Médécinales, & toutes les diverses Especes d'animaux qu'on y trouve, &c. Enrichie de Figures, & d'une Carte Topographique du païs. Par Philippe Fermin, Docteur en Médicine. *Amsterdam: E. van Harrevelt.* MDCCLXIX. 2 vols., 8vo, pp. xxiv, 252; (2), 352. 1 Map and 3 Plates.

"One of the best books, *at the time it was written*, in regard to the colonies."—Rich.

Fermin. Dissertation sur la Question s'il est permis d'avoir en sa possession des esclaves, et de s'en servir comme tels, dans les colonies de l'Amérique. *Maestricht.* 1770. 8vo, pp. 88.

Fermin. Histoire naturelle de la Hollande équinoxiale: ou. Déscription des animaux, plantes, fruits, et autres curiosités, qui se trouvent dans la colonie de Surinam; avec Leurs Noms différents, tant François, que Latins, Hollandois, Indiens & Nègre-Anglois. Par Philippe Fermin. ... *Amsterdam: M. Magerus.* MDCCLXV. 8vo, pp. xii, 239, (2). Plate. C., H. 24114

Fermin. D. Philipp Fermin's Ausführliche historisch-physikalische Beschreibung der Kolonie Surinam auf Beranlassung der Gesellschaft Naturforschender Freunde in Berlin. Aus dem Französischen übersetzet und mit Anmerkungen begaleitet. *Berlin: Joachim Pauli.* 1775. 8vo, 40 sheets. Plates and Map.

Fermin. Ph. Fermin's Historisch politische Uebersicht des gegenwärtigen und ehemaligen Zustandes der Kolonie Surinam in Südamerika. Aus dem Englischen mit einigen Zusazzen von Friedrich Gottlieb Canzler. *Göttingen: Viktorinus Bossiegel.* 1788. 8vo, 2 l., pp. 6, (2), 159. H. 24116

A German translation of the supplement to Fermin's "Surinam," printed in 1769.

Fermin. Tableau historique et politique de l'état ancien et actuel de la Colonie de Surinam, et des causes de sa décadence; Par Philippe Fermin ... . *Maestricht: Jeane-Edme Dufour & Philippe Roux.* M. DCC. LXXVIII. 8vo, pp. xxiv, 392. H. 24117

A supplement to our No. 24112, *supra*.

[Fermin.] An Historical and Political View of the Present and Ancient State of the Colony of Surinam, in South America; with the settlements of Demerary and Issequibo; Together with an account of its Produce for twenty-five Years past. By a Person who lived there ten Years. *London: W. Nicoll.* 1781. 8vo, pp. 149. 24118

A translation from the "Tableau Historique." *See* No. 24117, and "M. Rev.," LXVI. 148.

Fermin. Nieuwe algemeene beschryving van de colonie van Suriname. Behelzende et het merkwaardige van deselve, met betrekkinge tot de historie, aardryks — en natuurkunde. *Harlingen: Ter Drukkerye van V. van der Plaats Junior.* 1770. 2 vols., 8vo, xx l., pp. 228, Map; pp. 323, Table 3 l., 3 Plates. + 2de druk. *Amsterdam.* 1785. 2 vols., 8vo. 24119

Fermin. Reise durch Surinam. Aus dem Französischen übersetzt. ... *Potsdam: Carl Christian Horvath.* 1782. 2 vols., 8vo, 4 l., pp. 246; 336, 25 l. 1 Map and 2 Plates. C. 24120

Also: Remarques sur le tableau historique et politique de Surinam, de M. Fermin. *Amsterdam.* 1779. 8vo.

Fermin. Traité des Maladies de plus fréquentes à Surinam, et des remèdes les plus propres à les guérir. Suivi d'une dissertation sur le Fameux Crapaud de Surinam, nommé Pipa, et sur sa génération en particulier, avec Figures en Tailledouce. Par M. Phelippe Fermin. *Maestricht: Jacques Lekens.* 1764. 12mo, viii l, pp. 157. 2 Plates. + *Amsterdam.* 1765. 12mo. Plates.

Also: Développement parfait du mystère de la génération du fameux crapaud de Surinam, Nommé Pipa, par Philippe Fermin ... . *Maestricht: Jacques Lekens.* M. DCC. LXV. 8vo, 3 l., pp. 75, (1). 4 Plates. H.

Fermin (del Rey). Hernan Cortez en Tobasco, por Fermin del Rey. 1622. 24122

A play. *See* Ternaux, No. 443.

Fern (Fanny), *pseudonym.* *See* Parton (*Mrs.* P. S.)

[Fernagus de Gelone.] Manual Guide des Voyageurs aux Etats-Unis de l'Amérique du Nord, ou l'on trouve tous les renseignements necessaires et fondés sur des faits pour y commercer avec sureté et profit, pour s'y établir avec avantage dans toutes sortes de situations; ouvrage dans lequel on combat quelques opinions erronées répandues en Europe sur ces pays et ou l'on presente quelques idées simples et pratiques sur l'État politique actuel et l'avenir probable de la Floride Orientale, des Iles sous le vent et de toutes les Colonies ou anciens domaines de la couronne d'Espagne: addressé particulièrement aux commerçans, aux agriculteurs et aux personnes de toutes les métiers sur le continent de l'Europe. Par M. F. D. G——., Americain Naturalisé ancien élève ingénieur. *Paris.* 1818. 12mo, 8½ sheets. P. 24123

[Fernagus de Gelone.] Relation de la Déportation et de l'Exil à Cayenne d'un jeune Français sous le Consulat de Buonaparte, en 1802. *Paris.* 1816. 8vo. P. 24124

Fernambuco. *See* Pernambuco.

Fernand (Jacques). John Brown Mort pour l'Affranchisement des Noires Emancipation graduelle — Oswald — États-Unis ... . *Paris.* 1861. 16mo, pp. 107. C., H. 24125

Fernand-Michel. Dix-huit ans chez les sauvages; voyages et missions de Mgr. Henry Faraud, évêque d'Anemour, vicaire apostolique de Mackensie, dans l'extrême nord de l'Amérique britannique, d'après les documents de Mgr. l'évêque d'Anemour; avec la biographie et le portrait de Mgr. Faraud. *Paris: Ruffet et Cie.* 1865. 8vo. 24126

Fernand-Michel. Dix-huit ans chez les sauvages, voyages et missions dans l'extrême nord de l'Amérique britannique, d'après les documents de Mgr Henry Faraud, évêque d'Anemour. *Paris: Ruffet.* 1870. 18mo, pp. xix, 364. 24127

Fernandez (A.) Historia | eclesiastica | de nvestros | tiempos, qve es | compendio de los ex- | celentes frvtos que en ellos el estado | Eclesiastico y sagradas Religiones han hecho y hazen, en la conuersion de idola- | tras y reducion de hereges, Y de los ilustres martirios de varones | Apostolicos, que en estas heroicas empressas | han padecido. | Por el P. F. Alonso Fernandez, | de la Orden de santo Domingo ... | [4 lines, Engraving, 1 line.] | *En Toledo, Por la viuda de Pedro Rodriguez* | ... 1611. | Folio, 4 l., pp. 496. H. 24128

A large portion of this interesting and rare volume relates to Guatemala and Yucatan, and Mexico, and gives an account of the earliest printed books in the Indian languages. Sold at Puttick's, in 1860, for £2 5s.

Fernandez (A F. de L.) Imposto sobre os vencimentos. Decreto N. 3977 de 12 de Octubre de 1867 que regula a cobrança do imposto de tres por cento sobre os vencimentos com todas as circulares, avisos, instrucções, portarias e modelos, não só de governo geral, mas tambem do provincial, que tem havido atá hoje. Collecionado por Antonio Ferreira de Lara Fernandes. *Rio de Janeiro.* 1868. 8vo, pp. 36. 24129

Fernandez (Benito). Doctrina christiana en lengua mixteca. *Mexico.* 1550. 4to. 24130

An elaborate and learned disquisition, by Señor Icazbalceta, concerning this volume, which is one of the rarest books in existence, no known copy being to be "found in any public or private library in America, or in Europe," will be found in [Harrisse's] "Bibl. Am. Vetust.," p. 445–450. *See also* Ternaux, No. 56, Brunet, Vol. II., and Græsse, Vol. I.

Fernandez. [Another Edition. Colophon.] A gloria y ala | bança de Nuestro Redẽp | tor Iesu Christo, y de su | vendita Madre Sancta | Maria, y prouecho de- | los proximos. Aqui se aca | ba la Doctrina en lengua | misteca: compuesta por el | muy Reuerando Padre | fray Benito Hernandez | Vicario prouincial de la | Misteca de la orden de | los Predicadores en esta nueua España. *Fue im- | pressa en Mexico en casa | de Pedro Ocharte | impresor de libros | acabose a 22. de | Nouiembre.* | *de* 1567. | *años.* | *Laus Deo.* | 4to, clxxxix leaves. 24131

Fernandez. [Another Edition. Colophon.] A gloria y alabança de nuestro Re- | dẽptor Iesu Xpo. Aqui se acaba la Doctrĩa Xpia | na en lengua Misteca: cõpuesta por el muy R. | padre fray Benito Hernandez. *Fue impre* | *ssa en Mexico, en casa de Pedro O-* | *charte, impressor de libros. A-* | *cabose, a veynte y quatro* | *dias d'l mes d' Enero d'* | 1568. *Años.* | 4to, folios II and cc.

Consult also Icazbalceta's catalogue, Nos. 106–107. These other editions are almost equally rare with that of 1550. The only known copy that we can trace is that of Señor Icazbalceta's in Mexico.

Fernandez (D.) Primera [y segunda] parte, de la historia de Peru que se mando escrivir a Diego Fernandez. Contiene la primera lo succedido en la Nueva España y en el Peru, sobre la execucion de las nuevas leyes, y e allanamiento, y castigo, que hizo el presidente Gasca, de Gonçalo Piçarro y sus sequaces. La segunda contiene la tyrannia y alçamiento de los

Contreras, y Don Sebastian de Castilla con otros muchos acaescimientos y successos. *Sevilla: en Casa de Hernando Diaz.* 1571. 2 vols., folio, 4 l., 142 l.; 130 l. 24133

This work was forbidden to be circulated, and ordered to be destroyed by the Council of the Indies. *See* the "Biblioteca Oriental" of Leon Pinelo, also Brunet.

Fernandez (J.) Sermon que se hizo en Mextitlan de la Sierra alta el 8 de Enero con motivo de la jura de obediencia a nuestra emperador D. Augustino I. *Mexico.* 1823. 4to, 10 leaves. 24134

Fernandez (J. P.) Relacion | Historical | de las missiones de los | Indios, que llaman Chiquitos, que es- | tàn à cargo de los Padres de la Compa- | ñia de Jesvs de la Provincia del | Paraguay. | Escrita | Por el Padre Juan Patricio Fernandez, de la misma | Compañia. | Sacade a luz | Por el Padre Geronimo Herràn ... | [4 lines.] | Año 1726. | ... | *En Madrid: Por Manuel Fernandez* ... | ... | Sm. 4to, pp. 452, (3). C., H. 24135

The original edition of this interesting work. *See* "Bibliotheca Grenvilliana." There is an extract from his "Relacion" in the "Lettres édificantes et curieuses," *Paris.* 1839, II. 153–168. This highly esteemed work was printed fifty-four years after the death of the author, who was one of the most zealous and active missionaries among the Chiquito Indians of Paraguay. It contains interesting details concerning this large tribe, as well as of the tribes adjacent. Father Fernandez died in 1672, just as he was making arrangements for founding a mission in the Grand Chaco.

Fernandez. Relazione Istorica della Nuova Christianità degl' Indiani detti Chichiti scritta in Spagnuola, ... e tradotta in Italiano da Gio. Battista Memmi ambidue della compagnia di Gesù. Coll' aggiunta d'un 'Indice delle cose più notabili. *In Roma: per Antonio de Rossi.* MDCCXXIX. 4to, 5 l., pp. 233, Table, 5 l. 24136

Fernandez. Historica relatio de Apostolicis Missionibus patrum soc. Jes. apud Chiquitos, a P. Joan Patricio Fernandez, anno 1726, Paraquaria populos ... hodie in linguam latinam primo hispano idomate conscripta translata ab alio ejusdem soc. Jes. sacerdote. *Augustæ Vindelacorum: M. Wolff.* 1733. 4to, 19 l., pp. 276, 9 l. 24137

Fernandez. Erbauliche und angenehme Geschichten derer Chiquitos, samt einem ausführlichen Bericht von dem Amazonen-Strom. *Wien.* 1729. 8vo. 24138

Fernandez. Manuel arreglado al ritual romano, para el uso reformado de los Religiosos Franciscos Descalzos de la Mexicana provincia de San Diego. *Mexico.* 1748. 4to. 24139

Fernandez (Mariano). Baluartes de México, description historica de las Cuatro Milagrosas Imágines de Nuestra Señora, que se veneran en la Ciudad de México. *Mejico.* 1820. 4to.

Fernandez Cuesta (N.) Nuevo Viajero universal. Enciclopedia de viajes modernos, etc. *Madrid.* 1859–1862. 5 vols., 4to. Plates. 24141

Fernandez de Cordoba (M.) Discursos pronunciados en Mexico el 16 de Setiembre de 1863 por Manuel Fernandez de Cordoba. *Mexico.* 1863. 8vo. 24142

Fernandez de Cordova (D. Felipe Colmenares). El dia deseado. Relacion de la Solemnidad con que se estrenó la Iglesia del Santo Cristo de los Milagros, patron jurado por esta ciudad contra los temblores de que es amenazada, y titular del monasterio de Nazarenas Carmelitas Descalzas del señor San Joachin, ecc. *Lima: officina de la Calle de San Jacinto.* 1771. 4to, 10 l., pp. 58. 24143

Fernandez de Madrid (D. J.) Memoria sobre el comercio, cultivo y elaboration del tabaco da esta isla. Por el Dr. D. J. Fernandez de Madrid. *Habana.* 1821. Sm. 4to, pp. 18, 19.

Fernandez de San Salvador (A. P.) La America llorando por la temprana muerte de su amado, su padre, su bien y sus delicias el Señor B. de Galvez, gobernador de Nueva España. *Mexico.* 1787. 4to, 3 l., pp. 25. + *Mexico.* 1787. 4to, 16 l.

Fernandez de San Salvador. Desengaños que a los insurgentes de N. España seducidos por los fracmazones agentes de Napoleon, dirige la Verdad de la religion catolica y la experencia. Escritos por el Dr. D. Agustin Pomposo Fernandez de San Salvador. *Mexico.* 1812. Sm. 8vo, pp. 162. 24146

Fernandez de San Salvador. Los Jesuitas, quitados y restituidos al mundo. Historia de la Antigua California. Por el Dr. D. Augustin Pomposo Fernandez de San Salvador. *Mexico: Mariana Ontiveros.* 1816. 16mo, 5 l., pp. 213. 24147

At the end of this most curious book, written for the glorification of the Jesuits in California, is a list of the persons to whom it has been distributed, according to which only a very few copies have been sold.

Fernandez de San Salvador. El modelo de los cristianos presentado á los insurgentes de América, y una introduccion ... en la qual se funta el derecho de la soberania propia e Fernando VII, etc. *Mexico.* 1814. 8vo. 24148

Fernandez de Santa Cruz (M.) Octava Maravilla del Nuevo Mundo en la Gran Capilla del Rosario. Por Manuel Fernandez de Santa Cruz, Obispo de la Puebla. *Puebla: por de Fernandez de Leon.* 1690. 4to. 24149

Fernandez de Santa Cruz. Regla de S. Augustin, que han de guardar las religiosas del convento del maximo doct. S. Geronimo de la Puebla de los Angeles. Con las de ordenanças, y constituciones [del convento]. *Puebla: herederos J. de Villa Real.* 1701. 8vo, pp. 46, 21, C. 24150

Fernandez de Suosa (J. de Dios). Carta consolatorio a la Ciudad de Guanajuato en la sensible Muerte de su Zeloso Apostol el Padre Rector Ignacio Raphael Coromina. Su Author el Dr. Don Juan de Dios Fernandez de Suosa. *Mexico: Impressa en el Real, y mas Antiguo Colegio de S. Ildefonso.* 1764. Sm. 4to, pp. 38, 210. Portrait of Coromina. 24151

Fernandez de Uribe (J. P. de). Solemnes exequias de D. Matias de Galvez, Virey del Reyno de Nueva España, celebradas en la Iglesia Catedral de Mexico en los dias 4. y 5. de Marzo de 1785. *Mexico.* 1785. Con dos oraciones funebres. Folio, pp. 31, 23, 42. Portrait. 24152

Fernandez y Gonzalez (M. Amparo). Memorias de un loco. *Mexico.* 1864. 8vo. 24153

Also: Obispo, casada y rey. Leyenda historica. *Mexico.* 1862. 8vo. — Historia de un hombre con contada por su esqueleto. *Mexico.* 1861. 2 vols., 12mo. — La cabeza del rey Don Pedro. Tradicion historica original. *Mexico.* 1862. 8vo.

Fernando VI. Augusto Iluminado, justa Literaria Palestra Metrica ... la Coronacion de Fernando VI. Rey de las España, y Emperador de este Nuevo Mundo. *Mexico.* 1747. 24154

Fernando VI. Consudos Funerales, que la Ciudad de Antequera Ministre à la Catholica Magested en Señ. D. Fernando VI. Emperador de las Indias, en las dos Oraciones Funebres, en las Exequias de sú Esposa, la Señora Dona Maria Barbara de Portugal. *Imprenta de la Bibliotheca Mexicana.* 1759. 4to. 24155

Fernando VI. El Iris Diadema Immortal. Descripcion de los Festivos aplausos conque celebró la Feliz Elevacion al Trono de N. Rey del Fernando VI. Emperador de las Indias. El Real Tribunal del Protomedicato de esta Nueva España. A direcion del Fidelissimo zelo del D. N. J. Torres Escribiala, por D. J. G. de Campos y Martinez. 24156

Prose and verse, with curious plates of emblems.

Fernando VI. Festivas Aclamaciones de la Ciudad de Mexico. El Sol en Leon Solemnes aplausos conque, el Rey N. S. D. Fernando VI. Sol de las Españas, fué celebrado el dia 11 Febrero del Año de 1747. Por J. M. de Abarça, y J. F. de Cuevas, Aguirre, y Espinosa. *Mexico.* 1748. 4to. 24157

Fernando VII. Copia de la Representacion al Rey N. S. Don Fernando VII. por el Cabildo y Ayuntamiento de la Ciudad de Santa Fe, en el Nuevo Reino de Granada. *Mexico.* 1820. 4to, pp. 12. 24158

Fernando VII. Decretos expedidos desde su restitucion al trone español hasta el restablecimiento de la constitucion de 1812. *Megico.* 1836. 4to. 24159

Fernan (—), *and* Heydefuss. Die gesammten Vereinigten Staaten von Nord-Amerika. Vollstandiges Hand- und Reisebuch ... . *Berlin: Sacco.* [1854.] 8vo, 1 l., pp. 532. Map.

Ferrall (S. A.) A Ramble of Six Thousand Miles through the United States of America. By S. A. Ferrall, Esq. *London: Effingham Wilson.* 1832. 8vo, pp. xii, 360. Facsimile of a Cherokee Phœnix Newspaper. 24161

Ferrar (A. S.) Alexandri Sardi Ferrariensis, De moribus ac ritibus gentium libr. III omni rerum varietate referti iterum impressi. — ejusd. de Rerum inventorum libr. II &c. *Moguntia.* 1577. 24162

Ferrari (F.) Novum Lexicon Geographicum, Michael Antonivs Bavdrand auctiorem fecit. Accesserunt Dominici Magri Appendices & Correctiones. *Isenaci.* M.DC.LXXVII. Folio, pp. (10), 539, (2), 484, (22). B. 24163

Under "America," this lexicon gives a list of the countries described.

Ferrario (G.) Il Costume antico e moderno, o Storia del Governo, della Milizia, della Religione, delle Arti, Scienze ed Usanze di tutti i popoli antichi e moderni provata coi Monumenti dell' Antichitá ... Aggiunte e Rettificazione all' Opera. *Milano.* 1815–1834. 21 vols., folio. A. 24164

Vols. XVI.–XVII. relate to America; XXI.–XXII. Supplement to America and Europe. There is also an edition, *Firenze.* 1828–37. 34 vols., 8vo. Also, *Napoli.* 1831–32. 21 vols., 8vo.

Ferraz (L. P. de C.) Relatorio apresentado á assembléa geral legislativa na quarta sessão da nona legislatura pelo ministro e secret. d'estado dos negocios do imperio Luiz Pedreira de Coutto Ferraz. *Rio de Janeiro: typografia Nacional.* 1856. 4to, pp. 98, 52, (11). 2 Tables. 24165

[Also], for 1857, 528 pages in all.

FERREIRA (A. J. D.) O Infeliz Banqueiro Antonio José Domingues Ferreira, Justificado perante a Opinao publica. *Rio de Janeiro.* 1867. 16mo, pp. 36. 24166

FERREIRA E SOUZA (B. A.) Relaçao dos festejos, que a feliz acclamaçao do muito alto, muito poderoso, e fidelissimo Senhor D. João VI. rei do Reino Unido de Portugal, Brasil, e Algarves, como respeito votarao os habitantes do Rio de Janeiro. Seguido das poesias dedicadas ao mesmo Venerando Objecto, collegida por Bernardo Avellino Ferreira e Souza. *Rio de Janeiro: typographia real.* 1818. 4to, pp. 52, (2). 24167

FERREIRA (E.) Chrestomathia de Lingua Brazilica. Pelo Dr. Ernesto Ferreira França. *Leipzig.* 1859. 12mo, pp. xviii, 230. 24168

FERREIRA (M. J.) Promptuario eleitoral. Compilaçao alphabetica e chronologica das leis, decretos, e avisos sobre materia de eleiçoes, etc., organisada por Manoel Jesuino Ferreira. *Rio de Janeiro.* 1866. 8vo, pp. 520. 24169

FERREIRA (R.) Rejistro nacional de la Republica Argentina. Compilado por Ramon Ferreira. [1851–61.] *Buenos-Aires.* 1863–64. 3 vols., 4to, pp. xxxviii, 1060; 940; 892. 24170

FERREIRA (Silvestre Pinheiro). Breves observaçães sobre o tractado concluido em 1826; entre Suas Magestades o Imperador do Brasil e o Rei de França. *Lisboa.* 1845. 8vo. 24171

FERREIRA. Indicações de utilidade publica, offerecidas ás Assembléas legislativas do Brasil e de Portugal. *Paris: Cassimir.* 1834. 12mo, pp. vi, 56. 24172

FERREIRA DA SILVA (S.) Relaciõ|do sitio,|que o|governador de Buenos Aires|D. Miguel de Salcedo pox no anno de 1735 a Praça|da|Nova Colonia|do Sacramento,|Sendo Governador da mesma Praça Antonio Pedro de Vascon-|cellos, Brigadeiro dos Exercitos de S. Magestade;|Com algumas Plantas necessarias para a intelligencia de mes-|ma Relaçiõ.| [3 lines] |por|Silvestre Ferreira|da Sylva,| [2 lines.] *Lisboa:*|(11) *Na Officina de Francisco Luiz Ameno,*| ... | M. DCC. XLVIII.| ... | 4to, 4 l., pp. 107. 2 Plates and 3 Maps. H., J.C.B. 24173

FERRER (Jaime). Sentencias cathólicas del Divi poeta Dant. *Barcelona.* MDXLV. 24174

Concerning this, and how little it relates to America, *see* [Harrisse's] "Bibl. Am. Vet.," page 406.

FERRER DE COUTO (José). America y España consideradas en sus intereses de raza, ante la republica de los Estados Unidos del Norte. *Cadiz.* 1859. 4to, pp. 156. 24175

FERRER DE COUTO. Comentarios sobre le cuestion de Mejico. [n. p. n. d.] 4to, pp. 48. 24176

FERRER DE COUTO. Cuestiones de Méjico, Venezuela, y América en general. *Madrid.* 1861. 4to, pp. 660. 24177

FERRER DE COUTO. ... The Question of Slavery Conclusively and Satisfactorily solved as regards humanity at large, and the Permanent Interests of Present Owners. *New York: S. Hallett.* 1864. 8vo, pp. 312. + [*Ibid.*] 1865. 8vo, pp. 312. 24178

FERRER (M. R.) El Tabaco Habano. Por M. R. Ferrer. *Madrid.* 1851. 12mo. A. 24179

FERRI-PISANI (M. V. P. C.) Lettres sur États-Unis d'Amérique. *Paris: Hachette et Cie.* 1862. 18mo. C. 24180

FERRIE (A.) Appendix to Captain Synge's Pamphlet, entitled "Canada in 1848, &c. ..." Being a Letter to Earl Grey, by the Hon. Adam Ferrie. *Montreal.* 1847. 8vo, pp. 7. 24181

FERRIN (M. U.) Woman's Defence: a Reply to Horace Greeley's Lecture, ... in Providence, R. I. Written by Mary Upton Ferrin. ... *Peabody: Charles D. Howard.* 1869. 8vo, pp. 16. H. 24182

FERRIS (B.) A History of the Original Settlements on the Delaware, from its Discovery by Hudson to the Colonization under William Penn. To which is added an Account of the Ecclesiastical Affairs of the Swedish Settlers, and a History of Wilmington, from its First Settlement to the Present Time. Illustrated by Drawings. By Benjamin Ferris. ... *Wilmington: Wilson & Heald.* 1846. 8vo, pp. 312. Maps, 2 Plans, and 4 Plates. H. 24183

FERRIS (B. G.) Utah and the Mormons. — The History, Government, Doctrines, Customs, and Prospects of the Latter-Day Saints. From Personal Observation during a Six Months' Residence at Great Salt Lake City. By Benjamin G. Ferris, late Secretary of Utah Territory. *New York: Harper & Brothers.* 1854. 12mo, pp. 347. Woodcuts. H. 24184

[FERRIS (*Mrs.* B. G.)] Female Life among the Mormons. A Narrative of many Years' Personal Experiences. By the Wife of a Mormon Elder, recently from Utah. *New York: J. C. Derby.* 1855. 12mo, pp. x, 9–449. Plate. 24185

FERRIS. The Mormons at Home; With some Incidents of Travel from Missouri to California, 1852–53. In a Series of Letters. By Mrs. B. G. Ferris. *New York.* 1856. 12mo, pp. viii, 299. C., H. 24186

Also issued with the title: "The Mormons at Home; or, a Residence at the Great Salt Lake City. By Mrs. G. B. Ferris. ... *New York.*" 12mo.

FERRIS (C. G.) Speech of ... Charles G. Ferris ... February 3, 1835, on ... repealing the Duty on Foreign Coal. *Washington.* 1835. 8vo, pp. 7. H. 24187

FERRIS (D.) Trial of Captain David Ferris before a Court of Inquiry for Misconduct. *New York.* 1808. 8vo. 24188

FERRIS. Memoirs of the Life of David Ferris, An Approved Minister of the Society of Friends: Late of Wilmington ... . *Philadelphia: John Simmons.* 1825. 12mo, pp. 99. + *York.* 1825. 12mo, pp. 136. 24189

FERRIS (J.) A Discourse, in Commemoration of the Life and Character of the late George W. Bethune, D.D., ... By Isaac Ferris. *New York.* [1862.] 8vo, pp. 48. 24190

FERRIS. The Duties of the Times: Preached on the National Thanksgiving, August 6, 1863 ... By Isaac Ferris, D.D. ... *New York: John A. Gray & Green, Printers.* 1863. 8vo, pp. 24. H.

Address at the Funeral of Lieut. Col. A. R. Thompson, of the United States army, delivered May 25, 1838 ... *New York.* 1838. 8vo. — Address Delivered 27th April, 1839, at the Opening of the Rutgers Female Institute, New York. ... . *New York: printed by William Osborn.* 1839. 8vo, pp. 24. H. — Address ... at the Opening of the Law Department of the University of the City of New York ... 25th October, 1858. ... . *New York.* 1858. 8vo, pp. 31. H. — Jubilee Memorial of the American Bible Society; being a Review of its first Fifty Years' Work. ... *New York.* 1867 8vo. — Semi-Centennial Memorial Discourse of the New York Sunday School Union, delivered on the 25th of February, 1866 ... *New York.* 1866. 12mo, pp. 120. — Sermon ... Characteristics of the Reformed Dutch Church. *New York.* 1848. 12mo.

FERRIS (J.) The States and Territories of the Great West; including Ohio, Indiana, Illinois, Missouri, Michigan, Wisconsin, Iowa, Minesota, Kansas, and Nebraska; their Geography, History, Advantages, Resources, and Prospects; comprising their Local History, Institutions, and Laws. Giving a Table of Distances, and the most Direct Routes and Modes of Conveyance; also, pointing out the best Districts for Agriculture, Commercial,

Lumbering, and Mining Operations. With a Map and numerous Illustrations. By Jacob Ferris. *New York and Auburn: Miller, Orton, and Mulligan.* 1856. 12mo, pp. 352. C. 24192

FERRIS (J. A.) The Financial Economy of the United States Illustrated; and some of the causes which Retard the Progress of California. By John A. Ferris. *San Francisco: A. Roman & Co.* 1867. 12mo, pp. 356. Plate. 24193

FERRIS (O.) Purchase of Alaska. Speech of Hon. Orange Ferris ... in the House of Representatives, July 1, 1868. [*Washington.* 1868.] 8vo, pp. 12. H. 24194

FERRUFINO (J. B.) Relacion del martirio de los Padres Roque Gonçalez de Santa Cruz, Alonso Rodriguez, Juan del Castillo, de la Compañia de Jesvs. Padecido En el Paraguay, a 16 de Noviembre de 1628. Por Juan Baptista Ferufino, Procurador general de la Provincia del Paraguay. [*Madrid: Imprenta Real.* 1629?] 4to, 29 l. 24195

"Cette pièce fort rare n'est pas citée dans la bibliothèque des PP. de Backer et Pinelo ne l'indique que manuscrite, dans la bibliothèque du Roi." — LECLERC.

FERRY (G.), *pseudonym.* *See* Bellemare, Vol. II., Nos. 4518, 4523, and 4524.

FERRY (G.) Escenas de la vida militar en Mexico. Escrita en Francés [y] trad. *Mexico.* 1853. 12mo. 24196

FERRY (I.) La California, descrizione geografica, politica e morale. *Venezia.* 1851. 8vo. 24197

FERRY. Description de la Nouvelle-Californie géographique, politique et morale, contenant l'historique de la découverte de cette contrée, etc. *Paris: Maison.* 1850. 12mo, pp. 386. 7 Plates and 1 Map. 24198

FERRY (O. S.) Reconstruction. Speech of the Hon. Orris S. Ferry ... delivered in the Senate ... February 3, 1868. *Washington.* 1868. 8vo, pp. 15. H. 24199

FERRY (T. W.) Duty on Lumber paid by Canadians — Folly of Repeal. Speech of Hon. Thomas W. Ferry ... in the House ... May 24, 1870. *Washington.* 1870. 8vo, pp. 15. H. 24200

Also: Speech ... delivered ... February 10, 1860. [*Washington.* 1860.] 8vo, pp. 7. H.

The Ferry Boy. *See* [Trowbridge (J. T.)]

FÉRUSSAC (André E. J. P. J. F. d'Audebard, *le Baron de*). Observat. sur la synonymie des coquilles bivalves de l'Amérique septentrionale, etc. *Paris.* 1835. 8vo, pp. 36. 24201

FESCOURT (—). Histoire de la double conspiration de 1800, contre le gouvernement consulaire, et de la déportation, qui eut lieu dans la deuxième année du consulat: contenant des détails authentiques et curieux sur la machine infernale et sur les déportés, ... *Paris: Guillaume & Cie.* 1819. 8vo, 2 l., pp. xii, 330. 2 Maps. C. 24202

FESSENDEN (B.) ... Sermon at the Ordination of Rev. Samuel Tobey, Berkley, Nov. 23, 1737. By Rev. Benjamin Fessenden. *Boston.* 1739. 16mo, pp. 66. M. 24203

FESSSENDEN (C. P.) Oration at Conway [N. H.], July 4, 1798. By Caleb Page Fessenden. *Fryeburg, Me.* 1798. 8vo.

FESSENDEN (G. M.) A Genealogical Memoir of the Descendants of William Bradford, second Governor of New Plymouth, in New England. Principally Collected by Guy M. Fessenden. ... *Boston: Printed by Coolidge & Wiley.* 1850. 8vo, pp. 27. B., S. 24205

FESSENDEN (G. M.) The History of Warren, Rhode Island, from the Earliest Times, with particular Notices of Massasoit and his Family. By G. M. Fessenden. *Providence: H. H. Brown.* 1845. 18mo, pp. 125. 24206

See Tustin (J. P.) *See also* Vol. II., No. 6768, *note.*

FESSENDEN (J. M.) Report on the Surveys and Definite Location of the Eastern Railroad. By John M. Fessenden ... . *Boston: Freeman and Bolles, Printers.* 1836. 8vo, pp. 18.

FESSENDEN (Samuel). An Address, ... at the Annual Communication of the Grand Lodge of Maine, January 28, 1830 ... . *Portland: Shirley & Hyde.* 1830. 12mo, pp. 11. H. 24208

FESSENDEN (S. C.) The Issues of United States Notes, Feb. 12, 1862. [n. p. n. d.] 8vo, pp. 15. 24209

Also: Issues of the Rebellion. Speech ... in House of Representatives, January 20, 1862. *Washington.* 1862. 8vo, pp. 8. H. — Speech ... on the Abolition of Slavery in the District of Colûmbia. ... April 1, 1862. [n. p. n. p.] 8vo, pp. 8.

FESSENDEN. Selections from the Sermons, Addresses, etc., of S. C. Fessenden. *New York: W. P. Tomlinson.* 12mo, pp. 267. Portrait. 24210

FESSENDEN (T.) Sermon delivered July 4, 1802. *Walpole, N. H.* 1802. 8vo, pp. 31. 24211

Also: [Masonic] Sermon at Keene, N. H. June 24, 1789. 8vo.

[FESSENDEN (Thomas Green).] Democracy Unveiled; or, Tyranny stripped of the Garb of Patriotism. By Christopher Caustic, L. L. D. &c. ... . *Boston: David Carlisle.* 1805. 12mo, pp. viii, 220. + Second Edition. *Boston: the Author.* 1805. 12mo, pp. viii, 220. H. + Third Edition, with Large Additions. *New-York.* 1806. 2 vols., 12mo, pp. 179; 238. C.

[FESSENDEN.] The Modern Philosopher; or Terrible Tractoration! In Four Cantos, most respectfully addressed to the Royal College of Physicians, London. By Christopher Caustick, M.D., A.S.S., Fellow of the Royal College of Physicians, Aberdeen, and Honorary Member of no less than Nineteen very Learned Societies. *Philadelphia.* 1806. 8vo. 24213

A defence of Perkins's metallic tractors. For other editions, *see* No. 24218, *infra.*

FESSENDEN. Original Poems. By Thomas Green Fessenden, Esq. ... . *Philadelphia: E. Bronson.* 1806. 12mo, pp. xii, 203. H. + *London: Hurst.* Cr. 8vo, pp. 100. 24214

See "M. Rev.," XLVII. 103.

FESSENDEN. Register of Arts; or, a Compendious View of some of the most Useful Modern Discoveries and Inventions. *Philadelphia.* 1808. 8vo, pp. 404. C. 24215

With an appendix, giving a list of American patentees from 1790 to 1804.

FESSENDEN. Reply to Strictures on Fessenden's Essay on the Law of Patents for New Inventions. [*Boston.* 1823.] 8vo, pp. 7.

An answer to a severe criticism in the "N. Am. Rev.," XVI. 199.

FESSENDEN. Some Thoughts on the Present Dispute between Great Britain and America. By Thomas Green Fessenden. *Philadelphia.* 1807. 8vo, pp. 91. 24217

[FESSENDEN.] Terrible Tractoration!! A Poetical Petition against Galvanizing Trumpery, and the Perkinistic Institution. In Four Cantos. Most Respectfully addressed to the Royal College of Physicians, by Christopher Caustic, M.D., LL.D., A.S.S., etc. *London.* 1803. 12mo. Frontispiece. + Second Edition. *London.* 1803. 12mo. + First American, From the Second London Edition, Revised and Corrected by the Author, with Additional Notes. *New York: Samuel Stansbury.* 1804. 12mo, pp. xxxv, 192. 24218

[FESSENDEN.] Terrible Tractoration! Second American Edition, Revised, Corrected, and much Enlarged, by the Author. *Philadelphia: E. Bronson.* 1806. 8vo, pp. xxxii, 271. + Third American Edition. *Boston: Russell, Shattuck & Co.* 1836. 16mo, pp. viii, 264. Plate. + Fourth American Edition. To which is prefixed, Caustic's Wooden Booksellers and Miseries of Authorship. *Boston.* 1837. 12mo. 24219

FESSENDEN. The Weekly Inspector: Aug. 30, 1806, to Aug. 22, 1807. *New York.* 2 vols., 8vo. 24220

The first publication established to advocate the modern know-nothing principles. *See* Duyckinck's "Cyclopædia." Also: Address ... before the Charlestown Temperance Society, Jan. 31, 1831. ... *Charlestown: William W. Wheildon.* 1831. 8vo, pp. 46. H., M. — The American Kitchen Gardener, ... Revised from the Thirty-Fifth Edition ... By a Practical Gardener. *New York.* 1852. — The Complete Farmer and Rural Economist. Fifth Edition. ... *Boston.* 1840. 12mo. — Essay on the Law of Patents and New Inventions, ... *Boston.* 1810. 8vo. + Second Edition. *Boston.* 1822. 8vo, pp. 425. — The Ladies' Monitor, A Poem. *Bellows Falls, Vermont: Blake & Co.* 1818. 12mo, pp. 180. — The New American Gardener. ... *Boston.* 1828. 12mo. + Sixth Edition. *Boston: Carter and Hendee, and John B. Russell.* 1832. 12mo, pp. 306, (1). H. + *Philadelphia.* 1839. 12mo, pp. 306. + *Boston.* 1842. 12mo. — New-England Farmer's Almanack, for 1828. *Boston.* 8vo. Continued. — Practical Farmer, and Silk Manual. *Boston.* 1835. 8vo.

[FESSENDEN (William).] The Political Farrago, or a Miscellaneous Review of the Politics of the United States, from the Administration of Washington, to that of Mr. Jefferson, in 1806, including a Short History of the "Pittsburgh Insurrection," Remarks on the "Louisiana Purchase," Mammoth Cheese," Federalism and Republicanism, Atheism and Deism, Illuminism and Witchcraftism, &c., &c., &c., &c., by Peter Dobbins, Esq., R. C. U. S. A., First Edition, with privilege of Copyright. *Brattleboro', Vt.* 1807. pp. 59. W. 24221

I have seen a catalogue in which the "Biographical Memoir of George Washington" (*Brattleborough.* 1814) is attributed to W. Fessenden.

FESSENDEN (W. P.) Speech of W. P. Fessenden, ... against The Repeal of the Missouri Prohibition, North of 36° 30′ ... on the Senate ... March 3, 1854, on the Bill to Establish Territorial Governments in Nebraska and Kansas. [*Washington.* 1854.] 8vo, pp. 16. 24222

Also: Report of the Joint Committee on Reconstruction. ... [*Washington.* 1865?] 8vo, pp. 16. (Signed by W. P. Fessenden and 8 others.) H. — Final Report of the Congressional Committee upon the Question of Reconstruction, ... [*Washington.* 1865.] 8vo, pp. 24. H. — Speech ... on the Bankrupt Bill. ... August 11, 1841. *Washington.* 1841. 8vo, pp. 15. H. — Speech ... upon the Army Appropriation Bill ... May 31, 1842. *Washington.* 1842. 8vo, pp. 16. H. — Speech ... on the President's Message; ... Dec. 4, 1856. *Washington.* 1856. 8vo, pp. 16. H. —

Speech ... on the Issue of United States Notes. ... February 12, 1862. [*Washington.* 1862.] 8vo, pp. 15. H. — Speech ... on the Message of the President, transmitting the Lecompton Constitution ... February 8, 1858. *Washington.* 1858. 8vo, pp. 24. H.

FESSENDEN. Memorial Addresses on W. P. Fessenden, in the Senate and House of Representatives, Dec. 14, 1869. *Washington.* 1870. 8vo, pp. 82. B. 24223

Festival. *See* Connecticut, Vol. IV., No. 15738. *See also* Pilgrim Society, New Hampshire, and Virgil, N. Y.

FEUILLÉE (L.) Journal|des observations|physiques,|mathematiques|et botaniques,|Faites par l'ordre du Roy sur les Côtes Orientales|de l'Amérique Meridionale, & dans les Indes|Occidentales,|depuis l'année 1707. jusques en 1712.|Par le R. P. Louis Feuillée ... . | *Paris: Pierre Giffart.* M. DCC. XIV.–XXV. 3 vols., 4to, 8 l., pp. 504; 4 l., pp. 503–767, (1); 2 l., pp. xxix, (1), 426, (4), xlviii, (1), 71, (5). Maps and 103 Plates. H.

"Not elegant in style, but valuable for solid information upon all the subjects announced in its title, with various incidental matter besides. What relates to Peru makes a principal part of these volumes." — CHALMERS.

FEUILLÉE. Journal | des | Observations | Physiques, Mathematiques, et Botaniques,|fait par l'ordre du Roi sur les Côtes Orientales|de l'Amérique Meriodinale, & aux Indes Occidentales; et dans une autre Voyage par le mème auteur à la Nouvelle Espagne, & aux Isles de l'Amérique. Par le R. P. Louis Feuillée ... *Paris: Jean Mariette.* 1725. 4to, pp. (2), xlix, (4), xxxix, (1), 426, (2), 71, (3). 30 Plates. 24225

This is really Vol. III. of the preceding work. Some copies have colored plates, and the collation of two copies I have seen differs, as indicated in No. 24224.

FEUILLÉE. Beschreibung zur Arzeney dienlicher Pflanzen welche in den Reichen des mittägigen America in Peru und Chily vorzüglich im Gebrauch sind, in dem land selbst auf Königlichen Befehl, in den Jahren von 1709, 1710 und 1711 aufgesetzt. *Nürnberg: Johann Michel Seeligman.* 1756–7. 2 vols., 4to, pp. (6), 136, Table, (6); pp. (2), 208, Table, (12). 100 Plates. *Nürnberg: bei denen Seligmännischen Erben.* 1766. 2 vols., 4to. 100 Colored Plates of Plants. 24226

The edition of 1766 only differs from that of 1756 in the imprint.

[FEUILLET (J. B.)] Abregé de la vie de la B. sœvr Rose de Sainte Marie, religieuse du tiers ordre de S. Dominique, originaire dv Perov dans les Indes Occidentales. Avec le bref de nostre

S. Pere le Pape Clement IX. Ensemble l'antienne et l'oraison de cette bienheureuse. *Paris: André Cramoisy.* 1668. 12mo, pp. 29, (6). 24227

"Petite pièce fort rare non citée par Ternaux. Au bas de la dernière page on y lit l'annonce d'une réimpression de la vie de la sainte, divisée en 24 chapitres, par le P. J. B. Feuillet, de l'ordre des ff. Prêcheurs. L'abrégé que nous annonçons est sans doute extrait du mss. de cet ouvrage, l'impression n'ayant été faite qu'en 1671." — LECLERC.

Fever; an Elegiac Poem. Dedicated to the Citizens of Philadelphia, by a Citizen. *Philadelphia: Printed for the Author, By John Ormrod.* 1799. 12mo, pp. 24. 24228

A Few Considerations in Relation to the Choice of President. By Atticus. 1822. 24229

Relates to General Jackson.

A Few Days at Nashotah. *See* [Kip (W. I.)]

A Few Brief Facts concerning the Two Routes from Boston to the Hudson River. [n. p. 1853.] 8vo, pp. 4. H. 24230

A Few Facts and Documents relating to the Origin and Progress of the Anti-Church Party in Bridgewater, Mass. *Boston.* 1850. 12mo, pp. 27. 24231

A Few Facts and Reasons why Orange and Ulster Counties should not be Divided. *Goshen, N. Y.* 1859. 8vo, pp. 8. S.

A Few Facts regarding the Geological Survey of Pennsylvania, Exposing the Erroneous Statements and Claims of J. P. Lesley. [By an Assistant.] *Philadelphia: Author.* 1859. 8vo, pp. 22.

A Few Historical Records of the Church in the Diocese of Texas during the Rebellion. Together with a Correspondence between Right Rev. Alexander Gregg, D.D., and the Rev. Charles Gillette. *New York.* 1866. 8vo, pp. 131. 24234

A Few Observations on Canada. *See* Vol. III., No. 10446.

A Few Observations on the Government of the State of Rhode Island. By a Citizen. *Providence: John Carter.* 1809. 8vo, pp. 18. 24235

A Few Observations on the Importation of Slave Grown Sugar into the British Market, London, 5th Month 29th, 1844. By "An Abolitionist." [n. p.] 1844. 4to, pp. 4. 24236

A Few Plain Directions. *See* Vol. III., No. 10447.

A Few Plain Words with the Rank and File of the Union Armies. *Published by the Union Congressional Committee.* [1864.] 8vo, pp. 7. 24237

A Few Political Reflections; submitted to the Considerations of the British Colonies. By a Citizen of Philadelphia. *Philadelphia.* 1774. 12mo, pp. 86. N. 24238

A Few Reasons in favor of the Restoration of the Original Policy of the General Government, in relation to Railroads. [n. p.] 1856. 8vo, pp. 44. H. 24239

A Few Remarks on the Operations of the Companies, at present organized, for the Digging & Smelting of Copper and other Ores, on Lake Superior and the Saint Croix River. By an Explorer. [n. p. n. d.] 16mo, pp. 16. H. 24240

A Few Remarks. *See* Congress, Vol. IV., No. 15529.

A Few Remarks upon the Subject of a Railroad to the Pacific. By a Member of the Philadelphia Bar. *Philadelphia.* 1853. 8vo, pp. 13. 24241

A Few Thoughts on Intervention. By a Citizen of Pennsylvania. *Philadelphia: King and Baird.* MDCCCLII. 8vo, pp. 40.

A Few Thoughts on the Artillery. Its condition and Requirements. By an Artillery Officer. *New York.* 1871. 8vo, pp. (2), 30. 24243

A Few Thoughts on the Duties, Difficulties, and Relations of the Protestant Episcopal Church in the United States, in A Letter to the Commission of Bishops to whom was referred the Memorial of Dr. Muhlenberg and Others. By Catholicus. *New York: Stanford & Swords.* 1855. 12mo. 24244

A Few Thoughts on the Hard Times. By an Observer. [*Boston.* 1857.] 8vo, pp. 12. H. 24245

A Few Thoughts on Three Subjects of Public Interests. — The Bay of Samana, the Darien Canal, and the Subsidizing of American Steamers. [*New York.* 1870.] 8vo, pp. 10. H.

A Few Words on the Crisis. *New York.* [n. d.] pp. 8.

A Few Words. *See* [Clark (Charles)], Vol. VI., No. 13257.

A Few Words to Democrats, By a Democrat. 8vo, pp. 8.

A Few Words to Emigrants. *Leeds.* [n. d.] 12mo, pp. 4.

An English anti-slavery document.

A Few Words for Honest Pennsylvania Democrats. [*Philadelphia.* 1861.] 8vo, pp. 16. H. 24250

A Few Words in behalf of the Loyal Women of the United States. By one of themselves. New York, May, 1863. *New York: William C. Bryant & Co.* 1863. 8vo, pp. 23. C. 24251

Loyal Publication Society, No. 10.

A Few Words on the Nature of the Slave Trade; and the Measures which ought to be adopted. *London: Walter.* 1791. 8vo, pp. 60. 24252

See "M. Rev.," IV. 339.

A Few Words on the Objects and Prospects of the Bolivian Association. *London.* 1843. 8vo. Map. 24253

A Few Words to Loyal Democrats, by one who Knows and who Honors them. *Philadelphia.* [n. d.] 8vo, pp. 24. 24254

A Few Words to the Thinking and Judicious Voters of Pennsylvania. [n. p. 1855?] 8vo, pp. 39. H. 24255

Few Words upon Canada. *See* Vol. III., No. 20449.

FEYERABEND (S.), *Editor.* *See* Schmidt (U.)

FEYJOO DE SOSA (M.) Relacion | descriptiva | de la ciudad y provincia | de Truxillo | del Peru, | con noticias exactas de su estado politico, | segun el Real orden dirigido al Excelentisimo Señor Virrey | Conde de Super-Unda. | Escrita por el Doctor Don Miguel Feyjoo, | Corregidor (que fue) de dicha Ciudad, ... | [4 lines.] | *En Madrid: En la Imprenta del Real, y Supremo Consejo de las Indias.* | ... | *Año de* 1763. | Folio, 5 l., pp. 164. 3 Maps, and Portrait of Charles III. A., H. 24256

Le Fibrilia substitut pratique et économique du Coton. Trad. de l'Américain par H. Vattemare. *Paris.* 1861. 8vo. S.

FICKLIN (O. B.) Speech of Hon. O. B. Ficklin, of Illinois, on the Oregon Question. Delivered ... February 6, 1846. *Washington: Blair & Rives.* 1846. 8vo, pp. 13. H. 24258

Also: Speech on the Public Land Bill: ... December 19, 1844. *Washington.* 1844. 8vo, pp. 7. H. — Speech ... on the Annexation of Texas ... Jan. 23, 1845. *Washington.* 1845. 8vo. — Speech ... on the Cumberland Road Bill, ... April 3, 1846. *Washington.* 1846. 8vo, pp. 7. H. — Speech ... Democratic Meeting, ... Philadelphia, ... First of May, 1846. *Washington.* 1846. 8vo, pp. 13. H. — Speech ... on the Reduction of the Tariff, ... July 1, 1846. *Washington.* 1846. 8vo, pp. 15.

A Fidelidade Maranhense, demonstrada na sumptuosa festividade que no dia 12 de Outubro e seguintes, a solicitaçüo do ill.mo e ex.mo sr. presidente Pedro José da Costa Barros fez a camara di cidade, solemnisando os augustos objectos que n'ella tiveram logar, etc. *Maranhão: Typ. Nacional.* 1826. 4to, pp. 155. 24259

FIDFADDY (F. A.), *pseudonym.* The Adventures of Uncle Sam, in Search after his Lost Honor. By Frederick Augustus Fidfaddy, Esq. Member of the Legion of Honor, Scratch-etar-y to Uncle Sam, and Privy Counsellor to Himself. ... *Middletown: Printed by Seth Richards.* 1816. 12mo, pp. 142. BA. 24260

A political squib against the Democrats.

FIDLER (I.) Observations on Professions, Literature, Manners, and Emigration, in the United States and Canada, made during a Residence there in 1832. By the Rev. Isaac Fidler. *London: Whittaker, Treacher and Co.* 1833. Post 8vo, pp. viii, 434. B., BA. + *New York: J. & J. Harper.* MDCCCXXXIII. 12mo, pp. 247. 24261

The author, known as the Critic of the Mustard Pot, was a professor of Sanscrit, and failing to establish an academy for instruction in this popular study, abused the Americans. *See* "N. Am. Rev.," XXXVII. 273, and [Greene (Asa)].

FIDLER (J. M.) Speech of ... Jas. M. Fidler, at Lebanon, Ky., at the Dedication of "Runkle Institute." *Louisville, Ky.* 1869. 8vo, pp. 8. H. 24262

Also: Speech ... before the "Marion Grand Club," at Lebanon, Kentucky ... 7th ... September 1868. [n. p. 1868.] 8vo, pp. 23. H.

FIELD (A. S.) Report of the Trial of Albert S. Field, ... for the Murder of Jonathan Gray, ... Providence, ... 1826. *Providence: Miller & Grattan.* 1826. 8vo, pp. 48. 24263

FIELD (A. R.) The Hoosac Tunnel Route compared with the Western Railroad. By Alfred R. Field. *Lowell, Mass.: Stone & Huse.* 1866. 8vo, pp. 16. H. 24264

FIELD (C. W.) Prospects of the Atlantic Telegraph. A Paper read before the American Geographical and Statistical Society, ... New York, May 1, 1862. By Cyrus W. Field. [*New York.* 1862.] 8vo, pp. 14, (1). 24265

Also: The Atlantic Telegraph. Report of the Proceedings at a Banquet, given to Mr. Cyrus W. Field, by the Chamber of Commerce of New-York, ... November 15th, 1866. *New York.* 1866. 8vo. (Also on large paper.) S. — Proceedings at the Banquet held in Honor of C. W. Field, Esq., of New York, in Willis's Rooms, London, on Wednesday, 1st July, 1868 ... ["as an acknowledgment of his Devotion to the interests of Atlantic Telegraphy"]. *London: Metchim & Son.* 1868. 12mo, pp. 80.

FIELD (David D.) Brief Memoirs of the Members of the Class Graduated at Yale College, 1802. By D. D. Field. *New Haven.* 1863. 8vo. 24266

FIELD. Centennial Address, by David D. Field, D.D. With Historical Sketches of Cromwell, Portland, Chatham, Middle-Haddam, Middletown and its Parishes. *Middletown, Conn.: William B. Casey.* 1853. 12mo, pp. (2), 295, (1). Plate. BA.

FIELD. The Genealogy of the Brainerd Family, in the United States, with numerous Sketches of Individuals. By Rev. David D. Field, D.D., ... *New York: John F. Trow, Printer.* 1857. 8vo, pp. 303. Portrait. B., BA., S. 24268

FIELD. An Historical Sketch ... of the Church in Stockbridge, Mass. By Rev. David D. Field, D.D. ... *New York: John A. Gray.* 1853. 8vo, pp. 30. B. 24269

[FIELD.] A History of the County of Berkshire, Massachusetts; In Two Parts. The First being a General View of the County: the Second, an Account of the Several Towns. By Gentlemen in the County, Clergymen [the Berkshire Association of Congregational Ministers], and Laymen. *Pittsfield: Printed by Samuel W. Bush.* 1829. 12mo, pp. 468. 2 Maps, Portraits, and Plate. B., H. 24270

Very scarce. Edited, and partly written, by the Rev. D. D. Field; pp. 5–197 are by Rev. Chester Dewey.

FIELD. A History of the Town of Pittsfield, in Berkshire County, Mass. ... By Rev. David D. Field. ... *Hartford: Press of Case, Tiffany and Burnham.* 1844. 8vo, pp. 80. Map. BA.

FIELD. History of the Towns of Haddam and East Haddam. *Boston.* 1814. 24272

Title from the "New England Genealogical Register."

FIELD. A Statistical Account of the County of Middlesex, in Connecticut. By David D. Field, D.D. Published by the Connecticut Academy of Arts and Sciences. *Middletown: printed by Clark & Lyman.* 1819. 8vo, pp. 154. B., BA., C., H. 24273

See our No. 15702, and strike out "All that was published." Also: ... A Sermon preached at Chester, in Saybrook, Jan. 3, 1816, at the Ordination of Rev. Nehemiah B. Beardsley ... *Middletown.* 1816. 8vo, pp. 16. M. — Sermon at Middletown, June 20, 1816, the day of the Execution of Peter Ling, for the Murder of his Wife. *Middletown.* 1816. 8vo, pp. 28. — Sermon at Haddam, [Con.] Dec. 14, 1813, on the Death of Mrs. Elizabeth, Relict of Dr. Hezekiah Brainerd. ... *Middletown.* 1814. 8vo. Dr. Field was the father of Cyrus Field, David Dudley Field, Rev. H. M. Field, and Judge Field, of the United States Supreme Court.

FIELD (David Dudley). Argument upon the Constitutionality of the Act of Congress, passed Feb. 25, 1862, making United States Notes a Legal Tender ... Court of Appeals, New York, June Term, 1863. *New York.* 1863. 8vo. 24274

Also: ... An Address, ... Chicago ... September 31st, 1859. ... *New York: printed by William J. Read.* [1859.] 8vo, pp. 20. H. — The Danger of throwing the Election of President into Congress. Speech of David Dudley Field. ... Philadelphia, August 20, 1860. [*Washington.* 1860.] 8vo, pp. 7. B., H. — An International Code: Address on this subject before the Social Science Association at Manchester, Oct. 5, 1866. *New York.* 1867. S. — Legal Reform. An Address ... University of Albany, delivered March 23, 1855. ... *Albany: W. C. Little & Co.* 1855. 8vo, pp. 36. H. — A Letter to Gulian C. Verplanck, on the Reform of the Judicial System of this State. *New York.* 1840. 8vo, pp. 45. — Reorganization of the Judiciary: Five Articles originally published in the Evening Post, on that subject. *New-York. January,* 1846. — Speech ... at the Chicago Convention. ... *New-York.* 1847. 8vo, pp. 16. BA., H. — Suggestions respecting the Revision of the Constitution of New York. ... May, 1867. *New York: W. J. Read, Printer.* 1867. 8vo, pp. 29. — What shall be done with the Practice of the Courts? Shall it be wholly reformed? Questions addressed to Lawyers. *New York.* 1847. 8vo, pp. 38.

FIELD (E.) A Charge delivered to the Clergy of Bermuda, in the Easter Week of 1849. By the Rt. Rev. Edward Field, D.D., Bishop of Newfoundland. *St. John's.* 1850. 8vo, pp. 50.

FIELD (H. M.) The Family of Rev. David D. Field, D.D. of Stockbridge, Mass., with their Ancestors, from the time of Emigration to America. By his youngest son, Henry M. Field. *Not published, but printed privately for the use of the Family.* 1860. 12mo, pp. 105. 24276

Appendix to the Field Genealogy. 1864. 12mo, pp. 15.

FIELD. History of the American Telegraph, by Henry M. Field, D.D. ... *New York: Charles Scribner & Co.* 1866. 12mo, pp. 364. Plate. B., BA. + Second Edition. *New York: Scribner & Co.* 1867. 12mo, pp. 435. 2 Plates. 24277

FIELD (J.) Light and Truth, Discovering and Detecting Sophistry and Deceit; or a Reply to a Book called, "A Plain Discovery of many Gross Falshoods, &c." By George Keith. Together with Animadversions to G. K.'s Answer to his own Queries, concerning the Sacrament of the Lord's Supper (so called). By John Field. *London: J. Sowle.* 1701. 4to, 6½ sheets. 24278

FIELD. Piety Promoted, in a Collection of Dying Sayings Of many of the People called Quakers, with a Brief Account of some of their Labours in the Gospel, and Sufferings for the same. The 4th Part. By John Field. *London: J. Sowle.* 1711. 12mo,

pp. 240. + The Second Edition. *London: Luke Hinde.* 1754. 12mo. + The Fifth Part. (With a Preface by T. Raylton.) *London: Assigns of J. Sowle.* 1717. 12mo, pp. 276. + The Second Edition. 1718. 12mo, pp. 252. + The Third Edition. *London: Luke Hinde.* 1754. 12mo. + The Fourth Edition. *London: Mary Hinde.* 1775. 12mo, pp. 252. + The Sixth Part. *Assigns of J. Sowle.* 1728. 12mo, pp. 228. + The Second Edition. *London: Luke Hinde.* 1766. 12mo, pp. 228. 24279

FIELD (Joseph). Clerical Discipline, exemplified by the Franklin Association, in the late Measures adopted by them towards the Author. *Greenfield.* 1822. 8vo, pp. 23. M. 24280

FIELD. Historical Sketches of the Spirit of Orthodoxy: being Second Part of the above. *Springfield.* 1823. 8vo. W. 24281

[FIELD (J. M.)] The Drama in Pokerville; the Bench and the Bar of Jurytown, and other Stories. By "Everpoint." ... *Philadelphia: Carey & Hart.* 1847. 12mo, pp. 200. 8 Plates. + *Philadelphia: Getz & Buck.* 1854. 12mo, pp. 200. + *Philadelphia: T. B. Peterson and Brothers.* [n. d.] 24282

FIELD (J. E.) Texas. A View of the Texas Revolution, an Account of the Principal Battles, and Geographical, Historical and other important information. By Dr. Joseph E. Field ... . *Springfield, Mass.: Justin Jones.* 1836. 12mo, pp. 47. 24283

Cover title. The printed title differs.

FIELD (L. A.) An Historical Sketch of the First Congregational Church in Marlborough, Mass. ... By Levi A. Field. *Worcester.* 1859. 12mo, pp. 82, 52. S. 24284

FIELD (M.) City Architecture. By M. Field. *New-York: G. P. Putnam.* 1853. 8vo. 20 Plates. 24285

The illustrations include actual views.

FIELD (M. W.) The Currency Question. A Plea for Greenbacks. Remarks of ... Moses W. Field ... in the National Commercial Covention held at Boston, February, 1868. ... *Detroit.* 1868. 8vo, pp. 12. H. 24286

[FIELD.] Wages of American & English Workmen. Resolution of the "National Labor Congress" for Protection to Home Industry. [*Detroit.* 1869.] 8vo, pp. 8. H. 24287

Also: Protection vs. Free Trade. Address ... before the Legislature of Michigan. ... [*Detroit.* 1871.] 8vo, pp. 8. H.

FIELD (O.) Sketch of the Family of Field of the West Riding of Yorkshire, England, and of Flushing and Newtown, Long Island, New York. By Osgood Field, Esq., of London, England. *Albany: J. Munsell.* 1864. 8vo, pp. 12. 24288

FIELD (R. S.) Address on the Life and Character of Abraham Lincoln, By the Hon. Richard S. Field. Delivered before the Legislature of New Jersey, February 12, 1866. *Trenton, N. J.* 1866. 8vo, pp. 40. 24289

FIELD. "The Constitution not a Compact between Sovereign States." An Oration, delivered at Princeton, New Jersey, on the 4th of July, 1861, by Richard S. Field. *Princeton, N. J.: J. T. Robinson.* 1861. 8vo, pp. 27. B. 24290

FIELD. The Provincial Courts of New Jersey, with Sketches of the Bench and Bar. A Discourse, read before the New Jersey Historical Society. By Richard S. Field. *New York: Bartlett & Welford.* 1849. 8vo, pp. xi, (1), 311. B., BA. 24291

Forms Vol. III. of the "Collections of the New Jersey Historical Society." Also: Address before the Surviving Members of the Constitutional Convention, of the State of New Jersey. ... February 1st, 1853. ... *Princeton, N. J.: John T. Robinson.* 1853. 8vo, pp. 42. B. — A Charge to the Grand Jury in the District Court of the United States for the District of New Jersey, April 21, 1863. ... *Trenton, N. J.* 1863. 8vo, pp. 24. H. — Speech ... on the Discharge of State Prisoners. ... in the Senate ... ... January 7, 1863. *Washington.* 1863. 8vo, pp. 16. H.

FIELD (Samuel). Miscellaneous Productions in Poetry and Prose. With a Sketch of the Author's Life and Character. By Rodolphus Dickinson. *Greenfield.* 1818. 12mo, pp. 284.

FIELD (T. W.) The Battle of Long Island, with connected Preceding Events, and the Subsequent American Retreat. Introductory Narrative, with Authentic Documents. By Thomas W. Field. *Brooklyn.* 1869. 8vo, pp. ix, 549, xiii. 7 Plates.

Also on large paper, impl. 8vo. Two editions were issued at the same time, with the title as above; another forms Vol. II. of the "Memoirs of the Long Island Historical Society."

FIELD. An Essay towards an Indian Bibliography, being a Catalogue of Books relating to the History, Antiquities, Languages, Customs, Religion, Wars, Literature, and Origin of the American Indians, in the Library of Thomas W. Field, with Bibliographical and Historical Notes, and Synopses of Contents of some of the Works least known. *New York: Scribner, Armstrong & Co.* 1873. 8vo, pp. iv, 430. 24294

So far the most extensive list of books on this subject. Mr. Field has devoted many years to the acquisition of the books, and his notes, which are numerous, convey much valuable information concerning not only the books, but the Indians themselves. An appendix of additional items is now (May, 1873) in the press.

Field. Historic and Antiquarian Scenes in Brooklyn and its Vicinity, with Illustrations of some of its Antiquities. By T. W. Field. *Brooklyn.* 1868. Imp. 8vo, pp. iv, 2 l., pp. 96. 11 Plates and 1 Map. 24295

One hundred copies printed for private distribution. Also: The Minstrel Pilgrim. [A Poem.] *New York.* 1848. Sm. 4to, pp. 50.

Field (T.) Sermon, at the Dedication of a New Meeting-House in Westminster, Vt., in 1829. By Timothy Field. *Brattleborough.* 1830. 8vo. 24296

The Field of Mars: Being an Alphabetical Digestion of the Principal Naval and Military Engagements, in Europe, Asia, Africa, and America, particularly of Great Britain and her Allies, from the Ninth Century to the Present Period. ... *London: J. Macgowan, and W. Davis.* M,DCC,LXXX. 2 vols., 4to. B. + *London.* 1801. 2 vols., 4to. A. 24297

See "M. Rev.," XXXIX. 205.

Field Record of the Officers of the Veteran Reserve Corps, from the Commencement to the Close of the Rebellion. *Washington: Scriver & Swing.* 8vo, pp. 39. 24298

Fielder (H.) The Disunionist: A Brief Treatise upon the Evils of the Union between the North and the South, and the Propriety of Separation and the Formation of A Southern United States. By Herbert Fielding, Esq., of Georgia. [n. p.] *Printed for the Author.* 1858. 8vo, pp. 72. C. 24299

[Fields (James T.)] A Few Verses for a Few Friends. *Printed at the Riverside Press, Cambridge.* 16mo, pp. 78. B., BA.

For a caustic review of these verses, see Philes' "Philobiblion."

Fields. Poems, by James T. Fields. *Cambridge: Metcalf and Company, University Press.* [n. d.] 16mo, pp. 128. B., BA. + *Boston: William D. Ticknor & Company.* MDCCCXLIX. 8vo, pp. vi, (2), 99. B., BA. 24301

Also: Anniversary Poem, ... Mercantile Library Association of Boston, September 13, 1838. ... *Boston: William D. Ticknor.* 1838. 8vo, pp. 17. B., BA., M. His "Yesterday with Authors. *Boston.* 1872," includes Hawthorne.

Fields (R.) A Practical Treatise upon the Bankrupt Law of the United States. By R. Fields. *Boston.* 1800. 16mo, pp. 56. M. 24302

Fields (W.) The Scrap Book; consisting of Tales and Anecdotes, Biographical, Historical, Patriotic, ... in Prose and Poetry. By William Fields. *Philadelphia.* 1851. 8vo, pp. 544. + *Philadelphia: J. B. Lippincott & Co.* 1855. 8vo, pp. 544. + Second Edition. [*Ibid.*] 1858. 8vo, pp. 544. 24303

The Fiery Cross; a Tale of the great American War. ... *London: C. Clarke.* [1866.] 18mo, pp. 411. C. 24304

Fiestas en la beatification de Santa Rosa de Santa Maria en el convento del Rosario de Lima. [n. p.] 1662. 24305

Title from Ternaux, No. 802.

Las Fiestas nacionales. *Bogotá.* 1866. 18mo, pp. 16. 24306

Fifield (N.) An Address delivered before the Society for the Reformation of Morals, in Weymouth and Braintree ... April 13, 1818. By Dr. Noah Fifield ... . *Boston: Printed by Parmenter and Norton.* 1818. 8vo, pp. 23. BA., H. 24307

Fifteen Gallons: or the Tyranny and Injustice of Sumptuary Law: An Appeal to the Good Sense of the People. *Boston.* 1838. 8vo, pp. 38. B., H. 24308

Fifty Years in Chains; or, The Life of an American Slave. *New York: H. Dayton.* 1858. 12mo, pp. 430. 24309

Fifty Years of a Play-Goer's Journal; or, Annals of the New-York Stage, from 1798 to 1848, with Biographical Sketches of all the Principal Performers. *New York.* 1860. 12mo. 24310

Figsbee (—). Maritime Flags of all Nations. With a Geographical Description of every Empire, Kingdom, and Republic in the World. *New York: the Author.* 1856. 18mo, pp. 50. C. + *New York.* 1869. 16mo. C. 24311

Figuecoa (B. D. A. ...) Arte de la Lengua Mexicana, compuesto por el Bachiller Don Antonio Vasquez Gastelu El Rey de Figuecoa, Cathedrático de dicha Lengua en los Reales Collegios de San Pedro y San Juan. Sacado a luz por orden del illustr. Sr. Dr. D. Manuel Fernandez de Santa Cruz, Obisbo de Puebla. *Puebla de los Angelos.* 1689. 4to, 53 l. + [Reprinted.] *Mexico.* 1693. 4to. + [Reprinted.] Corregido segun su original, por el Br. D. Antonio de Olmeda y Torre. *Mexico.* 1716. 4to. [Another Edition.] *Puebla.* 1726. 8vo, pp. 55. 24312

Figueira (L.) Arte da Grammatica da Lingua do Brasil. Composto pelo P. Luiz Figueira, Natural de Almodovar. *Lisboa.*

1681. 8vo. + [2ª edição.] *Lisboa: Miguel Deslandes.* 1687. 8vo, pp. viii, 168. + Quarta impressaõ. *Lisboa.* 1754. 8vo, pp. 108. + [Another] Quarta impressaõ. *Lisboa: na officina Patriarcal.* 1795. 4to, 2 l., pp. 103. 24313

A volume of extreme rarity, not included in the "Bibl. Lusitana" of Barbosa Machado.

Figueira. Grammatica da lingua geral dos Indios do Brasil, reimpressa pela primeira vez n'este continente, depois de tão longo tempo de sua publicação em Lisboa, offerecida a Sua Magestade Imperial, attenta a sua augusta vontade, manifestada ao Instituto Historico Brasileiro ... por João Joaquim da Silva Guimarães, natural da Bahia. *Bahia: Typ. de Manuel Feliciano Supulveda.* 1851. 8vo, pp. xii, vi, 105, 12, (3). 24314

Figueira was born at Almodovar in 1573, and joined the Jesuits in 1592. He was sent to Brazil with Francis Pinto, who was put to death by the Indians. Figueira escaped and returned to France, after spending twenty years in the missions, with other missionaries. On his return he was shipwrecked at the mouth of the Amazon, and was massacred, with thirty of his companions, in July, 1643.

Figueiredo e Mello (P. A.) Arseos historico e analyse esthetigraphica do quadro de um episodio da batalha de Campo Grande, planejado e executado pelo Dr. Pedro Americo de Figueiredo e Mello. *Rio de Janeiro: typographia nacional.* 1871. 8vo, 1 l., pp. 101. Portrait. C. 24315

Figuereido (M.) Hydrographia. Examen de pilotos com os reteiros de Portugal para o Brasil, rio da Prata, etc., composto por Manoel de Figuereido. *Lisboa: Vicente Alvarez.* 1614. 4to.

Title from Ternaux, No. 368.

Figueroa (C. S. de). Hechos de Garcia Hurtado de Mendoza, quarto marquez de Cañete, por el doctor Cristoval Suarez de Figueroa. *Madrid: Imprenta real.* 1613. 4to, pp. 324.

"D. Garcia de Mendoça fut le conquérent et le pacificateur du Chili." — *See* Ternaux, No. 359.

Figueroa (F. A. de). Mosaico poetico de Don Francisco A. de Figueroa. *Montevideo.* 1857–58. 2 vols., 4to, pp. 432; 208. 24318

Figueroa (Francisco de), *a Jesuit.* Memorial de ocho Padres de la Compañia de Jesus y algunos otros Españoles y Indios martyrizados en la Provincia de Mexico el año de 1616. *Barcelona.* 1616. 4to. 24319

Sotwel says that this was translated into French, German, and other languages, but the Backers, from whose work and from Ternaux this title is taken, had only met with the French translation in E. Trigault's "Histoire du massacre," etc. *Valenciennes.* 1620. 8vo. Carayon No, 1249,12, says [s. l.] 1617, and No. 1252, *Mexico,* 1627.

Figuerao. Tratado breve del dvlcissimo nombre de Maria, repartido en cincuenta discursos; compuesto por el P. F. F. de Figueroa, difinidor de la prouincia de Santa Juan Bautista del Peru de la orden de Predicadores ... *Impresso en Lima: por Josef de Contreras.* 1642. 4to, Title, on the verso of which is a plate of the Virgin, 1 l., pp. 334, 14 l. 24320

Figueroa (F. A. R.) Tesoro Catequistico Indiano. Espejo de Doctrina cristiana y politica para la instruccion de los Indios, en el idioma castellano y mexicano, por Fr. Francisco Antº de la Rosa Figueroa. 4to. 24321

Figueroa (Jose). Manifesto a la Republica Mejicana. *Monterey.* 1835. 16mo. 24322

Filisola (V.) Evacuation of Texas. Translation of the Representation addressed to the Supreme Government in Defence of his Honor, and Explanation of his Operations as Commander-in-Chief of the Army against Texas. *Columbia.* 1837. 8vo. BA. 24323

Translated by G. L. H. The first book printed in Texas.

Filisola. Memorias para la historia de la Guerra de Tejas, por el General de Division, D. Vincente Filisola, actual Presidente del Supremo Tribunal de Guerra y marina de la República ... *Mexico: Imprenta de Ignacio Cumplido.* 1849. 2 vols., crown 8vo, pp. x, 587; xi, 625. BA. 24324

An account of the first campaign of the United States.

Filisola. A José Francisco Barrundia, emisario de la facción Sansalvadoreña en Guemala, en contestacion á su libelo de 10 de agosto del presente año, ó sean apuntes para la historia de la libertad de aquellas provincias. *Puebla.* 1824. 12mo. 24325

Replied to by "Notas se que citan en el cuaderno que dio a luz el general Vic. Filisola, en contestacion al libelo que contra el publico el 10 de agosto del presente año J. F. Barrundia, emisario de la facción Sansalvadoreña en Guatemala. *Puebla.* 1824." 12mo, 224 leaves.

Filisola. Representacion dirigida al Suprema Gobierno, por el General N. Filisola, en defensa de sú honor y aclaracion de sus operaciones como General en Gefe del ejercito sobre Tejas. *Mexico.* 1836. 4to, pp. 82. 24326

Fillebrown (Thomas). Circular. [*Washington.* 1833.] 8vo.

Concerning claims against the Navy Hospital Fund of the United States for official services.

Filley (W.) Life and Adventures of William Filley, who was Stolen from his Home in Jackson, Mich., by the Indians, August 3d, 1837, and his Safe Return from Captivity, October 19, 1866. After an Absence of 29 Years. *Chicago: Filley & Ballard.* 1867. 8vo, pp. 112. Plates. 24328

The cover title reads: "The Indian Captive, or the Long Lost Jackson Boy, William Filley, Abducted from his Parents at Jackson, Michigan, Aug. 3, 1837, at the tender age of Five Years, ... Edited by J. B. Ballard."

Fillmore (J.) A Narration of the Captivity of John Fillmore, and his Escape from the Pirates. *Johnston.* 1806. 8vo. + Second Edition. *Johnston: Abraham Taylor.* 1809. 8vo, pp. 18.

Fillmore. A True Account of the singular Sufferings of John Fillmore on board a noted Pirate Ship; with a Biography of Millard Fillmore of Buffalo. *Utica.* 1848. 12mo. S. 24330

Fillmore (M.) Biography of Millard Fillmore. *Buffalo: Thomas & Lathrops.* 1856. 12mo, pp. xv, 215. S. 24331

Fillmore. The Executive Acts of Ex-President Fillmore: with reasons for his Election, and a Memoir of his Life and Administration. ... and a Sketch of the Life of Andrew Jackson Donelson, ... *New York: Edward Walker.* 1856. 8vo, pp. 48.

This is the cover title. The inner title reads: "The Life and Administration of Ex-President Fillmore. (From Walker's Statesman's Manual.) To which are added, Reasons for his Election to the Presidency, Extracts from his recent Speeches, ..."

Fillmore. Life of Millard Fillmore, and Andrew Jackson Donelson. [n. p. n. d.] Rl. 8vo, pp. 32. + *New York: R. M. De Witt.* [1856.] 8vo, pp. 32. 24333

Also: Speech ... on the Revenue Bill, ... July 24, 1841. [*Washington.* 1841.] 16mo, pp. 8. H., S. — Speech ... on the Tariff Bill. ... June 9, 1842. *Washington.* 1842. 8vo, pp. 24. H. — Speeches ... at New-York, Newburgh, Albany, Rochester, Buffalo, &c. ... June 1856. 8vo, pp. 24. S. — Fillmore State Address to the People of Rhode Island, 1856. [n. p.] 1856. Folio, 1 l. — Great Fillmore Meeting, ... New York. Also, a Message from President Fillmore, on the 6th August, 1850. *New York: M. B. Wynkoop, Printer.* 1856. 8vo, pp. 20. S. — Is Millard Fillmore an Abolitionist? *Boston: American Patriot Office.* 1856. 8vo, pp. 29. B., BA., H. — Mr. Fillmore at Home. His Reception at New York and Brooklyn, and Progress through the State to his Residence in Buffalo. [*Buffalo.* n. d.] 8vo, pp. 24. H.

Filmore (J.) The Blessings of Peace: A Sermon preached in Christ's Church, New York, on the Fourth of July, 1794, at the joint Request of the Tammany Society, or Columbian Order and the Society of Mechanics. By the Rev. Joseph Filmore. *New York: Printed by John Buel.* 1794. 8vo, pp. 32. 24334

Filomeno (F.) Elogio del Excmo. Sr. Marqués de Someruelos D. Salvador del Muro y Salazar, Teniente General de los Reales Ejércitos &c., por D. Francisco Filomeno, ... *Habana: oficina de Arazoza y Soler.* 1814. 4to, pp. 27. 24335

Filson (J.) The Discovery, Settlement And present state of Kentucke: and An Essay towards the Topography, and Natural History of that important Country. To which is added, An Appendix, Containing, I. The Adventures of Col. Daniel Boon, one of the first Settlers, comprehending every important Occurrence in the political History of that Province. II. The Minutes of the Piankashaw Council, held at Post St. Vincents, April 15, 1784. III. An Account of the Indian Nations inhabiting within the Limits of the Thirteen United States, their Manners and Customs, and Reflections on their Origin. IV. The Stages and Distances between Philadelphia and the Falls of the Ohio, from Pittsburg to Pensacola, and several other Places. — The Whole illustrated by a new and accurate Map of Kentucke and the Country adjoining, drawn from actual Surveys. By John Filson. *Wilmington: Printed by James Adams.* 1784. 8vo, pp. 118. Map. B., BA., H., P. 24336

The map is usually wanting, and has been supposed not to exist; it is in the copy in the Philadelphia Library. It is a rare book, and worth from twenty to thirty dollars. It was reprinted with the following title:

Filson. The Discovery, Settlement, and Present State of Kentucky. And an Introduction to the Topography and Natural History of that Rich and Important Country; also, Colonel Daniel Boon's Narrative of the Wars of Kentucky: with An Account of the Indian Nations within the Limits of the United States, their Manners, Customs, Religion, and their Origin; and the Stages and Distances between Philadelphia and the Falls of the Ohio; from Pittsburgh to Pensacola, and several other Places. By John Filson. Illustrated with a large whole sheet Map of Kentucky from actual Surveys, and a Plan with a Descripton of the Rapids of the River Ohio. By Capt. Thomas Hutchins, Geographer to the Congress. *London: John Stockdale.* 1793. 8vo, pp. 67. Map. BA. 24337

It is also included in Imlay's "Topographical Description of the Western Territory," second and third editions. Filson believed in the existence of a Welsh settlement in this colony, under Prince Madoc, in 1170. *See* "M. Rev.," XIV. 148; *also* Herbert (J.)

Filson. Histoire de Kentucke, nouvelle colonie à l'ouest de la Virginie: contenant, 1°. La Découverte, l'Acquisition, l'Établissement, la Description topographique, l'Histoire Naturelle, &c. du Territoire: 2°. La Relation historique du Colonel Boon, un des premiers Colons, dans ses guerres contre les Naturels: 3°. l'Assemblée des Piankashaws au Poste Saint Vincent: 4°. Un exposé succinct des Nations Indiennes qui habitent dans les limites des Treize États-Unis, de leurs mœurs & coûtumes, & des Réflexions sur leur Origine; & autres Pièces: Avec une carte. Ouvrage pour servir de suite aux Lettres d'un Cultivateur Américain. Traduit de l'Anglois, de M. John Filson; Par M. Parraud, de l'Académie des Arcades de Rome. *A Paris: Chez Buisson, Libraire, Hôtel de Mesgrigny, rue des Poitevins, Nº.* 13. M. DCC. LXXXV. Avec Approbation et Permission. 8vo, pp. (4), xvj, 234. Map and Plate. BA., H. 24338

The translator has made some additions; but the map is often deficient — being extracted for insertion as a substitute in the Wilmington edition.

Filson. Reise nach Kentucke und Nachrichten von dieser neu angebaueten Landschaft in Nordamerika. Aus dem Englischen übersetzt. *Leipzig: Chr. Weigel.* 1790. 24mo, pp. 124.

Fin de la Guerre. | Dialogus, of t' Samen-sprekinge, | P. Scipio Africanus raedt den | Romeynen datmen naer Africam | most | trecken om Carthago te bekrygen ende bestryden, so | verre men Hannibal uyt Italien wilde jagen. | Q. Fabius Maximus raed datmẽ niet naer Carthago trec- | ken most, maer datmen Hannibal in Italien met alle | macht most aen vellen ende daer uyt slaen. | Dienende tot een Exemplaer, of Spiegel om te bewysẽ dat de West- | Indische Interprinse d'eenige, ende beste middele is, niet alleeneijck om de | Spangiaerden uyt den Nederlanden te jagen, en dese langdurige Oorloge | t'eyndigen, de geheele Christenheyt to bevredighen: De ghepreten- | deerde Spaensche Monarchie ende hooghmoet te krencken, | ende te dempen: Maer dat daer en boven noch six cinq | op den Teerling loopt, om de West-Indien voor | een kans te strijcken. | Audaces Fortuna juvat timidosque repellit. | *t' Amsterdam,* | *Ghedruckt by Paulus Aertsz. van Ravesteyn.* | 4to, pp. 43. 24340

This dialogue was written to encourage the Dutch in their war with Spain, and suggests the probability of gaining the West Indies. *See* Asher, No. 101.

Finan (P.) Journal of a Voyage to Quebec, In the Year 1825, with Recollections of Canada, during the late American War, in the Years 1812–13. By P. Finan. *Newry: Printed by Alexander Peacock.* 1828. 12mo, pp. v, 400. S. 24341

Finance. A Letter addressed to the House Committee of Ways and Means, January 1, 1862. ... . [*Washington.* 1862.] 8vo, pp. 7. H. 24342

Finance. — No. II. — Bill — Synopsis — and Explanatory Remarks. — "A Bill to establish a National System of Finance, based on Demand Notes, Currency Bonds, and Loan Bonds." [*Washington?* 1863.] 8vo, pp. 6. H. 24343

Sur les finances. 1802. *See* [Micoud d'Umons (C. E.)]

See also Report of the Secretary of the Treasury.

Financial Affairs in the United States during the first Two Years of the Southern Insurrection. By a Member of the Chamber of Commerce. *New York: J. W. Amerman.* 1862. 8vo, pp. 10. 23444

The Financial Condition and Resources of the United States. *New York: John Medole, Printer.* 1865. 8vo. 24345

The Financial Credit of the United States; how it can be sustained. A Report made to the American Geographical and Statistical Society, January 16, 1862. *New York.* 1862. 8vo, pp. 29. 24346

The Financial Measures of the United States Government. A Letter to Moses Taylor, Esq., New York. *New York: E. B. Clayton's Sons.* 1865. 12mo. 24347

The Financial Problem. [*Washington.* 1865.] 8vo, pp. 7.

Financial Register of the United States; devoted chiefly to Finance and Currency, and to Banking and Commercial Statistics. By Condy Raguet. *Philadelphia: Wirtz & Salem.* 1838. 2 vols., 8vo, pp. (2), 414; (4), 416. A., B., BA. 24349

Financial Review. United States Bonds, the Various Issues; as an Investment compared with each other. Paper Money, and the Rights and Advantages of the Public. Savings Banks, Life Insurance, and other Papers. ... *New York.* 1871. 8vo, pp. 24.

Financial Scheme for the Government. [*New York.* 1862.] 8vo, pp. 8. 24351

From "The Bankers' Magazine and Statistical Register."

The Financial Situation. [Signed, A Patriot. *New York.* *January* 9, 1865.] 8vo, pp. 15. H. 24352

Finch (John). Travels in the United States of America and Canada, containing some Account of their Scientific Institutions, and a few Notices of the Geology and Mineralogy of those Countries. To which is added, an Essay on the Natural Boundaries of Empires. By J. Finch, Esq., ... *London: Longman, Rees, Orme, Brown, Green and Longman.* 1833. 8vo, pp. xv, 455, and Errata. A., B., BA., C., P. 24353

Finch (M.) An Englishwoman's Experience in America. By Marianne Finch. *London.* 1853. Post 8vo. + *London: Ward & Lock.* 1857. Post 8vo. P. 24354

Finch (R. P.) A Sermon preached December 13. 1776, being the Fast Day, on account of the Troubles in America. ... St. Michael, Cornhill, London. By Robert Pool Finch, Rector. *London: J. Rivington.* 1771. 4to. 24355

See "M. Rev.," LVI. 77.

Fincke (F. G.) The Early History of the Original Charter of the Grand Lodge of New York; Critically Examined. By F. Gustav Fincke. *New York.* 1856. 8vo. 24356

Findlay (A. G.) A Description of the Bermudas or Somers' Islands; with Nautical Directions ... By A. G. Findlay. ... *London: R. H. Laurie.* 1847. 8vo, pp. (2), 19. Plate.

Findlay. A Directory for the Navigation of the Pacific Ocean; with Description of the Coasts, Islands, &c., from Strait of Magalhaens to the Arctic Sea, and those of Asia and Australia; its Winds, Currents, and other Phenomena. By Alexander G. Findlay. In Two Parts. Part I. The Coasts of the Pacific Ocean. Part II. The Islands, &c. of the Pacific Ocean. *London: R. H. Laurie.* 1851. 2 vols., 8vo, pp. 1472. C. 24358

Findlay. Notes Explanatory of a Chart of the North Atlantic Ocean. By Alex. G. Findlay, F.R.G.S. *London: Richard Holmes Laurie.* 1859. 8vo, pp. 15. B. 24359

Findley (W.) History of the Insurrection, in the Four Western Counties of Pennsylvania: In the Year M.DCC.XCIV. With a Recital of the Circumstances specially connected therewith: and an Historical View of the Previous Situation of the Country. By William Findley, Member of the House of Representatives of the United States. *Philadelphia: printed by Samuel Harrison Smith.* M.DCC.XCVI. 8vo, pp. 328. BA., H., P.

Known as the "Whiskey Rebellion," now scarce, and sells for upwards of fifteen dollars. *See also* Brackenridge (H. M.), Vol. II., No. 7166.

Findley. Observations on "The Two Sons of Oil;" containing a Vindication of the American Constitutions, and Defending the Blessings of Religious Liberty and Toleration, against the Illiberal Strictures of the Rev. Samuel B. Wylie. By William Findley, Esq. *Pittsburgh.* 1812. 12mo, pp. 366. C.

[Findley.] The Parole and Documentary Evidence delivered before a Committee of the House of Representatives, appointed to inquire into the Conduct of the Governor of the Commonwealth of Pennsylvania. [*Harrisburgh:*] *J. Wyeth.* [n. d.] 8vo. 275. 24362

[Findley.] A Review of the Revenue System adopted by the First Congress under the Federal Constitution ... . By a Citizen. *Philadelphia: T. Dobson.* M DCC XCIV. 8vo, pp. ii, 33.

Fine (J.) Letter of Hon. John Fine to his Constituents, August, 1840. [*Ogdensburgh, N. Y.* 1840.] 16mo, pp. 16. BA.

Also: Remarks, ... N. Y. Senate, on Slavery in New-Mexico, 1848. 8vo. S.

The Finest Part of America. To be Sold, or Lett from Eight Hundred to Four Thousand Acres, in a Farm, All that Entire Estate, called Long Island, in New Albion, Lying near New York: Belonging to the Earl Palatine, of Albion, Granted to his Predecessor, Earl Palatine, of Albion, by King Charles the First, ... [*London.* n. d.] 24365

This is a single octavo leaf, with a description of New Albion. At the foot of the leaf appears the following: "Just Published, and may be had as above, (Price One Shilling) A True Copy of the above Charter, With the Conditions of Letting, &c." This charter forms thirty pages, quarto.

The Finger-Post to Public Business: containing the Mode of Forming and Conducting Societies, Clubs and other Organized Associations, Full Rules of Order for the Government of their Debates and Business; and the Manner of Managing Conventions, Public Meetings, Celebrations, Dinners, Barbecues, and Pic-nics, etc. etc. etc. By an Ex-Member of the Philadelphia Bar. *New York: Dick & Fitzgerald.* 186–. 12mo, pp. 377.

Fink (W. W.) Valley Forge. [A Poem.] *Des Moines: Mills & Co.* 1870. 16mo, 4 l., pp. 111. 24367

[Finlason (W. F.)] Commentaries upon Martial Law, with Special Reference to its Regulation and Restraint; with ... Comments upon the Charge of the Lord Chief Justice. ... *London: Stevens and Sons.* 1867. 8vo, pp. (2), 287. 24368

Relates to the Jamaica troubles and Governor Eyre.

Finlason. The History of the Jamaica Case; being an Account, founded upon Official Documents, of the Rebellion in Jamaica: The Causes which led to it, and the Measures taken for its Suppression; ... and the Debates in Parliament, and the Criminal Prosecutions, arising out of it. Second Edition, Enlarged and Corrected. By W. F. Finlason, Esq. ... *London: Chapman and Hall.* 1869. 8vo, pp. viii, xcvi, 691. 24369

Finlason. Justice to a Colonial Governor; or, some Considerations on the Case of Mr. Eyre: containing the Substance of all the Documents, Discussions, and Proceedings relating thereto. By W. F. Finlason, Esq. ... *London: Chapman and Hall.* [1868.] 8vo, pp. viii, clxxvi. 24370

Finlason. Report of the Case of the Queen v. Edward John Eyre ... for High crimes ... committed by him in his office as Governor of Jamaica; containing the Evidence, ... and the Charge of Mr. Justice Blackburn. By W. F. Finlason, Esq. ... *London: Chapman and Hall.* MDCCCLXVIII. 8vo, pp. (6), xl, 111. B., BA. 24371

Finlason. A Review of the Authorities as to the Repression of Riot or Rebellion; with Special Reference to Criminal or Civil Liability. By W. F. Finlason, Esq. ... *London: Stevens & Sons.* 1868. 8vo, pp. vi, (1), 224. B., BA. 24372

Relates to the Jamaica case.

Finlason. Treatise on Martial Law, as allowed by the Law of England in time of Rebellion; with Practical Illustrations, drawn from the Official Documents in the Jamaica Case, and the Evidence taken by the Royal Commission of Inquiry; with Comments, Constitutional and Legal. *London.* 1866. 8vo. C.

Finlay (D. L.) Observations on West India Fevers. By D. L. Finlay. *London.* 1853. 24374

Finlay (H.) Journal kept by Hugh Finlay, Surveyor of the Post Roads of North America, during his Survey of the Post Offices between Falmouth and Casco Bay and Savannah, begun 13th September, 1773, & ended 26th June, 1774. [With Introduction by F. H. Norton.] *Brooklyn: Privately Printed for F. H. Norton.* 4to, pp. xxv, 94. C. 24375

One hundred and fifty copies printed.

Finlay (J. B.) Inaugural Address delivered at the Opening of the University of Kittanning ... 21st November, 1858; by John B. Finlay ... . *Pittsburgh: printed by J. T. Shryock.* 1859. 8vo, pp. 42. H. 24376

Finley (E. L.) An Address, delivered by Request of the Humane Impartial Society, at their Annual Meeting, held ... 24th January, 1831 ... . *Baltimore: printed by Lucas & Deaver.* 1831. 12mo, pp. 12. B.A., H. 24377

Also: An Address ... Sunday School Union, ... Maryland, ... 30th ... Nov. 1830 ... . *Baltimore: printed by Lucas & Deaver.* 1831. pp. 11. BA., H.

Finley (J. B.) Autobiography of Rev. James B. Finley; or, Pioneer Life in the West. Edited by W. P. Strickland, D.D. *Cincinnati: the Author.* 1854. 12mo, pp. 455. Portrait. BA., C.

Finley. History of the Wyandott Mission at Upper Sandusky, Ohio, under the Direction of the Methodist Episcopal Church. By Rev. James B. Finley, ... *J. F. Wright and L. Swormstedt.* 1840. 12mo, pp. 432. BA., S. 24379

Finley. Life Among the Indians; or, Personal Reminiscences and Historical Incidents illustrative of Indian Life and Character. By Rev. James B. Finley. ... . Edited by Rev. D. W. Clark, D.D. *Cincinnati: For the Author.* 1857. 12mo, pp. 548. Portrait and Plates. BA., C. + *Cincinnati.* 1860. 12mo, pp. 548. 24380

Finley. Memorials of Prison Life, by Rev. James B. Finley. Edited by Rev. B. F. Teft, D.D. *Cincinnati: L. Swormstedt.* 1860. 12mo, pp. 354. 2 Plates. C. 24381

Finley. Sketches of Western Methodism; Biographical, Historical and Miscellaneous: Illustrative of Pioneer Life. Edited by W. P. Strickland, D.D. *Cincinnati: Methodist Book Concern.* 1854. 12mo, pp. 452. S. + [*Ibid.*] 1856. 24382

Finley (R.) Account of the Proceedings in the House of Representatives of the United States, respecting the Contested Election for the Eastern District of Georgia. *Philadelphia.* 1792. 8vo. P. 24383

Finley (R.) Biography of the Rev. Robert Finley, D.D., of Basking Ridge, N. J. Second Edition, Enlarged. With an Account of his Agency as the Author of The American Colonization Society; also a Sketch of the Slave Trade ... . With an Appendix. By Rev. Isaac V. Brown, A.M. *Philadelphia: John W. Moore.* 1857. 12mo, pp. 336. 24384

Finley. Memoirs of the Rev. Robert Finley, of Georgia: with Sketches of his Contemporaries. *New Brunswick.* 1819. 8vo.

Finley (Samuel). Christ Triumphing, and Satan Raging. A Sermon on Matth. xii. 28. Wherein is proven that the Kingdom of God is come unto us at this Day. Preached at Nottingham in Pensilvania, Jan. 20, 1740. By Samuel Finley ... . *Philadelphia: B. Franklin.* 1741. 8vo, pp. 43. BA. + *Philadelphia Printed, Boston Printed, London Printed,* 1741. *Boston: Rogers and Fowle.* 1742. 8vo, pp. 32. H. 24386

Finley. Clear Light put out in Obscure Darkness. Being an Examination and Refutation of Mr. Thompson's Sermon, entituled, The Doctrine of Convictions set in a Clear Light. By Samuel Finley, Minister of the Gospel. *Philadelphia: printed by B. Franklin.* 1743. 12mo, pp. 71. P. 24387

Finley. The Curse of Meroz; | or, | The Danger of Neutrality, in the | Cause of God, and our Country. | A | Sermon, | Preached the 2d of October, 1757. | By Samuel Finley, A.M. Minister of | the Gospel in Nottingham, Pennsylvania. | Published at the Desire of many. | [Motto.] *Philadelphia: | Printed and Sold by James Chattin, at the Newest- | Printing-Office, on the South Side of the Jersey- | Market.* 1757. | 4to, pp. 32. 24388

Finley. The Madness of Mankind, represented in a Sermon preached in the New Presbyterian Church in Philadelphia, June 9, 1754. *Philadelphia.* 1754. 8vo, pp. 22. + Second Edition. *New York: Hugh Gaine.* 1758. 8vo, pp. 22. 24389

Finley. The Successful Minister of Christ distinguished in Glory. — A Sermon occasioned by the Death of the Late Reverend Mr. Gilbert Tennent: [with Eulogy, by another Author.] *Philadelphia: William Bradford.* 1764. 8vo, pp. 28, xv, xii.

Finley. A Vindication of the Charitable Plea for the Speechless: in answer to Mr. Abel Morgan's Antipœdorantism. Wherein the points in controversy are more largely opened, and his Objections particularly Considered, and Refuted. The whole is freely submitted to the Judgment of Common Sense. By Samuel Finley, V.D.M. at Nottingham, in Pennsylvania. *Philadelphia: William Bradford.* MDCCXLVIII. 8vo, pp. viii, 113. P. 24391

Also: The Approved Minister of God. A Sermon Preached at the Ordination of the Reverend J. Rodgers ... *Philadelphia.* [1749.] 8vo. — A Letter to a Friend [in defence of George Whitefield. About 1742.] 12mo, pp. 12. B., M. — Satan strip'd of his Angelic Robe: the Substance of several Sermons at Philadelphia, January 1742–3. Shewing the Nature of Delusion. With an Application to the Moravians. *Philadelphia.* [n. d.] 8vo, pp. xii, 42. B.

Finn (H. J.) Montgomery; or, the Falls of Montmorency; A ... Drama, in Three Acts: By Henry J. Finn. *Boston: Wells and Lilly.* 1821. 8vo, pp. (2), 56. BA. 24392

Finney (C. G.) A Fourth Voice from America; or, Two Sermons, preached by the Rev. C. G. Finney. *London.* 1850. 12mo, pp. 46. 24393

Fiora (P. M. da S.) Vita e Miracoli del Fr. Sebastiano d'Apparisio, Patriarca S. Francesco, e Figlio del Messico, nella Nuoua Spagna, dal Fr. Paolo Mariani da S. Fiora. *Roma.* 1696. 4to. 24394

Fiorentino (F. C.) Supplementi de le Chroniche vulgare, nouamente dal frate Jacobo Philippo, al anno 1503 vulgarizz., per Francesco C. Fiorentino. *Vinegia.* 1508. Folio, pp. 342, 343. 24395

Contains a relation of Columbus' discovery of America.

Fiorentino (M. L.) L'Elogio di Amerigo Vespucci Composto dal Proposto Marco Lastri Fiorentino. *Firenze.* 1787.

Also on large paper.

The Firelands Pioneer. Published by the Firelands Historical Society. *Sandusky, O.* 1858. 8vo. 24397

The later volumes are published at Norwalk, Ohio. *See* "Hist. Mag.," III. 324.

Firey (Lewis P.) Speech ... in the Senate of Maryland, February 5, 1862, on the Compromise Resolutions proposed by him. [n. p. n. d.] 8vo, pp. 11. 24398

Firm (Henry). American Comic Annual. Illustrated by D. C. Johnson. *Boston.* MDCCCXXXI. 16mo. 24399

Firmin (G.) The Real Christian, or a Treatise of Effectual Calling. By Giles Firmin, of New England. *London.* 1670. 4to, pp. (48), 321 [329]. B. + *Boston: Printed by Rogers and Fowle.* MDCCXLII. 12mo, 4 l., pp. 38. W. 24400

Contains references to various American authors.

Firmin. Of Schism. Parochial Congregations in England, and Ordination by Imposition of Hands. Wherein Dr. Owen's Discovery of The True Nature of Schism is briefly and friendly examined, with Mr. Noyes of New England his Arguments against Imposition of Hands in Ordination. By Giles Firmin ... . *London: Nathanael Webb, and William Grantham.* 1658. 8vo, pp. (10), 157, (1). BA. 24401

Also: A Serious Question Stated, ... *London.* 1651. 4to. — Weighty Questions Discussed. ... . *Printed for the Author.* 1692. 4to. Mr. Firmin came to New England, where he practiced physic at Ipswich, married the daughter of "Simple Cobler" Ward, returned to England, became a preacher, and was one of the ejected ministers of 1662. For a list of his works, *see* a paper by J. W. Dean, in the "New England Genealogical Register."

Firmin del Rey. Hernan Cortez en Tobasco. Por Firmin del Rey. [About 1622.] 24402

A theatrical piece on the conquest of the New World. *See* Ternaux, No. 443.

Firmin (M. C.), *and* Lacroix (F.) Amérique Méridionale iles diverses de L'Ocean et Régions circompolaires, par M. C. Firmin et F. Lacroix. *Paris.* 1840. 8vo. Maps and Plates.

The First Book of the American Chronicles of the Times. *Norwich.* 1774. 8vo. W. + *Boston.* 1775. 8vo, pp. 32. + *Philadelphia.* 1775. 8vo. + *Newbern: J. Davis.* [n. d.] 8vo, pp. 15. 24404

Relates chiefly to events in 1774, and is written in Scriptural style.

The First Duty of a Citizen. [n. p. n. d.] pp. 8. 24405

Showing the importance of a deeper interest by the people in the elections.

The First Duty of the Citizen. The Grandeur of the Struggle and its Responsibilities. Southern Principles. *Philadelphia: Printed for Gratuitous Distribution.* 1863. 8vo, pp. 16. H. + [Another Edition. 1863.] 8vo, pp. 8. 24406

First Impressions of the New World on Two Travellers from the Old in the Autumn of 1858. *London: Longman.* 1859. Post 8vo, pp. 320. C. 24407

The First Jubilee of American Independence and Tribute to John Adams and Thomas Jefferson. *Newark, N. J.* 1826.

First Lessons in the History of the United States. *Boston.* 1856. 12mo. B. 24409

First Letter to the People of England. *See* Letter to, &c.

First — in many cases where this word commences the title of a book, *see* under the next word as above.

The First Measures necessary to be taken in the American Department. *London.* 1768. 4to. 24410

The First of a Series of a Work in favor of the Constitutionality of a National Bank. By The Belarius of Cymbeline. *Washington: L. Towers & Co.* 1862. 8vo, pp. 31. 24411

The First of the Knickerbockers. *See* [Paulding (J. K.)]

The First Reader for Southern Schools. *Raleigh, (N. C.): Christian Advocate Publishing Co.* 1864. 12mo, pp. 24. C.

The First Settlers of New-England. *See* [Child], Vol. IV., No. 12714.

First Settlers of Virginia. *See* [Davis], Vol. V., No. 18849.

The Fiscal Convention. Hints for the People, &c., in proforma Debates of a Convention of Delegates from different Classes and Interests, with a Platform of Principles unanimously recommended to the National Government. *New York: J. M. Sherwood.* 1865. 8vo, pp. 90. 24413

Fisch (G.) Brief Notice of the Evangelical Church of Lyons. 1845. 24414

Fisch (G.) États-Unis en 1861. Par Georges Fisch. *Paris: Librarie E. Dentu.* 1862. 12mo, pp. 238. B., BA., C. 24415

Fisch. Nine Months in the United States during the Crisis. By the Rev. Georges Fisch, D.D. ... With an Introduction by the Hon. Arthur Kinnaird, M.P., and a Preface by the Rev. W. Arthur. ... *London: James Nesbit & Co.* M.DCCC.LXII. Crown 8vo, pp. xvi, 166. B. 24416

[Fischer (Augustin).] Bibliotheca Mejicana. A Catalogue of an extraordinary Collection of Books & Manuscripts, almost wholly relating to the History and Literature of North and South America, particularly Mexico. *London: Puttick & Simpson.* 1869. 8vo, 4 l., pp. 312, 41, (1). 24417

Father Fischer was chaplain to the Emperor Maximilian. This is a catalogue of his library, which was sold by auction.

Fischer (C. A.) Beyträge zur genauern Kenntniss der Spanischen Besitzungen in Amerika aus dem Spanischen übersetzt und mit einigen Anmerkungen begleitet von Christian August Fischer. *Dresden: Heinrich Gerlach.* 1802. 8vo, pp. xvi, 276.

"Ich diese verworrenen Materialien geordnet und das Ganze so gut als neu geschrieben habe."

Fischer. Bijdraagen tot eene meer naauwkeurige kennis der Spaansche Bezittingen in Amerika. Uit het Spaansch in het Hoogduitsch overgezet, et met eenige aanmerkingen voorzien. *Leyden: D. Du Mortier & zoon.* 1804. 8vo, pp. vi, 220. Plate.

Contributions to the knowledge of the Spanish colonies in America.

Fischer. Tafereelen van Braziliê. Naar het Hoogduitsch. *Haarlem.* 1819. 8vo. c. 24420

Sketches of Brazil. From the German.

Fischer (J. E.) De l'Origine des Américains. Par Jean-Eberhard Fischer, Professeur d'Histoire. *Pétersbourgh.* 1771.

Title from Faribault, No. 230.

Fischer (Johann G.) Reise-Beschreibung der Saltzburg Nürnberger Emigranten nach Holland. *Leipzig.* 1734. 4to, pp. 40. B. 24422

[Fischer (Johannes Jacob Gottlob).] Die Geschichte von der Marterwoche, Auferstehung und Hemmelfahrt unsers Herrn und Heilandes Jesu Christ. Übersetzt in die Aruwackische Sprache, und erklärend umschrieben. *Philadelphia: Carl Cest.* 1799. 8vo, pp. 213. 24423

The Indian title is long; commences "Wadaijahun Wuussa-goanti Wappusida-goanti baddia Jesus Christus," etc. It is a history of the passion, resurrection, and ascension of the Savior, in the Arrawak language.

Fischer (P.) Recherches zoologiques pour servir à l'histoire de la faune de l'Amérique centrale et du Mexique. Publiées sous la direction de Milne Edwards. 7e partie. *Paris: imprimerie impériale.* 1870. 4to, 3 l., pp. 152, 6 l. 6 Plates. c.

Fischer (P.), *and* Crosse (H.) Études sur les mollusques terrestres et fluviatiles du Mexique et du Guatémala. Par P. Fischer et H. Crosse. [*Paris: imprimerie impériale.* 1870.] 4to, pp. 152. 6 Plates. c. 24425

Forms part of the account of the scientific expedition sent to Mexico by France.

Fish (E.) The Art of War Lawful and Necessary for a Christian People. Considered and Enforced. Sermon to a Military Company, Upton, May 26, 1773. By Elisha Fish, A.M. *Boston.* 1773. 8vo, pp. 17. M., W. 24426

Fish. Japhet Dwelling in the Tents of Shem; or Infant Baptism Vindicated, in A Discourse ... at Upton, January 5, 1772. ... By Elisha Fish, A.M. ... . *Boston.* 1772. 8vo. + Second Edition. *Boston: Thomas and John Fleet.* 1773. 8vo, pp. 47. H. 24427

Fish. Thanksgiving Sermon at Upton, [Mass.] May 28, 1766, on the Repeal of the Stamp Act. *Providence, R. I.* 1767. 12mo. P. 24428

Also: Discourse at Worcester, [Mass.] March 28, 1775, at the Desire of the Convention of Committees for the County of Worcester. *Worcester.* 1775. 8vo.

Fish, *and* Crane (*Rev.* John). The Baptism of Jesus Christ not to be Imitated by Christians. Essay. *Boston.* [n. d.] 8vo, pp. 22. 24429

Fish (Hamilton). Communication from the Governor of New York, transmitting certain Proceedings of the Seneca Nation. [n. p. n. d.] 8vo. B. 24430

Fish. Fremont, the Conservative Candidate. Correspondence between Hon. Hamilton Fish and Hon. Jas. A. Hamilton [Respecting Presidential Candidates. [n. p. 1856.] 8vo, pp. 20.

Also: ... Reasons for supporting Fremont: A Letter, Sept. 12, 1856. *See* Marsh (E.) — Report of the Committee in Assembly in New York, to Examine the Claim of W. W. Niles. [n. p. n. d.] 8vo. B.

Fish (H. C.) History and Repository of Pulpit Eloquence, containing the Masterpieces of ... Edwards, Davies, John M. Mason, ... with ... Historical Sketches of Preaching in the different countries represented, and Biographical and Critical Notices of the several Preachers and their Discourses, By the Rev. Henry C. Fish. *New York: W. M. Dodd.* 1856. 2 vols., 8vo, pp. 1244. Portrait. 24432

Fish. Pulpit Eloquence of the Nineteenth Century: being Supplementary to the History and Repository of Pulpit Eloquence, and containing Discourses of Eminent Living Ministers in Europe and America, with Sketches, Biographical and Descriptive, By the Rev. Henry C. Fish. *New York: W. M. Dodd.* 1857. 8vo, pp. x, 815. 24433

Fish. A Semi-Centennial Sermon, preached June Twenty-Second and Twenty-Ninth, M,DCCCLI, upon the History of The First Baptist Church in Newark, N. J., for the First Half Century of its Ecclesiastical Existence, by ... Henry C. Fish. *New-York: Lewis Colby.* 1851. 18mo, pp. 108. 24434

Fish. The Valley of Achor a Door of Hope; or, the Grand Issues of the War. A discourse, delivered on Thanksgiving Day, Nov. 26, 1863. By Henry Clay Fish, D.D., ... *New-York: Sheldon & Co.* 1863. 8vo, pp. 24. C. 24435

Also: The Characteristics of Successful Benevolent Effort. ... The "Circular Letter" of the East New Jersey Baptist Association, printed with the Minutes of their Seventh Anniversary, June, 1848. ... *New-York: G. B. Maigne.* 1848. 8vo, pp. 8.

Fish (H. C.) The Agent's Manual of Life Assurance. By Henry C. Fish. *New York: Wynkoop & Hallenbeck.* 1868. 12mo, pp. 165. c. 24436

Fish (J.) Christ ... Sermon ... before the General Assembly of ... Connecticut ... Anniversary Election, May 8. 1760. By Joseph Fish ... . *New London: Timothy Green.* 1760. 8vo, pp. 66. C., H. 24437

Fish. The Church of Christ a firm and durable House. Shown in a Number of Sermons On Matth. xvi. 18. ... The Substance of which Was delivered At Stonington, Anno Domini, 1765. By Joseph Fish, A.M. And Pastor of a Church there. *New-London: Printed and sold by Timothy Green.* 1767. 8vo, pp. viii, (1), 196. 24438

Fish. The Examiner Examined. Remarks On a Piece wrote by Mr. Isaac Backus, of Middleborough; printed in 1768. (Called, "An Examination of Nine Sermons from Matth. 16. 18. published last Year, by Mr. Joseph Fish, of Stonington.") Wherein Those Sermons are vindicated, from the Exceptions taken against them by Backus ... Many of his Errors confuted, and his Mistakes corrected. By Joseph Fish, A.M. Pastor of a Church in Stonington, And Author of said Sermons. *New-London: Printed and Sold by Timothy Green.* M.DCC.LXXI. 8vo, pp. 127. C., H. 24439

Fish. Love ... Sermon ... Ordination Of the Reverend Mr. William Vinal ... Newport, October 29. 1746. ... By Joseph Fish ... . *Newport: Printed by the Widow Franklin.* 1747. 8vo, pp. 55. B., BA., H. 24440

Fish. A Sermon preached at Westerly in the Colony of Rhode Island, August 27, 1755, in the South Meeting House, to a number of Religious People, on a Day of Fasting and Prayer (observed by them) for Success to our Armies, with a more particular reference to the Expedition against Crown Point, in which some of them had near Relations. By Joseph Fish ... *Newport: J. Franklin.* [1755.] 8vo, pp. 32. W. 24441

Fish (P.) The Excellency of the Righteous. A Discourse occasioned by the Death of Hon. Elisha Doane, who died at Yarmouth, Mass., October 8, 1848. By Phineas Fish, A.M. *Yarmouth: W. S. Fisher.* 1849. 8vo, pp. 16. B., H. 24442

Fish. A Sermon, delivered at the Ordination of the Reverend Abner Morse ... in Nantucket, Dec. 16, 1819. By Phineas Fish, A.M. ... *Boston: Charles Ewer.* 1820. 8vo, pp. 32. BA.

Fish (S.) An Address, showing the Means to prevent Wars among all Nations of the Earth; The Cause of Zion defended; and a New Year's Gift; on the subject of Peace and Union. By Samuel Fish. *Windham.* 1796. 8vo. c. 24444

Also: A Discourse showing the certainty of Christ's Personal Appearance. *Windham.* 1793. 8vo. S. — An humble Address to every Christian of every Nation ... *Norwich.* 1793. 8vo. S.

Fish (T. G.) St. Ann's Church, Brooklyn, New York, from the Year 1784 to the Year 1845, with a Brief Notice of the other Episcopal Churches in Brooklyn. By T. G. Fish. *Brooklyn.* 1845. 12mo. 24445

Fish (W. H.) Orthodoxy *versus* Spiritualism and Liberalism. By Rev. W. H. Fish, Cortland, N. Y. *Hopedale Press.* 1857. 8vo, pp. 22. 24446

Fish (W. S.) Defence of William S. Fish, Submitted by his Counsel, Milton Whitney, Esq., Washington, April 11, 1864. *Washington.* 1864. 8vo. 24447

Fish. Report of Commissioners Appointed under Resolve of 1856, Chap. 58, Concerning the Artificial Propagation of Fish, with other Documents. *Boston: William White.* 1857. 8vo, pp. 55. 24448

The Massachusetts "Commissioners on Inland Fisheries" presented their fifth annual report in 1871.

Fishback (J.) ... The necessary dependence of the American Republics upon the Christian Religion, for their Origin, and continuance, evinced. By James Fishback. *Lexington, Ky.: Printed by Thomas T. Skillman.* 1813. 8vo, pp. (4), 306, (2).

Also: An Oration ... Lexington, Ky. ... July, 1816. ... *Lexington, Ky.: Thomas T. Skillman.* 1816. 8vo, pp. 34. BA.

Fishback (William M.) Letter to the Hon. James H. Lane giving a detailed account of his Conduct during the present Rebellion, and in defence of Himself against the Charge of Disloyalty. 8vo, pp. 4. (Senate Doc., No. 129, 38th Cong., 1st. Sess., 1864.) 24450

Fisher (A.) Sermon at Bellingham, [Mass.] Oct. 13, 1816. By Abiel Fisher. *Worcester.* 1817. 8vo. W. 24451

Fisher (A.), *Junr.* Century Sermons. Two Discourses delivered at Bellingham, Mass., in the Year 1822. By Rev. Abiel Fisher, Jr. *Worcester.* 1822. 8vo, pp. 28. 24452

Fisher (A.) A Journal of a Voyage of Discovery to the Arctic Regions, in his Majesty's Ships Hecla and Griper, in the Years 1819 & 1820. By Alexander Fisher, Surgeon R. N. *London: Longman.* 1821. 8vo, pp. xi, 320. 2 Maps. BA. + Second Edition. [*Ibid.*] 1821. 8vo, pp. xi, 320. 2 Maps. + Third Edition. [*Ibid.*] 1821. 8vo, pp. xi, 320. 2 Maps. + Fourth Edition, Corrected. [*Ibid.*] 1821. 8vo, pp. xi, 320. 2 Maps and 5 Plates. C., H. 24453

Fisher (C. M.) Report to the Brown Association, U. S. A., made by C. M. Fisher, A.D. 1866. Published by order of the Brown Association. *Middlebury.* 1866. 8vo, pp. 8. 24454

Fisher (C.) A Serious Expostulation with the Followers of Elias Hicks, called by themselves Tolerants; particularly addressed to those who live within the limits of Springborough Monthly Meeting, ... By Charles Fisher. 1829. 24455

Republished in Elisha Bates' "Miscellaneous Repository," II. 252.

[Fisher (Charles Edward).] Kansas and the Constitution. By "Cecil." *Boston: Damrell & Moore.* 1856. 8vo, pp. 16.

Fisher (E. C.) The English Branch of the United States Sanitary Commission. The Motive of its Establishment and Results of its Work. By Edmund C. Fisher. *London.* 1862. 8vo, pp. 31. 8vo. 24457

Fisher (E.) Lecture on the North and the South, ... Cincinnati, Ohio, January 16, 1849, By Elwood Fisher. *Charleston: A. J. Burke.* 1849. 8vo, pp. 24. B., H. + *Richmond.* 1849. 8vo. B. 24458

Also: Review of Ellwood Fisher's Lecture on the North and South. [*Louisville.* 1849?] 8vo, pp. 20. H. (Signed "Justice.") — The South and the North: being a Reply to a Lecture on the North and the South, By Ellwood Fisher. By a Carolinian. *Washington: Buel & Blanchard.* 1849. 8vo, pp. 32. B., BA. (*See also* Mussey (O.)

Fisher (G.) The American Instructor: Or, Young Men's Best Companion. Containing Spelling, Reading, Writing, and Arithmetick, in an easier way than any yet published, and how to qualify any Person for Business, without the aid of a Master. Instructions to write Variety of Hands, with Copies both in Prose and Verse. How to write Letters on Business or Friendship. Forms of Indentures, Bonds, Bills of Sale, Receipts, Wills, Leases, Releases, &c. Also Merchants' Accompts, and a short and easy Method of Shop and Book-Keeping; with a

Description of the several American Colonies. Together with the Carpenter's plain and exact Rule, shewing how to Measure Carpenters, Joyners, Sawers, Bricklayers, Plaisterers, Plumbers, Masons, Glasiers, and Painters' Work. How to undertake each work, and at what Price, the Rates of each commodity, and the common Wages of Journeymen; with Gunter's Line, and Coggeshal's Description of the Sliding-Rule. Likewise the Practical Guage made Easy: the Art of Dialling, and how to erect and fix any Dial; with Instructions for Dying, Colouring and making Colours. To which is added, The Poor Painter's Physician. With Instructions for marking on Linnen; how to Pickle and Preserve; to make divers sorts of Wine; and many excellent Plaisters, and Medecines, necessary in all Families. And also, Prudent Advice to Young Tradesmen and Dealers. The whole better adapted to these American Colonies, than any other book of the like kind. By George Fisher, Accomptant. The Ninth Edition, Revised and Corrected. *Philadelphia: Printed by B. Franklin and D. Hall, at the New-Printing-Office, in Market-Street.* 1748. 12mo, pp. v, 378. C., P. + The Tenth Edition, Revised and Corrected. *Philadelphia: B. Franklin and D. Hall.* 1753. 12mo, pp. v, 384, (2). + *Worcester: Isaiah Thomas.* MDCCLXXXVI. 12mo. + *Philddelphia: Jos. Crukshank.* MDCCLXXXVII. 12mo. W. + *Walpole: I. Thomas and D. Carlisle.* 1794. 12mo. W. 24459

Fisher (G.) Memorials of George Fisher, late Secretary to the Expedition of Gen. Mexia, against Tampico, in 1835, presented to the Congress of Texas, praying for Relief of the Members of said Expedition. *Houston, (Texas).* 1840. 8vo. C. S. 24460

Fisher (G. A.) The Yankee Conscript; or, Eighteen Months in Dixie. By George Adams Fisher. With an Introduction by Rev. William Dickson. *Philadelphia: J. W. Daughaday.* 1864. 12mo, pp. 251. Portrait. B., BA., C., S. 24461

The author was a compulsory soldier in the Rebel Army.

Fisher (G. E.) ... A Farewell Discourse, to the Congregational Church ... Rutland, Mass. ... May 16, 1852. By Rev. George E. Fisher. ... *Worcester: Chas. Hamilton.* 1852. 8vo, pp. 24. H. 24462

Fisher (G. J.) Biographies of Deceased Physicians of Westchester County, N. Y. By G. J. Fisher, M.D. *New York.* 1861. 8vo. S. 24463

Fisher (G. P.) A Discourse, Commemorative of the History of the Church of Christ in Yale College, during the first century of its existence. Preached in the College Chapel, November 22, 1857. With Notes and an Appendix. By George P. Fisher, ... *New Haven: Thomas H. Pease.* 1858. 8vo, pp. 98, (1). B. 24464

Fisher. Life of Benjamin Silliman, M.D., LL.D., ... Chiefly from his Manuscript Reminiscences, Diaries, and Correspondence. By George P. Fisher, Professor in Yale College. *New York: Charles Scribner & Co.* 1866. 2 vols., 12mo, pp. xvi, 407; ix, 408. Portrait and Plate. B. 24465

Also: A Discourse Commemorative of the Life and Services of Josiah Willard Gibbs ... Yale College. Delivered ... March 31st, 1861. ... *New Haven: Thomas J. Stafford.* 1861. 8vo, pp. 20. BA., H. — National Faults. A Sermon ... Yale College ... Fast Day, April 6, 1860. ... *New Haven: Tuttle & Morehouse.* 1860. 8vo, pp. 14 — Thoughts proper to the Present Crisis. A Sermon, ... Yale College, ... Fast Day, January 4, 1861. ... *New Haven: Thomas H. Pease.* 1861. 8vo, pp. 21. B.

Fisher (G. P.) Speech of Hon. George P. Fisher. ... on the Prohibition of Slavery. Delivered in the House of Representatives, May 12, 1862. [*Washington.* 1866.] 8vo, pp. 8. H.

Fisher (G. S.) The Great Issues of the Day. Speech of Hon. Geo. S. Fisher at the Mass Meeting at Angola, September 26th, 1868. [n. p. 1868.] 8vo, pp. 13. H. 24467

Fisher (H. W.) Considerations on the Origin of the American War. By Herbert W. Fisher, M.A. *London & Cambridge: Macmillan & Co.* 1865. Fcap 8vo, pp. vi, 97. B., BA. 24468

Fisher (H.) The Divine Right of Private Judgment. ... A Reply to ... Josiah Smith's Answer to a Postscript ... to A Preservative ... With Remarks on Mr. Nathan Bassett's Appendix. By Hugh Fisher. *Boston.* 1731. 8vo, pp. (2), 101.

Fisher. A Preservative from Damnable Errors, in the Unction of the Holy One. A Sermon at the opening of a Presbytery, at Charlestown in S. Carolina. With Remarks, upon Mr. Smith's Preface and Sermon. [n. p.] MDCCXXX. 8vo, pp. (2), 84. B., W. 24470

Fisher (J.) An Oration ... at Kennebunk, on the Fourth day of July, 1799 ... . By Dr. Jacob Fisher. ... *Portland: E. A. Jenks.* 1799. 8vo, pp. 20. BA., W. 24471

Fisher (J. H.) The Federal Constitution; its Claims upon the Educated Men of the Country. An Address before the Alumni of Hobart College. Delivered in Geneva, July 16, 1862. By James H. Fisher. *Geneva.* 1862. 8vo, pp. 6 *or* 8. 24472

Fisher (J.) Sermon preached at Machias, [Me.] September 3, 1800, at the Ordination of Rev. Marshfield Steele. By Jonathan Fisher. *Boston: E. Lincoln.* 1801. 8vo, pp. 28. BA., H.

Fisher (Joshua). A Medical Discourse, on several Narcotic Vegetable Substances, ... June 4th, 1806. *Salem: Joshua Cushing.* 1806. 8vo, pp. 14. H. 24474

[Fisher (Joshua Francis).] Concessions and Compromises. [Dated Philadelphia, December 8, 1860. *Philadelphia: E. Sherman & Son.* 1860.] 8vo, pp. 14. H. 24475

Fisher. A Discourse, delivered before the Historical Society of Pennsylvania, the Ninth Day of April, 1836, on the Private Life and Domestic Habits of William Penn. By J. Francis Fisher. *Philadelphia: printed for McCarty & Davis.* 1836. 8vo, pp. 40. 24476

Fisher. Memoir of Samuel Breck, late President of the Pennsylvania Institution for the Instruction of the Blind. ... By J. Francis Fisher. *Philadelphia: C. Sherman, Son & Co.* 1863. 8vo, pp. 45. C., H. 24477

See also "Pennsylvania Hist. Soc.," Vol. II., Part 2. Also: The Degradation of our Representative System and Reform. ... *Philadelphia: C. Sherman & Co.* 1863. 8vo, pp. 47. H. — Reform in our Municipal Elections, a Plan suggested to the Tax Payers of Philadelphia and New York. ... *Philadelphia: William P. Kildare.* 1866. 8vo, pp. 28. B.

Fisher (L. P.) Fisher's Advertiser's Guide, containing a Short Description of those Towns and Cities on the Pacific Coast in which Newspapers are published. *San Francisco: L. P. Fisher.* 1870. Sq. 16mo, pp. 116, 44. 24478

Fisher (N.) An Oration at Brookfield, Mass., on the Capture of Lord Cornwallis and his whole Army at Yorktown by the combined Army under the Command of Washington. By Nathaniel Fisher. *Boston.* 1781. 4to. 24479

Fisher. A Sermon preached December 29, 1799, in St. Peter's Church, Salem, the Sunday after the Melancholy Tidings were received of the Death of General Washington. By Nathaniel Fisher, A.M. Published by Desire of the Town. *Salem: Printed by Thomas C. Cushing.* 1800. 8vo, pp. 24. C.

Also: An Address delivered to the Pupils of Henry Dean's Writing School, at their First Annual Exhibition in ... Salem, October 26, 1804. ... *Salem: Joshua Cushing.* [1804.] 4to, pp. 8. B., H. — Sermon delivered at Salem, January 14, 1796, occasioned by the Execution of Henry Blackburn ... for the Murder of George Wilkinson. *Boston: J. Dabney.* 1796. 8vo, pp. 21. BA., H.

FISHER (P.) History of New Brunswick. By Peter Fisher. 1829. 24481

This imperfect title is from Morgan's "Bibliotheca Canadensis."

FISHER (R.) The Great Rebellion. By the Rev. R. Fisher, New Jersey. *New York: American Tract Society.* 186–. 18mo.

FISHER (R.) Fisher's Magazine and Industrial Record. *New York: Reduval Cushing.* 1845–6. 3 vols., 8vo, 2 l., pp. 1180; 592. BA., C. 24483

Put forth as a rival to "Hunt's Merchants' Magazine."

[FISHER (R.)] Seventeen Numbers, the Signature of Neckar, upon the Causes of the Present Distress of the Country, with a Proposed Remedy. By a Citizen of New York. *New York. August*, 1837. 8vo, pp. 68. 24484

FISHER (R. S.) The Book of the World: being an Account of all Republics, Empires, Kingdoms, and Nations, in Reference to their Geography, Statistics, Commerce, &c.; together with a Brief Historical Outline of their Rise, Progress, and Present Condition, &c. By Richard S. Fisher, M.D. *New York: J. H. Colton.* 1849. 2 vols., 8vo, pp. viii, 614; 705. BA. + Second Edition. [*Ibid.*] 1852. 2 vols., 8vo. C. + Third Edition, Corrected by the Census of 1851–52. [*Ibid.*] 1853. 2 vols., 8vo. B. 24485

FISHER. A Chronological History of the Civil War in America. Illustrated with A. J. Johnson's and J. H. Colton's Steel Plate Maps and Plans of the Southern States and Harbors. By Richard Swainson Fisher, M.D., Editor, &c. *New York: Johnson & Ward.* 1863. 8vo, pp. 160. 10 Maps. S. 24486

FISHER. Colton's Traveler and Tourist's Route-Book through the United States ... the British Provinces, etc. containing the Routes and Distances on the Great Lines of Travel by Railroads, Stage-Roads, Canals, Lakes, and Rivers. By Richard S. Fisher, M.D. ... . *New York: Johnson & Browning.* 1859. 18mo, pp. xix, 227. 24487

FISHER. Gazetteer of the State of Maryland, Compiled from the Returns of the Seventh Census of the United States, and

other Official Documents. To which is added, a General Account of the District of Columbia. By R. S. Fisher, M.D. ... . *J. H. Colton, New-York, and James S. Waters, Baltimore.* 1852. 8vo, pp. 122. BA., C. 24488

FISHER. Indiana: in relation to its Geography, Statistics, Institutions, County Topography, etc. ... By Richard S. Fisher, M.D. ... . *New York: J. H. Colton.* 1852. + 1854. 8vo, pp. 126. 24489

FISHER. A New and Complete Statistical Gazetteer of the United States of America, founded on and compiled from Official Federal and State Returns, and the Seventh National Census. By Richard Swainson Fisher, M.D. ... *New York: J. H. Colton.* 1853. 8vo, pp. 960. B., C. + [*Ibid.*] 1855. 8vo. C. 24490

FISHER. The Progress of the United States of America, from the Earliest Periods, Geographical, Statistical, and Historical. Compiled from Official Returns, &c. By R. Swainson Fisher, M.D. *New York.* 1854. 8vo, pp. 432. Plates and Map. C. 24491

FISHER. The Seventh Census of the United States ... 1850: Compiled from Official Sources. By R. S. Fisher. Fourth Edition. *New York.* 1851. 18mo. S. 24492

FISHER. Statistical Account of the West India Islands. By R. S. Fisher, M.D. *New York.* 1856. 12mo, pp. 68. Map.

See La Torre (J. M. de), *and* O'Neil (J. T.)

FISHER (R. S.), *and* COLBY (C.) American Statistical Annual for the Year 1854; [and 1855] Compiled from Authentic Sources. By Richard Swainson Fisher, M.D., and Charles Colby, A.M. *New York.* 1854–5. 12mo, pp. 537. C. 24494

FISHER (*Prof.*) Report on the Alcinda Gold Mine, Va. 1839.

FISHER (S.) Christ's Light springing, arising up, shineing forth, and displaying itself through the whole world. Being a Treatise wrote by Samuel Fisher. *London: printed in the Year* 1660. *Philadelphia: reprinted by William Bradford.* 1744. 12mo, pp. 35. 24496

FISHER (S.) A Sermon; ... Feb. 24th, 1808, at the Ordination of the Rev. Andrew Eliot ... New-Milford. By Samuel Fisher, A.M. ... . *Danbury, (Conn.): John A. Gray.* 1808. 8vo, pp. 21. BA. 24497

Also: Sermon, before the Presbyterian Education Society, in New York. *Newark.* 1821. 8vo. — ... A Sermon, ... at the Opening of the Session of the General Assembly of the Presbyterian Church in the United States, in ... Philadelphia, May 16, 1839. ... *Philadelphia: Isaac Ashmead & Co.* 1839. 8vo, pp. 28. H. — Two Sermons delivered at Morris-Town, N. J.; to which is annexed an Address to the Presbyterian Congregation in that place. *Morris-Town.* 1814. 8vo. S.

FISHER (S. H.) Address before the New York State Agricultural Society ... at Utica ... September 18, 1863. *Albany: Van Benthuysen.* 1863. 8vo, pp. 34. H. 24498

FISHER (S. W.) Report of the Committee on the Complaint of George Logan against Samuel W. Fisher, for a Breach of Privilege; with Documents. *Lancaster.* 1800. 8vo. P. 24499

FISHER (S. W.) God's Purpose in Planting the American Church. A Sermon, before the American Board of Commissioners for Foreign Missions ... October 2, 1860. By Samuel W. Fisher, D.D. ... *Boston: T. R. Marvin & Son.* 1860. 8vo, pp. 55. B. 24500

FISHER. Light in Darkness. A Discourse delivered in Clinton, N. Y., before the Methodist, Baptist and Congregational Churches, November 27, 1862. By S. W. Fisher. *Clinton: M. D. Raymond.* 1862. 8vo, pp. 23. 24501

FISHER. Public Exercises at the Inauguration of Rev. Samuel Ware Fisher, D.D., as the Sixth President of Hamilton College, ... November 4, 1858. ... *Utica: Roberts, Printer.* 1858. 8vo, pp. 62. BA., S. 24502

FISHER. William Curtis Noyes. *Utica, N. Y.* 1866. 8vo, pp. 59. 24503

Also: Female Education. An Address ... Dedication of the Ohio Female College, September 4th, 1849. *Cincinnati.* 1849. 8vo, pp. 44. BA. — Historical Discourse, Hamilton College. [n. p. n. d.] 8vo, pp. 43. S. — Our Country, its Position, Obligation, and Power; a Sermon ... Albany, ... a Plea for Home Missions, June 23, 1844. ... *Albany: Erastus H. Pease,* 1844. 8vo, pp. 29. B. — ... A Sermon, occasioned by the Death of Miss Mary S. Dwight, a Teacher in the Albany Female Academy, ... March 2, 1845. ... *Albany: Erastus H. Pease.* 1845. 8vo, pp. 32. B., BA. — ... A Sermon delivered in ... Albany, on the occasion of the Funeral of Capt. Richard Winslow, January 10th, 1847, ... *New York: William Van Norden, Printer.* 1847. pp. 28. — The Supremacy of Mind: a Lecture ... . *Albany: Munsell and Tanner.* 1845. 8vo, pp. 49. B., H.

FISHER (S. G.) A National Currency. By Sidney George Fisher. ... Reprinted from the North American Review for July, 1864. *Philadelphia: J. B. Lippincott & Co.* 1864. 8vo, pp. 83. 24504

Reply to a pamphlet recently published by Sidney George Fisher, Esq., entitled, "A National Currency." *Philadelphia: John Campbell.* 1865. 8vo, pp. (2), 18.

FISHER. The Law of the Territories. By Sidney George Fisher. *Philadelphia.* 1859. 12mo, pp. 127. 24505

FISHER. The Trial of the Constitution. By Sidney George Fisher. ... *Philadelphia: J. B. Lippincott & Co.* 1862. 8vo, pp. 391. B., BA. 24506

Also: Address ... before the Chester County Agricultural Society, ... West-Chester, September 26, 1857, ... *Philadelphia: Merrihew & Thompson, Printers.* 1857. 8vo, pp. 27. H. — Address before the Agricultural Society of New Castle County, Delaware, ... October 7, 1860. ... *Philadelphia: C. Sherman & Son.* 1860. 8vo, pp. 26.

FISHER (W.) The Travels of Captains Lewis and Clark, by order of the Government of the United States, in the Years 1804–6, from St. Louis, by way of the Missouri and Columbia Rivers, to the Pacific Ocean: with Delineations of the Manners, Customs, Religion, etc., of the Indians. By William Fisher. *Philadelphia: H. Lester.* 1809. 12mo, pp. 300. 5 Plates. C.

FISHER. An Interesting Account of the Voyages and Travels of Captains Lewis and Clark, in the Years 1804, 1805, and 1806. Giving a Faithful Description of the River Missouri, and its Source, the various Tribes of Indians through which they passed. Manners and Customs, Soil, Climate, Commerce, Gold and Silver Mines, Animal and Vegetable Productions, interspersed with very Entertaining Anecdotes, and a variety of other Useful and Pleasing Information, remarkably calculated to Delight and Instruct the Readers. To which is added a Complete Dictionary of the Indian Tongue. By William Fisher, Esq. *Baltimore: Anthony Miltenberger.* 1812. 12mo, pp. 326. 2 Plates. + *Baltimore: Mauro.* 1813. 16mo, pp. 262. 2 Plates. 24508

FISHER. New Travels among the Indians of North America; being a Compilation, taken partly from the Communications already published, of Captains Lewis and Clark, to the President of the United States; and partly from other authors who travelled among the various Tribes of Indians. With ... A Dictionary of the Indian Tongue. Compiled by William Fisher, Esqr. *Philadelphia: James Sharan.* 1812. pp. 300. 2 Wood-cut Portraits. 24509

FISHER (W. L.) The History of the Institution of the Sabbath Day, its Uses and Abuses, with Notices of the Puritans, the Quakers, the National and other Sabbath Conventions, and of the Union between Church and State. By William Logan Fisher. *Philadelphia: John Penington.* 1845. 8vo, pp. 194, (1). BA. + Second Edition, Revised. *Philadelphia.* 1859. 12mo.

FISHER. An Inquiry into the Laws of Organized Societies, as applied to the alleged decline of the Society of Friends. By William Logan Fisher. *Philadelphia: T. Ellwood Zell.* 1860. 12mo, pp. 64. 24511

FISHER. Progressive Friends. An Account of the Fourth Annual Meeting of the ... Friends, with some Observations on their Principles and Prospects. ... [*Wakefield.* 1856.] 12mo, pp. 32. H. 24512

FISHERIES. Report of the Secretary of State, on the Subject of the Cod and Whale Fisheries; House of Representatives, Feb. 1, 1791. *Philadelphia.* 1792. 8vo, pp. 45. 24513

FISK (A.) An Oration, ... September 3d, 1811: before the Philermenian Society, at Providence. By Amasa Fisk, Esq. [*Providence:*] *Jones & Wheeler.* [1811.] 12mo, pp. 12. BA.

FISK (C. B.), *and* HUGHES (G. W.) Report on the Examination of Canal Routes from the Potomac River to ... Baltimore, especially in relation to the Supply of Water for their summit levels, by Charles B. Fisk and George W. Hughes, to the Governor of Maryland. *Annapolis.* 1837. 8vo. 24515

FISK (C. B.) Plain Counsels for Freedmen: in Sixteen Brief Lectures. By ... Clinton B. Fisk. *Boston: American Tract Society.* [1866.] 12mo, pp. 79. Woodcuts. H. 24516

FISK (E.) Joy and Gladness: a Thanksgiving Discourse, preached in Upton, Wednesday, May 28, 1766; occasioned by the Repeal of the Stamp-Act. By Elisha Fisk, A.M. Pastor of the Church there. *Providence in New-England: Printed and sold by Sarah Goddard, and Company, at the Post-Office.* MDCCLXVII. 8vo, pp. 17. P. 24517

FISK. (E.) Wrentham Jubilee. A Sermon Preached in Wrentham, Mass. June 12, 1849, by Rev. Elisha Fisk, on the Fiftieth Anniversary of his Ordination, as Pastor of the Original Congregational Church in said Town. With an Appendix. *Boston: printed by C. C. P. Moody.* 1850. 8vo, pp. 64. 24518

FISK. A Sermon, preached in Franklin, March 16, 1820, at the Funeral of Major Erastus Emmons. By Elisha Fisk, A.M. ... *Boston: Munroe and Francis.* 1820. 8vo, pp. 19. B. 24519

Also: Anniversary Sermon, delivered June 14, 1846, at Wrentham. [n. p. n. d.] 8vo, pp. 25. — A Sermon, delivered at the Ordination of the Rev. Martin Moore, in Natick, February 16, 1814. ... . *Dedham.* 1814. 8vo, pp. 28. BA., H. — A Sermon, preached in Braintree, before the Norfolk Auxiliary Society for the Education of Pious Youth, ... June 9, 1819. ... *Dedham.* [n. d.] 8vo, pp. 36. B. — A Sermon, ... at Boston, May 29, 1822, before the Massachusetts Society for Promoting Christian Knowledge. ... *Boston: Crocker and Brewster.* 1823. 8vo, pp. 23. BA., W. — A Sermon, occasioned by the Sudden Death of Mrs. A. Fisher, Wife of David Fisher ... . Preached Feb. 18, 1827. ... . *Providence: Miller & Hammond.* 1827. 8vo, pp. 18. B., H.

FISK (E.) Oration before the Alumni of Williams College, Sept. 7, 1825. By Ezra Fisk. *New York.* 1825. 8vo, pp. 20.

Also: Sermon at the Funeral of Rev. George Stewart. *Goshen.* 1819. 8vo.

FISK (F.) Recollections of Mary Lyon, with Selections from her Instructions to the Pupils in Mt. Holyoke Female Seminary. By Fidelia Fisk. *Boston: Am. Tract Society.* [1866.] 12mo, pp. 333. Plate. BA., C. 24521

FISK (H.), *and* HATCH (C. B.) The Chesapeake and Ohio Railroad as a Short, Economical, and Profitable Line, from the Atlantic Coast to the Great West. *New York.* 1871. 8vo, pp. 36. H. 24522

FISK *and* HATCH. To the Bondholders of the Central and Western Pacific Railroad Companies. January 2, 1871. [Circular. *New York.* 1871.] 8vo, pp. 24. H. 24523

FISK (I.) An Eulogy on Mr. Samuel Smith Adams, ... Brown University, ... Pronounced at the University Hall, April 18, 1812. By Isaac Fisk ... *Providence: Jones & Wheeler.* 1812. 8vo, pp. 16. 24524

FISK (J.) A Life of James Fisk, Jun. Being a Full and Accurate Narrative of all the Enterprises in which he has been engaged. *New York.* 1868. 12mo, pp. 300. Portraits. 24525

FISK (James L.) ... Expedition of Captain Fisk to the Rocky Mountains. ... Report of ... his ... Expedition to the Rocky Mountains and Idaho. [*Washington.* 1864.] 8vo, pp. 38. (38th Cong., 1st Sess. Senate, Ex. Doc., No. 45.) H. 24526

FISK (L. R.) An Address on the Condition and Office of the Agricultural College of ... Michigan, delivered in the ... House of Representatives, Jan. 14, 1861 ... *Lansing: Hosmer & Kerr.* 1861. 8vo, pp. 35. (Legislature, 1861. House Doc., No. 3.)

Also: Address ... delivered before the Macomb County Agricultural Society, at Romeo, October 4th, 1861. *Romeo: Michigan.* 1861. 8vo, pp. 15. H.

FISK (*Mrs.*) A Plea before the Ecclesiastical Council at Stockbridge, in the Cause of Mrs. Fisk, who was Excommunicated for Marrying a Man whom they called Immoral and Profane, October 6 and 7. 1779. By a Gentleman of Connecticut ... *Norwich.* 1779. 4to. + *Norwich.* 1780. 8vo. W. + *Boston.* 1782. 8vo. BA., W. 24528

FISK (P.) The Good Subject's Wish; or, The Desirableness of the Divine Providence with Civil Rulers. [An Election] Sermon, at Hartford, May 12th, 1726. By Phineas Fisk. *New London.* 1726. 12mo, pp. (4), 38. B. 24529

FISK (R.) Address, Hudson Literary Society. By Richmond Fisk, Jr. *Hudson, N. Y.* 1859. 8vo. S. 24530

FISK (S.) The Character of the Candidates for Civil Government, especially for Council. ... [an Election] Sermon ... May 26th. MDCCXXXI. By Samuel Fisk. ... *Boston: Printed by T. Fleet.* 1731. 8vo, pp. 50. B., BA., H., M. 24531

FISK. A Faithful Narrative of the Proceedings of the Ecclesiastical Council, convened at Salem in 1734, occasioned by the Scandalous Divisions in the First Church in that town. By Samuel Fisk. *Boston: printed by D. Henchman.* 1735. 8vo, pp. (6), 94. 24532

FISK. A Just and Impartial Narrative of the Controversy between the Rev. Mr. Samuel Fisk the Pastor, and a Number of the Brethren of the First Church of Christ ... in Salem. *Boston: Printed by Thomas Fleet.* 1735. 8vo, pp. (2), 115. BA.

FISK. Remarks on the Contents of a Letter relating to the Divisions of the First Church of Salem. *Boston.* 1735. 8vo, pp. 16. 24534

FISK (T.) The Banking Bubble Burst; ... being a History of the ... American Banking System. ... By Theophilus Fisk. *Charleston, S. C.* 1837. 8vo, pp. 88. BA., C. 24535

FISK. Oration on the Anniversary of the Glorious Victory at Fort Moultrie, June 28th, 1776. By Theophilus Fisk. *Charleston.* 1836. C. 24536

Also: Capital against Labor. An Address, delivered ... before the Mechanics of Boston ... May 20 [1835]. ... *Boston.* 1835. 8vo, pp. 16. H. — Labor the only True Source of Wealth: or the Rottenness of the Paper Money Banking System Exposed ... . An Oration ... Charleston, S. C., July 4th, 1837. ... [n. p. n. d.] 8vo, pp. 32. BA. — ... An Oration upon the Freedom of the Press, delivered at Danbury, Conn., December 5, 1832, on the Liberation, from Imprisonment, of P. T. Barnum, Esq., for an Alleged Libel ... *New Haven.* [n. p. n. d.] pp. 33–39. BA. — Our Country; its Dangers and Destiny. An Address delivered before the Cadets of the Norwich University, at the Annual Commencement, August 20, 1840. ... *Washington, D. C.* 1845. 8vo, pp. 16. BA., H.

FISK (W.) A Sermon delivered before His Excellency Levi Lincoln, Governor ... of ... Massachusetts, on the Day of General Election, May 27, 1829. By Wilbur Fisk, A.M. ... *Boston: True and Green, State Printers.* 1829. 8vo, pp. 27. B., BA.

Also: An Introductory Address, delivered at the Opening of the Wesleyan Academy, in Wilbraham, Mass. Nov. 8, 1825. ... *Springfield: A. G. Tannatt.* 1825. 8vo, pp. 23. BA. — Science of Education: Inaugural Address at Middletown, [Conn.] Sept. 21, 1831, as President of the Wesleyan University. ... *New York.* 1832. 8vo. W. — Substance of an Address delivered before the Middletown Colonization Society, ... July 4, 1835 ... *Middletown.* 1835. 8vo.

FISKE (A.) A Sermon, ... October 28, 1795, at the Ordination of the Rev. Abiel Abbot, ... in Coventry, Connecticut. By Abel Fiske, A.M., ... *Amherst, New Hampshire: Biglow and Cushing.* MDCCXCVI. 8vo, pp. 26. BA. 24538

FISKE. A Sermon, ... August 15, 1798, at the Ordination of the Rev. Jacob Abbot ... Hampton-Falls. By Abel Fiske, A.M. ... . *Newburyport: Edmund M. Blunt.* 1798. 8vo, pp. 28. BA.

Also: Discourse in Lyndeborough, February 26, 1801, at a Singing Lecture. ... *Amherst, N. H.* 1801. 8vo, pp. 20. N. — Masonic Discourse at Amherst, N. H. June 25, 1798. *Amherst.* 1798. 8vo. W. — Thanksgiving Sermon at Wilton, N. H. Nov. 15, 1798, To which are added Two other Discourses. *Amherst.* 1799. 8vo.

FISKE (A. A.) A History of the Family (Ancestral, and Descendant) of the Hon. William Fiske of Amherst, N. H., with Brief Notices of those connected with them by Marriage. Compiled and Published by Albert A. Fiske, a Grandson. *Chicago, Ill.* 1865. 12mo, pp. 151. 24540

From page 33, this edition is identical with the second edition described, *infra*.

FISKE. A History of the Family (Ancestral and Descendant) of William Fiske, Senr., of Amherst, N. H., with Brief Notices of other Branches springing from the same Ancestry. Second and Complete Edition. Compiled and Published by Albert A. Fiske, a Descendant. *Chicago, Ill.* 1867. 8vo, pp. 209. B.

FISKE (A.) A Confession of Faith; or a Seminary of Divinity. By Mrs. Ann Fiske. *Boston.* 1704. 8vo, pp. 8. 24542

FISKE (D. T.) An Old Disciple. A Discourse occasioned by the Death of Dea. Moses Little, delivered in ... Newburyport, May 17, 1857. ... By D. T. Fiske. *Newburyport: M. Otis Hall.* 1857. 8vo, pp. 15. H. 24543

Fiske (D. W.) The Book of the First American Chess Congress; containing the Proceedings of that Celebrated Assemblage, held in New York, in the Year 1857; together with Sketches of the History of Chess in the Old and New Worlds. By Daniel Willard Fiske, M.A. *New York: Rudd & Carleton.* 1858. 12mo, pp. 563. C. 24544

Fiske (J.) ... A Sermon, preached at Brooklyn, (Conn.) June 9th, 1813. At the Ordination of the Rev. Luther Wilson ... . By John Fiske ... . *Hartford: B. & J. Russell.* 1814. 8vo, pp. 20. B., H. 24545

Fiske. Sermon at New Braintree, Mass., Aug. 20, 1812 [Fast Day]. *Brookfield.* 8vo. W. 24546

Also: A Semi-Centennial Sermon. ... *Greenfield.* 1816. pp. 34.

Fiske (J. O.) Discourse on the Death of Zachary Taylor, By John O. Fiske. *Bath (Me.)* 1850. 8vo. 24547

Fiske. ... Discourse delivered in Bath, June 20, 1852, on the Occasion of the Death of General William King. By John O. Fiske ... . *Bath: Haines & Freeman.* 1852. 8vo, pp. 32.

Also: A Sermon on the Present National Troubles, delivered in the Winter Street Church, January 4, 1861. ... *Bath.* 1861. 8vo, pp. 19. B.

Fiske (N.) The Moral Monitor, or a Collection of Essays on Various Subjects, Accommodated to the State of Society in the United States of America. ... By the Late Reverend Nathan Fiske, D.D. ... *Worcester: Isaiah Thomas, Jun.* 1801. 2 vols., 12mo, pp. 300; iv, 296. BA., W. 24549

Seventy-four essays published in the "Massachusetts Spy," under the title of the "Worcester Speculator."

Fiske. Oration ... at Brookfield, Nov. 14, 1781. In Celebration of the Capture of Lord Cornwallis. By Nathan Fiske. *Boston: Thomas and John Fleet.* 1781. 4to, pp. 8. H., W.

Fiske. ... A Sermon, Preached at Brookfield on the last Day of the Year 1775. Together with some Marginal Notes, & Giving an Account of the First Settling of the Town in the Year 1660; its Desolation by the Indians in Philip's War, in 1675; its Distresses in Queen Anne's War; and its Increase and Improvements to the Present Time. By Nathan Fiske, A.M. ... *Boston, New-England: Thomas and John Fleet.* 1776. 8vo, pp. 31, v. B., BA., W. + *West Brookfield.* 1860. 8vo.

See also "Mass. Hist. Coll.," I. 257–275.

Fiske. A Sermon Preached at Brookfield, March 6, 1778. On the Day of the Interment of Mr. Joshua Spooner, Who was most Barbarously Murdered at his own Gate on the Lord's Day preceding, by three Ruffians, who were Hired for the Purpose by his Wife. By Nathan Fiske, A.M. ... . With an account of the Murder. *Boston: Printed by Thomas & John Fleet.* 1778. 8vo, pp. 20. BA. 24552

Fiske. ... Two Discourses Delivered at Brookfield, July 4. 1774. ... A Day of Fasting and Prayer, on Account of the Threatening Aspect of our Public Affairs. By Nathan Fisk, A.M. ... *Boston: Printed by John Kneeland.* MDCCLXXIV. 8vo, pp. 40. BA. 24553

Also: .. A Sermon delivered at Brookfield, October 19, 1779, at the Funeral of the Honorable Jedediah Foster ... . *Providence: Bennett Wheeler.* pp. 30. BA. — ... A Sermon at Brookfield, April 1, 1784, at the Funeral of Josiah Hobbs, Jun. who was Killed by Lightning ... *Worcester.* 1784. 8vo. W. — A Sermon preached at the Dudleian Lecture, ... September 7, 1796. ... *Boston: Printed by Manning & Loring.* 1796. 8vo, pp. 19. BA., H., W. — Twenty-Two Sermons, on Various and Important Subjects; chiefly Practical. ... *Worcester: Isaiah Thomas.* 1794. 8vo, pp. 417.

Fiske (O.) Address ... before the Worcester Agricultural Society, Oct. 8, 1823. By Oliver Fiske. *Worcester: William Manning.* [1823.] 8vo, pp. 36. B., H. 24554

Also: An Address delivered before the Worcester Agricultural Society, October 20, 1831. ... . *Worcester: M. W. Grout.* 1831. 8vo, pp. 16. H. — Oration ... at Douglass, July 5th, 1802. [n. p. n. d.] 8vo. B. — An Oration, pronounced at Worcester, ... July 4. 1797. *Worcester: Isaiah Thomas, Jr.* 1797. 4to, pp. 15.

Fiske (S.) Mr. Dunn Browne's Experiences in the Army. By Samuel Fiske, Captain 14th Conn. Volunteers. *Boston: Nichols and Noyes.* 1866. 12mo, pp. (2), 390. Portrait. B.

Fiske (T.) A Sermon, Delivered Dec. 29, 1799. At the Second Parish in Cambridge, Being the Lord's Day, Immediately following the Melancholy Intelligence of the Death of General George Washington, Late President of the United States of America. By Thadeus Fiske, A.M. Pastor of the Second Church in Cambridge. *Boston: Printed by James Cutler.* 1800. 8vo, pp. 21. BA., W. 24556

Fiske. Thanksgiving and Prayer for Public Rulers ... Discourse ... in Cambridge, February 19, 1795, being the Day of National Thanksgiving in the United States. By Thaddeus Fiske, A.M. ... . *Boston.* MDCCXCV. 8vo, pp. 20. BA., M., W.

Also: A Sermon, to which is Appended the Family Record, with an Extract from his Diary. *Boston.* 1843. 8vo, pp. 40.

Fiske Family. *See* [Poor (Alfred)].

Fisler (L. F.) A Local History of Camden, commencing with its Early Settlement, Incorporation, and Public and Private Improvements, brought up to the Present Day. By L. F. Fisler, M.D. *Camden, N. J.: Francis A. Cassedy.* 1858. pp. 62, (1).

Fitch (A. F.) Report of the Great Conspiracy Case. The People of the State of Michigan, versus Abel F. Fitch and others, commonly called the Railroad Conspirators: ... Tried at the May Term, 1851. *Detroit: Advertiser and Free Press.* 1851. 8vo, pp. 399, 8. B., S. 24559

Fitch (A.) Memorial of A. Fitch in behalf of Fitch Brothers & Co. ... Navy Agents at Marseilles, Feb. 5, 1845. *Washington. Cong. Doc.* 8vo, pp. 36. S. 24560

Fitch. Memorial of A. Fitch, being a Rejoinder to a Monument placed before the Senate by Charles Gould. [*Washington.* 1845.] 8vo, pp. 20. H. 24561

Fitch (A.) First Report on the Noxious, Beneficial and other Insects, of the State of New York, made to the State Agricultural Society, ... By Asa Fitch, M.D., .. *Albany: C. Van Benthuysen, Printer.* 1855. 8vo, pp. 180. B., BA., S. + First and Second Reports. *Albany.* 1856. 8vo, pp. 336. 4 Plates. + Third, Fourth, and Fifth Reports. *Albany.* 1859. 8vo, pp. 172, 67, 74, xi. 4 Plates. + Sixth, Seventh, Eighth, and Ninth Reports. *Albany.* 1865. 8vo, pp. 259. 4 Plates. 24562

Fitch. Winter Insects of Eastern New York. [n. d.] 8vo, pp. 11. 24563

From the "American Quarterly Journal of Agriculture."

Fitch (C.) The Safety of this Nation. A Sermon delivered in Holliston, on the Day of the Annual Thanksgiving, November 26, 1829. By Charles Fitch ... . *Boston: T. R. Marvin.* 1830. 8vo, pp. 14. BA. 24564

Fitch. View of Holliston in its First Century. A Century Sermon, delivered in Holliston, Mass. December 4, 1826. By Charles Fitch ... . *Dedham: H. & W. H. Mann.* 1827. 8vo, pp. 36. BA., M. 24565

Also: Slaveholding weighed in the Balance of Truth, and its Guilt Illustrated. ... *Boston.* 1837. 8vo.

Fitch (C. E.) The National Problem. An Oration delivered at Delphi, New York, July 4, 1861. By Charles Fitch. *Syracuse: Summers & Co.* 1861. 12mo, pp. 19. 24566

Fitch. The Press of Onondaga: a Lecture delivered before the Onondaga Historical Association. By Charles E. Fitch. *Syracuse.* 1868. 8vo. S. 24567

Fitch (E.) Discourse addressed to the Candidates for the Baccalaureate, in Williams College, September 1, 1799. By Ebenezer Fitch. *Pittsfield.* [n. d.] 8vo, pp. 34. N. 24568

Fitch (E. T.) National Prosperity Perpetuated. A Discourse: delivered in the Chapel of Yale College; on the day of Annual Thanksgiving: November 29, 1827. By Eleazer T. Fitch. *New Haven: Treadway and Adams.* 1828. 8vo, pp. 34.

Also: A Sermon: preached at the Funeral of the Rev. John Elliott, D.D.; Late Pastor of a Church in East Guilford ... *New Haven: Nathan Whiting.* 1825. 8vo, pp. 19. H. — ... A Sermon; preached at the Ordination of the Rev. William C. Fowler ... in Greenfield, Mass. Aug. 31, 1825. ... *New-Haven: T. G. Woodward & Co.* 1825. 8vo, pp. 44. BA.

Fitch (E.) Discourse at Hopkinton, March 24, 1776, after the Flight of the British Troops from Boston. By Elijah Fitch. *Boston.* 1776. 8vo, pp. 30. M. 24570

Also: The Beauties of Religion. A Poem addressed to Youth, in Five Books, By Elijah Fitch, A.M. *Providence: John Carter.* 1789. 8vo, pp. 129. — The Choice. *Providence.* 1789.

Fitch (H. S.) The Lawyer's Test Oath. U. S. District Court. — Southern Dis't Georgia, May Term, 1866. Ex Parte William Law. Argument of Hon. Henry S. Fitch ... . *Savannah, Ga.* 1866. 8vo, pp. 22. H. 24571

Fitch. Pacific Railroad. An Essay on the Pacific Railway, by Henry S. Fitch; ... . *San Francisco: Frank Eastman.* 1859. 8vo, pp. 19. H. 24572

[Fitch (Jabez).] An Account of the Numbers that have died of the Distemper in the Throat Within the Province of New Hampshire; with some Reflections thereon. July 26, 1736. *Boston: Eleazer Russell.* 1736. 8vo, pp. (2), 14. BA., M. 24573

Fitch. Gospel Ministers considered under the Similitude of Fishers of Men. A Sermon Preach'd at Gosport, or the Shoals, July 26th, 1732. At the Ordination of the Reverend John Tucke. By Jabez Fitch, M.A. ... . *Boston: S. Kneeland and T. Green.* 1732. 8vo, pp. 19. BA., N. 24574

Fitch. Two Sermons, on Occasion of the Fatal Distemper, etc. [Sore Throat]. *Boston.* 1736. 8vo, pp. 27. N. 24575

Fitch. The Work of the Lord in the Earthquake to be duly regarded by us. A Discourse on the Earthquake which happened on the night after the 29th Oct. 1727. *Boston.* [1727.] 12mo, pp. 17. M., W. 24576

Also: Discourse On Serious Piety, A ... Sermon ... upon the Death of Mrs. Mary Martyn. ... Added, A Sermon on the Golden Rule of Justice. *Boston.* 1725. 8vo, pp. (4), ii, 37. B.

Fitch (J.) An Explanation of the Solemn Advice, ... by the Council in Connecticut Colony, to the Inhabitants ... Respecting the Reformation of those Evils, which have been the Cause of the late Judgments upon New-England. By Mr. James Fitch ... . *Boston: L. Usher.* 1683. 8vo, Title, 3 l., pp. 133. B., BA., W. 24577

"A Brief Discourse Proving that the First Day of the Week is the Christian Sabbath," pp. 73–133 has a separate title-page.

Fitch. The First Principles of the Doctrine of Christ; Together with stronger Meat for them that are skil'd in the Word of Righteousness. Or The Doctrine of living unto God, wherein the Body of Divinity Is Briefly and methodically handled by way of Question and Answer. Published at the desire, and for the use of the Church of Christ in Norwich in New-England. By James Fitch, Pastor of that Church. ... *Boston: Printed by John Foster.* 1679. 16mo, Title, "To the Reader," signed Increase Mather, 3 l., pp. 76, (2). 24578

Fitch. An Holy Connexion, Or a true Agreement Between Jehovah's being a Wall of Fire to his People, and the Glory in the midst thereof: ... . [an Election] Sermon ... at Hartford on Conecticut in N. E. May 14. 1674. ... *Cambridge: Printed by Samuel Green.* 1674. 4to, pp. (4), 20. B., H., M. 24579

An address to the "Christian Reader," pp. 4, is signed "John Whiting. Joseph Haines." Mr. J. H. Trumbull, of Hartford, in the "Historical Magazine," Vol. III., page 52, notices two historical pamphlets by James Fitch, justifying the revolution which displaced Sir Edmund Andros, "A Plain Short Discourse, 1691," and "A Little of the Much, 1692," which he has not as yet seen.

Fitch (J.) Sermon at the Funeral of Mrs. Anne Mason, wife of Major Mason. By James Fitch. *Cambridge, Mass.* 1842. 4to. W. 24580

Fitch (J.) The Original Steam-Boat supported; or, A Reply to Mr. James Rumsey's Pamphlet. Shewing the true Priority of John Fitch, and the False Datings, &c. of James Rumsey.

Philadelphia: Zachariah Poulson, Jun'r. MDCCLXXXVIII. 8vo, pp. 20. 24582

Includes a reprint of Mr. Rumsey's plan. Also reprinted in the "Documentary History of New York," Vol. II. *See also* Barnes (J.), Vol. I., No. 3521, and Rumsey (J.)

Fitch (J.) Sermon delivered at the Request of Harmony Lodge; as a Tribute of Respect for the Memory of the Late General George Washington, February 26th, 1800. By John Fitch. *Peacham, Vermont.* 1800. 8vo, pp. 24. 24583

Fitch. A Sermon delivered before ... the Representatives of Vermont ... Nov. 10 ... being the Day of ... Election. *Peacham.* 1805. 8vo. 24584

[Fitch (John).] Annals of the Army of the Cumberland; comprising Biographies, Descriptions of Departments, Accounts of Expeditions, Skirmishes, and Battles; also its Police Record of Spies, Smugglers, and Prominent Rebel Emissaries ... By an Officer. *Philadelphia: J. B. Lippincott & Co.* 1864. 8vo, pp. 716. 24585

[Fitch.] Chickamauga, the Price of Chattanooga. A Description of the Strategic Plans, Marches and Battles of the Campaign of Chattanooga. ... *Philadelphia: J. B. Lippincott & Co.* 1864. 8vo, pp. 451–482; 703–716. Map. 24586

Forms part of the "Annals," *supra.*

[Fitch.] Police Record of the Spies, Smugglers, and Rebel Emissaries in Tennessee. Being Selections from the "Annals of the Army of the Cumberland." *Philadelphia.* 1863. 8vo.

[Fitch (Thomas).] Reasons why The British Colonies, in America, should not be charged with Internal Taxes, by Authority of Parliament: Humbly offered, For Consideration, In Behalf of the Colony of Connecticut. *New-Haven: B. Mecom.* M,DCC,LXIV. 8vo, pp. 39. BA., S. 24588

Concerning this, *see* Pitkins' "United States," I. 165, and Ingersoll's "Letters," page 2.

[Fitch.] Some Reasons that influenced the Governor ... to administer the Oath, required by the Act of Parliament; commonly called the Stamp-Act. ... *Hartford: Thomas Green.* MDCCLXVI. pp. 14. B. 24589

Fitch (T.) Address on the Life and Character of Colonel Edward D. Baker. By Thomas Fitch. Delivered at Placerville, California, February 6, 1862. *Placerville.* 1862. 8vo, pp. 7. H. 24590

Also: Cuba and the Alabama Claims. Speech of Hon. Thomas Fitch ... in the House ... December 16, 1869. ... [*Washington.* 1869.] 8vo, pp. 7. H. — Reconstruction of Mississippi. Speech of Hon. Thomas Fitch ... in the House ... April 1, 1869. ... [*Washington.* 1869.] 8vo, pp. 7. H. — The Utah Problem. Review of the Course of Judge James B. McKean, and an Appeal for the Surrender of Polygamy. Speech ... February 20, 1872. [*Salt Lake City.*] 1872. 8vo, pp. 20. H.

Fitchburg, *Mass.* By-Laws to be observed by the Town of Fitchburg. [*Fitchburg.* 1848.] 8vo, pp. 7. H. 24591

Expenditures of the Town of Fitchburg, for ... 1842. [*Fitchburg.* 1842.] 8vo, pp. 7. H. 24592

Facts and Documents, Exhibiting a Summary View of the Ecclesiastical Affairs lately transacted in Fitchburg. *Boston.* 1802. 12mo, pp. 118. W. 24593

Facts and Documents on the Ecclesiastical Affairs of Fitchburg. Result of the Late Party Council, &c. *Boston.* 1802. 12mo. 24594

Facts relative to the Brief Statement of proposed Railroad from Fitchburg to Brattleborough ... . *Boston: Dutton and Wentworth.* 1844. 8vo, pp. 24. B. 24595

Fitchburg Almanac, Directory, and Business Advertiser for 1871. *Fitchburg: Shepley & Co.* 32mo, pp. 69, 120. 24596

The Fitchburg Directory, for the Year commencing July, 1871. *Fitchburg (Mass.): L. G. Corbin.* 1871. 8vo, pp. 244, 3 leaves. C. 24597

Fitchburg and Worcester Railroad Company. Annual Report. 1848. 8vo. Continued to 1854. 24598

Fitchburg Railroad. Annual Report, 1843. *Boston.* 8vo. Continued. B. 24599

Also: Report of a Committee of the Directors, September, 1842. *Boston.* 1842. 8vo, pp. 15. — Report of the Committee of Investigation, 1856. *Boston.* 1856. 8vo, pp. 44.

A Narrative of the Religious Controversy in Fitchburg. With Comments on a Pamphlet, entitled "Facts and Documents," &c. ... *Worcester: Isaiah Thomas, Jun. September,* 1804. 12mo, pp. 71. H. 24600

The Principles and Rules, with the Articles of Faith and Covenant of the Trinitarian Church, Fitchburg; with a List of the Officers and Members. *Fitchburg: W. J. Merriam.* 1843. 32mo, pp. 15. H. 24601

Report of Selectmen, also Report of the Auditing Committee and School Committee. From 1848, etc. [*Fitchburg.* 1848.] 8vo. H. 24602

[Fitton (James).] Influence of Catholic Christian Doctrines on the Emancipation of Slaves. By a Member of the Sodality of the B. V. Mary, Church of the Most Holy Redeemer, East Boston. *Boston: Patrick Donohoe.* 1863. 12mo, pp. 35. H.

Fitts (J. H.) Genealogy of the Fitts or Fitz Family in America, by James Hill Fitts ... . *Clinton: printed by Wm. J. Coulter.* 1869. 8vo, pp. vi, 91. B., H. 24604

Also: Manual of the Congregational Church in West Boylston, Mass. ... Prepared by James H. Fitts ... *Clinton: printed by W. J. Coulter.* 1870. 8vo, pp. 64, 9. H.

Fitz (D.) A Sermon delivered November 13, 1855, at the Interment of Rev. Robert Cowell, D.D. ... By Daniel Fitz ... . *Boston: J. R. Butts.* 1856. 8vo, pp. 24. H. 24605

Fitz. Thirtieth Anniversary Discourse, delivered in Ipswich, June 29, 1856. By Rev. Daniel Fitz, ... *Boston: William White, Printer.* 1856. 8vo, pp. 23. 24606

Also: A Sermon delivered in Essex, February 11, 1837, at the Funeral of Mrs. Hannah C. Crowell ... . *Boston: Dutton and Wentworth.* 1837. 8vo, pp. 30. BA., H. — ... A Sermon, delivered at the Funeral of Rev. David Tenney Kimball ... February 8, 1860. ... *Boston: T. R. Marvin & Son.* 1860. 8vo, pp. 27. H.

Fitz (J.) Modern Presbyterianism Unmasked, and Arrant Bigotry and Rank Fanaticism Exposed, in a Review of the Administration of Church Government, in the Session of the First Presbyterian Church in Newburyport; and of the Arbitrary and Infamous Transaction of the Newburyport Presbytery ... . By John Fitz. *Boston.* 1830. 8vo, pp. 72. H. 24607

Fitz-Geffrey (C.) The Life and Death of Sir Francis Drake: Poem. By the Rev. Charles Fitz-Geffrey. *Lee Priory (Kent): John Warwick.* 1819. 12mo, pp. xxiii, 101. C. 24608

Eighty copies printed.

Fitzgerald (J. E.) An Examination of the Charter and Proceedings of the Hudson's Bay Company, with reference to the Grant of Vancouver's Island. By James Edward Fitzgerald. *London.* 1849. 12mo, pp. 310. Map. C. 24609

Also: Vancouver's Island, the Hudson's Bay Company and the Government. *London.* 1848. 8vo, pp. 30.

Fitzgerald (C.) Christian Slaveholders Disobedient to Christ; or, Ten Thousand Christians Invited to Protest actively against the Church's Sin in the United States, and to cease from the Purchase of Slave Grown Cotton. By the Rev. John Fitzgerald. *London: Dalton.* 1854. 8vo. 24610

FITZGERALD (E.) A Hand-Book for the Albany Rural Cemetery, with an Appendix of Emblems. By Edward Fitzgerald. *Albany: Van Benthuysen Printing House.* 1871. 12mo, 1 l., pp. 141. 12 Plates and 1 Map. C. 24611

FITZGERALD (R.) A Visit to the Cities and Camps of the Confederate States. By Ross Fitzgerald, Captain in the Imperial Austrian Service. *London: W. Blackwood & Sons.* 1865. 12mo, pp. vi, 300. Map. 24612

FITZGERALD (W.) An Ode to the Memory of the late Captain James Cook. By W. Fitzgerald, of Gray's Inn. *London: J. Robinson.* 1780. 4to. 24613

See "M. Rev.," LXIII. 72.

FITZGERALD (W. P. N.) A Scriptural View of Slavery and Abolition. By W. P. N. Fitzgerald, Esq. *New Haven.* 1839. 8vo, pp. 24. + Second Edition. [*Ibid.*] N. 24614

A pro-slavery argument.

FITZGIBBON (J.) An Appeal to the People of the late Province of Upper Canada, by Col. Fitzgibbon, on his Claims for Public Services. *Montreal.* 1847. 8vo, pp. 65. 24615

FITZGIBBON. Documents, selected from several others, showing the Services rendered by Col. Fitzgibbon, while serving in Upper Canada, between the Years 1812 and 1837. *Windsor.* 1859. 8vo, pp. 15. 24616

FITZHUGH (G.) Cannibals All! or, Slaves without Masters. By George Fitzhugh, of Port Royal, Carolina, Va. ... *Richmond, Va.: A. Morris.* 1857. 12mo, pp. 379. BA., C. 24617

FITZHUGH. Sociology for the South, or the Failure of Free Society. By George Fitzhugh ... *Richmond, Va.: A. Morris.* 1854. 12mo, pp. 310. B., C. 24618

FITZHUGH (W. M.) Cash and Credit. ... *Baltimore: Sherwood & Co.* 1868. 8vo, pp. 14. H. 24619

FITZHUGH. Speech at the Ninth Anniversary of the American Colonization Society ... By William Henry Fitzhugh.

Imperfect title, from Allibone's dictionary.

FITZ-JAMES (Z.) ... An Autobiographical Narrative. By Zillah Fitz-James. *Little Rock, Arkansas.* 1855. 8vo, pp. 32.

FITZPATRICK (J.) Suggestions on the Slave Trade, for the Consideration of the Legislature of Great Britain. By Sir Jeremiah Fitzpatrick, Knt. M.D. ... *London: J. Stockdale.* 8vo.

See "M. Rev.," XXIII. 347.

FITZPATRICK (J. B.) In Memoriam of Rt. Rev. John B. Fitzpatrick. *Boston: Patrick Donahoe.* 1866. 8vo, pp. 45. B.

Familiar Letters to John B. Fitzpatrick, the Catholic Bishop of Boston. By an Independent Irishman. *Boston: J. P. Mendum.* 1854. pp. 72. BA., S.

FITZROY (Alex.) The Discovery, Purchase, and Settlement of the County of Kentuckie, in North America. 1786. 8vo. Map. 24624

Title from J. R. Smith's catalogue. I have not been able to find the book; it is probably an edition of Filson (*see our* No. 24337, *ante*) erroneously described.

FITZROY (R.) Report to the Earl of Clarendon on the proposed Honduras Interoceanic Railway. By Robert Fitzroy, Captain R. N. [Dated] *London. May 13th,* 1856. Confidential.

FITZROY (Robert). Instructions nautiques sur les côtes occidentales de l'Amérique du Sud, comprise entre le golfe de Peñas et Payta; traduites de l'anglais par M. Jules Lafont. *Paris: Ledoyen.* 1853. 8vo. 24626

FITZROY. Instructions nautiques sur les côtes occidentales d'Amérique, de la rivière Tumbez à Panama; traduit de l'anglais par M. Mac-Dermott. *Paris: Bossange.* 1863. 8vo.

FITZROY. Instructions nautiques sur les côtes occidentales d'Amérique, du golfe de Peñas à la rivière Tumbez; traduit de l'anglais par M. Mac-Dermott. *Paris: Bossange.* 1864. 8vo.

FITZROY (R.) *See* Darwin (C.), *also* King (P. P.)

FITZSIMMONS, *pseudonym.* Essays upon French Spoliations, with some observations upon the Importance of Commerce. By Fitzsimmons, a Native of Pennsylvania. *Philadelphia: James G. Watt & Co.* 1826. 8vo, pp. 31. 24629

[FITZWILLIAM (William Wentworth–).] A History of the San Juan Water Boundary Question, as affecting the division of Territory between Great Britain and the United States. Collected and Compiled from Official Papers and Documents printed

under the authority of the Governments respectively of Great Britain and Ireland and of the United States of America, and from other Sources. By Viscount Milton. *London: Cassell, Petter & Galpin.* 1869. 8vo, 2 l., pp. 442. 2 Maps. C. 24630

[FITZWILLIAM], *and* CHEADLE (W. B.) The Northwest Passage by Land. Being the Narrative of an Expedition from the Atlantic to the Pacific, undertaken with the View of Exploring a Route across the Continent to British Columbia through British Territory, by one of the Northern Passes to the Rocky Mountains. By Viscount Milton ... and W. B. Cheadle. ... *London: Cassell, Petter, and Galpin.* [1865.] 8vo, pp. xviii, 397. Map and Engravings. B. + Second Edition. [*Ibid.*] 8vo, pp. xix, 400. + Third Edition. [*Ibid.* 1865.] 8vo, pp. xxiv, 400. + Sixth Edition. [*Ibid.*] 1866. 8vo, pp. xxiv, 400. 24631

The Five Cotton States and New York. *See* [Colwell], Vol. IV., No. 14909.

Five Lessons for Young Men. *See* [Southwick (Solomon)].

Five Letters, 1792. *See* [Laughan (*Dr.*)]

Five Letters to my Neighbour Smith, touching the Fifteen-gallon Jug. *Boston.* 1838. 12mo, pp. 36. M. 24632

Relates to liquor laws.

Five Months in the New York State Lunatic Asylum. *Buffalo.* 1849. 16mo, pp. 63. C. 24633

Five Points Monthly Record. The New Charitable Monthly, or, "What is done for the Poor." ... *New York.* [1854.] 8vo. Continued. B. 24634

Five Years in the Alleghanies. [By a Colporteur.] *New York: American Tract Society.* [1863.] 18mo, pp. 206. Plate.

Five Years' Progress of the Slave Power, a Series of Papers first published in the Boston Commonwealth in 1851. *Boston.* 1852. 8vo. 24636

A Five Years' Residence in Buenos Ayres. *See* Vol. III., No. 9014.

FIX (T.) Conférence sur la guerre du Paraguay. Par M. Théodore Fix, capitaine d'état major. *Paris: Dumaine.* 1870. 18mo, pp. 94. 24637

FLACCUS, *pseudonym.* *See* [Ward (Thomas)].

FLACHAT (J.) Notes sur le fleuve du Darien, et sur les différents projets de canaux interocéaniques du Centre Amérique. Par M. Jules Flachat. Extrait des mémoires de la Société des ingénieurs civils. *Paris: Eugène Lacroix.* 1866. 8vo, pp. 133. 3 Maps. B., C. 24638

FLACK (*Captain*). A Hunter's Experiences in the Southern States of America, being an Account of the Natural History of various Quadrupeds and Birds which are the Objects of Chase in those Countries. By Captain Flack ("The Ranger"). *London: Longmans, Green & Co.* 1866. Post 8vo, pp. (6), 359. C.

FLACK. Texan Ranger; or, Real Life in the Backwoods. *London: Darton & Co.* 1866. Fcap 8vo, pp. 319. 24640

Also another edition, with illustrations, *London*, 1866.

FLACK. The Texan Rifle Hunter; or, Field Sports on the Prairie. By Captain Flack. *London: J. Maxwell & Co.* 1866. 12mo, pp. viii, 333. C. 24641

FLACOURT (Étienne de). Histoire de la grande isle Madagascar, composé par M. Flacourt, avec Discours de l'Amérique, et recet sommaire du voyage et Retour en France de l'Antheur, &c. *Paris: G. de Luyne.* 1658. 2 vols., 12mo, 8 l., pp. 384, 42, 9 l. 7 Maps and 7 Plates. C. + *Paris.* 1660. 4to. C.

The Flag of Truce. By the Chaplain. *Baltimore: James Young.* 1862. 12mo, pp. 12. 24643

The Flag of Truce. Dedicated to the Emperor of the French. By a White Republican. *London: James Ridgway.* 1862. Post 8vo, pp. 52. 24644

FLAGET (*M.*) Évêque de Bardstown et Louisville. Sa vie, son esprit et ses vertus: par le prêtre qui accompagnait le prélat pendant le voyage qu'il fit en Europe. *Paris.* 1851. 8vo. S.

FLAGG (A. H.) Obituary Notices of Mrs. Abigail H. Flagg. [n. p.] 1870. 8vo, pp. 11. H. 24646

FLAGG (A. C.) Banks and Banking in New York, from 1777 to 1864. By Azariah C. Flagg, Late Comptroller. *Brooklyn.* 1868. 8vo. S. 24647

[FLAGG.] Internal Improvements in the State of New-York. From Hunt's Merchants' Magazine. 8vo, pp. 34. S. 24648

Also: Circular to the Stockholders of the Chicago and Rock-Island Railroad Company, Dec. 1, 1857. *New York.* 1857. 8vo. S. — A few Historical Facts respecting the Establishment and Progress of Banks ... in the State of New York. 1868. 8vo.

FLAGG (C. E. B.) Oration delivered before the '76 Association and Society of the Cincinnati, Charleston, S. C., July 5, 1858. By Charles E. B. Flagg. *Charleston, S. C.* 1858. 8vo, pp. 22. 24649

FLAGG (E.) Report on the Commercial Relations of the United States with all Foreign Nations. By Edmund Flagg, Superintendent. Prepared and Printed under the Direction of the Secretary of State ... . *Washington.* 1856–7. 2 vols., 4to, pp. 827; xv, 623. Continued. 24650

[FLAGG (Edward).] The Far West: or, a Tour beyond the Mountains. Embracing outlines of Western Life and Scenery; Sketches of the Prairies, Rivers, Ancient Mounds, Early Settlements of the French, etc. etc. ... *New York: Harper & Brothers.* 1838. 2 vols., 12mo, pp. xvi, 13–263; xi, 9–241. B., C. 24651

Mr. Rich quotes a London edition, and attributes the work to —— Flint, which is an error.

FLAGG (H. C.) An Oration on the Republican Celebration of the 44th Anniversary of American Independence. By Henry C. Flagg ... . *New-Haven: John C. Gray.* 1820. 8vo, pp. 20.

FLAGG (M.) Remarks on the Culture of the Grape, and the Manufacture of Wine, in the Western States ... May 2, 1846. By Melzer Flagg ... . *Cincinnati: L'Hommedieu & Co.* 1846. 8vo, pp. 17. 24653

FLAGG (J.) A Collection of the Best Psalm Tunes, in Two, Three, and Four Parts. By Josiah Flagg. *Boston.* 1764. 8vo.

Engraved by Paul Revere, and very rare.

FLAGG (W.) A Good Investment, a Story of the Upper Ohio. By William Flagg ... . With Illustrations. *New York: Harper & Brothers.* 12mo, pp. 116. B., BA. 24655

Reprinted from "Harper's Magazine."

FLAGG (W. J.) Hand-Book of the Sulphur-Cure, as Applicable to the Vine Disease in America, and Diseases of Apple and other Fruit Trees. By William J. Flagg ... . *New York: Harper & Brothers.* 1870. 12mo, pp. 99. B. 24656

FLAGG (William J.) Abuses in the Navy. Case of Lieutenant Flagg. [*Cincinnati.* 1851.] 8vo, pp. 15. H. 24657

FLAGG (W. J.) Speech of Hon. William J. Flagg ... in the Ohio House of Representatives on the Resolution ... to Expel the Hon. Otto Drexel, March 25, 1863. [n. p. n. d.] 8vo, pp. 16. 24658

Relates to General G. B. McClellan. Also: Remarks ... delivered in the Ohio House of Representatives, February 20, 1860. *Columbus.* 1860. 8vo, pp. 7. H.

FLAGG (W.) Mount Auburn; its Scenes, its Beauties, and its Lessons. Edited By Wilson Flagg. *Boston and Cambridge: James Munroe and Company.* 1851. 12mo, pp. xii, 471. 12 Plates. + *Boston.* 1861. 12mo. C. 24659

FLAGG. Studies in the Field and Forest. By Wilson Flagg ... *Boston: Little, Brown & Co.* 1857. 12mo, pp. vi, 330. BA.

FLAGG. The Tailor's Shop: or, Crowns of Thorns and Coats of Thistles. Designed to tickle some and nettle others; intended chiefly for Politicians ... By Wilson Flagg. [A Poem.] *Boston: W. B. Kimball.* 1844. 18mo, pp. 58. B. 24661

FLAGG. The Woods and By-Ways of New England. By Wilson Flagg ... . *Boston: James R. Osgood and Company.* 1872. pp. xviii, 442. Photographs. B., BA., H. 24662

FLAMINIO (Gian Antonio). Epistola ad Paulum III. Pont. Max. initio Pontificatus. Eivsdem belli recentis Aphricani descriptio ad Ampliss. P. Antonium Puccium Sanctorum Quatuor Cardinalem. Eivsdem de qvibvsdam memorabilibus noui Orbis nuper ad nos transmissis ad eundem. Eivsdem Conflictvs ille Pannonicus cum Turcis, in quo Pannoniæ rex interijt. [Colophon:] *Bononiæ apud Vencentiū Bonardum Parmen. et Marcū Antoniū Carpen. socios. Anno salutis* M. D. XXXVI. *Mensis Martii.* 4to, 19 leaves. 24663

A volume of extreme rarity, not mentioned by Ternaux. Mr. Harrisse cites it from Panzer. It relates the discovery of America. Sold for 32 francs, in Paris, in 186–. "The reader will find a full account of John Anthony Flaminius (*i. e.* Zarrabini de Colignola, 1464–1536), in Vossius, Fabricius and Tiraboschi. We suppose that this epistle *de quibusdam in Nova Orbe*, is also to be found in Capponi's edition of Flaminius' Letters." — HARRISSE.

FLANAGAN (C.) Conversation and Conduct of John Young, who was Executed for the Murder of Robert Barwick. ... By Christopher Flanagan. *New York.* 1797. 8vo. 24664

FLANAGAN (J. W.) The Texas Pan-Handle. Speech of ... J. W. Flanagan ... in the Senate of the United States, March 7, 1872. [*Washington.* 1872.] 8vo, pp. 7. H. 24665

[FLANAGAN (John J.)] Memorial. Claims against Venezuela. [*New York.* 1871.] 8vo, pp. 12. 24666

FLANDERS (C. W.) ... Address ... before the Concord Temperance Society ... Fast Day, April 8, 1858. By Charles W. Flanders. ... *Concord: Jones & Cogswell, Printers.* 1858. 8vo, pp. 20. 24667

FLANDERS. The Opening Address delivered before the Concord Young Men's Christian Association ... January 16, 1853. By Charles W. Flanders ... . *Concord: McFarland & Jenks.* [1853.] 8vo, pp. 20. H. 24668

FLANDERS (H.) An Exposition of the Constitution of the United States. Designed as a Manual of Instruction. By Henry Flanders, ... *Philadelphia: E. H. Butler & Co.* 1860. 12mo, pp. 311. B., C. 24669

FLANDERS (H.) The Lives and Times of the Chief Justices of the Supreme Court of the United States. By Henry Flanders. *Philadelphia: Lippincott, Grambo & Co.* 1855–8. 2 vols., 8vo, pp. xxv, 11–645; xvi, (1), 11–560. B., BA., C. 24670

FLANDERS. Must the War go on? An Inquiry whether the Union can be restored by any other Means than War, and whether Peace upon any other Basis would be Safe or Durable. By Henry Flanders. *Philadelphia: William S. & Alfred Martien.* 1863. 8vo, pp. 23. B., BA. + [Another Edition. *Ibid.*] 8vo, pp. 16. H. 24671

FLANDERS. Observations on Reconstruction. By Henry Flanders, ... *Philadelphia.* 1866. 8vo, pp. 31. H. 24672

Against negro suffrage and the disfranchisement of the Rebels.

FLANDERS. A Treatise on Maritime Law. By Henry Flanders. *Boston: Little, Brown & Co.* 1852. 8vo. B. + [*Ibid.*] 1858. 8vo, pp. xvi, 444. 24673

FLANIGAN (J. H.) Mormonism Triumphant. By J. H. Flanigan. *Liverpool.* 1849. 8vo. 24674

FLASSAN (*Le Comte* Gaëtan de Raxis de). Histoire Générale et Raisonnée de la Diplomatie Française, depuis la Fondation de la Monarchie, jusqu'à la Fin du Règne de Louis XVI, avec des Tables Chronologiques de tous les Traités conclus par la France. *Paris.* 1809. 6 vols., 8vo. C. + Seconde édition. *Paris.* 1811. 7 vols., 8vo. S. 24675

FLATLANDS. List of Persons Enrolled in the Town of Flatlands, Kings County, N. Y. [1864.] 8vo, pp. 9. 24676

FLAUVEL GOURAUD (J. B. G.) Les hommes d'état de la France constitutionnelle comparés aux hommes d'état de la grande république des États-Unis, ou la haute politique du jour des deux gouvernements. Documents officiels en forme de dépêches ... . *Paris: Blondeau.* [1847.] 4to, pp. 26. Portrait. 24677

FLAUVEL GOURAUD, 1840. *See* Fauvel Gouraud (J. B. G.)

FLAVEL (J.) Exposition of the Assemblies' Catechism, &c., and carried on in the Lord's Day's Exercises in Dartmouth in the First Year of Liberty, 1688. By John Flavell of Dartmouth. *Salisbury, N. E.* 1767. 24678

The "Address to the Reader" is by Increase Mather, in which he says the author's "name is precious in both Englands, and it will be so as long as the earth shall endure."

FLAVEL. The | Great Design and Scope | of the | Gospel Opened. | An Extract from the Rev. | Mr. Flavel's, Englands's Duty. | ... With a Preface by the Reverend | Mr. Byles. | *Boston, H. Foster.* 1741. | 12mo, pp. (8), 28, (2). B., C. 24679

FLAVEL. Navigation Spiritualized: or a New Compass for Sea-Men, By John Flavel, ... *Boston: Re-Printed by Nich. Boone.* 1726. 12mo, pp. xviii, 220, (4). + *Newburyport.* 1796. 12mo.

FLAVEL. Prophane Swearing Condemn'd at the Bar of Reason. Taken from the Works of Flavel. Particularly recommended to the Merchants of Boston, &c. As proper to be given to their Mariners. *Boston.* 1731. 8vo, pp. (2), 22. B. 24681

FLAVEL. A Word to the Well-Wishers Of the Good Work of God in this Land. *Boston: Rogers & Fowle.* 1742. 8vo, pp. 23. B., C. 24682

An extract from his "Blow at the Root." Also: Discourse shewing Christ's Tender Care of his Mother. ... *Boston.* 1728. 12mo, pp. 20. — The Reasonableness of Personal Reformation, and the Necessity of Conversion. *Boston.* 1725. 12mo, pp. (12), 144. — A Saint indeed; or the Great Work of Salvation Opened and Pressed. *Boston.* 1726. 12mo. — A Token for Mourners. *Boston.* 1729. 16mo. + 1730. 16mo. — A Touchstone of Sincerity. *Boston.* 1831. 12mo.

FLAX CULTURE. A Manual of Flax Culture and Manufacture; embracing Directions for Preparing the Ground, Sowing the Seed, Harvesting the Crop, &c. Also, an Essay, by a

Western Man, on Hemp and Flax in the West; Amount Grown, Modes of Culture, Preparation for Market, &c. With Botanical Descriptions and Illustrations. *Rochester: D. T. Moore.* 1863. 8vo, pp. iv, 48. 24683

Moore's "Rural Manuals," No. 1.

Flecknoe (Richard). A Relation of Ten Years Travells in Europe, Asia, Affrique, and America. All by way of Letters written to divers Noble Personages, from place to place; and continued to this present year. By Richard Fleckno. With divers other Historical, Moral and Poetical Pieces of the same Author. *London: printed for the Author.* [1654.] Sm. 8vo, pp. 184. 24684

The most interesting and scarce of all the author's productions.

Fleeming (J.) Fleeming's Register for New-England and Nova-Scotia. With All the British Lists; and An Almanack for 1772, Being Leap Year. Calculated for the Meridian of Boston. *Boston: Printed by John Fleeming, and to be sold at his Shop in King-Street, opposite the South-Door of the Town-House.* [1772.] 12mo, pp. 97 *for* 96. 24685

Fleet (J.) A Discourse relative to the Subject of Animation, delivered before the Humane Society of ... Massachusetts ... June 13th, 1797. By John Fleet, Jun. ... *Boston: John & Thomas Fleet.* 1797. 4to, pp. 25. B., BA. 24686

Fleet (T.) MDCCXX. An Almanack ... for the Year ... 1720 ... *Boston: Printed for T. Fleet.* 1720. 18mo, 8 l. BA.

Fleet (T. *and* J.) A Pocket Almanack for the Year ... 1779 ... Calculated for the Use of the State of Massachusetts-Bay ... *Boston: T. & J. Fleet.* 16mo, 26 l. Continued. BA.

In 1792, entitled "Fleet's Pocket Almanack;" in 1798, entitled "Fleet's Register and Pocket Almanack."

[Fleet (William Henry).] How I came to be Governor of the Island of Cacona: with a Particular Account of my Administration of the Affairs of that Island. Respectfully Dedicated to my Fellow-Labourers in the Colonial Vineyard. By the Hon. Francis Thistleton, late Governor of the Island of Cacona. *Montreal.* 1853. + *New York.* 1854. 8vo, pp. 218. 24689

A satire upon Colonial Governors and their administrations, and upon the Canadian Government in particular.

[Fleetwood (W.)] A Sermon Preached before the Society for the Propagation of the Gospel in Foreign Parts, At the Parish-Church of St. Mary-le-Bow, On Friday the 16th of February, 17 1/2. Being the Day of their Anniversary Meeting. By the Right Reverend Father in God, William Lord Bishop of St. Asaph. *London: J. Downing.* MDCCXI. 8vo, pp. 32. + Second Edition. *London.* 1725. 8vo, pp. 43. 24690

Fleharty (S. F.) Our Regiment: a History of the 102d Illinois Infantry Volunteers, with Sketches of the Atlanta Campaign, the Georgia Raid, and the Campaign of the Carolinas. *Chicago.* 1865. 16mo. C. 24691

Fleischauer. Die Naturkräfte im Dienste des Menschen. ... *Langensalza: Schulbuchhandlung d. Thür. Lehrervereins.* 8vo.

Nr. 8 is "Die Polarexpeditionen und die dabei gemachten wichtigern Entdeckungen des magnetischen Nordpols ... . Nebst einer Zugabe: die unglückliche Nordpolreise Franklin's und Crozier's betrachtend. 1854." 8vo, pp. iv, 86. 3 Maps.

Fleischmann (C. L.) Erwerbsweige, Fabrikwesen und Handel der Vereinigten Staaten von Nordamerika. Mit besonderer Rücksicht auf Deutsche Auswanderer. ... von C. L. Fleischmann ... . *Stuttgart: Fr. Kohler.* 1850. 8vo, pp. x, 616. BA.

Fleischmann. Les États-Unis et le Russie considérés au point de vue de la grande culture et du travail libre. Par Ch. L. Fleischmann ... . *Paris: A. Franck.* 1858. 8vo, pp. 64.

Fleischmann. Neueste officielle Berichte an die Regier. der Verein. Staaten über die Lage und Zukunft Californiens. *Stuttgart.* 1850. 8vo. 24695

Fleischmann. Der Nordamerikanische Landwirth. Ein Handbuch für Ansiedler in den Vereinigten Staaten. Von C. L. Fleischmann ... . *Frankfurt am Main.* 1848. 8vo, pp. xiv, 399. Map and Plates. BA., C. + *New York: Rudolph Garrigue.* 1848. 8vo. 24696

Fleischmann. Wegweiser und Rathgeber nach und in den Vereinigten Staaten von Nord-Amerika. *Stuttgart.* 1852. 8vo.

Fleishman (S. L.) Free Trade and Protection. By S. L. Fleishman. ... *Philadelphia: Collins, Printer.* 1869. 8vo, pp. 67.

Fleming (A. C.) A Year in Canada, and other Poems, By Ann Cuthbert Fleming. *Edinburgh.* 1816. 12mo, pp. 126.

Fleming (J.) A Short Sermon: Also Hymns, in the Muskokee or Creek Language. By the Rev. John Fleming ... . *Boston: Crocker & Brewster.* 12mo, pp. 35. B. 24700

[Fleming (John).] The Political Annals of Lower Canada; being a Review of the Political and Legislative History of that Province, under the Act of the Imperial Parliament, ... which established a House of Assembly and Legislative Council; shewing ... its practical Discouragement of British Colonization. With an Introductory Chapter on the Previous History of Canada, and an Appendix of Documents, etc. By a British Settler. *Montreal: Montreal Herald Office.* 1828. 8vo, pp. lxxviii, 180. C.

"First published in the 'Canadian Review.' Designed exclusively for the Colonial Office, and a few private friends of the author in England. A work as full of information as it is of prejudice against the French Canadians." — Laterrière.

Fleming (*Dr.*) Letters on the state of Religion in Newfoundland to Dr. A. O'Connell. By Dr. Fleming. *Dublin.* 1844. 8vo. 24702

Fleming. Stato della religione cattolica in Terra-Nuova ricavato da due lettere di Monsig. Fleming vicario da Terra-Nuova al P. Giovanni Spratt. *Roma.* 1836. 4to, pp. 24.

Extracted from the "Annales religieuses de Rome," Vol. II.

Fleming (Peter). On the St. Lawrence Canal, and Gradual Diminution of the Discharge of the St. Lawrence. *Montreal.* 1849. 8vo. 24704

Fleming. Report to the President and Directors of the Mohawk and Hudson Railway Company. By Peter Fleming. *New York.* 1829. 8vo, pp. 15. N. 24705

Fleming (Sandford). Preliminary Report on the projected North West Railway of Canada, with a Description of the Extent, Physical Features, Soil and Settlement of the Country through which it is proposed to be constructed, showing the importance of the Valley of the Saugeen, as a field for Commerce and Railway Enterprise. *Toronto.* 1857. pp. 35. 24706

Fleming. Report on the Intercolonial Railway Exploratory Survey, made under instructions from the Canadian Government in the Year 1864. *Quebec.* 1865. 8vo, pp. 160. Maps.

Fleming (W. *and* E.) A Narrative of the Sufferings and Surprising Deliverance of William and Elizabeth Fleming, Who were taken captive by Capt. Jacob, Commander of the Indians, who lately made an Excursion on the Inhabitants of the

Great Cove, near Conecochieg, in Pennsylvania, as related by themselves. *Philadelphia: Printed for the Benefit of the unhappy Sufferers.* [n. d.] 12mo, pp. 28. + *Boston: Green & Russell.* 1756. 8vo, pp. 20. M. 24708

Fleming (W.) Four Days at the Falls of Niagara. By William Fleming, M.D. *Manchester: Privately Printed.* 1835. 12mo, pp. 30. 24709

Fletcher (A.) The History, Objects and Principles of the Order of the Sons of Temperance: an Address, ... Richmond, Va., December 2, 1844. By Abel Fletcher, ... *Gihon & Porter, Printers, Philadelphia.* 1845. 8vo, pp. 28. 24710

Fletcher (A.) The Tendency of Infidelity and Christianity Contrasted; in Two Sermons, Preached after the Conclusion of the Treaty of Peace with Great Britain and the United States of America. By the Rev. Alexander Fletcher. *London.* 1815. 8vo.

Fletcher (B.) An Account of the Treaty between His Excellency Benjamin Fletcher, Captain General and Governor in Chief of the Province of New-York and the Indians of the Five Nations, viz. the Mohoques, Oneydes, Onnondages, Cajonges, and Sennekes, at Albany, beginning the 15th of August, 1694. *Printed and Sold by William Bradford, Printer to their Majesties, King William and Queen Mary, at the Sign of the Bible, in New-York.* 1694. 4to. BM. 24712

Fletcher. A Journal of what passed in the Expedition of His Excellency Colonel Benjamin Fletcher, Captain General of New-York, to Albany, to renew the Covenant Chain with the Five Canton Nations of Indians. ... [*New-York.* 1694.] 4to.

Fletcher. Proclamation by His Excellency, Benj. Fletcher, Captain General and Governor-in-Chief of New-York, etc. to the Inhabitants of the Province of New-York, to erect a Beacon: Given at Fort William Henry, the 25th day of August, 1693. *Printed and sold by William Bradford, Printer, to their Majesties King William and Queen Mary, at the City of New-York.* 1693.

This is the earliest known specimen of printing in the province of New York. On the 23d of March, 1693, the Council passed a resolution encouraging a printer to settle in New York, "for the printing of our Acts of Assembley and public papers," (Coun. Min., VI. 182). On the 24th of April following, Gov. Fletcher set out from New York for Philadelphia, whence he returned on the fifth June, 1693, (Coun. Min., VI. 194, 202). Thomas, in his "History of Printing," Vol. II., gives a relation of the persecutions which drove Bradford from Pennsylvania to New York in 1693. It is presumed, from the above data, that he was induced by Gov. Fletcher to remove here, and that he accompanied his excellency on the latter's return to New York in June, 1693.

Fletcher (C. F.) A Plan for the Formation of a Society to Assist the Government in the Suppression of this Rebellion. By Charles Fosdick Fletcher. *Philadelphia.* 1863. 16mo, pp. 12.

Fletcher. A Plan of Peace. In Time of War prepare for Peace. ... By Charles Fosdick Fletcher ... . *Washington, D. C.: printed by Scammel & Co.* 1862. 24mo, pp. 12. H. 24716

Fletcher (C.) Much in Little: a History of the Charters, Government, etc., of the Colonies; of Political Parties, and American Slavery; with Curiosities of Literature. By Cyrus Fletcher. *Boston.* 1857. 18mo. 24717

Fletcher (E.) A Narrative of the Captivity & Sufferings of Ebenezer Fletcher, of New-Ipswich, Who was severely wounded and taken prisoner at the battle of Hubbardston, Vt. in the year 1777, by the British and Indians ... . Written by himself ... . Fourth Edition, Revised and Enlarged. *New-Ipswich, N. H.: printed by S. Wilder.* 1827. 12mo, pp. 24. C. 24718

Another edition is entitled:

Fletcher. The Narrative of Ebenezer Fletcher, a Soldier of the Revolution, Written by Himself, with An Introduction and Notes, by Charles I. Bushnell. *New York: Privately Printed.* 1866. 8vo, pp. 86. C. 24719

Fletcher (E. H.) Explanations, and Biographical Notes, designed to accompany a Genealogical Chart of the Descendants of Robert Fletcher. Compiled by Edward H. Fletcher. *New York: published by Edward H. Fletcher.* 1849. 24mo, pp. 24.

Fletcher. Fletcher Genealogy: an Account of the Descendants of Robert Fletcher, of Concord, Mass. By Edward H. Fletcher ... . *Boston: For the Author.* 1871. 8vo, pp. 271. Portrait. B. 24721

Fletcher (F.) The World Encompassed. *See* Drake, Vol. v., Nos. 20854 and 20855.

Fletcher (Henry Charles). History of the American War. By Lieut.-Colonel Fletcher ... . *London: Richard Bentley.* 1865–66. 3 vols., 8vo, pp. xi, (1), 445; xiii, (1), 549. 2 Maps. B.

Fletcher (J. C.), *and* Kidder (J. P.) Brazil and the Brazilians, Portrayed in Historical and Descriptive Sketches. By Rev. James C. Fletcher, and Rev. D. P. Kidder, D.D. Sixth

Edition, Revised and Enlarged. *Boston: Little, Brown & Co.* 1866. 8vo, pp. viii, 640. Map and Plates. B., BA. + [*Ibid.*] 1867. 24723

First appeared in 1857. *See* Kidder (D. P.)

Fletcher (J.) American Patriotism Farther confronted with Reason, Scripture, and the Constitution: Being Observations on the Dangerous Politicks Taught by the Rev. Mr. Evans, M.A. And the Rev. Dr. Price. With a Scriptural Plea for the Revolted Colonies. By J. Fletcher, Vicar of Madeley, Salop. *Shrewsbury: J. Eddowes.* MDCCLXXVI. 12mo, pp. viii, 130. BA.

The writer takes issue against Evans and Price, and defends the right of Great Britain to tax the colonies. *See* Evans (Caleb), No. 21539, for a reply.

Fletcher. An Essay upon the Peace of 1783, Dedicated to the Archbishop of Paris. Translated from the French of the Rev. J. Fletcher, late Vicar of Madeley, Salop. By the Rev. J. Gilpin, ... *London: Hindmarsh.* 1785. 4to. 24725

See "M. Rev.," LXXIV. 147.

Fletcher. A Vindication of the Rev. Mr. Wesley's "Calm Address to our American Colonies:" In some Letters to Mr. Caleb Evans. By John Fletcher, Vicar of Madeley, Salop. *London: Printed and sold at the Foundry.* [1776.] 12mo, pp. iv, 70. + *Dublin.* 1776. 8vo. 24726

The author claims that the doctrine of taxation maintained by Mr. Wesley "is rational, Scriptural, and constitutional," while that of Mr. Evans "is highly unconstitutional, and draws after it a long train of absurd consequences." *See* "M. Rev.," LIV. 325. Included in Vol. v. of Fletcher's works: *London.* 1825. 7 vols., 16mo.

[Fletcher.] The Rev. John Fletcher's Arguments, contained in his "Vindication of the Calm Address" in Defence of the Assumed Right of the British Parliament to Tax America, Considered. By a Member of the Rev. Mr. Wesley's Society. *London.* MDCCLXXVI. 8vo, pp. 70. 24727

Fletcher (J.) Remarks on the Case and Trial of T. O. Selfridge, for Shooting C. Austin. By John Fletcher. *Boston.* 1807. 8vo. 24728

Fletcher (J.) Studies on Slavery, in Easy Lessons. Compiled into Eight Studies, and subdivided into Short Sermons, for the Convenience of Readers. By John Fletcher, of Louisiana. ... *Natchez: Jackson Warner.* 1852. 8vo, pp. xiv, 7–637. B., BA., C. + Fourth Edition. [*Ibid.*] 1852. 8vo. 24729

Some copies have the imprint, *Charleston,* 1852. A "Fifth thousand" appears on the title of another issue.

Fletcher (J.) The American War. A Lecture. By the Rev. Joseph Fletcher. *Manchester: W. Irwin & Co.* 1863. 8vo, pp. 16. 24730

Fletcher (*Judge*). Address to the Grand Jury of Wexford, showing the Necessity of Putting Down Orange Societies, to which is added several Charges Against Captain O. H. Perry, of the United States Navy. [n. d.] 16mo. 24731

Fletcher (M.) The Methodist; or, Incidents and Characters from Life in the Baltimore Conference. By Miriam Fletcher. With an Introduction by W. P. Strickland, D.D. *New York.* 1859. 2 vols., 12mo. 24732

Fletcher (N. H.) A Sermon, delivered at Buxton, June 8th, 1821, at the Funeral of the Rev. Paul Coffin, D.D. By Nathaniel H. Fletcher ... . *Kennebunk: printed by James K. Remich.* 1821. 8vo, pp. 33. H. 24733

Fletcher (R.) The Lamentable State of New England: Being an Account of the Beginning, or Original of the Separates in New England, and their Progress with their Errors and Faults. Also an Account of the Beginning or Original of the Standing Churches in New-England, and their Progress, with their Errors and Faults. By Reuben Fletcher. *Boston: Printed for the Author.* 1772. 8vo, pp. 47. W. 24734

Fletcher (R.) Speech of Richard Fletcher to his Constituents ... in Faneuil Hall ... Nov. 6, 1837. [*Boston.* 1837.] 8vo, pp. 16. B., BA. 24735

On currency and banking. Also: Mr. Fletcher's Address to his Constituents, relative to the Speech delivered by him in Faneuil Hall. [*Washington.* 1837.] 8vo, pp. 15. H.

Fletcher (R.) Copy of the Record, in the Case, Robert Fletcher *vs.* John Peck; ... Circuit Court of the United States ... Boston, 1807. *Boston: printed by Munroe, Francis, & Parker. Dec.* 1808. 8vo, pp. 38. BA., H. 24736

Fletcher. Proceedings in the Case of Robert Fletcher. [Georgia Land Claim. n. p. n. d.] 8vo, pp. 38. 24737

Fletcher (S. S.) A Sermon, on the Fanaticism of the Present Age, ... brought to bear upon the Fatal Delusion of Millerism. Delivered in ... New Bedford, Mass., Oct. 29, 1844. By Silas S. Fletcher. *New Bedford: Press of Benj. Lindsey.* 1844. 8vo, pp. 16. 24738

Fletcher (T.) Letters in Vindication of the Rights of the British West India Colonies, originally addressed to the Editors of the Liverpool Mercury, in Answer to Mr. James Cropper's Letters to W. Wilberforce, Esq., M.P. By Thomas Fletcher. *Liverpool.* 1822. 8vo, pp. 68. 24739

Fletcher (T.) An Oration, delivered on the Fourth of July ... 1841 ... [at] Natchez. ... By Thomas Fletcher. *Natchez.* 1841. 8vo, pp. 16. H. 24740

Also: An Oration, delivered before the various Lodges ... of ... Odd Fellows of ... Natchez ... 26th ... April, 1843. ... *Natchez.* 1843. 12mo, pp. 12. H.

Fletcher (Thomas C.) Inaugural Message of Governor Fletcher to the Twenty-Third General Assembly of the State of Missouri, Jan. 2, 1865. *Jefferson City: W. A. Curry.* 1865. 8vo, pp. 13. 24741

Fletcher. Missouri's Jubilee. Speech ... delivered in the State Capital, on the Reception, by the Legislature, of the News of the Passage of the Convention Ordinance abolishing Slavery in Missouri. *Jefferson City: W. A. Curry.* 1865. 8vo, pp. 8.

Fletcher (W.) The Dying Words of William Fletcher. *Philadelphia: Printed by Reinier Jansen.* 1699. 24743

All works bearing this imprint are of extreme rarity.

Fletcher (W.) The State of the Action Brought by William Fletcher against William Vassall, For Defaming him: tried In the Superiour Court at Boston, August Term, A.D. 1752, and now Pending by Appeal to His Majesty in Council. *Boston.* 1753. 4to, pp. (4), 39. H., M. 24744

Fleuriau (B. G.) La Vie du vénérable Père Pierre Claver, de la Compagnie de Jésus, apôtre de Carthagène et des Indes orientales. Par Bertrand Gabriel Fleuriau. *Paris: chez Bordelet.* 1731. 12mo, pp. 199. + Nouvelle édition, revue avec soin, et augmentée de notes. *Paris: imprimerie de Béthune.* 1830. 2 vols., 18mo. + *Paris: Clermont-Ferrand, Thibaud-Landriot.* 1834–5. 2 vols., 12mo, pp. 311; 328. + Nouvelle édition. *Liége: Imprimerie de L. Grandmont-Donders.* 1851. 12mo, pp. 371. 24745

Fleuriau. Lebensgeschichte des Ehrwürdigen Vaters Peter Claver ... verfasst von Vater Bertrand Gabriel Fleuriau aus derselben Gesellschaft. Ins Deutsche übersetzt von Dominikus Schelke ... . Mit einer vorrede begleitet von Karl Egger ... . *Augsburg: bey Nicolaus Doll.* 1833. 8vo, pp. xxiv, 383.

[FLEURIAU.] The Life of the Venerable Father Claver, S.J., Apostle of the West Indies; ... *London: Thomas Richardson.* 1849. 12mo, pp. xxiv, 421. 24747

This is an abridged translation. Concerning Claver, *see* Bacher, III. 301.

[FLEURIEU (Charles Pierre Claret de, *Comte de*).] Découvertes des François, en 1768 & 1769, dans le sud-est de la nouvelle Guinée. Et reconnoissances postérieures des mêmes Terres par des Navigateurs Anglois qui leur ont imposé de nouveaux noms; précédées de l'Abrégé historique des Navigations & des Découvertes des Espagnols dans les mêmes Parages. Par M. * * *, ancien Capitaine de Vaisseau. *Paris: de l'Imprimerie Royale.* M.DCC.XC. 4to, pp. xvi, iv, 309. 12 Maps. BA. 24748

[FLEURIEU.] Discoveries of the French In 1768 and 1769, to the South-East of New-Guinea, with the Subsequent Visits to the same Lands by English Navigators, who gave them new Names. To which is prefixed, An Historical Abridgement of the Voyages and Discoveries of the Spaniards in the same Seas. By M. * * *, formerly a Captain in the French Navy. Translated from the French. *London: John Stockdale.* M.DCC.XCI. 4to, pp. xxiv, 323, (1). 12 Maps, and Plates. BA. 24749

There are copies on large paper. *See* "M. Rev.," VII. 174, 250.

FLEURIEU. Voyage fait par ordre du Roi en 1768 et 1769, à différentes parties du monde, pour épreuver en mer les Horloges marines inventées par M. Ferdinand Berthoud. Première partie contenant. 1°. Le Journal des Horloges marines ... . 2°. Le Journal de la Navigation, ... d'ou suit un examen critique de plusieurs Cartes publiées au Dépôt des plans & journaux de la Marine ... Par M. d'Eveux de Fleurieu ... . *Paris: Imprimerie Royale.* M. DCCLXXIII. 2 vols., 4to, 2 l., pp. lxxix, 803, 3 Maps; 2 l., pp. 622, 4 l. folded, pp. xl. A., H. 24750

FLEURIEU. Voyage autour du monde, pendant les années 1790, 1791, et 1792, Par Etiénne Marchand, précédé d'une introduction historique, auquel on a joint des recherches sur les terres australes de Drake, et un exam̃en critique du voyage de Roggeween, avec cartes et figures. Par C. L. Claret Fleurieu. ... *Paris: Imprimerie de la Republique. An* VI. [1798]. 5 vols., imp. 8vo, pp. viii, ccl, (1), 294, (1); vi, 529, (1); viii, 474, (1); viii, 494, (2); xii, 559, (4). Charts. 24751

See "M. Rev.," XXXIII. 523; XXXIV. 449; and XXXV. 496.

FLEURIEU. A Voyage round the World, performed during the Years 1790, 1791, and 1792; By Etienne Marchand. Preceded by a Historical Introduction, and Illustrated by Charts, etc. Translated from the French of C. P. Claret Fleurieu, of the National Institute of Arts and Sciences, &c. *London: T. N. Longman and O. Rees.* 1801. 2 vols., 4to, 6 l., pp. cxxviii, 361; xi, 503, 105. 8 Charts. + [*Ibid.*] 2 vols., 8vo, pp. cxci, 536; xiii, 663, 105. 8 Charts in 4to. 24752

Valuable for its scientific observations, and the learned researches of the author on the early navigators.

FLEURY (L.) L'histoire de la découverte de l'Amérique, racontée au jeune age par M. Lamé Fleury. *Paris: P. Dufart.* 1836. 12mo, pp. iv, 260. + Troisième édition, ornée de figures. *Bruxelles.* 1837. 12mo, pp. 204. 24753

FLEURY. L'histoire de la découverte de l'Amérique. Zum Schulgebrauch mit einem Wörterbuche herausgegeben von H. Robolsky. *Berlin: Renger.* 1857. 8vo, pp. xvi, 162. 24754

FLEURY. Historia del descubrimiento de la América, ... Por M. Lamé Fleury, traducida al castellano por M. J. J. *Paris.* 1836. 18mo. 24755

FLEURY. History of the Discovery of America, Written Expressly for Children. From the French. *London.* 1849. 12mo, pp. 142. S. 24756

Fliegendes Blatt. *See* Heyn (P. P.)

The Flight of Freedom; a Fragment. *London: Williams.* 1776. 4to. 24757

"Freedom emigrates at last to America." — *M. Rev.*, LV. 159.

FLINDERS (M.) A Voyage to Terra Australis, undertaken for the purpose of Completing the Discovery of that vast Country, and prosecuted in the years 1801, 1802, and 1803, in His Majesty's Ship the Investigator, and subsequently in the Armed Vessel Porpoise and Cumberland Schooner. With an account of the Shipwreck of the Porpoise, Arrival of the Cumberland at Mauritius, and Imprisonment of the Commander during Six Years and a Half in that Island. By Matthew Flinders, Commander of the Investigator. *London: G. & W. Nicol.* 1814. 2 vols., 4to, pp. ix, 5 l., pp. cciv, 269; (2), 613. Maps and Plates in folio. B.

Some copies on large paper. *See* Dibdin's "Literary Companion," also "Q. Rev.," XXXI., and "M. Rev.," LXXVI. 152; LXXVII, 35. There is a Dutch translation, en titled, "Ontdekkings-Reis naar het Groote Zuidland, anders Nieuw-Holland. Uit het Engelsch. *Haarlem.* 1815–16." 8 vols., 8vo. Map.

FLINN (A.) A Sermon occasioned by the Death of the Honble. Judge Wilds, delivered by desire of the Gentlemen of the Bar of Charleston, in the First Presbyterian Church in this City, On the 1st day of April, 1810. By the Rev. Andrew Flinn, A.M. *Charleston: Printed and Sold by J. Hoff.* 1810. 8vo, pp. 23.

Also: Sermon, 3d April, 1811, at the Dedication of the Second Presbyterian Church, Charleston, S. C. *Charleston.* 1811. 8vo. N.

FLINT (A.) A Charity Sermon, delivered in the North Presbyterian Meeting-House in Hartford, ... October 7th, 1810. ... By Abel Flint ... . *Hartford: Charles Hosmer.* 1810. 8vo, pp. 12.

FLINT. A Discourse, Delivered at Hartford, Feb. 22, 1800, The Day set apart by Recommendation of Congress, to pay a Tribute of Respect to the Memory of General George Washington, who Died, December 14th, 1799. By Abel Flint. ... *Hartford: Printed by Hudson and Goodwin.* 1800. 8vo, pp. (4), 22. BA., H., W. 24761

FLINT. A Discourse occasioned by the News of Peace, delivered in Hartford, February 14, 1815. By Abel Flint. *Hartford.* 1815. 8vo, pp. 11. 24762

FLINT. A Sermon, preached at the Anniversary Election, Hartford, May 9, 1816. By Abel Flint, ... *Hartford: George Goodwin and Sons, Printers.* 1816. 8vo, pp. 27. BA. 24763

Also: A Sermon ... at the Ordination of the Rev. Josiah B. Andrews ... April 21, 1802. ... . *Hartford: Printed by Hudson & Goodwin.* 1802. 8vo, pp. 27. B. — ... A Sermon, delivered at Hartford, Sept. 17, 1806, at the Funeral of John M'Curdy Strong, son of the Rev. Nathan Strong, D.D. ... *Hartford: Lincoln and Gleason.* 1806. 8vo, pp. 16. B., BA. — Sermon at East-Hartford, Nov. 3, 1806, at the Funeral of Mrs. Mary Yates. ... *Hartford.* 1806. 8vo. — Sermon at East Haddam, Oct. 23, 1816, at the Ordination of Rev. Isaac Parsons. ... *Hartford.* 1816. 8vo. — Sermon at the Ordination of Rev. W. B. Sprague, a Colleague Pastor with the Rev. Jos. Lathrop, at West Springfield. ... *Hartford.* 1819. 8vo, pp. 30. B.

FLINT (A.) The Reciprocal Duties and Obligations of the Medical Profession and the Public; a ... Lecture delivered at the Rush Medical College at the Commencement of the Session 1844–5. By Austin Flint, M.D. ... *Chicago: Z. Eastman.* 1844. 8vo, pp. 24. 24764

Also: An Address delivered before the Buffalo Young Men's Temperance Society ... April 1, 1841. ... *Buffalo: Thomas & Co.* 1841. 8vo, pp. 40. H.

FLINT (C. L.) The Agriculture of Massachusetts, as shown in Returns of the Agricultural Societies, 1853. Prepared by Charles L. Flint. To which is prefixed the First Annual Report

of the Secretary of the Board of Agriculture, Boston, Mass.; together with the Reports of Committees appointed to visit the County Societies. *Boston.* 1853–56. 8vo, pp. 678. 7 Engrs.

Mr. Flint continued these reports to 1866?

FLINT. A Practical Treatise on Grasses and Forage Plants, comprising their Natural History, Comparative Nutritive Value, Methods of Cultivating, Cutting, and Curing, and the Management of Grass Lands. By Charles L. Flint, A.M. *New York.* 1857. 8vo, pp. iv, 236. BA. + Third Edition, Revised and Enlarged. *New-York.* 1859. 12mo, pp. 398. + Fifth Edition. *Boston: Crosby, Nichols, Lee & Co.* 1860. B. 24766

Also: Address ... Annual Fair of the Hampden Co. Agricultural Society, ... Springfield, October 4th & 5th, 1855. *Springfield: Samuel Bowles & Co., Printers.* 1856. 8vo, pp. 27. H. — Agriculture: Its Past, Present, and Future. An Address delivered before the Hampshire Co. Agricultural Society ... October 11, 1855. ... *Amherts, Mass.* 1855. 8vo, pp. 26. H. — The Board of Agriculture and State Farm. An Address ... at Greenfield, October 2, 1856. ... . *Greenfield: printed by Charles A. Mirick.* 1856. 8vo, pp. 16. H. — Pleuro-Pneumonia. A Letter to ... John A. Andrew. ... . [*Boston.* 1863.] 8vo, pp. 15. — The State Board of Agriculture, and the Management of the State Farm at Westborough. An Address ... October 2, 1856. ... . *Greenfield: printed by Charles A. Mirick.* 1856. 8vo, pp. 34. H.

FLINT (H.) *See* Flynt (H.)

FLINT (H. M.) Life of Stephen A. Douglas: to which are added his Speeches and Reports. By H. M. Flint. *New York.* 1860. 12mo. + *Philadelphia: John E. Potter.* 1863. 12mo, pp. 408. Portrait. 24767

FLINT. Mexico under Maximilian. By Henry M. Flint, Esq., ... *Philadelphia,* [*etc.*] *National Pub. Co.* [1867.] 12mo, pp. 258. B., C. 24768

Written prior to the death of Maximilian. It aimed to convince the American public that the wisest national policy was to recognize the then Emperor of Mexico.

FLINT. The Railroads of the United States; their History and Statistics: Comprising the Progress and Present Condition of the various Lines with their Earnings and Expenses, and showing their Wonderful Power in Developing the Resources of the Country. To which are added a Synopsis of the Railroad Laws of the United States, ... By Henry M. Flint ... . *Philadelphia: John E. Potter and Company.* 1868. 12mo, pp. 452. B. 24769

FLINT (J.) An Address on the Character and Services of George Washington ... February 22, 1832, ... By Jacob Flint ... . *Boston: Leonard C. Bowles.* 1832. 8vo, pp. 18. BA.

FLINT. Two Discourses, containing the History of the Church and Society in Cohasset, delivered December 16, 1821. ... With a Geographical Sketch of Cohasset. By Jacob Flint ... . *Boston: Munroe and Francis.* 1822. 8vo, pp. 28. BA. 24771

See the "Christian Disciple," New Series, Vol. IV. 125–119. *See also* "Mass. Hist. Soc. Coll.," Vol. II., Third Series. Also: A Discourse ... at Cohasset, 9 June, 1816, ... after the Interment of Mrs. Sylvia Flint, ... *Boston: John Eliot.* 1816. 8vo, pp. 16. B., BA. — A Sermon ... at the Ordination of the Reverend Joshua Bates, ... to the ... First Church in Dedham. *Dedham: R. Mann.* 1803. 8vo. BA. — A Sermon ... at the Ordination of the Rev. James Flint ... October 29th, 1806. ... [*Boston*]: *Russell & Cutler.* 1806. 8vo, pp. 31. BA.

FLINT (J.) A Discourse ... at Plymouth, December 22, 1815, at the Anniversary Commemoration of the First Landing of our Ancestors at that Place. By James Flint ... . *Boston: James Avery.* 1816. 8vo, pp. 24. B., BA., W. 24772

FLINT. A Discourse, ... on the Anniversary Election, May 1815. By James Flint ... . *Boston: Benjamin Russell.* 1815. 8vo, pp. 31. B., BA., M. 24773

Mainly on the war, and the turn of affairs in Europe.

FLINT. God a Refuge, &c. Discourse, Nov. 6, 1814, before the Bridgewater Light Infantry. *Boston.* 1814. 8vo, pp. 20.

[FLINT.] Farewell Hymn, on leaving the Old Meeting-house at Quincy. [n. d.] Broadside. 24775

[FLINT.] Historical Address [by J. F.] and Poem [by Lilley Eaton] delivered at the Bi-Centennial Celebration of the Old Town of Reading, May 29, 1844. *Boston.* 1844. 12mo.

FLINT. Verses on Many Occasions, with others for which it may be thought there was no Occasion. By James Flint. *Lynn.* 1851. 4to. 24777

FLINT. Times of Birth and Death the Appointment and Ordering of God: a Sermon delivered in the East Church, in Salem, July 21, 1850, on Occasion of the Death of President Taylor, July 10, 1850; and of the Death of the Hon. Nathaniel Silsbee, July 14, 1850. By James Flint, D.D. ... *Salem.* 1850. 8vo, pp. 16. BA., H. 24778

FLINT. Two Discourses delivered on Taking Leave of the Old Church ... in Salem, December 28, 1845. By James Flint, D.D. ... . *Salem: Observer Office.* 8vo, pp. 18. B., BA. 24779

Also: The Deceased Pastor ... A Discourse delivered March 14, 1846, in ... Salem ... after the Decease of the Rev. John Brazer, D.D. ... *Salem.* 1846. 8vo, pp. 22. BA., H. — A Discourse, ... November 3, 1819, at the Ordination of the Rev. Seth Alden to the Pastoral Care of the Church and Society in ... Marlborough. ... . *Worcester: printed by Manning & Trumbull.* 1820. 8vo, pp. 40. BA., H. — A Discourse delivered ... at the Dedication of the New Church, Jan. 1, 1846. *Salem.* 1846. 8vo. — A Sermon ... at the Ordination of the Rev. Nathaniel Whitman, ... Billerica, Jan. 26, 1814. *Cambridge: printed by Hilliard and Metcalf.* 1814. 8vo, pp. 39. BA., H. — A Sermon delivered in ... Beverly, June 18, 1828, on the Occasion of the ... Death of the Rev. Abiel Abbot, D.D. ... *Salem: Foote & Brown.* 1828. 8vo, pp. 32. BA., W. — A Sermon delivered ... in Marblehead, February 11, 1849, ... after the Funeral of the Late Rev. John Bartlett ... *Salem.* 1849. 8vo, pp. 14. H. — The Vanity and Unsatisfactory Nature of Earthly Possessions, Pursuits and Pleasures: A Discourse. *Salem.* 1844. 8vo. S.

FLINT (J.) Letters from America, Containing Observations on the Climate and Agriculture of the Western States, the Manners of the People, the Prospects of Emigrants, &c. &c. By James Flint. ... *Edinburgh: W. & C. Tait.* 1822. 8vo, pp. viii, 330. B., BA., C., H. 24780

FLINT (J.), *and* STONE (J. H.) A Genealogical Register of the Descendants of Thomas Flint, of Salem, with a Copy of the Wills and Inventories of the Estates of the first two Generations. Compiled by John Flint and John H. Stone. *Andover: Printed by Warren F. Draper.* 1860. 8vo, pp. 150. 24781

FLINT (J. Barker). An Address delivered before the Massachusetts Society for the Suppression of Intemperance, May 29, 1828. By Joshua B. Flint ... . *Boston: Bowles & Dearborn.* 1828. 8vo, pp. 43. B., BA., H. 24782

Also: An Address ... Louisville Medical Institute ... at the Commencement ... November 13th, 1838. ... *Louisville, Ky.: Prentice and Weissenger.* 1838. 8vo, pp. 31. B., BA., H. — A Discourse delivered to the Class of the Kentucky School of Medicine, November 3, 1852 ... . *Louisville: Haldeman & Co.* 1852. 8vo, pp. 36. BA. — A Discourse, ... Kentucky State Medical Society, at its Annual Meeting, Lebanon, April 18, 1859. ... . *Louisville, Ky.: Hanna & Co., Printers.* 1859. 8vo, pp. 23. B., H.

FLINT (M. P.) The Hunter, and other Poems. By Micah P. Flint. *Boston: Cummings, Hilliard & Co.* 1826. 12mo, pp. 147. BA., S. 24783

FLINT (T.) Biographical Memoir of Daniel Boone, the First Settler of Kentucky, Interspersed with Incidents in the Early Annals of the Country. By Timothy Flint. *Cincinnati.* 1833. 12mo. + [*Ibid.*] 1834. 12mo, pp. 267. + [*Ibid.*] 1840. + [*Ibid.*] 1841. + *Cincinnati: George Conclin.* 1842. 12mo, pp. 252. C. + [*Ibid.*] 1846. 12mo. + [*Ibid.*] 1849. 12mo. +

[*Ibid.*] 1850. 12mo, pp. 252. + [*Ibid.*] 1851. 12mo. + *Cincinnati: Applegate & Co.* 1855. 12mo, pp. 252. 24784

It was afterwards reproduced as

FLINT. The First White Man of the West, or the Life and Exploits of Col. Dan'l Boone, the First Settler of Kentucky; interspersed with Incidents in the Early Annals of the Country. By Timothy Flint. *Cincinnati: Applegate & Company.* 1854. 12mo, pp. 252. Woodcut. BA. + [*Ibid.*] 1856. 12mo. + [*Ibid.*] 1858. 12mo. BA., C. 24785

FLINT. A Condensed Geography and History of the Western States, or the Mississippi Valley. By Timothy Flint. ... *Cincinnati: E. H. Flint.* 1828. 8vo, pp. 592; 520. BA., C.

[FLINT.] Francis Berrian, or the Mexican Patriot. ... *Boston: Cummings, Hilliard and Company.* 1826. 2 vols., 12mo, pp. 299; 285. B., BA. 24787

The autobiography of a New England adventurer.

[FLINT.] George Mason, the Young Backwoodsman; or, 'Don't Give up the Ship.' A Story of the Mississippi. By the Author of 'Francis Berrian.' *Boston: Hilliard, Gray, Little, and Wilkins.* 1829. 12mo, pp. 167. H. 24788

FLINT. The History and Geography of the Mississippi Valley. To which is appended a Condensed Physical Geography of the Atlantic United States, and the Whole American Continent. Second Edition. By Timothy Flint ... *Cincinnati: E. H. Flint and L. R. Lincoln.* 1832. 2 vols., 8vo, pp. 464; 276. B., BA., C., H. + Third Edition. [*Ibid.*] 1833. 2 vols., 8vo, pp. 469; 310. 24789

Some copies have the title: "The United States and other Divisions of the American Continent." Although written in "a most uncouth style," is highly commended in Ward's "Mexico," and the "N. Am. Rev."

FLINT. Indian Wars of the West: containing Biographical Sketches of those Pioneers who headed the Western Settlers in Repelling the Attacks of the Savages, together with a View of the Character, Manners, Monuments, and Antiquities of the Western Indians. By Timothy Flint. *Cincinnati: E. H. Fleet.* 1833. 12mo, pp. 240. B., BA., C. 24790

Stevens, in his "Bibliotheca Historia," quotes an edition, *Cincinnati.* 1830.

FLINT. Lectures upon Natural History, ... and Discoveries in the Arts. By Timothy Flint. *Boston.* 1833. 12mo. P. 24791

[FLINT.] The Life and Adventures of Arthur Clenning, ... *Philadelphia: Towar & Hogan.* 1828. 2 vols., 12mo, pp. 236; 175. BA., 24792

FLINT. The Life and Adventures of Daniel Boone, the First Settler of Kentucky, interspersed with Incidents in the Early Annals of the Country. By Timothy Flint. New Edition. To which is added an Account of Captain Estill's Defeat. *Cincinnati: U. P. James.* 1868. 16mo, pp. 256. Map and 3 Plates.

FLINT. Recollections of the last Ten Years, passed in Occasional Residences and Journeyings in the Valley of the Mississippi, from Pittsburg and the Missouri to the Gulf of Mexico, and from Florida to the Spanish Frontier; in a Serier of Letters to the Rev. James Flint, of Salem, Massachusetts. By Timothy Flint, Principal of the Seminary of Rapide, Louisiana. ... *Boston: Cummings, Hilliard and Company.* 1826. 8vo, pp. (2), 395.

See "M. Rev.," IV. 460; "N. Am. Rev.," XXIII. 355–368; and "Q. Rev.," XLVIII. 201. Allibone quotes a *second* edition, 1831, 8vo, for which his authority is Rich's "Bibl. Am.," Vol. II., pp. 182 and 230 — probably an error.

FLINT. A Sermon preached May 11, 1808, at the Ordination of the Rev. Ebenezer Hubbard, ... Newbury. By Timothy Flint ... . *Newburyport: E. W. Allen.* 1808. 8vo, pp. 36. H.

Also: The Shoshonee Valley. A Romance. *Cincinnati.* 1830. 2 vols., 12mo. *See also* Pattie (J. O.), and "Western Monthly Review."

[FLINT (Waldo).] Some Strictures on an Act to provide a National Currency, secured by a Pledge of United States Stocks: and to provide for the Circulation and Redemption thereof . ... *Boston: printed by John Wilson and Son.* 1863. 8vo, pp. 18. H.

Also: An Address ... before the Leicester Temperance Society, ... April 9, 1829. ... *Worcester: M. Spooner, Printer.* 1829. 8vo, pp. 22. H. — An Address ... before the Worcester Agricultural Society, ... Oct. 10, 1832. ... *Worcester: printed by S. H. Colton & Co.* 1832. 8vo, pp. 16. H., W.

FLINT. By-Laws of the Flint-Steel Mining Company, Lake Superior. ... *New-York: Francis Hart, Printer.* 1853. 8vo, pp. 154. H. 24797

FLINTER (George Dawson). An Account of the Present State of the Island of Puerto Rico ... and Documents Illustrative of the State of Commerce and Agriculture, ... Population ... By Colonel Flinter ... . *London: Longman.* 1834. 8vo, pp. xii, 392.

FLINTER. Exámen del estado actual de los esclavos de la Isla de Puerto Rico bajo el Gobierno español: ... Por Don Jorge D. Flinter ... . *Nueva York: Española del Redactor.* 1832. 8vo, 2 l., pp. 124. BA. 24799

FLINTER. A History of the Revolution of Caraccas, comprising an Impartial Narrative of the Atrocities committed by the contending Parties, illustrating the real State of the Contest, &c., with a Description of the Llaneros, or People of the Plains of South America. By Major Flinter. *London: T. and J. Allman.* 1819. 8vo, pp. xii, 213. B., BA. 24800

FLINTER. A View of the Present Condition of the Slave Population in the Island of Puerto Rico, under the Spanish Government. Showing the Impolicy and Danger of Prematurely Emancipating the West India Slaves. ... By George Dawson Flinter ... . *Philadelphia: printed by Adam Waldie.* 1832. 8vo, pp. 117. C. 24801

Floræ Fluminensis. *See* [Vellozo de Miranda (J.)]

Flore de terre Neuve, et des Isles St. Pierre et Miclon, avec figures dessinées par l'auteur sur la plante vivante. *Paris: Didot.* 1829. 4to, 16 sheets. 24802

FLORENCE (T. B.) The Principles of Democracy. Speech of Hon. Thos. B. Florence, of Pennsylvania. ... April 12, 1860. 8vo, pp. 11. 24803

[Another edition, [n. p. n. d.] 8vo, pp. 16. Also: The Tariff Question. Remarks ... April 25th, 1860. 8vo, pp. 4.

FLORENCE. Plan and Charters of the Florence and Keyport Companies, Incorporated by the State of New Jersey. *New York: Baker, Godwin & Co., Printers.* 1853. 8vo, pp. 12.

FLORENCIA (Francisco de). Descripcion Historica y Moral del Yermo de S. Miguel de las Cuevas en el Reyno de Nueva-España, ... con un Breve compendio de la Vida del V. Anachoreta Fray Bartholomè de Jesus Maria. *Cadiz: por Cristoval de Requena.* [1689.] 4to. 24805

FLORENCIA. La Estrella de el Norte de Mexico, aparecida al rayar el dia de la luz Evangelica en este Nuevo-Mundo, en la Historia de la milagrosa imagen de N. Señora de Guadalupe de Mexico, por Francisco de Florencia. *Mexico: Benavides.* 1688. 4to, pp. 830. Plate. 24806

FLORENCIA. La Estrella de el Norte de Mexico, aparecida al rayar el dia de la luz evangelica en este Nuevo Mundo, en la cumbre del cerro de Tepeyac, orilla del mar Tezcucano, à un Naturel recien convertido; pintada tres dias despues en su tilma, ò capa de lienzo, delante del Obispo, y de su familia, en su Casa Obispal: Para a luz en la Fè à los Indios, etc. *Mexico: Imprenta de Ant. Velazquez, à costa del dicho D. Juan Leonardo.* 1741. 4to, 10 l., pp. 260, (4). 24807

This edition is dedicated to the Empress and Angels of Men.

FLORENCIA. La Estrella del Norte de Mexico, aparacida al rayar el dia de la luz Evangelica en este Nuevo Mundo, en la cumbre del cerro de Tepeyacac, orilla del mar Tezcucano, à un Natural recien convertido; pintada tres dias despues milagrosamente en su Tilma ó Capa de Lienzo delante del Obispo y de su familia, en su Casa Obispal, para luz en la Fé à los Indios. ... En la historia de la milagrosa imagin de Nuestra Señora de Guadalupe de Mexico, que se apareció en la Manta de Juan Diego. Compusola el Padre Francisco de Florencia, de la extinguida Compañia de Jesus. *Madrid: En la Imprenta de Lorenzo de San Martin.* 1785. 4to, pp. 829, (10). J.C.B. 24808

This Madrid reprint is a finer book than the Mexican original. The Empress is dropped, and the dedication made to the Archbishop of Mexico.

FLORENCIA. Exemplar Vida y gloriosa muerte en odio de la fe del venerable padre Luis de Medina, martyrizado en las islas que llaman de los Ladrones o Marianos. *Sevilla: Juan Francisco de Blas.* 1673. 4to, 54 l. Portrait. 24809

FLORENCIA. Historia de la Provincia de la compañia de Jesus, de Nueva España, Tomo Primero [yunico] dividida en ocho libros. *Mexico: por J. Guillena Carrascoso.* 1694. Folio, Frontispiece, 9 l., pp. 409, 1 l. 24810

This history of the Order of the Jesuits in Mexico is amongst the most esteemed and rarest of this author's works.

FLORENCIA. Menologio de los Varones mas señalados en perfeccion religiosa de la Compañia de Jesus de la Provincia de Nueva España. *En Barcelona: por Jacinto Andres.* 1661. 4to. + *Barcelona: H. Andrea.* 1671. 4to. 24811

FLORENCIA. Menologio de los Varones mas señalados en perfeccion religiosa de la Provincia de la Compañia de Jesus de la Nueva-España, escrita por el Padre Francisco de Florencia, y

aprobado por N. M. R. P. Juan Paulo Oliva, ... Nuevamente añadido ... por P. Juan Antonio de Oviedo. ... [*Mexico.* 1747.] 4to, pp. (8), 228. 24812

FLORENCIA. La Milagrosa invencion de un tesoro escondido en un campo ... De los remedios en su admirable imagen de N. Señora de Mexico, etc. *Mexico.* 1685. 4to. Plate. 24813

FLORENCIA. La milagrosa invencion de un thesoro escondido en un campo, que hallò un venturoso cazique, y escondiò en su casa, para gozarlo á sus solas; patente ya en el Santuario de los Remedios en su admirable imagen de Ntra Señora, señalada en Milagros, invocada por patrona de las lluvias y temporales; ... Noticias de su origen, y venidas a Mexico; Marabillas, que ha obrado, con los que la invocan; Descripcion de su casa, y Meditaciones para sus Novenas. Por el P. Francisco de Florencia, de la Compañia de Jesus. Dalas a la estampa el Licenciado Don Lorenzo de Mendoza Capellan. ... Dedicalas a el Señor Don Gonzalo Suarez de San Martin. ... Con licentia. *En Sevilla: en la Imprenta de las Siete Revueltas. A costa de D. Jvan Leonardo Malo Manrique. Año de* 1745. 4to, Engraved Frontispiece, pp. (14), 160. 24814

Backer, II. 197, quotes an edition, *Mexico.* 1686.

FLORENCIA. Narracion de la Mirabillosa Aparicion que hizo el Archangel de San Miguel a un Indio [en Tzopiloatl]. *Sevilla.* [1692.] 4to, pp. (8), 194, (6). 24815

FLORENCIA. Origin de los celebros Santuarios de la Nueva Galicia, Obispado de Guadalaxara en la America Septentrional. *Mexico: por Carrascoso.* 1694. 4to. + *Imprenta de la Bibliotheca Mexicana.* 1757. 4to. 3 Plates. + *Reimpreso en Mexico.* 1783. + *Mexico.* 1796. 12mo. + *Mexico.* 1801. 12mo, pp. (8), 220.

FLORENCIA. Panegirico del Apostel S. Pedro, predicado en la Catedral de Pueblo. *Mexico: Lupercio.* 1680. 4to. 24817

FLORENCIA. Relacion de la exemplar, y Religiosa Vida del Padre Nicolas de Guadalaxara, ... *Mexico: por J. de Ribera.* 1684. 4to. 24818

FLORENCIA. Zodiaco Mariano, en que el sol de justicia Christo Con la salud en las alas visita como Signos, y Casas proprios para beneficio de los hombres los templos, y lugares dedicados á los cultos de su SS. Madre por medio de las mas celebres y mylagrosas imagines de la misma Señora, que se veneran en

esta America Septentrional, y Reynos de la Nueva España. Obra posthuma de el Padre Francisco de Florencia, de la Compañia de Jesus, reducida á compendio, y en gran parte añadida por el P. Juan Antonio de Oviedo de la misma Compañia, Calificador del Sto. Oficio, y Prefecto de la ilustre congregacion de la Purissima en el Colegio Maximo de S. Pedro, y San Pablo de Mexico. Quien la dedica al sacrosanto y dulcissimo nombre de Maria. Con Licencia. *En Mexico en la nueva imprenta del Real y mas Antiguo Colegio de San Ildefonsa año de* 1755. 4to, pp. (24), 328. 24819

"A work of considerable importance for the ecclesiastical history of Spanish North America. The details are narrated with great fullness, with names, dates, and circumstances, with authorities and bibliographical citations." — STEVENS. Florence was a native of Florida, and perhaps his own name as well as that of his native country formed the chief reason for his persistent and often recorded worship of the "florida imagen." His works contain historical matter burdened with much idolatry. This last work was a posthumous publication. Also: La casa peregrina, o Historia de Nuestra Señora de Loreto. *Mexico: por Calderon.* 1689. 4to. — Historia admirable de la Aparicion de S. Miguel al Indio Diego Lazaro en la Barranca de los Sopilotes de la Provincia de Tlaxcala, y fundacion de su magnifico Santuario. *En Sevilla: por Lopez de Haro.* 1692. 4to. — Milagroso hallazgo del tesoro escondido: Historia de la Imagen de Nuestra Señora de los Remedios de Megico. *En Mexico.* 1686. + *En Sevilla.* 1743. 4to. — Panegirico del Bienaventurado Luis Gonzaga. *Mexico: por Ribera.* 1683. 4to. — Sermon en la solemne dedicacion del templo de Tepozotlan. *Mexico: Lupercio.* 1682. 4to. — Sermon en la dedicacion de la Iglesia de Religiosas Carmelitas de S. José de Megico. *Mexico: por J. de Ribera.* 1684. 4to. — Vida admirable del Religioso P. Geronimo Figueroa, Jesuita, misionero quarenta añas entre los Indios Tarahumares. *Mexico: por Benavides.* 1689. 4to.

FLORES (A.) Discurso del Doctor Antonio Flores, ... al suceder en la Academia Nacional Cientifica Literaria del Ecuador á Mr. Sebastian Wine Ingeniero ea Jefe de la Republica el 21 de Junio de 1863. *Quito.* 1863. 24820

FLORES (F. F.) Sermon panegyrico al celestial cingulo de la Pureza del Angelico Doctor Santo Tomas, que en la solemne festividad, celebrada por la Ilustra Congregacion de las Castidad ... el dia 9 de Junio de 1794 ... predico el Doctor D. Francisco Fernando de Flores. ... *Mexico.* 1795. 4to, pp. (12), 46.

FLORES (L.) Memorial qve el Padre predicador fray Lvis Flores, padre de la Provincia de Santiago, en los reynos de Castilla, comissario general, que fue de todas las Provincias de la Nueva España, del Xapô, y Custodias de la Florida, Tampico, Rio verde, y Nuevo Mexico ... Remite á su Magestad, dandole cuenta del estado que tiene la obra del desague de Gueguetoca. [*Mexico.* 1653?] Folio, 27 l., 1 l. 24822

"Cette pièce n'est pas indiquée dans Pinelo. Nous trouvons dans son ouvrage qu'un P. Louis Flores, dominicain, fut martyrisé au Japon. Qu'il écrivit étant en prison, une relation des missions de ce pays jusqu'au 24 mai 1622. Le mss. original se conservait dans la bibliothèque de Lorenço Ramirez de Prado, du conseil des Indes. Orfanel le fit imprimer dans son histoire ecclésiastique du Japon (*Madrid*, 1833)." — LECLERC.

FLORES (P. F. A.) Arte de la lengua Kakchiquel y paralelo de las quatro Lenguas Metropolitanas que hoy integran en el reyno de Goathemala. Por P. F. Alonzo Flores. *Antigua, Guatemala.* 1753. 24823

Considered apocryphal until recently, when the Abbé Brasseur de Bourbourg wrote from Guatemala that he had obtained four copies. *See* a letter by G. Squier in the London "Athenæum," Dec. 8, 1855, No. 1467.

FLORES DE RIBERA (Jos. Ant.) Manifesto Juridico, en que por parte de D. Nicolas Benitez Coronel, como Marido de Doña Maria Josepha de Paz Cortes y Monroy, etc. *Mexico: J. R. de Hogal.* 1740. Folio. 24824

Also: Elogios Funebres: Oratio y Sermon Funebre en las Honras del J. A. de Flores y Ribera, Obispo de S. Iglesia de Leon de Nicaragua, 20 y 30 de Octobre de 1756. *Imprenta de la Bibliotheca Mexicana.* 1757. 4to.

FLORES DE PASCUA. Coleccion de composiciones escritas por Venezolanos. Aguinaldo para 1852. *Carácas.* 1851. 8vo, pp. 140. + Para 1866. *Carácas.* 1866. 8vo, pp. 113. 24825

FLORES DE PASCUA. Coleccion de Producciones originales en prosa y verso. *Carácas.* 1855. 8vo, pp. 95. + *Carácas.* 1849. 8vo, pp. 142. 24826

FLORES Y AGUILAR (Nic.) Oracion Panegyrica Gratulatoria al D. Luis Enriquez de Guzman Conde de Alva. *Lima.* [n. d.] 4to.

Sold at Puttick's, in 1860, for 9s.

FLORES DE VALDES (Roderigo Garcia). Sermon en las Honras Funebres que hizo el Religiosissimo convento de S. Phelippe de Jesus, de Madres Capuchinas de Mexico á la V. M. Sor Teresa Maria de Guzman, Fondadora de dicho Convento. *Mexico: por R. Calderon.* 1707. 4to. 24828

FLORES (V.) Rasgos biograficos de Venancio Flores. *Buenos-Aires.* 1864. 8vo, pp. 48. Frontispiece. 24829

Flores illustrium Epitaphiorum Cura P. A. Canonherio. *Antwerpiæ.* 1613. 8vo. 24830

Contains epitaphs on Christopher Columbus.

La Floresta. Periódico Semanario, de ciencias, artes, historia y americo literatura. 4to, pp. 72. *Mexico.* 1845. Plates and Portraits. 24831

La Floresta Espanola Peruana. *Lima.* 1848. 8vo, pp. 108.

FLOREZ (Fr. H.) Medallas de las Colonias, Municipios y Pueblos Antiguos de España. Coleccion de las que se hallan en diversos autores, y de otras hasta hoy nunca publicadas; con explication y dibujo de cada una. Por R. P. M. Henrique Florez. *Madrid: A. Marin.* 1757–73. 3 vols., 4to. Maps, and 67 Plates. 24833

"Cet ouvrage du savant Florez est le plus complet qui existe sur la numismatique espagnole." — SALVA. It includes the coinage of the Spanish colonies in America.

FLOREZ (Henrique). España Sagrada: theatro geographico-historico de Iglesia de España. Originen, Divisiones, y Terminos de todas sus Provincias. Antiguedad, traslaciones, y Estado antiguo y presente de sus Sillas ... . Con varios dissertaciones criticas para ilustrar la Historia Eclesiastica ... . Tomo I. ... Su autor el P. M. Fr. Henrique Florez ... . *Madrid: Miguel Francisco Rodriguez.* MDCCXLVII. 4to. Plates. BA. 24834

An important set of books, by the greatest antiquary Spain has produced, called by Mr. Ford, in his "Handbook of Spain," "The Dugdale, Muratori, and Montfauçon of Spain," was originally commenced in 1747, on the plan of the "Gallia Christiana," and the "Italia Sacra" of Ughelli, and continued throughout all political vicissitudes. It is at present "continuada por la Real Academia de la Historia." It is not finished, but Tomo I. was published in 1866. It is useful for the ecclesiastical history of the Spanish American colonies.

FLOREZ DE OCARIZ (J.) Genealogias del Nuevo Reyno de Granada. Por Don Juan Florez de Ocariz. *Madrid.* 1674. 2 vols., folio. 24835

Ternaux, No. 923, says of this work, "il est très important pour l'histoire de la colonisation de la Nouvelle-Grenade, car il entrait naturellement dans son plan de donner les détails les plus exacts sur l'époque de la fondation des diverses colonies et la personne des premiers fondateurs. Sold at Puttick's, in 1860, for £8 5s.

FLOREZ (Pedro Celestino). Guia de forasteros del departemento del Cuzco. *Cuzco: Evaristo Gonzalez.* 1833. 12mo, pp. 122. + *Lima: Corral.* 1834. pp. 99. + *Cuzco: J. Bautista de Sta. Cruz.* 1835. 8vo, pp. 89. 24836

FLOREZ (P.) La mas noble Montañesa Nuestra Señora del Brezo, su prodigiosa Aparicion, y algunos de los innumerables milagros que ha obrado y abra el Señor por la piados y continuado intercesion du su Santisima Madre en este divino Simulacio, en beneficio y consuelo de todo los fieles, sus devotos. Por El P. Mro. Fr. Plácido Florez. *Mexico.* 1807. 16mo, 6 l., pp. 126, 3 l. Plate. 24837

"A sort of 'Memorable Providences' of New England, calculated for the latitude and priestcraft of Mexico." — STEVENS.

FLOREZ (D. de Ribera). *See* Ribera Florez (D.)

FLOREZ ESTRADA (A.) *See* Estrada (A. F.), No. 23058.

The Floriad. Vol. I. *Schenectady.* 1811. 8vo. 24838

The Florian Claim. [n. p. 1852.] 8vo, pp. 15. H. 24839

FLORIDA. An Account of East Florida. With Remarks on its Future Importance to Trade and Commerce. *London.* [1766.] 8vo. 24840

See [Stork (W.)]; *see also* "M. Rev.," XXXIV. 478.

An Account of the First Discovery, and Natural History of Florida. 4to, pp. 32. N. 24841

An Act to Incorporate the Union Bank of Florida, &c. *Tallahassee.* 1834. 8vo. 24842

Acts of the Legislative Council of the Territory of Florida, passed at their First Session, 1822, ... Organizing the Government of Florida, &c. *Pensacola.* 1823. 8vo. + Third Session [1824]; with former Acts now in Force, and the Laws of Congress Organizing the Territory and Acts of the Legislative Council, passed at the Fourth Session [1825]. *Tallahassee.* 1825–26. 8vo. S. 24843

The Acts and Resolutions of the General Assembly of the State of Florida, passed at its First Session, ... November, 1845. *Tallahassee: Jones & Dyke.* 1845. 8vo. Continued. B. 24844

... The Acts and Resolutions adopted at the 1st Session of the 12th General Assembly of Florida ... November 17, 1862. ... *Tallahassee: Printed by Dyke & Carlisle.* 1862. 8vo, pp. iv.

These are the Confederate Acts.

Articles of Agreement and Association of the Florida Peninsula Land Company. *New York.* [n. d.] N. 24846

The Case and Petition of His Majesty's Loyal Subjects, late of West Florida. [*London.*] M.DCC.LXXXVII. 8vo. 24847

Case of the Inhabitants of East Florida, with Appendix, containing Papers, by which all the Facts stated in the Case are Supported. *St. Augustine.* 1784. 8vo. 24848

Coleccion de Varios Documentos. *See* [Smith (B.)]

Compilation of Militia Laws, and Patrol Laws, now in Force in Florida. *Tallahassee: J. B. Webb.* 1839. 8vo, pp. 80. C.

Compilation of the Public Acts of the Legislative Council of the Territory of Florida, passed prior to 1840. By John P. Duval. *Tallahassee.* 1839. 8vo. 24850

Constitution or Form of Government for the People of Florida. ... *Tallahassee: printed by Charles E. Dyke.* 1851. 8vo, pp. 27, iii. H. 24851

Constitution or Form of Government for the People of Florida, as Revised and Amended, At a Convention of the People begun and holden at the City of Tallahassee on the Third Day of January, A.D. 1861. Together with the Ordinances adopted by said Convention. *Tallahassee: Printed by Dyke and Carlisle.* 1861. 8vo, pp. 68. 24852

The Confederate Constitution.

Constitution of the State of Florida, framed at a Convention of the People, ... Tallahassee ... 20th ... January, 1868. Together with the Ordinances adopted by said Convention. ... *Jacksonville, Fla.: printed by Edw. M. Cheney.* 1868. 8vo, pp. 12.

Coppie d'une lettre venant de la Floride envoyée a Rouen, et depuis au Seigneur d'Everon: Ensemble le plan et portraict du fort que les Francois y ont faict. *Paris: Pour Vincent Normant et Jeanne Bruneau.* 1565. 12mo, 8 l. 24854

Copie d'vne lettre missive envoyée avx govuerneurs de la Rochelle, par les Capitaines des Galleres de France, sur la victoire qu'ils ont obtenue contre les Mores et Sauuages faisant le voyage de l'Isle de Floride, et du Bresil. Ensemble les manières de viures ... des Sauuages ... . *Suivant la coppie imprimée à la Rochelle par Jean Porteau.* 1853. 24855

Reprinted in Cimber [Danjou]'s "Archives curieuses," 1e sér., v. ix. pp. 327–339. 1836.

Crisis del ensayo ... Florida. *See* [Salazar (Joseph de)].

A Description of East and West Florida and the Bahama Islands, etc. 1813. 8vo. Map. N. 24856

From the American edition of Edwards' "West Indies."

A Description of the Windward Passage, and Gulf of Florida, with the Course of the British Trading Ships to and from Jamaica, Account of the Trade Winds, etc. Chart of the Coast of Florida, Bahama, Cuba, etc. Second Edition, with Additions. *London.* 1739. 4to. 24857

Discours de l'histoire de la Floride. *See* [Le Challeux].

The Discovery and Conquest of Terra Florida, by Don Ferdinando de Soto, and Six Hundred Spaniards, his Followers. Written by a Gentleman of Elvas, employed in all the Action, and translated out of Portuguese, by Richard Hakluyt. Reprinted from the Edition of 1601. Edited, with Notes and an Introduction, and a Translation of a Narrative of the Expedition of Luis Hernandez de Biedma, Factor to the Same. By William B. Rye ... . *London: Printed for the Hakluyt Society.* M.DCCC.LI. 8vo, 3 l., pp. lxvii, 1 l., pp. 200, v. Map. BA. 24858

See also A Relation, *infra*, and Kerr's "Voyages," v. 42.

Documents Accompanying the Message of the President, [relative to Florida] Dec. 5, 1821. *Washington.* 1821. 8vo, pp. 70. S. 24859

Documents in Proof of the Climate and Soil of Florida, particularly the Southern Section. *New York: Printed by Peter Van Pelt.* 1832. 8vo, pp. 28. BA. 24860

Documents in Proof of the Climate and Soil of Florida, particularly East Florida. *New York: W. Lunt Bradbury, Printer.* 1835. 8vo, pp. 70. 24861

An Extract, etc. *See* [Stork (J.)]

Florida: its Climate, Soil, and Productions, with a Sketch of its History, Natural Features and Social Condition: a Manual of Reliable Information concerning the Resources of the State and the Inducements to Immigrants. ... *Jacksonville: printed by Edw. M. Cheney.* 1869. 8vo, pp. 151. 24862

Also: The Florida Colonist, or Settler's Guide. Answers to the question "Where in Florida shall we locate?" Second Edition, Enlarged [By J. S. Adams]. *Jacksonville (Fla.)* 1871. 8vo, 1 l., pp. 86. Map. C.

The Florida Pirate, or, an Account of a Cruise in the Schooner Esperanza; with a Sketch of the Life of her Commander. ... *New York: Johnstone & Van Norden.* 1823. 12mo, pp. 24. 2 Plates. BA. 24863

Histoire de la Conqueste de la Floride, par les Espagnols, sous Ferdinand de Soto. Ecrite en Portugais par un Gentil-homme de la ville d'Elvas. [Traduite] par M. D. C. [Citri de la Gùette]. *Paris: Denys Thierry.* 1685. 12mo, 13 l., pp. 300. P. + *Paris: Edme Couterot.* 1699. 12mo, 13 l., pp. 300.

The only difference between these editions consist in the imprint. For the original, *see* Relaçàm, *infra.* The following is an English translation of this French version. It is "erroneous as to numbers, distances, and names of places, and very inferior to that by Hakluyt," published in 1609, as "Virginia richly valued," and in 1611 as "Discovery and Conquest of Terra Florida," our No. 24858.

A Relation of the Invasion and Conquest of Florida by the Spaniards, Under the Command of Fernando de Soto. Written in Portuguese, by a Gentleman of the Town of Elvas. Now Englished. To which is Subjoyned Two Journeys of the present Emperour of China into Tartary in the Years 1682 and 1683. With some Discoveries made by the Spaniards in the Island of California, in the Year 1683. *London: John Lawrence.* 1686. 16mo, Imprimatur Title, Preface, and Table, 8 l., pp. 273. C.

Kennett's "Bibl. Am. Prim.," gives this title, with some variations, dated 1687. *See also* Purchas, III. 807; 1532, 1603.

Historical Sketch of the Third Annual Conquest of Florida. Captain Le Diable. *Port Royal, S. C.* 1864. 12mo, pp. 19.

A satire upon the operations of the Union army in the occupancy of Florida.

Historical Society of Florida: organized in St. Augustine, 1856. Constitution. *New-York: Printed by John A. Gray.* 1856. 16mo, pp. 11. B. 24867

Investigation into the Conduct, Acts and Doings of Harrison Reed, Governor of Florida, by a Committee of the Assembly. [n. p. 1877.] 8vo, pp. 36. H. 24868

Journal of a Traveller to Florida. *Charleston: printed by A. J. Burke.* 1836. 8vo, pp. 20. H. 24869

Journal of the Proceedings of a Convention of Delegates to form a Constitution for the People of Florida, held at St. Joseph, December, 1838. *St. Joseph.* 1839. 8vo, pp. 120, 20. C.

Journal of the Proceedings of the Constitutional Convention, begun Jan. 20th, 1868. *Tallahassee: E. M. Cheney.* 1868. 8vo, pp. 134. C. 24871

Journal of the Proceedings of the House of Representatives of the State of Florida, from its First Session in 1845 to the end of the Fourth Session in 1849. *Tallahassee.* 1845–1848. 5 vols., 8vo. Continued. 24872

Journal of the Proceedings of the Legislative Council of the Territory of Florida for 1832. *Tallahassee.* 1832. 8vo. Continued. C. 24873

A Journal of the Proceedings of the Senate of the General Assembly of the State of Florida. Eighth Session, ... November 24, 1856. *Tallahassee: Printed by Benj. F. Allen.* 1856. 8vo.

Journal of the Proceedings of the Senate of the Territory of Florida, 1840. *Tallahassee.* 1840. 8vo. Continued. 24875

Laws Establishing a Common School System, and to provide a School Fund in the State of Florida: Passed at the Fourth Session of the General Assembly, 1848–9. *Tallahassee.* 1849. 8vo. 24876

Laws of the Territory of Florida, for 1822. *Tallahassee.* 1822. 8vo. Continued. 24877

Laws of the United States relative to the Territory of Florida, passed prior to 1828, now in Force. *Tallahassee.* 1829. 8vo.

Laws of the United States relative to the Territory of Florida, passed by Congress prior to 1838. *Tallahassee: S. S. Sibley.* 1837. 8vo, pp. 80. 24879

Session Laws of the Legislative Council of the Territory of Florida, passed at the 11th Session. *Tallahassee.* 1833. Continued. 24880

Laws of the State of Florida. First Session, 1845. *Tallahassee.* 1845. 8vo. Continued. 24881

Letters on Florida. [n. p. n. d.] 8vo, pp. 19. 24882

A Manual or Digest of the Statute Law of the State of Florida, ... in Force January 6, 1847. Digested and Arranged by Leslie A. Thompson, Esq. *Boston.* 1847. 8vo, pp. 686. C.

Memoir upon the Negociations between Spain and the United States, which led to the Treaty of 1819, with a Statistical Notice of that Country [Florida]. *Washington.* 1821. 8vo. 24884

Message of the Governor of Florida to the General Assembly, November 25, A.D. 1850. *Tallahassee.* 1850. 8vo, pp. 65. Continued. B. 24885

Message from the President ... Relative to the Proceedings of the Commissioner for Running the Boundary Line between the United States and East and West Florida. *Philadelphia.* 1797. 8vo. P. 24886

Message from the President, ... transmitting Sundry Papers relating to Transactions in East and West-Florida, April 19, 1822. [*Washington.* 1822.] pp. 46. 24887

Message from the President ... relating to the Treaty with Spain for the Cession of Florida ... Feb. 2, 1844. [n. p. n. d.] pp. 48. 24888

Notices of East Florida, with an Account of the Seminole Nation of Indians. By a recent Traveller in the Province. *Charleston: For the Author.* 1822. 12mo, pp. 105, (1). B., P.

Contains a Vocabulary of the Seminole Language.

Opinions of the Justices of the Supreme Court of Florida, in Reply to Gov. Reed and Lieut. Gov. Gleason's Letters relative to the Regularity of the Organization of the Called Session of the Legislature in November, 1868, and the Validity of the Impeachment of the Governor. [n. p. 1868.] 8vo, pp. 34. H.

An Original Memoir on the Floridas, with A General Description, from the best Authorities. By a Gentleman of the South. *Baltimore: Edward J. Coale. March* 1821. 8vo, pp. 43.

Private Land Claims — Florida. Message from the President of the United States, transmitting Information in Relation to the Execution of the Act of the 23d May last, Supplementary to the Several Acts provided for, the Settlement and Confirmation of Private Land Claims in Florida. *Washington: Gales & Seaton.* 1828. 8vo, pp. 277, xiv. 24892

Proceedings of a General Court-Martial, held at Pensacola in West Florida, March 16–April 20. 1768. *London: Johnston.* 1770. 8vo. 24893

The trial of Major Farmer. *See* "M. Rev.," XLIV. 77.

Recueil de Pièces sur la Floride, contenant Mémoire par Fontanedo, Relations par de Biedma et de Beteta. Lettre de Luis de Valasco au Roi d'Espagne. Mémoire par Lopez de Mendoz. Histoire du Voyage por Capitaine J. Ribaut. *Paris: A. Bertrand.* 1841. 8vo. 24894

Forms Vol. XX. of Ternaux-Compan's "Recueil de Voyages."

Relaçam verdadei|ra dos trabalhos *que*|ho gouernador|dõ Fernãdo d'|souto e cer|tos fidal|gos|portugueses passarom|no d'scobrimẽto da|prouincia da Fro|lida. Agora|nouamẽte feita por hũ|fidalgo Deluas.|Foy vista por ho señor inquisidor.|[Colophon:] *Foy impressa esta relaçam do|descoubrimento da Frolida|em casa de andree de Bur|gos impressor & cauallei|ro da casa do se-|nhor Cardẽal|iffante.|acabouse aos des dias de Febrei-|ro do anno de mil & quinhentos|& cincoenta & sete annos.|na nobre & sempre leal|cidade de Euora.*|[1557.] 8vo, clxxx leaves. L. 24895

A volume of the greatest rarity. The only known copy in America is in Mr. Lenox's library. Rich priced it, in 1830, at thirty guineas, and says "Frodida," which is an error, repeated by Ternaux, No. 76, and Brunet. It is reprinted in facsimile in Vol. I. of

"Collecção de opusculos reimpressos relativos à historia das navigações. ... *Lisboa.* 1844." 4to, pp. 8, xii, 139. For a French translation, *see* Histoire, 24864, *supra.* The following translation differs from our No. 24865, *supra, i. e.,* A Relation.

Virginia|richly valued,|By the description of the maine land of|Florida, her next neighbour:|Out of the foure yeeres continuall trauell and discouerie,|for above one thousand miles East and West, of|Don Ferdinando de Soto, and sixe hundred|able men in his companie.|Wherein are truly obserued the riches and fertilitie of those parts,|abounding with things necessarie, pleasant, and profitable|for the life of man: with the natures and dispo-|sitions of the Inhabitants.|Written by a Portugall gentleman of Eluas, emploied in|all the action, and translated out of Portugese|by Richard Hakluyt.|*At London*|*Printed by Felix Kyngston for Matthew Lownes,*|*and are to be sold at the signe of the Bishops*|*head in Pauls Churchyard.*|1609.| 4to, pp. (8), 180.

A rare volume, priced, in the "Nuggets," at five guineas. It is reprinted in Force's "Tracts," Vol. IV., No. I., in the supplement to Hakluyt's "Voyages," 4to, and omitting Hakluyt's preface, in French's "Hist. Coll.," Vol. II. The introduction says that Hakluyt's intention in this translation "was to encourage the young colony in Virginia." The title, under which his second edition appeared is,

The|Worthye and Famovs His-|tory of the Travailes, Discouery, & Conquest, of that Great|Continent of Terra Florida, being liuely|Paraleld, with that of our now Inha-|bited Virginia.|As also|The Comodities of the said Country,|with diuers Excellent and rich Mynes, of Golde,|Siluer, and other Mettals, &c. which cannot but|giue vs a great and exceeding hope of our|Virginia, being so neere|of one Continent.|Accomplished and effected, by that worthy|Generall and Captaine, Don Ferdinando|de Soto, and six hundreth Spaniards, his followers.|*London*|*Printed for Mathew Lownes,*| ... 1611.| 4to. 24897

Relation or Journal. *See* [Campbell (G. L.)], Vol. III., No. 10218.

Remarks on the Cession of the Floridas to the United States, and on the Necessity of Acquiring the Island of Cuba. 1819. 8vo. C. 24898

Rules of the Superior Court for the Southern Judicial District of Florida in Admiralty. *New York.* 1840. N. 24899

Titles, and Legal Opinions thereon, of Lands in East Florida, belonging to Richard S. Hackley, Esq. *Brooklyn: Printed by G. I. Birch.* 1822. 8vo, pp. 122. + *Fayetteville, N. C.* 1826. 8vo, pp. 71. 24900

Relates to the Duke of Alazon's grant. *See* "N. Am. Rev.," XXXIII. 232.

A True and Authentic Account of the Indian War in Florida, giving the particulars respecting the Murder of the Widow Robbins, and the Providential Escape of her Daughter Aurelia and her Lover, Mr. Charles Somers, after Suffering innumerable Hardships. The whole Compiled from the most Authentic Sources. ... *New York: Saunders & Van Welt.* 1836. 8vo, pp. 28. Plate. 24901

Verscheyde Scheeps-togten Na Florida, Door Pontius, Ribald, Laudonniere, Gourgues En Andere: Gedaan in het Jaar 1562. en vervolgens. Waar in veele zeldsame ontmoetingen zijn voor-gevallen, van sware Nederlagen, Wreedheeden, Hongers-nood-den, Wraak-oeffeningen, onderlinge Verdeeld-heeden, Muyteryen en wonderbaarlijke Ont-koomingen, van eenige gevlugte Franssen, uyt de handen der Spanjaards. Als mede een nette eñ naauw-keurige Aanteekening, van de geleegenheyd van dit Landschap, de Godsdienst, Zeden, Gewoontens, Levens-manier, Oorlogen, Dieren, Vogelen, Vrugten, Veld-gewassen en andere by sonderheeden. Door de Reysigers selfs opgeteekend, en door haar aan sijn Koninglijke Majesteyt van Vrankrijk, Karel de IX, persoonelijk verslag gedaan, en nu uyt die Taal aldereerst overgeset. Met noodig Register en Konst-Printen verrijkt. *Te Leyden, By Pieter Vander Aa, Boekverkooper,* 1706. Met Privilegie. 8vo, pp. (2), 171, Register, pp. 18. Map and 33 Plates. 24902

The War in Florida. *See* [Potter (W.)]

West Florida. Ordinances adopted by the Convention. *Natchez.* 1810. 8vo. 24903

FLORIDA TELEGRAPH Co. International Ocean Telegraph Company Monopoly. Extortionate Charges for Messages between Cuba and the United States. *Washington.* 1870. 8vo, pp. 21. H. 24904

FLORIDA, *N. Y.* Catalogue and Circular of the S. S. Seward Institute at Florida, Orange County, N. Y., 1846. *Albany: J. Munsell.* 1846. 8vo, pp. 8. Continued. 24905

Florist and Horticultural Journal, and Monthly Magazine of Horticulture, Agriculture, Botany, Agricultural Chemistry, Entomology, &c. Edited by H. C. Hanson. *Philadelphia.* 1852–4. 3 vols., 8vo. 24906

FLOURNOY (J. J.) An Essay on the Origin, Habits, &c., of the African Race: Incidental to the Propriety of having Nothing

to do with Negroes. ... By J. Jacobus Flournoy. *New-York.* 1835. 8vo, pp. 56. BA., H. 24907

FLOURNOY (J. J.) An Essay on the Eminent Services and Illustrious Character of Henry Clay. ... By John James Flournoy. *Athens, Georgia: Whig Office.* MDCCCXL. 8vo, pp. 46.

[FLOURNOY (J. J.)] Expulsion; the Best Earthly Conservative of Peace in our Country. *Athens.* 1837. 8vo, pp. 19. H.

Also: An Earnest Appeal for Peace, ... *Athens, Geo.* 1838. 8vo, pp. 19. H. — A Reply, to a Pamphlet, entitled "Bondage, a Moral Institution, sanctioned by the Scriptures and the Saviour, &c., &c.," so far as it attacks the Principles of Expulsion. With no Defence, however, of Abolitionism. ... *Athens. Ga.* 1838. 8vo, pp. 67. BA., H. — A Speech on our Indian Relations, and International Policies; elicited by the Seminole War ... February 4, 1836 ... . *Athens.* 1836. 8vo, pp. 15. H.

FLOWER (R.) Letters from L ington and the Illinois; containing a Brief Account of the English Settlement in the latter Territory, and a Refutation of the Misrepresentations of Mr. Cobbett. By Richard Flower. *London.* 1819. 8vo, pp. 32.

Speaks well of the country and its inhabitants.

FLOWER. Letters from the Illinois, 1820, 1821; containing an Account of the English Settlement at Albion and its Vicinity, and a Refutation of various Misrepresentations. By Richard Flower. With a Letter from M. Birkbeck, and a Preface and Notes by Benjamin Flower. ... *London: J. Ridgway.* 1822. 8vo, pp. 76. H., S. 24911

The "Quarterly Review," XXVII. 71, has an article on this book, and those of Harris, Welby, and Miss Wright, in which all the passages are selected which, by the ingenuity and misrepresentations of the reviewer, can be made to represent America in the most unfavorable light, followed immediately by another, representing in the brightest colors the advantages of Van Dieman's Land. *See also* "M. Rev.," Aug., 1822, and Ingersoll (C. J.)

FLOWERDEW (D. C.) Exposition of the Three Orders in Council, 11th Nov. 1807, on the Trade regulated by the new System of Blockade. *London.* 1807. 8vo. 24912

FLOYD (J. B.) Abstracted Indian Trust Bonds. Report of the Select Committee in relation to the Fraudulent Abstraction of certain Bonds, held by the Government in trust for the Indian Tribes, and to whom was referred the Communication of Hon. John B. Floyd, late Secretary of War. 8vo, pp. 352. (36th Congress, 2d Sess., House of Reps., Report No. 68.) 24913

FLOYD. The Acceptances of The War Department given in favor of Russell, Majors, and Waddell. Statement of Ex-Secretary Floyd. *Washington: Samuel Towers.* 1861. 8vo, pp. 16.

FLOYD. Floyd's Acceptances. *See* Duncan & Co., No. 21264.

FLOYD (J. G.) Speech of John G. Floyd ... on the Slavery and Compromise Questions. *Washington.* 1852. 8vo, pp. 14.

Also: Speech, ... Independent Treasury Bill. 1840. S.

FLÜGEL (Felix). Die englische Philologie in Nordamerika: ... [Extract] *Leipzig.* 1852. 8vo, pp. 20. H., S. 24916

FLURANCE (R. de). Les Estats, esquels il est discouru du Prince, du Noble et du tiers Estat, conformément à nostre temps. *Lyon.* 1595. 12mo. 24917

In this very curious and rare work the author has attempted to prove that America was known to the ancients by the name of *Tharsis.* He also shows that America was governed by kings.

FLUSHING, *N. Y.* Address to the Whigs of Flushing, October, 1857. [n. d.] 8vo, pp. 4. M. 24918

Annual Report of the Board of Education in District No. 5, New York. *Flushing.* 1849. 8vo. P. 24919

Celebration at Flushing, of the Birth-Day of Linnæus, by the New York Branch of the Linnæan Society of Paris. *May,* 1824. 8vo. 24920

Journal of the Institute at Flushing. [n. p.] *April,* 1833. 8vo. 24921

Studies and Discipline of the Flushing Institute, L. I., 1837. [n. p. n. d.] 12mo, pp. 19. B. 24922

Also: Catalogue. 1849. 8vo.

FLUSSER (C. T.) Address before Annapolis Lodge, June 24, 1826. By Charles T. Flusser. [n. p.] 1826. 8vo, pp. 9.

A Flying Bird from Missouri, to the Members of the Convention at Louisville, Ky. [n. p. n. d.] 8vo, pp. 8. H.

The Flying Roll: or, The Miscellaneous Writings of Redemptio. *Windsor, Vt.* 1805. 12mo. 24925

FLYNT (H.) An Appeal to the Consciences of a Degenerate People, for the Vindication of God's Proceedings with them. A Sermon ... in Boston, ... April 3, 1729. By Henry Flynt, N.A. *Boston: Samuel Gerrish.* 1729. 8vo, pp. (4), 19. B., BA., M.

FLYNT. A Caution to Sinners ... . A Sermon ... to the Scholars in the College Hall, February 8th. 1735, 6 ... . *Boston: S. Kneeland and T. Green.* 1736. 8vo, 2 l., pp. 20. B., H.

FLYNT. The Doctrine of the Last Judgment, Asserted and Explained, In Two Discourses. By Henry Flynt. ... *Boston.* 1714. 4to, pp. (2), ii, 28. B., W. 24928

An address "To the Reader" is signed "Increase Mather," pp. ii.

FLYNT. Oratio Funebris in Obitum Reverendi Domini Benjaminis Wadsworth, ... Collegii Harvardini Præsidis ... . Habita in Aula Academiæ, Ab Henrico Flynt ... . *Bostoni.* MDCCXXXVII. 8vo, Title, pp. 9. B., BA., H., M. 24929

FLYNT. Twenty Sermons on Various Subjects, Preach'd and Publish'd. By Henry Flynt ... . *Boston: Kneeland and T. Green.* MDCCXXXIX. 8vo, pp. (2), iv, 312. B., C., H. 24930

FOBES (P.) A Sermon ... in the Baptist Meeting-House in Providence, July 31, A.D. 1791. Occasioned by the Death of the Rev. James Manning, D.D. President of Rhode Island College. By Perez Fobes, A.M. ... *Providence: J. Carter.* [1791.] 8vo, pp. 40. H. 24931

FOBES. A Sermon, preached ... in May 27th, 1795: the Day of General Election. By Perez Fobes ... . *Boston: Young & Minns.* 1795. 8vo, pp. 42. B., H. 24932

Also: A Sermon ... at Taunton, Nov. 11, 1784, upon the ... Execution of John Dixson, for Burglary, ... With an Appendix ... and a Sketch of Dixson's Life. *Providence: Printed by Bennett Wheeler.* [1784.] 8vo, pp. 34, 14. — A Sermon ... January 7, 1789, at the Ordination of the Rev. Elijah Leonard ... Marshfield. ... *Boston: Printed by Thomas and John Fleet.* M.DCC.LXXXIX. 8vo, pp. 43. B., BA., H. — A Sermon ... to Youth; ... at Wrentham, Mass. August 4, 1793. ... *Hanover.* 1809. 8vo, pp. 23. — A Sermon delivered January 26, 1803, at the Ordination of George Barstow, Colleague Pastor with the Rev. Gad Hitchcock, D.D. over the Second Church and Society in Pembroke. ... *Boston.* 1803. 8vo. BA., H., W.

[FOCARD (Jacques).] Paraphrase | de l'Astro- | labe. | contenant | Les Principes de Géométrie, | La Sphere, | L'Astrolabe, ou, déclaration | des choses celestes, | Le Miroir du Monde, ou, | exposition des parties de | la terre. | *A Lyon, par Jean de Tournes* | M.D.XLVI. | 8vo, pp. (16), 187. 24933

See the passage on page 155; reprinted in Harrisse's "Bibl. Am. Vet.," p. 421.

FOCHER (J.) Itinerarvm Catholicvm Proficientium, ad infideles cõuertendos. Fratere Ioãe Focher minorita autore. Nuper summa cura & diligẽtia auctũ, expurgatum, limatũ ac prælo mãdatũ, per fratrem Didacum Valadesium, ejusdem instituti, ac provintiæ Sancti Euangelij in noua Hyspania, professorem. Ad Reverendissimom Patrem, F. Franciscum Guzmanum, omnium Indiarum maris Occeani Commissarium generalium. *Hispali: Apud Alfonsum Scribanum.* 1574. 8vo, 8 l., Text, 99 l., 9 l.

"This excessively rare book is wholly unknown to the American historian, though it has played no inconsiderable part in the conversion of the Indians of Mexico, especially the nation of the Chichimecas. Fray Focher was a Frenchman, but his book on the conversion of infidels generally was abridged, altered, and adapted by the Mexican missionaries to their use among the Indians." — STEVENS.

FOCHT (D. H.) Our Country: A Sermon ... On Thanksgiving Day ... New Bloomfield, Pa., Nov. 28, 1861. By Rev. D. H. Focht, A.M. *Gettysburg: H. C. Neinstedt, Printer.* 1862. 8vo, pp. 80. 24935

Also: Our National Day. An Address delivered at Ikesburg, Penn., on the 4th Day of July, 1862. *Selinsgrove: Kirchenbote Office.* 1862. 8vo, pp. 28.

FOCKE (H. C.) Neger-Engelsch Woordenboek, door Mr. H. C. Focke. *Leyden: P. H. v. d. Heuvel.* 1855. 8vo, pp. xiii, 160. 24936

Also: Enumeratio diagnostica quarundam Orchidearum Surinamensium. *Paramaribo.* 1848. 8vo. (Extract.) — Togte naar Para in Suriname. 1830. 8vo. (Extract.)

FOCKE (H. C.), *and others.* Bijdragen tot de Bevordering van de Kenniss de Nederlandsch West Indische Koloniën. Onder redactie van de Heeren H. C. Focke, Ch. Landré, C. A. van Sypesteyn, F. A. C. Dumoutier. *Haarlem.* 1855. 8vo.

Fœderal Constitution of the United States, agreed upon in Convention of the States in 1787, with Alterations and Additions made since that period. *London.* 1795. 8vo. 24938

See also "Constitution of the United States," Vol. IV.

The Fœderalist. *See* The Federalist.

FOERSTER (Fr.) Christoph Columbus, der Entdecker der neuen Welt. Ein Volksbuch ... . Bearbeitet nach den besten Originalquellen. *Leipzig: Teubner.* 1842, 43. 16mo. 23 Engravings and 2 Maps. + Zweite Stereotyp-Ausgabe. + [*Ibid.*] 16mo, 20 Engravings, 3 Maps, and 1 Facsimile. 24939

FOGG (T. B.) A Memorial Sermon delivered by Thomas Brinley Fogg in Old Trinity Church, Brooklyn, Conn., on the Hundredth Anniversary of its Opening, April 12th, 1871. [n. p. n. d.] 8vo, pp. 48, Errata. 24940

[FOGG (William).] A Short Genealogical Account of a few Families of the Early Settlers in Eliot, and of a Branch of the Moody Family: from the time they Emigrated to this Country to the year 1850. *Printed at Saco by A. A. Hanscomb.* 1850. 16mo, pp. 22. 24941

FOGLIETTA (Uberto). Clarorum Ligurum Elogia, Opuscula Nonnulla. Ad Joannem Andream auream ducem clarissimum. *Romæ: Apud heredes Antonii Bladii Impressores Camerales.* 1573. 4to, pp. (8), 265, (3). 24942

Contains some particulars relating to Columbus, and his discovery of America. *See* J. C. Brown's catalogue, No. 166. Lord Guildford's copy sold for £8 8s. Reprinted in his "Opera subcisiva, ... *Romæ: F. Zanetti.* 1579." 4to. "Recueil rare, et qui mérite d'etre recherchée." — BRUNET.

FOGUERAS (J.) Satisfacion que se da sobre el derecho, fundado á la devolucion que declaro de las Elecciones del Capitulo que se dexó de celebrar en la Provincia de Santa Elena de la Florida, el dia 23 de Enero del año de 1745, en que estaba legitimamente convocado, y los Vocales ya juntos. Por Juan Fogueras. *Mexico.* 1747. Folio, pp. 14. 24943

Fok: a Greenlander's Travels in Europe, in Greenlandish. *Nongme.* 1857. 8vo. 24944

With rude comic cuts, colored.

FOKKENS (F.), *and* OTTERLOO (A. van). Algemeene, beschrijving, van vreemde havens en zeeplaatsen buiten Europa. ... 2e deel. Amerika, benevens de omliggende eilanden. Bewerkt door F. Fokkens en A. van Otterloo. 1862. 8vo. 24945

FOLEY (D.) Account of the People and Institutions of the United States of America, from Personal Observations, during a Three Months' Summer Tour, in 1857. By Rev. Daniel Foley, D.D. *London.* 1858. 12mo. 24946

FOLEY (F.), *pseudonym.* Romance of the Ocean; A Narrative of the Voyage of the Wildfire to California; ... By Fanny Foley, one of the Passengers, ... *Philadelphia: Lindsay & Blakiston.* 1850. 12mo, pp. 218. 24947

FOLGER (P.) A Looking Glass for the Times, etc., to which is added the Report from the Lords of the Committee of Councils, and the King's Order relating to the People called Quakers in New England. By Peter Folger. 1677. + *Reprinted.* 1763.

Both editions are of extreme rarity. I have never seen the first. Mr. Duyckinck, in compiling his Cyclopædia, had recourse to a manuscript copy. The author resided at Sherburne Town, *i. e.*, Nantucket, and was Dr. Benj. Franklin's maternal grandfather. Franklin says the poems are written with "a manly freedom." *See* "Bibl. Ang. Poetica," p. 30, and Duyckinck, I. 73, where the poem is reprinted.

FOLGER (R. M.) Exchange Tables of British Sterling, showing the Value in the United States Currency, ... By Robert M. Folger. *New York: Edward O. Jenkins.* 1848. 8vo, pp. 59. + *New York: the Author.* 1849. 8vo, pp. 211. C. 24949

Folhinha da Guerra, para el anno de 1867 contendo a chronica nacional noticias curiosas e interessantes e a retaçao dos factos notaveis da guerra do Brasil e seus alliados contra o Paraguay. Primeira parte, Julho a Dezembro de 1865. *Rio de Janeiro.* 12mo, pp. lxiv, 216, 72, 64. Continued. 24950

The almanacs for 1860–70 contain a detailed chronicle of the Paraguayan war.

FOLIETA (Ubertus). *See* Foglietta (Uberto), No. 24942.

FOLKINGHAM (W.) Fendigraphia, the Synopsis or Epitome of Surveying Methodized, Anatomizing the whole Crops of the Faculte ... and no lesse remarkable for all undertakers in the Plantation of Ireland or Virginia ... By W. Folkingham. *London: Richard Moore.* 1610. 4to. 24951

This rare black letter tract sold at Puttick's, in 1860, for 9s.

FOLLANSBEE (J.) Case of Chief Engineer Joshua Follansbee, before a Navy General Court Martial, Convened at the Philadelphia Navy Yard, May, 1863. *Philadelphia.* 1863. 8vo, pp. 22. 24952

FOLLEN (C.) Inaugural Discourse, delivered before the University in Cambridge, Massachusetts, September 3, 1831. By Charles Follen. *Cambridge: Hilliard and Brown.* 1831. 8vo, pp. 28. H. 24953

Also: An Address Introductory to the Fourth Course of the Franklin Lectures. Nov. 3, 1834. ... *Boston.* 1835. 8vo, pp. 30. BA., H. — Funeral Oration: delivered ... Boston, ... Nov. 17, [1832], at the Burial of Gaspar Spurzheim, M.D. ... *Boston: Marsh, Capen & Lyon.* 1832. 8vo, pp. 32. B., BA., H. — Religion and the Church, ... Number 1. *Boston: James Munroe and Co.* 1836. 12mo, pp. 42. H. — Suggestions on Landscape Gardening; ... . *Boston: Phillips, Sampson, and Co.* 1859. 8vo, pp. 20. H.

FOLLEN (E. L.) The Liberty Cap. By Eliza Lee Follen. *Boston: Leonard C. Bowles.* 1846. 8vo, pp. 36. H. 24954

FOLLEN. Life of Charles Follen. By Mrs. Eliza Follen. *Boston.* 1844. 12mo. W. 24955

Also: Poems. ... *Boston: William Crosby & Company.* 1839. 12mo, pp. 192. — ... To Mothers in the Free States. *New York: American Anti-Slavery Society.* [n. d.] 12mo, pp. 4.

Del Follètin. *See* Mexico.

FOLLETT (F.) History of the Press of Western New-York ... by Frederick Follett ... with the Proceedings of the Printers' Festival, held ... in ... Rochester ... Jan. 18, 1847. *Rochester: printed by Jerome & Brother.* 1847. 8vo, 1 l., pp. 76. H., S.

The following Address, and particular instances as to the Duties demanded on Prize Goods brought into Jamaica, were sent from that Island by the Governor, Council and Assembly, in March 17 9/10: Whereupon an Act pass'd in the Ninth Year of Her Majesty's Reign, That Prize Goods should not be liable to the Demand of Duties by Vertue of an Act, Entituled, An Act to Encourage to Trade to America for the future: And all Proceedings upon the Bonds enter'd into were ordered to be staid until a clear State of those Bonds could be had from Jamaica, and laid before this present Parliament. Since then an Account of the said Bonds has been transmitted by the Governor, Council and Assembly of Jamaica to the Lords Commissioners of Trade and Plantations, as well as by the Collector of Her Majesty's Duties in the said Island, to the Commissioners of Her Majesty's Customs in Great Britain; which Account is hereunto annexed. Folio, pp. 4, Account, a folded sheet.

A reply to this is entitled, "An Answer to some False and Malicious Objections given out, to prevent the Duties on Prize Goods being remitted, with some Observations."

The Following Publication, which shows the Rancourous Disposition of the American Republicans against His Majesty's Loyal Subjects, is Republished at the particular request of a number of Loyalists, William Smith, Charles Inglis, and Others. *New York.* 1783. 8vo, 4 leaves. 24958

Following the Flag. *See* [Coffin (C. C.)], Vol. IV., No. 14165.

FOLSOM (A. H.) A Letter from a Member of the Boston Bar to an Avaricious Landlord; with an Expression of Sentiments. By Mrs. Abby H. Folsom. *Boston: printed by Abner Forbes.* 1851. 8vo, pp. 16. H. 24959

FOLSOM (B.) A Compilation of Biographical Sketches of Distinguished Officers in the American Navy. By Benjamin Folsom. *Newburyport: Horatio G. Allen.* 1814. 8vo, pp. 127.

[FOLSOM (Charles).] Remarks on a Latin Inscription found at Castine, in the State of Maine. From the "Proceedings of the American Antiquarian Society" for April, 1864. [n. p. 1864.] 8vo, pp. 8. B., H. 24961

FOLSOM (C. L.) An Oration, pronounced before the Handel Society of Dartmouth College, at the Anniversary Exhibition, August, 1820. By Charles L. Folsom. ... *Hanover: Printed by Bannister and Thurston.* 1821. 8vo, pp. 16. H. 24962

FOLSOM (G.) An Address delivered at Brunswick before the Maine Historical Society, at the Anniversary, Sept. 6, 1846. By George Folsom. *Portland.* 1847. 8vo, pp. 79. C. 24963

FOLSOM. The Annual Discourse Delivered before the New York Historical Society, on the 20th of December, 1859, By George Folsom, LL.D. *Ventnor: Printed by Fletcher Moor.* 1866. 8vo, pp. 48. 24963*a*

[FOLSOM.] A Catalogue of Original Documents in the English Archives, relating to the Early History of the State of Maine. ... *New York: Privately Printed.* 1858. Rl., 8vo, pp. iv, 127.

FOLSOM. A Discourse ... before the Maine Historical Society, ... September 6th, 1846. By George Folsom. ... *Portland: the Society.* 1847. 8vo, pp. 80. B., BA., C. 24965

FOLSOM. History of Saco and Biddeford, with Notices of other Early Settlements, and of the other Early Settlements, and of the Proprietary Governments in Maine, including the Provinces of New Somersetshire and Lygdonia. By George Folsom. *Saco: Printed by Alex. C. Putnam.* 1830. 12mo, pp. 331. Plate and Map. B., C., H. 24966

FOLSOM. Memoirs of T. L. Winthrop. [n. p. n. d.] 8vo, pp. 25. B. 24967

Also: Address delivered at the Nineteenth Annual Fair of the American Institute ... *New York.* 1846. 8vo. *See also* Cortes, Vol. IV., No. 16964.

[FOLSOM (George F.)] Mexico in 1842: Description of the Country, its Natural and Political Features; with a Sketch of its History, brought down to the Present Year. To which is added, an Account of Texas and Yucatan; and of the Santa Fé Expedition. ... *New York: Charles J. Folsom.* 1842. 18mo, pp. 256.

FOLSOM (J. M.) Heroes and Martyrs of Georgia. Georgia's Record in the Revolution of 1861. Volume First. By James M. Folsom, ... *Macon, Ga.: Burke, Boykin & Company.* 1864. 8vo, pp. 164. No more published. BA. 24969

FOLSOM (P.) An Eulogy on George Washington, late Commander-in-Chief of the Armies of the United States of America, who died Dec. 14, A.D. 1799; delivered in the Academy, February, 22, A.D. 1800, before the Inhabitants of Gilmanton, agreeably to their previous request. By Peter Folsom, 4th Preceptor of said Academy. *Gilmanton: Printed by E. Russell. March,* 1800. 12mo, pp. 12. H. 24970

FOLSOM (N. S.) Discourse before the R. I. State Temperance Society, ... Providence, January 11, 1839. By the Rev. Nathaniel Smith Folsom. *Providence: Knowles, Vose & Co.* 1839. 12mo, pp. 35. H. 24971

FOLSOM. Folsom's New Pocket Almanac for the Year 1789. *Boston.* 16mo. 24972

FOLTZ (J. M.) The Endemic Influence of Evil Government; illustrated ... with Medical Statistics of a Voyage of Circumnavigation of the Globe, and an account of other Service, both Ashore and Afloat. By J. M. Foltz, A.M., M.D., Surgeon, U. S. Navy. *New York.* 1843. 8vo, pp. 65. S. 24973

From the "New York Journal of Medicine."

FOMBONO (Evaristo). España y Venezuela. *Carácas.* 1863. 8vo, pp. 32. 24974

FONBLANQUE (A.) England under Seven Administrations. By Albany Fonblanque. *London.* 1837. 3 vols., post 8vo. C.

Contains many incidental references to American topics.

[FONBLANQUE (*Mr.*)] *See* An Enquiry, No. 22551.

FONDA (S. F.) Analysis of Sharon Waters, Schoharie County; also of Avon, Richfield, and Bedford Mineral Waters. With Directions for Invalids. By Sebastian F. Fonda, M.D., Resident Physician. *New York: John J. Schroeder.* 1854. 12mo, pp. 96. S. + *New York: R. Craighead, Printer.* 1860. 12mo, pp. 96. 24976

FONDEY (W. H.) An Oration before the Young Men's Association ... Albany, delivered July 4, 1838. By William H. Fondey. *Albany: J. Munsell.* [1838.] 8vo, pp. 40. S.

FONSECA (F. de), *and* URRUTIA (C. de). Historia general de real hacienda, obra hasta ahora inedita, escrita por Orden del Virey Conde de Revillagigedo. Por Fabian de Fonseca y Carlos de Urrutia. *Mexico: V. G. Torres.* 1845–53. 6 vols., 4to.

A rare work, containing statistical information on the condition of Mexico under the Spanish Government. It was not intended for publication, but the manuscript having been found in the Archives of Mexico after the Declaration of Independence, it was printed by permission of the supreme Government.

FONSECA (Joaquim Bento da). Memoria hydrographica, contendo reflexões sobre as viagens dos mais celebres navegadores, que têem feito o giro do globo, e a necessidade de uma nova viagem do mesmo genero, etc. *Lisboa: Typ. Lacerdina.* 1824. 4to, pp. viii–76. 24979

FONSECA. Memoria sobre as ilhas de S. Thomé e Principe, etc. *Lisboa: na Imp. Regia.* 1828. 24980

One hundred copies printed.

FONSECA (M. da). Vida do veneravel Padre Belchior de Pontes, da companhia de Jesus Da Provincia do Brasil. Composta pelo Padre Manvel da Fonseca da mesma companhia ... . *Lisboa: Francisco da Silva.* MDCCCLII. 4to, 12 l., pp. 266. H.

FONSECA (Y. G. da). Navegacão feita da Cida de do Gram Pará até a Bocca do Rio da Madeira pelo escolto que por este Rio subio às Minas do Mate Grassa escripta por Yose Gonsalvez da Fonseca. 1749. *Lisboa.* 1826. 4to. 24982

FONSECA. A Voyage to the New Island Fonseca, near Barbadoes. With some Observations made in a Cruize among the Leward Islands. In Letters from Two Captains of Turkish Men of War, driven thither in the Year 1707. Translated out of Turkish and French. *London: Printed in the Year* 1708. pp. (4), 44. 24983

See also [S. (J.)], *infra.*

FONTAINE (E.) Address of E. Fontaine, to the Voters of the District composed of the Counties of Fluvanna, Goochland, Louisa and Hanover. *Richmond: Bailie & Gallagher, Printers.* [1830.] pp. 7. 24984

Also: Address of ... Edward Fontaine ... Austin ... 22d January, 1852, at the Installation of the Officers of the Grand Lodge of Texas. *Austin: Chishney & Hampton, Printers.* 1852. 8vo, pp. 15.

FONTAINE (F. G. de). American Abolitionism, from 1787 to 1861. A Compendium of Historical Facts, embracing Legislation in Congress and Agitation without. (Originally Published in the New York Herald.) By F. G. De Fontaine. *New York: D. Appleton & Co.* 1861. 8vo, pp. 66. 24985

Also issued with the title: "History of American Abolitionism; Its Four Great Epochs, ... Together with a History of the Southern Confederacy."

FONTAINE (J.) A Tale of the Huguenots; or, the Memoirs of a French Refugee Family. Translated and Compiled from the Original Manuscripts of James Fontaine. By Ann Maury, one of his Descendants. With an Introduction by F. L. Hawks, D.D. *New York: J. S. Taylor.* 1838. 12mo, pp. 266. 24986

Another edition has the following title:

FONTAINE. Memoirs of a Huguenot Family: Translated and Compiled from the Original Autobiography of Rev. James

Fontaine and other Family MSS. Comprising an Original Journal of Travels in Virginia, New York, &c. in 1715. By Ann Maury. With an Appendix, ... *New York: Gorge P. Putnam & Co.* 1853. pp. 512. Portrait. 24987

FONTANA (F.) Traité sur le Vénin de la Vipere sur les poisons Américains sur le laurier-cerise et sur quelques antres poisons végetaux. On y a joint des observations sur la structure primitive du corps animal. Différentes expériences sur la reproduction des nerfs et la description d'un nouveau canal de l'œil. Par Mr. Felix Fontana ... . *Florence.* M.DCC.LXXXI. 2 vols., 4to, xxviii, 329; xi, 373. 10 Plates. B. 24988

FONTANA. Treatise on the Venom of the Viper; on the American Poisons ... To which are Annexed, Observations on the Primitive Structure of the Animal Body ... and a Description of a New Canal of the Eye. With Ten Descriptive Plates. ... From the ... French of Felix Fontana ... by Joseph Skinner ... *London: J. Murray.* M,DCC,LXXXVII. 2 vols., 8vo, pp. (2), xix, 409, xiv; (6), 395, xi, xxii. 10 Plates. + *London: John Cutbell.* M.DCC.XCV. 2 vols., 8vo, pp. (2), xix, 409, xiv; (6), 395, xiv, xxii. 10 Plates. BA. 24989

See "M. Rev.," LXXX. 267.

FONTANA. Trattato del veleno della vipera de' veleni americani, di quello del lauro-regio e di altri veleni vegetabili. Vi si aggiungono alcune osservazioni sopra la struttura primitiva del corpo animale, varie sperienze su la riproduzione de' nervi; e la descrizione d'un nuovo canale dell' occhio. *Napoli: Nuova società litteraria e tipografica.* 1787. 12mo, pp. 179; 248. C.

FONTANE (M.) La Guerre d'Amérique récit d'un soldat du sud. Par Marius Fontane. *Paris: Adrien le Clerc et Cr.* 2 vols., 12mo, pp. (3), 304; (2), 265. Map. B., BA. 24991

FONTANEDA. *See* Escalante Fontaneda (H.)

FONTANÈS (L.) Éloge funèbre de Washington: prononcé dans le Temple de Mars. Par Louis Fontanès, le 20 pluviôse an VII. *Paris. An* VIII. [1800.] 8vo, pp. 29. BA., H. 24992

For an English translation, *see* "Columbian Phenix." There is also a Dutch translation, "Lijkede af George Washington." [*Amsterdam.* 1800.] 8vo. Portrait.

FONTANÈS (L.), *and* DUBROCA (Louis). Éloges funèbres de Washington. [Avec une préface par Isaiah Townsend, jr. d'Albany, N. Y.] *Paris: Casimir.* 1835. 12mo, pp. 72. B.

FONTANI (A. D.) Guadalupana B. M. V. Imago, quæ Mexici colitur, carmine descripta. *Faventiæ,* 1773, *ex typographia Episcopali.* 8vo, pp. 51. Plate. 24994

FONTE (Pedro José). Representacion del Ilmo. Sr. Arzobispo de Mejico concermente a algunos sucesos anteriores a la independencia proclamada en aquella capital. *Habana: Impreso por Campe en la oficina liberal.* 1822. 8vo, pp. 43. BA. 24995

[FONTENAY (*l'Abbé*).] *See* La Porte.

FONTENAY (Marie). L'Autre Monde. *Paris.* 1855. 12mo, 3 l., pp. 259, 1 l. 24996

A curious attack on America.

FONTICELLO (Antonio). Americologia ossia osservazioni storiche e fisiologiche sopra gli Americani. Con un Breve Ragguaglio delle ultime Scoperte fatte dai Russi nel Mar Pacifico. *Genova: Adamo Scionico.* 1790. 12mo, pp. 123. 24997

FOOS (C.). State of the Accounts of Conrad Foos, Collector of Excise, Berks County, from ... 1781, to ... 1783 ... *Philadelphia: Printed by Robert Aitken.* M.DCCL.XXXIV. 8vo, pp. 6.

FOOS (J.) The Highway of all Nations. By Joseph Foos. *Columbus: Printed by P. H. Olmsted.* 1820. 8vo, pp. 24. BA.

FOOT (E.), *and* SPENCER (A.) Correspondence between Ebenezer Foot and Ambrose Spencer. Published originally in the Albany Centinel and Register. 12mo, pp. 48. 25000

FOOT (G.) An Address, embracing the Early History of Delaware: the Settlement of its Boundaries, and of the Drawyer's Congregation. By Rev. Geo. Foot. *Philadelphia.* 1842. 8vo, pp. 68. P. 25001

FOOT (J.) A Defence of the Planters in the West-Indies; comprised in Four Arguments, I. On Comparative Humanity; II. On Comparative Slavery; III. On the African Slave Trade, and IV. On the Condition of Negroes in the West-Indies. By Jesse Foot, Surgeon. ... *London: J. Debrett.* 1792. 8vo, pp. iv, 101. BA. 25002

See "M. Rev.," VIII. 217.

FOOT (John). Discourse, Jan. 8, 1769, occasioned by the Death of Joseph Hall, jr. who died Dec. 31, 1768. *New Haven.* [n. d.] 8vo. W. 25003

FOOT (J.) Memorial of John Foot, late Captain of Second Regiment of Minnesota Volunteers. *New York.* 1862. Port.

FOOT (J. I.) An Address, prepared by Rev. Joseph I. Foot, D.D., for his Inauguration as President of Washington College, East Tennessee. *Knoxville: Jac. C. Moses and Company.* 1840. 8vo, pp. 12. H. 25005

FOOT. An Historical Discourse ... at Brookfield, Mass. Nov. 27, 1828, the Day of the Annual Thanksgiving. By Joseph I. Foot ... . *Brookfield: Printed by E. and G. Merriam.* MDCCCXXIX. 8vo, pp. 64. BA. 25006

FOOT. An Historical Discourse delivered at West Brookfield, Massachusetts, November 27, 1828; on the Day of the Annual Thanksgiving. By Joseph I. Foot. With Captain Thomas Wheeler's Narrative now annexed, and Additional Notices of Occurrences in the Town since the first publication of the Discourse. *West Brookfield: Merriam & Wood.* 1843. 12mo, pp. 96. C. 25007

FOOT (J. J.) Sermons of Rev. Joseph J. Foot, D.D. With a Biographical Sketch by Rev. George F. Foot. *Philadelphia.* 1841. 8vo, pp. 600. 25008

FOOT (S. A.) An Examination of the Case of Dred Scott in the Supreme Court against Sandford, ... and a Full and Fair Exposition of the Decision of the Court, and of the Opinions of the Majority of the Judges. ... By the Hon. Samuel A. Foot, late Judge of the Court of Appeals. ... *New York: W. C. Bryant & Co.* 1859. 8vo, pp. 19. H. 25009

Also: An Address ... Geneva College, August 1, 1832. ... *Geneva: Printed by J. C. Merrell.* 1832. 8vo, pp. 23. B., BA. — An Argument, in Favor of the Constitutionality of the General Banking Law of this State, delivered before the Supreme Court, at the July Term, 1839 ... . *Geneva: Ira Merrell, Printer.* 1839. 8vo, pp. 101 (1). BA. — A Lecture on True Mercantile Character, and its influence on our Political Institutions ... . *New York: Jonathan Leavitt.* MDCCCXXXIII. 12mo, pp. 53. B. — Reasons for Joining the Republican Party. Reasons ... for accepting a Republican Nomination. [n. p. n. d.] 8vo, pp. 7. — Speech ... at the Mass Meeting at Millstone, New Jersey, August 7th, 1844. ... *Somerville: S. L. Bladwin, Printer.* 1844. 8vo, pp. 16. BA., H.

FOOT (S.) Speech of Mr. Solomon Foot, of Vermont, on the Origin and Causes of the Mexican War. Delivered ... July 16, 1846. *Washington: Printed by J. & G. S. Gideon.* 1846. 8vo, pp. 16. H. 25010

Also: Speech ... on the Oregon Question ... Feb. 6, 1840. [*Washington.* 1846.] 8vo, pp. 16. — Speech ... Character and Objects of the Mexican War. ... Feb. 10, 1847. [*Washington.* 1847.] 8vo, pp. 16. H.

FOOT. Proceedings on the Death of Hon. Solomon Foot, including the Addresses delivered in the Senate and House of Representatives ... April 12, 1866. *Washington: Government Printing Office.* 1866. 8vo, pp. 120. B., BA. 25011

FOOT. Funeral Sermon. Obituary Notices and Testimonials of Respect. By the Citizens of Rutland on the occason of the Death of Hon. Solomon Foot, LL.D. Late United States Senator For the State of Vermont. *Rutland: Tuttle, Gay & Company.* 1866. 8vo, pp. 26. 25012

FOOTE (A. H.) Africa and the American Flag. By Commander Andrew H. Foote, U. S. N., Lieut. Commanding U. S. Brig Perry on the Coast of Africa, A.D. 1850–51. *New York: D. Appleton & Co.* MDCCCLIV. 12mo, pp. 390. Plates. B., BA.

FOOTE. The African Squadron: Ashburton Treaty: Consular Sea Letters, Reviewed, in an Address by Commander A. H. Foote, U. S. N. *Philadelphia: William F. Geddes, Printer.* 1855. 8vo, pp. 16. BA., H. 25014

FOOTE (C. C.) American Women Responsible for the Existence of American Slavery: A Conversation between An Anti-Slavery Lecturer and A Lady. By C. C. Foote. *Rochester: E. Shepard.* 1846. 8vo, pp. 24. + Third Edition. *Rochester.* 1846. 25015

FOOTE (H.) Table of Monthly and Annual Pay, Tax, and Organization of the Army of the United States. Compiled and Arranged by Major Henry Foote, Additional Paymaster, U. S. A. *Cincinnati: Moore, Wilstach, Keys & Co.* 186–. Folio. 25016

FOOTE (H. G.) An Oration, ... July 4, 1856, By Henry G. Foote, at Ogdensburgh, N. Y. *Ogdensburgh.* 1858. 8vo.

FOOTE (H. Stuart). Report of the Special Committee, on the Recent Military Disaster at Forts Henry and Donelson, and the Evacuation of Nashville. Hon. H. S. Foote, Chairman; H. C. McLaughlin, Clerk. *Richmond: Enquirer Press.* 1862. 8vo, pp. 193, (1). 25018

FOOTE. Texas and the Texans: or, Advance of the Anglo-Americans to the South-West; Including a History of Leading Events in Mexico, from the Conquest by Fernando Cortez, to the Termination of the Texan Revolution ... By Henry Stuart Foote. ... *Philadelphia: Thomas Cowperthwaite & Co.* 1841. 2 vols., 12mo, pp. viii, 13–314; 403. Portrait. B. 25019

FOOTE. War of the Rebellion; or, Scylla and Charybdis. Consisting of Observations upon the Causes, Course, and Consequences of the Late Civil War in the United States. By H. S. Foote. ... *New York: Harper & Brothers.* 1866. 12mo, pp. (2), 440. Portrait. B., BA. 25020

Also: An Address, ... Franklin Institute and Union Literary Societies of Centenary College, Louisiana ... July 27, 1852. ... *Jackson.* 1852. 16mo, pp. 16. H. — Eulogy upon the Life and Character of James K. Polk, Late President ... at Washington City, July 9, 1849. ... *Washington.* 1849. 8vo, pp. 16. H. — Lectures on Popular Subjects, delivered in the Musical Fund Hall, to aid in Rebuilding the Southwark Church. I. ... [Second Title-Page:] A Lecture on the Value of the American Union. ... . December 30, 1850. *Philadelphia: J. K. Collins, Jr.* 1851. 8vo, pp. 18. BA. — Speech ... in the Senate ... February 16, 1848, on the Resolution of Thanks to General Taylor. [*Washington.* 1848.] 8vo, pp. 7. H. — Speech of Mr. Foote ... on the Admission of California ... in the Senate, Aug. 1, 1850. *Washington.* [n. d.] 8vo, pp. 16. H. — Speech ... in the Senate ... December 18, 19, 1851, on the Resolution Reaffirming the Compromise Measures. [n. p. n. d.] 8vo, pp. 24. S.

FOOTE (H. W.) ... A Sermon preached at King's Chapel, Boston ... May 29th, 1870, with a List of the Sons of the Church who entered the Service of the Country. By Henry W. Foote. ... *Boston: Barker, Colter & Co.* 1870. 8vo, pp. 28.

Also: ... A Discourse ... in ... Boston, ... after the Death of George Peabody, November 7th, 1869. ... *Boston: Barker, Colter & Co., Printers.* 1867. 8vo, pp. 19. B., H. — ... A Sermon ... in ... Boston, February 2, 1862, ... Funeral of the Hon. Samuel A. Eliot. ... *Cambridge.* 1862. 8vo, pp. 16. H.

FOOTE (J. J.) Chenango Canal Extension: Speech of John J. Foote ... in [N. Y.] Senate, March 11, 1859. 8vo, pp. 6.

FOOTE (John P.) Memoirs of the Life of Samuel E. Foote, by his Brother. *Cincinnati: R. Clarke & Co.* 1860. 12mo, pp. 307. C. 25023

FOOTE. The Schools of Cincinnati, and its Vicinity. By John P. Foote. ... *Cincinnati: C. F. Bradley & Co.'s Power Press.* 1855. 8vo, pp. vi, (4), 232. B., BA., C. 25024

FOOTE (*Mrs.*) Recollections of Central America and the West Coast of Africa. By Mrs. Foote. [*London:*] *T. Cautley Newby.* 1869. Sq. 12mo, pp. (6), 221. 25025

FOOTE (T. M.) National Characteristics: An Address delivered before the Literary Societies of Hamilton College, July 24, 1848. By Thomas M. Foote. *Buffalo: Jewett, Thomas & Co.* 1848. 8vo, pp. 38. B., BA., H. 25026

FOOTE (W. H.) The Huguenots; or, Reformed French Church. [etc.] In Three Parts: I. ... Part III. The Huguenots at Home in America. With an Appendix. By William Henry Foote, D.D. *Richmond: Presbyterian Committee of Publication.* [1870.] 8vo, 1 l., pp. xx, 627. 25027

FOOTE. Sketches of North Carolina, Historical and Biographical, Illustrative of the Principles of a Portion of her Early Settlers. By Rev. William Henry Foote. *New York: Robert Carter.* 1846. 8vo, pp. 557. BA., S. 25028

FOOTE. Sketches of Virginia, Historical and Biographical. By the Rev. William Henry Foote, D.D. ... *Philadelphia: William S. Martien.* 1850. 8vo, pp. v, (1), 568. + Second Series. *Philadelphia: J. B. Lippincott & Co.* 1855. 8vo, pp. 596. Portrait. B., BA. 25029

The first series is scarce.

Footprints of Travellers. Africa and America. *London: J. Cassell.* 1853. 12mo, pp. 144. 25030

For the Benefit of the Widows and Orphans of the Army. *** Folio, p. 1. P. 25031

Notices of theatrical performances by the British officers at Philadelphia, on 19th Jan. 1778. Printed by J. Humphreys.

For the Colony in Virginea Britannia. *See* Virginia.

For the Contemplation of Honorable and Just Legislators. In Addition to the Laws and Facts, stated in the Memorial now before the Legislature, to support the Demand for Payment of the Bills of Credit ... . [n. p. 1812.] 8vo, pp. 7. H. 25032

For Whom will you Vote? For Whom ought you to Vote? [n. p. n. d.] 8vo. 25033

Relates to Lincoln and McClellan.

FORBES (Abner), *and* GREENE (J. W.) The Rich Men of Massachusetts; containing a Statement of the Reputed Wealth of about Fifteen Hundred Persons, with Brief Sketches. ... By A. Forbes and J. W. Green. *Boston: W. F. Spencer.* 1851. 8vo, pp. 208. B., H., S. + Second Edition. *Boston.* 1852.

FORBES (A.) California: A History of Upper and Lower California from their First Discovery to the Present Time, comprising an Account of the Climate, Soil, Natural Productions, ... A Full View of the Missionary Establishments and Condition of

the Free and Domesticated Indians. With an Appendix ... . By Alexander Forbes, Esq. *London: Smith, Elder & Co.* 1839. 8vo, pp. xvi, 352. Portrait, Map, and 10 Plates. B., BA. 25035

The author was one of the first of the Anglo-Saxon race to explore this, till lately, unknown country; he reaped the reward of his enterprise by securing the possession of the great quicksilver mines, now worked by the firm of which he is the head. Mr. Forbes says that "if the country round St. Francisco bay were only peopled, that port would engross the commerce of the coast." He also refers to the total absence of gold and silver in the region! *Tempora mutantur.*

FORBES (C.) Vancouver Island; its Resources and Capabilities as a Colony. By Charles Forbes, M.D. [*Victoria:*] *Colonial Government.* 1862. 8vo, 2 l., pp. 63, 18, 1 l. 25036

FORBES (D.) A Manual of the Pension Laws of the United States of America, with the Forms and Instructions now in use and under the authority of the Pension Office; with a Digest of Decisions, etc. By Darius Forbes, late Chief Examiner in the Pension Office. *Washington: W. H. & O. H. Morrison.* 1865. 8vo, pp. x, 258. 25037

FORBES (Edward). *See* Richardson (John).

FORBES (E.) The Christian Ambassador. A Sermon, preached in the Tabernacle at Salem, ... 26th of February, 1784. By Eli Forbes. The Annexed Result of an Ecclesiastical Council. ... By Eli Forbes, A.M. ... . *Salem: Printed by Samuel Hall.* 1784. 8vo, pp. 27. BA. 25038

FORBES. The Dignity and Importance of the Military Character Illustrated. A Sermon Preached to the Ancient and Honorable Artillery Company, in Boston, New-England, June 3d. 1771. ... By Eli Forbes, A.M. ... . *Boston, New-England: Printed by Richard Draper.* M,DCC,LXXI. 8vo, pp. (2), ii, ii, 23.

FORBES. An Eulogy moralized on the Illustrious Character of the late General George Washington, Who died on Saturday, the 14th day of December, 1799. Delivered at Gloucester, on the 22d of February, 1800, in compliance with the Recommendation of Congress, the Legislature of the Commonwealth, and the Unanimous Vote of the town aforesaid. By Eli Forbes, A.M. Pastor of the First Church in said Town. Now made Public at the desire of the Hearers. To which is added, General Washington's Affectionate Address to the United States, declining their future suffrages for the Presidency. *Printed at Newburyport, by Edmund M. Blunt.* 1800. 8vo, pp. 40. BA. 25040

FORBES. God the Strength and Salvation of his People ... a Sermon Preached October 9, 1760. Being a day of Publick Thanksgiving. Appointed by Authority, For the Success of the British Arms in North-America, especially In the total Reduction of Canada to the Crown of Great-Britain. By Eli Forbes, M.A. ... *Boston: Edes & Gill.* 1761. 8vo, pp. 35. BA., H.

FORBES. The Name of God Recorded in his House. A Sermon, preached at the Desire of the Committee, appointed for Repairing of the Meeting-House, in ... Gloucester, from ... the Wanton Spoliations of Captain Lynzey in the Falcon Sloop of War ... on the 13th of September, 1792, by Eli Forbes, A.M. ... *Salem: Thomas C. Cushing.* 1795. 8vo, pp. 19. B. 25042

Also: A Family Book; containing Discourses on Various Subjects. *Salem.* 1801. 12mo. — ... A Sermon ... occasioned by the Dedication Of a Grammar School House ... in ... Gloucester, on the 5th of March, 1795, ... *Newburyport: printed by Blunt and March.* 1795. 8vo, pp. 15. B., BA., H. — The Inoffensive Ministry described, in a Sermon ... before the Convention of the Clergy of Massachusetts, In Boston, May 30, 1799. ... *Charlestown: printed by Samuel Etheridge.* 1799. 8vo, pp. 22. B., BA., H. — The Righteous ... Sermon ... at the Funeral of John Low, Esquire, on the 6th Day of November, 1796. ... *Newburyport: printed by Edmund M. Blunt.* 1797. 8vo, pp. 21. B., H. — Sermon at New Braintree, [Mass.] June 13, 1769, at the Funeral of Timothy Ware. ... *Worcester.* 1784. 8vo. W. — ... A Sermon, ... Tenth of May, MDCCXC, at the Funeral of the Rev. Benjamin Tappan, A.M. ... Manchester; ... . *Salem: Thomas C. Cushing.* 8vo, pp. 14. BA.

FORBES (E.) Diary of a Soldier, and Prisoner of War in the Rebel Prisons. By E. Forbes. *Trenton.* 1865. 8vo, pp. 68.

FORBES (M.) Manual for the Patriotic Volunteers on Active Service in Regular or Irregular War; being the Art and Science of obtaining and maintaining Liberty and Independence. Second Edition. *New-York.* 1855. 2 vols., 18mo. S. 25044

FORBES (J. G.) Report of the Trial of Brig.-General William Hull; commanding the North-Western Army of the United States. By a Court Martial held at Albany on Monday, January 3d, 1814, and succeeding days. Taken by Lieut. Col. Forbes, of the Forty-Second Regt. U. S. Infantry, and a Supernumerary Member of the Court. *New York: Eastburn.* 1814. 8vo, pp. (4), 156, 119, 29. BA., C., S. 25045

FORBES (J. G.) Sketches, Historical and Topographical, of the Floridas; more Particularly of East Florida. By James Grant Forbes. *New York: C. S. Van Winkle.* 1821. 8vo, pp. 226, 1 l. C. 25046

"A wretched compilation from old works." — *N. Am. Rev.*, XXVI. 482. "Contains much valuable information." — *N. Am. Rev.*, XIII. 98.

[Forbes (—.)] A Trip to Mexico; or, Recollections of A Ten-Months' Ramble in 1849–50. By A Barrister. *London: Smith, Elder and Co.* 1851. Post 8vo, pp. xii, 256. 25047

Forbes (Robert). *See* Vol. ii., No. 7288.

Forbes (R. B.) On the Establishment of a Line of Mail Steamers from the Western Coast of the United States on the Pacific to China. By Robert B. Forbes. *Boston.* 1855. 8vo, pp. 16. B., H. 25048

[Forbes.] The Prize Steamer "Cherokee," formerly the "Thistle." *Boston: printed by John Wilson and Son.* 1864. 8vo, pp. 33. H. 25049

[Forbes.] To Merchants, Underwriters, and others interested in the Welfare of our Maritime Interests. [n. p. 1852.] 8vo, pp. 8. H. 25050

[Forbes.] The Voyage of the Jamestown on her Errand of Mercy [to Ireland]. *Boston: Eastburn's Press.* 1847. 8vo, pp. ix, 7–27, cliv. B., BA. 25051

Also: An Appeal to Merchants and Ship Owners, on the Subject af Seamen: A Lecture ... March 7, 1854, ... *Boston: printed by Sleeper & Rogers.* 1854. 8vo, pp. 27. B. — The Memorial ... [to Congress] on the Subject of "Floating Mercantile Schools." [n. p. n. d.] 8vo, pp. 9. B., H. — Remarks on Ocean Steam-Navigation. *Boston.* 1855. 8vo, pp. 15. B., BA. — Remarks on the Steam-Power, Rig, &c., of the United-States Steam Sloops Building, 1864–5. ... . *Boston: Press of John Wilson and Son.* 1865. 8vo, pp. 16. 5 Plates. B.

Forbin (Louis Nicolas Philippe Auguste, *comte de*). Charles Barimore, suivi des œuvres inédites. [Le quaker de Philadelphie; romances en verse; réflexions detachées.] *Paris: Challamel.* 1843. 8vo, pp. xv, 298. C. 25052

Forbisser (Martin). *See* Frobisher (M.)

Force (Peter). American Archives: consisting of a Collection of Authentick Records, State Papers, ... and Letters and other Notices of Publick Affairs, the Whole forming a Documentary History of the Origin and Progress of the North American Colonies; of the Causes and Accomplishment of the American Revolution; and of the Constitution of Government for the United States, to the Final Rati on thereof. In Six Series. Published by M. St. Clair Clarke and Peter Force. ... [First title; the second title is] American Archives: Fourth Series ... from ... March 7, 1774, to the Declaration of Independence ... . *Washington.* 1837–1846. 6 vols., folio. +

Fifth Series. ... to ... September 3, 1783. ... *Washington.* 1848–1853. 3 vols., folio. 25053

This great storehouse of British Colonial and American history was printed by order of the United States Government. It was the intention to divide the work into six series, from 1493 to 1789. The nine volumes described are all that have appeared, and the further progress of the work is suspended. The manuscript of the unpublished series is in the Library of Congress. *See* "N. Am. Rev.," xlvi. 475.

Force. The Declaration of Independence, or Notes on Lord Mahon's History of the American Declaration of Independence. By Peter Force, Esq. ... *London: G. Willis.* 1855. 8vo, pp. 66.

This remarkable piece of criticism, by one who knew well whereof he was writing, first appeared in a series of articles in the "Daily National Intelligencer." The papers having been revised by the author, were sent to a friend in London, who, out of compliment to Mr. Force, had a few copies privately printed.

Force. Grinnell Land. Remarks on the English Maps of Arctic Discoveries, in 1850 and 1851, made at the Ordinary Meeting of the National Institute, Washington, in May, 1852, By Peter Force. [*Washington: printed for Private Distribution.* 1852.] 8vo, pp. 23. Map. B., BA. 25055

Also: Supplement to Grinnell Land. Read at ... the National Institute, July, 1853. ... [*Washington.*] 1853. 8vo, pp. 52. B., BA.

Force. The National Calendar, and Annals of the United States; for mdcccxx. ... *Washington: Davis & Force.* 1820. 12mo. 25056

Continued to 1838 or later. None published in 1825, 1826, and 1827.

Force. National Government Journal, and Register of Official Papers, from December, 1823, to December, 1824. *Washington City.* 1823–24. 4to. C. 25057

Force. Register of the Army and Navy of the United States. No. 1. 1830. By Peter Force. *Washington: Peter Force.* 1830. 16mo, pp. 204. BA., C., S. 25058

Force. Tracts and other Papers, relating principally to the Origin, Settlement, and Progress of the Colonies in North America, from the Discovery of the Country to the Year 1776. Collected by Peter Force. *Washington: Printed by Peter Force.* 1836–1846. 4 vols., 8vo. B., BA. 25059

A most interesting and valuable series of reprints of the rarest of tracts relating to America, all of which are noticed in this dictionary, under their respective names. *See* "N. Am. Rev.," xliii. 274. Also: A Directory for the Public Officers, the Library, Offices, and Committee Rooms, in the Capital; ... *Washington City: Davis & Force.* 1820. 12mo, pp. 20. BA. Mr. Force collected a very large library, mostly relative to American history, which he sold to the Library of Congress.

Force (W. Q.) Army and Navy Chronicle of the United States. January, 1843, to June, 1844. *Washington: W. Q. Force.* 1843–44. 3 vols. 25060

Force. Picture of Washington and its Vicinity, for 1845. With Forty-One Embellishments on Steel and Lithograph. To which is added the Washington Guide ... *Washington: W. Q. Force.* 1845. 16mo. C. + [*Ibid.*] 1850. 18mo, pp. 188. 38 Plates. C. 25061

Les Forces de l'Europe, Asie, Afrique and Amérique, ou description des principles villes avec leurs forteresses, etc. Nouvelle édition mis en meilleur ordre que les précédentes, beaucoup augmentée et divisée en 20 tomes. Enrichie de plusieurs magnifique Edifices, Jardins, etc. *A Paris: chez l'autheur et se vend à Leide chez P. van der Aa.* [1726.] 20 pts. in 2 vols. 25062

This very rare work is a collection of plans and views of the most remarkable cities and fortresses in Europe. In this edition sixteen plates of American subjects are added, mostly published before in other works, and afterwards reproduced anew (but with large borders and cartouches) in the "Galerie agréable du monde." It was originally published by N. de Fer, at Paris, in 8 vols., containing 170 plates; these were copied by P. Mortier, at Amsterdam, and augmented to 249 plates, in 14 vols. These copies were bought by P. van der Aa, who reissued them with other plates, augmented to the number of 509 in this edition. *See* Muller's "Books on America," No. 2.

Ford (D.) Journal of an Expedition made in the Autumn of 1794, with a Detachment of New Jersey Troops, into Western Pennsylvania, to aid in Suppressing the Whiskey Rebellion. By Captain David Ford. Communicated by Dr. Franklin B. Hough, of Albany. [n. p. n. d.] 8vo, pp. 14. 25063

A few copies separately printed from "New Jersey Hist. Coll.," Vol. viii.

Ford (H.) Oration delivered in the Presbyterian Church at Morristown, July 4, 1806. By Henry Ford. *Morristown.* 1806. 8vo. N. 25064

Ford (H. A.) The History of Putnam and Marshall Counties; embracing an Account of the Settlement, Early Progress, and Formation of Bureau and Stark Counties. With Appendix, containing Notices of old Letters and of the Antiquities, etc. By Henry A. Ford. *Lacon, Ill.: The Author.* 1860. 18mo, pp. vii, 160. BA., C., S. 25065

Ford (J.) A Sermon preached April 4th, 1820, at Orange, N. J., before the Executive Committee for the Counties of Essex and Morris. By John Ford, A.M. *Newark.* 1820. 8vo, pp. 32. 25066

Ford (P.) A Vindication of William Penn, Proprietary of Pennsilvania, from the late Aspersions spread abroad on purpose to Defame him. By Philip Ford. *London: Benjamin Clark.* 1683. Folio, 1 leaf. 25067

Ford (S. H.) The Battle of Freedom, including Seven Letters on Religious Liberty, addressed to Bishop Spalding. By S. H. Ford. *Louisville, Ky.: printed by J. F. Brennan.* 1855. 12mo, pp. 156. 25068

Ford (S. R.) Raids and Romance of Morgan and his Men, by Sally Ford ... *Mobile: S. H. Goetzel.* 1864. pp. 332. BA. + Second Edition. Reprinted from the Mobile Edition. *New York: Charles B. Richardson.* 1864. 12mo, pp. 417. Portrait. BA. + [*Ibid.*] 1864. 8vo. BA. 25069

Ford (T.) A History of Illinois, from its Commencement as a State in 1818 to 1847. Containing a Full Account of the Black Hawk War, the Rise, Progress, and Fall of Mormonism, the Alton and Lovejoy Riots, and other Important and Interesting Events. By the late Gov. Thomas Ford. *Chicago, S. C.: Griggs & Co.* 1854. 12mo, pp. 447. B., BA. 25070

Ford (T.) Eulogy on John Adams, delivered September 14, 1826, in St. Michael's Church, by Timothy Ford, Esq. at the request of the Honorable the Intendant and Wardens of the City of Charleston. *Charleston: Ellis and Neufville, Printers.* 1826. 8vo, pp. 39. BA., H. 25071

Ford (W.) American Republicanism ... its Success, its Perils, and the Duty of its present Supporters. Sermon delivered before the Citizens of Brandon, on the Occasion of the National Fast, September 26, 1861. By Rev. William Ford. *Rutland: George A. Tuttle & Co.* 1861. 8vo. pp. 24. B. 25072

Foreign Conspiracy against the United States. *See* [Morse (S. F. B.)]

Foreign Emigrant Society. [*Boston.* 1864.] 8vo, pp. 11. H.

The Foreign Slave Trade, A Brief Account of its State, of the Treaties which have been Entered into, and of the Laws Enacted for its Suppression, from the date of the English Abolition Act to the present time. *London: John Hatchard and Son.* 1837. 8vo, pp. 64. P. 25074

A Forensic Dispute on the Legality of Enslaving the Africans, held at the Public Commencement in Cambridge, New-England, July 21st. 1773. ... *Boston: Thomas Leverett.* MDCCLXXIII. 8vo, pp. 48. BA., M., W. 25075

Forest (P.) Voyage aux États-Unis de l'Amérique, en 1831. Par P. Forest. *Lyon.* 1834. 8vo, pp. 95. S. 25076

The Forest Arcadia of Northern New York; embracing a view of its Mineral, Agricultural, and Timber Resources. *Boston: T. O. H. P. Burnham.* 1864. 18mo. 25077

Forest Hills Cemetery: its Establishment, Progress, Scenery, Monuments, &c. With Ten Illustrations. *Roxbury: John Backup.* 1855. 12mo, pp. 237. C. 25078

Order of Exercises at the Consecration of Forest-Hills Cemetery. *Roxbury, Mass.* [n. d.] 8vo, pp. 4. 25079

Forest Lawn Cemetery Association. *Buffalo, New-York.* 1856. 8vo, pp. 92. S. 25080

Forest Life. *See* [Kirkland (*Mrs.* M.)]

Forest Mining Company. Report of the Directors of the Forest Mining Company, made at the Annual Meeting of the Stockholders, December 13, 1852, and Charter and By-Laws of the Company. Second Edition, with Supplementary Report. *Boston.* 1853. 8vo, pp. 43. Map. H. + *Boston.* 1854. 8vo, pp. 14. H. 25081

Forest Scenes and Incidents in the Wilds of North America, being a Winter's Route from Halifax to the Canadas. *London.* 1838. 8vo. 25082

Forester (Frank), *pseudonym.* *See* [Herbert (H. W.)]

The Foresters. *See* [Belknap (J.)], Vol. ii., No. 4433.

Foresti (J. P.) Nouissime hystoria*rū* omniū repercussio-|nes nouiter a Reuerendissimo patre Ja|cobo philippo Bergomēse, ordinis He|remitarum edite: que Supplementum|supplementi Cronicarū nuncupantur.|Incipiendo ab exordio mundi, vsq3 in|Annum salutis nostre. Mcccccij.|Cum gratia & Priuilegio.| [Colophon:] *Explicit Supplementum Chronicarum Diligenter Et|Accurate Reuisum Atque Correctū Venetiis Im|pressum Per Albertinū De Lissona Vercellē|sem. Regnā. Leonardo Loredano Ve|netiarum Principe. A Natiui-|tate Christi. M. ccccc.|iii. Die. iiii. Maii.|Cum Gratia Et|Priuilegio.|* Folio, 425 l., Tabla, 9 l. C. 25083

Printed in Gothic letter. The chapter, "De Insulis in India," on leaf 441, relates to Columbus and his voyages. We believe this to be the earliest considerable recognition of that important discoverer by any general author.

Foresti. Nouissime historiarū|omniū repercussiões: noui|ter a Reuerendissimo patre Jacobo philip|po Bergomense ordinis Heremitarum|edite: que Supplementum supple|menti Cronicarū nuncupan|tur Incipiendo ab exor|dio mūdi vsq3 in An|nū Salutis nostre.|Mccccc vi|Cum gratia & Priuilegio.| [Colophon:] ... *Vene|tiis impressum Opere & impensa Georgii de Ru-|sconibus Anno a Natiuitate Christi. M. D.|vi. Die iiii Maii: Regnante Leonar-|do Loredano Venetia-|rum Principe.|* Folio, 13 l., Text, 4–449 leaves. J.C.B. 25084

Concerning this, *see* Harrisse's "Bibl. Am. Vet.," p. 86. There was also an edition printed at Nuremberg this year [1506].

Foresti. Svpplementum supplementi de le Chroniche Vulgare nouamente dal venerando patre frate Jacobo Philippo del ordine heremitano primo auctore agionto & emendato: el qual comenza da principio del mōdo infino al anno de la nostra salute mccccciii. diligētemēte vulgarizato per miser Frācesco C. Fiorentino. Cum Gratia & Privilegio. [Colophon:] *Impresso nella inclita Citta de Venetia per me Georgio de Rusconi Milanese ne lanno della nostra salute.* 1508. *adi.* 7. *de Augusto: regnāte lo iclito Prīcipe Leonardo Lauredano.* Folio, 12 unnumbered l., cccl leaves. C.

Foresti. Svpplementvm | Supplementi Chronica | rum ab ipso Mundi Exordio usq3 ad redemptio|nis Nostræ Annum .M. ccccc.x. editum. Et nouissime recognitum.|Et castigatum a Venerando Patre Jacobo Phillipo Bergomate ordinis Heremitarum. Additis per eū|dem Auctorē q*uæ* pluribus vtilissimis & necessa|rijs additionibus. Nec nō elegāti tabula|nouiter excogitata quæ omnia mirfice demonstrat.|Cū Gratia & Privilegio.| [Colophon:] ... *Vene|tiis impressum Opere & impensa Georgii de Ru|sconibus Anno a Naitiuitate Xpi* .M.D.|XIII. *Die* .XX. *Augusti. Regnāte Leonardo Lauredano|Venetiarum Principe.|* Folio, cccxxxv leaves. BA. 25086

The chapter, "De quattuor p'maximis insulis in india extra orbem nuper inuentis," commences on the verso of folio 329.

Foresti. Svpplementvm|Svpplementi|De le Chroniche del Uenerando padre Fra-|te Jacobo Phillipo del ordine Heremitano| Primo Authore. Ulgarizato & Hystoriato.|cum la giunta per insino. 1524.| [Colophon:] ... *Impresso in Venetia|per Ioāne Francischo & Ioanne Antonio Fratelli di Rusconi.|Regnante lo Inclyto Principe Andrea Griti. Nel an-|no del Signore.* 1524. *del mese di Nouēbrio.|* Folio, ccclxvi leaves. BM. 25087

Foresti. Supplementum Chronicorum, Omnes Fere Historias quae ab orbe condito hactenus gestae sunt iucunda admodum dicendi breuitate complectens. Opus sanè quam vtilissimum, & cuiusuis conditionis viro pernecessarium: primum quidem à Venerando patre Jacobo Philippo Bergomate ordinem Eremitarum professo conscriptum, deinde vero eruditorum quorundam diligentia, multis mendis, ac superfuis quibusdam rebus diligentissime repurgatum, in studiosorum omnium gratiam atque vtilitatem. Cui insuper addita est nostrorum temporum breuis quaedam accessio eorum annorum historias ac res tum priuatas tum externas complectens quae ab anno. 1500. ad annum 1535. hic, tum etiam alibi gestae sunt. *Parisiis*, M.D.XXXV. *Apud Simonem Colineum, in vico D. Joannis Bellouacensis.* Folio, 443 leaves. 25088

"Quoique cette Edition soit furieusement tronquée, on ne la doit pas tout à fait rejetter, à cause du Livre xvii. qui sert de Suplément à l'Ouvrage, & qui contient certains articles, qui ne sont pas à mépriser: comme ceux d'Aldus Manutius, Christophorus Longolius, Jo. Calphurnius, Janus Lascaris, &c., mais il faut absolument l'accompagner d'une Edition plus ancienne: entre lesquelles je choisirais celle de l'an 1506. in Fol." — Clement. "The chapter 'de iv permaximis insulis,' &c., is on folio 412. This truncated edition, with the valuable chapter xvii, however, was republished at Venice, 1547, folio." — Harrisse. The Spanish translation of Foresti does not contain the chapter relating to Columbus. This writer belonged to the noble family of Foresti of Bergamo. On entering the monastery of the Augustines at that place, he assumed the name of Jacopo Filippo. As his books bear on the title "a Jacobo Philippo Bergomense," or "Bergomate," *i. e.* of Bergamo, he is often called simply Bergomensis or Bergomas, as if that were a family name.

Les forêts intérieures du Canada. *See* [Traill (C. P.)]

Forfaits des Jésuites au Paraguay, Extrait du Mémorial présénté au Roi d'Espagne. *Au Paraguay.* 1759. 12mo. 25089

Form of Consecration of the British Chapel and Burial Ground, according to the Rites and Ceremonies of the Church of England, by the Right Reverend Father in God William Hart Coleridge, D.D., Lord Bishop of Barbados and the Leeward Islands. *Carácas* 1834. Folio, English Text, pp. 10, Spanish Translation, pp. 10. 25090

Form of Prayer. *See* Jamaica, New York, etc.

A Form of Prayer, Proper to be used In the Churches throughout the Province of New-York, On Friday the Twelfth of May, being the Day appointed by Proclamation, for a General Fast and Humiliation: To supplicate the Pardon of our Sins, and to implore the Divine Protection and Blessing of His Majesty's

Sacred Person, His illustrious Family, His Kingdoms and Colonies, His Fleets and Armies. *New-York: Printed and Sold by J. Parker and Weyman, in Beaver-street.* MDCCLVIII. 4to, pp. 12.

Also: Form of Prayer, Proper to be used in the Churches in the Province of New York, 13 July, 1757, for a General Fast. — A Form of Prayer for the Fast, May 7, 1762. *New York.* 1762. 8vo, pp. 8. — Form of Prayer for Feb. 27th, for a General Fast and Humiliation before God, to restore tranquility among our subjects in America, that they may again return to Duty. [n. p. 177–.] + *Chester: J. Poole.* [177–.] 12mo. — A Form of Prayer to be used in all Churches and Chapels in Ireland, 7th of February, being the Day for a General Fast, ... on behalf "of our Subjects in America, who despitefully use us, now in open Rebellion," ... *Dublin.* 1778. 4to. — Form ... for the 27th February, 1778, being the day appointed for a General Fast, on account of the troubles in America. 1778. — Form of Prayer to be used in all Churches and Chapels, on the General Fast, to supplicate the Divine Majesty for assistance of our Arms against our deluded subjects in America. By Command, Feb. 10, 1779. 12mo. — A Form of Prayer, ... for a General Fast. *Dublin.* 1779. 4to, pp. 22. (The prayer for our enemies relates to the American Revolution.) — Form of Prayer ... 21 Feb., 1781 ... a General Fast, ... on behalf of "our fellow subjects in America, who have been unhappily misled into Rebellion." 1781. 8vo. — A Form of Prayer, for a General Fast, &c., on 5th February, 1812. 8vo, pp. 16. + On 10th March, 1813. 8vo, pp. 16.

Forma y modo de fundar las cofradias del cordon de N. P. S. Francisco. *Mexico.* 1589. 8vo. 25092

Forma,|y|Modo Breve|para tener a Punto|de guerra vna nao en ocasion de|dar vista al enemigo en esta mar,|segun la instruccion y orden,|con que Guarnecio|el Galeon llamado S. Joseph Almi-|ranta Real deste mar del Sur, al se-|gundo dia que salio del Puer-|to del Callao para el|de Panama,|A Conducir el Teso-|ro de su Magestad, y par-|ticulares|El Almirante|D. Ivan Zorrilla|de la Gandara,|Año de 1672.| [*Lima*] Con licencia del Real Gouierno.|*Año de* 1674.| [End] *Fecha en esta Almiranta Real San Ioseph en*|13. *de Iunio de* 672.| 4to, 13 l. 25093

Formaleoni (V.) Saggio sulla nautica antica de' Veneziani, con una illustrazione d'alcune carte idrografiche antiche della biblioteca di S. Marco, che dimonstrano l'isole Antille prima della scoperta di Cristoforo Colombo, di Vincenzio Formaleoni. *Venezia.* 1783. 8vo. Map. 25094

Facsimile of an ancient map of America, 1436. Llewell, in his "History of Geography," remarks that he was never able to see a copy of this rare book.

Formaleoni. Essai sur la Marine Ancienne des Venitiens dans lequel on a mis au jour plusieurs cartes tirées de la Bibliothèque de St. Marc, anterieures à la découverte de Cristophe Colomb et qui indiquent clairement l'existence des Antilles par Vicenzo Formaleoni. Traduite de l'Italien par le Chevalier D'Henin. *Venise: Formaleoni.* 1788. 8vo, pp. 186. Maps and Plates. 25095

FORMAN (J. G.) The Christian Martyrs; or, the Conditions of Obedience to the Civil Government; a Discourse by J. G. Forman ... . To which is added, a Friendly Letter ... on the Pro-Slavery Influences that occasioned his Removal. *Boston: Wm. Crosby and H. P. Nichols.* 1851. 8vo, pp. 51. B., BA., H.

FORMAN. The Western Sanitary Commission; a Sketch of its Origin, History, ... with Incidents of Hospital Life. By J. G. Forman. *St. Louis: R. P. Studley & Co.* 1864. 8vo, pp. (2), iii, 144. Plate. B., BA., H. 25097

Also: A Discourse preached at the Funeral of the late Mr. Samuel Fessenden ... Oct. 21, 1856. ... *Boston: Printed by John Wilson and Son.* 1857. 8vo, pp. 16. H. — The Fugitive Slave Law. A Discourse delivered in ... West Bridgewater, Mass., ... November 17th, 1850. ... *Boston: Wm. Crosby and H. P. Nichols.* 1850. 8vo, pp. 36. B., BA., H., M. — ... Two Sermons, delivered on the 19th and 26th April, 1848. *Boston.* 1848. 8vo.

FORMAN (*Mr.*) Mr. Forman's Letter to the Rt. Hon. W. Pulteney, Esq., shewing how Pernicious, the Imperial Company of Commerce and Navigation lately established in the Austrian Netherlands, is likely to prove to Great Britain, as well as to Holland. *London.* 1725. 8vo. 25098

Refers to the Scotch colony of Darien, etc.

Forms of Government of all the States in the World. 1791. 8vo. 25099

FORNARIS (J.) Cantos populares por José Fornaris. *Habana.* 1863. 8vo, pp. xx, 216. 25100

FORNARIS. Flores y lagrimas, por José Fornaris. *Habana.* 1860. 8vo, pp. xvi, 342. 25101

FORNEY (J. W.) Eulogy upon the Hon. Stephen A. Douglas, delivered at the Smithsonian Institute, Washington, July 3, 1861. By John W. Forney. *Philadelphia: Ringwalt & Brown.* 1861. 8vo, pp. 28. H. 25102

Also: Address on Religious Intollerance and Political Proscription, ... at Lancaster, Pa., ... 24th of September. ... *Washington.* 1855. 8vo, pp. 51. B. — Speech ... Delivered at the Union Meeting held at Mifflintown, Juniata County, Pennsylvania, on Tuesday, September 8, 1863. 8vo, pp. 7.

El Foro, de la Habana y sus misterios, ó un oficial de causas. *Madrid.* 1846. 2 vols., 8vo. 25103

El Foro. Revista de legislacion y jurisprudencia. Fundada por el Colegio de Abogados. Comision de redaction, Dres. D. José B. Gorostiaga, D. José Dominguez, D. Manuel R. Garcia. *Buenos Aires.* 1859. 4to. 25104

FORREST (Christopher). Captain Bob, the Mountain Devil. *New York: R. M. DeWitt.* 1867. 16mo, pp. 100. 25105

Also: Leatherskin; or, the Prairie Guide. *New York: R. M. DeWitt.* 1868. 16mo, pp. 100 — Old Pike, the Indian Trader. *New York: R. M. DeWitt.* 1868. 16mo, pp. 100. Those are Nos. 9, 15, and 18, of DeWitt's ten-cent romances, and are entirely fictitious.

FORREST (E.) The Biography of Mr. Edwin Forrest: the distinguished American Tragedian. ... *Philadelphia: Turner and Fisher.* 1835. 16mo, pp. 16. Portrait by W. H. Ellis.

Signed E. T. W.

FORREST. The History of Edwin Forrest, the Celebrated American Tragedian, from his Childhood to his present elevated station as a Performer. Written by an individual who has known him from his boyhood. *New York.* 1837. 8vo, pp. 24.

FORREST. Oration delivered at the Democratic Republican Celebration of the Sixty-Second Anniversary of the Independence of the United States, in the City of New York, Fourth of July, 1838. By Edwin Forrest, Esq. ... *New York: Jared W. Bell.* MDCCCXXXVIII. 1838. 8vo, pp. 24. B., H. 25108

Said to have been written for Mr. Forrest by Mr. Leggat. For the Forrest-Macready Tracts, *see* New York City.

FORREST DIVORCE CASE. Report of the Trial of Catharine N. Forrest *vs.* Edwin Forrest, for Divorce. *New York.* 1851. 8vo, pp. 185. 25109

Report of the Forrest Divorce Case. Containing the Full and Unabridged Testimony of all the Witnesses, the Affidavits and Depositions, together with the Consuelo and Forney Letters, *New York: DeWitt and Davenport.* [1852.] 8vo, pp. 187.

Catharine N. Forrest, Respondent, against Edwin Forrest, Appellant, Argument of John Van Buren for the Appellant, January 10th, 11th, 15th, 16th and 29th, 1856. *New York.* 1858. 8vo, pp. 234. 25111

Testimony in the Forrest Divorce Case. *Philadelphia.* 1850. 12mo, pp. 34. 25112

Testimony in the Forrest Divorce Case. Verbatim Report. *New York.* [1852.] 8vo, pp. 185. 25113

FORREST (M.) Women of the South Distinguished in Literature. By Mary Forrest. *New York: Derby & Jackson.* 1861. 4to, pp. 576. Portraits. 25114

The characters are Madame Le Vert, Anna Cora Ritchie, Marion Harland, L. Virginia French, Augusta J. Evans, Maria J. McIntosh, and Rosa Vertner Johnson.

FORREST (M.) Travels through America. A Poem. By Michael Forrest. *Philadelphia: Printed by Johnstone & Justice.* M.DCC.XCIII. 12mo, pp. 50. B., BA. 25115

Poor stuff, by an Irishman of Germantown. Suppressed. Many typographical errors.

FORREST (R.) ... A Sermon, ... before the Northern Missionary Society, ... in Lansingburgh, September 6, 1815. ... By Robert Forrest ... . *Albany: Printed by E. and E. Hosford.* 1815. 8vo, pp. 24. B., S. 25116

FORREST (W. S.) The Great Pestilence in Virginia; being an Historical Account of the Origin, General Character, and Ravages of the Yellow Fever in Norfolk and Portsmouth in 1855; together with Sketches of some of the Victims, Incidents of the Scourge, etc. By William S. Forrest. ... *New York: Derby & Jackson.* 1856. 12mo, pp. xiii, 326. Plate. H. 25117

FORREST. Historical and Descriptive Sketches of Norfolk and Vicinity, including Portsmouth and the Adjacent Counties, during a Period of Two Hundred Years. Also, Sketches of Williamsburg, Hampton, Suffolk, Smithfield, and other Places, with Descriptions of some of the Principal Objects of Interest in Eastern Virginia. By William S. Forrest. *Philadelphia: Lindsay and Blakiston.* 1853. 8vo, pp. 496. Plate. B., BA., H.

FORRESTER (A.) Duty of the Legislature of Nova Scotia with respect to Collegiate Education. By the Rev. Alexander Forrest, D.D. *Halifax.* 1852. 8vo, pp. 18. 25119

See Morgan's "Bibl. Canad.," p. 129.

[FORRESTER (Alfred Henry).] Goodnatured Hint about California. By Alfred Crowquill. *London.* [About 1849.] Obl. 24mo. 9 Plates. C. 25120

FORRY (S.) The Climate of the United States and its Endemic Influences. Based chiefly on the Records of the Medical Department and Adjutant General's Office, United States Army. By Samuel Forry, M.D. ... *New York: J. & H. G. Langley.* 1842. 8vo. Map. BA. + Second Edition. *New York.* 1842. 8vo, pp. 378, (3). Map. 25121

FORRY. Meteorology: comprising ... the Laws of Climate in general, and especially the Climatic Features peculiar to the Region of the United States; ... By Samuel Forry, M.D. ... *New York.* 1843. Sm. folio, pp. 48. B. 25122

Dr. Forry wrote an article on the "Natural History of the American Aborigines" in the "Biblical Repository."

FORS (L. R.) Miscelanea americana por Luis Ricardo Fors escritos publicados en la prensa americana, sobre politica, administracion filosophia, artes, etc. de la America Méridional. *Paris: E. Denné Schmitz.* 1872. 12mo, pp. 450. 25123

FORSEY (T.) The Report of an Action of Assault, Battery and Wounding, tried in the Supreme Court of Judicature for the Province of New-York, in the Term of October 1764, between Thomas Forsey, Plaintiff, and Waddel Cunningham, Defendant. *New-York: printed by John Holt, in the Year* 1764. 4to, pp. iv, 68. BA. 25124

Concerning this, *see* Sedgwick's "Life of Livingston."

[FORSTALL (E. J.)] An Analytical Index of the whole of the Documents relative to Louisiana, deposited in the Archives of the Department "De la Marine et des Colonies" at Paris, ... *New Orleans: E. Johns & Co.* 1841. 8vo. 25125

See also French's "Hist Coll.," Vol. II.

FORSTER (Johann G. Adam). Geschichte der Reisen, die seit Cook an der Nordwest- und Nordost- Küste von Amerika und in dem Nördlichsten Amerika selbst von Meares, Dixon, Portlock, Coxe, Long u. a. m. unternommen worden sind. Mit vielen Karten und Kupfern. Aus dem Englischen, mit Zuziehung aller anderweitigen Hulfsquellen, ausgearbietet von Georg Forster. *Berlin: in der Vossischen Buchandlung.* 1791. 3 vols., 4to, pp. x, 380; xx, 314; ix, 302. 4 Maps and 24 Plates. 25126

FORSTER. A Letter to the Right Honourable the Earl of Sandwich, first Lord Commissioner of the Board of Admiralty, &c. from George Forster, F.R.S. *London: G. Robinson.* MDCCLXXVIII. 4to, pp. 25, 6. 25127

Complaining of the bad treatment the writer and his father had received after their return from their voyage round the world.

FORSTER. Reply to Mr. Wales's Remarks. By George Forster, F.R.S., Naturalist on the late Voyage round the World, by the King's Appointment. *London: B. White.* MDCCLXXVIII. 4to, pp. 53. P. 25128

FORSTER. Sämmtliche Schriften ... Herausgegeben von dessen Tochter und begleitet mit einer Charakteristik Forster's von G. G. Gervinus. *Leipzig: F. A. Brockhaus.* 1843. 9 vols., 12mo. B., BA 25129

Vols. I.-II. contain "Johann Reinhold Forster's und Georg Forster's Reise um die Welt in den Jahren 1772 bis 1775." Vol. IV. contains "Die Nordwestküste von Amerika und der dortige Pelzhandel; Schilderung des Nordens von Amerika."

FORSTER. A Voyage Round the World, in his Britannic Majesty's Sloop, Resolution, commanded by Capt. James Cook, during the years 1772, 3, 4, and 5. By George Forster, F.R.S. ... *London: B. White.* MDCCLXXVII. 2 vols., 4to, pp. xviii, (25), 6, 1 l., pp. 602, 2 Maps; 2 l., pp. 607. BA., H. 25130

"This account of the second voyage of Capt. Cook is chiefly devoted to the description of scientific and philosophical subjects." — LOWNDES. The author's father was a naturalist to the expedition, and his account anticipated the official report, and forms a necessary adjunct to Capt. Cook's voyages.

FORSTER. Reise um die Welt während den Jahren 1772 bis 1775, in dem Schiffe the Resolution unternommen, beschrieben und herausgegeben von dessen Sohn und Reisegefährten Georg Forster, vom Verfasser selbst aus dem Englischen übersetzt, mit dem Wesentlichsten aus Capit. Cook's Tagebüchern und andern Zusätzen für den deutschen Leser vermehret, und durch Kupfer erläutert. *Berlin: Haude und Spener.* 1778. 4to, pp. 451. 4 Plates. 25131

George Forster, the son of J. R. Forster, who accompanied Capt. Cook in his voyages, edited and published these volumes. It was to this same George Forster, and to this same work that Humboldt, in his "Cosmos," acknowledges his indebtedness more than to all other sources, for his early love of nature and tropical beauty. *See* Forster (J. R.), and Meares (John).

FORSTER (J. R.) Bemerkungen auf seiner Reise um die Welt *Berlin.* 1783. 8vo, pp. 254. 25132

FORSTER. A Catalogue of the Animals of North America. Containing An Enumeration of the known Quadrupeds, Birds, Reptiles, Fish, Insects, Crustaceous and Testaceous Animals; many of which are new, and never described before. To which are added, Short Directions for Collecting, Preserving, and Transporting, all Kinds of Natural History Curiosities. By John Reinhold Forster, F.A.S. ... *London: B. White.* M.DCC.-LXXI. 8vo, pp. 43. Plate. BA., H. 25133

See "M. Rev.," XLV. 327. Faribault says there is a German version, *Berlin* or *Halle*, 1770 — probably part of our No. 6468.

FORSTER. Characteres generum Plantarum, quas in itinere ad insulas maris Australis. Colligerunt, Descripserunt, Delin-

earunt, Annis 1772–1775. Jo. R. Forster, LL.D., et Georgius Forster. *Londini: B. White.* MDCCLXXVI. 4to, xviii l., pp. 150. 75 Plates. N. 25134

Forms part of a complete set of Cook's voyages.

FORSTER. Floræ Americæ Septentrionalis; or a Catalogue of the Plants of North America. Containing An Enumeration of the known Herbs, Shrubs, and Trees, many of which are but lately discovered; Together with Their English Names, the Places where they grow, their Different Uses, and the Authors who have Described and Figured them. By John Reinhold Forster, F.A.S. ... *London: B. White.* MDCCLXXI. 8vo, pp. viii, 51. BA., H. 25135

Also included in Bossu's "Louisiana," translated by Forster. Faribault quotes a French version, *Londres.* 1771. 8vo.

FORSTER. Geschichte der Entdeckungen und Schiffahrten im Norden. *Frankfort.* 1784. 25136

FORSTER. Histoire des Découvertes et des Voyages faits dans le Nord. Par M. J. R. Forster. Mise en Français par M. Broussonet. Avec trois Cartes Géographiques. *Paris: Cuchet.* M.DCC.LXXXVIII. 2 vols., 8vo, pp. xv, 399; xii, 410. 3 Maps.

FORSTER. History of the Voyages and Discoveries made in the North. Translated from the German of John Reinhold Forster, I.U.D. and elucidated by several New and Original Maps. *London: G. J. and J. Robinson.* M.DCC.LXXXVI. 4to, pp. (6), xvi, 489, (16). 3 Maps. + Elucidated by a New and Original Map of the Countries situated about the North Pole. ... *Dublin: Luke White and Pat. Byrne.* MDCCLXXXVI. 8vo, pp. (8), xvi, 489, (30). B., BA 25138

A learned account of the various expeditions for discovering the North-West and North-East Passages.

FORSTER. Magazin von merkwürdigen neuen Reisebeschreibungen aus fremden Sprachen übersetzt und mit erläuternden Anmerkungen begleitet. ... *Berlin.* 1792. Vol. VII., 8vo, pp. xvi, 230. 25139

German translation of Brissot's "Travels in North America." *See our* Vol. II., No. 8033.

FORSTER. Observations made during a Voyage Round the World, on Physical Geography, Natural History, and Ethic Philosophy. ... By John Reinhold Forster, LL.D., F.R.S., &c. ... *London: G. Robinson.* MDCCLXXVIII. 4to, pp. iii, 9–649, folded Table, (2). B., BA., H. 25140

See Kalm (Peter), and "M. Rev.," LIX. 401.

FORSTER. Observations faites pendant le Second Voyage du Capitaine Cook: traduite de l'anglois. *Paris.* 1778. 4to.

FORSTER. Tagebuch einer Entdeckungs-Reise nach der Südsee in den Jahren 1776 bis 1780, unter Anführung d. Capitains Cook, Clarke, Gore, and King. *Berlin.* 1781. 8vo. 25142

FORSTER (J.) Piety Promoted; in Brief Biographical Memorials of some of the Religious Society of Friends, commonly called Quakers, the Eleventh Part. By Josiah Forster. *London: Harvey and Darton.* 1829. 12mo, pp. 444. + Second Edition. *Philadelphia.* 1830. 12mo. 25143

FORSTER (R. P.) A Collection of the most Celebrated Voyayes and Travel, from the Discovery of America to the Present Time, Arranged in Systematic Order, Geographical and Chronological, by R. P. Forster. *Newcastle.* 1818. 4 vols., 8vo. Maps and Plates. 25144

FORSTER (T. G.) Address of Thomas Gales Forster at the Music Hall, ... July 26, 1857. [*Boston.* 1857.] 12mo, pp. (2), 16. B., H. 25145

FORSTER (W. E.) William Penn and Thomas B. Macaulay; being Brief Observations on the Charges made in Mr. Macaulay's History of England, against the Character of William Penn. By W. E. Forster. *London: Charles Gilpin.* 1849. 8vo, pp. 54. B., BA., H. + American Edition. *Philadelphia: Henry Longstreet.* 1850. 8vo, pp. 48. 25146

Reprinted in a new edition of Clarkson's "Life of William Penn." "Review of Forster's Observations on the Charge made in Macaulay's History of England against William Penn. 1849." Folio, 2 leaves.

FORSTER. Speech of W. E. Forster on the Slaveholder's Rebellion, and Prof. Goldwin Smith's Letter on the Morality of the Emancipation Proclamation. *Manchester: Union and Emancipation Society.* 1863. 8vo, pp. 15. 25147

FORSYTH (J.) Eulogium, on Adams and Jefferson, delivered at the Request of the Citizens of Augusta. By the Hon. John Forsyth. ... *Augusta: Printed by Brantly & Clarke.* 1826. 8vo.

[FORSYTH.] Observaciones sobre la Memoria del Señor Onis, relativa à la Negociacion con los Estados Unidos. *Madrid.* 1822. Sm. 8vo. 25149

Written in English by the Hon. J. Forsyth, Minister of the United States to Spain, and translated into Spanish from the original manuscript, by Father Thomas Gough.

FORSYTH. Speech of Mr. Forsyth ... on the Bill ... for the Removal of the Indians ... May, 1830. *Washington.* 1830. 8vo, pp. 32. 25150

The appendix consists of the laws of Georgia relating to the Indians. Also: Speech ... on the subject of the Removal of the Public Deposites; January, 1834. *Washington: Francis Preston Blair.* 1834. 8vo, pp. 22. S.

FORSYTH. Speech of the Hon. John Forsyth, ... on the Bill to authorize a Loan ... not exceeding Twenty-Five Millions, ... 23d of February, 1814. *Washington: J. Crossfield.* 1814. 16mo, pp. 32. BA. 25151

FORSYTH (J.) Memoirs of the late Rev. Alexander Proudfit, D.D. By John Forsyth, D.D. With Selections from his Diary and Correspondence, and Recollections of his Life, &c., by his Son. *New York: Harper & Brothers.* 1846. 12mo, pp. 384. Portrait. C., S. + [*Ibid.*] 1855. 12mo. 25152

Also: Presbyterianism since the Reformation: Discourse, Presbyterian Historical Society, 1858. ... *Philadelphia.* 1858. 8vo, pp. 20. S.

FORSYTH (J.), *Junr.* Address, ... before the ... Societies of Rutgers College. ... 26th July, 1848. By John Forsyth, Jr., D.D. ... *New York: R. Craighead.* 1848. 8vo, pp. 25. B.

Also: Address, before the Alumni Association of Rutgers College. ... *New Brunswick.* 1836. 8vo.

FORSYTH (W.) An Epitome of Mr. Forsyth's Treatise on the Culture and Management of Fruit-Trees. By William Forsyth. Also, Notes on American Gardening and Fruit: &c., &c. By an American Farmer [W. Cobbett]. *Philadelphia.* 1803. 8vo. Plates. 25154

FORSYTH. A Treatise on the Culture and Management of Fruit Trees; ... To which are added, an Introduction and Notes, adapting the Rules of Treatise to the Climates and Seasons of the United States of America, by William Cobbett. *Philadelphia.* 1802. 8vo. + *Albany.* 1803. 8vo. C. 25155

FORSYTH (W.) [Masonic] Sermon at Danville [Vt.], June 25, 1798. By William Forsyth. *Boston.* 1798. 8vo. W.

FORSYTH (W.) Plats of Subdivisions of the City of Washington, D. C. By William Forsyth, Surveyor. *Washington: R. A. Waters.* 1856. Folio, 4 l. 62 Plates. C. 25157

FORT (G.) We Four Villagers. A Tale of Domestic Life in Pennsylvania. By G. Fort. *Philadelphia: J. S. McCalla.* 1861. 12mo, pp. 339. C. 25158

Fort Adams. Papers accompanying Joint Resolution in relation to the Arming of Fort Adams, Narragansett Bay. 8vo. (37th Cong., 2d Sess. Miscell. Doc., No. 79.) 25159

Fort Braddock Letters; or, a Tale of the French and Indian Wars, in America, at the Beginning of the Eighteenth Century. *Worcester: Dorr & Howland.* 1827. 18mo, pp. 98. H. 25160

Fort Chartres. Affairs at Fort Chartres 1768–1781. *Albany: J. Munsell.* 1864. 4to, pp. 12. 25161

Fifty copies reprinted from the "Historical Magazine."

Fort Edward Institute Magazine. B. D. Ames, Editor. Vol. 1, 1856–57. *Fort Edward.* 1856–7. 8vo. S. 25162

Fort Fillmore. Stephenson's Silver Mine. *See* Sprague (J. T.)

"Fort-La-Fayette Life." 1863–64. In Extracts from the "Right Flanker," A Manuscript Sheet circulating among the Southern Prisoners in Fort-La-Fayette, in 1863–64. ... *Liverpool: Edward Howell.* 1865. Fcap 8vo, pp. (2), 102. B., BA.

Fort Pillow. ... Report of the Joint Committee on the Conduct of the War. .. Massacre at Fort Pillow. [With] Report ... on the condition of Returned Prisoners. *Washington.* 1864. 8vo, pp. 128, 34. 4 Plates. 25164

Fort Pitt. *See* Pittsburgh.

Fort-Plain Seminary and Female Collegiate Institute, Montgomery County, New York. Catalogue, 1858. 8vo. S. 25165

The Fort Riley & Santa Fé Steam Traction Engine Company. Transportation by Steam across the Plains, from the Missouri River to the Rocky Mountains. *New York: Lange & Brother.* 1866. 8vo, pp. 16. H. 25166

Fort Sumter. Programme of the Order of Exercises at the Re-Raising of the United States Flag on Fort Sumter, April 14, 1865. *Port Royal, (S. C.): New South Office.* 1865. 8vo, pp. 4.

See also Vol. I., No. 3966, Vol. VI., No. 23752, and Sumter.

Within Fort Sumter; or, A View of Major Anderson's Garrison Family for One Hundred and Ten Days. By One of the Company. *New York: N. Tibbals & Company.* 1861. 12mo, pp. 72. 25168

Fort Wayne. Williams' Fort Wayne Directory for 1866–67, to which is appended a United States Post-Office Directory. Fourth Issue. Compiled by Williams & Co. *Fort Wayne, Ind.: N. P. Stockbridge.* 8vo, pp. 240, 106. 25169

Forten (J.) An Address delivered before the Ladies' Anti-Slavery Society of Philadelphia ... 14th of April, 1836. By James Forten, Jr. *Philadelphia: Printed by Merrihew and Gunn.* 1836. 8vo, pp. 16. H. 25170

[Fortescue (William).] A Short Relation concerning the Life and Death of William Simpson, who laid down his body in the Island of Barbadoes, the Eighth Day of the Twelfth Month. 1670. *London.* 1671. 4to. 25171

Written in Barbadoes. Contains an elegy written in the same island by Oliver Hooton; also curious particulars of Simpson's going to Cambridge stark naked with a blacked face.

Forthcoming, *pseudonym.* President Holley not the Transylvania University: in a Letter to William Gibbs Hunt, Esq., in Consequence of the Attacks made by him in his "Appeal;" By Forthcoming. *Lexington.* 1824. 12mo. 25172

Fortia d'Urban (Agricole Jos. Fr. Xav. Pierre Esprit Simon Paul Ant., *Marquis de*). Maximes de Washington; discours 1840. 12mo. 25173

The Marquis also edited the "Chronologie historique de l'Amérique," which forms the third and fourth volumes (*Paris: A. J. Denain.* 1830–38. 4to), of the third part of "L'art de vérifier les dates."

Fortifications. Report of the Committee on Military Affairs, upon Permanent Fortifications and Sea-Coast Defences. 8vo, pp. 528. (House of Reps., Report No. 86, 37th Cong., 2d Sess., 1862.) 25174

Fortin (P.) Annual Reports of Pierre Fortin, Esq., ... for the Protection of the Fisheries in the Gulf of St. Lawrence ... 1861 and 1862. ... *Quebec: Printed by Hunter, Rose & Lemieux.* 1863. 8vo, pp. (4), 123, (1). H. 25175

Fortin. Return To an Address from the Legislative Assembly for Copies of Reports or Correspondence of Pierre Fortin, Esquire, commanding the Forces charged with the Protection of the Fisheries of the Gulf of St. Lawrence, ... 1856. [*Toronto.* 1857.] 8vo, pp. 36. H., S. 25176

Fortique (Mariano Fernandez). Oracion fúnebre que en las exequias hechas por el clero de Carácas al ilustrísimo señor Dr. Manuel José Mosqueras Arzobispo de Santa Fé de Bogotá, pronunció en la S. T. M. el ilustrísimo Señor M. F. Fortique Obispo de Guayana, el dia 23 de Marzo de 1854. *Carácas.* 1854. 8vo, pp. 24. 25177

Also: Exequias hechas al Ilustrisimo Señor Doctor Mariano Fernandez Fortique, Antiquo Obispo de Guayana, en la S. T. Metropolitana el dia 11 de Diciembre. *Carácas.* 1866. 8vo, pp. 15. The funeral sermon is by Dr. Nicanar Rivero.

Fortsetzung der Zeytungen ... auss den ... Japonischen und Chineischen Königreichen ... wie auch ... ausz den Orientalischen als occidentalischen Indien etc. *Ingoldstadt: David Sartorius.* 1593. 8vo, pp. 477. J.C.B. 25178

Includes a translation of D'Abienza.

Fortune (E. F. T.) Epitome of the Stocks and Public Funds, English, Foreign, and American. To which is added, an Account of the English and Foreign Railways, ... Fourteenth Edition. By John Field. *London.* 1838. 16mo. + Seventeenth Edition, Enlarged and Revised by D. Morier Evans. *London.* 1856. 16mo. C. 25179

The Fortunes of Moll Flanders. *See* [Defoe], Vol. v., No. 19279.

Fortunio. Chicago avant, pendant et après l'incendie. Par Fortunio, témoin actif dans ce grand drame de feu. *Paris: imp. Masquin et Cie.* 1871. 18mo, pp. 35. 25180

The Forty-Third Regiment United States Colored Troops. *Gettysburg: J. E. Wible, Printer.* 1866. 8vo, pp. 8. 25181

Forward (W.) Speech of Walter Forward, to the Association of the Pittsburgh Board of Trade, on the Occasion of the Fifth Anniversary. *Pittsburgh: Advocate Office.* 1840. 8vo, pp. 16. BA. 25182

Forward or Backward? *See* [Pell (A.)]

Forwood (W. S.) An Historical and Descriptive Narrative of the Mammoth Cave of Kentucky. Including Explanations of the Causes concerned in its Formation, its Atmosphere, Chemistry, Geology, Zoology, &c. With full Scientific Details of the Eyeless Fishes. By W. Stump Forwood, M.D. ... *Philadelphia: J. B. Lippincott & Co.* 1870. 12mo, pp. 235. 11 Plates.

Fosdick (D.) The Anniversary and Farewell Sermon preached in the Hollis-Street Meeting-House, the former, March 3, the latter, September 19, 1847. By Daniel Fosdick, Jr. ... *Boston: Benjamin H. Greene.* 1847. 8vo, pp. 40. B., BA., H. 25184

Fosdick. ... A Sermon preached Sept. 5, 1855, at the Dedication of a new Meeting-house belonging to the "South-Groton Christian Union." By David Fosdick, Jr. ... . *Boston: Phillips, Sampson, and Company.* 1855. 12mo, pp. 48. B., BA., H.

See Putnam (George). Also: ... A Farewell Sermon preached July 1, 1860, in the Meeting-House recently belonging to the "South-Groton Christian Union," ... *Boston: Crosby, Nichols, Lee, and Company.* 1861. 8vo, pp. 30. BA. — Scriptural Temperance. A Sermon, delivered in the Hollis Street Meeting-House, Boston, on Thanksgiving Day, Nov. 26, 1846. ... *Boston: W. Warland Clapp & Son.* 1846. 8vo, pp. 26. BA.

Fosdick (B.) Crime and Punishment. By Blanchard Fosgate, M.D., ... *Auburn: W. J. Moses.* 1866. 12mo, pp. 48. H.

Foss (A. T.), *and* Mathews (E.) Facts for Baptist Churches. Collected, Arranged, and Reviewed by A. T. Foss, of New-hampshire, and E. Mathews, of Wisconsin. ... *Utica: Roberts & Sherman, Printers.* 1850. 12mo, pp. 408. Plate. B. 25187

Foss (J.) Journal of the Captivity and Sufferings of John Foss; several Years a Prisoner in Algiers: &c. *Newburyport.* 1798. 12mo. C. + Second Edition. [*Ibid.* n. d.] 12mo.

Foss. A Journal of the Shipwreck and Sufferings of Daniel Foss, A Native of Elkton, Maryland, Who was the only person saved from on board the Brig Negociator, of Philadelphia, which Foundered in the Pacific Ocean, on the 26th Nov. 1811. ... *Boston.* [1812.] 12mo, pp. 24. Plate. 25189

Fossetier de la Glorieuse Victoire divinement obtenue devant Pavie. Par lempereur Charles-Quint de ce nom. Des iles et q. il possesse en Aphrique. Chant royal à la loenge dycelluy. [*Anvers.* 1525.] 4to, pp. 24. 25190

Of this very rare tract, twenty copies were printed in facsimile, on vellum, by Messrs. Enschede and Sons, at Haarlem. The writer speaks of Christophe Coulon (Columbus), of the cannibal islands of Jocatan, etc.

Fossey (M. de). Le Mexique. Par Mathieu de Fossey. *Paris: Plon.* 1857. 8vo, pp. 581. + Seconde édition. [*Ibid.*] 1863. + Troisième édition. *Paris: E. Dentu.* 1865. 25191

Fossey. Viage á Méjico. Traducido del francés. *Méjico.* 1844. 8vo. Plate. 25192

Foster (A.) Liberty, the Nation, the Occasion. By Aaron Foster. *Greenfield, Mass.: Printed by C. J. J. Ingersoll.* 1854. 24mo, pp. 50. B., H. 25193

Foster (A.) Mr. Abiel Foster's Motion for an Amendment to the Constitution of the United States, 4th February, 1800. ... [n. p. n. d.] 8vo, pp. 4. B. 25194

Foster (A.) ... A Sermon delivered in Henniker, New-Hampshire, at the Ordination of Rev. Eden Burroughs Foster, August 18, 1841. By Rev. Amos Foster ... . *Concord: Printed by Asa McFarland.* 1841. 8vo, pp. 22. BA. 25195

Foster (A.) Documents relating to the Dissolution of his Connexion with the Congregational Church of Charleston, S. C. By Anthony Foster. *Charleston.* 1817. 8vo. W. 25196

Also: Sermons, chiefly of a Practical Nature, to which is prefixed a Memoir of the Author's Life. *Raleigh.* 1821. 8vo.

Foster (A.) Digest of the Laws of the State of Georgia; containing all Statutes, and the Substance of all Resolutions of a general and public nature, and now in force, which have been passed in said State from the year 1820 to the year 1829, inclusive: By Arthur Foster. *Philadelphia.* 1831. 8vo. C. 25197

Foster (A. J.) Notes on the United States. By the Right Hon. Sir Augustus J. Foster, Bart. *London.* 1841. 8vo.

This was not published, and all that is known of it appears in the "Quarterly Review," LXVIII. 20. The author was Secretary of Legation at Washington, 1804–6, and Envoy from 1811 to the declaration of war in 1812.

Foster (B.) A Dissertation on the Seventy Weeks of Daniel: the particular and exact Fulfilment of which Prophecy is considered and proved. By Benjamin Foster. *Newport, (Rhode Island).* 1787. 8vo. W. 25199

Also: ... Remarks on a printed Discourse of Rev. Mr. Fish, of Upton, entitled, Japhet dwelling in the Tents of Shem, &c. *Worcester, Mass.* [n. d.] 12mo. W.

Foster (B. F.) Education Reform. A Review of Wyse on the Necessity of a National System of Education ... By B. F. Foster. *New York: Wiley and Putnam.* 1837. 8vo, pp. 108.

Also: Prospectus of the Commercial Academy, 183 Broadway, New York. *New York.* 1837. 8vo, pp. 14.

Foster (B. F.) An Account of the Conflagration of the principal part of the First Ward of the City of New York, ... 16th of December, 1835. ... To which is added a List of Names of the Persons Burnt out, and of Removals. By Benjamin F. Foster. [*New York.* 1835.] 8vo, pp. 54. BM. 25201

Foster (C. H.) Exposition of the Conduct of Charles Henry Foster, in regard to the Election of Congressmen from the Second District of North Carolina, on January 1, 1863. [n. p. n. d.] 8vo, pp. 15. 25202

Foster (D.) An Election Sermon; delivered before the Honorable Legislature of the State of Vermont; convened at Westminster, October 8th, 1789. By Dan Foster, A.M. *Printed in Windsor, by Alden Spooner.* MDCCXC. 8vo, pp. 26. BA., H.

Also: A Funeral Sermon on the Death of Jeduthan Baldwin. *Worcester, Mass.* 1789.

Foster (D.) The Duty of Gospel Ministers ... Sermon, preached at the Ordination of the Rev. Oliver Dodge, A.B. ... in Pomfret, February 6, 1793. By Daniel Foster, A.M. ... *Windham: Printed by John Byrne.* M,DCC,XCIII. 8vo, pp. 21. B.

Foster. A Sermon preached before ... the Council, Senate, and House of Representatives, of the Commonwealth of Massachusetts, May 26, 1790. Being the day of General Election. By Daniel Foster, A.M. ... *Boston, Mass.: Printed by Thomas Adams.* M,DCC,XC. 8vo, pp. 35. B., BA 25205

Foster. A Sermon preached at the Ordination of the Rev. Joshua Crosby to the Pastoral Care of the Church of ... Greenwich ... Dec. 2d, 1789. By Daniel Foster, A.M. Pastor of the Church in New-Braintree. *Springfield.* 1791. 8vo. W. 25206

Also: His Doctrines Unscriptural, with the result of an Ecclesiastical Council, at his Ordination at New Braintree, Mass. *Worcester.* 1799. 12mo. W.

Foster. An Address on Slavery. Delivered in Danvers, Mass., By Daniel Foster, Pastor ... of North Danvers ... . *Boston: Bela Marsh.* 1849. 12mo, pp. 44. B. 25207

Foster (D.) The Constitution of the United States, With A Lecture, By Daniel Foster. Showing that A Fair Interpretation and Appreciation of Said Constitution will Abolish Slavery and Establish Liberty. *Springfield: Samuel Bowles & Company.* 1855. 12mo, pp. 62. H. 25208

Foster. Farewell Sermon, preached October 20, 1850, to the Union Evangelical Church, of Chester, Mass. By ... Daniel Foster. *Springfield: Printed by George W. Wilson.* 1850. 12mo, pp. 57. B. 25209

Foster. Our Nation's Sins and the Christian's Duty. A Fast Day Discourse, by Daniel Foster, ... April 10th, 1851. *Boston: White & Potter.* 1851. 8vo, pp. 34. B., H. 25210

Foster (E. B.) The Constitution Our Ark in the Storm. A Discourse ... in ... West Springfield, on Thanksgiving Day, Nov. 27, 1862. By Eden B. Foster, D.D. ... *Springfield: Samuel Bowles & Company.* 1862. 8vo, pp. 36. H. 25211

Foster. A North-Side View of Slavery. A Sermon on the Crime against Freedom, in Kansas and Washington, ... August 31, 1856. By Eden B. Foster ... . *Concord: Jones & Cogswell, Printers.* 1856. pp. 39. B. 25212

Foster. ... A Sermon, ... October 25, 1849, at the Installation of Rev. William C. Foster, as Pastor of the Shawmut Congregational Church, Boston. By Eden B. Foster, ... *Boston: Geo. C. Rand & Co., Printers.* 1850. 8vo, pp. 44.

Foster (E.) A Discourse pronounced before the Middlesex Martial Band ... at Westford, March 3, 1808. By Edmund Foster, A.M. ... *Cambridge: Printed by William Hilliard.* 1808. 8vo, pp. 14. BA., H. 25214

Foster. A Sermon, preached before his Excellency the Governor ... May 27, 1812, being the Day of Annual Election. By Edmund Foster, A.M. ... *Boston: Russell & Cutter.* 1812. 8vo, pp. 22. B., BA., H. 25215

A justification of the impending war.

Foster. A Sermon, preached at Littleton, Dec. 4, 1815. On the Completion of a Century from the Incorporation of that Town. By Edmund Foster, A.M. ... *Concord: Printed by Joseph T. Peters.* 1815. 8vo, pp. 28. BA., H. 25216

Also: An Oration, ... at Westford, ... July 4, 1804. *Boston: Adams and Rhodes.* 1804. 8vo, pp. 25. H. — An Oration ... at Littleton, July 4, 1806; ... *Cambridge: Printed by William Hilliard.* 1806. 8vo, pp. 23. BA., H. — ... A Sermon, preached at the Ordination of the Rev Jonathan Osgood, ... in Gardner, October 19, MDCCXCI. ... *Worcester: Isaiah Thomas & Leonard Worcester.* MDCCXCII. 8vo, pp. 40. BA., H. — A Sermon, occasioned by the Death of Josiah Hartwell, ... May 20, 1791. ... *Boston: Belknap and Hall.* MDCCXCIII. 8vo, pp. 23. BA., H. — Sermon at Littleton, on the Death of Dea. Daniel Kimball, who died May 24, 1813. *Boston.* [n. d.] 8vo. W. — Thanksgiving Sermon at Littleton, April 18, 1815, for the Restoration of Peace. *Boston.* 1815. 8vo. W.

Foster (E. H.) A Communication to the General Assembly of Tennessee, touching Several Instructions. By Ephraim H. Foster. *Athens.* 1839. 8vo. N. 25217

Foster. Funeral Oration by Ephraim H. Foster; delivered in ... Nashville, Tennessee, on the Occasion of the Celebration of the Obsequies of Henry Clay; July 28th, 1852. *Nashville, Tenn.: W. F. Bang & Co.* 1852. 8vo, pp. 21. BA., H. 25218

Foster (E.) An Examination of E. L.'s [Enoch Lewis's] "Review of the Causes and Course of the Division in the Yearly Meeting of Ohio." By Ethan Foster. *Boston: Press of T. R. Marvin.* 1855. 8vo, pp. 26. 25219

Foster (F.) Documents, Elucidating the Nature and Character of the Opposition made to the Rev. Mr. Foster, by a Portion of the Inhabitants of Petersham. Compiled and Published by Festus Foster, A.M. ... *Brookfield: Printed by Merriam & Co.* 1817. 8vo, pp. 46. BA., H. 25220

Foster. The Watchman's Warning to the House of Israel: A Sermon, delivered ... in Petersham, November 21, 1811, being the Day Appointed for Thanksgiving ... . By Festus Foster, A.M. ... . *Worcester: Isaiah Thomas.* 1861. 8vo, pp. 24. H.

Also: Address at the Ichthyon Feast, at Greenwich Village, Mass. Aug. 23, 1826. ... *Amherst.* [n. d.] 8vo. W. — Address before Hampshire, Franklin and Hampden Agricultural Society at Northampton, [Mass.] Oct. 29, 1829. ... *Northampton.* 1829. 8vo. W. — An Oration, ... at Hardwick, July 4th, 1812 ... *Brookfield: Printed by E. Merriam & Co.* 1812. 8vo, pp. 17. H. — An Oration pronounced ... in the Town of Northfield, ... July 5, 1813, ... *Brattleborough: Printed by William Fessenden.* 1813. 8vo, pp. 22. — A Preached Gospel, succeeded by the United Efforts of Pastor and People; A Sermon, ... *Greenfield.* 1802. 8vo. — ... Sermon, ... at the Interment of Mrs. Lydia Kilburn ... October 11, 1803 ... . *Greenfield, Mass.: Printed by John Denis.* 1804. 8vo, pp. 17. BA., H.

Foster (G. G.) Celio; or, New York above-ground and under-ground. By G. G. Foster, Esq. *New York.* [1850.] 8vo, pp. 144. 25222

Foster. Fifteen Minutes around New York. *New York: DeWitt and Davenport.* [About 1850.] 8vo, pp. 111. C.

Foster. The Gold Mines of California; and also a Geographical, Topographical and Historical View of that Country. Edited by G. G. Foster. *New York: DeWitt & Davenport.* 1848. 8vo, pp. 80. Map. 25224

Reproduced with a new title as:

Foster. The Gold Regions of California; being a Succinct Description of the Geography, History, Topography, and General Features of California: including ... the Gold Regions ... Edited by G. G. Foster. Third Edition. *New York: DeWitt & Davenport.* 1848. 8vo, pp. 80. Map. B., H. 25225

FOSTER. New York by Gas Light; with here and there a Streak of Sunshine. By G. G. Foster, ... *New York: DeWitt & Davenport.* 1850. 8vo, pp. 127, (1). BA., H. 25226

[FOSTER.] New York in Slices: by an Experienced Carver: being the Original Slices Published in the N. Y. Tribune. Revised, Enlarged, and Corrected by the Author. *New York: William H. Graham.* 1849. 8vo, pp. 128. 25227

Mr. Ludewig quotes, in a manuscript in my possession, "New York Naked. By G. G. Foster. *New York: DeWitt & Davenport.* 1838." 8vo, pp. 50, which is perhaps a mistake.

FOSTER (G. L.) The Past of Ypsilanti: A Discourse, Sept. 20, 1857. By Rev. G. L. Foster. *Detroit.* 1857. 8vo. S.

FOSTER (H.) Voyage. *See* Webster (W. H. B.)

[FOSTER (Hannah).] The Coquette; or, the History of Eliza Wharton. A Novel: founded on Fact. By a Lady of Massachusetts. *Boston.* 1797. + Fourth Edition. *Newburyport: Charles Whipple.* 1824. 12mo, pp. 303. BA. + Eleventh Edition. *Exeter.* 1828. 25229

See "New England Historical and Genealogical Register," IX. 191. Finally reprinted as "The Coquette, or, the Life and Letters of Eliza Wharton. A True Tale in Real Life, with Historical Preface and a Memoir of the Author. By a Lady of Massachusetts [Jane E. Locke]. *Philadelphia.* 1866." 12mo, pp. 302. B., BA., H.

FOSTER (I.) Defence of Religious Liberty. By Rev. Isaac Foster, M.A. *Worcester.* 1780. 8vo. W. 25230

FOSTER. Fallen Sinners of Men able to do well. A Sermon, Preached at the Ordination of the Reverend Daniel Foster ... in New-Braintree, ... On the 29th Day October, 1773. By his Father the Reverend Isaac Foster, M.A. ... *Worcester: Printed by Isaiah Thomas.* 16mo, pp. 36. B., BA. 25231

FOSTER. Misrepresentation and Falsehood Detected and Exposed, in Answer to D. S. Rowland and T. Hinsdale. By Isaac Foster. *Hartford, Con.* 1781. 8vo. 25232

FOSTER. Sermon at the Ordination of Joel Foster, at New Salem, Mass. June 9, 1779. By Isaac Foster. *Worcester.* [1779.] 8vo. 25233

Also: Letter to Rev. Joseph Buckminster, in Reply to his Paraphrase of Romans X. 4. and to Mr. Foster's Sermon at the Ordination of his Son at New Braintree. *Worcester.* 1780. 12mo.

FOSTER (J. J.) *See* Shotwell (T. L.)

FOSTER (J.) ... A Sermon, preached at the Ordination of the Rev. John Foster, November 1st, 1784. To the Pastoral Office in ... Cambridge. By his Brother Joel Foster, A.M. ... . *Boston: Printed by Benjamin Edes & Son.* M,DCC,LXXXV. 8vo, pp. 23. BA., H. 25234

Also: An Oration ... at New Salem, July 4th, 1797: ... *Northampton: Printed by William Butler.* 8vo, pp. 16. H.

FOSTER (J. H.) A Full Account of the Great Fire at Pittsburgh, on the Tenth Day of April, 1845; with the Individual Losses, and Contributions for Relief. Compiled by J. Heron Foster. *Pittsburgh: J. W. Cook.* 1845. 8vo, pp. 92. 25235

FOSTER (J.) A Discourse Delivered December 29, 1799; Occasioned by the Melancholy Death of George Washington, Lieutenant General and Commander in Chief of the Armies of the United States of America; Who departed this life, December 14, 1799. By John Foster, A.M. Pastor of the Third Church and Society in Cambridge. Published at the Request of the hearers. *Boston: Printed by Samuel Hall.* 1800. 8vo, pp. 22.

FOSTER. A Sermon delivered to the First and Third Societies in Cambridge, on the Anniversary Fast in Massachusetts, 4 April, 1805; By John Foster, A.M. ... *Cambridge: Printed by W. Hilliard.* MDCCCV. 8vo, pp. 26. BA., H. 25237

FOSTER. A Sermon, preached before the Ancient and Honourable Artillery Company, in Boston, June 5, 1809, being the Anniversary of their Election of Officers. By John Foster, A.M. ... *Boston: Printed by Munroe, Francis and Parker.* 1809. 8vo, pp. 27, (1). BA., H. 25238

FOSTER. A Sermon, preached 6 November, 1817, In ... Boston, before the Society for Propagating the Gospel among the Indians and others in North America. By John Foster, D.D. ... *Cambridge: Printed by Hilliard and Metcalf.* 1817. 8vo, pp. 44.

Also: A Discourse, on Church Musick, delivered in Brighton, March 29, 1811. ... *Brighton: Printed by D. Bowen.* 1811. 8vo, pp. 18. BA., H. — A Sermon, preached, June 22, 1809, at the Dedication of a New House of Worship, in Brighton. By John Foster, A.M. ... *Boston: Printed by B. True.* 8vo, pp. 31. BA., H. — A Sermon, preached before the Roxbury Charitable Society, ... September 16, 1799. *Boston: Printed by Samuel Hall.* 1799. 8vo, pp. 22. BA. — A Sermon, delivered September 7, 1803; at the Installation of the Reverend Joel Foster, A.M. to the Pastoral Office in East Sudbury ... *Cambridge: William Hilliard.* 1803. 8vo, pp. 39. BA., N., W. — A Sermon, delivered December 10, 1806, at the Ordination of the Rev. Samuel Venzie, A.M. to the Pastoral Office in Freeport. ... *Portland: Gazette Press.* 1807. 8vo, pp. 21. BA., H. — A Sermon, preached in Cambridge and Brighton, April 11,

1811, the Anniversary Fast in Massachusetts. ... *Cambridge: Printed by Hilliard and Metcalf.* 1811. 8vo, pp. 31. B., BA., H. — A Sermon preached in Brighton, January 12, 1815, a Day of National Fasting ... . *Boston: Printed by John Eliot.* 1815. 8vo, pp. 18 or 31. BA., H. — Sermon at the Installation of Rev. Ezekiel L. Bascom, at Ashby, Mass. Jan. 3, 1831. *Worcester.* [n. d.] W.

FOSTER (J.) Oration, at Stonington-Borough, July 5, 1802. By John Foster. *Stonington.* 1802. 25240

Also: Oration, pronounced July 4, 1808. [n. p.] 1808. 8vo, pp. 14.

FOSTER (J.) Fosteriana, consisting of Thoughts and Criticisms selected from Periodical Papers. [By John Foster.] ... Edited by H. G. Bohn. *London: H. G. Bohn.* 1858. 8vo.

Contains some Americana. Vol. II. of Foster's "Essays," *London,* 1856, contains an article on Geo. Whitfield.

FOSTER (J.) A Sketch of the Tour of General Lafayette, on his late Visit to the United States. By John Foster. *Portland.* 1824. 8vo. Portrait. S. 25242

FOSTER (J. Welch). Address on the Seventy-Fifth Anniversary of the South Parish Sunday School, June 11, 1843. By J. W. Foster ... . *Portsmouth, N. H.* 1843. 8vo, pp. 26. BA., H.

FOSTER. Memorial of John W. Foster. [Letters, Addresses, and Religious Writings.] Edited by Andrew P. Peabody. *Portsmouth (N. H.): J. F. Shores, Jr.* 1852. 12mo, pp. vi, 400.

FOSTER (J. W.) The Mississippi Valley: its Physical Geography, including Sketches of the Topography, Botany, Climate, Geology, and Mineral Resources; and of the Progress of Development in Population and Material Wealth. By J. W. Foster, LL.D. ... . *Chicago: S. C. Griggs and Company.* 1869. 8vo, pp. xvi, 443. 2 Maps. B., BA., H. 25245

FOSTER. Report upon the Mineral Resources of the Illinois Central Railroad ... By J. W. Foster. March 4th, 1856. *New-York: George Scott Roe.* 1856. 8vo, pp. 29. Map. H. 25246

FOSTER (J. W.), *and* KIMBALL (J. P.) Iron Cliffs Company. Geology and Metallurgy of the Iron Ores of Lake Superior. Reports of J. W. Foster and J. P. Kimball, PH. D., and other Papers. *New York: Wm. C. Bryant & Co., Printers.* 1865. 8vo, pp. 98. 25247

FOSTER (J. W.), *and* WHITNEY (J. D.) Description of the Lands and Mines of the Great Western Copper Mining Co. of Lake Superior. ... Reports and Maps by Professors J. W. Foster and J. D. Whitney ... . *New York: Pudney & Russell.* 1852. 8vo, pp. 47. H. 25248

FOSTER *and* WHITNEY. Report on the Geology and Topography of a Portion of the Lake Superior Land District, in the State of Michigan. Part I, Copper Lands; Part 2, The Iron Region, together with the General Geology. By J. W. Foster and J. D. Whitney, U. S. Geologists. *Washington: Printed by A. Boyd Hamilton.* 1850–51. 2 vols., 8vo. B., BA., H. 25249

Two parts. Forms Part I., House Doc. No. 69, 31st Congress, 1st Session; Part II., Senate Doc. No. 4, Special Session, 1851.

FOSTER (J. W.) War and Christianity Irreconcilable. An Address to Christians. By John W. Foster. *Providence: For the Author.* 1861. 8vo, pp. 46. 25250

FOSTER (J. Y.) New Jersey and the Rebellion: a History of the Services of the Troops and People of New Jersey in Aid of the Union Cause. By John Y. Foster. ... *Newark, (N. J.): Martin R. Dennis & Co.* 1868. 8vo, pp. viii, 872. Portrait and 4 Maps. B., BA. 25251

FOSTER (L. F. S.) Admission of Kansas. Speech of Hon. L. F. S. Foster, of Connecticut, in the Senate of the United States, June 25, 1856. [*Washington: Buell & Blanchard.* 1856.] 8vo, pp. 16. H. 25252

Also: Speech ... on the Lecompton Constitution; ... March 8 and 19, 1858. ... *Washington.* 1858. 8vo, pp. 15. H. — Speech ... on the Bill to Repeal the Fugitive Slave Law, ... April 27, 1864. [n. p. n. d.] 8vo, pp. 16. B.

FOSTER (L.) Andrew Johnson, President of the United States; his Life and Speeches. By Lillian Foster. *New York: Richardson & Co.* 1866. 12mo, pp. 316. C. 25253

FOSTER. Wayside Glimpses, North and South. By Lillian Foster. *New York: Rudd & Carleton.* MDCCCLX. 12mo, pp. 250. C. 25254

FOSTER (L. B.) Sermon delivered at Northborough, Mass. By Luke B. Foster. 1814. 8vo. 25255

FOSTER (N. G.) Speech of N. G. Foster, of Georgia, on the Presidential Issues. Delivered ... on the 9th of August, 1856. *Washington.* 1856. 8vo, pp. 15. H. 25256

FOSTER (Nathan W.), *and* ATKINS (Charles G.) Report of Commission on Fisheries. [*Augusta:*] *Stevens & Sayward.* 1868. 8vo, pp. 128. C. 25257

On the restoration of sea fish to the rivers and inland waters of Maine.

FOSTER (N.) The Young Freemason's Guide, ... An Address ... before the Members of St. Alban's Lodge, at Brooklyn, the 27th December, 1797. ... By Brother Nathaniel Foster, J.W. *New York: Printed by J. Buell.* 1797. 8vo, pp. 23. B.

FOSTER (N.) Trial of Nathaniel Foster for the Murder of his Wife, at Delhi, N. Y., in 1819. *Kingston.* [n. d.] 8vo.

FOSTER (N.) A Briefe | Relation | of the late | Horrid Rebellion | Acted in the Island | Barbadas, | In the West Indias. | Wherein is contained, | Their Inhumane Acts and | Actions, in Fining and Banishing the | Well affected to the Parliament of | England (both Men and Women) with- | out the least cause given them so to doe: | Dispossessing all such as any way op- | posed these mischievous actions. | Acted by the Waldronds and their | Abettors, Anno 1650. | Written at Sea by Nicholas Foster. | *London, Printed by I. G. for Richard Lowndes on Ludgate-hill: | and Robert Boydell in the Bulwarke neere the Tower.* | MDCL. | 16mo, pp. (4), 112. H. 25260

FOSTER (R. B.) Lincoln Institute. Full History of its Conception, Struggles and Triumph. ... . [Cover reads:] Historical Sketch of Lincoln Institute, by Prof. R. B. Foster. And Speech of Colonel David Branson, upon the Dedication of the New Building, July 4th, 1871. *Jefferson City, Mo.* 12mo, pp. 15.

FOSTER (S. C.) History of the Legislation of Congress upon the American Fisheries. Speech of Hon. Stephen C. Foster, of Maine. Delivered in the United States House of Representatives, May 25, 1858. [n. p. n. d.] 8vo, pp. 8. H. 25262

FOSTER. The Brotherhood of Thieves; or, a True Picture of the American Church and Clergy: ... By Stephen S. Foster. *London.* 1843. 12mo, pp. 68. + *Boston: Anti-Slavery Office.* 1844. 12mo, pp. 72. B., BA. 25263

FOSTER (T.) A Narrative of the Proceedings in America, of the Society called Quakers, in the Case of Hannah Barnard. ... By Thomas Foster. *London.* 1804. 8vo, pp. 162. 25264

FOSTER (T. F.) Speech of Hon. Thomas F. Foster, on a Memorial, &c., relative to the Missionaries (Worcester and Butler) Imprisoned in Georgia; House of Representatives of the United States, June 11, 1832. *Washington.* 1832. 8vo, pp. 16. 25265

FOSTER (V.) ... Work and Wages: or, the Penny Emigrant's Guide to the United States and Canada ... . By Vere Foster. *London: W. & F. G. Cash.* 12mo, pp. 16. H.

FOSTER (W.) True Fortitude Delineated. A Sermon, preached at Fags Manor, to Captain Taylor's Company of Recruits, on the Lord's Day, February 18th, 1776, (And now published by Request). By the Rev. William Foster, A.M. *Philadelphia: printed by John Dunlap.* M,DCC,LXXVI. 8vo, pp. 24. P. 25267

Dedicated to Colonel Wayne, his officers and men.

[FOSTER (William).] A Society for the Especial Study of Political Economy, the Philosophy of History, and the Science of Government. *Boston: Printed by Alfred Mudge & Son.* 1857. 8vo, pp. 19. H. 25268

With especial reference to the United States.

FOSTER (W. C.) Poetry on Different Subjects, written under the Signature of Timothy Spectacles. By William C. Foster. *Salem, (N. Y.)* 1805. 12mo, pp. xii, 144. 25269

Includes poems on the death of Washington, Adams, etc.

FOTHERGILL (J.) An Account of the Life and Travels in the Work of the Ministry, of John Fothergill. To which are added, Divers Epistles to Friends in Great Britain and America, on various Occasions. *London: Luke Hinde.* 1753. 8vo, pp. 372. + *London: Mary Hinde.* 1773. 8vo, pp. 376. + *London: Printed. Philadelphia: Reprinted and sold by James Chattin.* 1754. 12mo, pp. iv, 280. C. 25270

[FOTHERGILL (John).] Considerations relative to the North American Colonies. *London: Printed by Henry Kent.* MDCCLXV. 8vo, pp. 48. 25271

"One of the most important pamphlets published at this important period." — RICH. Reprinted in the works of John Fothergill, M.D. *London: Charles Dilly.* 1783–4. 3 vols., 8vo; and 1784. 4to. *See* "M. Rev.," XLIII. 249.

[FOTHERGILL (Samuel).] The Necessity and Divine Excellency of a Life of Purity and Holiness. ... In Seven Discourses and Three Prayers, and an Epistle to his Brethren in Religious Profession in the Island of Tortola; to which is prefixed an Account of the Life and Character of the Author. *Philadelphia.* 1780. 8vo, pp. 112. BA., C. + Second Edition. *Philadelphia.* 1783. 8vo. + The First Salem Edition. ... *Salem: Printed by Thomas C. Cushing.* M.DCC.XCII. 25272

FOTHERGILL. To Friends of the Island of Tortola. [1760.] 4to, pp. 4. 25273

Reprinted in "Memoirs, &c., of S. Fothergill."

FOUCAUD (Edouard). The Book of Illustrious Mechanics of Europe and America: Translated from the French, Edited By John Frost. *New-York.* 1846. 12mo. + 1847. 12mo.

FOUCHER (V.) Code Criminel de l'Empire du Brésil adopté dans la Session de 1830 ... . *Paris.* 1834. 8vo. A. 25275

FOULKE (W. P.) Considerations respecting the Policy of some Recent Legislation in Pennsylvania. By William Parker Foulke ... . *Philadelphia.* 1861. 8vo, pp. 35. H. 25276

FOULKE. ... Nôtes respecting the Indians of Lancaster County, Pennsylvania. By William Parker Foulke. [n. p. n. d.] 8vo, pp. 32. H. 25277

Also: Discourse in Commemoration of the Founding of the Academy of Natural Sciences ... March 20, 1854 ... . *Philadelphia.* 1854. 8vo, pp. 58. H. — Remarks on Cellular Separation. ... *Philadelphia: Privately Printed.* 1861. 8vo, pp. iv, 112. B., BA., C., H. — Remarks on the Penal System of Pennsylvania, particularly with Reference to County Prisons. ... *Philadelphia.* 1855. 8vo, pp. 52. Plates. H., P., S. — The Right Use of History. *Philadelphia.* 1856. 8vo.

FOULLOUZE (J.) *See* Louisiana.

The Fountain and the Bottle; comprising Thrilling Examples of the opposite effects of Temperance and Intemperance. Edited by a Son of Temperance. *Hartford: Case, Tiffany & Co.* 1850. 8vo, Engr. Title, pp. 448. 18 Plates. 25278

Four Dissertations, on the Reciprocal Advantages of a Perpetual Union between Great-Britain and her American Colonies. Written for Mr. Sargent's Prize-Medal. To which, (by Desire) is Prefixed, An Eulogium, Spoken on the Delivery of the Medal at the Public Commencement in the College of Philadelphia, May 20th, 1766. *Philadelphia: printed by William and Thomas Bradford.* M,DCC,LXVI. 8vo, pp. x, viii, 12, (2), 112. + *London, Re-printed: T. Payne and D. Wilson.* [1766.] 8vo, pp. (2), x, viii, 12, (4), 112. BA., C. 25279

The successful essay is by John Morgan, M.D., F.R.S., etc., a professor in the college. No. 2 is by Stephen Watts, M.A. No. 3 is anonymous. No. 4 is by Francis Hopkinson, Esq. The eulogium is by Dr. W. Smith, provost of the college. *See* "M. Rev.," XXXVI. 24.

Four Essays on the Right and Propriety of Secession by Southern States. By a Member of the Bar of Richmond. *Richmond, Va.: Ritchie & Dunnavant, Printers.* 1861. 8vo, pp. 36.

The Four Gospels and the Acts of the Holy Apostles, Translated into the Malayan Tongue, by Thomas Hyde. *Oxford.* 1677. 4to. 25281

Dedicated to the "Hon. Robert Boyle, Esq. ... Governor of the Corporation for the Propagating of the Gospel and the Conversion of the American Natives in New England," at whose cost the translation was made; contains allusions to the labors of Mr. Eliot, and the progress of printing in New England.

The Four Kings | of | Canada. | Being | A Succinct Account of the | Four Indian Princes lately arriv'd | from North-America, | With | A particular Description of their Country, | their strange and remarkable Religion, Feasts, | Marriages, Burials, Remedies for their Sick, | Customs, Manners, Constitution, Habits, | Sports, War, Peace, Policy, Hunting, Fish- | ing, Utensils belonging to the Savages, with | several other Extraordinary Things worthy | Observation, as to the natural or curious | Productions, Beauty or Fertility of that | Part of the World. | ... *London,* | ... *John Baker* ... | 1710. | 12mo, pp. 47. 25282

The Four Indian Kings' Speech to Her Majesty on the 20th April, Translated into Verse by T. S., with their Effigies taken from the Life and Curiously Engraved by S. N. *London.* 1710.

One folio sheet, containing four portraits, and the speech underneath. Very rare. Here is a specimen of the poetry:

"Great Queen!
A tedious voyage from near Canada,
On that vast continent, America,
A voyage our predecessors ne'er did make,
Nor could prevailed with be to undertake," etc.

These Indian chiefs went to England with Colonel Schuyler of New York, and attracted great observation throughout the kingdom, giving rise to a paper in the "Spectator," No. 50. Dean Swift, in his letters to Stella, also makes reference to the subject. For other particulars, *see* Smith's "Hist. of New Jersey," p. 366, and "Proceedings of the New Jersey Hist. Soc.," IX. 16. The Antiquarian Society, at Worcester, has a set of their portraits.

Four Letters. *See* Adams (J.), Vol. I., No. 242, and [Shebbeare (John)].

Four Letters, from the London Weekly History of the Progress of the Gospel; with a large Postscript vindicating the late Revival and its Promoters. *Edinburgh.* 1743. pp. 64. 25284

Relates entirely to Mr. Whitefield and the affairs of Georgia.

Four Letters on Interesting Subjects. *Philadelphia: Printed by Styner and Cist.* MDCCLXXVI. 8vo, pp. 24. C., P. 25285

A Whig tract. Relates to the American Revolution.

Four Years at Yale. By a Graduate of '69. *New Haven: Charles C. Chatfield & Co.* 1871. 12mo, pp. xiv, 713. C.

Four Years' Residence in the West Indies, during the Years 1826, 7, 8, and 9. By the Son of a Military Officer. Third Edition, enlarged with Engravings. To which is now added A Faithful Narrative, Derived from Official Documents and Private Letters of the dreadful Hurricanes in Barbados, St Vincent, and St. Lucia in August, M.DCCC.XXXI. *London: William Kidd.* MDCCCXXXIII. 8vo, pp. xiii, 742. 25287

FOURNEL (H.) Coup-d'oeil historique et statistique sur le Texas. Par Henri Fournel. *Paris: Delloye.* 1841. 8vo, pp. 57. Map. 25288

FOURNIER (C.) Dénonciation aux États généraux, des vexations abus d'Authorité et déni de justice commis envers lui à Saint-Domingue. [n. p.] 1789. 25289

FOURNIER (Jules). Les Assurances au Canada. *Montréal.* 1865. 8vo, pp. 47. 25290

FOURNIER. Le Canada, son présent et son avenir; Politique et Finance. *Montréal.* 1865. pp. 14. 25291

FOURNIER (L. M.) Topographie, ou Description Succincte, Naturelle et Medicale de l'État de la Louisiane. Par L. M. Fournier. Prospectus. *Paris: Huzard.* 1826. 25292

See Rich, Vol. II. Probably never published.

FOURQUET-D'HACHETTE. Constitution des Etats-Unis d'Amérique, par G. Washington; dédiée au général Lafayette. *Paris: Boulland.* 1830. 8vo, pp. 32. 25293

Fourteen Months in American Bastiles. *Baltimore.* 1863. 8vo, pp. 89. 25294

The Fourth Book of "Washington Benevolents," otherwise called, the Book of Knaves. *Boston: Printed by N. Coverly.* 1814. 12mo, pp. 24. 25295

The War of 1812, written in Scripture style, with a curious dedication.

A Fourth Essay. *See* [Webster (P.)]

A Fourth Letter. *See* [Shebbeare (*Dr.* John)].

FOWLE (D.) A Total Eclipse of Liberty: being a True and Faithful Account of the Arraignment, and Examination of Daniel

Fowle before the Honourable House of Representatives of the Province of the Massachusetts Bay in New-England, Octob. 24th. 1754, barely on Suspicion of his being concern'd in Printing and Publishing a Pamphlet, intitled, the Monster of Monsters: Also, his Imprisonment and Sufferings in a Stinking Stone Goal, without the Liberty of Pen, Ink or Paper, and not allowed to see his Nearest Friends, nor to Write a Line to his Wife; with many other Incidents and Aggravations; which shews it to be Monstrous Treatment. Written by Himself. ... *Boston.* 1755. 12mo, pp. 32, Appendix, 24. BA., C. 25296

See the "Journal of Massachusetts Bay" for this year. *See also our* No. 17745.

FOWLE (R.) An Oration, delivered at Plymouth, in New-Hampshire ... July 4th, 1800. By Robert Fowle. ... *Concord: Printed by Geo. Hough.* 1800. 8vo, pp. 15. BA. 25297

FOWLE (W. B.) An Elementary Geography for Massachusetts Children. By William Bentley Fowle ... *Boston.* [18—.] 16mo, pp. 72. H. 25298

Also: Report of the Monitorial School, Boston. .. *Boston.* 1826.

FOWLER (A.) Discourse at Goshen in Lebanon, upon the Ordination of Rev. W. T. Stone. By Amos Fowler. 1768. 8vo. 25299

FOWLER (A.) *See* [Fowler (W. C.)]

FOWLER (A.) Sketch of the Life and Death of Miss Hannah Dyckman, King's Ferry. By Andrew Fowler. *Danbury.* 1795. 8vo. 25300

FOWLER (B.) An Oration on the Death of Mr. Ebenezer Grant Marsh, ... in Yale College, ... on the 10th of January, 1804. By Bancroft Fowler ... *Hartford: Printed by Hudson & Goodwin.* 1804. 8vo, pp. 13. BA., H. 25301

FOWLER (B.) Tableau Geographical, Commercial, Geological and Sanitary of New Orleans. By Bernard Fowler, M.D. *New Orleans: Delta Office.* 1854. 25302

Title from a manuscript note by Herman Ludewig.

[FOWLER (Daniel W.)] A Genealogical Memoir of the Descendants of Capt. William Fowler, of New Haven, Connecticut. ... *Milwaukee: Starr & Son.* 1870. 8vo, pp. 42. H.

FOWLER (G.), *Editor.* The Wandering Philanthropist; or, Letters from a Chinese. Written during his Residence in the United States. Discovered and Edited by George Fowler, of Virginia. *Philadelphia: Geo. Fowler and B. Graves.* 1810. pp. 300. BA., H. 25304

FOWLER (H.) The American Pulpit: Sketches, Biographical and Descriptive, of Living American Preachers, and of the Religious Movements and Distinctive Ideas which they represent. By Henry Fowler ... *New York: J. M. Fairchild & Co.* 1856. 8vo, pp. 515. 10 Portraits. 25305

FOWLER. Character and Death of Abraham Lincoln. A Discourse preached at Auburn, N. Y., April 23, 1865. By Rev. Henry Fowler. ... *Auburn, N. Y.: Wm. J. Moses.* 1865. 8vo, pp. 16. B. 25306

FOWLER. History of the Church of Christ in Auburn: A Discourse, Thanksgiving, 1867. *Auburn: C. P. Williams.* 1867. 8vo, pp. 38. 25307

FOWLER (James H.) A Sermon on the State of the Country, delivered in ... Savannah, Ga., on Fast Day, June 1st, 1865, by Chaplain J. H. Fowler. ... *Savannah, Ga.* 1865. 8vo, pp. 16.

[FOWLER (John).] A Summary Account of the Present Flourishing State of the respectable Colony of Tobago, in the British West Indies. Illustrated with a Map of the Island, and a Plan of its Settlement agreeably to the Sales by his Majesty's Commissioners. *London.* MDCCLXXIV. 8vo, pp. 80. Map and Plan. + *London: S. Hooper.* MDCCLXXVII. 8vo, pp. iv, 7–80.

FOWLER (J.) Journal of a Tour in the State of New York in the year 1830; with Remarks on Agriculture, in those Parts most Eligible for Settlers; and Return to England by the Western Islands, in Consequence of Shipwreck in the Robert Fulton. By John Fowler. *London: Whittaker, Treacher and Arnot.* 1831. 12mo, pp. (11), 333. C. 25310

FOWLER (J.) An Address on the Death of President Lincoln, delivered at the Request of the Citizens of New Rochelle, Westchester Co., N. Y. By John Fowler, Jr., ... April 20, 1865. ... *New York: John A. Gray & Green, Printers.* 1865. 8vo, pp. 28. 25311

FOWLER (M. F.) Protest or Remonstrance of M. Field Fowler, against Opening the Doors of the Public Library, Bos-

ton, on the Lord's Day. ... *Boston: Rockwell & Rollins.* 1867. 8vo, pp. 7. B., BA., H. 25312

FOWLER (*Mr.*) A General Account of the Calamities occasioned by the Late Tremendous Hurricanes and Earthquakes in the West-India Islands, Foreign as well as Domestic: With The Petitions to, and Resolutions of, the House of Commons, in Behalf of the Sufferers at Jamaica and Barbados. ... Carefully Collated from Authentic Papers. By Mr. Fowler. ... *London: J. Stockdale.* MDCCLXXXI. 8vo, 2 l., pp. 86, (1). H. 25313

See "M. Rev.," Feb., 1781. Some copies are dated 1791. Allibone attributes this to William Fowle, M.D., and quotes "Fevers in the West Indies, 1800." 8vo.

FOWLER (O.) An Historical Sketch of Fall River, from 1620 to the present time; with Notices of Freetown and Tiverton: in Three Discourses, delivered January 24, 1841. By Orin Fowler, A.M. ... *Fall River.* 1841. 8vo, pp. 64, (2).

FOWLER. History of Fall River, with Notices of Freetown and Tiverton, as Published in 1841. By Rev. Orin Fowler, A.M., Together with a Sketch of the Life of Rev. Orin Fowler; an Epitome of the Massachusetts and Rhode Island Boundary Question; an Account of the Great Fire of 1843: and Ecclesiastical, Manufacturing, and other Statistics. *Fall River: Almy & Milne.* 1862. 8vo, pp. 100. B., BA., H. 25315

Also: A Disquisition on the Evils of using Tobacco. ... Third Edition. *Boston: Geo. Gregory.* 1842. 8vo, pp. 27. BA. — Slavery in California and New Mexico. Speech ... in ... March 11, 1850. ... [n. p. n. d.] 8vo, pp. 15. B., BA., H., M. — Speech ... on the Legislation of Massachusetts, our Government, ... House of Representatives of the United States, ... March 31, 1852. [*Washington.* n. d.] 8vo, pp. 16. BA., H.

FOWLER (P. H.) National Destruction Threatens us; and Repentance of Sin and Reformation our only Hope of Escape. A Discourse delivered in Utica, New York, July 28, 1861. By P. H. Fowler, D.D. *Utica, (N. Y.): Roberts.* 1861. 8vo, pp. 16.

Also: Employers and the Employed; their Relation and Duties to each other. ... *Utica: Wm. S. Taylor.* 1865. 8vo, pp. 180.

FOWLER (R.) Hither and Thither; or, Sketches of Travels on Both Sides of the Atlantic: By Reginald Fowler, Esq., Barrister at Law. *London: F. R. Daldy.* 1854. 8vo, pp. viii, 272, Errata. S. 25317

FOWLER (R.) A Quaker's Sea-Journal: being a True Relation of a Voyage to New-England. Performed by Robert Fowler of the Town of Burlington, in Yorkshire, in the Year 1658.

London: Printed for Francis Cossinet, at the Anchor and Mariner, in Tower-street. Anno 1659. 4to, pp. 8. 25318

This relation is inserted in "Collectitia," page 313. 1824. 8vo.

FOWLER (S. M.) Letters, Addressed to Joel Mann, Pliny Merrick, Thomas H. Smith, Augustus B. Read, Seceding Masons. By Samuel M. Fowler, Editor of the Pawtucket Chronicle. To which is added Mr. Mann's Reply, and a rejoinder to the same. *Pawtucket.* 1830. 12mo, pp. 34. 25319

FOWLER (S. P.) An Account of the Life, Character, &c., of the Rev. Samuel Parris, ... and of his Connection with the Witchcraft Delusion of 1692. Read ... Nov'r 14, 1856. By Samuel P. Fowler. *Salem: Samuel P. Ives and George W. Pease.* 1857. 8vo, pp. 20. BA., H. 25320

See "Salem Witchcraft."

FOWLER (S. W.), *and* HOWELL (W. T.) Speeches (Michigan Legislature, February 10 and 13, 1863.) [n. p. n. d.] 8vo.

FOWLER (T.) The Journal of a Tour through British America to the Falls of Niagara. By Thomas Fowler. *Aberdeen.* 1832. 12mo. 25322

FOWLER (W.) *See* [Fowler (D. W.)], No. 25303.

FOWLER (W. C.) Conditions of Success in Genealogical Investigations, illustrated in the Character of Nathaniel Chauncey. ... By William Chauncey Fowler, LL.D. *Boston.* MDCCCLXVI. 8vo, pp. 28. H. 25323

[FOWLER.] A Genealogical Memoir of the Descendants of Ambrose Fowler of Windsor, and Capt. Wm. Fowler of New Haven, Connecticut. ... *Boston: H. W. Dutton & Son, Printers.* 1857. 8vo, pp. 27. 25324

FOWLER. History of Durham, Connecticut, from the First Grant of Land in 1662 to 1866. By William Chauncey Fowler, LL.D. ... With an Appendix. *Hartford: Wiley, Waterman & Eaton.* MDCCCLXVI. 8vo, pp. 144. B., BA., H. 25325

FOWLER. Local Law in Massachusetts and Connecticut, Historically Considered. By William Chauncey Fowler, LL.D. ... *Albany: Joel Munsell.* 1872. 8vo, pp. 104. B. 25326

FOWLER. Memorials of the Chaunceys, including President Chauncey, his Ancestors and Descendants. By William Chauncey Fowler. [With Appendix.] *Boston: Henry W. Dutton & Son, Printers.* M.DCCC.LVIII. 8vo, pp. vii–304. Portrait. B., BA., H.

F[OWLER]. Printed but not Published. 8vo, pp. 32. 25328

A tract relating to Webster's Dictionary.

FOWLER. The Sectional Controversy; or, Passages in the Political History of the United States, including the Causes of the War between the Sections. By William Chauncey Fowler, LL.D. *New York: Charles Scribner.* 1862. 8vo, pp. 269. B., BA., C., S. + Second Edition. *New York.* 1868. 8vo. 25329

FOWLER. William Fowler, the Magistrate, and One Line of his Descendants. By William Chauncey Fowler. [n. p. n. d.] 8vo, pp. 12. B. 25330

Also: The Clergy and Common Schools. Letter, republished from Barnard's American Journal of Education. *Hartford.* 1868. 8vo, pp. 224. — A Discourse, delivered at Montpelier, October 17, 1834, before the Vermont Colonization Society. ... *Middlebury: Knapp & Jewett, Printers.* 1834. 8vo, pp. 24–32. BA., H. — A Sermon ... at the Dedication of the South Congregational Church in Durham, Conn., December 29, 1847. ... *Amherst: J. S. and C. Adams.* MDCCCXLVIII. 8vo, pp. 67.

FOWLER (W. H.) Guide for Claimants of Deceased Soldiers; Being Instructions to Army Officers and to Claimants, with a Collation of the Laws of Congress and the Orders from the War Department, and the Rules of Practice in the Offices of the Second Auditor and Comptroller of the Treasury, concerning the Settlement of the Claims of Deceased Officers and Soldiers. By Col. W. H. Fowler, Superintendent Army Records and Agent to Adjust the Claims of Deceased Soldiers for the State of Alabama. Revised and approved By the Second Auditor and Comptroller of the Treasury, and adapted to General Use. *Richmond, Va.: Geo. P. Evans & Co., Printers.* 1864. 8vo, pp. 72. B., BA.

FOWLER (William W.) Ten Years in Wall Street; or, Revelations of Inside Life and Experience on 'Change. ... By Wm. Worthington Fowler. ... *Hartford, (Conn.): Worthington, Dustin & Co.* 1870. 8vo, pp. xx, 19–536. 15 Plates. B., C., H.

FOX (C.) A Portrait of George Washington, from an Original Drawing, as he appeared while Reviewing the Continental Army on Boston Common, in 1776; A History of the Portrait, and Documentary Evidence in Proof of the Correctness of the Likeness. By Charles Fox. ... *Boston: Crocker & Brewster.* 1851. 8vo, pp. 37. Portrait. B., BA. 25333

[FOX (Charles Barnard).] Record of the Service of the Fifty-Fifth Regiment of Massachusetts Volunteer Infantry. ... *Cambridge: John Wilson and Son.* 1868. 8vo, pp. (4), 144. B., BA.

FOX (C. J.) The Speech of the Right Honourable Charles James Fox on American Independence: spoken in the House of Commons on Tuesday, July 2, 1782. *London: M. Folingsby.* [1782.] 8vo, pp. viii, 27. 25335

"This speech was made in consequence of Sir George Saville making a motion to exclude the word 'America' from the Colonial Place Bill, then before the consideration of the House. His reasons were, that, in his opinion, unless the word was excluded, it would be a revival of the dispute which had been the cause of all the differences between Great Britain and America." — *Advertisement.*

FOX. The Speech of the Right Hon. Charles James Fox, on Tuesday the 9th Inst., in Defence of his Resignation. *London: J. Debrett.* 1782. 8vo, pp. 30. 25336

FOX. The Speech of the Right Honourable Charles James Fox, at a General Meeting of e Electors of Westminster, July 17, 1782, in which is accurately given the Reasons for Withdrawing himself from the Cabinet; also an Account of the whole Proceedings on that day. *London: J. Debrett.* [1782.] 8vo, pp. 36. 25337

Also: An Accurate Account of the Important Debate, in the House of Commons, July 9, 1782; in which the cause of Mr. Fox's Resignation, and the great question of American Independence came under Consideration. Second Edition. *London.* 1782. 8vo. P., S. — The Celebrated Speech of the Right Hon. C. Fox, at the Shakespeare Tavern, with two admired Songs. *London.* [n. d.] 8vo. — History of the Political Life and Public Services, as a Senator and a Statesman, of the Right Honourable Charles James Fox, One of his Majesty's Principal Secretaries of State. *London: J. Debrett.* 1783. 8vo. *See* "M. Rev.," LVIII. 391, and LXIX. 429.

FOX. A Letter to the Hon. Mr. Ch——s F—x, upon his proceedings in P——t, on that Memorable Day, Feb. 17, 1778. *London: Fielding and Walker.* 1778. 8vo. 25338

FOX. Letter in Defence of Mr. Fox and others; in answer to Cicero, Lucius Catiline, or the American Deputy. ... *London.* [1784?] 8vo, pp. 31. + Second Edition. *London: J. Debrett.* [1784.] 25339

See "M. Rev.," LVIII. 39, and LXVIII. 78.

FOX. The Life of Charles James Fox, with some Account of his Principal Contemporaries. *London.* 1807. 12mo. Portrs.

FOX, NORTH, *and* BURKE. The Beauties and Deformities of Fox, North and Burke, selected from their Speeches, from ... 1774, down to the Present Time. With a Copious Index to the Whole, and an Address to the Public. ... *London: J. Stockdale.* D,DCC,LXXXIV. 8vo, pp. viii, 92, (10). BA. + Second Edition. + [*Ibid.*] 8vo. + [*Ibid.*] 8vo, pp. x, 83, (12). 25341

Designed to show the insincerity of the coalition between them.

FOX (C. J.) History of the Old Township of Dunstable: including Nashua, Nashville, Hollis, Hudson, Litchfield, and Merrimac, N. H., Dunstable and Tyngsborough, Mass. By Charles J. Fox. *Nashua: Charles T. Gill.* 1846. 12mo, pp. xiv, 278. Plate. B., BA., C., H. 25342

See New Hampshire Book.

FOX (E.) The Adventures of Ebenezer Fox, in the Revolutionary War. ... *Boston: Charles Fox.* 1848. 24mo, pp. 240. Portraits and Plates. B., BA. 25343

FOX. The Revolutionary Adventures of Ebenezer Fox, of Roxbury, Massachusetts. *Boston: Munroe & Francis.* 1838. 8vo, pp. 238. Portrait. B., H. 25344

F[OX] (G.) An | Answer | To several New | Laws and Orders | Made by the | Rulers of Boston | in | New-England. | The Tenth Day of the Eighth | Moneth, 1677. | By G. F. | [*London.*] *Printed in the Year* 1678. | 4to, pp. 7. 25345

FOX. Cain against Abel, representing New-England's Church-Hierarchy, in Opposition to her Christian Protestant Dissenters. By George Fox. *Printed in the Year* 1675. 4to, pp. 48.

The preface is addressed "To the New England Professors, that hanged the servants of the Lord for Religion," etc.

FOX. A Collection of many Select and Christian Epistles, Letters and Testimonies, written on Sundry Occasions, by that Antient, Eminent, Faithful Friend, and Minister of Christ Jesus, George Fox. The Second Volume. *London: T. Sowle.* 1698. Folio, pp. 576. 25347

Forms Vols. VII. and VIII. of "The Works of George Fox." *Philadelphia.* 1831. Many of the epistles are addressed to persons in America.

FOX. An Epistle to all my dear Friends, Elect and Precious in America. [n. p. n. d.] Folio, 1 leaf. 25348

FOX. An Epistle to all Planters, and such who are transporting themselves into Foreign Plantations in America, &c. London, 22nd 9th month, 1681. *London: Ben. Clark.* 1682. Folio, pp. 2. 25349

FOX. An | Epistle | To all | Professors | in | New-England, Germany, and other | Parts of the called | Christian VVorld. | Also | To the Jews and Turks throughout the | World. | That they may see who are the True Worshippers of God, | that he seeks, and in what he is worshipped. | An Exhortation to them to read it over, that they may | see what they have all grieved, vext and quenched, and what | they have walked despightfully, and rebelled, and kickt, | and stopt their Ears, and closed their Eyes to; so that they | may all return again, and turn within, and see what they have | profest, and not possest; so that they may come to be the true Pos- | sessors of the Truth, and true Worshippers in the Spirit of the | True and Living God, who is a Spirit, which is the perfect | Worship, which Christ the Truth and perfect One set up | above 1600 Years since. | George Fox. | *[London.] Printed in the year* 1673. | 4to, pp. 16. B., C. 25350

Fox. Gospel Family-Order, being a Short Discourse concerning the Ordering of Families, both of Whites, Blacks, and Indians. By G. F. *Printed in the Year* 1674. 4to, pp. 23. + *Reprinted, [Philadelphia: by Reinier Jansen], in the Year* 1701. 4to, pp. 23. P. 25351

A tract of great rarity. Translated into French in 1684.

Fox. A Journal, or Historical Account of the Life, Travels, Sufferings, Christian Experiences, and Labour of Love, in the Work of the Ministry, of that Ancient, Eminent, and Faithful Servant of Jesus Christ, George Fox. Who Departed this Life in great Peace with the Lord the 13th of the 11th Month, 1690. *London: Thomas Northcott.* 1694. Folio, pp. 724. + [Second Edition.] *London: J. Sowle.* 1709. 2 vols., 8vo, pp. lxxii, 592; 580, Tables, 18 l. + The Third Edition. *London: Luke Hinde.* M.DCC.LXV. Folio, pp. lix, 679, 14 l. C. + *New York: Collins.* 1800. 2 vols., 8vo. + Fifth Edition, Corrected. *Philadelphia: Baw & Kite.* 1808. 2 vols., 8vo. + Reprinted from the First Edition. *London: Printed by W. Phillips.* 1827. 2 vols., 8vo, pp. (2), 506; 487. + Sixth Edition. *Leeds: Printed by Anthony Pickard.* 1836. 2 vols., 12mo. + *Philadelphia and New York.* 1831. 8vo. BA., C. + Seventh Edition, with Notes — Biographical and Historical, &c., by Wilson Armistead. *London: W. & F. G. Cash.* 1852. 2 vols., 8vo. 25352

"One of the most extraordinary and instructive narratives in the World." — Sir James Mackintosh.

Fox. Selections from the Epistles of George Fox. By Samuel Tuke. Second Edition, with Additions. *London.* 1848. 12mo.

Fox. Something in Answer to a Law lately made at the First Sessions of the General Court held at Boston in New-England May the 28th, 1679. And Published by their Order, Edw. Rawson, Secretary. [n. p. 1679.] 4to, pp. 20. 25354

[Fox.] Some thing in | Answer | to a Letter | (which I have seen) of John Leverat, Governour of Boston, | To | William Coddington Governour of Rode-Island, | Dated 1677 | wherever he mentions my Name, and also | wherein John Leverat justifies Roger Williams's | Book of Lyes. | [n. p. n. d.] 4to, pp. 11.

A reply to Williams' "George Fox Digged out of his Burrows." This tract is sometimes found at the end of "Cæsar's Due | Rendered unto Him ... | ... | By G. F. *Printed in the Year* 1679. |" 4to, pp. 35.

[Fox.] To Friends in Barbadoes, Virginia, | Maryland, New-England, and els- | where. | [n. p. n. d.] 4to, pp. 3. C. 25356

Dated "*London, 29th of the 9th Month,* 1666." Signed "G. F."

[Fox.] A | Vision | Concerning | The | Mischievous Separation | among | Friends | in | Old England. | *Printed and sold by Will. Bradford at Philadelphia.* 1692. | 4to, pp. 7. 25357

Fox. The Works of George Fox. *Philadelphia: Marcus T. C. Gould.* 1831. 8 vols., 8vo, pp. 437; 393; 616; 414; 455; 496; 350; 318. 25358

Fox. A Brief Memoir of the Life of George Fox, an eminent Minister in the Society of Friends. *Sunderland: Printed by Hewitt Burnett.* 1842. 12mo, pp. 60. 25359

Reprinted, with alterations, and entitled, "A Brief Memoir of the Life of George Fox, an eminent Instrument in the Divine Hand, in Gathering the Religious Society of Friends, ... *Sunderland: Printed by H. J. Dixon.* 1843. 12mo, pp. 60. Also in Danish.

Fox. A Brief Memoir of George Fox. *London.* 1856. 18mo, pp. 78. 25360

Fox. A Memoir of the Life, Travels and Gospel Labor of George Fox, an Eminent Minister of the Society of Friends. *London: Harvey and Darton.* 1839. 8vo, pp. 408. + *London: Edward Marsh.* 1850. 8vo, pp. 400. + *London.* 1865. 8vo. + *London.* 1867. 8vo. 25361

Also in "The Friends' Library," Vol. I. There are also translations into German and into Danish. *See also* "The Biographical Magazine" for July, 1853.

Fox. A Short Account of George Fox, prepared for Young Children. *Philadelphia: Uriah Hunt.* 1842. 25362

George Fox was the founder of the Society of Friends or Quakers. In the course of his public ministrations he visited America twice, where he spent two years. He was a voluminous writer. A list of his works fills no less than fifty-one pages in Smith's "Catalogue of Friends' Books." *London.* 1867. 2 vols., 8vo. Charles Lamb speaks highly of Fox's writings.

Fox (G.), *and* Burnyeat (J.) A New-England-Fire-Brand Quenched, being Something in Answer unto a Lying, Slanderous Book, Entituled; George Fox Digged out of his Burrows, &c. Printed at Boston in the Year 1676. of One Roger Williams of Providence in New-England. Which he dedicateth to the King, with Desires, That, if the Most-High please, Old and New-England may Flourish, when the Pope & Mahomet, Rome & Constantinople are in their Ashes. Of a Dispute upon XIV. of his Proposals held and debated betwixt him, the said Roger Williams, on the one Part, and John Stubs, William Edmundson and John Burnyeat, on the other. At Providence and Newport in Rode-Island, in the Year 1672. Where his Proposals are turn'd upon his own Head, and there he was and is sufficiently confvted. In Two Parts. As also, Something in Answer to R. W.'s Appendix, &c. With a Post-Script Confuting his Blasphemous Assertions, viz. Of the Blood of Christ, that was Shed, its being Corruptible and Corrupted; and that Salvation was by a Man, that was Corruptible, &c. Where-unto is added, A Catalogue of his Railery, Lies, Scorn & Blasphemies: And his Temporizing Spirit made manifest. Also, The Letters of W. Coddington of Rode-Island, and R. Scot of Providence in New-England, Concerning R. W. And Lastly, Some Testimonies of Antient & Modern Authors concerning the Light, Scriptvres, Rvle & the Sovl of Man. By George Fox and John Bvrnyeat. *Printed in the Year* M DC LXXVIII. 2 pts., 4to, 14 l., pp. 233; (1), 255, (1). BA. 25363

This was reissued with a new title-page, in which the following changes occur:

Fox *and* Burnyeat. A New-England-Fire-Brand Quenched, Being an Answer unto a Slanderous Book, Entituled; George Fox Digged out of his Burrows, &c. Printed at Boston in the Year 1676. by Roger Williams ... In which his Cavils are Refuted, & his Reflections Reproved. In Two Parts. ... *Printed in the Year* MDCLXXIX. 2 pts., 4to, 14 l., pp. 235; (2), 255.

[Fox *and others.*] Here is Declared The manner of the naming of Children in The Old Time, without a Priest sprinkling them with Water, which now is, and hath been in these times, yet they have the Scriptures, but shews their contrary walking to Scripture. Given forth by G. F. *London: Printed for Thomas Simmons.* 1658. 4to, pp. 30. 25365

Fox (G. T.) Memoir of the Rev. C. Colden Hoffman ... . By the Rev. George Townshend Fox, M.A. ... . *New York: A. D. F. Randolph.* 1868. 8vo, pp. xxiii, 365. Plates, Portrait, and Map. B. 25366

[Fox (H. R.)] An Inquiry into the State of the Nation at the Commencement of the Present Administration. *London: Longman.* 1806. 8vo, pp. (2), 219, xviii. + Third Edition. *[Ibid.]* + Fourth Edition. *[Ibid.]* S. 25367

Partly relates to the American colonies, trade, etc.

Fox (J.) Seizure of the Ship Industry, By a Conspiracy, And the Consequent Sufferings of Capt. James Fox and his Companions; Their Captivity Among the Esquimaux Indians in North America; and the Miraculous Escape of the Captain; The Disasters which attended the Mutineers, Interspersed with Anecdotes, Descriptions, &c. Also, the Providential Escape and Sufferings of Captain Boyce In the Year 1727. *London: Thomas Tegg.* [n. d.] 12mo, pp. 28. Folded Plate. 25368

Fox (J.) God by his Power causes the Earth and its Inhabitants to Tremble. The Substance of Two Sermons, on I. Sam. xiv. 15. Preached soon after the Earthquake, at Wobourn. By John Fox. *Boston.* 1728. 8vo, pp. (2), 58. BM. 25369

Fox. Time and the End of Time, In Two Discourses; The first about Redemption of Time; The second about Consideration of our Latter End. By John Fox. *Boston: Samuel Philips.* 1701. 8vo, pp. (2), 234, (1). B. 25370

Also: The Door of Heaven Opened and Shut. *Newport: R. I.* 1731. 12mo.

Fox (J.) Opinion of The Hon. John Fox ... against the exercise of Negro Suffrage in Pennsylvania. Also; The Vote of the Members of the Pennsylvania Convention, on the Motion of Mr. Martin to insert the word "White" as one of the proposed Amendments to the Constitution. *Harrisburg.* 1838. 12mo, pp. 15. 25371

Fox (J.) Trial of John Fox, for the Murder of John Henry, ... at New-Brunswick, N. J., May, 1856. ... *New-Brunswick.* 1856. 8vo. 25372

Fox (M.) The Love-Life of Dr. Kane; containing the Correspondence, and a History of the Acquaintance, Engagement, and Secret Marriage between Elisha K. Kane and Margaret Fox, with Fac-similes of Letters, and her Portrait. *New York: Carleton.* M DCCC LXVI. 16mo, pp. 288. BA. 25373

Fox (S. M.) The Important and Interesting Trial of Samuel M. Fox, Esq., Jonathan Smith, Esq., John C. Stocker, at the

Suit of Patrick Lyon, to recover Damages for False Imprisonment on a Charge of Robbing the Bank of Pennsylvania, in 1798. *Philadelphia.* 1799. 8vo, pp. 181. 25374

Fox (T.) The Wilmington Almanac or Ephemeris, &c. for the year ... 1774. By Thomas Fox. *Washington: Printed and sold by James Adams.* 12mo. Continued. 25375

Fox (T. B.) Memorial of Henry Ware Hall, Adjutant 51st Regiment Illinois Infantry Volunteers. An Address delivered in ... Dorchester ... July 17, 1864. By Thomas B. Fox. ... *Boston: Printed by John Wilson and Son.* 1864. 8vo, pp. 35.

Also: ... A Discourse, delivered at the Fourth Anniversary of the Warren Street Chapel, January 26, 1840. ... *Boston: Printed by Tuttle, Dennett & Chisholm.* 1840. 12mo, pp. 16. B., BA. — ... A Sermon ... at the Dedication of the Indian Street Congregational Church, ... December 12, 1847. ... *Boston: Wm. Crosby and H. P. Nichols.* 1847. 8vo, pp. 28. B., BA., H. — An Oration, delivered at the Request of the Washington Light Infantry Company, in Newburyport, Feb. 22, 1832: ... *Newburyport: J. B. and E. L. White.* 1832. 8vo, pp. 22. B., BA., H.

[Fox (William).] Address to the People of Great Britain on the Propriety of Abstaining from West India Sugur and Rum. *London.* 1791. 8vo. + Seventh Edition. *London.* 1791. 8vo. + Fourteenth Edition. *London.* 1791. 12mo. + Ninth Edition. *Boston.* 1792. 8vo. + A Second Address ... Second Edition. *London.* 1792. 8vo. 25378

Fox. Defence of the National Convention of France for Emancipating the Slaves in the West Indies. *London.* 8vo.

[Fox.] Summary View of the Evidence before the House of Commons, relating to the Slave Trade. *London.* 1792. 12mo.

Fox's Martyrs. An Entire New Work. A New Book of the Sufferings of the Faithful. *London: J. Whitaker.* M,DCC,-LXXXIV. 8vo, pp. (4), 70. 25381

Fox and Hoyt's Quadrennial Register of the Methodist Episcopal Church, and Universal Church Gazetteer. ... 1852–6. *Hartford.* 1852. 12mo, pp. 311. BA., H. 25382

Fox and Wisconsin Improvement Company. Exhibit of the Fox and Wisconsin Improvement Company ... . August 1, 1853. *New York: Printed by R. Craighead.* 1853. 8vo, pp. 32. Map. H. 25383

Report of the Fox and Wisconsin Improvement Company, Dec. 1856. *New-York.* 1857. 4to, pp. 17, xxiv. 25384

Foxcroft (F.) Transcript Pieces. By Frank Foxcroft. *North Adams (Mass.): J. T. Robinson & Co.* 1856. 18mo, pp. 92.

Foxcroft (T.) An Apology In Behalf of the Revd. Mr. Whitefield, offering a Fair Solution of Certain Difficulties, objected against some Parts of his Publick Conduct, ... as the said Objections are set forth in a Late Pamphlet, intituled, "A Letter to the Reverend Mr. George Whitefield, publickly calling upon him to vindicate his conduct or confess his faults." By Thomas Foxcroft, A.M. ... *Boston: Printed by Rogers and Fowle.* 1745. 4to, pp. 38. B. 25386

This elicited "A Letter, To the Reverend Mr. Foxcroft, Being an Examination of his Apology for the Rev. Mr. Whitefield. By A. C----d and J. J. C. *Boston.* 1745." 4to, pp. 18. Probably by the Rev. Aaron Cleveland.

Foxcroft. The Day of a Godly Man's Death, Better than the Day of his Birth, shewed in a Sermon, Feb. 25. 1722. *Boston, N. E.: B. Green.* 1722. 8vo, pp. (2), ii, 196, (1). B.

Paged continuously with this (pp. 46–126 and 127–191), but having separate titles, are his "Two Sermons shewing How to Begin," etc., and "The Duty of the Godly."

Foxcroft. The Divine Right of Deacons. A Sermon ... On occasion of the Ordination of Mr. Zachariah Thayer to the Office of a Deacon ... May 23. 1731. *Boston: D. Henchman and J. Phillips.* 1731. 8vo, pp. (4), 42, (1). B., BA., H. 25388

Foxcroft. The Duty of the Godly. *See* No. 25387, *supra.*

Foxcroft. The Earthquake a Divine Visitation. A Sermon Preached to the Old Church in Boston, Jan. 8th, 1756, Being a Day of Publick Humiliation and Prayer, upon Occasion of the Repeated Shock of an Earthquake upon this Continent. *Boston: S. Kneeland.* 1756. 8vo, pp. 51. M. 25389

Foxcroft. Eli the Priest Dying Suddenly. A Sermon Preach'd at the Thursday-Lecture in Boston, June 19. 1729. Upon Occasion of the Sudden Death of the Reverend Mr. John Williams, who died June 12th, In the 65th Year of his Age. And of the Reverend Mr. Thomas Blowers, who died June 17th In the 52d Year of his Age. By Thomas Foxcroft M.A. Pastor to the Old Church in Boston. *Boston, N. E.: Printed for S. Gerrish in Cornhil.* MDCCXXIX. 8vo, pp. (2), ii, 36, (5). B., BA., H. 25390

Foxcroft. Elisha Lamenting after the God of Elijah. A Funeral Sermon Preach'd at Boston, March 27, 1737. Occasion'd by the Death of the Reverend Mr. Benjamin Wadsworth ... . By Thomas Foxcroft. ... . *Boston: Samuel Eliot.* 1737. 8vo, pp. (2), vi, 69. B., BA., H., M. 25391

[Foxcroft.] Eusebius Inerамatus. Just Remarks On a late Book, Intitled, "Eleutherius Enervatus, Or an Answer to a Pamphlet, Intituled, The Divine Right of Presbyterian Ordination, &c. argued. Done by way of Dialogue between Eusebius and Eleutherius; together with two Letters on this Subject. By Phileluth. Bangor, V. E. B. ... *Boston: Printed for D. Henchman.* MDCCXXXIII. 8vo, pp. (2), 158 [156]. B., BA., H.

F[oxcroft]. A Funeral Sermon occasion'd by Several Mournful Deaths, and preach'd on the Decease of Mr. John Coney, ... who died, August 20. 1722. ... By T. F. ... . *Boston: Printed by B. Green.* 1722. 12mo, pp. (1), vii, 67. B., BA., H., M., W.

Foxcroft. God the Judge, putting down One, and setting up Another. A Sermon Upon ... the Death of our late Sovereign Lord King George, And the Accession of ... George, II. ... By Thomas Foxcroft, A.M. ... *Boston: S. Gerrish.* MDCCXXVII. 4to, pp. (4), iv, 39. BA., H. 25394

Foxcroft. Grateful Reflexions on the Signal Appearances of Divine Providences for Great Britain and its Colonies in America, which diffuse a General Joy. A Sermon preached in the Old Church in Boston, October 9, 1760. Being the Thanksgiving Day, On Occasion of the Surrender of Montreal, and the Complete Conquest of Canada, by the Blessing of Heaven on his Britannic Majesty's brave Troops, under the Auspicious Conduct of that truly Great and Amiable Commander, General Amherst. By Thomas Foxcroft, A.M. One of the Pastors of the said Church. ... *Boston, N. E.: S. Kneeland.* 1760. 8vo, pp. (4), 36. B., BA., H. 25395

Foxcroft. The Importance of Ministers being Men in Christ: ... A Sermon Preach'd at Milton, Nov. 13. 1728. Upon ... the Ordination of the Rev. Mr. John Taylor ... . By Thomas Foxcroft ... . *Boston: D. Henchman.* 1728. 8vo, pp. (4), 59. BA., H. 25396

Foxcroft. Lessons of Caution to Young Sinners. A Sermon Preach'd ... Sept. 23. 1733. Upon the Affecting Occasion

of an Unhappy Young Woman ... under Sentence of Death. By Thomas Foxcroft, M.A. ... With a Preface by Mr. Cooper, and Mr. Byles's Conference with the Prisoner. *Boston: Printed by S. Kneeland and T. Green.* MDCCXXXIII. 8vo, pp. (2), iv, 68, (4). BA., H. 25397

Foxcroft. Ministers, Spiritual Parents, or Fathers in the Church of God. A Sermon preach'd at the Ordination of the Rev. Mr. John Lowell, at Newbury, Jan. 19. 1725, 6. By Thomas Foxcroft, Pastor of a Church in Boston. ... *Boston: S. Gerrish.* 1726. 8vo, pp. (2), 60. BA., H. 25398

Foxcroft. Observations, Historical and Practical, on the Rise and Primitive State of New-England. With a Special Reference to The Old or first gather'd Church in Boston. A Sermon, preach'd ... Aug. 23. 1730. Being the last Sabbath of the First Century, since its Settlement. By Thomas Foxcroft, M.A. ... *Boston: S. Gerrish.* M DCC XXX. 8vo, pp. (6), 46. BA.

A valuable tract, compiled from original sources.

Foxcroft. The Pleas of the Gospel-Impenitents Examin'd & Refuted. In Two Sermons At The Thursday-Lecture In Boston. On Febr. 5. & April 23. 1730. By Thomas Foxcroft, Pastor to the Old Church. Publish'd by Desire of some of the Hearers. *Boston: Printed by S. Kneeland, and T. Green, for S. Gerrish, in Cornhil.* 1730. 16mo, pp. (4), 76. S. 25400

Foxcroft. A Practical Discourse Relating to the Gospel-Ministry. Preach'd by Thomas Foxcroft, A.M. At His Ordination to the Office of Pastor of a Church in Boston, on Wednesday, November 20. 1717. Published and Enlarged at the Urgent Request of a Gentleman of his Auditory. With a Preface by the Reverend Mr. Benjamin Wadsworth, Pastor of the said Church. *Boston: Printed for Nicholas Buttolph, at his Shop at the lower end of Corn-Hill.* 1718. Sm. 8vo, pp. (2), iv, 65, Errata.

[Foxcroft.] The Ruling & Ordaining Power of Congregational Bishops, or Presbyters, Defended. Being Remarks on some Part of Mr. P. Barclay's Persuasive, lately distributed in New-England. By an Impartial Hand. In a Letter to a Friend. *Boston: Printed for Samuel Gerrish and Sold at his Shop near the Brick Meeting-House in Cornhill.* 1724. 8vo, pp. (2), 45. BA.

This is to be considered as an appendix to E. Wigglesworth's "Sober Remarks," and is so called in a note to the publisher's address in the second edition of that work. *See also* Foxcroft's Vindication, No. 25407.

FOXCROFT. A Seasonable Memento for New-Year's Day. A Sermon at the Old Church Lecture ... January 1. 1746, 7. ... By Thomas Foxcroft, A.M. ... *Boston: S. Kneeland and T. Green.* 1747. 8vo, pp. 76. B., BA., H. 25403

FOXCROFT. Sermon at Cambridge, After the Funeral of Mrs. Elizabeth Foxcroft. With an Addition, referring to Her Death. Also a Funeral Poem of the Reverend John Danforth. *Boston.* 1721. 8vo, pp. (4), iv, 55. B. 25404

FOXCROFT. Some Seasonable Thoughts on Evangelic Preaching; its Nature, Usefulness, and Obligation. A Sermon ... in Boston, ... Oct 23. 1740. ... Occasion'd By the late Visit, ... of the Rev. Mr. Whitefield. ... By James Foxcroft. ... *Boston: S. Eliot.* 1740. 4to, pp. (4), 47. B., BA., H., M., W. 25405

FOXCROFT. Survivors Inquiring after the God of their Pious Predecessors. Sermon occasioned by the Death of Rev. Benjamin Wadsworth, 1737. *Boston.* 1737. 8vo, pp. 68 or 69. B.

FOXCROFT. Two Sermons. *See* The Day, etc., No. 25387.

FOXCROFT. A Vindication of the Appendix to the Sober Remarks. A Reply to the Defence of the Modest Proof. *Boston.* MDCCXXV. 8vo, pp. (4), 59. 25407

See above, The Ruling & Ordaining Power, No. 25402, *supra*.

FOXCROFT. The Voice of the Lord, From The Deep Places of the Earth. A Sermon ... in Boston, in the Audience of the General Court, at the Opening of the Sessions, Nov. 23. 1727. ... By Thomas Foxcroft. ... *Boston: S. Gerrish.* MDCCXXVII. 8vo, pp. (4), 52. BA., H. 25408

Also: The Blessings of a Soul in Health, and prospering to be supremely wish'd for. A Sermon deliver'd (in Part) at a Family-Meeting in Private, Boston, Mar. 3. 1741, 2. ... *Boston: Printed and sold by S. Kneeland and T. Green.* 1742. 8vo, pp. (4), 52. B., BA., H. — A Brief Display of Mordecai's Character. In a Sermon ... after the Funeral of the Honourable Penn Townsend, Esq. ... *Boston: S. Gerrish.* 1727. 8vo, pp. (4), 42. B., BA., M., W. — The Character of Anna, the Prophetess. A Sermon after the Funeral of Dame Bridget Usher. With a Preface by the Reverend Mr. Wadsworth. *Boston: S. Kneeland.* MDCCXXIII. 8vo, pp. (4), iii, (1), 62. BA. — Cleansing our Way in Youth Press'd ... And Observing the Word of God Recommended. ... A Discourse ... *Boston: S. Gerrish.* 1719. 8vo, pp. (8), 192. H. — Death the Destroyer of Earthly and False Hopes, under the Divine Dominion. A Sermon ... January 30. 1725. ... *Boston: Samuel Gerrish.* 1726. 12mo, pp. (2), 25. BA. — A Discourse concerning Kindness. ... A Sermon ... in Boston, ... Febr. 28th. 1719, 20. ... *Boston: S. Gerrish.* 1720. 8vo, pp. (2), 364. BA., H. — A Discourse preparatory To the Choice of a Minister. ... The Substance of two Sermons, ... June 11. 1727. ... *Boston: Samuel Gerrish.* 1727. 8vo, pp. (2), 67. B., BA., H., W. — Divine Providence Ador'd Justify'd, in the Early Death of God's Children Servants. A Sermon ... on the Day of the Interment of the Reverend Mr. William Waldron ... *Boston: S. Gerrish and S. Kneeland.* 1727. 8vo, pp. (2), 20, 47. B., BA., H., M. — *Edinburgh.* 1746. 8vo. — God's Face set against an Incorrigible People. A Sermon, ... July 30. 1724. ... *Boston: John Eliot.* 1724. 8vo, pp. (2), v, (1), 50. BA., H. — Humillis Confessio: The Saints united Confession, in Disparagement of their own Righteousness. A Sermon, ... Jan. 30. 1749, 50. ... *Boston.* MDCCL. 8vo, pp. (4), 64. B., BA., H. — Like Precious Faith obtained, ... by all the True Servants of Christ. A Sermon, preached ... at the Old-Church Lecture, in Boston ... March 25th. 1756. ... *Boston, New-England: Green & Russell.* M,DCC,LVI. 8vo, pp. (2), 36. B., BA., C., H.

FOXBOROUGH. The Covenant, Doctrinal Articles and Articles of Discipline; adopted by the Church, in Foxborough, March 2, A.D. 1820. *Providence: Printed by Miller & Hutchens.* 1820. 12mo, pp. 15. 25409

FOXE (L.) North-VVest Fox, | or, | Fox from the North-west passage. | Beginning | VVith King Arthvr, Malga, Octhvr, | the two Zeni's of Iseland, Estotiland, and Dorgia; | Following with briefe Abstracts of the Voyages of Cabot, | Frobisher, Davis, Waymouth, Knight, Hudson, Button, Gib- | bons, Bylot, Baffin, Hawkridge: Together with the | Courses, Distances, Latitudes, Longitudes, Variations, | Depths of Seas, Sets of Tydes, Currents, Races, | and over-Falls; vvith other Observations, Accidents | and remarkable things, as our Miseries and | sufferings | Mr. Iames Hall's three Voyages to Groynland, with a | Topographicall description of the Countries, the Salvages | lives and Treacheries, how our Men have been slayne | by them there, with the Commodities of all those | parts; whereby the Merchant may have Trade, and | the Mariner Imployment. | Demonstrated in a Polar Card, wherein are all the Maines, Seas, | and Islands, herein mentioned. | With the Author his owne Voyage, being the XVIth. | with the opinions and Collections of the most famous Ma- | thematicians, and Cosmographers; with a Probabilitie to | prove the same by Marine Remonstrations, compa- | red by the Ebbing and Flovving of the Sea, experimented | vvith places of our ovvn Coast. | By Captaine Lvke Foxe of Kingstone vpon Hull, Capt. | and Pylot for the Voyage, in his Majesties Pinnace | the Charles. | Printed by his Majesties Command. | *London,* | *Printed by B. Alsop and Tho. Favvcet, dwelling in Grubstreet.* | 1635. | 4to, Plate of a Sphere 1 l, 5 l., pp. 269, (3). Map. H. 25410

After page 168 are two leaves paged 170, 172, 170, and blank, which are said to be cancelled leaves. There are several other errors in the pagination. After page 79 the next is page 100, and the *hiatus* is not supplied; the other errors are corrected by duplication; signature Bb is incorrectly paged 225–232 instead of 205–212. This

very rare collection of early voyages towards making a discovery of the North-West Passage, contains many important facts and judicious observations on the ice, tides, compass, northern lights, etc. Fox started on this expedition on the 28th April, 1631, and the result of his exploration is related in this very rare volume. The map is often deficient, or supplied by a facsimile. A perfect copy is worth over a hundred dollars.

FRACASTORIUS (Hieronymus). Opera omnia, in unum collecta. *Venetiis: apud Juntas.* 1754. 4to. 25411

"Dans le poème sur la Siphylis on trouve plusieurs passages relatifs à l'Amérique." — TROSS.

Foyer Canadien. *See* Vol. III., No. 10455.

[FRACKER (George).] A Voyage to South America, with an Account of a shipwreck in the River La Plata, in the Year 1817. By the Sole Survivor. *Boston: Printed by Ingraham and Hewes.* 1826. 12mo, pp. 128. H. 25412

Fragment. *See* [Carey (M.)], Vol. III., No. 10889, *note.*

A Fragment of the Chronicles of Nathan Ben Saddi; A Rabbi of the Jews. Lately discovered in the Ruins of Herculaneum: And Translated from the Original, into the Italian Language. By the Command of the King of the Two-Sicilies. And now first publish'd in English. *Constantinople: Printed, in the Year of the Vulgar Æra,* 5707. 8vo. P. 25413

By *Jews*, are meant Quakers; *Adonis* is Joseph Galloway; *Daniel* is Mr. Roberdeau. It is said to be by Robert Dodsley.

Fragment of an Essay towards the most Ancient Histories of the Old and New World [in blank verse]. *London.* 1765. 8vo.

Fragment of a Journal of a Sentimental Philosopher, during his Residence in the City of New-York ... . *New-York.* 1809. 8vo, pp. 38. S., W. 25415

A Fragment on Government; being an Examination of what is delivered on the subject of Government in general, in the Introduction to Sir William Blackstone's Commentaries: with a Preface, in which is given a Critique on the work at large. *London.* 1776. 8vo, pp. (2), lvii, 208. 25416

Included in a list of Americana made by Horace Rodd.

Fragments of the History of Bawldfredonia. *See* [Clopper (J.)], Vol. IV., No. 13770.

Fragments on the Confederation of the American States. *Philadelphia.* 1787. 12mo, pp. 22. P. 25417

FRAGOSO (J.) Aromatvm, | frvctvvm, et sim- | plicivm Aliqvot Medi- | camentorvm Ex India Vtraqve, | et Orientali et Occidentali, in Europam | delatorum, quorum iam vsus pluri- | mus, Historia brevis, vti- | lis, et iucunda. | Conscripta primvm | Hispanice A Ioanne Fragoso | Philippi II. Hispan. Regis Me- | dico et Chirurgo. | Nvnc latine edita ope- | ra Ac Stvdio Israelis Spachii | Med. D. & Prof. Argentinensis cum | Notis marginalibus atque | Indice. | Plura indicat ad Lectorem | Præfatio. | *Argentinæ* | *Excudebat Iodocvs Martinvs.* | *Anno* M. DC. | 8vo, 8 l., 115 l., 1 l.

This is a Latin translation of the

FRAGOSO. Discursos de las cosas aromaticas, arboles y frutales y de otras muchas medicinas simples, que se traen de la India oriental y sirven al uso de medicina. *Madrid: Francisco Sanchez.* 1572. Folio, pp. 8, 211. 25418*a*

See Pritzel's "Thesaurus literaturæ botanicæ."

FRALEY (F.) National Board of Trade. An Address delivered at St. Louis, December 6, 1871. By Frederick Fraley ... . *Boston: Barker, Cutter & Co.* 1872. 8vo, pp. 8. H. 25419

[FRAME (*Miss* Eliza).] Descriptive Sketches of Nova Scotia. By a Nova Scotian. *Halifax.* 1864. 12mo, pp. 250. 25420

FRAME (R.) A Short Description of Pennsilvania, By Richard Frame. *Philadelphia: Printed by W. Bradford.* 1692. 4to, pp. 16. P. 25421

Reprinted in 1869 in facsimile, from the supposed unique copy in the Philadelphia Library, with an introduction by Horatio Gates Jones, Esq. Sm. 4to, pp. 16. Edition, 118 copies, of which 16 are on large paper.

FRAMINGHAM, *Mass.* *See* [Ballard (W.)], Vol. I., No. 2958.

Annual Report of the Financial Affairs of the Town of Framingham, 1864–5. *Framingham: Asa W. Kingsbury.* 1865. 8vo, pp. 22. Continued. 25422

Reports of the Treasurer for the Years 1854–55. *Framingham.* 1855. 8vo. S. 25423

Report of the School Committee of the Town of Framingham, for the Year 1853–54. *Boston: T. R. Marvin.* 1854. 8vo, pp. 64. Continued. H. 25424

FRAMPTON (J.), *Translator.* *See* Monardes (Nicolo).

FRANÇA (E. F.) Brasilien und Deutschland. Ein offener Brief an die Redactionen der deutschen Tagespresse. *Leipzig:* 1858. 8vo, pp. 39. 25425

FRANÇA. Chrestomathia da lingua Brazilica. *Leipzig: F. A. Brockhaus.* 1859. 12mo, pp. xviii, 230. 25426

FRANCA (L. de). Compendio da Geographia da Provincia do Paraná. Adaptado ao ensino da mocidade brazileira, e acompanhado de cento e trienta notas instructivas por Luiz de Franca Almeida e Sá. *Rio de Janeiro.* 1871. 16mo, pp. 88. 25427

France and Mexico. Examination of the Difficulties between those Powers. By a Citizen of the United States. 1839. 8vo.

La France, le Mexico, et les États Confédéres. *Paris.* 1863. 8vo, pp. 42. 25429

Also: Message of the President ... on our Relations with France, including the Debates in the French Chambers, Jan. 1836. *Washington.* 8vo.

FRANCFORT (E.) The Simsbury Copper Mine. A Report on the Mines of the Connecticut Copper Company, in Granby, Hartford County, Connecticut. By Dr. E. Francfort. *Hartford.* 1857. 8vo, pp. 19. 25430

Also: Report of the Mines of the Chatham Cobalt Mining Company. *Middletown.* 1853. 8vo, pp. 22.

FRANCHÈRE (G.) Relation d'un Voyage à la Côte du Nord-Ouest de l'Amérique Septentrionale dans les années 1810–1814. Par Gabriel Franchère. [Redigé par Michel Bibaud.] *Montréal.* 1820. 8vo, pp. 284. 25431

FRANCHÈRE. Narrative of a Voyage to the North West Coast of America, in the Years 1811, 1812, 1813, and 1814; or the First American Settlement on the Pacific. By Gabriel Franchère. Translated and Edited by J. V. Huntington. *Redfield: New York.* 1854. 12mo, pp. 376. Plate. B., BA., H. + Second Edition. [*Ibid.*] 25432

The author was one of the party sent out by Mr. Asher, and this work is the basis of Washington Irving's "Astoria."

FRANCIA (T.) A Narrative of Facts connected with the change effected in the Political Condition and Relations of Paraguay under the Directions of Dr. Thomas Francia. *London.* 1826. 8vo. 25433

FRANCILLON (J.) Description of a Rare Scarabæus, from Potosi, in South America; with Engraved Representations of the same, Coloured from Nature. By John Francillon. *London: Printed by C. Whittington.* 1795. 4to, pp. (4). Plate. 25434

FRANCIS. La Letera | Mandata dal R. Padre frate Francesco da Bo | logna, da Lindia, ouer noua Spagna: & dalla | Cittã di Mexico al. R. P. frate Clemẽte da Mo | nelia, Ministro della Prouincia di Bologna, | & ã tutti li Venerãdi padri di essa prouin | cia Tradotta in vulgare da vno frate | dil prefato ordine de minori d' osser | uanza. Doue si narra la moltitu- | dine de la persone che sono cõ | uertite & che si conuertano | alla fede, & il grande pre | sente che li hanno mã | dato al nostro Papa | Paulo terzo, la qualita dell' aere di detto mon | do nouo, la grãdezza del paese, l'oro, l'argẽto, | e pietre preciose, la bõta delle acque, i costumi | del vino, di monti, boschi, animali, & grã | de abondantia di formento, & altri | grani, La qualitã de gli huomi | ni & dõne, gli essercitii, la | fede, la ruina de loro | Idoli, & modi | che tenea | no prima, & altre infinite cose piace | uole da intendere. | [Colophon:] *In Venetia per Paulo Danza.* | [1534.] 4to, 7 unnumbered l., 1 l. blank. 25435

Ternaux published a French translation of this interesting letter. *See* Harrisse's "Bibl. Am. Vet.," p. 307.

FRANCIS (B.) Elegy by Benjamin Francis. [1771.] Folio, 1 leaf. 25436

On George Whitefield.

FRANCIS (C.) A Discourse Delivered at Plymouth, Mass., Dec. 22, 1832, in Commemoration of the Landing of the Fathers. By Convers Francis, ... *Plymouth: Printed By Allen Danforth.* 1832. 8vo, pp. 56. B., BA., H. 25437

FRANCIS. An Historical Sketch of Watertown, in Massachusetts, from the First Settlement of the Town to the Close of its Second Century. By Convers Francis ... . *Cambridge: E. W. Metcalf and Company.* M DCCC XXX. 8vo, pp. 151. B., BA., H.

FRANCIS. Life of John Eliot, the Apostle to the Indians. By Convers Francis. *Boston: Hilliard, Gray, and Co.* 1831. 12mo, pp. (2), xii, (2), 357. B. + [*Ibid.*] 1836. 25439

Forms Vol. v. of Sparks' "Library of American Biography." Dr. F. also wrote the "Life of Sebastian Rale," in v. 17, and general memoirs in the "Mass. Hist. Soc.'s Collections."

FRANCIS. Three Discourses preached before the Congregational Society in Watertown: two, upon leaving the Old Meeting-House; and one, at the Dedication of the New. By Convers Francis, Pastor of the Congregational Society in Watertown. *Cambridge: Folsom, Wells, and Thurston, Printers.* 1836. 8vo, pp. 79, (1). B., BA., H. 25440

Also: An Address delivered on the Fourth of July, 1828, at Watertown. ... *Cambridge: Hilliard and Brown.* 1828. 8vo, pp. 23. B., H. — The Death of the Aged. A Discourse preached ... in Concord, ... September 26, 1841, ... Funeral of their late Senior Pastor, Rev. Ezra Ripley, D.D. ... *Boston: James Munroe and Company.* 1841. 8vo, pp. (2), 43. B., H. — The Dust to Earth, the Spirit to God. A Discourse delivered ... in Watertown, ... March 17, 1833. ... *Boston: I. R. Butts.* 1833. 8vo, pp. 16. BA. — Errors in Education: A Discourse, delivered at the Anniversary of the Derby Academy, in Hingham, May 21, 1828. ... *Hingham: Farmer & Brown.* 1828. 8vo, pp. 36. B., BA. + Second Edition. *Boston.* 1828. 8vo, pp. 36. B. — Memoir of Rev. John Allyn, of Duxbury. [n. p. n. d.] 8vo, pp. 8. B. — Memoir of Hon. John Davis, LL.D. ... *Cambridge: Metcalf and Company.* 1848. 8vo, pp. 20. BA. — A Sermon ... at the Ordination of the Rev. Benjamin Kent, ... Duxbury, June 1, 1826. ... *Cambridge: Printed by Hilliard and Metcalf.* 1826. 8vo, pp. 42. H. — A Sermon ... at the Ordination of the Rev. Samuel Stearns, ... Northampton, Nov. 9, 1831. ... *Northampton: T. W. Shepard.* 1831. 8vo, pp. 36. H. — A Sermon on the Inscription over the Entrance to Mount Auburn, 17th March, 1833. *Boston.* 8vo.

FRANCIS (C. S.) *See* New York City.

FRANCIS (J. B.) Lowell Hydraulic Experiments ... . Made at Lowell, Massachusetts. By James B. Francis, Civil Engineer ... *Boston: Little, Brown & Company.* 1855. 4to, pp. xi, 156. 15 Plates. BA. + Second Edition, Revised and Enlarged, ... *New York: D. Van Nostrand.* 1868. 4to, pp. xi, 251. 23 Plates. B. 25441

FRANCIS (J. W.) An Address delivered on the Anniversary of the Philolexian Society of Columbia College, May 15, 1831. By John W. Francis, M.D. *New York: G. & C. & H. Carvill.* M,DCCC,XXXI. 8vo, pp. 43. B., H. 25442

On the life and character of Chancellor Livingston.

[FRANCIS.] Historical Sketch of the College of Physicians and Surgeons of the University of the State of New York. *New York.* 1813. 8vo, pp. 52. 25443

FRANCIS. A Memorial of the Life and Character of J. W. Francis, Jr. *New York.* 1856. 8vo. Portrait. 25444

FRANCIS. New York during the last Half Century: A Discourse in Commemoration of the Fifty-Third Anniversary of the New York Historical Society, and of the Dedication of their New Edifice (November 17, 1857). By John W. Francis, M.D. ... *New York: John F. Trow.* 1857. 8vo, pp. 232, 27.

FRANCIS. Old New York; or, Reminiscences of the Past Sixty Years, being an Enlarged and Revised Edition of the Anniversary Discourse delivered before the New York Historical Society, (November 17, 1857). By John W. Francis, M.D., ... *New York: Charles Roe.* 1858. 12mo, pp. 384. B., BA., H.

FRANCIS. Old New York: or, Reminiscences of the Past Sixty Years. By John W. Francis, M.D., LL.D. With a Memoir of the Author, by Henry T. Tuckerman. *New York: W. J. Widdleton.* MDCCCLXV. 12mo, pp. cxxxvi, 400. 2 Portraits and 1 Plate. 25447

One hundred copies printed on large paper, in imp. 8vo. Reissued with a new title-page only in 1866.

FRANCIS. Reminiscences of Samuel Latham Mitchell, M.D., LL.D. By John W. Francis, M.D., ... *New York: John F. Trow.* 1859. 8vo, pp. 31. H. 25448

Also: An Address delivered before the New-York Horticultural Society, ... on the Eighth of September, 1829. ... *New York: Printed by E. Conrad.* 1830. 8vo, pp. 31. H. — Anniversary Discourse before the New-York Academy of Medicine. ... November 10th, 1847. ... *New-York: printed by Henry Ludwig.* 1847. 8vo, pp. 112. H. — A Discourse: ... Opening of the New Hall of the New-York Lyceum of Natural History. [Dec. 28, 1836.] ... *New-York: H. Ludwig, Printer.* M DCCC XLI. 8vo, pp. 93. H. — Inaugural Discourse before the New York Academy of Medicine on the Election of Professor Mott ... 1849. 8vo, pp. 8. — Observations on the Mineral Waters of Avon, Livingston County, N. Y. ... *New York.* 1834. 8vo, pp. 36.

FRANCIS (*Miss* L. M.) *See* [Child (L. M.)], Vol. IV.

FRANCIS (P.) Proceedings in the House of Commons, on the Slave Trade, and the State of Negroes in the West India Islands. With an Appendix. By Philip Francis, Esq. *London: J. Ridgway.* 1796. 8vo, pp. 106. N. 25449

See "M. R.," XXI. 218.

FRANCIS (S. W.) Biographical Sketches of Distinguished New York Surgeons. By Samuel W. Francis, A.M., M.D., etc. *New York: J. Bradburn.* 1866. 12mo, pp. 220. Portrait. + *New York: G. P. Putnam & Son.* 1867. 16mo, pp. 28. C.

[FRANCIS.] "Inside Out;" a Curious Book. By a Singular Man. *New York: Miller, Mathews & Clasback.* 1862. 16mo, 4 l., pp. 364. C., H. 25451

FRANCIS. Memoir of the Life and Character of Prof. Valentine Mott, Facile Princeps. By Dr. Samuel W. Francis, ... *New York.* 1865. + Second Edition. *New York: W. J. Widdleton.* 1865. Rl. 8vo, pp. 32. Portrait. 25452

FRANCIS (V. M.) The Fight for the Union. A Poem. By Valentine Mott Francis, M.D. *New York: John F. Trow.* 1863. 8vo, pp. 14. H. 25453

FRANCIS (—), *and* HALEY (Thomas). Trotting Record for 1869. Containing a Complete and Reliable Record of all the Trotting Events of the past season, Compiled and Arranged with great care. *New York.* 1870. 12mo, 2 l., pp. 142. 25454

Francis Berrian. *See* [Flint (T.)], No. 24787.

Francis, Lord Bacon: or, the Case of Private and National Corruption, and Bribery, Impartially Consider'd. Address'd to all South-Sea Directors, Members of Parliament, Members of State, and Church Dignitaries. By an Englishman. ... Seventh Edition. *London: J. Roberts.* MDCCXXI. 8vo, pp. xvi, 62.

Francis Tamo; the Indian Girl; and other Poems. By a Colonist of New Brunswick. [n. p. n. d.?] 12mo. 25456

FRANCISCIA (Julia). Letter to General Andrew Jackson. *Philadelphia.* 1831. 8vo, pp. 24. 25557

FRANCISCO DE SAN JOSEPH. Historia universal de la primitiva, y milagroso imagen de Nuestra Señora de Guadalupe etc. Refierense las historias de las plausibles imagenes de N. S. de Guadalupe de Mexico, la del Valle de Pacasmayo en el Peru, la de la Ciudad de la Plata ... la de Potosi, y se toca la milagrosisima imagen de la Ciudad del Cuzco. *Madrid: A. Marin.* 1738. Folio, 28 l., pp. 332. + [*Ibid.*] 1743. 25458

FRANCISCO DE P. SANTANDER. El vicepresidente de Colombia da cuenta a la Republica de su conducta en la negociacion, i manèjo del emprestito de 1824. *Bogota.* 1828. Sm. 4to, pp. 118.

FRANCISCUS (E.) Acerra exoticorum oder historisches Rauchfass darinnen mancherley fremde Fälle und Geschichte nebens andern Erzählungen etc. an Weihrauch statt gestreuet und auss Sina Cochinchina America etc. zusammengesucht. *Franckfurt: Schiele.* 1672. 8vo, 224 sheets. 25460

FRANCISCUS. Erasmi Francisci | Guineischer und Americanischer | Blumen-Busch: | Welcher | Einen ergetzlichen Geruch man- | cherley mercklicher Eigenschafften, wun- | derlicher Thiere, Vögel, Fische, fremder Wei- | sen, Sitten, Gebräuche selbiger Länder; u. a. m. | imgleichen aller Könige in Peru und Mexico Ge- | schichten und denckwürdigen Verrichtungen | von sich streuet. | Nebenst beygedrucktem Anhang | der, hiebey zugleich neu-auffgelegten, | Michael Hemmersams sel. Guineisch- und | West-Indianischen Reisebe- | schreibung. | *Nürnberg, In Verlegung Paul Fürstens,* | *Kunst- und Buchh. seel Wittib und Erben.* | *Gedruckt daselbst bey Christoph Gerhard,* | *Anno* M. DC. LXIX. | 18mo, Engraved Title, 3 l., pp. 399, (9), 110, 13 l. 23 Plates. C.

This work is divided into two parts. The first is the "Bouquet of Flowers," by Erasmus Franciscus. The second is the voyage of Michael Hemmersam to Brazil, by Christoph Ludwig Diether.

FRANCISCUS. Neu-polirter Geschichte- kunst- und Sittenspiegel ausländischer Völcker, der Sineser Japaner, Indostaner, Javaner, Malabarer, Peruaner, Mexicaner, Brassilianer, Guineer, etc. In Sechs Büchern. *Nürnberg: J. A. Endter.* 1670. Folio, 15 l., pp. 1550, 15 l. 52 Plates. 25462

The materials for this "newly polished mirror" are gathered from a whole library of voyages and travels. The notice of American matters are not together in one place, but are here and there throughout the volume. They form more than a hundred pages. Many of the engravings illustrate American subjects.

FRANCISCUS. Ost-und West-Indischer so wie auch Sinesischer Lust-und Stats-Garten, mit einem Vorgespräch von mancherley lustigen Discursen; In Drey Haupt-Theile unterschieden. ... *Nürnberg: Johann Andreæ Endter.* M. DC. LXVIII. Folio, 19 l., pp. 1762, 36. Plates. BA. 25463

Divided into three parts: the first and second containing the natural history of the West and East Indias, with an account of all the fabulous creatures, monstrosities, etc., which were said to live there. The third part treats at large of the various aboriginal people of America and the East Indies, their government, manners, and institutions, with many very curious details. "Orné de figures; ce n'est qu'une compilation sans intérêt." — TERNAUX.

FRANCISCUS. See-Helden, Admiralen und Land Erfinder unserer Zeiten, etc. *Hamburg.* 1681. 4to. Map and Plates. + *Nürnberg: J. A. Endter.* 1681. Folio, 187 sheets. 25464

This rare book contains a life of Columbus, Vesputius, De Reuter, etc., and many documents respecting the surrender of New Netherland or New York, to the English.

FRANCISCUS. De Orbis | sitv ac descriptione, ad re | uerendiss. D. archiepiscopum Panormitanum, | Francisci, Monachi ordinis Frãciscani, epistola sane quã luculenta. In qua | Ptolemæi, cæterorumq*ue*; supe | riorũ geographorum hal | lucinatio refellitur. | aliaq*ue*; præterea | de recens | inuen | tis | terris, mari, insulis. Deditione papæ Ioannis De situ | Paradisi, & dimensione miliarum ad pro | portionẽ graduum cœli, præclara | & memoratu digna recen | sentur | [Colophon:] *Excvdebat Martinvs Cae- | sar, expensis honesti viri Rolandi Bollaert, com- | morantis Antuerpiæ iuxta portam Ca- | merẽ sub intersignio maio- | ris falconis albi.* | [1524.] 12mo, 15 leaves. B., J.C.B. 25465

On the verso of the title-page is a map; on the recto of the following leaf another map. It relates to the dominions of Prester John. The edition mentioned by Laire is 12mo, printed by Withagius, and numbers nineteen leaves. *See* "Bibliotheca Browniana," p. 40, No. 145.

FRANCK (A.) Catalogue de livres, manuscrits et cartes relatifs a l'Amérique en vente ... à la Librairie A. Franck. *Paris.* [n. d.] 8vo. 25466

FRANCK (R.) A Philosophical Treatise of the Original and Production of Things. Writ in America in a Time of Solitudes. By R. Franck. *London: Printed by John Gain.* 1687. 12mo, 13 l., pp. 170. 25467

A very scarce and singular work. The only copy I have seen belonged to Mr. J. C. Brevoort. Joseph Lilly priced it at £2 12s. 6d.

FRANCK (S.) Weltbŭch: spiegel | vnbildenisz des gantzen | erdtbodens von Sebastiano Franco | Wördẽsi in vier bücher nemlich in Asi- | am Aphricã Europam vnd Americã gstelt vnd abteilt Auch aller dariñ be- | griffner Lãnder nation Prouintzẽ vnd Inseln gelegenheit grösse weite ge | wächsz eygenschafft vnd der darinn gelegener völcker vnd einwoner nam | men gestalt leben wesen religion glauben ceremonien gsatz regimẽt | pollicey sitten brauch krieg gewerb frŭcht thier kleidung vñ ver | enderung eygentlich für die augen gestelt Auch etwas võ new | gefundenen welten vnd Inseln nitt ausz Berosa Joanne | de monte villa S. Brandons Histori vñ dergleichen | fabeln sund ausz angenumnen glaubwirdigen | erfarnẽ weltschreibern mŭselig zŭ hauff tra | gẽ vñ ausz vilen weitleŭffigen bŭchern in | ein handebŭch engeleibt vnd ver- | fasst vormals dergleichen | in Teŭtch nie ausz- | gangen. | Mit einem zŭ end augehenckten Register alles innhaltes. | ... | *Anno* M.D.XXXIIII. | [Verso of folio ccxxxvij:] *Getruckt zŭ Tübingen durch Ulrich Morhart im tausent funff* | *hundert vier vnd dreyssigten jar.* | Folio, 6 unnumbered l., iii–ccxxxvii, 7 unnumbered l. C.

The account of America begins on folio ccx. Concerning this, *see* Bayle's "Dictionary," and Harrisse's "Bib. Am. Vet.," p. 325. First edition of the "Weltbuch." The description of America comprises fifty-four pages.

FRANCK. Weltbŭch spie- | gel und bildtnis des gan- | tzen Erdtbodens von Sebastiano | Franco Wördensi inn vier bŭcher | nämlich in Asiam Aphricam Eu- | ropam und Americam gestelt und abteylt auch aller dariñ begriffner län | der nation Prouintzen und Inseln gelegenheyt grösse weitte gewächs eygenschafft. | ... [*Frankfort?*] MDXLII. Folio, 5 unnumbered l., l. numbered iii–ccxxxvii, 7 unnumbered l. J.C.B. 25469

"This edition is *not* merely a reissue of the original, with a fresh title, as Harrisse asserts, but is entirely a new setting-up of the text." — B. QUARITCH's *Catalogue*. The alterations are slight, however. *See* Harrisse's "Bibl. Am. Vet.," No. 238.

FRANCK. Wereltboeck, Spieghel ende Beletenisse des gheheelen Aertbodems ... te weten Asia, Aphrica, Europa ende America. Oock wat van Nieugheuonden Werelden ende Eylanden, niet wt Berosa, Joa. de Monte Villa ... ende dierghelijcke fabulen, maer uit gheloofweerdighe Wereltbeschrijvers te

samen ghedraghen. [*Amsterdam.* 1558.] Folio. + [*Amsterdam?*] *Ghedruckt int Jaer* 1562. Folio, 198 l., Tables, 9 l.

The first Dutch translation. The fourth book, pp. 44, relates to America. The edition dated 1562 is an exact reprint of the one printed in 1558. There is another edition, *Amsterdam: Corn. Claesz.* 1595. Folio.

FRANCK. Erst theil dieses Welt- | buchs, von Newen | erfundnen Landt- | schafften. | Warhafftige Be- | schreibunge aller | theil der Welt, darinn nicht allein etli- | che alte Landtschafften, Königreich, Prouintzen, Insulen, auch | fürnehme Stedt vnd Märckte (so denn allen Weltbeschreibern bekant seind) mit | fleisz beschrieben werden, sondern auch sehr viel neuwe, so zu vnsern zeiten, zu Wasser, | durch vil sorgliche vnd vormals vngebrauchte Schiffarten, erfunden seyn, welche im andern, disem nachfolgen- | den Buch von Schiffarten geñant, ausz rechtem grundt der Cosmography vnd Geometry erfunden, augezigt | werden. Deszgleichen auch etwas von New gefundenen Welten, vnd aller darinn gelegnen Völcker, jhrer Reli- | gion vnd Glaubens sachen, jhren Regiment, Pollicey, Gewerb, handtierung vnd andern gebruchen | mehr, etc. ausz etlichen glaubwirdigen (fürnehmer Scribenten) Büchern, mit | grosser mühe vnd arbeyt, etc. | Durch Sebastian Franck von Wörd, zum ersten an tag | geben, jetzt aber mit sondern fleisz auff ein neuwes vbersehen, | vnd in ein wolgeformtes Handt- | buch vefasset. *Anno.* M.D.LXVII. | Folio, 6 l., pp. ccxlii, 8 l., one blank l.; followed by "Ander Theil," etc., 4 l., one blank l., pp. 110, 59, (1). 25471

A large portion of this volume relates to America. The second part of the volume, with separate title, consists of Ulric Smith's "Indian Voyages," which was afterwards printed as a distinct volume.

FRANCK. Warhaftige Beschreibung aller und mancherley sorgfeltigen Schiffarten, auch viler unbekanten erfundenen Landtschafften, Insulen, etc. Auch von mancherley gefahr, Streytt und Scharmuzeln so sich zu Wasser und Land zugetragen. Item von Straubingen. [Hans Staden von Homburg's Reise, etc.] *Francfurt: Sig. Feyrabend.* 1567. 2 vols., folio, 6 l., pp. ccxliii, 7 l.; 5 l., pp. 110, 59, (1). C. 25472

FRANCK. Werelt-Spiegel, Beschryvinge des gehelen Aertbodems, met sijn vier gedeelten, Europa, Asia, Africa, America, etc. Verbetert en vermeerd ... door J. Phocylides Holwarda. *Bolswart: S. v. Haringhouck.* 1649. 4to. 25473

"The corrections and additions of Holwarda are placed at the end of the description of each part of the world. Those to America fill four pages. Holwarda speaks here somewhat disdainfully of Frank's geographical notions of America. He calls them perfectly confused, and we must agree with him on seeing that in the description of America, Frank inserts an account of Senegambia, Cap-Verde, etc." — MULLER.

FRANCKE (A. H.) Vita Franckii: Cui adjecta est, Narratio Rerum Memorabilium in Ecclesiis Evangelicis per Germaniam &c. Revisa, et, Cura Samuelis Mather, Edita. *Bostoni.* MDCCXXXIII. 8vo, pp. (4), iv, 31, 11, (1). B. 25474

Francke's life, begun by himself, is concluded by Michael Alberti, who is also the author of the "Narratio."

FRANCKEAN EVANGELIC LUTHERAN SYNOD. Journal of the Annual Session of the Franckean Evangelic Lutheran Synod, 1837. *Albany.* 1837. 8vo. Continued. 25475

FRANCKENBERG (H.) Versuch einer Darstellung der politischen Verhältnisse der la Plata Staaten, und besonders der Republik Uruguay; mit Rücksicht auf eine Kolonisation derselben. Von Hans von Franckenberg. *Buenos Ayres.* 1866. 8vo, pp. 176.

The first book in German printed in Buenos Ayres.

FRANCKLIN (T.) A Sermon Preached before the Honourable Trustees For Establishing the Colony of Georgia in America, and the Associates of the late Rev. Dr. Bray, at their Anniversary Meeting, March 16, 1749–50. ... By Thomas Francklin, M.A. *London: R. Francklin.* MDCCL. 4to, pp. 20. 25477

FRANCKLYN (G.) An Answer to the Rev. Mr. Clarkson's Essay on the Slavery and Commerce of the Human Species, particularly the African, ... In Letters, from a Gentleman in Jamaica, to his Friend in London; Wherein many of the Mistakes and Misrepresentations of Mr. Clarkson are pointed out, both with Regard to the Manner in which that Commerce is carried on in Africa, and the Treatment of the Slaves in the West Indies. Shewing, at the Same Time, the Antiquity, Universality, and Lawfulness of Slavery, as ever having been one of the States and Conditions of Mankind. By Gilbert Francklyn, Esq. ... *London: J. Walter.* M.DCC.LXXXIX. 8vo, pp. xvi, 263. BA., H.

FRANCKLYN. Observations, Occasioned by the Attempts made in England to effect the Abolition of the Slave Trade; shewing, the manner in which Negroes are treated in the British Colonies in the West-Indies: And also, some Particular Remarks on a Letter addressed to the ... Society for effecting such Abolition, from the Rev. Robert Boucher Nicholls. By G. Francklyn, Esq. ... *Kingston, Jamaica: Printed. London: Reprinted, J. Walker.* M.DCC.LXXXIX. 8vo, pp. xx, 87. C., H. 25479

Some copies have no date. *See* "M. Rev.," LXXXI. 91, 92.

FRANCO (A.) Alegato de defensa en favor de los Srs. Esteves, que ante un consejo de guerra de Oficiales del ejercito de los

Estados-Unidos del Norte pronunció el dia 14 de Febrero de 1848. *Toluca.* 1848. 4to, pp. 19. 25480

FRANCO (A. *and* J.) Manifesto de la Justicia de D. Abraham y Jacob Franco, Comerciantes de la Ciudad de Londres en el Pleyto que tienen pendiente en Sala de Justicia del Supremo Consejo de las Indias de Vista con les herederos de Don Jos. Aguerre Acharan y otros. *Madrid.* 1777. Folio. 25481

Respecting the transportation of the negroes of Guinea to Buenos Ayres.

FRANCO (Bernardo de Sousa). Os Bancos do Brazil, e sua Historia. *Rio de Janeiro.* 1848. 8vo. 25482

FRANCO (Francisco Soares). Ensaio sobre os melhoramentos de Portugal e Brasil. *Lisboa: na Imp. Reg.* 1820. 4to, pp. 32.

FRANCO (Harry). Bankrupt Stories. By Henry Franco. Second Edition. *New York.* 1844. 8vo. 25484

By Charles F. Briggs. The stories relate, in part, to New York city.

Frank; or, Who's the Croaker? *New York.* 1820. 25485

FRANKENSTEIN (J.) American Art: Its Awful Altitude. A Satire. By John Frankenstein. *Cincinnati: The Author.* 186–. 16mo, pp. 112. 25486

FRANKENSTEIN (Jacob August). Gedancken über das Emigrations-Recht. wegen der Religion, bey Gelegenheit der Saltzburgischen Protestanten. *Leipzig.* 1734. 4to, pp. 60. 25487

Frankfort Literary Society. First Anniversary. *Ilion, N. Y.* 1857. 8vo, pp. 24. 25488

FRANKLIN (A. W.) American Cottage Library; ... Containing ... Statistics of the United States, ... Edited by A. W. Franklin. *New York: Burgess, Stringer & Co.* 1848. 8vo, pp. (2), 190. 4 Plates. B. 25489

END OF VOLUME SIX.

A DICTIONARY OF BOOKS

RELATING TO AMERICA.

RANKLIN (Benjamin).] An Account of the New Invented Pennsylvanian Fire-Places; Wherein their Construction and Manner of Operation is particularly explained; Their Advantage above every other Method of Warming Rooms obviated. With Directions for putting them up, and for Using them to the best Advantage. And a Copper-Plate, in which the several Parts of the Machine are exactly laid down, from a scale of equal Parts. *Philadelphia: Printed and Sold by B. Franklin.* 1744. 8vo, pp. 37. Folded Plate. P. 25490

This is doubtless the Franklin Stove, invented (?) by Franklin, and the pamphlet is probably written by him. Frequently reprinted in Europe and America. *See* Sparks' Franklin, VI. 34.

[FRANKLIN.] An Appeal, 1775. *See* Vol. I., No. 1783.

FRANKLIN. Autobiography of Benjamin Franklin, Published by W. T. Franklin. Edited by Jared Sparks. *London: H. G. Bohn.* 1850. 12mo, pp. vi, 154. 25491

Of another edition of this there was a Dutch translation published at the Hague in 1828, 12mo.

FRANKLIN. Autobiography of Benjamin Franklin. Edited from his Manuscript, with Notes and an Introduction. By John Bigelow. *Philadelphia: J. B. Lippincott & Co.* 1868. 12mo, pp. 410. Portrait. H. 25492

One hundred copies printed on large paper, imp. 8vo.

FRANKLIN. Benjamin Franklin, his Autobiography, with a Narrative of his Public Life and Services, by Rev. H. Hastings Weld. *New York: Harper & Brothers.* [1848.] 8vo, pp. xvi, (2), 549. B. 25493

First issued in monthly parts. Frequently reprinted; the last, *New York.* 1859.

[FRANKLIN.] A Brief History. *See* Vol. II., No. 7876.

FRANKLIN. A Collection of the Familiar Letters and Miscellaneous Papers of Benjamin Franklin; now for the first time Published. *Boston: Charles Bowen.* 1833. 12mo, pp. xvi, 295.

Issued at the same time in *London* as Familiar Letters. *See* No. 25507, *infra.*

FRANKLIN. The Complete Works, in Philosophy, Politics, and Morals, of the late Dr. Benjamin Franklin, now first Collected and Arranged; With Memoirs of his Early Life, written by Himself. *London: J. Johnson.* 1806. 3 vols., 8vo, pp. xiv, (1), 440, 18 l.; pp. vi, (1), 468; (2), vi, 562. 12 Plates. BA.

[FRANKLIN.] Continuation, 1761. *See* No. 25588.

[FRANKLIN.] Cool Thoughts on the Present Situation of our Public Affairs, In a Letter to a Friend in the Country. *Philadelphia: Printed by W. Dunlap.* M,DCC,LXIV. 8vo, pp. 22. S.

FRANKLIN. Correspondance inédite et secrète du Docteur B. Franklin, Ministre Plénipotentiaire des États-Unis d'Amérique près la Cour de France. Depuis l'année 1753 jusqu'en 1790; offrant, en trois parties complètes et bien distinctes, 1° les mémoires de sa vie privée; 2° les causes premières de la révolution d'Amérique; 3° l'histoire des diverses négociations entre l'Angleterre, la France et les États-Unis. Publiée, pour la première fois, en France, avec des notes, additions, etc. *Paris.* M. DCCC.-XVII. 2 vols., 8vo. Portrait. [*Ibid.*] 1827. 25497

[FRANKLIN.] A | Dissertation | on | Liberty and Necessity, | Pleasure and Pain. | *London:* | *Printed in the Year* MDCCXXV. | 8vo, pp. 32. 25498

So rare, that in Puttick's catalogue 1860, it is said to be "unique. This is the long-lost and much sought-for *wicked* tract of the youth, Benjamin Franklin. It eluded even the research of Mr. Sparks, who ransacked European and American libraries for it, and says" (Vol. VIII., p. 405), "No copy of this tract is now known to be in existence." Franklin, in his autobiography, says, "I printed a small number. It occasioned my being more considered by Mr. Palmer as a young man of some ingenuity, though he seriously expostulated with me upon the principles of my pamphlet." In a letter to his friend Benjamin Vaughan, he wrote, "There were only a hundred copies printed, of which I gave a few to friends; and afterwards ... burnt the rest, except one copy, ... I was not nineteen years of age when it was written. In 1730, I wrote a piece on the other side of the question. ... This pamphlet was never printed." *See* "Notes and Queries," Jan. 3, 1852, from which it appears it was reprinted in sixteen pages. It has never been reprinted in any of the editions of Dr. Franklin's works. It is priced in the Nuggets, No. 1098, at £10 10s. Twenty-five copies were reprinted, in facsimile, by Charles Whittingham, for Henry Stevens, of London, about 1854.

[FRANKLIN.] An Essay on the African Slave Trade. *Philadelphia: Printed by Daniel Humphreys.* M.DCC.XC. 8vo, pp. 15.

FRANKLIN. Essays Humourous, Moral and Literary. By Benjamin Franklin. *Boston.* 1811. 12mo, pp. 182, (2). + *London.* [n. d.] 18mo, pp. 144. 25500

Frequently reprinted in America and England. Also translated into French, *Paris.* 1867. 16mo.

FRANKLIN. The Examination of Doctor Benjamin Franklin, before an August Assembly, relating to the Repeal of the Stamp-Act, &c. [n. p. 1766.] 8vo, pp. 16. P. 25501

No title-page; probably printed at Philadelphia. Another edition, also without date or place, has 23 pages, 8vo. It was reprinted in London as

FRANKLIN. The | Examination | of | Doctor Benjamin Franklin, | Relative to the | Repeal | of the | American Stamp Act, | in MDCCLXVI. *London,* MDCCLXVII. | 8vo, pp. (2), 50. BA., H.

Mr. Rich quotes this title with the words, "before an Honourable Assembly." This edition we have not seen. *See* Sparks' Franklin, IV. 199, and "M. Rev.," XXXVII. 73.

FRANKLIN. Die Verhörung Doctor Benjamin Franklin's vor der Hohen Versammlung des Hauses der Gemeinen von Groszbrittannien, die Stämpel-Act, &c. betreffend. *Philadelphia: Gedruckt bey S. Miller.* 1766. 8vo, pp. 43. P. 25503

A German translation of the preceding.

FRANKLIN. Interrogatoire de Mr Franklin Deputé de Pensilvanie au Parlement de la Grande Bretagne. Traduit de l'Anglois par Ch .... D. H .... Maitre de la langue Angloise à Strasbourg. Prix 24 sols. [Colophon:] *A Strasbourg: de l'Imprimerie de Simon Kürsner.* [n. d.] Avec Approbation. 8vo, pp. 35. C. 25504

FRANKLIN. Experiments and Observations on Electricity made at Philadelphia, in America, By Mr. Benjamin Franklin, Esq. *London: E. Cave.* 1751. 4to. Plates. 25505

For the second and third editions, *see* New Experiments, No. 25559, *infra.*

FRANKLIN. Experiments and Observations on Electricity, made at Philadelphia in America, by Benjamin Franklin, LL.D. and F.R.S. To which are added, Letters and Papers on Philosophical Subjects. The Whole Corrected, Methodized and Improved, and now first collected into one Volume, And Illustrated with Copper-Plates. [Fourth Edition.] *London: Printea for David Henry.* MDCCLXIX. 4to, pp. (iii), 496, (16). 7 Plates. C., H. + The Fifth Edition. *London: J. Newbery.* M.DCC.-LXXIV. 4to, pp. (2), vi, 514, (16). 7 Plates. 25506

FRANKLIN. Familiar Letters and Miscellaneous Papers of Benjamin Franklin; now for the first time Published. Edited by Jared Sparks. ... With Explanatory Notes. *London: Jackson and Walford.* 1833. Cr. 8vo, pp. xvi, 295. B. 25507

See "N. Am. Rev.," XXXVII. 249, and our No. 25494, *supra.*

FRANKLIN. Father Abraham's Speech To a Great Number of People, at a Vendue of Merchant-Goods; Introduced to the Public by Poor Richard, A Famous Pennsylvania Conjurer, and Almanack-Maker, In Answer to the following Questions; Pray, Father Abraham, what think you of the Times? Won't these heavy Taxes quite ruin the Country? How shall we be ever able to pay them? What would you advise us to? To which are added, several curious Pieces of Writing. *Dedham: Printed by H. Mann, for Wm. Tileston Clapp, Boston.* 1807. 12mo, pp. 24. H. + *New London.* [n. d.] + *New Haven.* [n. d.] 12mo, pp. 16. 25508

There are many other editions of this popular piece.

[FRANKLIN.] A few Reasons in favour of Vendues. [*Printed by B. Franklin and D. Hall.* About 1772.] Folio, 1 l. P.

FRANKLIN. Franklin before the Privy Council, Whitehall Chapel, London, 1774, on behalf of the Province of Massachusetts, to Advocate the Removal of Hutchinson and Oliver. *Philadelphia: John M. Butler.* 1859. 8vo, pp. v, 134. Plate.

Privately printed, and scarce.

FRANKLIN. Franklin's Letters to his Kinsfolk, Written during the Years 1818, '19 & '20, from Edinburgh, London, the Highlands of Scotland, and Ireland. *Philadelphia: J. Maxwell.* 1822. 2 vols., 18mo, pp. ——; 200. 25511

[FRANKLIN.] An Historical Review of the Constitution and Government of Pennsylvania, From its Origin; So far as regards

the several Points of Controversy, which have, from Time to Time, arisen between the several Governors of that Province, and Their several Assemblies. Founded on Authentic Documents. ... *London: R. Griffiths.* MDCCLIX. 8vo, pp. viii, 9 l., pp. 444. 25512

Generally attributed to Franklin, but perhaps by his son William. "It has recently been ascertained, however, that he was not, in fact, the author, although it was written under his direction, and doubtless from copious material furnished by him." — SPARKS' *Franklin,* III. 109. *See also* "M. Rev.," XXI. 367. Mr. Rice's copy is printed on very thick paper, and is perhaps unique. The editor of the following edition apparently had no doubt as to the authorship:

FRANKLIN. An Historical Review of Pennsylvania, From its Origin, Embracing, among other subjects, the Various Points of Controversy which have arisen, from time to time, between the several Governors and the Assemblies. Founded on Authentic Documents. By Benjamin Franklin, LL.D. [Originally Published in London.] *Philadelphia: Published by E. Olmsted and W. Power.* 1812. 8vo, pp. xv–xxxvi, 431. C. 25513

Forms Vol. II. of the edition of Franklin's Works, in 6 vols. Some copies have the imprint, *Philadelphia: W. Duane.* 1808.

FRANKLIN. Information for those who would remove to America. By Dr. Benjamin Franklin. *London: M. Gurney.* 1794. 8vo, pp. 23. + *London.* 1796. 4to. H. 25514

Sparks says it was first published in England in 1784, and afterward 1787, included in Dilly's edition of Franklin's Works. *See* Sparks' Franklin, II. 453.

FRANKLIN. Bericht für Diejenigen so sich nach Nordamerika begehen wollen: aus dem Englischen. *Hamburg: Herold.* 1786. 8vo. 25515

[FRANKLIN.] Interest of Great Britain, 1760. *See* [Jackson (Richard)].

FRANKLIN. Internal State of America. Being a True Description of the Interest and Policy of that vast Continent. *London.* 1784. 8vo. 25516

I have never seen this pamphlet, and infer the title from Sparks' Franklin, II. 453, where it is said to be reprinted in Dilly's edition of Franklin's Works, in 1787.

FRANKLIN. Jugenbjahre, von ihm selbst beschrieben und aus dem Englischen übersetzt von G. U. Bürger. *Berlin: Rottmann.* 1792. 8vo. 25517

FRANKLIN. Kleine Schriften meist in der Manier de Zuschauers nebst seinem Leben. Aus dem Englischen von G.

Schatz. Mit Franklins doppelten Bildnitze. *Weimar: Im Verlage des Industrie Comptoirs.* 1794. 2 vols., 8vo, 7 l., pp. 352; 428. 2 Portraits of Franklin. + [*Ibid.*] 1802. + *Weimar: Industrie Comptoir.* 1802. 2 vols., 8vo. Portrait. + *Rotweil.* 1822. 8vo. 25520

FRANKLIN. Leben und Schriften. Aus dem Englischen übersetzt. *Weimar.* 1818. 2 vols., 8vo. 25521

Forms Vols. III. and IV. of Franklin's works in German.

[FRANKLIN.] Die Lautere Wahrheit, oder ernsliche Betrachtung des gegenwärtigen Zustandes der Stadt Philadelphia, und der Provintz Pensylvanien. Von einem Handwercksmann in Philadelphia. Aus dem Englischen übersetzt durch J. Crell. [*Philadelphia:*] *Gedrucht, und zu finden bey Gotthard Armbrüster.* 8vo, pp. 20. 25422

Title in German text. A translation of Plain Truth. *See* No. 25563, *infra.*

FRANKLIN. Leben und Schriften, nach der von seinem Enkel W. T. Franklin, veranstalten neuen London. Ausgabe mit Benutzung des bei derselben bekannt gemachten nachlasses und früherer Quellen zeitgemass bearbeitet von A. Binzer. *Kiel.* 1829. 4 vols., 12mo. 25523

FRANKLIN. Leben des Benjamin Franklin, von ihm selbst beschrieben. *Leipzig: Geo. Wigand.* 1839. 16mo. (Geschichtsbibliothek fur's Volk, 3 Bd.) 25524

FRANKLIN. Leben und Ausgewählte Schriften ... . *Leipzig: G. Wigand.* 1838. 16mo. 25525

FRANKLIN. A Letter from Benjamin Franklin to a Gentleman in New Jersey, dated Philadelphia, June 6th, 1753. *Nottingham* [*England.* n. d.] Folio, 1 l. 25526

[FRANKLIN.] A Letter to a Friend in the Country, Containing the Substance of a Sermon Preached at Philadelphia, in the Congregation of The Rev. Mr. Hemphill, concerning the Terms of Christian and Ministerial Communion. *Printed and sold by B. Franklin: Philadelphia.* 1735. 25527

See Sparks' "Life of Franklin," p. 125.

[FRANKLIN?] Letters | between | Theophilus and Eugenio, | on the | Moral Pravity of Man, | and the | Means of His Restoration. | Wrote in the East-Indies, | And now First Published from

the Original Manuscript. | *Philadelphia:* | *Printed and Sold by B. Franklin.* | MDCCXLVII. | 4to, pp. iv, 64. 25528

Very rare. This is attributed to Franklin, on the authority of an auction sale catalogue.

FRANKLIN. Letters and Essays. *London.* 1820. 8vo. A.

Also many other editions.

FRANKLIN. The Life and Essays of Dr. Franklin. *London: T. Kinnersly.* [n. d.] 2 vols., 12mo, Engraved Title, pp. vi, 471. + *New York.* 1807. 12mo. + *London.* 1816. 8vo. + *New York.* 1858. 12mo, pp. 375. 25530

Reprinted as Life and Essays, Humorous, Moral and Literary. *Dublin.* 1793. 8vo. Portrait. + Third Edition. *London.* 1800. 2 vols., 8vo; and afterwards in numerous forms.

FRANKLIN. The Life of Benjamin Franklin, LL.D. *Printed and sold by George Nicholson, Poughnell, near Ludlow.* [n. d.] 12mo, Engraved Title, pp. 56. Portrait. 25531

FRANKLIN. The Life of Dr. Benjamin Franklin. Written by Himself. Second American Edition. *Philadelphia: Benjamin Johnson.* 1794. 16mo, pp. 197. + Third American Edition. *New-York: T. and J. Swords.* 1794. 16mo, pp. 214. Portrait. + *Salem: Cushing and Carleton.* 1796. 16mo, pp. 132. C. + *Albany.* 1797. 16mo. + *Montpelier, Vt.* [n. d.] 16mo. + *Montpelier: printed by Samuel Goss, for Joseph Parks.* 1809. 16mo. + *New-York: Printed by Clayton & Van Norden.* 1824. 16mo. + [*Ibid.*] 1825. W. 25532

FRANKLIN. The Life of the late Doctor Benjamin Franklin. Written by Himself. *Philadelphia: Johnson & Warner.* 1811. 12mo, pp. 104. + [*Ibid.*] 1812. + *Edinburgh.* 1839. + *Philadelphia.* 1864. BA. + *New York.* [n. d.] 25533

FRANKLIN. Life of Dr. Benjamin Franklin, Written by Himself; with Essays, Humorous, Moral, and Literary. *Boston.* 1815. 16mo. Portrait. W. 25534

FRANKLIN. The Life of Benjamin Franklin, including a Sketch of the Rise and Progress of the War of Independence, and of the Various Negotiations at Paris for Peace; with the History of his Political and other Writings. *London.* 1826. 12mo. 25535

FRANKLIN. Life of Benjamin Franklin, Written by Himself. Together with his Essays, Humorous, Moral and Literary. *Auburn, N. N.* [sic] *Derby, Miller & Co.* 1848. 12mo. 25536

Reprinted. *Auburn, N. Y.* 1853. 12mo. Also issued in 8vo.

FRANKLIN. The Life of Benjamin Franklins. Vol. I. B. Franklin's Autobiography. With an Appendix. *Leipzig: A. Dürr.* 185–. 8vo, pp. x, 239. 1 Lithograph. (Dürr's Coll. of Stand. Amer. Auth., Vol. II.) 25537

FRANKLIN. The Life of Benjamin Franklin; containing the Autobiography; with Notes and a Continuation. By Jared Sparks. *Boston.* 1845. 8vo, pp. 612. + *Dessau.* 1854. 8vo.

FRANKLIN. The Life of Benjamin Franklin. Illustrated by Tales, Sketches, and Anecdotes. Adapted to the Use of Schools. *Philadelphia: Thomas, Cowperthwait & Co.* 1838. 12mo.

FRANKLIN. Franklin's Leben. *Tübingen.* 1795. 8vo.

FRANKLIN. Het Leven van Benjamin Franklin, door hemzelven beschreven. Benevens deszelfs zede-, staat-, letterkundige en geestige schriften. Uit het Engelsch. *Groningen: W. Zuidema.* 1798–1800. 2 vols. in 1, 8vo, 6 l., pp. 258; 5 l., pp. 432. C. 25541

FRANKLIN. Der Weg zum Glück, oder Leben und Meynungen des Dr. Benjamin Franklin. Von ihm selbst geschrieben. *Reading, (Pa.): Heinrich B. Sage.* 1820. 18mo, pp. 128. C. + *'s Hage.* 1828. 8vo. 25542

FRANKLIN. Vie de Benjamin Franklin: écrite par lui-même, suivie de ses œuvres morales, politiques et littéraires, dont la plus grand partie n'avoit pas encore été publiée. Traduite de l'Anglais, avec des notes, par J. Castéra. *Paris: F. Buisson An* VI. *de la République.* [1799.] 8vo, pp. viii, 438. 25543

FRANKLIN. Mélanges de morale, d'économie et de politique, extraits des ouvrages de Benjamin Franklin ... . *Paris: Chez Antoine-Augustin Renouard.* 1824. 2 vols., 12mo, pp. vi, 252; (2), 182. Portrait. B. 25544

FRANKLIN. Memoirs of the Life and Writings of Benjamin Franklin, LL.D., F.R.S., &c. Minister Plenipotentiary from the United States of America, at the Court of France, and for the Treaty of Peace and Independence with Great Britain, &c. &c. Written by Himself to à late Period, and continued to the time of his Death, by his Grandson; William Temple Franklin. Now first published from the original MSS. Comprising the Private Correspondence and Public Negociations of Dr. Franklin, and a selection from his Political, Philosophical, and Miscellaneous Works. *London: Henry Colburn.* 1818–19. 6 vols., 8vo, pp. xii, 542; (2), 450; xvi, 456; xii, 392; xvi, 493; viii,

523. 10 Plates. H. + Second [and Third] Edition. [*Ibid.*] 3 vols., 4to, pp. x, 450, lxxxviii, (1), Map; xxiv, 449; (2), xii, 570, 10 Plates. + New Edition. *London: published for Henry Colburn by R. Bentley.* 1833. 6 vols., 8vo. C. 25545

All of these sets are often broken up, and the three series of Life, Correspondence, and Posthumous Writings sold separately with the same general title, and the editions are sometimes mixed. "*Caveat emptor.*" The so-called new edition of 1833 is the first edition of 1818, with new title-pages only. *See* "M. Rev.," LXXXIII. 18 and 133; LXXXVIII. 409; and "N. Am. Rev.," VII. 289.

FRANKLIN. Memoirs of Benjamin Franklin, Written by Himself and Continued by his Grandson, with his Correspondence, Essays, Diplomatic Transactions, &c. with a Postliminious Preface. *Philadelphia.* 1834. 2 vols., 8vo, pp. xxxviii, 624; vii, 517. + *New York.* 1861. 2 vols., 8vo. 25546

FRANKLIN. Memoirs of Benjamin Franklin; Written by Himself. With his most Interesting Essays, Letters, and Miscellaneous Writings; Familiar, Moral, Political, Economical, and Philosophical. Selected with care from all his Published Productions, and comprising whatever is most Entertaining and Valuable to the General Reader. *New-York: Harper & Brothers.* 1839. 2 vols., 18mo, pp. 287; (2), 288. B., BA. + [*Ibid.*] 1840. + [*Ibid.*] 1845. 25547

FRANKLIN. Memoirs of the Life of Benjamin Franklin, Written by Himself. Illustrated Edition. *New-York: John Doggett, Jr.* 1850. 8vo. 25548

FRANKLIN. Mémoires de la vie privée de Benj. Franklin écrits par lui-même, suivis d'un précis historique de sa vie po tique. *Paris.* 1791. 8vo. 25549

FRANKLIN. Mémoires sur la vie et les écrits de Benjamin Franklin, ... Publiés sur le manuscrit origina rédigée par lui-même en grande partie, et continué jusqu'a sa mort, Par William Temple Franklin, son petit-fils. Tome Premier, Avec une Portrait de B. Franklin. *A Paris: Chez Treuttel et Würtz, Libraires, rue de Bourbon, no 17; Et à Strasbourg, même Maison de Commerce. A Londres: Chez H. Colburne.* 1818. 3 vols., 4to, 10 l., pp. 390; (6), 435; 16 l., pp. 410. 25550

This translation was by M. Le Veillard. *See* Sparks' Frank n, x. 231

FRANKLIN. Mémoires complets, œuvres morales et littéraires, traduites d'après la dernière édition publiée à New-York. *Paris.* 1841. 8vo. 25551

FRANKLIN. Mémoires écrits par lui-même. Traduite de l'Anglais, et annotés par Édouard Laboulaye. *Paris: L. Hachette et Ce.* 12mo. 25552

FRANKLIN. Gedenkschriften van Benjamin Franklin; bestaande in uitgelezen brieven. Naar het Engelsch. *Haarlem.* MDCCCXVII. 8vo, pp. viii, 338. B. 25553

[FRANKLIN.] A Memorial of the Case of the German Emigrants settled in the British Colonies of Pennsilvania, and the back Parts of Maryland, Virginia, &c. *London: Printed in the Year* MDCCLIV. 4to, pp. 20, 8. 25554

FRANKLIN. Miscelanea de Economia, Politica, y Moral, extractada de las Obras de Benjamin Franklin, y precedida de una Noticia sobre su Vida. Traducida del Frances por R. Mangino. *Paris.* 1825. 2 vols., 18mo. 25555

[FRANKLIN.] A Modest Enquiry into the Nature and Necessity of a Paper Currency. *Philadelphia: Printed and sold at the New Printing-Office, near the Market.* 1729. 8vo, pp. 36.

Written and printed by B. Franklin, to encourage making more paper money, which was done. Signed "B. B. *April* 3. 1729." His first published tract, which was well received by the common people, but disliked by the rich.

FRANKLIN. Nachgelassene Schriften und Correspondenz; nebst einem Leben. Aus dem Englischen. *Weimar: Industrie-Comptoir.* 1817–19. 5 vols., 8vo. 25556*a*

Vols. III. and IV. are entitled "Franklin's Leben;" Vol. V., "Aufsätze vermischen Inhalts."

[FRANKLIN.] A Narrative of the Late Massacres, in Lancaster County, of a Number of Indians, Friends of this Province, By Persons unknown. With some Observations on the same. *Printed in the Year* M,DCC,LXIV. 8vo, pp. 31. P. 25557

Written and printed by B. Franklin. Shehaes, one of the slain, had assisted in the second treaty (1701) with Wm. Penn. Twenty-two unoffending, innocent Indians, old men, women, and children, who had long lived at peace with and among the whites, were murdered, with every circumstance of cowardly cruelty, by a mob of the Presbyterian settlers, calling themselves the Paxton Boys, led on by the Rev. Mr. Elder, persuading themselves they were doing God's work. Mr. Field, in his "Indian Bibliography," characterizes this massacre as "the most horrible picture of human phrensy this continent ever saw "

[FRANKLIN.] Necessary Truth; or Seasonable Considerations for the Inhabitants of the City of Philadelphia, and Province of Pennsylvania. In relation to the Pamphlet call'd Plain Truth: and Two other Writers in the News-Paper. *Philadelphia: printed in the Year* MDCCXLVIII. 8vo, pp. 16. P. 25558

In the type of Franklin and Hall, and probably written by Franklin.

Franklin. New Experiments and Observations on Electricity. Made at Philadelphia in America. By Benjamin Franklin, Esq.; ... The Second Edition. *London: D. Henry and R. Cave.* 1754. 4to, pp. (2), 154. + Third Edition. *London: D. Henry and R. Cave.* 1760. 4to, pp. (6), 154. 25559

There are, in all, three parts of these experiments, and copies are sometimes made up with the dates of 1760, 1762, and 1754. *See* Experiments, No. 25505, *supra*.

Franklin. Osservazione a chiunque desideri passare in America. *Padova.* 1785. 8vo. 25560

Franklin. A Paper supposed to have been Written by Dr. Benj. Franklin at Paris, for the purpose of Borrowing Money for the Use of the United States. [About 1776.] 8vo.

Title from J. R. Smith's sale catalogue.

Franklin. Philosophical and Miscellaneous Papers. Lately written by B. Franklin, LL.D. ... *London: C. Dilly.* M.DCC.LXXXVII. 8vo, pp. (6), 186. Plates. H. 25562

[Franklin.] *See* Plain Facts.

[Franklin.] Plain Truth: or, Serious Considerations on the Present State of the City of Philadelphia and Province of Pennsylvania. By a Tradesman of Philadelphia. *Printed in the Year* MDCCXLVII. 8vo, pp. 22. P. 25563

Written and printed by Benjamin Franklin. On the back of the title-page is a rude woodcut of Hercules and the Waggoner. A second edition in the same year, which contains an extra leaf, unpaged, pp. 2. *Printed and sold by Godhard Armbruster: Philadelphia.* 1747. 8vo. Both editions are very rare. For a Reply, *see* A Treatise, etc., 1748, and "Sundry Christian Truths, and Short Views of a Pamphlet lately Published, entitled, 'Plain Truth.' In German. By a Tradesman of Germantown. *Germantown: printed by C. Sower.* 1748."

Franklin. A Pocket | Almanack | For the Year 1742. | Fitted for the Use of Penn- | sylvania, and the neigh- | bouring Provinces. | By Richard Saunders, Phil. | *Philadelphia:* | *Printed by B. Franklin.* | 32mo, pp. 16. 25564

Continued to 1749; after that date, printed by *B. Franklin and D. Hall*, to 1766 or later.

Franklin. Political, Miscellaneous, and Philosophical Pieces; Arranged under the following Heads, and Distinguished by Initial Letters in each Leaf: [G. P.] General Politics; [A. 13. P.] American Politics before the Troubles; [A. D. F.] American Politics during the Troubles; [P. P.] Provincial of Colony

Politics; and [M. P.] Miscellaneous and Philosophical Pieces; Written by Benj. Franklin, LL.D. ... Now first Collected, With Explanatory Plates, Notes, And an Index to the Whole. *London: J. Johnson.* M DCC LXXIX. 4to, pp. xi, (1), 567, (7). Portrait, 3 Plates, and Table. BA. 25565

See "M. Rev.," LXII. 194. Also printed on large paper.

Franklin. Poor Richard, 1733. An Almanack For the Year of Christ 1733, Being the First after Leap Year, and makes since the Creation ... Wherein is contained The Lunations, Eclipses, Judgment of the Weather, Spring Tides, Planets Motions & mutual Aspects, Sun and Moon's Rising and Setting, Length of Days, Time of High Water, Fairs, Courts, and observable Days. Fitted to the Latitude of Forty Degrees, and a Meridian of Five Hours West from London, but may without sensible Error, serve all the adjacent Places, even from Newfoundland to South-Carolina. By Richard Saunders, Philom. *Philadelphia: Printed and sold by B. Franklin, at the New Printing-Office near the Market.* [n. d.] 12mo, 12 l. P. 25566

Reprinted in facsimile, *Philadelphia: George S. Appleton.* 1847? 12mo. This is the first of this series of almanacs, of which a complete set is almost unknown. The issues for 1733 to 1749, inclusive, all consist of 12 leaves each. The almanac for 1748 is entitled,

Franklin. Note, This Almanack us'd to contain but 24 Pages, and | now has 36; yet the Price is very little advanc'd. | Poor Richard improved: | Being an | Almanack | and Ephemeris | of the | Motions of the Sun and Moon; | the True | Places and Aspects of the Planets; | the | Rising and Setting of the Sun; | and the | Rising, Setting and Southing of the Moon, | for the | Bissextile Year, 1748. | Containing also, | The Lunations, Conjunctions, Eclipses, Judg- | ment of the Weather, Rising and Setting of the | Planets, Length of Days and Nights, Fairs, Courts, | Roads, &c. Together with useful Tables, chro- | nological Observations, and entertaining Remarks. | Fitted to the Latitude of Forty Degrees, and a Meridian of near | five Hours West from London; but may, without sensible Error, | serve all the Northern Colonies. | By Richard Saunders, Philom. | *Philadelphia: Printed and Sold by B. Franklin.* | 12mo, pp. 36. 25567

Continued to 1761 by B. Franklin; after this year, to 1766, it was *Printed and sold by B. Franklin and D. Hall.* 12mo, all with pp. 36. It was continued by *Hall and Sellers, Philadelphia*, to 1794 or later. To the almanac for 1758 is prefixed a collection of the Proverbs, etc., scattered through the previous numbers. These sayings were frequently reprinted in England as the "Way to Wealth," and in

French as the "La science du bonhomme Richard." Stevens, in his "Nuggets," No. 1110, has also reprinted them. *The almanac for 1758 is the most rare and valuable of the series.* The almanacs for 1733–1741 were reprinted and adapted to the years 1850, 1851, and 1852, as below:

Franklin. "Poor Richard." Poor Richard's Almanac for 1850, [1851], [1852] as Written by Benjamin Franklin, for the Years 1733–1734–1735. [1736–1737] ... The Astronomical Calculations ... adapted to Boston, New-York, ... To which is added, ... the Life of the Great Philosopher, Written by Himself. ... *New-York: John Doggett, Jr.* 1849–50. 3 vols., 12mo, pp. 60. B., H. 25568

Franklin. Posthumous and other Writings, (not contained in his Collected Works, Published from the Originals, by his Grandson, W. T. Franklin). *London: H. Colburn.* 1819. 2 vols., 8vo. 25569

These are Vol. v. of vi. of our No. 25545, *supra*, with new title-pages.

Franklin. The Private Correspondence of Benjamin Franklin, ... comprising a Series of Letters ... Illustrating the Memoirs of his Public and Private Life. ... Published from the Originals, by his Grandson, Wm. Temple Franklin. *London: Henry Colburn.* 1817. 4to, pp. xxiii, (2), 449. H. + Second Edition, with Additions. *London: H. Colburn.* 1817. 2 vols., 8vo, pp. xxiv, 486; xi, 475. Plate. C. 25571

The quarto edition forms Vol. II. of our No. 25545, *supra*. The 8vo forms Vols. III. and IV. The title-pages of the fourth edition sometimes vary.

Franklin. Correspondance choisie, suivie de ses mémoires, publiés par son petit-fils W. Temple Franklin, traduit Français. *Strassbourg.* 25572

Franklin. The Private Life of the late Benjamin Franklin, LL.D. Late Minister Plenipotentiary from the United States of America to France, &c. ... Originally written by Himself, and now Translated from the French. To which are added, Some Account of his Public Life, a variety of Anecdotes concerning him, by MM. Brissot, Condorcet, Rochefaucault, Le Roy, &c. and the Eulogium of M. Fauchet. ... *London: J. Parsons.* 1793. 8vo, pp. xvi, 324. 25573

See "M. Rev.," XIII. 307.

[Franklin.] Proposal for Promoting Useful Knowledge, &c. *Phila.* 14 *May*, 1743. 25574

Originally printed as a circular. *See* Sparks' Franklin, VI. 14.

[Franklin.] Proposals relating to the Education of Youth in Pennsylvania. *Philadelphia.* M.DCC.XLIX. 8vo, pp. 32. BA.

In the advertisement prefixed to this pamphlet, letters on the subject are requested to be addressed to B. Franklin, Printer, &c., from which it appears probable that Franklin was the author.

[Franklin.] Remarks on a late Protest against the Appointment of Mr. Franklin an Agent for this Province. [*B. Franklin: Philadelphia. Nov. 5th*, 1764.] 8vo, pp. 7. C. 25576

This was an answer to "A Protest against the Appointment of Mr. Franklin an Agent for Pennsylvania. 1764." 8vo, which, in its turn, was answered by

Franklin. An Answer to Mr. Franklin's Remarks, on a late Protest. *Philadelphia: William Bradford.* M.DCC.LXIV. 8vo, pp. 22. P. 25577

A very furious attack on Dr. Franklin. "There is ample room to show how diametrically opposite his principles have been at different times; how he has paid servile court to all sides, deceived all, calumniated all!" — Page 21.

[Franklin.] Remarks concerning the Savages of North America. *Birmingham.* 1784. 8vo. 25578

In an advertisement to this tract it is stated that it was written by Dr. Franklin, and taken from a copy printed by himself, for his own amusement, at his house at Passy. "It is strongly marked by that plainness and simplicity of manner, accompanied by that point and poignancy, which distinguish the doctor's writings, whenever he chooses to indulge his vein of pleasantry." — *M. Rev.*, LXXI. 70. Reprinted in Two Tracts. *See our* No. 25594, *supra*.

[Franklin.] Report of Dr. Benjamin Franklin, and other Commissioners, charged by the King of France, with the Examination of the Animal Magnetism, as now practised at Paris. Translated from the French. With an Historical Introduction. *London: J. Johnson.* 1785. pp. xx, 123. 25579

Franklin. Rules for Reducing a Great Empire to a Small one. By the late Benjamin Franklin, L.L.D. F.R.S. Dedicated to the Right Honourable Alexander, Lord Loughborough. To which is subjoined The Declaration of Independence by the Representatives of the United States of America in General Congress assembled. *London: James Ridgway.* 1793. 8vo, pp. 16. 25580

Written for "The Public Advertiser" (London), Oct. 1772. The Earl of Hillsborough is alluded to. The dedication to this edition is ironical.

Franklin. ... Sämmtliche Werke. Aus dem Englischen und Französischen ubersetzt. ... von G. T. Wenzel. *Dresden: Walther.* 1780. 3 vols., 8vo, pp. (12), 502, Portrait; (12), 442, Plates; (12), 636. B. 25581

Franklin. Sämmtliche Werke. Nebst dessin Lebens-beschreibung. *Hamburg: Schuberth.* 1845. 32mo. 25582

Franklin. La science du bonhomme Richard, ou moyen facile de payer les impôts, dans les Possessions de l'Amérique Angloise; contenant un Discours de Mr. J. Hancock, M. Francklinn, &c. Traduit de l'Anglois. *A Philadelphie, et se trouve à Lausanne.* 1778. 12mo. + Seconde édition, exactement semblable à la première. *Philadelphie et Paris: Renault.* 1778. 12mo, pp. 151. + Troisième édition. [*Ibid.*] + *à Riom.* 1799. 12mo. + *Paris.* 1830. 12mo, pp. 30. H. + *Paris.* 1852. 18mo, pp. 35. H. + *Paris: Jules Renouard.* 1865. 32mo, 2 l., pp. 34. H. 25583

Contains also the examination of Dr. Franklin before the British Parliament, in 1766. Translated by Dupont de Nemours. The Constitution of Pennsylvania, as established in 1776. And the examination of Mr. Penn, at the bar of Parliament, in 1776. Translated by MM. Quetant and Lecuy. There are many other editions.

Franklin. La science du bonhomme Richard. [Précédée de l'histoire typographique de l'auteur.] *Paris: C. L. F. Pankoucke.* 1827. Folio, pp. xvi, 16. S. 25584

A splendid edition, and but few printed.

Franklin. La Science du Bonhomme Richard, précédée d'un Abrégé de la vie de Franklin, et suivie de sur Interrogatoire devant la Chambre des Communes. *Paris. l'An* II. [1794.] 16mo. 25585

Franklin. La Ciencia del buen Ricardo ó el Camino de la fortuna. Y Pensamientos sobre moral, politica, literatura, religion y costumbres por J. M. Samper. *Carácas.* 1858. 8vo, pp. 88. 25586

Franklin. The Select Works of Benjamin Franklin, including his Autobiography; with Notes and Memoirs. By Epes Sargent. *Boston.* 1858. 12mo, pp. 502. Portrait. 25587

Franklin. *See* Second Appeal, *infra*.

[Franklin.] Some Account of the Pennsylvania Hospital; From its first Rise, to the Beginning of the Fifth Month, called May, 1754. *Philadelphia: Printed by B. Franklin and D. Hall.* MDCCLIV. 4to, pp. 40. + Continuation of the Account of the Pennsylvania Hospital; From the First of May 1754, to the Fifth of May 1761, With an Alphabetical List of the Contributors, and of the Legacies which have been bequeathed, for Promotion and Support thereof, from its first Rise to that Time. *Philadelphia: Printed by B. Franklin and D. Hall.* MDCCLXI. 4to, pp. 41–77. 25588

[Franklin.] Some Account of the Success of Inoculation for the Small-Pox in England and America. Together with Plain Instructions. ... *London: Printed by W. Strahan.* M,DCC,-LIX. 8vo, pp. 8, 12. H. 25589

[Franklin.] Some Observations concerning the Increase of Mankind, Peopling of Countries, &c. [n. p. n. d.] 8vo, pp. 15. H. 25590

[Franklin.] Some | Observations | on the | Proceedings | against the Rev. Mr. Hemphill; | with a | Vindication of his Sermons. | *Philadelphia: Printed and sold by B. Franklin.* 1735. | 12mo, pp. 32. + The Second Edition. [*Ibid.*] 25591

Ascribed positively to Franklin in Webster's "Presbyterian Church in America," p. 111.

[Franklin.] The True Root of Scarcity; or Sure Road to Competence in times of Dearth, And to Riches in times of Plenty. *Edinburgh: C. Stewart & Co.* M,DCCC,I. 12mo, pp. 23.

[Franklin.] True State of Proceedings. *See* [Lee (A.)]

Franklin. Tvær aefisögur. *Copenhagen.* 1839. 8vo.

Lives of Franklin and Oberlin in Icelandic.

[Franklin.] Two Tracts: Information to those who would remove to America. And, Remarks concerning the Savages of North America. *London: John Stockdale.* MDCCLXXXIV. 8vo, pp. 39. + Second Edition. [*Ibid.*] 8vo, pp. 39. + Third Edition. [*Ibid.*] 8vo, pp. 39. + *Dublin.* 1784. 8vo, pp. 30.

The first of these tracts was written by Dr. Franklin, on account of numerous applications made to him by persons desirous of emigrating to America, with sanguine expectations, in order that they might not be disappointed on their arrival. The second is a reprint of our No. 25578, *supra*.

[Franklin?] View of the Title to Indiana, a Tract of Country on the River Ohio. Containing Indian Conferences at Johnson-Hall, in May, 1765 — the Deed of the Six Nations to the Proprietors of Indiana, settling the Boundary Line between the English and Indians Lands — and the Opinion of Counsel on the Title of the Proprietors of Indiana. *Philadelphia: Printed by Styner and Cist.* MDCCLXXVI. 8vo, pp. 46. P. 25595

This was a favorite scheme of Dr. Franklin's, from which he counted on large profits. At the conclusion, to Counsellor Dagge's and Mr. Serjeant Glynn's opinions in its favor, he added his own and that of Patrick Henry, junr., dated Phila. July, 1775.

Franklin. The Way to Wealth, or Poor Richard Improved. La Science du Bonnehomme Richard, ou moyen facile de payer les impôts. Lettres de Franklin. Dialogue entre la goutre et Franklin. Quelques mots sur l'Amérique. Avis à ceux qui voudroient aller s'établir dans cette contrée. Observations sur les sauvages du Nord de l'Amérique. *Paris: Printed for Ant. Aug. Renouard.* 1795. 18mo, pp. 181, 28. Portrait. 25596

Beautifully printed. The letters to Franklin above mentioned are private, and addressed to Madame * *, dated Passy, 1778 and 1779.

Franklin. The Way to Wealth as clearly shown in the Preface of an old Pennsylvania Almanac, intitled, Poor Richard Improved. [n. p. n. d.] 8vo, pp. 16. + *Paisley.* 1784. 12mo, pp. 16. + *Worcester.* 1790. 12mo. + *London.* 1823. 12mo. + *Newburyport, Mass.* [n. d.] 12mo. + *Windsor, Vt.* 1826. 24mo. 25597

Franklin. The Way to Wealth; or, the Admonition of Poor Richard. ... The Whistle, a Story. ... By Dr. Franklin. ... *Printed by J. Marshall, Newcastle.* [1817.] 12mo, pp. 24. + Way to Wealth, to which is added the Prompter, or Maxims and Common Sayings, by Noah Webster. 1808. 12mo. Plate.

Also issued with various other titles; one is called "Advice to a Young Tradesman, ... 1748. *Philadelphia: printed by Danl. Humphreys.*" [n. d.] Folio, 1 l.

Franklin. Works of Dr. Benjamin Franklin. *London: C. Dilly.* [1785?] 25599

Concerning this edition, which I have not seen, *see* Sparks' Franklin, x. 240. *See also* the same, VIII. 404, for a notice of an edition by Benjamin Vaughan, 1779.

Franklin. Works of the late Doctor Franklin: Consisting of his Life. Written by Himself, together with Essays, Humorous, Moral & Literary, Chiefly in the manner of the Spectator. *London: G. G. J. and J. Robinson.* 1793. 2 vols., 12mo, Engraved Titles, pp. ix, (2), 317; 3 l., pp. 268. + Second Edition. [*Ibid.*] + Third Edition. [*Ibid.*] + *Dublin: P. Wogan, P. Byrne, J. Moore.* 1793. 8vo, pp. vi, (2), 303. Portrait. H.

This edition was edited by Dr. Price. *See* "M. Rev.," XIII. 304.

Franklin. Works of the late Dr. Benjamin Franklin; consisting of his Life, written by himself, together with Essays, Humourous, Moral & Literary; chiefly in the manner of the Spectator. The Second American Edition. *New York: Printed by Samuel Campbell.* 1794. 2 vols., 12mo, pp. 206; 142. H.

This edition contains "The Eulogium," by the Abbé Fauchet.

Franklin. Works of the late Dr. Benjamin Franklin. Consisting of his Life, written by Himself. Together with Essays, Humorous, Moral, and Literary, chiefly in the Manner of the Spectator. *Fairhaven, Vt.: J. Lyon.* 1798. 12mo, pp. 254. BA. + *Charlestown: Printed by John Lawson.* 1798. 12mo, pp. 300. Portrait. + *London: A. Millar.* 1799. 2 vols., 18mo, pp. vi, (2), 207; v, 201. + *Huntington.* 1800. 2 vols., 12mo. W. + *Philadelphia.* 1801. 2 vols., 12mo. Portrait. + *London.* 1802. 2 vols., 12mo. + *London.* 1806. 16mo. Portrait. H. + *New York.* 1807. 16mo. + *London.* 1809. 24mo. + *Edinburgh: Printed by D. Schaw & Son.* 1809. 2 vols., 16mo, pp. (8), 5–233; (4), 186. + [*Ibid.*] 1814. + *Philadelphia.* 1815. 12mo, pp. 335. + [*Ibid.*] 1818. P. + *Edinburgh: Oliver & Boyd.* 1818. 18mo, pp. 204, 228. + *Chiswick: C. Whittingham.* 1824. 16mo, pp. viii, 295. + *Peekskill, N. Y.* 1834. 18mo. B. + *London.* 1843. 16mo. + *Hartford: S. Andrus and Son.* 1847. 18mo, pp. 304. 25602

And many other editions

Franklin. Works of the late Dr. Benjamin Franklin: Consisting of Memoirs of his Early Life, Written by Himself; together with a Collection of his Essays, Humorous, Moral and Literary, chiefly in the manner of the Spectator. A New Edition Revised and Enlarged. *Easton: Henry W. Gibbs.* 1810. 12mo, pp. 274. 25603

Franklin. The Works of Dr. Benjamin Franklin, consisting of Essays, Humorous, Moral, and Literary, with His Life, Written by Himself. *New York: W. Van Norden.* 1825. 18mo. + *Boston.* 1825. 2 vols., 16mo. + *Baltimore: N. Hickman.* 1835. 18mo, pp. 304. 25604

Franklin. The Works of Dr. Benjamin Franklin, in Philosophy, Politics, and Morals; containing, besides all the Writings Published in Former Collections, his Diplomatic Correspondence, as Minister of the United States, at the Court of Versailles; a Variety of Literary Articles, and Epistolary Correspondence, never before published; with Memoirs and Anecdotes of his Life. *Philadelphia: William Duane.* 1809–1818. 6 vols., 8vo, pp. xxii, 519; (2), xxxv, 431; (6), 477; (6), 407; viii, 434; xxiii, 564. 25605

Some copies of this, and all the English editions, read Memoirs, etc., as in our No. 25547, *sup a.*

FRANKLIN. The Works of Benjamin Franklin; containing several Political and Historical Tracts not included in any Former Edition, and many Letters, Official and Private not hitherto published; with Notes and A Life of the Author. By Jared Sparks. *Boston: Hilliard, Gray and Company.* 1836–40. 10 vols., 8vo, pp. xxxvii, (2), 612; ix, (2), 557; xv, 577; ix. (2), 539; xv, 516; xiii, (2), 578; xxxi, (2), 568; xxii, (2), 554; xxi, (2), 550; xix, (2), 540, Corrigenda, 1 l., 3 canceled l. 22 Plates. B., BA., H. 25606

One hundred copies printed on large paper. Reprinted, *Boston.* 1844–1856, and new edition, *Philadelphia: Childs & Peterson.* 1858. The stereotype plates were sold to Mr. Henry Stevens, of London, who proposes to issue a new edition, with many additions from MSS. in his possession. *See* "N. Am. Rev.," VII. 289; XXXVII, 249; LIX, 446; "Ed. Rev.," Vols. II., VIII., and XXVIII.

FRANKLIN. Œuvres de M. Franklin, Docteur es Loix, Membre de l'Académie Royale des Sciences de Paris, des Sociétés Royalès de Londres & de Gottingue, des Sociétés Philosophiques d'Édimbourg & de Rotterdam, Président de la Société Philosophique de Philadelphe, & Résident à la Cour de la Grand Bretagne pour plusieurs Colonies Britanniques Américaines. Traduites de l'Anglois sur la quatrième édition. Par M. Barbeu Dubourg. Avec des Additions Nouvelles et des Figures en Taille douce. ... *A Paris: Chez Quillau l'aîné.* M.DCC.LXXIII. 2 vols., 4to, pp. xxiv, 338; xv, 320. 12 Plates. 25607

"The friendship of the author for me has induced him to draw from his portfolio some papers which had not yet appeared, to enrich the French edition." — *Preface.*

[FRANKLIN (B.), *and* NEUFVILLE (J.)] Letters to the Merchant's Committee of Philadelphia, Submitted to the Consideration of the Public. Folio, pp. 1. P. 25608

Published Monday morning, May 14, 1770. From B. Franklin and John Neufville, of So. Ca. The following relate to Franklin:

FRANKLIN. Benjamin Franklin. A Book for All. *Cambridge: printed for the Author.* 1855. 12mo, pp. 36. 25609

FRANKLIN. Franklin the Apprentice. *New York: Harper & Brothers.* 1856. 12mo. 25610

FRANKLIN. The Boy's Life and Essays of Franklin. *Philadelphia.* [n. d.] 18mo. 25611

FRANKLIN. A Letter to Benjamin Franklin, LL.D. F.R.S. In which his pretensions to the title of Natural Philosopher are Considered. *London: J. Bew.* 1777. 8vo. 25612

A pompous attempt to undervalue the merits of Franklin.

FRANKLIN. A Letter to Mr. Franklin, on a single sheet, in support of Mr. Tennant's Sermon of 24 Dec. 1747. Folio, pp. 2.

No title, year, date, or printer's name, but apparently printed by Franklin.

FRANKLIN. Letters to Benjamin Franklin from his Family and Friends, 1751–1790. *New York: C. B. Richardson.* 1858. Rl. 8vo, pp. 195. 3 Plates. 25614

Edited by W. J. Duane. Some copies are dated *New York.* 1859. Edition, 250 copies rl. 8vo, and 10 in 4to. Scarce. *See* "Athenæum," No. 1656.

FRANKLIN. Memoirs of the Late Dr. Benjamin Franklin; With a Review of his Pamphlet, entitled "Information to those who would wish to remove to America." *London: A. Grant.* 1790. 8vo, pp. 94. Portrait. N. 25615

An endeavor to depreciate the Doctor, and a flat contradiction of his representations as to emigration. *See* "M. Rev.," IX. 83.

FRANKLIN. Memorial of the Inauguration of the Statue of Franklin. *See* [Shurtleff (N. B.)]

FRANKLIN. The Printer Boy; or, How Ben Franklin made his Mark. An Example for Youth. *Boston: J. E. Tilton.* 1864. 12mo, pp. xvi, 261. 25616

FRANKLIN. Die Vater unserer Republik in ihrem Leben und Wirken. Leben Benjamin Franklins. *New York.* 1847. 8vo.

FRANKLIN. Euskildta lefeverne Öfwersättn. *Stockholm.* 1792. 8vo. Portrait. 25618

FRANKLIN. Proceedings at the Printers' Banquet, held by the N. Y. Typographical Society, on the occasion of Franklin's Birth-Day, Jan. 17, 1850. At Niblo's, ... *New York: Charles B. Norton.* 1850. 8vo, pp. 64. 25619

FRANKLIN (J.) The Philosophical and Political History of the Thirteen United States of America, comprehending New Hampshire, Massachusetts-Bay, Rhode Island and Providence Plantation, Connecticut, New York, New Jersey, Pennsylvania, Delaware, Maryland, Virginia, North Carolina, South Carolina and Georgia, containing a Concise Account of their First Settlement, Principal Cities and Towns, Air, Soil, Produce, Manufactures, and Commerce, with a Short View of the Independent State of Vermont, and of East and West Florida. Also a General Survey of the Remains of British North America, and of the British American and West Indian Islands. To which is prefixed An Account of the Persons, Singular Customs and Manners of the Original Inhabitants of America. By James Franklin, Esq. *London: S. Hinton and W. Adams.* MDCCLXXXIV. 8vo, pp. (12), 156. H. 25620

FRANKLIN (J.) The Present State of Hayti, (Saint Domingo) with Remarks on its Agriculture, Commerce, Laws, Religion, Finances, and Population, etc. By James Franklin. *London: John Murray.* MDCCCXXVIII. 8vo, pp. viii, 411, (1). B., BA., H.

See Rich, Vol. II., for an extract from the "N. Am. Rev."

FRANKLIN. View of the West India Question; with Remarks on Mr. Huskisson's Letter to Sir John Keane, Governor of Jamaica. By James Franklin. *London.* 1828. 8vo, pp. 119.

FRANKLIN (J.) United States Album. Embellished with the Arms of each State, and other appropriate Engravings, containing the Autographs of the President and Cabinet, Twenty-Eighth Congress, Supreme Court Judges, Ministers, and other officers of Government, Arranged and Designed by J. Franklin. *Lancaster, Pa.* 1844. 4to. 25623

FRANKLIN (J.) Narrative of a Journey to the Shores of the Polar Sea, in the Years 1819, 20, 21 and 22. By John Franklin, Captain R. N. ... and Commander of the Expedition. With an Appendix on various Subjects relating to Science and Natural History. Illustrated by numerous Plates and Maps. ... *London: John Murray.* 1823. 4to, pp. xv, 784. 34 Plates and 4 Maps.

The plates are engraved by Finden (some of them being colored), from drawings by Lieuts. Hood and Back. The valuable appendix on natural history is by Sir John Richardson, Col. Sabine, Lieut. Hood, etc.

FRANKLIN. Narrative [as above]. Second Edition. *London: John Murray.* MDCCCXXIV. 2 vols., 8vo, pp. xix, 370; iv, (1), 399. 5 Maps. B., BA., H. + Third Edition. [*Ibid.*]

These octavo editions do not contain the appendices.

FRANKLIN. Narrative of a Journey, ... &c., in the Years 1819–20–21–22. By John Franklin, ... With an Appendix containing Geognostical Observations and Remarks on the Aurora Borealis. *Philadelphia: Carey & Lea.* 1824. 8vo, pp. 482. Plate and Map. 25626

FRANKLIN. Narrative of a Journey to the Shores of the Polar Sea, in the Years 1819–20–21–22; with A Brief Account of the Second Journey In 1825–26–27. By John Franklin, Capt. R. N., F.R.S., and Commander of the Expedition. With Plates [by Finden]. *London: John Murray.* M DCC XXIX. 4 vols., 18mo, pp. xxi, 255; vi, 248; vi, 265; 2 l., pp. 249. 24 Plates. 25627

FRANKLIN. Narrative of a Second Expedition to the Shores of the Polar Sea, in the Years 1825, 1826, and 1827, by John Franklin, Captain R. N., ... Including an Account of the Progress of a Detachment to the Eastward. By John Richardson, M.D., F.R.S., ... Surgeon and Naturalist to the Expedition. Illustrated by Numerous Plates and Maps. ... *London: John Murray.* MDCCCXXVIII. 4to, pp. xxiv, 320, Appendix, clvii, (1). 7 Maps and 31 Plates. B., BA., H. 26228

There are copies on fine paper, with proofs of the plates on India paper. "The views of Arctic scenery with which these volumes are both illustrated and embellished, are of extreme beauty." — *Quart. Rev. See also* "Edinb. Rev."

FRANKLIN. [Another Edition.] *Philadelphia: Carey, Lea and Carey.* 1828. 8vo, pp. 318. Map. 25629

FRANKLIN. Zweite Reise an die Küsten des Polarmeeres. Aus dem Englischen. *Weimar.* 1829. 8vo. Map. 25630

FRANKLIN. Histoire des deux voyages entrepris par ordre du gouvernement Anglais, par Franklin et Parry, pour la découverte d'un passage de l'Océan Atlantique dans la Mer Pacifique. Traduite de l'Anglaise. *Paris.* 1824. 8vo. Map. 25631

FRANKLIN. Thirty Years in the Arctic Regions; or the Adventures of Sir John Franklin. *New York: H. Dayton.* 1859. 12mo. 25632

FRANKLIN. Die Franklin-Expedition und ihr Ausgang; Entdeckung der nordwestl. Durchfahrt durch Mac Clure, sowie Auffindung der Ueberreste von Franklin's Expedition durch M'Clintock. *Leipzig.* 1861. 8vo. Plates. 25633

Concerning Franklin's expedition, *see our* Vol. I., No. 1920, and Vol. IV., No. 13200. Also: Arctic Expeditions. Return ... 5 February, 1850, pp. vi. Papers relating to the Arctic Relief Expedition. Folio, pp. 157. — Papers relative to the Recent Arctic Expeditions in Search of Sir John Franklin and the Crews of H. M. S. "Erebus" and "Terror." ... *London: Printed by Eyre and Spottiswoode.* 1854. Folio, pp. (2), 225. + Further Papers. [*Ibid.*] 1855. Folio, pp. iv, 958. — Report of he Committee appointed by the Lords Commissioners of the Admiralty to Inquire and Report on the Recent Arctic Expeditions in Search of Sir J. Franklin. *London.* 1852. 2 vols., folio, pp. 560. Maps. — Report from the Select Committee on Arctic Expedition; together with the Proceedings of the Committee, Evidence and Appendix. ... 20 July, 1855. Folio, pp. xx, 35. — Vessels on the North Atlantic Return ... 4 June, 1852. [*London.* 1852.] Folio, pp. 38. (Relates to Franklin's Polar Expedition.)

FRANKLIN (*Lady*). A Letter to Viscount Palmerston, K.G., from Lady Franklin; with an Appendix. *London: J. Ridgway.* 1857. 8vo, pp. 36. 25634

FRANKLIN (S. F.) Life and Character of Abraham Lincoln. A Memorial Oration, delivered at Franklin, N. Y., June 1, 1865. By S. F. Franklin. *Delhi: Sturtevant & Co.* 1865. 8vo, pp. 16. 25635

FRANKLIN (W.) The Answer of his Excellency William Franklin, Esq; Governor of His Majesty's Province of New Jersey, to the invidious charges of the Proprietary Party, contained in a Libel, read by Mr. James Biddle, Clerk of the Common Pleas for the County of Philadelphia, On Saturday last, and afterwards published and industriously dispersed through the Province. [*Philadelphia.* n. d.] Folio, 1 l. P. 25636

[FRANKLIN.] A Humble Attempt at Scurrility, in Imitation of Those Great Masters of the Art, The Rev. Dr. S—th; the Rev. Dr. Al—n; the Rev. Mr. Ew—n; the Reverend D. J. D—oe, and the Heroic J—n D—n, Esq; Being a full Answer to the Observations on Mr. H—s's Advertisement. By Jack Retort, Student in Scurrility. *Quilsilvania; Printed.* 1765. 8vo, pp. 48. P. 25637

A defence of Dr. Franklin, by his son, W. Franklin. Printed at Philadelphia. The initials in the title severally signify: Smith, Allison, Ewing, Dove, John Dickinson, and Hughes. A large copperplate caricature of the election scene was published in the same vein.

FRANKLIN (W.) The Building Associations of Connecticut and other States Examined, with a Review of the New York and Massachusetts systems. ... To which is added, for the Management of such Institutions, a Model Plan. *New-Haven, Conn.: William Franklin.* 1864. 4to, pp. 225, iv. B., C. 25638

FRANKLIN (W. B.) A Reply of Maj.-Gen. William B. Franklin, to the Report of the Joint Committee of Congress on the Conduct of the War, submitted to the Public on the 6th of April, 1863. *New York: D. Van Nostrand.* 1863. 8vo, pp. 31. 2 Maps. BA., H. + Second Edition. *New York.* 1867. pp. (1), 14. 2 Maps. 25639

FRANKLIN. *See also* Francklin.

FRANKLIN, *pseudonym.* Letters of Franklin on the Conduct of the Executive and the Treaty negotiated by the Chief Justice of the United States with the Court of Great Britain. *Philadelphia.* 1795. 8vo, pp. 56. C., N. 25640

[FRANKLIN], *pseudonym.* An Examination of Mr. Bradish's Answer to the Interrogatories presented to him by a Committee of the State Anti-Slavery Society, October 1, 1838. [Also Correspondence with W. Jay and Gerritt Smith.] *Albany: Printed by Hoffman & White.* 1838. 8vo, pp. 30. BA. 25641

The Franklin Almanack for 1819. Calculated by John Armstrong. *Pittsburgh.* 1819. 12mo. 25642

Continued, under various editors.

Franklin Almanac and Diary, for 1868. *Cincinnati.* [1868.] 4to, pp. 32. 25643

FRANKLIN AND MARSHALL COLLEGE. Formal Opening of Franklin and Marshall College, in the City of Lancaster, June 7, 1853: Together with Addresses ... . *Lancaster, Pa.* 1853. 8vo, pp. 44. H. 25644

Dedication of Franklin and Marshall College. ... May 16th, 1856. ... *Chambersburg, Pa.: Printed by M. Kuffer & Co.* 1856. 8vo, pp. 24. H. 25645

Also: Catalogue of the Officers and Students, 1865. + Triennial Catalogue, 1866. 8vo.

FRANKLIN ASSOCIATION, *Mass.* The Constitution of the Charitable Society, instituted by the Franklin Association of Ministers, and the Address of their Committee. *Greenfield (Ms.): Printed by Ansel Phelps.* 1816. 8vo, pp. 16. H. 25646

FRANKLIN BAPTIST ASSOCIATION, *Delaware County, N. Y.* Minutes for 1815. 8vo. Continued annually. 25647

FRANKLIN CANAL. Message of Governor Bigler in Relation to the Franklin Canal Company. *Harrisburg.* 1854. 8vo. P.

FRANKLIN COLLEGE, *Athens, Ga.* Catalogue of the Trustees, Officers, and Graduates of Franklin College, from its Establishment in 1801, to the Annual Commencement in 1836. *Athens.* 1837. 8vo. 25649

FRANKLIN, *Conn.* The Celebration of the One Hundred and Fiftieth Anniversary of the Primitive Organization of the Congregational Church and Society, in Franklin, Connecticut, October 14th, 1868. *New Haven: Tuttle, Morehouse & Taylor.* 8vo, pp. 151. Map and 3 Portraits. B., BA., H. 25650

FRANKLIN COUNTY, *N. Y.* Proceedings of the Board of Supervisors of the County of Franklin, for 1869. *Malone.* 1869. 8vo. Continued. S. 25651

FRANKLIN COUNTY GRAMMAR SCHOOL, *Vt.* Catalogue ... 1840, 1841. *St. Albans.* 1840, 41. 8vo. 25652

Franklin Fund. *See* Vol. II., No. 6707.

FRANKLIN INSTITUTE. Catalogue of the Books belonging to the Library of the Franklin Institute. *Philadelphia.* 1851. 12mo.

Charter, Constitution, and By-Laws of the Franklin Institute of Pennsylvania, &c. With the First Quarterly Report, &c. *Philadelphia.* 1824. 12mo. P. 25654

The Franklin Journal, and American Mechanics' Magazine; devoted to the Useful Arts, Internal Improvements, and General Science. Edited by Thomas P. Jones. *Philadelphia.* 1826. 8vo.

Continued monthly. After Vol. IV. a second series was commenced, and the title was changed to "Journal of the Franklin Institute of the State of Pennsylvania, devoted to the Mechanic Arts, Manufactures, General Science, and the Recording of American and other Patented Inventions." This second series forms 25 vols. A third series was commenced in 1841, and is continued. This publication was edited, Jan., 1826–Jan., 1848 (Jan., 1841–July, 1842, jointly with Prof. J. J. Mapes), by T P. Jones, M.D.; Jan., 1848–1850, by Committee on Publications; subsequently by Prof. J. F. Frazer, assisted by the Committee on Publications.

First Annual Report of the Proceedings of the Franklin Institute of the State of Pennsylvania ... . *Philadelphia: J. Harding* 1825. 8vo, pp. 107. Continued. 25656

Also: Report of the Second Annual Exhibition of the Franklin Institute of the State of Pennsylvania, etc. *Philadelphia.* 1825. — Address of the Committee on Premiums and Exhibitions of the Franklin Institute of the State of Pennsylvania ... October, 1832. *Philadelphia: J. Harding.* 1832. 8vo, pp. 4. BA. — Letter from the Corresponding Secretary of the Franklin Institute of the State of Pennsylvania, for the Promotion of the Mechanic Arts. *Philadelphia.* 1824. 8vo. P. — Proceedings of Franklin Institute ... relative to the Establishment of a School of Design for Women. *Philadelphia.* 1851. 8vo.

FRANKLIN LIBRARY. *See* Lawrence, *Mass.*

FRANKLIN, *Mass.* Annual Report of the School Committee of the Town of Franklin, for the Year ending 1862–63. *Boston: Geo. C. Rand & Avery.* 1863. 8vo, pp. 16. Continued. H.

Annual Report of the Benevolent Societies of Franklin County for the Year 1840. *Greenfield: Phelps & Ingersoll.* 12mo, pp. 11.

Also: Condensed Report of the Benevolent Societies of Franklin County, Mass *Greenfield.* 1839. 12mo.

Annual Report of the Franklin Domestic Missionary Society. *Greenfield.* 1826–27. 12mo. Continued. 25659

Constitution, By-Laws and Code of Ethics of the Franklin Medical Association ... January 1, 1851. *Greenfield: Printed by Charles A. Mirick.* 1851. 8vo, pp. 28. H. 25660

Receipts and Expenditures of the Town of Franklin, from March 1st, 1859, to March 1st, 1860. *Boston: Printed by J. B. Chisholm.* 1860. 8vo, pp. 16. Continued. H. 25661

Transactions of the Franklin County Agricultural Society, for the Year 1854. *Greenfield: Printed by Charles A. Mirick.* 1854. 8vo, pp. 93. Continued. H. 25662

FRANKLIN MINING COMPANY. First Report of the Directors ... of the Franklin Mining Company, Issued April 10, 1861. 8vo, pp. 45. Continued. H. 25663

Franklin Ore and Iron ... also, the Proper Location for a National Foundry ... . *New York: George F. Nesbitt & Co.* 1862. 8vo, pp. 16. H. 25664

FRANKLIN RAILROAD. ... Plan of the Franklin Rail Road Company ... . *Boston: Press of John H. Eastburn.* 1830. 8vo, pp. 7. Map. 25665

Franklin Typographical Society. Proceedings at the Printers' Festival, January 15, 1848. *Boston.* 1848. 8vo. B. 25666

Franklin's Legacy; or the New-York & Vermont Almanack. *Troy.* 1802. 12mo. Continued. 25667

Frankliniana, ou Recueil d'Anecdotes, bons mots, Réflexions, Maximes et Observations de Benjamin Franklin; Par un American. *Paris: Tiger.* [About 1820.] 18mo, pp. 108. Portrait.

FRANKLINVILLE ACADEMY. Annual Catalogue of the Franklinville Academy, Franklinville, L. I. 1857–1858. *New York.* 1862. 8vo. Continued. 25669

FRANKS (David). *See* New York City.

FRANSHAM (J.) The World in Miniature, or the Entertaining Traveller. By John Fransham. *London.* 1740. — Second Edition. *London: John Torbuck.* 1741. 12mo, pp. 275. Plates.

Vol. II. contains America, and the Isles thereof.. Reprinted in 1745, 1752, and 1767.

FRANSIOLI (J.) Patriotism, a Christian Virtue. A Sermon preached ... by the Rev. Joseph Fransioli, at St. Peter's (Catholic) Church, Brooklyn, July 26th, 1863. *New York: W. C. Bryant & Co.* 1863. 8vo, pp. 8. B., N. 25671

Loyal Publication Society, No. 24.

The Frantic Conduct of John Bull, for a Century past: or a Review of his Wars and Debts. A Poem, in Two Cantos. ... *London: J. Ridgway.* 1803. 8vo. 25672

See "M. Rev.," new series, XLI. 101.

The Frantic Maid; or a Tale of Wyoming, a Poem, in Five Cantos. *Wilkesbarre.* 1819. pp. 201. 25673

FRASANS (Hippolyte de), *and* LANGLOIS (Jean Thomas). Mémoire pour le chef de brigade Magliore Pélage et pour les habitants de la Guadaloupe, chargés par cette colonie, de l'administration provisoire, après le depart du capitaine-général Lacrosse. *Paris: Dessene, etc.* 1802–03. 2 vols., 8vo, 2 l., pp. 326, xl; vii, 358, 1 l. C. 25674

FRASER (C.) Reminiscences of Charleston, lately published in the Charleston Courier, and now Revised and Enlarged by the Author, Charles Fraser. *Charleston: John Russell.* 1854. 8vo, pp. 119. 25675

Also: An Address, delivered before the Citizens of Charleston ... at the Laying of the Corner-Stone of a New College Edifice ... 12th January, 1858. ... *Charleston: Printed by J. S. Burges.* 1828. 8vo, pp. 24. H. — Address at Charleston, [S. C.] Sep. 19, 1834, before the Euphradian Society. ... *Charleston.* 1834. 8vo. — Address on the Birth-Day of General Washington, delivered at the request of the Washington Light Infantry, on the 22d of February, 1845, ... *Charleston.* 1845. 8vo, pp. 31. — Address ... on the Dedication of Magnolia Cemetery, on the 19th November, 1850. ... *Charleston: Walker & James.* 1850. 8vo, pp. 23. B., BA. — An Oration ... before the Inhabitants of Charleston, on the 4th of July, 1808 ... . *Charleston: Printed by J. Hoff.* 1808. 8vo, pp. 40. BA.

FRASER (D.) The American Magazine of Wonders, and Marvelous Chronicle. By Donald Fraser. *New York: Southwick & Pelsue.* 1809. 2 vols., 8vo, pp. 508, 2 l.; pp. 510, 2 l. 8 Plates. C. 25676

FRASER. A Collection of Select Biography; or, the Bulwark of Truth: ... By D. Fraser. *New York: Printed for the Author.* 1798. 12mo, pp. vi, (1), 255, (9). 25677

Includes life of George Fox, William Penn, etc.

FRASER. The Columbian Monitor: ... By Donald Fraser ... . *New-York: Printed for the Author by Loudon and Brewer.* M,DCC,XCIV. 12mo, 6 l., pp. 149, 7. H. 25678

Also: Compendium of the History of all Nations ... *New York.* 1807. 8vo. — Young Gentleman's and Lady's Assistant. *New York.* 1791. 12mo.

FRASER (D.) Leaves from a Minister's Portfolio. By Rev. Donald Fraser. *Montreal.* 1858? 25679

FRASER (E.) Narrative of the Capture, Sufferings and Miraculous Escape of Mrs. Eliza Fraser, Wrecked on an Unknown Island, inhabited by Savages, by whom Captain Fraser and his First Mate were barbarously Murdered, and Mrs. Fraser ... was ... compelled to take up her abode in a Wigwam, and to become the adopted Wife of one of the Chiefs, Mrs. F. was providentially rescued from her perilous situation ... *Newark: Charles S. Webb.* 1837. 8vo, pp. 24. 3 Plates. 25680

"Little or nothing to do with American Indians." — T. W. FIELD.

FRASER (J.) Papers on the Colonial Questions, extracted from Fraser's Magazine. *London: J. Fraser.* 1830. 8vo.

Fraser's Magazine (*London: James Fraser.* 1830, etc. 8vo), contains many articles on American topics.

FRASER (J.) ... Report ... on the Common School System of the United States and ... . Canada. By the Rev. James Fraser, M.A., Assistant Commissioner. ... . *London: Printed by George E. Eyre and William Spottiswoode.* 1866. Folio, pp. 435, v. 14 Plates. B., BA., H. 25682

FRASER (J.) A Short History of the Agrostis Cornucopiæ, or the New American Grass; and a new Botanical Description of the Plant. To which are added, Experiments to point out the Proper Mode of Cultivating this Plant; and also some account of a Journey to the Cherokee Nation, in search of New Plants. By John Fraser. *London: Wenman.* 1789. Folio, pp. 8. Plate.

FRASER (M.) Extract from a Manuscript Journal relating to the Siege of Quebec in 1759, kept by Col. Malcom Fraser. *Quebec.* 1865. 8vo, pp. 37. 25684

FRASER (Thomas). Inoculation in Antigua. 1755–56. *London.* 1778. 8vo. 25685

Title from Allibone's Dictionary.

FRASER RIVER. Guide to Fraser River, with Vocabulary of Indian Words. *New York.* 1858. 18mo. 25686

FRASSO (P.) De Regio Petronatu Indiarum. Quæstiones aliquæ desumptæ et disputatæ, in alia quinquaginta capita partitæ. Auctore D. Petro Frasso Juris-consulto Turritano, in Regio Limano Senatu fisci patrono. *Matriti: Ex Typographia Blaisii Roman.* MDCCLXXV. 2 vols., folio, pp. 328, xc; cxv, 383.

First printed in 1677, which edition I have not seen. Important as connected with Spanish-American law.

FRAUNCES (A. G.) An Appeal to the Legislature of the United States, and to the Citizens, etc., against the Conduct of the Secretary of the Treasury. By Andrew G. Fraunces. *New York.* 1793. 12mo. N. 25688

Fray Serapio, Escenas de la vida Mejicana. Traduccion del francés por R. d. Z. *Veracruz.* 1849. 12mo. 25689

FRAZEE (B.) An Appeal to the Methodist Episcopal Church, North and South, on the Course of the Christian Advocate and Journal. By Bradford Frazee. *New York.* 1844. pp. 29.

FRAZEE (J.) A Refutation of the Charges against John Frazee, Architect of the New-York Custom House. *New York.* 1844. 8vo, pp. 21. M. 25691

[FRAZER (John).] To the Committee of the Washington Monument Association. [June 8, 1848.] 8vo, pp. 7. 25692

FRAZER (W. C.) A Funeral Oration in Memory of George Washington, delivered at Lancaster, before Lodge 43, on the 22nd of February. By William Clark Frazer. *Wilmington.* 1800. 8vo, pp. 15. 25693

FRAZIER (T. H.), *Judge, etc.* Proceedings of the High Court of Impeachment in the case of the People of the State of Tennessee *vs.* Thomas W. Frazier. Begun and held at Nashville, May 11, 1867. *Nashville: C. S. Mercer.* 1867. 8vo, pp. 124, 8, 207. C. 25694

FREBLE (Thomas M.) The Voice of God: or, an Account of the Unparalleled Fires, Hurricanes, Floods and Earthquakes, commencing with 1845; also, some Account of Pestilence, Famine, and Increase of Crime. *Albany: J. Munsell.* 1847. 12mo, pp. 84. 25695

"Written to show that these calamities were the result of the wickedness of the times. The author was a Second Advent preacher, in haste to bring the world to a close." — J. MUNSELL.

FREDERICKSBURG. Report of the Operations of the Inspectors and Relief Agents, after the Battle of Fredericksburg, December 13, 1862. [n. p. 1863.] 8vo, pp. 31. 25696

"United States Sanitary Commission Tract," No. 57.

FREDERICTON. A Charge delivered at his Primary Visitation held in Christ Church Cathedral, Fredericton, August 24, 1847, by John, Bishop of Fredericton. *Fredericton: John Simpson, Printer.* 1847. 8vo, pp. 46. 25697

FREDONIA ACADEMY. Annual Catalogue ... of Fredonia Academy, at Fredonia, Chautauque County, N. Y., for the Year 1844. *Fredonia.* 1844. 8vo, pp. 22. Continued. B. 25698

Also: Proceedings of the Fredonia Academy Re-union, March 12, 1867. 8vo.

A Free and Calm Consideration. *See* [Presscott (Benj.)]

A Free and Candid Address to the Right Hon. William Pitt, on the present Posture of Affairs, both at Home and Abroad. *London: Cooke.* 1765. Folio. 25699

See "M. Rev.," XXXIII. 486.

Free and Candid Remarks on a Late Celebrated Oration; with Some Few Occasional Thoughts on the Late Commotions in America. In a Letter to ——. *London: B. Law.* M,DCC,-LXVI. 8vo, pp. 32. BA. 25700

"Censures Mr. Pitt's speech against the American Stamp-Act." — *M. Rev.*, XXXIV. 482.

Free and Candid Review. *See* [Holroyd (John)].

The Free and Impartial Examiner: Being a Candid Enquiry ... with regard both to Domestick and Foreign Affairs ... *London.* 1745. 8vo, pp. vii, 52. 25701

A Free and Impartial Examination of the Preliminary Articles of Pacification, With a Retrospective Review of the Rise, and various Stages of the War. By a Member of Parliament. *London: Fielding.* 1783. 8vo, pp. 50. 25702

See "M. Rev.," LXVIII. 178.

Free and Impartial Remarks on the real Importance of the Whale Fishery: ... By a Merchant. *London: M. Cooper.* [n. d.] 8vo. 25703

A Free Appeal to the People of Great Britain, on the Conduct of the Present Administration, since the Thirtieth of July, 1766. *London: J. Almon.* MDCCLXVII. 8vo, pp. 45. BA. + Second Edition. [*Ibid.*] 25704

See "M. Rev.," XXXVI. 129.

Free Blacks and Slaves. Would Immediate Abolition be a Blessing? A Letter to the Editor of the Anti-Slavery Advocate. By a Cambridge Man. ... *London: Arthur, Hall, Virtue & Co.* 1853. 8vo, pp. 27. B. 25705

The Free Briton's Memorial. *See* [Bollan (W.)], Vol. II., No. 6212.

FUGL (Ulrich Nicolai). Oplysninger angaande de dansk vestindiske Øers nuværende commercielle Forhold. I. St. Thomas. *Kjobenhavn.* 1840. 26135

Also: Om Negerslaveriet i Vestindien, og sammes Ophör; med specielt Hensyn til de danske Besiddelser, in the "Juridisk Tidsskrift," 1835, XXIV. 1–60.

FULFORD (F.) Five Occasional Lectures, delivered in Montreal. By Francis Fulford, D.D. *Montreal.* 1859. 8vo, pp. 118.

FULFORD. The Sermon at the Consecration of Horatio Potter, D.D., to the Episcopate. Preached by Appointment in Trinity Church, New York, November 22, 1854. By Francis Fulford, D.D. ... . *New-York: Daniel Dana, Jr.* M,DCCC,LIV. 8vo, pp. 31. B. 26137

FULFORD. Sermon ... Triennial Meeting of the General Convention of the Protestant Episcopal Church ... in ... Philadelphia, October 4th, 1865. By the Most Reverend Francis Fulford, D.D. ... . *Philadelphia: King and Baird.* 1865. 8vo, pp. 14. B., H. 26138

FULFORD. Sermons, Addresses and Statistics of the Diocese in Montreal. *Montreal, London, and Cambridge.* 1865. 8vo, pp. xiv–308. 26139

Also: Pastoral Letter addressed to the Clergy of the Diocese. ... *Montreal.* 1851 pp. 16. — An Address ... in the Chapel of the General Theological Seminary of the Protestant Episcopal Church ... November 13th, 1852. ... . *New York.* MDCCCLII. 8vo, pp. iv, (2), 15, (1). B., H. — A Charge delivered to the Clergy of the Diocese of Montreal, at the Primary Visitation. ... *Montreal.* 1852. pp. 25. — A Charge delivered to the Clergy of the Diocese of Montreal, at the Triennial Visitation. ... *Montreal.* 1855. pp. 38. — A Letter to the Bishops and Clergy of the United Church of England and Ireland in Canada. ... *Montreal.* pp. 30.

FULGOSIS (B.) Baptistæ Fulgosi de dictis factils que memorabilibus collectanea a Camillo Galino latina facta. [Colophon:] *Jacobus Ferrarius Mediolane* . x . *Kl. Julius a redemptione christana anno* MDVIII *impressit.* Folio, 366 unnumbered l. 26140

On signature llii is a short chapter on Columbus. Reprinted in *Paris, by Peter Vidoux.* 1518. 4to; *Antwerp.* 1565; *Basle.* 1567; *Cologne.* 1604. 4to.

A Full and Authentic Report of tbe [*sic*] Debates in Faneuil Hall, Dec. 31, Jan. 1, & 2, 1821–2; On changing the form of Government of the Town ... Including the Speeches of Messrs. Clough, Emmons, &c. ... *Boston: William Emmons.* 1822. 12mo, pp. 48. H. 26141

Free Thoughts on Despotic and Free Governments, as connected with the Happiness of the Governor and the Governed. *London.* 1781. 8vo. 25719

Free Thoughts on the Continuance of the American War, and the Necessity of its Termination. Addressed to the Inhabitants of Great Britain. By a Gentleman of Lincoln's Inn. *London: T. Payne.* 1781. 8vo, pp. 22. P. 25720

See "M. Rev.," LXV. 468.

Free Thoughts. *See* [Seabury (Sam.)], [Wilkins (I.)], *and* [Wesley (John)].

Free Trade and Farmer's Rights, or the "Market Wagon War." *Cincinnati.* 1839. 8vo. 25721

Free Trade and Sailor's Rights. American Glory. The Victories of Hull, Jones, Decatur, Bainbridge; as detailed in their Official Letters and the Letters of other Officers. Together with ... the Public Testimonials of Respect, and the Songs and Odes written in Celebration of those Events ... With [wood] Engravings of the Actions. The Designs by Woodside, the Engravings by Mason. *Philadelphia: [Thomas Palmer], Dennis Heartt, Printer.* 1813. 8vo, pp. 58. H. 25722

Free Trade in Negroes. *London.* 1849. 8vo, pp. 52.

Free Trade and the American System; a Dialogue between a Merchant and a Planter. *Columbia.* 1832. 8vo, pp. 12. 25724

Free Trade Policy, examined with respect to ... our Colonial System, ... By a Liverpool Merchant. *London.* 1846. 8vo, pp. 36. 25725

The Free-Trader. *New York: J. Savell.* 1867–71. 5 vols., folio. C. 25726

Organ of the "American Free-Trade League." Vol. I. is "The League."

Free-Will Baptist Register for 1847. *Dover, N. H.* 1847. 18mo. Continued. S. 25727

General Conference of the Free-Will Baptist Connection in North America. Minutes. 1828. 12mo. Continued.

The Freeborn Englishman's Unmasked Battery; containing Remarks on the Preliminary Articles of Peace grounded upon undeniable Facts, shewing the Fatal tendency of granting the French a Fishery and restoring our most important Conquests. *London: P. Hunt.* MDCCLXII. 8vo, pp. 73. J.C.B. 25729

FREEDLEY (E. T.) Leading Pursuits and Leading Men. A Treatise on the Principal Trades and Manufactures of the United States, showing the Progress, State and Prospects of Business: and Illustrated by Sketches of Distinguished Mercantile and Manufacturing Firms. Edited by Edwin T. Freedley, ... *Philadelphia: Lippincott, Grambo, and Co.* [1856.] 8vo, pp. 188.

FREEDLEY. Philadelphia and its Manufactures: a Hand-Book exhibiting the Development, Variety, and Statistics of the Manufacturing Industry of Philadelphia in 1857. Together with Sketches of Remarkable Manufactories; and a List of Articles now made in Philadelphia. By Edwin T. Freedley, ... *Philadelphia: Edward Young.* 1858. 12mo, pp. 490. + [*Ibid.*] 1859. 12mo, pp. 504. 25731

FREEDLEY. Philadelphia and its Manufactories and Representative Mercantile Houses of Philadelphia in 1867. By Edwin T. Freedley ... . *Philadelphia: Edward Young & Co.* [1867.] 8vo, pp. 634. 6 Plates. B. 25732

FREEDLEY. Geschäft, Verkehr und Arbeit in den Vereinigten Staaten, oder praktische Anleitung in Amerika Geld zu erwerben, zu sparen, anzuwenden und zu hinterlassen. Nach dem Englischen ... . *Göttingen: Wigand.* 1853. 16mo, pp. 125.

Also: The Issue, and its Consequences. ... *Philadelphia: King & Band.* 1856. 8vo, pp. (2), 20. B., BA., H. — Opportunities for Industry and the Safe Investment of Capital; or, a thousand chances to make Money. ... *Philadelphia.* 1859. 12mo. — A Practical Treatise on Business: or, how to Get, Save, Spend, Give, Lend, and Bequeath Money; ... Second Edition. *Philadelphia: Lippincott & Co.* 1856. 8vo, pp. 336. C., H. — United States Mercantile Guide. Leading Pursuits and Leading Men. A Treatise on the Principal Trades and Manufactures of the United States ... . *Philadelphia: Edward Young.* 1856. 8vo. B.

FREEDMAN (J. J.) Argument in Favor of the Repeal of the Excise Law, delivered in ... Albany, February 12, 1868 ... . By John J. Freedman. *New York.* 1868. 8vo, pp. 24. H.

FREEDMAN. Is the Act entitled "An Act for enrolling and calling out the National Forces, and for other purposes," passed March 3, 1863, Constitutional or not? *New York: George S. Diossy.* 1863. 8vo, pp. 62. 25735

The Freed-Man: a Monthly Magazine, Devoted to the Interests of the Freed Colored People. ... *London: S. W. Partridge.* MDCCCLXVI. pp. 16. Continued. B., H. 25736

FREEDMEN. An Act to Incorporate the Freedmen's Saving

and Trust Company, Approved March 3, 1865. *New York: W. C. Bryant & Co.* 1865. 8vo, pp. 8. 25737

... The American Freedmen's Aid Commission. Its Origin [Purpose, Policy, etc. n. p. 1865.] 8vo, pp. 11, (1). H.

First Annual Report of the Educational Commission For Freedmen. May, 1863. *Boston: Prentiss & Deland.* 1863. 8vo, pp. 22. + The same, with Extracts from Letters of Teachers. *Boston: David Clapp.* 1863. 8vo, pp. 28. B. 25739

The Freedmen's Bulletin. *Chicago.* 186–. 8vo. 25740

The Freedman's Harp: ... Patriotic Hymns, ... *Providence: A. Crawford Greene.* [n. d.] 12mo, pp. 36. 25741

The Freedmen's Journal, [afterwards] the Freedmen's Record. *Boston.* 1865. 8vo. Monthly. 25742

Semi-Annual Report on Schools for Freedmen, 1866. By J. W. Alvord, General Superintendent. *Washington: Government Printing Office.* 1869. 8vo. Continued. 25743

See also [Eaton], Vol. VI., No. 21729.

Freedman's Savings and Trust Company. ... *New York: Wm. C. Bryant & Co.* 1865. 8vo, pp. 20. H. 25744

Minutes of the Convention of Freedmen's Commissions, held at Indianapolis, July 19 and 20, 1864. *Cincinnati: R. P. Thompson.* 1864. 8vo, pp. 28. H. 25745

Report of the General Superintendent of Freedmen Department of the Tennessee and State of Arkansas For 1864. *Memphis, Tenn.* 1865. 8vo, pp. 38. 25746

Also: First Annual Report of the National Freedmen's Relief Association. *New York. February* 19, 1863. 4to, pp. 3. — Monthly Report of the same, No. 2. 4to, pp. 4. — Report of the National Freedmen's Relief Association. *New York.* 1864. 8vo.

The Freedom of Commerce of the Subjects of the Netherlands, a Confutation of the Arguments advanced by the West Indian Company. [n. p. 1725?] 4to. 25747

Relates to trading to the coasts of America.

The Freedom of Speech and Writing upon Public Affairs, considered; with an Historical View of the Roman Imperial Laws against Libels ... *London.* 1766. 4to. 25748

Relates in part to the American Colonies. *See* A Succinct View.

Freedom The first of Blessings. [Colophon:] *Sold at the Heart and Crown in Cornhill, Boston.* [n. d.] 4to, pp. 7.

This rare tract relates to the Massachusetts Excise Bill.

Freedom's Journal. Devoted to the Improvement of the Coloured Population. *New-York.* 1828. 8vo. Continued. B.

Freeholder. An Appeal to the People of the United States. By a Freeholder. ... *Boston: Hilliard, Gray, Little & Wilkins.* 1831. 8vo, pp. 88. B. 25751

A Freeholder's Address to the Freeholders of the Southern District. [n. p.] 1789. 16mo. 25752

The Freeholder's Political Catechism. Very necessary to be Studied by every Freeman in America. *London: Printed. New-York: Re-printed by T. Green.* 1769. 8vo, pp. 23. BA. 25753

Freeland (W. H.) Address delivered before the Library Association of Hudson, Jan. 27, 1836. By William H. Freeland. *Hudson, N. Y.* 8vo. 25754

Freeman (B.) Verdeediging | van | D. Bernardus Freeman | wegens | Het gene hem voornamlyk ten laste | gelegt word in zeeker BOek, | Genaamt | Klagte, &c. | *Te Nieuw York,* | *Gedrukt by J. Peter Zenger, in't Jaar* | 1726 |. 16mo, pp. 125. 25755

The author was a Dutch dominie at Midwood, N. Y. He wrote his name Freerman, but it is not so printed.

Freeman (E. A.) History of Federal Government, from the Foundation of the Achaian League to the Disruption of the United States. By Edward A. Freeman, M.A. Volume I. ... *Macmillan and Co.: London and Cambridge.* 1863. pp. xl, 721. Maps. B., C., H., S. 25756

Freeman (F.) Yaradee; a Plea for Africa. ... *Philadelphia: J. Whetham.* 1836. 12mo, pp. 360. BA., H., P. + Third Edition. 1838. BA. 25757

Freeman (F.) Africa's Redemption the Salvation of Our Country. By Rev. F. Freeman ... *New-York: For the Author.* 1852. 8vo, pp. 383. H. 25758

Freeman. Religious Liberty. A Discourse delivered in the Congregational Church at Hanson, on the Fourth of July, 1832. By F. Freeman, ... *Plymouth, Mass.: Printed by Benjamin Drew, Jr.* 1832. 8vo, pp. 32. 25759

Freeman (F.) The History of Cape Cod: The Annals of Barnstable County and of its Several Towns, including the District of Mashpee. By Frederick Freeman. *Boston: The Author.* 1860–62. 2 vols., rl. 8vo, pp. 803; 803. Portraits. B., BA.

First published in ten parts.

[Freeman (James).] The Character of Rev. John Eliot, D.D. ... who Died Feb. 14, 1813. A Discourse delivered at the New North Church, Boston, March 7, 1813. *Boston: Thomas Wells.* 1813. 8vo, pp. 23. B., BA., H. 25761

[Freeman.] A Description of the Eastern Coast of the County of Barnstable, from Cape Cod, or Race Point, ... to Cape Malebarre ... . By a Member of the Humane Society. *Boston: Printed by Hosea Sprague.* 1802. 8vo, pp. 15. B., BA.

[Freeman.] Eighteen Sermons and a Charge. *Cambridge.* 1829. 8vo, pp. iv, 276. H. 25763

F[reeman.] Remarks on the American Universal Geography. By J. F. *Boston: Belknap and Hall.* 1793. 8vo, pp. 61, (1). B., BA., H., M., W. 25764

Adverse criticism on Morse's "Geography."

[Freeman.] A Sermon for December 15, 1796; the Day of Public Thanksgiving. ... *Boston: William Spottswood.* 1796. 8vo, pp. 21. H. 25765

Freeman. Sermons and Charges. By James Freeman. New Edition. *Boston: Carter, Hendee and Co.* 1832. 12mo. 25766

[Freeman.] Sermons on Particular Occasions. ... *Boston: Printed by Manning and Loring.* 1812. 8vo, pp. 296. B., BA., H. + Third Edition. *Boston.* 1821. 25767

Also: A Description of Marshpee, in the County of Barnstable, September 16th' 1802. 8vo, pp. 96. *See* [Cary (S.)]

Freeman, *and* Cary (S.) Funeral Sermons, preached at King's Chapel, Boston. By James Freeman and Samuel Cary. *Boston: Printed by Sewell Phelps.* 1820. 8vo, pp. 68. BA., H.

Occasioned by the deaths of Mrs. Susan Bulfinch, Rev. Samuel Cary, and Joseph Coolidge.

Freeman (J.) A Copy of a Letter from J. Freeman, together with a Letter and Extracts of Letters from Settlers in the Huron Tract, and other Parts of Upper Canada, containing Useful Information respecting that Country. *Framlingham.* 1832. 12mo, pp. 12. 25769

Freeman (M.), *pseudonym.* A Word in Season to All True Lovers of their Liberty and their Country. By Mylo Freeman. *Boston.* 1748. 8vo, pp. 16. M., W. 25770

Freeman (N.) A Charge to the Grand Jury, at the Court of General Sessions of the Peace, holden at Barnstable, ... March Term, A.D. 1802. By Nathaniel Freeman, Esq. ... . *Boston: Printed by Manning & Loring.* 1802. 8vo, pp. 30. B.

Freeman (N.) Tables of the Pay, Emoluments, and Supplies of the Army and Militia of the United States, corrected to Sept. 1, 1814. By Nehemiah Freeman. *Boston.* 1814. 16mo, pp. 40. 25772

Freeman (Nicholas). Le Glaneur. *See* Jay (A.)

Freeman (O. S.) Letters on Slavery, addressed to the Pro-Slavery Men of America; showing its Illegality in all Ages and Nations; its Destructive War upon Society and Government, Morals, and Religion. By O. S. Freeman. ... [*Bela Marsh, Boston.*] 1853. 12mo, pp. 108. B., BA., C., H. 25773

Freeman (P. R.) An Oration Pronounced at Portsmouth, N. H. on the Fourth Day of July, 1810 ... . By Peyton Randolph Freeman, Esq. *Portsmouth, N. H.: Printed by William Treadwell.* [1810.] 8vo, pp. 23. BA., M., W. 25774

Freeman. A Refutation of Sundry Aspersions in the "Vindication" of the Present Trustees of Dartmouth College, on the Memory of their Predecessors. By Peyton R. Freeman. *Portsmouth: Printed by Beck & Foster.* 1816. 8vo, pp. 32. BA., H.

Freeman (Philo), *pseudonym.* The Essex Almanack for the Years 1770 and 1771. *Salem.* [n. d.] 12mo. Continued.

Freeman (S.) The Emigrant's Hand Book, and Guide to Wisconsin, comprising information respecting Agricultural and Manufacturing Employment, ... By Samuel Freeman, ... *Milwaukee.* 1851. 8vo, pp. 148. 25777

Freeman (Theresa J.) Silver Lake; or, the Belle of Bayou Luie. A Tale of the South. *Saint Louis: P. M. Pinckard.* 1867. 12mo, pp. 344. C. 25778

Freeman (T.) Address to the Inhabitants of Pennsylvania. By Thomas Freeman. [n. p. n. d.] 8vo. 25779

Freeman (T.) Adventures of Mr. Thos. Freeman, who was Shipwrecked on the Coast of St. Domingo in the Year 1806, and received into the Family of Orizo, an African. [n. d.] 12mo.

Freeman (W.) Copy of the Petition of William Freeman, Esq., in behalf of himself, Mr. Mead, and others, owners of several tracts of Land in the Charibbee Islands in America, against Colonel Codrington, Governor of the Leeward Islands, presented to the House of Commons, with remarks thereon. *London.* 1702. 4to. 25781

Freeman (W.) An Address delivered at Limerick, Me., February, 1815, on the Celebration of Peace, between Great Britain and the United States. By William Freeman. *Bangor: Smith & Sayward.* 1846. 8vo, pp. 16. B. 25782

Freeman. An Oration, delivered at ... Portland, July 4th, 1808. By William Freeman. *Portland.* 1808. 8vo, pp. 16.

Freeman. Genealogy of the Freeman Family. [*Portland.* 1861.] 8vo. 25784

Freeman (W.) Trial of William Freeman for the Murder of John G. Van Nest, ... Reported by Benjamin F. Hall. *Auburn.* 1848. 8vo. 25785

Freeman (W. P.) Biography of Isaac W. Ambler. By William P. Freeman. Second Edition. *Biddeford (Me.): Horton Brothers.* 1860. 12mo, pp. 240. C. 25786

Freeman *and* Custis. An Account of the Red River in Louisiana, drawn up from the Returns of Messrs. Freeman & Custis to the War Office, in the United States, who Explored the same in the Year 1806. [n. p. n. d.] 8vo, pp. 63. 2 folded Tables. 25787

Freeman, *pseudonym.* A Letter from Freeman of South-Carolina, to the Deputies of North-America, assembled in the High Court of Congress at Philadelphia. *South-Carolina, Charles-Town: Printed by Peter Timothy.* M,DCC,LXXXIV. Sm. 4to, pp. 47.

Reprinted in London. Written by William Henry Drayton, Christopher Gadsden, John Mackenzie, and others; they originally appeared in Peter Timothy's "South Carolina Gazette."

Freeman's Address to the North Americans; proving that their Present Embarrassments are owing to their Federal Union, their Sovereign States, their Constitutions, and their Statesmen; and containing some Propositions for Relief. ... Property of the Author, secured by Public Faith. [1840 or 1846.] 8vo, pp. 29.

The Freeman's Guide: containing the Federal Constitution, and the Constitutions of the Different States ... . *Charlestown: Solomon B. Brega.* 1812. 12mo, pp. 294. BA., H. 25790

The Freeman's Oath. 1839. 25791

Thomas's "History of Printing" says, "In January, 1639, printing was first performed in that part of North America which extends from the gulph of Mexico to the frozen ocean." The first press and font of type were imported by Rev. Jesse Glover, who defrayed a part of the expense, the balance being contributed by several gentlemen in New England and Amsterdam. A London printer, called Stephen Daye, came at the same time with the printing apparatus, in 1638, and the office was located in Cambridge, Massachusetts. "The first thing which was printed," says Winthrop, "was 'The Freeman's Oath;' the next was an almanac made for New England, by Mr. William Peirce, mariner," both of which, according to Thomas, were issued in 1639. We have been unable to ascertain whether there are any copies in existence of these two publications. Mr. S. F. Haven is of opinion that "The Freeman's Oath" was printed on one side of a sheet of small paper. *See* Harrisse's "Bibl. Am. Vetustissima."

Freemen, Awake!! Declaration and Protest of Liberty against Usurpation and Tyranny. [n. p. 186–.] 8vo, pp. 4. 25792

Freemasonry. Apologie des Franc-Maçons par, Le Frère **** Membre, de la Loge ** Ecossaise de P. * *à Philadelphie l'an* 5651, 1779. 12mo, 4 l., pp. 119. 25793

See also Knights Templars, Masonry, and also under the names of the respective States.

A Collection of Letters on Freemasonry, in Chronological Order. *Boston: T. R. Marvin.* 1849. 8vo, pp. 103. B., C.

By J. C. Spencer, R. Rush, H. Tatem, and E. Everett.

Constitution of the Grand Royal Arch Chapter of the United States. *Hartford.* 1794. 12mo. W. 25795

Freemasons. Constitution of the General Grand Royal Arch Chapter, of the Northern States of America. *Albany: Thomas S. Webb.* 1799. 8vo, pp. 19. H. 25796

Several other editions, with additional by-laws.

The Constitutions of the Free Masons. Containing the History, Charges, Regulations, &c., of that most Ancient and Right Worshipful Fraternity. For the use of the Lodges. *London: Printed Anno* 5723. *Re-printed in Philadelphia by Special Order, for the Use of the Brethren in North America. In the Year of Masonry* 5734, *Anno Domini* 1734. 4to. 25797

Printed by Benjamin Franklin, and very rare.

The Constitutions of the Ancient and Honourable Fraternity of Free and Accepted Masons: containing their History, Charges, Addresses, &c., Collected and Digested from their old Records, Faithful Traditions, and Lodge Books, for the Use of Masons. To which are added, the History of Masonry in Massachusetts, and the Constitution, Laws, and Regulations of their Grand Lodge. Together with a large Collection of Songs, Epilogues, &c. *Printed at Worcester, by Brother Isaiah Thomas. In the Christian Era* MDCCXCII.; *in the Year of Light* VMDCCXCII. 4to, pp. 228. Plate. M. 25798

Very rare. A later edition differs.

Disclosures relating to the "A. B. C." Affair. ... [n. p. n. d.] 8vo, pp. 8, 12. B., BA. 25799

A Freeman on Freemasonry [*Boston?* n. d.] 8vo, pp. 8.

The Freemason; a Monthly Magazine, ... Conducted by R. C. F. Rayhouser, and an able staff of contributors. *Indianapolis: Indianapolis Journal Company.* 1860. 25801

Six numbers published.

The Freemason; A Masonic Monthly Journal. ... Edited By George Frank Gouley ... . *St. Louis, Mo.* 1867. 4to. Continued. 25802

Freemasonry; A Poem, ... with Notes, illustrative of the History, Policy, Principles, &c., of the Masonic Institution, ... Circumstances relative to the Abduction of Capt. Morgan; and of the present prospects of Anti-Masonry in various parts of the Union ... . By a Citizen of Massachusetts. *Leicester: Samuel A. Whittemore.* 1830. 12mo, pp. 216. 25803

Freemasonry and the War. Report of the Committee under the Resolutions of 1862, Grand Lodge of Virginia ... . *Richmond: Charles H. Wynne.* 1865. 8vo, pp. 31. H. 25804

Free-Masonry in Reply to Anti-Masonry, in the American Quarterly Review, for March, 1830. *Boston.* 1830. 12mo, pp. 40. B., H. 25805

Freemasonry in New York: its Troubles & their Causes Impartially Reviewed. By an Inactive Member. *New York.* 1856. 8vo, pp. 48. 25806

Freemasonry Unmasked: ... *Gettysburg, Pa.: R. W. Middleton.* 1835. Sm. 8vo, pp. 93. B. 25807

The Freemasons' Magazine and General Miscellany. *Philadelphia.* 1811. 2 vols., 8vo. Plates and Portraits. N. 25808

The Freemasons' Magazine, Edited By Chas. W. Moore ... *Boston: Printed by Tuttle & Dermott.* 1842. 8vo. Continued.

The Freemasons' Monitor; or, Illustrations of Masonry: ... *Albany: Spencer and Webb.* 1797. 12mo, 6 l., pp. 284. B., H.

The Freemasons' Repository. ... *Providence: Ferrin & Hammond.* 1870. Rl. 8vo. 25811

The Freemasons' Vocal Assistant and Register of Lodges in South Carolina and Georgia. *Charleston.* 1807. 12mo. 25812

Proceedings of the General Grand Chapter of the United States, at the Triennial Meeting, September 11, A.L. 1829. *New York.* 1829. 8vo. B. 25813

Rules and Orders for establishing a Fund of Charity, for the ... Relief of Free and Accepted Masons ... . *Boston: Printed by Ezekiel Russell.* MMMMM,VII,LXXIV. 4to, pp. 15. BA. 25814

Freemen, Awake! the Devil is in the Camp! *Philadelphia.* 1839. 8vo, pp. 24. 25815

The Freemen's Glee-Book: a Collection of Songs, Odes, Glees, and Ballads, with Music, [etc.] Edited by H. Camp. Published under the auspices of the Central Fremont and Dayton Glee Club of the city of New York. *New York: Miller, Orton & Mulligan.* 1856. 18mo, pp. 108. C. 25816

Freeport (A.) Case of the Hudson's Bay Company. By Andrew Freeport. *London.* 1857. 8vo. 25817

Freeport. Edwards' Annual Director to the Inhabitants, etc., in Freeport. *Chicago: Edwards, Greenough & Deved.* 1867. 8vo, pp. 183. C. 25818

Present Advantages and Future Prospects of the City of Freeport, Ill. 12mo, pp. 44. 25819

Freese (J. R.) Report on School-Houses, and the means of promoting Popular Education. By Jacob R. Freese. *Washington: Government Printing Office.* 1868. 8vo, pp. 13. C. 25820

Freidlander (Julius R.) Observations on the Institution for Blind Persons. *Philadelphia.* 1833. 8vo. W. 25821

Also: Address to the Public, on the first Exhibition of the Pupils of the Pennsylvania Institution for the Instruction of the Blind. *Philadelphia.* 1833. 8vo. W.

Freiheitskampf im spanischen America. *See* Palacio (—).

Freiligrath (F.) F. Freiligrath's Epistle an Audubon nebst einer Antwort aus Amerika an Freiligrath. *Philadelphia.* 1844. 12mo. P. 25822

Freira (F. do Brito). *See* Vol. II., No. 7644.

Freire (J. de N.) *See* Noronha Freire (J. de).

Freisach (Karl). Geographische und magnetische Beobachtungen in Nord- und Süd-Amerika, angestellt in den Jahren 1856 und 1857. (Aus d. Sitzungsberichten d. I. Akad. d. W.) *Wien: Gerold im Comm.* 1858. 8vo, pp. 46. 25823

Freistaat Costa Rica. *See* Vol. V., No. 17016.

Freire (José Rodrigues). Relação da conquista do gentio Xavante, conseguida pelo ill.mo e ex.mo da sr. Tristão Cunha Menezes, governador e capitão general da capitania de Goyaz. *Lisboa: Typ. Nunesiana.* 1790. 4to, pp. 27. 25824

Frejes (F.) Historia breve de la conquista de los estados independientes del Imperio Mejicano, escrita por Fr. Francisco Frejes. *Zacatecas.* 1838. Sm. 4to, pp. vi, 166, (2). 25825

Very rare, and of little moment. Some copies have a different imprint.

Frelich (J. H.) The True Position, Interests, and Policy of the South. Union or Secession: which is Best? *Memphis. January,* 1861. 8vo, pp. 35. 25826

Frelinghuysen (F.) An Oration on the Death of Gen. George Washington: delivered in the Dutch Church, in New-Brunswick, on the 22d of February, 1800. By Major-General Frederick Frelinghuysen. ... *New-Brunswick, New Jersey: Printed by Abraham Blauvelt.* 1800. 8vo, pp. 23. C., H., P. 25827

Also: An Address before the Literary Societies of Rutgers College, July 26 ... *Newark, N. J.* 1853. 8vo. B.

Frelinghuysen (F. T.) Obsequies of Abraham Lincoln, in Newark, N. J., 1865. Oration by Frederick T. Frelinghuysen, Esq. *Newark, N. J.: Daily Advertiser Office.* 1865. 8vo, pp. 23. B. 25828

Also: Reconstruction. Speech ... in the Senate of the United States, January 28, 1868. *Washington: F. & J. Rives & Geo. A. Bailey.* 1868. 8vo, pp. 14. H.

Frelinghuysen (T.) An Address ... before the Philoclean and Peithessophian Societies, of Rutgers College. ... By Theodore Frelinghuysen. *New-Brunswick, N. J.: Printed by Van Doorn and M'Cready.* 1831. 8vo, pp. 24. B., BA., C., H. 25829

Frelinghuysen. Speech of Mr. Frelinghuysen, of New Jersey, delivered in the Senate ... April 6, 1830, on ... an Exchange of Lands with the Indians residing in any of the States or Territories, and for their Removal West of the Mississippi. *Washington.* 1830. 8vo, pp. 44. B., BA., H. 25830

Frelinghuysen. A Sketch of the Life and Public Services of Theodore Frelinghuysen. [n. p. n. d.] 8vo, pp. 12.

Also: Speech ... on ... the Resolutions concerning Sabbath Mails. ... May 8, 1830. *Washington: Printed by Rothwell & Ustick.* 1830. 8vo, pp. 15. BA., H. — Speech ... on the Removal of the Deposites; ... Senate of the United States, ... January, 1834. *Washington.* 1834. 8vo, pp. 16. M. *See* Rutgers College.

Fremantle (Arthur James). Three Months in the Southern States, April–June, 1863. By Lieut.-Col. Fremantle, Coldstream Guards. *Edinburgh: William Blackwood and Sons.* MDCCCLXIII. Post 8vo, pp. ix, 316. B., H. + *New York: John Bradburn.* 1864. 12mo, pp. 309. Portrait of Jefferson Davis. BA., H. + *Mobile: S. H. Goetzel.* 1864. 8vo, pp. 158. BA., C. 25832

The cover to the Mobile edition is printed on wall paper.

Fréminville (*Chev. De*). *See* La Poix de Freminville.

Fremond (S. P.) The Negroes and Anglo-Africans, as Freedmen and Soldiers. By Sarah Parker Fremond. *London: Ladies' Emancipation Society.* 1864. 12mo, pp. 30. 25833

Fremont (J. B.) The Story of the Guard: A Chronicle of the War. By Jessie Benton Frémont. ... *Boston: Ticknor & Fields.* 1863. 12mo, pp. 227, (2). B., BA., H. + Knapsack Edition. [*Ibid.*] 25834

Fremont. Die Leibgarde. Eine Geschichte aus dem Kriege. Von Jessie Benton Frémont. ... *Boston: Ticknor und Fields.* 1863. 18mo, pp. 187. 25835

Fremont (J. C.) The California Guide Book; comprising Col. Fremont's Geographical Account of Upper California; Major Emory's Overland Journey from Fort Leavenworth, in Missouri, to San Diego, in California; including parts of the Arkansas, Del Norte and Gila Rivers; and Captain Fremont's

Narrative of the Exploring Expedition to the Rocky Mountains, and to Oregon and North California; ... *New York: D. Appleton & Co.* 1849. 8vo, pp. 29, 83, 186. 2 Maps. 25836

Fremont. Geographical Memoir upon Upper California, in Illustration of his Map of Oregon and California. By Hon. Charles Frémont; addressed to the Senate of the United States. *Washington: Wendell & Van Benthuysen.* 1848. 8vo, pp. 67. B., BA., H. + *Washington.* 1849. 8vo, pp. 40. 25837

This is the third expedition, and is sometimes found with Emory's "Notes of a Military Reconnoisance," etc.

Fremont. Life, Explorations, and Public Services of John Charles Fremont. With Illustrations. *Boston: Ticknor and Fields.* MDCCCLVI. 12mo, pp. 355. + [Another Edition.] *New York.* 1856. 12mo, pp. 114. 25838

Fremont. The Life of Col. John Charles Fremont, and his Narrative of Explorations and Adventures in Kansas, Nebraska, Oregon, and California. The Memoir by Samuel V. N. Smucker, A.M. *New York and Auburn.* 1856. 12mo, pp. 494. Portrait and Plates. 25839

Fremont. Message from the President, communicating the Proceedings of the Court-Martial in the Trial of Lieut. Col. Fremont, with his Defence, and Speeches and Documents on the California Claims, 1846–'7. *Washington.* 1848. 8vo, pp. 447. C., S. 25840

Fremont. Narrative of the Exploring Expedition to the Rocky Mountains in the Year 1842, and to Oregon and North California in the Years 1843–44. By Brevet Capt. J. C. Fremont ... . *Washington.* 1845. 8vo, pp. 324. Map and Plates. P. + *Syracuse: L. W. Hall.* 1846. 12mo, pp. 305. BA. + *New York: D. Appleton & Company.* 1846. 8vo, pp. 186. BA. + Reprinted from the Official Report ordered to be published by the United States Senate. *London.* 1846. 8vo. Plates.

Also included with our No. 25836, *supra.*

Fremont. Oregon and California. The Exploring Expedition to the Rocky Mountains, Oregon and California. By Brevet Col. J. C. Fremont. To which is added a Description of the Physical Geography of California, with recent notices of the Gold Region, from the latest and most Authentic Sources. *Buffalo: Geo. H. Derby & Co.* 1849. 12mo, pp. 456. 25842

Fremont. Report of an Exploration of the Country lying between the Missouri River and the Rocky Mountains on the line of the Kansas and the Great Platte Rivers. *Washington: Printed for the Senate.* 1843. 8vo, pp. 207. Map and Plate. 25843

Fremont. Report of the Committee on Military Affairs, to which was referred the Memorial of J. C. Fremont, praying an Investigation of the Claims of Citizens of California ... for ... Supplies furnished by them for the use of the United States. [*Washington.*] 1848. pp. 83. (Sen. Doc.) S. 25844

Fremont. Report of the Exploring Expedition to the Rocky Mountains in the Year 1842. To Oregon and North California in the Years 1843–'44. By Brevet Capt. J. C. Frémont, ... *Washington: Gales and Seaton.* 1845. 8vo, pp. 693. 23 Plates and 2 Maps. BA. + Printed by Order of the House of Representatives. *Washington: Blair and Rives, Printers.* 1845. 8vo, pp. 583. 23 Plates and 2 Maps. BA. + Second Edition. *Washington: Taylor, Wilde & Co.* [1845?] 8vo, pp. 278. C. + *New York: D. Appleton & Co.* 1849. 8vo, pp. 83, 185.

Included in our No. 25836, *supra.* The following relate to Fremont: *See* No. 5741, and add *James S. Thomas, St. Louis, May* 3, 1862. — Fremont & Dayton Central Club of the City of New-York. *Republican Bulletin, No.* 8. 1856. 4to, pp. 4. S. — Fremont and McClellan. [*Washington.* 1862.] 8vo, pp. 6. H. (*See* McClellan for a reply.) — J. C. Fremont's Record, 1856. 8vo, pp. 16. — Fremont's Romanism Established. 8vo, pp. 16. — Fremont a Protestant! 8vo, pp. 8. — Col. Fremont's Religion. 8vo, pp. 10. — Col. Fremont not a Roman Catholic. 8vo, pp. 4. — Kein Slaven territorium, 1856. 8vo, pp. 16. — ... Fremont Songs for the People, Original and Selected. Compiled by Thomas Drew, ... *Boston: John Jewett and Company.* 1856. 24mo. — John C. Fremont! "Is he honest? is he capable?" [n. p. n. d.] 8vo, pp. 8 H. — John C. Fremont! Ist er ehrlich? Ist er sähig? [n. p. n. d.] 8vo, pp. 8. — Life of Col. Fremont. [n. p. 1856.] 8vo, pp. 32. + *New-York: Greeley & M'Elrath.* [1856.] 8vo, pp. 32. — Das Leben des Obersten. *New-York: Greeley & MacElrath.* 1856. 8vo, pp. 32. — The Life of Fremont. Published by Levison & Haney. *New-York.* [1856.] 24mo, pp. 17. — Only Seventeen Working Days in the United States Senate. His Whole Civil Life. ... [n. p. n. d.] 8vo, pp. 15. H. — Republican Bulletins in favor of Fremont & Dayton, published during the Canvass preceding the Presidential Election. 1856. Nos. 1 to 9 or more. — The Romish Intrigue! Fremont a Catholic!! [n. p. n. d.] 8vo, pp. 16. H. *See* Purchase of Arms. Dr. Allibone notices an edition of Fremont's Exploration, 2 vols., 8vo, 1859, which does not exist.

Fremont *and* Emory. Notes of Travel in California; comprising the Prominent Geographical, Agricultural, Geological, and Mineralogical Features of the Country; also, the Route from Fort Leavenworth, in Missouri, to San Diego, in California, including parts of the Arkansas, Del Norte, and Gila Rivers. From the Official Reports of Col. Fremont and Maj. Emory.

New-York: D. Appleton & Company. MDCCCXLIX. 8vo, pp. 186. Map. BA. + *London: M'Glashan.* 1849. Fcap 8vo, pp. 312. *London.* 1856. 2 vols., post 8vo. 25846

French (A. M.) Slavery in South Carolina, and the Ex-Slaves, or the Port Royal Mission. By Mrs. A. M. French. *New York: Winchell M. French.* MDCCCLXII. 12mo, pp. 312.

French (B.) History of the Evangelical Churches in New York. By B. French. *New York.* 1839. 18mo, pp. 122.

French (Benjamin Brown). Address delivered before the ... Grand Lodge of the District of Columbia, at the Tomb of Washington, ... June 24, 1857. ... By ... B. B. French. ... *Washington: Robert A. Waters.* 1857. 8vo, pp. 24. 25849

French. A Compendium of the Proceedings of the General Grand Chapter of Royal Arch Masons of the United States. From the 24th day of October, 1797, to the Second Tuesday of September, 1856. Compiled ... by B. B. French ... . *Baltimore: Printed by Joseph Robinson.* 1859. 25850

Also: Address delivered at Portland, before the Grand Lodge of the State of Maine, June 26, 1849. ... *Portland.* 1849. 8vo, pp. 24. — Address ... Grand Lodge of the District of Columbia, at its Annual Meeting, November 5, 1850. *Washington.* 1850. 8vo, pp. 15. — An Address delivered before Richmond Encampment of Knights Templars ... May 16, 1853. ... *Richmond, Va.: C. H. Wynne.* 1853. 8vo, pp. 21. H. — Eulogy on the Life and Character of Oliver Whittlesey; pronounced ... Jan. 15, 1856. *Washington.* 1856. 8vo, pp. 18. — Eulogy on the Life and Character of Yelverton Peyton Page, Esq., ... *Washington: H. Polkinhorn.* 1863. 8vo, pp. 22. H. — Washington's Masonic Character and Standing. An Address ... *Washington.* 1851. 8vo.

[French (Benjamin Franklin).] Biographia Americana; or, an Historical and Critical Account of the Lives, Actions, and Writings, of the most Distinguished Persons in North America. ... By a Gentleman of Philadelphia. *New York: D. Mallory.* 1825. 8vo, pp. vii, 356. Portraits. C., H. 25851

French. Historical Collections of Louisiana, embracing many Rare and Valuable Documents relating to the Natural, Civil and Political History of that State. Compiled with Historical and Biographical Notes, and an Introduction, By B. F. French. ... *New York: Wiley & Putnam.* 1846. 5 vols., 8vo, pp. ix, (1), 222; vi, (1), 301, Map; 252. B., BA., H. 25852

Part I. Historical Documents from 1678–1691. Part II. *Philadelphia: Daniels and Smith.* 1850. Part III. *New York: D. Appleton & Company.* 1851. Part IV. *See* Shea (J. G.) Part V. has the following title:

French. Historical Memoirs of Louisiana, from the First Settlement of the Colony to the Departure of Governor O'Reilly in 1770, with Historical and Biographical Notes, forming the Fifth of the Series of Historical Collections of Louisiana. By B. F. French ... . *New York: Lamport, Blakeman & Law.* 1853. 8vo, pp. vii, 291. Maps and Portraits. BA., H. 25853

"This collection is remarkable for the immense amount of material relating to the aborigines of America, being almost wholly composed of memoirs and narratives, in the language of the original explorers." — Field. Vol. I. contains, with other historical material, La Salle's memoir of the discovery of the Mississippi, Joutel's journal, and Hennepin's account of the Mississippi. Vol. II. Marquette and Joliet's voyage to discover the Mississippi, De Soto's expedition, and Coxe's "Carolana." Vol. III. La Harpe's journal of the establishment of the French in Louisiana, Charlevoix's journal, etc. Vol. IV. Narratives of the voyages, missions, and travels among the Indians, by Marquette, Joliet, Dablon, Allouez, Le Clercq, La Salle, Hennepin, Membre, and Douay, with biographical and bibliographical notices of these missionaries and their works. By J. G. Shea. Vol. V. Dumont's memoir of transactions with the Indians of Louisiana, from 1712 to 1740, and Champégny's memoirs.

French. Historical Collections of Louisiana and Florida, including Translations of Original Manuscripts relating to their Discovery and Settlement, with Numerous Historical and Biographical Notes. By B. F. French ... New Series. *New York: J. Sabin & Sons.* 1869. 8vo, 2 l., pp. ii, 1 l., pp. 362. B.

Contents: M. de Rémonville on the importance of establishing a colony in Louisiana; The expedition of P. Le Moyne d'Iberville to Louisiana; Annals of Louisiana, 1698–1722, by M. Penicaut; History of the first attempt of the Huguenots to colonize Florida, by Réné Laudonnière, translated by R. Hakluyt. 500 copies printed.

French. History of the Rise and Progress of the Iron Trade of the United States, from 1621 to 1857. With Numerous Statistical Tables, relating to the Manufacture, Importation, Exportation, and Prices of Iron for more than a Century. By B. F. French, ... *New York: Wiley & Halsted.* 1858. 8vo, pp. xvi, 179. B., C., H. 25855

[French.] Memoirs of Eminent Female Writers, of all Ages and Countries. *Philadelphia: T. Desilver.* 1827. 24mo, pp. vii, 183. 2 Plates. C. 25856

French (E.) An Oration, pronounced July 4th, 1805, Before the Young Democratic Republicans, of the Town of Boston, in Commemoration of the Anniversary of American Independence. By Ebenezer French. ... Second Edition. *Boston: Printed by J. Ball.* 1805. 8vo, pp. 23. BA., H. 25857

Also: An Oration pronounced before the Republican Inhabitants of Portland, July 4, 1806. *Portland.* 1806. 8vo, pp. 12. M.

French (E. W.) Our Present Duty: A Sermon, Preached in the First Presbyterian Church, South Bergen, N. J., by Edward W. French, Pastor, July 20th, 1862. *New York: Wm. C. Bryant & Co., Printers.* 1862. 8vo, pp. 16. 25858

French (G.) An Answer to a Scurrilous Libel, intitled a Letter to Mr. French, occasion'd by his History of Col. Parke's Administration, &c. To which is added the Character and Conduct, as well of Walter Hamilton, the present Captain General of the Leeward Islands, as of the Principal Actors and Fomentors in the Rebellion & Murder mentioned in that History. By George French. *London: J. Bettenham.* 1719. 8vo, pp. xxiv, 239. 25859

French. The History of Col. Parke's Administration Whilst he was Captain-General and Chief Governor of the Leeward Islands; with an Account of the Rebellion in Antegoa, wherein he, with several others, were murther'd on the 7th of December, 1710. By Mr. George French. *London.* MDCCXVII. 8vo, 6 l., pp. 427. Portrait of Daniel Parke. J.C.B., C. 25860

French (H. F.) An Address delivered before the York County Agricultural Society, Oct. 7, 1852. By Henry F. French ... . *Saco: William Noyes.* 1853. 8vo, pp. 31. H.

French (J. W.) Gazetteer of the State of New-York: embracing a Comprehensive View of the Geography, Geology, and General History of the State, and a Complete History and Description of Every County, City, Town, Village and Locality. With Full Tables of Statistics. By J. H. French ... Illustrated by Original Steel Engravings, and accompanied by a New Map of the State from Accurate Surveys. Tenth Edition. *Syracuse: R. Pearsall Smith.* 1861. 8vo, pp. 739. B., C. 25862

[French (James Clark), *and* Carey (Edward).] The Trip of the Oceanus to Fort Sumter and Charleston, S. C. Comprising the Incidents of the Excursion, the Appearance at that time of the City, and the entire Programme of Exercises at the Re-raising of the Flag over the ruins of Fort Sumter, April 14th, 1865. By a Committee appointed by the Passengers of the Oceanus. *Brooklyn: "The Union" Steam Printing House.* 1865. 8vo, pp. 172, (2). 6 Plates. 25863

[French (James S.)] Elkswatawa; or, the Prophet of the West. A Tale of the Frontier. *New York: Harper & Brothers.* 1836. 2 vols., 12mo, pp. 246; 254. C. 25864

French. Life and Adventures of David Crockett, of West Tennessee. By J. S. French. *Cincinnati.* 1833. 12mo.

French (J. R.) Equal Suffrage and the Material Development of the Country. Speech of Hon. John R. French, of North Carolina ... February 9, 1869. [n. p. n. d.] 8vo, pp. 7.

French (J.) A Discourse ... at an Evening Lecture, in Portsmouth, N. H. 31 July, 1805. It being the Evening succeeding the Session of an Ecclesiastical Council convened respecting the Separation of the Reverend Timothy Alden, Junior, from his Pastoral Relation to the South Church and Congregation in that Town. By the Reverend Jonathan French, A.M. ... *Portsmouth: Printed by William and Daniel Treadwell.* 1805. 8vo, pp. 15. BA., N. 25867

French. A Sermon Preached before his Excellency Samuel Adams, Esq. Governour: ... May 25, 1796. Being the Day of General Election. By Jonathan French, A.M. ... *Boston: Printed by Adams & Larkin.* M,DCC,XCVI. 8vo, pp. 23. B., BA., H.

French. A Sermon delivered on the Anniversary Thanksgiving, November 29, 1798. With Some Additions in the Historical Part. By Jonathan French, A.M. ... *Andover: Printed by Ames and Parker.* 1799. 8vo, pp. 31. BA. 25869

French. A Sermon preached at the Ordination of the Rev. Jonathan French, Jun. ... in Northampton, ... November 18, 1801. By Jonathan French, A.M. ... *Portsmouth: Printed by William Treadwell.* 1802. 8vo, pp. 32. B., BA., H., M., W.

Also: A Practical Discourse against Extortion, from Ezekiel xxii. 12. Delivered ... in Andover, January 1, 1777. ... *Boston: Printed by T. & J. Fleet.* 1777. 8vo, pp. 38. BA. — A Sermon, ... at the Ordination of the Reverend Mr. Daniel Oliver, ... in Beverly, October 3, 1787 ... . *Newbury Port: Printed by John Mycall.* [1787.] 8vo, pp. 48. BA., H., W. — A Sermon ... at the Ordination of the Rev. Abiel Abbot, ... in Haverhill, June 3d, 1795 ... . *Haverhill: Printed by Benjamin Edes, Jun.* 1795. 8vo, pp. 36. B., BA., M. — A Sermon ... at the Ordination of the Reverend James Kendall, ... Plymouth, January 1, 1800. ... *Boston: Printed by Samuel Hull.* 1800. 8vo, pp. 28. BA.

French (J.), *Junr.* A Discourse on the Anniversary Thanksgiving, delivered in Andover, December 1, 1803. ... . By Jonathan French ... . *Printed by E. M. Blunt.* 1804. 8vo, pp. 20.

French. A Discourse delivered at Northampton, N. H. Nov. 18, 1821, being twenty years from the Author's Settlement in the Christian Ministry in that place. By Jonathan French, A.M. *Portsmouth: T. H. Miller.* 1822. pp. 11. 25872

French. Historical Notices of the Piscataqua Association, ... By Jonathan French ... . *Boston: Charles C. P. Moody.* 1850. 8vo, pp. 24. B. 25873

French. Reminiscences of a Fifty-Years' Pastorate. A Half-Century Discourse, delivered in North-Hampton, N. H. November 18, 1851. By Jonathan French, D.D., Pastor of the Congregational Church. *Portsmouth: C. W. Brewster & Son.* 1852. 8vo, pp. 46. B., BA. 25874

See also "Mass. Hist. Coll.," XIV. 189–192.

French. A Sermon preached ... before ... the ... Concord Senate, and House of Representatives of ... New Hampshire, June 6, being the Anniversary Election. *Concord.* 1822. 8vo, pp. 27. M. 25875

Also: An Address ... before the Rockingham Sacred Music Society, at Portsmouth, May 8, 1816. ... *Exeter: Printed by C. Norris & Co.* 1816. 8vo, pp. 16. H. — ... A Discourse at the Funeral of Mrs. Harriot Putnam. *Portsmouth.* 1832. 8vo. — Sermon at the Installation of the Rev. Isaac Briggs, Boxford, September 28, 1808. *Haverhill.* 1809. 8vo, pp. 20. — [Fast] Sermon, delivered on the 20th of August, 1812, Northampton, New Hampshire. *Exeter.* 8vo, pp. 28. — A Sermon ... at the Installation of the Rev. Ebenezer Peck Sperry ... in Wenham, March 29, 1820. ... *Portsmouth: Printed by S. Whidden.* 1820. 8vo, pp. 28. BA.

French (J.) The True Republican, containing the Inaugural Addresses, with the First Annual Addresses and Messages of all the Presidents of the United States, from 1789 to 1841, with their Farewell Addresses. By Jonathan French. *Philadelphia.* 1842. 12mo. Portraits. + [*Philadelphia:*] *Daniels & Getz.* 1853. 12mo, pp. 280, 198. 25876

[French (*Mrs.* L. Virginia).] Kernwood; or, after many Days. A Historical Romance, founded on the Events of the Late War, from the Manuscript of a Confederate Spy. By L'Inconnue. *Louisville, (Ky.): for the Author.* 1867. 12mo, pp. 390. C. 25877

French (Rodney). Facts and Documents in the case of Rev. Charles Morgridge; with the Report of his Committee. By R. French. *Fall River.* 1848. 8vo, pp. 56. 25878

French (T. P.) Information for Emigrants on the Ottawa and Opeongo Road, and its Vicinity. By T. P. French, Crown Land Agent. *Ottawa.* 1857. 8vo pp. 36. 25879

French (W.) Petition, Report and Bill on the subject of a Monument in honor of William French. In the House of Representatives [of Vermont], November 9, 1852. *Montpelier: E. P. Walton & Son.* 1852. 8vo, pp. 16. 25880

French Arrogance. *See* [Cobbett], Vol. IV., No. 13883.

French Canadian Missions. *See* VOL. III., No. 10523.

French Claims. To the People of the United States. *Philadelphia.* 1807. 8vo. 25881

A statement of the transactions of the American commissioners at Paris relative to the French spoliations.

The French Convert, being a True Relation of the Conversion of a Noble French Lady from the Superstition of Popery to the Reformed Religion, wherein is showed her great Sufferings, and her Extraordinary Deliverance, from two Assassins; and of her Wonderful Preservation in a Wood for Two Years, &c. To which is added, A brief account of the Persecution in France. With an Abstract of the present French King's Edict against the Protestants in France. *Sold by W. Bradford in New-York. Price, Bound,* 18*d.* 25882

Unseen by me. Copied from advertisement at the end of Row's Collection (N. Y. 1725), and inserted here on account of the imprint.

The French Encroachments Exposed; or, Britain's original Right to all that part of the American Continent claimed by France fully Asserted; Wherein it appears, that the Honour and Interest of Great Britain are equally concerned, from the Conduct of the French, for more than a Century past, to Vindicate her Right; ... In Two Letters from a Merchant retired from business, to his Friend in London. ... *London: George Keith.* 1756. 8vo, pp. 44. 25883

"The author's zeal for his country is expressed in furious declamation against its enemies, and in these declamations his merit, as a writer, seems chiefly to consist." — *M. Rev.*, XIII. 508.

The | French Flogged, | or, the | British Sailors in America, | a Farce of two Acts, | As it was performed | at the | Theatre Royal, Covent Garden. | *London:* | ... *J. Williams,* ... | ... 1767. | 8vo, 2 l., pp. 22. 25884

See "M. Rev.," XXXV. 238.

French Guiana. *See* Guiana.

French Influence upon English Counsels Demonstrated from an Impartial Examination of our Measures for Twenty Years Past. *London: T. Cooper.* MDCCXL. 8vo, pp. 72. 25885

Principally on American affairs.

A French-Onondaga Dictionary. *See* Shea (J. G.)

French Originals of all the Documents, Translations of which accompanied the Message of the President of the United States, of the 18th January, 1799, relative to the Affairs of the United States with the French Republic, &c., &c. *Philadelphia.* 1799. 8vo. C., P. 25886

French Policy Defeated. Being, an Account of all the Hostile Proceedings of the French, Against the Inhabitants of the British Colonies in North America, For the last Seven Years. Also, The Vigorous Measures pursued both in England and America, to vindicate the Rights of the British Subjects, and the Honour of the Crown, from the Insults and Invasions of their perfidious Enemies. With an Authentic Account of the Naval Engagement off Newfoundland, and the Taking of the Forts in the Bay of Fundy. Embellished with Two curious Maps, Describing all the Coasts, Bays, Lakes, Rivers, Soundings, principal Towns and Forts, confining on the British Plantations in America. *London: M. Cooper.* MDCCLV. 8vo, 1 l., pp. 114. 2 Maps. B.

Running title, "Gallica Fides, or French, &c." It was reproduced with a new title-page only in 1760.

The French Revolution; including a Story, founded in Fact, of Leontine and Matilda: a Drama. Written & Exhibited in the United Fraternity, at Dartmouth College, 1790; Exhibited also at Windsor, Vermont, May, 1791. *Printed at New Bedford, Massachusetts, by John Spooner.* 1793. 8vo, pp. 67.

Inserted here as partly illustrative of the history of the stage in America.

French Spoliations prior to 1800. [*Washington.* 1832?] 8vo. + [1858?] C., H. 25889

Also: Report of Select Committee of the Senate, to whom were referred the severas Petitions and Memorials of those persons who have lost property by F.ench Spoliation; prior to the year 1800, praying Indemnity from the United States. Made May 24, 1828. 8vo. C.

French Universal Exposition for 1867. ... Official Correspondence on the Subject, published by the Department of State, for the Information of Citizens of the United States, ... *Washington: Government Printing Office.* 1865. 8vo. 25890

[FRENEAU (Philip).] The British Prison-Ship: | A | Poem, | In four Cantoes. | Viz. Canto 1. The Capture, | 2. The Prison-Ship, | 3. The Prison Ship, continued, | 4. The Hospital-Prison-Ship. | To which is added, | A Poem on the Death of Capt. N. Biddle. |

who was blown up, in an Engagement with the | Yarmouth, near Barbadoes. | ... | *Philadelphia: Printed by F. Bailey.* ... | M.DCC.-LXXXI. | 8vo, pp. 23. 25891

FRENEAU. A Collection of Poems, on American Affairs. ... Written Between the Year 1797 and the Present Time. By Philip Freneau ... . *New York: David Longworth.* 1815. 2 vols., 18mo, pp. viii, 13–188; (4), 9–176. B., BA., C. 25892

[FRENEAU.] A Journey from Philadelphia to New-York, by way of Burlington and South-Amboy. [In Verse.] By Robert Slender, Stocking Weaver. *Philadelphia: F. Bailey.* 1787. 8vo, pp. 28. C., N. 25893

Reprinted with the following title:

FRENEAU. A Laughable Poem; | or | Robert Slender's | Journey | from | Philadelphia to New York, | by | Way of Burlington and South Amboy. | By Philip Freneau, | ... | *Philadelphia:* | *Printed for Thomas Neversink.* | *Dec.* 20, 1809. | 12mo, pp. 24. P.

[FRENEAU.] Letters on Various Interesting and Important Subjects, many of which have appeared in the Aurora. Corrected and much Enlarged. By Robert Slender, O. S. U. *Philadelphia: R. Slender.* 1799. 8vo, pp. 142. 25895

FRENEAU. The Miscellaneous Works of Mr. Philip Freneau; containing his Essays, and Additional Poems. *Philadelphia: F. Bailey.* MDCCLXXXVIII. 8vo, pp. xii, 429. C. 25896

FRENEAU. The Poems of Philip Freneau. Written chiefly during the late War. *Philadelphia: Printed by Francis Bailey.* M DCC LXXXVI. 8vo, pp. viii, 407. 25897

FRENEAU. Poems Written between the Years 1768 & 1794, by Philip Freneau of New Jersey: A New Edition, Revised and Corrected by the Author; Including a Considerable Number of Pieces never before Published. ... *Monmouth, (N. J.): printed at the press of the Author, at Mount Pleasant, near Middletown-Point;* M,DCC,XCV: *and, of American Independence* XIX. 8vo, pp. (4), ix–xv, 455, (1). BA., C., H. 25898

FRENEAU. Poems Written and Published during the American Revolutionary War, and now Republished from the Original Manuscripts, interspersed with Translations from the Ancients, and other pieces not heretofore in Print. By Philip Freneau. ... The Third Edition, ... *Philadelphia: From the Press of Lydia Bailey.* 1809. 2 vols., 12mo, pp. 4, 280; 302, xii. 2 Plates.

FRENEAU. Poems on Various Subjects, but chiefly Illustrative of the Events and Actors in the American War of Independence. By Philip Freneau. Reprinted from the Rare Edition printed at Philadelphia in 1786. With a Preface. *London: J. R. Smith.* 1861. Fcap 8vo, pp. xxii, 362. 25900

FRENEAU. Poems relating to the American Revolution. By Philip Freneau. With an Introductory Memoir and Notes, By Evert A. Duyckinck. *New York: W. J. Widdleton.* M.DCCC.-LXV. 12mo, pp. xxviii, 288. Portrait. B. 25901

One hundred copies printed on large paper.

FRENEAU. The Village Merchant: A Poem. To which is added the Country Printer. ... *Philadelphia: Printed by Hoff and Derrick.* M,DCC,XCIV. 12mo, pp. 16. 25902

FRENEAU. Voyage to Boston: A Poem. By Philip Freneau. *Philadelphia: Woodhouse.* 1775. 8vo, pp. 24. 25903

This is a visionary voyage in verse. The author does not say whence he came, but arrives at a river in Massachusetts; the native genius of North America presents him with a mantle which renders him invisible; he then proceeds to General Gage's mansion, and makes his observations on General Gage, Admiral Greaves, Lord Percy, and others. I am indebted to Mr. C. F. Harris, of Providence, for corrections of this list.

[FRENEAU *and* BRACKENRIDGE (H. H.)] A Poem, on the Rising Glory of America; Being an Exercise delivered at the Public Commencement at Nassau-Hall, September 25, 1771. ... *Philadelphia: R. Aitken.* M,DCC,LXXII. 8vo, pp. 27. 25904

See also [Brackenridge (H. H.)], Vol. II., No. 7190.

FRENZEL. Der Belus auf den Anden, oder Kelten in Amerika. Von Pastor Frenzel. *Leipzig: Denicke.* 1867. 8vo.

FRÉNILLY (*le marquis* A. F. de). Opinions prononcées dans la discussion du projet de loi relatif à l'indemnité des colons de Saint-Domingue, dans la séance du 7 mars 1820. *Paris: imp. de Boucher.* 1826. 8vo, pp. 48. 25906

[FRERE (H.)] *See* Vol. I., Nos. 3288 and 3289.

FRERE (J.) Mormonites, or Latter Day Saints: A short History of this Sect. With an Account of the Real Origin of the Book of Mormon. Compiled from various sources. By the Rev. J. Frere, M.A. *London.* 1850. 12mo, pp. 24. 25907

A Fresh Catalogue of Southern Outrages upon Northern Citizens. *New York: American Anti-Slavery Society.* 1860. 25908

FRESNEL (R. F.) Que l'Europe soit attentive aux événements possibles en Amérique; par R. F. Fresnel. *Paris: E. Dentu.* 1862. 8vo, pp. 61. BA., C. 25909

FRESNEL. Recherches qui ont été faites depuis Fernand Cortez jusqu'à présent, afin de découvrir le passage de la jonction maritime des océans Atlantique et Pacifique. *Paris: Dentu.* 1865. 8vo. Map. 25910

FRESNILLO. Notices of the Silver Mines of Fresnillo in the State of Zacatecas, Mexico. 1834. 8vo. Map and Plates.

FRESNOY. *See* Du Fresnoy (L.)

FRÉVILLE (A. F. J.) Les Droits de la Grande-Bretagne etablis contre les pretentions des Americains. Pour Servir de Reponse a la Declaration du Congres General. Ouvrage traduit de l'Anglois, sur la Seconde Edition. *A. la Haye.* 1776. 8vo.

Translated from Dalrymple. Our title, No. 18348, is incomplete.

FRÉVILLE. Histoire des Nouvelles Découvertes Faites dans la Mer du Sud en 1767, 1768, 1769, 1770. Rédigée d'après les dernières relations. Par M. de Fréville. Accompagnée d'un Carte dressée par M. de Vaugondy. *A Paris: Chez Hansy, le jeune.* M.DCC.LXXIV. 2 vols., 8vo, xlvii, 522, Errata, 1 l.; 2 l., 572, Approbation, 2 l. Map. C. 25913

Mr. Rich gives this title as

FRÉVILLE. Hydrographie de la Mer du Sud, ou histoire de nouvelles découvertes faites dans la mer du Sud, rédigée d'après les diverses relations Angloises et Francaises, avec une carte dressée par Vaugondy. Par M. de Fréville. *Paris: de Hansy.* M.DCC.LXXIV. 2 vols., 8vo. N. 25814

FREY (Alfred A.) Report of the Case of the Canadian Prisoners. With Introduction on the Writ of Habeas Corpus. *London.* 1839. 8vo. C. 25915

FREYCINET (L. Claude Desaulses de). Voyage autour du Monde, entrepris par ordre du Roi, sous le Ministère et conformément aux Instructions de ... M. le Vicomte de Bouchage ... . Exécuté sur les Corvettes de S. M. l'Uranie et la Physicienne, pendant les Années 1817, 18, 19, et 20, &c., par Louis de Freycinet. *Paris: Pillet.* 1824–44. 8 vols., 4to, and 4 vols., folio, containing 358 Plates and Maps. A., B., H. 25916

This splendid work is divided as follows: Zoologie, par Quoy et Gaimard, 1824, 2 vols., 4to, atlas; folio, 96 plates. Botanique, par M. Gaudichaud, 1826, 4to, atlas;

120 plates. Historique, par M. de Freycinet, 1826, 4 vols. in 2, 4to, atlas; folio, 120 plates. Navigation et Hydrographie, 1826, 2 vols., 4to, atlas; 22 maps. Observations du pendule, 1826, 4to, pp. (6), 292. Météorologique, 4to; atlas, folio. Magnetique, 4to. Many of the plates are colored. *See* Arago, Vol. I., No. 1867, and Peron.

FREYCINET. De découvertes aux térres Australe sur la corvette le Geographe, sous les ordres du capitaine Baudin, pendant les années 1801 a 1804. Exécuté par Ordre de sa Majesté l'Empereur et roi ... . Navigation et géographie, par M. L. Freycinet. *Paris.* M.DCCC.VII. 4to, 2 l., pp. xv, 496, (2), and Atlas of 32 Charts in folio. B., N. 25917

Freyheit die treue Liebe, zu alle Americanische Bürger und Einwohner. *Gedruckt für den Liebhaber.* 1809. 12mo, pp. 60.

FREYLINGHAUSEN (D. Gotlieb Anastasius), *and* SCHULZE (D. Johann Ludewig). Neuere Geschichte der Evangelishen Missions-Anstalter zu Belehrung der Heiden in Ostindien, etc. *Halle.* 1784–99. 4to. N. 25919

Periodical missionary accounts from the United States, relating chiefly to the history of Germans, memoirs of eminent Lutheran divines in the United States, etc.

FREYRE (A.) Piratas de la America. *See* Exquemelin (J.)

FREYRE (Domingos). Vida admiravel e morte preciosa da bemaventurada Santa Rosa de Santa Maria, natural da cidade de Lima, religiosa da terceira orden de Santo Domingo. *Lisboa: J. Dacosta.* 1669. 4to. 25920

FREYRE (Francisco de Brito). *See* Brito Freire, Vol. II.

FREYRE (Ramon). Manifiesto a sus conciudadanos. *Lima.* 1830. 8vo. 25921

FREYREISS (Georg Wilhelm). Beiträge zur näheren Kenntniss des Kraiserthums Brazilien, nebst einer Schilderung der neuen Colonie Leopoldina, Erster Theil. *Frankfurt am Main: J. D. Sauerländer.* 1824. 8vo, pp. xii, 170, 1 l. C. 25922

No more published.

FREYTAG (J. D.) Mémoires, contenant des détails sur les déportés du 18 fructidor à la Guyane française; la relation des principaux événements qui se sont passés dans cette colonie pendant la révolution ... ses voyages dans les diverses parties de l'Amérique; l'histoire de son séjour parmi les Indiens de ce continent; accompagnés de notes historiques, topographiques et critiques par M. C. de B. [Couvray de Beauregard]. *Paris: Nepveu.* 1824. 2 vols., 8vo. 25823

Quérard appears to think that Couvray de Beauregard is more than the annotator of these memoirs.

FREZIER (Amédée François). Relation du Voyage de la Mer du Sud aux côtes du Chily et du Perou, Faits pendant les années 1712, 1713 & 1714. ... Par M. Frezier, Ingenieur Ordinaire du Roy. ... Ouvrage enrichi de quantité de Planche, en Tailledouce. *Paris: Jean-Geoffròy Nyon.* M DCC XVI. 4to, pp. xix, 298, (2). 23 Maps and 14 Plates. + *Amsterdam: Pierre Humbert.* M,DCC,XVII. 2 vols., 12mo, pp. xx, 294; Title, pp. 297–600. 37 Maps, and Plates. B., C. 25924

At page 577 of the Amsterdam edition will be found a "Mémoire touchant l'etablissement des P. P. Jésuites dans les Indes d'Espagne." This curious relation relative to the missions of Paraguay is not by Frezier. It originally appeared [at Amsterdam] in 1712, as a separate publication.

FREZIER. Relation du Voyage de la Mer du Sud aux Côtes du Chily et du Perou, Fait pendant les années 1712, 1713, & 1714. Dediée à S. A. R. Monseigneur Le Duc D'Orleans, Regent du Royaume. Avec une Réponse a la Preface critique Du Livre intitulé, Journal des Observations Physiques, Mathematiques & Botaniques du R. P. Fevillée, contre la Relation du Voyage de la Mer du Sud, & une Chronologie des Vicerois du Perou, depuis son établissement jusqu'au tems de la Relation du Voyage de la Mer du Sud. Par M. Frezier, Ingenieur Ordinaire du Roy. Ouvrage enrichi de quantité de Planches en Tailledouce. *A Paris: Nyon, Didot, Quillau.* M.DCC.XXXII. 4to, Half-Title, 14 l., pp. 298, (2), 63. 37 Maps, and Plates.

Merely a new title-page, and a supplement of sixty-three pages added to the quarto edition of 1716. The supplement consists of Frezier's reply to Father Feuillée's criticisms in the preface to his third volume (1725).

FREZIER. A Voyage to the South Sea, And along the Coasts of Chili and Peru, in the Years 1712, 1713, and 1714. Particularly describing The Genius and Constitution of the Inhabitants, as well Indians as Spaniards: Their Customs and Manners; their Natural History, Mines, Commodities, Traffick with Evrope, &c. By Monsieur Frezier, Engineer in Ordinary to the French King. Illustrated with 37 Copper-Cutts of the Coast, Harbours, Cities, Plants and other Curiosities: Printed from the Author's Original Plates inserted in the Paris Edition. With a Postscript by Dr. Edmund Halley, Savilian Professor of Geometry in the University of Oxford. And an Account of the Settlement, Commerce, and Riches of the Jesuites in Paraguay. *London: Jonah Bowyer.* MDCCXVII. 4to, pp. (14), 335, (9). 37 Plates.

This English translation contains the same engravings as the original, and is preferable to the latter by reason of Halley's postscript, in which some geographical errors of Frezier are corrected. On page 147 is an interesting account of Guano. There are copies with the date 1735, which are the same edition, with a new title-page.

FREZIER. Reis-Beschryving door de Zuid-Zee langs de Kusten van Chili, Peru en Brazil, opgestelt op eene Reistocht gedaan in de jaren 1712, 1713 en 1714. Nevens eene Beschryvinge van de Regeringe der Yncas, Koningen van Peru, en hun ryk, zo als het was voor den komst der Spanjaarden aldaar. Het eene uit het Fransch vertaalt, en het andere opgemaakt uit verscheide Schryveren. Door Isaac Verburg. ... *Te Amsterdam: R. en G. Wetstein.* 1718. 4to, 7 l., pp. 406, (9). 19 Maps and 13 Plates. C. 25927

Also on thick paper. There are copies dated 1727, which are the same edition, with a new title-page.

FREZIER. Allerneueste Reise nach der Süd See und denen Kusten von Chili, Peru und Brasilien. Aus dem Frantzösischen übersetzet und mit vielen saubern Kupfern versehen. *Hamburg: Thomas von Wierings.* 1718. 12mo, pp. 416. Maps and Plates.

FREZIER. Reise nach der Süd-See und denen Kusten von Chili, Peru, und Brasilien. Aus dem Französischen übersetzet und mit vielen saubern Kupfern versehen. Zum andernmal herausgegeben, und mit einem Anhang aus der in den Jahren 1740 bis 1744 von dem beruhmten Engl. Commandeur Georg Anson, nach der Süd See, oder meistens um die ganze welt, gethanenen reise vermehret. *Hamburg: Thomas von Wietings Erben.* 1745. 8vo, 2 l., pp. 640. 5 Maps and 6 Plates. 25929

FREZIER. Reponse à préface critique du livre intitulé: Journal des observations physiques, etc., du P. Feuillée, contre la Relation du voyage de la mer du Sud. *Paris: Ravenel.* 1727. 4to. 25930

This is also added to the second edition of the "Relation du voyage," etc. "Frezier was not a sea-commander, but an officer of engineers in the French service. His Journal is one of observation and description, his researches being professedly directed to supply what was wanting in the Journal of Pere Feuillée. His Relation contains much, both of the natural and civil history of Chili and Peru." — BARTLETT.

FRIAS (F.) El Liberalismo revolucionario y el Matrimonio civil, por Felix Frias. *Buenos Aires.* 1867. 12mo, pp. 84.

FRIBERT (Lauritz Jacob). Haandbog for Emigranter til Amerikas Vest med Anviisning for Overreisen samt Beskrivelse af Livet og Agerdyrkningsmaaden naermest i Viskonsin. [*Christiania.* 1847.] 8vo, pp. 100. 25932

FRIC (Karel). Príspevky ku poznání amerického petroleje. *Prag: J. Petrík.* 1863. 8vo, pp. 19. 25933

Contributions towards a knowledge of petroleum.

Friccius (V.) Indianischer Religionstandt der gantzen newen Welt, beider Indien gegen Auff vnd Nidergang der Sonnen. Schleinigister Form ausz gründtlichen Historien, Sonderbar desz Hochwirdigen Vatters Francisci Gonzagen Barfüsserischẽ Ordens croniken, vnd Didaci Vallades, geistlicher. Rhetoric zusammen gezogen, vnd auszm Latein in hochteutsch verwendet: Durch F. Valentinum Fricium, Barfüsser Ordens, F. D. Matthiassen Ertz Hertzogen in Oesterreich, etc. ... *Getruckt zu Ingolstadt, durch Wolffgang Eder.* 1588. 8vo, 16 l., pp. 200. c. 25934

"Cet ouvrage inconnu à Ternaux et à Brunet, est cite par Pinelo, sous la date de 1688. C'est en partie une traduction de l'ouvrage de Franc. Gonzagæ, *de Origine Seraphicæ religionis Franciscanæ ... Romæ*, 1587, et de celui de Valades, *Rhetorica Christiana. Perusiæ*, 1579." — Leclerc, No. 590.

Frick (W.) An Address preparatory to Opening the Department of the Arts and Sciences in the University of Maryland. ... By William Frick. ... *Baltimore: Printed by John D. Toy.* 1831. 8vo, pp. 37. H. 25935

Frickmann (A.) Côte occidentale de l'Amérique du Nord. Côtes de l'Orégon et du territoire de Washington. De la baie Pélican à l'entrée du détroit de Juan de Fuca. Instructions traduites de l'américain et corrigées d'après les documents les plus récents, par A. Frickmann ... . *Paris: imp. Lainé.* 1872. 8vo, pp. 112. 25936

Friedel (L.) Les émigrants au Brésil. Imité de Mme Amélie Schoppe. Par Louis Friedel. Neuvième édition. *Tours: Mame et fils.* 1870. 18mo, pp. 144. Illustrated. 25937

Friedlander (Julius R.) An Address to the Public at the First Exhibition of the Pupils of the Pennsylvania Institution for the Instruction of the Blind. Second Edition. *Philadelphia.* 1833. 8vo. 25938

Friedmann (S.) Niederländisch Ost- und Westindien. Ihre neueste Gestaltung in geographischer, statistischer, und culturhistorischer hinsicht, mit besonderer Darstellung der klimatischen und sanitätischen Verhältnisse. *München: G. Franz.* 1860. 8vo, 1 l., pp. viii, 274. Plate. c. 25939

Frielenhuysen (T.) Wars, and Rumors of Wars, Heaven's Decree over the World. Sermon to the New-England Forces on the Expedition against Crown Point. By Theodorus Frielenhuysen, A.M. *New York.* 1755. 8vo, pp. 47. M. 25940

The Friend. An Essay to do Good; or, Relief from the Pressure: Addressed to ... the Wealthy Classes of New-York. *New York.* 1837. 8vo, pp. 16. S. 25941

The Friend, an Independent Monthly. *New York: Friend Association.* 1865. 8vo. Continued. B., C., H. 25942

The Friend: A Religious and Literary Journal. Edited by R. Smith. *Philadelphia.* 1820. 8vo. Continued. 25943

The Friend of Peace. By Philo-pacificus [Noah Worcester]. *Boston.* 1815–26 or later. 25944

See also [Worcester (Noah)].

The Friend of Progress. *New York.* 1864–5. 8vo. 25945

A Friend to the Constitution. Nos. I. to V. [n. p. n. d.] 12mo, pp. 60. 25946

A Friendly Address, 1774. *See* [Cooper (Myles)], Vol. VI.

Friendly Advice to the Gentlemen-Planters of the East and West Indies. In Three Parts. I. A brief Treatise of the most principal Fruits and Herbs that grow in the East & West Indies; giving an Account of their respective Vertues both for Food and Physick, and what Planet and Sign they are under. Together with some Directions for the Preservation of Health and Life in those Hot Climates. II. The Complaints of the Negro Slaves against the hard Usages and Barbarous Cruelties inflicted upon them. III. A Discourse in way of Dialogues between an Ethiopian or Negro-Slave, and a Christian that was his Master in America. By Philotheos Physiologus. *Printed by Andrew Sowle, in the Year* 1684. 8vo. 25947

A Friendly Check from a New Relation to the Chief Cannoneer, founded on a late Information, dated N. E. Castle William, 1720. *Boston.* 1721. 16mo, pp. 7. B. 25948

Signed "Americus Patriar." This very rare tract is a satirical answer to "A Word of Comfort to a Melancholy Country — Massachusetts Bay."

A Friendly Debate. *See* Douglas (W.), Vol. V., *note* to No. 20724.

Friendly Letter to Parents and Heads of Families, particularly those residing in the Country Towns and Villages of America. *Boston.* 1827. 12mo. 25949

Friendly Remarks to the People of Connecticut, upon their Colleges and Schools. [n. p.] 1799. 8vo, pp. 42. H. 25950

A Brief Account of the Society of the Friendly Sons of St. Patrick; with Biographical Notices of some of the Members, ... *Philadelphia: Hibernian Society.* 1844. 12mo, pp. 112. Plate.

Friendly Voice from England. *See* [Cobden (R.)], Vol. IV.

Friends (W.) Guide Book to Mr. Washington Friends' great American Tour, with the words of the Songs and Melodies sung by him in his Unrivalled Entertainment. *Nottingham.* [1857.] 8vo. 25952

Friends, Brethren, and Countrymen, &c. 4to, pp. 1. P.

Printed at Philadelphia, Sept. 30, 1766. An appeal against B. Franklin's election, as being the author of the Stamp Act.

Friends of Human Progress. Proceedings of the Annual Meeting, ... held at Waterloo, N. Y., ... 1855. *Syracuse.* 1855. 8vo, pp. 27. B. + Proceedings ... 1857 ... Waterloo ... . *Rochester: Curtis, Butts & Co.* 1857. 8vo, pp. 30. B.

The Friends of Liberty and Justice think it necessary, at this Juncture, to republish the following Piece, which made its appearance some Time ago in the New-York Journal, and which was written by a Gentleman of Distinguished Merit in the City of New-York. [About *October*, 1772.] Folio, pp. 1. P.

The original letters are dated Oct. 8, 1771. Refers to Goddard and the "Pennsylvania Chronicle."

Friends. *See also* Indians, Quakers, Slavery, and Society of Friends.

The Friends' Library: comprising Journals, Doctrinal Treatises, and other Writings of Members of the Religious Society of Friends. Edited by William Evans and Thomas Evans. *Philadeelphia: Printed by Joseph Rakestraw.* 1837–1850. 14 vols.

Each volume contains from 486 to 490 pages.

The Friends' Pocket Almanac, for 1852. *Philadelphia.* 1852. 24mo. Continued. 25957

Frierson (M. S.) An Address .. Nov. 10, 1860, by Madison S. Frierson, Esq., to the Maury County Horticultural Society, ... Columbia, Tenn. ... *Columbia: Tenn.: Mirror Office.* 1860. 8vo, pp. 5. H. 25958

Fries (E.) Novæ symbolæ mycologicæ. [*Upsal.* 1851.] 4to, pp. 128. 25959

Fungi collected in Mexico, Costa Rica, and the West Indies.

Fries (G.) Speech of Hon. George Fries, of Ohio, on the Oregon Question. Delivered in the House of Representatives, Saturday, February 7, 1846. [n. p. n. d.] 8vo, pp. 7. H.

Fries (J.) The Two Trials of John Fries, on an Indictment for Treason; together with a Brief Report of the Trials of several other Persons, for Treason and Insurrection, in the Counties of Bucks, Northampton and Montgomery ... Begun at ... Philadelphia, April 11, 1799; continued at Norristown, October 11, 1799, and concluded at Philadelphia, April 11, 1800; before the Hon. Judges, Iredell, Peters, Washington and Chase. ... Taken in Short Hand by Thomas Carpenter. *Philadelphia: William W. Woodward.* 1800. 8vo, pp, 4, 226, 51. B., BA.

Friese (P. C.) An Essay on Wages ... showing the Necessity of a Workingman's Tariff ... . By Philip C. Friese. *New York: Fowler and Wells.* 1853. 12mo, pp. 35. H. 25962

[Friese.] Statement for the Consideration of Workingmen ... and a Workingman's Tariff. *Baltimore: Printed by Wm. Wooddy & Son.* 1851. 8vo, pp. 6. H. 25963

Also: Letter to the President and People of the United States, showing that the President cannot lawfully execute an Unconstitutional Law ... By [Philip] C. Friese ... . *Baltimore: Sun Job Office.* 1869. 8vo, pp. 31. H. — The Unconstitutonality of Congressional Action; An Essay, on the Paramount Unwritten Law: ... . By Philip C. Friese ... . *Baltimore: Murphy & Co.* 1867. 8vo, pp. 42. B., H.

[Friess (Lorenz *or* Laurentius).] Aslegung der Mer|carthen oder Cartha Marina|Darin man sehen mag|wa einer in der welt sey|vnd wa ein ietlich|Laud Wasser vnd Stat gelegẽ ist. Das als in de bũchlin zefiudẽ.| [Colophon:] *Getruckt: zũ Strassburg von|Johannes Grieninger vnd|vollandet vff vnser Lie-|ben frawen abent der|geburt. Im Iar|* 1.5.2.5.| Folio. c. 25964

Title, 4 lines; preface, on verso of title, 38 lines; 29 leaves, folioed irregularly, from ii to xxxiii. 2 folded maps, and numerous woodcuts, all colored. One of the maps delineates Cadamosto's first voyage. The first chapter of this very rare work relates wholly to America, beginning "Das nëuw laud hie beschriben America genant ist gar nakendt als gros als ein vierdes teil der gantzen welt," etc.

Friess. Ynderweisung|vnd|vszlegung|Der Cartha Marina oder die mer|cartẽ Darin man sehen mag|wa einer in d' welt sy vnd wa ein ytlich|land wasser vnd stet ligẽ als in de bũ chlin angezögt vn in d' chartẽ zuschen.| [Colophon:] *Gedruckt* zũ

Strasburg von|Johannes Grieninger vnd|vollende vff Sant Yõrgẽ| abent Ym. Jar . . M . D . XXX.| Folio, Title, 1 l., 21 unnumbered l. 25965

The first Gazeetter. *See* Graesse, Vol. II., p. 635, and Harrisse. "*See* the verso of the last leaf for the chapter: 'Von America ein teyl dauonhie beschriben.'" — Harrisse.

Frieze (J.) A Concise History of the Efforts to obtain an Extension of Suffrage in Rhode Island, from the Year 1811 to 1842. By Jacob Frieze. *Providence: Benjamin F. Moore.* 1842. 12mo, pp. 171. BA., C., H. + Second Edition. [Enlarged. *Ibid.*] 1842. 12mo, pp. 179. 25966

[Frieze.] Facts for the People: containing a Comparison and Exposition of Votes on occasions relating to the Free Suffrage Movements in Rhode-Island. *Providence: Knowles & Vose, Printers.* 1842. 12mo, pp. 12. BA., H. 25967

Frieze (R.) An Address delivered before the Grand Lodge of Rhode Island, at their Anniversary ... at East Greenwich, R. I., Friday, June 24, 1831. By Robert Frieze, Grand Chaplain. *Providence: B. Cranston.* 1831. 8vo, pp. 24. 25968

Frignet (E.) La Californie. Histoire des Progrès de l'Un des États-Unis d'Amérique, et des Institutions qui font sa Prospérité. Par Ernest Frignet ... . *Paris: Schlessinger frères.* 1865. 8vo, 2 l., pp. xxvi, 479. Map. C. + Second Edition. [*Ibid.*] 1867. 8vo, pp. xxvi, 479. Map. B. 25969

Frignet (E.), *and* Carrey (E.) Etats-Unis d'Amérique. Les Etats du Nord-West et Chicago. Par Ernest Frignet et Edward Carrey. *Paris: imp. Jouast.* 1871. 8vo, pp. 88. 10 Plates. 25970

Frilinghuisen *or* Freijlinghausen (Theodorus Jacobus). Eenige Predicatien. *Nieuw York: W. Bradford.* 1721. 12mo.

Frilinghuisen. Sermons. Translated from the Dutch. And Prefaced by a Sketch of the Author's Life, by Rev. William Demarest. With an Introduction by the Rev Thomas De Witt, D.D. *New York: Board of Publication of the Reformed Protestant Dutch Church.* 1856. 12mo, pp. vi, 3–422. C. 25972

Frilinghuisen. Jeugd-oeffening|of|Verhandeling|van de| godlyke waarheden,|der christelyk religie.|by wyze van|vragen en antwoorden,|tot onderwgs der ionkeyd.|Door|Theodorus

Frielinghuyzen,|Predicant tot Albany, in Noord-America.|De Tweede Druck.|*Gedruckt by W. Weyman, te Nieuw-York, voor| den Autheur.*| [1748.] 12mo, 3 l., pp. 103. 25973

The following complaint relates chiefly to Frilinghuisen:

[Frilinghuisen.] Klagte|Van Eenige Leeden der|Nederduytse Hervormde Kerk,|Woonende op Raretans, &c., in der Provincie van|Nieu-Jersey, in Noord-America,|Onder de Kroon van Groot-Brittanje.|Over het Gedrag, Aldaar en Elders,|van| Do. Theodorus Jacobus Frilinghuisen,|Met syn Kerken-Raaden. |Ten|Antwoord|Op hunne|Bau-Dreygende Daag-Brieven, &c. Aan|Alle Liefhebbers der Waarheyd,|ter ondersoek, voorgesteld,|Hoe Die Gregronds zun ef Niet.|Met een|Noodige Voor-Reeden, tot opheldering van de Klagte.|Uytzegeven Door|De Gevolmag tigden der gemelde Leeden.|*Te Nieu-York, Gedrukt by William Bradford en J. Peter Zenger.* 1725.| 4to, 5 l., pp. xvi, 146. J.C.B. 25974

"This complaint of some of the members of the Low Dutch Reformed Church, in regard to the conduct of Dominie Jacobus Frilinghuysen, in conjunction with his consistories, is a vindication of certain members of the Dutch churches on and near the Raritan River, who had been expelled from the Church by sentence of Mr. Frilinghuysen. These members had accused him of preaching false doctrine in insisting upon the necessity of regeneration, and of unjustly excluding them from partaking of the Holy Communion in consequence of their alleged unworthiness. He first admonished them of their conduct, and then cited them to appear before the consistories, and on their failure to do so, expelled them. Hence this published reply. The book was written by a lawyer of New York, the brother of Henricus Boel, of that city, who took sides with the members of the Church." — J. R. Bartlett. "The preface is signed in the name of sixty-five members of the Dutch Reformed Church, whose names are all given, by their representatives: Pieter Dumont, Justice of Peace at Raritans; Simon Wyckof, Deacon at Drie Myl Run; and Daniel Sebering, Treasurer of the church at Nord-Branch. Very rare." — F. Muller.

Frilinghuisen. Verdeediging. *See* Freeman (B.), No. 25755.

Frink (S.) The Marvellous Works of Creation and Providence, Illustrated. Being the Substance of a Sermon preached at ... Shrewsbury ... 7th of October, 1762. A Day of Public Thanksgiving, occasioned by the Reduction of the Havannah. By Samuel Frink, A.M. ... *Boston: Printed by S. Kneeland.* 1763. 8vo, pp. 39. BA. 25975

Frink (T.) A King Reigning in Righteousness, and Princes Ruling in Judgment. A Sermon preached before ... Governour, ... being the Anniversary for the Election of His Majesty's Council, ... May 31, 1758. By Thomas Frink, M.A. ... *Boston: Printed by S. Kneeland.* 1758. 8vo, pp. 36. B., BA., C., H., M.

Frink. ... A Sermon at Stafford In Connecticut, March 23d. 1757. When Mr. John Willard was Ordained. By Thomas Frink, A.M. *Boston: S. Kneeland.* 1757. 8vo, pp. (4), 45.

Also: Discourse at Giving the Right Hand of Fellowship at the Installation of Rev. Edward Billing, at Greenfield District [Mass.] March 28, 1754. ... *Boston.* 12mo.

Frisbie (B.) The History of Middletown, Vermont, in Three Discourses ... By the Hon. Barnes Frisbie ... . *Rutland: Tuttle & Company.* 1867. 8vo, pp. 130. B., BA., H. 25977

Frisbie (Levi). A Collection of the Miscellaneous Writings of Professor Frisbie. With some Notices of his Life and Character. By Andrews Norton. *Boston.* 1823. 8vo, pp. 235. C.

Frisbie. A Discourse, before the Society for Propagating the Gospel among the Indians, and others, in North-America. Delivered on the 1st of November, 1804. By Rev. Levi Frisbie, A.M. ... *Charlestown: Printed by Samuel Etheridge.* 1804. 8vo, pp. 38. B., BA., H., N., W. 25979

The second of the addresses before this society. *See* Wheelock (E.)

Frisbie. An Eulogy on the Illustrious Character of the late General George Washington ... delivered at Ipswich, on the 7th day of January, 1800. By Levi Frisbie, A.M. ... To which is added, General Washington's Parential and Affectionate Address to his Country ... . *Newburyport: Printed by Edmund M. Blunt.* 8vo, pp. 61. BA., C., M., N., W. 25980

Frisbie. An Oration, Delivered at Ipswich, At the Request of a Number of the Inhabitants, On the Twenth-Ninth of April, 1783: On Account of the Happy Restoration of Peace, Between Great-Britain and the United States of America. By Levi Frisbie, A.M. ... *Boston, in America: Printed and Sold by E. Russell, near Liberty Pole.* M,DCC,LXXXIII. 4to, pp. 24. BA.

Also: Inaugural Address, delivered in the Chapel of the University at Cambridge, November 5, 1817. ... *Cambridge: Printed by Hilliard & Metcalf.* 1817. 8vo, pp. 28. BA., H. + Second Edition. *Cambridge.* 1818. 8vo, pp. 28. B., BA. — An Oration ... at the Interment of the Rev. Moses Parsons ... [n. p. n. d.] 8vo, pp. 19. H. — A Sermon ... February 19, 1795, the Day of Public Thanksgiving ... . *Newburyport: Printed by Blunt and March.* 8vo, pp. 28. BA. — ... Two Discourses ... in Ipswich, April 4, 1799 ... Fast Day ... *Newburyport: Printed by Angier March.* MDCCXCIX. 8vo, pp. 42. BA.

Frisch (P.) Die Staaten von Mexico, Mittel-und Südamerica in ihren geschichtlich-politischen, administrativen, Handels-und Cultur-Beziehungen, seit ihrer Unabhängigkeitserklärung bis zum Jahre 1850, bearbeitet von Dr. P. Frisch. *Lübeck: A. Dittmer.* 1853. 8vo, pp. 297. C. 25982

Frisius (G.) *See* Gemma Phyrsius.

Fristoe (W.) A Concise History of the Ketockton Baptist Association: ... By William Fristoe. *Staunton: Printed by William Gilman Lifford.* 1808. 12mo, pp. 162. 25983

Fritsch (J. G.) Demonstratio historico-geographica per quam efficitur veteres Americam ignorasse. Auctore Joanne Gottlobio Fritsch. *Vitebergæ.* 1798. 8vo, pp. 116. 25984

Mr. Rich gives the title:

Fritsch. Disputatio historico-geographica, in qua quæritur; utrum veteres Americam noverint, nec ne? Auctore Joanne Gottlobio Fritsch. 1798. 8vo. 25985

Fritz (J. P.) Orientalisch und Occidentalisches Sprachmeister. *Leipzig:* 1748. 8vo. 25986

Contains the Lord's Prayer, in eight North American dialects.

Fröbel (J.) America, Europa und die politischen Gesichtspunkte der Gegenwart. Von Julius Fröbel. *Berlin: J. Springer.* 1859. 12mo, pp. x, 213. C. 25987

Fröel. Aus Amerika. Erfahrungen, Reisen und Studien. Von Julius Fröbel. *Leipzig: Weber.* 1857–58. 2 vols., 8vo, pp. xvi, (1), 550; xvi, 616. B. 25988

Fröbel. Die deutsche Auswanderung und ihre culturhistorische Bedeutung. ... *Leipzig: Franz Wagner.* 1858. 8vo, 3 l., pp. 103. 25989

Fröbel. Geographisch-statistische Beschreibung von Ober- und Nieder-Peru od. den Freistaaten Peru und Bolivia a Julius Fröbel. *Weimar.* 1831. 8vo. 25990

Fröbel. Geographisch-statistische Beschreibung der Argentinischen Republik, etc. *Weimar.* 1832. 8vo. 25991

Fröbel. Seven Years' Travel in Central America, Northern Mexico, and the Far West of the United States. By Julius Fröbel. ... With Illustrations. *London: Richard Bentley.* M.DCCC.LIX. 8vo, pp. xiv, 587. B., BA., C., H. 25992

See also "Report of the Smithsonian Institute." 1854.

Fröbel. A travers l'Amérique par Julius Frœbel. Traduction de l'Allemand, par Émile Tandel. *Bruxelles: Lacroix, Van Menen. Paris: E. Jung-Treuttel.* 1861. 3 vols., 12mo, pp. 344; 380; 358. B., H. 25993

FROBISHER (M.) De | Martini | Forbisseri | Angli Navigati- | one in Regiones Occi- | dentis et Septen- | trionis | Narratio historica, | Ex Gallico sermone in La- | tinum translata | per | D. Joan. Tho. Freigivm. | Cum gratia & privilegio Imperiali. | CIↃ. IↃ. XXC. [Colophon :] *Noribergæ | Imprimebatur, in officina Ca- | tharinæ Gerlachin, & Hære- | dum Iohannis Mon- | tani.* | *Anno* | CIↃ IↃ XXC. | 8vo, 44 leaves. Woodcut. 25994

The woodcut represents Frobisher in a canoe, throwing darts at wild fowl, and the Greenlanders in their costume. This woodcut is sometimes supplied from the later edition, described below. This is the first Latin edition of his second voyage in 1577. It is translated from Chippin's French version of George Best's discourse (*see our* Vol. II., No. 5051), is not easily found, and scarcely ever with the plate. *See* "Bibliotheca Grenvilliana."

FROBISHER. Historia navigationis Martini Frobisseri Angli Prætoris sive Capitanei, A. C. 1577, Maio, Junio, Julio, Augusto & Septembri mensibus, jussu Reginæ Elizabethæ, ex Angliâ, in Septemtrionis & Occidentis tractum susceptæ, ephemeridis sive diarii more conscripta & Stilo, triennioq: post, ex gallico in latinum sermonem Joh. Thoma Freigio translata, et Noribergergæ, antè A. 94, cum præfatione utili, observationib9 aliquot et appendicè edita, denuò prodit, é Muséo D. Capelli, P. P. *Hamburghi: Georgievolffh.* 1675. 4to, 8 l., (1), pp. 37. Plate. B.

This Hamburg reprint contains some augmentations, and is very rare. In Dr. Hamel's "Notes on Russia," many notices are given on this voyage and its results.

FROBISHER. Beschreibung der schiffart des Haubtmans Martini Forbisher ausz Engelland, in die Lender gegen West und Nordt-west, im Tar 1577 etc. *Nürnberg: Katharina Gerlachin und Johanns vom Berg Erben.* 1580. 4to, 13 unpaged l. 25996

FROBISHER. Ausführliche Beschreibung des theils bewohnt theils unbewohnt-sogenannten Grönlands, nebenst einem Begriff der seltsamen Reisen, so M. Forbeisser, Gotzke Lindenau, Christ. Richard, und die Kopenhagen-Grönländ. Gesellsch. gethan. Mit Anfügung dss Tagebuchs eines die Durchfahrt zwischen Grönland und America suchenden Dänischen Schiffs etc. Durch S. von V. *Nürnberg.* 1679. 4to. 2 Maps and Engraved Title. 25997

FROBISHER. Drie Seldsame Scheeps-togten. De Eerste na China ondernoomen. In 't Jaar 1576. De Tweede, om in het Noord-Westen een nieuwe doorgang na Cataye, in 1577–1578, etc. Door een Reysigers in het Engels beschreeven, etc. *Leyden: Pieter van der Aa.* 1706. 8vo, pp. 73 and Register. Map and 2 Plates. 25998

Forms part of van der Aa's collection of voyages; also in folio.

FROBISHER. Les trois Navigations pour chercher un Passage à la Chine et au Japon par la Mer Glaciale en 1756, '57, '58, trad. de l'Anglais. *Amsterdam: Chez Jean Frederic Bernard.* M.DCCXX. 12mo. C. 25999

Included in the "Recueil de Arrests." *See* Bernard (J. F.), Vol. II. *See also* Hakluyt's "Voyages," Vol. III.; Pinkerton, Vol. XII., p. 202; "Relations de la Louisiane;" Brydges' "Restituta," Vol. II.; "Biogr. Universelle;" etc.

FROBISHER. Frobisher's Three Voyages in Search of a Passage to Cathaia and India, by the North-West, 1576–8. Edited by Admiral R. Collinson. *London: Printed for the Hakluyt Society.* 1867. 8vo, pp. xxvi, 376. Portrait. BA. 26000

Forms Vol. XXXVIII. of the "Hakluyt Society Publications." *See also* Settle (D.) The author was born near Doncaster, in Yorkshire, and acquired great skill in navigation. The discovery of a north-west passage to the Indies excited his ambition, and after many attempts, he was enabled, by the ministers of Queen Elizabeth, to fit out a private adventure of two barks and a pinnace, in which he entered the strait ever since called by his name; he returned to England with some ore, supposed to contain gold, which induced Queen Elizabeth to patronise a second and third voyage, but without success. He accompanied Sir Francis Drake to the West Indies, and at the defeat of the Spanish Armada he commanded one of the largest ships in the fleet, and was knighted by Queen Elizabeth for his services.

FROGER (F.) Relation d'un voyage fait en 1695. 1696 & 1697. Aux côtes d'Afrique, Détroit de Magellan, Brezil, Cayenne et Isles Antilles, par une escadre des vaisseaux du Roy, commandée par M. de Gennes. Par le Sieur Froger. Imprimée par les soins et aux frais de Fer. *Paris: dans l'isle du Palais et Michel Brunet.* 1698. 12mo, pp. (12), 219. P. 26001

Original edition. Engraved frontispieces, and 29 plates and maps. There are copies of this edition dated *Paris*, 1699.

FROGER. Relation | d'un voyage | Fait en 1695. 1696. & 1697. | Aux côtes d'Afrique, | Détroit de | Magellan, Bresil, Cayenne | et Isles Antilles, | Par une Escadre des Vaisseaux du Roi, commandée par | M. de Gennes. | Faite par le Sieur Froger Ingenieur Volontaire | sur le Vaisseau de Faucon Anglois. | Enrichie de grand nombre de Figures | dessinées sur les lieux. | *A Amsterdam, | Chez les Héritiers, | d'Antoine Schelte,* | M. DC. XCIX. | 12mo, 7 l., pp. 227. 16 Plates and 12 Maps. + *Paris: N. le Gras.* 1700. 12mo, pp. (12), 219. 29 Plates and Maps. + *Lyons: Jean Viret.* 1702. 12mo, pp. (8), 152. Engraved Frontispiece. + *Amsterdam.* 1702. 12mo. Maps and Plates. 26002

The edition of 1699 has two titles, one of which is engraved.

FROGER. Relation d'un Voyage de la Mer du Sud, Détroit de Magellan, Brésil, Cayenne et les Isles Antilles. Où l'on voit

les Observations que l'Auteur a faites sur la Religion, Mœurs & Coûtumes des Peuples qui y habitent, Et sur les divers Animaux qui s'y trouvent, de même que des Fruits & des Plantes qui y croissent. Par Le Sr. Froger. Enrichie de Figures dessinées sur les lieux, & gravées fort proprement. *A Amsterdam: Chez L'Honoré et Chatelain.* M.DCC.XV. 12mo, pp. (12), 227. 28 Maps and Plates. C. 26003

Title in red and black. A reprint, almost page for page, of the edition of 1699; but the dedication to Count Maurepas, and nearly all the dates of the year, are omitted, so as to make the book read as if the events narrated might have been recent.

FROGER. A | Relation | of a | Voyage | Made in the Years 1695, 1696, | 1697, on the Coasts of Africa, | Streights of Magellan, Brasil Ca- | yenna, and the Antilles, by a Squa- | dron of French Men of War, under | the Command of M. de Gennes. | By the Sieur Froger, Voluntier-Engineer | on board the English Falcon. | Illustrated with divers strange Figures, | drawn to the Life. | *London, | Printed for M. Gillyflower in Westminster- | Hall; W. Freeman, M. Wotton in Fleet- | street; J. Walthoe in the Temple; and | R. Parker in Cornhill.* 1698. | 8vo, pp. (12), 173, (2). A., C., H.

FROGOSO (J.) Aromatum Fructuum et Simplicium, aliquot Medicamentorum ex India vtraque et Orientali et Occidentali Historia brevis. *Argent.* 1600. 8vo. 26005

From Canada. *See* Vol. III., No. 10456.

From Dawn to Daylight. *See* [Beecher (H. W.)], Vol. II.

From our Yearly-Meeting, held at Philadelphia, for Pennsylvania, and New-Jersey, from the 17th to the 21st day of the 7th Month, 1737. To the Quarterly and Monthly Meetings. ... 1737. Folio, pp. 4. + *Re-printed at Leeds, for James Lister.* [n. d.] Folio, pp. 4. 26006

From the Meeting for Sufferings for New England, to the several Quarterly and Monthly Meetings belonging to the Yearly-Meeting. Signed by Moses Brown, Clerk. *Providence: Printed by John Carter.* [1782.] 4to, pp. 19. 26007

From the United States Gazette. Important Slave Case. [n. p. n. d.] 8vo, pp. 8. 26008

FROMELDEN, *pseudonym.* *See* Vol. IV., No. 13639.

FROMENTIN (E.) Dominique. Par Eugène Fromentin. *Paris: Hachette et Cie.* 1863. 12mo. 26009

The Frontenac Lead Mining Company ... in Bedford ... Canada West ... . *New York.* 1864. 8vo, pp. 8. 26010

Frontier Maid; or, a Tale of Wyoming: a Poem ... . *Wilkes-barre, Penn.: Printed by Steuben Butler & Samuel Maffet.* 1819. 12mo, pp. 208. H. 26011

Frontier Sketches, Selected and Arranged. *New York.* 1850. 12mo. 26012

FROSSARD (Benjamin Sigismond). La cause des esclaves nègres et habitans de la Guinée, portée au tribunal de la justice, de la religion, de la politique; ou histoire de la traite & de l'esclavage des nègres, preuves de leur illégitimité, moyens de les abolir sans nuire ni aux colonies ni aux colons. Par M. Frossard ... . *A Lyon: De l'imprimerie d'Aimé de la Roche, imprimeur de la Société Royale d'Agriculture.* M.DCC.LXXXIX. Avec approbation & Privilége du Roi. 2 vols., 8vo. C., A., P. 26013

Collation: Vol. I. (with a spirited frontispiece on steel), pp. v, (1), 367; II., pp. vii, 403. This volume should also contain the "Approbation de la Société Royale d'Agriculture de Lyon," and the "Privilége du Roi," printed on two leaves, unpaged. An esteemed and valuable work, and one of the earliest on the evils of the slave trade; rare.

FROSSARD. De Zaak der Negerslaaven, 'en der inwooneren van Guinea. *Gravenhaage.* 1790. 2 vols., 8vo. B. 26014

FROST (B.) The Church. A Discourse delivered at the Dedication of the New Church of the first Parish in Concord, Mass., Dec. 29, 1841. By Barzillai Frost. *Boston.* 1842. 8vo, pp. 31. B., BA., H., M. 26015

FROST. A Sermon delivered at the Funeral of the Rev. Ezra Ripley, D.D. By Barzillai Frost ... . *Boston: James Munroe and Company.* 1841. 8vo, pp. 22. B. 26016

FROST. A Sermon ... Concord, November 9th, 1856, being the Sunday succeeding the Death of Hon. Samuel Hoar, LL.D. By the Pastor, Barzillai Frost. ... *Concord: Benjamin Tolman.* 1856. 8vo, pp. 20. C., H 26017

FROST (D.) An Address, delivered before the Canterbury Temperance Society. By Daniel Frost, Jr. *New Bedford: Re-printed by B. Lindsey & Son.* 1829. 8vo, pp. 24. H. + *Brooklyn, Con.: Wm. H. Bigelow.* 1829. 8vo, pp. 26. H. 26018

FROST (G.) Camp and Prison Journal, embracing Scenes in Camp, on the March, and in Prisons: [etc., during the Rebellion]. By Griffin Frost. *Quincy, (Ill.)* 1867. 12mo, pp. vi, 393. C. 26020

FROST (J. B.) The Rebellion in the United States; or, the War of 1861; being a Complete History of its Rise and Progress ... . By Mrs. J. Blakeslee Frost. *Boston: Degen, Estes and Priest.* 1862. 8vo, pp. xiv, 11–388. Portraits and Plates.

FROST. (J.) The American Generals, from the founding of the Republic to the Present Time, comprising Lives of the Great Commanders, and Other Distinguished Officers who have acted in the Service of the United States. ... By John Frost, LL.D. ... *Philadelphia: J. W. Bradley.* 1848. 8vo, pp. 916. B. 26022

FROST. American Naval Biography; comprising Lives of the Commodores and other Commanders distinguished in the History of the American Navy. Compiled ... by John Frost, LL.D. ... *Philadelphia.* 1844. 8vo, pp. 450. 26023

FROST. The Book of the Army: comprising a General Military History of the United States ... . By John Frost, LL.D. ... *New-York: D. Appleton & Co.* 1845. 12mo, pp. 446. C., H.

FROST. The Book of the Colonies; comprising a History of the Colonies composing the United States, from the Discovery in the Tenth Century until the Commencement of the Revolutionary War ... By John Frost, LL.D. ... *New York and Philadelphia: D. Appleton & Co.* 1846. 12mo, pp. 280. Plates. C., H., S. + *Hartford.* 1849. 12mo, pp. 280. 26025

FROST. The Book of the Indians of North America: illustrating their Manners, Customs, and Present State. Edited by John Frost, LL.D. ... . *New York: D. Appleton & Co.* MDCCCXLV. 12mo, pp. 283. C., H. + [*Ibid.*] MDCCCXLVIII. 12mo.

FROST. The Book of the Navy; Comprising a General History of the American Marine; and Particular Accounts of all the most Celebrated Naval Battles, from the Declaration of Independence to the Present Time. Compiled from the best Authorities, by John Frost, A.M. ... With an Appendix. ... *New York: D. Appleton & Co.* MDCCCXLIII. 12mo, pp. 344. 12 Plates. B., C., H., P. + [*Ibid.*] MDCCCLVI. 26027

FROST. Border Wars of the West; comprising the Frontier Wars of Pennsylvania, Virginia, Kentucky, Ohio, Indiana, Illinois, Tennessee, and Wisconsin. And embracing Individual Adventures among the Indians, and Exploits of Boon, Kenton, Clark, Logan, Brady, Poe, Morgan, the Whetzel's, and other Border Heroes of the West. By John Frost ... *Auburn: Derby & Miller.* 1853. 8vo, pp. 608. + [*Ibid.*] 1856. C. + *New York.* 1859. 8vo. 26028

The plates are highly and horribly colored.

FROST. Heroes of the Revolution. By John Frost. Third Edition. *New-York.* 1844. 12mo. C. 26029

FROST. Heroic Women of the West; comprising Thrilling Examples of Courage, Fortitude, Devotedness, and Self-Sacrifice, among the Pioneer Mothers of the Western Country. By John Frost, LL.D. *Philadelphia: A. Hart.* 1854. 12mo, pp. 348. 5 Plates. C. 26030

FROST. Historical Collections of all Nations; ... with Special Notices of the Heroes of the West. *Hartford: Tiffany & Co.* 1852. 8vo, pp. 1008, including 71 Plates. C. 26031

FROST. Historical Sketches of the Indians: exhibiting their Manners and Customs on the Battle Field and in the Wigwam. With numerous Anecdotes and Speeches, from the Best Authorities. By John Frost. *Hartford.* 1852. 12mo, pp. 400.

FROST. History of the State of California; from the Period of the Conquest by Spain to her Occupation by the United States of America. By John Frost, LL.D. Also, Advice to Emigrants on the Best Routes. *Auburn.* 1853. 12mo, pp. 508. + *Auburn and Buffalo.* 1853. 8vo. + [*Ibid.*] 1855. 26033

A so-called new edition is entitled, "Pictorial History of California."

FROST. A History of the United States of North America. By John Frost ... A New Edition, Revised and Corrected. *Philadelphia: E. C. Biddle.* 1835. 12mo, pp. 461. + [*Ibid.*] 1837. 16mo, pp. 324. + New Edition. [*Ibid.*] 1837. 12mo, pp. 432. + *London: C. Tilt.* 1838. P. + *Philadelphia.* 1843. 12mo. + *Philadelphia.* 1846. 12mo. + *Philadelphia.* 1860. 12mo. 26034

FROST. Illustrated Historical Sketches of the Indians: exhibiting their Manners and Customs on the Battle Field and in the Wigwam. With numerous Anecdotes and Speeches. *Hart-*

ford: E. Hunt & Son. 1854. + *Hartford: L. E. Hunt.* 1857. 12mo, pp. 400. 37 Plates. C. + [*Ibid.*] 1857. 8vo, pp. 400.

FROST. An Illustrated History of Washington and his Times: embracing a History of the Seven Years' War, Revolutionary War, the Formation of the Federal Constitution, and the Administrations of Washington. By John Frost. Edited by Rev. W. Hutchison. *Norwich, (Conn.): H. Bill.* 1868. 8vo, pp. 626. 23 Plates. C. 26036

FROST. Indian Battles, Captivities and Adventures from the Earliest Period to the Present Time. Edited by John Frost, LL.D. ... *New York: J. C. Derby.* 1856. 12mo, pp. 408. 2 Plates. + [*Ibid.*] 1858. 12mo, pp. 408. 26037

FROST. The Indians on the Battle Field and in the Wigwam. By John Frost. *Boston.* 1860. 12mo. 26038

[FROST.] Indian Wars of the United States, from the Discovery to the Present Time. From the best Authorities. By William V. Moore. *Philadelphia: R. W. Pomeroy.* 1840. 12mo, pp. 321. 26039

This is the first work of its prolific author, if such a term can be applied to a notorious pilferer. He afterwards reprinted it as

FROST. Indian Wars of the United States, from the Earliest Period to the Present Time. By John Frost ... *New York and Auburn: Miller, Orton and Mulligan.* 1856. 12mo, pp. 300. 52 Plates. + [*Ibid.*] 1859. 26040

FROST. The Life of William Penn, with a Sketch of the Early History of Pennsylvania. By John Frost. *Philadelphia: Orrin Rogers.* 1839. 18mo, pp. xii, 239. Plate. C. 26041

FROST. Life of Major General Zachary Taylor; with Notices of the War in New-Mexico, California, and in Southern Mexico; and Biographical Sketches of Officers who have distinguished themselves in the War with Mexico. By John Frost ... . *New York: D. Appleton & Co.* 1847. 8vo, pp. 346. 26042

[FROST.] Lives of American Merchants, Eminent for Integrity, Enterprise, and Public Spirit. Seventh Edition. *Auburn: Alden & Markham.* 1848. 12mo, pp. 240. 26043

FROST. The Lives of the Presidents of the United States, from Washington to Pierce, comprising their Personal and Political History ... By John Frost. *Boston.* 1854. 12mo, pp. 455. + [*Ibid.*] 1860. 26044

FROST. The Mexican War and its Warriors; ... Biographical Sketches and Anecdotes of the most Distinguished Officers in the Regular Army and Volunteer Force. By John Frost ... *New Haven and Philadelphia: H. Mansfield.* 1850. pp. 332, 11.

FROST. The Pictorial Book of the Commodores, comprising Lives of Distinguished Commanders in the Navy of the United States, ... By John Frost, LL.D. ... *New York: Nafis & Cornish.* [1845.] 8vo, 1 l., pp. xiv, 9–440. H. 26046

FROST. Pictorial History of the American Navy: comprising Lives of its Distinguished Commanders. Compiled from the best Authorities. By John Frost ... *New York: Leavitt & Allen.* [1854.] 8vo, pp. xv, 9–440. 7 Plates. 26047

FROST. Pictorial History of Mexico and the Mexican War: Comprising an Account of the Ancient Aztec Empire, the Conquest by Cortes, Mexico under the Spaniards, the Mexican Revolution, the Republic, the Texan War, and the Recent War with the United States. By John Frost, LL.D. ... Embellished with Five Hundred Engravings, from Designs of W. Croome and other Distinguished Artists. *Philadelphia: Thomas Cowperthwait and Co.* 1848. 8vo, pp. 652. + [*Ibid.*] 1849. 8vo. + [*Ibid.*] 1862. 8vo. 26048

FROST. The Pictorial History of the United States of America, from the Discovery by the Northmen in the Tenth Century to the Present Time. By John Frost, ... *Philadelphia.* 1843–4. 4 vols., 8vo. + *Hartford: Case, Tiffany and Burnham.* 1848.

First issued in parts; reprinted in London; also republished as "Remarkable Events," 8vo, various dates.

FROST. Illustrische Geschichte der Vereinigten Staaten Amerika's. Aus den Englischen von Rally. *Philadelphia.* 1845. 8vo.

FROST. Pictorial Life of George Washington. Embracing a Complete History of the Seven Years' War, the Revolutionary War, the Formation of the Federal Constitution, and the Administration of Washington. ... *Philadelphia: Charles J. Gillis.* 1847. 8vo, pp. iv, 588. + *Philadelphia: Leary & Getz.* 1853.

FROST. Remarkable Events in the History of America, from the Earliest Times to the Year 1848, Compiled from the Best Authorities. By John Frost, LL.D. ... *Philadelphia: William A. Leary & Co.* 1848. 2 vols., 8vo. B. + [*Ibid.*] 1849. + [*Ibid.*] 1852. + [*Ibid.*] 1857. 26052

FROST. Thrilling Adventures among the Indians, ... as well as of Incidents in the recent Indian Hostilities in Mexico and Texas. *Philadelphia: J. W. Bradley.* 1849. 8vo, pp. 448. 46 Plates. c. 26053

[FROST.] Thrilling Incidents of the Wars of the United States, ... *Philadelphia: Carey & Hart.* 1848. 8vo, pp. 600.

Also: The Book of Anecdotes; or, the Moral of History ... . By John Frost, LL.D. ... . *New-York: D. Appleton & Co.* 1846. 12mo, pp. 252. + *Hartford.* 1851. — The Book of Good Examples. ... *New-York.* 1846. 12mo. — The Chess Book of American Literature. *Boston.* 1826. 12mo. — The Duty of the American Scholar to the Literature of his Country. An Address, ... Marshall College, ... September 28, 1841. *Philadelphia: J. Crissy, Printer.* 1841. 8vo, pp. 22. BA., H. — Grand Illustrated Encyclopædia of Animated Nature; embracing a full description of the different Races of Men, and of the Characteristic Habits and Modes of Life of the various Beasts, Birds, Fishes, Insects, Reptiles, &c. *Auburn.* 1855. 4to. c. — Great Events in Modern History. ... *Philadelphia.* 1851. 8vo. c. — Incidents and Narratives of Travel in Europe, Asia, Africa, and America. ... *Auburn and Buffalo.* 12mo, pp. 544. — Lives of Eminent Christians of various Denominations ... *Philadelphia.* 1852. 8vo. — An Oration, at Middlebury, before the Alumni of the College ... August 19th, 1829. ... *Utica: Printed by Hastings and Wary.* 1829. 8vo, pp. 23. — Panorama of Nations, comprising the Characteristics of Courage, Perseverance, etc., by the Principal Nations of the World. *Auburn and Buffalo.* [n. d.] 12mo. — Pictorial Family Encyclopædia of History, Biography and Travels. New Edition. *Auburn.* 1855. 8vo, pp. 648. — Pictorial Life of Andrew Jackson. Embellished with Numerous Engravings ... . *Hartford: Belknap and Hamersly.* 1847. 8vo, pp. 512. B., C. — Pictorial Modern History; From the Discovery of America by Columbus to the Present Time. *Philadelphia.* 1846. 8vo, pp. 560. c. — Wild Scenes of a Hunter's Life, or the Hunters and Hunting of all Nations. *New York.* 1855. 8vo. c. — *New York.* 1860. 12mo, pp. 467.

FROST (J.), *and* DRAKE (S. G.) Indian Wars and Captivities of the United States, embracing the Early Wars of the Colonies and Revolution, King Philip's, the French and Indian, the North-Western Black Hawk, Seminole War, &c., together with Indian Captivities; being Narratives of Captives who have been carried away by the Indians from the Frontier Settlements of the United States, from the Earliest Period to the Present Time, by John Frost, LL.D., and Samuel G. Drake, M.D. *Auburn.* 1855. 8vo, pp. 670. 290 Engravings. 26055

FROST. Genealogy of the Frost Family. *See* [Parsons (U.)]

FROSTBURG. Report of the Examination and Survey of the Coal Fields and Iron Ore belonging to the Boston and New-York Coal Company, at Frostburg, Alleghany County, in the State of Maryland. *New-York: E. B. Clayton.* 1837. 12mo, pp. 18.

FROTHINGHAM (C. W.) Six Hours in a Convent: ... A Tale of Charlestown in 1834. By Charles W. Frothingham. *Boston: Graves & Weston.* 1855. 8vo, pp. 44. H. 26057

FROTHINGHAM (E.) A Key to Unlock the Door, That leads in, to Take a Fair View of the Religious Constitution established by Law in the Colony of Connecticut. By Ebenezer Frothingham. *Printed in the Year* 1767. 16mo. W. 26058

FROTHINGHAM (F.) The Lord's Freedman. A Discourse. By Frederick Frothingham, of Buffalo, N. Y. ... *New York: Wm. P. Tomlinson.* 1868. 12mo, pp. 13. H. 26059

FROTHINGHAM. Tribute to the Memory of William Czar Bradley of Westminster, Vermont, who died March 3, 1867. By Fred'k Frothingham. ... *Cambridge: John Wilson and Son.* 1867. 8vo, pp. 15. H. 26060

Also: ... A Sermon ... at the Dedication of the Church of the Messiah, in Montpelier, January 25, 1866. *Montpelier: Ballou, Loveland & Co.* 1866. 8vo, pp. 11, (1). H. — Significance of the Struggle between Liberty and Slavery in America. A Discourse ... April 16th, 1857. *New York.* 1857. 16mo, pp. 21. B., H.

FROTHINGHAM (F. E.) The Boston Fire, November 9th and 10th, 1872. Its History ... . By F. E. Frothingham ... . *Boston: Lee & Shepard.* 1873. pp. 115. Map. B., BA. 26061

FROTHINGHAM (N.) Short Account of the Conversion, Life and Death of N. Frothingham. *Boston.* 1811. 12mo. 26062

FROTHINGHAM (N. L.) Christian Patriotism. ... A Sermon on Occasion of the Death of John Adams, ... July 9th, 1826. By N. L. Frothingham ... . *Boston: Printed by Munroe and Francis.* 1826. 8vo, pp. 20. B., H. 26063

FROTHINGHAM. Farewell: A Sermon preached to the First Church, on resigning its Pastoral Charge, ... March 10, 1850. By N. L. Frothingham. *Boston: Printed by John Wilson.* 1850. 8vo, pp. 26. B., BA., H., M. 26064

FROTHINGHAM. "Gathered to his People." A Sermon preached ... June 5th, 1847. At the Funeral of Rev. Thomas Gray, D.D. By N. L. Frothingham ... . *Boston: Printed by Joseph G. Torrey.* 1847. 8vo, pp. 14. B., BA., H. 26065

FROTHINGHAM. Memoir of Rev. Thaddeus Mason Harris, D.D. By Nathaniel L. Frothingham. *Cambridge: Metcalf and Company.* 1855. 8vo, pp. 28. B., H. 26066

FROTHINGHAM. A Memoir of William Parsons Lunt, D.D. By Nathaniel L. Frothingham, D.D. *Boston: privately printed.* 8vo, pp. 16. B., H. 26067

[FROTHINGHAM.] Recollections of Rev. F. W. P. Greenwood, D.D. A Sermon preached after his Death, and Selections from his Writings. ... *Boston: James Munroe & Co.* 1845. 12mo, pp. 46. 26068

FROTHINGHAM. A Sermon, delivered before the Ancient and Honourable Artillery Company, June 6th, 1825 ... By N. L. Frothingham ... . *Boston: For the Company, by E. G. House.* 1825. 8vo, pp. 21, 1 l. B., BA., H., M. 20669

FROTHINGHAM. A Sermon on the Death of General Lafayette, preached to the First Church in Boston, on Sunday, the 29th of June, 1834. By N. L. Frothingham ... . *Boston: Munroe and Francis.* 1834. 8vo, pp. 16. B., BA., H. 26070

FROTHINGHAM. A Sermon, preached to the First Church, by its Minister, N. L. Frothingham, on the Twentieth Anniversary of his Ordination, March 15, 1835. ... *Boston: Munroe and Francis* 1835. 8vo, pp. 16. B., BA., H. 26071

FROTHINGHAM. The Shades of the Past. For the Celebration of the Close of the Second Century, since the Establishment of the Thursday Lecture. By N. L. Frothingham, ... *Boston: Russell, Odiorne, and Metcalf.* 1833. 8vo, pp. 13, (1). B., BA.

FROTHINGHAM. Two Hundred Years Ago. A Sermon preached to the First Church, on the Close of the Second Century, 29 August, 1830. By N. L. Frothingham. *Boston: For the Society.* 1830. pp. 20. B., BA., H., M. 26073

[FROTHINGHAM.] A Tribute to the Memory of Thomas B. Wales. *Boston.* M DCCC LIII. 8vo, pp. 11. H. 26074

Also: The Duties of Hard Times. A Sermon, ... April 23, 1837. ... *Boston: Munroe & Francis.* 1837. 8vo, pp. 20. B., BA., H. — The Duty of the Citizen to the Law. A Sermon. ... *Boston: Leonard C. Bowles.* 1844. 8vo, pp. 14. B., BA., H. — Funeral Sermon, on the Death of the Rev. Joseph McKean, D.D. delivered ... April 19, 1818. ... . *Boston: Printed by J. T. Buckingham.* 1818. 8vo, pp. 19. B., BA., H. — God with the Aged: A Sermon preached, ... Jan. 7, 1849, after the Death of Hon. Peter C. Brooks. ... . *Boston: Printed by John Wilson.* 1849. 8vo, pp. 15. B., BA., H. — The Memory and Example of the Just. A Sermon preached on All Saints' Day ... *Boston: Printed by Joseph T. Buckingham.* 1840. 8vo, pp. 15. B., BA., H. — Mourning Days. A Sermon, [after the Death of Daniel Webster. n. p. n. d.] 8vo, pp. 73–79. B. — The New Idolatry. A Sermon, ... 22nd November, 1840. ... *Boston: Printed by J. T. Buckingham.* 8vo, pp. 15. — Our Religious Terms. An Address ... before the ... Alumni of Cambridge ... July 12, 1844. *Boston: William Crosby.* 1844. 8vo, pp. 23. B., BA., H. — Ruffian Released: A Sermon Preached ... 21st Feb., 1836. ... *Boston.* 1836. 8vo, pp. 15. B. — ... A Sermon ... at the Ordination of Mr. Edgar Buckingham ... in Dover, N. H. December 30, 1835. ... .

Boston: Printed by J. T. Buckingham. 1836. 8vo, pp. 31, (1). B., H. — ... A Sermon ... after the Death of J. G. Stevenson, M.D. ... *Boston: Printed by Isaac R. Butts.* 1835. 8vo, pp. 15. B., BA., H. — ... A Sermon, preached at the Installation of Rev. William Parsons Lunt ... in Quincy, June 3, 1835. ... . *Boston: Leonard C. Bowles.* 1835. 8vo, pp. 40. B., BA., H. — ... A Sermon, ... after the Death of Joseph P. Bradlee, 25 February, 1838. *Boston: Munroe and Francis.* 1838. 8vo, pp. 16. B., BA., H. — ... A Sermon ... after the Funerals of the Rev. Dr. Harris, and the Hon. Daniel Sargent. ... *Boston: Printed by J. T. Buckingham.* 1842. 8vo, pp. 14. — B., BA., H., P. — A Sermon preached in King's Chapel, August 6, 1843, the Sunday after the Funeral of the Rev. F. W. P. Greenwood, D.D. ... . *Boston: Charles C. Little and James Brown.* 1843. 8vo, pp. 27. B., H. — A Sermon, ... at the Ordination of Rev. O. B. Frothingham ... in Salem. ... . *Salem: Gazette Office.* 1847. 8vo, pp. 30. BA., H. — Sermon at the Funeral of Rev. T. Gray. *Boston.* 1847. 8vo. — The Solemn Week. A Sermon, preached ... on Fast-Day, April 8th, 1841. ... *Boston: Printed by J. T. Buckingham.* 1841. 8vo, pp. 14. B., H.

FROTHINGHAM (O. B.) ... A Discourse delivered at the Installation of J. K. Karcher ... October 5, 1859. By O. B. Frothingham ... . *Philadelphia: T. B. Pugh.* 1859. 8vo, pp. 39. H. 26075

FROTHINGHAM. The Last Signs. A Sermon preached at the Unitarian Church in Jersey City, ... June 1, 1856. By O. B. Frothingham. *New York: Printed by John A. Gray.* 1856. 8vo, pp. 22. B. 26076

FROTHINGHAM. The Morality of the Riot. Sermon of Rev. O. B. Frothingham, at Ebbit Hall, Sunday, July 19, 1863. *New York: David G. Francis.* 1863. 18mo, pp. 20. 26077

FROTHINGHAM. The New Year's Gifts of the Spirit. Two Discourses. By O. Frothingham ... . *New York: David G. Francis.* 1865. 8vo, pp. 44. B. 26078

This discourse has reference to the great successes that attended the Union armies during a short period previous to January, 1865.

FROTHINGHAM. ... Seeds and Shells: A Sermon in New York, Nov. 17, 1861. By O. B. Frothingham. *New York: Wyncoop & Co.* 1862. 8vo, pp. 22. B., H. 26079

Also: Allegiance and Patronage. Sermon ... June 17, 1866. ... *New York: James Miller.* 1866. 12mo, pp. 16. — Colonization [Anti-Slavery]. *New York.* [n. d.] — The Let-Alone Policy. A Sermon, ... June 9, 1861. *New York.* [1861.] 12mo, pp. 16. B., H. — Speech ... before the American Anti-Slavery Society, in New York, May 8th, 1856. *New York.* 1856. 16mo, pp. 26. B., H. — Theodore Parker: A Sermon ... New York, June 10, 1860. ... *Boston: Walker, Wise, and Company.* 1860. 8vo, pp. 20. B., H. — ... A Sermon ... at the Dedication of the Unitarian Church in Jersey City ... September 19, 1855. ... *New York: Printed by John A. Gray.* 1855. 8vo, pp. 24. B. — The Worship of Tools. A Sermon. ... *New York: James Miller.* 16mo, pp. 22. H.

FROTHINGHAM (R.) The Command in the Battle of Bunker Hill, with a Reply to "Remarks on Frothingham's History of the Battle, by S. Swett." ... By Richard Frothingham, Jr., ... *Boston: Charles C. Little and James Brown.* 1850. 8vo, pp. 56. View of the Battle, and Key. B., BA., H. 26080

FROTHINGHAM. The History of Charlestown, Massachusetts. By Richard Frothingham, Jr. ... . *Charlestown: Charles P. Emmons.* 1845–49. 8vo, 368. Maps and Plates. B., BA., H.

Seven parts, all published.

FROTHINGHAM. History of the Siege of Boston, and of the Battles of Lexington, Concord, and Bunker Hill: Also, an Account of the Bunker Hill Monument. With Illustrative Documents. By Richard Frothingham, Jr., ... *Boston: Charles C. Little and James Brown.* 1849. 8vo, pp. ix, (1), 420. Maps. B., BA., C., H., P. + Second Edition. [*Ibid.*] 1851. 8vo. B.

See "N. Am. Rev.," LXX. 405.

FROTHINGHAM. Life and Times of Joseph Warren. By Richard Frothingham. *Boston: Little, Brown & Company.* 1865. 8vo, pp. xix, 558. Portrait and Facsimile. B., BA., H., C.

FROTHINGHAM. Life and Services of Joseph Warren. By Richard Frothingham. *Boston: Little, Brown, and Company.* 1866. 8vo, pp. xix, 558. 26084

FROTHINGHAM. Oration delivered in Newburyport on the Fourth of July, 1851 ... By Richard Frothingham, Jr. ... [*Boston.* 1851.] 8vo, pp. 12. H. 26085

FROTHINGHAM. The Rise of the Republic of the United States. By Richard Frothingham. *Boston: Little, Brown, and Company.* 1872. 8vo, pp. xxii, 1 l., pp. 640. B., BA., H. 26086

FROTHINGHAM. A Tribute to Thomas Starr King. By Richard Frothingham. *Boston: Ticknor and Fields.* 1865. 16mo, pp. 247. B., BA., C., S. 26087

FROUT DE FONTPERTUIS (A.) Les Etats-Unis de l'Amérique Septentrionale, leurs origines, leur émancipation et leurs progrès. Par Adalbert Frout de Fontpertuis. *Paris: Guillaumin et Cie.* 1873. 8vo, pp. viii, 619. 26088

FROUT DE FONTPERTUIS. Les Français en Amérique. Le Canada. *Paris: J. Albanel.* 1867. 16mo, 2 l., pp. xi, 264. C.

FRÜHAUF (D.) Beschreibung der bevorstehenden Partial Monds-Finsterniss, so aus dem meridian zu Philadelphia und America sichtbar seyn wird, den 7ten April, im Jahr 1773. Von Daniel Frühauf. *Philadelphia: Gedruckt bey Henrich Miller.* 1773. 4to, pp. 16. P. 26090

FRUHBECK (F. J.) Skizze meiner Reise nach Brasilien in S: A: im Yahre 1817. Von F. J. Fruhbeck. *Wien.* 1830. 8vo.

Fruits of Colonization. [*Boston.* n. d.] 8vo, pp. 12. M.

FRY (B. St. J.) The Life of Robert A. Roberts, one of the Bishops of the Methodist Episcopal Church. By Benjamin St. James Fry. *New York: Carlton & Phillips.* 1856. 18mo, pp. 126. C. 26093

FRY (E.) Pantographia; containing Accurate Copies of all the known Alphabets in the World. ... By Edmund Fry. *London.* 1799. Imp. 8vo, pp. xxxvi, 320. W. 26094

Includes some North American Indian alphabets, vocabularies, etc.

FRY (F.) Fry's Travellers' Guide and Descriptive Journal of the Great North-Western Territories of the United States of America. Comprising the Territories of Idaho, Washington, Montana, and the State of Oregon, with Sketches of Colorado, Utah, Nebraska, and British America; the Grain, Pastoral, and Gold Regions defined, with some new Views of their future greatness. By F. Fry. *Cincinnati.* 1865. pp. vi, 264.

FRY (Frinkle, *pseudonym*). "Wooden Nutmegs" at Bull Run. A Humorous Account of some of the Exploits of the Three Months' Connecticut Brigade, and the part they bore in the National Stampede. *Hartford: G. L. Coburn.* 1872. 8vo, pp. 86. C. 26096

FRY (H.) To the Hon. The House of Representatives ... the Memorial of Henry Fry. [*Philadelphia.* 1835.] 8vo.

Relates to his dismissal as purser.

FRY (J.) ... The Danger and Duty of the Church in the Present Crisis. A Sermon, preached in ... Dec. 30, 1860. By Rev. Jacob Fry, ... *Carlisle: E. Cornman.* 1861. 8vo, pp. 21.

FRY (J. B.) *See* Provost Marshal, *infra.*

FRY (J. R.) A Life of Gen. Zachary Taylor; comprising a Narrative of Events connected with his Professional Career, derived from Public Documents and Private Correspondence; by J. Reese Fry; and Authentic Incidents ... by Robert T. Conrad. ... *Philadelphia: Grigg, Elliot & Co.* 1847. 12mo, pp. 332. Portrait. B., H. + [*Ibid.*] 1848. 12mo, pp. 332. 26099

FRY (Lewis). On the Slavery of the Old World and the Relations of Christianity to it. [A Lecture.] Lithographed.

FRY (W. H.) Republican Campaign Text Book for 1860. *New York.* 1860. 12mo. 26101

FRYE (G.) Case of Capt. Geo. Frye, President of the Council in the Island of Montserrat, containing an Impartial Narrative of his Behaviour in that Station, his Impeachment and Answer, with the Assembly's Replication. *London.* 1754. 8vo. 26102

[FRYE (Isaac W.)] The Charlestown Convent; its Destruction by a Mob, on the Night of August 11, 1834. ... . *Boston: New England News Company.* 1870. 8vo, pp. 98. B. 26103

FRYEBURG, *Me.* The Centennial Celebration of the Settlement of Fryeburg, Me., with the Historical Address, By Rev. Samuel Souther, of Worcester, Mass. *Worcester: printed by Tyler & Seagrave.* [1863.] 8vo, pp. 79. 26104

FRYER (A.) The Sugar Duties. An Examination of the Letter addressed by Edward Potter, M.P. to the Rt. Hon. W. E. Gladstone, M.P. By Alfred Fryer. *Manchester: Galt & Co.* 1864. 8vo, pp. 44. 26105

FUCHSII (S.) Metoposcopia et Ophthalmoscopia. *Argentorate.* 1615. 8vo. 26106

Includes a portrait of Christopher Columbus.

The Fudge Family in Washington. Edited by Harry Nimrod. ... *Baltimore: Joseph Robinson.* 1820. 12mo, pp. 109. BA.

FUENTE (F. de la). De lo bveno lo mejor, govierno espiritval politico. Por el capitan Francisco de la Fvente, sindico apostolico general de las conuersiones de la serafica orden en este reyno del Perú, y natural de el. *Lima: Joseph de Contreras y Alvarado.* 1693. 2 vols., folio, 6 l., pp. 693, 19 l.; 5 l., pp. 657, 15 l. 26108

"Livre fort rare, non cité par Antonio, par Brunet et Salva." — LECLERC.

FUENTE (G. de la). (Estudios estadísticos.) Censo de poblacion en la Republica Argentina (Algunos antecedentes para su organizacion). Por D. G. De La Fuente. *Buenos Aires.* 1869. Sm. 4to, pp. 42. 26109

FUENTE (R. de la). Biografia del ilustre general americano Don José de San Martin, resumida de documentos autenticos. Por Don Romualdo de La Fuente. *Paris: Rosa y Bouret.* 1872. 18mo, pp. 180. Vignette. 26110

FUENTE (V. de la). Historia Eclesiástica de España. Por Vicente de la Fuente. *Barcelona.* 1855–59. 4 vols. 26111

Contains valuable information on the Spanish dominions in America.

FUENTE (V. de). Villar de Fuente y Dion. Capáz. Manifiesto de las sesiones tenidas en el pueblo de Miraflores para las transaciones intentadas con el General San Martin y Docomentos de los Comisionados en ellas. *Lima.* 1820. 8vo. 26112

FUENTES (J. M. de). El Combate Naval del 21 de Octobre, por D. Jos. Mor de Fuentes. [In verse.] *Mexico.* 1806. 4to, 2 l., pp. 18. 26113

FUENTES (M. A.) Biblioteca Peruana de historia, ciencias y literatura. Coleccion de escritos del anterior y presente siglo de los mas acreditados autores Peruanos por Manuel A. Fuentes. Antiguo Mercurio Peruano. *Lima.* 1861–1864. 9 vols., 8vo, pp. vi, 318; 360; 332; 322; 318; 328; 363; 386; 326.

FUENTES. Coleccion de causas celebres contemporaneas, civiles y criminales, del Foro Peruano y extrangero por Manuel A. Fuentes. *Lima.* 1860–62. 10 vols., 8vo, pp. 298; 400; 432; 430; 390; 408; 388; 422; 492; 422. 26115

FUENTES. Guia historico-descriptiva administrativa, judicial y de domicilio de Lima por Manuel A. Fuentes. Publicada por Felipe Bailly. Segunda edicion. *Lima.* 1861. 8vo, pp. 362.

FUENTES. Lima, esquisses historiques, statistiques, administratives, commerciales et morales. Par Manuel A. Fuentes ... *Paris: Firmin Didot frères, fils et Cie.* 1866. 8vo, pp. ix, 243. Portraits, Views, etc. 26117

FUENTES. Lima Sketches of the Capital of Peru, Historical, Statistical, Administrative, Commercial and Moral. By Manuel A. Fuentes. *Paris: Firmin Didot frères, fils et Cie.* 1866. 8vo, pp. ix, 228. 26118

[FUENTES.] Memorias de los Vireyes que han gobernado el Peru, durante el Tiempo del Coloniaje Español, impresas de orden suprema. *Lima.* 1859. 6 vols., 4to, pp. xxx, 379, 2 l.; pp. 428; 391; 540; 392, 1 blank l., pp. 17, 1 l.; pp. 394. Map and 12 Plates. 26119

A work of extreme interest, edited by M. A. Fuentes, at the desire of the Government, from important manuscript relations existing in the archives of Peru. It ranges from the earliest time to 1790.

FUENTES. Mémoire sur le coca du Pérou, ses caractères botaniques, sa culture, ses propriétés hygiéniques et thérapeutiques. Par Manuel A. Fuentes (de Lima). *Paris: imp. Lainé et Havard.* 1866. 8vo, pp. 24. 26120

FUENTES (P.) Guia del estado eclesiastico de España y de los dominios de S. M. en América y Asia para el año de 1851. *Madrid.* 1851. 8vo. 26121

FUERTE (C.) Alegacion juridica en defensa del capitan Don Joseph Diego de Medina y Saravia, Tesorero proprietario de la Real Casa de Moneda de Mexico, Don Manuel de Pereda Palacio, su Teniente, yà difunto, etc. etc. en los Autos de visita, o pesquisa principiados contra los referidos, y otros Oficiales Majores de dicha Casa de Mexico, y Mercaderes de plata de la misma Ciudad, por el Virrey Marquis de Casa Fuerte, y continuados por don Joseph Fernandez de Veytia Linage etc. Sobre defectos de ley, y peso en monedas fabricadas en la referida Casa de Mexico, y otras cosas, de que se formò cargo à los expressados en los mismos Autos, por le respectivo al ministerio, y obrar de cada uno. [*Mexico.* 1728.] Folio, 1126 l. 26122

Fugitive Political Essays which have appeared in the Public Advertiser, 1769, '70, under the several names of Old Sly Boots, Hortensius, ... etc. *London.* 1770. 8vo, pp. 112. 26123

Partly relates to American affairs.

The Fugitive Slave Bill. Enacted by the United States Congress, and approved by the President, Millard Fillmore, September 18, 1850. *Boston.* 1854. 8vo, pp. 7. B., H. 26124

The Fugitive Slave Bill; its History and Unconstitutionality; with an Account of the Seizure and Enslavement of James Hamlet, and his Subsequent Restoration to Liberty. *New York: William Harned.* 1850. 8vo, pp. 36. B., BA., H. 26125

FUGITIVE SLAVE BILL. Proceedings of the United States Senate, on the Fugitive Slave Bill ... Speeches of Messrs. Davis, Winthrop and others. *Boston: J. R. Marvin.* [n. d.] 8vo, pp. 68. B., BA. 26126

Fugitive Slave Case. District Court of the United States for the Southern Division of Iowa, June Term, 1850. Ruel Daggs *vs.* Elihu Frazier *et als.* Rep. by George Frazee. *Burlington.* 1850. 12mo, pp. 40. H. 26127

The Fugitive Slave Law, and its Victims. *New York: American Anti-Slavery Society.* 1856. 12mo, pp. 48. + Revised and Enlarged Edition. [*Ibid.*] 1861. 12mo, pp. 168. B. 26128

The Fugitive Slave Law of 1850. 8vo, pp. 3. 26129

The Fugitive Slave Law. Unconstitutionality of the Fugitive Slave Act. Decisions of the Supreme Court of Wisconsin in the Cases of Booth and Rycraft. *Milwaukee: Rufus King & Co., Printers.* 1856. 8vo, pp. 218. 26130

Fugitive Slaves. N. Y. Court of Appeals. Report of the Lemmon Slave Case: Containing Points and Arguments of Counsel on Both Sides, and Opinions of all the Judges. *New York: Horace Greeley & Co.* 1860. 8vo, pp. 146. 26131

Fugitive Thoughts on the African Slave Trade, interspersed with Cursory Remarks on the Manners, Customs, and Commerce of the African and American Indians. *Liverpool, Printed.* 1796. 8vo, pp. 66. 26132

Written to advocate slavery, and dedicated to those merchants who trafficked in negroes. Every act of oppression and barbarity practised in Great Britain is brought forward to exhibit the slave owner and planter as among the mildest of masters. Title and note from J. C. Hotten's catalogue.

FUGITT (J. P.) ... Is Slaveholding Constitutional and Scriptural? By the Rev. James Preston Fugitt. *Baltimore: Printed by John D. Toy.* 1862. 12mo, pp. 35. 26133

FUGITT. ... Our Country and Slavery. A Friendly Word to the Rev. Francis L. Hawks, ... And Other Northern Clergymen. By the Rev. James Preston Fugitt. *Baltimore: Printed by Joseph Robinson.* 1861. 12mo, pp. 33. B. 26134

Also: A Plea for Peace. A Sermon preached in Baltimore, September 26, 1861. ... *Baltimore: John D. Toy.* 1861. 8vo, pp. 17. — The Union of Patriots for the sake of the Union. An Oration on the Union. Delivered at Cantonsville, June 30, 1860. ... *Baltimore: Joseph Robinson.* 1860. 8vo, pp. 16.

FUGL (Ulrich Nicolai). Oplysninger angaande de dansk vestindiske Oers nuværende commercielle Forhold. I. St. Thomas. *Kjobenhavn.* 1840. 26135

Also: Om Negerslaveriet i Vestindien, og sammes Ophör; med specielt Hensyn til de danske Besiddelser, in the "Juridisk Tidsskrift," 1835, XXIV. 1–60.

FULFORD (F.) Five Occasional Lectures, delivered in Montreal. By Francis Fulford, D.D. *Montreal.* 1859. 8vo, pp. 118.

FULFORD. The Sermon at the Consecration of Horatio Potter, D.D., to the Episcopate. Preached by Appointment in Trinity Church, New York, November 22, 1854. By Francis Fulford, D.D. ... . *New-York: Daniel Dana, Jr.* M,DCCC,LIV. 8vo, pp. 31. B. 26137

FULFORD. Sermon ... Triennial Meeting of the General Convention of the Protestant Episcopal Church ... in ... Philadelphia, October 4th, 1865. By the Most Reverend Francis Fulford, D.D. ... . *Philadelphia: King and Baird.* 1865. 8vo, pp. 14. B., H. 26138

FULFORD. Sermons, Addresses and Statistics of the Diocese in Montreal. *Montreal, London, and Cambridge.* 1865. 8vo, pp. xiv–308. 26139

Also: Pastoral Letter addressed to the Clergy of the Diocese. ... *Montreal.* 1851 pp. 16. — An Address ... in the Chapel of the General Theological Seminary of the Protestant Episcopal Church ... November 13th, 1852. ... . *New York.* MDCCCLII. 8vo, pp. iv, (2), 15, (1). B., H. — A Charge delivered to the Clergy of the Diocese of Montreal, at the Primary Visitation. ... *Montreal.* 1852. pp. 25. — A Charge delivered to the Clergy of the Diocese of Montreal, at the Triennial Visitation. ... *Montreal.* 1855. pp. 38. — A Letter to the Bishops and Clergy of the United Church of England and Ireland in Canada. ... *Montreal.* pp. 30.

FULGOSIS (B.) Baptistæ Fulgosi de dictis factils que memorabilibus collectanea a Camillo Galino latina facta. [Colophon:] *Jacobus Ferrarius Mediolane* . x . *Kl. Julius a redemptione christana anno* MDVIII *impressit.* Folio, 366 unnumbered l. 26140

On signature llii is a short chapter on Columbus. Reprinted in *Paris, by Peter Vidoux.* 1518. 4to; *Antwerp.* 1565; *Basle.* 1567; *Cologne.* 1604. 4to.

A Full and Authentic Report of tbe [*sic*] Debates in Faneuil Hall, Dec. 31, Jan. 1, & 2, 1821–2; On changing the form of Government of the Town ... Including the Speeches of Messrs. Clough, Emmons, &c. ... *Boston: William Emmons.* 1822. 12mo, pp. 48. H. 26141

A Full and Exact. *See* Vol. v., Nos. 18554 and 18555.

A Full and Faithful Report of the Debates in both Houses of Parliament, on Monday the 17th of February, and Friday the 21st of February, 1783, on the Articles of Peace. *London: S. Bladon.* [1783.] 8vo, pp. 116, 72. + [*Ibid.*] N. 26142

A Full and Free Inquiry into the Merits of the Peace; with some Strictures on the Spirit of the Party. *London: T. Payne.* MDCCLXV. 8vo, pp. (4), 160. 26143

A Full and Impartial Account of the Company of Mississippi, otherwise call'd the French-East-India Company, Projected and Settled by Mr. Law. Wherein the Nature of that Establishment and the almost incredible Advantages thereby accruing to the French King, and a great Number of his Subjects, are clearly explain'd and made out. ... To which are added a Description of the country of the Mississippi, and a Relation of the Discovery of it, in Two Letters from a Gentleman to his Friend. *London: Printed for R. Francklin.* 1720. 8vo, pp. 80. C. 26144

In French and English. One of the tracts that induced so many to embark in the famous "Mississippi Bubble." The Company "had the sole privilege of the trade of the Mississippi. Mr. Law, a Scotch gentleman, whose genius always carried him to the study of trade and money, contrived the plan of this establishment, of which he was appointed the principal director," etc.

A Full & just Discovery of the weak &|slender foundation of a most Pernicious|Slander|Raised against the|French Protestant Refugees|Inhabiting the Province of New-York generally, but more|particularly affecting|Capt. Benj. Faniel [*sic*],| A Person of considerable Note amongst them.|Printed and Published by Licence of his Excellency Edward Viscount Cornbury,|Capt. General and Governour in chief of the said Province, in favour| of Justice.| [n. p. 1708.] Folio, pp. 6. S. 26145

A tract of the greatest rarity. Consists of memorials signed by the French, affidavits and doings of the council. The original manuscript is in the office of the Secretary of the State of New York. The only known copy is in the State Library at Albany, N. Y. Faneuil's name is signed Faniel.

A Full and Particular Account of all the Circumstances attending the Loss of the Steamboat Lexington, in Long Island Sound, on the night of January 13, 1840; as elicited in the evidences of the Witnesses examined before the Jury of Inquest, held in New York, immediately after the lamentable event. ... *Providence: H. H. Brown & Stillwell.* 1840. 8vo, pp. 32.

A Full and Particular Answer to all the Calumnies, Misrepresentations and Falsehoods contained in a Pamphlet called a Fourth Letter to the People of England. *London.* 1756. 8vo, pp. 61.

See [Shebbeare (John)], for the Fourth Letter, and an answer to this pamphlet.

A Full Answer to the King of Spain's last Manifesto, respecting the Bay of Honduras, and the Mosquito-Shore: in which all the Accusations brought against the Subjects of Great Britain settled in the Bay of Honduras; and against the ancient British Settlements in the Free and Independent Dominions of the Mosquito-Shore, are candidly stated and refuted; and the Importance of the Mosquito-Shore to Great Britain Delineated and Ascertained. *London: T. Cadell.* MDCCLXXIX. 8vo, pp. 75. 26148

"A very sensible and spirited refutation of the King of Spain's manifesto, so far as regards subjects mentioned in the title-page. The author, however, zealously presses our perseverance in carrying on the ruinous and (in the opinion of many well-informed people) hopeless war in America." — *M. Rev.*, LXI. 472.

A Full, Clear, and Succinct Discussion of the Preliminary Articles of Peace, as Published by Authority. By an Eminent Citizen. *London: S. Williams.* [1763.] 4to, pp. 20. 26149

Respecting the treaty for ceding Nova Scotia, Canada, Cape Breton, etc., to the British.

A Full Exposition of a Pamphlet entitled Observations on the Papers relative to the Rupture with Spain ... *London: Williams.* 1762. 8vo, pp. 47. S. 26150

A Full State of the Dispute betwixt the Governor and the Commons House of Assembly Of His Majesty's Province of South Carolina, in America. With the Proper Vouchers and Reasons in Support of the Proceedings of the House of Assembly, As Transmitted to their Agent in Great Britain. *Printed in the Year* MDCCLXIII. Sm. folio, pp. (2), 78. N. 26151

A Full Statement of the Reasons offered to the Committee of the Legislature of Massachusetts, against Penal Laws respecting Abolitionists and Anti-Slavery Societies. *Boston.* 1836. 8vo, pp. 46. 26152

Full Vindication. *See* [Howe (*General*)].

Full Vindication of ... Congress. *See* [Hamilton (A.)]

FULLARTON [(William)]. A Letter to Lord ******, on the Subjects of Torture introduced into the British Colonies, as connected with the Laws of Old Spain. By Colonel Fullarton. *London.* 1806. 4to. 26153

FULLARTON. A Refutation of the Pamphlet which Colonel Picton lately addressed to Lord Hobart. By Colonel Fullarton. *London: J. Stockdale.* 1805. 4to. 26154

Relates to the governorship of Trinidad. *See* "M. Rev.," New Series, XLVII. 222.

FULLARTON. A Statement, Letters, and Documents respecting the Affairs of Trinidad: including a Reply to Colonel Picton's Address to the Council of that Island; submitted to the Consideration of the Lords of His Majesty's Most Honourable Privy Council. By Colonel Fullarton. *London: B. McMillan.* 1804. 4to, 1 l., pp. 201, 25–94. C. 26155

FULLER (A. S.) The Forest Tree Culturist; a Treatise on the Cultivation of American Forest Trees, with Notes on the most Valuable Foreign Species. By Andrew S. Fuller, Horticulturist ... . *New York: George E. Woodward.* 1866. pp. iv, 184.

Also: The Small Fruit Culturist. *New York: O. Judd & Co.* [1867.] 12mo, pp. 276.

FULLER (A. B.) An Historical Discourse, delivered in the New North Church, [Boston] October 1, 1854. By Arthur B. Fuller. ... *Boston: Crosby, Nichols, and Company.* 1854. 8vo, pp. 33. BA., H. 26157

Also: A Discourse, occasioned by the Death of Richard Hazen Ayer, delivered ... February 13, 1853. ... . *Manchester, N. H.* 1853. 8vo, pp. 15. B., H. A Discourse, occasioned by the Death of Miss Mirey Tufts ... Jan. 24, 1858. ... . *Boston: Printed by John Wilson and Son.* 1858. 8vo, pp. 21. B., H.

FULLER (D.) A Familiar Exposition of the Constitution of Pennsylvania, for the Use of Schools and for the People. By Daniel Fuller. *Philadelphia.* 1840. 12mo, pp. 105. 26158

Also: Political Class-Book of the State of Pennsylvania. *Philadelphia: Biddle.* 1853. 12mo, pp. 120. C.

FULLER (H.) The Causes and Consequences of the Civil War in America. A Discourse. By H. Fuller. ... *London: James Ridgway.* [1861.] 8vo, pp. 30. B., C., H. 26159

FULLER (H. M.) National Politics. Speech of Hon. Henry M. Fuller ... in the House ... May 10, 1856. [n. p. n. d.] 8vo.

[FULLER (Henry W.)] The Woodlawn Cemetery in North Chelsea and Malden. ... *Boston: Higgins and Bradley.* 1856. 8vo, pp. 125. BA. 26161

[FULLER (Hiram).] Belle Brittan on a Tour, At Newport, and Here and There. *New-York: Derby & Jackson.* 1858. 12mo, pp. 359. B. 26162

[FULLER.] North and South. By the White Republican ... . *London: Chapman & Hall.* 1863. 12mo, pp. (6), 336. BA.

FULLER (J. C.) A Letter addressed by James Cannings Fuller, of Skaneateles, N. Y., to the Editor of the London "Friend," relative to ... the recent Secession from the Yearly Meeting of Indiana: also, a Letter from three Friends of Indiana to James C. Fuller, on the same subject: and the Declaration issued by the Yearly Meeting of Anti-Slavery Friends of Indiana, in Justification of their Secession. *Dublin: Printed by Webb and Chapman.* 1843. 12mo, pp. 27. 26164

Also: Letters to the Farmers of Somerset. *Bristol: John Wright.* 1836. 12mo, pp. 24.

FULLER (J. G.) Bending Willow: a Tale of Missionary Life in the North-West. By Jane Gay Fuller. *New York: R. Carter & Brothers.* 16mo, pp. 305. 3 Plates. 26165

FULLER. The Grahams. A Story of the Florida War. By Jane Gay Fuller. *New York: M. W. Dodd.* 1864. 16mo.

Also: The Brownings: a Tale of the great Rebellion [With] Lucy Lee; or All Things for Christ. ... *New York: M. W. Dodd.* 1867. 16mo, pp. 310. 3 Plates.

FULLER (Metta Victoria). *See* [Victor (M. V. F.)]

FULLER (R.) A City or House Divided Against Itself. A Discourse, delivered by Rev. Richard Fuller, June 1, 1865, the Day of National Fasting and Humiliation. *Baltimore: G. E. Weishampel.* 1865. 8vo, pp. 20. 26167

FULLER. Mercy remembered in Wrath. A Sermon Preached by the Rev. Dr. Fuller, on Thursday, September 26, 1861, being the Day of National Fasting, Humiliation and Prayer. *Baltimore: Henry Taylor.* 1861. 8vo, pp. 24. H. 26168

FULLER. Wrong and Right Dispositions under National Judgments. A Sermon preached by the Rev. Dr. Fuller. On Thursday, April 30, 1863. Being the Day of National Fasting, Humiliation and Prayer. *Baltimore: Printed by W. M. Innes.* 1863. 8vo, pp. 27, (1). B., H. 26169

Also: Address before the American Colonization Society. Washington, D. C., January 21, 1851. ... *Office of the True Union.* 1851. 8vo, pp. 17. B. — A Discourse delivered before the General Convention of the Baptist Denomination April 28th, 1841. ... *Philadelphia.* 1841. 8vo, pp. 38. — Our Duty to the African Race. An Address delivered at Washington, D. C., January 21, 1851. ...*Baltimore: Printed by W. M. Innes.* 1851. 8vo, pp. 17. H.

FULLER (R.), *and* WAYLAND (F.) Domestic Slavery considered as a Scriptural Institution: in a Correspondence between the Rev. Richard Fuller, of Beaufort, S. C., and the Rev. Francis Wayland, of Providence, R. I. Revised and Corrected by the Authors. *New York: Lewis Colby.* 1845. 18mo, pp. viii, 254.

Reissued in 1850 and 1860. For a Review, *see* Hague (—).

FULLER (R. F.) Chaplain Fuller: Being a Life Sketch of a New England Clergyman and Army Chaplain [Arthur B. Fuller]. By Richard B. Fuller. ... *Boston: Walker, Wise & Company.* 1863. 12mo, pp. vi, 342. Portrait. B., BA., C., H. 26171

FULLER (R.) An Account of the Imprisonment and Sufferings of Robert Fuller, of Cambridge ... . *Boston: Printed for the Author.* 1833. 8vo, pp. 30. BA., H. 26172

The author was seized and detained in the M'Lean Asylum at Charlestown, Mass., for sixty-five days.

FULLER (M.) *See* Ossoli (M. *Countess*).

FULLER (S.) Early Days of the Church in the Hilderberg. Two Sermons preached in ... Rensselaerville, N. Y., ... April 24, 1842, on the Death of its Founder and First Rector, the Rev. Samuel Fuller ... By his Son, the Rev. Samuel Fuller ... . *Andover: Printed by Allen, Morrill and Wardwell.* 1843. 8vo, pp. 52. B., H., S. 26173

FULLER. Education in the Two Andovers. Address at the Dedication of the Punchard Free School, ... September 2nd, 1856. By Rev. Samuel Fuller, D.D., ... *Andover: Printed by W. F. Draper.* 1856. 8vo, pp. 42. B., BA., H. 26174

FULLER. Effects of the War of the Revolution upon the Protestant Episcopal Church. Discourse, July 4, 1858. ... *Andover.* 1858. 8vo, pp. 31. B. 26175

FULLER. Memorial to Peter Smith Byers, A.M. ... at his Funeral, ... Andover, ... March 21, 1856. By the Rector, Rev. Samuel Fuller, D.D. ... *Cambridge: Printed by Allen and Farnham.* 1856. 8vo, pp. 16. BA., H. 26176

FULLER. The Speaking Dead. A Discourse, delivered in ... Litchfield, Sept. 19, 1849, on the Death of Major General Francis Bacon ... . By the Rector, Rev. Samuel Fuller, D.D. *New York: S. W. Benedict.* 1849. 8vo, pp. 24. B., H. 26177

[Fuller (Samuel), *and others*.] Memoir of Benjamin Hanover Punchard, the Founder of the Punchard Free School, Andover, Mass. ... *Andover: Printed by Warren F. Draper*. 1847. 8vo, pp. 43. H. 26178

Fuller (S.) The Representation of Stephen Fuller, Agent for Jamaica to his Majesty's Ministers. [n. p. n. d.] 4to, pp. 4.

See also Jamaica.

Fuller. Sermon at Oxford, N. H. May 20, 1801, at the Ordination of Sylvester Dana. By Stephen Fuller. *Hanover*. [n. d.] 8vo. W. 26180

Fuller (T.) The Holy and Profane State (a Collection of Characters, Moral Essays and Lives, Ancient, Foreign and Domestic). By Thomas Fuller. *Cambridge*. 1642. Folio.

Contains the life of Sir Francis Drake, of Tavistock, in Devonshire, with account of his voyages to various parts of America. Repeatedly reprinted. The latest edition is edited, with notes, by J. C. Nichols. *London: W. Tegg*. 1841. 8vo.

Fuller (T.) Historical Notices of Thomas Fuller and his Descendants, with a Genealogy of the Fuller Family. ... *Boston: Henry W. Dutton & Son, Printers*. M.DCCC.LIX. 8vo, pp. 16.

Fuller (T. J. D.) Speech of Hon. T. J. D. Fuller, of Maine, in the House of Representatives, March 30, 1852, on the Homestead Bill. [n. p. n. d.] 8vo, pp. 8. H. 26183

Fuller (T.) Remarks on that part of the Strictures on Mr. Thacher's Pamphlet which relates to the Controversy between Mr. Fuller and the People of Princeton. By Timothy Fuller, A.M., Pastor of the Church of Princeton, &c. *Boston: Norman & Co.* [1776.] 8vo, pp. 23. W. 26184

Fuller (T.) Address ... at the Eleventh Anniversary of the Massachusetts Peace Society, December 25, 1826. By Timothy Fuller. *Boston: Printed by C. S. Hamilton*. 1827. 8vo, pp. 27.

Fuller. Oration, delivered at Faneuil Hall, Boston, July 11, 1831, at the Request of the Suffolk Anti-Masonic Committee. By Timothy Fuller. *Boston: Benton Press*. 1831. 8vo, pp. 11.

Fuller. An Oration pronounced at Watertown, July 4, 1809. At the Request of the Republicans of Watertown and the adjacent Towns, in Commemoration of the Anniversary of American Independence ... By Timothy Fuller, Esq. *Boston: J. Beecher*. 1809. 8vo, pp. 16. B., BA., H., M. 26187

Fuller. An Oration ... at Lexington ... Fourth of July, A.D. 1814 .... By Hon. Timothy Fuller. *Boston: Rome & Hooper*. 1814. 8vo, pp. 23. BA., H. 26188

Fullerton (A.) Coercion a Failure, Necessarily and Actually. By Alexander Fullerton Jr. *Philadelphia*. 1863. 8vo, pp. 16. 26189

Fullonton (J.) The History of Acton, Me. By Joseph Fullonton. *Dover, N. H.* 1847. Sm. 8vo, pp. 36. 26190

Fullom (S. W.) The Great Highway: a Story of the World's Struggles. By S. W. Fullom. *London: Longman*. 1852. 3 vols., post 8vo. + Third Edition. *London: G. Routledge & Co.* 1854. Post 8vo, pp. vii, 428. 4 Plates. 26191

Contains incidental reference to American topics. The author's "History of Woman" also contains some American examples

Fulton. (A. R.) The Free Lands of Iowa. Being an Accurate Description of the Sioux City Land District. A General View of Iowa: her Resources and Advantages; ... By A. R. Fullom, ... *Des Moines, Iowa: Mills & Co.* 1869. 8vo, pp. 44, (3). Map. 26192

Fulton (J. A.) Peach Culture. By James Alexander Fulton, Dover, Delaware. Illustrated. *New York*. 1870. 12mo, pp. 190. 26193

Fulton (J. D.) Memoir of Timothy Gilbert. By Justin D. Fulton. ... *Boston: Lee & Shepard*. 1866. 16mo, pp. (2), 255. B., BA. 26194

Fulton. Outlook of Freedom; or, the Roman Catholic Element in American History. *Cincinnati*. 1856. 12mo. C. + *New York*. 1857. 12mo. 26195

Also: The True Woman. ... . To which is added Women *vs.* Ballot. ... *Boston: Lee and Shepard*. 1869. 12mo, pp. xii, 3–48, (2). B., H. — "Who is my Neighbor?" A Sermon preached in the Baptist Church, Albany, N. Y., September 14, 1862. 8vo, pp. 8.

Fulton (R.) Letter from Robert Fulton to the Secretary of the Navy; ... [on] the Practical Use of the Torpedo, or Sub-Marine Explosion, Feb. 4th, 1811; ... *Washington*. 1811. 8vo, pp. 55. 26196

Fulton. Letters ... on Sub-Marine Navigation and Attack; ... By Robert Fulton, Citizen of the United States of America, and Author of the System for Destroying Ships of War. *London. September 23d*, 1806. 8vo, pp. vii, 37. 26197

Fulton. Report on the Practicability of Navigating with Steamboats on the Southern Waters of the United States, from the Chesapeake to the River St. Mary's, ... By Robert Fulton ... . *New-York: Printed by E. Conrad*. 1813. 8vo, pp. 13. B.

Fulton. Torpedo War, and Submarine Explosions. By Robert Fulton, ... *New-York: Printed by William Elliott*. 1810. Oblong 4to, pp. 57, (3). 5 Plates. B., H. 26199

Fulton. De la machine infernale ... expériences faites en Angleterre et aux États-Unis, sur la manière d'en faire usage. Traduit de l'anglois par M. E. Nunez de Taboada. *Paris; Demonville; Magimel*. 1811. 8vo, pp. 104. 26200

Fulton. A Treatise on the Improvement of Canal Navigation; exhibiting the numerous Advantages to be derived from Small Canals, and Boats of Two to Five feet wide, containing from Two to Five Tons Burthen. ... including Observations on the great importance of Water Communications, with Thoughts on, and Designs for Aqueducts and Bridges of Iron and Wood. By R. Fulton, Engineer. ... *London: I. and J. Taylor*. 1796. 4to, pp. xvi, 144. Portrait and 17 Plates. 26201

The New York Historical Society has a unique copy, with all the original drawings executed by Fulton himself, from which the engravings were afterwards made, also the original joint letter of Fulton and his colleague, Chancellor Livingston, asking the undisputed right to the use of steam navigation upon the waters of the Mississippi for a term of years.

Fulton. Recherches sur les Moyens de perfectionner les Canaux de Navigation. *Paris*. 1799. 8vo. A. 26202

Fulton (R.), *and* Livingston (E. P.) Memorial of Robert Fulton and E. P. Livingston, in regard to Steamboats. *Albany*. 1814. 8vo. 26203

Fulton City, *Ill.* Sketches of the Early History and present advantages of Fulton City, Ill., showing its Resources and Prospects; to which is added a brief Sketch of Whiteside Co. *Fulton City*. 1856. 8vo, pp. 32. 26204

Fulton County. Proceedings of the Board of Supervisors of the County of Fulton, for 1857. *Johnstown*. 1858. 8vo. Continued. S. 26205

Fun for the Camp. *New York*. 1862. Oblong 8vo. S.

Funch (Johan Christian Vilhelm). Syv Aar i Nord-Grönland. *Viborg*. 1840. 8vo. 26207

The Fundamental Constitutions. *See* Carolina, Vol. III.

Fundamentos de hecho y de derecho por la Testamentaria del Presbitero D. Sib. Lecaros para que la di D. Jose Toribio Larrian le devuelva la hacienda de Molina con sus frutos los del vinculo di Viluco en dos anos diez mesis cinco dias y se le declane posesion proindeviso en Viluco y tierra de Campasano hasta ser reintegrado de la parte hereditaria con frutos que tiene en ellas. *Santiago de Chile*. 1838. Sm. 4to. 26208

Funeral Gratitud con que la Religiosa communidad del convento de N. S. P. San Francisco de la Ciudad de la Puebla de los Angeles, contribuye â las Exequias de D. Andre de Arce. *Puebla*. 1774. 4to. 26209

A Funeral Sermon, on Michel Morin, Master and Verger of the Church of Beausejour, in Champagne, Deceas'd the first of May, 1718. Preached by the Parson of the aforesaid Parish, before the body of the deceased, in presence of the Parishioners. ... *New-York: printed by James Parker*. 1748. 12mo, pp. 7.

A burlesque production. There was a Morin family in the province at that time; but I cannot perceive any local allusions in the piece.

Funes (G.) Ensayo de la Historia Civil del Paraguay, Buenos-Ayres y Tucuman escrita por el Doctor D. Gregorio Funes, Dean de la Santa Iglesia Catedral de Cordova. Tomo Secundo [y Tercio]. *Buenos-Ayres: Imprenta de M. J. Gandarillas y socios*. [1816–17.] 3 vols., 8vo, 2 l., pp. xi, 368, (14); (4), 409, 7 l.; pp. 532, 6 l. BA. + Segunda edicion. *Buenos Aires*. 1856. 2 vols., 4to, pp. 390; 478. 26211

Composed from original documents. *See* Leclerc's catalogue, No. 597. There is a new edition, by Maeso, in one volume, with a life of the author. Also: Arenga ... sobre la victoria de Ayacucho; [and] Resumen sucinto de la vida del Gen. Sucre. *Buenos-Aires*. 1825. 12mo.

Funk (*Mr.*) Copperheads under the Heel of an Illinois Farmer. [n. p. n. d.] pp. 3. H. 26212

Funnell (W.) A | Voyage | Round the World. | Containing an Account of | Captain Dampier's Expedition | Into the South Seas in the Ship St. George, | in the Years 1703 and 1704. | With his various Adventures, Engagements, &c. | And a particular and exact Description of se- | veral Islands in the Atlantick Ocean, the Brazil- | ian Coast, the Passage round Cape Horn, and | the Coasts of Chili, Peru and Mexico. | Together with the | Author's Voyage from Amapalla, | On the West-Coast of Mexico, | To

East-India. | His passing by Three Unknown Islands, and thro' | a New-discover'd Streight near the Coast of New-Guinea. | His Arrival at Amboyna: | With a large Description of that and other Spice Islands; | as also of Batavia, the Cape of Good Hope, &c. | Their Rivers, Harbours, Plants, Animals, Inhabitants, &c. | With Divers Maps, Draughts, Figures of Plants and Animals. | By William Funnell, Mate to Captain Dampier. | *London: James Knapton*. 1707. | 8vo, 12 l., pp. 300, (17). 9 Plates and 5 Maps.

Generally considered as the fourth volume of Dampier's collection, although there is no indication that it was intended for such at the time of its publication. Funnell "arrived in England before Dampier, and seized on the opportunity to compose a relation of his voyage, a task for which he was ill qualified, and which he performed with disadvantage to the public. Knapton, the publisher of Dampier's voyages, tempted by the favorable reception of the latter, added Funnell's voyage to them as a fourth." His narrative contained much that was disapproved by Captain Dampier, who immediately after published a "Vindication of his Voyage," pointing out the misrepresentations of Funnell. This brought out "An Answer" from John Welbe, a midshipman on board Captain Dampier's ship, in which he charges the captain with barbarous treatment of his crew. *See* Dampier (W.), Vol. v.

Fur, Fin, and Feather: Containing the Game Laws of the Principal States of the United States and Canada. ... *New York: M. B. Brown & Co.* 1868. 8vo, pp. 219. B., C., H. 26214

Furber (G. C.) Camp Stories; or, Incidents in the Life of a Soldier, designed to give correct ideas of a Soldier's Life. By George C. Furber. *Cincinnati: J. A. & U. P. James*. 1849. 8vo, pp. 96. 26215

Furber. History of Mexico; continued from the Capture of Vera Cruz to the Termination of the War with the United States; containing the Treaty of Peace, &c.; being a Continuation of "Young's History of Mexico." *Cincinnati: J. A. and U. P. James*. 1848. 8vo. + [*Ibid.*] 1850. C. 26216

Furber. The Twelve Months' Volunteer; or, Journal of a Private, in the Tennessee Regiment of Cavalry, in the Campaign in Mexico, 1846–7; ... including a Complete History of the War with Mexico. ... By George C. Furber. *Cincinnati: J. A. & U. P. James*. 1848. 8vo, pp. 640. Map and Engravings. BA. + [*Ibid.*] 1850. + [*Ibid.*] 1851. + [*Ibid.*] 1857.

Furlong (L.) The American Coast Pilot. By Lawrence Furlong. *Newburyport*. 1796. 8vo. 26218

Furlong. The American Pilot; containing the Courses and Distances between the Principal Harbours, Capes and Headlands from Passamaquoddy through the Gulph of Florida, ... By

Capt. Lawrence Furlong ... Second Edition. 1798. B. + Third Edition. *Newburyport: Printed by Edmund M. Blunt*. 1800. 8vo, pp. 251. B. + Fourth Edition. [*Ibid.*] 1804. 8vo. BA., C. + The American Coast Pilot. Sixth Edition. [*Ibid.*] 1809. 8vo, pp. 389. 15 Plans and Charts. BA. + Seventh Edition. *New York: Printed by Edmund M. Blunt*. [1812.] 8vo, pp. 321, 65. 15 Plans and Charts. 26219

Furman (G.) Notes, Geographical and Historical, relating to the Town of Brooklyn, in Kings County on Long-Island. By Gabriel Furman. *Brooklyn: Printed by A. Spooner*. 1824. 12mo, pp. 116, (4). BA. + With Notes, and a Memoir of the Author. *Brooklyn: Reprinted for the Faust Club*. 1865. 4to, pp. xxxiv, 116, (4), xxxix. BA., H. 26220

Edition, 120 copies, of which 20 are on excessively large paper. The "Faust Club" consisted of one person. Also: Address delivered before the American Institute ... during the Sixteenth Annual Fair, October 25th, 1843. ... *New York: Robert Craighead*. 1843. 8vo, pp. 12. B. — Address before the Queen's County Agricultural Society. *Jamaica*. 1845. 8vo. B. And other addresses.

[Furman (Garrit.] The Maspeth Poems. *New York: Published by Connor & Cooke*. 1837. Square 12mo, pp. 128. 10 Plates.

[Furman.] Rural Hours; a Poem. [*Maspeth*. 1824.] 12mo.

The plates are designed by G. Furman, and engraved by A. B. Durand. The author thus sings of steamboats:

Safe wafted now by heat's hydraulic steam
Which late to man did but in vision seem (!)

Furman (G.) The Medical Register of the City of New York, for ... 1866. ... Guido Furman, M.D., Editor. *New York: The Author*. 1866. 18mo, pp. 306. 26223

Furman (M.) To the Public ... Moore Furman. *Philadelphia. July* 31, 1771. Folio, pp. 2. P. 26224

Relates to an affair with Isaac Wikoff. *See* Irwin (T.)

Furman (R.) Humble Submission to Divine Sovereignty, the duty of a Bereaved Nation: A Sermon occasioned by the Death of His Excellency General George Washington, late Commander-in-Chief of the Armies, and formerly President of the United States of America, Preached in the Baptist Church in Charleston, S. C., on the 22nd of February, before the American Revolution Society, the State Society of the Cincinnati, and a numerous assemblage of Citizens. By Richard Furman, A.M., Pastor of said Church, and a Member of American Revolution Society. ... *Charleston*. MDCCC. 8vo, pp. 28. 26225

Furman. An Oration. Delivered at the Charleston Orphan-Asylum, before the Intendant and Wardens of the City ... and a Large Assemblage of the Benefactors to the Institution ... October the 18th, 1796 ... . By Richard Furman, A.M. ... *Charleston: Printed by W. P. Young*. M.DCC.XCVI. 8vo, 1 l., pp. 28. H. 26226

Furman. Rev. Dr. Richard Furman's Exposition of the Views of the Baptists relative to the Coloured Population in the United States, in a Communication to the Governor of South-Carolina. *Charleston: Printed by A. E. Miller*. 1823. pp. 24.

Also: Sermon preached at the High Hills of Santee before the Charleston Association of Baptist Churches. *Charleston*. 1794. 8vo. — A Sermon preached at the Baptist Church in Charlestown, South-Carolina, on the 4th day of July 1802, before the State Society of Cincinnati, the American Revolution Society ... *Charleston*. 1802. 8vo. C., S. — A Sermon Occasioned by the Decease of the Rev. Oliver Hart. *Charleston*. 1796. 8vo.

Furman (W.) A History of the Charleston Association of Baptist Churches in the State of South Carolina, with an Appendix, containing the principal Circular Letters to the Churches. Compiled by Wood Furman. *Charleston, S. C.: Press of J. Hoff*. 1811. 8vo, pp. 238, (2). C. 26228

Furneaux (John). An Abridged History of the principal Treaties of Peace, commencing generally after the Peace of Westphalia, and at an earlier period, with reference to the question of the Neutral Flag protecting the Property of an Enemy. By Captain Furneaux, R. N. *London*. 1837. 8vo. C. 26229

Furneaux (P.) The Duty of Benevolence and Public Spirit: A Sermon at Salter's Hall, April 7, 1775, before the Correspondent Board, in London, of the Society in Scotland for Propagating Christian Knowledge, and for Spreading the Gospel among the Indians in America. By Philip Furneaux, D.D. *London*. 1775. 8vo, pp. 33. C., H., N. 26230

Furness (William Henry). The Blessings of Revolution. A Discourse delivered in the First Congregational Unitarian Church, ... July 1, 1860. By W. H. Furness ... . *Philadelphia: C. Sherman & Sons*. 1860. 8vo, pp. 26. BA. 26231

Furness. The Declaration of Independence. A Discourse delivered in ... Philadelphia, June 29, 1862. By W. H. Furness, Minister. *Philadelphia: C. Sherman & Sons*. 1862. 8vo, pp. 18. B. 26232

Furness. A Discourse, ... at the Dedication of the First Congregational Unitarian Church, Philadelphia, November 5, 1828. By William Henry Furness. *Philadelphia*. 1828. 8vo, pp. 40. H. 26233

Furness. A Discourse ... January 19, 1840, in the First Congregational Church, occasioned by the Loss of the Lexington. By W. H. Furness ... . *Philadelphia: C. A. Elliott*. 1840. 8vo, pp. 16. BA., H. 26234

Furness. A Discourse delivered on the Occasion of the National Fast, September 26th, 1861, in ... Philadelphia. By W. H. Furness, Minister. *Philadelphia: T. B. Pugh*. 1861. 8vo, pp. 20. B., BA., H. 26235

Furness. England and America. A Discourse ... Dec. 22, 1861, delivered by W. H. Furness ... [*Philadelphia*. 1861.] 8vo, pp. 51. H. 26236

[Furness.] In Memoriam ... . [Occasioned by the Death of his Son William H. Furness. *Philadelphia*. 1867.] 8vo, pp. 10. H. 26237

Furness. A Sermon occasioned by the Destruction of Pennsylvania Hall ... May 20, 1838 ... . *Philadelphia: Printed by John C. Clark*. 1838. 8vo, pp. 12. BA. 26238

Furness. A Thanksgiving Discourse delivered ... in Philadelphia, April 13th, 1862. By W. H. Furness, D.D. In Accordance with the Recommendation of the President of the United States. *Philadelphia: T. B. Pugh*. 1862. 8vo, pp. 17. H.

Furness. A Word of Consolation for the Kindred of those who have Fallen in Battle. A Discourse ... September 28, 1862. Together with the Funeral Services at the Burial of Lieut. A. W. Peabody, Sept. 26, 1862. By W. H. Furness ... *Philadelphia: Crissy & Markley*. [1862.] 8vo, pp. 13. B.

Also: An Address delivered before the Art-Union of Philadelphia ... October 12th, 1848. ... *Philadelphia: Printed by Griggs & Adams*. 1848. 8vo, pp. 32. H. — An Address ... before ... the Members and Friends of the Pennsylvania Anti-Slave Society ... December 19, 1849. ... *Philadelphia: Merrihew & Thompson*. 1850. 8vo, pp. 16. B., H. — Christianity a Spirit. Discourse delivered at the Ordination of William J. Potter, as Pastor ... in New Bedford, Dec. 28, 1859. ... *New Bedford: Printed for the Society*. 1860. 8vo, pp. 31. H. — A Discourse for the Time ... January 4, 1852 ... *Philadelphia: C. Sherman*. 1852. 8vo, pp. 23. BA. — A Discourse ... March 17, 1844, concerning the use of the Bible in the Public Schools ... *Philadelphia*.

1844. 8vo. — ... A Discourse ... April 17, 1859. ... *Philadelphia: C. Sherman & Son.* 1859. 8vo, pp. (2), 18. — ... A Discourse delivered at the Anniversary of the Derby Academy, in Higham, May 19, 1847. ... . *New-York: W. S. Dorr.* 1847. 8vo, pp. 20. BA. — ... Three Discourses ... May 28th, June 4th and June 11th, 1854. ... with Reference to the Recent Execution of the Fugitive Slave Law in Boston and New York. *Philadelphia: Merrihew & Thompson.* 1854. 8vo, pp. 42. — A Discourse delivered on the ... Erection in the Church of Tablets in Memory of John Vaughan, Ralph Eddowes, and William Y. Birch, Aug. 20th, 1842. ... . [*Philadelphia.* 1842.] 8vo, pp. 16. B., H., M. — A Discourse occasioned by the Boston Fugitive Slave Case, delivered in ... Philadelphia, April 13, 1851. ... . *Philadelphia: Merrihew and Thompson.* 1851. 8vo, pp. 15. B., BA., H. — ... A Discourse ... at the Ordination of the Rev. Charles E. Hodges ... in Barre, Mass., June 11, 1851. ... . *Boston: Wm. Crosby & H. P. Nichols.* 1851. 8vo, pp. 30. H., BA., H. — A Discourse delivered on the Occasion of the Death of John Vaughan ... Jan. 16, 1842. ... *Philadelphia: J. Crissy.* 1842. 8vo, pp. 32. B. — A Funeral Discourse, May 4th, 1845. *Philadelphia.* 1845. 8vo. — The Memory of the Just. A Discourse, ... in Philadelphia, February 27, 1848. .. *Philadelphia: Crissy and Markley.* 1848. 8vo, pp. 16. BA. — The Moving Power. A Discourse delivered in Philadelphia, ... Feb. 9, 1851, after the Occurrence of a Fugitive Slave Case. ... *Philadelphia: Merrihew and Thompson.* 1851. 8vo, pp. 16. BA., H. — Our Duty as Conservatives. A Discourse ... November 25, 1860, occasioned by the Threatened Secession of some of the Southern States. ... *Philadelphia: C. Sherman & Son.* 1860. 8vo, pp. 20. B. — Our Benevolent Institutions. A Discourse occasioned by the Death of Julius R. Friedlander, Principal of the Pennsylvania Institution for the Blind. ... March 24, 1839. ... . *Philadelphia: C. Sherman & Co.* 1839. 8vo, pp. 24. B., BA., H., M., P. — Our American Institutions. A Thanksgiving Discourse delivered ... in Philadelphia, August 6th, 1863. ... *Philadelphia: T. B. Pugh.* 1863. 8vo, pp. 21. H. — Put up thy Sword. A Discourse delivered before Theodore Parker's Society, at the Music Hall, Boston, Sunday, March 11, 1860. ... . *Boston: R. F. Wallcut.* 1860. 8vo, pp. 23. B., BA., H. — Religion and Politics. A Discourse ... March 20th, 1859. ... *Philadelphia: T. B. Pugh.* 1859. 8vo, pp. 21. BA. — Religion, a Principle, not a Form. A Discourse, delivered ... March 17, 1844 ... concerning the Use of the Bible in the Public Schools. ... *Philadelphia: J. Crissy.* 1844. 8vo, pp. 16. H. — The Revivals. A Discourse ... in Philadelphia ... April 11, 1858. ... *Philadelphia: Crissy & Markley.* 1858. 8vo, pp. 21. 8vo. B. — The Rights of Property in Man. A Discourse delivered ... July 3, 1859 ... . *Philadelphia: C. Sherman & Son.* 1859. 8vo, pp. 23. B., BA. — A Sermon, delivered May 14, 1841, on the occasion of the National Fast recommended by the President. ... *Philadelphia: Printed by John C. Clark.* 1841. 12mo, pp. 12. H., M. — ... A Sermon at the Installation of Rev. John T. Sargent, ... in Somerville, Mass., ... February 18, 1846. ... *Somerville: Edmund Tufts.* 1846. 8vo, pp. 48. B., BA., H. — The Spirit of Jesus. ... A Sermon preached at the Installation of Rev. D. H. Barlow, in Brooklyn, New-York, September 17, 1834. ... . *Brooklyn: A. Spooner.* 1834. B., H., M. — The Spirit of the Pilgrims. An Oration delivered before the Society of the Sons of New England of Philadelphia, December 22d, 1846. ... *Philadelphia: Printed by John C. Clark.* 1846. 8vo, pp. 23. H. — Sunday Travel. A Discourse delivered ... April 28, 1850 ... . *Philadelphia: C. Sherman.* 1850. 8vo, pp. 16. B., H. — A Thanksgiving Discourse. Nov. 27th, 1845. [*Philadelphia.* n. d.] 8vo, pp. 20. B., H. — Two Discourses, occasioned by the Approaching Anniversary of the Declaration of Independence. Delivered June 25, A. M., and July 2, A. M., 1843. *Philadelphia.* 1843. 8vo, pp. 23. BA., M. — Two Discourses, ... January 26, and February 2, 1845. ... . *Philadelphia: J. Crissy.* 1845. 8vo, pp. 28. BA. + *Boston.* 1845. 8vo. B. — A Voice of the Hour. A Discourse ... January 10, 1864. *Philadelphia: Crissy & Markley.* 1864. 8vo, pp. 15. H. — A Word for Peace. A Christmas Discourse ... December 25th, 1845. ... *Philadelphia: J. Crissy.* 1845. 8vo, pp. 14. B., BA., H., M.

FURNESS. Proceedings of a Meeting of the ... First Congregational Society of ... in the City of Philadelphia: Held on the 28th September, 1846, to receive and act upon a Communication from the First Congregational Society of New Bedford, Massachusetts, relative to an Invitation given by that Society to the Rev. W. H. Furness, to become their Pastor. *Philadelphia: Printed for the Society.* 1848. 8vo, pp. 18. 26241

FURST (M.) Proceedings of the Engagement between Moritz Furst and the United States Consul at Leghorn. 1825. 12mo.

FÜRSTENWARTHER (M. von). Der Deutsche in Nord America. *Stuttgart: v. Cotta.* 1818. 12mo, pp. 124. 26243

"M. Von Fürstenwärther, was sent to America by his half brother Von Gagern, to look into the condition of the poor German emigrants to the United States. This work consists of M. Von Gagern's instructions to M. Von Fürstenwärther, a report drawn up from the letters of the latter, and an appendix of the various articles of information relative to the country." — *N. Am. Rev.*, XI. p. 1.

FURTADO (J.) O Conselheiro Francisco José Furtado. Biographia e Estudo de Historia politica contemporanea pelo conselheiro Tito Franco de Almeida. *Rio de Janeiro.* 1867. 8vo, pp. viii, 486. Portrait of Furtado. 26244

A Further Accompt. *See* [Eliot], Vol. VI., No. 22149.

A Further Account of New Jersey, in an Abstract of Letters lately writ from thence, by several Inhabitants there resident. *Printed in the Year* 1676. 4to. 26245

One of the earliest accounts of New Jersey. It is signed by Richard Hartshorne, Martha S—, Robert Wade, Ester Huckens, and Roger Pæderick, all being among the first settlers in the province.

A Further Account of the Province of Pennsylvania, and its Improvements, for the Satisfaction of those that are Adventurers, and inclined to be so. [*London.* 1685.] 4to. 26246

Further and still More Important Suppressed Documents. [*Boston.* 1808.] 8vo, pp. 24. BA., H., N. + *Flatbush, N. Y.* 1809. 8vo, pp. 24. 26247

Relates to the Milan decree of Napoleon.

A Further Appeal to the Unprejudiced Judgment of Mankind in behalf of the Indians. Containing, 1. Animadversions upon some late Arguments of a Right Reverend Prelate of the Church of England, in reference to our sending Missionaries from hence to convert the Indians. Written in the Year 1760. 2. Thoughts upon the Proper Means and Measures of Converting the Indians to true Christianity. Written in the Year 1764. To which are added, Considerations relative to the Subject of the foregoing Proposals, particularly that of appointing Bishops or Superintendents in our Colonies abroad; By another Hand; both Jointwriters in the Free and Candid Disquisitions relating to the Church of England, &c. *London: J. Millar.* 1766. 8vo.

"This appeal is written with spirit and judgment, and contains several smart and pertinent observations relating to the propagation of the Gospel among the Indians, and the Episcopizing of our Colonies." — *M. Rev.*, XXXIV. 326.

Further Considerations for Encouraging the Woollen Manufactures by sending them to America, and utterly denying them Callicoes. [n. p. n. d.] Folio, 1 l. 26249

A Further Consideration of the Dangerous Condition of the Country, the Causes which have led to it, And the Duty of the People. By a Marylander. *Baltimore.* 1867. 8vo, pp. 21 or 23.

Further Considerations on our Insurance of the French Commerce, in the present Juncture. *London.* 1758. 8vo. 26251

Further Considerations. *See* [Lyttelton (*Lord*)].

Further Correspondence respecting the proposed Union of the British North American Provinces. *London.* 1867. Folio.

Further Examination. *See* [Robinson (Mathew)].

A Further Illustration of the Case of the Seneca Indians in the State of New York, in a Review of a Pamphlet entitled An Appeal ... by Nathaniel T. Strong ... Printed by Direction of the Joint Committees on Indian Affairs, of the four Yearly Meetings of Friends of Genesee, New York, Philadelphia, and Baltimore. *Philadelphia.* 1841. 8vo, pp. 84. 26253

Further Information respecting the Aborigines; containing Extracts from the Proceedings of the Meeting for Sufferings in London, and of the Committee on Indian Affairs, of the Yearly Meetings of Philadelphia and Baltimore, together with some Particulars relative to the Seminole War. ... *London.* 1859. Crown 8vo, pp. 34. + Second Edition. [*Ibid.*] 26254

Forms No 3 of Tracts relative to the Aborigines.

Further Information respecting the Aborigines; containing Reports of the Committee on Indian Affairs at Philadelphia, Extracts from the Proceedings of the Yearly Meetings of Philadelphia, New York, New England, Maryland, Virginia, and Ohio. ... Published by Direction of the Aborigines' Committee of the Meeting for Sufferings. *London: Edward Marsh.* 1842. Crown 8vo, pp. 40. 26255

Forms No. 8 of Tracts relative to the Aborigines.

A Further Manifestation. *See* [Eliot (J.)], Vol. VI.

Further Observations intended for Improving the Culture and Curing of Indigo in South Carolina, 1746. [*London.* 1747.] 8vo. 26256

Privately printed. Probably edited by James Crokatt.

Further Papers. *See* Franklin (J.), *note* to No. 25633.

Further Papers and Returns, relating to the Slave Population of Jamaica, St. Christopher's, and the Bahamas. *London.* 1823. Folio. 26257

Further Papers relating to American Loyalists. [Parliamentary.] *London.* 1821. Folio, pp. 31. 26258

Further Proceedings. *See* Seneca Indians.

Further Report of the Committee on that part of the President's Message which relates to the Defence of our Sea-Port Towns and Harbors, December 3, 1807. *Washington.* 1807. 8vo. N. 26259

A Further Report from Committee of Secrecy, appointed to Enquire into the Conduct of Robert, Earl of Orford. *London.* 1742. 8vo. 26260

On the currency of Jamaica, etc.

A Further Salutation of Brotherly Love, from the Monthly Meetings of Friends of Philadelphia, to the Members of our Religious Society, in and near the said City. *Philadelphia.* 1795. 8vo, pp. 8. 26261

FUSÉE D'AUBLET. *See* Aublet (J. B. C. F.), Vol. I.

The Future of the Country. By a Patriot. [n. p. 1864.] 8vo, pp. 28. B., H. 26262

The Future of the North-West. *See* [Owen (R. D.)]

FYFE (A. G.) Suggestions respecting Sugar, with a Plan for a Central Sugar Factory at Annotto Bay. By Alexander Gordon Fyfe. *London: Wilson.* 1846. 26263

Printed for private circulation.

FYFE (J. H.) British Enterprise Beyond the Seas; or, our Colonies. By J. Hamilton Fyfe. *London: T. Nelson & Sons.* 1863. 12mo. 26264

Contents: Newfoundland, Virginia, New England, Pennsylvania, Darien, Canada, Pitcairn's Island, and Jamaica.

FYFE. Merchant Enterprise; or, the History of Commerce from the Earliest Times. By J. Hamilton Fyfe ... . *London: T. Nelson & Sons.* 1864. 12mo, pp. viii, 15–289. B., H. 26265

* * *. *See* Vol. I., No. 4202.

G. (B. J.) Memoria sobre las principaes causas per que deve o Brazil reassami os recit directos, par B. J. G. *Rio de Janeiro.* 1822. 4to. 26266

G. (C. J.) Ansdale Hall; or, "Stand by your Colors." By C. J. G. *Boston: American Tract Society.* [1868.] 18mo, pp. 224. 3 Plates. 26267

[G. (E.)] The Compromise, the Constitution, and the Union. [n. p. n. d.] 8vo, pp. 35. BA. 26268

Signed E. G. *W. L., K. & Q., Va.*

G. (F. D.) *See* [Fernagus de Gelone], Vol. VI., No. 24123.

G. (G.) *See* G[renville] (G[eorge]).

G. (J.) White Acre *vs.* Black Acre. A Case at Law. Reported by J. G., Esq., a retired Barrister of Lincolnshire, England. *Richmond, (Va.): J. W. Randolph.* 1856. 16mo, pp. 251. C. 26269

A romance of colonial life in the reign of Queen Anne.

G. (I. C.) Lee's Last Campaign. By Captain J. C. G. *Raleigh, N. C.: William B. Smith & Company.* MDCCCLXVI. 16mo, pp. 59. BA. 26270

G. (J. J. S. P.) Gedancken über die Burnuck Kunfft der Französischen Escadren aus Amerika. *Anno* 1741. 4to, pp. 15.

Reflections on the return of the French fleet from America, April, 1741; the result, in the opinion of the writer, of an agreement between France and Spain, after the death of the Emperor, Charles VI., relating to the sovereignty of the Netherlands.

G. (I. A.) Breeden-Raedt | Aende | Vereenichde Nederlandsche | Provintien. | Gelreland. | Holland. | Zeeland. | Wtrecht. | Vriesland. | Over-Yssel. | Groeningen. | Gamaeckt ende gestelt uyt diverse ware en waerachtige | memorien Door I. A. G., W. C. | *Tot Antwerpen,* | *Ghedruct by Francoys van Duynen, Boeckverkooper by* | *de Beurs in Erasmus.* 1649. | 4to, 24 l. 26272

This homely advice to the United Dutch provinces, made up from divers true and faithful documents, is an excessively rare pamphlet, and is, no doubt, the most important document existing on New Netherland; its importance was discovered by Mr. Asher. *See* Asher's "Essay," pp. 183–200. It was translated by Henry C. Murphy, and printed at the expense of James Lenox, for private circulation. Priced, by Mr. F. Muller, at 175 florins.

G. (L. C. D. L.) *See* Vol. I., No. 1290.

G. (M. R.) Respuesta á las cartas del Doctor Alberdi á sus amigos y compatriotas sobre los intereses argentinos en la guerra del Paraguay y el Brazil, por M. R. G. *Buenos-Aires.* 1865. 8vo, pp. 46. 26273

G. (M.) *See* G[odwyn] (M[organ]).

G. (N.) *See* Brazil, Vol. II., No. 7633.

G. (R.) Virginia's Cure: or an Advisive Narrative concerning Virginia. Discovering the true Ground of that Churches Unhappiness, and the only true Remedy. As it was presented to the Right Reverend Father in God Gvilbert Lord Bishop of London. September 2. 1661. Now publish'd to further the Welfare of that and the like Plantations: By R. G. *London: printed by W. Godbid for Henry Brome, at the Sign of the Gun in Ivy Lane.* 1662. 4to, pp. 20. 26274

A tract of extreme rarity. I have never seen a copy. It is reprinted in Force's "Tracts," Vol. III., No. 15.

G. (S.) *See* G[roome] (S.)

G. (T.) *See* G[ib] (T.)

G. (W.) *See* G[auntley] (W[illiam]).

G. (W.) Letter of W. G., dated Saratoga Springs, 20th June, 1822, on the Great Western Canal. 8vo, pp. 8. N.

G. (W.) Sketches of Newfoundland and Labrador, taken in 1857, by W. G. *Ipswich.* [n. d.] Oblong 4to. 24 Plates.

G. (W. D.) *See* G[allagher] (W. D.)

Gaa-na-shoh-ne Deowaahsaonyohgwah Na wen ni yuh. *Dosyowa* [*Buffalo Creek*:] *Mission Press.* 1843. 18mo, pp. 136.

Hymns in the Seneca dialect. Rev. A. Wright's System of Writing the Seneca is included in the preface.

GABB (W. M.) Catalogue of the Invertebrate Fossils of the Cretaceous Formation of the United States. By W. M. Gabb. [n. p.] 1859. 8vo, pp. 20. B. 26278

See also California, Vol. III., No. 10008.

GABELENTZ (H. C. v. d.) Grammatik der Dakota Sprache. Von H. C. von der Gabelentz. *Leipzig: F. A. Brockhaus.* 1852. 8vo, pp. 64. 26279

GABELENTZ. Kürze Grammatik der Tscherokesischen Sprache. 8vo, pp. 42. 26280

From Hoefer's "Zeitschrift," III. 3. 257–300.

El Gabinete de lectura. Periódico literario, político, arístico, industrial y de teatros, ó miscelánea instructiva de variedades y costumbres de ambos mundos, y en particular de la Republica Mexicana. Tomo I. *Mexico.* 1845. 4to, pp. 288. 26281

GABRIAC (*Comte de*). Promenade à travers l'Amérique du Sud ... . *Paris: Michel Lévy Frères.* 1868. Rl. 8vo, pp. (4), 304. Plates. B. 26282

GABRIELII EUGUBINI (J.) Orationes et Epistolæ. Accedit Epistola de Rebus Indicis a quodam Soc. Jesu Presbyter Italice scripta et nunc primum in Latinum conversa a J. Gabrielio. *Venetiis.* 1569. 4to. 26283

Partly relates to Brazil.

Gacetas de Literatura. *See* Vol. I., No. 989.

GADDIS (M. P.) Brief Recollections of the late Rev. George W. Walker. By Maxwell Pierson Gaddis. With an Introduction by Charles Elliott. *Cincinnati.* 1857. 12mo. C.

GADDIS. Sermon upon the Assassination of Abraham Lincoln. By the Rev. M. P. Gaddis ... delivered [at Cincinnati], April 16, 1865. ... *Cincinnati: Times Office.* 1865. 8vo, pp. 15.

Also: Foot-Prints of an Itinerant. *Cincinnati.* 1855. 12mo. Portrait. C.

GADSDEN (C. E.) A Discourse ... on the Occasion of the Death of Bishop Dehon. By Christopher E. Gadsden ... . *Charleston: Printed by A. E. Miller.* 1817. 8vo, pp. 36. H.

[GADSDEN.] A Discourse on the ... Death of the Right Rev. Nathaniel Bowen, D.D. Late Bishop ... of South Carolina ... . *Charleston: Printed by A. E. Miller.* 1840. 8vo, pp. 50.

GADSDEN. An Essay on the Life of the Right Reverend Theodore Dehon, D.D. Late Bishop of the Protestant Episcopal Church, in the Diocese of South-Carolina. By Christopher E. Gadsden, D.D. ... . With an Appendix. *Charleston, (S. C.): A. E. Miller, For the Author.* 1833. 8vo, pp. v, (1), 341. C.

GADSDEN. A Sermon ... August 21, 1825, by Christopher E. Gadsden, on the Occasion of the Decease of Gen. Charles Cotesworth Pinckney. ... *Charleston: Printed by A. E. Miller.* 1825. 8vo, pp. 31. BA., H. 26289

[Gadsden.] The Sermon preached at St. Philip's Church ... on the Fast-Day, May 14th, 1841. ... *Charleston: A. E. Miller.* 1841. 8vo, pp. 18. H. 26290

Gadsden. The Times, morally considered, in a Charge, from the Bishop, to the Clergy of the Diocese of South-Carolina, delivered ... Charleston ... 13 February, 1843. *Charleston: Miller & Browne.* 1843. 8vo, pp. 28. B., H. 26291

Gadsden (C. P.) Duty to God not to be overlooked in Duty to the State. A Sermon ... Charleston ... November 11, 1860. By the Rev. Christopher P. Gadsden, Rector. *Charleston: Evans & Cogswell.* 1860. 8vo, pp. 15. B. 26292

Gadsden (J.) An Eulogy on the late Keating Lewis Simons, Esq. Pronounced ... on the Tenth of September, 1819; by appointment of the Revolution Society, ... By John Gadsden. *Charleston: W. P. Young & Son, Print.* [1819.] 8vo, pp. (1), 25. BA., H., M. 26293

Gaffarel (P.) Étude sur les rapports de l'Amérique et de l'ancien continent avant Christophe Colomb. Par Paul Gaffarel ... . *Paris: Ernest Thorin.* 1869. 8vo, pp. viii, 346. B. 26294

Gage (N.) A Discourse delivered in Windham, N. H., November 5, 1834, at the Interment of Rev. Jacob Abbot and Capt. John Dinsmore, who were drowned Nov. 2. By Nathaniel Gage ... . *Nashua, N. H.: Printed by Alfred Beard.* 1835. 8vo, pp. 24. H. 26295

Gage. A Sermon delivered at the Installation of Rev. A. Dumont Jones, over the Congregational Church in Wilton, January 1, 1834. By Rev. Nathaniel Gage. ... *Nashua, N. H.: Printed by Alfred Beard.* 1834. 8vo, pp. 32. BA., H., N. 26296

Gage. Sins and Dangers of the Times. A Sermon, delivered in Haverhill, Mass., on Fast Day, April 5, 1838. By Nathaniel Gage, ... *Haverhill: E. H. Safford.* 1838. 8vo, pp. 28. B., BA. 26297

Also: An Address before the Essex Agricultural Society, at Topsfield, September 27, 1837. ... *Salem: Gazette Office.* 1838. 8vo, pp. 27. H.

Gage (T.) The English-American his Travail by Sea and Land; | Or, | A New Svrvey | of the | VVest-India's, | containing | A Journall of Three thousand and Three hundred | Miles within the main Land of America. | Wherein is set forth his Voyage

from Spain to St. John de Vlbus; | and from thence to Xalappa, to Tlaxcalla, the City of Angeles, and | forward to Mexico; With the description of that great City, | as it was in former times, and also at this present. | Likewise his Journey from Mexico through the Provinces of Guaxaca, | Chiapa, Guatemala, Vera Paz, Truxillo, Comayagua; with his | abode Twelve years about Guatemala, and especially in the | Indian-towns of Mixco, Pinola, Petapa, Amatitlan. | As also his strange and wonderfull Conversion, and Calling from those | remote Parts to his Native Countrey. With his return through the Province of Nicaragua, and Costa Rica, | to Nicoya, Panama, Portobelo, Cartagena, and Havana, with divers | ocurrents and dangers that did befal in the said Journey. | Also, | A New and exact Discovery of the Spanish Navigation to | those Parts; And of their Dominions, Government, Religion, Forts, | Castles, Ports, Havens, Commodities, fashions, behaviour of | Spaniards, Priests, and Friers, Blackmores, Mulatto's, Mestiso's, | Indians; and of their Feasts and Solemnities. | With a Grammar, or some few Rudiments of the Indian Tongue, | called, Poconchi, or Pocoman. | By the true and painfull endevours of Thomas Gage, now Preacher of | the Word of God at Acris in the County of Kent, Anno Dom. 1648. | *London: Printed by R. Cotes*, ... | ... 1648. | Folio, pp. (10), 220, Contents, (12).

First edition of this curious work, which "appears to have been much celebrated in its time." — Rich. "The author was probably 'Parson of Deale.' In the second and third editions, after expurging from the dedication certain passages in honor of Fairfax, the remainder were dexterously converted into a preface; and the twenty-second chapter, as containing particulars relative to the artifices used by the 'Pafulins' to convert the writer, totally omitted. This preface was afterwards printed separately." — Wrangham. Southey's "Omniana," I. 113–119, informs us that part of the book is taken, *verbatim et literatim*, from Thomas Nicholas' translation of Gomara. Gage uses the word "party" in its modern slang sense of "individual." He belonged to the Dominican order, originally, but joined the English Church before he wrote his travels. He appears to have been a believer in witchcraft and sorcery, and admits into his work many curious relations on those subjects. Priced, in the "Nuggets," at £1 11s. 6d.

Gage. A New Survey | of the | West-India's: | Or, | The English American his Travail by Sea and Land: | Containing | A Journal of Three thousand and Three hundred Miles within the main Land of America. | Whereupon is set forth his Voyage from Spain to St. John de Vlhua; | and from thence to Xalappa, to Tlaxcalla, the City of Angels, and | forward to Mexico; With the description of that great City, | as it was in former times, and also at this present. | Likewise, his Journey from Mexico, through the Provinces of Guaxaca, | Chiapa, Guatemala, Vera Paz, Truxillo, Comayagua; with his | abode Twelve years about Guate-

mala, and especially in the | Indian-Towns of Mixco, Pinola, Petapa, Amatitlan. | As also his strange and wonderfull Conversion and Calling from those | remote Parts, to his Native Countrey. | With his return through the Province of Nicaragua, and Costa Rica, to | Nicoya, Panama, Portobelo, Cartagena, and Havana, with divers | Occurrents and dangers that did befal in the said Journey. | Also, | A New and Exact Discovery of the Spanish Navigation | to those Parts: And of their Dominions, Government, Religion, Forts, | Castles, Ports, Havens, Commodities, Fashions, Behaviour of | Spaniards, Priests and Friers, Blackmores, Mulatto's, Mestiso's, | Indians; and of their Feasts and Solemnities. | With a Grammar, or some few Rudiments of the Indian Tongue, | called Pochonci, or Pocoman. | The Second Edition enlarged by the Author, and beautified with Maps. | By the true and painful endevours of Thomas Gage, Preacher of the | Word of God at Deal in the County of Kent. | *London, Printed by E. Cotes, and sold by John Sweeting | at the Angel in Popes-head-alley*, M. DC. LV. | Folio, pp. 220, Contents, (12). BA.

Gage. A New Survey of the West-Indies: ... . The Third Edition, Enlarged by the Author, with a New and Accurate Map. *London: Printed by A. Clark.* 1667. 8vo, pp. 577, Contents, (18). C. 26300

"The twenty-second chapter, relating to the author's journey to Rome, was omitted in this edition, owing, as it is said, to its reflecting on the character of Archbishop Laud." — Lowndes.

Gage. A New Survey of the West Indies. ... The Fourth Edition. *London: Printed for J. Nicholson.* 1699. 8vo, pp. (7), 477, Contents, (18). Map of Mexico. BA. 26301

Gage. A Survey of the Spanish West Indies. ... The Fourth Edition, Enlarged ... *London: Thomas Horne.* 1702. 8vo, pp. (6), 477, Contents, (18). Map of Mexico. + The Fourth Edition, Enlarged by the Author. *London: T. Horne.* 1711. 12mo, pp. (6), 477, Contents, (18). Map. 26302

Gage. Nouvelle relation des Indes Occidentales, contenant ses voyages de Thomas Gage, dans la Nouvelle Espagne, ses diverses avantures; et son retour par la province de Nicaragua, jusques à la Havane. Avec la description de la ville de Mexique telle qu'elle estoit autrefois, et comme elle est à present. Le tout traduit de l'anglois par le Sieur de Beaulieu Hues O'Neil. *Paris: Gervais Clouzier.* 1676. 4 vols., 12mo, 12 l., pp. 246, 2 l.; 3 l., pp. 240; 3 l., pp. 297, (5); 3 l., pp. 153, (5). 26303

The translator is said to have been Adrien Baillet. Usually found bound up in two volumes. The Pocochi Grammar is sometimes found separately. *See* Brunet. This French translation has often been reprinted. In addition to those we have described, *infra*, there are others, viz.: *Paris.* 1677; *Amsterdam: Moret.* 1680. 2 vols., 12mo; [*Ibid.*] 1687; [*Ibid.*] 1694.

Gage. Nouvelle | Relation, | Contenant | les Voyages de Thomas Gage | dans la Nouvelle Espagne, ses diverses avan- | tures; & son retour par la Province de Ni- | caragua, jusques à la Havane. | Avec | la Description de la Ville | de Mexique telle qu'elle estoit autrefois, | & comme elle est à present. | Ensemble vne Description | exacte des Terres & Provinces que possedent les E- | spagnols en toute l'Amérique, de la forme de leur | Gouvernement Ecclesiastique & Politique, de leur | Commerce, de leurs Mœurs, & de celles des Criol- | les, des Metifs, des Mulatres, des Indiens, & | des Negres. | ... | *A Amsterdam, | Chez Paul Marret, dans le Beurs-straat | proche le Dam à la Renommée.* | M. DC. LXXXXV. | 2 vols., 12mo, pp. (24), 200, 178; (14), 1 l. blank, pp. 318. 16 Maps and Plates. B., BA., H. 26304

Gage. Nouvelle | Relation, | contenant | les voyages de Thomas Gage | dans la Nouvelle Espagne, ses diverses avan- | tures; & son retour par la Province de Ni- | caragua, jusques à la Havane. | Avec | la description de la ville | de Mexique telle qu'elle estoit autrefois, | & comme elle est à present. | Ensemble une description | exacte des Terres & Provinces que possedent les Espagnols en | toute l'Amérique, de la forme de leur Gouvernement Eccle- | sia- | stique & Politique, de leur Commerce, de leurs Mœurs, & | de celles des Criolles, des Metifs, des Mulatres des Indiens, | & des Negres. | ... | Troisième Edition Reveuë & Corrigée. | *A Amsterdam, | Chez Paul Marret, dans le Beurs-straat | proche le Dam à la Renommée.* | M. DC. XC IX. | 2 vols., 12mo, Engraved Title-Pages, pp. (24), 200, 176; (14), 1 l. blank, pp. 318. 16 Maps and Plates. S. 26305

Gage. Nouvelle Relation, contenant les Voyages de Thomas Gage dans la Nouvelle Espagne, ses diverses avantures, & son retour par la Province de Nicaragua, jusques à la Havane. Avec la Description de la Ville de Mexique, telle qu'elle étoit autrefois, & comme elle est à present. Ensemble une Description exacte des terres & provinces que possedent les Espagnols en toute l'Amérique, de la forme de leur Gouvernement Ecclesiastique & Politique, de leur Commerce, de leurs Mœurs, & de celles des Criolles, des Metifs, des Mulatres, des Indiens, & des Negres. Avec Figures. ... Quatrième Edition revûë & corrigée. [Vig-

nette:] *A Amsterdam: chez Paul Marret dans le Beurs-straat, proche le Dam, à la Renommée.* M.DCCXX. 2 vols., sm. 8vo, Engraved Half-Title and Title, 12 l., pp. 431, 8 Maps or Engraved Plates; Title and Half-Title, 4 l., pp. 432, 8 Maps or Plates. C. 26306

The translator changed the title, and altered the divisions of the chapters.

Gage. Nouvelle | Relation, | Contenant | les Voyages de Thomas Gage | dans le nouvelle Espagne, ses diverses avan- | tures, & son retour dans la Province de Ni- | caragua jusqu'à la Havane. | Avec | la Description de la Ville | de Mexique, telle qu'elle étoit autrefois, & | comme elle est à present. | Ensemble vne Description | exacte des | Terres & Provinces que possedent les Espagnols en toute l'Amérique, de la for- | me de leur Gouvernement Ecclesiastique & | Politique, de leur Commerce, de leurs Mœurs, | & de celles des Creoles, des Metifs, | des Mu- | lâtres, des Indiens, & des Négres. | ... *A Amsterdam, | Chez Paul Marret, Marchand Libraire | dans le Beurs-straat.* | M.DCC.XXI. | 2 vols., 12mo, pp. (24), 200, 178; (12), 316. 16 Maps and Plates. + *Amsterdam.* 1722. 2 vols., 12mo. 26307

Gage. Nouvelle Relation contenant les Voyages de Thomas Gage ... Traduite de l'Anglois par H. O'Neil. *Paris.* MDCC-LXXVI. 2 vols., 12mo. + *Amsterdam.* MDCCLXXXV. 2 vols., 12mo. 26308

A part of this work in included in Thevenot's "Collection of Voyages," Vol. II *Paris.* 1696. Folio.

Gage. Neue merckwürdige Reise-Beschreibung | Nach | Neu Spanien, | Was ihm daselbst seltsames begegnet, und | wie er durch die Provintz Nicaragua wider zurück | nach der Havana gekehret: | In welcher zu finden ist | Ein ausführlicher Bericht von der Stadt Mexico, | wie selbte so wol vor Alters gewesen, als auch wie sie ietzo | beschaffen sey: | Ingleichen | Eine vollkommene Beschreibung aller Län- | der und Provinzen, welche die Spanier in gantz Ame- | rica besitzen; von ihrem Kirchen- und Policey-Regiment: ihrem | Handel: wie auch von ihren und der Criollen, Mestifen, | Mulaten, Indianer und Schwartzen, Sitten | und Lebens-Art. | Deme allem zum Beschluss noch beygefüget ist | Ein kurtzer, Unterricht von der Poconchischen oder | Pocomanischen Sprache, | Aus dem Frantzöschen ins Deutsch übersetzt | *Leipzig, | Verlegts Johann Herbordt Kloss, Buchändl.* | *Anno* M. DC. XCIII. | 4to, pp. (6), 471. Plate. C. 26309

Gage. Nieuwe en seer Nauwkeurige | Reyse | door de Spaensche Westindien | van | Thomas Gage | met verscheyde Curieuse plaeten | Voorsien overgeset door | H. V. Q. | *t' Utrecht by Ioannes Ribbius, A°.* 1682. | 4to, Engraved Title, 9 l., pp. 450, 34 l. 3 Maps. 26310

This Dutch translation is by H. V. Quellenburgh.

Gage. Nieuwe ende seer naeuwkeurige | Reyse | Door de Spaensche | West-Indien | van | Thomas Gage; | Met seer curieuse soo Land-kaerten als Historische Figue- | ren verciert ende met twee Registers voorsien. | Overgeset door | H. V. Q. | Den Tweeden Druck. | *t' Amsterdam, By Willem de Coup, Willem Lamsvelt, Philip | Verbeek en Johannes Lamsvelt, | Boekverkoopers, Anno* 1700. | 4to, Engraved Title, 10 l., pp. 450, 34 l. 26311

Gage. Nueva Relacion que contiene los Viages de Tomas Gage en la Nueva España durante el año 1625 y siguientes. *Paris: Rosa.* 1838. 2 vols., 12mo, 29 sheets. 26312

Gage. Viages en la Nueva-España, durante el año 1625 y siguientes. *Paris: Rose.* 1838. 2 vols., 12mo, 29 sheets.

The first Spanish translation. Gage was a Catholic, but became Protestant before his travels were published. Its circulation was not permitted in Spain.

Gage. A full Survey | of | Sion and Babylon, | And | A clear Vindication of the Parish-Churches and Pa- | rochial-Ministers of England, from the uncharitable | Censure, the infamous Title, and the inju- | rious Nick-name of Babylonish. | Or, A Scripture Disproof, and Syllogistical Conviction of M. Charles | Nichols, of Kent, his Erroneous Assertions, Justifying his | Separated Congregation for the true House of God; | and branding all the Parochial Churches, and the | Parish Officiating Ministers in England, with | the infamous Title of Babylonish. | Delivered in three Sabbath-dayes Sermons, in the Parish Church | of Deal, in Kent, after a Publick Dispute in the same | Church with the said Mr. Charles Nichols, upon | the 20. day of October 1653. | By Thomas Gage, Preacher of the Word, to the Church within the | Bounds and Limits of Deal in Kent. | *London, Printed by W. Bentley, and are to be sold by Joshuah | Kirton, at the Kings Arms in St. Pauls Church-yard.* 1654. | 8vo, pp. xvi, 86. 26314

A curious and scarce piece, being all Gage published in addition to the travels. The introduction contains poems by W. Stanley and Henry Harlete.

Gage. Some Remarkable Passages Relating to Archbishop Laud, particularly of his Affection to the Church of Rome, being

the Twenty-Second Chapter of Gage's Survey of the West Indies, as 'twas Printed in the Folio Edition before the Restoration, but Suppressed in the Octavo size. *London.* 1712. 8vo.

Gage. The Traveller. Part I. Containing, A Journal of Three Thousand Three Hundred Miles, through the Main Land of South-America. By Mr. Thomas Gage, an Englishman; and a Missionary Friar in New-Spain, twelve Years. In which is set forth, His Journey from St. John de Ulva to Mexico, with a Description of that great City as in former Times, and at present; as also his Travels through many other Parts of New-Spain; with an Account of their Government, Castles, Ports and Commodities; as also their ecclesiastical State, in which the lascivious Intrigues, and wicked Lives of the Jesuits in those Parts, and their grand Impositions upon the poor ignorant Natives, are truly delineated. To which is added, The Policy, Manners, Behaviour, Arts and Sciences, religious Rites and Ceremonies, Feasts and Solemnities of the Native Indians. Concluding with The Wonderful Conversion of the Author to the Protestant Religion; his Escape from the Spaniards, in South-America; his Return to England, his Native Country; and the Reception he met with there by his Relations, after an Absence of four-and-twenty Years. To be published Monthly in the New American Magazine. *Woodbridge, in New-Jersey: Printed and Sold by James Parker.* 1758. 8vo, pp. 136. 26316

Gage (Thomas). General Gage's Instructions, of 22d February 1775, to Captain Brown and Ensign de Berniere, (of the Army under his Command) whom he ordered to take a Sketch of the Roads, Passes, Heights, &c., from Boston to Worcester, and to make other Observations: With a Curious Narrative of Occurrences during their Mission. ... Together with an Account of their Doings, in Consequence of further Orders ... from General Gage, ... to proceed to Concord, to Reconnoitre and find out the State of the Provincial Magazines, ... Also, An Account of the Transactions of the British Troops, from the Time they marched out of Boston, on the Evening of the 18th, 'till their Confused Retreat back, on the ... Nineteenth of April, 1775; and a Return of the ... Killed, Wounded ... . *Boston: J. Gill.* MDCCLXXV. 8vo, pp. 20. BA., N. 26317

Gage. Narrative of the Excursion and Ravages of the King's Troops [at Lexington] under Command of Gen. Gage, April 19, 1775, with the Depositions taken by order of Congress. *Worcester.* 1775. 8vo. W. 26318

Gage. Letters. *See* Bernard, Vol. II., No. 4923, and Vol. V., No. 19774.

Gage. General Gage's Confession, Being the Substance of His Excellency's last Conference, with his Ghostly Father, Friar Francis. ... By the Author of the Voyage to Boston. A Poem, &c. *Printed in the Year*, 1775. 8vo, pp. 8. P. 26319

Published October, 1775; consists of 624 lines. *See our* Vol. II., No. 6571.

Gage. Letters of the Two Commanders-in-Chief, Generals Gage and Washington, and Major-Generals Burgoyne and Lee; with the Manifesto of General Washington to the Inhabitants of Canada. *New York: James Rivington.* 1775. 8vo, pp. (2), 8.

Also: Letter to P. Randolph. *Boston.* 1774. 8vo.

Gage (*Viscount*). Speech of Viscount Gage in Parliament, against the Convention with Spain. *London.* 1739. 4to.

Gage (T.) The History of Rowley, anciently including Bradford, Boxford, and Georgetown, from the Year 1639 to the Present Time. By Thomas Gage. With an Address, delivered September 5, 1839, at the Celebration of the Second Centennial Anniversary of its Settlement. By Rev. James Bradford, *Boston: Ferdinand Andrews.* 12mo, pp. xx, 483, (1). Plate. BA.

Gage (W. L.) A Discourse Occasioned by the Death of Dr. Warren F. Chamberlin, delivered November 30, 1856, Manchester ... By Rev. William L. Gage ... *Manchester, N. H.: E. Bartholomew.* 1857. 8vo, pp 10. B., H. 26323

Also: The Spirit of Human Liberty ... A Sermon ... November 2, 1856, and another Sermon ... November 9, 1856. ... *Manchester: Press of J. H. Goodale.* 1856. 8vo, pp. 11. B. — The Spiritual Life ... . Valedictory Sermon ... April 4, 1858. ... . *Manchester, N. H.: Chas. H. Livingston.* 1858. 8vo, pp. 15. B., H. — The War; its Necessity, ... A Discourse ... before the New Hampshire Volunteers ... Portsmouth, May 5, 1861 ... [*Portsmouth.* 1861.] 8vo, pp. 4. H.

Gagern (C.) Apelacion de los Mexicanos a la Europa bien informada de la Europa mal informada. Por Carlos de Gagern. *Mexico.* 1862. 4to, pp. 86. 3 Portraits. 26324

Gagnon (E.) Chansons populaires du Canada. Recueillies et publiées avec annotations par Ernest Gagnon. *Quebec.* 1865. 8vo, pp. 376 26325

Gail (G. W.) Suggestions for Taxing Tobacco in its Raw State, ... By G. W. Gail, of Baltimore. *Baltimore: Printed by John Murphy & Co.* 1865. 8vo, pp. 16. H. 26326

Gailland (Maurice), *Compiler*. Potewatemi nemēmiseniŭkin ipi nemēnigamowinin. *Cincinnatinag: wewikaneitidjik Benziger*. 1868. 18mo, pp. 550. 36 Plates. c. 26327

Gaillard (H.) La Constitution Universelle. Renfermant las Matiēres suivantes: Dévelopement du Sophisme de Thomas Jefferson ... contre la Race Africaine ... *Port-au-Prince: Jb. Courtois*. 1836. Sm. 4to, pp. 16. H. 26328

Gaillardet (Frédéric). Profession de foi et considérations sur le système républicain des États-Unis. *Paris: Dupont*. 1848. 8vo. 26329

Gaimard (P.) Voyage en Islande et au Groënland, exécuté pendant les années 1823 et 1836 sur la corvette "la Recherche", commandée par M. Tréhouart, lieutenant de vaisseau, dans le but de découvrir les traces de la "Lilloise"; publié par ordre du roi sous la direction de M. Paul Gaimard. *Paris: Arthus Bertrand*. 1838–1851. 7 vols., 8vo, 2 Atlases in folio, 1 Atlas in 8vo. 246 Plates. B., H. 26330

This work is divided into — Histoire du voyage, par P. Gaimard et E. Robert, 2 vols., 8vo, 2 atlases, folio; Histoire del Islande, par X. Marmier, 8vo; Littérature Islandaise, par X. Marmier, 8vo; Physique, par Lottin, 8vo; Géologie, minéralogie et botanique, par E. Robert, atlas, rl. 8vo, text in 8vo; Zoologie et Médecine, par E. Robert, avec notice statistique, par la Roquette, 8vo.

Gaine (H.) New York Pocket Almanac for 1761. *New York: H. Gaine*. 1762. 26331

Continued to 1803 or later; after 1805 known as "Ming's Almanack."

Gaine's Universal Register, or, American and British Kalendar, for the Year 1775. *New-York: Printed by H. Gaine*. 1774. 18mo, pp. 168. BA. 26332

Continued as "Gaine's Universal Register, or, Columbian Kalendar."

Gaines (E. P.) Memorial of Edmund Pendleton Gaines, to the Senate and House of Representatives of the United States ... [on National Defence]. *Memphis, Tenn*. 1840. 8vo, pp. 30.

Gaines. To the Young Men ... of the American Union, Civil and Military ... 1838. [*Fort Jackson*, (*La.*) 1838.] 8vo, pp. 88. B., BA., H. 26334

Also: Letter ... to the Common Council ... of New York ... on ... assuming the Command of the Eastern Division. [*New York:*] *W. C. Bryant & Co.* [1846.] 8vo, pp. 24. B.

Gaines (George S.), *and others*. Report of the Affairs and Condition of the Branch of the Bank of the State of Alabama at Mobile, and accompanying Documents. *Tuscaloosa*. 1837. 8vo.

Gaines (Myra Clark) *v.* De La Croix (F. D.) *et al.* Supreme Court of the United States. Appeal from the Circuit Court of the United States for the Eastern District of Louisiana. [Record] filed December 19, 1865. *Washington: Government Printing Office*. [1867.] 2 vols., 8vo, pp. xvi, 948; iv, 1120.

Gair (T.) A Sermon ... at the Ordination of the Reverend Thomas Green, in Cambridge, [Mass.] November 17, 1783. By Thomas Gair, A.M. *Boston: Printed by Benjamin Edes and Sons*. M, DCC, LXXXIV. 8vo, pp. 36, (2). BA. 26337

Gaisford (S.) An Essay on the good Effects which may be derived in the British West Indies in consequence of the Abolition of the African Slave Trade: including an Inquiry into the present Insular Policy of those Colonies. By Stephen Gaisford, Esq. *London: Baldwin, Cradock & Co.* 1811. 8vo, pp. 236 or 136. 26338

See "M. Rev.," New Series, LXXI. 281.

Gala (I.), *Editor*. Memorias de la Colonia Francesa de Santo Domingo, con algunas reflexionas relativas a la Isla de Cuba, por un Viagero Español. Publicalas Ignacio Gala. *Madrid: En la oficina de Hilario Santos Alonzo*. MDCCLXXXVII. 12mo, 4 l., pp. 180. C., H. 26339

[Galard de Terraube.] Tableau de Cayenne ou de la Guiane française, contenant des Renseignemens Exacts sur son Climat, ses Productions, les Naturels du Pays, les Différentes Ressources que l'on y trouve, et le Degré de Prospérité dont cette Colonie est Susceptible. ... *Paris: Tilliard et Fils, an* VII. [1799.] 8vo, pp. 230. BA. 26340

[Galard de Terraube.] Tafereel van Cayenne, of Fransch Guiana: naar het Fransch; door Joannes van der Linden. *Leyden*. 1800. 8vo. 26341

Galardi (P. Ferdinand de). Traicté politique touchant les Ambassades, Ligues et les Ordres Militaires d'Espagne. *Cologne:* [*Elzevier.*] 1666. Frontispiece. 26342

Very rare. Title and note from an English catalogue. "With a long dedication to Don Pedro Nuno Colon, Duc de Veraguas, respecting his ancestors of the family of Columbus. In it Galardi relates, not as a rumor, but as a positive fact, that a ship-wrecked pilot, on his death-bed, communicated the existence of unknown lands to Christopher Columbus. It is evident Mr. Irving could never have seen this very scarce work, or he would not have ventured to have treated as a mere fable a circumstance here minutely detailed as the descendant of the family who held the high station of Grand Admiral of the Indies, and who must have been well aware whether his ancestor had received such information or not. If the fact had not been too well known

and believed as true, Galardi would hardly have dared to insult the Duke by the insertion of a tale derogatory to the discoverer of America." Mr. Stevens, in his "Bliblio-theca Geographica," gives the date as 1660, and adds a note: "This extraordinary little book, though compiled from Herera and other good Spanish authorities, is valued chiefly for its long and quaint dedication to Don Pedro Columbus, who is styled Grand Admiral of the Indies, Duke of Veragua, Duke of La Vega (in Santo Domingo), ... But the odd part of this dedication of Galardi is the cool repetition of the story of the Pilot of Madeira dying in the house of Columbus, and in gratitude for kindness revealing to him the discoveries he had made of lands in the West, thus relieving Columbus of the originality and honor of his discovery."

Galatian (A. B.) History of Elmira, Horseheads, and the Chemung Valley, with Sketches of the Churches, Schools, Societies, Railroads, etc. Also, Directory and Business Advertiser for 1868. By Andrew B. Galatian. *Elmira*, (*N. Y.*): *Wheeler & Watts*. 1868. 8vo, 4 l., pp. 280, 33. 26343

Galatian. History of Scranton, Providence, Dunmore, Waverly, and Humphreysville, with accounts of the Coal Companies [etc.] Also, Directory and Business Advertiser for 1867–68. By Andrew B. Galatian. *Scranton*, (*Pa.*): *Author*. 1867. 8vo, pp. 416.

The Galaxy. An Illustrated Magazine of Entertaining Reading. *New York: W. C. & F. P. French*. 1866. 8vo. B., BA.

Continued. Contains many articles of historical interest.

Galbraith (J.) Speech of the Hon. John Galbraith, of Pennsylvania, on the United States Bank, and the Removal of the Deposites, delivered ... the 6th, 7th, 14th, & 16th May, on the Resolution of Mr. Mardis, of Alabama, and the Amendment offered thereto. *City of Washington: John Francis Blair*. 1834. 8vo, pp. 36. 26346

Gale (A.) History of the Town of Lee, Mass. A Lecture, ... March 22d, 1854. By Rev. Amory Gale. *Lee: Printed by French & Royce*. 1854. 8vo, pp. 48. BA., H. 26347

Gale (B.) A Calm and full Vindication of a Letter, wrote to a Member of the Lower House of Assembly of Connecticut ... Being a full Answer to a Letter wrote to a Member of the House of Representatives in Vindication of Yale-College, with some further Remarks on the Laws and Government of that Society ... . By Benjamin Gale, A.M. *New Haven*. 1759. 4to, pp. 32. M. 26348

Gale. A Few Brief Remarks on Mr. Graham's Answer; and on his Vindication of Mr. President Clap ... . By Benjamin Gale, A.M. *New-Haven: Printed by J. Parker, and Company*. 1790. 8vo, pp. 15. B., M. 26349

[Gale.] A Letter to a Member of the Lower House of Assembly ... shewing that the Taxes of Yale College, are stated Higher than is Necessary. ... *New-Haven: Printed by James Parker, and Company*. 1759. 4to, pp. 23. BA. 26350

Gale. Doctor Gale's Letter, to J. W., Esquire, Containing a Narrative of the Principal Matters, of a Public and Interesting Nature, which were Subjects of the Debates and Resolves of the General Assembly of the Colony of Connecticut, during their Sessions in May, 1769. ... *Hartford: Printed by Green & Watson*. 1769. 8vo or 12mo, pp. 34. BA. 26351

Dated Killingworth, 25 July, 1769. *See* [Dyer (E.)], Vol. VI., No. 21587.

Gale. Observations | On a Pamphlet, entitled | Remarks on Dr. Gale's Letter to J. W. Esq; | Signed E. D. | Of which | the Hon. Eliphalet Dyer | is the Reputed Author. | Shewing, from the Matters therein contained, | that such an Imputation is highly Injurious to | the Character of that Worthy Patriot. | By Benjamin Gale, A.M. | ... | *Hartford: Printed by Green & Watson*, | ... | [1769.] 8vo, pp. 40. BA., P. 26352

Interesting as regards the Susquehanna Company and the Paxton Men.

[Gale.] The Present State of the Colony of Connecticut considered. In a Letter from a Gentleman in the Eastern part of said Colony, to his Friend in the Western part of same. [*New London:*] *Printed* [*by T. Green*] *in the Year* 1755. 4to, pp. (1), 21. H. 26353

Signed A. Z. It consists of answers to the four following queries: I. What the common and ordinary expenses of this government are annually? II. Whether some of the same may not, without inconveniency to the government, be reduced, particularly the annuity to Yale College. III. What the state of our treasury is, and why the knowledge of its true state is so long retarded? IV. Whether we in the Eastern part of this Colony, exceed you in the Western part of the same so much in our lists and number of Freemen, as we do in men of capacity and integrity, and the best turned and qualified for government? *See* [Dyer (E.)], Vol. VI., No. 21587.

Gale. A Reply to a Pamphlet, entitled "The Answer of a Friend in the West, &c." With a Prefatory Address to the Freemen of His Majesty's English Colony of Connecticut. By A. Z. [*New London:*] *Printed* MDCCLV. Sm. 4to, pp. 63.

Also: A Brief Essay; or, An Attempt to Prove, from the Prophetic Writings of the Old and New Testaments, what Period of Prophecy the Church of God is now under, etc. *New Haven*. [n. d.] 8vo, pp. 63. N.

Gale (G.) The Gale Family Records in England and the United States; to which are added, the Tottingham Family of

New England, and some Account of the Bogardus, Waldron, and Young Families of New York. By George Gale, LL.D. *Galesville, Wisconsin: Leith & Gale, Printers*. 1866. 16mo, pp. 254. 4 Plates. C., H. 26355

[Gale (George).] [Genealogy of the Gale Family. n. p. n. d.] 8vo, pp. 9. B. 26356

Gale. Upper Mississippi; or, Historical Sketches of the Mound Builders, the Indian Tribes, and the Progress of Civilization in the Northwest. From A.D. 1600 to the Present Time. By George Gale. *Chicago: Clarke and Company*. 1867. 12mo, pp. 460. Portrait. B., H. 26357

Gale (G. W.) History of Knox College and Galesburgh, Ill. By George W. Gale. *Cincinnati*. 1845. C. 26358

Also: Claims of Colleges to Public Favor — Knox College. An Address, ... delivered ... July 23, 1847. *Galesburg: Southwick Davis, Printer*. 1847. 8vo, pp. 15.

Gale (N.) ... A Discourse ... in ... Lee, Mass., Thanksgiving Day, November 27, 1856. By Rev. Nahum Gale. *Pittsfield, Mass.: Chickering and Davis*. 1857. 8vo, pp. 25. H.

Gale. The Pilgrims' First Year in New England. By Rev. Nahum Gale. ... . *Boston*. [1865.] 16mo, pp. viii, 7–336. 4 Maps and 1 Plate. B., H. 26360

Also: An Inaugural Address, delivered in ... Connecticut ... August 7, 1851. ... . *Hartford: Case, Tiffany and Company*. 1851. 8vo, pp. 23. H.

[Gale (S.)] An Essay on the Nature and Principles of Public Credit. *London*. 1784. 8vo, pp. vi, 234. Essay II. *London*. 1785. Essay III. *London*. 1786. 8vo, pp. xviii, 60. Essay IV. *London*. 1787. 8vo, pp. vii, 142. N. 26361

The author was a resident of Charleston, South Carolina. The subject of a so-called sinking fund is here discussed.

The Galena City Directory for 1854. *Galena: H. H. Houghton & Co.* 1854. 8vo, pp. 128. Continued. B., BA. 26362

Galena and Chicago Union Railroad: Report of Survey ... by R. P. Morgan: and Charter. *Chicago*. 1847. 8vo. 26363

Also: Annual Reports. *Chicago*. 1848. Continued.

Galena Theological Seminary: Charter. *Galena, Ill*. 1853. 8vo. S. 26364

Galeria Americana. *Mejico*. [n. d.] Folio. 26365

"Collection de 64 belles gravures s. acier exécutées Mexico, a représant. des faits du Nouveau Testament et differents Saints et Saintes principalement de l'Amérique." — Andrade.

Galeria Pittoresca da historia portugueza, ou Victorias, Conquistas, Façanhas e Factos memoraveis da historia Portugal et do Brasil; obra destinada á instrucção da mocidade portugueza e brasilienze; ... 4 vols., 8vo. 36 Plates. 26366

La Galerie Agréable du Monde où l'on voit les principaux empires, royaumes, villes, les côtes, rivières, habillements, et mœurs des peuples, leur religion, les jeux, cérémonies ainsi que les animaux, plantes et autres raretés de l'Univers. *Leide: P. van der Aa*. [1729.] 66 vols., folio. 26367

This stupendous publication contains above three thousand plates and maps, many by the best Dutch engravers, as Luiken, Mulder, Goeree, Stoopendaal, etc. Four volumes relate to America. It was edited by its publisher, Peter van der Aa.

Galerm (J. B.) A Relation of the Misfortunes of the French Neutrals, as laid before the Assembly of the Province of Pennsylvania, by John Baptiste Galerm, and of the said People. Folio, p. 1. P. 26368

Printed by Franklin and Hall. These neutrals were Canadian exiles.

[Gales (J.)] The Past, the Present, and the Future. [n. p. n. d.] 8vo, pp. 40. H. 26369

Gales (J.) A Sketch of the Personal Character & Qualities of General Zachary Taylor. By Joseph Gales, Esq., ... [n. p.] 1848. 8vo, pp. 8. H., S. 26370

Gales (J.), *Reporter*. *See* Vol. IV., Nos. 15519 and 15587.

Galiano (D. A.) Cuba en 1858. Por D. A. Galiano. *Madrid*. 1859. 8vo. 26371

Galibi. *See* S[auvagé de la] (M.)

Galicia (Ant. Miguel). Manual del Sagrado Orden de Charidad de S. Hypolito Martyr, Provincia en esta Nueva-España. *Madrid: por J. Ibarra*. 1766. 4to. 26372

Galicia (F. C.) Silibario de Idioma Mexicano. Por el Lic. D. Faustino Chimalpopocatl Galicia. *Mexico: 1849. Imprenta de las Escalerillas n. 7, dirigida por M. Castro*. 8vo, pp. 16. + *Mexico: Manuel Castro*. 1859. 8vo, pp. 32. 26373

Galisteo (J.) Remedio Natural para precaverse de los Rayos, y de sus funestos efectos. Secreto tan util, como curioso, sacado de las repetidas observaciones, y experiencias, que sobre la analogia de la electricidad con la materia de los rayos, ha estampado en Madrid año de 1757, en su Diario Philosophico Don Juan Galisteo. [Colophon:] *Reimpresso en Mexico*. [1758?] 4to, pp. 8. 26374

"This tract treats of Dr. Franklin's discovery of the use of the lightning rod, and the use of the electrical machine, as set forth in his publication in London in 1751, how the matter was immediately taken up in France and Spain, and subsequently in Mexico, particularly in Puebla de los Angeles, where there is usually much lightning. The writer differs from Franklin and other philosophers as to the form and shape of the lightning rods. Instead of being pointed or square, as discussed in the Royal Society of London, this writer thinks the form of a cross would better secure the desired protection. The Holy Cross always strikes certain terror into the malignant spirits of the clouds, so that if Franklin's steel points were arranged in the form of a cross, they would become a more secure protection against the insults of the lightning!" — Stevens.

Galitzin (*le Prince* Dmitri). Un missionnaire russe en Amérique. ... Précédée d'une notice ... et traduit de l'anglais par le prince Aug. Galitzin. *Paris: Dounioul*. 1856. 8vo.

Galitzin (E.) Le Nord de la Sibérie. Voyage parmi les peuplades de la Russie asiatique et dans la mer Glaciale, entrepris par ordre du gouvernement russe, et exécuté par MM. de Wrangell, chef de l'expédition, Matiouchkine. Traduit du russe par le prince Emmanuel Galitzin. *Paris: Amyot*. 1843. 2 vols., 8vo. Map and 2 Plates. 26376

Galitzin (E.) Notice sur Madame Elizabeth Galitzin, Religieuse du Sacré Cœur 1795–1843. *Tours: Bouserez*. 1858. 8vo, pp. 39. 26377

One hundred copies printed. She was Superior of the Convents of the Sacred Heart in the United States.

Gall (J.) The First Initiatory Catechism, By James Gall, with the Ten Commandments and the Lord's Prayer in the Ojibwa [Chippeway] Language. Translated by Rev. P. Dougherty, aided by D. Rodd. *Printed for the Presbyterian Church: Grand Traverse Bay*, [*Mich.*] 1847. 16mo, pp. 69. C. 26378

Gall (Ludwig). Meine Auswanderung nach den Vereinigten Staaten in Nord Amerika im Frühjahr 1819 ... und 1820. Von Ludwig Gall. ... *Trier*. 1822. 2 vols., 8vo, pp. (3), 428, (2), Maps and Plates; vi, (4), 408; 5 Plates. BA. 26379

See "N. Am. Rev.," XVIII. 91.

Gallagher (J.) The Western Sketch-Book. By Rev. James Gallagher. *Boston*. 1850. 8vo. S. 26380

Gallagher (W. D.) Facts and Conditions of Progress in the North West. Being the Annual Discourse for 1850, before the Historical and Philosophical Society of Ohio, delivered April 8, the Sixty-Third Anniversary of the First Settlement of the State. By William D. Gallagher. With an Appendix ... . *Cincinnati: H. W. Derby & Co*. 1850. 8vo, pp. 85. BA., H. 26381

G[allagher]. Selections from the Poetical Literature of the West ... Edited by W. D. G. *Cincinnati: U. P. James*. 1841. 12mo, pp. 264. B., H., S. 26382

Also: Erato, Number II. *Cincinnati*. 1835. 12mo. + Number III. *Cincinnati: Alexander Flash*. 1837. 16mo, pp. 60. C., S.

Galland (I.) Iowa Emigrant; containing a Map and General Description of Iowa Territory. By I. Galland. *Chillicothe*. 1840. 8vo, pp. 32. 26383

Gallardo (A. L.) Corona funebre á la memoria de la celebre poetisa Zacatecana D. Josefa Letechipia de Gonzalez. *Guadalaxara*. 1854. Folio, pp. 18. 26384

Gallardo (B. J.) Ensayo de la Biblioteca Española de Libros Raros y Curiosos, formados con los Apuntamientos de D. B. J. Gallardo, coordinados y aumentados por Zarco del Valle y J. Sancho Rayon. *Madrid*. 1863–66. 2 vols., 8vo. 26385

Gallardo (Basilio Perez). Breve reseña de los sucesos de Guadalajara y de las Lomas de Calderon, ó Diario de las operaciones del ejercito federal, despues de la batalla de Silao, etc. *Mexico*. 1861. 4to, pp. 70. 26386

Gallardo (Jo.) Sermon Funebre que en las Exequias, que el Convento de San Francisco Xavier de Religiosos Bethlemitas de la Ciudad de Mexico hizo á sú difunto General el Rmô. P. Fr. Juan Angel de San Ignacio. *Mexico*. 1786. 8vo. 26387

Also: Sermon Fúnebre en las solemn. exequias de Señ Cayet Ant. de Torres. *Mexico*. 1787. 4to, 17 leaves.

[Gallatin (Albert).] An Examination of the Conduct of the Executive of the United States towards the French Republic; likewise an Analysis of the Explanatory Article of the British Treaty — In a Series of Letters. By a Citizen of Pennsylvania. *Philadelphia: Francis and Robert Hill*. 1797. 8vo, pp. vi, 72.

GALLATIN. Letters of Albert Gallatin on the Oregon Question, January, 1846. *Washington.* 1846. 8vo, pp. 30. BA., M.

GALLATIN. A Memoir of the North-Eastern Boundary, in Connection with Mr. Jay's Map, by the Hon. Albert Gallatin, LL.D., ... Together with a Speech on the Same Subject, by the Hon. Daniel Webster, LL.D. ... delivered at a Special Meeting of the New-York Historical Society, April 15th, 1843. Illustrated by a Copy of the "Jay Map." *New York: Printed for the Society.* 1843. 8vo, pp. 74. B., BA., H. 26390

Included in the "Collections of the New York Historical Society."

GALLATIN. The Oregon Question. By Albert Gallatin [Nos. 1–5. With Appendix.] *New York: Bartlett & Welford.* 1846. 8vo, pp. 78. B., H. 26391

GALLATIN. Peace with Mexico. By Albert Gallatin. *New York: Bartlett & Welford.* 1847. 8vo, pp. 16, (1). B., BA., H. + *New York: O. Jenkins.* [n. d.] 8vo, pp. 16. 26392

GALLATIN. The Right of the United States of America to the North-Eastern Boundary claimed by them. Principally Extracted from the Statements laid before the King of the Netherlands, and Revised by Albert Gallatin, with an Appendix and Eight Maps. *New York: Samuel Adams, Printer.* 1840. 8vo, pp. x, 179, (1). 8 Maps and 6 Plates. B., H. 26393

GALLATIN. A Sketch of the Finances of the United States. By Albert Gallatin. *New York: Printed by William A. Davis.* 1796. 8vo, pp. (4), 9–205, 3 Tables. B., BA., H. 26394

GALLATIN. The Speech of Albert Gallatin, a Representative from the County of Fayette, in the House of Representatives of the General Assembly of Pennsylvania, on the Important Question touching the Validity of the Elections held in the Four Western Counties of the State, on the 14th Day of October, 1794. With Notes and an Appendix, containing Sundry Documents Relative to the Western Insurrection. *Philadelphia: Printed by William W. Woodward.* 1795. 12mo, pp. 66. B., BA.

GALLATIN. The Speech of Albert Gallatin, delivered in the House of Representatives ... on the First of March, 1798. Upon the Foreign Intercourse Bill. [n. p. 1798?] 8vo, pp. 48. P. + [*Washington.*] 1798. 8vo, pp. 28. M. + Second Edition. With an Appendix. *Philadelphia: Printed by Richard Folwell.* 1798. 8vo, pp. 48. BA., H. 26396

For a reply, *see* Addison (Alex.), Vol. I., No. 378.

GALLATIN. Suggestions on the Banks and Currency of the Several United States, in Reference principally to the Suspension of Specie Payments. By Albert Gallatin. *New-York: Wiley and Putnam.* 1841. 8vo, pp. (4), 9–124. B., BA. 26397

[GALLATIN.] The United States Coast Survey. [n. p. n. d.] 8vo, pp. 20. H. 26398

GALLATIN. Views of the Public Debt, Receipts & Expenditures of the United States. By Albert Gallatin. *New-York: Printed by M. L. & W. A. Davis.* 1800. 8vo, pp. 61, (5). BA., H. + Second Edition. *Philadelphia: M. Carey.* 1801. 8vo, pp. 72. 26399

Also: Considerations on the Currency and Banking System of the United States. .. *Philadelphia: Carey & Lea.* 1831. 8vo, pp. 108. B., H. — Expenses of the War ... [*Washington.* 1848.] 8vo, pp. 16. H. — Inaugural Address ... on taking the Chair as President of the New-York Historical Society, ... Feb. 7th, 1843. *New-York: Printed for the Society.* 1843. 8vo, pp. 21, (1). B., BA., H. — Letter from the Secretary of the Treasury in reply to the Memorial of the President of the United States. *Washington.* 1811. 8vo, pp. 8. — Memorial of the Committee appointed by the "Free Trade Convention," held at Philadelphia, in September and October, 1831, to prepare and present a Memorial to Congress, remonstrating against the existing Tariff of Duties; ... *New York: Wm. A. Mercein, Printer.* 1832. 8vo, pp. 87. — Report from the Secretary of the Treasury, on the Subject of American Manufactures, prepared in Obedience to a Resolution of the House of Representatives, April 19, 1810. ... . *Boston: Farrand, Mallory & Co.* 1810. 8vo, pp. 62. H. + *Washington.* 1810. — Report of the Secretary of the Treasury, to whom was referred the Memorial of the United States Bank for a Renewal of their Charter. *Washington.* 1809. 8vo, pp. 18 — Report of the Secretary of the Treasury on the subject of the National Bank. 8vo, pp. 62. — Report of the "Union Committee" on the National Bank, appointed by the Signers of the Memorial to Congress, New York, Feb. 11, 1834. *New York.* 1834. 8vo, pp. 34. — Report of the Secretary of the Treasury on the subject of Public Roads and Canals, ... March 2, 1807. *Philadelphia.* 1808. + *Washington.* 1808. 8vo. — Report of the Secretary of the Treasury ... respecting the Direct Tax, December 28th, 1807 ... . *Washington: Printed by Roger C. Weightman.* 1809. 8vo, pp. 14. B. — Speech ... on the Alien and Sedition Laws. *Philadelphia.* 1799. 8vo. — The Substance of Two Speeches of Mr. Gallatin, on the Bill for Augmenting the Navy Establishment of the United States. ... 7th and 11th of February, 1799. *Philadelphia: Printed by Joseph Gales.* 1799. 8vo, pp. 28. — War Expenses. ... *Bartlett & Welford.* 1848. 8vo, pp. 22. B., BA. Mr. Gallatin also contributed an essay on the Indian languages to the "Transactions of the American Antiquarian Society," constituting its second volume. He was President of the New York Historical Society, and furnished interesting papers to the first and second volumes of the Transactions of the latter. He died in 1849, aged eighty-eight years. *See* Duyckinck's "Cyclopædia of American Literature," I. 492.

GALLATIN (J.) Address by Hon. James Gallatin, before the Democratic Union Association, October 18, 1864. George B. McClellan as a Patriot, a Warriot, and a Statesman. Course of the Administration, State of the Finances, etc., etc. [n. p. n. d.] 8vo, pp. 14. B., BA. 26400

GALLATIN. Government Finances and the Currency. Letters ... By James Gallatin, ... *New York: Hall, Clayton & Medole, Printers.* 1862. 8vo, pp. 31. H. 26401

GALLATIN. The National Debt, Taxation, Currency, and Banking System of the United States. With some Remarks on the Report of the Secretary of the Treasury. By James Gallatin. *New York: Hosford & Ketcham.* 1864. 8vo, pp. 61. BA.

GALLATIN. The National Finances, Currency, Banking, &c., By James Gallatin, being a Reply to a Speech in Congress, by Hon. Samuel Hooper. *New York: Clayton & Medole, Printers.* 1864. 8vo, pp. 34. 26403

Also: An Address on the subject of the Usury Laws: An Answer to the Hon. J. Whipple ... *New York.* 1859. 8vo, pp. 21. S. — The Financial Economy of the United States, with Suggestions for Restoring Specie Payments. ... *New York: W. C. Bryant & Co.* 1868. 8vo, pp. 25. H. — Letter ... on Financial Affairs; ... June 14, 1862. 4to, pp. 3. — Letter ... [on] The Proposed United States Banking System, and further Issues of Legal Tender. *New York: John W. Amerman.* 1863. 8vo, pp. 11. H. — Letter on Financial Affairs, to A. Stockley, Esq., President of the Bank of Smyrna. *New York. June* 24, 1865. 4to, pp. 2. — Letter to Hon. Samuel Hooper, of Massachusetts, Member of the Committee of Ways and Means of the United States House of Representatives, ... [*New York: Hall, Clayton & Medole?*] 1863. 8vo, pp. 8. B. — The Public Debt ... and Finances of the United States. Letter to Hon. James R. Doolittle ... *New-York: John W. Amerman.* 1866. 8vo, pp. 22. H. — Two Letters to the Hon. S. P. Chase, Secretary of the Treasury, ... *Printed by Particular Request, for Private Circulation only, by Hosford & Ketcham.* 1861. 8vo, pp. 21. H. *See* Sedgwick (Theodore).

GALLAUDET (E. M.) An Address in Behalf of the Columbia Institution for the Instruction of the Deaf and Dumb and the Blind. By Edward M. Gallaudet ... . *Washington: Henry Polkinghorn.* 1858. 8vo, pp. 11. H. 26404

GALLAUDET (T.) A Discourse, delivered by Rev. Thomas Gallaudet, at ... New York, on the National Fast Day, ... September 26th, 1861. *New York: Henry Spear.* 1861. 8vo, pp. 8. H. 26405

GALLAUDET (T. H.) An Address on Female Education, ... Nov. 21st, 1827, at the Opening of the Edifice ... for the Accommodation of the Hartford Female Seminary. By T. H. Gallaudet ... . *Hartford: H. & F. J. Huntington.* MDCCCXXVIII. 8vo, pp. 34. B., BA., H. 26406

GALLAUDET. Plan of a Seminary for the Education of Instructors of Youth. By Thomas H. Gallaudet ... . *Boston: Cummings, Hilliard, and Co.* 1825. 8vo, pp. 29. B., BA., H.

GALLAUDET. A Sermon at the Opening of the Connecticut Asylum for the Education and Instruction of Deaf and Dumb Persons, ... April 20th, 1817, in ... Hartford. By Thomas H. Gallaudet. *Hartford: Hudson and Co.* 1817. 8vo, pp. 15. B.

GALLAUDET. Gallaudet's Picture defining and Reading-Book; Also, New-Testament Stories, in the Ojibua [Chippeway] Language. *Boston.* 1835. 16mo, pp. 123. BA., H. + Bible Stories, ... on the Fall. By T. H. Gallaudet ... . *Park Hill, Cherokee Nation: John Candy and John F. Wheeler.* 1845. 18mo, pp. 24. + Scripture Biography; from Adam to Noah. By Rev. J. H. Gallaudet. *New York.* [About 1850.] 18mo, pp. 88. S. + History of Abraham. *New York.* [About 1860.] 8vo, pp. 88. S. + History of Joseph. *New York.* [n. d.] 18mo, pp. 42. + History of Moses. *New York.* [About 1850.] 18mo, pp. 207. S. 26409

All in the Choctaw language. Also: A Discourse, delivered at the Dedication of the American Asylum, for the Education of Deaf and Dumb Persons, May 22d, 1821. By Thomas Gallaudet ... . *Hartford: Printed by Hudson and Co.* 1821. 8vo, pp. 15. B. — Sermon on the Duty and Advantages of Affording Instruction to the Deaf and Dumb. *Concord.* 1824. 8vo. B.

GALLEGOS (C.) Catechismo y doctrina cristiana en los idiomas castellano y qquechua. Le da nuavemente a luz el DD. Carlos Gallegos. *Cazko.* 1829. 4to, pp. 34. 26410

GALLEGOS (Estevan Joseph). El Moyses Lusitano. Oracion Funebre, que a la Memoria del fidelissimo Señor D. Juan V. Rey de Portugal, en las reales exequias, solemnizadas por el Excmo Señor De Joseph Manso de Velasco, Governador de los Reynos del Peru y Chile. [*Lima.*] 1752. 4to, 29 l. 26411

GALLEGOS (J.) Dechado de la Castidad, oracion panegyrica, que en la ... fiesta ... del celestial Cingulo del Doctor Angelico Santo Thomas, ... dia 28 de enero del año de 1771. El R. P. Fr. Joseph Gallegos. *Mexico: Jauregaí.* 1771. 4to, pp. 17.

GALLEGOS. La Monarquia dischosa. Oracion panegyrica que en la Santa Iglesia Cathedral de Mexico dixo el dia XII. de Octubre de este año de MDCCCLXX. El R. P. Fr. Joseph Gallegos. *Impressa en Mexico, en la Imprenta de la Biblioteca Mexicana.* [1770.] 4to, 9 l., pp. 11. 26413

Gallegos praises Spain as the happiest kingdom in the world, for its having embraced the Catholic religion, and excluded the other creeds. Also: Glorias de España deduc. de su restauracion milagrosa. Oracion panegyrico. *Mexico.* 1774. 4to, 25 l.

Gallery of British and Foreign Portraits, with Memoirs by Distinguished Biographers. *London: Charles Knight.* 1833–38. 7 vols., imp. 8vo. 26414

Includes Kosciusko, Franklin, Washington, Raleigh, Penn, and Jefferson.

Gallery of Illustrious Americans; containing the Portraits and Biographical Sketches of Twenty-Four of the most Eminent Citizens of the Republic, since the Death of Washington. Daguerreotypes by Brady, Engraved by D'Avignon. Edited by C. Edwards Lester, assisted by an Association of Literary Men. *New York.* 1850. Imp. folio. 24 Plates. 26415

GALLÈS (E.) Du Brésil, ou Observations generales sur le Commerce et les Douanes de ce pays, suivie d'an tarif de droits d'entrèe, etc. Par Ed. Gallès. *Paris.* 1828. 8vo, pp. 108.

Gallica Fides. *See* French Policy, etc., No. 25587.

[GALLIFFET (*le Marquis de*).] Les Bivouacs de Vera-Cruz à Mexico, par un zouave; avec une carte spéciale dressée sur place par l'auteur. Préface par Aurélien Scholl. *Paris: Librairie centrale.* 1864. 12mo. 26417

GALLISON (J.) Memoir of John Gallison, Esq. From the Christian Disciple. *Boston: Wells and Lilly.* 1821. 8vo, pp. 15.

[GALLISON.] A Proposed Memorial to the Congress of the United States, [on Privateering]. *Boston. May* 1819. 8vo, pp. 7.

Also: Address, delivered at the Fourth Anniversary of the Massachusetts Peace Society, December 25th, 1819. *Cambridge: Printed by Hilliard & Metcalf.* 1820. 8vo, pp. 18. B., BA., H.

GALIANI NAPIONE. *See* Napione.

[GALLOWAY (Joseph).] An Account of the Conduct of the War in the Middle Colonies. Extracted from a late Author. The Second Edition. *London: Printed in the Year* MDCCLXXX. 12mo, pp. 28. 26420

An attempt having been made in the House of Commons to show that the colonists are almost universally disaffected to the British government, and that their subjugation is impracticable, this tract attempts to prove the reverse of these statements. *See* Letters to a Nobleman, No. 26436, *infra.*

GALLOWAY. Advertisement. *Philadelphia. December* 20, 1865. ... Joseph Galloway. Folio, p. 1. P. 26421

[GALLOWAY.] A Candid Examination of the Mutual Claims of Great-Britain, and the Colonies; with a Plan of Accommo-

dation, on Constitutional Principles. By the Author of Letters to a Nobleman on the Conduct of the American War. *New York: Printed by James Rivington.* M.DCC.LXXV. 8vo, pp. 62. B., BA., H., P. + [*London:*] *Republished by G. Wilkie, and R. Faulder.* MDCCLXXX. 8vo, pp. 116. 26422

A well-written Tory tract. "The effect of illiberal motives and unworthy passions. A principal object of this pamphlet is to reprobate the proceedings of the Congress; and for this purpose the author labors to maintain the unlimited supremacy of Parliament over all the dominions of the crown, by arguments which have been often alleged, and sufficiently answered." — *M. Rev.*, LII. 537. *See also* "M. Rev.," LXII. 492.

[GALLOWAY.] A Candid Examination ... With a Reply to an Address to the Author. *New York.* 1780. 12mo. BA.

[GALLOWAY.] The Claim of the American Loyalists Reviewed and Maintained upon Incontrovertible Principles of Law and Justice. *London: Printed by J. Almon.* [1783.] 8vo, pp. vi, (2), 5–126. + *London: Printed by G. and T. Wilkie.* M DCC-LXXXIII. 8vo, pp. viii, 138. BA. 26424

[GALLOWAY.] Cool Thoughts on the Consequences to Great Britain of American Independence. On the Expense of Great Britain in the Settlement and Defence of the American Colonies On the Value and Importance of the American Colonies. On the Value and Importance of the American Colonies and the West Indies to the British Empire. *London: J. Wilkie.* MDCC-LXXX. 8vo, pp. iv, 70. BA., C., H., S. 26425

"Its object is 'to show the ruinous consequences to Great Britain of acknowledging the independence of the American Colonies.' It is written in a decent and dispassionate, though very earnest and serious strain." — *M. Rev.*, LXII. 88. It was translated as below:

[GALLOWAY.] Réflexions Impartiales sur les Conséquences qui doivent résulter pour la Grande Bretagne, de l'Indépendance des Amériquains; sur les dépenses qu'elle a faites pour l'établissement et la conservation de ses colonies de l'Amérique; enfin, sur l'importance dont ces mêmes colonies Amériquaines et les Indes Occidentales sont pour l'empire Britannique. Ouvrage traduit de l'Anglois. *Londres.* 1780. 12mo. C. 26426

GALLOWAY. The Examination of Joseph Galloway, Esq; Late Speaker of the House of Assembly of Pennsylvania. Before the House of Commons, in a Committee on the American Papers. With Explanatory Notes. *London: J. Wilkie.* MDCC-LXXIX. 8vo, pp. (2), 85. + The Second Edition. *London: J. Wilkie.* M DCC LXXX. 8vo, pp. (2), 85. BA., H. 26427

GALLOWAY. The Examination of Joseph Galloway, Esq., by a Committee of the House of Commons. Edited by Thomas Balch. Two Hundred and Fifty Copies Printed. *Philadelphia: Printed for the Seventy-Six Society.* 1855. 8vo, 2 l., pp. 86.

"Besides Mr. Galloway's very important evidence, this pamphlet contains many useful and interesting notes relative to the conduct of the war in America." — *M. Rev.* *See also* Rich, I. 276.

[GALLOWAY.] An Extract from a Reply to the Observations of Lieut. General William Howe, on a Pamphlet, entitled Letters to a Nobleman. *London: J. Paramore.* MDCCLXXXI. 12mo, pp. 104. 26429

Published by the Rev. John Wesley.

[GALLOWAY.] Fabricius: Or, Letters to the People of Great Britain: on The Absurdity and Mischiefs of Defensive Operations only in the American War; and on The Causes of the Failure in the Southern Operations. *London: G. Wilkie.* MDCC-LXXXII. 8vo, 2 l., pp. 111. 26430

See "M. Rev.," LXVI. 303.

[GALLOWAY.] Historical and Political Reflections on the Rise and Progress of the American Rebellion. In which The Causes of that Rebellion are pointed out, and the Policy and Necessity of offering to the Americans a System of Government founded in the Principles of the British Constitution, are clearly demonstrated. By The Author of Letters to a Nobleman, on the Conduct of the American War. *London: G. Wilkie.* MDCCLXXX. 8vo, 4 l., pp. 135. BA., H. 26431

"His zeal for a solid reunion of the two countries is as laudable as it is warm, and seems to be really founded in his sincere wishes for the permanent welfare and happiness of all parties." — *M. Rev.*, LXII. 407.

[GALLOWAY.] A Letter from Cicero to the Right Hon. Lord Viscount H—e occasioned by His late Speech in the H—e of C—ns. *London: J. Bew.* MDCCLXXXI. 8vo, pp. (4), 43.

Mr. Galloway here accuses Lord Howe, and his brother Sir William, of having most flagrantly, shamefully, and wickedly betrayed the trust reposed in them, in the command of the British naval and land forces in America." — *M. Rev.* "A thorough roasting and toasting of the two brothers, Lord and Sir William Howe, commanding in America, for their blunders, selfishness, and misconduct, especially at Brooklyn on Long Island, at White Plains, the Brandywine, Germantown, Valley Forge, Princeton, New York, on the Raritan, the Delaware, etc." — STEVENS.

[GALLOWAY.] Letter from Cicero to Cataline the Second. With Corrections and Explanatory Notes. *London: J. Bew.* MDCCLXXXI. 8vo, pp. 104. 26433

Under the assumed name of Cicero, Mr. Galloway attacks the Hon. Charles James Fox (whom he calls Cataline the Second), and the leaders of the opposition, with the view of exposing them to the indignation of the public. Mr. Galloway was attacked in return, as below:

[GALLOWAY.] A Letter to Cicero, Lucius Cataline, or the American Deputy; with Two Letters in Defence of the present, and more general Association of Protestants in England, ... *London: John Stockdale.* 1781. 8vo. 26434

"A zealous friend to religious and civil liberty, but a very indifferent writer, who attacks Mr. Galloway with much asperity, stigmatizing him as a 'traitor, who has quitted one injured country to injure another.'" — *M. Rev.*, LXIV. 225.

[GALLOWAY.] A Letter to the Right Honourable Viscount H—e, on His Naval Conduct in the American War. *London: J. Wilkie.* MDCCLXXIX. 8vo, 2 l., pp. 50. + The Second Edition, Corrected. *London: G. Wilkie.* MDCCLXXXI. 8vo, 2 l., pp. 50. B., BA., H. 26435

"The conduct of Admiral Howe is severely criticised. He is charged with the most palpable and criminal negligence and misconduct, in regard to the prosecution of the American war, leaving the reader to account for it, if he can, from connections with opposition at home, from secret favor to the American defection, from views of private interest, or from coöperation of all these unworthy principles." *See* "M. Rev.," LXI. 467.

[GALLOWAY.] Letters to a Nobleman, on the Conduct of the War in the Middle Colonies. *London: J. Wilkie.* M DCC-LXXIX. 8vo, pp. viii, 101. Plan. BA., H. + The Second Edition. [*Ibid.*] + The Third Edition. *London: J. Wilkie.* M DCC LXXX. 8vo, pp. viii, 101. Map. + The Fourth Edition. [*Ibid.*] 26436

Written to demonstrate the shameful misconduct of the English generals in the American war. *See* "M. Rev.," LXI. 228; *also* Rich, I. 277.

[GALLOWAY.] Observations on the Fift [*sic*] Article of the Treaty with America: And on The Necessity of appointing a Judicial Enquiry into the Merits and Losses of the American Loyalists. Printed by Order of their Agents. *London: G. Wilkie.* MDCCLXXXIII. 8vo, pp. 19. 26437

The article referred to is that which relates to the restitution of their property to persons who had not borne arms against the United States.

[GALLOWAY.] Observations upon the Conduct of S—r W—m H—e at the White Plains, as related in the Gazette of Dec. 30th, 1776. *London.* 1779. 8vo. Map. 26438

GALLOWAY. Observations on the Conduct of Sir William Howe. By J. Galloway. *Philadelphia.* 1780. 12mo. P.

[GALLOWAY.] Plain Truth: or, a Letter to the Author of Dispassionate Thoughts on the American War, In which the Principles and Arguments of that Author are Refuted, and the necessity of carrying on that War clearly demonstrated. By the Author of Letters to a Nobleman, ... *London: G. Wilkie.* MDCCLXXX. 8vo, pp. vii, 76. BA., J.C.B., C., H. 26440

The object of the writer is to show that Great Britain cannot, consistent with her own safety, give up her American colonies, while the other powers of Europe retain their colonies. He points out the causes of the want of success by the British army, with the means by which future success may attend them. "Strongly recommends a spirited prosecution of the war, in which he has not the least doubt of the complete success of the British arms; and he points out the policy by which America may be firmly and perfectly united with Great Britain." — *M. Rev.*, LXIII. 66.

[GALLOWAY.] Political Reflections on the late Colonial Government, ... *London.* 1783. 8vo. N. 26441

[GALLOWAY.] A Reply to an Address to the Author of a Pamphlet, entitled, "A Candid Examination," &c. By the Author of the Candid Examination. *New York: Printed by James Rivington.* 1775. 8vo. 26442

[GALLOWAY.] A Reply to the Observations of Lieut. Gen. Sir William Howe, on a Pamphlet, entitled Letters to a Nobleman; in which His Misrepresentations are Detected, and those Letters are Supported, by a Variety of New Matter and Argument. To which is added, An Appendix, Containing, I. A Letter to Sir William Howe upon his Strictures on Mr. Galloway's Private Character. II. A Letter from Mr. Kirk to Sir William Howe, and his Answer. III. A Letter from a Committee to the President of the Congress, on the State of the Rebel Army at Valley Forge, preserved among the Papers of Henry Laurens, Esq. By the Author of Letters to a Nobleman. *London: G. Wilkie.* M DCC LXXX. 8vo, pp. (2), 149, (3.) + The Second Edition, with Additions. *London: G. Wilkie.* MDCCLXXXI. 8vo, pp. (4), 157. C., H. 26443

"Mr. Galloway's defence of his own character and conduct against Sir William Howe." — *M. Rev.*, LXIII. 465. The "Additions to the First Edition of the Reply, etc. *London.* 1780." 8vo, pp. 8, were issued separately. It was reprinted, with the title slightly altered, as "A Short History of the War in America, during the Command of Sir William Howe. ... By Joseph Galloway, Esq. *Philadelphia: Re-printed and Sold by Enoch Story.*" The next leaf to this title-page is the following: "A Reply to the Observations of Lieut. Gen. Sir William Howe. ... . III. A Letter from a Committee to the President of the Congress, on the State of the American Army at Valley Forge, found among the Papers of Henry Laurens, Esq. By Joseph Galloway ... . *Philadelphia: Re-printed and Sold by Enoch Story.* 1787." 8vo. pp. 105. BA.

GALLOWAY. The Speech of Joseph Galloway, Esq; ... In Answer to the Speech of John Dickinson, Esq; Delivered in the House of Assembly, of the Province of Pennsylvania, May 24, 1764. On Occasion of a Petition drawn up by Order, and then under the Consideration of the House; praying his Majesty for a Royal, in Liew of a Proprietary Government. *Philadelphia: Printed by W. Dunlap.* MDCCLXIV. 8vo, pp. xxxv, (iv), 45. BA.

GALLOWAY. The Speech of Joseph Galloway, Esq; ... With a Preface by a Member of the Assembly [Benjamin Franklin]. *Philadelphia, Printed; London, Reprinted and Sold by W. Nicoll.* M DCC LXV. 8vo, pp. (2), 92. C. 26445

"A manly and spirited, though not a very correct production." — *M. Rev.*, XXXII. 67. *See* Dickinson (John), Vol. V., No. 20051. Galloway at first espoused American Independency, but subsequently joined the home party and wrote against the Americans. He was undoubtedly the most distinguished and influential man among the American Loyalists. He abandoned his estate and property in Pennsylvania to the value of £40,000 sterling. "John Adams, in his 'Diary,' describes him as 'sensible and learned, but a cold speaker.' Franklin had confidence in his patriotism, and left in his charge in America a valuable collection of letter-books and papers, which were lost. His defection, from his well-known talents, was severely commented upon by the friends of the Revolution. Stiles, in his manuscript diary of the date of October 1, 1775, says: 'Mr. Galloway has also fallen from a great height into contempt and infamy; but he never was entirely confided in as a thorough son of liberty.' Trumbull, too, tells the story in 'McFingal,' how Galloway began by being a flaming patriot; but, being disgusted with his own want of influence, and the greater popularity of others, he turned Tory, wrote against the measures of Congress, and absconded." — DUYCKINCK'S *Cyclopædia of American Literature*, I. 172. *See* Sparks' "Franklin," Vol. III.

[GALLOWAY (Samuel).] *See* [Cooper (M.)], Vol. IV., *note* to No. 16590.

GALLOWAY (S.) Kansas Contested Election. Speech of Hon. S. Galloway, of Ohio, in the House of Representatives, March 17, 1856. On the Resolution Reported by the Committee of Election in the Contested Election Case from the Territory of Kansas. [n. p. n. d.] 8vo, pp. 7. 26446

GALLUCCI (J. M.) Vida del Ven. Padre Antonio Baldinucci, Missionero Apostolico de la Compañia de Jesus. Escrita en Italiano, por Jos. Maria Gallucci, y traducida al castellano. *Mexico Imprenta del Real, y mas Antiguo Colegio de S. Ildefonso.* 1760. 4to, 7 l., pp. 277, 1 l. Portrait. 26447

GALLUP (J. A.) Sketches of Epidemic Diseases in the State of Vermont; from its First Settlement to the Year 1815. With a Consideration of their Causes, Phenomena, and Treatment.

To which is added Remarks on Pulmonary Consumption. By Joseph A. Gallup ... . *Boston: Printed by T. B. Wait & Sons.* 1815. 8vo, pp. 49. BA., H. 26448

The Galphin Case. The Danger of Electing an Incompetent Man as President. 1852. 8vo, pp. 8. S. 26449

GALPINE (C.) Funeral Sermon Preached on Walterhouse Fernley, Esq., of Kingston. By Calvin Galpine. *Kingston, (Jamaica).* 1723. 4to. 26450

GALPINE. Vindication of the Rev. Calvin Galpine, Rector of Spanish Town, Jamaica; also an Account of his Trial for Perjury. *London.* 1742. 8vo. 26451

GALT (Alexander Tilloch). Canada: 1849 to 1859. By the Hon. A. T. Galt, Finance Minister of Canada. *London: Robert Hardwicke.* 1860. 8vo, pp. (1), 54. B. + Second Edition. *Quebec.* 1860. 8vo, pp. 44. 26452

[GALT.] The Saint Lawrence and Atlantic Railroad. A Letter to the Chairman ... of the North American Colonial Association ... . *London.* MDCCCXLVII. 8vo, pp. 40. Map.

GALT. Speech on the Proposed Union of the British North American Provinces, ... by the Hon. A. T. Galt ... 23rd November, 1864. ... *Montreal: Printed by M. Longmore & Co.* 1864. 8vo, pp. 24. B. 26454

Also: Letter to the Chairman, &c., of the North American Colonial Association on the St. Lawrence and Atlantic Railroad, with Appendix and a Map of the British Possessions in North America. ... *London.* 1847. pp. 40. — Report upon the Memorial of the Chamber of Commerce of Sheffield. ... *Quebec.* 1859. — Speech at the Chamber of Commerce, Manchester. ... *London.* 1862. pp. 18. — Speech on introducing the Budget, together with Statistical and Financial Statements. ... *Quebec.* 1862. 8vo, pp. 48. — Speech ... on bringing down the Financial Statement, August 29th, 1865. [n. p. n. d.] 8vo, pp. 12. B., H. — Speech on introducing the Budget. ... *Ottawa.* 1866. 12mo, pp. 43.

GALT (J.) The Canadas. *See* Picken (Andrew).

GALT (J.) The Autobiography of John Galt. *London: Cochrane and M'Crone.* 1833. 2 vols., 8vo, pp. xii, 311; 375. Portrait. H. 26455

Contains his services in the Canada Company, travels in America, founding the city of Guelph, U. C., etc.

GALT. Lawrie Todd; or, The Settlers in the Woods. By John Galt, Esq. ... *London: R. Bentley.* 1830. B., BA., H. +

New-York: J. & J. Harper. 1830. 2 vols., 12mo, pp. 203; 202. + With an Original Preface by Grant Thorburn. *New York.* 1845. 8vo, pp. 174. + Revised ... Sixteenth Edition. Edited by Grant Thorburn. *New-York: D. Fanshaw.* 1847. 18mo, pp. 404. + *London: R. Bentley.* 1849. Fcap 8vo, pp. vii, 452. P. 26456

Repeatedly reprinted. The subject of these sketches is Grant Thorburn, seedsman of New York. *See* Thorburn (Grant).

GALT. The Life and Studies of Benjamin West, Esq., President of the Royal Academy of London, prior to his arrival in England. Compiled from Materials furnished by himself. By John Galt. *London: T. Cadell and W. Davis.* 1816. 8vo, pp. xii, (1), 160. + *Philadelphia: Moses Thomas.* 1816. 8vo, pp. iv, 196. C. + Second Edition. *London: T. Cadell and W. Davis.* 1820. 8vo, pp. xii, (1), 160. P. 26457

Some copies of the London edition were printed on large paper.

GALT. The Life and Works of Benjamin West, Esq. ... Subsequent to his Arrival in this Country. Composed from Materials furnished by himself. By John Galt, Esq. Part II. *London: T. Cadell and W. Davis.* 1820. 8vo, pp. xv, (1), 251.

GALT (J. M.) Essays on Asylums for Persons of Unsound Mind. By John M. Galt, M.D. ... *Richmond: H. K. Ellyson's Power Press.* 1850. 8vo, pp. 22. B., BA. + Second Series. *Richmond.* 1853. 8vo, pp. 44. 26459

GALT. Political Essays. [n. p. n. d.] 8vo, pp. 38.

GALTON (F.) The Art of Travel; or, Shifts and Contrivances available in Wild Countries. By Francis Galton. ... *London: John Murray.* 1854. Post 8vo, pp. viii, 196. B., H. 26461

GALTON. Narration of an Explorer in Tropical South America. By Francis Galton. *London.* 1853. 12mo. C. 26462

GALVAN RIVERA (Mariano). Calendario de las Señoritas megicanas, para el año 1838. *Megico.* 1838. 12mo. 26463

GALVAN RIVERA. Calendario manual y Guia de forasteros de Mexico para el año de 1831. [*Mexico.* 1830?] *Impresa de Mariano Arevalo.* 18mo, pp. 277, 8 l. Continued. 26464

GALVAN RIVERA. Historia de México, Guatemala, Estados-Unidos del Norte, Perú, y otras naciones del continente Americano. *Mexico.* 1852. 2 vols., 8vo, pp. 719; 72. Portraits.

GALVAN RIVERA. Ordenanzas de tierras y aguas ó sea formulario geométricó-judicial para la designacion, establecimiento, mensura, amojonamiento y deslinde de las poblaciones y todas suertes de tierras, sitios, cabellerias y criaderos de ganados mayores y menores, y mercedes de Agua. Cuarto Edicion. *Mexico.* 1851. 4to. + Quinto Edicion. Corr. y aument. *Mexico.* 1855. 8vo. 26466

GALVAÕ (A.) Tratado que compôs o nobre e notauel capitão Antonio Galuão, dos diuersos e desuayrados caminhos, por onde nos tempos passados a pimenta e especearia veyo da India ás nossas partes, e assi de todos os descobrimentos antigos e modernos que são feitos em a era de mil e quinhentos e cincoenta cõ os nomes particulares das pessoas que os fizeram; e em que tempos, e as suas alturas, obra certo muy notauel e copiosa ... Impressa na casa de João da Barreira. (â la fin): se acabou o liuro dos descobrimentos das Antilhas e India. *Imprimio-se* [*Lisboa*] *en casa de Joham da Barreira, impressor del Rey nosso senhor. Aos quinze de dezembro de mil e quinhentos e sessenta e tres annos* [1563]. 8vo, 4 l., Text, 80 leaves. J.C.B. 26467

So rare, that three copies only are known to exist. *See* J. C. Brown's Catalogue, Part I., No. 134, and Graesse's "Tresor." It was reprinted with the following title:

GALVAÕ. Tratados dos Descobrimientos Antigos, e Modernos, Feitos até a Era de 1550. com os nomes particulares das pessoas que os fizeraõ: e em que tempos, e as suas alturas, e dos desvairados caminhos por onde a pimenta, e especiaria veyo da India ás nossas partes: obra certo muy notavel, e copiosa. Composto pelo famoso Antonio Galvaõ, Offerecido ao Excellentissimo Senhor Dom Luiz de Menezes, Quinto Conde da Ericeira, do Concelho de Sua Magestade, Coronel, e Brigadeiro de Infantaria, Viso Rey, e Capitaõ General, que foy dos Estados India, &c. *Lisboa Occidental: Na Officina Ferreiriana.* M DCC.XXXI. Com todas as licenças necessarias. Folio, 8 l., pp. 100. Portrait.

This second edition is also rare, the greater portion having been destroyed by an earthquake.

GALVAÕ. The | Discoveries | of the World from their | first originall vnto the | yeere of our Lord | 1555. | Briefly written in the Por- | tugall tongue by Antonie Galvano, Gouvernour of | Ternate, the chiefe Island | of the Malucos: | Corrected, quoted, and now | published in English by Richard | Hakluyt, sometimes student | of Christ-church in | Oxford. | *Londini,* | *Impensis G. Bishop.* | 1601. | 4to, 1 l., pp. 5, (1), 4, 97. C. 26469

This translation is also a rare book, but is reprinted in the additions to the edition of Hakluyt's voyages, published by Evans in 1809. Hakluyt, in his preface, says, "The worke, though small in bulke, containeth so much rare and profitable matter, as I know not where to seeke the like, within so narrow and streite a compasse. ... Now touching the translation, it may please you sir, to be aduertised that it was first done into our language by some honest and well affected marchant of our nation, whose name by no meanes I could attain vnto. For it hath lien by me aboue these twelue yeares. In all which space though I have made much inquirie, and sent to Lisbon, where it seemeth it was printed, yet to this day I could neuer obtaine the originall copie; whereby I might reform the manifold errours of the translator." — HAKLUYT'S *Dedicatory Epistle.* It is included in Osborn's "Collection of Voyages." Jadis' copy sold for eight pounds.

GALVAÕ. The Discoveries of the World from their First Original to the Year of our Lord 1555, by Antonio Galvano, Governor of Semate. Corrected, Quoted, and Published in England, by Richard Hakluyt, (1607). Now Reprinted, With the Original Portuguese Text; and Edited by Vice Admiral Bethune, C.B. *London: Printed for the Hakluyt Society.* M.DCCCLXII. 8vo, pp. (6), viii, 212. C. 26470

This edition includes the Portuguese text. Antonio Galvano was born at Lisbon in 1503. He embarked for India in 1527, where he soon distinguished himself. He was selected by the Viceroy Don Nunho da Cunha to reduce and govern the Moluccas. After a time he succeeded, as much by valor as by judicious conduct, in bringing these islands under Portuguese sway; and by exercising strict justice and kind dealing towards the natives, both rare in those days, he earned the title of "father of the country." Galvano was a man of rare talent, well versed in religious and secular knowledge, and also well instructed in warlike arts, both military and naval. Faria y Sousa sums up his high qualities in these words: "His fame will never perish so long as the world endures; for neither weak kings, nor wicked ministers, nor blind fortune, nor ages of ignorance, can damage a reputation so justly merited."

GALVAÕ. Reflexões sobre o Correio Brasiliense. *Lisboa: Na Imp. Regia.* 1809. 8vo. 26471

GALVESTON. Articles of Association of the City of Galveston. *Washington: Printed by J. & G. S. Gideon.* 1846. 8vo, pp. 20. BA. + *New York.* 1847. BA. 26472

First Semi-Annual Report of the Public Schools of Galveston. ... *Galveston: News Office.* 1847. 8vo, pp. 34. H. 26473

Address to the Reader of the Documents Relating to the Galveston Bay & Texas Land Company, which are contained in the Appendix. *New-York: Printed by G. F. Hopkins & Son.* 1831. 8vo, pp. 37, (1), 28. B., H. 26474

GALVEZ. Diario de las operaciones contra la plaza de Panzacola concluida por las armas de S. M. C. baxo las ordenes del Mariscal de campo D. Bernardo de Galvez. [n. p. n. d.] 4to, pp. 48. 26475

"Apparently printed at Madrid about 1781." — RICH.

GALVEZ. Reglamento concerniente al Teatro de Mexico y la representacion de comedias etc. *Mexico.* 1786. Folio, pp. 28.

GALVEZ (B.) Demonstracion y Lamentable muerte del Conde de Galvez. [In Verse.] 1787. 4to. 26477

On the death of Bernardo de Galvez, Governor of Louisiana and Florida. *See* San Salvador.

GALVEZ. Poema Epico la Rendicion de Panzacola y conquista de la Florida Occidental, por el Exmo. Señor Conde de Galvez. *Mexico.* 1785. 4to. 26478

GALVEZ (Francisca de Paula de Perez). Representacion á la Camara de Diputados con motivo de los denuncios de vertientes y pozos de agua salada hechos en Haciendas de su pertenencia, y de la testamentaria de su hermano De Juan de Dios Perez Galvez. *Mexico.* 1851. 4to, pp. 68. 26479

GALVEZ (J. B.) Causas del atraso de dere chopenal relativamente al civil hasta el Siglo XVIII., por Don Jesus Benigno Galvez. *Habana.* 1864. 8vo, pp. 52. 26480

[GALVEZ (J. de).] Informe del Visitador General de Nueva España al ... Marques de Croix, Virrey, ... del mismo reyno. Sobre los motivos de la expedicion hecha en las provincias internas, causas que ha formado y Providencias que deja dadas para su pacificacion. [Colophon: *Mexico. Dec.* 25, 1767.] 4to, 1 l., pp. 149. H. 26481

"Signed 'Joseph de Galvez,' apparently a different person from the minister of the same name who was sent to Mexico a few years later, to settle a dispute between the Viceroy and the Audencia. The expedition to which the present work relates was undertaken to take preparatory measures for expelling the Jesuits." — RICH.

[GALVEZ.] Leyes de la recompilacion de Indias, cédulas reales, ordenanzas y otras soberanas declaraciones, que deben gobernar para el cumplimiento de lo que se dispone en los articulos de la Instruccion, que irán citados. 68 l., pp. 24.

[GALVEZ.] Ordenanza Real para el establecimiento é instruccion de Intendentes de exército y provincia en el virreinato de Buenos-Aires. Año de 1782. De orden de S. M. *Madrid: Imprenta Real.* [1782.] Folio, Arms of Spain, 1 l., 29 l., pp. 326. 26483

This and the former are signed "Josef de Galvez."

GALVEZ (M.) El Doctor Mariano Galvez, sobre la cuestion de Tehuantepec. *Mexico.* 1853. 8vo, pp. 55. 26484

Also: El Provincial del Carmen. *Mexico.* 1851. + [*Ibid.*] 1852.

GALWAY, *N. Y.* Confession of Faith of the Second Baptist Church of Galway Saratago, County, N. Y. *Albany: Joel Munsell.* 1848. 16mo, pp. 18. 26485

GAMA (A. de). *See* Leon y Gama (A. de).

GAMA (A. L.) Saggio dell' Astronomia, Cronologia e Mitologia degli Antichi Messicani. *Roma.* 1804. 8vo. Plates.

GAMA (José Basilio da). O Uraguay: Poema. *Lisboa: na Reg. Offic. Typ.* 1769. 8vo. 26487

GAMA (José Vicente da). Almanach civil, ecclesiastico, historico-administrativo da provincia de Moçambique, para o anno de 1859. *Moçambique: na Imp. Nac.* 1859. 8vo, pp. 199.

GAMA (J. Bern. Fern.) Memorias historicas da provincia de Pernambuco. *Pernamouco.* 1844–48. 4 vols., 8vo. 26489

GAMA (J. de S. da). Configuraçao e descripçao de todos os orgaos fundamentaes das principaes madeiras de cerne e brancas da Provincia do Rio de Janeiro e suas applicaçoes na engenharia, industria, medecina, e artes com umo tabella de pesos especificos. Por José de Saldanha da Gama Filho. *Rio de Janeiro.* 1865. Vol. I., 8vo, pp. 158; 11 Plates in 4to. 26490

GAMA (Manuel Jacinto Nogueira da). Memoria sobre a absoluta necessidade que ha de nitreiras nacionaes para a independencia e defesa dos estados: com a descripção da origem, estado e vantagens da real nitreira artificial de Braço de Prata. *Lisboa: na Imp. Regia.* 1803. 4to, pp. 73. 26491

GAMA (Nicolau Antonio Nogueira Valle da). Genealogia das familias Botelho, Arruda, Sampaio, Horta, Paes Leme, Gama e Villas-boas, até seus actuaes descendentes, etc. *Rio de Janeiro: Typ. Univ. de Laemmert.* 1859. 8vo, pp. 184. 26492

[GAMA E CASTRO (Josê de).] Memoria sobre a nobreza no Brasil, por un brasileiro. *Rio de Janeiro.* 1841. 8vo. 26493

GAMA LOBO (O. de). Direitos e Deveres dos Estrangeiros no Brasil. Pelo Bacharel Ovidio da Gama Lobo, Secretario do Governo da Provincia do Maranhão. *Maranhão.* 1868. 8vo, pp. 2, 252. 26494

GAMA LOBO. Indice alphabetico das leis, decretos e avisos relativos á incompatibilidade na accumulaçao dos cargos e empregos publicos por Ovidio da Gama Lobo. *Maranhão.* 1862. 8vo, pp. 96, 16. 26495

Gama Lobo. Os jesuitas perante a historia, por Ovidio da Gama Lobo. *Maranhão.* 1860. 8vo, pp. xiii, 271. 26496

Gama *or* Gamma. *See* Vasco de Gama.

Gamage (W.) Some Account of the Fever which existed in Boston ... 1817 and 1818. With ... Remarks on Typhus Fever. By W. Gamagé, Jr., M.D. ... *Boston: Printed by Wells and Lilly.* 1818. 8vo, pp. 86. B. 26497

Gamarra y Dávalos (J. B. Diaz de). Elogio Funebre del P. Luis Felipe Neri de Alfaro, Misionero Apostolico. *Mexico: J. de Jauregui.* 1776. 4to. 26498

Gamarra y Dávalos. Exemplar vida de la muy rev. madre sor Maria Josefa Sina de la santissima trinidad, fundadora del convento de la Purisima Concepcion, en la Ciudad de San Miguel de Allende, Obispado de Michoacan. *Mexico.* 1831. 4to, 4 l., pp. 102. 26499

Gambara (L.) Laurentii | Gambaræ | Brixiani | De Navigatione Christophori Co | lumbi libri quattuor. | ... | ... | *Romæ,* | *Apud Franciscum Zannettum.* | MDLXXXI. | 8vo, 8 l., pp. 112.

Gambara. De Navigatione Christophori Columbi, libri quattuor. Ad Ant. Perenottvm card. Granvellanvm. *Romæ: Typis Barth. Bonfadini, et Titi Diani.* 1583. 4to, 3 l., 63 l., 4–64 l.

The verso of the fifteenth leaf is occupied by a map of the discoveries of Columbus.

Gambara. De Navigatione Christophori Columbi libri quatuor accedit epitaphia Hippol. Capilupi in Chr. Columbum, editio copiosior, etc. *Romæ.* 1585. 18mo. + *Romæ.* 1683. 4to.

A Latin poem on the discovery of Cuba, etc.

Gambara. Poemata omnia in vnum collecta. *Romæ.* 1551. 8vo. + Poemata nunc primum impressa. *Romæ: Ant. Bladum.* 1555. 4to. + *Romæ: Zannettus.* 1581. 8vo. *Romæ: T. & P. Diani.* 1586. 18mo, 4 l., pp. 439. C. + *Antverpiæ.* 1669. Sm. 8vo. 26503

An interesting volume to the collector of early voyages, as it contains a long poem, in four books, on the "Voyage of Columbus and his Discovery of America. Gambara was one of the best poets of the sixteenth century. He studied at Rome, and wrote some eclogues, and other amatory poems, which, on taking priest's orders (about 1556), he suppressed and burnt.

Gambier (*Vice-Admiral*). A Narrative of Facts relative to the Conduct of Vice-Admiral Gambier, during his late Command in North America. Written by the Admiral himself. *London: M. Scott.* MDCCLXXXII. 8vo, pp. (4), 73. 26504

Gambier, *Ohio.* Interesting Report of the Rise and Progress of the Protestant Episcopal Church, Kenyon College, and the New Town of Gambier, in the Diocese of Ohio, ... 1827. 8vo, pp. 64. 26505

See also Kenyon College.

Gambino (P. J.) Piadoso Devocionario en honor del Sagrado Corazon de Jesus, por Teodoro de Almeida. Traducido al idioma mexicano, ... por D. Pedro J. Gambino. *Orizava: F. Mendarte.* 1839. 8vo, 4 l., pp. 128. 26506

Gamble (J. M.) The Memorial of Lieut. Colonel J. M. Gamble, of the United States Marine Corps, to Congress, 1828. *New York: Printed by Geo. F. Hopkins & Son.* 1828. 8vo, pp. 16.

The Gambler, or Memoirs of a British Officer, Distinguished in the War of the American Revolution. The Second Edition. *Washington.* 1802. 12mo, pp. 94. 26508

Gamboa (F. X. de). Comentarios a las Ordenanzas de minas dedicados al Catholico Rey nuestro Señor Don Carlos III. (Qui Dios garde.) Siempre magnanimo, siempre felix, siempre augusto. Por Don Francisco Xavier de Gamboa, Colegial de el Real, y mas antiguo de San Ildefonso de Mexico, etc. Con aprobacion y privilegio del Rey. *Madrid: En la Oficiana de Joachin Ibarra. Año de* MDCCLXI. Folio, 12 l., pp. 534. 3 folded Plates. 26509

"Livre intéressant et très estimé, qui traite aussi les mines de l'Amérique." — Andrade.

Gamboa. Commentaries on the Mining Ordinances of Spain; Translated from the Original Spanish by Richard Heathfield. *London.* 1830. 2 vols., rl. 8vo. Plates. C. 26510

Gamboa (J. L.) Lamentos Americanos por la sensible Muerte del D. Bernardo Galvez, por D. J. J. L. Xaso, Gamboa y Villavicenzio. 1786. 4to. 26511

Gamboa (P.) *See* Sarmiento de Gamboa (P.)

Gamboa (Ramon). Impugnacion al informe del General Santa-Anna, y constancias en que se apoyan las ampliaciones de la acusacion del Diputado Gamboa. *Mexico.* 1849. 8vo, pp. 71.

Gamboa. Informe que el General Santa-Anna dió por acuerdo de la seccion del gran Jurado sobre las acusaciones presentadas por el Diputado D. Ramon Gamboa. *Mexico.* 1849. pp. viii, 71, 184. 26513

[Gamboa.] Memoría económica de la municipalidad de Mexico. *Mexico.* 1830. 4to. 26514

Gamma. *See* Vasco de Gama.

Gammage (W. L.) The Camp, the Bivouac, and the Battle-Field. By W. L. Gammage, Surg'n, C. S. A. *Selma, Ala.* 12mo, pp. 184. 26515

This is the title to the cover; the title proper is much longer.

Gammell (W.) A History of American Baptist Missions in ... North America, under the Care of the American Baptist Missionary Union. By William Gammell, A.M. ... . Sixth Thousand. *Boston: Gould and Lincoln.* 1849. 12mo, pp. xii, 350. + Seventh Thousand. [*Ibid.*] 1850. 8vo. 26516

Gammell. Life of Roger Williams, Founder of the State of Rhode Island, with Portrait of Williams. By William Gammell, A.M. *Boston.* 1845. 12mo. + *Boston: Gould, Kendall & Lincoln.* 1850. 12mo, pp. ix, 221. + *Boston: Little, Brown & Co.* 1854. 16mo, pp. ix, 221. 26517

Forms Vol. XIV. of Sparks' "American Biography." Also: Address delivered before the Rhode-Island Historical Society, at the opening of their Cabinet ... Nov. 20, 1844. ... *Providence: B. Cranston and Company.* 1844. 8vo, pp. 30. B., BA., H., M., S. — ... A Sermon ... at Medfield, ... Feb. 6, 1820. Occasioned by the Death of Mrs. Rebecca Balch ... . *Dedham: Printed by H. & W. H. Mann.* 1820. 8vo, pp. 24. BA. — Sketch of the Educational and other Benefactions, of the Late Hon. Nicholas Brown. ... [*Providence.*] 1857. 8vo, pp. 26. Portrait. B., H.

Gamond (T.), *and* Belly (F.) Carte d'étude pour le tracé et le profil du canal de Nicaragua, par M. Thomé de Gamond, ingénieur civil; précédée de documents publiés sur cette question par M. Félix Belly. *Paris: Dalmont et Dunod.* 1858. 4to, pp. 91 or 90. Map. C. 26518

Gan Eden! 1854. *See* [Hurlbut (W. H.)]

Gándara (M. M.) Esposicion que eleva al supremo gobierno D. Bartolomé E. Almada, Apoderado por Sonora, sobre los ultimos acontecimientos de aquel Estado, a consecuencia de la revolucion promovida por D. Manuel Maria Gándara. *Mexico.* 1856. 8vo, pp. 80. 26519

Gándara. Exposicion al supremo Gobierno sobre su conducta politica y demás sucesos antiguos y recientes acaecidos en aquel Departamento. *Mexico.* 1842. 8vo. 26520

Gándara. Manifestacion que hace al gefe supremo de la republica, D. Manuel Maria Gándara, en la que espresa las causas que le obligaron a salir del estado de Sonora y los de la revolucion de dicho estado. *Mexico.* 1857. 8vo, pp. 27, 21, 42.

Gándara (S. de la). Carta, sobre la Vida y Muerte de el Padre Doctor Francisco Xavier Lazcano, Dirige á los Padres de la Compania de Jesus de la Provincia de Mexico el P. Salvador de la Gándara. *Mexico: [En el Rl., y mas antiguo Colegio de S. Ildefonso].* 1763. 8vo, pp. 130. 26522

Gandavo *See* Magalhaes de Gandavo (Pero de).

Gandobruganus (L.) *See* Apollonius, Vol. I., Nos. 1761, 2.

Gane (William). Memoirs of Don Pedro, Ex-Emperor of Brazil. 26523

Title from Morgan's "Bibliotheca Canadensis."

Ganilh (A.) Odes, and Fugitive Poetry. By Rev. Anthony Ganilh. *Boston: W. Smith.* 1830. 12mo, pp. 36. C. 26524

Gannet (D.) An Address ... at the Federal-Street Theatre, Boston, ... March 22, 1802 ... By Mrs. Deborah Gannet, the American Heroine, who served Three Years with Reputation ... in the Late American Army. ... *Dedham: Mrs. Gannet.* 1802. 8vo, pp. 29. B. 26525

Gannett (C.) Sketch of the Life and Character of Caleb Gannett, Esq. [n. p. n. d.] 8vo, pp. 9. BA. 26526

Gannett (E. S.) The Atlantic Telegraph: a Discourse ... August 8, 1858. By Ezra S. Gannett. ... *Boston: Crosby, Nichols, and Company.* 1858. 8vo, pp. 19. B. 26527

Gannett. A Discourse, occasioned by the Death of the Hon. Josiah Quincey, delivered in ... Boston, ... July 10, 1864, By Ezra S. Gannett. *Boston: Printed by John Wilson and Son.* 1864. 8vo, pp. 37. B., BA., H. 26528

Gannett. "A Memorial of the Federal-Street Meeting-House." A Discourse ... March 13, 1859, By Rev. Ezra S. Gannett; and Addresses ... . With an Appendix. March 13, 1859. *Boston: Crosby, Nichols, Lee, and Co.* 1860. 8vo, pp. 89.

Gannett. Peace—not War. A Sermon Preached in the Federal Street Meeting-house, December 14, 1845. By Ezra S. Gannett. ... *Boston: Joseph Dowe.* 1845. 8vo, pp. 24. B.

Gannett. Relation of the North to Slavery. A Discourse preached ... in Boston, ... June 11, 1854. By Ezra S. Gannett, ... *Boston: Crosby, Nichols & Company.* M DCCC LIV. 8vo, pp. 23. B., BA., H., M. 26531

For a reply, *see* [Curtis], Vol. V., No. 10842.

Gannett. The Religion of Politics. A Sermon delivered before ... The Legislature of Massachusetts, at the Annual Election, January 5, 1842. By Ezra S. Gannett, ... *Boston: Dutton and Wentworth, Printers to the State.* 1842. 8vo, pp. 46.

Gannett. A Sermon ... in the Arlington-Street Church, Boston, ... July 3, 1864, at the Close of the Fortieth Year of his Ministry. By Ezra S. Gannett. *Boston: Printed by John Wilson and Son.* 1864. 8vo, pp. 22. B., H. 26533

Gannett. The State of the Country: A Discourse preached ... in Boston, ... June 8, 1856. By Ezra S. Gannett. ... *Boston: Crosby, Nichols, and Company.* 1856. 8vo, pp. 20. B.

Gannett. Thanksgiving for the Union. A Discourse delivered in the Federal-Street Meeting-House in Boston, on Thanksgiving-Day, November 28, 1850. By Ezra S. Gannett. ... *Boston: Wm. Crosby and H. P. Nichols.* 1850. 8vo, pp. 22.

Gannett. Services in Memory of Rev. Ezra Stiles Gannett, D.D. Late Pastor of the Arlington-Street Church. *Boston: John Wilson and Son.* 1871. 8vo, pp. 71. B., H. 26536

Also: An Address ... on the Celebration of the Fiftieth Anniversary of the Sunday School Institution ... September 14, 1831. ... *Boston.* 1831. 12mo, pp. 42. B., BA., H., W. — An Address ... at the Funeral of Rev. William Ellery Channing, D.D. October 7, 1842. *Boston: William Crosby and Company.* 1842. 8vo, pp. 41. + *Boston: James Munroe & Co.* 1843. 12mo, pp. 30. — An Address ... at the Fourth Convention of the Graduates and Members of the West-Newton State Normal School, July 24, 1850. ... . *Boston: Charles C. P. Moody.* 1850. 8vo, pp. 20. BA., H. — An Address delivered at the Semi-Centennial Celebration of the Cambridge Divinity School, July 17, 1867. ... *Boston: Leonard C. Bowles.* 1867. 8vo, pp. 31. B., H. — The Arrival of the Britannia. A Sermon delivered ... in Boston, July 19, 1840. ... *Boston: Joseph Dowe.* 1840. 8vo, pp. 23. B., BA., M. — A Devoted Ministry. A Sermon delivered at the Ordination of Rev. James I. T. Coolidge, ... Boston, February 9, 1842. ... *Boston: Benjamin H. Greene.* MDCCCXLII. 8vo, pp. 53. BA. — ... A Discourse ... at the Ordination of Rev. Artemas B. Muzzey, ... in Framingham, June 10, 1830. ... *Boston: Gray and Brown.* 1830. 8vo, pp. 43. B., H. — A Discourse ... on ... Thanksgiving Day, December 2, 1830. ... *Boston.* 1830. 8vo, pp. 24. BA. — A Discourse ... at the Dedication of the Meeting-House erected by the

Independent Congregational Society in Ipswich, October 23, 1833. ... *Boston: Leonard C. Bowles.* 1833. 8vo, pp. 24. B. — ... A Discourse ... at the Installation of the Rev. John Parkman, ... at Dover, N. H., April 22, 1840. ... *Boston: William Crosby and Company.* 1840. 8vo, pp. 56. B., BA. — ... A Discourse ... Fast-Day, April 8, 1852 ... . *Boston: Printed by Dutton & Wentworth.* 12mo, pp. 16. H. — A Discourse, ... at the Funeral of William B. O. Peabody, D.D., in Springfield, June 1, 1847. ... *Springfield: Samuel Bowles.* 1847. 8vo, pp. 34. B. — A Discourse, ... March 20, 1854, at the Funeral of the late Rev. Alexander Young, D.D. ... Boston, 1854. ... *Boston: Crosby, Nichols, and Company.* 1854. 8vo, pp. 24. B., BA., S. — ... A Discourse ... at the Dedication of the Church on Arlington Street, Boston, December 11, 1861. ... *Boston: Crosby and Nichols.* 1862. 8vo, pp. 83. BA. — A Discourse delivered in ... Dedham, ... July 31, 1864, after the Death of Alvan Lamson, D.D. ... *Boston: Printed by John Wilson and Son.* 1864. 8vo, pp. 28. BA. — Dissipation; A Sermon ... on the Federal-Street Meeting-House ... May 17, 1857. ... *Boston: Crosby, Nichols, and Company.* 1857. 18mo, pp. 24. B., H. — A Discourse ... at the Installation of Rev. Alfred P. Putnam ... in Brooklyn, N. Y., September 28, 1864. ... *New York: E. S. Dodge & Co.* 1864. 8vo, pp. 28. BA., H. — A Discourse ... Dec. 25, 1870, the Sunday succeeding the Death of Robert B. Storer. ... *Cambridge: John Wilson and Son.* 1871. 8vo, pp. 22. H. — A Discourse delivered at the Dedication of the Unitarian Church, Montreal, ... May 11, 1845. ... *Boston: Wm. Crosby & H. P. Nichols.* [1845.] 8vo, pp. 40. BA. + Second Edition. *Boston.* [1845.] 8vo, pp. 36. — A Good Old Age. A Sermon occasioned by the Death of Hon. John Davis, LL.D., and preached in Boston, January 24, 1847. *Boston: Wm. Crosby and H. P. Nichols.* 1847. 8vo, pp. 42. B., BA. — National Commercial Convention. A Discourse ... in Boston ... Feb. 16, 1868. ... *Boston: John Wilson and Son.* 1868. 8vo, pp. 16. BA., H. — The Object, Subjects, and Methods of the Ministry at Large. A Discourse, delivered before the Benevolent Fraternity of Churches ... April 9, 1848. ... *Boston: Printed by John Wilson.* 1848. 8vo, pp. 36. B., BA., H., M. — Our Help is in God. A Discourse, delivered ... in Boston ... February 24, 1850. ... *Boston: Wm. Crosby and H. P. Nichols.* 1850. 8vo, pp. 19. B., BA., H. — The Prince's Visit: A Discourse ... October 21, 1860. ... *Boston: Crosby, Nichols, Lee and Company.* 1860. 8vo, pp. 19. BA., H. — Repentance amidst Deliverance: and Mobs. Two Discourses preached ... July 12 and July 19, 1863. ... *Boston: Crosby & Nichols.* 1863. 8vo, pp. 31. B., BA., H. — A Sermon delivered ... in Boston, October 9, 1842, the Sunday after the Death of Rev. William Ellery Channing, D.D. ... *Boston: William Crosby and Company.* 1842. 8vo, pp. 32. B., BA., H. — ... A Sermon ... October 17, 1847, After the Death of Hon. Artemas Ward, LL.D. ... *Boston: Wm. Crosby and H. P. Nichols.* 1847. 8vo, pp. 24. B., BA., H. — A Sermon preached before the Fatherless and Widows' Society ... October 25, 1849. ... . *Boston: Ticknor, Reed, and Fields.* MDCCCXLIX. 8vo, pp. 28. B., BA., H. — ... A Sermon ... May 2, 1852, after the Death of Thomas Tarbell, Esq. ... *Boston: Printed by John Wilson & Son.* 1852. 8vo, pp. 16. BA. — A Sermon ... in Baltimore ... September 18, 1859, after the Death of Rev. George W. Burnap, D.D. ... *Boston: Crosby, Nichols, and Company.* 1859. 8vo, pp. 32. BA., H. — ... A Sermon ... after the Death of Marshall Sears Perry, M.D. ... *Boston: Crosby, Nichols, and Company* 1859. 8vo, pp. 20. B., BA. — ... A Sermon ... at the Ordination of John C. Kimball ... at Beverly, Mass., ... Dec. 29, 1859. *Boston: Printed by John Wilson and Son.* 1860. 8vo, pp. 44. BA. — ... A Sermon ... July 21, 1861 ... after the Funeral of the late Hon. Nathan Appleton, of Boston. ... *Boston: J. H. Eastburn's Press.* 1861. 8vo, pp. 18. B. — A Sermon ... in the Arlington-Street Church, November 29, 1863, after the Death of Mrs. Susan L. Torrey. ... *Boston.* 1864. 12mo, pp. 20. BA., H. — Services at the Ordination of Mr. James de Normandie, in Portsmouth, N. H., October 1, 1862. Sermon by Rev. Ezra S. Gannett. ... . *Boston: Walker, Wise, and Company.* 1862. 8vo, pp. 52. BA. — The Temperance Cause. A Discourse delivered before the Boston Young Men's Total Abstinence Society, ... November 8, 1846. ... *Boston: Wm. Crosby and H. P. Nichols.* 1846. 8vo, pp. 23.

B., BA. + Third Edition. [*Ibid.*] 1846. 8vo. — Unitarianism not a Negative System. A Discourse ... at the Dedication of the Meeting-House ... in Ipswich, October 23, 1833. *Boston: Leonard C. Bowles.* 1833. 8vo, pp. 24. BA. — The Useful Man. A Sermon delivered at the Funeral of Hon. Charles Paine, at Northfield, Vt., Sept. 1, 1853. ... *Northfield: Printed by Woodworth & Gould.* 1853. 8vo, pp. 63. B., BA., H.

Gannett (E. S.), *and* Heywood (J. H.) Discourses in Memory of Robert Waterston. By Rev. E. S. Gannett, D.D. ... and by the Rev. John H. Heywood ... Sept. 12, 1869. ... *Boston.* 1869. 8vo, pp. 72, (1). BA., H. 26537

Gano (J.) Biographical Memoirs of the late John Gano, of Frankfort, (Kentucky) formerly of the City of New-York. Written principally by himself. *New York: John Tiebout.* 1806. + *New York: Southwick & Hardcastle.* 1806. 16mo, pp. 151.

Contains many incidents of Revolutionary history.

Gano (S.) A Sermon on the Death of General George Washington; delivered Lord's Day, January 5, 1800, before the Baptist Society in Providence. By Stephen Gano, Pastor of the Baptist Church and Congregation. *Providence: Printed by John Carter, Jun.* 1800. 8vo, pp. 20. 26539

Also: ... A Sermon, occasioned by the Death of the Rev. Joseph Snow, ... Providence, Rhode-Island, ... preached ... April 17, 1803. ... *Providence: Printed by J. Carter.* 1803. 8vo, pp. 24. B.

Gans (G. W.) ... Nov. 19, 1861. The War for the Union, or the Rights of the Republic. [n. p. n. d.] 8vo, pp. 7. H.

Gans (S.) Sermon at the Ordination of Joshua Bradley, at Newport, R. I. May 13, 1801. By Stephen Gans. 1801. 8vo.

Ganse (H. D.) Bible Slaveholding not Sinful. By H. D. Ganse. *New York.* 1856. 8vo. 26542

Gantt (E. W.) Address of Brig.-Gen. E. W. Gantt, C. S. A. First Published Oct. 7, 1860, at Little Rock, Arkansas. *Union League of Philadelphia, No.* 36. [n. d.] 8vo, pp. 29. 26543

Gaona (Joan de). Colloqvios de-|la paz, y tranquilidad Chri-|stiana, en lengua|Mexicana.|Con Licencia, y|Priuilegio.| *En Mexico: Casa ẽ d Pedro Ocharte.* M.D.LXXXII. 16mo, pp. (30), Text, 121 leaves. 26544

Garangula, the Ongua-honwa Chief: A Tale of Indian Life among the Mohawks and Onondagas, Two Hundred Years Ago. By a Citizen of Milwaukee. *Milwaukee: Strickland & Co.* 1857. 8vo, pp. 160. BA., H., S. 26545

"A romance, without value."—T. W. Field.

Garay (J. de). An Account of the Isthmus of Tehuantepec in the Republic of Mexico; with Proposals for Establishing a Communication between the Atlantic and Pacific Oceans, based upon the Surveys and Reports of a Scientific Commission, Appointed by the Projector, Don José de Garay. *London: J. D. Smith and Co.* 1846. 8vo, pp. 128. 2 Plans of Mexico. C., P.

Also published at the same time in Spanish.

[Garay.] Memoria instructiva de los derechos y justas causas que tiene el gobierno de los Estados-Unidos Mexicanos, para no reconocer ni la subsistencia del privilegio concedido a Don José Garay para abrir una via de Comunicacion entre los Oceanos Atlantico y Pacifico por el Istmo de Tehuantepec, ni la legitimidad de la cesion que a quel hizo del mismo privilegio a ciudadanos de los Estados-Unidos de la America del Norte. La publica el ministro de relaciones. *Mexico.* 1852. 8vo, pp. 39.

Also in English, with the following title:

[Garay.] A Memorial, setting forth the Rights and just Reasons which the Government of the United States of Mexico has, for not recognising the validity of the privilege granted to D. José Garay, for opening a way of Communication between the Atlantic and Pacific Oceans, by the Isthmus of Tehuantepec ... *Nueva York: W. G. Stewart.* 1852. 8vo, pp. iv, 39.

Garay. Survey of the Isthmus of Tehuantepec, Executed in the Years 1842 and 1843, with the Intent of Establishing a Communication between the Atlantic and Pacific Oceans, and under the Superintendence of a Scientific Commission appointed by the Projector, Don José De Garay. *London: Ackermann and Co.* 1844. 8vo, pp. (3), 188. 5 Maps. BA. 26549

Also in Spanish, as below:

Garay. Reconocimiento del Istmo de Tehuantepec, practicado en los años 1842 y 1843, con el objeto de una comunicacion oceánica, por la comision científica que nombró al efecto el empresario D. José de Garay. *Mexico.* 1844. Folio, pp. 40. Map. 26550

Also: Dictamen de la comision especial de la Camara de Diputados del Congreso General, sobre el privilegio concedido á D. José Garay, para la apertura de una via de comunicacion inter-oceanica por el istmo de Tehuantepec. *Mexico.* 1851. 4to, pp. 46. — Dictamen de la comision especial de Tehuantepec del Senado, encargada de ecsaminar las varias resoluciones dictadas con motivo del privilegio concedido á D. José Garay. *Mexico.* 1851. 4to, pp. 51. — Dictamen de la comision especial sobre el mismo asunto. *Mexico.* 1852. 4to, pp. 18. — Fundacion de la Ciudad de Buenos Aires, por D. Juan de Garay, con otros documentos de aquella epoca. *Buenos Aires.* 1836. Folio, pp. 30.

Garces y Eguia (J.) ... Beneficio de ... oro y plata por fundicion y amalgamacion ... . Don Joseph Garces y Eguia ... . *Mexico: En la oficina de D. Mariano de Zúñiga y Ontiveros.* 1802. Sm. 4to, 5 l., pp. 168. B. 26551

Garcia ab Horto. *See* Orto (G. de).

Garcia (Andres). Sermon en Honras del D. Juan Ant. de Lardizabal. *En la Puebla.* 1733. 8vo. 26552

Garcia de Cespedes. *See* Cespedes (A. G. de), Vol. III.

Garcia de Palacio (Diego). *See* Palacios (D. G. de).

Garcia (P. A. X.) Carta edificativa, en que el P. Andres Xavier Garcia, Proposito de la Cava professa de la Sagrada Compañia de Jesus, participa a todos los Superiores, y Colegios de ella, la fervorosa vida, y religiosas virtudes del P. Martin Larrainzar. *Mexico.* 1763. 4to, pp. 24. 26553

Garcia de Cubas (Antonio). Atlas, Geográphico, Estadístico é Historico de la Republica Mexicana. *Mexico: imprenta de José M. Lara.* 1858. Imp. folio. 33 Maps. 26554

Three hundred copies printed.

Garcia y Cubas. Compendio de Geographia de la Republica Mexicana. Arreglado en Cincuenta y cinco lecciones para uso de los establecimientos de Instruccion publica, por Antonio Garcia y Cubas. *Mexico.* 1861. 12mo, pp. 210.

Garcia y Cubas. Memoria para servir á la carta general de la república mexicana. *Méxixo: Andrade y Escalante.* 1861. 8vo, pp 106. Map. C. 26556

Also: Curso elemental de Geografia universal ... *Mexico.* 1870. 8vo, pp. xiv, 466. — Noticias geograficas y estadisticas de la republica Mexicana. *Mexico.* 1857. 4to, pp. 27.

Garcia (A. J.) Kalendario Manual y Guia de Forasteros, en Santa Fé de Bogotà, capital del Nuevo Reyno de Granada para el año 1806. Compuesto de orden del superior gobierno por el Dr. D. Ant. Jos. Garcia de la Guardia, &c. *Santa Fe.* 1806. 16mo. H. 26557

Garcia y Garcia (A.) Instructions nautiques sur la côte du Pérou; d'après Aurelio Garcia y Garcia ... avec additions dues à Fitz-Roy, Lartigue ... . *Paris: Bossange.* 1872. 8vo, pp. vii, 211. 26558

Garcia y Garcia (A.) Peruvian Coast Pilot. By Captain Aurelio Garcia y Garcia. Translated from the Spanish. *New York: E. & G. W. Blunt.* 1866. 8vo, 1 l., pp. 112. Map.

Garcia (B.) Manual para Administrar los Santos Sacramentos de Penitencia, Eucharistia, Extrema-Uncion y Matrimonio: dar Gracias despues de Comulgar, y Ayudar a Bien Morir á los Indios de las Naciones: Pajalates, Orejones, Pacaos, Pacóas, Tilijayas, Alasapas, Pausanes, y otras muchas diferentes que se hallen en las Missiones del Rio de San Antonio, y Rio Grande, pertenecientes à el Colegio de la Santissima Cruz de la Ciudad de Queretaro como son ... Compuesto por el P. Fr. Bartholomé Garcia ... . [*Mexico?*] *Impresso con las Licencias.* 1760. 4to, 8 l., pp. 88. H. 26560

I have seen it quoted with the imprint, *Mexico: herederos de Doña Maria de Rivera.* 1760. 4to, 8 l., pp. 88. *See* Icazbalceta, No 32, for the title at greater length.

Garcia Yannez (Christopher). Acoluthia, seu Argumentum operis, hoc est cohærens, et apta sedes clavis Scientiæ, et Potestatis, Juris naturalis, Divini, Gentium, Pontificii, Cæsarei, Hispanici, ac Americi, seu novi Orbis. 26561

The Backers give no imprint. The author died in 1646.

Garcia (Domingo). Demonstracion generosa de la mas agradecida piedad. Sermon Panegyrico en las magnificas Honras celebro à la memoria del D. Juan Antonio de Bizarron y Egmarreta, Virrey de la Nueva España. *Sevilla.* 1749. 4to. 26562

[Garcia (E.)] Lucia. Novela, sacada de la Historia Argentina, por Daniel. *Buenos Aires.* 1860. 4to, pp. 110.

The name of the writer, disguised under the *pseudonym* of Daniel, is Eduarda Garcia, a niece of the notorious Juan Manoel de Rosas. Her novels have met with great applause in her native country.

Garcia (E.), *Editor.* Elogia Selecta é varijs, quæ Mexicearum Scholarum more ab alumnis Academiæ S. Philippinerij elaborata sunt, præfixaque thesibus propugnatis. Olim sparsim edita, collecta modò, notisque aucta ab ipsius academiæ Præside D. Emmanuele Garcia de Arellano, etc. *Mexici: ex nova Typographiâ.* MDCCLV. 4to, 11 l., pp. 91. 26564

Garcia (Fr.) Vida y Martyrio de el Ven. Padre Diego Lvis de Sanvitores de la Compañia de Jesus. Primer Apostol de las Islas Marianas, y Sucessos de estas Islas, &c. *Madrid.* 1683. 4to. 26565

Includes much respecting Central America, Guatemala, etc.

Garcia (G.) Origen de los Indios del Nuevo Mundo, e Indias Occidentales. Averiguado con discurso de opiniones, por el Padre Presentado Fr. Gregorio Garcia, ... Tratanse en este libro varias cosas y puntos curiosos tocantes à diversas ciencias y facultades con que se hace varia historia, de mucho gusto para el ingenio y entendimiento de hombres agudos y curiosos. *Valencia: Pedro Patricio Mey.* 1607. Sm. 8vo, 14 l., pp 535. C.

First edition, of great rarity. It has not been translated into any other language. The first license to print (2 pages) is in the Valencia dialect. *See* Ternaux, No. 303.

Garcia (G.) Origen de los Indios de el Nuevo Mundo, e Indias Occidentales, averiguado con discurso de opiniones por el Padre Presentado Fr. Gregorio Garcia, de la Orden de Predicadores. Tratanse en este Libro varias cosas, y puntos curiosos, tocantes à diversas Ciencias, i Facultades, con que se hace varia Historia, de mucho gusto para el Ingenio, i Entendimiento de Hombres agudos, i curiosos. Segunda Impresion. Enmendada, y añadida de algunas opiniones, ò cosas notables, en maior prueba de lo que contiene, con Tres Tablas mui puntuales de los Capitulos, de las Materias, y Autores, que las tratan. Dirigido al Angelico Doct. Sto. Tomas de Aquino. Con Privilegio Real. *En Madrid: En la Imprenta de Francisco Martinez Abad. Año de* 1729. Folio, 15 l., pp. 336, Tabla, 40 l. Portrait of St. Thomas. B., BA., C., H., P. 26567

This second edition has many notes and additions by the editor, And. Gonzalez de Garcia. Clavigero pronounces it "a work of vast erudition, but almost totally useless, as it gives little or no assistance in discovering truth; the foundation for the opinions which he maintains concerning the origin of the Americans are, for the most part, weak conjectures founded on the resemblance of some of their customs and words, and those of other nations."—*History of Mexico*, Vol. I., p. xxv. "All that has ever been imagined as to the origin of the Americans, and the manner in which this New World was peopled, is gathered here, and set forth with endless, but not always necessary erudition."—Charlevoix's *New France*, Vol. I. The fifth book contains the various native accounts of the origin of the Indians. The others comprise the experience of Garcia during many years sojourn in America, a summary of the various opinions of others, and his own deductions. Barcia's additions are considerable. This edition forms part of Barcia's collection, and some copies are printed on large paper.

Garcia. Predicacion del Evangelio en el Nvevo Mvndo, viuiẽdo los Apostoles, por Gregorio Garcia. *Imp. en Baeça por Pedro de la Cuesta.* 1625. Sm. 8vo. 26568

For an account of the rarity of this work, *see* Lord Kingsborough's "Mexican Antiquities," Vol. III., Suppl. Extracts, p. 13. Sold at Puttick's (No. 425), in 1860, for £4 15s. Ternaux, No. 502, gives the date 1628.

Garcia. Solemnes Exêquias del D. Motias de Galvez Garcia, Madrid y Cabrera, celebradas en la Santa Iglesia Catedral de

la Imperial Corte Mexicana 4 de Marzo de 1783. *Mexico.* 1785. 4to. 26569

Garcia de Arboleya (Dn José G.) Manual de la Isla de Cuba. Compendio de su historia, geografia, estadística y administracion. *Habana: imprenta del Tiempo.* 1859. 8vo, pp. 418. 5 Plans and 32 Plates. 26570

Garcia de Concepcion (Joseph). Historia Bethlehemitica. Vida exemplar y admirable del venerable siervo de Dios, y Padre de San Joseph Betancvr, fvndador de el regvlar instituto de Bethlehen en las Indias Occidentales; frvtos singvlares de sv fecvndo espiritv, y successos varios de esta religion. ... *En Sevilla: por Jvan de la Pverta.* 1723. Folio, 18 l., pp. 216. Plate, "Christi Nativitatis." 26571

In the same volume are the following: Libro Segundo. Vida del Rmo P. Fr. Rodrigo de la Cruz, ... pp. 203. Libro Tercero. Continvase de los successos de la Religion Bethlehemitica hasta la muerta de el Rmo P. Fr. Rodrigo de la Cruz. pp. 173. Libro Quarto. ... Vidas y Virtudes de algvnos Varones, que floricieron en el, institvto Bethlehemitico, ... pp. 39, indice, 15 l. "Bethlehemite Brothers" was the name of an order of monks at Cambridge, England, in the thirteenth century; also of an order founded in Guatemala in 1673, of which latter the above is a history.

Garcia del Rio (J.) Documentos relativos a la deneyacion de pasaporte para Mejico a J. G. del Rio. *New York.* 1828. 8vo. BM. 26572

Garcia de la Vega (Jos. Ant.) El gran piscator de la Nueva-España. Explicacion del eclypse de Sol, y sus efectos, que será el dia 25. de Agosto de este presente año de 1756. [*Mexico.* 1756.] 4to, 2 l. 26573

Garcia y Garcia (José Ant.) Relaciones de los vireyes del Nuevo Reino de Granada, ahora Estados Unidos de Venezuela, Estados Unidos de Colombía y Ecuador, compiladas y publicadas por el Sr. Dr. D. J. A. García y Garcia. *Nueva York: [Hallet and Brown.]* 1869. 8vo, pp. xx, 705. 26574

Garcia y Garcia. Un viaje del Atlántico á Bogotá por José Antonio Garcia y Garcia. *Bogotá.* 1863. 18mo, pp. xvi, 60.

Garcia (José Gabriel). Compendio de la historia de Santo Domingo, arreglada para el uso de las escuelas de la republica Dominicana. *Santo Domingo: Garcio Hermanos.* 1868. 18mo, pp. 300, ix, 1 l. C. 26576

Garcia de Torres (J. J.) Vindicacion del Clero Mexicano vulnerado en los Anotaciones que publicó el M. R. P. Fr. José Joaquin Oyarzabal contra la representacion que el mismo Clero dirigió al Illmo. y Venerable Cabildo Sede-vacante promoviendo la defensa de su immunidad personal, formola el Dr. y Mtro. Don Joseph Julio Garcia de Torres. *Mexico.* 1812. 4to, pp. 18.—El Vindicador del Clero Mexicano, a su antagonista. *Mexico.* 1812. 4to, pp. 18. 26577

Also: Prosperidades de la Union y Desastres del Vico Opuesto, Impresas de Orden de este Superior Gobierno. *Mexico.* 1810. — Manifesto del Ilustre de la Real y Pontificia Universidad de Mexico. *Mexico.* 1810. — Elogio Historico del S. D. J. A. del Castillo y Llata, por D. Ant. Perez Velasco. *Mexico.* 1818.

Garcia Barreras (D. Juan). Oracion funebre del D. A. M. Bucareli. *Havana.* [1779.] 4to. 26578

Garcia (J.) Justification de la conducta publica seguida por D. Juan Garcia del Rio i D. Diego Paroissien ex ministros Plenip. del Gobierno del Peru cerca de las Cortes de Europa. 1825. 8vo. 26579

Garcia (J. M.) Oracion funebre en las sol. exequias que hizo la S. iglesia catedr. de Valladolid de Michoacan por el Señ. Don Carlos IV. *Valladolid.* 1819. 4to, 19 l. 26580

Garcia de Prado (Joseph). Compendio General de las Contribuciones, que en particular ocasionan las Mercaderias ... que se trafican entre España, y la America ... como en la Real Aduana de Cadiz ... . *Cadiz.* 1745. 4to, pp. 59. H. 26581

Garcia (Juan de la Cruz). La Seudo-Defensa que el Señor Virgil hace de los Gobiernos refutada por el Misma. *Lima.* 1866. 4to. 26582

Garcia y Reveron (Luis Felipe). Noticia biográfica del Doctor y General Gonzalo Cárdenas. *Carácas.* 1869. 4to, pp. vi, 46. Portrait. 26583

Garcia (M.) Reflecsiones sobre el Artículo primero del decreto emitido por la Asamblea de Guatemala, en viente de Julio de 1826. *Guatemala.* 1826. 26584

Garcia de Sena (Manuel). Historia Concisa de los Estados Unidos. *Philadelphia.* 1812. 8vo. 26585

Garcia (M. R.) Estudios sobre la aplicacion de la justicia federal Norte-Americana a la orginizacion constitucional Argentina por Manuel Rafael Garcia. 1863. 4to, pp. 104. 26586

Garcia (M.) Por el Maestro Martin Garcia de Gastizabal, Chantre desta santa Iglesia Catedral de Guatemala, Prouisor, y Vicario General de todo su Obispado, por la Sedeuacante. Con el Señor Obispo de Ariquipa don Agustin de Vgarte y Sarabia. *Año de* 1641. Folio, 12 l. 26587

Garcia (Pablo). Manifiesto á sus conciudadanos, refiriendo los motivos que le obligaron á separarse de la Legislatura del Estado. *Campeche.* 1857. 4to, pp. 15. 26588

Garcia (P. A.) Diario de la Expedicion de 1822 a los campos del sud de Buenos-Aires, desde Moron hasta la Sierra de la Ventana, ... D. Pedro Andres Garcia. Con las observaciones, descripciones y demas trabajos cientificos, egecutados por el oficial de Ingenieros de Jose Maria de los Reyes. *Buenos-Aires. Imprenta del Estada.* 1836. Folio, pp. (1), vi, 3–178, iii. H.

Garcia. Diario de un viage a Salinas Grandes, en los campos del Sud de Buenos-Aires, por Pedro Andrés Garcia. *Buenos-Aires.* 1836. 4to, pp. xxii, 72. C. 26590

Garcia (P. F.) Istoria della Conversione alla nostra Santa Fede dell' isole Mariane dette prima de' Ladroni, nella vita, Predicatione, e morte gloriosa per Christo del Ven. P. Diego Lerigi di Sanvitores. *Napoli.* 1686. 4to. 26591

Contains some curious particulars of Mexico, which was visited by the Holy Father on his way to the Ladrones.

Garcia Despones *and* Kern. Representacion elevada al Soberano Congreso, por los Sres. Garcia Despones y Kern. Sobre que les concedan los medios que proponen para el pago de la deuda que les reconoce el gobierno. *Mexico.* 1852. 8vo, pp. 8. 26592

Garcia (J. M. N.) Nova forma de apreciar os ferimentos do peito com offensa duvidosa das entranhas: Memoria extrahida da "Gazeta dos Tribunæs" e dedicada ao ill.mo sr. José Mauricio Nunes Garcia, etc., por um Advogado da Justica. *Rio de Janeiro: Typ. Imparcial de Paula Brito.* 1847. 8vo, pp. 117.

Garcilasso de la Vega. *See* Vega (Garcilasso de la).

Garden (A.) A Brief Account of the Deluded Dutartres; extracted From a Sermon, Preached by the Rev. Mr. Alexander Garden, A.M. at Charlestown, in South Carolina. *New-Haven: James Parker and Company.* 1762. 8vo, pp. 6. 26594

Garden. Regeneration and the Testimony of the Spirit. Being the Substance of Two Sermons Lately preached in the Parish Church of St. Philip Charles-Town, in South-Carolina. Occasioned by some erroneous Notions of certain Men who call themselves Methodists. By Alexander Garden, M.A. Rector of the said Parish. *South-Carolina, Charles-Town: Printed by Peter Timothy.* 1740. 12mo, pp. (2), iii, 33. + *Boston.* 1741. 12mo. W. + *New-York: Printed by John Peter Zenger.* 1742. 12mo.

A violent attack upon Whitefield, who had then landed. The author calls him, derisively, "that Angel! that Seraphim! the wondrous Whitefield!" Then, again, he says, "I see the *Wolf* coming."

Garden. Six Letters to the Rev. Mr. George Whitefield. The First, Second and Third, on the Subject of Justification. The Fourth containing Remarks on a Pamphlet, entitled, The Case between Mr. Whitefield and Dr. Stebbing stated, &c. The Fifth containing Remarks on Mr. Whitefield's Two Letters concerning Archbishop Tillotson, and the Book entitled, The Whole Duty of Man. The Sixth, containing Remarks on Mr. Whitefield's Second Letter, concerning Archbishop Tillotson, and on his Letter concerning the Negroes. By Alexander Garden, M.A., Rector of St. Philip's, Charlestown, and Commissary in South-Carolina. Together with, Mr. Whitefield's Answer to the First Letter. The Second Edition. *Boston: Re-printed by T. Fleet.* 1740. 8vo, pp. 54. BA., H., S. 26596

"Mr. Garden's Letters seem full of Mistake, Misconstru[ction], Misrepresentation, Cavil, Ill-Nature, Ill-manners, S[corn?], & Virulence."—*MS. note in Prince's copy in the Public Library of Boston.* Also: The Doctrine of Justification ... Explained and Vindicated. In a Letter to Mr. A. Crosswell ... . *South-Carolina, Charles-Town: Printed by Peter Timothy.* MDCCXLII. 8vo, pp. 70, (1). BA., H. (For an Answer to an earlier tract, in which Crosswell's name appears, *see* (Crosswell *and* Prince.) — Take Heed How Ye Hear. Sermon at Charleston, July 13, 1740. ... With Remarks on Whitefield's Journals. *Charleston.* 1741. 12mo. W.

Garden (A.) Anecdotes of the Revolutionary War In America, with Sketches of Character of Persons the most Distinguished, in the Southern States, for Civil and Military Services. By Alexander Garden, ... *Charleston.* 1822. 8vo, pp. xi, 459.

Garden. Anecdotes of the American Revolution, illustrative of the talents and virtues of the Heroes and Patriots, who acted the most Conspicuous parts Therein. By Alexander Garden, of Lee's Legion. Second Series. *Charleston: Printed by A. E. Miller.* 1828. 12mo, pp. ix, 240, Errata, 1 l. 26598

See "N. Am. Rev.," XV. 455, for a commendatory notice, qualified by the remark that it is disfigured by numerous typographical errors.

Garden. Anecdotes of the American Revolution, Illustrative of the Talents and Virtues of the Heroes of the Revolution, who acted the most conspicuous parts therein. By Alexander Garden of Lee's Legion. *Reprinted: Brooklyn, N. Y.* 1865. 3 vols., 4to, pp. vii, 438; xxxii, v; ix, 223, vi. 26599

150 copies printed; 25 copies printed in folio. This edition contains additional anecdotes, collected by Thomas W. Field.

Garden. Eulogy on Gen. Chs. Cotesworth Pinckney, President-General of the Society of the Cincinnati, Delivered, By Appointment of the Society of the Cincinnati of South-Carolina, on Tuesday, the 1st of November, 1825 ... . By Alexander Garden ... . *Charleston: Printed by A. E. Miller.* 1825. 8vo, pp. 48. BA. W. 26600

Garden (*Le Comte* de). Histoire générale des traités de Paix et autres transactions principales entre toutes les Puissances de l'Europe, depuis la paix de Westphalie. Ouvrage comprenant les travaux de Koch, Schoell, etc.; entièrement refondus et continués jusqu'à ce Jour. *Paris.* [n. d.] 14 vols., 8vo. 26601

Some of these treaties relate to America.

The Garden of the Soul; or, a Manual of Spiritual Exercises and Instructions for Christians, who (living in the world) aspire to Devotion. The Seventh Edition, Corrected. *London: printed. Philadelphia: reprinted by Joseph Crukshank.* [1774?] 18mo, pp. 167. 26602

Said to be the first Catholic Prayer-Book printed in this country.

The Garden of the World, or the Great West; its History, its Wealth, its Natural Advantages, and its Future. ... comprising a Complete Guide to Emigrants, ... By an Old Settler. ... *Boston: Wentworth and Company.* 1856. 12mo, pp. 296. B., C.

Gardener (H.) New-England's Vindication. Shewing the Mis-understanding of the Apprehension to take all that Vast Countrey under the Nation of a Particular Place of One Pattent of Boston, the Metropolitan of the Machechusets there, who in these Late Times have acted as a Free State and Illegal Proceeding ... . By Henry Gardener ... . *London: For the Author.* 1660. Sm. 4to, 2 l., pp. 8. H. 26604

A tract of the greatest rarity.

Gardenier (Barent). *See* The Examiner, Vol. VI., No. 23374.

Gardenier. Mr. Gardenier's Speech in the House of Representatives of the United States, on Foreign Relations, ... December, 1808. *Boston.* [n. d.] 8vo, pp. 32. B., H. 26605

Also: Speech ... on Foreign Relations. *Georgetown.* 1809. — Speech in the House of Representatives on the Embargo, 1808.

GARDENIER. The Speeches of Messieurs Gardenier & Tallmadge, on the Resolution for removing the Seat of Government to Philadelphia. Delivered ... on the Third and Eighth of February, 1808. [n. p.] 1808. 8vo. pp. 32. BA., H. 26606

GARDETTE (Charles D.) The Whole Truth in the Question of "The Fire Fiend" between Dr. R. Shelton Mackenzie ... and C. D. Gardette, briefly stated by the Latter. *Philadelphia: Sherman & Co.* 1864. 8vo, pp. 24. H. 26607

GARDETTE. The Fire Fiend, and other Poems. By Charles D. Gardette. *New York.* 1866. 12mo, pp. 104. 26608

The first poem in this volume was written in the manner of "The Raven," and was issued as "from an unpublished MS. of Edgar A. Poe's." So close was the resemblance in style and manner, that it has been reprinted in collections of poetry as an undoubted poem by Poe.

GARDETTE (E. B.) A Biographical Memoir of Dr. William D. Brinckle. ... By Dr. E. B. Gardette. *Philadelphia.* 1863. 8vo, pp. 55. 26609

GARDINER (A.) An Address, delivered in Wales, Mass., October 5, 1862, being the Centennial Anniversary of Organization of the Town; to which is annexed a "Roll of Honor," being a Catalogue of the names, etc., of Soldiers from this Town, who Served in the late Civil War. By Absalom Gardiner. *Springfield.* 1866. 8vo, pp. 44. 26610

GARDINER (A. F.) A Visit to the Indians on the Frontiers of Chila. By Captain Allen F. Gardiner, R.N. *London: R. B. Seeley and W. Burnside.* MDCCCXLI. 12mo, pp. (4), 194, Table, 1 l. 3 Plates and Map. B., BA., C., M. 26611

The author died of starvation in Patagonia.

GARDINER. A Voice from South America. By Capt. A. F. Gardiner. 1847. 12mo. 26612

GARDINER (D.) Chronicles of the Town of Easthampton, County of Suffolk, New York. By David Gardiner. *New York: [Bowne & Co.]* 1871. 8vo, 4 l., pp. 121. C. 26613

GARDINER (Edmund). The Trial of Tobacco. *London.* 1610. 4to. BM. 26614

GARDINER (G. A.) ... . A Brief and Correct Account of an Earthquake which happened in South America. By G. A. Gardiner, M.D. ... . *Poughkeepsie: Printed by P. Potter.* 1820. 8vo, pp. 24. B., P. 26615

GARDINER (H.) The Anglo-American; or, Memoirs of Capt. Henry Gardiner. ... . *Liverpool: Printed by G. Wood.* 1813. 12mo, pp. xvi, 3–249. BA., C., S. 26616

GARDINER (J.) Memoirs of Christian Missionaries; ... By the Rev. James Gardiner ... *Edinburgh: John Johnstone.* M.DCCC.XLVIII. Post 8vo, pp. xv, 384. 26617

Includes John Eliot, Pliny Fisk, etc.

GARDINER (J.) Memoirs of Eminent Christians. By Rev. James Gardiner, A.M. *Aberdeen: George & Robert King.* [n. d.] Fcap 8vo, pp. 360. 26617*a*

Includes Brainerd, Payson, etc.

GARDINER (J.) Argument or Speech of John Gardiner, Esq., Barrister-at-Law, who stood committed by the pretended Assembly of this Island for a pretended Contempt. *St. Christopher.* 1770. 8vo. 26618

GARDINER. An Oration, delivered July 4, 1785, at the Request of the Inhabitants of the Town of Boston, in Celebration of the Anniversary of American Independence. *Boston: Printed by Peter Edes, State Street.* [1785.] 4to, pp. 37, (1), xxii. BA.

The first Fourth of July oration delivered in Boston.

GARDINER. The Speech of John Gardiner, Esquire, Delivered in the House of Representatives. On Thursday, the 26th of January, 1792; On the Subject of the Report of the Committee, appointed to consider the Expediency of Repealing the Law against Theatrical Exhibitions within this Commonwealth. ... . *Printed at the Apollo Press, in Boston, for the Author.* MDCCXCII. 8vo, pp. 159, (1). B., BA., C., H., P. 26620

Probably the first American defence of theatres and stage plays. *See* Duyckinck's "Cyclopædia," I. 535, and Dunlap's "American Theatre," Chap. XI.

GARDINER (John), *and* HEPBURN (David). The American Gardener. Third Edition. *Washington: W. Cooper, jr.* 1826. 16mo, pp. viii, 308. C. 26621

GARDINER (J. S. J.) A Discourse, delivered, ... July 23, 1812, on the Day of Publick Fast in Massachusetts, upon the Declaration of War against Great-Britain. By John S. J. Gardiner, A.M. Rector. *Boston: Munroe & Francis.* 1812. 8vo, pp. 19.

Opposed to the war.

GARDINER. Remarks on the Jacobiniad. Revised and Corrected by the Author; and Embellished with Carricatures. Part First. ... *Printed at Boston, by E. W. Weld and W. Greenough.* 1795. 8vo, pp. 54. + Part Second. 1798. 8vo, pp. 52. B.

First appeared in the "Federal Orrery."

GARDINER. The Christian Soldier. A Sermon ... before ... Artillery Company, on June 2d, 1823. ... By John S. J. Gardiner, D.D. ... *Boston: Printed by Munroe and Francis.* 1823. 8vo, pp. 19, (1). BA., H., M. 26624

Also: An Address ... Massachusetts Charitable Fire Society, ... May 28, 1803. ... *Boston: Printed by Russell and Cutler.* 1803. 8vo, pp. 21, (2). B., BA., H. — Christian's Victory ... . A Sermon, delivered ... November 5, 1809, on the Decease of Elizabeth Lady Temple. ... *Boston: Printed by Munroe, Francis and Parker.* 1809. 4to, pp. 22. BA., H. — An Epistle to Zenas. A Poem. ... *Boston.* 4to. W. — A Sermon ... May 25, 1802 ... Ordination of the Rev. James Bowers, ... Marblehead. ... *Boston: Printed by H. Sprague.* 1802. 8vo, pp. 3–16. BA., H. — A Sermon ... before the Humane Society, ... of ... June 14, 1803. ... *Boston: Printed by Hosea Sprague.* 1803. 8vo, pp. 43. BA., H. — A Sermon ... on the Death of the Right Reverend Samuel Parker, D.D., Bishop ... of Massachusetts. ... . *Boston: Printed by Gilbert & Dean.* 1804. 8vo, pp. 16. B., BA., H., N. — A Sermon ... in Boston, on Fast Day, April 7, 1808. *Boston: Printed by Munroe, Francis & Parker.* 1808. 8vo, pp. 22. B., N. — Life a Journey, and Man a Traveller. A New-Year's Sermon, preached ... January 4th, 1824 ... January 2nd, 1825. ... *Boston: Samuel H. Parker.* 1825. 8vo, pp. 19. — A Sermon ... at Trinity Church, in Boston, on the Day appointed for Publick Thanksgiving ... *Boston: Munroe, Francis and Parker.* 1808. 8vo, pp. 23. BA. — A Sermon ... September 22nd, 1809, before the ... Boston Female Asylum ... their Ninth Anniversary. ... . *Boston: Munroe, Francis & Parker.* 1809. 8vo, pp. 23. BA. — A Sermon ... at Trinity Church, March 25, 1810, On the Decease of Doctor James Lloyd. ... *Boston: Printed by Munroe and Francis.* 1810. 8vo, pp. 22. BA. — A Sermon, preached at Trinity Church, April 6, 1810, being the Day of Publick Fast. ... *Boston: Printed by Munroe and Francis.* 1810. 8vo, pp. 24. BA. — A Sermon ... before the African Society, on the 14th of July, 1810, The Anniversary of the Abolition of the Slave Trade. ... *Boston: Printed by Munroe and Francis.* 1810. 8vo, pp. 20. BA. — A Discourse ... at Trinity Church, Boston, April 9, 1812, on the Day of Publick Fast. ... *Boston: Munroe and Francis.* 1812. 8vo, pp. 19. BA., H. — A Sermon, ... November 22, 1812; the Sunday after the Interment of Thomas Amory, Esq. ... *Boston: Printed by Munroe and Francis.* 1812. 8vo, pp. 20. BA. — A Sermon, ... March 21, 1812, on the Decease of Mr. George Higginson. ... *Boston: Printed by Munroe and Francis.* 1812. 8vo, pp. 19. BA. — A Sermon ... at Boston, Nov. 10, 1816, on the Death of David Sears, Esq. ... *Boston: Printed by John Eliot.* 1816. 8vo, pp. 19. BA.

GARDINER (L.) A History of the Pequot War. By Lieut. Lion Gardiner. *Cincinnati: J. Harpel.* 1860. 4to, pp. 36.

Appended to Penhallow's "Indian War," Cincinnati edition; also included in the "Mass. Hist. Soc. Coll.," Vols. III. and X., 3d Series.

GARDINER (O. C.) The Great Issue; or, the Three Presidential Candidates; [Taylor, Cass, and Van Buren] being a

Brief Historical Sketch of the Free Soil Question in the United States, from the Congress of 1774 and '78 to the Present Time. By O. C. Gardiner. ... *New York: Wm. C. Bryant & Co.* 1848. 8vo, pp. 176. BA., C., H. 26626

GARDINER (R.) An Account of the Expedition to the West Indies, against Martinico, Guadelupe, and other the Leeward Islands; Subject to the French King, 1759. By Richard Gardiner, Esq; Captain of the Marines on board His Majesty's Ship Rippon, on the Expedition. *London: Zech. Stuart.* 1759. 4to, 2 l., pp. 75. Map and Plan. C., H. + The Second Edition. *London: Zech. Stuart.* 1760. 8vo, pp. vi, 75. Map. 26627

GARDINER. An Account of the Expedition to the West Indies, against Martinico, With the Reduction of Guadelupe, And other the Leeward Islands; Subject to the French King, 1759. By Captain Gardiner of the King's Royal Musqueteers, late Captain of Marines on Board his Majesty's Ship Rippon, employed on this Expedition. The Third Edition. *Birmingham: John Baskerville.* 1762. 4to, pp. (6), 91. Map and 3 Plans. BA., C.

A beautiful specimen of typography. There are copies on large paper. A French translation, occupying the same number of pages, is usually bound up with it. *See* "M. Rev.," XXI. 423.

GARDINER. Relation de l'Expédition aux Indes Occidentales, contre la Martinique, Avec la Reduction de la Guadelupe, Et autres Isles sous Vent, Appartenant au Roi de France, en 1759. Par Mons. Gardiner Capitaine des Mousquetaires Royaux de S. M. Autrefois des Troupes de Marine à bord le Rippon, Vaisseau de S. M. employé á cette Expedition. Troisième édition. *A' Birmingham: Jean Baskerville.* 1762. 4to, pp. (6), 91. BA., C.

Usually bound up with the preceding.

GARDINER. Memoirs of the Siege of Quebec, Capital of all Canada, and of the Retreat of Monsieur De Bourlemaque, from Carillon to the Isle aux Noix in Lake Champlain. From the Journal of a French Officer on Board the Chezine Frigate, taken by His Majesty's Ship Rippon. Compared with the Accounts transmitted hence by Major-General Wolfe and Vice-Admiral Saunders; with Occasional Remarks. By Richard Gardiner, Esq., Captain of Marines in the Rippon. ... *London: R. and J. Dodsley.* MDCCLXI. 4to, Title, pp. 39. H. 26630

A very rare tract. Compiled by Gardiner. *See* "M. Rev.," XXIV. 348.

GARDINER (S.) Address to the Public. By Doctor Sylvester Gardiner. [n. p. n. d.] 8vo, pp. 8. M. 26630*a*

In answer to James Flagg. Also: A Full Answer to the Pamphlet intitled "A Short Vindication of the Conduct of the Referees in the Case of Gardiner *versus* Flagg," &c. [n. p. n. d.] 8vo, pp. 44. BA., H. — Dr. Gardiner *versus* James Flagg, Merchant. *Boston.* 1767. 8vo, pp. 28. H., M., W. — To Messieurs Edward Payne & Henderson Inches. [n. p. n. d.] 8vo, pp. 14. BA., H. — Letter to the Public. [n. p. n. d.] 12mo, pp. 18. — Proposal to Build an Inoculating Hospital for Small Pox at Boston, addressed to the Freeholders and other Inhabitants of that Town, March, 1761. Folio, 1 leaf. — A Short Vindication of the Conduct of the Referees in the Case of Gardiner *versus* Flagg. [n. p. n. d.] 8vo, pp. 22. — Statement in relation to the Case between Sylvester Gardiner and James Flagg. *Boston.* 4to. W.

GARDINER (W. C.) Letter to the Corporation of Trinity Church, accompanied with Documents relative to the Episcopal Church, at Hudson. By Walter Clarke Gardiner. 1802. 8vo, pp. 33. N. 26631

Also: Oration at Hudson, N. Y., at the Dedication of the Masonic Hall. *Hudson.* 1797. 12mo.

GARDINER (*Mrs.* William). Brief Memoir of Harriet [M. Gardiner], with some of her Essays in Prose and Verse. By her Mother. *Oberlin: J. M. Fitch.* 1855. 18mo, pp. iv, 129. Portrait. C. 26632

GARDINER (W. H.) An Address ... before the Phi Beta Kappa Society of Harvard University, 28 August, 1834. ... . By William Howard Gardiner ... . *Cambridge: James Munroe and Company.* 1834. 8vo, pp. (1), 68. BA., H. 26633

GARDINER LYCEUM, *Me.* An Address to the Public from the Trustees of the Gardiner Lyceum. *Hallowell: Printed by Goodale, Glazier & Co.* 1822. 8vo, pp. 8. BA. 26634

Also: Laws and Catalogue. *Gardiner.* 1829. 8vo.

[GARDNER (Alexander).] Photographic Sketch Book of the [American] War. *Washington: Philp & Solomons.* [1865–6.] 2 vols., imp. oblong folio, 53 l., 50 Plates; 53 l., 50 Plates. BA.

Two volumes, containing one hundred photographs of the operations of the Army of the Potomac, including scenes in Richmond, etc.. Each plate is accompanied with a page of letter-press description.

GARDNER. Rays of Sunlight from South America. By Alexander Gardner. *Washington: Philp & Solomons.* Folio.

A collection of seventy photographs of scenes in South America.

GARDNER (A. K.) Eulogy on John W. Francis, March 7, 1861. By A. K. Gardner. *New York.* 1861. 8vo, pp. 24.

GARDNER (C. K.) A Dictionary of all Officers, who have been Commissioned, or have been appointed and Served, in the Army of the United States, since the Inauguration of their First President, in 1789, to the first of January, 1853, ... including the Distinguished Officers of the Volunteers and Militia of the States, who have served in any Campaign, or Conflict with an Enemy ... . and of the Navy and Marine Corps, who have served with the Land Forces. By Charles K. Gardner ... . *New York: G. P. Putnam.* 1853. 12mo, pp. 587. B., BA., H. + Second Edition. *New York: D. Van Nostrand.* 1860. 8vo, pp. 640. H., P. 26638

GARDNER. ... Proceedings of a General Court-Martial held at Fort Independence, ... for the Trial of Major Charles K. Gardner, ... upon Charges of Misbehaviour, Cowardice ... preferred against him by Major-General Ripley. [*Boston.*] 1816. 8vo, pp. 157. B., BA., H., S. 26639

Also: Regulations for Light Infantry and Riflemen. ... *New York: William A. Mercier.* 1820. 12mo, pp. 108.

GARDNER (D.) Institutes of International Law, Public and Private, as settled by the Supreme Court of the United States, and by our Republic. With References to Judicial Decisions. By Daniel Gardner, Esq., ... *New-York; John S. Voorhies.* 1860. 8vo, pp. xix, 719. B., C. 26640

GARDNER. A Treatise on International Law, and a Short Explanation of the Jurisdiction and Duty of the Government of the Republic of the United States. By Daniel Gardner, Esq. ... *Troy: N. Tuttle.* 1844. 12mo, pp. 315. B., BA., C., H. 26641

Also: A Treatise on the Law of the American Rebellion, and our True Policy, Domestic and Foreign. ... *New York: John W. Amerman.* 1862. 8vo, pp. 20. H. — A Treatise on the Martial Power of the President of the U. S. [n. p. n. d.] 8vo, pp. 8. H.

GARDINER (D. P.) Address of Dr. D. P. Gardner, before the National Convention of Farmers and Gardeners, held at the Repository of the American Institute. [*New York.* 1844.] 8vo.

GARDNER. The Fall of Fort Morgan. A Poem. Delivered at the Celebration of the Birthday of Washington, by the Cooper Union, February 20, 1865. By D. T. Gardner. 18mo, pp. 8. 26643

GARDNER (F.) A Discourse, in Two Parts. Delivered in Leominster, December 27, 1812. By the Rev. Francis Gardner,

... The Son-Day after the close of the Fiftieth Year of his Ministry. *Leominster, (Mass.): By Salmon Wilder. January,* 1813. 8vo, pp. 34. H., S. 26644

Also: A Sermon ... on the Day of Annual Thanksgiving, November 19, 1795. ... *Leominster: Printed by Charles Prentiss.* 1796. 8vo, pp. 23. BA.

GARDNER (G.) Travels in the Interior of Brazil, principally through the Northern Provinces, and the Gold and Diamond Districts, during the Years 1836–41. By George Gardner, F.L.S., Superintendent of the Royal Botanic Gardens of Ceylon. ... *London: Reeve, Brothers.* 1846. 8vo, pp. xvi, 562. Plate and Map. B., BA., S. + Second Edition. [*Ibid.*] 1849. 8vo, pp. 578. Plate and Map. B. 26645

GARDNER. Reisen im Innern Brasiliens ... übergesetz von M. B. Lindau. *Dresden.* 1848. 2 vols., 8vo, pp. xii, 298; vi, 374. Map. 26646

GARDNER (G. W.) Treason and the Fate of Traitors. A Sermon preached in ... Charlestown, ... April 13, 1862. By George W. Gardner ... . 1862. *Boston: Davis and Farmer, Printers.* 1862. 8vo, pp. 20. B. 26647

Also: ... A Sermon, ... Annual Fast, April 7, 1859. ... *Concord: P. B. Cogswell.* 1859. 8vo, pp. 20.

GARDNER (H. W.) Correspondence with the Secretary of the Navy, relative to certain Work for the Navy. By H. W. Gardner, Agent of the Providence Steam Engine Company. pp. 15. 26648

[GARDNER (John).] A Brief Consideration of the Important Services and Distinguished Virtues and Talents which Recommend Mr. Adams for the Presidency of the United States. [Signed "Aurelius."] *Boston.* 1796. 12mo, pp. 31. S. 26649

[GARDNER (John L.) Military Control, or Command and Government of the Army. By an Officer of the Line. *Washington: Printed by A. B. Claxton & Co.* 1839. 8vo, pp. 82.

GARDNER (O. A. A.) Description of the Climate, Soil, Production and Advantages, offered to Settlers, and Information to many Inquirers about Audrain County, Missouri ... written by and printed for O. A. A. Gardner ... . *Mexico, Mo.* [n. d.] 8vo, pp. 8. H. 26651

GARDNER (R.) Descendants of Richard Gardner of Woburn, of the name of Gardner. *Boston: printed for Private Circulation.* MDCCCLVIII. 8vo, pp. 14. 26652

GARDNER (S. J.) Autumn Leaves. By Samuel Jackson Gardner. *New York: Hurd and Houghton.* 1865. 8vo, pp. 301.

Fifty copies printed.

GARDNER (T.) Historical Memoirs of the Life of Thomas Gardner. *New York.* 1805. 12mo, pp. 84. N. 26654

GARDNER. The Way to Grow Rich, or Historical Memoirs of the Life of Tom Gardner, a Citizen of New York. Showing how ... he acquired a great estate, ... *Frankford: Coale & Gilbert.* 1811. 18mo, pp. 35. C., N. 26655

GARDNER (W. S.) Address upon Henry Price, Esquire, First Provincial Grand Master of New England ... December 27th, 1871. By William Sewall Gardner ... . *Boston: Press of Rockwell & Churchill.* 1872. 8vo, pp. 112. Portrait and Plate. B.

Also other Masonic addresses.

GARDNER, *Me.* Annual Report of the Selectmen and Overseers of the Poor, of the Town of Gardner, for the Year ending February 25, 1868. *Athol Depot: Printed by R. William Waterman.* 1868. 8vo, pp. 16. H. 26657

GARDWELL (G.) Currency: the Evil and the Remedy. By Godek Gardwell. Fourth Edition ... . [n. p. n. d.] pp. (1), 43. + Fifth Edition. *New York.* 1844. 26658

GARDYNER (G.) A | Description | Of the New | World. | Or, | America Islands and Continent: | and by what people those Regions | are now inhabited. | And what places are there desolate and | without Inhabitants. | And the Bays, Rivers, Capes, Forts, Cities and | their Latitudes, the Seas of their Coasts: | the Trade, Winds, the North-west Passage, | and the Commerce of the English Nation, as | they were all in the Year 1649. Faithfully de- | scribed for information of such of his Coun- | trey as desire Intelligence of these perticulars. | By George Gardyner of Peck- | ham, in the County of Surrey Esq. | *London: Printed for Robert Leybourn, and are to be Sold* | *by Thomas Pirrepont, at the Sun in S. Pauls* | *Churchyard,* 1651. | 8vo, pp. (16), 187. [Colophon:] *November* 18. 1650. | *Imprimatur* | *Nathanael Brent.* | 1 p., reverse blank. H. 26659

A volume of extreme rarity Foster's copy sold, in 1857, for £6 10s.

GARELLA (N.) Projet d'un Canal de Jonction de l'Océan Pacifique et de l'Océan Atlantique à Travers l'Isthme de Panama par Napoléon Garella, Ingénieur en Chef au Corps Royal des Mines. *Paris: Carilian-Gœury et Vor Dalmont.* 1845. 8vo, pp. viii, 233. Plans on a large sheet. A., B., C. 26660

Garella. Uber die Strassenverbindungen der beiden Meere bei Panama. [n. d.] 4to. Map. 26661

Gareschè (*M.*) Mémoire pour Mm. Garesché frères négocians à la Rochelle, consignataires de la gôelette américaine la Reward, Capitaine William Goss; ... . [n. p.] *De l'imprimerie d'Ant. Bailleul.* [n. d.] Sm. 4to, pp. 12. BA. 26662

Garfield (J. A.) The Currency. Speech of Hon. James A. Garfield, of Ohio, delivered in the House of Representatives, May 15, 1868. ... *Washington: F. & J. Rives & Geo. A. Bailey.* 1868. 8vo, pp. 16. H. 26663

Garfield. Free Commerce between the States. Speech of Hon. James A. Garfield of Ohio, ... March 24th and 31st, 1864. The House having under Consideration the Bill to declare the Raritan and Atlantic Railroad, a Legal Structure for Commerce between New York and Philadelphia. *New York.* 1864. 8vo, pp. 15. H. 26664

Also: ... Address ... Consolidated Business College, Washington, D. C. June 29, 1869. ... [*Washington:*] *Gibson Brothers.* 1869. 8vo, pp. 8. — ... An Address ... Eclectic Institute, at Hiram, Ohio, June 14, 1867. ... *Cleveland: Fairbanks, Benedict & Co.* 1867. 8vo, pp. 22. H. — The Campaign on the Reserve. Speech ... at Warren, Ohio, July 31, 1872. [n. p. n. d.] 8vo, pp. 8. H. — National Politics. ... Speech ... at Warren, O., Sept. 1, 1866. [n. p. n. d.] 8vo, pp. 8. — Ninth Census. Speech ... December 16, 1869. ... *Washington.* 1869. 8vo, pp. 16. H. — Oration ... at Arlington, Va., May 30, 1868, on the Occasion of Strewing Flowers on the Graves of Union Soldiers. *Cleveland, O.: Fairbanks, Benedict & Co.* 1868. 8vo, pp. 8. H. — Public Expenditures ... Speech ... January 23, 1872. [n. p. n. d.] 8vo, pp. 8. H. — Remarks ... April 14, 1866, in Memory of Abrahrm Lincoln. *Washington, D. C.: Hudson Taylor.* 1866. 8vo, pp. 4. H. — Speech ... on the Confiscation of Property of Rebels. ... January 28, 1864. [n. p. n. d.] 8vo, pp. 8. — Speech ... on the ... Amendment to Abolish Slavery, ... January 13, 1865. [n. p. n. d.] 8vo, pp. 8. H. — Speech ... on the Public Debt and Specie Payments; ... March 16, 1866. ... *Washington.* 1866. 8vo, pp. 14. H. — Speech ... June 8th, 1866, on a Bill "To Establish a National Bureau of Education" ... . [n. p. n. d.] 8vo, pp. 16. — Speech ... on the Garrahan Claim ... Feb'y 20, 1871. [n. p. n. d.] 8vo, pp. 16. H. — Treason in Congress. Speech ... in Reply to Alexander Long, in favor of Abandoning the War and Recognizing the Southern Confederacy. ... April 8, 1864. [n. p. n. d.] 8vo, pp. 8.

Garfielde (S[elucius]). The North-West Coast: A Lecture ... in Washington ... November 15th, 1869 ... By Hon. S. Garfielde ... . *Washington: Joseph L. Pearson.* 1869. 8vo, pp. 26. H. 26665

Garibay y Camálloa (E. de). Los quarenta libros d'el Compendio Historial de las Chronicas y Universal Historia de todos los Reynos de España. Compuestos por Estevan de Garibay. *Anvers.* 1571. 4 vols., folio. C. 26666

"The author's autograph is written on the back of the title-page. Where the copyright was of great importance (as the numerous privileges affixed to it show), it was not uncommon for the author thus to sign every copy. I am glad to possess a relic of Garibay, whom I love for his laborious life, and for the excellent simplicity with which he requests Phillp II. to employ a few of his leisure moments in reading these four volumes. Gave him my thanks, too; for I have borrowed his motto, which is as applicable to me as it was to him." — Robert Southey.

Garibay y Camálloa. Compendio Historial [as in No. 26667]. *Barcelona.* 1628. 4 vols., sm. 4to. 26667

"A work of great intrinsic worth, and rare occurrence in a perfect condition. Meuseulius' account (borrowed from Antonio) of the plan, energies, judgments, and talent of Garibay, will make the 'young man' sigh, the 'old man' weep, if he do not speedily become master of it — *and yet I look in vain for a copy of Garibay in many of our richest bibliopolistic* catalogues." — Dibdin's *Library Companion.* "Garibay, one of the most distinguished among the Spanish historians." — Washington Irving.

Garimberto (H.) Problemi | natvrali, e morali | di Heronimo Garimberto. | Con gratia, & priuilegio di Papa | Paolo III. & dell' Illustrissima | Signoria di Vinegia | per anni X. | *In Vinegia | nella Bottega d'Erasmo | di Vicenzo Valgrisi.* | M. D. L. | 8vo, Title, 1 l., pp. 239, 7 l. BM. 26668

"The 70th Problem (pp. 119–122) is most interesting, as it explains the reason why, at the discovery of America, many laws and customs were found similar to those of the Old World." — *Libri Catalogue.* His Problems were translated into French by Jean Louveau. Harrisse quotes an edition, *Venet.* 1549.

Garin (R. P.) Catechisme recueil de prières et de cantiques à l'usage des sauvages d'Albany, (Baie d'Hudson). *Montreal: L. Perrault.* 1854. 12mo, 1 l., pp. 94. C. 26669

Garland (H. A.) The Life of John Randolph of Roanoke. By Hugh A. Garland. *New York: D. Appleton & Company.* M.DCCC.L. 2 vols., 8vo, pp. xii, 311; 375. 2 Portraits. + Eleventh Edition. [*Ibid.*] 1851. BA. + [*Ibid.*] 1857. B., H.

Also: Speech ... Sub-Treasury Scheme. ... September 25, 1837. *Washington.* 1837. 8vo, pp. 48. H. — An Oration in Celebration of the 2d Declaration of Independence; or, the Independent Treasury Bill, pronounced in Castle Garden, July 27, 1840. 8vo. N.

Garland (J.) Eulogy on J. K. Polk, late President. *Lynchburg.* 1849. 8vo. 26671

The Garland of Freedom; a Collection of Poems, chiefly Anti-Slavery. Selected from Various Authors, by a Friend to the Negro. [Wilson Armistead.] In Three Parts. *London: W. and F. L. Cash.* MDCCCLIII. 12mo, pt. II., pp. 3–203. Plate.

The Garland of Gratitude; Respectfully Dedicated to the Constitutional Suffrage Ladies of Rhode Island. *Providence.* 1842. 8vo, pp. 12. 26673

Garlick (Theodatus), *M.D.* A Treatise on the Artificial Propagation of certain kinds of Fish, with the Description and Habits of such kinds as are the most suitable for Pisciculture. *Cleveland, O.* 1857. 8vo, pp. 142. 26674

Garneau (F. X.) Histoire du Canada depuis sa Découverte jusqu'a nos jours. Par F. X. Garneau. *Quebec: N. Aubin.* 1845–1852. 3 vols., 8vo, pp. (4), 558; (4), 577, (1); (4), 566, (1). C. + Seconde édition. *Quebec: Imprimé par John Lovell.* 1852. 3 vols., 8vo, pp. iii–xxii, 377; 454; 5–410, (2). B. + Troisième édition, corrigée. [*Ibid.*] 1859. 3 vols., 8vo.

For notices of this able work, *see* Morgan's "Bibl. Canad.," p. 135–6.

Garneau. History of Canada, from the Time of its First Discovery till the Union Year 1840–41. Translated from "l'Histoire du Canada," of F. X. Garneau, Esq. ... By Andrew Bell, and Accompanied with Illustrative Notes ... *Montreal: Richard Worthington.* 1862. 2 vols., 8vo, pp. 556; 499. B., BA. + Third Edition, Revised. *Montreal.* 1866. 2 vols., 8vo, pp. 556; 499. Woodcut. C. 26676

An indifferent translation. *See* Morgan's "Bibl. Canad." Also: Abrégé de l'histoire du Canada depuis sa découverte jusqu'à 1840. ... *Quebec.* 1856. 12mo. *See* "N. Am. Rev.," LXXIV. 261; "La Revue des Deux-Mondes, seconde série de la nouvelle période," III. 278 (1853); "Le Correspondant," XXXIII, 243.

Garnet (H. H.) A Memorial Discourse; by Rev. Henry Highland Garnet, delivered in the ... House of Representatives, Washington ... February 12, 1865. With an Introduction, by James McCune Smith, M.D. *Philadelphia: Joesph M. Wilson.* 1865. 8vo, pp. 13–91. Portrait. BA., H. 26677

Garnett (J. M.) An Address ... delivered before the ... Hampden Sidney College, at their Last Commencement. By James M. Garnett. ... *Richmond: Printed by Thomas W. White.* 1835. 8vo, pp. 11. H. 26678

Garnett (J. M.) Constitutional Charts, or, Comparative Views of the Legislative, Executive and Judiciary Departments, in the Constitutions of all the States in the Union, including that of the United States. With an Appendix. By James M. Garnett. *Richmond: Thomas W. White.* 1829. 4to, pp. 64.

Garnett. A Reply to the Inquiries of a Freeholder ... on the Subject of the Convention: soliciting the Several Persons ... to delare "The Fundamental Principles which they are for laying down our Future Government." *Richmond: T. W. White.* 1829. 8vo, pp. 12. H. 26680

Garnett (M. R. H.) Speech of Mr. Garnett, of Virginia, on the Admission of Kansas into the Union. Delivered in the House of Representatives, March 22d, 1858. [n. p. n. d.] 8vo, pp. 8. H. 26681

Also: Speech ... on the State of the Union, ... January 16, 1861. ... *Washington: M'Gill & Witherow, Printers.* 1861. 8vo, pp. 16. H. — Letters on the Calamitous State of Affairs.

Garnier (Pierre). Voyage médical en Californie. *Paris: Aux bureau de l'Union médicale.* 1854. 26682

Garnier (E.) Nouvel abrégé de tous les voyages autour du monde depuis Magellan jusqu'à d'Urville et Laplace (1519–1832). Par E. Garnier. ... *Bruxelles: Meline, Cans et Cie.* 1837. 2 vols., 8vo, pp. (3), ii, (1), 288); (3), 295. Plates. BA. 26683

Garran (J. Ph.) Opinion sur les dénonciations formées contre les agens du Directoire, à Saint Domingue. Séance du 16 Prairial, an V. *Paris: De l'imprimerie nationale an* V. [1797.] 8vo, pp. 24. 26684

Garran. Rapport sur les Troubles de Saint Domingue. Fait au nom de la Commission des Colonies des Comités de Salut Public, de Législation, et de Marine, réunis. Par J. Ph. Garran. Imprimé par ordre de la Convention Nationale, et distribué au Corps législatif en Ventôse, an V. *Paris: Imprimerie nationale. An V de la République.* [1797.] 4 vols., 8vo, pp. 374, (2); 625, (2); 498, (2); (1), 666, Tables, pp. vi. C. 26685

The report was made to the National Convention by the Committees of Public Safety, Legislation and Marine. It is the fullest and most authoritative work on the Revolution in St. Domingo. *See also* St. Domingo.

Garrard (L. H.) Chambersburg in the Colony and the Revolution. A Sketch. By Lewis H. Garrard ... . *Philadelphia: J. B. Lippincott & Co.* 1856. 8vo, pp. 16, v, (1), 60. B., BA.

Garrard. Wah-to-Yah, and the Taos Trail; or, Prairie Travel and Scalp Dances, with a Look at Los Rancheros from Muleback and the Rocky Mountain Camp Fire. By Lewis H. Garrard. *Cincinnati: H. W. Derby.* 1850. 12mo, pp. vi, (1), 349. 26687

Garrard (K.) Explanation of the Difficulty between Lieut. Kenner Garrard, 2d Cavalry, and M. Charles E. Travis, Late Captain 2d Cavalry. [n. p. n. d.] 8vo, pp. 4. H. 26688

Garrard (T. T.) Letter from the Secretary of War, transmitting papers relative to General T. T. Garrard's Claim for the Destruction of Salt Works, by Order of General Buell, in 1862. (H. of R., Ex. Doc., 38th Cong., 1st Sess., 1864.) pp. 30.

Garreau (A.) Louisiana; épisode emprunta á la domination française en Amérique. *Paris: Lacroix.* 1862. 12mo. 26690

Garret (J.) Report of the Committee on the Public Lands, on the Petition of Joab Garret. *Washington.* 1810. 8vo. H.

Garretson (F. V. D.) Carmina Yalensia. Yale College Songs. With Pianoforte Accompaniments. Compiled and Arranged by F. V. D. Garretson. *New York: Taintor Broths. & Co.* [1867.] 8vo, pp. 90. C. 26692

Garretson (F.) Dialogue between Do Justice and Professing-Christians. By Freeborn Garretson. *Wilmington, Del.* [n. d.] 16mo. 26693

An early abolition document. Published before 1827, in which year Garretson died.

Garretson. A Letter to the Rev. Lyman Beecher, containing Strictures and Animadversions on a Pamphlet entitled an Address ... for the Education of Indigent Pious Young Men for the Ministry ... . By the Rev. Freeborn Garretson. *New York.* 1816. 12mo. H. + *Boston: Re-printed by Thomas Rowe.* 1817. 12mo, pp. 24. BA. 26694

Garretson (G. J.) A Discourse Delivered in the Reformed Dutch Church, Jamaica, L. I. February 15, and Repeated in Newtown, February 20, 1842, at the Quadrigenian Anniversary of the Ministry of the Rev. Jacob Schonemaker, D.D., as Senior Pastor of the Collegiate Reformed Dutch Churches of Jamaica and Newtown. By Garret J. Garretson, Junior, Pastor of said Church. *Flushing: Charles R. Lincoln.* MDCCCXLII. 8vo, pp. 29. 26695

Garretson. Certified Report of the Investigation of the case of Rev. Garret J. Garretson, ... of Lodi, Seneca Co., N. Y., before the Classis of Geneva, ... April 27, 1853, relative to a charge of Immoral Conduct; together with the proceedings of the Civil Courts in the same case. *New York.* 1853. 8vo.

Garrett (J. W.) Letter ... from John W. Garrett, President of the Baltimore and Ohio Railroad Company, to the Comptroller of Maryland, in Relation to the Obligation of the State, to provide for Remitting to England the Interest due on Certain Sterling Bonds of the State. ... *Baltimore: Printed by Kelly & Piet.* 1865. 8vo, pp. 16. H. 26697

Also: Remarks ... embracing a Statement of the Necessity for ... an Additional ... Railway between Baltimore, ... Philadelphia and New York, ... 11th of January, 1871 ... . *Baltimore,* 1871. 8vo, pp. 9. H. — Remarks ... 14th of February, 1866 ... in Relation to the Annual Message of the Mayor of Baltimore, of January 15th, 1866, ... *Baltimore.* 1866. 8vo, pp. 20. H. — Statement ... made before the Committ.e on Military Affairs ... 25th of April, 1862, in Opposition to the "Proposition" of the Metropolitan Railroad Company, to "Build a Road ... between Washington City and New York. ... *Baltimore: Printed by Kelly, Hedian & Piet.* 1862. 8vo, pp. 20. H. Also several addresses, etc., relating to the Baltimore and Ohio Railroad.

Garrett (L Recollections of the West. By L. Garrett ... *Nashville: Western Metooaist Office.* 1834. 24mo, pp. 240.

Garrett (W.) A Tabular Statement of the Census of Alabama, taken in the Year 1844; also, the Census ... of 1838 and 1840, ... Compiled by W. Garrett. *Tuscaloosa.* 1844. 26699

Garrey (E.) Grandeur et Avenir des Etats-Unis. Par Emile Garrey. *Paris: Dentu.* 1863. 8vo, pp. 48. 26700

Garrich (R. P.) Balanza general del comercio de la Isla de Cuba, en los años de 1836 y 1838. *Habana.* 1837–39. Folio.

Garrison (J. F.) The Teachings of the Crisis. Address delivered in ... Camden, N. J., on the occasion of the Funeral of Abraham Lincoln, April 19, 1865. By Rev. J. F. Garrison, M.D. *Camden, N. J.: Printed by S. Chew.* 1865. 8vo, pp. 20. + Second Edition. [*Ibid.*] 1865. 8vo, pp. 20. 26702

[Garrison (Wendell Phillips).] The Benson Family of Newport, Rhode Island. ... . *New York.* 1872. 8vo, pp. 65.

Garrison (W. L.) An Address, delivered before the Free People of Color, in Philadelphia, New-York, and other Cities,

during the Month of June, 1831. By Wm. Lloyd Garrison. ... *Boston: Printed by Stephen Foster.* 1831. 8vo. + Second Edition. [*Ibid.*] 1831. 8vo. + Third Edition. [*Ibid.*] 1831. 8vo. + *New York.* 1833. 8vo. 26704

Garrison. A Brief Sketch of the Trial of William Lloyd Garrison, for an Alleged Libel on Francis Todd, of Newburyport, Mass. *Boston: Printed by Garrison and Knapp.* 1834. 8vo, pp. 24. H. + [Also. n. p. n. d.] 8vo, pp. 8. BA. 26705

[Garrison.] Henry Ward Beecher and Theodore Parker. ... [n. p. n. d.] 12mo, pp. 16. H. 26706

Garrison. Selections from the Writings and Speeches of William Lloyd Garrison. With an Appendix. ... *Boston: R. F. Wallcut.* 1852. 12mo, pp. 416. B., BA., H. 26707

Garrison. Thoughts on African Colonization: or an Impartial Exhibition of the Doctrines, Principles and Purposes of the American Colonization Society. Together with the Resolutions, Addresses and Remonstrances of the Free People of Color. ... By Wm. Lloyd Garrison. *Boston: Garrison and Knapp.* 1832. 2 pts., 8vo, pp. 160; 76. B., BA., C., H., S.

Garrison. Papers relating to the Garrison Mob. Edited by Theodore Lyman. *Cambridge: Welch, Bigelow, and Company.* 1870. 8vo, pp. 73. B., BA. 26709

Garrison. Proceedings against William Lloyd Garrison, for a Libel. *Baltimore: Printed by William Woody.* 1847. 8vo, pp. 32. B. 26710

Garrison. Proceedings at the Public Breakfast held in Honour of William Lloyd Garrison, Esq., of Boston, Massachusetts, in ... London, on Saturday, June 29th, 1867. ... *London: William Tweedie.* 1868. 8vo, pp. 96. B., BA., H. 26711

Garrison. Sketch of the Character, etc., of William Lloyd Garrison. *New York.* 1833. 26712

Also: The Abolitionists, and their Relations to the War. An Address ... delivered ... January 14, 1862 ... *New York: E. D. Barker.* 1862. 12mo, pp. 31–54. B. — ... The Abolition Conspiracy to Destroy the Union; or, a Ten Years' Record of the "Republican" Party. The Opinions of William Lloyd Garrison ... . *New York: Van Evrie, Horton & Company.* 1868. 8vo, pp. 31. H. — An Address ... in Marlboro' Chapel, Boston, July 4, 1838. ... *Boston: Isaac Knapp.* 1838. 12mo, pp. 48. BA., H. — An Address ... New York, August 1, 1838, by request of the People of Colour ... in Commemoration of the ... Emancipation of 600,000 Slaves on that day, in the British West Indies. *Boston.* 1838. 12mo. — An Address ... before the

Old Colony Anti-Slavery Society, at South Scituate, Mass., July 4, 1839. ... *Boston: Dowd & Jackson.* 1839. 16mo, pp. 40. H. — The "Infidelity" of Abolitionism. ... *New York: American Anti-Slavery Society.* 1816. 12mo, pp. 12. B., H. — Letter to Louis Kossuth, concerning Freedom and Slavery in the United States. ... . *Boston: R. F. Wallcut.* 1852. 8vo, pp. 112. B., H. — No Compromise with Slavery: An Address, New-York, Feb. 14, 1854. ... 18mo. — ... Principles and Mode of Action of the American Anti-Slavery Society: A Speech ... *London: William Tweedie.* [n. d.] 12mo, pp. 16. H. — Sonnets and other Poems. ... *Boston: Oliver Johnson.* 1843. 12mo, pp. 96. B., H. — Speech ... In Support of ... a Law to Prevent the Recapture of Fugitive Slaves, ... Feb. 24, 1859. *Boston: F. W. Wallcut.* 1859. 18mo, pp. 24. — West India Emancipation. A Speech ... at Abington, Mass., on the First Day of August, 1854. ... *Boston.* 1854. 24mo, pp. 48. H.

[Garthwaite (J. O.)] A Few Words touching a Late Pamphlet, strangely entitled "A Word of Self-Defence." [*Newark.* 1850.] 8vo, pp. 13. B., P. 26713

Gartrell (L. J.) The Dangers of Black-Republicanism and the Duty of the South. Speech of Hon. L. J. Gartrell, of Georgia, in the House of Representatives, January 10, 1860. [n. p.:] *Printed by Lemuel Towers.* [n. d.] 8vo, pp. 16. H.

Garus y Eguia (J.) Nueva Téorica y Practica de los Metales de Oro y Plata por Fundicion y Amalgamacion, &c. Por Don J. Garus y Eguia ... . *Mexico.* 1802. Sm. 4to. 26715

Garver (D.) Our Country in the Light of History. An Address ... Pennsylvania College, ... Gettysburg, Pa., September 18, 1861. By Rev. D. Garver ... . *Gettysburg: A. D. Beuhler.* 1861. 8vo, pp. 32. B., H. 26716

[Garvie (William).] Barney Rooney's Letters on Confederation, Botheration, and Political Transmogrification. *Halifax, N. S.* 1865. 12mo, pp. 56. 26717

Garza (J. J.) Correspondencia recogida á los agentes de Santa-Anna, al ser aprehendidos en Tampico por el General D. Juan José de la Garza. *Zacatecas.* 1858. 4to, pp. 20. 26718

Garza y Ballesteros (L.) Carta pastoral del Illmo. Sr. Arzobispo de México, Dr. D. Lázaro de la Garza y Ballesteros. Dirigida al V. Clero y fieles de este arzobispado con motivo de los proyectos contra la Iglesia publicados en Vera Cruz por D. Benito Juarez, Antiguo Presidente del Supreme Tribunal de la Nacion. *Mexico.* 1859. 8vo, pp. 15. + Segunda, Tercera, Cuerta, Quinta Carta Pastoral. *Mexico.* 1859. 4 pts., 8vo, pp. 16; 12; 16; 20. 26719

Against Juarez and his Vera Cruz manifesto.

GARZA Y BALLESTEROS. Defensa de la Manifestacion de los Arzobispos y Obispos de la Republica Mexicana. *Mexico.* 1860. 4to. 26720

GARZA Y BALLESTEROS. Varias Cartas sobre diversas materias, que el Yllmo. Sr. Dr. D. Lázaro de la Garza y Ballesteros, Arzobispo de Mexico, dirigio al Clero de Aquella Diocesis, y hoy dedica al de la Iglesia Mexicana. *Mexico.* 1851. 8vo, pp. 148. 26721

Also: Edicto para la publicacion del Santo Jubileo, concedido por Pio IX. *Mexico.* 1852. 4to, pp. 22; and other pieces on religious controversies, pastoral letters, etc.

GASCOYNE (P.) Pétition aux membres de l'Assemblée Nationale, sur les actes de spoliation et de persécution exécutés contre lui par le gouvernement argentin, présidé par le Gal Rosas, et sur la violation, à son égard, par ce même gouvernement, du traité du 29 octobre, 1840. *Paris: Lacombe.* 1851. 26722

GASKELL (W.) ... A Sermon on the Death of Mrs. Thomas Worthington ... March 14th, 1869 ... By William Gaskell ... . *Manchester: Johnson and Rawson.* 1869. 8vo, pp. 22. H.

GASPAR DA MADRE DE DEOS. Memorias para a historia da Capitania de S. Vicente, hoje Chamada de S. Paulo, do estado do Brazil publicadas de ordem da Academia R. das Sciencias. Por Gaspar da Madre de Deos, Monge Benedictino, e Correspondente da mesma Academia. *Lisboa: na topographia da Academia.* 1797. 4to, pp. (4), 242, (1). BA., C., H. 26724

GASPARIN (A. de). L'Amérique devant l'Europe. Principes et Intérêts. Par le Cte Agénor de Gasparin. *Paris: Michel Lévy frères.* 1862. 8vo, pp. 553. B., BA., C. 26725

Written with great ability, in defence of the North.

GASPARIN. America before Europe. Principles and Interests. By Count Agénor de Gasparin. Translated by Mary L. Booth. *New-York: C. Scribner.* 1862. 12mo, pp. xi, 419. + Third Edition. [*Ibid.*] 1862. 12mo, pp. xi, 419. B., BA., C. 26726

GASPARIN. Esclavage et traite. Par Agénor de Gasparin ... . *Paris: Joubert, Librairie-Éditeur.* 1838. 8vo, pp. xvi, 261, (1). B., BA. 26727

GASPARIN. Les États-Unis en 1861. Un grand peuple qui se relèvo. Par le Cte Agénor de Gasparin. 1861. *Paris: Michel Lévy frères.* 1861. 8vo, pp. viii, 414, Table, 1 l. + Seconde édition, revue et corrigée. [*Ibid.*] 1862. B., BA., H. 26728

GASPARIN. Une Parole de paix, sur le différend entre l'Anglettere et les États-Unis. Par le C[te.] A. de Gasparin, M.L. *Paris: Michel Lévy frères.* 1862. 8vo, pp. 31. B., BA., H.

Relates to the Trent affair, and advises the return of Messrs. Mason and Slidell.

GASPARIN. Reconstruction, a Letter to President Johnson. By Count A. de Gasparin. Translated by Mary L. Booth. Second Edition. *New York: Loyal Publication Society, No.* 87. 1865. 8vo, pp. 70. 26730

GASPARIN. The Uprising of a Great People. The United States in 1861. To which is added, A Word of Peace on the Difference between England and the United States. From the French of Count Agénor de Gasparin. *New York: C. Scribner.* 1861. 12mo, pp. 298. S. 26731

GASPARIN. The Uprising of a Great People. ... Abridged. ... With Appendices. *London: Sampson, Low, Son & Co.* 1861. 12mo, pp. vi, 82. B., C., H. 26732

GASPARIN. Een groot volk dat zich verheft. De Vereenigten Staten in 1861. Uit het fransch. *Utrecht.* 1861. 8vo.

Also: A Word of Peace on the American Question. Translated from the French of Gasparin, by the Rev. J. McClintock, D.D. *London: Sampson, Low & Co.* 1861. 12mo, pp. 24.

GASPARIN, *and others.* Réponse de MM. de Gasparin, Laboulaye, Martin et Cochin, à la ligue loyale et nationale de New York, 1863. *New York: Loyal Publication Society, No.* 41. 1864. 8vo, pp. 20. B., H. 26734

Also, in English, as a Reply. *New York.* 1863. 8vo, pp. 30. + *Liverpool: D. Marples.* 1864. 12mo, pp. 17. — Letter to Count Gasparin, Edward Laboulaye, Henri Martin, Augustin Cochin, and other Friends of America, in France. pp. 10. — Antwort der Herren Agenor de Gasparin, Edouard Laboulaye, Henri Martin, Augustin Cochin und anderer Freunde Amerikas in Frankreich an die Loyal National League. ... . *Loyal Publication Society, No.* 43. 1864. 8vo, pp. 11. B. — Science *v.* Modern Spiritualism; a Treatise on Turning Tables, the Supernatural in General, and Spirits. ... Translated by C. W. Robert; with Introduction, by Robert Baird. *New York.* 1861. 2 vols. C.

GASPÉ (P. A. de). Les Anciens Canadiens. Par Philippe Aubert de Gaspé. *Québec: G. et G. E. Desbarats.* 1864. 8vo, pp. 407, (2). BA. 26735

GASPÉ. The Canadians of Old. Translated By G. M. Pennée. *Quebec.* 1864. 8vo. S. 26736

Highly commended by the "Dublin Review."

GASPÉ. Mémoires par Philippe A. de Gaspé ... *Ottawa: G. E. Desbarats.* 1866. 8vo, pp. 563. B. 26737

GASPÉ (P. A. de), *Junr.* L'Influence d'un Livre, roman de Mœurs Canadiennes. Par Philippe Aubert de Gaspé. *Quebec.* 1837. 12mo. 26739

GASPE, *Canada.* Reports of the Inspectors of the Free Ports of Gaspe and Sault Ste. Marie ... . *Quebec: Printed by Hunter, Rose & Co.* 1865. 8vo, pp. 50. B., H. 26740

GASS (P.) A Journal of the Voyages and Travels of a Corps of Discovery, under the Command of Captain Lewis and Captain Clarke, of the Army of the United States; from the Mouth of the River Missouri, through the Interior Parts of North America, to the Pacific Ocean; during the Years 1804, 1805, & 1806. Containing An Authentic Relation of the most interesting Transactions during the Expedition: A Description of the Country: And an Account of its Inhabitants, Soil, Climate, Curiosities, and Vegetable and Animal Productions. By Patrick Gass. One of the Persons employed in the Expedition. With Geographical and Explanatory Notes by the Publisher. *Pittsburgh: David M'Keehan.* 1807. 12mo. C., P. + *London: Re-Printed for J. Rudd.* 1808. 8vo, pp. iv, 381. H. + Second Edition, with Six Engravings. *Philadelphia: Mathew Carey.* 1810. 12mo, pp. xii, 262. S. + Third Edition. [*Ibid.*] 1811. + Fourth Edition. [*Ibid.*] 1812. 12mo. [*Ibid.*] 1815. 12mo. + *Dayton, Ohio.* 1847, &c. 12mo, pp. 238. 26741

GASS. Voyage des Capitaines Lewis et Clarke, depuis l'embouchure du Missouri, jusqu'à l'entrée de la Colombia dans l'Océan Pacifique; fait dans les années 1804, 1805 et 1806, par ordre du gouvernement des États-Unis. ... Rédigé en anglais par Patrice Gass, ... et traduit en francais par A. J. N. Lallemant ... avec des notes ... par J. B. Tardieu. *Paris: Arthus Bertrand.* 1810. 8vo, pp. xviii, 443. Map. C., H., P. 26742

This translation contains notes and additions, and a map, by Tardieu. *See* "Edinb. Rev.," XXIV. 412, and "Lond. Q. Rev.," XII. 317. Finotti thinks there is a Dutch translation.

GASSAWAY (S. G.) The Limits of Episcopal Prerogative at a Canonical Visitation: being the Substance of an Argument delivered before the Convention of the Diocese of Maryland, May 31, 1850. By the Rev. S. G. Gassaway, ... Together with a Sketch of the Proceedings of the Convention in relation to that

subject. *Washington: printed by John T. Towers.* 1850. 8vo, pp. 47. H. 26743

GASSETT (H. M.) Categorical Account of the Female Medical College, ... By Helen M. Gassett. *Boston: For the Author.* 1855. 8vo, pp. 138, (1). B., H. 26744

[GASSETT (Henry).] Catalogue of Books on the Masonic Institution, in Public Libraries of Twenty-Eight States of the Union, Anti-Masonic in Arguments and Conclusions. By Distinguished Literary Gentlemen, Citizens of the United States. With Introductory Remarks, and a Compilation of Records. By a Member of the Suffolk Committee of 1829. *Boston: Printed by Damrell & Moore.* 1852. 8vo, pp. xi, 270. B., BA., 26745

GASTELU (A. V.) Arte de Lengua Mexicana compuesto por el Bachiller Don Antonio Vazquez Gastelu el Rey de Figueroa: Cathedrático de dicha Lengua en los Reales Collegios de S. Pedro y S. Juan. Sacalo á luz por orden del Illustrissimo Señor Doctor Don Manuel Fernandez de Sancta Cruz, ... *Con Liçencia en la Puebla de los Angeles, en la Imprenta nueva de Diego Fernandez de Leon, año de* 1689. *Impresso à su costa: Hallarase en su Libreria.* 4to, 6 l., 42 l. + Segunda Impression. *Puebla de los Angeles* [*Mexico*]. 1693. 4to. 26746

Both of these editions are of extreme rarity.

GASTELU. Arte de Lengua Mexicana compuesto por el Bachiller D. Antonio Vasquez Gastelu, ... *Con liçēcia en la Puebla, por Diego Fernādez de Leō, y por su original en la Imprenta de Francisco Xavier de Morales, y Salazar, Impressor, y Mercader de libros en el Portal de Borja, donde se vende. Año de* 1716. 4to, 2 l., 54 l. 26747

GASTELU. Arte de Lengua Mexicana, ... correjido segun su original por el Br. D. Antonio de Almedo y Torre. ... *Con licençia en la Puebla, por Diego Fernandez de Leon.* 1726. 4to, 2 l., 54 l. 26748

GASTELU. Cathecismo Breve, que precisamente deve saber el Christiano. Dispuesto en Lengua Mexicana por el Licenciado Don Antonio Vasquez Castelu [*sic*] el Rev de Figueroa, Cathedrático que fuè, de dicha Lengua, en los Reales Colegios de S. Pedro y S. Juan. ... *Reimpresso en la Puebla: Por la Viuda de Miguel de Ortega, e. el Portal de las Flores, donde se vende. Año de* 1733. 4to, pp. 1, 2. + *Puebla,* [*Mexico*]. 1838. + *Reimpreso en Orizava. Impr. de la Caja de ahorros por J. Ramon Matos.* 1846. 8vo, pp. 16. 26749

GASTELU. Catecismo in idioma Mexicano por Ant. Varguez Gastelu. *Puebla.* 1854. 8vo. 26750

GASTELU. Breve Catecismo de la Doctrina Cristiana, traducido al Mexicano. *Orizaba: B. Aburto.* 1865. 8vo, pp. 19.

GASTINE (Civique de), *pseudon.* *See* [Toulette (E. L. J.)]

GASTON (W.) Speech of the Hon. William Gaston, ... on the Bill to Authorize A Loan of Twenty-Five Millions of Dollars, delivered, ... February 1814. *Washington City.* [n. d.] 8vo, pp 53. + [Another Edition.] *Washington.* [n. d.] 12mo, pp. 48. + *Georgetown: Printed by Robert Allison.* 1814. 8vo, pp. 36. B., H. 26752

The proposed loan was for the purchase of Canada. Also: Address before the Philanthropic and Dialectic Societies ... June 20, 1832. ... *Raleigh: Printed by Jas. Gales & Son.* 1832. 8vo, pp. 16. + Second Edition. *Richmond.* 1832. B., H. — An Address ... before the American Whig and Cliosohpic Societies of the College of New Jersey. September, 29, 1835. ... *Princeton: printed by John Bogart.* MDCCCXXXV. 8vo, pp. 42. B., H. + Second Edition. *Princeton: R. E. Hornor.* 1835. — Speech ... in Support of the Proposition ... to Expunge from the Rules of the House ... the "Previous Question." *Georgetown, D. C.: James B. Carter.* 1816. 8vo, pp. 31. B., S. — Speech ... on the Recent State Convention of North Carolina ... for ... revising the Constitution. *Baltimore.* [1835.] 8vo, pp. 50. BA.

GATCHEL (S.) A Contrast to the Reverend Nathaniel Whitaker, D.D. his Confutation of the Reverend John Wise, A.M. Vindication of the New-England Churches; and the Churches' Quarrel Espoused. By Samuel Gatchel. ... *Danvers: Printed by E. Russell.* M,DCC,LXXVIII. 8vo, pp. 23. BA. 26753

GATCHEL. The Signs of the Times: ... Remarks ... relative to the Remarkable Phenomenon, or Dark-Day which appeared in New-England on the Nineteenth of May, 1780: ... By Samuel Gatchel ... . *Danvers: Printed by E. Russell.* M,DCC,-LXXXI. 12mo, pp. 16. H. 26754

GATCHELL (J.) The Disenthralled; being Reminiscences of the Life of Joseph Gatchell. *Troy.* 1843. 8vo. 26755

GATEREAU (*M.*) Histoire des troubles de St. Domingue, depuis le mois d'Octobre 1789, jusqu'au 16 Juillet 1791. Par M. Gatereau, Citoyen du Cap François. *Paris.* 1792. 8vo, pp. 153. 26756

GATES (H.) King George's Right to the Crown of Great Britain displayed. Being a Collection from History, from the First Known Times to the Present Year, 1769. ... Extracted by

Hezekiah Gates ... . *Boston: Printed by W. McAlpine.* M,DCC,-LXXII. BA., H. 26757

GATES (T. R.) The Trials, Experience, Exercises of Mind, and First Travels of Theophilus R. Gates. Written by himself. *Poughkeepsie: printed by C. C. Adams and Co. for the Author.* 1810. 18mo, pp. 214, (1). + The Second Edition, with Additions. *New York: Enoch Johnston, Junr.* 1818. 12mo, pp. 514.

GATES (W.) Proceedings of the Court-Martial for the Trial of Major W. Gates. *New-York.* 1837. 8vo. 26759

[GATFORD (Lionel).] Publick|Good|Without Private|Interests:|Or,|A Compendious Remonstrance of the|present sad State and Condition of the English|Colonie in Virginia.|With|A Modest Declaration of the severall Causes|(so far as by the Rules of Right, Reason and Religious Obser-|vation may be Collected) why it hath not prospered better hitherto|As also,|A Submissive suggestion of the most prudentiall probable wayes, and|meanes, both Divine and Civill (that the inexpert Remembrancer could|for the present recall to minde) for its happyer improvement|and advancement for the future.|Humbly presented to His Highness the Lord Protectour,|By a Person zealously devoted,|To the more effectual propagating of the Gospel in that Nation,|and to the inlargement of the Honour and Benefit, both of the said|Colonie, and this whole Nation, from whence they|have been transplanted.|*London,*|*Printed for Henry Marsh, and are to be sold at*|*the Crown in S. Paul's Church-yard.* 1657.| 4to, pp. (20), 26. 26760

A volume of extreme rarity. Reprinted in facsimile at Vienna for E. Tross, of Paris. The reprint is also scarce.

Gathered Leaves. *See* [Dana (Eliza A.)], Vol. v., No. 18409.

GATINE (Adolphe Ambroise Alexandre). Abolition de l'esclavage á la Guadeloupe.—Quatre mois de gouvernement dans cette colonie. *Paris.* 1849. 8vo. 26761

Also: Situation des affranchis à l'ile de la Réunion. [*Ibid.*] 1850. 4to.

GATTERER (J. Chr.) De belli Romanorum socialis caussis et eventu, respectu ad bellum cum Coloniis Americanis gestum habito. *Gottingen.* 1783. Sm. Folio, pp. 8. 26762

"Of the highest rarity. It is reprinted in the works of C. G. Heyne."—MULLER.

GAUDICHAUD-BEAUPRÉ. *See* Vaillant.

GAULD (George). An Account of the Surveys of Florida, &c. With Directions for Sailing from Jamaica or the West Indies, by the West End of Cuba, and through the Gulf of Florida. To accompany Mr. Gauld's Charts. *London: W. Faden.* 1790. 4to, pp. 27. Map. 26763

The author served as a volunteer during the siege of Pensacola, by the French and Spanish navy, and the French, Spanish, and American troops. *See* extract from his journal in the introduction to this work.

GAULD. Observations on the Florida Kays, Reef, and Gulf; with Directions for Sailing along the Kays, From Jamaica by the Grand Cayman and the West End of Cuba; also, a Description ... of ... West Florida, ... By George Gauld, to accompany his Charts. ... *London: W. Faden.* 1796. 4to, pp. 28. 26764

GAUME (J. A.) Dónde vamos á parar? Ojeada sobre las tendencias de la epoca actual. *Mexico.* 1851. 4to. 26765

G[AUNTLEY] (W[illiam]). Remarks on a Certain Publication, entitled, Macaulay's Portrait of the Founder of Quakerism, 1856. *Sheffield: Rogers, Printer.* 1856. 12mo, pp. 12.

Signed W. G. Another edition has the auther's name on the title.

GAUSSOIN (E.) Memoir on the Island of Navassa, W. I. By Eugene Gaussoin. *Baltimore.* 1866. 8vo, pp. 32. 26767

GAUSSOIN. The Island of Navassa, Illustrated in Six Large Folio Chromo-Lithograph Plates. By Eugene Gaussoin. *Baltimore.* 1866. 26768

GAUTIER. Plan d'une colonie, à la Guyane française sur les bords d'Ayapack et d'Ouenay. 1794. 4to. 26769

[GAUTIER DU TRONCHOY.] Journal de la campagne des isles de l'Amérique, qu' a fait Monsieur D—— La prise & possession de l'isle saint Christophe, avec une description exacte des animaux, des arbres, et des plantes les plus curieuses de l'Amérique. La manière de vivre des sauvages, leurs mœurs, leur police & religion. Avec la relation de la surprise que voulut faire la Garrison de Fribourg sur des deux Brissack. Par G. D. T. Ensigne dans le vaisseau du roy, le Zeripsée. *Troyes: Jacques le Febre.* 1709. 12mo, pp. 274. 26770

GAUTTIER (G. A.) Recherches sur l'organization de la peau de l'homme et sur les causes de sa coloration. *Paris.* 1819. pp. 83. 26771

The Gavel, and Freemason's Journal. ... Bro. Robt. Ramsay, Editor. *Orillia and Montreal.* 1870–71. 2 vols., 8vo. 26772

The Gavel: a Monthly Periodical devoted to Odd Fellowship and General Literature. By C. C. Burr and John Tanner. *Albany: J. Munsell.* 1845. 8vo, pp. 324. Portraits. 26773

GAVET (D.), *and* BOUCHER (P.) Jakaré-Ouassou, ou les Tupinambas: Chronique Brésilienne. *Paris.* 1830. 8vo. S.

GAVOCK (R. W.) A Tennessean Abroad; or Letters from Europe, Africa and Asia. By Randall W. Gavock. *New York.* 1854. 12mo. 26775

GAY (B.) The Accomplished Judge; or, A Compleat Dress for Magistrates. A Sermon ... at Keene, at the First Opening of the Inferior Court, ... October 8, 1771. By Bunker Gay, A.M. ... *Portsmouth: Printed by D. Fowle.* 1773. 8vo, pp. 29.

GAY. A Genuine and Correct Account of the Captivity; Sufferings, and Deliverance of Mrs. Jemima Howe. By Bunker Gay. *Boston.* 1792. 8vo, pp. 20. 26777

Also: A Discourse ... at Hinsdale, July 29, 1792 ... occasioned by the Death of Mrs. Abigail Gay. ... *Greenfield: Printed by Thomas Dickman.* MDCCXCII. 8vo, pp. 24. H. — Sermon at the Interment of the Rev. Lemuel Hedge, at Warwick, [Mass.] who died Oct. 15, 1777. ... *Hartford, Con.* 1778. 8vo. S. — To Sing of Mercy and Judgment Recommended and Exemplified. Thanksgiving Discourse. ... . *Greenfield.* 1793. 8vo, pp. 19.

GAY (C.) Fragment d'un Voyage dans le Chili et au Cusco, patrie des anciens Incas. Par Claude Gay. *Paris.* 1843. 8vo, pp. 24. 26778

GAY. Historia Fisica y Politica de Chile, segun documentos adquiridos en esta Republica durante doce annos de residencia en ella, y publicado bajo los auspicios del Supremo Gobierno: por Claudio Gay, Ciudadano Chileno. *Paris.* 1844–62. 8vo.

This grand work forms 24 vols., 8vo, and 2 vols., 4to, of plates, divided as follows: Botanica. *Paris.* 1845. 8 vols., 8vo; Documentos sobre la Historia, la Estadistica y la Geografia. *Paris.* 1846. 2 vols., 8vo; Zoologia. *Paris.* 1847. 8 vols., 8vo; Historia, 6 vols.; Atlas, 2 vols., folio.

GAY (E.) The Alienation of Affections from Ministers consider'd and improv'd. A Sermon Preach'd at the Ordination of the Reverend Mr. Jonathan Mayhew ... June 17. 1747. By Ebenezer Gay, A.M. ... *Boston, N. E.: Printed by Rogers and Fowle.* MDCCXLVII. 8vo, pp. 28, (4). BA., H. 26780

GAY. A Beloved Disciple of Jesus characterized. In a Sermon Preached at the West-Church in Boston, July 27. A.M. 1766. The Third Lord's-Day from the Decease of ... Jonathan Mayhew, D.D. By Ebenezer Gay, A.M. ... *Boston: Printed by R. and S. Draper, T. and J. Fleet, and Edes and Gill.* MDCCLXVI. 8vo, pp. 30. BA., H. 26781

Also: St. John's Vision ... In a Discourse ... July 27, P.M., 1766 ... of the Decease of the Reverend Jonathan Mayhew, D.D. By Ebenezer Gay, A.M. Pastor. ... *Boston: Printed by R. and S. Draper.* 1766. 8vo, pp. 40. BA., H.

GAY. The Character and Work of a Good Ruler, and the Duty of an Obliged People. ... A Sermon, preach'd before his Excellency William Shirley, Esq; May 29th, 1745. ... By Ebenezer Gay, A.M. ... *Boston: Daniel Gookin.* 1745. 8vo, pp. 33. B., BA., H., M. 26782

GAY. Natural Religion, ... Dudleian-Lecture, at Harvard-College, ... May 9, 1759. By Ebenezer Gay, A.M. ... *Boston, New-England: John Draper.* 1759. 8vo, pp. 34. BA., H., M.

GAY. The Old Man's Calendar. A Discourse ... delivered in the first Parish of Hingham, on the Lord's-Day, August 26, 1781, The Birth-Day of the Author, Ebenezer Gay. *Boston: Printed by John Boyle.* MDCCLXXXI. 8vo, pp. 24. B. + Second Edition. *London.* 1783. + The Fourth Edition. *Dover, N. H.* MDCCXCIII. 8vo, pp. 32. BA. + *Stockbridge: Re-printed by Loring Andrews.* M,DCC,XCIV. 8vo, pp. 16. + *Salem: J. D. Cushing.* 1822. 8vo, pp. 36. + *Hingham: Jedediah Farmer.* 1846. 8vo, pp. 32. 26784

The edition of 1846 contains an historical, genealogical, and biographical appendix. Drake says it went through several editions in England, and was translated into one or two of the languages of continental Europe. We have only seen one English edition.

GAY. Well-Accomplish'd Soldiers, a Glory to their King, and Defence to their Country. A Sermon preach'd at Hingham ... May 10. 1738. In the Audience of Four Military Companies; ... By Ebenezer Gay, V.D.M. ... *Boston: David Henchman.* 1738. 12mo, pp. (1), 29. BA., H. 26785

Also: A Call from Macedonia. A Sermon ... at Hingham, ... October 12. 1768, at the Ordination of the Reverend Caleb Gannett ... in the Town of Cumberland, and Province of Nova-Scotia. [Ch., William Rand; R. H.; Daniel Shute.] ... . *Boston: Printed by Richard Draper, and Thomas and John Fleet.* MDCCLXVIII. 8vo, pp. 39. BA., H. — The Devotions of God's People. A Sermon ... Hingham, December 6, 1770. ... a Day of Public Thanksgiving and Prayer. ... *Boston: Printed by Richard Draper.* MCCLXXI [*sic*]. 8vo, pp. 23. B., BA. — A Discourse on ... A Pillar of Salt, To Season a Corrupt Age. A Sermon to bring Lot's Wife to Remembrance. ... . *Boston: D. Henchman.* MDCCXXVIII. 8vo, pp. (3), 64. BA., H. — The Duty of People to Pray for and Praise their Rulers. A Sermon ... in Hingham, August 12. 1730. On Occasion of the Arrival of His Excellency Jonathan Belcher, Esq; to his Government. ... *Boston: Printed by Thomas Fleet.* 1730. 8vo, pp. 35. BA., H. — The Evangelical Preacher. A Sermon ... at the Ordination of the Rev'd Mr. Bunker Gay, at Hinsdale, August 17th, 1763. ... *Boston: Printed by Richard & Samuel Draper.* 1763. 8vo, pp. 43. — Jesus Christ the Wise Master-builder ... A Sermon Preached at the Installment of the Reverend Mr. Ezra Carpenter ... in Keene and Swanzey, ... New-Hampshire. ... October 4th, 1753. *Boston: Printed by S. Kneeland.* 1753. 2 l., pp. ii, 26. — The Levite not to be Forsaken. A Sermon ... at the Installment of the Rev. Grindal Rawson ... in Yarmouth, December 10th, 1755. ... *Boston.* 1756. 8vo, pp. 29. B. + The Second Edition. *Dover, (N. H.): Printed by E. Ladd.* M,DCC,XCIII. 8vo. — Ministers are Men of Like Passions with Others. A Sermon Preachd at Barnstable, May 12, 1725. The Day on which a Church was gathered ... and Mr. Joseph Green was ordained Pastor of it. ... *Boston: Printed by B. Green.* 1725. 8vo, pp. 41. BA., M., W. — ... A Sermon Preach'd at the Ordination of the Rev. Mr. Ebenezer Gay, Junior. In Suffield, Jan. 13, 1741, 2. And Publish'd at the Desire of the People there. *Boston: S. Eliot.* 1742. 8vo, pp. 39. BA. — The Mystery of the Seven Stars in Christ's Right Hand. ... in a Sermon ... at the Ordination of the Reverend Mr. Jonathan Dorby, ... in Scituate; November 13, 1751. *Boston: Printed by J. D. Draper.* 1752. 8vo, pp. 31. BA. — A Sermon Preached at Hingham on a Training Day there, May 10, 1738. ... *Boston: Printed by T. Fleet.* 1738. 12mo. — Sermon at the Installment of Ezra Carpenter, as Pastor at Keene and Swanzey, N. H. Oct. 4, 1753. ... *Boston.* [n. d.] 12mo. W. — ... A Sermon preach'd before the Ministers of the Province of the Massachusetts-Bay in New-England, at their Annual Convention in Boston; May 29. 1746. ... *Boston: Printed for D. Gookin.* 1746. 8vo, pp. 33, (1). BA. — The Untimely Death of a Man of God Lamented. In a Sermon Preach'd at the Funeral of the Reverend Mr. John Hancock ... in Braintree; Who Died May 7th, 1744. ... *Boston: Printed by S. Kneeland and T. Green.* MDCCXLIV. 12mo, pp. (4), 25. BA. — Zechariah's Vision of Christ's Martial Glory ... In a Sermon preach'd at the Desire of the Honourable Artillery-Company in Boston, June 3, 1728. ... *Boston: J. Eliot, J. Phillips, and B. Lone.* 1728. 8vo, pp. 38. BA., H.

GAY (E.) An Oration pronounced at Suffield, on Saturday, the 22d of Feb. A.D. 1800, the day recommended by Congress for the people to assemble publickly, to testify their Grief for the Death of General George Washington. By the Rev. Ebenezer Gay. *Suffield.* 1800. 8vo, pp. 16. N. 26786

Also: Oration on American Independence, July 5, 1790.

GAY (F. A.) For Gratuitous Distribution. Sketches of California. An Account of the Life, Manners and Customs of the Inhabitants. Its History, ... By Frederick Gay. Also Interesting information in Relation to the Canchalagua, a Californian Plant of Rare Medicinal Virtues. *Boston: Redding & Co.* 1848. 8vo, pp. 16. B., H. 26787

[GAY (John).] The Mohocks; a Tragi-Comical Farce. *London: Bernard Lintott.* 1712. 12mo, 4 l., pp. 21. + [*Ibid.*] 1717. 26788

GAY (M. M.) Gleanings from Real Life. By Mr. M. M. Gay. *Buffalo.* 1858. 12mo. C. 26789

[GAYARRÉ (Charles).] Address on the "Religious Test" to the Convention of the American Party assembly in Philadelphia on the 5th June, 1855. 1855. 8vo, pp. 34. H. 26790

GAYARRÉ. Essai Historique sur Louisiane. Par Charles Gayarré. *Nouvelle Orléans.* 1830. 2 vols., 8vo. 26791

GAYARRÉ. Histoire de la Louisiane. By Charles Gayarré. ... *Nouvelle-Orléans: Magne et Weisse.* 18-4647. 2 vols., 8vo, pp. (2), xi, 377; vii, 427. C., H. 26792

GAYARRÉ. History of Louisiana. The French Domination. By Charles Gayarré. *New York.* 1854. 2 vols., 8vo, pp. 540; xi, 380. Map. + The Spanish Domination. *New York: Redfield.* 1854. 8vo, pp. xii, 649. + The American Domination. *New York: William J. Widdleton.* 1866. 8vo, pp. viii, 693. B., C. 26793

GAYARRÉ. Letter from Judge Gayarré. The Cession of Louisiana to the United States. [n. p. n. d.] 8vo, pp. 4.

Written to sustain the secession of Louisiana from the United States.

GAYARRÉ. Louisiana; its Colonial History and Romance. By Charles Gayarré. *New York: Harper & Brothers.* 1851. 8vo, pp. 546. B., H. 26795

GAYARRÉ. Louisiana: Its History as a French Colony. Third Series of Lectures. By Charles Gayarré. *New York: John Wiley.* 1852. 8vo, pp. 380. Map. H. 26796

GAYARRÉ. Romance of the History of Louisiana. A Series of Lectures. By Charles Gayarré. ... *New York: D. Appleton & Company.* M DCC XLVIII. 12mo, pp. 265. B., BA. 26797

Also: Address ... On the Late Frauds ... at the Election ... 7th November, 1853, in ... New Orleans. *New Orleans: Printed by Sherman & Wharton.* 1853. 8vo, pp. 16. BA., H. — Address to the People of Louisiana on the State of Parties. ... *New Orleans: Printed by Sherman, Wharton & Company.* 1855. 8vo, pp. (1), 40. H. — General Jackson. A Sketch. *New Orleans.* 1857. 8vo. — A Lecture on Oaths, Amnesties, and Rebellion, delivered ... January 25, 1866. ... . *New Orleans.* 1866. 8vo, pp. 26. H. — Influence of the Mechanic Arts on the Human Race. Two Lectures. ... *New York: John Wiley.* 1854. 12mo, pp. (2), 86. H. — The School for Politics: A Dramatic Novel. *New York: D. Appleton and Co.* 1854. 12mo, pp. 158. C., H. ("An exhibition of party frauds." — DUYCKINCK, II. 401. Mr. Duyckinck refers to two other tracts by Mr. Gayarré, which I have not seen.)

GAYLE [(John)]. Speech of Mr. Gayle, of Alabama, on ... a Territorial Government in Oregon. Delivered ... March 28, 1848. *Washington.* 1848. 8vo, pp. 14. H. 26798

GAYLER (C.) Out of the Streets. A Story of New York Life. By C. Gayler. *New York: R. M. DeWitt.* 1869. 12mo, pp. 360. B. 26799

GAYLEY (J. F.) A History of the Jefferson Medical College of Philadelphia. With Biographical Sketches of the Early Professors. By James F. Gayley. *Philadelphia.* 1858. 4to, pp. 61.

GAYLORD (N. M.) Kossuth and the American Jesuits. A Lecture ... in Lowell, Jan. 4, 1852. By N. M. Gaylord. ... *Lowell: Merrill & Strair.* 1852. 8vo, pp. 48. H. 26801

Also: Letter ... containing Reasons for refusing to sign a Protest against American Slavery. ... *Memphis: Enquirer Office.* 1846. 8vo, pp. 31. BA.

GAYLORD (W. L.) The Soldier, God's Minister. A Discourse delivered in Fitzwilliam, N. H., October 5, 1862, on the Departure of a Company of Volunteers for the Seat of War. By William Gaylord. *Fitchburg: "Rollstone Office."* 1862. 8vo, pp. 21. 26802

GAYLORD (W.), *and* TUCKER (L.) American Husbandry; being a Series of Essays on Agriculture; Compiled principally from "The Cultivator" and "The Genesee Farmer," with Additions, by Willis Gaylord and Luther Tucker. *New York.* 1840. 2 vols., 12mo. + *New York.* 1843. + *New York.* 1847. 2 vols., 18mo. 26803

GAYOSO (Jose de Souza). Compendio Historico-Politico dos principios da lavoura do Maranhão, suas producçoens, et progressos que tem tido até ao prezente, entraves que à vao deteri orando [etc.] Por Raymundo José de Souza Gayoso. *Paris: Imprimerie de Rougeron.* 1818. 8vo, pp. 344. 26804

GAYTAN DE TORRES (M.) Relacion de las minas de cobre que hay en las serranias de Cocorote en la provincia de Venezuela y modo de beneficiar las, por D. Manuel de Torres. Fol.

Title from Ternaux, who gives no place of publication.

GAZAIGNES (Jean Antoine). Annales de la société des soi-disans Jésuites; ou recueil historique-chronologique de tous les actes, écrites, dénonciations, avis doctrinaux, [etc.] contre la doctrine, l'enseignement, les entreprises et les forfaits des soi-disans Jésuites, depuis 1552, époque de leur naissance en France, jusqu'en 1763. *Paris.* 1764–1771. 5 vols., 4to. C. 26806

Gazelle, a True Tale of the Great Rebellion; and other Poems. [By John B. Rich?] *Boston: Lee & Shepard.* 1866. 16mo, pp. 194. BA. 26807

GAZER (G.), *pseudonym.* Frederick de Algeroy, the Hero of Camden Plains. A Revolutionary Tale. By Giles Gazer. *New York: Collins & Hannay.* 1825. 12mo, pp. 235. C. 26808

Gazeta de Columbia. *Cucuta.* 1821. 26809

The first twelve numbers were published at *Cucuta*, in 4to, the rest, called "Gaceta de Colombia," at *Bogota*, in folio.

Gazeta de Literatura de Mexico. *See* Alzate, Vol. I.

Gazette de Leyde. Nouvelles de livers endroits. *Leyde: Et. Luzac.* 1778–97. 20 vols., 4to. 26810

"This valuable journal is of the highest importance for the history of America. Each number is divided into two parts, each of four pages, the second of them bearing the title 'Supplement aux Nouvelles' is very often entirely filled by the news from America. The editor of this Gazette, Mr. Luzac, was a very learned man, of high, liberal principles, who fostered and encouraged to his utmost the contest of American United States against England. He was in correspondence with the heads of the American Revolution, and especially with J. Adams. These relations enabled him to publish many of the most important documents, as he himself says, 'le premier en Europe.'" — MULLER.

The Gazette of the United States. A National Paper, Published at the Seat of Government. ... *New York and Philadelphia: John Fenno.* 1789–92. Folio. B. 26811

Continued as Gazette of the United States, and Daily Evening Advertiser. *New York and Philadelphia: John Fenno.* 1794.

Gazetteer of the World, or Dictionary of Geographical Knowledge, ... Edited by a Member of the Royal Geographical Society. Compiled from the most recent Authorities. *Edinburgh: A. Fullerton & Co.* 1851–56. 7 vols., rl. 8vo. Maps and 120 Engravings. B., BA. 26812

The best and most complete of all Gazetteers, and forming a complete body of modern geography, physical, political, statistical, historical, and ethnographical.

Gazlay's Business Directory of the Five Great Cities of California and Oregon. 1864–65. *San Francisco and New York: D. Gazlay.* 4to, pp. 430. 26813

Il Gazzettiere Americano Contenente un distinto ragguaglio di tutte le parti del Nuovo Mondo, della loro Situazione, Clima, Terreno, Prodotti, Stato antico e moderno, Merci, Manifatture, e Commercio. Con una esatta descrizione delle Città, Piazze, Porti, Baje, Fiumi, Laghi, Montagne, Passi, e Fortificazioni.

Il tutto destinato ad esporre lo stato presente delle cose en quella parte di Globo, e le mire, e interessi delle diverse Potenze, che hanno degli stabilimenti in America. Tradotto dall' Inglese e arricchito di Aggiunte, Note, Carte, e Rami. *Livorno: per Marco Coltellini.* MDCCLXIII. 3 vols., 4to, pp. xxiii, 216, (1); 256; 253. 21 Maps and 57 Plates. B., BA. 26814

For the English version, *see* American Gazetteer, Vol. I., No. 1090.

Het geamplieerde Octroy | Van de | Oost-Indische | Compagnie, | By de Hoogh. Mogh. Heeren | Staten Generael, tot wech-nem-inge van alle disputen ende questien, den 13. Martij deses jaers gearresteert. | Midtsgaders: | Eene corte verthooninge vande noot-sakelickheyt | vande geoctroyeerde West Indische Navigatie, by mid- | del vande welcke de vrye Nederlandtsche Republicque, met Godes | hulpe tot de hoogste prosperiteyt int stuc vande al-derrijckste waren | vande geheele werelt, tot hare ende der Partici-panten voordeel syn | te gheraecken. | ... | *Ghedruckt Int laer ons Heeren.* 1623. | 4to, 12 leaves. 26815

This enlarged charter of the East India Company includes a short demonstration of the necessity of the chartered West India navigation. *See* Asher, No. 82.

GEAR (A. S.) National Bank Note Detector. Fourth Edition. *New Haven.* 1866. 18mo. 26816

GEAR. The Nation's Grief for its Fallen Chief, A Sermon preached in the First Congregation at Chapel, Philadelphia, Sabbath Evening, April 23d, 1865. By the Pastor, Rev. D. L. Gear. Published by Request. *Philadelphia: Ringwalt & Brown, Printers.* 1865. 8vo, pp. 8. 26817

GEARE (A.) Eben Ezer; Or a Monument of Thankfulness: Being a true Account of a late miraculous Preservation of 9 Men in a small Boat, which was inclosed within Islands of Ice about 70 Leagues from Land, and continuing in Distress 20 Days; with the most remarkable Passages which happened in their Voyage from Plymouth to the Newfoundland, in the Ship called the Langdon Frigate, Capt. Arthur Holdsworth Commander; with a List of the Names of those that survived, and can witness to the Truth of this Relation. Written by Allen Geare, Chief Mate of the Ship, who was a Principal Sharer both in the Misery and the Mercy. *London: Printed by Sam. Smith.* 1708. 8vo, pp. 8. 26818

GEARY (J. W.) A Sketch of the Early Life and of the Civil and Military Services of Maj. Gen. John W. Geary, Candidate of the National Union Party for Governor of Pennsylvania. [n. p.] 1866. 8vo, pp. 32. H. 26819

Also: Correspondence ... relating to the Foreign Commerce of the United States. [*Harrisburg.* 1870.] 8vo, pp. 13. H.

GEBEL TEIR. *See* [Tudor (William)].

GEBELIN. *See* Court de Gebelin, Vol. v., No. 17174.

GEBHARD (F.) Illinois as it Is. By F. Gébhard. *Chicago.* 1857. 12mo. Maps. 26820

[GEBHARDT (A. G.)] Actes et Mémoires concernant les négociations qui ont en lieu entre la France et les États-Unis de l'Amérique, depuis 1793, jusqu'à ... 30 septembre 1800. *Londres: De l'Imprimerie de J. B. G. Vogel.* 1807. 3 vols., 8vo, pp. vi, 368; 451; 481, 2, (1). BA. 26821

GEBHARDT. State Papers relating to the Diplomatick Transactions between the American and French Governments, From the Year 1793, to the Conclusion of the Convention, on the 30th of September, 1800. Collected by A. G. Gebhardt, ... *London.* 1816. 3 vols., 12mo, pp. vi, 368; 451; 481, 2. 26822

GEDDES [(Alexander)]. An Apology for Slavery; or, Six Cogent Arguments against Abolition of Slave Trade. *London.* 1792. 8vo. C. 26823

GEDDES (G.) Origin and History of the Measures that led to the Construction of the Erie Canal ... By George Geddes, 1866. *Syracuse.* 1866. 8vo. 26824

Also: Observations upon Plank Roads, ... *Syracuse.* 1850. C. — Report on the Agriculture and Industry of the County of Onondaga, N. Y., with an Introductory Account of the Aborigines. *Albany.* 1860. 8vo. — Address ... N. Y. State Agricultural Society, Albany, February 3, 1862. ... and Address of Ezra Cornell, on taking the Chair as President Elect, ... *Albany: Printed by Charles Van Benthuysen.* 1862. 8vo, pp. 38. H.

GEDDES (James). Report to the Canal Commissioners of Ohio of the Surveys and Examinations of the Country between Lake Erie and the Ohio River. *Columbus.* 1823. 8vo. 26825

GEDDES (M.), *Translator.* *See* History of the Church.

GEDDIE (J.) Memorial to the Very Reverend the Synod of the Presbyterian Church of Nova Scotia. By John Geddie. *Pictou.* 1844. 4to, pp. 4. 26826

[GEE (Joshua).] The Trade and Navigation of Great-Britain considered: Shewing That the surest Way for a Nation to increase in Riches, is to prevent the Importation of such Foreign Commodities as may be rais'd at Home. That this Kingdom is capable of raising within itself, and its Colonies, Materials for employing all our Poor in those Manufactures, which we now import from such of our Neighbours who refuse the Admission of ours. Some Account of the Commodities each Country we trade with takes from us, and what we take from them; with Observations on the Balance. *London.* 1729. 8vo. + The Second Edition. *London: Sam. Buckley.* 1730. 8vo, pp. (18), 147. + The Third Edition. To which is added, A Supplement. *London: Sam. Buckley.* 1731. 8vo, pp. (24), 164. + The Fourth Edition. *London: A. Bettesworth and C. Hitch.* 1738. 12mo, pp. (24), 164 + Fifth Edition. *Glasgow: R. & A. Foulis.* 1750. 12mo, 12 l., pp. 180. + Sixth Edition. [*Ibid.*] 1755. 12mo. P. + [*Ibid.*] 1760. 12mo. + New Edition, with Interesting Additions by a Merchant. *London.* 1767. 12mo. BA. + [*Ibid.*] 1768. 8vo. 26827

The author states that the work was printed for private distribution. This probably relates to the first edition only, which was anonymous. A great part of it relates to the trade of the plantations in America. "A small but excellent treatise." — ANDERSON's *Hist. Comm.*, I. xxv–xlviii.

GEE. Sur le Commerce et la Navigation de la Grande-Bretagne. *Paris.* 1749. 12mo. 26828

GEE. Two Curious Papers written in 1739, by Mr. Joshua Gee, and others. *London: J. Almon.* 1767. 26829

Forms No. IV. of Vol. III. of Almon's Tracts on Taxing the British Colonies.

GEE (J.) Israel's Mourning For Aaron's Death. A Sermon Preached on the Lord's-Day After the Death of the very Reverend and Learned Cotton Mather, DD. ... By Joshua Gee ... . *Boston: S. Gerrish.* MDCCXXVIII. 12mo, pp. (4), 34. B., BA.

GEE. A Letter To the Reverend Mr. Nathaniel Eells, Moderator of the Late Convention of Pastors, ... Containing Some Remarks on their Printed Testimony ... . By Joshua Gee ... . *Boston: N. Proctor.* 1743. 8vo, pp. 17. BA., H., M. 26831

For an Answer, *see* Hanwich (J.)

[GEE.] The Straight Gate and the Narrow Way. ... Two Sermons. ... *Boston: D. Henchman.* 1729. 12mo, pp. (1), 103.

GEER (G. P.) Geer's Express Directory and Railway Forwarder's Guide. ... By Geo. P. Geer ... . New England States. Vol. I. *Springfield, (Mass.): C. R. Chaffee & Co.* 1858. 8vo, 3 l., pp. 271. c., H. 26833

GEER (J.) Historical Sketch and Genealogy of George and Thomas Geer, from 1621 to 1856. By James Geer. *Hartford: Elihu Geer, Printer.* 1856. 12mo, pp. 84. 26834

GEER (J. J.) Beyond the Lines: or, a Yankee Prisoner loose in Dixie. By Captain J. J. Geer. With an Introduction by Rev. Alexander Clark. ... *Philadelphia: J. W. Daughaday.* 1863. 12mo, pp. 285. Illustrations. B., BA. 26835

Gegenwart und Zukunft der Plata-Länder fur Deutschen Handel und Colonisation. *Hamburg.* 1852. 26836

Relates to Buenos Aires.

Gegenwärtiger Zustand derer Finantzen von Franckreich, worinnen die bissherigen Unternehmungen des Herrn Law ... angeführt und erlautert werden; als ein ander Theil der Beschreibung des mississipischen Handels, und Supplement zu der europäischen Fama. *Leipzig: I. F. Gleditsch.* 1720. 18mo, 5 l., pp. 252. Portrait. 26837

Gegenwärtiger Zustand der Colonie von St. Domingo, aus den Französischen. *Leipzig.* 1779. 2 vols. 26838

Geheime anecdotes, betreffende den agttienden Fructidor, en nieuwe gedenkschriften der gedeporteerden naar Guiana, door hen zelven geschreeven, zijnde het vervolg van het dagverhaal van Ramel. Uit het Fransch vertaald. *In den Haag: Isaac van Cleef.* 1800. 8vo, pp. 198. 26839

GEIJER. Öfver Europeiska colonial-väldets grundläggning. *Upsal.* 1834. 4to. 26840

GEIKIE (J. C.) George Stanley; or, Life in the Woods: a Boy's Narrative of the Adventures of a Settler's Family in Canada. Edited by John C. Geikie. *London: G. Routledge & Co.* 1864. 12mo, pp. 420. B. 26841

Reprinted in Boston as "Life in the Woods; a Narrative of the Adventures of a Settler's Family in Canada."

GEINITZ (H. B.), *and* LIEBE (Carl). Ueber ein Aequivalent der takonischen Schiefar Nordamerikas, in Deutschland und dessen geologische Stellung. *Dresden: K. Leopold. Carol. deutsche Akad.* 1866. 4to, pp. 25–52 (Extract), iv, 52, 8 l. 8 Plates.

GEISLER (Adam Friedrich). Kurze Karakter-und Thatenschilderungen von hundert und siebenfunfzig sich in leztern amerikanischen Kriege vorzüglich ausgezeichneter brittischer Offiziere wie auch einiger Offiziere von den deutschen Hülfstruppen. *Dresden und Leipzig.* 1784. 8vo. 26843

Among the sketches are the characters of André, Arnold, Asgill, Burgoyne, Carleton, Clinton, Cornwallis, Gage, Howe, Sir William Howe, Governor Hutchinson, Johnstone, Kempenfeld, Keppel, Prescott, Rodney, Tarleton, etc.

GELDARD (D.) Handbook on Cotton Manufacture: ... By James Geldard. *New York.* 1867. 12mo, pp. 298. Plates.

GELLATLY (A.) Some Observations upon a late piece, entitled, "The Detection detected," showing how the Rev. Mess. S. Finley and R. Smith, handle the obligation of the Solemn League. By A. Gellatly. *Germantown.* 1758. 8vo. 26845

GELLINE (P. L.) Journal de mer d'un voyage à la Nouvelle Orleans, capitale de la Louisiane; depart et retour àbord des trois mâts le Severn et le Chateaubriand, du 2 Octobre 1841 au 21 Fevrier 1842. Par P. L. Gelline. *Paris: l'auteur.* 1842. 8vo, pp. 40. 26846

G[ELONE] (F.) *See* [Fernagus de Gelone], Vol. VI.

Geluckwenschinghe aen de West Indische Vlote. Afghevaren uyt Nederl. in Januario 1624. *Amsterdam.* 1624. 4to. 26847

Felicitation to the West India fleet, that set sail from Netherland in January, 1624. *See* Asher, No. 103.

Gem of the Western World, for all Seasons ... Edited by M. E. Hewitt. *New York.* [1850?] 8vo. 26848

Gemälde der Länder uud Völker mit Bezug auf ihre Geschichte. Rechtmässige deutsche Ausgabe des Univers pittoresque mit den Original-Stahlstichen. Zweite Serie. Columbien und Guyana, Italien, Aegypten. *Frankfurt: Schwerber.* 183–. 8vo. 26848*a*

GEMELING (Joh. George). Disputatio geographica de vero Californiae situ et conditione. *Marburgi.* [n. d.] 8vo, 30 l.

GEMELLI-CARERI (Giovanni Francesco). Giro del Mundo. *Napoli.* 1699. + *Venezia.* 1719. 9 vols., 12mo. Portraits and Plates. 26850

These travels were considered, for a long time, as fictitious; and Goldsmith, in his "Citizen of the World" (Letter 108), treats them as such. Baron von Humboldt, however, has proved that he certainly was in Mexico and at Acapulco, and that his descriptions have the charm of local tint which could only have been given by an ocular witness.

GEMELLI-CARERI. Voyage autour du monde, traduit de l'italien de Gemelli-Careri. Par [Eustache Lenoble]. *Paris: Étienne Ganeau.* 1719. 6 vols., 16mo. Maps and Plates. + [*Ibid.*] 1727. 6 vols., 16mo. 60 Plates. B., C. 26851

The part relating to South America, New Spain, etc., is very curious. An English translation will be found in the "Compendium of Authentic Voyages," 7 vols., 1756, and in Churchill's collection.

Gemma Phrysius de Principiis Astronomiæ et Cosmographiæ deque Usu Globi ab eodem editi. Item de Orbis Divisione et Insulis Rebusque nuper inventis. [*Antverpiæ.* 1850.] 4to.

This edition is not mentioned by Harrisse.

Gemma Phrysivs de Principiis Astronomiæ & Cosmographiæ; de usu Globi; di Orbis divisione ac Insulis. *Joan: Grapheus typis excudebat. Antverp.* 1530. 4to. 26853

"*Mense Octobr. Væneunt cum Globis* Lovanii *apud* Gregorium Zassenum, & Antverpiæ *apud* Gregorium Bontium *sub Scuto Basiliensi.*" — MAITTAIRE.

Gemmam | Phrysium, apud Louanienses Medicum ac Mathema- | ticum insignem, restituta. Additis de adem re ipsius Gemmæ Phry. libellis, vt sequens pagina docet. | *Væneunt Antuerpiæ in pingui gallina Arnoldo Berckmāno.* 1 . 5 . 3 . 9 . | 4to, 61 l., 1 l.

Gemma | Phrysius de Princi | -pijs astronomiæ & Cosmographie, | Deq; vsu Globi ab eodem edi- | ti. Item de Orbis diuisione, | & Insulis, rebusq; nu- | per inuentis. | *Antuerpiæ excudebat Ioannes Richard. An. D.* 1544. | Sm. 8vo, Title, 1 l., 88 unnumbered l., Tables, 3 l. 26855

See "Caput. XXX. De America. 'America ab inuentore Amerio [*sic*] Vesputio numen habet,'" etc.

Gemma Phrysivs | De Principiis | Astronomiae et | Cosmographiae, deqve vsv | Globi Cosmographici ab eodem editi. | de Orbis diuisione & Insulis, rebusq; nuper inuentis. | eivsdem De Annuli Astronomica vsu. | Ioannis Schoneri | De vsv Globi Astriferi opusculum. | *Antverpiæ,* | *In ædibus Ioan. Steelsii. Anno* | M.D.XLVIII. | [Second title-page, on the recto of unnumbered leaf 73:] Vsvs Annuli Astro- | nomici Gemma Frisio Mathematico | Authore. | *Antverpiæ, In ædibus Ioannis Steelsii.* | M.D.XLVIII. | [Third title-page on recto of unnumbered leaf:] Ioannis Schoneri | de vsv Globi Astriferi | Opusculum. | ... M.D.XLVIII. [Colophon:] *Typis Ioan. Graphei Anno à Christo hu- | manæ salutis Authore nato,* | M.D.XLVIII. | Sm. 8vo, 3 l., 116 numbered l., 1 unnumbered l.

Gems from the American Poets. Sixth Edition. *London: Thomas Tegg.* MDCCCXL. 32mo, pp. xii, 188. + *New York: D. Appleton and Company.* [1842.] 32mo, pp. 222. H. 26857

GENDRON (*Le Sieur*). Quelqves Particvlaritez | dv pays | des Hvrons | en la novvelle France | Remarqvées par le Sieur Gendron, | Docteur en Medecine, qui a demeuré | dans ce Pays- | là fort long-temps. | Redigees par Iean Baptiste de Rocoles, | Conseiller & Aumosnier du Roy, & | Historiographe de sa Majesté. | *A Troyes, &* | *A Paris,* | *Chez* | *Denys Bechet et Lovis Billaine.* | M.DC.LX. | 8vo, pp. 26. 26858

Of this very rare book, twenty-five copies were reprinted at *Albany, N. Y.: J. Munsell.* 1860. 8vo, pp. (1), 26.

A Genealogical Register of the Descendants in the Male line of David Atwater, one of the Original Planters of New Haven, Conn., to the Fifth Generation. *New Haven: Printed by J. H. Benham.* 1851. 8vo, pp. 30. 26859

Genealogical Registry of the United States. Incorporated under the Laws of the State of New York. ... *New York.* [1871.] 8vo, pp. 23. B., H. 26860

Genealogy of the Adam Family, by William Adam of Canaan, Litchfield Co., Conn. *Albany: Printed by Joel Munsell.* 1848. 8vo, pp. 16. 26861

Genealogy of the Adams Family of Kingston, Mass. ... by George Adams of Boston. *Boston: Printed by David Clapp.* 1861. 8vo, pp. 64. 26862

Genealogical Sketch of the Bird Family, having its Origin in Hartford, Conn. *Hartford.* 1855. 8vo, pp. 24. 26863

General Accompt. *See* Georgia, *infra.*

A General Account of Miranda's Expedition. *See* [Sheerman (John H.)]

The General Address (in Two Parts) Of the Outinian Lecturer to his Auditors, Periodically read by him as a Lecture, during the Season in London, and Descriptive of the Institution of the Outinian Society in the Hundredth Year after the Death of the Benevolent William Penn, and the Year of the Second Peace of Aix-la-Chapelle, to secure the Advantages of Justice and Benevolence, with the aid of Ethical and Critical Lectures, when no other provision can easily be made for that purpose. *London: W. Nicol.* 1822. 8vo, Title, pp. (2), 56. 6 Plates. 26864

General Address to the Freemen of New-Hampshire; or the General Government and the Leaders of the New-England Opposition contrasted. [n. p. n. d.] 8vo, pp. 35. H. 26865

General Assembly of the Presbyterian Church. *See* Presbyterian Church.

General and Private Laws, and Memorials and Resolutions of the Territory of Dakota, passed ... March 17–May 15, 1862. To which is Prefixed a Brief Description of the Territory and its Government, ... *Yankton: J. C. Trask.* 1862. 8vo, pp. xvii, 558; iv l., pp. 38. 26866

The General Attacked by a Subaltern; or, the "Strictures on the Friendly Address" Examined and a Refutation of its Principles Attempted. *Boston.* 1744. 8vo. + *New York: James Rivington.* [1775.] 8vo, pp. 11. C., N. 26867

This is in Reply to General [Charles Lee's] Strictures on [Myles Cooper's] Friendly Address. Its author was probably Lieutenant Henry Barry.

A General Atlas for the Present War ... in Europe and the West Indies, ... *Philadelphia: Printed by Mathew Carey.* 1796.

This is one of the earliest attempts at an atlas in the United States.

General Armstrong. Documents in relation to the Attack on the private Armed Brig General Armstrong, of New York. 12mo. 26869

General Assembly's State. *See* [Duane], Vol. v., No. 20987.

General Chronica das ist; wahrhaffte eigentliche und kurtze Beschreibung, vieler namhaffter, und zum theil bisz daher vnbekannter landtschafften, erstlich des priester Johanns, königs in Morenlandt, ... zum andern ein gemeine beschreibung des gantzen erdbodems, ... Zum dritten ein beschreibung der neuw erfundenen inselen Americe und Magellane. *Frankfurt am Mayn: S. Feyrabendt.* 1576. 3 pts. in 1 vol., folio, pp. 143; 94; 45. C. 26870

"The publisher, Feyerabend, issued this work in three parts. 1st. The 'General Chronicle,' containing the 'Account of Priester John's Country,' etc. 2d. The 'Cosmographia', a general account of 'Europe, Asia, Affrice, vnd die nach Petolomeo neuw erfunden Inseln, America vnd Magellane (so jetz die neuwe Welt genennt),' etc. 3d. The 'Chronicle of Paulus Orosius.' It was his opinion that all these properly came together, and yet they are printed in three distinct books (each having its own title and pagination), to suit the convenience of purchasers." — STEVENS.

A General Circular to all Persons of Good Character, who want to Emigrate to the Oregon Territory, ... *Charlestown.* 1831. 8vo, pp. 27, (1). 26871

A General Collection of Treatys, Declarations of War, Manifestos, and other Publick Papers, Relating to Peace and War,

Among the Potentates of Europe, from 1648 to the Present Time ... between England, France, Spain and Holland. ... The Right of the Crown of England to Hudson's-Bay. ... To which is prefix'd, An Historical Account of the French King's Breach of the most Solemn Treatys. *London: J. Darby.* 1710. 8vo, pp. 44, 448. 26872

A General Collection of Treatys, Declarations of War, Manifestos, and other Publick Papers, relating to Peace and War. The Second Edition. *London: J. J. and P. Knapton.* M.DCC.XXXII. 4 vols., 8vo, pp. 32, 448; xxii, Errata, 1, 560, 23; xxxix, 492; 4 l., pp. 458 [490], 13. 26873

Many of these treaties relate to American territory.

A General Collection of Voyages, undertaken either for Discovery, Conquest, Settlement, or The Opening of Trade, from the Commencement of the Portuguese Discoveries to the Present Times. Vol. I. *London: W. Richardson.* [1789.] 4to, pp. (x), 518. 9 Maps and Plates. 26874

This volume, the only one published, contains, among others, the voyages of Cada Mosto, Dias, Vasco de Gama, Columbus, Americus Vespucius, Albuquerque, and Magellan. Some copies have a different title, as follows:

A General Collection of Voyages and Discoveries, made by the Portuguese and the Spaniards during the Fifteenth and Sixteenth Centuries. ... *London: W. Richardson.* MDCCLXXXIX. 4to, pp. (10), 518. Maps and Plates. 26875

General Convention of Agriculturists and Manufacturers and others Friendly to the Encouragement and Support of the Domestic Industry of the United States, ... July 30, 1827. [n. p. n. d.] 8vo, pp. 76. B., C. 26876

General Description of Nova Scotia. *See* Nova Scotia.

A General Epistle given forth by the People of the Lord called Quakers. 1685. *Philadelphia.* 1686. 8vo, pp. 24.

Title from Smith's "Bibliography of Friends' Books."

The General Fast. A Lyric Ode; With a Form of Prayer proper for the Occasion, and a Dedication to the King. *London.* 1777. 4to. 26878

"Ridicules the Fast, and insults the Government." — *M. Rev.*, LV. 481.

General Hints to Emigrants: containing Notices of the Various Fields for Emigration, with Practical Hints ... *London: Virtue Brothers & Co.* 1866. 12mo, pp. iv, 209. B. 26879

General History of all Voyages and Travels throughout the Old and New World. *London: Edmund Curll.* 1708. 8vo.

General History of North and South America, including the Celebrated Work by Robertson. Continued by a Complete History of the United States to the Present Time. *London.* 1834. Rl. 8vo. 26881

The General History of the late War: containing its Rise, Progress, and Event, in Europe, Asia, Africa, and America, and exhibiting the State of the Belligerent Powers at the Commencement of the War; their Interests and Objects in its Continuation; and Remarks on the Measures, which led Great Britain to Victory and Conquest. Interspersed with the Characters of the able and disinterested Statesmen, to whose Wisdom and Integrity, and of the Heroes, to whose Courage and Conduct we are indebted for that Naval and Military Success, which is not to be equalled in the Annals of this, or of any other Nation. And with Accurate Descriptions of the Seat of War, the Nature and Description of our Conquests, and of the most remarkable Battles by Sea and Land. Illustrated with a variety of Heads, Plans, Maps, and Charts, ... The Third Edition, Corrected. *London: Printed for Edward and Charles Dilly, and John Millan.* M.DCC.LXVI. 4 vols., 8vo, pp. (ii), 495; 464; 480; 480. 31 Heads and 7 Maps. 26882

Very full on America.

The General History of the Cruelties and Proceedings of the Inquisition. *London.* 1737. 12mo. Plates. 26883

Contains accounts of the Inquisition in Mexico, and the sufferings and imprisonment of Louis Ramez for heresy, at Vera Cruz, etc.

A General History of Trade, and especially considered as it respects British Commerce, as well at Home as to all parts of the World, with a Discourse on the use of Harbours and Roads for Shipping, as it relates particularly to the filling up of the Harbour of Dunkirk. *London: J. Baker.* 1713. 2 pts., 8vo, pp. 48; 48. 26884

Containing interesting matter relative to America.

General Idea of the College of Miramia. *See* [Smith (W.)]

General Index. *See* Congress, Vol. IV., No. 15531.

General Instructions for the Government of the Consular and Commercial Agents of the Republic of Texas. ... *Houston.* 1838. 8vo. 26885

The General Laws of the Improved Order of the Red Men; ... *Washington, D. C.: Printed by William Q. Force.* 5606. 12mo, pp. 23. 26886

These *red men* are usually *white.*

The General Magazine, and Historical Chronicle, for all the British Plantations in America. [To be continued Monthly.] *Philadelphia: printed and sold by B. Franklin.* 1741. 12mo, pp. 426.

The General Magazine of Arts and Sciences. By Benjamin Martin. *London: W. Owen.* 1755, etc. 4 vols., 8vo. 26888

Contains many notices of events in America during the French and Indian War, with maps of the parts in contention.

The General Opposition of the Colonies to the Payment of the Stamp Duty; and the Consequence of Enforcing Obedience by Military Measures; Impartially Considered. Also a Plan for uniting them to this Kingdom, in such a manner as to make their Interest inseparable from ours, for the future. In a Letter to a Member of Parliament. *London: T. Payne.* M. DCC. LXVI. Sm. 4to, pp. 40. H. 26889

Also on large paper in 4to. "An ingenious dissuasive from violent measures with the colonies, on account of the stamp act, written partly in a serious and partly in a ludicrous vein." — *M. Rev.*, XXXIV. 68.

General Order Regulating the Uniform of the Militia. *Albany.* 1842. 8vo, pp. 17. 26890

General Orders affecting the Volunteer Force. 1861. *Washington.* 1862. 12mo, pp. xvi, 60. Table. + For 1862, pp. lvi, 158. Table. + For 1863, pp. xlix, iiii, 214. Table. 26891

General Orders of the War Department; embracing the Years 1861, 1862 and 1863, adapted for the use of the Army and Navy of the United States. Chronologically Arranged, with an Alphabetical Index. By T. O'Brien and O. Diefendorf. *New York: Derby & Miller.* 1864. 2 vols., 8vo, pp. xxiv, 472; xxxi, 710.

General Orders. *See* Roll of Honor.

General Orders. Department of the East. Head-Quarters, New York City. Jan. 12, 1862, to Dec. 30, 1864. Nos. 1 to 102. 12mo. 26893

General Orders of the War Department, from January 18, 1861, to December 26, 1861. Nos. 1–110. + For 1862. Nos. 1–217. + For 1863. Nos. 1–400. + For 1864. Nos. 1–300. Continued. 26894

The Orders are all issued from the Adjutant-General's Office at Washington.

General Orders from Adjutant and Inspector-General's Office, Confederate States Army, From January, 1862, to December, 1863, (both inclusive.) In Two Series. Prepared from Files of Head-Quarters, Department of S. C., Ga., and Fla. With Full Indexes. *Columbia: Presses of Evans & Cogswell.* 1864. 8vo, Index, pp. xlvii, 159; lviii, 276. 26895

General Orders from the Adjutant and Inspector-General's Office, Confederate States Army, For the Year 1863, With a Full Index. Compiled and Corrected under Authority of Gen'l S. Cooper, A. & I. G. By R. H. P. Robinson, of the Adjutant and Inspector-General's Office. ... *Richmond: A. Morris, Publisher.* 1864. 8vo, pp. 240. 26896

A General Outline of the United States of North America, her Resources and Prospects, with a Statistical Comparison, shewing at one view the Advance she has made in National Opulence in the period of 30 years, &c. Being the result of Letters addressed from Philadelphia, 1823, to a Friend in England; and some additional matter. Illustrated with Engravings, &c. *Philadelphia.* 1824. 8vo, pp. 238. + [*Ibid.*] 1825. P.

This work does not accord with its promising title, being — according to the "North American Review," xx. 446 — a miserable attempt at book-making.

A General Plan for Laying Out Town and Townships on the new-acquired Lands in the East Indies, America, or elsewhere, in order to promote Cultivation, and raise the Value of all the Adjoining Land. *London.* 1794. 8vo. c. 26898

General Public Acts of Congress respecting the Sale and Disposition of the Public Lands, with Instructions ... and Official Opinions of the Attorney-General ... In Two Parts. ... *Washington.* 1838. 2 vols., 8vo, 1 l., pp. 615, 24; 8, 1117. 26899

General Reflections occasioned by the Letter to Two Great Men, and the Remarks on that Letter. *London: C. Dilly.* 1760. 8vo, pp. 20. c. 26900

See "M. Rev.," xxii. 246.

The General Register of Politics and Literature in Europe and America, for the Year 1827. Preceded by a Memoir of ... George Canning. *Edinburgh: Constable & Co.* 1828. 12mo, pp. (1), 335. Portrait. B. 26901

General Regulations for the Army; or, Military Institutes. *Philadelphia: M. Carey and Sons.* 1821. 8vo, 10 l., pp. 13–355.

w. + *Washington.* 1825. 8vo. c. + *Washington: F. P. Blair.* 1834. 12mo, pp. xxxix, 236. c. 26902

General Regulations for the Army of the United States; also, the Rules and Articles of War, ... *City of Washington.* MDCCCXXXV. 12mo. Continued. 26903

General Regulations for the Navy and Marine Corps. *Washington.* 1841. 8vo. Continued. 26904

General Regulation for the Organizing of Congregations, &c., of the Roman-Catholic Churches in the Diocese of Kentucky. *Bardstown.* 1836. 12mo, pp. iii, 19. 26905

General Remarks on the Proceedings lately had in the adjacent Country, relative to Infidelity. Comprehending the Writings of D. N., the Conduct of the Goshen Printer, with some Observations on the Consequence of Persecution. *Newburgh, N. Y.: David Denniston.* 1798. 8vo. 26906

General Report of the Colonial Land and Emigration Commissioners. *London.* 1840. Folio and 8vo. Continued, after 1842, in 8vo. 26907

The General Repository and Review ... *Cambridge: William Hilliard.* 1812–13. 8vo, pp. (1), 474, iv. Continued. B., BA.

General Republican Address. *Albany.* 1820. 8vo. 26908

The General Stud-Book, containing Pedigrees of English Race Horses. With an Appendix giving extended Pedigrees of Stallions Imported into the United States, and of their most noted Progeny. *Baltimore.* 1834. 8vo. 26909

The General Theological Seminary of the Protestant Episcopal Church in the United States. Proceedings of the Board of Trustees, 1828. *New York.* 1828. Continued. 26910

Also: An Abstract of the First Annual Report of the Directors ... Boston, April 20th, 1863 ... . *Boston: Printed by Alfred Mudge & Son.* 1863. 8vo, pp. 26. Continued. H. — The Act of Incorporation, Constitution and Statutes. *New York.* 1832. 8vo, pp. 22. + *New York.* 1855. 8vo, pp. 40. — Catalogue of the Officers and Students, with Catalogue of the Alumni, 1835. *New York.* 1836. 8vo. Continued. — The Constitution, Act of Incorporation, and Statutes, of the General Theological Seminary of the Protestant Episcopal Church in the United States. *New York.* 1829. 8vo, pp. 19. — Constitution of the General Theological Seminary, with Address and Resolutions, New York, December, 1821. *New York.* 1822. 8vo, pp. 12. — Report of the Joint Committee of the House of Bishops, and of the House of Clerical and Lay Deputies ... on the General Theological Seminary ... Nov. 14, 1826. 12mo, pp. 11.

General Theological Seminary of the Protestant Episcopal Church in the United States of America. Proceedings relating to the Organization of the General Theological Seminary from its inception to its final Establishment in the City of New York; together with the Regular Proceedings of the Board of Trustees, 1821–38. Compiled by a Member of the Board. *New York: D. Dana, jr.* 1854. 8vo, pp. x, 668. c. 26911

A General Treatise of Monies & Exchanges, with a General Discourse of Commerce, being a View of the Commodities & Merchandizes produced in all Countries of Trade. *London.* 1707. 4to. 26912

New England is said to be much of the same climate and soil as Old England, etc.

A General Treatise of Naval Trade and Commerce. *London.* 1739. 2 vols., 8vo. 26913

Chapters iv., vii., and xvii. relate to the Greenland and Newfoundland Fishery, the South-Sea Company, and the American Plantations.

The Address of the General Union for Promoting the Observance of the Christian Sabbath, to the People of the United States ... *New York: Printed by Daniel Fanshaw.* 8vo, pp. 16. H.

Also: First Annual Report of the General Union for Promoting the Observance of the Christian Sabbath. *New York.* 1829. 8vo. Continued. W.

A General Review of the African Slave Trade, demonstrating its Injustice and Impolicy: With Hints Towards a Bill for its Abolition. *London: R. Faulder.* M DCC LXXXVIII. 8vo, pp. 39.

See "M. Rev.," LXXVIII. 160.

A General View of the Origin and Nature of the Constitution and Government of the United States, deduced from the Political History and Condition of the Colonies and States, and their public Acts in Congress and Conventions, from 1774 till 1788; together with their Exposition by the Supreme Court of the United States; and Rules of Construction, in relation to such provisions of the Constitution as impose Restraints on the Powers of the States. *Philadelphia.* 1838. 8vo. 26916

A General View of the Rise ... of the American Navy, down to the Present Time. *Brooklyn.* MDCCCXVIII. 12mo. 26917

General View of the United States. *See* [Rich (O.)]

General View of the World, comprising a Physical, Political, and Statistical Account of its Five Grand Divisions: America, with their various Republics, Empires, Kingdoms, ... *Philadelphia.* 8vo. 26918

Generaliteits-Rapport op de klagten over het nemen van Nederl. scheepen door de Engelschen, 6 Nov. 1778. Folio. 26919

Report of the Generality of the complaints concerning the capture of Dutch vessels by the English at St. Eustatius.

GENESEE. Description of the Settlement of the Genesee. *See* [Williamson (Charles)].

Genesee College: Laws. *Lima, N. Y.* 1856. 8vo. + Catalogue. 1857. Continued. 26920

A Reply of the Genesee Consociation, to the Letter of the Rev. Joseph Emerson ... on the Subject of ... Masonic Ministers, and Masonic Candidates for the Ministry. *Rochester, N. Y.: Edwin Scranton.* 1829. 8vo, pp. 43. + *Hartford: Hudson and Skinner.* 1829. 8vo, pp. 34. H. 26921

The Genesee Farmer and Gardener's Journal. A Weekly Paper, devoted to Agriculture, Horticulture, and Rural Economy, N. Goodsell, Editor. Jan. 1831, to Dec. 1832. *Rochester: L. Tucker & Co.* 1831–32. 4to. + The Same. A Monthly Journal. Second Series. *Rochester: J. Harris.* 1840. 4to. Continued. H. 26922

Vols I.–V., Second Series, are known as the "New Genesee Farmer." *See also* New Genesee.

Genesee Missionary Society in the State of New York. Constitution, with an Address. *Philadelphia.* 1812. 8vo, pp. 12.

Genesee Wesleyan Seminary, Lima, N. Y. Catalogue, 1849. 8vo. Continued. H. 26924

GENESEE RIVER. Memorial of the Owners of Water of the Genesee River at Rochester to the Legislature. *Rochester.* 1853. pp. 16. 26925

GENESEE TRACT. An Account of the Soil, Growing Timber, and other Productions, of the Lands ... in North America. And particularly the Lands ... known by the Name of the Genesee Tract ... . [n. p.] 1791. Sm. 4to, pp. (1), 37. Map. 26926

Appeal to the People of the State of New York in favor of Constructing the Genesee and Alleghany Canal. *New York.* 1833. 8vo. 26927

Genesis in various Languages. *See* under the language.

[GENET (Edmund Charles).] Communications on the Next Election for President of the United States, and on the Late Measures of the Federal Administration. ... . [n. p.:] *For the Author.* 1808. 8vo, pp. 70. BA. 26928

GENET. The Correspondence between Citizen Genet, Minister of the French Republic, to the United States of North America, and the Officers of the Federal Government; to which are prefixed the Instructions from the Constituted Authorities of France to the said Minister. *Philadelphia: Printed by Benjamin Franklin Bache.* M,DCC,XCIII. 4to, pp. (3), 9. B., BA., N. + *Charleston, S. C.* 1794. 8vo, pp. 19. M. 26929

GENET. Correspondance entre le Citoyen Genet, Ministre Plenipotentiaire de la Republique Française pres les Etats-Unis, et les Membres du Gouvernement Féderal, Précedée des Instructions données à ce Ministre par les Autorités constituées de la France. Tirée des Originaux. *Philadelphie: De l'Imprimerie de Benjamin Franklin Bache.* M. DCC. XCIV. 4to, pp. 32. 26930

[GENET.] Letter to the Electors of President and Vice-President of the United States. By a Citizen of New-York. ... *New-York: Printed by Henry C. Southwick.* 1808. 8vo, pp. 22.

Also: Address on the Means of Opening New Sources of Wealth for the Northern States ... *Troy: Printed by Francis Adamourt.* 1821. 8vo, pp. 56. B., C., S. — Address on the Several Subjects of Science ... Public Improvements, Finances, ... Rivers, Canals, Navigation, and Commerce ... *Albany: Printed by Packard & Van Benthuysen.* 1825. 8vo, pp. 43. — Growth and Manufacture of Silk. [With] Letter from the Secretary of the Treasury in relation to the Growth and Manufacture of Silk, adapted to the different parts of the Union. *Washington: Gales & Seaton.* 1828. 8vo, pp. 8, 220, 1 Table. 5 Plates. C. — Instructions to Citizen Genet, from the Executive Council and the Minister of Marine. 4to, pp. 9. — Memorial of the Alluvions, or Obstructions, at the Head of the Navigation of the River Hudson ... *Albany: Printed by J. W. Clark.* 1818. 8vo, pp. 46, (1). B., BA. *See also* Reasons.

GENET (H. W.) Practical Directions for the Holding of Elections ... principally applicable to the City of New York, ... By Henry W. Genet, County Clerk. *New York: W. D. Roe & Co.* 1864. 26932

Genethliaco, Eloglo, Prognostico felice, en la expectacion del real augusto Parto, que esperamos segun lo denota el benigno a specto de la mas brillante Americana Estrella Mario Virgen, que

venera esta Nueva-España con la advocacion de los Remedios. Predicolo D. Miguel Gonzales de Valdeosera. *Mexico.* 1707.

The titles of the author occupy one-half of the title-page.

GENEVA. Celebration of the Ninetieth Anniversary of American Independence in Geneva (Suisse), July 4th, 1866. ... [n. p. 1866.] 8vo, pp. 41. H. 26934

GENEVA. Articles of Association of the Farmers' Bank of Geneva; ... *Geneva.* 1839. 12mo, pp. 16. 26935

Directory for the Village of Geneva. W. G. Rodney, Compiler. For 1857–1858. *Geneva.* 1857. 12mo, pp. 47. H.

Geneva, Seneca Falls and Waterloo Directory for 1862–63, with Histories of the Towns. By A. Delany Brigham. *Geneva, N. Y.* 8vo. 26937

Catalogue of the Trustees, Faculty and Students of Geneva College, Dec. 28, 1826. *Geneva, N. Y.* 1827. 8vo, pp. 8. Continued. 26938

Also: Catalogue of the Medical Institution ... *Geneva.* 1835. Continued.

Medical Institution in Geneva College. Letter of the Board of Professors to the Board of Trustees on the Rights and Relations of the two Boards. *Geneva.* 1843. 8vo. B. 26939

Catalogue of the Medical Institution of Geneva College, ... of 1841–42. *Geneva: Stair & Mazee.* 8vo, pp. 24. Continued. B. 26940

Catalogue of the Geneva Lyceum, N. Y., 1835. 8vo. Continued. 26941

Geneva. *See* Hobart College.

Geneva, Tribunal of Arbitration. A Complete Collection of the Forensic Discussions on the Part of the United States and of Great Britain, before the Tribunal of Arbitration under the Treaty of Washington. *New York: D. Appleton and Co.* 1873. 8vo, pp. xvi, 653. B. 26942

Also: Correspondence respecting the Geneva Arb'tration. [*London.* 1872.] pp. 155. B.

GENIN (S.) Selections from the Works of the Late Sylvester Genin, Esq., in Poetry, Prose and Historical Design. With a Biographical Sketch. Portrait and Illustrations. *New York: Maigne & Hall.* 1855. 8vo, pp. 252. B. 26943

A most singular work, with curious plates. Privately printed.

GENIN (T. H.) Selections from the Writings of the Late Thomas Hedges Genin. With a Biographical Sketch. *New York: Edward O. Jenkins.* 1869. 8vo, pp. (1), 615. Portrait.

GENIO (A.) The Mystic Mount, and the Voice ... By Arthur Genio, Esq. *New-York: For the Author.* 1823. 8vo, pp. 22.

The Genius of America to General Carlton, an Ode. *London.* 1778. 4to, pp. 23. 26946

Written upon hearing the news of the General having been recalled.

The Genius of Britain to General Howe, the Night before the Battle at Long Island. An Ode. *London: Sewell.* 1776. 4to.

Tolerable, on so melancholy a subject.

The Genius of Columbia — a Poem. [n. p. n. d.] Folio.

The Genius of Erin, Columbia's Freedom, ... Being Part I. of a Series of Poems, by a Citizen of South Carolin. *Charleston: D. J. Dowling.* 1836. 12mo, pp. 190. 26949

The Genius of Great Britain, an Ode. In Allusion to the Present Times. *London: Almon.* 1775. 8vo. 26950

Genius of Universal Emancipation; a Weekly Publication, containing Documents, Essays and Facts relative to the Subject of African Slavery, together with Notices of the Events of the Times. Edited by Benjamin Lundy [and W. Lloyd Garrison]. *Baltimore.* 1830–49. 4to. 26951

GENLIS (Stéphanie Félicité Ducrest de Saint-Aubin, *comtesse* de). A Selection from the Annals of Virtue, containing the most important and interesting Anecdotes from the Histories of Spain ... and America; ... From the French, by E. M. James. *Bath: S. Hazard.* 1794. 8vo, 4 l., pp. 255, 4 l. 26952

GENNES (De). Voyage, 1695. *See* Froger (F.)

GENTIL (Le). *See* Barbinais (L. G. de).

The Gentlemen and Ladies' Town and Country Magazine: ... *Boston.* 1784. 8vo. Continued. 26953

The Gentleman's Magazine, or Monthly Intelligencer. Volume I., For the Year M.DCC.XXXI. ... Collected chiefly from the Public Papers by Silvanus Urban. [Motto] E Pluribus Unum. *London: F. Jefferies.* MDCCXXXII. 8vo. Continued. B., BA.

The motto, *E Pluribus Unum*, was discontinued in 1790, *et seq.* Many of the articles in the earlier volumes are on American topics.

Gentleman's Law Magazine, containing a variety of the most useful Practical Forms of Writing. *Middlebury, Vt.* 1804. 12mo.

"One of the rarest books printed in Vermont." — STEVENS.

GENTRY (Meredith P.) Speech of Mr. M. P. Gentry, of Tennessee, on the Admission of California: Delivered in the House of Representatives, ... June 10, 1850. *Washington.* [n. d.] 8vo, pp. 8. 26956

Also: Speech on the Mexican War ... Dec. 16, 1846. [n. d.] 8vo, pp. 16. — Speech on the Oregon Question ... Feb. 5, 1846. [n. p. 1846.] — Speech ... on the Tariff, delivered ... July 2, 1846. *Washington.* 1846. 8vo.

GENTY (L., *l'Abbé*). L'influence de la découverte de l'Amérque sur le bonheur du genre-humain. Par M. l'Abbé Genty. *Orléans: Jacob.* 1789. 2 vols., 12mo, pp. viij, xxxvj, 292; 296.

"That the discovery in question was neither advantageous to America nor to Europe, is a proposition that many believe; and this author illustrates it, and renders it striking; but that it might have been, and may even yet be made useful to both, is equally credible. The principal object of this judicious writer is to point out the manner of diminishing the evils occasioned by the discovery of the New World, and of multiplying the advantages that may result from it. The work breathes a liberal spirit, and is worthy of attention." — *Monthly Review.*

GENTZ (F. von). The Origin and Principles of the American Revolution, compared with the Origin and Principles of the French Revolution. Translated from the German. *Philadelphia: Asbury Dickens.* 1800. 8vo, pp. 73. BA. 26958

A Genuine Account of Earthquakes, especially ... [a] Terrible One at Port-Royal, in Jamaica, In ... 1692. *London: Henry Slater.* M.DCC.L. 8vo, pp. viii, 24. 26959

Genuine Account of Nova Scotia. *See* Nova Scotia.

A Genuine Account of the late Secret Expedition to Martinico and Guadeloupe, under Commodore Moore and General Hopson. Written at Guadeloupe, By a Sea-Officer who went out with Commodore Hughes. [*London:*] *R. Griffiths.* 1759. 8vo, pp. 23. J.C.B. 26960

A reprint of newspaper articles. *See* "M. Rev.," for 1759.

A Genuine Dialogue, Facetious and Pathetic, Amorous and Political, full of Strange and Surprizing Adventures, Written by the Author of the Curious Maid. 1736. 8vo. 26961

Many of these adventures are located in America.

Genuine Letters and Memoirs. *See* [Pichon (Thos.)]

A Genuine History of the Family of the Great Negroes of G****. 1756. 12mo. 26962

Title from a catalogue of Americana.

Genuine Letters from a Volunteer, in the British Service, at Quebec. *London: H. Whitridge.* [1760.] 8vo, pp. viii, 39.

See "M. Rev.," xxi. 367.

The Genuine Principles of the Ancient Saxon, or English Constitution. Carefully Collected from the Best Authorities; [A. Ramsay] With some Observations on their Peculiar Fitness for the United Colonies in General, and Pennsylvania in Particular. By Demophilus. *Philadelphia: Printed by Robert Bell.* MDCCLXXVI. 8vo, pp. 36. BA. 26964

GENUNG (Abram P.) The Frauds of the New York City Government Exposed. Sketches of the Members of the Ring and their Confederates; ... *New York: Author.* 1871. 8vo, pp. 52. 26965

GENOVESE (J. M.) Carta de la Vida del Joseph Maria Genovese, Missionerio de Californias. *Mexico.* 1758. 26966

GEOFFROY (W.) Facts connected with the Cruise of the United States Steam Frigate Merrimac, commanded by R. B. Hitchcock, Commander, ... during the Years 1857, 1858, 1859 & 1860. By William Geoffroy ... . *Baltimore: Printed by Kelly, Hedian & Piet.* 1860. 8vo, pp. 40. Plate. B. 26967

Geografia General. *See* [Colon (F. M.)], Vol. v., No. 14678.

Geografische bijdragen tot de kennis der bezittenen van de Europeanen, in Azië, Afrika en Amerika. Uit het Hoogduitsch. *Rotterdam: J. Meyer.* 1792. 8vo. 26968

A Geographic, Historical Summary; or Narrative of the present Controversy with the Wappinger [N. Y.] Tribe of Indians. *Hartford, Con.* 1767. 12mo. W. 26969

Geographical and Commercial Gazette: A Monthly Publication ... Edited by an Association: Published by J. Disturnell. *New York.* 1855. Folio. S. 26970

Geograph cal, Commercial, and Political Essays: including Statistical Details of Various Countries. *London: J. Valpy.* 1812. 8vo, pp. 323. P. 26971

There are several papers in this volume relating to America. It was edited by E. H. Barker, of Thetford.

Geographical Description, 1740. *See* [Smith (Caleb)].

Geographical Dictionary, of all the Countries, Provinces, Remarkable Cities, etc., of the World. 1688. 8vo. Plate.

America, New England, etc., occupies a large share of the work.

A Geographical and Historical Description of the Principal Objects of the Present War in the West-Indies, viz. Cartagena, Puerto-Bello, La Vera Cruz, The Havana, and San Augustin. Shewing their Situation, Strength, Trade, &c. With An Account of the many Sieges they have Undergone to the present Time. The whole Compiled from the most Authentic Memoirs, and Enlarged with many Curious Particulars not to be met with in former Authors. To which is prefix'd An Accurate Map of the West-Indies adapted to the Work. *London: T. Gardner.* 1741. 8vo, pp. (8), 192. Map. 26973

A Geographical, Historical, Commercial, and Agricultural View of the United States of America; forming a Complete Emigrant's Directory through every part of the Republic: likewise an Account of Upper and Lower Canada. Compiled by several Gentlemen, from a variety of Original Manuscripts, and from the Latest and Best Authorities. *London.* 1820. 8vo, pp. 146. Maps and Plates. A., C. 26974

A Geographical History of Nova Scotia. *See* Nova Scotia.

A Geographical Sketch of St. Domingo, Cuba, and Nicaragua, with Remarks on the Past and Present Policy of Great Britain affecting those Countries. By a Traveller. *Boston.* 1850. 8vo, pp. 36. 26975

A Geographical View of the United States. *Boston. A. K. White.* 1827. 8vo, pp. 130, 1 l. 26976

La Geographie en Estampes. *Paris: Rougerons.* [1800?] Oblong 8vo. 26977

Costumes of the various nations, in copperplates, with descriptive text, including Canadians, Greenlanders, United Statesmen, Natchez Indians, Mexicans, Californians, Brazilians, Peruvians, Patagonians, Chilians, etc. Curious.

Geographische, natuurkundige en historische berigten over Asie, Afrika en Amerika. Getrokken uit de stigtelyke brieven, en Reisbeschryvingen der Jesuiten, ter voortplantinge van den Christelyken Godsdienst, naar die Gewesten gezonden. Uit het Fransch vertaald. 3 deelen. *Harlingen: V. van der Plaats.* 1769. 8vo. 26978

A translation of the "Mémoires géographiques et historiques sur l'Asie," etc. *Paris.* 1767. 4 vols., 12mo.

Geographisches Jahrbuch zur Mittheilung aller wichtigen neuen Erforschungen von Heinrich Brockhaus. *Gotha: J. Perthes.* 1850–52. 4 pts., 4to, pp. 64; 64; 66; 64. 13 Charts.

Includes accounts of several American Indians, and other articles relating to this continent.

Geographische Belustigungen zur Erläuterung der neuesten Weltgeschichte. Mit Landkarten, Planen und Kupfern nach den neuesten und besten Originalen. 1. Stück. Allgemeine Beschreibung der engländischen Colonien in Nord-Amerika, nebst einem Plane von Boston. *Leipzig: Joh. Carl Müllerschen.* 1776. 4to. 26980

Geographische vnd Historische Beschreibung der vberausz grosser Landtschafft America: welche auch West India, vnd jhrer grösse halben die New Welt genennet wirt. *Cölln: Johann Christoffel.* 1598. Folio, pp. (4), 51. 20 Maps, with two pages of text on the verso of each. 26981

Geographische-statistische Beiträge zur Kenntniss aller auswartigen Besitzungen in Asien, Afrika und Amerika. *Essen: Badeker.* 1790. 8vo. 26982

Geography Epitomized, Or A Tour round the World. Being A Short but Comprehensive Description of the Terraqueous Globe: Attempted in Verse (For the sake of the Memory:) and principally designed for the Use of Schools. By an American. *Philadelphia: Joseph Cruikshank.* M DCC LXXXIV. 8vo, pp. 60.

The Geography of America and the West Indies. *London.* 1841. 8vo, pp. xii, 648. 3 Maps. 26984

A Geological Survey of the County of Albany, taken under the Direction of the Agricultural Society of the County. *Albany.* [1820.] 8vo, pp. 55. 26985

A Geological Survey. *See* [Eaton (Amos)], Vol. VI.

Geological Survey of Canada. Descriptive Catalogue of .. Minerals ... sent to the London ... Exhibition for 1862. *Montreal: Printed by John Sewell.* [n. d.] 8vo, pp. 83, (5). 26986

Geological Survey of Canada. *See* Billings (E.), Vol. II.

Geological Society of Pennsylvania. Transactions. *Philadelphia.* 1834. 8vo. Continued? 26987

Geology of North America: with Two Reports on the Prairies of Arkansas and Texas, the Rocky Mountains of New Mexico, and the Sierra Nevada of California. *Zurich.* 1858? 4to. Map and Plates. 26988

GEORGE (D.) An Almanack, for ... 1777. ... By Daniel George ... *Boston: Printed by Draper and Phillips.* 12mo, 5 l., pp. xii. Continued. 26989

GEORGE (J. H.) Speech of John H. George on Franklin Pierce, at Concord, N. H. 1852. 8vo. S. 26990

GEORGE (N. J. T.) A Pocket Gazetteer of Vermont. By N. J. T. George. *Haverhill, N. H.* 1823. 18mo. 26991

GEORGE (W.) Sermon before the Society for the Propagation of the Gospel in Foreign Parts, February, 1748. By the Rev. William George, D.D., Dean of Lincoln. *London.* 1749. 4to, pp. 67. M., S. 26992

GEORGE III. (*King of England*). The Annals of Administration, containing the General History of Georgiana the Queen-Mother, and Prince Coloninus, her son, a Biographical Fragment, Written about the Year 1575 [*sic*], Inscribed by the Proprietor of the Authentic Papers to Edmund Burke, Esq. 1775. 8vo.

A curious parody.

GEORGE III. The Correspondence of King George the Third with Lord North from 1768 to 1783. Edited from the Originals ... with an Introduction and Notes, By W. Bodham Donne. *London: John Murray.* 1867. 2 vols., 8vo, pp. xcii, 370, (2); 752. B., BA. 26994

GEORGE III. George the Third, his Court and Family. ... . *London: Henry Colburn and Co.* 1821. 2 vols., 8vo, pp. xv, (1), 447; (3), 454. Portraits. B., BA., C. 26995

[GEORGE III.] His Majesty's ... Speech to both Houses of Parliament, October 26, 1775. *Boston.* 1775. Folio. 26996

GEORGE III. The History of the First Ten Years of the Reign of George the Third, from his Accession to the Throne in 1760 to 1770, to which is Prefixed a Review of the War, which was terminated by the Peace of Paris in 1769. *London: Evans.* 1770. + Second Edition. *London: for the Author.* 1783. 8vo, pp. 402. + 1794. 26997

GEORGE III. The History of the Second Ten Years of the Reign of George the Third, King of Great Britain, &c. From the Conclusion of the Third Session of the Thirteenth Parliament, in 1770, to the End of the Last Session of the Fourteenth Parliament of Great Britain, in 1780. ... *London: Evans, For the Author.* MDCCLXXXII. 8vo, pp. 463. BA. 26998

"The most important part of this work is that which relates to the commencement and prosecution of the war with America. The author aims at impartiality, and nowhere discovers the zeal of a partisan. He is neither a determined Whig nor a pertinacious Tory, but seems to have made it a rule to steer a middle course. This volume is intended as a continuation to the history of the *first* ten years of the reign of George III., written apparently by a different author." *See* "M. Rev.," LXVII. 420.

GEORGE III. The King's Speech. [Nov. 30, 1774.] *Newport.* 1775. Folio, 1 leaf. 26999

GEORGE III. A Sketch of the Reign of George the Third, from 1780, to the Close of the Year 1790. *London: J. Debrett.* 1791. 8vo, pp. 206. + Second Edition. [*Ibid.*] M DCC XCI. 8vo, pp. (2), 206. BA. 27000

See "M. Rev.," IV. 224.

GEORGE III. Another Sketch of the Reign of George III., from the Year 1780 to 1790. Being an Answer to a Sketch, &c. *Dublin: P. Byrne, J. Moore.* M. DCC. XCI. 8vo, pp. (2), 82.

See also Eustace (J. S.), Vol. VI., No. 23117.

George Mason. *See* [Flint (Timothy)], Vol. VI., No. 24788.

GEORGETOWN, *D. C.* The United States *versus* the Corporation of Georgetown. Opinion of Hon. Thos. H. Crawford, Judge of the Criminal Court, District of Columbia. [n. p. n. d.] 8vo, pp. 24. H. 27003

Ordinances of the Corporation of Georgetown. With an Appendix, containing the Law for laying out the Town, the Original and Supplementary Charters, the Act of Cession, ... *Georgetown, D. C.: Printed by James C. Dunn.* 1821. 8vo, pp. (1), 126, 64, xv. BA. 27004

Petition of the Sisters of the Visitation of George Town, District of Columbia, praying that an Act of Incorporation may be passed in their favour. *Washington.* 1828. 8vo. 27005

GEORGETOWN COLLEGE, *Ky.* The Laws of Georgetown College, Kentucky, Revised, 1840. *Georgetown, Ky.* 1840. 8vo, pp. 20. 27006

Also: Catalogue of the Officers and Students, for the Year 1853–'54, 1854–'55 *Georgetown.* 1855. 8vo.

GEORGIA. Account of the Proceedings at the Countess of Huntington's College in Wales relative to the Students called to the College to go to Georgia, with Farewell Sermons by Mr. Piercy, President of Georgia College. *Printed* 1772. 27007

An Account of Georgia, 1741. *See* [Martyn (Benjamin)].

An Account Shewing what Money has been received by the Trustees for the use of the Colony of Georgia. 174–. Folio, 1 leaf. 27008

Acts of the General Assembly ... of ... Georgia ... 1837. *Milledgeville: P. L. Robinson.* 1838. 8vo, pp. 287, 37, 16. B.

Acts of the General Assembly [Sessional], 1801. *Louisville.* 1802. 8vo. Continued. 27010

Acts of the General Assembly of the State of Georgia, ... Session of 1866. *Macon.* 1867. 8vo. 27011

Act for the Better Settling of Intestate Estates. *Savannah, Georgia.* 1777. 4to. P. 27012

Acts of the State of Georgia, passed at Augusta, December, 1794, and January, 1795. *Augusta: printed by John E. Smith.* 1795. 8vo, pp. 31. 27013

Analysis of the Constitution of Georgia. ... By John N. Conley. *Atlanta.* 1870. 8vo. 27014

Appendix to the [Georgia] Senate Journal of the Session of 1826–27, containing Messages and Documents relative to the Controversy between Georgia and the Creek Indians. *Harrisburg.* 1827. 8vo. 27015

The Books of the Chronicles of the Land of Georgia as written in the Archives of the State, by Rabbi Ben-Ansel. *Published by the Rome Courier Office, Rome, Ga.* 1872. pp. 68. 27016

Both Sides of the Question, or a Candid & Impartial Enquiry into a Certain Doubtful Character, in a Letter to a General Officer, remarkably Acquitted by a C—t M—l. *London: J. Mechell.* [1749.] 8vo, pp. 28. 27017

Relates to Georgia and South Carolina.

Brief Account. *See* [Stephens (T.), *and* Everhard (*Sir* R.)]

A Brief Account of the Establishment of the Colony of Georgia, under Gen. James Oglethorpe, February 1, 1733. *Washington: Printed by Peter Force.* 1835. 8vo, pp. 15. B., BA.

Forms No. 2 of Vol. I. of Force's Tracts. Not heretofore published.

Campaign Document for 1870. The Barbarism of Gov. Bullock's Chain Gang Slavery exhibited from the Proceedings of the Joint Committee to Investigate the condition of the Georgia Penitentiary. *Atlanta, Georgia.* 1870. pp. 8. 27019

Can a Negro Hold Office in Georgia? Decided in Supreme Court, June Term, 1869. Arguments of Counsel, with the Opinions of the Judges, and the Decision of the Court in the case of Richard W. White, Clerk of Superior Court of Chatham Co., Plaintiff in Error, *versus* the State of Georgia, ex relatione Wm. J. Clements, Defendant in Error. Phonographically Reported by Eugene Davis. *Atlanta (Ga.): Daily Intelligencer Office.* 1869. 8vo, pp. 179. 27020

The Case of the Georgia Sales on the Mississippi Considered. With a Reference to Law Authorities and Public Acts, and an Appendix, Containing Certain Extracts, Records, and Official Papers. *Philadelphia: Printed for Benjamin Davies.* 1797. 8vo, pp. (4), 109. B. 27021

Catalogue of Books in the Library of the University of Georgia. *Athens.* 1850. 8vo, pp. 146, Index, 1. + *Athens, (Ga.) College.* 1858. 8vo, pp. 192. 27022

Catalogue of the State Library ... *Milledgeville (Georgia).* 1859. 8vo, pp. 144. + Catalogue of the Georgia State Library, 1869. *Atlanta.* 1869. 8vo. 27023

Catalogue of the Trustees, Officers, and Students of the Georgia Female College [at Macon]. *New York.* [1844.] 8vo. 27024

The Chain of Lorenzo; By the Request of his Friends, as his Farewell to Georgia. ... *Augusta: Printed by G. F. Randolph.* pp. 32. 27025

A Codification of the Statute Law of Georgia, including the English Statutes of Force: ... Compiled, Digested, and Arranged, by William A. Hotchkiss. *Savannah.* 1845. 8vo, pp. 990.

Collections of the Georgia Historical Society. *Savannah: Printed for the Society.* MDCCCXL–XLII. 2 vols., 8vo, pp. xii, 307, (1); 6, 336. B. 27027

Vol. III., Part I., consists of Colonel Benjamin Hawkins' Sketch of the Creek Confederacy, being Collections of the Georgia Historical Society. *Savannah.* MDCCCXLVIII. 8vo, pp. 88. No more published.

Communication from the Governor of Georgia, relative to the Abolitionists of the South, to the Executive of Maryland. *Annapolis.* 1836. 8vo. 27028

Compilation of the Laws of Georgia, from 1800 to 1810. By A. S. Clayton. *Augusta.* 1842. 4to. 27029

A Compilation of the Laws of the State of Georgia, passed ... since the Year 1819 to 1829. ... To which are added ... Resolutions ... of a General, Local, or Private Nature. By William C. Dawson. ... *Milledgeville.* 1831. 4to. 27030

Constitution, By-Laws, and List of Members of the Georgia Historical Society. *Savannah.* 1859. 8vo, pp. 15. 27031

The Constitution of the State of Georgia. *Savannah: W. Lancaster.* 1777. 4to, pp. 11. C. 27032

The Constitution of the State of Georgia, with Full Marginal Notes, and a Copious and analytical Index thereto. By John L. Conley. *Atlanta: New Era Establishment.* 1870. 8vo, pp. 88. 27033

The Contract for the Purchase of Western Territory, made with the Legislature of Georgia in the Year 1765; considered with reference to the Subsequent Attempts of the State to Impair its Obligations. By John E. Anderson and William J. Horrey. *Augusta: Randolph and Bunce.* 1799. 4to, pp. 93. 27034

Controller-General's Statement, March 31, 1863. *Milledgeville.* 1863. 8vo. BA. 27035

Cursory Remarks. *See* Vol. v., No. 18013.

Debates and Proceedings of the Georgia Convention, Assembled in Milledgeville, December 10, 1850, as to the Admission of California. By A. E. Marshall. *Milledgeville.* 1850. 8vo, pp. 28. B. 27036

A Description of Georgia, By a Gentleman who has resided there upwards of Seven Years, and was one of the first Settlers. *London: Printed for C. Corbett.* MDCCXLI. Folio, pp. 8. 27037

Ludewig says [*Ibid.*] 1761 — probably an error. Reprinted in Force's Tracts, Vol II., No. 12, 8vo, pp. 6.

Description of the Soil. *See* Morse (J.)

A Digest of the Laws, containing all Statutes and the Substance of Resolutions passed in this State previous to December, 1820. With Notes and References. ... Compiled by Oliver H. Prince. *Milledgeville.* 1822. 8vo, pp. 669. 27038

A Digest of the Laws of ... Georgia ... previous to ... December, 1837. With ... Notes ... Connecting References [and] an Appendix. Second Edition. Compiled by O. H. Prince. *Athens.* 1837. 8vo. 27039

A Digest of the Statute Laws of the State of Georgia, in Force prior to the Session of 1851, with Notes and References; ... Compiled by Thomas R. R. Cobb. *Athens.* 1851. 8vo, pp. 1252. 27040

Directions for the Officers of His Majesty's General Court and Session of Oyer and Terminer, and general Gaol Delivery of the Province of Georgia. Compiled by the Chief Justice. *Savannah: James Johnston.* 1771. 4to, pp. 24. 27041

Documents ... accompaning the Report of the Commissioners appointed for the Amicable Settlement of Limits with the State of Georgia, 10th February, 1803. ... *Washington: Printed by William Duane & Son.* 1803. 8vo, pp. 27. B. 27042

Document accompanying Report of the Commissioners on the Georgia-Mississippi Territory, Ceded to the United States. [*Washington.*] 1803. 8vo, pp. 92. 27043

Documents relating to the Boundary between Georgia and Florida. *Washington.* 1826. 8vo. 27044

Examination of the Controversy. *See* Vol. VI., No. 23357.

Facts shewing the Right of Certain Companies to the Lands Purchased from the State of Georgia. *United States.* 1795.

The General Account of all the Monies and Effects Received and Expended by the Trustees for Establishing the Colony of Georgia in America: ... *London.* 1736. Folio, pp. 29. 27046

Georgia. A Poem. Tomo Chachi. An Ode. A Copy of Verses on Mr. Oglethorpe's Second Voyage to Georgia. ... *London: J. Roberts.* MDCCXXXVI. Folio, pp. 19. 27047

The first of these poems is a praise of the Colony of Georgia. The second refers to Tomo Chachi, a celebrated Indian chief of the country, who, with his son, was sent to England by General Oglethorpe. *See* Bancroft, Vol. III.

Georgia *against* Florida. To the Supreme Court of the United States of America. The Bill of Complaint of the State of Florida, Complainant, against the State of Georgia, Defendant. [*Washington.* 1849.] 8vo. 27048

The Georgia Analytical Repository, by Henry Holcombe, ... *Savannah.* 1802. 8vo. Continued to 2 or more vols. 27049

Georgia and Carolina Almanac, For 1865. 27050

Georgia Justice; being a convenient Directory for the Justices of the Peace, and various other Civil Officers known to the Laws of the State of Georgia. By Rhodom A. Greene and John W. Lumpkin. *Milledgeville.* 1835. 8vo. 27051

Georgia Republican Extra, Savannah, 25th April, 1804, refusing to publish the Charge of Judge Jabez Bowen to the Grand Jury. 27052

Georgia Scenes. *See* [Longstreet (A. B.)]

Georgia Sketches. *See* [Johnston (Richard M.)]

Governor's Communication Transmitting Documents from Georgia, January, 1862. [*Richmond.* 1862.] 8vo, pp. 11.

Grant to the Georgia Mississippi Company, The Constitution thereof, And Extracts Relative to the Situation, Soil, Climate, and Navigation of the Western Territory of the State of Georgia; And particularly of that Part thereof in which the Company's Lands are Situated. Published by Order of the Directors. *Augusta: Printed by John Erdman Smith.* MDCCXCV. 8vo, pp. 40. B., C., W. 27054

Reprinted, with an appendix, by desire of the purchasers in Connecticut. pp. 39.

The Hard Case of the Distressed People of Georgia. 1742. Folio, pp. 4. 27055

Signed "Thomas Stephens, Agent for the people of Georgia."

Historical Account, 1779. *See* [Hewatt (Alexander)].

Impartial Enquiry into, 1741. *See* [Martyn (Benjamin)].

Journal of the Congress of the Four Southern Governors, and the Superintendent of that District, with the Five Nations of Indians, at Augusta, 1763. *South-Carolina, Charles-Town: Printed by Peter Timothy.* M,DCC,LXIV. Folio, Half-Title, pp. 45.

Journal of the House of Representatives, at the Biennial Session. *Milledgeville.* 1855. 8vo. Published biennally. 27057

Journal of the House of Representatives, at the Annual Sessions of the General Assembly, at Milledgeville, 1861. *Milledgeville.* 1861. 8vo. Continued. 27058

Journal of the Proceedings of the Commons House of Assembly of the Province of Georgia, at the First Session of the Seventh General Assembly of the said Province, convened at the Town of Savannah on Monday the 30th October, 1769. By H. E. James Wright, Captain General, and Governor in Chief of the Province aforesaid. [1777.] 27059

No title-page; probably printed at Savannah.

Journal of Proceedings of the Convention of the People, held at Milledgeville in Oct. and Nov., 1865. With the Ordinances and Resolutions adopted. *Milledgeville.* 1865. 8vo. 27060

Journal of the Public and Secret Proceedings of the Convocation of the People of Georgia, Held in Milledgeville, and Savannah in 1861. Together with the Ordinances Adopted. Published by Order of the Convention. *Milledgeville, Ga.: Boughton, Nisbet & Barnes, State Printers.* 1861. 8vo, pp. 416.

Journal of the Senate of Georgia. 8vo. 27062

Published biennially till 1860; afterwards annually.

Keeps of Kanphy? A Georgia Book, in Warp and Woof, containing Tales, Incidents, &c., of the "Empire State of the South," with a Slight Sketch of that well-known and eccentric "colored gemman," Old Jack C. *Athens: J. S. Peterson.* 1853. 12mo, pp. 108. 27063

Laws of Georgia, passed from Nov., 1862, to April, 1863. ... *Milledgeville.* 1863. 8vo. BA. 27064

Also: Laws passed from Nov., 1863, to March, 1864. ... *Milledgeville.* 1864. 8vo. These are known as the Confederate laws.

Letter from the Secretary of War, respecting Claims against the United States, for Services of the Militia of the State of Georgia, in the Creek War of 1792. *Washington.* 1803. 8vo, pp. 32. 27065

The Letters of a Farmer to the People of Georgia: or, the Constitutionality, Policy, and Legality of the Late Sales of Western Lands examined. ... . *Charleston: Printed by W. P. Young.* 1796. 8vo, pp. 41. B. 27066

Letters of Sicilius to the Citizens of the State of Georgia, on the Constitutionality, the Policy and the Legality of the late Sale of Western Lands in the State. 1795. 8vo, pp. 64. 27067

A List of the Lords, Spiritual and Temporal — to which are added the Names of the Trustees of Georgia, and place of Abode. *London.* 1734. 24mo. 27068

Memorial of Claimants under Georgia, &c., to the President of the United States. [n. p. n. d.] 8vo, pp. 19. 27069

Memorial on the Subject of the late Tariff: Addressed by the General Assembly of Georgia to the Anti-Tariff States. 1828. 8vo. 27070

Memorial of the Legislature of the State of Georgia to Congress, Nov. 29, 1805. *Washington.* 1806. 8vo, pp. 45.

Relates to unclaimed lands, etc., ceded to Georgia by the United States, but claimed by North Carolina.

Message from the President of the United States Accompanying Certain Articles of Agreement and Cession ... entered into ... by the Commissioners of the United States, and the Commissioners of Georgia ... . 26th April, 1802. [n. p. n. d.] 8vo, pp. 140. B. 27072

Message from the President of the United States, transmitting sundry Documents in relation to the Extinguishment of the Indian Title within the limits of Georgia. *Washington: Gales and Seaton.* 1824. 8vo. P. 27073

Message of Governor Troup, transmitted May 23, 1825, to the Legislature of Georgia, specially convened by Proclamation. *Milledgeville.* 1825. 27074

Relates to the Creek Indians.

Message of His Excellency Joseph E. Brown, ... March 10th, 1864 ... . *Milledgeville: Boughton, Nisbet, Barnes & Moore.* 1864. 8vo, pp. 48. BA. + Nov. 3rd, 1864. . [*Ibid.*] 8vo, pp. 27.

These messages relate chiefly to Confederate affairs.

Message of the Governor to the General Assembly of Georgia, at Extra Session, May 23, 1825. *Milledgeville.* 1825. 8vo, pp. 128. 27076

Minutes of the Georgia Association. ... Clark's Station, October, 1788. 4to, pp. 4. + At Powell's Creek, ... October [1794]. ... *New York: Printed by Alexander M'Millan.* 1794.

12mo, pp. 12. + At Whatley's Mill, October, 1803. *Augusta: Printed by William J. Bunce.* 1804. 8vo, pp. 8. + At Kioke, MDCCCIV. *Savannah: Printed by Lyon & Morse.* 1804. 12mo, pp. 24. + at Newford, ... October, 1804. *Augusta: Printed by Hobby and Bunce.* 1804. 8vo, pp. 8. 27077

Minutes of the ... Georgia Convention. 1821. 8vo. Continued. 27078

Neueste und richtigste nachricht. *See* [Oglethorpe (J.)]

A New Voyage to Georgia. | By a Young Gentleman. | Giving an Account of his Travels to South Carolina, | and part of North Carolina. | To which is added, | a Curious Account of the Indians, | By an Honourable Person. | And a Poem to James Oglethorpe, Esq. | On his Arrival | from Georgia. | *London: J. Wilford.* 1735. | 8vo, pp. 62. + The Second Edition. *London: J. Wilford.* 1737. 8vo, pp. (1), 62. BA. 27079

The second edition has merely a new title-page. Also in "Georgia Hist. Soc. Collections," II. 37–66. *See* Bancroft, Vol. III.

Observations upon Georgia. *See* [Walton (George)].

Official Documents, containing a Message of the State of Georgia to the Legislature, with the Correspondence between the Special Agent of the United States, Governor Troup, and the Secretary of War. *Milledgeville.* 1825. 8vo. 27080

Opinion of the Supreme Court of the United States at January Term, 1832, Delivered by Mr. Chief Justice Marshall, Together with the Opinion of Mr. Justice McLean, In the Case of Samuel A. Worcester, Plaintiff in Error *versus* The State of Georgia. With a Statement of the Case, extracted from the Records of the Supreme Court of the United States. Printed from Authenticated Copies. *Washington: Gales and Seaton.* 1832. 8vo, pp. 39. W. 27081

Relates to the Cherokee Indians.

The Particular Case of the Georgia Loyalists; in addition to the General Case and Claim of the American Loyalists, which was lately published by order of their Agents. [*February.* 1783.] 8vo, pp. 16. 27082

The Penal Code of the State of Georgia, as enacted December 19, 1816. With Reflections on the Same, and on Imprisonment for Debt. *Philadelphia.* 1817. 8vo, pp. 96. 27083

De præstantia coloniæ Georgico-Anglicanæ, præ coloniis aliis. *Aug. Vind.* 1747. 4to. 27084

Proceedings in the House of Representatives of the United States of America, Respecting the Contested Election for the Eastern District of the State of Georgia. *Philadelphia: Printed by Parry Hall.* BA. 27085

Proceedings of the Anti-Tariff Convention, held at Milledgeville. *Milledgeville.* 1832. 8vo. 27086

Progress of the Colony of Georgia, in America, a proper contrast to "State of the Colony of Georgia." *Privately Printed.* 1743. 8vo, pp. 24, 10. 27087

Public Laws of Georgia, passed ... in November and December, 1861 ... *Milledgeville.* 1861. 8vo, pp. 47, (1). Continued.

The Confederate laws; the last is dated March, 1864.

Public Laws passed by the General Assembly of the State of Georgia, at the Sessions of 1870 and 1871, with an Appendix, containing the Government of Georgia and Court Calendar, etc. *Atlanta (Georgia).* 1870–71. 2 vols., 8vo. 27089

Reasons for Establishing ... Georgia. *See* [Martyn (Benjamin)].

Regulations for the Quartermaster's Department of the State of Georgia, 1861. Regulations for the Commissariat of ... Georgia. 1861. *Milledgeville: Boughton, Nisbet & Barnes.* 1861. 8vo, pp. 80, 43. B. 27090

Remarks upon [Martyn's] Georgia. *See* [Percival (John)].

Reminiscences of Georgia. *See* Burke (E. P.), Vol. III.

Report from the Committee ... to enquire into the Expediency of extending the Time for Claimants to Lands under the State of Georgia, lying South of the State of Tennessee ... . 4th December, 1804. ... *Washington City: Printed by William Duane and Son.* 1804. 8vo, pp. 4. BA. 27091

Report from the Committee of Claims, on Memorials of Citizens of Massachusetts, purchasers under the Georgia Company, &c. *Washington.* 1805. 8vo. 27092

Report on the Address of ... Members of the General Assembly of Georgia. *Charleston: Evans and Cogswell.* 1860. 8vo, pp. 6. BA. 27093

Report of the Adjutant and Inspector General ... for ... 1862–63. *Milledgeville: Boughton, Nisbet & Barnes.* 1863. 8vo, pp. 44. BA. + October 26, 1864. BA. 27094

A Report of the Attorney-General to Congress, relative to Land situated in the Southwest part of the United States, claimed under a Law of Georgia. *Philadelphia.* 1796. 8vo. P. 27095

Report of the Board of Public Works to the Assembly. *Milledgeville.* 1826. 8vo, pp. 14. 27096

Report of the Commissioners ... for the Amicable Settlement of Limits with the State of Georgia, and authorizing the Establishment of a Government in the Mississippi Territory, February 10th, 1803. *Washington City.* 1803. pp. 92. M. 27097

... Report of the Comptroller-General of the State of Georgia ... October 20, 1860. *Milledgeville: Boughton, Nisbet & Barnes.* 1860. 8vo, pp. 118. Continued. BA. 27098

... Report ... of the Georgia Penitentiary ... 1st October, 1862. *Milledgeville: Boughton, Nisbet & Barnes.* 1862. 8vo, pp. 29. Continued. BA. 27099

Report of ... the Georgia Relief & Hospital Association ... October 29, 1862. *Augusta: Press of Chronicle & Sentinel.* 1862. 8vo, pp. 39. BA. + [For] 1863. *Augusta.* 1863. 8vo, pp. 49. BA. 27100

Report of the Treasurer of the State of Georgia, October 16, 1863. [*Milledgeville.* 1863.] 8vo, pp. 12. Continued. BA.

Report on the Address of a Portion of the Members of the General Assembly of Georgia. *Charleston: Evans & Cogswell, Printers.* 1860. 8vo, pp. 6. 27102

Resolutions ... by the General Assembly of Georgia, on the 19th Day of March, 1864 ... . *Milledgeville: Boughton, Nisbet, Barnes & Moore.* 1864. 8vo, pp. 8. BA. 27103

The Resolutions of the Trustees for Establishing the Colony of Georgia in America, in Common Council assembled, Relating to the Grants and Tenure of Lands within the said Colony. *London.* 1741. Folio, pp. 4. 27104

Resolutions of the Legislature of Georgia, relating to Lands Occupied by Cherokees. *Washington.* 1829. 8vo. C. 27105

Rules of the District Courts of the Confederate States of America, for the Districts of Georgia, under the Act entitled "An Act for the Sequestration of the Estates, Property and Effects of Alien Enemies." Together with the Act of Congress. *Savannah: W. Thorne Williams.* 1861. 12mo, pp. 29. BA.

Rules of the House of Representatives for the Session of 1864 ... *Milledgeville: Boughton, Nisbet, Barnes & Moore.* 1864. 8vo, pp. 7. BA. 27107

Slave Life in Georgia. *London.* 1853. 12mo. 27108

Some Account of the Design of the Trustees for Georgia. *London.* 1732. Folio. BM. 27109

Special Message of Gov. Joseph E. Brown ... November 7th, 1860. *Milledgeville: Boughton, Nisbet & Barnes.* 1860. 8vo, pp. 22. BA. 27110

Speeches, Letters, &c., by Distinguished Georgians. 8vo, pp. 45. 27111

State of Facts, showing the Right of certain Companies to the Lands lately Purchased by them from the State of Georgia. *United States: printed in the Year* 1795. 8vo, pp. 64. S., W.

A State | of the | Province of Georgia, | Attested upon Oath | in the Court of Savannah, | November 10, 1740. | *London, W. Meadows.* MDCCXLII. | 8vo, pp. 32. BA. 27113

Reprinted in Stephens' "Journal," Vol. II.; also in George Hart's "Collection," and Force's "Tracts," Vol. I., No. 3. *Washington.* 1836. 8vo, pp. 20.

UNIVERSITY OF GEORGIA. Catalogue of Books in the Library. By Williams Rutherford, jr. *Athens (Ga.), College.* 1858. 8vo, pp. 192. C. 27114

The Georgian Era. Memoirs of the most Eminent Persons, who have flourished in Great Britain, from the Accession of George the First to the Demise of George the Fourth. *London: Vizetelly, Brandon and Co.* MDCCCXXXII. 4 vols., crown 8vo, pp. 582, (2); 588, (2); 588; 588. 4 Portraits. BA. 27115

GARALDINI (A.) Itinerarivm | ad | Regiones svb Æqvinoctiali | plaga constitvtas | Alexandri Geraldini | Epi. S. Dominici apud Indos Occid^{es}. | Ad | Em^{um}. et R^{um}. Principem | Franciscum S. R. E. Card^{em}. | Barberinum | Opus posthumum. | [Colophon:]

Romæ, | *Typis Guilelmi Facciotti.* M.DC.XXXI. | Sm. 8vo, Engraved Title, pp. (10), 284, 36. 27116

A very scarce and curious volume on the discovery of the West Indies, written in 1524. Its writer was the intimate friend of Columbus, the one whose interest prevailed over Ferdinand to fit out the first expedition in search of unknown lands, and proved the feasibility of discovery by mathematical demonstration. Previous to being appointed Bishop of St. Domingo, he had been Ambassador to the Court of Henry VIII. of England. We learn from the twelve leaves of verses in commendation of the author and his travels by various writers, in Greek, Latin, Italian, French, German, Spanish, Hungarian, and English languages, the latter written by John Walker, that the bishop had had the charge of four queens, the greatest of whom was Catherine of Arragon, queen of Henry VIII.

GERANO. Considerations sur les divers methodes à suivre dans l'observations des peuples sauvages. *Paris. An* VIII [1800]. 4to. 27117

GERARD (G.) Clytia: a Tale of the Southern States. With other Poems. By G. Gerard. *London: Bosworth.* 1856. 12mo, pp. 176. 27118

GERARD (J. W.) London and New-York; their Crime and Police. *New-York.* 1853. 8vo. S. 27119

[GERARDUS DE MYST.] Veloren Arbeyt ofte klaar en kortbondigh vertoogh van de in de Lantstreeke Guyana aan de vaste kuste van Amerika op de rivier Wiapoca gelegen colonie. *Amsterdam.* [1678.] 4to. Map. 27120

Lost labor, or clear and concise account of the colony, situated on the river Wiapoca, in Guiana, on the coast of America. "This little recital contains the whole history of the colony sent out by the States General in 1676 to the banks of the river Wiapoca, the hardships they underwent, and the reasons which prevented them from succeeding. The river Wiapoca is the principal boundary between Guiana and Brazil." — MULLER.

GERBER (H.) Noçoes geographicas e administrativas da Provincia de Minas Geraes. Por Henrique Gerber. Com uma planta topographica do Ouro Preto. "Carta da Provincia de Minas Geraes." *Rio de Janeiro.* 1863. 4to, pp. 86. 27121

GERBIER (B.) Copye van het mandement von d'Edele Hove van Hollant. [1657.] 4to, pp. 4. 27122

Order of the Court of Holland to the shareholders of Gerbier's company to fulfil their duties. Not mentioned by Asher.

GERBIER. Extract | en | Copye | van | Verklaringen | op | eede | Voor den Achtbaren Magistraet van de Stadt. | Amsterdam, den 9. September 1660, gedaen | volgens Interrogatorien. | [n. p. n. d.] 4to, 4 leaves. 27123

From the "Sommier Verhael," *infra.*

GERBIER. Gebedt, | Van den Ridder | Balthazar Gerbier, | Baron Douvilly, | Patroon ende Commandeur | Van de Geoctroyeerde | Guiaense Colonie, | Op 't Schip | St. Jan Euangelist, ende 't Landt van Beloften. || *t'Amsterdam,* | *Gedruckt by Gillis Joosten, Boeckdrucker en Boeck-* | *verkooper in de Nieuwe-straet. Anno* 1659. | 4to, 4 leaves. 27124

Prayer of Balthazar Berbier, commander of the Guiana colony.

GERBIER. Informatie | Voorde Rechtsgeleerde die van wegen d' Edele Heeren | Bewinthebbers vande gheoctroyeerde West-In- | dische Compagnye gherequireert syn hare ad- | visen te geven op den | Moorde in Cajany | Begaen, en waer van gemelt is in het Sommier | verhael door den | Baron Douvily, | In druck contbaer gemaeckt. | [n. p. n. d.] 4to, pp. 8, 1 l. 27125

Information for the lawyers delegated to give their advice on the murder in Guiana, related in the account of Baron Gerbier.

GERBIER. Octroy, | Van de Hoog: Moog: Heeren | Staten Generael, aengaende de | Colonie op de Wilde Kust | Van | America. | Onder het beleyt van den Ridder | Balthasar Gerbier Baron Douvily. | *Gedruckt in 't laer ons Heeren,* 1659. | 4to, 4 l. 27126

GERBIER. Sommier Verhael, | Van sekere | Amerikaensche | Voyagie, | Gedaen | Door den Ridder | Balthasar Gerbier, | Baron Douuily, | Door Haer Ho: Mo: d'Heeren Staten Generael van de | Vereenighde Nederlanden, en d'Edele Heeren Bewint- | hebberen van de Geoctroydeerde generale West-Indi- | sche Compagnie, Opperhooft Commandeur van | een Guajaensche Colonie gekoosen, ge- | committeert ende gestelt. | *Gedruckt voor den Autheur. Anno* 1660. | 4to, 5 leaves. 27127

See Asher, No. 11. Summary account of a certain American voyage, done by the Chevalier Balthazar Gerbier.

GERBIER. Sommier Verhael, | Van sekere | Amerikaensche | Voyagie, | Gedaen | Door den Ridder | Balthasar Gerbier, | Baron Douuily, | ... *Gedruckt voor den Autheur. Anno* 1660. | 4to, pp. (12). 2 Plates. 27128

Muller quotes another edition, with addition of the protocol of the Amsterdam Court in the affair of Gerbier. 1660. 4to, pp. 18. 2 Plates.

GERBIER. Waerachtige | Verklaringe | Nopende de | Goude en Silvere Mijne, Waer van den Ridder | Balthasar Gerbier, Douvily | gecontracteert heeft met eenige geasossieerde | In Zeelant. | *In 'sGraven-Hage,* | *Gedruckt by Iohannes Rammazeyn, Boeck-drucker*

woonende | *op de Veer-kaey, naest de bestelder inde Boeckdruckerye.* 1656. | 4to, 4 l. Portrait of Gerbier. 27129

True declaration concerning the gold and silver mines, for which the Chevalier B. Gerbier has made a contract.

GERBIER. Waaractige | Verklaringe vanden Ridder | Balthasar Gerbier, | B: Douvilij; | Noopende sijn saecke van Goude | en Silvere Mynen, waer | over hy ghecontracteert hadde | met sekere Persoonen in | Zeelant. | [n. p. n. d.] 4to, 8 l. 27130

True declaration of B. Gerbier on his affair of gold and silver mines. Muller describes a copy with twenty pages.

GERBIER. Tweede Deel | Vande | Waeractige | Verclaringe | Nopende de | Goude en Silvere Mijne, | Waer van den Ridder | Balthazar Gerbier, Douvily | gecontracteert heeft met eenige geasossieerde | in Zeelant. | *In 'sGraven-Hage* | *Gedruckt by Iohannes Rammazeyn,* ... 1656. | 4to, 5 l. 27131

Second part of the true declaration.

GERBIER. Derde | Verclaringe | Aengaende de | Goude ende Silvere Mijne | Aenghewesen door den Ridder | Balthasar Gerbier, | Baron Douvily, | ... *In 'sGraven-Hage* | *Gedruct by Iohannes Rammazeyn,* ... 1656. | 4to, 2 l. 27132

GERHARD (F.) Illinois as it Is; its History, Geography, Statistics, Constitution, Laws, Government, Finances, Climate, Soil, Plants, &c., &c. By Fred. Gerhard. With [3] Maps, and other Illustrations. *Chicago, Ill.: Keen and Lee.* [1857.] 12mo, pp. 451. BA. 27133

GERHARD. Will the People of the United States be Benefited by an International Copyright Law, or will such a law be an injury to them? By Frederick Gerhard. *New York.* 1868. 8vo, pp. 28. 27134

GERHART (E. V.) ... An Address, delivered at the Opening of the New Diagnothian Hall, July 2nd, 1847. By Rev. E. V. Gerhart. *Mercersburg, Pa.* MDCCCXLVII. 8vo, pp. 19. BA.

GÉRIN (E.) La Gazette de Québec. Par Elzear Gérin. *Québec.* 1864. 8vo, pp. 65. 27136

GÉRIN-LAJOIE (A.) Catéchisme politique, ou élémens du droit public et constitutionnel du Canada, mis à la portée du peuple. *Montreal.* 1851. 8vo. 27137

GERKE (H. C.) Der Nordamerikanische Rathgeber, nebst den, in den Jahren 1831 und 1832, in der Union gemachten Reisebeobachtungen und Taschenbuch für deutsche Auswanderer jeder Art, von Heinrich Christian Gerke. *Hamburg: Perthes, Besser und Mauke.* 1833. 12mo, pp. 598. 27138

A Germ of Severe Ethical Analysis, Pure Philosophy and Nationality, and the only Practical Basis for restored Peace. *Danbury, Connecticut.* 1862. 8vo, pp. 7. 27139

GERMAIN (George). Correspondance du lord G. Germain; avec les Généraux Clinton, Cornwallis, & les Amiraux dans la station de l'Amérique, avec plusieurs lettres interceptées du général Washington, du marquis de la Fayette, & de M. de Barras, chef d'Escadre. Traduit de l'anglois sur les originaux publiés par ordre de la Chambre des Pairs. *Berne: Chez la nouvelle société typographique.* 1782. 8vo, pp. xvi, 304. Portrait of Washington by Desrais. S. + *Londres et Versailles: chez Poincot.* 1784. 8vo, pp. xvi, 304. 2 Tables. 27140

GERMAINE (G.) Epistle to Lord George Germaine, in Verse, relating to the American War, &c. *London.* 1778. 4to.

GERMAINE. A Letter to Lord George Germaine. *London: J. Almon.* MDCCLXXVI. 8vo, pp. 38, Advt., 1 l. B., BA. 27142

"This writer sets forth, very circumstantially, the prodigious numbers and alarming power of the United Colonists by sea and land, and enumerates the unsurmountable difficulties that will impede in particular the operations of our land forces in every province. In short, that it will be impossible for us to succeed in the attempt of forcing the Americans to submission. Urges on Great Britain a discontinuance of the contest in America." — *M. Rev.*, LIV. 328.

GERMAINE. A Letter to Lord George Germaine giving an Account of the Origin of the Dispute between Great Britain and the Colonies, with some Remarks on the Manner in which the War has been conducted. To which are added, certain Terms, humbly proposed as a ground-work of a Reconciliation. By a Gentleman for many years a resident in America. *London: T. Whieldon.* MDCCLXXVIII. 8vo, pp. 84. 27143

"A defense of the measures of the British government, in which the writer recommends that the independency of the Americans should never be acceded to." — *M. Rev.*, LVIII. 477.

[GERMAINE.] A Reply to Lieutenant General Burgoyne's Letter to his Constituents. *London: J. Wilkie.* MDCCLXXIX. 8vo, pp. (1), 46. BA. + Second Edition. [*Ibid.*] 27144

This has also been ascribed to Sir John Dalrymple.

[GERMAINE.] The Rights of Great Britain Asserted against the Claim of America; Being an Answer to the Declaration of the General Congress; Said to be Written by Lord George Germaine. *London, Printed; Philadelphia, Re-Printed, and Sold by R. Bell.* M DCC LXXVI. 8vo, pp. 92, (4), Appendix, folded. P. + The Second Edition, with Additions. [*Ibid.*] + The Third Edition, with Additions. *London: T. Cadell.* MDCCLXXVI. 8vo, pp. 96. + *Glasgow: Printed from the Third London Edition.* M DCC LXXVI. 12mo, pp. 76. Table. + The Fourth Edition, with Additions. *London: T. Cadell.* MDCCLXXVI. + The Fifth Edition, with Additions. [*Ibid.*] + Sixth Edition, with Additions. *Edinburgh.* 1776. 8vo. + Seventh Edition. *London: T. Cadell.* M DCC LXXVI. + The Eighth Edition. To which is now added, a Refutation of Dr. Price's Statement of the National Debt. *London: T. Cadell.* M DCC LXXVI. 8vo, pp. 123. + The Ninth Edition. To which is now added, a Further Refutation of Dr. Price's State of the National Debt. *London: Printed for T. Cadell.* M DCC LXXVI. 8vo, pp. 131. + The Tenth Edition. *London: T. Cadell.* MDCCLXXVI. 8vo, pp. (4), 131, Appendix, a folded sheet at p. 99. 27145

For a translation, *see* Réponse a la Declaration, etc. It has been variously ascribed to Sir John Dalrymple, on the authority of Sir James Mackintosh; Lord George Germaine, James Macpherson, the translator of "Ossian," and Henry Mackenzie, the author of "The Man of Feeling."

The German Charitable Society's Lottery, on Petty's Island, (etc.) [*Philadelphia.* About *April,* 1773.] Folio, pp. 1. P.

A German Freeholder to his Countrymen. ... *Germantown. September* 22, 1770. 4to, pp. 1. 27147

An attack upon Mr. Galloway.

German Evangelical Lutheran Ministerium of Pennsylvania. Verhandlungen der 100sten jährlichen versammlung, *Reading, Pa.* 1847. 8vo. 27148

German Evangelical Lutheran Zion's Church, Boston, Mass. Kirchenordnung. *Albany.* 1857. 18mo, pp. 11. 27149

German Reformed Church, in the United States Army. Acts and Proceedings ... at Reading, Pa. 1841. *Chambersburg, Penn.* 1842. 8vo, pp. 84. 27150

Catalogue of the Library of the German Society contributing for the Relief of Distressed Germans in Pennsylvania; with the Rules of the Library. *Philadelphia.* 1839. 8vo. + [*Ibid.*] 1850. 8vo. 24151

Also an additional catalogue.

Charter and By-Laws of the German Society, with a List of Members. *New York.* 1799. 8vo. 27152

GERMANICUS, *pseudonym. See* [Randolph (Edmund)].

GERMANTOWN, *Pa.* Abdruck einiger wahrhafften Berichte aus Germanton in Pensylvanien vom 17. Nov. 1738. Betreffende den inn- und äusserl. Zustand dererjenigen die dahin gezogen etc. *Berlenburg.* 1739. 4to, pp. 16. 27153

Acts relating to the Germantown and Norristown Railroad. Company. *Philadelphia.* 1847. 8vo. 27154

Centennial Anniversary of the Foundation of the Germantown Academy, 1860. *Printed for the Germantown Academy.* 1860. 4to, pp. xvii, 59. + [Another Edition.] *Philadelphia: C. Sherman.* 1860. 8vo, pp. xv, 53. 27155

Certain Agreements and Concessions, Made, concluded and agreed on by and between the Contributors to a Sum of Money for erecting and establishing a School-House and School in Germantown, this Twenty-Fifth Day of January, In the Year of our Lord One Thousand Seven Hundred and Sixty. [n. p. n. d.] 4to, pp. 8. 27156

Constitution of the Germantown Society for Promoting Domestic Manufactures. *Philadelphia.* 1790. 8vo. C. 27157

Copia eines Send-Schreibens auss der neuen Welt betreffend, etc. 1695. 4to. 27158

This letter recounts the dangerous voyage and happy delivery of certain Christian missionaries who journeyed to America to propagate the knowledge of the true faith. The letter is dated from Germantown, Pennsylvania, August 7, 1694.

Germantown: a Tale of the Quaker City during the Revolution. By the Author of the "Child of Song." *New York: Irwin & Co.* 1866. 18mo, pp. 100. 27159

Nachricht von einer Hochteutschen Evangelischen Colonie zu Germantown, in Nord-Virginien in America, und derselben dringendliches Ansuchen an ihre Glaubens-Genossen in Europa. [n. p.] 1720. 4to. 27160

Prospectus of the Lyceum at Mount Airy, near Germantown. *Philadelphia.* 1825. 12mo. 27161

Also: Prospectus of the American Classical and Military Academy at Mount Airy, near Germantown. [n. p. n. d.] 12mo.

Der alte Germantown Calendar, 1854. *Philadelphia.* 1854. 4to. 27162

De la Gerontocratie en Haiti. *Paris: Dentu.* 1860. 8vo.

GERRALD (J.) Address to the People of England on the Necessity of a Convention. By Joseph Gerrald. *London.* 1796. 8vo. 27164

By an enthusiastic admirer of American institutions, who resided a considerable time in the United States. Contains an account of the American Revolution.

GERRISH (J.), *and* BARRELL (J.) The State of Gerrish and Barrell's Accounts and Disputes, deliver'd to Mr. Robert Sanderson, and Mr. Nathaniel Bethune, June, 1751. *Boston: Printed by D. Fowle.* 1751. 4to, pp. 46. BA. 27165

GERRISH (M.) The Happiness of a Holy Life, Exemplified in the Sickness and Death Of the Pious Mrs Martha Gerrish, Of Boston in New-England, Who died April the 14th, 1736. Ætat. 48. With A Collection of very Pathetick Letters written by Her, during her Languishing Indisposition, to her Children, Relations, and Friends, to comfort them under all Afflictions; and defending several Important Points of the Christian Religion, in opposition to some late Deistical Writings. To which is added, Her Funeral Sermon [By Nathaniel Appleton]. *London: C. Rivington.* M,DCCXL. 12mo, pp. (1), xxii, 207, (5). 27166

GERSHOM, *pseudonym.* Emigration for the Million; being the Digest of a Plan for more equally locating the Population of Great Britain and Ireland throughout the British Empire. By Gershom. *London.* 1849. 8vo, pp. 36. 27167

GERSON (J.) Tripartito del | Christianissimo y consolato | rio doctor Iuan Gerson de | doctrina Christiana: a qual- | quiera muy puechosa. Tra- | duzido de latī en lēgua Cas | tellana para el diē d' muchos | necessario. *Impresso en Me-* | *xico: en casa de Iuan crom-* | *berger. Por mādado y a cos* | *ta del R. S. obispo de la mes* | *ma ciudad Fray Iuā çumar* | *raga. Reuisto y examinado* | *por su mandado.* | *Año de.* M. d. xliiij. | [Colophon:] *Acabose el Tripartito de Iuan* | *gerson: a gloria y loor de la sanctissima trinidad: y d'* | *la sacratissima virgē sancta Maria reyna d' los an-* | *geles. Y de los gloriosissimos sant Iuan Baptista:* | *Y sant Ioseph. Y sant Frācisco. El qual se impri-* | *mio en la grā ciudad d' Tenuchtiltlan Mexico de* | *sta nueua España en casa de Iuā crōberger que dios* | *aya. Acabose de imprimir. Año de.* M. d. xliiij. | 4to, 28 unnumbered l. 27168

See "Bulletin du Bibliophile," 1859, p. 183, and "Diccionario Univ. de Hist. y Geogr." A volume of the highest interest for its imprint. It is among the earliest books printed in the New World.

GERSTAECKER (F.) Achtzehn Monate in Süd-Amerika und dessen deutschen Colonien von Friedrich Gerstäcker. *Leipzig: Hermann Costenoble.* 1862. 3 vols., 8vo. + 1863. B. 27169

GERSTAECKER. Amerikanische Wald- und Strombilder. Von Friedrich Gerstäcker. *Leipzig.* 1862. 2 vols., 12mo, pp. (4), 218; (4), 219. B. 27170

GERSTAECKER. Die Blauen und Gelben. Venezuelanisches Charakterbild aus der letzten Revolution von 1868. *Jena: Costenoble.* 1870. 3 vols., 8vo, pp. v, 356; v, 348; v, 339.

GERSTAECKER. Californische Skizzen. *Leipzig: Arnold.* 1856. 8vo, 2 l., pp. 379. 27172

GERSTAECKER. Die Colonie. Brasilianisches Lebensbild. *Jena: Costenoble.* 1864. 3 vols., 8vo, pp. 120. 27173

GERSTAECKER. Der deutschen Auswanderer Fahrten und Schicksale. Mit einer Karte der Vereinigten Staaten von Nordamerika, von F. Gerstäcker. *Leipzig.* 1847. 8vo, pp. 334. + Same. *Leipzig.* 1849. + Same. 1854. 27174

GERSTAECKER. Lotgevallen en Ontmoetingen van een gezelschap duitsche landverhuizers naar en in Noord-Amerika. Naar het Hoogduitsch. *Amsterdam: H. Frijlink.* 1847. 8vo, pp, (4), 352. Map and Plate. C. 27175

GERSTAECKER. The Wanderings and Fortunes of some German Emigrants. By Frederick Gerstæcker. Translated by David Black. *New-York: D. Appleton & Company.* M DCCCXLVIII. Square 12mo, pp. 3–270. B., BA. + *London: D. Bogue.* 1848. Square 12mo, pp. viii, 310. C. 27176

GERSTAECKER. Der Flatbootmann. Amerikanische Erzählung. *Prag: Kober und Markgraf.* 1858. 16mo. + Album. Bibliothek deutscher Originalromane. 2. Aufl. *Schwerin: Hildebrand.* 1870. 8vo, pp. 244. 27177

GERSTAECKER. Frank Wildman's Adventures on Land and Water. By E. Gerstaecker. Translated by Lascelles Wraxall. *London: Routledge & Co.* 1853. 12mo, pp. 296. 27178

GERSTAECKER. Gerstäcker's Travels: Rio de Janeiro, Buenos Ayres, Ride through the Pampas, Winter Journey across the Cordilleras, Chili, Valparaiso, California, and the Gold Fields. Translated from the German. *London: Nelson & Sons.* 1854. Post 8vo, pp. 290. 27179

GERSTAECKER. In Amerika. Amerikanisches Lebensbild aus neuerer Zeit im Anschluss an "Nach Amerika." *Jena: Hermann Costenoble.* 27180

GERSTAECKER. In Mexico. Charakterbild aus den Jahren 1864–67, von Friedrich Gerstäcker. *Jena: Hermann Costenoble.* 1872. 2 vols., 8vo, pp. (6), 374; (6), 380. 27181

GERSTAECKER. Nach Amerika! Ein Volksbuch. Illustrirt von Theodor Hosemann und Karl Reinhardt. *Jena: Hermann Costenoble. Leipzig.* 1855. 3 vols., 8vo, pp. pp. xi, 260; 258; 296; 268; 274; 252. 27182

GERSTAECKER. Narrative of a Journey round the World. Comprising a Winter Passage across the Andes to Chili, with a Visit to the Gold Regions of California and Australia, the South Sea Islands, Java, &c. By F. Gerstaecker. *London.* 1853. 12mo, pp. 624. C., P. + *London.* 1854. 12mo. *New York: Harper & Brothers.* 1854. 27183

GERSTAECKER. Neue Reisen durch die Vereinigten Staaten, Mexiko, Ecuador, Westindien und Venezuela, von Friedrich Gerstäcker. ... . *Jena: Hermann Costenoble.* 1868. 3 vols., 18mo, pp. 414; 422; 443. B. 27184

GERSTAECKER. Mississippi-Bilder, Licht- und Schaltenseiten transatlantischen Lebens, von Friedrich Gerstaecker. *Dresden und Leipzig.* 1847. 2 vols., pp. (4), 343; (3), 386. BA. + *Leipzig.* 1853. 3 vols., 4 l., pp. 352; 3 l., pp. 414; 3 l., pp. 363. B. 27185

GERSTAECKER. Reisen. *Stuttgart und Tübingen.* 1853–54. 5 vols., 8vo. 27186

Contents: Vol. I. Süd America; II. Californien; III. Die Südsee Inseln. IV. Australien; V. Java.

GERSTAECKER. Reisen um die Welt. Ein Familienbuch. 3 verbesserte Auflage. *Leipzig.* 1870. 8vo, pp. viii, 172. Continued. 27187

GERSTAECKER. Scènes de la vie californien; traduites de l'Allemand par Gustave Revilliod. *Genève: J. G. Fick.* 1860. 8vo. 27188

GERSTAECKER. Western Lands and Western Waters. By Frederick Gerstäcker. With Illustrations from Designs by Eminent Artists. *London: S. O. Beeton.* 8vo, pp. xii, 388. 27189

GERSTAECKER. Wie ist es denn nun eigentlich in Amerika? Eine kurze Schilderung dessen, was der Auswanderer zu thun and dafür zu hoffen und zu erwarten hat. *Leipzig.* 1849. 16mo, pp. viii, 127. + [*Ibid.*] 1853. 16mo, pp. viii, 127. 27190

GERSTAECKER. Wild Sports in the Far West. By Frederick Gerstaecker. Translated from the German, by Harrison Weir. *London: Routledge.* 1854. 12mo, pp. 314. C., P. + *London.* 1862. 16mo. + *Boston.* 1866. 12mo. 27191

GERSTAECKER. Der Wahnsinnige. Erzählung aus Sud-Amerika. 2 Auflage. *Schwerin: Hildebrand.* 1870. 8vo, pp. iii, 226. 27192

GERSTAECKER. Zwei Republiken. *Jena: Costenoble.* 1865. 8vo. 27193

GERRSTAECKER. Aus Zwei Welttheilen. Gesammelte Erzählungen. *Leipzig: Arnold.* 1854. 2 vols., 8vo, 3 l., pp. 428; 3 l., pp. 316. 27194

Also: Aventures d'une colonie d'émigrants en Amérique. Traduites de l'allemand par X. Marmiér. *Paris: Hachette et Cie.* 1855. 12mo. — Echos aus dem Urwäldern oder Skizzen transatlantischen Lebens. Nach englischen Quellen bearbeitet. *Leipzig: Gerhard.* 1847. 8vo. — Die Flusspiraten des Mississippi. Aus dem Waldleben Amerika's. *Jena: Hermann Costenoble.* — Der kleine Goldgraber in Californien. Eine Erzählung für die Jugend. *Jena: Hermann Costenoble.* 8vo. 6 Colored Plates. — Gold! Ein Californisches Lebensbild aus dem Jahre 1849. *Leipzig.* 1858. 8vo. — How a Bride was Won; or, A Chase across the Pampas. ... Translated by F. Jordan. *New York: D. Appleton & Co.* 1869. 8vo, pp. 274. 8 Plates. C. — Les pirates du Mississippi. ... Roman allemand traduit par Bénédict H. Révoil. *Paris: Hachette et Cie.* 1858. 18mo, pp. viii, 406. + [*Ibid.*] 1872. — Pirates of the Mississippi. ... Translated from the German. *London: G. Routledge & Co.* 1856. 16mo, pp. 276. — Die Regulatoren in Arkansas. Aus dem Waldleben Amerika's. *Leipzig: Vereinsverlags buchhandlung.* 1846. 3 vols., 8vo. — Streif- und Jagdzüge durch die Vereinigten Staaten Nord-Amerikas. Mit einer Vorworte von Th. Bromme. *Dresden und Leipzig: Arnoldische Buchhandlung.* 1844. 12mo. — Unter den Penchuenden. Chilenischer Roman. 3 Bde. *Jena.* 1867. 8vo, pp. 984. — The Young Gold-Digger; or, a Boy's Adventures in the Gold Regions. *London.* 1860. 16mo.

GERSTNER, *geb.* von EPPLEN HARTENSTEIN (Clara von). Beschreibung einer Reise die Vereinigten Staaten von Nordamerica, in den Jahren 1838 bis 1840. In Gesellschaft des Ritters Franz Anton von Gerstner unternommen. *Leipzig: J. C. Heinrich.* 1842. 12mo, pp. xii, 456. C., S. 27195

GERSTNER (Franz Anton *Ritter* von). Berichte aus den Vereinigten Staaten von Nordamerika üb. Eisenbahnen, Dampfschifffahrten, Banken, etc. *Leipzig.* 1839. 4to. 27196

GERSTNER. Die innern Communicationen der Vereinigten Staaten von Nordamerika. Nach dessen Tode aufgesetzt, redigirt und herausgegeben von L. Klein. *Wien: Forster.* 1842–43. 2 vols., 4to, pp. iv, 376; 2 l., pp. 339. Map and 15 Plates. 27197

GERTRUDES MAGNA (Fr. Francisco de Paula de Sancta). Canto poetico aos faustos annos de S. M. I. o sr. D. Pedro de Alcantara, Imperador do Brasil. *Rio de Janeiro: na Imp. Reg.* 1827. 4to. 27198

GERTRUDES MAGNA. Canto Poetico: o grande poder dos vates, e o retrato de uma senhora. *Rio de Janeiro: na Imp. Reg.* 1825. 8vo. 27199

GERTRUDES MAGNA. Sermão em memoria do faustissimo dia, em que Sua Alteza Real desembarcou n'esta cidade da Bahia, recitado no antigo collegio dos Jesuitas a 23 de Janeiro de 1815. *Rio de Janeiro: na Imp. Reg.* 1816. 4to, pp. 18. 27200

GERVINUS (G. G.) Geschichte des neunzehnten Jahrhunderts seit den Wiener Verträgen. *Leipzig.* 1858. 8vo, pp. 512. 27201

Partly relates to America.

GERVINUS. Histoire du XIXe siècle. Edition belge en publication. *Bruxelles: Lacroix.* 1865. 27202

Vols. VII. and VIII. relate to America.

GERVINUS. Introduction to the History of the Nineteenth Century. By G. G. Gervinus. From the German. With a Brief Notice of the Author by the Translator. *London: Henry G. Bohn.* M,DCCC,LIII. Post 8vo, pp. xx, 137. P. 27203

Gesammelte Aktenstücke des Vereins zum Schutze deutscher Einwanderer in Texas. Nebst e. Karte. *Mainz.* 1845. 8vo. 27204

Gesammlete Nachrichten von den Englischen Kolonien in Nordamerika, bis auf jetzige Zeiten. *Hamburg: bey Buchenroder und Ritter.* 1776. 8vo, 2½ sheets. 27205

Geschichte allgemeine, du Länder und Völker von America. *Halle.* 1752. 4to. 27206

Geschichte von Californien. *See* [Venegas].

Geschichte des Americanischen Kriegs von 1812, ... an dem glorreichen achten ... 1815 vor New-Orleans. ... *Reading.* 1817. 8vo, pp. vii, (1), 273. Portrait. B. 27207

Geschichte du aussereuropäischen Staaten. Herausgegeben von mehrerer Gelehrten. *Quedlinberg: Basse.* 1836, etc. 8vo. 27208

Vols. III. and IV. are Solis' "Mexico Aus. d. Span. übers. von L. G. Förster. 1838."

Geschichte der Colonisation. *See* [Robinson (Theresa)].

Geschichte der englischen Kolonien in Nordamerika, von der ersten Entdeckung dieser Länder durch Sebastian Cabot, bis auf den Frieden 1763. Aus dem Englischen [von Anton Ernst Klausing]. *Leipzig: Caspar Fritsch.* 1775–76. 2 vols., 16mo, 8 l., pp. 452; 4 l., pp. 424, 4 l. Map. B. 27209

Geschichte der Entdekkung von Amerika. Ein durchaus verständliches Lesebuch für Jedermann. Mit einem historischen Kupferstich. *Halle.* 1795. 8vo, pp. 400. 27210

Die Geschichte der Errichtung und des Handels der Englischen Colonien im mitternächtlichen Amerika. Aus dem Französischen. *Rostock.* 1756. 12mo. A. 27211

Geschichte der europäischen. Pflanzstädte auf den Antillischen Inseln ... . *Stuttgart: Metzler.* 1760. 8vo. 27212

Geschichte der Kriege in und ausser Europa, vom Aufange des Austandes der Brittischen Kolonien in Nordamerika an ... 1776. [*Nürnberg:*] *bey Gabriel Nicolaus Raspe.* 1777–1784. 4to, pp. (8), 112; 84; (2), 127; (5), 122; (3), 134; 111; (3), 109; (2), 117, (1). 8 Plates or Maps. 27213

These volumes described relate exclusively to America. A set forms thirty parts.

Geschichte der Vereinigten Staaten von Nord Amerika. Aus dem Englischen übersetzt von Aug. Lebr. Herrmann. *Leipzig: Hartleben's Verlags-Expedition.* 1835. 8vo. Plate. 27214

A translation of the article "America" in the "Penny Cyclopædia."

Geschichte und Handlung der Englischen Colonien in dem nördlichen Amerika, worinnen man den jetzigen Zustand ihren Bevölkerung und besondere Umstände von ihrer Regierungsform bevorab von Neu England, Pensilvanien, Carolina und Georgien findet; verdeutscht durch A. G. U. *Frankfurt am Mayn: J. B. Andrea.* 1755. 12mo, 2 l., pp. 238. 27215

See [Butel-Dumont], Vol. III., No. 9604.

Geschichte und Handlung der französischen Pflanzstädte in Nordamerika, nebst einer zuverlässigen Nachricht von deren Be-

völkerung, ihren Einwohnern [etc.] wie auch einer kurzen Einleitung in die jezige Streittigkeiten der Engländer und Franzosen wegen Akadien. *Stuttgart: J. B. Mezler.* 1756. 16mo, pp. (8), 376. Map. C. 27216

Geschichte der Kolonisirung der freyen staaten des Alterthums, angewandt auf den gegenwärtigen Streit zwischen Grossbritannien und seinen amerikanischen Kolonien. Aus dem Englischen. *Leipzig: Weygand.* 1778. 27217

Colonization in ancient times, applied to the present difficulties between Great Britain and the American colonies.

Die Geschichte von der Marterwoche. *See* [Fischer (J. G.)]

Geschied en handelkundig tafereel van de Bataav. West-Ind. Coloniën bijzonderlijk van Suriname. *Amsterdam.* 1802. 8vo. 27218

Geschiedenis der kolonie van Suriname. *See* Suriname.

De Geschillen der Engelschen met hunne volkplantingen in America. Uit het Engelsch. *Leyden.* 1777. 8vo, pp. 106. 27219

Differences of the English with their colonies in America. Contains translations of W. Smith on the present state of America, J. Wesley's address, and two refutations of Wesley.

Geschwinde Rechner, oder des Handlers rutzlicher Gehulfe. *Chestnut-Hill: Samuel Saur.* 1793. 12mo, 67 l. 27220

Federal Reckoner. A very rare imprint. No printing has been done there since this date.

GESNER (Abraham). The Gold Fields of Nova Scotia. *Halifax.* 1862. 12mo, pp. 8. 27221

GESNER. New Brunswick; with Notes for Emigrants. Comprehending the Early History, an Account of the Indians, Settlement, Topography, Statistics, Commerce, Timber, Manufactures, Agriculture, Fisheries, Geology, Natural History, Social and Political State, Immigrants, and contemplated Railways of that Province. By Abraham Gesner, Esq. ... *London: Simmons & Ward.* 1847. 8vo, pp. xv, 388. 27222

GESNER. The Industrial Resources of Nova Scotia, comprehending the Physical Geography, Topography, Geology, Agriculture, Commerce, contemplated Railways, &c., of the Province. By Abraham Gesner. *Halifax.* 1849. 8vo, pp. 341. Map and Plate. C. 27222

GESNER. A Practical Treatise on Coal, Petroleum, and other Distilled Oils. By Abraham Gesner, M.D., F.G.S. Second Edition, Revised and Enlarged, by George Weltden Gesner. *New York.* 1865. 8vo, pp. 181. 27224

GESNER. Remarks on the Geology and Mineralogy of Nova Scotia. By Abraham Gesner, Esq. ... *Halifax, N. S.: Printed by Gossip and Coade.* 1836. 8vo, pp. xl, 272. Maps and Plates. 27225

GESNER. [Second, Third, and Fourth] Report on the Geological Survey of the Province of New Brunswick. By Abraham Gesner. *Saint John.* 1836–42. 2 vols., 8vo, pp. xii, 76; xiv, 88, 101. BA. 27226

Also: Report on the Geological Survey of the Province of New Brunswick, with Topographical Account of the Public Lands and the Districts Explored in 1842. *St. John.* 1843. 8vo. — Report on the Londonderry Iron and Coal Deposits. *Halifax.* 1846. 8vo. C.

GESNER (Conrad). Historiæ Animalium. *Francofurti.* 1585–1606. 3 vols., folio. Woodcuts. 27227

On the title is a portrait [?] of a Patagonian su [sow].

GESNER. History of Animals. Translated by Edward Toprell. *London: J. Jaggard.* 1607–8. 2 vols., folio. + *London.* 1658. Folio. 27228

The "su" is reproduced and described on page 660.

GESSNER (L.) Le Droit des Neutres sur Mer. *Berlin.* 1865. Rl. 8vo, pp. xiv, 437. 27229

Discusses questions arising out of the Civil War of 1861.

Getrouw Vervaal van de opkomst en tegenwoord. toestand der zo genaamde Methodisten in Engeland. *Workum: D. Balk.* 1752. 8vo. 27230

This true account of the Methodists contains an account of the voyage of John Charles Wesley to Georgia, and their residence there.

GETTYSBURG. Address of Hon. Edward Everett, at the Consecration of the National Cemetery at Gettysburg, 19th November, 1863, with the Dedicatory Speech of President Lincoln, and the other Exercises of the Occasion; accompanied by an Account of the Origin of the Undertaking and of the Arrangement of the Cemetery Grounds, and a Map of the Battle-Field and a Plan of the Cemetery. Published for the Benefit of the Cemetery Monument Fund. *Boston: Little, Brown & Co.* 1864. 8vo, pp. 87, (1). B., BA. 27231

The Diary of a Lady of Gettysburg, Pennsylvania, from June 15 to July 15, 1863. 8vo, pp. 29. 27232

Not published.

First Annual Meeting ... Proceedings of the Commissioners of the Soldiers' National Cemetery Association, held at Philadelphia, on the 7th of December, 1864. *Providence: Knowles, Anthony & Co., Printers.* 1864. 27233

First Annual Report of the Commissioners composing the Board of Managers of the Soldiers' National Cemetery, at Gettysburg, Pennsylvania, made December 7, 1864. *Philadelphia: King & Baird.* 1864. 8vo, pp. 32. 27234

Charter and Proceedings of the Board of Commissioners of the Soldiers' National Cemetery Association. Incorporated by the State of Pennsylvania. *Providence: Knowles, Anthony & Co., Printers.* 1864. 8vo, pp. 20. 27235

Jenny Wade, of Gettysburg. *Philadelphia: J. B. Lippincott & Co.* 1863. 12mo, pp. 33. 27236

Hospital Scenes after the Battle of Gettysburg, July, 1863. ... By the Patriot Daughters of Lancaster. [*Lancaster.*] 1864. 8vo, pp. 33. B., BA., 27237

Names of the Officers and Privates who fell in the Battle of Gettysburg, and in the Skirmishes incident thereto, or who Died of Wounds received in that Battle. [n. p.:] *Printed for the National Cemetery Association.* [1864.] Folio, pp. 153. C. 27238

Oration of Major General O. O. Howard and Speech of Governor Curtin, at the Laying of the Corner Stone of the Monument in the Soldiers' National Cemetery, at Gettysburg, July 4, 1865; with the other Exercises of the Occasion. *Gettysburg: Auginbaugh & Wible.* 1865. 8vo. 27239

Order of Masonic Ceremonies for Laying the Foundation Stone of the Monument in the Soldiers' National Cemetery at Gettysburg, Pa., July 4, 1865. *Philadelphia: J. B. Chandler, printer.* 1865. 8vo, pp. 12. 27240

See also "The Soldiers' Casket," August, 1865.

Our Campaign around Gettysburg: being a Memorial of what was Endured, Suffered, and Accomplished by the Twenty-Third Regiment (N. Y. S. N. G.), and other Regiments associated with

Them, in their Pennsylvania and Maryland Campaign, during the Second Rebel Invasion of the Loyal States in June–July, 1863. ... *Brooklyn: O. H. Rome & Brothers.* 12mo, pp. 168. BA. 27241

Proceedings of the Commissioners of the Soldiers' National Cemetery at Gettysburg, December, 1863. 8vo, pp. 5. + Proceedings and Second Annual Report. *Gettysburg: J. E. Wible.* 1865. 8vo, pp. 28. 27242

Report of John R. Bartlett, Commissioner of Rhode Island, to the General Assembly of Rhode Island, on the Soldiers' National Monument or Cemetery, at Gettysburg, January, 1866. pp. 6. 27243

Report of the Committee [of the State of Maine], on the Soldiers' National Cemetery. [n. p.] 1865. 8vo, pp. 8. 27244

Report of the Operations of the Sanitary Commission, during and after the Battles at Gettysburg, July 1, 2 and 3, 1854. *New York: W. C. Bryant & Co.* 1863. 8vo, pp. 29. 27245

Report of the Select Committee relative to the Soldiers' National Cemetery, together with the Accompanying Documents, as Reported to the House of Representatives of the Commonwealth of Pennsylvania, March 31, 1864. *Harrisburg: Singerly & Myers.* 1864. 8vo, pp. 108, (3). Map. B., BA. 27246

Revised Report of the Select Committee relative to the Soldiers' National Cemetery, together with the Accompanying Documents, as Reported to the House of Representatives of the Commonwealth of Pennsylvania. ... *Harrisburg: Singerly & Myers.* 1865. 8vo, pp. 212. Plate and Maps. B. 27247

Report of the Joint Special Committee on the Burial of Massachusetts Dead at Gettysburg; ... with the Oration of Edward Everett, at the Consecration of the National Cemetery ... . *Boston: J. E. Farwell and Company.* 1863. 8vo, pp. 93. Map. 27248

Three Weeks at Gettysburg. *See* [Woolsey (G.)]

What we did at Gettysburg. *New York: Anson D. F. Ran dolph.* 1863. 16mo, pp. 24. 27249

Also: Prayer at the Dedication of the National Cemetery at Gettysburg, Thursday November 19th, 1863. *Philadelphia: Martien.* 4to. — Report to the Governor of the State of Michigan, on the Soldiers' National Monument at Gettysburg, 1864. [n. p. n. d.] 8vo, pp. 6. — Report of W. G. Veazey, Agent of the State of Vermont, in relation to the National Cemetery, 1864. [n. p. n. d.] 8vo, pp. 3.

Gevangenhuizen van Philadelphia, door een Europeër in Philadelphia. Uit het franschoiszen. *Philadelphia.* 1796. 8vo.

Gevers Deynoot (W. T.) Reis door de Vereeningten Staten van Nord Amerika en Canada. *'s Hage.* 1860. 8vo. 27251

Gewichtige aanmerkingen over het verval van Neerlands zeevaard en koophandel ... opgedragen aan de reeders der te wapene schepen geschikt voor de West-Ind. Colonien. *Rotterdam.* 1781. 8vo, pp. 72. 27252

Important notices on the decline of Netherland's navigation and commerce, addressed to the owners of the armed vessels, fit for the West India colonies.

Geyer (H. S.) Speech of Hon. Henry S. Geyer, of Missouri ... February 24 and 25, 1852, on the Bill granting Land to the State of Iowa in Aid of Constructing Certain Railroads. [n. p. n. d.] 8vo, pp. 16. 8vo. BA. 27253

The Geysers. San Francisco and around the Bay (north). *San Francisco: A. L. Bancroft & Co.* 1871. 16mo, pp. 227, (4), lxxx.

Gezelius (G.) Försök til et biographiskt lexicon ofver namnkunnige och lärde Svenske Man. *Stockholm.* 1778–80. 3 vols., 8vo. 27255

Contains (Vol. II., pp. 346–349) the best biography extant of Johan Biörnsson Printz, Governor of Nova Suecia (Delaware). The materials for this biography are derived partly from Stiernman and partly from the Svensk Mercurius, Jan., 1760.

Gerling (C. L.) Naval Astronomical Observations in Chili: Report from the Committee on Naval Affairs, of Correspondence of Dr. C. L. Gerling, Lieut. G. M. Gilliss and others. 8vo, pp. 56. (House of Reps. Doc., April 13, 1848. 27256

Ghega (Carl). Die Baltimore-Ohio-Eisenbahn über das Alleghany-Gebirg mit besonderer Berücksichtigung der Steigungs- und Krummungsverhältnisse untersucht auf seiner Reise in den Vereinigten Staaten von Nordamerika. *Wien: Kaulfuss Wwe; Prandel u. Comp.* Map and Atlas of 19 Plates. 27257

Ghega. Ueber nordamerikanischen Brückenbau und Berechnung des Trauungsvermögens der Howe'schen Brücken. ... *Wien: Kaulfuss Wwe; Prandel u. Comp.* 1845. 4to. 2 Plates.

Gheluck-wenschinghe | Aan de | West-Indische Vlote. | Afghevaren uyt Nederland in de | Maand Januario, des Jaars 1624. | *T' Amsterdam | Ghedruckt by Broer Jansz woonende op de nieu- | zijds achter Borchwal in de Silvere Kan.* 1624. | 4to, pp. 8. 27259

Felicitation to the West India fleet that sails from Netherland in January, 1624.

De Ghemeene Directeurs, gestelt tot het formeren van de Capitalen van de West-Indische Compagnie. 1622. 27260

Ghillany (Friedrich Wilhelm). Geschichte des Seefahrers Ritter Martin Behaim, nach den ältesten vorhandenen Urkunden bearbeitet von Dr. F. W. Ghillany ... . Eingeleitet durch eine Abhandlung: Ueber die ältesten Karten des neuen Continents und den Namen Amerika, von Alexander von Humboldt. ... Mit einer genauen Abbildung des Behaim'schen Globus von Jahr 1492 in zwei Planigloben nach seiner natürlichen Grosser und drei der ältesten Karten von Amerika. *Nürnberg: Bauer und Raspe.* 1853. 4to, pp. iv, (4), 122. 3 Maps and Portrait. B.

Ghillany. Manuel diplomatique. Recueil des traités de paix européens les plus importants, des actes de congrès et autres documents relatifs à la politique internationale, depuis le traité de Westphalie jusqu'à cest dernier temps. Augmenté de traductions françaises et d'une introduction générale par J. H. Schurtzer. *Noerdlingen, Paris et Bruxelles: C. H. Beek.* 1856. 2 vols., 8vo, pp. xvi, 344; 547, 2 l. C. 27262

Gholson (T. S.) Speech of Hon. Thomas S. Gholson, of Virginia, on the Policy of Employing Negro Troops, and the Duty of all Classes to aid in the Prosecution of the War. Delivered in the House of Representatives of the Confederate States, February 1, 1865. *Richmond: G. P. Evans & Co.* 1865. 8vo, pp. 20. 27263

Gholson (W. Y.) Speeches of Hon. W. Y. Gholson, on the Payment of the Principal of the National Debt, and on the Reconstruction of the Southern States. *Cincinnati: C. Clarke & Co.* 1868. 8vo, pp. 32, 20. 27264

Giambullari (P. F.) Pier Fran | cesco Giambvl | lari accademi | co fior. | De'l Sito, Forma, & Misure, dello | Inferno di Dante. | [Motto.] *In Firenze per Nèri Dortelata* M. D. XLIII. | Sm. 8vo, pp. 153, (28). 27265

"It requires no little stretch of imagination to place it among the books relating to America, on the strength of a small fanciful map on page 18, which exhibits on the West a kind of promontory, with the inscription: TERRA INCOGNITA, and on the South: MONTE DEL PVRGATORIO." — Harrisse.

Gianetti (F.) Cosmus Philosophicus seu Aristotelicæ Philosophiæ de Mundo Explanatio. *Florentiæ.* 1683. 2 vols., 12mo. 27266

In this curious commentary on Aristotle's "de Mundo," chapters XXIV. and XXV. treat of "de America et Insulis adjacentibus." The author was not a Copernican.

Gianetti (M. A.) Eulogy of Captain James Cook. Composed and publicly recited before the Royal Academy of Florence, by Michel Angelo Gianetti. Translated into English by a Member of the Royal Academy of Florence. *Florence.* 1785. 4to, 2 Titles, pp. 87. 27267

The Giant Spy of Bunker Hill. By the author of "The Tory Outwitted," etc. *New York: George Munro & Co.* [n. d.] 16mo, pp. 96. 27268

Gib (A.) Sermon at the Ordination of Thomas Beveridge upon a Mission to North America. By Adam Gib. *Edinburgh.* 1783. 27269

[Gib (T.)] Remarks on the Rev. Mr. Whitefield's Journal, his many inconsistencies are pointed out, and his tenets considered; the whole shewing the Dangerous Tendency of his Doctrine. Addressed to the Religious Societies. *London: Brett.* [1738.] 8vo, pp. 32. 27270

Preface signed "T. D." No date, but evidently printed this year. Relates to "Whitefield's Journal," Part I.

G[ib]. [The Same.] With an Appendix, containing Accounts of the Disorders in matters of Religion lately introduced into New England and Carolina, with a reply to Mr Whitefield's Remarks on the First Edition. *Glasgow.* 1742. 8vo. 27271

Gibb (G. D.) The Canadian Caverns. ... By Sir George Duncan Gibb, Bart. *London.* 1861. 8vo, pp. 28. 27272

See Morgan's "Bibliotheca Canadensis," pages 141–150, for a list of papers by this prolific writer.

[Gibbes (George M.)] A Letter to the American Peace Society, from a Member of the Committee of Peace in Paris. *Paris.* 1842. 8vo, pp. 31. 27273

Gibbes (Georges). Traité du 4 juillet 1831 entre la France et les Etats-Unis. *Paris.* 1835. 4to. 27274

Also: Documents relatifs au même traité, communiqués par le ministre des affaires étrangères de France. *Paris.* 1835. 3 pts., 4to. — Memorial of a Citizen of the United States (George W. Gibbes) to the Chamber of Deputies, on the Treaty, July 4, 1831.

Gibbes (Lewis R.) On the Carcinological Collections of the Cabinet of Natural History in the United States. With an Examination of the Species contained therein, and Descriptions of New Species. *Charleston.* 1850. 8vo. 27275

Also: Plants near Columbia, S. C. 1835. 8vo. S.

Gibbes (R. W.) Cuba for Invalids. By R. W. Gibbes, M.D., Columbia, S. C. *New Lock: W. A. Townsend and Company.* 1860. 12mo, pp. xii, 214. C. 27276

Gibbes. Documentary History of the American Revolution: Consisting of Letters and Papers Relating to the Contest for Liberty, Chiefly in South Carolina, from Originals in the Possession of the Editor and other Sources. 1774–1776. + 1776–1782. By R. W. Gibbes, M.D. *New York: D. Appleton & Co.* 1855–57. 2 vols., 8vo, pp. xi, 292; xii, 93. + [Vol. III.] *Columbia, S. C.: Banner Press.* 1853. 8vo, pp. xv, 288.

Gibbes. A Memoir of James de Veaux, of Charleston, S. C. Member of the National Academy of Design, New-York. By Robert William W. Gibbes, M.D. ... *Columbia, S. C.: I. C. Morgan's Letter Press Print.* 1846. 12mo, pp. 258. Portrait.

Gibbes. Memoir of the Fossil Genus Basilosaurus; with a Notice of Specimens from the Eocene Green Sand of South Carolina. By Robert W. Gibbes, M.D. *Philadelphia.* 1847. 4to, pp. 13. Plates. 27279

Gibbes. A Memoir on Mososaurus, and the three allied new Genera, Holcodus, Conosaurus, and Amphorosteus. By Robert W. Gibbes, M.D. *Washington.* 1850. 4to, pp. 14. 3 Plates.

Gibbes. Monograph of the Fossil Squalidæ of the United States. By Robert W. Gibbes, M.D. *Philadelphia.* 1848. 4to.

Also: Description of the Teeth of a New Fossil Animal found in the Green Sand of South Carolina. 1845. 8vo.

[Gibbon (Edward)]. Exposition of the Motives of the Conduct of the King of France towards England, with the Justifying Memorial in Answer to the Exposition of the Court of France. French and English. 1780. 4to. 27282

Isaac Reed's copy has the following note in his handwriting: "This masterly performance [the 'Justifying Memorial'] was written by Edward Gibbon, the historian. In the collection of his works lately published by Lord Sheffield, the original French only is published, without the translation. The 'Observer' at the end (*an article in a newspaper in reply*) may, I believe, be ascribed with certainty to Mr. Wilkes."

[Gibbon.] Mémoire justificatif pour servir de réponse à l'Exposé, etc., de la Cour de France. *London.* 1780. 4to. 27283

Relates to the assistance given by France to the Americans. It is a reply to the "Exposé des motifs de la conduite de sa Majesté très chrétienne," etc., published at *Madrid.* 1779. 4to. This Mémoire must not be confounded with the "Mémoire justificat de la conduite de la Grande Bretagne," published by Sir James Marriott. *Londres.* 1779. 4to. "A Short History of the Opposition" is also attributed to Gibbon.

Gibbon (J.) Introductio ad Blasoniam, or Essay to a more Correct Blason than hath formerly been used. By John Gibbon. *London.* 1682. 8vo. 27284

A curious book, by an ancestor of the great historian (*see* his autobiography for an account of it). The author passed a year in Virginia, 1659, "being most hospitably entertained by the Hon. Col. Richard Lee, Secretary of State there," and gives a singular account of the war dances, etc., of the Indians, which he saw in America.

Gibbon (J. H.) Report on a Uniform System in Weights, Measures, &c., for Commercial Nations, &c. *Philadelphia.* 1854. 8vo. C. 27285

Gibbons (C.) An Address delivered before the Northern Lyceum ... Philadelphia, At their Anniversary Meeting, November, 1839. By Charles Gibbons, Esq. *Philadelphia.* [1839.] 8vo, pp. 26, (1). 27286

On the Aborigines of America. Also: The Charges against the Collector and Surveyor of the Port of Philadelphia. Reply of Charles Gibbons to the Argument of David Paul Brown, Esq. ... . [*Philadelphia.*] 1851. 8vo. pp. viii, 96. BA. — Proceedings in Commemoration of the 89th Anniversary American of Independence, 1865. Oration by Chas. Gibbons, Esq. *Philadelphia: King & Baird.* 1865. 8vo, pp. 32. — Oration before the Union League of Philadelphia, on July 4, 1865. *Philadelphia: King & Baird.* 1865. 8vo, pp. 32. — Speech ... October 5th, 1860, In Reply to ... Hon. W. B. Reid, ... on the Presidential Question. *Philadelphia: King & Baird.* 1860. 8vo, pp. 30. — The Truth Plainly Spoken. Speech ... April 19, 1865. [n. p. n. d.] 8vo, pp. 4.

Gibbon (Lardner). *See* Herndon (W. L.)

Gibbons (I.) Crescent-Shine: or Gleams of Light on all Sorts of Subjects from The Collections of the "New Orleans Crescent." By Israel Gibbons. ... *New-Orleans: J. O. Nixon.* 1866. 8vo, pp. 194. 27287

Gibbons (J.) Miscellaneous and Patriotic Poems. By James Gibbons. *Philadelphia: Printed for Private Circulation.* 1870. 16mo, pp. 64. 27288

Gibbons (J. S.) The Banks of New-York, their Dealers, the Clearing House, and the Panic of 1857. With a Financial Chart. By J. S. Gibbons. *New York:* 1858. 12mo, pp. 399. B. + *New York: D. Appleton & Co.* 1870. 8vo, pp. 399. B.

Gibbons. The Public Debt of the United States. Its Organization: its Liquidation: Administration of the Treasury. The Financial System. By J. S. Gibbons ... . *New York: Charles Scribner & Co.* 1867. Crown 8vo, pp. xii, 276. B., BA. 27290

Gibbons (T.) Divine Conduct Vindicated, or the Operations of God shewn to the Operations of Wisdom: In the Substance of Two Discourses, preached at Haberdasher's-Hall, London, March 29, 1761; Occasioned by the Decease of The Rev. Mr. Samuel Davies, M.A. And President of the College of Nassau-Hall in New-Jersey, February 4, 1761. By Thomas Gibbons, M.A. In which are contained Some Memoirs of Mr. Davies, and some Extracts from his Letters. *London: J. Buckland.* 1761. 8vo, pp. 31. S. 27291

Gibbons. Simpathy with our Suffering Brethren, etc. Two Discourses occasioned by the Cruel Oppression of the Protestants in France, to which are prefixed some Serious Reflections on the Present State of our American Colonies. By Thomas Gibbons. *London.* 1755. 8vo. 27292

These reflections relate chiefly to the beginning of the old French war in America and "Braddock's Defeat," communicated to the writer by the clergymen of Hanover Co., Virginia. Also: Memoirs of Eminent Pious Women, ... *London: J. Buckland.* 1777. 2 vols., 8vo, pp. lxiv, 436, 6 Plates; 2 l., pp. 528, 5 Portraits.

Gibbons *vs.* Ogden. Steamboat Controversy: Opinion of the Supreme Court of the United States in the Case of Gibbons *vs.* Ogden, delivered by Chief Justice Marshall, March 28, 1824. *Albany.* 1824. 8vo, pp. 28. S. 27293

Gibbs (C.) Horrible Confessions of the Pirate and Murderer, Charles Gibbs, who acknowledges to taking the lives of no less than Four Hundred Human Beings. *Printed for the Purchasers.* 1831. 12mo, pp. 24. 27294

Gibbs. Mutiny and Murder. Confessions and Life of C. Gibbs, alias J. J. Jeffers, who ... was hung in New York ... for the Murder of the Captain and Mate of the Brig Vineyard ... *Dover.* 1831. 12mo. + *Providence: Israel Smith.* 1831. 12mo, pp. 36. + *New York.* [n. d.] 8vo. 27295

Gibbs (David), *and others.* Report for their Examination for the Alledged Murder of Sally Burdick, at Coventry, R. I. *Hartford, R. I.* 1833. 12mo. 27296

Gibbs (F. W.) The Foreign Enlistment Act. By Frederick Waymouth Gibbs, C.B. The Second Edition. *London: William Ridgway.* 1863. 8vo, pp. (1), 74. B., BA. 27297

Gibbs. Recognition. A Chapter from the History of the North American & South American States. By Frederick Waymouth Gibbs, C.B. *London: William Ridgway.* 1863. 8vo, pp. (2), 46. B., BA., C. 27298

Gibbs (G.) Alphabetical Vocabulary of the Chinook Language. By George Gibbs. *Cramoisy Press, New York: J. G. Shea.* Imp. 8vo, pp. 23. 27299

Shea's "Library of American Linguistics," XIII. Of this and the two following works one hundred copies were printed, of which ten are on large paper.

Gibbs. Alphabetical Vocabularies of the Clallam and Lummi [Languages]. By George Gibbs. *New York: Cramoisy Press.* 1863. 4to, pp. 40. B., BA. 27300

The Clallams reside on the shore of the Straits of Fuca, the Lummi in the Gulph of Georgia, near Vancouver's Island. *See* Leclerc's Catalogue, No. 636.

Gibbs. A Dictionary of the Chinook Jargon, or, Trade Language of Oregon. By George Gibbs. *New York: Cramoisy Press.* 1863. Imp. 8vo, pp. xiv, (2), 43, (1). B., BA. 27301

Shea's "Library of American Linguistics," XII. Also included in the "Miscellaneous Collections of the Smithsonian Institute."

[Gibbs.] The Judicial Chronicle, being a List of the Judges of the Courts of Common Law and Chancery in England and America, and of the Contemporary Reports ... *Cambridge: James Munroe & Company.* 1834. 8vo, pp. iv, (4), 55. B., BA., C.

Also: Instructions for research relative to the Ethnology and Philology of America. *Washington.* 1863. 8vo, pp. iii, 51. "Smithsonian Miscellaneous Collections," Vol. VII. *See* Wolcott (Oliver).

[Gibbs (George M.)] Traité du 4 Juillet, 1831, entre la France et les Etats-Unis. Mémoire aux Chambres par un Citoyen des Etats-Unis. *Paris.* 1835. 4to, pp. 70. 27303

Signed "George M. Gibbs."

Gibbs (H.) The Right Method of Safety, or, The Just concern of the People of God. Massachusetts Artillery Election Sermon. By Henry Gibbs. *Boston.* 1704. 16mo. W. 27304

Gibbs (J.) Cotton Cultivation in its various details, the Barrage of great Rivers, and Instructions for Irrigating, Embanking, Draining, and Tilling Land in Tropical and other Countries ... especially adapted to ... India. By Joseph Gibbs. *London: E. & N. Spon.* 1862. Crown 8vo. C. 27305

Gibbs (P.) Letter to John Beckles, Esq., Attorney General at Barbadoes, and Correspondence between them on the subject of the Conveyance of the Kendal Plantation being Unfairly obtained. By Sir Philip Gibbs. *London.* 1802. 8vo. 27306

Gibbs (W.) Family Notices collected by William Gibbs, of Lexington, Mass. [n. p. 1845.] pp. 8. B. 27307

Gibbs (W. H.) Address delivered before the Ladies Association, Blandford, Mass., September 21, 1850, upon the History of that Town. By William H. Gibbs. *Springfield.* 1850. 12mo, pp. 76. 27308

Gilbert (P.) A Report of the Trial of Pedro Gilbert, Bernardo de Soto, Francisco Ruiz, and others, before the United States Circuit Court, charging them with the Commission of an act of Piracy on board the Brig Mexico, of Salem. By a Congressional Stenographer. *Boston.* 1834 8vo. C. 27309

[Gibson (Edmund)]. The Bishop of London's Pastoral Letter to the People of his Diocese, ... occasioned by some late Writings in favour of Infidelity. *London: Sam. Buckley.* 1728. 8vo, pp. (1), 54. B., BA. + Sixth Edition. *Boston, Reprinted.* M,DCC,XXX. 8vo, pp. (4), 48. 27310

This diocese included New England.

[Gibson.] Lettre Pastorale de l'Eveque de Londres aux fideles de son diocese; à l'occasion de quelques ouvrages qui ont paru depuis peu en faveur de l'incrédulité. On y a joint deux lettres du même prélat: dont la première est adressée aux chefs de famille dans les Colonies Angloises de l'Amérique; et la seconde aux missionnaires qui sont dans ces Colonies. Ces deux dernieres lettres sont précédées d'une Exhortation adressée à tous les Chrétiens de ce royaume d'assister la Société évangélique à travailler à l'instruction des nègres qui sont dans les plantations Angloises. Traduit de l'Anglois. *Londres: J. P. Conderc.* 1729. 8vo, pp. 115. 27311

Gibson. Two | Letters | of the | Lord Bishop of London: | The First, | To the Masters and Mistresses of Families in | the English Plantations abroad; Exhorting | them to Encourage and Promote the Instruction | of their Negroes in the Christian Faith. | The Second, | To the Missionaries there; directing them to | distribute the Said Letter, and Exhorting them | to give their Assistance towards the Instruction | of the Negroes within their Several Parishes. | *London: | Printed by Joseph Downing.* M.DCC.XXVII. | 4to, pp. 20. B., C. + [With] an Address to the Serious Christians among ourselves, to assist the Society for Propagating the Gospel. [*Ibid.*] 8vo, pp. 31. + Second Edition. *London.* M DCC XXIX. 8vo, pp. 31. B. 27312

See Humphrey's "Hist. Soc. Prop. C. K." Also, a Sermon, 19th May, 1727. *See* Bancroft, III. 409.

Gibson. A Letter to the Lord Bishop of London from an Inhabitant of the Leeward Caribbee Islands, containing some Considerations on his Lordship's Two Letters of May 19, 1727. The First to the Masters and Mistresses of Families in the English Plantations; the Second to the Missionaries there. With a Short Essay concerning the Conversion of the Negro Slaves in our Sugar Colonies. *London: J. Wilford.* 1730. 8vo, pp. 103.

The "Essay on the Conversion of the Negro Slaves" fills ninety-nine pages.

Gibson (E. B.) Biographical Sketches of the Bordley Family, of Maryland, for their Descendants. Part First. By Mrs. Elizabeth Bordley Gibson, Edited by her Niece, Elizabeth Mifflin. *Philadelphia: Printed by Henry B. Ashmead.* 1865. 8vo, pp. 158, (1). B., C. 27314

Gibson (J.) A Journal Of the Late Siege by the Troops from North-America, against The French at Cape Breton, the City of Louisbourg, and the Territories thereunto belonging. Surrendered to the English, on the 17th of June, 1745, after a Siege of Forty-eight Days. By James Gibson, Gentleman Voluntier [*sic*] at the above Siege. *London: J. Newbery* [*sic*]. MDCCXLV. 8vo, pp. (1), 49. Plate. C. 27315

For another edition *see* [Johnson (Lorenzo D.)]

Gibson (J.) Speech of the Hon. James Gibson, in the Senate ... March 20, 1867. For the Enlargement of the Champlain Canal and the Improvement of the Hudson River. *Albany.* 1867. 8vo. 27316

Gibson (J.) Gibson's Guide and Directory of the State of Louisiana, and the Cities of New Orleans & Lafayette, ... *New Orleans: John Gibson.* 1838. 8vo, pp. 334. 27317

Gibson. Trial for Libel. State of Louisiana *vs.* John Gibson. Before the ... Criminal Court of the First Judicial District of ... Louisiana ... Reported by T. W. Collens ... & W. G. Snethen. ... *New Orleans: John Gibson. July,* 1839. 8vo, pp. 70, (1). H. 27318

Gibson (L.) The Isthmus of Darien in 1852. Journal of the Expedition of Inquiry for the Junction of the Atlantic and Pacific Oceans. By Lionel Gibson. *London.* 1853. 12mo. 4 Maps. 27319

Gibson (R.) Strictures on a Pamphlet published by a Minority of the Eastern Subordinate Synod. By Robert Gibson. *New York.* 1832. 8vo. 27320

Gibson (R.) A Treatise of Practical Surveying, ... The whole illustrated with Copperplates. The Fourth Edition. By Robert Gibson. With Illustrations and Amendments, adapted to the Use of American Surveyors. *Philadelphia: Joseph Crukshank.* M.DCC.LXXXV. 8vo, pp. viii, 272, 90. 12 Plates.

One of the earliest publications of its kind in the United States. Abridged from the British edition, and a set of tables, etc., introduced, with separate title.

Gibson (T. A.) Geography of Canada. By T. A. Gibson. *Montreal.* 1854. 12mo. 27322

Gibson (W.) Strictures on "Mr. Pattison's Reply to Certain Oral and Written Criticisms." By William Gibson. *Philadelphia: Printed by James Maxwell.* 1820. 8vo, pp. 56. BA.

Gibstone (H.) L'esclavage aux États-Unis. Dean le quarteron. Par Henri Gibstone. *Paris: E. Dentu.* 1863. 16mo, 3 l., pp. 340. 27324

Giddinge (G. P.) An Address, Palmyra, Missouri, June 29, 1855, at the Commencement of St. Paul's College. By Rev. George P. Giddinge. [Also], a Brief Account of St. Paul's College, &c. *Quincey, Ill.* 1855. 8vo. 27325

Giddinge (J. R.) American Piracy. Speech ... June 7, 1858. [n. p. n. d.] 8vo, pp. 8. B. 27326

Upon the joint resolutions proposing hostilities with England.

Giddings (J. R.) The Exiles of Florida: or, the Crimes committed by our Government against the Maroons, who fled from South Carolina and other Slave States, seeking Protection under Spanish Laws. By Joshua R. Giddings. ... Ninth Thousand. *Columbus, Ohio: Follett, Foster and Company.* 1858. 12mo, pp. viii, 338. B., BA. 27327

A severe attack upon the government of the United States for its complicity with slavery.

Giddings. History of the Rebellion: Its Authors and Causes. By Joshua R. Giddings. *New York: Follett, Foster & Co.* 1864 8vo, pp. 498. B., BA. 27328

Giddings. Speeches in Congress. By Joshua R. Giddings. *Boston: John P. Jewett and Company.* 1853. 12mo, pp. ix, 511. Portrait. B., C. 27329

Also: Amistad Claim. History of the Case: ... Speech of Mr. Giddings, of Ohio ... Dec. 21, 1853 ... . [n. p. n. d.] 8vo, pp. 7. B. — Baltimore Platforms — Slavery Question. Speech ... in the House of Representatives, June 25, 1852. [*Washington.*] 1852. 8vo, pp. 8. B., BA. — The Conflict between Religious Truths and American Infidelity. [n. p. n. d.] 8vo. — Speech ... upon the Issues ... before the American People, in Regard to Freedom and Slavery, ... February 26, 1858. 8vo, pp. 8. B. — Executive Influence. Speech ... March 16, 1854 ... upon our Relations with Spain. [n. p. n. d.] 8vo, pp. 7. B., BA. — Freedom of Speech Vindicated. Speech ... on the President's Message ... December 10, 1856. [n. p. n. d.] 8vo, pp. 8. B. — Organization of the House. Speech ... Dec. 18, 1855. [n. p. n. d.] 8vo, pp. 8. B. — Privileges of Members of Congress. Speech ... April 25, 1848. [n. p. n. d.] 8vo, pp. 15. B. — ... Remarks ... in the House ... June 7, 1854, in Defense of the Hon. John Quincy Adams and himself, against the Assault of Mr. Smith, of Virginia, of the 27th April, 1854. [n. p. n. d.] 8vo, pp. 8. B. — The Rights and Duties of Representatives. ... December 27, 1849, ... [n. p. n. d.] 8vo, pp. 8. B. — Speech ... on the Motion of Mr. C. T. Ingersoll ... in favor of paying for the Negroes on board the Schooner Amistad. Delivered in the House ... April 18, 1844. *Washington.* 1844. 8vo, pp. 11. H. — Speech ... upon the Improvement of the Harbors on the Lakes; ... Jan. 12, 1844. [*Washington.* 1844.] 8vo, pp. 8. C. — Speech ... upon the Annexation of Texas. ... May 21, 1844. [*Washington.* 1844.] 8vo, pp. 16. BA. — Speech ... January 5, 1846. *Washington: Blair & Rives.* 1846. 8vo, pp. 8. — Speech ... on the Resolution to refer so much of the President's Message as relates to the Mexican War, to the Committee on Military Affairs ... December 15, 1846. *Washington: Printed by J. & G. S. Gideon.* 1846. 8vo, pp. 16. B. — Speech ... on his Motion to reconsider the Vote [on] the "Bill for the Relief of the Owners of Slaves lost from on Board the Comet and Encomium." ... February 13, 1843. [n. p. n. d.] 8vo, pp. 8. BA. — Speech ... upon the Bill to Supply the Deficiency of Appropriations for the year ending June 30, 1848. ... February 28, 1848. *Washington: Printed by J. & G. S. Gideon.* 1848. 8vo, pp. 15. B., BA. — Speech ... on the Bill to Pay ... for a Slave sent West ... with the Seminole Indians in 1838. ... Dec. 28, 1848, and Jan. 6, 1849. *Washington: Printed by Buell & Blanchard.* 1849. 8vo, pp. 14. B. — ... Speech ... on the Bill Organizing Territorial Governments in Kansas and Nebraska, ... May 17, 1854. [n. p. n. d.] 8vo, pp. 8. B. — Speech ... on the Relation of the Federal Government to Slavery; ... February 17, 1849. *Washington.* 1849. 8vo, pp. 12. B. — ... Speech ... on the Trial of Preston S. Brooks, for an Assault on Senator Sumner. ... July 11, 1856. [n. p. n. d.] 8vo, pp. 8. B. — Speech ... on the Compromise Measures. 1852. [n. p. n. d.] 8vo, pp. 8. — Speech ... upon the Issues ... Freedom and Slavery, Feb. 26, 1858. 8vo. — Speech ... on Cuban Annexation ... December 14, 1862. [n. p. n. d.] 8vo, pp. 12.

[Giddings (L.)] Sketches of the Campaign in Northern Mexico, in 1846–7, by an Officer of the First Regiment of Ohio Volunteers. *New York.* 1853. 12mo. 27330

Giddins (E.) Account of the Savage Treatment of Captain William Morgan, in Fort Niagara, who was ... murdered by the Masons, and sunk in Lake Ontario, for Publishing the Secrets of Masonry. By Edward Giddins ... . Seventh Edition. *Boston.* 1830. 12mo, pp. 13–24. B. 27331

Giddins. An Inquiry into the Causes of the Rise and Fall of the Lakes, embracing an Account of the Floods and Ebbs of Lake Ontario as determined by a long series of Actual Observations, and an Examination of the various Opinions in regard to the late Unprecedented Flood throughout the Chain of great Lakes. ... By Edward Giddins. *Lockport, N. Y.* 1838. 8vo, pp. 31. S. 27332

Also: The Anti-Masonic Almanac for ... 1829. *Rochester.* [1830.] 12mo, pp. 48. Also issued as the Pennsylvania Anti-Masonic Almanac. 12mo, pp. 48. Continued to 1833 or later.

Giesy (S. H.) The Crowning Event: a Discourse on the occasion of the Fall of Richmond, preached on Sunday, April 9, 1865, in ... Philadelphia. ... By ... Rev. Samuel H. Giesy, *Philadelphia: Jas. B. Rogers, Printer.* 1865. 8vo. 27333

Gifford (C. H.) History of the Wars occasioned by the French Revolution, ... comprising ... the American War; ... Peace of Europe, ... By C. H. Gifford, Esq. ... *London: W. Lewis.* 1817. 2 vols., 4to, pp. x, 874; vii, (1), 875–1741. Map, Plate, and Portraits. BA. 27334

A large portion of Vol. II. is devoted to the War of 1812.

Gifford (G.) An Address on the Patent Laws Delivered on Invitation of the American Institute, ... By George Gifford, Esq., of New York. *New York: Jennings & Harrison.* 1849. 8vo, pp. 23. BA. 27335

Gifford (J.) The History of England, from the Earliest Times to the Peace of 1783. By John Gifford, Esq. *London: Harrison and Co.* M DCC XC. 2 vols., folio. 27336

Includes the American Revolution.

Gifford (John), *pseudonym. See* Green (J. R.)

Giguet (*M.*) Anecdotes Secrètes sur la Révolution du 18 Fructidor: et nouveaux mémoires des déportés à la Guiane, écrits par eux-mêmes: contenant des Lettres du Gén. Murinais, ... Mémoires de Barbé Marbois, &c. Faisant suit au Journal du Gén. Ramel. Seconde edition. *Paris.* 1799. 8vo, pp. 215.

Gihon (J. H.) Geary and Kansas. Governor Geary's Administration in Kansas: With a Complete History of the Territory until July, 1857; Embracing a Full Account of ... its Organization as a Territory, ... Election Frauds, Battles and Outrages

... All fully Authenticated. By John H. Gihon, M.D., Private Secretary of Governor Geary. *Philadelphia: Chas. C. Rhodes.* 1857. 8vo, pp. xii, 348. B., BA. 27338

Gijon y Leon (T.) Compendio Historico de la prodigiosa vida, virtudes, y milagros de la Venerable sierra de Dios Mariana de Jesus, Flores y Paredes, conocida con el justo renombre de la Azucena de Quito. Por Thomas de Gijon y Leon. *Madrid: Joseph de Orga.* 1754. 4to pp. (42), 217. 27339

Gil (F.) Fundacion de la obra pia, que para el mayor culto, y veneracion del augustisimo sacramento del altar, hace D. Francisco Gil, Vezino de la Nueva Vera-Cruz. *Mexico.* 1745. Folio, pp. 31, 5 l. 27340

Gil de Jaz (Isid.) Por el Colegio Mayor de Santa Maria de todos Santos de la Ciudad de Mexico ... con la real universidad, sobre la observancia de diferentes privilegios del Colegio Mayor. [*Mexico.* About 1750.] Folio, 27 l. 27341

Gil de Gama (Leonarda). Astro Brillante en el Nuevo Mundo, Fragrante Fior de el Parayso Plantada en el Jardin de la America: Historia Panegyrica y Vida Prodigiosa de Santa Rosa de Santa Maria. *Manila: Imprimiose por Thomas Adriano.* 1755. 4to. Portrait. 27342

Gil Gelpi y Ferro. Estudios sobre la América. Conquista, colonizacion, gobiernos coloniales y gobiernos independientes. *Habana.* 1864. 8vo. 27343

Gil y Garces (D. Martin). Dean de la santa iglesia catedral de Michoacan, manifiesta los hechos é irrefragables constancias que evidencian la escandalosa arbietrad con que su Cabildo lo ha despojado del Beneficio que canonicamente obtiene. *Mexico.* 1831. 4to, pp. 52, 11. 27344

Gilbart (J. W.) The History of Banking in America; with an Inquiry how far the Banking Institutions of America are adapted to this Country; ... By James William Gilbart. *London: Longman.* 1837. 8vo. + *Philadelphia: H. C. Baird.* 1849? 8vo. 27345

Gilbert (A. G.) From Montreal to the Maritime Provinces and Back. By A. G. Gilbert. *Montreal.* 1867. 12mo.

Gilbert (A.) Memoir of Frances Wright, the Pioneer Woman in the Cause of Human Rights. By Amos Gilbert. *Cincinnati.* 1855. 16mo, pp. 86. 27347

Gilbert (B.) A Narrative of the Captivity and Sufferings of Benjamin Gilbert and his Family; Who was surprised by the Indians, and taken from their Farms, on the Frontiers of Pennsylvania, in the Spring, 1780. *Philadelphia: Joseph Crukshank.* M DCC LXXXIV. 8vo, pp. 96. P. + *Philadelphia, Printed: London, Reprinted and Sold by James Phillips.* M.DCCLXXXV. 12mo, pp. 123. + [*Ibid.*] MDCCXC. + Third Edition, Revised and Enlarged. To which is Prefixed a Short Account of the Gilbert Family who settled at Byberry. And an Appendix, giving some account of the Captives after their return. *Philadelphia: Printed by John Richards.* 1848. 12mo, pp. 240. C. 27348

Verbally narrated by Gilbert to William Walton, who wrote the narrative. *See* Hazard's "Register of Penn.," III. 276.

Gilbert (F.) Funeral Sermon preached by F. Gilbert, May 1, 1774, in St. John, Antigua, on the Death of Nathanael Gilbert Esq. of the said Island. *Antigua: R. Mearns.* 1774. 4to.

Gilbert (C. N. P.) Histoire médicale de l'armée française à Saint-Domingue en l'an dix; ou Mémoire sur la fièvre jaune, avec un aperçu de la topographie médicale de cette colonie; par le C. N. P. Gilbert ... . *Paris: Gabon. an* XI–1803. 8vo.

Also in German, with notes by J. E. Aronsson.

Gilbert (H.) A Discovrse | Of a Discouerie | for a new Pas- | sage to Cataia. | VVritten bv Sir Hvm- | frey Gilbert, Knight. | *Imprinted at* | *London by Hen-* | *ry Middleton,* | *for Richarde* | *Ihones.* | *Anno Domini.* | 1576. | *Aprilis.* 12. | 4to, Title, 1 l., George Gascoigne Esquire to the Reader, pp. 16, Sonet, p. 1, A Letter, pp. 6, Table, pp. 2, Text, 29 l., Faultes escaped, 1 p. 27351

Excessively rare. Jadis' copy sold for £26 5s. *See* Wood's "Athenæ Oxoniensis," edited by Bliss, and Hakluyt's "Voyages," Vol. III.

Gilbert (J.) A Sermon ... before the ... Society for the Propagation of the Gospel in Foreign Parts ... February 17, 1743–4. By John, Lord Bishop of Llandaff. *London: Printed for J. and H. Pemberton.* MDCCXLIV. 4to, pp. 76. BA., J.C.B.

Gilbert (L.) ... A Sermon ... at the Dedication of the New House of Worship ... Second Congregational Society in Newton, Ms., March 29, 1848. By Lyman Gilbert, A.M., ... *Boston: T. R. Marvin.* 1848. 8vo, pp. 32. BA. 27353

Gilbert (R.) Sermon at Northampton, Nov. 29, 1759, on a Day of Thanksgiving for Successes in America. By R. Gilbert. 1759. 8vo. 27354

Gilbert (W.) The Hurricane: A Theological and Western Eclogue ... By William Gilbert. *Bath.* 1796. 12mo. 27355

"The story of the poem is allegorical, typifying, by the figure of a hurricane in the Island of Antigua, the final conflict which is to terminate in the subversion of Europe by America, and the annihilation of the artificial system of society."—*Retrospective Review*, x. 160–172.

Gilberti Colchestrensis de Magnete Magneticisque Corporibus, et de magno Magnete Tellure, phisiologia nova. *Londini: Short.* 1600. Folio. 27356

"Ouvrage curieux dans lequel, selon Lalande, Kepler aurait puisé une parte des dées sur l'attraction et la physique céleste. Après la dédicace on trouve une préface d'Edward Wright, dans laquelle on parle des voyages de Drake, Candish, Linschoten, et des différents voyages aux Açores." — Tross.

Gilberti (M.) Arte en lengua de Míchoacan. ... R. padre Fr. Maturino Gilbertí de la ordẽ del Seraphico padre sant Frãcisco: ... y tambíen podra seruir para los Indios de Mechuacan para aprender la lengua Castellana. *Acabose de imprimir a ocho de Octubre de* 1558. *Años.* 8vo. 27357

Gilberti. Dialogo de Doctrina Christiana en la lengua de Mechuacã. ... por el muy Reuerendo padre Fray Maturino Gylberti de la orden del seraphico Padre san Frãcisco. ... *Acabose de imprimir a* xv. *dias del mes de Iunio de* 1559. *Años.* 4to, pp. 6.

Gilberti. Evangelios en Tarasco. 8vo, pp. 224. 27359

Gilberti. Thesoro spiritual de pobres en lẽgua de Michuacã: ... Por el muy. R. Padre Fray Maturino Gilberti de la ordẽ de los menores. *En Mexico. Con licencia, por Antonio de Spinosa.* 1575. 8vo, pp. 1, 302. 27360

Gilberti. Vocabulario en lengua de Mechuacan. Compvesto por el reuerendo padre Fray Maturino Gilberti de la ordẽ del seraphico Padre sant Francisco. ... Dirigido al muy Illustre y reuerẽdissimo Señor Dõ Vasco de Quiroga Obispo de Mechuacan. *Año de.* 1559. 4to, pp. 2, 79. 27361

These works of Gilberti are all of excessive rarity and interest, being early examples of printing in the New World. The author was one of the earliest missionaries amongst the Indians in Spanish America, and chose for the field of his exertions the province of Michoacan.

Gilchrist (R. C.) The Duties of a Church Advocate. ... By Captain R. C. Gilchrist ... . *Columbia, S. C.: Evans and Cogswell.* 1864. 8vo, pp. 47. BA. 27362

Gildemeister (J. C. F.) Verfahren und Erkenntniss des Bremischen Obergerichts in Untersuchungsachen wider den Capitan des Bremischen Schiffs Julius u. Eduard und Cons. wegen Sklavenhandels. Nach den Acten. *Bremen: Heyse.* 1842. 8vo. 27363

Gildon (C.) History of the Head-Longs and the Long-Heads. By Charles Gildon. *London.* 1720. 27364

Relates to the South Sea Company.

Giles (C.) The Convention of Drunkards: an Oration on the Anniversary of American Independence: and an Ode on the Completion of the Erie Canal. By Charles Giles. *Utica.* 1852. 18mo, pp. 126. 27365

Giles (Charles). Pioneer: A Narrative of the Nativity, Experience, Travels, and Ministerial Labors of Rev. C. Giles. ... *New York: G. Lane & P. P. Sandford.* 1844. 12mo, pp. 333.

Giles (C.) The Problem of American Nationality, and the Evils which hinder its Solution. A Discourse delivered April 30, 1863. By Rev. Chauncey Giles. *Cincinnati: Wrightson & Co.* 1863. 8vo, pp. 24. 27367

Also: The True Source of National Prosperity. A Discourse delivered on Thanksgiving Day. ... *New York: C. S. Westcott & Co.* 1864. 8vo, pp. 22.

Giles (J. A.) American History. By Dr. J. A. Giles. *London.* 1853. 18mo. 27368

Giles (J.) Practical Liberty. An Oration delivered before the City Authorities of Boston, ... July 4, 1848. By Joel Giles. *Boston: Eastburn's Press.* 1848. 8vo, pp. 24. B., BA. 27369

Giles (J.) Memoirs of Odd Adventures, Strange Deliverances, etc., in the Captivity of John Giles, Esq., Commander of the Garrison on Saint George River, in the District of Maine. Written by Himself. *Boston.* 1736. + *Cincinnati: William Dodge.* 1869. 8vo, pp. 64. 27370

The original edition is extremely rare. The reprint includes notes and an appendix.

Giles. Two Discourses, delivered to the Second Presbyterian Society in Newburyport, August 20, 1812, The Day recommended ... for National Humiliation and Prayer. By the Rev. John Giles. *Haverhill: Printed by W. B. & H. G. Allen.* 1812. 8vo, pp. 28. BA. + Third Edition. *Newburyport.* 1812. 8vo, pp. 20. + *Bridgeport.* 1812. 8vo. 27371

Also: An Address, ... before the Republican Citizens of Newburyport, ... on the Fourth of July, 1809 ... Second Edition. *Newburyport: W. and J. Gilman.* 1809. 8vo, pp. 16. BA.

Giles (W. B.) Address of the Hon. William Branch Giles to the People of Virginia. 1813. 8vo, pp. 123. 27372

Giles. Letter from W. B. Giles to the Legislature of Virginia. [*Washington?* 1812.] 8vo. 27373

Relates to their censure of his action concerning the United States Bank.

Giles. Political Miscellanies. [*Richmond.* 1827.] 8vo, pp. 189. BA., C. 27374

Following the contents is a full title, which reads:

Giles. Mr. Clay's Speech upon the Tariff: or the "American Question," so called; ... Mr. Giles' Speech upon the Resolutions of Inquiry in the House of Delegates of Virginia, in Reply to Mr. Clay's Speech; also, his Speech in Reply to Gen. Taylor's; ... . *Richmond: Printed by Thomas W. White.* 1827. 8vo, pp. (2), iv, 189. BA. 27375

[Giles.] Public Defaulters brought to Light, &c. [By a Native of Virginia.] *New York.* 1822. 8vo. 27376

Also: Speech ... in the Senate ... on the Bill for Renewing the Charter of the United States Bank. [n. p. n. d.] 8vo, pp. 32. BA. — Speech ... On the Bill ... entitled, "An Act to Repeal Certain Acts respecting the Organization of the Courts of the U. States," Delivered ... February 18, 1802. [n. p. n. d.] 4to, pp. 20. BA. + *Washington.* 1802. 8vo. + *Boston.* 1802. 8vo. — Speech ... in ... Senate of the United States, on ... 24 November, 1808, on the Resolution of Mr. Hillhouse, to Repeal the Embargo Laws. [n. p. n. d.] 8vo, pp. 36. BA. + *Washington.* 1808. 8vo, pp. 20. + [Another Edition. n. p. n. d.] 8vo, pp. 23. N. [Another. n. p. n. d.] 8vo, pp. 20. BA. + *Baltimore.* 1808. 8vo, pp. 28. + *Salem, Mass.* 1808. 8vo. — Second Speech on the same Subject, Dec. 2, 1808. 8vo. — The New Embargo Law, and Hon. Mr. Giles' Speech on the Same. [n. p. n. d.] 8vo, pp. 23. BA., C. — Speech ... on ... Raising an Additional Military Force. *Washington.* 1811. 8vo.

Giles (W. B.), *and* Bayard (A. W.) The Speeches of Mr. Giles and Mr. Bayard, in the House ... February, 1802, on the Bill received from the Senate, entitled, "An Act to Repeal Certain Acts respecting the Organization of the Courts of the United States." *Boston: printed by Munroe & Francis.* 1802. 8vo, pp. 56. BA., H. + *Hartford: Hudson & Goodwin.* 1802. 8vo, pp. 48. W. 27377

Speeches in Congress by W. B. Giles, S. Smith, and Judge Anderson, on Repeal of Embargo Laws. *Washington.* 1808. 8vo. C.

Giles (W. F.) The Annual Address delivered before the Maryland Historical Society, December 17, 1866. By the Hon. Wm. Fell Giles. *Baltimore.* 1867. 8vo, pp. 29. 27378

Also: Speech ... on the Oregon Question. Delivered ... January 9, 1846. *Washington: Blair & Rives.* 1846. 8vo, pp. 7.

Gilham (W.) Instruction for Field Artillery, Extracted from Gilham's Memorial for Volunteers and Militia. *Richmond, Va.: West & Johnston.* 1862. 12mo, pp. 78. 27379

Gilham. Report on the Soils of Powhatan County. By W. Gilham. *Richmond.* 1857. 8vo. Map. 27380

Gili (Ph. S.) Nachrichten vom Lande Guiana, dem Oronocofluss und den dortigen Wilden. Aus dem italiänischen übersetz von M. C. Sprengel. *Hamburg.* 1785. 8vo. 27381

Gilij (F. S.) Saggio | di Storia Americana | ó sia | Storia naturale, civile, e sacra | De regni, e delle provincie Spagnuole di Terra-Ferma | nelle' America meridionale. | Descritta dall' Abate | Filippo Salvadore Gilij | E conderata alla santita di N. S. | Papa Pio sesto | felicimente regnaute. | *Roma: Luigi Perego Erede Salvioni.* MDCCLXXX–LXXXIV. 4 vols., 8vo. 27382

Contents: Vol. I. Della storia geografica e naturale della provincia dell' Oronoco, pp. xliv, 355, map and 3 plates; II. De costumi degli Orinochesi, 1781, pp. xvi, 400, map and 4 plates; III. Della religione e delle lingue degli Orinochesi e di altri Americani 1782, pp. xvi, 430; IV. Stato presente di terra ferma 1784, pp. xx, 497, map. The author was one of the Jesuits banished to America, with the rest of his order, in 1767. Charles III. honored him with a pension for having vindicated, in this work, the Spanish government from the attacks of foreigners. The third volume, which relates to the language of the Aborigines, is often referred to by philologists.

Gill (J.) State of the Accounts of John Gill, Esquire, late Sub-Lieutenant of Bucks County. *Philadelphia: Printed by John Dunlap.* MDCCLXXXIII. 8vo, pp. 17. P. 27383

[Gill (O.), *and others.*] Some Few Remarks, upon A Scandalous Book, against the Government and Ministry of New England. Written, By one Robert Calif. Detecting the Unparallel'd Malice & Falsehood, of the said Book; and Defending the Names of several particular Gentlemen ... aspersed ... . Composed ... by several Persons belonging to the Flock of some of the Injured Pastors ... . *Boston: Nicholas Boone.* 1701. Sm. 8vo, pp. 71. 27384

By Obadiah Gill and six others, with a postscript by Increase and Cotton Mather. An extremely rare pamphlet. It was answered by "Remarks on Some Few Remarks upon a Scandalous Book against the Government and Ministry of New England. *Boston.* 1701." 16mo, according to a Boston catalogue. I have not seen the book.

Gill (Theodore Nicholas). Catalogue of the Fishes of the Eastern Coast of North America, from Greenland to Georgia. *Philadelphia: [Academy of Natural Science.* 1861.] 8vo, pp. 63.

Gill. Synopsis of the Fresh Water Fishes of the Western Portion of the Island of Trinidad, (W. I.) *New York: H. Baillière.* 1858. 8vo, pp. 70. 28386

Also: Synopsis of the Fishes of the Gulf of St. Lawrence and the Bay of Fundy. *Montreal.* 1865. 8vo, pp. 24.

Gill (J.), *and* Lee (F.) Legends of New England. By Julia Gill and Frances Lee. *New York: Carleton & Porter.* 16mo, pp. 171. Illustrated. 27387

Gilleland (J. C.) History of the Late War between the United States and Great Britain. Containing an Accurate Account of the most important Engagements by Sea and Land, interspersed with Geographical Sketches of the Country where the Principal Battles were Fought. By J. C. Gilleland. *Baltimore.* 1817. 8vo. + Second Edition. *Baltimore: Schaeffer & Maund.* 1817. 12mo, pp. 190. B., BA. + Third Edition. [*Ibid.*] 1818. 18mo, pp. 175. C. 27388

Gilleland. The Ohio and Mississippi Pilot. Consisting of a set of Charts of those rivers. ... with Directions for the use of Navigators. To which is added A Geography of the States and Territories, West and South of the Allegheny Mountains. By J. C. Gilleland. *Pittsburgh: R. Patterson & Lambdin.* 1820. 12mo, pp. 274. 27389

Mostly founded on Zadok Cramer. *See* our Vol. v. The geography has a separate title-page.

Gillelen (F. M. L.) The Oil Regions of Pennsylvania: with Maps and Charts of Oil Creek, Alleghany River, etc. ... By F. M. L. Gillelen. *Pittsburgh.* 1865. 8vo, pp. 67. 27390

Gillespie (A.) Gleanings and Remarks: Collected during many months of residence at Buenos Ayres, and within the Upper Country; with a prefatory account of the Expedition from England, until the Surrender of the Colony of the Cape of Good Hope, under the Joint Command of Sir D. Baird, G.C.B. K.C. and Sir Home Popham, K.C.B. By Major Alexander Gillespie, Now upon the Full-Pay Retired List of the Royal Marines. Illustrated with a Map of South America, and a Chart of Rio de la Plata, with Pilotage Directions. *Leeds: B. Dewhurst.* 1818. 8vo, pp. (4), 243, [*i. e.*] 342. C. 27391

Gillespie. Bermerkungen auf einer Reise im Innern von La Plata. [n. d.] 12mo. 27392

Gillespie. Historical Review of the Royal Marine Corps, from its original Institution down to the Present Era. *Birmingham.* 1803. 4to. C. 27393

Includes its services in America.

Gillespie (L.) Advice to the Commanders and Officers of his Majesty's Fleet serving in the West-Indies, on the Preservation of the Health of Seamen. By Leonard Gillespie. *London: Cuthell.* 1798. 8vo. 27394

See "M. Rev.," XXIX, 456.

Gillespie. Observations on the Diseases which prevailed on board a Part of his Majesty's Squadron, on the Leeward Island Station, between Nov. 1794, and April 1796. By Leonard Gillespie, M.D. *London: Cuthell.* 1800. 8vo, pp. 240. 27395

See "M. Rev.," XXXVII. 434.

Gillespy (E.) The Columbian Naval Songster; Being a Collection of Original Songs, Odes, &c., composed in Honor of the five great Naval Victories obtained by Hull, Jones, Decatur, Bainbridge, and Lawrence. By Edward Gillespy. *New York.* 1813. 12mo, pp. 96. N. 27396

Gillespy (G.) A | Letter | to the | Rev. Brethren of the Presbytery of | New-York, or of Elizabeth- | Town; | In which is shewn | The Unjustness of the Synod's Pro- | test, entered last May at Philadelphia, | against some of the Rev. Brethren. As also | Some of the Causes of the great Decay of | Vital Religion, and Practical Holiness, in | our Presbyterial Church; | With Proof of God's remarkable Appearance, for | the Good of Many Souls, in our Land of late. | By George Gillespy, Member of the Gospel at | the Head of Christiana-Creek, ... in America. | *Philadelphia: Printed by B. Franklin, for the Author,* 1740. | 12mo, pp. 23. 27397

An extremely rare and very early Franklin imprint.

Gillet (E.) A Discourse, delivered at Hallowell, April 25th, 1799. Being the Day Appointed by the Chief Magistrate of the United States for a National Fast. By Eliphalet Gillet, A.M. ... *Hallowell.* 1799. 8vo, pp. 27. BA. + *Augusta: Printed by Peter Edes.* 1799. 8vo, pp. 32. + *New York: Reprinted.* 1799. 27398

Gillet. A Discourse delivered on the Annual Fast in Massachusetts, April 7, 1808. By Eliphalet Gillet, A.M. ... *Augusta: Printed by Peter Edes.* 1808. 8vo, pp. 24. BA. 27399

Gillet. An Oration, delivered January 8, 1800, before the Citizens of Hollowell ... in Commemoration of the ... Death of General George Washington ... . By Eliphalet Gillet, A.M. ... *Hallowell.* 1800. 8vo, pp. 19. N. 27400

Gillet. The Patriot. A Sermon delivered on the Annual Fast in Massachusetts, April 11, 1811. By Eliphalet Gillet ... . *Hallowell: Printed by N. Cheever.* 1811. 8vo, pp. 20. 27401

Also: Discourse ... on the Annual Thanksgiving in Massachusetts, November 29, 1804. ... . *Augusta: Printed by Peter Edes.* 1804. 8vo, pp. 20. BA. — Discourse at Hallowell. Thanksgiving, March 21, 1811 ... *Hallowell.* 1811. 8vo, pp. 20. — A Discourse ... at Hallowell and ... Augusta, on the Day of the National Fast, August 20, 1812. ... . *Hallowell: E. Goodale.* 1812. 8vo, pp. 23. BA. — Evils of Intemperance. A Sermon ... Hallowell, on the Day of the Annual Fast in Maine, April 12, 1821. ... *Hallowell: Printed by Goodale, Glazier & Co.* 1821. 8vo, pp. 19. — A Sermon, ... at the Ordination of the Rev. Hugh Wallis ... December 9, 1795. By Eliphalet Gillett, [*sic*] A.M. ... *Hallowell: Printed by Wait and Baker.* 8vo, pp. 32. BA. — Sermon at the Ordination of John Dane ... *Augusta.* 1803. — A Sermon delivered before the Maine Missionary Society, ... in Bath, June 27, 1810. ... . *Hallowell: Printed by N. Cheever.* 1810. 8vo, pp. 30. BA. — Sermon at the Ordination of Harvey Loomis, ... *Buckstown.* 1812. 8vo. — Sermon at the Dedication of the New Meeting-house in Vassalboro. *Hallowell.* 1817. 8vo, pp. 34. — Thanksgiving. A Discourse delivered at Hallowell, on the Day of the Annual Thanksgiving in Massachusetts, Dec. 2, 1819. ... . *Hallowell: Printed by E. Goodale.* 1819. 8vo, pp. 16. BA.

Gillet (R. H.) Democracy in the United States: What it has Done, What it is Doing, and What it will Do. By R. H. Gillet. *New York: D. Appleton & Co.* 1868. 12mo, pp. xiv, 414. 2 Plates. 27402

Gillet. The Federal Government; its Officers and their Duties. By Ransom H. Gillet. *New York: Woodworth, Ainsworth & Co.* 1871. 12mo, pp. 444. 27403

Also: Oration on the Anniversary of the Adoption of the Federal Constitution ... *Washington.* 1855. 8vo. — Speech ... on the Resolutions of the Legislature of New York relating to the Militia. *Washington.* 1836. 8vo.

Gillett (Ezra H.) History of the Presbyterian Church in the United States of America. By E. H. Gillett, ... *Philadelphia.* 1864. 2 vols., 12mo, pp. xxiv, 576; xii, 605. 27404

Also: Thanksgiving Sermon preached at Harlem, November 27, 1862. ... *New York: A. J. Brady.* 1863. 8vo, pp. 16. — *See* Hours at Home.

Gillett (F.) Address delivered in Windsor, Conn., Feb. 10. By Francis Gillett. *Hartford.* 8vo. 27405

Gillette (A. D.) God Seen Above All. National Calamities, A Sermon on the Death of President Lincoln, April 23, 1865. By A. D. Gillette, D.D. ... *Washington: McGill & Witherow, Printers.* 1865. 8vo, pp. 15. 27406

Gillette. Minutes of the Philadelphia Baptist Association, from 1707 to 1807; being the first one hundred years of its existence. Edited by Rev. A. D. Gillette. *Philadelphia: American Baptist Publication Society.* 1851. 8vo, pp. 476. 27407

More than local in its range. Mr. Bartlett quotes it as "a most important contribution to the Baptist history of Rhode Island." Also: Memoir of Joseph Wistar. ... *Philadelphia.* 1852. 16mo. — A Sketch of the Labours, Sufferings, and Death of the Rev. A. Judson. ... *Philadelphia.* 1851. 16mo.

Gillette (C.) A Few Historic Records of the Church in the Diocese of Texas, during the Rebellion. Together with a Correspondence between the Right Rev. Alexander Gregg, D.D., and the Rev. Charles Gillette ... . *New York: John A. Gray & Green, Printers.* 1865. 8vo, pp. 131. BA. 27408

Gillette (F.) A Review of the Rev. Horace Bushnell's Discourse of The Slavery Question ... By Francis Gillette. *Hartford: S. S. Cowles.* 1839. 8vo, pp. 49. 27409

Also: National Slavery and National Responsibility. Speech ... in the Senate of the United States, February 23d, 1855. *Washington, D. C.: Buell & Blanchard, Printers.* 1855. 8vo, pp. 15.

Gillette (U. B.) Memoir of Rev. Daniel Holbrook Gillette, of Mobile, Alabama. By his Brother, Rev. U. B. Gillette, of Piscataway, and Rev. A. D. Gillette, of Philadelphia. *Philadelphia: J. B. Lippincott & Co.* 1846. 12mo, pp. vi, 234. Portrait. 27410

Gilley (William B.) The Olio; Being a Collection of Poems, Fables, Epigrams, &c., including Tributes to the Memory of Lieut. Allen, the Hon. Wm. W. Van Ness, and the Hon. Brockholst Livingston. *New York.* 1823. 12mo.

Gilliam (A. M.) Travels over the Table Lands and Cordilleras of Mexico. During the Years 1843 and '44; including a Description of California, the Principal Cities and Mining Districts of that Republic. And the Biographies of Iturbide and Santa Anna. By Albert M. Gilliam, Late U. S. Consul to California. *Philadelphia: John W. Moore.* 1846. 8vo, pp. 455. BA., C. + [Same.] A New Edition. *Aberdeen: George Clark and Son.* MDCCCXLVII. 12mo, pp. 312. [*Ibid.*] + MDCCCLVII.

Gillies (J.) Historical Collections relating to Remarkable Periods of the Success of the Gospel, and Eminent Instruments employed in promoting it. ... Compiled by John Gillies, ... *Glasgow: Printed by Robert and Andrew Foulis.* MDCCLIV. 2

vols., 8vo, pp. x, (6), 464; xii, 468. + Appendix. *Glasgow: John Orr.* 1761. 12mo, pp. (4), 250. 27413

Vol. I. contains the reports of the speeches of the Indians, collected and taken down by Daniel Gookin, and translated into English by Eliot. Notices of missionary operations in the various British colonies in America from the year 1705, fill the larger portion of the second volume.

Gillies. Historical Collections ... With a Continuation to the Present Time, By Rev. Horatius Bonar. *Kelso.* 1845. Rl. 8vo. C. 27414

Gillies. Memoirs of the Life of the Reverend George Whitefield, M.A. ... To which are added, A Particular Account of his Death and Funeral; and Extracts from the Sermons, which were preached on that occasion. Compiled by the Rev. John Gillies, D.D. *London: Edward and Charles Dilly.* MDCCLXXII. 8vo, pp. xvi, 357. Portrait. + *New-York: Printed by Hodge and Shober.* M.DCC.LXXIV. 12mo, pp. 312. Portrait by Gillandet. + To which is now added, An Extract from Mr. Whitefield's Tracts. *New-London, Conn.: S. Green, for Cornelius Davis, New-York.* 1798. 12mo, pp. xii, 275. + *Falkirk: printed for Mr. Burns, Preacher of the Gospel.* 1798. + *Printed by Joshua Cushing, for Cushing & Appleton, Salem.* 1801. 8vo, pp. xii, 231. + *New Haven.* 1812. 12mo. + First American, from the Third European Edition. Revised and Corrected, with Large Additions, by Aaron C. Seymour. *Philadelphia.* 1812. + Fifth Edition, Revised ... by Aaron C. Seymour. *Boston: Samuel T. Armstrong.* 1813. 12mo, pp. xix, 13, 268. Portrait. + *New Haven.* 1834. 8vo, pp. 648. + With an Introduction, by C. E. Stowe. [Also] Collection of his Sermons, etc. *Hartford.* 1853. 8vo, pp. 666. B. 27415

Also included in the "Christian Library," Vol. II.

Gillies (M.) The Voyage of the Constance: a Tale of the Arctic Seas. By Mary Gillies, ... With an Appendix, containing the Story of "The Fox." *London.* 1860. Fcap 8vo.

Gilliland (W.) Pioneer History of the Champlain Valley; being an Account of the Settlement of the Town of Willsborough, ... By William Gilliland, together with his Journal and other Papers, and a Memoir, and Historical and Illustrative Notes, by Winslow C. Watson. *Albany, N. Y.: J. Munsell.* 1863. 8vo, pp. 231. BA. 27417

Twenty-six copies printed on large paper in royal octavo.

Gilliss (James Melville). Magnetical and Meteorological Observations made at Washington, under orders of the Hon. Secretary of the Navy, ... August 13, 1838. By Lieutenant J. M. Gilliss, U. S. N. ... *Washington: Gales and Seaton.* 1845. 8vo, pp. xxviii, 648. Plates. BA. 27418

Gillis. The U. S. Naval Astronomical Expedition to the Southern Hemisphere, during the years 1849–'50–'51–'52. Lieut. J. M. Gilliss, Superintendent. *Washington: A. O. P. Nicholson.* MDCCCLV–VI. 4 vols., 4to. 27419

Contents: Vol. I. Chile: its Geography, Climate, Earthquakes, Government, Social Condition, Mineral and Agricultural Resources, Commerce, etc. pp. xiii, 556, 3 Maps and 11 Plates. II. The Andes and Pampas, by A. MacRae; Minerals, by J. L. Smith; Indian Remains, by T. Ewbank; Mammals, by S. F. Baird; Birds, by J. Cassin; Reptiles, Fishes, and Crustacea, by C. Girard; Shells, by A. A. Gould; Dried Plants, by A. Gray; Living Plants and Seeds, by W. D. Brackenridge; Fossil Mammals, by J. Wyman; Fossil Shells, by T. A. Conrad. pp. ix, 300, 2 Maps and 35 Plates. III. Observations to Determine the Solar Parallax, by J. M. Gilliss. pp. cclxxxviii, 492. VI. Magnetical and Meteorological Observations. pp. xlviii, 420. Vols. IV, and V. not published. Also: ... An Account of the Total Eclipse of the Sun on September 7, 1858, as observed near Olmos, Peru. ... April, 1859. *Washington: Smithsonian Contribution, Vol.* XI. 4to, pp. 24. Plates. BA. — Account of the U. S. Naval Observatory at Washington and its Instruments, etc. *Washington.* 1845. — Astronomical and Meteorological Observations, made at the United States Naval Observatory during the year 1862. Capt. J. M. Gilliss, U. S. N., Superintendent. *Washington: Government Pr.* 4to, pp. lii, 699. — Circular ... in relation to the Astronomical Expedition to Chile. Astronomical Tables. *Washington.* 1849. 4to. — On the Longitude of Washington ... *Philadelphia.* 1849. 4to. — Origin and Operations of the United States Naval Astronomical Expedition. *Washington.* 1854. 4to, pp. xiii.

[Gillmore (Parker)]. Gun, Rod, and Saddle. Personal Experiences. By Ubique. *London: Chapman and Hall.* 1869. 8vo, pp. viii, 295. + *New York: W. A. Townsend & Adams.* 1869. 16mo, pp. 275. Plate. 27420

Gillmore (P.) A Hunter's Adventures in the Great West. By Parker Gillmore ... . *London: Hurst and Blackett.* 1871. 8vo, pp. 10, 336. Plate. B., BA. 27421

Gillmore (Q. A.) Engineer and Artillery Operations against the Defences of Charleston Harbor in 1863 ... . By Q. A. Gillmore, Major of Engineers ... and Commanding General of the Land Forces ... *New York: D. Van Nostrand.* 1865. 8vo, pp. viii, 7–314; Supplement, pp. 172. 76 Plates and Views. BA.

Also, published with the following title:

Gillmore. Professional Papers, Corps of Engineers, No. 16. Engineer and Artillery Operations ... with a Supplement. By

Q. A. Gillmore ... . *New York: D. Van Nostrand.* 1868. 8vo, pp. viii, 7–314, 172. 83 Plates and Views. BA. 27423

Each edition contains some matter not in the other.

GILLMORE. ... Official Report to the United States Engineer Department of the Siege and Reduction of Fort Pulaski, Georgia, February, March, and April, 1862. By Brig.-Gen. Q. A. Gillmore, ... *New York: D. Van Nostrand.* 1865. 8vo, pp. 96. Illustrated by 76 Plates. BA. 27424

GILLMORE (R. H.) The Thrilling Narrative of Edgell, Pierson Gatwood and Savage, who were Rescued, after having been Buried Alive Seven Hundred Feet Under Ground, For Fourteen Days and Thirteen Hours, Without Food, in the Blue Rock Coal Mines. By Robert H. Gillmore. 1856. 18mo, pp. 48. 27425

GILLPATRICK (J.) ... An Address ... before the Mount Desert Temperance Society, July 4th, 1832. By James Gillpatrick ... . *Boston: Lincoln and Edmands.* 1832. 8vo, pp. 19.

GILMAN (A.) Genealogical and Biographical Record of the Branch of the Family of Gilman, descended from the Honourable Counsellor John Gilman of Exeter, N. H. ... Compiled by Arthur Gilman. *Printed for the use of the Family, by J. Munsell, Albany.* 1863. Rl. 8vo, pp. 51. 27427

GILMAN. Genealogy of the Gilman Family in England and America; traced in the Line of Hon. John Gilman, of Exeter, of N. H. By Arthur Gilman, of Glywllyn. *Albany: J. Munsell.* 1864. Sm. 4to, pp. 24. Portrait and 2 Cuts. S. 27428

GILMAN (C.) The Poetry of Travelling in the United States. By Caroline Gilman. With Additional Sketches, by a few Friends; and a Week among Autographs, by Rev. S. Gilman. *New York: S. Colman.* 1838. 12mo, pp. (10), 430. 27429

GILMAN. Recollections of a New England Bride and of a Southern Matron. By Caroline Gilman. *New York: G. C. Putnam & Co.* 1852. 12mo, pp. (2), 403. Plate. B., BA.

GILMAN. Recollections of a Southern Matron. *New York: Harper & Brothers.* 1838. 12mo, pp. 272. + [*Ibid.*] 1839. + *Charleston: Walker, Richards and Co.* MDCCCLIX. 12mo, pp. 268. 27431

Also: Tales and Ballads. ... *Boston: W. Crosby & Co.* 1839. 12mo, pp. 190.— Verses of a Lifetime. ... *Boston: James Munroe and Company.* MDCCCXLIX. 16mo, pp. viii, 263 BA. *See* Wilkinson (Eliza).

GILMAN (D. C.) A Historical Discourse, delivered in Norwich, Connecticut, Sept. 7, 1859, at the Bi-Centennial Celebration of the Settlement of the Town. By Daniel Coit Gilman, ... Second Edition, with Additional Notes. *Boston: Geo. C. Rand and Avery, Printers.* 1859. 8vo, pp. 128. BA., C. 27432

For first edition, *See* Norwich Jubilee.

GILMAN. Our National Schools of Science. By Daniel C. Gilman, ... Reprinted from the "North American Review" for October, 1867. *Boston.* 1867. 8vo, pp. 28. 27433

Also: Scientific Schools in Europe: Considered in reference to their Prevalence, Utility, Scope and Desirability in America. *New Haven.* 1856. 8vo.

GILMAN (S.) Contributions to Literature, Descriptive, Critical, Humorous, Biographical, Philosophical, and Poetical. By Samuel Gilman, D.D. *Boston.* 1856. 12mo, pp. 564. 27434

GILMAN. Funeral Address, delivered at ... Charleston, (South-Carolina) at the Interment of Edward Peter Simons. By Samuel Gilman, ... Accompanied with other Testimonials of Respect. *Charleston: printed by A. E. Miller.* 1823. 8vo, pp. 31. 27435

GILMAN. Monody on the Victims and Sufferers by the Late Conflagration in the City of Richmond, Virginia. By Samuel Gilman. *Boston: Charles Williams.* 1812. 8vo, pp. 24. BA.

Also: The Memoirs of a New England Village Choir.—Pleasures and Pains of the Student's Life. Two Poems, one delivered in 1811, ... and the Other, a Sequel to the Former, delivered in 1852, ... *Boston: Ticknor, Reed, and Fields.* M DCCC LII. 8vo.—A Sermon ... at the Dedication of the Unitarian Church in Augusta, Geo., Dec. 27, 1827. ... *Charleston.* 1828. 8vo, pp. 43.—A Week among Autographs. *See* Gilman (Caroline), No. 27429, *supra.*

GILMAN (T.) Sermon on the Death of the Hon. David Mitchell, Esq., at North Yarmouth, [Me.] March 20, 1796. By Tristram Gilman. *Portland.* [n. d.] 8vo. 27437

GILMAN (W. S.) Trial of Winthrop S. Gilman, who was indicted with Enoch Long, Amos B. Roff, and others, for the crime of Riot, committed on the night of the 7th of November, 1837, while engaged in defending a Printing Press, from an attack made on it at that time, by an Armed Mob, ... *New York.* 1838. 12mo. 27438

Relates to a pro-slavery riot at Alton, Ill.

GILMER (F. W.) An Oration ... in Winchester on the Fortieth Anniversary of American Independence. By Francis W. Gilmer, Esq. *Winchester, Va.: J. Foster.* 1816. 8vo, pp. 14.

Also: Sketches, Essays, and Translations. *Baltimore.* 1828. 12mo. C.

[GILMER (George R.)] Sketches of Some of the First Settlers of Upper Georgia, of the Cherokees, and the Author. *New York: D. Appleton & Co.* MDCCCLV. 8vo, pp. 587. Patriot. C.

Also: The Literary Prospects of Georgia: An Address ... at Athens before the ... Alumni ... August 7, 1851, being the Semi-Centennial Anniversary of Franklin College ... *Athens, Geo.: White & Brother.* 1851. 8vo.

GILMER (J. A.) Speech of John A. Gilmer, of North Carolina, on the State of the Union, delivered in the House of Representatives, January 26, 1861. 8vo, pp. 8. 27441

Also: Speech ... on the Kansas Question. *Washington.* 1858. 8vo, pp. 8.

GILMER (J. H.) Letter Addressed to Hon. Wm. C. Rives, by John H. Gilmer, on the Existing Status of the Revolution, &c. [*Richmond.* 1864.] 8vo, pp. 16. BA. 27442

[GILMER.] Southern Politics! What we are and what we will be. Considered in a Letter from a Virginian to a New Yorker. *Richmond: J. Wall Turner, Printer.* 1867. 8vo, pp. 18. 27443

GILMER. War of Races; by whom it is sought to be brought about. In Two Letters. By John H. Gilmer. *Richmond.* 1867. 8vo, pp. 16. 27444

GILMOR (H.) Four Years in the Saddle. By Colonel Harry Gilmor. ... *London: Longmans, Green & Co.* 1866. 8vo, pp. viii, 310. BA. + *New York: Harper & Brothers.* 1866. 12mo, Title, pp. xi, 291. B., BA. 27445

This book has something of the dash of a centaur. His revelation of himself shows him to have had a good deal of fondness for adventure, an unreflecting courage, and no little addictedness to swearing, boasting, and brandy.

GILMORE (J. H.) ... A Thanksgiving Sermon ... Fisherville, N. H., Nov. 26, 1863. By J. H. Gilmore ... . *Concord: P. B. Cogswell.* 1864. 8vo, pp. 14. BA. 27446

[GILMORE (James R.)] Among the Guerillas. By Edmund Kirke. *New York.* 1866. 12mo, pp. 286. 27447

[GILMORE.] Among the Pines; or, South in Secession-Time. By Edmund Kirke. *New York: J. R. Gilmore.* 1862. 12mo, pp. 310. B., BA. + [*Ibid.*] MDCCCLXIV. B., BA., S. 27448

Reprinted from the "Continental Magazine."

[GILMORE.] Down in Tennessee, and Back by Way of Richmond. By Edmund Kirke ... . *New York: Carleton.* M.DCCC.LXIV. 12mo, pp. 282. B., BA. 27449

[GILMORE.] My Southern Friends. ... By Edmund Kirke ... . *New York: Carleton.* M.DCCC.LXIII. 12mo, pp. 308. [*Ibid.*] MDCCCLXIV. BA. 27450

[GILMORE.] Les noirs et les petits blancs dans les états du Sud de l'Amérique du Nord. Traduit par F. Bertin. *Paris.* 1863. 8vo. 27451

[GILMORE.] On the Border. By Edmund Kirke ... . *Boston: Lee & Shepard.* 1867. 12mo, pp. 333. B., BA., C. 27452

[GILMORE.] Patriot Boys and Prison Pictures. By Edmund Kirke ... . *Boston: Ticknor & Fields.* 1866. 16mo, pp. 306.

Also: Col. Jacques. What Jeff. Davis Said. The North must Yield—the South Nothing. 8vo, pp. 7.

GILMORE (Patrick S.) History of the National Peace Jubilee and Great Musical Festival, held in the City of Boston, June, 1869, to Commemorate the Restoration of Peace throughout the Land. By P. S. Gilmore. ... *Boston: for the Author.* 1871. 8vo, pp. x, 758. 4 Plates and 1 Portrait. B., BA. 27454

GILPIN (H. D.) The Character of Franklin. Address before the Franklin Institute ... the Fourth of December, 1856. By Henry D. Gilpin. *Philadelphia: King & Baird.* 1857. 8vo, pp. 50. BA. 27455

GILPIN. The Eulogy on Silas Wright, delivered ... [at] ... Philadelphia ... 12th November, 1847. By Henry D. Gilpin. *Philadelphia.* 1847. 8vo, pp. 30. C. 27456

[GILPIN.] A Northern Tour; being a Guide to Saratoga, Lake George, Niagara, Canada, Boston, &c. *Philadelphia.* 1825. 24mo. 27457

GILPIN. A Speech ... at the Democratic Celebration ... of the Fifty-Eighth Anniversary of the Declaration of Independence, July 4, 1834. By Hy. D. Gilpin. [*Philadelphia.* 1834.] 8vo, pp. 27. 27458

Also: Address before the Philomathean Society of the University of Pennsylvania, ... 1845. *Philadelphia.* 1845. 8vo.—Address before the Alumni of the University of Pennsylvania, November, ... 1851. *Philadelphia.* 1851. 8vo.—An Annual Discourse before the Pennsylvania Academy of the Fine Arts, ... on the 29th of November, ... *Philadelphia: H. C. Carey and J. Lea.* 1827. 8vo, pp. 58.—A Biographical Sketch of Thomas Jefferson. ... *Philadelphia.* 1828. 8vo.—A Biographical Notice of Edward Livingston, read before the American Phil. Society. ... *Philadelphia.* 1843. 8vo. C. *See* "Historical Society of Penn. Mem.," Vol. IV.. *See also* Madison (James), and Bank of the United States, Vol. I., *note* to No. 3189.

GILPIN (*Mrs.* H. D.) A Memorial of Henry D. Gilpin. *Philadelphia.* 1860. Rl. 8vo, pp. 111, 211. Portraits. 27459

GILPIN (J. B.) Lecture on Sable Island; its Past History, Present Appearance, Natural History, &c. ... By J. Bernard Gilpin. ... *Halifax.* 1859. 12mo, pp. 24. 27460

GILPIN (J.) A Memoir on the Rise, Progress, and Present State of the Chesapeake and Delaware Canal, accompanied with Original Documents and Maps. By Joshua Gilpin. *Wilmington.* 1821. 8vo, pp. 50, 72. 27461

GILPIN. A Monument of Parental Affection to a Dear and Only Son: or, a Memoir of J. R. Gilpin. ... *Philadelphia.* 1814. 12mo. + *New Haven.* 1814. 18mo. 27462

GILPIN (Joshua), *and* LATROBE (B. H.). Letters to the Hon. Albert Gallatin, Secretary of the Treasury of the United States; and other Papers, relative to the Chesapeake and Delaware Canal. *Philadelphia: Jno. W. Scott.* 8vo, pp. 46. 27463

[GILPIN (Thomas).] Exiles in Virginia, with Observations on the Conduct of the Society of Friends during the Revolutionary War, comprising the Official Papers of the Government Relating to that Period, 1777–1778. *Philadelphia: Published for the Subscribers.* 1848. 8vo, pp. 302. BA., P. 27464

[GILPIN.] On the Representation of Minorities of Electors to act with the Majority in Elected Assemblies. *Philadelphia: John C. Clark.* 1844. 8vo, pp. 15. BA. 27465

GILPIN. An Essay on Organic Remains, as connected with an Ancient Tropical Region of the Earth. By Thomas Gilpin. *Philadelphia: E. H. Butler.* 1843. 8vo, pp. 39. 27466

GILPIN (W.) Memoirs of Josias Rogers, Esq., Commander of his Majesty's Ship Quebec. By the late William Gilpin, A.M. *London.* 1808. 8vo. 27467

Contains a curious account of his shipwreck in Virginia, and imprisonment and suffering at Williamsburgh, during the Revolutionary War, Siege of Charleston, account of Block Island, etc.

GILPIN (W.) The Central Gold Region. The Grain, Pastoral, and Gold Regions of North America. With some New Views of its Physical Geography; and Observations on the Pacific Railroad. By William Gilpin. Illustrated with Maps. *Philadelphia: Sower, Barnes & Co.* 1860. 8vo, pp. 194. 6 Maps.

GILPIN. Mission of the North American People, Geological, Social, and Political. Illustrated by 6 Charts delineating the Physical Architecture and Thermal Laws of all the Continents. By William Gilpin, late Governor of Colorado. *Philadelphia.* 1870? 8vo, pp. 217. 27469

GIMENEZ FRIAS (Josef Antonio). Oracion Funebre, que en esta Santa Iglesia Catedral de Mexico el 12 Nov. 1770, en que se celebró el primer aniversario de las Honras de los Señores Sacerdotes. *Mexico.* 1770. 4to. 27470

GIORDAN (F.) Description et Colonisation de l'Isthme de Tehuantepec, précédées d'une notice historique, par François Giordan. *Paris: Le Douen.* 1838. 8vo, pp. (4), 144, (4). Map and Table. S. 27471

GIORDAN (P.) Beschreibung und Kolonisation der Landenge von Tehuantepec; aus dem Französischen. *Karlsruhe.* 1840. 8vo. C. 27472

GIORGINI (G.) Il|Mondo Nvovo|del Sig. Giovanni|Giorgini da Iesi,|All Inuittissimo Principe de Spagna, e sue|Serenissime Sorelle.|Con gli argomenti in ottaua rima del Sig. Gio. Pietro|Coloni, & in prosa del Sig. Girolamo Ghisileri.|*In Iesi,*|*Appresso Pietro Farri,* M.D.XCVI.|4to, Title, 1 l., pp. 2–153, 5 l. 27473

A very rare Italian poem on the discovery of America, etc. Unknown to Haym, and other bibliographers; nor was Dr. Cotton able to find any book printed at Jesi in the sixteenth century. Heber's copy sold for £1 11s. In the second edition of Cotton's "Typographical Gazetteer," under *Esium*, he speaks of the existence of a press there from 1472 to 1475, but adds, "The duration of this establishment appears to have been very limited; we have no book before 1472, nor after 1475: nor is anything heard of a Jesi press in the following century."

GIOSEPPE DI S. TERESA (P. F. G.) Istoria delle Guerre del Regno del Brasile, accadute tra la Corona di Portogallo e la Republica di Olanda. Composta da P. F. Gio. Gioseppe de S. Teresa, carmelitano. *Roma.* 1520. 2 vols., folio. 23 Maps and 2 Portraits. S. 27474

A well-written book, by an author thoroughly acquainted with the country he described. Other editions, *Roma: Ant. de Rossi.* 1698 and 1700. *See* Brunet, 1617.

GIOVAGNOLI (A. F.) Vita di S. Rosa de Lima Domenicana descritta e dedicata alle nobilissime religiose di S. Caterina da Siena. Per Anton Francisco Giovagnoli. *Roma: S. Michele a Ripa.* 1768. 4to, pp. xii, 242. 27475

GIOVANNI (*Mme*). Journal de Mme Giovanni, en Australie, aux îles Marquises, à Taïti, à la Nouvelle-Calédonie, en Californie et au Mexique. *Paris: Dufour, Mulat et Boulanger.* 1858. 8vo. 8 Plates. 27476

GIOVANNI. Taïti.—Marquises.—Californie. Journal de Mme Giovanni, rédigée et publié par Alexandre Dumas. *Paris: Cadot.* 1855. 4 vols., 8vo. 27477

GIOVIO (Paolo). Gli Elogi Vite brevemente scritte d'huomini illustri di guerra, antichi et moderni, tradotti per L. Domenichi. *Fiorenza: Torrentino.* 1554. 4to. + *Venetia: F. Bindoni.* 1858. 8vo. + *Vinezia.* 1559. 8vo. 27478

Contains lives of Columbus, Cortez, Tristan d'Acugna, etc.

GIRALDO (J.) Compendio de la Ystoria General del origen, viajes y monarquia de los Indios de la America Septentrional fundada sobre las mejores noticias que se hallan de el Nuevo Mundo, dondo manifiesta la Ystoria Indiana à la España sucesos de sus peregrinaciones y casos mas memorables asta el estado presente. Por Josef Giraldo, grabador de laminas, etc. *Madrid.* 1780. Sm. 4to. 27479

"This work consists merely of six plates, representing the ancient history of the Mexicans, with an engraved account at the bottom of each, of their emigrations, etc. A work of no sort of authority."—RICH.

[GIRARD (C.)] Les états confédérés d'Amérique visités en 1863. *Paris: E. Dantu.* 1864. 8vo, pp. 160. Map. B., BA.

GIRARD (C.) Bibliographia Americana Historico Naturalis, or Bibliography of American Natural History for the year 1851. By Charles Girard ... . *Washington: Smithsonian Institute.* 1852. 8vo, pp. iv, (2), 66. BA. 27481

GIRARD. Contributions to the Natural History of the Fresh Water Fishes of North America. By Charles Girard. *Washington.* 1850. 4to, pp. 88. 3 Plates. 27482

GIRARD. Contributions to the Fauna of Chili (Reptiles, Fishes, and Crustacea). By Charles Girard. *Washington.* 1856. 4to, pp. 60. 12 Plates. 27483

GIRARD. United States Exploring Expedition ... Herpetology. By Charles Girard ... . With a folio Atlas. *Philadelphia: J. B. Lippincott & Co.* 1858. 4to, pp. xvii, 496. Atlas, folio, pp. x. 32 Plates. BA. 27484

Forms Vol. XX. of the United States Exploring Expedition. The edition consists of only 150 copies. It was first published as: Herpetology. Prepared under the super-

intendence of S. F. Baird ... *Philadelphia: Printed by C. Sherman & Sons.* 1858. 4to, pp. xv, 492. Atlas in folio, pp. x. 32 Plates.—*See* Smithsonian Contributions, Vol. III.—Also: Researches upon Nemertians and Planarians. I. Embryonic Development of Planocera Elliptica. *Philadelphia.* 1854. 4to, pp. 28. Plates.

GIRARD (J.) Excursion d'un touriste au Mexique pendant l'année 1854. Par Just Girard. *Tours: Mame & Cie.* 1859. 8vo, 1 l., pp. 188. Plate. 27485

GIRARD (S.) The Will of the late Stephen Girard, Esq., procured from the Office for the Probate of Wills. With a short Biography of his Life. ... *Philadelphia: Thomas and Robert Desilver.* 1832. 8vo, pp. 36. + [*Ibid.*] 1839. 8vo, pp. 55. B. + *Philadelphia: Thomas Desilver.* 1848. 8vo, pp. 32; [*Ibid.*] pp. 44. 27486

GIRARD. The Decision of the Supreme Court of Pennsylvania, relative to the After-Purchased Real Estate of the Late S. Girard ... . [n. p. n. d.] 8vo, pp. 35. BA. 27487

GIRARD. Will of Stephen Girard. Opinion of the Supreme Court of the United States, delivered February 27, 1844. By Mr. Justice Story. *Philadelphia: J. Crissy.* 1844. 8vo, pp. 35. BA. 27488

Also: Arguments of the Defendants' Counsel, Judgment in the case of Vidal ... *vs.* . ... Printed by order of the Commissioners of the Girard Estates. *Philadelphia: J. Crissy, Printer.* 1844. 8vo, pp. (4), 307. BA., M.—Bill in Chancery, filed in the Circuit Court of the United States in Behalf of the Heirs of Stephen Girard, to Recover all the Real and Personal Estate, &c. *Philadelphia.* 1836. 8vo, pp. 12.

GIRARD (S.) The Merchants' Sketch Book and Guide to New York City. ... Particularly Intended for the Merchant visiting New York. By Stephen Girard, a Western Merchant. *New York.* 1844. 27489

Part III. ends with page 74.

GIRARD BANK. Act to Incorporate the Girard Bank ... 1832 ... and the Act Supplementary, 1836. *Philadelphia,* 1836. 8vo. 27490

GIRARD COLLEGE. Account of the Proceedings on Laying the Corner-stone of the Girard College for Orphans, on July 4, 1833; together with the Address ... by Nicholas Biddle. *Philadelphia.* 1833. 8vo, pp. 28. 27491

First Anniversary of the Opening of the Girard College for Orphans. Address of Hon. Noel Jones, Address of Joseph R. Chandler, and Discourse by Job R. Tyson, Esq., January 1st, 1849. *Philadelphia: Crissy & Markley.* 1849. 8vo, pp. 42.

A Description of the Girard College for Orphans, Contained in a final Report of the Building Committee to the Select and Common Councils of Philadelphia. *Philadelphia.* 1848. 8vo, pp. 64, 92. 27493

Girard College and its Founder. *Philadelphia.* 1856. 12mo.

The First Annual Report of the Board of Directors of the Girard College for Orphans, December, 1848 *Philadelphia: Crissy & Markley.* 1848. 8vo, pp. 48. Continued.—Accounts of the Receipts and Payments of the Mayor and Aldermen in trust for the Girard Fund. *Philadelphia.* 1832. Folio. Continued.—Communication from the Board of Trustees of the Girard College ... to the ... Councils of Philadelphia. *Philadelphia.* 1840. 8vo.—First Report of the Building Committee and the Architect ... to the Councils of Philadelphia. *Philadelphia.* 1848. 8vo.—Constitution and Plan of Education. By F. Lieber. *Philadelphia.* 1834. 8vo.—Addresses on the Occasion of Opening the Girard College for Orphans, January, 1848.—Digests of the Acts of Assembly and Ordinances of Councils relating to. *Philadelphia.* 1849. 8vo.—Report of the Managers of the Girard Trust. *Philadelphia.* 1832. Folio.—Copy of the Inventory of his Personal Estate; with 1st to 5th Settlements of the Estate. Auditor's Reports. 1836. Continued.—The Decision of the Supreme Court in the Girard Will Case Considered. *Philadelphia.* 1833. 8vo.—Report of a Special Committee to the Commissioners of the Girard Estate, on the Subject of Opening the Girard College for Orphans. *Philadelphia.* 1847. 8vo.—Report of the Special Committee appointed by the Common Council on a Communication from the Board of Trustees of the Girard College ... read ... August 27, 1840. *Philadelphia.* 1840. 8vo.

GIRARDEAU (J. L.) Conscience and Civil Government: An Oration before the Society of Alumni of the College of Charleston. *Charleston.* 1860. 8vo. B. 27495

GIRARDIN (L. H.) History of Virginia. *See* Burk (J.)

GIRARDOT (Auguste Théodore, *Baron de*). L'Ordre Américain de Cincinnatus en France. Règlements et correspondances de Washington. *Nantes.* [n. p. n. d.] 8vo. 27496

GIRAUD. Fleurs des Antilles: Poésies. *Paris: Poulet-Malassis.* 1862. 12mo. 27497

GIRAUD (J. P.) The Birds of Long Island. By J. P. Giraud, Jr., ... *New York: Wiley & Putnam.* 1844. 8vo, pp. xxii, 379.

GIRAUD (C. F. F. J.) Mémoire sur la colonie de la Guyane française et sur les advantages politiques et commerciaux de sa possession, rédigé sur les notes d'un colon [M. Vidal]. *Paris, an XII.* 8vo. 27499

GIRAUD. Mémoire sur les causes du peu de produit des terres de Cayenne et sur les moyens d'y remédier. 1767. 4to.

GIRAUD (Octave). L'abolition de l'esclavage réflexions sur le livre de M. Cochin. *Paris: Aubry.* 1861. 27501

GIRAULT (A. N.) Vie de George Washington. Pris de l'Anglais, et dédié a la jeunesse Américaine. Par A. N. Girault. *Philadelphia.* [1834.] 18mo, pp. 321, 6 l. + Quatrième édition. *Philadelphia: H. Perkins.* 1836. 18mo, pp. 321. + Dixième édition. *Philadelphia: Henry Perkins.* 1840. 18mo, pp. 320, (3). BA. + *Philadelphia: Perkins and Purves.* 1843. pp. 321. 27502

A twenty-fourth edition. *Philadelphia.* 1856.

GIRAULT. ... Discours Funèbre prononcé a la mémoire de M. President Lincoln, par le Grand President Girault. ... [n. p. n. d.] 8vo, pp. 3. 27503

GIRAVA (Hieronymo). La Cosmographia, y geographia. En la qual se contiene la Descripcion de todo el mundo, y de sus partes, y particularmente de las yndias, y tierra nueua. Islas de España, y de las otros partes del mundo; con la nauegacion, longitud, latitud, grandeza, y circuito de todas ellas. *En Venetia, por Jordan Zileti, y su compañero.* 1570. 4to, pp. (8), 272, (10). Map. 27504

This rare volume is printed in singular Italic letters. The map is often wanting; all after page 186, Part II., relates to America. Leclerc's copy sold for 60 francs.

GIRD (H. H.) State Exaltation: An Address delivered before the Philomathic Society of the College of Louisiana, June 13, 1837. By Professor H. H. Gird. *Jackson, La.* 1837. 16mo, pp. 38. 27505

GIRDLESTONE (T.) Facts tending to Prove that General Lee was Never Absent from this Country for any length of time during the years 1767, 1768, 1769, 1770, 1771, 1772, and that he was the Author of Junius. By Thomas Girdlestone, M.D. *London: P. Martin.* 1813. 8vo, pp. vii, 138, Errata, 8 lines. Portrait and 2 Fac-similes. BA., C., S. 27506

GIRDWOOD (J.) An Address delivered before the New Bedford Port Society, on the occasion of its Twenty-eighth Anniversary, February 28th, 1858. By Rev. John Girdwood. *New Bedford: Printed by Benj. Lindsey.* 1858. 8vo, pp. 24. 27507

GIROD (A.) Notes diverses sur le Bas-Canada. Par Amury Girod. ... *Village Debartzch.* 1835. 8vo, pp. 129. 27508

GIROD (J. F.) A Reply to Messrs. Daniel W. Coxe and Henry Turner's Remarks on my Exposition relating to the Title of a Concession of Thirty Leagues of Land claimed by those Gentlemen, in the name of the Marquis of Maison Rouge. By John Francis Girod, of Quachita. *New Orleans.* 1820. 8vo, pp. 12. 27509

[GIROD-CHANTRANS.] Voyage | d'un Suisse | dans | différentes Colonies | d'Amérique | pendant la dernière guerre, | avec une table | D'Observations météorologiques faites à Saint- | Domingue. ... *A Neuchatel: De l'Imprimerie de la Société Typographique.* MDCCLXXXV. 8vo, pp. vii, 416. 27510

This is, no doubt, the work mentioned by Barbier and Quérard, as printed in 1787, "Aux verreries suisses," attributed by them to Girod-Chantrans. It relates principally to St. Domingo.

GIROT-POUZOL. Corps Législatif. Conseil des Anciens. Rapport fait par Girot-Pouzol, au nom d'une Commission composée des Representans Ligeret, Courtois & Girot-Pouzol. Séance du Germinal, an v. [1797]. 8vo, pp. 7. P. 27511

Relates to the manner of elections in St. Domingo and the other colonies.

GISBORNE (L.) The Isthmus of Darien in 1852. Journal of the Expedition of Inquiry for the Junction of the Atlantic and Pacific Oceans. By Lionel Gisborne. *London: Saunders and Stanford.* 1853. Post 8vo, pp. vi, 238. 4 Maps. + *Philadelphia: Lippincott, Grambo and Co.* 1854. 12mo, pp. vi, 238.

See Dublin "Univ. Mag.," XII. 718. Also, "Fraser's Magazine."

GISBORNE (T.) Remarks on the late Decision of the House of Commons respecting the Abolition of the Slave-trade. By Thomas Gisborne. Second Edition. *London: B. White.* 1792. 8vo, pp. 49. A., M. 27513

See "M. Rev.," VIII. 216.

GISSON Y LEON (T.) Vida, Virdudes, y Milagros de la venerable Sierva de Dios, Mariana de Jesus, Virg. Americana. Por D. Thomas Gisson y Leon. *Madrid.* 1754. 4to. 27514

GIST (C.) Journal of Christopher Gist; who accompanied George Washington on his first visit to the French Commander of the Troops on the Ohio, 1753. *Boston.* 1836. 8vo. C.

Also included in the Mass. Hist. Soc. Coll., Vol. v, 3d Series.

GITTERMANN (J. C. H.) Revolution oder Abolition frei bearbeitet nach H. R. Helper's die dem Süden bevorstehende Crisis. *Stuttgart: J. G. Cotta.* 8vo, pp. 112. 27516

GIUSEPPE (Fr.) Storia della vita, virtù, doni, e grazie del ven. servo di Dio P. F. Pietro di S. Giuseppe Betancur, fondatore dell' ordine Betlemitico nelle Indie Occidentali. Por Fr. Giuseppe della madre di Dio. Cavata da' processi ordinarij fatti per la sua beatificazione. *Roma: Ant. de' Rossi.* 1739. 4to, pp. (22), 332, (36). Portrait of Béthencourt and Vignettes. 27517

GIUSTINIANI (A.) Castigatissimi annali con la loro copiosa tavola | della Eccelsa & Illustrissima Republi. di Genoa, da fideli & approuati Scrit- | tori, per el Reuerēdo Monsignore Agostino Giustiniano Genoese Vescouo di | Nebio accuratamente racolti. Opera certamēte molto laudeuole, a Stu- | diosi assai comoda, & communemente a tutti vtilissima. Facēdo per | la varieta delle opere chiaramente conoscere, quanto si deb | ba da tutti riprouare el male, & constantemente pro- | curare el bene della sua Republica. | *Genoa.* | M.D.XXXVII. | Cum gratia & priuilegio. Folio, pp. (28), 282 l. 27518

Contains on fol. 249 an interesting account of Columbus, and a mention of the bequest supposed to have been made by the Admiral. *See* Harrisse's "Bib. Am. Vet.," No. 220; also, "Psalterium."

GIUSTINIANI (L.) Intrigues of Jesuits in the United States of America. By L. Giustiniani, D.D. *Camden, N. J.* 8vo.

GIVRY (M.) Eclaircissemens sur les Positions Géographiques déterminées en 1821, 1822, et 1823, sur les côtes de l'Amerique Méridionale. Par M. Givry. *Paris.* 1825. 8vo, pp. 28

"Not printed for sale."—RICH, II. 178.

GLACKMEYER (E.) An Alphabetical List of the Laws of Canada. *Toronto.* 1859. 8vo, pp. 16. 27521

Glad Tidings; or, An Account of the State of Religion within the Bounds of the General Assembly of the Presbyterian Church in the United States. *Philadelphia.* 1804. 8vo, pp. 48.

GLADDEN (W.) From the Hub to the Hudson. With Sketches of Nature, History and Industry in Northwestern Massachusetts. By Washington Gladden. *Boston: New England News Co.* 1869. 16mo, pp. 149. C. 27523

GLADSTONE (J.) The Correspondence between John Gladstone, Esq., M.P., and James Cropper, Esq., on the Present State of Slavery in the British West Indies and in the United States of America; and on the Importation of Sugar from the British

Settlements in India. With an Appendix, containing several Papers on the Subject of Slavery. *Liverpool.* 1824. 8vo, pp. 184. C. 27524

GLADSTONE. Facts Relating to Slavery in the West Indies and America ... Second Edition. *London.* 1830. 8vo, pp. 30.

GLADSTONE. Letters to the Earl of Clancarty, President of the Board of Trade, on the Inexpediency of permitting the Importation of Cotton Wool from the United States, during the Present War. By John Gladstone, of Liverpool. *London: Richardson.* 1813. 8vo, pp. 35. BA. 27526

Also: Statement ... on the Present State of Slavery in the British Sugar and Coffee Colonies, and in the United States. *London: Baldwin and Cradock.* 1830. 8vo, pp. 30. BA.

GLADSTONE (T. H.) Kansas; or, Squatter Life and Border Warfare in the Far West. By Thomas H. Gladstone. Reprinted, by permission, from "The Times," with Additions and Corrections. *London: G. Routledge & Co.* 1857. 12mo, pp. viii, 295. 2 Plates and Map. C. 27527

GLADSTONE. The Englishman in Kansas; or, Squatter Life and Border Warfare. By T. H. Gladstone, Esq. ... With an Introduction by Fred. Law Olmsted. *New York: Miller & Company.* 1857. 12mo, pp. 328. 27528

GLADSTONE. Bilder und Skizzen aus Kansas während des jüngsten Bürgerkriegs. *Leipzig.* 1857. 8vo. 27529

GLADSTONE (William Evarts). Speech of the Hon. W. E. Gladstone in the House of Commons ... Abolition of the Negro Apprenticeship, March 30, 1838. *London.* 1838. 8vo.

Also: Our Colonies: An Address, Mechanic's Institute, Chester, November, 1855. *London.* 1855.

A Glance at State Rights; their Misconstructions, their Wrongs, and their Rightful Protections against the "Irrepressible Conflict." By a State Rights Republican. *Richmond.* 1860. 27531

A Glance at the Nations; with other Poems. *Boston.* 1835. 12mo. 27532

A Glance at the Times. ... By a Yankee. ... *Philadelphia: Richard R. Small.* 1827. 12mo, pp. 52. BA., P. 27533

Glances at the Metropolis. A Hundred Illustrated Gems. *New York.* 1854. 4to. C. 27534

Contains a hundred plates from the London Art Journal, interspersed with notices of mercantile establishments in New York. Edited by C. E. Lester. *See also* New York City.

GLANDORFF (H.) Carta del P. Bartholome Braun, Visitador de la Provincia Tarahumara a los PP. Superiores de esta Provincia de Nueva-España sobre la apostolica vida, virtudes, y santa Muerte del P. Francisco Hermano Glandorff. *Mexico.* 1764. 4to, pp. 33. 27535

GLAREANUS (H.) D. Hen | rici Glareani | Poetae Lavrea | ti de Geogra- | phia Liber | vnvs. ¶ Basileae, anno | M. D. XXVII. | [Colophon:] ¶ *Basileae, Anno* M. D. XXVII. | *Excvdebat Ioannes Fa | ber Emmevs Jvliacensis.* | Folio, 36 leaves, the last being blank.

The passage relating to America will be found on the recto of leaf 35: "*Porro ad occidentem terra est, quam Americam vocant,*" etc.

GLAREANUS. Henrici | Glareani, Poetæ Lav | reati de Geogra- | phia Liber vnvs, ab ipso Avthore | iam recognitvs. | Basileae. | [Colophon:] *Basileae . Anno* | M . D . XXVIII . | *Excvdebat Ioannes Fa- | ber Emmevs Ivliacensis.* | Sm. 4to, 32 l. 27537

"In the copy before us, folios 31 and 32 are printed on one side only, and these blank pages are those which should contain the passages mentioned in the edition of 1527."—HARRISSE, No. 143. *See also* Troemel's "Bibliothèque Américaine," No. 3.

GLAREANUS. Henrici | Glareani Poetae Lav- | reati de Geogra- | phia Liber vnvs, | ab ipso Avtore | recognitvs. | Apud Fribvrgvm Brisgavdiae. | [Colophon:] *Apvd Fribvrgvm Bisgoicvm* | *Anno.* M. D. XXX. | *Excvdebat Ioannes Fa- | ber Emmeus Ivliacensis.* | 4to, 35 leaves, and one with a woodcut on the verso. 27538

GLAREANUS. Henrici Gla | reani Helvetii, Poetae Lav- | reati, de Geographia Li- | ber vnvs, ab ipso Av- | thore iam tertio | recog- nitvs. | Apvd Fribvrgvm Bris- | goiae, An. M.D.XXXIII. | [Colophon:] *Apvd Fribvrgvm Brisgoicvm* | *Anno* M.D.XXXIII. | *Excvdebat Ioannes Faber* | *Emmevs Ivliacensis.* | 4to, 35 leaves, and one with woodcut on the reverse. F. 27539

GLAREANUS. Henrici | Glareani Helvetii, | Poetae Lavreati de | Geographia Liber unus ab ipso | authore iam tertio re- | cognitvs. | [Colophon:] *Venetijs apud Ioan. Amt. de Nicolinis de Sabio* | *Sumptu & requisitione D. Melchioris Sessæ. An* | *no Domini* M.D. XXXIIII. | *Mense Augusto.* | 8vo, Title and 46 leaves. 27540

GLAREANUS. De Geographia Liber unus, ab ipso autore iam tertio recognitus. Apud Friburgium Brisgoiae An. M.D.XXXVI. Dicavit autor Joanni a Lasco Poloniae baroni. [Colophon:] *Apud Friburgum Brisgoicum Anno.* M.D.XXXVI. *Excudebat Joannes Faber Emmeus Juliacensis.* 4to, 35 l. 27541

See Panzer's "Annales Typogr.," Vol. VII., p. 61, No. 29. Also: Harrisse, No. 228. Another Edition. *Venitiis.* 1537. 4to.

GLAREANUS. Henrici | Glareani Helvetii | Poetae Lavreati de Geographia Liber vnvs ab | ipso authore iam tertio | recognitvs. | Venitiis. | [Colophon:] *Venetijs apud Ioan. Ant. de Nicolinis de Sabio. Sum | ptu uero & requisitione D. Melchioris Sessæ.* | *Anno Domini* MDXXXVIII. | *Mense Augusto.* | 8vo, Title and 39 leaves.

GLAREANUS. Henrici Gla | reani Helvetii, Poetae Lav- | reati de Geographia Liber | vnvs, ab ipso Avthore | iam novissime re- | cognitvs. | Apud Fribvrgvm Bris- | goiae, An. M.D.XXXIX. | [Colophon:] *Apvd Fribvrgvm Brisgoicum.* | *Anno.* M.D.XXXIX. | *Excvdebat Ioannes Faber* | *Emmevs Ivliacensis.* | 4to, Title and 34 pp.

GLAREANUS. Henrici | Glareani Helvetii, | Poetae Lavreati de Geogra | phia Liber unus, ab ipso Authore iam no | uissime recognitus. ¶ *Friburgi Brisgoiae* | *Stephanus Melechus Grauius excu- | debat, Anno* | M.D.XLIII. 4to, Title and 35 leaves. 27544

GLAREANUS. De Geographia Liber unus ab ipso Aucthore jam tertio recognitus. *Venetiis, apud Petrum et Jo. Mariam fratres et Cornelium nepotem de Nicolinis de Sabio, ad instantiam Melchioris Sessae, anno Dñi* M . D . XLIV. 8vo. 27545

Title from Lancetti as quoted by Harrisse.—Heber's Catalogue, Part I., No. 2767, notices an edition *Venetiis: J. A. de Sabio.* 1538. 8vo.

GLAREANUS. Henrici | Glareani Helvetii, | Poetae Lavreati de Geogra | phia Liber unus, ab ipso Authore iam no | uissime recognitus. | *Friburgi Brisgoiæ,* | *Stephanus Grauius excudebat,* | *Anno* | M.D.LI. | 4to, 33 leaves. C. 27546

GLAS (G.) *See* [Abreu de Galineo], Vol. I., No. 79.

For Collation add, 8 l., pp. 368. Map and 2 Charts. It was reprinted *Dublin: D. Chamberlaine.* 1767. 2 vols., 18mo, pp. xvi, 227; 223, Map. A. *See* "M. Rev.," XXXI. 54.

[GLASCOCK (William N.)] Naval Sketch Book; or, the Service Afloat and Ashore. *London: H. Colburn.* 1826. 2 vols., 12mo, pp. xxiv, 251; 286. C. 27547

GLASCOTT (Rev. C.) The best Method of putting an End to the American War. Being the Substance of a Sermon Preached on the 13th of December, 1776; The Day of the General Fast, at Tottenham-Court Chapel (Erected by the Rev. Mr. George Whitefield). By the Rev. Cradock Glascott, A.M. ... With an Address from Henry Peckwell, A.M., and Chaplain to the Marchioness Dowager of Lothian, to his Fellow Subjects on that Solemn Occasion. *London: Printed by J. W. Pasham, ... and sold at ... J. Mathew's, Bookseller, in the Strand.* 1776. 8vo, pp. 31. BA. 27548

A silly thing. J. Mathews, by the way, at whose shop this tract was to be obtained, was the father of the late Mr. Charles Mathews, of facetious memory. *See* "M. Rev.," LVI. 77.

GLASGOW (J.) Imprisonment and Enslavement of British Colored Seamen. Illustrated in the case of John Glasgow. [*Leeds.* 1853.] 8vo, pp. 8. 27549

GLASGOW EMANCIPATION SOCIETY. The American Board of Commissioners for Foreign Missions and the Rev. Dr. Chalmers, on Christian Fellowship with Slaveholders. An Address. *Glasgow.* 1845. 12mo, pp. 11. 27550

Also: Annual Report of the Glasgow Emancipation Society. *Glasgow.* 1835. 8vo. Continued.—Annual Report of the Glasgow New Association for the Abolition of Slavery. *Glasgow.* MDCCCLI. 8vo, pp. 15. Continued.

GLASS (F.) A Life of George Washington in Latin Prose. By Francis Glass, A.M., of Ohio. Edited by J. N. Reynolds. *New York: Harper & Brothers.* 1835. 12mo, pp. 233. Portrait. + Third Edition. [*Ibid.*] 1836. 12mo. C. 27551

Severely handled in the "N. Am. Rev.," XLIII. 37; XLIV. 270. Defended in the "Knickerbocker Mag.," VIII. 473.

The Glass; or, Speculation: A Poem. Containing an Account of the Ancient, and Genius of Modern Speculators. *New York: Printed for the Author.* 1791. 12mo, pp. 12. 27552

GLASSCOCK (L.) The Life and Travels of Lemuel Glasscock. [*Maysville, Ky.* 1841.]? 8vo, pp. 27. C. 27553

GLASTENBURY. Catalogue of the First Church of Christ in Glastenbury; Together with a Brief Outline of its History, and its Articles of Faith and Covenant. *Hartford.* 1859. 8vo, pp. 24. 27554

Glaubwürdiger Bericht der emigrirenden Saltburger. [n. p.] 1732. 4to, pp. 15. B. 27555

Glavery (F. R.) Report of the Select Committee of the Senate, to whom was referred the Petition of Francis R. Glavery and others, sufferers by French spoliations prior to the 30th September, 1800. Made February 22, 1830. 8vo. 27556

Glazier (L.) History of Gardner, Massachusetts, from its Earliest Settlement to 1860. By Lewis Glazier. *Worcester: Printed by Charles Hamilton.* 1860. 12mo, pp. 163. BA., H.

Glazier. The Capture, the Prison Pen, and the Escape: Giving an Account of Prison Life in the South, Principally at Richmond, ... [etc.] describing the Arrival of Prisoners, Plans of Escape, with Incidents and Anecdotes of Prison Life; embracing, also ... an Escape from Columbia, S. C., Recapture, Trial as Spy, and Final Escape from Sylvania, Georgia. By Willard W. Glazier. *Albany: J. Munsell.* 1866. pp. 353. BA., B. + *New York.* 1870. 12mo. B., H. 27558

The Gleaner. A Miscellaneous Production. ... By Constantia. *Printed at Boston, by I. Thomas and P. T. Andrews* ... 1798. 3 vols., 12mo, pp. xii, 348; iv, 321; iv, 328. BA., S.

A collection of papers, in part originally published in the Massachusetts "Monthly Museum," by the wife of the Rev. John Murray. It contains some curious information on the condition of the stage at Boston and elsewhere; and some dramatic compositions.

The Gleaner. Sustained by the Senior Department of the Girls' High School, Providence, Rhode Island. *Providence.* 1855–1857. 4 vols., 8vo. 27560

Gleanings in America. Interspersed with Sketches Selected from the Portfolio of a Traveller. *Cork.* 1821. 8vo. Part I.

Died from the effects of its own severity.

Gleason (B.) Anniversary Oration ... Charlestown, July 5, 1819. By Benjamin Gleason, Esq. ... *Charlestown: T. Green.* 1819. 8vo, pp. 16. BA. 27562

Gleason. An Oration ... in Wrentham, February 22, 1800 ... in Memory of Gen. George Washington ... . By Benjamin Gleason. *Wrentham: Printed by Nathaniel and Benjamin Heaton.* 1800. 8vo, pp. 31 (1). B., BA., H. 27563

Gleason An Oration on the Anniversary of American Independence. Pronounced before the Senior Class of Rhode Island College, in College Chapel, ... July 5, 1802. By Benjamin Gleason. *Boston: Munroe & Francis.* 1802. 8vo, pp. 16. H.

Also: An Oration, Charlestown ... July 4, 1805. Second Edition. *Boston.* 1805. 8vo, pp. 24. BA., H.—Oration before the Bristol Lodge, Norton, June 24, 1806. ... *Boston.* 1806. 8vo, pp. 22. BA., H.—Oration ... before the Republican Citizens of ... Hingham ... July 4, 1807 ... Second Edition. *Boston.* 1807. 8vo, pp. 22. BA., H.—Oration at Charlestown, Mass., July 5, 1809. ... *Charlestown.* [n. d.] 8vo.—Oration before the Republican Citizens of Charlestown, July 5, 1813. ... *Boston.* 1813. 8vo, pp. 16. BA., M.—Oration, Cambridge, Mass., July 4, 1826 ... *Boston.* 1826. 8vo, pp. 35. B., BA.—Oration before St. Paul's and Union Lodges, Montreal, June 24, 1812. Second Edition. *Boston.* 1812. 8vo. BA. And other Masonic Addresses.

Gleason (J.) Oration ... at Boston, ... July 4, 1806. By Joseph Gleason, Jr. Second Edition. *Boston: Printed by Oliver & Munroe.* 1806. 8vo, pp. 24. BA., W. 27565

Gleason (L.) An Impartial Narrative of the Trial of Luther Gleason, before the Congregational Convention of Long Island, at Brookhaven, April 13, 1808. To which is added, a Brief Account of the said Luther Gleason, from the time of his coming into this part of the Church. *Sag Harbor.* 1808. 12mo. N.

Glegg (*Col.*) Correspondence between Lt.-Col. Glegg, Secretary of His Excellency Lord Aylmer, Governor-in-Chief of Lower Canada, and James Stuart, Esq., Attorney-General for the said Province, relating: (1.) To the case of Cowie, Davis & Boucher, in the Service of the Hudson's Bay Company, ... (2.) Respecting the Establishments of Boundaries between the King's Posts Territory, and the Seigniory of "Mille Vaches;" (3.) Relating to the Suspension of Attorney-General Stuart from his Office ... With a Memorial from Mr. Stuart ... Folio. 1827–1831. 27567

Title from the Catalogue of the Library of Parliament, Canada.

[Gleig (George Robert)]. A Narrative of the Campaign of the British Army at Washington and New Orleans, under Generals Ross, Pakenham, and Lambert, in the years 1814 and 1815, with some Account of the Countries visited. By an Officer who served in the Expedition. *London: John Murray.* 1821. 8vo, pp. (iv), 377, (1). BA., H. + Second Edition. [*Ibid.*] 1826. P. + Third Edition, corrected and revised. [*Ibid.*] 1827. 12mo, pp. 387. 27568

By the author of the "Subaltern," who has a great dislike to the Americans, and having been at the battle of New Orleans, has doubtless good reasons for it.—*Ed. Rev.*, XLV., p. 368. Reprinted with the following titles:

[Gleig.] A Narrative of the Campaigns of the British Army, at Washington, Baltimore, and New Orleans, under Generals Ross, Pakenham, and Lambert, in the years 1814 and 1815; with some Account of the Countries visited. By an Officer who served in the Expedition. To which is annexed an Appendix, containing an Exposition of sundry Errors in the Work. *Philadelphia: M. Carey.* 1821. 8vo, pp. 431. B. 27569

[Gleig.] A Subaltern in America; Comprising the Narrative of the Campaigns of the British Army at Baltimore, Washington, etc., etc., during the late War. *Philadelphia: Carey & Hart.* 1833. 12mo, pp. 266. B. 27570

[Gleig.] The Campaigns of the British Army at Washington and New Orleans, in the years 1814–1815. By the Author of The Subaltern. Fourth Edition, corrected and revised. *London: J. Murray.* MDCCCXXXVI. 12mo, pp. iv, 389. H. + [*Ibid.*] 1847. 27571

[Glen (*Dr.*)] A Description of South Carolina; Containing many Curious and Interesting Particulars relating to the Civil, Natural, and Commercial History of that Colony, viz.: The Succession of European Settlers there; Grants of English Charters; Boundaries; Constitution of the Government; Taxes; Number of Inhabitants, and of the neighboring Indian Nations, &c. ... The Culture and Product of Rice, Indian Corn and Indigo; The Process of Extracting Tar and Turpentine; The State of their Maritime Trade in the years 1710, 1723, 1740, and 1748, with the number or tonnage of shipping employed, and the Species, Qualities and Values of their Produce exported in one year. To which is added a very Particular Account of their Rice Trade for twenty years, with their Exports of Raw Silk and Imports of British Silk Manufactures for twenty-five years. *London: R. and J. Dodsley.* MDCCLXI. 8vo, pp. viii, 110. H. 27572

Reprinted in the "Historical Collections of South Carolina," etc. Vol. II., 1836. This work has been attributed to Governor Glenn of South Carolina. "With the exception of Hewatt's history, it is the most complete early history of the State we have. It is divided into ten sections, in which are respectively treated the succession of European settlers in the province; grants of English charters; boundaries, and government; the history of neighboring Indians; nature of climate and soil; barometical accounts," etc.—*Preface to South Carolina Historical Collections.*

[Glendinning (W.)] A Short Account of the Exemplary Life and Triumphant Death of Theodosia Marxly, a Young Woman of Virginia, whose Death happened on the 3d day of March, 1793. [Motto.] *Philadelphia: Printed for William Glendinning, Preacher of the Gospel—By William W. Woodward.* 1794. 12mo, pp. 40. 27573

Glenelg (*Lord*). *See* [Grant (Charles)].

Glenn (J.) The City and Country Contrasted: A Poem by Dr. James Glenn of New York. *New York: Privately printed.* 1845. 8vo. 27574

Glenn (S. F.) Gravities and Gaieties. By Samuel F. Glenn. *Washington: R. Farnham.* 16mo, pp. (4), 116. 27575

Glenn. The New Constitution of Louisiana, adopted in 1845; with a Comparative View of the Old and New Constitutions of the State. By Samuel F. Glenn. *New Orleans.* 1845. 8vo. N. 27576

Glennie (A.) Sermons Preached on Plantations to Congregations of Negroes. By Rev. Alexander Glennie. *Charleston, (S. C.): A. K. Miller.* 1844. 18mo, pp. viii, 161. C. 27577

Glen's Falls Academy, *N. Y.*: Catalogue. 1858. 8vo.

Glentworth (J. B.) A Statement of the Frauds on the Elective Franchise in the City of New York, in ... 1838 and ... 1839. By James B. Glentworth. *New York.* [1840.] 8vo. pp. 79. B., BA., N. 27578

Relates to the "Pipe Laying" fraud.

Glezen (L.) An Oration delivered at Lexington, the 22d February, 1800. By Levi Glezen. *Stockbridge.* 1800. 8vo. pp. 20. GB. 27579

Relates to the Death of George Washington. Also: Oration (4th July, 1802), at Lenox, Mass. *Pittsfield.* [1802.] 8vo, pp. 24. N.

"Glimmerings": a Quarterly Journal, conducted by the Knights of Richmond Castle. Vol. I., No. I. *Portland.* 1860. 8vo, pp. 16. H. 27580

A Glimpse of Hayti and her Negro Chief. *Liverpool.* 1850. Square 12mo, pp. 140. 27581

Glimpses of New York City. By a South Carolinian, [William M. Bobo?]. *Charleston, S. C.* 1852. 12mo, pp. 215.

The Globe. Vol. I. *New York.* 1819. 8vo, pp. 384.

Edited by J. O'Connor.

Globus mundi | Declaratio siue descriptio mundi | et totius orbis terrarum. globulo rotundo comparati vt spera soli | da. Qua cuiuis etiã mediocriter docto ad oculũ videre licet an | tipodes esse, quoR pedes nostris oppositi sunt. Et qualiter in vna- | quaq; orbis parte homines vitam agere queunt salutarẽ, sole

sin- | gula terre loca illustrante: que tamen terra in vacuo aere pendere | videtur: solo dei nutu sustẽtata, alijs q; permultis de quarta orbis | terrarũ parte nuper ab Americo reperta. | [Colophon:] *Valete Feliciter ex | Argentina vltima Augusti. Anno post natũ salutatorẽ.* M.D.IX. *Joannes grüniger impri | mebat. Adelpho castigatore.* | Small 4to, 14 leaves. H. 27583

Concerning this World's Globe, *see* Humboldt's "Examen," Brunet's "Manuel," p. 1626, and Harrisse's "Bib. Am. Vet.," No. 61.

Glocester *or* Gloucester (*Bp. of*). *See* Benson (M.), Johnson (J.), Warburton (W.), Waugh (*Dr.*), Wilcoks (*Dr.*)

Glocester, *Mass.* Letters from the First Church in Glocester to the Second in Bradford, with their Answer. To which is added an Appendix, Containing the Result of the Council at Bradford, and Mr. Balch's Reply to the Articles of Error alledg'd against him. *Boston: J. Edwards.* 1744. 8vo, pp. 32. 27584

See also Gloucester, Mass.

Glocester *R. I.* Report of the Committee appointed by the General Assembly of the State of Rhode-Island and Providence Plantations, ... to Inquire into the Situation of the Farmers' Exchange Bank in Glocester ... . *Providence: "American Office."* 1809. 8vo, pp. 56. BA. + *Gloucester, R. I.* 1809. 8vo, pp. 43. + [n. p.] 1809. 8vo, pp. 43. BA. 27585

A Gloria y loor de dios. *See* Meneses (F. de), *and* Olave (A. S. de).

Gloria Britannorum; or, the British Worthies. A Poem. Being an Essay on the Character of the Most Illustrious Persons in Camp or Cabinet, Since the Glorious Revolution to this present Time. More Particularly, of this present Ministry, under our most renowned Sovereign Lord King George. To which is added an Ode on his Majesty's Coronation, and an Elegy on the Death of the late Glorious Duke of Marlborough. By a Lover of the present happy Constitution. *Boston: Printed by J. Franklin for A. Buttolph, and Sold at his Shop in Cornhill.* 1723. 12mo, pp. 30. M., W. 27586

Incidentally refers to Harvard College. Very rare.

Gloriosa coroa de esforçados religiosos da companhia de Jesus morbos pela se catholica nas conquistas dos reynos da coroa de Portugal. *Lisboa: A. Alvarez.* 1642. Folio. 27587

Title from Ternaux, No. 618.

Glorious Manifestation. *See* Whitfield (H.)

Glorious News. A Brief Account of the late Revivals of Religion in a Number of Towns in the New-England States, and also Nova Scotia; extracted chiefly from letters written by several Gentlemen of unquestionable Veracity. To which is added, a very interesting Letter from a Minister in London to his friend in Massachusetts. With several important and additional Extracts. *Philadelphia: S. C. Ustich.* 1800. 12mo, pp. 28. + *New York: Printed by I. Seaver and J. Sutton.* 1800. 12mo, pp. 28. 27588

The Glory of America. *See* [Humphreys (David)].

The Glory of America. Comprising Memoirs of the Lives and Glorious Exploits of some of the Distinguished Officers engaged in the late War with Great Britain. *New York.* 1834. 8vo. 27589

The Glory of Columbia. *See* [Dunlap (William)].

Gloster (A.) Narrative of some recent Facts in the Colony of Dominica. By Archibald Gloster, of Roseau. *Printed in the Year* 1814. 4to. 27590

Gloucester (*Dean of*). *See* Tucker (J.), *and* (Waugh (*Dr.*)

Gloucester, *Mass.* An Appeal to the Impartial Publick, by the Society of Christian Independents congregating in Glocester. *Boston: Printed by Benjamin Edes & Son.* M,DCC,LXXXV. 8vo, pp. 39. BA., H. M. 27591

An Answer to a Piece, entitled, "An Appeal to the Impartial Publick," by an Association calling themselves "Christian Independents, in Glocester." *Salem.* 1785. 8vo, pp. 23. H. 27592

By-Laws of the Town of Gloucester. *Gloucester.* 1853. 12mo, pp. 10. 27593

The Gloucester Directory ... 1859, an Almanac for 1860. *Gloucester: Proctor Brothers.* 1860. 18mo, 1 l., pp. 192 (2). B.

The Gloucester and Rockport Directory for 1869. By Sampson, Davenport & Co. *Gloucester: Proctor Brothers.* 1868. 8vo, pp. 206. Continued. C. 27595

Report of the Board of Health of the Town of Gloucester ... . *Gloucester: John S. E. Rogers.* 1855. 8vo, pp. 9. H.

Report of the Case of Gloucester Election, January, 1811. *Boston.* 8vo. 27597

Rules and Orders of the Masonic Fire Society in Gloucester. *Boston.* 1789. 12mo. 27598

Gloucester County, *N. J.* Proceedings of the Democratic Association of Gloucester County, New Jersey, March, 1801. [n. p.] 1801. 8vo. C. 27599

Gloucester, *Pa.* Memoirs of the Gloucester Fox Hunting Club near Philadelphia. *Philadelphia.* 1830. 8vo, pp. 56, and Errata. BA., H. 27600

Glover (A.) Glover Memorials and Genealogies. An Account of John Glover of Dorchester and his Descendants. With a brief Sketch of some of the Glovers who first settled in New Jersey, Virginia, and other places. By Anna Glover. *Boston: David Clapp & Son, Printers.* 1867. 8vo, pp. ix, 602. B., BA., H.

Glover (H.) An Essay to discover the principal causes | of the Anger of God against New-England. | By Habakkuk Glover of Boston in New-England. | [*London.* 1665.] 4to, pp. 8.

Glover (J.) An Oration ... before the Medical Society of South-Carolina. ... 24th December, 1809 ... . By Joseph Glover, M.D. ... *Charleston, S. C.: J. Hoff.* 1810. 8vo, pp. 32, Table. H. 27603

Glover (L. M.) The Character of Abraham Lincoln. A Discourse Delivered April 23d, 1865, at ... Jacksonville, Ill. By Rev. L. M. Glover, D.D., ... *Jacksonville.* 1865. 8vo, pp. 21. B. 27604

Glover. ... A Discourse ... at the Funeral of John Adams, LL.D. April 26th, 1863. By L. M. Glover ... . *Jacksonville.* [n. d.] 8vo, pp. 18. BA. 27605

Also: Our Country Vindicated. A Thanksgiving Discourse. Delivered November 29, 1860. ... *Jacksonville: Catlin & Co.* 1860. 8vo, pp. 22. H.—National Sin and Retribution. A Discourse delivered on the ... National Fast, January 4, 1861 ... *Jacksonville: Catlin & Co.* 1861. 8vo, pp. 19.

Glover [Richard]. The Evidence Delivered on the Petition Presented by the West-India Planters and Merchants to the Hon. House of Commons, as it was Introduc'd at the Bar and Summ'd up by Mr. Glover. [*London.* 1775.] 8vo, pp. (2), 95. J.C.B., H

Without date or place. The petition is dated February 2, 1775.

[Glover.] Remarks on the Evidence delivered on the Petition presented by the West-India Planters and Merchants, to the House of Commons, On the 16th of March, 1775, As it was Introduced and summed up By Mr. Glover, So far as the same respects Barbadoes and the Leeward Islands. In a Letter to a Member of Parliament. By a West-India Planter. *London: J. Bew.* MDCCLXXVII. 8vo, pp. iv, 50, (2). H. 27607

Glover. A Short Account Of the late Application to Parliament Made by the Merchants of London Upon the Neglect of their Trade: With The Substance of the Evidence Thereupon; As sum'd up by Mr. Glover. The Second Edition. *London: T. Cooper.* M.DCC.XLII. 8vo, pp. 61. BA. + The Fourth Edition. *Dublin: George Ewing.* M,DCC,XLII. H. + The Sixth Edition. *London: J. Wilkie,* MDCCLXXIV. 8vo, pp. 71. 27608

A portion relates to the neglect of our Trade on the coast of North America.

Glover. The Substance of the Evidence Delivered to a Committee of the Honourable House of Commons by the Merchants and Traders of London, Concerned in the Trade to Germany and Holland, and of the Dealers in Foreign Linens, As Summed up By Mr. Glover. To which is Annexed, His Speech, Introductory to the Proposals Laid before the Annuitants of Mess. Douglas, Heron and Co. At the King's-Arms Tavern, Cornhill, on the Ninth of February, 1774. *London: J. Wilkie.* MDCCLXXIV. 8vo, pp. (4), 72. C., H., S. 27609

Glover. The Substance of the Evidence on the Petition Presented by the West-India Planters and Merchants to the Hon. House of Commons, As it was introduc'd at the Bar, and summ'd up By Mr. Glover On Thursday the 16th of March, 1775. *London: H. S. Woodfall.* [1775.] 8vo, pp. (4), 47. C. + *New York.* 1775. 8vo, pp. 75. B. + [*Ibid.*] 1778. 8vo. B.

"Contains many important facts and observations respecting the situation, mutual relations, and commerce of the British American colonies."—*Monthly Review.* *See also* our Vol. I., No. 1783.

Glover (S. T.) Slavery in the United States; Emancipation in Missouri. Speech of Samuel T. Glover at the Ratification Meeting, St. Louis, July 22, 1863. *St. Louis: "Daily Union Office."* 1863. 8vo, pp. 18. B., H. 27611

Also: Speech, July 26, 1860. *St. Louis.* 1860. 8vo, pp. 8. H. *See also* Lincoln (A.)

Glover. Emancipation in Missouri. Speech of Samuel T. Glover, Esq., ... St. Louis ... June 25th, 1862. [n. p. n. d.] 8vo, pp. 16. H. 27612

Glover. Proceedings in the Criminal Court of St. Louis Co. The State of Missouri *vs.* Samuel T. Glover. Indictment for practising Law without taking the New Constitution Oath. ... *St. Louis: George Knapp & Co.* 1865. 8vo, pp. 16. H.

Glover. Missouri Test Oath. Argument of Samuel T. Glover, Esq., in the Circuit Court of Saint Louis County. ... *St. Louis: George Knapp & Co.* 1866. 8vo, pp. 26. H. 27614

Glyndon (Howard), *pseudonym.* *See* [Redden (Laura C.)]

[Goadby (Robert).] An Apology for the Life of Mr. Bampfylde-Moor Carew, Son of the Rev. Mr. Carew, of Bickley, commonly known by the Title of King of the Beggars; Account of his leaving Tiverton School at the age of fifteen and entering the Society of Gypsies, his many comical Adventures, Travels through America, Living with the Wild Indians, return Home, and Travels through England, Wales, Scotland, and Ireland. *London.* [1749.] 8vo, pp. 149. C. + The Second Edition. [With Dedication of 17 pages to Henry Fielding.] *London: R. Goadby.* [n. d.] 8vo. + Sixth Edition, with Additions. *London: R. Goadby.* 1756. 12mo. [Another] Sixth Edition. *London: R. Goadby.* [n. d.] 12mo, pp. xxviii, iv, 350. Portrait. C. + Eighth Edition. [*Ibid.*] 1768. 12mo. + The Ninth Edition. [*Ibid.*] MDCCLXXV. Large folded Portrait. + *London: A. Millar* ... MDCCLXXXII. 12mo, pp. 246. Portrait. + *London.* 1789. + *London: W. Wright.* [n. d.] 12mo, pp. 282. + *London: J. Barker.* [n. d.] 12mo, pp. (4), 212. + *Bath.* 1802. 12mo. + A New Edition, corrected and much improved. *Tiverton: W. Salter.* 1812. 12mo, pp. 288. Portrait and Engraved Title. S. + *London.* 1827. 12mo. Plate. + *London: Printed for Owen.* [n. d.] 8vo, pp. 149. Portrait. 27615

Owen's Edition recites in its title "his bold attempt in Swimming the River Delaware."— Another purports to be Collected and Amended from his own Writings, by Thomas Price, of Poole, in Devon. *London.* [n. d.] 12mo. Portrait.— An Edition, *Newcastle* [1812], 12mo, pp. 24, does not contain his adventures in America.—"Carew was born in Devonshire, was tried at Exeter about 1739 or 1740, and banished to Maryland, where he went at the cost of the public. He gives an amusing account of the country, and his adventures in Maryland, Virginia, New Jersey, New York, and Connecticut, till he embarked at New London for England. His accounts how he bamboozled and bled Whitfield, Thos. Penn, Gov. Thomas, and many others of good repute, are amazing, true or not."—Stevens.

Goadby (J.) Discourse, Education Society of the Saratoga Baptist Association, Ballston Spa, June 26, 1844. By Rev. John Goadby. *Schenectady.* 1844. 8vo. S. 27616

Go-ahead Louisiana and Texas Almanac for 1839. *New Orleans.* 8vo. W. 27617

Goazacoalco. Colonie du Goazacoalco. [Prospectus.] 8vo, pp. 16. Map. 27618

The Go-Between, or Two Edged Sword; being an Impartial Address to the Citizens of the United States. By a Gentleman from South Carolina [Mr. Devot?]. *New York.* 1807. 8vo, pp. 37. 27619

Gobat (P. G.), *Translator.* *See* Raguenau (P.)

Gobineau (*Le Comte* Joseph Arthur de). Voyage a Terre-Neuve. *Paris: Hachette et Cie.* 1861. 8vo, pp. 309. 27620

Gobright (J. C.) The New-York Sketch Book and Merchants' Guide: ... A Description of the Leading Firms. By John C. Gobright. *New York: J. C. Gobright & Co.* 1858. 12mo, pp. 169, (1), xxi. B., H. 27621

Gobright. The New-York Hand Book and Merchants' Guide. ... Compiled from Authentic Sources. By John C. Gobright. *New York: Pudney & Russell.* 1859. 12mo, pp. 131.

Gobright. The Union Sketch-Book: A Reliable Guide, Exhibiting the History and Business Resources of the Leading Mercantile and Manufacturing Firms of New York. To which is added, a Directory to the Principal Objects of Interest in New York. ... By Gobright and Dawes. *New York: Rudd & Carleton.* M DCCC LXI. 8vo. 27623

Gobright (L. A.) Recollections of Men and Things at Washington, during the third of a Century. By L. A. Gobright. *Philadelphia: Claxton, Remsen & Haffelfinger.* 1869. 12mo, pp. 420. B., BA., C., H. 27624

Gock (Carl). Die Vertheidigung der freyen Kirche von Nord-Amerika, [etc.] *Reading,* (*Pa.*): *C. Gock.* 1822. 16mo, pp. 120. 27625

Gockelivs (C. L.) ... Dissertatio Inavgvralis Medica de Serpentaria Virginiana. ... Examini submittit Christophorvs Lvdovicus Gockelivs, Hersprvcko-Noricvs ... Ad diem Iun. A. CIↃ IↃCCX. *Ienæ: Litteris Christophori Krebsii.* 4to, pp. (viii), 40. P. 27626

Göcking (G. G. G.) Emigrations-Geschichte von denen aus dem Ertz-Bissthum Saltzburg vertriebenen Lutheranern. *Franckfurt.* 1734–37. 2 vols., 4to. B. 27627

God *or* Our Country. *See* [Bowditch (W. I.)], No. 7008.

God's Image in Ebony: A Series of Sketches demonstrative of the Mental Powers and Intellectual Capacities of the Negro Race. Edited by H. G. Adams. With a Sketch by F. W. Chesson, and a Chapter by Wilson Armistead. *London: Partridge & Okey.* 1854. 12mo, pp. 188. 27628

God's Wonders in the Great Deep, Recorded in several Wonderful and Amazing Accounts of Sailors, who have met with unexpected Deliverances from Death, when in the greatest Dangers. To which is added the Seaman's Spiritual Directory. *Gravesend.* 1803. 12mo. Frontispiece. 27629

Relates several shipwrecks (1670, &c.) on the New England coast.

Godard-Lange. La Congrégation ou une Mission chez les Iroquois; poëme ... par Godard-Lange. *Paris.* 1846. 8vo, pp. xiv, 397. 27630

"A satire, without a word regarding the Iroquois or any other savages, except those of Paris".—T. W. Field.

Goddard (D. A.) The Mathers Weighed in the Balances, and Found not Wanting. By Delano A. Goddard, M.A. *Boston: "Daily Advertiser Press."* 1870. Square 16mo, pp. 32. BA.

A few copies only printed.

Goddard (Edward). A Brief Account of the Formation and Settlement of the Second Church and Congregation in Framingham. [*Boston.* 1750.] 8vo, pp. 4. M. 27632

Goddard (F. B.) Where to Emigrate, and Why; describes the Climate, Soil, Productions, Minerals, and general Resources ... of the United States; and contains a Description of the Pacific Railroad, ... etc. By Frederick B. Goddard. *New York: F. B. Goddard.* 1869. 8vo, pp. xvi, 591. 4 Plates, 19 Maps. B.

Also issued, with the title changed to: Homes and Fortunes in the Boundless West and the Sunny South; their Climate, Scenery, etc. *Philadelphia: The People's Publishing Company.* 1869.

Goddard (K.) The Present Crisis: A Sermon ... Thanksgiving Day, December 8, 1842. By the Rev. Kingston Goddard. *Brooklyn.* 1842. 8vo, pp. 19. 27634

Goddard (J.) An Oration ... at Conway, on the Fourth of July, 1804. By Elder Josiah Goddard. *Northampton: Printed by Andrew Wright.* 1804. 8vo, pp. 24. BA. 27635

Goddard. Oration at Goshen, [Mass.] July 4, 1805. By Josiah Goddard. *Northampton.* [1805.] 8vo. W. 27636

Goddard (N.) Report of a Committee of the Citizens of Boston ... opposed to an Increase of Duties. *Boston: Nathan Hale.* 1827. 8vo, pp. 196. B., BA. + *Philadelphia: Reprinted by S. Parker.* 1828. 8vo, pp. 180. H. 27637

For a reply see our note to Carey (M.) in Vol. III.

Goddard (S. A.) The American Rebellion. Letters on the American Rebellion. By Samuel A. Goddard ... . 1860 to 1865, &c. *London: Simpkin, Marshall & Co.* 1870 8vo, pp. xvi, 583. B., BA., H. 27638

Goddard. Reply to Mr. Roebuck's Speech at Sheffield, on the American Question. *Birmingham.* [1863.] 8vo, pp. 9. B., H.

Goddard. Reply to Mr. Lindsay's Speech at Sunderland, August, 1864, on the American Questions. *Birmingham,* [*Eng.*]: *E. C. Osborne.* 8vo, pp. 16. B., H. 27640

Goddard (T. A.) A General History of the most prominent Banks in Europe: Particularly the Banks of England and France; the Rise and Progress of the Bank of North America; a full History of the late and present Bank of the United States; to which is added, A Statistical and Comparative View of the Moneyed Institutions of New York, and Twenty-four other Principal Cities of the United States, Compiled from various standard works, official sources, and private correspondence. Also, A. Hamilton's Report to Congress on Currency ... and McDuffie's Report on Currency ... By Thomas H. Goddard. *New York: H. C. Sleight.* 1831. 8vo, pp. 254. A., BA., C.

[Goddard (William).] Advertisement ... *Philadelphia, August* 1, 1770. Folio, 1 l. P. 27642

Signed, William Goddard—relates to his quarrel with Towne—it is in reply to [Towne's] "To the Public."

Goddard. The Partnership: or the History of the Rise and Progress of the Pennsylvania Chronicle, &c. Wherein the Conduct of Joseph Galloway, Esq; Speaker of the Honourable House of Representatives of the Province of Pennsylvania, Mr. Thomas Wharton, Sen. and their Man Benjamin Towne, my late Partners, with my own, is properly delineated, and their Calumnies against me fully refuted. By William Goddard. *Philadelphia: William Goddard.* M,DCC,LXX. 8vo, pp. 72. BA., H., W.

This consists of the Soliloquy, Advertisement, &c., find issued separately, but now paged consecutively.

Goddard. The Prowess of the Whig Club, and the Manœuvres of Legion. *Baltimore: Printed for the Author.* [1777.] 12mo, pp. 16, 4. BA., W. 27644

Contains the defense of William Goddard against the action of the Whig Club of Baltimore, which drove him from that city. *See* J. C. Brown's Catalogue.

[Goddard.] A Soliloquy. *Printed in the year* 1770. 4to, pp. 15. P. 27645

Probably printed at Philadelphia. Relates to local politics.

Goddard (W. A.) A Genealogy of the Descendants of Edward Goddard. By William Augustus Goddard. *Worcester: M. Spooner, Printer.* 1833. 12mo, pp. 96. B., S. 27646

Goddard (W. Giles). An Address to the People of Rhode-Island, delivered in Newport ... on May 3, 1843, in presence of the General Assembly, on the Occasion of the Change in the Civil Government of Rhode-Island, by the adoption of the Constitution, which superseded the Charter of 1663. With Appendix. By William G. Goddard. *Providence: Knowles and Vose.* 1843. 8vo, pp. 80. B., BA., C., H., P. 27647

Goddard. Memoir of the Rev. James Manning, D.D., first President of Brown University; with Biographical Notices of some of his Pupils. By William G. Goddard. ... *Boston: Perkins & Marvin.* 1839. 8vo, pp. 24. Portrait. B., BA. 27648

Goddard. Political and Miscellaneous Writings. By William Giles Goddard. Edited by his Son, Francis W. Goddard. *Providence: S. S. Rider & Brother.* 1870. 2 vols., 8vo, pp. xxxii, 568, Portrait; viii, pp. 535. B., C., H. 27649

Also: Address to the Phi Beta Kappa Society of Rhode Island, delivered September 7, 1836. ... *Boston: John H. Eastburn.* 1837. 8vo, pp. 30.— Address in Commemoration of the Death of William Henry Harrison, delivered before the City Council and Citizens of Providence, on the National Fast, May 14, 1841. *Providence.* 1841.

8vo, pp. 30.— Brief Notices of the Life and Character of the late Nicholas Brown. ... *Providence.* 1841. 12mo, pp. 15.— Obituary Notice of Thomas Poynton Ives, who died April 30th, 1835. ... *Providence.* 1835. 8vo, pp. 6.

Godefroy (F.) Recueil d'estampes représentant les différents événemens de la guerre ... de l'indépendance des États Unis. Par F. Godefroy. *Paris.* 4to, pp. 16. H. 27650

Goden (Julius). Die Spanier in Peru. *Berlin: Bei Friedrich Maurer.* 1794. 2 vols., 12mo, pp. (4), 308; 260. 27651

Godet (J. A.) Notes sur le Golfe du Mexique et les mouillages compris entre Tampico et Vera Cruz. Par J. A. Godet. *Bordeaux: Lafargne.* 1856. 8vo. 27652

Godet (T. L.) Bermuda: Its History, Geology, Climate, Products, Agriculture, Commerce and Government; From the Earliest Period to the Present Time; with Hints to Invalids. By Theodore L. Godet, M.D. *London: Smith, Elder & Co.* MDCCCLX. 8vo, pp. xv, 271. B., C., H. 27653

Godfrey (A. W.) Letters and Correspondence on the Halifax and Quebec Railroad ... *Halifax.* 1847. 8vo. 27654

Godfrey (M.) Authentic Narrative of the Seminole War and Miraculous Escape of Mrs. Mary Godfrey and her four female Children, [also] Massacre of Whites by Indians and Negroes in Florida. *Providence, R. I.* 1836. 8vo, pp. 24. C.

Godfrey (T.) The Pennsylvania Almanack for 1733. By T. Godfrey. *Philadelphia: Printed and Sold by A. Bradford.* [n. d.] Continued. 27656

Godfrey. The Court of Fancy: A Poem. By Thomas Godfrey. [Motto.] *Philadelphia: William Dunlap.* M.DCC.LXII. 4to, pp. 24. P. 27657

Godfrey (T., Jr.) Juvenile Poems on Various Subjects. With the Prince of Parthia, a Tragedy. By the late Mr. Thomas Godfrey, Jr., of Philadelphia. To which is prefixed some Account of the Author and his Writings. [By N. Evans.] *Philadelphia: Henry Miller.* MDCCLXV. 4to, pp. xxv, (2), 223. P.

The author served as lieutenant against Fort Duquesne in 1758 in the Pennsylvania forces; he died in North Carolina, August 3, 1763.

Godfrey (W. C.) Godfrey's Narrative of the Last Grinnell Arctic Exploring Expedition, in Search of Sir John Franklin, 1853–4–5. Biography of Dr. Elisha K. Kane, from the Cradle to the Grave. By William C. Godfrey, one of the Survivors of the Expedition. *Philadelphia: J. T. Lloyd & Co.* 1857. 8vo, pp. 267. + [*Ibid.*] 1860. 8vo, pp. 295. 27659

Godin (M.) Naufrage d'Isabelle de Grand Maison et Bruno, epouse de M. Godin des Odonais, et de sa famille sur les bords du fleuve des Amazones. *Paris: Imp. de Delalain.* 1827. 8vo, pp. 16. 27660

"This relation is an abridgment of the letter of M. Godin, printed with the letter of M. D. L. C. (de la Condamine) *sur le sort des Astronomes, etc.,* an 8vo of 30 pages, without date, but printed in 1773 or 1774, and also at the end of La Condamine's 'Relation,'" etc., 1778. An English version will be found on pp. 307–334 of "Constable's Miscellany," Vol. xi.

Godinez (M.) Practica de la Theologia Mystica. Por Miguel Godinez y San Pablo ... *Mexico.* 1682. Sm. 8vo. 27661

Godley (J. R.) Letters from America. By John Robert Godley. *London: John Murray.* 1844. 2 vols., post 8vo, pp. xxxv, 272; 243. B., BA., H. 27662

Godman (J. D.) American Natural History. Part I. Mastology. By John D. Godman, M.D. *Philadelphia: H. C. Carey & I. Lea.* 1826–28. 3 vols., 8vo, pp. 362; 331; 264. 73 Plates. + [*Ibid.*] 1828–31. + Second Edition. *Philadelphia: Key & Mickle.* 1831. + Third Edition. To which is added, his last work, the Rambles of a Naturalist; with a Biographical Sketch of the Author. *Philadelphia.* 1842. 2 vols., 8vo. 38 Plates. + [*Ibid.*] 1846. + New Edition. *Philadelphia: U. Hunt.* 1855. 8vo. 27663

Godman. Rambles of a Naturalist. By the late Dr. John D. Godman. To which are added Reminiscences of a Voyage to India. By Reynell Coates, M.D. *Philadelphia: T. T. Ash.* 1836. 12mo, pp. 151. C. + *Philadelphia: Association of Friends.* 1859. 12mo, pp. 124. 27664

Godman. A Letter to Dr. Thomas P. Jones, Editor of the Franklin Journal. By John D. Godman, M.D. *Philadelphia.* 1826. 8vo, pp. 28. B., P. 27665

Relates to Harlan's "Fauna Americana."— Also: Description of a New Genus and New Species of Extinct Mammiferous Quadrupeds. 4to.— Addresses delivered on various Public Occasions. With Appendix. *Philadelphia.* 1829. 8vo, pp. 194. B., H.— Professional Reputation: An Oration before the Philadelphia Medical Society ... February 8, 1826. *Philadelphia: Benjamin & Thomas Kill.* 1826. 8vo, pp. 24. B., BA.— A Sketch of the Life and Character of the late Dr. John D. Godman. ... *Bristol.* [n. d.] 12mo, pp. 18.— Also published by the London Tract Association, No. 70, 1848, and again in 1857. 12mo.

Godman (S. A.) The Ocean-Born: A Tale of the Southern Seas. By Stuart Adair Godman. *New York.* [1852.] 8vo, pp. 100. H. 27666

Godoy (Manuel de). Memorias de don M. Godoy, principe de la Paz, ó sea cuenta de su vida politica; para servir a la historia del reinado del señor don Carlos IV. de Borbon. Reimpresa sobre la edicion original, publicada en Paris por el mismo principe. *Gerona: Vicente Oliva.* 1839. 6 vols., 12mo. 27667

Many of the issues treated relate to American questions.

Godoy. Memoirs of Don Manuel de Godoy, Prince of the Peace, ... written by himself. Edited ... by Lieut.-Colonel J. B. D'Esménard. With an Introduction, Historical and Biographical Notes, &c. *London: Richard Bentley.* 1836. 2 vols., 8vo, pp. viii, 492; viii, 428. 2 Portraits. BA., C. 27668

Godoy. An Exact and Impartial Account of the Most Important Events which have occurred in Aranjuez, Madrid, &c., 1808. Translated from the Spanish. *New York.* 1808. 8vo, pp. 46. M. 27669

Godoy (Nicholas de). Pompa Funeral en la muerte, y Exequias del Dr. Joan de Salzedo, Dean de la Iglesia Metropolitana de Mexico, Oratio Funebri, &c. *Mexico.* 1626. 4to. 27670

Godwin (B.) Sabstance of a Course of Lectures on British Colonial Slavery, delivered at Bradford, York, and Scarborough. By Rev. Benjamin Godwin. *London.* 1830. 8vo. + *Boston: James B. Dow.* 1836. 12mo, pp. 258. BA., H. 27671

Godwin (Morgan). *See* Godwyn (Morgan).

Godwin (P.) Cyclopedia of Universal Biography. By Parke Godwin. *New York: G. P. Putnam.* 1852. 12mo. + [*Ibid.*] 1855. + New Edition, with a Supplement brought down to the Present Time. *New York: Hurd & Houghton.* 1866. Cr. 8vo, pp. 821, 158. 27672

First published as a Hand-book of Universal Biography. 8vo.— Also: An Address to the People of the United States. ...— Democracy, Constructive and Pacific. 12mo.

Godwin. Political Essay. By Parke Godwin. [From Contributions to Putnam's Magazine.] *New York: Dix, Edwards & Co.* 1856. 8vo, 3 l., pp. 345. B., H. 27673

Godwin (W.) A Letter of Advice to a Young American, on the Course of Studies most advantageous for him to pursue. *London.* 1818. 8vo. 27674

GODWIN. Lives of the Necromancers. ... By William Godwin. *London.* 1834. 8vo, pp. xxi, 465. B. + *New York.* 1835. 12mo. 27675

Includes a chapter on Witchcraft in New England, p. 454.

GODWIN. Of Population. An Enquiry concerning the Power of Increase in the Numbers of Mankind, in Answer to Malthus's Essay on that Subject. *London: Longman, Hurst* ... 1820. 8vo, pp. 22, 626. B., H. 27676

This elicited the following reply: Question of Population as it relates to the Increase in the Inhabitants of the United States, carefully considered, in Answer to Godwin. *London.* 1821. 8vo. — His novel, entitled Cloudesley, is founded on the Annesley story, see our Vol. I., Nos. 1599–1603. His Life of the Earl of Chatham contains some details of Pitt's efforts in favor of the Colonists.

GODWYN (M.) The | Negro's & Indians | Advocate, | Suing for their Admission into the | Church: | Or | A Persuasive to the Instructing | and Baptizing of the Negro's and | Indians in our Plantations. | Shewing, | That as the Compliance therewith can prejudice | no Mans just Interest; So the wilful Neglecting | and Opposing of it, is no less than a manifest | Apostacy from the Christian Faith. | To which is added, A brief Account of Religion in Virginia. | By Morgan Godwyn, | Sometime St. of Ch. Ch. Oxon. | *London: Printed for the Author, by J. D. and are* | *to be Sold by most Booksellers.* 1680. | 8vo, 7 l., pp. 174. H. 27677

Containing a curious article on the "style of religion in Virginia as it was before the late rebellion."

G[ODWYN] (M[organ]). A Supplement to the Negro's and Indian's Advocate: or Some further Considerations and Proposals for the effectual and speedy carrying out of the Negro's Christianity in our Plantations (notwithstanding the late pretended Impossibilities) without any prejudice to their owners. By M. G. a Presbyter of the Church of England. *London: Printed by J. D[unton].* 1681. Sm. 4to, pp. 12. C., H. 27678

GODWYN. Trade Preferred before Religion, and Christ made to give place to Mammon; Represented in a Sermon relating to the Plantations. First preached at Westminster-Abbey, and afterwards in divers Churches in London. By Morgan Godwyn. *London: B. Tooke.* 1685. 4to, pp. 34. C. 27679

Goede nieuwe tijdinghe ghecomen met het | Jacht de Vos ghenaemt, afghesonden von den generael Jacob | Wilckens uyt Bresilien, aen de Heeren Bewint-Hebbers | vande gheoctroyeerde West-Indische Compagnie. | *Ghedruckt by Broer Jansz. Out Courantier in't Legher van syn Princelycke Ex-* | *cellentie* | *woonende op de Nieu-zyds achter Borchwal* | *in de Silvere Kan* | *by de Brouwerie* | *van den Hoy-Bergh* | *den* 27 *Augustus* | *Anno* 1624. | 4to, 1 l. 27680

Good news ... from Brazil to the Directors of the West-India Company.

GOEDEL (C.) Sklaverei und Emancipation der schwarzen Rasse in den Vereinigten Staaten von Nordamerika. ... von C. Goedel. ... *Zurich: Schabelitz'sche Buchhandlung (Cäsar Schmidt).* 1866. 8vo, 2 l., pp. 149. B., BA., H. 27681

GOELLM (J. v.) D. D. Dissertatio Medico-Botanica, sistens Specifica Canadensium, qvæ, consensu ampliss. Facult. Medicæ in Regia Academia Upsaliensi ... submittit Johannes von Goellm Vestro-Gothus R. A. S. adscriptus in Auditorio Carolino Majori D. *Anno* MDCCLXVI. 4to, pp. (iii), 28. P. 27682

[GOENS (R. M. van).] Politiek Vertoog over het waar Systema van Amsterdam met relatie tot de algemeene belangen der Republiek, benevens consideratien over den tegenwoord. oorlog, en het voorgevallene in 1777–80, mitsg. Deductie over de geheime onderhandelingen tusschen d. Pensionaris van Berkel en de Engelsche Colonien in Amerika, en het tractaat met dezelve gesloten te Aken 4 Sept. 1778. [*Utrecht.*] 1781. Folio, pp. 151. 27683

This political discussion relates to the secret negotiations between the Pensionary v. Berkel and the English colonies, and the treaty at Aix-La-Chapelle in 1778. "Extremely scarce, being printed privately at the author's expense, and only a very small number of copies. A counterfeit edition in 8vo, published against the will of the author, appeared in the same year. It strongly condemns the help indirectly granted by Amsterdam to the Americans."—F. MULLER. The peculiar views of this writer caused much controversy, and many pamphlets exist which relate partly to the aid rendered the Americans from Amsterdam. The autobiography (Eigen levensbeschryving) edited by H. W. T. Tydeman, and another biography by B. Ten Brink, will throw light on the subject.

GOEPP (C.) The National Club on the Reconstruction of the Union, February 4, 1864. By Charles Goepp. *New York: G. B. Teubner.* 1864. 8vo, pp. 16. H. 27684

GŒRTZ (*Comte* J. de). Mémoire, ou Précis Historique sur la Neutralité armée et son origine, suivi de pièces justificatives. *Basle.* 1801. 12mo, pp. 127. S. 27685

Included in Warden's "Bib. Am. Sept."

GOES (D. de). Chroni | ca do felicissimo rei dom Ema | nvel, composta per Damiani de | Goes, dividida em quatro partes, | das quaes esta he ha primeira. | ¶ Foi vista, & approuada per ho R. P. F. Emanuel da veiga examinador dos liuros. | ¶ *Em Lisboa em casa de Francisco correa, impressor do Serenissi* | *mo, Cardeal Infante, ahos xvii dias do mes de Julho de* 1566. ... *Com privilegio Real.* Folio, Title, 107 l., Tabla, 2 l. Segunda parte. Title, 75 l., Tabla, 2 l. Terceira parte. Title, 138 l., Tabla and Errata, 3 l. Quarta parte. Title, 112 l., Tabla and Errata, 3 l. 28686

The four parts form one volume. The work includes the voyage of Contreal. There are several reprints, in which Chaps. 23–27 of the third part have been altered and mutilated by order of the Government.

GOES. Chronica do felicissimo rei D. Manuel de gloriosa memoria. A qual por mandado de serenissimo principe o infante D. Henrique seu filho, o Cardeal de Portugal do titulo dos Sanctos quatro coroados, Damião de Goes collegia e compoz de novo. *Lisboa p. Ant. Alvarez.* 1619. Folio, pp. viii, 609. + *Lisboa: M. Manescal da Costa.* 1749. Sm. folio, 4 l., pp. 609. B. + *Coimbra na off. da Univ.* 1790. 2 vols., 4to. 27687

Chap. LXVI. has voyage of the Contreals.

GOES. Fides, Reli- | gio, Moresqve Aethi- | opvm svb Imperio Pre- | ciosi Ioannis (quem vulgò Presbyterum Ioan- | nem vocant) degentium, vnà cum enarratione | confoederationis ac amicitiæ inter ipsos Aethiopium Imperatores, & Re- | ges Lusitaniæ initæ, Damiano à Goes Equite Lu | sitano autore ac | interprete. | ... *Parisiis.* | *Apud Christianum Wechelum sub scuto Basi* | *liensi, in vico Iacobæo: & sub Pegaso in vice* | *Bellouacensi.* M. D. XLI. | 8vo, Title and 95 pp. 27688

See page 8.

GOES. Hispania | Damiani a Goes, | Eqvitis Lvsitani | *Lovanii* | *Excudebat Rutgerus Rescius Anno* | M. D. XLII. | 4to, 30 l.

"This Opuscule, addressed to Petrus Nannius, Latin Professor at Louvain, was intended to correct Münster's account of Spain. On fol. 19, verso, are brief notices of Cortes and Pizarro, and of American products on fols. 29 and 30. It appeared again, much amended and somewhat enlarged, with 'De Rebus Oceanicis,' of Peter Martyr, at Cologne, 1574."—J. C. BREVOORT.

GOES. Damiani | a Goes Eqvitis Lv | sitani Aliqvot Opvscvla. | Fides, Religio, moresq; Aethiopum. | ... [Colophon:] *Lovanii* | ¶ *Ex officina Rutgeri Rescij, Anno* 1544. *Mensi Decemb.* 4to, pp. 134. 27690

See the verso of the sixth leaf. The first edition, which I have not seen, is Lovanii, 1540, 4to, and is extremely rare.

GOES. De Rebus Hispanicis, Lvsitanicis, Aragonicis, Indicis et Æthiopicis Damiani à Goes, Hieronymi Pauli, Hier. Blanci, Iacobi Tevij opera. *Coloniæ Agrippinæ: In officina Birckmannica.* 1602. 8vo, 12 l., pp. 442. 27691

Portrait of Damianus a Goes on page 7.

GOETHE (Louise). Les Esclaves; étude de mœurs contemporaines; précédé d'une lettre de M. Victor Hugo. *Paris: Levy frères.* 1862. 12mo, pp. 360. B., BA. 27692

GOFF (A. W.) Lecture ... delivered at the Capitol. [n. p. n. d.] 8vo, pp. 20. B. 27693

On the Resources of the United States. Also: Oration on General George Washington ... in ... Philadelphia. *New York.* 1855. 8vo, pp. 16. B.

GOFFE (J.) ... Sermon ... at Holden, Mass., September 4th, 1816. By Joseph Goffe. ... *Worcester: Printed by William Manning.* [1816.] 8vo, pp. 23. BA., H., W. 27694

GOFFE. Result of an Ecclesiastical Council ... at Princeton, Mass., March 7, 1817, and the Protest of the Minority; with Remarks, Notes, and Observations. By Joseph Goffe. *Worcester.* 1817. pp. 24. BA., H., W. 27695

Also: Review of Dr. Bancroft's Vindication of the "Result," &c. *Worcester.* 1817. 8vo, pp. 44. BA., W.

GOFFE (W.) *See* Hough (F. B.), Philagathus, *and* Stiles (E.)

GOFFELMAN (C. A.) Reise zwischen Süd- und Nord-Amerika. *Rostock.* 1834. 8vo. 27696

GOGGIN. ... Remarks of Mr. Goggin, of Virginia, in the House of Representatives, December 30, 1847, and January 6 & 7, 1848, on the Joint Resolution for the Transportation of the Great Northern and Southern Mail. [n. p. n. d.] 8vo, pp. 18. H. 27697

GOGGIN. Speech of William L. Goggin, of Virginia, on the Veto Power. ... July 21, 1848. [n. p. n. d.] 8vo, pp. 16. H.

GOGGIN. Speech of Hon. W. L. Goggin, of Virginia, in Favor of Uniform Postal Charges ... February 21, 1849. *Washington: "Globe Office."* 1849. 8vo, pp. 13. H. 27699

GOGGIN. Speech of Mr. Goggin, of Virginia, on the War with Mexico. Delivered in the House of Representatives, February 1, 1848. [*Washington.*] [1848.] 8vo, pp. 16. B., H.

GOIN (J. W.) An Apprentice System for the United States Merchant Service. ... By John W. Goin. *New-York: J. P. Wright.* 1855. 12mo, pp. 36. H., S. 27701

GOING (J.) A Discourse delivered at Worcester, December 11, 1825, the Sabbath after the Execution of Horace Carter, ... By Jonathan Going. *Worcester.* [1825.] 8vo, pp. 22. H., W.

[GOING.] Outline of a Plan for establishing a Baptist Literary and Theological Institution in a Central Situation in New-England. ... *Worcester: Printed by William Manning.* 1819. 8vo, pp. 16. BA. 27703

Also: Discourse at Belchertown, Mass., June 24, 1816. *Worcester.* 8vo.

GOLD (Thomas R.) To the People of the County of Oneida. ... 1800. Sm. 4to, pp. 28. B., N., S. 27704

Respecting the location of the Court-house. Also: Address ... Berkshire Association for the Promotion of Agriculture and Manufactures, October 2, 1817. *Pittsfield.* [n. d.] 8vo, pp. 32. B., BA., H. — Address ... Berkshire Agricultural Society, October 3, 1816; ... 8vo, pp. 22, (2). B., N. — Address ... before the Agricultural Society for the County of Oneida, at Whitestown, October 18, 1820. *Utica.* 1820. N.

Gold. Report, No. 31. House of Representatives. Gold Panic Investigation. *Washington.* 1871. 8vo, pp. 484. W.

Gold. American Gold Quotations, 1862–66, and Members of the New York Gold Exchange, Stock Exchange, Open Board, and Petroleum Board of Brokers. *New York.* 1866. 18mo, pp. 36. 27706

Gold and Silver Mining in Sonora, Mexico. ... *Cincinnati: Wrightson & Co.* 1867. 8vo, pp. 16. H. 27707

Gold. Highest and Lowest Prices of Gold for Four Years. *New York.* 18mo. 27708

Gold Fields. Notes on the Distribution of Gold throughout the World, including Australia, California, and Russia. *London.* 1853. 8vo. 27709

The Golden Age, or Future Glory of America discovered by an Angel to Caledon in Visions. [n. p.] 1785. 8vo. 27701

The Golden Fleece. *See* [Vaughan (W.)]

Golden Hills News: June 3, 1854. *San Francisco.* 27711

In Chinese; for the Celestials in California.

GOLDER (J.) Life of the Honourable William Tilghman, Late Chief Justice of the State of Pennsylvania. Compiled from the Eulogies of Two distinguished Members of the Philadelphia Bar, who delivered them in commemoration of his Virtues. By John Golder, Esq. *Philadelphia: Printed for the Author.* 1829. 8vo, pp. 148. Portrait. C. 27712

Also: The American Teacher's Lessons; being ... Select Speeches ... from the most eminent American Authors. *Philadelphia.* 1827. 8vo.

GOLDING (W.) Servants on | Horse-Back: | Or, | A Free-People bestrided in their per- | sons, and Liberties, by worthlesse men: | Being | A Representation of the dejected state | of the Inhabitants of Summer Islands. | Containing | Short Illustrations upon a Petition pre- | sented to the High Court of Parliament | for Redresse. | Published by Will. Golding Master of Arts, and | Teacher to the Congregation in that Island. | [*London:*] *Printed in the Yeare*, 1648. | 4to, pp. (4), 24). 27713

This writer complains bitterly of the Governor's tyranny manifested towards himself and "other poor plantours." Priced by Lilly at £6 6s.

GOLDMANN (Fr.) Briefe aus Wisconsin in Nord-Amerika. *Leipzig.* 1849. 8vo. 27714

GOLDSBOROUGH (C. W.) The United States Naval Chronicle. By Charles W. Goldsborough. *Washington City: James Wilson.* 1824. 8vo, pp. 395, Index, xii, Errata, 11 lines. B., BA., C., H.

All published; exhibits a very interesting historical view of Naval affairs during the Revolution. *See* "N. Am. Rev.," XXI. I. — Also: Original and Correct List of the United States Navy, contains a list of the Ships in Commission and their respective Force, List of Officers, etc. 1800. 18mo. — To the Public. 1813. 8vo.

GOLDSBOROUGH (L. M.) A Reply by L. M. Goldsborough to an Attack made upon the Navy of the United States by Samuel Coues ... *Portsmouth: C. W. Brewster.* 1845. 8vo, pp. 23. H. 27716

GOLDSBOROUGH (W. W.) The Maryland Line in the Confederate States Army. By W. W. Goldsborough. *Baltimore: Kelly, Piet & Co.* 1869. 12mo, pp. 357. 9 Portraits. B., C.

[GOLDSMITH (J.)] The Present State of the British Empire in Europe, Asia, Africa, and America; containing a Concise Account of our possessions in every part of the Globe. ... *London: Griffin & Co.* M DCC LXVII. 8vo, pp. (8), 486. 5 Maps, 1 Plate. C. 27718

140 pages are devoted to America. *See* "M. Rev.," XXXIX. 405; *also* [Smollett (T.)]

GOLDSMITH (L.) An Exposition of the Conduct of France towards America, illustrated by Cases decided in the Council of Prizes in Paris. By Lewis Goldsmith. *London: J. M. Richardson.* 1810. 8vo, pp. iv, 133. B. + Second Edition. *London.* 1810. 8vo. + Second Edition. *New-York.* 1810. 8vo, pp. 99. B., H. + Third Edition. *London.* 1810. 8vo, pp. iv, 133. BA. 27719

The author was a German Jew.

GOLDSMITH (O.) The Rising Village, with other Poems. By Oliver Goldsmith, a Descendant of the Author of "The Deserted Village." *Saint John, (N. B.): John M'Millan.* ... MDCCCXXXIV. 18mo, pp. 144. 27720

GOLDSMITH (Z.) Three Lectures delivered at Southold, L. I., February, 1826. By Z. Goldsmith. *New York.* 1826. 8vo, pp. 40. 27721

GOLDSON (William). Observations on the Passage between the Atlantic and Pacific Oceans, in two Memoirs of the Straits of Anian, and the Discoveries of De Fonte. Elucidated by a New and Original Map. To which is prefixed an Historical Abridgement of Discoveries in the North of America. By William Goldson. *Portsmouth: W. Mowbray.* M,DCC,XCIII. 4to, pp. xii, 162. Map. 27722

"The large 'Chart on Mercator's projection exhibiting the Tracks of Maldonado in 1598 and De Fonte in 1640, compared with the modern discoveries,' is very curious, considering it was made after much study in 1793. It shows that geographical lies are difficult to kill permanently dead as any others. Both the book and the map have and will have an increasing interest to those exploring the north-west coasts of North America. The bibliographical research of this author is as commendable as his judgment is untrustworthy."—STEVENS. *See also* "M. Rev.," XVI. 18.

GOLOVIN (I.) Stars and Stripes; or, American Impressions. By Ivan Golovin. *London: W. Freeman.* 1856. 12mo, pp. 312.

[GOMARA (Francisco Lopez de).] | ¶ Con priuilegio de su Alteza. Por diez años. | [Large woodcut with Arms of the Emperor, nearly filling the page.] ¶ Primera y segunda parte dela his- | toria general de las Indias con todo el descubrimiento y cosas nota | bles que han acaecido dende que se ganaron ata [*sic*] et año de 1551. Con la cõquista de | Mexico Y de la nueua España. *En Caragoça.* 1553. | *A costa de Miguel Capila mercader de libros vezino de Caragoça.* | Part I., folio, 122 l., Woodcut Map of the World on 2 l., not counted. Dedicated to the Emperor. [Followed by] | ¶ La conquista de Mexico. | 1552. | Con licencia y preuilegio del Principe nuestro señor. | [Under a cut with arms of Cortez.] [Colophon:] ¶ *Fue impressa la presente* | *istoria de Indias y conquista de Mexico en* | *casa de Agustin Millan. Y acabose vis* | *pera de Nauidad Año de Mil y* | *quinientos y cinquenta y dos* | [1552] *en la muy noble y leal Ciu-* | *dad de Caragoça.* | ·.· | 140 l., the last not numbered, contains "Priuilegio," on recto and colophon on verso. J.C.B., J.C.BT. 27724

The first edition, of extreme rarity, and a work of the highest importance, concerning which see Ternaux, No. 61, Ticknor's "Spanish Literature," Vol. I., Prescott's "Conquest of Mexico," Vol. I., Robertson's "History," and Muñoz' "New World."

"Affords us the most authentic views of the primitive condition of the Indians before tyranny had crushed, or civilization had corrupted them."—T. W. FIELD. The work is indispensable to the student of Spanish affairs in America after the conquest, notwithstanding the charges made by Bernal Diaz against Gomara of occasional inaccuracy. The dedication to Charles V. begins with these remarkable words: "The greatest event which has happened since the creation of the world (leaving aside the incarnation and death of Him who created it) is the discovery of the Indies." Gomara prefixes a curious address to intending translators, warning them to be accurate and to measure the full significance of the pregnant Spanish phrases, also to pay special attention to proper names. He further declares that he is writing the book in Latin, and much fuller, so that the translators may take no trouble to put it into that language. His Latin version has never appeared. Antonio de Leon, p. 70, says: "It is a free history (historia libre), and was ordered by an ancient 'Cedula' of the Council of the Indies." He adds that Frisius made use of the geographical part in his edition of the Cosmography of Apianus. Reprinted by Barcia and Vedia.

[GOMARA.] Hispania Victrix. [Large woodcut of the King's Arms, nearly filling the page.] Primera y segunda par | te de la historia general de las Indias cõ todo el descu | brimiento, y cosas notables que han acaescido dende que se ganaron hasta el año | de 1551. Con la conquista de Mexico, y de la nueua España. | *En Medina del Campo, por Guillermo de Millis.* 1553. Folio, 122 l. [Followed by] Conquista de Mexico. [Woodcut of King's Arms, varied, filling half the page.] Segunda parte de la | Chronica general delas Indias, que trata de | la conquista de Mexico. Nueuamen- | te y con licencia impressa. | *Año de* 1553. | [Colophon:] *Fue impressa la presente historia de Indias* | *y conquista de Mexico en Medina del Campo, en casa de Gui-* | *llermo de Millis. Acabose a veynte dias del mes de Ago-* | *sto. Año de mil y quinientos y cinquenta y tres.* 139 l. J.C.BT. 27725

Although the title and the collation of this and our No. 27724, are almost identical, it is absolutely another edition, as a comparison will show.

[GOMARA.] Conquista de Mexico. Segvnda parte de la Chronica general de las Indias Occidentales, su Historia, Geografia, Temperamento, Producciones, Usos, y Costumbres de los Naturales de ellas. *Madrid.* 1553. Folio. 27726

Called in by a Decree of the Council of the Indies, and long considered as a prohibited book, which may account for its mutilation. Title and note from a catalogue of Puttick & Simpson's, 1860. We have not seen this edition, and are at a loss to understand why it should be called in by a Decree of the Council, as the original edition bears the usual privileges. Perhaps the arms of Cortez in the second part of our No. 27724 caused some offence, for in our No. 27725 they are replaced by the Royal arms. Meusel III. 227, says that Gomara was prohibited by the Council of the Indies, but gives no authority, while Antonio states the contrary.

[GOMARA.] Con priuilegio del Principe nuestro Señor por diez años. | [Arms of Spain, nearly filling the page.] La historia general de las In | dias y nueuo mundo, con mas la conquista del Pe | ru y de Mexico agora nueuamente añadida y emendada por el mismo autor, con vna ta-|bla muy complida de los capitulos, y muchas figuras que en otras impressiones no llena. *Vendeu se en Çaragoça en casa de Miguel de Capila mercador de libros.* 1554. Folio, 4 l., Text, 99 l., Colophon 1 l. J.C.B. 27727

[GOMARA.] Con priuilegio del Principe nuestro Señor.| [Arms of Spain, nearly filling the page.] Cronica de la nueua españa|con la conquista de Mexico, y otras notables : hechas| por el valoroso Hernando Cortes, Marques del Valle, Capitan| de sa Magestad en aquellas partes.|Con mucha diligencia corregida, y añadida por el mesmo autor.|*En Caragoça.* 1554. Folio, 113 l. Gothic letter. 27728

[GOMARA.] La Historia ge|neral de las In-|dias, y todo lo acaescido enellas|dende què se ganaron|hasta agora.|Y|La conquista de Mexico|y dela nueua España.| *En Anuers por Martin Nucio.*|*Con preuilegio Imperial.*|M.D.LIIII.| Sm. 8vo, 300 leaves. J.C.BT., P. 27729

GOMARA. La Historia|general delas Indias,|con todos los descubrimientos, y cosas nota|bles que han acaesido enellas, dende|que se ganaron hasta agora, escri|ta por Francisco Lopez| de Gomara, clerigo.| Añadiose de nueuo la descripcion y traça de las Indias,|con vna tabla alphabetica de las Prouincias, Islas,| Puereos, [*sic*] Ciudades, y nombres de conquistadores|y varones principales que alla han passado. *En Anvers.*|*En casa de Iuan Steelsio.*|*Año* M.D.LIIII. Sm. 8vo, pp. (32), Text, 287 l. + *En Anvers, Iuan Bellero.* 1554. Sm. 8vo, pp. (32), Text, 287 l. C.

These editions are alike, except in the imprint. The title calls for a "traça," but the map is not always present. Uricochea, Mapotheca Colombiana, *Londres*, 1860, p. 2, speaks of this map as "Very well engraved and extremely exact as compared with cotemporary ones." It is a woodcut 6x5 inches, and is one of the first maps of America of Spanish origin. This map is only found in the Bellero editions, and also in his edition of Levinus Appollonius of 1565 and 1567.

GOMARA. Historia de|Mexico, con el descv-|brimiento dela nueva España, conquistada|por el muy illustre y valeroso Principe| don Fernando Cortes, Marques|del Valle, Escrita por Fran-| cisco Lopez de Go-|mara, clerigo.| Añadiose de la nueuo descripcion y traça de todas las Indias,|con vna Tabla Alphabetica de las materias, y haza-|ñas memorables enella contenidas.| ¶ *En Anvers,*|*Por Iuan Bellero, al Salmon.* 1554.|*Con priuilegio.*| [Colophon:] ¶ *Impresso en Anuers por Juan*|*Lacio.* 1554. 8vo, 349 l., Tabla, 11 l. C. + *En Anvers,*|*En casa de Iuan Steelsio,* 1554.| 8vo, 349 l., Tabla, 11 l. P. 27731

Forms the Second Part of the History of the Indies. *See* a note in Trömel's "Bibl. Américaine, No. 17. The only difference in these two editions consists in the *imprint*.

[GOMARA.] La segunda par|te dela histo-|ria general delas Indias.|que contiene|La conquista de Mexico,|y dela nueua España.| *En Anuers por Martin Nucio.*|*Con priuilegio Imperial.*| M.D.LIIII.| 12mo, 340 leaves. J.C.BT., C. 27732

GOMARA. Conquista de Mejico. Historia general de las Indias 1º y 2a parte. *Madrid.* 1852. C. 27733

Forms Vol. LI. of "Bibl. de Autores Espagnoles." The "Chronica" also forms part of Barcia's "Historiadores Primitivos."

GOMARA. Historia|di Mexico,|et|qvando si discoperse|la Nvova Hispagna, conqvi|stata per l'illvstriss. et|valoroso Principe|Don Ferdinando Cortes,|Marchese del Valle. ... Tradotta nel|volgare Italiano per|Avgvstino de Cravaliz. *In Roma, Appresso Valerio & Luigi Dorico fratelli.* M.D.LV. Sm. 4to, 8 l., Text, 240 l. J.C.B., BA., H. 27734

For some reason this title-page was cancelled, and the work was put forth with the following title :

GOMARA. Historia del|illvstriss. et valorosiss.|capitano Don Ferdinando Cortes marchese della Valle,|et qvando discoperse, et acqvisto|la Nvova Hispagna.|Scritta per Francesco Lopes de Gomara,|in lingua Spagnuola, & hora tradotta nella Italiana per Avgvstino de Cravaliz.| ... *Roma: Valerio, & Luigi Dorici fratelli.* MDLVI. 4to, 8 l., Text, 240 l. H. 27735

GOMARA. La Historia|Generale delle Indie|Occídentalí, con tutti lí díscopri-|mentí, & cose notabílí, che|ín esse sonno successe,|da che si acquí-|storno fino|a hora.|Scritta per Francesco Lopez|de Gomara ín língua Spagnuola,|&|Tradotta nel volgare| Italíano per|Avgvstino de Cravaliz.|Co'l Príuílegío del sommo Pontefice, & della|maesta Cesarea per díece anní : si come si|puo uedere nella príma parte della|Historía del Peru, gía da noí| Stampata.|*In Roma*|*Per Valerío, & Luigí Doríci, l'anno*|MDLVI.| 4to, 2 l., Text, 211 leaves, and one leaf with woodcut bookmark. J.C.BT. 27736

This translation of the first part of Gomara is dedicated to Cosmo de Medici.

GOMARA. La Seconda Parte|delle Historie generali dell' India,|Con tutte le cose notabili|accadute in esse dal principio fin' à questo|giorno,|& nuouamente tradotte|di Spagnuolo in Italiano.|Nelle quali, oltre|all' imprese del Colombo|et di Magalanes, e si tratta|particolarmente della presa del Re Atabalippa,|delle Perle, dell'oro, delle spetierie, ritro-|uate alle Malucche, & delle gue-|rre ciuili tra|gli Spagnuoli.| Con privilegio.

In Venetia. M.D.LVII.|*Appresso Andrea Arrivabene.* Sm. 8vo, 18 l., Text, 324 l. + [*Ibid:*] *Appresso Giordano Ziletti.* 1564. + 1565, *et al.* J.C.BT. 27737

These two imprints are exactly alike. The *Prima Parte*, published in 1556, contains Cieza di Leone. We cannot find Arrivabene's edition of the third part, but Ziletti's (with 32 l., 402 l.) is quoted by Græsse and Leclerc. Arrivabene used Lucio Mauro's version, but Ziletti has it only in the second and third parts, in which last his name appears as translator. Ziletti's Cieza, and the three parts of the other four publishers, are from the version of Cravaliz, who, according to Pinelo, was a native of St. Sebastian.

GOMARA. Historia|delle Nvove Indie|Occidentali,|con tvtti i discoprimenti,|& cose notabili, auuenute dopo l'acquisto di esse.| Parte seconda.|Composta da Francesco Lopez di|Gomara in lingua Spagnuola,|Tradotta nella Italiana da Agostino di Cravaliz.| *In Venetia,*|*Per Francesco Lorenzini da Turino,*|MDLX. 8vo, 10 l., Text, 306 l. J.C.BT. 27738

This volume is called *Parte Seconda*, because it formed the second volume of the series of Italian translations in which Cieça's chronicle of Peru was the first, and Gomara's Mexico the third. It contains the same matter as the Spanish volume printed by Nucio in 1554.

GOMARA. Historia di Don Fernando Cortes, Marchese della Valle, Capitano Valorosissimo, con le sve maravigliose prodezze nel tempo, che discoprì, & acquistò la nuoua Spagna. Composta da Francesco Lopez di Gomara in Lingua Spagnuola. Tradotta nella Italiana da Agostino di Cravaliz. ... *In Venetia, Per Francesco Lorenzini da Turino.* MDLX. 11 l., Text, 348 l. 27739

See Leclerc's Catalogue, Nos. 1627–9; *also*, Cieça, in our Vol. IV., No. 13053, in which for Crauliz read Craualiz.

GOMARA. Historia,|delle nvove Indie|occidentali,|con tvtti i discoprimenti & cose notabili, auuenute do-|po l'acquisto di esse.|Parte seconda. Composta da Francesco Lopez|di Gomara in lingua Spagnuola, & Tradotta|nell' Italiana per Agostino di Craualiz. *In Venetia per Giouanni Bonadio.* 1564. 8vo, 8 l., Text, 312 l. 27740

GOMARA. Historia, di Don Ferdinando|Cortes, Marchese della Valle, Capitano valorosissimo.|Parte Terza.|Con le sve maravigliose|prodezze nel tempo, che discoprì, & ac-|quistò la Nuoua Spagna. ... Tradotta ... da Ag. di Cravaliz. *Venetia per G. Bonadio* 1564. 8vo, 8 l., Text, 355 l. + *Venezia.* 1570. 8vo. J.C.BT. 27741

GOMARA. Historia de Messico con il discoprimento della Nuova Spagna. *Venetia.* 1573. Sm. 8vo, 404 leaves, and Map.

Forms the third part of Ziletti's edition.

GOMARA. Historia|delle nvove|Indie Occidentali.|Con tutti discoprimenti|& cose notabili auuenute, dopò|l'acquisto di esse.| Parte seconda.|Composta da Francesco Lopez di|Gomara in lingua Spagnuola,|Tradotta nella Italiana per Agostino di Craualiz.|*In Venetia, Appresso Camillo Franceschini.* 1576. 8vo.

GOMARA. Historia di|Don Ferdinando|Cortes, marchese| della Valle, Capitano Valorosissimo,|Con le sue marauigliose prodezze, nel tempo che discopri,|& acquistò la nuoua Spagna.| Parte terza.|Composta da Francesco Lopez di|Gomara in lingua Spagnuola.|Tradotta nella Italiana per Agostino di Craualiz.| *In Venetia, Appresso Camillo Franceschini.* 1576. 8vo, 8 l., Text, 343 l. J.C.BT. 27744

[GOMARA.] Historia|dell' Indie|Occidentali,|ouero|Conqvista|della Provincia|d'Ivcatan,|Della marauigliosa Città di Messico, & d'altre|Prouincie ad essa sottoposte.|Nellaquale particolarmente si tratta dello scoprimento|della nuoua Spagna, dell'usanze & costumi di quelli|Indiani; accrescimento della fede Christiana, & d'altre|cose degne di memorial.|Tradotta di Lingua Spagnuola, da Lucio Mauro.|Con la Tauola delle cose più notabili, & con Priuilegio.| *In Venetia, Appresso Barezzo Barezzi.* 1599.| Sm. 8vo, 6 l., 2 l. blank, Tavola, 26 l., Text, 402 l.

This appears to be the last of the Italian editions, of which, with the trifling variations we have indicated, make no less than eighteen in twenty years, showing how much interest was felt in Italy respecting the conquests by Cortez and Pizarro.

[GOMARA.] Histoire|Generalle|des Indes Occidentales|& Terres neuues, qui jusque à present|ont esté descouuertes.|Traduite en françois par M. Fumée; Sieur|de Marly le Chastel.| *Paris: Michel Sonnius.* 1569. 8vo, 6 l., Text, 258 l. [mispaged 252], Table, 19 l. + *Paris: Bernard Turrisan.* 1569. Sm. 8vo, 6 l., Text, 252 l., Table, 12 l. 27746

Both editions are alike, except in the imprint. Mr. Lenox reports an edition dated 1568. Also quoted by Stück, No. 3314.

[GOMARA.] Histoire|Generalle|des Indes Occiden-|tales et Terres Nevves,|qui iusques à present ont|esté descouuertes.| Traduite en françois par M. Fumée Sieur|de Marley le Chastel.| *A Paris.*|*Chez Michel Sonnius, rue sainct Iacques*|*à l'enseigne de l'Escu de Basle.*|M.D.LXXVII.|*Auec Priuilege dv Roy.*| 8vo, 6 l., Text, 355 l., Table, 29 l. + [*Ibid.*] M.D.LXXVIII. + [*Ibid.*] 1580. C. 27747

Ternaux, No. 169, quotes an edition, *Paris*, 1597; another, *Paris*, 1604.

GOMARA. Histoire|generalle|des Indes Occiden|tales, et terres|neuues, qui iusques à présent|ont esté descouuertes.|Augmentee en cette cinquiesme edition de la description de|la nouuelle Espagne, et de la grande ville de Me|xicque, autrement nommee,|Tenuctilan.|Composée en Espagnol par Fr. Lopez de Gomara et traduite en François par le S. de Genillé, Mart. Fumée. *Paris: Michel Sonnius.* MDLXXXIV. 8vo, 4 l., Text, 485 l., Table, 19 l. + [*Ibid.*] M.D.LXXXVII. + [*Ibid.*] 1605. C.

The last French version has the following title :

GOMARA. Histoire|Generalle|des Indes Occiden-|tales, et Terres|neuues, qui iusques à present|ont esté decouuertes.|Augmentee en ceste cinquiesme edition de la description de|la nouuelle Espagne, & de la grande ville de Me|xicque, autrement nommee,|Tenuctilan.|Composee en Espagnol par François Lopez de Go|mara, & traduite en François par le|S. de Genillé Mart. Fumée.|*A Paris.*|*Chez Michel Sonnius, ruë sainct Iaques à l'enseigne*|*de l'escu de Basle.*|1606.| 8vo, 4 l., Text, 485 l., Table, 19 l. 27749

This contains more than the edition of 1578, pp. 67–198 being additional.

GOMARA. Voyages et|Conqvêtes dv|Capitaine Ferdinand| Courtois, es Indes|Occidentales.|Histoire, traduite de langue Espagnole|par Guillaume le Breton, Niuernois.|*Paris: Abel l'Angelier.* 1588. 12mo, 8 l., Text, 416 l. J.C.B. 27750

This translation of the Second Part of Gomara is very rare.

GOMARA. The|Pleasant Historie of the|Conquest of the VVeast India,|now called new Spayne,|Atchieued by the worthy Prince|Hernando Cortes Marques of the valley of| Huaxatac, most delectable to Reade:|Translated out of the Spa-|nishe tongue, by T. N[icholas].|Anno 1578.|¶ *Imprinted at London by Henry Bynneman.* [n. d.] 4to, pp. (12), 405, Table, pp. 3. Gothic Letter. J.C.B., BA. 27751

[GOMARA.] The|Pleasant Historie of|the Conquest of the| West India, now called|new Spaine.|Atchieued by the most woorthie Prince|Hernando Cortes, Marques of the Valley of| Huaxacac, most delectable to reade.|Translated out of the Spanish tongue, by T. N. Anno. 1578.|*London:*|*Printed by Thomas Creede.*|1596.| 4to, pp. (12), 405, (6). Gothic letter. C., H. 27752

The "Epistle" is signed Thomas Nicholas. Lowndes erroneously calls this a translation of Bernal Diaz. It is the Second Part of Gomara's "Chronica de Nueva Espana," and is the only portion of the works of the "Father of American history"

in English. *See* Beloe's "Anecdotes," Vol. VI., p. 11. The Laudatory Verses are by Stephen Gosson, author of "The School of Abuse." Although the two English editions have the same number of pages, they differ throughout.

GOMARA. Historia de la conquista de Hernando Cortés, escrita en español por Fr. Lopez de Gomara, traducida al mexicano y aprobada por verdadera por D. Juan Bautista de San Anton Muñon Chimalpain Quauhtlehuanitzin, India Mexicano. Publícala Carlos Maria de Bustamente. *México: Ontiveros.* 1826. 2 vols., 4to, pp. xiii, 315; (2), Title, pp. 187, (1). "Para immortalizar el valor heróico de los Indios Cascanes por causa de su libertad" ... 1827. pp. 39, Table, pp. (4). 27753

"The statement on the title of 'translated by Chimalpain' is merely parenthetical. Bustamente, when he had in his hands the MS. from which he printed the book, supposed it to be an original work by Chimalplain, but afterwards discovered that this Mexican, who flourished at the beginning of the seventeenth century, had only rendered Gomara's book into his own tongue. It is not clear from what original Bustamente has published the above volumes; he does not appear to have seen the Mexican text, and there is nothing, except a few words in chapter 62, to show any connection between the Spanish publication of Bustamente and the work of Chimalpain. As for the text it seems rather like a modern improvement of Gomara, than like a fresh translation from the Mexican version. However this may be, the editor's notes are copious and valuable. It should be stated, indeed, that a MS. professing to contain the Mexican text of Chimalpain's history, but according to the description, differing in its character from that of Gomara, was sold at the Abbé Fischer's sale in 1869." —QUARITCH. *See also* Brunet's "Manuel" and Trömel's "Bibl. Américaine." For further particulars, concerning Gomara, *see* Brydges' "Censura Literaria," III. 359, 368; Beloe's "Anecdotes," VI. 121; Clarke's "Progress of Maritime Discovery," p. 186.

GOMBERVILLE. Relation de la Rivière. *See* Rogers (W.)

GOMES DE BRITO (Bernardo). Historia tragico-maritima, em que se escrevem chronologicamente os naufragios que tiveraõ as náos de Portugal depois que se poz em exercicio à navegaçaõ da India. *Lisboa na. off. da Congregação do Oratorio.* 1735–36. 2 vols., 4to, pp. xvi, 479; xvi, 538. A., BA. 27754

Vol. II. includes: Relaçao do naufragio que passon Jorge de Albuquerque Coelho, vindo do Brasil; por Bento Teixeira Pinto. 1565. *See* "Silva Dic. Bib. Port.," I. 377.

GOMEZ DE AVELLANEDA (G.) Dolores. Novela historica. *Mexico.* 1851. 12mo. 27755

GOMEZ DE AVELLANEDA. Guatimozin, último Emperador de Méjico. Novela histórica por la Senorita Gomez de Avellaneda. *Méjico: Imprenta de Juan R. Navarro.* 1853. Folio, pp. 178. 27756

GOMEZ DE AVELLANEDA. Viage à la Havana por la Condesa de Merlin, precedido de una biografia de esta ilustre Cubana.

Por la Señorita Doña Gertrudis Gomez de Avellaneda. *Madrid.* 1844. Sm. 8vo. 27757

Also: Poesias. *Mejico.* 1852. 4to.

GOMEZ (C.) Defensa legal que el Ciudadano Coronel Cirilo Gomez y Anaya hizo por el Exmo. Señor General de Division D. Pedro Celestino Negrete, en el conseyo de guerra que conoció en la causa que se le formó sobre atribuírsele el crimen de infidencia. *Mexico.* 1828. 12mo, pp. 53. 27758

GOMEZ (D.) Discursos sobre los Comercios de las dos Indias, donde se tratan materias importantes de Estado, y Guerra. Autor Duarte Gomez ... Natural de Lisboa. *Año de* MDCXXII. 4to.

Concerning this *see* Ternaux's "Bibl.," No. 442. Sold at Puttick's, 1860, for 5s.

GOMEZ (J.) Biografia d. D. José M. Justo Gomez de la Cortina Conte de la Cortina, escrita por una Comision de la Sociedad Mexicana de geografia y estadistica. *Mexico.* 1860. 4to, pp. 19. Portrait. 27760

GOMEZ (J.) Vida de la venerable madre Antonio de San Jacinto, monja professa del velo negro de el conv. de Santa Clara de Jesus de la ciudad de Santiago de Queretaro. *Mexico: Calderon.* 1689. 4to, 10 l., Text, 62 l. 27761

GOMEZ DE CERVANTES (Nic.) Sermones Varios. *Sevilla.* 1674. Sm. 4to. 27762

"L'auteur de ces sermons était Mexicain; le livre contient un sermon 'de la aparicion de la milagrosa imagen de Guadelupe de Mexico.'" —ANDRADE.

GOMEZ DE LA PARRA (J.) Fundacion y primero siglo del ... convento de S. Joseph de Religiosas Carmelitas Descalzas de la ciudad de la Puebla de los Angeles, que se fundo en la nueva España, el primero que se fundo en la America Septemtrional en 27. de Diziembre de 1604. Por Jose Gomez de la Parra, ... *Puebla de los Angeles.* 1732. Folio, pp. (18), 603, (8). 27763

GOMEZ DE LA PARRA. Panegyrico funeral de la vida en la muerte de el Señ. Man. Fern. de S. Cruz. *Puebla de los Angeles.* 1699. 4to, 82 l. 27764

GOMEZ DE MORA (Juan). Relacion de Juramenso que hizieron los Reinos de Castilla, i Leon al Principe de las Españas i Nuevo Mondo. *Madrid.* 1632. 4to. 27765

GOMEZ (J. B.) El Coloniaje. Dedica a la H. Municipalidad de Tacna este Pequeno Trabajo, con Apéndice. *Tacna.* 1861. 4to. 27766

An abridged history, the only known work published at Tacna, an important town of Southern Peru.

GOMEZ (J. M.) Oratio Funebris Caroli III. Hispaniarum et Indiarum Regis, habita Guadalaxaræ, etc., 1789. *Mexico.* 1789. Folio. 27767

GOMEZ (M. M.) Defensa Guadalupana, contra la disertacion de J. B. Muñoz. *Méjico.* 1819. 4to. 27768

GOMEZ (Manuel). Biografia del Gral. de Division C. Ignacio Zaragoza. *Mexico.* 1862. 4to, pp. 50. Portrait. 27769

GOMEZ PEDRAZA (M.) Manifiesto que Manuel Gomez Pedraza, ciudadano de Mejico, dedica a sus compatriotas; o sea, una reseña de su vida publica. *Nueva-Orleans: B. Levy.* 1831. 16mo, 1 l., pp. 129. C. 27770

GOMEZ PARADA (Vicente). Segunda esposicion que dirige al Soberano Congreso. *Mexico.* 1841. 4to, pp. 18. 27771

GONÇALEZ DE CUETO (Damiano). Oratio Fvne-|bris Habita a Magistro Da-|miano Gonçalez de Cveto, eorvm,|qui ad Philosophiæ lauream ascendunt exa-|minatore, & in Apolliniea scientia denuo li-|centiando, in exequijs Religiosissimi|Patris Antonij Arias è Socie-|tate Iesu| ... |Sacræ Theologiæ Interpre-|tis, & Congregationis Annuntiatæ primarij, ac vigilentissimi Du-|cis, quas eadem congregatio cohonestauit, in Collegio Mexi-|cano eiusdem Societatis, decimo Kalendas Iulij.| Anni 1603 ...| ¶ *Mexici: Svperiorvm Permissv,*|*Apud Henricum Martinez* ...| 4to, 9 l. 27772

GONÇALEZ DE ESLAVA. Coloquios Espirituales y Sacramentales y Canciones divinas, recopiladas por Vello de Bustamente. *Mexico.* 1610. Sm. 4to. 27773

Excessively rare. This writer, the earliest poet of Mexico, is not mentioned by Ticknor, Salva, Antonio, Ternaux, Brunet, nor other bibliographers.

GONCALEZ MOLGUIN (Diego de). Libro primero del Vocabulario ... la lengua general del Peru. 1808. 4to.—Gramatica y lengua general del Peru. 1607. 4to, pp. 374, 332, 4 l., (1), 140. H. 27774

Gonçalez de Mendoça (Fr. Juan). Historia de las cosas mas notables, ritos y costvmbres del gran Reyno de la China, sabidas assi por los libros de los mesmos Chinos, como por relacion de Religiosos y otras personas que han estado en el dicho Reyno. ... por Fr. Juan Gonçalez de Mendoça de la orden de S. Agustin. Con vn Itinerario del nuevo Mundo. *En Roma, a costa de Bartholome Grassi.* 1585. 8vo, 16 l., pp. 440. 27775

"Ouvrage tiré du Chinois, et dans lequel parurent pour la première fois, en Europe, les caractères de cette langue. L'édition de Rome est rare."—Brunet. In order of publication, this is the first European book in which Chinese characters occur; but actually it is the second, as one of Ortelius' maps, engraved in 1584, but not published till 1590, bears two Chinese words in the native character. According to Nicholas Antonio, the above Itinerary of the New World (which occupies leaves 268–368) was written by F. Martin Ignacio, and was never published separately. Translations were made into Latin, French, Italian, German, and English. The Itinerary gives curious details concerning the Canaries, St. Domingo, Jamaica, Cuba, Porto Rico, and especially Mexico. Ortelius, in his Atlas, declared that he had received more information concerning America, from this Itinerary than from any other single book. We have not seen the German or Flemish versions referred to in our note to 27782.

Gonçalez de Mendoça. Historia | de las cosas | mas notables, Ritos | y costumbres del gran Reyno dela China, sa | bidas assi por los libros delos mesmos Chinas, | como por relacion de Religiosos, y otras | personas que han estado enel | dicho Reyno. | Hecha y ordenada por | el muy Reuerendo Padre Maestro Fray Iuan | Gonçalez de Mendoça ... Con vn Itinerario del Nueuo Mundo. | Con Privilegio. | *Impressa en Madrid, en casa de Querino Ge | rardo Flamenio. Año de* 1586. *A costa de Blas de Robles librero.* | 12mo, 12 l., Text, 368 l. (erroneously printed 268 l.), Tabla, 8 l. + *Madrid: Pedro Madrigal.* 1586. 8vo, pp. (24), 245, (24). + *Zaragoça, L. y D. Robles.* 1587. 8vo, pp. 556. + *Barcelona: Juan Pablo Mareschal.* 1588. 8vo. + *Medina del Campo, por Sanctiago del Canto.* 1595. Sm. 8vo. + *[Ibid.:] per los herederos de Benito Boyer.* 1595. 8vo. c. 27776

Gonçalez. Historia | de las cosas | mas notables, | ritos y costvmbres, | Del gran Reyno de la China, sabidas assi por los li- | bros de los mesmos Chinas, | como por relacion de | Religiosos y otras personas que an estado en el di- | cho Reyno. | Hecha y ordenada por el mvy r. p. | maestro Fr. Ioan Gonçalez de Mendoça de la Orden de S. Au- | gustin, y penitenciario Apostolico a quien la Magestad Ca- | tholica embio con su real carta y otras cosas para el Rey de a- | quel Reyno el año. 1580. | Con vn Itinerario del nueuo Mundo. || ¶ *En Anvers, | En casa de Pedro Bellero,* | 1596. | *Con Priuilegio.* | 8vo, pp. (24), 380, 1 l. + *Amberes.* 1598. 8vo. B., H. 27777

Gonçalez. Dell' historia della China ... tradotta nell' italiana, da Francesco Auanzo cittadino di Venetia. *Roma: B. Grassi.* 1586. 4to, 23 l., pp. 379. 27778

Gonçalez. Dell' Historia Della China, Dove è descrive il sito, e lo stato di quel gran Regno, e si tratta della religione, de i costumi, e della disposition de' suoi popoli, e d'altri luochi piu conosciuti del Mondo Nuovo, tradotta nell' Italiana, dal Magn. M. Francesco Auanzo, cittadino di Venetia. *In Venetia, Appresso Andrea Muschio.* 1586. 8vo, 15 l., pp. 462, 20 l. + *[Ibid.]* 1587. + *[Ibid.]* 1588. + *[Ibid.]* 1590. 12mo. + *Genova.* 1586. 4to. 27779

Gonçalez. Histoire | dv grand royavme de la | Chine, sitvé avx | Indes orientales, diuisée | en deux parties : | Contenant en la Première, la situation, antiquité, fertilité, re- | ligion, ceremonies, sacrifices; rois, magistrats, etc.: Et en la Seconde, trois voyages faits vers iceluy en l'an 1577. | 1579. & 1581. auec les singularitez plus remarquables y | veuës & entenduës: ensemble vn Itineraire du | nouueau monde, et le descouurement du | nouueau Mexique en l'an 1583 ... mise en françois ... par Luc de la Porte, Parisien. *Paris: Jeremie Perier.* 1588. 8vo, 12 l., Text, 323 l., 25 l. c. + *Paris: N. du Fossé.* 1589. 8vo, 11 l., pp. 419, (48). + *Paris.* 1600. + *[Genève:] Pour Jean Arnavd.* 1606. 8vo, 12 l., the last blank, pp. 419, (48). + *Rouen: Nicolas Angot.* 1614. 8vo, 8 l., pp. 388, 14 l., Descr. de la Chine, pp. 25. 27780

Gonçalez. Nova et succincta ... historia ... de amplissimo regno China. Translata a [Marco] Henningio. *Franckfurt: Sig. Feyrabend.* [1589.] Sm. 8vo. 27781

Stück, 2751, says that this is translated from the German and Italian versions. Under 927 he quotes a German version, *Frankfurt: J. Kellner,* 1589, translated from the Italian, and adds that it contains only the first part of the original work, the American portion being in the second part. Adelung, "Forts. zu Jöcher's Lexicon," mentions the German version, same place and date. Græsse quotes a Flemish edition. *Delft.* 1656. 12mo.

Gonçalez. Rerum morumque in regno Chinensi maximè notabilium historia ... ex hipan. P. J. G. de Mendoza, latinè transtulit Joachim Brullius. *Antuerpiæ: F. Frickaërt.* 1655. 4to. 27782

Gonçalez. The Historie of the | Great and Mightie Kingdome | of China, and the Situation | thereof: | Togither with the great riches, huge | citties, politike gouernment, and | rare inuentions in the same. | Translated out of Spanish by R. Parke. | *London: | Printed by I. Wolfe for Edward White, and are to be sold at the little North | doore of Paules, at the signe | of the Gun.* | 1588. | 8vo. 27783

Title from the following reprint. It is so rare that we have never seen it.

Gonçalez. The History of the Great and Mighty Kingdom of China and the Situation Thereof. Compiled by the Padre Juan Gonzales de Mendoza. ... Edited by Sir George T. Staunton. With an Introduction by R. H. Major. *London: Hakluyt Society.* M,DCCC,LIII–LIV. 2 vols., 8vo, pp. (6), lxxxiii, 172; 4, (6), 350. BA. 27784

Goncalez de Nagera (Alonzo). El Qvinto, y Sexto Pvnto de la Relacion del Desengaño de la guerra de Chile, facados de 14. de su declaracion, cuyos titulos han de ferlos que estan puestos al fin. Por el Maestre de Campo Alonzo Gonçalez de Nagera. *[Madrid.* 1647?] 4to, 16 l. 27785

Gongora. Glorias de Queretaro en la Foundacion de la Congregacion de Presbiteros Seculares de Maria Santissima de Guadalupe por Gongora. *Mexico.* 1803. 4to. Plates. c.

Gongara y Siguenza. Primavera Indiana, Poema sacro de N. S. de Guadaloupe. 1668. 8vo. 27787

One of a series of "miserable productions."—[Harrisse] "Bibl. Am. Vet.," 210.

[Gonneville (Binot Paulmier de).] Campagne du Navire L'Espoir de Honfleur 1503–1505. Relation authentique du voyage du Capitaine de Gonneville ès nouvelles terres des Indes, publiée intégralement pour la première fois avec une Introduction et des Éclaircissements par M. D'Avesac, Membre de L'Institut. *Paris: Challamel.* 1869. 8vo, pp. 115. 27788

From the "Annales des Voyages," 1869. This memoir contains the last discovered document relating to the above voyage, together with a full *resumé* and critical investigations of it, which leave no doubt that the "Land of De Gonneville" was on the East coast of Brazil, about the R. San Francisco do Sul. Although the title below properly belongs to the letter P, we give it here. The author of it was a lineal descendent of Essomneric, the young native brought to France by De Gonneville.

[Gonneville (Jean Binot Paulmyer de).] Mémoires touchant l'établissement d'une Mission chrestienne dans le Troisième monde autrement appelé la Terre Australe, Méridionale, Antartique, et Inconnuë. Dediez à Nostre S. Père le Pape Alexandre VII. Par un Ecclesiastique Originaire de cette mesme Terre. [Jean Paulmyer de Courtonne.] *Paris: Gabriel Cramoisy.* 1663. 8vo, 12 l., 6 l., pp. 216. Map. 27798

An earlier issue, not authorized by Paulmyer, has *Presentez* instead of *Dediez* in title, and a Dedication signed in full, which was cut out and replaced by one signed with initials. One copy of the first, and three of the second, are in public libraries in Paris. For more details relating to this rare book, see Margry's "Navigations Françaises," 1867, and the Memoir above. Title quoted in Nyon's "La Vallière," 21395. In the "Additions," by Chaudon, to the "Nouveau Dictionnaire Historique," in 1772, and in other editions of them, this book figures under the curious title of Myer (Paul).

Gonzaga. Fr. de Gonzaga de origine seraphicae religionis Franciscanae ejusque progressibus, de regularis observantiae institutione, forma administrationis ac legibus admirabilique ejus Propagatione. *Romae: D. Basa.* 1587. 2 vols., folio. 27790

Not only relating to the rise and progress of the Franciscans in the Old World, but particularly also in the New, and enumerating their religious houses and establishments both in Mexico and Peru, as well as in Yucatan, Chili, and the Brazils. With beautiful portraits and plates.

Gonzaga (L.) Discorso Filosofico, di Don Luigi Gonzaga. 1776. 4to. Portrait. 27791

On the back of the title of a copy of this work is the following inscription: "To the most eloquent Orator of the British Senate, from an Anti-American Author."

Gonzaga (Luis). Sermon historico apologético de nuestra señora de Guadeloupe. *Puebla.* 1836. 4to. 27792

[Gonzalez (Antonio).] La vie | de la bienhevrevse | epovse | de Jesus-Christ | Soevr Rose | de Sainte Marie, | Religieuse du Tiers Ordre | de S. Dominique, | originaire dv Perov | Dans les Indes Occidentales. | Traduite du Latin imprimé à Rome. | Par le R. P. Jean Baptiste Feüillet, | de l'Ordre des FF. Prêcheurs de la Province Re- | formée de S. Louis, & Missionaire Apostolique | dans les Antisles de l'Amerique. ¶ *A Paris, | Chez André Cramoisy, rüe | S. Iacques, au Sacrifice d'Abraham, | proche S. Severin.* | M. DC. LXVIII. | *Avec Pivilege & Approbation.* | 12mo, 12 l., pp. 277, 5 l. Portrait of Soeur Rose. 27793

"Feuillet, dans la préface de cet opuscule, dit l'avoir traduit de l'original latin du P. Antonio Gonzalez, imprimé à Rome en 1665 à l'occasion de la béatification de la Sœur Rose."—Trœmel.

Gonzalez. Traduccion de el Cathecismo Castellaño del G. de Ripalda, en el Idioma Mexicana por Fr. Antonio Gonzales. *Puebla: (Mexico) M. de Orttega, año* 1719. 8vo. 27794

Gonzalez de Candamo. Sermon de honras de su difunto Arzobispo D. Alonzo Nuñez de Haro y Peralta. *Mexico.* 1800. 4to, 25 l. 27795

Gonzalez de la Vega. Pesames y parabienes por la muerte del D. Bern. de Galuez. *[Mexico.]* 1787. 4to, 9 l. 27796

Gonzalez (Cabrera Bueno). Navegacion especulativa y practica con la Explication de algunos Instrumentos, Tabla de las declinaciones del Sol, etc. *Manila.* 1734. Sm. folio. 27797

The work of a Spanish Admiral, a native of Tenerife. It contains Routes or Sailing Directions through the Eastern Archipelago, from the Philippine Islands to California, thence from Cape Mendocino to Acapulco, back and forward between Acapulco and Panama, from Panama to Callao.

Gonzalez de Bustos (F. de). Los Españoles en Chile por Don Francisco Gonzalez de Bustos. *Madrid.* 1736. 4to.

Gonzalez Carranza (Domingo). A Geographical Description of the Coasts, Harbours, and Sea Ports of the Spanish West-Indies; particularly of Porto Bello, Cartagena, and the Island of Cuba. With Observations of the Currents, and the Variations of the Compass in the Bay of Mexico, and the North Sea of America. Translated from A Curious and authentic Manuscript, written in Spanish by Domingo Gonzales Carranza, his Catholick Majesty's principal Pilot of the Flota in New Spain, Anno 1718. To which is added, An Appendix, containing Capt. Parker's own Account of his taking the town of Porto Bello, in the Year 1601. With an Index, and a New and Correct Chart of the Whole; as also Plans of the Havannah, Porto-Bello, Cartagena, and La Vera Cruz. *London: Caleb Smith.* M.DCC.XL. 8vo, pp. 136, Index, 8 pp. 5 Maps. 27899

Gonzalez de Estava (Fernan). Coloquios Espirituales y Sacramentales y Canciones Divinas, compuestos por el Divino Poeta Fernan Gonzalez de Estava, Clerigo Presbytero, recopiladas por el Fernando Vello de Bustamente; de la Orden de S. Austin. *Mexico: Diego Lopez Daualos.* 1610. 4to. 27800

A very scarce collection of the productions of the earliest Mexican poet.

Gonzalez (F.) Lecciones de derecho constitucional por Florentino Gonzalez ... [With an Appendix:] Constitucion reformada de la nacion Argentina. *Buenos Aires.* 1869. Imp. 8vo, pp. 480, xxxviii, 2. 27801

Gonzalez Davila (Gil.) *See* Davila, Vol. v., No. 18777.

Gonzalez (H. V.) Carta de la Vida y Virtudes del H. Vicente Gonzalez, Novico Estudiante del la Colegio de Tepotzotlàn, 1754. 4to. 27802

Gonzalez (J.) Sermon panegirico de Santa Ines virgen y martir. *Mexico.* 1816. 4to, 23 l. 27803

Gonzalez. Sermon panegirico del gran Padre S. Francisco de Avés. ... *Mexico.* 1816. 4to, 30 l. 27804

Gonzalez (J.) Sermon Funebre, que en las Honras que hizo la Insigne Real Colegiata de Nuestra Señora de Guadalupe de Mexico, á sú Primero Abad el Sr. D. Juan Antonio de Alarcon y Ocaña, el dia 30 Sept. 1757 años, el Dr. D. Joseph Gonzalez del Pino. *Mexico.* 1758. 4to. 27805

Gonzalez y Montoya (Josef). Rasgos Sueltos para la Constitucion de America. *Cadiz.* 1811. 8vo, pp. 16. c., H. 27806

Gonzalez (J.) Palos de nueva invencion, ó carta que dirige D. José Gonzalez á D. José de Arango sobre las ocurrencias del dia. *[Habana:] Imprenta del Gobierno.* 1812. 27807

Gonzalez de la Puente (J.) Historia de S. Agostin de la province de Mechosacan, por Fray Juan Gonzalez de la Puente. 1624. Folio. 27808

Gonzalez de Quiroga. El nuevo apostol de Galicia, el venerable padre Fray Joseph de Corabantes, ... y missionari apostoliso en la America, y Europa ... Por el Lic. Don Diego Gonzalez de Quiroga ... . *Madrid: panerico Lasso.* 1705. Sm. 4to, 8 l., pp. 400, 10 l. H. 27809

Gonzalez (J.) Oracion fúnebre ... pronunciada en la iglesia del convento de San Agustin por el M. R. P. presentado fray Juan Gonzalez, del orden de predicadores. *Havana, Imprenta de la capitania general.* Folio, pp. 23. 27810

Gonzalez Bustillo (Don Juan). Extracto ò Relacion de los Autos de Reconocimiento practicado en Virtud de Commision del Señor Presidente de la Real Audiencia de estos Reino de Guatemala. *Impreso en la Oficiana de D. Antonio Sanchez Cubillas en el Pueblo de Mixco en la Casa que llaman de Comunidad de Santo Domingo Año de* 1774. 27811

Also: Razon puntual de los Successos mas memorables, y de los Estragos y Daños que ha padecido la Ciudad de Guatemala y su Vecindaria. *Mixco.* 1774.—Razon particular de los Templos, Casas de Comunidades y Edificios publicos y por Mayor del Numero de los Vecinos de la Capital Guatemala, etc., por los Terremontos. *Mixco.* 1774.—Demonstracion de las Proporciones è Improporciones que ofrece el Pueblo ó Valle de Xalapa. *Mixco.* 1774.—Demonstracion de las Proporciones ó Defectos que ofrece el Pueblo ó Valle de la Hermita. *Mixco.* 1774. Folio. These rare tracts are among the earliest works printed at Mixco, a place not mentioned by Archdeacon Cotton.

Gonzalez de la Requera (Juan Domingo). Fama postuma del Excelentisimo é ilust. Señor Dr. D. J. D. Gonzalez de la Requera: del Consejo de su Majestad: caballero gran cruz de la real y distinguida orden Española de Carlos III. Dignisimo XVI. Arzobispo de los Reyes. Por el mismo Autor de la Oracion Funebre [Dr. D. Joseph Manuel Bermudez]. *Lima, en la Imprenta Real de los Huérfanos.* 1805. 4to. Portrait. 27812

Gonzalez (J. F.) Coleccion de las Ciudades, Villas, y Lugares, que Comprehende la Capitania General de Castilla la Nueva; Creada Ultimamente por S. M. y encargado su mando, y gobierno al Excelentissimo Señor Conde de Aranda, Presidente del Consejo. Compuesto, y Ordenado Por Don Juan Francisco Gonzalez, Escribano principal de la Auditoria de ella. Con Superior Permiso. *Se hallará en la Libreria de Josef Batanero calle del Arenal.* Sm. 8vo, pp. 48. 27813

Gonzalez (J. F. de C.) Relacion del Restablecimiento de la Sagrada Compañia de Jesus en el Reyno de Nueva España, y de la entrega á sus religiosos del real Seminario de San Ildefonso de México. Dispuesta y publicada por el Illmo. Sr. Dr. D. Juan Francisco de Castañiza Gonzalez de Aguero. *Mexico.* 1816. 4to, pp. 47. 27814

A most curious and important paper for the History of the Jesuits. There are copies on large paper.

Gonzalez (J. V.) Manual de historia universal. Por Juan Vicente Gonzalez. *Caracas.* 1863. 8vo, pp. xiv, 760. 27815

[Gonzalez.] Para la Historia. Manifesto del General J. C. Falcon. Su Contestacion, Biografia de aquel. *Carácas.* 1860. 8vo, pp. 24. 27816

[Gonzalez.] Venezuela y los Monagas. Vasquez A. T. Unipersonal. Por J. V. G. *Carácas.* 1838. 8vo, pp. 37.

Also: Biografia del Doctor José Cecilio Avila. *Carácas.* 1858. 8vo, pp. 67.—Revista literaria, por J. V. G. *Carácas.* 1865. 8vo, pp. 560.

Gonzalez (M. J.) Exêquias del Señor D. Manuel Ignacio Gonzalez del Campillo, dignisimo Obispo de la Puebla de los Angeles celebradas 26 y 27 de Nov. 1813. *Mexico.* 1814. 4to.

Gonzalez de Acuna. Elogio del Ilust. Señor Dr. D. Manuel J. Gonzalez de Acuna, y Sanz Merino, Dignismo Obispo de Panamá. Dixola en la Universidad de San Marcos, 31 de Agosto, 1803. *Lima.* 1803. 4to, pp. 16. 27819

Gonzalez (M. D.) Memoria historica de la Villa de Santa Clara y su jurisdiccion, por D. Manuel Dionisio Gonzalez. *Villaclara.* 1858. 4to. 27820

Gonzalez (P.) Elementos de Geografia General. *Habana.* 1852. 12mo. s. 27821

Gonzalez de Agueros. Descripcion Historial de la Provincia y Archipielago de Chilóe, en el Reyno de Chile, y Obispado de la Concepcion. Por El Padre Fray Pedro Gonzalez de Agueros. ... *En la Imprenta de Don Benito Cano.* 1791. 4to, pp. (8), 318. Plate and Map. 27822

Gonzalez Araujo (Pedro). Impugnacion de algunos impios, blasfemos, sac ilegos, y sediciosos Articulos del Codigo de Anarquia, cuyo Titulo es: Decreto Constitucional para la Libertad de la America. *Mexico.* 1816. 4to. + *Reimpresso en Madrid.* 1817. 4to. 27823

Gonzalez (Tho.) Epigrammata. *Mexici: [Circa.* 1641.]

Gonzalo Pinero (Maestro Fr.) Sermon en las Honras de el Doctor Don Andres Gonzalez Calderon Arcediano de la Santa Iglesia de Oaxaca, en Puebla. *Imprenta Nueva Plantiniana de Diego Fernandez de León.* 1689. 4to. 27825

Gonzalo (V. L.) Carta pastoral de D. Victoriano Lopez Gonzalo, Obispo de la Puebla de los Angeles. *[Puebla.]* 1748. 4to, pp. 101. 27826

Gooch (D. W.) The Lecompton Constitution, and the Admission of Kansas into the Union. Speech of Hon. D. W. Gooch, of Massachusetts. ... March 29, 1858. [n. p. n. d.] 8vo, pp. 8. H. 27827

Gooch. Polygamy in Utah. Speech of Hon. Daniel W. Gooch, of Massachusetts. Delivered in the House of Representatives, April 4, 1860. [n. p. n. d.] 8vo, pp. 8. 27828

Also: The Supreme Court and Dred Scott. ... Speech ... May 3, 1860. [n. p. n. d.] 8vo, pp. 8. H.—Any Compromise a Surrender. Speech ... February 23, 1861. [n. p. n. d.] 8vo, pp. 8. H.—Recognition of Hayti and Liberia. Speech ... June 2, 1862. [n. p. n. d.] 8vo, pp. 8. H.

The Good Indian Missionary. Written for the American Sunday School Union ... *Philadelphia.* [n. d.] 18mo, pp. 36.

Good Humor; or, away with the Colonies. Wherein is occasionally enquired into, Mr. P——t's claim to Popularity; and the principles of virtuous Liberty as taught in the School of Mr. Wilkes, and other Peripatetics. *London: W. Nicoll.* 1766. 8vo.

A fiery attack upon the colonies and their defenders. The so-called Liberty preached by such scoundrels as "Mr. P——" (Lord Chatham), with whom are associated Wilkes and Churchill, is real Slavery! The colonists are worse than thieves, to resist the Stamp-Act, or any taxes imposed by their gracious monarch. *See* "M. Rev.," XXXIV. 238; *also*, Sparks' "Franklin," IV. 215.

Good News! Good News from Home. *Providence: The Author.* 1862. 12mo, pp. 16. 27831

Good news from | Nevv-England: | with | An exact relation of the first plan- | ting that Country: A description of the | profits accruing by the Worke. | Together with a briefe, but true | discovery of their Order both in Church | and Common-wealth, and maintenance al- | lowed the painfull Labourer's in that Vineyard | of the Lord. | With | The names of the severall Towns, | and who be Preachers to Them. | *London:* | *Printed by Matthew Simmons,* | 1648. | 4to, Title, 1 l., pp. 25. W. 27832

Reprinted in "Mass. Hist. Collection," Fourth Series, Vol. I.

The Good of the Community Impartially Considered, In a Letter to a Merchant in Boston, In Answer to one received respecting the Excise Bill. By a True Friend to Liberty. *Boston.* 1754. 12mo, pp. 50. M., W. 27833

Good Old Age, a Brief Essay on the Glories of Aged Piety, humbly commended and presented to them whose arrival at or near Sixty makes them among the Aged. *Boston.* 1726. 12mo.

Good Old Virginia Almanac. *Richmond.* 1803. 12mo. Continued. 27835

Good Public Roads. [About March, 1773.] 4to, pp. 1. P.

Appeal in favor of a road from Philadelphia to Strasburg.

A | Good Speed | to Virginia. | *London: Printed by Felix Kyngston for William | Welbie, and are to be Sold at his Shop at the Signe | of the Greyhound in Pauls Church- | yard.* 1609. | Sm. 4to, 14 l. J.C.B.

Printed in black letter, and one of the rarest of tracts relative to Virginia. Lowndes is unable to refer to the sale of a single copy. It is dedicated "To the Noblemen, Merchants, and Gentlemen Adventurers to the Plantations of Virginia," by R. G.

Goodale (E.) Record of the Proceedings of a General Court Martial holden at the Court House in Salem, Sept. 28, 1812, by Order of his Excellency Caleb Strong, Governor, ... on the Complaint of Lieut.-Col. Samuel Brimblecome and

others against Ebenezer Goodale, Major-General of the Second Division. *Cambridge: Hilliard and Metcalf.* 1812. 8vo, pp. 80. BA., H., M., N. 27838

Goodale (John, *and others*). Report of the Committee sent to Georgia, to examine the Cedar Shoals Water-Power, October 29th, 1855. *Boston: Farwell & Co.* 1855. 8vo, pp. 16. H.

Goodale (M. S.) A Discourse ... in Amsterdam Village, May 14, 1841. ... in View of the ... Death of William Henry Harrison, Late President of the United States. By M. S. Goodale. ... [n. p.] *Printed by S. B. Marsh.* 1841. 80, pp. 17.

Goodale. A Historical Discourse of the Presbyterian Church of Amsterdam Village; delivered July 6, 1851. ... *Albany: J. Munsell.* 1851. 8vo, pp. 22. 27841

Goodale (S. L.) *See* Maine (State of).

Goodall (B.) The Tryall of Trauell, or 1. The Wonders in Trauell, 2. The Worthes of Trauell, 3. The Way to Trauell. In three bookes Epitomized, By Baptist Goodall, Merchant. *London: Printed by Iohn Norton.* 1630. 4to, 40 l. 27842

An excessively rare volume of poems. Midgeley's copy sold for £10 15s. Among the Worthies of Travel the author records:

"Collumbus and Magellian prowdly ventur'd,
Then Drake, Vesputius, and our Forbish enter'd:
Peruana and the Mexican are clear'd,
But the South regiones what they are unheard,
The words of wealth thence to our Lands accrue
And the many fertile Colonies insue."

It is dedicated to Elizabeth, Queen of Bohemia. Priced in the "Bibl. Angl. Poet.," at £12 12s.

Goode (T.) The Invalid's Guide to the Virginia Hot Springs, Containing an Account of the Medical Properties of these Waters ... By Thomas Goode, M.D. *Richmond: Printed by P. D. Bernard.* 1839. 18mo, pp. 44. BA. + *Richmond: T. D. Derrand, Printer.* 1846. 18mo, pp. 95. + *Richmond: P. D. Bernard.* 1851. 18mo, pp. 88. 27843

Goode was the proprietor of these Springs.

Goode (W. O.) The Speech of William O. Goode, on the Abolition of Slavery; ... January 24, 1832. *Richmond: Printed by Thomas W. White.* 1832. 8vo, pp. 33. B. 27844

Goodell (C. L.) Sermon ... New Britain, Conn., Thanksgiving Day, November 26, 1863. By C. L. Goodell. 8vo.

Goodell (W.) The American Slave Code in Theory and Practice: Its Distinctive Features Shown by Its Statutes, Judicial Decisions, and Illustrative Facts. By William Goodell, ... *New-York: ... Anti-Slavery Society.* 1853. 12mo, pp. 431. B., BA., H. + Second Edition. [*Ibid.*] + Third Edition. [*Ibid.*] + *London: Clarke, Beeton, and Co.* [1853.] 16mo, pp. xii, 411. B.

Goodell. Our National Charters; for the Millions. ... With Notes, showing their bearing on Slavery, and the relative Powers of the State and National Governments. By William Goodell. *New York: William Goodell.* 1861. 12mo, pp. 144. BA. + *New York: J. W. Alden.* 1863. 12mo, pp. 144. H.

Goodell. ... The Rights and the Wrongs of Rhode Island. By William Goodell. [*Oneida:*] *Institute Press.* [1842.] 8vo, pp. 120. N. 27848

From the "Christian Investigator," No. 8, Whitesboro, N. Y., Sept., MDCCCXLII.

Goodell. Slavery and Anti-Slavery. A History of the great Struggle in both Hemispheres; with a View of the Slavery Question in the United States. By William Goodell. *New York: William Harned.* 1852. pp. x, 604. + Third Edition. *New York.* 1855. 8vo. C., S. 27849

Goodell. Views of American Constitutional Law, in its bearing upon American Slavery. By William Goodell. + Second Edition, Revised ... *Utica, N. Y.* 1845. 12mo. pp. 162. B., H., S. 27850

Also: American Slavery. A Formidable Obstacle to the Conversion of the World. ... *New York.* 1856. 12mo, pp. 24. — Address of the Macedon Convention. ... And Letters of Gerrit Smith. *Albany: S. W. Green.* 1847. Rl. 8vo, pp. 16. B., H. — Come-out-erism. ... *New York.* 1845. pp. 38. B. — The Nationalities. Their Origin, Elements, Mission, Responsibilities, Duties, and Destinies. A Discourse delivered in Williamsburg, New York (and in other places), April 28 to September 1, 1861. 12mo, pp. 15. — One more Appeal to Professors of Religion. *New-England Anti-Slavery Tract Association* (Tract No. 7). — Reasons why distilled Spirits should be Banished from the Land. Address ... *New York.* 1830. 8vo. — ... A Sermon ... at Reading ... August 13, 1851, at the Funeral of the Rev. Daniel Temple. ... . *Boston: T. R. Marvin.* 1851. 8vo, pp. 30. B., H.

[Goodenow (John M.)] ... American Jurisprudence in Contrast with the Doctrine of English Common Law. ... *Steubenville, O.: Printed by James Wilson.* 1819. 8vo, 1 l., pp. vii, (1), 426, iv. BA. 27851

A very rare book, relating to the Ohio Courts.

Goodenow. Historical Record of the Proceedings of Court of Common Pleas and "The Bar" of Hamilton County, Ohio,

in Reference to the Appointment of Clerk of said Court, 1833, 1834. *Cincinnati.* 1834. 8vo. 27852

Goodenow. Letter of the Hon. John M. Goodenow on the subject of the Northern Boundary of Ohio. *St. Clairsville.* 1835. 8vo, pp. 15. 27853

[Goodenow (Sterling).] A Brief Topographical and Statistical Manual of the State of New-York ... *Albany: J. Frary.* 1811. 12mo, pp. 34. B., S. 27854

Goodenow. A brief Topographical and Statistical Manual of the State of New York; and an Account of the Grand Canals. By Stirling Goodenow. Second Edition ... enlarged. *New York.* 1822. 8vo. A., P. 27855

Goodfellow (W.) Discourse on the Death of Abraham Lincoln, Delivered at Buenos Aires, June 11, 1865. By Rev. William Goodfellow. *Buenos Aires: German Printing Office.* 1865. 8vo, pp. 25. 27856

Goodhue (J. F.) History of the Town of Shoreham, Vermont, from the date of its Charter, October 8th, 1761, to the present time. By Rev. Josiah F. Goodhue. *Middlebury: A. H. Copeland.* 1861. 8vo, pp. vi, 198, Contents, 1 l. B., H.

With an account of the County of Addison, by Samuel Swift, LL.D.

Goodhue (S.) [Biography of the first Settlement of the Family of the Name of Goodhue, at Ipswich, in 1636, and Genealogy to 1833; together with an Address by Deacon Samuel Goodhue, to his Descendants. *Boston.* 1846.] 12mo, pp. 16. H.

The address was written by a grandson, and was also printed in 1770, 1805, and 1850.

Goodhue (S.) The Copy of a Valedictory and Monitory Writing, left by Sarah Goodhue, of Joseph Goodhue, of Ipswich. ... *Cambridge.* 1681. 27859

Reprinted in 1770, 1805, and lastly as edited by David Pulsifer. *Boston.* 1850. 16mo, pp. 13. B., H.

[Goodloe (D. R.)] ... Causes that have retarded the Accumulation of Wealth and Increase of Population in the Southern States. ... *Washington: W. Blanchard.* 1846. 8vo, pp. 27. B.

Goodloe. Federalism Unmasked: or the Rights of the States, the Congress, the Executive, and the People ... . By Daniel R. Goodloe. [*Washington: Buell & Blanchard.* 1860.] 8vo, pp. 15. B., H. 27861

Goodloe. Letter of Daniel R. Goodloe [May 7th, 1868,] to Hon. Charles Sumner, on the Situation of Affairs in North Carolina. [n. p. n. d.] 8vo, pp. 16. B., H. 27862

Goodloe. The Marshalship in North Carolina, being a Reply to Charges made by Messrs. Abbott, Pool, Heaton ... . [*Washington?* 1869.] 8vo, pp. 12. H. 27863

Goodloe. The Southern Platform: or, Manual of Southern Sentiment on the Subject of Slavery. By Daniel R. Goodloe. *Boston: John P. Jewett & Co.* 1858. 8vo, pp. 79, (1). B., BA.

Also: Emancipation and the War. 8vo. — Is it Expedient to introduce Slavery into Kansas? ... [*Cincinnati.*] [n. d.] 12mo, pp. 24. H. — "Negro Slavery No Evil," etc. *Boston: Alfred Mudge and Son.* 1855. 8vo, pp. 55. H.

Goodman (J. R.) Pennsylvania Biography; or Memoirs of Eminent Pennsylvanians. By John R. Goodman. *Philadelphia.* 1840 18mo. C. + *Philadelphia: J. Crissy.* 1842. pp. 276.

Goodman (R.) Address ... before the Berkshire Agricultural Society, October 8th, 1868. By Richard Goodman. *Pittsfield: Chickering & Axtell.* 1868. 8vo, pp. 20. B. 27866

Goodman (W.) The Social History of Great Britain during the Reigns of the Stuarts, beginning with the Seventeenth Century, being the Period of settling the United States. ... By William Goodman. *New-York: William H. Colyer.* 1843–44. 2 vols., 12mo, 2 l., pp. 324; 1 l., 349, ix. BA. + Third Edition. [*Ibid.*] 1847. 27867

Goodman (W F.) Contrast of British America with the United States and Texas. By W. F. Goodman. *London.* 1846. 8vo. 27868

Goodrich (Charles A.) The Family Tourist: A Visit to the Principal Cities of the Western Continent; embracing an account of the Situation, Origin, Plan, Extent, their Inhabitants, Manners, Customs, and Amusements, and Public Works, Institutions, Edifices, &c., together with Sketches of Historical Events. By C. A. Goodrich. *Philadelphia.* 1848. 8vo, pp. 640. 68 Illustrations. 27869

Goodrich. The Child's History of the United States ... Improved from the Twenty-first Edition. *Philadelphia.* 1846.

Goodrich. History of the United States of America. By Rev. Charles A. Goodrich. *Hartford.* 1823. 12mo. + Third

Edition. *Hartford: Barber & Robinson.* 1824. 12mo, pp. 400. Plates. 27871

Also: A History ... of America, from the First Discovery to the Fourth of March, 1825. ... *Hartford: Barber & Robinson.* 1825. 12mo, pp. 418, (4). 12 Plates. + Second Edition. *New-York: Collins & Co.* Sm. 12mo, pp. 296, 20. B. + Fourth Edition. *Greenfield.* 1825. 18mo, pp. 296, 20. H. + Fifth Edition. *Bellows Falls, Vt.* 1825. 18mo, pp. 296, 20. B. + Ninth Edition. *Bellows Falls, Vt.: James I. Cutler and Co.* 1826. 12mo, pp. 396, 20. + Twelfth Edition. [*Ibid.*] 1827. + To the Year 1827. *Boston.* 1828. 12mo, pp. 432. + [*Ibid.*] 1832. + Thirty-fifth Edition. *Brattleborough, Vt.* 1832. 12mo. + *Bellows Falls: James I. Cutler & Co.* 1833. pp. 296, 20. H. + *Boston: Carter, Hendee & Co.* 1833. 16mo, pp. 296. + *Boston: John B. Russell.* [1834.] 16mo, pp. 352. H. + Sixty-Fourth Edition. *Boston.* [n. d.] B. + To the present time, embracing an Account of the Aboriginal Tribes ... *Hartford.* 1840. 12mo. + Enlarged from the One Hundreth Edition. *Boston.* 1844. 12mo, pp. 384. + Enlarged from the One Hundred and Fiftieth Edition, and brought down to 1847. *Boston: Jenks, Palmer and Co.* [1847.] 12mo, pp. 412. B., H. + [*Ibid.*] 1852. 12mo. C. + *Boston: Jenks, Hickling & Swan.* 1853. 12mo, pp. 425. B., H. + *Boston.* 1854. 12mo, pp. 426. + *Boston: Hickling, Swan & Brown.* 1857. pp. 433. + Revised ... by W. H. Seavy. *Boston.* 1867. 12mo, pp. 320, 28. B., BA., H.

Goodrich. The Land we Live In; or, Travels, Sketches, and Adventures, in North and South America, with Descriptions of the Towns, Cities, States, and Territories, their Inhabitants, Manners, Customs, &c.; together with Sketches of Historical Events. By Charles A. Goodrich. Revised, Corrected, Enlarged, &c. *Cincinnati.* 1857. Rl. 8vo. 27872

Goodrich. Lives of the Signers to the Declaration of Independence. By the Rev. Charles A. Goodrich. *New York: William Reid & Co.* 1829. 8vo, pp. 460. C., H. + Third Edition. [*Ibid.*] 1832. 12mo. + Fourth Edition. *Boston: Thomas Mather.* 1834. 12mo, pp. 460. Portraits and Plate. B. + Eighth Edition. *New York: Thomas Mather.* 1840. 8vo, pp. 460. H. 27873

Goodrich. Outlines of Modern Geography on a New Plan. *Brattleborough: Holbrook and Fessenden.* 1827. Sm. 12mo, pp. 252. Plates. B. 27874

Goodrich. Stories on the History of Connecticut, designed for the Instruction of Young Persons. By Charles A. Goodrich. *Hartford: Robinson & Co.* 1829. 12mo, pp. 203. 27875

Republished with a new title as follows: A History of Connecticut, Designed for Schools; ... *Hartford: D. F. Robinson & Co.* 1833. 12mo. — Address before the Female Charitable Society at Worcester, [Mass.] June 26, 1817 ... *Worcester.* 1817. 8vo. W. — Address before the Hartford County Agricultural Society, Oct. 12, 1826. ... *Hartford, Conn.* 1826. 8vo. — Cabinet of Curiosities, Natural, Artificial, and Historical, selected from the most authentic records, ancient and modern. *Hartford.* 1822 2 vols.,

12mo. — Pictorial and Descriptive View of all Religions; embracing the Forms of Worship practised by the several Nations of the Known World; also, a ... *Hartford.* 1829. 8vo. — Religious Ceremonies and Customs. *Louisville, Ky.* 1840. — The Universal Traveller ... with woodcuts. *Hartford.* 1850. 12mo. *See also* Worcester, *Mass.*

Goodrich (C. B.) Opinion of Charles B. Goodrich, upon the Legal and Equitable Rights of a Bona Fide Holder for Value of Sundry Drafts made by Army Contractors upon, and accepted by, the Secretary of the War Department. *Washington: Scammell & Co.* 1862. 8vo, pp. 21. H. 27876

Goodrich. Lowell Lectures. The Science of Government as exhibited in the Institutions of the United States. ... By Charles B. Goodrich. *Boston: Little, Brown and Company.* 1853. 8vo, pp. viii, 343. A., B., BA., C. 27877

Goodrich (Chauncy). Northern Fruit Culture; or, Farmers' Guide to the Orchard and Fruit Garden. *Burlington, Vt.* 1850. 12mo, pp. 112. 27878

Goodrich. Speech of Mr. Goodrich, in the Senate, December 19th, 1808, on the ... Embargo. [n. p. n. d.] 8vo, pp. 7.

Goodrich (C. A.) Travels and Sketches in North and South America; embracing an account of their Situation, Origin, Plan, Extent, their Inhabitants, Manners, Customs, and Amusements, and Public Works, Institutions, Edifices, &c., together with Sketches of Historical Events. By Chauncy A. Goodrich. *Hartford: Case, Tiffany & Co.* 1852. 8vo, 2 l., pp. 704. Illustrated with Engravings. C. 27880

Goodrich (Chauncy E.) A Sermon on the Death of Dr. A. Brigham. *New York: J. F. Trow.* 1850. 8vo, pp. 35. B.

Goodrich (E.) The Duty of Gospel-Ministers, to take Heed to themselves, and their Flock. A Sermon Preached at the Ordination of the Reverend Mr. Roger Newton, at Greenfield, Nov. 18, 1761. By Elizur Goodrich. *Boston: Edes & Gill.* M.DCC.LXII. 8vo, pp. 30. 27882

Goodrich. The Principles of civil Union and Happiness considered and recommended. A Sermon before ... the General Assembly of Connecticut, at Hartford, on the Day of Election, May 10th, 1787. ... *Hartford: Hudson & Goodwin.* 1787. 8vo, pp. 58. BA., C., H., M. 27883

Goodrich. A Sermon, delivered at the Ordination of the Reverend Matthew Noyes, A.M., to the Pastoral Charge of the Church of Christ, in Northford, August 18, 1790. By Elizur Goodrich, D.D. *New-Haven: Printed by A. Morse.* M.DCC.XC. 8vo, pp. 31. 27884

Also: Sermon at the Installation of the Rev. B. Boardman, at Hartford, May 5, 1754. ... *Hartford.* 1784. 8vo, pp. 29. BA. + Sermon at the Ordination of Samuel Goodrich. ... *Fairfield.* 1787. 8vo, pp. 29. BA. + Sermon ... on the Day of Election, 1817 ... *Hartford.* 1817. 8vo. W.

Goodrich (F. B.) Man Upon the Sea; or, a History of Maritime Adventure, Exploration, and Discovery, from the earliest ages to the present time; comprising a detailed account of Remarkable Voyages, Ancient as well as Modern. By Frank B. Goodrich. *Philadelphia: Lippincott & Co.* 1858. 8vo, 1 l., pp. 560. Plates. B., BA., H. 27885

Abridged, and issued with the title:

Goodrich. The Sea and her Famous Sailors. By Frank B. Goodrich. *London: Hogg & Sons.* 1859. 12mo, pp. 290.

Goodrich. The Tribute Book. A Record of Munificence, Self-Sacrifice, and Patriotism of the American People during the War for the Union. Illustrated by Frank B. Goodrich. *New York: Derby & Miller.* 1865. Impl. 8vo, pp. 512. 7 Plates. C., S.

His "Women of Beauty and Heroism, *New York,* 1859"—4to, pp. 424, 19 Plates—includes a Portrait and Memoir of Pocahontas. This was also reproduced as: World-famous Women. *Cincinnati: W. H. Moore & Co.* 1871.

Goodrich (J. W.) A Continuation of the Maritime History of Connecticut, By Capt. James W. Goodrich, delivered before the New Haven Colony Historical Society, December 31st, 1866. [n. p. n. d.] 8vo, pp. 40. H. 27888

Goodrich (J. Z.) Exposition of the J. D. & M. Williams Fraud, and of its Settlement: ... By J. Z. Goodrich. ... . *Boston: Rockwell and Rollins.* 1866. 8vo, pp. 48. B., H. 27889

Goodrich. Nebraska and Kansas. Speech of Hon. John Z. Goodrich, of Massachusetts, ... House of Representatives, May 20, 1854. ... *Washington: Congressional Globe Office.* 1854. 8vo, pp. 16. H. 27890

Goodrich. The Pro-Slavery Policy Tactics, false fraudulent, and dishonest: Letter to R. Toombs. *Boston.* [1856.] 8vo, pp. 16. B., H. 27891

Goodrich. A Reply to the Statements of Hon. Samuel Hooper, in a pamphlet fancifully entitled "A Defence of the Merchants of Boston," which justify the Wine Frauds of J. D. & M. Williams, and the official Misconduct of Timothy B. Dix, and asperse the Character of "John Z. Goodrich, Ex-Collector of Customs." By J. Z. Goodrich. *Boston: Rockwell & Rollins, Printers.* 1867. 8vo, pp. 44. B., H. 27892

Also: Speech on the Tariff and Revenue Questions; House of Representatives, Jan. 24, 1855. ... *Washington.* 1855. 8vo, pp. 8. H. + Speech delivered on the Peace Convention in Washington, February, 1861. ... *Boston: J. E. Farwell & Co.* 1864. 8vo, pp. 31. B., H.—Speech ... in the House of Representatives, May 27, 1852. [n. p. n. d.] 8vo, pp. 16. B., BA.

Goodrich (S.) ... Sermon ... at Worcester, Mass., October 9, 1816, at the Ordination and Installation of his Son, the Rev. Charles Augustus Goodrich ... . By Samuel Goodrich ... . *Worcester: Printed by William Manning.* 1816. 8vo, pp. 24.

Goodrich (S. G.) Comprehensive Geography and History, Ancient and Modern. By Samuel G. Goodrich. *New-York.* 1855. 4to. + *New York.* 1860. 4to, pp. 272. 27894

Pages 25 to 174 relate to America.

[Goodrich.] Curiosities of Human Nature ... . *Boston: Bradbury, Soden & Co.* MDCCCXLIV. 18mo, pp. 320. S. 27895

[Goodrich.] Les contes de Pierre Parley sur l'Amérique. ... *Boston: Carter and Hendee.* 1832. 16mo, pp. 144. B., BA.

Goodrich. Les États-Unis d'Amérique. Aperçu statistique, historique, géographique, industriel et social, a l'usage de ceux qui recherchent des renseignements précis sur cette partie du Nouveau-Monde. Par S. G. Goodrich. ... *Paris: Guillaumin et Cie.* 1852. 8vo, pp. xvi, 376. H. 27897

[Goodrich.] Five Letters to my Neighbor Smith, touching the Fifteen Gallon Jug: ... By O. B. Second Edition. 1838. 8vo, pp. 36. + Fifth Edition, to which is added a Sixth Letter. *Boston: Weeks, Jordan and Company.* 1838. 8vo, pp. 36. H.

Goodrich. Histoire des États-Unis d'Amérique. ... *Philadelphie: E. H. Butler et Cie.* 1855. 12mo, pp. 352. 27899

Goodrich. A History of all Nations, from the Earliest Periods to the Present Time; or, Universal History: in which the History of every Nation, Ancient and Modern, is separately given. ... By S. G. Goodrich. *Boston: Wilkins, Carter & Co.*

1849–51. 2 vols., 8vo, pp. 600; x, 601–1207. + *Auburn, N. Y.* 1855. 2 vols., rl. 8vo. + Revised Edition. *New-York.* 1857. 2 vols., 4to. 27900

Goodrich. History of South America and the West Indies. ... 1846. 18mo. 27901

[Goodrich.] History of the Indians of North and South America. *Boston: Bradbury, Soden & Co.* 1844. 12mo, pp. (2), 315. B. + *Boston: George C. Rand.* 1855. 18mo, pp. 320.

Goodrich. History of the United States of America, from the Discovery of the Continent by Columbus to the present time. ... *Hartford.* 1842. 8vo. 27903

Goodrich. Illustrated Natural History of the Animal Kingdom, ... By S. G. Goodrich. With 1400 Engravings. *New York: Derby & Jackson.* 1859. 2 vols., impl. 8vo, pp. xvi, 680; viii, 680. B. 27904

American Natural History forms a large portion.

Goodrich. A Letter to Moses Williams, of Roxbury. By S. G. Goodrich. *Boston: Weeks, Jordan & Co.* 1838. 8vo, pp. 12. B., H. 27905

Goodrich. Lights and Shadows of American History. ... *Boston: Bradbury, Soden and Co.* 1844. 16mo, pp. 336. B., H. + [*Ibid.*] 1848. 27906

Goodrich. The Life of Benjamin Franklin. Illustrated by Tales, Sketches, and Anecdotes. ... *Philadelphia.* 1844.

The edition of 1832 is spurious, and, perhaps, this is also.

[Goodrich.] Lives of Celebrated American Indians: ... *Boston: Bradbury, Soden & Co.* MDCCCXLIII. 12mo, pp. (2), 315.

[Goodrich.] The Manners, Customs, and Antiquities of the Indians of North and South America. *Boston: Bradbury, Soden and Co.* MDCCCXLIV. 12mo. B. + [*Ibid.*] 1848. 18mo, pp. 336. 27909

[Goodrich.] Peter Parley's Tales about New York. 1832. Square 16mo. 27910

[Goodrich.] Peter Parley's Tales about America. *Boston.* 1827. BA. + South America. *Baltimore: J. Jewett.* 1832. Square 16mo, pp. 166. Map. 27911

[Goodrich.] Peter Parley's Tales of Animals, ... *Boston: Carter and Hendee.* 1830. 12mo, 2 l., pp. 342 BA. + *Louisville: Morton & Smith.* 1836. 12mo, pp. 360. 27912

[Goodrich.] Parley's Cabinet Library for Schools and Families. *Boston.* 1843, 1844. 20 vols., 16mo. B. + *Philadelphia.* 1846. 20 vols. Illustrated. + *Boston.* 1848. 27913

The works composing the above series have no general title-page. The serial number occurs on signature-pages only of each volume. Titled: Vol. I. Famous Men of Modern Times. II. Curiosities of Human Nature. III. Eccentric and Wonderful Persons. IV. Lives of Benefactors. V. Famous American Indians. VI. Celebrated Women. VII. American History. VIII. European History. IX. Asiatic History. X. African History. XI. History of the Indians. XII. Customs of the Indians. XIII. A Glance at the Sciences. XIV. Wonders of Geology. XV. The Animal Kingdom. XVI. A Glance at Philosophy. XVII. Book of Literature. XVIII. Enterprise and Art of Man. XIX. Customs of all Nations. XX. The World and its Inhabitants. The arrangement of some sets I have seen does not agree with the above order.

[Goodrich.] Peter Parley's Common School History. ... Second Edition. *Boston: J. B. Russell.* 1838. 8vo, pp. 411.

Also: First, Second, and Third Books of History.

[Goodrich.] Peter Parley's Universal History. ... *New York: Mark H. Newman & Co.* 1850. 2 vols., pp. viii, 1 l., 380; 380.—Elohi nulistanitolv kanohesgi. [Common school history. Translated into Cherokee. 53 Chaps. in Cherokee Messenger. *Cherokee.* 1844–1846. 8vo.] C. 27915

Goodrich (S. G.) A Pictorial History of America, embracing both the Northern and Southern Portions of the New World. Illustrated with more than 300 Engravings. *Hartford.* 1845. 8vo. + [*Ibid.*] 1846. pp. 813. + *Hartford.* 1850. pp. 836, and Appendix on the Aborigines, pp. 48. + [*Ibid.*] 1853.

Goodrich. Pictorial History of the United States; with Notices of other portions of America. *Philadelphia: Sorin & Ball.* 1844. 12mo, pp. 354. + Revised and Improved Edition. *Philadelphia.* 1854. 12mo. 27917

[Goodrich.] Popular Biography. By Peter Parley. Embracing the most eminent Characters of every Age, Nation, and Profession. ... *New York: Leavitt & Allen.* [n. d.] 12mo, pp. 326. 27918

Goodrich. Recollections of a Lifetime; or, Men and Things I have Seen: in a Series of Familiar Letters to a Friend; Historical, Biographical, Anecdotical, and Descriptive. By S. G. Goodrich. Illustrated with many Engravings. *New York.* 1851.

2 vols., post 8vo, pp. 542; 563. + *New York: Miller.* MDCCCLVI. + [*Ibid.*] MDCCCLVII. B., C. 27919

[Goodrich.] Stories about Captain John Smith of Virginia, for the Instruction and Amusement of Children. *Hartford: H. & F. J. Huntington.* 1829. 18mo, pp. 100. 27920

Goodrich. De Vereenigde Staaten van Amerika. Een algemeen overzicht van hun Statistiek, Geschiedenis, Aardrijks- en Luchts-Gesteldheid, Nyverheid en onderscheiden maatschappelijk Karakter. *Amsterdam.* 8vo. Map. 27921

Goodrich. Who are the Aggressors? A Letter from S. G. Goodrich to a Friend in Kentucky. [*New-York.*] [1856.] 8vo, pp. 8. B. 27922

Also: Adventures of Billy Bump in Boston and California. ... Being the Life of a Boy in America. *London.* 1852. 18mo, pp. 210.—The Captive of Nootka Sound; or, Adventures of John R. Jewett. 1832. 16mo, pp. 259.—Common School History. New Edition. *Philadelphia.* 1854. 12mo. C.—The Child's Book of American Geography ... *Boston: Wait & Dow.* 1831. 8vo, pp. 64. B. + Second Edition. *Boston: James B. Dow.* 1837. 8vo, pp. 64.—Dick Boldhero; or, a Tale of Adventures in South America ... *Philadelphia.* 1845. 16mo.—First Book of History, for Children and Youth. *Boston: Richardson, Lord & Holbrook.* 1832. 12mo, pp. 180. Maps. + Fourth Revised Edition. *Boston.* 1849. 12mo. + *Boston: Jenks, Hickling & Swan.* 1853. 16mo, pp. 224. H.—National Geography for Schools. ... *New York: Huntington & Savage.* 1848. 4to, pp. 112.—A Pictorial Geography of the World ... 1831. Impl. 8vo. + 1840. + *Boston: Charles D. Strong.* 1856. 2 vols., pp. ——; 775. B.—Outlines of Chronology. Fourth Edition. *Boston.* 1828. pp. 232. + *Boston.* 1832. 16mo.—Peter Parley's Tales about America. Second Edition. *Boston.* 1829. 12mo.—A Pictorial Geography. ... *Otis Broaders & Co.* 1840. Rl. 8vo, pp. 1008. B., BA.—A Pictorial Natural History ... *Boston: J. Munroe & Co.* 1842. 12mo, pp. 415.—Sketches from a Student's Window. *Boston: W. D. Ticknor.* 1841. 12mo, pp. 311. H.—A System of Universal Geography; comprising a Physical, Political, and Statistic Account of the World and its Various Divisions, &c. *Cincinnati: Roff & Young.* 1832. 8vo, pp. 920, (2). C.—A Tale of the Revolution, and other Sketches. ... *Philadelphia.* 1845. 18mo.—Tales about the World; containing Europe, Asia, Africa, America, and Australia. Edited by Rev. T. Wilson. 1857. 18mo.—Universal History on the basis of Geography. *Boston.* 1837. 2 vols., 18mo.—The World as it Is, and as it Has Been: A Comprehensive Geography and History. *New York.* 1855. 4to.—The Young American: or Book of Government and Law; showing their History, Nature, and Necessity. ... *New York: W. Robinson.* 1842. 16mo, 2 l., pp. 282. + Fourth Edition. *New York.* 1844. 12mo. The following are believed to be spurious issues under the name of Peter Parley:

Goodrich. The Life of C. Columbus, ... G. Washington, and B. Franklin. *Philadelphia.* 1844. 12mo. 27923

Goodrich. Peter Parley's Tales about Canada. *London.* 1839. 16mo. 27924

A large number of the English editions of Peter Parley's Tales are not by Goodrich, and being uncertain as to their authenticity, we have omitted most of them from our list. *See* Allibone's "Dictionary."

Goodrich (W. H.) The Education of Divine Providence. A Sermon by William H. Goodrich. *Cleveland.* 1861. 8vo, pp. 7. 27925

Relates to the Rebellion in the Southern States. Also: A Sermon on the Christian Necessity of War, preached in Cleveland, April 21, 1861. ... *Cleveland: Fairbanks, Benedict & Co.* 1861. 8vo, pp. 15.— ... A Sermon ... at Bristol, Conn., on the Day of Annual Fast, 1852. ... . *New Haven: Printed by J. H. Benham.* 1852. 8vo, pp. 24. B.

[Goodricke (Henry).] Observations|on|Dr. Price's|Theory and Principles|of|Civil Liberty and Government,|preceded by a Letter to a Friend,|on the Pretentions of the American Colonies|in respect of Right and Equity. *York: Printed by A. Ward.* 1776. 8vo, pp. (8), 147. J.C.B., H. 27926

The author asserts that "there cannot be a more evident truth, than that the right of taxing any part of the British empire, and consequently the American colonies, unless particularly exempted by grant or compact, is legally and constitutionally resident in the Parliament."—Page 7. Maryland alone he excepts from this general subjection. *See* "M. Rev.," LV. 239.

[Goodricke.] Aenmerkingen op Price's leer- en grondbeginselen van burgerlijke vryheit en regeering enz., voorafgegaan door een brief aan eenen vriend over de vermeende voorrechten der Americaensche volkplantingen. *Leyden.* 1777. 8vo.

[Goodricke.] A Speech on some Political Topics, the substance of which was intended to have been delivered in the House of Commons, on Monday the 14th of December, 1778. When the Estimates ... were agreed to ... *Cadell.* 1779. 8vo.

The author, Henry Goodricke, Esq., ranges the whole field of our American disputes, he defends the Government on the main question, but condemns them on subordinate points. *See* "M. Rev.," LX. 155.

Goodridge (C. M.) Narrative of a Voyage to the South Seas, and the Shipwreck of the Princess of Wales' Cutter, with an Account of a Two Years' Residence on an Uninhabited Island, by One of the Survivors, Charles Medyett Goodridge, ... Second Edition. *Exeter: W. C. Featherstone.* 1838. 12mo, pp. 180, (10). Plate. 27929

Goodridge (E. P.) The Sham-Robbery, committed by Elijah Putnam Goodridge, on his own Person, in Newbury, Dec. 19, 1816, with a History of his Journey to the place where he Robbed Himself ... . *Concord, N. H.* 1819. 12mo, pp. 152.

Contains the Trial of Ebenezer Pearson and Levi and Seban Kenniston. *Concord, N. H.* 1819. 12mo. W.

Goodsir (Robert Anstruther). An Arctic Voyage to Baffin's Bay and Lancaster Sound, in Search of Friends with Sir John Franklin. By R. A. Goodsir. *London: J. Van Voorst.* 1850. Post 8vo. Map and Plate. A., C. 27931

Goodspeed (E. J.) Funeral Discourse on the Death of Abraham Lincoln, Preached ... April 23d, 1865, in ... Chicago. By Rev. E. J. Goodspeed, Pastor. ... *Chicago.* 1865. 8vo, pp. 37. 27932

Goodwell (G.) Currency; the Evil and the Remedy. By Godek Goodwell. Third Edition. *New York: Wm. H. Graham.* 1846. 8vo, pp. 48. H. 27933

Goodwin (B.) Discourse delivered at South Canaan, Conn., on the one hundredth Anniversary of the Birthday of Widow Margaret Higby. By B. Goodwin. *Hartford.* 1848. 27934

Goodwin (*Dr.*) Speech of Dr. Goodwin in Reply to Dr. Hawks, Dr. Mahan, and others, delivered in Convention, October 14, 1862. *New York: John A. Gray.* 1862. 18mo, pp. 35.

Relates to the Rebellion of the Southern States.

Goodwin (D. R.) Southern Slavery in its Present Aspects; containing a Reply to a late Work of the Bishop of Vermont on Slavery. By Daniel R. Goodwin. *Philadelphia: J. B. Lippincott & Co.* 1864. 12mo, pp. 343. B., BA., C., H. 27936

Goodwin (E. C.) Wayside Songs. By Edward C. Goodwin. *New York: Mason Brothers.* 1856. 12mo, pp. 185.

Goodwin (E. S.) An Address delivered at the third Anniversary of Barnstable Peace Society, December 25, 1830. By Rev. Ezra Shaw Goodwin. *Barnstable.* 1831. 12mo, pp. 23.

Also: Sermons ... in Sandwich, Mass., with a Memoir. *Boston: Benjamin H. Greene.* 1834. 12mo, pp. 268. B., H.

Goodwin (F. J.) Farewell Sermon on Resignation, at St. George's Church, Flushing, L. I. By Frederick J. Goodwin. *Flushing.* 1844. 27939

Goodwin (H.) A Vision ... of the Departed Spirit of Mr. Yeamans. By H. Goodwin. *Brattleboro, Vt.* 1800. 12mo, pp. 11. S. 27940

Goodwin (H. C.) Ithaca as it was, and Ithaca as it is, with Thoughts suggestive of the Future. By H. C. Goodwin. *Ithaca, N. Y.: Andrus, Gauntlett & Company.* 1853. 8vo, pp. 64. N., S.

Goodwin. Pioneer History; or Cortland County and the Border Wars of New York, from the Earliest Period to the Present Time. By H. C. Goodwin. *New York: A. B. Burdick.* 1859. 12mo, pp. 456. 3 Plates. B., BA., C., H. 27942

Also: Speech ... on the Territorial Policy, February 27, 1855. 8vo. S.—The Lecompton Constitution. Speech ... February 24, 1858. [n. p. n. d.] 8vo, pp. 8. BA., H.—Life of John Jacob Astor.—Edgar Wentworth: A Prize Story of the Second American Revolution.

Goodwin (H. M.) The Pilgrim Fathers. ... Two Memorial Discourses ... Rockford, May 22, 1870. By Rev. H. M. Goodwin, ... *Rockford, Ill.: Bird, Conick & Flint.* 1870. 8vo, pp. 36.

Goodwin (I.) An Oration delivered at Lancaster, February 21, 1826, in Commemoration of the One Hundred and Fiftieth Anniversary of the Destruction of that Town by the Indians. By Isaac Goodwin. *Worcester: Rogers & Griffin, Printers.* 1826. 8vo, pp. 15. B. 27944

Goodwin. Town Officer: or Laws of Massachusetts relative to the Duties of Municipal Officers. ... Second Edition, Revised and Enlarged. ... *Worcester.* 1829. 12mo. 27945

Also: An Address ... at Worcester, August 24, 1820, before the American Antiquarian Society, at the opening of the Antiquarian Hall. *Worcester: Printed by Manning & Trumbull.* 1820. 8vo, pp. 17, (1). BA., H., W.—Address ... before the Worcester Agricultural Society, October 13, 1824. *Worcester: Printed by William Manning.* [1824.] 8vo, pp. 32. BA., H. *See also* "Worcester Magazine."

Goodwin (L. S.) The Mysterious Miner; or, The Gold Diggers of California. A Story of the Atlantic and Pacific Shores. By Mrs. L. S. Goodwin. *Boston: Elliott, Thomes & Talbot.* 16mo, pp. 128. 27946

Goodwin (N.) Descendants of Thomas Olcott, one of the First Settlers of Hartford, Connecticut. By Nathaniel Goodwin, ... *Hartford: Press of Case, Tiffany & Burnham.* 1845. 8vo, pp. xii, 64. H., S. 27947

Goodwin. The Foote Family: or the Descendants of Nathaniel Foote, one of the First Settlers of Wethersfield, Conn., with Genealogical Notes of Pasco Foote, who settled in Salem, Mass., and John Foote and others of the name, who settled more recently in New York. By Nathaniel Goodwin, ... *Hartford: Press of Case, Tiffany & Co.* 1849. 8vo, pp. 360. C., S.

Goodwin. Genealogical Notes, or Contributions to the Family History of some of the First Settlers of Connecticut and

Massachusetts. By the Late Nathaniel Goodwin. [Edited by Daniel Goodwin.] *Hartford: F. A. Brown.* 1856. 8vo, pp. xx, 362. B., BA., C., H. 27949

Goodwin (P. A.) Biography of Andrew Jackson, President of the United States, formerly Major-General in the Army of the United States. By Philo A. Goodwin. *Hartford.* 1832. 12mo, pp. xi, 422. H. + [Another Edition.] *New York: R. Hart Towner.* 1833. 12mo, pp. xi, 456. B., C. + *Hartford.* 1852. 12mo. S. 27950

Goodwin (R. M.) Trial of Robert M. Goodwin, on an Indictment of Manslaughter for killing James Stoughton, Esq., in ... New York, ... December, 1819. Taken in Short-hand by William Sampson. *New York: Printed by G. L. Birch & Co.* 1820. 8vo, pp. 33. BA., C. 27951

Also: Summary of the Trial of Robert M. Goodwin for the killing of James Stoughton, ... Taken in Short-hand. *New York.* 1820. 8vo.

Goodwin (T.) An|Apologeticall Narration,|hvmbly svbmitted|to the|Honourable Houses|of|Parliament.| By|Tho: Goodwin,|Philip Nye,|William Bridge,|Jer: Burroughes,| Sidrach Simpson.|*London,*|*Printed for Robert Dawlman.*|M.DC.XLIII. 4to, pp. (4), 31. BA. 27952

This was answered by

Goodwin. An Anatomy of Independency, or A Briefe Commentary, and Moderate Discourse upon The Apologeticall Narration of Mr. Thomas Goodwin, and Mr. Philip Nye, &c. By Argument, laying naked the dangers of their Positions, and From Experience, discovering their spirits and wayes. Published by Authority. *London Printed for Robert Bostock, dwelling in Pauls Church-yard, at the sign of the Kings head,* 1644. 4to, pp. (4), 52.

Connected with the disputes about Church Government, with allusion to those in New England. Also: Some Observations and Annotations upon the Apologeticall Narration [of Thomas Goodwin, etc.] *London: C. Meredith.* 1643. 4to.

Goodwin. A Copy of a|Remonstrance|lately delivered|in to the|Asssembly.|By
Thomas Goodwin. Ierem: Burroughs. William Greenhill. } William Bridge.| Philip Nie.| Sidrach Simpson.| and William Carter.|
Declaring the Grounds and Rea-|sons of their declining to bring in to the As-|sembly, their Modell of Church-|Government.| *London:*|*Printed in the Yeer,* 1645.| 4to, pp. 8. BA. 27954

Goodwin (T. S.) The Natural History of Secession; or, Despotism and Democracy at Necessary, Eternal, Exterminating War. By Thomas Shepard Goodwin, A.M. *New York: John Bradburn.* 1864. 12mo, pp. 328. B., BA., C., H., S. 27955

Goodwin (W.) Statistics of the Senate and House of Representatives of Connecticut, May Session, 1848; ... Compiled by William Goodwin. *New Haven: Printed by T. J. Stafford.* 1848. 8vo, pp 7, (1). Continued. 27956

Goodyear (C.) Speech of Hon. C. Goodyear, of New York, ... in the House of Representatives ... June 29, 1846. [n. p. n. d.] 8vo, pp. 7. H. 27957

Gookin (D.) An Historical Account of the Doings of the Christian Indians in New England in the years 1675, 1676, 1677, impartially drawn by one well acquainted with that affair, and presented unto the Right Honourable the Corporation residing in London, appointed by the King's Most Excellent Majesty for promoting the Gospel among the Indians in America. *Cambridge.* 1836. 8vo. C. 27958

Included in the "Archæologia Americana," Vol. II.

Gookin. Historical Collections of the Indians in New England. Of their several Nations, Numbers, Customs, Manners, Religion, and Government, before the English planted there. Also a true and faithful account of the present state and condition of the praying Indians, (or those who have visibly received the Gospel in New England:) declaring the number of that people, the situation and place of their towns and Churches, and their manner of worshipping God, ... briefly declaring the prudent and faithful endeavors of the Right Honorable the Corporation of London, for promoting that affair; also suggesting some expedients for their further civilizing and propogating the Christian Faith among them. By Daniel Gookin. *Apollo Press: By Belknap and Hall.* MDCCXCII. 8vo, pp. 89. B., BA. 27959

Also included in the first volume of the "Massachusetts Historical Collections."

Gookin (N.) The Day of Trouble near, The Tokens, and a Due Preparation; Three Sermons. By Nathaniel Gookin. Added, A Sermon on Deuteronomy v. 29. And an account of the Earthquake, in Hampton, And something Remarkable of Thunder and Lightning, in 1727. *Boston.* M.DCC.XXVIII. 8vo, pp. (8), 75. B., W. 27960

See "Mass. Hist. Collections," Vol. VII. 55.

Goold (T.) Address, before the Berkshire Agricultural Association for the Promotion of Agriculture and Manufactures. By Thomas Goold. ... And the Address of Elkanah Watson, Esq. *Pittsfield.* 1816. 8vo. 27961

[Goos (P.)] Zee-Atlas, ofte Waterwereld, waer in vertoont werden alle de zee-kusten van het bekende des aerd-bodems. *Amsterdam: P. Goos.* 1666. 27962

This Sea Atlas, or the Watter World, contains ten colored maps relating to America, and one representing California as an island.

Gopsill's Directory of Reading, Allentown, Easton, Pottsville, and Bethlehem (Pa.), 1864–65. *Jersey City: Jas. Gopsill.* 1864. 8vo, pp. vi, 188. 27963

Gopsill's Westchester County Directory, containing Names in the Towns of Peekskill, Sing Sing, Tarrytown, White Plains, and Yonkers, together with a Business Directory of the whole County. *Jersey City: J. Gopsill.* 1866. 12mo, pp. 283.

Goram (R.) Political Inquiries. To which is added a Plan for the General Establishment of Schools throughout the United States. By Robert Goram. *Wilmington.* 1791. 8vo. 27965

Gordoa (J.) Esposicion publica. Por J. Gordoa, Cura propio de Ahualulco. *San Luis Potosi.* 1859. 8vo, pp. 58. Map.

[Gordon] *of Lochinvar.* Encouragements for such as shall have Intention to bee Undertakers in the new Plantation of Cape Briton, now New Galloway, in America, by mee Lochinvar. *Edinburgh.* 1620. Sm. 4to. 27967

Sold at the Gordonstown sale for £3. Very rare, and worth ten times that amount.

Gordon (A. H.) Wilderness Journeys in New Brunswick, in 1862–63. By Hon. A. H. Gordon. *St. John, N. B.* 1864. 12mo, pp. 64. 27968

Gordon (A. J.) Address [by A. J. Gordon] and Reply [by S. P. Chase] on the Presentation of a Testimonial to S. P. Chase by the Coloured People of Cincinnati: with some account of the Case of J. Watson. [*Cincinnati.* 1845.] 8vo. 27969

Gordon (A. J.) ... A Discourse commemorative of the Life and Character of Hon. Richard Fletcher ... July 11, 1869. By Rev. A. J. Gordon. *Boston: Gould and Lincoln.* 1869. 8vo, pp. 24. B., H. 27970

Gordon. ... A Discourse ... in Jamaica Plain, on the Occasion of the State Fast ... April 13th, 1865. By A. J. Gordon ... . *Boston: N. P. Kemp.* 1865. 8vo, pp. 17. B. 27971

Gordon (C.) The Trial of the Hon. Colonel Cosmo Gordon, of the Third Regiment of Foot Guards, for neglect of duty before the enemy, on the 23d of June 1780, near Springfield, in the Jerseys; containing the whole proceedings of a General Court Martial held at the City of New York on the 22d of August, and continued by several adjournments to the 24th of September 1782. *London: Geo. Harlow.* MDCCLXXXIII. 8vo, pp. 118. 27972

See "M. Rev.," LXVIII. 269.

Gordon (G.) In the Matter of George Gordon's Petition for Pardon. *Cincinnati.* 1862. 8vo, pp. 56. 27973

Gordon was convicted for a violation of the Fugitive Slave Law, in Ohio, in 1861.

Gordon (G. A.) ... An Essay, ... October 27, 1863, for the Benefit of the Wayside Home. ... By G. A. Gordon. *Savannah: George N. Nichols.* 1863. 8vo, pp. 28. BA. 27974

Gordon (G. H.) On the Currency. By George H. Gordon. *Boston: Alfred Mudge & Son.* 1867. 8vo, pp. 25. H. 27975

Also: Speech of Gen. Geo. H. Gordon, ... at Newburyport, Mass., October 28, 1863. [n. p. n. d.] 8vo, pp. 16. H.

Gordon (G. F.) Oration delivered on ... July 5, 1858. By George F. Gordon, Esq., in ... Philadelphia, ... *Philadelphia.* 1858. 8vo, pp. 14. H. 27976

Gordon (G. W.) Correspondence respecting the Removal of G. W. Gordon from the Magistracy, and the circumstances connected with the Morant Bay Lock-up Case. *London.* 1866. Folio. 27977

Gordon (G. W.) A Lecture before the Boston Young Men's Society, on the Subject of Lotteries, delivered March 12, 1833. By George William Gordon. *Boston.* 1833. 8vo, pp. 79.

Also: The Record of George Wm. Gordon. The Slave Trade at Rio Janeiro—Seisure of Slave Vessels—Conviction of Slave Dealers ... *Boston: Printed by J. E. Farwell & Co.* 1856. 8vo, pp. 16. H.

Gordon (J. B.) An Historical and Geographical Memoir of the North American Continent; its Nations and Tribes. By the Rev. James Bentley Gordon. With a summary account of

his Life, Writings, and Opinions. *Dublin: Printed by John Jones.* 1820. 4to, pp. civ, x, (2), 305. B., H. 27979

Edited by Thomas Jones. Also on large paper.

Gordon (J. D.) Halifax: its Sins and Sorrows. By Rev. James D. Gordon. *Halifax.* 1862. 12mo, pp. 41. 27980

Gordon (J.) Sermon on the Suppression of the late Unnatural Rebellion. By John Gordon. *Annapolis.* 1746. 4to.

Gordon (J.) The Case of Mr. John Gordon, with respect to the Title to certain Lands in East Florida, purchased of his Catholic Majesty's Subjects by him and Mr. Jesse Fish for themselves, and of other His Britannic Majesty's Subjects, in conformity with the twentieth Article of the last definitive Treaty of Peace. With an Appendix. *London: Printed in the Year* MDCCLXXII. 4to, pp. 32, Appendix, 22 l. C. 27981

Privately printed, for the use of the persons interested.

Gordon (J.) Proceedings of the General Court-Martial in the Trial of Major John Gordon, of the late 8th West India Regiment. *London.* 1804. 8vo. 27982

Gordon (J. *and* W.) A full Report of the Trial of John Gordon and William Gordon, charged with the Murder of Amaza Sprague; ... 1844; ... Reported by Edward C. Larned and William Knowles. *Providence: Transcript Office.* 1844. 8vo, pp. 45.

Gordon. Synopsis of the Trial of John and Wm. Gordon, for the Murder of Amaza Sprague ... together with the Full Particulars of the Execution of John Gordon, on the 14th of February, 1845. ... *Boston: Skinner & Blanchard.* 1845. 12mo, pp. 64. H. 27984

Gordon. A full Report of the Arguments ... in the case of The State *vs.* John and William Gordon, ... Reported by Edward C. Larned. *Providence: Transcript Office.* 8vo, pp. 38.

Gordon. Last Days of Gordon; being the Trial of John and William Gordon, ... the full Particulars of the Execution of John Gordon, on the 14th of February, 1845. By an Eye Witness. Also, William's full Disclosure of what he avers to be Facts in regard to the Murder. *Boston: Skinner & Blanchard.* 1845. 12mo, pp. 64. 27986

Gordon. Petition of John Gordon to His Excellency, James Fenner, Governor of the State of Rhode Island. February 10, 1845. 8vo, pp. 8. 27987

Gordon J. W.) The Hon. Edward Bates, of Missouri, is he Fit ... is he Available, as the Republican Candidate for the Presidency? By J. W. Gordon. *Indianapolis.* 1860. 8vo, pp. 15. H. 27988

Gordon. ... Origin of the Troubles in Kansas, and the Remedy therefor; Speech delivered in ... Indianapolis, September 29, 1856. *Indianapolis: Indiana State Journal.* 1856. 8vo, pp. 56. B., H. 27989

Gordon (N. M.) Alleghan; a Poem in Nine Books. By N. M. Gordon. *Cincinnati.* 1856. 12mo, pp. 343. C. 27990

Gordon (P.) Geography Anatomiz'd. The Third Edition, Corrected. By Pat. Gordon, ... *London: Robert Morden.* 1702. 8vo, pp. (24), 428, (1). 16 Maps. + *London: S. and J. Sprint.* 1704. 12mo, 12 l., pp. 428. H. + Fifth Edition. [*Ibid.*] 1708. + Sixth Edition. [*Ibid.:*] *J. Nicholson.* 1711. 12 l., pp. 428. H. + Seventh Edition. [*Ibid.*] 1716. 12mo. + Eighth Edition. [*Ibid.:*] *J. and B. Sprint.* 1719. 12 l., pp. 428. H. + Eleventh Edition. [*Ibid.*] 1728. + Twelfth Edition. [*Ibid.*] 1730. H. + *London: Knapton.* 1733. 8vo, pp. (24), 432. 17 Maps. BA., C. + *London: J. and P. Knapton.* 1737. pp. 432. B. + Eighteenth Edition. [*Ibid.*] 1744. + Nineteenth Edition. *London.* M.DCC.XLIX. 10 l., pp. 432. Maps. B., BA. 27991

Chapter IV. relates to America and the West Indies.

Gordon (*Hon.* Patrick). *See* Philadelphia.

Gordon (P.) History of the War in America, from its Commencement to the Conclusion in 1783. *Dublin.* 1785–9. 3 vols., 8vo. 27992

Title from Lowndes' "Bibliographer's Manual." Probably an anonymous work.

Gordon (S.) Speech ... on the Bankrupt Law ... January 5, 1843. *Washington.* 1843. 8vo. 27993

Also: The Mexican War; Speech ... December 24, 1846. [n. p. n. d.] 8vo. B.

Gordon (T. F.) A Digest of the Laws of the United States, including an Abstract of the Judicial Decisions relating to Constitutional and Statutory Law. By Thomas F. Gordon. With Notes explanatory and historical. *Philadelphia.* 1827. 8vo, pp. 884. + Second Edition. [*Ibid.*] 1837. 8vo, pp. 822. + Third Edition. [*Ibid.*] 1844. 8vo, pp. xx, 998. BA. + Fourth Edition. [*Ibid.*] 1851. 8vo. 27994

Gordon. A Digest of the Treaties and Statutes of the United States, relating to Commerce, Navigation, and Revenue, compiled at the instance of the Secretary of the Treasury. By Thomas F. Gordon. *Philadelphia.* 1830. 8vo, pp. xix, 302, 319, and Index. 27995

Gordon. A Gazetteer of the State of New-Jersey. Comprehending A General View of its Physical and Moral Condition, together with A Topographical and Statistical Account of its Counties, Towns, Villages, Canals, Rail Roads, &c. ... By Thomas F. Gordon. *Trenton, N. J.: Daniel Fenton.* 1834. 8vo, pp. iv, 266. Map. B., BA., H., P. 27996

Gordon. Gazetteer of the State of New York: Comprehending its Colonial History; General Geography, Geology, and Internal Improvements; Its Political State; A Minute Description of its several Counties, Towns, and Villages; Statistical Tables, exhibiting the Area, Improved Lands, Population, Stock, Taxes, Manufactures, Schools, and Cost of Public Instruction, in each Town. ... By Thomas F. Gordon. *Philadelphia: The Author.* 1836 8vo, pp. xii, 102, 801. 2 Maps. B., BA., H.

Gordon. Gazetteer of the State of Pennsylvania. Part First, contains a general Description of the State, its Situation and Extent, General Geological Construction, Canals and Railroads, Bridges, Revenue, Expenditures, Public Debt, &c., &c. Part Second, embraces ample Descriptions of its Counties, Towns, Cities, Villages, Mountains, Lakes, Rivers, Creeks, &c., alphabetically arranged. By Thomas F. Gordon. ... *Philadelphia: T. Belknap.* 1832. 8vo, pp. 65, 508. Map. + [*Ibid.*] 1833. 27998

Ludewig says, "Reprinted 1839." I have not seen it so dated.

Gordon. The History of America. By Thomas F. Gordon. ... Containing the History of the Spanish Discoveries prior to 1520. *Philadelphia: The Author.* [n. d.] 2 vols., 12mo, pp. xx, 297; 252. 2 Plates. C. + [*Ibid.:*] *Carey & Lea.* 1831. pp. xx, 297; 252. Plate. B., H. + [*Ibid.*] 1832. 27999

Gordon. The History of Ancient Mexico; from the Foundation of that Empire to its Destruction by the Spaniards. ... By Thomas F. Gordon. *Philadelphia: The Author.* 1832. 2 vols., 12mo, pp. xiv, 363; xi, 265. Plates. B., H. 28000

This, with the preceding work, forms all that was published of a projected "Cabinet of American History."

Gordon. The History of New Jersey; from its Discovery by Europeans to the Adoption of the Federal Constitution. By Thomas F. Gordon. *Trenton: Daniel Fenton.* 1834. 8vo, pp. xii, 339. B., BA., H. 28001

The Gazetteer described *supra*, is usually bound up with this.

Gordon. The History of Pennsylvania, from its Discovery by Europeans to the Declaration of Independence in 1776. By Thomas F. Gordon, Esq. *Philadelphia: M. Carey.* 1829. 8vo, pp. vii, 628. B., BA., C., H. 28002

[Gordon.] The War on the Bank of the United States; or, A Review of the Measures of the Administration against that Institution and the Prosperity of the Country. ... *Philadelphia: Key & Biddle* 1834. 8vo, pp. 155. H. 28003

Also: An Inquiry into the Propriety and Means of Consolidating and Digesting the Laws of Pennsylvania. ... *Philadelphia.* 1827. 8vo. P.

Gordon (W.) Sermon at the Funeral of Col. C. Codrington, late Governor of the Carribee Islands, at St. Michael's Barbadoes. By W. Gordon, M.A. 1710. 4to. 28004

Gordon (W.) A Discourse Preached December 15th 1774. Being the day recommended By the Provincial Congress; And Afterwards at the Boston Lecture. By William Gordon, Pastor of the Third Church in Roxbury. ... *Boston: Thomas Leverett.* 1775. 8vo, pp 32, (1). BA., H., P. + *London: Edward and Charles Dilly.* MDCCLXXV. 8vo, pp. 36. BA. 28005

The author says, there "are special times and seasons when the pulpit may treat of politics," and that the present occasion is one in which he shall dedicate his discourse to "the service of the public, the situation of whose affairs is, both distressing and alarming." Reprinted in Thornton's "Pulpit of the Revolution." The remarks of the patriotic minister was so severe on the government that they called forth the following two tracts.

Gordon. Remarks upon a Discourse Preached December 15th 1774. Being the Day recommended by the Provincial Congress: And afterwards at the Boston Lecture. By William Gordon, Pastor of the third Church in Roxbury. In a Letter from a Gentleman in the Country to his Friend in Boston. [*Boston:*] *Printed in the Year* MDCCLXXV. 8vo, pp. 11. J.C.B., M.

Gordon. Observations on the Rev. Pastor of Roxbury's Thanksgiving Discourse. *Boston.* 1776 or 1777. 8vo, pp. 8.

Gordon. The Plan of a Society for Making Provision for Widows, by Annuities for the remainder of Life, And, For Granting Annuities to Persons after certain Ages, With the

Proper Tables for calculating what must be paid by the several members in order to secure the said Advantages. By William Gordon. *Boston: Sold by Joseph Edwards and John Fleeming,* MDCCLXXII. 8vo, pp. vi, 35. B., BA., H., P. 28008

Dated Roxbury, 20 May, 1772, copies are found signed by M. G., and these words inserted in his autograph after the word "expulsion," in the ninth line of p. 5, viz.: "and the monies received from him be retained." A very interesting account of the first life assurance scheme projected in America.

Gordon. The Separation of the Jewish Tribes, after the Death of Solomon, accounted for, and applied to the Present Day, In a Sermon preached before the General Court, on Friday, July the 4th, 1777, Being the Anniversary of the Declaration of Independency, by William Gordon, ... *Boston: Printed by J. Gill, Printer to the General Assembly.* M.DCC.LXXVII. 8vo, pp. 37. BA. 28009

Perhaps the *first* oration commemorating the Declaration of Independence.

Gordon. A Sermon preached before the Honorable House of Representatives, on the day [July 19, 1775,] intended for the choice of Counsellors, agreeable to the Advice of the Continental Congress. By William Gordon, Pastor of the Third Church in Roxbury. *Watertown: Benjamin Edes.* MDCCLXXV. 8vo, pp. 29. B., BA., H. 28010

Publishrd by request of the Massachusetts House of Representatives. This celebrated sermon was delivered at Watertown on the 19th July, about a month after the Battle of Bunker's Hill, and nearly a year before the Declaration of Independence, while the General Court was in Session there, having been driven out of Boston by the British troops. The truly republican text was from Jer. XXX. 20, 21—"And I will punish all that oppress them; and their nobles shall be of themselves, and their governor shall proceed from the midst of them."

Gordon (W.) The History of the Rise, Progress, and Establishment, of the Independence of the United States of America: Including an Account of the late War; and of the Thirteen Colonies, from their Origin to that Period. By William Gordon, D.D. ... *London: Printed for the Author,* MD CC LXXXVIII. 4 vols., 8vo, pp. (26), 504; (8), 584; (8), 499; (8), 445, Index, 17 l. 8 Plates, 5 Maps. B., BA., H. + *New York: Hodge, Allen, and Campbell.* M.DCC.LXXXIX. 3 vols., 8vo, pp. (12), 25–443; (10), 25–474; (36), 17–446. 2 Maps. H. + Second American Edition. *New York: Samuel Campbell.* MDCCCXCIV. 3 vols., 8vo, pp. 431; 460; 448. B. + The Third American Edition. *New York: S. Campbell.* MDCCCI. 3 vols., 8vo, pp. 431; 460; 414, 15 l. B. 28011

There are copies of the English edition on fine and thick paper; the first American edition has a long list of subscribers' names. Gordon is deservedly reckoned as one of the most impartial and reliable of the numerous historians of the American Revolution. "This work deserves little encomium, but the merit of fidelity is the first qualification in a historian, and to that claim, we believe, the present dispassionate writer is fully entitled."—*Monthly Review*, LXXX. 441. The "Critical Review" says that "there arises some suspicion that Dr. Gordon actually wrote under the influence of American prejudice." A suspicion which might perhaps have been confirmed had the reviewer been aware that the author was aided by Thomas Jefferson. *See* Tucker's "Life," Vol. I. 260. Prof. Smyth characterizes the work as "an immense collection of facts presented with great impartiality." Sedgwick, in his "Life of Livingston" (*see* pp. 128, 208) says, Gordon is generally inaccurate, and Bancroft, Vol. IV. 376, calls him inquisitive, but credulous. *See also* Rich's "Bib. Am.," I. 346; Biographie Universelle, &c.

GORDON (W. A.) A Compilation of the Registers of the Army of the United States from 1815 to 1837 [inclusive]. To which is appended a List of Officers on whom Brevets were conferred for Services during the War with Great Britain. By William A. Gordon. *Washington.* 1837. 8vo, pp. 5, 601. B., C., P., S.

GORDON (W. R.) The Peril of our Ship of State. A Sermon preached on Fast Day, January 4, 1861. The Folly of our Speculations. A New Year's Sermon, January 6, 1861. Strictures on a Sermon by Rev. H. J. Van Dyke, on the Character and Influence of Abolitionism. By W. R. Gordon, D.D. ... *New York: John A. Gray.* 1861. 8vo, pp. 38. W. 28013

GORDON. Reliance on God, our Hope of Victory. A Sermon preached on the Day of Fasting and Prayer, September 26th, 1861. By Rev. W. R. Gordon, D.D., ... Schraalenburgh, N. J. *New-York: John A. Gray, Printer.* 1861. 8vo, pp. 30. 28014

GORDON. The Sin of Reviling, and its Work. A Funeral Sermon, occasioned by the Assassination of President Lincoln, April 14, 1865. By W. R. Gordon, D.D., ... Preached ... May 7, 1865. *New York: John A. Gray & Green, Printers.* 1865. 8vo, pp. 24. B. 28015

[GORE (C.)] Manlius; with Notes and References. [*Boston.* 1794.] 8vo, pp. 54. B., BA., H., M. 28016

GORE. An Oration: delivered at the Chapel in Boston, before the Ancient and Honourable Society of Free and Accepted Masons, June 24, 1783. The day appointed for the Installation of John Warren, Esq., Most Worshipful Grand Master of Massachusetts. By Christopher Gore. *Boston: Printed for Brother William Green.* [1783.] 4to, pp. 12. B., BA., H. 28017

Also: Speech to the Legislature of Massachusetts. ... *Boston.* 1809. 8vo. *See* "Mass. Hist. Coll., Third Series, Vol. III."

GORE (M.) Observations on the Disturbances in Canada. By Montague Gore, Esq. *London: Saunders and Ottley.* 1838. 8vo, pp. 38. 28018

GORE. Reflections on the Present State and Prosperity of the British West Indies. By Montague Gore. *London.* 1848. 8vo. 28019

GORGES (F.) America | Painted to the Life. | The true | History | of | The Spaniards Proceedings in the Conquests of the | Indians, and of their Civil Wars among them- | selves, from Columbus his first Discovery, | to these later Times. | As also, | Of the Original Undertakings of the Advancement of | Plantations into those parts; | With a perfect Relation of our English Discoveries, shewing | their Beginning, Progress and Continuance, from the Year | 1628. to 1658. Declaring the forms of their Govern- | ment, Policies, Religions, Manners, Customs, Military Disci- | pline, Wars with the Indians, the Commodities of their | Countries, a Description of their Towns and Havens, | the Increase of their Trading, with the Names of | their Governors and Magistrates. | More especially, an absolute Narrative of the North | parts of America, and of the Discoveries and | Plantations of our English in | Virginia, New-England, and Berbadoes. | Publisht by Ferdinando Gorges, Esq; | A Work now at last exposed for the publick good, to stir up the Heroick and | Active Spirits of these times, to benefit their Countrey, and Eternize | their Names by such Honourable Attempts. | For the Readers clearer understanding of the Countreys, they are lively | described in a compleat and exquisite Map. | *London, Printed for Nath. Brook at the Angel in Cornhil.* 1659. | Title, pp. (4), 51. Portrait and Map. Part II. A | Briefe Narration | of the | Originall Undertakings | of the | Advancement | of | Plantations | Into the parts of | America. | Especially, | Shewing the beginning, progress | and continuance of that of | New-England. | Written by the right Worshipfull, Sir Ferdinando Gorges | Knight and Governour of the Fort and Island of | Plymouth in Devonshire. | *London: | Printed by E. Brudenell, for Nath. Brook at the | Angell in Corn-hill.* 1658. | Title, pp. 57. Part III. America | Painted to the Life. | A | True History of the Originall undertakings of the advancement | of Plantations into those parts, with a perfect relation of | our English Discoveries, shewing their beginning, progress, and | continuance, from the Year, 1628. to 1658. declaring the forms of | their Government, Policies, Religions, Manners, Costumes, Military | Discipline, Warres with the Indians, the Commodities of their |

Countries, a Description of their Townes, and Havens, the increase | of their trading with the names of their Governours and Magistrates. | More | Especially an absolute Narrative of the North parts of America, and | of the discoveries and plantations of our English in | New-England. | Written by Sir Ferdinando Gorges Knight | and Governour of the Fort and Island of Plimouth in | Devonshire, one of the first and chiefest pro- | moters of those Plantations. | Publisht since his decease, by his Grandchild Ferdinando Gorges Esquire, | who hath much enlarged it and added severall accurate Descripti- | ons of his owne. | A work now at last exposed for the publick good, to stir up the heroick and active spirits | of these times, to benefit their Country, and Eternize their names, | by such honourable attempts. | For the Readers clearer understanding of the Country's they are lively described in a | compleat, and exquisite Map. | *London: Printed by E. Brudenell, for Nathaniel Brook dwelling at | the Angel in Cornhill.* 1658 | Title, pp. (2), 236. Part IV. America | Painted to the Life. | The | History | of the | Spaniards Proceedings in America, their Con- | quests of the Indians, and of their | Civil Wars among themselves. | From | Columbus his first Discovery, to these | later Times. | By | Ferdinando Gorges, Esq; | *London, Printed by T. J. for Nath. Brook at the Angel | in Cornhil.* 1659. | Title, pp. (2), 52, Table, 10 l. BA., H. 28020

This "Briefe Narration of the Originall Undertakings of the Advancement of Plantations in America," was printed in the "Maine Hist. Soc. Coll.," Vol. II., also, "Mass. Hist. Soc. Coll.," Vol. VI., Third Series. "These four works were all printed separately (the second and third in 1658), but I believe are always found together. There is an Index at the end, which refers to the four parts, but without any distinguishing mark, by which the reader may ascertain in which book the article referred to is to be found. It is altogether a very singular performance, containing a great deal of important information relative to the early history of New England, and particularly of the district of Maine, which was granted originally to the author's grandfather, by whom the second work was written. Not the least singular circumstance relating to this work, perhaps, is the manner in which Ferdinando Gorges, Esq., has appropriated to himself the authorship of a work written by another, as appears by the following extract from Prince's 'New England.': 'When I went to England, I met with a great variety of Books and Pamphlets relating to this country. Among others, in a history of New England, from 1628 to 1651, printed in 4to, London, 1654, I found many particulars of the beginning of our several churches, towns and colonies, which appear in no other writer. The running title of the book is, 'Wonder working Providence,' &c., and in the genuine title-page no author is named. Some of the books were faced with a false title-page, wherein the work is wrongly assigned to Sir F. Gorges: but the true author was Mr. Johnson, of Woburn, in New England, as the late Judge Sewall assured me, as of a thing familiarly known among the fathers of the Massachusett's Colony.' The third of these books being neither more nor less than the identical history of New England, with merely a new title-page and dedication. The first and second books are spoken of in the 'North American Review,' Vol. II., p. 289, &c., but in an inverted order. The title of the first book, as given there, is

the same as the title to the third, in my copy. Besides the map, there is a portrait of a young Indian woman, with a human leg in her hand; a folded plate, inscribed

AMERICA.

'Tis I, in tempting divers, for to try,
By sundry meanes, t' obtaine me, caus' de them dye;
And, last discover'd, undiscover'd am;
For men, to treade my soyle, as yet, are lame."

—RICH'S *Catalogue*, No. 314.

GORGES. The Seventeenth Jewel of the United States of America: Shining in its Meridian Splendor; in the Latitude and Longitude of the Intended State of Maine. 1797. 12mo. W.

GORHAM (G. C.) Speech ... by George C. Gorham of San Francisco, Union Nominee for Governor, ... San Francisco, July 10th, 1867. [n. p. n. d.] 8vo, pp. 16. H. 28022

GORHAM (J.) Inaugural Address ... of John Gorham, in the Chapel of the University at Cambridge, December 11, 1816. *Boston: Printed by Wells and Lilly.* 1817. pp. 23. B., BA., H.

GORHAM (R.) Political Inquiries, to which is added a plan for the general establishment of Schools throughout the United States. By Robert Gorham. *Wilmington.* 1791. 8vo, pp. 107.

GORHAM, *Me.* "Dead on the Field of Honor." Dedication of the Soldier's Monument, October 18, 1866, Addresses, Poems, &c. *Portland.* 1866. 8vo, pp. 32. 28025

GORHAM SEMINARY, *Maine.* Catalogue. 1839. Continued.

GORISITO (Fr. de). Sermon de N. P. San Pedro Nolasco. *Puebla.* 1687. 4to, 14 leaves. 28027

Title from Andrade's Catalogue. An early Mexican imprint.

GÖRLING (Adolph). Die Neue Welt. Skizzen von Land und Leuten der Nord-Amerikanischen Freistaaten. *Leipzig.* 1848. 12mo. C. 28028

[GORMAN (Charles O.)] An Irish Catholic Whig to his Fellow Countrymen in the United States. ... [*Providence.* 1852.] 8vo, pp. 8. H. 28029

GORMAN (J. B.) Philosophy of Animated Existence. By John B. Gorman. To which is added a brief Medical Account of the Middle Regions of Georgia. *Philadelphia.* 1845. 8vo, pp. 570. 28030

GORMAN (J. C.) Lee's Last Campaign, with an Accurate History of Stonewall Jackson's Last Wound. By Capt. J. C. Gorman. Second Edition—Tenth Thousand. *Raleigh, N. C.: Wm. B. Smith & Company.* 1866. 18mo, pp. 71. B. 28031

[GOROSTIZA.] Trois Lettres addressée par un Mexicain, a Mess. les Rédacteurs du Courrier des Pays-Bas. [*Paris.* 1829.] 8vo, pp. 32. 28032

Privately printed. Relates to the War of Independence of the Spanish Colonies. The author was Consul General of Mexico.

GORRIE (P. D.) The Black River Conference Memorial: containing Sketches of the Life and Character of the Deceased Members of the Black River Conference of the M. E. Church. With Portraits and an Introduction. By Rev. P. Douglass Gorrie. *New York: Carlton & Phillips.* 1852. 12mo, pp. 351. 10 Portraits. C. 28033

GORRIE. The Churches and Sects of the United States: containing a brief Account of the Origin, History, Doctrines, Church Government, Mode of Worship, Usages, and Statistics of each Religious Denomination, so far as known. By the Rev. P. Douglass Gorrie. *New York.* 1850. 12mo, pp. 240.

GORRIE. Episcopal Methodism, as it Was and Is: or, an Account of the Origin, Progress, ... and Statistics of the Methodist Episcopal Church in the United States. Embracing also a Sketch of the Rise of Methodism in ... Canada. *Auburn: Derby and Miller.* 1852. 8vo, pp. xxii, 354. 28035

GORRIE. The History of the Methodist Episcopal Church in the United States and Canada. By the Rev. P. D. Gorrie. *New York.* 12mo. 28036

GORRIE. The Lives of Eminent Methodist Ministers, containing Biographical Sketches, Incidents, Anecdotes, Records of Travel, &c. By Rev. P. Douglass Gorrie. *Auburn: Derby and Miller.* 1852. 12mo, pp. 408. Portraits. B. 28037

GORRINGE (Henry H.) Argument ... in Favor of "A Bill for the Relief of Certain Officers in the United States Navy." Read before the Senate Naval Committee. [*Washington.* 186–.] 8vo, pp. 7. H. 28038

GORRITI (J. M.) Suenos y realidades. Obras completas de la Senora Dona Juana Manuela Gorriti, publicada bajo la direccion de Vicente G. Quesada. *Buenos-Aires.* 1865. 2 vols., 4to, pp. xvi, 352; 344. Frontispiece. 28039

GORTON (B.) A View of Spiritual, or Anti-Typical Babylon, with its Downfall Exhibited, by a Vision of Elisha Peck; as well as by sundry Scripture Prophecies and Revelations. Interpreted and Explained, ... for a Warning ... of the near Approach of the Great and Terrible Day of the Lord. By Benjamin Gorton. *Troy: Printed by Oliver Lyon.* [1808.] 12mo, pp. 179, (1). 28040

Also: Scriptural Account of the Millennium. *Troy.* 1802. 12mo.

[GORTON (S.)] An Antidote against the Common Plague of the World, or an Answer to a small Treatise (as in water face answereth to face), entituled Saltmarsh returned from the Dead; and by transplacing the letters of his name, is Smartlash, ascend unto the Throne of Equity, for the Arraignment of false Interpretours of the Word of God. Summoning out of all the Ages to appear under Penalty of Death, challenging the Consent, or forbidding to gainsay the common approved Priesthood of this Age. *London: Printed by J. M., for A. C.* 1657. 4to, pp. 18, 62, 296, Addenda, (3), Appendix, 30. 28041

A very curious volume, with long epistle dedicatory to Oliver Cromwell, signed Samuel Gorton, and appendix of certain copies of letters which passed betwixt the penman of this treatise and certain men nearly come out of Old England into New, and imprisoned in the common goal of Boston (being Quakers), lest the churches of New England should be defiled with error. The letters are dated from Warwick, in the Nanhyganset Bay, Sept. 16, 1656, and the answers signed by W. Brend, Thos. Thurston, Christopher Holder, and John Copeland. The addenda of three pages consists of faults in printing "Saltmarsh returned." *See* Bartlett's "Bibliography of Rhode Island."

GORTON. An Incorruptible Key composed of the CX. Psalme, wherewith You may open the rest of the Holy Scriptures; Turning itselfe onely according to the Composure and Art of that Lock, of the Closure and Secrecy of that great Mystery of God manifest in the Flesh, but justified only by the Spirit which it evidently Openeth and Revealeth out of Fall and Resurrection; ... By Samuel Gorton, Gent., and at the time of the penning hereof, in the Place of Judicature (upon Aquethneck, alias Road Island) of Providence Plantations in the Nanhygansett Bay, New England. *Printed in the Yeere* 1647. 4to, pp. (2), 6, (24), 120, 119. B. 28042

Appears to have been written at the request of some hearers of Mr. Cotton, who were dissatisfied with his exposition of this Scripture. Query—Is there any record of Mr. Cotton's exposition beyond what is contained in Gorton's animadversions? *See* Bartlett's "Bibliography of Rhode Island."

[GORTON.] Saltmarsh returned from the Dead. In amico Philalethe, or, the Resurrection of James the Apostle, out of the

grave of Cavnall Glosses, for the Correction of the Universall Apostacy, which cruelly buryed him, who yet liveth. Appearing in the comely Ornaments of his Fifth Chapter, in an Exercise, June 4, 1654. Having laid by his grave clothes, in a despised village remote from England, but wishing well, and heartily desiring the true Prosperity thereof. *London: Printed for Giles Calvert, and are to be sold at the black Spread Eagle, at the west end of Pauls.* 1655. 4to, pp. xiv, 198. J.C.B. 28043

Five pages of errata are printed at the end of the "Incorruptible Key."

[GORTON.] Simplicities Defence | against | Seven-headed Policy. | Or | Innocency Vindicated, | being unjustly Accused, | and sorely Censured, by that | Seven-headed Church-Government | United in | New-England: | or | That Servant so Imperious in his Masters Absence | Revived, and now thus re-acting in Nevv-England. | Or | The combate of the United Colonies, not onely against | some of the Natives and Subjects, but against the Authority also | of the Kingdome of England, | with their execution of Laws, in the name and | Authority of the Servant, (or of themselves) and not in the Name and | Authority of the Lord, or fountain of the Government. | Wherein is declared an Act of a great people and Country | of the Indians in those parts, both Princes and People (unanimously) | in their voluntary Submission and Subjection unto the Protection | and Government of Old England (from the Fame they hear thereof) toge- | ther with the true manner and forme of it, as it appears under their own | hands and seals, being stirred up, and provoked thereto, by | the Combate and Courses above-said. | Throughout which Treatise is secretly intermingled, that | great Opposition, which is in the goings forth of those two grand | Spirits, that are, and ever have been, extant in the World | (through the sons of men) from the beginning and | foundation thereof. | *London.* | *Printed by John Macock, and are to be sold by Luke Favvne, | at his shop in Pauls Church yard, at the sign of the Parrot.* 1646. | 4to, pp. (16), 111. B., C., H.

"This very rare and important volume contains the entire early history of the settlement of Warwick, Rhode Island, including the treaties with the Indian Princes, with facsimiles of their 'Markes;' the ordinances issued against Gorton at Boston, and the various documents necessary to substantiate the claims of the Colony, against the persecutions of the Governor and Council. John Cotton seems to have played an important part in these transactions."—STEVENS. It was reproduced with the following title:

[GORTON.] Simplicities Defence against Seven-headed Policy, or a True Complaint of a Peaceable People, Being Part of the English in New England, Made unto the State of Old England, Against Cruell Persecutors, United in Church Government in

those parts. Wherein is made manifest the manifold Outrages, Cruelties, Oppressions and Taxations, by cruell and close Imprisonments, Fire and Sword, Deprivation of Goods, Lands, and Livelyhood; and such like Barbarous Inhumanities, exercised upon the People of Providence Plantations in the Nanhyganset Bay, by those of the Massachusetts, with the rest of the United Colonies, stretching themselves beyond the bounds of all their own jurisdictions, perpetrated and acted in such an unreasonable and barbarous manner, as many thereby have lost their lives. As it hath been faithfully declared to the Honorable Committee of Lords and Commons for Forrain Plantations; whereupon they gave present order for redress. The sight and consideration whereof hath moved a great Country of the Indians and Natives in those parts, Princes and people, to submit unto the Crown of England, and earnestly to sue to the State thereof, for Safeguard and Shelter from like Cruelties. *London: Printed by John Macock, and are to be sold by George Wittington, at the Blue Anchor, neer the Royal Exchange, in Cornhill.* 1647. 4to. 28045

GORTON. Simplicity's Defence. A New Edition, with Notes explanatory of the Text, and an Appendix containing Original Documents, referred to in the work. By William R. Staples. *Providence: Marshall, Brown & Co.* 1835. 8vo, pp. 278. BA.

Forms Vol. II. of the "Rhode Island Historical Collections." B. Also reprinted in Force's "Tracts," Vol. IV., No. 6. Gorton also wrote an "Answer to Nathaniel Morton of New Plimouth, concerning some part of his booke intitutled New Englands Memorial," which exists in MS., and of which Hutchinson printed a portion in the Appendix to Vol. I. of his "History," which has also been reprinted by Mr. Force, in his "Tracts," Vol. IV., No. 7, pp. 17. Concerning Gorton, *see* notes in Bartlett's "Bibliography of Rhode Island." For an answer *see* Winslow (E.)

GÖRTZ (C. G. von). Reise um die Welt, in den Jahren 1844–47. *Stuttgart und Tübingen.* 1852–54. 3 vols., 8vo. A.

GOSCH (L.) Washington und die Nordamerikanische Revolution. *Giesen.* 1817. 12mo. 28048

Title from M. Ellinger's Catalogue.

GÖSHEN (G. J.) Amerika dargestellt durch sich selbst, herausgegeben von George Joachim Göschen. *Leipzig.* 1818–20. 3 vols., 4to. 28049

GOSNOLD (B.) Voyage. *See* Brereton (J.), and for a Dutch version *see* Van der Aa's Collection, Vol. XXII. 8vo.

The Gospel according to Matthew. *See* Cherokee, Vol. III.

For other Indian versions of the Gospel, *see* under the respective Languages or Transators.

Gospel Music, Or the singing of David's Psalms, &c., in the publick Congregation, or private Families asserted and vindicated. By the loving Brothers NHDDMMS. Unto which is added, the judgment of our worthy Brethren of New England touching singing of Psalms as it is learned by and gravely set forth in the preface to the singing Psalms by them translated into Metre. *London: Henry Overton.* 1644. 4to. 28050

Gospel in Central America. *See* [Crowe (Frederick)].

The Gospel of Slavery. A Primer of Freedom. By Iron Gray [*i. e.* Abel C. Thomas?]. *New York: T. W. Strong.* 1864. 12mo, 14 l. 28051

Gospel Order | Revived, | Being an Answer to a Book lately set | forth by the Reverend Mr. Increase Mather, President | of Harvard Colledge, &c., | Entituled, The Order of the Gospel, &c. | Dedicated to the Churches of Christ in New-England, By sundry Ministers of the Gospel in New-England. ... *Printed in the Year* 1700. 4to. Advertisement, 1 l., Epistle Dedicatory, 4 l., Text, pp. 40, Errata, 1 l. 28052

Printed by William Bradford. Thomas says: "This is the only book printed in New York, prior to 1700, that contained more than twenty pages." *See* "History of Printing, Vol. II. 90, 458, for an interesting account of this work. The following title appears in the Catalogue of the Massachusetts Historical Society: Gospel Order Revived. Answer to Increase Mather's "Order of the Gospel." [With Depositions of T. Brattle, Z. Tuthill, and Bart. Green.] *Boston.* 1700. 4to, pp. 40.

Gospel Reminiscences in the West Indies. The Condemned Negro; or, Man's Victim God's Chosen. *Bath.* 1850. 18mo, pp. 40. 28053

Goss (C. C.) Statistical History of the First Century of American Methodism: With a Summary of the Origin and Present Operations of Other Denominations. By Rev. C. C. Goss. *New York: Carlton & Porter.* 1866. 16mo, pp. 188. H.

Goss (E.) Supervisor's Book; containing an Abstract of all Laws ... relating to ... Supervisors of ... New York, ... By Ephraim Goss. *Rochester: D. M. Dewey.* 1849. 8vo, pp. 212.

Goss (E. H.) The Melrose Memorial. The Annals of Melrose, ... Massachusetts, in the Great Rebellion of 1861–1865. By Elbridge H. Goss. *Boston: Mudge & Son.* 1868. Sm. 4to, pp. 270. B., BA., H. 28056

Goss (W. L.) The Soldier's Story of his Captivity at Andersonville, Belle Isle, and other Rebel Prisons. By Warren Lee Goss. *Boston: Lee & Shepard.* 1867. 12mo, pp. 274. BA., C., H. + *Boston: Lee & Shepard.* 1868. 8vo, pp. 274. Plates. + *Boston: Lee & Shepard.* 1869. 8vo, pp. (2), 357. Portrait, 16 Plates, 2 Maps. 28057

Gosse (L. A.) Dissertation sur les races qui composaient l'ancienne population du Pérou, par L. A. Gosse ... *Paris: Claye.* 1861. 8vo. 3 Plates. 28058

An extract from Vol. I. of the "Mémoires de la Société d'Anthropologie."

Gosse. Rapport sur les questions ethnologiques et médicales, relatives au Pérou, ... par M. le Dr. L. A. Gosse ... *Paris: Hennuyer.* 1861. 8vo. 28059

Also: Monographie de l'erythroxylon coca. ... *Bruxelles: M. Hayes.* 1861. 8vo. 2 Plates.

Gosse (P. H.) The Birds of Jamaica. By Philip Henry Gosse; Assisted by Richard Hill, Esq., of Spanish-Town. *London: J. Van Voorst.* 1847. Post 8vo, pp. x, 447. A., C. 28060

Also: Illustrations of the Birds of Jamaica. *London: J. Van Voorst.* 1849. 8vo, 2 l., 52 colored Plates. C.

Gosse. The Canadian Naturalist, a Series of Conversations on the Natural History of Lower Canada. By Philip H. Gosse. *London: J. Van Voorst.* 1840. Post 8vo, pp. 360. A., B., BA., H.

Gosse. Letters from Alabama, chiefly relating to Natural History. By Philip Henry Gosse. *London: Morgan & Co.* 1859. Post 8vo, pp. 310. B., BA., C. 28062

Gosse. A Naturalist's Sojourn in Jamaica. By Philip Henry Gosse; Assisted by Richard Hill, Esq. With coloured Plates. *London: J. Van Voorst.* 1851. Post 8vo, pp. 506. BA. 28063

Gosse. The Romance of Natural History. By Philip Henry Gosse, ... *Boston: Gould and Lincoln.* 1861. 8vo, pp. xiv, (1), 372. BA. + Sixth Edition. *London: James Nisbet and Co.* M.DCCC.LXIII. Post 8vo, pp. xi, 372. 28064

Includes many references to American Natural History. Also, his "Life." *London.* 1857. 12mo; and, The Ocean. *London.* 1849. 12mo, pp. xii, 360.

Gosselman (Carl August). Resa i Colombia, åren 1825 och 1826. *Nyköping.* 1828. 8vo. Map and Plate. + Andra uppl. *Stockholm: J. Hörberg.* 1830. 2 vols., 8vo, pp. 275; 302. 2 Plates, 1 Map. A., C. 28065

Gosselman. Reise in Columbien, in den Jahren 1825 und 1826. Aus dem Schwedischen übersetz von A. G. F. Freese. *Stralsund: Löffler.* 1829–31. 2 vols., 12mo, pp. (2), 230, Map; (2), 312, (2), Plate. C. 28066

Gosselman. Reis naar Columbia, in de Jaren 1825 en 1826. *Haarlem: de wed. A. Loosjes.* 1832. 2 vols., 8vo, pp. viii, 254, Map; vi, 344, Plate. C. 28067

Gosselman. Reise zwischen Süd- und Nord-Amerika. *Rostock.* 1834. 8vo. 28068

[Gostich (J.)] *See* Chambers (R.), Vol. III., No. 11800.

Gostling (G.) Extracts from the Treaties between Great-Britain and other Kingdoms and States of such Articles as relate to the Duty and Conduct of the Commanders of His Majesty's Ships of War. By George Gostling. *London.* MDCCXCII. 4to, pp. lix, 379. J.C.B. 28069

This beautifully printed volume includes the Treaty with America.

Gotham. *See* [Judah], and [Paulding (J. K.)]

Gottfriedt (Johann Ludwig). *See* Aa (P. v. d.), Vol. I., No. 3, and Abelin (J. P.), Vol. I., No. 50.

The following should have appeared under Avity (P. de).

Gottfriedt. Archontologia cosmica; sive, imperiorvm, regnorvm, principatvvm, rervmqve pvblicarvm omnivm per totvm terrarvm orbem commentarii lvcvlentissimi, [etc.] Opera et studio Jo. Lvdovici Gotofredi, qui eos primo gallice per D. T. V. Y. [id est Petrum d'Avitium] conscriptos in sermonem latinum conuertit, locupletavit, etc. *Francofvrti ad Moenum: L. Jennisivs.* 1628. 2 vols., folio, 22 l., pp. 690; 267, 81, 42 l. C. + *Francofvrti: M. Meriani.* 1649. Folio. [Also] 1695. Folio.

This interesting work forms a Geography and Pictorial Atlas of the World. It is, perhaps, the first of that useful class of books called Gazetteers, which it resembles more than anything else.

Gouge (W. M.) The Fiscal History of Texas; embracing an Account of its Revenues, Debts, and Currency, from the Commencement of the Revolution in 1834, to 1851–52. With Remarks on American Debts. By William M. Gouge. *Philadelphia: Lippincott, Grambo & Co.* 1852. 8vo, pp. 347. B., BA.

Gouge. An Inquiry into the Expediency of Dispensing with Bank Agency and with Bank Paper in the Fiscal Contracts of the United States. 1837. 8vo, pp. 56. 28072

Gouge. The Journal of Banking, from July, 1841, to July, 1842; with a short History of Paper Money and Banking. By W. M. Gouge. *Philadelphia.* 1842. 8vo. P., S. 28073

Gouge. A Short History of Paper-Money and Banking in the United States. Including an Account of Provincial and Continental Paper-Money. To which is prefixed an Inquiry into the Principles of the System, ... By William M. Gouge. *Philadelphia.* 1833. 12mo, pp. xii, 240. BA., C., H. + Second Edition. *New-York: B. & S. Collins.* 1835. 8vo, pp. 64. B., H. + Third Edition. [*Ibid.*] 1840. + Fourth Edition. *New York.* 1840. S. 28074

Cobbett reproduced this in London under the title of "The Curse of Paper-Money." Also: History of the Banking System. *New York.* 1835. 12mo.

Gougenot des Mousseaux (Henri Roger). L'Emancipation aux Antilles françaises, état actuel des colonies. *Paris: Dauvin et Fontaine.* 1844. 8vo. A. 28075

[Gough (James).] Britannia: a Poem. With Historical Notes. Inscribed to the King, Queen, and Royal Family. The Lords and Commons of Great Britain and Ireland. The Governors and Members of British Colonies. *London: A. Millar.* 1764. 4to, pp. 32. 28076

Gough (J.) A History of the People called Quakers, from their first Rise to the present Time. Compiled from Authentic Records, and from the Writings of that People. By John Gough. *Dublin: Robert Jackson.* M, DCC, LXXXIX–XC. 4 vols., 8vo, pp. x, (1), 546, (7); (2), 557, (10); 526, (9). B., C.

Gough. The History of the People called Quakers. Abridged from the Writings of John Gough, William Sewell, &c. *London: Darton and Harvey.* 1799. 2 vols., 8vo. 28078

Supposed to be abridged by Thomas Bradley.

Gough (J. B.) The Autobiography of John B. Gough. *Boston.* 1845. 18mo, pp. 172. + Fourteenth Thousand. [*Ibid.*] 1845. + *London.* 1845. 18mo. + *Boston.* 1848. + [*Ibid.*] 1853. 18mo, pp. 180. 28079

Gough. The Autobiography of John B. Gough, with Continuation to the Present Time. *London: W. Tweedie & Co.* 1855. 12mo, pp. 172. 28080

Gough. Autobiography of John B. Gough, and Orations. *London: W. Tweedie & Co.* 1855. 12mo, pp. 395. 28081

Gough. Autobiography and Personal Recollections, with Twenty-Six Years' Experience as a Public Speaker. By John B. Gough. *Springfield, Mass.: Bill, Nichols & Co.* 1869. 8vo, pp. 552. 8 Plates, 1 Portrait. B. 28082

See Pound (J.) Alliance Weekly News. The True Position of the Controversy regarding Mr. Gough's Dead Letter: August 8, 15, 1857. The Final Word of the Alliance as regards the Gough Controversy: September 19, 1857. Folio, pp. 8.

Gough. ... Narrative of the Conduct and Conversation ... during ... his late Absence. ... *New York: Lewis C. Donald.* 1845. 8vo, pp. 16. B. 28083

Gould (Albert P.) Speech ... delivered in the House of Representatives of Maine, March 6th and 7th, 1862. *Augusta.* 1862. 8vo, pp. 48. B., H. 28084

Gould (A. Addison). Otia Conchologica: Descriptions of Shells and Mollusks, from 1839 to 1862. By Augustus A. Gould. *Boston: Gould & Lincoln.* 1862. 8vo, 2 l., pp. 256. C.

[Gould.] Report on the Invertebrata of Massachusetts, comprising the Mollusca, Crustacea, Annelida, and Radiata. *Cambridge: Folsom, Wells & Thurston.* 1841. 8vo, pp. xiii, 373. 15 Plates. B., BA., C., H. 28086

Gould. Report on the Invertebrata of Massachusetts, published agreeably to an Order of the Legislature. Second Edition, comprising the Mollusca. Edited by W. G. Binney. *Boston: Wright & Potter, State Printers.* 1870. 8vo, 1 l., pp. vii, 524, 12 l. 12 Plates, Nos. xvi.–xxvii. B., H. 28087

Of this there was an extra edition, containing a Notice of Dr. Gould.

Gould. Results of an Examination of the Shells of Massachusetts. By Augustus A. Gould. *Boston.* 1841. pp. 13.

From the "Boston Journal of Natural History," Vol. v.

Gould. ... Mollusca and Shells. By Augustus A. Gould, M.D. With an Atlas of Plates. *Philadelphia: Printed by C. Sherman.* 1852. 4to, pp. xv, 510; Atlas, pp. 16, 52 colored Plates. 28089

Forms Vol. XII. of the "United States Exploring Expedition." The Atlas is dated 1856, but was not issued till 1862. Some copies of the text have the imprint *Boston: Gould and Lincoln.* 1852. Also: Address in Commemoration of Professor J. W. Bailey, August 19, 1857. *Boston.* 1857. 8vo. B.—Descriptions and Notices of some of the Land Shells of Cuba. [n. p. n. d.] 8vo, pp. 12. B.—Description of the Principal Fruits of Cuba. [*Boston.* n. d.] 8vo, pp. 41.—Descriptions of Shells from the Gulf of California and the Pacific Coasts of Mexico and California. [n. p. n. d.]

8vo, pp. 35. 3 Plates. B.—Memoir of Dr. Amos Binney. *Boston.* 1850. 8vo, pp. 21. B.—Origin, Progress, and Present Condition of the Boston Society of Natural History ... *Boston.* 1842. 8vo, pp. 8. B.

[Gould (Augustus A.), *and* Kidder (Frederic).] The History of New Ipswich, from its First Grant in MDCCXXXVI, to the Present Time: with Genealogical Notices of the Principal Families, and also the Proceedings of the Centennial Celebration, September 11, 1850. *Boston: Gould and Lincoln.* 1852. 8vo, pp. (4), 488, iv. Map and Plates. 28090

Gould (B. A.) Biographical Notice of James Melville Gilliss. By Benjamin Apthorp Gould. ... *Cambridge: Welch, Bigelow and Company.* 1867. 8vo, pp. 57. H. 28091

Gould. ... Boston Harbor: A Series of Communications to the Boston Daily Advertiser. By Benjamin A. Gould. ... *Boston: J. E. Farwell & Co.* 1863. 8vo, pp. 65. B., H. 28092

Gould. Defence of Dr. Gould, by the Scientific Council of the Dudley Observatory. *Albany: Weed, Parsons and Company.* 1858. 8vo, pp. 91. B., BA. + Second Edition. [*Ibid.*] + Third Edition. [*Ibid.*] pp. 93. B. 28093

Gould. Eulogy on Joseph S. Hubbard. [*Cambridge: Printed by Welch, Bigelow & Co.* 1864.] 8vo, pp. 44. B., H. 28094

Gould. Investigations in the Military and Anthropological Statistics of American Soldiers. By Benjamin Apthorp Gould, ... Actuary to the U. S. Sanitary Commission. *New York.* 1869. 8vo, pp. xiv, 655. BA., H. 28095

Gould. Reply to the "Statement of the Trustees" of the Dudley Observatory. By Benj. Apthorp Gould, Jr. *Albany: Printed by Charles Van Benthuysen.* 1859. 8vo, pp. v, (2), 366.

[Gould.] Specimens of the Garblings of Letters by the Majority of the Trustees of the Dudley Observatory. *Albany.* 1858. pp. 19. B., H. 28097

Signed, B. A. Gould, J. Also: ... Address to the American Association ... on retiring from the Office of President, August 20, 1869. *Salem: Essex Institute Press.* 1869. 8vo, pp. 39. B., H.—An Address in Commemoration of Alexander Dallas Bache ... August 6, 1868, ... *Salem: Essex Institute Press.* 1868. 8vo, pp. 56. B., H.—An Address in Commemoration of Sears Cook Walker, delivered before the American Association for the Advancement of Science, April 29, 1854. ... *Cambridge: Joseph Lovering.* 1854. 8vo, pp. 28. B., H.—An American University. An Oration before the Connecticut Beta of the Phi Beta Kappa Fraternity, Trinity College, Hartford, 1856, July 15. ... *Hartford: Case, Tiffany and Company.* M.DCCC.LVI. 8vo, pp. 32. B., H.—Deposition in relation to the Claims of Prof. Samuel F. B. Morse to

the Invention of the Electro-Magnetic Telegraph, Circuit Court of the United States, April, 1850. ... [n. p. n. d.] 4to, pp. 16.— ... The Transatlantic Longitude, as determined by the Coast Survey Expedition of 1866. A Report to the Superintendent of the U. S. Coast Survey. ... *Washington.* 1869. Imp. 4to, pp. 102. B., BA.

Gould (C.) Appeal of Charles Gould from the Session of the Madison Square Presbyterian Church. *New-York: George F. Nesbitt & Co., Printers.* 1864. 8vo, pp. 54. 28098

[Gould (Daniel).] A Brief Narration of the Sufferings of the People called Quakers; who were put to death at Boston in New-England. Also An account from their own hands, of their Coming to Boston, and of their staying in their Iurisdiction after Banishment. With a Precious Epistle of William Robinson, to us his fellow Prisoners, and other Epistles hereunto Annexed. [n. p.: 1700.] 4to, pp. 38. M. 28099

Gould wrote his name on the copies circulated in England. He died on Rhode-Island, 1716, aged about ninety-one, and was a minister forty-five years.

Gould (D.) Life of Robert Morris. ... With Extracts from his Speeches, illustrating his Biography, and the Early History of Finance, Banking, and Commerce in the United States. By David Gould. *Boston: Leonard W. Kimball.* 1834. 12mo, pp. 126. B., BA. 28100

Gould (E. S.) ... American Criticism on American Literature. A Lecture delivered before the Mercantile Library Association, Clinton Hall, December 29, 1835. By Edward S. Gould, Esq., ... *New York.* 1836. 8vo, pp. 26. N. 28101

Gould. John Doe and Richard Roe; or, Episodes of Life in New York. By Edward S. Gould. *New York: Carleton.* 1862. 12mo, pp. 312. C. 28102

Also: "The Very Age." A Comedy in five Acts. ... *New York.* 1850. 12mo, pp. 153. *See also* Gourlie (J. H.)

Gould (E.) Report of the Committee on the Petition of Elijah Gould, and others, with Counter Statement. 1830. 8vo, pp. 14, 4. 28103

Relates to some affairs at Antrim, N. H.

Gould (G. H.) Sermon at the Funeral of Hon. W. W. Ellsworth. By Rev. G. H. Gould. *Hartford: R. P. Wales, Printer.* 1868. 8vo, pp. 20. 28104

Gould (H. F.) Poems. By Hannah Flagg Gould. *Boston: Hilliard, Gray, Little & Wilkins.* 1832. 16mo, pp. viii, 174. Plate. C., H. + Second Edition, with Additions. *Boston.* 1833.

24mo. + *Boston: Hilliard, Gray & Co.* 1835. pp. viii, 239. P. + *Boston: Hilliard, Gray & Co.* 1836. pp. viii, 239; x, 192. H. + *Boston: Hilliard, Gray & Co.* 1839–41. 3 vols., 12mo, pp. viii, 239; vii, 240; vii, 240. BA. 28105

Also: New Poems. *Boston: William J. Reynolds & Co.* 1850. 12mo, pp. viii, 286. BA.

Gould (J.) An Oration Pronounced before the Connecticut Alpha of the Phi Beta Kappa Society, September 13th, 1825. By James Gould. *New Haven.* 1825. pp. 31. 28106

Gould. An Oration at Litchfield, on the Anniversary of the Independence of the United States of America, in the Year M,DCC,XCVIII. By James Gould. *Printed by T. Collier.* [1798.] 8vo, pp. 32. BA. 28107

Gould (J.) History of Delaware County and Border Wars of New York. Containing a Sketch of the Early Settlements in the County, and a History of the Late Anti-Rent Difficulties in Delaware, with other Historical and Miscellaneous Matter, never before Pulished. By Jay Gould. *Roxbury: Keeny & Gould.* 1856. 12mo, pp. xvi, 426. Portrait of Z. Pratt. S. 28108

Very rare. The author is widely known in connection with the Erie Railway. The book was really printed in Philadelphia; almost the entire edition was destroyed by fire.

Gould (J.) A Monograph of the Odontophorinæ, or Partridges of America. By John Gould. *London.* 1844–50. 3 vols., folio. 28109

Gould. A Monograph of the Ramphastidæ, or Family of Toucans. By John Gould. *London.* 1854. Folio. C., S. + Supplement to the First Edition. *London.* 1855. 2 Parts, folio.

Gould. A Monograph of the Trogonidæ, or Family of Trogons. By John Gould. *London.* 1838. Folio. Descriptive Letter-Press, with 36 Plates. A. 28111

Gould. A Monograph of the Trochilidæ, or Humming-Birds. By John Gould. *London.* 1852–61. 5 vols., folio. C., S.

Many of the animals described are American, and this series of works is probably one of the grandest ever attempted by one naturalist. *See also* Darwin (C.), Vol. v., No. 18694.

Gould (J. S.) Address Delivered at the Annual Meeting of the New York State Agricultural Society, Albany, February 13, 1867. By John Stanton Gould, President. *Albany.* 1867. 8vo.

Gould. Eulogium on the late Gov. John A. King, delivered ... at Buffalo, October 3d, 1867. By John Stanton Gould. *Albany: Van Benthuysen & Sons.* 1867. 8vo, pp. 42. H., S.

Also: A Report on Food and Diet ... suited for Almshouses, Prisons, and Hospitals. ... *New-York: Wm. C. Bryant & Co.* 1852. 8vo, pp. 99. B., H., S. — Address ... before the Cayuga County Agricultural Society ... Auburn, September 14, 15 & 16, 1859. *Auburn: Knapp & Peck.* 1859. 8vo, pp. 31. B.

Gould (J.) Digest of the Statutes of Arkansas; embracing all the Laws of a General and Permanent Character in force at the close of the Session of the General Assembly of 1856; ... with Notes, &c., ... By Josiah Gould. ... *Little Rock.* 1858. 8vo. C. 28115

Gould (J. W.) John W. Gould's Private Journal of a Voyage from New York to Rio De Janeiro, together with a brief Sketch of his Life. Edited by his Brother. Printed for private circulation only. *New-York.* 1839. 8vo, pp. 207. Map. C., S.

Gould (L. S.) The Origin and Present Condition of Freemasonry in Melrose. ... June 25th, A.D. 1866. By Levi S. Gould ... . *Boston: McIntire & Moulton.* 1866. 8vo, pp. 20.

Gould (M. T. C.) Debate in the Senate of New York on Mr. Granger's Motion ... Increasing the Number of Delegates. Reported by M. T. C. Gould. *Albany: Printed by E. & E. Hosford.* 1821. 8vo, pp. 37, (2). B. 28118

Gould. Report of the Trial of Friends, at Steubenville, Ohio, from the 15th to the 26th of October, 1828. ... By Marcus T. C. Gould, Stenographer. *Philadelphia: Jesper Harding, Printer.* 1829. 8vo, pp. 338. B., S. 28119

This trial grew out of the Hicksite Controversy.

Gould. Report of the Trial of Friends, in the City of Philadelphia, June, 1828, ... or the Case of Edmund Shotwell, Joseph Lukins, Charles Middleton, and two others, ... Taken in Short-hand, by M. T. C. Gould, Stenographer. *Philadelphia: J. Harding, Printer.* 1828. 8vo, pp. 156. 28120

Gould. Trial of Twenty-four Journeymen Tailors charged with a Conspiracy, before the Mayor's Court of the City of Philadelphia, September, 1827. Reported by M. T. C. Gould. *Philadelphia.* 1827. 8vo. N., S. 28121

Gould (N.) A Sketch of the Trade of British America. By N. Gould. *London.* 1835. 8vo, pp. 20. 28122

Gould (N. D.) History of Church Music in America: treating of its Peculiarities at different Periods; its Legitimate Use and Abuse: with Criticisms, Cursory Remarks, and Notices. ... By Nathaniel D. Gould. *Boston: Gould & Lincoln.* 1853. 12mo, pp. 240. B., BA., H. 28123

Gould (Roland F.) The Life of Gould, an Ex-Man-of-War's-Man, with Incidents of Sea and Shore, including the Three Years' Cruise of the Battle-Ship Ohio, under Commodore Hull. *Claremont (N. H.) Manufacturing Co.* 1867. 16mo, pp. 240. Portrait. C. 28124

Gould (T. B.) Selections from the Letters of Thomas B. Gould, a Minister ... in the Society of Friends. With Memoir of his Life. By William Hodgson. *Philadelphia.* 1860. 8vo, pp. 448. 28125

Gould (V.) Sermon, at Westhampton, in Time of Sickness, 1802. By Vinson Gould. *Northampton, Mass.* 1804. 8vo. S.

Gould. A Sermon ... at East-Haven [Connecticut], January 13, 1808, at the Ordination of the Reverend Saul Clark ... . By Vinson Gould ... *New-Haven: Printed by Oliver Steel & Co.* 1808. 8v, pp. 24. 28127

Gould (W., *Senr.*) A History of the Emigration and Settlement of our Predecessors. By William Gould, Sen., of Albany. [*Albany: J. Munsell.* 1841.] 8vo, pp. 2. 28128

Gould (W.) New York and the White Mountains. Map. *Boston.* 1852. 12mo, pp. 80. 28129

Goulding (F. R.) Robert and Harold; or, the Young Marooners on the Florida Coast. By F. R. Goulding. *Philadelphia.* 1852. 12mo. + *London.* 1853. + Second Edition. *Philadelphia.* 1853. + Fifth Edition. *Philadelphia.* 1856. 12mo, pp. 422. + *Macon, Ga.: Burke, Boykin & Co.* 1862. + New and Enlarged Edition. *Philadelphia: J. S. Claxton.* 1866. 16mo, pp. 446. 11 Plates. C. 28130

Also: Marooner's Island; or, Dr. Gordon in search of his Children. ... *Philadelphia: Claxton, Remsen & Haffelfinger.* 1869. 16mo, pp. 493. 6 Plates. B., C. — Sal-o-quah; or, Boy-Life Among the Cherokees. ... *Philadelphia: Claxton, Remsen & Haffelfinger.* 1870. 16mo, pp. 265. 4 Plates. C.

Goulty (J. N.) A Discourse on Colonial Slavery. By J. Nelson Goulty. 1826. 8vo. 28131

Gouly (B.) Opinions et Réflexions Morales, Physiques et Politiques, de B. Gouly, Représentant du Peuple, sur le rapport de la Commission des onze, relatif au régime constitutionnel des Colonies françaises; Imprimées par ordre de la Convention Nationale. *A Paris, de l'imprimerie Nationale, Thermidor, an III.* 8vo, pp. 26. 28132

Gouraud (J. B. G. Fauvel). Les hommes d'état de la France constitutionnelle comparés aux hommes d'état de la grande république des États-Unis, ou la haute politique du jour des deux gouvernements. Documents officiels en forme de dépêches, [etc.] *Paris: Blondeau.* [1847.] 4to, pp. 26. Portrait. 28133

See also our Vol. VI., No. 23932.

Gouraud (Francis Fauvel). Cosmophonography: or the Lord's Prayer in One Hundred Languages. *New York.* 185–. 8vo. 28134

Includes some American languages.

Gourdin (T. S.) Historical Sketch of the Order of Knights Templar: An Address ... at Charleston, S. C., on March 23, A.·.O.·.737, A. D. 1865. By Theodore S. Gourdin, ... *Charleston.* 1865. 8vo, pp. 34. 28135

Also: The Reviewer Reviewed, or A Reply to ... The Southern Presbyterian Review for April, 1857. *Charleston: Harper & Calvo, Printers.* 1857. 8vo.

Gourges (D. de). *See* Ternaux, Vol. XX., and Aa (v. der), Vol. XVI.

Gourlay (R. F.) A Banished Briton. Appellant and Mediator. No. 1.—A Record. *Cleveland.* 1836. 8vo, pp. 28, 16.

Gourlay. The Banished Briton and Neptunian; being a Record of the Life, Writings, Principles, and Projects of Robert Gourlay, Esq., now Robert Fleming Gourlay. *Boston: Redding & Company.* 1843. 8vo, pp. 16, 232. B., BA., H. 28137

Gourlay. General Introduction to Statistical Account of Upper Canada, compiled with a View to a Grand System of Emigration, in connection with a reform of the Poor Laws. *London: Simpkin & Co.* 1822. 8vo, pp. div–47. A., W. 28138

Forms Vol. I. of No. 28143, with a separate title.

Gourlay. On Emigration and Settlement on Wild Land. *Cupar-Fife.* 1849. 8vo. 28139

Gourlay. Letters, &c., by Robert Gourlay, on Emigration Societies in Scotland, written in 1828 and 1829. 8vo, pp. 32.

Gourlay. Principles and Proceedings of the Inhabitants of the District of Niagara ... respecting Claims of Sufferers in the War. Lands to Militia-Men, and the General Benefit of Upper Canada. *Niagara.* 1818. 8vo. 28141

Gourlay. Plans for beautifying New York, and for enlarging and improving the City of Boston. Being Studies to illustrate the Science of City Building. By Robert Fleming Gourlay. *Boston: Crocker & Brewster.* 1844. 8vo, pp. 38, 381–384. Plans and Map. BA., H. 28142

Gourlay. Statistical Account of Upper Canada, compiled with a View to a Grand System of Emigration. By Robert Gourlay. *London: Simpkin & Co.* 1822. 3 vols., 8vo, pp. (1), xx, (2), 625; (3), xxii, 704; Appendix, cxxix, (1), General Introduction, xii, div, Index, 47. Plates and Maps. B., C., H.

Also: Canada and Common Laws, or no Common Laws, no Canada. *Edinburgh.* 1852. 12mo, pp. 12. — Chronicle of Canada, 1818. *St. Catherines, N. C.* 1842. 12mo, pp. 40. — Case before the Legislature, with his Speech, delivered on 1st July, 1858. ... *Toronto.* 1858. 8vo, pp. 29.

Gourlay (W.) Guide to the Canadas, containing Useful and Practical Information for those who propose Emigrating to the British Possessions in North America. By William Gourlay. *Ayr.* 1833. 12mo, pp. 82. 28144

Gourlie (J. H.) An Address, ... before the Mercantile Library Association ... January 8, 1839. (Embodying a History of the Association.) By John H. Gourlie. *New-York: Printed by James Van Norden.* 1839. 8vo, pp. 20. BA. 28145

See Gould (E. S.) Also: The Origin and History of "The Century" [Club], 1856. *New-York: Wm. C. Bryant & Co.* 1856. 8vo, pp. 30, (1). H., S. — The Benefits and Influences of Commerce. A Lecture delivered before the Mercantile Library Association, ... January 5, 1836. ... *New York.* 1836. 8vo, pp. 23. N.

Gouroff (M.) Récherches sur les Enfants trouvés, et les Enfants illégitimes, en Russie, dans le Reste de l'Europe, en Asie et en Amérique. *Paris.* 1839. 8vo. A. 28146

Gouverneur (Isaac) *and* Kemble (Peter). Report of the Case in the Court of Errors, for the State of New York, between Isaac Gouverneur and Peter Kemble, Plaintiffs in Error, and Louis Le Guen, Defendant in Error. *Albany: Printed by Charles R. & George Webster.* 1798. 8vo, pp. 135. 28147

Gouverneur (L. D.) America the Land of Emanuel; or Constitutional Liberty a Refuge for the Gathering to Shiloh.

By Lorenzo D. Gouverneur of the Shaker Community ... *Boston: Williams & Co.* 28148

Gouverneur, *pseudonym.* Remarks on the Life Insurance Laws of New-York. ... *Boston.* 1852. 12mo, pp. 12. H. + *New-York.* 1852. 12mo, pp. 12. S. 28149

Gouverneur Wesleyan Seminary: Catalogue. 1842. *Ogdensburgh, N. Y.* 8vo. Continued. 28150

Goux (M.) Catéchisme en langue Créole, précédé d'un essai de Grammaire sur l'idiome usité dans les colonies françaises. Par M. Goux, Missionnaire apostolique à la Martinique. *Paris: Imp. de Vrayet de Surcy.* 1842. 18mo, pp. 72. 28151

Gouy (*Comte* de). Première Dénonciation Solemnelle d'un Ministre, faite a l'Assemblée Nationale, en la personne du Comte de la Luzerne, Ministre d'Etat, de la Marine, et des Colonies; par le Comte de Gouy, Député de Saint-Domingue, au nom de la Députation & de ses Commettans: Signée par les Représentants de la Colonie; Approuvée & confirmée par les trois Assemblées Provinciales, & par l'Assemblée Coloniale de Saint-Domingue. Dédiée a la Nation, a la Loi, au Roi, a la partie Française de Saint-Domingue, a toutes les Colonies, aux Sociétés des Amis de la Constitution, a tous les bons Citoyens, et aux Ministres de toutes les Puissances. *Imprimée pour l'Assemblée Nationale. Chez Denonville, l'an second de la Liberté. Paris.* 1790. 8vo, pp. 166. 28152

With it should also be found a sort of appendix, entitled "Extrait des pieces justificatives a l'appui de la denonciation," &c., pp. 141. They are both very rare.

Goüy d'Arsy (*Marquis* de). Lettre du Comité Colonial de France, au Comité Colonial de Saint-Domingue, contenant le journal historique de toutes les assemblées. *Paris.* 1788. 8vo, pp. 135. S. 28153

Gouy d'Arsy. Opinion de M. le Marquis de Gouy d'Arsy, député de Saint-Domingue, sur le rétablissement du Conseil supérieur du Cap, et sur le renvoi de M. le Comte de Luzerne, Ministre actuel de la Marine, prononcée à l'Assemblée Nationale, au nom de la députation de la colonie. [n. p.:] *Mars,* 1790. 8vo, pp. 22. 28154

[Gouy (Louis Marthe de).] Idées Sommaires sur la restauration de Saint-Domingue, présentées à la Nation, au Roi et à la Colonie. *Paris: Boulard.* 1792. 8vo, pp. (1), iv, 88. J.C.B., H.

Goveo de Victoria. *See* Victoria (Pedro Goveo de).

The Governing Race. A Book for the Time. *Washington.* 1860. 8vo. 28156

Government Contracts. Report of the Special Committee of the House, appointed to enquire into all the Facts and Circumstances connected with Contracts and Agreements by, or with, the Government, growing out of its Operations in suppressing the Rebellion, December 7, 1861. House of Representatives, 37th Congress, 2d Session, Report No. 2, 1861. 8vo, pp. 1119. + December 18, 1861. 8vo, pp. 84. + March 3, 1863. 8vo, pp. 29, 184. 28157

Government of Canada. *See* Cavendish (H.), Vol. IV.

On Government, 1777. *See* [Wycliffe (T.)]

"Government, or no Government;" or, The Question of State Allegiance. A Tract for Churchmen. *Mobile: Farrow & Dennett.* 1861. 8vo, pp. 8. BA. 28158

Government Sale. Catalogue of ... Books to be sold at Auction ... November 17th, 1862. ... [*New York.* 1862.] 8vo, pp. 95. 28159

This was the Public Library of Beaufort, S. C., seized by the Federal army during the Rebellion, but through the remonstrances of E. A. Duyckinck, Prof. Lieber, and others, the sale was prevented. The books were sent to the Smithsonian Institution at Washington, and were burnt at the fire which destroyed a portion of that building.

All Goverments derive their Just Powers from the Consent of the Governed. ... Under this Declaration, Free Suffrage, tried for the First Time, succeeds; Aristocracy and Caste, ... tried for the Thousandth Time, fails as Usual. *Cleveland: For the Author.* 1865. 8vo, pp. 20. H. 28160

Governor and Company of Connecticut. *See* Vol. IV.

Govin (D. Joseph). Informe presentado en juntas generales celebradas por la Rl. Sociedad económica de la Havana, el 12 de diciembre de 1805. *Havana: Imprenta de la Capitania general.* [1805.] 8vo, pp. 8. 28161

Govin. Denuncia de los autores del asesinato del Dr. D. José Govin, por los Filantrópicos. *Habana: Oficina del ciudadano D. José Boloña.* 1821. 4to. 28162

"Una declamacion vaga para hacer odiosa una fraccion. Supone que lo asesinaron los *serviles* por sus ideas liberales."—Bachiller.

Gow (D.) Civil War in America: A Lecture, ... November 24th, 1862. ... By Dan. Gow. *Manchester: Abel Heywood.* 1862. 18mo, pp. 34. B. 28163

Gowahas Goyadoh. 1836. 12mo. 28164

Gowan (J.) Speeches of James Gowan and Mr. Haly at the Irish Anti-Jackson Meeting, August 6th, 1832. [n. p. n. d.] 8vo, pp. 12. 28165

Gowan (O. R.) Responsible or Parliamentary Government; ... By Ogle R. Gowan. *Toronto.* 1830. 8vo. + Second Edition. [*Ibid.*] 1839. 8vo. 28166

Gowan (William, *Publisher*). Gowan's Bibliotheca Americana. *See* Budd (T.), Denton (D.), Miller (J.), and Wooley (C.)

Mr. Gowan published many Catalogues of Books on American History, which are enlivened by his own notes, written under the *pseudonym* of "Western Memorabilia." The notes are distinguished by much originality, some personality, and not a little bad grammar.

Gowan. Letter on Responsible Government. By Lieut.-Col. Gowan, M.P.C. *Toronto.* 1839. 8vo. 28167

Gó-wana Gwó-ih sat' hah yon dé yas dah' gwah—a Spelling-Book in the Seneca Language, with English Definitions. *Buffalo Creek Reservation: Mission Press.* 1842. 12mo, pp. 112. C.

Gowanas Hotel and Wharf Company. *Brooklyn.* 1836. 8vo, pp. 8. Map. S. 28169

Gowen (A. C.) An Address ... Calvert College, New Windsor, Carroll County, Md., September 18, 1851. *Baltimore.* 1851. 8vo. 28170

Gowen [James.] A Statement of Facts in the Matter betwixt Mr. Gowen and the Philadelphia Exchange Company, together with the Expression of Feeling against the Company for erecting that Public Nuisance, the Ugly Wall: ... [n. p. 1839.] 8vo, pp. 21. H. 28171

Gower (F.) Account of the Loss of H. M. Sloop "Swift," on the Coast of Patagonia, March 13, 1770. *Privately printed* 1803. 8vo. Map. 28172

Goycoechea (J. A.) Oracion Funebre, Dedicada à la Memoria del D. Mathias de Galvez, Governador, y Capitan General de Nueva España. Par J. A. Goycoechea. [n. p.:] 1787. 4to. 28173

Goyeneche (J. Sebastian, *Arzobispo de Lima*). Exposicion sobre el Proyecto de Lei de Desamortizacion des Bienes Eclesiasticos. *Trujillo.* 1867. 4to. 28174

Gozosa descripcion de las festibus demonstraciones con que esta Ciudad Capital de la America meridional celebro la real proclamacion de el nombre del Señor Don Carlos III. *En Lima.* 1760. 4to. 28175

Graaff (Nicolaus de). Reysen na de vier gedeeltens des werelds, als Asia, Africa, America en Europa. ... Als ook een mette dog korte beschrijving van China. ... Hier agter is by gevœgt D'oostindise spiegel. *Hoorn: F. Rijp.* 1704. 2 vols., 4to, 5 l., pp. 222, 4 l., 6 Plates; 3 l., pp. 84. C. 28176

A portion of the work was translated into French, and published at *Amsterdam*, 1719.

Graah (Wilhelm August). Beskrivelse til det vorende Situations-Kart over den vestlige Kyst af Grönland. 1823–24. *Kjöbenhavn.* 1825. 4to. 28177

Graah. Undersögelses-Reise til Östkysten af Grönland, efter kongelig Befaling, udförd i Aarene 1828–31. *Kiöbenhavn: J. D. Quist.* 1832. 4to, pp. xviii, 216. 8 colored Plates. Map.

Graah. Narrative of an Expedition to the East Coast of Greenland, sent by order of the King of Denmark, in search of the Lost Colonies, under the command of Captn W. A. Graah of the Danish Royal Navy. ... Translated from the Danish by the late G. Gordon Macdougall. ... With the original Danish Chart. ... *London: John W. Parker.* 1837. 8vo, pp. xvi or xxi, 199. Map. A., B., P., S. 28179

Grabe. Ueber die Bedeutung des ersten Kampfes von Panzerschiffen für die künftig gebotene Bauart der Kriegsschiffe. *Berlin: Strikken.* 1862. 8vo, pp. 73. 28180

Relates to the Civil War in the United States.

Gräberg di Hemsö (Jacopo). "Recueil de Voyages," etc. Historical Researches by John Ranking. Estratto dall' Antologia, No. 104. [Review. n. p.] 1829. 8vo, pp. 37. M.

Grabowski (Stanislaus). Der gegenwärtige Krieg in Nord-Amerika. *Berlin: Grosse.* 1865. 16mo, pp. iii, 212. 28182

Grabowski. Die Rosas'sche Schreckensperiode in Süd-Amerika. *Berlin: Grosse.* 1865. 16mo, pp. iii, 187. 28183

Also: Die Rose von Puebla. Historische Novelle. *Berlin: Behrend.* 186–. 16mo, pp. 175.—Santa Anna. Historischer Roman aus dem Bürgerkriege in Mexico. *Berlin Grosse.* 1865. 16mo, pp. iii, 131.

GRACE (H.) The History of the Life and Adventures of Henry Grace of Basingstoke in the County of Southampton, being a Narrative of the Hardships he underwent during several Years' Captivity among the Savages in North America, and of the Cruelties they practised to their unhappy Prisoners, with Account of the several Customs and Manners of the different Nations of Indians, as well as a Compendious Description of the Soil, Produce, and Various Animals of those Parts. Written by Himself. *Reading: For the Author.* M DCC LXIV. 8vo, pp. 56.

"The author's recital of the various hardships he underwent affords that painful entertainment we find in historical details of distress, especially when they have anything of adventure in them, as is the case with the present artless but affecting narrative."—*Monthly Review.* One of the scarcest of Indian narratives. I have only seen one copy.

[GRACE (J.)?] Memoranda respecting the Families of Quincy and Adams, ... [*Havana.* 1841.] 8vo, pp. (2), 9. H. 28185

GRACE CHURCH, Albany. [To the Parishioners.] 1851. 8vo. S. 28186

See Boston; New York; Providence.

GRACERIE (De la). De la République des États-Unis de l'Amérique du Nord. *Paris.* 1857. 8vo. A. 28187

GRACEY (S. L.) Annals of the Sixth Pennsylvania Cavalry. By Rev. S. L. Gracey, Chaplain of the Regiment. *For the Officers of the Regiment.* MDCCLXVIII. 8vo, pp. 5–371, (1). Map.

GRACIE (Pierre) dit Ferrande. Grant Routier et Pilotage et enseignement pour ancrer tant es portez, haures, que autres lieux de la mer. *Rouen, pour J. Burges.* 1525. 4to. 28189

First edition, with very rude woodcuts representing the shapes of headlands and harbors, with the objects visible upon them from the sea; very rare. "There is little to connect this work with America, but as it is an early Mariner's Guide-book, and contains at least a mention of the New World, which has not been discovered by the bibliographers, it deserves a place in this list. On the reverse of T i, the author refers to the wanderings of sailors, 'es terres neufves, es isles trouvees, es isles de madere, es isles novantes.' His superstitions, his rude spelling and language, his description of the English coasts (including the *isle douhic*, in which the Isle of Wight is sadly disguised), make the volume an interesting one for the English collector. This edition is mentioned by Brunet as having fetched £16 at one of Libri's sales. The work is full of curious maritime information, and was composed at St. Gilles in 1483–84, but was not published till the year 1525, as will appear by the preface to the Calendar (T i reverse) 'Et ya de temps depuys quil nasquit jusques a cette annee Mil cinq centz xxv.' The first example in the Calendar refers to the year 1521, through which Brunet has fallen into error with regard to the age of the undated edition, which he places before this. The citation from Du Verdier of a Poitiers edition of 1520, is probably no less incorrect as to date, and we must look upon the Rouen edition of 1525 as the Princeps, until there is satisfactory evidence of an earlier."—QUARITCH'S *Catalogue.*

GRADIN (A.) A Short History of the Bohemian-Moravian Protestant Church of the United Brethren. Translated from the Latin Manuscript. *London.* MDCCXLIII. 8vo, pp. (2), 62. B.

Contains allusions to America, pp. 43, 55–58, 60, 61.

... Gradual Abolishment of Slavery. Message from the President of the United States, in relation to Co-operating with any State for the Gradual Abolishment of Slavery. 37th Congress, 2d Session. Ex. Doc., No. 69. 1862. 8vo, pp. 8, 1 l. 28191

[GRAFFIGNY (Frances d'Isembourg d'Happoncourt, *Dame de*).] Lettres d'une Peruvienne. *A Peine.* [1747.] + *Amsterdam.* M.DCC.LX. 2 vols., 12mo, pp. xii, 240; viii, 124. + *Paris.* 1761. + *Amsterdam.* MDCCLXIV. 2 vols., 12mo. P. 28192

This popular romance was first published in 1747, but I have not seen that edition. For a defence of some of the author's statements, concerning the Quipus, *see* "Lettera Apologetica."

GRAFFIGNY. Lettres d'une Péruvienne, par Mme De Graffigny, Traduites du Français en Italien par M. Deodati. Édition ornée du portrait de l'auteur, gravé par M. Gaucher, et de six gravures exécutées par les meilleurs artistes, d'après les dessins de M. le Barbier l'ainé. *Paris: Migneret.* 1792. 8vo, pp. 487. + *Paris: Migneret.* MDCCXCVII. 8vo, pp. 487. 6 Plates. + *Paris: imprimerie de P. Didot l'aine, an V.* 2 vols., 18mo. + Nouvelle Edition. *London: Printed by Da Ponte.* 1801. 12mo, pp. (2), 459. B. + Augmentées et suivies des Lettres d'Aza. *Paris.* 1813. 8vo. Plates. C. 28193

Some copies of the Paris editions of 1797 and 1798 were printed on large paper, two of the latter edition on vellum.

GRAFFIGNY. Lettere d'una Peruviana tradotte ... dal Francése in Italiano ... dal Signor Deodati. Nueva edizione. *Londra.* 1774. 12mo. P. + *Parigi: Duchesne.* [1799.] C. + *Avignone: Fr. Seguin aîné.* 1817. pp. 214. B., H. + *A Londres: G. et W. B. Whittaker.* 1821. 18mo, pp. 162. + *Parigi: Presso H. Seguin.* MDCCCXXIV. 18mo, pp. 114. 28194

[GRAFIGNY.] Letters written by a Peruvian Princess. Translated from the French. *London: M. Cooper.* MDCCLXVIII. 12mo, pp. viii, (4), 186. + New Edition. *London: I. Robson.* MDCCLXXI. 2 vols., 12mo, Engraved Titles, pp. liv, 170; 263. C. + *St. Christopher.* 1773. 12mo. W. 28195

GRAFIGNY. Letters of a Peruvian Princess, with the Sequel. Translated from the French of Madame de Grafigny. *London.*

1795. 12mo. P. + *London: Hatchard.* 1805. 12mo, pp. xx, vi, 191; 204. + French and English. *Paris.* 1807. 2 vols., 8vo. Portrait and Plates. 28196

GRAFIGNY. The Letters of a Peruvian Princess. By Madame de Grafigny. Also, as a Sequel, the Letters of Aza, by Ignatius Hungari de la Marche-Courmont. To which are prefixed, a Life of Madame de Grafigny, and a Short Biographical Notice of Marche-Courmont. Translated from the French by William Mudford. *London: Sherwood, Neely & Jones.* 1809. 12mo, pp. xxi, 221. 28197

GRAFIGNY. Cartas de huma peruviana. Traduzidas do francez na lingua portugueza. *Lisboa.* 1802. 12mo. 28198

GRAFTON (J.) A Sermon delivered at Newton, ... October, 1802, occasioned by the Death of Miss Sally Grafton, ... By her Father, Joseph Grafton, A.M. *Boston: Printed by Manning & Loring.* 1803. 8vo, pp. 20. B., BA. + Third Edition *Boston: Printed by Manning & Loring.* 1805. pp. 20. B. 28199

Also: "The Godly and Faithful Man" Delineated. A Sermon at Newton [Mass.], January, 1804, occasioned by the Death of Samuel Richardson. ... *Boston.* [1804.] 8vo. H.

GRAFTON, *Mass.* A Result of a Council of Churches at Grafton, October 2d, 1744. [n. p. n. d.] 8vo, pp. 11. B.

GRAFTON. An Address from the Grafton and Coos Counsellor Convention, to the Independent Electors of the District. [n. p. n. d.] 8vo, pp. 8. H. 28201

GRAHAM (C.) A Sermon against Profane Cursing and Swearing, delivered to the New York Forces in their Camp. By the Rev. Chauncey Graham. *New York.* 1761. 8vo. 28202

GRAHAM (D.) The Pioneer, consisting of Essays, Literary, Moral, and Theological. By Rev. David Graham. *Pittsburg.* 1812. 8vo, pp. 301. W. 28203

GRAHAM. Narrative of the Proceedings of the ... Reformed Church ... relative to the Reverend David Graham; with a Narrative Part of the Trial and Defense of Mr. Graham, before the Reformed Presbytery in Pittsburg, ... *Pittsburg.* 1811. 8vo.

GRAHAM (D., Jr.) A Treatise on the Organization and Jurisdiction of the Courts of Law and Equity in the State of New York. By David Graham, Jr. *New York.* 1839. 8vo.

Also other Law Books.

GRAHAM (G.) Inaugural Address of Geo. Graham, Esq., President American Wine Growers' Association. Delivered Saturday, March 29, 1862. ... *Cincinnati: Morse, Wilstach, Keys & Co.* 1862. 8vo, pp. 12. H. 28206

GRAHAM (G. R.) Graham's American Monthly Magazine, for November, 1846. *Philadelphia: Published by George R. Graham.* Rl. 8vo. 28207

GRAHAM (H.) Sermon and Address ... at the Induction of the Rev. John Waddell ... Truro ... By Hugh Graham. *Halifax.* 1799. 8vo. 28208

GRAHAM (I.) Life and Writings of the late Mrs. Isabella Graham, of New York. Second Edition. *New York: Kirk & Mercein.* 1817. 12mo, pp. 428. Portrait. + Fourth Edition. *New-York:* [*Ibid.*] 1819. 12mo, pp. 336. H. + Eighth Edition. *New-York: William A. Mercein.* 1834. 12mo, pp. 303, (1).

GRAHAM. Power of Faith Exemplified in the Life and Writings of ... Mrs. Isabella Graham of New York. *New York: Printed by J. Seymour.* 1816. 8vo, pp. 411. B. 28210

GRAHAM. The Power of Faith, Exemplified in the Life and Writings of the late Mrs. Isabella Graham. A New Edition, Enriched by her Narrative of her Husband's Death, and other Select Correspondence. [Compiled by Joanna Bethune.] *New York: American Tract Society.* 1843. 12mo, pp. 440. B., H.

GRAHAM. The Unpublished Letters and Correspondence of Mrs. Isabella Graham, from ... 1767 to 1814; ... Selected and Arranged by her Daughter, Mrs. Bethune. *New-York: John S. Taylor.* 1838. 12mo, pp. 314. C., S. + *London.* 1839. 12mo. 28212

GRAHAM (J.) Trial of James Graham ... for the Murder of Hugh Cameron and Alexander M'Gillavrae, in Delhi, Delaware County, July 14th, 1813. Taken during the Trial by Aaron Clark. ... *Albany: Printed by J. Buel.* 1814. 8vo, pp. 24.

GRAHAM (J.) The Life of General Daniel Morgan, of the Virginia Line of the Army of the United States; with Portions of his Correspondence, compiled from Authentic Sources. By James Graham. *New York: Derby and Jackson.* 1856. 12mo, pp. 475. Portrait. B., BA., C., H. + [*Ibid.*] 1858. + [*Ibid.*] 1859. C. 28214

GRAHAM (James D.) ... Report of Lieutenant-Colonel Graham on the Subject of the Boundary Line between the United States and Mexico. 32d Congress, 1st Session. Ex. Doc., No. 121. *Washington, Aug.* 25, 1852. 8vo, pp. 250. Map. C., M.

GRAHAM. A Report upon the Military and Hydrographical Chart of the Extremity of Cape Cod, ... from Surveys executed during 1833, 1834, and 1835, under the Direction of James D. Graham. ... Folio, not paged. [n. p. n. d.] B., BA., M. 28216

GRAHAM. ... Report from Lt.-Col. Graham of the Harbors in Wisconsin, Illinois, Indiana, and Michigan. Sen. Doc. *Washington.* 1856. 8vo, pp. 479. 28217

GRAHAM. Report on the Commerce and Improvement of Western Lake Harbors. Part I., 1854–55; Part II., 1856. Sen. Doc. 16, 34th Congress, 3d Session. *Washington.* [n. d.] 8vo.

GRAHAM. Report on the Improvement of Lake Harbors, September 30, 1857. Sen. Doc. 42, 35th Congress, 1st Session. *Washington.* [1858.] 8vo. 28219

See Peirce (Benjamin). Message of Governor of Pennsylvania. Also: Lunar Tidal Wave in the North American Lakes, Demonstrated. *Cambridge: Allen and Farnham.* 1861. 8vo, pp. 11. Plates. B., H.—A Lunar Tidal Wave in Lake Michigan, Demonstrated. With [3] Plates. *Philadelphia.* [1860.] 8vo, pp. 7.—On the Latitude and Longitude of Milwaukee, Prairie Du Chien, Racine and Madison, Wisconsin. ... [*Milwaukee.* 1859.] 8vo, pp. 88. H.

GRAHAM (James T.) *See* Graham (Samuel).

GRAHAM (J.) An Answer to Mr. Gales' Pamphlet; entituled, A Calm and Full Vindication, &c., Relating to Yale College. Wherein is clearly shewn, that he has no Ways vindicated himself from the Misrepresentation made in his former piece; and in his last, has made sundry more, as foreign from the Truth: And his Injurious and Abusive Reflections, on the worthy Governors of the College, are censured, in as Calm and Soft Terms, as the nature of the case can allow. By John Graham, A.M., And Pastor of the Church in Southbury. *New Haven: James Parker & Co.* 1759. pp. 28. BA., H., W. 28220

GRAHAM. A Few Remarks on the Remarks, etc. By Rev John Graham. *New Haven.* 1760. 8vo. J.C.B. 28221

[GRAHAM.] A Letter to a Member of the House of Representatives ... in Vindication of Yale College. [*New Haven.*] 1759. 8vo. J.C.B. 28222

GRAHAM. The Obligations which the Profession of the Christian Religion lays Men under. Sermon at his Ordination, Stafford, May 29, 1723. *New London.* 1725. 12mo, pp. 43.

GRAHAM. ... Sermon at the Ordination of Rev. Nathan Strong, Coventry, Oct. 9, 1745. *Boston.* 1746. 12mo, pp. 55.

See Gale (Benjamin). Also: The Duty of Renewing their Baptismal Covenant Proved and Urged upon the Adult Children of Professing Parents. *Boston.* 1734. 8vo, pp. (6), 13. B.

GRAHAM (J.) The Flowers of Melody: A Select Collection of Scottish, English, Irish, and American Songs. Selected and Arranged by John Graham. Vol I. *New York.* 1825. 18mo. 28225

GRAHAM (J.) Autobiography and Reminiscences of Rev. John Graham, late Pastor of the Associate, now the United Presbyterian Congregation of Bovina, Delaware County, N. Y. [With] Sermons. *Philadelphia: W. S. Rentoul.* 1870. 12mo, pp. vi, 206. C. 28226

GRAHAM (J.) Opening Speech of John Graham on the Trial of Daniel E. Sickles, in the Criminal Court of the District of Columbia, 1859. *New York.* [1859.] 8vo. S. 28227

Also other Speeches on public occasions.

GRAHAM (J. A.) An Address to the Public; together with a Copy of a Letter to Stephen R. Bradley, Esq., Senator in Congress from Vermont. By John A. Graham. *New York.* 1805. 8vo. C. 28228

GRAHAM. A Descriptive Sketch of the Present State of Vermont. One of the United States of America. By J. A. Graham, LL.D. late Lieutenant-Colonel in the Service of the above State. *London: Printed and sold for the Author, by Henry Frey.* 1797. 8vo, pp. vii, 186, (1). Portrait. Woodcuts by Bewick. B., BA., H. 28229

"This work is beautifully printed; the author, at the time it was published, was in England, as agent from the Episcopal Church of Vermont to the Society for Propogating the Gospel in Foreign Parts."—RICH, I. 401.

GRAHAM. A True Copy of the Proceedings of John A. Graham, Esq., LL.D., Agent to the Protestant Episcopal Church of the State of Vermont, in North America, at the Court of London, A.D. 1795. *Boston: Printed by Young and Minns.* 1795. 8vo, pp. 56. H., M. 28230

Also: The Correspondence of John A. Graham with his Grace of Canterbury ... *New York.* 1835. 8vo, pp. 26.—His "Memoirs of John Horne Tooke" contain

some notices of Tooke's connection with American Politics. *New York: Stephen Gould.* 1828. 8vo, pp. 242. Portrait. H.

GRAHAM (J. A.) Speeches delivered at the City Hall ... New York, in the Courts of Oyer and Terminer and Common Pleas. *New York.* 1812. 8vo, pp. 140. Portrait. + Second Edition. *New York: George Forman.* 1812. 8ov, pp. 140. BA.

Also: Speech before the Court of General Sessions, on the Trial of Hiram Maxwell. *New York.* 1823. 8vo.

GRAHAM (J. H.) Letters on Public Education in Canada. *Montreal.* 1866. 8vo, pp. 28. 28232

Also: Letters in reply to the Superintendent of Education for Lower Canada. ... *Montreal.* 1865. 8vo, pp. 16.

GRAHAM (J. L.) Appeal of John Lorimer Graham from the Decision of the Auditor of the Post Office Department, rejecting Expenditures for fitting up New Post Office Buildings in Nassau Street and Chatham Square. *New York.* 1846. 8vo. S.

GRAHAM (M.) Journal of a Residence in Chile, during the year 1822. And a Voyage from Chile to Brazil in 1823. By Maria Graham. *London: Longman & Co.* 1824. 4to, pp. (2), v, 512. 14 Plates, 10 Vignettes. B., BA., C., H., P. 28234

GRAHAM. Journal of a Voyage to Brazil, and Residence there, during part of the years 1821, 1822, 1823. By Maria Graham. *London: Longman & Co.* 1824. 4to, pp. v, 335. 11 Plates 9 Vignettes. B., C. 28235

The plates are by Finden, from drawings by the authoress. Highly praised by Sir James Mackintosh. The authoress was afterwards Lady Calcott.

[GRAHAM (Patrick).] *See* Georgia, Vol. VII, No. 27113.

GRAHAM (S.) Letter to ... Daniel Webster, on the Compromises of the Constitution. By S. Graham. *Northampton: Hopkins, Bridgeman & Co.* 1850. 8vo, pp. 10. B., BA., H.

GRAHAM (Samuel). Memoir of General Graham, with Notices of the Campaigns in which he was engaged from 1779 to 1801. Edited by his Son, Colonel James J. Graham. *Edinburgh: Privately printed by R. & R. Clark.* 1862. Crown 8vo, pp. xix, 318. 2 Maps, 4 Plates. BA. 28237

One hundred copies only printed. Contains a graphic account of the romantic incidents connected with Captain Charles Asgill during the American Revolution

GRAHAM (W.) State of the Accounts of William Graham, Esquire, Collector of Excise, for the Counties of Westmoreland, Washington, and Fayette; From April, 1785, till July, 1786. *Philadelphia: Printed by Robert Aitken.* M. DCC. LXXXVI. 8vo, pp. 3. P. 28238

GRAHAM (W.) The Contrast, or the Bible and Abolitionism. ... By Rev. William Graham. *Cincinnati.* 1844. 12mo, pp. 48.

GRAHAM (W. A.) Discourse in Memory of the Life and Character of the Hon. Geo. E. Badger. ... By William A. Graham, of Orange, ... July 19th, 1866. *Raleigh: Nichols, Gorman & Neathery.* 1866. 8vo, pp. 34. H. 28240

GRAHAM. Speech of Hon. William Graham, of Orange, in the Convention of North-Carolina, Dec. 7th, 1861, on the Ordinance concerning Test Oaths and Sedition. *Raleigh: W. W. Holden, Printer.* 1862. 12mo, pp. 31. H. 28241

Also: Message from the Governor in relation to the History of North Carolina. *Raleigh.* 1846. 8vo. N.—Speech ... April 13, 1842, on the Loan Bill. *Washington.* 1842. 8vo.—Speech ... June 3, 1842, on the Apportionment Bill. *Washington.* 1842. 8vo.

GRAHAM (W. S.) Remains of William Sloan Graham. With a Memoir. ... Edited by George Allen. *Philadelphia: J. W. Moore.* 1849. 12mo, pp. viii, 13–278. Portrait. H. 28242

GRAHAME (J.) The History of the Rise and Progress of the United States of North America, till the British Revolution in 1688. By James Grahame, Esq. *London: Longman.* 1827. 2 vols., 8vo, pp. xvi, (1), 531; viii, 528, (1). B., BA. + *New York.* 1830. 2vols., 8vo. + *Boston.* 1833. 2 vols., 8vo. 28243

Reprinted in Knapp's "Library of American History."

GRAHAME. The History of the United States of North America, from the Plantation of the British Colonies till their Revolt and Declaration of Independence. By James Grahame. *London: Smith, Elder and Co.* 1836. 4 vols., 8vo, pp. xxiii, 451; viii, 448; viii, 436; vii, 462. BA., H. 28244

"This historical work is the fruit of more than eleven years of intense meditation, eager research, industrious composition, and solicitous revisal."—*Author's Preface.* "Mr. Grahame has published the best book that has anywhere appeared upon the History of the United States. He has corrected the mistakes, whether of error or malignity, which his predecessors in the same labors had committed."—*North American Review*, Vol. XXXII. 174. *See also* "Am. Quarterly," 1832.

Grahame. The History of the United States of North America, from the Plantation of the British Colonies till their Assumption of National Independence. By James Grahame, LL.D. ... Second Edition, Enlarged and Amended. *Philadelphia: Lea and Blanchard.* 1845. 8vo, pp. lxix, 468; ix, 457; viii, 446; vii, 510. 28245

Some copies have the imprint, *Boston: Little & Brown.* 1845. There are also copies printed on thick paper; this edition was edited with a memoir and preface by Josiah Quincy. It was reprinted, *Philadelphia: Lea & Blanchard.* 1846. 2 vols., 8vo, pp. xli, 25–598; vi, 619. Portrait. + [*Ibid.*] 1850. + *Philadelphia: Blanchard and Lea.* 1852. 2 vols., 8vo, pp. xli, 25–598; vi, 619. *See* "Mass. Hist. Soc. Collections," Vol. xxxix; Montgomery (James); also, Quincy (Josiah), for a vindication of this work from the aspersions of Mr. Bancroft.

Grahame. Who is to Blame? or Cursory Review of the "American Apology for American Accession to Negro Slavery." ... By James Grahame, Esq. *London: Smith, Elder and Co.* 1842. 8vo, pp. 112. B., H., S. 28246

Grailhe (Alexandre). Mémoire à plaider devant la cour suprême de la Louisiane, pour les villes de la Nouvelle-Orléans et de Baltimore, dans le procès sur le testament de M. McDonogh. *Nouvelle-Orléans.* 1852. 8vo, 1 l., pp. 323. C. 28247

[Grainger (J.)] An Essay on the More Common West-India Diseases, and the Remedies which that Country itself produces; with Hints on the Management of Negroes. By a Physician in the West Indies. *London: T. Becket and P. A. De Hondt.* MDCCLXIV. 8vo, 4 l., pp. 75. H. + Second Edition. By James Grainger, M.D. Notes and Index by William Wright, M.D. *Edinburgh.* 1802. 8vo. M. 28248

Grainger. The Sugar Cane: A Poem. In Four Books. With Notes. By James Grainger, M.D., &c. *London: R. and J. Dodsley.* MDCCLXIV. 4to, pp. vii, 167. Plate. B., C., H., P. + *London: For the Booksellers.* MDCCLXVI. 12mo, pp. ix, 180.

Reprinted in Anderson's "Poets of Great Britain."

Grainger. The Sugar Cane, and other Poems. By James Grainger. *Chiswick.* 1822. 12mo. 28250

See the "Monthly Review," xxxi. 105; also, the "London Chronicle," for 1764, in which is a review by Dr. S. Johnson.

Gram (H.) Sacred Lines for Thanksgiving Day, November 7, 1793. By Hans Gram. With Several Psalm Tunes. *Boston.* 1793. 8vo. 28251

A Grammatical Sketch of the Heve Language, Translated from an Unpublished Spanish Manuscript. With a Vocabulary by Buckingham Smith. *New York: Cramoisy Press.* 1861. 8vo, pp. 26. C., H. 28252

One hundred copies printed. Forms No. III. of Shea's "Library of American Linguistics."

The Grammar School System of Ontario. A Correspondence between the Board of Trustees of the Clinton County Grammar School and the Rev. E. Ryerson, D.D. ... Second Edition. *Clinton: Re-Printed from the Clinton New Era.* 1868. 16mo, pp. 26. 28253

Granada, *Nicaragua.* Reales Exequias, por el Señor Don Carlos III. Rey de las Espanas, y Americas, y Real Proclamacion de su Augusto hijo el Señor D. Carlos IV. por la muy Noble, y muy leal Ciudad de Granada, Provincia de Nicaragua, Reyno de Guatemala. 1790. Plates. 28254

See also Nueva Granada.

Granados y Galvez (J. J.) Tardes | Americanas: | Gobierno Gentil y Catolico: | Breve y particular Noticia | de toda la Historia Indiana: | Sucesos, cosas notables, y cosas ignoradas, desde la | entrada de la Gran Nacion Tulteca, á esta tierra | de Anahuac, | hasta los presentes tiempos. | Trabajadas | por un Indio, y un Español. | Sacalas a Luz | El M. R. P. Fr. Joseph Joaquin Granados | y Galvez, ... *Mexico: En la nueva Imprenta Matritense de D. Felipe | de Zuñiga y Ontiveros, ... año de* 1778. | 4to, 36 l., Text, pp. 540. 3 Plates. A., BA., H. 28255

Purports to be "an account or history of the early people of Mexico, from the first coming of the great Toltec nation to Anahuac to the present time, in the form of a dialogue between an Indian and a Spaniard. The author lived in Michoacan, and was guardian of a convent and superintendent of the Missions among the Indians in that department. The work contains much respecting the early Mexican Archæology and Antiquities. It is a book of some rarity, and seems to have escaped the notice of Clavigero. It has lately been reprinted in Mexico, edited by Bustamente."—J. R. Bartlett. "A scarce and curious work relating to the early history of the Mexicans, unknown to Clavigero, and not mentioned by Meusel."—Rich. Prescott refers to it as containing the original Mexican text of the Poems of Ixtlilxochitl, &c. It is styled by Salva, "Ouvrage aussi rare qu'important pour connaitre à fond l'histoire primitive de la Nouvelle Espagne." *See* Leclerc's Catalogue, No. 1147. Fischer's copy sold for £4 15s.

Grand Arcanum. *See* [Green (Joseph)].

Grand Army of the Republic. *See* Massachusetts, Michigan, New York, &c.

Grand Celebration in honor of the Passage of the Ordinance of Emancipation, by the Free State Convention, May 11, 1864. Held in New Orleans, June 11; with the Programme, Proceedings and Speeches. *New Orleans: H. R. Lathrop.* 1864. 8vo, pp. 32. 28256

Grand Celebration in the City of St. Paul, the Capital of the State of Minnesota, United States, 1st September, 1858, Commemorative of the Successful Laying and Working of the Atlantic Telegraph Cable. *St. Paul, Minnesota.* 1858. Rl. 8vo.

The successful working lasted a few hours only on this occasion.

A Grand Chorus, to be sung on the Fourth of June, being His Majesty's Birth Day; at an Entertainment on the Banks of Schuylkill, by a large Company of the Inhabitants of the City of Philadelphia. [n. p. 1766] Folio, pp. 1. 28258

The Grand Encampment of Knights Templar, and appendant Orders of Massachusetts and Rhode Island. Its History; Edicts; Past and Present Grand Officers; and Organizations of its Subordinates. *Boston: J. Wilson & Son.* 1864. 8vo, pp. 68.

Grand Jurors Duty Considered. *Boston.* 1724. 8vo, pp. 16.

Grand Lodges of Alabama: Proceedings of the Annual Communication. ... December 1853. *Montgomery.* 1853. pp. 162, 26, 21. M. 28261

We purposely omit the proceedings of most of the Grand Lodges, as possessing but little of interest outside of the organization.

The Grand Mistakes. [n. p. n. d.] 8vo, pp. 4. 28262

Relates to the Rebellion.

Grand National Peace Jubilee. Official Monthly Bulletin. No. 1. February. 28263

The Grand Question, whether War or no War with Spain, impartially considered: In Defence of the present Measures against those that delight in War. *London: J. Roberts.* MDCCXXXIX. 8vo, pp. 32. B., W. 28264

Contains allusions to America on pp. 18–20, 24, 29.

Grand Rapids. Holland's Grand Rapids City Directory for 1867–68. With a Business Directory. *Chicago: Western Publishing Company.* 1867. 8vo, pp. 276. 28265

Le Grand Routier de Mer qu'il convient tenir en la Navigation des Indes Orientales et au Voyage de la Coste du Brazil des Antilles et du Cap de Lopo Gonsalves. *Amsterdam.* 1638.

Contains a narrative of Sir Francis Drake's Voyage.

Grand Trunk Railway Company of Cañada. Report of Vice-President and Managing Directors of the Grand Trunk Railway, for the year 1856. *Toronto.* 1856. 8vo. Continued. S.

Certain Papers connected with the Affairs of the Grand Trunk Railroad Company of Canada. *Quebec.* 1855. 8vo. pp. 66.

Report of the Special Committee appointed to Enquire and Report as to the Condition, Management, and Prospects of the Grand Trunk Railway Company. *Toronto.* 1857. 8vo, pp. 263.

Also: Liste des actionnaires de la compagnie du Grand Tronc de chemin de fer, et des autres compagnies associées avec elle. *Québec.* 1855. 8vo, pp. 20.—Report of the Commission ... [on] the Affairs of the Grand Trunk Railway. *Quebec.* 1861. 8vo, pp. 179, 1 l. H.—Return of all Documents relating to the Postal Service by the Grand Trunk Railway Company. ... *Quebec.* 1863. 8vo, pp. 107. H.—Return for Statements relative to Applications of the Grand Trunk Railway Company, for Releases of Provincial Debentures, and Copy of any Memorial from the Company since January 1, 1856. *Toronto.* 1856. 8vo, pp. 32.—Statements, Reports, and Accounts of the Grand Trunk Railway Company of Canada, presented 23d April, 1857. *Toronto.* 1857. 8vo, pp. 72. M.

El Grande Miseno en la America. *Puebla.* 1821. 8vo, 4 or more numbers. 28270

Grandguillot (A.) La Reconnaissance du Sud. Par A. Grandguillot. *Paris: Michel Lévy Frères.* 1861. 8vo, 1 l., pp. 310, (1). B. 28271

A defence of the right of the South to secede.

Grandidier (E.) Voyage dans l'Amérique du sud Pérou et Bolivie. Par M. Ernest Grandidier. *Paris.* 1861. 8vo. B.

Grand Pierre (Dralse de). Relation de Divers Voyages faits dans ... l'Amérique, & aux Indes Occidentales. La Description du Royaume de Juda & quelques particularitez touchant la vie du Roy regnant. ... *A Paris, chez Claude Jombert, rue S. Jacques au coin de la rue des Mathuvins, a l'Image Notre Dame* MDCCXVIII. 12mo, pp. (10), 352, (4). C., H. 28273

Grand-Pierre (J. H.) Quelques Mois de Séjour aux États-Unis d'Amérique. Par J. H. Grand-Pierre. ... *Paris: Chez. Grassart.* 1854. 12mo, pp. 207, 2 l. H. 28274

Grand Pierre. Eenige maanden in de Vereenigten Staten van Noord-Amerika. Naar het Fransch. *Amsterdam.* 1854. 8vo. 28275

Grand Pierre. A Parisian Pastor's Glance at America. By Rev. J. H. Grand Pierre. ... *Boston: Gould & Lincoln.* 1854. 16mo, pp. 132. H., S. 28276

Grandy (M.) Narrative of the Life of Moses Grandy, formerly a Slave in the United States. ... Second American from the Last London Edition. *Boston: Oliver Johnson.* 1844. 16mo, pp. 45, (1). H., M. 28277

[Grange de Chessieux (De la).] *See* La Grange de Chessieux.

Granger (A.) ... A Sermon ... at the Dedication of the Orthodox Congregational Meeting House in Medfield, April 17, 1832. By Arthur Granger. ... *Boston: Printed by Peirce & Parker.* 1832. 8vo, pp. 24. H. 28278

Granger (A. H.) The Voice of Christ in the Storm. A Sermon delivered in the Fourth Baptist Church, Providence, on the Morning of April 21st, 1861. By Rev. A. H. Granger. *Providence: Knowles, Anthony & Co., Printers.* 1861. 8vo, pp. 16.

Relates to the Rebellion.

Granger (A. P.) The Slavery Question. Speech of Hon. Amos P. Granger, of New York, in the House of Representatives, April 4, 1856. The House being in the Committee of the Whole on the state of the Union. [n. p. n. d.] 8vo, pp. 8.

Another edition is entitled: Slavery Unconstitutional. [n. p. n. d.] 8vo, pp. 8. Also: State Sovereignty ... Slavery: Remarks, ... February 17, 1859. [n. p. n. d.] 8vo, pp. 8. H., S.—Kansas—The Lecompton Constitution. Speech ... March 24, 1858. *Washington: Buell & Blanchard.* 1858. 8vo, pp. 8. H.—A Protective Tariff. Speech ... February 24, 1859. [*Washington: Buell & Blanchard.*] 8vo, pp. 8. H. —Speech ... on the Finances; ... January 25, 1858. *Washington.* 1858. 8vo, pp. 5.

[Granger (Gideon).] An Address to the People of New-England [in Defence of the Administration of Mr. Jefferson.] By Algernon Sidney. *Washington: Printed by Dinmore and Cooper.* 1808. 8vo, pp. 38. B., S. + [n. p.] 1809. 12mo. + *Albany.* 1809. 8vo. S. + [n. p. n. d.] 12mo, pp. 36. B., H.

[Granger.] The Address of Epaminondas to the Citizens of ... New York. *Albany: Printed by Jeremiah Tryon.* 1819. 8vo, pp. 8. BA. 28282

[Granger.] A Vindication of the Measures of the Present Administration. By Algernon Sidney. ... Taken from the "National Intelligencer." *Trenton: Wilson & Blackwell, May* 16, 1803. 4to, pp. 16. H. + *Hartford.* 1802. 8vo. + Second Edition. *Wilmington, Del.: James Wilson.* 1803. 12mo, pp. 36. + *Washington: Printed by Samuel H. Smith.* 1803. 8vo, pp. 20.

Also: Address delivered before the Ontario Agricultural Society; ... *Canandaigua: Printed by J. D. Bemis & Co.* [1820.] 8vo, pp. 23, (1). B.—Mr. Granger's Reasons for voting against the Grant of $11,870.50 to Governor Tompkins. [*Albany: F. & E. Hosford.*] 1820. 8vo, pp. 12. B., BA., S.—An Oration Spoken ... July 4, 1797, at ... Suffield. *Suffield.* 1797. 8vo. W.—Speech ... before a Convention of the People of Ontario County, N. Y., ... in 1817, on the Subject of a Canal from Lake Erie to Hudson's River. *Canandaigua: Printed by J. D. Bemis.* [1817.] 8vo, pp. 24. B.—Speeches ... on Increasing the Number of Delegates; and Address to the Convention of the Two Republican Parties in the Western District. *Albany.* 1821. 8vo.

Granger (J. N.) A Sermon occasioned by the Death of the Rev. Zabdiel Bradford, delivered ... in Providence, June 10, 1849. By Rev. James N. Granger. *Providence: Weeden & Peck.* 1849. 8vo, pp. 23. H. 28284

Also: ... A Thanksgiving Sermon ... in ... Providence, November 26th, 1846. *Providence: George P. Daniels.* 1847. 8vo, pp. 27. BA.

Granier (J. E.) Forfaits de Sonthonax, Victor Hugues et Lebas, ex-Agens particuliers de l'ex-Directoire exécutif à Saint Domingue et á la Guadeloupe; Devoilés par J. E. Granier, une de leurs principales victimes. *Paris: An* 7 [1799]. 8vo, pp. 22.

Granier. Suite de l'Examen de la conduite de Sonthonax, Polverel, et Nilhaud. [n. p. 1799?] 8vo, pp. 33–64. 28286

Granier de Cassagnac (Adolphe de). Voyages aux Antilles françaises, anglaises, danoises, espagnoles, à Saint-Domingue et aux États-Unis d'Amérique. ... Par A. Granier de Cassagnac. *Paris.* 1842–44. 2 vols., 8vo. A. 28287

Granite Club. Constitution and By-Laws of the Granite Club, No. 1. Organized in Boston, June 29, 1852. *Boston: Printed by Robert Wier.* 1852. 12mo, pp. 8. H. 28288

Graniteville, *S. C.* Report of the President and Treasurer of the Graniteville Manufacturing Company ... 1854. *Charleston, S. C.: Walker & Evans.* 1855. 8vo, pp. 23. H. 28289

Grant (Abraham P.) Mr. Grant, from the Committee on Roads and Canals, made the following Report: ... of the result

of the survey of the several routes of a ship canal around the Falls of Niagara, to connect the navigable waters of the Lakes Erie and Ontario, ... [n. p. 1838.] 8vo, pp. 35. 28290

Grant (A.) History of Brazil, comprising a Geographical Account of that Country, together with a Narrative of the most remarkable Events which have occurred there since its Discovery; A Description of the Manners, Customs, Religion, &c., of the Natives and Colonists; Interspersed with Remarks on the Nature of its Soil, Climate, Productions, and Foreign and Internal Commerce. To which are subjoined Cautions to new Settlers for the Preservation of Health. By Andrew Grant, M.D. *London: Henry Colburn.* 1809. 8vo, pp. vi, 304. BA., H. 28291

See "M. Rev.," New Series, LXIV. 52.

Grant. Histoire du Brésil, contenant un précis des Événemens le plus remarquables, depuis sa découverte; la Description des mœurs, des coûtumes et de la religion des habitants; des Observations sur la nature du sol, du climat, des Productions Naturelles et des Cultures Coloniales; suivi d'un Tableau du Commerce intérieur et extérieur de cette colonie; de la réduction de ses monnaies en livres sterling et en roubles d'argent; de quelques avis de l'auteur sur les moyens de préserver la santé en passant au Brésil ou autres climats du Trophique, etc. etc. Traduit de l'Anglais d'Andrew Grant, M.D. On a joint à cette traduction des notes et le traité d'amitié et de commerce entre S. M. Britannique et S. A. R. le Prince-Régent de Portugal, signé à Rio Janeiro le 19 Février 1810. *St.-Petersbourg: de l'Imprimerie de Pluchart et Comp.* 1811. 8vo, pp. viii, 55. + *Braunschweig: Pluchart.* 1811. 8vo. 28292

Grant. Beschreibung von Brasilien, mit Berichtigungen des Herrn Navarro d'Andrade. Aus dem Französischen. *Weimar.* 1814. 8vo. 28293

Grant (A.) Case before the House of Lords, betwixt the Trustees of Andrew Grant, of Grenada, and Douglas Heron & Co., relative to Monetary Transactions connected with the Grenada Estate. *Privately printed.* 1796. Folio. 28294

Grant (A.) The Ramsden Sermon on the Extension of the Church in the Colonies and Dependencies of the British Empire. By A. Grant. *London.* 1852. 8vo, pp. 24. 28295

[Grant (Anne).] Memoirs of an American Lady; with Sketches of Manners and Scenery in America, as they existed previous to the Revolution. By the author of "Letters from the Mountains." *London: Longman.* 1808. 2 vols., 12mo, pp. xii, 322; v, (1), 344. + Second Edition. [*Ibid.*] 1809. + *Boston: B. W. Wells.* 1809. pp. (4), 158; (2), 161. BA. + *New-York: Samuel Campbell.* 1809. 12mo, pp. viii, 344. B. + Third Edition. *London: A. K. Newman and Co.* 1817. pp. xii, 322; vii, 344. C., H. + *New York.* 1836. 12mo, pp. 354. + *New York: D. Appleton & Co.* 1846. 12mo, pp. 295. B., BA.

"The 'American Lady' means Mrs. Schuyler. Mrs. Grant passed many years of her youth in the family of General Schuyler, of Albany, of whom and of Provinc' Life her book is a most delightful picture."

Grant. Memoir and Correspondence of Mrs. Grant, of Laggan, ... Edited by her Son, J. P. Grant, Esq. *London: Longman.* 1845. 3 vols., post 8vo, pp. xvi, 320; xv, 335, (1); xv, 316, (1). Portrait. B., BA., S. + Second Edition. [*Ibid.*] 1853. 28297

Her Letters from the Mountains—being the Real Correspondence of a Lady, between the years 1773 and 1807. *London: Longman.* 1807. 3 vols., 12mo, pp. xii, 216; (4), 280; (4), 224. BA. + *Boston: Printed by Greenough and Stebbins.* 1809. 2 vols., 12mo, pp. 275; 268. B., H.—contains some reference to America. The American edition was printed at the suggestion of the Rev. Dr. Lowell, and the proceeds sent to the authoress in Scotland.

Grant (Charles, *Vicomte de Vaux.*) Addresse à toutes les puissances de l'Europe, sur l'état présent et futur de la noblesse, et du clergé Français. Particulièrement au Gouvernement Britannique, sur les moyens d'assurer à ces deux corps l'existence la plus convenable aux circonstances, moyennant un plan d'établissemens dans le Canada, les plus advantageux possibles, soit au Commerce Britannique soit aux Loyalistes. *Londres.* 1794. 8vo, pp. 109. Portrait and Map. 28298

Grant. Proposals for a Subscription to form Colonies in Canada of French Emigrant Loyalists, and Ecclesiastics now in England. By Charles Grant, Viscount de Vaux. [n. p. 1793?] 8vo, pp. 8. H. 28299

[Grant (Charles).] A Despatch from ... Lord Glenelg ... containing H. M.'s Answer to the separate Addresses ... from the Legislative Council. *Toronto.* 1836. 8vo, pp. 36. S.

On the government of the Province.

[Grant.] Lord Glenelg's Despatches to Sir F. B. Head, Bart, during his Administration of the Government of Upper

Canada. Abstracted from the Papers laid before Parliament. *London: James Ridgway and Sons.* 1839. 8vo, pp. iv, 193. C., S.

GRANT (D.) An Essay on the Yellow Fever of Jamaica. By David Grant, M.D. *London: Robinsons.* 1801. 8vo, pp. 65.

See "M. Rev.," New Series, XXXVIII 316.

GRANT (E. B.) Beet-Root Sugar, and the Cultivation of the Beet. By E. B. Grant. *Boston: Lee & Shepard.* 1866. 16mo, pp. 158. C. 28303

Also: Boston Railways, their Condition and Prospects. *Boston: Little, Brown and Company.* 1856. 8vo, pp. iv, 3–138. B.

GRANT (J.) A Sermon Preached December 13, 1776, being the Fast Day, on account of the Troubles in America, at Oxenden Chapel. By James Grant. *London: Whitaker.* 8vo.

A flaming invective against the revolted colonies. See "M. Rev.," LVI. 76.

GRANT (J. M.) Three Letters to the New York "Herald," from J. M. Grant of Utah [Mayor of Great Salt Lake City. n. p. n. d.] 8vo, pp. 64. B., H. 28305

GRANT (J.) The Narrative of a Voyage of Discovery, performed in H. M. Vessel the Lady Nelson, of sixty tons burthen, with sliding keels, in the years 1800, 1801, and 1802, to New South Wales. By James Grant, ... With elegant Engravings. *London: Egerton.* 1803. 4to, pp. 220. BA. 28306

Included in Mr. Rich's "Bibliotheca Americana," Vol. II.

GRANT (J.) The Peregrinations of Jeremiah Grant, Esq., the West Indian. ... *London: G. Burnet.* MDCCLXIII. 12mo, 3 l., pp. 327, (1). H. 28307

GRANT (J. W.) The Flying Regiment. Journal of the Campaigns of the 12th Regt. Rhode Island Volunteers. By Captain J. W. Grant. *Providence: Sidney S. Rider & Brother.* 1865. 12mo, pp. 152. B., BA. 28308

GRANT (M.) Matthew Grant's Old Church Record. *Albany: Printed by J. Munsell.* 1859. 8vo, pp. 14. 28309

Relates to Windsor, Conn. Fifty copies printed.

GRANT (*Mrs.*) *See* [Grant (Anne)].

GRANT (Ulysses S.) Illustrated Life, Campaigns, and Public Services of Lieut.-General Grant. *Philadelphia: T. B. Peterson & Bros.* [1865.] 12mo, pp. 15–271. B. 28310

[GRANT.] [Letters upon the Advantages of Point Lookout for an Establishment of an Asylum for Disabled Soldiers and Sailors. n. p. 1865.] 4to, pp. (3). H. 28311

GRANT. The Life, Campaigns, and Battles of Gen. U. S. Grant. With Introduction by B. J. Lossing. *New York: L. Bill.* 1868. 8vo, pp. 502. Portrait. C. 28312

GRANT. The Life and Services as a Soldier of Major-General Grant, the Hero of Fort Donelson, Vicksburg, and Chattanooga; Commander of the Military Division of the Mississippi; and Captor of Four Hundred and Seventy-two Cannon and over Ninety Thousand Rebel Prisoners. *Philadelphia: T. B. Peterson & Bros.* 1864. 12mo, pp. 17–66. B. 28313

GRANT. Life and Services of Gen. U. S. Grant, Conqueror of the Rebellion, and Eighteenth President of the United States. *Washington: Philip & Solomons.* 1868. 8vo, pp. 160. B., H., S.

GRANT. Official Report of Lieut.-Gen. Ulysses S. Grant, embracing the ... Operations of the Armies of the Union from March, 1862, to the Closing Scene of the Rebellion. *New York: Beadle & Co.* [1866.] 16mo, pp. 87. H. 28315

GRANT. Report of Lieutenant-General U. S. Grant, of the Armies of the United States—1864–'65. *New York: D. Appleton and Company.* 1865. 8vo, pp. 77. Portrait. B., BA., H. + *Washington: Government Printing Office.* 1866. 8vo, pp. 44. B.

GRANT. Public Honors to Lieutenant-General Grant, by the Citizens of New-York. Fifth Avenue Hotel, November 20th, 1865. Printed for the Citizen's Committee. *New-York: Geo. F. Nesbit & Co.* 1865. Impl. 8vo, pp. 39. 28317

Also: The Grant Campaign Songster. *New York: Robert M. De Witt.* [1868.] 12mo, pp. 72. B.—The Grant Songster. *New York: Haney & Co.* 1868. 18mo, pp. 63.—The Grant Songster. A Collection of Campaign Songs for 1868. *Chicago: Root & Cady.* 1868. Square 18mo, pp. 42, (1). B.—General Grant's Lady Detective. A most Singular Narrative. *Philadelphia: C. W. Alexander.* 1868. 8vo, pp. 99.—Lively Life of General Grant. *New York.* 1868.—Speeches of General U. S. Grant, Republican Candidate for Eighteenth President of the United States ... . *Washington: Gibson Brothers.* 1868. 8vo, pp. 16. H. Also a host of Campaign Text Books, Documents, &c., relating to the presidential elections of 1864 and 1868.

GRANT *and* COLFAX. The Lives of Gen. U. S. Grant and S. Colfax. *Philadelphia: T. B. Peterson & Bros.* 1868. 12mo, pp. 362. Portraits. B. 28318

GRANT *and* COLFAX. Sketches of the Lives and Services of Ulysses S. Grant and Schuyler Colfax, National Republican Candidates for President and Vice-President of the United States. [n. p. n. d.] 8vo, pp. 8. H. 28319

Also: Lives of U. S. Grant and S. Colfax. *Cincinnati: Padrick & Co.* 1868. 8vo, pp. 104. Portrait. B.

GRANT (T.) Oration at Flemington, July 4, 1799. *Trenton.* 1799. 8vo. 28320

GRANT (W. H.) ... Observations on the Western Trade, and its Influence upon the Growth and Prosperity of the Cities of New York, Boston, and Philadelphia, through the several Competing Lines of Communication and the Hudson River Railroad. By William H. Grant. *Poughkeepsie.* 1846. 8vo, pp. 40. H., S.

GRANT (W. R.) Sketch of the Life and Character of S. G. Morton, M.D., October 13, 1851. By William R. Grant. *Philadelphia.* 1852. 8vo. Portrait. S. 28322

Grant and Release. *See* Carolina, Vol. III, No. 10971.

Grant to the Georgia Mississippi Company. *See* Georgia.

GRANTHAM (T.) An Historical | Account | of some | Memorable Actions, | Particularly in Virginia; | Also | Against the Admiral of Algier, | and in the East Indies: | Perform'd for the Service of his | Prince and Country, | By | S[r] Thomas Grantham, K[t]. | *London: | J. Roberts,* ... | MDCCXVI. 8vo, pp. 71. 28323

A very rare piece. I have only seen one copy.

GRANTLAND (Seaton). Speech of Mr. Grantland of Georgia ... [on] ... the Cherokee Treaty, delivered in the House ... June 29, 1836. *Washington.* 1836. 8vo, pp. 7. 28324

GRANVILLE (J.) History of St. Domingo, from its Discovery by Columbus. *New York.* 1821. 8vo. 28325

GRANVILLE, *Mass.* Account of the Classical School in Granville, Mass. *Albany.* 1831. 12mo. 28326

The Granville Jubilee, Celebrated at Granville, Mass., August 27 and 28, 1845. *Springfield: Printed by Horace S. Taylor.* 1845. 8vo, pp. 139. BA., H., S. 28327

Contains an historical discourse by the Rev. Dr. Cowley, pp. 26–79.

GRANVILLE, *O.* ... Annual Meeting of the Trustees of the Granville Literary and Theological Institution, and of the Ohio

Baptist Education Society, August 13th and 14th, 1834. *Cincinnati: Printed by N. S. Johnson.* 1834. 8vo, pp. 23. H. 28328

GRANVILLE, *O.* Biennial Catalogue of the Teachers and Pupils of the Granville Female Seminary, 1850–52. *Granville, O.* 1852. 8vo, pp. 16. 28329

Graphic Sketches. *See* Wyth (John).

GRASSE-TILLY (François Joseph Paul, *comte*, afterwards *marquis* de). Notice biographique sur l'amiral comte de Grasse, d'après les documents inédits communiqués par M. le comte Alexandre-François-Auguste de Grasse, son fils. *Paris: imprimerie de Bailly.* 1840. 8vo, pp. 48. 28330

[GRASSE.] Journal d'un Officier de l'armée navale en Amérique en 1781 & 1782. *A Amsterdam.* M.DCC.LXXXIII. 8vo, pp. 72. N. 28331

It was translated, as below, for the Bradford Club.

GRASSE. The Operations of the French Fleet under the Count de Grasse, in 1781–82, as described in two Contemporaneous Journals. *New York.* MDCCCLXIV. Rl. 8vo, pp. 216. Portrait and Plate. 28332

Bradford Club Series, No. III. 150 copies printed.

GRASSE. Mémoire du Compte de Grasse, sur le Combat Naval du 12 Avril, 1782, avec les plans des positions principales des Armées respectives. [n. p. n. d.] 4to, pp. 27. With 8 large folded Plans. BA., S. 28333

A very full account of Rodney's famous victory in the West Indies, by the defeated commander. Privately printed, and very rare.

GRASSET DE SAINT SAUVEUR (Jacques). Tableau cosmographique de l'Europe, de l'Asie, de l'Afrique, et de l'Amérique, avec histoire générale et détaillée des peuples sauvages. *Paris.* 1787. 4to. 28334

GRASSET DE SAINT SAUVEUR. Voyages pittoresques dans les quatre parties du monde. *Paris.* 1806. 4to. 28335

GRASSI (G.) Notizie varie sullo stato presente della Repubblica degli Stati Uniti dell' America settentrionale, scritte al principio del 1818. Dal P. Giovanni Grassi della Compagnia di Gesu. *In Roma* 1818. *Presso Luigi Perego Salvioni.* 12mo, pp. viii, 120. + Edizione seconda. *Milano.* 1819. 8vo, pp. 146. H.

+ Terza Edizione Accresciuta di recenti Memorie dello stesso Autore. *Torino Tipografia Chirio e Mina.* 1822. 8vo, pp. 140.

See "N. A. Rev.," XVI. 209. The author resided some years at Georgetown in the District of Columbia, as superior of the Catholic seminary at that place.

Grateful Reflections On the Divine Goodness vouchsaf'd to the American Arms in their Remarkable Successes in the Northern Department, after giving up our Fortresses at Ticonderoga on the 6th of July, A. D. 1777. [A Poem.] *Hartford, Conn.* [n. d.] 12mo. W. 28337

[GRATTAN (Peachy R.)] Letter on the Constitutional Power of the General Assembly to extend the Boundaries of the City of Richmond ... . *Richmond: H. K. Ellyson.* 1861. 8vo, pp. 14. H. 28338

Also: Speech ... in the General Assembly at Cleveland, June 2, 1857. *Richmond: H. K. Ellyson.* 1857. 8vo, pp. 22. BA.

GRATTAN (T. C.) Civilized America. By Thomas Colley Grattan. *London: Bradbury and Evans.* 1859. 2 vols., 8vo, pp. xix, 444, Map; vii, 517, (1). B., BA. + Second Edition. [*Ibid.*] 2 vols., 8vo, pp. xxiv, xviii, 444; vii, 517, Errata, Map. 28339

GRATTAN. England and the Disrupted States of America. By Thomas Colley Grattan. *London: Ridgway.* 1861. 8vo, pp. 42. + Second Edition. [*Ibid.*] 1861. pp. 42. B., H. + Third Edition. [*Ibid.*] 1862. 8vo, pp. 47. C. 28340

Also: The Boundary Question Revised; and Dr. Franklin's Red Line shown to be the Right One. By a British Subject. ... *New York: Albion Office.* 1843. 8vo, pp. 24. H.

GRATTON (J.) A Journal of the Life of that Ancient Servant of Christ, John Gratton. ... *London: J. Sowle.* 1720. 8vo.

Includes, An Epistle to Friends in Pennsylvania. Written at Monyash, in the 7th month, 1693. Reprinted, *London: James Phillips.* 1779. 8vo. + *London.* [*Ibid.*] 1795. 12mo. + *Stockport: Printed by Thomas Claye.* 1823. 12mo. + Republished in "The Friends' Library," Vol. IX. *Philadelphia.* 1845.

A Gratulatory Address | delivered July 5th 1790. before the | Society of the | Cincinnati, | of the | Commonwealth of Massachusetts. | Published by their Order. | *Printed in Boston,* | *By Benjamin Russell,* ... | M,DCC,XC. | Sm. 4to, pp. 14. 28342

GRAU (J.) Catecismo politico arreglado á la constitucion de la república de Colombia de 30 de Agosto de 1821. Para el uso de las escuelas de primeras letras del departamento de Orinoco. .. *Caracas: reimpreso por Tomas Antero.* 1824. 8vo, pp. 38, (1).

[GRAVE (John).] A Song of Sion. Written by a Citizen thereof, whose outward Habitation is in Virginia; and being sent over to some of his Friends in England, the same is found fitting to be published, for to warn the Seed of Evil-doers. With an Additional Postcript from another hand. [M. M., *i. e.* Martin Mason?] *Printed in the Year* 1662. 4to, pp. 12. 28344

A copy of this rare and curious poetical Quaker tract sold at Puttick's, in 1860, for two guineas.

GRAVES (A. J.) Girlhood and Womanhood: or, Sketches of my Schoolmates. By Mrs. A. J. Graves. *Boston: T. H. Carter & Co.* 1844. 12mo, pp. 216. 28345

GRAVES. Woman in America; being an Examination into the Moral and Intellectual Condition of American Female Society. By Mrs. A. J. Graves. *New York: Harper and Brothers.* [1841.] 12mo, pp. 262. B., BA., 28346

GRAVES (A. T.) Address by Allen T. Graves, Miami University, August 9, 1843. 28347

GRAVES (J.) A Memorial; or a Short Account of the Bahama-Islands; Of their Situation, Product, Conveniency of Trading with the Spaniards; The Benefit that ariseth by the great Quantities of Salt that is made by the Sun; and the Safety all Ships that are in distress near those parts do find, by having so good a Harbour as Providence to bare away to for Succour. Delivered to the Lords, Proprietors of the said Islands, and the Hon. Commissioners of Her Majesty's Customs. By John Graves, Collector of Customs in those Islands, and now Humbly Presented to both Houses of Parliament. *London: Printed in the Year* 1708. 4to, pp. 8. + The Same, without date. 4to, pp. 8.

The author of this pamphlet (John Graves, Esq.) has prefixed to it the following advertisement: "This is no *Catchpenny* pamphlet, for not a copy of it ever has been, nor (we trust) ever will be *sold*." Mr. Rich places this under the date 1789.

GRAVES (J.) Truth against Error. A Defence of Slavery: being a Review of a Letter written by the Rev. Charles T. Torrey, now confined in the Baltimore Jail, upon the Charges of Abducting Slaves from their Masters, in Maryland and Virginia. By J. Graves. *Baltimore: Woods & Crane.* 1844. 8vo, pp. 32.

GRAVES (J. R.) The Great Iron Wheel; or, Republicanism Backwards and Christianity Reversed. In a Series of Letters addressed to J. Soule, Senior Bishop of the M. E. Church, South. By J. R. Graves, ... *Nashville.* 1855. 12mo, pp. 574. C. + Thirtieth Thousand. [*Ibid.*] 1860. 12mo, pp. 586. 28350

GRAVES (R. S.) To the People of Mississippi. By Richard Stanford Graves. [n. p. n. d.] 8vo, pp. 29. BA. 28351

GRAVES (R.) A Statement of the Claim of Rear-Admiral R. Graves, and Louisa Carolina his Wife, on the Bahama Islands. ... *London: Printed by J. Gillet.* 1815. 8vo, pp. 40. BA.

Privately printed. Title from J. R. Smith's Catalogue.

GRAVES (W.) A Sermon ... at the Funeral of Mr. Silas May ... December 26, 1805 ... . By William Graves, A.M. ... . *Hartford: Printed by Lincoln & Gleason.* 1807. 8vo, pp. 16. B.

Also: A Sermon ... at the Funeral of Mr. Alpha Child ... Jan. 20, 1809 ... . *Hartford: Peter B. Gleason.* 1810. 8vo, pp. 16. BA.

GRAVES (W.) Two Letters from W. Graves, Esq.; respecting the Conduct of Rear-Admiral Thomas Graves, in North America, during his Accidental Command there for Four Months in 1781. [n. p. n. d.] 4to, pp. 48. With three Appendixes, pp. 29; Plan of Sea-fight, Sept. 5, 1781. 28354

In Hotten's Catalogue, No. 339, it is described as pp. 40, and No. 340 describes "Another Edition, with considerable alterations and additions. 1782. 4to, pp. 68." Mr. H. B. Dawson reprinted the work with the following title:

GRAVES. Two Letters respecting the Conduct of Rear-Admiral Graves on the Coast of the United States, July to November, 1781. By William Graves, Esq., of the Inner Temple. *Morrisania, N. Y.* 1865. 4to, 2 l., pp. 39. B., BA.

One hundred copies only printed.

The Graves of the Indians, with other Poems. *Boston: Hilliard, Gray & Co.* 1827. 12mo, pp. 72. 28356

GRAVESEND. List of Persons Enrolled for the Draft in the Town of Gravesend, Kings County, N. Y. [1862.] 8vo, pp. 6.

GRAVIER (G.) Découvertes et établissements de Cavelier de la Salle de Rouen dans L'Amérique du Nord (lacs Ontario, Érié, Huron, Michigan, Vallées de l'Ohio et du Mississippi et Texas). Par Gabriel Gravier, ... *Paris: Maisonneuve et Ce.* ... 1870. Rl. 8vo, pp. xii, 411. 2 Plates and 2 Maps. B., BA. 28358

GRAVIER (J.) Lettre du Père Jacques Gravier, de la Compagnie de Jésus, le 23 Février 1708. Sur les Affaires de la Louisiane. *Nouvelle-York: de la presse Cramoisy de Jean-Marie Shea.* M D CCC LXV. 8vo, pp. 18. BA., C. 28359

Forms part of No. XIX. of Shea's Cramoisy Series.

GRAVIER. Relation de ce qui s'est passé dans la Mission de l'Immaculée Conception au pays des Illinois, depuis le mois de Mars 1693, jusqu'en Février 1694. Par le R. Père Jacques Gravier, de la Compagnie de Jésus. *À Manate: de la Presse Cramoisy de Jean-Marie Shea,* M,DCCC,LVII. Sm. 8vo, pp. 65, (1).

Forms No. I. of Shea's Cramoisy Series. See "Hist. Mag.," I. 318.

GRAVIER. Relation ou Journal du Voyage de R. P. Jacques Gravier, de la Compagnie de Jésus, en 1700, depuis le pays des Illinois jusqu'à l'embouchure du Mississippi. *Nouvelle-York, Isle de Manate, de la Presse Cramoisy de Jean-Marie Shea,* M.DCCC.LIX. Sm. 8vo, pp. 68. B., BA., C., H., S. 28361

Forms No. XI. of Shea's Cramoisy Series.

GRAVIER (Jean). Documents in support of the Right of the Inhabitants of the City of New Orleans, to the Alluvion in front of the Suburb St. Mary, Contested. *City of Washington: A. & G. Way.* 1809. 8vo, pp. 53. H. 28362

GRAVIER. Examination of the Judgment rendered in the Cause between Jean Gravier and the City of New Orleans. *City of Washington: A. & G. Way.* 1809. 8vo, pp. 19. H.

GRAY (A.) Elements of Geology. By Alonzo Gray, A.M., and C. B. Adams, A.M. *New York.* 1852. 8vo. + *New York: Harper & Brothers.* 1853. 8vo, pp. xv, 354. H. 28364

[GRAY.] The Smithsonian Institution. [n. p. n. d] 8vo, pp. 21. H. 28365

Also: An Address before the Essex Agricultural Society, at Georgetown, September 30, 1841. ... *Salem: Salem Gazette Office.* 1842. 8vo, pp. 30. B., H.—Address on Female Education. *New York.* 1854. 8vo.

GRAY (A.) A Manual of the Botany of the Northern United States, from New England to Wisconsin, and South to Ohio and Pennsylvania inclusive. [The Mosses and Liverworts by W. S. Sullivant.] By Asa Gray, M.D. *Boston and Cambridge.* 1848. 12mo, pp, 782. B., C. + Second Edition; including Virginia, Kentucky, and all East of the Mississippi. *New York: George P. Putnam & Co.* 1856. 8vo, pp. xxviii, 739. 14 Plates. BA., H. + *New York: Ivison & Phinney.* 1857. 8vo, pp. xxiv, 631. Plates. B. + *New York: Ivison & Co.* 1859. 8vo, pp. 739. 14 Plates. C. + Third Revised Edition *New York: Ivison, Phinney & Co.* 1862. 12mo, pp. xcviii, 606, 13 l. 6 Plates. + Fifth Edition. *New York: Ivison, Phinney & Co.* 1867. 8vo, pp. 701. 20 Plates. C. 28366

GRAY *et* SULLIVANT (W. S.) Musci Alleghanienses, sive Spicilegia Muscorum atque Hepaticarum quos in itinere a Marylandia usque ad Georgiam per tractatus montium decerpserunt. *Columbus.* MDCCCXLV. 8vo, pp. 69. A., H. 28367

GRAY (A.) ... Botany. Phanerogamia. By Asa Gray, M.D. With a folio Atlas of One Hundred Plates. *Philadelphia: Printed by C. Sherman.* 1854. 4to, pp. (4), 777. Atlas, dated 1857, 100 Plates, folio. 28368

Forms Vol. XV. of the United States Exploring Expedition. Some copies have the imprint *New York: George P. Putnam,* 1854; and owing to some mistake, a large number of copies of the Atlas were sold by auction, unbound and without the letter-press, the result is that odd volumes are comparatively common—whole sets are scarce. Also: The Botanical Text-Book ... *New York: Wiley and Putnam.* 1842. 12mo, pp. 413. B., BA. H. + [*Ibid.*] 1845. 12mo, pp. 5–506. BA. + Third Edition. *New York: George P. Putnam & Co.* 1850. 8vo, pp. 520. + Fourth Edition. [*Ibid.*] 1853. 8vo, pp. 528. B.—Botany for Young People ... With a Popular Flora, or an Arrangement and Description of Common Plants, both Wild and Cultivated. *New York: Ivison and Phinney.* 1858. Small 4to, 1 l., pp. 233. B. + *New York.* 1869 Square 12mo, pp. 234. *See also* Pacific Railroad Surveys, Vols. II. and XII.; Ives' Report on Colorado, and Torrey (John).

GRAY. Chloris Boreali-Americana: Illustrations of New, Rare, or otherwise interesting North-American Plants. By Asa Gray. Decade I. *Cambridge.* 1846. 4to. 10 colored Plates. + *Boston.* 1848. 28369

GRAY. Field, Forest, and Garden Botany; a Simple Introduction to the Common Plants of the United States East of the Mississippi, both Wild and Cultivated. By Asa Gray. *New York: Ivison, Phinney, Blakeman & Co.* 1868. 8vo, pp. 386. C.

GRAY. Genera Floræ Americæ Boreali-Orientalis illustrata. Vol. I. *Boston.* 1848–49. 2 vols., rl. 8vo. H. 28371

GRAY. ... The Genera of the Plants of the United States, illustrated by Figures and Analyses from Nature, by Isaac Sprague, ... Superintended, and with Descriptions, &c., By Asa Gray, M.D. Vol. I. *Boston: James Munroe and Company.* Vol. II. *New York: Geo. P. Putnam.* 1848–49. 2 vols., 8vo, pp. 230, 100 Plates; 229, (1), 186 Plates. B., BA. 28372

GRAY. Plantæ Wrightianæ Texano Neo-Mexicanæ. By Asa Gray, M.D. Part I. *Washington.* 1852. 4to, pp. 146. 10 Plates. 28373

GRAY. Plantæ Wrightianæ Texano Neo-Mexicanæ. Part II. An Account of a Collection of Plants made by Charles Wright

in Western Texas, New Mexico, and Sonora, in the years 1851 and 1852. By Asa Gray, M.D. *Washington.* 1853. 4to, pp. 120. 4 Plates. 28374

Also included in the "Smithsonian Collections," Vols. III. and IV. BA., H.

GRAY (A. B.) Southern Pacific Railroad. Survey of a Route for the Southern Pacific R. R., on the 32nd Parallel, by A. B. Gray for the Texas Western R. R. Company. *Cincinnati, O.: Wrightson & Co.'s Print.* 1856. 8vo, pp. 110, Errata, 1 slip. 33 Plates, 2 Maps. BA. 28375

GRAY. Explanatory Report ... of his Proceedings while a Member of the "United States and Mexican Boundary Commission," appointed to run and mark the Boundary Line under the Treaty of Guadalupe Hidalgo, 1853. Ex. Doc., 1855. 8vo, pp. 50. Map. S. 28376

GRAY (B.) ... Account of the Captivity ... & Deliverance of Mrs. Jemima Howe. ... By the Rev. Bunker Gray ... . *Boston: Printed by Belknap and Young.* MDCCXCII. 8vo, pp. 20.

GRAY (B. G.) Extra-Territorial Incidents of Colonial Legislation. By B. G. Gray. *Boston.* 1836. 12mo, pp. 22. 28378

GRAY (David.) Gray's Narrative [of his Services as Spy], 1776–82. [n. p. n. d.] 8vo, pp. 8. S. 28379

GRAY (E. H.) Assaults upon Freedom; or, Kidnapping an Outrage upon Humanity and Abhorrent to God. A Discourse occasioned by the Rendition of Anthony Burns. By E. H. Gray. *Shelburne Falls: D. B. Gunn.* 1854. 8vo, pp. 22. B., H.

Also: A Discourse on the Imperative Duties of the Hour ... Washington, D. C., July 5, 1863. *Washington: H. Polkinhorn.* 1863. 8vo, pp. 15. B., H.

GRAY (E.) An Oration, delivered July 5, 1790. At ... Boston ... By Edward Gray, Esq. *Boston: Printed by Samuel Hall.* M.DCC.XC. 8vo, pp. 16. BA., M. 28381

Also: Address ... before the Members of the Massachusetts Charitable Fire Society, ... June 1, 1804; with Odes, &c. ... *Boston: Printed by Russell and Cutler.* 1804. 8vo, pp. 31. BA., H.

GRAY (Edwin). Mr. Gray's Motion, January 24, 1806. [*Washington.* 1806.] 8vo. 28382

Relative to representatives being contractors for the public service.

GRAY (Ellis). The Fidelity of Ministers to Themselves, and to the Flock of God. ... A Sermon ... at the Ordination

of the Reverend Mr. Thaddeus Maccarty, ... in Kingston, Nov. 3, 1742. *Boston: M. Dennis.* 1742. 8vo, pp. 40. B., BA., H.

Also: The Design of the Institution of the Gospel-Ministry. A Sermon, ... September 27, 1741, ... in Boston. ... *Boston: M. Dennis.* 1741. 8vo, pp. 23. B., BA.

GRAY (F. C.) Letter to Governor Lincoln, in relation to Harvard University. [By Francis C. Gray.] *Boston: W. L. Lewis.* M DCCC XXI. 8vo, pp. 48. B., BA., H. + Second Edition. *Boston: Carter, Hendee and Babcock.* 1831. 8vo, pp. 60. B., BA., H. + Third Edition. [*Ibid.*] 1831. 8vo, pp. 63. B.

GRAY. Oration delivered before the Legislature of Massachusetts, At their Request, on the One Hundredth Anniversary of the Birth of George Washington. By Francis C. Gray. *Boston: Dutton & Wentworth, Printers* ... 1832. 8vo, pp. 80. B., BA.

GRAY. Report of the Committee of Merchants and others on the Tariff, October 2, 1820. 28386

The resolutions appended were drawn up by Mr. Webster.

GRAY. Remarks on the Early Laws of Massachusetts Bay. With the Code adopted in the year 1641, and called the Body of Liberties, now first printed. By Francis C. Gray. *Boston: Charles C. Little and James Brown.* 1843. 8vo, pp. 49. B., BA.

See also "Mass. Hist. Soc. Coll.," Vol. III., Third Series. Also: An Address to the Massachusetts Charitable Fire Society, ... Oct. 10, 1817. *Boston: Printed by Chester Stebbins.* 1817. 8vo, pp 21. BA., H., M.—Discourse at Plymouth, Mass., on the ... Anniversary of the Landing of the Pilgrims, December 22, 1829. ... 8vo.—A Discourse before the American Institute, ... August 23, 1832. *Boston: Carter, Hendee and Co.* 1832, 8vo, pp. 21. B.—Oration, pronounced July 4, 1818, at ... Boston. *Boston: Charles Callender.* 1818. 8vo, pp. 24. B., BA., H.—Oration before the Phi Beta Kappa Society of Brown University, Providence, R. I., ... September 7, 1842. ... *Providence: B. Cranston & Co.* 1842. 8vo, pp. 40. B., BA., H., M.—Poem spoken at Cambridge, before the Phi Beta Kappa Society of Harvard University, August 27, 1840. *Boston: Charles C. Little and James Brown.* MDCCCXL. 8vo, pp. 36. B., BA., M., W.—Prison Discipline in America. ... *Boston: Charles C. Little and James Brown.* MDCCCXLVII. 8vo, pp. 203. B., BA. + *London: John Murray.* 1848. 8vo, pp. 203. B., C., H., S. For a review of this *see* [Packard (F. A.)]—Speech ... in the House of Representatives of Massachusetts, March 19, 1836, on the Bill to abolish Capital Punishment. *Boston: James Loring.* 1836. 8vo, pp. 19. B. And many articles in the "North American Review."

GRAY (F. Turell). Extract from a Sermon delivered at the Bulfinch-Street Church, Boston, Jan. 9, 1853, the Sunday following the Interment of ... Amos Lawrence. By Rev. F. T. Gray. *Boston: John Wilson & Son.* 1853. 16mo, pp. 16. B.

GRAY. ... A Sermon ... at the Friend Street, Chapel, the Sunday Evening after the Execution of Russell and Crockett. By Frederick T. Gray. ... *Boston: S. G. Simpkins.* 1836. 8vo, pp. 16. BA. 28389

[GRAY.] The Sunday-School Teacher's Reward. Address before the Teachers of the Hancock Sunday School, March 31, 1832. *Boston.* 1832. 12mo, pp. 25. H. 28390

Also: An Address delivered ... before the Society for the Prevention of Pauperism, January 14, 1839. ... *Boston: Weeks, Jordan and Company.* 1839. 12mo, pp. 22, (1). B., BA., H.—New Years' Sermons preached in ... Bulfinch Street Church, ... January 3, 1847. *Boston: Printed by William A. Hall & Co.* 1847. 8vo, pp. 24. B., H.—Two Sermons, November 29, 1841. Being the close of the second year of [his] Ministry. With an Appendix. *Boston: James Munroe and Company.* 1841. 8vo, pp. 56. B., H.—A Sermon on the Death of the Rev. Henry Ware, Jr., D.D., in Bulfinch Street Church, October 1, 1843. *Boston: James Munroe & Co.* 1843. 8vo, pp. 16. H., W.—Letter to the Friends of Rev. F. T. Gray, and the Bulfinch Street Society, occasioned by "Strictures" on Two Sermons ... November 27, 1841 ... . By a Proprietor. *Boston: James Munroe & Co.* 1842. 8vo, pp. 64. H., BA.

[GRAY (Harrison).] A Few Remarks upon some of the Votes and Resolutions of the Continental Congress ... at Philadelphia in September, and the Provincial Congress ... at Cambridge in November 1774. By a Friend to Peace at Good Order. ... *For the Purchasers in* 1775. 8vo, pp. 20. BA. 28391

GRAY (H.) Memoirs of Rev. Benjamin C. Cutler, D.D. ... By Rev. Horatio Gray, A.M. *New York: Anson D. F. Randolph.* 1865. 12mo, pp. 439. B. 28392

GRAY (H.) Letters from Canada, written during a Residence there in the Years 1806, 1807, 1808; showing the Present State of Canada, its Productions, Trade, Commercial Importance, and Political Relations. Illustrative of the Laws, the Manners of the People, and the Peculiarities of the Country and Climate. Exhibiting also, the Commercial Importance of Nova-Scotia, New Brunswick, & Cape-Breton; and their increasing Ability, in Conjunction with Canada, to furnish the necessary Supplies of Lumber and Provisions to our West-India Islands. By Hugh Gray. *London: Longman & Co.* 1809. 8vo, pp. (16), 406. Map and Table. BA., H. + Second Edition. [*Ibid.*] 1814. C., P.

See "M. Rev.," New Series, LXI. 23.

GRAY (J. W. D.) A Reply to the Statement of the Rev. Mr. Wiggins, A.M., showing the Causes which have led to his Retirement from the Curacy of St. John. By Rev. J. W. D. Gray. *St. John.* 1851. 8vo. 28394

GRAY (J.) Concio ad Clerum: A Sketch of the Condition and Prospects of the Christian Church, delivered Baltimore, April 20, 1821. By James Gray. *Baltimore.* 1821. 8vo, pp. 108. 28395

GRAY (J.) ... A Discourse ... 31st of December, 1808; ... a Day of Thanksgiving and Prayer ... in ... Philadelphia. By James Gray, D.D. ... *Philadelphia: Printed by Jane Aitken.* 1809. 8vo, pp. 36. H. 28396

[GRAY (John).] Doctor Price's Notions of the Nature of Civil Liberty, shewn to be contradictory to Reason and Scripture. *London: T. Becket.* MDCCLXXVII. 8vo, 2 l., pp. 123. BA.

"Mr. John Gray, the author of this pamphlet, appears to have bestowed great attention on the several important topics on which the patriotic Dr. Price had given his opinion, and many of his arguments come recommended by their novelty as well as by the ingenuity with which they are enforced."—*M. Rev.*, LVI. 152.

GRAY (J.) A Brief, Historical, Statistical, and Descriptive Review of East Tennessee, United States of America: developing its Immense Agricultural, Mining, and Manufacturing Advantages, with Remarks to Emigrants. Accompanied with a Map and Lithographed Sketch of a Tennessee Farm, Mansion House, and Buildings. By J. Gray, a Naturalized Citizen of the United States of America. *Leith.* 1842. 8vo, pp. 71. Map and Plates. 28398

GRAY (J. Chipman). An Oration, pronounced on the Fourth of July, 1822, at ... the Request of the Inhabitants of ... Boston. ... By John C. Gray. *Boston: Charles Callender.* 1822. 8vo, pp. 20. B., BA., H., M., W. 28399

Also: Address before the Massachusetts Horticultural Society, ... Sixth Anniversary, September 17, 1834. ... *Boston: Printed by J. T. Buckingham.* MDCCCXXXIV. 8vo, pp. 40. B.—Address delivered at Concord, October 4, 1848, before the Middlesex Society of Husbandmen and Manufacturers. ... *Boston: Printed by Freeman and Bolles.* 1848. 8vo, pp. 19. B., BA., H.—Essays, Agricultural and Literary. ... *Boston: Little, Brown and Company.* 1856. 12mo, pp. ix, 1 l., 386. B., BA., H.

GRAY (J. Edward). Zoology of the Voyage of H.M.S. Samarang, under the Command of Sir Edward Belcher, during the Years 1843–1846. By John E. Gray, Sir John Richardson, Professor Owen, Arthur Adams, Lovell Reeve, and Adam White. Edited by Arthur Adams, F.L.S. *London.* 1850. Rl. 4to, pp. 250. 32 colored and 22 plain Plates. 28400

GRAY. The Zoology of the Voyage of H.M.S. Erebus and Terror, under the Command of Captain Sir James Clark Ross, during the Years 1839–1843, etc. Parts 1–16. *London: Longman, Brown, Green & Longmans.* 1844–48. 4to. C. 28401

Contents: Mammalia. By J. E. Gray. Parts 1, 4, 13, 14, 15. Birds. By G. R. Gray. Parts 3, 8, 9, 10. Reptiles. By J. E. Gray. Part 6. Fishes. By Sir John Richardson. Parts 2, 5, 7, 12, 16. Insects of New Zealand. By Adam White. Part 11. *See also* Richardson (John).

GRAY (M. W.) Remarks by M. W. Gray in the House of Representatives of South Carolina. *Columbia, S. C.* 1860. 8vo.

Relates to the impending secession of the State.

[GRAY (R.)] *See* A Good Speed, Vol. VII., No. 27837

GRAY (R.) A Discourse delivered in Dover, November 15th, 1798, a Day observed as an Anniversary Thanksgiving. By Robert Gray, A.B. *Dover: Samuel Bragg, Jun.* [1798.] 8vo.

GRAY. A Sermon delivered at Hopkinton, before the Hon. General Court of the State of New-Hampshire, at the Annual Election, ... June, 1798. By Robert Gray, A.B. ... *Dover: Printed by Samuel Bragg, Jun., for the General Court.* [1798.] 8vo, pp. 29. N. 28404

GRAY. A Sermon ... at the Ordination of the Reverend Daniel Stone, ... Hallowell, October 21st, 1795, to the First Church in Hallowell. By Robert Gray, A.B. *Hallowell: Peter Edes.* 1796. 8vo, pp. 36. BA. 28405

GRAY (Robert A.) Speech to the Loyal Refugees from Virginia, in Convention at Alexandria, February 22d, 1865. *Baltimore: James Young.* 1865. 8vo, pp. 20. 28406

GRAY (S. B.) The Revival of Bishop Berkeley's Bermuda College: A Letter ... on the Plan which has been lately promulgated with the above Title. By S. Brownlow Gray. *London: Whittaker & Co.* 1853. 8vo, pp. 31. 28407

GRAY (T.) California Politics. Letter of Thomas Gray, of San Francisco, California, to the Secretary of the Treasury. [*Washington.* 1861.] 8vo, pp. 15. H 28408

GRAY (T.) Half Century Sermon, delivered ... April 24, 1842, at Jamaica Plain. By Thomas Gray, D.D. ... *Boston: Printed by I. R. Butts.* 1842. 8vo, pp. 44. B., BA., H. 28409

[GRAY.] Obituary Notice of Rev. John Bradford, with a Brief Historical Sketch of the Congregational Churches in Roxbury. *Boston: F. Y. Carlile.* [1825.] 8vo, pp. 12. H. 28410

GRAY. A Sermon on the Death of ... William Eustis, Late Governor ... of Massachusetts; preached ... in Roxbury, February 13, 1825. ... By Thomas Gray. ... *Boston: Francis Y Carlile.* 1825. 8vo, pp. 26. B., H., M. 28411

GRAY. The Value of Life and Charitable Institutions. A Discourse ... before the Humane Society of ... Massachusetts, ... June 11th, 1805. ... By Thomas Gray. ... *Boston: Printed by Hosea Sprague.* 1805. 8vo, pp. 46. BA., H. 28412

Also: A Sermon, delivered in Boston, before the African Society, on the 14th Day of July, 1818, the Anniversary of the Abolition of the Slave-trade. *Boston: Printed by Parmenter and Norton.* 1818. 8vo, pp. 16. B., BA., H.—A Sermon ... before the Ancient and Honourable Artillery Company, in Boston, June 7, 1819. ... *Boston: E. G. House.* 1819. 8vo, pp. 22, (1). B., BA., H.—A Sermon, delivered ... the Afternoon ... immediately succeeding the Twelfth Anniversary of his Ordination, March 31, 1805. ... *Boston: Printed by Russell and Cutler.* 1805. 8vo, pp. 22. B., BA., H.—A Tribute to the Memory of Benjamin Bussey, Esq., who died January 13, 1842. *Boston.* 1842. 8vo, pp. 12. B., H.

GRAY (T.) Change: a Poem pronounced at Roxbury, October VIII, MDCCCXXX, in Commemoration of the First Settlement of that Town. By Thomas Gray, Jr., M.D. *Roxbury: Charles P. Emmons.* MDCCCXXX. 8vo, pp. 25. B., BA., H. W.

GRAY (W. C.) Life of Abraham Lincoln; for the Home Circle and Sabbath School. By William C. Gray. *Cincinnati: Western Tract and Book Society.* 1867. 16mo, pp. 200. 3 Plates.

[GRAY (William Farley).] Letter to his Excellency William H. Seward, Governor of the State of New York, touching a Controversy with the Governor of Virginia respecting the Surrender of certain Fugitives from Justice from that State, charged with the Stealing of Slaves. *New York.* 1841. 8vo, pp. 100.

GRAY (W. H.) A History of Oregon, 1792–1849, drawn from Personal Observation and Authentic Information. By W. H. Gray. *Portland: Author [printed at New York.]* 1870. 8vo, pp. 624. Plate. C., S. 28416

GRAY (W. S.) Better Days of Joseph Barker. *Akron, Ohio: Tusdale, Elkins & Co, Printers.* 1855. 16mo, pp. 32. 28417

[GRAYDON (Alexander).] Memoirs of a Life, Chiefly Passed in Pennsylvania, within the Last Sixty Years. With Occasional Remarks upon the General Occurrences, Character and Spirit of that Eventful Period. *Harrisburgh: Printed by John Wyeth.* 1811. 12mo, pp. 378, Errata, 1 l. B., BA. 28418

[GRAYDON.] Memoirs of a Life, Chiefly Passed in Pennsylvania, within the Last Sixty Years. *Edinburgh: Blackwood.* 1822. 8vo, pp. vii, 431. 28419

This edition was edited by John Galt, and owing to this circumstance it is often catalogued as by Galt. The author was a captain in the United States army (not in

the navy, as stated by Allen). J. Galt says "it is, perhaps, the best personal narrative that has yet appeared relative to the history of that great conflict which terminated in establishing the independence of the United States. The "Quarterly Review" (xxvi., p. 364) calls Mr. Galt to account, for his high opinion of this work, which, it "ventures to pronounce to be in matter almost worthless, and in manner wholly contemptible. *See* "M. Rev.," New Series, May, 1822, and Rich, Vol. II.

GRAYDON. Memoirs of his Own Time. With Reminiscences of the Men and Events of the Revolution. By Alexander Graydon. Edited by John Stockton Littell. ... *Philadelphia: Lindsay & Blakiston.* 1845. 8vo, pp. xxiv, 13–504. + [*Ibid.*] 1846. B., BA., C., H. 28420

GRAYDON (W.) An Abridgment of the Laws of the United States. Or a Complete Digest of all such Acts of Congress as concern the United States at large. To which is added an Appendix, containing all Existing Treaties, the Declaration of Independence, the Articles of Confederation, the Rules and Articles for the Government of the Army, and the Ordinance for the Government of the Territory North-west of the Ohio. By William Graydon, Esq. *Harrisburgh: Printed by John Wyeth.* 1803. 2 vols., 8vo, pp. liii, (3), 476; 163, (1), 8 l. BA., C., H. 28421

Vol. II. contains all such treaties as have been made since the publication of the former volume. Also: Justices and Constables Assistant. *Harrisburg, Penn.* 1805. 8vo.

GRAYSON (E. T.) Argument in Defense of Edward T. Grayson, before a Navy General Court Martial, convened at the Philadelphia Navy Yard, March 23d, 1863. [n. p. n. d.] 8vo, pp. 13. 28422

GRAYSON (Eldred, *pseudon*). Standish, the Puritan. A Tale of the American Revolution. By Eldred Grayson, Esq. *New York: Harper & Brothers.* 1850. 12mo, pp. 320. B., C., H.

GRAYSON (W. J.) The Hireling and the Slave, Chicora, and other Poems. By William J. Grayson. ... *Charleston, S. C.: McCarter & Co.* 1854. 12mo, pp. 169. + Second Edition. [*Ibid.*] 1855. 12mo. + [*Ibid.*] 1856. 12mo, pp. 169. B.

"An idyllic picture of rural life at the South."—DUYCKINCK, II. 103.

GRAYSON. James Louis Petigru, of South Carolina. A Biographical Sketch. By William J. Grayson. *New York: Harper & Brothers.* 1866. 12mo, pp. 178. Portrait. B., BA., H.

The author was a supporter of State rights, but strongly opposed to secession.

GRAYSON. Letter to ... Whitemarsh B. Seabrook ... on the Dissolution of the Union. *Charleston: A. E. Miller. Re-printed by George N. Nichols, Savannah, Ga.* 1850. 8vo, pp. 16.

[GRAYSON.] Letters of Curtins. Published originally in the Charleston Courier. *Charleston, S. C.: Printed by A. E. Miller.* 1851. 8vo, pp. 53. BA., H. 28427

Also: Reply to Dr. Dewey's Address, delivered at the Elm Tree, Sheffield, Mass. ... *Charleston, S. C.* 1856. 8vo, pp. 32.—Reply to Professor Hodge, on the "State of the Country." *Charleston: Evans & Cogswell.* 1861. 8vo, pp. 32. B.

Great and Important Meeting of Democratic Republicans; with an Address. *New York.* 1838. 8vo. 28428

The Great Arctic Mystery. 1856. 8vo. 28429

Great Auction Sale of Slaves. Sequel to Mrs. Kemble's Journal. *Union League of Philadelphia.* [n. d.] 8vo. 28430

GREAT BARRINGTON, *Mass.* Catalogue of the Officers and Students of Great Barrington Academy, for the Academic Year 1851–52. *Albany: J. Munsell, Printer.* 1852. 8vo, pp. 12. Plate. 28431

GREAT BRITAIN. ... Correspondence respecting the Proposed Union of the British North American Provinces. ... 8th February, 1867. *London: Printed by George Edward Eyre and William Spottiswoode.* 1867. 8vo, 2 l., pp. 170. B. 28432

Etat Militaire de la Grande Bretagne pour l'Année MDCCLXXIV. Quinzieme Edition Corrigée & Augmentée de l'Etat Major. *A Paris. Quai des Augustins, Avec Approbation & Privilege du Roi.* [1774.] 16mo, pp. 76. Engraved Title. 28433

Great Britain and the United States, with a View to their Future Commercial Connection, with Observations on Canada, Nova Scotia, and the Fisheries. *London.* 1784. 8vo. 28434

Title from an auctioneer's catalogue.

Great Britain Undeceived in the Conduct of Government and the Views of America. Including, Occasional Strictures on the Prevailing Sects, a Cursory Hint for Regulating the Police of London, and a Plan for the Speedy Termination of the Present Unhappy Contest. In an Epistle to the Right Honourable Lord N * * * *, suggested by the late Proposal for an Accommodation. *London: T. Cadell.* 1778. 12mo. 28435

"The writer contends for the most determined persecution of the American war, in order, at all hazards, and at whatever expense, to reduce the colonies to unconditional submission. The means he points out are to 'lay waste, burn, and destroy, through all the coasts of the thirteen States,' but on New England in particular this good Christian soul would pour the utmost severity of vengeance; and *Delenda est Bostonia!* is repeatedly sounded in the ears of the noble statesman to whom this burning, sinking, and destroying proposal is addressed."—*M. Rev.*, LIX. 389.

Great Britain's Complaints against Spain Impartially Examined. *London.* 1740. 28436

Chiefly relating to America. Title from Sparks' Catalogue.

Great Britain's Right to Tax her Colonies; Placed in the clearest Light, by a Swiss. *London: Printed by J. Delegal.* M.DCC.LXXIV. 8vo, pp. (4), 55. + *Philadelphia.* [n. d.] 28437

"This Swiss is an advocate for the people of America, chiefly on grounds which have before been trodden by others."—*M. Rev.*, LI. 479. Another copy I have seen has neither place or date.

Great Britain's Speediest Sinking Fund is a Powerful Maritime War, rightly manag'd, and especially in the West-Indies. *London.* 1727. 8vo, pp. (2), 30. 28438

Great Central Route. Blue Line. General Managers' Report ... 1867. *Detroit.* 1868. 8vo, pp. 12. H. 28439

The Great Conspiracy. Full Account of the Assassination Plot. John H. Surratt and his Mother. With Biographical Sketches of J. B. Booth and J. Wilkes, and the Life and Extraordinary Adventures of John H. Surratt. *Philadelphia: Barclay & Co.* 1866. 8vo, pp. 201. C. 28440

A catchpenny affair; relates to the assassination of Abraham Lincoln.

The Great Controversy of States and People. *Boston: Wm. Crosby and H. P. Nichols.* 1851. 8vo, pp. 45. B., BA., H.

The Great Cotton Question: Where are the Spoils of the Slave? Addressed to the Upper and Middle Classes of Great Britain. By λ. *Cambridge: Macmillan & Co.* 1861. 8vo, pp. 21. 28442

The Great Difficulty, and Distinguishing Reward of the Faithful Discharger of the Ministerial Office. A Discourse on 2 Cor. 11: 15, 16, delivered at an Association Meeting. By one of the Reverend Members. *Boston.* 1762. 8vo, pp. 12. B.

Separately paged, but with continuous signatures, and apparently by the same author, is, "The Necessity of Brotherly Love."

The Great Dutch Flat Swindle!! The City of San Francisco demands Justice!! ... An Address to the Board of Supervisors, Officers and People of San Francisco. [n. p. n. d.] 8vo, pp. 131, (1). H. 28444

Great Exhibition of the Works of Industry of all Nations, 1851. Official and Illustrated Catalogue. *London.* 1851. 3 vols., rl. 8vo. 28445

American industry forms an important part of this and the subsequent World's Fairs.

GREAT FALLS. The Act of the Legislature of New-Hampshire Incorporating the Great Falls Manufacturing Company, and the By-Laws of the Corporation. *Dover: For the Corporation.* 1824. 18mo, pp. 14. H. 28446

GREAT FALLS MANUFACTURING COMPANY. Report of the Investigating Committee, September 1, 1858. [n. p. n. d.] 8vo, pp. 9. 28447

Great Falls [N. H.] Directory. *See* Dover, Vol. v., No. 20745.

The Great Importance of Cape Breton Demonstrated and Exemplified, by Extracts from the best writers, French and English, who have treated of that Colony. The whole containing, besides the most accurate Description of the Place, a Series of the Arguments that induced the French Court to settle and fortify it; the Plan laid down for making the Establishment, and the great Progress made in the Execution of that Plan: With the Reasons that induced the People of New England to subdue this formidable and dangerous Rival, and that should determine the British Nation never to part with it again on any consideration whatever. In this Pamphlet is included all that Father Charlevoix says of this Island in his celebrated History of New France, etc. Also additional Remarks by the Compiler, with a Map and Plan from Charlevoix, and References giving a distinct idea of the late Siege. *London: John Brindley.* MDCCXLVI. 8vo, pp. viii, 72. 2 Maps. H., J.C.B. 28448

The Great Indian Chief of the West, or Life and Adventures of Black Hawk. *Cincinnati.* 1845. 12mo. Portrait. 28449

The title was afterwards changed. *See* our Vol. II., No. 5677.

The Great Issue to be Decided in November next! Shall the Constitution and the Union Stand or Fall, Shall Sectionalism Triumph? Lincoln and his Supporters. *Washington: McGill & Witherow, Printers.* [1860.] 8vo, pp. 24. 28450

The Great Issue, or Rebellion against Democracy. *New York.* 1863. 8vo. 28451

The Great Mass Meeting of Loyal Citizens, at Cooper Institute, ... March 6, 1863. Speeches of Judge Daly [and others.] *Loyal Publication Society, No.* 3. [1863.] 8vo, pp. 16. 28452

The Great Metropolis. *See* New York City.

The Great Mystery of Foxcraft Discovered. And the Quaker Plainness and Sincerity Demonstrated. First to their great

Apostle, George Fox, Secondly, In their late subscribing the Oath or Act of Abjuration. Introduced with two letters written by George Fox to Coll. Lewis Morris, deceased, exactly Spelled and Pointed as in the Originals, which are now to be seen in the Library at Burlington in New Jersey, and will be proved (by the likeness of the Hand, &c.) to be the Hand-writing of the Quakers Learned Fox, if desired. To which is added, A Postscript with some Remarks on the Quakers' Almanach for the Year 1705. *New York: Printed by William Bradford.* 1705. 4to, pp. 16. 28453

Great National Object. Proposed Connection of the Eastern and Western Waters, by a Communication through the Potomac Country. [n. p. n. d.] 8vo, pp. 38. 28454

A very rare tract on the subject, sometimes followed by a "Report of the Commissioners appointed to Survey the River Potomac." 8vo, pp. 92.

Great National Thoroughfare from the West and South-West, into New England, by the Northern, or Lake Route, from New Orleans to New York, Boston and Portland. [n. p.] 1847. 8vo, pp. 16. H. 28455

Great News from Jamaica in the West Indies, giving an Account of a Bloody Fight between Admiral Bembow and the Spanish Plate-Fleet. 1702. Folio, single leaf. 28456

Great News from the Barbadoes. *See* Vol. I., No. 3270.

The Great Northern Conspiracy of the O. S. L. [n. p. n. d.] 8vo, pp. 15. 28457

Charter of the Great Northern Turnpike Company. *Albany.* 1805. 8vo. 28458

A | Great Plot | Discovered, | or | The notorious and wicked Design | upon the River of Thames, put | in execution on Monday last, | With a Hu-and-Cry after the Condemned Pri- | soners that made their escape upon their re- | moving from Newgate to be transported for | Jamaica; And the manner how they made their | escape, and got ashore in Essex, the killing of | the Steer-man, the pursuing of them by Soul- | diers, and the Names and Number of those since | re-taken, which are now to be executed upon | several Gibbets. | Likewise the apprehending of the wicked Vil- | lains ill-affected to his Gracious Majesty, and | his Royal Highnesse the Duke of York. | *London, Printed for G. Horton.* 1661. | 4to, pp. 7. 28459

The Great Probability of a North West Passage: deducted from Observations on the Letter of Admiral De Fonte, Who sailed from the Callao of Lima on the Discovery of a Communication between the South Sea and the Atlantic Ocean; And to intercept some Navigators from Boston in New England, whom he met with, Then in Search of a North West Passage. Proving the Authenticity of the Admiral's Letter. With Three Explanatory Maps. 1st. A Copy of an authentic Spanish Map of America, published in 1608. 2d. The Discoveries made in Hudson's Bay, by Capt. Smith, in 1746 and 1747. 3d. A General Map of the Discoveries of Admiral De Fonte. By Thomas Jefferys, Geographer to the King. With an Appendix. Containing the Account of a Discovery of Part of the Coast and Inland Country of Labrador, made in 1753. The Whole intended for The Advancement of Trade and Commerce. *London: Thomas Jefferys.* MDCCLXVIII. 4to, pp. xxiv, 154. 3 Maps. 28460

Often catalogued under the name of Jefferys, who copied the maps, was the publisher and, perhaps, the editor. The author, according to Meusel, was Theodore Swindrage; but is named by Watts, Dragge. The authenticity of De Fonte's voyage is a disputed question, the Spanish original has never been published. Murray, the geographer, decides in its favor. *See* "M. Rev.," XXXIX. 240.

The Great Questions of the Times, discussed in a Brief Report of Proceedings at the Great Inaugural Mass Meeting of the Loyal National League, in ... New York, ... April 11, 1863. *New York: Printed for the Loyal National League.* 1863. 8vo, pp. 32. 28461

The Great Republic. Description of the Largest Ship in the World, the ... Great Republic, of Boston. ... With Illustrated Designs of her Construction. ... *Boston.* 1853. 8vo, pp. 24. B.

The Great Republic Monthly. A National Magazine. Vol. I. *New York.* 1859. 8vo. H. 28463

GREAT SALT LAKE CITY. Charter of Great Salt Lake City and Ordinances and Resolutions of the City Council, with Constitution of the United States, and Organic Act of the Territory of Utah. ... *Desert News Print.* 1860. 8vo, pp. xliv, 75, 6. B.

The Great Steam-Duck. Description of an Invention for Aerial Navigation. *Louisville.* 1841. 16mo, pp. 32. M. 28465

The first American affair of the kind.

The Great Struggle between Democracy and Absolutism impending. Being the Alarm Bell published in 1863 ... . America Threatened. By a Constitutionalist. *New York.* [1865.] 8vo, pp. 16. H. 28466

The Great Surrender to the Rebels in Arms. The Armistice. [*Washington.* 1864.] 8vo, pp. 7. 28467

Great Trans-Continental Railroad Guide, containing a full and authentic Description of over Five Hundred Cities, Towns, Villages, Stations, Government Forts, etc., from the Atlantic to the Pacific Ocean. *Chicago: G. A. Crofutt & Co.* 1869. 16mo, pp. 244. 16 Plates. 28468

Reprinted, and title changed to read:

Great Trans-Continental Tourists' Guide. [etc.] *New York: G. A. Crofutt & Co.* 1870. Square 16mo, pp. 208. 16 Plates, 1 Map. H. 28469

Great Union Meeting, New York, December 19th, 1859. *New York.* 1859. 8vo, pp. 176. 28470

Great Union Meeting, Philadelphia, December 7, 1859. *Philadelphia: Crissy & Markley.* [1859.] 8vo, pp. 59. 28471

Great Union War Ratification Meeting, at the Cooper Institute, October 8, 1862. One Country! One Constitution! One Destiny. Speeches of W. Curtis Noyes, D. S. Dickinson, and Lyman Tremaine. [n. p. 1862.] 8vo, pp. 19. 28472

Great Utility of Inland Navigation. With a Map of Pennsylvania, Delaware, New Jersey, and Maryland. *Philadelphia.* 1805. 8vo. 28473

A Great Victory Obtained by the English against the Dutch, And the pursuance of the Dutch Fleets by General Blake and Sir George Ayscue. ... Also the number of ships coming up the river of Thames for London, richly laden from the East Indies, the Streights, Virginia and Barbadoes. Die Septembris 27, 1652. Extracted out of the original papers, sent, from Captain Stoaks. ... *Imprinted at London for George Horton.* 1652. 4to, pp. 8.

Reprinted in the "Harlean Tracts," Vol. VI. 8vo.

Great Western. *See* Erie Canal, Vol. VI., and [Haines (C. G.)]

Great Western Almanac, 1842. *Philadelphia.* 12mo. Continued. 28475

GREAT WESTERN IRON COMPANY. Charter and By-Laws of the Great Western Iron Company; also, an Act to encourage the Manufacture of Iron in the State of Pennsylvania. [n. p. n. d.] 8vo, pp. 16. H. 28476

The Great Western Magazine and Anglo-American Journal of Literature, Science, Art ... . *London: Simpkin, Marshall, and Co.* 1842. B. 28477

GREAT WESTERN RAILROAD COMPANY, *Canada.* Acts incorporating ... Act Empowering Municipal Corporations to subscribe for Stock in the Great Western Railway. *Hamilton, C. W.* 1850. 8vo. S. 28478

Also: Report to be submitted by the Board of Directors to the Shareholders, 15th May, 1854. *Hamilton.* 1854. 12mo, pp. 15.—Report of the Directors of the Great Western Railway of Canada. *London.* 1852. 8vo.—Report upon the Merits of the Great Western Railroad, Canada West. By a Committee of its American Friends. *Boston.* 1851. 8vo, pp. 20.—Report; Half Year, ending January 31, 1856. *Hamilton, C. W.* Continued.—Report on ... to the President and Directors. By Charles B. Stuart, Chief-Engineer. September, 1847. 8vo. S.

GRECE (C. F.) Essays on Husbandry, addressed to the Canadian Farmers. By Charles Frederick Grece. *Montreal.* 1817. 12mo. 28479

GRECE. Facts and Observations respecting Canada, and the United States of America: Affording a Comparative View of the Inducements to Emigration presented in those Countries. To which is added An Appendix of Practical Instructions to Emigrant Settlers in the British Colonies. By Charles F. Grece, Member of the Montreal and Quebec Agricultural Societies; and Author of Essays on Husbandry, addressed to the Canadian Farmers. *London: J. Harding.* 1819. 8vo, pp. xv, 172. C., H.

Puffs Canada, and underrates the United States. *See* "M. Rev.," New Series, XC. 248.

The Grecian Wreath of Victory. *New York.* 1824. 18mo.

Contributions in Prose and Verse by eminent New Yorkers, including Professors Moore and Anthon, Gov. Dewitt Clinton, Dr. Hosack, Col. Trumbull, etc.

GREELEY (H.) The American Conflict: A History of the Great Rebellion in the United States of America 1860–64; Its Causes, Incidents, and Results; Intended to exhibit especially its Moral and Political Phases, with the Drift and Progress of American Opinion respecting Human Slavery from 1776 to the close of the War for the Union. By Horace Greeley. Illustrated by Portraits in Steel of Generals, Statesmen, and other Eminent Men, Views of Places of Historic Interest, Maps, Diagrams of Battle Fields, Naval Actions, etc. From Official Sources ... *Hartford: O. D. Case & Company.* 1864–66. 2 vols., rl. 8vo, pp. 4–648; 782. Plates. B. BA., H. 28482

Notwithstanding the author had been a life-long antagonist of slavery and its kindred consequences, he has written a tolerably fair and certainly honest history of the events attempted to be described. It remains for the next generation to treat the subject philosophically.

GREELEY. Der grosse Conflikt in Amerika. Die Geschichte der grossen Rebellion in den Vereinigten Staaten von Nord-Amerika, nach ihren Ursachen, Fortschritten und Resultaten. Aus dem Englischen übersetzt von W. Grauert. *Hartford: O. D. Case & Co.* 1867. 2 vols., 8vo, pp. 749. 10 Plates, 1 Map.

GREELEY. Art and Industry, as represented in the Exhibition at the Crystal Palace, New York, 1853–54; showing the Progress and State of the various Useful and Æsthetic Pursuits. From the New York Tribune; revised and edited by Horace Greeley. *New York: Redfield.* 1853. 12mo, pp. xxv, 13–386.

GREELEY. Aunt Sally Come Up; or, the Nigger Sale. By Horace Greeley. *London: Ward and Lock.* 1859. 12mo, pp. 136.

[GREELEY.] Controversy between New York Tribune and Gerrit Smith. *New York: John A. Gray.* 1855. 8vo, pp. 32.

GREELEY. Hints towards Reforms, in Lectures, Addresses, and other Writings. By Horace Greeley. *New York: Harper & Brothers.* 1850. 12mo, pp. 400. B., H. 28487

GREELEY. A History of the Struggle for Slavery Extension or Restriction in the United States, from the Declaration of Independence to the Present Day. Mainly compiled ... from the Journals of Congress and other Official Records, and showing the Votes by Yeas and Nays of the most important Divisions in either House. By Horace Greeley. *New York: Dix, Edwards & Co.* 1856. Rl. 8vo, pp. iv, 164. B., BA., H. 28488

GREELEY. Letter of Horace Greeley to ... Members of the Union League Club. Privately printed. [*New York.*] 1867.] 8vo. 28489

"Once for all I *dare* you and *defy* you."—*Extract.*

GREELEY. An Overland Journey from New York to San Francisco in the Summer of 1859. By Horace Greeley. *New York: C. M. Saxton.* 1860. 12mo, pp. 386. B., C., H. 28490

GREELEY. Recollections of a Busy Life. Including Reminiscences of American Politics and Politicians, from the Opening of the Missouri Contest to the Downfall of Slavery; to which are added Miscellanies: "Literature as a Vocation," "Poets and Poetry," "Reforms and Reformers," "A Defence of Protection," etc. Also, a Discussion with Robert Dale Owen of the Law of Divorce. By Horace Greeley. *New York: J. B. Ford & Co.* 1868. Rl. 8vo, pp. 624. Portrait. B., BA., H. 28491

[GREELEY.] Why I am a Whig. Reply to an Inquiring Friend. [*New York.* 1852.] 8vo, pp. 16. H. 28492

Also: Address before the Literary Societies of Hamilton College, Clinton, N. Y., July 23, 1844. ... *New York.* 1844. 8vo, pp. 40. B., BA., H.—An Address on Success in Business, delivered at the Cooper Union, November 11, 1867. ... *New York: S. S. Packard.* 1868. 8vo, pp. 38. 2 Plates. B.—The Crystal Palace and its Lessons; A Lecture. ... [*New York.* 1851.] 8vo, pp. 32. H.—Essays designed to Elucidate the Science of Political Economy, while serving to explain and defend the Policy of Protection to Home Industry, as a System of National Co-operation for the Elevation of Labor. ... *Boston: Fields, Osgood & Co.* 1870. 16mo, pp. 384. B., BA., C., H., S.—Protection and Free Trade. The Question Stated and Considered. [n. p. n. d.] 8vo, pp. 16. H.—The Tariff as it Is, compared with the Substitute proposed ... by Gen. McKay. ... [n. p. n. d.] 8vo, pp. 16. H.—The Tariff Question Protection and Free Trade Considered. *New York.* [n. d.] 8vo, pp. 24. H.—The True Issues of the Presidential Campaign. Speeches of Horace Greeley during his Western Trip and at Portland, Maine. Also, Ex-President's Mahan's Letters. [n. p. n. d.] 8vo, pp. 32. H.— ... An Address before the Indiana State Agricultural Society ... Lafayette, Indiana, October 13th, 1853. ... *New York: Fowlers and Wells.* 1853. 8vo, pp. 33.

GREELEY *and* CLEVELAND. A Political Text-Book for 1860: comprising a Brief View of Presidential Nominations and Elections: Including all the National Platforms ever yet adopted; Also, A History of the Struggle respecting Slavery in the Territories, and of the Action of Congress as to the Freedom of the Public Lands, with the most notable Speeches and Letters of Messrs. Lincoln, Douglas, Bell, Cass, Seward, Everett, Breckinridge, H. V. Johnson, etc, etc., Touching the Questions of the Day; and Returns of all Presidential Elections since 1836. Compiled by Horace Greeley and John F. Cleveland. *New-York: Published by the Tribune Association.* 1860. 8vo, pp. 248. 28493

GREELEY *and* H. J. RAYMOND. Association Discussed; or the Socialism of the Tribune Examined, being a Controversy between the New York Tribune and the Courier and Enquirer. By H. Greeley and H. J. Raymond. *New York.* 1847. 8vo, pp. 83. S. 28494

GREELEY, BEECHER, GARRISON, etc., the Great Perversionists of the Constitution. Jeff. Davis and the Rebels justified by the Friends of Freedom. The Constitution interpreted in Favor of Criminals and the worst form of Opposition, etc. [n. p. 1864.] 8vo, pp. 8. H. 28495

Greeley *and* Bennett, or Banjo and Bones' Comic Song Book. *New York: Geo. Munroe & Co.* 1864. 28496

GREELY (A.) A Sermon Delivered in Bangor, June 23d, 1824, before the Maine Missionary Society at the 17th Anniversary. By Allen Greely. *Hallowell.* 1824. pp. 32. H.

GREEN (A.) A Discourse Delivered at Malden, January 8, 1800. A Day, Devoted by the Inhabitants, Publicly to Respect The Memory of the Illustrious George Washington. Who died December 14, 1799. ... By Aaron Green, A.M. ... *Medford: Printed by Nathaniel Coverly.* ... [1800.] 8vo, pp. 23. BA., H.

Also: A Sermon ... in Malden, November 25th, 1821. ... after the Interment of Capt. Jonathan Barrett, ... *Boston: Ezra Lincoln.* 1822. 8vo, pp. 16. H.

GREEN (A. H.) Communication to the Commissioners of the Central Park, relative to Improvements West of 6th and 7th Avenues, &c. By Andrew H. Green. *New York.* 1866. 8vo.

Mr. Green is probably the author of the earlier Reports on the New York Central Park.

GREEN (A.) Advice and Exhortation, addressed to the People of the Second Presbyterian Congregation in Philadelphia, on Resigning the Pastoral Charge. By Ashbel Green. *Philadelphia.* 1812. 8vo, pp. 32. 28500

GREEN. Discourses, delivered in the College of New Jersey; addressed chiefly to Candidates for the First Degree in the Arts; with Notes and Illustrations, including an Historical Sketch of the College, from its Origin to the Accession of President Witherspoon. By Ashbel Green, D.D. ... *Philadelphia: E. Littell.* 1822. pp. xi, 419. BA., C. 28501

GREEN. A Historical Sketch or Compendious View of Domestic and Foreign Missions in the Presbyterian Church of the United States of America. By Ashbel Green, D.D. *Philadelphia: W. S. Martien.* 1838. 12mo, pp. 214. H. 28502

GREEN. The Life of the Rev. Ashbel Green ... begun ... by himself in his eighty-second year and continued to his eighty-fourth [by the editor]. Prepared for the Press ... by J. H. Jones. *New York: Robert Carter and Brothers.* 1849. 8vo, pp. 628. Portrait. B., C., H. 28503

Contains reminiscences of the Revolutionary War.

GREEN. Memoirs of the Rev. Joseph Eastburn, Stated Preacher in the Mariner's Church, Philadelphia. Who departed this Life, January 30th, 1828. By Ashbel Green, D.D. *Philadelphia: G. W. Mentz.* 1828. 12mo, pp. 208. Portrait. H.

GREEN. A Report to the Trustees of the College of New Jersey; relative to A Revival of Religion among the Students of said College, in the winter and spring of the year 1815. With an Appendix. By Ashbel Green, D.D. ... President of the College. ... *Philadelphia: Benjamin B. Hopkins.* 1815. 8vo, pp. 28.

Also: An Address to the Students and Faculty of the College of New-Jersey, ... May 6th, 1802. ... *Trenton: Printed by Sherman & Mershon.* 1802. 8vo, pp. 16. BA.—Address ... at the Funeral of the Rev. Dr. William M. Tennent. ... *Philadelphia.* 1811. 8vo, pp. 27. B.—Address at the Interment of Robert Ralston, Esq., August 13, 1836. ... *Philadelphia.* 1836. 8vo, pp. 23. H., W.—Discourse at the Opening of the Presbyterian Church in the Northern Liberties, Philadelphia, April 7, 1805. ... *Philadelphia: Printed by Thomas and William Bradford.* 1805. 8vo, pp. 21. B., M.—Obedience to the Law of God, the Sure and Indispensable Defence of Nations. National-Fast Sermon, May 9, 1798. *Philadelphia.* [1798.] 8vo, pp. 51. M.—Oration, July 4, 1789, at Philadelphia. ... *Philadelphia.* 1789.—Sermon at the Funeral of the Rev. George Duffield, D.D., at Philadelphia, February 2, 1790. ... *Philadelphia: Printed by Daniel Humphreys.* 1790. 8vo, pp. 24. B., M., W.—Sermon occasioned by the Death of Rev. Dr. James Sproat, late the Senior Pastor of the Second Presbyterian Congregation, in the City of Philadelphia. ... *Philadelphia: Printed by William Young.* M,DCC,XCIV. 8vo, pp. 30. B., P.—A Sermon, ... Second Presbyterian Church in the City of Philadelphia, on the 19th of February, 1795, being the Day of General Thanksgiving throughout the United States. ... *Philadelphia: Printed by John Fenns.* 1795. 8vo, pp. 48. BA., H., M., S., W.

GREEN (Bartholomew). Deposition, [relating to his refusing to print a pamphlet called "Gospel Order Revived."] *Boston.* 1701. 4to. W. 28506

GREEN (B.) An Eulogy on George Washington, late Commander-in-Chief of the American Armies, who Died December 14th, 1799. Pronounced at Berwick, January 4, 1800. By Benjamin Green, A.M. *Portsmouth: Printed by J. Melchers.* 1800. 8vo, pp. 16. H. 28507

GREEN. An Oration, ... before the ... Philanthropic Lodge of Free and Accepted Masons ... in Marblehead ... June 24, 1797. By Brother Benjamin Green. *Salem: Printed by Thomas C. Cushing.* 1797. 8vo, pp. 23. H. 28508

GREEN. The True Believer's Vade-mecum; or Shakerism Exposed. With the Life of the Author. By Benjamin Green. *Concord, N. H.* 1831. 12mo. 28509

GREEN (B.) The Martyr; A Discourse in Commemoration of the Martyrdom of the Rev. Elijah P. Lovejoy. Delivered in New York, By Beriah Green. [*New York.*] 1838. 8vo, pp. 18.

GREEN. The Miscellaneous Writings of Beriah Green. *Whitesboro: Published by the Oneida Institute.* [n. d.] 12mo, pp. vii, 408. B. 28511

GREEN. Sketches of the Life and Writings of James Gillespie Birney. By Beriah Green. *Utica, N. Y.: Jackson & Chaplin.* 1844. 12mo, pp. (4), 119. 28512

Also: Address delivered at Whitesborough. *Utica.* 1833. 8vo.—A Memorial of Ann Parker Green Hough. *Utica.* 1844.—An Oration, pronounced at Middlebury, before the Associated Alumni of the College ... August 16th, 1826. ... *Castleton: Printed by Ovid Miner.* 1826. 8vo, pp. 39.—Sermon at the Funeral of Henry D. Ward, July 24, 1858. ... *Rome, N. Y.: R. R. Meredith.* 8vo, pp. 16.—Sermons and Addresses, ... *Cleveland.* 1833. 8vo.—Success. A Valedictory Address, delivered at the Anniversary of the Oneida Institute, November 1, 1843. *Utica, N. Y.: R. W. Roberts.* 1843. 8vo, pp. 16.—Things for Northern Men to Do; A Discourse, July 17, 1836, in Whitesboro, N. Y. ... *New York.* 1836. 8vo, pp. 22. B.—Valedictory Address, delivered September 13, 1837. ... *Whitesboro.*—Valedictory Address to the Senior Class of Oneida Institute, September 12, 1838. *Whitesboro, N. Y.* 1838. 8vo.

[GREEN (Calvin) *and* WELLS (Seth Y.)] A Summary View of the Millennial Church, or United Society of Believers (commonly called Shakers). Comprising the Rise, Progress, and Practical Order of the Society; together with the General Principles of their Faith and Testimony. ... *Albany: Printed by Packard & Van Benthuysen.* 1823. 12mo, pp. xvi, 320. B., C. + Second Edition, Revised and Improved. *Albany: C. Van Benthuysen.* 1848. 8vo, pp. viii, 384. B., C. 28513

GREEN (D.) Facts and Suggestions, Biographical, Historical, Financial, and Political. Addressed to the People of the United States. By Duff Green. *New York: Richardson & Co.* 186–. 8vo, pp. vi, 234. H. 28514

GREEN. Facts and Suggestions relative to Finance & Currency addressed to the President of the Confederate States. By Duff Green. *Augusta, Ga.: J. T. Paterson.* 1864. 8vo, pp. 80.

[GREEN.] Protest of the Columbia Typographical Society ... against the Washington Institute. ... *Washington: Printed by Francis Preston Blair.* 1834. 8vo, pp. 21. 28516

See also Reply of the Columbia Typographical Society, to the Strictures of Gen. Duff Green, upon the Protest of that Body ... *Washington: Printed by Francis Preston Blair.* 1834. 8vo, pp. 8. BA.

GREEN. Register of Debates; being a Report of the Speeches delivered in the two Houses of Congress, reported for the U. S. Telegraph. By Duff Green. *Washington.* 1834–35. 3 vols., 8vo. C., S. 28517

[GREEN.] The United States and England. By an American. (Extracted from The Great Western Magazine, for September, 1842. Vol. II., No. 6. *London.* 1842. 8vo, pp. 122.)

See also Tucker's "Partisan Leader," United States Telegraph, &c.

GREEN (D. *and* Benj. C.) Memorial to the Congress ... praying Repeal or Modification of the Act 30th January, 1779, one of the "Alien and Sedition" Laws. [n. p. n. d.] 8vo, pp. 14.

GREEN (E.) Shall we Suffocate Ed. Green? By a Citizen of Walden. *Boston: Jas. Redpath.* 1864. 8vo, pp. 61. H.

GREEN (E.) Sermon occasioned by the Death of Rev. William Ramsay, Fairfield, December 9, 1771. By Enoch Green. *Philadelphia.* 1772. 8vo, pp. 32. N. 28521

GREEN (F. H.) Biography of Mrs. Semantha Mettler, the Clairvoyant; being a History of Spiritual Development, ... By Francis H. Green. *New York.* 1853. 16mo. C. 28522

GREEN (F. H.) *and* CONGDON (J. W.) Analytical Class-Book of Botany, By Francis H. Green. Illustrated by a Compendious Flora of the Northern States, By Joseph W. Congdon. *New York.* 4to, pp. 234. 28523

GREEN (H. G.) Trial of Henry G. Green, for the Murder of his Wife. *New York.* 1845. 8vo, pp. 32. H. 28524

GREEN (I. L.) Barnstable Congressional Nomination, and Statement of Votes in Congress, By Isaiah L. Green, Esq. ... *Boston: Printed by Russell & Cutler.* 1812. 8vo, pp. 16. M.

GREEN (J.) An Address on the Botany of the United States, delivered before the Society for the Promotion of Useful Arts. ... To which is added a Catalogue of Plants Indigenous to the State of New York. By Jacob Green. *Albany.* 1814. 8vo, pp. 76. N., P. 28526

GREEN. A Monograph of the Trilobites of North America; with Coloured Models of the Species, By Jacob Green, M.D. *Philadelphia: Joseph Brano.* 1832. 12mo, pp. 93. + A Supplement ... *Philadelphia.* 1835. 12mo, pp. 24. 28527

The supplement ends abruptly at page 24, the MS. having been lost. This book was published to accompany the models made by Joseph Brano, the publisher of the work. Also: The Inferior Surface of the Trilobite Discovered. *Philadelphia.* 1839. 12mo. S.

GREEN (J. D.) An Oration delivered at Malden on the Two Hundredth Anniversary of the Incorporation of the Town, May 23, 1849. By James D. Green. *Boston: Geo. C. Rand and Co.* 1850. 8vo, pp. 53. B., BA., H., M. 28528

GREEN. Remarks on the Connection of the City of Cambridge with the Cambridge Water Works. *Boston: Geo. C. Rand & Avery.* 1858. 8vo, pp. 32. H. 28529

Also: An Address delivered at the ... Organization of the Boston Phrenological Society. ... *Boston: Marsh, Capen and Lyon.* 1837. 8vo, pp. 27. H., M.— ... An Address ... before the Malden Temperance Society, January 21, 1838. ... *Boston: J. Howe.* 1838. 8vo, pp. 24. H.

GREEN (J. D.) Narrative of the Life of J. D. Green, a Runaway Slave. 1864. 12mo. 28530

GREEN (James S.) An Address ... before the Washington Benevolent Societies of Cranbury and Princeton, ... New Jersey, on the 22nd of February, 1815. *New Brunswick: Printed by Lewis Deare.* 1815. 8vo, pp. 21. B. 28531

GREEN. Communication from J. S. Green and W. P. Hall in relation to the St. Joseph and Hannibal Railroad, June 19, 1848. [Cong. Doc.] 1848. 8vo. 28532

GREEN. Speech of the Hon. J. S. Green, of Missouri, on the Constitution of Kansas; delivered in the Senate ... December 16, 1857. *Washington.* 1857. 8vo, pp. 14. B. 28533

Also: Speech on the Admission of Kansas, March 23, 1858. [n. p. n. d.] 8vo, pp. 32.—Speech ... April 4, 1850, on the Admission of California and New Mexico. [n. p. n. d.] 8vo.—Territorial Policy. Speech ... In the Senate ... January 10 and 11, 1860. *Washington: H. Polkinhorn.* [1860.] 8vo, pp. 32. H.

GREEN (J. H.) The Secret Band of Brothers; or, the American Outlaws. ... By J. H. Green. ... *Philadelphia: G. B. Zieber & Co.* 1847. pp. 192. Plates. B., P. + *Philadelphia: For the Author.* 1848. pp. 312. B. 28534

GREEN. Twelve Days in the Tombs; or, A Sketch of the Last Eight Years of the Reformed Gambler's Life. *New York.* 1850. 12mo, pp. 240. 28535

Also: Gambling Unmasked. *Philadelphia.* 1847. 12mo. C.—A Report on Gambling in New York: made by J. H. Green ... . *New York: J. H. Green.* 1851 8vo, pp. 96. H.

GREEN (J. H.) The Life, Trial, and Confessions of Samuel H. Calhoun, for the Murder of William Sutherland, of Bardstown, Ky. By Captain J. H. Green. *Cincinnati.* 1862. 12mo, pp. 96. 28536

Calhoun was a private in Company A, Second Kentucky Infantry.

[GREEN (John).] Explanation for the New Map of Nova Scotia and Cape Britain, With the Adjacent Parts of New England and Canada. *London: T. Jefferys,* MDCCLV. 4to, pp. 22.

GREEN. Remarks in Support of the New Chart of North and South America; In Six Sheets. By J. Green. *London: Thomas Jefferys.* 1753. 4to, pp. 48. H., S. 28538

[GREEN (J.)] A New General Collection of Voyages and Travels: ... Comprehending every Thing remarkable in its Kind, in Europe, Asia, Africa, and America, ... Also the Manners and Customs of the Several Inhabitants; their Religion and Government, Arts and Sciences, Trades and Manufactures: ... *London: Printed for Thomas Astley.* M.DCC.XLV–VII. 4 vols., 4to, pp. (24), 680, Frontispiece; (12), 730; (8), 605, Frontispiece; (14), 751; Index 21 l. 227 Maps and Plates. H. 28539

Usually known as Astley's Collection. It was originally published in weekly numbers, and gave rise to the more extensive collection of the Abbé Prévost. Other editions were issued by substituting a new title-page only. The project was grand, and the execution, so far as it goes, is admirable, but so far as "Americana" is concerned it is of little value. It includes the Voyage of Capt. George Roberts to the Canaries, and Bermuda in 1721; and a Voyage to Guinea, Brazil, and the West Indies in 1721, by John Atkins. The contents of these volumes have been translated three times, twice into French and once into Dutch. They form the first nine volumes of Abbé Prévost's "Histoire des Voyages," published at *Paris*, 1746–89, in 20 vols., 4to, also in 18mo.

GREEN (J.) A Sermon before the Society for the Propagation of the Gospel ... February 19, 1768. By John, Lord Bishop of Lincoln. With Proceedings. *London.* 1768. 4to, pp. 94.

GREEN (J.) City Hospitals. By John Green ... . With Illustrations. *Boston: Little, Brown, and Company.* 1861. 8vo, pp. 66. B., BA., H. 28541

GREEN (J. A., *Jr.*) Letter to the Publisher of the Daily Courier and Union. An Appeal for Peace. By John A. Green, Jr. *Syracuse, N. Y., May,* 1861. pp. 14. 28542

GREEN (*Rev.* John B.) An Address at the Funeral of Hon. Henry Wyles Cushman, ... in Bernardston, Mass., Nov. 24, 1863. *Boston: Printed by John Wilson and Son.* 1864. 8vo, pp. 23. BA. 28543

GREEN (J. O.) The Factory System, in its Hygienic Relations. An Address ... Massachusetts Medical Society, May 27, 1846. By John O. Green, M.D. *Boston: Printed by Wm. S. Damrell.* 1846. 8vo, pp. 34. BA., H. 28544

GREEN. A Memorial of John C. Dalton, M.D. An Address ... before the Middlesex North District Medical Society, April 27, 1864. By John O. Green, M.D., Lowell. *Cambridge: University Press.* 1864. 8vo, pp. 35. B., H. 28545

[GREEN (Joseph).] An Eclogue Sacred to the Memory of the Rev. Dr. Jonathan Mayhew, who departed this Life July 9, ... 1766, Ætatis 46. *Boston: Printed by Thomas and John Fleet.* [1766.] 28546

[GREEN.] Entertainment for a Winter's Evening: Being A Full and True Account Of a very strange and wonderful Sight seen in Boston, on the Twenty-seventh of December, 1749. At Noon-Day. The Truth of which can be attested by a Great Number of People, who actually saw the same With their own Eyes. By Me, the Hon. B. B. Esq; *Boston: G. Rogers.* [1750.] 8vo, pp. ii, 5–15. + Second Edition. [*Ibid.*] + *Boston: Printed in the Year* 1750, *Reprinted* 1795. 8vo, pp. 12. BA., H. 28547

A versified satire on a masonic procession, &c., which caused in its day much ill feeling. The last edition supplies in foot-notes the names of the actors. *See* Drake's "Boston," p. 629.

[GREEN.] The Grand Arcanum Detected; or a Wonderful Phenomenon Explained, which has baffled the Scrutiny of many Ages. By Me, Phil Arcanos, Gent. Student in Astrology. *Printed in the Year* 1755. 12mo, pp. 14. W. 28548

[GREEN.] A | Mournful Lamentation | For the sad and deplorable Death of | Mr. Old Tenor, | A Native of New-England, who, after a long Confinement, by a deep and mortal Wound which he received above Twelve Months before, expired on the 31st Day of March, 1750. | He lived beloved, and died lamented. | To the Mournful Tune of, Chevy-Chace. | [n. p. n. d.] Folio, 1 l.

Relates to the colonial paper currency of New England, which was instituted in 1702 and abolished in 1750.

GREEN (J.) ... Sermon ... at Marshfield, Feb. 21, 1753, at the Ordination of Mr. Joseph Green, Jun. ... [By Rev. Joseph Green, A.M., of Barnstable, Mass.] *Boston: Printed by S. Kneeland.* 1753. 8vo, 1 l., pp. 26. B., BA., H. 28550

GREEN (J. C.) An Appeal to the Christian Public. Containing the Discipline of the Trinitarian Church in Concord, Mass. With Joseph C. Green, also his Defence. ... . *Boston: For the Author.* 1828. 8vo, pp. 35, (1). B., M., W. 28551

GREEN (Matthew). The Spleen: An Epistle to Mr. Jackson ... . *Boston.* 1804. 12mo, pp. 31. 28552

GREEN (N. W.) Fifteen Years among the Mormons: Being the Narrative of Mrs. Mary Ettie V. Smith, late of Great Salt Lake City: A Sister of one of the Mormon High Priests, she having been personally acquainted with most of the Mormon Leaders, and long in the Confidence of the "Prophet" Brigham Young. By Nelson Winch Green. *New York: Charles Scribner.* 1858. 12mo, pp. 388. Plate. B., BA., C. 28553

GREEN. Mormonism: Its Rise, Progress, and Present Condition. Embracing the Narrative of Mrs. Mary Ettie V. Smith, of her Residence and Experience of Fifteen Years with the Mormons; containing a Full and Authentic Account of their Social Condition, their Religious Doctrines, and Political Government. *Hartford: Belknap & Bliss.* 1870. 12mo, pp. 472. Portraits. B., C. 28554

See also Smith (M. E. V.)

GREEN (S.) A Discourse ... at Plymouth, Dec. 20, 1828, on the Two Hundred and Eighth Anniversary of the Landing of the Pilgrim Fathers. By Samuel Green. ... *Boston: Peirce & Williams.* 1829. 8vo, pp. 36. B. 28555

Also: ... Sermon ... at the Dedication of the Trinitarian Church, in Concord, Massachusetts, Dec. 6, 1826. ... *Concord: Allen & Atwill.* 1827. 8vo, pp. 34, (1).

GREEN (S.) Life of Samuel Green, executed at Boston, April 25, 1822, for the Murder of Billy Williams, a Fellow Convict with Green, in the State Prison. Written by Himself. ... *Boston: David Felt.* 1822. 8vo, pp. (1), 47, (1). Portrait.

[GREEN (Samuel A.) Genealogy of] Percival and Ellen Green. [*Boston.* 1861.] 8vo, pp. 5. B., H. 28557

Also: A Bibliography of the Massachusetts Historical Society. *Boston: John Wilson and Son.* 1871. 8vo, pp. 10. B., H.—The Story of a Famous Book: an Account of Dr. ... Franklin's Autobiography. ... *Boston.* 1871. 8vo, pp. 14. B., BA.

GREEN (S. B.) A Pamphlet on Equal Rights and Privileges, to the People of the United States. By Samuel B. Green ... November 1, 1856. *St. Joseph, Mo.: Printed by Pfouts and Cuncliff.* 1857. 8vo, pp. 24. B. 28558

GREEN (S. M.) Proposed Revision of the General Statutes of the State of Michigan, as reported to the Legislature ... in 1846. By Sanford M. Green ... . *Detroit: Bagg & Harmon.* Folio, pp. viii, 1023. H. 28559

GREEN (T.) Green's Register for the State of Connecticut: with an Almanack for the Year of our Lord 1794, calculated by Nathan Daboll for the Meridian of New London. *New-London: T. Green.* [1793.] 16mo. Continued. 28560

Commenced 1789—this is the earliest I have seen.

GREEN (T. J.) Reply of Gen. Thomas J. Green to the Speech of Gen. Sam. Houston in the Senate, August 1, 1854. [*Washington.* 1854.] 8vo, pp. 67. S. 28561

GREEN. Journal of the Texian Expedition against Mier. Subsequent Imprisonment of the Author; his Sufferings, and final Escape from the Castle of Perote. With Reflections upon the present Political and probable future Relations of Texas, Mexico, and the United States. By Thomas J. Green. Illustrated by Drawings taken from Life by Charles M'Laughlin, a Fellow-prisoner. *New York: Harper & Brothers.* 1845. 8vo, pp. 482. B., H. 28562

GREEN (W.) The Sufferings of William Green; being a Sorrowful Account of his Seven Years Transportation to Marblehead, Massachusetts. *London.* 1774. 12mo. 28563

In J. R. Smith's Catalogue his sufferings are located in Maryland.

GREEN (W.) Annals of George the Third; from his Majesty's Accession to the Throne, to the Peace of 1801. By William Green, A.M. *London.* 1805. 2 vols., 8vo. + To the Victory of Trafalgar, in 1805. *London.* 1808. 2 vols., 8vo. P.

Contains some details of American events, so also does his Chronological History of the Reign of George III. 1819.

GREEN (W.) Narrative of Events in the Life of William Green (formerly a Slave). Written by Himself. *Springfield: L. M. Guernsey.* 1853. 8vo, pp. 23. H. 28565

GREEN (W.) Review of Mr. Calhoun's Report on the Memphis Memorial. From the American Review for January, 1848. By W. Green, Esq., Cincinnati, Ohio. [n. p. n. d.] 8vo, pp. 15–30. BA., H. 28566

GREEN (W. H.) Our National Union, a Sermon. By William H. Green. *Philadelphia.* 1850. 8vo, pp. 48. 28567

GREEN. ... A Sermon ... at Newburyport, Dec. 30, 1856, on Occasion of the Installation of Rev. Heman R. Timlow ... . By William Henry Green ... . *Newburyport: Moulton & Clark.* 8vo, pp. 23. H. 28568

GREEN (W. L.) Plea for the Supremacy of Christ: Two Sermons on the Presbyterian Church, Madison, Wis., March 18, 1860. By Rev. William L. Green. *Madison.* 1860. 8vo.

Relates to the Slavery Question.

Green-Back to his Country Friends. To the Constituents of the 37th Congress, now assembled in Washington. New York, June 20, 1862. [*New York.* 1862.] 8vo, pp. 17. B., H.

Greenbacks: The Evils and Remedy for using Promises to pay as a Measure of Value. [n. p. n. d.] 28571

Greenbank's Periodical Library; a Republication of Voyages, Travels, History, Biography, Science, Tales, and Poems. *Philadelphia: T. K. Greenbank.* 1833. 3 vols., 8vo, pp. 622; 622.

Contains: Domestic Manners, etc., of the West Indies, by A. C. Carmichael.

GREEN BAY AND LAKE SUPERIOR RAILROAD COMPANY. Articles of Association. *Cleveland.* 1851. 8vo. 28573

Green Box of M. de Sartine. *See* [Tickell (Richard)].

The Green Hand; a "Short" Yarn. *New-York.* 1850. 8vo.

A Green Hand's First Cruise; Roughed out from the Log-Book of Memory, of Twenty-five Years Standing, together with a Residence of Five Months in Dartmoor. By a Younker. *Baltimore.* 1841. 2 vols., 12mo. 28575

Green Mount Cemetery. *See* Baltimore.

The Green Mountain Boys. *See* [Thompson (Daniel P)].

Green Mountain Liberal Institute, South-Woodstock, Vt. Catalogue, 1856. 8vo. 28576

Green Mountain Mining Company, Vermont. ... *Boston: Morrill & Son.* 1863. 8vo, pp. 18. H. 28577

The Green Mountain Repository for the Year 1832. Edited by Zadoc Thompson. Vol. I. *Burlington: Edward Smith.* 1832. 12mo, pp. 284. 28578

The Green Mountain Slate and File Company. ... *Boston: Alfred Mudge & Son.* 1865. 8vo, pp. 24. H. 28579

Green Peas. *See* [Crippen (William G.)] No. 17509.

GREENBUSH, *N. Y.* Charter of the Village of Greenbush, with all the Amendments. *Albany: J. Munsell.* 1852. 8vo, pp. 11. 28580

GREENE (A. G.) An Address to the Citizens of Providence, [R. I.] on the Anniversary Celebration of the Birth Day or

Washington, February 22, 1825, ... By Albert G. Greene. *Providence: J. B. Yerrington.* 1825. 8vo, pp. 22. W. 28581

GREENE. Recollections of the Jersey Prison Ship: Taken, and prepared for Publication, from the Original Manuscript of the late Captain Thomas Dring, of Providence, R. I., One of the Prisoners. By Albert G. Greene. *New York: P. M. Davis.* 1831. 12mo. WM. 28582

For two other editions *see* Dring (T.), Vol. v., Nos. 20948, 20949. Also: Address to the Patrons of the Manufacturer's and Farmer's Journal and Independent Inquirer, for the New Year, 1826. *Providence.* 1826. 8vo, pp. 8. W.—Anniversary Poem pronounced before the Philhermenian Society at their Thirty-fourth Celebration, September 2d, 1828. ... *Providence: Smith & Parmenter.* 1829. 8vo, pp. 24. B., W. —An Ode for the Celebration of the Philhermenian Society, September 6, 1825. ... 8vo.—Old Grimes. Illustrated by A. Hoppin. *Providence.* 1867. 4to, pp. 30.—An Oration delivered in Commemoration of the Forty-seventh Anniversary of the Declaration of American Independence, July 4, 1823, before the Citizens of Providence. ... *Providence: John Miller.* 1823. 8vo, pp. 16.—Oration ... Providence, July 4, 1827. ... *Providence: Smith & Parmenter.* 1827. 8vo, pp. 28. H., W.—The Catalogue of his Library, which was sold in New York at auction, enumerates nearly two thousand lots of American Poetry, and is useful to Collectors in that Department of Literature. *New York: Bangs, Merwin & Co.* 1869. 8vo, pp. 521. B., BA., H.

[GREENE (Asa).] A Glance at New York. ... *New York: Asa Greene.* 1837. 18mo, pp. 264. 28583

The author of this and the following items was a physician, and afterwards became a bookseller.

[GREENE.] The Perils of Pearl Street, including a Taste of the Dangers of Wall-Street. By a Late Merchant. *New York.* 1834. 12mo. 28584

[GREENE.] Travels in America. By George Fibbleton, Esq., Ex-barber. ... *New York.* 1833. 12mo. 28585

A satire on the Rev. Isaac Fidler's "Travels in America."

[GREENE.] A Yankee among the Nullifiers: An Auto-biography. By Elnathan Elmwood, Esq. ... *New-York: William Stodart.* 1833. 18mo, pp. 152. BA. + Second Edition. *New-York: William Pearson.* 1833. 18mo, pp. 143. 28586

GREENE (B.) A Farewell Discourse to the First Church and Society in Medway, delivered March 17, 1793. By Benjamin Greene. *Boston: T. and J. Fleet.* [1793.] 8vo, pp. 33. BA.

GREENE. An Oration ... at Kittery, the Fourth of July, 1808. By Benjamin Greene, Esq. ... *Portsmouth: S. Sewall.* 1808. 8vo, pp. 16. BA. 28588

GREENE. An Oration, pronounced at Lexington, July 4, 1809. ... By Benj. Greene, Esq. *Boston: Munroe, Francis & Parker.* 1809. 8vo, pp 24. 28589

Also: Oration before the Members of Murray's Lodge, No. XVII., at Festival of St. John. *Montreal.* 1817. 12mo, pp. 15. *See also* Green (B.)

GREENE (C. R.) An Oration ... in ... Charleston, South-Carolina; ... the Fourth of July, 1815; ... . By Christopher R. Greene ... . *Charleston: Printed by W. P. Young.* 1815. 8vo, pp. (2), 26. BA. 28590

GREENE (C. S.) Thrilling Stories of the Great Rebellion: comprising Heroic Adventures of Soldiers, Scouts, Spies, and Refugees; ... with an Account of the Death of President Lincoln and Fate of the Assassins. By Lieutenant-Colonel Charles S. Greene. With Illustrations. *Philadelphia: J. E. Potter.* 1866. 12mo, pp. 494. 28591

GREENE (D.) Ministerial Fidelity Exemplified: A Sermon at the Funeral of the Rev. Daniel Crosby ... of ... Charlestown. By David Greene. *Boston: T. R. Marvin.* 1843. 8vo, pp. 39.

GREENE (E. B.) Political Tracts, from November, 1779, to April, 1780. Inscribed to the Right Hon. Lord North. By Edward Burnaby Greene. *London.* 1780. 8vo. N. 28593

Also: The Prophecy of Andree: an Ode Written in the Year 1780. *London: G. Kearsly.* MDCCLXXXII. pp. 22.

GREENE (F.) Shahmah in Pursuit of Freedom; or the Branded Hand. By Mrs. Frances Greene. *New York: Thatcher & Hutchinson.* 1858. 12mo, pp. 599. 28594

GREENE (G. W.) Biographical Studies. By George Washington Greene. *New York: G. P. Putnam.* 1860. 12mo, pp. 233. C., H. 28595

GREENE. A Discourse delivered before the Rhode-Island Historical Society, ... February 8, 1849. By George Washington Greene. ... *Providence: Gladding & Proud.* 1849. 8vo, pp. 22, (1). B., H. 28596

GREENE. Historical Studies. By George Washington Greene, ... *New York: G. P. Putnam.* 1850. 12mo, pp. xi, 468. BA.

GREENE. Historical View of the American Revolution. By George Washington Greene. *Boston: Ticknor & Fields.* 1865. 12mo, pp. xi, 459. B., BA., H., S. 28598

Contains a series of lectures delivered before the Lowell Institute in Boston in 1863, with other papers.

GREENE. The Life of Nathanael Greene, Major-General in the Army of the Revolution. By George Washington Greene. *New York: G. P. Putnam & Son.* 1867–71. 3 vols., 8vo, pp. xxiv, 582, (1); ix, 514; (2), xi, 571. Map. B., BA. 28599

GREENE. Nathaniel Greene. An Examination of some Statements concerning Major-General Greene, in the ninth volume of Bancroft's "History of the United States." By George Washington Greene. *Boston: Ticknor & Fields.* 1866. 8vo, pp. 86. B., BA. H. 28600

GREENE. Proceedings in Congress attending the Reception of the Statue of Maj.-Gen. Nathaniel Greene, ... for the Capitol at Washington ... *Providence.* 1870. 8vo, pp. 41. H.

Twenty copies printed in 4to. Also a Life of Nathaniel Greene in Sparks' "Libr. of Am. Biog.," Vol. XX.—The Debate on the Constitutional Amendment. Substance of Remarks ... in the Senate of Rhode Island, January 30 and 31, 1867, on the Proposed Amendment of the United States Constitution. *Providence.* 1867. 8vo, pp. 8. —The Fifteenth Amendment to the Constitution of the United States. Speech ... May 28, 1869. [n. p. n. d.] 8vo, pp. 8. H.—The Proposed Constitutional Amendment. Speech ... February 7th, ... *Providence.* 1867. 8vo, pp. 4. H.

GREENE (H.) An Address delivered at Whitsborough, Sept. 5th, 1833. By Hiram Greene. *Utica.* 1833. pp. 20. 28602

GREENE (H. W.) Letters addressed to Francis O. J. Smith ... being a Defence of the Writer against the Attacks made on him by that Individual—and a Sketch of Mr. Smith's Political Life. By H. W. Greene ... . [n. p.] 1839. 8vo, pp. 22. H.

GREENE (Jerome B.) The World's Progress, and other Poems. *Worcester: Author.* 1856. 12mo, pp. vi, 112. C.

GREENE (J.) The Crown Won but not Worn; or, M. Louise Greene, a Student of Five Years at Kent's Hill, Me. By Jonas Greene. *Boston.* 1867. 8vo, pp. 162. 28605

Answered by the following: Libel Refuted: a Reply to Greene's Pamphlet, by the Trustees of the Maine Wesleyan Seminary and Female College, Kent's Hill. *Lewiston: Printed at the Journal Office.* 1868. 8vo, pp. 95; which Greene followed with: A Rejoinder to Reply on the Kent's Hill Tragedy. *Lewiston.* 1868. 8vo.

GREENE (J. P.) Facts relative to the Expulsion of the Mormons, or Latter-Day Saints, from the State of Missouri, under the "Exterminating Order." By John P. Greene. *Cincinnati.* 1839. 8vo, pp. 43. 28606

GREENE (M.) The Kansas Region: Forest, Prairie, Desert, Mountain, Vale, and River. Descriptions of Scenery, Climate, Wild Productions, Capabilities of Soil, and Commercial Re-

sources; Interspersed with Incidents of Travel, and Anecdotes illustrative of the Character of the Traders and Red Men; to which are added ... By Max Greene. *New York: Fowler and Wells.* 1856. 12mo, pp. 192. B., C., H. 28607

GREENE (N.) An Address delivered at ... Boston, January 8, 1828. By Nathaniel Greene. *Boston.* 1828. 8vo. 28608

In celebration of the Anniversary of the Battle of New Orleans Also: Address before the Massachusetts Charitable Mechanic Association at Boston, ... October 10, 1833. ... *Boston.* 1833. 8vo, pp. 16. B., H., M.—Reply to a Letter published by Henry Orne. ... With an Appendix. ... *Boston: Printed by True and Greene.* 1829. 8vo, pp. 39. H.

GREENE (R. H.) The Todd Genealogy; or, Register of the Descendants of Adam Todd. By Richard Henry Greene. *New York: Wilbur & Hastings.* 1867. 8vo, pp. xvii, 143. B., C.

GREENE (S. D.) Appeal of Samuel D. Greene, in Vindication of Himself against the False Swearing of Johnson Goodwill, a Morgan Conspirator, in the Case of Commonwealth *vs.* Moore & Sevey ... for a Libel on said Greene. *Boston.* 1834. 8vo, pp. 64.

GREENE. The Broken Seal; or, Personal Reminiscences of the Morgan Abduction and Murder. By Samuel D. Greene. *Boston: H. H. and T. W. Carter.* 1870. 12mo, pp. 304. C.

GREENE (S. S.) A Genealogical Sketch of the Descendants of Thomas Green[e], of Malden, Mass. By Samuel S. Greene, Providence, R. I. *Boston: Henry W. Dutton & Son, Printers.* 1858. 8vo, pp. 80. S. 28612

Mr. Greene is also the author of "Remarks on Mr. Horace Mann's Report on Education."

GREENE (T.) American Nights' Entertainments: compiled from Pencilings of a United States Senator: entitled, A Winter in the Federal City. With a Supplement. By Talbot Greene. *Jonesborough, Tenn.: Wm. A. Sparks & Co.* 1860. S. 28613

GREENE (T.) A Sermon ... before the ... Society for Propagation of the Gospel in Foreign Parts, ... February 21, 1723. By the Right Rev. ... Thomas [Greene], ... Bishop of Ely. *London.* 1723. 4to, pp. 36. + *London: Printed by Joseph Downing.* 1724. 8vo, pp. 69, (3). B., BA., M. 28614

GREENE (T. A.) An Address, delivered before the ... New Bedford Lyceum, at their First Meeting, December 18th, 1828. By Thomas A. Greene. ... *New Bedford: Printed by Benj. T. Congdon.* 1829. 8vo, pp. 19. BA., W. 28615

GREENE (W.) An Oration on the Life and Character of John Quincy Adams. Delivered at Cincinnati, 25 March, 1848, ... before the Bar of Hamilton County. By William Greene. *Cincinnati.* 1848. 8vo, pp. 35. B., H. 28616

GREENE. Some of the Difficulties in the Administration of a Free Government. A Discourse pronounced before the Rhode-Island Alpha of the Phi Beta Kappa Society, July 8, 1851. By William Greene. *Providence: John T. Moore.* 1851. 8vo, pp. 40. B., H., M. 28617

GREENE (W. B.) ... Letter from Wm. B. Greene to Edward Atkinson, Esq., on the State of the Currency. [*Brookline, Mass.* 1868.] 8vo, pp. 8. H. 28618

GREENE. The Radical Deficiency of the Existing Circulating Medium, and the Advantages of a Mutual Currency. By William B. Greene. *Boston: B. H. Greene.* 1857. 24mo, pp. xix, (1), 239. B., BA., H. 28619

GREENE. The Sovereignty of the People. By William B. Greene. *Boston: A. Williams & Co.* 1868. 8vo, pp. 35.

Also: Trancendentalism. *West Brookfield, Mass.* 1849. 12mo, pp. 49. B., BA.

GREENE *vs.* BRIGGS. Report in the Case of William H. Greene *vs.* Nathan M. Briggs, *et al.* The Plaintiff's Opening Argument, and the Opinion of the U. S. Circuit Court for the Rhode Island District. By Joseph S. Pitman, ... *Boston: Little, Brown & Co.* 1853. 8vo, pp. 60. BA., H. 28621

Relates to the Maine Liquor Laws.

GREENE CO., *N. Y.* Proceedings of the Greene County Agricultural Society. Address of B. P. Johnson. *Albany.* 1837. 8vo. 28622

Proceedings of the Board of Supervisors of the County of Greene, for 1861. *Catskill.* 1862. 8vo. Continued. S.

Constitution of the "Greene and Delaware Society for the Promotion of Good Morals;" with an Address to the Public. *Catskill.* 1815. 16mo. 28624

GREENFIELD (W.) Defence of the Surinam Negro-English Version of the New Testament, ... By William Greenfield. *London: S. Bagster.* 1830. 8vo, pp. 80. 28625

Contains a Philological Analysis of the Negro-English language.

GREENFIELD, *Mass.* Outline of the Plan of Education pursued at the Greenfield High School for Young Ladies, with a Catalogue. ... *Greenfield, Mass.: Phelps and Ingersoll.* 1829. 8vo, pp. 20, (1). Continued. BA., M., W. 28626

A Just Account of an Ecclesiastical Council met at Greenfield, December 12, 1753. 12mo. W. 28627

Results of two Ecclesiastical Councils; Rev. Samuel Willard's Confession of Faith, &c. *Greenfield: Printed by Ansel Phelps.* 1813. 12mo, pp. 18. BA., W. 28628

Also: An Address to the Christian Public, In two Parts. In Answer to the above. *Greenfield: Printed by Ansel Phelps.* 1814. 12mo, pp. 20. BA., W.—Report of a Boarding School, conducted on the Self-Supporting System of Education. *Greenfield.* 1832. 8vo. W.

GREENHALGH (T.) Incidents of the Slave Trade. *London.* 1856. Post 8vo. 28629

GREENHOW (R.) Answer to the Strictures of Mr. Thomas Falconer, ... on the History of Oregon and California. By Robert Greenhow. [*Washington.* 1845.] 8vo, pp. 7. B., N.

GREENHOW. The Geography of Oregon and California, and the other Territories on the North-west Coast of North America. ... By Robert Greenhow. *Boston: Printed for the Author.* 1845. 8vo, pp. 140. Map. + *New York.* 1845. 8vo. N. 28631

GREENHOW. The History of Oregon and California, and the other Territories on the North-west Coast of North America, accompanied by a Geographical View and Map of those Countries, and a number of Documents as Proofs, and Illustrations of the History. By Robert Greenhow. ... *Boston: Little & Brown.* 1844. 8vo, pp. xviii, 482. Map. C. + *London: John Murray.* 1844. 8vo, pp. xviii, 482. Map. + Second Edition, Revised and Enlarged. *Boston: Little & Brown.* 1845. 8vo, pp. (2), xviii, 492. Map. S. + Third Edition. *New York.* 1845. pp. xx, 492. Map. + Fourth Edition. *Boston.* 1847. 8vo.

The second edition contains an answer to Falconer's "Strictures." Murray's edition is the Boston edition of 1844, with a new title only.

GREENHOW. Memoir, Historical and Political, on the Northwest Coast of North America, and the adjacent Territories. Illustrated by a Map and a Geographical View of those Countries. By Robert Greenhow. ... *Washington: Blair & Rives, Printers.* 1840. 8vo, pp. xii, 228. Map. BA., H. 28633

Sen. Doc., No. 174, 26th Cong., 1st Session. Also: The Tri-Color; Devoted to Political Literature, etc. *New York.* 1830. 8vo. Four or more numbers.

GREENHOW (R. O'N.) My Imprisonment, and the First Year of Abolition Rule in Washington. By Rose O'Neill Greenhow. *London: Richard Bentley.* 1863. 12mo, pp. x, 352. Portrait. B., BA., H. 28634

GREENLAND. Ajokaersutit illuartut ... *See* Vol. VI., No. 22847.

Alphabetun Gronlandicun. *Kjøbv.* 1796. 8vo. 28635

Ajokœrsoirsun Atuagekseit ... *See* Vol. VI., No. 22846.

Artikler hvorefter Commandeurerne og Mandskabet paa Skibene, der udsendes for den Gronlandske Handel og Fiskefangst, skulle rette sig. Artikeln wornach die Commandeuren etc. sich zu richten haben. *Odensime.* [1776.] 4to. 28636

Beschryving van Groenland. *See* Vries (S. de).

Bibelingoak. *See* Vol. II., No. 5164.

The Books of Genesis, Psalms, and Isaiah, in the Language of Greenland. By N. G. Wolf. *Copenhagen.* 1822–25. 8vo.

These translations were made for the Moravian Mission to Greenland.

Case of the Merchants who have raised a Joint Stock for Recovery and carrying on the Greenland Whale Fishery with Vigor. 1720. Folio, 1 l. 28638

Customs and Anecdotes of the Greenlanders. *New York.* [n. d.] 18mo. 28639

Domestic Scenes in Greenland and Iceland. Second Edition. *London.* 1850. 24mo. C. 28640

Drie Voyagien gedaen na Groenlandt om te ondersoecken of men door de naeuwte Hudsons soude kunnen seylen, ten versoecke v. Christianus IV. v. Denem.: 1°. door J. Monnick, 2°. door M. Forbisser, en 3° door G. Lindenau. Mit korte beschryv. v. Groenl., manieren en hoedan. d. inwoond. *Amsterdam: G. J. Saeghman.* [1663.] 4to. 28641

These three voyages to Greenland, to investigate whether there is a passage to East-India through the Hudson Straits, and containing a short description of Greenland, the manners and condition of the inhabitants, etc., were made in 1577, 1605, and 1619. *See* Tiele, No. 256.

Echt Historisch Verhaal van drie zeelieden ... wegens het verongelukken van hun schip ... in Groenland. *Amsterdam: D. Schuurman.* 1778. 4to. 28642

This is a true historical account of three sailors shipwrecked in Greenland.

Geschichte der Shiffbrüche und Ueberwinterungen in Grönland, Nova Sembla und Spitzberg. *Prag.* 1798. 8vo. 28643

Greenlandic Psalm-Book, translated in Verse, by K. Kjer. *Odensime.* 1834. 8vo. A. 28644

En Groenlandsk A B D Bog. *Kjöbenhavn.* 1760. 8vo. [Reprinted,] Kattitsiomarsut attuaromarsullo Malligekseit. *Gnadau.* 1835. 8vo. Nye udg. ved Steenberg. *Kjöbenhavn: Missions Collegium.* 1849. 8vo, pp. 20. 28645

Gronlandia, edur Grœnlands Saga. *Skalholte.* 1688. 4to.

Greenland and Iceland. *London: J. Van Voorst.* 1850. 18mo.

A Greenland Family, or the Power of the Gospel: A Narrative of Facts. *Dublin.* 1830. 18mo, pp. 54. 28648

Greenland Missions, with Biographical Sketches of some of the Principal Converts. Second Edition, Revised and Enlarged. *Dublin.* MDCCCXXXI. 18mo. 28649

Grönlands Historiske Mindesmærker udgivne af det Kongelige nordiske oldskrift-selskab. *Kjöbenhavn: Brünnich & Möller.* 1838–45. 3 vols., 8vo, pp. xvi, 797; 717; 950. 12 Plates.

Published by the Society of Antiquaries at Copenhagen.

Jungerutit Tuksiutidlo kaladlinnut Okertunnut Attuaegeksaet. *Kjöbenhavnime.* [n. d.] 28651

Psalms and Prayers in Greenlandish.

Lost Greenland, or Uncle Philip's Conversations about the Lost Colonies of Greenland. *New York.* 1840. 16mo.

Marcus Boss aus Travemünde seine beschwerliche Reise nach Grönland, er gieng von Hause ab anno 1777 den 23sten Februar, und kam nach vielem ausgestandenen Elende und Ungemach, Hunger und Durst, etc., den 26sten Juny 1778. *Hamburg: Joh. Mart Ripke.* 1778. 12mo, pp. 23. 28653

Title from Mr. Bartlett's Catalogue of J. C. Brown's Library.

Naukeerige Beschriving van Groenland. *Amsterdam.* 1675. 4to. 28654

Title from Ternaux's Catalogue, No. 951.

Pok: a Greenlander. *See* Vol. VI., Nos. 22866, 24944.

Relation du Groenland, 1647. *See* [La Peyrere (Isaac de)].

Schediasma hocce ... *See* Vol. VI., No. 22867.

Spellingbook for Greenlanders. Fifth Edition. *Kiöbenhavnime.* 1837. 28655

Strange and Wonderful News from Greenland. 1674. 4to.

Title from Ternaux's Catalogue, No. 913.

Testamentitokab. Makpérsegejsa illanoet Mosesim Aglegèjsa ardlejit Tedlimejdlo, Jobib, Esrab, Nehemiab, Esterib, Rutiblo Aglegejt. Okàuzeenut Petermit-Kraghmit. *Kiövenhavnime.* 1832. 28657

The Old Testament. Translated by Peter Kragh.

Testamentitokab. Profetib mingnerit Danieliblo aglèit; okàuzeenut Pellesimit Petermit Kraghmit. *Kiobenhavn.* 1829.

The Old Testament. The Minor Prophets—Daniel; translated by Peter Kragh.

New Testament. *See* Vol. VI., Note to No. 22875.

A View of the Greenland Trade and Whale Fishery, with the National and Private Advantages thereof. *London: Printed for J. Roberts.* MDCCXXII. 8vo, pp. 68. J.C.B. 28659

The Annaler for Nordisk oldkyndighed, *Kjöbenhavn*, 1843, 8vo, contains: Antiquariske efterretninger fra Groenland, redig. af Dr. C. Pingel. Many anonymous works, relating to Greenland, will be found under the first word of the title. *See also* Eskimo.

GREENLEAF (A.) An Address ... Society of Associated Mechanics and Manufacturers of ... New Hampshire, at ... their Anniversary ... By Abner Greenleaf. *Portsmouth.* 1826. 8vo. 28660

GREENLEAF (J.) A History of the Churches of all Denominations in the City of New York, from the First Settlement to the Year 1846. By Jonathan Greenleaf. *New York: E. French.* 1846. 18mo, pp. 379. BA., C. + To the Year 1850. Second Edition. [*Ibid.*] 1850. 12mo, pp. 430. S. 28661

GREENLEAF. Sketches of the Ecclesiastical History of the State of Maine, from the Earliest Settlement to the Present Time. By Jonathan Greenleaf, Pastor of Wells. *Portsmouth, [N. H.]: Harrison Gray.* 1821. 12mo, pp. 293, Appendix, 78.

Also: Memoir of Rev. Jonathan Parsons, M.A., First Pastor of the Presbyterian Church in Newburyport. ... *Boston: Press of T. R. Marvin.* 1841. 8vo, pp. 12. Portrait. H., M.

GREENLEAF (J.) A Genealogy of the Greenleaf Family. By Jonathan Greenleaf, of Brooklyn, N. Y. *Printed for the use of the Family, by Edward O. Jenkins, ... New York.* 1854. 8vo, pp. 116. B., H. 28663

GREENLEAF (L. N.) King Sham, and other Atrocities in Verse; including a Humorous History of the Pike's Peak Excitement. By Lawrence N. Greenleaf. *New York: Hurd & Houghton.* 1868. 16mo, pp. 139. B., C. 28664

GREENLEAF (M.) A Statistical View of the District of Maine: more especially with reference to the Value and Importance of its Interior. Addressed to the Consideration of the Legislators of Massachusetts. By Moses Greenleaf, Esq. *Boston: Cummings & Hilliard.* 1816. 8vo, pp. 154. Map. B., C.

Reviewed by Benjamin Rand, of Boston, in the "North American Review," Vol. III. 369.

GREENLEAF. A Survey of the State of Maine in reference to its Geographical Features, Statistics, and Political Economy. Illustrated by Maps. By Moses Greenleaf. *Portland: Shirley and Hyde.* 1829. 8vo, pp. 468. BA., C., H., W. 28666

Also: Atlas accompanying Greenleaf's Map and Statistical Survey of Maine. ... *Portland.* [1829.] Folded sheets.

GREENLEAF (P. H.) An Address at the Laying of the Corner Stone of the Church of the Advent, Walnut Hills, December 12, 1855. By P. H. Greenleaf, D.D. ... . *Cincinnati: Moore, Wilstach, Keys & Overend.* 1855. 8vo, pp. 7, (1). H. 28667

[GREENLEAF (Simon).] A Brief Inquiry into the Origin and Principles of Free Masonry. *Portland: Printed by Arthur Shirley.* 1820. 8vo, 1 l., pp. 117. B., BA., C., H. 28668

GREENLEAF. A Discourse commemorative of the Life and Character of the Hon. Joseph Story, LL.D.; ... pronounced ... on the eighteenth of September, A.D. 1845. ... *Boston: Charles C. Little and James Brown.* 1845. 8vo, pp. 48. B., BA., H., M.

[GREENLEAF.] The Right of the Eastern Diocese to elect an Assistant Bishop. *Cambridge.* 1837. 8vo, pp. 26. M., S.

Also: Discourse ... at the Inauguration of the Author as Royall Professor of Law in Harvard University, August 26, 1834. *Cambridge: James Munroe and Company.* 1834. 8vo, pp. 28. B., BA., H., S.

Greenleaf's New-York, Connecticut & New-Jersey Almanack. *New York.* 1797. + *Brooklyn: T. Kirk.* 1800. Continued. S. 28671

GREENOUGH (H.) Æsthetics at Washington. No. I. By Horatio Greenough ... . *Washington: Printed by Jno. T. Towers.* 1851. 8vo, pp. 22. H. 28672

[GREENOUGH (W. W.)] Descendants of Richard Gardner of Woburn, of the name of Gardner. *Boston: Printed for Private Circulation.* 1858. 8vo, pp. 14. 28673

GREENOUGH. "The Conquering Republic." An Oration ... Boston, July 4, 1849. ... *Boston: J. H. Eastburn.* 1849. 8vo, pp. 39. B., BA., H. 28674

GREENSBURGH, *Pa.* Proceedings of a Meeting of the Friends of the General Administration, held in the Borough of Greensburgh, Westmoreland County, Pennsylvania. ... 20th November, 1827. ... [n. p.] 1827. 8vo, pp. 16. BA. 28675

GREENVILLE, *Ala.* To the Citizens of Greenville District. 8vo. 28676

An Address on Secession, signed J. C. Furman, T. S. Arthur, W. H. Campbell, W. M. Thomas.

GREENWICH, *Conn.* Statement of Facts and Remarks, in Relation to the Proceedings of the Consociation of the Western District of Fairfield County, in the Dismission of the Rev. Noah Coe from the Second Congregational Church and Society in Greenwich, 1845. *Printed for the Church.* pp. 21. 28677

GREENWICH, *N. Y.* Congregational Church Manual. *Albany.* 1860. 28678

GREENWOOD (A.) An | Oration, | composed at the request of the | Selectmen, | and delivered before the | Inhabitants | of the Town of Bath | on Saturday, 22nd February, 1800. | By Andrew Greenwood, Esq. | *Hallowell (District of Maine)* | *Printed by Peter Edes.* | 1800. 4to, pp. 16. GB. 28679

GREENWOOD (F.) Geluk op reis, aan de uitgaande Groenlantsche vloot. [A Poem.] *Rotterdam.* 1715. 1 l. Plate.

GREENWOOD (Francis William Pitt). A Description of the Principal Fruits of Cuba. By F. W. P. Greenwood. ... [n. d. n. p.] 8vo, pp. 41. B., H. 28681

GREENWOOD. ... A Discourse occasioned by the Death of James Freeman Curtis; ... April 21, 1839. By F. W. P. Greenwood. ... *Boston: James Munroe and Company.* 1839. 8vo, pp. 20. BA. 28682

GREENWOOD. A Funeral Sermon on the late Hon. Christopher Gove, Formerly Governor of Massachusetts. Preached at King's

Chapel, Boston, March 11, 1827. By F. W. P. Greenwood. *Boston: Wells & Lilly.* 1827. 8vo, pp. 19. B., H., M. 28683

GREENWOOD. A History of King's Chapel in Boston, the First Episcopal Church in New England. Comprising Notices of the Introduction of Episcopacy into the Northern Colonies. By F. W. P. Greenwood, ... *Boston: Carter.* 1833. 12mo, pp. xii, 215. Plate. B., BA., C., H. 28684

GREENWOOD. The Miscellaneous Writings of F. W. P. Greenwood, D.D. Edited by F. W. Greenwood. *Boston.* [1846.] 12mo, pp. iv, 2 l., 393. A., B., BA., H. 28685

GREENWOOD. Prayer for the Sick. ... Sermon, preached ... August 9, 1832, being the Fast Day appointed by the Governor of Massachusetts, on account of the Appearance of Cholera in the United States. *Boston: Leonard C. Bowles.* 1832. 8vo, pp. 13. B., BA., C., H. 28686

GREENWOOD. Recollections of. *See* [Frothingham (N. L.)]

GREENWOOD. ... A Sermon, ... at the Dedication of the Meeting House of the Second Parish in Saco, and the Installation of the Rev. Thomas Tracy ... November 21, 1827. By F. W. P. Greenwood. ... *Kennebunk: Printed by James K. Remich.* 1827. 12mo, pp. 22. BA., H. 28687

Also: Character of the Puritans. Massachusetts Artillery-Election Sermon. ... *Boston.* 1826. 8vo, pp. 22. M., W.—The Christian and National Church. Sermon at Installation of Rev. James W. Thompson, Salem, March 7, 1832. ... *Boston.* 1832. 8vo, pp. 39.— ... A Discourse ... at the Ordination of the Rev. William Newell ... Cambridge, May 19, 1830. ... *Cambridge.* 1830. 8vo, pp. 40. C., M.— ... Sermon at the Ordination of Samuel May, Jr., at Leicester, August 13, 1834. ... *Worcester.* 1834. 8vo, pp. 14. M., W.—Sermon, March 7, 1841, on the Death of J. May. ... *Boston: Printed by S. N. Dickinson.* 1841. 8vo, pp. 23.. B., BA.—A Sermon ... at the Ordination of the Rev. William Parsons Lunt as Pastor of the Second Congregational Unitarian Society in ... New York, June 19, 1828. ... *New York: David Felt.* 1828. 8vo, pp. 50. B., BA., H.—A Sermon ... November 22d, 1835, the Sunday after the Funeral of the Rev. James Freeman, D.D., ... *Boston.* 1835. 8vo, pp. 25. B., BA., H.—Sermon at the Ordination of J. T. Sargeant, as Minister ... in Boston ... October 29, 1837. *Boston: Weeks, Jordan and Company.* 1837. 8vo, pp. 32. B., BA.—A Sermon on the Death of John Lowell, LL.D., ... in King's Chapel, Boston, March 22, 1840. *Boston: Charles C. Little and James Brown.* 1840. 8vo, pp. 36. B., BA.—Sermon ... on the Twenty-fifth Anniversary of the Boston Female Asylum, September 23, 1825. ... *Boston.* [1825.] 8vo, pp. 20. B., BA., H., W.— ... A Sermon ... at the Ordination of the Rev. Warren Benton ... in Cambridge; March 5, 1828. *Boston: Bowles and Dearborn.* 1828. 12mo, pp. 22. H.

GREENWOOD (F. W.) A Sketch of the Life of Francis William Greenwood. From the Monthly Religious Magazine. *Boston.* 1847. 8vo, pp. 26. H. 28688

GREENWOOD (Grace, *pseudon.*) *See* Clark (S. J.), and Lippincott (Mrs. S. J.)

GREENWOOD (I.) A Philosophical Discourse concerning the Mutability and Changes of the Material World; Read to the Students of Harvard-College, April 7. 1731. Upon the News of the Death of Thomas Hollis, Esq; of London, The most bountiful Benefactor to that Society. By Isaac Greenwood, A.M. Hollisian Professor of Philosophy and the Mathematicks. Made Public, At the Desire of the Reverend the President and Fellows of that Society. *Boston: S. Gerrish.* MDCCXXXI. 8vo, pp. (4), 24. B., BA., C., H., W. 28689

See Wigglesworth (E.) The Blessedness. Also: An Account of an Aurora Borealis seen in New-England on the 22d October, 1730. 4to, pp. 53–78 of Philosophical Transactions.—Arithmetick Vulgar and Decimal. *Boston.* MDCCXXIX. 8vo, pp. (6), 138, (4). B., M.

GREENWOOD (J.) The Philadelphia Vocabulary; English and Latin; ... By James Greenwood. *Philadelphia: Printed by Carey & Co.* M,DCC,LXXXVII. 12mo, pp. viii, 123. 28690

An early American school-book, with poor woodcuts.

GREENWOOD (J.) Curiosities of Savage Life. By James Greenwood. Third Edition. *London: S. O. Beeton.* 1865. 8vo, pp. xiv, 418. 8 Plates. + Second Series. *London.* 1864. 8vo. B. 28691

Includes many details relating to the American Indians.

GREENWOOD (J.) The Temple of God to be Measur'd by his Ministers. A Sermon at Southborough, October 21, 1730. At the Ordination of Nathan Stone. By John Greenwood. *Boston.* M,DCC,XXXI. 8vo, pp. (4), 34. B. 28692

Greenwood Cemetery. Surveyed by E. Boyle. 1850. 18mo.

Green-Wood Cemetery, its Rules, Regulations, &c. *New-York: John Douglas, Printer.* 1843. + [*Ibid.*] 1846. P. 28694

Greenwood Illustrated. In a Series of Picturesque and Monumental Views, in highly finished Line Engravings. From Drawings taken on the Spot, by James Smillie; the Literary Department by N. Cleaveland. *New York.* [1847.] 4to.

See also our Vol. VI., No. 13606. It forms the first portion of the Rural Cemeteries of America, and was also issued in folio, with proof impressions of the plates.

Rambling Reflections in Greenwood; with a Description of the same, By Campeador. *New York: Printed by George W. Wood.* 1853. 12mo, pp. 60. 28696

A Report of the Receipts and Expenditures of the Green-Wood Cemetery, from 1839 to 1861. ... *New-York: Joseph Russell, Printer.* 1861. 8vo, pp. 94. 28697

Rules and Regulations of the Green-Wood Cemetery. 8vo, pp. 23. + With an Appendix. *New York.* 1844. 8vo, pp. 40. + With a Catalogue of Proprietors. *New York.* 1845. 8vo, pp. 67. + [*Ibid.*] 1846. 8vo, pp. 72. + [*Ibid.*] 1852. 8vo, pp. 55. + [*Ibid.*] 1854. 8vo, pp. 78. + [*Ibid.*] 1860. 8vo, pp. 123. c. 28698

Rules and Regulations ... with Suggestions respecting the Purchases and Improvements of Lots, &c. *New York.* 1860. 8vo, pp. 46. c. 28699

Rules and Regulations ... with ... Mr. Cleaveland's Descriptive Notices. ... *New York.* 1847. 8vo. A. + *New York.* 1849. 8vo, pp. 120. 28700

Also: Exposition of the Plan and Objects of the Green-Wood Cemetery. ... *New York: Printed by Narine & Co.* 1839. 8vo, pp. 28. P.

Greepe (T.) The true and perfect Newes of the woorthy and valiaunt Exploytes perfoormed and doone by that valiaunt Knight, Syr Frauncis Drake: not onely at Sancto Domingo and Carthagena, but also now at Cales and vpon the Coast of Spayne. By Thomas Greepe. *London: Imprinted by Charlewood.* 1587. 4to, 12 l. B., M. 28701

In verse, and extremely rare; Strettell's copy sold for £7 16s, White Knight's, £10.

Greer (George P.) Express Directory, and Railway Forwarder's Guide. New England States. *Springfield.* 1858. 8vo. Vol. I. 28702

Gregg (A.) A Few Historic Records of the Church in the Diocese of Texas, during the Rebellion. Together with a Correspondence between Rt. Rev. Alexander Gregg, D.D., and the Rev. Charles Gillette. *New York: Gray & Green, Printers.* 8vo, pp. 131. c. 28703

Gregg. History of the Old Cheraws; containing an Account of the Aborigines of the Pedee, the First White Settlements, their Subsequent Progress, Civil Changes, the Struggle of the Revolution, and Growth of the Country afterwards. Extending from about A.D. 1730 to 1810, with Notices of Families and Sketches of Individuals. By the Rt. Rev. Alexander Gregg, Bishop of Texas. *New York: Richardson & Co.* 1867. 8vo, pp. viii, 546. 4 Maps. BA., C. 28704

Really printed in London, probably some copies have an English imprint.

Gregg (Andrew). Mr. Gregg's Motion [on Land Grants], December 6, 1805. *Washington.* 1805. 8vo. 28705

Also: Mr. Gregg's Motion to suspend Commercial Intercourse with Great Britain and her Dependencies, January 29, 1806. *Washington.* 1806. 8vo.

Gregg (D. H.) An Address ... before the Newton Temperance Society, July 4, 1828. By Daniel H. Gregg, M.D. ... *Boston: True and Greene.* 1828. 8vo, pp. 26, (2). BA., H.

Gregg (G. O.) Pittsburgh, her Advantageous Position, and Great Resources as a Manufacturing and Commercial City, embraced in a Notice of Sale of Real Estate. By G. Ormsby Gregg. *Pittsburgh: Johnston & Stockton.* 1845. 8vo, pp. 40.

Gregg (J.) The Sermon for the Times. Preached at Jacksonville, Fla., May 22d, 1864. By James Gregg. *Baltimore: Lucas & Son.* 1864. 8vo, pp. 16. 28708

Relates to the Civil War, 1861-65.

Gregg (J.) An Address, delivered before the New-Hampshire State Lyceum ... at their Second Annual Meeting. ... By Jarvis Gregg. *Concord: Marsh, Capen and Lyon.* 1834. 8vo, pp. 32. BA., H. 28709

Gregg. Eulogy on Lafayette, delivered in ... Dartmouth College, July 4, 1834. By Jarvis Gregg. *Hanover, N. H.: Thomas Mann.* 1834. 8vo, pp. 28. B., BA., M. 28710

Gregg (J. I.) History of the 16th Regiment Pennsylvania Cavalry, for 1863. By Col. John I. Gregg. 8vo. 28711

Gregg (J.) Commerce of the Prairies: or the Journal of a Santa Fé Trader, during Eight Expeditions across the Great Western Prairies, and a Residence of nearly Nine Years in Northern Mexico. Illustrated with Maps and Engravings. By Josiah Gregg. *New York: Henry G. Langley; London: Wiley & Putnam.* M,DCC,XLIV. 2 vols., 12mo, pp. 320, Map; 318, 2 Maps, 6 Plates. C. + Second Edition. *New York: J. & H. G. Langley.* 1845. 2 vols., 12mo, pp. 323, Map and Plate; 327, Map and Plate. + Third Edition. [*Ibid.*] 1845. + Fourth Edition. *Philadelphia: J. W. Moore.* 1850. 2 vols., 12mo, pp. 320; 318. 1 Map, 6 Plates. B., BA. + [*Ibid.*] 1851. + Fifth Edition. [*Ibid.*] 1855. 28712

The title was afterwards changed to read:

Gregg. Scenes and Incidents in the Western Prairies; during Eight Expeditions and including a Residence of nearly Nine

Years in Northern Mexico. By Josiah Gregg. *Philadelphia: John W. Moore.* 1857. 2 vols., 12mo, pp. 3-320; 318. Map.

Gregg. Karawanenzüge durch die westlichen Prärien, und Wanderungen in Nord-Mexico. Nach dem Tagebuche des Amerikaner J. Gregg bearbeitet von M. B. Lindau. *Dresden & Leipzig: Arnold.* 1845. 8vo, pp. x, 208. Plate and Map. C.

Gregg. Karawanenzüge durch die westlichen Prärien, und Wanderungen in Nord-Mexico. Nach des Verfassers Tagebuch bearbeitet von M. B. Lindau. *Leipzig: Arnold.* 1845. 8vo, pp. xvi, 453. 28715

Gregg. Wanderungen durch Prärien und das nördliche Mexico. Aus dem Englischen von G. Fink. *Stuttgart.* 1847. 16mo, pp. xii, 548. + [*Ibid.*] 1851. 2 vols., 12mo. 28716

Gregg (S.) The History of Methodism within the Bounds of the Erie Annual Conference of the Methodist Episcopal Church. By Rev. Samuel Gregg. Vol. I. *New York: Carlton & Porter.* 1865. 12mo, pp. 354. 28717

Gregg (T. C.) Life in the Army, in the Departments of Virginia and the Gulf. Including Observations in New Orleans, with an Account of the Author's Life and Experience in the Ministry. By Rev. T. Chandler Gregg. *Philadelphia: Perkinpine & Higgins.* 1866. 12mo, pp. 231. 28718

Gregg (W.) Essays on Domestic Industry; or, an Enquiry into the Expediency of Establishing Cotton Manufactures in South Carolina. Originally published in the Charleston Courier, ... By William Gregg. *Charleston: Burges & James.* 1845. 8vo, pp. 63. B., H. 28719

Gregg. Speech of William Gregg ... in the Legislature of South Carolina, Dec., 1857, on the Bank Question. *Columbia, S. C.: R. W. Gibbes.* 1857. 8vo, pp. 43. B. 28720

Gregg (W. H.) Catalogue of the Birds of Chemung County, N. Y. By W. H. Gregg, M.D. *Elmira.* 1870. 8vo. S.

Gregg (W. P.), *and* Pond (Benjamin). The Railroad Laws and Charters of the United States, ... Vol. I. Containing the Laws, &c., of Maine, New Hampshire, and Vermont. | ... Vol. II. Massachusetts, Rhode Island, and Connecticut. *Boston: Charles C. Little and James Brown.* 1851. 2 vols., 8vo, pp. xx, 954; xix, 1192. B., BA. 28722

Grégoire (Henri). Apologie de Barthelemy de Las Casas, Évêque de Chiappa. Par Le Citoyen Grégoire. *Paris.* [1800.] 4to. 28723

Extracted from the "Memoires de Morale et de Politique."

Gregoire. A Defence of Bartholomew Las-Casas, Bishop of Chiapa. By Henry Gregoire, ex Bishop of Blois, Senator of France, and Member of the National Institute. To which are added, the Ruins of Port Royal in 1801, by the same Author. Translated from the French, by H. R. Yorke, Esq. With a Short Sketch of his Writings, &c. By the Translator. *London H. D. Symonds.* 1802. 12mo, pp. 125. 28724

Grégoire. De la Liberté de Conscience et de Culte à Haïti. *Paris.* 1824. 12mo, pp. 43. A., S. 28725

Grégoire. Lettre aux Philantropes sur les malheurs, les droits et les réclamations des Gens de Couleur de Saint Domingue, et des autres Iles Françoises de l'Amérique. Par M. Grégoire. *Paris: Belin.* 1790. 8vo, pp. 21. C. 28726

Grégoire. De la Littérature des Nègres ou recherches sur leurs Facultés intellectuelles, leurs Qualités morales, leur Littérature; suivies de Notices sur la Vie et les Ouvrages des Nègres qui se sont distingués dans les Sciences, les Lettres et les Arts. Par H. Grégoire. ... *Paris: Chez Maradan.* M. DCCC. VIII. 8vo, pp. xvi, 287, (1). A., C., H. 28727

Gregoire. An Enquiry concerning the Intellectual and Moral Faculties, and Literature of Negroes. Followed with an Account of the Life and Works of Fifteen Negroes & Mulattoes, distinguished in Science, Literature and the Arts. By H. Gregoire. ... Translated by D. B. Warden. *Brooklyn: Printed by Thomas Kirk.* 1810. 8vo, pp. (2), 253, (1 l.) B., BA., C., H.

Gregoire. Ueber die Literatur der Neger. *Tübingen.* 1809. 8vo. 28729

Grégoire. Mémoire en faveur des Gens de Couleur, ou Sang-Mêlés de St. Dominique, et des autres Isles Françoises de l'Amérique ... . *Paris: Chez Belin.* 1789. 8vo, pp. 52. H.

Grégoire. Mémoires ecclesiastiques, politiques et littéraires, précédés d'une Notice historique sur l'Auteur par M. H. Carnot. *Paris.* 1840. 2 vols., 8vo. A. 28731

Grégoire. Observations d'un habitant des Colonies sur le Mémoire en faveur des Gens de Couleur, ou Sang-Mêlés, de Saint Domingue & des autres Isles Françoises de l'Amérique, adressé à l'Assemblée Nationale, par M. Grégoire, Curé d'Embermenil Depute de Lorraine. *Paris.* 1789. 8vo, pp. 68.

This elicited the following reply, the title to which is imperfectly given in our No. 17167.

Grégoire. Réponse aux Observations d'un habitant des Colonies, sur le Mémoire en faveur des Gens de Couleur, ou Sang-Mêlés, de Saint Domingue, et des autres Isles Françoises de l'Amérique, adressé à l'Assemblée Nationale, par M. Grégoire. Par l'Abbé de Cournaud. [n. p. 1789.] 8vo, pp. 37. H., J.C.B.

Grégoire. Observations Critiques sur le Poëme de M. Joel Barlow, "The Colombiad." Par M. Grégoire, ancien évêque, ... *Paris: Chez Maradan.* 1809. 8vo, pp. 16. BA., H. 28734

Gregoire. Critical Observations on the Poem of Mr. Joel Barlow, the Columbiad. By M. Gregoire ... . *Washington City: Printed by Roger Chew Weightman.* 1809. 8vo, pp. 15. H.

[Grégoire.] Observations sur un pamphlet ayant pour titre: Réclamation des Nègres Libres, Colons Américains. *Paris: Le Clerc.* 1789. 8vo, pp. 17. 28736

Gregoire. On the Slave Trade, and on the Slavery of the Blacks and of the Whites. By a Friend of Men of all Colours. Translated from the ... French of M. Gregoire, ... To which are annexed Prefatory Observations and Notes; By the Translator. *London: J. Conder.* 1815. 8vo, pp. xi, 89. H. 28737

See "Monthly Review," LXXVII. 443. Also: De la Noblesse de la Peau ou du Préjugé des Blancs contre la Couleur des Africains et celle de leurs Descendants. *Paris.* 1826. 8vo. A.—De la traite et de l'esclavage des noirs et des blancs. ... *Paris: Adrien Égron.* 1815. 8vo, pp. 84. BA., H.

Gregorius (S. G.) Die curieuse Geographia, oder accurate Beschreibung derer berühmsten Berge in Europa, Asia, Afrika und Amerika. *Frankfurt.* 1715. 8vo. 28738

Gregorio de Argaiz. Chronista de la Religion de San Benito. Vida, y escritos del venerable varon Gregorio Lopez, por Fr. Gregorio de Argaiz. *Madrid, A. Franc. de Zafra.* 1678. 4to, pp. (32), 121, (6). 28739

Concerning this, *see* Leclerc's Catalogue, No. 78.

Gregory (J.) Industrial Resources of Wisconsin. By John Gregory, Esq., C.E. *Chicago.* 1853. 18mo. + *Milwaukee, U. S. America.* 1855. 18mo, pp. 329. B., BA. 28740

Gregory (J.) The Life and Character of John Brown: a Sermon ... at ... Pittsburgh ... December 4, 1859. By Rev. John Gregory ... . *Pittsburgh: Printed by A. A. Anderson.* 1860. 8vo, pp. 16. BA., H. 28741

Gregory (J. M.) The Handbook of History and Chronology. ... both European and American ... Sixteenth [to the] Nineteenth Centuries. ... By Rev. J. M. Gregory. *Chicago: Adams, Blackmer & Lyon.* 1867. 12mo, pp. 175. 28742

Also: ... Inaugural Address ... Kalamazoo College. Delivered at the Jubilee Meeting ... September 20th, 1864. *Kalamazoo: Walden, Ames & Co.* 1865. 8vo, pp. 23.

Gregory (O. H.) Memoir of Andrew Meneely, ... Elder in the Reformed Protestant Dutch Church of West Troy, N. Y. By Rev. Oscar H. Gregory, D.D. ... *American Tract Society,* ... *New York.* 18mo, pp. 159. 28743

Also: The Glory of God's House: A Sermon, Dedication of Reformed Dutch Church, Farmerville, N. Y. *Albany.* 1857. 12mo, pp. 46. S.

Gregory (S.) Gregory's History of Mexico. ... from the Earliest Times to the Present, ... By Samuel Gregory, A.M. ... *Boston: F. Gleason.* 1847. 8vo, pp. 100. B., BA., C., H. 28744

With a long catchpenny title-page, not worth transcribing. Also: Gregory's Guide to California. *New York.* 1850. 8vo.

Gregory. The War against the New England Female Medical College. By Samuel Gregory, A.M. ... . *Boston: Printed by Alfred Mudge & Son.* 1866. 8vo, pp. 27. H. 28745

Gregory (W.) A Visible Display of Divine Providence; or, the Journal of a Captured Missionary, designated to the Southern Pacific Ocean, in the second voyage of the Duff, ... Captain Thomas Robson, captured by Le Grand Buonaparte off Cape Frio; including every remarkable occurrence which took place on board the ... Duff, le Grand Buonaparte, &c., in the Province of Paraguay, Spanish South America, and .. Portugal, on the return home, in 1798 and 1799. By William Gregory, one of the Missionaries, &c. *London: Symonds.* 1799. 8vo. + *London: Printed by T. Gillet.* 1800. 8vo, pp. viii, 328. Map. H., P. + The Second Edition. *London.* [1801.] 8vo. Map and Plates. 28746

First published in numbers.

Gregory XVI. (*Pope*). Bull for the Abolition of the Slave Trade, and the Words of Daniel O'Connell. *New York.* 1856. 8vo, pp. 8. S. 28747

Grellet (S.) Memoirs of the Life and Gospel Labours of Stephen Grellet, Edited by Benjamin Seebohm. ... *London: A. W. Bennett.* 1860. 2 vols., 8vo. Portrait. + Second Edition. [*Ibid.*] 1861. Sm. 8vo. + Third Edition. [*Ibid.*] 1862. 8vo. + *Philadelphia: Henry Longstreth.* 1862. 2 vols., 8vo, pp. viii, 478, Portrait; viii, 492, Plate. H. 28748

Grellet was a native of Limoges, France, but emigrated to America, and was a minister at Burlington, N. J.

Grenada, *Island of.* Audi alteram Partem; or A Counter-Letter to the Right Hon. the E—l of H—ll—gh, his M——'s P——l S——y of State for the Colonies, on the late and present State of Affairs in the Island of Grenada. In which it is clearly demonstrated, that the Troubles and Confusion which have so long subsisted in that Island, to the Distraction of Government, and to the irreparable Loss of the long-suffering Inhabitants, took their Rise, originally and solely from the arbitrary and partial Disposition of Governor M——ll; from his total Ignorance of the British Constitution, and the Interests of the People whom he was appointed to govern; and from his perverting or dispensing with the Laws. And that these Disturbances have since been kept up by a continuance of the same causes, ... *London: W. Nicoll.* MDCCLXX. 8vo, pp. 123, Appendix, 91. H. 28749

See the "Monthly Review," Vol. XLII. 150.

Denombrement des Habitations de Grenade. [n. p.] 1763. 8vo. 28750

Explication du plan de l'Isle de la Grenade. [n. p.] 1763.

The Grenada Planter; or, A Full and Impartial Answer to a Letter in the Gazetteer of October 22, 1768, relative to the Conduct of his Ex——cy G——r M——le. ... *London: J. Almon.* [1768.] 8vo, pp. 59. H. 28751

Governor Melvill is referred to. *See* "M. Rev.," XL. 92.

... Inquiry into the Causes of ... the Insurrection in Grenada. *London: R. Faulder.* 1796. 8vo, 1 l., pp. 196, (1). Map. H.

The Laws of the Legislature of the Islands of Grenada and the Grenadines, from the first Establishment of a Legislature to the Dissolution of the last Assembly on the Fifth day of September, one thousand seven hundred and seventy-four. Volume I.

This volume contains only such Laws as are now in force. *Grenada: William Wayland.* 1774 4to, pp. 288. J.C.B. 28753

The Laws of the Legislature of the Islands of Grenada and the Grenadines. *Grenada: Printed for Alexander Middleton.* MDCCLXXVIII. 2 vols., folio, pp. 294, Index, 22 l. Vol. II.: MDCCLXXIX. pp. 289, Index, 7 l. H. 28754

A rare and beautifully printed volume. In speaking of the book, Mr. Rich adds the following from a manuscript note: "This book is so rare that the author of the new edition never saw it. See his preface. The reason of its rarity, is the French capturing the island a few months after it was printed, and of course destroying them. This is supposed to be the only copy in England."

The Laws of Grenada, from 1763 to 1805, with Tables of all the Statutes passed in that Period, and of all the Originals yet remaining in the Public Office, and Index of Contents, Collected and Arranged by George Smith. 1808. 4to. 28755

The Laws of Grenada and the Grenadines, from the Year 1766: in which those Acts and Parts of Acts, only, are printed, which were in force at the period of the publication of this work. With numerous Notes of Reference, and a Copious Analytical Index, by a Professional Gentleman. *Grenada: A. McCombie.* 1830. 4to, pp. xxv, 412, (2). C. 28756

A Letter to the Right Honourable The Earl of H---B----H, ... on the Present Situation of Affairs in the Island of Gr–n–da. *London: J. Wilkie.* M.DCC.LXIX. 8vo, pp. 54. H. 28757

Letters to the Earl of Hillsborough, Secretary of State for the Colonies, The Marquis of Rockingham, and the Archbishops and Bishops; on the late Subversion of the Political System, of the Glorious Revolution; and the manifest violation of the Act of Settlement; by authorising and appointing persons professing the Roman Catholic Religion, to hold Legislative and Executive Offices, in the Government of His Majesty's Islands of Grenada and the Grenadines, ... By Pliny, Junior. *London: J. Wilkie.* 1770. 8vo, pp. viii, 63. M. 28758

A Narrative of the Proceedings upon the Complaint against Governor Melvill. *London: T. Becket and P. A. De Hondt.* MDCCLXX. 8vo, pp. xlviii, 132. H., M. 28759

Eight charges were preferred against Governor Melvill, from which it appears that he was guilty of illegal, grievous, cruel, oppressive, and unjust acts towards his Majesty's subjects. He was, however, acquitted. The charges, the reply, and all the proceedings in the case are set forth in this volume.

Narrative of the Revolt. *See* Trumbull (*Mr.*)

Observations upon the Report made by the Board of Trade against the Grenada Laws. *London: W. Flexney.* 1770. 8vo, pp. vii, 62. H., M. 28760

In the "Monthly Review," Vol. XLIII., the author is called a sensible and spirited writer.

Proceedings of the Grenada Agricultural Society. 1820. 8vo. Continued. 28761

A Review, 1795. *See* [Wise (Thomas Turner.)]

GRENARD (L.) A Book for the Times; or Shots from the Monitor. By Leo Grenard. *New York: Sinclair Tousey.* 1863. 8vo, pp. 22. 28762

Reproduced as: Shots from the Monitor; or, Facts for the Times. ... *New York: Sinclair Tousey.* 1864. 16mo, pp. 22. H.

GRENIER (*Chev.*) Mémoires de la Compagne des Découvertes dans les Mers de l'Inde. *Brest.* 1772. 8vo. 28763

GRENNELL (G.) An Oration ... at Northampton, on the Anniversary of American Independence, 1811. By George Grennell, Jun. ... *Northampton: Printed by William Butler.* 1811. 8vo, pp. 24. BA., H. 28764

[GRENVILLE (G.)] The Conduct of the Late Administration. *See* our Vol. IV., Nos. 15202, 15203.

An Epistle to the Right Honourable Lord G—— G——. 4to. *London: J. Almon.* 1778. 28765

Title from the "Monthly Review," Vol. LVIII. 237. *See also* our Vol. I., No. 1849.

G[RENVILLE]. A Letter to G. G. "Stiff in Opinions, always in the Wrong." *London: J. Williams.* MDCCLXVII. 8vo, pp. (4), 96. 28766

"This letter to Lord George Grenville, if not the most elegant, or the most correct of our late political disquisitions, is one of the most solid and most intelligent, and is evidently the produce of no vulgar pen, no ill-instructed hand. It is intended as an answer to some publications in defense of Mr. Grenville's ministerial measures."—*Monthly Review*, XXXVII. 143. The letter is dated Richmond, January 18, 1767, relates entirely to American affairs, and is signed L.

GRENVILLE. Letter to the Right Hon. G. Grenville, occasioned by his Speech in the House of Commons, on the Motion for Expelling Mr. Wilkes, February 3, 1769. To which is added, a Letter on the Public Conduct of Mr. Wilkes. *London: I. Fell.* 1769. 8vo, pp. (2), 131. C., S., W. 28767

[GRENVILLE (George), *and* KNOX (William).] The Present State of the Nation, particularly with respect to its Trade, Finances, &c., &c., addressed to the King and Both Houses of Parliament. *London: J. Almon.* 1768. 8vo, pp. 100. + Fourth Edition, Corrected. [*Ibid.*] 1769. 8vo, pp. (4), 9–107. BA., S.

Partly relating to America. *See* "M. Rev.," XXXIX. 388. It elicited a reply by Mr Burke [*see our* No. 9294] in which most of Mr. Grenville's positions were successfully assailed, and the following is a reply to Burke:

GRENVILLE *and* KNOX. An Appendix to the Present State of the Nation. Containing a Reply to the Observations on that Pamphlet. *London: J. Almon.* MDCCLXIX. 8vo, pp. 68. S.

See "Monthly Review," Vol. XL. 252, and McCulloch's "Literature of Political Economy," pp. 353–354.

[GRENVILLE.] The Regulations Lately Made concerning the Colonies, and the Taxes Imposed upon Them, considered. *London: J. Wilkie.* 1765. 8vo, pp. (2), 114. BA., H. 28770

This pamphlet has also been ascribed to Dr. Campbell and John Dickinson. *See* Bancroft's "United States," v. 157. The following title settles the question:

GRENVILLE. The Regulations Lately Made concerning the Colonies, and the Taxes Imposed upon Them, considered. By the late Right Hon. George Grenville. The Third Edition. *London: J. Wilkie.* 1775. 8vo, pp. 114. 28771

GRENVILLE. The Speech of a Right Honorable Gentleman on the Motion for Expelling Mr. Wilkes, Friday, February 3, 1769. Fourth Edition. *London: J. Almon.* 1769. 8vo, pp. 54.

[GRENVILLE (Richard), *Earl Temple.*] A Letter to His Grace the Duke of Grafton, on the Present Situation of Public Affairs ... . *London: J. Almon.* [1768.] 8vo, pp. 30. S. 28773

[GRENVILLE?] The Principles of the Late Changes Impartially Examined; in a Letter from a Son of Candor to the Public Advertiser. *London: J. Almon.* 1764. 8vo, pp. 85, (1). + Second Edition. [*Ibid.*] 1765. 8vo, pp. 89. 28774

Also: Enquiry into the Conduct of Pitt, 1766.

GRENVILLE (*Sir* R.) *See* Hariot (T.)

GRENVILLE. Address to the House of Representatives of the United States on Lord Grenville's Treaty. *Philadelphia: Mathew Carey.* 1796. 8vo, pp. 48. C. 28775

The Grenville Papers; being the Correspondence of Richard Grenville, Earl Temple, K.G., and the Right Hon. George Grenville, their Friends and Contemporaries: now first published from the Original MSS. formerly preserved at Stowe. Edited, with Notes, by William James Smith. *London: Payne.* 1852–53. 4 vols., 8vo, pp. (2), xliii, (2), 494; xx, 535; ccxxviii, 397; xviii, 592. B., BA., C., H., S. 28776

GRENVILLE (*Lord*). *See* Wyndham (William.)

GREVELINK (A. H., *Bisschop.*) Bemerkingen betreffende de Nederlandsche West-Indische eilanden. II. Emancipatie der Slaven. *Rotterdam.* 1848. 8vo. 28777

Notices of the Dutch West-India islands, and on the emancipation of slaves.

GREVELINK. Beschrijving van het Eiland Sint Eustatius. [n. p.] 1846. 8vo. 28778

GREVELINK. De volkplanting op het eiland St. Eustatius van 1816 tot op den tegenwoordigen tijd. [*Utrecht.* 1847.] 8vo.

GREW (H.) Address delivered before the Peace Society of Hartford and the Vicinity, Sept. 7, 1828. By Henry Grew. ... *Hartford: Printed by P. Canfield.* 1828. 8vo, pp. 22. 28780

GREW. A Narrative of Proceedings in the Bank Street Ch., Philadelphia, relative to the Reception of an Adhering Freemason. With an Examination of Masonic Oaths, &c. By Henry Grew. *Philadelphia.* 1836. 12mo, pp. 36. 28781

GREW (M.) James Mott: a Biographical Sketch. By Mary Grew. With Tributes from Wendell Phillips. *New York: W. P. Tomlinson.* 1868. 18mo, pp. 40. H. 28782

GREW (T.) The Barbados Almanack, For the Year of our Lord 1752: Being Bissextile, or Leap-Year. By Theophilus Grew, Professor of the Mathematicks. ... *Philadelphia: Printed by B. Franklin, and D. Hall.* Folio, 1 l. P. 28783

In black and red. The probably unique copy in the Philadelphia library, has MS. notes by Dr. Franklin. Also: The Description and Use of the Globes, Celestial and Terrestial. ... *Germantown: Printed by Christopher Sower.* 1753. 16mo.

GREWINGK (C.) Beitrag zur Kenntniss der orographischen und geognostischen Beschaffenheit der Nord-West-Küste Amerikas mit den anliegenden Inseln. Von Dr. C. Grewingk. ... *St. Petersburg: Gedruckt bey Karl Kray.* 1850. 8vo, pp. iv. 3–351. 7 Maps. 28784

GREWINGK. Beitrag zur Kenntniss der geognostischen Beschaffenheit Californiens. *St. Petersburg.* 1847. 8vo. A.

Both of these pieces of Grewingk's first appeared in the "Verhandlungen der Mineralogischen Gesellschaft."

GREY (B. E.) New Mexico ... . Speech of Hon. Ben Edwards Grey, of Kentucky, on the Compromise. Delivered in the House of Representatives, May 17, 1852. [*Washington.* n. d.] 8vo, pp. 15. H. 28786

[GREY (*Sir* Charles Edward).] Remarks on the Proceedings as to Canada in the Present Session of Parliament: By one of the Commissioners. *London.* 1837. 8vo, pp. 67. 28787

GREY (G.) Speech of Sir George Grey in the House of Commons, March 29, 1838, on Abolition of Negro Apprenticeship. *London.* 1838. 8vo. S. 28788

GREY [(Henry George)]. The Colonial Policy of Lord John Russell's Administration. By Earl Grey. *London: Richard Bentley.* 1853. 2 vols., 8vo, pp. xxvii, 447; xii, 508. B., BA., S. + Second Edition, with Additions. [*Ibid.*] 1853. 2 vols., 8vo.

"A handbook of modern colonial policy, which no person desirous of understanding the present state and future prospect of our colonies can omit to read."—*Edinburgh Review*, Vol. XCVII., p. 92. *See also* "Fraser's Magazine," Vol. XLVII., p. 485.

[GREY (Isaac).] A Serious Address to such of the People called Quakers, on the Continent of North-America, as profess Scruples relative to the Present Government: Exhibiting the ancient real Testimony of that People, concerning Obedience to Civil Authority. Written before the Departure of the British Army from Philadelphia, 1778, by a Native of Pennsylvania. To which are added, for the Information of all rational Enquirers, an Appendix, consisting of Extracts from an Essay concerning Obedience to the Supreme Powers, and the Duty of Subjects in all Revolutions, published in England soon after the Revolution of 1688. The Second Edition. *Philadelphia: Printed by Steiner & Cist.* MDCCLXXVIII. 8vo, pp. 48. P. 28790

Justifies obedience to the American Government.

GREY (R.) Sermon at Hallowell, [Me.] October 21, 1795, at the Ordination of Daniel Stone. By Robert Grey. *Hallowell.* 1796. 8vo. W. 28791

GREY (Z.) An Impartial Examination of the Second Volume of Mr. Daniel Neal's History of the Puritans. In which the Reflections of that Author, upon King James I. and King

Charles I. are proved to be groundless: His Misrepresentations of the Conduct of the Prelates of those Times, fully detected; And his numerous Mistakes in History, and unfair Way of quoting his Authorities, exposed to Publick View. By Zackary Grey, LL.D. With an Appendix, in Answer to two Common, but Unreasonable Complaints of the Dissenters, against the Establish'd Church, etc. ... *London: R. Gosling.* M.DCC.XXXVI. 8vo, pp. 434. Examination of the Third Volume ... MDCCXXXVII. pp. 404, 143. Examination of the Fourth Volume ... *Printed by J. Beltenham.* 1739. pp. 427, 176. H. 28792

The titles of each volume vary; for an examination of Neal, Vol. I., *see* Madox (Isaac).

[GREY.] A Serious Address to Lay-Methodists to beware of the False Pretences of their Teachers. With an Appendix, containing an Account of the Fatal and Bloody Effects of Enthusiasm, in the case of the Family of the Dutartres in South Carolina, which was attended with the Murder of two Persons, and the Execution of four others. By a Sincere Protestant. *London.* 1745.

[GREY.] The Quaker and Methodist Compared, in an Abstract of Geo. Fox's Journal, with his Will, and of the Rev. Geo. Whitefield's Journal, with Historical Notes. *London.* 1740. 8vo. 28794

The Greyjackets, and How they Lived, Fought, and Died for Dixie. With Incidents and Sketches of Life in the Confederacy. By a Confederate. *Philadelphia: Jones, Brothers & Co.* 1867. 8vo, pp. 574. 11 Maps, 5 Plates. C. 28795

GREYLOCK (Godfrey), *pseudonym.* Taghconic; or, Letters and Legends about our Summer Home. By Godfrey Greylock. [J. E. A. Smith?] *Boston.* 1852. 12mo. 28796

GREYTOWN, *Nicaragua.* Bombardement, et entière Destruction de Grey-Town. *Paris.* 1856. 8vo. 28797

Lettre du Délégué de la Population Française de Grey-Town, Amérique Centrale. *Paris.* 1856. + 2me Lettre du Délégué de la Population Française de Grey-Town, Royaume Mosquite, Amérique Centrale, au Commerce Français, Britannique, Sarde, Espagnol, et Allemand, etc. (Recueil a reproduisant les documents indiqués dans la lettre du 15 Juin, 1856, etc.) *Paris.* 1856. 8vo. 28798

A Memorial to the Congress of the United States, on behalf of the Sufferers from the Bombardment and Destruction of Grey-

town, or San Juan del Norte, by the U. S. Sloop-of-war Cyane, on the 13th July, A.D. 1854; and Narrative of Events which transpired at that Place between the years 1852 and 1854. By S. S. Wood, Commissioner, ... *New-York: John A. Gray, Printer.* 1859. 8vo, pp. 40. S. 28799

GRIBBLE (C. B.) Slavery a Sin; or, Aunt Phillis's Cabin Reviewed. By Charles B. Gribble. 1853. 12mo, pp. 53.

GRIDER (H.) Speech of Mr. Henry Grider, of Kentucky, on the Sub-Treasury Bill. Delivered in the House of Representatives ... April 1st, 1846. *Washington: J. & G. S. Gideon.* 1846. 8vo, pp. 15. H. 28801

Also: Speech ... on the Mexican War ... May 18, 1846. *Washington: Printed by J. & G. S. Gideon.* 1846. 8vo, pp. 16. H.

GRIDLEY (J.) History of Montpelier. A Discourse delivered in the Brick Church, Montpelier, Vt., on Thanksgiving Day, December 8, 1842. By Rev. John Gridley. *Montpelier: E. P. Walton & Sons.* 1843. 8vo, pp. 48. C., H. 28802

GRIDLEY (P.) An Address ... before the Literary Societies of Hamilton College, July 22, 1845, Clinton, N. Y. By Hon. Philo Gridley. *Utica: R. W. Roberts.* 1845. 8vo, pp. 29. H.

GRIEBEN (A. H.) Instrucciones para la cria cientifica de Ovejas en los rebanos de la América del Sud, por A. H. Grieben. *Buenos Aires.* 1866. 8vo, pp. 22. 28804

GRIER (R.) The Georgia Almanac, for ... 1834. ... By Robert Grier. *Augusta, Ga.* 1833. 12mo, pp. 45. H.

Grier's Southern Almanac for the States of Georgia, Alabama, South Carolina, and Tennessee, for the Year ... 1862. *Savannah: E. Knapp & Co.* 8vo, pp. 23. Continued. S. 28806

GRIESINGER (T.) Freiheit und Sklaverei unter dem Sternenbanner, oder Land und Leute in Amerika. *Stuttgart: A. Kröner.* 1862. 2 vols., 8vo. 28807

GRIESINGER. Land und Leute in Amerika. Skizzen aus dem Amerikanischen Leben. Von Theodor Griesinger. ... *Stuttgart: A. Kröner.* 1863. 8vo, pp. (4), 882. Map. B. 28808

GRIESINGER. Lebende Bilder aus Amerika. *Stuttgart.* 1858. 8vo. 28809

GRIEVE (J.) *See* Kracheninnikow.

Grievances of the ... Colonies. *See* [Hopkins (Stephen)].

GRIEVOUS (Peter), *pseudonym.* *See* [Hopkinson], *also*, Vol. IV., No. 14025.

GRIFFEN (P.) A Short Memoir of Phebe Griffen. *New York: Press of M. Day & Co.* 1841. 12mo, pp. 12. 28810

GRIFFIN (A.) Griffin's Journal. First Settlers of Southold. The Names of the Heads of those Families, being only thirteen at the time of their landing; First Proprietors of Orient; Biographical Sketches, &c., &c., &c. By Augustus Griffin. *Orient, L. I.: Augustus Griffin.* 1857. 12mo, pp. 312. Portrait.

[GRIFFIN (Benjamin).] Whig and Tory. [A Play.] [n. p. n. d.] 8vo, pp. 82. BA. 28812

GRIFFIN (*Rev.* Cornelius). Letter to Lord Bathurst, on his Missionary Labors [in Canada], 1828. C., S. 28813

GRIFFIN (E.) Speech of the Hon. Ebenezer Griffin ... Oct. 30, 1860, in Reply to the Address of Hon. Wm. L. Yancey ... Oct. 17, 1860. ... *Rochester, N. Y.: C. D. Tracy & Co.* 1860. 8vo, pp. 23. H. 28814

GRIFFIN (E.) Testimony of Purchase Monthly Meeting, concerning Esther Griffin, deceased, a Minister in the Religious Society of Friends. *London.* 1833. 12mo, pp. 12. 28815

GRIFFIN (E. D.) Remains of the Rev. Edmund D. Griffin, Compiled by Francis Griffin: with a Biographical Memoir of the Deceased, by the Rev. John McVickar, D.D. ... *New-York: G. & C. & H. Carvill.* 1831. 2 vols., 8vo, pp. xiii, 11–455; 466.

GRIFFIN (E. D.) A Farewell Sermon, preached May 28, 1809, at Newark, New-Jersey. By Edward D. Griffin. *Newark: Printed by E. B. Gould.* 1809. 8vo, pp. 29. B., BA., H. + Second Edition. *Newburyport, Mass.* 1809. 8vo, pp. 16. B., BA., H. + *Reprinted, Pittsfield.* 1809. 8vo, pp. 20. 28817

GRIFFIN. A Sermon ... September 2, 1828, at the Dedication of the New Chapel connected with Williams College Massachusetts. By Edward D. Griffin, D.D. President ... *Williamstown: Printed by Ridley Bannister.* 1828. 8vo, pp. 37, Errata, 1 slip. H. 28818

Also: Address before the American Education Society, at Boston, May 25, 1825. ... *Boston.* 1825. 8vo.—Address, May 26, 1829. .. American Bible Class Society, at Philadelphia. ... *Williamstown,* [*Mass.:*] *Printed by Ridley Bannister.* 1830. 8vo, pp. 11. B., BA., W.—An Address ... to the ... Graduates of Williams College, at the Commencement, Sept. 4, 1822. ... . *Pittsfield: Printed by Phinehas Allen.* 1822. 8vo,

pp. 12. H.— ... A Missionary Sermon ... Philadelphia, May 23, 1805. ... *Philadelphia: Printed by Jane Aitken.* 1805. 8vo, pp. 30. B., BA., H. + *Greenfield, Mass.* 1808. 8vo. + *Andover: Flagg and Gould.* 1821. 8vo, pp. 24. BA.—A Letter to the Rev. Ansel D. Eddy ... on the Narratives of the Revivals of Religion in the Presbytery of Geneva. *Williamstown: Printed by Ridley Bannister* 1832. 8vo, pp. 12. BA., H., S.—A Plea for Africa: a Sermon, October 26, 1817, before the Synod of New York and New Jersey. ... *New York.* 1817. 8vo, pp. 76. B., BA., N.—Poem in Latin and English. *New York.* 1821. 4to. W.—Poema in Comitiis Collegii Columbiani pronuntiatum. *New York.* 1823. 4to. W.—Sermon, July 22, 1807, at the Funeral of the Rev. Alexander Macwhorter, D.D., Newark, N. J. ... *New York: S. Gould.* 1807. 8vo, pp. 52. B., BA., H., S.—A Sermon preached January 10th, 1810, at the Dedication of the Church in Park Street, Boston. ... *Boston.* [1810.] 8vo, pp. 34. B., BA., M.—Sermon ... for the Benefit of the Portsmouth Female Asylum, and for the Roxbury Charitable Society, 1811. *Boston: Munroe & Francis.* 1811. 8vo, pp. 47. BA., H. + Second Edition. *Boston: Printed by Samuel T. Armstrong.* 1812. 8vo, pp. 24. BA., H.—A Sermon ... May 9, 1819, at the Anniversary of the United Foreign Missionary Society. ... New York ... *New York.* 1819. 8vo, pp. 27. N.—Sermon at Sandwich, [Mass.] October 20, 1813, at the Dedication of the New Meetinghouse. ... *Boston.* 1813. 8vo, pp. 35. H.—Sermon, "The Claims of Seamen," ... November 7, 1819. ... *New York: Printed by J. Seymour.* 1819. 8vo, pp. 22. BA.—Sermon ... September 14, 1826, before the American Board of Missions at Middletown, Conn. ... *Middletown: Printed by E. & H. Clark.* 1826. 8vo, pp. 27. B.—A Sermon ... before the Annual Convention of the Congregational Ministers of Massachusetts, in Boston, May 29, 1828. ... *Boston.* 1828. 8vo, pp. 24. B., H.—Sermons ... . To which is prefixed a Memoir of his Life, by William B. Sprague, D.D. *Albany: Printed by Packard, Van Benthuysen & Co.* 1838. 2 vols., 8vo, vi, (1), 597; vi, (1), 596. Portrait. B.—Strictures on a Sermon by E. D. Griffin. By a Friend to Revivals. *New York.* 1832. 8vo.—Remarks on Dr. Griffin's Requisition for Seven Hundred Thousand Ministers. *New Haven, Conn.* 1824. 8vo. W.

GRIFFIN (F.) Junius Discovered. By Frederick Griffin. *Boston: Little, Brown and Company.* 1854. 12mo, pp. 310, (1).

The evidence educed is in favor of Thomas Pownall, Governor of Massachusetts Bay.

GRIFFIN (J.) Memoirs of Captain James Wilson, containing an Account of his Enterprises ... his Missionary Voyage to the South Seas, ... By John Griffin. *London: T. Williams.* [n d.] 8vo. + [n. p. n. d.] pp. 230. BA. + *Boston: Samuel T. Armstrong.* 1822. 12mo, pp. iv, 9–219. Portrait. BA. + Second American Edition, with an Appendix. *Portland: James Adams, Jr.* 1827. 12mo, pp. 220. B. 28820

Captain Wilson served in the Battles of Bunker-Hill and Long-Island. *See* "M. Rev.," LXXIV. 217. An abridgment of the work was published, *Philadelphia.* 1841. 16mo.

[GRIFFIN (John Q. A.)] Some Fresh Suggestions on the Project of Annexing Charlestown to Boston. By a Bunker Hill Boy. *Charlestown.* 1855. 8vo, pp. 18. H., N. 28821

GRIFFIN (N.) Gathering of Descendants of Nathan Griffin at the Old Homestead, at Stockton, Me. *Belfast, Me.* 1863. 18mo. 28822

GRIFFITH (D.) Passive Obedience Considered: in a Sermon preached at Williamsburg, December 31st, 1775. By the Reverend David Griffith, Rector of Shelburne Parish, Virginia. Published at the Request of the General Convention. *Williamsburg: Printed by Alexander Purdie.* [n. d.] 8vo, pp. 26. P.

GRIFFITH (Francis P.) A Chart, containing the Names of Senators ... from every State in the Union, from the Commencement of the Federal Government to the Present Period; also, the Names of Presidents and Vice-Presidents, Cabinet Officers, &c. *Columbus: F. W. Murray & Co.* 1849. 28824

GRIFFITH (J.) A Journal of the Life, Travels and Labours in the Work of the Ministry of John Griffith. *London: James Phillips.* M DCC LXXIX. 8vo, pp. iv, 427. BA., H. + *Philadelphia: Joseph Crukshank.* M DCC LXXX. 8vo, pp. (2), iv, 426. H., P. + *York: Printed by W. Alexander & Co.* 1830. 12mo, pp. 296.

Griffith was a Quaker missionary, born in Wales. He travelled through parts of New England, New York, New Jersey, Pennsylvania, and Maryland, in 1736 and the following year. *See* "M. Rev.," LXI. 571. Reprinted in "The Friend's Library," Vol. v. *Philadelphia.* 1841. 8vo. Also reprinted with: Some Brief Remarks upon Sundry Important Subjects, etc.; principally addressed to the People called Quakers. ... *London.* 1764. 8vo, pp. 100. + [*Ibid.*] 1765. + *Dublin.* 1765. 8vo. + *London, Printed; and Wilmington, Reprinted by James Adams.* 1768. 8vo. P. + *Philadelphia: Joseph Crukshank.* M DCC LXXXI. pp. (8), 112. + *London: Phillips and Fardon.* 1805. 8vo. + *York.* 1830.

GRIFFITH (J. F.) Remarks on Bridging the Upper Mississippi and other Large Navigable Streams. ... Submitted to Congress by James F. Griffith ... . [n. p. n. d.] 8vo, pp. 4. H.

GRIFFITH (T. W.) Annals of Baltimore. By Thomas W. Griffith. *Baltimore: Printed by William Wooddy.* 1824. 8vo, pp. 296, Errata, 1 l. Portrait. BA. 28827

GRIFFITH. Sketches of the Early History of Maryland. By Thomas W. Griffith. *Baltimore: Printed [for the Author] by Frederick G. Schaeffer.* 1821. 8vo, pp. 77. Portrait and Plate.

[GRIFFITH (William).] Eumenes: Being a Collection of Papers, written for the purpose of Exhibiting some of the more Prominent Errors and Omissions of the Constitution of New Jersey, as established on the Second Day of July, One Thousand Seven Hundred and Seventy-Six; and to Prove the Necessity of Calling a Convention, for Revision and Amendment. *Trenton: Printed by G. Craft.* 1799. 8vo, pp. 149, (6). 28829

[GRIFFITH.] Historical Notes. [n. p. 1825.] 8vo.

"This book was never published. The author was W. Griffith of New Jersey, whose death prevented the continuance of the work, and the completion of this unfinished volume."—J. SPARKS. It was afterwards issued as a posthumous work, viz.:

GRIFFITH. Historical Notes of the American Colonies and Revolution, from 1754 to 1775. By William Griffith, Esq., of New Jersey. Published by his Executors. *Burlington, N. J., Jos. L. Powell.* 1843. 8vo, pp. 300, Note, 3 l. B., BA., C., H.

GRIFFITH. An Oration, delivered To the Citizens of Burlington, on the 22d of February, 1800, In Commemoration of Gen. George Washington, ... By William Griffith, Esq. To which is added A Prayer, on the same occasion. By Charles H. Wharton, D.D. ... *Trenton: Printed by G. Craft.* MDCCC. 8vo, pp. 25. BA., P. 28832

Also: Annual Law Register of the United States—Vols. III., IV. *Burlington: David Allinson.* 1822. 2 vols., 8vo, pp. iv, 564; 1 l., 565–1452. BA., H., S.—which contains much political information.—A Treatise on the Jurisdiction and Proceedings of Justices of the Peace in Civil Suits, ... *Newark.* 1797. 12mo.

GRIFFITHS (D., *Jr.*) Two Years Residence in the New Settlements of Ohio, North America: With Directions to Emigrants. By D. Griffiths, Jr. *London.* 1835. 12mo. C. 28833

GRIFFITHS (John W.) Treatise on Marine and Naval Architecture ... *New-York.* 1851. 4to. 28834

Contains some historical data.

[GRIFFITHS (Julia).] Autographs for Freedom. *Boston: John P. Jewett & Company.* 1853. 12mo, pp. viii, 263. + Second Series. Edited by Julia Griffiths. *Auburn: Alden, Beardsley & Co.* 1854. 12mo, pp. 309. Portrait. B., BA., H. 28835

A collection of articles from the pens of William H. Seward and numerous other persons of eminence, male and female, with their signatures in facsimile appended.

[GRIFFITHS (Mattie).] Autobiography of a Female Slave. *Redfield, New York.* 1857. 12mo, pp. 401. B., C., H. 28836

Also: Poems. Now first Collected. ... *New York: D. Appleton & Co.* M. DCCC-LIII. 12mo, pp. 167. B., H.

GRIGG (J.) ... A Sermon, preached on the Fifth Day of September, 1832, ... Athens, Greene Co. On a Day appointed by the Rector for Humilation and Prayer to Almighty God, that he would be pleased to avert the prevailing Epidemic. By the Rev. John Grigg, A.M. ... *Hudson: Crawford Livingston.* 1832. 8vo, pp. 23. 28837

GRIGG (John, *publisher*). Grigg's Southern and Western Songster; being a Choice Collection of the most Fashionable Songs. ... New Edition. *Philadelphia.* 1835. 24mo. + [*Ibid.*] 1836. + [*Ibid.*] 1839. Plate. 28838

GRIGGS (William N.) The Celebrated "Moon Story," its Origin and Incidents; with a Memoir of the Author. [J. Adams Locke.] *New York.* 1852. 12mo. C. 28839

[GRIGGS (*Rev. Mr.*)] The Manuscript. *New York: G. and C. Carvill and Elam Bliss.* 1828. 2 vols., 8vo, pp. 192; 188. Plate of Trenton Falls, N. Y. 28840

A periodical; six numbers in each volume. Vol. I. reached a second edition—nearly all the articles relate to America.

GRIGNON. Vindication of Col. Grignon, and the Western Interior Regiment, during the Rebellion, 1831–32. *Jamaica: Office of the St. Jago Gazette.* 1833. 2 Plates. 28841

GRIGSBY (H. B.) Discourse on the Life and Character of the Hon. Littleton Waller Tazewell, delivered ... before the Bar of Norfolk, Virginia, and the Citizens Generally, on the 29th day of June, 1860. By Hugh Blair Grigsby, LL.D. *Norfolk: J. D. Ghiselin, Jr.* 1860. 8vo, pp. 124. B., BA., C., H., S.

GRIGSBY. The Virginia Convention of 1829–30, a Discourse delivered before the Virginia Historical Society, ... December 15th, 1853. By Hugh Blair Grigsby. *Richmond: Macfarlane and Fergusson.* 1854. 12mo, pp. 104. B., M. 28843

GRIGSBY. The Virginia Convention of 1776. A Discourse delivered before the Virginia Alpha of the Phi Beta Kappa Society, in the Chapel of William and Mary College in the City of Williamsburg, July 3, 1855. ... By Hugh Blair Grigsby. *Richmond: J. W. Randolph.* 1855. 8vo, pp. 206. B., H.

Also: Oration, delivered before the Students of William and Mary College, July 4, 1859. [n. p. 1859.] 8vo, pp. 16. B., H.

GRIJALUA (J. de). Cronica de la Orden de N. P. S. Augustin en las Prouincias de la Nueua España, en quatro decades desde el año de 1533 hasta el de 1592. Por M. F. Joan de Grijalva, Prior del Convente de N. P. S. Augustin de Mexico. *Mexico en el Religiosisimo Conuento de S. Augustin, y Imprenta de Joan Ruyz.* 1624. Folio, Engraved Title, 3 l., 218 l., (9 l.) H.

The author was a native of Colima, on the Pacific Coast; born about 1559, and was for many years the Rector of St. Paul's College; died at Puebla in 1627. "Es

Historia bien escrita, i que no sale de lo que en el *Titulo* promete."—PINELO-BARCIA. A rare work; the Andrade copy sold for 145 thalers. Priced by Tross, in 1872, at 600 francs.

GRILLET *and* BECHAMEL. *See* Acuña (Ch. de). Vol. I.

GRIMALDI. Respuesta del Marques de Grimaldi sobre la cuestion de limiter en la banda oriental del Rio de la Plata, y noticias sobre los dos sitios de la colonia del Sacramento en 1762 y 1773. *Montevideo.* 1849. 4to, pp. 72. 28846

[GRIM (Charles Frederic).] An Essay towards an Improved Register of Deeds, City and County of New York, to December 31, 1790, inclusive. *New-York.* 1832. 8vo, pp. 371.

Mr. Gowan marked his copy as "Rare; $50.00."

Grim Dick, the One-Eyed Robber. A Tale of Hunters, Indians, and Banditti. *New York: Geo. Munro & Co.* 1866. 16mo, pp. 100. 28848

GRIMES (G.) The Lily of the West, On Human Nature, Education ... . By G. Grimes, an Inmate of the Lunatic Asylum in Tennessee. *Nashville, Tenn.* 1846. 8vo, pp. 96. 28849

GRIMES (J. S.) The National Crisis. A Sermon preached at Columbia, Pa., and repeated ... in Wrightsville, Pa., on the National Fast Day, January 4th, A.D. 1861; ... by Rev. J. S. Grimes, A.M., Pastor. *Wrightsville: Robert W. Smith, Printer.* 1861. 8vo, pp. 16. 28850

Also: The Nation's Last Hope. A Sermon preached in the First Presbyterian Church, on the Day of National Humiliation, August 4, 1864. ... *Newcastle (Pa.): E. S. Durban.* 8vo, pp. 20.

GRIMES (J. W.) Address to the People of Iowa, April 8, 1854. By James W. Grimes. [n. p. n. d.] 8vo, pp. 7.

GRIMES. Opinion of James W. Grimes, of Iowa, ... in the United States Senate ... for the Trial of Andrew Johnson ... . *Washington: F. & J. Rives & Geo. A. Bailey.* 1868. 8vo, pp. 14.

Also: Achievements of the Western Naval Flotilla. Remarks in the Senate, March 13, 1862. [n. p. n. d.] 8vo, pp. 8.—The Surrender of Slaves by the Army. Speech ... April 14, 1862. 8vo, pp. 7.

GRIMKÉ (A. E.) Appeal to the Christian Women of the South. By Angelina E. Grimké. *New York.* [1836.] 8vo, pp. 36. + *Edinburgh: Printed by Willm. Oliphant, Junr. & Co.* 1837. 8vo, pp. 36. P. 28853

On Slavery. *See* "Anti-Slavery Examiner," Vol. I.

GRIMKÉ. Letters to Catharine E. Beecher, in Reply to an Essay on Slavery and Abolitionism, addressed to A. E. Grimké: Revised by the Author. *Boston: Isaac Knapp.* 1838. 12mo, pp. 130. C., N. 28854

GRIMKÉ (F.) Considerations upon the Nature and Tendency of Free Institutions. By Frederick Grimké. *Cincinnati: H. W. Derby & Co.* 1848. 8vo, pp. viii, 544. + Second Edition, Corrected. [*Ibid.*] 1856. 8vo, pp. 670. 28855

GRIMKÉ (S. M.) An Epistle to the Clergy of the Southern States. By Sarah M. Grimké. [n. p. n. d.] 8vo, pp. 20. S.

Also: Letters on the Equality of the Sexes, and the Condition of Woman. Addressed to Mary S. Parker. ... *Boston: Isaac Knapp.* 1838. 8vo, pp. 128. B., C.

GRIMKÉ (T. S.) A Letter [on Nullification] to the Honorable John C. Calhoun, Vice-President ... Robert Y. Hayne, ... George M'Duffie, ... and James Hamilton, Jr., Governor of the State of South Carolina. By Thomas S. Grimké. *Philadelphia: Thomas Kite and Co.* 1832. 8vo, pp. 17. W. + Second Edition. *Charleston: Printed by James S. Burges.* 1832. 8vo, pp. 15. 28857

GRIMKÉ. An Oration delivered in ... Charleston on the Fourth of July, 1809, by the Appointment of the South Carolina State Society of Cincinnati. ... By Thomas S. Grimké. ... *Charleston.* 1809. 8vo, pp. 32. + *Re-printed by Wm. Riley.* 1829. 8vo, pp. 32. 28858

GRIMKÉ. Oration on the Absolute Necessity of Union, and the Folly and Madness of Disunion. Delivered Fourth of July, 1809. By Thomas S. Grimké. Speech of Thomas S. Grimké, delivered in December, 1828, On The Constitutionality of the Tariff, and on the True Nature of State Sovereignty. ... *Charleston: Printed by W. Riley.* 1829. 12mo, pp. 129. 28859

This is the cover title, the printed titles differ. The oration was first published separately. 8vo, pp. 32.

GRIMKÉ. Oration on the Principal Duties of Americans; delivered before the Washington Society, and other Citizens of Charleston ... 4th of July [1833]. By T. S. Grimké. With the Farewell Address of the Hon. Wm. Drayton, to the Washington Society. ... *Charleston: Printed by William Estill.* 1833. 8vo, pp. 39. P. 28860

GRIMKÉ. Report of Committee of Senate of South-Carolina, on the Practicability ... of reducing the Law to the Form of a

Code ... 1827. By Thomas S. Grimké. *Columbia: Printed by D. & J. M. Faust.* 1827. 8vo, pp. 26. B., H. 28861

GRIMKÉ. Speech of Thomas Smith Grimké ... delivered in the Senate of South Carolina, In December, 1828, during the Debate on Sundry Resolutions of the Senate and House of Representatives Respecting the Tariff. ... *Charleston: Printed by W. Riley.* 1829. 8vo, pp. 129. C. 28862

Also: Address at the Dedication of the Building in Chalmers Street, ... April 8, 1829. *Charleston.* [1829.] 8vo, pp. 32. W.—Address at Charleston, ... March 29, 1831, to consider the Resolution of ... Sunday Schools in the Valley of the Mississippi. ... *Philadelphia.* 1831. 8vo, pp. 15.— ... Address at the Celebration of the Sunday School Jubilee, Charleston, S. C., ... September 14, 1831. *Charleston.* 1831. 8vo, pp. 20. + *Philadelphia.* 1834. 8vo, pp. 16.—Address on ... Peace, and ... War: delivered ... at New-Haven, ... 6th of May, 1832. ... *Hartford: Printed by George F. Olmsted.* 1832. 8vo, pp. 56.—Address on the Patriot Character of the Temperance Reformation, delivered before the Charleston Temperance Society, etc., 26th February, 1833. ... *Charleston.* 1833. 8vo, pp. 35. N., P.—Argument delivered in the Court of Appeals of the State of South Carolina ... April 2 and 3, 1834, ... on the Constitutionality of the Oath in the Act for the Military Organization of this State, passed December 19, 1833. ... *Charleston.* 1834. 8vo, pp. 28.—Correspondence, on the Principles of Peace, Manual Labor Schools, &c. *Charleston.* 1833. 8vo, pp. 16.—Letter to John Mathour and Others. ... *Philadelphia.* 1832. 16mo, pp. 17.—A Letter to the People of South Carolina. ... [*Charleston:*] *Printed by J. S. Burges.* [1832.] 8vo, pp. 16.—Oration ... before the Connecticut Alpha of the Phi Beta Kappa Society, September 7, 1830. ... *New Haven.* 1830. 8vo, pp. 76. P.—Oration on American Education ... before the Western Literary Institute ... October, 1834. ... *Cincinnati: Josiah Drake.* 1835. 8vo, pp. 43.—Oration on ... Grecian and American Eloquence ... Oxford, Ohio; ... *Cincinnati: Truman and Smith.* 1834. 8vo, pp. 56, (2).—Oration on the Practicability and Expediency of reducing the whole body of the Law to a Code, ... 17th March, 1827. *Charleston.* 1827. 8vo, pp. 31.—Oration ... before the Euphradian Society of the College of Charleston, 13th August, 1832. *Charleston: Printed by A. E. Miller.* 1832. 8vo, pp. 28. BA., M.—Reflections on the ... Objects of all Science and Literature, and on the Relative Excellence and Value of Religious and Secular Education and of Sacred and Classical Literature, in Two Addresses and an Oration. ... *New Haven: Hezekiah Howe.* 1831. 12mo, pp. xii, 201. W.—Report to the Legislature of South Carolina on the Expediency of a Code of the Statute and Common Law. *Charleston.* 1827. 8vo.—The Temperance Reformation the Cause of Christian Morals. Address before the Charleston Temperance Society, and the Young Men's Temperance Society of Charleston, February 25, 1834. *Charleston.* 1834. 8vo, pp. 26.—Extracts from Newspapers relative to the Decease of Thomas S. Grimké. *Philadelphia.* 1834. 12mo.

GRIMM (W.) Central-Amerika. *See* Baily (J.), Vol. I.

GRIMOULT (*Lieut.*) Renseignements nautiques sur la Nouvelle-Caledonie et les isles Loyality. *Paris: Bossange et Fils.* 1859. 8vo, pp. 47. 28863

GRIMSHAW (W.) An Exposition of the Situation, Character, and Interests of the American Republic. By William Grimshaw. *Philadelphia.* 1822. 8vo, pp. 31. C., M. 28864

GRIMSHAW. The History of South America, from the Discovery of the New World by Columbus, to the Conquest of Peru by Pizarro. By William Grimshaw. *New-York: Collins & Hannay.* 1830. 12mo, pp. 252. + *Philadelphia.* 1833. 12mo.

GRIMSHAW. The History of the United States, from their First Settlement to the Peace of Ghent. By William Grimshaw. *Philadelphia.* 1820. 12mo, pp. 306. C. 28866

GRIMSHAW. History of the United States ... to the Cession of Florida, ... comprising every Important Political Event; with a Progressive View of the Aborigines, etc., ... By William Grimshaw. Second Edition. *Philadelphia: Benjamin Warner.* 1821. 12mo, pp. (2), 271, (5). + Third Edition. *Philadelphia: L. R. Bailey.* 1822. 12mo, pp. 308. + A Revised Edition. *Philadelphia: John Grigg.* 1826. 12mo, pp. (2), 308. B. + To the Fifth Census. *Philadelphia.* 1832. 12mo. + To the Sixth Census in 1840. *Philadelphia: Grigg, Elliot & Co.* 1847. 12mo, pp. 336. C. + To the Peace with Mexico, in 1848. *Philadelphia: Grigg, Elliot & Co.* 1849. 12mo, pp. 371. C. + Revised and Corrected, with Additional Chapters, By A. H. Grimshaw, A.M., M.D. *Philadelphia: Lippincott, Grambo & Co.* 1853. 12mo. C. + [*Ibid.*] 1856. 28867

Frequently reprinted. Also: Questions adapted to Grimshaw's History of the United States. *Philadelphia.* 1847. 12mo.—Incidents Recalled. *Philadelphia.* 1848. 8vo, pp. 84.

GRINDROD (R. B.) A Prize Essay on Intemperance. By R. B. Grindrod. First American Edition. *New-York.* 1840. 12mo. S. 28868

Contains Statistics of Intemperance, &c., in the United States.

GRINNELL (G.) An Oration ... at Northampton, on the Anniversary of American Independence, 1811. By George Grinnell, Jun. *Northampton: William Butler.* 1811. 8vo, pp. 24.

GRINNELL (J.) Memoir of Joseph Grinnell, read at a Dinner at William T. Russell's, March 7th, 1863. Privately printed. *New York.* 8vo. 28870

GRINNELL (Joseph). Speech of Mr. Grinnell, of Massachusetts, on the Tariff; with Statistical Tables on the Whale Fishery of the United States. Delivered ... May 1, 1844. *Washington.* 1844. 8vo, pp. 16. 28871

GRINNELL (J. B.) Early and Modern Democracy Reviewed. Speech of Josiah B. Grinnell, of Iowa, in the House of Representatives, March 5, 1864. [n. p. n. d.] 8vo, pp. 14. 28872

GRISCOM (J.) Address ... before the Newark Mechanics' Association, on their Third Anniversary, January 25, 1831. By John Griscom, LL.D. ... *Newark: Printed by William Tuttle.* 1831. 8vo, pp. 39. 28873

[GRISCOM.] Considerations relative to an Establishment for perfecting the Education of Young Men within the Society of Friends. ... *New-York: Printed by Samuel Ward & Sons.* 1815. 8vo, pp. 24, (1). BA. 28874

GRISCOM. A Discourse on the Importance of Character and Education, in the United States, delivered on the 20th of 11th Mo. (November,) 1822, ... By John Griscom, ... *New-York: Printed by Mahlon Day.* 1823. 8vo, pp. 26, (1). B. 28875

GRISCOM (J. H.) A History ... of the Visitations of Yellow Fever at New York. By John H. Griscom, M.D., ... *New York: Hall, Clayton & Co.* 1858. 8vo, pp. 36. 28876

GRISCOM. Memoir of John Griscom, LL.D., with an Account of the New York High School; Society for the Prevention of Pauperism; the House of Refuge; and other Institutions. By John H. Griscom. *New-York.* 1859. 8vo, pp. 427. 28877

GRISCOM. The Sanitary Condition of the Laboring Population of New York. With Suggestions for its Improvement. A Discourse ... 1844, ... By John H. Griscom, M.D. ... *New York: Harper & Brothers.* 1845. 8vo, pp. 58. 28878

Also: Monitorial Instruction. An Address ... at the Opening of the New-York High-School. ... *New York: Printed by Mahlon Day.* 1825. 12mo, pp. 216. Plate.

GRISEBACH (*Dr.*) Flora of the British West Indian Islands. By A. H. R. Grisebach, M.D. ... *London: Lovell Reeve & Co.* 1864. 8vo, pp. xvi, 789. H. 28879

Contains complete systematic descriptions of the Flowering Plants and Ferns of the British West India Islands, accompanied by an elaborate index of reference, and a list of Colonial names.

GRISSON (Wilhelm). Beiträge zur Charakteristik der Vereinigten Staaten von Nord-Amerika. *Hamburg.* 1844. 8vo, pp. 480. C., S. 28880

GRISWOLD (A. V.) A Sermon delivered in ... Boston, at the First Meeting of the Convention of the Eastern Diocese, 19th September, 1810. By Alexander Viets Griswold. With Constitution of the Protestant Episcopal Church of the Eastern Diocese, &c. *Boston: Printed by Munroe & Francis.* 1811. 8vo, pp. 19, 15.

Also: Address to the Diocesan Convention at Windsor, Vt., September 25, 1816 ... [n. p. n. d.] 12mo, pp. 14, (2). W. — Address to the Biennial Convention at Greenfield, Massachusetts, September 30, 1818. ... *Providence, R. I.* 1818. 8vo, pp 20. BA., W. — A Charge ... to the Clergy of the Protestant Episcopal Church in the Eastern Diocese ... in Portsmouth, N. H., Sept. 28, 1814; ... *Boston: Printed by Munroe, Francis & Parker.* 1816. 8vo, pp. 52. — ... Discourse ... on ... the Decease of F. L. D'Wolf, September 25, 1825. ... *Providence: Miller and Grattan.* 1826. 8vo, pp. 15. B. + *Bristol, R. I.* 1838. 12mo. B. — A Discourse ... February 11, 1838, occasioned by the Decease of the Hon. James D'Wolf and Mrs. Ann B. D'Wolf, his Wife. *Bristol: W. H. S. Bayley.* 1838. 12mo, pp. 14. B. — A Discourse ... at Harwinton, on the 5th Day of January, 1797, occasioned by the Death of Mr. Lent Munson. ... *Litchfield: Printed by T. Collier.* MDCCXCVII. 8vo, pp. 16. — A Discourse ... in Rhode Island, November 13, 1833, on ... the Ordination of the Rev. James C. Richmond. ... *Philadelphia: William Stavely.* 1835. 12mo, pp. 12. B. — A Pastoral Letter addressed to the Members of the Protestant Episcopal Church in the Eastern Diocese. ... *Boston: Joseph W. Ingraham.* 1821. 8vo, pp. 68. + Second Edition. *Boston.* 1821. 8vo, pp. 68. — A Sermon preached at Bristol, R. I., July 9, 1808, at the Funeral of the Hon. William Bradford, Esq. ... *Bristol: Golden Dearth.* 1808. 8vo, pp. 15. — ... A Sermon at the ... General Convention of the Protestant Episcopal Church in the United States ... in ... New York, May 21st, A.D. 1817. ... *New York: Printed by T. and J. Swords.* 1817. 8vo, pp. 30. H. — A Short Sketch of the Life of Mr. Lent Munson. *Litchfield: Printed by T. Collier.* 8vo, pp. 8.

GRISWOLD (C.) An Address in Commemoration of ... Ledyard and his Brave Associates, who fell at Groton Heights, Sept. 6, 1781, in Defence of their Country, delivered at Groton (Conn.), September 6th, 1826 ... By Charles Griswold, Esq. *New London: Printed by J. B. Clapp.* 1826. 8vo, pp. 19. B.

GRISWOLD (C. D.) The Isthmus of Panama, and What I Saw There. By C. D. Griswold, M.D. ... *New York: Dewitt & Davenport.* 1852. 12mo, pp. 180. 2 Maps. C., S. 28883

GRISWOLD (E.) Answer to Mr. Gillett's Letter. *Hartford.* 1793. 8vo. 28884

Also: Letter in Answer to the Rev. Daniel Perry's Short View. ... *Hartford: Printed by Hudson & Goodwin.* 1796. 8vo, pp. 27. B.

GRISWOLD (F.) James' Railroad and Route Book, for the Western and North Western States. Compiled by F. Griswold. *Cincinnati: J. A. & U. P. James.* 1854. 16mo, pp. 93.

GRISWOLD (J.) ... A Sermon, preached at Pawlet, on the Anniversary Thanksgiving of Vermont, December 6, 1804, ... By John Griswold, A.M. ... *Benington: Haswell & Smead, Printers.* [n. d.] 12mo, pp. 60. 28886

GRISWOLD (M.) [Descendants of Matthew Griswold. *Chicago.* 1856.] 4to, pp. 6. 28887

GRISWOLD (Roger). Speech of Mr. Griswold, on the Bill for the Repeal of the Internal Taxes, delivered in the House of Representatives of the United States, on Thursday, the 18th of March. *Philadelphia: E. Bronson.* 1802. 8vo, pp. 27. 28888

GRISWOLD. Message of his Excellency to the General Assembly of Connecticut, at their Special Session, August 25, 1812. With Documents accompanying the same. *New Haven.* 1812. 8vo. N. 28889

GRISWOLD. Report of a Committee of the United States House of Representatives on the Expulsion of Roger Griswold and Matthew Lyon. 1798. 28890

GRISWOLD (R. W.) The Biographical Annual; consisting of Memoirs of Eminent Persons [Americans], recently Deceased. Edited by Rufus W. Griswold. *New-York: Linen and Fennell.* 1841. 12mo, pp. vii–307. 2 Portraits. C. 28891

[GRISWOLD.] The Cyclopedia of American Literature, by Evart A. Duyckinck and George L. Duyckinck. A Review. *New York.* 1856. 8vo, pp. 32. 28892

Reprinted from the New York "Herald," of February 13, 1856. A malignant review of a useful work.

GRISWOLD. The Female Poets of America. By R. W. Griswold. *Philadelphia.* 1849. 8vo, pp. 400. Portraits. + Second Edition. *Philadelphia: Henry C. Baird.* 1853. 8vo, pp. 3–400. Plates. + New Edition. *Philadelphia.* 1859. 8vo. C. + Revised and brought down to the Present Time by R. H. Stoddard. *New York.* 1869. 8vo, pp. 487. 28893

GRISWOLD. Gems from American Female Poets, with Brief Biographical Notices. By Rufus W. Griswold. *Philadelphia: H. Hooker.* 1842. 32mo, pp. 192. Plate. C. 28894

GRISWOLD. The Poets and Poetry of America. With an Historical Introduction. By Rufus W. Griswold. *Philadelphia: Carey and Hart.* MDCCCXLII. 12mo, pp. xxiv, 468. + Second Edition, Revised. *London and Philadelphia.* MDCCCXLII. 12mo. + Third Edition, Revised. *Philadelphia.* 1843. 12mo. + Seventh Edition, Revised. *[Ibid.]* 1847. + Tenth Edition. *Philadelphia: Carey and Hart.* 1850. pp. 550. Portraits. B., C.

+ Sixteenth Edition. *Philadelphia: Parry & McMillan.* 1855. 8vo, pp. 622. 10 Portraits. C. + *[Ibid.]* 1856. pp. 620, (1). Portrait. H. + Seventeenth Edition, Revised. *[Ibid.]* 1856. Rl. 8vo, pp. 622. + New Edition, Revised, Enlarged, and brought down to the Present Time. *[Ibid.]* 1860. Rl. 8vo.

GRISWOLD. The Prose Writers of America, with a Survey of the ... History, Condition and Prospects of American Literature. By Rufus Wilmot Griswold. *Philadelphia: Carey & Hart.* 1847. 8vo, pp. 552. + Fourth Edition, Revised. *Philadelphia: A. Hart.* 1853. 8vo, pp. (2), 552. Plates. + *[Ibid.]* 1854. C. + *Philadelphia: Parry & McMillan.* 1857. pp. 552. + *Philadelphia: Porter & Coates.* 1870. pp. 669, (1). Plates. 28896

GRISWOLD. The Republican Court, or American Society in the Days of Washington. By Rufus Wilmot Griswold. With Twenty-One Portraits of Distinguished Women, engraved from Original Pictures by Woolaston, Copley, Gainsborough, Stuart, Trumbull, Pine, Malbone, and other Contemporary Painters. *New York: D. Appleton and Company.* M.DCCC.LV. Rl. 8vo, pp. iv, (4), 408. 21 Portraits. + New Edition. *[Ibid.]* M.DCCC.LVI. 8vo. C. + New and Revised Edition. *[Ibid.]* M.DCCC.LXI. Rl. 8vo, pp. iv, (4), 490, (1 l.) 25 Portraits. + *[Ibid.]* MDCCCLXVI. 28897

Also issued in twelve parts.

GRISWOLD. Sacred Poets of England and America, from the Earliest to the Present Time. A New Improved Edition. *New-York: D. Appleton & Co.* MDCCCXLIV. 8vo, pp. 552. Plate.

GRISWOLD. Statement of the Relations of Rufus W. Griswold with Charlotte Meyers [called Charlotte Griswold], Elizabeth F. Ellet, Ann S. Stephens, Samuel J. Waring, Hamilton R. Searles, and Charles D. Lewis, with particular reference to their late unsuccessful attempt to have set aside the Decree granted ... in the Case of Griswold *vs.* Griswold. *Philadelphia.* 1856. 8vo, pp. 32. 28899

Contains some very curious particulars in relation to this scandalous affair.

[GRISWOLD.] Washington and the Generals of the American Revolution. *Philadelphia: Carey & Hart.* 1847. 2 vols., 12mo, pp. 324; 336. 16 Portraits. 28900

Said to have been suppressed in consequence of a controversy concerning J. T. Headley's work with a similar title-page. Also: The Cypress Wreath: a Book of Consolation for those who Mourn. *Boston: Gould, Kendall & Lincoln.* 1844. 32mo, pp. 128. C.

[GRISWOLD (Rufus W.) *and* LOSSING (Benson J.)] Washington: A Biography: Personal, Military, and Political. *New York: Virtue & Co.* 1856–60. 3 vols., rl. 8vo, pp. vi, (1), 17–768; 4, 740; (4), 652. Plates. BA. 28901

GRISWOLD (S. O.) Speech of Hon. S. O. Griswold on the Resolutions relative to the Suspension of the Writ of Habeas Corpus and Arrest of Disloyal Persons. Delivered in the Ohio House of Representatives, January 29, 1863. [n. p. n. d.] 8vo, pp. 7. 28902

GRISWOLD (S.) Church and State: a Political Union, formed by the Enemies of both. Illustrated in Correspondence between the Rev. Stanley Griswold and the Rev. Dan Huntington, and between Col. Ephraim Kirby, and the Rev. Joseph Lyman. MDCCCII. 8vo, pp. 60. B., BA., N. 28903

GRISWOLD. A Discourse delivered at New Milford, October 12, 1800. By Stanley Griswold. *Bridgeport.* 1800. 8vo, pp. 31.

GRISWOLD. A Funeral Eulogium, pronounced at New-Milford on the Twenty-second of February, 1800; Being the day recommended by Congress for publicly testifying respect to the Memory of George Washington, ... By Stanley Griswold. ... *Printed at Litchfield, by T. Collier.* [1800.] 8vo, pp. 24. 28905

GRISWOLD. The Good Land we live in. A Sermon, delivered at Suffield, July 7, 1802. ... *Suffield.* 1802. 8vo, pp. 29.

GRISWOLD. Overcoming Evil with Good. A Sermon, delivered at Wallingford, Connecticut, March 11, 1801, before a numerous Collection of the Friends of the Constitution, of Thomas Jefferson, President, and of Aaron Burr, Vice-President of the United States. By Stanley Griswold, A.M., of New-Milford. *Hartford: Printed by Elisha Babcock.* 1801. 8vo, pp. 36. G. + *Suffield.* 1801. 12mo. 28907

GRISWOLD. A Statement of the Singular Manner of Proceeding of the Reverend Association of the South Part of Litchfield County. By Rev. Stanley Griswold. With an Address by Nehemiah Strong, Esq. *Hartford.* 1798. 8vo, pp. 32. M.

Also: Two Discourses on the Death of Rev. Nathanael Taylor. *Litchfield.* 1801. 8vo.

GRISWOLD (W.) Letter of Hon. Whiting Griswold, in reply to the Speech of Hon. Benjamin F. Butler, delivered at Lowell,

May 15, 1860, on the Proceedings of the Charleston Convention. *[Greenfield,] June* 8, 1860. 8vo, pp. 16. 28909

Also: Oration ... at the Firemen's Celebration in Greenfield, July 4, 1862. ... *[Greenfield.* 1862.] 8vo, pp. 8. — Speech ... before the Massachusetts Constitutional Convention, June 14, 1853, on the Subject of the Basis of the House of Representatives. [n. p. n. d.] 8vo, pp. 25. — Speech ... on ... loaning the Credit of the State to the Amount of Two Million Dollars ... for ... tunneling the Hoosac Mountain, ... April 9th and 11th, 1851. *[Boston: A. Forbes.* n. d.] 8vo, pp. 20.

GRISWOLD (W.) A Sermon ... January 1st, 1811, at the Dedication of the Presbyterian Meeting-House, in Hartwick, Otsego County ... New York. By Rev. Whiting Griswold. ... *Cooperstown, N. Y.: Printed by J. H. Prentiss.* 1815. 8vo, pp. 24.

GRISWOLD COLLEGE. ... The First Catalogue of Griswold College, Preparatory Department, 1859–60. *Davenport: Luse, Lane & Co.* 1860. 8vo, pp. 21, (1). Continued. 28911

Grizzly Jake; or, The White Tiger of the Woods and Prairies. By an Old Hunter. *New York: G. Munro & Co.* [1864.] 18mo, pp. 100. 28912

GROAM (R.) Political Inquiries; to which is added a General Plan for the Establishment of Schools throughout the United States. By Robert Groam. *Wilmington.* 1791. 8vo. 28913

The Groans of Jamaica, express'd in a Letter from a Gentleman residing there, to his Friend in London; containing a Clear Detection, and most Convincing Narrative of some of the Crying Grievances and Fraudulent Oppressions, which gave the first Rise to the present Growing Discontents and Animosities among the Inhabitants of that Island. As also Particular Characters of the chief Authors and Promoters of these Distractions. *London: Printed in the Year* 1714. 8vo, pp. viii, 48. 28914

Groans of the Plantations. *See* Vol. I., No. 3271.

See also McCulloch's "Literature of Political Economy," p. 87.

GROCER (J. R.) The Society of Friends. A Domestic Narrative, illustrating the Peculiar Doctrines of George Fox. By Mrs. J. R. Grocer. *New York.* 1853. 12mo. 28915

GROENWALL (And.) Dissertatio grad. de Platatione Ecclesiæ Svecanæ in Amerika. *Upsal.* 1731. 28916

GROESBECK (H. J.) Address delivered at the Second Anniversary Celebration of the Alpha Delta Phi Society of Miami University, August 10, 1837. By Herman J. Groesbeck. *Cincinnati.* 1837. 8vo, pp. 24. M. 28917

GROESBECK (W. S.) Speech of Hon. William S. Groesbeck, of Ohio, against the Admission of Kansas under the Lecompton Constitution. Delivered ... March 31, 1858. *Washington: Printed by Lemuel Towers.* 1858. 8vo, pp. 14. 28918

Also: Speech ... on Walker's Expedition to Nicaragua. ... January 11, 1858. *Washington: Printed by Lemuel Towers.* 1858. 8vo, pp. 15.

GRONE (C. von). Briefe über Nord-Amerika und Mexico, und den zwischen beiden geführten Krieg. Herausgegeben und mit einem Vorworte begleitet von A. C. E. von Grone. *Braunschweig.* 1850. 8vo. 28919

GRONEWEG (L.) Meteorological Observations made in Montgomery County, Southern Ohio, and a Condensed Treatise on Meteorology in general. By L. Groneweg. *Germantown, O.* 1856. 8vo, pp. 29. 28920

De Grondwet van de Vereenigde Staten van Noord-Amerika en van de Fransche Republyk, vertaald door R. Posthumus. *Leeuwarden.* 1850. 8vo, pp. 60. 28921

GRÖNLAND. *See* Greenland.

GRONNOIOSAW (J. A. U.) Narrative of the most Remarkable Particulars in the Life of James Albert Ukawsaw Gronnoiosaw, an African Prince. *Bath.* [n. d.] 12mo. 28922

Relates his long and perilous journey to the Coast of Guinea, his being sold and carried to New York, his situation there, etc.

GRONOVIUS (Johann Friedrich). Flora Virginica Exhibens Plantas quas V. C. Johannes Clayton In Virginia Observavit atque collegit. Easdem Methodo Sexuali disposuit, ad Genera propria retulit, Nominibus specificis insignivit, & minus cognitas descripsit Joh. Fred. Gronovius. Pars Prima. || Secunda. *Lugduni Batavorum, Apud Cornelium Haak.* 1743. 8vo, pp. (4), 128, (6); Title, pp. (4), 129–206, (4). 28923

Reprinted in 1762 with additions, as below:

GRONOVIUS. Flora Virginica exhibens Plantas, quas nobilissimus Vir D. D. Johannes Claytonus, Med. Doct. etc. etc. in Virginia Crescentes observavit, collegit & obtulit D. Joh. Fred. Gronovio, cujus studio & opera descriptæ & in ordinem sexualem systematicum radactæ sistuntur. *Lugduni Batavorum.* CIↃIↃCCLXII. 4to, pp. (12), 176, (8). Map. B., C., H., P. 28924

A valuable and correct work. *See* Jefferson's "Virginia," 276, and Rich's "Bib. Amer.," I. 73.

GRONOW (L.) State of the Accounts of Lewis Gronow, Esquire, late a Sub-Lieutenant of Chester County, From March 1777, to March 1780, ... *Philadelphia: Printed by Robert Aitken.* M. DCC. LXXXIII. 8vo, pp. 22. P. 28925

G[ROOME] (S.) A | Glass | For the People of | New-England, | in which | They may see themselves and Spirits, and | if not too late, Repent and Turn from their | Abominable Ways and Cursed Contrivances: | That so the Lord God may turn away his Wrath, | which he will bring upon them (if they Repent not) for | their Blasphemies against himself, and for all the Mur- | ders and Cruelties done to his tender People, ever since | they usurped Authority, to Banish, Hang, Whip, and | Cut Off Ears, and Spoil Goods of Dissenters from | them in Religious Matters, while themselves disown | Infallibility in those things. | By S. G. | *[London:] Printed in the Year*, 1676. | 4to, pp. 43. 28926

This rare tract contains curious extracts from a book called "The Elder Tenents in the Bay," also "Queries for the New England Priests by another hand," G[eorge] F[ox], and letters to Bellingham, and "Increase Madder," from Jno. Tyso, dated Boston, Prison-House.

GROOT (J. J.) Beknopt en getrouw Verhaal, van de Reys van Commandeur Jeldert Jansz Groot, uit Texel na en in Groenland etc. Deszelfs Verblyf op de Kust van Oud-Groenland, naa het Verongelukken van deszelfs onderhebbend Schip; tusschen Ysland en Staatenhoek. Voorgevallen in Ao. 1777 en 1778. *Amsterdam.* [1779.] 4to, pp. 16. 28927

This account of a voyage from Texel to and in Greenland, his sojourn in Old-Greenland, etc., is scarce.

GROOT (Jose M.) Los Misioneros de la Herejia. *Bogatá.* 1869. 28928

GROOT (Olaus de). Tooneel der Noordsche Landen met een korte beschryvingh van Yslandt en Groenlandt door Dithmarus Blefkenius, beyde uyt het Latijn vertaelt. *Amsterdam: Nicl. van Ravesteyn.* 1652. 8vo. 28929

The maps in this Dutch edition of the famous history of Olaus Magnus, are curious and valuable, especially the one of the North Polar regions. The addition of the important work of Blefkens on Greenland renders this altogether a desirable geographical volume on the high North.

Groot Placcaetboek inhoudende de Placaten ende Ordonnantien van de Staten van Holland en West-Vrieslandt. *s' Gravenb.* 1658–1796. 10 vols., folio. 28930

This great placard-book, containing all the ordonnances of the States General, and of the States of Holland and of Zealand, contains all the documents of public law relating to the West-India-Company, Brazil, etc., from 1581 to 1795.

Groote Schrijf-Almanach ... op het jaer 1641. Ghecalculeert door D. Origanus. *Amsterdam: C. L. van der Plasse.* 1641. 8vo.

This very rare Almanac contains "a memorable account of the discovery of the New World, not longer ago than one hundred and fifty years, by Christopher Columbus."

Het Groote Tafereel | der Dwaasheid, | vertoonende de opkomst, voortgang en ondergang der Actie, | Bubbel en Windnegotie, in Vrankryk, Engeland, en | de Nederlanden, gepleegt in dem | Jaare MDCCXX. | Zynde een Versameling van alle de | condities en projecten | van de opgeregte Compagnien van Assurantie, Navigatie, Commercie, &c. | in Nederland, zo wel die in gebruik zyn gebragt, als die door de | H. Staten van eenige Provintien zyn verworpen: | als meede | Konst-Plaaten | Comedien en Gedigten, | ... Gedrukt tot waarschouwinge voor de Nakomelingen, in't noodlottige Jaar, voor veel Zotte en Wyze, 1720. *[Amsterdam: D. Onder de Linden.]* 1720. Folio, Engraved Frontispiece, pp. 25, 52, 31, 8, 9. Portrait of John Law and 73 Plates. A., C. 28932

This great Theatre of Folly, representing the origin, progress, and downfall of the South Sea Bubble in France, England, and Holland, is an exceedingly curious collection of emblematical plates and caricatures on the scheme of J. Law and the Mississippi Company and the imitations of it in Holland, with their fatal results. Not a few of the scenes here depicted have been reproduced in the New York Exchange. The engravings, which illustrate the rise and fall of the great speculation, are full of humor; many of them are exceedingly ludicrous, and some very obscene. They are finely engraved on copper, and are accompanied with full descriptions in prose and poetry. So much offence was given to the English and French by this book that medals were struck by them in ridicule of the Dutch, which was perhaps the beginning of the hostility which long existed in the minds of the English against the latter. The number of the plates in copies varies from sixty to seventy-four.

De Groote Wonderlijcke Wereldt. *See* [Joosten (T. J.)]

GROS (J. D.) Natural Principles of Rectitude, for the Conduct of Man in all States and Situations of Life, Demonstrated and Explained in a Systematic Treatise on Moral Philosophy. By John Daniel Gros. *New York.* 1795. 8vo, pp. 456. C.

The first treatise on Moral Philosophy written and published in America.

The Gros Mosqueton Diplomatique. *See* [Cobbett (W.)]

[GROSE (Francis).] Advice to the Officers of the British Army: With the Addition of some Hints to the Drummer and Private Soldier. ... The Sixth Edition. *London: G. Kearsley.* MDCCLXXXIII. 12mo, pp. (6), iv, 134, (2). Plate. + Facsimile Reprint ... With Introduction and Notes. *New York: Agathynian Club.* 1867. 8vo. 28934

One hundred and twenty-three copies printed, three of which were on thin paper. It is an imitation of Swift's "Advice to Servants," which was probably derived from a German source, "Dedekindus de Morum Simplicitate." It refers to the officers the serving in New York.

GROSETT (J. R.) Remarks on West India Affairs. By J. R. Grosett, Esq., M.P. *London: Richardson.* 1824. 8vo, pp. 114. 28935

[GROSS (Charles H.)] A Reply to Horace Binney's Pamphlet on the Habeas Corpus. *Philadelphia.* 1862. 8vo, pp. 40.

GROSS (S. D.) A Discourse on the Life, Character, and Services of Daniel Drake, M.D. Delivered ... [at] Louisville, January 27, 1853. By S. D. Gross, M.D. *Louisville.* 1853. 8vo, pp. 92. BA. 28937

GROSS. Lives of Eminent American Physicians and Surgeons of the Nineteenth Century. Edited by Samuel D. Gross, ... *Philadelphia: Lindsay & Blakiston.* 1861. 8vo, pp. 836. Portrait. 28938

GROSS. Memoir of Valentine Mott, M.D. ... By S. D. Gross, M.D., LL.D. *New York: D. Appleton and Co.* 1868. 8vo, pp. 96. Portrait. H. 28939

Also: Report on the Causes which Retard the Progress of American Medical Literature. 1856. 8vo. *See* "Allibone's Dictionary."

GROSS (*Mr.*) Speech of Mr. Gross on the Missouri Question. *Washington.* 1820. 12mo. P. 28940

GROSS (W.) The Last Words and Dying Confession of William Gross, who was Executed February 7, 1823, for the Murder of Kesiah Stow. *Philadelphia.* 1823. 8vo, pp. 20.

GROSS-BRITANNISCHES AMERIKA. *See* [Oldmixon (John)].

[GROSSOURDY (Renato de).] El Médico botánico criollo. *Paris.* [n. d.] 28942

Parte primera: Floral medical y útil de las Antillas y de la parte correspondiente del Continente Americano. 2 vols., 8vo, pp. 426; 512. Parte segunda: Compendio de Terapéutica vejetal de las Antillas y de la parte correspondiente del Continente Americano. 2 vols., 8vo, pp. 416; 511.

GROSVENOR (C. P.) Address before the Anti-Slavery Society of Salem and the Vicinity, in the South Meeting House, in Salem, February 24th, 1834. By Cyrus Pitt Grosvenor. *Salem: W. & S. B. Ives.* 1834. 8vo, pp. 48. 28943

GROSVENOR. A Review of the "Correspondence" of Messrs. Fuller & Wayland on the Subject of American Slavery: By Cyrus Pitt Grosvenor. ... To which is added a Discourse, by

Roger Williams, Printed, London, 1652, on "The Hireling Ministry." *Utica, N. Y.: H. H. Curtiss, Printer.* 1847. 18mo, pp. 187. 28944

Also: National Blessings of Christians. [Thanksgiving] Discourse in the First Baptist Church, ... November 26, 1829. ... *Boston: Printed by True and Greene.* 1829. 8vo, pp. 15. B.—A Discourse. ... Second Baptist Church ... Salem, January 13, 1833. *Boston.* [1833.] 8vo, pp. 23.—Freedom's Defence: a Candid Examination of Mr. Calhoun's Report on the Freedom of the Press, made in the Senate of the United States, February 4, 1836. ... *Worcester.* 1836. 8vo.

GROSVENOR (D.) A Sermon ... at the Ordination of the Rev. Mr. Isaac Bailey, in Ward, November 3, MDCCLXXXIV. By Daniel Grosvenor, A.M. ... *Worcester: Printed by Isaiah Thomas.* MDCCLXXXV. 8vo, pp. 24. BA., W. 28945

GROSVENOR (D. A.) ... A Discourse occasioned by the Death of Mrs. Mary Harris Ely, ... March 4th, 1849. By David A. Grosvenor ... . *Cleveland: M. C. Younglove & Co.* 1849. 8vo, pp. 13. B. 28946

Also: A Discourse on the Death of Hon. Heman Ely ... Feb'y 8th, 1852. ... *Cleveland, Ohio: Sanford & Hayward's Press.* 1852. 8vo, pp. 22.

GROSVENOR (E.) A Sermon ... at the Ordination of the Rev. Mr. Daniel Grosvenor, ... Grafton, October 19, 1774. By Ebenezer Grosvenor, A.M. ... *Boston: Printed by Thomas and John Fleet.* 1774. 8vo, pp. 31. M., W. 28947

GROSVENOR (L.) ... Address before the Sigma Phi Society of Illinois College, at Anniversary, July 12, 1848. By Rev. L. Grosvenor. *St. Louis: Brewster & Casamayou.* 1848. 8vo, pp. 16. B. 28948

GROSVENOR. History of the First Congregational Church and Society, of Woodstock, Conn. By L. Grosvenor. *Worcester.* 1860. 8vo, pp. 28. S. W. 28949

GROSVENOR. The Life and Character of Major-General Putnam. An Address delivered at a Meeting of the Descendants of Major-General Israel Putnam, at Putnam, Conn., October 25, 1855. By L. Grosvenor. *Boston: Farwell & Co.* 1855. 8vo, pp. 37. B. 28950

"An important tract, recording much biographical material, and planting many genealogical trees of the Putnam families. Old Put's right position at the Battle of Bunker's Hill is defined and fortified."—HENRY STEVENS.

GROSVENOR (L. D.) America, the "Land of Emanuel." Constitutional Liberty a Refuge for the Gathering to Shiloh. By Lorenzo D. Grosvenor ... . [*Boston.* n. d.] 8vo, pp. 8.

GROSVENOR (T. P.) An Oration, delivered in ... Hudson, on the 4th of July, 1808. [With Explanatory Notes.] By Thomas P. Grosvenor, Esq. *Hudson.* 1808. 8vo, pp. 80.

GROSVENOR. A Sketch of the Life, last Sickness and Death, of Mrs. Mary Jane Grosvenor. Left among the Papers of the Late Hon. Thomas P. Grosvenor. Second Edition. ... *Baltimore: Edward J. Coale.* 1817. 16mo, pp. 86. 28953

GROSVENOR (W. M.) The Rights of the Nation, and the Duty of Congress. By Col. W. M. Grosvenor, New Haven, Conn. ... 1865. [n. p. n. d.] 8vo, pp. 23. 28954

GROTE (A. R.) Notes on the Sphingidæ of Cuba. By Augustus Radcliffe Grote, Curator of Entomology, Buffalo Society of Natural Sciences. *Philadelphia: Entomological Society.* 1865. 8vo, pp. 52. Colored Plates. 28955

GROTIUS (H.) Annales et Historiae de Rebus Belgicis, 1566–1609. *Amsterdam: Joannis Blaue.* M DC LVIII. 24mo, 8 l., pp. 812, 16 l. H. 28956

"Important for the history of the events which impeded the execution of Usselincx's plan to form the East- and West-India Companies, from 1591–1609."—F. MULLER.

GROTIUS. Hugonis Grotii de Origine Gentium Americanarum dissertatio. *Amsterdam.* 1642. 8vo. + [*Paris.*] 1642. 8vo, pp. 15. + [n. p.] 1642. Sm. 4to. + *Paris: G. Pele.* 1643.

Another edition was included in Albinus (P.) Commentatio de linguis peregrinis atque insulis ignotis ed. S. Cnauthius. *Vitemb.* 1714. 8vo. The New York Historical Society Catalogue places under the name of Grotius: Dissertatio altera de Origine Gentium Americanarum, adversus obtrectatorem, opaca quem bonum facit barba. [*Paris: Carmoisy.*] 1643. 8vo, pp. 30. For a refutation of this work *see infra* Horn (G.) and Laet (J. de).

GROTIUS, *pseudon.* Pills for the Delegates; or the Chairman Chastised, in a Series of Letters addressed to Peyton Randolph, Esq.; on his Conduct as President of the General Congress: held at the City of Philadelphia, September 5, 1774. By Grotius. Originally published in the "Massachusetts Gazette," and now first collected. *New York: Printed by James Rivington.* 1775. 8vo, pp. 32. 28958

GROTIUS, *pseudon.* *See* [Clinton (De Witt)], Vol. IV.

GROTON, [*Mass.*] An Act of the Commonwealth of Massachusetts, A.D. 1827, to provide for the Instruction of Youth; together with the By-Laws of the Town of Groton, in Relation to Schools. *Boston: Christian Register Office.* 1828. 8vo, pp. 22. Continued. H. 28959

Bye-Laws of Groton, relative to Schools; and Instructions of the School Committee, 1805. *Cambridge: Printed by William Hilliard.* 1806. 8vo, pp. 12, 3. + *Boston.* 1828. + By-Laws ... reported April 7, 1856. *Groton.* 1856. 8vo, pp. 9. M.

Catalogue of the Groton Public Library, with By-Laws. *Groton: Geo. H. Brown.* 1855. 12mo, pp. 26. B. + *Groton Junction: Henry L. Brown.* 1862. 8vo, pp. 53. + 1868. 8vo. B.

Catalogue of the First Parish Library, Groton, instituted 1841. *Lowell: Stearns & Taylor.* 1844. 12mo, pp. 12. 28962

Catalogue of the Congregational Library of the Union Church and Society, Groton. [n. d.] 16mo, pp. 16. 28963

Catalogue of the Officers and Students of Groton Academy. *Groton.* 1843. 8vo, pp. 16. 28964

A Collection of Facts and Documents relating to Ecclesiastical Affairs in Groton, Mass., occasioned by the publication of the "Result of an Ecclesiastical Council Convened at Groton, Massachusetts, July 17, 1826." And intended to correct misstatements made, and supply material Facts, suppressed by the Authors of the Result. [By Caleb Butler.] *Boston: Stephen Foster, Printer.* 1827. 8vo, pp. vi, 44. C., H., W. 28965

Constitution and By-Laws of the Groton Invincible Club, founded 1843. *Groton, Mass.* 1846. 12mo, pp. 18, (2). B., P.

Covenant of the First Church, Groton, Mass., as adopted July 23, 1826. *Groton.* [n. d.] 12mo, pp. 9. M. 28967

Expenditures of the Town of Groton, for the Year ending February 28, 1850. *Groton.* 1850. Folio, 1 l. 28968

Extracts from the Revised Statutes, Ch. XXIII.; with the By-Laws of the Town in relation to Schools. *Lowell.* 1837. 8vo, pp. 17. 28969

Groton Soapstone Quarry and Manufactory. Statement regarding Property, Location, Value, etc. *Boston: Printed by Alfred Mudge & Son.* 1864. 8vo, pp. 16. 28970

Receipts and Expenditures of the Town of Groton, for the Year 1861. *Groton Junction.* 1861. 8vo. S. 28971

Report of a Committee of the Town of Groton, appointed ... November, 1855, to consider the Expediency of Establishing a High School. *Boston: William White.* 1856. 8vo, pp. 15. M.

The Annual Report of the School Committee of the Town of Groton, for the Year 1841–42. *Lowell: S. O. Dearborn.* 1842. 12mo, pp. 10. Continued. 28973

Report of the Selectmen, Overseers of Poor ... of the Town of Groton, for ... 1859. [n. p. n. d.] 8vo, pp. 15. Continued.

Report of the Superintending School Committee. 1855–56. 8vo, pp. 7. Continued. 28975

The Rights of the Congregational Churches of Massachusetts. ... The Result of an Ecclesiastical Council convened at Groton, Mass., July 17, 1826. ... *Boston: T. R. Marvin.* 1827. 8vo, pp. 63. + From the Christian Examiner. *Boston: Bowles and Dearborn.* 1827. 8vo, pp. 32. + Second Edition. *Boston: Bowles and Dearborn.* 1827. 8vo, pp. 36. + [Another] Second Edition. [*Ibid.*] pp. 47. 28976

For a review of the above *see* [Lowell (J.)]

The Group. *See* [Warren (Mrs. Mary)].

The Group; or, an Elegant Representation Illustrated. *Philadelphia: T. Stephens.* 1796. 4to, pp. 35. 28977

GROUT (J.) Sermon at Cummington, [Mass.] March, 1811. By Jonathan Grout. *Northampton.* 1812. 8vo. W. 28978

Also: Song of Zion: a Sermon preached at Cummington, Mass. ... *Northampton.* 1825. 8vo.

GROUT (H. M.) Commemorative of Hon. Edward Southworth ... December 11, 1869. Prepared by Rev. Henry M. Grout ... . *Springfield: Samuel Bowles and Company.* 1870. 8vo, pp. 38. Portrait. 28979

GROUT (W. W.) An Oration before the Re-union Society of Vermont Officers, ... November 4, 1869. By Gen. William W. Grout. ... *Rutland: Tuttle & Co.* 1869. 8vo, pp. 29. H.

GROUVEL. Faits historiques sur Saint-Domingue, depuis 1786 jusqu'en 1805, et résultats des moyens employés par les Colons de la partie de l'Ouest pour s'opposer à l'entière dévastation de l'île, ainsi que de ceux mis en usage par les Anglais, en 1796–98, pour la soumettre à leur domination. Par Grouvel. *Paris: Delaunay.* 1814. 8vo, pp. 151. 28981

Leclerc describes a copy with "2 brochures supplémentaires que l'auteur fit paraître la même année et qui manquent presque toujours."

GROUX (D. E.) Description of the Franklin Medallion, struck for the Inauguration of the Statue of Franklin, Boston, September 17, 1856. By Daniel E. Groux. *Boston.* 1856. 8vo, pp. 4. Plate. 28982

GROUX. Prospectus of an Important Work in Three Volumes, to be called Numismatical History of the United States ... By Professor Daniel E. Groux. *Boston.* 8vo, pp. 16. 28983

GROULX (L. T.) Epitre à Son Altesse Royale le Prince de Galles. [n. p.] 1860. pp. 40. 28984

Also: Epitre à Son Altesse Royale le Prince Alfred Ernest Albert, en visite au Canada. [n. p.] 1860. pp. 19.

GROVE (J. P.) Life and Reminiscences, with Early Sketches of John S. Moseby. Late Lieutenant Colonel in the Rebel Army. By James P. Grove. Urbana, Ohio. [n. p. n. d.]

GROVE (Joseph). *See* Bishope (George).

GROVE (*Miss*). Little Grace; or Scenes in Nova Scotia. By Miss Grove. *Halifax.* 1846. 8vo, pp. 178. 28986

GROVE (*Mr.*) A Letter to a Right Honorable Patriot; Upon the Glorious Success at Quebec. In which is drawn a parallel, between a good and a bad General, a scene exhibited, wherein are introduced (besides others), three of the Greatest Names in Britain; and a Particular Account of the Manner of General Wolfe's Death. ... By Mr. Grove of Richmond. *London: J. Burd.* MDCCLIX. 8vo, pp. (1), 58. C., P. 28987

See "M. Rev.," Second Series, XXI. 536.

GROVELAND. Annual Report of the Auditors of the Town of Groveland, ... 1869. *Haverhill: E. G. Frothingham.* 1869. 8vo, pp. 16. 28988

GROVER (L.) The Oregon Archives, including the Journals, Governor's Messages and Public Papers of Oregon, from the earliest Attempt on the Part of the People to form a Government, down to, and inclusive of the Session of the Territorial Legislature, held in the Year 1849. ... By La Fayette Grover. ... *Salem.* 1853. 8vo. 28989

GROVER (M.) Speech of Mr. Grover, of New York, on the Oregon Question. Delivered in the House of Representatives,

Monday, January 26, 1846. *Washington: Blair & Rives.* 1846. 8vo, pp. 8. 28990

Also: Speech ... on the Wilmot Proviso .. January 7, 1847. *Washington: Blair and Rives.* 1847. 8vo, pp. 8. B., S.

GROVER (W.) Biographical Memoir of William Grover; with Selections from his Letters and other Papers. *Philadelphia.* 1831. 12mo. 28991

GROVES (R.) Gleanings: or, A Collection of some Memorable Passages, both Antient and Moderne. By Robert Groves. Second Edition. *London: Printed by R. I.* M DC LI. 8vo, pp. (6), 163 [179], (10). B. 28992

A curious and amusing volume, full of witty and humorous sayings; it contains, also, short accounts of Mrs. Hutchinson and Mrs. Dyer, of Boston, fearful monsters, and other notices relating to America. *See* pp. 24, 106.

GROW (Galusha A.) Admission of Kansas. Speech of Hon. G. A. Grow, of Pennsylvania, in the House ... June 30, 1856, on ... the Admission of Kansas into the Union ... . [n. p. n. d.] 8vo, pp. 8. 28993

GROW. ... Free Homes for Free Men. Speech of Hon. G. A. Grow, ... February 29, 1860. [n. p. n. d.] 8vo, pp. 8.

GROW. Land for the Landless. Speech of Hon. G. A. Grow, of Pennsylvania, in the House of Representatives, February 29, 1860. 8vo, pp. 14. 28995

"Tribune Tracts," No. 5.

GROW. Remarks ... December 1, 1856, on the Question of administering the Oath of Office to John W. Whitfield as Delegate from Kansas Territory. [*Washington: Buell & Blanchard.*] 1856. 8vo, pp. 7. 28996

GROW. Responsibility for Organizing the House, and for the Defeat of the Post Office Appropriation Bill. Remarks of Hon. Galusha A. Grow ... 1859. [n. p. n. d.] 8vo, pp. 8. 28997

Also: Kansas—The Lecompton Constitution. Speech ... in the House of Representatives, March 25, 1858. [n. p. n. d.] 8vo, pp. 8. H.—Nebraska and Kansas. Speech ... May 10, 1854. [n. p. n. d.] 8vo, pp. 8.— ... Speech ... March 30, 1852, on the Homestead Bill. [n. p. n. d.] 8vo, pp. 8.—Speech ... February 21, 1854, on the Homestead Bill. [n. p. n. d.] 8vo, pp. 7. B.

The Growth of New York. *New York: Geo. W. Wood.* 1865. 8vo, pp. 49. 28998

GRUBE (A. W.) Abraham Lincoln, der grosse Staatsman und edle Menschenfreund. Eine biographische Skizze. Von August Wilhelm Grube. *Stuttgart: J. F. Steinkopf.* 1868. 16mo, pp. 130. Plate. B. 28999

GRUBER (J.) Trial of Jacob Gruber, Minister of the Methodist Episcopal Church. Reported by James Martin. *Fredericktown.* 1819. 16mo. 29000

GRUBER (J. G.) Beschreibung von Grönland und Spitzbergen mit den Wundern der Natur und Menschenwelt um den Nordpol. *Zürich und Leipzig.* 1803. 4to. 3 Maps, 5 Plates.

GRUMBLER, *pseudon.* *See* [Hoffman (D.)]

GRUND (F. J.) The Americans in their Moral, Social, and Political Relations. By Francis J. Grund. *London: Longman & Co.* MDCCCXXXVII. 2 vols., 8vo, pp. viii, 365; iv, 418. + *Boston.* 1837. 12mo, pp. 423. C. 29002

See Rich, Vol. II. 289; also, "North American Review," Vol. XLVI. 106.

GRUND. Die Amerikaner in ihren moralischen, politischen und gesellschaftlichen Verhältnissen. In's Deutsche übersetzt vom Verfasser. *Stuttgart und Tübingen: J. G. Cotta.* 1837. 8vo, 4 l., pp. 444. C. 29003

GRUND. Aristocracy in America. From the Sketch-Book of a German Nobleman. Edited by Francis J. Grund. ... *London: Richard Bentley.* 1839. 2 vols., post 8vo, pp. xii, 319; vii, 331. 2 Portraits. 29004

Highly commended by the "North American Review." "We assume this work to be written by Mr. Grund, though he is professedly only the editor. He has given two whole volumes of sketches of manners, but the vast majority are caricatures without point, truth, or even vraisemblance."—*Athenæum*, 1839, p. 947. *See* Rich, II. 289.

GRUND. Die Aristokratie in Amerika. ... *Stuttgart.* 1839. 2 vols., 8vo, pp. (4), 223; 240. 2 Portraits. S. 29005

GRUND. Aufruf an die deutschen Wähler. General Harrison's Leben und Wirken. *Philadelphia: C. F. Stollmeyer.* 1840. 8vo, pp. 30. 3 Plates. 29006

GRUND. Handbuch und Wegweiser für Auswanderer nach den Vereinigten Staaten von Nord-Amerika. *Stuttgart und Tübingen: J. G. Cotta.* 1843. 8vo, pp. 251. Map. 29007

GRUND. Martin Van Buren als Staatsman und künftiger Präsident der Vereinigten Staaten von Nord-Amerika. [n. p.] 1835. 8vo, pp. 29. B., M. + *Boston.* 1835. 8vo, pp. viii, 29. H., S.

Grund. Thoughts and Reflections on the present Position of Europe, and its probable Consequences to the United States. *Philadelphia: Childs & Peterson.* 1860. 12mo, pp. iv, ii, 5–245.

Also: Grund's Speech from the "North American." *Union League of Philadelphia.* [n. d.] Mr. Grund was for some years the editor of the Philadelphia "Ledger."

Gründliche | An- und Aufforderung | an die | Ehmahlig erweckte hier und dar zerstreuete | Seelen dieses Landes, | In oder ausser Partheyen, | zur | Neuen Umfassung, | Gliedlicher Vereinigung, | und | Gebets-Gemeinschaft; | Dargelegt aus dringendem Herzen eines um Heilung | der Brüche Zions ängstlich bekümmerten Gemüths, | im Jahr 1736. | *Philadelphia,* | *Gedruckt und zu haben* | *bey B. Franklin,* | M DCC XLII. | 4to, pp. 14. 29010

Gründlicher Bericht von Beschaffenheit und Eigenschaft, Cultivirung und Bewohnung, Privilegien und Benificien Dess in Amerika Zwischen dem Rio Orinoque und Rio de la Amazones an der vesten Küst in der Landschafft Guiana gelegenen, sich dreissig Meil wegs breit an der See und hundert Meil wegs in der Tieffe erstreckenden Strich Landes, Welchen Die Edle privilegirte West-Indischen Compagnie der vereinigten Niederlanden, mit Authentischer Schrifftlicher Ratification und Permission Der Hochvermögenden Herren Staten General An den Hochgebohrnen, gegenwertig regirenden Herrn, Herrn Friederich Casimir, Grafen zu Hanaw, Rieneck, Zweybrücken, Herrn zu Müntzenburg, Liechtenberg und Ochsenstein, ... wie auch an das gesämptliche Hochgräft Hauss von Hanaw, mit allen Regalien und Jurisdictionen, ewig und erblich, unter gewissen in dieser Deduction publicirten Articular den 18 Julii 1669 cedirt und überlassen hat. *Franckfurt, bey Johan Kuchenbecker, Anno* 1669. 4to. Map of Guiana. 29011

This is a report on the state of the country, situated between the Orinoco and the Amazon, which the West India Company of the United Netherlands ceded to the Count of Hanau, on the 18th July, 1669. It was distributed gratuitously among the German peasantry to induce them to emigrate to Guiana.

Grundriss von Nordamerika, entworfen von I. N. C. B. *Hamburg, in der Möllerschen Buchhandlung.* 1778. 8vo. 29012

Grundverfassung der evangelischen-lutherischen General-Synode in den Vereinigten Staaten von Nord-Amerika, nebst dem Protokoll der Versammlung die sie entworfen. *Baltimore.* [1820.] 8vo. 29013

Grundy (Felix). Speech of Mr. Grundy, of Tennessee, on ... Abolishing the Office of Surveyor-General of Public Lands,

... Delivered ... February 29, 1830. *Washington: Printed by Duff Green.* 1830. 8vo, pp. 16. B. 29014

Grundy. Speech of Mr. Grundy. ... In the Senate of the United States on the 4th and 5th of March, 1840 ... against the Assumption, by the General Government, of the States' Debts, contracted for Local Internal Improvements ... . [n. p. n. d.] 8vo, pp. 16. H. 29015

Grundy. Speech of Mr. Grundy, ... on the ... Protest of the President of the United States. [n. p. 1834.] 8vo, pp. 8.

Also: Speeches of Hon. Mr. Grundy ... and the Hon. Mr. Yancey. ... 1813, on Mr. Webster's Resolutions. *Baltimore: E. French & Co.* 8vo, pp. 16.—Speech ... on Public Lands, 1840.—Speech ... on the Tariff. ... February 15, 1832. ... *Washington.* 1832. 8vo, pp. 27. B.—Speech ... on the Removal of the Public Deposites. *Washington.* 1834. 8vo.

Grundy (R. C.) The Temporal Power of the Pope Dangerous to the Religious and Civil Liberties of the American Republic: delivered in Maysville, Ky., ... February 11, 1855. By ... Rev. Robert C. Grundy, D.D. *Maysville, Ky.* 1855. 8vo, pp. 13. H. 29017

Gryalva (J. de). *See* Grijalva (J.)

Gryneus (Simon). *See* [Huttich (John)].

Guadalajara (J. E.) Oracion panegirici en la titular de la S. Veracruz. *Mejico.* 1834. 4to, 10 l. 29018

Guadalajara. Carta Pastoral que el Illmo. Sr. Obispo de Guadalajara dirige a sus Diocesanos, con motivo de la Ley penal publicada en Zacatecas en 16 de Junio del presente año de 1859. *Guadalajara.* 1859. 4to, pp. 15. 29019

This pastoral letter is a valuable contribution towards the history of the civil war in Mexico. It is directed against the laws decreed by Gonzales Ortega (of Juarez party), ordering capital punishment on all priests, "que, ante uno ó mas testigos, exijan retractacion del juramento de la constitucion de 1857," etc.

Circular a todos los Sacerdotes de la Diocesis Gobierno eclesiastico de Guadalajara. *Guadalajara.* 1859. 8vo, pp. 16. [Colophon:] *Guadalajara, Julio 19 de 1859. Pedro. Obispo de Guadalajara.* 29020

Containing the protest of the Bishop of Guadalajara against the laws of the "Gobierno del Estado de Zacatecas," dated July 2d, 1859.

Coleccion de documentos relativos á la conducta del Cabildo eclesiastico de la Diocesi de Guadalaxara y del clero misma, en

cuanto á reusar el juramento de la segunda parte del articulo setimo de la Constitucion del Estado libre de Jalisco. [n. p.] 1825. 4to, pp. 136. 29021

Consulta del Cabildo Eclesiastico de Guadalajara. *Imprenta de Rodriguez.* 1849. 8vo. 29022

Contestacion del Comisionado por el Ven. Cabildo de Guadalajara a las Observaciones de los del Hon. Congreso de Zacatecas. sobre administracion de Diezmos. *Guadalajara.* 1831. 4to.

Defensa del Cabildo eclesiastico de Guadalajara, contra el informe que ha hecho en ofensa suya la junta directiva de diezmos y el gobierno civil de Jalisco. *Mexico.* 1827. 4to, pp. 41.

Elogios Fúnebres con que la Santa Iglesia Catedral de Guadalaxara ha celebrado la Buena Memoria del Fr. Antonio Alcade. *Guadalaxara.* 1793. 4to. 29025

Esposicion del Sr. Gobernador de la Mitra sobre la esclusiva concedida al Gobierno. *Guadalaxara.* 1826. 4to, pp. 36.

Fundacion y Descripcion de la Santa Iglesia Catedral de Guadalajara. *Mexico.* 1852. 29027

Real Cedula de ereccion del Consulado de Guadalaxara, expedida en Aranjuez a 6. de Junio de 1795. *Guadalajara.* 1795. Folio, pp. 50. 29028

Real Cedula de S. M. y Señores del Real y Supremo Consejo de las Indias, por la qual se aprueban las Constituciones formadas para la direccion y gobierno de la Real Universidad literaria de Guadalaxara, capital de la Nueva-Galicia. [n. p.] 1816. Folio, 56 l. 29029

Representacion de la junto de Fomento de Comercio de Guadalajara, en que promueve la libertad del Tobaco en el Estado de Jalisco. *Guadalajara.* 1852. 29030

Representacion que los eclesiasticos de Guadalajara diriges al soberano congreso constituyente, etc. [Por M. España.] *Guadalajara.* 1856. 8vo. 29031

Representacion que los eclesiasticos de Guadalajara dirigen al Congreso Constituyente, sobre que en la Carta Fundamental que se discute, no quede consignada la tolerancia de cultos en la Republica. *Guadalajara.* 1846. 4to, pp. 18. 29032

Guadalaxara (N.) Relacion de la Exemplar, y Religiosa Vida del Padre Nicolas de Guadalaxara, Professo de Nuestra Compañia de Jesus, á los Rev. Padre y Charissimos Hermanos de la V. y Religiosa Provincia de Nueva España. *Mexico.* 1684. 4to. 29033

Guadaloupe: A Tale of Love and War. By One who served in the late War with Mexico. *Philadelphia: J. B. Smith & Co.* 1860. 12mo, pp. 156. Plate. 29034

Guadalupe (A. de). Historia de la Santa Provincia de los Angeles de la regular observancia y orden de nuestro serafico San Francisco. Por Fray Andres de Guadalupe, Comissario General de las Indias ... *Madrid, M. Fernandez.* 1662. Folio. Frontispiece and large folded Plate. 29035

The author was a native of the province whose history he writes; being also a *padre* or priest, he jokes upon this circumstance in the title, by calling himself *hijo y padre de mesma provincia.*

Guadalupe. Breve Ragguaglio della prodigiosa e rinomata immagine della donna di Guadalupe del Messico. *Cesena: G. Biasini.* 1782. 8vo, pp. xxxix. 29036

Guadalupe Ramirez. *See* Ramirez (G.)

Guadeloupe. Almanach de la Guadeloupe et dépendance. 1822. *Basse-Terre Guadeloupe.* 1822. 8vo. Continued.

Candid Answer to a Pamphlet called Reasons for keeping Guadaloupe at a Peace, etc. *London.* 1761. 29038

Title from an auction catalogue. *See* Vol. v., No. 19779; *also*, Reasons.

Conseil de la Guadeloupe. *Pointe-à-Pitre.* 1837. 8vo.

Desastres de la Guadeloupe, et Précis Historique sur la Pointe-à-Pitre. *Paris.* 1843. 12mo, pp. 12. 29040

Genuine Account. *See* Vol. vii., No. 26960.

La Guadeloupe, Basse-Terre, la Soufrière, Pointe-à-Pitre, Histoire, Description. Catastrophe du 8 Février. *Paris.* 1843. 18mo, pp. 72. 2 Maps and Plates. 29041

Mémoire pour le chef de Brigade Magloire Pelage et pour les habitants de la Guadeloupe chargés par cette colonie, de l'administration provisoire après le depart du Capitaine-General Lacrosse, dans le mois de Brumaire an X. *Paris.* 1803. 2 vols., 8vo.

Reasons for not restoring Guadaloupe at a Peace. In a Letter ... to the ... Earl of Hallifax, ... In answer to certain Animadversions contained in a Letter to Two Great Men. *London: Williams.* 1760. 8vo, pp. 46. M. 29043

See "M. Rev.," xxii. 165.

Reasons for keeping Guadaloupe at a Peace, preferable to Canada, explained in Five Letters from a Gentleman in Guadaloupe, to his Friend in London. *London: M. Cooper.* M. DCC.-LXI. 8vo, pp. 79. 29044

The writer thinks that it is more desirable that Great Britain should retain Guadaloupe than Canada. The former, he thinks, can furnish as much sugar, cotton, rum, and coffee, as all the islands we have put together, and consume a vast quantity of British goods, while the latter can yield but little extension of the fur trade. He thinks, too, that if the French are permitted to hold Canada, they will be a check upon the British colonies and prevent a revolt, an event which he thought very distant. *See* "Monthly Review," Vol. xxiv., p. 440.

Guaireño (A.) Flores de Mar ó Aguinaldo Guaireño. *Carácas.* 1854. 8vo, pp. 15. + *Carácas.* 1855. 8vo, pp. 26. + *Carácas.* 1856. 8vo, pp. 24. 29045

Gual i Jean (Ricardo). Biografia, el Jeneral San Martin. *Londres* 1823. 8vo. M. 29046

[Gualberto de Ortega (Juan).] À los Cubanos. [*Philadelphia.* 1825?] 8vo, pp. 7. B. 29047

Gualdi (P.) Monumentos de Mejico tomados del natural y lithographiados. *Mejico.* 1841. Folio. 12 Plates. 29048

Gualdo (Diego de). Arte de la Lengua Aymara, con una silva de sus frases i su declaracion. *Chicuitu* 1612. 8vo.

See Barcia-Pinelo, and Ternaux, No 349.

Gualterotti (R.) L'America, de Raffael Gualterotti. *Firenze: Giunti.* 1611. 18mo, 14 l. 29050

A poetical piece in one hundred and four octaves. Amerigo Vespucci is the hero. It was reprinted with Stagio Dati, *Firenze*, 1859, and *Milan*, 1865. 8vo.

Guamanga, *Peru.* Constituciones para la Diocesis en el Peru. *Lima.* 1795. 4to. 29051

Guanajuato. Actos administrativos del Gobernador de Guanajuato, D. Lorenzo Arellano, contados por dos perros. *Mexico.* 1848. Sm. 4to, pp. 34. 29052

Constitucion Politica del estado libre de Guanajuato. Sancionada 14 Ab. 1826. *Mexico.* 1826. 12mo, pp. 82. S. 29053

Guano. Account of the Manure Guano, with Instructions for Using it, etc. *Liverpool.* 1843. 8vo. 29054

Guano, its Origin, Properties and Uses ... . *New-York: Wiley and Putnam.* 184–. 8vo, pp. 80. B. + Second Edition, with an Appendix. [*Ibid.*] 1845. 8vo, pp. 92. BA. + *New Bedford.*

Report of the United States Guano Company. *New York.* 1859. 8vo, pp. 40. S. 29056

Statements made in Congress, on the Duty on Importation of Peruvian Guano. [n. p. n. d.] 8vo. 29057

Guard (Theodore de la). *See* [Ward (Nathaniel).]

G[uardia] (H[eraclio] M[artin] de la). Oda á la desventurada Cumaná. *Caracás.* 1853. 8vo, pp. 17. 29058

Also: Güelfos y Gibelinos, Dramá en cuatro actos. *Caracás.* 1859. 8vo, pp. 60.—Don Fadrique, Gran Maestre de Santiago. Drama en 4 actos y en verso. *Caracás.* 1863. 8vo, pp. 64.

Guardia (J.) Les Républiques de l'Amérique espagnole. *Paris: L. Hachette et Cie.* 1862. 8vo, pp. 61. B. 29059

The Guardian; or Youth's Religious Instructor. *New Haven.* 1819–20. 2 vols., 12mo. S. 29060

Continued as the "Guardian and Monitor."

First Annual Report of the "Guardian for Friendless Girls," ... May, 1855. [By John T. Sargent.] *Boston: Printed by Prentiss and Sawyer.* 1855. 8vo, pp. 24. H. 29061

The Guardian Genius of the Federal Union; or Patriotic Admonitions on the Signs of the Times, in relation to the evil spirit of party, arising from the Root of all our Evils—Human Slavery. By a Philanthropist. [Julius R. Ames.] *New York.* 1839. 12mo, pp. 103. + [*Ibid.*] 1842. P. 29062

Guareña (J. B.) La Mayor Gloria y felicidad de Cantabria baxo la proteccion de Maria Sant. en su soberana imágen de Aranzazu: panegirei artificial. *Guadalaxara.* 1797. 4to, pp. (8), 38. 29063

Guatemala. Almanaque para el año de 1837, arreglado al meridiano de Guatemala. *Guatemala.* 1837. 18mo, 40 l. Continued. 29064

Aranceles formados de orden de la Real Audiencia del Reyno de Guatemala, para el mejor gobierno de sus ministros subalternos,

en virtud de Reales Cedulas. *Guatemala de la Asuncion.* [1779.] Folio. 29065

Arancel provisional para las aduanas de Guatemala. *Guatemala.* 1822. Folio, 8 l. 29066

El Banco de Guatemala. [n. p. n. d.] 12mo, pp. 36.

Die Belgischen Colonien in Guatemala und Brasilien. *Cöln.* 1844. 8vo. 29068

Brief Statement, supported by Original Documents of the Important Grants conceded to the Eastern Coast of Central America Commercial and Agricultural Company, by the State of Guatemala. *London: Whittaker & Co.* 1839. 8vo, pp. 132. 2 Maps.

Calendario de Guatemala, para el año de 1842. *Sucre, Castillo.* 12mo, pp. 24. Continued. 29070

Catalogo de los Individuos que componen la Real Sociedad de amantes de la Patria de Guatemala en el Año de 1799. [n. p. n. d.] 29071

Coleccion de documentos antiguos del archivo del ayuntamicuto de la ciudad de Guatemala, formado por su secretario D. Rafael de Arevalo. *Guatemala.* 1857. 4to. 29072

Decretos del Gefe del Estado [Agustin Prado], Mar. 1827. *Guatemala.* 1827. Folio, 1 l. M. 29073

Dissertacion canonica sobre los justos motivos que representa el Reyno de Guatemala, para que el consejo se sirva de erigir en Metropoli Eclesiastica la Sta. Iglesia Catedral de la Ciudad de Santiago su Cabeza. [n. p. n. d.] Folio, pp. 36. 29074

Estado politico de Guatemala. Derrota del general Morazan. *Mexico.* 1840. 8vo. 29075

Estado del Hospital Gral de S. Juan de Dios de Guatemala del Año de 1826. *Guatemala.* [1826.] M. 29076

Extracto, ô Relacion Methodica, y Puntual de los autos de reconocimiento, practicada en virtud de Comission del Señor Presidente de la Real audiencia de este Reino de Guatemala. *Impressa con Superior permiso en la Officina de D. Antonio Sanchez Cabillas en el Pueblo de Mixco en el Casa que Claman de Comunidad de Santo Domingo. Año de* 1774. Folio, pp. (2), 86. 29077

Gazeta de Guatemala, de 1797. [*Guatemala.*] 1779. 4to.

Continued to 1807, or later. Important for the history and geography of Central America.

El Gefe del Estado [Mariano Aycinena] a los Pueblos de su Mando. [*Guatemala.* 1827.] Folio, 1 l. M. 29079

Guatemala; Geographical, Historical and Topographical. *London.* 1835. 29080

Forms Vol. xxvi. of Conder's "Modern Traveller."

Guatemala por Fernando Septimo el dia 12 de Diciembre de 1808. [*Guatemala.* 1809.] 4to, pp. 166, Oracion Eucaristica que pronunció el Dr. D. Sicilia y Montoya, ... pp. (3), 19. 21 Plates.

This rare volume relates to the fetes at the City of Guatemala on the accession of Ferdinand vii. to the throne. The plates are well executed.

El Indicador. 1824–1827. *Guatemala.* 1824–27. 29082

Informe de Guatemala sobre la ereccion de Obispo, y nombramiento de Obispo, que hizo el Estado de San Salvador, etc. *Guatemala.* 1827. 4to. 29083

Also: Informe que el Cabildo Eclesiastico de la Catedral de Guatemala, etc. 1827.

Instruccion para el arreglo de conoscer y proceder las causas correspondientes al juzgado general de bienes de defuntos Reyno de Guatemala. *Nueva Guatemala.* 1799. Folio, pp. (2), 24.

Segunda Junta Publica de la Real Sociedad Economica de Guatemala, 1797; Tercera Junta, 1798; Quarta Junta, 1798; Quinta Junta, *Nueva Guatemala*, 1799; Octava Junta, 1811; Novena Junta, 1812. 29085

Kalendario y Guia de Forasteros de Guatemala y sus provincias para el año de 1805. *Guatemala.* 1805. 12mo. Continued.

Manifiesto del Gefe del Estado de Guatemala. [*Guatemala.* 1827.] Folio, pp. 16. 29087

Mémoire contenant. *See* [Obert (*M.*)]

Memoria de los trabajos de la sociedad Economica de Amigos de Guatemala; con que dió cuenta en la junta general celebrada el 10 de Enero de 1864, su Secretario D. Felipe Andreu. *Guatemala.* 1864. 8vo, pp. 16. 29088

Memoria sobre los medios de destruir la mendicidad, y descorrer los verdaderos probres de esta capital. *Nueva Guatemala.* 1797. 8vo. 29089

Noticia de los premios aplicados a las mejores hilanderas al torno ens. en la Escuela de la Nueva Guatemala. 1796. 4to.

Papeles curiosos de Guatemala. *Habana.* [n. d.] 2 vols., folio.

A collection from old MS. chronicles.

Proyecto de constitucion del estado de Guatemala uno de los de Centro-America, presentado a la asamblea constituyente, reunida en virtud del decreto de convocatoria expidido en 25 de Julio de 1838. *Imprenta de de la Paz.* 1842. 4to, pp. 18.

Reclamacion y protesta del supremo gobierno del estado de Guatemala, sobre la ocupacion de Soconusco, por las tropas de la Republica Mexicana, con los documentos en que se fundan. *Guatemala: Imprenta de la Paz.* 1843. Folio, pp. 18, (6).

Reglamento para la propagacion y estabilidad de la Vacuna en el reyno de Guatemala dispuesto, de orden de S. M, por el superior gobierno del mismo reyno. *Nueva Guatemala: D. Ignacio Beteta.* 1805. Folio, 3 l., pp. 29, 1 l., Adiciones, 2 l. 29094

Relacion d'l espãtable terremoto que agora nueuamente ha acontecido en la cibdad d' Guatimala: es cosa de grãde admiracion y de grãde exemplo para que todos nos emendemos d' nuestros pecados y estemos apresciuidos para quãdo Dios fuere seruido de nos llamar. [Colophon:] *Fue impressa en la grã ciudad d' Mexico en casa de Iuã Cromberger año d' mill y quiniẽtos y quarẽta y vno* [1541.] 4to, 4 l. 29095

A volume of the greatest rarity, of which the only known copy is at Madrid. It is one of the earliest books printed in Mexico. "An edition of the same plaquette was also published in Spain, four leaves, 4to."—HARRISSE's *Bib. Am. Vet.*

Representacion del M. N. Y. L. Ayuntamiento de Guatemala al exmo. Señor D. José de Bustamente, teniente general de la real armada, presidente, gobernador, y capitan general de este reyno, ecc., en contestacion á su oficio circular de XXIV. de Marzo, y á su sabio manifiesto de XIII. de Abril de 1811. *Guatemala, en casa de Beteta.* [1811.] 4to, pp. 36. 29096

GUAYAQUIL. El Concordato il la esposicion del concejo cantonal de Guayaquil. *Guayaquil.* 1863. 4to, pp. 108. 29097

GUAY-TROUIN. Mémoires de Monsieur du Guay-Trouin ... *Amsterdam: Pierre Mortierre.* M.DCC.XL. 12mo, 1 l., pp. xxxvi, 279. Portrait, Maps. H. 29198

GUAZACOALCO. Colonie de Guazacoalco ... au Mexique. Projet de société. *Paris: Tastu.* [1827.] 29199

Prospectus, published by Villevêque, Giordan and Baradère. *See* Bristol.

GUELEN (A. de). Brieve Relation | de l'Estat | de Phernambucq. | Dedié à l'assemblée de XIX. pour | la tresnoble Compagnie d'West-Inde. | Par Auguste de Gvelen. | *A Amsterdam,* | *Chez Louys Elzevier.* 1640. | 4to, pp. 44. 29100

Relates to the war with Spain concerning Brazil, and is a very rare piece. In the following, a Dutch translation, the name is changed to Quelen:

GUELEN. Kort Verhael | Vanden staet | van | Fernanbvc, | Toege-eygens de E. Heeren Gecommitteerde | ter Vergaederinghe, vande Negenthiene, inde Geo- | ctroyeerde West-Indische Compagnie, ter Camere van | Amstelredam. | Door Augustus van Quelen. | Wt het Francois int Nederduytsch vertaeldt. ¶ *T'Amsterdam,* | *Ghedruckt in 't laer ons Heeren.* 1640. | 4to, 15 l.

See Asher's "Bibliographical Essays," Nos. 155 and 156.

GÜELL Y RENTÉ (J.) Leyendas americanas. Por José Güell y Renté. *Madrid: Imprenta de las Novedades é Ilustracion.* 1856. 12mo, pp. (2), 283. Portrait. BA., C. 29102

GÜELL Y RENTÉ. Traditions américaines. Par José Güell y Renté. *Paris: M. Lévy frères.* 1861. 12mo, pp. (4), 295, (1).

GUEMES (J. F. de). Cedula del Virey de la Nueva-España, D. Juan Francisco de Guemes, sobre el arrendamiento de la bebida del Pulque blanco en la ciudad de Mexico y sus cinco leguas en contorno. *Mexico, 9. de Julio de* 1753. Folio, pp. 39. + Otra Cedula del mismo, sobre el mismo asunto. *Mexico,* 16 *Mayo de* 1753. Folio, pp. 32. 29104

GUEMES (P. G. de). Defensas de vn ministro afligido, al rey nvestro señor. Por el doctor Don Pedro Gonçalez de Guemes, Oydor del Nueuo Reyno de Granada. *Año de mil y seiscientos cinquenta y tres* [1653]. 4to, 14 l., 214 l. 29105

"Cet ouvrage, ainsi que ceux qui étaient addressés au roi, sous forme de mémoire, sont généralement dépourvus des privilèges et des licences ordinaires en autorisant l'impression, attendu que, dirigés contre de puissants personnages, ils étaient imprimés secrètement à très-peu d'exempl. et distribués seulement aux membres du conseil des Indes. Le volume en question doit être imprimé à Madrid; Antonio ne fait pas mention de son auteur, qui était auditeur de Santa-Fé, et Ternaux l'a omis dans sa "Bibliothèque Américaine."—LECLERC.

GÜEMEZ (V.) Solemnes Exequias del S. D. J. Vicente Güemez, Conde de Revilla Gigedo. *En la N. Guatemala.* 1800. 4to. 29106

GÜEN (G.) Salud, por el Br. Genaro Güen. *Imprenta de D. Francisco Mas.* 1821. 4to. 29107

In reply to Arango's "Independencia de la Isla de Cuba."

GUENEBAULT (J. H.) Natural History of the Negro Race, extracted from the French. *Charleston, S. C.* 1837. 12mo, pp. 176. M. 29108

GUÉRIN (L.) Histoire Maritime de France et des Colonies, depuis les temps anciens jusqu'à nos jours, par Léon Guérin. *Paris.* 2 vols., 8vo. 31 Plates. + Troisième Édition. *Paris.* 1846–48. 3 vols., 8vo. A. 29109

Vol. IV. of his "Tour du Monde" is entitled "Les trois Fils du Capitaine Amérique du Sud Antilles."

GUÉRIN-MÉNEVILLE (F. E.) Histoire naturelle de l'Ile de Cuba. Par F. E. Guérin-Méneville. I. Animaux articulés à pieds articulés. *Paris.* 1857. Rl. 8vo, pp. 868. Folio Atlas of 20 colored Plates. 29110

GUÉRIN-MÉNEVILLE (F. E.), *et* PERROTTET (S.) Mémoire sur un Insecte et un Champignon qui ravagent les Cafiers aux Antilles. *Paris.* 1842. 8vo. 29111

[GUERINI (Aloise).] L'Ammiraglio dell' Indie Poema di Ormildo Emeressio. *Venetia.* 1759. 4to. Plates. 29112

GUERNSEY (A. H.), *and* ALDEN (H. M.) Harper's Pictorial History of the Great Rebellion. By Alfred H. Guernsey and Henry M. Alden. Part First. To the Close of the Peninsular Campaign of 1862. || Part Second. *New York: Harper & Bros.* 1866–68. Folio, pp. (iv), 380; iv, 381–836. B., BA. 29113

GUERNSEY (C. F.) The Silver Rifle: a Story of the Saranac Lakes. By Clara F. Guernsey. *Philadelphia: American Sunday-School Union.* [1871.] 16mo, pp. 256. 3 Plates. 29114

GUERNSEY (E.) History of the United States of America, designed for Schools. ... By Egbert Guernsey, A.M. Second Edition. *New York.* 1848. + Fifth Edition. 1848. + Together with a Notice of American Antiquities and the Indian Tribes. Seventh Edition. *New York: Cady & Burgess.* 1850. 12mo, pp. 456. + New Edition. *Philadelphia.* 1863. 12mo, pp. 515. + Revised Edition. *Philadelphia: Moss & Co.* 1869. 12mo, pp. 589. Plate. C. 29115

GUERNSEY. Primary History of the United States of America. *New York: D. Burgess & Co.* 1854. 16mo, pp. 206. C. 29116

GUERNSEY (O.), *and* WILLARD (J. F.) History of Rock County, and Transactions of the Rock County Agricultural Society and Mechanics' Institute. Edited and Compiled by Orrin Guernsey and Josiah F. Willard. *Janesville, Wis.* 1856. 8vo, pp. xii, 350. 3 Plates, 1 Portrait. B., H., S. 29117

GUERRA (Fr. Joan). Art de la Lengua Mexicana segun la acostumbran hablar los Indios en todo el Obispado de Guadalaxara, parte del de Guadiana, y del de Mechbacan; dispuesto por orden y Mandato de Fr. Joseph de Alcaras. *Con licencia, en Mexico, por la Viuda de Francisco Rodriguez Lupercio, en la puente de Palacio año de* 1692. 4to. 29118

A volume of great rarity. Ludewig quotes the following title:

GUERRA. Arte de la Lengua Megicana segun el Dialecto de los Pueblos de la Nueva Gallicia, por Fr. Juan Guerra. *Mexico.* 1699. 4to. 29119

GUERRA (José). Fecunda Nube del Cielo Guadalupano, y Mystica Paloma del estrecho Palomar, de el Colegio Apostolico de Nuestra Señora de Guadalupe. Relacion Breve de la Vida exemplar de F. A. Margil de Jesus. *Mexico, por J. B. de Hogal.* 1726. 8vo. 29120

GUERRA (José). *See* [Norriega y Guerra].

GUERRA (José Maria). Pastoral del Ilustrisimo Señor Obispo, dirigida a los Indigenos de esta dióceso. *Merida de Yucatan, impreso por Antonio Petra.* 1848. 4to. Portrait. 29121

"Le présent opuscule est une lettre pastoral en *maya*, addressée par cet évêque aux indigènes rebelles."—BRASSEUR DE BOURBOURG.

GUERRA (R.) Clemencia. Drama original en verso y en tres actos de Rosa Guerra, dedicado al General D. Bartolomé Mitre. *Buenos Aires.* 1862. 8vo, pp. 90. 29122

Guerra do Paraguay, a nova phase. (Carta a um amigo) por * * *. Primera e segunda carta. *Montevideo.* 1869. 12mo, pp. 43. 29123

Guerre d'Amérique. *Paris.* 1863. *See* [Joinville, (*Prince de*)].

La Guerre Civile, aux États-Unis. Par A. D.... *Paris.* 1862. 8vo, pp. 32. 29124

Guerra de España con Mejico. *Paris.* 1856–57. 8vo, pp. 154, 58. 29125

GUERREIRO (B.) Tornado dos vassalas de Coroa de Portugal, pera se recuperar a Cidade de S. Salvador na Bahya de Todas os Santos, tomado pollos Olandezes, a oito de Mayo de 1624 & recuparado no primeiro de Mayo 1625; Feita pollo Padre Bartolomeu Guerreiro de Companhia de Jesu. *Lisboa: Mathieu Pinheiro.* 1625. 4to. Plate folded. 29126

GUERREIRO. Gloriosa Coroa d'esforçados religiosos da Companhia de Jesu. Mortos polla fe Catholica nas Conquistas dos Reynos da Coroa de Portugal. Por P. Bertholamey, da Companhia de Jesu. *Em Lisboa, por Antonio Alvarez.* 1642. Folio, Title, Arms of Portugal, 1 l., 6 l., pp. 736, Printer's Mark, 1 l., 6 l. 29127

"Ce Martyrologe est divisé en quatre parties; celle qui nous intéresse particulièrement, est la troisième (pp. 301–387), dans laquelle l'auteur traite des Missions du Brésil, et de l'histoire des religieux de la Compagnie morts dans cet empire."—LECLERC.

GUERREIRO. Relaçam Anual | das Covsas | que Fezeram | os Padres da Companhia | de Iesvs nas Partes da India | Oriental, & no Brasil, Angola, Cabo Verde, Guine, nos annos | de seiscentos & dous & seiscentos & tres, & do pro- | cesso da conuersam, & christandade daquellas par- | tes, tirada das cartas dos mesmos padres | que de là vieram. | Pelo padre Fernam Guerreiro da mesma | Companhia, natural de Almodouuar | de Portugal. | Vay diuidido em quatro liuros. O primeiro de Iapã | O II. da China & Maluco. O III. da India. | O IIII. do Brasil, Angola, & Guiné. | *Em Lisboa: Per Iorge Rodrigues im- | pressor de liuros.* | *Anno* M.D.CV. | 4to, pp. (7), Text, Livro Primeero, Signatures A–N in fours, O in two; Livro Segvndo, Signatures A–Nnn in fours. 29128

GUERRERO (B. Sanches). Oracion Sacropolitica Panegyrico, Mistico, Dogmatico, Moral que en la Fiesta de accion de Gracias, por Excel. S. D. Manuel de Guirior, Virrey del Peru, 4 Diziembre 1776. *Lima: En la Imprenta de la calle de Juan de Medina.* 1778. 4to. 29129

Also: Oracion Panegyrico Polemica que en la Fiesta de la SS. Trinidad ... *Lima.* 1779. 4to, pp. 80.

GUERRERO (C. E.) Oratio in Funere S. P. ac D. N. Clementis XIV. Por R. P. Fr. Cosma Enriquez Guerrero. [*In Almo et Imp. Fratrum Prædicatorum Mexicano Conventu dicta* 3 *Apr.* 1775.] Sm. 4to. 29130

GUERRERO (D. B. L.) Constituciones Synodales del Arcobispado de los Reyes, en el Peru. ... Senor D. Bartholomé Lobo

Guerrero ... *San Christoval: Juan Joseph Morel.* 1754. 8vo, pp. (25), 96, (1); Second title-page, pp. 83, (1), 63, (3). H.

GUERRERO (José Maria). Dictamen teologico, contra el ensayo sobre tolerancia religiosa, publicado en Mexico por Vicente Rocafuerte. *Mexico.* 1831. 4to, pp. 60. 29132

GUERRERO (T.) Historia intima de seis mujeres. Cuadros sociales. Por Teodoro Guerrero. *Mexico.* 1862. 8vo, pp. 578.

GUERRERO (V.) Elogia a la Muerte de J. M. Morelos. *Puebla.* 1821. 12mo, pp. 7. 29134

[GUERRERO.] El soberano Estado de Oajaca al Benemerito de la Patria Vicente Guerrero.—Con el Elogio funebre, pronunciado en sus magnificas ecsequias por José Juan Canseco el dia 2 de Mayo de 1833. *Oajaca.* 1833. 4to, pp. 61. 29135

GUERRERO. Manifiesto á sus Compatriotas, por Vicente Guerrero, Segundo Presidente de los Estados-Unidos Mexicanos. *Mexico.* 1829. 4to, pp. 20. 29136

GUERRERO. Manifiesto de su conducta publica en la Camara en eleccion de Presidente celebrada en favor de D. Vicente Guerrero. Por José Maria Apulche, Diputado de Tabasco. *New-York.* 1830. 4to, pp. 19. 29137

GUERRERO. Sumaria Averiguacion contra el General D. Vicente Guerrero, y socios por el delito de conspiracion contra el supremo Gobierno. *Oaxaca.* 1831. Folio, pp. 25. 29138

GUEST (M.) Poems on Several Occasions; to which are annexed; Extracts from a Journal kept by the Author while he followed the Sea, and during a Journey from New Brunswick, in New Jersey, to Montreal and Quebec. By Moses Guest. *Cincinnati: Looker & Reynolds.* 1823. 12mo, pp. (4), 160. Plate. + Second Edition. [*Ibid.*] 1824. C. 29139

Guest commanded the party of militia which captured the noted partisan, Col. Lincoln, in New Jersey, in October, 1779. Several of the Poems relate to Washington.

GUEST (R.) A Compendious History of the Cotton Manufacture; with a Disproval of the Claim of Sir Richard Arkwright to the Invention of its Ingenious Machinery. By Richard Guest. *Manchester: J. Pratt.* 1823. 4to, pp. (1), 70, 3. 12 Plates. C. 29140

GUEUDEVILLE (M.) Atlas Historique, ou nouvelle introduction à l'Histoire, à la Chronologie, et à la Géographie Ancienne et Moderne, avec Dissertations sur l'Histoire de chaque Etat. *Amsterdam.* 1739. 7 vols., impl. folio. 29141

Includes copious details relative to America.

GUEUDEVILLE (Nicolas). Suite du voyage de l'Amérique, ou dialogues de Monsieur le Baron de Lahontan et d'un sauvage dans l'Amérique. Avec les voyages du même en Portugal et en Danemarc. *Amsterdam: Boeteman.* 1704. 16mo, pp. (16), 222. 2 Maps, 4 Plates. C. 29142

The Travels of La Hontan have been attributed to this author.

[GUEULLETTE (Thomas Simon).] Peruvian Tales, related, in One Thousand and One Hours, by one of the Select Virgins of Cusco, to the Yncka of Peru; ... with ... Historical Remarks. ... Translated from the ... French by Samuel Humphreys, Esq.; The Third Edition. *London: J. Hodges.* MDCCXLV. 4 vols., 12mo, pp. (8), xiv, (2), 275; (1), 334; vii, (1), 362; (10), 84, (1); xii, 94. 3 Plates. BA. + *London.* 1749. 3 vols., 12mo. + Fourth Edition. *London.* 1764. 3 vols., 12mo. + *London: J. Walker.* 1817. 18mo, pp. (4), 571. Plate. C. 29143

Also included in the "Novelists Magazine," Vol. XXI.

GUEVARA (Ant. Ladron de). Noticias de los Poblados de que se Componen el Nuevo Reyno de Leon, Provincia de Coaguila, Nueva-Estremadura, y de la Texas, Nuevas Philipinas: despoblados que ay en sus Cercanias y los Indios que las habitan, y causa de los pocas, ò ningunos aumentos. *Año de* 1739. Folio.

GUEVARA (D. L. de). Aplavso Reverente y Afectuoso de la Real Universidad de S. Marcos de la Ciudad de Lima, al D. Diego Ladron de Guevara, Obispo de Quito, y Uirrey del Perù, etc. 1711—Carta Pastoral, que escribio el D. Diego Ladron de Guevara; etc. *Lima, por Joseph de Contreras y Alvarado.* 1711. Folio. 29145

GUEVARA (M. de). Arte doctrinal y modo general para aprender la lengua Matlatzinga, para la administracion de los santos sacramentos ... Hecho y ordenado por el padre Fr. Miguel de Guevara, Ministro predicador ... en las tres lenguas que generalmente corren en esta provincia de Michoacan Mexicana, Tarasca y Matlatzinga, prior actual del convento de Santiago Undoméo. Año de 1638. [*Mexico, imprenta de Vicente Garcia Torres.* 1862.] 4to, pp. (8), 64. 29146

GUEVARA (M. T. de). Oracion Funebre en las exequias que el religiosisimo Convento de Corpus Christi de Mexico, consagró á la venerable memoria de su exemplar Fundadora, y dignisima Prelada la M. R. M. Sor Maria Teresa de Sr. S. Josef Vetancurt, el 22 de Abril de 1773. Y dixo El R. P. Fr. Miguel Thadeo de Guevara. *Mexico.* 1773. 4to, 10 l., pp. 20. 29147

GUEVARA. Sumario de las Indulgencias, Gracias y Privilegios Autenticos que ganan y gozan los Hermanos de la Tercera Orden de Penitencia de N. P. S. Francisco, ... tenor de la Bulla de Benedicto XIII. que llamamos el Mare Magnum, ... *Mexico: F. de Zuñiga.* 1787. 4to, pp. 58. 29148

A reimpression from the "Bulletin de la Société de Géographie et de Statistique de Mexico."

GUEVARA (P.) Historia del Paraguay, Rio de la Plata y Tucuman que redactó el P. Guevara jesuita. *Buenos Aires.* 1854.

A continuation of the "Historia Argentina," by Rui Diaz de Guzman, 1612.

GUEVARA (S. B. L. de). Sermon en las honras del S. B. Ladron de Guevara. *Mexico.* 1804. Portrait. 29150

[GUÉZENEC (Alfred).] Histoires d'amour au Mexique, en Californie, dans la Nouvelle-Grenade et dans l'Inde. Par Alfred de Bréhat. *Paris: Hachette et Cie.* 1861. 12mo. 29151

Lorenz gives the publisher as Hetzel.

Guia de Nueva York y los Estados Unidos, para uso de los Españoles y Sudamericanos, dende se esplica cuanto puede interessar a un Viajero. *Nueva York.* 1856. 18mo, pp. 134. Map.

Guia del Estado Ecclesiástico, seglar, y Regular de España é Indias. 1817. 18mo. 29253

Guia del Viajero en los Estados Unidos. *Nueva York.* 1859. 12mo. Plates. 29154

GUIACUM. Eyn bewert Recept, wie man das Holtz Guayacan brauchen soll. [*Augspurg.* 1524.] 4to, 4 l. 29155

Relates to the American wood called Guiacum.

GUIANA. *See also* British Guiana and Surinam.

Almanach de Guyane française. *Cayenne.* 1822. 8vo. Continued. 29156

Anecdotes sur le 18 fructidor et nouveaux mémoires des deportés de Guyane. [n. p. n. d.] 29157

Title from Muller's Catalogue, No. 949.

Annuaire de la Guyane française pour 1866. *Paris: Challamel aîné.* 1866. 18mo. 29158

Arrêt du conseil d'état, qui prolonge jusqu'au 1er juillet 1792, l'effet des lettres patentes du 1er mai 1768, qui accordoient à l'isle de Cayenne et à la Guyane françoise, la liberté de commerce avec toutes les nations. Du 15 mai 1784. *Paris: Impr. Royale.* pp. 2. 29159

Beschrijving van de Kust van Guyana. *Amsterdam: Weduwe G. Hulst van Keulen.* 1824. 8vo. 29160

Beschrijvinge van | Guiana; | Des selfs Cituatie, Gesontheyt, Vruchtbaerheyt ende | ongemeene Profijten en Voordeelen boven andere Landen. | Discourerender wijse voorgestelt, tusschen | Een Boer ofte Landt-man, | Een Burger ofte Stee-man, | Een Schipper ofte Zee-man en | Een Haeghsche Bode. | Waer inne sy-luyden malkander voor-houden | 1. Den slechten toestant en verval in Koop-handel, Zee-vaert, Ambachten en | Boeren handel, ende wat daer van de oorsaek is. | 2. Door wat middelen dit is te her-stellen. | 3. Hoe, en op wat manier deselve moesten aengevangen en uytgevoert werden. | Mitsgaders 't gene van onsen Staet daer op is geresol- | veert; dienende tot narichtinge van vele Koop-luyden, Bur- | gers, | Huys-luyden en alle Zee-varende Persoonen.|| ¶ *Tot Hoorn, Gedruckt by Stoffel Iansz. Kortingh.* 1676. | 4to, pp. 46. 29161

A description of Guiana, its situation, healthiness, fertility, and advantages, especially treats of the bad state of commerce and navigation to Guiana, the means of restoration, etc. "Cette description de la Guyane, inconnue aux bibliographes a été faite à l'occasion des débats qui s'étaient élevés à l'égard de la fondation d'une colonie sur la rivière Wiapoca et pour démontrer l'importance de la Guyane, aussi bien pour la colonisation que pour le commerce de la mère-patrie. Dans la préface l'auteur fait mention des démarches, que déjà en 1659, Otto Keye avait faites pour diriger l'attention publique sur ce pays." — TRŒMEL.

Beschriving van Guyana, geleegen an het vast Kust van America. *Amsterdam.* 1676. 4to. 29162

Beschryving van Guiana. *See* [Bancroft (Edward)], No. 3109.

Cartilla de doctrina cristiana para uso de los niños americanos de la Guyana inglesa. *Roma.* 1864. 18mo, pp. 35. 29163

Catalogue de la Guyane anglaise. 29164

Relates to the World's Fair in London, 1851.

Ceylon and British Guiana. Minutes of Evidence, etc. Folio.

Church in the Colonies. *See* Vol. IV., No. 13007.

Code de procédure civile adopté à la Guyana française, publié à Cayenne le 18 août, 1821. 29166

Codes de la Guyane française, avec les ordonnances portant leur application. *Paris.* 1828–29. 3 vols., 4to. 29167

Collection of Pieces relating to the French Emigrations to Guyana. 1844. 8vo. 29168

"Not published." — MULLER'S *Catalogue*, No. 961.

Compagnie pour l'exploitation des bois de construction civile et maritime, et autres produits de la Guyane française. *Paris.* 1826. 8vo. 29169

Conditien de welcke by de Ed. Groot Mog. Heeren Staten van Hollandt ende West Vrieslandt, etc. [1675.] 4to. 29170

First impression of the proposals offered by the States General to intending emigrants to the American coast.

Considérations sur la Guyane. *See* Vol. IV., No. 16027.

De la Guyane française. *See* [Catineau-Laroche (P. M. S.)]

Délibération du Conseil colonial de la Guiane française. *Paris.* 1839. 8vo. A. 29171

Dialogue ... between a Planter. *See* Vol. V., No. 19945.

Eigendliche Beschreibung des Lands Guiana, welches gelegen an der vesten meergrentzenden Landschafft America. *Bärn: S. Kneubüler.* 1677. Sm. 4to, pp. 63. Map. 29172

Eight Years Residence. *See* Vol. VI., No. 22082.

Essay on Guiana. *See* [Bancroft (Edward)], Vol. I., No. 3100.

Feuille de la Guyane française. *Cayenne.* 1820. Sm. 4to.

Forêts vierges de la Guyane française, considérées sous le rapport des produits qu'on peut en retirer pour les chantiers maritimes de la France. *Paris.* 1827. 8vo. 29174

Instructions nautiques sur les côtes de la Guyane française. *Imprimerie Impériale.* 1808. 4to. 29175

Letter to Chas. Jas. Fox, on the Importance of the Colonies on the Coast of Guiana. By a British Merchant. *London.* 1806. 8vo. 29176

Mémoire à Consulter pour les Colons de la Guyane française, spoliés par la violation de la Capitulation, du 12 Janvier, 1809, avec le Portugal. *Paris.* 1839. 8vo, pp. 24. 29177

Mémoire sur la Colonie de la Guyane française, et sur les avantages politiques et commerciaux de sa possession. *Paris.* 1803. 8vo, pp. 67. 29178

Mémoire sur la Guyane française. *Cayenne.* 1824. 8vo.

Mémoire sur l'exploitation des bois de la Guyane française. *Cayenne.* 1785. 4to. 29180

Notes sur les Colonies de Surinam et de Demerary. [n. p.] 1835. 8vo. A. 29181

Notice statistique sur l'Isle Bourbon et Guyane française, imprimée par ordre de M. le Ministre de la Marine et des Colonies. *Paris.* 1838. 8vo. 29182

For another edition *see* [Ternaux (H.)]

Notice sur la transportation à la Guyane française et à la Nouvelle-Calédonie, ... *Paris: Imprimerie Impériale.* 1867. 8vo, pp. (2), 95. 2 Maps. C. 29183

Observations sur la multiplication des bestiaux dans la Guiane françoise. *Cayenne: de l'Imprimerie du Roi.* 1787. 4to, pp. 4.

Ordonnance du Roi portant application du code pénal à la Guiane française. *Paris: Imprimerie Royale.* 1828. 4to.

Pertinente Beschrijvinge | Van | Guiana. | Gelegen aen de vaste Kust van | America. | Waer in kortelijck verhaelt wordt, het aenmerckelijckste dat in en om- | trent het Landt van Guiana valt, als de Limiten, het Klimaet en | stoffen der Landen, de Mineralen, Edele Gesteenten, Vruchten | Dieren, ende overvloedigheyt der Vissen, nevens der selver | Inwoonderen alderer. | Hier is bygevoeght | Der Participanten uytschot ende profijten, die daer uyt te | volgen staen. | Als oock de Conditien van mijn Heeren de Staten van Hollandt en West- | Vrieslandt, voor die gene die nae Guiana begeeren te varen.|| ¶ *t'Amsterdam,* | *By Jan Claesz. ten Hoorn, Boeckverkooper tegen over* | *'t Oude Heeren Logement.* 1676. | 4to, pp. 55. A., C., H. 29186

"Autre description de la Guyane, inconnue aux bibliographes, et tirée des ouvrages de Laet, Keye, David Pietersz Vries et autres. Elle est ornée d'une carte du pays et porte en tête les conditions accordées aux colons par les États de Hollande et la Frise occidentale." — TRŒMEL.

Précis Historique de l'Expedition du Kouru, Guyane française, 1762–1765. *Paris: Arthur Bertrand.* 1842. 8vo, pp. 79.

Précis sur la Colonisation des Bords de la Mana, Guyane française. *Paris: Bertrand.* 1835. 8vo, pp. 70. 29188

This, the foregoing, and the following, were published by the Minister of Marine.

Procès-verbaux des Séances de la Commission de Colonisation de la Guyane. *Paris: Imprimerie Royale.* 1842. 4to, pp. xliv, 236.

A Publication of Gviana's Plantation, newly undertaken by the Right Honourable the Earl of Barkshire (Knight of the most Noble Order of the Garter) and Company, for that most famous River of the Amazones in America. Wherein is briefly shewed the Lawfulness of Plantations in Foreign Countries; Hope of the Natives Conversion; Nature of the River; Qualitie of the Land, Climate, and People of Gviana: With the Provisions for Man's Sustenance, and Commodities therein growing for the Trade of Merchandise, and manner of the Adventure. With an Answer to some Objections touching feare of the Enemy. *London: Printed by William Jones.* 1632. 4to, pp. 24. 29190

Publication de la Société d'Études pour la Colonisation de la Guyane. No. 3. Note sur la fondation d'une nouvelle colonie dans la Guyane française, ou premier aperçu d'un nouveau mode de population et de culture, pour l'exploitation des regions tropicales; suivi de plusieurs pièces et documens, etc. *Paris: Didot.* 1844. 8vo, pp. 288. 29191

Rapport sur les Questions Coloniales, à la suite d'un voyage fait aux Antilles et aux Guyanes. *Paris.* 1843–44. 2 vols., folio.

Réflexions sur la colonie françoise de la Guyane. [*Paris.*] 1788. 8vo. 29193

Réflexions sur le projet d'une colonie de cultivateurs européens à Mana dans la Guyane française. 29194

Réglement de police sur les nègres de la Guyane, du 6 janvier 1750. *Cayenne.* 1785. Folio. 29195

Reise nach Guiana und Cayenne, nebst einer Uebersicht der ältern dahin gemachten Reisen und neuern Nachrichten von diesem Lande, dessen Bewohnern und den dortigen europäischen Colonien, besonders den französischen. Aus dem Französischen. *Hamburg: Benjamin Gottlob Hoffman.* 1799. 8vo, pp. vi, 317. Map and Plate. 29196

Thoughts on British Guiana. By a Planter. Second Edition. *Demerara.* 1847. 8vo, pp. 42. 29197

Verloren Arbeyt. *See* [Mijst (G. de)].

Voyage à la Guiane. *See* [Prudhomme (L.)]

Guide Book of the Atlantic and St. Lawrence, and St. Lawrence and Atlantic Rail Roads, including a Full Description of all the Interesting Features of the White Mountains, By S. B. Beckett; with Illustrations ... By C. E. Beckett, ... *Portland: Sanborn & Carter, and H. J. Little & Co.* 1853. 12mo, pp. 180.

Guide-Book of the Central Railroad of New Jersey, and its Connections through the Coal-Fields of Pennsylvania. *New York: Harper & Brothers.* 1864. 12mo, pp. 120. B. 29299

Guide Book to the Gold Regions of Fraser River, with Map, etc. *New York.* 1858. 24mo, pp. 55. 29200

Contains some specimens of the Chinook Jargon.

Guide-Book for Investments in Petroleum Stocks. *New York: American News Company.* 1865. 16mo, pp. 80. 29201

Guide des Emigrés au Texas, dans l'Amérique Septentrionale, contenant la description de ce pays, d'après des Documents officiels. *Paris.* 1836. 8vo, pp. 16. 29202

Guide des Emigrants aux États-Unis. Traduit de l'Allemand par J. B. Bettinger. *Havre: J. Morlent.* 1834. 12mo, pp. xii, 127. H. 29203

Guide des Emigrants Français dans les États de Kentucky et d'Indiana, ou renseignements fidèles sur les États-Unis de l'Amérique Septentrionale en générale et sur les États de Kentucky et Indiana en particulier, indiquant les mesures et précautions à prendre avant de s'embarquer, ainsi que les moyens d'y émigrer agréablement, d'y doubler sa fortune, etc. *Paris: Arthus Bertrand.* 1834. 8vo, pp. 66. 29204

Guide du Commerce. *See* Ch[ambon] (M.)] Vol. III.

Guide from Montreal and Quebec to the Eastern Townships of Lower Canada and to Portland (Maine). *Montreal.* 1853. 12mo, pp. 42. Map and Woodcuts. 29205

The Guide, or Counsellor, of Human Life, containing Miscellaneous Pieces ... The First [and perhaps the last] Edition.

By the Editor, ... *Springfield: Printed by Edward Gray.* M,DCC,-XCIV. 12mo, pp. 191, (6). 29206

Guide Politique pour la campagne présidentielle de 1860. [n. p. n. d.] 8vo, pp. 15. H. 29207

Guide to Emigrants proceeding to Australia and the Canadas; comprehending General Instructions, Regulations on board the Transports, and Useful Receipts for the Settlers and various Classes of Labourers, Carpenters, &c., residing in those Colonies. *Oxford.* 1844. 18mo, pp. 72. 29208

Guide to Government Situations; showing the Extent, Nature, and Value of the Government Civil Patronage at Home and Abroad. Ninth Edition. *London.* 1852. 16mo. 29209

The American colonial situations are pointed out.

Guide to the New Gold Region of Western Kansas and Nebraska, with ... Map. *New-York.* 1859. 18mo, pp. 32. S.

Guide to Northern Archæology. By the Royal Society of Northern Antiquarians of Copenhagen. Edited for the Use of English Readers, by the Right Hon. the Earl of Ellesmere. *London.* 1848. 8vo, pp. 128. Plates. 29211

Contains some reference to the Discovery of America by the Northmen.

A Guide to South Bend, Notre Dame du Lac, and Saint Mary's, Indiana. ... *Baltimore: Printed by John Murphy & Co.* 1859. 8vo, pp. 16. Plate. H. 29212

Guide to the Lakes and Mountains of New-Hampshire, via the Several Routes connecting with the Boston, Concord & Montreal Railroad at Concord, N. H. *Concord: Printed by Tripp & Osgood.* 1852. 12mo, pp. 45. H. 29213

A Guide to the Virginia Springs; ... a Description of the Springs ... the Natural Curiosities of the State. *Staunton, Va.: Robert Cowan.* 1851. Sm. 8vo, pp. 9–141. Map. B. 29214

Guide to the White Mountains and Lakes of New Hampshire: with Minute and Accurate Descriptions of the Scenery and Objects of Interests on the Route; ... *Concord, N. H.: Tripp & Morril.* 1850. 16mo, pp. 48. + *Concord [N. H.]: Tripp & Osgood.* 1851. 16mo, pp. 72. C. 29215

Guides to States, Cities or Towns will be found under their respective names.

GUIDÉE (Archille). Vie du R. P. Joseph Varin, suivie de notices sur quelques uns de ses confrères. *Paris: Poussielgue Rusaud.* 1845. 12mo, pp. 415. 29216

Contains sketches of Archbishop John Carroll, Rev. Anthony Kohlman, &c.

GUIGNARD. Notice Historique sur la vie et les travaux de M. Fevret de Saint-Memin par Ph. Guignard ... *Dijon: Imprimerie Loireau-Feuchot* ... MDCCCLIII. 8vo, pp. 22. 29217

Saint-Memin was an artist who resided for sometime in America, and published a series of Portraits of Americans. *See* Saint-Memin.

GUILBERT (E.) A Reminiscence of Sleepy Hollow. By the Rev. Edmund Guilbert, M.A. [n. p. n. d.] 8vo, pp. 8. H.

GUILD (*Junr.*) The Central Park Photographed by —— Guild, Junr., with Descriptions by —— Perkins. *New York.* 1864. 4to. 29219

GUILD (C.) Genealogy of the Descendants of John Guild, Dedham, Massachusetts. By Calvin Guild. *Providence: Printed by the Providence Press Company.* 1867. 12mo, pp. xii, 120.

[GUILD (Reuben Aldridge).] An Account of the Writings of Roger Williams. [*Providence: S. S. Rider.* 1862.] 8vo, pp. 11. 29221

GUILD. History of Brown University, with Illustrative Documents. By Reuben Aldridge Guild, ... *Providence: The Author.* 1867. Sm. 4to, pp. iv, 443. 5 Plates. 29222

Edition 310 copies, of which 10 are on large paper. Also: Historical Sketch of the Library of Brown University, with Regulations. ... [1861.] *New Haven: Tuttle, Morehouse & Taylor.* 1861. 8vo, pp. 253–272. B.

GUILD. The Librarian's Manual; A Treatise on Bibliography, comprising a Select and Descriptive List of Bibliographical Works; to which are added, Sketches of Publick Libraries. Illustrated with Engravings. By Reuben A. Guild, A.M. ... *New York: Charles B. Norton.* MDCCCLVIII. 4to, pp. 304.

Edition 500 copies in fcp. 4to, and 10 copies on large paper, demy 4to.

GUILD. Life, Times, and Correspondence of James Manning, and the Early History of Brown University. By Reuben Aldridge Guild. *Boston: Gould & Lincoln.* 1864. 8vo, pp. xxii, 523.

The circular announcing the work contained the following *unique* statement: "Three hundred copies, large paper, ten copies. Paper covers, $10.00; cloth, $11.00; half red Goat, marbled edges, $12.00; half red Goat, Roxburgh style, upper edges gilt, $12.50; Full Goat, $15.00." It is presumed that half goat means half morocco. *See* Cotton (John), Staples (W. R.), Narraganset Club.

[GUILD (Samuel Eliot).] The Question before us. *Boston: Printed by John Wilson and Son.* 1862. 8vo, pp. 12. H. 29225

Relates to the Rebellion.

GUILD (W.) A Chart and Description of the Boston and Worcester and Western Rail Roads, ... *Boston: Bradbury & Guild.* 1847. 12mo, pp. 84. Illustrations. S. 29226

GUILD. New York and the White Mountains; with a ... Map, and Wood-cut Views ... By William Guild. *Boston: Bradbury & Guild.* 1852. 12mo, pp. 80. Map. 29227

Also: A Chart and Description of the Railroad from Boston to New-York. *Boston.* 1850. 12mo.

GUILDING (J.) Sermon preached before his Excellency the Governor, etc., of the Island of St. Vincent, the Day appointed for the Observance of the Jubilee in celebrating the Fiftieth Anniversary of the Accession of George III. to the Throne. By the Rev. J. Guilding. *Saint Vincent.* 1810. 4to. 29228

Guilford Mineral Spring Water. ... *Boston.* [1869.] 12mo, pp. 30. 29229

GUILLAUME, *pseudonym.* Lettre de Guillaume-le-Disputeur au Cousin Jacques, sur l'état présent de nos colonies. *Paris: Maret An IV. de la République Française.* [1796.] 8vo, pp. 45. J.C.B.

GUILLEMAN TARAYRE (M. E.) Exploration minéralogique des régions mexicaines suivie des notes archéologiques et ethnographiques par M. E. Guilleman Tarayre ... *Paris: Imprimerie Impériale.* 1869. 8vo. 8 Plans, 2 Plates. 29231

GUILLEN (Fr. Pedro Rodriguez). El sol y año feliz del Perù San Francisco Solano, apostol y patron universal de dicho reyno, glorificado, adorado, y festejado en su templo y convento maximo de Jesus de la Ciudad de los Reyes Lima, etc. *Madrid.* 1735. Folio. 29232

GUILLERMIN (G.) Journal historique de la révolution de la partie de l'Est de Saint-Domingue, commencée le 10 Août 1808, avec des notes statistiques sur cette partie. Par Gilbert Guillermin, chef d'escadron, etc. *Philadelphie: M. Lafourcade.* 1810. 8vo, pp. (6), xii, 314, (2). Table, Portrait of Gen. Ferrand. B.

GUILLERMIN. Précis historique des derniers événemens de la partie de l'Est de Saint-Domingue, depuis le 10 Août 1808, jusqu'à la capitulation de Santo Domingo. Avec des notes historiques, politiques, et statistiques sur cette partie ; des réflexions sur l'Amérique septentrionale, &c. Par M. Gilbert Guillermin. *Paris: A. Bertrand.* 1811. 8vo, pp. (2), 494. Portrait of Ferrand, Map and Plate. H. 29234

The plate is a view of the ruins of the *chateau* built by Columbus in Santo Domingo.

GUILLERMIN. Considerations sur l'état moral et physique de l'Amérique Espagnole et sur son Independance. Par M. Guillermin. *Paris.* 1824. 8vo, pp. 64. S. 29235

The Guillotina. *See* Cobbett, Vol III., No. 13885.

"Guilty or Not Guilty." A Few Facts and Feelings regarding the Religious Bodies of America in the Matter of Slavery. A Report of an Anti-Slavery Meeting in Leeds. *Leeds, Printed.* 1855. 12mo. + Second Edition, with Additions. *Leeds.* 1855. 12mo, pp. 20. 29236

GUIMARÃES (B.) Lendas e Romances por Bernardo Guimarães. Uma historia de Quilombolas. A Garganta do Inferno. A Dansa dos Ossos. *Rio de Janeiro.* 12mo, pp. 229. 29237

GUIMARÃES (Luiz, *Jr.*) Galeria Brazileira. Pedro Americo. *Rio de Janeiro: H. Brown e J. de Almeida.* 1871. 18mo, pp. 128.

GUINAN-LAOUREIM (M.) De l'influence Anglaise par Guinan-Laoureim. *Bruxelles.* 1817. 8vo. 29239

Relating partly to the American colonies.

GUINES (*Count de*). Memorial of the Count de Guines, the French Ambassador to the Court of London: against Messieurs Tort and Roger, formerly his Secretaries, and against Mr. Delpech. [Translated from the Paris copy. n. p. n. d., probably 1777.] 8vo, pp. 48. S. 29240

There are in the New York State Library three other tracts on the same subject in French: Réplique ... au premier Mémoire du Sieur Tort. *Paris.* 1775. pp. 175.—Procès ... discuté ... 1775. pp. 175.—Mémoire sur la nature, origine et les progrès de l'affaire. pp. 96. In 1 vol., 4to. The reference to America is indirect.

GUINNARD (A.) Trois ans d'Esclavage chez les Patagons. Récit de ma Captivité par A. Guinnard ... . Deuxième Édition. *Paris: P. Brunet.* 1864. 12mo, pp. (4), v, 340. Map, Portrait.

GUINNARD. Three Years Slavery among the Patagonians: An Account of his Captivity, By A. Guinnard, Member of the Geographical Society of France. From the Third French Edi-

tion, by Charles S. Cheltnam. *London: Richard Bentley and Son.* 1871. Post 8vo, pp. x, 375. Map. 29242

"The English translator speaks with some confidence of the authenticity and truthfulness of M. Guinnard's narration of the incidents of his captivity, and I am inclined to believe them veritable, but it lacks so notably that Anglo-Saxon simplicity, which marks and distinguishes unalloyed historical relations, that we may subject it to an unjust suspicion. With true French exaltation of style, he so begilds his narrative, as to give his true story the color of fiction. It is, however, a very valuable collection of material relative to the habits, religion, and mode of life of the but little known race of savages inhabiting the vast Pampas between Buenos Ayres, Chili, and Northern Patagonia."—T. W. FIELD.

GUINNESS (H. G.) The Duty of Christians in the Present Crisis. A Letter to a Christian Brother. By H. Grattan Guinness. *Philadelphia: Collins.* 1861. 16mo, pp. 22. 29243

GUINNESS (*Mrs.* H. G.) An Answer to the Question "Who are the Plymouth Brethren?" By Mrs. H. Grattan Guinness. *Philadelphia: J. B. Lippincott & Co.* 1861. 12mo, pp. 47. BA.

GUION (A.) Report of the Establishment of Grace Free Church, Williamsburgh, Brooklyn. By the Rev. Alvah Guion ... . *New York: Daniel Dana, Jr.* M.DCCC.LIX. 12mo, pp. 31. Plate. 29245

GUION (E.) Sermon on the Scriptural, Ecclesiastical, and Political Obligations, in regard to the use of certain Prayers in the Liturgy of the Protestant Episcopal Church, Preached in New Orleans, April 9, 1864. By Rev. Elijah Guion. *New Orleans.* 1864. 8vo, pp. 25. 29246

Relates to the prayers for the United States during the Rebellion.

GUION (J. M.) Sermon on the Death of Bishop J. H. Hobart, St. Marks, N. Y. By Rev. John M. Guion. *New York.* 1830. 8vo. 29247

GUION (T. T.) Sermon on the National Fast Day, January 4, 1861. *New York.* 8vo. 29248

GUIONA (J.) Colloquios en Lengua Mexicano. Por Juan Guiona. *Mexico.* 1593. 29249

Title from Ternaux, No. 190.

GUIOT (C.) La Louiseiziade; poëme en seize chants, de chacun 330 vers, sur l'affranchissement de l'Amérique et la réunion des États généraux; par Charles Guiot (de Pontille). Précédé de la Vie de l'auteur, écrite par lui-même, pour servir à l'intelligence des personnes qui verront ses œuvres artistiques et littéraires. *Paris: Sirou.* 1845. 12mo, pp. 224. + Seconde édition. *Paris: E. Dentu.* 1853. 18mo, pp. 252. 29250

GUIPUZCOANA. Contestacion veridica, y formal, que se hace al manifiesto, que ha dado al publico la Compañia Guipuzcoana de Caracas, sobre los Beneficios, que de su establecimiento han redundado al Estado, a la Real Hacienda, al bien publico, y los verdaderos interesses de la Provincia de Caracas, fundada en hechos de tan inexorable verdad, que los mas se pueden diferir a lo que sabe, y ha experimentado el mismo Director, Autor del Manifiesto. [*Carácas.* 1748.] Folio, 31 l. 29251

GUIREY (W.) A Funeral Sermon on the Death of General George Washington ... Delivered ... at Lynn, January 7, 1800. ... By the Rev. William Guirey. ... *Salem: Printed by Joshua Cushing.* 1800. 8vo, pp. 22. B. 29252

GUIREY. The History of Episcopacy. In four parts; from its Rise to the Present Day, among the Methodists in America. By William Guirey. [n. p. n. d.] 8vo, pp. 385. 29253

The preface ends as follows: "This work was principally intended for the information of the Inhabitants of the Backwoods of Ga.;" and it is probable that the book was printed in some of the Southern States.

GUIREY. The Pattern in the Mount ... Sermon ... on the Ordination of J. Lockhart. Second Edition. *Raleigh, Printed; Philadelphia, Reprinted.* 1808. 8vo, pp. 22. 29254

LA GUIRNALDA. Semanario de historia, geografia, costumbres, literatura y variedades. Vol. I. *Mexico.* 1844. 4to.

GUISAN (*M.*) Traité sur les Terres noyées de la Guiane, appellées communèment Terres-Basses, sur leur desséchement, leur défrichement, leur culture et l'exploitation de leur productions, avec les réflexions sur la régie des esclaves et autres objets. Par M. Guisan, capitaine d'infanterie, etc. *Cayenne: De l'Imprimerie du Roi.* 1788. 4to, pp. 346. J.C.B., H., S. 29256

GUISE (C.) Légende Canadienne. Le Cap au Diable. Par Charles De Guise, M.D. *St. Anne de la Pocatière.* 1863. 12mo, pp. 45. 29257

GUITEMEZ (D.) Relacion del Pleyto Seguido por el Ilust. S Obispo de Arequipa, con la Illma. corte superior dela mism Ciudad, con motivo de los expedidos por esta en favor de Doña Domingo Guitemez, etc. *Arequipa.* 1832. 4to, pp. 28. 29258

GUITERAS (P. J.) Historia de la Conquista de la Habana (1762). Escrita por Pedro J. Guiteras. *Filadelfia: Parry and McMillan.* 1856. 8vo, pp. 188. B. 29259

GUITERAS. Historia de la Isla de Cuba. Con Notas e Ilus traciones. Por Dn. Pedro J. Guiteras. *Nueva York: Jorje R. Lockwood.* 1865–66. 2 vols., 12mo, pp. xvi, 417; vi, 421. B.

[GUITERRES.] Le Mexique, principes de l'ère nouvelle, journal publié à Mexico. 29261

GUITTEREZ DE ESTRADA (J. M.) Mexico en 1840 y en 1847, por J. M. Guitterez de Estrada. *Mexico.* 1848. 29262

GUIZOT (François Pierre Guillaume). Etude Historique sur Washington. *See* Witt (C. de).

GUIZOT. An Essay on the Character of Washington and his Influence in the Revolution of the United States of America. By M. Guizot. Translated from the French [by G. S. Hillard]. *Boston: J. Munroe & Co.* 1840. 16mo, pp. xxi, 188. C. + Second Edition. *Boston and Cambridge: James Munroe & Company.* 1851. 16mo, pp. 160. Portrait. + *New York: James Miller.* 1863. 16mo, pp. 160. 29263

See "North American Review," LI. 69.

GUIZOT. Life and Times of Washington. *London.* 1840. 12mo. 29264

GUIZOT. Monk and Washington: Historical Sketches. *London.* 1851. 18mo. S. 29265

GUIZOT. On the Causes of the Success of the English and American Revolutions. By M. Guizot. With a Biographical Sketch of the Author. Translated by A. R. Scoble. New Edition. *London: E. Kent & Co.* 1856. 12mo, pp. 50.

GUIZOT. Report upon the International Exchanges undertaken by M. Alexandre Vattemare, and upon the Actual State of Letters and Especially of Historical Investigations in the United States of America. By M. Guizot. ... [French and English.] *Paris: Paul Dupont.* 1855. 8vo, pp. 55, (1). B., H.

GUIZOT. Washington. Par M. Guizot, Membre de l'Institut. *Paris: Charles Gosselin.* 1841. 12mo, pp. 228. Portrait of M. Guizot. + [*Ibid.*] MDCCCXLIV. 12mo, pp. (3), 216. Portrait. B. + *Bruxelles: Meline & Co.* 1851. 12mo, pp. (2), 173, (1). H. + *Paris.* 1851. 2 vols., 8vo. 2 Portraits. 29268

GUIZOT. Washington. By Monsieur Guizot ... Translated by Henry Reeve, Esq. *London: John Murray.* MDCCCXL. Post

8vo, pp. xvi, 230. + *Paris: Galignani & Co.* 1840. 16mo. Portrait. 29269

Jared Sparks is the real author of this work. *See* Ellis's "Memoirs of Sparks."

GUIZOT. Washington. Por M. Guizot. *Madrid: Espinosa y Ca.* 1846. 16mo, pp. (2), xxi, 148. C. 29270

GULLIVER (J. P.) The Lioness and her Whelps: A Sermon on Slavery, ... Norwich, Ct., December 18, 1857. By Rev. J. P. Gulliver. ... *Norwich: Manning Perry.* 1860. 8vo, pp. 12.

Also: ... An Address at the Dedication of the Free Academy in Norwich ... *Norwich: L. & E. Edwards.* 1856. 8vo, 56. B.— ... A Discourse occasioned by the Death of Mrs. Mary Hooker. ... *Norwich, Conn.: J. G. Cooley.* 1853. 8vo, pp. 17.

GUMERSBAC (J.) Carta de la Vida del P. Juan Gumersbac. *Mexico.* 1737. 29272

GUMILLA (J. Informe, que hace a su Magestad, en su Real y Supremo Consejo de las Indias, el Padre Joseph Gumilla, de la Compañia de Jesus, sobre impeder à los Indios Caribes, y à los Olandeses las hostilidades, que experimentan las Colonias del gran Rio Orinoco y los medios mas oportunos para este fin. [*Madrid.* 1740?] Folio, pp. 16. H., J.C.B. 29273

Apparently a privately printed book.

GUMILLA. El Orinoco Ilustrado, historia, natural, civil y geographica de este gran Rio y de sus caudalosas vertientes; govierno, usos y costumbres de los Indios sus habitadores, con nuevas y utiles noticias de animales, arboles, frutos, aceytes, resinas yervas y raices medicinales: y sobre todo se hallaran conversiones muy singulares à nuestra Santa Fé y casos de mucha edificacion. Escrita por el P. Joseph Gumilla de la Compañia de Jesus, missionero y superior de las missiones del Orinoco, &c. *En Madrid: Por Manuel Fernandez.* 1741. 4to, 19 l., pp. 580, Index, 10 l. Map, 2 Plates. C., M. 29274

"At the time it was published, the good father was supposed to have availed himself of the traveller's privilege; but later discoveries have proved the truth of his assertions, and his work has received the credit to which it is entitled."—ALCEDO'S *MS.*

GUMILLA. El Orinoco | Ilustrado, y Defendido, | Historia Natural, | Civil, y Geographica | de este Gran Rio, | y de sus Caudalosas Vertientes; | Govierno, Usos, y Costumbres de los Indios | sus habitadores, con nuevas, y utiles noticias de Animales, Arboles, | Frutos, Aceytes, Resinas, Yervas, y Raices medicinales; y sobre | todo, se hallaràn conversiones muy singulares à N. Santa

Fé, | y casos de mucha edificacion. | Escrita | por el Padre Joseph Gumilla, ... Segunda Impression, Revista, y Aumentada | por su mismo Autor, y dividida en dos Partes. | ... *En Madrid: Por Manuel Fernandez, ... Año* M.DCC.XLV. 2 vols., 4to, 24 l., pp. 403, Indice, 4, Map and Plate; 4 l., pp. 412, Indice, 16, Plate.

GUMILLA. Historia Natural, Civil y Geografica de las naciones situadas en las riveras del Rio Orinoco. Sué autor el Padre Joseph Gumilla, Missionero que fué de las Missiones del Orinoco, Meta y Casanare. Nueva impression; mucho mas correcta que las anteriores, y adornada don ocho laminas finas, que manifiestan las costumbres y ritos de aquellos Americanos. Corregido por P. Ignacio Obregon. *Barcelona: En la Imprenta de Carlos Gilbert y Tuto.* MDCCLXXXXI. 2 vols., 4to, xvi, 360; 352. Portrait, Map and 7 Plates. H. 29276

"D'après l'avis qui se trouve en tête du tome II., ce volume a été revu et corrigé sur l'édition de 1745, par le Dr. A. D. Antonio Jugla y Font, par suite d'une indisposition du P. Ignacio Obregon."—LECLERC. The work of Father Gumilla is one of the most curious and interesting hitherto published upon the country of the Orinoco. Although the reverend Father passed many years of his life in America, his work is derived principally from the historic MSS. of the Fathers Mercado and Ribera. Of this last edition in Spanish there are copies on large paper.

GUMILLA. Histoire Naturelle, Civile et Géographique de l'Orenoque; Et des principales Rivières qui s'y jettent. Dans laquelle on traite du Gouvernement, des Usages & des Coûtumes des Indiens qui l'habitent, des Animaux, des Arbres, des Fruits, des Résines, des Herbes & des Racines Médicinales qui naissent dans le Païs. On y a joint le détail du plusieurs conversions remarquables et édifiantes. Par le P. Joseph Gumilla, de la Compagnie de Jesus, Supérieur des Missions de l'Orenoque. Traduite de l'Espagnol sur la seconde Edition, par M. Eidous, ci devant Ingenieur des Armées de S. M. C. *A Avignon: Desaint & Saillant,* M.DCC.LVIII. 3 vols., 12mo, pp. xviii, (7), 388, Table, 4, Map and Plate; (2), 334, Table, 4, Plate; (2), 332, Table, 4.

This French version is abridged.

Gun & Co.'s Index to Advertisements which have appeared in the Newspapers published in ... [the] United States of America, &c., since 1600, for next of Kin, Heirs at Law, Legatees, and cases of Unclaimed Money. *London.* 1865–69. 8vo. 29278

GUNCKEL (L. B.) Speech of Hon. Lewis B. Gunckel, of Montgomery County, delivered in the Senate of Ohio, March 2, 1863, on the Resolutions of Mr. Welch in favor of the Union. [n. p. n. d.] 8vo, pp. 11. 29279

GUNN (A.) Memoirs of the Rev. John H. Livingston. ... Prepared in compliance with a request of the General Synod of the Reformed Dutch Church of North America. By Alexander Gunn. ... *New-York: William A. Mercein.* 1829. 8vo, pp. 540. Portrait. C. + A New Edition ... with New Matter. *New-York: Ref. Prot. Dutch Church Board of Publication.* 1856. 12mo, pp. 405. S. 29280

GUNN. A Sermon, occasioned by the Death of ... Rev. Dr. John N. Abeel, ... containing a short Account of [his] Life and Character ... Preached the 26th January, 1812, ... By Alexander Gunn, A.M. *New-York: Whiting & Watson.* 1812. 8vo, pp. 24. 29281

Also: Sermon on the Prevailing Vice of Intemperate Drinking, Bloomingdale, January 1, 1813. ... *New York.* 1813. 8vo, pp. 24. N.

GUNN (O. B.) New Map and Hand-Book of Kansas & the Gold Mines. Containing Descriptions ... of the Indian Tribes ... Soil ... with Descriptions of all the Routes to the New Gold Mines ... . By O. B. Gunn ... . *Pittsburgh: Printed by W. S. Haven.* 1859. 12mo, pp. 71. BA. 29282

GUNN (T. B.) The Physiology of New York Boarding-Houses. By Thomas Butler Gunn. ... *New York: Mason Brothers.* 1857. 12mo, pp. 300. 29283

GUNNING (B.) Funeral Oration upon the Death of General George Washington, prepared at the request of Masonic Lodge No. 14, of Wilmington, State of Delaware, &c. By Bedford Gunning, A.M. *Wilmington: Printed at the Franklin Press, by Jas. Wilson.* 1800. Sm. 4to, pp. 19. 29284

GUNNISON (J. W.) The Mormons, or, Latter-Day Saints, in the Valley of The Great Salt Lake: A History of their Rise and Progress, Peculiar Doctrines, Present Condition and Prospects, derived from Personal Observation, during a Residence among them. By Lieut. J. W. Gunnison. ... *Philadelphia: Lippincott, Grambo & Co.* 1853. 12mo, pp. 168. Plate. C., P.

Some copies have a London imprint.

GUNNISON. Die Mormonen im Thale des grossen Salzsees. Deutsch von M. B. Lindau. *Dresden.* 1857. 29286

GÜNTHER (F. B.) Berichte über Ost-Tennessee und die deutsche Ansiedelung. *Stuttgart: Hoffman.* 1849. 8vo, pp. 48.

GURGEL (M. J. do A.) O conselheiro Manoel Joaquim do Amaral Gurgel. Elogio historico e noticia dos successos politicos que precederão e seguirão-se á proclamação da Independencia na Provincia de S. Paulo, pelo Dr. Olegario Herculano de Aquino e Castro. *Rio de Janeiro.* 1871. 8vo, pp. x, 164. 29288

GURIDI ALCOCER (J. M.) Apología de la Aparicion de Nuestra Senora de Guadalupe de Méjico en respuesta á la disertacion que la impugna. Su autor el Dr. D. José Miguel Guridi Alcocer. *Mejico, Año de* 1820, *en la Oficina de Don Alejandro Valdes.* 4to, 4 l., pp. 201, (9). 29289

Also: Exortacion para el juramento de la constitucion en la parroquia del sagrario. *Mejico.* 1820. 4to, 16 l.

[GURIDI Y ALCOZER (J. M.)] Ley, justicia y verdad, resplandecen en la suprema corte de justicia de Mexico, por la inocencia del regidor Paz. *Mexico.* 1828. 4to. 29290

GURLEY (G. H.) Catalogue of ... Books ... relating to American History. Sold April [1844?] *New York.* [1844?] 8vo, pp. 44. 29291

GURLEY [Henry H.] Speech of Mr. Gurley, ... delivered ... in Support of ... the Bill for the Relief of Marigny D'Auterive. January 11, 1828. *Washington: Printed by Peter Force.* 1828. 8vo, pp. 16. 29292

GURLEY (J. A.) Confiscation and Emancipation. Speech ... May 26, 1862. *Washington.* 1862. 8vo, pp. 8. 29293

GURLEY. Money and Paper. Bank Bill. Soldiers must be Paid. Why not Paid. Speech ... in House of Representatives, January 15th, 1863. [n. p. n. d.] 8vo, pp. 8. 29294

GURLEY. ... Speech ... on ... the Public Printing. Delivered ... May 30, 1860. [n. p. n. d.] 8vo, pp. 14. 29295

GURLEY. The War must be Prosecuted with more Vigor. Speech ... in House of Representatives, January 29, 1862. [n. p. n. d.] 8vo, pp. 8. 29296

Also: The West for the Union, now and forever. Speech ... January 16, 1861. [n. p. n. d.]

GURLEY (J. Ward). An Address delivered before the Grand Lodge of Massachusetts, ... December, 27, 5802. By Brother John W. Gurley. *Boston: Printed by Brothers Russell and Culter.* 5803. 8vo, pp. 20. 29297

Largely devoted to a notice of Washington.

GURLEY (L. B.) Sermon on the Victory at Fort Donelson, and Moral Aspects of the Rebellion. Delivered in Galion, Ohio, February 23, 1862. By Rev. L. B. Gurley. *Cincinnati: Methodist Book Concern.* 1862. 8vo, pp. 28. 29298

GURLEY (P. D.) Man's Projects and God's Results. A Sermon: Preached by the Rev. P. D. Gurley, D.D., on Thursday, August 6, 1863, being the Day of National Thanksgiving, Praise and Prayer. *Washington, D. C.: Wm. Ballantyne.* 1863. 8vo, pp. 20. 29299

GURLEY. The Voice of the Rod. A Sermon: Preached on Thursday, June 1, 1865, on The New York Avenue Presbyterian Church, Washington, D. C., By Rev. P. D. Gurley, D.D., ... *Washington: William Ballantyne.* 1865. 8vo, pp. 16. B.

See also the "National Preacher."

GURLEY (R. R.) A Discourse, delivered on the Fourth of July, 1825, in the City of Washington. By Ralph Randolph Gurley. *Washington: Printed by Gales & Seaton.* 1825. 8vo, pp. 21. 29301

On colonization and slavery.

GURLEY. Life and Eloquence of the Rev. Sylvester Larned, ... [in which is contained his Portrait.] By R. R. Gurley. *New York: Wiley and Putnam.* 1844. 8vo, pp. 412. C. 29302

GURLEY. Life of Jehudi Ashmun, Late Colonial Agent in Liberia. With an Appendix, containing Extracts from his Journal and other Writings, with a brief Sketch of the Life of the Rev. Lott Carey. By Ralph Randolph Gurley. *Washington: J. C. Dunn.* 1835. 8vo, pp. 396, 160. Portrait. [Some copies have the imprint:] *New York: Leavitt, Lord & Co.* 1835. pp. vii, 17–396, (1), 160. + Second Edition. [*Ibid.*] 1840.

Also: Address at the Annual Meeting of the Pennsylvania Colonization Society, November 11, 1839. ... *Philadelphia: Hermann Hooker.* 1839. 8vo, pp. 40.—Letter ... on the American Colonization Society. ... Washington, April 9, 1833. [n. p. n. d.] 8vo, pp. 8.—Memorial to Congress for the Purchase of Catlin's Collection of Indian Portraits, 1848. 8vo.—Mission to England, in behalf of the American Colonization Society. *Washington: Wm. W. Morrison.* 1841. 12mo, pp. xii, 264.

GURLEY (R.) *and Co.* Catalogues of Books on American History, sold by Auction. *New-York.* 1849. S. 29304

GURNEE (L.) The Modern Inquisition: or Popery Outdone. The Infallibility of the Clergy and Officers of the Presbyterian Church, and their Authority over Private Members: As Assumed

and Maintained in the Trial and Suspension of Lucien Gurnee, a Member of the First Presbyterian Church in Romulus, N. Y. *Waterloo: Charles Sentell.* 1844. 8vo, pp. 48. 29305

GURNEY (D.) A Sermon ... December 5, 1792, at the Ordination of the Rev. Edward Richmond, ... Stoughton. By David Gurney ... *Boston: Printed by Thomas and John Fleet.* [1793.] 8vo, pp. 42. M., N. 29306

GURNEY (J.) A Funeral Sermon ... of Miss Sarah Coffin Whitney ... 1810 ... 14th January. By James Gurney, A.B. ... *New-Bedford: Printed by Benjamin Lindsey.* 1810. 8vo, pp. 27.

GURNEY (Joseph). Arguments of Counsel in the Cases of the Snipe, the Martha, the Vesta, and other American Vessels, detained under the orders in council, and brought to Adjudication in the High Court of Admiralty, before the R: H. Sir Wm. Scott, in July, 1812. Taken in Short-hand by Mr. Gurney. *London.* 1812. 8vo, pp. 296. 29308

GURNEY (J. J.) Familiar Letters to Henry Clay of Kentucky, describing A Winter in the West Indies. By Joseph John Gurney. ... *New-York: Mahlon Day & Co.* 1840. 8vo, pp. 203. C. 29309

For the English edition, *see* "A Winter," etc., *infra.*

GURNEY. A Journey in North America, described in Familiar Letters to Amelia Opie. By Joseph John Gurney. Not to be Reprinted in Part or Whole without the Author's Permission. *Norwich: Printed for Private Circulation, by Josiah Fletcher.* 1841. 8vo, pp. 416. 29310

GURNEY. Reconciliation respectfully recommended to all Parties in the Colony of Jamaica. A Letter addressed to the Planters. By Joseph John Gurney. *London: George Wightman.* 1840. 12mo, pp. 24. 29311

Reprinted from his "Winter in the West Indies." *See* Appendix C.

GURNEY. A Winter in the West Indies, described in Familiar Letters to Henry Clay of Kentucky. By Joseph John Gurney. *London: John Murray.* 1840. 8vo, pp. 304. + The Second Edition. [*Ibid.*] s. + The Third Edition. [*Ibid.*] 1841. 8vo, pp. xvi, 282. Illustrations. B. + The Fourth Edition. 1841. 12mo. 29312

GURNEY. Un Hiver aux Antilles en 1839–40, ou lettres sur les résultats de l'abolition de l'esclavage dans les colonies anglaises

des Indes occidentales, adressées à Henri Clay, du Kentucky, et traduites de l'anglais sur la 3e édition, par J. J. Pacaud. *Paris: Firmin Didot frères.* 1842. 8vo, pp. xi, 358. C. 29313

GURNEY. Een Winter in de West-Indiën, beschreven in gemeenzame brieven aan Henry Clay van Kentucky. Naar den vierden druk, uit het Engelsch vertaald door C. J. Zweerts. *Amsterdam: M. H. Binger.* 1843. 8vo, pp. (2), vi, (2), 248.

Also: Brief Memoirs of Thomas Fowell Buxton and Elizabeth Fry. ... *London: Charles Gilpin.* 1845. Sm. 8vo, pp. 74.—Familiar Sketch of William Wilberforce. 1840. 18mo.—A Letter to the Followers of Elias Hicks, in the City of Baltimore and its Vicinity. *Baltimore Printed.* 1839. 8vo, pp. 56. + The Second Edition. [*Ibid.*] 1840.—Letter to Friends of the Monthly Meeting of Adrian, Michigan. ... *New York Printed.* 1839. 8vo, pp. 15. S. + *Bristol: George Davey.* 1846. 8vo, pp. 15. Also reprinted in a work entitled "Calumny Refuted." 1846. 8vo.—Observations on the Distinguishing Views and Practices of the Society of Friends. ... First American, from the Seventh London Edition. *New York: Mahlon Day & Co.* 1840. 8vo, pp. viii, 338. B.—Speech ... on the Abolition of Negro Slavery, ... 28th January, 1824. *Liverpool: Rushton and Melling, Printers.* [1824.] 8vo, pp. 16.—Substance of a Speech ... Norwich ... 28th January, 1824, on the subject of British Colonial Slavery. *London: Printed by Ellerton and Henderson.* 1824. 8vo, pp. 16 + *Norwich: Printed by Burks and Kinnebrook.* 1824. 12mo, pp. 30.—Free and Friendly Remarks on a Speech lately delivered to the Senate of the United States, by Henry Clay, of Kentucky, on the Subject of the Abolition of North American Slavery. 1839. Reprinted at the end of his "Winter in the West Indies," &c.

GURNEY. A Defence of the Religious Society of Friends, who constitute the Yearly Meeting of Baltimore, against Certain Charges circulated by Joseph John Gurney. *Baltimore: Printed by William Wooddy.* 1839. 8vo, pp. 18. 29315

GURNEY. Mrs. Gurney's Apology, in Justification of Mrs. ——'s Friendship. *Philadelphia: William Brotherhead.* MDCCCLX. Rl. 8vo, pp. (4), 51. B. 29316

Relates to a scandalous affair of the free-love order.

GURNEY (S.) Epitome of Proceedings at a Telegraphic Soiree on the great Advantages for Communication with America, by Samuel Gurney, M.P., Princes Gate, Hyde Park, March 26th, 1862. *Privately printed.* 1842. 8vo. 29317

GUROWSKI (*Count* A. G. de). America and Europe. By Adam G. De Gurowski. *New York: D. Appleton and Company.* M.DCCC.LVII. 12mo, pp. viii, 411. S. 29318

GUROWSKI. Diary, from March 4, 1861, to November 12, 1862. By Adam Gurowski. *Boston: Lee and Shepard.* 1862. 12mo, pp. (2), 315. + Diary, from November 18, 1862, to October 18, 1863. ... Volume Second. *New-York: Carleton.* M DCCC LXIV. 12mo, pp. 348. 29319

GUROWSKI. Diary, 1863, '64, '65. By Adam Gurowski. ... *Washington: W. H. & O. H. Morrison.* 1866. 12mo, pp. 413.

GUROWSKI. Slavery in History. By Adam Gurowski. *New York: A. B. Burdick.* 1860. 12mo, pp. xiv, 260. B., C. 29321

GUSMÃO (P. Alexandre de). Sermão na Cathedral da Bahia de todas os Sanctos nas Exequias de Illmo Sr. D. Fr. João de Madre de Deus, primeiro Arcobispo da Bahia. *Lisboa, por Miguel Manescal.* 1686. 4to, pp. iv, 19. 29322

GUSS (A. L.) The Coward's Curse and Patriot's Duty: A Discourse ... Sept. 18, 1861, before Capt. McCullough's Military Company, in ... Centreville, Cumb'd. Co., Pa. By Rev. A. L. Guss, A.B., ... *Carlisle, Pa.: Printed at the "Herald" Office.* 1861. 8vo. 29323

GUSTAVUS VASSA. *See* Equiano (Olaudah), Vol. IV.

[GUTHRIE (Abelard).] The Shawnee Indians. [*Kansas.* 1868.] 8vo, pp. 11. 29324

GUTHRIE. To the Public. [Assailing the Character of Charles Robinson. Dated Quindaro, Kansas Territory, Dec. 31, 1860.] 8vo, pp. 16. 29325

GUTHRIE (J.) Speech of the Hon. James Guthrie in the Senate of Kentucky, on the Proposition to confer Banking Privileges on the Charleston and Cincinnati Railroad Company. [n. p. n. d.]. 8vo, pp. 16. M. 29326

GUTHRIE (W.) A New System of Modern Geography, ... By William Guthrie, Esq. ... *London.* 1770. 4to. + A New Edition. *London: C. Dilly, &c.* 1780. 4to. + [*Ibid.*] 1786. 4to. + Fourth Edition. [*Ibid.*] 1788. 4to. S. + Sixth Edition. [*Ibid.*] MDCCXCV. pp. (11), 1098, (28). H. + The First American Edition. *Philadelphia: Mathew Carey.* M.DCC.XCIV–M.DCC.XCV. 2 vols., 4to, pp. 572; iv, 704, 43. 49 Maps. C.

Frequently reprinted. The American edition contains twenty-one maps of th States, &c., not in the English edition, also much matter relating to America. *See* "M. Rev.," LXII. 490. A Spanish version was published at *Madrid.* 1804–1808. 12 vols., 12mo. It was reproduced as: A New Geographical, Historical and Commercial Grammar; and Present State of the several Kingdoms of the World. ... Eighth Edition. *London: Charles Dilly.* 1783. 8vo, pp. 848. Map. + Ninth Edition. [*Ibid.*] 1785. 8vo, pp. 928. Map. + Eleventh Edition. *London.* 1788. + Fourteenth Edition, Corrected, &c. *London: Charles Dilly.* 1794. 2 vols., 8vo, pp. 12, (4), 965. + Sixteenth Edition. *London.* 1796. 8vo, pp. xii, 971. + Eighteenth Edition. *London.* 1801. 8vo, pp. 6, (1), 1076. + *Montrose.* 1805. 8vo. + First American Edition. *Philadelphia: Johnson & Warner.* 1809. 2 vols., 8vo, pp. 7, 556; 3, 496. + *Philadelphia.* 1815. 2 vols., 8vo. + Twenty-fourth Edition. *London.* 1827. 8vo.

GUTHRIE. General History of the World, from the Creation to the Present Time, including all the Empires, Kingdoms, and States, etc., with their Chronology, Antiquities, Curiosities, etc. By W. Guthrie, assisted by other eminent writers. *London: J. Newberry.* MDCCLXIV. 12 vols., 8vo. H. 29328

Dr. Samuel Johnson is said to have contributed to this work. *See* [Knox (J.)]

GUTHRIE (W. E.) Oration on the Death of Abraham Lincoln. Addressed to the American People, By Dr. W. E. Guthrie. *Philadelphia: John Penington & Sons.* 1865. 18mo, pp. 9.

GUTIERRES CORONEL (R. J.) ... Sermon panegyrico, que en ocasion de estarse celebrando el quarto concilio Provincial Mexicano predico, ... el Dr. Ricardo Josef Gutierres Coronel. *Mexico.* 1771. 4to, 10 l., pp. 21. 29330

[GUTIERREZ (Alonzo).] Speculum Conjugiorum dictum per R. P. F. Illephonsum a Veracruce Instituti Hæremitarum Sancti Augustini, Artium ac Sacræ Theologiæ doctorē Cathed. primariæ in inclyta Mexicana Academia Moderatorem. *Mexici in Ædibus Joannis Pauli Brissensis.* 1556. 4to. 29331

An extremely rare volume, being one of the earliest specimens of printing in the New World.

[GUTIERREZ.] Speculum Conjugiorum cum Indicibus locupletissimis et Appendix. *Ex Officina Jo. Graciani.* 1572. 4to.

The author went to Mexico in 1535, where he joined the order of St. Augustine, and became the founder of the celebrated library of that order. During a period of many years, he dedicated himself to the conversion of the Indians, and being a perfect master of the Mexican and Tarascan languages, he met with considerable success, and was undoubtedly one of the most acute and distinguished theologians of the New World.

GUTIERREZ (B. J.) Vindicacion del juez de Circuito de Sinora, Sinaloa y Baja California, Blas J. Gutierrez, acusado de perturbador del orden publico por D. Pomposo Verdugo. *Mexico.* 1856. 4to, pp. 31. 29333

GUTIERREZ (C.) Relacion de las fiestas triumphales que la insigne universidad de Lima hizo a la immaculada Conception de Nuestra Señora, por Diego Cano Gutierrez. *Lima: por Francisco Lasso.* 1619. 4to. 29334

[GUTIERREZ (Eusebio).] Esposicion que presenta en Bolivia el ministro de estado, en el despacho del interior, à la convencion nacional. *En* 1843. *Imprenta de Beeche y Cia.* 4to, pp. 18.

GUTIERREZ (Fr.) Poesias en la vistosa porteria del convento parroquial de S. Francisco de Toluca de nuestra deseada independencia. [*Mexico.*] 1822. 4to, 5 l. 29336

GUTIERREZ (J. J.) Voto a favor de los primeros caudillos de la libertad americana. [*Mexico.*] 1822. 12mo. 29337

GUTIERREZ (J. M.) Apuntes biograficos de escritores, oradores y hombres de estado de la Republica Argentina, por José Maria Gutierrez. *Buenos-Aires.* 1860. 8vo, pp. 294. 29338

GUTIERREZ. Bibliographia de la primera imprenta de Buenos Aires desde su fundacion hasta el año de 1810 inclusive o Catalogo de las producciones de la Imprenta de Ninos Espositos, con observaciones y noticias curiosas. Precedida de una biografia del virey Don Juan José de Vertiz y de una disertacion sobre el orijen del arte de imprimír en America y especialmente en el Rio de la Plata. Por el Dr. D. Juan Maria Gutierrez. Orijenes del arte de imprimir en la America Espanola, Introduccion a la Bibliografia de la imprenta de Ninos Espositos desde su fundacion en 1781 hasta Mayo de 1819. ... *Buenos Aires: Imprenta de Mayo.* 1866. 8vo, pp. (2), 43, 246. B. 29339

Fifty copies only printed.

GUTIERREZ. Bosquejo Biográfico del General D. José de San Martin por Juan Maria Gutierrez. Nueva Edicion correjida y aumentada con un rapido parablo entre San Martin y Bolivar, por el mismo autor. *Buenos Aires: Imprenta de Mayo.* 1868. 12mo, pp. 143, (2). B. 29340

GUTIERREZ. El doctor don Baltazar Maziel, Primer cancelario de los estudios públicos de Buenos-Aires. Por Don Juan Maria Gutierrez. ... *Buenos-Aires: Imprenta de Mayo.* 1864. 8vo, pp. 52. 29341

GUTIERREZ. Estudios biograficos y criticos sobre algunos poetas Sud-Americanos anteriores al siglo XIX. Por Juan Maria Gutierrez. *Buenos Aires.* 1865. 8vo, pp. viii, 358. 29342

Contains biographical and critical studies on eight South American poets, most of whom flourished in the sixteenth and seventeenth century. Written with great taste and considerable judgment.

GUTIERREZ. Frai Domingo de Neyra. Hyo de Buenos-Aires: Sus viajes por España, Italia, Francia, Inglaterra y el Brasil durante el primer tercio del siglo XVIII. Por Juan Maria Gutierrez. ... *Buenos-Aires: Imprenta de Mayo.* 1865. 8vo, pp. 67. B. 29343

[GUTIERREZ.] Noticia sobre la persona y escritos del Sr. D. Avelino Diaz ... . *Buenos Aires: Imprenta de La Revista.* [n. d.] Sm. 8vo, pp. 40. B. 29344

GUTIERREZ. Noticias historicas sobre le Orijen y Desarrollo de la Enseñanza Pública Superior en Buenos Aires, desde la Epoca de la Estincion de la Compañia de Jesus en el año 1767 hasta poco despues de fundada la Universidad en 1821. Con Notas, biografias, datos, estadisticos y documentos curiosos inéditos ó poco conocidos. Por Juan Maria Gutierrez. *Buenos Aires: Imprenta del Siglo.* 1868. Folio, pp. xvii, (3), 941. B.

GUTIERREZ. Pensamientos, maximas, sentencia, etc., de escritores, oradores y hombres de estado de la republica Argentina, con notas y biografias por Juan Maria Gutierrez. Prima parte (Pensamientos). *Buenos Aires.* 1859. 8vo, pp. iv, 312. 29346

GUTIERREZ. Poesia Americana. Composiciones selectas escritas por poetas Sud-Americanos de fama, tanto modernos como antiguos. Publicadas por la imprenta del siglo bajo la direccion de D. Juan Maria Gutierrez. *Buenos Aires: Imprenta del Siglo.* 1866–67. 2 vols., 8vo, pp. (2), 191, ii–vi; viii, 192, v. B., H.

Fifty copies only printed.

GUTIERREZ. Poesias de Juan Maria Gutierrez. *Buenos Aires.* 1869. 8vo, pp. x, 336. 29348

GUTIÉRREZ (J. P.) Memorias Histórico-Politicas. Tomo I. *Bogotá.* 1865. Rl. 8vo. 29349

No more published.

GUTIERREZ (R.) La fibra salvage. Canto al Dr. D. Miguel Cané, por Ricardo Gutierrez. *Buenos Aires.* 1860. 8vo, pp. 66.

GUTIERREZ. Lázaro. Poema de Ricardo Gutierrez. *Buenos Aires.* 1862. 18mo, pp. 112. 29351

GUTIERREZ DE ALBA (José M.) Fábulos politicas dedicadas al pueblo libre. *Carácas.* 1857. 12mo, pp. 92. 29352

GUTIERREZ DAVILA (J.) *See* Davila (J. G.), Vol. V., No. 18778.

Add to the collation, 1 Plate, and to No. 18779 add for collation pp. (36), 400, (8)

GUTIERREZ ESTRADA (J. M.) Carta dirigida al Escino Sr. Presidente de la Republica, sobre necessidad de buscar en una Convencion el posible remedio de los males que aquejan à la República. *Mexico.* 1840. 8vo. 29353

Also: Algunas reflecsiones acerca de los dolorosos sucesos ocuridos [en Mexico] durante la ultima mitad del mes de julio [de 1840].

GUTIERREZ DE ESTRADA. Discurso pronunciado en el Palacio de Miramar el 3 de Octubre de 1863 por el presidente de la diputacion mejicana, encargada á ofrecer la corona de Mejico al Archiduque Maximiliano, y contestacion del Archiduque. *Paris.* 1863. 8vo. 29354

GUTIERREZ DE ESTRADA. Mexico en 1840 y en 1847. Por D. J. M. Gutierrez de Estrada. *Mexico.* 1848. Sm. 8vo, pp. 40.

GUTIERREZ DE ESTRADA. Méjico y el Archiduque Fernando Maximiliano. *Paris.* 1862. 8vo. 2 Portraits. + *Mexico.* 1863. 8vo. 29356

GUTIERREZ DE ESTRADA. Le Mexique et l'archiduc Fernand Maximilien d'Autriche. *Paris: Garnier frères.* 1862. 8vo. 2 Portraits. 29357

GUTIERREZ DE LÀ HUERTA (Francisco). Dictamen leido y presentado en el Consejo de Castilla sobre el restablecimiento de los Jesuitas. *Méxice: R. Rafael.* 1849. 8vo, pp. v, 178.

GUTIERREZ DE RUBALCAVA (J.) Proyecto para galeones y flotas de el Peru, y Nueva España, y para navios de registro, y avisos, que navegaren a ambos reynos. *Cadiz.* 1720. 12mo, pp. 60. 29359

This was reproduced with the following work.

GUTIERREZ DE RUBALCAVA. Tratado historico, politico y legal de el comercio de las Indias Occidentales, pertenecientes a los Reyes Catholicos, conforme al tiempo de Paz, y Guerra, en interpretacion de las Leyes de la Nueva Recopilacion à ellas, Compendio historico del Comercio de las Indias, desde su principio hasta su actual Estado. Su autor Don Joseph Gutierrez de Rubalcava ... [Colophon:] *Impresso en Cadiz, en la Imprenta Real de Marina de Don Manuel Espinosa de los Monteros.* [1750.] 12mo, 32 l., pp. 351. C. 29360

No date on the title, but the several licences and dedication are dated 1750. At the end, with separate title and paging, is "*Proyecto para Galeones.*"

GUTS-MUTHS (J. Ch. F.) Vollständige Erdbeschreibung von Chile, Arauca, Patagonien, der Falklandinseln und der Süd-Polar Eilande. *Weimar.* 1830. 8vo. 29361

GUTS-MUTHS. Vollständige und neueste Erdbeschreibung des britischen, niederländischen und französischen Guyana's und des Kaiserthums Brasilien mit einer Einleitung zu Südamerika bearbeitet von J. Ch. F. Guts-Muths. *Weimar.* 1827. 8vo, pp. 1254.

Guts-Muths. Vollständige Erdbeschreibung des Staats Columbia. *Weimar.* 1830. 8vo. 29363

Guyane Française. *See* Cayenne *and* Guiana.

Guyer (I. D.) History of Chicago; its Commercial and Manufacturing Interests and Industry; ... . By I. D. Guyer. *Chicago: Church, Goodman & Cushing.* 1862. 8vo, pp. 200. Plates. 29365

Guyho (M. C.) L'armée son histoire ... à Rome, en France, en Europe et aux États-Unis ... . Par M. Corentin Guyho ... . *Paris: Ernest Thorin.* 1870. 8vo, pp. (2), 498. B. 29364

Guyon (*l'abbé*). Histoire des Amazones anciennes et modernes ... . En deux parties. *Paris.* 1740. 12mo. + *Bruxelles: Jean Leonard.* 1741. 8vo, pp. (4), lxlvii, (1), 210. Plates. B.

Includes an account of the American Amazons. *See also* "Putnam's Magazine," Vol. VI. 252.

Guzman (A. E. de). The Life and Acts of Don Alonzo Enriquez de Guzman, a Knight of Seville of the Order of Santiago, A.D. 1518 to 1543, Translated from an Original and Inedited Manuscript in the National Library at Madrid; With Notes and an Introduction By Clements R. Markham. ... *London: For the Hakluyt Society.* M DCCC LXII. 8vo, pp. xxv, (1), 168. 29367

Forms Vol. XXIX of the Publications of the Hakluyt Society.

Guzman (A. Leocadio). El Evangelio liberal. El defensa de la causa liberal. *Curazao, Oct.* 1869. 8vo, pp. 48. + Reprinted, *Carácas.* 1869. Pt. II. *Curazao, Nov.* 1869. pp. 32. + Pt. III. (*Curazao*), *Carácas.* 1870. 29368

G[uzman]. Ojeada al proyecto de Constitucion que el Libertador ha presentado á la República Bolivar. Por A. L. G. *Lima.* 1826. 4to, pp. 52. + *Carácas: Reimpresso por Devisme.* 1826–28. 4to, 2 l., pp. 64, 108. 29369

The second part of the Caracas edition consists of decrees and proclamations by Bolivar.

[Guzman.] Informe del Secretario de Estado en los Despachos del Interior y Justicia y Relaciones Exteriores á S. E. es Presidente de la República. *Carácas.* 1848. 8vo, pp. 8. 29370

Guzman. Venezuela Loan, 1862. A Letter [translated] addressed to Messrs. Baring Brothers and Co., by Antonio L.

Guzman, Fiscal Agent of the Republic of Venezuela; with copies of Documents referred to therein. *London.* 1865. 8vo, pp. 38. 29371

Also: Aniversario de la entrada de los restos del inmortal Bolivar, Libertador, Padre de cinco Naciones, en su patria la Ciudad de Carácas. *Carácas.* 1845. 8vo, pp. 13.—Inmunidades consulares. *Carácas.* 1852. 8vo, pp. ii, 51.

Guzman (D. de G.) Arte Mexicano, ò Grammatica de la Lengua Mexicana. Por Diego de Galdo Guzman, Proprietario de las Lenguas Mexicana, y Otomi, en la Real Universidad de Mexico. *En Mexico, por la Viuda de Bernardo Calderon.* 1642. 8vo. 29372

Extremely rare. Ternaux, Brunet, and Ludewig give the date of this scarce volume as 1643. *See* Adelung.

Guzman (Diego Rodriguez). Ilvstracion de la destreza Indiana epistola officiosa qve escribio Don Francisco Santos de la Paz al maestro de campo, Don Francisco Lorenz de Rada. *En Lima: Ger. de Contreras y Alvarado.* 1712. 4to. 29373

Guzman (Jos. Javier). El Chileno instruido en la Historia topografica, civil y politica de su pais. *Santiago de Chile.* 1834. 8vo, pp. xvi, 927, 8. 29374

Guzman (J. M. V. de). Las Naves de Cortés Destruidas. Canto premiado por la Real Academia Española en Junta que celebró el dia 13 de Agosto de 1778. Su autor Don José Maria Vaca de Guzman. *Madrid: Joachin Ibarra.* [1778.] 4to, pp. 21. H. 29375

A poem founded upon the destruction of the ships of Cortés by his order, after disembarking his forces upon the coast of Mexico.

Guzman (J. P. de). Breve Epitome de la restavracion de la isle de Santa Catalina, en las Indias Occidentales, executada por la buena disposicion del Maestro de Campo D. Juan Perez de Guzman, governador y capitan general del reyno de Tierra-Firme, y presidente de Panamà: sacandola del poder de los Ingleses, que la tenian tiranizada a los Españoles. [Colophon:] *Impresso en Sevilla, por Juan Gomez de Blas, su Impressor mayor. Año* 1667. 4to, 4 l. 29376

Not mentioned by Pinelo. "Le sujet de l'ouvrage est la prise de l'île de la Providence, nommée Santa-Catalina par les Espagnols, sur les boucaniers anglais qui s'étaient établis en 1629."—Leclerc.

Guzman (Fray Pedro José). La Religion perseguida por los anarquistas en la Nueva Granada. *Carácas.* 1851. 8vo, pp. 14.

Guzman (R. D. de). Historia del Descubrimiento, Conquista Poblacion del Rio de la Plata. *Asuncion.* 1854. Sm. 4to.

Guzman. Historia Argentina del descubrimiento, poblacion y conquista de las provincias del Rio de la Plata, escrita por Rui Diaz de Guzman, en el año 1612. Ilustrada con disertaciones y un indice ... *Reimpressa en Buenos Aires.* 1854. 3 vols., 4to, pp. 346; 358; 416. 29379

Consists of the works of Guevara, Gonzalez de Doblas, Thomas Falkner, Luis de la Cruz, and Barco Centenera.

Guzman (S.) El Peregrino Indiano, Poema de los Hechos de Hernan Cortes; por Antoine de Saavedra Guzman: viznieto del conde del Castellar, nacido en Mexico. *Madrid: Pedro de Madrigal.* 1599. 12mo. 29380

"A very rare Poem, celebrating the actions of Cortés."—Rich, who gives the date 1597. There was to have been a second part, which was never published. *See also* Ternaux, No. 232.

Gwatkin (T.) A Letter to the Clergy of New York and New Jersey, occasioned by an Address to the Episcopalians in Virginia. By the Rev. John Gwatkin, Prof. of Mathemathics in William and Mary College. *Williamsburg, Va.: Printed by Alex. Purdie and John Dixon.* 1772. Sm. 4to. 29381

See Shroeder's "Hobart," 57.

[Gwinn (C. J. M.)] The Washington Conspiracy against the Railroad Interests of Maryland. [n. p. n. d.] 8vo, pp. 20.

Gwin (W. M.) Remarks of the Hon. William M. Gwin in the Senate ... April 19 and 20, 1852, on the Deficiency Appropriation Bill, &c. *Washington.* [n. d.] 8vo, pp. 16. M. 29383

Also: Speech ... May, 1842, on Navy Appropriation. *Washington.* 1842. 8vo.—Speech ... July 8, 1842, on the Tariff. *Washington.* 1842. 8vo.—Speech ... August 2, 1852, on Public Lands. [n. p. n. d.]—Speech ... on the Bill to establish a Railway to the Pacific ... in the Senate, January 13, 1853. [n. p. n. d.] 8vo, pp. 8.—Speech ... on the Pacific Railroad. ... April 10, 1854. Railroad from the Mississippi to the Pacific. *Washington: Geo. S. Gideon.* 1854. 8vo, pp. 35. S.—Speeches ... on the Pacific Railroad Bill, April 8, and December 13, 1858. *Washington: Congressional Globe Office.* 1858. 8vo, pp. 22.

Gwinett (A.) The Life, Strange Voyages, and Uncommon Adventures of Ambrose Gwinett, Formerly known to the Public as The Lame Beggar, ... Containing an Account of ... His Voyage to the West-Indies ... *London: J. Barker.* [about 1750.]

A curious and perhaps apocryphal performance—possibly by Daniel De Foe.

Gwinett. The Life and Adventures of Ambrose Gwinett, ... Who for a Murder which he never committed, was tried, condemned, executed, and hung in chains, in old England; yet lived many Years afterwards, and in his Travels found the Man in the West-Indies actually alive, for the supposed Murder of whom he had been really executed. ... *Boston: Printed by J. White.* 1800. 8vo, pp. 24. BA. + [With] A Narrative of the extraordinary Adventures of four Russian Sailors, who were cast away, and lived for six Years, on the Desert Island of East-Spitzbergen. As related by themselves. *Philadelphia: Robert Bell.* M, DCC, LXXIV. 8vo, pp. 32. P. + *Newcastle: Angus.* [1817.] 12mo, pp. 24. 29385

Gwynn (S.) Official Report of Col. L. C. Baker, ... in the Case of Stuart Gwynn and S. M. Clarke. Also the Minority Report of the Treasury Investigating Committee, with accompanying Documents. June, 1864. *New York: Henry A. Oliver.* 1864. 8vo, pp. 48. 29386

See also Lyon (S. S.)

Gyles (J.) Memoirs of Odd Adventures, Strange Deliverances, etc., in the Captivity of John Gyles, Esq., Commander of the Garrison on St. George's River. Written by Himself. ... *Boston: Printed by S. Kneeland and T. Green.* MDCCXXXVI. 4to, pp. (3), 40, 4. B., H., M. 29387

A very rare pamphlet, which was republished with other narratives, *Boston: Samuel G. Drake.* 1846. 12mo.

H. (A. J.) *See* H[amilton] (A[ndrew] J.)

H. (E. A. W.) Ella Lincoln; or Western Prairie Life; An Autobiography, by Mrs. E. A. W. H. *Boston.* 1857. 12mo.

H. (G.) The World Surveyed: or, a Brief Account of many Remarkable Passages, wherein the Omnipotent Works of God are brought to our Knowledge. 1675. 12mo. 29389

Includes some account of America.

H. (G.) The American Mines, shewing their Importance with the Progress and Position of the Real del Monte Company. By G. H. *London.* 1834. 8vo. 29390

H. (I.) Faction, a Sketch; or, a Summary of the Causes of the Present most Unnatural and Indefensible of all Rebellion's; ... Written at New-York, February, 1776. By I. H. *New-York.* 1777. 8vo, pp. 8. BA. 29391

H. (J.) *See* H[ardy] (J.)

H. (J.) El Liberalismo y sus efectos en la republica mexicana. Por J. H. *Mexico: A. Boix.* 1858. 12mo, pp. 14. C.

H. (J.) *See* Häfkens (J.)

H. (J.) Morgan Lewis. [n. p. n. d.] 8vo, pp. 12. Portrait.

H. (J. A.) Examination of the Power of the President to remove from Office during the Recess of the Senate. *New York: Wynkoop, Hallenbeck & Thomas.* 1861. 8vo, pp. 23. H.

H.... (L. F. l'). Le champ-d'asile, Tableau topographique et historique du Texas, contenant ... . Par L. F. l'H...., (de l'ain,) l'un des auteurs des Fastes de la gloire. *Paris: Ladvocat.* 1819. 8vo, pp. 247. + Seconde édition augmentée d'une Description du Tombechbé et accompagné d'une carte de Texas, ainsi que de l'état de Marengo, dessinée par P. Ladvocat ... . [*Ibid.*] 1819. 8vo. 29395

Published for the benefit of the emigrants (to Texas?)

H. (M.) A Miscellaneous Collection, consisting of an Original Letter of Columbus, Original Poetry, etc. With Selections, by M. H. *London: T. Davison.* 1803. 4to, pp. 132. 29396

H. (M. J.) The Rivals: a Chickahominy Story. By Miss M. J. H. of Virginia. Illustrated. *Richmond: Ayres & Wade.* 1864. 8vo, pp. 61. 29397

H. (M. S.) The Soldier's Sacrifice. A Poem for the Times. ... By M. S. H. *Stoughton: The Author.* 1865. 16mo, pp. 38.

H. (*Mrs.*) Three Years in Field Hospitals of the Army of the Potomac. By Mrs. H. *Philadelphia: J. B. Lippincott & Co.* 1867. 16mo, pp. 131. 29399

H. (P. A.) Field, Gunboat, Hospital, and Prison; or, Thrilling Records of the Heroism, Endurance, and Patriotism displayed in the Union Army and Navy during the Rebellion. By Mrs. P. A. H. *Boston.* 1866. 12mo, pp. 379. 29400

H. (R.) *See* H[akluyt] (R[ichard]).

H. (R.) An Examination of Sundry Scriptures, alleadged by our Brethren (of New England) in Defence of some Particulars of their Churchway, by R. H., M.A. of Magd. Col. Camb. *London.* 1645. 4to. 29401

Chiefly in reply to Cotton on the Keys. It elicited the following reply:

H. (R.) Defence of Sundry Positions and Scriptures alleged to Justifie the Congregationall Way, charged at first to be weak therein, impertinent and unsufficient, by R. H., M.A., of Magd. Coll. Camb., in his Examination of them. But upon further Examination cleerly manifested to be sufficient pertinent and full of power, by Samuel Eaton and Timothy Taylor, of the Church in Duckenfield, in Cheshire. *London.* 1645. 4to. 29402

Connected with the controversy on the Question of Church Government in New England.

H. (R. G.) Memoria sobre la Propriedad Eclesiastica, Riqueza publica destruida y victimas hechas por los Demagogos de 858 hasta Junio, 1863. Escritas por R. G. H. *Mexico.* 1864. 12mo, pp. v, 52. 29403

H. (S.) *See* H[ume] (S[ophia]).

H. (T.) *See* [Johnson (Edward)].

H. (T.) A Short Way to know the World; or, The Rudiments of Geography. Second Edition. *London.* 1712. 16mo.

Haag (E. *and* E.) La France protestante ... par MM. Eugène et Émile Haag. ... *Paris.* 1846–58. 10 vols., 8vo.

Some of the lives relate to this country, that of Ribaut for instance.

[Haagensen.] Beskrivelse over Eylandet St. Croix i America i West-Indien. *Kiobenhavn: L. H. Lillies Enke.* 1758. 4to, pp. 72. J.C.B. 29406

The author's name is given on the authority of Meusel.

Haan (Lourens Feykes). Beschryving van de straat Davids, van de Zuydbay, tot om het eyland Disko. Als meede van de Z. O. bogt tot door het Waygat. *Amsterdam: G. van Keulen.* 1719. Sm. 4to, pp. 14. 29407

First edition; very rare. The following is an amplification of the same work.

Haan. Beschryving van de Straat Davids, benevens des zelven Inwooners, Zede, Gestalte, en Gewoonte, misgaders hunne Vischvangst, en andere Handelingen. Als mede een kort en keknopt verhaal van de Westkust van de zelfde Straat, of anders Noord-Amerika. *Amsterdam: Gerald van Keulen.* 1720. 4to, pp. 40. C. 29408

A description of the Strait of Davids, its inhabitants, manners, fishery; with an account of its Western coast or North America.

Haas (C. de). Nordamerika, Wisconsin, Calumet. Winke für Auswanderer. Zweite Auflage. *Elberfeld: Bädeker.* 1848. 8vo, pp. 96. View and Map. + Zweite vermehrte Auflage. [*Ibid.*] 8vo, pp. xii, 92. 3 Views and Map. 29409

Haas. Nordamerika. Wisconsin. Zwei Abtheilungen. Beschreibung von Wisconsin. Nebst Reisebildern von Alexander Ziegler. 1849. 8vo, pp. iv, 140. 29410

Haas (J. C.) Geographie von Amerika und insbesondere von den Vereinigten Staaten. *Philadelphia & Leipzig: Schäfer & Koradi.* 1867. 12mo, pp. 69. 29411

Habana. *See also* Havana.

Actas de las juntas generales que celebro la Real Sociedad economiga de amigos del pais de la Habana, en los dias 14, 15, y 16 de Diciembre de 1829. Ympressa de acuerdo de la misma Sociedad. *Habana.* 1830. pp. 366. Continued. 29412

Agricultura y comercio de la Habana. Estados varios. *Habana.* 1808. 4to, pp. 34. 29413

Anales de las reales junta de fomento y Sociedad economica de la Habana. Periodico mensual, dirigido por D. Francisco de P. Serrano, con real aprobacion. Tom. I. *Habana.* 1849. Continued. 29414

Anecdota de la Havana. [*Havana.* 1803.] 4to, pp. 22.

Apuntaciones sobre el Habanero. Periódico. 1824. 29416

Archivo de la Habana. Obra por entregas de literatura, ciencias y artes, consagrada á los intereses de todas clases de esta ciudad y su vecindurio. Por Manuel Zapatero. *Habana.* 1856–1857. 2 vols., 4to, pp. 196; 96. 29417

An Authentic Account of the Reduction of the Havana. *London.* 1762. 8vo. 29418

Title from Rich; perhaps the same as our No. 2450, Vol. I.

Bando de buen gobierno para la ciudad de la Havana 1792. *Reimpreso en la Imprenta de la capitania general.* 4to, pp. 42.

Categorias de la parte fisico-moral con relacion al Hombre Público, ó sea Anatomía racional de los miembros, que componen el Ayuntamiento constitucional de la Habana, en el presente año de 1821. 8vo, pp. 31. 29420

Coleccion de los partes y otros documentos publicados en la Gaceta Oficial de la Habana referentes à la invasion de la gavilla de piratas capitaneada por el traidor Narcisco Lopez. *Habana.* 1851. Sm. 4to, pp. 80. 29421

Copia de la Real Cedula de su Magestad, expedida para que en la Ciudad de San Christoval de la Habana se forme una Compania a cuyo Cargo este la Conduccion de Tabacos, Azucar, Corambres, y otros Frutos de la Isla de Cuba, con la Direccion, Reglas, Exempciones, y Obligaciones que se expressan. *Madrid.* 1740. 12mo. 29422

Declamation del Comercio de la Habana. *Imprenta de D. Juan Pablo en* 1813. 29423

Defensa de Don Diego Tabares Caballero del Orden de Santiago Mariscal de Campo de los Reales Exercitos, Contra los Cargos formados sobre el Sitio y Rendition de la Habana. [*Madrid.* 1764.] Folio, pp. 89. 29424

Defensa y Satisfaccion, que por la de su obligacion, y honor proprio expone. El Marques del R[l]. Transporte, Gefe de Esquadra de la Real Armada, y Comandante Principal de todos los Batallones de ella. A los Cargos que se han formado en la causa, mandada instruir, en virtud de Real Orden, por la Junta de Generales, que S. M. se ha dignado nombrar por ello. Sobre la conducta que tuvieron en la Defensa, Capitulacion, Perdida y Rendicion de la Plaza de la Habana, y Esquadra que se hallaba en su Puerto. Los Gefes, y oficiales comprehendidos en ella, y en la Junta de Guerra, que en la misma Plaza se havia tambien formado, en consequencia de otra Real Orden. *Madrid.* 1764. Folio, 74 l. 29425

Descripcion de la Iglesia parroquial de Ntra. Sra. de Guadalupe situada extramuros de la ciudad de la Habana, segun debe quedar conforme al proyecto formado por disposicion de Illmo. Sr. Obispo Diocesano actual. *Habana: Imprenta de D. Pedro Nolasco Palmer é hijo.* 1812. 4to, pp. 9. 29426

Descripcion histórica del Triunfo fúnebre de los manes de Portier-Laci, Vidal, el jóven Beltran de Lis y demas víctimas de la Patria que les consagra la Habana el 8 de Agosto de 1822. *Oficina Liberal de Campe.* 1822. 4to, pp. 57. 29427

Directorio de Artes, Comercio e Industrías de la Habana, 1860. *Habana.* 1860. 8vo, pp. vi, 264. 29428

Directorio de la Ciudad de la Habana. 1841. 12mo.

Estafas escandalosas de la hacienda pública de la Habana. Diálogo entre D. Toribio y Venancio. *Imprenta de D. P. N. Boloña.* 1822. 29430

Estatutos de la Sociedad anónima denominada Banco Industrial. *Habana.* 1865. 8vo, pp. 20. 29431

Estracto alfabetico de los Acuerdos generales é interesantes de la Junta superior de Hacienda, formado por orden del conde de Villannueva. *Habana.* 1846. 8vo. 29432

Exhortacion a los Fieles de la Ciudad de la Havana, hecha por su prelado diocesano, sobre el Cementerio General de ella; y su Reglamento, aprobado por el Gobierno, con el correspondiente de Policía. *Havana: En la Imprenta de Don Estevan Joseph Boloña.* MDCCCV. 4to, pp. 42. 29433

An Explanation. *See* Vol. VI., No. 23421.

Exposicion de las honras fúnebres que en la muerte del Sr. D. Fernando VII. de Borbon, Rey de España y de las Indias celebró el Excmo. Ayuntamiento de la Habana en 30 de Diciembre de 1833 en la santa iglesia Catedral en la oracion que en ella se pronunció. *Imprenta Fraternal.* 1834. 4to, pp. 25. 29434

Exposicion de la fiesta de gracias al arcángel S. Rafael por haber cesado la epidemia del cólera en el barrio de la parroquia del Santo Angel Custodia y de las exequias que los feligreses que fallecieron celebraron en junta de caridad é individuos calificadores, con los sermones que se predicaron en ellas. *Oficina de D. José Boloña impresor de la Real Marina por S. M.* [1834.] 4to, pp. 34. 29435

Exposicion del Intendente de ejército al público de la Habana. *En la Imprenta del Gobierno Constitucional.* 1820. Folio. 29436

A justification of the conduct of Sr. D. Alejandro Ramirez.

Exposicion que presenta. *See* Vol. VI., No. 23443.

La Farola de la Habana. *Imprenta de Boloña.* 1821. 29437

Informe que sobre el empedrado y limpieza de las calles de la Habana presentó a Su Exmo. Ayuntamiento el alcalde ordinario D. José de Pizarro y Gardin. *Habana.* 1831. 4to, pp. 28.

Letters from the Havana, during the year 1820; containing an Account of the Present State of the Island of Cuba, and Observations on the Slave Trade. *London: J. Miller.* 1821. Cr. 8vo, pp. x, 135. Map. C., P. 29439

Memoria acerca del estado de la enseñanza en la universidad de la Habana desde su fundacion hasta Octubre de 1864. *Habana.* 1865. 8vo, pp. 162. C. 29440

Memorias de la clase de derecho patrio del Real y Conciliar Colegio Seminario de la Habana. *Imprenta de Marina.* 1819. 4to, pp. 63. 29441

Memorias de la Real Sociedad Economica de la Habana. *Habana.* 1817. Sm. 4to. Continued. 29442

Contains valuable papers on the agriculture, productions, &c., of Cuba.

Memorias de la Real Sociedad Patriotica de la Habana. *Havana.* 1835. 8vo. Continued. 29443

After 1848 the title was changed to read: "Memorias de la Real Sociedad Economica de la Habana."

Notorias escandalosas injusticias del Tribunal mercantil de la Habana, protector de delincuentes. *Imprenta de Palmer.* 1820.

Observatorio fisico-meteorico de la Habana. Anuario publicado por d. Andres Poëy. Año primero. 1862. Tomo I. Barometria. *Habana: Viuda de Barcina & Comp.* 1869. Folio, 1 l., 7 l. C. 29445

Also: Observaciones magnéticas y meteorológicas hechas por los alumnos del colegio de Belen. Año meteorologico de 30 noviembre de 1869 a 30 de noviembre de 1870. *Habana: Imprenta y libreria religiosa.* 1870. 8vo. C.

Oracion del funeral que hizo la muy noble y leal ciudad de la Habana á las cenizas del gran descubridor de las Américas, &c. *Impresa por Boloña.* 1796. 29446

Ordenanzas de Comisarios de barrio de esta ciudad, aprobados por Real Cédula fecha en S. Lorenzo en 19 de Noviembre de 1769. *Reimpresas por D. José Boloña.* 1820. 29447

Ordenanzas para el Gobierno de la casa de beneficencia de la siempre fidelisima ciudad de la Habana. *Habana.* 1828. 8vo, pp. 30. 29448

Proceso formado de Orden S. M. á las autoridades de Cuba, cuando la toma de la plaza de la Habana, por los Ingleses. Folio.

Real Cédula de ereccion del Consulado de la Habana expedida en Aranjuez á 4 de Abril en 1794. *Reimpresa ... Arazoza y Soler.* 1820. 4to, pp. 59. 29450

Permiso para fabricar extramuros. *Imprenta Fraternal.* 1821. 4to. 29451

El Rayo á lo que quiere la Habana. *Imprenta de Boloña.* 1821.

Reglamento de los mayorales y mayordomos de ingenios. *Imprenta Fraternal.* 1821. 29453

Reglamento de policía de la Habana por el Excmo. Sr. Conde de Ricla, Gobernador y Capitan General. *Imprenta del Gobierno.* 1763. 29454

Relacion de las obras y fiestas públicas que para los dias 18, 19 y 20 de Marzo de 1828 se han dispuesto y ejecutado en la ciudad de la Habana, en memoria de la primera misa y del primer cabildo celebrado á la orilla de su puerto en 1519—y en justo y debido obsequio de los dias de la Reina Ntr. Sra. *Imprenta de D. José Severino Boloña.* 1828. 4to, pp. 33. 29455

Repique particular ó Memoria sobre peticion con dos proyectos, uno para sellar un millon de pesos en cuartillos y otro para una loteria municipal, todo por cuenta de la municipalidad de la Habana. *Imprenta de D. Antonio Valdés.* 1821. 29456

Revista de administracion de comercio y de jurisprudencia. Causa sobre falsificacion de Sellos de Franqueo y Billetos del Banco espanol de la Habana. *Habana.* 1860. 8vo, pp. 28.

Satisfaccion del Coronel Don Dionysio Solér, Theniente del Rey de la Habana, à los Cargos del Señor Fiscal, de la Excma. Junta de Guerra formada de ordende S. M. para conocer de la Defensa, rendicion, y pèrdida de aquella Plaza. [*Madrid.* 1764.] Folio, pp. 32. 29458

Satisfaccion del Mariscal de Campo D. Juan de Prado, Governador que ha sido de la Plaza de la Habana y Capitan General de la Isle de Cuba, a los Cargos, que se han formado en la causa pendiente en la Junta de Generales nombrados por S. M. Sobre la conducta, que tuvieron en la Defensa, Capitulacion, Rendicion y Perdida de la misma Plaza, y Esquadra surta en su Puerto, los Gefes y Oficiales de que compuso la Junta de Guerra, formada en ella en virtud de Real orden. [*Madrid.* 1764.] Folio, pp. 104. 29459

During the war between Great Britain and Spain in 1762, the port of Havana was surrendered to the English. These documents, described in 29458 and 29459, embrace the defence of the Spanish officers who were in command at the time, and who surrendered the city, the proceedings of the Court of Inquiry on the capitulation, with various letters and papers connected therewith. The city was restored to Spain the following year. They are without place or date, and were evidently intended only for the court and government, and not for sale. The proceedings took place in 1764. Two other documents on the subject are thus described in the Sobolewski Catalogue: Satisfaccion del coronel D. Dion. Soler à los cargos del Señor fiscal, de la junta de guerra formada de ordende S. M. para conocer de la defensa, rendicion y perdida de aquella plaza. pp. 36.—Satisfaccion del conde de Superunda, theniente general, y Virrey del Peru, etc. pp. 42.

A Todo el mundo entero dice la Habana. *Imprenta de D. Miguel de Oro.* 1821. 29460

The Habeas Corpus. [n. p. n. d.] 8vo, pp. 6. 29461

See [Johnston (James F.)], *also*, [Vaux (Richard)].

The Habeas Corpus. [The Act, the Writ, and the Privilege.] Its Death, and How it came by it. [Poetical.] *Printed by John Doe.* 1862. 4to, pp. 8. 29462

Habeas Corpus. The Proceedings in the Case of John Merryman of Baltimore County, Maryland, before the Hon. Roger Brooke Taney. ... *Baltimore: Lucas Brothers.* 1861. 8vo, pp. 24.

The Benefit of the Writ of Habeas Corpus is naturally Suspended until granted, and the Suspension is Lawful until made Unlawful. [n. p. n. d.] 8vo, pp. 6. 29464

The Suspending Power and Writ of Habeas Corpus. *Philadelphia: John Campbell.* 1862. 8vo, pp. 48. 29465

Habersham (A. W.) The North Pacific Surveying and Exploring Expedition; or, My Last Cruise. Where we Went and What we Saw: ... By A. W. Habersham, Lieut. U. S. Navy ... *Philadelphia: J. B. Lippincott & Co.* 1857. 8vo, pp. 507. C., S.

Habersham (R. W.) Speech of R. W. Habersham on the Tariff Bill; delivered in the House ... June 22, 1842. *Washington.* 1842. 8vo. 29467

Habersham (*Mr.*) A Letter from Mr. Habersham, (Super-Intendent of Temporal Affairs at the Orphan-House in Georgia,) To the Reverend Mr. Whitefield: containing A Particular Account of the Spiritual and Temporal State thereof. Dated March 2, 1744, and sent with others, bearing Date June 7. Publish'd at the Request of his Friends. *London: Printed by J. Lewis, in Bartholomew-Close; and Sold by J. Syms in Ironmonger-Row, near St. Luke's Church in Old-Street; and at the Tabernacle,* 1744. 12mo, pp. 16. 29468

Habersham (S. E.) Health and Profit: as found in the Hilly Pine Region of Georgia and South Carolina. Together with an Account of its Horticultural, Agricultural, and Manufacturing Resources, and the Topography, Geology, Botany, and Climatology of the Region. By S. E. Habersham, M.D. *Augusta* [*Ga.*] 1869. 12mo, pp. 147. C. 29469

Habrechti (J.) Planiglobium Terrestre. *Argentorati.* 1629. 4to. Plate and Maps. 29470

Title from Libri's Catalogue. Includes America.

[Hachard (Marie Madeleine).] Relation du voyage des dames religieuses ursulines de Rouen à la Nouvelle-Orléans, avec introduction et des notes par Gabriel Gravier. *Paris.* 1872. 4to, pp. lix, 122. B. 29471

An interesting set of letters from Louisiana by a young nun, who went out to America in 1727. The first edition, which I have not seen, was printed at Rouen in 1728.

Hacienda Pública. *Carácas.* 1858. 8vo, pp. 56. 29472

Hacke (W.) A | Collection | of | Original Voyages: | Containing | I. Capt. Cowley's Voyage round the Globe. | II. Captain Sharp's Journey over the Isthmus of | Darien, and the Expedition into the South Seas, | Written by himself. | III. Capt. Wood's Voyage thro' the Streights of | Magellan. | IV. Mr. Roberts' Adventures among the Cor- | sairs of the Levant; his Account of their | Way of Living; Description of the Archi- | pelago Islands, Taking of Scio, &c. | Illustrated with several Maps and Draughts. | Published by Capt. William Hacke. *London, Printed for James Knapton, at the | Crown in St. Paul's Church-Yard.* 1699. | 8vo, pp. xvi, 45, 100, 53. 3 Plates, 2 Maps. BA., C., P. 29473

Part of the original material for the History of the Buccaneers, now scarce.

Hackelton (M. W.) Jamestown of Pemaquid: a Poem. By Mrs. Maria W. Hackelton. [With Prefatory Notice by E. Ballard, and Historic Sketch by M. W. Hackelton.] *New York: Hurd and Houghton.* 1869. 16mo, pp. 40. 29474

Hackett (H. B.) Christian Memorials of the War; or, Scenes and Incidents illustrative of Religious Faith and Principle, Patriotism and Bravery in our Army. With Historical Notes. By Horatio B. Hackett, Professor of Biblical Literature, &c. *Boston: Gould & Lincoln.* 1864. 12mo, pp. 3–252.

Hackett (J.) Narrative of the Expedition which sailed from England in 1817, to join the South American Patriots, comprising every particular connected with its Formation, History, and Fate; with Observations and Authentic Information, elucidating the real Character of the Contest, Mode of Warfare, State of the Armies, &c. By James Hackett, First Lieutenant of the late Venezuelan Artillery Brigade. *London: John Murray.* 1818. 8vo, pp. (2), xv, 144. C., H. 29476

See "M. Rev.," New Series, XCIII. 109. The following is a French translation:

Hackett. Relation de l'expédition partie d'Angleterre en 1817, pour joindre les Patriotes de Vénézuela: traduit de l'anglois par N. Perrin. *Paris.* 1819. 12mo, pp. 159. S. 29477

Hackley (R. S.) Titles, and Legal Opinions thereon, of Lands in East Florida, belonging to Richard S. Hackley, Esq. *Brooklyn: Printed by G. I. Birch.* 1822. 8vo, pp. 122. + *Fayetteville, N. C.* 1826. 8vo, pp. 71. + *New York.* 1831. 8vo.

Hackley. Legal Opinions on the Title of Richard Hackley to Lands in East Florida, with Documents in relation to the Climate and Soil of Florida. *London.* 1841. 8vo. 29479

Relates to the famous grant of the King of Spain to the Duke of Alagon, previous to the cession of the Floridas to the United States. This grant includes nearly one half of East Florida, on the side of the Gulf of Mexico. *See* "N. A. R.," XXIII. 232.

Hackley. Petition and Protest of Richard S. Hackley, a Citizen of the United States, addressed to the President of the United States, 1842. [n. p. n. d.] 8vo, pp. 7. 29480

Haco (D.) J. Wilkes Booth, the Assassinator of President Lincoln. By Dion Haco. *New York: T. R. Dawley.* 1865. 12mo, pp. 102. 29481

Haco. Osgood, the Damon Refugee. *New York: T. R. Dawley.* 1865. 18mo, pp. 92. 29482

Also: Larry, the Army Dog Robber. *New York: T. R. Dawley.* 1865. 18mo, pp. 106.—Cheatham, or the Swamp Dragons. [*Ibid.*] 18mo, pp. 94.—Perdita ... [*Ibid.*] 18mo, pp. 93.—Hawks, the Conscript. [*Ibid.*] 18mo, pp. 106.—Sue Munday, the Guerilla Spy. [*Ibid.*] 1865. 12mo, pp. 13–66.—Rob. Cobb Kennedy, the Incendiary Spy. [*Ibid.*] 16mo, pp. 13–71.

Haddock (C. B.) A Discourse delivered at Hanover, N. H., May 7, 1841, on the Occasion of the Death of William Henry Harrison, late President of the United States. By Charles B. Hadduck. ... *Windsor, Vt.: Printed by Tracy & Severance.* 1841. 8vo, pp. 24. 29483

Haddock. A Discourse delivered before the New England Society of the City of New York, December 22, 1841. By Charles Bricket Haddock. *New York.* 1842. 8vo, pp. 24. N.

Also: An Address ... before the Railroad Convention, at Lebanon, N. H., October 10, 1843. ... *Hanover: J. E. Hood.* 1843. 8vo, pp. 31.— ... An Address ... for the Promotion of Collegiate and Theological Education at the West ... in ... Boston, May 31, 1848. ... *Boston: T. R. Marvin.* 1848. 8vo, pp. 20.—Addresses and Miscellaneous Writings ... *Cambridge: Metcalf and Company.* 1846. 8vo, pp. ix, 574.—An Oration before the Phi Beta Kappa Society of Dartmouth College, August 25, 1825. By Charles B. Hadduck. [*sic.*] ... *Concord: Printed by Jacob B. Moore.* 1825. 8vo, pp. 35. Portrait. M.— ... An Oration ... before the Phi Beta Kappa at Yale College ... August 16, 1848. ... *New Haven: Printed by B. L. Hamlen.* 1848. 8vo, pp. 24. B.

Hadelich. America ante Columbum veteribus Rabbinis nota. 8vo, pp. 30. 29485

Hadfield (W.) Brazil, the River Plate, and the Falkland Islands; with the Cape Horn Route to Australia. Including Notices of Lisbon, Madeira, the Canaries and Cape Verds. By William Hadfield. Illustrated ... from the South American Sketches of Sir W. Gore Ouseley, ... and from the Drawings of Sir Charles Hotham, ... during his recent Visit to Paraguay, of which Country much new information is supplied; as also of the Region of the Amazon. *London: Longman, Brown, Green, and Longmans.* 1854. 8vo, pp. (2), vi, 384. Portrait, 2 Maps, Plates. BA., C., H. 29486

See "Dublin University Magazine," Vol XLIV.

Hadfield. Brazil and the River Plate in 1868; By William Hadfield. Showing the Progress of those Countries since his former Visit in 1853. *London: Bates, Hendy & Co.* 1869. 8vo, pp. 271. 4 Plates. C. 29487

Hadley (A.) The Literary Labors of the Laboring Man; Early History of Dunbarton. Two Addresses [with Additions and Emendations], before the Dunbarton Lyceum, October 18, 1844, and January 31, 1845. By Amos Hadley. *Concord: Asa McFarland.* 1845. pp. 27. 29488

Hadley (S. A.) No More, the Senior's Farewell, a Poem. By Samuel A. Hadley. *Winchester.* 1861. 29489

Hadley (W. H.) The American Citizen's Manual of Reference: being a Comprehensive Historical, Statistical, Topographical, and Political View of the United States of North America, and of the several States and Territories. ... By W. Hobart Hadley. *New-York: Printed by S. W. Benedict.* 1840. 8vo, pp. 102. C., P. 29490

Hadley. The United States Historical and Statistical Index. *New-York.* 1840. 8vo. 29491

Also published as a broadside.

Hadley, *Mass.* Celebration of the Two Hundredth Anniversary of the Settlement of Hadley, Massachusetts, at Hadley, June 8, 1859; including the Address by Rev. Prof. F. D. Huntington, ... Poem by Edward C. Porter, ... and the other Exercises of the occasion. *Northampton: Bridgman & Childs.* 1859. 8vo, pp. 98. 29492

Hadley Falls. A Report on the History and Present Condition of the Hadley Falls Company. ... *Boston: Printed by John Wilson & Son.* 1853. 8vo, pp. 22. 2 Maps. H. 29493

Also: Report of the Directors, May, 1854. *Boston.* 1854. 4to, pp. 3. M.—Report of the Committee appointed by the Stockholders, ... March 1, 1854. *Boston: Printed by Moore & Crosby.* 1854. 8vo, pp. 18. H., S.

Hadley Families. *See* [Boltwood (L. M.)], Vol. II., No. 6253.

[Haeberlin (Carl Ludwig).] Die Auswanderer nach Texas. Historisch-romantisches Gemälde aus der neuesten Zeit. *Leipzig: C. L. Fritzsche.* 1841. 3 vols., 8vo. 29494

[Haeberlin.] De landverhuizers naar Texas. Histor. romant. verhaal uit den jongsten tijd. Uit het Hoogduitsch. *Groningen: R. J. Schierbeek.* 1842. 2 vols., 8vo. 29495

[HAEBERLIN.] Geschichte der Entdeckung und Eroberung von Mexico. ... *Berlin: C. H. Schultze.* 1847. 8vo, pp. 230.

Perhaps the following work relates to America: "Die Emigranten. Novelle. *Leipzig: Fritzsche.* 1850." 8vo, pp. 268. All published under the *pseudonym* of Balani.

Hæc sunt Acta Capitali Generalis Bononiæ, celebrati in Conuento Sancti Dominici in festo Sanctiss. Pentecostes Anno Domini Milesimo quingentesimo quarto: Die Vigesimo Maij. Sub Reverendissimo Patre Frate Vincentio Justiniano Chiense Sacræ S. Theologie Professore Magistro Generali Ordinis Predicatorū Diffinientibus Reverendis Diffinitoribus: videlicet ... . *Impressa sunt hæc Acta, Mexici apud Petrum Ocharte, Typographum, Anno Domino*, 1567, *Die quinto decima mensis Aprilis.* 29497

"Of excessive rarity, and probably unique; we have been unable to trace notice of it by any bibliographer, and it appears hitherto to have been unknown. As a specimen of typography and wood engraving in the infancy of printing in the New World, it is of peculiar interest, also for biographical notices of members of the Dominican order then living in Mexico." Title and note from an English catalogue. Also: Hæc sunt Provisiones pro bono Regimine Provincialium Indiarum Occidentalium Ordinis Fratrum Prædicatorum, etc. *Hispali, excudebat Franciscus de Lira, Año* 1619.

HAECKER (L.) Amerikanische Reise-Skizzen aus dem Gebiete der Technik, Landwirthschaft und des socialen Lebens. Von Ludwig Häcker. *Braunschweig: Friedrich Vieweg und Sohn.* 1867. 8vo, pp. iii–x, 199, (1). B., C. 29498

HAEFKENS (J.) Centraal Amerika, uit een geschiedkundig, aardrijkskundig en statistiek Oogpunt beschouwd. *Dordrecht.* 1832. 8vo. Maps and Plates. C. 29499

This Central America, considered from a historical, geographical, and statistical point of view, is a revised and augmented edition of the author's book on Guatimala.

H[AEFKENS] (J.) Reise naar Guatemala, door J. H. *Gravenhage: W. K. Mandemaker.* 1827. 2 vols., 8vo, pp. (2), 120; (4), 113. 2 Plates. C. + Tweede Stuk; behelzende eene Reise door de Provincie San Salvador, als mede een Verslag der geschiedenis en des Handels van Centraal-Amerika. *'s Gravenhage.* 1828. 8vo. 29500

HAEFKENS. Reise naar Guatemala in 1829, Central-Amerika beschouwd uit een geschiedkundig en statistiek Oogpunt. *Dordrecht.* 1832. 8vo. 29501

HAEGHOORT (G.) Keter Der Goddelyke Waarheden, Die men geloven en betrachten moet Om Salig te worden, in haar natuurlyk verband kortlyk te same-geschakelt. Door Gerard Haeghoort, predikant te Second River. *Te Nieuw York, Gedruckt by J. Peter Zenger.* 1738. 12mo, pp. (8), 36. S. 29502

HÆNKE (T.) Reliquiæ Hænkeanæ, seu descriptiones et icones Plantarum, quas in America meridionali et boreali, in insulis Philippinis et Marianis collegit Th. Hænke. Redegit C. B. *Prag.* 1825–30. Folio. 48 Plates. B., C. 29503

HAERLEM, *N. Y.* Constitution of the Friendly Society of the Town of Haerlem. *New York.* 1807. pp. 13. N. 29504

Haerlems | Schuyt-praetjen, | op 't | Redres | Vande | West-Indische Compagnie. ¶ *Gedruct op 't Jaer* 1649. | 4to, 12 l. C.

Haerlem's boat-talk on the reformation of the West India Company's affairs in Brazil. *See* Asher, No. 262.

HAERNE (Le Chanoine de). La question américaine dans ses rapports avec les mœurs, l'esclavage, l'industrie et la politique. Par Le Chanoine de Haerne. ... *Bruxelles: La Revue Belge.* 1862. 8vo, pp. (2), 72. H. 29506

A collection of facts from all the best authorities, American and foreign, relative to the political history, rise and progress of the United States, indicating the value of the Union to Europe, and especially to Belgium, whose Constitution has been in a measure formed upon it.

HAERNE. The American Question. ... Translated by Thomas Ray. *London: William Ridgway.* 1863. 8vo, pp. 114.

HAGADORN (W.) A Comparison of American and British Slavery. By William Hagadorn, Jr. *New York: Printed by E. B. Thomas.* 1851. 8vo, pp. 32. H. 29508

[HAGEN (F. F.)] The Moravian Mission among the Germans in the City of New York. *Bethlehem, Pa.* 1866. 8vo, pp. 14.

HAGEN (H.) Synopsis of the described Neuroptera of North America. With a List of the South-American Species. Prepared for the Smithsonian Institution by Hermann Hagen. *Washington, July,* 1861. 8vo, pp. xx, 348. C. 29510

Included in the "Smithsonian Miscellaneous Collection," Vol. IV.

HAGEN (J. C.) Footprints of Truth, or Voice of Humanity. By John C. Hagen. With Illustrations. *New York.* 1853. 8vo.

HAGENBACH (C. F.) Tentamen floræ Brasiliensis ... adjectis Casp. Bauhini Synonymis ... . *Basel: Neukirch.* 1821–34. 2 vols., 12mo. 29512

HAGER (A. D.) The Marbles of Vermont: An Address, ... before the Vermont Historical Society. ... By Albert D. Hager. *Burlington.* 1858. 8vo, pp. 16. 29513

See "Vermont Geological Survey."

HAGERMAN (H. B.) Trial of Henry B. Hagerman, Esq., on an Indictment for an Assault and Battery, with intent to Murder; Committed on William Coleman, Esq., Editor of the New York Evening Post. Taken in Short-hand by David Bacon, Esq. *New York.* 1818. 8vo, pp. 68. C. 29514

HAGERSTOWN, *Md.* Opening of St. James' Hall, Hagerstown, Md., 1842. 29515

Also: Studies, Discipline, etc., of St. James' Hall.

HAGEWISCH. Americanisches Magazin, herausgegeben von Prof. Hagewisch und Ebeling. *Hamburg.* 1795–97. 4 vols., 8vo. W. 29516

HAGGARD (*Dr.*) The Judgment of Lord Stowell, respecting the Slavery of the Mongrel Woman Grace, on an Appeal from the Vice-Admiralty Court of Antigua, given in 1827. By Dr. Haggard. *London.* 1827. 8vo, pp. 49. 29517

HAGGENMACHER (Johann Heinrich). Ueber die Auswanderungen nach Amerika. ... *Heilbronn.* 1839. 8vo. 29518

HAGGERTY (J.) Report of the Trial and Conviction of John Haggerty for the Murder of Melchior Fordney, ... Lancaster, Pennsylvania. ... By a Member of the Bar. *Lancaster.* 1847. 8vo. C. 29519

HAGNER (C. V.) Early History of the Falls of Skuylkill, Manayunk, Schuylkill and Lehigh Navigation Companies, Fairmount Water-Works, etc. By Charles V. Hagner. *Philadelphia: Claxton, Remsen & Haffelfinger.* 1869. 8vo, pp. 102. 2 Plates. C. 29520

HAGNER (T. H.) An Address ... in Senate Chamber of Maryland, 4th July, 1837. By Thomas Holme Hagner. *Annapolis: Printed by J. Hughes.* 1837. 8vo, pp. 32. H. 29521

HAGTHORPE (J.) England's-Exchequer. | or A Discovrse of | the Sea and Navigation, | with some things thereto coinci- | dent concerning Plantations. | Likewise | Some particular Remonstrances, how | a Sea-force might be profitably imployed. | Wherein by the way, is likewise set downe the | great Commodities and Victories the Portingalls, Spa- | niards, Dutch, and others, haue gotton by Naui- | gation and Plantations, in the West-Indies, | and elsewhere. | Written as an incouragement | to our English Nation, to af- | fect the like, who are better prouided then any of those. | By | Iohn Hagthorpe Gent. | *London,* | *Printed for Nathaniel Butter, and* | *Nicholas Bowne.* 1625. | 4to, pp. (4), 49. J.C.B. 29522

HAGUE *and* KING. United States Geological Exploration of the Fortieth Parallel, Clarence King, Geologist in Charge. Mining Industry, by James D. Hague, with Geological Contributions by Clarence King. Submitted to the Chief of Engineers, and Published by Order of the Secretary of War, under Authority of Congress. Illustrated by 37 Plates, and accompanying Atlas of 14 Plates and Maps. *Washington.* 1870. Impl. 4to, pp. xvi, 648. 29523

HAGUE (W.) ... An Address delivered before the ... Alumni of Newton Theological Institution, August 18, 1835. By William Hague. ... *Boston: William D. Ticknor.* 1835. 8vo, pp. 32.

HAGUE. The Baptist Church Transplanted from the Old World to the New One. The substance of Discourses delivered in Celebration of the Two Hundredth Anniversary of the First Baptist Church in Providence, November 1839. By Rev. William Hague. *New York.* 1846. 12mo, pp. 192. 29525

HAGUE. Christianity and Slavery: A Review of the Correspondence between Richard Fuller ... and Francis Wayland. ... By William Hague, D.D. *Boston: Gould, Kendall & Lincoln.* 1847. 12mo, pp. 54. B., H. 29526

A vindication of the Bible from the charge of sanctioning slavery.

HAGUE. Christianity and Statesmanship. With Kindred Topics. By William Hague. ... *New-York.* 1855. 12mo, pp. 420. C., S. + *Boston: Gould and Lincoln.* 1865. 8vo, pp. 414.

HAGUE. A Discourse ... Death of the Hon. John Quincy Adams ... February 27, 1848. By William Hague ... *Boston: William D. Ticknor & Company.* MDCCCXLVIII. 8vo, pp. 22. B.

HAGUE. An Historical Discourse; delivered at the Celebration of the Second Centennial Anniversary of the First Baptist Church in Providence, November 7th, 1839. By William Hague, Pastor of the Church. *Providence: B. Cranston & Co.* 1839. 12mo, pp. 192. C., S. 29529

See "N. A. Rev.," L. 525.

HAGUE. ... A Discourse delivered at the Dedication of the Baptist Church in Bowdoin Square, Boston, November 5, 1840. By William Hague, ... *Boston: Gould, Kendall, and Lincoln.* 1840. 8vo, pp. 38. S. 29530

Also: ... A Discourse ... in ... Albany ... March 19th, 1854, the Day following the Funeral Solemnities of the Hon. Friend Humphrey. ... *New York: Sheldon, Lam-*

port & Blakeman. 1854. 8vo, pp. 41.— ... A Discourse on the Life and Character of Rev. Irah Chase ... June 27, 1865. ... *Boston: Gould and Lincoln.* 1866. 8vo, pp. 46. H.—Life and Character of Adoniram Judson, late Missionary to Burmah. ... *Boston: Gould and Lincoln.* 1851. 8vo, pp. 38. B.—The Relation of Christianity to Politics. A Discourse ... Thanksgiving, November 28, 1844. ... *Boston: William D. Ticknor & Co.* 1845. 12mo, pp. 32.—True Friendship: A Discourse Commemorative of the Life and Character of the Rev. John Overton Choules, D.D. ... Newport, R. I. ... February 24, 1856. *New-York: Sheldon, Blakeman & Co.* 1856. 8vo, pp. 76. S.—Religion and Business: A Discourse Commemorative of Isaac Newton, Esq. ... *New-York.* 1859. 8vo.—Addresses of Drs. Wm. Hague and E. N. Kirk at ... the Educational Commission for Freedmen, ... May 28, 1863. *Boston: Printed by David Clapp.* 1863. 8vo, pp. 16. B., H.

HAHN (Christoph Ulrich). Die grosse Erweckung in den Vereinigten Staaten von Nordamerika. Sammlung von Gedanken und Thatsachen ... . *Basel: Bahnmaier.* 1859. 8vo, pp. iv, 42. 29531

HAHN (C. W.) Vögel aus Asien, Afrika, Amerika und Neuholland, in Abbildungen nach der Natur, mit Beschreibungen. *Nürnberg, Lechner, und Leipzig, Fleischer.* 1819–20. 4to. Plates.

Issued in parts, with plain, also, with colored plates. 1818–36, 114 colored plates.

HAHN (Michael). ... Speech ... before the National Equal Suffrage Association of Washington ... November 17, 1865. [*Washington.* 1865.] 8vo, pp. 8. 29533

Also: ... On Louisiana Legislation relating to Freedmen. [*Washington.* 1866.] 8vo, pp. 8.—Speech ... on the Louisiana Election. ... February 17, 1863. [*Washington.* 1863.] 8vo, pp. 8.—The Political Record of Hon. Michael Hahn. ... [n. p. 1864.] 8vo, pp. (4).—What is Unconditional Unionism? Speech ... before the Union Association of New Orleans ... November 14, 1863. *New Orleans.* 1863. 8vo, pp. 12. H.

HAIDEKOPER (H. T.) Opinion of the Supreme Court on the Act of the 3rd of April, 1792, in the Case of H. T. Haidekoper *vs.* James Douglas. *Philadelphia.* 1805. 8vo. W. 29534

HAIG (F.) Notes on the River Navigations of North America. By F. Haig, R.E. *Madras.* 1863. Rl. 8vo. 29535

HAIGH (S.) Sketches of Buenos Ayres and Chile. By Samuel Haigh. *London: James Carpenter.* 1829. 8vo, pp. xviii, (1), 316. Map. BA., H. 29536

HAIGH. Sketches of Buenos Ayres, Chile, and Peru. By Samuel Haigh, Esq. *London: Effingham Wilson.* 1831. 8vo, pp. iii–x, (1), 434. Map. BA. 29537

The preface is omitted in this edition. The additional 118 pages relate entirely to Peru "Faithful and picturesque."—*Athenæum.*

HAIGHT (B. I.) Address to the Students of the General Theological Seminary of the Protestant Episcopal Church ... at the Annual Matriculation, ... 1848. By Benjamin I. Haight, D.D. ... *New-York: Daniel Dana, Jr.* MDCCCXLIX. 8vo, pp. 20.

Also: An Address delivered before the Philolexian Society of Columbia College, May 17th, 1840. ... *New York: William C. Martin.* 1840. 8vo, pp. 27. BA., N.—A Letter to a Parishioner relative to the recent Ordination of Mr. Arthur Carey. *New York: James A. Sparks.* 1843. 8vo, pp. 22. B., N.

HAIGHT (N.) Argument and Appeal in behalf of the Remains of the Revolutionary Patriots who died in the Sugar-House Prison in Liberty Street, and others, Soldiers of the War of 1812, and those of our Citizens; before the Street Committee of the Corporation, ... for the Repeal of the Ordinance passed to open Albany Street through Trinity Church-Yard to Broadway. By Nicholas Haight, General-in-Chief of the Veterans of the War of 1812 ... also the Remarks of Col. John Alwaise, before the same Committee, together with Affidavits and Names of Persons interred in said Grave-Yard, etc. *New York: A. Baptist, Jr.* 1854. 8vo, pp. 31. 29539

HAIGHT. Practical Treatise on the Water delivered by the Manhattan Company; with Observations on Waters surrounding the City of New York. By Nicholas Haight. 1825. 8vo.

[HAIGHT (*Mrs.* R. K.)] Letters from the Old World. By a Lady of New York. *New York.* 1840. 2 vols., 12mo. + Second Edition. [*Ibid.*] 29541

HAIGHT (S. G.) Reply to Col. Troup's Defence of the Agency of the Pulteney Estate, &c. By Samuel G. Haight. 1822. 8vo. 29542

HAILE (L.) An Oration ... before the Citizens of Warren, R. I., July 4, 1821 ... . By Levi Haile ... . *Warren, R. I.: Printed by S. Randall.* 1821. 8vo, pp. 16. 29543

HAIN (A. H. F.) A Brief Essay on the Civil Service of the United States. By Augustus H. F. Hain. *Washington, D. C.: R. Beresford.* 1869. 8vo, pp. 8. 29544

HAINES (A. M.) Original Papers relating to Samuel Haines and his Descendants. By Andrew M. Haines. *Boston: David Clapp & Son.* 1869. 8vo, pp. 34. B. 29545

HAINES (C. G.) An Appeal to the People of ... New-York on ... Abolishing the Council of Appointment. By Charles G. Haines. *New York: Printed by E. Conrad.* 1819. 8vo, pp. 83.

[HAINES.] Considerations on the Great Western Canal, from the Hudson to Lake Erie; with a View of its Expense, Advantages, and Progress. Published by Order of the New York Corresponding Association for the Promotion of Internal Improvements. *Brooklyn: Spooner & Worthington.* 1818. 8vo, pp. 58. + Second Edition. [*Ibid.*] 8vo, pp. 81. B., H., N. 29547

HAINES. Examination into the Expediency of Establishing a Board of Agriculture in the State of New York. By C. G. Haines. *Brooklyn.* 1819. 8vo. 29548

HAINES. A Letter to the Hon. Micah Sterling, ... on the Expediency of adopting a Uniform System of Bankruptcy in the United States. *New York: Printed by E. Conrad.* 1822. 8vo, pp. 52. B., H., W. 29549

HAINES. Memoir of Thomas Addis Emmet; by Charles Glidden Haines, with a Biographical Notice of Mr. Haines. *New York: G. & C. & H. Carvill.* 1829. 12mo, pp. 128. C.

[HAINES.] Public Documents relating to the New York Canals, which are to connect the Western and Northern Lakes with the Atlantic Ocean. With an Introduction. Printed under the direction of the New York Corresponding Association, for the Promotion of Internal Improvements. *New York.* 1821. 8vo, pp. iii, 485. Map. 29551

"Not printed for sale."

[HAINES.] Report on the Penitentiary System in the United States; Prepared under a Resolution of the Society for the Prevention of Pauperism in the City of New York. *New York: Printed by Mahlon Day.* 1822. 8vo, pp. 101, Appendix, 107.

Also: Two Speeches, delivered in the New-York State Convention, September, 1824. With the Proceedings. *New-York: Printed by G. F. Hopkins.* 1824. 8vo, pp. 88. B., BA., H., W.

HAINES (E. M.) A Compilation of all the General Laws of the State of Illinois, relative to Township Organization. ... By Elijah M. Haines. *Chicago.* 1855. 8vo. + [*Ibid.*] 1857. 8vo. + [*Ibid.*] 1865. 8vo. + *Chicago: E. B. Myers & Co.* 1870. 8vo, pp. 392. 29553

HAINES. Historical and Statistical Sketches of Lake County, ... Illinois. By Elijah M. Haines. *Waukegan (Ill.): E. G. Howe.* 1852. 16mo, pp. 112. Plate. 29554

HAINES. Laws of Wisconsin ... and Duties of Town Officers ... . By Elijah M. Haines. *Chicago: Wm. B. Keen.* 1858. 8vo, pp. 189. 29555

Also: ... The American Law Directory ... . *Chicago: E. B. Myers.* 1862. 8vo, pp. 56. B.—Haines' Treatise, for Justices of the Peace. A Practical Treatise on the Powers and Duties of Justices of the Peace, Police Magistrates and Constables in the State of Illinois. 1868. 8vo, pp. xxxvi, 804.

HAINES (H.) L'état d'Alabama, ... ses ressources minérales, agricoles et industrielles ... par Hiram Haines. *Paris: Raçon et Cie.* 1867. 8vo, pp. 128. 29556

HAINES. The State of Alabama; ... its Mineral, Agricultural and Manufacturing Resources ... By Hiram Haines, C.E. ... *Paris: Simon Raçon et Cie.* 1867. 8vo, pp. 120. H. 29557

HAINES (S.) A Biographical Sketch of the Class of 1826, Yale College. ... By Shelden Haines ... . *Utica, N. Y.: Roberts ... Printer.* 1866. 8vo, pp. 99. B. 29558

HAINES (W. A.) Catalogue of the Terrestrial Shells in the Collection of William A. Haines. *New York: New York Printing Co.* 1868. 8vo, pp. 119. C. 29559

[HAINES (Zenas T.)] Letters from the Forty-Fourth Regiment M. V. M.: a Record of the Experience of a Nine Months' Regiment in ... North Carolina in 1862–3. By "Corporal." *Boston: Printed at the Herald Job Office.* 1863. 8vo, pp. 121.

HAIR (J. T.) Iowa State Gazetteer; embracing Descriptive and Historical Sketches of Countries, Cities, Towns, and Villages, which include much valuable information respecting the Agriculture, Manufactories, Commerce, Educational and Religious Institutions; Population and History of the State. ... and a Classified Business Directory ... . Compiled and Edited by James T. Hair. *Chicago.* 1865. 8vo, pp. 722. + [*Ibid.*] 1866. 8vo, pp. 76, 722. 29561

The Hairbreadth Escapes and Humorous Adventures of a Volunteer in the Cavalry Service. By One of Them ... . *Cincinnati: P. C. Browne.* 1865. 8vo, pp. 200. 29562

HAITI. *See also* Hayti, Dominica, *and* St. Domingo.

Abécédaire Haytien; suivi d'un Précis Historique, Chronologique et Géographique sur l'Isle de Haiti. *Paris.* 1839. 8vo.

Adresses de l'Assemblée Provinciale du Nord de St. Domiuique du 15 Juillet, 1791, à l'Assemblée Nationale au Roi au 83 départements et au directoire du département de la Gironde. *Paris.* 1791. 8vo. A. 29564

Affaire d'Haiti. *Paris.* 1836. 8vo. A. 29565

Almanach national de la République d'Haïti, pour l'année 1827. *Port-au-Prince.* 1826. 12mo. B., M. 29566

Almanach Royal d'Hayti pour l'année 1815, douzième de l'Indépendance et la Quatrième du Régne de sa Majesté, par P. Roux. *Au Cap Henry.* 8vo. Continued. 29567

Code-Civil d'Haiti. *Port-au-Prince.* 1826. 4to. + *Paris.* 1826. 8vo. A. 29568

Code des Colons de St. Domingue, avec des Notes par Vanufel et Villeneuve, avocats. *Paris.* 1826. 8vo. 29569

Code Henry, Loi de Commerce, Loi Penale. *Au Cap Henry.* 1812. Post 8vo. 29570

Communications received at the Foreign Office relative to Hayti. Printed by order of the House of Commons. *London.* 1829. Folio. A. 29571

Compagnie d'Haïti pour la culture du café et autres produits. Haïti sa fertilité, ses ressources commerciales D'après Peuchet et divers documents anciens et modernes. *Paris: Imprimerie de E. Brière.* 1867. 8vo, pp. 22. BA. 29572

Constitution de la République d'Hayti, du 14 Novembre, 1846. *Port-au-Prince.* [n. d.] 8vo, pp. 24. M. 29573

Constitution de l'Empire d'Haiti: Septembre 18, 1849. *Port-au-Prince: De l'Imprimerie Nationale.* 8vo. S. 29574

Constitution of the Republic of Hayti. To which is added Documents, &c. *New York.* 1818. 12mo. W. 29575

Copies des Pièces des Agens du Gouvernement Français, etc. *Cap Henry.* 1814. 8vo, pp. 14. C. 29576

Correspondence relative to the Emigration to Hayti, of the Free People of Colour, in the United States. Together with the Instructions to the Agent sent out by President Boyer. *New-York: Printed by Mahlon Day.* 1824. 8vo, pp. 32 N., W.

... Haytian Papers. A Collection of the very interesting Proclamations, and other Official Documents, together with some Account of the Rise, Progress, and Present State of the Kingdom of Hayti. With a Preface by Prince Sanders, Esq., Agent to the King of Hayti. *London: W. Reed.* 1816. 8vo, pp. xvi, 228. + *Boston.* 1818. 12mo, pp. 156. 29578

"Prince Sanders was 'a gentleman of color,' born and bred in Boston."—RICH.

Loi et ordinances relatives a la République d'Haiti. [1826.]

Manifeste du Roi (Henri Christophe). *Cap Henry.* [1814.] 8vo, pp. 44. 29580

L'Organisation Judiciare et sur la Police des Tribunaux sur Hayti. 29581

Pièces Officielles relatives aux négotiations du Gouvernement Français avec le Gouvernement Haïtien, pour traiter de la formalité de la reconnaissance de l'Indépendance d'Haiti. *Port-au-Prince: Imprimerie du Gouvernement, Octobre,* 1824, *An* 21 *de l'Indépendance d'Haïti.* 4to, pp. 84. + *Paris.* 1825. 8vo, pp. 88.

Plan général de défense du Royaume. *Cap Henry.* 1814. 8vo, pp. 8. 29583

Le Propagateur Haïtien, Journal politique et littéraire, rédigé par plusieurs Haïtiens. *Imprimé au Port-au-Prince.* 1822. 4to, pp. 200. 29584

Recueil général des lois et actes du Gouvernement d'Haiti. *Paris: Auguste Durard.* 1851. 8vo. 29585

The Rural Code of Haïti; in French in English. With a Prefatory Letter to the Right Hon. The Earl Bathurst, K.G. ... *London: James Ridgway.* 1827. 8vo, pp. (2), xviii, 100. A.

The Rural Code of Haïti. Literally Translated from a Publication by the Government Press; together with Letters from that Country, by a Southern Planter. *Granville, Middletown, N. J.* 1837. 8vo, pp. 48. M. 29587

Les Six Codes d'Haïti, suivis d'une table raisonnée des matières. *Au Port-au-Prince.* 1828. 12mo, pp. 738. C. 29588

Translation of an Official Communication from the Government of Hayti, February 16th, 1816. 4to. 29589

See also on Hayti: "Revue des Deux Mondes," 15 Novembre 1845; "Blackwood's Magazine," IV. 130 and X. 545; "Quart. Rev.," XXI. 430; "North Amer. Rev.," XII. and XXVIII.; "Pamphleteer," XIII. 150

[HAKEN (J. Chr. L.)] Schiffbruch und Drangsale von John Byron. Neu erzählt. *Berlin.* 1793. 8vo. 29590

HAKEWILL (J.) A Picturesque Tour of the Island of Jamaica, from Drawings made in the Years 1820 and 1821. By James Hakewill ... *London: Hurst and Robinson.* 1825. Folio, pp. (5), 16, 13, (28). 21 colored Plates. C., H. 29591

[HAKLUYT (Richard).] Divers | voyages, touching the discouerie of | America, and the Ilands adiacent | vnto the same, made first of all by our | Englishmen, and afterward by the French- | men and Britons: | And certaine notes of aduertisements for obserua- | tions, necessarie for such as shall heereafter | make the like attempt. | With two mappes, annexed heereunto for the | plainer vnderstanding of the whole matter. | *Imprinted at Lon- | don for Thomas Woodcocke, | dwelling in paules Church-yard, | at the signe of the blacke beare.* | 1582. | [Colophon:] *Imprinted at London, at the | three Cranes, in the Vine- | tree, by Thomas Daw- | son.* | 1582.] 4to, Title, Names of Travellers, Dedication to Sir Philip Sydney, signed R. H., Patent to Cabot, Note on Cabot, Thorne's Address, To Dr. Ley, in all 16 leaves, Text, 37 leaves. 2 Maps. BA., H., J.C.B., H.C.M. 29592

A tract of excessive rarity, only one or two perfect copies being known, and of the deepest interest, having been published for the purpose of inducing the English nation to establish colonies in America. It is Hakluyt's first publication. The "two mappes" mentioned in the title are rarely found with the work. The first of these is introduced with a notice: "This is the Forme of a Mappe sent 1527, from Sivill in Spayne, by Maister R. Thorne, Merchaunt, &c." The second, is dedicated to Sir Philip Sydney by "Michael Lok"—1582. It relates to attempts to discover a North-west passage, the discoveries of the Cabots, Ribault's adventures in Florida, &c., from the scarce English edition of 1563, which Hakluyt omitted in his later collections; and contains the first translation into English of the letter attributed to Verazzano. *See* Ribault (J.) It was reprinted with the following title:

HAKLUYT. Divers Voyages touching the Discovery of America and the Islands adjacent, Collected and Published by Richard Hakluyt. ... Edited, with Notes and an Introduction, by John Winter Jones, of the British Museum. *London: Printed for the Hakluyt Society.* M.DCCC.L. 8vo, pp. (6), cxi, 171, 6. 2 Maps, 1 Facsimile. B., BA. 29593

HAKLUYT. The Principall | Navigations, Voia- | ges, and Discoveries of the | English nation, made by Sea or ouer Land, | to the most remote and farthest distant Quarters of | the earth at any time within the compasse | of these 1500. yeeres: Deuided into three | seuerall parts, according to the po- | sitions of the Regions whereun- | to they were directed. | *** | The first, conteining the

personall trauels of the English vnto Iudæa, Syria, A- | rabia, the riuer Euphrates, Babylon, Balsara, the Persian Gulfe, Ormuz, Chaul, | Goa, India, and many Islands adioyning to the South parts of Asia: toge- | ther with the like vnto Egypt, the chiefest ports and places of Africa with- | in and without the Streight of Gibraltar, and about the famous Promon- | torie of Buona Esperanza. | The Second, comprehending the worthy discoueries of the English towards | the North and Northeast by Sea, as of Lapland, Scrikfinia, Corelia, the Baie | of S. Nicholas, the Isles of Colgoieue, Vaigats, and Noua Zembla toward the | great riuer Ob, with the mightie Empire of Russia, the Caspian Sea, Georgia, | Armenia, Media, Persia, Boghar in Bactria, & diuers Kingdoms of Tartaria. | The third and last, including the English valiant attempts in searching al- | most all the corners of the vaste and new world of America, from 73. de- | grees of Northerly latitude Southward, to Meta Incognita, Newfoundland, | the maine of Virginia, the point of Florida, the Baie of Mexico, all the In- | land of Noua Hispania, the coast of Terrafirma, Brasill, the riuer of Plate, to | the Streight of Magellan: and through it, and from it in the South Sea to | Chili, Peru, Xalisco, the Gulfe of California, Noua Albion vpon the backside | of Canada, further than euer any Christian hitherto hath pierced. | Whereunto is added the last most renowmed English Nauigation, | round about the whole Globe of the Earth. | By Richard Hakluyt Master of Artes, and Student sometime | of Christ-church in Oxford. | *Imprinted at London by George Bishop | and Ralph Newberie, Deputies to | Christopher Barker, Printer to the | Queenes most excellent Maiestie.* | 1589. | Folio, 8 l., viz.: Title, reverse blank; 'To the Right Hono- | rable Sir Francis Walsingham |' etc., pp. 3; 'Richard Hakluyt to the fauourable Reader,' 3; Epigrams, 1; 'The order of all the voyages comprised in this whole worke in | generall,' etc., 7; Text, 825; 'A Table Alphabeticall,' etc., 9. Map, entitled "Typvs Orbis Terrarvm." [Colophon:] *Imprinted at London by the | Deputies of Christopher Barker, Printer to | the Queenes most excellent Maiestie.* | *Anno Dom.* 1589. | H.

This is the first edition of Hakluyt's collection of voyages, which, in their second form, were recast and amplified into three volumes, as described *infra.* At p. 597 there should be a map $25\frac{1}{4}$ by $17\frac{1}{4}$ inches, which can be recognized by the royal arms and the word Virginia, and references to the recent expeditions sent thither by Sir Walter Raleigh, but it is rarely found with the work, and there is sometimes substituted another edition of the same map from the English version of Linschoten's Voyages, and occasionally a half-sheet woodcut map entitled "A general map made onelye for the particular declaration of this Discovery," to illustrate Sir Humfrey Gilbert's Discourse to prove a passage by the North-west to Cathaia and the East Indies; it belongs to Sir Humfrey Gilbert's Discourse described in our Vol. IV., *supra.* The uncertainty as to

the map arises perhaps from the fact that the one which was at first intended to be inserted does not appear to have been published. Hakluyt, at the end of his preface, says: "I have contented myselfe with inserting into the worke one of the best general mappes of the world onely, vntill the comming out of a very large and most exact terrestriall Globe, collected and reformed according to the newest, secretest, and latest discoueries ... composed by M. Emmerie Mollineux, of Lambeth, a rare Gentleman in his profession, being therein for diuers yeeres, greatly supported by the purse and liberalitie of the worshipfull marchant M. William Sanderson." The voyage of Sir Jerome Bowes, Knight, to Muscovy in 1582, was in some particulars erroneous; it was, therefore, "printed this second time, according to the True copie, I received of a gentleman that went in the same voyage, for the correction of the errors in the former impression." This reprinted portion commences at p. 491 and ends at p. 501; thus concluding the second part. The third part beginning at p. 506. Hakluyt, on the last page of his address "to the Reader," notices with regret his being compelled to comply with the request of certain friends, in the suppression of Sir Francis Drake's Voyage, "wherein I must confesse to have taken more than ordinarie paines, meaning to have inserted it in this worke." He, however, appears to have printed a few copies privately; and the Voyage thus suppressed, is sometimes inserted after p. 643. This portion consists of three sheets, or six leaves, bearing the signatures M m m. 4, 5, and 6; followed by a broadside or sheet, a Journal or Extract, from the Logbook of the Voyage, from the departure from Plymouth Road, September 14, 1585, the progress minutely detailed till the return to Portsmouth, July 22, 1586. This sheet is of extreme rarity. It is scarcely necessary to suggest that the addition of the original version of Bowes' and Drake's Voyages add greatly to the value of any copy of the work in which they happen to be. "His volume contains an invaluable treasure of material information, which even at this day affix to the name of Hakluyt a brilliancy of reputation which a series of ages can never efface or obscure."—ZOUCH'S *Life of Sir Philip Sidney.*

HAKLUYT. The | Principal Navi- | gations, Voiages, | Traffiqves and Disco- | ueries of the English Nation, made by Sea | or ouer-land, to the remote, and farthest di- | stant quarters of the Earth, on any time within | the compasse of these 1500 yeeres; Deuided | into three seuerall volumes, according to the | positions of the Regions, whereunto | they were directed. This first volume containing the woorthy Discoueries, | &c., of the English toward the North and Northest by Sea, | as of Lapland, Scriksinia, Corelia, the Baie of S. Nicolas, the Isles of Col- | goieue, Vaigatz, and Noua Zembla, toward the great riuer Ob, | with the the mighty Empire of Russia, the Caspian Sea, Geor- | gia, Armenia, Media, Persia, Boghar in Bactria, | and diuers kingdoms of Tartaria; | Together with many notable monuments and testimo- | nies of the ancient forren trades, and of the warrelike and | other shipping of this realme of England in former ages. | VVhereunto is annexed also a briefe Commentarie of the true | state of Island, and of the Northren Seas and | lands situate that way. | And, lastly, the memorable defeate of the Spanish huge | Armada, Anno 1588. and the famous victorie | atchieued at the citie of Cadiz, 1596. | are described. By Richard Haklvyt Master of | Artes, and sometime Student of Christ- | Church in Oxford. |

Imprinted at London by George | Bishop Ralph Newberie and Robert Barker. | 1598. | Folio, Title, Dedication, Preface, Sonnets, and Catalogue, pp. (24), 619. 29595

This is the title of the first issue of the first volume of this amplified edition of the former work. The original voyage to Cadiz, on p. 607, was suppressed by order of Queen Elizabeth, on the disgrace of Essex, and is therefore often supplied by a reprint. Owing to this suppression the title was changed in the particulars indicated in the following title, in which we have omitted only such words as are mere repetitions of the former title; it will be noticed there is no mention of the voyage to Cadiz.

HAKLUYT. The | Principal Navi- | gations, Voyages, | Traffiqves and Discove- | ries of the English Nation, ... at any time within the compasse of these 1600 yeres: | ... The first Volume containeth the worthy Discoueries | &c. of the English ... . | VVhereunto is annexed a briefe Commentary of the true state of Island, ... As also the | memorable defeat of the Spanish huge Armada, Anno 1588. | ¶ The second Volume comprehendeth the principall | Nauigations, Voyages, Traffiques, and discoueries of the English | Nation made by Sea or ouer-land, to the South and South-east | parts of the World, as well within as without the Streight of | Gibraltar, at any time within the compasse of these 1600. | yeres: Diuided into two seueral parts, &c. | ¶ By Richard Hakluyt Preacher, and | sometime Student of Christ-Church, in Oxford. | *Imprinted at London by George | Bishop, Ralph Newberie, | and Robert Barker.* | *Anno* 1599. | Folio, pp. (24), 619.

It will be observed that this title-page includes an abridgment of the title which follows. We may add that Vols. I. and II. are usually found together when in their original binding, and should, in fact, be so bound.

HAKLUYT. The | Second Volvme | of the Principal Na- | vigations, Voyages, Traf- | fiques and Discoueries of the English Nation, made by | Sea or ouer-land, to the South and South-east parts of the | World, at any time within the compasse of these 1600. yeres: | Diuided into two seuerall parts: | Whereof the first containeth the personall trauels, &c. | of the English, through and within the Streight of Gibraltar, to Al- | ger, Tunis, and Tripolis in Barbary, to Alexandria and Cairo in AEgypt, to the Isles | of Sicilia, Zante, Candia, Rhodus, Cyprus, and Chio, to the Citie of Constantinople, to diuers parts | of Asia Minor, to Syria and Armenia, to Ierusalem and other places in Iudea; As also to A- | rabia, downe the Riuer of Euphrates, to Babylon and Balsara, and so through the Per- | sian gulph to Ormuz, Chaul, Goa, and to many Islands adioyning vpon the | South parts of Asia; And likewise from Goa to Cambaia, and to all the | dominions of Zelabdim Echebar the great Mogor, to the mighty | Riuer

of Ganges to Bengala, Aracan, Bacola and Chon- | deri, to Pegu, to Iamahaí in the kingdome of Si- | am, and almost to the very fron- | tiers of China. | The second comprehendeth the Voyages, Trafficks, &c., of the English Nation, made without the Streight of Gibral- | tar, to the Islands of the Açores, of Porto Santo, Madera, and the Canaries, | to the kingdomes of Barbary, to the Isles of Capo Verde, to the Riuers of Senega, Gam- | bra, Madrabumba, and Sierra Leona, to the coast of Guinea and Benin, to the Isles | of S. Thomé and Santa Helena, to the parts about the Cape of Buona Espe- | ranza, to Quitangone near Mozambique, to the Isles of Comoro and | Zanzibar, to the citie of Goa, beyond Cape Comori, to the Isles | of Nicubar, Gomes Polo, and Pulo Pinaom, to the | maine land of Malacca, and to the king- | dome of Iunsalaon. By Richard Hackluyt Preacher, and sometime Stu- | dent of Christ-Church in Oxford. | *Imprinted at London by George Bishop, | Ralph Newbery, and Robert Barker* | *Anno* 1599. Folio, Title, Dedication, and Catalogue, pp. (16), 321; Part II, pp. 204. H. 29597

HAKLUYT. The | Third and Last | Volvme of the Voy- | ages, Navigations, Traf- | fiques, and Discoueries of the English Nation, and in | some few places, where they have not been, of strangers, per- | formed within and before the time of these hundred yeeres, to all | parts of the Newfound world of America, or the West Indies, from 73. | degrees of Northerly to 57. of Southerly latitude: | As namely to Engronland, Meta Incognita, Estotiland, Tierra de Labrador, Newfoundland, vp The grand bay, the gulfe of S. Lau- | rence, and the Riuer of Canada to Hochelaga and Saguenay, along the coast of Aram- | bec, to the shores and maines of Virginia and Florida, and on the West or backside of them | both, to the rich and pleasant countries of Nueua Biscaya, Cibola, Tiguex, Cicuic, | Quiuira, to the 15. prouinces of the kingdome of New Mexico, to the | bottome of the gulfe of California, and vp the | Riuer of Buena Guia: | And likewise to all the ysles both small and great lying before the | cape of Florida, The bay of Mexico, and Tierra firma, to the coasts and Inlands | of Newe Spaine, Tierra firma, and Guiana, vp the mighty Riuers of Orenoque, | Dessekebe, and Marannion, to euery part of the coast of Brasil, to the Riuer of Plate, | through the Streights of Magellan forward and backward, and to the | South of the said Streights as farre as 57. degrees: | And from thence on the backside of America, along the coastes, harbours, | and capes of Chili, Peru, Nicaragua, Nueua Espanna, Nueua Galicia, Culiacan, |

California, Noua Albion, and more Northerly as farre as 43. degrees: | Together with the two renowmed, and prosperous voyages of Sir Francis Drake | and M. Thomas Candish round about the circumference of the whole earth, and | diuers other voyages intended and set forth for that course. Collected by Richard Haklvyt Preacher, and sometimes | student of Christ-Church in Oxford. *Imprinted at London by George Bishop, Ralfe | Newberie, and Robert Barker.* | *Anno Dom.* 1600. Folio, Title, Dedication, and Catalogue, pp. (18), 868. H. 29598

A fine set of this grand series of Voyages is one of the desiderata in an American collection. The largest I have seen, measured $12\frac{1}{8}$ by $8\frac{1}{4}$ inches, and contained many rough leaves; the third volume in the set referred to measured only $11\frac{7}{8}$ by $7\frac{3}{4}$ inches, and that had many rough leaves, which circumstance, inclines me to believe that vols. I. and II. were printed on paper somewhat larger than the third. It is difficult to overrate the importance and value of this extraordinary collection of voyages. Mr. Bancroft characterizes "Richard Hakluyt as the enlightened friend and able documentary historian of these commercial enterprises, a man whose fame should be vindicated and asserted in the land which he helped to colonize," while Oldys, in his British Library, devotes fifty pages to an analysis of his works, and remarks that his collection "redounds as much to the glory of the English nation as any book that ever was published," and Mr. Dibdin is in an ecstacy of delight in his famous passage, beginning "All hail to thee, Richard Hakluyt," &c. The great rarity and value of the series suggested the following edition:

HAKLUYT. Hakluyt's Collection of the Early Voyages, Travels, and Discoveries of the English Nation. A New Edition, with Additions. *London: R. H. Evans.* 1809–12. 5 vols., 4to, pp. xxvii, (5), 670; (4), ix, (viii), 684; viii, (viii), 623; (6), 612; (4), v, 595; (4), 595. B., BA., H. 29599

This is an accurate reprint of the 3 vols., folio, 1598–1600, with the addition of those voyages which were published in the first edition and omitted in the second, also, a supplement containing all the voyages and travels printed by Hakluyt or at his suggestion. 325 copies only were printed, of which 75 are on large paper. This reprint is now very scarce, and commands more than its original price. An additional number of copies of vol. v. were printed with the following title:

HAKLUYT. A Selection of Curious, Rare, and Early Voyages and Histories of Interesting Discoveries, chiefly published by Hakluyt, or at his suggestion, but not included in his celebrated compilation, to which, to Purchas and other General Collections, this is intended as a Supplement. *London: R. H. Evans.* 1812. 4to, pp. 807. B., C., S. 29600

Contains fourteen rare works not easily accessible in any other form, and is quite as important as either of the volumes published in his time. It includes "Virginia Richly Valued," Anghiera's "West Indies," &c. Hakluyt was the translator of other works which we have already noticed. *See* our Vol. I., No. 1564; Vol. VI., Nos. 24896, 24897; Laudonniere (M.), and Ribault (J.), *infra.*

Hakluyt. Some Observations on Richard Hakluyt and American Discoveries. Communicated to the Society of Antiquaries, by J. Payne Collier. *London.* 1850. 4to. 29601

A few copies privately issued.

Hakluyt Society.

This Society was formed in 1847, and has, up to this date, 1875, published about forty volumes. A detailed list will be found in Part xi. of Bohn's Edition of Lowndes' "Manual." It is a very desirable series of books, and so many as relate to American topics are described in this dictionary under the names of their respective authors.

Halbert (H.) The last Speech and Confession of Henry Halbert, who was executed at Philadelphia, October 19, 1765, for the Murder of the Son of Jacob Woolman. *Philadelphia.* 1765. 8vo. P. 29602

Halberstadt (A.) Vrijmoedige gedachten over de oorzaken van den tegenwoordigen staat van verval der kolonie Suriname, en over de gebreken in het stelsel van regering dier kolonie. [n. p.] 1838. 8vo. 29603

Halcyon Luminary and Theological Repository ... By a Society of Gentlemen. *New-York: E. Riley.* 1812–13. 2 vols., 8vo, pp. 590. B., H. 29604

Haldeman (R. J.) African Slavery regarded from an Unusual Stand-Point. Territorial Abstractions ignored ... and a more Radical Issue raised. ... [n. p. n. d.] 8vo, pp. 8. 29605

Haldeman. Remarks on the Census Bill of ... Dec. 8th, 13th, and 15th. 1869. [n. p. n. d.] 8vo, pp. 6. 29606

Haldeman (S. S.) A Description of several New and Interesting Animals. ... *Albany: J. Munsell.* 1847. 8vo, pp. 7.

Haldeman. Haldeman's Zoological Contributions. With Colored Plates. *New York.* 1843–44. 8vo. 29608

Haldeman. A Monograph of the Limniades, or Fresh-water Univalve Shells of North America. By S. S. Haldeman, ... Also Supplement. *Philadelphia.* 1842. 8vo. 40 colored Plates.

Haldeman. A Monograph of the Freshwater Univalve Mollusca of the United States, including Notices of Species in other parts of North America. By S. Stehman Haldeman. *Philadelphia.* 1870. 8vo. 8 colored Plates. 29610

Haldrick. Banks, Banking, and Paper Currencies. By Haldrick. *Boston.* 1840. 8vo. 29611

Hale (A.) Two Discourses on ... the War between the U. States and Mexico; ... Springfield ... 11th July, 1847. By Albert Hale. ... *Springfield.* 1847. 8vo, pp. 16. B. 29612

Hale (B.) An Inaugural Address, delivered in the Chapel of Geneva College, December 21, 1836. By Benjamin Hale, D.D. ... *Geneva, N. Y.: Printed by J. J. Mattison.* 1837. 8vo, pp. 31. + Second Edition. *Albany: J. Munsell.* 1837. 8vo, pp. 32.

Hale. A Sermon ... at the Opening of the Convention of the Protestant Episcopal Church in ... New Hampshire, holden in ... Hopkinton, ... September 8, 1830. *Concord: Printed by Asa M'Farland.* 1830. 8vo, pp. 23. 29614

Hale. Valedictory Letter to the Trustees of Dartmouth College. [*Hanover.* 1835.] 12mo, pp. 24. 29615

Also: A Baccalaureate Address ... Geneva College, August 1, 1838. ... *Geneva, N. Y.* 1838. 8vo, pp. 30. H.—A Baccalaureate Address ... August 7, 1839. ... [*Ibid.:*] *Printed by Stow & Frazee.* MDCCCXXXIX. 8vo, pp. 32. H.—Baccalaureate Address ... at ... Geneva College, August 4, 1847. *Geneva.* 1847. 8vo, pp. 24.—An Inaugural Address, ... at Gardiner, ... Jan. 1, 1823. *Hallowell.* 1823. 8vo, pp. 16. B., H.—Lecture ... before the Young Men's Association in Geneva, New-York, November 8, 1837; ... *Geneva.* 1838. 8vo, pp. 24.—Sermon, occasioned by the Death of David Bates Douglass, ... Geneva College, ... 1849. *Geneva.* 1850. 8vo, pp. 19. BA., S.—What is Education? A Lecture before the Teachers' Institute of Yates and Ontario Counties, N. Y., October 1846. *Geneva.* 1846. 8vo, pp. 24. M.—Professor Hale and Dartmouth College. [n. p. n. d.] 12mo, pp. 23. M.—Remarks on a Pamphlet entitled "Prof. Hale and Dartmouth College." [n. p. n. d.] 12mo, pp. 34. BA., M.

Hale (B. E.) Familiar Conversations upon the Constitution of the United States. By B. E. Hale. *West Bradford* [*Mass.*]: *Hale & Co.* 1835. 18mo, pp. 132. B., C. 29616

Hale (B. F.) Opinions of the Attorney Generals of the United States, advising the President and Heads of Departments: Compiled by B. F. Hale, and published with Indices and Digest, by Robert Farnham. *Washington.* 1852. 5 vols., 8vo. C.

Hale (C.) All Men are Born Equal. Speech of Charles Hale, in the House of Representatives of ... Massachusetts, ... March 27, 1856, on a Proposition for Amending the Constitution. ... *Boston.* 1856. 8vo, pp. 7. 29618

Hale. Debates and Proceedings in the Massachusetts Legislature. January, 1856, to June, 1856. ... *Boston.* 1856. 8vo.

Hale. Our Houses are our Castles. A Review of the Proceedings of the Nunnery Committee of the Massachusetts Legislature, and especially their Conduct, and that of their Companions, on occasion of their Visit to the School in Roxbury, March 26th, 1855, with an Appendix ... . [*Boston: Daily Advertiser Office.* 1855.] 8vo, pp. 62. 29620

Also: Debates and Proceedings in the Massachusetts Legislature at the Regular Session, January–May; and also at the Special Session, July, 1857. *Boston.* 1857. 8vo.

Hale (*Mrs.* C. L.) Woodland Lays, Legends, and Charades. *Philadelphia: Lippincott & Co., for the Author.* 1868. 12mo, pp. 282. 29621

Hale (C. S.) The Exciting Crisis: an Exposition of the Signs of the Times. By C. S. Hale. [n. p. n. d.] 12mo, pp. 4.

Hale (D.) An Oration ... Portland ... July 4th, 1800 ... By David Hale ... . *Portland: E. A. Jenks.* 1800. 8vo, pp. 28, (1). B., H. 29623

Hale (E. Everett). Kansas and Nebraska: the History, Geographical and Physical Characteristics, and Political Position of those Territories; an Account of the Emigrant Aid Companies, and Directions to Emigrants. By Edward E. Hale *Boston: Phillips, Sampson & Co.* 1854. 8vo, pp. 256. Map. B., C.

See "N. A. Rev.," LXXX. 91.

Hale. The Desert and the Promised Land. A Sermon. By E. E. Hale. *Boston: C. C. P. Moody.* 1863. 12mo, pp. 22. + *Hartford: L. E. Hunt.* 1863. 12mo, pp. 22. 29625

Hale. ... How to conquer Texas, before Texas conquers us. *Boston: Redding & Co.* 1845. 8vo, pp. 16. H. 29626

Hale. Man without a Country. *Boston: Ticknor & Fields.* 1865. 16mo, pp. 23. 29627

[Hale.] The President's Words. A Selection of Passages from the Speeches, Addresses, and Letters of Abraham Lincoln. *Boston: Walker, Fuller & Co.* 1865. 16mo, pp. 186. 29628

Hale. The Public Duty of a Private Citizen: A Sermon, preached in the South Congregational Church, Boston, September 3, 1865, the Sunday following the Death of Mr. George Livermore. By Edward E. Hale. *Cambridge: Printed by John Wilson & Sons.* 1865. 8vo, pp. 14. 29629

Hale. Puritan Politics in England and New England: a Lecture ... Feb. 12, 1869. By Edward E. Hale. *Boston: John Wilson and Son.* 1869. 8vo, pp. 22. H. 29630

Hale. A Sermon delivered before ... the General Court of Massachusetts, at the Annual Election, ... Jan. 5, 1859. By Edward E. Hale, ... *Boston: William White, Printer.* 1859. 8vo, pp. 37. S. 29631

Hale. Thirty Years of Boston. ... By Edward E. Hale. [n. p. n. d.] 8vo, pp. 7. 29632

Also: Christian Duty to Emigrants. A Sermon ... before the Boston Society for the Prevention of Pauperism. May 9, 1852. *Boston.* 1852. 8vo, pp. 24.—Edward Everett in the Ministry of Reconciliation. A Sermon preached in South Congregational Church, Boston, Jan. 22, 1865. ... *Boston: Alfred Mudge & Son.* 1865. 8vo, pp. 15.—The Future Civilization of the South. A Sermon, preached April 13, 1862, at ... Boston. *Boston.* 12mo, pp. 17.—Letters on Irish Emigration. First published in the Boston Daily Advertiser. ... *Boston.* 1852. 8vo, pp. 64. N.— ... A Sermon ... at the Installation of Rev. E. B. Willson ... West Roxbury, July 18, 1852. ... *Boston: Printed by John Wilson & Son.* 1852. 8vo, pp. 20.— ... A Sermon ... at the Ordination of Mr. Chas. B. Ferry ... Peterborough, N. H., June 13, 1860. ... *Peterborough: Printed by K. C. Scott.* 1860. 8vo, pp. 12.

Hale (E.) Sermon, in Westhampton, Fast-Day, 1804. By Enoch Hale. *Northampton* [*Mass.*] 1804. 8vo. S. 29633

Hale. History and Description of an Epidemic Fever, commonly called Spotted Fever, which prevailed at Gardiner, Maine, in the Spring of 1814. By Enoch Hale, Jr., M.D. *Boston: Wells & Lilly.* 1818. 8vo, pp. xvi, 246. C. 29634

Hale (H.) United States Exploring Expedition ... Ethnography and Philology. By Horatio Hale, Philologist to the Expedition. *Philadelphia: Printed by C. Sherman.* 1846. 4to, pp. xii, 666. 3 Charts. 29635

150 copies only printed. Forms Vol. VII. of the "United States Exploring Expedition." Very scare. Contains many Vocabularies and Grammars of the Oceanic Islands, besides a general Polynesian Lexicon. Some copies have the imprint: *Philadelphia: Lea & Blanchard.*

Hale. Remarks on the Language of the St. John's or Wlastukweek Indians, with a Penobscot Vocabulary. [By H. E. Hale.] *Boston.* 1834. 8vo, pp. 8. 29636

See also "Transactions of the American Ethnological Society," Vol. II.

Hale (J.) A Modest Enquiry | into the Nature of | Witchcraft, And | How Persons Guilty of that Crime | may be Convicted: And the means | used for this Discovery Discussed, both

Negatively and Affirmatively, | according to Scripture and | Experience. | By John Hale, | Pastor of the Church of Christ in Beverly, | Anno Domini, 1697. *Boston in N. E.* | *Printed by B. Green and J. Allen for* | *Benjamin Eliot under the Town House.* 1702. | Small 8vo, pp. 176. H., M. 29637

One of the rarest of the books relating to the New England witchcraft delusion. Also: A Massachusetts Election Sermon, 1684. 8vo.

[Hale (John).] A Statement of the Cause of the McClary Owners and Doane and Doane's Administrators. *Portsmouth, N. H.* 1795. 16mo, pp. 67. M. 29638

Hale (J.) Six Months' Residence and Travels in Central America. By J. Hale. *New York.* 1826. 8vo. S. 29639

Hale (J. P.) Relations with Mexico. Speech ... February 15, 1853. *Washington, D. C.: Buell & Blanchard.* 1853. 8vo, pp. 15. B., H. 29640

Hale. The Wrongs of Kansas. Speech of Hon. John P. Hale, of New Hampshire. In the United States Senate, February [26], 1856. [n. p. n. d.] 8vo, pp. 16. 29641

Also: Frauds and Corruption in the Navy Department. A Speech ... delivered ... January 18 and 31, and February 1 and 17, 1865. [n. p. n. d.] 8vo, pp. 32. H.—Letter ... to his Constituents on the proposed Annexation of Texas. *Washington.* 1845. 8vo, pp. 8. M.—Remarks ... on the Increase of the Army. ... January 26 and 28, and February 2, 1858. [*Washington: Buell & Blanchard.* 1858.] 8vo, pp. 8.—Speech ... upon the Slavery Resolutions, June 25, 1846. [*Boston.* n. d.] 8vo, pp. 12.—Speech ... on the Increase of the Army in Mexico; ... January 6, 1848. *Washington.* [n. d.] 8vo, pp. 16. M—Speech ... on the Territorial Question; ... March 19, 1850. *Washington.* [n. d.] 8vo, pp. 16. M.—Speech ... and Comments of the National Era on the President's Message. ... January 3, 1856. [*Washington.*] 1856. 8vo, pp. 8.—Kansas and the Supreme Court. Speech ... January 19 and 21, 1858. [*Washington.* 1858.] 8vo, pp. 16.—Speech ... in the Senate ... February 14, 1869. [n. p. n. d.] 8vo, pp. 15. H.—Speech ... on the Ten Regiment Bill ... United States Senate ... Jan. 6. [n. p. n. d.] 8vo, pp. 8.—Speech ... on the State of the Union, January 31, 1861. [n. p. n. d.] 8vo, pp. 16.—Speech ... on the Purchase of Vessels by Geo. D. Morgan. ... February 7, 1862. [n. p. n. d.] 8vo, pp. 8.—Speech ... on the Abolition of Slavery in the District of Columbia. Delivered ... March 18, 1862. [n. p. n. d.] 8vo, pp. 8.—Speech on Frauds in Naval Contracts, ... May 23, 1864. *Washington.* 1864. 8vo, pp. 16. H.

Hale (M.) Some Necessary and Important Considerations Directed To All Sorts of People. Taken out of the Writings of that late Worthy and Renowned Judge, Sir Mathew Hales. Wherein is described his own Experience of the Inward and Invisible Guidance of the Spirit of God. The Tenth Edition. *New York: Printed and Sold by William Bradford.* 1736. 8vo, pp. 24. M. 29642

Hale (M.) Spring Water versus River Water, for Supplying the City of New York, containing a Compendious Examination of the Internal Supplies, the Method, and Actual Expense of obtaining them. By M. Hale. *New York: Marsh and Harrison.* 1835. 8vo, pp. 50. N. 29643

Hale (M.) A Genealogical Memoir of the Families of Lawrences. With a direct male line from Sir Robert Lawrence, of Lancashire, A.D. 1190, down to John Lawrence, of Watertown, A.D. 1636. With Notices of Others of the same name in different States. By Mercy Hale. ... *Boston: Printed for the Author.* 1856. 8vo, pp. 20. B., H. 29644

Hale (M.) A Sermon ... at ... Ordination of the Reverend Mr. Joseph Woodman, ... Sanborntown, ... New Hampshire, November 13, 1771. By Moses Hale, M.A. *Salem: Printed by Samuel and Ebenezer Hall.* MDCCLXXII. 8vo, pp. 36. BA., M.

Hale (M. P.) Summer at Walnut Ridge. By M. P. Hale. *New York: Carlton & Lanahan.* [1869.] 18mo, pp. 259. 4 Plates. C. 29646

Hale (N.) Hale Monument Association. Memoir of Captain Nathan Hale. *New Haven: Printed by S. Babcock.* 1844. 8vo, pp. 16. 29647

[Hale (Nathan).] The American System, or the Effects of High Duties on Imports, designed for the Encouragement of Domestic Industry: With Remarks on the late Treasury Report. *Boston: Printed by Nathan Hale.* 1828. 8vo, pp. 86. B. 29648

[Hale.] The North-Eastern Boundary of the United States. *Boston.* 1832. 18mo. 29649

[Hale.] Notes made during an Excursion to the Highlands of New Hampshire and Lake Winnipiseogee. By a Gentleman of Boston. *Andover: Flagg, Gould & Co.; Boston: Hilliard, Gray & Co.* 1833. 12mo, pp. 184. 29650

[Hale.] Remarks on the Banks and Currency of the New England States ... . *Boston: William L. Lewis.* 1826. 8vo, pp. 40. BA. 29651

[Hale.] Remarks relative to the Construction of a Rail Road from the City of Boston to the Hudson River. [n. p. n. d.] 8vo, pp. 20. B., H. 29652

[Hale.] Remarks on the Practicability and Expediency of Establishing a Rail Road on one or more Routes from Boston to the Connecticut River. By the Editor of the Boston Daily Advertiser. *Boston: William L. Lewis.* 1827. 8vo, pp. 71.

One of the earliest works of its class—suggests a horse railroad.

[Hale.] Journal of Debates and Proceedings in the Convention to revise the Constitution of Massachusetts. November 15, 1820, to January 9, 1821. [By Nathan Hale and Charles Hall.] ... *Boston.* 1821. 8vo. + New Edition, Revised and Corrected. *Boston.* 1853. 8vo, pp. vii, (1), 677. H. 29654

See also our Vol. II., No. 6785, and note to 6786.

Hale (N.), *and* Davis (John). Loan for the Completion of the Chesapeake and Ohio Canal, July, 1847. [*Boston.* 1847.] 8vo, pp. 13. M. 29655

Hale (N.), *and* Swift (William H.) Report on the Present State of the Chesapeake and Ohio Canal. With an Appendix. *Boston.* 1846. 8vo. M. 29656

Hale (N.) The Moral Significance of the Contrast between Slavery and Freedom: A Discourse Preached in the First Church, Dorchester, May 10, 1864. By Nathaniel Hale. ... *Boston: Walker, Wise, and Company.* 1864. 8vo, pp. 15. 29657

Hale (R. W.) A Comparison of the Fitchburg Railroad, with other Massachusetts Railroads. ... By Robert Ward Hale. *Boston: M. Stevens.* 1863. 8vo, pp. 11. 29658

[Hale (Salma).] The Administration and the Opposition. ... By Algernon Sidney. *Concord: Printed by Jacob B. Moore.* 1826. 8vo, pp. 20. H. 29659

Hale. Annals of the Town of Keene, from its First Settlement, in 1734, to the Year 1790. By Salma Hale. *Concord, N. H.: J. B. Moore.* 1826. 8vo, pp. 69. B., BA., W. + With Corrections, Additions, and a Continuation from 1790 to 1815. *Keene, N. H.: Printed by J. W. Prentiss and Company.* 1851. 8vo, pp. 120. Map. BA., C., H. 29660

[Hale.] History of the United States of America. By a Citizen of Massachusetts. Second Edition. *Keene, N. H.* 1821. 12mo. + [*Ibid.*] 1823. 12mo. + [*Ibid.* n. d.] + *Keene, N. H.: J. and J. W. Prentiss.* 1830. 12mo, pp. 298, 24. BA.

[Hale.] History of the United States, from their First Settlement as Colonies, to the Close of the War with Great Britain in 1815. *New York.* 1825. 12mo, pp. 236. + [*Ibid.*] 1826. + *London: J. Miller.* 1826. 8vo, pp. 467. + Second Edition. [*Ibid.*] 1827. + *New York: Collins and Hannay.* 1827. 18mo, pp. 280, 24. H. + [*Ibid.*] 1830. + *London: J. Miller.* 1836. 8vo. B. + *Cooperstown, N. Y.* 1838. 16mo. 29662

See "N. A. Rev.," XXII., p. 221. Methodical and correct. "A valuable compendium."—*Bishop* A. Potter.

Hale. History of the United States, from their First Settlement as Colonies, to the Close of the Administration of Mr. Madison in 1817. By Salma Hale. *New York: Harper & Brothers.* 1840. 2 vols., 12mo, pp. xii, 295; xi, 5–292. B., BA. + [*Ibid.*] 1841. + [*Ibid.*] 1843. + [*Ibid.*] 1845. + [*Ibid.*] 1857. + *Aberdeen.* [n. d.] 29663

Hale. History of the United States, from their First Settlement as Colonies to the Close of Mr. Tyler's Administration in 1845. ... By Salma Hale. *Cooperstown* [*N. Y.*]: *H. & E. Phinney.* 1846. 12mo, pp. 326, 28. C. 29664

Hale. An Oration delivered at Keene, N. H., February 22, 1832, being the Centennial Anniversary of the Birthday of Washington. By Salma Hale. *Keene.* 1832. 8vo, pp. 28. 29665

Hale (*Mrs.* S. J.) Liberia; or, Mr. Peyton's Experiments. Edited by Sarah Josepha Hale. ... *New-York: Harper & Brothers.* 1853. 12mo, pp. 304. C. 29666

Some copies have a London imprint, 1854.

Hale. Northwood; or, Life North and South; showing the true character of both. By Mrs. Sarah J. Hale. *New York.* 1852. pp. 408. P. + *London.* 1852. + Second Edition. *New York.* [1852.] 29667

Hale. Sketches of American Character. By Mrs. Sarah J. Hale. ... *Boston: Freeman Hunt.* 1829. 18mo, pp. 287. + Second Edition. [*Ibid.*] 1830. 18mo. B. + Fourth Edition. [*Ibid.*] 1831. + [Another] Fourth Edition. *Boston: Russell, Odiorne & Co.* 1833. pp. 287. B. + *Philadelphia.* 1843. 18mo, pp. 287. 29668

Hale. Traits of American Life. By Mrs. Sarah J. Hale. *Philadelphia: E. L. Carey & A. Hart.* 1835. 12mo, pp. 298.

HALE. Woman's Record; or Sketches of all Distinguished Women, from "The Beginning" until A.D. 1850; arranged in Four Eras; with Selections from Female Writers of every Age. By Sarah Josepha Hale. *New York: Harper & Brothers.* 1853. Impl. 8vo, pp. 952. + New and Enlarged Edition. *New York.* 1855. 8vo. + Third Edition, Revised. *New York: Harper & Brothers.* 1870. 8vo, pp. xlviii, 918. Portrait. C., P. 29670

Also: Alice Roy. A Romance in Rhyme. *Philadelphia.* 1845. 12mo, pp. 37. — The Genius of Oblivion; and other Original Poems. By a Lady of New-Hampshire. *Concord: J. B. Moore.* 1823. 16mo, pp. 147. — Flora's Interpreter: or, the American Book of Flowers and Sentiments. Sixth Improved Edition. *Boston: Marsh, Capen & Lyon.* 1838. 12mo, pp. (2), 262. Colored Plate. + Ninth Edition. [*Ibid.*] 1840. 8vo, pp. 262, (2). H. — Flora's Interpreter, and Fortuna Flora. Third Revision. *Boston: Chase, Nichols & Hill.* 1860. 12mo, pp. 288. 2 colored Plates. — The Ladies' Wreath: a Selection from the Female Poetic Writers of England and America. With Original Notices and Notes; ... *Boston: Marsh, Capen & Lyon.* 1837. 12mo, pp. 408. + Second Edition ... Enlarged. *Boston.* 1839. 12mo, pp. (1), 436. Portrait. H. — Love; or Woman's Destiny. A Poem in Two Parts: with other Poems. *Philadelphia: D. Ashmead.* 1870. Square 16mo, pp. 112. — Manners; or, Happy Homes and Good Society all the Year Round. *Boston: J. E. Tilton & Co.* 1867. 12mo, pp. 377. Her "Grosvenor, a Tragedy," relates to the execution of Col. Hays of South Carolina.

[HALE (William).] Relations between the Boston and Maine and Cocheco Railroads. [n. p. n. d.] 8vo, pp. 8. B. 29671

HALES (J. G.) A Survey of Boston and its Vicinity. Showing the Distance from the Old State House ... to all the Towns and Villages not exceeding fifteen miles therefrom; also the intermediate distance from one place to another, Together with a short Topographical Sketch of the Country. The whole taken from actual survey and lineal measure in the years 1818, 1819, and 1820. By John G. Hales. *Boston: Printed by Ezra Lincoln.* 1821. 12mo, pp. 156. Map and Plate. B., BA., C. 29672

HALES (*M.*) *See* Individual y Verdadera.

HALES (S.) A Sermon preached before the Trustees for Establishing the Colony of Georgia in America; and before the Associates of the late Dr. Thomas Bray, for converting the Negroes in the British Plantations. ... At their Anniversary Meeting ... March 21, 1734. By Stephen Hales, D.D. ... To which is Annex'd the General Account for one whole Year, &c., Exhibited by the ... Trustees, &c. *London: T. Woodward.* MDCCXXXIV. 4to, pp. 16. BA., H. 29673

HALEY (T.) Trotting Record for 1869. Revised and Corrected. Containing a complete and reliable Record of all the

Trotting Events of the Past Season. By Thomas Haley. *New York: Torrey Brothers.* 1870. 12mo, pp. 144. 29674

HALFELD (Fernando). Atlas e relatorio concernente a exploração do Rio de S. Francisco, desde a Cachoeira da Pirapóra até ao oceano Atlantico, levantado por odem, ... Dom Pedro II., em 1852, 1853 e 1854. ... *Rio de Janeiro.* 1860. Folio, pp. 57. 46 Maps, 2 Plates, with Explanatory Text. A., B., H. 29675

HALFERN (Albert von). Scenen aus den Kämpfen der Indianer Floridas gegen die Weissen; oder, der Letzte der Seminolen. Nebst Rückblick auf die Zustände der Vereinigten Staaten. *Dresden & Leipzig: Arnoldsche Buchhandlung.* 1846. 16mo, pp. 311. + Zweite Ausgabe. [*Ibid.*] 1848. 29676

HALIBURTON (R. G.) Intercolonial Trade our only Safeguard against Disunion. By R. G. Haliburton. *Ottawa: G. E. Desbarats.* 1868. 8vo, pp. 42. C. 29677

HALIBURTON. The Past and the Future of Nova Scotia: an Address on the One Hundred and Thirtieth Anniversary of the Settlement of that Province. By Robert G. Haliburton. *Halifax.* 1862. 8vo, pp. 27. 29678

Also: Confederation or Annexation? An Address on the proposed Federation of the British North American Provinces. *Halifax.* 1865. 8vo. — Voices from the Street. A Series of Poems. *Halifax.* [n. d.] 12mo, pp. 20.

HALIBURTON (Thomas Chandler). An Address on the Present Condition, Resources, and Prospects of British North America: delivered ... at ... Glasgow. By the Hon. Mr. Justice Haliburton. *London: Hurst & Blackett.* 1857. 8vo. + *Montreal.* 1857. 8vo, pp. 47. C., P. 29679

[HALIBURTON.] The Americans at Home; or, Byeways, Backwoods, and Prairies. Edited by the Author of "Sam Slick." *London.* 1843. + New Edition. *London: Hurst & Blackett.* 1854. 3 vols., post 8vo. C., P. 29680

HALIBURTON. British North America; its Condition, &c. By Thomas C. Haliburton. *London: Hurst & Blackett.* 1857.

[HALIBURTON.] The Bubbles of Canada. By the Author of "The Clockmaker." *London: Richard Bentley.* 1839. 8vo, pp. (6), 332. BA. + Second Edition. [*Ibid.*] 8vo. 29682

Reprinted with the following title:

[HALIBURTON.] The Bubbles of Canada. By the Author of "Sam Slick." ... *Philadelphia: Lea & Blanchard.* 1839. 12mo, pp. 262. P. 29683

[HALIBURTON.] The Clock-maker; or the Sayings and Doings of Samuel Slick, of Slickville. *London.* 1837–46. Three Series each in 3 vols., post 8vo. C. + Reprinted. 1838–43. + *Paris.* 1841. 8vo, pp. vi, 199. H. + New Edition. 1845. + First Series. *New York: William H. Colyer.* 1840. 8vo, pp. 11–114. H. + Second Series. [*Ibid.*] pp. 115–240. H. + Third Series. *Philadelphia: Lea and Blanchard.* 1840. 8vo, pp. iv, 13–215. BA. 29684

These very clever sketches of Yankee and colonial life are, of course, somewhat overdrawn. They were immensely and deservedly popular, for under the guise of satire there was a rich vein of sound practical common sense. They first appeared in a Nova Scotian newspaper, from which they were reprinted into a 12mo volume, which I have not seen, and afterwards repeatedly reprinted both in England and the United States. The first American edition of the first series was printed *Philadelphia: Lea & Blanchard.* 1837. 12mo. They have been reprinted in London in Bentley's "Cabinet Library," also, by *Hurst and Blackett,* in post 8vo, by *Routledge,* in 12mo; in *Concord: William White.* 1838. 18mo, pp. vi, 262. BA. + [*Ibid.:*] *Israel S. Boyd.* 1839. 18mo, pp. 262; and lastly, *New York: Hurd & Houghton.* 1872. 18mo, pp. xi, 271. 6 Plates. *See* the "N. A. Rev.," LVIII. 312.

[HALIBURTON.] The English in America. ... *London: Colburn and Co.* 1851. 2 vols., post 8vo, pp. xix, 351; xi, 272. C.

A General View of American History up to the Independence of the United States.

HALIBURTON. A General Description of Nova Scotia. New Edition. *Halifax.* 1825. 8vo, pp. 192. 29686

HALIBURTON. An Historical and Statistical Account of Nova-Scotia, ... Illustrated by a Map of the Province, and several Engravings. By Thomas C. Haliburton, Esq. ... *Halifax: Joseph Howe.* 1829. 2 vols., 8vo. B., BA., C., H. 29687

Collation: pp. (14), 340, viii; (6), 453, (3); 10 Maps and Plates; the Publisher's Apology for the view of Halifax, on a small slip; 3 folded sheets. *See* "N. A. Rev.," XXX. 121. Some copies which vary from this collation in the preliminary leaves, seem to be perfect.

[HALIBURTON.] Kentucky; A Tale. *London: A. K. Newman & Co.* 1834. 2 vols., 12mo. 29688

[HALIBURTON.] The Letter-Bag of the Great Western; or, Life in a Steamer. ... *London.* 1839. 12mo. S. + *Halifax.* 1840. 8vo, pp. 189. + *Philadelphia: Lea & Blanchard.* 1840. 8vo, pp. 187. H. + *New York: William H. Colyer.* 1840. 8vo, pp. viii, 112, [88]. B. + *London.* 1843. + *New York.* 1847. 12mo, pp. 189. + *London: Bryce.* 1856. 12mo, pp.

232. + [*Ibid.*] 1862. + New Edition. *London: Geo. Routledge & Co.* 1865. Fcap. 8vo, pp. xxiii–232. 29689

[HALIBURTON.] The Letters of Sam Slick; or, Life in a Steamer. From the Letter-Bag of the Great Western. ... *Philadelphia: T. B. Petersen.* 1850. 12mo, pp. 189. BA. 29690

[HALIBURTON.] Nature and Human Nature. *London.* 1855. 2 vols., post 8vo. C. + *New York.* 1855. 12mo, pp. 336. + New Edition. *London: Hurst & Blackett.* 1858. 29691

[HALIBURTON.] The Old Judge: or Life in a Colony. *London: H. Colburn.* 1843. 2 vols., post 8vo, pp. 642. + New Edition. *London.* 1849. + *New York: Stringer & Townsend.* 1849. 8vo, pp. 239. C., H. + New Edition. *London: Hurst & Blackett.* 1860. Post 8vo, pp. 476. 29692

[HALIBURTON.] A Reply to the Report of the Earl of Durham. By a Colonist. *London: Richard Bentley.* 1839. 8vo, pp. 91. + *Halifax.* 1839. 8vo, pp. 28. 29693

[HALIBURTON.] Rule and Misrule of the English in America. *London.* 1843. + New Edition. *London.* 1851. 2 vols., post 8vo, pp. 351; 372. + *New York: Harper & Brothers.* 1851. 12mo, pp. ix–379. BA., H. 29694

See "Quarterly Review," Vol. XCIV.

HALIBURTON. The Sayings and Doings of Samuel Slick, Esq. ... By Judge Haliburton. *New York: Dick & Fitzgerald.* 1858. 12mo, pp. 11–263. B. 29695

This is the "Clockmaker" with a different title.

HALIBURTON. Traits of American Humour. By Native Authors. Edited by Judge Haliburton. *London: Colburn.* 1843. 3 vols., post 8vo. + [*Ibid.*] 1852. 29696

Also: The Attaché; or Sam Slick in England. New Edition. *New York.* 1856. 12mo—does not strictly belong to our plan, it being the author's observations on the aspects of British society. — Speech ... 21st April, 1860, on ... Duties on Foreign and Colonial Wool. *London.* 1860. 8vo, pp. 39. — Wise Saws; or, Sam Slick in Search of a Wife. *New York.* 1855. 12mo, pp. 336. — Yankee Stories and Yankee Letters. *Philadelphia: T. B. Peterson.* [1852.] 2 vols., 12mo. B.

[HALIBURTON (William).] Effects of the Stage on the Manners of a People and the Propriety of Encouraging and Establishing a Virtuous Theatre. By a Bostonian. *Boston: Printed by Young and Etheridge.* MDCCXCII. 8vo, pp. 75, (1). Plate. W.

See Clapp's "History of the Boston Stage," p. 15.

HALIFAX, *N. S.* Acta et Decreta Primi Concilii Provincialis Halifaxiensis habiti in Ecclesia Metropolitana S. Mariæ, Mense Septembri MDCCCLVII. *Halifaxiæ: Compton et Bowden.* 1860. 8vo, pp. 76. 29698

Annual Report of ... City Government of Halifax, Nova Scotia, ... 1861–62. *Halifax: Printed by Compton & Co.* 1862. 8vo, pp. (1), 71. 29699

Catalogue with the Constitution and Rules of the Citizens' Free Library ... . *Halifax, N. S.: Printed by James Bowes & Sons.* 1864. 16mo, pp. 87. B. 29700

The Charter and Ordinances of the City. [Appended, Supplement 1, 2, containing the Acts passed 1851–56.] *Halifax.* 1851–56. 29701

A Defence of the Letter from a Gentleman at Halifax, to his Friend in Rhode-Island. With Appendix. *Newport: S. Hall.* 1765. Sm. 4to, pp. 30. C., P. 29702

Halifax Libel. *See* Vol. II., No. 7889, *also* [Howard (M.)], [Otis (J.)], and Vindication.

Letters and Papers on Agriculture: Extracted from the Correspondence of a Society instituted at Halifax, for Promoting Agriculture in the Province of Nova-Scotia. To which is added a selection of Papers on various branches of Husbandry, from some of the best publications on the subject in Europe and America. Vol. I. [all published?] *Halifax: Printed by John Howe.* M.DCC.XCI. 8vo, pp. 139, (2). 29703

Origin and Formation of the Baptist Church in Halifax, N. S., 1828. 8vo. 29704

Provincial Agricultural Society, Halifax, N. S. An Abstract of the Proceedings at the Two Meetings during the Session of 1823. *Halifax, N. S.* 1823. 8vo, pp. 40. 29705

The Report of the Committee of Aldermen respecting the Recent Explosion of the Gunpowder Magazine, at Halifax ... . *Halifax.* 1857. 8vo, pp. 40. H. 29706

Reports on the Halifax and Quebec Railway, by George R. Young, January 24, 1849. [n. p. n. d.] 4to, pp. 52. M.

HALKETT (J.) Historical Notes respecting the Indians of North America: with Remarks on the Attempts made to Convert and Civilize them. ... By John Halkett, Esq. *London: Printed for Archibald Constable & Co.* 1825. 8vo, pp. viii, 408.

"A compilation from standard writers, containing an impartial and temperate account of the former condition of the Indians, and a review of the efforts, which have been made for their improvement. The author feels like a man of humanity, and writes like a man of sense."—*N. A. Rev.* XXII. 108. *See also* [Douglas (T.)], Vol. V., Nos. 20703 and 20704. Dr. E. B. O'Callaghan, in the "Hist. Mag.," III. 50, attributes these to Halkett.

HALL (A.) Oration at Keene, N. H., June 30, 1788, to Celebrate the Ratification of the Federal Constitution by the State of New Hampshire. By Aaron Hall. *Keene.* 1788. 8vo.

HALL. A Sermon preached ... June 2d, 1803, before ... the Governor ... Council ... of ... New Hampshire. By Aaron Hall. ... *Concord: Printed by George Hough.* 1803. 8vo, pp. 23.

HALL (A. H.) Equal Rights of the Rich and Poor. *Boston: Jas. French & Co.* 1855? 18mo, pp. 148. 29711

HALL (A. O.) Horace Greeley Decently Dissected, in a Letter on Horace Greeley, addressed by A. Oakey Hall to Joseph Hoxie, Esq., Republished [with an Alphabet of Notes] by Popular Request. ... *New York: Ross & Tousey.* 1862. 8vo, pp. 38. B., BA., H. 29712

HALL. The Manhattaner in New-Orleans; or, Phases of "Crescent City" Life. By A. O. Hall. *New-York: J. S. Redfield.* 1851. 12mo, pp. 10, 190. C., S. 29713

Also: Address ... before ... the Sigma Phi Fraternity ... July 17, 1855. *Geneva, N. Y.* 1855. 8vo, pp. 23. H. — The People of the State of New York *vs.* John A. Dix, and Five Others. Outlines of Argument of District Attorney Hall for Prosecution. *New York: Baker & Godwin.* 1864. 8vo, pp. 10.

HALL (A.) Life and Confession of Andrew Hall, as given by Himself to Rev. George C. Baldwin. *Troy.* 1849. 8vo. S.

HALL (A. M.) The Buccaneer. A Tale. By Mrs. Anna Maria Hall. *London.* 1832. 2 vols., 12mo. + *Philadelphia.* 1833. 2 vols., 12mo. 29715

Founded on some expeditions to America.

HALL (A.) Letters on Medical Education addressed to the Members of the Provincial Legislature of Canada. By Archibald Hall, M.D. *Montreal.* 1842. 8vo, pp. 30. 29716

Also: Biographical Sketch of ... A. F. Holmes, M.D. *Montreal.* 1860. 8vo, pp. 21. — Letters on the Medical Faculty of McGill College. *Montreal.* 1845. 8vo, pp. 7.

[HALL (*Miss* Arethusa).] Life and Character of the Rev. Sylvester Judd. *Boston: Crosby, Nichols & Co.* 1854. 12mo, pp. x, (1), 531. Portrait. C. 29717

HALL (B.) Extracts from A Journal, written on the Coasts of Chili, Peru, and Mexico, in the Years 1820, 1821, 1822, By Captain Basil Hall, ... *Edinburgh: Constable.* 1824. 2 vols., post 8vo. + Second Edition. [*Ibid.*] 1824. + Third Edition. [*Ibid.*] 1824. C. + Fourth Edition. [*Ibid.*] 1825. 2 vols., post 8vo, pp. xx, 379; xii, 320, 80. Map. BA., H. + *Philadelphia: E. Littell.* 1824. 2 vols., 12mo, pp. 244; vii, 230. BA. + *Boston: Wells and Lilly.* 1824. 2 vols., 12mo, pp. 244; vii, 230. B. + *Edinburgh: Constable.* 1826. 2 vols., 12mo, pp. xii, v–viii, 313. B. + *London: William Smith.* 1848. Rl. 8vo, pp. 166. 29718

Highly commended by Lowndes. *See* "Edinb. Rev.," XL. 31, 43.

HALL. Voyage au Chili, au Pérou, et au Mexique, pendant les années 1820, 21, et 22, entrepris par ordre du gouvernement anglais. *Paris.* 1825. + *Paris: A. Bertrand.* 1834. 2 vols., 8vo, pp. 359; 382. Map. C., P. + *La Haye.* 1835. 2 vols., 8vo. 29719

This translation was made by M. Leroy.

HALL. Dagboek, gehouden op eene reize langs de kusten van Chili, Peru en Mexico, gedurende de jaren 1820, 1821, 1822. Uit het Engelsch. *Delft.* 1826. 2 vols., 8vo. Map. 29720

HALL. Forty Etchings from Sketches made with the Camera Lucida, in North America, in 1827 and 1828. By Captain Basil Hall, R.N. *Cadell & Co., Edinburgh.* 1829. 4to, 42 l. 40 Plates. + Second Edition. [*Ibid.*] 29721

HALL. Fragments of Voyages and Travels. ... *Edinburgh: Robert Cadell.* 1831. 3 vols., 18mo, pp. iv, (1), 338; (3), 371; (3), 320. BA. + Second Series. *Edinburgh.* 1832. 3 vols., 18mo, pp. (6), 334; (5), 312; (5), 339. BA. + Third Series. *Edinburgh.* 1833. 3 vols., 18mo, pp. viii, (2), 363; (5), 325; (6), 328. BA. + *Philadelphia: Carey and Lea.* 1831. 2 vols., pp. (2), 247; 235. H. + *Philadelphia.* 1831–33. 6 vols., 12mo. + New Edition. *London: William Smith.* 1844. Rl. 8vo, pp. 499. + [*Ibid.*] 1850. + *London: Edward Moxon.* 1852. 8vo, pp. (8), 165; Second Series (4), 160; Third Series (4), 169, (1).

"As true as nature itself."—*Athenæum.* *See* "Quarterly Review," XLVII. 133, and Waldie's Circulating Library, Vol. II.

HALL. Zee- en Landreizen. Vertolkt door J. Olivier. *Amsterdam.* 1826. 2 vols., 8vo. 29723

HALL. The Lieutenant and Commander; being Autobiographical Sketches of his own Career, from Fragments of Voyages and Travels. By Captain Basil Hall, R.N. *London: E. Bell.* 186–. 24mo. 29724

HALL. Travels in North America, in the Years 1827 and 1828. By Captain Basil Hall. *Edinburgh: Robert Cadell.* MDCCCXXIX. 3 vols., post 8vo, pp. (2), iv, ii, 421, Map; (2), iv, ii, 421; vii, 436, Table. C. + *Philadelphia: Carey, Lea & Carey.* 1829. 2 vols., 12mo, pp. 322; iv, 9–329. + Third Edition. *Edinburgh: Robert Cadell.* MDCCCXXX. Post 8vo, pp. xiv, 421, Map; vi, 432; vii, 436, Table, 1 sheet, Appendix, pp. 9.

Capt. Hall "is apt to see one side of a thing so vividly as to forget that there is another side at all.—*Quart. Rev.* XLV. 145. For a review *see* [Biddle (R.)], Vol. II., No. 5247. For opinions of this work *see* "N. A. Rev.," XXIX. 323; "Quart. Rev.," XII. 417; Blackwood, XXXIV. 288; "Western Review," XI. 416; "M. Rev.," CXVII. 503.

HALL. Voyage dans les États-Unis de l'Amérique du Nord, et dans le Haut et le Bas-Canada: Par le Capitaine Basil-Hall, ... Chargé par le Gouvernement anglais de missions secrètes dans ces états. *Paris.* 1834. 2 vols., 8vo. P. + *Berlin.* 1834. 2 vols., 8vo. Map. + *Bruxelles: H. Dumont.* 1835. 2 vols., 12mo.

HALL (B. R.) Frank Freeman's Barber Shop. A Tale for the South and North. By Rev. Baynard R. Hall, D.D. *New York.* 1852. 12mo. C. 29727

[HALL.] The New Purchase: or, Seven and a Half Years in the Far West. By Robert Carlton, Esq. *New York: D. Appleton & Co.* MDCCCXLIII. 2 vols., 12mo, pp. xii, 300; viii, 316. + *New Albany, Ind.: J. R. Nunemacher.* [1855.] 12mo, pp. 471. Portrait. H. 29728

Reprinted in England as:

[HALL.] The New Purchase; or, Early Years in the Far West. By Robert Carlton, Esq. *London.* 1855. 12mo, pp. 471. 29729

[HALL.] Something for Every Body: Gleaned in The Old Purchase, from Fields Often Reaped. By Robert Carlton, Esq., ... *New-York: D. Appleton & Company.* MDCCCXLVI. 12mo, pp. 223. 29730

Also: ... An Oration ... before the ... Societies of the College of New Jersey. *New York: Charles Scribner.* 1852. 8vo, pp. 40. B.

Hall (B. F.) The Early History of the Northwestern States, embracing New-York, Ohio, Indiana, Illinois, Michigan, Iowa, and Wisconsin, with their Land-Laws, &c. And an Appendix containing the Constitutions of those States. *Buffalo: G. H. Derby & Co.* 1849. 8vo, pp. 477. c. 29731

This is the Land Owners Manual with a new title-page.

Hall. The Land Owner's Manual. Containing a Summary of Statute Regulations in New York [and other States]. With an Appendix, containing the Constitutions of the said States. By Benjamin F. Hall. *Auburn, N. Y.: Derby & Co.* 1847. 8vo, pp. 477. 29732

Hall. The Republican Party and its Presidential Candidates: comprising an Accurate Descriptive History of the Republican Party ... from ... 1796 to ... 1832; of the Whig and Democratic Parties during the Interregnum; and of its Re-formation in 1856, to ... resist the Aggressions of the Slave Power. With Biographical Sketches ... of Fremont and Dayton. By Benjamin F. Hall. *New York and Auburn: Miller, Orton & Mulligan.* 1856. 12mo, pp. 512. 2 Portraits. BA., C. 29733

See Official Opinions of the Attorney Generals. Also: Address to the Friendly Sons of St. Patrick, at Auburn. ... *Auburn.* 1849. 8vo. s.

Hall (B. H.) A Collection of College Words and Customs. By Benjamin H. Hall. Revised and Enlarged Edition. *Cambridge: John Bartlett.* 1856. 12mo, pp. 506. C., S. 29734

First published anonymously in 1851.

Hall. History of Eastern Vermont, from its earliest Settlement to the Close of the Eighteenth Century, with a Biographical Chapter and Appendixes. By Benjamin H. Hall. *New York: D. Appleton & Co.* 1858. 8vo, pp. xii, (2), 799. BA., C. + *Albany, N. Y.: J. Munsell.* 1865. 2 vols., rl. 8vo, pp. xii, (2), 799. 29735

The Albany imprint, of which fifty copies were prined on large paper, is the same as Appleton's. *See* "Hist. Mag.," I. 64; II. 190, 191; III. 133-143.

[Hall.] A Tribute of Respect by the Citizens of Troy, to the Memory of Abraham Lincoln. *Albany, N. Y.: J. Munsell.* 1865. 8vo, pp. 342. 29736

Fifty copies printed on large paper in 4to. Also: "Bibliography of Vermont; a Descriptive Catalogue of Books and Pamphlets relating to the History and Statistics of Vermont," included in Norton's "Literary Letter," New Series, No. 2. 1860.

Hall (B. M.) Life of Rev. John Clark. By Rev. B. M. Hall. With an Introduction by Bishop Morris. *New-York.* 1857. 12mo. C., S. 29737

Also: Sermon on the Fugitive Slave Law. ... *Schenectady.* 1850. 8vo.

Hall (C. F.) Arctic Researches and Life among the Esquimaux: Being the Narrative of an Expedition in Search of Sir John Franklin, in the Years 1860, 1861, and 1862. By Charles Francis Hall. ... *New York: Harper & Brothers.* 1865. 8vo, pp. (1), 595. Maps and Plates. B., BA., C., S. 29738

Hall. Life with the Esquimaux: A Narrative of Arctic Experience in Search of Survivors of Sir John Franklin's Expedition. From May 29, 1860, to September 13, 1862. Popular Edition. With Maps, colored Illustrations and Woodcuts. *London: S. Low, Son & Co.* Post 8vo, pp. x-547. 29739

[Hall (*Captain*).] The History of the Civil War in America. Vol. I. Comprehending the Campaigns of 1775, 1776, and 1777. By an Officer of the Army. *London: J. Sewall.* M.DCC.LXXX. 8vo, pp. (10), 467. Map. N. + The Second Edition. *London: T. Payne & Son.* M.DCCC.LXXX. 8vo, pp. (10), 467. Map.

Attributed to Major Hall, of General Howe's army. It is rather a vindication of the measures of the mother country, and consequently a condemnation of the Americans, than an impartial history. Although this Vol. I. reached a so-called second edition, it was never completed.

Hall (C. H.) A Mournful Easter, A Discourse Delivered in the Church of Epiphany, Washington, D. C. On Easter Day, April 19 [16th], 1865. By the Rector, Rev. Charles H. Hall, D.D. Being the Second Day after the Assassination of the President of the United States ... *Washington: Gideon & Pearson, Printers.* 1865. 8vo, pp. 15. B., H. 29741

Also: ... A Discourse ... on ... the National Fast Day, January 4, 1861, in ... Washington, D. C., ... *Washington: McGill & Witherow, Printers.* 1861. 8vo, pp. 10.

Hall (C. W.) Court Martial of Charles W. Hall, at Cincinnati, October, 1863. *Cincinnati: Robert Clarke & Co.* 1863. 8vo, pp. 28. 29742

Hall (C. W.) Legends of the Gulf ... By Charles W. Hall ... . *Charlottetown, P. E. I.: Printed by William H. Bremner.* 1870. 12mo, pp. 81. H. 29743

Hall. Twice Taken: an Historical Romance of the Maritime British Provinces. By C. W. Hall. *Boston: Lee & Shepard.* 1867. 16mo, pp. 242. C., H. 29744

Hall (D. W.) Arctic Rovings; or The Adventures of a New Bedford Boy on Sea and Land. By Daniel Weston Hall. *Boston.* 1861. 12mo, pp. 171. 29745

Hall (D.) Imported in the last Vessel from England, and to be Sold by David Hall, at the New Printing Office, in Market-Street, Philadelphia, the following Books, &c. [*Philadelphia.* 1768.] Folio, 1 l. H. 29746

One of the earliest catalogues issued in Pennsylvania. Also: David Hall, At the New Printing-Office, in Market-street, Philadelphia, has to dispose of, Wholesale and Retail, the following Books, &c. [1770.] Folio, pp. 2. H., P.

Hall (D.) A Mite into the Treasury; or, Some serious Remarks on that solemn and indispensable Duty of duly attending Assemblies for divine Worship, incumbent upon all Persons come to Years of Understanding (especially the Professors of Truth) whilst favoured with Health, Strength, and Liberty. Together with some due Animadversions upon the Neglect thereof; as also a Word of Consolation to such sincere hearted Friends, as are rendered incapable of personally attending there, by reason of Old Age, some bodily Disorder or Confinement, &c. To which is subjoined, an Epistle to Friends of Knaresborough Monthly-Meeting. By David Hall. *London, Printed; Philadelphia: Re-printed by B. Franklin, and D. Hall.* 1758. 8vo, pp. x, 53. 29747

Introduced here on account of the imprint; the first edition is *London: Luke Hinde.* 1756. 8vo. Also: An Epistle of Love and Caution to the Quarterly and Monthly Meeting of Friends in Great Britain, or elsewhere. Third Edition. ... *London: L. Hinde.* 1750. 12mo, pp. 46. C. — A Compassionate Call, and Hand reached for the in Tender Gospel Love, ... *Philadelphia: Printed by Benjamin & Jacob Johnson.* 1799. 8vo, pp. 12. C., H., P.

Hall (D.) Thanksgiving Sermon for the Entire Reduction of Canada, etc., delivered October 9, 1760. By David Hall of Sutton. *Boston.* 1761. 29748

Hall. ... A Sermon Preach'd at the Ordination of Mr. Joshua Eaton. ... in Leicester, November 7th. 1744. By David Hall, A.M. ... *Boston: Printed by S. Kneeland and T. Green.* 1745. 8vo. pp. 23. BA. 29749

Hall. A Sermon Preached at Sutton (County of Worcester), By David Hall, D.D., October 24th, 1779. Being Fifty Years after his Ordination there. *Worcester: Isaiah Thomas.* MDCCLXXXI. 12mo, pp. 28. BA. 29750

Hall (E. B.) A Discourse ... before the Rhode-Island Historical Society, February 6, 1855, On the Life and Times of John Howland, late President of the Society. By Edward B. Hall, D.D. *Providence: Geo. H. Whitney.* 1855. 8vo, pp. 36.

Hall. Discourses, comprising a History of the First Congregational Church in Providence. Delivered June 19th, 1836, after the Close of a Century from the formation of the Church. By Edward B. Hall, Pastor. *Providence: Knowles, Vose & Co.* 1836. 8vo, pp. 62. M. 29752

See "N. A. Rev.," January, 1837.

Hall. Memoir of Mary L. Ware. By Edward B. Hall. Third Thousand. *Boston: Crosby, Nichols and Company.* 1853. 12mo, pp. vii, (1), 434. Portrait. BA. + Eleventh Thousand. *Boston: Am. Unit. Assoc.* 1867. 12mo, pp. vii, 434. Plate.

Also: An Address before the Rhode Island Peace Society at its Twenty-seventh Annual Meeting, June 30, 1844. ... *Providence: H. H. Brown.* 1844. 8vo, pp. 24. — A Discourse occasioned by the Death of William Ellery Chauncey ... Providence, ... October 12, 1842. ... *Providence: B. Cranston & Co.* 1842. 8vo, pp. 32, (2). BA. — ... Discourse ... at the Dedication of the New Divinity Hall, ... Meadville, Pa. ... [*Cambridge.*] 1854. 8vo, pp. 43. — Discourse in behalf of the Children's Friend Society, ... Providence, October 7, 1845. ... *Providence: C. Burnett, Jr.* 1845. 8vo, pp. 16. — A Lecture on the Pleasures and Vices of the City, delivered Sunday evening, March 30, 1856. ... *Providence: Knowles, Anthony & Co.* 1856. 8vo, pp. 31. — Sermon preached May 14, 1841; being the National Fast, occasioned by the Death of President Harrison. ... *Providence.* 1841. 8vo, pp. 16. — The Value of a Man. A Discourse occasioned by the Death of the Hon. Henry Wheaton; delivered Sunday evening, March 19, 1848, in the First Congregational Church, Providence, R. I. ... *Providence: Charles Burnett, Jr.* 1848. 8vo, pp. 23. B., H.

Hall. A Memorial of Rev. E. B. Hall, D.D., late Pastor of the First Congregational Society, Providence, R. I. *Providence: S. S. Rider & Bro.* 1867. Sm. 4to, pp. 176. Portrait. C.

Hall (E. Hepple). Appleton's Handbook of American Travel: Northern Tour. Northern States, and British Provinces. With Descriptive Sketches, and Maps. By Edward H. Hall. Ninth Annual Edition. *New York: D. Appleton & Co.* 1867. 12mo, pp. 288, 435-456, viii. 11 Maps. 29755

Hall. Appleton's Handbook of American Travel. The Southern Tour, being a Guide through Maryland, District of Columbia, Virginia, North Carolina, South Carolina, Georgia, Florida, Alabama, Mississippi, Louisiana, Texas, Arkansas, Tennessee, and Kentucky, with descriptive Sketches ... By Edward H. Hall. *New York: D. Appleton & Co.* 1866. 12mo, pp. xii, 142, 32. 8 Maps. 29756

These two works are usually found together.

Hall. Third Edition. ... The Traveller and Emigrants' Hand-Book to Canada and the North-West of the American Union ... By Edward H. Hall ... . *London: Algar & Street.* 1858. 8vo, pp. 32. H. 29757

Hall. The Great West: Travellers', Miners', and Emigrants' Guide and Hand-Book to the Western, North-Western, and Pacific States and Territories. ... By Edward H. Hall, ... *New York: D. Appleton and Company.* 1865. 12mo, pp. 198.

Hall. The Great West; Railroad, Steamboat, and Stage Guide and Hand-Book, for Travellers, Miners, and Emigrants ... By Edward H. Hall. *New York: D. Appleton & Co.* [1866.] 12mo, pp. 181. H. 29759

Hall. The Northern Counties Gazetteer and Directory, for 1855-6: a ... Guide to Northern Illinois. Containing a concise description of the Cities, Towns & Principal Villages, with the Names of the Public Officers, Professional and Business Men, ... and a variety of other useful and interesting information. ... E. H. Hall, Compiler. *Chicago: Robert Fergus, Printer.* 1855. 8vo, pp. (2), iv, iii-vi, v-vii, (1), vii, (1), 17-208, Advertisements, 128. BA., H. 29760

Hall. The Great West. Emigrants', Settlers', and Travellers' Guide and Handbook to the States of California and Oregon, and the Territories ... By Edward H. Hall. *New York: Tribune Office.* 186-. 16mo, pp. 89. Map. 29761

Hall. The Summer Tourist's Pocket Guide to American Watering Places. With Map and Tables of Distances. *New York: Cathcart & Hall.* 1869. 16mo, pp. (10), xxx, 156, (22). Map. 29762

Also: Ho! for the West. [n. p. n. d.] — The National Tax Law as Amended. *New York.* 1863. 12mo. s. — Illinois Gazetteer. 1858. 8vo. — Western Gazetteer.

Hall (E.) The Ancient Historical Records of Norwalk, Conn.; with a Plan of the Ancient Settlement, and of the Town in 1847. Compiled by Edwin Hall. *Norwalk: James Mallory & Co.* 1847. 12mo, pp. 320. 3 Maps, 4 Plates. B., H.

Hall. The Puritans and their Principles. By Edwin Hall. *New York: Baker and Scribner.* 1846. 8vo, pp. 440. B. + Second Edition. [*Ibid.*] pp. 440. H. + Fourth Edition. [*Ibid.*] 1851. 8vo. C. 29764

Also: Colleges Essential to Home Missions: Discourse ... Society for the Protection of Collegiate and Theological Education at the West. *Boston.* 1852. + *New-York.*

1853. 8vo, pp. 30. H., S. — ... A Sermon ... North Fairfield, Connecticut, April 24, 1833, at the Ordination of George H. Hulin. ... *New York: S. W. Benedict & Co.* MDCCCXXXIII. 8vo, pp. 22. B. — A Sermon, ... Norwalk, Conn., October 12, 1834. ... *New York.* 8vo, pp. 20.

Hall (E. J.) Observations and Documents relative to a Calumny circulated by John Brown to the prejudice of Elisha J. Hall. [n. p. 1802.] 8vo. C., W. 29765

[Hall (F.)] The Importance of the British Plantations in America to this Kingdom; with The State of their Trade, and Methods for Improving it; As Also A Description of the several Colonies there. *London: J. Peele.* MDCCXXXI. 8vo, pp. (6), 114.

Anderson ("Hist. of Commerce," Vol. III. 167,) gives an abstract of this "judicious tract."

Hall (F. *and* H.) Narrative of the Capture and Providential Escape of Misses Frances and Almira Hall, Two respectable young Women (Sisters), of the ages of 16 and 18,—who were taken prisoners by the Savages, at a Frontier settlement, near Indian Creek, in May last, when fifteen of the Inhabitants fell victims to the bloody Tomahawk and Scalping Knife; among whom were the parents of the unfortunate females. Likewise, is added, the Interesting Narrative of the Captivity and Sufferings of Philip Brigdon, a Kentuckian, who fell into the hands of the merciless savages, on their return to their Settlement, three days after the Bloody Massacre. ... [*St. Louis.*] 1832. 8vo, pp. 24. Plate. 29767

Hall (F.) Colombia: its Present State, in respect of Climate, Soil, Productions, Population, Government, Commerce, Revenue, Manufactures, Arts, Literature, Manners, Education, and Inducements to Emigration, with Itineraries, partly from Spanish Surveys, partly from actual observation. By Colonel Francis Hall, Hydrographer in the Service of Colombia. *London: Baldwin, Cradock & Jay.* 1824. 8vo, pp. vi, (2), 179. + *Philadelphia: A. Small.* 1825. 12mo, pp. 131. B., BA., H., P. + Second Edition, with a Tariff. *London: Baldwin.* 1827. 8vo, pp. vi, (2), 179. Map. BA., H. 29768

Hall. Travels in Canada, and the United States, in 1816 and 1817. By Lieut. Francis Hall, 14th Light Dragoons, H.P. *London: Longman.* 1818. 8vo, pp. (4), 543. Map. + *Boston: Wells & Lilly.* 1818. 8vo, pp. 332. B., BA. + Second Edition. *London: Longman.* 1819. 8vo, pp. xii, 421. Map. C., H.

Shrewd, clever, humorous, and without prejudice. *See* "Edinb. Rev.," XXXI. 133; "N. A. Rev.," IX. 135.

Hall (F.) Catalogue of Minerals found in the State of Vermont, and in the adjacent States, together with their Localities; including a Number of the most interesting Minerals which have been discovered in other parts of the United States; Arranged alphabetically. By Frederick Hall, ... *Hartford: P. B. Goodsell, Printer.* 1824. 8vo, pp. 44. P. 29770

Hall. Eulogy on the late Solomon Metcalf Allen, Professor of Languages in Middlebury College, March 17, 1818. By Frederick Hall, A.A.S. *Middlebury, Vt.* 1818. 8vo, pp. 16. N.

Hall. Letters from the East and from the West. By Frederick Hall, M.D. ... *Washington City: F. Taylor and William M. Morrison.* [1840.] 8vo, pp. xi, 168. C., S. 29772

Relates in part to the Geology and Mineralogy of the Connecticut River.

Hall. Statistical Account of the Town of Middlebury, in the State of Vermont. Part First. By Frederick Hall. ... *Boston: Printed by Sewell Phelps.* 1821. 8vo, pp. 38. BA., N., S.

Also included in the "Mass. Hist. Soc. Coll.," 1822, Vol. XIX. 123-158.

Hall (F.), *lawyer*. Life of Maximilian I., late Emperor of Mexico, with a Sketch of the Empress Carlota. By Frederic Hall ... . *New York: James Miller.* 1868. 12mo, pp. 317. Portrait. B., BA. 29774

Hall (G. M.) Sermon delivered at the Semi-Annual Meeting of the Associate Presbytery of Miami. By George M. Hall. *Xenia, Ohio.* 1843? 12mo, pp. 12. 29775

Hall (G.) Divine Mercy a Cause for Humiliation. A Discourse Preached on the Occasion of the State Fast, April 13, 1865. By Gordon Hall, D.D., ... *Northampton, Mass.: Trumbull & Gere, Printers.* 1865. 8vo, pp. 15. 29776

Hall. President Lincoln's Death. Its Voice to the People. A Discourse by Gordon Hall, D.D., Pastor of Edwards Church. Preached in the First Church, Northampton, April 19, 1865. *Northampton, Mass.: Trumbull & Gere, Printers.* 1865. 8vo, pp. 16. 29777

Also: Discourse, Edwards Church, Thanksgiving Day, November 27, 1856. ... *Northampton, Mass.* 1857. 8vo. s.

Hall (H.) The History of Auburn. By Henry Hall. *Auburn: Dennis Brothers & Co.* 1869. 12mo, pp. xvi, 580. C., S.

Chapter I. relates to the Cayuga Indians.

Hall (H.) The Capture of Ticonderoga in 1775. ... By Hiland Hall. *Montpelier.* 1869. 8vo. S. 29779

Hall. The History of Vermont, from its Discovery to its Admission into the Union in 1791. By Hiland Hall, ... *Albany: Joel Munsell.* 1868. 8vo, pp. xii, 521, (1). Map. 29780

An exhaustive work on that interesting portion of the history of Vermont, relating to the severe struggle which it carried on with the government of New York for the maintenance of its title.

Hall. Remarks of Hiland Hall ... in the House ... May 5, 1834, on presenting a Memorial from Windham County, Vermont, on the ... Removal of the ... Deposites. *Washington.* 1834. 8vo. 29781

Also: Reports on Revolutionary Claims. *Washington.* 1840-43. 8vo. — Speech ... on the Fortification Bill; ... May 24, 1836. [n. p. 1836.] 8vo, pp. 8. — Speeches ... June 16 and 25, 1842, on the Virginia Bounty Land Claims ... *Washington.* 1842. 8vo. — Vindication of Volume First of the Collections of the Vermont Historical Society, from the Attacks of the New York Historical Magazine. ... *Montpelier.* 1871. 8vo, pp. 28. — Why the Early Inhabitants of Vermont disclaimed the Jurisdiction of New York. Address delivered December 4, 1860. *Bennington.* 1872. 8vo.

Hall (H. C. van). Verhandeling over de noodzakelijkheid der verbetering van den landbouw in de Nederlandisch West Indien, inzonderheid in den gegenwaerdigen tijd. [*Haarlem.* 1857.] 8vo. 29782

Hall (J.) A Brief History of the Mississippi Territory; to which is prefixed a Summary View of the Country between the Settlements on the Cumberland River and the Territory. By the Rev. James Hall, of North Carolina. *Salisbury: Francis Coupee.* 1801. 12mo, pp. (2), 70. C. 29783

An extremely rare pamphlet.

Hall. A Narrative of a most Extraordinary Work of Religion in North Carolina. By Rev. James Hall. *Philadelphia.* 1802. 8vo. S. 29784

Hall (J.) An Oration ... 24th. June 1818, before ... Ancient York Masons ... in ... Pittsburgh. By James Hall ... . *Pittsburgh: Butler & Lambdin.* 1818. 8vo, pp. 17. BA. 29785

Hall (J.) The Harpe's Head; a Legend of Kentucky. By James Hall. *Philadelphia.* 1833. C., P., S. 29786

Hall (J.) Legends of the West. By James Hall ... . *Philadelphia: Harrison Hall.* 1832. 12mo, pp. (6), 265. C. + Second Edition. *Philadelphia: Key & Biddle.* 1833. 12mo, pp.

257. + Author's Revised Edition. *New York: G. P. Putnam & Co.* 1853. 12mo, pp. 435. + *New York: T. L. Magagnos & Co.* 1854. 12mo, pp. 435. 2 Plates. C. + *Cincinnati.* 1857. 12mo. 29787

HALL. Legends of the West: Sketches Illustrative of the Habits, Occupation, Privations, Adventures and Sports of the Pioneers of the West. By James Hall. *Cincinnati: Robert Clarke & Co.* 1869. 12mo. 29788

HALL. Letters from the West; containing Sketches of Scenery, Manners, and Customs; and Anecdotes connected with the First Settlements of the Western Sections of the United States. By the Hon. Judge Hall. *London: Henry Colburn.* 1828. 8vo, pp. vi, 385. + [*Ibid.*] 1830. 29789

First appeared in the Port Folio. *See* "Quart. Rev.," XXXIX. 345; "N. Am. Rev.," XLV. 234, XLVII, 4-6, 499-501.

HALL. A Memoir of the Public Services of William Henry Harrison, of Ohio. By James Hall. *Philadelphia: Key & Biddle.* 1835. 18mo, pp. vi, 323. Portrait. + [*Ibid.*] 1836. P.

HALL. Notes on the Western States; Containing Descriptive Sketches of their Soil, Climate, Resources, and Scenery. By James Hall ... *Philadelphia: Harrison Hall.* 1838. 12mo, pp. xxiii, 13-304. 29791

This is "Statistics of the West," 1836, with a new title.—*N. Am. Rev.*, XLVII. 499. The preface was issued separately as a reply to strictures in the "North Am. Review."

HALL. The Romance of Western History: or, Sketches of History, Life and Manners, in the Far West. By James Hall ... *Cincinnati: Applegate & Company.* 1857. 12mo, pp. 420. Portrait. C. + *Cincinnati.* 1869. 12mo. 29792

HALL. Sketches of History, Life and Manners, in the West; containing Accurate Descriptions of the Country and Modes of Life in the Western States and Territories of North America. By James Hall. Vol. I. *Cincinnati: Hubbard & Edmonds.* 1834. 12mo, pp. 263. P. 29793

Of this edition, we believe, Vol. I. was published. It was reissued as:

HALL. Sketches of History, Life and Manners, in the West. By James Hall. ... *Philadelphia: Harrison Hall.* [1835.] 2 vols., 12mo, pp. 282, Explanation, 1 l., Plate; 276. P. 29794

See "N. A. Rev.," XLIII. 1, XLV. 234, XLVII. 499.

HALL. Statistics of the West, at the Close of the Year 1836. By James Hall. *Cincinnati: J. A. James & Co.* 1836. 12mo, pp. xviii, (2), 9-284. + [*Ibid.*] 1837. C., P. 29795

HALL. Tales of the Border. By James Hall. *Philadelphia: Harrison Hall.* 1834. 12mo, pp. 276. + [*Ibid.*] 1835. C., P.

Mr. Ludewig quotes the date of 1832 to the first issue.

HALL. The West: its Commerce and Navigation. By James Hall. *Cincinnati: H. W. Derby & Co.* 1848. 12mo, pp. vii, 328. C. 29797

HALL. The West: its Soil, Surface, and Productions. By James Hall. *Cincinnati: Robinson & Jones.* 1848. 12mo, pp. 260. P. 29798

Some copies have the imprint, *Cincinnati: Derby, Bradley & Co.* 1848.

HALL. The Western Souvenir. A Christmas and New Year's Gift. For 1829. Edited by James Hall. *Cincinnati.* 1829. 18mo, pp. 324. 4 Plates. 29799

The first annual published in the Western States. The contributors are all Western authors.

HALL. The Wilderness and the War-Path. By James Hall. *New York: Wiley & Putnam.* 1846. 12mo, pp. 174. S. 29800

Some copies have a London imprint. Also: Address before the ... Mercantile Library Association of Cincinnati, ... April 18, 1846. ... *Cincinnati.* 1846. 8vo, pp. 32. —The Soldier's Bride, and other Tales. ... *Philadelphia.* 1833. 12mo. C., P. *See* "Illinois Monthly Magazine," "Western Monthly Magazine," McKinney (T. L.), Sparks (J.)

HALL (James). Report ... of a Route for a Railroad from Portland to Montreal. *Portland.* 1844. 8vo. 29801

HALL (J.) Address to the Free People of Color. By James Hall. *Baltimore.* 1858. 8vo. S. 29802

HALL (J.) An Address delivered at the Anniversary Meeting of the Harvard Natural-History Society, May 24, 1848. By James Hall. *Cambridge: Metcalf and Company.* 1848. 8vo, pp. 39. B., M. 29803

HALL (J.) Contributions to the Palæontology of New York, being some of the Results of Investigations made during the Years 1855, '56, '57, and '58. With Woodcuts. *New York: B. Westerman and Co.* 1859. 29804

HALL (J.) Geological Survey of Canada. Figures and Descriptions of Canadian Organic Remains. Decade II. Graptolites of the Quebec Group. By James Hall. *Montreal: Dawson Bros.* 1865. 8vo, pp. 151. 21 Plates. 29805

HALL (J.) Key to a Chart of the successive Geological Formations, with an actual section from the Atlantic to the Pacific Ocean. By Professor James Hall. *Boston: Gould & Lincoln.* 1852. 18mo, pp. 72. C. 29806

HALL. Niagara Falls, their Physical Changes and the Geology and Topography of the Surrounding Country. [n. p. n. d.] 8vo. B. 29807

HALL. Notes upon the Geology of the Western States. [n. p.] 1841. 18mo. B., S. 29808

Also: An Address before the Society of Natural History of the Auburn Theological Seminary, August 15, 1843. ... *Auburn.* 1844. 8vo. B., S.—Explorations, Surveys and Reports from Belfast to Quebec.—Plants of Troy, N. Y. [n. p. n. d.] S.—*See* Emory (W. H.), Fremont (J. C.), Iowa, New York, Wisconsin.

HALL (J.) The Young Patriot; a Memorial of James Hall. *Boston, Mass.: Sabbath School Society.* [1862.] 18mo, pp. 192. 2 Portraits. C. 29809

HALL (J.) History of the Presbyterian Church in Trenton, N. J., from the First Settlement of the Town. By John Hall, D.D. *New York: A. D. F. Randolph.* 1859. 12mo, pp. vii, 453. Plate. S. 29810

HALL (J.) An Oration delivered at Tolland, Conn., before the Washington Benevolent Society, February 22d, 1814. By John Hall. *Hartford.* 1814. 8vo. 29811

HALL (J. E.) The American Law Journal and Miscellaneous Repertory ... By John E. Hall, Esq. ... *Philadelphia: William P. Ferrand & Co.* 1808. 8vo. 29812

[HALL (J. E.)] Memoirs of Eminent Persons, with Portraits and Facsimiles: Written, and in part Selected by the Editor of the Port Folio. *Philadelphia.* 1827. 8vo. S. 29813

See also Baltimore, Vol. I., No. 3038.

HALL (J. E.) The Philadelphia Souvenir; a Collection of Fugitive Pieces from the Philadelphia Press. With Biographical and Explanatory Notes, By J. E. Hall. *Philadelphia: Harrison Hall.* 1826. 12mo. P. 29814

HALL (J. K.) A Geographical Sketch of that Part of North America called Oregon. ... *Boston: J. Howe.* 1838. 8vo, pp. 80. Map. 29815

See Ludewig's "Literature of American Local History," p. 167.

HALL (J. P.) A Discourse delivered before the New England Society in the City of New York, December 22, 1847. By J. Prescott Hall. *New York.* 1848. 8vo, pp. 77. 29816

Also: An Address delivered at Middletown, R. I., on the 21st of September, 1854, before the Aquidneck Agricultural Society. ... *Newport: Cranston & Norman.* 1854. 8vo. S.

HALL (J. T.) Memorial of Lewis and Susan Benedict. By John Tayler Hall. [n. p.:] *Printed for the Family.* 1870. 8vo, pp. 55. 2 Portraits. C., S. 29817

H[ALL] (J[oseph]). A | Common | Apologie of | the Chvrch of | England: | Against the vniust Chal- | lenges of the ouer-iust Sect, | commonly called | Brownists. | Wherein the grounds and De- | fences, of the Separation are | largely discussed: | Occasioned, by a | Late Pamphlet published vnder the | name, Of an Answer to a Censorious Epistle, | Which the Reader shall finde | in the Margent. | By J. H. | *London.* | *Printed for Samuel Macham, and* | *are to be sold at his Shop in Pauls* | *Church-yard, at the Signe of* | *the Bull-head.* | 1610. | 4to, Title, pp. (4), 145, (4). 29818

END OF VOLUME SEVEN.

A DICTIONARY OF BOOKS

RELATING TO AMERICA.

[H]ALL (Joseph).] Mundus Alter et Idem siue Terra Australis ante hac semper incognita longis itineribus peregrini Academici nuperrime lustrata. Authore Mercurio Britannico. *Hannoviæ: G. Antonium.* 1607. 8vo, Engraved Title, 5 Maps. + *Francoforti: apud heredes ascanii de Reinalme.* [n. d.] 8vo, Engraved Title, pp. (12), 224. 2 Maps. BA. + [*Ibid.*] 1648. + Accessit propter affinitatem materiæ Thomæ Campanellæ, Civitas Solis et Nova Atlantis, Franc. Baconis. *Ultrajecti: Jo. a Waesberge.* 1643. 12mo. C.

A satirical romance in the style of Gulliver's Travels (of which it is said to have been the prototype), by Bishop Hall, the author of the Virgidemiæ. It obtains a place here because two of the maps include a delineation of America.

[HALL.] Discovery of the New World, or a Description of the South Indies, hetherto unknowne (Tenter-belly, Shee-land, Fooliana, Theevingen). By an English Mercury. *Imprinted for Ed. Blount and W. Barrett.* [n. d.] 8vo. Frontispiece. 29820

A humorous translation of the foregoing work, by John Healey. The first edition is 1643. Brand's copy of this very curious and amusing old work sold for £3. 7s. *See* Wraugham's Catalogue, 260.

HALL (J.) An Oration Pronounced July 4, 1800, at the Request of the Inhabitants of the Town of Boston, in Commemoration of the Anniversary of American Independence. By Joseph Hall. *Boston: Manning & Loring.* [1800.] 8vo, pp. 24.

George Washington forms the principal topic.

HALL (J.) Gems from Greenwood. Photographed by Joseph Hall, Brooklyn. Part I. *New York: Caldwell & Co.* 1868. Obl. folio, 18 leaves. 12 Photographs. C. 29822

HALL (J. W.) Marine Disasters on the Western Lakes, during the Navigation of 1869, with the Loss of Life and Property; Vessels Bought and Sold; new Vessels and their Tonnage; also, those which have passed out of existence; with the Names of Vessels laid up at various lake ports. By Capt J. W. Hall. *Detroit (Mich.): W. E. Tunis.* 1870. 16mo, pp. 120.

HALL (J. G.) Encomium on the Ladies ... at Sutton, Mass., March 22, 1809. By Joseph G. Hall. *Sutton.* 8vo. W.

HALL (M.) The Two-Fold Slavery of the United States; with a Project of Self-Emancipation. With two Maps. By Marshall Hall. *London: Adam Scott.* 1854. 12mo, pp. xiii, 159. 2 Maps. C. 29825

HALL (M.) Oration at Saugus, Mass., July 4, 1815. By M. Hall. *Boston.* [n. d.] 8vo. W. 29826

HALL (N.) A Discourse delivered ... [at] Dorchester, at the Funeral of ... Rev. Richard Pike, February 20, 1863. By Rev. Nathaniel Hall. *Boston: Walker, Wise & Co.* 1863. 8vo, pp. 29. 29827

To this is appended a Sermon by Rev. Caleb Bradlee. pp. 33-47.

HALL. The Moral Significance of the Contrasts between Slavery and Freedom: A Discourse ... Dorchester, May 10, 1864. By Nathaniel Hall. ... *Boston: Walker, Wise, and Company.* 1864. 8vo, pp. 15. 29828

HALL. The Proclamation of Freedom. A Sermon ... Dorchester, January 4, 1863, By Nathaniel Hall. ... *Boston: Crosby and Nichols.* 1863. 8vo, pp. 15. 29829

HALL. ... Slavery and its Hero-Victim. The Iniquity. A Sermon preached in ... Dorchester, ... Dec. 11, 1859. By Nathaniel Hall. *Boston: John Wilson & Son.* 1859. 8vo, pp. 19.

Paged continuously with "Slavery," but with a separate title-page: The Man, the Deed, the Event: A Sermon preached in the First Church, Dorchester, ... Dec. 4, and repeated Dec. 11, 1859. ... *Boston: John Wilson & Son.* 1859. 8vo, pp. 20-37. B. Also: An Address delivered in the First Church, Dorchester, April 7, 1842, at the Funeral of Rev. Thaddeus Mason Harris. ... *Boston: B. H. Greene.* 1842. 8vo, pp. 28. B.—An Address ... Dorchester, February 1, 1863. At the Funeral of George Francis Boynton. ... *Boston: Alfred Mudge & Son.* 1865. 8vo, pp. 20.—An Address ... Dorchester, June 19th, 1864, Commemorative of Walter Humphreys. ... *Boston: Printed by Alfred Mudge & Son.* 1864. 8vo, pp. 19.—The Christian Ministry. Sermon ... at Ordination of Rev. Hiram Withington, Leominster, December 25, 1844. ... *Boston.* 1845. 8vo, pp. 30.—Discourse delivered in Dorchester, on the Sunday succeeding the Funeral of Robert Thaxter, M.D. ... *Boston.* 1852. 8vo, pp. 23. B., H., M.— ... A Discourse ... February 10, 1869, ... the Installation of Rev. H. Hall ...

Worcester: Printed by Charles Hamilton. [1869.] 8vo, pp. 18.—A Discourse on the Life ... of Rev. John Pierpont ... Sept. 2, 1866. ... *Boston: Walker, Fuller, and Company.* 1866. 8vo, pp. 16.—Discourse ... September 30th, 1855. ... 8vo, pp. 27.—Discourse at Dorchester, Mass., May 10, 1864. 8vo.—Discourses, ... July 19, 1835, being the First Sabbath after his Ordination. ... *Boston.* 1835. 8vo, pp. 31. BA.—The Limits of Civil Obedience. A Sermon preached in ... Dorchester, January 12, 1851. ... *Boston.* 1851. 8vo, pp. 26. BA., M.—A Memorial of Edward Everett: A Discourse ... Dorchester ... Jan. 22, 1865. ... *Boston: Walker, Wise, and Company.* 1865. 8vo, pp. 16.—A Sermon ... in ... Dorchester, ... June 19, 1870, being the Two Hundred and Fortieth Anniversary ... of the Church ... after its Landing in America. ... *Boston: Ebenezer Clapp.* 1870. 8vo, pp. 27.—A Sermon ... Dorchester, (October 8, 1866,) ... upon the Decease of Maria S. Cummins. ... *Cambridge: Riverside Press.* 1866. 8vo, pp. 19.— ... A Sermon ... at Dorchester ... following the Decease of Mrs. Rebecca Stetson. ... *Boston: Printed by John Wilson and Son.* 1856. 8vo, pp. 16.— ... A Sermon ... at the Ordination of Mr. Frank P. Appleton ... in Danvers, January 14th, 1846. ... *Danvers: G. R. Carlton.* 1846. 8vo, pp. 34. B.—A Sermon ... following the Death of Rev. James F. Brown ... June 19th, 1853. ... *Boston: White & Potter.* 1853. 8vo, pp. 38.— ... A Sermon ... April 16, 1857; being the Day of the Annual Fast. ... *Boston: Crosby, Nichols and Co.* 1857. 8vo, pp. 17.—[A Tribute to the Memory of James Pierce.] A Sermon ... June 12th, 1853, ... *Boston: David Clapp.* 1853. 8vo, pp. 22.—Truth not to be overthrown. ... A Sermon ... at Dorchester, ... Jan. 27, 1861. ... *Boston: Printed by John Wilson and Son.* 1861. 8vo, pp. 19. B., BA., H. *See also* Everett (Edward).

HALL (N. K.) Opinion of Judge N. K. Hall, ... on Habeas Corpus in the Case of Rev. Judson D. Benedict. *New York: Comstock and Cassidy.* 1862. 8vo, pp. 15. + [With] Documents and Statements of Facts relating thereto. *Buffalo: Joseph Warren & Co.* 1862. 8vo, pp. 34. + [*Ibid.*] 1863. 29831

Relates to the Rebellion.

HALL (N.) The American War, by Newman Hall, LL.D. A Lecture to Working Men, Delivered in London, October 20, 1862. *London: James Nisbet & Co.* 1862. 12mo, pp. 31. + *Boston: American Tract Society.* [n. d.] 12mo, pp. 32. + *New York: Anson D. F. Randolph.* 1862. 12mo, pp. 48. B. 29832

HALL. Assassination of Abraham Lincoln. A Lecture. By Newman Hall, LL.B. *London: J. Snow.* 1866. 32mo, pp. 31.

HALL. From Liverpool to St. Louis. By Newman Hall, LL.B. *London: G. Routledge & Sons.* 1870. 16mo, pp. xxv, 294.

HALL. George Peabody. A Funeral Sermon. By Newman Hall, LL.B. ... November 14 ... Second Edition. *London: J. Nisbet & Co.* [n. d.] 12mo, pp. 16. H. 29835

HALL. Newman Hall in America. Rev. Dr. Hall's Lectures, etc. Reported by Wm. Anderson. *New York: New York News Co.* 1867. 16mo, pp. 137. 29836

HALL. A Sermon on the Assassination of Abraham Lincoln, preached ... London, ... May 14, 1865. By Rev. Newman Hall. *Boston: Bartlett and Halliday.* 1865. 8vo, pp. 16. B.

Also: A Parting Word. ... *New York: Sheldon & Co.* 1867. 18mo, pp. 88.—No War with America. A Lecture on the Affair of the Trent. ... December 9, 1861. *London: Eliot Stock.* 1861. 12mo, pp. 8.—A Reply to the Pro-Slavery Wail. ... *London: John Sents.* 1863. 8vo, pp. 15.—The Pro-Slavery Religion of the South. To the Editors of ... Religious Periodicals which have admitted the Appeal from the Clergy of the Confederates States. *Manchester Union and Emancipation Society:* [1863.] 8vo, pp. 2.—Sermons. ... With a History of Surrey Chapel. ... *New York: Sheldon & Co.* 1868. 12mo, pp. 309. Portrait. B.

HALL (P.) A Charge delivered to the Brethren of the African Lodge, ... 25th of June, 1792. ... By Prince Hall. *Boston.* [n. d.] 8vo, pp. 13. H., M. 29838

Also: Charge ... to the African Grand Lodge, June 24, 1797, at Menotomy. [*Boston.*] 1797. 16mo, pp. 18. B., BA., H., M.

HALL (P.) Dangers and Duties of the Present Hour. A Sermon preached at Indianapolis, Ind., April 28, 1861. By Rev. P. Hall. *Indianapolis: "Journal Co."* 1861. 8vo, pp. 15.

Also: What Shall we Do? A Sermon delivered January 13, 1861. ... *Indianapolis: "Journal Co."* 1861. 8vo, pp. 16.

HALL (R.) Acts Passed in the Island of Barbados, from 1643 to 1762, Inclusive; carefully Revised, innumerable errors Corrected; and the whole Compared and Examined, with the Original Acts, in the Secretary's Office. By the late Richard Hall, Esquire; ... and since his Death continued by his Son, Richard Hall. To which is added An Index; and Abridgment: with many useful Notes, References and Observations, never before published. And also a List of Laws, passed from the Settlement of the Island. *London: Richard Hall.* MDCCLXIV. Folio, pp xi, iv, 526, 84. J.C.B. 29840

HALL (R. B.) ... Speech of Hon. Robert B. Hall ... in the Senate of Massachusetts, April 24th, 1855, on the Address for the Removal of Edward G. Loring from the office of Judge of Probate. *Boston: Wright & Hasty.* 1855. 8vo, pp. 32. B., S.

Also: Admission of Kansas. Speech ... March 27, 1858. [n. p. n. d.] 8vo, pp. 8.—Speech ... on the Assault on Senator Sumner. *Washington.* 1856. 8vo, pp. 8.

HALL (S.) *See* Ojibway.

HALL (S.) Sermon, in which is shewed, What are Not, and What Are the Evidences of Any One's being in the Favor of

God: New Cheshire, January, 1746–7. By Samuel Hall. *New London.* 1747. 8vo, pp. 26. N. 29842

Also: ... Election Sermon, Hartford ... May 8th, 1746. *New London: Printed by Timothy Green.* 1746. 12mo, pp. (4), 28. B., H., W.

Hall (S. H.) The Tried Stability of our Government, a Cause for Thanksgiving. A Sermon preached in Oswego, New York, November 28, 1861. By Samuel H. Hall. *New York: A. D. F. Randolph.* 1861. 8vo, pp. 18. 29843

Hall (S. R.) ... History of the United States ... By Samuel R. Hall and A. R. Baker. *Boston: William Peirce.* 1836. 12mo, pp. xxxv, 290. B. + *Andover.* 1839. 12mo. 29844

Also: Lectures on School-keeping. *Boston: Richardson, Lord and Holbrook.* 1829. 12mo, pp. 135. B. + Second Edition. [*Ibid.*] 1830. 12mo, pp. 136. BA., H. + Fourth Edition. *Boston & Albany.* 1832. 12mo, pp. 100. B. + *Boston: Benjamin B. Murray.* 1843. 12mo, pp. 368. Plate. H.

Hall (S. E.) Selections from the Writings of Mrs. Sarah Hall, ... with a Memoir of her Life. [By Harrison Hall.] *Philadelphia: Harrison Hall.* 1832. pp. xxxiv, 180. + [*Ibid.*] 1833. pp. xxxiv, (1), 180. Portrait. B., C. 29845

Hall (S. H.) In Memoriam Sarah Hills Hall. ... [*Cambridge:*] *Printed by Welch, Bigelow & Co.* [1866.] 8vo, pp. 16.

Hall (Silas). Discourse before the Baptist Church in Abington. *Boston.* 1830. 12mo. 29847

Hall. A Sermon ... at the Ordination of Rev. William W. Hall ... North Marshfield, Mass., Feb. 9, 1831. By Rev. Silas Hall, A.M. ... *Plymouth: Allen Danforth.* 1831. 8vo, pp. 24.

Also: A Sermon ... at the Ordination of Rev. C. Tingley ... in Foxborough, Mass., July 14, 1831. ... *Dedham: Mann & Tolman.* 1831. 8vo, pp. 16. H.

Hall (S. W.) ... Report on the Petition of S. W. Hall, that the Water from Lake Cochituate, may be carried to East Boston. ... [*Boston.*] 1848. 8vo, pp. 14. 29849

Hall (T. B.) Gold and the Currency. Specie better than Small Bills. [By Thomas B. Hall, Esq.] *Boston: Printed by Evans & Plumer.* 1855. 8vo, pp. 16. H. 29850

[Hall.] ... Hearing before the Committee on Banks and Banking ... to suppress Bank Bills under Five Dollars ... Feb. 1856. *Boston: Printed by Evans and Plumer.* 1856. 8vo, pp. 12.

Hall (T. D.) Hudson, and its Tributary Region. By T. Dwight Hall. *Hudson (Wis.), May,* 1867. 12mo. Map.

Hall (W.) An Answer to "Colonel Choate's Reasons of Dissent, from the Judgment of a Council, in a Controversy, respecting some Doctrines, advanc'd by the Rev. Mr. Bacheller of Haverhill." ... By Willard Hall. ... *Boston: Printed by Edes and Gill.* 1761. 8vo, pp. 23. BA., H. 29853

Hall (W.) A Defence of the American Sunday School Union, against the Charges of its Opponents. ... By Willard Hall. *Philadelphia: Printed by John Clarke.* 1831. 8vo, pp. 18.

Hall. Lecture on the Nature, Character and Value of our Civil Institutions ... before the Elkton Lyceum. By Hon. Willard Hall. *Elkton.* 1839. 8vo, pp. 16. 29855

Also: Address before the Literary Societies of Delaware College, ... June 25, 1845. .. *Philadelphia: Isaac Ashmead.* 1845. 8vo, pp. 40. H.

Hall (W. P.) Admission of California: Speech of Willard P. Hall, of Missouri, March 5, 1850. [n. p. n. d.] 8vo. S.

Also: Instructions to Mr. Slidell. Speech ... House of Representatives, January 19, 1848. ... [*Washington.* n. d.] 8vo, pp. 8.—Speech ... December 11, 1851, on Public Lands. [n. p. n. d.]—Territorial Government in Oregon. Speech ... July 28, 1848 ... . [*Washington.* n. d.] 8vo, pp. 8.

Hall (W.) Statement of some of the Principal Facts which took place in the Revolutionary War, in and about the County of Barnstable on Cape Cod. By William Hall. *Boston.* 1831. 8vo, pp. 4. H. 29857

Hall (W.) The Abominations of Mormonism Exposed; containing Facts and Doctrines concerning that singular People, during seven years' membership with them from 1840 to 1847. By William Hall. *Cincinnati: I. Hart & Co.* 1852. 16mo, pp. 155. C. 29858

Hall (W. A.) Remarks of Hon. W. A. Hall, of Missouri, on the Slavery Question, in the House ... May 13, 1862. [n. p. n. d.] 8vo, pp. 8. 29859

Hall (W. A.) The Historic Significance of the Southern Revolution. A Lecture Delivered by Invitation in Petersburg, Va., March 14th and April 29th, 1864. ... By Rev. William A. Hall, of New Orleans Battalion Washington Artillery. *Petersburgh: Printed by A. F. Crutchfield & Co.* ... 1864. 8vo, pp. 45.

[Hall (William M.)] Bribery and Piracy. ... Wilful and Malicious Loss of the Steamship Shooting Star. ... *New York.* 1870. 8vo, pp. 57, (1). H. 29861

Hall (W. M.) Speech of William M. Hall ... Railroad to the Pacific ... July 7. *Chicago.* 1847. 8vo. S. + *New York.* 1853. 8vo, pp. 68. B., H. 29862

Hall (W. W.) Take care of your Health. [Advice to Soldiers.] By W. W. Hall, M.D. *Boston: American Tract Society.* [n. d.] 16mo, pp. 15. 29863

Published for the benefit of the volunteers and soldiers. Reissued as: Soldiers' Health. Third Edition. *New York.* 1862. 8vo, pp. 31. + Fifth Edition. [*Ibid.*] 1863. The author's "Journal of Health" contains many articles of historical interest.

Hall (W.) The Opinion of [Willis Hall] on the Legality of the Conduct of Robert H. Morris, Recorder of the City of New-York, in going to the house of one Pierce, in the Night Time, and seizing certain Private Papers: Given on the requisition of Gov. Seward. *Albany: Printed by Hoffman, White, and Visscher.* 1841. 8vo, pp. 12. BA., S. 29864

Also: An Address delivered August 14, 1844, before the Society of the Phi Beta Kappa in Yale College. ... *New Haven: Printed by B. L. Hamlin.* 1844. 8vo, pp. 32. B., H.—Letter to the Whigs. ... [*Boston.* 1848.] 8vo, pp. 8.—Speech ... in Committee ... on the Governor's Message. *Albany: Printed by W. and A. White.* 1843. 8vo, pp. 15. H., S.

Hallager (Morten). Udförlige og trœværdige efterretninger om de fra Rusland af langs med kysterne af Jishavet til söes giorte opdagelser; lilligemed de i russiske tieneste værende danske söe-officerers, commandeur-capitain Vitus Berings og capitain Morten Spangbergs söe-reiser, foretagne i aarene 1728, 1729, 1738, 1741 til 1743, paa det østlige ocean fra Kamtschatka af til Japon og Amerika; samt en beskrivelse over de siden den tid i dette hav fundne öer ... uddragne af ovenmeldte söefareres dagböger og af Müllers, Stellers, de l'Isle's, Pallas's beretninger og skrifter, ... *Kiöbenhavn: M. Hallager.* 1784. 16mo, pp. (2), xiv, 350. C. 29865

Hallam (R. A.) National Unity. A Sermon preached in ... New London, The Day of the National Fast, September 26th, 1861. By Robert A. Hallam, D.D., Rector. ... *D. S. Ruddock, Printer, New London, Conn.* 8vo, pp. 15. 29866

Also: ... A Discourse ... at the Funeral of Mr. Ichabod Pease ... New-London, March 5th, 1842. ... *New-London: Bolles & Williams.* 1842. 8vo, pp. 16. BA.—... Sermon preached in St. John's Church, Bridgeport, April 22d, 1866, in Commemoration of the Rev. Junius Marshall Willey, M.A. ... *New-Haven: Printed by Tuttle, Morehouse & Taylor.* 1866. 8vo, pp. 24. H.

[Halleck (Fitz-Greene).] Alnwick Castle, with other Poems. *New York: G. & C. Carvill.* 1827. 8vo, pp. 64. C.

First edition; very scarce.

Halleck. Alnwick Castle with other Poems. [By Fitz-Greene Halleck.] *New York: George Dearborn.* M DCCC XXXVI. 8vo, pp. 3–98, (1). H. + *New York: Harper & Brothers.* 1845. 12mo, pp. 15–104, (1). Plate. 29868

Halleck. Fanny; [a Poem.] [By Fitz-Greene Halleck.] *New York: C. Wiley & Co.* 1819. 8vo, pp. 64. B., BA., H.

Original edition, different from all subsequent issues.

Halleck. Fanny, a Poem. By Fitz-Greene Halleck. Second Edition. *New York.* 1821. 8vo, pp. 67. B., BA.

Halleck. Fanny: with other Poems. *New York: Harper & Brothers.* 1839. 8vo, pp. 130, (1). BA., H. 29871

Halleck. Fanny: a Poem. With Notes. *New York: W. L. Andrews.* 1866. Imp. 8vo, pp. 84. Portrait. 29872

Seventy-five copies printed, of which five are on India paper on one side of the paper, and two on paper of various colors.

[Halleck.] Fanny, Continued. *New York: Printed by William Grattan.* 1820. 12mo. 29873

Halleck. Lines to the Recorder. By Fitz-Greene Halleck. *New York: W. L. Andrews.* 1866. Imp. 8vo. 29874

Only seventy-five copies printed, of which five are on India paper and two on colored paper.

Halleck. The Poetical Works of Fitz-Greene Halleck. Now first collected. *New York.* 1847. 8vo. + [*Ibid.*] 1850. 8vo, pp. 286. + *New York: Redfield.* 1852. 8vo, pp. (2), iv, 9–232. BA. + [Another Edition.] *New York.* 1856. 12mo, pp. 204. 29875

Halleck. Poetical Writings, ... with Extracts from those of Joseph Rodman Drake. Edited by James Grant Wilson. *New York: D. Appleton & Co.* 1869. 12mo, pp. (2), xviii, 11–389. Portrait. B. 29876

Fifty copies printed on large paper.

Halleck. Young America. A Poem. By Fitz-Greene Halleck. *New York: D. Appleton & Co.* 1865. 16mo, pp. 49.

Halleck. A Description of the Dedication of the Monument at Guilford City, in honor of Fitz-Greene Halleck. ... *New York: D. Appleton & Co.* 1869. 8vo, pp. 39. H. 29878

Halleck (H. W.) Collection of Mining Laws of Spain and Mexico. By H. W. Halleck. *San Francisco.* 1859. 8vo. C.

Halleck. Elements of International Law and Laws of War. By H. W. Halleck ... . *Philadelphia: J. B. Lippincott & Co.* 1866. 8vo, pp. xxviii, 17–380. B. 29880

Halleck. International Law; or, Rules Regulating the Intercourse of States in Peace and War. By H. W. Halleck, A.M. ... *New York: D. Van Nostrand.* 1861. 8vo, pp. xxxv, (1), 907. + *San Francisco.* 1861. 8vo, pp. xxxvi, 908. C.

Also: Laws of War, and Martial Law: ... Extracts from General Halleck's Work on International Law, and their Application to Passing Events. *Boston: A. Williams & Co.* 1863. 12mo, pp. 15. B.

Halleck. Report of H. W. Halleck, ... on the Treatment of Kansas Troops by the Rebels. 1864. 8vo. Senate Executive Document, No. 4, 37th Congress. 29882

Halleck. Annual Report of H. W. Halleck, General-in Chief. ... Washington, D. C., November 15, 1863. 8vo, pp. 15–46. 29883

Accompanies Report of the Secretary of War.

Halleck. General H. W. Halleck's Report Reviewed in the Light of Facts. *New York: Anson D. F. Randolph.* 1862. 8vo, pp. 23. 29884

Halleck. General Halleck and General Burnside. A Reprint, with additions of two articles originally communicated to the Providence Journal, December 18, 1863, and July 16, 1864. *Boston: John Wilson & Co., Printers.* 1864. 8vo, pp. 23.

Haller (G. O.) The Dismissal of Major Granville O. Haller, of the Regular Army, ... by order of the Secretary of War, ... July 25th, 1863. Also, A Brief Memoir of his Military Services, and A Few Observations. *Paterson, N. J.* 1863. 8vo, pp. 84. 29886

Hallett (B. F.) ... A Full Report of the Trial of Ephraim K. Avery, charged with the Murder of Sarah Maria Cornell, ... at ... Newport ... 1833; with ... the Testimony ... and a ... Map ... . Reported by Benjamin F. Hallett. ... *Boston: Daily Advocate, May,* 1833. 8vo, pp. 191, 40. Map. + Second Edition. *Boston: Russell, Odiorne and Co.* [and] *David H. Lea.* 1833. 8vo, pp. 143. 29887

Of the edition with pp. 207, 40, there was another issue with the title changed. *See also* Avery (E. K.), Vol. I.

Hallett. Legislative Investigation into Masonry; being a Correct History of the Investigation of more than Fifty Adhering and Seceding Masons, before a Committee of the General Assembly of Rhode Island, ... between December 7, 1831, and January 7, 1832. Reported from Minutes taken at the time. By Benjamin F. Hallett, George Turner, and Others, and carefully compared. *Boston: Daily Advocate.* 1832. 8vo, pp. 85, and Index. 29888

Hallett. The Right of the People to establish Forms of Government. Mr. Hallett's Argument in the Rhode Island Causes before the Supreme Court of the United States, January, 1848. ... Martin Luther *vs.* Luther M. Borden and Others. ... Rachel Luther *vs.* the same. *Boston: Beals & Greene.* 1848. 8vo, pp. 71. H. 29889

Hallett. Rights of the Marshpee Indians. Argument of Benjamin F. Hallett ... before a ... Committee of the Legislature of Massachusetts ... To whom the Complaints of Indians ... were referred ... *Boston: J. Howe, Printer.* [1834.] 8vo, pp. 36. M. 29890

Also: Address to the People of Massachusetts, in Relation to the Political Influence of Freemasonry. ... 1833. Folio, 1 l.—Oration delivered July 4th, 1836, at Palmer ... Mass., [before the] Democratic Citizens of ... the Eighth Congressional District. ... *Boston: Printed by Beals & Greene.* 1836. 8vo, pp. 52. M.—Oration, ... July 4th, 1838, at Middleborough. ... *Boston: Printed by Beals and Greene.* 1838. 8vo, pp. 48. H., W.—Oration ... at Millbury, July 4, 1839. ... *Worcester: E. W. Bartlett.* 1839. 8vo, pp. 48. H.—Oration ... Oxford ... July 5, 1841. ... *Boston: Printed by Beals and Greene.* 1841. 8vo, pp. 39. BA.—Report of the Trial of Robert S. Field for the Murder of Jonathan Gray. *Providence, R. I.* 1826. 8vo. W.—Speech ... October 17, 1856, at the Grand Rally of the Democracy. [*Boston.* 1856.] 8vo, pp. 4.—Speech ... Oct. 21, 1853, in Favor ... of the New Constitution [n. p. n. d.] 8vo, pp. 12.—Speech ... before the Massachusetts Democratic Convention. *Boston.* 1860. 8vo. C.— ... Speech ... Washington ... June 25, 1860. Minority Report of Mr. Stevens ... Mr. Leach's Protest. [*Washington.* 1860.] 8vo, pp. 8.—Three Letters ... to Col. C. G. Greene, ... on ... the Democratic Party of Massachusetts ... . [*Boston.* 1852.] 8vo, pp. 12. H.

Hallett (J. W.) Address before the Ontario Agricultural Society. By Jacob W. Hallett. *Canandaigua.* 1821. 8vo. S.

Hallett (S.) Industrial and Financial Resources of the United States, ... as developed by Official, Federal and State Returns; ... With an Appendix, ... Also, The Federal and State Laws Relating to the Union Pacific Railroads. Companion to Samuel Hallett's American Circular. *New York: Samuel Hallett.* 1864. Rl. 8vo, pp. 312. 29892

Halley (E.) Sermon, in Argyle, County of Washington, on the Interment of the Rev. George Mairs. By Ebenezer Halley. *Schenectady.* 1842. 8vo. 29893

Also: Address, before the Theological Society, at Union College. ... *Albany: J. Munsell.* 1847. 8vo.—Lecture on Colonial Slavery. 1833.—Sermon at Troy, on the Death of General Zachary Taylor. ... *Troy.* 1850. 8vo. S.

Halley (E.) Atlas Maritimus et Commercialis. General View of the Trade and Navigation of the World. By Dr. Edmund Halley. *London.* 1728. 2 vols., folio. 50 Maps and Charts. 29894

Contains full accounts of the American colonies, &c.

Halley (R.) The Sinfulness of Colonial Slavery. A Lecture ... February 7th, 1833. By Robert Halley. Second Edition. *London: Hamilton, Adams, and Co.* 1833. 8vo, pp. 28. Portrait. B. 29895

Halley (W.) The Irish Race, at Home and Abroad. A Speech by William Halley. *Toronto.* 1860. 8vo. 29896

[Halliburton (*Sir* Brenton).] Observations upon the Importance of the North American Colonies to Great Britain. By an Old Inhabitant of British North America. *Halifax: Printed at the Royal Gazette Office.* [1825.] 8vo, pp. vi, 34. + Second Edition. *London.* 1831. 8vo, pp. 49. J.C.BT. 29897

See "Quart. Review," XXXIII. 410.

[Halliburton.] Reflections on Passing Events. A Poem. With Notes. By an Octogenarian. *Printed for private Circulation. Halifax.* 1856. 29898

Halliday (A.) The West Indies: The Natural and Physical History of the Windward and Leeward Colonies; with some Account of the Moral, Social, and Political Condition of their Inhabitants, immediately before and after the Abolition of Negro Slavery: By Sir Andrew Halliday, ... *London: John William Parker.* M,DCCC,XXXVII. Post 8vo, pp. viii, 408. 2 Maps and Table. A., B., BA., C., P. 29899

"Of modest pretensions, but replete with interesting and instructive information."—*Athenæum,* 1837, p. 242. In some copies the title reads:

Halliday. The West Indies: ... with the History of the Past and Present State of British Guiana: a Geological Map of the Barbadoes, and a Catalogue of Plants, by J. D. Maycock, M.D. *London.* 1837. Post 8vo. 29900

Also: Letter to the Secretary at War on Sickness and Mortality in the West Indies. *London.* 1839. 8vo.

Halliday (C. K.) Petition by C. K. Halliday, to the U. S Senate, in relation to the Osage Indian Reservation. *Washington.* 1869. 8vo. 29901

Halliday (J.) Life of William late Earl of Mansfield. *London.* 1797. 4to. Portrait. 29902

Contains observations relating incidentally to America.

Halliday (S. B.) The Lost and Found; or Life among the Poor. By Samuel B. Halliday. ... *New York: Blakeman & Mason.* 1859. 12mo, pp. 356. H. 29903

Hallock (G.) History of the South Congregational Church, New Haven, from its Origin in 1852, till January 1, 1865. By Gerard Hallock. ... *New Haven: Printed by Tuttle, Morehouse and Taylor.* 1865. 12mo, pp. 257, 48. Plate. B. 29904

Hallock (J.) Narratives of Reformations in Canton and Norfolk, Conn., in Four Letters. By Rev. Jeremiah Hallock. [*Providence: Barnum, Field & Co.* n. d.] 12mo, pp. 20. H.

Two Letters by Hallock and two by Ammi Robbins.

Hallock (M. A.) Beasts and Birds of America, Europe, Asia and Africa. By Mrs. M. A. Hallock. *New York: American Tract Society.* 1870. Sq. 12mo, pp. 64, 62, (2). 9 Plates.

Hallock (R. T.) ... An Oration ... in New York, on the Fourth of July, 1856. ... *New York: Ellinwood and Hills.* 1856. 8vo, pp. 37. B. 29907

[Hallock (W. A.)] The Hallock Ancestry. For the Memoir of Rev. Jeremiah Hallock of Connecticut and Rev. Moses Hallock of Massachusetts. [*New York.*] 1863. 12mo, pp. 8. S. 29908

An extract, being paged 389–396, but with a separate title.

Hallock. Memoir of Harlan Page. ... By William A. Hallock. *New York: American Tract Society.* [1835.] 18mo, pp. (2), 230. S. 29909

Hallock. ... A Sketch of the Life and Labors of the Rev. Justin Edwards, D.D. ... By Rev. W. A. Hallock. *New York.* [1855.] 12mo, pp. 556. Portrait. 29910

Hallock (W. H.) Life of Gerard Hallock, Thirty-three Years Editor of the "Journal of Commerce." Illustrated in Biography, Professional Writings, Correspondence, Controverses, &c. By W. H. Hallock. *New York: Oakley, Mason & Co.* 1869. 12mo, pp. 287. 29911

HALLORAN (L. B.) Rescued Fragments of Cabin Memorandums (South America). By Lieut. L. B. Halloran. *Plymouth.* 1826. 12mo. 29912

HALLOWELL (B.) Address ... Agricultural Society of Loudon County, Virginia. By B. Hallowell. *Washington.* 1853.

Also: Address ... Agricultural Society of Montgomery County, Md., ... September 9, 1852. ... *Washington.* 1852. 8vo, pp. 16. B.

HALLOWELL (E.) Report upon the Reptilia of the North Pacific Exploring Expedition, under Command of Captain John Rogers, U. S. N. By Edward Hallowell, M.D. Edited by E. D. Cope. *Philadelphia.* 1860. 8vo, pp. 30. 29914

HALLOWELL, *Me.* Mayor's Address, and Annual Reports made to the City Council of Hallowell ... 1860 ... *Hallowell: Masters, Smith & Co.* 1860. 12mo, pp. 36. 29915

Order of Exercises at the Dedication of the New Meeting-house in Hallowell, and Ordination of Rev. S. Everett, September 15, 1824. *Broadside.* [n. d.] 29916

Halls of the Montezumas: or, Mexico in Ancient and Modern Times. *New York: J. C. Burdick.* 1848. 8vo, pp. 136. 4 Plates. C. 29917

[HALPINE (Charles Grahame).] Baked Meats of the Funeral. A Collection of Essays, Poems, Speeches, Histories, and Banquets. By Private Miles O'Reilly, Late of the ... New York Volunteer Infantry, ... Collected, Revised, and Edited ... by an Ex-Colonel of the Adjutant-General's Department, with whom the Private formerly served as Lance-Corporal of Orderlies. *New York: Carleton.* M DCCC LXVI. 12mo, pp. viii, 3–378. BA.

[HALPINE.] The Life and Adventures, Songs, Services, and Speeches of Private Miles O'Reilly. ... With Comic Illustrations by Mullen ... *New York: Carleton.* MDCCCLXIV. 12mo, pp. (2), 237. C. 29919

HALPINE. The Poetical Works of Charles G. Halpine (Miles O'Reilly). Consisting of Odes, Poems, Sonnets, Epics, and Lyrical Effusions ... not heretofore ... collected. ... With Biographical Sketch and ... Notes. Edited by Robert B. Roosevelt. *New York: Harper & Brothers.* 1869. 8vo, pp. 352. Portrait.

Also: Lyrics by the Letter H. *New York.* 1854. 12mo. C.—Poem, at the Laying of the Corner Stone of the Soldiers' National Monument at Gettysburg, July 4, 1865. [n. p. n. d.] pp. 5.

HALSEY (L.) The Falls of Taughannock; a Complete Description. ... in the State of New York ... . By Lewis Halsey. *New York: John A. Gray & Green.* MDCCCLXVI. Sq. 18mo, pp. 95. B., S. 29921

HALSEY (Le Roy J.) Memoir of the Life and Character of Rev. Lewis Warner Green, D.D. With a Selection from his Sermons. By Leroy J. Halsey, D.D. *New York: C. Scribner & Co.* 1871. 12mo, pp. xi, 491. 2 Portraits. 29922

Also: Address ... University of Nashville ... with ... a Catalogue of the Alumni and Certain Proceedings of the Society. *Nashville.* 1841. 8vo.—Life and Educational Labors of P. Lindsley. [*Hartford.*] 1859. 8vo, pp. 46. B.

HALSEY (W.) An Oration, Delivered the Twenty-Second of February MDCCC, Before the Brethren and a Select Audience in the Hall of St. John's Lodge, No. 2, Newark, New-Jersey. By William Halsey, Esq. *Newark: Printed by Jacob Halsey.* 1800. 8vo, pp. 23. N. 29923

HALSTEAD (M.) Caucuses of 1860. A History of the National Political Conventions of the Current Presidential Campaign: ... By M. Halstead, an Eye-Witness of them all. *Columbus: Follett, Foster and Company.* 1860. 8vo, pp. (4), 232, Errata, 4 lines. BA., C. 29924

HALSTEAD (*Mr.*) Speech ... May 23, 1842, on the Bill making Appropriations for Civil and Diplomatic Expenses of the Government. *Washington.* 1842. 8vo. 29925

HALSTEAD (William H.) Little Pieces: Verse and Prose. By Quilp, Jr. *Norfolk (Va.): Office of the "Norfolk Virginian."* 1868. 8vo, pp. 63. C. 29926

HALSTED (Fred.) Letters addressed to President Lincoln and others, on the War. [n. p. n. d.] 29927

HALSTED (O. S.) Address upon the Character of the late Hon. Isaac H. Williamson, delivered before the Bar of New Jersey, September 3, 1844. By Oliver S. Halsted. *Newark.* 1844. 8vo. N. 29928

HALSTED (O. S.), *Jun.* Finance. A Letter addressed to the House Committee of Ways and Means, January 1, 1862. [n. p. n. d.] 8vo, pp. 7. 29929

Also: Finance, No. 3. Should the Interest on the National Debt be forced by Congressional Enactment to be paid in Coin? [n. p. n. d.] 8vo, pp. 5.

HALY (F. L.) Trotting Record for 1869. Containing a Complete and Reliable Record of all the Trotting Events of the Past Season. Compiled and Arranged ... by Francis L. Haly. *New York: The Author.* 1870. 12mo, pp. 136. 29930

HALZINGLER. The Three Sisters; or, the Life, Confession, and Execution of Amy, Elizabeth, and Cynthia Halzingler, who were tried, convicted, and executed, at Elizabethtown, Ark., November 30, 1855, for the wilful and horrible Murder of the Edmonds Family, consisting of seven members. Edited by the Rev. O. R. Arthur. *Philadelphia.* 1856. 8vo. 29931

HAMBDEN, *pseudonym.* First Reflections on reading the President's Message to Congress, of December 7, 1830. By "Hambden." ... *Washington: Printed by Gales & Seaton.* 1831. 8vo, pp. 15. B., BA. 29932

HAMBLETON (J. P.) A Biographical Sketch of Henry A. Wise, with a History of the Political Campaign in Virginia in 1855. To which is added, A Review of the Position of Parties in the Union. ... By James P. Hambleton, M.D. *Richmond, Va. J. W. Randolph.* 1856. 8vo, pp. xxxvi, 509. B., C., S. 29933

HAMBLIN (E.) The Life and Amours of Thomas S. Hamblin, as communicated by his loyal wife, Mrs. Elizabeth Hamblin. *New York.* [n. d.] 8vo, pp. 40. 29934

Hamblin was the proprietor of the Bowery Theatre, New York.

HAMBLIN (P. K.) United States Criminal History; By P. K. Hamblin. *Fayetteville.* 1826. 8vo, pp. 560. 29935

HAMBURG, *S. C.* Origin of the Town of Hamburg, South Carolina, founded ... July 4, 1821 ... *Augusta: Printed by Benj. Brantley.* 1837. 8vo, pp. 18, 18, 2. 29936

Part of a long title; proposing a direct trade between Hamburg in America, and Hamburg in Prussia.

HAMCONII (Mart.) Frisia seu de viris rebusque Frisiae illustribus. *Franekerae: Joa. Lamrinck.* 1620. 4to. 29937

Pages 74–75 contain an account of a voyage of the Frisons to America and Chili long before Columbus. As to the probability of such a voyage, *see* "Memoir on the Discovery of America by Van der Bergh." Title and note from F. Muller's Catalogue.

[HAMEL (*M.* DU).] Acoubar, ou la Loyauté trahie. Tragédie tirée des amoùrs de Pistion & de Fortunie en leur voyage de Canada, avec des chœurs, dediée á Philippes Desportes, Abbé de Tyron. [n. p.] 1586. 12mo. 29938

Reprinted with the author's name as below. Also in the "Bibliothèque du Théâtre françáis," Vol. I. 279. It should have appeared under Du Hamel.

HAMEL, DU. Acoubar, tragédie, tirée des amours de Pistion et Fortunie, en leur voyage du Canada, par maistre Du Hamel, advocat en la Cour de Parlement. *Rouen: Raphael du Petit Val.* 1603. 12mo, pp. 71. 29939

HAMEL (J.) Tradescant der Aeltere, 1618, in Russland. Der Handelsverkehr zwischen England und Russland in seiner Entstehung. Rückblick auf einige der älteren Reisen im Norden. *St. Petersburg.* 1847. 4to. Portrait and Map. 29940

This very interesting work abounds with valuable notices of the early voyages to the North.

HAMEL. England and Russia; comprising the Voyages of John Tradescant, the Elder, Sir Hugh Willoughby, Richard Chancellor, Nelson, and Others, to the White Sea, etc. By Dr. J. Hamel. Translated by John Studdy Leigh. *London: Richard Bentley.* 1854. 8vo, pp. xi, 422. BA., C. 29941

HAMER (T. L.) Speech of Thomas L. Hamer in the House ... March 2, 1837, on the ... Civil and Diplomatic Expenses ... [*Washington.* 1837.] 8vo. 29942

Also: Speech of Mr. Hamer ... on the Bill ... for a Survey and Exploring Expedition to the South Sea. ... May, 1836. *Washington: Blair & Rives.* 1836. 8vo, pp. 8.

HAMERSLY (L. R.) The Records of Living Officers of the United States Navy and Marine Corps; with a History of Naval Operations during the Rebellion of 1861–65, and a List of the Ships and Officers participating in the great Battles, Compiled from Official Sources. By Lewis R. Hamersly. *Philadelphia: J. B. Lippincott & Co.* 1870. 8vo, pp. 350. B. 29943

HAMET (C.) Documents respecting the Application of Caramalli, Ex-Bashaw of Tripoli. 1806. 12mo. W. 29944

HAMIL (E. J.), *and* HENDERSON (Samuel). Discussion on Methodist Episcopacy. *Charleston.* 1856. Post 8vo. C. 29945

HAMIL (S. M.) President Lincoln, a Faithful Son. An Address delivered before the High School, at Laurenceville, N. J., By Samuel M. Hamel, M.D., June 1st, 1865. *Trenton: Murphy & Bechtel, Printers.* 1865. 8vo, pp. 11. 29946

[HAMILTON (Alexander).] An Address to the Electors of the State of New York. *Albany.* [1801.] 12mo, pp. 23. B., N. + *Re-printed, April.* 1801. 8vo, pp. 22. 29947

[HAMILTON.] American Arguments for British Rights; being a Republication of the celebrated Letters of Phocion, on the subject of Neutral Trade. *Charleston, S. C.* 1806. 8vo. + Reprinted, with a Preface by the English Editor. *London.* 1806. 8vo, pp. xii. 29948

HAMILTON. American Budget, 1794. The Income and Expenditure of the United States of America, as presented to the House of Representatives, in Sundry Estimates and Statements relative to Appropriations for the Service of the Year 1794. By Alexander Hamilton, Esq. ... To which is added: The Report to the Congress of the United States of America on the Nature and Extent of the Privileges and Restrictions of the Commercial Intercourse of the United States with Foreign Nations, * * * &c. By Thomas Jefferson, Esq. *London: J. Debrett.* 1794. 8vo, pp. (4), 42. BA., C. 29949

See "M. Rev.," XV. 203.

[HAMILTON.] The Argument of ... upon the Constitutionality of a National Bank. [*Philadelphia.* 1791.] 8vo, pp. 40.

[HAMILTON.] A Defence of the Treaty of Amity, Commerce, and Navigation, entered into between the United States of America & Great Britain, as it has appeared in the Papers under the signature of Camillus. *New York: Francis Childs and Co.* 1795. 8vo, pp. 139. C., H., N., P. 29951

Relates to Jay's Treaty. *See* Tucker's "Life of Jefferson," I. 300.

[HAMILTON.] An Examination of the late Proceedings in Congress, respecting the Official Conduct of the Secretary of the Treasury [Alexander Hamilton]. *Printed within the United States* [*March*] M.D.CC.XCIII. 8vo, pp. 28. N., S. 29952

[HAMILTON.] The Examination of the President's [Jefferson's] Message, at the Opening of Congress, December 7, 1801, Revised and Corrected by the Author. *New-York.* 1802. 8vo, pp. 127. N. 29953

First appeared in the *Evening Post*, under the signature of Lucius Crassus.

[HAMILTON.] Examination of the Treaty of Amity, Commerce, and Navigation, between the United States and Great Britain, In Several Numbers: By Cato. [n. p.:] *Re-published, from the Argus, by Thomas Greenleaf.* 1795. 8vo, pp. 96. N.

[HAMILTON.] The Farmer Refuted: Or, A more impartial and Comprehensive View of the Dispute between Great-Britain

and the Colonies, intended as a Further Vindication of the Congress: In Answer to a Letter from *A. W.*, Farmer, intitled A View of the Controversy between Great-Britain and her Colonies: Including, A Mode of determining the present Disputes finally and effectually, &c. ... *New-York: Printed by James Rivington.* 1775. 8vo, pp. iv, 78. BA., C., H. N., P. 29955

Written by Hamilton when only eighteen years old. A copy in the New York Historical Society, which formerly belonged to Dr. T. B. Chandler of Elizabeth-Town, contains a MS. note stating that "An Answer to the preceding piece by A. W., Farmer, was advertised to be in the Press with the following title: 'The Republican Dissected; or, the Anatomy of an American Whig;' but, by a sudden and unexpected Revolution, the Liberty of the Press was totally destroyed, and nothing could be printed on the side of Government." This refers to the seizure and destruction of Rivington's press and types by Captain Isaac Sears, with a party from Connecticut.

[HAMILTON.] The Federalist. *See* Vol. VI., pp. 376–379.

[HAMILTON.] A Full Vindication of the Measures of the Congress, from The Calumnies of their Enemies; In Answer to a Letter, under the Signature of *A. W.* Farmer, Whereby His Sophistry is exposed, his Cavils confuted, his Artifices detected, and his Wit ridiculed; In a General Address To the Inhabitants of America. And A Particular Address To the Farmers of the Province of New-York. *New-York: Printed by James Rivington.* 1774. 8vo, pp. 35. 29956

In reply to "The Congress Canvassed;" remarkable as having been the first published production of Alexander Hamilton; and the more extraordinary as having been written at so early an age. Hamilton was born January 11th, 1757.

HAMILTON. A Letter by Alexander Hamilton, ... on ... Banks and the Currency, proposing the creation of a State Bank of Issues, and the restriction of Private Banks to Circulation, Discount, and Deposits. *New-York.* 1839. 8vo, pp. 22. P. + [*Ibid.*] pp. 25. H. 29957

HAMILTON. Letter to Congress on a Plan of a Fiscal Agent. *Washington.* 1841. 8vo. 29958

HAMILTON. Letter from Alexander Hamilton, concerning the Public Conduct and Character of John Adams, Esq., President of the United States. *New York: Printed for John Lang, by George F. Hopkins.* 1800. ... 8vo, pp. 54. + Second Edition. *New York: Printed for John Lang, by John Furman.* 1800. 8vo, pp. 54. BA. + Third Edition. *New York: Printed for John Lang, by Furman & Loudon.* 1800. 8vo, pp. 54. BA., C., H. + Fourth Edition. [*Ibid.*] 8vo, pp. 58. + [Another Edition.] *New York: Printed for John Lang, by George F. Hopkins.* 1800.

Philadelphia: Re-printed Pro Bono Publico. 8vo, pp. 54, 8. + New Edition, with a Preface. *Boston: Printed by E. G. House.* 1809. 8vo, pp. 56. BA., H., S. 29959

This elicited several replies as below:

HAMILTON. A Letter to General Hamilton, occasioned by his Letter to President Adams. By a Federalist. [n. p. n. d.] 8vo, pp. 8. N. + pp. 10. BA. + *New York.* 1800. 12mo. H. + *Philadelphia.* 1800. 8vo, pp. 10. + [*Boston.* 1809.] 8vo, pp. 10. 29960

Signed Aristides—perhaps by W. P. Van Ness.

HAMILTON. Vindication of the Conduct and Character of John Adams, Esq., in Reply to the Letter of General Hamilton addressed to the Federal Citizens of the Union. *New York.* 1800. 8vo. W. 29961

For other replies *see* Caius, Vol. III., No. 9863, and Cincinnatus, Vol. IV., No. 13135.

[HAMILTON.] A Letter from Phocion to the Considerate Citizens of New-York, on the Politics of the Day. [Said to be written by Colonel Hamilton, late Aid to his Excellency General Washington, and a Member of the American Congress.] *New York: S. Loudon.* 1784. 8vo, pp. 23. N. + [*Ibid.*] pp. 19. BA. + [Another Edition.] *New York.* 1784. 12mo, pp. 12. + *Newport, Reprinted.* 1784. 12mo, pp. 12. + *Philadelphia: Robert Bell.* M.DCC.LXXXIV. 8vo, pp. 15. H. + *Boston.* 1784. 8vo, pp. 23. S. + [Another Edition.] *Boston.* 1784. 8vo, pp. 19. H. 29962

[HAMILTON.] Mentor's Reply to Phocion's Letter; with some observations on Trade. Addressed to the Citizens of New York. *New York: Shepard Kollock.* 1784. 8vo, pp. 18. N. + *Philadelphia.* 1784. 8vo, pp. 17–24. H. 29963

[HAMILTON.] A Second Letter from Phocion to the Considerate Citizens of New-York; containing Remarks on Mentor's Reply. *New York: Loudon.* 1784. 8vo, pp. 43. C.

Reprinted with the following title:

HAMILTON. Colonel Hamilton's Second Letter from Phocion to the Considerate Citizens of New-York, on the Politics of the Times, in Consequence of the Peace: Containing Remarks on Mentor's Reply. *Philadelphia: Robert Bell.* M, DCC, LXXXIV. pp. 25–48. BA., H. 29965

HAMILTON. Letters addressed to the Yeomanry of the United States. By A. Hamilton. *Philadelphia.* 1792. 8vo. 29966

[HAMILTON.] Letters of Pacificus, Written in Justification of the President's Proclamation of Neutrality. Published Originally in the Year 1793. *Philadelphia.* 1796. 8vo, pp. 60. P.

See "Federalist," edition of 1802, Vol. VI., No. 23981.

HAMILTON *and* MADISON (James). Letters of Pacificus and Helvidius on the Proclamation of Neutrality of 1793, [with] the Proclamation. *Washington: J. and G. S. Gideon.* 1845. 8vo, pp. 102. C. 29968

HAMILTON. Observations on Certain Documents contained in Nos. V. and VI. of "The History of the United States, for the year 1796," in which the Charge of Speculation against Alexander Hamilton, late Secretary of the Treasury, is Fully Refuted. Written by Himself. *Philadelphia: Printed for John Fenno.* 1797. 8vo, pp. 37, lviii. BA. + [*Ibid.*] 1800. BA., H.

The Author's Edition, usually known as the "Reynold's Pamphlet," in which Hamilton explains his public conduct at the expense of his private character. *See* Callender (J. T.) This edition was afterwards bought up by Hamilton's family and destroyed. Concerning this, *see* a notice in Stevens's "Bibliotheca Historica" which concludes, "Truth never appeared so naked as in these confessions of Alexander Hamilton." It is not included in Hamilton's Works, but was reprinted as below:

HAMILTON. Observations [&c.] *New York: Printed for John Lang, by George F. Hopkins.* 1800. 8vo, pp. 37, lviii. + *Philadelphia: Reprinted Pro Bono Publico.* [1800.] 8vo, pp. 37, lviii. + *New York: Printed for the Hamilton Club.* 1865. 8vo, pp. (6), 157. 29970

This last edition forms "Hamilton Club Series," No. II., of which fifty copies were printed in 8vo, twenty-five in 4to, and five on drawing paper in 4to.

HAMILTON. The Official and other Papers of the late Major-General Alexander Hamilton. Compiled chiefly from the Originals in the possession of Mrs. Hamilton. Vol. I. *New York: Wiley & Putnam.* 1842. 8vo, pp. iv, 496. BA., C., M. 29971

Compiled by Francis L. Hawks. No more published.

HAMILTON. Official Reports on Public Credit, a National Bank, Manufactures and a Mint. *Philadelphia.* 1821. 8vo.

See Carey (M.)

[HAMILTON.] The Politicks and Views of a Certain Party Displayed. *Printed in the Year* M.DCC.XCII. 8vo, pp. 36.

HAMILTON. Propositions of Alexander Hamilton in Convention, for Establishing a Constitution of the United States, with a Summary of the Political Opinions of John Adams, and a Discussion between John Adams and Samuel Adams. *Pittsfield.* 1802. 8vo, pp. 32. 29974

Hamilton. Report of the Secretary of the Treasury on the Privileges and Restrictions on the Commerce of the United States in Foreign Countries. *Philadelphia: Childs & Swaine.* 1793. 8vo, pp. 20. 29975

Hamilton. Extract of a Report ... on the Subject of Manufactures ... of the 15th Day of January, 1790. *New-York: Printed by George Largin.* 1816. 8vo, pp. 32. BA. 29976

Hamilton. Report of the Secretary of the Treasury on the Subject of Manufactures, made the fifth of December, 1791. *Philadelphia.* 1824. 4to, pp. 58. 29977

This famous report is highly commended in the "Monthly Review," XII. 211, and was reprinted as below:

Hamilton. Report of the Secretary of the Treasury of the United States on the Subject of Manufactures. Presented to the House of Representatives, December 5, 1791. *London: J. Debrett.* 1793. 8vo, pp. (4), 129. + *Dublin.* MDCCXCIII. 8vo, pp. 88. + *Philadelphia: Printed by Joseph R. A. Skerrett. Jan.* 1. 1824. 18mo, pp. 143. P. 29978

Hamilton. Alexander Hamilton's Report on the Subject of Manufactures, made in his capacity of Secretary of the Treasury, on the 5th December, 1791. Sixth Edition; To which are prefixed, two Prefaces by the Editor [Mathew Carey]. *Philadelphia: Mathew Carey.* 1827. 8vo, pp. 80. BA., H. 29979

Hamilton. Report of the Secretary of the Treasury, read in the House of Representatives of the United States, January 19th, 1795; containing a Plan for the further support of Public Credit. Printed by Order of the House of Representatives. [*Philadelphia:*] *John Fenno.* 1795. 8vo, pp. 90. Tables.

Hamilton. Reports of Alexander Hamilton, Esq., Secretary of the Treasury of the United States, January 19, 1795. Containing, I. A Plan for the further Support of the Public Credit. II. For the Improvement and better Management of the Revenues of the United States. To which is added an Act for making Provision for the Support of Public Credit & the Redemption of the Debt. ... *London: J. Debrett.* 1795. 4to, pp. 96. J.C.B.

See "Monthly Review."

[Hamilton.] Reflections on Monroe's View ... as published in the Gazette of the United States under the Signature of Scipio. ... [n. p. n. d.] 8vo, pp. 88. BA. 29982

[Hamilton.] [Scipio's] Reflections on Monroe's View of the Conduct of the Executive, connected with a Mission to the French Republic, in the years 1794, '95, '96. *Boston: C. P. Wayne.* 1798. 8vo, pp. 140. C., M. 29983

Sometimes ascribed to Alexander Hamilton.

Hamilton. The Soundness of the Policy of Protecting Domestic Manufactures; fully established by Alexander Hamilton, in his Report to Congress on the Subject, and by Thomas Jefferson in his Letter to Benjamin Austin. *Philadelphia: Printed by J. R. A. Skerrett.* 1817. 8vo, pp. 24. BA. 29984

Hamilton. Sundry Statements by the Secretary of the Treasury; in conformity with the Resolution of the House of Representatives of the 23d of January 1793. [*Philadelphia:*] *Printed by Childs and Swaine.* Folio, pp. 31. 29985

These various reports of the Secretary of the Treasury are introduced here in deference to the fact that the Treasury was, in fact, organized by Hamilton; and we may add that so well considered were his plans that *to-day* the regulations which he introduced are the regulations now in practice, with but little alteration.

Hamilton *and others.* The Speeches ... of Mr. Van Ness, Mr. Caines, ... Mr. Harrison, and General Hamilton, in the Great Cause of the People, against Harry Croswell, on an Indictment for a Libel on Thomas Jefferson. *New York.* 1804. 8vo.

Hamilton. The Works of Alexander Hamilton, comprising his most important Official Reports; an improved Edition of the Federalist, on the New Constitution, written in 1788; and Pacificus, on the Proclamation of Neutrality; Written in 1793. *New York.* 1810. 3 vols., 8vo, pp. vii, 325; iv, 368; iv, 368. 3 Portraits. C., H. 29987

Some of the contents of these volumes are not included in the new edition of Hamilton's Works, noticed below:

Hamilton. The Works of Alexander Hamilton; comprising his Correspondence, and his Political and Official Writings, exclusive of the Federalist, Civic and Military. Published from the Original Manuscripts deposited in the Department of State, by order of the Joint Library Committee of Congress. Edited by John C. Hamilton, ... *New York: John F. Trow,* ... M.DCCC.L. 7 vols., 8vo, pp. (6), 492; (6), 495; (4), 590; (4), 652; (4),

604; (4), 635; (4), 894, (2). Portrait. + *New York: Charles S. Francis & Co.* M.DCCC.LI. 7 vols., 8vo. BA. 29988

For other of Hamilton's Reports, *see* Reports; *also*, Williston (E. B.), Vols. I. and IV. The following relate to Hamilton:

A Collection of Facts and Documents relative to the Death of Major-General Alexander Hamilton; with Comments and Eulogies, &c., on his Life and Character. *New York.* 1804. 8vo, pp. 46. M. 29989

For another Collection *see* [Coleman (W.),] Vol. IV., No. 14311.

Particulars of the late Duel fought at Hoboken, July 11th, between Aaron Burr and Alexander Hamilton, in which the Latter unfortunately Fell: containing all the Papers relating to that Event. *New York.* 1804. 8vo, pp. 32. 29990

Presentation of the Statue of Alexander Hamilton to the City of Boston, by Thomas Lee. *Boston: Printed for the City Council.* 1865. 8vo, pp. 11. 29991

A Sketch of the Character of Alexander Hamilton. ... [*Boston.* 1804.] 8vo, pp. 15. M. 29992

Hamilton (A. J.) An Address to the People of Texas. By A. J. Hamilton, Military Governor. *New Orleans: "Era" Office.* 1864. 8vo, pp. 19. + [*Ibid.*] pp. 8. H. 29993

Hamilton. An Address on "Suffrage and Reconstruction," ... By Hon. A. J. Hamilton, of Texas. ... December 3, 1866. *Boston: Impartial-Suffrage League.* 1866. 8vo, pp. 40. 29994

Hamilton. Letter of General A. J. Hamilton, of Texas, to the President of the United States, New York, October, 1863. *New York: W. C. Bryant & Co.* 1863. 8vo, pp. 18. + *Loyal Publication Society.* 1863. 8vo, pp. 18. 29995

Hamilton. Origin and Objects of the Slaveholders' Conspiracy against Democratic Principles, as well as against the National Union, Illustrated in the Speeches of Andrew Jackson Hamilton, the Statements of Lorenzo Sherwood, &c. *New York: Baker & Godwin.* 1862. 8vo, pp. 16, 8. 29996

Also: Fœderal Monthly. A Party of the Future. By A. J. H.—Memorial to Congress on the Texas Election Frauds. *Austin.* 1870. 8vo.— ... Political Situation in Texas ... Speech at Benham, February 18, 1869. [n. p. 1869.] 8vo, pp. 7.—Speech ... On the Condition of the South, under Rebel Rule, and the Necessity of early Relief to the Union Men of Western Texas. October 3, 1862. *New York: National War Committee.* 1862. 8vo, pp. 19.—Speech ... on the State of the Union. Delivered in the House of Representatives ... February 1, 1861. *Washington.* 1861. 8vo, pp. 16.—Speech ... at the War Meeting at Faneuil Hall ... April 18, 1863. *Boston.* 1863. 8vo, pp. 63.

Hamilton (A.) Articles Exhibited against Lord Archibald Hamilton, Late Governour of Jamaica. With Sundry Depositions and Proofs relating to the same. *London: Printed in the Year* M.DCC.XVII. 8vo, pp. viii, 32. A. 29997

Hamilton. An Answer to an Anonymous Libel, entitled, Articles exhibited against Lord Archibald Hamilton, late Governour of Jamaica; with sundry Depositions and Proofs relating to the same. By Lord Archibald Hamilton. *London: Printed in the Year* MDCCXVIII. 8vo, pp. 92. P. 29998

Hamilton (A.) Marriage Rites, Customs, and Ceremonies of all Nations in the Universe. By Lady Augusta Hamilton. *London.* 1822. 8vo, pp. viii, 400. Portrait. C., H. 29999

See pages 278–378 for American ceremonies.

Hamilton (C.) An Epitome of Universal Chronology, History and Biography, forming a Companion to Irving's Stream of History, from the German of F. Strass, and Continued to the Year 1826. By Charles Hamilton. *London: G. B. Whitaker.* 1826. 12mo, pp. 116. 30000

Hamilton (C.) Report of the Trial of an Action by Mr. W. Dawe, against Vice-Admiral Sir Charles Hamilton, Governor of Newfoundland. *London.* 1824. 8vo. 30001

Hamilton (C.) The Problem of Freedom and Slavery in the United States. A Lecture before the Literary and Scientific Institution of Smyrna (Turkey). By Rev. C. Hamilton. *Smyrna: Damian.* 1862. 8vo, pp. 28. 30002

Hamilton (Charles James). Defence of a Liberal Construction of the Powers of Congress as regards Internal Improvement, &c. By Major (now Gov.) Hamilton. *Philadelphia.* 1831. 8vo. P. 30003

Hamilton. Important Correspondence on the Subject of State Interposition, between ... Gov. Hamilton and Hon. John C. Calhoun. ... *Charleston: Printed by A. E. Miller.* 1832. 12mo, pp. 27. BA., C., M. 30004

Relates to Nullification.

Hamilton (Charles M.) Right of Suffrage. Speech ... delivered in the House of Representatives, January 29, 1869. *Washington.* 1869. 8vo, pp. 8. 30005

Hamilton (D. H.) National Thanksgiving Sermon. "Thy Prayer is heard." *Jacksonville.* 1866. 8vo, pp. 30. 30006

Hamilton (E.) The Life of Rear-Admiral Paul Jones. By Edward Hamilton. *Aberdeen: G. Clark & Son.* 1848. 12mo, pp. 304. + *Philadelphia.* 1858. 12mo. 30007

Hamilton (F. H.) Eulogy on the Life and Character of Theodoric Romeyn Beck, M.D., LL.D., before the Medical Society of the State of New York. By Frank Hastings Hamilton, M.D. *Albany.* 1856. 8vo, pp. 90. Portrait. 30008

Hamilton. Life of Nathaniel T. Otis, Jun. Introductory Lecture, delivered at the University of Buffalo, Session 1849–50. By F. H. Hamilton, M.D. *Buffalo.* 1850. 8vo, pp. 14. 30009

Also other addresses on medical and miscellaneous topics.

Hamilton (Gail), *pseudonym. See* [Dodge (Mary Abigail)].

[Hamilton (George).] [Poetical] Epistle from the Marquis de La Fayette to General Washington. *Edinburgh.* 1800. 12mo.

Hamilton (G.) A Voyage round the World, in His Majesty's Frigate Pandora. Performed under the Direction of Captain Edwards In the Years 1790, 1791, and 1792. By Mr. George Hamilton, late Surgeon of the Pandora. With the Discoveries made in the South-Sea; and the many Distresses experienced by the Crew from Shipwreck and Famine, in a Voyage of Eleven Hundred Miles in open Boats, between Endeavour Straits and the Island of Timor. *Berwick: W. Phorson.* M DCCXCIII. 8vo, pp. 164. Portrait. J.C.B. 30011

The *Pandora* was sent out to discover and bring to England for trial the mutineers of the *Bounty. See* "M. Rev.," XIV. 417.

Hamilton (H. W.) Rural Sketches of Minnesota: also, Letters upon Northern Wisconsin. By H. W. Hamilton. *Milan* (O.) 1850. 8vo. C. 30012

[Hamilton (James),] *Junr.* An Account of the Late Intended Insurrection among a Portion of the Blacks of this City. Published by the Authority of the Corporation of Charleston. *Charleston: A. E. Miller.* 1822. 8vo, pp. 48. BA. + Second Edition. [*Ibid.*] + Negro Plot. An Account [etc.] *Boston: J. W. Ingraham.* 1822. 8vo, pp. 50. BA. + Second Edition. ... [*Ibid.*] + Third Edition. *Charleston.* 1822. 4to, pp. 49.

Hamilton. Important Correspondence on ... State Interposition, between ... Gov. Hamilton, and Hon. John C. Calhoun ... from the Pendleton Messenger of 15th Sept. 1832. *Charleston: A. E. Miller.* 1832. 12mo, pp. 27. BA. 30014

Hamilton. Oration, ... Fourth of July, 1821, before the Cincinnati and Revolution Societies. By James Hamilton, Jun. A Member of the Cincinnati. ... *Charleston: Printed by A. E. Miller.* 1821. 8vo, pp. 32. BA. 30015

Hamilton. The Substance of General Hamilton's Remarks, delivered May 31, 1838, in the Senate of South Carolina, on the Resolution of respecting the Sub-Treasury. [*Charleston.* 1838.] 8vo, pp. 8. 30016

Also: An Eulogium on Robert J. Turnbull ... . *Charleston: A. E. Miller.* 1834. 8vo, pp. 35. BA.— ... The Memorial of James Hamilton [and others, on modifying the Boundary Act respecting Texas]. [n. p. n. d.] 8vo, pp. 8.—A Letter to Hon. James Hamilton, Jun. ... to whom was referred "so much of the Governor's Message as relates to the affairs of the College," 1822. ... [n. p.] 1823. 8vo, pp. 16.—Five Letters to Governor Hamilton, by Anti-Guillotine. ... *Charleston.* 1831. 12mo, pp. 32.—The Introductory Address ... at the First Meeting of the Charleston State Rights and Free Trade Association of South-Carolina .... August 1, 1831. ... *Charleston: The Association.* 1831. 8vo, pp. 15. BA.—Obituary Addresses on the ... Death of General James Hamilton ... delivered in the Supreme Court, Senate, and House of Representatives of ... Texas. *Austin.* 1857. 8vo, pp. 32.—Speech ... April 6, 1824, on the Tariff Bill. *Washington.* 1824. 12mo.—Speech ... against the Tariff, at Walterborough, S. C. 1828. S.—Speech ... February 5, 1827, on the Abuses of a Government Press. [n. p. n. d.] 8vo, pp. 12.

Hamilton (J.) A Memoir of Richard Williams, Surgeon; Catechist to the Patagonian Missionary Society in Terra del Fuego. By James Hamilton, D.D. *London: James Nisbet & Co.* MDCCCLIV. 12mo, pp. viii, 255. Portrait. + *New York.* 1854. 12mo. S. 30017

Hamilton (J. A.) Reminiscences of James A. Hamilton; or, Men and Events, at Home and Abroad, during three quarters of a Century. *New York: C. Scribner & Co.* 1869. 8vo, pp. ix. 647. C. 30018

Hamilton. State Sovereignty. Rebellion against the United States by the People of a State Is Its Political Suicide. By James A. Hamilton. ... *New York: Baker & Godwin, Printers.* 1862. 8vo, pp. 32. 30019

Also: Address ... Naval Academy, Newport, 1864. 8vo.—The Constitution Vindicated, Nationality, Secession, Slavery. ... May, 1864. *New York: Loyal Publication Society.* No. 50. 1864. 8vo, pp. 12. C.—Letter. To the Hon. E. D. Morgan, dated Nevis, Dobbs' Ferry, N. Y., January 6th, 1868. [*Nevis.* 1868.] 8vo, pp. 7.

Hamilton (J. E.) ... Remarks on the Prospects of a Russian War and a Canada Bill. By James Edward Hamilton. *London.* 1791. 8vo. 30020

Hamilton (J. C.) History of the Republic of the United States of America, as traced in the Writings of Alexander Ham-

ilton and of his Contemporaries. By John C. Hamilton. ... *Philadelphia: J. B. Lippincott & Co.* 1857–64. 7 vols., 8vo. C.

This must not be mistaken for Alexander Hamilton's Works, which also fill 7 vols., and are published at *Philadelphia.* We have seen a Vol. VII. of this, which purports to be "Second Edition," which surprises us, as we think the merits of the work scarcely demanded its republication.

Hamilton. The Life of Alexander Hamilton. By His Son, John C. Hamilton. Vol. I. *New York: Halsted & Voorhies.* 1834. 8vo, pp. viii, 422. Vol. II. *New-York: D. Appleton & Co.* 1840. 8vo, pp. vi, 563. Portrait. C. 30022

Also: Coercion Completed, or Treason Triumphant. Remarks, ... September, 1864. *New York.* 1864. 8vo, pp. 25. + *Loyal Publication Society.* No. 66. 8vo, pp. 25.—The Slave Power: its Heresies and Injuries to the American People. A Speech ... November, 1864. *New York: J. A. Gray & Green.* 1864. 8vo, pp. 23. + *Loyal Publication Society.* No. 74. 1864. Mr. Hamilton also edited an edition of the "Federalist," which met with review by Horace Binney. *See our* Vol. II., No. 5494.

Hamilton (J. P.) Travels through the Interior Provinces of Colombia. By J. P. Hamilton, late Chief Commissioner from H. B. M. to the Republic of Colombia. *London: John Murray.* MDCCCXXVII. 2 vols., post 8vo, pp. (4), 352; 256. Plates by Finden. C. 30023

Highly commended by the "Monthly Review." *See* Rich, Vol. II. The following is a German translation:

Hamilton. Reise durch die innern Provinzen von Columbien. ... *Jena: Bran.* 1827. 8vo. + *Weimar: Ind.-Comptoir.* 1828. 8vo. 30024

Forms Vol. XLVII of "Bibliotek der neuesten Reisebeschreibungen."

Hamilton (J. S.) The Army, Navy and Militia Volunteer Guide to Health, Valor, and Victory. By John S. Hamilton, M.D. *Albany.* 1851. 12mo. S. 30025

Hamilton (L.) "Worship God." Sermon at the Dedication of the Church of the First Congregational Society in Taunton, Mass., October 7, 1830. By Luther Hamilton. *Boston.* 1830. 8vo. W. 30026

Hamilton (P. S.) Nova-Scotia Considered as a Field for Emigration. By Pierce Stevens Hamilton. *London.* 1858. 8vo, pp. 91. S. 30027

Hamilton. Union of the Colonies of British North America; ... By P. S. Hamilton, ... Chief Commissioner of Mines for Nova Scotia. *Montreal.* 1864. 8vo, pp. 103. 30028

Also: Letter to ... the Duke of Newcastle upon a Union of the Colonies of British North America. *Halifax.* 1860.—Observations upon a Union of the Colonies ... .

Halifax. 1855. 8vo.—A Review of Hon. Joseph Howe's Essay, entitled: "Confederation Considered ... ." *Halifax.* 1866. 8vo, pp. 25.—Union of the Colonies ... *Halifax.* 1856. 8vo.

Hamilton (Sarah). A Narrative of the Life of Mrs. Hamilton. [n. p. n. d.] 8vo, pp. 8. S. 30029

Hamilton (S. S.) Indian Treaties, and Laws and Regulations relating to Indian Affairs. *Washington.* 1826. 8vo. C.

Hamilton (S.) Address to and by Schuyler Hamilton on the Presentation of a Sword to him, for Services in Mexico. [n. p. n. d.] 12mo, pp. 7. 30031

Hamilton. History of the National Flag of the United States of America. By Schuyler Hamilton, U.S.A. *Philadelphia: J. B. Lippincott.* 1852. 12mo, pp. viii, 13–115. 15 colored Plates. BA., C. + [*Ibid.*] 1853. S. 30032

Hamilton (S.) Life and Confessions of Sophia Hamilton, who was Tried, Condemned, and Sentenced to be Hung at Montreal, L. C., January 22, 1845. [n. p.] 1845. 8vo. 30033

[Hamilton (Thomas).] Men and Manners in America. By the Author of Cyril Thornton, etc. ... *Edinburgh: William Blackwood.* M.D.CCC.XXXIII. 2 vols., post 8vo, pp. (1), ix, (1), 393; (4), 402. BA. + Second Edition. [*Ibid.*] 1834. 2 vols., post 8vo, pp. xi, 384; (6), 402. C., P. + Third Edition. [*Ibid.*] 2 vols., post 8vo, pp. xi, (1), 393; (6), 402. + *Philadelphia: Carey, Lea & Blanchard.* 1833. 8vo, pp. 410. + Second American Edition. [*Ibid.*] 1833. 12mo, pp. vi, 208. 30034

Hamilton. Men and Manners in America. By Thomas Hamilton, Esq. New Edition, with ... Letters written by him during his Journey through the United States. *Blackwood, Edinburgh.* 1843. Post 8vo, pp. 490. 30035

For a review *see* [Norton (Andrew)]. *See also* "Dublin University Magazine," II. 444 and 558; Fraser's "Magazine," IX. 42; Blackwood's "Magazine," XXXIV. 285; "North American Review," XXXVIII. 210; "American Quarterly Review," XIV. 320.

Hamilton. Les hommes et les mœurs aux États-Unis d'Amérique. Traduit de l'Anglais sur la 3e édition par le comte D. L. C. *Paris: H. Fournier.* 1834. 2 vols., 8vo, pp. xv, 311; (4), 380. 2 Plates. C. 30036

Hamilton. Die Menschen und die Sitten in den Vereinigten Staaten von Nord-Amerika. Nach der dritten englischen Auflage übersetzt von L. Hout. *Mannheim.* 1834. 2 vols., 8vo.

HAMILTON (W.) An Oration delivered in the African Zion Church ... in Commemoration of the Abolition of Domestic Slavery in this State. By William Hamilton. *New York.* 1827. 8vo. 30038

Also: Address to the New-York African Society for Mutual Relief ... . *New York.* 1809. 8vo, pp. 12. BA.—Address to the Fourth Annual Convention of Free People of Color of the United States. ... June 2, 1834. *New-York.* 1834. 8vo, pp. 8. BA.

HAMILTON (W.) Report of the Trial and Acquittal of Edward Shippen, Esquire, Chief Justice, and Jasper Yeates and Thomas Smith, Esquires, Assistant Justices of the Supreme Court of Pennsylvania, on an Impeachment, before the Senate of the Commonwealth, January, 1805. By William Hamilton ... . *Lancaster: Printed by the Reporter.* 1805. 8vo, pp. 491, 96. C.

Also: Debates of the Legislature of Pennsylvania on the case of Gideon Olmstead. Reported by William and Hugh Hamilton, Lancaster, Pa. 1810. 8vo.

HAMILTON *and* IRWIN. An Elementary Book of the Ioway Language, with an English Translation. By Wm. Hamilton and S. M. Irwin ... . J. B. Roy, Interpreter. *Ioway and Sac Mission Press, Indian Territory.* 1843. 16mo, pp. 101. BA. 30040

HAMILTON *and* IRWIN. An Ioway Grammar, illustrating the Principles of the Language used by the Ioway, Otoe, and Missouri Indians. Prepared and printed by Rev. Wm. Hamilton and Rev. S. M. Irwin. *Ioway and Sac Mission Press.* 1848. 16mo, pp. xi [ix], (3), 9–152. BA., C. 30041

HAMILTON (W.) A Plea for the Union and the War. An Address, occasioned by the death of David Mould, of Ulsterville, Ulster County, N. Y. Who fell in Battle at Chancellorsville, ... May 3, 1863. By Rev. W. Hamilton. *New York: Gray & Green, Printers.* 1863. 12mo, pp. 24. 30042

HAMILTON (W.) Prodromus Plantarum Indiæ Occidentalis hucusque cognitarum tam in oris Americæ Meridionalis, quam in Insulis Anticillis sponte crescentium. *Londini.* 1825. Post 8vo, pp. 67. Colored Plate. B. 30043

HAMILTON (W. J.) Big Foot, the Guide; or, The Surveyors. A Tale of the Carolina Settlements. By W. J. Hamilton. *New York: Beadle & Co.* 1866. 12mo, pp. 91. 30044

This and the following are rather trashy stories, based on American topics: The Shawnees' Foe; or, The Hunter of the Juniata. ... *New York: Beadle & Co.* 1866. 16mo, pp. 100.—The Peddler Spy; or, Dutchmen and Yankees. ... *New York: Beadle & Co.* 1867. 18mo, pp. 100.—Eph. Peters; or, The Scout of the Mohawk Valley. ... *New York: Beadle & Co.* 1866. 12mo, pp. 98.

HAMILTON (W. R.) No Mistake; or, a Vindication of the Negociators of the Treaty of 1783, respecting the North-Eastern Boundary of the United States, in a Conversation between John Bull and Jonathan. By W. R. Hamilton. *London: Privately printed.* 1842. 8vo, pp. 20. 30045

HAMILTON (W. T.) A Discourse delivered in the First Presbyterian Church, Newark, N. J. December 8th, 1831, on the Occasion of Public Thanksgiving. By William T. Hamilton, A.M. *Newark.* 1832. 8vo, pp. 20. 30046

HAMILTON. A Word for the African. A Sermon, ... Newark, July 24th, 1825. By Rev. William T. Hamilton. *Newark.* 1825. 8vo, pp. 27. C. 30047

Also: Oration before Euphemian and Philomathian Society of Erskine College, September 15, 1847. ... *Charleston.* And other orations and addresses.

HAMILTON *vs.* EATON. Case respecting British Debts lately determined in the Circuit Court in the United States, for North Carolina District, presided by C. J. Ellsworth. *Newbern.* 1797. 8vo. C. 30048

HAMILTON, *pseudon.* Address on the Tendency of our System of Intercourse with Foreign Nations. Nos. I. and V. *Philadelphia.* 1852. 30049

HAMILTON, *pseudon.* The Bishops' Fund and Phœnix Bonus: a Collection of the Pieces on this Subject, from the Connecticut Herald; With an Explanatory Preface, Notes, &c., and an Additional Piece by Hamilton ... . *New Haven: Printed at the Journal Office.* 1816. 8vo, pp. 76. H., W. 30050

HAMILTON, *pseudon.* Thoughts on the Constitution; and Strictures on the Court of Chancery. By Hamilton. *Albany.* 1821. 8vo. 30051

"Hamilton" to the Friends of Peace and Good Order; and a Review of the Address of the Free Trade Convention. [n. p. n. d.] 8vo. P. 30052

HAMILTON, *pseudon.* The New Olive Branch. A Solemn Warning on the Banks of the Rubicon. By Hamilton. [n. p. n. d.] 8vo, pp. 8. 30053

HAMILTON. Eleventh Series. No. I. [1826.] 8vo, pp. 19. No. IX. 8vo, pp. 8. No. V. Second Edition. Letter to Edward Livingston, Esq. [n. p. n. d.] 8vo, pp. 4. M. 30054

For others *see* [Carey (M.),] Vol. III., page 340.

HAMILTON, *pseudon.* Review of a Late Pamphlet, under signature of "Brutus," by Hamilton. *Charleston.* 1828. 8vo.

HAMILTON, *pseudon.* To the Editors of the National Intelligencer. [Nine or more numbers.] 1822. 30056

"HAMILTON," *pseudon.* To the Federalists of the United States, on the Choice of a President. *New York.* 1812. 8vo.

HAMILTON, *pseudon.* The Whig Party; its objects—its principles—its candidates—its duties—and its prospects. An Address to the People of Rhode-Island, published in the Providence Journal, in a series of articles during the months of September and October, 1844. By Hamilton. [n. p. 1844.] 8vo, pp. 44. + *Providence: Knowles & Vose.* 1844. 8vo, pp. 31. 30058

Supposed to be by W. R. Watson.

HAMILTON, *C. W.* Report on Supplying the City of Hamilton, C. W., with Water. *New York: Baker & Godwin.* 1855. 8vo, pp. 34. 30059

HAMILTON CLUB. *See* Callendar (J. T.), Hamilton (A.), Williams (John).

This series consists of 4 vols., 4to, printed for Francis S. Hoffman, now of Philadelphia; they are well printed, twenty sets only in 4to, and forty in 8vo. Of some of the series a few additional copies were printed.

HAMILTON COLLEGE, *N. Y.* Catalogue of the Corporation, Officers, and Students of Hamilton College, 1855–56. *Clinton, N. Y.* 1855. 8vo, pp. 30. Continued. M. 30060

Catalogus Senatus Academici, et eorum qui munera et officia academica gesserunt, quique aliquo gradu exornati fuerunt, in Collegio Hamiltonensi ... *Romæ.* 1840. 8vo. Continued.

A Memorial of the Semi-Centennial Celebration of the Founding of Hamilton College, Clinton, N. Y. *Utica: Ellis H. Roberts.* 1862. 8vo, pp. 232. S. 30062

Public Exercises at the Inauguration of Samuel Ware Fisher, D.D., as Sixth President ... November 4, 1858. ... *Utica.* 1858. 8vo, pp. 71. BA. 30063

Public Exercises at the Inauguration of President S. G. Brown, 1867. *Utica.* 1867. 8vo. 30064

Triennial Catalogue of the Members, Library and Catalogue of the Union Society, 1851. *Utica.* 8vo. 30065

HAMILTON CO., *N. Y.* Proceedings of the Board of Supervisors of the County of Hamilton, for 1868, '69. *Johnstown.* 1869–70. 8vo. S. 30066

HAMILTON CO., *Ohio.* First Annual Report of the Hamilton County Sabbath School Association, issued October, 1863. *Cincinnati: Moore, Wilstach, Keys & Co., Printers.* 1863. 8vo, pp. 24. Continued. 30067

HAMILTON FEMALE SEMINARY, *N. Y.* Catalogue, 1858. *Utica.* 1859. 8vo. S. 30068

HAMILTON LITERARY AND THEOLOGICAL INSTITUTION. Catalogue of the Officers and Students, for 1832. *Hamilton.* 1832. 8vo. Continued. 30069

HAMILTON, *Ohio.* Williams's Hamilton Directory for 1866–7. With a U. S. Post Office Directory. *Hamilton, Ohio: Williams & Co.* 1866. 8vo, pp. 120, 108. 30070

Proceedings of the Buckeye Celebration, in Commemoration of the Day on which General St. Clair named 'Fort Hamilton;' at Hamilton, Ohio ... Thirtieth ... September, 1835. [n. p. n. d.] 8vo, pp. 60. BA. 30071

HAMILTONIAD: or, The Effects of Discord. An Original Poem. In Two Books. With an Appendix; containing a Number of Interesting Papers relative to the late Unfortunate Duel. By a Young Gentleman of Philadelphia. ... *Philadelphia: Printed for the Author, August* 3, 1804. 8vo, pp. 55. BA. 30072

For another "Hamiltoniad" *see* [Williams (John)].

HAMLIN (A. C.) Martyria; or Andersonville Prison. By Augustus C. Hamlin, ... Illustrated by the Author. *Boston: Lee & Shepard.* 1866. 12mo, pp. 256. 30073

HAMLIN (E. S.) Speech of E. S. Hamlin, of Ohio, on the Annexation of Texas. [n. p. n. d.] 8vo, pp. 15. 30074

HAMLIN (H.) Speech of Hon. Hannibal Hamlin, of Maine, in the ... Senate, March 9 and 10th, 1858, in reply to Governor Hammond, and in defence of the North and Northern Laborers. [n. p. n. d.] 8vo, pp. 12. 30075

Also: Remarks ... on resigning his position as Chairman of the Committee on Commerce; and the Tests of the Cincinnati Convention, in the Senate of the United States, January 12, 1856. [n. p. n. d.] 8vo, pp. 8.

HAMLINE (L. L.) Address delivered by Rev. L. L. Hamline, A.M., ... before the Jefferson and Union Literary Societies of Augusta College, August, 1836. *Cincinnati: J. F. Wright and L. Swormstedt.* 1836. 8vo. 30076

HAMLINE. Works of Rev. Leonidas L. Hamline, D.D., late one of the Bishops of the Methodist Episcopal Church. Edited by the Rev. F. G. Hibbard, D.D. *Cincinnati.* 186–. 2 vols., 12mo. 30077

HAMME (T. V.) Het leven van Pater Petrus Thom. v. Hamme, Missionaris in Mexico en in China [1651–1727]. *Gent.* 1871. 8vo. Plate. 30078

Life of Father P. Thom. van Hamme, Missionary in Mexico and China. Published by Prof. C. P. Serrure for the Society of Flemish Bibliophiles. A few copies only printed.

HAMMEN Y LEON (Lorenzo Vander). Don Filipe el Prvdente, segvndo deste nombre, Rey de las Españas y Nuevo-Mvndo. *Año* 1625. *Madrid, por Vivda de Alonso Martin.* 8 l., 152 l., 10 l. 30079

HAMMERDÖRFER *und* KOSCHE. Nord- und Südamerika, geographische historische ... *Leipzig.* 1788. 2 vols., 8vo. 30080

[HAMMETT (Charles E.), *Jr.*] *See* [Brooks (C. T.)], Vol. II.

HAMMETT (J.) John Hammett's Vindication and Relation: Giving an Account, 1. Wherein he was misrepresented in a letter lately printed in his Name. 2. Of his withdrawing from the Baptist's Communion. 3. Of his uniting to them again. 4. Of his separating himself wholly from the Baptists, and joining himself in Unity with the People called Quakers. (With an Introduction by Jacob Mott, Samuel Bownas, John Wanton.) *Newport, Rhode Island: Printed and sold by James Franklin.* 1727. 8vo, pp. 24. 30081

Also: Answer to Nat. Stone's (of Harwich) Cautions to Erring Christians, relating to the Ministry. 1739. 8vo, pp. 32. N.—Promiscuous Singing, No Divine Institution. 1793. 12mo. W.

[HAMMITT (Samuel A.)] Piney Woods Tavern; or, Sam Slick in Texas. *Philadelphia: T. B. Peterson.* [1858.] 12mo, pp. 309. 30082

[HAMMITT.] A Stray Yankee in Texas. By Philip Paxton. *New York.* 1853. 12mo. C. 30083

[HAMMITT.] The Wonderful Adventures of Captain Priest. By Philip Paxton. 1855. 30084

HAMMON (J.) An Address to the Negroes in the State of New York. By Jupiter Hammon, servant of John Lloyd, Esq. of the Manor of Queen's Village, Long Island. *New York: Carroll & Patterson.* 1787. 8vo, pp. 20. + *Philadelphia.* 1787. + *New-York.* 1806. 18mo. P., S., W. 30085

HAMMON. A Winter Piece; being a Serious Exhortation. With a Call to the Unconverted. By Jupiter Hammon. *Hartford: Printed for the Author.* 1782. 8vo, pp. 24. M. 30086

HAMMOND (A.) An Address delivered before the Agricultural Society of the County of West Chester, New York, October 26, 1820. By Abijah Hammond. *Mount Pleasant.* 1821. 8vo, pp. 23. 30087

Also: Address, before the Westchester Agricultural Society. ... *New York.* 1824. 8vo.

HAMMOND (C.) Light from the Spirit World—the Pilgrimage of Thomas Paine, and others, to the Seventh Circle in the Spirit World. *Rochester.* 1852. 12mo. C. 30088

[HAMMOND (C.)] Review of the Opinion of the Supreme Court of the United States in the Case of Cohens *vs.* Virginia. [By Charles Hammond.] ... To which is added, a Letter ... [By E. A. Brown.] *Steubenville, O.* 1821. 8vo, pp. 78. W.

[HAMMOND.] State of the Case and Argument for the Appellants, in the Case of the Bank of the United States, versus the Auditor and Treasurer of the State of Ohio, and others, in the Supreme Court of the United States. *Cincinnati: Morgan and Lodge, Printers.* 1823. 8vo, pp. 98. BA. 30090

HAMMOND (C.) A Sermon on the Life and Character of Abraham Lincoln, Preached at Monson, at the United Service of the Congregational and Methodist Churches, on the Occasion of the National Fast, June 1, 1865. By Charles Hammond, Principal of Monson Academy. *Springfield: Samuel Bowles & Co., Printers.* 1865. 8vo, pp. 21. H. 30091

HAMMOND. Sermon preached at the Re-dedication of the Congregational Church in Union, Conn., July 25, 1866. *Springfield.* 1867. 8vo, pp. 39. S. 30092

Also: Address before the Citizens of Union, Conn., and Neighboring Towns, July 4, 1853. .. *Worcester, Mass.* 1853. 8vo.—An Address delivered at the Re-dedication of Monson Academy, July 12, 1864. *Springfield.* 1865. 8vo, pp. 32.—Secondary Education. I. New England Academies and Classical Schools. ... 1868. 8vo, pp. ii. 119 (403–522).

HAMMOND (J.) Catalogue of James Hammond's Circulating Library, ... Newport, R. I. ... *Newport, R. I.* 1853. 8vo, pp. 108. 30093

HAMMOND (J. D.) The History of the Political Parties in the State of New-York, from the Ratification of the Federal Constitution to December, 1840. By Jabez D. Hammond. *Albany: E. Van Benthuysen.* 1842. 2 vols., 8vo, pp. 588; 551. P., S. + Second Edition. [*Ibid.*] + Third Edition. *Cooperstown: H. & E. Phinney.* 1844. 2 vols., 8vo, pp. 588; 551; 10 Portraits. + Fourth Edition, Corrected and Enlarged, to which are added Notes by Gen. Root. *Cooperstown: H. & E. Phinney.* 1846. 2 vols., 8vo, pp. 594; 553; Portraits. + *Syracuse: Hall & Dickson.* 1849. + *Buffalo.* 1850. 2 vols., 8vo. A. + *Syracuse: Hall, Mills & Co.* 1852. 3 vols., 8vo, pp. xiii, 596; v, 553; 758. Portraits. BA. 30094

The third volume is the Life of Silas Wright.

[HAMMOND.] Letter to the Hon. John C. Calhoun on the Annexation of Texas. *Cooperstown.* 1844. 8vo, pp. 34. 30095

HAMMOND. Life and Times of Silas Wright, Late Governor of the State of New York. By Jabez D. Hammond. *Syracuse: Hall & Dickson.* M DCCC XLVIII. 8vo, pp. 749. BA., C. 30096

Forms Vol. III. of our No. 30094, *supra*.

HAMMOND. Life and Opinions of Julius Melbourn; with Sketches of the Lives and Characters of T. Jefferson, J. Q. Adams, J. Randolph, etc.: Edited by a late Member of Congress. *Syracuse.* 1847. 12mo. 30097

Also: Address delivered on the occasion of the Dedication of the New York Conference Academy, at Charlotteville, Schoharie Co., November 8, 1850. *Albany: J. Munsell.* 1851. 8vo, pp. 20. B., S.—Letters on the Repeal of the Restraining Law. ... *New-York: John Windt.* 1836. 8vo, pp. 31.—Letter to Daniel Webster [relating to his Speech of March 7, 1850.] [n. p. n. d.] 8vo. B.—Oration on the Revocation of the British Orders in Council. *Otsego, N. Y.* 1809. 8vo. C.

HAMMOND (James Hamilton). Governor Hammond's Letters on Southern Slavery, addressed to Thomas Clarkson, the English Abolitionist. *Charleston.* [1845.] Rl. 8vo, pp. 32. M.

Republished from "The South Carolinian." Another edition is entitled:

HAMMOND. Two Letters on Slavery in the United States, addressed to Thomas Clarkson, Esq. ... By J. H. Hammond. *Columbia.* 1845. 8vo, pp. 51. BA., H., N., P. + *Charleston, S. C.* 1852. 12mo. C. 30099

A reply was entitled: Slavery in the South: a Review of Hammond's ... Letters ... From the Oct. No. (1845) of the Southern Quarterly. [*Charleston.* n. d.] 8vo pp. 24. BA.

HAMMOND. An Oration on the Life, Character, and Services of John Caldwell Calhoun. By J. H. Hammond. *Charleston.* 1850. 8vo, pp. 73. BA., H., P. 30100

HAMMOND. To the People of the South. Senator Hammond and The Tribune. By Troup. *Charleston: Printed by Evans & Cogswell.* 1860. 8vo, pp. 24. H. 30101

Also: An Address delivered before the South Carolina Institute, at its First Annual Fair, 20th November, 1849. *Charleston, S. C.* 1849. 8vo, pp. 54. N.—Letter of Gov. Hammond to the Free Church in Glasgow, on the Subject of Slavery. *Columbia.* 1844. 8vo, pp. 7. BA., P.—Marl: A Letter addressed to the Agricultural Society of Jefferson County, Georgia. ... *Augusta.* 1846. 8vo. C., P.—Message, ... of his Excellency, ... November 28, 1843. [*Columbia.* 1843.] 8vo, pp. 15.—Message ... November 26, 1844. [*Columbia.* 1844.] 8vo, pp. 14. N.—An Oration before the two Societies of South Carolina College. *Charleston.* 1850. 8vo. P.—Remarks ... on the Question of receiving Petitions for the Abolition of Slavery in the District of Columbia. *Washington.* 1836. 8vo. P.—Speech ... on the Admission of Kansas under the Lecompton Constitution, March 4, 1858. *Washington.* 1858. 8vo, pp. 15. —Speech ... delivered at Barnwell C. H., October 29th, 1858. *Charleston.* 1858. 8vo, pp. 28. + *Washington.* 1858. 8vo, pp. 16.

HAMMOND (J.) Leah and Rachel, | Or, | the Two Fruitfull Sisters | Virginia, | and Mary-Land: | Their Present Condition, Im- | partially stated and related. | VVith | A Removall of such Imputations as are scandalously | cast on those Countries, whereby many deceived | Souls, chose rather to Beg, Steal, rot in Prison, | and come to shamefull deaths, then to better their being | by going thither, wherein is plenty of all things | necessary for Humane subsistance. | By John Hammond. | *London,* | *Printed by T. Mabb, and are* | *to be sold by Nich. Bourn, neer the Royall* | *Exchange,* 1656. | 4to, pp. (6), 32. H., P. 30102

A volume of extreme rarity, worth $150 to $200. Reprinted in Force's "Tracts," Vol. III., No. 14.

HAMMOND (J. P.) The Army Chaplains' Manual, Designed as a Help to Chaplains in the Discharge of their Various Duties, both Temporal and Spiritual. ... By Rev. J. Pinkney Hammond, M.A., Chaplain U. S. Army. *Philadelphia.* 1863. 12mo, pp. 286.

HAMMOND (J. W.) A Tabular View of the Financial Affairs of Pennsylvania, from the Commencement of her Public Works to the Present Time; in which are included the Cost, Revenue, and Expenditures of the ... Canals and Railroads, &c.; ... prepared from the Official Records. By J. W. Hammond. *Philadelphia.* 1844. 8vo. S. 30104

HAMMOND (M. M.) Memoir of Captain M. M. Hammond. *New York.* 1858. 12mo. 30105

HAMMOND (M. C. M.) An Oration on the Duties and Requirements of an American Officer, delivered before the ... Military Academy at West Point, June 5, 1852. *New York.* 1852. 8vo, pp. 30. H. 30106

HAMMOND (Samuel H.) Hills, Lakes, and Forest Streams; or, a Tramp in the Chateaugay Woods. By S. H. Hammond. *New-York.* 1854. 12mo, pp. 340. BA., H., C., S. 30107

Republished with new titles as:

HAMMOND. Hunting Adventures in the Northern Wilds; or, a Tramp in the Chateaugay Woods, over Hills, Lakes, and Forest Streams. By S. H. Hammond. *New York: J. C. Derby.* 1855. 12mo, pp. 340. + *London: Beadle & Co.* 1857. Fcp. 8vo. 30108

HAMMOND. Wild Northern Scenes; or, Sporting Adventures with the Rifle and the Rod. *New York: Derby & Jackson.* 1857. 12mo, pp. 341. 4 Plates. + [*Ibid.*] 1858. C., S. 30109

Also: Freedom National—Slavery Sectional. Speech ... on the Governor's Message. In Senate, February, 1860. *Albany: Weed, Parsons & Co.* 1860. 8vo, pp. 14; Chicago Platform, 1 leaf.

HAMMOND (S. H.) *and* MANSFIELD (L. W.) Country Margins, and Rambles of a Journalist. By S. L. Hammond and L. W. Mansfield. *New York: J. C. Derby.* 1855. 12mo, pp. 356.

HAMMOND (W. S.) Oration delivered at Cherry Valley, on the Fourth of July, 1839. By Wells S. Hammond. *Albany: J. Munsell.* 1839. 8vo, pp. 16. 30111

HAMMOND (W. A.) Defence of Brig. Gen'l Wm. A. Hammond, Surgeon General U. S. Army. [n. p. n. d.] 8vo, pp. 61.

HAMMOND. Military, Medical and Surgical Essays; prepared for the United States Sanitary Commission. Edited by William A. Hammond, M.D., Surgeon General U. S. A. *Philadelphia: J. B. Lippincott & Co.* 8vo, pp. viii, 552. H. 30113

These essays are prepared by eminent medical men, selected for their presumed acquaintance with the subjects upon which they were desired to write, and were originally published as separate monographs for distribution to the Medical Officers of the army.

HAMMOND. Robert Severne, His Friends and His Enemies. A Novel. By W. A. Hammond, M.D. *Philadelphia.* 1867. 16mo. 30114

Contains some interesting bibliographical and personal sketches.

HAMMOND. A Statement of the Causes which Led to the Dismissal of Surgeon-General William A. Hammond from the Army; with a Review of the Evidence adduced before the Court. *New York: September,* 1864. 8vo, pp. 73. H. 30115

HAMMOND. Surgeon General's Office. Reports on the Extent and Nature of the Materials available for the Preparation of a Medical and Surgical History of the Rebellion. *Philadelphia: J. B. Lippincott & Co.* 1865. Imp. 4to, pp. 166. 30116

Also: Letter to the President of the United States. Removal of the Surgeon-General. [n. p. n. d.] 8vo, pp. 4.—Review by the Judge Advocate General, of the Case of Surgeon General Hammond. [n. p. n. d.] 8vo, pp. 6. *See also* Bingham (J. A.), Vol. II., No. 5452.

HAMMOND (W. G.) Abraham Lincoln: A Eulogy delivered at Anamosa, Iowa, on the Day of the State Fast, April 27, 1865. By William G. Hammond. ... *Davenport: Luse & Griggs.* 1865. 8vo, pp. 16. 30117

HAMON (A.) Des Colonies et de la Législation sur les Sucres. Par Amédée Hamon, Docteur en Droit. *Paris.* 1839. 8vo, pp. 230. 30118

HAMON (H.) New York Stock Exchange Manual, containing its Principles, Rules, and its different Modes of Speculation; also, a Review of the Stocks dealt in on 'Change, Government and State Securities, Railway, Mining, Petroleum, &c., &c. By Henry Hamon. *New York: John F. Trow.* 186–. 12mo, pp. 405. C. 30119

HAMOR (R.) A Trve | Discovrse of the | Present Estate Of Vir-|ginia, and the successe of the affaires | there till the 18 of Iune. 1614. | Together. | with a Relation of the | seuerall English Townes and fortes, the assu-|red hopes of that countrie | and the peace | concluded with the Indians. | The Christening of Powhatans daughter | and her mariage with an English-man. | Written by Raphe Hamor the yon-|ger, late Secretarie in that Colony. | ... [Motto and Woodcut.] | *Printed at London by Iohn Beale, for Wil-|liam Welby dwelling at the signe of the | Swanne in Pauls Church-yard* 1615. | 4to, pp. (8), 69, Errata, 1 p. H.

Very rare, and worth about $200. Contains "minute relations of the Characteristics of the Indians of Virginia."—T. W. FIELD. It was reprinted as below:

HAMOR. A Trve Discovrse [as before]. [*Albany: by J. Munsell.* 1860.] Folio, pp. (10), 69, (2). BA. 30121

Two hundred copies privately [re]printed for Chas. Gorham Barney, of Richmond, Va., 1860. The recto of the first leaf reads, "Presented to;" by which it is to be

understood the entire edition was reprinted for presents only; but the book was used for exchanges. It is conspicuous for its ridiculously large margin.

HAMOR. Dreyzehente Schiffahrt | Darinnen | Ein Warhafftiger und | Gründtlicher Bericht, von dem jtzigen | Zustandt der Landschafft Virginien; Auch wie nun-|mehr der Friede mit den Indianern beschlossen: Vnd wie etliche | Stätte vnd Vestunge alda zum Schutz des Landts von den Enge-|lischen auffgebawet worden. | Sampt | Einer Relation, wie König Powhatans in Virginien | Tochter | Pocahuntas genant | Christlichen getaufft vnd mit einen | Engelischen verheurahtet worden | sehr anmütig zu lesen. | Erstlichen in Englischer Sprach durch Raphe Hamor, &c. Secretarium | daselbst beschrieben | auss deren | durch einen Liebhaber der Historien, in | Teutsch vbergesetzt. | Pierate Fiedes Gaudet. | *Gedruckt zu Hanaw In Verlegung der Hulsischen. Anno.* M.DC.XVII. | 4to, pp. 76. 4 Plates. 30122

This is the XIIIth Part of Hulsius's Collection. A Latin version is included in Part X. of Bry's "Voyages."

HAMPDEN (A.) Hartley Norman. A Tale of the Times. By Allen Hampden. *New York. Rudd & Carleton.* MDCCCLIX. 12mo, pp. vi, 9–429. 30123

"Hampden"'s Letters. *See* [Jervis (J. B.)]

HAMPDEN, *pseudon.* The Genuine Book of Nullification ... . By Hampden. ... *Charleston: ... State Rights Association.* 1831. 8vo, pp. (4), 155. BA. 30124

HAMPDEN, *pseudon.* A Letter to the President of the United States touching the Prosecutions under his Patronage before the Circuit Court in the District of Connecticut. *New Haven.* 1808. 8vo, pp. 28. H., N. 30125

HAMPDEN, *Mass.* Mechanic Association, instituted February 5, 1824. *Springfield.* 1832. 12mo. W. 30126

Report of the Missionary Society, Hampden ... for 1832. *Springfield.* 1832. 12mo. W. 30127

HAMPDEN CO., *Mass.* Address of Hampden County Society. *Springfield.* 1820. 12mo. 30128

Annual Reports of the Benevolent Association of the County of Hampden, ... October 16, 1846. *Springfield.* 1846. 12mo, pp. 36. 30129

Sketches of the Churches and Pastors in Hampden County, Mass.; also an Address by Rev. T. M. Cooley. By a Committee of Pastors. *Westfield: S. W. Edson.* 1854. 12mo, pp. 144. BA., S. 30130

Historical, biographical, genealogical, and statistical.

The Transactions of the Hampden County Agricultural Society, for the Year 1853–1854, including the Reports of the Several Committees, and the List of Premiums awarded. *Springfield.* 1853–54. 8vo. Continued. 30131

HAMPDEN DISTRICT. Medical Police; with the Rules and Regulations adopted by the Hampden-District Medical Society, 1841. *Springfield.* 1842. 12mo, pp. 12. M. 30132

HAMPDEN SIDNEY COLLEGE, *Prince Edward Co., Va.* Catalogue, 1851. *Richmond.* 8vo. S. 30133

Laws of Hampden Sidney College. [*Richmond.* n. d.] pp. 15.

HAMPSHIRE, *Mass.* Address by the Hampshire Convention of the Friends of the License Law. 1838. 12mo, pp. 12. H.

A Letter to the Author of the Pamphlet Called An Answeer to the Hampshire Narrative. *Boston.* 1737. 8vo, pp. (2), 84. B.

Report of the Trustees of the Hampshire Missionary Society, ... August, 1802. *Northampton.* 1802. 8vo, pp. 12. Continued.

Transactions of the Hampshire Agricultural Society for 1851. *Amherst.* 1851. 8vo, pp. 85. Continued. 30138

HAMPSHIRE CO., *Mass.* An Address to the People of the County of Hampshire, by a Committee appointed for that Purpose. *Northampton.* 1809. 8vo, pp. 20. H., N., W. 30139

The Address, etc., of the Charitable Society, instituted by the Central Association of Ministers in the County. *Northampton.* 1815. 8vo, pp. 12. N. 30140

Address to the Friends of Sabbath Schools in the County of Hampshire, 1839. [n. p. n. d.] 8vo, pp. 4. 30141

See Breck (R.), Vol. II., No. 7660.

An Address, of the Ministers of the Northern Association in the County of Hampshire, ... upon the Subjects of a Due Observation of the Lord's Day, and of a Virtuous and Religious Education of Children and Youth. *Northampton (Massachusetts),* 1801. 8vo, pp. 15. H. 30142

HAMPSHIRE EDUCATION SOCIETY. Report of the Directors, Nov. 5, 1817. *Northampton.* 1818. 8vo, pp. 8. Continued.

Also: The Constitution of the Hampshire Education Society, and Rules of the Directors, &c. A.D. 1818. *Northampton.* 1818. 8vo, pp. 19. H.

HAMPSHIRE AND HAMPDEN CANAL COMPANY. Report of J. Hurd, Engineer. *Northampton.* 1826. 8vo. W. 30144

Hampshire, Franklin and Hampden Agricultural Society. Thirty-Seventh Report ... for the Year 1855. *Northampton.* 1855. 8vo, pp. 84. 30145

Transactions of the Hampshire, Franklin and Hampden Agricultural Society, for the Year 1858. *Northampton.* 1858. 8vo, pp. 66. Continued. 30146

HAMPSON (J.) Memoirs of the late Rev. John Wesley, A.M., with a Review of his Life and Writings, and a History of Methodism from its Commencement in 1729, to the Present Time. By John Hampson, A.B. *Sunderland.* 1791. 3 vols., 12mo. P.

[HAMPSON.] Observations on the Present War, the Projected Invasion, and a Decree of the National Convention, for the Emancipation of the Slaves in the French Colonies. [By the Rev. John Hampson.] *Sunderland.* [1793.] 8vo, pp. (2), 61.

HAMPSON. Reflections on the Present State of the American War. By the Rev. J. Hampson. *London.* 1776. 8vo.

HAMPTON (G.) Candid Remarks upon the Rev. Mr. Taylor's Discourse, entitled The Scripture Doctrine of Atonement Examined. In a Letter to Mr. Taylor. By George Hampton ... . *London.* [1801.] 8vo, pp. (2), 96. H. 30150

HAMPTON (M.) Speech of Moses Hampton of Pa. ... on Rivers and Harbors, and the Policy of Protection and Free Trade. *Washington.* 1848. 8vo, pp. 16. S. 30151

Also: Speech ... on the Tariff Question, January 22, 1851. 8vo. S.

HAMPTON (W.) Memorial of the Representatives of Wade Hampton, For the Confirmation of their Claims to Land in Louisiana. *Washington.* 1831. 8vo, pp. 31. 30152

Also: An Appeal to the Honorable the Senate of the United States. *Columbia, S. C.* 1868. 8vo, pp. 16.

HAMPTON, *N. H.* Three Sermons on the Earth Quake of 1727, with an Account of it at Hampton, and something Remarkable of Thunder and Lightning in that Town the same Year. *Boston.* 1728. 8vo. 30153

HAMPTON ACADEMY, *N. H.* Catalogue, 1847, 8vo. Continued. 30154

HAMPTON, *Va.*, Normal and Agricultural Institute. Report ... by President Hopkins and others, 1869. 30155

Also: Catalogue. 1870–71. 8vo. Continued.

HANAFORD (J. L.) History of Princeton, Worcester County, Massachusetts, Civil and Ecclesiastical, from its First Settlement in 1739 to April, 1852. By Jeremiah Lyford Hanaford. *Worcester.* 1852. 8vo, pp. 204. S. 30156

HANAFORD (P. A.) Abraham Lincoln: his Life and Public Services. By Mrs. P. A. Hanaford. *Boston.* 1865. 12mo. Portrait and Plates. 30157

HANAFORD. Abraham Lincoln, sein Leben und seine öffentlichen Dienste. Nach dem Englischen frei bearbeitet von J. W. Würzburger. *New York.* 1865. 12mo. 30158

HANAFORD. The Captive Boy in Terra del Fuego; being an Authentic Narrative of the Loss of the Ship Manchester, and the Adventures of the Sole White Survivor. By Mrs. Phebe Ann Hanaford. *New York: Carlton & Porter.* [1867.] 16mo, pp. 231. 4 Plates. C. 30159

HANAFORD. Field, Gunboat [&c.] *See* Vol. VII., No. 29400.

HANAFORD. The Life of George Peabody. By Mrs. P. A. Hanaford. *Boston.* 1870. 12mo. S. 30160

HANAFORD. Our Martyred President. By Mrs. P. A. Hana ford. Abraham Lincoln, Born February 12, 1809; Died April 15, 1865. [Mottoes.] *Boston: B. B. Russell and Company.* 1865. 8vo, pp. 24. Portrait by Smith. 30161

HANAFORD. The Young Captain: a Memorial of Captain Richard C. Derby, 15th Regiment Massachusetts Volunteers, who fell at Antietam. By Mrs. P. A. Hanaford. *Boston: Degen, Estes & Co.* 1865. Post 16mo, pp. 226. Portrait. 30162

Also: Frank Nelson; or, the Runaway Boy. *Boston: W. H. Hill.* 1866. 16mo, pp. 296. C.

HANBURY (B.) Historical Memorials relating to the Independents or Congregationalists, from their Rise to the Restoration of the Monarchy, A. D. 1660. *London.* 1839–1844. 3 vols., 8vo. C. 30163

HANCKEL (T. M.) Oration delivered on the Fifth Anniversary of the South Carolina Historical Society ... in Charleston, ... May 23, 1860. By Thomas M. Hanckel. *Charleston.* 1860. 8vo, pp. 34. 30164

HANCOCK (J.), *of Lexington, b.* 1671, *d.* 1752. The Gaining of Souls the Most Joyful Gain to Faithful Ministers. A Sermon preached 16th November, 1748, at the Instalment of Rev. Timothy Harrington, in Lancaster. By Rev. John Hancock, of Lexington. *Boston.* 1748. 8vo, pp. 22. B., BA., M., W.

HANCOCK. The Lord's Ministers are the People's Helpers. A Sermon preached at the Ordination of Rev. Ebenezer Hancock, at Lexington, January 2d, 1733–34. *Boston.* 1735. 8vo, pp. (4), iv, 21. B., BA., M. 30166

HANCOCK. The Prophet Jeremiah's Resolution to get him unto Great Men, and to speak unto them, Considered and Applied: in a Sermon ... Boston, November 21. 1734. ... By John Hancock ... Lexington. ... *Boston: S. Kneeland.* MDCCXXXIV. 8vo, pp. (4), 26. B., BA. 30167

HANCOCK. Rulers should be Benefactors. [An Election] Sermon. *Boston.* 1722. 16mo, pp. (4), 30. B., BA., M. 30168

HANCOCK. A Sermon at the Ordination of [his Son] John Hancock. In the North Precinct of Braintree [Mass.]; November 2, 1726. *Boston.* 1726. 8vo, pp. (4), 36. B., BA., M., W.

HANCOCK (J.), *of Braintree, b.* 1702, *d.* 1744. The Danger of an Unqualified Ministry. Sermon at Ordination of Rev. John Bass, Ashford, Conn., Sept. 7, 1743. By the Rev. John Hancock. *Boston.* 1743. 8vo, pp. 31. BA., H., M., W. 30170

HANCOCK. A Discourse upon the Good Work, Delivered at the Monthly Tuesday Lecture in Pembrook, September 7th, 1742. By John Hancock. *Boston.* 1743. 8vo, pp. 38. B., W.

[HANCOCK.] The Examiner; or Gilbert against Tennent. Containing a Confutation of the Rev. Mr. Gilbert Tennent and his Adherents: from his own writings. With Strictures on the Preface to Tennent's Five Sermons. By Philalethes. *Boston.* 1743. 8vo, pp. 32. BA., H. 30172

HANCOCK. Expostulatory and Pacifick Letter. By Way of Reply to ... Mr. Gee's Letter of Remarks, on the printed Testimony of the late Convention of Pastors in Boston, against sev-

eral Errors and Disorders in the Land ... . By John Hancock ... Braintree. ... *Boston: Rogers & Fowle.* 1743. 8vo, pp. 15. B.

HANCOCK. The Instability of Humane Greatness. A Discourse At Braintree, April 23, 1738. Upon the much lamented Death Of Edmund Quincy, Esq. who died of the Small Pox at London. Feb. 23, 1737–8. By John Hancock ... Braintree. *Boston.* MDCCXXXVIII. 8vo, pp. (4), 31, (1). B., BA., H. 30174

The last two pages contain "Addenda, from the Weekly Journal. April 11."

HANCOCK. A Memorial of God's Goodness. Being the Substance of Two Sermons, Preach'd in the first Church of Christ in Braintree, Sept. 16th. 1739. On compleating the first Century since the Gathering of it. By John Hancock, M.A. ... *Boston: S Kneeland & T. Green.* 1739. 8vo, pp. 37. BA., M., W. + *Boston, reprinted.* 1811. 8vo, pp. 35. BA. 30175

HANCOCK (J.), *LL.D., b.* 1737, *d.* 1793. Discours de son Excellence Monsieur Jean Hancock, President du Congres de Philadelphie. *A Philadelphie.* MDCCLXXVI. 8vo, pp. 32. N. 30176

A rare and curious satirical brochure.

HANCOCK. An Oration; delivered March 5, 1774, at the Request of the Inhabitants of the Town of Boston; to commemorate the Bloody Tragedy of the Fifth of March, 1770. By The Honorable John Hancock Esq: [Motto.] *Boston: Printed by Edes and Gill,* ... M,DCC,LXXIV. 4to, pp. 20. BA., H. + The Second Edition. [*Ibid.*] H. + *New-Haven: Re-Printed by Thomas and Samuel Green.* 8vo, pp. 15. 30177

Also included in the "Boston Orations."

HANCOCK. E Pluribus Unum. British Cruelty, Oppression, and Murder. Two Orations. An Oration delivered by John Hancock, Esq. at Boston, in Commemoration of the Evening of the 5th of March, 1770, when a number of Citizens were killed by a party of British Troops, quartered among them in a time of peace. [Also,] An Oration delivered by Dr. Joseph Warren, at Boston, On The Same Subject. The principles of which ought to be handed down from Father to Son, to the latest posterity, that they may know how to appreciate the Government whose mercy is cruelty, and whose touch is poison. To which is added An Account of the Captivity of Mrs. Jemimah Howe, Taken by the Indians at Hinsdale, N. H., July 27, 1755. [n. p.:] *P. M. Davis, Publisher, Formerly Adjutant of the 31st Regiment Infantry. M. M.* 1824. 12mo, pp. 23. 30178

Hancock. The Twelve United Colonies, By their Delegates in Congress to the Inhabitants of Great Britain. [n. p. n. d.] 8vo, pp. 8. 30179

Signed "John Hancock, July 8, 1775." *See* [Higginson (Stephen)], and [Sullivan (J.)]

Hancock. Biographical Sketch of the Life & Character of His Late Excellency Governor Hancock. *Boston: Chronicle-Office.* [1793.] 16mo, pp. 16. BA. 30180

Hancock. Report of the Committee Relative to the Purchase of the Hancock Estate. *Boston.* [1859.] 8vo, pp. 13.

Hancock (J.) Observations on the Climate, Soil, and Productions of British Guiana, and on the Advantages of Emigration to, and Colonizing the Interior of, that Country: Together with Incidental Remarks on the Diseases, their Treatment and Prevention: Founded on a long experience within the Tropics. By John Hancock, M.D. *London.* 1835. 8vo. + Second Edition. *London: Published for the Author.* 1840. 8vo, pp. (4), 92.

Hancock. Plan for the Reconciliation of all Interests in the Emancipation of West India Slaves. By John Hancock, M.D. *London.* 1833. 8vo, pp. 16. S. 30183

Hancock (J.) The Constitution and Government of the United States; with Questions and Answers. With the late Amendments. By John Hancock. *Philadelphia: King & Baird.* 1867. 18mo, pp. xiv, 130. Plate. C. 30184

Hancock. Counter-Statement in Support of the Petition of John Hancock and another for a Modification of the Statute of 1840, Ch. 97. [n. p. n. d.] 8vo, pp. 4. BA., H. 30185

Hancock. Essays on the Elective Franchise; or, Who has a Right to Vote? Second Edition. *Philadelphia.* 1865. 8vo, pp. 40. H. 30186

Hancock (John), *pseudon.* De Witt Clinton and the Late War. [n. p. n. d.] 8vo, pp. 16. BA. 30187

Hancock (J.) Merchant's and Trader's Guide ... for Boston ... *Boston: J. Hancock ... John Ford.* 1836. 24mo, pp. 118.

Hancock (J. W.) A Synoptical Index of the Statutes of Canada and Upper Canada with Notices of the later Acts which affect them. By J. W. Hancock, Esq., LL.B. *Toronto.* 1865. 8vo. 30189

Hancock (S. J.) The Montanas, or under the Stars. A Romance. By Sallie J. Hancock, of Kentucky. *New York: Carleton.* 1866. 12mo, pp. 320. C. 30190

Hancock. Etna Van de Noir. A Romance of Kentucky, and "The Great Uprising." By Sallie J. Hancock, of Kentucky. *New York: Cutter, Tower & Co.* 1863. 12mo, pp. 366.

Hancock (W.) An Emigrant's Five Years in the Free States of America. By William Hancock. ... *London: T. Cautley Newby.* 1860. Post 8vo, pp. (6), 321. Map. 30192

Hancock (W. S.) Major-General W. S. Hancock. His Civil Record during his Administration in Louisiana and Texas. 1871. [n. p. n. d.] 8vo, pp. 32. H. 30193

Also: Reports on Indian Affairs, 1866–67.

Hancock, *pseudon.* Essays on Texas, By Hancock. *New York: Printed by Thomas W. McGowran.* 1837. 8vo, pp. 20.

Hancock, *pseudon.* A Letter to the Hon. Samuel A. Eliot, Representative in Congress from Boston, in Reply to his Apology for Voting for the Fugitive Slave Bill. By Hancock. *Boston: Wm. Crosby & H. P. Nichols.* 1851. 8vo, pp. 57. B., BA., S.

Hancock, *pseudon.* The Whole Truth. Address to the Freemen of New England, Nov. 1, 1808. By Hancock. 12mo.

Also: Essex Junta Exposed. The Whole Truth. *New York.* 1809. 8vo.

Hancock Mining Company. Report of the Directors ... of the Hancock Mining Company ... March 20, 1863. *Boston.* 1863. 8vo, pp. 15. Continued. 30197

Hand (W. M.) The House Surgeon and Physician ... with Concise Directions for the Preparation and Use of a Numerous Collection of the best American Remedies ... . By William M. Hand. Second Edition, Revised and Enlarged. *New-Haven.* 1820. 12mo, pp. xii, 288. H. 30198

Hand-Boeck, 1630. *See* Viverus (J.)

Hand-Book for Active Service. *Richmond, Va.: J. W. Randolph.* 1861. 16mo, pp. 68. 30199

Hand-Book Almanach for the Pacific States; an Official Register and Business Directory, for the year 1862. Edited by W. H. Knight. *San Francisco: H. H. Bancroft & Co.* 1862. 16mo.

Continued to 1864, or later.

Hand-Book to Canada and the United States, with Descent of Niagara and the St. Lawrence. ... *London.* 1854. 8vo, pp. 40.

The Hand Book of Chicago, or Stranger's Guide to Points of Interest ... . *Chicago.* 1859. 16mo, pp. 129. 30202

The Hand-Book of Civil Rights: Collated and Digested from Original Manuscripts and other Sources. By Anachoreta. *Cincinnati.* 1849. 12mo, pp. 86. H. 30203

Hand-Book of the Democracy, for 1863–64. *New York.* 1864. 8vo. BA. 30204

Hand Book for Emigrants to the Province of New Brunswick, Containing the average price of Land, Provisions, Clothing, Farm Stock, Building and other Materials, &c., and the rate of Wages to Mechanics, Labourers, &c. With other necessary information for persons with Capital, as well as for Mechanics, Farm Servants, Labourers, &c. intending to settle in the Province. Compiled From Returns in the Office of the Provincial Secretary. *Fredericton: John Simpson,* ... 1841. 8vo, pp. 15.

Hand-Book for Immigrants to the United States. Prepared by the American Social Science Association. *New York. Hurd and Houghton.* 12mo, pp. vi, 118. Maps. 30206

Hand Book to Ogdensburgh, Montreal, Quebec ... . *Buffalo.* 1858. 32mo, pp. 8. Map. 30207

Hand-Book of the Oneida Community: with a Sketch of its Founder and an Outline of its Constitution and Doctrines. *Wallingford, Conn.: Circular Office.* 1867. 8vo, pp. 71. Plate. C.

A Hand-Book for Passengers over the Cambridge Railroad, with a Description of Mount Auburn Cemetery. *Boston: W. V. Spencer.* 1858. 18mo, pp. 70. Map and Plate. C. 30209

Hand Book of Practical Receipts; or Useful Hints in every Day Life. By an American Gentleman and Lady. *New York.* 1860. 18mo, pp. (2), x, 3–153. 30210

Hand-Book of Stevens' Point and the Upper Wisconsin. *Stevens' Point.* 1857. 12mo. 30211

Hand-Book for the Stranger in Philadelphia ... . By a Philadelphian. *Philadelphia: Geo. S. Appleton.* 1849. 16mo, pp. 113. Map. 30212

Handbook for Strangers, June 17, 1857. Containing a Sketch and Portrait of Gen. Scott, &c. *Boston.* 1857. 32mo, pp. 32.

Hand-Book for Travelers to Niagara Falls, Montreal and Quebec, and through Lake Champlain to Saratoga Springs. *Buffalo, N. Y.* 1853. 12mo. Map. 30214

Hand-Book for the Visiter [*sic*] to Lowell. ... *Lowell.* 1848. 24mo, pp. 45. 30215

Hand-Book for the War. [n. p. n. d.] 12mo, pp. 23.

Ein Handbuch für Deutsche Auswanderer. *Bremen.* 1845.

Relates to Texas.

Handelmann (Heinrich). Geschichte von Brazilien. *Berlin: J. Springer.* 1860. 8vo, pp. xxiv, 989. 30218

Handelmann. Geschichte der Insel Hayti. Zweite Ausgabe. *Kiel: Homann.* 1860. 8vo, pp. 192. 30219

Handelmann. Geschichte der Vereinigten Staaten. Erster Theil. Die historische Entwickelung des Landes, des Volkes und der Verfassung. Zweite Ausgabe. *Kiel: Homann.* 1860. 8vo, pp. xvi, 688. 30220

Handey (W. H.) Political Equilibrium. By William H. Handey. *Hagerstown, Md.* 1842. 18mo. C. 30221

Handlin (W. W.) American Politics. A Moral and Political Work, treating of the Causes of the Civil War, the Nature of Government, and the Necessity for Reform. By W. W. Handlin. *New Orleans: Isaac T. Hinton.* 1864. 8vo, pp. 107.

Handy (G.) Poem, upon the Great Disaster, at Lawrence, Mass. By George Handy. *Boston.* 1860. 8vo, pp. 16.

Handy (I. W. K.) Our National Sins. A Sermon, ... Portsmouth, Va. On the Day of Fasting ... January 4, 1861. By Rev. Isaac W. K. Handy, D.D. *Portsmouth, Va.* 1861. 8vo, pp. 20. C. 30224

Handy (W. W.) Speech of William W. Handy ... House of Delegates, Maryland, April 4, 1839, ... on the ... Eastern Shore Railroad .. *Baltimore.* 1839. 8vo. 30225

Hanger (G.) An Address to the Army; in reply to Strictures, by Roderick M'Kenzie (late Lieutenant in the 71st Regiment), on Tarleton's History of the Campaigns of 1780 and 1781.

By the Hon. George Hanger. ... *London: James Ridgway.* MDCCLXXXIX. 8vo, pp. xvi, 138, 8. 30226

Hanger. The Life, Adventures, and Opinions of Col. George Hanger. Written by Himself. With Advice to the Lovely Cyprians, and to the Fair Sex in general. Adventures in America, &c. *London: J. Debrett.* 1801. 2 vols., 8vo. Portrait. C. + *New York.* 1801. 2 vols., 8vo. 30227

Col. Hanger (afterward Lord Coleraine) served with distinction in the American war. The following curious prophecy will be found on p. 427 of Vol. II.: "One of these days the Northern and Southern powers will fight as vigorously against each other as the both have united to do against the British."

Hankins (M. L.) Women of New York. Written and Illustrated. By Marie L. Hankins. *New York: M. L. Hankins & Co.* 1861. 12mo, pp. 349. 36 Plates. 30228

Hanly (P.) The Life of Peter Hanly, otherwise Peter Robertson, ... containing an Account of his Travels and Adventures to America, the East and West Indies, &c. ... Written by Himself. *Calne: W. Burly.* 1799? 8vo, pp. 64. 30229

Hanna (J. M.) The Acts of Kings: a Biblical Narrative of the Acts of First and Second Kings of the First Province, once Virginia. By J. M. Hanna. *New York.* 1868. 12mo, pp. 74. 30230

Hanna (J. S.) A History of the Life and Services of Captain Samuel Dewees, a Native of Pennsylvania, and Soldier of the Revolutionary and Last Wars. Also, Reminiscences of the Revolutionary Struggle (Indian War, Western Expedition, Liberty Insurrection in Northampton County, Pa.) and Late War with Great Britain, in all of which he was Patriotically Engaged. The whole written (in part from manuscript in the handwriting of Captain Dewees) and compiled By John Smith Hanna. ... *Baltimore: Printed by Robert Neilson.* 1844. 12mo, pp. 360. Portrait. 30231

Hanna (S. W.) Notes of a Visit to some Part of Haiti, Jan.–Feb., 1835. By Rev. S. W. Hanna ... of St. George's, Jamaica. *London: Seeley.* 1836. 12mo, pp. lxii, 153. 30232

Hannaford (Edwin). The Story of a Regiment: a History of the Campaigns, and Associations in the Field, of the Sixth Regiment Ohio Volunteer Infantry. By E. Hannaford ... . *Cincinnati: The Author.* 1868. 8vo, pp. 622. Map. C. 30233

Hannay (C. J. J.) The Maritime Rights and Obligations of Belligerents, as between themselves, their allies, and neutrals, as recognized by English Maritime Courts. By Charles J. J. Hannay. *London.* 1862. 16mo. C. 30234

Hannay (R.) True Account of the Proceedings, Sense and Advice of the People called Quakers in London, in order to put an end to the divisions and differences among some of the People called Quakers in America, with the Proceedings of the Yearly Meeting at Burlington, N. Jersey. By Robert Hannay. *London.* 1694. 30235

This scarce little volume relates to the Quaker persecutions and quarrels in Pennsylvania, and East and West Jersey.

Hannegan (Edward A.) Speech of Mr. Hannegan ... on the Oregon Question. ... Senate ... February 16, 1846. *Washington.* 1846. 8vo, pp. 12. H. 30236

Hannibal (Julius Cæsar), *pseudon.* Black Diamonds; or Humor, Satire, and Sentiment treated scientifically. *New York.* 1855. 12mo. 30237

Hannibal & St. Joseph R. R. Co. Circular in regard to the Company. *Hannibal.* 1863. 8vo. 30238

Hanning (J.) Two Sermons—one on Beneficence, or Universal Charity; the other, The Rights of Women Vindicated. Preached in Jefferson Co., Indiana. By John Hanning. *Savannah, Ga.* 1846. 12mo, pp. 36. 30239

In E. P. Boon's Auction Catalogue a copy of the "Rights of Women" is quoted as printed at *New York.* 1807. 8vo.

Hanover College, *Indiana.* A Catalogue of the Officers and Students of Hanover College. *Madison.* 1840. 12mo, pp. 14. Continued. M. 30240

The Twentieth Annual Circular of Hanover College; comprising the Triennial and Annual Catalogues, Course of Studies, &c. August, 1852. *Cincinnati.* 1852. 8vo. 30241

Hanover College, *Hanover, Ind.* Second Triennial Catalogue. For the Year 1849. *Madison.* 1849. 8vo. 30242

Hanover, *Mass.* The Selectmen's Report ... of the Town of Hanover, from February 1, 1854, to February 1, 1855. ... *Centre Abington.* 1855. 8vo. Continued. 30243

The Annual Report of the School Committee of the Town of Hanover, for A.D. 1858–9. *Abington.* 1859. 8vo, pp. 14.

An Hanoverian. *See* [Toplady (A.)]

Hansard (T. C.) The Parliamentary Debates, from the Year 1803, to the Present Time, forming a Continuation of the Work, entitled "The Parliamentary History of England, from the Earliest Period to the Year 1803," begun by W. Cobbet, and continued under the Superintendence of T. C. Hansard. First Series, 1803 to 1820, 41 vols. Second Series, 1820 to 1830, 25 vols. Third Series, 1830. Continued. 30245

It is scarcely necessary to say that in any great collection of Americana this series should have a place. The intimate relation between the two countries necessarily involve many public discussions concerning their respective interests.

Hansard's Analytical Parliamentary Digest. In two parts: Part 2, Vol. I., being an Index to the sixty-three vols. of Hansard's Parliamentary Debates from 1803 to 1830: *London.* 1832. 8vo. S. 30246

No more published.

Hanscom (S. P.) [A Letter] to His Excellency Henry J. Gardner, Governor of ... Massachusetts. [n. p. n. d.] 8vo, pp. 8. 30247

Hansen (C.) To ... the Senate and House of Representatives in Congress assembled.—Postal and Commercial Statistical Information, in relation to the Connecting Lines of Mail Steamers, proposed to be established by Christian Hansen, between the City of Brooklyn ... New York, and Antwerp, Belgium, ... [*Brooklyn, N. Y.* 1854.] 8vo, pp. 26. 30248

Hansen (L.) [Engraved title:] Rosa Pervana | Vita Mirabilis et Mors | Pretiosa | Ven^lis. Sororis Rosæ de S. Maria | Limensis ex tertio Ordine S. P. Dominici | Ad S^m. D. N. Alexandrum VII. | Pont Max. | 1664 | [Printed title:] Vita mirabilis | et Mors pretiosa | venerabilis Sororis | Rosæ de S. Maria | Limensis, | Ex Tertio Ordine S. P. Dominici, | ad Sanctissimvm D. N. | Alexandrvm VII. | Pontificem Max. Excerpta & collecta | Per P. M. F. Leonardvm Hansen | Prouincialem Angliæ, & Socium | Reueren- | dissimi P. Magist. Generalis Ord. Præd. | *Romæ, Typis Nicolai Angeli Tinassij* M. DC. LXIV. | *Superiorum permissu.* | 4to, pp. (10), 360, (4). + [*Ibid.*] 1664. 12mo, pp. x, 452, (4) H.

The subject of this memoir is the only American female saint

Hansen. [Engraved title:] Vita | Beatæ | Rosæ | Lovanij, | Typis H. Nempei A: 1668. | [Printed title:] Vita | Mirabilis | et | mors pretiosa | B. Rosæ | de S. Maria | Limensis, | Ex Tertio Ordine S. P. Dominici, | Excerpta & collecta, | Per Eximium | P. F. Leonardum Hansen | S. Th. Magist. Provincialem Angliæ, & So- | cium Reverendissimi P. Magist. | Gener. Ord. Præd. | Post Romanam secundam editio tertia. | *Lovanii,* | *Typis H. Nempæi.* 1668. | *Superiorum permissu.* | 12mo, pp. (24), 549, (6). 30250

Hansen. Vita Mirabilis mors pretiosa Sanctitas thaumaturgæ inclytæ Virginis Sponsæ Christi B. Rosæ à S. Maria Peruanæ, ex tertio ordine S. P. Dominici. ... per F. Leonard Hansen. Editio tertia ac novissima. *Romæ, Nicolai Angeli Tinassi.* 1680. Folio, pp. (6), 321, (4). 30251

Hansen. Dass Wunderbarliche Leben vnd vil werther Todt der Ehrwürdigen Schwester Rosa De S. Maria von Lima, gebürtig ausz der dritten Regel desz Vatters Dominici. *Insprugg: Michael Wagner.* 1667. 4to, pp. (14), 203, 60. 30252

Hansen (T.) List of the Attorneys and Counselors of the Supreme Court of the State of New York, together with the places of their Residences, and the names of their respective Agents, residing in New York, Albany and Utica. *Albany.* 1821. 8vo, pp. 55. 30253

Hanson (Alexander C.) An Accurate Report of the Argument, on a Motion of Attachment, against Baptis Irvine, Editor of the Whig, for a Contempt against the Court of Oyer and Terminer for Baltimore County. By A. Contee Hanson ... . *Baltimore: P. K. Wagner.* 1808. 8vo, pp. viii, 116. BA. 30254

[Hanson.] Considerations on the Proposed Removal of the Seat of Government, Addressed to the Citizens of Maryland, By Aristides. *Annapolis: Printed by Frederick Green.* [1786.] 12mo, pp. 62. 30255

[Hanson.] Political Schemes and Calculations, Addressed to the Citizens of Maryland, By a Native Citizen and Servant of the State. *Annapolis: Printed by F. & S. Green.* MDCCLXXXIV. 8vo, pp. vi, 38. 30256

[Hanson.] Reflections upon the late Correspondence between Mr. Secretary Smith and Francis James Jackson, Esq., Minister Plenipotentiary of His Britannic Majesty. Originally published in the Federal Republican of Baltimore. *Baltimore: Published for the Author.* 1810. 8vo, pp. 97. BA., N. 30257

[Hanson.] Remarks on the Proposed Plan of a Federal Government, Addressed to the Citizens of the United States of America, and Particularly to the People of Maryland, By Aristides. *Annapolis: Printed by Frederick Green.* [1788.] 12mo, pp. 42. 30258

Dedicated to George Washington, Esq.

[Hanson.] Remarks on the Proposed Plan of an Emission of Paper, and on the Means of Effecting it, Addressed to the Citizens of Maryland, By Aristides. *Annapolis: Printed by Frederick Green.* [1787.] 12mo, pp. 43. N. 30259

Hanson. Speech ... on the Loan Bill ... House of Representatives, February 14, 1814 ... . *Georgetown: Printed by Robert Allison.* 1814. 8vo, pp. 37. BA. 30260

Hanson. Trial of Alexander Contee Hanson, Esq., a Lieutenant ... of Militia attached to the thirty-ninth Regiment, upon a Charge "conceived to be Mutinous and Highly Reproachful to the President, and founded upon a Political Piece published in The Federal Republican ... ." *Baltimore: Printed by J. Robinson, March,* 1809. 8vo, pp. 56. BA. + *Boston.* 1809. 8vo, pp. 56.

Hanson (C. W.) Oration before the Washington Benevolent Society of Maryland. By Charles W. Hanson. *Baltimore.* 1811. 8vo. S., W. 30262

Hanson (E.) God's Mercy surmounting Man's Cruelty, exemplified in the Captivity and Redemption of Elizabeth Hanson, Wife of John Hanson of Knoxmarsh at Keacheachy in Dover Township, who was taken Captive with her Children and maid servants by the Indians in New England in 1724. *To be sold by Samuel Keimer in Philadelphia and by Hewston Goldsmith in New York,* 1724, *Dec.* 24. Small 8vo. 30263

Hanson. God's Mercy surmounting Man's Cruelty, exemplified in the Captivity and Redemption of Elizabeth Hanson, Wife of John Hanson, of Knoxmarsh at Kecheachy, in Dover Township, who was taken captive with her children, and Maid-Servant, by the Indians in New England, in the year 1724. In which are inserted, Sundry remarkable Preservations, Deliverances, and Marks of the Care and Kindness of Providence over her and her children, worthy to be remembered. The substance of which was taken from her own mouth, and now published for general service, by Samuel Bownas. The Second Edition. *Philadelphia: Printed and sold by James Chattin.* 1754. Small 8vo, pp. 24. 30264

Hanson. An Account of the Captivity of Elizabeth Hanson, Now or Late of Kachecky, in New-England: Who, with Four of her Children and Servant-Maid was taken captive by the Indians, and carried into Canada. Setting forth the various remarkable Occurrences, sore Trials, and wonderful Deliverances which befel them after their Departure, to the Time of their Redemption. Taken in Substance from her own Mouth, by Samuel Bownas. Second Edition. *London: Samuel Clark.* M.D.CCLX. Small 8vo, pp. 28. + A New Edition. *London: James Phillips.* 1782. 12mo, pp. 26, (2). S. + [*Ibid.*] 1787.

Hanson. God's Mercy surmounting Man's Cruelty, exemplified in the Captivity and Redemption of Elizabeth Hanson. ... Third Edition. *Danvers, reprinted.* 1780. 8vo, pp. 32. M. + *Stanford, N. Y.* 1803. 18mo. 30266

Reprinted in Drake's "Tragedies of the Wilderness."

Hanson (J. H.) The Lost Prince: Facts tending to prove the Identity of Louis XVII., of France, and the Rev. Eleazer Williams, Missionary among the Indians of North America. By John H. Hanson. *New York.* 1854. 12mo, pp. 479. 3 Portraits. H., S. 30267

"More traditional than circumstantial, and more circumstantial than positive."—T. W. Field.—*See* Putnam's Magazine, 1853 and 1854; *also,* Williams (John).

Hanson. Poems; By the Rev. John H. Hanson. With a Memoir, by his Sister, C. Hanson. *New York: Pott & Amery.* 1869. 12mo, pp. 167. C. 30268

Hanson (J. W.) Historical Sketch of the Old Sixth Regiment of Massachusetts Volunteers, during its Three Campaigns in 1861, 1862, 1863, and 1864. ... By John W. Hanson, Chaplain. *Boston: Lee & Shepard.* 1866. 12mo, pp. 352. 3 Photographs. C., H., S. 30269

Hanson. History of Gardiner, Pittston and West Gardiner, with a Sketch of the Kenebec Indians & New Plymouth Purchase, comprising Historical Matter from 1602 to 1852; with genealogical Sketches of many families. By J. W. Hanson, ∴ *Gardiner: William Palmer.* 1852. 12mo, pp. 343. Engravings.

Hanson. History of the Old Towns Norridgewock and Canaan, comprising Norridgewock, Canaan, Starks, Skowhegan, and Bloomfield [Maine], from their early settlement, to the year 1849. Including a Sketch of the Abnakis Indians. By J. W. Hanson, ... *Boston: The Author.* 1849. 12mo, pp. 371, (1). 4 Plates. BA., C., H., S. 30271

Hanson. History of the Town of Danvers, from its Early Settlement to the Year 1848. By J. W. Hanson. *Danvers: The Author.* 1848. 8vo, pp. 304. B., BA., H., S. 30272

Hanson (S.) Case of Samuel Hanson, Merchant and Planter in Barbadoes, against the Prejudice and Injustice of Sir Richard Dutton, the several Verdicts, Judgements, Appeals, Reversals, &c. 1682. Folio. 30273

Title from one of Thomas Thorpe's catalogues, No. 1195.

Hanson (T.) The Prussian Evolutions in Actual Engagements ... also The Theory and Practice of Gunnery. By Thomas Hanson ... Teacher of part of the American Militia. *Philadelphia: The Author.* [1775.] 4to, pp. (8), iv, 64, 30 Plates; pp. 56. BA. 30275

This obtains a place here as an early American work on military science. The second paging has a separate title, "Book the Second ... Gunnery. ..."

Hanway (C.) *and others.* A History of the Trial of Castner Hanway and others, for Treason, at Philadelphia in November, 1851. With an Introduction upon the History of the Slave Question. By a Member of the Philadelphia Bar. *Philadelphia.* 1852. 8vo, pp. 86. H. 30274

[Hanway (Jonas).] An Account | of the | Society | For the Encouragement of the | British Troops, | In Germany and North America. | With the Motives to the making a present to those troops, | also to the widows and orphans of such of them as have died | in defence of their country, particularly at the battles of | Thonhausen | Quebec, &c. | With an Alphabetical List of the Subscribers to this benevolent De- | sign; and a State of the Receipts and Disbursements of the Society. | *London.* M.DCC.LX. | 8vo, pp. viii, 91, 55. H., P. 30276

Title in red and black. Contains a curious account of the hardships and difficulties of North American warfare, the taking of Quebec, &c.

Happel (E. G.) E. G. Happelii | grösseste | Denkwürdigkeiten der Welt | oder so genandte | Relationes | Curiosæ. | Worinnen fürgestellet, | und aus dem Grund der gesunden Vernunfft examiniret werden, | allerhand | Antiquitäten, Curiositäten, Critische, Historische, Physicalische, | Mathematische, Künstliche und andere | Merckwürdige Seltzamkeiten | Welche auff dieser Unter-Welt, in der Lufft, auff | der See oder Land jemahlen zu finden gewesen, oder | sich noch täglich zeigen. | Einem jeden curieusen Liebhaber zur Lust und Erbauung in | Druck verfertiget, und mit erforderten

schönen Kupfern und andern | Figuren erläutert. | Mit Käyserl. Mayst. allergnädigstem Privilegio. | *Hamburg.* | *Gedruckt und verlegt durch Thomas von Wiering* ... 1683–1708. 8 vols., 4to.

Happel's Relations are a miscellany of popular information, containing short notices of curious phenomena in every part of the globe, as well as of curious historical events. The notices of American matters are numerous in all the volumes. They are rarely original, still they are interesting enough. Many portraits and plates are included.

Happel. Mundus Mirabilis tripartitus oder Wunderbare Welt in einer kurtzen Cosmographia fürgestellet. *Ulm: Wagner.* 1687–88. 3 vols., 4to. Maps and Plates. + *Ulm: Barthel.* 1708. 4to. 30278

"This very interesting work, full of the most various curiosities, etc, contains a description of America; an account of the manners, customs, etc., of the inhabitants of Canada, Virginia, Florida, Peru, Brazil, etc.; superstitions of these people; American languages, etc."—F. Muller.

Happel. Thesaurus Exoticorum. | Oder eine mit Ausländischen | Raritäten und Geschichten | Wohlversehene | Schatz-Kammer | Fürstellend | die Asiatische, Africanische und | Americanische | Nationes | der Perser, Indianer, Sinesen, Tartarn, | Egypter, Barbarn, Libyer, Nigriten, Guineer, Hottentotten, | Abyssiner, Canadenser, Virgenier, Floridaner, Mexicaner, Peruaner, | Chilenser, Magellanier und Brasilianer, etc. Nach ihren Königreichen | Policeyen, Kleydungen, Sitten und Gottes-Dienst. | Darauff folget eine Umständliche | von Türckey Beschreibung: | Der Türcken Ankunfft; aller Sultanen Lebens-Lauff und Bildnüss; Aller hohen | Staats-Bedienten; Des Sultans Hoff, Regierung, Intraden, Macht und | Vasallen; Wie auch ihres Propheten Mahomets Lebens-Beschreibung, und sein | Verfluchtes Gesetz-Buch oder Alkoran. | Alssdann eine Kürtzbündige | Beschreibung von Ungarn: | Nach seiner Grösse, Fruchtbarkeit, Macht, Städten und vielen Vestungen | von Wien biss nach Constantinopel hinaus. | Da es dann Gelegenheit gibt zu Reden | Von den 4 Monarchien, der Assyrer, Perser, Griechen und Römer: Aller | Käysern, von Nimrod an biss auff den grossen Leopoldum, und so dann | von allen Hertzogen und Königen von Ungarn sampt ihren Bildnüssen. | Hiernechst eine umbständliche Beschreibung des Lebens-Lauffs | Ihrer Käyserl. Mayest. Leopoldi I. | Und des itzo annoch wehrenden bluthigen Türcken-Krieges, und was in demselben | Denckwürdiges in Ungarn, Pohlen und Morea passiret. | Alles mit grosser Mühe und Fleiss aus den berühmtesten Scribenten zusammen | getragen, mit schönen Kupfern und Landkarten, auch andern Figuren in sehr grosser | Anzahl aussgezieret, und denen Liebhabern zur Ergetzligkeit heraussgegeben | Von

Everhardo Gvernero Happelio. ¶ *Hamburg,* | *Gedruckt und Verlegt durch Thomas von Wiering,* ... 1688. | Folio, pp. (18), 120; (2), 160; (2), 192; (2), 288; (4), 115. 3 Maps; 2 Titles, one of which is engraved. 30279

The greater part of this work, which is a sort of German Coryat, is filled with a history of the wars between Hungary and Turkey, but it has also a special interest for the American collector, as it contains a series of fifteen curious representations of the aborigines of America, all with detailed descriptions of their manners, customs, religion, etc. We find among them representations of the natives of New-France, New-Netherland, Virginia, a King of Florida, Californians, Peruvians, Chilians, Mexicans, etc.

The Happy Briton, or his Country's Friend; shewing the superior Advantages of being a Subject of this Country; with a few Hints to the People of North America, and a Description of the very fatal Earthquake at Caracca, in South America; ... [*London:*] *Sherwood and Co.* 1812. 8vo. 30280

Title from the "Monthly Review," LXIX. 217.

Haralson (H. A.) Speech of Hon. H. A. Haralson, of Georgia, on the Oregon Question. ... February 9, 1846. [n. p. n. d.] 8vo, pp. 8. 30281

Also: Speech ... on the Mexican War. ... Thursday, July 16, 1846. *Washington.* 1846. 8vo, pp. 8.

[Haraszthy (A.), *and* Warner (J. J.)] Report of Commissioners on the Culture of the Grape-Vine in California. *San Francisco.* 1862. 8vo, pp. 30. 30282

Harbach (F.) Cleveland, Painsville and Ashtabula R. R. Company. Ohio Section: Report on the Preliminary Surveys, By F. Harbach, Chief Engineer. March 28, 1850. *Cleveland.* 1850. 8vo. S. 30283

Harbaugh (H.) Fathers of the German Reformed Church in Europe and America. By Henry Harbaugh. *Lancaster, Pennsylvania.* 1857–58. 3 vols., 12mo. C., S. 30284

Harbaugh. The Life of Rev. Michael Schlatter; with a full account of his Travels and Labors among the Germans in Pennsylvania, New Jersey, Maryland and Virginia; including his Services as Chaplain in the French and Indian War, and in the War of the Revolution. 1716 to 1790. By Rev. H. Harbaugh. ... *Philadelphia.* 1857. 12mo, pp. xxxi, 26–375. C., S.

Harbaugh. A Tract for the Time. The Religious Character of Washington, By Rev. H. Harbaugh, D.D. ... *Chambersburg, Pa.: M. Kieffer & Co.* 1863. 12mo, pp. 24. 30286

Harbaugh. Treason and Law. A Discourse, delivered at Clearspring, Maryland, June 1, 1865, the Day of National Mourning, By H. Harbaugh, D.D. *Philadelphia: Jas. B. Rogers.* 1865. 12mo, pp. 31. 30287

The Harbinger of Peace. ... *New-York.* [1828–31.] Vols. I.–III. 12mo. H. 30288

The Harbinger, devoted to Social and Political Progress. ... Published by the Brook Farm Phalanx. *New-York* [also] *Boston.* 1845–48. 5 vols., I.–V., 8vo. Vol. VI., published by the American Union of Associationists. Folio. C., H., S. 30289

The Harbinger: a May Gift, dedicated to the Ladies who ... aided the New England Institution for the Blind. *Boston: Carter, Hendee and Co.* 1833. 12mo, pp. vi, (1), 96. H. 30290

By Oliver Wendell Holmes, Park Benjamin, and Epes Sargent.

Harbison (M.) A Narrative of the Sufferings of Massy Harbison, from Indian Barbarity, giving an Account of her Captivity, the Murder of her Two Children, her Escape, with an Infant at her Breast; Together With some account of the Cruelties of the Indians, on the Allegheny River, &c., during the years 1790, '91, '92, '93, '94. Communicated by Herself. *Pittsburgh: Printed by S. Engles.* 1825. 12mo, pp. 98. + *Pittsburgh: D. and M. Maclean.* 1828. 12mo, pp. 98. H. + Together, with some account of the History, Laws, Religion, Wars, and Cruelties of the Indians, particularly in this Western Country. Fourth Edition, much Enlarged. Edited by John Winter. *Beaver, Pa.* 1836. 18mo, pp. 192. C. 30291

Harbor Defences. Report from Select Committee of U. S. House of Representatives on Harbor Defences of the Great Lakes and Rivers. 1862. 8vo. 30292

The Harbor Excursion and Intemperance in Boston. [*Boston.* 1851.] 12mo, pp. 12. H. 30293

Harby (I.) A Selection from the Miscellaneous Writings of the late Isaac Harby, with a Memoir by Ab. Moise. *Charleston.* 1829. 8vo, pp. 288. C. 30294

Includes Political Essays, Dramatic and Shakespearian Criticisms, etc. Also: Discourse before the Reformed Society of Israelites; Charleston, S. C., Nov. 21, 1825. ... *Charleston.* 1825. 8vo, pp. 40. M., W.

Harcort (E.) Noticias Geograf.-polit. del territorio de Colima, publicato por R. de la Tega. *Mexico.* 1842. 12mo, pp. 23.

Harcourt (R.) A | Relation | of a Voyage | to Gviana. | Describing the Climat, | Scituation, fertilitie, prouisions and commodities | of that Country, containing seuen Prouinces, and | other Signiories within that Territory: Together, | with the manners, customes, behauiors, and | dispositions of the people. | Performed by Robert Harcovrt, of | Stanton Harcourt Esquire. | The Pattent for the Plantation of which Country, | His Maiestie hath granted to the said Robert | Harcovrt vnder the Great Seale. | *At London* | *Printed by Iohn Beale, for W. Welby, and* | *are to be sold at his shop in Pauls Churchyard at the* | *signe of the Swan.* 1613. | 4to, pp. (16), 71. C., H. 30296

Harcourt. The | Relation | of a Voyage | To Gviana. | Describing the Climate, Situation, | Fertilitie, & Commodities of that | Country: Together with the | Manner, and Customes of | the People. | Performed by Robert Harcovrt, | of Stanton Harcourt Esquier. | 1619. | Now newly reviewed, & enlarged, by addition | of some necessary Notes, for the more ample explai- | ning of some things mentioned in the said Relation: Together, with a larger declaration of the famous | Riuer of the Amazones and the Coun- | try thereabout. | Gathered from the moderne experience of | our owne Country-men. | The Patent for the Plantation of which Country, | His Maiestie hath lately Granted | to a Corporation. | *London,* | *Printed by Edw: Allde, dwelling neere Christ-* | *Church.* 1626. | 4to, pp. (16), 84. 30297

Both editions are very rare. Reprinted in Purchas, Vol. I., and in the "Harleian Miscellany," Vol. III. A Dutch version is included in Van der Aa's Collection, Vol. XXIV. 8vo. The patent for the plantation of Guiana was granted to the said Harcourt, of Stanton Harcourt, in Oxfordshire.

[Harcourt (William George Granville Vernon).] Additional Letters on some Questions of International Law. [Belligerent rights of maritime capture; The doctrine of continuous voyages.] By Historicus. *London: Macmillan & Co.* 1863. 8vo, pp. xvi, 44.

[Harcourt.] American Neutrality. By Historicus. From the London Times of December 22, 1864. *New York.* 1865. 8vo, pp. 11. 30299

[Harcourt.] Belligerent Rights of Maritime Capture. By Historicus. *Liverpool: Webb & Hunt.* 1863. 8vo, pp. 4, 22.

[Harcourt.] Letters by Historicus on some Questions of International Law. Reprinted from 'The Times' with Considerable Additions. ... *London: Macmillan & Co.* 1863. 8vo, pp. xiii, 98. BA., S. 30301

Hard Cider and Log Cabin Almanac, for Harrison and Tyler. *New York.* 1841. 12mo. 30302

Hard Cider: a Poem, descriptive of the Nashville Convention. *Louisville, Ky.* 1840. 16mo, pp. 56. 30303

Hard Times. Important Suggestions to Laborers ... . *Boston.* 1855. 8vo, pp. 24. M. 30304

Hardcastle's Annual Masonic Register for 5812. *New York.* [1812.] 12mo. 30305

Hardcastle. Fiftieth Anniversary of a Marriage-Day. Dedicated to the Members and Friends of the Hardcastle Family. *Philadelphia: For Private Circulation.* 1855. 12mo. 30306

Hardee (W. J.) Rifle and Infantry Tactics, Revised and Improved. By Lieut.-General William J. Hardee, ... Ninth Edition. *Mobile: S. H. Goetzel.* 1863. 2 vols., square 32mo, pp. 228, 32 Plates; pp. 232, 37 Plates. C. 30307

A standard work on the subject. First published in Philadelphia; frequently reprinted in Mobile and elsewhere in the South during the rebellion.

Hardeman (T.) Speech of T. Hardeman, of Georgia, on the Rights of the South. Delivered in the House of Representatives, April 12, 1860. [n. p. 1860.] 8vo, pp. 8. 30308

Harden (E. J.) A Eulogy on the Life and Character of the late Hon. Robert M. Charlton, delivered ... Savannah, March 8th, 1854. By Edward J. Harden, Esq. *Savannah: George N. Nichols, Printer.* 1854. 8vo, pp. 16. 30309

Harden. The Life of George M[ichael] Troup, ex-Governor of Georgia. By Edward J. Harden. *Savannah: E. J. Purse.* 1859. 8vo, pp. xxii, 536. Portrait. C. 30310

[Harden.] Notes of a Short Northern Tour. For Private Circulation only. *Savannah:* ... 1869. 8vo, pp. 38. 30311

In English and Latin. A trifling performance, read before the Georgia Historical Society.

Harden (J. S.) Life, Confession, and Letters of Courtship of Jacob S. Harden, of the M. E. Church, Mount Lebanon, ... N. J. Executed for the Murder of his Wife, ... *Hackettstown, Warren Co., N. J.: E. Winton, Printer.* 1860. 8vo, pp. 48. S.

Hardie (*Col.*) Letter from Col. Hardie to the Secretary of War, in regard to the Murder of Capt. [Theodore] Reed of

Philadelphia, by the Citizens of Accomack County, Va., May 25, 1864. [*Washington.*] 1864. 8vo. 30313

38th Congress, 1st Session, Executive Document, No. 93.

HARDIE (J.) An Account of the Malignant Fever, lately prevalent in the City of New-York. Containing I. A Narrative of its Rise, Progress and Decline ... II. The Manner in which the Poor were relieved ... III. A List of the Donations, which have been presented ... for ... the Indigent. IV. A List of the Names of the Dead ... V. A Comparative View of the Fever of ... 1798, with that of ... 1795. By James Hardie, A.M. ... *New-York: Printed by Hurtin and M'Farlane.* 1799. 8vo, pp. 139, (9). H. 30314

HARDIE. An Account of the Malignant Fever, which prevailed in the City of New-York, ... 1805. Containing ... an Account of the ... Hospitals, ... Record of Deaths, &c. ... By James Hardy, A.M. *New York: Southwick & Hardcastle.* 1805. 8vo, pp. vii, 196. 30315

HARDIE. An Account of the Yellow Fever which occurred in the City of New York, in ... 1822. To which is prefixed a brief Sketch of the different Pestilential Diseases, with which this City was afflicted in the Years 1798, 1799, 1803 & 1805, ... To which is added ... List of all the Deaths ... during the late Season. ... By James Hardie, A.M. *New York: Samuel Marks.* 1822. 12mo, pp. iv, 120. 30316

HARDIE. The American Remembrancer, and Universal Tablet of Memory: containing a list of the most eminent men, ... also the most memorable events in history, from the earliest period to the year 1795. ... By James Hardie. ... *Philadelphia.* M,DCC,XCV. 12mo, pp. vi, (1), 259. C., H. 30317

HARDIE. A Census of the New Buildings erected in the City of New York in the year 1824. ... By James Hardy, A.M. *New York: Samuel Marks.* 1825. 12mo, pp. 48. 30318

HARDIE. The Description of the City of New-York; containing its Population, Institutions, Commerce, Manufactures, Public Buildings, Courts of Justice, Places of Amusements, &c. To which is prefixed, A Brief Account of its First Settlement by the Dutch, in the Year 1629, And of the most Remarkable Events, which have occurred in its History, from that to the Present Period. By James Hardie, A.M. *New-York: Samuel Marks.* 1827. 12mo, pp. (6), 360. C., H., N. 30319

HARDIE. A Dictionary of the Most Uncommon Wonders of the Works of Art and Nature, particularly of those, which are the most remarkable in America; ... By James Hardie, A.M. ... *New York: Printed by Samuel Marks.* 1819. 12mo, pp. xii, 338.

HARDIE. The History of the Tread Mill, containing an Account of its Origin, etc. With a General View of the Penitentiary System, etc. *New York.* 1824. 12mo, pp. 70. Plate.

HARDIE. The New Universal Biographical Dictionary and American Remembrancer of Departed Merit, containing Complete and Impartial Accounts of the Lives and Writings of Eminent Persons of every Age and Nation, but more especially those who have signalized themselves in America; Embellished with Portraits. *New York.* 1801. 4 vols., 8vo 30322

HARDIE. The Philadelphia Directory and Register ... . By James Hardie, A.M. *Philadelphia: The Author.* 1793. 8vo, pp. x, 234. BA., H. + The Second Edition. ... *Philadelphia: Jacob Johnson & Co.* 1794. 8vo, pp. (8), 232. Plan. H. 30323

HARDIE. A Short Account of the City of Philadelphia, and of the Different Charitable and Literary Institutions Therein. Embellished with a Correct Plan of the City. By James Hardie, A.M. *Philadelphia: Jacob Johnson & Co.* 1794. 8vo, pp. 40. Map. BA. 30324

HARDIMAN (H. M.) The Free Flag of Cuba; or, the Martyrdom of Lopez: a Tale of the Liberating Expedition of 1851, By H. M. Hardiman. *New York.* 1855. 12mo, pp. 206.

HARDIN (Benjamin). Speech of Mr. Hardin ... on Mr. Adams's Resolutions concerning the Loss of the Fortification Bill ... January 28, 1836. *Washington.* 1836. 8vo, pp. 28.

HARDIN (J. P.) Remarks of James P. Hardin in the House of Representatives of Kentucky, on the Importation of Slaves. [n. p. n. d.] 8vo, pp. 13. M. 30327

HARDIN (John J.) Speech of Mr. J. J. Hardin, ... reviewing the Public Life & Political Principles of Mr. Van Buren. ... March 21, 1844. *Washington.* [1844.] 8vo, pp. 32. C., M.

HARDING (A.) Speech of A. Harding of Kentucky, on Emancipation of Slaves in Rebel States. ... Dec. 17, 1861. [n. p. n. d.] 8vo, pp. 16. 30329

Also: Speech ... on the President's Two Proclamations, and the Two Rebellions, in the House of Representatives, January 21, 1863. [n. p. n. d.] 8vo, pp. 15.

HARDING (A.) Address, before the "Franklin R. A. Chapter," at Greenfield, Mass., on St. John's Day. By Alpheus Harding. *Wendell.* 1832. 8vo. 30330

Also: The Farewell Discourse ... Jan. 5, 1845, to the Congregational Church and Society in New Salem. *Barre: Albert Tyler.* 1845. 8vo, pp. 20.—Masonic Discourse at Princeton [Mass.], July 24, 1823. *Wendell.* 1823. 8vo. W.

HARDING (B.) A Tour through the Western Country, A.D. 1818 & 1819. By Benjamin Harding, Surveyor. Published for the Use of Emigrants. *New-London: Printed by Samuel Green for the Author.* 1819. 8vo, pp. (1), 17. C., H., W. 30331

HARDING (C.) My Egotistigraphy. By Chester Harding. Prepared for his Family and Friends, by one of his Children [M. E. White]. *Cambridge: Press of John Wilson and Son.* 1866. 12mo, pp. 185. C., H. 30332

Privately printed. Mr. Harding was an eminent artist.

HARDING (G.) Argument for the Complainant, in the Case of the State of Pennsylvania, *vs.* The Wheeling and Belmont Bridge Company ... . In Reply to Mr. Russell, by George Harding. *Washington.* 1851. 8vo, pp. 16. 30333

[HARDING.] ... In the Matter of Application of Samuel F. B. Morse, for an Extension for Seven Years of Letters Patent granted to him June 20th, 1840, reissued January 15th, 1846, and ... June 13th, 1848, for the Electro-Magnetic Recording Telegraph. Argument in Favor of the Extension. *Washington.* 1854. 8vo, pp. 40. 30334

[HARDING (J. D.)] ... Report of the Law Officers of the Crown ... in a Memorandum ... on the subject of the Fishery Convention with the Government of the United States in 1818, ... *London.* 1852. 8vo, pp. 6. H. 30335

Signed by J. D. Harding, Fred. T. Hesiger, Fitzroy Kelly.

HARDING (S. S.) Oration by Hon. S. S. Harding, Chief Justice of Colorado, delivered ... in the City of Denver, February 22d, 1864. *Denver, Colorado.* 1864. 8vo, pp. 36. 30336

[HARDING (W. M.)] Trans-Atlantic Sketches, by "Porte Plume." *New York: G. F. Nesbitt & Co.* 1870. 8vo, pp. 87.

[HARDINGE (B.)] Belle Boyd, in Camp and Prison. With an Introduction by a Friend to the South. *London: Saunders & Otley.* 1865. 2 vols., post 8vo, pp. xi, 291; xv, 280. Portrait.

[HARDINGE.] Belle Boyd in Camp and Prison. Written by Herself. With an Introduction by George Augustus Sala. *New York: Blelock & Co.* 1865. 12mo, pp. 464. BA. 30339

"Belle Boyd was a young woman of Martinsburg, Virginia; who was notorious as a skillful spy for Stonewall Jackson and other Rebel Generals, and she cloaked her career by seducing one Hardinge, a lieutenant of our navy, who fell in love with her; and for her sake, suffered the escape of a prisoner in his hands, and afterward deserted to the enemy and married Miss Boyd."—*Evening Post, Aug.* 3, 1865.

HARDINGE (E.) "America and her Destiny:" Inspirational Discourse given extemporaneously at Dodworth's Hall, New York, ... August 25, 1861, through Emma Hardinge, by the Spirits. *New York: Robert M. De Witt.* [1861.] 8vo, pp. 15. + Second Edition. [*Ibid.*] 30340

HARDINGE. The Great Funeral Oration on Abraham Lincoln. By Miss Emma Hardinge. Delivered April 16, 1865, at Cooper Institute, New York, before upwards of three thousand persons. *New York: American News Company.* [1865.] 8vo, pp. 28. 30341

HARDINGE. Modern American Spiritualism; a Twenty Years' Record of the Communion between Earth and the World of Spirits. By Emma Hardinge. *New York: The Author.* 1870. 8vo, pp. 565. 2 Plates, 13 Portraits. C. 30342

A record of infatuation would be a better title.

HARDMAN (F.) Scenes and Adventures in Central America. Edited by Frederick Hardman ... . *Edinburgh and London.* 1852. 8vo, pp. (7), 298. C., H., P. 30343

Principally adventures in Louisiana, Texas and Northern Mexico. *See* Jerrmann (Edward). Reprinted as:

HARDMAN. Frontier Life; or, Scenes and Adventures in the Southwest. By F. Hardman. *Auburn: Derby & Miller.* 1853. 12mo. + New Edition. [*Ibid.*] 12mo, pp. 376. 30344

Hard-Scrabble Callendar. Report of the Trials of Oliver Cummins, Nathaniel G. Metcalf, Gilbert Humes and Arthur Farrier, who were indicted with six others for a Riot, and for aiding in pulling down a Dwelling House, on the 18th October, at Hard-Scrabble. *Providence: Printed for the Purchaser.* 1824. 8vo, pp. 32. 30345

HARDWICK, *Mass.* Report of the Selectmen of Hardwick, for the Year ending March 1 1867. ... *Boston.* 1867. 8vo, pp. 60.

Report of the Selectmen and Overseers of the Poor of Hardwick, ... February 15, 1868. *Barre.* [1868.] 8vo, pp. 14.

HARDY (Arthur S.) Oration delivered in the Chapel of the U. S. Military Academy, July 4th, 1868, by Cadet Hardy. ... [*West Point.* 1868.] 8vo, pp. 15. 30348

HARDY (C.) Forest Life in Acadie. Sketches of Sport and Natural History in the Lower Provinces of the Canadian Dominion. By Captain Campbell Hardy, ... *London: Chapman & Hall.* 1869. 8vo, pp. viii, (1), 371. 12 Plates. 30349

Includes many incidents of personal association with the Micmac and Milicete Indians. Some copies have the imprint, *New York: D. Appleton & Co.* 1869.

HARDY. Sporting Adventures in the New World; or, Days and Nights of Moose-Hunting in the Pine Forests of Acadia. By Lieut. Campbell Hardy, ... *London: Hurst & Blackett.* 1855. 2 vols., post 8vo, pp. xii, 304; viii, 299. H. 30350

Contains many particulars concerning the Micmac Indians.

HARDY (*Sir* Charles). Chronological List of the Captains of the Royal Navy, from June 1673 to 1788. By Rear Admiral Hardy. 1779. Oblg. 4to. 30351

HARDY. An Address to his Excellency Sir Charles Hardy, Captain General and Governor in Chief of the Province of New-York ... By the Author of a Weekly Paper, entitled, The Watch-Tower. [J. P. Zenger.] *New York.* 1755. Folio, pp. xiii.

HARDY (D.) Poems. By D. Hardy, Jr. With a Biographical Sketch. *New York.* 1858. 18mo, pp. 260. S. 30353

H[ARDY] (J[ohn]). A | Description | of the | Last Voyage | to | Bermudas, | In the Ship | Marygold, | S. P. Commander; | By J. H. φιλοχειρηρνεία. | Begun November the twelfth, 1670. And ending | May the third, 1671. | With Allowance. | *London, printed for Rowland Reynald at the Sun and Bible | in the Poultrey* 1671. | 4to, pp. (8), 24 [in verse]. 30354

Ternaux (No. 796) quotes this under the date 1661.

HARDY (John). Startling Developments of Crim. Con.! Or Two Mormon Apostles exposed ... in Boston ... . *Boston.* 1844. 8vo, pp. 12. 30355

HARDY (——). The History and Adventures of the Cuban Expedition, from the first movements down to the dispersion of the army at Key West, and the Arrest of General Lopez. Also;

an account of the ten Deserters at Isla de Mugeres. By Lieutenant Hardy, of the Kentucky Battalion. *Lorenzo Stratton Cincinnati.* 1856. 8vo, pp. 94. 30356

HARDY (R. W. H.) Travels in the Interior of Mexico, in 1825, 1826, 1827, & 1828. By Lieut. R. W. H. Hardy, R.N. *London: Henry Colburn and Richard Bentley.* 1829. 8vo, pp. xiv, 540. Map and 7 Plates. C., S. 30357

"Mr. Hardy was sent out to search for pearls in the Gulf of California. His book is full of information on the little-known regions of Sonora and Lower California."

[HARDY (S.)] A Guide to Heaven From the Word: or, Good Counsel How to close savingly with Christ. *Boston: Samuel Green.* 1689. 8vo. + *Boston.* 1717. 48mo, pp. 72. B.

"Ye author of this Book was one Mr. Hardy. vid Calamy's acct. of eiected ministers."—*MS. Note of Mr. Prince.* A book with this title is mentioned at page 283 of Calamy's "Account," but the meaning ascribed by Calamy to that title is so very inappropriate to the present work, as to suggest a doubt whether Mr. Prince was correct in identifying the two.

HARDY (W.) Sketch of the Proceedings and Trial of William Hardy, on an Indictment for the Murder of an Infant, November 27, 1806, ... at Boston. *Boston.* 1807. 8vo, pp. 47.

HARE (C. W.) An Address to the Citizens of Pennsylvania relative to the Election for Governor. By C. W. Hare, Esq. *Philadelphia.* 1808. 8vo. P. 30360

HARE. Oration delivered before the Washington Benevolent Society of Pennsylvania. At their first Anniversary Meeting, February 22d, 1813. By Charles W. Hare, Esq ... *Philadelphia: Printed for the Society by T. J. Stiles.* 1813. 8vo, pp. 20.

[HARE (*Dr.*)] Sermon ... Society for the Propagation of Christian Knowledge. By Dr. Hare, Bishop of Chichester. [n. p.] 1735. 4to, pp. 86. M. 30362

[HARE (Francis).] *See* Vol. I., No. 915.

HARE (J. I. C.) Opinion of Hon. J. I. Clark Hare, of ... Philadelphia, upon the Constitutionality of the Acts of Congress of February 5th, 1862. Declaring United States Notes "Lawful Money" and a "Legal Tender." [*Philadelphia:*] *King & Baird.* [n. d.] 8vo, pp. 16. H. 30363

HARE (J. T.) The Life and Adventures of Joseph T. Hare, the ... Highwayman ... *New York.* [n. d.] 8vo. 30364

HARE. Trials of the Mail Robbers [John] Hare, Alexander and [Lewis] Hare, with the Testimony, the Proceedings, ... reported by Edward J. Coale; ... with the Trial ... of William Wood, an Accessary before the Fact. ... *Baltimore: Edward J. Coale.* 1818. 8vo, pp. 220. BA. 30665

HARE (R.) A Brief Exposition of the Injury done to the Community, and especially to the Poor, by the Prohibition of Bills under Five Dollars, while such Bills are permitted to Circulate in adjoining States. In a Letter to William B. Reed, Esq. Also, a Subsequent Letter on the Failure of the late Effort to Resume Specie Payments. To which is annexed a Scheme for a National Currency. By Robert Hare. *Philadelphia.* 1841. 8vo, pp. 12. B., N. 30366

[HARE.] Defence of the American Character: ... . *Philadelphia.* 1819. 8vo, pp. 12. BA. 30367

HARE. Suggestions respecting the Reformation of the Banking System. By R. Hare, M.D. *Philadelphia: John C. Clark.* 1837. 8vo, pp. 29. BA., C., H., N. 30368

[HARE.] A Brief View of the Policy and Resources of the United States; comprising ... Strictures on a Letter on the Genius and Dispositions of the French Government. ... *Philadelphia: Bradford & Inskeep.* 1810. 8vo, pp. viii, 3–133. BA.

Also: An Effort to Refute the Opinion that no Addition is made to the Capital of a Community by Banking.—Proofs that Credit as Money ... is ... preferable to Coin. *Philadelphia.* 1834. 8vo, pp. 12.—Testimonials ... submitted to the Trustees of the University of Pennsylvania. *Philadelphia.* 12mo. *See* "Vindication of the Cherokee Claims," Vol. IV., No. 12476, which has been attributed to Dr. Hare.

HAREWOOD IRON AND MINING CO., *St. Lawrence County, New York.* Report of Directors ... . *Boston: Geo. C. Rand & Avery.* 1864. 8vo, pp. 16. 30370

HARFORD (J.) Merchants' Directory for 1865 and 1866, containing a List of the Principal Manufacturers and Wholesale Dealers in New York City, with Map, etc. By Joseph Harford. *New York.* 1865. 18mo. C. 30371

Also, for 1866 and 1867. *New York: Harford & Co.* 1866. 24mo, pp. 208.

HARFORD (J. S.) Some Account of the Life, Death and Principles of Thomas Paine, together with Remarks on his Writings; and on their intimate connection with the avowed objects of the Revolutionists of 1793 and of the Radicals in 1819. By John S. Harford Esq. *Bristol: J. M. Gutch.* 1819. 8vo, pp. viii, 93. 30372

HARFORD, *Pa.* First Annual Catalogue of the Officers and Students of Harford University, Harford, Susquehanna County, Pa., From Sept. 1, 1849, to June 1, 1851. *"Montrose Democrat" Print, Montrose, Pa.* 1851. 8vo, pp. 18, (1). 30373

HARGRAVE (Francis). An Argument in the case of James Sommersett a Negro, Lately determined by the Court of King's Bench: Wherein it is attempted to demonstrate the present Unlawfulness of Domestic Slavery in England. To which is prefixed a State of the Case. By Mr. Hargrave, one of the Counsel for the Negro. *London: Printed for the Author:* ... M. DCC. LXXII. 8vo, pp. 32. BA. + *Boston, reprinted.* 1774. 8vo, pp. 56. + *London.* MDCCLXXVIII. 4to. A., C., P. 30374

"In this tract we meet with considerable learning, and with much precision of thought and expression. It appears not however in our opinion, to exhibit a very masterly view of its subject."—*Monthly Review,* XLVII. 421. This case decided the freedom of every man of color on his landing in Great Britain.

HARGROVE (J.) The Substance of a Sermon, on the Leading Doctrines of the New Jerusalem Church; ... the 26th December, 1802, before the President of the United States, and ... Congress ... Washington. By John Hargrove. [n. p.:] *Printed by Warner & Hanna.* 1803. 8vo, pp. 24. N. 30375

HARIOT (T.) Artis Analyticæ Praxis ad æquationes Algebraicas nova, expedita et generali methodi resolvendas: Tractatus e posthumis T. H. schediasmatis descriptus. [Edente W. Warner.] *Londini: Barker.* 1631. Folio. 30376

This posthumous work of Hariot contains interesting information concerning the personal history of that author. It was edited by Walter Warner.

HARIOT. A briefe and true re- | port of the new found land of Virginia: of | the commodities there found and to be raysed, as well mar- | chantable, as others for victuall, building and other necessa- | rie vses for those that are and shalbe [*sic*] the planters there, and of the na- | ture and manners of the naturall inhabitants: Discouered by the | English Colony there seated by Sir Richard Greinuile Knight in the yeere 1585, which remained· vnder the gouernment of Rafe Lane Esqui- | er, one of her Maiesties Esquieres, during the space of twelue monethes: at | the speciall charge and direction of the Honourable Sir | Walter Raleigh Knight, Lord Warden of | the stanneries; who therein hath been fauou- | red and authorised by her Maiestie and | her letters patent: | Directed to the Adventurers, Fauourers, | and Welwillers of the action, for the inhabi- | ting and planting there: | By

Thomas Hariot; seruant to the abouenamed | Sir Walter, a member of the Colony, and | there employed in discouering. | *Imprinted at London* 1588. | 4to, 23 leaves. 30377

A work of great rarity. We have seen only one copy, belonging to Mr. James Lenox. There is a copy in the Grenville Library at the British Museum, and another in the Bodleian Library at Oxford; and strange to relate a copy was sold at Dublin, in December, 1873, with five other rare pieces relating to America, for less than £25—the real value was at least ten times that sum. Lowndes does not even so much as mention Hariot, and in searching the works of other eminent bibliographers our success has been *nil*; the ominous gap remained unfilled. Rich silently passes over "anno 1588," and Stevens, in all his "Nuggets," had it not. It remained for Brunet alone to describe the work. Heber did not let it escape his all-devouring, still insatiate maw, and from that source Brunet gets his title. It is included in De Bry's Collection, and forms the rarest volume of that series, which is described in *our* Vol. III., pp. 24–30. An abridged English version is included in Hakluyt's Collection, Vol. III. For a German version *see* Dresser, Vol. v., No. 20926.

[HARISON (Francis).] The Report of the Committee of His Majesty's Council, To whom it was Referred, To Examine and make Enquiry, touching a Letter found in the House of Mr. Alexander in New-York, on Friday the First Day of February, 1733–4. In Order To Make the fullest Discovery concerning the Author of the same. *New-York: Printed and Sold by William Bradford.* 1734. Folio, pp. 11. P. 30378

New York arms on title. A threatening letter to Mrs. Alexander, to extort money, was left at Mr. James Alexander's, and was attributed by him to the Hon. Francis Harison, a political opponent. *See* Zenger's "New York Journal," of February 4 and 19; and March 11 and 19, 1733.

HARISON. To the Right Worshipful, the Mayor, Aldermen and Commonalty of the City of New-York. ... Francis Harison. *Printed and Sold by William Bradford in New-York.* 1734. Folio, pp. 9. P., S. 30379

No title-page; dated March 12, 1733–4. Mr. Harison's vindication.

HARISON. The Vindication of James Alexander, one of His Majesty's Council for the Province of New-York; and of William Smith, Attorney at Law. From the Matters charged and suggested against them in two Pamphlets lately published. The One a Paper addressed to the Mayor, Aldermen and Commonalty of the City of New-York, by the Honourable Francis Harison, Esq; one of His Majesty's Council for the Province of New-York. The Other a Report of the Committee of His Majesty's Council, to whom it was referred to examine and make enquiry touching a Letter found in the House of Mr. Alexander, on Fryday the 1st of February, 1733–4, in order to make the fullest Discovery concerning the Author of the same. To which is added a Supplement containing a brief Account of the Case of

William Trusdell, Plaintiff, against the Honourable Francis Harison, Esq; Defendant. For Arresting and imprisoning the Plaintiff and keeping him 9 Weeks in Prison, at the Suit of Joseph Weldon, without the Assent, Consent, or Knowledge of the same Joseph Weldon. Which Cause was tried in the Supreme Court of New-York, on the 19th of April, 1734. wherein the Jury found for the Plaintiff Trusdell £150 Damages, and Costs of Suit. *Printed by John Peter Zenger, and to be sold by him at his House in Broad Street, near the upper End of the long Bridge, in New-York.* 1734. Folio, pp. 20. P. 30380

[HARISON (W. H.)] Trinity Church Title. An Exposure of Miller's Letter, with Documents, &c., Addressed to the late Commissioners of the Land Office. *Albany: Joel Munsell.* MDCCCLVI. 8vo, pp. 46. S. 30381

HARIZON (A. de). Vozes que hizieron eco, en la religiosa pyra, que en las honras del V. P. Fr. Antonio Margil de Jesus, erigió N. R. P. Fr. Antonio de Harizon, el dia 21 de Agosto de 1726 en el Convento de N. S. P. S. Francisco de la Imperial Ciudad de Mexico. *Mexico.* [1726.] 4to, pp. (34), 56.

HARKER (*Rev.* Samuel). An Appeal from the Synod of New-York and Philadelphia, to the Christian World ... Written by Himself. *Philadelphia: Printed by William Dunlap.* M,DCC,-LXIII. 8vo, pp. 40. BA., M. 30383

HARKNESS (E.) The Disposition of the Mineral Lands. By Edson Harkness, of Eldorado County, California. *Washington, D. C.: McGill & Witherow, Printers.* 1865. 8vo, pp. 16. H.

Harlaem River: its Use previous to and since the Revolutionary War. ... *New York.* 1857. 8vo. S. 30385

HARLAN (J.) Admission of Kansas. Speech of Hon. James Harlan, of Iowa, in the Senate ... March 27, 1856. [n. p. n. d.] 8vo, pp. 14. 30386

Also: The Constitution Upheld and Maintained. Speech ... [n. p. 1864.] 8vo, pp. 8.—The Democratic Party: ... Speech ... June 22nd, 1859 ... . *Mt. Pleasant, Iowa.* 1859. 8vo, pp. 13.—Legal Title to Property in Slaves. Speech ... on the Amendment to the Constitution, delivered in the United States Senate, April 6, 1864. [n. p. n. d.] 8vo, pp. 8.—Reconstruction. Speech ... February 10, 1868. *Washington: F. & J. Rives & Geo. A. Bailey.* 1868. 8vo, pp. 16. H.—"Service of the Militia." Speech ... July 11, 1862. [n. p. n. d.] 8vo, pp. 16.—Shall the Territories be Africanized? Speech ... January 4, 1860. [n. p. n. d.] 8vo, pp. 8. H.—Speech ... April 14, 1856, on the Kansas Legislative Petition.—Speech ... on the Lecompton Constitution ... January 25, 1858. *Washington.* 1858. 8vo, pp. 14.—State of the Union. Speech ... January 11, 1861. [n. p. n. d.] 8vo, pp. 15. H.

HARLAN (M. B.) Ellen; or, the Chained Mother, and Pictures of Kentucky Slavery, Drawn from Real Life. By Mrs. Mary B. Harlan. *Cincinnati: Applegate & Co.* 1853. 12mo, pp. 260. C. 30387

HARLAN (R.) American Herpetology; or, Genera of the North American Reptilia, with a Synopsis of the Species. By Richard Harlan, M.D. *Philadelphia.* 1827. 8vo, pp. 88. P.

HARLAN. Beschreibung der in der grossen Knochen Höhle—Tennessee (Nord-America) Gefundenen Fossilen Knochen des Megalonyx Lagueatus. Von R. Harlan, M.D. ... [n. p. n. d.] 8vo, pp. 28. H. 30389

HARLAN. Fauna Americana: being a Description of the Mammiferous Animals inhabiting North America. By Richard Harlan, M.D. ... *Philadelphia: Anthony Finley.* 1825. 8vo, pp. 318, (2). BA., P. 30390

HARLAN. Genera of the North American Reptilia, and a Synopsis of the Species in Medical and Physical Researches. By Richard Harlan, M.D. *Philadelphia.* 1835. 8vo. A. 30391

HARLAN. Medical and Physical Researches; or, Original Memoirs in Medicine, Surgery, Physiology, Geology, Zoology, and Comparative Anatomy. By Richard Harlan, M.D. *Philadelphia: Printed by Lydia R. Bailey.* 1835. 8vo, pp. xxxix, 653. 1 Table, 39 Plates. A., C. 30392

[HARLAN.] Refutation of Certain Misrepresentations issued against the Author of "Fauna Americana," in the Philadelphia Franklin Journal, No. 1, 1826, and in the North American Review, No. 50. *Philadelphia: William Stavely.* 1826. 8vo, pp. 42.

See Godman (John D.), Jackson (Samuel). Also: Description of the Elephant Tortoise. ... *Philadelphia.* 1826. 8vo.—Description of an Hermaphrodite Orang-Outang lately in Philadelphia. ... *Philadelphia.* 1826. 8vo.—Observations on the Genus Salamandra, and Description of a New Genus of Quadrupeds of the order Edentata (Chlamyphorus) ... *New York.* 1824. 8vo. P.—Zoological and Medical Miscellany. ... *Philadelphia.* 1826. 8vo. P.

HARLAND (Marion), *pseudon.* *See* Terhune (Mary V. H.)

THE HARLEIAN MISCELLANY; or a collection of scarce, curious and entertaining Pamphlets and Tracts, as well in Manuscript as in Print, found in the late Earl of Oxford's Library, inspersed with Historical, Political and Critical Notes. ... [By W. Oldys.] *London: T. Osborne.* 1744–46. 8 vols., 4to. H.

+ [The Same.] *London.* 1753. 8 vols., 8vo. H. + With Additional Notes by Thomas Park. *London.* 1808–13. 10 vols., 4to. + *London: Robert Dutton.* 1808–11. B., BA. 30394

12 vols., 8vo, pp. xx, 547, (3); viii, 566, (4); xi, 561, (5); viii, 571, (4); xii, 582, (5); vii, 552, (6); xii, 9–608, (4); xii, 574, (6); x, 561, (4); viii, 568, (4); iv, 557, (6); 284, (7), cxxxi. The 8vo edition, 1808, was edited by J. Malham, and also published on large paper. It includes reprints of Harcourt's "Voyage to Guiana," "The Trades Increase," "Declaration of the Demeanor of Sir W. Raleigh," and other Tracts on America. Dibdin observes, "I hardly know of any one collection or set of volumes, likely to be productive of more varied entertainment." Park's is the best edition, as it contains two additional volumes. *See also* "A Selection."

[HARLOW (Laurence).] The Conversion of an Indian: In a Letter to a Friend. *Printed in the Year* 1774. 12mo. + The Third Edition. *Printed in the Year* 1788. 12mo, pp. 18.

HARLOW (S. R.), *and* BOONE (H. H.) Life Sketches of the State Officers, Senators, and Members of the Assembly of the State of New York, in 1867. By Samuel R. Harlow and H. H. Boone. *Albany: Weed, Parsons & Co.* 1867. 8vo, pp. 418. Plate. C., S. 30396

HARLOW *and* HUTCHINS (S. C.) Life Sketches of the State Officers, Senators, and Members of the Assembly of the State of New York, in 1868. By S. R. Harlow and S. C. Hutchins. *Albany: Weed, Parsons & Co.* 1868. 8vo, pp. 402. Portrait. S.

HARMAN (J.) The Crooked Disciple's Remarks upon the Blind Guide's Method of Preaching; the Rhapsodies, Hyperboles, and incongruities of the Sacred and Profane, made use of by the Rev. Dr. Squintum at Tottenham-Court, etc., by Mr. John Harman, Regulator of Enthusiasts. [*London.* n. d.]

This is an attack upon the Rev. George Whitefield.

HARMAN. Remarks upon the Life, Character and Behaviour of the Rev. George Whitefield, as written by Himself, from the time of his Birth, to the time he departed from his Tabernacle. Demonstrating by Astronomical Calculation, that his Ascension, Meridian, and Declination were necessarily actuated by Planetary Influence; and that his Doctrine was not from Divine Mission, but from a mere Fatality, evident as daily seen in the Fatal Catastrophe of his unhappy, gloomy, and misguided followers. The whole being a choice New Year's Gift for Methodists. By John Harman, Astronomer. *London: Printed for the Author.* MDCCLXIV. 8vo, pp. 48. 30399

HARMANSON (John H.) Speech ... June 24, 1846, ... [on] the Tariff. [*Washington.* 1846.] 8vo, pp. 8. 30400

Also: Speech ... on the Independent Treasury Bill. ... April 1, 1846. *Washington: Blair and Rives.* 1846. 8vo, pp. 8.

HARMAR (J.) The Proceedings of a Court of Inquiry, Held at the Special Request of Bregadier-General Josiah Harmar, to investigate his Conduct, as Commanding Officer of the Expedition against the Miami Indians, 1790; The same having been transmitted by Major-General St. Clair, to the Secretary of the United States, for the Department of War. Published by Authority. *Philadelphia: Printed by John Fenno.* M.DCC.XCI. Folio, pp. (4), 31. S. 30401

An extremely rare, and somewhat important trial.

HARMER (J.) Address, on St. John's Day, before Fortitude Lodge, No. 84. By John Harmer. *Brooklyn.* 1811. 16mo.

HARMON. A Manual of the Pension Laws of the United States of America, embracing all the Laws under which Pensions, Bounties, and Bounty Lands are now Granted, with Forms and Instructions. To this is added a Digest of the Most Important Decisions, etc., etc. *Washington: W. H. & O. H. Morrison.* 186–. 8vo, pp. x, 397. 30403

HARMON (D. W.) A Journal of Voyages and Travels in the interiour of North America, between the 47th and 58th Degrees of North Latitude, extending from Montreal nearly to the Pacific Ocean, a distance of about 5,000 miles, Including an account of the Principal Occurrences, during a Residence of nineteen Years, in different parts of the Country. To which is added a concise description of the face of the Country, its Inhabitants, their Manners, Customs, Religion, etc., and considerable specimens of the two Languages, Most extensively Spoken; together with an account of the Principal Animals, to be found in the Forests and Prairies of this extensive Region. Illustrated by a Map of the Country. By Daniel Williams Harmon, a Partner in the North-West Company. *Andover: Flagg and Gould.* 1820. 8vo, pp. 432. Portrait and Map. B., BA., C., S. 30404

"Revised and edited by Mr. Daniel Haskell, who is said to have introduced religious reflections not made by the author. Harmon's narration of events among, and peculiarities of, the Indian tribes is believed by those familiar with him, and the regions he visited, to be correct; but the life of a fur-trader, dispensing fire-water to the Indians, while daily witnessing the murders it produced, was not favorable to religious emotions. Mr. Haskell makes the writer reject the proffer of an Indian concubine by her father, with very proper pious emotions; but Mr. Schoolcraft intimates that the latter were not more consonant with his character than the story of his continence."—FIELD. *See also* Greenhow's "Oregon," p. 291.

HARMON (J.), *Jr.* The Columbian Sacred Minstrel. By John Harmon, Jr. *Northampton, Mass.* 1809. Oblong 4to. N.

Harmony Grove. *See* Salem, *Mass.*

The Harmony of Interests. *See* [Carey (H. C.)]

Harmony of Wisdom and Felicity in relation to our Civil, Moral, and Spiritual Behaviour. *Boston.* 1743. 12mo. 30406

Harmony Society. *See* Raph (G.)

HARNDEN (H.) Narrative of the Apprehension in Ridge, N. H., of the Rev. E. K. Avery, charged with the Murder of Sarah M. Cornell: together with the Proceedings of the Inhabitants of Fall River. By Harvey Harnden. *Providence: W. Marshall & Co.* 1833. 8vo, pp. 36. 30407

HARNEY (E. E.) Speech of Hon. E. E. Harney on the Bell Resolutions ... February 7, 1858. [n. p. n. d.] 8vo. 30408

HARNEY (W[illiam] S.) Official Correspondence of Brig. Gen. W. S. Harney, U. S. Army, and First Lt. Geo. Ihrie, Late U. S. Army, with the U. S. War Department ... . [*Washington.* 1861.] 8vo, pp. 16. 30409

[HARO (Cristoffel de).] Copia der Newen Zeytung. *See* Vol. II, Nos. 7559 and 7560.

HARO (D. L. de). Constitvciones sinodales, hechas por e Ill. y Reuer. señor Don fray Damian Lopez de Haro, Obispo de la ciudad de San Juã de Puerto-Rico, Islas de Barlouento, Prouincia de Cumana, y demas anexas à ella. *Madrid, por Catalina de Barrio y Angulo,* 1647. Folio, 3 l., Text, 128 l. 30410

"Ces constitutions diocésaines, destinées, à être distribuées dans le diocèse, sont par cette raison très-rares en Europe, aussi ni Antonio, ni Ternaux n'en font mention."—LECLERC, whose copy sold for 50 francs.

HARO Y PERALTA (A. N. de). Constituciones para el mejor regimen y govierno del real colegio seminario ... fundado en el Pueblo de Tepotzotlan. Por Alonso Nunez de Haro y Peralta ... *Mexico: Zuñiga.* 1777. 4to, pp. (8), 87. 30411

Also: Carta Pastoral al Rector, &c., del Real Colegio de Tepotzotlan, y à todos los Sacerdotes y demás Clerigos en nuestro Arzobispado. *Mexico.* 1776. 4to.—Carta Pastoral a todos sus amados diocesanos, sobre la Doctrina sana, y à las mas esenciales obligaciones que tene mos para con Dios y para con el Rey. *Mexico.* 1777. 4to.—Relacion de la funebre Ceremonia y Exequias del ilustrisimo Señor Doctor Don Ildefonso Nuñez de Haro y Peralta, Arzobispo que fue de esta santa iglesia Metropolitana de Mexico. Virey y Capitan General de esta Nueva España, etc., dispuesta por un Presbitero de este Arzobispado. *Mexico.* 1802. 4to, pp. 80, 26, xlviii.

HARO Y TAMARIZ (Antonio de). Á sus compatriotas. [n. p.] 1856. 4to, pp. 20. 30412

HAROLD (J.) The Unanimous Decision and Action of the Presbytery of Nassau, January 14th and January 25th, 1865, in the judicial case of John Harold, *versus* The Session of Christ's First Church, Hempstead, L. I. *New York: G. A. Whitehorne, Printer.* 1865. 8vo. 30413

HAROLD (William Vincent). Sermon ... in the Catholic Church ... Baltimore, November 1st, 1810, on Occasion of the Consecration of the Rt. Rd. Dr. John Cheverus, Bishop of Boston. By the Rev. W. V. Harold, one of the Pastors of St. Mary's Church, Philadelphia. ... *Baltimore: Bernard Dornin.* 1810. 8vo, pp. 20. BA., H., W. 30414

See [Carey (M.)], Vol. III., and add to the "Rejoinder" Second Edition: [*Ibid.*] 1822.

HAROLDVS (F. Franciscvs). Lima Limata conciliis, constitvtionibvs synodalibvs, et aliis monvmentis. Qvibvs venerab. servvs dei Toribivs Alphonsvs Mogroveivs archiepisc. Limanvs prouinciam Limensem, seu Peruanum Imperium elimanuit et ad normam SS. Canonum composuit. Omnia ferè ex hispanico sermone latina reddidit, apparatu historico, notis, scholiis, et indicibus illustravit Fr. Fr. Haroldvs Hibernvs Limericensis ord. minor. *Romæ, Josephi Corvi,* 1673. Folio, pp. (32), xxxiv, Portrait of D. Torribio, pp. 379, (22). 30415

"Volume fort rare, traduit de l'espagnol en latin, par un moine Irlandais. Non cité par Ternaux. Lowndes, dans son "Manuel bibliographique," ne fait pas mention de cet ouvrage, quoique il indique une vie de S. Torribio de Lima par le même auteur, imprimée à Rome en 1680 (1684 Pinelo, qui cite une autre édition des Constitutions synodales des conciles de Lima, sous la date de 1725)." Title and note from Leclerc. Bohn's edition of Lowndes makes no mention of the work referred to.

HAROLDVS. Thuribi Alphonsi Mogroveii Archiepiscopi Limensis, Vita exemplaris per Fr. F. Haroldum, Ord. Minor. Hibernum Limericensem conscripta. *Romæ,* 1680. 4to. Portrait.

This rare volume contains the history of the ecclesiastical affairs of Peru during a great part of the sixteenth century, and an account of the modes employed for the conversion of the Indians.

Harp of the Beech Woods. Original Poems. *Montrose, Pa.: Adam Waldie.* 1822. 12mo, pp. xi, 156. 30417

Harp and the Plow. *See* [Canning (J. D.)]

HARPER (C.) Memoir on Slavery, read before the Society for the Advancement of Learning, of South Carolina ... at Co-

lumbia. 1837. By Chancellor Harper. *Charleston: James S. Burges.* 1838. 8vo, pp. 61. B. 3 418

HARPER (C. C.) An Address ... at the ... Meeting of the Maryland State Colonization Society ... of Annapolis, January 23, 1835. By Charles C. Harper. *Baltimore: Printed by Sands & Neilson.* 1835. 8vo, pp. 12. H. 30419

HARPER [Joseph M.] Mr. Harper's Report to the Legislature of ... New-Hampshire on the Culture of Silk. [*Canterbury.* 1830.] 8vo, pp. 32. H. 30420

HARPER (L.) Preliminary Report of the Geology and Agriculture of the State of Mississippi. By L. Harper, LL.D. *Jackson, State Printer.* 1857. 8vo, pp. vii, 351. Colored Map, 7 Plates, etc. C. 30421

HARPER (R. D.) The Church Manual, containing Important Historical Facts and Reminiscences connected with the Associate and Associated Reformed Churches, previous to their union as the United Presbyterian Church of North America. By Rev. R. D. Harper ... Xenia, Ohio. *Fleming & Hamill, Xenia, Ohio.* 1859. 30422

HARPER (R. G.) An Address from Robert Goodloe Harper, of South-Carolina to his Constituents. Containing his Reasons for Approving of the Treaty of Amity, Commerce, and Navigation, with Great-Britain. *Philadelphia.* 1795. 8vo, pp. 35. S. + *Boston: Young & Minns.* 1796. 12mo, pp. 36. B., BA., H.

HARPER. Address ... to his Constituents; ... with a Letter from Governor Jay, explaining his Sentiments respecting the French Revolution. *New York.* 1796. 8vo. N. + *Philadelphia.* 1796. 8vo, pp. 44. M. 30424

HARPER. An Argument against the Policy of re-opening the African Slave Trade. By Robert G. Harper, Esq. *Atlanta, Georgia: Printed by C. R. Hanleiter.* 1858. 8vo, pp. 78. B.

HARPER. Correspondence respecting Russia, between Robert Goodloe Harper, Esq. and Robert Walsh, Jr. together with the Speech of Mr. Harper, Commemorative of the Russian Victories, delivered at Georgetown, D. C., June 5th, 1813, and an Essay on the Future States of Europe. *Philadelphia.* 1813. 8vo, pp. 140. B., H. 30426

HARPER. General Harper's Speech to the Citizens of Baltimore on the Expediency of promoting a Connexion between the Ohio, at Pittsburgh, and of the Waters of the Chesapeake, at Baltimore, by a Canal through the District of Columbia, with his Reply to some of the Objections of Mr. Winchester, delivered ... on the 20th day of December, 1823. *Baltimore: E. T. Coale.* 1824. 8vo, pp. 78. Map. C., P. 30427

HARPER. A Letter from Robert Goodloe Harper ... to his Constituents. ... *Portsmouth: Printed by Charles Peirce.* 1801. 8vo, pp. 16. B., H., N., W. + [*Cambridge:*] *William Hilliard, Printer.* 1801. 8vo, pp. 16. B., BA., H., M. 30428

Probably a reprint of our No. 30443, *infra.*

HARPER. A Letter from General Harper, of Maryland, to Elias B. Caldwell. *Baltimore.* 1818. 8vo, pp. 32. 30429

HARPER. Mr. Harper's Speech on the Foreign Intercourse Bill, in Reply to Mr. Nicholas and Mr. Gallatin. Delivered in ... House of Representatives of the United States, on ... the second of March, 1798. [n. p. n. d.] 8vo, pp. 43. B., H. + [n. p. n. d.] 8vo, pp. 57. H. + *Washington.* 1798. M., N.

See "M. Rev.," XXVI. 225. Reprinted as: Speech of R. Goodloe Harper, Esq. ... on Friday, March 2, 1798. *London: J. Wright.* 8vo, pp. 73. P.

HARPER. Observations on the Dispute between the United States and France, addressed by Robert Goodloe Harper, of South Carolina, to his Constituents, in May, 1797. *Philadelphia: Thomas Bradford.* 1797. 8vo, pp. 102. BA., H., P. + Second Edition. 1797. 12mo. P. + *London: John Stockdale.* 1797. 8vo, pp. 162. + *Philadelphia: William Cobbett.* 1798. 8vo, pp. 112. + [Another Edition.] *Philadelphia.* 1798. 8vo, pp. 92. + Third Edition. *Philadelphia.* 1798. 8vo, pp. 104. + Third American Edition. *Philadelphia: William Cobbett.* 1798. 8vo, pp. 96. H.

HARPER. Observations on the Dispute between the United States and France, addressed by Robert Goodloe Harper, Esq. One of the Delegates of South Carolina (a State at one time, the most devoted to the French interest of any in the Union) to his Constituents, in May, 1797. *London: Philanthropic Press.* 1797. 8vo, pp. 162. + Second Edition. [*Ibid.*] 8vo, pp. viii, 5–109, (2). + Third Edition. *Philadelphia, Printed. Dublin, Reprinted: P. Byrne.* M,DCC,XCVIII. 8vo, pp. 160. + [Another] Third Edition. *Dublin: William Walter and Son.* M.DCC.XCVIII. 8vo, pp. 160. + Fourth Edition. *Dublin.* M,DCC,XCVIII. 8vo, pp. 91. + Fifth Edition. *London: John Stockdale.* 1798. 8vo, pp. 109.

HARPER. Observations on the Dispute between the United States and France, addressed By Robert Goodloe Harper, Esq. One of the Representatives in Congress for the State of South Carolina, To his Constituents, in May 1797, ... Second Edition. *Philadelphia Printed. London Reprinted ... and Sold by Debrett and Wright, ... and by all other Booksellers Except John Stockdale,* 1789. 8vo, pp. viii, 5–109, (1). + Third Edition. [*Ibid.*] + Fourth Edition. [*Ibid.*] 8vo, pp. viii, 5–109, (2). B. + Fifth Edition. [*Ibid.*] 12mo, pp. (8), 7–86. + Sixth Edition. [*Ibid.*] 8vo, pp. viii, 5–109, (1). 30433

See an explanation of the note "sold by all booksellers except by John Stockdale" at back of title-page.

HARPER. Observations on the Dispute between the United States and France, addressed By Robert Goodloe Harper, Esq. One of the Representatives in Congress for the State of South Carolina, to his Constituents, in May 1797. Fifth Edition. *Philadelphia Printed. London Reprinted John Stockdale,* 1798. 8vo, Title and Text, pp. 5–109. 30434

HARPER. Observations on the Dispute between the United States and France addressed By Robert Goodloe Harper, Esq. One of the Representatives in Congress for the State of South Carolina, to his Constituents, in May, 1797. Tenth Edition. *Philadelphia printed. Edinburgh reprinted. Arch. Constable, Cross.* 1798. 12mo, pp. 89. 30435

HARPER. Observations on the Dispute between the United States & France, addressed by Robert Goodloe Harper, of South Carolina, to his Constituents, in May 1797. Fourth American Edition. To which is annexed, His Speech, in Congress, on the Foreign Intercourse Bill, in Reply to Mr. Nicholas, Mr. Gallatin, and Others, delivered March 2, 1798. *Boston, Printed for the Subscribers, April,* 1798. 8vo. pp. 151. B., BA., H., N. 30436

HARPER. Observations on the North American Land Company, lately instituted in Philadelphia; containing an Illustration of the Object of the Company's Plan, the Articles of Association, with a succinct Account of the States wherein their lands lie; to which are added, Remarks on American Lands in general, more particularly the Pine Lands of the Southern and Western States, in Two Letters from Robert G. Harper, Esq. of South Carolina, to a Gentleman in Philadelphia. *London: H. L. Galabin.* MDCCXCVI. 8vo, pp. 149. M. 30437

HARPER. Observations on the North American Land Company, lately instituted in Philadelphia: containing an Illustration of the Company's Plan, the Articles of Association, with an account of the States where the lands lie: to which are added, remarks on American lands in general, more particularly the pine-lands of the Southern and Western States, in two letters from Robert G. Harper, Esq., Member of Congress from South Carolina. *London: H. L. Galabin.* 1796. 8vo, pp. xviii, 145.

HARPER. Observations on the North-American Land-Company, lately instituted in Philadelphia: Containing an Illustration of the Object of the Company's Plan, the Articles of Association, with a succinct Account of the States wherein the Lands lie: To which are added, Remarks on the American Lands in general, more particularly the Pine-Lands of the Southern and Western States, in Two Letters from Robert G. Harper, Esquire, Member of Congress, for South Carolina, to a Gentleman in Philadelphia. *London: C. Bannell and H. Savante, and sold by J. Debrett,* M,DCC,XCVI. 8vo, pp. 149. 30439

"Mr. Harper's letters are sensibly written, and his remarks on the *pine-barrens* are very satisfactory, and prove that these lands, when brought into cultivation, will be very valuable."—*Monthly Review,* XX. 211.

HARPER. Observations sur les Démêlés entre les États-Unis et la France; adresseés par Robert Goodloe Harper, Esq. l'un des Représentans au Congrès pour la Caroline Méridionale ... en Mai 1797. ... *Londres: T. Baylis.* 1798. 8vo, pp. (1), 11, vi, 126, (1). BA. 30440

HARPER. An Oration, on the Birth of Washington. ... before the Washington Society of Alexandria, ... on the 22d. of February, A. D. 1810. ... *Alexandria: Printed by S. Snowden.* 1810. 8vo, pp. 18. B., S. 30441

HARPER. Select Works of Robert Goodloe Harper: Consisting of Speeches on Political and Forensic Subjects; with the Answer drawn up by him to the Articles of Impeachment against Judge Chase. ... Vol. I. *Baltimore: O. H. Neilson.* 1814. 8vo, pp. iv, 400. B., C., H., N. 30442

No more published. Highly commended in Blackwood's "Magazine," XVII. 56.

HARPER. A Short Account of the Principal Proceedings of Congress, in the late Session, and a Sketch of the state of Affairs between the United States and France in July, 1798; in a Letter from Robert Goodloe Harper, Esq., of South Carolina, to one of his Constituents. *Philadelphia: William Cobbett.* 1798. 8vo,

pp. 22. B., BA., H., M. + *London: J. Wright.* 1798. 8vo, pp. 25. + [*Ibid.*] 1799. 30443

Mr. Rich suggests that this is the same as the "Observations on the Dispute," in which he is mistaken. "The Proceedings" relate to the affairs of France, involved in the W. X. Y. Z. Question.

HARPER. Speech of R. G. Harper, Esq., at the Celebration of the Recent Triumphs of the Cause of Mankind, in Germany; delivered at Annapolis, January 20, 1814. ... *Boston: Russell, Cutler & Co.* 1814. 8vo, pp. 81, (1). B., BA., H. + *Alexandria, D. C.: Printed by S. Snowden and J. D. Simms.* [1814.] 8vo, pp. 68. BA., H., N. + *New Haven: Printed by Oliver Steele.* 1814. 8vo, pp. 59. B., M. 30444

Also: Mr. Harper's Speech on the Navy: Opposition to the Motion of Mr. Gallatin ... February 8, 1799. To which is annexed a Speech of the Same Gentleman ... April 18, 1798 ... . *Philadelphia: Printed by Joseph Gales.* 1799. 8vo, pp. 24. BA. —Oration ... before the Washington Society of Maryland, on the Fourth of July, 1810. ... *Baltimore: Printed by John L. Cook.* 1810. 8vo, pp. 12. BA.—Speech ... on the Navy, Feb. 8, 1796. *Philadelphia.* [n. d.] 8vo. W.—Speech ... 29 May 1797, ... on the Conduct of France towards the United States. *Philadelphia: William Cobbett.* 1798. 8vo, pp. 44. H., S.—Speech ... on the War with Great Britain. [n. p. n. d.] 8vo, pp. 81. M.—Speech ... on the Reduction of the Army. *Philadelphia.* 1800. 12mo, pp. 44. BA., H., N.—Speeches, ... on the Necessity of granting Convoy: and on Augmenting the Navy. *Philadelphia.* 1797. 8vo. *See also* Williston (E. B.) Mr. Harper was a member of Congress from South Carolina in 1795. After his marriage to the daughter of Charles Carroll, he removed to Maryland, which State sent him to the Senate of the United States. "His writings are energetic, manly, profound, satisfactory. We hold him to be, altogether, one of the ablest men that North America has produced."—BLACKWOOD'S *Magazine,* VII. 56. *See also* "M. Rev.," XXV. 230.

HARPER (W.) Memoir of the Life ... of the Late Hon. Henry Wm. De Saussure ... read on the 15th February, 1841, ... Charleston. By the Hon. William Harper. ... *Charleston: Printed by W. Riley.* 1841. 8vo, pp. 38. H. 30445

HARPER. The Remedy by State Interposition, or Nullification, Explained and Advocated. By William Harper. *Charleston.* 1832. 12mo. 30446

Also: The South Carolina Society for the Advancement of Learning ... Anniversary Oration, delivered by the Hon. William Harper, ... Dec. 9, 1835. *Washington: Duff Green.* 1836. 8vo, pp. 23. B., BA., M.—Speech ... before the Charleston State Rights and Free Trade Association, April 1, 1832. *Charleston.* 1832. 8vo. *See also* Pro-Slavery Argument.

Harper's New Monthly Magazine. Vol. I., July to November, 1850. *New York: Harper and Brothers.* MDCCCL. Rl. 8vo. Continued. 30447

This serial contains many articles of historical, biographical, topographical, and political interest.

Harper Establishment; or, How the Story Books are made. *New York: Harper & Brothers.* 1856. 12mo, pp. 160. 30448

Harper's New York and Erie Rail-Road Guide Book: containing a description of the scenery, rivers, towns, villages, and most important works on the road. ... By Lossing and Barrett, ... *New York: Harper & Brothers.* [1851.] 12mo, pp. 173. C. + Eighth Edition, Revised, Enlarged, and Corrected. [*Ibid.*] 1855. 12mo. C. 30449

Harper's Pictorial History of the Rebellion. *See* Guernsey.

HARPER'S FERRY, *Md.* Report of the Select Committee of the Senate appointed to inquire into the late Invasion and seizure of the Public Property at Harper's Ferry. *Washington.* 1860. 8vo, pp. 255, (1). 30450

John Brown's Raid. *See* [Drew], Vol. V. No. 20935.

Rise and Progress of the Bloody Outbreak at Harper's Ferry. Published by Direction of the New York Democratic Vigilant Association. *John F. Trow, Printer.* [1860.] 8vo, pp. 20.

HARPONVILLE (le Vte.) *See* Hespel d'Harponville (G.)

[HARRINGTON (*Miss*).] Narrative of the Barbarous Treatment of Two Unfortunate Females ... of ... Louisiana ... by Two Runaway Blacks. ... *New York: For the Publisher.* 1844. 8vo, pp. 24. H. 30452

HARRINGTON (G. F.) Inside: a Chronicle of Secession. By George F. Harrington. With Illustrations by Thomas Nast. *New York: Harper & Brothers.* 1866. 8vo, pp. 223. C. 30453

HARRINGTON (H. F.) The Comparative Importance of Foreign and Domestic Missions; including Statistics of Education, &c., in Albany. A Discourse preached Jan. 7, 1846. By Rev. Henry F. Harrington. *Albany: Printed by C. Van Benthuysen and Co.* 1846. 8vo, pp. 30. B., BA., H., M. 30454

HARRINGTON. The Moral Influence of the American Government: an Oration ... Albany, N. Y., July 4, 1846 ... By Henry F. Harrington. *Albany: Printed by C. Van Benthuysen and Co.* 1846. 8vo, pp. 8. 30455

Also: Our Grammar Schools: Why do they not furnish more and better Material to our High Schools? A Lecture ... Springfield, October 19th, 1867. ... *Boston: Crosby and Ainsworth.* 1867. 8vo, pp. 38. B.— ... A Sermon ... on ... the "Anti-rent" Disturbances ... December 22, 1844. *Albany: Weare C. Little.* 1845. 8vo, pp. 23. BA., S.

HARRINGTON (J.) A Discourse ... on the ... Death of Caleb A. Buckingham, Esq., ... Jan. 15, 1841. By Joseph Harrington ... . *Chicago: Holcomb & Company.* 1841. 8vo, pp. 13, (1).

HARRINGTON (T.) A Century Sermon, preached at the First-Parish in Lancaster, May 28th, 1753. By Timothy Harrington, ... *Boston, N. E.: S. Kneeland.* 1753. 4to, pp. (4), 29. B., P. + *Leominster: Printed by S. & J. Wilder.* 1806. 8vo, pp. 25, (1).

Contains an account of the settlement of Lancaster, Mass.

HARRINGTON. A Peaceable Temper and Conduct divinely enjoined. Discourse delivered at Princetown, Dec. 23, 1759. By Timothy Harrington. *Boston.* 1760. 8vo, pp. 22. M.

HARRINGTON. Prevailing Wickedness, and Distressing Judgments, Ill-boding Symptoms on a Stupid People. A Discourse, ... Lancaster, ... September 5th, 1756. By Timothy Harrington. ... *Boston: Printed by Edes and Gill.* M,DCC,LVI. 8vo, pp. 32.

HARRINGTON (William H.) Harrington's Oration [delivered in New Bedford, July 4, 1833. *New Bedford.* 1833.] Folio, 1 l.

Also: Speech ... at the Company Election, Dec. 26, 1829. *New Bedford.* 1829. 12mo.

HARRIOTT (J.) Struggles through Life, Examplified in Various Travels and Adventures in Europe, Asia, Africa, & America, of Lieut. John Harriott, now Resident-Magistrate of the Thames Police. ... *London: Hatchard.* 1807. 2 vols., 12mo, pp. xxiv, 375; xi, 347. Portrait. H., S. + *London Printed. Philadelphia reprinted by James Humphreys.* 1809. 2 vols., 12mo, pp. iii–304; 267. B. + *New York: Inskeep & Bradford.* 1809. 2 vols., 12mo, pp. 304; 267. + *Philadelphia.* [*Ibid.*] P. + Third Edition. *London: Longman, for the Author.* 1815. 3 vols., 12mo, pp. xxv, 443, Portrait; xii, 428; vii, (1), 479. B., BA., C.

A large portion of this curious book relates to America, and especially Long Island, the author having passed much of his life there.

HARRIS (A.) A Geographical Hand Book ... . By Alex. Harris. *Lancaster (Pa.)* 1862. 12mo, pp. 427, (1). C. 30462

HARRIS (B.) Case of Benjamin Harris, Bookseller, lately come from New England, a Citizen of London, who had been exposed in the Pillory before his own house, near the Royal Exchange, imprisoned two years, and fined £500 by Lord Chief Justice Scroggs, and other Judges, for Reprinting and Selling "An Appeal from the Country to the City," &c. 1681. Folio, 1 l.

HARRIS (B. G.) Speech of Hon. Benjamin G. Harris, of Maryland, ... April 9, 1864, on the Resolution to expel Mr Long. *Washington: Constitutional Union Office.* 1864. 8vo pp. 7. 30464

Also: Speech ... June 14, 1866. [n. p. n. d.] 8vo.—Speech ... on Secret Societies, ... House of Delegates of Maryland. [n. p. n. d.] 8vo. C.

HARRIS (B. W.) The Annexation Question. Closing Argument of B. W. Harris, Esq. ... against the Annexation .. Roxbury to Boston ... April 27, 1869. *Boston: Rockwell & Rollins.* 1869. 8vo, pp. 51. H. 3046[illegible]

HARRIS (C.) History of the Captivity and Providential release therefrom of Mrs. Caroline Harris, Wife of the late Mr. Richard Harris, of Franklin County, State of New York: who with Mrs Clarissa Plummer, wife of Mr. James Plummer, were in the Spring of 1835 (with their unfortunate husbands) taken prisoners by the Camanche tribe of Indians, while emigrating from said Franklin County (N. Y.) to Texas, and after having been made to witness the tragical deaths of their husbands, and held nearly two years in bondage, were providentially redeemed therefrom by two of their country-men attached to a Company of Santa Fé Fur Traders. *New York: Perry & Cook.* 1838. 8vo, pp. 24 Plate. 3046[illegible]

HARRIS (C. H.) History of the Venango Oil Regions: .. and other Places of Note in the Oil Regions. By Charles H Harris. *Titusville, Pa.* 1866. 12mo, pp. v, 108. 2 Plates. C

[HARRIS (D. L.)] The Hoosac Tunnel and Troy and Green field Rail Road. [n. p.] 1862. 8vo, pp. 24. H. 3046[illegible]

HARRIS (E. D.) An Account of some of the Descendants of Capt. Thomas Brattle, Compiled by Edward Doubleday Harris. [*Boston:*] *D. Clapp and Son.* 1867. 4to, pp. 90. B

HARRIS. A Genealogical Record of Thomas Bascom and his Descendants. By E. D. Harris. *Boston: William Parsons Lunt* 1870. 8vo, pp. 79. B., S. 3047[illegible]

HARRIS. The Vassalls of New England and their Immediate Descendants. ... By Edward D. Harris. ... *Albany: J. Munsell* 1862. 8vo, pp. 26. B., H., S. 3047[illegible]

HARRIS (E.) Observations in Hospitals in Shenandoah Valley October, 1864. By Elisha Harris, M.D. [n. p. n. d.] pp. 12

Also: Pestilential Diseases, and the Laws which govern their Propagation. A Letter ... [to] the Quarantine Commissioners ... *Albany.* 1858. 8vo, pp. 23. S. -

Tobacco, N. Y. 1853. 12mo, pp. 43. S.—Sanitary Qualities of the Water-Supply of New York and Brooklyn. ... *New York: C. S. Westcott & Co., Printers.* 1868. 8vo, pp. 16. H.

HARRIS (G.) The Economy and Policy of a Christian Education. ... By George Harris. *Baltimore.* 1823. 12mo, pp. 282.

HARRIS (I.) Speech upon the Anti-Rent Question ... Assembly [New York], February 4, 1846. [n. p n. d.] 8vo. B.

HARRIS (I.) Confiscation of Rebel Property. Speech of Hon. Ira Harris ... in the Senate ... April 14, 1862. *Washington: D. C. Scammell & Co.* 1862. 8vo, pp. 8. B., H. 30475

HARRIS. The Expulsion of Senator Bright. Speeches ... in the Senate ... January 24 and February 25, 1862. [n. p. n. d.] 8vo, pp. 7. 30476

HARRIS (Isaac). *See* Pittsburgh, *Pa.*

HARRIS (J. D.) A Summer on the Borders of the Caribbean Sea. By J. Dennis Harris. With an Introduction by George William Curtis. *New York: A. B. Burdick.* 1860. 12mo, pp. 179. C., H. 30477

HARRIS (J. H.) Speech of James H. Harris ... August 14th, 1868, in Support of the Militia Bill. [n. p. n. d.] 8vo, pp. 3.

HARRIS (J. H.) A Letter to Archdeacon Strahan, in reply to some passages in his "Letter to Dr. Chalmers, on the Life and Character of Bishop Hobart," respecting ... the Bible Society. By J. H. Harris, D.D. *York, U. C.* 1833. 8vo, pp. 23. S.

HARRIS (J. M.) Discourse on the Life and Character of Sir Walter Raleigh, delivered by J. Morrison Harris before the Maryland Historical Society, May 19, 1846 ... . *Baltimore: Printed ... by John D. Toy* ... MDCCCXLVI. 8vo, pp. 71. 30480

HARRIS. A Paper upon California: read before the Maryland Historical Society, by J. Morrison Harris ... March, 1849. *Baltimore: Printed ... by John D. Toy* ... MDCCCXLIX. 8vo, pp. 32.

Also: State of the Union. Speech ... January 29, 1861. [n. p. n. d.] 8vo, pp 8.

HARRIS (J.) Navigantium atque Itinerantium Bibliotheca; or a Compleat Collection of Voyages and Travels: Consisting of above Four Hundred of the most Authentick Writers; beginning with Hackluit, Purchass, &c. in English; Ramusio in Italian: Thevenot, &c. in French; De Bry, and Grynæi Novus Orbis in Latin; the Dutch East-India Company in Dutch: And Continued with Others of Note that have Published Histories, Voyages,

Travels, or Discoveries, in the English, Latin, French, Italian, Spanish, Portuguese, German, or Dutch Tongues; relating To any part of Asia, Africa, America, Europe, or the Islands thereof, to this present Time. With the Heads of several of our most Considerable Sea-Commanders; and a great Number of Excellent Maps of all Parts of the World, and Cuts of most Curious Things in all the Voyages. ... To which is Prefixed, a History of the Peopling of the several Parts of the World, and particularly of America ... &c. By John Harris, A.M. ... *London: T. Bennet.* M DCC V. 2 vols., folio, pp. (14), lxvii, 862, (14); (6), 928, 56, (12). 9 Maps, 23 Plates. BA., C. 30482

First edition. "It appears to have been got up in competition with Churchill's Collection, but differs entirely from that work, being a *history* of all the known voyages and travels, whereas Churchill's is a *collection* of some particular relations and histories." —RICH *Bib. Am.* I. 9.

HARRIS. Navigantium atque Itinerantium Bibliotheca; or, a Complete Collection of Voyages and Travels; consisting of above Six Hundred of the most Authentic Writers; beginning with Hakluit, Purchas, &c., in English; Ramusio, ... Carreri, &c., in Italian; Thevenot, ... Labat, &c., in French; De Brye and Grynæus, Maffeus, &c., in Latin; Herrera, Oviedo, Coreal, &c., in Spanish, and the Voyages ... of the East India Company in Holland, in Dutch, together with such other Histories, Voyages, Travels, or Discoveries, ... in English, Latin, French, Italian, Spanish, Portuguese, High and Low Dutch, or in any other European language. Containing whatever has been observed worthy of notice, in Europe, Asia, Africa and America; in respect to the Extent and Situation of Empires, Kingdoms, Provinces, &c. The Climate, Soil, Produce, whether Animal, Vegetable, or Mineral of each country; Likewise the Religion, Manners, and Customs of the several Inhabitants, their Government, Arts and Sciences, ... Mountains, Rivers, Harbours, &c. Illustrated by proper ... Maps and Cuts. To which is prefixed a copious introduction, [on] the Rise and Progress of ... Navigation. ... Now carefully revised, with large additions, and continued down to the present time. [By Dr. John Campbell.] *London: Printed for T. Osborne and others.* M.DCC.LXIV. 2 vols., folio, pp. (10), xvi, (4), 984, 17 Plates and 5 Maps; (10), 1056, Index, 11 l., 10 Maps and 33 Plates. BA., C., P. 30483

This edition was first issued in 1743–4. "As to Harris's Collection, let any one inspect the curious contents only of the first volume as exhibited by Mr. Harris, in hi valuable Catalogue of the Library of the Royal Institution, p. 260, and he will not hesitate a moment respecting the importance of this work."—DIBDIN's *Library Companion.* There are copies on large paper.

HARRIS (J. O.) Report to the Mayor of New Orleans on the Charitable Institutions in the Cities of New Orleans and Jefferson. By J. O. Harris. *New Orleans.* 1868. 8vo, pp. 44.

HARRIS (J. S.) Levees of the Mississippi. Speech of Hon. John S. Harris ... June 2, 1870. [*Washington.* 1870.] 8vo, pp. 7. H. 30485

HARRIS (J. S.) ... A Memorial Sermon ... the Death of Rev. Pierpont E. Bishop ... March 20th, 1859. By Rev. Jno. S. Harris ... . *Charleston: Walker, Evans & Co.'s.* 1859. 8vo, pp. 35. H. 30486

[HARRIS (Luther M.)] A Branch of the Whitney Family. [*Boston.* 1858.] 8vo, pp. 7. 30487

HARRIS. Robert Harris and his Descendants. With Notices of the Morey and Metcalf Families. Compiled by Luther M. Harris, M.D. *Boston: Printed by Henry W. Dutton & Son.* 1861. 8vo, pp. 56. S. 30488

HARRIS (M.) Lettre de M. Harris, Citoyen de la Pennsylvanie ... sur les Finances des États-Unis ... . [n. p. n. d.] 8vo, pp. 32. BA. 30489

HARRIS (M.) Official Report of the Trial of Mary Harris, indicted for the Murder of Adoniram J. Burroughs, ... July 3, 1865. Prepared by James O. Clephane, Official Reporter. *Washington: W. H. & O. H. Morrison.* 1865. 8vo, pp. 181.

[HARRIS (N. S.)] Journal of a Tour in the "Indian Territory," performed by order of the Domestic Committee of the Board of Missions of the Protestant Episcopal Church, in the Spring of 1844, by their Secretary and General Agent. *New York: Daniel Dana, Jr.* 1844. 8vo, pp. (6), 74. 3 Maps. C.

HARRIS (R.) Scriptural Researches on the Licitness of the Slave-Trade, showing its conformity with the Principles of Natural and Revealed Religion delineated in the Sacred Writings of the Word of God. By the Rev. Raymond Harris. *London: Lowndes.* 1788. 8vo. A., C., S. + *Liverpool.* 1788. 8vo. C.

This elicited several epistles, among them: A Scriptural Refutation of a Pamphlet lately published by the Rev. Raymond Harris, intituled, "Scriptural Researches on the Licitness of the Slave Trade." *London: Law.* 1788. 8vo.—Scripture the Friend of Freedom, exemplified by a Refutation of the [above] Defence of Slavery in the Scriptural Researches on the Licitness of the Slave Trade. *London.* 1789. 8vo. A. *See* "M. Rev." LXXVIII. 344; LXXIX, 71; and Ramsay (James).

HARRIS (R. W.) A Sermon occasioned by the Death of the Rev. Alexander H. Crosby, A.M. And preached ... in ... Yonkers, ... March 10, 1839. By Robert William Harris, ... *New-York: W. H. Vermilye.* M DCCC XXXIX. 8vo, pp. 29. 30493

Also: Sermon preached at the Opening of St. Mark's Church, New York, Jan. 25, 1852. ... *New York.* 1852. 8vo.

HARRIS (*Mr.*) Christmas Sermon at Boston. *Boston.* 1712. 4to. W. 30494

HARRIS (*Mr.*) Sermon at Boston, August 15, 1713, at the Funeral of Charles Dyer, Esq. *Boston.* 1713. 4to. W. 30495

HARRIS (*Mr.*) Removal of the Cherokees west of the Mississippi ... Mr. Harris ... Report ... [*Washington.* 1842.] 8vo, pp. 100. 30496

HARRIS (S. W.) Speech of Hon. Sampson W. Harris (of Alabama), ... to Organize a Territorial Government for the Territory of Oregon. ... July 25, 1848. *Washington: Printed by J. & G. S. Gideon.* 1848. 8vo, pp. 15. H. 30497

HARRIS (S.) A Farewell Sermon to the People of Windham, N. H. At the Close of the Author's Ministry, January 7, 1827. By Samuel Harris. *Amherst: R. Boylston.* 1827. 8vo, pp. 24.

HARRIS. Inaugural Address ... by Samuel Harris at his Induction into the Presidency of Bowdoin College, August 6, 1867. *Brunswick: Joseph Griffin.* 1867. 8vo, pp. 45. B., S. 30499

HARRIS. ... A Sermon ... at the Dedication of the Congregational Church in Hatfield, Mass., 17th January, 1850. By Samuel Harris. *Northampton.* 1850. 8vo, pp. 23. H. 30500

Also: ... A Sermon ... at the Ordination of Rev. Oliver M. Sears ... Dalton, Mass., September 29, 1847. ... *Pittsfield: Printed by Charles Montague.* 1847. 8vo, pp. 22. BA., H.— ... A Sermon ... National Independence, 1852. ... *Pittsfield: Printed by W. D. Axtell.* 1852. 8vo, pp. 22. H.

HARRIS (S. F.) Class of 1858. An Oration By Samuel F. Harris, and a Poem by John M. Hay, of Warsaw, Illinois, delivered in ... Brown University, on Class day, June 1858. Printed for Private Distribution. *Providence: Knowles, Anthony & Co.* 1858. 8vo, pp. 43. 30501

[HARRIS (*Mrs.* Sidney S.)] Louie's Last Term at St. Mary's. *New York: Derby & Jackson.* 1860. 12mo, pp. 239. + *New York: C. Scribner & Co.* 1871. 12mo, pp. 239. 30502

A story of St. Mary's Hall, Burlington, N. J. The authoress' maiden name was Miriam Cole.

HARRIS (S. W.) Speech of Hon. S. W. Harris, June 10, 1850, on the Compromise Bill. [n. p. n. d.] 8vo. 30503

HARRIS (T. M.) An Address delivered before the Washington Benevolent Society, in Dorchester, February 22d, 1813. By Rev. Thaddeus Mason Harris. ... *Boston: J. Belcher.* 1813. 8vo, pp. 15. B., H. 30504

HARRIS. Biographical Memorials of James Oglethorpe, Founder of the Colony of Georgia, in North America. By Thaddeus Mason Harris, D.D., ... *Boston: Printed for the Author.* MDCCCXLI. 8vo, pp. xxii, 424. Portrait and Maps. B., BA., H.

HARRIS. Chronological and Topographical Account of Dorchester, Mass. *Boston: Munroe & Francis.* [n. d.] 8vo, pp. 55.

Also included in the "Mass. Hist. Soc. Collections," IX. 147–199.

HARRIS. Constitutions of the ... Fraternity of Free and Accepted Masons; collected and digested from their old Records, faithful Traditions, and Lodge Books ... Together with the History and General Regulations of the Grand-Lodge of Massachusetts. By Thaddeus Mason Harris. *Worcester.* 1792. 4to. W. + Second Edition, Revised and Corrected, with large Additions. *Worcester.* 1798. 4to. Plate. C., W. 30507

HARRIS. A Discourse addressed to the Religious Society of Young Men in Dorchester, on the Termination of One Hundred Years from the Time of its Establishment. By Thaddeus Mason Harris. *Charlestown: Printed by Samuel Etheridge.* 1799. 8vo, pp. 24. H., N., S., W. 30508

HARRIS. A Discourse, delivered at Dorchester, Dec. 29, 1799, Being the Lord's Day after hearing the Distressing Intelligence of the Death of General George Washington, ... By Thaddeus Mason Harris, A.M. *Charlestown: Printed by Samuel Etheridge.* M,DCCC. 8vo, pp. 16. B., BA., H. 30509

Forms part of our No. 20623, Vol. V. Some copies were issued as a separate publication.

HARRIS. A Discourse ... before the Humane Society ... of Massachusetts, June 10, 1806. *Boston: Printed by E. Lincoln.* 1806. 8vo, pp. 40. B., BA., H., M. 30510

With "The Life-Boat," a Poem by Samuel Davis; and Appendix of Proceedings.

HARRIS. Discourse delivered at Plymouth, Dec. 22, 1808, at the Anniversary Commemoration of the Landing of our Ances-

tors at that Place. By Thaddeus Mason Harris. *Boston: Printed by J. Belcher.* 1808. 8vo, pp. 32. H., M. 30511

HARRIS. A Discourse ... before the African Society in Boston, 15th of July, 1822, on the Anniversary ... of the Abolition of the Slave Trade. By Thaddeus Mason Harris. *Boston: Printed by Phelps and Farnham.* 1822. 8vo, pp. 27. B., BA., W.

HARRIS. A Discourse delivered before the Society for propagating the Gospel among the Indians and others in North America, 6th November, 1823. By Thaddeus Mason Harris. ... With the Report of the Select Committee. *Cambridge: [Printed] by Hilliard and Metcalf.* 1823. 8vo, pp. 50. B., BA., S., W. 30513

HARRIS. Discourses ... Illustrating the Principles, Displaying the Tendency, and Vindicating the Design, of Freemasonry. By Thaddeus Mason Harris, ... *Printed at Charlestown, by Samuel Etheridge,* A.L. 5801. 8vo, pp. 328. Plate. B., S. + *Philadelphia.* 5819. 8vo, pp. 376. + With Notes and Observations, by the Rev. George Oliver, D.D. 1850. 8vo. 30514

HARRIS. The Journal of a Tour into the Territory North west of the Alleghany Mountains; made in the Spring of the Year 1803. With a Geographical and Historical Account of the State of Ohio. Illustrated with Original Maps and Views. By Thaddeus Mason Harris, ... *Boston: Printed by Manning & Loring.* 1805. 8vo, pp. 271. 5 Plates and Maps. B., BA., H.

HARRIS. Memorials of the First Church in Dorchester, from its Settlement in New England, to the End of the Second Century; in Two Discourses, delivered July 4, 1830. By ... Thaddeus Mason Harris ... . *Boston: W. L. Lewis, Printer.* 1830. 8vo, pp. 67. BA., S., W. 30516

HARRIS. Remarks on the Charges made against the Religion and Morals of the People of Boston, and its Vicinity, by the Rev. Gardner Spring, D.D., in a Sermon preached before the New England Society of New York, December 22, 1820. *New York.* 1820. 8vo, pp. 21. 30517

HARRIS. A Sermon, delivered at the Dedication of the South Meeting House in Dorchester, October 30, 1806. ... *Boston: Printed by Belcher and Armstrong.* 1806. 8vo, pp. 20. M., W.

HARRIS. A Tribute of Respect, to the Memory of the Hon. James Bowdoin, Esq. in a Sermon, preached at Dorchester, Oc-

tober 27, 1811. With Extract from a Discourse by Rev. J. S. Buckminster. By Thaddeus Mason Harris ... . *Boston: Printed by Joshua Belcher.* 1811. 4to, pp. 32. B., BA., H. 30519

One hundred copies privately printed.

[HARRIS.] Triumphs of Superstition: an Elegy. By a Student of Harvard University. *Boston.* 1790. 4to. W. 30520

HARRIS. A Valedictory Discourse, preached to the First Church and Society in Dorchester, 23d. of October, 1836. *Boston: Printed by D. Clapp, Jr.* 1836. 8vo, pp. 24. B., H. 30521

Also: Address at the Interment of R. W. James Davenport ... July 17, 1824. ... *Boston: John B. Russell, Printer.* 1824. 8vo, pp. 15. H.—An Address ... Dec. 28, 1803, ... at the Interment of Three Persons who were drowned in the Harbour between Boston and Dorchester. ... *Boston: Printed by Manning & Loring.* 1804. 8vo, pp. 12. BA., H.—[Artillery-Election] ... Sermon, ... 1805 ... . *Boston.* 1805. 8vo, pp. 20. H., M., W.—The Approved Minister. Sermon preached at the Ordination of Rev. Enoch Pratt, in Barnstable, Mass. *Boston.* 1807. 8vo, pp. 32. H.—Beauties of Nature Delineated. ... *Charlestown.* 1800. 16mo, pp. 223. B. + Second Edition. [*Ibid.*] 1801. 16mo, pp. 237. B.—Charge before the Massachusetts Grand Lodge, June 24, 1795. ... *Worcester.* 1795. 4to. W.—Discourse at Bridgewater, November 3, 1797, before the Fellowship Lodge. *Boston.* 1797. 8vo, pp. 20. H., N.—Discourse at Brookfield, Mass., September 12, 1798. ... *Brookfield.* [n. d.] 12mo. W.—Discourse ... at Dorchester, October 10, 1804, at the Funeral of Dea. Abijah White. ... *Boston: Printed by Manning & Loring.* 1804. 8vo, pp. 23. B., BA., H., W.—A Discourse preached before the Members of the Boston Female Asylum, September 24th, 1813. ... *Boston.* 1813. 8vo, pp. 32. BA., M., N.—Discourse at Dorchester, March 5, 1813, at the Funeral of Ebenezer Wales, Esq. ... *Boston.* 1813. 8vo, pp. 20. N., W.—Discourse delivered at Dorchester, March 29, 1813, at the Funeral of Moses Everett, Esq. *Boston.* 1813. 8vo, pp. 18. B., H.—A Discourse ... at Marblehead, June 24, 1822, before the ... Philanthropic Lodge ... . *Cambridge: Printed by Hilliard and Metcalf.* 1822. 8vo, pp. 24. B., H.—Discourse ... at Plymouth [Mass.], Dec. 22d. 1808. ... *Boston: Printed by J. Belcher.* 1808. 8vo, pp. 32. BA., W.—Discourse ... at Stoughton, before the Rising Star Lodge, ... June 24, ... 1818. ... *Boston.* 1818. 8vo, pp. 16. BA., H., M.—Masonic Emblems Explained. In a Sermon, preached before the Members of King Solomon's Lodge, in Charlestown, June 24, 5796. ... *Boston.* 5796. 8vo, pp. 24. BA., H. + Second Edition. *Boston.* 1796. 8vo. W.—Masonic Sermon at Groton [Mass.], August 9, 1797. *Leominster.* 1797. 8vo.—A Masonick Eulogy, pronounced 24th June, 1794, before the Morning-Star Lodge, Worcester, and Trinity Lodge, Lancaster. *Worcester: Isaiah Thomas.* 1794. 4to, pp. 16. C.—The Minor Encyclopedia; or, Cabinet of General Knowledge. *Boston.* 1803. 4 vols., 12mo. B., BA., H.—A New Year's Wish of an Affectionate Minister for the People of his Charge. Sermon at Dorchester, Mass., January 1, 1796. ... *Boston.* 1796. 8vo, pp. 24. H., W.—A Selected Catalogue of Publications in the English Language, proper to form a Social Library. *Boston.* 1793. 12mo, pp. 23.—A Sermon Preached at the Ordination of Rev. John Pierce, ... Brookline, March 15, 1797. ... *Boston.* 1797. 8vo, pp. 39. BA., H., W.— ... A Sermon at the Consecration of Saint Paul's Lodge in Groton, and the Installation of its Officers ... August 9th, A.L. 5797. ... *Leominster: Printed by Brother Charles Prentiss.* A.L. 5797. 8vo, pp. 28. BA., H.—Sermon preached at Milton ... and Dorchester, May 9th, 1798, on the National Fast. ... *Boston.* 1798. 8vo, pp. 24. BA., H., W.—Sermon at Oxford, Mass., September 13, 1798. ... *Worcester.* 1799. 8vo. W.—A Sermon ... in Dedham, September 13, 1801. ... after the Execution of Jason Fairbanks. ... *Dedham: Printed by Herman Mann.* 1801. 8vo, pp. 24. BA., H.—Sermon at Beverly [Mass.], December 14, 1803, at

the Installation of Rev. Abiel Abbot. ... *Salem.* 1804. 8vo, pp. 36. BA., N., W.—A Sermon ... at the Ordination of the Rev. Caleb Hamilton Shearman ... in Dover, New-Hampshire, May 6, 1807. ... *Dover, N. H.: Printed by Samuel Bragg, Jr.* 1807. 8vo, pp. 16. H.—A Sermon ... at Dorchester, Nov. 26, 1807. ... *Boston.* 1807. 8vo, pp. 16. BA., W.—A Sermon ... at the Ordination of the Rev. Samuel Osgood ... in Springfield, January 25, 1809. ... *Springfield: Printed by Thomas Dickman.* 1809. 8vo, pp. 36. BA., H.—A Sermon preached at New Bedford, October 26, 1814, at the Ordination of Rev. Ephraim Randall. ... *New Bedford: Printed by Benj. Lindsey.* 1814. 8vo, pp. 39. BA.—A Sermon at the Ordination of Lemuel Capen, at Sterling, Mass., March 22d, 1815. ... *Boston.* 1815. 8vo, pp. 44. H., W.—A Sermon ... at Dorchester ... after the Interment of Mr. Nathaniel Topliff ... 4th December, 1819. ... *Boston: Printed by Sewell Phelps.* 1820. 8vo, pp. 27. BA.—A Tribute of Filial Respect to the Memory of his Mother ... Feb. 8, 1801 ... . *Charlestown: Printed by Samuel Etheridge.* 1801. 8vo, pp. 20. H., M., N., W.—A Tribute of Respect to the Memory of Mrs. Sarah Bowdoin Dearborn; ... delivered ... in Boston, June 4, 1826. ... *Boston.* 1826. 8vo, pp. 24. BA., M.—A Valedictory Sermon ... in Dorchester, 1st December 1816; and a Dedicatory Sermon ... the Next Day. ... *Boston: Printed by John Eliot.* 1817. 8vo, pp. 36. BA., H. *See also* "Mass. Hist. Soc. Collections," Second Series, Vol. VIII., Fourth Series, Vol. II.

HARRIS (T. W.) Remarks upon the North American Insects belonging to the Genus Cychrus of Fabricius, with description of some newly detected Species. *Cambridge.* 1839. BM. 30522

[HARRIS.] A Report on the Insects of Massachusetts Injurious to Vegetation. Published agreeably to an Order of the Legislature, by the Commissioners on the Zoological and Botanical Survey of the State. *Cambridge: Folsom, Wells, and Thurston.* 1841. 8vo, pp. viii, 459. B., BA., 30523

HARRIS. A Treatise on some of the Insects of New England, which are injurious to vegetation. By Thaddeus William Harris, M.D. *Cambridge: John Owen.* 1842. 8vo, pp. (4), 459. + Second Edition. *Boston: Wright & Potter.* 1852. 8vo, pp. viii, 513. C. + Third Edition. *Boston: William White.* 1862. 8vo, pp. xi, 640. Plates. BA. + New Edition, Enlarged and Improved, with Additions from the Author's Manuscripts and Original Notes. Illustrated by Engravings drawn from Nature under the Supervision of Professor Agassiz. Edited by Charles L. Flint. ... *Boston.* 1862. 8vo, pp. xi, 640. B., C. + *Philadelphia: Porter and Coates.* 1869. 8vo, pp. xi, 640. Plates. B.

See "N. A. Rev.," LIV. 73–101; LXXVI. 255. Also: Characteristics of some previously-described North American Coleopterous Insects, etc. *Hartford.* 1836. 8vo, pp. 28. Plate.—A Discourse ... before the Massachusetts Horticultural Society, on the Celebration of its Fourth Anniversary, October 3, 1832. ... *Cambridge: E. W. Metcalf.* 1832. 8vo, pp. 96. H. + *Boston.* 1832. 8vo, pp. 96.

HARRIS (T.) Account of the Spanish Butcheries on the Native Indians, ... *London.* 1745. 8vo. 30525

Title from a bookseller's catalogue; probably "Old England for Ever" with a new title-page.

HARRIS (T.) The Life and Services of Commodore William Bainbridge, United States Navy. By Thomas Harris, M.D. *Philadelphia: Carey, Lea & Blanchard.* 1837. 8vo, pp. 254, Errata, 1 l. Portrait. C. 30526

Also: An Oration ... before the Philadelphia Medical Society, February, 19, 1831 ... *Philadelphia: Printed by James Kay, Jun. & Co.* 1831. 8vo, pp. 28. BA., P.

HARRIS (T. L.) Juvenile Depravity and Crime in our City. A Sermon, by Thomas L. Harris, ... January 13th, 1850. With an Appendix embodying the Recent Report of the Chief of Police concerning Destitution and Crime among Children in the City. *New-York: Charles B. Norton.* 1850. 8vo, pp. 15. BA.

Also: Letter on the Repeal of the Fugitive Slave Law. 1851. [n. p. n. d.] 8vo. —Speech ... March 25, 1850, on the Admission of California. [n. p. n. d.] 8vo.

HARRIS (T. S.) *See* Mohawk, *also* Seneca.

HARRIS (W.) A Discourse at Dunbarton, New Hampshire, on Thanksgiving Day, Nov. 12, 1812. By Walter Harris, A.M. *Concord.* 1812. 8vo, pp. 18. 30528

Also: Sermon at Installation of Stephen Chapin. Mount Vernon, N. H., November 15, 1809. [n. p. n. d.] 8vo.

HARRIS (W. P.) Speech of Hon. Wiley P. Harris on the Nebraska and Kansas Bill; ... April 24 and 26, 1854. *Washington.* 1854. 8vo, pp. 8. M. 30529

HARRIS (W.) Sermon at the Funeral of Mrs. Martha Roads, September 26, 1792. By William Harris, M.A. *Boston.* 1795. 8vo, pp. 19. H., M., W. 30530

Also: Sermon before the Annual Convention of the Protestant Episcopal Church in Massachusetts, May 28, 1799. ... *Boston.* 1799. 4to, pp. 22. B., BA., H.—A Sermon delivered in Trinity Church, New York, ... before the Convention of the Protestant Episcopal Church. ... *New York.* 1810. 8vo, pp. 24. H., N.

HARRIS (W. C.) Prison-Life in the Tobacco Warehouse at Richmond. By a Ball's Bluff Prisoner, Lieut. Wm. C. Harris, of Col. Baker's California Regiment. *Philadelphia: George W. Childs.* 1862. 12mo, pp. 175. 30531

HARRIS (W. L.) Address of Hon. Wm. L. Harris, before the Agricultural Association, Jackson, November 12, 1858. ... *Jackson: E. Barksdale.* 1858. 8vo, pp. 24. H. 30532

HARRIS (W. T.) Remarks made during a Tour through the United States of America, in the years 1817, 1818, and 1819. By William Tell Harris. In a series of Letters to a Friend in

England. *Liverpool.* 1819. 8vo, pp. 74. H., S. + *London: Sherwood & Co.* 1821. 12mo, pp. 196. C. 30533

See "M. Rev.," XCVII. 201.

HARRIS. Bemerkungen auf einer Reise durch die Vereinigten Staaten von Nord-Amerika, in den Jahren 1817, 1818, und 1819, in einer Reihe von Briefen an Freunde in England. Aus dem Englischen übersetzt von Dr. C. Fl. Leidenfrost. *Weimar: Landes-Industrie-Comptoir.* 1822. 8vo, pp. viii, 236. C. 30534

HARRIS (W. T.) Epitaphs from the Old Burying-Ground in Cambridge. With Notes by William Thaddeus Harris. ... *Cambridge: John Owen.* 1845. 12mo, pp. vii, 192. C. 30535

HARRIS. Epitaphs from the Old Burying-Ground in Watertown. Collected by William Thaddeus Harris, LL.B., ... With Notes by Edward Doubleday Harris. *Boston.* 1869. 8vo, pp. (2), iii, 70. 30536

HARRIS. Sketches of the Early History of the Town of Middleborough, County of Plymouth, Mass. *Boston.* 1849. 8vo.

See [Child (F. L.)], *also* "Historical and Genealogical Register," Vol. III.

HARRIS (W. A.) The Record of Fort Sumter, from its Occupation by Major Anderson, to its Reduction by South Carolina Troops during the Administration of Governor Pickens. Compiled by W. A. Harris. *Columbia, S. C.: South Carolinian Steam Job Printing Office.* 1862. 8vo, pp. 50. 30538

HARRIS (W. W.) The Battle of Groton Heights: a Collection of Narratives, Official Reports, Records, &c., of the Storming of Fort Griswold, and the Burning of New London by British Troops, under the Command of Brig.-Gen. Benedict Arnold, on the Sixth of September, 1781. With an Introduction and Notes. By William W. Harris. *New London.* 1870. 8vo, pp. (2), x, 123. C. 30539

HARRISBURG, *Pa.* The Harrisburg Business Directory, and Stranger's Guide, with a Sketch of its First Early Settlement. By H. Napey. [n. p.:] *The Author.* 1842. 8vo, pp. 64. Map.

The Directory for 1843 was edited by J. A. Spofford, for 1867–68 by W. J. Divine.

"The Patriot" Harrisburg Directory, and a Business Directory of Carlisle, Chambersburg, Greencastle, Middletown, Mechanicsburg, Newville, Shippensburg, etc. 1871–72. [*Harrisburg:*] *A. & W. H. Boyd.* [1871.] 8vo. 30541

Harrisburg and Hamburg Railroad; First Annual Report. *Philadelphia.* 1855. C. 30542

Harrisburg and Lancaster Railroad; Charter ... passed June 9, 1832. 8vo. 30543

Also: Controversy between the Canal Commissioners and the Harrisburg and Lancaster and the Pennsylvania Railroad Companies. *Philadelphia.* 1852. 8vo. C.

Harrisburg Cemetery Association; Charter, History and By-Laws; with the Address of Rev. W. R. De Witt at the Ceremony of its Dedication, September 30, 1845. 8vo. 30544

Harrisburg Convention. Proceedings of the Democratic Whig National Convention, which assembled at Harrisburg, Penn., on 4th December, 1839, for the purpose of Nominating Candidates, President and Vice-President of the United States. *Harrisburg.* 1839. 8vo. N. 30545

Harrisburg Insurrection. Address of the Hon. Charles B. Penrose, Speaker of the Senate; and the Speeches of Fraley (City), Williams, Pearson, and Penrose, delivered in the Senate of Pennsylvania, on the Subject of the Insurrection at Harrisburg ... in December, 1838. *Harrisburg: Printed by E. Guyer.* 1839. 8vo, pp. 207. BA., C. 30546

Harrisburg National Democratic Union Club. Address. *Philadelphia.* 1860. 8vo. 30547

Harrisburg, Portsmouth, Mount Joy and Lancaster Railroad; Report of the President and Directors to the Stockholders. *Philadelphia.* 1840. Continued. 30548

Harrisburg Water Works. Reports of the Town Council on the Expenses incurred in their Construction, from June, 1840, to January, 1844. [n. p. n. d.] 8vo. 30549

Pastoral Letter to the Churches under the Care of the Harrisburg Presbytery. *Philadelphia.* 1840. 8vo. 30550

HARRISON (D.) The Melancholy Narrative of the Distressful Voyage and Miraculous Deliverance of Captain David Harrison of the Sloop Peggy, of New York, on his Voyage from Fayal ... to New York, until relieved by Capt. Evers of the Virginia Trade. Written by Himself. *London: Printed for James Harrison.* 1766. 8vo, pp. (2), 67. N. 30551

See "M. Rev.," XXXV. 72.

HARRISON. Droevig Verhaal z. ongel. reis en wonderl. verlossinge, komende van Fyal en gaande naar Niew-York. *Hoorn.* 1769. 8vo, pp. 50. 30552

HARRISON (Edward). A Paper, headed, "In the Days of Tiberius Cæsar, the Governors of the several Provinces were wont to advertise the Senate of such occurrences as happen'd in their Countries, and Publius Lentulus, President of Judæa, writ the following Epistle to the Senate and People of Rome." E. H. [n. p. n. d.] Folio, pp. 2. 30553

HARRISON (E.) A Funeral Discourse ... on the ... Death of ... J. Muir ... By Elias Harrison. *Alexandria.* 1820. 8vo.

[HARRISON (George).] An Address to the Right Reverend the Prelates of England and Wales, on the subject of the Slave-Trade. *London: J. Parsons.* 1792. 8vo. + A Second Address ... *London: J. Johnson.* 1795. 8vo. 30555

[HARRISON.] Notices on the Slave Trade in reference to the present state of the British Isles. 1804. 8vo. 30556

HARRISON (H.) Hydraulicus; or Improvement of the Mississippi: offering a Plan for the reduction of its overflow, and that of its alluvial tributary Streams ... By H. Harrison. *Cincinnati.* 1828. 12mo. B., M. 30557

HARRISON (H. B.) Obituary Notice of Hon. R. S. Baldwin. By Henry B. Harrison. *Hartford.* 1863. 8vo, pp. 7. 30558

HARRISON (H. W.) The Battle-Fields of the Republic, from Lexington to the City of Mexico. By Henry W. Harrison. Illustrated by ... Engravings of Medals, Portraits, and Battle-Fields. *Philadelphia.* 1857. Rl. 8vo, pp. 464. 30559

HARRISON (J.) Sketches of Upper Canada, Domestic, Local, and Characteristic, &c. By John Harrison, Esq. *London.* 1822. 8vo. 30560

HARRISON (J. B.) A Discourse on the Prospects of Letters and Taste in Virginia, pronounced before the Literary and Philosophical Society of Hampden-Sydney College, in September, 1827. By J. B. Harrison. *Cambridge.* 1828. 8vo, pp. 42. N.

HARRISON (J. S.) Pioneer Life at North Bend. An Address before the Whitewater and Miami Valley Pioneer Association, at Cleves, Ohio, Sept. 8, 1866. By J. Scott Harrison. *Cincinnati.* 1867. 8vo. 30562

HARRISON (*Mr.*) The Life of the Right Honourable Horatio Lord Vis-count Nelson, K.B. ... By Mr. Harrison. *London: Chapple.* 1806. 8vo. 30563

Details his services in the West Indies. *See* "M. Rev.," LVI. 291.

HARRISON (*Mr.*) Proposal of Mr. Harrison for the application of part of the funds of the New England Company within the territories of the Hudson's Bay Company. *London.* 1815. 8vo, pp. 15. 30564

HARRISON (R.) Colonial Sketches. By R. Harrison. *London.* 1865. 12mo. 30565

HARRISON (R.) Reasons in Support of an Opinion offered to the Public, respecting the Votes of Otsego County. By Richard Harrison and others. *New York.* 1792. 8vo. 30566

HARRISON (R. A.) Oration delivered at Pleasant Valley, Ohio, July 14, 1863. By R. A. Harrison. *London* [*Ohio*]: "*Union Print.*" 1863. 12mo, pp. 22. C. 30567

HARRISON. The Principles of Representation in Congress. Substance of Remarks made by Hon. Richard A. Harrison in the House of Representatives, February 27, 1862. [n. p. n. d.] 8vo. 30568

Also: Speech ... January 28, 1862, on the Suppression of the Rebellion. [n. p. n. d.] 8vo. — Speech ... February 27, 1862, on Claims of C. H. Upton. [n. p. n. d.] 8vo. — The Suppression of the Rebellion. Speech ... June 23, 1862. [n. p. n. d.] 8vo, pp. 8.

HARRISON (S.) Songs in the Night, by a young Woman under heavy Afflictions. By Susannah Harrison. First American Edition. *Exeter, N. H.* 1802. 18mo, pp. xii, 202. S.

An early New Hampshire imprint.

HARRISON (W.) Pickett's Men: a Fragment of War History. ... By Walter Harrison. *New York: D. Van Nostrand.* 1870. 12mo, pp. 202. 2 Plates. C. 30570

HARRISON (W. H.) A Discourse on the Aborigines of the Valley of the Ohio. In which the Opinions of the Conquest of that Valley by the Iroquois, or Six Nations, in the Seventeenth Century, supported by Cadwallader Colden, of New York, Governor Pownall, of Massachusetts, Dr. Franklin, the Hon. De Witt Clinton, of New York, and Judge Haywood, of Tennessee, are examined and contested. ... By William Henry Harrison. ... *Cincinnati.* 1838. 8vo, pp. 51. + *Boston: William D. Ticknor.* 1840. 12mo, pp. 47. 30571

Included in the "Transactions of the Historical Society of Ohio," Vol. I. *See* "N. A. Rev.," LI. 46.

HARRISON. Remarks of General Harrison, late Envoy Extraordinary and Minister Plenipotentiary of the United States to the Republic of Columbia, on certain Charges made against him by that Government. To which is added an Unofficial Letter from General Harrison to General Bolivar on the Affairs of Columbia; with Notes, explanatory of his views of the present State of that Country. *Washington: Gales & Seaton.* 1830. 8vo, pp. 69. 30572

HARRISON. Speech of Mr. Harrison, on the Bill for the relief of the Surviving Officers of the Revolution. Delivered in the Senate ... January 28, 1828. [n. p. n. d.] 8vo, pp. 12.

Also: Speech ... at the Dayton Convention, September 10, 1840. *Boston.* [1840.] 8vo, pp. 8. The following works relate to Harrison, many of them are merely electioneering affairs:

A Brief Sketch of the Life and Public Services of William Henry Harrison, ... with a Succinct Account of the Battles of Tippecanoe and the Thames. Compiled from Official Documents. *New-York: T. & C. Wood.* 1835. 8vo, pp. 31. N. + *New York.* 1839. 8vo. 30574

The Campaign for President, William H. Harrison. *Frankfort, Ky.: Brown and Hodges.* 1840. 8vo. Portrait. 30575

Condensed Memoir of the Services of William Henry Harrison. 8vo. N. 30576

The Contrast, or Plain Reasons why William Henry Harrison should be elected President ... and why Martin Van Buren should not be elected. By an old Democrat. [n. p. 1840.] 8vo, pp. 16. 30577

General Harrison in Congress, originally Compiled for and Published in the National Intelligencer. *Washington.* 1840. 8vo. Portrait. B., M. 30578

The Harrison Almanac. *New-York: J. P. Gipping.* 1841. 8vo. C. 30579

The Harrison and Log Cabin Song Book. *Columbus: I. N. Whiting.* 1840. 18mo, pp. 108. Portrait. 30580

The Harrison Medal Minstrel. ... Songs, Illustrations of the Enthusiastic Feelings of a Grateful, but Power-ridden People towards the Gallant Defender of their Country. ... *Philadelphia: Grigg & Elliot.* 1840. 18mo, pp. 192, cover, pp. 4, with Portrait. 30581

Harrison Melodies, Original and Selected. ... *Boston: Weeks, Jordan and Company.* 1840. 18mo, pp. 72. 30582

Illustrated Incidents in the Life of William Henry Harrison. *New York.* 1840. 8vo. N. 30583

Incidents in the Life of W. Henry Harrison. *Albany.* 1839. 8vo. N. 30584

The Life of Major-General William Henry Harrison, comprising a brief account of his Important Civil and Military Services, and an accurate description of the Council at Vincennes with Tecumseh, as well as the Victories of Tippecanoe, Fort Meigs, and the Thames. *Philadelphia: Grigg & Elliot.* 1840. 8vo, pp. 96. 4 Plates. 30585

The Life of William H. Harrison (of Ohio), the People's Candidate for the Presidency. With a History of the Wars with the British and Indians on our North Western Frontier. *Philadelphia.* 1840. 12mo, pp. 212. 30586

The Life of General William Henry Harrison, from the 8th No. of Haddy and Duval's Magazine. [n. p. n. d.] 8vo, pp. 16.

Outlines of the Life and Public Services, Civil and Military, of William Henry Harrison. *Newark.* 1840. 8vo. 30588

See also Cushing (C.), Vol. V., No. 18092. The following is also attributed to Cushing:

The People's Presidential Candidate; or the Life of William Henry Harrison, of Ohio. *Boston: Weeks, Jordan and Company.* 1839. 18mo, pp. 211. 30589

Plain Reasons why William Henry Harrison should be Elected President. *New York.* 1840. 8vo. 30590

Proceedings of the Common Council of New York in relation to the Funeral Ceremonies of W. H. Harrison, late President. *New York.* 1841. 8vo. 30591

Proceedings of the American Citizens at Paris, upon the Death of General Harrison, late President of the United States. *Paris: Printed by E. Briere ... .* 1841. 8vo, pp. 31. 30592

Report of the Committee ... of the Common Council of the City of New York, for the Funeral Obsequies in Memory of William H. Harrison, Late President ... with an Oration by the Hon. Theodore Frelinghuysen, Chancellor ... . [*New York: Bryant & Boggs, Printers.* [1841.] 8vo, Title, pp. 937–1034.

A Sketch of the Life and Public Services of William Henry Harrison. Commander in Chief of the North Western Army, during the War of 1812, &c. *New York: Printed by Harper & Brothers.* MDCCCXXXVI. 8vo, pp. 32. S. + *Philadelphia.* 1836. 8vo, pp. 36. C. + *Lexington, Ky.* 1836. 8vo. + *New York.* 1839. 8vo, pp. 32. + *Harrisburgh.* 1840. 8vo. + *Hartford: Printed by John B. Eldredge.* 1840. 8vo, pp. 32. 30594

Sketch of the Life of Major General William Henry Harrison, comprising a brief account of his important Civil and Military Services, including a description of the Victories, Tippecanoe, Fort Meigs, and the Thames. 1836. [n. p. n. d.] 12mo, pp. 39.

A Sketch of the Life and Public Services of Gen. William Henry Harrison, Candidate of the People of the United States, to which is annexed an Appendix. *Washington: J. Gideon.* 1840. 8vo, pp. 15. C. 30596

See also Burr (S. J.), Dawson (M.), Niles (W. O.)

HARRISON *and* DODDRIDGE (*Va.*) Contested Election. Report of Committee, January, 1848. [n. p. n. d.] 8vo. 30597

[HARRISS (Julia Mildred).] Wild Shrubs of Alabama; or, Rhapsodies of Restless Hours. By the Minstrel Maiden of Mobile. *New York: C. B. Norton.* 1852. 12mo, pp. 180. Portrait. C. 30598

[HARRISSE (Henry).] Bibliotheca Americana Vetustissima A Description of Works relating to America published between the Years 1492 and 1551 *New-York Geo. P. Philes*, MDCCCLXVI. Imp. 8vo, pp. (8), liv, 519. 30599

Four hundred copies printed in imp. 8vo, ninety-nine in 4to, and ten on Holland paper. Undertaken at the suggestion of Mr. S. L. M. Barlow, of New York, and contains the titles of over three hundred books. As as specimen of American typography, has probably never been surpassed. In regard to its merits it has received at the hands of some members of the Geographical Society of Paris very high praise, of which an English version (in part) will be found in Stevens's "Bibliotheca Historica," followed by some rather severe criticism on the work by Mr. Stevens, who, writing in the third person, quotes largely from an article in the "Athenæum" of the 6th of October, 1866, of which Mr. Stevens is the author. The writer of this notice does not presume to enter into a controversy with, or a criticism upon, the works of either of these bibliographers, but he cannot help regretting that a work so elaborate, learned, and useful to the American bibliographer, as is this "Bibliotheca," should have had any blemish, which looks like the exhibition of personal pique. We have been assured on very good authority that the blunder of "Ander Schiffahrt's" was really due to some proof-reader, and that the Index, in which Schiffahrt (Ander) is made to appear once more in *propria persona*, was not the work of Mr. Harrisse at all. Let it suffice for us to remark that for the student of the earliest of books relating to America, this book is indispensably necessary. Let us add that Mr. Harrisse has, in some instances,

quoted works from White Kennett's "Bibliothecæ Americanæ Primordia," and made the remark that he has found nothing in the works so quoted relating to America. This has arisen from the fact that he has misapprehended the nature of that work, which purposely introduces many books which had no relation to America. The following is a continuation:

[HARRISSE.] Bibliotheca Americana Vetustissima A Description of Works relating to America published between the Years 1492 and 1551 Additions *Paris Librairie Tross* M. DCCC.-LXXII. Imp. 8vo, pp. (iv), 40, 199, (1). 30600

Two hundred copies printed in 8vo, and fifty copies in 4to. In the matter of printing and paper this volume exceeds in beauty that of its predecessor. Its contents cover the same ground; some titles contained in the former work are further elaborated, and many are entirely new. It will, perhaps, not be saying too much that many of them are only remotely related to America, but the author's careful researches and elaborate dissertations have combined to render the volume a very desirable addition to an American bibliographical collection.

[HARRISSE.] A Brief Disquisition Concerning the Early History of Printing in America. *New York: Privately Printed.* 1866. Imp. 8vo. 30601

Twenty-five copies printed, of which five are on drawing paper. It forms part of the introduction to the "Bib. Am. Vetustissima." A Spanish version has been printed.

[HARRISSE.] Fernand Colomb Sa Vie, ses Œuvres Essai critique par l'auteur de la Bibliotheca Americana Vetustissima. *Paris* M DCCC LXXII Imp. 8vo, pp. (vii), 230, (1). 30602

Two hundred and fifty copies printed, of which twenty-five are on Whatman's paper.

[HARRISSE.] Notes on Columbus. *New York: Privately Printed.* 1866. Sm. folio, pp. vii, 227. 30603

Ninety copies only printed for presentation, at the expense of Samuel L. M. Barlow, of New York. It is one of the finest specimen of printing by the Riverside Press, and having been privately printed, is as rare as it is beautiful. It is both bibliographical and historical, and in each department is a specimen of zeal and erudition.

[HARRISSE.] Notes pour servir à l'histoire, à la bibliographie et à la cartographie de la Nouvelle-France et des pays adjacents 1540–1700 Par l'auteur de la Bibliotheca Americana Vetustissima *Paris Librairie Tross* 1872 Crown 8vo, pp. (6), xxxiii, (1), 367. 30604

This is a capital resumé of the Bibliography of Canada up to 1700. The volume is very handsomely printed; some copies are printed on vellum paper, and others on Dutch paper. Also: Les Colombo de France et d'Italie fameux marins du XVe siècle 1461–1492 D'après des documents nouveaux ou inédits tirés des Archives de Milan, de Paris et de Venise ... *Paris: Tross.* 1873. 4to, pp. 136. — L'Histoire de Christophe Colomb attribuée a son fils Fernand Examen Critique du Mémoire lu par M. D'Avezac, Membre de l'Institut de France a l'Académie des Inscriptions et Belles-Lettres dans ses séances des 8, 13 et 22 Aout 1873. ... *Paris.* 1875. 8vo, pp. 59.

HARRISSON (D.), *Jr.* A Voice from the Washingtonian Home. Being a History ... an Institution ... at ... Boston, for the Reformation of the Inebriate. ... Together with a Sketch of the Temperance Reform in America. By David Harrisson, Jr. ... *Boston: Redding & Co.* 1860. 8vo, pp. xii, 322, (1). Portrait. B., BA., C. 30605

HARRO-HARRING (Paul). Dolores: a Historical Novel of South America: with Episodes on Politics, Religion, Socialism, Psychology, Magnetism, and Sphereology. By P. Harro-Harring. *New York.* 1847. 8vo. 30606

HARROWER (D.) A Sermon on the Death of Mr. William Steile ... August 10, 1851. By David Harrower, A.M. *New York: Printed by Edward O. Jenkins.* MDCCCLII. 8vo, pp. 24.

HARSHA (D. A.) Life of the Rev. George Whitefield. By D. A. Harsha, ... *Albany: J. Munsell.* 1864. 8vo. 30608

Thirty-two copies on large paper.

HARSHA. The Life of Charles Sumner; with choice Specimens of his Eloquence, a Delineation of his oratorial Character, and his great Speech on Kansas. By David A. Harsha. *New York: Dayton & Burdick.* 1856. 12mo, pp. 329. Portrait and Plate. C. 30609

HARSHA. The Most Eminent Orators and Statesmen of Ancient and Modern Times; containing Sketches of their Lives, Specimens of their Eloquence, ... By David A. Harsha. *New York: Charles Scribner.* MDCCCLV. 8vo, pp. viii, 518. Portrait of Webster. B. 30610

HART (Abram). Two for One; or, a Shilling's Worth of Good Sense and a Shilling's Worth of Common Sense, for Twelve-and-a-Half Cents. *New York.* 1813. 8vo. N. 30611

HART (A. M.) History of the Discovery of the Valley of the Mississippi. By Adolphus M. Hart. *Saint Louis, Mo.: A. M. Hart.* 1852. 12mo, pp. 155. B. + Second Edition. *Cincinnati: A. M. Hart.* 1852. 12mo, pp. 155. C., H. 30612

[HART.] History of the Issues of Paper-Money in the American Colonies, Anterior to the Revolution, Explanatory of the Historical Chart of the Paper Money of that Period. *St. Louis.* 1851. 8vo. C. 30613

HART. History of the Valley of the Mississippi. By Adolphus M. Hart ... *Cincinnati: Moore, Anderson, Wilstach & Keys.* 1853. 12mo, pp. 286. B., BA., C., P. 30614

HART. Life in the Far West; or, the Comical, Quizzical, and Tragical Adventures of a Hoosier. By Adolphus M. Hart. *Cincinnati: H. B. Pearson.* [about 1854.] 8vo, pp. 131. C.

HART. Uncle Tom in Paris; or, Views of Slavery outside the Cabin. By Adolphus M. Hart ... . *Baltimore: William Taylor & Company.* 1854. 12mo, pp. 87. B. 30616

Also: Practical Suggestions on Mining Rights and Privileges in Lower Canada. *Montreal.* 1867.

HART (A. A.) The Traveler's Own Book. A Souvenir of Overland Travel, via the ... Chicago, Burlington & Quincy R. R. to Burlington; Union Pacific Railroad, to Ogden; Central Pacific Railroad, [etc.] with maps of each of the Railroads. ... By Alfred A. Hart. [*Chicago.*] 1870. Obl. 16mo, pp. 34, (10). 12 Colored Plates, 2 Photographs, 3 Maps. C. 30617

Also: Hart's Pathfinder. 1846. S.

HART (A. W.) "Our Colonies." By Arthur Wellington Hart. *Montreal.* 1849. 8vo. C. 30618

HART (B.) A Discourse on the Death of William K. Townsend, Esq. ... Sept. 30, 1849. By Rev. Burdett Hart ... . *New Haven: Durrie & Peck.* 1849. 8vo, pp. 16. 30619

HART. The Mexican War. A Discourse ... in Fair Haven, on the Annual Fast of 1847. By Rev. Burdett Hart. *New Haven: Peck & Stafford.* 1847. 8vo, pp. 16. 30620

HART (C. H.) A Biographical Sketch of ... Abraham Lincoln ... By Charles Henry Hart ... *Albany: Joel Munsell.* 1870. Sm. folio, pp. 21. S. 30621

HART. Memoir of William H. Prescott ... . By Charles H. Hart ... . *Boston: David Clapp & Son, Printers.* 1868. Rl. 8vo, pp. 13. Portrait. H. 30622

One hundred copies on large paper. Also: A Historical Sketch of the National Medals issued ... 1776–1815. ... *Philadelphia: H. B. Ashmead, Printer.* 1867. 8vo, pp. 24.—A Discourse on the Life and Services of the late Gulian Crommelin Verplanck, LL.D. ... *New York.* 1870. 8vo, pp. 20. S.—A Memoir of George Ticknor. ... *Philadelphia.* 1870. 8vo. S.—A Necrological Notice of the Hon. Richard Stockton Field, LL.D. ... *Philadelphia.* 1870. 8vo, pp. 10.—Remarks on Tabasco, Mexico, occasioned by the reported Discovery of Remains of Ancient Cities being found in that Locality. ... *Philadelphia: H. B. Ashmead, Printer.* 1867. 8vo, pp. 12. S.—A Tribute to the Memory of Hon. William Willis, LL.D. ... *Philadelphia.* 1870. 8vo, pp. 8. B., H., S.

HART (C.) De Cortice Peruviano. Auctore Cheney Hart. *Edinburgh.* 1748. 4to. P. 30623

HART (E. S.), *and* STREET (O.) *See* Whitman.

HART (F. W.) Argument on the Houmas Land Claim. By Dr. Frederic W. Hart ... . *Washington: Thomas McGill.* 1860. 8vo, pp. 14 H. 30624

[HART *and* TILLOTSON (Romants).] Exposition of the Houmas Land Claim, and of the Second Section of the Missouri Land Bill ... June 2, 1858. ... *Washington.* 1859. 8vo, pp. 30.

HART (G.) Trial of George Hart for the Murder of Mary Van Housen. New York ... Nov., 1811. With his Life and Confession. [n. p. n. d.] 8vo. S. 30626

HART (J. Seely). A Brief Exposition of the Constitution of the United States. For the use of Common Schools. By John S. Hart, A.M. ... *Philadelphia: Butler & Williams.* 1845. 12mo, pp. 100. H. + *Philadelphia.* 1858. + [*Ibid.*] 1860. 30627

HART. The Female Prose Writers of America. With Portraits, Biographical Notices, and Specimens of their Writings. By John S. Hart ... *Philadelphia: E. H. Butler & Co.* 1852. 8vo, pp. 432. BA. + New Edition, Revised and Enlarged. *Philadelphia.* 1855. 8vo, pp. 620. C. + Fourth Edition. *Philadelphia: E. H. Butler & Co.* 1864. 8vo, pp. 436. B. 30628

See "N. A. Rev.," LXXX. 261. Also: The Common School Journal of the State of Pennsylvania. Vol. I. *Philadelphia.* 1844. Continued.

HART (J.) State of the Accounts of Joseph Hart, Esquire, Lieutenant of Bucks County, From ... 1780, to ... 1783; In which is set forth the amount of the fines incurred within that period by delinquents of the 1st battallion, for non-performance of militia duty and exercise ... . *Philadelphia: Printed by Robert Aitken.* M DCC LXXXIII. 8vo, pp. 24. P. 30629

Also: State of the Accounts of Joseph Hart, Esq. Late Lieutenant ... . From ... March, to ... November, 1783. *Philadelphia: Printed by John Steele.* M,DCC,LXXXV. 8vo, pp. 11. P.

HART (J. C.) The Romance of Yachting: Voyage the First. By Joseph C. Hart ... . *New York: Harper & Brothers.* 1848. 12mo, pp. 332. H., N. 30630

Many chapters relate to America, and some to Shakespeare, sustaining the Baconian theory.

HART (L.) A Christian Minister described and distinguished from a Pleaser of Men, in a discourse ... at the Ordination of Reverend Abiel Holmes ... . By Levi Hart ... . *New Haven: Printed by Meigs & Dana.* M.DCC.LXXXVII. 8vo, pp. 56. BA., M.

Includes a Memoir of the Church.

HART. The Christian Minister ... described. A Sermon Delivered at the Ordination of the Reverend Mr. Joel Benedict, At Newent, in Norwich, On the 21st of February, 1771. By Levi Hart, A.M. ... *New-London: Printed by Timothy Green.* 1771. 8vo, pp. (2), 31. 30632

HART. A Discourse ... at Newport, Rhode Island, at the Funeral of the Rev. Samuel Hopkins, D.D., Pastor ... there, who died on the 20th of December, A.D. 1803, in the Eighty-Third Year of his Age, and Sixtieth of his Ministry. By Levi Hart, A.M. [*Newport.*] 1804. 12mo, pp. 24. 30633

HART. Liberty described and recommended, in a Sermon to the Corporation of Freemen in Farmington, Sep. 20, 1774. By Levi Hart. *Hartford: Eben. Watson.* 1775. 8vo. + *Boston.* 1775. 8vo. 30634

"The general assembly (preaches Levi) of a neighbouring Colony [Rhode Island] have prohibited the importation of Negro slaves under a large penalty, and have enacted that such slaves shall be free as soon as they set foot on the shore within the Colony. Can this Colony [Connecticut] want motives from reason, justice, religion, or public spirit to follow the example?"

HART. Religious Improvement of the Death of Great Men. A Discourse ... in Preston ... Dec. 29, 1799, Occasioned by the Death of Gen. George Washington ... By Levi Hart, A.M. *Norwich: Printed by Thomas Hubbard.* 1800. 8vo, pp. (4), 26.

One of the rarest of Washington orations.

HART. ... Discourse at the Funeral of the Reverend Timothy Stone, Pastor of the Church at Goshen in Lebanon; Who died, May 12th, 1797, in the 56th year of his age, and 30th of his Ministry. By Levi Hart, A.M. ... *Printed in Norwich (Connecticut) by John Trumbull.* M,DCC,XCVIII. 8vo, pp. 22. 30636

HART. The Resurrection ... illustrated. In a Discourse ... Addressed to the Second Congregational Church ... Newport, Rhode-Island, at the Ordination of the Reverend William Patten ... May 24, 1786. By Levi Hart, A.M., Pastor of a Church in Preston, Connecticut. *Providence: Printed by John Carter.* 1786. 8vo, pp. 30, 19, (1). BA. 30637

Also: The Description of a Good Character. Election Sermon, 1786. *Hartford.* [1786.] 8vo, pp. 30. M.—Discourse occasioned by the Death of the Hon. Jabez Huntington, Esq., delivered at Norwich, October 8, 1786. ... *New London: Printed by T. Green.* 1786. 8vo.— ... A Discourse at the Ordination of the Reverend John Wilder, ... Attleborough, January 27, 1790. *Providence: Printed by Bennett Wheeler.* [n. d.] 8vo, pp. 27. H., N.—Discourse at the Funeral of N. Eells, July 3, 1786. *New London.* 8vo.— ... Discourse: Delivered at Chelsea in Norwich, May 22, 1791. ... [on] the death and funeral of Mrs. Sarah King. ... *Norwich: Printed by Ebenezer Russell Bushnell.* M,DCC,XCII. 8vo, pp. 34.—The Important Objects of the Evangelical Ministry considered; ... In a Discourse at the Ordination of the Rev. Mr. Amos Chase, ... June 27th, 1787. ... *Litchfield: Printed by Thomas Collier.* M.DCC.LXXXVIII. 8vo, pp. 26.—Sermon ... January 4, 1789 ... on the Death of his Wife: ... *New-London.* 1789. 8vo. S.

HART (L.) A Memoir of the Life of the Rev. Amos Pettengil. ... By Rev. Luther Hart ... . *Boston.* 1834. 12mo, pp. (4), 264. H. 30638

[HART (*Miss*).] Letters from the Bahama Islands, Written in 1823–4. *Philadelphia.* 1827. 12mo. P. 30639

HART (N. C.) Documents relative to the House of Refuge, instituted by the Society for the Reformation of Juvenile Delinquents in the City of New York, in 1824. ... By Nathaniel C. Hart, Superintendent. *New York: Printed by Mahlon Day.* 1832. 8vo, pp. 311. Plate. BA. 30640

HART (O. B.) Argument by O. B. Hart. [n. p. n. d.] 8vo, pp. 12. 30641

Application for a Seat in the Senate as Senator of Florida.

HART (O.) America's Remembrancer, with respect to her Blessedness and Duty. A Sermon ... in Hopewell, New Jersey, on Thanksgiving Day, November 26, 1789. By Oliver Hart, A.M. ... *Philadelphia: Printed by T. Dobson.* M,DCC,XCI. 8vo, pp. 24. BA., P. 30642

Also: Dancing Exploded: a Sermon in Charleston, S. C., March 22, 1778. *Charleston.* 1778. 8vo, pp. 32. N.—A Gospel Church portrayed. ... A Sermon delivered in Philadelphia at the opening of the Baptist Association, October 4, 1791. *Trenton.* 1791. 8vo, pp. 38.—Sermon at Charleston, S. C., on the Death of Rev. William Tennent. *Charleston.* 1777. 12mo. W.—Sermon before the Association at Philadelphia, October 21, 1783. ... *Philadelphia.* 1785? 12mo.

HART (R.) Reconstruction. Speech of Hon. Roswell Hart, of New York ... March 24, 1866. [*Washington.* n. d.] 8vo, pp. 8. 30643

HART (S.) Elegy to the Memory of Miss Sarah Hart, Daughter to Rev. William Hart, of Saybrook; who departed this Life, June 24, 1788. *Hartford.* 1790. 8vo, pp. 7. M. 30644

HART (S.) A Sermon, preached in (the newly rebuilt) St. George's Church, Hempstead ... September 21, 1823. To which is prefixed a short Historical Sketch of the most Important Events relative to the said Church, for a Century past. By the Reverend Seth Hart, Rector. *New York: Printed by T. and J. Swords.* 1823. 8vo, pp. 16. H. 30645

HART (W.) Brief Remarks on a number of False Propositions, and Dangerous Errors, Which are spreading in the Country; Collected out of sundry Discourses publish'd, wrote by Dr. Whitaker and Mr. Hopkins. Written by Way of Dialogue, By William Hart, A.M. ... *New-London: Printed and Sold by Timothy Green.* 1769. 8vo, pp. 71, (1). BA., H., N., W. 30646

HART. A Few Remarks, upon the Ordination of the Rev'd Mr. James Dana, and the Doings of the Consociation, respecting the Same: Being a Letter to the Author of the Faithful Narrative, &c. By William Hart ... . *New Haven: Printed by James Parker and Company.* 1759. 8vo, pp. 46, xv, (3). BA., M., W.

HART. Remarks on a late Pamphlet, Wrote by Mr. Hobart, Entitled, The Principles of Congregational Churches, relating to the Constitution and Authority of Ecclesiastical Councils; considered, and applied to the case of the late Ordination at Wallingford, [Conn.] ... By William Hart ... . *New Haven: Printed by J. Parker, and Company.* 1760. 8vo, pp. 59, iii, (5). BA., W.

Also: A Discourse concerning the Nature of Regeneration, and the Way Wherein it is Wrought. *N. London: T. Green.* 1742. Sm. 8vo, pp. (6), 57.—Letter to Rev. Sam. Hopkins. *New London: T. Green.* 1770. 8vo.—A Letter to the Reverend Nathaniel Whitaker, D.D., wherein Some of his ... Misrepresentations ... are detected ... . *New London: Printed by T. Green.* 1771. 8vo, pp. 63. BA., M.—Remarks on President Edwards's Dissertations concerning the Nature of True Virtue ... . *New-Haven: Printed by T. and S. Green.* 1771. 8vo, pp. 52. BA.—A Scriptural Answer to this Question, ... What are the necessary Qualifications for a lawful and approved Attendance on the Sacraments of the New Covenant? ... *New London: Printed by Timothy Green.* 1772. 8vo, pp. 80, (2). BA.

HART (W.) The Travelling Book-Agent's Guide and Instructor ... By William Harte ... . *Boston: D. C. Colesworthy.* 1865. 12mo, pp. 16. 30649

HARTE (F. B.) The Luck of Roaring Camp, and other Sketches. By Francis Bret Harte. *Boston: Fields, Osgood & Co.* 1870. 16mo, pp. iv, (2), 239. BA., C. 30650

Mr. Harte has also published Mrs. Skagg's Husbands, and other Sketches. *Boston: Osgood.* 1873. 16mo, and Echoes of the Foot-Hills. [*Ibid.*] 1875 [1874]. 16mo, the first a collection of stories, the second of poems illustrative of Western life, &c.

[HARTE (Walter).] Essays on Husbandry: ... *London: W. Frederick.* MDCCLXIV. 8vo, pp. xviii, (3), 213. B., H. + Second Edition. [*Ibid.*] M.DCC.LXX. 8vo, pp. xxvi, (2), 232. H. 30651

Relates to the husbandry of the North American colonies, &c.

HARTFORD, *Conn.* Addresses ... on the ... Dedication of the Hartford Hospital ... Conn., ... 18th of April, 1859. *Hartford: Case, Lockwood and Company.* 1859. 8vo, pp. 40. 30652

Also: The First Annual Report of the Executive Committee of the Hartford Hospital ... 1855–56. *Hartford: Case, Tiffany and Company.* 1856. 8vo, pp. 18. Continued. H.

First Report of the Directors of the American Asylum at Hartford, for the Education and Instruction of the Deaf and Dumb ... 1817. *Hartford: Hudson and Co.* 1817. 8vo, pp. 15. Continued. H. 30653

Annual Report of the Hartford Evangelical Tract Society. [*Hartford.* 1817.] 12mo, pp. 10, (1). BA. 30654

By Laws of the City of Hartford relative to Fire, and Names of the Officers of the Fire Department. [*Hartford.*] 1832. 8vo, pp. 19. 30655

Catalogue of the North Church, Hartford. *Hartford.* 1839.

The Charter of the City of Hartford. ... *Hartford.* 1862. 8vo, pp. 36, 10. Continued. 30657

Also: The Ordinances of the City of Hartford ... 1863. ... *Hartford: Williams, Wiley & Waterman.* 1863. 8vo, pp. 144. Continued. S.

Copy of the Report of the Joint Committee of the Legislature of Connecticut on the Petition of C. Stockbridge and others against the Hartford Bridge Company. [*Hartford.* 1839.] 8vo.

Constitution of the Hartford Auxiliary of the American Colonization Society. *Hartford.* 1819. 8vo, pp. 16. 30659

Directory. Gardner's Hartford City Directory. Published Annually. 1838. 12mo. 30660

Continued to 1841; followed by Geer's Hartford Directory from 1842.

Education. The Annual Catalogue of the Hartford Female Seminary for 1828. [n. p. n. d.] 8vo, pp. 15. Continued.

Also: African Mission-School Society. Address of the Executive Committee, with Record of Proceedings, &c. *Hartford.* 1828. 8vo, pp. 11.—Catalogue of the Hartford Public High School, for the Year 1862–3. *Hartford: Press of Case, Lockwood & Company.* 1862. 8vo, pp. 19, (1).—Circular of Hartford Female Seminary, Hartford, Conn. Founded A.D. 1823. Incorporated A.D. 1827. *Hartford: Press of Williams, Wiley and Turner.* 1862. 8vo, pp. 24.—Hartford Female Seminary. Prospectus: By Catharine E. Beecher. 1827. 8vo, pp. 9.—Report of the Board of School Visitors to First School Society of Hartford ... 1856. ... *Hartford: Case, Tiffany and Company.* 1857. 8vo, pp. 23. H.

The Hartford | Convention | in an Uproar! | And the | Wise Men of the East | Confounded! | Together with a | Short History of the | Peter Washingtonians; | being | the First Book of the Chronicles | of the | Children of Disobedience; | otherwise falsely called | "Washington Benevolents." | By Hector Benevolus, Esq. | *Windsor, Vt.*, | ... 1815. | 8vo, pp. 46. 30662

Very rare. The only copy we know belongs to E. G. Asay of Chicago. *See also* Cabot (G.), Dwight (T.), Massachusetts, Proceedings, Public Documents.

... The Identity of the Old Hartford Convention Federalists with the Modern Whig, Harrison Party. ... [*Boston.* 1840.] 8vo, pp. 14. 30663

HARTFORD ARGILLO MANUFACTURING COMPANY. Report, United States Senate [on the] Memorial; July 31, 1848. [n. p. n. d.] 8vo, pp. 6. 30664

Hartford in the Olden Time: Its First Thirty Years. By Scæva. Edited by W. M. B. Hartley. With Illustrations. *Hartford: F. A. Brown.* 1853. 8vo, pp. (2), 316. 5 Plates and Map. H. 30665

HARTFORD TRACT SOCIETY. Speeches of Judges Williams, Parsons, and Ellsworth. *Hartford.* 1859. 8vo, pp. 26. S.

Hartford War Debt Bonds. Town Meeting. *Hartford, December 23d,* 1862. 12mo, pp. 7. 30667

Also: Report of Special Committee relative to War Debt Bonds. 1862.

Historical Notices of Hartford. *Hartford.* 1842. 8vo.

Proceedings at the Dedication of Charter Oak Hall, at Hartford, Conn. *Hartford.* 1856. 8vo, pp. 15. 30669

Edited by J. Deane Alden.

Railroads. Report of the Engineer upon the several definite Locations for the Hartford and Springfield Railroad; with the Acts of Incorporation in Connecticut and Massachusetts. *Hartford.* 1841. 8vo. Map. 30670

Report of Joint Committee upon Petition of Hartford and New Haven Railroad Company. 8vo, pp. 7. 30671

Report of the Committee on the Petition of the Town of East Hartford and others, against the Hartford Bridge Company. *Hartford.* 1843. 8vo. 30672

Also: Report of the Joint Standing Committee on the Petition of the Hartford-Bridge Company; General Assembly, May, 1841. *Hartford.* 1841. 8vo, pp. 9.

First Annual Report of the Hartford Soldiers' Aid Association, January 1, 1863. *Hartford.* 1863. 8vo, pp. 20. 30673

Retreat for the Insane at Hartford, Conn.: Third Report of the Directors, ... May 11, 1827. *Hartford.* 1827. 8vo, pp. 11. Continued. 30674

Also: Society for the Relief of the Insane ... At Hartford. ... *Hartford: W. Hudson and L. Skinner.* 1823. 8vo, pp. 32. BA.

Transactions of the Natural History Society of Hartford. No. 1. *Hartford: Case, Tiffany & Co.* M DCCC XXXVI. 8vo, pp. 91. B., H. 30675

A Unanimous Remonstrance of the Fourth Congregational Church, Hartford, Conn., against the Policy of the American Tract Society on the Subject of Slavery. *Hartford: Foundry of Silas Andrus & Son.* 1855. 12mo, pp. 34. + *New York: Anti-Slavery Society.* 1855. 30676

Young Men's Institute, Hartford. First Annual Report of the Executive Committee ... together with the Charter, By Laws ... . *Hartford: Printed by Case, Tiffany & Burnham.* 1839. 8vo, pp. 14, (2). Continued. B., S. 30677

Catalogue of the Library and Reading Room of the Young Men's Institute, Hartford. *Hartford: Case, Tiffany & Burnham.* 1844. 8vo, pp. 359. H. + Catalogue of Books added to the Library since 1844. *Hartford: Case, Tiffany & Burnham.* 1848. 8vo, pp. 32. + Catalogue of Books added ... since 1847. *Hartford.* 1852. 8vo. + Catalogue ... . *Hartford: The Institute.* 1873. 8vo, pp. vi, 471, (1). BA. 30678

See also Trinity and Washington Colleges.

Hartford County Agricultural Society. Transactions for 1843 and 1844. *Hartford: E. Geer.* 1845. 8vo, pp. 110. C.

HARTGERTS *or* HARTGERS (Joost). [Engraved Title:] Oost en West-indische | Voyagien: | Met de | Beschrijvingen van | Indien. | Eerste Deel. | *t'Amsterdam, bij Ioost Hartgers. Inde Gasthuys-steech bij't Stad-huys.* 1648. | [Printed Title:] Oost-Indische Voyagien | Door dien | Begin en Voortgangh, van de Vereenighde | Nederlandtsche Geoctroyeerde | Oost-Indische | Compagnie. | Vervatende de voornaemste Reysen, by de Inwoonderen der | selver Provintien derwaerts ghedaem. | ... | Erste Deel. Daer in begrepen zijn 16 Voyagien. | *t'Amstelredam,* | *Voor Joost Hartgerts, Boeck-verkooper in de Gasthuys-Streegh, bezijden* | *het Stadt-huys, in de Boeck-winckel, Anno,* 1648. | 4to. C. 30680

This extraordinary Collection of Voyages by Joost Hartgerts is sometimes called the "Dutch De Bry" or the "Dutch Hulsius;" for in beauty of execution and intrinsic interest it rivals both of those famous collections. In point of rarity there is no comparison; this being scarcely known to bibliographers. How many parts Hartgerts published, it is even now uncertain, although the most active research has for many years been made by Collectors of Voyages and Travels. The parts were probably issued and sold separately, and their collection into sets, with a collective title, preface, etc., was an afterthought. This collection has an advantage over De Bry and Hulsius, that many of the voyages are in the language in which they were originally written, while most of those by De Bry and Hulsius are translations. *See* Stevens' "Nuggets," No. 1339, for complete titles and collations. Of so many as relate to America, Parts VI., VIII., and X., we give the titles at length under the names of their respective authors.

HARTLEY (C. B.) Heroes and Patriots of the South; comprising Lives of General Francis Marion, General William Moultrie, General Andrew Pickens, and Governor John Rutledge. With Sketches of other distinguished Heroes and Patriots who served in the Revolutionary War in the Southern States. By Cecil B. Hartley. *Philadelphia: G. G. Evans.* 1860. 12mo, pp. 320. Plate. C., H. 30681

Reprinted as: The Life of Gen. Francis Marion: also, Lives of Generals Moultrie and Pickens, and Governor Rutledge. ... *Philadelphia: Davis, Porter & Coates.* 1866. 12mo, pp. 320. B.

HARTLEY. Life and Adventures of Lewis Wetzel, The Virginia Ranger, to which are added Biographical Sketches of General Simon Kenton, General Benjamin Logan, Captain Samuel Brady, Governor Isaac Shelby and other Heroes of the West. ... By Cecil B. Hartley. ... *Philadelphia: G. G. Evans.* 1860. 12mo, pp. 320. 30682

An edition dated 1869 differs slightly in the title-page only.

HARTLEY. Life and Times of Colonel Daniel Boone, comprising a History of the Early Settlement of Kentucky. By Cecil B. Hartley. To which is added Colonel Boone's Autobiography complete, as dictated to John Filson, and published in 1784. ... *Philadelphia: G. G. Evans.* 1859. + [*Ibid.*] 1860. 12mo, pp. 351. 30683

HARTLEY. Life of Major General Henry Lee, Commander of Lee's Legion in the Revolutionary War, and subsequently Governor of Virginia; to which is added the Life of General Thomas Sumter, of South Carolina. By Cecil B. Hartley. *Philadelphia: G. G. Evans.* 1859. 12mo. S. + *New York.* 1859. 12mo. C. 30684

Also: The Three Mrs. Judsons, the celebrated Female Missionaries. A New Edition. *Philadelphia: G. G. Evans.* 1860. 12mo, pp. 419. 2 Portraits. C.

HARTLEY (D.) An Address to the Committee of Association of the County of York, on the State of Public Affairs. By David Hartley Esq. January 3, 1781. The Second Edition. *York: A. Ward.* 1781. 8vo, pp. 46. N. 30685

Chiefly relating to the War with the American Colonies.

HARTLEY. An Address to the Committee of the County of York, on the State of Public Affairs. By David Hartley, Esq. *London: J. Stockdale.* MDCCLXXXI. 8vo, pp. 63. BA., H., M., P.

A reprint of the preceding, with the addition of "The Address of the Committee of Association for the County of York." *See* "M. Rev." for February, 1781.

HARTLEY. An Address to the ... Mayor and Corporation ... the Wardens ... of Trinity House, and to the Worthy Burgesses of ... Kingston. By David Hartley, Esq. *London: J. Debrett.* 1784. 8vo, pp. 31. BA. 30687

HARTLEY. Addresses and Letters on the State of Public Affairs. *York.* 1781. C. 30688

"The Budget," *our* No. 8964, is perhaps by Hartley.

HARTLEY. Letters on the American War. Addressed to the ... Mayor and Corporation; ... the Wardens and Corporation of the Trinity-House, and to the Worthy Burgesses of ... Kingston-upon-Hull. By David Hartley, Esq., Member of Parliament for ... Hull. *London: J. Almon.* MDCCLXXVII. 4to, pp. 92. + Second Edition. [*Ibid.*] MDCCLXXVIII B. + Third Edition. [*Ibid.*] MDCCLXXVIII. H. + Fifth Edition. *London: J. Almon.* MDCCLXXIX. 8vo, pp. 126. C. + Sixth Edition. [*Ibid.*] MDCCLXXIX. 8vo. C. + Eighth Edition. [*Ibid.*] MDCCLXXIX. 8vo, pp. (2), ii, 126. BA. 30689

The autograph signature of the author is affixed to each letter of the 4to editions. "In these letters Mr. Hartley endeavors to prove, that whatever pretexts may have been held out, coercion, and not reconciliation, was from the very first the secret and adopted plan, and this plan hath ever since been systematically and inflexibly pursued." —*Monthly Review.* *See* Sparks' "Franklin," VIII. 312.

[HARTLEY.] Motions | made in the | House of Commons, | on | Monday, the 27th of March, 1775. | Together with a | Draught | of a | Letter of Requisition | to the | Colonies. | [*London:*] *J. Almon.* [1775.] 4to, pp. (2), 14. 30690

These motions and the proposed letter of requisition, were the parts of a plan offered by Mr. Hartley, for restoring peace between Great Britain and her American colonies. *See* "M. Rev.," LII. 548.

HARTLEY. Speech and Motions made in the House of Commons on Monday March 27th 1775 together with a Draught of a Letter of Requisition to the Colonies. By David Hartley. *London.* 1775. 8vo, pp. 32. C. + Second Edition. [*Ibid.*]

HARTLEY. Substance of a Speech in Parliament, Upon the State of the Nation and the Present Civil War with America, ... April 1, 1776. By David Hartley, Esq. *London: J. Almon.* MDCCLXXVI. 4to, pp. (2), 24. + Second Edition. [*Ibid.*] BA.

See "M. Rev.," LIV. 403.

HARTLEY. Two Letters from D. Hartley Esq: M.P. addressed to the Committee of the County of York. *London: J. Almon.* M,DCC,LXXX. 8vo, pp. 21. BA., N. 30693

On American Affairs. *See* "M. Rev.," LXII. 486. Also: Address to the Authorities of the Town of Kingston-upon-Hull. 1784. 8vo, pp. 15. N.

HARTLEY (O. C.) A Digest of the Laws of Texas: to which is subjoined an Appendix containing the Acts of Congress of the United States on the Subjects of the Naturalization of Aliens, and the Authentication of Records, &c., in each State or Territory, so as to take effect in every other State or Territory; and to which are prefixed the Constitutions of the United States, of the Provisional Government of Texas, of the Republic of Texas, and of the State of Texas. By Oliver C. Hartley, of Galveston. *Philadelphia: Thomas, Cowperthwait & Co.* 1850. 8vo, pp. viii, 1041, (1). BA., C. 30694

HARTLEY (R. M.) Intemperance in Cities ... . By Robert M. Hartley. *New York: John F. Trow.* M.DCCCLI. 12mo, pp. 209. B., H. 30695

HARTLEY (T.) A Discourse on Mistakes concerning Religion, Enthusiasm, Experience, &c. By Thomas Hartley, A.M. ... *London printed. Germantown, reprinted by Christopher Sower.* 1759. 8vo, pp. 168. P. 30696

Another edition, pp. 74, is usually found with Bromley's (T.) "Way to ... Rest."

[HARTLEY (Thomas).] Observations on the Propriety of Fixing upon a Central and Inland Situation for the Permanent Residence of Congress. Humbly offered to the Consideration of the Honorable the Members of the Senate and House of Representatives of the United States. By the Author. *Printed in the Year* MDCCLXXXIX. 8vo, pp. 11. P. 30697

Written by Thomas Hartley; published at New York, August 25th, 1789; signed Phocion; and urges York, in Pennsylvania, as the best site.

HARTLEY (W. M. B.) The Neoshoo Valley. By W. M. B. Hartley. 8vo, pp. 10. 30698

See also "Hartford in the Olden Time."

[HARTLIB (Samuel).] Glory be to God on high, Peace on Earth, Good will amongst men. | A Rare and New | Discovery | of | A speedy way, and easie means, found out by a | young Lady in England, she having made full proofe | therof in May, Anno 1652. | For the feeding of Silk-worms in the Woods, | on the Mulberry-Tree-leaves in Virginia: Who after fourty | dayes time present their most rich golden-coloured silken | Fleece, to the instant wonderfull enriching of all | the Planters there, requiring from them | neither cost, labour, or hindrance in any | of their other employments | whatsoever. | And also to the good hopes that the Indians, | Seeing and finding that there is neither Art, Skill or Pains in | the thing: they will readily set upon it, being by the benefit | therof inabled to buy of the English (in way of | Truck for their Silk-bottomes) all those | things that they most desire. | So that not only their Civilizing will follow, | thereupon, but by the infinite mercie of God, their Conversion | to the Christian Faith, the Glory of our Nation, which | is the daily humble prayer | Of | Virginia for Virginia. | With two Propositions tending to England's and the | Colonies infinite advantage. | *Printed for Richard Woodenothe in Leaden-hall street.* 1652. | 4to. 30699

Title 1 l., To the Reader, signed Samuel Hartlib, and Instructions, 3 l., Verses, 4 l., Text, 12 pp. On the title-page of a copy, once in my possession, after the word Virginia, is written "being the Daughter of Mr. Ananias Dare born 18 of Augt 1587 On the Island of Roanak who being the first Child born there of English Parents was Christened Virginia." One of the poems, however, is "By her Brother," and is signed "John Ferran," which is inconsistent with the name of "Dare," unless he was her brother-in-law. Afterwards reprinted with the following title:

[HARTLIB.] The Reformed | Virginian | Silk-Worm, | Or, a Rare and New | Discovery | of | A speedy way, and easie means, found out | by a young Lady in England, she having made | full proof thereof in May, | Anno 1652. | For the feeding of Silk-worms in the Woods, on the | Mulberry-Tree-leaves in Virginia: Who after forty dayes | time, present their most rich golden-coloured silken | Fleece, to the instant wonderful enriching of | all the Planters there, requiring from | them neither cost, labour, or

hindrance | in any of their other employ- | ments whatsoever. | And also to the good hopes, that the Indians, see- | ing and finding that there is neither Art, Skill, or Pains | in the thing: they will readily set upon it, being | by the benefit thereof inabled to buy of the | English (in way of Truck for their | Silk-bottoms) all those things | that they most desire. | *London,* | *Printed by John Streater, for Giles Calvert at the* | *Black-Spread-Eagle at the West end* | *of Pauls,* 1655. | 4to, pp. (4), 40. 30700

Reprinted with additions as below:

HARTLIB. The Reformed | Common-wealth | of | Bees | Presented in severall Letters and | Observations to Samuel Hartlib, Esq. | with | The Reformed Virginian Silk-Worm. | Containing | Many Excellent and Choice Secrets, Experiments, | and Discoveries for Attaining of Natio- | nal and Private Profits | and Riches. | *London,* | *Printed for Giles Calvert at the Black-Spread-Eagle at* | *the West-end of Pauls,* 1655. | Small 4to, pp. (4), 62, (2).

Scarce; at the end are some curious poems by Du Bartas and others. *See* Force' "Tracts," Vol. III., No. 13.

HARTLIB. Samuel Hartlib, his Legacie; or an enlargement of the Discourse of Husbandry used in Brabant and Flaunders; wherein are bequeathed to the Commonwealth of England more Outlandish and Domestick Experiments and Secrets in reference to Universal Husbandry. *London: H. Hills.* 1651. Small 4to, pp. (8), 131. C. 30702

Really written by Robert Child at Hartlib's request; relates to silk-worms, etc., and includes many references to New England husbandry.

HARTMAN (G. W.) A Private's Journal in the Battles in Mexico, under General Scott. *Greencastle (Pa.)* 1849. 12mo.

HARTMANN (C.) Geographisch-statistische Beschreibung von Californien. Aufschlüsse über die Lage, den Boden und das Clima des Landes, über seine Bewohner, ihr Leben, Sitten und Gebräuche, etc. *Weimar.* 1849. 2 vols., 8vo. Map. 30704

HARTMANN (J. A.) Dissertatio geographica de vero Californiæ situ et conditione: aucthore Joh. Adolph. Hartmann. *Marburg.* 1739. 4to. 30705

Title from Meusel, III. 1, 351.

HARTMANN *et* MILLARD. Le Texas, ou Notice Historique sur le Champ d'Asile; comprenant tout ce qui s'est passé depuis la formation jusqu'à la dissolution de cette colonie, les causes qui l'ont amenée, et la liste de tous les colons français, avec des renseignemens utiles à leurs familles, et le plan du camp, Dédié à Messieurs les Souscripteurs en faveur des Réfugiés. Par MM. Hartmann et Millard, Membres du Champ d'Asile, nouvellement de retour en France. *A Paris, chez Béguin, Juin,* 1819. 8vo, pp. (10), 135. Map. A., B., H. 30706

HARTPENCE (A.) Our National Crisis: A Sermon Preached in ... Holmesburg, Pa., September 14, 1862, By Rev. A. Hartpence, A.M. ... *Philadelphia.* 1862. 8vo, pp. 8. 30707

Hartroerende, Stigtelyke Bespiegeling behelzende de Memorie van Ridder Yorke (10 Nov.), met aanmerkingen van Will. Penn Sec., Quaker. [1780.] 8vo, pp. 22. 30708

Cordial and edifying contemplation of the Memorial of Chev. York, with notes by W. Penn.

HARTSHORN (C. W.) The New England Sheriff; being a Digest of the Laws of Massachusetts ... . Second Edition ... . *Worcester: Enos Dorr & Company.* 1855. 8vo, pp. 416. B.

[HARTSHORNE (Richard), *and others.*] A further Account of New Jersey, in an abstract of Letters lately writ from thence, By several Inhabitants there resident. *Printed in the Year* 1676. 4to, pp. 16. 30710

A volume of the greatest rarity—*presque unique.* The first letter is by Richard Hartshorne, dated, New Jersie, Midleton, 12th of the 9th month, 1675; the second is by Martha S., New Jersey, the 22nd of 9th month, 1675; the third is by Robert Wade, Delarware River, the place called Upland, the 2nd of the 2nd month, 1676; the fourth is by Ester Huckens, New Jersey, Delaware, April the 4th, 1676; the fifth is by Robert Wade, 17th of 4th month, 1676; the sixth is by Roger Pederick, From Delaware River, the 14th day of the 4th month, 1676. "Richard Hartshorne lived in Middletown, in East-Jersey; he was one of the People called Quakers, of good reputation, public character, and of a benevolent disposition, in those early times. He came thither from London, in the 7th month, old style 1669; where he lived many years." —SMITH'S *Quakers.* *See* Proud's "History of Pennsylvania," I. 138, note.

HARTSHORNE (R. T.) American Lloyd's Register of American and Foreign Shipping. R. T. Hartshorne & J. F. H. King, Proprietors. *New York: J. W. Pratt & Co.* 1867. pp. xxxii, 730. 5 Plates. C. 30711

Continued as "United States Lloyd's Register of American and Foreign Shipping."

HARTSINCK (J. J.) Beschryving van Guiana, of de Wildekust, in Zuid-America, Betreffende de Aardrykskunde en Historie des Lands, de Zeeden en Gewoontes der Inwooners, de Dieren, Vogels, Visschen, Boomen en Gewassen, als mede de eerste Ontdekking dier Kust, de Bezittingen der Spanjaarden, Franschen en Portugeezen en voornaamelyk de Volkplantingen der Nederlanderen, als Essequebo, Demerary, Berbice, Suriname en derzelver Rivieren, met de noodige Kaarten en Afbeeldingen der Forten. Waarby komt eene Verhandeling over den Aart en de Gewoontes der Neger-Slaaven. Alles uit echte stukken opgesteld door M^r. Jan Jacob Hartsinck ... . *Amsterdam: Gerrit Tielenburg.* MDCCLXX. 2 vols., 4to, pp. xii, (4), 520; (1), 521–962, (15). 14 Maps and Plates. BA., H. 30712

This description of Guiana or the wild coast of South America, its geography, history, inhabitants, animals, with an account of its discovery and the colonies of the Spaniards, French and Portuguese, is said by Mr. Warden to be "by far the best work ever published on the countries described." The author was Director of the East India Company, and a man of very high standing, who had access to all the authorities. Quaritch remarks: "It will serve to temper the warm colouring of Stedman's narrative." There are copies on large paper. The following is a German translation:

HARTSINCK. Beschreibung von Guiana oder der wilden Küste in Südamerika ... . Aus dem Holländischen übersetzt. *Berlin: bei Johann Friedrich Unger.* 1784. 8vo, pp. xiv, 472. 4 Maps.

HARTT (C. F.) Thayer Expedition. Scientific Results of a Journey in Brazil, by Louis Agassiz and his Travelling Companions. Geology and Physical Geography of Brazil. By Ch. Fred. Hartt ... . *Boston: Fields, Osgood & Co.* 1870. 8vo, pp. xxiii, 620. 8 Plates, 3 Maps. B., BA., C., H. 30714

HARTWELL (A.) Memoir of the Late Rev. John Pierce. By Abraham Hartwell. ... *Lunenburg: The Author.* 1842. 8vo, pp. 180. Portrait. H. 30715

HARTWELL (H.), BLAIR *and* CHILTON. The Present State of Virginia, and the College: By Messieurs Hartwell, Blair, and Chilton. To which is added, The Charter for Erecting the said College, granted by their late Majesties King William and Queen Mary of Ever Glorious and Pious Memory. *London: John Wyatt.* M.DCC.XXVII. 8vo, pp. (4), 95. C., H., P. 30716

Very rare. The authors were Henry Hartwell, Esq., of the Royal Council of Virginia, the Rev. James Blair, President of William and Mary College, and Edw. Chilton, Esq., Attorney General of Virginia, and afterwards of Barbadoes.

HARTWICK SEMINARY. Annual Catalogue of the Officers and Students of Hartwick Theological and Classical Seminary. *Albany.* 1827. 8vo. Continued. 30717

HARTWICK SYNOD. Minutes of the ... Annual Session of the Hartwick Synod, of the Evangelical Lutheran Church, in the State of New York. 1809. 8vo. Continued. 30718

Also: Constitution of the Hartwick Synod of the Evangelical Lutheran Church. *Albany.* 1858. 8vo.

HARTWIG (George). The Polar World: A Popular Account of Nature and Man in the Arctic and Antarctic Regions ... . By Dr. G. Hartwig, ... *London: Longmans, Green, and Co.* 1869. 8vo, pp. xviii, 548. 2 Maps. B., BA. + With Additional Chapters. *New York: Harper & Brothers.* 1869. 8vo, pp. 486. Plate.

HARTWIG. The Tropical World: A Popular Scientific Account of the Natural History of the Animal and Vegetable Kingdoms in the Equatorial Regions. By Dr. G. Hartwig, ... With eight chromoxylographic plates and ... woodcuts. *London: Longman[s].* 1863. 8vo, pp. xx, 566. 30720

Both of these were reprinted *Springfield, Mass.*, 1871. The author's "Harmonies of Nature," and "The Sea and its Living Wonders," touch on American Natural History.

HARVARD (*Rev.* W. M.) Letter to His Excellency Sir George Arthur, K.C.H., Gov. and Commander-in-Chief, &c., on that portion of the Clergy Reserve Property (Landed and Funded) of Upper Canada, not specifically appropriated to any particular Church. *Quebec.* 1839. pp. 46. + Second Edition. [*Ibid.*]

HARVARD COLLEGE *or* HARVARD UNIVERSITY.

The following *anonymous* works, relative to this institution, are arranged in alphabetical order; works by known authors under their respective names; minor pieces arranged as notes.

An Account of the Constitution and Government of Harvard-College, from its First Formation in the Year 1636 to the Year 1742. [n. p. n. d.] 4to, pp. 43. 30722

An Account of the "Society for the Promotion of Theological Education in Harvard University;" ... with Constitution. *Boston: Printed by John Eliot.* 1816. 12mo, pp. 24. H., M.

Addresses at the Inauguration of ... Hon. Edward Everett as President ... April 30, 1846. *Boston.* 1846. 8vo, pp. 66. H.

Also: Addresses ... Inauguration of Jared Sparks, LL.D., ... June 20, 1849. *Cambridge: John Bartlett.* 1849. 8vo, pp. 60. H.—Addresses ... Inauguration of the Rev. James Walker, D.D., ... May 24, 1853. *Cambridge: John Bartlett.* 1853. 8vo, pp. 69. H.—Addresses ... Inauguration of Charles Conway Felton ... July 19, 1860. *Cambridge: Sever & Francis.* 1860. 8vo, pp. 149. BA., H.—Addresses ... Inauguration of Thomas Hill, D.D., ... March 4, 1863. *Cambridge: Sever & Francis.* 1863. 8vo, pp. 39. H.—Addresses ... Inauguration of Charles William Eliot ... October 19, 1869. *Cambridge.* 1869. 8vo, pp. 65. H.

Annals of the Astronomical Observatory of Harvard College. Vol. I.—Pt. I. *Cambridge.* 1856. 4to. 30725

The Annual Report of the President of Harvard University to the Overseers on the State of the University for the Academical Year 1825–6. *Cambridge: Hilliard, Metcalf & Co.* 1827. 8vo, pp. 52. Continued to Vol. V., 1867. BA., H., W. 30726

Catalogue of the ... Institute of 1770. ... *Cambridge: E. W. Metcalf & Co.* 1832. 8vo, pp. 44. Continued. H., W. 30727

Catalogus Librorum Bibliothecæ Collegij Harvardini Quod est Cantabrigiæ in Nova Anglia. *Bostoni: Typis B. Green.* MDCCXXIII. 4to, pp. (2), ii, 102. B., BA., H. + Continuatio Supplementi Catalogi Librorum Biblioth. Coll. Harv. *Boston.* 1725. 4to, pp. 10. M. 30728

Also: Catalogus Librorum in Bibliotheca Cantabrigiensi selectus, frequentiorem in usum Harvardinatum, qui Gradu Baccalaurei in Artibus nondum sunt donati. *Bostoniæ.* 1773. 8vo, pp. 27. M.—Catalogus Bibliothecæ Harvardianæ Cantabrigiæ Nov-Anglorum. *Bostoniæ: Typis Thomæ et Johannis Fleet.* MDCCXC. 8vo, pp. (2), iii, 358. H.

A Catalogue of the Library of Harvard University in Cambridge, Massachusetts. ... [By B. Peirce.] *Cambridge: E. W. Metcalf.* 1830–34. pp. xvii, (2), 490; Vol. II. pp. (2), 493–952, (2); Vol. III. [Index,] pp. xii, 223. BA., H., C. + First Supplement. [By T. W. Harris.] *Cambridge: Chas. Folsom.* 1834. pp. (4), 260. BA. 30729

A Catalogue of the Maps and Charts in the Library of Harvard University in Cambridge, Massachusetts. *Cambridge: E. W. Metcalf and Company.* 1831. 8vo, pp. viii, 224. BA. 30730

Compiled by B. Peirce; edited by T. W. Harris. Forms Vol. IV. of the catalogue. Also: Considerations relative to the Library of Harvard University, submitted to the Legislature by Josiah Quincy, President. *Cambridge.* 1833. 8vo, pp. 16.—Letter of the Librarian [J. L. Sibley] to the Committee of the Association of the Alumni appointed to take into Consideration the State of the College Library. *Cambridge.* 1859. 8vo, pp. 8.—The Annual Report of the Librarian ... 1864 ... *Cambridge: Welch, Bigelow & Co.* 1865. 8vo, pp. 40. H.—Report of the Committee of the Overseers ... appointed to visit the Library in 1850. ... *Boston: Printed by John Wilson and Son.* 1851. 8vo, pp. 11. Continued. H.—Report of the Committee ... apointed to take into consideration the State of the College Library, ... July 16, 1857. *Cambridge: Metcalf and Company.* 1858. 8vo, pp. 44. BA.—Report of the Committee of the Overseers of Harvard College appointed to visit the Library for the year 1861; ... *Boston: Press of Geo. C. Rand & Avery.* 1862. 8vo.

Catalogue of the Library of the Law School of Harvard University. *Cambridge: Hilliard and Metalf.* 1826. 8vo, pp. 25.

Catalogue of the Law Library of Harvard University in Cambridge, Massachusetts. [By Charles Sumner.] *Cambridge.* 1834. 8vo, pp. viii, 80. 30732

With historical sketch. + A Catalogue of the Law Library ... . [By William R. Woodward.] Second Edition. *Cambridge.* 1841. 8vo. + Fourth Edition. *Cambridge: Metcalf & Co.* 1846. 8vo, pp. 354. C.

Catalogue of the Officers and Students of the University in Cambridge, October, 1819. *Cambridge: Hilliard and Metcalf.* 1819. 8vo, pp. 16. Continued. H. 30733

A Catalogue of the Members of the Hasty-Pudding Club ... Instituted 1795. *Cambridge: E. W. Metcalf & Co.* 1829. 8vo, pp. 13. H., W. 30734

Also: A Catalogue of the Members and Library of the Hasty-Pudding Club in Harvard University ... *Cambridge.* 1841. 8vo, pp. 48.—Catalogue of the Officers and Members of the Hasty-Pudding Club ... *Cambridge.* 1856. 12mo, pp. 68.

Catalogue of the Members and of the Library of the Porcellian Club of Harvard University ... *Boston.* 1839. 8vo, pp. 95. + *Cambridge: Printed by Allen and Farnham.* 1857. 8vo, pp. 103. BA. 30735

Also: Catalogue of Books in the Library of the Porcellian Club. *Cambridge: Printed by Hilliard and Metcalf.* 1816. 8vo, pp. 12. Continued H., M.—Catalogue of the Honorary and Immediate Members of the Porcellian Club ... . *Cambridge: Printed by Hilliard and Metcalf.* 1819. 8vo, pp. 18, (2). Continued. H.—Catalogue of the Members of the Boylston Medical Society of Harvard University. *Boston: True & Greene.* 1825. 8vo, pp. 8. Continued. H.—Catalogue of the Officers and Members of the Boylston Medical Society of Harvard University. *Boston.* 1837. 8vo, pp. 16.—Catalogue of the Officers and Members of the Harvard Natural History Society. *Cambridge: Metcalf and Company.* 1845. 12mo, pp. 17, (2). H.—Catalogue of the Officers and Members of the Rumford Society in Harvard College. *Cambridge: Metcalf & Co.* 1851. 12mo, pp. 8. H.—Catalogue of the ... Members of the Pierian Sodality ... *Cambridge: Metcalf* ... . MDCCCXXXIX. 8vo, pp. 15, (1). H. Catalogue of the Students in the Law School of the University at Cambridge, from the Establishment of the School to the end of the Year 1836. *Cambridge.* 1836. 12mo. Continued.

Catalogus Collegii Harvardini, 1776. *Bostoniæ.* 1776. 8vo, pp. 32. Continued. 30736

Catalogus eorum qui in Collegio Harvardino, ... Nov-Anglorum, Anno 1642, ad Annum 1700, alicujus Gradus Laurea donati sunt. *Cantabrigiæ Nov. Anglorum.* MDCC. Folio. H. 30737

These triennial catalogues were issued in 8vo after 1751.

Catalogus Senatus Academici, eorum qui Munera et Officia gesserunt, quique alicujus gradus Laurea donati sunt, in Universitate Harvardiana, Cantabrigiæ. ... *Cantabrigiæ: Hilliard et Metcalf.* MDCCCXII. 8vo, pp. 70. Continued. H. 30738

Also: Catalogus Senatus Facultatis eorum qui munera et officia gesserunt, quique alicujus gradus laurea donati sunt in facultate medicinæ in universitate Harvardiana ... . *Cantabrigiæ: Hilliard, Metcalf, et Soc.* MDCCCXXVII. 8vo, pp. 25, (2). BA.—Catalogus Universitatis Harvardianæ, 1782. *Bostoniæ.* 1782. 8vo, pp. 34. Continued. M.

The Collegian. *Cambridge.* 1830. 8vo, pp. 290. 30739

A periodical published by the students.

The Constitution and Government of Harvard College, from its First Formation in ... 1636 to ... 1742. [n. p. n. d.] 4to, pp. 40. BA., W. 30740

Also: The Constitution of the University at Cambridge. With an Appendix. *Cambridge: For the University.* 1812. 8vo, pp. 33. BA., H., M.—Consitution of the Society for the Promotion of Theological Education in Harvard College. *Boston: F. Y. Carlile.* [1825.] 8vo, pp. 17. BA., H.

A Descriptive Catalogue of the Warren Anatomical Museum. By J. B. S. Jackson, M.D. *Boston: A. Williams & Co.* 1870. 8vo, pp. xii, 759. Plate. C. 30741

Don Quixote at College. *See* [Tufts (Joseph)].

Further Remarks [&c.] *See* [Lowell (J.)]

Harvard College and its Benefactors. *Boston: Charles C. Little and James Brown.* 1846. 8vo, pp. 37. BA., H. 30742

The Harvard Lyceum. Vol. I., Nos. 1 and 2. *Cambridge.* 1810. 8vo, pp. 48. BA., H. 30743

The Harvard Magazine. Vol. I. *Cambridge: John Bartlett.* 1855. 8vo, pp. iv, 488. Continued. BA., H. 30744

Harvard Memorial Biographies. Edited by T. W. Higginson. *Cambridge: Sever & Francis.* 1866 8vo, pp. xix, 477; iv, 512. BA. + [*Ibid.*] 1867. 2 vols., crown 8vo, pp. xix, 445, iv; 483.

The Harvard Register. 1827–28. ... *Cambridge: Hilliard and Brown.* 1828. 8vo, pp. (2), 384. BA. 30746

No more published. Edited by Undergraduates of the University.

Harvardiana. Vol. I. ... *Cambridge and Boston: James Munroe and Company.* MDCCCXXXV. 8vo, pp. vi, (1), 384, (1). Continued. BA., H. 30747

Illustrated Catalogue of the Museum of Comparative Zoology, at Harvard College. *Cambridge: Printed for the Museum of Comparative Zoology.* 1871. 8vo. C. 30748

The Laws of Harvard College. *Boston: Printed by Samuel Hall.* M.DCC.XC. 8vo, pp. 66. H. + *Boston.* MDCCXCVIII. 8vo, pp. 67. + *Cambridge: Printed by W. Hilliard.* MDCCCVII. 8vo, pp. 71. + *Cambridge.* 1814. 8vo, pp. 67, 14. + [*Ibid.*] 1820. + [*Ibid.*] 1824. 8vo, pp. 26. + [*Ibid.*] 1841. 8vo, pp. 40.

Also: By-Baws, Rules, and Regulations of the Overseers of Harvard University, now in force. *Cambridge: Metcalf, Keith, and Nichols.* 1842. 8vo, pp. 12. H.—Constitutional Articles and Legislative Enactments relative to the Board of Overseers and the Corporation of Harvard University. Also Rules and Regulations of the Over-

seers. *Cambridge: Charles Folsom, Printer.* 1835. 8vo, pp. 38. BA., H.—Regulations adopted by the Corporation ... 1838. [n. p.] 1838 8vo, pp. 7.—Report of the Committee of the Overseers ... to revise the By-Laws and Rules. *Boston: Printed by John Wilson & Son.* 1851. 18mo, pp. 18. H.—Report of the Committee of the Overseers appointed to confer with a like Committee of the President and Fellows, and agree upon Certain Joint Rules, ... January 29, 1857. *Boston: T. R. Marvin.* 1857. 8vo, pp. 28. H.—Revised Code of College Laws reported to the Corporation by the Immediate Government. [n. p. n. d.] 8vo, pp. 23.—A Revision of the Statutes and Laws ... . *Cambridge.* 1847. 8vo, pp. 43. H.—The Rules and Orders of the Overseers of Harvard College. To which is appended the Charter, ... *Boston: Printed by John Wilson & Son.* 16mo, pp. 47, (1). M., H.—Rules and By-Laws of the Overseers of Harvard College; with the Charter. *Boston.* 1852. 12mo, pp. 56. + *Boston.* 1857. 16mo. M.—Rules and Statutes of the Professorships in the University at Cambridge. *Cambridge: Metcalf and Company.* 1846. 8vo, pp. (2), 64. BA., H.—Rules and Regulations of the Theological School at Cambridge. [n. p. n. d.] 8vo, pp. 4. H.—Rules and Regulations of Harvard College. [n. p.] 1833. 12mo.—Statutes and Laws of the University in Cambridge, Mass. *Cambridge: Hilliard and Metcalf.* 1825. 8vo, pp. 43. Continued. BA., H.—Statutes and Laws of Harvard University relative to Undergraduates. *Cambridge: E. W. Metcalf and Company.* 1832. 12mo, pp. 40, (7). Continued. BA., H.

A Letter to the President. *See* [Eliot (S. A.)]

Also: Letter to the Corporation and Overseers of Harvard College on the proposed Change in the Constitution of that Seminary. By an Alumnus. *Boston: Russell, Odiorne, and Metcalf.* 1835. 8vo, pp. 24. BA., H.—Letters to a Student in the University of Cambridge, Massachusetts. *Boston.* 1796.

A Memorial concerning the Recent History and the Constitutional Rights and Privileges of Harvard College. Presented by the President and Fellows to the Legislature, January 17, 1851. Third Edition. *Cambridge: John Bartlett.* 1851. 8vo, pp. 56.

Memorials of the Graduates of Harvard University. *August*, 1833. 30751

Also: Memorial [to the Legislature] of the ... President and Fellows of Harvard College, in behalf of the Corporation and Overseers of Said College. [Feb. 24, 1812.] [n. p. n. d.] 8vo, pp. 8.—Memorial of the Professors and Tutors of Harvard University to the Corporation. [n. p.] 1824. 8vo, pp. 30. M.

A Narrative of the Proceedings of the Corporation of Harvard College, relative to the late Disorders in that Seminary. *Cambridge: Printed by W. Hilliard.* 1807. 8vo, pp. 19. BA., H., W.

Also: Proceedings of the Overseers of Harvard University, the Report accepted, and the Resolutions adopted by them on the 25th of August, 1834, relative to the late Disturbances in that Seminary. *Boston: Press of James Loring.* [1834.] 8vo, pp. (2), 47. BA., H.—Circular [Letter, dated June 4, 1834, relating to disturbances, &c. n. p. n. d.] 8vo.—Circular [Letter of the Senior Class upon the same Subject, dated June 11, 1834. n. p. n. d.] 8vo, pp. 12. H., W.—Remarks occasioned by the ... Pamphlet entitled Proceedings of the Overseers of Harvard University relative to the late Disturbances in that Seminary. *Boston: Dutton & Wentworth.* 1834. 8vo, pp. 36. H.—Statement of Faculty to Parents and Guardians of Students, relative to late Disturbances in College, June 4, 1834. [n. p. n. d.] 8vo, pp. 8.—Statement of Senior Class relative to the late Disturbances in College; with Statement of President Quincy, June 4, 1834. [n. p. n. d.] 8vo, pp. 12.

Orders and Regulations of the Faculty of Harvard University. *Cambridge.* 1841. 8vo, pp. 13. Continued. 30753

Pietas et Gratulatio Collegii Cantabrigiensis apud Novanglos. *Bostoni-Massachusettensium: Typis J. Green & J. Russell.* MDCCLXI. 4to, pp. xiv, (1), 106, (1). BA., C., H. 30754

A Collection of Poems in Latin, Greek and English, on the Death of George II. and the accession of George III., preceded by a fulsome address written by Governor Bernard. "The inevitable condition of such a work," says Mr. Duychinck, "is eulogy; so the departing guest is sped and the coming welcomed, in the most rapturous figments of poetry."—*Cyclopædia American Literature*, I. 11. The authors were Edward Holyoke, Sir Francis Bernard, Governor; Stephen Sewall, Benjamin Church, John Lovell, and others. *See* "Monthly Anthology" for June, 1809, also the "Monthly Review" for July, 1763, where it is said to "contain some indifferent performances; but these, though they cannot be well excused when they come from ancient and established seats of learning, may at least be connived at here; and what we could not endure from an illustrious University, we can pardon in an infant Seminary." It contains the first specimen of printing with Greek type executed in the North American colonies.

A Plea for Harvard. *See* [Quincy (J.)]

The Rebelliad; or Terrible Transactions at the Seat of the Muses; a Poem. Auctore enginæ societatis poeta. Edited and patronized by the Pi Tau. *Boston.* 1842. 8vo. 30755

Remarks on a Pamphlet printed by the Professors and Tutors of Harvard University. By an Alumnus. [J. Lowell.] *Boston.* 1824. 8vo, pp. 58. M. 30756

Remarks [&c.] *See* [Dabney (J.)] *and* [Ticknor (G.)]

Remarks on a Report of a Committee of the Overseers of Harvard College, ... May 4th, 1824. ... By one lately a Member ... . *Cambridge: Hilliard and Metcalf.* 1824. 8vo, pp. 12.

Report of a Committee of the Board of Overseers respecting the State of the University and the Changes it would be expedient to recommend to the Corporation for its adoption. May 4, 1824. [n. p. n. d.] 8vo. W. 30758

Report of the Committee of the Association of the Members of the Federal-street Society for Benevolent Purposes on the ... Theological School in Cambridge. *Cambridge: Printed by Hilliard and Metcalf.* 1825. 8vo, pp. 15. BA., H. 30759

Report on the Rights and Duties. *See* [Walker (J.)]

Also: Report upon the Constitutional Rights and Privileges of Harvard College; and upon the Donations that have been made to it by this Commonwealth. ... 1820. [*Boston:*] *Order of the Convention.* 1821. 8vo, pp. 16. H., W.— ... Report of Committee on the Petition of the President and Fellows of Harvard College.

[n. p. 1832.] 8vo, pp. 15, (1). BA.—Report of the Committee of the Overseers, on the State of the University, appointed July 24, 1823. [*Boston.* n. d.] 8vo, pp. 11.—Report of the Committee relative to a New Organization, Oct. 7, 1824. *Boston.* 1824. 8vo, pp. 14.—Report of the President of Harvard College to the Overseers ... *Cambridge.* 1824. 8vo.—Report of a Committee of the Overseers of Harvard College, January 6, 1825. *Cambridge: Hilliard and Metcalf.* 1825. 8vo, pp. xiv. BA., H.—Report of a Committee of the Overseers ... on the Memorial of the Resident Instructors. [n. p.] 1825. 8vo, pp. 23. H.—Report of the Committee on the College Studies [Dec. 23, 1839. n. p. n. d.] 8vo, pp. 12. H.—Report and Resolutions of the President and Fellows of Harvard University, respecting the Introduction of the Voluntary System in the Studies of the Mathematics, &c. and also the Report of the Visiting Committee ... January, 1841. *Cambridge: Folsom, Wells, and Thurston.* 1841. 8vo, pp. 16. BA., H.—Report on diminishing the Cost of Instruction in Harvard College, together with a Minority Report ... . [n. p. 1845.] 8vo, pp. 32. BA., H.—Report of a Committee ... concerning the Requirements for Admission to the University. *Salem: Gazette Office.* 1845. 8vo, pp. 12. BA.—Report of the Joint Special Committee of the Legislature ... to consider the Powers of the Legislature, under the Constitution, in regard to the Government of Harvard University. [*Boston.* 1849.] 8vo, pp. 23.—Report of the Committee of the Overseers ... appointed to visit the University in 1849. *Cambridge.* 1850. 8vo, pp. 13. Continued.—Report of the Visiting Committee of Harvard University, made to the Overseers. January, 1849. *Boston.* 1849. 8vo, pp. 39.—Report of the Committee of the Overseers ... appointed to visit the Lawrence Scientific School in 1849. *Cambridge.* 1850. 8vo, pp. 27.—Report of a Committee of the Overseers, and Memorial of the Corporation, of Harvard College, on the ... Theological School. *Boston: Printed by John Wilson & Son.* 1852. 8vo, pp. 30. H.—Report on the Relative Powers, Duties, and Responsibilities of the Corporation and Overseers of Harvard College, ... January 31, 1856. *Boston: T. R. Marvin.* 1856. 8vo, pp. 28. BA., H.—Report of the Committee of the Overseers appointed to consider what Measures, if any, may be adopted to reduce the Expenses incident to a Residence at Cambridge. *Boston.* 1858. 8vo, pp. 12.—Report of the Committee of the Overseers ... appointed to procure a Perfect Copy of the College Charter ... February 20, 1862. *Boston: Printed by Geo. C. Rand & Avery.* 1862. 8vo, pp. 91. H.—Report to the Board of Overseers ... on the Condition, Needs, and Prospects of the University. *Cambridge: Welch, Bigelow and Company.* 1869. 8vo, pp. 78. BA., H.

Roll of Students of Harvard University who served in the Army or Navy of the United States during the War of the Rebellion. Prepared by ... Francis H. Brown. *Cambridge: Welch, Bigelow & Co.* 1866. 8vo, pp. 47, (1). H. + Second Edition. [*Ibid.*] 1869. 8vo, pp. 52. BA., H. 30760

Selected Songs sung at Harvard College, from 1862 to 1866. *Cambridge: John Wilson & Son, Printers.* 1867. 8vo, pp. 100.

A Statement of Facts, relative to the Late Proceedings in Harvard College, Cambridge. Published by the Students. *Boston.* 1807. 12mo, pp. 12. BA., H. 30762

Strictures on Harvard University. ... By a Senior. *Boston: Printed by John W. Folsom.* M,DCCXCVIII. 12mo, pp. 35. H., M.

The Testimony of the President, Professors, Tutors, and Hebrew Instructor of Harvard College in Cambridge, against

the Reverend Mr. George Whitefield, and his Conduct. *Boston, N. E.: Printed by T. Fleet.* 1744. 8vo, pp. 15. B., BA., M., N.

... Theses ... quas sub ... Reverendi D. Crescentii Matheri, Collegii Harvardini, quod est Cantabrigiæ Nov-Anglorum, Rectoris vigilantissimi defendendas proponunt Juvenes in Artibus initiati ... *Cantabrigiæ, Nov-Anglorum.* MDC.LXXXVII. H. 30765

Also: Address of the Directors of the Society for promoting Theological Education; with the Act of Incorporation, By-Laws ... . *Boston: W. L. Lewis.* 1832. 8vo, pp. 16. H., M.—Alumni Hall: an Appeal to the Alumni and Friends ... . *Cambridge: John Wilson & Sons.* 1866. 8vo, pp. 23. H.—Annual Circular of the Massachusetts Medical College; with a History of the Medical Department of Harvard University. ... *Boston.* 1846. 8vo, pp. 32.—Answers of the Immediate Government. To Questions proposed by a Committee of the Overseers. [n. p. 1824.] 8vo, pp. 64. H., W.—Catalogue of the Students at the Law Institution ... since its First Establishment ... *Cambridge: Charles Folsom.* 1833. 8vo, pp. 4—A Catalogue of the Law School of the University at Cambridge, for the Academical Year 1848–49. *Cambridge.* 1849. 12mo.—Catalogue of the Alumni of the Divinity School of the University of Cambridge. [*Cambridge.*] 1836. 8vo, pp. 8.—A Catalogue of the Fraternity of Φ B K, Alpha of Massachusetts, Harvard University ... 1810. *Cambridge: Printed by W. Hilliard and E. W. Metcalf.* 1810. 8vo, pp. 14. Continued. H.—A Catalogue of the Members ... of Φ B K, 1806. *Cambridge: William Hilliard.* 1806. 12mo, pp. 15. H.—Catalogue of the Lawrence Scientific School, at Harvard College. 1850–51.—Catalogue of the Medical Society in Harvard College. *Cantabrigiæ.* 1827. 8vo. W. Catalogue of the Members of Harvard University, Oct. 1803. *Broadside.* [1803.]—Circular of the Directors of the Theological School, January, 1825. [n. p. n. d.] 8vo, pp. 17. M.—Course of Instruction for Undergraduates in Harvard College, Oct. 1820 ... [n. p. n. d.] 8vo, pp. 4. H.—Documents relating to Harvard College. To which are added a Few Cursory Remarks. *Boston.* 1820. 8vo, pp. 12. W.—Facts and Documents in relation to Harvard College. *Boston.* 1829. 12mo, pp. 96.—The Foundation of the Massachusetts Professorship of Natural History at Harvard College in Cambridge ... . *Boston: Printed by Russell and Culter.* 1805. 12mo, pp. 21. BA., H., W.—Foundations and Statutes of the Professorships and Tutorships at Harvard University. [n. p. 1824.] 8vo, pp. 56. H., W.—The New-Milk Cheese, No. 2, by Van Tromp. *Boston.* 1807. 8vo.—Observations on the Proposition for Increasing the Means of Theological Education at the University in Cambridge. *Cambridge: Printed by Hilliard and Metcalf.* 1816. 8vo, pp. 22. BA., W.—Opinion of the Supreme Judicial Court on the Question of separating the Divinity School from Harvard College. *Cambridge: Metcalf and Company.* 1856. 8vo, pp. 24. H.—Oration and Poem. Departure of Senior Class, July 31, 1811. *Cambridge.* 1811.—Order of Exercises, Commencement, 1813. *Cambridge.* 1813. 8vo, pp. 4. Continued.—Remarks at a Hearing before the Joint Committee of Education, 1 February, 1848, in Aid of the Memorial of the Colleges. *Cambridge: Metcalf and Company.* 1848. 8vo, pp. 32. BA., H.—Remarks on the Constitution of the Society for the Promotion of Theological Education in Harvard University. *Boston: I. R. Bults.* 1825. 8vo, pp. 8. BA., H., M.—Society of Christian Brethren in Harvard University, June, 1856. *Boston.* 1856. 12mo, pp. 16.—A Statement of the Course of Instruction, Terms of Admission, Expenses, &c., at Harvard University, Cambridge, Mass. [*Cambridge:*] *Hilliard and Metcalf.* 1823. 8vo, pp. 23. BA., H.—Statement of the Faculty in relation to Trespasses by the Students in May, 1834. [n. p. n. d.] 8vo, pp. 8.—Statement of the Income of Harvard College ... [Feb. 16, 1824. n. p. 1824.] 8vo, pp. 4.—Statement of the Immediate Government to the Corporation. 1824. 8vo.—Statement of the Senior Class, in Reply to the Circular of the Faculty, June 11, 1834. [n. p. n. d.] 8vo, pp. 12.—No. 1. Statement of the Treasurer of Harvard College [1824.

n. p. n. d.] 8vo, pp. 22. Continued. BA., H.—Votes of the Overseers and Corporation of Harvard University relating to Articles 60 and 28 of the Statutes. [n. p. n. d.] 8vo, pp. 11. BA., H.

HARVARD SILVER MINING ASSOCIATION. Prospectus of the Harvard Silver Mining Association: By Hon. Henry A. Gaston, of Austin, Nevada. ... *East Cambridge: Printed by Randolph C. Getchell.* 1865. 8vo, pp. 10. H. 30766

HARVEST (G.) A Sermon Preached before the Honourable Trustees For Establishing the Colony of Georgia in America, ... at their Anniversary Meeting, March 16, 1748–9, ... By George Harvest, M.A. *London: W. Meadows ... and M. Cooper ...* . 1749. 4to, pp. 22. S. 30767

Harvest Home Meeting of Chester and Montgomery Counties at Valley Forge, July 28, 1828. 8vo. P. 30768

HARVEY (Arthur). The Reciprocity Treaty; its Advantages to the United States and to Canada. [An Essay to which was awarded the first prize by the proprietors of the *Trade Review.*] Second Edition. *Quebec.* 1865. 8vo, pp. 29. 30769

See also "Year Book."

HARVEY (C. T.) Report of C. T. Harvey ... to the Directors of the Norwich Mining Company ... 1856. *New York: Sackett & Cobb.* 8vo, pp. 15. 30770

[HARVEY (Edward).] The Manual Exercise, as ordered by His Majesty, in the Year 1764, Together with Plans and Explanations of the method generally practised at Reviews and Field-Days, ... With Copperplates. *Boston, in New England*, 1774. 4to, pp. 40. + *New York.* 1775. 4to. + *Philadelphia: Sold by J. Humphreys, R. Bell, and R. Aitken.* MDCCLXXVI. 8vo, pp. 33. Two Plates. P. + *New York.* 1780. 4to, pp. 35. N. 30771

Also: Manual Exercise as Ordered by His Majesty in 1764, and now generally adopted in Connecticut, Rhode Island and Massachusetts Bay. *New Haven.* [n. d.] 12mo. W.

HARVEY (G.) Harvey's Scenes of the Primitive Forest of America, at the Four Periods of the Year, Spring, Summer, Autumn, & Winter. Engraved from his Original Paintings. Accompanied with Descriptive Letter Press. By George Harvey. *New York* [*i. e. London*]. 1841. Folio, pp. (6). 4 colored Plates. BA., 30772

HARVEY. Harvey's Illustrations of our Country ... an Epitome of ... Lectures ... on the Discovery, Resources & Progress of

North America, North of Virginia. *Boston.* 1851. Rl. 8vo, pp. 36. 30773

HARVEY (G.) Conclave of Physicians, detecting their Frauds, also peculiar Discourse of Jesuits' Bark, By Gideon Harvey. *London.* 1683. 12mo. 30774

Contains an account of the gathering and abuse of this bark in America.

HARVEY (H.) History of the Shawnee Indians, from the Year 1681 to 1854, inclusive. By Henry Harvey; a Member of the Society of Friends. *Cincinnati: Ephraim Morgan & Sons.* 1855. 12mo, pp. 316. Portrait. BA., C. 30775

One of the most simple and veritable narrations of facts relating to the Indians ever printed. *See* Field's "Essay," No. 663.

HARVEY (H.) Memoir of Alfred Bennett, First Pastor of the Baptist Church, Homer, New York. ... By H. Harvey. Third Edition. *New York: Edward Fletcher.* 1852. 12mo, pp. 231. Portraits. C. 30776

HARVEY (J.) Fast-Day Sermon. By James Harvey. *New York.* 1776. 8vo. 30777

HARVEY (M.) Lectures, Literary and Biographical. By Rev. M. Harvey, of St. John's, Newfoundland. *Edinburgh: A. Elliot.* 1864. 12mo, pp. 512. C. 30778

HARVEY (R. J.) Life of John Tyler ... including some of his most Important Speeches, etc. By R. J. Harvey. *New York.* 1843. 8vo. N. 30779

HARVEY (T.), *and* BREWIN (W.) Jamaica in 1866; a Narrative of a Tour through the Island, with Remarks on its Social, Educational, and Industrial Condition. By Thomas Harvey and William Brewin. *London: C. Bennett.* 1867. 8vo. 30780

HARVEY (W. H.) Nereis Australis, or Illustrations of the Algæ of the Southern Ocean; being Figures and Descriptions of new or imperfectly known Sea-Weeds, collected on the Shores of the Cape of Good Hope, the extra-tropical Australian Colonies, Tasmania, New Zealand, and the Antarctic Regions. *London.* 1847. Imp. 8vo. 100 colored Plates. 30781

HARVEY. Nereis Boreali-Americana; or, Contributions to a History of the Marine Algæ of North America. Part I. Melanospermeæ. By William Henry Harvey, M.D., M.R.I.A. *Washington.* 1852. 4to, pp. 152. 12 colored Plates. P. + Part II.

Rhodospermeæ. *Washington.* 1853. 4to, pp. 262. 24 colored Plates + Part III. Chlorospermeæ. *Washington.* 4to, pp. 142. 14 colored Plates. 30782

Forms a portion of the "Smithsonian Contributions to Knowledge," but the copies with colored plates are a separate publication.

HARVEY (W. W.) Sketches of Hayti; from the Expulsion of the French, to the Death of Christophe. By W. W. Harvey, of Queen's College, Cambridge. *L. B. Seeley, London.* MDCCCXXVII. 8vo, pp. xvi, 416. Plate. BA., P. 30783

Harvie's Prince Edward Island Almanack; for 1868. ... *Charlottetown, P. E. Island: Henry A. Harvie.* [1868.] 16mo, pp. 104. 30784

HARWARD (T.) Electuarium Novum Alexipharmacum. Or, A new Cordial, Alexiterial and Restorative Electuary; A succedaneum to the grand Theriaca Andromachi. By Thomas Harward. *Boston.* 1732. 8vo, pp. (6), 26. B., M. 30785

Also: The Fulness of Joy in the Presence of God; being the Substance of a Discourse preach'd lately in the Royal Chappel at Boston in New England. *Boston: B. Green.* 1732. 8vo, pp. (4), 23. B., M., W.

HARWOOD (A. A.) The Law and Practice of United States Naval Courts-Martial. By A. A. Harwood. *New York: D. Van Nostrand.* 1867. 8vo, pp. 325. 30786

Also: The Practice of Naval Summary Courts-Martial. *Washington* 1863. 8vo, pp. 29.

HARWOOD (E.) An Address made in New Haven, Nov. 1, 1863, Commemorative of the late Frederick Croswell. By Edwin Harwood, D.D. *New Haven: Thomas J. Stafford, Printer.* 1864. 8vo, pp. 19. 30787

Also: Canaan, Shem and Japheth. A Sermon preached in Trinity Church, New Haven, Oct. 25, 1863. ... *New Haven: T. H. Pease.* 1863. 8vo, pp. 28.

HARWOOD (J. E.) Poems. By John Edmund Harwood. *New-York: M. & W. Ward.* 1809. 12mo, pp. (2), 107. BA.

Has Religion anything to do with our Colleges? [n. p. n. d.] 8vo, pp. 31. 30789

On Unitarian Professorships in Columbia College, New York.

Has this Administration done any thing to put down the Rebellion? &c. [n. p. n. d.] pp. 4. 30790

Relates to the Connecticut Election, in April, 1863.

HASBROUCK (A. B.) Address by the Hon. A. Bruyn Hasbrouck, LL.D., ... before The Ulster Historical Society, Oct. 17th, 1859. ... *Kingston: ... Hommel & Lounsberry, Printers.* 1859. 8vo, pp. 20. 30791

Also: Addresses ... at the Inauguration ... as President of Rutgers' College, ... Sept. 15, 1840. ... *New York: Robert Carter.* 1840. 8vo, pp. 39. B.

HASELTINE (E.) ... A Discourse delivered at the Ordination of the Rev. David Lawrence Morrill, ... Presbyterian Congregational Church in Goffstown, March 3d, 1802. By Ebenezer Haseltine, A.B. *Concord.* 1802. 8vo. 30792

HASENCLEVER (P.) The Case of Peter Hasenclever, &c. *London.* 1774. 8vo, pp. 97. S. 30793

Relative to the establishment of iron foundries at Charlottenburg, Ringwood, Long-pond in New Jersey, and at Courtland and New Petersberg in the State of New York.

[HASKE (John).] The Present State of North America, ... Part I. *London: J. Dodsley.* 1755. + Second Edition, with Emendations. [*Ibid.*] 8vo, pp. (4), 88. 30794

[HASKE.] Present State of North America, the Rights and Possessions of Great Britain and of France, and the Encroachments and Depredations of the French, &c. *Boston.* 1755. 8vo, pp. 64. 30795

HASKEL (D), *and* SMITH (C.) A Complete Descriptive and Statistical Gazetteer of the United States of America, containing a particular Description of the States, Territories, Counties, Districts, Parishes, Cities, Towns, and Villages Mountains, Rivers, Lakes, Canals, and Railroads: with an Abstract of the Census and Statistics for 1840: exhibiting a complete view of the Agricultural, Commercial, Manufacturing, and Literary Condition and Resources of the Country. By Daniel Haskel, A.M., ... and J. Calvin Smith. ... *New York: Sherman and Smith.* 1843. 8vo, pp. 752. B., BA. + [*Ibid.*] 1844. B. + *New York.* 1847. 8vo, pp. 754. B. + [*Ibid.*] 1850. C. 30796

Also: Chronological View of the World ... . *New York.* 1845. 12mo. S. + *New York: J. H. Colton.* 1853. 12mo, pp. 278. C.

HASKELL (A.) An Oration before the Washington Benevolent Society at Fitchburgh, Mass., July 4, 1814. By Abraham Haskell. *Worcester.* 8vo. W. 30797

HASKELL (Daniel). Remarks on "Some Communications first published in the Brattleborough Paper;" by W. Wells. [*Burlington.* 1816.] 8vo, pp. 16. 30798

HASKELL. A Sermon ... at the Ordination of the Rev. Royal A. Avery ... Cambridge, Vermont, December 10th, 1823. By Daniel Haskell, A.M. ... *St. Albans: Printed by J. Spooner.* 1824. 8vo, pp. 36. BA. 30799

HASKELL (D. N.) Address ... before the Boston Mercantile Library Association, January 3, 1848. By Daniel N. Haskell ... . *Boston: For the Association.* 1848. 8vo, pp. 40. B., BA., S.

HASKELL (T. N.) ... A Sermon ... East Boston ... Fast Day, April 30, 1863. By Rev. T. N. Haskell ... . *Boston: Hollis & Gunn.* 1863. 8vo, pp. 40. B. 30801

HASKELL (William O. & Son). Illustrated Catalogue of the Boston School Furniture Manufactory. *Boston: S. Thornton.* 1870. 8vo, pp. 101. Plate. C. 30802

HASKETT (W. J.) Shakerism Unmasked, or the History of the Shakers; including a form politic of their government as Councils, Orders, Gifts, with an Exposition of the Five Orders of Shakerism, and Ann Lee's Grand Foundation Vision, in Sealed Pages. With some extracts from their private Hymns which have never appeared before the public. By William J. Haskett, formerly of the Society of Shakers. *Pittsfield: The Author.* 1828. 8vo, pp. 300. C., M. 30803

HASKINS (J. B.) Remarks of the Hon. John B. Haskin ... upon Anti-Lecompton Democrats ... . December, 1859. *Washington: Thomas McGill.* 1859. 8vo, pp. 16. 30804

Also: Speech ... on the Admission of Kansas, March 10, 1858. [n. p. n. d.] 8vo, pp. 16. S.

HASKINS (R. W.) New England and the West. By R. W. Haskins, A.M. ... *Buffalo: A. W. Wilgers.* 1843. 12mo, pp. 36.

Also: Effects ... of a Material Increase ... of the Money Metals. [*Buffalo.* 1850.] 8vo, pp. 8. B.

HASKINS (S. M.) A Pastoral Offering from the Rector of St. Mark's, Williamsburgh ... on the Twenty-First Anniversary of his Pastorate ... October 28th, 1860. *New York: Slote & Janes.* 1860. 8vo, pp. 36. B. 30806

Also: Sermon at Williamsburgh, N. Y., on the Thirtieth Anniversary of the Rectorship, 1869. ... *New York.* 1869. 8vo.

[HASSALL (*Miss*).] Secret History; or, the Horrors of St. Domingo, in a series of Letters, written by a Lady at Cape François to Colonel Burr, ... principally during the Command

of General Rochambeau. *Philadelphia: Bradford & Inskeep.* 1808. 12mo, pp. (4), 255. 30807

H[ASSAN] (A. B.) Contributions to the Rhymes of the War. *Baltimore.* 1865. 16mo. 30808

[HASSAN.] Our Military Experience, and What it Suggests. *Baltimore: Cushing & Bailey.* 1863. 8vo, pp. 24. 30809

HASSARD (J. R. G.) Life of the Most Reverend John Hughes, D.D., First Archbishop of New York, with Extracts from his Private Correspondence. By John R. G. Hassard. *New York: D. Appleton & Co.* 1866. 8vo, pp. 519. Portrait.

HASSARD (S.) An Oration delivered at the Union Meeting House, in Westerly, R. I., July 4, 1828. By Samuel Hassard, A.M. *Stonington: W. & J. B. Stone.* 1828. 8vo, pp. 24.

HASSAUREK (F.) Four Years among Spanish Americans. By F. Hassaurek, late United States Minister Resident to the Republic of Ecuador. *New York: Hurd & Houghton.* 1867. 12mo, pp. x, 401. B., BA., C. 30812

HASSEL (Johann Georg Heinrich). Vollständige und neueste Erdbeschreibung des Britischen und Russischen Amerika's. *Weimar: Geographisches Institut.* 1822. 8vo. 30813

This and the two following form Vols. XVI., XVII., and XVIII. of A. C. Gaspari's "Vollständiges Handbuch der neuesten Erdbeschreibung."

HASSEL. Vollständige und neueste Erdbeschreibung der Vereinigten Staaten von Nordamerika, mit einer Einleitung zur Statistik dieser Länder. *Weimar.* 1823. 8vo, pp. 1200. 30814

HASSEL *und* CANNABICH. Vollständige und neueste Erdbeschreibung vom Reiche Mexico, Guatemala und Westindien; bearbeitet von Dr. G. Hassel und J. G. Fr. Cannabich. *Weimar.* 1824. 8vo, pp. 866. 30815

This systematical and well-written treatise contains about all the material for the Geography and Statistics of Central America which were then at the disposal of the scholar. It is still a valuable book for the geographical and historical student.

HASSLER (F. R.) Coast Survey of the United States. [*Philadelphia.* 1842.] 30816

The author edited the Documents relative to the Coast Survey of the United States. *See* Vol. IV.

HASSLER. Investigation upon the Survey of the Coast ... and the Construction of Standards of Weights and Measures, by a Committee of Congress, 1842. *Washington.* 8vo. 30817

HASSLER. Papers on Various Subjects connected with the Survey of the Coast of the United States. By F. R. Hassler. *Philadelphia.* 1824. 4to. 30818

Also included in the "Trans. Am. Phil. Soc.," N. S., Vol. II.

HASSLER. Principal Documents relating to the Survey of the Coast of the United States, since 1816; ... by F. R. Hassler. *New York: William Van Norden.* 1834. 8vo, pp. 180, iii, (1). Map. B. 30819

See "N. A. Rev.," XLII. 75. Also: ... Principal Documents ... October, 1834, to November, 1835. *New York: William Van Norden.* 1835. 8vo, pp. 156, iii. B. — ... Principal Documents relating to the Survey of the Coast of the United States, and ... Construction of Uniform Standards of Weights and Measures ... from November, 1835, to November, 1836. *New York: Printed by John Windt.* 1836. 8vo, pp. 123, iii. A., B.—Survey of the Coast of the United States. Further rectification of facts alleged in the Discussion of Congress, in December, 1842. [*Washington.* 1843.] 8vo.—Comparison of Weights and Measures, reported to the Senate of the United States by the Treasury Department in 1832. *Washington.* 1832. 8vo, pp. 122. C.

HASTED (F.) A copy of a Letter written to the President of the United States [Franklin Pierce] on Slave Emancipation. By Frederick Hasted. Dated Indianapolis, Ind., Dec. 2, 1854. pp. 8. 30820

Also: Copy of a Letter written from Buffalo, State of New York, December 21st, 1860. To Abraham Lincoln. 8vo, pp. 8. The New York State Library possesses other tracts by this writer.

HASTINGS (D. K.) Major David K. Hastings. ... record of the trial by court-martial ... . [*Washington.* 1865.] 8vo, pp. 293. 30821

House of Representatives, 38th Congress, 2d Session, Executive Document, No. 54, 1865.

HASTINGS (H. P.) An Essay on Constitutional Reform. By Hiram P. Hastings. *New York.* 1846. 8vo, pp. 35. S. 30822

HASTINGS (J.) Speech of Mr. John Hastings, of Ohio, on the Revenue, or Tariff Bill: ... July 29, 1841. [n. p. n. d.] 8vo, pp. 8. BA. 30823

HASTINGS (L. E.) The Emigrants' Guide to Oregon and California; containing Scenes and Incidents of a party of Oregon Emigrants; a description of Oregon; Scenes ... of a party of California Emigrants; and a description of California; with ... Routes. By Lansford W. Hastings, Leader of the California Emigrants of 1842. *Cincinnati: George Conclin.* 1845. 8vo, pp. 152. 30824

Reproduced with a new title and some additions as follows:

HASTINGS. A New History of Oregon and California; containing complete description of those countries together with the Oregon Treaty and Correspondence and a vast amount of Information relating to the Soil, Climate, Productions, Rivers and Lakes and the various Routes over the Rocky Mountains. By Lansford W. Hastings. *Cincinnati: George Conclin.* 1847. 8vo, pp. 160. Plate. + [*Ibid.*] 1849. 30825

HASTINGS (S.) Poems, ... to which is added A Descriptive Account of a Family Tour to the West; in the year 1800. ... By Sally Hastings. *Lancaster: William Dickson.* 1808. 12mo, pp. 220. C. 30826

HASTINGS (S. D.) Address before the Hastings Invincibles, 30th Regiment Wis. Vols., Nov. 9, 1862, at Madison, Wis. By Samuel D. Hastings. *Madison: Willard G. Roberts.* 1862. 8vo, pp. 22. 30827

Also: Address at Sparta, Wis., July 4, 1863. ... *Madison.* 1863. 8vo.—Oration at Beaver Dam, July 4, 1865. ... *Madison.* 8vo. *See also* Wisconsin.

HASTINGS (W. S.), *and* PICKERING (John). Remarks made in the Senate [of Massachusetts] upon the Manufacturing Bill. By the Hon. Messrs. Hastings & Pickering. [n. p. n. d.] 8vo, pp. 20. B., BA., M., W. 30828

The Hastings Memorial. *See* [Buckminster (L. N. H.)]

"The Hasty Pudding." *See* [Barlow (J.)]

These are other editions: *Hallowell.* 1815. 12mo. + *Brooklyn.* 1833. 8vo, pp. 22.

HASWELL (A.) Memoirs and Adventures of Captain Matthew Phelps; formerly of Harwington in Connecticut, now resident in Newhaven in Vermont. Particularly in Two Voyages, from Connecticut to the River Mississippi, From December 1773 to October 1780. ... Compiled from the Original Journal and Minutes kept by Mr. Phelps, during his Voyages and Adventures, and revised and corrected according to his present recollection. By Anthony Haswell. *Anthony Haswell, Bennington in Vermont.* 1802. 12mo, pp. iv, 210, Appendix, 63, (1), 1 l., Subscribers, xii. BA., C., P. 30829

HASWELL (C. H.) Engineer's and Mechanic's Pocket Book, containing United States and Foreign Weights and Measures, ... By Charles H. Haswell. Fifth Edition. *New York: Harper & Brothers.* 1848. 16mo, pp. 296. + [*Ibid.*] 1858. 12mo, pp. 322. 30830

HATBOROUGH, *Pa.* The Charter, Laws, and Catalogue of Books of the Union Library Company of Hatborough; with a Short Account of the First Establishment thereof. *Philadelphia.* 1788. 8vo. P. + Sixth Edition. *Norristown.* 1858. 18mo, pp. 116. C. 30831

Address at the Inauguration of the Hatborough Monument, Commemorating the Battle of the Crooked Billet, Dec. 5, 1861. By Jacob Belville. *Doylestown, Pa.* 1862. 8vo, pp. 12. 30832

HATCH (C. L. V.) Two Lectures on the Present Crisis, by the late Theodore Parker and the late Hon. Henry Clay, delivered at Dodsworth Hall, ... Dec. 16, 1860. Mrs. C. L. V. Hatch, Medium. *New York: S. T. Munson.* [1861.] 8vo, pp. 44. 30833

Also: Lecture on Secession. By Andrew Jackson. *New York.* 1861.

HATCH (I. T.) Report of Hon. Israel T. Hatch upon the Operation of the Revenue Laws and The Reciprocity Treaty upon the Northern Frontier. Communicated to Congress, ... June 18th, 1860. *Washington.* 1860. 8vo, pp. 46. B. 30834

Also: The Canal Contracts: Speech ... January 19, 1852, on ... Inquiry in the Canal Contract Frauds. [n. p. n. d.] 8vo, pp. 8. S.—Maryland Contested Election Case: Speech ... 1858. [n. p. n. d.] 8vo. S.—Speech ... on Inland Commerce, 1858. [n. p. n. d.] 8vo. S.—Speech on the subject of the Admission of Kansas as a State, March 30, 1858. [n. p.] 1858. 8vo. *See also* Hayes (J. D.)

HATCH (J.) Historical Sketch of J. Hatch and Descendants. *Peterborough, N. H.* 1850. 8vo. S. 30835

HATCH (J.), *Jr.* Reminiscences, Anecdotes and Statistics of ... Sherburne, Chenango County, N. Y. By J. Hatch, Jr. *Utica.* 1862. 12mo. 30836

HATCH (N.) Claims of the Officers of the Revolution, under Resolve of Oct. 21, 1780. By Nathaniel Hatch. *Washington.* 1857. 8vo. 30837

HATCH (N.) Suggestions to the Creditors of the United States, their Relations as Constituents and Creditors. ... By Nathaniel Hatch ... *Washington: Henry Polkinhorn.* 1858. 8vo, pp. 40. B. 30838

HATCH (R.) Bible Servitude Re-examined; with special reference to Pro-Slavery Interpretations and Infidel Objections. By Rev. Reuben Hatch. *Cincinnati: Applegate & Co.* 1862. 12mo, pp. 284. C. 30839

HATCH (W. S.) A Chapter of the History of the War of 1812 in the Northwest, Embracing the Surrender of the North-western Army and Fort, at Detroit, August 16, 1812; with a Biographical Sketch of ... Tecumseh. By Colonel William Stanley Hatch. *Cincinnati.* 1872. 12mo, pp. 156. 30840

HATCHARD (J.) Report of the Trial of the King *v.* John Hatchard, for a Libel on the Aides-de-Camp of Sir James Leith, Governor of the Leeward Islands, and the Grand Jury of the Island of Antigua. *London.* 1817. 8vo. C. 30841

HATFIELD (E. F.) History of Elizabeth, New Jersey, including the Early History of Union County. By Rev. Edwin F. Hatfield, D.D. ... *New York: Carlton & Lanahan.* 1868. 8vo, pp. 701. Portrait and 7 Plates. B., BA., C. 30842

HATFIELD. Patient Continuance in Well-Doing; a Memoir of Elihu W. Baldwin, D.D. By Rev. Edwin F. Hatfield. With an Introduction by Samuel Hanson Cox, D.D. *New York: J. Leavitt.* 1843. 12mo, pp. 404. Portrait. C., N. 30843

Also: ... A Discourse occasioned by the Decease of Mr. Jacob Bell, of New-York, .. July 25th, 1852. ... *New-York: Printed by John A. Gray.* 1852. 8vo, pp. 32. B.— ... A Discourse, occasioned by the Death of Rev. Samuel Washburn, of Baltimore, Md. ... October 9th, 1853. ... *New-York: John A. Gray, Printer.* 1853. 8vo, pp. 38.—Twenty Years in the Seventh Presbyterian Church, New York City; Two Sermons, Delivered July 1st, 1855. ... *New York.* 1855. 12mo, pp. 66.—Universalism as it is; or, Text Book of Modern Universalism in America. *New York: J. A. Hoisington.* 1841. 12mo, pp. 341. B., N.

[HATFIELD (Julia).] The Bryant Homestead-Book. By the Idle Scholar. *New York: G. P. Putnam & Son.* 1870. Small 4to, pp. (10), 224. Portrait. B. 30844

HATFIELD *and* DEERFIELD. *See* Papers concerning

HATHAWAY (G. W.) A Lecture in Defence of the Maine Law ... Skowhegan, March 12, 1854. By G. W. Hathaway ... *Skowhegan.* 1854. 8vo, pp. 30, (1). BA. 30845

HATHAWAY (L.) The Narrative of Levi Hathaway, giving an Account of his Life, Experience, Call to the Ministry of the Gospel ... and Travels as such to the present time. *Providence: The Author.* 1820. 12mo, pp. 140. C. 30846

HATHAWAY (W.) A Discourse Occasioned by the Death of Abraham Lincoln: Preached at Coxsackie, on Wednesday, April 19, 1865, By Warren Hathaway. *Albany: J. Munsell.* 1865. 8vo, pp. 24. B. 30847

Five hundred copies printed.

[HATHEWAY (Calvin).] Sketches of New Brunswick; containing an Account of the First Settlement of the Province, with a Brief Description of the Country, Climate, Productions, Inhabitants, Government, Rivers, Towns, Settlements, Public Institutions, Trade, Revenue, Population, &c. By an Inhabitant of the Province. *St. John.* 1825. 8vo, pp. 108. 30848

HATIN (Eugène). Histoire pittoresque des voyages dans les cinq parties du monde. Recueil des descriptions pittoresques, des récits curieux, des scènes variées, des découvertes scientifiques, des mœurs et coutumes qui offrent un intérêt universel. Extrait des Voyages de Christophe Colomb, Pizarre, La Condamine, etc. *Limoges: Ardant frères.* 1843. 5 vols., 8vo. 30849

HATTERSLEY (J.) The Conquest of America, and Minor Poems, by John Hattersley. *London: Baldwin and Cradock.* MDCCCXXXI. 16mo, pp. viii, 207. 30850

HATTON (A. J.) The Songs of Tammany; or the Indian Chief: a Serious Opera. By Ann Julia Hatton. *New York.* [n. d.] 12mo. 30851

HAUCH (John Carsten). Robert Fulton; roman historique de C. Hauch. Traduit pour la première fois du danois en français par D. Soldi; avec une notice historique par Albert De Roy. *Paris: Alph. Taride.* 1859. 18mo, pp. x, 395. 30852

First published at Copenhagen in 1846, and translated as below:

HAUCH. Robert Fulton, An Historical Novel. By John Carsten Hauch, Dr. Ph. ... Translated by Paul C. Sinding ... . *New York: Macdonald & Palmer, Printers.* 1868. 12mo, pp. vii, (2), 450. B., C. 30853

HAUGHTON (J.) Slavery Immoral; being a Reply to a Letter in which an Attempt is made to prove that Slavery is not Immoral. By James Haughton. ... *Dublin: James McGlashan.* 1847. 8vo, pp. 23. BA. 30854

HAUGHTON (R. B.) Eulogy on William H. Harrison. By R. B. Haughton. *Tallahassee.* 1841. 8vo. C. 30855

HAUGHWOUT & Co. Report of the (28th) Anniversary Banquet. *New York.* 1860. 12mo. 30856

HAUPT (H.) A Consideration of the Plans proposed for the Improvement of the Ohio River. By Hermann Haupt. *Philadelphia.* 1855. 8vo. P., S. 30857

[HAUPT.] Hoosac Tunnel. Appeal to the People of Massachusetts [1865. n. p. n. d.] 8vo, pp. 14. B. 30858

HAUPT. Military Bridges; with Suggestions of New Expedients and Constructions for crossing Streams and Chasms, Including, also, Designs for Trestle and Truss Bridges for Military Railroads. ... By Hermann Haupt, A.M., Civil Engineer ... . *New York: D. Van Nostrand.* 1864. 8vo, pp. xix, 310. 69 Plates. B., BA., 30859

Also: Brief Review ... of the Errors ... in a Pamphlet ... by D. L. Harris. [n. p. n. d.] 8vo, pp. 10. B.—Closing Argument of ... on Behalf of the Troy and Greenfield Railroad Co. ... March 6, 1862. ... *Boston: Wright & Potter.* 1862. 8vo, pp. 38. B.—Committee of Investigation on the Hoosac Tunnel Loan. Communication of ... *Greenfield: Printed by H. D. Mirick & Co.* 1860. 8vo, pp. 24. B.—Communication ... to D. N. Carpenter, Esq., ... in Regard to the Suspension of Operation on the Hoosac Tunnel. [*Deerfield.*] 1861. 8vo, pp. 21. B.—[Communication to the] Chairman and Gentlemen of the Joint Committee. [*Cambridge.* 1861.] 8vo, pp. 31. B.— ... Final Settlement of the Claim of ... against the State of Massachusetts. ... *Boston: Wright & Potter.* 1869. 8vo, pp. 20. B.—Hoosac Tunnel ... Reply ... to ... Legislature of Massachusetts of 1868. *Boston: Wright & Potter.* 1868. 8vo, pp. 16. B.—Memorial to the [Legislature] of Massachusetts. [*Cambridge.* 1864.] 8vo, pp. 16. B.—Memorial of ... 1866, to the [Legislature] of Massachusetts. [n. p. n. d.] 8vo, pp. 6.— ... Remarks ... at a Public Meeting ... in ... Boston, June 9, 1857, ... upon ... prosecution of the Work upon the Hoosac Tunnel. *Boston.* [1857.] 8vo, pp. 7. B., M.—Report of ... Chief Engineer of the Pennsylvania Rail Road Company ... . *Philadelphia: Crissy & Markley.* 1854. 8vo, pp. 34. B.—Rise and Progress of the Hoosac Tunnel ... [*Cambridge.*] 1862. 8vo, pp. 24. B.—Statement ... on Troy and Greenfield Railroad and Hoosac Tunnel, 1864. [*Cambridge.*] 1864. 8vo, pp. 42. B.—Tunnel Loan Bill. An Answer to the Inquiry, why do the Contractors ask for more than the Tunnel costs? ... *Boston: Printed by Alfred Mudge and Son.* 1859. 8vo, pp. 22. B.—Claim of H. Haupt & Co. Statement of Case to ... [Legislature] of Massachusetts. [n. p. n. d.] 8vo, pp. 13. B.—Remarks on the Present Position of the Hoosac Tunnel Enterprise. *Boston: Printed by Alfred Mudge and Son.* 1858. 8vo, pp. 20. B.

HAUPTMANN (I. G.) Comparatio brevior Germanorum antiquorum et hodiernarum Americae borealis gentium. *Gera.* 1760. 4to. 30860

HAUSLEUTNER (Ph. W. G.) Gallerie der Nationen, Part I., Asia; Part II., America. *Stuttgart.* 1792. Folio. 30861

HAUT (Marc de). La Crise Américaine, ses Causes, ses Résultats probables, ses Rapports avec l'Europe et la France. Par Marc de Haut ... . *Paris: E. Dentu.* 1862. 8vo, pp. (7), 168.

Favors the South.

HAUTEFEUILLE (L. B.) Propriétés Privées des sujets Belligérants sur mer, par L. B. Hautefeuille. *Paris: A. Franck.* 1860. 8vo, pp. 39. 30863

HAUTEFEUILLE. Quelques Questions de Droit International Maritime, à propos de la guerre d'Amérique, par L. B. Hautefeuille ... . *Leipzig et Paris: A. Franck.* 1861. 8vo, pp. (2), 74.

HAUTEFEUILLE. Questions de droit maritime international. Par L. B. Hautefeuille ... . *Paris: Guillaume et Cie.* 1868. 8vo, pp. vii, 388. BA. 30865

Also: De la Legalité des Blocus Américaines. [n. p. n. d. From the "Revue Contemporaine," February 28, 1863.]—Nécessité d'une Loi Maritime pour régler les rapports des Neutres et des Belligérants. *Paris: Revue Contemporaine.* 1862.

HAUTERIVE (*Le Comte d'*) *et* CUSSY (Frédéric de). Recueil des Traités de Commerce et de Navigation de la France, avec les Puissances Etrangères, depuis la Paix de Westphalie, en 1648. Suivi du Recueil des Principaux Traités de même nature conclus par les Puissances Etrangères entre elles, depuis la même époque. *Paris.* 1834–1844. 10 vols., 8vo. C. 30866

HAVANA. *See* Vol. I., No. 2450, *also* Habana.

HAVANA, *N. Y.* People's College, Havana, N. Y. Circular and Act of Incorporation. *Buffalo.* 1853. 30867

Public Exercises at the Laying of the Corner Stone of the People's College, at Havana, N. Y. ... September 2d, A.D. 1858. *New York: John F. Trow, Printer.* 1858. 8vo, pp. 56.

HAVE (J. L. ten). De Noord-Amerik. Unie, hare wording, geschiedenis, geldmiddelen en toekomst. *Amsterdam.* 1867. 8vo.

•The North American Union, its origin, history, finances and future.

Have we the best possible Ambulance System? Reprinted from the Christian Examiner, January, 1864. *Boston: Walker, Wise & Co.* 1864. 8vo, pp. 18. 30870

HAVEN (A. B.) A Memoir of Cousin Alice B. Haven. *New York: D. Appleton and Company.* 1865. 12mo, pp. 392. Portrait.

HAVEN (C. C.) Annals of the City of Trenton [N. J.], with Random Remarks and Historic Reminiscences. By C. C. Haven. *Trenton, N. J.* 1866. 8vo, pp. 31. C. 30872

HAVEN. Gloria Majorum, Posteris Lumen. Washington and his Army during their March through and Return to New Jersey, ... December 1776 and January 1777. Read before the Literary and Philosophical Society of New Jersey. By C. C. Haven, one of its Vice-Presidents. *Trenton: C. Scott & Co.* 1856. 8vo, pp. 56. B. 30873

HAVEN. Thirty Days in New Jersey Ninety Years ago: An Essay revealing New Facts in Connection with Washington and his Army in 1776 and 1777. By C. C. Haven. *Trenton: State Gazette.* 1867. 8vo, pp. 72. Plate and Map. B., BA. 30874

HAVEN (C. W.) The Manhattan Souvenir, and New York Sketch Book, for 1851. *New York.* 1851. 12mo, pp. 96.

HAVEN (E. O.) ... A Baccalaureate Sermon ... June 23, 1867. By E. O. Haven, D.D. ... *Ann Arbor.* 1867. 8vo, pp. 16.

Also: Universities in America. An Inaugural Address ... Ann Arbor, Michigan, October 1st, 1863. ... *Ann Arbor: C. G. Clark, Jr.* 1863. 8vo, pp. 31.

HAVEN [E. O.] Speech ... on the Hoosac Tunnel Bill, in the Senate [Massachusetts] ... April 19. *Boston: Geo. C. Rand & Avery.* 1862. 8vo, pp. 11. B. 30877

HAVEN (E.) Christ's Agony Improved. In a Sermon preached at a Public Lecture in Attleborough, Jan. 5th, 1741, 2, By Elias Haven, Pastor of Second Church in Wrentham. *Boston: S. Kneeland and T. Green.* 1742. 12mo, pp. 31. C. 30878

Also: Youthful Pleasures must be accounted for, at the Day of Judgment. A Sermon in Wrentham, May 27. 1741. ... *Boston.* 1741. 8vo, pp. 32. B.

HAVEN (G.) Te Deum Laudamus. The Cause and the Consequence of the Election of Abraham Lincoln. A Thanksgiving Sermon ... November 11, 1860. By Rev. Gilbert Haven. ... *Boston: J. M. Hewes.* 1860. 8vo, pp. 44. B., BA., 30879

HAVEN. The Mission of America: A Discourse ... Charlestown ... State Fast, April 2d, 1863. By Rev. Gilbert Haven. ... *Boston: J. P. Magee.* 1863. 8vo, pp. 40. B. 30880

HAVEN. National Sermons. Sermons, Speeches and Letters on Slavery and its War: from the Passage of the Fugitive Slave Bill to the Election of President Grant. By Rev. Gilbert Haven. *Boston: Lee & Shepard.* 1869. 12mo, pp. xxiv, 656. Portrait.

HAVEN. The Uniter and Liberator of America. A Memorial Discourse on the Character and Career of Abraham Lincoln: Delivered in ... Boston ... April 23, 1865, By Gilbert Haven. ... *Boston: James P. Magee.* 1865. 8vo, pp. 32. B. 30882

HAVEN (G.), *Jr.* A Poem ... at Malden, on the Two Hundredth Anniversary of the Incorporation of the Town, May 23, 1849. By Gilbert Haven, Jr. ... *Boston: Printed by Geo. C. Rand & Co.* 1850. 8vo, pp. 22. B., BA. 30883

HAVEN (J.) A Sermon ... to the Ancient and Honorable Artillery Company in Boston, New England, June 1, 1761, ... the Anniversary ... Election of Officers. By Jason Haven, A.M. ... of Dedham. *Boston: Edes & Gill.* M,DCC,LXI. 8vo, pp. 35.

HAVEN. A Sermon Preached before His Excellency Sir Francis Bernard, Baronet, Governor; His Honor Thomas Hutchinson, Esq. Lieutenant-Governor, The Honorable His Majesty's Council, And the Honorable House of Representatives of the Province of the Massachusetts-Bay in New-England, May 31st, 1769. Being the Anniversary of the Election of His Majesty's Council for said Province. By Jason Haven, A.M. ... *Boston, New England: Printed by Richard Draper.* MDCCLXIX. 8vo, pp. 55. BA.

HAVEN. A Sermon preached in the First Society in Dedham, on the 7th Day of February, 1796. Forty years after the Author's Induction into the Work of the Gospel Ministry. By Jason Haven, A.M. ... *Boston: Printed by Thomas Fleet, Jun.* MDCCXCVI. 8vo, pp. 30. B., BA. 30886

HAVEN. A Sermon ... Stoughton ... 18th of June, 1783. At the Funeral of the Rev. Mr. Samuel Dunbar ... . By Jason Haven ... . *Boston: Printed by N. Willis.* MDCCLXXXIII. 8vo, pp. 23. BA. 30887

Also: A Discourse occasioned by the Death of Mrs. Hannah Richards, of Dedham, who departed this Life on the 8th of February, 1770. ... *Boston: Printed by Richard Draper.* M,DCC,LXX. 8vo, pp. 32. B., BA., M., W.—A Sermon ... at Needham [Mass.], November 7, 1792; when the Rev. Stephen Palmer was ordained ... . *Boston: Printed by Belknap and Hall.* MDCCXCII. 8vo, pp. 36. BA., W.

HAVEN (J.) A Sermon at the Ordination of Joseph Avery, at Holden, Mass., Dec. 21, 1774. By Joseph Haven. *Boston.* 1775. 12mo. 30888

Also: A Sermon preached July 4, 1764, at the Ordination of the Reverend Mr. Edward Brooks, ... North Yarmouth. ... *Boston: Printed by Richard and Samuel Draper.* MDCCLXIV. 8vo, pp. 55. B., BA., M.—A Sermon ... at the Ordination of the Rev. Mr. Moses Everett, ... Dorchester, September 28, 1774. ... *Boston: Printed by Mills and Hicks.* M,DCC,LXXV. 8vo, pp. 40. B., BA., M.—A Sermon ... at ... Ordination of the Reverend Mr. Ephraim Ward, ... Brookfield, October 23d. 1771. ... *Boston: Printed by Richard Draper.* M,DCC,LXXI. 8vo, pp. 46. BA., M.

HAVEN (J.) An Address ... before the Students of Amherst College ... in Amherst, Nov. 17, 1852. By Joseph Haven, A.M. ... *Amherst: J. S. & C. Adams.* 1853. 8vo, pp. 43. B., BA. + Second Edition. *Amherst.* 1853. 8vo. B. 30889

On the Life and Character of Daniel Webster. Also: Discourse, American Education Society. *Boston.* 1856. 8vo. S.

HAVEN (N. A.) The Remains of Nathaniel Appleton Haven. With a Memoir of his Life, by George Ticknor. [*Cambridge.*] MDCCCXXVII. 8vo, pp. xl, 351. B., BA., M. 30890

HAVEN (S.) Joy and Salvation by Christ. A Sermon preached in Portsmouth; occasioned by Success in the late War, and by the Happy Peace of 1763. By Samuel Haven. *Portsmouth, N. H.* 1763. 8vo, pp. 39. M. 30891

HAVEN. ... An Occasional Discourse, delivered soon after the Ordination of the Rev. Timothy Alden, Jun., A.M., ... South Church in Portsmouth. By Samuel Haven ... . *Portsmouth: Printed by Charles Peirce.* 1800. 8vo, pp. 28. BA., W. 30892

Also: Discourse on Hosea xiv. 9, delivered 24th August, 1794. *Newburyport.* 1794. 8vo, pp. 23. N.—An Election Sermon preached before the General Court of New Hampshire at Concord ... *Portsmouth.* 1786. 8vo, pp. 24. M.—Poetic Miscellany, on Subjects Moral and Religious. *Boston.* 1798. 8vo, pp. 23. N.—Preaching Christ the Great Business of the Gospel-Ministry. A Sermon at the Anniversary Convention of Congregational Ministers ... September 30, 1760. ... *Portsmouth: Printed by Daniel Fowle.* 1760. 8vo, pp. 40. BA., N., W.—Sermon occasioned by the Death of George II., delivered at Portsmouth, January 22, 1761. *Portsmouth.* 1761. 8vo, pp. 25. N.—A Sermon preached February 18, 1767, at the Ordination of the Rev. Mr. Jeremy Belknap ... Dover. ... *Portsmouth, N. H.: Printed by D. & N. Fowle.* M,DCC,LXVII. 8vo, pp. 36. BA., M., W.— ... Sermon on the Death of the Hon. Henry Shelburne, Esq. who died March 30, 1767. *Portsmouth.* 1767. 8vo, pp. 34.—Sermon ... after the Death of Nathaniel Ward, preached at Cambridge, 15th October, 1768. ... *Boston.* 1768. 8vo, pp. 35. N.—Sermon occasioned by the Death of Benjamin Stevens of Kittery Point. With Notes. *Portsmouth.* 1791. 8vo, pp. 32. N.—Slothful Servants neglecting their Talents inexcuseable. A Sermon preached at Medfield ... Jan. 27, 1771. ... *Boston.* 1771. 8vo, pp. 31. M.—The Validity of Presbyterian Ordination ... Illustrated in a Discourse ... at the Dudleian Lecture of Harvard College, September 5, 1798. ... *Boston: Printed by Manning & Loring.* 1798. 8vo, pp. 24. BA., N., W.

HAVEN (S. F.) Archæology of the United States, or Sketches, Historical, and Bibliographical of the Progress of Information and Opinion respecting Vestiges of Antiquity in the United States. By Samuel Haven. ... *New York: G. P. Putnam.* 1856. 4to, pp. v, 168. 30893

Forms part of Vol. VIII. of the "Smithsonian Contributions." On the importance of this contribution, *see* "North American Review," LXXXV. 468.

HAVEN. An Historical Address, delivered before the Citizens of the Town of Dedham, on the Twenty-First of September, 1836, being the Second Centennial Anniversary of the Incorporation of the Town. By Samuel F. Haven. *Dedham: Printed by Herman Mann.* 1837. 8vo, pp. 79. B., BA., C. 30894

Also on large paper.

Haven. History of Grants under the Great Council for New England. A Lecture ... before the Lowell Institute, January 15, 1869. By Samuel F. Haven. *Boston: John Wilson and Son.* 1869. 8vo, pp. 36. B. 30895

Haven. Remarks on the Popham Celebration of the Maine Historical Society. Read before the American Antiquarian Society, April 26, 1865. By S. F. Haven. *Boston: John Wilson and Son, Printers.* 1865. 8vo, pp. 32. 30896

Haven (S. G.) Remarks of Mr. S. G. Haven, of New York, on ... the Ten Million Mexican Treaty Bill; ... House of Representatives, June 27, 1854. *Washington: Printed by John T. and Lem. Towers.* 1854. 8vo, pp. 15. BA., M. 30897

Also: Remarks ... on Dunn's and Haven's Bills on Kansas ... *Buffalo.* 1856. 8vo, pp. 16. S.

Haven (T.) A Sermon ... at the Ordination of the Rev'd Mr. Jacob Burnap ... Merrimac, October the 14th, 1772. By Thomas Haven, A.M. ... *Salem: Printed by S. and E. Hall.* MDCCLXXIII. 8vo, pp. 28. BA., W. 30898

Haven's Nicodemus. Wonderful Vision of ... the City of New York ... wherein he was presented with a View of the Situation of the World, after the Dreadful Fourth of June, 1812, and shewing what Part of New York is to be Destroyed. [n. p. n. d.] 8vo, pp. 11. BA. 30899

Havens (J. S.) The Usurpations of the Federal Government. Speech of J. S. Havens on the Subject of Arbitrary Arrests, and the Suspension of the Writ of Habeas Corpus. Delivered in the Assembly at Albany, February 17, 1863. [n. p. n. d.] 8vo, pp. 8. 30900

Havens (P. E.) Review of Governor Seymour's Message, in the Assembly (of N. Y.), Feb. 6, 1863. By Hon. Palmer E. Havens. [n. p. n. d.] 8vo, pp. 12. 30901

Havens. Speech of Hon. Palmer E. Havens ... on the Constitutional Amendment Question, in the Senate, January 11, 1865. ... *Albany: Weed, Parsons and Company.* 1865. 8vo, pp. 12.

Also: Arbitrary Arrests. Speech in the House of Assembly, of New York, March 5, 1863. [n. p. n. d.] 8vo, pp. 7.

Haverford, *Pa.* Account of the Present State of the Asylum for the Relief of Persons deprived of their Reason. ... *Philadelphia.: Printed by W. Brown.* 1816. 8vo, pp. 24. Continued.

Account of Haverford School, near Philadelphia, with Constitution, By-Laws, etc. *Philadelphia.* 1835. 8vo. S. 30904

A Catalogue of the Officers and Students of Haverford School, 1852–53. *Philadelphia.* 1853. 8vo. 30905

Also: Report of the Managers ... 1839. *Philadelphia: Brown, Bicking & Guilbert.* 1839. 8vo, pp. 36. Continued.

Catalogue of the Haverford Loganian Library. *Philadelphia.* 1854. 8vo. 30906

Haverford Revisited; being a Memento of a day spent on the old grounds by a number of the former Pupils, and the Address of Isaac Serrill, May 29, 1846. *Philadelphia.* 1847. 8vo. P.

Haverhill, *Mass.* Account of the Difficulties in the Church of Haverhill. W. 30908

Haverhill Directory for 1865. By W. A. Greenough, Jr. *Haverhill: Smiley & Jaques.* 1865. 12mo, pp. 119, 24. 30909

Continued as the

Haverhill and Bradford Directory for 1867. By Langford & Chase. *Haverhill: J. V. Smiley.* 1867. 16mo, pp. 138, 20.

The Haversack. Published ... for the Great Central Fair, for the U. S. Sanitary Commission. *Philadelphia: Henry B. Ashmead.* 1864. 8vo, pp. 60. 30911

Havestadt (B.) Chilidúgú sive res Chilensis vel descriptio status tum naturalis, tum civilis, cum moralis regni populique Chilensis, inserta suis locis perfecta ad Chilensem linguam manuductioni, Deo O. M. multus ac miris modus juvante opera, sumptibus, periculisque Bernardi Havestadt. *Monasterii Westphaliæ. Typis Aschendorfianis.* 1777. 12mo, pp. (16), 952, Errata, 1 l., Lachrymæ Salutares, pp. 78. 4 Plates and Map. A., J.C.B.

Usually bound in two or three volumes. "The author passed twenty years as a missionary in Chili. The main object of the work is to promote a knowledge of the Chilian language, which he avers to be as much above all other languages, as the Chilian Andes are above the mountains of the rest of the earth. The work is divided into seven parts. The first is a very ample grammar of the Chilian tongue, amounting to near two hundred pages. The second is a translation into the Chilian tongue of Father Porney's 'Indiculus Universalis.' The third is a Chilian catechism, in verse and prose. The fourth is an ample vocabulary of the Chilian language. The fifth is a Latin vocabulary, corresponding with the preceding. The sixth contains the music for accompanying the organ, in chanting the poetical catechism. The seventh is the author's diary of a missionary excursion in the years 1751 and 1752."—*North American Review.*

Haviland (J. de). Le Mexique sous la maison de Habsbourg. Par John de Haviland. *Vienne: C. Gerold Fils.* 1863. Folio, pp. 34. C. 30913

Haw (W.) Fifteen Years in Canada: being a Series of Letters on its Early History and Settlement; its Boundaries, Divisions, Population, and General Routes; its Agricultural Progress and Wealth compared with the United States; its Religious and Educational Institutions; and its Present Political Condition and Relations; together with the Advantages it affords as a Desirable Field of Emigration. By the Rev. William Haw. *Edinburgh.* 1850. 8vo, pp. 128. 30914

Hawes (A. H.) The Grafted Bud; a Memoir of Angelica Irene Hawes. By Mrs. A. H. Hawes. *Redfield, New York.* 1853. 16mo, pp. 102. Plate. C. 30915

Hawes (B.) Tales of the North American Indians and Adventures of the Early Settlers in America. By Barbara Hawes. *London: Longman & Co.* 1844. Fcp. 8vo, pp. xii, 362. Plate. C. + Second Edition. *London: J. Jarrold.* 1853. 12mo, pp. 190. 30916

A collection of anecdotes and narratives of Indian life and warfare, some of which are from sources not now easily accessible.

Hawes (E.) The Harp of Acushnet: Poems by Mrs. Elizabeth Hawes. *Boston.* 1838. 12mo, pp. viii, 172. 30917

Written amid the scenery formerly laid waste in Philip's War.

Hawes (G. W.) United States Express Guide and Shipping Directory for 1866–7. *Baltimore: G. W. Hawes.* 1866. 8vo, pp. xxxvi, 572. 30918

See also Indiana, Kentucky, Maryland, and Ohio.

Hawes (J. H.) Manual of United States Surveying ... . [With] an Appendix ... in regard to Entering, Locating, Purchasing, and Settling Lands ... . By J. H. Hawes. *Philadelphia: J. B. Lippincott & Co.* 1868. 12mo, pp. 234. B., C.

Hawes (J.) An Address delivered at the request of the Citizens of Hartford, on the 9th of November, 1835, the Close of the Second Century from the First Settlement of the City. By Joel Hawes. *Hartford: Belknap & Hamersley.* 1835. 12mo, pp. 80. B., C., N. 30920

Hawes. Historical Sketches of the First Church in Hartford. A Centennial Discourse delivered in the First Church June 26,

1836. By Joel Hawes, D.D. *Hartford: Hudson and Skinner, Printers.* 1836. 8vo, pp. 35, (1). B., N. 30921

Hawes. Memoir of Normand Smith; or The Christian Serving God in his Business. By Rev. Joel Hawes, D.D. *American Tract Society, New-York.* [n. d.] 18mo, pp. 72. 30922

Hawes. North and South: or Four Questions Considered: .. A Sermon ... on the Day of the National Fast, Sept. 26th, 1861. By J. Hawes, D.D. *Hartford: Press of Case, Lockwood and Company.* 1861. 8vo, pp. 31. 30923

Hawes. A Tribute to the Memory of the Pilgrims, and a Vindication of the Congregational Churches of New England. By Joel Hawes, D.D. *Hartford.* 1830. 18mo, pp. 226. Plate. + Second Edition. *Hartford: Daniel Burgess & Co.* 1836. 12mo, pp. 176. B., BA., C. 30924

This elicited the following:

Review of the Tribute to the Pilgrims, &c., and the Centennial Address, of Joel Hawes, D.D. By Juris Consultus. *Hartford.* 1836. 12mo, pp. 19. 30925

Also: A Brief Review of Thirty Years in the Ministry. Two Discourses ... Hartford, March 5, 1848. ... *Hartford: Case, Tiffany & Co.* 1848. 8vo, pp. 42. B.— .. A Discourse ... in Hartford ... December 9th, 1844, on the Death of Mrs. Mary E. Van Lennep ... [n. p.:] *Printed by D. B. Moseley.* 1845. 8vo, pp. 30. B., BA.—A Discourse ... Dec. 20, 1836, at the Installation of Rev. John Storrs ... in Holliston, Mass. ... *Boston: Printed by Perkins & Marvin.* 1837. 8vo, pp. 34. BA.—Sermon at the Dedication of the North Congregational Church in Hartford, December 1, 1824. .. *Hartford,* 1825. 8vo. N.— ... A Sermon ... March 9th, 1825, at the Installation of the Rev. Leonard Bacon ... in New-Haven, Conn. ... *New-Haven: Printed by Nathan Whiting.* 1825. 8vo, pp. 23, (1). B., BA., W.— ... A Sermon ... at the Ordination of the Rev. Lyman Colman ... in Belchertown, Mass., Oct. 19, 1825. ... *Hartford: W. Hudson and L. Skinner.* 1825. 8vo, pp. 32. B., BA.—A Sermon ... at the Funeral of Rev. Elias Cornelius, at Hartford, Conn., Feb. 12, 1832. ... *Hartford: Hudson and Skinner.* 1832. 8vo, pp. 31. B., W.— ... A Sermon ... December 27th, 1832, at the Ordination of Rev. Cornelius C. Vanarsdalen ... in Hartford, Conn. ... *Hartford: D. F. Robinson.* 1833. 8vo, pp. 23. B.—A Sermon ... Death of Mrs. Delia Williams ... 28th of June, 1840. ... *Hartford: Lewis Skinner.* 1840. 8vo, pp. ·3. B.— ... A Sermon at the Ordination of Prof. Timothy Dwight ... New Haven, September 15, 1861. ... *New Haven: Printed by E. Hayes.* 1861. 8vo, pp. 24. B.

[Hawes (*Mrs.* J.)] Memoir of Mrs. Mary E. Van Lennep, only daughter of the Rev. Joel Hawes, D.D. and wife of the Rev. Henry J. Van Lennep, Missionary in Turkey. By her Mother. .. *Hartford: Belknap and Hamersley.* 1848. 12mo, pp. 382. Portrait. 30926

[Hawes (Mary Virginia).] *See* [Terhune (M. V.)]

Hawes (R.) [Address of the Hon. Richard Hawes] to my Constituents of the Counties of Clarke, Fayette, Woodford, and Franklin [Ky. *Washington.* 1841.] 8vo, pp. 8. 30927

Hawes. Speech of Mr. Hawes, of Kentucky, on the Sub-Treasury Bill. Delivered in the House of Representatives, June 30, 1840. *Washington: Printed by Gales and Seaton.* 1840. 8vo, pp. 30. 30928

[Hawes (William Post).] Sporting Scenes and Sundry Sketches; being the Miscellaneous Writings of J. Cypress, Jr. Edited by Frank Forrester [*i. e.* Henry William Herbert]. *New-York.* 1842. 2 vols., 12mo. Plates. S. 30929

Hawke (E.) Authentic Register of the British Successes; being a Collection of all the Extraordinary, and some of the Ordinary Gazettes from the Taking of Louisbourgh, July 26, 1758, by Admiral Boscawen and Gen. Amherst, to the Defeat of the French Fleet under M. Conflans, Nov. 21, 1759. By Sir Edward Hawke. To which is added a particular account of M. Thurot's Defeat by Capt. John Elliott. *London: G. Kearsly.* MDCCLX. 12mo, pp. vi, 126. 30930

Also: Form of Prayer and Thanksgiving for the Victory of Sir Edward Hawke, 20 Nov. 1759. *London.* 1759.

Hawker (Peter). Instructions to Young Sportsmen ... By Lieutenant Colonel P. Hawker. First American from the Ninth London Edition. [With] the Hunting and Shooting of North America ... By Wm. T. Porter. *Philadelphia: Lea & Blanchard.* 1846. 8vo, pp. 459. 12 Plates. C. 30931

Hawkes (J.) Steam Trip to the Tropics; or, the Description of a Visit to the West Indies. Including part of Central and South America. By J. Hawkes, M.D. *London: J. Skeet.* 1864. Post 8vo, pp. vii, 164. 30932

[Hawkes (J.)] *See* Vol. III., No. 6786.

Hawkes (T. H.) Our National Trials a Cause for Thankfulness. A Sermon preached in Cleveland, Nov. 28, 1861. By Rev. T. H. Hawkes. *Cleveland: Fairbanks, Benedict & Co.* 1861. 8vo, pp. 24. 30933

Hawkesbury (*Lord*). *See* Jenkinson (Charles).

Hawkesworth (J.) An Account of the Voyages undertaken by the Order of His Present Majesty for making Discoveries in

the Southern Hemisphere, And successively performed by Commodore Byron, Captain Wallis, Captain Carteret, And Captain Cook, In the Dolphin, the Swallow, and the Endeavour: Drawn up from the Journals which were kept by the several Commanders, And from the Papers of Joseph Banks, Esq. By John Hawkesworth, LL.D. ... Illustrated with Cuts, and a great variety of Charts and Maps, relative to Countries now first discovered, or hitherto but imperfectly known. *London: W. Strahan.* MDCCLXXIII. 3 vols., 4to, pp. (12), xxxvi, (3), 676; xv, (1), 410; (6), 411–799. 52 Maps and Plates. A., B., BA. 30934

This is the Narrative of Cook's First Voyage and forms an indispensable part of a Series of Cook's Voyages. The first edition, to be preferred for its plates, is known by the collation we have given. In the later issues the paging of Vol. III. commences *de novo.* For further particulars *see our* Vol. IV., pp. 468–474.

Hawkesworth. An Account of the Voyages undertaken by the Order of His Present Majesty for making Discoveries in the Southern Hemisphere, And successively performed by Commodore Byron, Captain Wallis, Captain Carteret, And Captain Cook, In the Dolphin, the Swallow, and the Endeavour: Drawn up from the Journals which were kept by the several Commanders, And from the Papers of Joseph Banks, Esq. By John Hawkesworth, LL.D. ... *Dublin: A. Leathley.* MDCCLXXIII. 3 vols., 8vo, pp. (12), xxxvi, 521; xiv, 456; (6), 456. 30935

Hawkesworth. New Voyage Round the World In the years 1768, 1769, 1770, and 1771; Undertaken by Order of his present Majesty, performed by Captain James Cook In the Ship Endeavour, Drawn up from his own Journal, and from the Papers of Joseph Banks, Esq. F.R.S. And published by the special Direction of the Right Honourable the Lords of the Admiralty, By John Hawkesworth, LL.D. ... With Cutts [*sic*] and a Map of the whole Navigation. *New-York: Printed by James Rivington.* 1774. 2 vols., 8vo, pp. (2), 260; (2), 250. 2 Plates and Map. P. 30936

Hawkesworth. An Account of the Voyages undertaken by the order of his present Majesty, for making Discoveries in the Southern Hemisphere, and successively performed by Commodore Byron, Captain Wallis, Captain Carteret, And Captain Cook, In the Dolphin, the Swallow, and the Endeavour: Drawn up from the Journals which were kept by the several Commanders, and from the Papers of Joseph Banks, Esq; By John Hawkesworth, LL.D. ... *Dublin: James Potts.* MDCCLXXV. 2 vols., 8vo, pp. (12), xxxviii, 3–489; (10), 539. Chart and 7 Plates. 30937

Hawkesworth. [Same title.] To which is added a Voyage to the North Pole. By Commodore Phipps. ... *Dublin: James Williams.* M DCC LXXV. 2 vols., 8vo, pp. (12), xxviii, 3–489; (10), 539; "A Voyage," etc., pp. 49. 2 Charts and 6 Plates.

Hawkesworth. [Same title as No. 30934.] Third Edition. *London: W. Strahan.* MDCCLXXXV. 4 vols., 8vo, pp. (12), liii, 362; (8), 447; (8), 416; (6), 420. 10 Plates. + *London.* 1789. 4 vols., 12mo. 30939

Hawkesworth. Relation des Voyages entrepris par ordre de sa Majesté Britannique, actuellement regnante; Pour faire des Découvertes dans l'Hémisphère Méridional, et successivement exécutés par le Commodore Byron, le Capitaine Carteret, le Capitaine Wallis & le Capitaine Cook, dans les Vaisseaux le Dauphin, le Swallow & l'Endeavour: Rédigés d'après les Journaux tenus par les différens Commandans & les Papiers de M. Banks, Par J. Hawkesworth ... . Et enriche de Figures, & d'un grand nombre de Plans, & de Cartes relatives aux Pays qui ont été nouvellement découverts, ou qui n'etoient qu'imparfaitement connus. Traduite de l'Anglois. [Par Suard.] *A Paris, Chez Saillant et Nyon,* M. DCC. LXXIV. 4 vols., 4to, pp. (4), xxxii, 388; (6), 536; (6), 394, (1); viii, 361, (1). 52 Plates and Maps. + [*Ibid.*] MDCCLXXIV. 4 vols., 8vo. + *A Lausanne.* M.DCC.LXXIV. 4 vols., 8vo, pp. xxxix, 419; (4), 594; (4), 431; (4), 366, (2). B. 30940

These editions should be accompanied by an Atlas entitled: Cartes et Figures *A Paris, Chez Saillant et Nyon,* ... M. DCC. LXXIV. 4to.

Hawkesworth. Voyages autour du Monde entrepris par ordre de sa Majesté Britannique actuellement regnante, pour faire des découvertes dans l'Hémisphère austral. Exécutées successivement par le Chef d'Escadre Byron, les Capitaines Wallis, Carteret & Cook, dans les Vaisseaux le Dauphin, l'Hirondelle & l'Endeavour. Rédigés par M. Jean Hawkesworth sur les Journeaux tenus par les divers Commanders, & après les papiers de Mr. Joseph Banks. Enrichi de figures, & d'un grand nombre de Plans & de Cartes. Traduit de l'Anglois. *Amsterdam: E. van Harrevelt & Changuion.* MDCCLXXIV. 4 vols., 4to, pp. (16), xxxii, 388; 530, (6); 394; viii, 367, including Index. 51 Maps and Plates. 30941

The same as the Paris edition, with a different title, and a privilege of the States General to the Dutch publisher, and preface. A complete series of Cook's Voyages in French forms 14 vols., 4to. *Paris.* 1774–89.

Hawkesworth. Geschichte der See-Reisen und Entdeckungen im Süd-Meer welche auf Befehl Sr. Grossbrittannischen Majestät unternommen, und von Commodore Byron Capitain Wallis Capitain Carteret und Capitain Coock im Dolphin, der Swallow, und dem Endeavour nach einander ausgeführet worden sind; aus den Tagebüchern der verschiedenen Befehlshaber und den Handschriften Joseph Banks Esq. in drey Bänden verfasst von Dr. Johann Hawkesworth. Mit des Herrn Verfassers Genehmhaltung aus dem Englischen übersetzt von Johann Friedrich Schiller. ... *Berlin, bey A. Haude und J. C. Spener.* 1774. 3 vols., 4to, pp. (8), 459; (2), 8, (4), 413. 30942

Hawkesworth. Ausführlich und glaubwürdige Geschichte der neuesten Reisen um die Welt welche auf Befehl und Kosten des jetztregierenden Königs von England in den Jahren 1764, bis 1772, ... aus dem Englischen [von J. F. Schiller]. *Berlin: Haude und Spener.* 1775. 4 vols., 8vo. Maps and Plates. J.C.B.

Hawkesworth. Geschichte der Seereisen nach dem Südmeere, von Hauckesworth beschrieben, und nun in einen Auszug gebracht. *Frankfurt, bey Fleischern.* 1775. 8vo. 30944

See Schwarz (J. L.)

Hawkesworth. Reis naar den Zuidpool en Rondom de Weereld, in den Jaaren 1772–75. Uit het Engelsch. *Rotterdam.* 1784. 30945

Hawkins (Alfred). Hawkins's Picture of Quebec; With Historical Recollections. *Quebec: For the Proprietor.* 1834. 12mo, pp. viii, (4), 477. 14 Plates. BA. 30946

See "N. A. Rev.," April, 1835; *also* Quebec.

Hawkins (B.) A Sketch of the Creek Country with a Description of the Tribes, Government, and Customs of the Creek Indians. By Colonel Benj. Hawkins, for Twenty Years Resident Agent of that Nation. Preceded by a Memoir of the Author and a History of the Creek Confederacy. ... *Savannah.* 1848. 8vo, pp. (2), 88. 30947

Some copies are entitled: A Sketch of the Creek Country, in 1798 and 1799. With an Introduction and Historic Sketch of the Creek Confederacy. By W. B. Hodgson. *New York: Bartlett & Welford.* 1848. The work also forms Part I. of Vol III. of the Collections of the Georgia Historical Society.

Hawkins (C.) The Adventures of Christopher Hawkins, containing "Details of his Captivity, a first and second time on the High Seas, in the Revolutionary War, by the British, and his consequent sufferings, and escape from the 'Jersey' Prison Ship, then lying in the Harbour of New York, by swimming." Now first Printed from the Original Manuscript. Written by Himself. With an Introduction and Notes by Chas. I. Bushnell. Illustrations. *New York: Privately Printed.* 1864. 8vo, pp. 316.

HAWKINS. The Life and Adventures of Christopher Hawkins, a Prisoner on Board the 'Old Jersey' Prison Ship during the Revolution. *New York: Printed for the Holland Club.* 1858. 8vo. 30949

HAWKINS (E. W.) The History and Confession of the Young Felon, who was executed in Estill Co., Ky., on the 29th day of May, 1857, for the Murder of James M. Land, and Jesse Arvine, ... [n. p. n. d.] 8vo, pp. 60. 30950

HAWKINS (E.) Annals of the Diocese of Toronto [and] Quebec. By Ernest Hawkins, B.D. *London: Society for Promoting Christian Knowledge.* 1848. 12mo, pp. xiv, 335. + [*Ibid.*] 1849. 30951

HAWKINS. Historical Notices of the Missions of the Church of England in the North American Colonies, previous to the Independence of the United States. Chiefly from the Documents of the Society for the Propagation of the Gospel in Foreign Parts. By Ernest Hawkins. *London.* 1845. 8vo. C., S. 30952

HAWKINS (J.) An Account of the Loss of His Majesty's Ship Deal Castle, commanded by Capt. James Hawkins, off the Island of Port Rico, during the Hurricane in the West-Indies, in the year 1780. *London: J. Murray.* M DCC LXXXVII. 8vo, pp. (6), 48. 30953

HAWKINS (*Sir* J.) A true Declaration of the troublesome Voyage (the second) of Mr. John Hawkins to the Partes of Guynea & the West Indies, 1567 and 1568. *London.* 1569. 8vo. 30954

See Hakluyt's Collection, Vol. III. Title and note from Lowndes' "Manual." We have never seen the book, and incline to the belief that this octavo edition does not exist, but that it is only to be found in Hakluyt's Collection. The first voyage is described in Kennett's "Bibl. Am. Prim.," page 17, and the third on page 18, and both these are from Hakluyt or Purchass.

[HAWKINS (John).] A Few Remarks on an Address to the Roman Catholics of the United States ... occasioned by a Letter ... to the Catholics of Worcester by Mr. Wharton ... By the Right Rev. Dr. Carroll. By a Fair Inquirer. *Worcester: J. Tymbs.* [1796.] 12mo, pp. 24. 30955

Concerning this controversy *see* Finotti's "Bibliog. Cath. Americana."

HAWKINS (J.) History of a Voyage to the Coast of Africa, and Travels into the Interior of that Country; containing ... Descriptions of the Climate and Inhabitants, and ... Particulars concerning the Slave Trade. By Joseph Hawkins of New York, ... *Philadelphia: S. C. Ustick & Co.* 1797. 18mo, pp. 179, (1). Plate. + Second Edition. *Troy: Printed for the Author by Luther Pratt.* 1797. 18mo, pp. 180. B., BA., C. 30956

Published for the benefit of the author, who had become blind.

HAWKINS (R.) The | Observations | of | Sir Richard Havv | kins Knight, in his | Voiage jnto the | South Sea. | Anno Domini 1593. | *London | Printed by I. D. for Iohn Iaggard, and are to be | sold at his shop at the Hand and Starre in Fleete-streete, | neere the Temple Gate.* 1622. | Folio, pp. (6), 169, Errata, 1 page, "The Table," etc., pp. 5. C., J.C.B., S. 30957

A volume of much rarity. Jadis' copy sold for £3 4s, Bolton Corney's, erroneously said to be on large paper, for £11 15s. The author was a son of the famous Sir John Hawkins, and was Admiral of New England in 1619. He narrates some particulars relating to the Indians of Florida, the Caribbean Islands, and parts of South America, which interest us, as data of their history and mode of life two and a half centuries ago. The work was reprinted as below:

HAWKINS. The Observations of Sir Richard Hawkins Knt in his Voyage into The South Sea in the Year 1593. Reprinted from the Edition of 1622, Edited by C. R. Drinkwater Bethune, Captain R. N. *London: Printed for the Hakluyt Society.* M.DCCC.XLVII. 8vo, pp. xvi, 246. B., BA. 30958

HAWKINS (R. C.) Testimonial to Col. Rush C. Hawkins, Ninth Regiment New York Volunteers. "Hawkins Zouaves." *New York: Latimer Brothers & Seymour.* 1863. 8vo, pp. 9.

HAWKINS (W. G.) Life of John H. W. Hawkins. Compiled by his Son Rev. William George Hawkins, A.M. ... *Boston: John P. Jewett and Company.* 1859. 12mo, pp. vii, 433. Portrait. B., BA., S. 30960

HAWKINS. Lunsford Lane; or, Another Helper from North Carolina. By the Rev. William G. Hawkins, A.M. ... *Boston: Crosby & Nichols.* 1863. 12mo, pp. 305. Portrait. B., BA.

[HAWKS (Francis Lester).] The American Forest; or Uncle Philip's Conversations ... about the Trees of America. *New York: Harper & Brothers.* 1834. 18mo, pp. 5–8, 250. B. + [*Ibid.*] 1841. 30962

HAWKS. Contributions to the Ecclesiastical History of the United States of America. By Francis L. Hawks. A Narrative of Events connected with the Rise and Progress of the Protestant Episcopal Church in Virginia. ... *New York: Harper & Brothers.* 1836. 8vo, pp. (2), 332. + In Maryland from 1632 to 1838. *New York.* 1839. 8vo, pp. 523. BA. 30963

[HAWKS.] The Early History of the Southern States: Virginia, North and South Carolina, and Georgia. Illustrated by Tales, Sketches, Anecdotes, and Adventures, ... By Lambert Lilly, Schoolmaster. *Philadelphia: Published by Key, Mielke and Biddle.* 1832. 12mo, pp. 192. Plate. + *Boston: Ticknor and Fields.* M DCCC LIV. 12mo, pp. 192. 30964

HAWKS. History of North Carolina: with Maps and Illustrations. By Francis L. Hawks, D.D., LL.D. *Fayetteville, N. C.: E. J. Hale & Son.* 1857–1858. 3 vols., 8vo, pp. 254; 591; 470. + Second Edition. [*Ibid.*] 1857–1858. Portrait and 5 Maps. BA. + Third Edition. [*Ibid.*] 1859. B. 30965

Some copies of Vol I. have the imprint *Raleigh.* 1857. I have given the collation of Vol III. on the authority of the late William Gowans, who assured me he had seen the volume, and that the entire edition was shipped to North Carolina during the earlier period of the Civil War, and was probably lost — but, *per contra*, the publishers assert it was never printed. The author's plan is to print some original document or a rare tract, and to it append his own historical narrative.

[HAWKS.] History of the United States, No. 2; or, Uncle Philip's Conversations with the Children about New York. *New York: Harper & Brothers.* 1835. 2 vols., 18mo. B.

HAWKS. Narrative of Events connected with the Rise and Progress of the Protestant Episcopal Church in Virginia, with Appendix of the Journals of the Conventions in Virginia, from the Commencement to the Present Time. *New York: Harper & Brothers.* 1836. 8vo, pp. (2), 332. 30957

Our No. 30963, *supra*, with a different title-page.

HAWKS. Narrative of the Expedition of an American Squadron to the China Seas and Japan, performed in the Years 1852, 1853, and 1854, under the Command of Commodore M. C. Perry, United States Navy, by Order of the Government of the United States. Compiled from the Original Notes and Journals of Commodore Perry and his Officers, at his Request, and under his Supervision, By Francis L. Hawks, ... With Numerous Illustrations. ... *Washington: A. O. P. Nicholson, Printer.* 1856. 3 vols., 4to, pp. xvii, (1), 537, 89 Plates; (6), 414, (2), 14 Fac-

similes, xi, (1), Maps; Vol. III., Observations on the Zodiacal Light ... by Rev. George Jones, A.M. pp. xliii, 705. BA.

Issued as Ex. Doc., 97, Sen. Doc., 79, 33d Congress, 2d Sess. The numerous plates represent objects of natural history, portraits and views. One of the plates, representing a bathing scene, at page 408 of Vol I., was suppressed; but it is found in many copies. In the editing of this work Dr. Hawks was assisted by Robert Tomes; Mr. J. C. Brevoort described the fish. Some copies of Vol I. bear the imprint: *New York: D. Appleton & Co.* 1857, without any mention of the number of volumes which constitute a complete work. This firm also issued the Narrative (Vol I.) in royal 8vo, 1846, pp. 642.

HAWKS. Revolutionary History of North Carolina, in Three Lectures, by Rev. Francis L. Hawks, D.D., LL.D., Hon. David L. Swain, LL.D., and Hon. Wm. A. Graham, LL.D. To which is prefixed a preliminary Sketch of the Battle of the Alamance. Compiled by William D. Cooke, A.M. Illustrated by Darley and Lossing. *Raleigh: William D. Cooke.* 1853. 12mo, pp. 237. P.

[HAWKS.] Uncle Philip's Conversations with Young Persons. History of Virginia. *New York: Harper & Brothers.* 1834. 16mo, pp. 4, 232. Plates. B. 30970

[HAWKS.] Uncle Philip's Conversations with the Children about the Whale Fishery and Polar Seas. *New York: Harper & Brothers.* 1836. 16mo, pp. (2), vi, xi–211. B. 30971

Also: The Adventures of Daniel Boone ... . *New York: D. Appleton & Co.* MDCCCXLIV. 12mo, pp. 174. Plate. B. Dr. Hawks also edited and amplified Elihu Rich's "Cyclopedia of Universal Biography," which was put forth as Appleton's "Cyclopedia of Biography ..." *New York: D. Appleton & Co.* 1856. Rl. 8vo, pp. 1058. *See also* Hamilton, Rivero & Tschudi, and Rich (E.)

HAWKS. A Tribute to the Memory of the Rev. Francis L. Hawks, D.D., LL.D. *New York.* 1867. 8vo, pp. 71. 30972

Contains a Sketch of his Life by Rev. N. L. Richardson, and an Address by Rev. W. F. Morgan, and Resolutions by the Diocesan Convention.

HAWKS *and* PERRY (W. S.) Documentary History of the Protestant Episcopal Church, in the United States of America. Containing Numerous hitherto Unpublished Documents concerning the Church in Connecticut. Francis L. Hawks, DD., LL.D., and William Stevens Perry, A.M., Editors. *New York: James Pott.* 1863–4. 2 vols., 8vo, pp. (2), 328; 359. B., BA. 30973

HAWKSHAW (J.) Reminiscences of South America: from Two and a Half Years' Residence in Venezuela. By John Hawkshaw, ... *London: Jackson & Walford.* 1838. Fcp. 8vo, pp. xii, 260, (8). BA., C., P. 30974

HAWKSLEY (John). The Security of God's People in Times of Trouble. A ...non. *Boston.* 1846. 8vo. 30975

[HAWLES (*Sir* John).] The Englishman's Right: a Dialogue between a Barrister and a Juryman. *London: Printed for Joseph White.* M.DCC.LXX. 8vo, pp. vii, 56. BA. + *London.* MDCCLXXI. 12mo, pp. vi, (1), 51. + *London.* M,DCC,LXXI. *Boston reprinted.* M,DCC,LXXII. 12mo, pp. 56. BA., M. + *Philadelphia: J. Thompson.* 1798. 8vo, pp. 70. 30976

HAWLEY (B.) Truth and Righteousness Triumphant. A Discourse Commemorative of the Death of President Lincoln: Preached in the Washington Avenue M. E. Church, April 20, 1865. By B. Hawley, D.D. *Albany, N. Y.: J. Munsell.* 1865. 8vo, pp. 20. B. 30977

HAWLEY (F. J.) Ten Years' Parochial Work in the Tropics; a Sermon, Santa Cruz, W. I. By Fletcher J. Hawley. *London.* 1856. 18mo. S. 30979

Also: "Let them Marry." A Tract for the Tropics. A Sermon preached at St. John's Church, Santa-Cruz West Indies. *London.* 1856. 18mo.—Tribute to the Memory of Rev. F. S. Mines, Rev. Edmund Richards and Rev. John Wade. ... *St. Croix*, 1853. 8vo.

HAWLEY (G.) Address at the Public Exercises of Albany Academy, ... August 6, 1835. By Gideon Hawley, LL.D. *Albany: Printed by E. W. and C. Skinner.* 1835. 8vo, pp. 19. S.

HAWLEY. Instructions for the better Government and Organization of Common Schools. *Albany.* 1819. 8vo. 30981

Also: Instructions from the Regents of the University of the State of New York, to the Several Colleges ... . *Albany: Printed by Croswell, Van Benthuysen and Burt.* 1835. 8vo, pp. (2), 8. B.

HAWLEY (J.) An Essay on the Enlargement of the Erie Canal, with Arguments in favor of retaining the present proposed size of seventy feet by seven. By Jesse Hawley. *Lockport, N. Y.* 1840. 8vo, pp. 16. S. 30982

HAWLEY (Joseph Roswell). The Brilliant Military Record of Maj.-General Hawley. [n. p. n. d.] 8vo, pp. 4. 30978

HAWLEY (S. C.) An Address ... before the Young Men's Association of ... Buffalo, ... March 22, 1836. By Seth C. Hawley ... . *Buffalo: Oliver G. Steele.* 1836. 8vo, pp. 20. B.

HAWLEY (S.) The Fall of Sumter: Its Intent and Portent. An Address given at ... St. Paul, ... April 12th, 1863, the Anni-

versary of the attack on Fort Sumter. By Rev. S. Hawley. ... *Saint Paul.* 1863. 8vo. 30984

HAWLEY (W.) A Letter to the Right Rev. James Kemp, D.D. Bishop of the Protestant Episcopal Church, in the Diocese of Maryland; an Address to the Congregation of St. John's Church, in the City of Washington; (occasioned by the appointment of a Unitarian Chaplain to Congress,) on Sunday, Dec. 9, 1821. By the Rev. William Hawley, ... *Washington City: Printed by Davis and Force.* 1822. 8vo, pp. 8. BA., M. 30985

HAWLEY (W. F.) Quebec. The Harp, and other Poems. By William Fitz Hawley. *Montreal.* 1829. 18mo, pp. 172.

HAWLEY. The Unknown, or Lays of the Forest. By William Fitz Hawley. *Montreal.* 1831. 12mo. 30987

Contains a description of the river St. Maurice and the falls of Shawenegan, Canada.

HAWLEY (Z.) A Journal of a Tour through Connecticut, Massachusetts, New York, the North Part of Pennsylvania and Ohio, including a Year's residence in that part of the State of Ohio, Styled New Connecticut, or Western Reserve. In which is given, a description of the Country, Climate, Soil, Productions, Animals, Buildings, Manners of the People, State of Society, Population, &c. From actual and careful Observation. By Zerah Hawley, A.M. *New-Haven: Printed by S. Converse.* 1822. 12mo, pp. 158. C. 30988

HAWLEY (Z. K.) Congregationalism and Methodism. By Z. K. Hawley. *New York: Leavitt, Trow & Co.* 1846. 12mo, pp. 311. 30989

HAWTHORNE (N.) Famous Old People: being the Second Epoch of Grandfather's Chair. By Nathaniel Hawthorne ... . Second Edition. *Boston: Tappan & Dennet.* 1842. Small 8vo, pp. 158. B. 30990

HAWTHORNE. Liberty Tree; with the Last Words of Grand Father's Chair. By Nathaniel Hawthorne. *Boston.* 1842. 18mo, pp. 156. 30991

HAWTHORNE. Life of Franklin Pierce. By Nathaniel Hawthorne. *Boston: Ticknor, Reed, and Fields.* M DCCC LII. 12mo, pp. 144 Portrait. B., BA., C. 30992

An electioneering piece.

HAWTHORNE. Passages from the American Note-Books of Nathaniel Hawthorne. *Boston: Ticknor & Fields.* 1868. 2 vols.,

12mo, pp. (2), 222; (2), 228. + *London.* 1868. 2 vols., post 8vo. + *Boston: Fields, Osgood & Co.* 1869. 30993

Also: Passages from the English Note-Books of Nathaniel Hawthorne. *Boston: Fields, Osgood & Co.* 1870. 2 vols., 16mo, pp. viii, 410; (2) 393. BA. + *London.* 1870. 2 vols., post 8vo.

HAWTHORNE. The Scarlet Letter. A Romance. By Nathaniel Hawthorne. *Boston: Ticknor & Fields.* 1855. 12mo, pp. vi, 307. BA., C. 30994

A story of Puritan times in New England. Frequently reprinted, both at Boston and London. Most of the following works are based on American Life and Manners: The Blithedale Romance. ... *Boston: Ticknor, Reed, and Fields.* M DCCC LII. 12mo, pp. 288. —Mosses from an Old Manse. ... *New York.* 1846. 12mo. + *Boston: Ticknor and Fields.* 1865–67. 2 vols., 12mo, pp. 286; 297.—The House of the Seven Gables; a Romance. ... *Boston: Ticknor, Reed, and Fields.* M DCCC LI. 12mo, pp. 344. + *Boston: Ticknor and Fields.* 1866. 12mo, pp. 344.—The Snow Image, and other Twice-Told-Tales. ... *Boston: Ticknor and Fields.* 1865. 12mo, pp. 5–273.—True Stories from History and Biography. ... *Boston: Ticknor and Fields.* 1868. 12mo, pp. 352. Plates. —Twice-Told Tales. ... *Boston: Ticknor, Reed, and Fields.* M DCCC LIII. 2 vols., 12mo, pp. 287; 288. Portrait. + *Boston: Ticknor & Fields.* 1864. 2 vols., 12mo. + [*Ibid.*] 1866.

HAY (D. G.) Apuntes del Distrito de Texcoco, por D. G. Hay. *Mexico.* 1866. 30995

HAY (G.) An Essay on Naturalization and Allegiance. By George Hay. *Washington.* 1816. 8vo. C. 30996

[HAY.] An Essay on the Liberty of the Press, respectfully inscribed to the Republican Printers throughout the United States. By Hortensius. *Philadelphia.* 1799. 8vo, pp. 51. + *Richmond: Reprinted by Samuel Pleasants, Jr.* 1803. 8vo, pp. 48. 30997

Written after his endurance of repeated libels from Callender, printed in the Recorder. Some copies are entitled: An Essay on the Liberty of the Press, shewing that the Requisition of Security for Good Behavior from Libellers is perfectly compatible with the Laws of Virginia. *Richmond: Printed by Samuel Pleasants, Junior.* 1803. 8vo, pp. 48.

[HAY.] A Treatise on Expatriation. *Washington: A. & G. Way, Printers.* 1814. 8vo, pp. (2), 90. B., BA., C. 30998

This elicited a "Review of a Treatise on Expatriation by George Hay, Esq. ... By a Massachusetts Lawyer." *Boston: Russell, Cutler & Co.* 1814. 8vo, pp. 39. B., S., W.

HAY (Henry). *See* Tariff.

HAY (J.) Narrative of the Insurrection in the Island of Grenada, in 1795. By John Hay. *London.* 1823. 8vo, pp. 177.

HAY (W.) Speech of William Hay delivered in the Legislature of Virginia, 1816, '17, concerning Usury. *Richmond.* 1817. 16mo, pp. 38. 31000

HAY (W.) An Address, ... before the Washington Benevolent Society ... By William Hay, Junr. *Glenn's Falls: Printed by J. Cunningham.* 1813. 8vo, pp. 16. B. 31001

[HAY (W.)] History of Temperance in Saratoga Co., N. Y. ... *Saratoga.* 1855. 12mo. S. 31002

HAYDEN (C. A.) Our Country's Martyr. A Tribute to Abraham Lincoln, our beloved and lamented President. By Mrs. Caroline A. Hayden. *Boston: Press of Dakin and Metcalf.* 1865. 12mo, pp. 23. B. 31003

This poem was written, published, and one edition sold within one week, another edition in the next. Also: Carry Emerson; or, Life at Cliftonville. Second Edition. *Boston: J. French & Co.* 1856. 12mo, pp. 360. C.

HAYDEN (Ferdinand Vanderveer). Geological Report of the Exploration of the Yellowstone and Missouri Rivers. By Dr. F. V. Hayden, Assistant, under the Direction of Captain (now Lieut.-Col. and Brev. Brig.-Gen.) W. T. Reynolds, Corps of Engineers, 1859–60. *Washington: Government Printing Office.* 1869. 8vo, pp. x, 174. Map. C. 31004

Includes a Report on the Cretaceous and Tertiary Plants, by J. S. Newberry.

HAYDEN. Preliminary Field Report of the United States Geological Survey of Colorado and New Mexico. Conducted under the Authority of Hon. John D. Cox, Secretary of the Interior. By F. V. Hayden, U. S. Geologist. *Washington: Government Printing Office.* 1869. 8vo, pp. 155. BA., C. 31005

HAYDEN. Preliminary Report of the United States Geological Survey of Wyoming, and Portions of Contiguous Territories (being a Second Annual Report of Progress), conducted under the Authority of the Secretary of the Interior. By F. V. Hayden ... . *Washington: Government Printing Office.* 1871. 8vo, pp. 511. C. 31006

HAYDEN. Sun Pictures of Rocky Mountain Scenery, with a Description of the Geographical and Geological Features, and some Account of the Resources of the Great West; containing Thirty Photographic Views along the Line of the Pacific Railroad, from Omaha to Sacramento. By F. V. Hayden ... *New York: J. Bien.* 1870. 4to, pp. viii, 150. 30 Photographs. B.

Also: Contributions to the Ethnography and Philology of the Indian Tribes of the Missouri Valley. ... *Philadelphia: C. Sherman & Son.* 1862. 4to, pp. 227–461. Map. — ... Notes ... illustrating the Geological Structure of the Country bordering on the Missouri River, from the Mouth of the Platte River to Fort Benton ... . *Philadelphia: Merrihew & Thompson.* 1857. 8vo, pp. 10. Map.

HAYDEN (H. H.) Geological Essays; or, an Inquiry into some of the Geological Phenomena, to be found in Various Parts of America, and elsewhere. By Horace H. Hayden, Esq. ... *Baltimore: J. Robinson, for the Author.* 1820. 8vo, pp. viii, 412.

See "N. A. Rev.," XII. 434.

HAYDEN (J. H.) Genealogy of the Hayden Family, from Stiles' History of Ancient Windsor. *Albany: J. Munsell.* 1859. 8vo, pp. 15. 31009

HAYDEN (L.) Caste among Masons: Address before ... Masons of ... Massachusetts ... December 27, 1865. By Lewis Hayden ... . *Boston: Printed by Edward S. Coombs & Company.* 1866. 8vo, pp. 72. 31010

Also: Grand Lodge Jurisdictional Claim: An Address before ... Masons ... June 24, 1868. ... *Boston: Printed by Edward S. Coombs.* 1868. 8vo, pp. 92.

HAYDEN (S.) Washington and his Masonic Compeers. By Sidney Hayden, ... with a ... Masonic Portrait of Washington, ... Third Edition. *New York: Masonic Publishing and Manufacturing Co.* ... 1866. 12mo, pp. 407. + Sixth Edition. [*Ibid.*] 1867. 31011

HAYDEN (W.) Narrative of William Hayden, containing a Faithful Account of his Travels for a Number of Years, whilst a Slave, in the South. Written by Himself. ... *Cincinnati.* 1846. 12mo, pp. 156. 31012

HAYDEN (W. B.) A Brief Abstract of Remarks by Rev. Wm. B. Hayden, at the New Jerusalem Church, on the Funeral of the President, April 19, 1865. *Cincinnati: Mallory & Co., Printers.* 1855. 8vo, pp. 10, cover, 2 l. 31013

Also: The Institution of Slavery, viewed in the Light of Divine Truth. A Lecture delivered in ... Portland, ... March 17, 1861. ... *Portland: Printed by David Tucker.* 1861. 8vo, pp. 28.

HAYDN (J.) Dictionary of Dates and Universal Reference relating to all Ages and Nations: ... By Joseph Haydn. Second Edition. *London: Edward Moxon.* 1844. 8vo, pp. 574. + Edited by Benjamin Vincent, and Revised for American Readers. *New York: Harper & Brothers.* 1869. 8vo, pp. 541. 31014

This very useful book has passed through many editions both in Europe and America. The following is the best for American topics:

Haydn's Dictionary of Dates. Edited by B. Vincent. Authorized American Edition, with Supplement on American Topics, and Biographical Index, by G. P. Putnam. *New York: G. P. Putnam & Son.* 1867. 8vo, pp. 100, viii, 833. C. 31015

HAYE (J.) De Rebvs Japonicis, Indicis, et Pervanis epistolæ recentiores. A Joanne Hayo Dalgattiensi Scoto, societatis Jesv, in librum vnum coacervatæ. *Antverpiæ, Martini Nutij.* 1605. 8vo, pp. (8), 968, (52). C., J.C.B. 31016

For a full account of this Scotch Jesuit, and the contents of this work, *see* Backer, I. 390. *See also* Carayon, No. 760. The part relative to Peru, occupies pp. 935–943.

HAYÈRE (J. T.) Éloge Funèbre du Président A. Lincoln, fait pas le très-puissant frère J. T. Hayère, ... *Paris: Imprimerie de E. Martinet.* 1865. 8vo, pp. 4. 31017

HAYES (G. E.) The Geology of Buffalo, ... By George E. Hayes. *Buffalo.* 1869. 8vo. 31018

HAYES (I. I.) An Arctic Boat Journey, in the Autumn of 1854. By Isaac I. Hayes, M.D. *Boston: Brown, Taggard & Chase.* 1860. 12mo, pp. xvii, 375. 2 Maps. B., BA. + With an Introduction and Notes by Dr. Norton Shaw. *London.* 1860. 12mo. Map. + New Edition, Enlarged and Illustrated. *Boston: Ticknor & Fields.* 1867. 12mo, pp. xxiii, 387. 12 Plates, 2 Charts. B., C. + *Boston.* 1869. 31019

HAYES. The Open Polar Sea: a Narrative of a Voyage of Discovery towards the North Pole, in the Schooner "United States. By Dr. I. I. Hayes. *New York: Hurd & Houghton.* 1867. 8vo, pp. xxiv, 454. Portrait and Plates. B., BA., C.

HAYES. ... Physical Observations in the Arctic Seas. By Isaac I. Hayes, M.D., ... Made on the west coast of North Greenland, the vicinity of Smith Strait, and the west side of Kennedy Channel, during 1860 and 1861. Reduced and discussed ... by Charles A. Schott, ... *Washington: Smithsonian Institution.* 1867. 4to, pp. xi, 270. 3 Maps and 3 Plates. C. 31021

Also included in the "Smithsonian Contributions," Vol. XV. Also: Cast Away in the Cold: an Old Man's Story of a Young Man's Adventures, as Related by Captain John Hardy, Mariner. ... *Boston: Ticknor & Fields.* 1869. Small 4to, pp. vi, 263. 2 Plates. B.—The Land of Desolation: being a Personal Narrative of Observation and Adventure in Greenland. ... *New York: Harper & Brothers.* 1872. 12mo, pp. 357.

HAYES (J. D.) *and* HATCH (Israel T.) "The Niagara Ship Canal:" and "Reciprocity:" Papers ... By J. D. Hayes, Esq. Together with the Speech of Hon. Israel T. Hatch, in the Convention at Detroit, July 14, 1865. ... *Buffalo: Matthews & Warren.* 1865. 8vo, pp. 58. C. 31022

HAYES (J.) Rural Poems. By John Hayes. *Carlisle.* 1807. 12mo. 31023

HAYES (J. J.) Remarks made at ... Portsmouth, ... January, 1845, in Defence of ... John P. Hale, ... in Relation to the Annexation of Texas. By John J. Hayes. [n. p. n. d.] 8vo, pp. 12. B., BA. 31024

HAYES (J. L.) Vindication of the Rights and Titles, Political and Territorial, of Alexander, Earl of Stirling & Dovan, ... and Lord Proprietor of Canada and Nova Scotia. By John L. Hayes. *Washington: Gideon & Co.* 1853. 8vo, pp. 52. B., C.

HAYES. Trial of Lord Stirling: being Part II. of the Vindication of the Rights and Titles ... . *Washington: Gideon & Co.* 1853. 8vo, pp. 76. Plates and Pedigree. B. 31026

Also: Address before the National Association of Wool Manufacturers. ... Sept. 6. 1865. ... *Cambridge: John Wilson and Sons.* 1865. 8vo, pp. 80. B.—Memorial of the Iron Manufacturers of New England, asking for a Modification of the Tariff of 1846. ... *Philadelphia: C. Sherman.* 1850. 8vo, pp. 39. C.—Protection a Boon to Consumers. An Address ... before the National Association of Knit Goods Manufacturers. ... New-York ... May 1, 1867. ... *Boston: J. Wilson & Son, Printers.* 1867. 8vo, pp. 55. B.—The Protective Question Abroad, and Remarks at the Indianapolis Exposition. ... *Cambridge: John Wilson and Son.* 1871. 8vo, pp. 66. B.—Statement of Facts relative to Canada Wools. *Boston.* 1866. 8vo.

HAYES (J. R.) Negrophobia "on the Brain" in White Men; or, An Essay upon the Origin and Progress, Mental and Physical, of the Negro Race, etc. By Dr. J. R. Hayes. *Washington.* 1869. 8vo, pp. 35. 31027

HAYES (R.) The Negociator's Magazine; or, the most Authentick Account yet published of the Monies, Weights, and Measures of the Principal Places of Trade in the World. ... *London.* 1740. 8vo. C. + *London: John Noon.* MDCCLIV. 8vo, pp. (16), 479. Table. BA. + To which are added, Curious Calculations, of great use in the West Indian and American Trades. *London.* 1777. 8vo. 31028

HAYES (S. S.) Taxation in the United States. Reply to the London Times, By S. S. Hayes, of the late United States Revenue Commission. *Chicago: Sinclair & Blair.* 1867. 8vo.

HAYES (W.) The Revision of the Laws; prepared ... by Wingate Hayes. *Providence: Knowles, Anthony & Co.* 1857. 8vo, pp. 12. 31030

A History of the several codes of Rhode Island, 1647–1857.

HAYGARTH (J.) An Inquiry how to prevent the Small-Pox. And Proceedings of a Society for Promoting General Inoculation, at stated Periods, and preventing the Natural Small-Pox, in

Chester. By John Haygarth, M.B.F.R.S. *Chester: Printed by J. Monk. For J. Johnson, ... London. and P. Broster, Chester.* MDCCLXXXV. 8vo, pp. xi, 223. P. 31031

Chiefly relating to English matters, but has a very interesting correspondence with Dr. Benj. Waterhouse relating to the municipal regulations concerning small-pox in America.

HAYGARTH. A Letter ... on the Prevention of Infectious Fevers; and an Address to the College of Physicians at Philadelphia, on the Prevention of the American Pestilence. ... By John Haygarth, M.D. *Bath.* 1801. 8vo, pp. (2), 188. B., P.

HAYLE (G. P.) Dissertatio Medico Inauguralis quædam de Cantharidum natura et usu complectens ... Eruditorum examini submittit Gulielmus Pusey Hayle, Jamaicensis. *Lugduni Batavorum, A. et J. Honkoop,* MDCCLXXXVI. 8vo, pp. (8), 38.

HAYLEY (T.) A Sermon before the Society for the Propagation of the Gospel in Foreign Parts. By Thomas Hayley. *London.* 1717. 8vo. J.C.B. 31034

HAYLEY (W.) The Triumphs of Temper; a Poem. In Six Cantos. By William Hayley, Esq. ... First American Edition, with Plates. *Newburyport: Printed by John Mycall for Joseph H. Seymour.* [1781.] 12mo, pp. 162. B. 31035

Merely inserted as illustrative of early American art.

H[AYMAN] (R[obert].) Certaine | Epigrams ovt | of the first fovre | Bookes of the Ex- | cellent Epigrammatist, Master | Iohn Owen: | Translated into English | at Harbor-Grace in | Bristol's Hope in Britaniola, anciently | called New-found-land: | By R. H. | *At London | Imprinted for Roger Michell,* ... 1628. 4to, pp. (6), 40.

The first translation made in Newfoundland, and forms part of the following work.

H[AYMAN]. Quodlibets, lately come over from New Britaniola, Old-Newfound-Land. Epigrams and other Small Parcels, both Morall and Divine. The first four Bookes being the Authors Owne; the rest Translated out of that Excellent Epigrammatist, Mr. John Owen, and other rare Authors; with two Epistles of that excellently Wittie Doctor, Francis Rablais; ... All of them Composed and done at Harbor-Grace in Britaniola, anciently called Newfound-Land. By R. H. ... *London: Roger Michell.* 1628. 4to, pp. (8), 64. BA., C. 31037

The author was some time governor of the plantations there. It is dedicated "To the King's Most Excellent Majestie, Charles ... King of Great-Britaine, France, and Ireland, &c., Emperour of South and North Virginia, King of Britaniola, or Newfound-

land, and the Iles adjacent, Fatner, Fauourer, and Furtherer of all his loyall Subjects right Honourable and Worthie Plantations." It is an extremely rare poetical volume divided into three parts, with separate title-pages, and some preliminary verses by William Vaughan, Richard Spicer, George Wither, and John Vicars.

HAYNE (A. P.) A Brief Sketch of the Life and Military Services of Arthur P. Hayne, of Charleston, South Carolina. *Philadelphia: Printed by T. K. & P. G. Collins.* 1837. 8vo, pp. 16.

HAYNE (Robert Y.) Defence of the South!! General Hayne, in Reply to Mr. Webster, of Massachusetts. *Charleston, S. C.: A. E. Miller.* 1830. 8vo, pp. 20. BA., M. 31039

HAYNE. An Oration Delivered in the Independent or Congregational Church, Charleston, before the State Rights & Free Trade Party, the State Society of Cincinnati, the Revolution Society, the '76 Association, and several Volunteer Companies of Militia, on the 4th of July, 1831, being the 55th Anniversary of American Independence. By the Hon. Robert Y. Hayne. *Charleston: A. E. Miller.* 1831. 8vo, pp. (iv), 47. 31040

HAYNE. Speech of the Hon. Robert Y. Hayne ... on the Reduction of the Tariff. Delivered January 9, 1832, ... on a Motion to Amend Mr. Clay's Resolution. *Washington: Printed by Jonathan Elliot.* [1832.] 8vo, pp. 47. BA., 31041

This elicited a reply entitled: Errors in Fact, advanced by Senator Hayne, in his Anti-Tariff Speech ... *Philadelphia: Printed by Henry Young.* 1832. 8vo, pp. 8. BA. Perhaps by Mathew Carey.

HAYNE. Speech of Mr. Hayne of Georgia ... January 21, 1831, in reply to Mr. Everett of Massachusetts on the Indian Question. *Washington: Printed by Duff Green.* 1831. 80, pp. 13.

Also: A Call upon the Stockholders of the Louisville, Cincinnati, and Charleston Railroad Company. *Charleston.* 1838. 8vo, pp. 39. M.—Letter ... to a Committee of the State's Rights and Free Trade Party, and a Reply to Col. Drayton's late Address. *Charleston.* 1832.—An Oration ... Charleston ... 4th of July, 1814. ... Second Edition. ... *Charleston.* 1814. 8vo, pp. 24. BA.—Remarks in the Senate ... May 1830, on the Pension Bill. *Washington.* 1830. 8vo. W.—Speech of Mr. Hayne, of South-Carolina, against the Tariff Bill; ... in the Senate ... April, 1824. *Charleston: Printed by A. E. Miller.* 1824. 8vo, pp. 48. BA.—Second Speech in Reply to Mr. Webster, on the Public Lands. *Washington.* 1830. 12mo, pp. 20. W.—Speech ... on the Mission to Panama, March, 1826. *Washington.* 1826. 8vo, pp. 32. C., W. + 12mo, pp. 36.—Speech ... on the Bill to Establish a Uniform System of Bankruptcy, Delivered ... May 1, 1826. *Washington.* 1826. 8vo, pp. 24.—Speech ... on the ... Improvement of the Navy. ... February 15, 1827. *Washington.* 1827. 8vo, pp. 21.—Speech ... in Support of his Amendment to Mr. Clay's Resolution proposing to Reduce the Duties on Imports, in Senate January 16, 1832. *Washington: Duff Green.* 1832. 8vo, pp. 20.—Speech of Gen. Hayne in Reply to the Hon. Henry Clay. In Senate ... Jan. 16, 1832. [n. p. n. d.] 8vo, pp. 18. B., BA.

HAYNE *and* WEBSTER. Several Speeches made during the Debate in the Senate of the United States, on Mr. Foot's Resolution proposing an Enquiry into the Expediency of Abolishing the Office of Surveyor General of Public Lands, and to suspend further Surveys, &c. By General Hayne, of South-Carolina, and Mr. Webster, of Massachusetts. *Charleston, S. C.: A. E. Miller.* 1830. 8vo, pp. 22, 36, 112. + *Washington.* 1830. 8vo.

Reprinted as: Speeches of the Hon. Robert Y. Hayne, and the Hon. Daniel Webster, delivered in the Senate of the United States, Jan. 21, and 26, 1830. With a Sketch of the Preceding Debate on the Resolution of Mr. Foot, Respecting the Sale, &c., of Public Lands. *Boston: Carter and Hendee.* MDCCCXXX. 8vo, pp. 136. B. Also: Speeches of Messrs. Hayne and Webster in the United States Senate, on the Resolution of Mr. Foot. January, 1830. *Washington.* 1833. P. + *New Haven: Printed by J. H. Benham.* 1849. 8vo, pp. 85. BA. + *Boston.* 1852. 8vo, pp. 84. + [n. p. n. d.] 8vo, pp. 40. B. These speeches elicited a

Review on the Article in the Southern Review, for 1830, on the Several Speeches made during the Debate on Mr. Foot's Resolution, by Mr. Hayne and Mr. Webster. [By Lucius Falkland.] *Baltimore.* 1830. 8vo. 31044

HAYNE (S.) An | Abstract | of all the | Statutes | Made Concerning | Aliens Trading | in | England | From the first year of K. Henry the VII. | Also, | Of all the Laws made for Securing | our Plantation Trade to our Selves. | With Observations thereon, proving that the | Jews (in their practical way of Trade at this time) | Break them all, to the great Damage of the King in | His Customs, the Merchants in their Trade, the | whole Kingdom, and His Majesties Plantations in | America in their Staple. | Together with the Hardships and Difficulties the Au- | thor hath already met with, in his Endeavouring to find out | and Detect the Ways and method they take to Effect it. | By Samuel Hayne, ... | [*London:*] *Printed by N. T. for the Author, and are to be Sold by Walter | Davis in Amen-Corner,* 1685. 4to, pp. (6), 38. 31045

HAYNER (——). Speech of Mr. Hayner on the Anti-Rent Question ... in the House of Assembly, January 17, 1846. [*Albany.*] 1846. 8vo. 31046

HAYNES (D. C.) The Baptist Denomination: its History, Doctrines, and Ordinances; its Polity, Persecutions, and Martyrs; Facts and Statistics of its Missionary Institutions, Schools of Learning, &c.; the Indebtedness of the World to Baptists, and their Duty to the World, by D. C. Haynes. With an Introduction by John Downing, D.D. *New York.* 1857. 12mo, pp. 356. C. 31047

HAYNES (C. E.) Speech of Charles E. Haynes on the Removal of the Indians West of the Mississippi. 8vo. 31048

HAYNES (E. M.) A History of the Tenth Regiment, Vermont Volunteers, with Biographical Sketches of the Officers who fell in Battle. ... By Chaplain E[dwin] M. Haynes. [n. p.] 1870. 8vo, pp. 249. B., BA. 31049

HAYNES (G.) Pictures from Prison Life. An Historical Sketch of the Massachusetts State Prison. With Narratives and Incidents, and Suggestions on Discipline. By Gideon Haynes. *Boston: Lee & Shepard.* 1869. 12mo, pp. 290. 2 Plates. C.

HAYNES. Speeches of the Hon. Gideon Haynes, Hon W. S. Brakenbridge, and Hugh W. Greene, on the Question as to Incorporating the Town of Belmont. ... *Boston: Printed by Alfred Mudge & Son.* 1857. Rl. 8vo, pp. 47. 31051

[HAYNES (Joseph).] ... XX Articles of Charge against the Rev[d] Mr. Bacheller ... Haverhill ... September 19, 1758. Also the ... Council's Result, with the Evidences ... . *Portsmouth: Printed by D. Fowle.* 1760. 8vo, pp. 87. B. 31052

HAYNES (J.) Poems. By Dr. J. Haynes. *Quebec: J. Hunter.* 1864. 12mo, pp. 152. 31053

HAYNES (L.) Mystery Developed, or Russell Colvin (supposed to be murdered), in full Life, and Stephen and Jesse Boorn (his convicted murderers), rescued from Ignominious Death by Wonderful Discoveries. Containing: I.—A Narrative of the whole Transaction, by Rev. Lemuel Haynes. II.—Rev. Mr. Haynes' Sermon. III.—A Succinct Account of the Indictment, Trial, and Conviction of Stephen and Jesse Boorn. Second Edition. *Hartford.* 1820. 8vo, pp. 48. 31054

HAYNES. The Prisoner Released. A Sermon ... at Manchester, Vermont, ... Jan. 9th, 1820, on the remarkable ... deliverance of Stephen and Jesse Boorn. By Lemuel Haynes. *Hartford.* 1848. 8vo, pp. 48. 31055

HAYNES. Universal Salvation: a very Ancient Doctrine, with Some Account of the Life and Character of its Author. A Sermon, ... at Rutland, ... 1805. Sixth Edition. *Boston.* 1807. 12mo. + Ninth Edition. *Boston: R. P. & C. Williams.* 1814. 12mo, pp. 12. BA. + Tenth Edition. *Boston.* 1821. B.

Also: Sermon at the Ordination of Reuben Parmelee. *Litchfield, Ct.* 1791. 8vo —Two Valedictory Discourses, at Rutland West Parish, May 24, 1818. *Bennington.* 1820. 8vo, pp. 27. N.

HAYNES (S.) A Sermon delivered before ... the Governor ... Council, and ... Representatives of Vermont ... Oct. 13, 1809, Being the Day of General Election. By Sylvanus Haynes. *Randolph.* 1809. 12mo. 31057

HAYNES (T. W.) Baptist Cyclopædia, or, Dictionary of Baptist Biography, Bibliography, Antiquities, History, Chronology, Theology, Polity, and Literature, By Thomas Wilson Haynes. Vol. I. *Charleston.* 1848. 8vo, pp. 294, 29. Portraits.

HAYS (G. P.) The Introduction of Religion into Politics right and needed. A Sermon ... Baptist Church, Thanksgiving ... November 24, 1864. By Rev. George P. Hays. *Baltimore: Sherwood & Co.* [1864.] 8vo, pp. 13. 31059

HAYS (I. N.) "Our Nation's Hope in the Present Crisis:" A Thanksgiving Sermon. By Rev. I. N. Hays. *Harrisburg.* 1857. 31060

HAYS (M.) Female Biography; or, Memoirs of Illustrious and Celebrated Women, of all Ages and Countries. By Mary Hays. *London.* 1803. 6 vols., 12mo. + First American Edition. *Philadelphia: Birch and Small.* 1807. 3 vols., 8vo, pp. vi, (2), 488; (4), 510; (4), 512. BA., P. 31061

HAYTER (T.) The Liberty of the Gospel explained. A Sermon preached before the Incorporated Society for the Promotion of the Gospel in Foreign Parts, 15th February, 1716. By Thomas Hayter, Bishop of Norwich. *London: Jos. Downing.* 1717. 4to, pp. 36. 31062

HAYTI. *See* Haiti, *also* Saint Domingo.

HAYWARD (C.) Address before the School Committee, School Masters, &c., of Mendon [Mass.], Nov. 19, 1827. By Caleb Hayward. *Worcester.* 1827. 8vo. W. 31063

HAYWARD (J.) Report on the Proposed Rail-Road between Boston and Ogdensburgh [N. Y.] By James Hayward. *Boston: Carter, Hendee and Babcock.* 1831. 8vo, pp. 46. Map. B., BA.

Also: Report of Surveys and Estimates for the Northern Railroad in New York. *Boston.* 1847. 8vo, pp. 27.—Report of a Survey for a Rail Road from the City of Boston to Lowell. [n. p.] 1830. 8vo, pp. 16. B., BA.

HAYWARD (J.) The Book of Religions; comprising the Views, Creeds, Sentiments, or Opinions, of all the Principal Religious Sects ... particularly ... in Europe and America; to which are added ... Statistics, together with Biographical Sketches. By John Hayward, ... *Boston: John Hayward.* 1842. 12mo, pp. 432. C. + [*Ibid.*] 1843. + *Concord: Boyd & Buswell.* 1843. 8vo, pp. 443. + *Boston: Albert Colby & Co.* 1859. 12mo, pp. 432. B. + *Boston.* 1861. 12mo, pp. 432. 31065

Reproduced as:

Hayward's History of all Religions in the United States and Europe, with Biographical Notices of Distinguished Divines and Theologians. Edited and Compiled by Samuel M. Smucker, A.M. *Philadelphia.* 1855. 12mo. 31066

HAYWARD. The Columbian Traveller and Statistical Register. Principally relating to the United States. By John Hayward. *Boston: J. Hayward.* 1833. 8vo, pp. 40. Maps and Plates. B., C. 31067

HAYWARD. A Gazetteer of Massachusetts, containing Descriptions of all the Counties, Towns and Districts in the Commonwealth; also, of its Principal Mountains, Rivers, Capes, Bays, Harbors, Islands, and Fashionable Resorts. To which are added, Statistical Accounts of its Agriculture, Commerce and Manufactures; with a great variety of other Useful Information. By John Hayward, ... *Boston: John Hayward.* 1846. 12mo, pp. 444. B. + [*Ibid.*] 1847. Plate. BA. + *Boston: John P. Jewett and Co.* 1849. 12mo, pp. 452. B. 31068

HAYWARD. The Gazetteer of the United States, comprising a Series of Gazetteers of the Several States and Territories.—Maine—By John Hayward. *Portland: S. H. Colesworthy.* 1843. 8vo, pp. 92. B. 31069

HAYWARD. A Gazetteer of the United States: ... With valuable statistical Tables, and a Map of the United States. By John Hayward. *Hartford: Case, Tiffany and Company.* 1853. 8vo, pp. 861. Portrait and Map. B., BA. 31070

HAYWARD. A Gazetteer of New Hampshire; containing a Description of all the Counties, Towns and Districts in the State; also of its Principal Mountains, Rivers, Waterfalls, ... With Statistics, ... By John Hayward. *Boston: John P. Jewett.* 1849. 12mo, pp. 264. Illustrated. B. 31071

HAYWARD. A Gazetteer of Vermont: containing Descriptions of all the Counties, Towns, and Districts in the State, and of its Principal Mountains, Rivers, Waterfalls, Harbors, Islands,

and curious places. To which are added, Statistical Accounts of its Agriculture, Commerce and Manufacture, with a great variety of other useful information. By John Hayward, ... *Boston: Tappan, Whittemore and Mason.* 1849. 12mo, pp. 216. Map. B., C., P. 31072

HAYWARD. The Massachusetts Directory; being the First Part of the New-England Directory, By John Hayward. *Boston: John Hayward.* 1835. 18mo, pp. 198. B., BA. 31073

HAYWARD. The New England Gazetteer; containing Descriptions of all the States, Counties and Towns in New England; also Descriptions of the Principal Mountains, Rivers, Lakes, Capes, Bays, Harbors, ... Alphabetically Arranged. By John Hayward ... *Boston: John Hayward.* 1839. 8vo, pp. (510). 3 Plates. C. + Second Edition. *Concord.* 1839. 12mo. B. + Third Edition. *Concord: Boyd & White.* 1839. 12mo. + Fourth Edition. [*Ibid.*] 12mo, pp. (521). Plate. BA. + Eighth Edition. [*Ibid.*] 1839. + Ninth Edition. [*Ibid.*] 1839. 12mo, pp. (514). C. + Tenth Edition. *Concord.* 1839. P. + Fourteenth Edition, Revised and Corrected, with an Appendix, containing the Census of 1840, and numerous other Additions. [*Ibid.*] 1841. 12mo, pp. 620. B. 31074

[HAYWARD.] Appendix to Hayward's New England Gazetteer; and Specimens of the Northern Register. [*Boston.* 1841.] 8vo, pp. 40. B. 31075

HAYWARD. The New-England and New-York Law-Register, for the year 1835: containing an Almanac, Descriptions of the Courts, and the Times of the Sessions, the Names of the Judges, Counsellors, &c., with other useful Information. By John Hayward, ... *Boston: John Hayward.* [1834.] 12mo, pp. 262, (2). B., BA. 31076

HAYWARD. The Religious Creeds and Statistics of every Christian Denomination in the United States and British Provinces. With some Account of the Religious Sentiments of the Jews, American Indians, Deists, Mahometans, &c. Alphabetically Arranged. By John Hayward. *Boston: John Hayward.* 1836. 12mo, pp. 156. B. 31077

See "N. A. Rev.," April, 1837, and "Book of Religions," *supra.*

HAYWARD. A View of the United States. By John Hayward. *New York.* 1832. 8vo. 31078

HAYWARD (J. H.) Poetical Pen-Pictures of the War. Selected from our Union Poets. By J. Henry Hayward. *New York: T. R. Dawley.* 1864. 12mo, pp. 408. + Third Edition. *New York: J. H. Hayward.* 1864. 12mo, pp. 408. 31079

HAYWARD (W. H.) Camp Songs for the Soldier, and Poems of Leisure Moments. By General William H. Hayward. *Baltimore.* 1864. 16mo. 31080

[HAYWARD (W. S.)] Fiery Cross. A Tale of the Great American War. *London: C. H. Clarke.* 1862. Fcp. 8vo, pp. 411. 31081

Also: Star of the South. New Edition. *London: Bryce.* 1862. Fcp. 8vo.

HAYWARDE (R.), *pseudon.* Prismatics. By Richard Haywarde. ... *New York: D. Appleton & Company.* MDCCCLIII. 12mo, pp. 235. 31082

Contains a poem on Bunker Hill.

HAYWOOD (E. G.) Speech delivered by Ed. Graham Haywood, Esq., of Wake County, ... December, 1858, in the House of Commons of North-Carolina, on his Eligibility to a Seat in that Body. *Raleigh: Holden & Wilson.* 1859. 8vo, pp. 54. 31083

Also: Trial of the Murderers of Archibald Beebe. Argument of Ed. Graham Haywood, Special Judge Advocate, in reply to the Arguments of the several Counsel for William J. Tolar, David Watkins and Thomas Powers, charged with the Murder of Archibald Beebe at Fayetteville, North Carolina. February 11th, 1867. Delivered September ... 1867, before the Military Commission, Raleigh, N. C. Published for Robert Avery, U. S. A., Judge Advocate. *Raleigh, N. C.* 1867. 8vo.

HAYWOOD (J.) The | Civil and Political | History | of the | State of Tennessee, | from its | Earliest Settlement | up to | the year 1796; | including the | Boundaries of the State. | By John Haywood. | *Printed for the Author* | *by Heiskell and Brown,* | *Knoxville, Tenn.* | 1823. 8vo, pp. (6), 504. Map. BA. 31084

This work, only less rare than the following, contains a large portion of material relating to the border warfare with the Indians, narrated in that work. The speculative and antiquarian portions and descriptions of mounds are omitted, but the story of Indian conflicts and massacres is narrated with greater detail and minuteness, filling much the larger portion of the work. The story of the formation of the State of Franklin, and the civil war which ensued, is a chapter of American history but little known, and scarcely exceeded in interest by any other. *See* Field's "Essay," No. 671.

HAYWOOD. The | Natural and Aboriginal | History | of | Tennessee, | up to the | First Settlements Therein | by the | White People | in the | year 1768. | By John Haywood | of the County of Davidson, in the State of Tennessee. | *Nashville:* | *Printed by George Wilson.* | 1823. 8vo, pp. viii, 390, liv. BA. 31085

A volume of much rarity. The author has brought together a large number of curious facts, relating to the origin and character of the natives of his State, prior to the

settlement by the whites. He does not favor the hypothesis of great antiquity in the Indian nations of America, but describes with great care the relics of the race which once inhabited this territory.

HAYWOOD. A Manual of the Laws of North Carolina. Arranged under distinct heads in Alphabetical Order, ... By John Haywood. *Raleigh.* 1819. 8vo, pp. 879. 31086

HAYWOOD *and* COBBS (Robert L.) Statute Laws of the State of Tennessee, of a Public and General Nature. *Knoxville.* 1831. 2 vols., 8vo. 31087

HAYWOOD (J. H.) A Discourse on the occasion of the Death of James H. Perkins; ... By the Rev. John H. Haywood. *Cincinnati.* 1850. 8vo. 31088

HAYWOOD (W. H.) Address of Hon. William H. Haywood, Jr., to the People of North Carolina. *Washington.* 1846. 8vo, pp. 29. 31089

Also: Speech ... on the Annexation of Texas. *Washington.* 1845. 8vo, pp. 13. —Speech ... on the Oregon Question. Delivered ... March 4 & 5, 1846. *Washington: Blair and Rives.* 1846. 8vo, pp. 22. BA.

HAYWOOD (W. S.) A Poem ... One Hundredth Anniversary of the Incorporation of Westminster, Mass. By William S. Haywood. *Boston: T. R. Marvin & Son.* 1860. 8vo, pp. 24. 31090

HAZARD (B.) Letters addressed to the Hon. John Quincy Adams, in Refutation of Charges made by that Gentleman against a Committee of the Legislature of Rhode-Island, and against the Legislature itself. By B. Hazard, Esq. ... *Providence: Marshall Brown & Co.* 1834. 8vo, pp. 46. B., S. 31091

Relates to masonry in Rhode Island.

[HAZARD.] Report of the Committee on the Subject of an Extension of Suffrage [to the General Assembly of Rhode Island, June, 1829. n. p. 1829.] 8vo, pp. 26. B. 31092

Signed B. Hazard, R. I. Schedule, James Lesser.

[HAZARD.] Report of the Committee appointed by the House of Representatives, of the State of Rhode Island, &c., to Inquire into the Expediency of Increasing the Banking Capital within said State. ... *Providence: Smith & Parmenter.* 1826. 8vo, pp. 40. 31093

A very able paper by Benjamin Hazard. Also: Argument in the Case Rhode Island against Massachusetts, Supreme Court of the United States, ... 1838. ... *Providence: Knowles, Vose & Co.* 1838. 8vo, pp. 60. *See* Providence R. I.

HAZARD (C. T.) To the People of Rhode Island: Ives *vs.* Hazard. By Charles T. Hazard. [*Providence.*] 1860. 8vo, pp. 4. 31094

Also: Majority Report of the Special Committee on the Petition of Charles T. Hazard. *Providence: Knowles, Anthony & Co.* 1860. 8vo, pp. 7.

HAZARD (E.) Historical Collections; Consisting of State Papers, and other Authentic Documents; Intended as Materials for an History of the United States of America. By Ebenezer Hazard, A.M. ... *Philadelphia: T. Dobson, for the Author.* M DCC-XCII-IV. 2 vols., 4to, pp. iv, 629, x; iv, 654. B., BA. 31095

This scarce and valuable collection embraces State Papers relating to Columbus, Cabot, Sir Humphrey Gilbert, and Sir Walter Raleigh. It includes various Patents and Charters of the several English colonies in America, with a variety of other documents relating to these colonies as well as to New France. Many of these papers are taken from Hakluyt's Voyages; Rymer's "Fœdera;" Rushworth's "Historical Collections;" the Public Records of the Colonies, and from rare works relating to America. Vol. II. is rarer than Vol. I. *See* "Mass. Hist. Collections," Second Series, Vol. IV., and Plymouth Records.

HAZARD (E.) Thoughts on Currency and Finance. By Erskine Hazard. Philadelphia, September 25th, 1863. [n. p. n. d.] 8vo, pp. 8. 31096

HAZARD (J.) The Conquest of Quebec. A Poem. By Joseph Hazard, of Lincoln College, Oxford. *Oxford: James Fletcher.* 1769. 4to, pp. 20. Plan of Quebec. 31097

See "M. Rev.," XL. 517.

HAZARD (J.) Poems on Various Subjects. By Joseph Hazard. *Brooklyn, N. Y.: The Author.* 1814. 18mo. 31098

HAZARD (R. G.) A Discourse delivered before the Rhode-Island Historical Society, ... January 18th, 1848; on the Character and Writings of Chief Justice Durfee. By Rowland G. Hazard. ... *Providence: Charles Burnett, Jr.* 1848. 8vo, pp. 45. 31099

HAZARD. Finance and Hours of Labour. By R. G. Hazard. *New York: Charles Scribner & Company.* 1868. 8vo, pp. 50. B. 31100

HAZARD. Our Resources. A Series of Articles on the Financial and Political Condition of the United States. By Rowland G. Hazard. *London: Trübner & Co.* 1864. 8vo, pp. 32. + Second Edition. *Providence: Sidney S. Rider & Brother.* 1864. 8vo, pp. 32. B. 31101

Some Dutch translations of extracts. This work appeared in *Amsterdam.* 1864. 8vo, pp. 4; also in the Dutch newspapers. Also: Acts relating to Public Schools in Rhode Island, 1839. *Providence.* 8vo.—Address before the Pawcatuck Tem-

perance Society at Westerly, July 4, 1843. ... *Providence: B. F. Moore.* 1863. 12mo, pp. 30.—Address before the Washington County Association for the Improvement of Public Schools, at Wickford, January 3d, 1845. ... *Providence: Benjamin F. Moore, Printer.* 1845. 8vo, pp. 42.—An Essay on the Philosophical Character of W. E. Chaning. *Boston: James Monroe & Co.* 1845. 8vo, pp. 40. B.—Lecture on the ... Decline of Political and National Morality. *Providence: H. Fuller.* 1841. 8vo, pp. 29.—Narragansett Speech. *October* 21, 1856. 8vo, pp. 15.—Remarks ... in the General Assembly, January, 1851, on the Act introduced by him to equalize the charges for carrying freight on the Stonington Rail Road. *Providence: Sayles & Miller.* 1851. 8vo, pp. 12.

HAZARD (S.) Annals of Pennsylvania, from the Discovery of the Delaware. 1609–1682. By Samuel Hazard. ... *Philadelphia: Hazard and Mitchell.* 1850. 8vo, pp. viii, 664. C., P. 31102

HAZARD. General Index to the Colonial Records, in 16 volumes, and to the Pennsylvania Archives, in 12 volumes, prepared and arranged by Samuel Hazard, under an Act of the General Assembly of Pennsylvania. *Philadelphia.* 1856. 8vo, pp. vi, 654. 31103

HAZARD. Minutes of the Provincial Council of Pennsylvania, from the Organization [on the 10th March, 1663,] to the Termination of the Proprietary Government; ... *Philadelphia: Printed by Joseph Severns & Co.* 1852. [Vol. I.–IX., March 10, 1683, to October 17, 1771; Vol. X. ... October 18, 1771, to September 27, 1775;] ... together with Minutes of the Council of Safety, from June 30, 1775 to 1776, Minutes of the Supreme Executive Council, from its Organization in 1777 to the Termination of the Revolution [*i. e.* to the 20th December, 1790]. [Vols. XI.–XVI.] *Philadelphia and Harrisburg.* 1852–53. 16 vols., 8vo. BA., C. 31104

Edited by Samuel Hazard, and usually known as the Colonial Records.

HAZARD. Pennsylvania Archives. Selected and Arranged from Original Documents in the Office of the Secretary of the Commonwealth, Conformably to Acts of the General Assembly, Feb. 15, 1851, & March 1, 1852. By Samuel Hazard. Commencing 1644. *Philadelphia: Printed by Joseph Severns & Co.* 1852–56. 12 vols., 8vo. B., BA. 31105

HAZARD. The Register of Pennsylvania; devoted to the Preservation of Facts and Documents, and every other kind of useful Information respecting the State of Pennsylvania. January, 1828, to January, 1836. Edited by Samuel Hazard. *Philadelphia.* 1828–36. 16 vols., imp. 8vo, pp. iv, 448; viii, 386; viii, 416; viii, 416; viii, 416; viii, 432; Vols. VII. to XVI. each pp. viii, 416. C. 31106

Issued in 390 numbers.

Hazard's United States Commercial and Statistical Register, Containing Documents, Facts, and other Useful Information, Illustrative of the History and Resources of the American Union, and of each State: Embracing Commerce—Manufactures—Agriculture—Internal Improvements—Banks—Currency— ... Education, &c. Edited by Samuel Hazard. *Philadelphia.* 1840–1842. 6 vols., rl. 8vo, pp. xix, 432; xv, 416; xvi, 432; xii, 416; xii, 416; xv, (1), 416. B., BA. 31107

Also: Report of Samuel Hazard, relative to the Pennsylvania Archives. *Harrisburg.* 1852. 8vo. P.

HAZARD (S. H.) Discourse delivered April 29, 1849, before the Iowa City California Emigrating Association. By Rev. S. H. Hazard. [n. p. n. d.] 8vo, pp. 7. 31108

HAZARD (T. R.) An Appeal to the People of Rhode Island, in behalf of the Constitution and Laws. By Thomas R. Hazard. *Providence.* 1857. 8vo, pp. 163. 31109

Relates to the case of Ives *vs.* Hazard.

[HAZARD.] A Constitutional Manual for the National American Party; in which is examined the Question of Negro Slavery, in connection with the Constitution of the United States. By a Northern Man with American Principles. *Providence: A. Crawford Greene & Brother, Printers.* 1856. 8vo, pp. 30. BA. 31110

[HAZARD.] Facts for the Laboring Man. By a Laboring Man. *Newport: James Atkinson.* 1840. 8vo, pp. 102. 31111

Contains many facts relative to the early history of manufactories in Rhode Island.

HAZARD. Report on the Poor and Insane in Rhode-Island; Made to the General Assembly at its January Session, 1851. By Thomas R. Hazard. ... *Providence: Joseph Knowles, State Printer.* 1851. 8vo, pp. 119. B. 31112

Also: Letter addressed to Robert H. Ives, in reply to his published statements in relation to the case in equity, Ives *vs.* Hazard. ... *Newport: George T. Hammond.* 1859. 8vo, pp. 48.—Memorial of Thomas R. Hazard asking for the Removal of the State Reporter, and the Impeachment of Chief Justice Ames, etc. *Providence: A. Crawford Greene.* [1861.] 8vo, pp. 16.

[HAZARD (Willis Pope).] The American Guide Book; being a Hand Book for Tourists and Travellers through every part of the United States ... Part I. Northern and Eastern States and Canada. *Philadelphia: G. L. Appleton.* 1846. 12mo. 31113

HAZART (C.) Kirchen-Geschichte, das ist: Catholisches Christenthum durch die gantze Welt auszgebreitet, Insonderheit

bey nächst verflossenen, und anjetzo fliessenden Jahrhundert ... *Wienn in Oesterreich, Leopoldam Voight,* 1678–1701. 3 vols., folio, pp. (8), 666, (16); (12), 606, (12); (12), 220, 159, 304, (6), 284, (24). 31114

Vol III. is in two parts, and the work is usually bound in two volumes. Vol II. relates to America. The plates are vivid representations of the sufferings and martyrdoms of the missionaries. The following is a Dutch translation:

HAZART. Kerckelycke Historie van de gheheele Wereldt ... Inde welcke verhaelt worden de gheleghentheden der landen, manieren, ceremonien, ende Religien der inwoonders, maer naemelijek de verbreydinghe des H. Gheloofs, Martelaren, ende andere Cloceke Roomsche Catholijcke daeden, inde vier ghewesten des wereldts, met over de 40 Copere platen verçiert. Beschreven Door den Eerw. P. Cornelius Hazart Priester der Societeyt Jesu. Het eerste deel. Vervattende de Rijcken ende landen van Joponien China Morgor Bisnagar, Peru, Mexico, Brasilien, Florida, Canada, Paraguarien, Maragnan. *T' Antwerpien: Michael Cnobbaert.* M.DC.LXVII. 4 vols., folio. + [*Ibid.*] M.DC.LXXXII. 4 vols., folio. 31115

Part of Vol I. and the whole of Vol II. relate to America.

HAZEL (Harry), *pseudon.* *See* [Jones (J.)]

HAZEL GREEN COLLEGIATE INSTITUTE, *Wis.* First Annual Catalogue, 1857. *Galena, Ill.* 1857. 8vo. Continued. 31116

HAZELIUS (E. L.) History of the American Lutheran Church, from its Commencement, in the Year of our Lord 1685, to the Year 1842. By Ernest L. Hazelius. *Zanesville, Ohio.* 1846. 12mo, pp. 300. C., S. 31117

HAZELTINE (*Lieut.-Col.*) The Border Spy; or the Beautiful Captive of the Rebel Camp. A Story of the War. By Lieut.-Col. Hazeltine. *New York: Sinclair Toucey.* 1864. 8vo, pp. 40. 31118

Also: The Freebooters: or, the Rivals of the Gulf. A Story of Land and Ocean ... *New York: American News Company.* 1865. 8vo, pp. 87.—The Prisoner of the Mill; or Captain Hayward's Body Guard. ... *New York: American News Company.* 1864. 8vo, pp. 46.

HAZELTINE (S. W.) The Traveller's Dream and other Poems. By Silas Wood Hazeltine. *Boston: The Author.* 1860. 12mo, pp. 150, (2). 31119

HAZELTON (H.) The Trail of Blood: a Tale of New York. By Harry Hazelton. *New York: American News Company.* 1866. 8vo, pp. 79. 31120

HAZEN (J. A.) Five Years Before the Mast; or, Life in the Forecastle, aboard of a Whaler, and a Man-of-War. By Jacob A. Hazen. Second Edition. *Philadelphia.* 1854. 12mo.

HAZEN (N. W.) An Oration delivered in Haverhill, Mass., on the Fifty-First Anniversary of American Independence, July 4, 1827. By Nathan W. Hazen. *Haverhill: Printed by A. W. Thayer* ... 1827. 8vo, pp. 28. M. 31122

Also: An Address before the Essex Agricultural Society, at Danvers, September 28, 1836 ... . *Salem: Gazette Office.* 1837. 8vo, pp. 23. B.

HAZLITT (W.) A Thanksgiving Discourse, preached at Hallowell, 15 December, 1785. By William Hazlitt, A.M. *Boston: Printed by Samuel Hall.* MCDDLXXXVI. [*sic.*] 8vo, pp. 19. BA.

[HAZLITT (William).] The Eloquence of the British Senate; ... being a Selection of the best Speeches of the most distinguished Parliamentary Speakers, ... with Notes, &c. *London: Thomas Ostell.* 1807–08. 2 vols., 8vo, pp. (2), 525; (2), 591. BA. + *Brooklyn.* 1810. 2 vols., 8vo, pp. iv, 525; viii, 591. C.

Vol II. includes many speeches on American affairs during the Revolution.

HAZLITT (W.), *and* ROCHE (H. P.) A Manual of Marine Warfare: embodying the Decisions of Lord Stowell and other English Judges, and of the American Courts, and the Opinions of the most eminent Jurists. *London: Stevens & Norton.* 1854. 12mo, pp. 457. 31125

HAZLITT (W. C.) British Columbia and Vancouver's Island. Comprising an Historical Sketch of the British Settlements on the N. W. Coast of America, and a Survey of the Physical Character, Capabilities, Climate, Topography, Natural History, Geology, and Ethnology of that Region. Compiled from Official and Authentic Sources. By William Carew Hazlitt. *London: Routledge & Co.* 1858. 12mo, pp. viii, 247. Map. C. 31126

Also: Great Gold Fields of Cariboo; with an Authentic Description brought down to the Latest Period, of British Columbia and Vancouver Island. ... *London: Routledge & Co.* 1862. Fcp. 8vo. Map.

HEACOCK (G. W.) Political Atheism. An Address ... before the Alumni ... of Western Reserve College, August 12, 1846, By Rev. Grosvenor W. Heacock. *Hudson: Observer Press.* 1846. 8vo, pp. 24. 31127

HEACOCK (J. W.) Speech of J. W. Heacock, April 6, 1863, in favor of a Vigorous Prosecution of the War; Sustaining the Administration in its Emancipation Policy ... [n. p. 1863.] 8vo.

The Heacock Family. Jonathan and Ann Heacock, who ... settled in Chester County, Pennsylvania, in 1711, and their Descendants. [n. p.] 1869. 8vo, pp. (4), 28. B. 31129

[HEAD (E. F.)] Poltroonius; a Tragic Farce. ... [Assault on Charles Sumner.] *Boston: A. Williams & Co.* 1856. 8vo, pp. 31. B., BA., H. 31130

HEAD (*Sir* Francis Bond). An Address to the House of Lords, against the Canada Re-Union Bill, and disclosing the improper means by which the consent of the Legislature of the Upper Province has been obtained ... By Sir F. B. Head, Bart. *London.* 1840. 8vo, pp. 52. 31131

HEAD. The Emigrant. By Sir Francis B. Head, Bart. ... *London: John Murray.* 1846. Post 8vo, pp. (6), 441. BA. + Fifth Edition. [*Ibid.*] 1847. + *New York: Harper & Brothers.* 1847. 12mo, pp. (4), 382, (1). B. + Sixth Edition. *London: John Murray.* 1852. Post 8vo, pp. (6), 233. H. + New Edition. [*Ibid.*] 1852. Post 8vo, pp. 233. B. + [*Ibid.*] 1853.

"Composed of political history [of the writer's administration in Canada], buoyed up by a few light sketches, solely written to make a dull subject fly."—*Preface.* *See* "Edinburgh Review," LXXXV. 358, for an adverse criticism.

HEAD. A Narrative. By Sir Francis B. Head. ... *London: John Murray.* MDCCCXXXIX. 8vo, pp. viii, Errata, 2 lines, 488, Appendix, 38. B. + Second Edition. [*Ibid.*] + Third Edition; with a Supplemental Chapter. [*Ibid.*] 8vo, pp. viii, 488, 38, 36.

The preface and supplemental chapter—*London: John Murray.* MDCCCXXXIX. 8vo, pp. 36—were issued separately. "A lively, pleasant, self-complacent piece of egotism. This narrative, although well worth perusal, is exactly opposite to the report of Lord Durham."—*Athenæum*, 1839, p. 169. It details the origin and suppression of the McKenzie rebellion, and is a vindication of the author's administration. *See* Dublin "University Magazine," XIII. 501; "Westminster Review," XXXII. 426; "Edinburgh Review," LXXX.; "Quarterly Review," LXIII. 457.

HEAD. Rough Notes taken during some Rapid Journeys across The Pampas, and among the Andes. By Captain F. B. Head. *London: John Murray.* MDCCCXXVI. 8vo, pp. xii, 309. H. + Second Edition. [*Ibid.*] + *Boston: Wells and Lilly.* 1827. 12mo, pp. 264. BA. + Fourth Edition. *London: John Murray.* 1846. 16mo, pp. ix, 166. B. 31134

This work obtained for its author the *soubriquet* of "Galloping Head," from the manner in which he scoured across the Pampas. It contains descriptions of the life of the savage Guachos, and the fearful atrocities of the Salteadores, both of the Creole or Mestizo race, and the Indians of the Pampas. *See* "Quarterly Review," XXXV. 114; "North American Review," XXIV. 295.

HEAD. Practical Arguments against Emigration. *London.* 1828. 8vo. 31135

HEAD. Reports Relating to the Failure of the Rio Plata Mining Association. By Captain F. B. Head. *London.* 1827. 8vo. P. 31136

For a reply to this *see* Bunster (G.), Vol. III., No. 9191. The following relate to Sir F. B. Head:

Addresses to Sir Francis B. Head, Bart, from the Legislatures of the British North American Colonies, &c., on his Resignation of the Government of Upper Canada. *Toronto.* 1838. 8vo, pp. 38. 31137

Canada. Sir F. B. Head. Return to an Address of the Hon. the House of Commons, dated 21 April, 1837; for—Copy of a Despatch from Sir F. B. Head, in Answer to Charges preferred against him by Dr. C. Duncombe, in a Petition presented to the House of Commons, 19th August, 1836; together with a Copy of Lord Glenelg's Reply thereto. Ordered by the House of Commons to be printed, 3 May, 1837. *London.* 1837. Folio, pp. 180. 31138

Copies or Extracts of Despatches from Sir F. B. Head, Bart, K.C.H., on the Subject of Canada: with Copies or Extracts of the Answers from the Secretary of State. Ordered, &c., 22 March, 1839. *London.* 1839. Folio, pp. 524. 31139

Governor Head's Message to the Assembly on the Subject of the Steamer "Caroline." *Toronto.* 1838. Folio. 31140

Report and Despatches (British North America). *London.* 1839. Small folio, pp. 430. 31141

The Speeches, Messages, and Replies of ... Sir Francis Bond Head ... Lieutenant-Governor of Upper Canada ... Together with Introductory Remarks, and a Brief Biographical Sketch. ... *Toronto, U. C.: Henry Rowsell.* 1836. 8vo, pp. 72. H. 31142

Also: Descriptive Essays Contributed to the Quarterly Review. ... *London: John Murray.* 1857. 2 vols., 8vo, pp. (6), 367; (2), 368. B., BA. Includes a chapter on Cornish miners in America.

HEAD (G.) Forest Scenes and Incidents, in the Wilds of North America; being a Diary of a Winter's Route from Halifax to the Canadas, and during Four Months' Residence in the Woods on the Borders of Lakes Huron and Simcoe. By George Head, Esq. *London: John Murray.* MDCCCXXIX. Post 8vo, pp. v, (1), 362. BA., H. + Second Edition. [*Ibid.*] 1838. 31143

See "Quarterly Review," XLII. 80.

[HEAD.] Remarks on the North Eastern Boundary Question between Great Britain and the United States of America. *London.* 1838. 8vo. 31144

Signed at the end by George Head.

HEAD (J.), *Jr.* Enthusiasm. An Occasional Poem, written by Appointment of the Society of Φ B K, and delivered at Cambridge on the Anniversary of their Institution, August 31, 1809, By Joseph Head, Jun. ... *Boston: T. B. Wait & Co.* 1809. 8vo, pp. 10. BA., H. 31145

HEADLAM (J.) Discovery of America; a Poem honored by the Prize given by the venerable Charles Thorp, D.D., Warden of Durham University. By John Headlam. *Richmond.* 1835. 8vo. C. 31146

HEADLEY (Joel Tyler). The Adirondack; or Life in the Woods. By J. T. Headley. *New York: Baker & Scribner.* 1849. 12mo, pp. 288. Plates. C., P. + [*Ibid.*] 1851. + [*Ibid.*] 1853. 12mo, pp. (10), ii, 5–288. + New and Enlarged Edition. *New York: Charles Scribner.* 1869. 12mo, pp. (16), 451. 8 Plates. C. 31147

HEADLEY. The Chaplains and Clergy of the Revolution. By J. T. Headley. ... *New York: Charles Scribner.* 1864. 12mo, pp. 402. B., S. 31148

HEADLEY. Farragut and our Naval Commanders. By Hon. J. T. Headley. ... *New York: E. B. Treat & Co.* 1867. 8vo, pp. 609. Portraits, Plates. B., BA. 31149

HEADLEY. Grant and Sherman: their Campaigns and Generals. By Hon. J. T. Headley ... . Comprising an Authentic Account of Battles and Sieges, Adventures and Incidents, including Biographies of the Prominent Generals who brought to a Triumphant Close the Great Rebellion of 1861–1865. *New York: E. B. Treat & Co.* 1865. 8vo, pp. 608. Portraits and Maps. B. 31150

HEADLEY. The Great Rebellion: a History of the Civil War in the United States. By J. T. Headley. ... *Hartford: Hurlbut, Williams & Co.* 1866. 2 vols., 8vo, pp. 502; 702. 27 Plates. B., BA. 31151

HEADLEY. Die Grosse Rebellion. Eine Geschichte des Bürgerkrieges in den Vereinigten Staaten. Von J. T. Headley, ... *Hartford, Connecticut.* 1863. 8vo, pp. 520. Portraits, Plates.

HEADLEY. Letters from the Backwoods and the Adirondac. By the Rev. J. T. Headley. *New York: John S. Taylor.* 1850. 12mo, pp. 105. Portrait. H. 31153

A spurious edition, not recognized by Headley.

HEADLEY. The Life of George Washington. By J. T. Headley. ... *New York: Charles Scribner.* 1856. 8vo, pp. 477. Plates. B., BA. 31154

HEADLEY. The Life of Ulysses S. Grant, General in Chief, U. S. A. By J. T. Headley. *New York: E. B. Treat & Co.* 1864. 12mo, pp. 458. 4 Plates. + [*Ibid.*] 1868. 8vo, pp. 458.

HEADLEY. The Life of Winfield Scott. By J. T. Headley. ... *New York: Charles Scribner.* 1861. 8vo, pp. viii, 13–202. Portrait. BA. 31156

HEADLEY. The Lives of Winfield Scott and Andrew Jackson. By J. T. Headley. ... *New York: Charles Scribner.* 1852. 12mo, pp. 341. Portraits. H. 31157

HEADLEY. Miscellaneous Works of J. T. Headley. With a Biographical Sketch and Portrait of the Author. *New York: J. S. Taylor.* 1849. 2 vols., 12mo, pp. 322; 319. C. 31158

HEADLEY. Miscellanies. By J. T. Headley. Authorized Edition. *New York: Baker and Scribner.* 1850. 12mo, pp. viii, 298. Portrait. C. 31159

The author, in his preface, repudiates the publication by J. S. Taylor, described *supra.*

HEADLEY. The Second War with England. By J. T. Headley. *New York: Baker and Scribner.* 1853. 2 vols., 12mo.

HEADLEY. Washington and his Generals. By J. T. Headley. ... *New York: Baker and Scribner.* 1847. 2 vols., 12mo, pp. 348; 372. Plates. B., BA., H. + *New York: Charles Scribner.* 1853. 2 vols., 12mo, pp. 348; 372. + [*Ibid.*] 1856. C. 31161

Also: The One Progressive Principle. ... Delivered before ... University of Vermont, August, 1846. ... *New York: John S. Taylor.* MDCCCXLVI. 8vo, pp. 32. BA. —An Oration delivered before the Literary Societies of the New-York Free Academy, July 25, 1853. ... *New York.* 1853. 8vo, pp. 16.—Report on Criminal Statistics of the State of New York, 1857. 8vo.

HEADLEY (Phineas Camp). The Hero Boy; or, The Life and Deeds of Lieut.-General Grant. By Rev. P. C. Headley. *New York: Wm. H. Appleton.* 1869. 12mo, pp. ix, 340. C.

HEADLEY. Life and Military Career of Major-General Philip Henry Sheridan. By Rev. P. C. Headley. ... *New York: William H. Appleton.* 1865. 16mo, pp. 358. Plates. B., BA., S.

HEADLEY. The Life and Campaigns of Lieut.-Gen. U. S. Grant ... including an ... Account of Sherman's Great March, ... and the Final Official Reports of Sheridan, Meade, Sherman, and Grant. ... *New York: Derby and Miller Publishing Company.* 1866. 8vo, pp. 720. Portraits, Plates. B., C. 31164

HEADLEY. Life and Military Career of Major-General William Tecumseh Sherman. By Rev. P. C. Headley ... *New York: Wm. H. Appleton.* 1865. 12mo, pp. 368. C., S. 31165

HEADLEY. Life and Naval Career of Vice-Admiral David Glascoe Farragut. By Rev. P. C. Headley. ... *New York: Wm. H. Appleton.* 1865. 16mo, pp. 342. Plates. B., BA. 31166

HEADLEY. The Life of General Lafayette. ... By P. C. Headley. *Auburn: Derby and Miller.* 1851. 12mo, pp. vi, 377. B. + *Auburn: Miller, Orton & Mulligan.* 1854. + New Edition. [*Ibid.*] 1855. 12mo, pp. 377. + [*Ibid.*] 1856. P.

HEADLEY. Massachusetts in the Rebellion. A Record of the Historical Position of the Commonwealth, and the Services of the leading Statesmen, the Military, the Colleges, and the People, in the Civil War of 1861–65. By P. C. Headley ... . *Boston: Walker, Fuller & Co.* 1866. 8vo, pp. xii, 688. 8 Plates.

HEADLEY. The Patriot Boy; or, The Life and Career of Major-General Ormsby M. Mitchel. By Rev. P. C. Headley. ... *New York: Wm. H. Appleton.* 1865. 16mo, pp. 278. 31169

Also: The Grand Army. P. C. Headley is brother to J. T. Headley, and like him is a prolific book-maker, but of a lower grade.

Heads of Inquiry. *See* Vol. IV., No. 15747.

[HEADY (Morrison).] The Farmer Boy [Washington], and how he became Commander-in-Chief. By Uncle Juvinell. Edited by William M. Thayer ... . *Boston: Walker, Wise & Co.* 1864. 12mo, pp. 321. 3 Plates. B., C. 31170

HEALD (J. G.), *and* WRIGHT (R.) The Choctaws and their Debts, due Joseph G. Heald and Reuben Wright. [n. p. n. d.] 8vo, pp. 20. H. 31171

HEALY (——). A Description of Mr. Healy's Picture of the Great Constitutional Debate in the Senate of the United States, January 26, 1830; with Biographical Sketches of Mr. Webster and General Hayne. *Cambridge: Metcalf and Company.* 1851. 8vo, pp. 35. H. 31172

HEALY (J.) An Appeal to the Public, by Joseph Healy, in Vindication of his own Character ... through the Slanderous Abuse of Ebenezer Paine. Also, an Exposition ... of the Prominent Features in the Character of Ebenezer Paine. *Boston.* [n. d.] 8vo, pp. 44. 31173

HEALY (W.) A Brief Account of the Life & Adventures of William Healy. *Boston.* 1832. 8vo, pp. (1), 17. H. 31174

HEAP (G. H.) Central Route to the Pacific, from the Valley of the Mississippi to California: Journal of the Expedition of E. F. Beale, Superintendent of Indian Affairs in California, and Gwinn Harris Heap, from Missouri to California, in 1853. By Gwinn Harris Heap. *Philadelphia: Lippincott, Grambo & Co.* 1854. 8vo, pp. 136. 13 Plates. B., BA., H., P. 31175

No. 1. Hear Both Sides, or an Address to all Impartial Men of all Parties. *New York: G. Hardcastle.* [1809.] 8vo, pp. 38.

Contains Hillhouse's Speech on the Embargo.

Hear Both Sides. Documents and Papers relating to the Late Camden and Amboy Railroad Accident, at Burlington, N. J. ... *Philadelphia: Joseph M. Wilson.* 1855. 8vo, pp. 30. B., BA.

HEARD (I. V. D.) History of the Sioux War and Massacres of 1862 and 1863. By Isaac V. D. Heard. *New York: Harper and Brothers.* 1863. 12mo, pp. 354. Portraits. BA. 31178

The old story, of the red man made desperate by a sense of unbearable wrongs, avenging them upon the innocent.

[HEARD (Jared M.)] Origin of the Free Public Library System of Massachusetts. [*Clinton.* 1860.] 8vo, pp. 15. B., H.

HEARD (J. T.) A Historical Account of Columbia Lodge of Free and Accepted Masons of Boston, Mass. By John T. Heard, ... *Boston: Printed by Alfred Mudge & Son.* 1856. 12mo, pp. xi, (1), 9–592. B., H. C. 31180

Also: The Annual Address and Accompanying Documents ... before the Grand Lodge of Massachusetts, December 28, 1857. ... *Boston: Hugh H. Tuttle, Printer.* 1858. 8vo, pp. 63. (1). H.—An Address ... before the Grand Lodge ... on the ... Dedication of Freemasons' Hall, in Boston, Dec. 27, 1859. ... *Boston: Wright & Potter.* 1860. 8vo, pp. 127. H.

HEARNE (S.) A Journey from Prince of Wales's Fort in Hudson's Bay, to The Northern Ocean. Undertaken by Order of the Hudson's Bay Company, for the Discovery of Copper Mines, A North-West Passage, &c., In the Years 1769, 1770, 1771, & 1772. By Samuel Hearne. *London: Printed for A. Strahan and T. Cadell.* 1795. 4to, pp. xliv, 458. 4 Maps and 8 Plates. B., BA., C., H., P. 31181

Of this first and best edition there are copies on large paper. It was the first of a long series of Arctic Voyages and Travels which reflect so much honor on the British Press. Its publication is due to the celebrated navigator La Perouse who captured Fort Albany, Hudson's Bay, and found the MS. of Hearne. The fort was afterwards surrendered to the British, but La Perouse stipulated for the publication of this work by the Hudson's Bay Company, which stipulation was honorably fulfilled in this beautiful volume. *See* Bartlett's Catalogue of J. C. Brown's Library; "M. Rev.," XX. 246, and Rich's "Bibliotheca Americana," I. 390. "The author will always be remembered as the first white man that ever gazed on the dreary expanse of the Arctic or Frozen Ocean from the northern shores of the Continent of America."

HEARNE. [Title as above.] *Dublin: Printed for P. Byrne and J. Rice.* 1796. 8vo, pp. 459. Map and 8 Plates. C. + *Philadelphia.* 1802. 8vo. 31182

HEARNE. Voyage du Fort du Prince de Galles dans la Baie de Hudson, à l'Océan Nord, Entrepris par ordre de la Compagnie de la Baie de Hudson, dans les années 1769, 1770, 1771, et 1772, et exécuté par terre pour la découverte d'un Passage au Nord Ouest. Par Samuel Hearne. Traduit de l'Anglais [par Lallement. *Paris:*] *Imprimerie de Patris, An VII* [1799]. 2 vols., 8vo, pp. lviii, 373; 332, xxix, (2). 5 Maps, 4 Plates. 31183

Brunet quotes an edition in 4to, and the Sobolewski catalogue describes an edition, *Paris*, 1797, 2 vols., which is probably an error as to the date. The preface to this edition confirms the legend as to the discovery of the journal referred to in our No. 31181.

HEARNE. Landreis van 't Prins van Wallis Fort aan Hudsons Baai, naar den Noorde-Oceaan, Ondernomen op Bevel van de Maatschappij der Hudsons Baai, ter ontdekkinge van Koper-Mijnen, een Noord-Westen Doortogt, enz. in de Jaren 1769, 1770, 1771 en 1772. Door Samuel Hearne. Uit het Engelsche vertaald, met Aanmerkingen van Johann Reinhold Forster. Met Plaaten en Kaarten. *In den Haage, bij J. C. Leenwestijn.* 1798. 2 vols., 8vo, pp. 247; (2), 289, (1). 4 Plates and Map. J.C.B.

HEARNE. Reise von dem Prinz vom Wallis Fort an der Hudsons Bay bis zu dem Eismeere, in den Jahren 1769 bis 1772. Aus dem Englischen übersetzt. Mit Anmerkungen von Johann Reinhold Forster. *Berlin: In der Vossischen Buchhandlung.* 1797. 8vo, pp. 284. 3 Plates. 31185

Vierter Theil of the "Magazin von merkwürdigen neuen Reisebeschreibungen."

HEARNE. Reise vom Fort Prinz Wallis in der Hudsonsbai nach dem nördlichen Weltmeer. Aus dem Englischen von M. Chr. Sprengel. *Halle: Renger.* 1797. 8vo. 31186

HEATH (H. H.) Address of General H. H. Heath, at Santa Fe, New Mexico, ... the 12th of November, '68, on the Occasion of the Republican Jubilee ... in Honor of Grant's Election to the Presidency. *Santa Fe, N. M.: Manderfield & Tucker, Printers.* 1869. 8vo, pp. 10. H. 31187

Also: Letter from Gen'l H. H. Heath. [*Washington.* 1870.] 8vo, pp. 8. H.

HEATH (J. P.) Reply of James P. Heath ... to a Pamphlet by H. May. [*Baltimore.* 1839.] 8vo. 31188

Relates to an intended duel between J. A. Young and J. H. Sotheron.

HEATH (J.) Serious Charges against Captain Oliver H. Perry, of the United States Navy. By John Heath, Late Captain of the Marine Corps. [*Washington, June* 15, 1817.] 12mo, pp. 24. BA. 31189

[HEATH (Labaw).] On Paper Money: its Influence on National Prosperity ... *Philadelphia.* 1825. 8vo, pp. 15. BA.

HEATH (U. S.) Oration ... before the Washington Society of Maryland, on the Twenty-Second February, 1812. By Upton S. Heath, Esq. *Baltimore: Printed by Magauran and Kennedy.* 1812. 8vo, pp. 23. BA., M. 31191

HEATH (William). Memoirs of Major-General Heath. Containing Anecdotes, Details of Skirmishes, Battles, and other Military Events, during the American War. Written by Himself. ... *Printed at Boston, By I. Thomas and E. T. Andrews, ... Aug.* 1798. 8vo, pp. 388. B., BA., H., P. 31192

A work of equal interest and authority; now scarce. An uncut copy sold for $95 at J. A. Rice's sale, ordinary copies are worth about $18.

[HEATHCOTE (George).] A Letter to the ... Lord Mayor; the Worshipful Aldermen, and Common-Council; the Merchants, Citizens and Inhabitants of the City of London. From an Old Servant. *London: W. Owen.* MDCCLXII. 8vo, pp. (2), 90. S. + The Second Edition. *London: W. Nicoll.* MDCCLXII. 8vo, pp. 90. BA. + The Third Edition. [*Ibid.*] 31193

Relates to the productions of several of the British Colonies and Plantations in America, including Newfoundland, Virginia, Maryland, the Carolinas, and the West India Islands, and the trade of Great Britain with these Colonies. It elicited a "Reply to Mr. Heathcote's Letter ... from an Honest Man, in which the Arguments are proved to be Delusive, and the Facts Untrue." *London.* [1763.] 8vo.

HEATHER (W.) New North-American Pilot. By William Heather. *London.* 1801. 8vo. S. + [*Ibid.*] 1805. 8vo. W.

HEATHERINGTON (A.) ... A Practical Guide for Tourists, Miners, and Investors, and all Persons interested in the Development of the Gold Fields of Nova Scotia. By A. Heatherington, ... *Montreal: Printed by John Lovell.* 1868. 12mo, pp. 177, (2). Plan. B. 31195

HEAVISIDE (J. T. C.) American Antiquities, or the New World the Old, and the Old World the New. By J. T. C. Heaviside. *London: Trübner & Co.* 1868. 8vo, pp. 46. C.

HEBBARD (W. W.) The Night of Freedom: An Appeal, in Verse, against the Great Crime of our Country, Human Bondage! By William Wallace Hebbard, ... *Boston: Sam'l Chism.* 1857. 8vo, pp. 42. B., H. 31197

Also: The Patriot's Hope, Toil and the Toilers, etc.

[HEBERDEN (William).] An Account of the Success of Inoculation for the Small-Pox in England and America. Together with Plain Instructions, By which any Person may be enabled to perform the Operation, and conduct the Patient through the Distemper. *London: Printed by W. Strahan.* M,DCC,LIX. 4to, pp. 8, 12. P. 31198

The preface is a letter by B. Franklin of Philadelphia, giving the substance of statistics on the subject.

HEBERT (W.) Visit to the Colony of Harmony, in Indiana. By William Hebert. *London.* 1825. 8vo. C. 31199

HEBERTON. Full and Complete Account of the Heberton Tragedy; to which is added Beauchamp, or the Kentucky Tragedy. *New York.* [n. d.] 18mo, pp. 68. 31200

HECHAVARRIA (Santiago Jos. de). Carta á todos los Medicos, y Cirujanos de Santiago de Cuba, de Jamayca, y Provincias de la Florida. [*Santiago de Cuba.* 1771.] 4to, pp. 13. 31201

Also: Carta Pastoral á los Curas, Beneficiados ... de Santiago de Cuba, etc. [*Santiago.* 1771.] 4to, pp. 13.

HECKE (J. Valentin). Reise durch die Vereinigten Staaten von Nord-Amerika in den Jahren 1818 und 1819. Nebst einer kurzen Uebersicht der neuesten Ereignisse auf dem Kriegsplatze in Süd-Amerika und West-Indien. *Berlin.* 1820-21. 2 vols., 8vo. Plate. C. 31202

HECKER (J.) Record of Visits to the Primary Schools of the City of New York ... . By John Hecker, School Inspector. *New York.* 1868. 8vo, pp. 28. S. 31203

HECKEWELDER (J.) Names given by the ... Delaware Indians to Rivers, Streams, Places, &c., in the now States of Pennsylvania, New Jersey, Maryland and Virginia; and also Names of Chieftains and Distinguished Men of that Nation: ... By the Late Rev. John Heckewelder ... . *Philadelphia: Printed by James Kay, Jun. and Co.* 1833. 4to. pp. 48. BA. 31204

HECKEWELDER. A Narrative of the Mission of the United Brethren among the Delaware and Mohegan Indians, from its Commencement, in the Year 1740, to the close of the Year 1808. Comprising all the Remarkable Incidents which took Place at their Missionary Stations during that Period. Interspersed with Anecdotes, Historical Facts, Speeches of Indians, and other Interesting Matter. By John Heckewelder, Who was many Years in the Service of that Mission. *Philadelphia: M'Carty & Davis.* 1820. 8vo, pp. xii, 17-429, Errata, 1 p. Portrait of Zeisberger.

A full and undoubtedly faithful record of all the details of the Mission, its wonderful success and its appalling destruction. It is at once an interesting story abounding in veritable incidents, and a valuable history, fortified by impregnable facts. *See* Field's "Essay," No. 678.

HECKEWELDER. Histoire Moeurs et Coutumes des Nations Indiennes qui habitaient autrefois la Pennsylvanie et les états voisins: par Jean Heckewelder, Missionnaire Morave, Traduit de l'Anglais par le Chevalier Du Ponceau. *Paris: J. De Bure.* 1822. 8vo, pp. (iv), 571. C., S. 31206

This is a translation of so much of the Transactions of the Historical and Literary Committee of the American Philosophical Society, Vol. I., as was written by Heckewelder, with additions by the translator. *See* Vol. I., No. 1183.

HECKEWELDER. Reise von Bethlehem in Pensilvanien bis zum Wabashflusz im nordwestlichen Gebiet der Vereinigten Staaten von Nordamerika. Mit Anmerkungen herausgegeben von M. C. Sprengel. *Halle.* 1797. 12mo, pp. 94. 31207

HECKEWELDER. Nachricht von der Geschichte, den Sitten und Gebräuchen der Indianischen Völkerschaften, welche ehemals Pennsylvanien und die benachbarten Staaten bewohnten. ... Aus dem Englischen übersetzt und mit den Angaben anderer Schriftsteller über eben dieselben Gegenstände vermehrt von F. Hesse. Nebst einem Zusatze von G. E. Schulze. *Göttingen: Vandenhoek & Ruprecht.* 1821. 8vo, pp. xlvi, (2), 582, (2). C.

HECKINGIO (G.) I. N. D. de Praestantia Coloniae Georgico-Anglicanae prae Coloniis aliis. Deo benigne opem ferente illvstri splendidissimoqve scholarcharvma. C. Collegio gratiose approbante a.d xviii. Septembris A. R. S. MDCCXXXXVII. horis antemeridianis in acroaterio bibliothecae pvblico, praeside M. Gottfrido Heckingio ... disseret postea vero gymnasio patriaeque carmine vernacvlo valedicet a.et r. Ioannes Avgvstvs Vrlspergervs Avgvstanvs, *Augustae Vindel.* [1747]. 4to, pp. (8), 52. J.C.B. 31209

Relates to the Saltsburger colony in Georgia.

HEDDING (E.) ... The Substance of a Sermon ... Bath, (Maine,) July 4, 1822, before the New-England Conference of Ministers of the Methodist Episcopal Church. By Elijah Hedding. ... *Boston: Printed by Lincoln & Edmands.* [1822.] 8vo, pp. 32. BA. 31210

The author was a Methodist Bishop, and has published many sermons and doctrinal pieces.

HEDDING LITERARY INSTITUTE. Catalogue, 1854. Ashland, Greene County, N. Y. *Albany.* 1855. 8vo. S. 31211

Hedendaagsche Historie, of tegenwoordige staat van Amerika. Behelzende de Historie der Ontdekkinge van dit Wereldsdeel en der Verovering van een gedeelte van't zelve door de Spanjaarden; de algemeene Beschryving van de Landsen Lugtsgesteldheid, de Ingezetenen en het gene tot de Natuurlyke Historie behoort; de byzondere Beschryving van een voornam gedeelte dar tegenwoordige Bezittingen van de Kroon van Spanje in Amerika: etc. *Amsterdam: Isaac Tirion.* 1766-69. 3 vols., 8vo, pp. 676, (22); 685, (18); 620, (16). Many Maps and Plates. 31212

A history of the present States of America, embracing chiefly notices of those settled by Spain, in both North and South America. The latter half of the third volume relates to Louisiana, Canada and the countries near Hudson's Bay. The numerous maps and plates are well executed. The entire series, relating to all parts of the world, forms 45 vols., 8vo.

HEDGE (F. H.) Conservatism and Reform. An Oration ... before the Peucinian Society, Bowdoin College, September 5, 1843. By Frederic Hedge. ... *Boston: Charles C. Little and James Brown.* MDCCCXLIII. 8vo, pp. 39. B., BA., H. 31213

HEDGE. A Discourse on the Death of William Henry Harrison; ... delivered ... on the Day of the National Fast, May 14, 1841. By Rev. Frederic H. Hedge. ... *Bangor: Printed by Samuel S. Smith.* 1841. 8vo, pp. 24. B., BA. 31214

HEDGE. Discourse on Edward Everett, delivered in ... Brookline, on the Twenty-Second January, 1865. By Frederic Henry Hedge. *Boston: Geo. C. Rand & Avery [Printers].* 1865. 8vo, pp. 23. B., H. 31215

HEDGE. The National Weakness: a Discourse ... in ... Brookline, on Fast Day, Sept. 26, 1861. By Rev. F. H. Hedge, D.D. *Boston: Walker, Wise, and Company.* 1861. 8vo, pp. 19.

HEDGE. A Sermon, preached to the Independent Congregational Society, March 3d, 1850, By Frederic H. Hedge, on closing his Pastoral Connexion with that Society. ... *Bangor: Samuel S. Smith, Printer.* 1850. 8vo, pp. 16. B., M. 31217

HEDGE. Seventeen Hundred Fifty-Eight and Eighteen Hundred Fifty-Eight. A New Year's Discourse, Preached at Brookline, ... 1858. By Frederic H. Hedge, D.D, ... *Boston: Phillips, Sampson and Company.* 1858. 8vo, pp. 20. B., H. 31218

Also: Artillery-Election Sermon, 1834. ... *Boston.* 1834. 8vo, pp. 30. B., M.— ... A Sermon ... at the Dedication of the Church presented to the Town of Stetson by the Hon. Amasa Stetson, of Dorchester, Mass., Feb. 22, 1844. ... *Bangor.* 1844. 8vo, pp. 16. M.—Conscience and the State. A Discourse preached in Providence, April 27, 1851. ... *Providence.* 1851. 8vo, pp. 15. B., H., M.—An Introductory Lecture delivered at the Opening of the Bangor Lyceum, Nov: 15th, 1836. ... *Bangor.* 1836. 8vo, pp. 29. BA., H., M.—Memoir of Nathaniel Langdon Frothingham, D.D. ... *Boston: Press of John Wilson and Son.* 1870. 8vo, pp. 20. Portrait. B.— ... A Sermon preached at Ordination of Rev. Joshua Young, Boston, Feb. 1, 1849. ... *Boston.* 1849. 8vo, pp. 32. B., BA., M.—The National Entail. A Sermon preached to the First Congregational Church in Brookline, 3d of July, 1864. ... *Boston: Wright & Potter, Printers.* 1864. 8vo, pp. 19.—An Oration ... Bangor, on the Fourth of July, 1838. ... *Bangor.* 1838. 8vo, pp. 38.—A Sermon on the ... Late William Ellery Channing ... November 17th, 1842. ... *Bangor: Samuel S. Smith, Printer.* 1842. 8vo, pp. 19. BA.— ... A Sermon ... in Brookline ... succeeding the Death of Mr. Benjamin Goddard, November 3, 1861. ... *Boston: Printed by H. W. Dutton & Son.* 1861. 8vo, pp. 22. B., BA.—The Sick Woman. A Sermon for the Time. ... *Boston: Prentiss & Deland, Printers.* 1863. 8vo, pp. 16.

HEDGE (L.) The Duty and Manner of Singing in Christian Churches considered and illustrated; in a Sermon preached at a Singing Lecture in Warwick, January 29th, 1772. By Lemuel Hedge ... *Boston: R. Draper.* 1772. 8vo. 31219

HEDGE (L.) Eulogy on the Rev. Joseph McKean, D.D. ... delivered before the University, Cambridge, April 22, 1818. By Levi Hedge. ... *Cambridge: Hilliard & Metcalf.* 1818. 8vo, pp. 20. H. 31220

HEDGES (H. P.) An Address, delivered on the 20th of December, 1849, on the Occasion of the Celebration of the Two Hundredth Anniversary of the Settlement of the Town of East-

Hampton, together with an Appendix, containing a General History of the Town from its Settlement to the Year 1800: By Henry P. Hedges. *Corrector Office, Sag-Harbor, L. I.* 1850. 8vo, pp. 100. 31221

Also: A History of the Excise Law of the State of New-York. ... An Address ... January 25, 1853. *New-York.* 1853. 8vo, pp. 15. BA., S.

HEDGES (I. A.) Sorgo; or, The Northern Sugar Plant. By Isaac A. Hedges, the Pioneer Investigator in the Northern Cane Enterprise. *Cincinnati: Applegate & Co.* 1863. 12mo, pp. 204.

HEDGES (P.) Stricture on the "Elementa Medicinæ" of Doctor Brown. By Phineas Hedge. *Goshen: David M. Westcott.* MDCCXCV. 18mo, pp. (6), 130, (1). 31223

A specimen of early printing in an interior town in the State of New York.

[HEDRICK (B. S.)] Are North Carolinians Freemen? ... [*Chapel Hill.* 1856.] 8vo, pp. 8. B., H. 31224

[HEECKEREN (*Baron van*).] Aanteekeningen betrekkelijk de kolonie Suriname. *Te Arnhem.* 1826. 8vo. 2 Maps. 31225

[HEECKEREN.] Verslag van den staat van h. Suriname landbouwkund. genootschap: Prodesse conamur. *Paramaribo.* 1832. 8vo. 31226

See Teenstra's "De Negerslaven," p. 333, concerning the author of these pieces.

HEEDE (J. van). Discours | ende | Beschrijvinge van het groot | Eylandt Canaria, ende Gomera, | midtsgaders het innemen, ende | verlaten van dien. | Alles ghetrouwelijc met grooten aerbeyt, wt diversche Journa- | liers by een ghebrocht, ende vergadert. Door Michiel Ioostens van Heede, | Schrijver op de Armade vande E. Heeren des Nederlants Staten, ghede- | stineert op Westen, onder tbevel ende commandement E. Jonc Heer Pieter | vander Doest, als Admirael Generael. | Begrijpende alle de courssen ghedaen in dese Zeevaert, van daghe tot daghe, be- | ghinnende vanden XXV. Meye 1599. tot op den tienden Septembris deszel- | ven Jaers, stilo novo. | Door Eendrachtich perseveren, en Wet- | telijc strijden, van Noodts Weghen | Wort met Eeren, ende verblijden. Gherech- | tighe Victorije verkreghen. | *Tot Rotterdam*, | *Bij Gillis Pietersz. Boec-verkooper op Steygher*, | *inden rooden Enghel.* M.D.-XCIX. | 4to, 12 l. 31227

An account of the Dutch Expedition under Van der Does, which comprised no less than seventy vessels, for the redress of certain grievances, and which resulted in the taking of Alligona (in the Canaries) and the infliction of great damage at St. Thomas. *See* Trömel, No. 51.

HEEMSKERCK (C. van). Journael | Oft Daghelijcx-register van de Voyagie na Rio | de Plata, ghedaen met het Schip ghenoemt de Silveren Werelt, het welcke onder | t'Admiraelschap van Laurens Bicker, ende het bevel van Cornelis van Heems-kerck als Commies die | Custen van Guinea versocht hebbende, ende van den Admirael daer na versteken zijnde, alleen voorts seylende | na Rio de Plata, daer in de voorsz. Rieviere by de 60. mijlen opwaerts gekomen wesende, tot Bonas Aeris den Commis (d'welcke op de val- | sche aen-biedinghe van den Gouverneur derselver Plaetsen, om vry te mooghen handelen, aen Landt voer) met noch 8. ander | Personen heeft moeten achter laten, ende van daer wederom wech varende, noch selven seer deyrlijcken na 't af-ster- | ven van bycans all het Volck met die Reste in de Bay Todos los Santos in der Portugijsen handen | ghevallen is, allen Zee-varende Luyden tot eenen Spieghel ende Excempel beschreven | Door den Schipper daer op gheweest zijnde Hendrick Ottsen. | Zeer weerdich om lesen eñ aenmerckelijck om der Spaengiaerden gruwelijcke wreetheyt wille; die trouw, eer ende geloof schandelijck mis-bruycken, | om alle andere Natien, ... uyt de niewe Werelt te sluyten, daer sy door sulcken middel de verste af werden sullen. | ... | *Gedruckt tot Amstelredam by Cornelis Claesz, op 't Water in 't Schrijf-boek, Anno* 1603. | Obl. 4to, pp. 49. 5 Plates. + *Tot Amstelredam by Michiel Colijn, Boeck-vercooper op 't Water by de Oude-brugge int Huys-boeck.* 1617. | Obl. 4to, pp. 54. 5 Plates. 31228

HEER (O.) Flora fossilis arctica. Die fossile Flora der Polarländer enthaltend die in Nordgrönland, auf der Melville-Insel, im Banksland, am Mackenzie, in Island und in Spitzbergen entdeckten fossilen Pflanzen. Von O. Heer. Mit einem Anhang über versteinerte Hölzer der arctischen Zone von Dr. Carl Cramer ... *Zurich: Friedrich Schultheiss.* 1868. 4to, pp. vii, 192. 50 Plates.

HEEREN (Arnold Hermann Ludwig). Handbuch der Geschichte des europäischen Staatensystems und seiner Colonieen. Dritte Ausgabe. ... *Göttingen: J. F. Röwer.* 1819. 8vo, pp. xxxviii, 880. C. 31230

HEEREN. History of the Political System of Europe, and its Colonies, From the Discovery of America to the Independence of the American Continent. From the German of A. H. L. Heeren. ... *Northampton, Mass.* 1828. 2 vols., 8vo. + *Northampton, Mass.: S. Butler and Son.* 1829. 2 vols., 8vo, pp. viii, 314; x, 406. B. + *Oxford: D. A. Talboys.* 31231

The translation is by George Bancroft. The English edition, described below, was edited by the publisher, D. A. Talboys, an eminent and learned bookseller at Oxford.

HEEREN. A Manual of the History of the Political System of Europe and its Colonies, from its Formation at the Close of the Fifteenth Century, to its Re-establishment upon the Fall of Napoleon. By A. H. L. Heeren. Translated from the Fifth German Edition. *Oxford: D. A. Talboys.* M DCCC XXXIV. 2 vols., 8vo, pp. xxix, 372; xvi, 464. H. + *Reprinted, London: Henry G. Bohn.* MDCCCXLVI. 8vo, pp. xxxii, 540. B., C. 31232

Some copies of the Oxford edition have the imprint *London: H. G. Bohn.*

HEEREN. Manuel Historique du Système Politique des États de l'Europe et de leurs Colonies: ... traduit de l'allemand. *Paris.* 1821. 8vo, pp. 364. + Traduit de l'allemand sur la troisième édition. *Paris: Videcocq.* 1841. 2 vols., 8vo. S. 31233

HEERMANS (J.) ... War Power of the President—Summary Imprisonment—Habeas Corpus. By J. Heermans. *New York: Loyal Publication Society.* 1863. 8vo, pp. 10. B. 31234

HEGEWISCH (*Prof.*) Amerikanisches Magazin. *See* Vol. I., No. 1287, add for collation, pp. (6), 190, 166; (4), 200; (4), 184.

[HEGNER (J. K.)] *See* Crantz, Vol. V., No. 17412.

HÉGUERTY (D'). Essai sur les Intérêts du commerce maritime. *La Haye.* 1754. 12mo, pp. 258. 31236

The | Heidelbergh Catechism | or | Method of Instruction, | in the | Christian Religion, | as | The same is taught in the Reformed Churches | and Schools of Holland. | Translated for the Use of the Reformed Protestant | Dutch Church, of the City of New-York. | *New-York: | Printed and Sold by John Holt, at the | Exchange.* | MDCCLXIV. | 8vo, pp. 46. + Sixth Edition. *Albany.* 1799. 8vo, pp. 60. N. 31237

The Heidelberg Catechism, in German, Latin, and English: With an Historical Introduction. Prepared and published by the Direction of the German Reformed Church in the United States of America. Tercentenary Edition. *New York: Charles Scribner.* 4to, pp. 277. 31238

HEIDELBERG COLLEGE, *Tiffin, Ohio.* Catalogue. 1857. *Sandusky.* 1858. 8vo. S. 31239

HEIJLIDIJ (C. J.) De modo procedendi Surinamensi in causis criminalibus, cum veteri tum novissimo. *Traject. a Rhenum.* 1857. 8vo. 31240

HEINE (Wilhelm). Reise um die Erde nach Japan an Bord der Expeditions-Escadron unter Com. Perry in den Jahren 1853, 54, und 55, unternommen im Auftrage der Regierung der Vereinigten Staaten. *Leipzig: H. Costenoble.* 1856. 2 vols., 8vo, pp. 321; 375. 31241

Translated into French, *Bruxelles: A. Lacroix*, ... 1859. 2 vols., 8vo. + Seconde édition. [*Ibid.*] 1863.

HEINE. Wanderbilder aus Central-Amerika. Skizzen eines deutschen Malers von Wilhelm Heine. Mit einem Vorwort von Friedrich Gerstäcker. Zweite Auflage. *Leipzig: Hermann Costenoble.* 1853. 18mo, pp. xvi, 264. B. + [*Ibid.*] 1857. 8vo.

Also: Graphic Scenes of the Japan Expedition. *New York: G. P. Putnam.* 1856. Folio. 10 Plates.

HEINECKE (S.) Genealogy from Adam to Christ; with the Genealogy of Adam Heinecke and Henry Vandersaal, from 1747 to 1868. By Rev. Samuel Heinecke. To which is added, a Brief Account of the Author's Travels as an Evangelist, with ten Sermons composed by Himself. *Philadelphia: Collins.* 1869. 12mo, pp. 231. C. 31243

HEINER (E.) Centenary Sermon ... December 8th, 1850, on the Occasion of the Centenary Celebration of the First German Reformed Congregation of Baltimore. By Rev. Elias Heiner, A.M. *Baltimore: Sherwood & Co.* 1850. 16mo, pp. 52. + Second Edition. [*Ibid.*] 31244

Also: Reminiscences of a Quarter of a Century: A Sermon ... in ... Baltimore, January 13, 1861. ... *Baltimore: Printed by John D. Toy.* 1861. 8vo, pp. 23, (1).

HEINRIACH (A. P.) The Dawnings of Music in Kentucky, or the Pleasures of Harmony, in the Solitudes of Nature. (Opera Prima.) *Philadelphia.* 1820. Folio, pp. 269. 31245

HEINZEN (K.) Die Teutschen und die Amerikaner. Von Karl Heinzen. Zweite Auflage. *Boston.* 1860. 8vo, pp. 59.

Also: A Few "Patriotic" Contemplations. ... Translated by C. P. [n. p. 1870?] 8vo, pp. 4. H. — Mankind the Criminal. A Lecture ... in Washington, D. C. ... *Roxbury, Mass.* [n. d.] 12mo, pp. 24. B., BA., H.

HEISING (A.) England und die Anglo-Sächsische Staatenbildung in Amerika, Westindien und Australien, vom Ursprung bis auf die Gegenwart. *Berlin: A. Sacco* [about 1835]. 8vo, pp. 258. C. 31247

HELDERBERGIA. *See* [Schoolcraft (H. R.)]

HELDRING (O. G.) Binnen- en buitenlandsche kolonisatie, in betrekking tot de armoede. *Amsterdam.* 1846. 8vo. 31248

Colonization at home and abroad, with relation to pauperism.

Helen Lason: A Peep at New-York Society. *Philadelphia.* 1855. 12mo. 31249

HELLENBROECK (A.) Specimen of Divine Truths, Fitted for the Use of those, of various Capacities, who desire to prepare themselves for a due Confession of their Faith. By the Rev. Mr. A. Hellenbroeck, Late Minister of the Gospel at Rotterdam. Translated from the Dutch, for the Use of the Reformed Protestant Dutch Church, of the City of New-York. *New-York: Printed by John Holt, opposite the Exchange.* MDCCLXV. 8vo, pp. 95. + *New Brunswick.* 1787. 12mo. + *Wilmington.* 1797.

HELLER (Carl Bartholomæus). Reisen in Mexiko in den Jahren 1845–48. *Leipzig: W. Engelmann.* 1853. 8vo, pp. xxiv, 432. Plate and 2 Maps. B., C., S. 31251

HELLIER (T.) The | Vain Prodigal Life, | and | Tragical Penitent Death | of | Thomas Hellier | Born at Whitchurch near Lyme | in Dorset-shire: | Who for Murdering his Master, | Mistress, and a Maid, was Executed accor- | ding to Law at Westover in Charles City, in | the Country of Virginia, neer the Plantation | called Hard Labour, where he perpetrated | the said Murders. | He Suffer'd on Munday the 5th of August, 1678. | And was after Hanged up in Chains at Windmill- | Point on James River. | *London: | Printed for Sam. Crouch at the Princes Arms, a corner-shop of | Popes-head-alley in Cornhil.* 1680. 4to, pp. (4), 40. J.C.B. 31252

Hellier & Co's Chicago Business Directory for 1859–60, with which is combined a Commercial Register of the Business Men of the City of New York. ... 1859. ... *Hellier & Co., New York.* [n. d.] 8vo, pp. 57. 31253

See also our Vol. IV., No. 12641.

HELLIMER (Régis). Épisodes de la guerre des États-Unis d'Amérique (1861–1862). Mémoires du Yankee James Trevor. *Limoges: Ardant frères.* [1863.] 8vo, pp. 288. Plate. B.

HELLMUTH (I.) A Reply to a Letter of the Rt. Rev. the Lord Bishop of Montreal and Metropolitan of Canada, addressed to the Bishops and Clergy of the United Church of England and Ireland in Canada. By I. Hellmuth, Archbishop of Huron. *Quebec.* 1862. 8vo, pp. 26. 31255

HELLO (J. M.) Relation de l'Expedition de la Corvette la Créole, au Mexique, en 1838 et 1839. Par J. M. Hello. *Paris: Dufart.* 1839. 8vo, pp. 60. 31256

HELLWALD (F. von). Die americanische Völkerwanderung. Eine Studie von Friedrich von Hellwald ... . *Wien: Adolf Holzhamer.* 1866. 12mo, pp. (2), iii, 54. BA. 31257

HELLWALD. Maximilian I. Kaiser von Mexico. Sein Leben, Wirken und Tod, nebst einem Abriss der Geschichte des Kaiserreichs. *Wien: Braumüller.* 1869. 2 parts, 8vo, pp. xvi, 617.

HELM (C. J.) Letter from Ch. J. Helm Esqr. on the Blockade and Rights of Neutrals. ... [n. p. n. d.] 8vo, pp. 19. H.

HELM (J. I.) Memoir of Martha Thompson Sharp. By James I. Helm. *Philadelphia.* 1849. 16mo. C. + *New York.* [1853.] 16mo. C. 31260

HELM (J. L.) Biographical Sketch of the Hon. John L[arue] Helm, late Governor of Kentucky. [By a Committee.] Published by Direction of the General Assembly of Kentucky. *Frankfort (Ky.): S. I. M. Major, Public Printer.* 1868. 8vo, pp. 144. Portrait. C. 31261

HELMER (C. D.) Two Sermons. I. Signs of our National Atheism. II. The War Begun. By C. D. Helmer, Milwaukee. ... April 21st and 28th, 1861. *Milwaukee: Terry & Cleaver.* 1861. 8vo, pp. 35. 31262

Also: The Stars and Stripes. A Poem pronounced before the Phi Beta Kappa Society, Yale College, July 30, 1862. ... *New Haven: E. Haynes.* 1862. 8vo, pp. 23–47.

HELMIG VAN DER VEGT (A.) Proeve eener Handleiding om het Neger-Engelsch, zoo als hetzelve over het algemeen binnen de Kolonie Suriname gesproken wordt, ... Door A. Helmig van der Vegt. *Amsterdam.* 1844. 8vo, pp. 56. 31263

HELMS (A. Z.) Tagebuch einer Reise durch Peru, von Buenos-Ayres auf dem grossen Plataflusse über Potosi nach Lima der Hauptstadt des Königreichs Peru. Vom Königlich Spanischen Huttendirektor Anton Zacharius Helms. *Dresden: In der Waltherischen Hofbuchhandlung.* 1798. 8vo, pp. 300. J.C.B.

HELMS. Travels from Buenos Ayres, by Potosi, to Lima. With Notes by the Translator, containing Topographical Descriptions of the Spanish Possessions in South America. Drawn

from the Last and Best Authorities. By Anthony Zachariah Helms, formerly Director of the Mines near Cracow in Poland, and late Director of the Mines, ... in Peru. *London: Richard Phillips.* 1806. 12mo, pp. xii, 287. Map. BA., H. + [Another Edition. *Ibid.*] 1807. 8vo, pp. 92. + Second Edition. *London.* 1807. 12mo, pp. 304. Plate and 2 Maps. 31265

An abridgment of Helms' travels, which occupies 108 pages and an appendix of 150 pages, consisting of extracts from Alcedo, Ulloa, &c. *See* "M. Rev.,' LIII. 148.

HELMS. Voyage dans l'Amérique Méridionale, commençant par Buenos Ayres et Potosi jusqu'à Lima, Avec un Appendice contenant la Description la plus complète et la plus exacte des Possessions ou Colonies espagnoles dans l'Amérique méridionale; Appendice formé de l'extrait des meilleurs Voyages les plus modernes; Par Antoine Zacharie Helms. Traduit de l'Anglais par M. B. B. D. V., member de plusieurs Academies. *Paris: Galignani.* 1812. 2 vols., 8vo, pp. (2), x, 257. 2 Maps. H., S.

HELMUTH (J. H. C.) Kurze Nachricht von dem gelben Fieber, Philadelphia, von J. H. C. Helmuth. *Philadelphia.* 1793. 8vo. B. 31267

HELMUTH. A Short Account of the Yellow Fever in Philadelphia, for the Reflecting Christian. By J. Henry C. Helmuth, ... Translated from the German by Charles Erdmann. ... *Philadelphia: Printed by Jones, Hoff & Derrick.* M,DCC,XCIV. 8vo, pp. (4), 55. B., P. 31268

Also: Kurze Andachten einer gottsuchenden Seele, auf alle Tage der Woche, und andere Umstände einrichtet. *Germantaun: M. Billmeyer.* 1795. 12mo, pp. 28. C.

A Help to a National Reformation. Containing An Abstract of the Penal-Laws against Prophaneness and Vice. Fifth Edition, Enlarged. *London.* 1706. 8vo, pp. (16), 131. B. 31269

Includes an account of the efforts for the reformation of morals in Jamaica and in New England, pp. 4, 9, 11–16.

HELPER (H. R.) Compendium of the Impending Crisis of the South. By Hinton Rowan Helper, of North Carolina. *New York: A. B. Burdick.* 1859. 8vo, pp. 214. + [*Ibid.*] 1860.

HELPER. The Impending Crisis of the South: how to meet it. By Hinton Rowan Helper, of North Carolina. *New York: Burdick Brothers.* 1857. 12mo, pp. 413. C. + Hundredth Thousand. *New York: A. B. Burdick.* 1860. 12mo, pp. 420.

For a reply *see* Peissner (E.), The Union, and Wolfe (*Judge*).

HELPER. The Land of Gold. Reality versus Fiction. By Hinton Rowan Helper ... . *Baltimore: For the Author.* 1855. 12mo, pp. 300. B., C. 31272

HELPER. The Negroes in Negroland; the Negroes in America; and Negroes Generally. Also, the Several Races of White Men, considered as the Involuntary and Predestined Supplanters of the Black Races. A Compilation. By Hinton Rowan Helper ... . *New York: G. W. Carleton.* MDCCCLXVIII 12mo, pp. 254. B. 31273

HELPER. Nojoque; A Question for a Continent. By Hinton Rowan Helper ... . *New York: George W. Carleton & Co.* MDCCCLXVII. 12mo, pp. 479. B., C. 31274

[HELPS (Arthur).] The Conquerors of the New World and their Bondsmen being a Narrative of the Principal Events which led to Negro Slavery in the West Indies and America. ... *London: William Pickering.* 1848–52. 2 vols., post 8vo, pp. x, (2), 264, (1); (4), 300. B. 31275

Now scarce. The author is said to have suppressed the work.

[HELPS.] A Letter on "Uncle Tom's Cabin." ... *Cambridge: John Bartlett.* 1852. 8vo, pp. 29. H. 31276

HELPS. The Life of Columbus, the Discoverer of America. Chiefly by Arthur Helps ... *London: Bell and Daldy.* 1869. Post 8vo, pp. xvi, 262, (1). B., BA. 31277

Some copies have the imprint *Philadelphia: J. B. Lippincott & Co.*

HELPS. The Life of Las Casas, "The Apostle of the Indies." By Arthur Helps. ... *London: Bell and Daldy.* 1868. 8vo, pp. xix, 292. Map. B. + Second Edition. [*Ibid.*] 1868. Map.

Some copies have the imprint *Philadelphia: J. B. Lippincott & Co.* 1868. In this work, reproduced with additions from the author's "Spanish Conquest," Mr. Helps has refuted the charge that Las Casas, in his anxiety to relieve the Indians from the slavery imposed upon them by the Spaniards, first suggested the institution of African slavery.

HELPS. The Life of Pizarro, with some Account of his Associates in the Conquest of Peru. By Arthur Helps. *London: Bell and Daldy.* 1869. 16mo, pp. xxii, 320. B., BA. + Second Edition. [*Ibid.*] 31279

HELPS. The Spanish Conquest in America and its Relation to the History of Slavery and to the Government of Colonies. By Arthur Helps. *London: John W. Parker & Son.* 1855–1861.

4 vols., 8vo, pp. xv, 528; vii, 526, (1); viii, 584; viii, 510, (1). B., BA. + *New York: Harper & Brothers.* 1857. 4 vols., 12mo, pp. 490; 470; 532; 456. Map. H. + *London: Parker, Son, & Bown.* 1861. 4 vols., 8vo. 31280

"The whole of this noble work is devoted to a history of the relations of the Indians of America to its Spanish invaders; and the effect of their occupation, and conquest upon the population, religion, and manners of the aborigines. The various narratives and histories, which describe the awful destruction of many Indian nations by the Spaniards, are criticised with true philosophical acumen, and the veracity and capability of their authors fairly examined." *See* Field's "Essay," No. 682; Fraser's "Magazine," LVI. 441, and "Westminster Review," New Series, VIII. 579.

Helvington; a Dramatic Story in Five Acts. *Memphis.* 1867. 8vo, pp. 187. B. 31281

[HELYOT (*le Père*).] Histoire des Ordres Monastiques, religieux et militaires, et des Congregations Seculieres de l'un & de l'autre sexe [continuée jusqu'à présent par M. Bullot, avec un Catalogue des livres qui traitent des ordres Monastiques]. *Paris: Chez Jean Baptiste Coignard.* 1714–19. 8 vols., 4to, pp. xcviii, (5), 399, (24); (7), 436, (31); xvi, (8), 456, (47); (8), 464, (42); (6), 488, (20); (8), 446, (26); (8), 493, (34); (8), 446, (38). Plates. B. + *Paris.* 1792. 8vo. H. 31282

Relates to their labors in America. "Cet ouvrage, fruit d'un travail de 25 ans, est plein de savantes recherches, et est plus exact, quoiqu'il ne le soit pas toujours, que ceux des écrivains qui l'avaient précédé."—FELLER. *See* Brunet's "Manuel" for other editions and other works by this author.

HEMENWAY (A. M.) Poets and Poetry of Vermont. Edited by Abby Maria Hemenway. ... *Rutland: George A. Tuttle & Company.* 1858. 12mo, pp. xii, 400. + Second Revised Edition. *Boston.* 1860. 12mo, pp. 514. S. 31283

Some copies of the Second Edition have the imprint *Brattleboro.* 1860.

HEMENWAY. The Vermont Historical Gazetteer: a Magazine, embracing a History of Each Town, Civil, Ecclesiastical, Biographical and Military. Edited by Abby Maria Hemenway. *Burlington, Vt.: Miss A. M. Hemenway.* 1867–71. 2 vols., 8vo, pp. xi, 1096; 1199. Portraits and Plates. BA., H. 31284

This is a series of Town Histories, grouped in Counties, and issued in quarterly numbers. Each number containing 100 pages in double columns, and portrait. It was first issued as the "Vermont Quarterly Gazetteer." *Ludlow, Vt.* 1860.

[HEMING] (T.) A Sermon ... before the Incorporated Society for the Propagation of the Gospel in Foreign Parts ... February 17, 1737–8. By Thomas, Lord Bishop of Bangor. *London: J. and J. Pemberton.* MDCCXXXVIII. 8vo, pp. 70, (1). BA. 31285

Since setting this up, and too late to alter, we discovered it should be under Herring.

The Hemisphere. English and French Journal; containing Literary and Biographical Varieties, dedicated to Americans, ... *Philadelphia.* 1810–11. 31286

HEMMENWAY (M.) A Discourse Delivered at Welles, on the 22d February, 1800, Occasioned by the Lamented Death of General George Washington. By Moses Hemmenway, D.D. ... *Portsmouth (N. H.): C. Peirce.* 1800. 8vo, pp. 16. C. 31287

HEMMENWAY. A Sermon, Preached ... May 26, 1784. Being the Day of General Election. By Moses Hemmenway, A.M. ... *Boston: ... Printed by Benjamin Edes and Sons*, ... M,DCC,LXXXIV. 8vo, pp. 52. B., BA., H. 31288

Also: Sermon at the Ordination of the Rev. John Kelly, Hempstead, December 5, 1792. ... *Dover.* 1793. 8vo. M. — ... Sermon ... at York, March 16, 1810, at the Interment of ... Rev. ... Isaac Lyman. ... *Boston: Press of John Eliot, Jun.* 1810. 8vo, pp. 31. BA., N., W. — A Sermon ... March 11th, at the Interment of the Reverend James Pike ... . *Dover: Printed by Eliphalet Ladd.* M,DCC,XCII. 8vo, pp. 28. B. — A Sermon ... at the Ordination of Mr. Jonathan Calef ... June 11, 1794. ... *Hallowell (District of Maine): Printed by Howard S. Robinson.* 1795. 8vo, pp. 31. H. And many sermons on religious and doctrinal topics.

HEMMERSAM (Michael). Guineische und West-Indianische Reissbeschreibung de An. 1639. biss 1645. Von Ambsterdam nach ... Brasilien ... . *Nürnberg: Paul Fürsten.* [1647.] 8vo, pp. 109. + Vermehrt durch C. L. Diethern. *Nürnberg: Paul Fürstens.* [1663.] 16mo, pp. (30), 109, (26). BA., H. 31289

Relates to Brazil, Guyana, Peru, Chile, Paraguay, etc. The edition of 1663 contains an Appendix, pp. 47, which seems to have been a separate publication. For other editions *see our* Vol. VI., p. 568, 569.

HEMMERSAM. West-Indianisk Reese-Beskriffning, från åhr 1639 till 1645. Ifrån Amsterdam till St. Foris de Mina, itt Castell i Africa: Förättat och beskrefvin aff Michael Hammersam, Borg. uthi Nurenberg. Och nu på wårt Swänska Språåk förwänd och tryckt ... *Wijsingborg ... Johan Kanckel. Anno* MDCLXXIV. Small 4to, pp. (8), 94. C. 31290

"Cet ouvrage ne se trouve pas cité par aucun bibliographe. Très-rare."—LECLERC.

HEMPHILL (J.) Eulogy on the Life and Character of the Hon. Thomas J. Rusk, Late U. S. Senator from Texas. Delivered in the Hall of the House of Representatives of the State of Texas, on the Seventh of November, 1857. By John Hemphill. ... *Austin: Printed by John Marshall & Co.* 1857. 8vo, pp. 24. H. 31291

Also: Speech ... on the State of the Union. ... In the Senate ... January 28, 1861 [n. p. n. d.] 8vo, pp. 16. H.

HEMPHILL (Joseph). Speech of Mr. Hemphill, on the Missouri Question ... . *Washington.* [1819.] 8vo, pp. 27. H., P., S.

Also: Speech ... on the subject of Roads and Canals. [*Washington.* 1823.] 8vo. W. — Mr. Hemphill's Speech on the Bill to Construct a National Road from Buffalo to New Orleans, ... March 23, 1830. [n. p. n. d.] 8vo, pp. 23. N. S.

HEMPHILL (Samuel). A Defence Of Mr. Hemphill's Observations: or, An Answer to the Vindication of the Rev. Commission. *Philadelphia: Printed and Sold by B. Franklin.* 1735. 8vo, pp. 47, (1). B., M. 31293

HEMPHILL. Extract of the Minutes of the Commission of the Synod, Relating to the Reverend Samuel Hemphill. *Philadelphia: Printed and sold by B. Franklin.* 1735. 12mo, pp. 13. B.

HEMPHILL. A Letter to a Friend in the Country, Containing the Substance of a Sermon Preached at Philadelphia, in the Congregation of The Rev. Mr. Hemphill, Concerning the Terms of Christian and Ministerial Communion. *Philadelphia: Printed and sold by B. Franklin, at the new Printing-Office near the Market.* 1735. 16mo, pp. 40. W. 31295

HEMPHILL. Remarks upon a Pamphlet, entitled A Letter to a Friend, &c., containing the Substance of a Sermon preached at Philadelphia, in the Congregation of Rev. Mr. Hemphill. *Philadelphia.* 1735. 16mo, pp. 32. M. 31296

HEMPHILL. A Vindication of the Reverend Commission of the Synod, in Answer to Observations on their proceedings against the Rev. Mr. Hemphill. *Philadelphia: Printed and sold by B. Franklin.* 1735. 16mo, pp. 63. M. 31297

These pieces, relative to Hemphill who was an Irishman, are introduced here because they are slightly historical; some of them are moreover early specimens of Franklin's press, and, in Sparks' judgment, some are written by Franklin. *See* [Franklin (B.)], Vol. VII., No. 25591. *See also* Sparks' "Life of Franklin," p. 125.

HEMPSTEAD (S.) Masonic Oration ... by S. Hempstead, Esq., on St. John's Day, June 24, 1846. *Dubuque, Iowa.* 12mo, pp. 6.

HEMPSTEAD CASE, *State of New York.* In the Court for the Trial of Impeachments and the Correction of Errors. Between Richard Bedell and others, Respondents, and Samuel Denton, Benjamin Tredwell and others, Appellants. On Appeal from the Court of Chancery. Case on behalf of the Respondents. *New York.* 1818. 8vo, pp. over 504. N. 31299

HEMPSTEAD CASE. In Error. The Town of North Hempstead, etc., Appellants, and the Town of Hempstead, etc., Respondents. Appellants' Case. *New York.* 1825. 8vo. N.

HEMPSTEAD INSTITUTE. Circular. *New York.* 1857. 8vo.

HENCHMAN (N.) A Letter to the Reverend Mr. William Hobby, Occasioned by sundry Passages in his ... Letter, In Vindication of Mr. Whitefield's Itinerancy and Conduct. By Nathaniel Henchman ... . *Boston: Printed by T. Fleet.* 1745. 4to, pp. 12. B., H., M., W. 31302

Also: Letter to Stephen Chase, stating why he will not admit G. Whitefield into his Pulpit. *Boston.* 1744. 8vo, pp. 12.—Reasons ... for declining to admit Mr. Whitefield into his Pulpit. *Boston: Printed by T. Fleet.* 1745. 8vo, pp. 12. B., BA., H., M., W.— ... Sermon occasioned by the Death of the Hon ... John Burrill, Esq ... Decemb. 10, 1721. ... *Boston.* 1721. 12mo, pp. iv, iv, 41, (2). B., M., W.— ... A Sermon ... at the Ordination of ... Mr. James Varney, in Wilmington, October 24 the ... 1733. ... *Boston: D. Henchman.* 1733. 8vo, pp. 29. (1). BA., W.

HENDERSON (A.) A Grammar of the Moskito Language. By Alexander Henderson, of Belize, Honduras. *New York: Printed by John A. Gray.* 1846. 8vo, pp. iv, 48. 31303

HENDERSON. The Gospel according to Mathew in the Charibbean Language. Translated by Alexander Henderson. *Edinburgh.* 1847. 8vo, pp. 88. 31304

HENDERSON. The Maya Primer. By Alexander Henderson, Belize, Honduras. *Birmingham: Printed by J. Showell.* [n. d.] 8vo, pp. 12. 31305

Also: Catecismo de los Metodistas. 8vo, pp. 17.—Breve Devocionario. 8vo, pp. 17. Each in the Maya language.

HENDERSON (A.) Canadian Views and Studies. By Alexander Henderson. *Montreal.* 1866. 8vo. 31306

HENDERSON (A. W.) Remember; a Word for Soldiers. By Rev. A. W. Henderson. *New York: American Tract Society.* 18mo, pp. 48. 31307

Also a series of seven tracts entitled "Glad Tidings for the Hospital;" all issued during the Civil War, 1861–65.

HENDERSON (George). An Account of the British Settlement of Honduras; being a View of its Commercial and Agricultural Resources, Soil, Climate, Natural History, &c. To which are added, Sketches of the Manners and Customs of the Mosquito Indians, preceded by the Journal of a Voyage to the Mosquito shore. Illustrated by a Map. By Capt. Henderson, of

his Majesty's 5th West India Regiment. *London: C. and R. Baldwin.* 1809. 8vo, pp. xi, 203. Map. C., P., S. + Second Edition, Enlarged. *London: R. Baldwin.* 1811. 8vo, pp. xi, 237, (1). Map. BA., H. 31308

See "M. Rev," LXIII. 396; LXXII. 443; LXXXII. 218; Field's "Essay," 682.

HENDERSON. A Brief View of the actual Condition and Treatment of the Negro Slaves in the British Colonies; ... By Captain Henderson, ... *London: Baldwin and Co.* 1816. 8vo, pp. 56. 31309

HENDERSON (G.) A Short View of the Administrations in the Government of America, under the Former Presidents, the Late General Washington, and John Adams; and of the Present Administration under Thomas Jefferson: with Cursory Observations on the Present State of the Revenue, ... of the United States. By George Henderson, Esq. ... *London: J. Hatchard.* 1802. 8vo, pp. viii, 71. B., H. 31310

See "M. Rev.," XL. 205.

HENDERSON (G. D.) Address on the Death of General Nathaniel Lyon. Delivered at Manhattan, Kansas, September 26, 1861. By Rev. George D. Henderson ... *Leavenworth.* 1861. 8vo, pp. 8. 31311

HENDERSON (H.) Fast Sermon, Civil War, Demopolis, Ala. By H. Henderson, A.M. 31312

This imperfect title is from the "Historical Magazine."

HENDERSON (J.) The Rev. Mr. Jacob Henderson's Fifth Letter to Daniel Dulany, Esq; In Relation to the Case and Petition of the Clergy of Maryland. *Printed for the Author, in the Year* MDCCXXXII. 8vo, pp. (2), 41. 31313

The only one of the series I have ever seen.

HENDERSON (J.) A History of the Brazil; comprising its Geography, Commerce, Colonization, Aboriginal Inhabitants, &c., &c., &c. By James Henderson, recently from South America. ... *London: Longman* ... 1821. 4to, pp. xxiii, 522. 28 Plates, 2 Maps. A., B., BA., H., P., S. 31314

Said to be compiled principally from Cazal. *See* Vol. III., No. 11640.

HENDERSON. A Series of Observations ... on the Expediency of Great Britain entering into Commercial Regulations with the South American States, accompanied by Brief Commercial Notices of the five Republics. By James Henderson, ... *London: J. M. Richardson.* 1822. 8vo, pp. 24. H. 31315

HENDERSON. Representacion à los Americanos del Sud y Mexicanos, para dissuadirles de que concedan ventajas commerciales a otras nacionas, en perjuicio de Inglaterra, por causa de su retardo en reconocer su independencia ... con un examen rapido de varios acontecimientos importantes, y rasgos patrioticos que han distinguido sus respectivas revoluciones, por James Henderson. *London.* 1822. 8vo, pp. 44. 31316

Also: An Address to the South Americans and Mexicans. ... *London: J. M. Richardson; and J. Hatchard.* 1822. 8vo, pp. (2), 45. H.

HENDERSON (J. B.) The Missouri Test Oath. Argument in the Supreme Court of the United States, March, 1866. *Washington Reporter, March* 19, 1866. 8vo, pp. 16. 31317

HENDERSON. Speech of Hon. J. B. Henderson, of Mo., on the Confiscation of Property. Delivered ... April 8, 1862, [n. p. n. d.] 8vo, pp. 16. H. 31318

HENDERSON. Speech delivered ... at Hannibal, Mo., before a Mass Meeting of the Citizens of Marion and Ralls Counties, 20th of August, 1862. [n. p. n. d.] 8vo, pp. 36. B. 31319

Also: Issues of the Day. Speech ... St. Louis ... Oct. 21. [n. p. 1868.] 8vo, pp. 11. H.—Letter ... to the Secretary of War. [June 1, 1865. n. p. n. d.] 8vo, pp. 7. H.—Reconstruction. Speech ... February 20th, 1867. [n. p. n. d.] 8vo, pp. 8.—The Funding Bill. Speech ... in the Senate, March 4, 1868. [n. p. n. d.] 8vo, pp. 16.—Speech ... on the Present Condition of the Country and the Remedy for Existing Evils; ... February 13 and 14, 1866. *Washington.* 1866. 8vo, pp. 40. Speech ... on the Proposed Amendment of the Constitution, to abolish Slavery throughout the United States, ... April 7, 1864. *Washington: M. Polkinhorn, Printer.* 1864. 8vo, pp. 30. B.—Speech ... on the Post Office Appropriation Bill; ... April 30 and May 1, 1866. *Washington.* 1866. 8vo, pp. 16. B.—Reconstruction. Speech ... in the Senate ... June 8, 1866. ... [n. p. n. d.] 8vo, pp. 12.—Speech ... on the Tax on Unmanufactured Cotton; ... in the Senate ... June 25, 1866. *Washington.* 1866. 8vo, pp. 15. H.—Speech ... on the Bill to provide Increased Revenue from Imports; ... in the Senate ... January 26, 1867. *Washington.* 1867. 8vo, pp. 14. H.—Speech ... on the Abolition of Slavery. ... Senate, ... March 27, 1862. [n. p. n. d.] 8vo, pp. 15.—Speech ... on the National Currency, ... May 6, 1864. [n. p. n. d.] 8vo, pp. 16. H.—Speech Feb. 13 and 14, 1866, on Apportionment. [n. p. n. d.]

HENDERSON (J.) Constitution and Regulations of the Society of Masons, in Virginia. *Richmond.* 1818. 31320

HENDERSON (J.) Letter of Hon. John Henderson to the Legislature of the State of Mississippi, Dec. 28, 1840. [n. p. n. d.] 8vo, pp. 16. M. 31321

Also: Remarks ... on the Bankrupt Bill. ... In the Senate ... 25th May, 1840. [n. p. n. d.] 8vo, pp. 7. H.

HENDERSON (J. H. D.) Reconstruction—Branch Mint in Oregon. Remarks of Hon. James H. D. Henderson ... House of Representatives, June 13, 1866. *Washington.* 1866. 8vo, pp. 8.

HENDERSON (J. J.) Annual Statement of the Trade and Commerce of Buffalo, for 1853. ... By John J. Henderson. *Buffalo: E. A. Maynard & Co., Printers.* 1854. 8vo, pp. 24. H. + For 1854. *Buffalo.* 1855. 8vo, pp. 56. 31323

HENDERSON (J. S.) The Unseen Hand; or, the Four Scouts of the Waccamaw. By J. Stanley Henderson. *New York: Beadle & Co.* [1868.] 16mo, pp. 100. C. 31324

Also: Missing Jo; or, the Mystery of Camp White. A Tale of the Tents. ... *New York: Beadle & Co.* 1865. 16mo, pp. 36.—The Willing Captive; or, The Woodyard Mystery. A Tale of Ohio River Life. ... *New York: Beadle & Co.* 1865. 16mo, pp. 39. All poor enough to be omitted.

HENDERSON (M. A.), *pseudon.* The Song of Milgenwater: Translated from the Original Feejee. By Marc Antony Henderson ... *Cincinnati: Jones, Brown & Robinson.* 1856. 12mo, pp. 96. H. + The Song of Milhanwatha. Second Edition. *Cincinnati: Tickell & Grinne.* 1856. 12mo, pp. 144. B., C.

One of the many travesties of Longfellow's "Hiawatha."

HENDERSON (M. H.) The Days of Old; a Centennial Discourse delivered in ... Newark, N. J., Feb. 22, 1846. By Mathew H. Henderson, M.A. *New York: Leavitt, Trow & Co.* 1846. 8vo, pp. 64. 31326

HENDERSON (S.) Suggestions for the Prevention ... in the West Indies ... [of] the Yellow Feaver. To which are added other Papers connected with the Subject. By Stewart Henderson, M.D. ... *London: J. Stockdale, Jr.* 1809. 8vo, pp. 114.

See "M. Rev.," New Series, LX. 203.

HENDERSON (T.) A Lecture delivered at the Opening of the Medical Department of the Columbian College, Washington, D. C. [n. p.] 1826. 8vo, pp. 8. M. 31328

HENDERSON (T.) *See* [Smith (Fr. H.)]

HENDRICKS (——). Speech of Mr. Hendricks, on the Bill to graduate the Price of the Public Lands. Delivered in the Senate ... January 28, 1828. *Washington: Printed by Gales & Seaton.* 1828. 8vo, pp. 26. H. 31329

HENDRICKS (T. A.) Reconstruction. Speech of Hon. Thomas A. Hendricks ... in the Senate ... January 30, 1868. *Washington: F. & J. Rives & Geo. A. Bailey.* 1868. 8vo, pp. 16

[HENDRICKS (William).] *See* Journal of the March.

HENDRICKSON (J.) Trial of John Hendrickson, Jr., for the Murder of his Wife, Maria, by poisoning, at Bethlehem, Albany

County, New York, March 6, 1853, tried in ... 1853. Reported and compiled by David M. Barnes, and W. S. Hevenor. *Albany.* 1853. 8vo. 31331

Also: Review, Opinions &c., of Dr. Charles A. Lee and Others, of the Testimony of Drs. Salisbury and Swinburne on the Trial of John Hendrickson, Jr., ... *New York.* 1855. 8vo, pp. 41, (3). B., H.

HENDRICKSON *vs.* SHOTWELL. The Decision. Chancery of New Jersey, between Joseph Hendrickson, Complainant, and Thos. L. Shotwell and Elizabeth his wife, Defendants, On Bill for Relief, &c.—and between Thos. L. Shotwell, Complainant, Joseph Hendrickson, and Stacy Decow, Defendants, On Bill of Interpleader, on the 10th July, 1832. *Philadelphia.* 1832. 8vo.

HENDSCHEL (Thomas). Relation von der freudenreichen Bekehrung des Königreichs Voxu in Japon. *Ingoldstat.* 1617. 4to. Frontispiece. 31333

Contains an account of Peru.

HENDY (J.) A Treatise on the Glandular Disease of Barbadoes, ... By James Hendy, M.D. ... *London: C. Dilly.* M.DCC.-LXXXIV. 8vo, pp. (2), vii, 140. 2 Plates. B., BA. 31334

HENDY. A Vindication of the Opinions and Facts, contained in a Treatise of the Glandular Disease of Barbadoes by James Hendy, M.D. ... *London: J. Kearsly.* 1789. 8vo, pp. 155.

See "M. Rev.," LXXXI. 553.

HENDY *und* ROLLO (John). Ueber die Drüsenkrankheit in Barbados oder über Wilhelm Hillary's Elephantiasis. *Frankfurt.* 1788. 8vo, pp. (10), 254. 2 Plates. H. 31336

HENEY (H.) Commentaire ou observations sur l'acte de la 31e année du règne de George III., chap. 31, communément appelé acte constitutionel du haut et bas Canada. Par H. Heney. *Montréal: Leclere et Jones.* 1832. 8vo, pp. 72, 4. 31337

HENFREY (B.) A Plan with Proposals for Forming a Company to work Mines in the United States; and to Smelt and Refine the Ores, whether of Copper, Lead, Tin, Silver, or Gold. By Benjamin Henfrey. ... *Philadelphia: Printed by Snowden & M'Corkle.* 1797. 8vo, pp. 34. BA., N., S. 31338

HENING (W. W.) The Statutes at Large; being a Collection of all the Laws of Virginia, from the first Session of the Legislature in 1619. ... By W. W. Hening. *New York, Philadelphia, & Richmond.* 1819–1823. 13 vols., 8vo. H. 31339

Bancroft remarks, that no other State in the Union possesses so excellent a work on its legislative history.

HENING. The New Virginia Justice. ... By William Waller Hening. ... *Richmond.* 1795. C., P. + The Third Edition. *Richmond for the Author.* 1820. 8vo, pp. 821. H. 31340

HENIS (T. X.) Diario historico de la rebelion y guerra de los pueblos Guaranis, situados en la costa oriental del Rio Uruguay, del año de 1754. Version castellana de la obra escrita en latin por el P. Tadeo Xavier Henis de la compañia de Jesus. *Buenos Aires.* 1836. Folio, pp. (2), vii, 60. H. 31341

HENKLE (M. M.) The Life of Henry Bidleman Bascom, D.D., LL.D., late Bishop of the Methodist Episcopal Church South. By Moses Montgomery Henkle, D.D. *Louisville: Morton & Griswold.* 1854. 12mo, pp. 408. Portrait. 31342

Also: Masonic Addresses. 1847. 8vo.

HENLEY (D.) The Proceedings of a General Court-Martial; Held at Cambridge, on Tuesday the Twentieth of January; and continued by several Adjournments to Wednesday the 25th of February, 1788: Upon the Trial of Colonel David Henley. *Boston: Printed by J. Gill.* MDCCLXXVIII. Small 4to, pp. 88. N.

Henley was an American officer, charged by Gen. Burgoyne with cruelty to the British prisoners. It was reprinted with the following title:

HENLEY. Proceedings of a Court Martial held at Cambridge, by Order of Major General Heath, Commanding the American Troops for the Northern District, for the Trial of Colonel David Henley, accused by General Burgoyne, of ill treatment of the British Soldiers, &c. Taken in Short Hand by an Officer who was present. *London: J. Almon.* MDCCLXXVIII. 8vo, pp. (4), 147. H. + The Second Edition. [*Ibid.*] 31344

HENLEY (S.) Sermon at Williamsburg, May v. 1777, for the Benefit of a Fund to support the Widows and Orphans of Clergymen in Virginia. By S. Henley, Professor in William and Mary College. *Williamsburg.* 1771. 4to. 31345

HENLEY. Distinct Claims of Government. Sermon preached before the Honourable House of Burgesses at Williamsburg, in Virginia, March 1, 1772. *Cambridge.* 1772. 4to. 31346

This sermon exposed its author to much obloquy. Also: A Candid Refutation of the Heresy imputed by Ro. C. Nicholas ... to the Reverend S. Henley. ... *Williamsburg: Printed for B. White in London, D. Prince in Oxford, and J. Woodver in Cambridge.* MDCCLXXIV. 8vo, pp. (6), 72. BA.

HENNEPIN (L.) Description | de la | Louisiane, | nouvellement decouverte | au Sud'Oüest de la Nouvelle France, | par ordre du roy. | Avec la Carte du Pays: Les Mœurs | & la Manière de vivre | des Sauvages. | Dedie'e a Sa Majeste'. | Par le R. P. Louis Hennepin, | Missionaire Recollet & | Notaire Apostolique. | *A Paris,* | *Chez la Veuve Sébastien Huré,* ... | M. DC. LXXXIII. | ... | 12mo, pp. (12), 312, "Mœurs des Sauvages," pp. 107. Map by Guerard. BA., C.

There are copies of this edition dated *Paris,* MDCLXXXIV. This is the first edition of the Travels of this famous friar, giving his voyage up the Mississippi from the Illinois river. He first described the Falls of Niagara, and, according to some authorities, named Louisiana after the then King of France, Louis XIV. But this fact is disputed by Harrisse and others; it is, however, the first printed account of Louisiana.

HENNEPIN. Description | de la | Lousiane | nouvellement decouverte | au Sud'Oüest de la Nouvelle France, | par ordre du roy. | Avec la Carte du Pays: Les Moeurs | & la Maniere de vivre | des Sauvages. | ... | Par le R. P. Loüis Hennepin, | Missionaire Recollet & | Notaire Apostolique. | *A Paris,* | *Chez Amable Auroy,* ... | M. DC. L. XXXVIII. | ... | 12mo, pp. (12), 312, 107. Map. BA., H.

An exact reproduction of the edition of 1683, but some slight verbal changes and typographical errors prove that it is a reprint. Both editions have a monogram AA above imprint.

HENNEPIN. [Engraved title:] Nouvelle decouverte | d'un tre grand | Pays | Situé dans L'Amerique | Par R. P. Louis de Hennepin. | *a Utrec* | *Chez Guiliaume Broedelet* | [Followed by printed title:] Nouvelle | decouverte | d'un tres grand | pays | Situé dans l'Amerique, | entre | Le Nouveau Mexique, | et | La Mer Glaciale, | Avec les Cartes, & les Figures necessaires, & de plus | l'Histoire Naturelle & Morale, & les avantages, | qu'on en peut tirer par l'établissement des Colonies. | Le tout dedie | à | Sa Majesté Britannique. | Guillaume III. | Par le | R. P. Louis Hennepin, | Missionaire Recollect & Notaire Apostolique. ¶ *A Utrecht,* | *Chez Guillaume Broedelet,* | *Marchand Libraire.* M DC XCVII. | 12mo, Engraved Title, pp. (70), 506. 2 Maps, 2 Plates, one of which is the first engraved view of Niagara Falls. BA., H., J.C.B., M. 31349

This is the first edition of the second part, it includes the substance of his first book, but gives, before the account of his voyage up the Mississippi, an account of a voyage he here claims to have made down to the mouth and up again. It is identical, in fact, with Membré's in Leclercq, which Hennepin says was taken from his account. The charges against Hennepin's veracity are based on this interpolation chiefly. The preface contains a narration of his embroglio with Mr. La Salle. *See* Trömel, No. 422. The following is the same work with a new title-page only.

HENNEPIN. Nouvelle | Découverte | d'un très grand | Pays Situé dans l'Amerique, | entre | Le Nouveau Mexique, | et La Mer Glaciale, | Avec les Cartes, et les Figures nécessaires, et de plus |

l'Histoire Naturelle et Morale, et les avantages | qu'on en peut tirer par l'établissem. des Colon. | Le tout dedié | à Sa Majesté Britannique, | Guillaume III | par le R. P. Louis Hennepin | ... *A Amsterdam, Chez Abraham van Someren* ... MDCXCVIII. 12mo, Engraved Title, pp. (70), 506. 2 Maps, 2 Plates. 31350

HENNEPIN. Nouveau | voyage | d'un Pais plus grand que | l'Europe | Avec les reflections des enterprises du Sieur | de la Salle, sur les Mines de St. Barbe, &c. | Enrichi de la Carte, de figures expressives, des mœurs | & manières de vivre des Sauvages du Nord, | & du Sud, de la prise de Quebec Ville Capital- | le de la Nouvelle France, par les Anglois, & des | avantages qu'on peut retirer du chemin recourci | de la Chine & du Japon, par le moien de tant | de Vastes Contrées & de Nouvelles Colonies. | Avec approbation & dedié à sa Majesté | Guillaume III. | Roy de la grande | Bretagne | par le | R. P. Louis Hennepin, | Missionaire Recollect & Notaire Apostolique. ¶ *A Utrecht,* | *Chez Antoine Schouten,* | *Marchand Libraire.* 1698. | 8vo, pp. (70), 1 leaf blank, pp. 389. 4 Plates, 1 Map. BA. 31351

This forms a third series of Hennepin's Travels. It is not a personal narrative, as he was but once in America. It gives an account of La Salle's unfortunate journey, and describes at greater length the manners, customs, and superstitions of the Indian tribes.

HENNEPIN. Voyage | ou Nouvelle decouverte | d'un tres-grand pays, | dans | l'Amerique, | entre le Nouveau | Mexique | et la Mer Glaciale, | Par le R. P. Louis Hennepin, | Avec toutes les particularitez de ce Païs, & de celui connu sous le nom de La Louisiane; | les avantages qu'on en peut tirer par | l'établissement des Colonies enrichie de Cartes Geographiques. | Augmenté de quelques figures en taille douce. | Avec un | voyage | Qui contient une Relation exacte de l'Origine, Mœurs, | Coutûmes, Religion, Guerres & Voyages des Caraibes, | Sauvages des Isles Antilles de L'Amerique, | Faite par la Sieur De la Borde, | Tirée du Cabinet de Monsr. Blondel. | *A Amsterdam, Chez Adriaan Braakman.* M. D. CCIV. | 12mo, Frontispiece, pp. (34), 604, (32). 2 Maps, 6 Plates. BA. 31352

Brunet says pp. 516, having probably an imperfect copy which did not include the "Voyage qui contient," etc., pp. 517–604.

HENNEPIN. Voyage Curieux | Du R. P. Louis Hennepin, | Missionaire Recollect, & Notaire Apostolique, | Qui contient une | Nouvelle Decouverte | D'un Tres-Grand Pays, | Situé dans l'Amerique, | Entre le Nouveau Mexique & la Mer Glaciale, | Avec | Toutes les particularitez de ce Pays, & les avantages qu'on | en peut tirer par l'établissement des Colonies, enrichi | de Cartes & augmenté de quelques figures | en taille douce necessaires. | Outre cela on a aussi ajoûté ici un | Voyage | Qui contient une Relation exacte de l'Origine, Mœurs, | Coûtumes, Religion, Guerres & Voyages | Des Caraibes, | Sauvages des Isles Antilles de l'Amerique, | Faite par le Sieur De La Borde, | Employé à la Conversion des Caraibes, | Et tirée du Cabinet de Mr. Blondel. | *A La Haye,* | *Chez Jean Kitto, Marchand Libraire, dans* | *le Spuy-straet.* 1704. 12mo, Two Titles, one of which is engraved, pp. (32), 604, (32). 2 Maps, 6 Plates. H.C.M. 31353

The engraved title reads, "Nouveaux Voyages du R P Louis Hennepin et de Sieur Dela Borde." This is a reprint of Hennepin's second publication entitled: "Nouvelle decouverte d'un tres grand pays situé dans l'Amerique &c." (*Utrecht,* 1697,) together with the voyage made by Sieur De la Borde to the Antilles, giving an account of the Caraibes, not elsewhere published, p. 517 (*our* No. 604), which was printed by Van der Aa. Brunet refers to this edition as a reprint of his "Nouveau Voyage," printed at *Utrecht* in 1698; and, at the same time, gives as his principal article on Hennepin this very edition containing La Borde with a different title, as if it were a different work and the first of the series. Some copies have the imprint, *A Leide: Chez Pierre van der Aa.* MDCCIV.

HENNEPIN. Voyages | curieux et nouveaux | de Messieurs Hennepin & De la Borde, | Ou l'on voit | Une Description très Particuliere, d'un Grand Pays dans L'Amérique, entre le | Nouveau Mexique, & la Mer Glaciale, avec une Relation Curieuse des | Caraibes sauvages des Isles Antilles de L'Amérique, | les Mœurs, Coutûmes, Religion, &c. | ... | *Amsterdam, Aux depens de la Compagnie.* M. DCCXI. | 12mo, oblong title, pp. (32), 604, (32). 2 Maps, 6 Plates. BA., H. 31354

The same as the edition of 1704, with a title printed in 4to.

HENNEPIN. Voyage | ou nouvelle découverte d'un très- | grand Pais, dans | l'Amérique, | entre le Nouveau Mexique | et la | Mer Glaciale. | ... Augmenté ... avec un voyage | qui contient une relation exacte de l'Origine, Mœurs, Coutûmes, Religion, Guerres et Voyages des Caraibes, | Sauvages des Isles Antilles de l'Amérique. Faite par le Sieur de la Borde. *Amsterdam: Jaques Desbordes.* 1712. 12mo, Frontispiece, pp. (34), 604. Map and Plates. 31355

Another French version (1720) is included in Bernard's "Recueil de Voyages du Nord," Vol. V. *See our* Vol. II., No. 4936, *note.*

HENNEPIN. Descrizione | della | Lvigiana ; | Paese nuouamente scoperto nel- | l'America Settentrionale, | sotto gl'auspicij | del Christianissimo | Lvigi XIV. | Con la Carta Geografica del mede- | simo; costumi, e manière di | vìuere di que' Seluaggi. Del P. Lvigi

Hennepin | Francescano Recolletto, e Missionario | Apostolico in questa Scoperta. Tradotta dal Francese, e Dedicata | al Reverendiss. P. D. Ludovico | de' Conti Gverra | Abbate Casinense de S. Procolo | di Bologna. | *In Bologna, per Giacomo Monti.* 1686. 12mo, pp. (8), 396. Map. J.C.B. 31356

This Italian translation is by Casimiro Freschot; it is a little remarkable that the first translation should have been into Italian. It does not appear ever to have been reprinted.

HENNEPIN. [Engraved title:] Ontdekking van | Louisania | Door den Vader L. Hennepin. | Benevens de Beschryving van Noord-America | door den Heer Denys. | *'tAmsterdam by Jan ten Hoorn ...* 1688. | [Printed title:] Beschryving | van | Louisania, | Nieuwelijks ontdekt ten Zuid-Westen | van | Nieuw-Vrankryk, | Door order van den Koning. | Met de Kaart des Landts, en een nauwkeurige verhande- | ling van de Zeden en manieren van leeven der Wilden. | Door Den | Vader Lodewyk Hennepin, | Recollet-sche Missionaris in die Gewesten, en | Apostolische Notaris. | Mitsgaders de | Geographische en Historische Beschrijving der Kusten | van | Noord-America, | Met de Natuurlijke Histoire des Landts. | Door den Heer Denys, | Gouverneur Lieutenant Generaal voor Zijn Allerchriste- | lijkste Majesteit, en Eigenaar van alle de Landen en Ei- | landen gelegen van Cap de Campseaux tot aan Cap des Roziers. | Verçiert met Kopere Figuren. ¶ *t'Amsterdam,* | *By Jan ten Hoorn, Boekverkooper over 't Oude | Heeren Logement, in de Histori-Schryver. A.* 1688. | 4to, Two Titles, one of which is engraved, pp. (4), 158, (5), Map and 6 Plates; followed by "Geographische ... Door den Heer Denys," pp. (4), 200, (4). J.C.B.

This first edition in Dutch consists of a translation of our No. 31347 [*Paris.* 1683], with the addition of Denys' geographical and historical description of the Coasts of North America, as described in our Vol. IV., Nos. 19615, 19616. The map is entitled: "Kaart van Nieuw Vrankrijk en van Louisania."

HENNEPIN. [Engraved title:] Reyse | door | Nieuwe Ondekte | Landen [Printed title:] Aenmerckelycke | Historische | Reys-Beschryvinge | Door verscheyde Landen veel grooter als die van geheel | Europa | onlanghs ontdeckt. | Behelsende een nauwkeurige Beschrijvinge van gelegentheyd, natuur, en | vrughtbaerheyd, van't Zuyder, en Noorder gedeelte van America; mitsgaders | de gedaente, aerd, manieren, kledingen, en't geloove der talrijke Wilde Natien | aldaer woonende. Het beleg en veroveringe van Quebek, de Hooft-stad van Cana- | da, door de Engelschen. De gewigtige aenmerkingen op de onderneminge van de | Heer de la Salle, op de Goud-Mijnen van St. Barbara, met veel meer andere | waeragtige en seldsame geschiedenissen. En in't besonder de

aenwijsingen om | door een korten wegh sonder de Linie Equinoctiael te passeeren, na China en | Japan te komen; en de groote voordeelen die men hier door, als mede door de | nieuwe Volckplantingen in dese vrughtbaare Landen sou konnen trecken. Alles | met een nette Kaert tot dese | aenwijsinge nodig, en kopere Platen verciert. | Met Approbatie van | Wilhelmus den III. | Koningh | van | Groot-Britanie. | En aan deselve sijne Majesteyt opgedragen | door | Lodewyck Hennepin, | Missionaris Recollect, en Notaris Apostoliek. | *Tot Utrecht,* | *By Anthony Schouten.* 1698. | 4to, Two Titles, one of which is engraved, pp. (28), 142 [misnumbered 242], (18). Map and 4 Plates. BA. 31358

This is a translation of the "Nouvelle découverte," No. 31349. *Utrecht.* 1697. The map is entitled: "Carte d'un Nouveau monde entre le Nouveau Mexique et la Mer Glaciale. Gasp. Bouttats fecit."

HENNEPIN. Nieuwe Ontdekkinge | Van een groot Land, gelegen in | America, | tusschen nieuw Mexico | en de | Ys-Zee. | Behelzende de gelegentheid der zelve nieuwe ontdekte Landen: de Rivieren en | groote Meeren in't zelve. En voor al van de groote Rivier Meschasipi genaamd. | De Kolonien die men by de zelve tot voordeel van dezen Staat, zo ten opzich- | te van den Koophandel, als tot verzekeringe der Spaansche Goud-Mijnen, | zou konnen oprechten. De uitneemende vruchtbaarheid van 't Land; over- | vloed der Visschen in den Rivieren. De gedaanten, inborst, geloove en oeffe- | ningen der Wilden aldaar woonende. De vreemde Dieren in haare Rosschen en | Velden. Met een korte aanmerkinge over de zo genaamde Straat Aniam; en | 't middel om door een korte weg, zonder de Linie Æquinoctiaal te passee- ren, | na China en Japan te komen met veele curieuse dingen meer. Alles met goede | Kaarten tot deze aanwijzinge nodig, en met Kopere Plaaten vercierd. | Met goed-vindinge van den | Koning van Engeland | Wilhelmus den III. | In 't licht gegeeven: | En aan de zelve zijne Majesteit opgedraagen, | door | Lodewyk Hennepin, | Missionaris Recollect en Notaris Apostoliek. ¶ *Tot Amsterdam,* | *By Abraham van Someren.* 1699. | 4to, pp. (26), 220, (14). 2 Maps, Plate. 31359

The maps are entitled: 1st. "Carte d'un très grand pais ... Chez A. v. Someren à Amsterdam;" 2d. "Amérique Septentrionalis [*sic.*] Carte d'un très grands pays ... Chez A. v. Someren à Amsterdam 1698. J. v. Vianen fecit."

. HENNEPIN. Nieuwe Ontdekkinge | Van een Groot Land, gelegen | in America, | Tusschen nieuw | Mexico en de Ys-Zee. | Behelzende de gelegenheid der zelve nieuwe ontdekte Landen, | de Rivieren en groote Meeren, en voor al de groote Rivier Me-

schasipi genaamd: | de Colonien die men by de zelve tot voordeel van dezen Staat, | zo ten opzichte van den Koophandel, als tot verzekeringe der Spaan- | sche Goud-Mijnen, zou konnen oprechten; ... . Benevens een Aanhangsel, behelzende een Reize door een | gedeelte van de Spaansche West-Indiën, en een Verhaal | van d'Expeditie der Franschen op Cartagena. | Door L[ouis] de C[apiné]. *Tot Amsterdam,* | *By Andries van Damme, Boekverkooper ...* 1702. | 4to, Two Titles, one of which is engraved, pp. (24), 220, (14). 2 Maps, the same as in our former number, and 2 Plates; "Aanhangsel," pp. 47, Map and Plate. BA. 31360

This is a translation of the "Nouvelle Découverte" of Hennepin, and has the two maps and two plates which are found in the original; it also contains an Appendix consisting of Capiné's Voyage through the Spanish West Indies, and an account of the French expedition to Cartagena. The engraved title reads, "Nieuwe Ontdekkinge in America Gedaan Door L. Hennepin."

HENNEPIN. Aenmerkelyke Voyagie | Gedaan na't | Gedeelte van Noorder America, | Behelzende een nieuwe ontdekkinge van een seer | Groot Land, gelegen tusschen | Nieuw Mexico en de Ys-Zee. | Vervattende de gelegentheid der zelve nieuwe ontdekte Lan- | den; de Revieren en groote Meeren in't zelve. En voor al van de groote Revier Meschasipi genaamd. Die Kolonien die men by de zelve tot voordeel van dezen Staat, zo ten opzichte van den | Koophandel, als tot verzekeringe der Spaansche Goud Mijnen | zou kunnen oprechten. De uitnemende vruchtbaarheid van't | Land, overvloed der Visschen in die Revieren. De gedaanten, | inborst, geloove en oeffeningen der Wilden aldaar woonende. | De vreemde Dieren in Haare Bosschen en Velden. Met een | korte aanmerkinge over de zogenaamde Straat Aniam; en't | middel om door een korte weg, zonder der Linie Æquinoctiaal | te passeeren, na China en Japan te komen met veele andere by- | sonderheden meer. Door Lodewyk Hennepin, | Missionaris Recollect en Notaris Apostoliek. | Desen laatsten Druk is niet alleen verçierd, met noodige Kaarten | maar ook met verscheide Kopere Printverbeeldingen, | noyt te vooren soo gesien. | *Te Leyden,* | *By Pieter van der Aa.* 1704. | 4to, pp. (22), 219, (13). 6 Plates, 2 Maps. 31361

HENNEPIN. Aanmerkelyke voyagie | gedaan na 't | gedeelde van | Noorder America, | behelzende een nieuwe ontdekkinge van een seer | groot land, gelegen tusschen | Nieuw-Mexico en de Ys-zee, | ... *Rotterdam: B. Bos.* 1704. Sm. 4to, pp. (22), 200, (14). 2 Maps, 6 Plates. C. 31362

Usually found with Benzoni (G.), "De gedenkwaardige West-Indise voyagien," etc., and is also included in Van der Aa's Collection of Voyages. *Leyden.* 1704.

HENNEPIN. Nieuwe Ontdekkinge, van groote Lande in Amerika, tusschen Nieuw Mexico en de Ys-Zee. ... Benevens ... een Reize door een gedeelte van de Spaanisch West Indien, door L. de Capiné. Met Kaarten en Kopere Plaat. *Amsterdam.* 1722. 4to. 31363

HENNEPIN. Beschreibung der Landschaft Louisiana welche auf Befehl des Königs in Frankreich neulich gegen Süd-Westen Neu Frankreichs in America gefunden. *Nürnberg: Andreas Otto.* 1692. 18mo, pp. 427. Map. J.C.B. 31364

HENNEPIN. Neue Entdeckungen vieler sehr grossen Landschaften in America zwischen Neu Mexico und dem Eis-Meer gelegen, übersetzt von J. G. Langen. *Bremen.* 1690. 31365

Title from Ternaux, No. 1049—perhaps an error as to place and date.

HENNEPIN. Neue | Reise Beschreibung | durch viele Länder weit grösser als gantz | Europa, | ... durch L. Hennepin. | *Bremen: Phil. Gottfr. Saurmans.* 1698. | 8vo, pp. (64), 288. J.C.B.

HENNEPIN. Neue | Entdeckung | vieler sehr grossen | Landschafften | in | America zwischen Neu-Mexico und dem Eyss- | Meer gelegen. ... Ins Teutsche übersetzt durch | M. J. G. Langen. | Mit Land-Charten und Kupffer Figuren. *Bremen: Philip Gottfr. Saurmans.* 1699. 12mo, pp. (66), 382. Map and Plates.

HENNEPIN. Neue | Reise | Beschreibung | nach | America, | und derer | bisher noch unbekandten Län- | der und Völcker, | vornemlich | von der Landschafft | Lovisiana, | und den Sitten und Lebens Art der Wil- | den in selbiger Landschafft. | Aus dem Französischen über- | setzt und mit Kupfern geziert. *Nürnberg.* 1739. *Im Verlag Christ. Fried. Feisze.* 18mo, pp. 425. 2 Maps.

HENNEPIN. Reisen | und seltsahme | Begebenheiten; Oder sonderbare Entdeckung | vieler sehr grossen | Länder | in Amerika. Welche biszhero noch unbekannt | gewesen, und an Grösse gantz Euro- | pa übertreffen, etc. *Bremen: Nathaniel Saurmann.* 1742. 18mo, pp. (24), 382. 2 Maps and Plate. J.C.B. 31369

HENNEPIN. A | New Discovery | of a | Vast Country in America, | Extending above Four Thousand Miles, | between | New France and New Mexico; | with a | Description of the Great Lakes, Cata- | racts, Rivers, Plants, and Animals. | Also, the Manners, Customs, and Languages of the se- | veral Native Indians; and the Advantage of Com- | merce with those different Nations. | With a | Continuation, | Giving an Account of the | Attempts of

the Sieur De la Salle upon the | Mines of St. Barbe, &c. The taking of | Quebec by the English; With the Advantages | of a Shorter Cut to China and Japan. | Both Parts Illustrated with Maps, and Figures, | and Dedicated to His Majesty K. William. | By L. Hennepin, now Resident in Holland. | To which are added, Several New Discoveries in North- | America, not publish'd in the French Edition. | *London, Printed for M. Bentley, J. Tonson,* | *H. Bonwick, T. Goodwin, and S. Manship.* 1698. | 8vo, Two Titles, one of which is engraved, pp. (20), 243; Pt. II., pp. (32), 228. 2 Maps, 7 Plates. H. 31370

HENNEPIN. [Same title.] *London: Printed for M. Bentley, J. Tonson, H. Bon- | wick, T. Goodwin and S. Manship.* 1698. | 8vo, Two Titles, one of which is engraved, pp. (20), 299, (1); Pt. II. pp. (32), 178, (2), 303–355. 2 Maps, 7 Plates. 31371

The only difference between the contents of these two editions, date 1698, is in their arrangement. In this edition the entire work fills 585 pages, and in the former only 525, the type being smaller.

HENNEPIN. A | New Discovery | of a | Vast Country in America, | Extending above Four Thousand Miles, | between | New France & New Mexico; | with a | Deseription [*sic*] of the Great Lakes, Cataracts, | Rivers, Plants, and Animals. | Also, the Manners, Customs, and Languages of the several | Native Indians; And the Advantage of Commerce with | those different Nations. | With a | Continuation | Giving an Account of the | Attempts of the Sieur de la Salle upon the | Mines of St. Barbe, &c. The Taking of Quebec | by the English; With the Advantages of a | shorter Cut to China and Japan. | Both Illustrated with Maps, and Figures; and Dedicated | to His Majesty King William. | By L. Hennepin now Resident in Holland. | To which are added, Several New Discoveries in North- | America, not Publish'd In [*sic*] the French Edition. | *London, Printed for Henry Bonwicke, at the Red Lion* | *in St. Paul's Church-Yard.* 1699. | 8vo, Engraved Title, pp. (20), 240; Pt. II. pp. (24), 216. 2 Maps, 6 Plates. BA.

The second paging has the title "A Continuation of the New Discovery ... ."

[HENNEPIN.] A | Discovery Of a Large, Rich, and Plentiful | Country | in the | North America; | Extending above 4000 Leagues. Wherein, | By a very short Passage, lately found | out, thro' the Mer-Barmejo into the South- | Sea; by which a considerable Trade might | be carry'd on, as well in the Northern as | the Southern Parts of America. | *London: W. Boreham.* [1720.] 8vo, pp. (2), 22. BA. 31373

Evidently an abridgment.

HENNEPIN. Relacion | de un pais | que nuevamente se ha descu- | bierto | en la | America | Septentrional | de mas estendido que es | la Europa. | Y que saca à luz en Castellano, debajo de la proteccion de ... Don Sebastian Fernandez de Medrano. | *Brusselas:* | *Lamberto Marchant.* | M.DC.XCIX. | 12mo, pp. (8), 86. Map and 2 Plates. J.C.B. 31374

This Spanish version, which is of course an abridgment, concludes our long list of the various editions of the work of this famed traveller, who was "the undoubted discoverer and explorer of the Upper Mississippi, and the first to lay open to the world that mighty region." That he should have made some mistakes is not to be wondered at, and that when he first saw the Falls of Niagara he should have overstated the "wonderful downfall of above 600 feet," is not very surprising; but his mistakes have not entitled him to receive the castigations which have been heaped upon him. Bancroft, Vol. III., 202, remarks: "Had he loved truth, he would have gained a noble reputation, who now is remembered, not merely as a light-hearted and daring discoverer, but also as a boastful liar. The Journal of a voyage down the Mississippi in this book is a lie by the author." Charlevoix was the first to attack the author, not so much with reference to the truth of his statements as to his manners. He remarks that Hennepin "vents his chagrin not only on the Sieur de la Sale, but on France also, by which he deemed himself ill used, and he tries to save his credit by declaring himself a born subject of the Catholic King. But he should have remembered that it was at the expense of France that he travelled in America, and that it was in the name of the most Christian King that he and the Sieur Dacan took possession of the countries which they had discovered. He does not even hesitate to aver that it was with the consent of the Catholic King, his first sovereign, that he dedicated his book to William III., King of England, and that he solicited that monarch to effect the conquest of those vast tracts, send colonies there, and have the gospel preached to the heathen. This step, which scandalized the Catholics, and made even Protestants laugh, surprised to see a *religieux*, calling himself Missionary and Apostolic Prothonotary, exhort a Protestant Prince to found a church in the New World. All these works are written in a declamatory style, offensive by its inflation, and revolting by the liberties which the author takes, and by his indecent invectives. As to substance, Father Hennepin believed himself entitled to take a traveller's license; he is accordingly much decried in Canada, his fellow-travellers often protesting that he was anything but truthful in his accounts."—*New France,* Vol. I. On which we remark that it must be recollected that Charlevoix (whose remarks are ungrammatical) was a Jesuit, and that Hennepin belonged to an order who were opposed to them, that he should have solicited the assistance of William III. is simply a proof that he was no bigot. Mr. Field very properly observes that "criticism [on Hennepin] proceeds from sources which entitle him to the benefit at least of a doubt of its impartiality," and adds, "The author lost the support of his own brethren of the order of Recollects by neglecting or refusing to return to his duties in America as a missionary." "This Reverend Father was the most impudent of liars, and the narrative is a rare monument of brazen mendacity. Hennepin, however, had seen much and dared much: for among his many failings fear had no part; and where his vanity or his spite was not involved he often told the truth. ... These fabrications occur, not in the early editions, which are comparatively truthful, but in the edition of 1697, and those which followed. La Salle was dead at the time of their publication."—PARKMAN'S *Discovery of the Great West,* p. 124. The question of Hennepin's veracity, as to his claim of descending the Mississippi, was first raised by Sparks' "Life of La Salle," "Amer. Biog.," II. 1, followed by Shea, Parkman, etc. A portion of Hennepin's first work is given in Shea's "Discovery of the Mississippi," and his "New Discovery" is included in the "Amer. Ant. Soc. Trans.," Vol. I. *See* Faribault's "Bibl.," *also* "N. Am. Rev.," XLVIII. 70; XLIX. 258.

HENNI (J. M.) Ein Blick in's Thal des Ohio oder Briefe über den Kampf und das Wiederaufleben der katholischen Kirche im fernen Westen der Vereinigten Staaten Nordamerikas. *München.* 1836. 8vo, pp. 128. 31375

The author is now Bishop of Milwaukie.

HENNIG (Christian Gottfried). Briefe über Amerika nach der neuesten, verbeszerten und mit dem dritten Theile vermehrten Ausgabe, aus dem Italianischen des Herrn Grafen Carlo Carli übersetzt, und mit einigen Anmerkungen versehen. *Gera: Christoph Friedrich Bekmann.* 1795. 3 vols., 12mo, pp. 468; 502; 368. Map. 31376

I have a memorandum of an edition, *Gera.* 1785. 2 vols., 12mo.

HENNING (T.) Slavery in the Churches, Religious Societies, &c. A Review by Thomas Henning, Esq. With Prefatory Remarks, By J. J. E. Linton, Esq., Stratford. *Toronto.* 1856. 12mo, pp. 39. 31377

HENNINGSEN (C. F.) Letter from Gen. C. F. Henningsen, in reply to the Letter of Victor Hugo on the Harper's Ferry Invasion; with an Extract from the Letter of the Rev. Nathan Lord, D.D. ... and an Article from the London "Times" on Slavery. *New York: Davies & Kent, Printers.* 1860. 8vo, pp. 32.

HENRION (*Le Baron* Mathieu R. A.) Histoire générale des Missions Catholiques depuis le XIIIe Siècle jusqu'à nos jours. Illustré par trois cents gravures. *Paris: Gaume frères.* 1844–47. 2 vols., imp. 8vo. 31379

HENRION. Historia general de las misiones, desde el siglo XIII. hasta nuestros dias. Traducida al castellano, ampliada y adicionada en lo perteneciente á España. *Barcelona.* 1863–65. 4 vols., 8vo. 117 Plates, 17 Portraits, 8 Maps. 31380

HENRIQUEZ. Don Henriquez | De | Castro. | Or, the Conquest | of the Indies. | A | Spanish Novel. | Translated out of Spanish, by a Person | of Honour. | *London,* | *Printed by R. E. for R. Bentley* | *and S. Magnes, in Russell-Street* | *in Covent-Garden.* [1685.] 12mo, pp. (12), 167. H. 31381

HENRIQUEZ (F.) Francisci Henriquez Soc. Jes. Epistola de duodecim sociis, pro catholica fide, in mari Brasilico interfectis anno de 1550. *Neapoli, Ap. J. Cochium.* 1572. 31382

Title from Ternaux, No. 117. Not in Carayon. The Backers, in the "Bibl. de la Soc.," have the following title: "Carta escrita a 5 de Dezembro de 1571, aos Padres Assistentes em Roma que relata largamente o glorioso martyrio de Padre Pedro Dias e seus companheiros em osmares de Brasil a 13 de Setembro de 1571," with the note "Traduite en Italien et *imprimée à Naples par Joseph Cochia*, 1572. Le P. Manoel da Costa l'a traduite en latin, p. 462 de: 'Rerum a Soc. Jesu in India Gestarum. *Coloniæ*, 1574.' 8vo. La même lettre a été traduite en latin par le P. Maffée, in Epistolis Indicis; à la fin de la seconde Epitre."

Henry (A.) Travels and Adventures in Canada and the Indian Territories, between the years 1760 and 1776. In Two Parts. By Alexander Henry Esq. *New York: I. Riley.* 1809. 8vo, pp. vi, (1), 330. Portrait. BA., H., P. 31383

Henry escaped almost miraculously from the massacre at Detroit, in the war occasioned by the conspiracy of Pontiac, of which he gives a thrilling account. "His perils, enterprise, and intrepidity excite deep interest."—*Chancellor* Kent. The narrative of his long captivity affords us the most authentic information we have, relative to the domestic habits of the northern Indians. *See* a long extract from the Preface in Rich, Vol. II. 42. *See also* "Hist. Mag.," III. 226.

Henry (A. A.) Direccion general de cartas de España à sus Indias; no solo segun el orden geografico general, sino por el particular que rige en el ramo de correos de unas administraciones à otras y caxas de las Americas à que deven remitirse, como tanbien á Canarias y a Filipinas, &c. Formada por D. Angel Ant° Henry, &c. *Madrid.* 1807. 2 vols., 4to. 31384

Henry (Caleb Sprague). American Advocate of Peace: Conducted by C. S. Henry, and Francis Fellowes. Vols. I. and II. *Hartford: William Watson.* 1834–36. 8vo. 31385

Henry. History and its Philosophy: The Address at the Sixty-Third Anniversary of the New-York Historical Society, Dec. 19, 1867. By C. S. Henry, D.D. *New-York: [New-York Historical Society].* 1868. 8vo, pp. 16. H. 31386

Henry. Patriotism and the Slaveholders' Rebellion. An Oration, By C. S. Henry. *New York: D. Appleton and Company.* 1861. 8vo, pp. 34. 31387

Henry. Politics and the Pulpit: A Tract for the Times. ... *New York: John F. Trow.* [1860.] 8vo, pp. (2), 355–400. H.

Also: Doctor Oldham at Greystones, and his Talk there. ... *New York: D. Appleton and Company.* 1860. 12mo, pp. viii, 342. Plate. B.—The Importance of Exalting the Intellectual Spirit of the Nation: and Need of a Learned Class. A Discourse pronounced before the Phi Sigma Nu Society of the University of Vermont, August 3, 1836. ... *Burlington.* 1836. 8vo, pp. 44. B., H. + Second Edition. *New York: George W. Holley.* 1837. 8vo, pp. 44. BA.—On Social Welfare and Human Progress. *New York.* 1861. 12mo.— ... Plain Reasons for the Great Republican Movement. .. Remarks ... at ... Geneva, N. Y., July 19, 1856. ... Second Edition. *New York: Dix, Edwards & Co.* 1856. 8vo, pp. 20. H., S.—The Position and Duties of the Educated Men of the Country. A Discourse pronounced before the Euglossian and Alpha Phi Delta Societies of Geneva College, Aug. 5, 1840. ... *New York.* MDCCCXL. 8vo, pp. 46. (1), H., N.—Principles and Prospects of the Friends of Peace. A Dis-

course pronounced before the Hartford County Peace Society. December, 25, 1833. ... *Hartford: J. Hubbard Wells, Print.* 1834. 8vo, pp. 27. BA. + 8vo, pp. 31. B.—The True Idea of the University, and its Relation to a Complete System of Public Instruction. An Address before the ... Alumni of the University of the City of New-York, June 28, 1852. ... *New-York.* 1853. 8vo, pp. 27. H., M.

[Henry (David).] An Historical Account of all the Voyages round the Word, performed by English Navigators; including those lately undertaken By Order of his Present Majesty. The whole Faithfully Extracted from the Journals of the Voyagers. Drake, undertaken in 1577–80. Cavendish, 1586–88. Cowley, 1683–86. Dampier, 1689–96. Cooke, 1708–11. Rogers, 1708–11. Clipperton and Shelvocke, 1719–22. Anson, undertaken in 1740–44. Byron, 1764–66. Wallis, 1766–68. Carteret, 1766–69, and Cook, 1768–71. Together with that of Sydney Parkinson, Draftsman to Joseph Banks, Esq; who circumnavigated the Globe with Capt. Cook, in his Majesty's Ship the Endeavour. And The Voyage of Mons. Bougainville round the World, Performed by Order of the French King. Illustrated with Maps, Charts, and Historical Prints. ... To which is added, An Appendix. Containing the Journal of a Voyage to the North Pole, by the Hon. Commodore Phipps, and Captain Lutwidge. *London: F. Newbery.* MDCCLXXIV–MDCCLXXIII. 4 vols., 8vo, pp. (1), l, (6), 480; (1), 440; (4), 470; (4), 364, (3); Supplement, 118. 43 Plates, 7 Maps and Charts. H. 31389

"The first two volumes were compiled by David Henry, a great contributor to the 'Gentleman's Magazine,' and who added a fifth volume in 1775, and a sixth in 1776, containing Capt. Cooke's second and third voyages; introduced by an admirable summary of all the voyages undertaken for discovery only, in both the Southern and Northern hemispheres, and in the Pacific and Atlantic Oceans."—Nichols' *Literary Anecdotes*, Vol. III., p. 425. In some copies the collation varies from our statement.

Henry (G.) Emigrants Guide. By George Henry. *Quebec.* [n. d.] 12mo. 31390

Henry (G. W.) Incidents in the Life of George W. Henry. Dictated by himself, being blind. *Utica: R. W. Roberts, Printer.* 1846. 18mo, pp. 305. 31391

The author was a peripatetic bookseller and preacher in Western New York.

Henry (G. A.) Speech of Hon. Gustavus A. Henry, of Tennessee, in the Senate of the Confederate States, November 29, 1864. [n. p. n. d.] 8vo, pp. 13. BA. 31392

Declaring a resolution to prosecute the war to independence.

Henry (G. V.) Military Record of Civilian Appointments in the United States Army. By Guy V. Henry ... . Vol. I. *Carleton, New York.* MDCCCLXIX. 8vo, pp. 527. B., C. 31393

[Henry (J.)] An Enquiry into the Evils of General Suffrage and Frequent Elections in Lower Canada. By Camillus. ... *Montreal: Printed by Nahum Mower.* 1810. 8vo, pp. 32. H.

Henry (J.) Sketches of Moravian Life and Character. Comprising a General View of the History, Life, Character, and Religious and Educational Institutions of the Unitas Fratrum. By James Henry ... . *Philadelphia: J. B. Lippincott & Co.* 1859. 12mo, pp. 316, (1). B., BA. 31395

Henry (J.), *Jr.* An Address upon Education and Common Schools, delivered at Cooperstown ... Otsego County, Sept. 21, [1843.] By James Henry, Jr. *Albany: Press of C. Van Benthuysen and Co.* 1843. 8vo, pp. (4), 58. B., M. + Second Edition. *New York: A. S. Barnes & Co.* 1846. 8vo, pp. 64. .B.

Also: The Mechanics' Institute—Past, Present and Future. *New York.* 1854. 8vo. S.

[Henry (John).] The Hand-book of the Nation: ... Dedicated to the People of America. *New-York.* 1852. 12mo, pp. 33.

Henry (J.) Report on the Criminal Law at Demerara, and in the ceded Dutch Colonies. *London.* 1821. 8vo. S. 31398

Also: Report of the Judgment of the Court of Demarara, in the Case of Odwin *v.* Forbes, on the Plea of the English Certificate of Bankruptcy, in Bar in a Foreign Jurisdiction, to the suit of a Foreign Creditor, as confirmed in Appeal; with the Authorities, and Foreign and English Cases. *London.* 1823. 8vo. S.

[Henry (John).] The Essex Junto and the British Spy: or, Treason Detected. *Printed at Salem, March,* 1812. 8vo, pp. 36.

Henry (J. J.) An Accurate and Interesting Account of the Hardships and Sufferings of that Band of Heroes, who Traversed the Wilderness in the Campaign against Quebec in 1775. By John Joseph Henry Esq ... *Lancaster: Printed by William Greer.* 1812. 12mo, pp. 225. B., BA., H. 31400

First and best edition of a narrative of rare interest, addressed to his children Reprinted with the following title:

Henry. Library Edition. Campaign against Quebec; being an Accurate and Interesting Account of the Hardships and Sufferings of that Band of Heroes who traversed the Wilderness, by the Route of the Kennebec and Chaudiere River, to Quebec, in the year 1775. By John Joseph Henry. Revised Edition, with Corrections and Alterations. *Watertown: Knowlton & Rice.* 1844. 12mo, pp. 212. C. 31401

Henry (J.) A Statement of Facts respecting the Condition & Treatment of Slaves, in the City of Vicksburg and its Vicinity in the State of Mississippi, in 1838 & 39. By Joseph Henry. *Medina, Ohio.* 1839. 12mo, pp. 24. 31402

Henry (J.) Eulogy on Prof. Alexander Dallas Bache, late Superintendent of the United States Coast Survey, ... By Prof. Joseph Henry, ... *Washington: Government Printing Office.* 1872. 8vo, pp. 28. 31403

Also: Smithsonian Bequest. Prof. Henry's Exposition before the New Jersey Historical Society at ... Princeton, ... September 27th, 1847. ... 8vo, pp. 8. H.—An Account of the Smithsonian Institution, ... Aug. 10th, 1853. ... *Newark.* 1854. 8vo, pp. 15. *See also* "Smithsonian Report," 1870, and "Smithsonian Collections."

Henry (M. S.) History of the Lehigh Valley, Containing a Copious Selection of the Most Interesting Facts, Traditions, Biographical Sketches, Anecdotes, etc., etc., relating to its History and Antiquities. With a Complete History of all its Internal Improvements, Progress of the Coal and Iron Trade, Manufactures, etc., By M. S. Henry. ... *Easton, Pa.: Bixler and Corwin.* 1860. 8vo, pp. xii, 436. 31404

First published in parts and now very scarce.

Henry (*Mr.*) American Documents relative to Mr. Henry's Mission, Collected and Re-Printed. *London: J. Ridgway.* 1812. 8vo, pp. 28. 31405

Henry (M. M.) Bibliothèque portative des voyages; traduite de l'anglais par M. M. Henry et Breton. Avec Gravures et Atlas. *Paris.* [v. d.] 42 vols., 18mo. 31406

This large collection of voyages and travels includes many relative to America.

Henry (P. F.) Tableau de la colonie de Cayenne, à la suite du voyage à Surinam, de Stedman. Par P. F. Henry. *Paris.* 1798. 8vo. 31407

Henry (P.) An Argument on the Powers, Duties, and Conduct, of the Hon. John C. Calhoun, A Vice-President of the United States, and President of the Senate. By Patrick Henry. *Washington: P. Force.* 1827. 8vo, pp. 56. 31408

See [Henry (W. W.)], Sparks (J.), Wirt (W.), and Williston (E. B.)

Henry (R.) ... A Sermon ... before the Society in Scotland for propagating Christian Knowledge ... June 5, 1773. By Robert Henry, D.D. ... *Edinburgh: Printed by A. Murray & J. Cochran.* MDCCLXXIII. 8vo, pp. (4), 29, 5, 3. H. 31409

Henry [Robert P.] Speech of Mr. Henry, on the Proposition to amend the Constitution ... respecting the Election of President and Vice-President. ... April 1, 1826. [n. p. n. d.] 8vo, pp. 15. H. 31410

Henry (R. R.) A Letter to the New-York Chamber of Commerce on "Discretionary Power," with An Appendix, ... By Robert R. Henry, one of the Inspectors of Pot and Pearl Ashes for New-York, ... *New-York: Printed for the Author.* 1830. 12mo, pp. 124. BA., W. 31411

Henry (S.) A New and Complete American Medical Family, Herbal. By Samuel Henry. *New York.* 1814. 8vo. S.

Henry (S. C.) Oration before the Cincinnati Society of New Jersey, Trenton, July 5, 1824. By Symmes C. Henry. *Trenton.* 1824. 8vo. N. 31413

Henry. The Pestilence ... A Sermon ... August the Third, 1849. The Day of National Fast. By Symmes C. Henry ... . *Princeton, N. J.: Printed by John T. Robinson.* 1849. 8vo, pp. 18.

Henry (T. C.) A Plea for the West: Sermon before the Missionary Society of the Synod of South Carolina and Georgia, Nov. 21, 1824. By T. Charlton Henry. *Charleston.* 1824. 12mo. W. 31415

Also: Farewell Discourse, Columbia, South Carolina, January 4, 1824. ... *Charleston.* 1824. 12mo, pp. 30. N.— ... A Sermon ... Third of April, 1825, being the Fourteenth Anniversary of the ... Second Presbyterian Church, in Charleston S. C. ... *Charleston: Printed by Wm. Riley.* 1825. 8vo, pp. 35. B.

[Henry (Walter).] Trifles from my Portfolio; or, Recollections of Scenes and Small Adventures during Twenty-Nine Years Military Service in the Peninsular War and Invasion of France, the East Indies, Campaign in Nepaul, St. Helena during the Detention and until the Death of Napoleon, and Upper and Lower Canada. By a Staff Surgeon. *Quebec.* 1839. 2 vols., 4to. 31416

Reprinted in England as:

Henry. Events of a Military Life. being Recollections after Service in the Peninsular War, Invasion of France, the East Indies, St. Helena, Canada, and elsewhere. By Walter Henry, ... Second Edition, Revised and Enlarged. *London: William Pickering.* 1843. 2 vols., post 8vo, pp. xii, 301; x, 384. H.

Henry (W. S.) Campaign Sketches of the War with Mexico. By Captain William S. Henry. ... With Engravings. *New York: Harper & Brothers.* 1847. 12mo, pp. 331. B. + [*Ibid.*] 1848.

[Henry (William Wirt).] Character and Public Career of Patrick Henry. Comments upon Mr. Jefferson's Letter. ... November 22, 1867. [n. p. n. d.] 8vo, pp. 8. H. 31419

Henry; or, the Juvenile Traveller, a Delineation of a Voyage across the Atlantic; a Description of a part of the United States [Lakes George and Champlain, etc.]; a Journey to Canada, etc. By the Wife of a British Officer in Canada. *London.* 1836. 8vo. 31420

Henry Roberts; or, Incidents of the War of 1861–62–63. By the Author of "Elfie Grafton," &c., &c. *Boston: Mass. Sunday School Society.* 1863. 16mo, pp. 120. Frontispiece.

Henshaw (D.) Letters on the Internal Improvements and Commerce of the West. By Hon. David Henshaw. *Boston: Dutton and Wentworth.* 1839. 8vo, pp. 29. B., BA., M. 31422

[Henshaw.] A Refutation, by his Friends, of the Calumnies against David Henshaw, in Relation to the Failure of the Commonwealth Bank, and the Transfer of South Boston Lands to the United States. *Boston: Beals and Greene.* 1844. 8vo, pp. 60.

[Henshaw.] Remarks upon the Bank of the United States, being an Examination of the Report of the Committee of Ways and Means, made to Congress, April, 1830. By a Merchant. *Boston: Printed by True and Greene, February,* 1831. 8vo, pp. 47.

[Henshaw.] Remarks upon the Rights and Powers of Corporations, and of the Rights, Powers, and Duties of the Legislature. ... *Boston: Beals and Greene.* 1837. 8vo, pp. 31. B.

Also: An Address ... before an Assembly of Citizens from all parts of the Commonwealth, at ... Boston, July 4, 1836. ... *Boston: Beals and Greene.* 1836. 8vo, pp. 39. B., BA.— ... The Exchequer and Currency ... recommended by the President of the United States, and the Effects of Paper Money upon the ... Whole Community. [*Boston.* 1842.] 8vo, pp. 8. BA.

Henshaw (J. C.) Proceedings of a General Court Martial which convened at Fort Washitaw (Indian Territory), on the 20th of November, 1855, for the Trial of Brevet Major John C. Henshaw, United States Army. Taken from the Official Records. Privately printed. *New York.* 1858. 8vo. C. 31426

Henshaw (John Prentis Hewley). Memoir of the Life of the Rt. Rev. Richard Channing Moore, D.D., Bishop of the Protestant Episcopal Church in the Diocese of Virginia. By J. P. K. Henshaw, D.D. Accompanied by a Selection of the Sermons of the late Bishop. *Philadelphia: W. Stavely & Co.* 1843. 8vo, pp. (2), x, 9–503. Portrait. C., P. 31427

Henshaw. ... A Sermon ... at the Consecration of the Rev. George Burgess, D.D. as Bishop of the Protestant Episcopal Church in Maine, ... October 31st, 1847, ... Hartford, Connecticut, By J. P. K. Henshaw, D.D., Bishop of Rhode-Island. *Providence: Charles Burnett, Jr.* 1847. 8vo, pp. 24. B. 31428

Henshaw. A Statement of Facts, relating to the late Ordination at Grace Church, with the Correspondence ... between the Rt. Rev. J. P. K. Henshaw, D.D. and the Rev. James W. Cooke, Rector of St. Michael's Church, Bristol, R. I. *Providence: Charles Burnett, Jr.* 1847. 8vo, pp. 72. H. 31429

Also: A Discourse delivered in ... Providence, on the occasion of the Third Jubilee, or One Hundred and Fiftieth Anniversary of the Society for the Propagation of the Gospel in Foreign Parts. ... June 22, 1851. ... *Providence: J. F. Moore.* 1851. 8vo, pp. 36.—Funeral Sermon occasioned by Death of W. H. Harrison, late President ... delivered April 25, 1841. ... *Baltimore.* 1841. 8vo.—An Oration ... before the ... Alumni of Middlebury College, at the ... Commencement ... 15th August, 1827. ... *Middlebury: Printed by J. W. Copeland.* 1827. 8vo, pp. 48. B.—The Right of the Clergy to Temporal Support. A Discourse ... *Boston: James B. Dow.* 1850. 8vo, pp. 28. BA.—A Vindication of the Protestant Episcopal Church, in an Address on the Occasion of the Laying of the Corner Stone of Grace Church in Providence, ... April 8, 1845. ... *Providence: B. F. Moore.* 1845. 12mo, pp. 16.

Henshaw (J. S.) A Manual for United States Consuls; embracing their Rights, Duties, Liabilities and Emoluments, the Laws and Judicial Decisions Governing them, ... By J. Sidney Henshaw. *New York: J. C. Riker.* 1849. 16mo, pp. 252. C.

Also: Around the World: ... . By an Officer of the U. S. Navy. ... *New York: Charles S. Francis.* 1840. 2 vols., 12mo, pp. 336; 344. 2 Plates. + Second Edition [*Ibid.*] 1846. BA.

Henshaw (S. E.) Our Branch and its Tributaries; being a History of the Work of the Northwestern Sanitary Commission and its Auxiliaries, during the War of the Rebellion. By Mrs. Sarah Edwards Henshaw. Including a full Report of Receipts and Disbursements, by E. W. Blatchford, Treasurer; and an Introductory Chapter, by Hon. Mark Skinner. *Chicago: Alfred L. Sewell.* 1868. 8vo, pp. 432. 2 Maps and Plate. B., C.

See "American Bibliopolist," Vol. I.

Henson (G.) The Civil, Political, and Mechanical History of the Framework Knitters in Europe and America. By Gravenor Henson. Vol. I. *Nottingham.* 1831. 8vo. 31434

No more published—shallow, prejudiced, curious and interesting. *See* McCulloch, 240.

Henson (J.) The Life of Josiah Henson, formerly a Slave, now an Inhabitant of Canada, as Narrated by Himself [to S. A. Eliot]. *Boston: Arthur D. Phelps.* 1849. 18mo, pp. iv, 76. B. + *London.* 1852. H. 31432

Henson. Father Henson's Story of his Own Life. With an Introduction by Mrs. H. B. Stowe. *Boston: John P. Jewett & Co.* 1858. 12mo, pp. xii, 212. Portrait. B., C. 31433

Hensseir. [Letter of Gen. Hensseir, Mayor of Tunis, explaining Moslem Slavery and the Causes which led to its Abolition, closing with an Appeal against American Slavery. *Arabic. Tunis?* 18—.] 8vo, pp. 7. H. 31435

Hentz (C.) Courtship and Marriage; or, the Joys and Sorrows of American Life. By Caroline Lee Hentz. *Philadelphia.* 1856. 12mo, pp. 467. B., BA., C. 31436

Also: Ernest Linwood. ... *Boston: John P. Jewett and Company.* 1856. 12mo, pp. 467.—Linda; or, the Young Pilot of the Belle Creole. A Tale of Southern Life. ... *Philadelphia: T. B. Peterson & Brothers.* [n. d.] 12mo, pp. xviii–13–276. B., C.—Marcus Warland; or the Long Moss Spring; a Tale of the South. ... *Philadelphia.* 1852. 12mo.—Planter's Northern Bride. ... *Philadelphia.* 1854. 2 vols., 12mo.—Robert Graham; A Sequel to Linda. ... *Philadelphia.* 1855. 12mo.

Hentz (N. M.) On the Alligator of North America. By N. M. Hentz. *Philadelphia.* 1821. 4to. P. 31437

Hentz. Tadeuskund, the last King of the Lenape. By N. M. Hentz. *Boston.* 1825. 12mo. W. 31438

Hentz. The Valley of Shenandoah; or, Memoirs of the Graysons. By N. M. Hentz. Second Edition. *New York.* 1828. 2 vols., 12mo. C. 31439

Heny (G. A.) Speech of G. A. Heny of Tennessee. [n. p.] 1864. 8vo. 31440

Hepburn (John). The American Defence Of The Christian Golden Rule. [n. p. 1714?] 8vo, pp. (5), 40. B. 31441

Hepburn (R. S. E.) Haïti as it is; being Notes of Five Months' Sojourn in the North ... of Haïti. By Robert S. E. Hepburn ... *Kingston, Jamaica: A. Decordova & Nephew.* MDCCCLXI. 8vo, pp. (8), 114. H. 31442

HEPWORTH (G. H.) The Criminal; The Crime; The Penalty. By George H. Hepworth. *Boston: Walker, Fuller and Company.* 1865. 12mo, pp. 31. B. 31443

On the punishment of Jefferson Davis.

HEPWORTH. A Sermon before the Ancient and Honorable Artillery Company on the CCXXI Anniversary, June 6, 1859. By George H. Hepworth. *Boston: William White, Printer.* 1859. 8vo, pp. 24. B. 31444

HEPWORTH. Two Sermons Preached ... April 23, 1865. I. On the Death of Abraham Lincoln. II. Duties Suggested by the National Grief. By George H. Hepworth ... . *Boston: Printed ... By John Wilson and Son.* 1865. 12mo, pp. 27.

HEPWORTH. The Whip, Hoe, and Sword; or, the Gulf-Department in '63. By George H. Hepworth. *Boston: Walker Wise and Company.* 1864. 12mo, pp. 298. B., BA. 31446

Also: The Appropriation of the Public Money for the Support of Sectarian Schools. ... *Boston.* 1870. 12mo. pp. 15. H.—A Discourse ... after the Death of Theodore Parker. ... *Boston: Crosby, Nichols* ... 1860. 8vo, pp. 20. B.—Oration ... Boston, July 4, 1867. ... *Boston: Alfred Mudge & Son.* 1867. 8vo, pp. 39. H.— ... A Sermon ... at the Dedication of the Church of the Unity, in Boston, November 6, 1859. ... *Boston: For the Society.* 1859. 8vo, pp. 42. H.

HERA (J. S. de la). Representaciones documentadas del aguntamiento de Santiago de Cuba y otras corporaciones à la reina, sobre los importantes servicios hechos á esta ciudad y provincia por D. José Santos de la Hera, gobernador. *Santiago de Cuba.* 1835. 4to. 31447

The Herald Almanac for the United States, for 1849. *New York.* 1849. 8vo, pp. 50. 31448

The first and last issue.

The Herald of Gospel Liberty. Vol. I. *Portsmouth, N. H.* 1808. 31449

Edited by Elias Smith; afterwards published at Philadelphia, and finally at Portsmouth again. The first religious newspaper published in the United States. *See* "Historical Magazine," II. 27.

The Herald of the New Jerusalem. Vol. I. *Philadelphia and New York.* 1854. 12mo. S. 31450

Herald of the Union. *New-York.* 1851. 31451

The Heraldic Journal; recording the Armorial Bearings and Genealogies of American Families. Vol. I. *Boston: J. K.*

Wiggin. 1865–68. 4 vols., 8vo, pp. x, 192; xii, 192; viii, 192; viii, 192. B., H. 31452

El Heraldo, Periódico politico, literario y comercial. *Mexico.* 1848–1849. 31453

HERARD-DUMESLE. Voyage dans le nord d'Hayti, ou revelations des lieux et des monumens historiques. Par Herard-Dumesle. *Aux Cayes de l'imprimerie du gouvernement.* 1824. 4to, pp. (8), 392. 31454

HERAS (Barth. M.) Discurso con Motivo de la Apertura y Benedicion Solemne del Cementerio General erigido en esta Capital. *Impresa en la casa de Niños Expósitos Año de* 1808. Folio, pp. 14. 31455

HERBERT (C.) A Relic of the Revolution, containing a Full and Particular Account of the Sufferings and Privations of all the American Prisoners captured on the High Seas, and Carried into Plymouth, England, during the Revolution of 1776. Also, an account of the Several Cruises of the Squadron under the Command of Commodore John Paul Jones, Prizes taken, etc., etc. By Charles Herbert, of Newburyport, Mass. *Boston: Charles Peirce.* 1847. 18mo, pp. (2), 258. B. 31456

HERBERT (G.) The Temple. Sacred Poems, and Private Ejaculations. By Mr. George Herbert. ... *Cambridge.* 1631. 16mo, pp. 204. + The Third Edition. ... *Cambridge: Printed by T. Buck, and R. Daniel.* 1634. 16mo, pp. (8), 192, (3). H.

The famous prophecy, relative to the church militant, entitles Herbert's poems to a place in this Dictionary. Frequently reprinted in England and America.

HERBERT (Henry John George), *Earl of Carnarvon.* Confederation of the British North American Provinces: the Speech of the Rt. Hon. Earl of Carnarvon. *London: John Murray.* 1867. 8vo, pp. 24. 31458

[HERBERT (Henry William).] American Game in its Seasons. By Frank Forester. *New York.* 1853. Illustrated. C., P.

[HERBERT.] The Complete Manual for Young Sportsmen: ... For the ... Youth of America. ... *New York: W. A. Townsend and Company.* 1859. 8vo, pp. (2), xiii, 17–480. Plates. H.

HERBERT. Frank Forester's Field Sports of the United States and British Provinces of North America. ... By Henry William Herbert ... . *New York: Stringer & Townsend.* [1848.] 2 vols.,

8vo, pp. 366; 381. Portrait and Plates. B., BA. + *London.* 1848. 2 vols., post 8vo. + *New York: Stringer & Townsend.* 1849. 2 vols., 8vo. + Fourth Edition. [*Ibid.*] 1852. 2 vols., 8vo. + New Edition, Revised. With Memoir of the Author. *New York: W. A. Townsend.* 1860. 2 vols., 8vo, pp. 366; 383.

HERBERT. Frank Forester and his Friends; or, Woodland Adventures in the Middle States of North America. By Henry William Herbert. *London.* 1849. 3 vols., post 8vo, pp. 932.

HERBERT. Frank Forester's Fish and Fishing in the United States and British Provinces of North America. By Henry William Herbert. ... *London: Richard Bentley.* 1849. 8vo, pp. xvi, 455. H., P. + *New York: Stringer & Townsend.* 1850. 8vo, pp. 359. 11 Plates. + Third Edition, with a Supplement. *New York.* 1851. 8vo. C. + New Edition. *New York: W. A. Townsend.* 1859. 8vo, pp. xxiv, 18–512. Plates. BA.

HERBERT. Supplement to Frank Forester's Fish and Fishing in the United States and British Provinces of North America. By Henry William Herbert. *New York: Stringer & Townsend.* 1850. 8vo, pp. 86. Colored Plate. 31464

HERBERT. Frank Forester's Horse and Horsemanship of the United States and British Provinces of North America. By Henry William Herbert. ... With Steel-engraved Portraits of Celebrated Horses. *New York: Stringer and Townsend.* 1857. Imp. 8vo, pp. 552; (1), 576. 16 Plates. B., BA. + Revised, Corrected, Enlarged, and Continued to 1871, by S. D. and B. G. Bruce. *New York: G. E. Woodward.* 1871. 2 vols., 8vo, pp. 657, (10); 601. 28 Plates. B., C. 31465

An admirable work on the subject. The author was an Englishman, of great talents, who, in a fit of despondency, shot himself.

HERBERT. Ringwood the Rover: A Tale of Florida. ... Second Edition. *Philadelphia.* 1843. 8vo, pp. 55. 31466

HERBERT (John C.) An Address ... Annapolis ... Society of the Alumni of St. John's College. *Annapolis.* 1828. 8vo.

HERBERT (Mary E.) Scenes in the Life of a Halifax Belle. *Halifax.* 1859. 12mo, pp. 60. 31468

HERBERT (S.) McClellan Campaign Melodist. A Collection of Patriotic Songs, in favor of the Constitution and the Union, the Election of Gen. McClellan, ... By Sidney Herbert. *New York: B. W. Hitchcock.* 1864. 16mo, pp. 32. 31469

HERBERT. Republican Campaign Melodist and Register. By S. Herbert. *New York: Dick & Fitzgerald.* 1868. 18mo, pp. 76. 31470

HERBERT (T.) A Relation of some yeares Travaile, Begvnne Anno 1626. Into Afrique and the greater Asia, especially the Territories of the Persian Monarchie; and some parts of the Orientall Indies and Iles adiacent. Of their Religion, Language, Habits, Discent, Ceremonies and other Matters Concerning them. By Sir Thomas Herbert. *London: W. Stansby.* 1634. Folio, Engraved Title by Marshall, pp. (8), 225, Index, 7 l. Plates by Hollar. C. + [Another Edition.] *London.* 1638. Folio. + Second Edition. [*Ibid.*] 1658. + Third Edition. *London.* 1665. Folio. + Fourth Impression, with many Additions. *London: R. Everingham.* 1677. Folio. 31471

Some copies of the first edition are entited: "A Description of the Persian Monarchy now beinge, the Orientall Indyes, Iles, and other parts of the greater Asia and Africk." In returning to England Herbert coasted the eastern shores of North America; which gives him occasion to display some erudition on the subject of the discovery of the New World. The last chapter is "A Discourse and proofe that Madoc ap Owen-Gwyned first found out that Continent now called America," illustrated with quotations from the early Welsh Bards in evidence of the departure of Madoc with a number of ships and men for an unknown country at the west. The analogies in language which the author gives to prove the identification of Cymric words in Mexican names is entirely fanciful. Nor are the manners and customs of the North American Indians, to which he refers, of any account as evidences of a Welsh colony in America. It is amusing that he points to the name of Cape Breton as a proof that his countrymen were there in the ninth century.

HERBERT. Zee- en lant-reyse na verscheyde deelen van Asie en Africa, Oost-Indien ... Beneffens een verhael van den eersten vinder van America. Uyt het Engelsch vert. door L. v. Bosch. *Dordrecht: Abr. Andriessz.* 1658. 4to. Plates. 31472

Pages 188–192 contain the "Discovery of America by Madoc ap Owen Gwyneth."

HERBERT. Relation du Voyage de Perse et des Indies ... traduit du flamand de Jérémie van Vliet [par Wicquefort]. *Paris.* 1663. 4to. 31473

HERBERT (William). Visit to the Colony of Harmony, in Indiana. *London.* 1825. 31474

Herbert Wendell. A Tale of the Revolution. *New York.* 1835. 2 vols., 12mo. 31475

HERCKMANS (Elias). Der | Zee-Vaert Lof | Handelende | vande gedenckwaerdighste Zee- | vaerden met de daeraenklevende op en onder- | ganghen der voornaemste Heerschappijen | der gantscher

Wereld: | Zedert haere beginselen tot op den | dagh van huyden. | In VI boecken | Beschreven. Door E. Herckmans. | *Tot Amsterdam bij Iacob Pieterss Wachter op den Dam* 1634. | Folio, Engraved Title, pp. (20), 236, (8). Plate. 31476

"The author of this excessively curious and rare work was Vice-Admiral of the celebrated expedition of the Dutch in 1643, under Admiral Hendrick Brouwer, against the Spaniards of Chili; first printed at Amsterdam in 1646, and three years later forming the 25th Part of the Collection of Hulsius. Brouwer dying on the passage out, the command fell upon Herckmans, who was probably the amateur compiler and editor of the various Journals. This Zee Vaert Lof is an elaborate historical poem in six books in honor of Navigation. All the celebrated voyages of the world from Noah to 1632 are recorded in chronological order. The voyages of discovery, leading up to the discovery of America, are mentioned with considerable detail, and after Columbus are recorded most of the voyages both to the east and the west, especially the expeditions of the Dutch navigators. The voyages to the north are all mentioned in the text and notes. The volume is beautifully illustrated by an engraved title and eighteen exquisite etchings in the text. The one at the beginning of the third book bears the mark of Rembrandt, with the date 1633."—STEVENS. "Le poème 'Louange de la Navigation,' par Elias Heerckmans, traite dans ses quatrième et cinquième livre de l'histoire des Indes depuis leur découverte jusqu'en 1588. Il contient beaucoup de gravures à l'eau forte de W. Basse et une gravure originale de Rembrandt."—TRÖMEL.

H[ERCKMANS?] Theatrum Victoriae, ofte het tooneel der zeeslagen, uytbeeld. alle de treffelycke overwinningen over de vyanden van onses vreyheyds. *'s Gravenhage.* 1641. 4to.

This poetical account of the naval war with Spain, the victories of P. Heyn, etc., represents all the victories over the enemies of the Dutch liberty.

HEREDIA (A.) Estudios sobre los Estados Unidos. Un folleto. Por Angulo Heredia. *Durán, Madrid.* 1865. 12mo.

HEREDIA Y SARMIENTO (José-Ignacio). Sermon panegirico de la gloriosa aparicion de Nuestra Señora de Guadelupe, que en el dia 12 de diciembre de 1801 dixio J. I. H. y S., cura de Metepec. [*Mexico*], *en la imprenta de dona Maria Fernandez Jauregui.* 1802. 4to, pp. 155. + [*Mexico*], *Calle de St. Domingo. D. M. F. Jauregui.* 1803. 4to, pp. 69. Plates and Plan of the Ancient City of Mexico. 31479

Also: Oracion Funebre en las sol. exequias par animas de los quo murieron en la reconquista y defensa de Montevideo y Buenos-Ayres, 5 de Julio de 1808. ... *Mexico.* 1808. 4to, pp. 18. Plate. Sermon panegirico del ang. doct. S. Tomas de Aquino que en la sol. Festividad por el Imperial Convento de Santo Domingo de Mexico. ... *Mexico.* 1804. 4to, pp. 66.

HEREDIA (J. M.) Discurso pronunciado en la festividad civica de Toluca, el 16 de Setiembre de 1836, por el Ciudadano J. M. Heredía, magistrado de la Exma. Audiencia. *Toluca.* 1836. Small 8vo, pp. 14. 31480

HEREDIA. Lecciones de historia universal y miscelanea. Por José Maria Heredia. *Toluca en Mexico.* 1831–1832. 6 vols., 12mo. 31481

HEREDIA. Poesias del ciudadano José M. Heredia, Ministro de la Audiencia del Estado de México. *Mexico.* 1852. 8vo, pp. vi, 316. + *Nueva York: Roe, Lockwood & Son.* [n. d.] 2 vols., 24mo, pp. xxiv, (4), 11–136; vii–viii, 181, Appendice, 30. B. + *New York: F. W. Christern.* 1858. pp. xxiv, (4) 11–138; 182, Appendice, 34. 31482

Also: Poesia inedita. ... *Mexico.* 1848. 8vo, pp. 4.

HEREFORD (*Bishop of*). *See* Bisse (P.), *and* Egerton (H.)

Heresiography, or a Description of the Hereticks and Sectaries sprang up in these later times. *London.* 1647. 4to. 31483

Contains an account of the "stirres" raised by the Antinomians and Familists in New England, the Synod of New England, etc.

HÉRICAULT (Charles). Maximilien et le Mexique. Histoire des derniers mois de l'empire Mexicain. *Paris: Garnier Frères.* 1869. 12mo, pp. (4), 419. Plate. B. 31484

HERING (C. J.) De kultuur en de bewerking van het suikerriet, bevattende de theoretische en practische beschrijving van het suikerriet en deszelfs bewerking met inbegrip van de laatste verbeteringen, zoowel in Amerika als in Europa, benevens eene beschrijving van al de toestellen tot de suikerbereiding en tot het distilleren van rum. *Rotterdam.* 1858. 3 vols., 8vo. Plates.

HERING (J. H.) Beschryving van het Eiland Curaçao, en daar onder hoorende Eilanden, Bon-Aire, Oroba en Klein-Curaçao. *Amsterdam: Joannes van Selm.* 1779. 8vo, pp. 89. Map and Plate. 31486

Herinneringen [etc.] 1829. *See* Vol. IV., No. 14582.

Herinneringen eener Reize naar Nieuw York gedaan in de Jaren 1831 en 1832. Benevens eenige bijzonderheden omtrent C. Polari. *Leiden.* 1833. 8vo, pp. 220. S. 31487

These recollections of a voyage to New York are by J. de Brauw.

HERIOT (G.) The History of Canada, from its First Discovery, comprehending an Account of the Original Establishment of the Colony of Louisiana. By George Heriot, Esq. ... Vol. I. *London: Longman & Co.* 1804. 8vo, pp. 616. 31488

"This work, which was not continued, is taken principally from Charlevoix."—RICH. *See* "M. Rev.," XLIX. 143.

HERIOT. Travels through the Canadas, Containing a Description of the Picturesque Scenery on Some of the Rivers and Lakes; with an Account of the Productions, Commerce, and Inhabitants of those Provinces. To which is subjoined a Comparative View of the Manners and Customs of the Indian Nations of North and South America. By George Heriot, Esq. ... Illustrated with a Map and Numerous Engravings, from Drawings made at the Several Places by the Author. *London: Richard Phillips.* 1807. 4to, pp. xii, 602, (1). 28 Tinted Plates and Map. BA. + *Philadelphia: M. Carey.* 1813. 12mo, pp. 282. B. 31489

Part Second contains a minute description of the peculiarities of various nations of American aborigines, principally derived from other printed works. The last thirty-one pages are filled with Father Raslé's Vocabulary of the Algonquin Language. An extended review, amounting to an abridgment of the book, in Phillips' Voyage, Vol. VII. *See also* "Edinburgh Review," XI. 212.

HERKIMER COUNTY AGRICULTURAL SOCIETY. Proceedings, 1857. *Ilion, N. Y.* 1857. 8vo. S. 31490

Proceedings of the Board of Supervisors of the County of Herkimer, for 1863–64. 8vo. S. 31491

HERKIMER COUNTY MUTUAL INSURANCE COMPANY. Act of Incorporation and By-Laws, 1836. *Little-falls.* 1839.

Also: Act of Incorporation, etc. ... *Albany.* 1851. 12mo. S.

HERKIMER MANUFACTURING AND HYDRAULIC COMPANY. Memorial, To the Legislature of New York [1849]. 8vo, pp. 8.

... Herkimer Convention: ... Proceedings, ... Oct. 26, 1847. ... Speeches of the Hon. David Wilmot, of Pa.; C. C. Cambreleng, John Van Buren, &c. [n. p. n. d.] 8vo, pp. 32. B., S.

H[ER]L[EIN] (J. D.) Beschrijvinge van de volkplantinge Zuriname. Opkomst dier zelver colonie, aanbouw der zuikerplantagien ... aard der inwoonders ... levensmanieren, afgodendienst, regering, enz. Mitsgad ... van de bosch-grond ... gedierten, vrugten, etc. *Leeuwarden: M. Injema.* 1718. 4to. Map and Plates. 31495

Description of the colony Surinam, her rise, etc., the cultivation of the sugar plantations, the inhabitants, animals and plants, etc. Dedicated to Mr. Paul van der Veen, Governor of Surinam. Pages 249–262 contain a Caraib Vocabulary.

HERLE (Charles). The Independency on Scriptures of the Independency of Churches. By C. Herle ... . *London.* 1643. 4to, pp. 44. M. 31496

Answered by Richard Mather, of Dorchester, New England, and William Tompson, of Braintree, New England.

HERMANN (——). A Continuation of the Letters of Hermann, as published in the Banner of the Constitution. [*Philadelphia.* 1832.] 8vo, pp. 33. 31497

HERMENEGILDO. Vida portentosa del Americano Septentrional Apostol, El V. P. fr. Antonio Margil de Jesus, Fundador, y Ex-guardian de los Colegios de la Santa Cruz de Queretaro, de Christo Crucificado de Guatemala, y de nuestra Senora de Guadalupe de Zacatecas. Relacion historica de sus nuevas, y antiques maravillas escrita por el Rev. Padre Fray Hermenegildo de Vilaplana. *Madrid.* 1775. Small 4to, pp. xii, 335. 31498

HERMES (K. H.) Die Entdeckung von America durch die Isländer im zehnten und eilften Jahrhunderte. *Braunschweig: Viewig & Sohn.* 1844. 8vo, pp. (1), iv, (1), 134. Plate. B., BA.

[HERMES.] The Oracle of Liberty, and Mode of establishing a Free Government. *Philadelphia: Printed by Parry Hall.* M DCC XCI. 8vo, pp. 39. BA. 31500

HERMITE (J. l') Verhael | Van 't ghene | Den Admirael l'Hermite in | zyne reyse naer de Custen van Peru ver- | richt, ende oock wat Schepen hij ghenomen | ende verbrandt heeft, inde Haven van | Callao, | Tot den 1 Julij 1624 toe. | Ghetranslateert uyt het Spaensch in onse | Neder-duytsche Tale. | *Tot Amsterdam,* | *By Christiaen Meulemans, Boeckvercooper, woonende* | *aen de Beurs, inden ghekroonden Hoedt, Anno* 1625. | 4to, pp. 8. 31501

HERMITE. Waerachtigh verhael, | Van het succes van de Vlote, onder den Admirael | Iaques l'Hermite, | In de Zuyt-zee, op de Custen van Peru, en | de Stadt | Lima in Indien. | Hier is | Een Spaensche Brief by-ghevoeght, de | Staet van Castilien, en op de Cust van Peru in | kort verhalende. | *Anno* M. DC. XXV. 4to, pp. 14.

This was translated into English and published in London the same year. *See* Ternaux's "Bibliothèque Asiatique," No. 1360, and 31510, *infra.*

HERMITE. Iournael | Vande | Nassausche Vloot, | Ofte | Beschryvingh vande Voyagie om | den gantschen Aerdt-kloot, ghedaen met | elf Schepen: | Onder 't beleyd vanden Admirael | Iaques l'Heremite, ende Vice-Admirael Geen Huy- | gen Schapenham, inde Iaeren 1623, | 1624, 1625, & 1626. | Waer in | De gantsche Historie, so wel haer wedervaren, als de ghelegent- | heyt der Landen ende des Volckx, so in woorden als in | Figuren voor gestelt wordt. | *T'Amstelredam,* | *By Hessel Gerritsz ende Iacob Pietersz Wachter.* | *'t Iaer* 1626. | 4to, pp. (6), 99. 31503

This forms the second part of our No. 11607, Vol. III. Another edition is included in [Commelin (Isaac)], "Begin ende," &c. *See* Vol. IV., p. 316. First and very rare edition of the complete journal. The eight plates and maps are sometimes taken from the second edition, being the same as those of the first edition but with altered numbers of pages. The journal gives the principal incidents which occurred every day. Jan. 1, 1624: "Januarius heeft de Heere Admiral aen yeder back een kanne Spaansche Wijn tot een Neuwe-Jaer laten geven." It contains maps of Terra del Fuego, a very curious view of Juan Fernandez Island, harbor of Acapulco, River Guayaquil, sea coast of Lima, and burning of the Spanish fleet in the Bay of Callao.

HERMITE. Iournael | Vande | Nassausche Vloot | Ofte | Beschryvingh vande Voyagie om den | gantschen Aerd-Kloot, ghedaen met elf Schepen: | Onder 't beleydt van den Admirael | Jaques l'Heremite, ende Vice-Admirael Gheen | Huygen Schapenham, in de Iaren 1623, | 1624, 1625, en 1626. | Wy hebben hier noch achter by gevoeght een Beschryvinghe vande Regeringe | van Peru, door Pedro de Madriga gebooren tot Lima. Als mede een | verhael van Pedro Fernandez de Quir, aengaende de ontdeckinge | van 't onbekent Austrialia, sijn grooten Rijckdom ende | vruchtbaerheyt. | *t'Amstelredam*, | *By Jacob Pietersz Wachter, Boeck-verkooper op den Dam*, | *inde Wachter*, *Anno* 1643. | 4to, pp. (6), 122. 31504

This is part of our No. 11607, but is issued with a separate title. Add for collation, pp. (4), 122; (4), 12.

HERMITE. Journael | van de | Nassausche Vloot, | ofte | Beschrijvingh van de Voyagie om den gantschen Aert- | Kloot, Gedaen met elf Schepen: | Onder 't beleydt van den Admirael | Iaques l'Heremite, ende Vice-Admirael Gheen Huy- | gen Schapenham, in de Iaren 1623. 1624. 1625. en 1626. | Noch is hier by gevoegt een Beschrijvinge van de Regeeringe van Peru, door | Pedro de Madriga geboren tot Lima. Als mede een verhael van Pedro | Fernandez de Quir, aengaende de ontdeckinge van 't onbekent Austrialia, syn grooten Rijckdom ende | vruchtbaerheyt. | Oock mede eenige Discoursen de Oost-Indische Vaert en de Coopmanschap betreffende. | *t'Amstelredam*, | *Voor Joost Hartgertsz, Boeckverkooper, woonende in de Gast-Huys-* | *steegh naest het Stadt-huys, in de Boeck-winckel.* *Anno* 1648. | 4to, pp. 76. 31505

Reprint of the edition of 1643, but with addition of the account of an English voyage to Guiana in 1596, and some other particulars relative to the navigation to the East Indies. The account of de Quir on Australia, announced on the title, is omitted. It is also included in Hartgerts' "Oost-Indische voyagien," Vol. I., Part IX.

HERMITE. Journael [as above] ... 1625. en 1626. | Noch is hier by gevoeght een Beschrijvinge van de Regeringhe van Peru, sijn | grooten Rijckdom ende vruchtbaerheydt. | Door Pedro de Madriga, ghebooren tot Lima. | *t'Amstelredam*, *Voor Joost Hartgersz* ... *Anno* 1652. | 4to, pp. 72. 31506

Reprint of the edition of 1648, but without de Quir's and the other accounts on navigation; with 5 small plates from the preceding edition printed in the text. De

Bry has given in the Latin "Pet. Voy." XII., chapt. 9, an extract of this journal, and in the German "Pet. Voy." XII., p. 37, a larger account. The best and only complete edition is that of Cavendish (T.), *see our* No. 11609. *See also* [Commelin (Isaac)] for other editions.

HERMITE. Journael van de | Nassausche | Vloot, | Zijnde een Beschryvingh van de | Voyagie om den gantschen Aerdt-kloot, | Gedaen met elf Scheepen onder 't beleydt van den Admirael | Jaques l'Heremite, | En Vice-Admirael Geen Huygen Schapenham, in de Jaren 1623. 1624. | 1625. en 1626. Verhalende veel vreemdicheden haer up de Reyse voor gevallen | en de Beschryvingh der Volckeren, Landen, Beesten, Voogels, etc. | *t'Amsterdam, Gedruckt* | *Bij Gillis Joosten Saeghman, in de Nieuwe straet* | *Ordinaris Drucker van de Journalen ter Zee*, | *en de Reysen te Lande.* [about 1663.] 4to, pp. 60. Map. 31507

A reprint of No. 31506, omitting the preface and the account of Peru. J. R. Bartlett places this edition under the date 1640, in his catalogue of J. C. Brown's library. The narrative of this voyage, during which both commanders perished, was drawn up and published by Adolph Decker, captain of marines in the expedition, under whose name we have described a German version in our Vol. V., No. 19152.

HERMITE. La furieuse defaite des Espagnols, et la sanglante Bataille donnée au Perou, tant par mer que par terre. Entre lesdits Espagnols et les Hollandois, conduits par leur Admiral, Jacques l'Hermite. *A Paris, Chez Jean Martin, rue de la vieille Bouclerie à l'Escu de Bretagne. Iouxte la copie Flamande imprimée à Anvers.* 1625. 8vo, pp. 16. 31508

HERMITE. La | furieuse | defaite des | Espagnols, et la | sanglante Bataille donnée | au Perou, tant par mer | que par terre. | Entre lesdits Espagnols et les Hollandois | conduits par leur Admiral, | Jaques l'Hermite. | *Tolose, de l'imprimerie de J. Boude, jouxte la coppie imprimée à Paris.* 1625. 8vo, pp. 15. 31509

"Piece rarissime qui tant que nous sachons n'est décrite nulle part."—TROSS.

HERMITE. A True Relation | of the Fleete which went vnder the | Admirall Jaquis Le Hermite through | the Straights of Magellane towards the | Coast of Peru, and the Towne of | Lima in the West-Indies. | With a Letter, Containing the present State | of Castile in Peru. | Herevnto is annexed an excellent Discourse | which sheweth by cleare and strong Arguments | how that it was both necessary and profitable for | the Vnited Provinces to erect a West-India | Company, and euery true subiect of | the same ought to aduance it accor- | ding to his power. | Written by a Well-willer of the | Common-wealth. | *London*, | *Printed for Mercurius* | *Britannicus.* 1625. | 4to, pp. (2), 36. 31510

HERMITAGE. The Life of Gen. Frank Pierce ... With a Biographical Sketch of Hon. William Rufus King ... By Hermitage. ... *New York: Cornish, Lamport & Co.* 1852. 8vo, pp. 96.

HERMOSA (J.) Manual de geografia y estadística de la Republica Mejicana. *Paris.* 1857. 12mo. 31512

[HERNANDEZ (Ant. del Valle).] Ensayo sobre el cultivo del café. [n. p. n. d.] 4to, pp. 32, and Index. 31513

HERNANDEZ (Francisco). Quatro Libros. De la naturaleza y virtudes de las Plantas y animales que estan recividos en el uso de Medicina en la Nueva Espana, y la methodo y coreccion y preparacion que para administrallas se requiere con lo que el Doctor Hernandez escrivio en lengua latina. Muy util para todo genero de gente que vive en estancias y Pueblos, do no ay Medicos ni Botica. Traduzido y aumentados muchos simples y compuestos y otros muchos secretos curativos por Fr. Francisco Ximenez. *Mexico, en casa de la Viuda de Diego Lopez Davalos.* 1615. Small 4to. 31514

Ximenes, in his introduction, remarks that the work of Hernandez, abridged by the Neapolitan physician Nardo Antônio Reccho, by strange ways reached the Indies, and fell into his hands; and that he was induced to publish this translation, adding such examples as fell into his way. This is probably the work referred to by Henry Stevens' "Bibliotheca Historica," No. 891, where the date is said to be 1604.

HERNANDEZ. Rerum Medicarum Novæ Hispaniæ Thesaurus, seu Plantarum Animalium Mineralium Mexicanorum historia ex Francisci Hernandi Noui orbis medici Primarij relationibus in ipsa Mexicana vrbe conscriptis à Nardo Antonio Reccho. ... Collecta ac in ordinem digesta à Joanne Terrentio Lynceo notis illustrata; cum Indice, et Historiæ Animalium et Mineralium libro. Nunc primum in naturaliũ rerũ studiosor gratiã et utilitatẽ studio et impensis Lynceorum Publici iuris facta Philippo magno dicata. *Romæ.* M.DCXXVIII *Ex Typographeio Jacobi Mascardi.* Folio, Engraved Title, pp. 950, 17 l., "Historiæ Animalium," pp. 90, (6).

This edition was abridged, and edited from the author's MS. by Dr. Reccho of Naples; pp. 345–455 are additions by Terrentius de Constance, pp. 460–840 by John Faber, pp. 841–899 are annotations by Fabio Colonno, the tables by Prince Cesi. Leclerc, No. 547, describes: Fabri (Joannis lyncei). Animalia Mexicana Descriptionibus, scholijsq. exposita. *Romæ*, 1628, folio, which is merely an extract, pp. 460–840, from the foregoing.

HERNANDEZ. Rervm medicarvm | Novæ Hispaniæ | thesavrvs | sev | plantarvm animalivm | mineralivm mexicanorvm | historia | ex Francisci Hernandez | Noui Orbis Medici Primarij relationibus | in ipsa Mexicana Vrbe conscriptis | a Nardo Antonio Reccho | Monte

Coruinate Cath. Maiest. Medico | Et Neap. Regni Archiatro Generali | Jussu Philippi II. Hisp. Ind. etc. regis | Collecta ac in ordinem digesta | A Ioanne Terrentio Lynceo | Constantiense Germº. Phõ ac Medico | Notis Illustrata | Nunc primũ in Naturaliũ reꝵ Studiosoꝵ gratiã | lucubrationibus Lynceorũ publici iuris facta. | Quibus Jam excussis accessere demum alia quoꝵ omnium Synopsis sequenti pagina ponitur | Opus duobus voluminibus diuisum | Philippo IIII Regi Catholico Magno | Hispaniaꝵ vtriusq3. Siciliæ et Indiarũ etc. Monarchæ | dicatum. || Cum Priuilegiis. ¶ *Romæ Superioꝵ permissu. Ex Typographeio Vitalis Mascardi.* M.DC.XXXXXI. | Folio, Engraved and Printed Titles, pp. (16), 950, (22), "Historiæ animalium et mineralium novæ Hispaniæ, liber Unicus," pp. 90, (6). A. 31516

The similarity of the collation of this with the preceding edition, suggests the possibility of its being a remainder with a new title-page. The printed title has the imprint *Romæ, Blasii Deuersini et Zanobij Masotti.* 1651.

HERNANDEZ. Francisci Hernandi, Medici atque Historici Philippi II. Hisp. et Indiar. Regis, et totius Novi Orbis Archiatri, Opera, cum edita, tum inedita, ad autographi fidem et integritatem expressa, impensa et jussu Regio. *Matriti: Ex typographia Ibarræ Heredium. Anno* MDCCLXXXX. 3 vols., 4to, pp. xviii, (6), 452, (2); 562, (2); 571. 31517

"Belle édition, publiée par J. B. Muñoz Casimire Ortega. Elle est augmentée de pièces jusqu'alors inédites et sauvées de l'incendie."—BRUNET. Of this edition there are copies on large paper. These volumes contain the "Historæ Plantarum Novæ Hispaniæ," Libri XXIV., much enlarged from the author's manuscript, the minerals, animals, and notes have not been reprinted. Stevens observes: "This edition is not to be compared with the work of Dr. Ricci. This is more of Hernandes without his editors, more correct, with many additions, but without any illustrations. Had Hernandes lived to edit and publish his own work, as Humboldt and Bonpland did theirs, two hundred years later, it is not likely that these two friends would have then laid before the public so much that was entirely new to the philosophers of the Old World." The author was a Spanish physician and naturalist sent to the North American Spanish possessions by order of Philip the Second, for the purpose of describing their productions, concerning whom Acosta remarks: "Doctor Francis Hernandes hath made a goodly worke uppon this subject, of Indian plants, liquors, and other phisicall things, by the King's expresse commission and commandement, causing all the plants at the Indies to be lively painted, which they say are above a thousand two hundred, and that the worke cost above three score thousand ducats." And Mr. Prescott says concerning the edition of 1651: "The work of Hernandez is a monument of industry and erudition, the more remarkable as being the first on this difficult subject; and after all the light from the labors of later Naturalists, it still holds its place as a book of the highest authority." The author's manuscripts were deposited in the library of the Escurial, and many of them were destroyed by fire in 1671. For further particulars concerning this "Third Pliny," *see* an article by Du Petit Thouars in the "Biographie Universelle," article Recchi. *See also* Trômel, No. 263, and Rich's Catalogue, No. 282, where some peculiarities and bibliographical variations are pointed out, but not fully explained. It is evident Rich had not seen the edition described No. 31515. Mr. Rich remarks, that "at page 460, there is an address to the reader, dated in Rome 1625, which appears to have been placed,

instead of an address to Cardinal Barberini, with the same date ... A dedication to the same Cardinal, at page 903 ... without date, is supplied in some copies by another to the Duke del Infantado, dated Rome, 1651. In some copies the figure of the Dragon, at page 816, is torn out, and the plates at pages 213 and 301 are often wanting: many copies have only the engraved title-page, in some dated 1649." Leon Pinelo says an edition was printed in Germany.

HERNANDEZ. A Philosophical and Practical Essay on the Gold and Silver Mines of Mexico and Peru; containing the Nature of the Ore, and the Manner of working the Mines. ... Translated from a Letter wrote in Spanish by Father James Hernandez of the Society of Jesus, employed by His Catholic Majesty to write the Natural History of the West Indies. *London: J. Scott.* 1755. 8vo, pp. 86. N. 31518

See "M. Rev.," XII. 80; XIII. 461.

HERNANDEZ (J. J.) Defensa que produjo el Dr. D. Juan José Hernandez en el juicio de jurados reunido para la calificacion de su impreso suscrito "El Guagiro." Segunda edicion. [n. p.] 1823. *Imprenta de la Union y el Comercio de D. A. M. Valdes.* 4to, pp. 28. 31519

HERNANDEZ. Legal resistencia al despotismo, hecha por el Dr. D. Juan José Hernandez. *Matanzas, imprenta de la Constitucion á cargo de Jimenez.* 1821. 4to. 31520

HERNANDEZ (J. M. P.) Discurso pronunciado por el Ciudadano lic. José Maria Perez y Hernandez, la tarde del 27 de Setiembre de 1850. *Mexico.* 1850. 8vo, pp. 24. 31521

HERNANDEZ. Estadística de la República Mejicana. *Guadalajara.* 1862. 4to. 31522

HERNANDEZ (José de la Luz). Memoir on the Salubrity of the Isle of Pines. *Habana: [Author.]* 1857. 8vo, pp. 56. C.

HERNDON (W. L.), *and* GIBBON (L.) Exploration of the Valley of the Amazon, made under Direction of the Navy Department, by William Lewis Herndon and Lardner Gibbon. Part I. By Lieut. Herndon. | ... Part II. By Lieut. L. Gibbon. *Washington: Robert Armstrong, Public Printer.* 1853–54. 2 vols., 8vo, pp. iv, 414; x, (1), 339. 52 Plates and Maps. C. 31524

Published as Ex. Doc., 2d Sess., 32d Cong., Vol. V.; Sen. Doc., 2d Sess., 32d Cong., Vol. VI., P. I., and contain minute, accurate, and very interesting accounts of the aborigines of the Andes, and the Amazon and its tributaries. The maps are usually found in two separate volumes.

Un Héroe. Historia contemporánea. *Mexico.* 1863. 8vo.

Relates to the French occupation of Mexico.

The Heroes and Battles of the American Revolution; or, Thrilling Stories and Anecdotes of that Eventful Period, By a Veteran Soldier. *Philadelphia.* 1845. 12mo, pp. 252. 31526

Scissors and paste—probably by John Frost.

Heroes and Hunters of the West; comprising Sketches and Adventures of Boone, Kenton, Brady, Logan, Whetzel, Fleehart, Hughes, Johnston, etc. ... *Philadelphia: Theodore Bliss & Co.* [1853.] 12mo, pp. 300. Illustrations. B. 31527

The Heroes of the Lake. A Poem, in Two Books, written in the Autumn of 1813. *New York.* 1814. 12mo, pp. 108. Plate. 31528

Heroes of the Last Lustre. *See* [Mines (J. F.)]

The Heroes of the Nineteenth Century. *Philadelphia.* 1859. 8vo, pp. 20. B. 31529

Heroic Address, for the Fourth of July, 1813. Inscribed to the Washington Benevolent Society in New Brunswick. By a Member. [n. p.] 1813. 8vo. W. 31530

Heroic Incidents of the Civil War in America, 1862. [n. p. n. d.] 8vo. W. 31531

L'Héroïne chrétienne. *See* [Faillon (*l'Abbé*)], Vol. VI.

L'Héroïne du Texas, ou Voyage de Madame *** aux États-Unis et au Mexique. ... Par Mr. G...n. F......n. *Paris: Chez Plancher.* 1819. 8vo, pp. 118. Plate. BA. 31532

Heroism and Adventure in the Nineteenth Century: as exemplified in the American Civil War. With numerous Anecdotes, a Map, and Portraits. *London: Warne & Co.* 1867. Fcp. 8vo, pp. viii, 264. 31533

HERON (R.) Letter to William Wilberforce, on the Justice and Expediency of Slavery and the Slave Trade; by Robert Heron. *London.* 1806. C. 31534

HERRAN (H.), *translator.* Historica | Relatio, | de | Apostolicis | Missionibus | patrum | Societatis Jesu | apud | Chiquitos, Paraquariæ populos, | primò | Hispano idomate conscripta | à | P. Joan: Patricio Fernandez, | dein ad typum promota | A. P. Hieronymo Herran, | Procuratore generali provinciæ Paraquariæ, | utroque Societatis Jesu Sacerdote, | Anno M.DCCXXVI. | Hodie in linguam Latinam translata | ab | alio ejusdem Societatis Jesu Sacerdote. | *Augustæ*

Vendelicorum Sumptibus Mathiæ Wolff, Bibliopolæ. M.DCCCXXXIII. 4to, pp. (40), 276, (18). J.C.B. 31535

This title is a substitute for our No. 24137, Vol. VI.

HERRAN (P. C.) Protesta del General Pedro Alcantara Herran, enviado extraordinario i ministro plenipotenciario de la Confederacion Granadina cerca del Gobierno de los Estados Unidos de America contra la dictadura del titulalo: "Presidente de los Estados Unidos de Colombia," Tomas C. de Mosquera. *Bogotá.* 1865. 8vo, pp. iv, 68. 31536

HERRERA (A. de C. de). Memorial por el licenciado D. Alonso de Castillo de Herrera, de la Real Audiencia de Quito. [n. p. n. d.] 31537

HERRERA (A. de). Cinco libros de la Historia de Portugal, y conquista de las Islas de los Açores en 1582 y 1583. Por Antonio de Herrera. *Madrid.* 1591. 4to. 31538

HERRERA. Descripcion de | las Indias Occide- | ntales de Antonio | de Herrera coro- | nista Mayor de | sv Magd. de las In- | dias y sv coronista | de Castilla. | Al Rey Nrõ Señor. | *En Mad: enla emplenta Real* 1601. | [Colophon:] *En Madrid*, | *Por Iuan Flamenco.* | *Año* M.DC.I. | Folio, Engraved Title, pp. (4), 96. 14 Maps. J.C.B. 31539

This work should go with the General History, and is usually bound at the end of the second volume after the fourth Decade. In the composition of this work the author had access to the most secret of the archives of Spain. It embraces the history from the discovery of America to 1555. The engraved title contains a miniature of the author, and representations of Mexican Deities. It was published in Latin, with additions from Le Maire and Cevallos, under the following title:

HERRERA. Novvs Orbis, | Sive | Descriptio | Indiæ Occi- | dentalis, | Auctore | Antonio de Herrera, | Supremo Castellæ & Indiarum authoritate Philippi III. | Hispaniarum Regis Historiographo. | Metaphraste C. Barlæo. | Accesserunt & aliorum Indiæ Occidentalis Descriptiones, & | Navigationis nuperæ Australis Jacobi le Maire Histo- | ria, uti & navigationum omnium per Fretum | Magellanicum succincta narratio. | *Amstelodami*, | *Apud Michaelem Colinivm Bibliopolam, ad* | *insigne Libri Domestici. Anno* M. D. C. XXII. *Cum Privilegio.* | Folio. BA., C., G., J.C.B., S. 31540

Six prel. leaves, including the engraved and printed titles; text, 44 leaves; followed by a half-title "Ephemerides," etc., 3 leaves and text, 46 to 81, 81 repeated, 1 leaf Followed by another half-title "Descriptio Indiæ Occidentalis, etc., Avthore Petro Ordonnez de Cevallos," 9 leaves; succeeded by a half-title "Brevis ac Succincta Americæ," 11 leaves. The first part has the 14 maps copied from the Madrid edition of 1601 of the "Indias Occidentales," and Le Maire is illustrated with the three maps taken from

De Bry, together with 4 plates in the text. Stevens observes "In the Preface to Barcia's reprint of Herrera, *Madrid*, 1726–30, the editor repudiates this edition, as being full of typographical errors, and encumbered with matters not pertaining to Herrera." On which Quaritch remarks: "It is erroneously stated in the 'American Nuggets' that Barcia, in the preface to his edition of Herrera, repudiates the edition by Colin as full of errors. The fact is, that Barcia makes nowhere any remark prejudicial to the above publication of 1622, which certainly contains a faithful translation of the 'Descripcion' of Herrera, and an equally faithful reproduction of the fourteen genuine maps. He alludes only to the Antwerp edition of 1728." But Mr. Quaritch's note is appended to the French version, described *infra*, yet the review is probably correct. It is reprinted in part, in Vol. XII. of De Bry's "Grands Voyages." *See* Camus' "Mémoire," 147–160; Tiele, No. 294.

HERRERA. Descripcionde | las Indias Ocide | ntales de Antonio | de Herrera coro- | nista mayorde | su Magd. de las | Indias, ysu coronista | de Castilla. Al Rey Nrõ. Señor. | *EnMadrid enla OficinaReal* | *de Nicolas Rodriguez Franco, Año de* 1730. | Folio, pp. (40), 78. 14 Maps. BA., P. 31541

This, which is Barcia's reprint of the first edition, usually accompanies the General History, and forms part of that work. *See our* note to No. 31539, *supra.* The title is engraved, and the final DE of the first line is one letter.

HERRERA. Nieuwe | Werelt, | Anders ghenaempt | West-Indien. | *t' Amsterdam*, | *By Michiel Colijn, Boeck-vercooper op t' Water* | *by de Oude Brugh, in 't Huys-Boeck.* | *Anno* 1622. | *Met Privilege.* | Folio, Two Titles, one of which is engraved, pp. (8), 111. 17 Maps, J.C.B. 31542

Usually followed by Ordonnez and Le Maire. *See* Tiele, p. 314–315.

HERRERA. Description | des | Indes Occidentales, | Qu'on appelle aujourdhuy | le | Novveau Monde. | Par | Antoine de Herrera, | Grand Chroniqueur des Indes, & Chroniqueur de Castille: | Translatee d'Espagnol en François. | A la quelle sont adjoustees | Quelques autres Descriptions des mesmes pays, | Avec | La Navigation du vaillant Capitaine de Mer Jaques le Maire, | & de plusieurs autres. | Le contenu de cest œuvre se veoit en la page suyvante. ¶ *A Amsterdam*, | *Chez Michel Colin, Libraire, demeurant au Livre* | *Domestique. Anno* M.D.C.XXII. | *Avec Privilege.* | Folio, Two Titles, one of which is engraved, pp. (4), 254. 17 Maps, + *A Amsterdam, chez Emmanuel Colin de Thovoyon, & à Paris, chez Michel Joly.* 1622. Folio, Two Titles, pp. (4), 254. 17 Maps. Portrait. J.C.B. 31543

The contents of this French version are the same as that of the preceding Dutch, except that the French translation has not the portrait of Le Maire. "The volume is valuable as containing the first edition of the genuine Voyage of Le Maire (also issued in Latin and Dutch in the same year) as distinguished from that which had been, through the Dutch India Company's jealousy of Le Maire, published by Blaeu under the name of Cornelius Schouten, who had commanded one of Le Maire's vessels. It concludes with the Spanish and English voyages to Magellan's Straits and the descriptions of America given by Ordoñez de Cevallos and Bertius."—QUARITCH. For a detailed list of the contents *see* Leclerc's Catalogue, No. 708. *See also* Ternaux, No. 447; Rich, No. 168; Camus, p. 162.

HERRERA. Historia Gene | ral de los hechos | de los Castellanos | en las Islas i tierra fi-|rme del Mar oceano esc | rita por Antonio de | Herrera coronista | mayor de sv M^d. delas | Indias y svcoronis-|ta de Castilia. | En quatro Decadas desde el Ano de | 1492. hasta el de 1531. | De Cada primera | Al Rey Nu^ro. Señor. | *En Ma^d. en la* | *Emplentarea* | 1601. | -15. Folio, Engraved Titles, pp. (12), 371, (20). C. 31544

Decada segvnda, 1601, pp. (4), 368, (16); Decada terzera, 1601, pp. (4), 377, (16); Decada qvarta, 1601, pp. (4), 293, (14); Decada quinta, 1615, pp. (8), 317, (20); Decada sesta, 1615, pp. (4), 302, (18); Decada setima, 1615, pp. (8), 316, (20); Decada octaua, 1615, pp. (4), 342, (16). 14 Maps. These eight decades are usually bound in four volumes.

HERRERA. Historia general de las Indias Occidentales ò de los Hechos de los Castellanos en las Islas y Tierra Firme del Mar Oceano en Ocho Decades. Escrita por Antonio de Herrera ... Sigue a la Ultima Decada la Description de las Indias Occidentales por el mismo Autor. Nueva Impression. *En Amberes Por Juan Bautista Verdussen*, M.D.CC.XXVIII. 4 vols., folio. H. 31545

Engraved titles, pp. 496, (23); 446, (16); 412, (20); 422, (22). "Descripcion de las Islas, y Tierra Firme del Mar Oceano, que llaman Indias Occidentales." Folio, pp. 68. 2 Maps. The Portraits and Plates in the text are copies from De Bry, by Bouttats, and are not so accurate as those which are used in Barcia's edition. This Antwerp edition was, in fact, brought out with a design to forestall Barcia's, to which it is very inferior, especially with regard to the absence of the maps, without which the "Descripcion" is almost valueless. This "Descripcion" is sometimes found at the beginning of Vol. I., but more frequently after the eighth decade.

HERRERA. Historia Gene | ral de los hechos | delos Castellanos | enlas Islas i Tierrafi | rme del Mar Oceano. Es | crita por Antonio de | Herrera Coronista | Mayor de su M^d. Ðlas | Indias y svCoronis-|tade Castilla | En quatro Decadas desde el Año de | 1492 hasta el de [1]531. | Decada primera | Al Rey Nu^ro. Señor. | *En Madrid*, | *en la Imprenta* | *Real* | *de Nicolas Rodiguez* | *franco* | *Año de* 1730. | 4 vols., folio. BA. 31546

Each decade has an engraved title. "Historia general de los Hechos de los Castellanos," pp. (40), 78, 14 Maps. Decada primera, 1725, pp. (12), 292; Decada segunda, 1726, pp. (6), 288; Decada terzera, 1726, pp. (4), 296; Decada quarta, 1730, pp. (6), 232; Decada quinta, *Franc. de Abad*, 1728, pp. (8), 252; Decada sexta, *Rodriguez Franco*, 1730, pp. (6), 236, [on the last leaf: *Imprenta de Francisco Martinez Abad*, 1727;] Decada setima, 1730, pp. (6), 245; Decada octavo, 1730, pp. (6), 251; "Tabla General," etc., 226 leaves, ending with the Colophon. *En Madrid: En la Imprenta de Francisco Martinez Abad. Año de* MDCCXXVIII. Each engraved title is divided into from ten to fourteen compartments, in which is represented some scene of the conquest of the Indians by the invading Spaniards, or a portrait of some eminent

Conquistador; seventy-two battle-scenes, views of human sacrifices, or Indian life, and thirty-nine portraits are thus exhibited. In some sets the "Descripcion de las Indias Occidentales," or "Historia general de los Hechos de los Castellanos," 1730, is found preceding the "Tabla" in Vol. IV., and in the LARGE PAPER copies it is usual to bind this "Descripcion" and "Tabla" together as a fifth volume, indeed, some small paper copies are thus divided. There are copies of this edition dated 1727, 1728, 1729, and 1730, which are all alike except as to the date—the work not having been completed till that year—the publishers changing the dates as circumstances suggested. It is merely a reprint of the original edition of 1601–1615, with the addition of a very copious index, compiled under the direction of Gonzales Barcia, but without a continuation, as erroneously stated by Meusel, and it is deservedly regarded as the *best edition*.

HERRERA. Histoire | generale | des Voyages | et Conqvestes | des Castillans, dans les Isles & Terre-ferme | des Indes Occidentales. | Traduite de l'Espagnol d'Antoine | d'Herrera, Historiographe de sa Maiesté Catholique, | tant des Indes, que des Royaumes de Castille. | Par N. de la Coste. | *A Paris* | *Chez Nicolas & Jean de la Coste.* M.DC.LIX. 4to, pp. (28), 776, (24). 31547

It was reprinted the next year with the following title:

HERRERA. Histoire generale des Voyages et Conqvestes des Castillans, dans les Isles & Terre-ferme des Indes Occidentales. Traduite de l'Espagnol d'Antoine d'Herrera, Historiographe de sa Maiesté Catholique, tant des Indes, que des Royaumes de Castille. Par N. de la Coste. Premier Decade, Contenant les Premiers Descouuertes du nouueau Monde par Christofle Colon, Les diuers combats qu'il eut contre les Indiens de Veragua, de Iamayca, & autres lieux, Les mauuais traitemens qu'il recent de ses gens dans les quatre voyages qu'il y sit, & les trauaux qu'il souffrit, Les voyages d'Americ Vespuce, La Descouuerte de la mer du Sud, Les diuers succés des armées Castillanes dans ces nouuelles terres; Et les soins qu'eurent les Rois Catholiques pour y establir la Police tant spirituelle, que temporelle. *A Paris Chez Nicolas & Jean de la Coste.* M.DC.LX. 4to, pp. (30), 776, (24). H., S. 31548

HERRERA. Histoire | generale | [as above]. Seconde Decade, Contenant les dif- | ferens Voyages de plusieurs Capitaines dans ce nouueau Monde, & les diuers | succés qu'ils eurent contre les Indiens, La descouuerte de la Riuiere de la Plata. | L'entrée de Fernand Cortés dans la nouuelle Espagne, Les batailles qu'il eut | contre la Republique Tlascala, Son entrée dans la ville de Mexique, La | prize du Roy, & sa mort, Les cruelles batailles que les Mexiquains liurerent | à Cortez pour le chaffer de leurs Terres, Sa retraite, & les preparatifs quil | fait pour le siege de çette grande ville. | *A Paris* | *Chez Nicolas & Jean de la Coste.* M'DC LX. 4to, pp. (24), 784, Table (28). 31549

HERRERA. Histoire | Generale | des Voyages et Conqvestes | des Castillans dans les Isles & Terre-ferme | des Indes Occidentales. | Traduite de l'Espagnol d'Antoine d'Herrera, | Historiographe de sa Majesté Catholique, tant | des Indes, que des Royaumes de Castille. | Par N. de la Coste. | Oú l'on voit la prise de la grande ville de Mexique, & autres | Provinces par Fernand Cortés; Sa fondation; le Rois qui | la gouvernerent; Le commencement & fin de cet Empire; | Leur coûtumes & ceremonies; Les grandes revoltes qui y | sont arrivez; Les contestations qu'eurent les Castillans & | les Portugais, sur l'assiette de la ligne de partarge de leurs | conquestes; La découverte des Isles Philippines par | Hernando de Magellan; Sa mort & autres choses remar- | quables. | Dediée à Monseigneur le premier President. | *A Paris*, [*Chez La Veuve Nicolas de la Coste, a l'Ecu* | *de Bretagne.* | *François Clovzier l'aisné, à l'Image nostre Dame* | *et* | *Pierre Avboüin, à la Fleur de Lys.* |] *demeurant tous* | *proche l'Hostel* | *de Monseigneur* | *le premier Pre-* | *sident.* | M. DC. LXXI | *Avec Privilege dv Roy.* | 4to, pp. xyiii, 790, (12). 31550

The three volumes having been published separately, with different titles, are rarely found together. The remaining five decades have not been translated. *See* Faribault, p. 62.

HERRERA. Verscheide zee en land-togten gedaan in de West-Indien: d'eerste, door Jean Ponce de Leon, naar Florida in 1512. De andere gedaan door Pamphilio de Narvaes op't eiland Cuba, in 1513. In't Spaans beschreven door Antonius Herrera en nu aller-eerst in't Nederduyts vertaald. *Leyden: P. Van der Aa.* 1706. Sm. 8vo, pp. 77, (6). 4 Plates. C. 31551

Forms part of Van der Aa's "Collection of Voyages." Also in folio. *See our* Vol. I.

HERRERA. Vevolg der Roemwaardige Zee en Land-Reysen des Dapperen Ferdinand Cortez; aan de Vaste Kust van Mexico en Nieuw-Spaanje. Gedaan in 't Jaar 1521, en vervolgens. Verhalende de Oorlagen en bloedige Gevegten, in 't verder bemagtigen der Mexicaansche Landschappen, het Beleegeren, en Innemen der beroemde Hoofdstad Mexico; nevens de seldsame Handelingen met de Koning Motezuma; sijn dood, en nagelaten Rijkdommen. *Te Leyden: By Pieter Van der Aa.* 1706. 8vo, pp. 418, Register (24). 31552

HERRERA. [Drie] scheeptogten van Kolumbus, Vasco de Gama, Amerikus Vesputius, Chr. Guerre en A. Nino. Uit het Spaansch. *Leyden: P. Van der Aa.* 1706. 8vo. Map. 31553

HERRERA. Zeetogten naar West-Indien, 1508, 1509: OCampa naar Kuba, Ponze de Leon naar de Borriquen, de Solis

d'Ojeda, Nicueza, etc. Uit het Spaansch. *Leyden: P. Van der Aa.* 1706. 8vo. Map. 31554

HERRERA. Drie togten ter zee en te land in de West-Indien in 1523 en vervolg. ... d. F. de Garay, van Jamaica na Panuco, ... d. P. d'Alvarado, van Mexico na Guatemala, ... d. D. de Goday, van Mexico ter ontdekking, enz. nu alder-eerst in 't Neder-duyts vertaald. *Leyden: P. Van der Aa.* 1707. 8vo. Map. 31555

HERRERA. Aankomst van Jean d'Ezquebel ter Bevolking van Jamaica door den Ammiraal Diego Kolumbus in't Jaar 1510. *Leyden: P. Van der Aa.* 1706. 31556

HERRERA. The General History of the Vast Continent and Islands of America, Commonly call'd The West-Indies, from The First Discovery thereof: With the Best Accounts the People could give of their Antiquities. Collected from the Original Relations sent to the Kings of Spain. By Antonio de Herrera, Historiographer to His Catholick Majesty. Translated into English by Capt. John Stevens. Illustrated with Cutts and Maps. *London: Jer. Batley* M.DCC.XXV–VI. 6 vols., 8vo, pp. (8), 379; (2), 436; Vol. III., dated 1726, (2), 418; (2), 422; (2), 430; (2), 408; Index, 30. 2 Maps, 15 Plates, and Portraits of Columbus and Cortez. H. 31557

HERRERA. The General History [same title and collation]. The Second Edition. *London: Wood & Woodward.* MDCCXL. 6 vols., 8vo. BA. 31558

This translation includes only the three first decades. This so-called second edition has new title-pages only. A portion of Herrera is included in Kerr's "Voyages," Vol. III. The following does not relate specially to America:

HERRERA. Historia general del Mundo, de XVII. años del tiempo del Señor Rey don Felipe II. el Prudente, desde el año de 1554, hasta el de 1598. *Valladolid: J. G. de Millis.* 1606–12. 3 vols., folio. S. 31559

"Histoire estimée."—BRUNET. "A work written under the influence of contemporary passions, and published before any of those passions had been much tranquilized."—TICKNOR, III. 142.

A grand chorus of writers, from Nicholas Antonio down to Thomas W. Field, unite in their testimony as to the fidelity of this Prince of Historians. He was successively employed as historiographer by Philip II., III., and IV., and having access to every available source of information, made free use of many original documents which had never before been printed, and which no longer exist in MS. His works embrace a large part of the MS. "Chronicle" of B. de las Casas, and almost the entire MS. "Relacion" of Palacio is incorporated with his fourth decade. A French bibliographer, quoted without name by Trömel, observes: "Parmi les historiens de l'Amérique, D. Antonio

de Herrera tient incontestablement le premier rang. Il naquit en 1559, et fut quelque temps secrétaire de Vespasien de Gonzague, vice-roi de Naples, et fut ensuite nommée par Philippe II. historiographe des Indes. Son ouvrage est ce que nous possédons de plus complet sur l'époque qu'il embrasse." The Spanish bibliographer Salva says: "Cet ouvrage est un des plus importants qu'on ait publiés sur les découvertes des Espagnols dans le Nouveau-Monde." Munoz, at the 22d page of the prologue to his "History of the New World," remarks: "Herrera eclipsed all other historians on the same subject which had till then been published, in fullness of matter, truth of narration, chronological arrangement, geographical accuracy, and beauty of style." J. Beldon de Guevara writes: "No one of all those who have writ on this subject has performed it with so much exactness as Ant. de Herrera." The Italian, Davila, observes: "This history is very useful for all sorts of people, because the author's method is very good, being at the same time brief and intelligible, joining profound knowledge and undoubted truth, and undeceiving us as to many errors into which other authors have led us." The Scotch historian Robertson remarks: "Of all the Spanish writers Herrera furnishes the fullest and most accurate informations concerning the conquest of Mexico, as well as every other transaction of America; his Decades may be ranked amongst the most judicious and useful collections." The English bibliographer Dibdin observes: "Antonio de Herrera is well designated by Bishop Kennett as the chief chronicler of the Indies and Castile; he stands in the foremost rank of early American Historians." Our own Washington Irving, in his "Life of Columbus," concludes a judicious criticism thus: "Herrera has left voluminous proofs of industrious research, extensive information, and great literary talent. His works bear the mark of candour, integrity, and a sincere desire to record the truth." Ticknor, in his "History of Spanish Literature" accords him equal praise; and Thomas W. Field's "Essay on Indian Bibliography" concludes our series of eulogizers with the statement that "His work is a perfect treasure-house of the most valuable details, regarding the original state of the religion and manners of the Indians."

HERRERA (Antonio M. de). Vindicacion que hace de los injustos cargos que ha formulado en su contra el Gobernador de Sinaloa D. Placido Vega. *Durango.* 1861. 4to, pp. 50.

HERRERA (Cypriani de). Mirabilis Vita et Mirabiliora Acta dei Vener. servi Toribii Alfonsi Mogrobesii Limani Archipræsulis. *Romæ.* 1670. Folio. Plate. 31561

The plate represents the archbishop healing the sick. Very valuable for the ecclesiastical history of Peru, embracing also a description of the country, etc. Mogrobesius was Archbishop of Lima from 1580 to 1624. For an abridgment *see* Nicoselli (A.)

HERRERA (D.) Agrimensura aplicada al sistema de medidas de la Isla de Cuba, por D. Desiderio Herrera, agrimensor público &. *Imprenta de Gobierno.* 1834. 4to, pp. 272. 31562

HERRERA. Memoria sobre los huracanes en la Isla de Cuba, por Don Desiderio Herrera. *Habana.* 1847. 8vo, pp. 72. Map.

[HERRERA (Hernando Alonso de).] Disputatio Aduersus Aristotelez Aristo | telicosqȝ | sequaces. [Colophon:] *Acabose esta obra ẽ salamãca bispera d'* | *corp9 xp̃i. Año d'l* | *misterio d'la ẽcarnaciõ d' hijo d'dios d'mil y* | *qniẽtos y dies y siete.* | 4to, Title, 1 l, 55 l.

Title from [Harrisse], Vol. II., No. 50. It contains a sketch of Peter Martyr.

HERRERA (I.) Contestaciones entre el Gobernador del estado de Jalisco, D. Ignazio Herrera y Cairo, y el Obispo de la Diocesis, D. Petro Espinosa, con motivo al prestamo forzoso decretado por el primero. *Mexico.* 1856. 4to, pp. 17. 31565

HERRERA (J. H.) Album de Ayacucho. Coleccion de los principales documentos de la guerra de la Independencia del Peru, y de los cantos de victoria y poesias relativas a ella, redactada por Jose Hipolito Herrera. *Lima.* 1862. 4to. 31566

HERRERA (J. J.) Discurso pronunciado por el Presidente de la Republico Mexicana, general de division Jose Joaquin, de Herrera, el die 1. de Enero de 1851, en la apertura de las sesiones del Congreso. *Mexico.* 1851. Rl. 8vo, pp. 24. 31567

Also: Discurso pronunciado por el Presidente de los Estados-Unidos Mexicanos, en la apertura de los sesiones ordinarias del Congreso el die 1. de Enero de 1852. *Mexico.* 1852. Rl. 8vo, pp. 30.

HERRERA (J. M. de) Correspondencia entre Jose Manuel de Herrera, Secretario de Estado, &c. del Imperio de Mexico y Miguel Santamana, Enviado, &c. de la Republica de Colombia, &c. &c. *Mexico.* 1822. 4to. P. 31568

HERRERA ASCANIO (N. de). Sermon Panegirico de Accion de Gracias por el deseado Nacimiento de nuestro Principe D. Luis Philipo, en la Cathedral de la Ciudad de Sanctiago de Leon de Caraccas. Predicolo D. Nicolas de Herrera Ascanio. *Mexico.* 1701. 4to. 31569

Contains some curious allusions to the Spanish nobility then resident in Mexico.

HERRERA (P.) Ensayo sobre la Historia de la Literatura Ecuatoriana por Pablo Herrera. *Quito.* 1860. 31570

HERRERA (R. V.) Poesias de Ramon Velez Herrera. *Habana.* 1833. 8vo, pp. 130, xxiv. 31571

HERRERO (A.) Doctrina y Oraciones cristianas en lengua Mosetena, traducidas en espanol palabra por palabra. Por P. F. Andres Herrero, misionero apostolico. *Roma: Imprenta de Propaganda.* 1834. 12mo, pp. 20. 31572

The Mosetana language is spoken in Peru.

HERRICK (A.) The Disunion Policy of the Administration. Speech of Anson Herrick ... March 26, 1864. [*Washington.* 1864.] 8vo, pp. 14. 31573

HERRICK (J.) A Genealogical Register of the Name and Family of Herrick, from the Settlement of Heneric Herricke, in Salem, Massachusetts, 1629 to 1846. With a Concise Notice of their English Ancestry. By Jedediah Herrick. ... *Bangor: Samuel S. Smith, Printer.* 1846. 8vo, pp. 69. Plate. BA., H.

HERRICK (W. A.) The Powers, Duties, and Liabilities of Town and Parish Officers in Massachusetts; ... By William A. Herrick ... . *Boston: Little, Brown & Co.* 1870. 12mo, pp. (2), x, 613. BA., C. 31575

HERRING (E.) An Oration on the Anniversary of the Battle of Lexington, delivered at the request of the "United Whig Club." By Elbert Herring. *New York.* 1809. 8vo, pp. 14.

Also: An Oration on the Death of George Clinton, late Vice-President. ... *New York.* 1812. 8vo. S.

HERRING (J.) The National Portrait Gallery of Distinguished Americans. Conducted by James Herring, New York, and James B. Longacre, Philadelphia, under the Superintendence of the American Academy of Fine Arts. *New York: Monson Bancroft.* 1834–39. 4 vols., rl. 8vo. 31577

Also on large paper, in 4to. Contains 144 portraits, accompanied by biographies written by John Quincy Adams, Prof. Ticknor, Dr. Francis, etc. Up to this date nothing had came from the hands of American engravers to equal in delicacy of handling, and beauty of finish, these fine portraits. The imprint given above describes the first and best issue of this work, which was frequently reproduced. Some copies have the imprint *Philadelphia: Henry Perkins.* 1834–39—a mere variation in the title. An edition dated 1837, has on the title-page Longacre & Herring. *Philadelphia: James B. Longacre.* 1837. 4 vols., rl. 8vo. More recently the work was issued with the imprint *Philadelphia: J. H. Rice*, much inferior as regards the impressions of the plates; still later—the date varying—copies have the imprint *Philadelphia: J. Rutter*; in these issues the copperplates seem to have had a little cleaning up, but the intelligent buyer will not take them. To this last publication there is added a fifth volume consisting of additional portraits and biographies of inferior personages and inferior art.

HERRING (J.) Eulogy on Maj. Gen. J. Morton and E. W. King, pronounced in St. Matthew's Church, June 7th, 1837, at the Request of the Grand Lodge. *New York.* 1837. 8vo, pp. 26.

[HERRING] (T.) A Sermon ... before the Incorporated Society for the Propagation of the Gospel in Foreign Parts; ... February 17, 1737–8. By Thomas, Lord Bishop of Bangor. *London: J. and J. Pemberton.* MDCCXXXVIII. 8vo, pp. 70, (1). BA. 31579

HERRINGTON (W. D.) The Deserter's Daughter. By W. D. Herrington, 3d N. C. Cav. ... *Raleigh: Wm. B. Smith & Co.* 1865. 8vo, pp. 27. H. 31580

Also: The Captain's Bride, The Refugee's Niece, and other Confederate stories.

HERRLIBERGER (David). Heilige Ceremonien, Gottes- und Götzen-Dienste aller Völcker der Welt. *Zürich.* 1748. 2 vols., folio. 31581

Contains 234 plates, engraved by Herrliberger after Picart's "Cérémonies religieuses," with a descriptive text, 34 of which represent the ceremonies of the American Indians, especially the Virginians, Floridans and Mexicans.

HERRMANN (F.) Die Deutschen in Nordamerika. ... Von Friedrich Herrmann ... . *Lübben: Gotsch.* 1806. 8vo, pp. (8), 191, (1). 31582

HERRNHUTERS. Candid Narrative of the Rise and Progress of the Herrnhuters. *London.* 1753. + Supplement to the Candid Narrative. *London.* 1755. 8vo. C. 31583

The Herrnhuters are a religious sect, somewhat of the Moravian order, some of whom settled in Pennsylvania.

HERRON (A. C. *and* J. W.) The Columbian Historian. Vol. I. *New Richmond, Ind.: A. C. & J. W. Herron.* 1824–25. 8vo. 31585

HERRON (J. P.) American Grammar: adapted to the National Language of the United States; with an Accompanying Panorama. By James P. Herron. *Columbus (O.): Osgood & Pearce.* 1859. 12mo, pp. 312. C. 31586

HERSEY (C.) History of Worcester, Massachusetts, from 1836 to 1861; with Interesting Reminiscences of the Public Men of Worcester. By Charles Hersey. *Worcester.* [1862.] Rl. 8vo. Plate. 31587

HERSEY. Reminiscences of the Military Life and Sufferings of Col. Timothy Bigelow ... in the Continental Army, during the ... Revolution. By Charles Hersey. *Worcester: Printed by Henry J. Howland.* 1860. 8vo, pp. 24. B., H. 31588

HERSEY (H.) Claims of Tufts College on its First Students. Oration ... Mathetican Society ... October 20, 1856. By Harvey Hersey. With a Poem by Heman A. Dearborn. ... *Boston: A. Tompkins.* 1856. 8vo, pp. 31. H., S. 31589

HERSEY (J.) An Appeal to Christians, on the Subject of Slavery. By John Hersey. Second Edition. *Baltimore: Armstrong & Plaskitt.* 1833. 18mo, pp. 124. 31590

De Herstelde Fabrikant. Tooneelspel. *Amsterdam.* 1782. 8vo, pp. 60. 31591

This drama of the "Re-established Manufacturer" is a continuation of the "Nieuwe Kolfspel." It relates to the Dutch question during the American Revolution.

HERTFORD (J.) Personals; or, Perils of the Period. By Joseph Hertford. *New York: The Author.* 1870. 12mo, pp. 339, viii. Plate. C. 31592

HERTHA. Zeitschrift für Erd-, Völker und Staatenkunde, besorgt von H. Berghaus und K. F. V. Hoffmann. *Stuttgart.* 1825. 8vo. Continued. 31593

A valuable periodical for recent geographical information, containing articles by A. v. Humboldt, H. Berghaus, Klaproth, Martens, K. v. Raumer, Martius, abbreviations of voyages, etc. The earlier volumes are out of print.

HERTSLET (L.) A Complete Collection of the Treaties and Conventions, at Present subsisting between Great Britain & Foreign Powers; so far as they relate to Commerce and Navigation, to the Repression and Abolition of the Slave Trade; and to the Privileges and Interests of the ... High Contracting Parties. ... Compiled from Authentic Documents, by Lewis Hertslet, Esq., Librarian and Keeper of the Papers, Foreign Office. *London.* 1840–71. 12 vols., 8vo. 31594

First issued in 1820–40. 5 vols., 8vo. The later volumes are edited by Edward Hertslet.

HERTTELL (T.) The Demurrer; or, Proofs of Error in the Decision of the Supreme Court of the State of New York, requiring Faith in Particular Religious Doctrines as a Legal Qualification of Witnesses. By Thomas Herttell. *New York.* 1828. 8vo, pp. 158. N. 31595

Also: The People's Rights Reclaimed ... *New York.* 1826.—Remarks on the Law of Imprisonment for Debt: showing its Unconstitutionality, and its Demoralizing Influence on the Community. ... *New York: Gould & Banks.* 1823. 8vo, pp. 67. + *Boston.* 1825. 8vo, pp. 47.—In Assembly, March 30, 1836. Remarks ... showing the Unconstitutionality ... of the Bill "to incorporate the Attica and Buffalo Rail-Road Company," as authorizes the taking of Private Property without the Consent of the Owner. [n. p. 1836.] 8vo, pp. 7. H.—Remarks comprising in substance Judge Herttell's Argument in the House of Assembly of the State of New-York, in the Session of 1837, in support of the Bill to Restore to Married Women "the Right of Property," as guaranteed by the Constitution of the State. ... *New-York: Henry Durell.* 1839. 12mo. + *Boston: J. P. Mendum.* 1867. 12mo, pp. 83. B., H.—Rights of Conscience Defended, ... Speech ... 7th of May, 1835, on ... Rights ... of Witnesses. Also, his reply to Mr. ... Humphrey's Remarks against the Bill. ... *New-York.* 1835. 12mo. + Second Edition. *New-York: G. W. & A. J. Matsell.* 1835. 12mo, pp. 64.

HERTY (T.) A Digest of the Laws of Maryland being an Abridgment, Alphabetically Arranged, of all the Public Acts of

Assembly now in Force, and of General Use, from the First Settlement of the State to the End of November Session, 1797, inclusive, with References to the Acts at Large. With an Appendix [containing Laws] passed November Session, 1798. By Thomas Herty. *Baltimore: The Editor.* 1799. 8vo, pp. xii, 524, 55. C. 31596

HERTY. A Digest of the Laws of the United States of America, ... Now in Force, from the Commencement of the Federal Government, to ... 1802, inclusive. By Thomas Herty. *Baltimore and Washington.* 1800–1813. 2 vols., 8vo. 31597

HERTZ (B.) Catalogue of the Collection of Assyrian, Babylonian, Egyptian, Greek, Etruscan, Roman, Indian, Peruvian and Mexican Antiquities. Formed by B. Hertz ... . *London.* 1851. 4to, pp. iv, 156, (2), Tables, vi, Errata, 4 lines. Plate.

HERTZ (H.) ... United States *vs.* Henry Hertz *et al.* charged with Hiring and Retaining Persons to go beyond the Jurisdiction of the United States, with the intent to enlist in the British Foreign Legion, for the Crimea. Taken in Short Hand ... By James B. Sheridan ... . *William Rice, Philadelphia.* 1855. 8vo, pp. 106. 31599

HERVAS (L.) Catalogo de las Lenguas de las Naciones Conocidas y numeracion, division y clases de estas segun la diversidad de sus idiomas y dialectos. Su Autor el Abate Don Lorenzo Hervas ... . *Madrid: En la Imprenta de la administracion del Real Arbitro de Beneficencia.* 1800–1805. 6 vols., 4to, pp. xvi, 396; 480; 359; 343; 315; 379. 31600

The first volume of this very learned work, similar in its object to Adelung's "Mithridates," is devoted to the aboriginal languages, and the people who spoke them. Latham remarks "His data he collected by means of an almost unlimited correspondence with the Jesuit missionaries of the Propaganda." And Balbi observes "Ouvrages, qui, malgré beaucoup de défauts et d'erreurs, dûs en partie à l'epoque où ils furent redigés et en partie au manque d'une saine critique dans le choix des matériaux n'en contiennent pas moins des trésors précieux pour l'histoire et la science des langues, surtout à l'égard de celles du Nouveau Monde." The other works of Hervas are: Historia de la Vida del Hombre. ... *Madrid.* 1789–99. 7 vols., 4to, pp. xxxii, 380; 434; 344; 384; 322; 456; 476.—Aritmetica delle Nazioni e Divisione del Tempo fra l'Orientali. ... *Cesena.* 1785. 4to. pp. 202.—Origine, Formazione, Meccanismo, ed Armonia degl' Idiomi. ... *Cesena.* 1785. 4to, pp. 180.—Catalogo delle Lingue conosciute e Noticia della loro Affinitá, e Diversitá. ... *Cesena.* 1784. 4to, pp. 260. They form an extremely learned series of philological researches, with comparative vocabularies, in many hundred languages, some of them American.

HÉRVE (Étienne A.) *et* LANOYE (F. de). Voyages dans les glaces du pôle arctique, à la recherche du passage nord-ouest. Extraits des relations de Sir John Ross, Edward Parry, John

Franklin, Beechey, Back, Mac Clure et autres navigateurs célèbres. *Paris: Hachette et Cie.* 1854. 16mo. + Nouvelle édition. [*Ibid.*] 1862. 12mo. Plates. 31601

HERVEY (Augustus John). Speech of the Earl of Bristol in the House of Lords, April 23, 1779. *London.* 1779. 4to, pp. 22.

HERVEY (E. W.) A Catalogue of the Plants found in New Bedford and its vicinity; arranged according to the Season of their Flowering. By E. W. Hervey. *New Bedford: Printed by E. Anthony.* 1860. 8vo, pp. 30. 31603

HERVEY (F.) Naval History of Great Britain, and Origin and Progress of the British Power at Sea, Account of all Battles, &c. By F. Hervey. *London.* 1779. 5 vols., 8vo. 31604

HERVEY (G. W.) Liberty, as a Cloak of Maliciousness. A Discourse delivered ... Canton, Mass., on the Day of the National Fast, Jan. 4th. 1861. By George Winfred Hervey. *New York: Sheldon & Co.* 1861. 8vo, pp. 21. B., H. 31605

[HERVEY (Henry M.)] Historical Sketches of The Presbyterian Church (O. S.), in Licking County, Ohio ... Read before the Licking County Pioneer Association. *Newark, Ohio: Wilson & Clark, Printers.* [1868.] 8vo, pp. 20. 31606

[HERVEY (John, *Lord.*)] Miscellaneous Thoughts on the Present Posture both of our Foreign and Domestic Affairs. ... *London: Roberts.* 1742. 8vo, pp. 80. P. 31607

[HERVEY (N.)] The Memory of Washington; with Biographical Sketches of his Mother and Wife. Relations of Lafayette to Washington; with Incidents and Anecdotes in the Lives of the Two Patriots. *Boston: J. Munroe & Co.* 1852. 12mo, pp. 320. 2 Plates. 31608

HERZ (H.) Mes Voyages en Amérique. Par Hénri Herz. *Paris: A. Faure.* 1866. 16mo, pp. 328. C. 31609

HESKITH (T.) Excellency and Advantages of Religion. A Sermon preach'd for the Reformation of Manners in St. John's, at Nevis, in America, July 21, 1701. By Thomas Heskith, M.A. ... *London: Thomas Speed.* 1701. 4to, pp. 26. 31610

HESKITH. Piety and Learning the Great Ornament and Character of Priesthood, a Farewell Sermon at St. John's, at Nevis, in America, May 25, 1701. ... *London: Thomas Speed.* 1702. 4to. 31611

HESKITH. Sermon at the Funeral of the Hon. Col. Francis Collingwood and of his Lady, who were both interred in St. John's Church, in the Island of Nevis, in America, May 29th and May 31st, 1699. ... 1700. 4to. 31612

Also: Divine Providence asserted and some Objections answered. Sermon at Annapolis Royal [N. S.], Oct. 10, 1710. *Boston.* 1710. 4to. W.

HESPEL D'HARPONVILLE (*Le Vicomte* Gustave d'). La reine des Antilles, ou Situation actuelle de l'île de Cuba. Précis topographique et statistique, histoire, géographie, agriculture, commerce, administration et mœurs. *Paris.* 1850. 8vo. 2 Maps, 4 Tables. 31613

The Hesperian. Edited by Mrs. F. H. Day. Containing Sketches of Early Settlers of California. *San Francisco.* 1859. 8vo. 31614

The Hesperian: or Western Monthly Magazine. Edited by William D. Gallagher and Otway Curry. *Columbus, Ohio.* 1838–1839. 8vo. 31615

Three or more volumes published.

HESS (William). *See* Mohawk Language.

HESSEL (A.) Kort Berettelse om then Swenska Kyrkios närwarande tilstånd i America samt oförgripeliga tankar om thess widare förkofring, Upstälte af Andrea Hesselio, för thetta probst ock Kyrkioherde i Pensilvanien. *Norkioping. Anno* 1725. 4to, pp. 23. J.C.B. 31616

This is a "Short account of the present situation of the Swedish church in America, with incontrovertible thoughts on its future progress, drawn up by And. Hessel, late its priest and pastor in Pennsylvania." Very scarce.

HESSIANS. Von den Hessen in Amerika, ihrem Fürsten und den Schreyern. 1782. 8vo. 31617

Title from an English bookseller's catalogue.

HESTON (J. F.) Moral and Political Truth; or, Reflections suggested by reading History and Biography. By Jacob Franklin Heston. *Philadelphia.* 1811. 12mo. N. 31618

HETH. A Report of the Arguments in the Case of the United States *vs.* Heth. *Richmond.* 8vo, pp. 23. 31619

HETH (J.) The Life of Joice Heth, the Nurse of Gen. George Washington ... now living at the Astonishing Age of 161 Years, and weighs only 46 Pounds. ... *New York: For the Publisher.* 1835. 12mo, pp. 12. H. 31620

HETZEL (A. R.) Military Laws of the United States, including those relating to the Army, Marine Corps, Volunteers, and to Bounty Lands and Pensions; to which is prefixed, the Rules and Articles of War, and the Constitution of the United States, By Capt. A. R. Hetzel, U. S. A. Third Edition. *Washington.* 1846. 8vo. C., P. 31621

Heuglyk vooruitzigt of vaderlandsche droom. [n. p. 1781.] 8vo, pp. 16. 31622

This "Joyful prospect, or patriotic dream," is a satirical poem against Van Goens and others of his party.

HEURNIUS (J.) De Legatione Evangelica ad Indos capessenda admonitio. *Lugduni Batavorum, ex officina Elzeviriana.* 1618. Small 8vo, pp. (20), 300, (2). S. 31623

Included in D. B. Warden's "Bibliotheca Americana."

HEURTIER (*M.*) Emigration Européenne. Rapport par M. Heurtier. *Paris.* 1854. 8vo. B. 31624

HEUSINGER (O.) Amerikanische Kriegsbilder. Aufzeichnungen aus den Jahren 1861–1865. Von Otto Heusinger ... . *Leipzig: Verlag von Friedr. Wilh. Grunow.* 1869. 16mo, pp. viii, 262, (2). B. 31625

HEUSSER (H.) *and* CLARAZ (G.) Ensayos de un Conocimiento Geognostico-Fisico de la Provincia de Buenos-Aires. I. La Cordillera. Por D. H. Heusser y Georges Claraz. *Buenos-Aires.* 1863. 8vo, pp. 20. Plate. H. 31626

HEUSTIS (D. D.) A Narrative of the Adventures and Sufferings of Capt. Daniel D. Heustis, and his Companions, in Canada and Van Dieman's Land, during a long captivity. With Travels in California, and Voyages at Sea. Second Edition. *Boston.* 1848. 8vo. 31627

HEUSTIS (J. W.) Physical Observations, and Medical Tracts and Researches, on the Topography and Diseases of Louisiana. By Jabez W. Heustis, M.D. *New York: Printed by T. and J. Swords.* 1817. 8vo, pp. 165. N., S. 31628

[HEUVELL (H. H. v. d.)] Onpartijdige raadgevinge tot eensgezindheid en moderatie. *Utrecht.* 1779. 8vo, pp. 22. 31629

This impartial advice for unanimity and moderation, relates to the American Revolution, and cautions the Dutch against a war with England.

[HEWATT (Alexander).] An Historical Account of the Rise and Progress of the Colonies of South Carolina and Georgia. ... *Printed for Alexander Donaldson, London.* M.DCC.LXXIX. 2 vols., 8vo, pp. xiv, 347; ix, 309. B., BA. 31630

Also forms Vol. II. of Carroll's "Historical Collections." The author was an Englishman who at one time resided at Charleston. *See* "M. Rev.," LXI. 444.

HEWES (G. R. T.) *See* Vol. III., No. 6786, *and* [Thatcher (B. B.)]

HEWES (G. W.) Ballads of the War, By George Whitfield Hewes. *New York: Carleton.* M DCCC LXII. 12mo, pp. 147.

Also: ... A New Plan to Resume Specie Payments and Pay the National Debt. ... *Philadelphia: H. B. Ashmead.* 1868. 8vo, pp. 27. B., H.

HEWES (Joseph). A Collection of Occurrences and Facts, known by living Evidences, and also recorded in a public Manner, in printed and written Papers, now in Being, and indisputably true. [*London.*] 1775. 8vo, pp. 46. 31632

HEWETT (D.) The American Traveller; or National Directory, containing an Account of the Roads in the United States, with a Description of the Country, and a Geographical and Statistical View of the United States. By D. Hewett. *Washington: Davis & Force.* 1825. 16mo, pp. 440. C., S. 31633

HEWETT. A Gazetteer of the New-England States. Concise and Comprehensive. By D. Hewett. *New-York: Charles S. Francis.* 1829. 12mo, pp. 84. C., S., W. 31634

Also: Universal Traveller and Commercial and Manufacturing Directory. ... *Philadelphia.* 1832. 8vo. W.

HEWETT (J. F. Napier). European Settlements on the West Coast of Africa; with Remarks on the Slave Trade and the Supply of Cotton. By Captain J. F. N. Hewett, ... *London: Chapman & Hall.* 186–. Post 8vo, pp. 374. 31635

HEWIT (N.) The Moral Law the Essential Element of American Liberty. ... Lecture to the Bridgeport Lyceum ... April 19, 1839. By N. Hewit. ... *Bridgeport: Stiles, Nichols & Co.* 1839. 8vo, pp. 12. BA. 31636

HEWITT (A. S.) The Production of Iron and Steel in its Economic and Social Relations. By Abram S. Hewitt, United States Commissioner to the Universal Exposition at Paris, 1867. *Washington.* 1868. 8vo, pp. iv, 104. 31637

HEWITT. On the Statistics and Geography of the Production of Iron: A Paper read before the American Geographical and Statistical Society, ... 21st February, A.D. 1856 ... By Abram S. Hewitt ... . *New York: Wm. C. Bryant & Co.* 1856. 8vo, pp. 37. Map. B., H. 31638

Also: ... The Production of Iron and Steel in its Economic and Social Relations. ... *Washington: Government Printing Office.* 1868. 8vo, pp. v, 183. Plate. B., H.

[HEWITT (Girart).] Minnesota; its Advantages to Settlers, ... Being a Brief Synopsis of its History and Progress, Climate, Soil, Agricultural and Manufacturing Facilities, Commercial Capacities, and Social Status; its Lakes, Rivers, and Railroads; Homestead and Exemption Laws ... . *Girart Hewitt, St. Paul, Minnesota.* 1867. 8vo, pp. 36. B., H. + [The Same.] New Series. Second Edition. *St. Paul.* 1868. 8vo, pp. 40. H. + First Edition. *St. Paul, (Minn.) [Published by the State.]* 1869. 8vo, pp. 41. C. + Sixth Edition. [*Ibid.*] pp. 30.

HEWITT (J.) Geography of the British Colonies and Dependencies, Physical, Political, Commercial, and Historical. By James Hewitt, F.R.G.S. *London: National Society.* 186–. Fcap 8vo, pp. 192. 31640

HEWITT (J. H.) Miscellaneous Poems. By John H. Hewitt. *Baltimore: N. Hickman.* 1838. 12mo, pp. 235. C., S. 31641

HEWITT (*Mrs.* Mary Elizabeth), *afterwards* Stebbins. Heroines of History. Edited by M. E. Hewitt. *New-York.* 1852. 12mo. Illustrated. C. 31642

HEWITT. The Memorial; written by the Friends of the late Mrs. Osgood, and edited by M. E. Hewitt. *New York.* 1851. 8vo. 31643

Also: The Songs of our Land, and other Poems. *Boston: William D. Ticknor & Co.* MDCCCXLVI. 12mo, pp. 156. B., H.—Gems of the Western World.

HEWITT (N.) Discourse delivered before the General Association of Connecticut, at its Annual Meetings, New-Haven, June, 1840. By Nathaniel Hewitt, D.D. *Hartford: Printed by Elihu Geer.* MDCCCXI. 12mo. 31644

HEWLETT (H.) Address on Slavery, and against Immediate Emancipation. *New-York.* 1834. S. 31645

HEWSON (J.) Brief History of the Revolution, with Sketch of Capt. John Hewson. *Philadelphia.* 1843. 8vo. C. 31646

HEWSON (W.) Principles and Practice of Embanking Lands from River-Floods, as applied to "Levees" of the Mississippi. By William Hewson, Civil Engineer. Assisted in the Engineering Remarks by Consultation with M. Butt Hewson, Esq. ... *New York: D. Van Nostrand.* 1860. 8vo, pp. 171. BA., C.

HEY (R.) Observations On the Nature of Civil Liberty, And the Principles of Government. By Richard Hey, M.A. ... *London: T. Cadell.* MDCCLXXVI. 8vo, pp. (4), 70. C. 31648

"Mr. Hey's observations are generally delivered in the candid liberal style of a gentleman, and many of them deserve particular attention."—*Monthly Review*, LV. 153.

HEYDEN (T.) A Memoir on the Life and Character of the Rev. Prince Demetrius A. de Gallitzin, Founder of ... Catholicity, in Pa. ... By Very Rev. Thomas Heyden ... . *Baltimore: John Murphy & Co.* 1869. 12mo, pp. 200. Portrait. 31649

HEYL (L.) Statutes of the United States relating to Revenue, Commerce, Navigation, and the Currency. With the Declaration of Independence and the Constitution. Compiled by Lewis Heyl. *Boston: Little, Brown & Co.* 1868. Rl. 8vo, pp. xviii, 960. C. 31650

HEYLEN (L.) The Progress of the Age, and the Danger of the Age. Two Lectures ... By the Rev. Louis Heylen. *Cincinnati: John P. Walsh.* 1865. 16mo, pp. 107. 31651

HEYLIDY (C. J.) Vroegere en hedendaagsche strafregtspleging in Suriname. *T.-a.-R.* 1857. 8vo. 31652

HEYLYN *or* HEYLIN (P.) Antidotum Lincolniense, or an answer to a Book entituled the Holy Table, Name, and Thing, etc. By Peter Heylin. *London.* 1637. 4to. 31653

Contains allusions to John Cotton of New England, and his Letter to the Vicar of Grantham. *See* [Williams (*Bishop.*)]

HEYLIN. Aulicus Coquinariæ; or Vindication, in answer to a pamphlet entitled, the Court and Character of James I., pretended to be penn'd by Sir Anthony Weldon. By Peter Heylin. *London.* 1650. 12mo. 31654

Contains observations on Sir Walter Raleigh's Voyage to Guiana, Virginia, and other plantations in America.

HEYLYN. Cosmographie, In four Books, containing the Chorographie and Historie of the Whole World, and all the Principal Kingdoms, Provinces, Seas and Isles thereof. By Peter Heylin. *London: Henry Seile* ... . 1652. Folio, pp. (12), 1052, (18). 4

Maps. c. + Second Edition. [*Ibid.*] 1657. Folio, pp. (12), 1007, (8). + [Another] Second Edition. [*Ibid.*] 1660. s. + Third Edition. [*Ibid.*] 1665. Folio, pp. (12), 1095, (8). + Fourth Edition. With an accurate and an approved Index of all the Kingdoms, Provinces, Countries, Inhabitants, People, Cities, Mountains, Rivers, Seas, Islands, Forts, Bays, Capes, Forests, &c., of any Remarque in the whole World; Much wanted and desired in the Former, and now annexed to this last Impression, Revised and Corrected by the Author himself immediately before his death. ... *London: Printed for Anne Seile.* M.DC.LX.VI. Folio, Engraved Title, pp. (14), 1098, (54). + Fifth Edition. [*Ibid.*] 1669. N. + Third [Sixth] Edition, Corrected and Inlarged by the Author. *London: P. Chetwind.* 1670. Folio, Engraved Title, pp. (14), 1110 [paged 1095], (12). 4 Maps. c. 31655

The fourth book of this work is devoted to the chorography of America. The title-pages of the separate books are dated from 1662–67. There are copies of the sixth edition dated 1673, 1674, and 1677. The last edition is "Improved, with an Historical Continuation to the present time, by Edmund Bohun, Esq." *London.* 1703. Folio. c.

HEYLYN. Μικρόκοσμος. A Little Description of the Great World. By Peter Heylin. *Oxford.* 1621. 4to. + The Second Edition, Augmented and Revised, By Peter Heylyn. *Oxford.* 1625. 4to. + The Third Edition, Revised, By Peter Heylyn. ... *Oxford, Printed by I. L. and W. T. for William Turner and Thomas Huggins.* 1627. 4to, pp. (8), 807, (4). + The Fourth Edition. [*Ibid.*] 1629. + The Fifth Edition ... [*Ibid.*] 1632. M. + The Sixth Edition. ... *Oxford, Printed for William Turner, and Robert Allott.* 1633. 4to, pp. (20), 807, (1). + Seventh Edition. [*Ibid.*] 1636. + [*Ibid.*] 1637. + [*Ibid.*] 1939 [for 1639]. 31656

In speaking of America, he remarks "this great tract of land ought, and that most aptly, to bee called the New World; New for the late discovery, and World, for the vast spaciousness of it: the most vsuall and yet somewhat improper name, is America." Dr. W. B. Stevens remarks, that it "illustrates the great deficiency of geographical knowledge concerning America, even as late as the settlement of the Plymouth pilgrims." Also: Examen Historicum; or, a Discovery and Examination of the Mistakes, Falsities and Defects in some Modern Histories. ... *London.* 1659. 8vo. N.

HEYLIN *and others.* A Pocket Commentary Of the first Settling of New-Jersey, by the Europeans; and An Account or Fair Detail Of the Original Indian Elizabeth-Town Grants: And other Rights of the like Tenure, in East New-Jersey, (Digested in Order) Wherein is intermixed a great part of the Annals (if they may be so called) of New-Jersey, in general; extracted out of the Reverend Doctor Peter Heylin; the accu-

rate and Facetious William Douglass, Esquire, Doctor of Physick; and other Authors; from its Beginning, to the Year 1745. *New York: Printed by Samuel Parker.* 1759. 8vo, pp. 19.

A tract of extreme rarity. I have seen only two copies. It is not mentioned in Mr. Whitehead's List of Books relating to New Jersey.

HEYN (P. P.) Extract uyt den Brief van den | E. Generael Pieter Pietersz. Heyn | aen de Geoctroyeerde West-Indische Compagnie, ghe-|schreven in 't Schip Amsterdam, ghedateerd den 26 Sep-|tember, 1628, 140 mylen by Westen Eyland Bermuda. [1628.] 4to, pp. 4. 31658

Extract from the letter of the noble General P. P. Heyn to the ... West India Company; written in the ship Amsterdam, 1628. *See* Asher's "Bibliographical Essay," *also* Frederick Muller's "Catalogue," 1872, p. 100, where Mr. Muller remarks, "Perhaps no success ever made so great a sensation in Holland as the capture of the Spanish Silverfleet at Matanca by P. Heyn, in 1628. ... This important capture not only enriched Holland, but inspired the West-India-Company with new courage; for immediately afterwards they began to elaborate the privileges of the colonists of New-Netherland; it was with the money gained in this affair, that the Company in a great measure defrayed the enormous but useless expenses of their North-American Colony." The various tracts which relate to the subject, are in this dictionary described under the names of the authors, or when anonymous, if not below, under the first word in the title-page, articles excepted.

HEYN. Lof-dicht, | Van alle de voornaemste Exploy-|ten, ghedaen onder het bewint van de Ghe-|octroyeerde Westindische Compagnie, | Door het cloeck beleyt van den Erntfesten ende Manhaf-|tighen Zee-helt den Generael | Pieter Pietersz Heyn, | Beginnende vanden Iare 1624. 1625. 1626. | ende 1628. | *Tot Dordrecht,* | *Gedruct by Francoys Bosselaer.* 1629. | 4to, pp. 16.

See our No. 3978a for the name of the author of this panegyric on the exploits of Heyn; the title there given is not exact—this is. *See also* [Pels (E.)], [Wynandts (W.)]

HEYN. Practiicke | van den | Spaenschen | Aes-Sack: | Aengevvesen | Op de Veroveringe, en Victorie van den | Loffelijken, Voorsienighen, Manlijck-hertighen | Heer Generael | Pieter Pietersz. Heyn. | Met By-voegingthe van noodighe Poëtische 't Samen-spraecke; | Ende | Aerdige Rijm-Vyeren, en VVellekomsten. | Mitsgaders | Eenighe Treur-Versen op het droevich ongheluck des | Coninckl: | M: van Bohemen. |

Let op het spel; Vignette. Want loos bedroch
En wachtje wel: Dat guychelt noch.

In 's Gravenhage, | *Gedruckt in 't Jaer ons Heeren* 1629. | 4to, 16 l.

"Le discours en vers qui commence cet écrit, porte en tête une gravure satirique. L'un des poèmes est signé 'Druck om geluck;' les 'Treurversen' par A. Duyrcant."—TRÖMEL.

HEYN. Practiicke | van den | Spaenschen | Aes-Sack: | Aengevvesen | Op de Veroveringe, en Victorie van den | Loffelijken, Voorsienighen, Manlijck-hertighen | Heer Generael | Pieter Pietersz. Heyn. | Met By-voegingthe van noodighe Poëtische 't Samen-spraecke; | Ende | Aerdige Rijm-Vyeren, en VVellekomsten. | Mitsgaders | Eenighe Treur-Versen op het droevich ongheluck des | Coninckl: | M: van Bohemen. |

Let op het spel; Vignette. Want loos bedroch
En wachtje wel: Dat guychelt noch.

In 's Gravenhage, | *Voor Anthonis Iansz. Tongerloo, Boeck-verkooper inde Veen-straet;* | *inde Thien-Geboden. Anno* 1629. | 4to, 16 l.

"Même impression que le précédent, avec la seule différence que le nom de l'éditeur y est indiqué sur le titre."—TRÖMEL.

HEYN. Samenspraak in het Rijck der dooden tusschen Admiraal Piet Heyn en de Schout-by-Nacht W. Krull, gesneuveld voor St. Eustatius. *Amsterdam.* 1781. 8vo, pp. 28. 31662

Dialogue in the Land of Shadows between Admiral P. Heyn and Rear-Admiral W. Krull, killed at St. Eustatius.

HEYN. Svvymel-Klacht. *See* Eibergen (Rutgerus), Vol. VI.

HEYN. Tekel | Ofte | VVeech-schale | vande groote monarchie | van Spaingien, waer bij ontdect | wert, dat de selve soo veel niet en | vermach, als sy haer onder-staet to doen. | Ter occasie vande Silver Vlote by | den Generael Pieter Pieterssen Heyn vero-|wert, neder-ghestelt. | ... | *Middleburgh.* | *Gedruckt by Hans van der Hellen.* | *Voor* | *Jacob vande Vivere. Boeck-*| *vercooper, woonende bij de nieuwe Beurse,* | *inde nieuwe Druckerie. Anno* 1629. | 4to, pp. 48. 31663

HEYN. Victorij Sang en Lof dicht ofer de heerlijcke veroveringe vande Spaensche Silver-vloot uyt Nova Spanje door den Generael Pieter Pietersz Heyn den 8. Sept. 1628. *Haerlem.* 1629. Folio, 1 l. 31664

HEYNE (Chr. G.) Opuscula Academica. *Göttingæ.* 1785–1812. 6 vols., 8vo. 31665

Contents: Vol. III., pp. 144–162. De belli Romani socialis caussis et eventu, respectu ad bellum cum Coloniis Americanis gestum habito. Vol. IV., pp. 268–286. Comparatur deportatio in Novam Cambriam australem cum deportatione Romanorum in insulam.

HEYNS (P.) Miroir du monde, reduict premièrement en rithme brabançonne, et maintenant tourné en prose françois, auquel se représente clairement et au vif ... la vray situation, nature et

propriété de la terre universelle. *Anvers: Plantin.* 1579. 4to. Map. 31666

HEYNS. Spieghel der werelt. Waer inne ... de gheleghentheyt, nature, ende aert aller landen claerlijck afgebeeldt ende beschreuen. *Antwerpiæ: Chr. Plantijn.* 1583. 4to. 5 Maps.

[HEYRICK (Elizabeth).] Immediate, not Gradual Abolition; or, an inquiry into the Shortest, Safest, and most Effectual Means of getting rid of West Indian Slavery. *London: Hatchard and Son.* 1824. 8vo, pp. 24. + *London: F. Westley.* [n. d.] 8vo, pp. 28. + *Philadelphia.* 1837. 12mo, pp. 36. + *Boston: Isaac Knapp.* 1838. 12mo, pp. 35. B., H. 31668

The American reprints give the name of the author.

HEYWOOD (B. A.) Disendowment Condemned by the Supreme Court of America. The Decisions in Terrett *v.* Taylor, The Society for the Propagation of the Gospel *v.* the Town of New Haven, and the Trustees of Dartmouth College *v.* Woodward. Edited by B. A. Heywood, M.A. *London: Hatchards.* 1869. 8vo. 31669

HEYWOOD (J. H.) The Spirit and Duty of Christian Citizenship. A Sermon preached in Louisville, Kentucky, September, 1862. By Rev. J. H. Heywood. *Louisville: Maxwell & Co.* 1862. 8vo, pp. 12. 31670

HEYWOOD. A Tribute to the Memory of James H. Perkins. Two Sermons; one delivered in ... Cincinnati, ... Dec. 23, 1849, by Rev. John H. Heywood; the other ... Dec. 30, 1849, by Rev. B. F. Barrett. *Cincinnati.* 1850. 8vo, pp. 47. 31671

Also: Discourse on the Life and Character of Joseph Brown Smith ... . *Louisville, Ky.: Hanna & Co, Printers.* 1859. 8vo, pp. 16. H.— ... A Discourse [Memory of Joshua B. Flint, M.D.] ... Louisville, Ky., March 21, 1864. ... *Louisville.* 1864. 8vo, pp. 14. B.—Discourse on the Life and Services of Daniel Webster ... Louisville ... October 31, 1852. ... *Louisville, Ky.: Printed by J. F. Brennan.* 1852. 8vo, pp. 14. —Two Sermons occasioned by the Death of William H. G. Butter ... November 6, 1853, and April 30, 1854. ... *Louisville: Morton & Griswold.* 1854. 8vo, pp. 24.

HEYWOOD (J.) ... A Sermon ... at Dunstable, Mass., ... Oct. 24th, 1813, ... the Death of Sergeant John Woodward, Jr. ... By Joshua Heywood, A.B. ... *Groton Junction: Printed by John H. Turner.* 1870. 8vo, pp. 12. B., H. 31672

HEYWOOD (L.) An Oration, ... at Worcester, Mass. ... July 4th, 1810. By Levi Heywood. ... *Worcester: Printed by Henry Rogers.* 1810. 8vo, pp. 15. B., W. 31673

HEYWOOD (P.) The Brazil Pilot. By Peter Heywood, Captain English Navy. *London: W. Faden.* 1818. 8vo, pp. iv, 107, 3. C. 31674

HIATT (J. M.) The Voter's Text Book; comprising a Collection of the most Important Documents and Statistics connected with the Political History of America. *Indianapolis.* 1868. 12mo. 31675

HIBBARD (A. G.) In Memory of Abraham Lincoln. A Discourse delivered ... in ... Detroit, Mich., ... April 17th, 1865, by A. G. Hibbard, ... *Detroit: O. S. Gulley's Office.* 1865. 8vo, pp. 12. 31676

HIBBARD (Billy). Memoirs of the Life and Travels of B. Hibbard, Minister of the Gospel, containing an Account of his Experience of Religion; and of his Call to and Labours in the Ministry, for nearly Thirty Years: in which are recorded many Important, Curious and Interesting Events, illustrative of the Providence and Grace of God. *New-York: The Author.* 1825. 12mo, pp. over 360. + *New York.* 1843. 31677

HIBBARD (H.) Nebraska and Kansas. Speech of Hon. Harry Hibbard, of N. H., ... May 8, 1854. [*Washington.* n. d.] 8vo, pp. 8. B. 31678

HIBBARD (J. R.) A Spiritual Ground of Hope for the Salvation of the Country. A Discourse delivered ... August 6, 1862. By Rev. J. R. Hibbard, ... *Chicago: Tribune Office.* 1862. 8vo, pp. 24. 31679

Also: A Sermon on the Causes and Uses of the Present Civil War, delivered in Chicago, April 11, 1862. ... [n. p. n. d.] 8vo, pp. 8.—War in Heaven. A Sermon preached April 21, 1861. ... *Chicago: Tribune Office.* 1861. 12mo, pp. 15.

HIBBARD (R. T.) Startling Disclosures concerning the Death of John N. Maffit. By Rufus T. Hibbard. *New York.* 1856. 8vo. C. 31680

HIBBERT (E.) Narrative of a Journey from Santiago de Chile to Buenos Ayres, in July and August, 1811. By Captain Edward Hibbert. *London.* 1824. Post 8vo. Map. 31681

Only a few copies privately printed.

HIBBERT (G.) Substance of three Speeches in Parliament, on the Bill for the Abolition of the Slave Trade. By George Hibbert. *London.* 1807. 8vo. C. 31682

HIBBERT (Mary?) *and* BUIST (Robert). The American Flower Garden Directory, ... With a Description of the Plants most Desirable in each ... *Philadelphia: For the Authors by Adam Waldie.* 1832. 8vo, pp. ix, 7–375, (1). Plate. C. 31683

HIBBERT (N.) An Abstract of the Case of the West India Dock Company ... By N. Hibbert ... . *London: Printed by J. Darling.* 1823. 8vo, pp. (4), 69. H. 31684

HIBBERT. Report of the Select Committee on Foreign Trade; with an Abstract of the Case of the West India Dock Company ... By N. Hibbert ... . *London: J. M. Richardson.* 1823. 8vo, pp. viii, 101. H. 31685

Hibernia Fire Engine Company, No. 1 [of Philadelphia]. Visit to the Cities of New York. Boston, Brooklyn, Charlestown, and Newark, in 1858. Memorial. *Philadelphia: J. B. Chandler.* 1859. 4to, pp. 108. 18 Plates. C. 31686

The Hibernian Provident Society of New York, or the Spanish Inquisition under Nine Directors. Address to the People of the State of New York. *New York.* 1809. 8vo. 31687

Hibernicus, or Memoirs of an Irishman now in America, containing an Account of the Principal Events of his Life, both before and since his Emigration, and interspersed with Anecdotes and Observations, Humorous, Political, and Moral. With a Supplement. *Pittsburg.* 1828. 12mo, pp. 251. 31688

HIBERNICUS, *pseudon.* *See* [Clinton (De Witt)], [Neilson (S.)]

HICHBORN (B.) An Oration, delivered March 5th, 1777, at the Request of the Inhabitants of the Town of Boston; to Commemorate the Bloody Tragedy of the Fifth of March, 1770. By Benjamin Hichborn ... . *Boston: Edes & Gill.* M.DCC.LXXVII. 4to, pp. 18. B., BA., C., M., W. 31689

HICHBORN. An Oration ... July 5, 1784, at ... Boston, in Celebration of ... American Independence. *Boston.* [1784.] 4to, pp. 19. M. 31690

HICKCOX (J. H.) An Historical Account of American Coinage. By John H. Hickcox. ... With Plates. *Albany, N. Y.: Joel Munsell.* 1858. Imp. 8vo, pp. viii, 151. 5 Plates. B., BA.

Two hundred copies printed, of which five are on large paper.

HICKCOX. A History of the Bills of Credit or Paper Money Issued by New York, From 1709 to 1789: With a Description of the Bills, and Catalogue of the Various Issues. By John H. Hickcox. ... *Albany, N. Y.: J. H. Hickcox & Co.* 1866. Rl. 8vo, pp. (6), 103. Scale. B., BA., C. 31692

Two hundred and fifty copies printed, of which fifty are large paper in quarto. Important chapter in the revolutionary history of New York.

H[ICKERINGILL] (E[dmond].) Jamaica | Viewed: | With | All the Ports, Harbours, | and their several Soundings, | Towns, and Settlements | thereunto belonging | Together, | With the nature of it's Climate, | fruitfulnesse of the Soile, | and it's suitablenesse to | English Complexions. | With several other collateral | Observations and Reflexions | upon the Island. | By E. H. | *London,* | *Printed for J. R.* 1661. | 16mo, pp. (6), 106. Map. C., J.C.B. + The Second Edition. *London, Printed for Iohn Williams,* ... 1661. 16mo, pp. (16), 87. Map. 31693

HICKERINGILL. Jamaica | Viewed: | With | All the Ports, Harbours, and their | several Soundings, Towns, and | Settlements thereunto belonging. | Together, | With the nature of its Climate, fruitfulness | of the Soil, and its suitableness to English | Complexions. | With several other collateral Observations | and Reflections upon the Island. | The Third Edition. | By Captain Hickeringill. | *London:* | *Printed: ... by B. Bragg,* ... MDCCV. | 4to, pp. (8), 44. Map. C., H. 31694

The author, who was an eccentric man, after having been an officer in the army, took orders and became a priest, "when he gave much offence to his brethren by his wild and often scurrilous attacks on the church, in a variety of pamphlets."—CHALMERS. Barcia says that "this work is a paraphrase of all that had been previously written on the subject." The map is often wanting.

HICKERINGILL. Miscellaneous Tracts, Essays, Satires, &c., in Prose and Verse, containing a Description of Jamaica, &c. *London.* 1707. 4to. Portrait and Map. 31695

Includes the foregoing work.

HICKEY (W.) The Constitution of the United States of America, with an alphabetical analysis; ... with a descriptive account of the State Papers, Public Documents, ... at the seat of Government. By William Hickey. Second Edition. *Philadelphia: T. K. & P. G. Collins.* 1847. 12mo, pp. (1), xl, (1), 497. H. + Third Edition. *Philadelphia.* 1848. 12mo, pp. 509. + Fourth Edition. [*Ibid.*] 1851. 12mo, pp. xlvi, (1), 521. Plate. BA., C. + Fifth Edition. [*Ibid.*] 1852. 8vo. S.

+ Sixth Edition. [*Ibid.*] 1853. 12mo, pp. (1), xlvi, (1), 521. H. + Seventh Edition. [*Ibid.*] 1854. 12mo, pp. xlvii, 521. B.

For the first edition *see our* Vol. IV., No. 16111.

HICKMAN (E. C.) Scraps of Poetry and Prose. By Edwin C. Hickman. *Lexington (Ky.): A. W. Elder.* 1854. 18mo, pp. 200. C. 31697

HICKMAN (G. H.) Life and Public Services of the Hon. James Knox Polk; with a Compendium of his Speeches on various public measures. Also a Sketch of the Life of the Hon. George M. Dallas. By George H. Hickman. *Baltimore.* 1844. 8vo. C. 31698

[HICKMAN.] The Life of General Lewis Cass, with his Letters and Speeches on Various Subjects. *Baltimore: N. Hickman.* 1848. 8vo, pp. 72. Portrait. 31699

This is a corrected title of *our* No. 11356.

[HICKMAN.] The New Tariff, of 1846 ... With a History of the Proceedings connected with the Passage of the Act; ... *Baltimore: N. Hickman.* 1846. 8vo, pp. 16. H. 31700

HICKMAN (H. H.) Oration ... at ... Detroit, to Zion Lodge ... Dec. 27. A.L. 5810. By Harris Hampden Hickman. *Pittsburgh, Penn.: Printed by Cramer, Spear & Eichbaum.* 1811. 8vo, pp. 10. H., W. 31701

HICKMAN (J. G.) The Life of John Howes, a Loyalist of the Memorable Revolution of 1776. ... By J. G. Hickman, Barrister at Law. *St. John, N. B.: Carrilton, Briggs & Co.* 1846. 8vo, pp. 32. B. 31702

HICKMAN (J.) Kansas Contested Election. Speech of Hon. John Hickman, of Pa., delivered in the House of Representatives, March 19, 1856. [n. p. n. d.] 8vo, pp. 7. 31703

Also: Democracy. The Old and the New. Speech ... on the Battle Ground of Brandywine, September 11, 1860. [n. p. n. d.] 8vo, pp. 5.—Political Issues and Presidential Candidates. Speech ... Philadelphia, ... July 24th, 1860. [n. p. n. d.] 8vo, pp. 11. + [Same.] Campaign Document, No. 3. Speech ... July 24th, 1860. [n. p. n. d.] 8vo, pp. 8.—Popular Sovereignty—The Will of the Majority against the Rule of a Minority. Speech ... January 28, 1858. [*Washington.* n. d.] 8vo, pp. 8.—Southern Sectionalism. Speech ... May 1, 1860. [n. p. n. d.] 8vo, pp. 8. H. —The "Joint Resolution" on the Subject of Emancipation. ... Speech ... March 11, 1862. [n. p. n. d.] 8vo, pp. 8.—Who have violated Compromises. Speech ... December 12, 1859. *Washington: D. C. Buell & Blanchard.* 1859. 8vo, pp. 8. H.

HICKMAN (N.) The Citizen Soldiers at North Point and Fort McHenry, Sept. 12, 13, 1814. ... By N. Hickman. *Baltimore: N. Hickman.* [1858.] 12mo, pp. 96. S. 31704

The muster rolls of those who defended Baltimore and parts adjacent.

[HICKMAN.] The Politician's Register, containing the Result of the Elections which have taken Place during the Years 1844, 1845, 1846, 1847, 1848 ... . *New York: Burgess, Stringer & Co.* 1848. 12mo, pp. 48. H. 31705

HICKMAN (W.) Sketches on the Nissisaguil, a River of New Brunswick. By William Hickman. *London.* 1861. Folio.

HICKOK (L. P.) A Nation saved from its Prosperity only by the Gospel. A Discourse in Behalf of the American Home Missionary Society, preached in the Cities of New York and Brooklyn, May, 1853. By Rev. Laurens P. Hickok, D.D. ... *New York: American Home Missionary Society.* 1853. 8vo, pp. 30.

Also: ... A Sermon ... December 5, 1832, at the Installation of the Rev. N. M. Urmstone ... in Newtown. ... *Litchfield: Printed by Henry Adams.* 1833. 8vo, pp. 18. H.—Sermon preached at Litchfield, Conn., at the Funeral of Colonel Benjamin Tallmadge, March 12, 1835. ... *New-York: Printed by J. M. Elliott.* 1835. 8vo, pp. 24. S.—A Sermon on the Death of Leonard E. Lathrop, D.D., ... at Sharon, Conn., August 23, 1857. ... *New-York: Baker and Godwin.* 1857. 8vo, pp. 22. BA., H., S. —The Sources of Military Delusion ... An Address before the Connecticut Peace Society ... May 5, 1833 in ... Hartford. ... *Hartford: Printed by Philemon Canfield.* 1833. 8vo, pp. 40. B., BA., H., W.

HICKOK (M. J.) ... A Thanksgiving Sermon: preached in ... Scranton, Pa., November 27, 1862. By M. J. Hickok, D.D., ... *New York: John F. Trow, Printer.* 1862. 8vo, pp. 28.

HICKS (A. W.) Life, Trial, Confession and Execution of the Pirate and Murderer Albert W. Hicks ... *New York.* [1860.] 8vo, pp. 84. Numerous Engravings. 31709

Also: Trial of Hicks, for Piracy, on board the Sloop Edwin A. Johnson. *New York.* 1860. 8vo, pp. 68.

HICKS (E.) The Answers, By Elias Hicks to the Six Queries addressed to him, With his Declarations upon the same Points, on other occasions, contrasted with each other, and with the Doctrines of the Society of Friends. *New-York: Printed by Mahlon Day.* 1831. 12mo, pp. 32. 31710

HICKS. Journal of the Life and Religious Labours of Elias Hicks. Written by Himself. Third Edition. *New York: Isaac T. Hopper.* 1832. 8vo, pp. 451. B. + Fifth Edition. [*Ibid.*] 1832. 8vo, pp. 451. H. 31711

HICKS. Letters of Elias Hicks, Including also a few short Essays, written on several Occasions, mostly illustrative of his Doctrinal Views. *New York: Isaac T. Hopper.* MDCCCXXXIV. 8vo. 31712

HICKS. Observations on the Slavery of the Africans and their Descendants. Recommended to the Serious Perusal, and Impartial Consideration of the Citizens of the United States of America, and Others concerned, By Elias Hicks. ... *New York: Printed by Samuel Wood.* 1811. 12mo, pp. 24. P. + [The Same, with many Alterations.] *New York: Samuel Wood.* 1814. 12mo, pp. 23. B., S. 31713

Reprinted in Hicks' "Letters," 1834.

HICKS. A Series of Extemporaneous Discourses, delivered in the several meetings of the Society of Friends, in Philadelphia, Germantown, Abington, Byberry, Newtown Falls, and Trenton. By Elias Hicks, a Minister in said Society. ... *Philadelphia: Joseph and Edward Parker.* 1825. 8vo, pp. 328. P. 31714

Also: Observations on the Sermons of Elias Hicks, in Several Letters ... by a Demi-Quaker. *Philadelphia.* 1826. 8vo, pp. 67.

HICKS. Sermons delivered by Elias Hicks & Edward Hicks; in Friends' Meetings, New-York, in 5th month, 1825. Taken in Short-hand, by L. H. Clarke, & M. T. C. Gould. ... *New-York: J. V. Seaman.* 1825. 8vo, pp. 138. BA., C., N. 31715

The Hicksite controversy elicited numerous books and pamphlets mostly relative to the doctrine of Elias Hicks and his opponents, a list of which can be found in Smith's "Catalogue of Friends' Books." We have introduced only so many as seem to be historical. The following relate to Hicks:

Account of the Life, Ministry, Last Sickness, and Death of Elias Hicks. [n. p. n. d.] 8vo. 31716

An Examination of an Epistle issued by a Meeting of the Followers of Elias Hicks, held ... in Philadelphia, ... 1827, being a Statement of Facts relative to their Separation from the Society of Friends. ... *Philadelphia.* 1827. 12mo, pp. 54. P. 31717

A Testimony from the Monthly Meeting of Friends of Jericho, concerning Elias Hicks, deceased. ... *New York: Printed by Isaac T. Hopper.* 1830. 8vo, pp. 8. B., W. 31718

For an account of Elias Hicks and his ministry, *see* Emanuel Howitt's "Tour through the United States," p. 9.

HICKS (G. E.) The Fair Maid of Wyoming. A Tale of the War of Independence. Compositions from Campbell's Gertrude of Wyoming, by G. E. Hicks. With Introduction and

Historical Notes, by Gabriel Alexander. *Art Union of London.* 1846. Oblong 4to. 13 Plates. 31719

HICKS (R.) The Lady Killer; a Tale of Virginia. By Miss R. Hicks. *Philadelphia.* 1857. 12mo. 31720

HICKS (T.) Thomas Crawford; his Career, Character, and Works. A Eulogy, By Thomas Hicks, N.A., read before the Century Club, ... New York, ... January 26, 1858. *New York: D. Appleton and Company.* 1858. 8vo, pp. 52. B., H. M. 31721

Reprinted for W. Loring Andrews as

HICKS. Eulogy on Thomas Crawford. By Thomas Hicks, N.A. *New York: Privately Printed for Subscribers.* 1865. 8vo, pp. 103. 3 Plates. B. 31722

Seventy copies only printed for subscribers, of which twenty-five are on large paper.

HICKS (T. H.) Addresses on the Death of Hon. T. H. Hicks, delivered in the Senate and House of Representatives, ... February 15, 1865. *Washington: Government Printing Office.* 1865. 8vo, pp. 48. B., BA. 31723

HIDALGA (L.) Paralelo y proyecto de penitenciarias. Aprobado por la junta directiva de carceles. *Mexico.* 1850. Folio. 7 Plates. 31724

HIDALGO (Ignacio Xavier). La Nueva Ruth de la Gracia, Sermon Funebre y Panegyrico en las Honras de Dña. Maria Rosa de la Peña lloró sú Primogenito D. Joseph Tagle Villegas de la Peña. *Mexico.* 1754. 4to. 31725

HIDALGO (J.) Apuntes para escribir la Historia de los Proyectos de Monarquia en México, desde el reinado de Carlos III. hasta la Instalacion del Emperador Maximiliano. Por José Hidalgo. *Paris.* 1868. 8vo. 31726

HIDALGO. Apuntes biograficos de D. Ignacio Valdivielso. Por José Hidalgo. *Paris.* 1861. 8vo. Portrait. 31727

HIDALGO (M.) Glorias Dominicanas en su esclarecido, é ilustre Militar tercer Orden. Por El M. R. P. Mrô. Fr. Miguel Hidalgo, Fundador de las quatro Missiones en la Provincia de Californias. Tomo 1º. Contiene el Origen de este Venerable Instituto, su antiqüedad, y precedencia á todas las Ordenes Terceras de la Militante Iglesia: &c. *Mexico.* 1795. Small 4to, pp. xi, 224. 2 Plates. 31728

No more printed?

HIDALGO *and* ALLENDE (I.) Pública Vindicacion del illustre Ayuntamiento de Santa Fé de Guanaxuato justificando su conducta moral y politica en la entrada y crimenes que cometieron en aquella Ciudad las huestes insurgentes agabilladas por sus corifeos M. Hidalgo y Ignacio Allende. *Mexico.* 1811. 4to.

HIDALGO *and* COSTELLA (M.) Cuadro Historico de la Revolucion de la America Mexicana, comenzada en quince de Sept. de Mil. Ochocientos Diez, por el ciudadano Miguel Hidalgo y Costella. *Mexico Imprenta.* 1823–24. 2 vols., 4to. 31730

Issued in tracts of twelve pages each, and highly interesting.

HIEMCKE (A. H.) Aanleiding tot de regte gebruik van he compas, bij militaire expeditien in de wildernissen van West-Indien. *Paramaribo.* 1817. 8vo. 31731

The Hierophant: or Monthly Journal of Sacred Symbols and Prophecy. Conducted by George Bush ... . *New York: Mark H. Newman.* 1844. 8vo, pp. (4), 288. B., BA., H. 31732

A Swedenborgian journal.

[HIESLER (William M.)] The Place of the Ringgold Light Artillery of Reading ... April, 1861. ... *Reading, Pa.* 1870. 8vo, pp. 16. H. 31733

HIGBEE (J.) Sermon at Alstead, N. H. April 24, 1803, Occasioned by the Death of Miss Persis Hatch. By Jeremiah Higbee. *Walpole.* 1803. 8vo. W. 31734

HIGBY (W.) Alaska. Speech of William Higby, 21st ... March, 1868, on the Treaty between the United States and the Russian Government for the Transfer of Alaska. [*Washington.* n. d.] 8vo, pp. 16. H. 31735

Also: Privileges and Immunities of Citizenship. Speech ... February 27, 1866. [n. p. n. d.] 8vo, pp. 7. H.

HIGGINS (B.) Observations and Advices for the Improvement of the Manufacture of Muscovado Sugar and Rum. Second Part. By Bryan Higgins, M.D. *St. Jago de la Vega: Printed by Alexander Aikman,* ... M. DCCC. 8vo, pp. (4), 132. 9 Plates. J.C.B. 31736

See Barrington (D.), Vol. I., No. 3632.

HIGGINS (G.) Anacalypsis, an attempt to draw aside the veil of the Saitic Isis, or an Inquiry into the Origin of Languages,

Nations and Religions. By Godfrey Higgins. *London.* 1833. 2 vols., 4to, pp. xxxii, 867. 5 Plates. 31737

Two hundred copies only printed. Its tendency is to overturn all the established systems of religion, and to destroy all received notions upon subjects generally considered sacred, and to substitute a simple unsacerdotal worship. Many of the articles refer to America.

HIGGINS (James). Reports. *See* Maryland.

[HIGGINS (Thomas W.)] The Crooked Elm; or, Life by the Way-Side. *Boston: Author.* 1857. 12mo, pp. 452. Plate.

[HIGGINSON (Francis).] New-Englands Plantation. Or, a Short and Trve Description of the Commodities and Discommodities of that Countrey. Written by a reuerend Diuine now there resident. *London, Printed by T. C. and R. C. for Michael Sparke,* ... 1630. 4to, pp. 20. 31739

This edition forms No. XII. of Force's "Tracts," Vol. I. *See also* "Mass. Hist. Society Collections," 1st Series, Vol. I.; 3d Series, Vol. VII.; *also*, Young (A.) "Chronicles of Massachusetts." Muller's Catalogue, No. 451, gives the date 1628.

HIGGINSON. New-Englands | Plantation. | Or, | a Short and Trve | Description of the | Commodities and | Discommodities | of that Covntrey. | Written by Mr. Higgeson, a reuerend Diuine | now there resident. | Wherevnto is added a Letter, sent by Mr. Graues | an Enginere, out of New-England, | The third Edition enlarged. | *London,* | *Printed by T. and R. Cotes. for Michael Sparke, dwelling* | *at the Signe of the Blue Bible in Greene-* | *Arbor.* 1630. | 4to, 13 l. C., H. 31740

Very rare, highly interesting, and important.

HIGGINSON (F.) Transatlantic Cable. By Lieut. Francis Higginson. *London.* 1847. 31741

[HIGGINSON (F. J.)] Remarks on Slavery and Emancipation. ... [*Boston.* n. d.] 12mo, pp. 105. B., BA. 31742

HIGGINSON (J.) The | Cause of God | and his People in New-England, | as it was | Stated and Discussed | in | A | Sermon Preached before the Honourable General | Court of the Massachusets Colony, | on the 27 day of May 1663. Being the Day | Of Election at Boston. | By John Higginson, Pastor of the Church | of Christ at Salem. ... *Cambridg: Printed by Samuel Green.* 1663. 4to, pp. (4), 24. H., BA. 31743

The preface is signed "John Wilson, Senior. Samuel Whiting." *See* Michel (J.) "This Reverend Person (John Higginson) has been always valued for his useful Preaching, and his holy Living, having formerly born his Testimony to the Cause of God, and his People in New-England, in a Sermon so entituled, which he preached on

the greatest Anniversary Solemnity, which occurr'd in the Land."—*Magnalia,* Book III., p. 76.

[HIGGINSON.] The Deplorable State of New-England. *See* Vol. V., No. 19639, and add [*Boston*], *reprinted.* 1721. 8vo, pp. 36.

HIGGINSON. A Direction for a Publick Profession in the Church Assembly, after a Private Examination by the Elders; with Confession of Faith agreed upon by the Church at Salem, 6th August, 1629. By John Higginson. [n. p. n. d.] 8vo, pp. 6. M. 31744

HIGGINSON. Our Dying Saviour's | Legacy of Peace | To His Disciples in a Troublesome | World, ... | Also a | Discourse | On the Two Witnesses, | Shewing that it is the Duty of all Christians | to be Witnesses unto Christ, ... | Unto which is added | Some Help to Self-Examination. | *Boston, Printed by Samuel Green for John Usher near the Town-House.* 1686. 8vo, pp. (14), 205. B.

HIGGINSON *and* HUBBARD (William). A Testimony, to the Order of the Gospel, In the Churches of New-England. *Boston.* 1701. 8vo, pp. 15. 31746

See also Wise (J.)

[HIGGINSON (Stephen).] Examination of the Treaty of Amity, Commerce, and Navigation, between the United States and Great Britain ... . By Cato. [*New York.*] 1795. 8vo, pp. 96. B.

[HIGGINSON.] The Writings of Laco, as Published in the Massachusetts Centinel, in the months of February and March, 1789—with the addition of No. VII. which was omitted. ... *Printed at Boston,* 1789. 8vo, pp. 39. B., BA., C., H., M. 31748

A bitter attack on Hancock. The author was "an Adams writer, who attracted great attention; but kept his own Secret; and it is not known who he was."—W. SULLIVAN'S *Public Men of the Revolution,* 145. The work was reprinted with the following title:

[HIGGINSON.] Ten Chapters in the Life of John Hancock. Now First Published since 1789. *New York.* 1857. 8vo, pp. 68.

One hundred and fifty copies printed, sixty of which were destroyed by fire.

HIGGINSON (S.) The Impartial Inquirer; being a Candid Examination of the Conduct of the President of the United States, &c. [*Boston?*] 1811. 8vo. 31750

HIGGINSON (Stephen), *Jun.* Some Notice of the Remarks on S. Higginson, Jun., contained in Dr. Morse's Appeal to the Publick. [*Boston.* 1814?] 8vo, pp. 3. BA. 31751

HIGGINSON (Thomas Wentworth). Army Life in a Black Regiment. By T. W. Higginson. *Boston: Fields, Osgood & Co.* 1870. 16mo, pp. iv, 296. 31752

HIGGINSON. Memoir of Thaddeus William Harris. By T. W. Higginson. *Boston.* 1869. 8vo, pp. ix–xlvii. H. 31753

HIGGINSON. Out-Door Papers. By Thomas Wentworth Higginson. *Boston: Ticknor & Fields.* 1863. 12mo, pp. (3), 370.

HIGGINSON. ... A Ride through Kansas. By Thomas Wentworth Higginson. [n. p. 1856.] 8vo, pp. 24. B., H. 31755

Also: Address to the Voters of the Third Congressional District of Massachusetts. ... *Lowell: C. L. Knapp, Printer.* 1850. 8vo, pp. 7. B.—Does Slavery Christianize the Negro? ... *New York: Anti-Slavery Society.* [n. d.] 12mo, pp. 8.—"Man shall not live by Bread alone." A Thanksgiving Sermon: preached in Newburyport, Nov. 30, 1848. ... *Newburyport.* 1848. + Second Edition. *Newburyport: Charles Whipple.* 1848. 12mo, pp. 12.—Malbone: An Oldport Romance. ... *Boston: Fields, Osgood & Co.* 1869. 8vo, pp. iv, 244. BA. + *London: Macmillan & Co.* 1869. 16mo, pp. viii, 272.—Massachusetts in Mourning. A Sermon ... in Worcester, June 4, 1854. ... *Boston: James Monroe & Co.* 1854. 8vo, pp. 15. B.—Merchants: A ... Lecture ... *Newburyport: A. A. Call.* 1857. 8vo, pp. 31.—The New Revolution: A Speech before the American Anti-Slavery Society, ... New York, May 12, 1857. ... *Boston: R. F. Wallcut.* 1857. 8vo, pp. 16.— ... Ought Women to learn the Alphabet? ... *Boston: C. K. Whipple.* 1869. 12mo, pp. 20.—Things New and Old: An Installation Sermon ... *Worcester: For the Society.* 1852. 8vo, pp. 30. B.—The Unitarian Autumnal Convention, a Sermon: *Boston: Benjamin B. Mussey & Co.* 1853. 8vo, pp. 14.—Woman and her Wishes: An Essay ... *Boston: Robert F. Wallcut.* 1853. 8vo, pp. 26. + Second Edition, with an Appendix. *New York: Fowlers and Wells.* 1853. 8vo, pp. 23. + Third Edition. [n. p. n. d.] 12mo, pp. 32. B. + *London.* 1854. 8vo, pp. 23. B. *See also* Harvard Memorial Biographies.

The "High Private." With a full and exciting History of the New York Volunteers, including the Mysteries and Miseries of the Mexican War. Part First. By "Corporal of the Guard." *New York.* 1848. 12mo, pp. 60. P. 31756

The Higher Law. [n. p. n. d.] 8vo, pp. 15. B. 31757

The Higher Law, tried by Reason and Authority. ... *New York: S. W. Benedict.* 1851. 8vo, pp. 54. B. 31758

The Highland Brigade. *See* [Elliott (S. M.)]

HIGHLAND COUNTY, *N. Y.* [Proposed] Remonstrance, 1856. 8vo, pp. 15. S. 31759

Also: Statistics, etc. *Newburgh.* 1858. 8vo, pp. 16. S.

The Highlands. A Tale of the Hudson. *Philadelphia.* 1826. 2 vols., 8vo. 31760

HILDEBRAND (S. S.) Autobiography of Samuel S. Hildebrand, the Renowned Missouri "Bushwhacker;" ... being his complete Confession, recently made to the Writers, and carefully compiled by James W. Evans and Wendell Keith, M.D. Together with all the Facts connected with his early History. *Jefferson City, (Mo.): State Times Printing House.* 1870. 12mo, pp. 312. 8 Plates. C. 31761

HILDRETH (F. A.) ... Lowell Patriot and Advertiser, and Lowell Republican. ... [*Lowell.*] 1846. 8vo, pp. 11. 31762

[HILDRETH (Hosea).] An Abridged History of the United States of America. For the Use of Schools. Intended as a Sequel to Hildreth's View of the United States. *Boston: Carter, Hendee & Babcock.* M DCC XXXI. 12mo, pp. xii, 248. C., H.

[HILDRETH.] A Book for Massachusetts Children, in Familiar Letters from a Father, for the use of Families and Schools. *Boston: Hilliard, Gray, Little & Wilkins.* 1829. 12mo, pp. iv, 132. Map. C., H., + Second Edition. [*Ibid.*] 1831. 12mo, pp. iv, 142. Map. B., H. + *Boston: John P. Jewett and Company.* 1857. 12mo, pp. 164. Map. H. 31764

[HILDRETH.] A Book for New-Hampshire Children, in Familiar Letters from a Father. Second Edition ... *Exeter: Francis Grant.* 1826. 12mo, pp. 106. Map. H. 31765

HILDRETH. A Discourse Delivered before the Washington Benevolent Society in Exeter, on the Day of their Anniversary, May 4th, 1813. By Hosea Hildreth. *Exeter: Printed by Charles Norris & Co.* 1813. 8vo, pp. 24. 31766

HILDRETH. Two Discourses on the most Important Duties of Townsmen. By H. Hildreth ... *Exeter: J. & B. Williams.* 1824. 12mo, pp. 23. + Second Edition. [*Ibid.*] 1824. BA.

HILDRETH. A View of the United States; for the use of Schools and Families. By Rev. Hosea Hildreth ... . *Boston: Carter & Hendee.* 1830. 16mo, pp. 162. Map. C. + Second Edition. [*Ibid.*] 1831. H. + [*Ibid.*] 1832. 31768

Also: A Discourse to the Students of Phillips' Exeter Academy, ... June 26, 1825, being the Sabbath succeeding the Death of Master Charles H. Hatch, a Member of the Academy. ... *Exeter: Printed by Gerrish & Tyle.* 1825. 8vo, pp. 16.—A Discourse occasioned by the Death of Dr. William Coffin ... June 24, 1827. ... *Gloucester.* 1827. 12mo, pp. 12.—A Dudleian Lecture, ... in Cambridge, May 13, 1829. ... *Cambridge: Printed by E. W. Metcalf & Co.* 1829. 8vo, pp. 24. B., H., M.

[HILDRETH (James).] Dragoon Campaigns to the Rocky Mountains; being a History of the Enlistment, Organization, and First Campaigns of the Regiment of United States Dragoons; together with Incidents of a Soldier's Life and Sketches of Scenery and Indian Character. By a Dragoon. ... *New York: Wiley & Long.* 1836. 8vo, pp. 288. B., H. 31769

Relates to the expedition under Colonel Dodge in 1834. The Official Report is annexed to the Message of the President, 28th Congress, 2d Session, Doc. II., p. 60.

HILDRETH (R.) Atrocious Judges. Lives of Judges Infamous as Tools of Tyrants and Instruments of Oppression. Compiled from ... Lord Campbell ... with an Appendix, containing the Case of Passmore Williamson. Edited, with an Introduction and Notes. By Richard Hildreth. *Boston.* 1856. 12mo, pp. 432. C. + *New York and Auburn: Miller, Orton & Mulligan.* 1856. 12mo, pp. 432. H. 31770

[HILDRETH.] Brief Remarks on Miss Catharine E. Beecher's Essay on Slavery. ... *Boston: Printed by Isaac Knapp.* 1837. 12mo, pp. 28. H. 31771

[HILDRETH.] The Contrast: or William Henry Harrison *versus* Martin Van Buren. ... *Boston: Weeks, Jordan & Company.* 1840. 8vo, pp. 72. BA., H. 31772

[HILDRETH.] Despotism in America; or an Inquiry into the Nature and Results of the Slave-Holding System in the United States ... *Boston: Whipple & Damrell.* 1840. 12mo, pp. 186. H. + Second Edition. *Boston: Mass. Anti-Slavery Society.* 1840. 12mo, pp. 186. B., BA. 31773

HILDRETH. Despotism in America: an Inquiry into the Nature, Results, and Legal Basis of the Slave-Holding System in the United States. By Richard Hildreth ... . *Boston: John P. Jewett and Company.* 1854. 12mo, pp. 307. B., BA., H. 31774

HILDRETH. The History of Banks: [and] Advantages ... of Free Competition in the Business of Banking. By Richard Hildreth. *Boston: Hilliard, Gray & Company.* 1837. 12mo, pp. 142.

Severely reviewed in McCulloch's Literature of Political Economy. Also: Banks, Banking, and Paper Currencies. ... *Boston: Whipple & Damrell.* 1840. 12mo, pp. 209. B., C.

HILDRETH. The History of the United States of America, from the Discovery of the Continent to the Organization of Government under the Federal Constitution. By Richard Hil-

dreth. *New York: Harper and Brothers.* 1849. 3 vols., 8vo, pp. xxvi, 33–570; 579; (2), 592, (1). B., BA. + Revised Edition. [*Ibid.*] 1854. 31776

HILDRETH. The History of the United States of America, from the Adoption of the Federal Constitution to the End of the Sixteenth Congress. ... *New York: Harper & Brothers.* 1851–52. 3 vols., 8vo, pp. 704; 686; 739, (1). B., BA. + [*Ibid.*] 1855.

A continuation of the preceding. The two works have also a uniform title: "The History of the United States of America." Vols. I.–VI. It concludes with the Administration of Madison and Monroe. The merits of this history are very considerable, and entitle it to a place in every extensive library. The author, in avoiding what he is pleased to call the Fourth of July style of Bancroft, perhaps, falls into the opposite extreme—great severity of style. *See* "Edinburgh Review," Vol. CII., "Westminster Review," New Series, Vol. II., "North American Review," Vol. LXXIII. 411. It was translated into Dutch with the following title:

HILDRETH. Geschiedenis van de Vereenigde Staten van Noord Amerika, sedert de ontdekking van Columbus. Uit het Engelsch, met aanteekeningen door M. Keijser. *'s Gravenhage.* 1854–57. 6 vols., 8vo. 31778

This translation has notes by M. Keijzer of Delft, and is an evidence of Dutch enterprise, deserving of respect and commendation.

HILDRETH. A Letter to Emory Washburn, Wm. M. Rogers, and Seventy-eight others, Dissentients from the Resolution Touching Political Action, adopted at the State Temperance Convention. By R. Hildreth ... . *Boston: Kidder & Wright.* 1840. 8vo, pp. 16. B., M. 31779

[HILDRETH.] Local Guide of British Guiana. ... *Demerary: Baum and Dallas.* 1843. 8vo, pp. 11, clvi, 828. BA. 31780

[HILDRETH.] Native-Americanism Detected and Exposed. By a Native American. *Boston: For the Author.* 1845. 12mo, pp. 36. 31781

HILDRETH. Origin and Genealogy of the American Hildreths; A Letter ... from Richard Hildreth. *Boston: Henry W. Dutton & Son, Printers.* 1857. 8vo, pp. 8. 31782

[HILDRETH.] The People's Presidential Candidate: or the Life of William Henry Harrison of Ohio. *Boston: Weeks, Jordan and Company.* 1839. 18mo, pp. 211. BA. 31783

[HILDRETH.] Strictures on Governor Morton's Message. ... Second Edition. *Boston: Printed by Cassady & March.* 1840. 8vo, pp. 16. H. 31784

HILDRETH. Theory of Politics: An Inquiry into the Foundations of Governments, and the Causes and Progress of Political Revolutions. By Richard Hildreth ... . *New York: Harper & Brothers.* 1853. 12mo, pp. 274. B., H. + [*Ibid.*] 1856.

[HILDRETH.] The White Slave; or, Memoirs of a Fugitive. ... *Boston: Tappan & Whittemore.* 1852. 12mo, pp. 408. BA.

Reprinted in London as

[HILDRETH.] The White Slave; or, Memoirs of a Fugitive, a new Picture of American Slave Life. ... *London.* 1852. 12mo.

Also as

[HILDRETH.] The White Slave; or Negro Life in the Slave States of America. ... *London.* 1853. 8vo, pp. 300. 31788

And again

[HILDRETH.] The Slave; or Memoirs of Archy Moore. ... *London.* 1836. 12mo. 31789

[HILDRETH.] The Slave: or Memoirs of Archy Moore. ... *Boston: John H. Eastburn.* 1836. 2 vols., 8vo, pp. (4), 170; 163. + Second Edition. ... *Boston: Whipple and Damrell.* 1840. 2 vols., 12mo, pp. 123; 115. H. + Third Edition. ... *Boston: Mass. Anti-Slavery Society.* 1840. 2 vols., 12mo, pp. 123; 115.

And lastly as

HILDRETH. Archy Moore, the White Slave; or, Memoirs of a Fugitive. By Richard Hildreth. *Auburn.* 1855. 12mo. + *New York.* 1857. 12mo. 31791

The following is a French translation:

HILDRETH. L'Esclave blanc, nouvelle peinture de l'esclavage en Amérique. Par M. Hildreth. Traduit par MM. Mornand et L. de Wailly. *Paris: Lecou.* 1853. 18mo. + Le compagnon du père Tom. L'esclave blanc. Traduit de E. de La Bédollière. *Paris: Barba.* 1853. 12mo. + [*Ibid.*] 1854. 4to. + Traduit par Henry Madinier. *Paris: Dupont.* 1853. 32mo. + Traduction F. Mornand. *Paris: Hachette et Cie.* 1858. 12mo.

Also: ... A Letter to Deacon Moses Grant, on Moral Suasion. ... [n. p. 1844.] 8vo, pp. 8. M. + Second Letter to Deacon Moses Grant. ... *Boston.* 1844. 8vo. pp. 4. M.—A Letter to his Excellency Marcus Morton, on Banking and the Currency. ... *Boston: Printed by Kidder & Wright.* 1840. 8vo, pp. 16. H.—My Connection with the Atlas Newspaper; including a Sketch of the History of the Amory Hall Party of 1838 ... . *Boston: Whipple and Damrell.* 1839. 12mo, pp. 24. B.—A Report of the Trial of the Rev. Ephraim K. Avery, ... on an Indictment for the Murder of Sarah Maria Cornell. ... Second Edition. *Boston: Russell, Odiorne and Co.* 1833. 8vo, pp. 143.—Anti-Slavery Tracts, No. 6.—The "Ruin" of Jamaica. ... [*New York.* n. d.] 12mo, pp. 12.—What can I do for the Abolition of Slavery? pp. 4. H.

HILDRETH (S. P.) Biographical and Historical Memoirs of the Early Pioneer Settlers of Ohio, with Narratives of Incidents and Occurrences in 1775, By S. P. Hildreth, M.D. To which is annexed "A Journal of Occurrences which happened, in the Circles of the Author's Personal Observation, in the Detachment commanded by Col. Benedict Arnold, consisting of Two Battalions from the United States Army at Cambridge, Mass., in A.D. 1775." By Colonel R. J. Meigs. *Cincinnati: H. W. Derby & Co.* 1852. 8vo, pp. 539. Portraits and Plate. B., BA., H.

I have never seen a copy of this work with the Meigs' "Journal," annexed on the title. To some copies are appended:

[HILDRETH.] Biographical Sketches of the Early Physicians of Marietta, Ohio. [n. p. n. d.] 8vo, pp. 19. B., H., M.

HILDRETH. Contributions to the Early History of the North-West, including the Moravian Missions in Ohio. By Samuel P. Hildreth, M.D. *Cincinnati: Poe & Hitchcock.* 1864. 12mo, pp. 240. C., S. 31795

Includes incidents of border warfare and Indian life.

[HILDRETH.] ... Miscellaneous Observations made during a Tour in ... 1835, to the Falls of Cuyahoga, near Lake Erie: ... [n. p. n. d.] 8vo, pp. 84. BA., H. 31796

HILDRETH. ... Observations on the Bituminous Coal Deposits of the Valley of the Ohio ... with Notices of the Fossil Organic Remains ... illustrated by a Geological Map. ... By Dr. S. P. Hildreth. ... [*New Haven.* 1836.] 8vo, pp. 156. 36 Plates. B., BA. 31797

HILDRETH. Original Contributions to the American Pioneer. By Dr. S. P. Hildreth. ... [*Cincinnati:*] *J. S. Williams.* 1844. 8vo, pp. (4), 144. BA., H. 31798

HILDRETH. Pioneer History: being an Account of the First Examinations of the Ohio Valley, and the Early Settlement of The Northwest Territory. Chiefly from Original Manuscripts; Containing the Papers of Col. George Morgan; those of Judge Barker; The Diaries of Joseph Buell and John Mathews; The Records of the Ohio Company, &c., &c., &c. By S. P. Hildreth. *Cincinnati: H. W. Derby & Co.* 1848. 8vo, pp. xiii, 525. 8 Plates and Map. B., BA., H., P. + [*Ibid.*] 1850. 31799

Forms Vol. I. of "Trans. of the Hist. Soc. of Cincinnati." Also: History of the Belville Settlement [in Western Virginia]. ... *Cincinnati: Published originally in the Hesperian.* 1839. 8vo, pp. 25–59. BA., H., M.

HILDRETH *and* SCHOTT (Charles Anthony). ... Results of Meteorological Observations, made at Marietta, Ohio, between 1826 and 1859, inclusive, By S. P. Hildreth, M.D. To which are added Results of Observations taken at Marietta, by Mr. Joseph Wood, between 1817 and 1823. Reduced and discussed ... by Charles A. Schott, ... *Washington.* 1868. Folio, pp. v, 46.

Also included in the "Smithsonian Contributions to Knowledge," Vol. XVI.

HILDROP (J.) An Essay on Honour, ... By John Hildrop, D.D. ... *Elizabeth-Town, Maryland. Reprinted by Stewart Herbert,* 1791. 8vo, pp. 37, Subscribers' Names, 2 l. 31801

Introduced on account of the imprint, which is very rare.

HILGARD (Eugene W.) *See* Louisiana, *also* Mississippi.

HILHOUSE W.) Indian Notices; or Sketches of the Habits, Characters, Languages, Superstitions, Soil and Climate of the several Nations. By William Hilhouse, late Quarter Master General of Indians. [*Demerara:*] *Printed for the Author.* 1825. 12mo. 31802

With a Vocabulary of eighty-two Nouns and Numerals in the four Indian Languages of British Guiana, also the Ichthyology of the fresh waters of the interior. Partly translated into French in the "Nouvelles Annales des Voyages," Vol. I., 1833; also "Annales des Voyages," Vol. I., 1835. *See also* "Journal of the Royal Geographical Society."

HILL (A. F.) Our Boys. The Personal Experiences of a Soldier in the Army of the Potomac. By A. F. Hill. *Philadelphia: J. E. Potter.* 1864. 12mo, pp. xii, 412. Frontispiece.

HILL (A. H.) *See* Mohawk Language.

HILL (A.) A Discourse on the Life and Character of the Rev. Nathaniel Thayer, D.D. ... Lancaster ... June 29, 1840. By Alonzo Hill ... . *Worcester: Printed by Spooner & Howland.* 1840. 8vo, pp. 40. BA., M. 31804

HILL. A Discourse delivered in The Ancient Meeting-House of the First Congregational Society in Hingham, on Sunday, September 8, 1850. By Alonzo Hill ... . *Boston: Wm. Crosby and H. P. Nichols.* 1850. 8vo, pp. 23. H., M. 31805

HILL. In Memoriam. A Discourse preached in Worcester, Oct. 5, 1862, Lieut. Thomas Jefferson Spurr, Fifteenth Massachusetts Volunteers, who, mortally wounded at the Battle of Antietam, died in Hagerstown, Sept. 27th, following. By Alonzo Hill. *Boston: Printed by John Wilson and Son.* 1862. 8vo, pp. 32.

Also: A Discourse on the Life and Character of the Rev. Aaron Bancroft, D.D. ... Worcester, ... August 22, 1839. ... *Worcester: Printed by T. W. & J. Butterfield.* 1839. 8vo, pp. 40.— ... A Commemorative Discourse on the Rev. Samuel Clarke ... Dec. 11, 1859. ... *Boston: Printed by John Wilson and Sons.* 1860. 8vo, pp. 36. — ... A Discourse ... in Worcester, on the ... Death of the Hon. John Waldo Lincoln, who died Oct. 2, 1852. ... *Boston: Printed by John Wilson & Son.* 1852. 8vo, pp. 33.— ... A Discourse on the Twenty-Fifth Anniversary of his Ordination ... in Worcester, March 28, 1852. ... *Worcester: Andrew Hutchinson.* 1852. 8vo, pp. 46.—A Discourse Commemorative of the Hon. Thomas Kinnicult, who died January 22, 1858 ... *Boston: Printed by John Wilson & Son.* 1858. 8vo, pp. 28. B.—The Glory of the Latter House: A Discourse delivered at the Dedication of the Second Congregational Society in Worcester, March 26, 1851. ... *Worcester: Andrew Hutchinson.* 1851. 8vo, pp. 55. M.—Life and Character of the Rev. Aaron Bancroft, D.D. ... *Boston: James Munroe & Co.* 1839. 12mo, pp. 30. BA.—The Maine Law: An Address ... in Sterling, April 13, 1853. ... [n. p. n. d.] 12mo, pp. 12.—A Sermon ... at the Ordination of Rev. Josiah Moore ... in Athol [Mass.], December 8, 1830. ... *Worcester: Spooner and Church, Printers.* 1831. 8vo, pp. 39.— ... A Sermon on the Death of Hon. John Davis ... at Worcester, Mass. April 23, 1854. ... *New York: Charles B. Norton.* 1854. 8vo, pp. 25.— ... A Sermon preached in Worcester, Aug. 17, 1862, ... after the Burial of Mr. William Hudson, a Private in the Twenty-Fifth Regiment of Massachusetts Volunteers. ... *Boston: Printed by John Wilson & Son.* 1862. 8vo, pp. 23. H.— ... A Sermon preached March 28, 1867, before the Second Congregational Society in Worcester, on the Fortieth Anniversary of his Settlement. ... Together with an Account of the Exercises on that Occasion. *Cambridge: John Wilson and Son.* 1867. 8vo, pp. 66. Portrait. B., BA., H.

HILL (A.) Afer Baptizatus: Or, the Negro turn'd Christian. Being a Short and Plain Discourse, shewing I. The Necessity of Instructing and Baptizing Slaves in English Plantations. II. The Folly of that Vulgar Opinion, That Slaves do cease to be Slaves when once baptized. Delivered (most of it) in a Sermon Preach'd at Stratford-le-Bow, in Middlesex, March 15th. 170½. By Anthony Hill, ... *London, Charles Broome,* MDCCII. 8vo, pp. (6), 55.

HILL (B. H.) Speech of B. H. Hill on the Condition of the Country. ... Atlanta ... July 16, 1867. And Letter of Ex-Governor Johnson. *Augusta, Ga.* 1867. 8vo, pp. 15. 31808

HILL (B. M.) Sermon delivered at the Dedication of the Baptist Meeting-House in New Haven. By Rev. Benjamin M. Hill, ... [n. p. n. d.] 8vo, pp. 23. 31809

Also: Sermon ... Annual Election. ... *New Haven.* 1829. 8vo. + Second Edition. *New Haven.* 1829. 8vo. W.

HILL (B. E.) Recollections of an Artillery Officer, or Scenes in Ireland, America, &c. By Benson Earle Hill. *London.* 1836. 2 vols., 8vo. 31810

[HILL (Charles W.)] ... Should Republicans vote for James M. Ashley? ... [*Toledo.* 1868.] 8vo, pp. 15. 31811

HILL (C. H.) Argument before ... the Legislature of Massachusetts, May 17, 1869, against the Establishment of a State Police in the City of Boston. By Clement Hugh Hill. ... *Boston: Alfred Mudge & Son.* 1869. 8vo, pp. 46. 31812

HILL (E.) The Substance of Two Lectures on the History of Mason, delivered before the Lyceum in Mason Village. By Rev. Ebenezer Hill. ... *Fitchburg: W. J. Merriam, Printer.* 1846. 8vo, pp. 16. 31813

Also: A Sermon ... at Mason, April 11, 1803, at the Funeral of Miss Persis Lawrence ... . *Amherst, N. H.: Printed by Joseph Cushing.* 1803. 8vo, pp. 24. H. —A Sermon ... at New-Ipswich [N. H.], June 3, 1811, at the Interment ... of Miss Ruthy Batcheller. ... *Boston: Printed by Munroe and Francis.* 1812. 8vo, pp. 46. W. —Sermon at New Ipswich, Aug. 6, 1811, at the Interment of William Kimbal Batcheller. ... *Boston.* 1812. 8vo. W.—A Sermon ... at Townsend, March 3, 1808, at the Interment ... of Lt. Jacob Blodget ... . *Amherst, N. H.: Printed by Joseph Cushing.* 1809. 8vo, pp. 18. H.

HILL (E.) The Widow's Offering: an Authentic Narrative of the Parentage, Life, Trials and Travels of Mrs. Elizabeth Hill. Written by Herself. *D. S. Ruddock, Printer, New London, Conn.* 1852. 12mo, pp. 179. B. + Second Edition. *Starr & Farnham, Printers, New London, Conn.* 1856. 12mo, pp. 281.

HILL (G.) Decade di alberi curiosi ed eleganti piante delle Indie Orientali, e dell' America. Dall' inglese rid. all' italian. *Roma.* 1786. 4to. Colored Plate. 31815

HILL (G. C.) Benedict Arnold, a Biography. By George Canning Hill. *Boston.* 1858. 16mo. Portrait. 31816

HILL. Capt. John Smith, a Biography. By George Canning Hill. *Boston: Hill and Libby.* 1858. 12mo, pp. 286. B., C.

HILL. Gen. Israel Putnam. ... A Biography. By George Canning Hill. *Boston.* 1858. 12mo. + *Philadelphia.* 1868. 12mo, pp. 270. B. 31818

HILL. Daniel Boone the Pioneer of Kentucky. A Biography. By George Canning Hill. *New York.* 1860. + *Philadelphia: J. B. Lippincott & Co.* 1863. 12mo, pp. 262. Plates. 31819

HILL (G. W.) Memoir of Sir Brenton Halliburton, Late Chief Justice ... of Nova Scotia. By Rev. George W. Hill ... *Halifax: Printed by James Bowes & Sons.* 1864. 8vo, pp. (4), 207.

HILL. Nova Scotia and Nova-Scotians: A Lecture ... By Rev. George W. Hill ... . *Halifax, N. S.: James Bowes & Sons.* 1858. 8vo, pp. 49, (1). BA., H. 31821

Also: Letter to the Parishioners of St. Paul's, Halifax. ... *Halifax.* 1866. 8vo, pp. 48.—Oration at the Inauguration of the Welsford and Parker Monument. ... *Halifax.* 1860. 8vo, pp. 24.—Records of the Church of England in Rawdon from its origin until the present date. ... *Halifax.* 1858. 8vo, pp. 28.—Review of the Rise and Progress of the Church of England in Nova Scotia; a Sermon. ... *Halifax.* 1858. 8vo, pp. 33.—A Sermon preached before the Hon. the Board of Governors and the Members of the University of King's College, Windsor. ... *Halifax.* 1855. 8vo, pp. 13.

HILL (H. A.) American Shipping: its Decline and the Remedies. By Hamilton A. Hill. *Boston: J. H. Eastburn's Press.* 1869. 8vo, pp. 31. 31822

HILL. Commercial Associations; their Uses and Opportunities. By Hamilton A. Hill. *Boston: J. H. Eastburn's Press.* 1869. 8vo, pp. 27. H. 31823

[HILL.] A Plea for our Foreign Commerce. [n. p. n. d.] 8vo, pp. 16. 31824

HILL. The Relations of the Business Men of the United States to the National Legislation. By Hamilton A. Hill. *Boston: Barker, Colter & Co., Printers.* 1870. 8vo, pp. 32. BA.

Also: Boston and Liverpool. Reports of the American Steamship Company for 1864 and 1865, with List of Officers, &c. ... *Boston: J. H. Eastburn's Press.* 1866. 8vo, pp. 16.—A Review of the Proceedings of the Detroit Convention. ... *Boston: J. H. Eastburn's Press.* 1866. 8vo, pp. 63.—Steam Navigation between Boston and Europe. A Paper read before the ... American Social Science Association, at Boston, January 30, 1867. ... *Boston: J. H. Eastburn's Press.* 1867. 8vo, pp. 17. B.—Also Reports to Boston Board of Trade. On stamping Freight Receipts, 1864; On the Northern Pacific Railroad, 1865; On the National Board of Trade, 1868; pp. 7. B. On Recommendation for a Department of Commerce ... . 1871; On Decision of the Supreme Court of the United States in the Case of Ward *vs.* the State of Maryland, 1872; On List of Boards of Trade, and other Commercial Associations in the United States, 1872. BA.

HILL (H.) A Legacy for Children, being some of the Last Expressions and Dying Sayings of Hannah Hill, Junr., of the City of Philadelphia, in the Province of Pensilvania, in America, aged Eleven years and near three months. *Printed by Andrew Bradford, at the Sign of the Bible, in Philadelphia.* [about 1714.] Small 8vo, pp. 36. + The Second Edition. [*Ibid.* n. d.] + The Third Edition. [*Ibid.*] 1717. Small 8vo. + *Dublin: Reprinted by Sam. Fairbrother.* 1719. Small 8vo, pp. 32. 31826

HILL (H. R.) Succinct View of the Importance and Practicability of forming a Ship Canal across the Isthmus of Panama. *London.* 1845. 8vo. Map and Plan. 31827

HILL (I.) Antiquities of America Explained. By Ira Hill, A.M. *Hagers-town: W. D. Bell.* 1831. 12mo, pp. 131.

Hill (I.) An Address, delivered at Concord, N. H., January 8, 1828, being The Thirteenth Anniversary of Jackson's Victory at New Orleans. By Isaac Hill. *Concord, N. H.: Printed by Manahan, Hoag & Co.* 1828. 8vo, pp. 44. B., BA.

Hill. Biography of Isaac Hill of New-Hampshire. With an Appendix, containing Selections from his Speeches, and Miscellaneous Writings. *Concord, N. H.: John F. Brown.* 1835. 18mo, pp. 245. B., C., H. 31830

[Hill.] Brief Sketch of the Life, Character and Services of Major General Andrew Jackson. ... *Concord, N. H.: Isaac Hill.* 1828. 12mo, pp. 51. Portrait. H. 31831

Hill. Congressional Reporter; containing a List of the Members of the 12th Congress, the President's Message, the Public Documents, and the Debates on all interesting questions agitated during the Session, commencing on the first Monday of November 1811: By Isaac Hill. *Concord.* 1811–12. 2 vols.

See also Vol. IV., No. 15609, *and* Farmer's Monthly Visitor, Vol. VI. Also: An Address ... Portsmouth ... July 4, 1828. ... *Concord: Horatio Hill and Co.* 1828. 8vo, pp. 14. BA.—Speech of Mr. Hill, of New Hampshire, on Mr. Clay's Resolutions in relation to the Tariff. [*Washington.* 1832.] 8vo, pp. 24. BA.—Speech ... May 10, 1832, on ... the Abolition of Postage on Newspapers. [n. p. n. d.] 8vo, pp. 12.—Speech ... on the Motion of Mr. Calhoun that the Senate refuse to receive a Petition from ... Friends ... of Pennsylvania, to abolish Slavery in the District of Columbia ... February 12, 1836. [n. p. n. d.] 8vo, pp. 8. H.—Speech ... on the ... Removal of the Deposits ... March 3 and 4, 1834. *Washington.* 1834. 8vo. S.—Speech on ... French Spoliations ... December 23, 1834. ... *Washington: Printed by Blair & Rives.* 1834. 8vo, pp. 14. H.—Speech ... on Mr. Benton's Expunging Resolutions, May 27, 1836. [*Washington.* 1836.] S.—Speech ... on Surplus Revenue ... January 28, 1836. [*Washington.* 1836.] 8vo, pp. 8. H., S.—Speech ... on ... distributing the Surplus Fund among the Several States, called the Land Bill ... March 17, 1836. [n. p. n. d.] 8vo, pp. 18. H.—Speech, at a Dinner given in his honor. [n. p. n. d.] 8vo.— ... Wise Sayings of the Honorable Isaac Hill. ... [from New Hampshire Journal Office, February 11, 1828.] 8vo, pp. 8. H.

Hill (J. J.) A Sketch of the 29th Regiment of Connecticut Colored Troops. By J. J. Hill. Giving a Full Account of its Formation; of all the Battles through which it passed, and its final Disbandment. *Baltimore: Daugherty, Maguire & Co.* 1867. 8vo, pp. 42. 31833

Hill (J.) By Authority. The Trial of James Hill, alias, John the Painter, for wilfully and maliciously setting Fire to the Rope-House, in the King's Yard at Portsmouth: Tried at Winchester, March 6th, 1777, Before the Hon. Sir Wil. Henry Ashurst, Knt. and Sir Beaumont Hotham. Taken in Short

Hand by a Gentleman at the Trial. *London: Sold by G. Corrall.* [1777.] 8vo, pp. 55. Portrait. 31834

Hill. John the Painter's Ghost. How he appeared on the Night of his Execution to Lord Temple, &c. *London: John Williams.* 1778. 4to. 31835

John the Painter's ghost rises to the tune of William and Margaret, and takes his revenge on Lord Temple and the rest of the courtiers.

Hill. The Life of James Aitken, commonly called John the Painter, an Incendiary, who was tried at the Castle of Winchester, on Thursday the 7th Day of March, 1777, and Convicted of Setting Fire to his Majesty's Dock Yard, at Portsmouth, Exhibiting a detail of Facts of the utmost importance to Great Britain. The whole faithfully taken down from the Convict's own mouth, on Friday, Saturday, and Sunday, preceding his Execution. The Third Edition. ... *Winton: Printed by J. Wilkes.* [n. d.] 8vo, pp. 62. Portrait. 31836

Hill. Life of James Aitken, commonly called John the Painter. *Portsmouth.* [n. d.] 31837

Hill. A Short Account of the Motives which determined the Man, called John the Painter; and a Justification of his Conduct; written by Himself, and sent to his Friend, Mr. A. Tomkins, with a request to publish it after his Execution. *London: John Williams.* M.DCC.LXXVII. 4to, pp. (4), 15. 31838

"They think it monstrous and terrible, and I do not know what, to attempt to burn the Dock Yard at Portsmouth. Not considering how many docks, and towns, and ships of ours, have been burned by their soldiers in America."—P. 11.

Hill. The Trial at Large of James Hill, otherwise James Hind, otherwise James Aitken, commonly known by the name of John the Painter, who was tried and convicted at the Assizes held at Winchester, on Thursday March 6, 1777, and Executed and Hung in Chains, at Portsmouth, on Monday March 10, for Setting Fire to the Rope-house in his Majesty's Dock-yard at Portsmouth, on Saturday the 7th of December, 1776. Together with the Confession he made before Magistrates, and to Commissioner Gambier; and an Account of his Behaviour at the time of his Execution. Also, the Particulars of his Life, previous to his Setting Fire to the Dock-yard, which he gave to Mr. White, Keeper of the Goal at Winchester. The Second Edition. [n. p.] 1777. Small 8vo, pp. 94. Copperplate Portrait of John the Painter, and figure of the machine by which he set Fire to the Rope-house. WM. 31839

Hill. The Trial (at large) of James Hill; otherwise, James Hind; otherwise, James Actzen: for Feloniously, Willfully, and Maliciously, Setting Fire to the Rope-House, in His Majesty's Dock-Yard at Portsmouth. ... March 6, 1777. Taken in Short Hand by Joseph Gurney. ... *London: G. Kearsly.* [n. d.] Folio, pp. 40. 31840

Hill. The Whole of the Proceedings upon the Trial of James Hill, otherwise James Hind, otherwise James Actzen, commonly called John "the Painter," on Thursday, March 6th, 1777. Taken in Short Hand by Wm. Blanchard. *London.* [n. d.] S. 31841

Hill or Aitken was a native of Scotland. With the privity of Silas Deane, whom he met and conferred with at Paris, the attempt to destroy the government property, stores, and shipping at Portsmouth, was determined upon, and, notwithstanding its apparently desperate and impracticable character, it partially succeeded. From Deane, who supplied him with a royal passport, and a sum of money in advance, he had assurances of a reward proportioned to the services he should render to the American cause. The counsel for the crown on the trial, publicly accused Benjamin Franklin and Silas Deane of complicity in the enterprise, and expressed a hope that they might be called to account for it. "The affair," says Gordon, "created much confusion, apprehension, and suspicion throughout England at the time of its occurrence." Stevens says "John the Painter was an American who, in the Revolutionary War, very cordially espoused the cause of his country, and resolved to secure a good name by some daring deed. He came to England and attempted to burn the Portsmouth Dock where were the chief shipping and stores to be used against America. He failed and was executed. In his defence, which is now of no inconsiderable rarity, he compares himself to many ancient victims self offered up for their country's good, especially to the assassin of Porsenna. 'Love of country was the motive of both,' he says, 'of me *John Moxam*, of him *Mutius Scævola.*' How different the result hitherto from that of André and of Hale." *See* "M. Rev.," LVI. 391, 398, 478.

Hill (J.) The Trial of Jeremiah Hill, Esq. for Heresy, before the Church ... in Biddeford [Me.], May 2, 1793. [n. p. n. d.] 12mo, pp. 24. BA., H., W. 31842

Hill (J.) De par Son Excellence M. Jean Hill, Général & Commandant en Chef les Troupes de Sa Majesté Britannique en Amérique. ... *A Boston, Chez B. Green.* 1711. 31843

A manifesto, "en assez mauvais François," for distribution in Canada during the nvasion under Hill and Nicholson. The whole impression seems to have been cast away with the fleet, and no copy of the original edition (which is probably a broadside n folio) is known. *See* Charlevoix, Liv. xx.

Hill (John). *See* Berkley (G.), Vol. II., No. 4888.

Hill (J. Boynton). History of the Town of Mason, N. H. from the First Grant in 1749, to ... 1858. By John B. Hill. *Boston: Lucius A. Elliot & Co.* 1858. 8vo, pp. 324. S. 31844

Hill. Memoir of the Rev. Ebenezer Hill, Pastor of the Congregational Church, in Mason, N. H. from November, 1790, to May, 1854. With Some of his Sermons, and his Discourse on the History of the Town. By John B. Hill. *Boston: Lucius A. Elliot & Co.* 1858. 8vo, pp. 113, (1). B., S. 31845

Hill. Proceedings at the Centennial Celebration of the One Hundredth Anniversary ... of the Town of Mason, N. H., August 26, 1868. ... By John B. Hill. *Boston: Elliott, Thomes & Talbot.* 1870. 8vo, pp. 115. Portrait. H. 31846

Hill (Joshua). The Union Record ... a Letter in reply to his Enemies. *Washington: Gibson Brothers.* 1870. 8vo, pp. 18.

Also: Letter ... on the Election of U. S. Senators. [*Madison, Ga.* 1866.] 12mo. pp. 15. H.

[Hill (Mark Langdon).] A Narrative shewing the Promises made to the Officers of the ... Continental Army, for their Services in the Revolutionary War; ... *Elizabeth-Town, N. J.: Printed by Edward Sanderson.* 1826. 8vo, pp. 47, (1). BA.

Hill. A Vindication of Mark Langdon Hill ... Collector of ... Bath ... Maine, Against the Aspersions in a Pamphlet entitled "Documents Relating to Violations and Evasions of the Laws, during the Commercial Restrictions, and late War, with Great Britain. [n. p. n. d.] 8vo, pp. 32. H., W. 31849

Hill (N.), *Jr.* Opinion ... on the Unconstitutionality of the Coercive Temperance Bill. *Albany.* 1855. S. 31850

Also: ... Argument ... in the Albany Bridge Case, before the United States Circuit Court, ... New York, in September, 1858. *Albany: Weed, Parsons & Co.* 1858. 8vo, pp. 48. BA., H.

Hill. Memoir of Nicholas Hill, a Member of the Bar of New-York ... Prepared ... by a Committee of the Bar of the City of New-York, 1859. [n. p. n. d.] 8vo, pp. 60. S.

Hill (P. G.) Fifty Days on board a Slave-Vessel in the Mozambique Channel, in ... 1843. By the Rev. Pascoe Grenfell Hill ... . *London: John Murray.* 1844. Post 8vo, pp. 115. Map. + *New-York: J. Winchester.* [1844.] 8vo, pp. 29. C.

Also: Voyage to the Slave Coast of Africa. *London.* 1849. Post 8vo.

Hill (P. C.) The United States and British Provinces Contrasted from personal Observations. A Lecture by Philip Carteret Hill, D.C.L. *Halifax.* 1859. 8vo, pp. 30. 31853

Hill (R.) A Sermon preached in ... Pittsburgh, Pa. On Thanksgiving Day, November 29, 1860. By Rev. R. Hill. *Pittsburgh: Printed by W. S. Haven.* MDCCCLX. 8vo, pp. 21.

Hill (R.) Reconstruction. Speech of Hon. Ralph Hill, of Indiana ... March 17, 1866. [n. p. n. d.] 8vo, pp. 8. 31855

Hill (R.) Haïti and Spain: A Memorial, By Richard Hill, dedicated to the Hon. W. H. Seward ... . *Jamaica: De Cordova & Co., Printers.* 1862. 8vo, pp. 14. H. 31856

Hill. A Week at Port Royal [Jamaica]. By Richard Hill of Jamaica. *Montego Bay.* 1855. 12mo, pp. (4), 109. C.

Hill (R.) Letters of Doctor Richard Hill and his Children, or the History of a Family as told by Themselves. Collected and Arranged by John Jay Smith. Privately printed for the Descendants. *Philadelphia.* 1854. 8vo, pp. xlv, 466. 6 Portraits, 2 Plates. 31858

Hill (R. W.) The Tendency of the Christian Religion to promote Genuine Liberty: A Sermon ... By Robert W. Hill. *Rochester: P. Canfield.* 1846. 8vo, pp. 19. 31859

Hill (S. S.) The Emigrant's Introduction to an Acquaintance with the British American Colonies, and the Present Condition and Prospects of the Colonists, &c. ... designed to fix the determination of all persons who may contemplate Emigrating, ... By S. S. Hill, Esq. *London: Parbury and Co.* 1837. 12mo. Map. P. 31860

[Hill.] A Short Account of Prince Edward Island, designed chiefly for the Information of Agriculturist and other Emigrants of Small Capital. ... *London: Madden & Co.* 1839. Post 8vo, pp. (4), vi, 90, Appendix, iii, (1). Map. B., C. 31861

Hill. Travels in Peru and Mexico. By S. S. Hill. ... *London: Longman, Green, Longman and Roberts.* 1860. 2 vols., post 8vo, pp. xiii, 330; xii, 312. B., BA. 31862

Hill (Theophilus H.) Hesper, and Other Poems, By Theo. H. Hill. ... *Raleigh.* 1861. + Second Edition. *Raleigh, N. C.: Branson, Farrar & Co.* 1863. 12mo, pp. 96. BA. 31863

The first collection of original poems published in the Confederate States. Also: Poems ... *New York: Hurd & Houghton.* 1869. 12mo, pp. vi, 155. C.

Hill (T.) Integral Education. An Inaugural Address, ... at Antioch College, Yellow Springs, ... Ohio, September 8, 1859. By Rev. Thomas Hill ... . *Boston: Little, Brown and Company.* 1859. 8vo, pp. 31. BA., H. 31864

Also: Address at the Funeral of Rev. Samuel Abbot Smith, ... With the Discourse by Rev. Rufus P. Stebbins. ... *Boston: Walker, Fuller and Company.* 1865. 8vo, pp. 32.—An Address ... to the Graduating Class at the Massachusetts Medical College, March 8, 1865. ... *Boston: Printed by David Clapp & Son.* 1865. 8vo, pp. 14. B.—The Annual Address before the Harvard Natural History Society, delivered ... May 19, 1853. *Cambridge: John Bartlett.* 1853. 8vo, pp. 26.—Liberal Education. An Address delivered before the Phi Beta Kappa Society of Harvard College, July 22, 1858. ... *Cambridge: John Bartlett.* 1858. 8vo, pp. 34. B., H.—Religion in Public Instruction: Baccalaureate Address ... before ... Antioch College, ... June 20, 1860. ... *Boston: Little, Brown and Company.* 1860. 8vo, pp. 31. H.—The Sin of Silence. A Sermon preached in the Unitarian Church at Waltham, April 13, 1865. ... *Waltham: Free Press, May 2,* 1865. 8vo.—Sermon ... Fast Day. *Waltham, Mass.* 1853. S.

Hill (T.) The White Mountain Notch, By Thomas Hill. Morning after the Catastrophe of the Willey Family. *Willard Felt & Co., Printers, N. Y.* [n. d.] 24mo, pp. 8. 31865

Describes a painting on exhibition.

Hill (W.) A History of the Rise, Progress, Genius, and Character of American Presbyterianism: together with a Review of "The Constitutional History of the Presbyterian Church in the United States of America, by Chas. Hodge, D.D. ..." By William Hill, D.D. ... *Washington City: J. Gideon, Jr.* 1839. 8vo, pp. xv, 224. C. 31866

[Hill (W. B.), *and others.*] Address of the Unconditional Union State Central Committee to the People of Maryland, September 16th, 1863. *Baltimore: Printed by Sherwood & Co.* [n. d.] 8vo, pp. 20. H. 31867

Hill (W. H.) Genealogical Table of the Lee Family, from the First Emigration to America in 1641. ... to ... 1851. Compiled from Information furnished by Hon. Martin Lee, of Granville, Washington County, N. Y., and from Other Sources, by the Rev. William H. Hill ... . [Printed for private circulation only.] *Albany: Weed, Parsons & Co.'s Print.* 1851. 8vo, pp. 31.

Hill & Savage's Confederate States Railroad Guide. *Griffin, Ga.* 1862. 16mo. 31869

Hill & Co.'s Confederate States Railroad Guide, April, 1863. *Griffin, Ga.* 1863. 12mo. BA. 31870

Hillard (E. B.) The Last Men of the Revolution. A Photograph of Each from Life, together with Views of their Homes ... Accompanied by Brief Biographical Sketches of the Men. By Rev. E. B. Hillard. *Hartford, Conn.: N. A. & R. A. Moore.* 1864. 12mo, pp. 64. BA. 31871

Hillard (G. Stillman). A Discourse Delivered before the New-England Society in the City of New-York, December 22, 1851. By George S. Hillard. ... *New-York: George F. Nesbitt and Co.* 1852. 8vo, pp. 31. H. 31872

Hillard. Life and Campaigns of George B. McClellan, Major-General U. S. Army. By George S. Hillard. *Philadelphia: J. B. Lippincott & Co.* 1864. 12mo, pp. 396. Portrait. C. + [*Ibid.*] 1865. 31873

Hillard. A Memoir of James Brown. With Obituary Notices and Tributes of Respect from Public Bodies. By George S. Hillard. *Boston: Privately Printed.* 1856. 8vo, pp. (8), 138. Portrait. 31874

The subject of this memoir was an eminent publisher at Boston.

[Hillard.] A Memorial of Daniel Webster, from The City of Boston. *Boston: Little, Brown and Company.* 1853. 8vo, pp. viii, 270. Portrait, Plate. BA. 31875

Also: ... An Address ... before the Mercantile Library Association, at its Thirtieth Anniversary, Nov. 13, 1850. ... *Boston: Ticknor, Reed, and Fields.* M DCCC L. 12mo, pp. 47.—Address before the Norfolk Agricultural Society, at Dedham, Sept. 26, 1860. ... [n. p. n. d.] 8vo, pp. 15. B.—Memoir of Joseph Story, LL.D. ... *Boston: Press of John Wilson and Son.* 1868. 8vo, pp. 32. H.—An Oration pronounced before the Inhabitants of Boston, July the Fourth, 1835. ... *Boston: John H. Eastburn.* 1835. 8vo, pp. 30.—The Political Duties of the Educated Classes. A Discourse ... before the Phi Beta Kappa Society of Amherst College, July 10, 1866. ... *Boston: Ticknor & Fields.* 1866. 8vo, pp. 48. B.—The Relation of the Poet to his Age. A Discourse delivered before the Phi Beta Kappa Society of Harvard University. ... August 24, 1843. ... *Boston: Charles C. Little and James Brown.* 1843. 8vo, pp. 53. + Second Edition. [*Ibid.*]

Hillary (W.) Observations on the Changes of the Air and the Concomitant Epidemical Diseases in the Island of Barbadoes, and other West India Islands. By William Hillary, M.D. *London.* 1754. + [*Ibid.*] 1759. 31876

Hillary. Observations on the Changes of the Air and the Concomitant Epidemical Diseases in the Island of Barbadoes. To which is added a Treatise on the ... Yellow Fever; and Such other Diseases as are Indigenous ... in the West India Islands. ... By William Hillary, M.D. Second Edition. *London:*

L. Hawes. M,DCC,LXVI. 8vo, pp. xiii, 360, (4). C. + With Notes, by Benjamin Rush ... *Philadelphia: B. & T. Kite.* 1811. 8vo, pp. (4), 260, (4). B., BA. 31877

See "M. Rev.," XXI. 369.

Hiller (J.) A Charge delivered at St. Peter's Church, in Salem, to the Brethren of the Essex Lodge of Ancient Free and Accepted Masons. By Joseph Hiller. *Salem.* [1781.] 4to, pp. 14. W. 31878

Hiller (O. P.) American National Lyrics, and Sonnets. By O. Prescott Hiller ... . *Boston: Otis Clapp.* 1860. 16mo, pp. vi, (1), 80. BA., H. 31879

Hiller. Pocahontas; or the Founding of Virginia. A Poem. In Three Cantos. By the Rev. O. Prescott Hiller. *London: Hatchard & Co.* 1865. 16mo, pp. 107. C., H. 31880

Also: A Chapter on Slavery ... *London: Hodson & Son.* 1860. 18mo, pp. v, (1), 175. H., S.

Hillhouse (J.) A Sermon ... on the occasion of the Death of Rachel Hillhouse, of Londonderry, Ireland, Jan. 7th, 1716. By Rev. James Hillhouse. *Boston, N. E. by B. Green.* 1721. 18mo, pp. (8), 135. B., M. 31881

With a Preface by Increase and Cotton Mather.

Hillhouse (James). Mr. Hillhouse's Speech on the Resolution to Repeal the Embargo, November 29, 1808. [*Washington.* 1808.] 8vo, pp. 15. B., BA. 31882

Hillhouse. Propositions for amending the Constitution of the United States; submitted by Mr. Hillhouse to the Senate, on the Twelfth Day of April, 1808. With his Explanatory Remarks. [*Washington.*] 1808. 12mo, pp. 52. B. + *New-Haven: Printed by Oliver Steele & Co.* 1808. 8vo, pp. 26, (1). BA., C. + *Troy.* 1808. 8vo. W. + Appendix. *New Haven.* 1808. 8vo, pp. 40. P. + *Washington: Printed by Gales & Seaton.* 1830. 8vo, pp. 40. H. 31883

Hillhouse. Speeches delivered in the Senate of the United States, on the Resolution offered by Mr. Hillhouse for repealing the Embargo Laws. *Albany.* 1809. 8vo, pp. 45. 31884

Also: Amendments to the Constitution of the United States, submitted for Consideration by Mr. Hillhouse. 1808. 12mo, pp. 7.—Remarks before the Joint Committee on the Petition of Samuel Hinkley and others for the Extension of the Hampshire and Hampden [Mass.], Canal. *Boston.* 1827. 8vo, pp. 11. M., W.—Remarks [upon the same Subject.] *Boston.* 1828. 8vo.—Speech in the Senate, Dec. 21 [1808], on the Bill making further Provision for enforcing the Embargo. [*Baltimore: Printed by*

J. Robinson. n. d.] 8vo, pp. 16. M.—Speech ... 12th April 1808. Explanatory of his proposed Amendments to the Constitution of the United States. ... *Troy, N. Y.: Printed by Wright, Goodenow, and Stockwell.* 1808. 8vo, pp. 39. B.—Speech, in the Senate ... February 21, 1809, on Mr. Giles' Non-Intercourse Bill. ... [n. p. n. d.] 8vo, pp. 12. W.—Speech ... on his Resolution to prevent an improper Expenditure of the Public Moneys. 1809. 8vo.

HILLHOUSE (J. A.) Dramas, Discourses, and other Pieces. By James A. Hillhouse. *Boston: Charles C. Little and James Brown.* 1839. 2 vols., 16mo, pp. xiv, (1), 296; (6), 247, (2).

HILLHOUSE. An Oration pronounced at New Haven, by Request of the Common Council, August 19, 1834; in Commemoration of the Life and Services of General LaFayette. By James A. Hillhouse. *New Haven: H. Howe & Co.* 1834. 8vo, pp. 40. Portrait. B., BA., H. 31886

Also: An Oration ... at New-Haven, before the Society of Phi Beta Kappa, September 12, 1826, on ... the Choice of an Era. ... *New-Haven: A. H. Maltby and Co.* 1826. 8vo, pp. 32.—On the Relation of Literature to a Republican Government. [n. p. 1836.]

HILLHOUSE (T.) The Conscription Act Vindicated. By Thomas Hillhouse, late Adjutant General. *Albany: Weed, Parsons & Co.* 1863. 8vo, pp. 27. 31887

HILLHOUSE (W.) The Crisis, No. 1, or Thoughts on Slavery occasioned by the Missouri Question. By William Hillhouse. *New Haven, Conn.* 1820. 8vo. + No. 2. [*Ibid.*] 1820. W.

HILLHOUSE (W.), *Jun.* A Dissertation, in Answer to a Late Lecture on the Political State of America, Read in New-Haven, January 12th, 1789, During the adjourned Sessions of the Honorable Legislature. By William Hillhouse, Jun ... . To which is added, A Short Poem spoken at the same time. *New Haven: Printed by T. & S. Green.* [1789.] 12mo, pp. 23. BA., C.

HILLIARD (H. W.) Speeches and Addresses. By Henry W. Hilliard. *New-York: Harper & Brothers.* 1855. 8vo, pp. 497.

Also: Address ... before the American Institute. ... October 14, 1850. With some Remarks, by Gen. Tallmadge, President ... *New York: Wm. L. S. Harrison, Printer.* 1850. 8vo, pp. 9.—De Vane: A Story of Plebeians and Patricians. ... *New York: Blelock & Co.* 1865. 2 vols., 12mo, pp. 552.—Letter on the Political Issues of the Day. ... *Montgomery.* 1858. 8vo, pp. 8.— ... Speech ... February 10, 1849. On ... providing Governments for the New Territories ... . [n. p. n. d.] 8vo, pp. 8.—Speech ... on the Mexican War; ... House of Representatives of the United States, January 5, 1847. ... *Washington: J. & G. S. Gideon, Printers.* 1847. 8vo, pp. 16. M.—Speech ... on the Bill to establish a Territorial Government in Oregon: ... March 30, 1848. *Washington: Printed by J. and G. S. Gideon.* 1848. 8vo, pp. 14.—Speech ... on the Oregon Question ... Jan. 6, 1844. *Washington: J. & G. S. Gideon, Printers.* 1846. 8vo, pp. 15. B.—Speech ... on the Boundary of Texas ... Aug. 28, 1850. *Washington: Printed at the Congressional Globe Office.* 1850. 8vo, pp.

12.—The Spirit of Liberty. An Oration ... before the Literary Societies of the University of Virginia, on the 27th July, 1859. ... *Montgomery, Ala.: Barrett & Wimbish, Printers.* 1860. 8vo, pp. 33.—[Woman.] Address delivered at the Commencement of La Grange Female College, ... 12th ... July, 1854. ... *Montgomery.* 1854. 8vo, pp. 20.

HILLIARD (I.) The Federal Pye [in verse]. By Isaac Hilliard. May, 1803. *Danbury.* 1804. 8vo, pp. (2), 16. 31891

HILLIARD. The New England Mountain in Labor. ... By Isaac Hilliard. [1814.] 12mo. W. 31892

Also: A Short Practical History of Fragments Collected from Past and Present Times. [A Poem.] *Danbury.* 1803. 12mo.

HILLIARD (J.) A Sermon ... May 14, 1817, at the Funeral of Mrs. Elizabeth Wentworth. By Joseph Hilliard ... . *Cambridge: Printed by Hilliard and Metcalf.* 1817. 8vo, pp. 12. H.

Also: Two Discourses to the Second Church and Society in Berwick, October 15, 1797. ... *Dover.* 1798. 8vo.

HILLIARD (T.) The Duty of a People, under the Oppression of Man, to seek Deliverance from God. The Substance of Two Sermons delivered at Barnstable, July 14, 1774. By Timothy Hilliard, A.M., Pastor. *Boston: T. Greenleaf.* 1774. 8vo, pp. 31.

HILLIARD. An Oration, pronounced before the Inhabitants of Portland, July 4th, 1803. Being the Twenty-Seventh Anniversary of American Independence. By Timothy Hilliard. *Portland: Printed by E. A. Jenks.* 1803. 8vo, pp. 20. BA., H., W.

Also: An Eulogy, delivered at the Funeral of the Hon. William Gorham, Esq. on the 25th July, 1804. ... *Portland: Printed by Jenks & Shirley.* [n. d.] 12mo, pp. 12.—A Sermon delivered December 10, 1788, at the Ordination of the Rev. John Andrews, ... in Newburyport [Mass.] ... *Newburyport: Printed by John Mycall.* MDCCLXXXIV. 8vo, pp. 52. [Printed in black, red, and blue.]—A Sermon ... October 24, 1787, at the Ordination of the Rev. Henry Ware, ... Hingham. ... *Salem: Printed by Dabney and Cushing.* MDCCLXXXVIII. 8vo, pp. 28. W. + Second Edition. *Cambridge: Hilliard, Metcalf and Company.* 1828. 8vo, pp. 22. M.—A Sermon, ... September 3, 1788, at the Dudleian Lecture in the Chapel of Harvard College, in Cambridge. ... *Boston: Printed by Edmund Freeman.* M,DCC,LXXXVIII. 8vo, pp. 30. H.—Sermon delivered April 27, 1785, at the Ordination of Rev. Bezaleel Howard, Springfield. ... *Springfield.* [1785.] 4to, pp. 18.— ... A Sermon ... at Cambridge, ... preceding the Execution of Alexander White, Richard Barrick and John Sullivan. With an Appendix, exhibiting some Account of their Conversation and Behavior in Prison, &c. ... *Boston: E. Russell.* M,DCC,LXXXV. 8vo, pp. 32. BA., C., H.

HILLIARD (W.) An Address delivered before the Massachusetts Charitable Mechanic Association, October 4, 1827, being the Anniversary ... . By William Hilliard. *Cambridge: Printed by Hilliard, Metcalf, and Co.* 1827. 8vo, pp. 48. M., W. 31896

Also: Address delivered at the ... Amicable Lodge in Cambridge, November 16, 1829. ... *Cambridge: E. W. Metcalf and Company.* 1829. 8vo, pp. 12. B., BA., H.

[HILLIARD D'AUBERTEUIL (Michel René).] Considérations sur l'état présent de la Colonie Française de Saint Domingue. Ouvrage politique et législatif; Presenté au Ministre de la Marine. Par Mr. H. Dl. *Paris: Chez Grangé.* MDCCLXXVI–VII. 2 vols., 8vo, pp. xvi, 327; (4), iv, 368. C., H. 31897

A third volume was commenced, but was not published. It was first answered by Du Buison in "Nouvelles considérations," and translated into German as:

HILLIARD D'AUBERTEUIL. Betrachtungen über den gegenwärten Zustand der Französischen Colonie zu San Domingo, aus dem Französischen übersetzt und mit einigen Anmerkungen versehen. *Leipzig.* 1779. 2 vols., 8vo. A. 31898

HILLIARD D'AUBERTEUIL. Essais historiques et politiques sur les Anglo-Américains. Par M. Hilliard d'Auberteuil. *Bruxelles.* M.DCC.LXXXI–II. 2 vols. in 4 pts., 8vo, pp. xvi, 198; xii, 199–441; xii, 208; xiv, 209–436. BA. + *Bruxelles.* MDCCLXXXIV. 2 vols., 8vo, pp. xii, 303; iv, 315. 17 Maps and Plates. H.

The second volume, printed in 1782, is entitled: "Essais Historiques et Politiques sur la Révolution de l'Amérique Septentrionale." The work was reprinted in a more elegant manner as below:

HILLIARD D'AUBERTEUIL. Essais Historiques et Politiques sur les Anglo-Américains. Par M. Hilliard d'Auberteuil. *A Bruxelles.* M. DCC. LXXXII. 2 vols., 4to, pp. xii, 303; vi, 307. 8 Maps, 10 Plates. 31900

The Plates in this edition, by Le Barbier and others, are finely engraved and include First Assembly of Congress, Portraits of Hancock, Washington, Franklin and Pitt, Death of Warren, Montgomery, Fire in New York, Plan of the Battle of Monmouth, etc. At the end of Vol. II. are a number of Epitaphs upon American officers.

[HILLIARD D'AUBERTEUIL.] Histoire de l'Administration de Lord North, Ministre des Finances en Angleterre, depuis 1770 jusqu'en 1782, et de la guerre de l'Amérique Septentrionale, jusqu'à la Paix: Suivie du Tableau Historique des Finances d'Angleterre, depuis Guillaume III. jusqu'en 1784. ... *A Londres: et se trouve a Paris: Couturier.* M.DCC.LXXXIV. 2 vols., 8vo, pp. xx, 276; (4), 180. + Nouveau Compte Rendu. pp. 80. C.

The author says, that after having translated the "View of the History of Great Britain during the Administration of Lord North," he thought he might substitute in its place a less prolix and more complete history, preserving all that was useful, agreeable, and interesting in the English work; and adding a narrative of events which would comprise a complete account of the American War.

HILLIARD D'AUBERTEUIL. Historischer und Politischer Versuch über die Anglo-Amerikaner und die Staatsveränderung in Nordamerika. In zwölf Büchern. Aus dem Französischen des

Herrn Hilliard d'Auberteuil übersetzt [von A. Wittenberg]. *Hamburg und Kiel: Bohn.* 1783. 2 vols., 8vo, pp. 148, 188; 178, 176. 31902

HILLIARD D'AUBERTEUIL. Historia de la administracion del lord North, primer ministro de Inglaterra, y de la guerra de la América septentrional hasta la paz. Obra escrita en Ingles, traducida al Frances, y de este al Castellano, con notas del traductor. Por d. P. P. de A. *Madrid: Imprenta real.* 1806. 16mo, pp. (14), 402. C. 31903

HILLIARD D'AUBERTEUIL. Mis Mac Rea, Roman Historique, Par M. Hilliard-D'Auberteuil. *A Philadelphie* [*i. e. Bruxelles*]. M. DCC. LXXXIV. 16mo, pp. xii, 146. C. 31904

A tale founded on the story of Jane McCrea, probably published at Brussels.

HILLIER (R.) Oration, on the Fourth of July, 1800. By Richard Hillier. *Mount Pleasant.* 1800. 8vo. 31905

HILLS (A. C.) Emancipation in Louisiana. Speech of Alfred C. Hills ... in the Constitutional Convention of Louisiana, May 4th and 5th, 1864. *New Orleans.* 1864. 8vo, pp. 21. BA.

HILLS. Macpherson, the Great Confederate Philosopher and Southern Blower. A Record of his Philosophy, his Career as a Warrior, Traveller, Clergyman, Poet, and Newspaper Publisher, his Death, Resuscitation, and Subsequent Election to the Office of Governor of Louisiana. ' By Alfred C. Hills, Editor of the New Orleans Era. *New York: James Miller.* MDCCCLXIV. 12mo, pp. 209. B., BA. 31907

Also: Yankees made Southerners ... Speech ... Nov. 28, 1863. [*New Orleans.* n. d.] 8vo, pp. 4. H.

HILLS (G.) A Sermon preached at the Farewell Service, celebrated at St. James's Church, Piccadilly, on Wednesday, Nov. 16, 1859, the Day previous to his Departure for his Diocese. By George Hills, D.D. With an Account of the Meeting held on the same Day at the Mansion House of the City of London, in Aid of the Columbia Mission. *London: J. & J. Rivington.* 1859. 8vo, pp. 55. 31908

HILLS (G. M.) ... A Sermon Commemorative of the Rt. Rev. ... William Heathcote De Lancey ... First Bishop of Western New York; preached in ... Syracuse ... . By the Reverend George Morgan Hills ... . *Syracuse, N. Y.* 1865. 8vo, pp. 19, (1). H. 31909

HILLS (J.) Plan of Philadelphia. By John Hills. *London.* 1796. 4to. P. 31910

HILLSBOROUGH (*Earl of*). A Letter to the Right Honourable Wills, Earl of Hillsborough, on the Connection between Great Britain and her American Colonies. ... *London: T. Beckett.* MDCCLXVIII. 8vo, pp. 47. B. 31911

See "M. Rev." XXXVIII. 500, *and our* Vol. VII., No. 28757.

HILLSBOROUGH. A Letter to the Right Honourable the Earl of Hillsborough, on the Present Situation of Affairs in America. In which the Arguments in Favour of the Colonies are placed in a New Point of View, and their Rights and Privileges are incontestibly demonstrated on Constitutional Principles, supported by Unanswerable Arguments, drawn from their Ancient Original Charters, and the Circumstances attending their first Settlement. Together with a Serious and Impartial Consideration of the Consequences which must necessarily result from the Exercise of Coercive Measures, to compel them to a Submission to the late Acts of Parliament. Also, an Appendix in Answer to a Pamphlet, intitled "The Constitutional Right of Great Britain to tax the Colonies." *London: J. Kearsly.* 1769. 8vo, pp. (1), 117. + *Boston: Reprinted by Edes & Gill.* 1769. 8vo, pp. 55. B., C.

The "Monthly Review," styles this "Another very spirited advocate for the liberties of America." It is perhaps by Samuel Adams. The author is particularly severe on the Earl of Hillsborough, whom he blames for the troubles in the colonies. "Your troops," he says "have been obliged to abandon their conquests; and all their laurels are blasted. Cushing still lives; Otis still harangues with spirited firmness; and the civil power begins to assume its hated offices; nay worse, the day of retribution approaches, and your Lordship must answer for having invaded the privileges of a free assembly, by a threatening letter, and having infringed an act of Parliament, in quartering troops in Boston, expressly contrary to law." *See also* Pliny, Junior.

HILLSBOROUGH, *Ill.* Order of Exercises at the Dedication of the First Congregational Church in the Town of Hillsborough, Aug. 29, 1841. *Alton, Ill.* 1841. 12mo, pp. 6. 31913

HILLSBOROUGH, *N. H.* A True Account of the Defalcation of the Hillsborough Bank. *Concord.* [n. d.] 8vo, pp. 16.

A fragment of political and local history.

HILLYARD (I.) A Wonderful and Horrible Thing is committed in the Land. The Prophets prophecy falsely, and the Priests rule by their means, and my people love to have it so; and what will ye do in the end thereof? By Isaac Hillyard. And also the Chronicles of Andrew, containing an accurate and brief

account of General Jackson's Victories in the South over the Creeks, also, his Victories over the British, at New Orleans, with a Biographical Sketch by Jesse Denson Bate, in the Historical Bible style. *Hamilton, Ohio.* 1822. 8vo. C. 31915

HILLYER (A.) A Sermon ... May 4th, 1820, in the Wall Street Church, New York, before the Presbyterian Educational Society. By Asa Hillyer, D.D. *Newark.* 1820. 8vo, pp. 21.

HILTON (J. T.) An Address, delivered before the African Grand Lodge, of Boston ... June 24th, 1828. By John T. Hilton ... . *Boston: Printed by David Hooton.* 1828. 8vo, pp. 16.

HILTON (R. B.) ... A Bill ... to levy Additional Taxes for ... 1865 for the Support of the Government. [n. p. n. d.] pp. 6.

HILTON (W.) A | Relation | Of | A Discovery lately made on the Coast of | Florida, | (From Lat. 31. to 33 Deg. 45 Min. North-Lat.) | By William Hilton Commander, and | Commissioner with Capt. Anthony Long, | and Peter Fabian, in the Ship Adventure, which set | Sayl from Spikes Bay, Aug. 10. 1663. and was | set forth by several Gentlemen and Mer- | chants of the Island of Barbadoes. | Giving an account of the nature and tempera- | ture of the Soyl, the manners and disposition | of the Natives, and whatsoever else is | remarkable therein. | Together with | Proposals made by the Commissioners | of the Lords Proprietors, to all such per- | sons as shall become the first Setlers on the | Rivers, Harbors, and Creeks there. | *London,* | *Printed by J. C. for Simon Miller at the Star neer the* | *West-end of St. Pauls,* 1646. | 4to, pp. 34. C.

Reprinted in Force's "Tracts," Vol. IV. The original edition is a pamphlet of great rarity.

HILTZHEIMER (B.) The Hermit; or, an account of Francis Adam Joseph Phyle. By B. Hiltzheimer. *Philadelphia.* 1811. 12mo. P. 31920

HIME (H. L.) Photographs taken at Lord Selkirk's Settlement on the Red River of the North, to illustrate a Narrative of the Canadian Exploring Expeditions in Rupert's Land, by Henry Youle Hind, in charge of the Assinniboine and Saskatchewan Expedition. By Humphrey Lloyd Hime. *London: J. Hogarth.* 1861. 4to. 30 Plates. C. 31921

HIMES (J. V.) Mormon Delusions and Monstrosities. A Review of the Book of Mormon ... . By Joshua V. Himes. *Boston: Joshua V. Himes.* 1842. 12mo, pp. 90 B., BA. 31922

Himnos Patrioticos.—Himno de la guerra de la América—Himno Nacional Oriental—Himno Nacional Argentino—Himno de Riego—Napoleon el Grande y Napoleon el Chico. *Buenos Aires.* 1863. 12mo, pp. 16. 31923

[HINCHETA (José).] Tactica nueva de administrar justicia y proceder en juicio de residencia. *Habana, imprenta de Arazoza y Soler.* 1813. 4to, pp. 29. 31924

HINCHLIFF (T. W.) South American Sketches; or a Visit to Rio Janeiro, the Organ Mountains, La Plata, and the Parana. By Thomas Woodbine Hinchliff, M.A. ... *London: Longman, Green* ... . 1863. Post 8vo, pp. xviii, (1), Errata, 1 slip, 414. Map, 4 Plates. B., BA., C. 31925

Highly commended by the "Saturday Review."

HINCHLIFFE (H. J.) Rules of Practice for the Vice-Admiralty Court of Jamaica; with a Digest and Notes, By Henry J. Hinchliffe. *London.* 1813. 8vo. C. 31926

HINCHLIFFE (J.) A Sermon preached before the ... Society for the Propagation of the Gospel in Foreign Parts, ... February 16, 1776. By the Right Reverend John, Lord Bishop of Peterborough. *London: Printed by T. Harrison and S. Brooke.* M DCCLXXVI. 8vo, pp. 76, (1). B., M. 31927

HINCHMAN. The Hinchman Conspiracy Case, in Letters to the New York Home Journal, with an Abstract of the Evidence for the Defence. *Philadelphia.* 1849. 8vo. 31928

HINCKLEY (A.) Traveller's Illustrated Pocket Guide. *New-York.* 1848–49. 18mo. S. 31929

HINCKLEY (F.) The Farmer and the Man; ... An Address ... before the Middlesex North Agricultural Society, at Lowell, Sept. 15, 1858. By Rev. Frederic Hinckley. *Lowell.* 1858. 8vo, pp. 21. B. 31930

HINCKS (F.) Canada: its Financial Position and Resources. By the Hon. Francis Hincks, M.P.P. *London.* 1849. 8vo, pp. viii, 32. 31931

[HINCKS.] The Seigniorial Question; its Present Position. By a Member of the Legislative Assembly from Upper Canada. *Quebec.* 1854. 8vo. 31932

Also: Religious Endowments in Canada. ... A Chapter of Canadian History. ... *London: Dalton & Lucy.* 1869. 8vo, pp. 105.—Review of Mr. Howe's Pamphlet on

the Organization of the Empire. *London.* 1855. 8vo.—Speech in the Legislative Assembly on the Financial Condition of the Province. *Toronto.* 1851. 8vo, pp. 16. *See also* our Vol. III., No. 10418.

HIND (H. Y.) Explorations in the Interior of The Labrador Peninsula the Country of the Montagnais and Nasquapee Indians. By Henry Youle Hind. ... *London: Longman, Green, Longman, Roberts & Green.* 1863. 2 vols., 8vo, pp. xv, (1), 351; xiii, (1), 304. 12 Plates, 2 Maps. B., BA. 31933

Almost entirely occupied with incidents of Indian life and character, particularly of the Montagnais, Abenakis, and Esquimaux. "All that Mr. Hind undertakes, is done so thoroughly that little more could be indicated, to complete the exhaustion of his subject."—T. W. FIELD.

HIND. Narrative of the Canadian Red River Exploring Expedition of 1857 and of the Assinniboine and Saskatchewan Exploring Expedition of 1858 By Henry Youle Hind ... In charge of the Assinniboine and Saskatchewan Expedition. *London: Longman, Green, Longman, and Roberts.* 1860. 2 vols., 8vo, pp. xx, 494; xvi, 472. 20 Plates, 11 Maps. B., BA., C. 31934

During this exploration, Mr. Hind lived almost constantly among the Crees and Chippeways, whose habits and peculiarities he was most eager to study, and prompt to record. Everything in their life had not only the charm of novelty to him, but as a man of science, he was anxious to observe all the facts which may prove stepping-stones in tracing their origin and their history.

HIND. A Preliminary Report on the Geology of New Brunswick, together with a special Report on the distribution of the "Quebec Group" in the Province. By Henry Youle Hind, M.A. ... *Fredericton: G. E. Fenety.* 1865. 8vo, pp. 293. C.

The maps named in the introductory note have not yet been published.

HIND. Report on the Sherbrooke Gold District, together with a Paper on the Gneisses of Nova Scotia, and an Abstract of a Paper on Gold Mining in Nova Scotia. By Henry Youle Hind, M.A. *Halifax.* [n. d.] 8vo, pp. 80. Tables. S. 31936

HIND. North West Territory. Reports of Progress; together with a Preliminary and General Report on the Assinniboine and Saskatchewan Exploring Expedition, made under Instructions from the Provincial Secretary, Canada. *Toronto: Printed by John Lovell.* 1859. 4to, pp. xii, 201. Plates and Maps. H. + *London: Stationery Office.* 1860. Folio, pp. 219. 5 Maps.

Also, with the text in French, "Rapports sur l'Expédition d'Exploration de l'Assiniboine et de la Saskatchewan." *Toronto.* 1859. 4to.

HIND. Report on the Waverley Gold District, with Geological Maps and Sections. By Henry Youle Hind, M.A. ... *Halifax.* 1869. 8vo, pp. 62. S. 31938

Also: A Comparative View of the Climate of Western Canada, Considered in Relation to its Influence upon Agriculture ... *Toronto: Printed by Brewer, McPhail & Co.* 1851. 8vo, pp. 38.—Essay on the Insects and Diseases Injurious to the Wheat Crops. ... To which was awarded, by the Bureau of Agriculture and Statistics, the First Prize. ... *Toronto: Printed by Lovell & Gibson.* 1857. 8vo, pp. 139, (1.) c.—Report on a Topographical and Geological Exploration of the Canoe Route between Fort William, Lake Superior and Fort Garry, Red River, and also of the Valley of the Red River, North of the 49th Parallel, in 1857. ... *Toronto.* 1858. 8vo, pp. 16.—A Sketch of the Overland Route to British Columbia. ... *Toronto.* 1862. 8vo. *See* Hime (H. L.), *ante.*

HIND, *and others.* Eighty Years Progress of British North America, by Messrs. Hind, Keefer, Robb, Perley and Murray. *Toronto.* 1836. 8vo, pp. 776. 31939

HINDES (S.) Trial of S. Hindes and Nicholas Wood, Police Commissioners of Baltimore. *Baltimore.* 1868. 8vo. 31940

Relates to the election troubles after the Civil War.

HINDMAN. Report of Major General Hindman, of his Operations in the Trans-Mississippi District. Published by Order of Congress. *Richmond: R. M. Smith, Public Printer.* 1864. 8vo, pp. 26. BA. 31941

HINDOBRO (F. G.) Nuevas Ordenenzas de Minas para e Reino de Chile qui de orden de su Majisdad ecribi Don Francisco Garcia de Hindobro, 1754. *Reimpresas Santiago de Chile.* 1838. Folio. 31942

HINDS (E.) History of Facts in Relation to Ebenezer Hinds. *Middleborough.* 1787. 8vo. 31943

HINDS (R. B.) Botany of the Voyage of H. M. S. Sulphur, under the command of Captain Sir Edward Belcher, R.N., &c. Edited and Superintended by R. B. Hinds. The Botanical Descriptions, by George Bentham, Esq. *London: Smith, Elder & Co.* 1844. Rl. 4to. 31944

HINDS. Zoology of the Voyage of H. M. S. Sulphur, under the command of Capt. Sir Edward Belcher, R. N., &c. Published under the authority of the Lords Commissioners of the Admiralty. Edited and Superintended by Richard Brinsley Hinds, Esq., Surgeon, R.N., attached to the Expedition. *London: Smith, Elder & Co.* 1844. [1843–45.] 2 vols., 4to, pp. (2), 150, 64 Plates; (2), 72, v, 21 colored Plates. C. 31945

Contents: Vol. I. Mammalia, by J. E. Gray; Birds, by J. Gould; Fish, by J. Richardson. Vol. II. Mollusca, by R. B. Hinds. "Among the countries visited by the 'Sulphur,' and which in the present state of science, are invested with more particular interest, may be mentioned the Californias, Columbia River, the North West Coast of America," &c. *See our* Vol. II., No. 3390, *and* Rich, Vol. II.

HINDE (W.) The very Singular Life of John Bruen, Esquire of Bruen Stapleford, Cheshire: ... By the Rev. William Hinde, .. *New York: Printed by Edward O. Jenkins.* 1857. 18mo, pp. 116. 31946

Title from Whittemore's "American Genealogy."

HINE (H.) An Oration on the Death of Jabez Backus, ... pronounced in Yale College Chapel, July 21st, 1794. By Homer Hine. ... *New-Haven: Printed by T. and S. Green.* [1794.] 8vo, pp. 14. B., M. 31947

HINE (L. A.) ... A Lecture on Garrisonian Politics ... in Cincinnati ... April 24th, 1853. By L. A. Hine. *Cincinnati: Printed by Longley & Brother.* [n. d.] 8vo, pp. 23. H. 31948

HINE. Hine's Progress Pamphlets. Part I. Earth and Man. *Cincinnati: L. A. Hine.* [1853.] 8vo, pp. (2), 224. C. 31949

HINES (D. T.) The Life, Adventures and Opinions of David Theo. Hines, of South Carolina; Master of Arts, and, sometimes, Doctor of Medicine; alias, Dr. Hamilton, Col. Hamilton, Dr. Haynes, Col. Hayne, Dr. Porcher, Col. Singleton, Rev. Mr. Beman, Rev. Dr. Baker, Col. Allston, Maj. Parker, Col. Benton, Maj. Middleton, Lieut. Pringle, Capt. Rutledge, Col. Pinckney, Dr. Brandreth, Major Moore, &c. &c. &c. in a Series of Letters to his Friends. Written by Himself. *New York: Bradley & Clark.* 1840. 12mo, pp. 195. 31950

HINES (G.) Oregon and its Institutions; comprising a Full History of the Willamette University, the first established on the Pacific Coast. By Rev. Gustavus Hines. With Four Engravings. *New York: Carlton & Porter.* [1868.] 12mo, pp. 326.

HINES. A Voyage Round the World: with a History of the Oregon Mission; and Notes of several years Residence on the Plains, bordering the Pacific Ocean, comprising an Account of interesting Adventures among the Indians West of the Rocky Mountains. To which is appended a full Description of Oregon Territory, its Geography, History, and Religion. By Rev. Gustavus Hines. *Buffalo: Geo. H. Derby.* 1850. 12mo, pp. 437.

Next year the publisher changed the title to read:

HINES. Life on the Plains of the Pacific. Oregon: its History, Condition, and Prospects: Containing a Description of the Geography, Climate and Productions with Personal Adventures among the Indians during a Residence of the Author on the

Plains bordering the Pacific while connected with the Oregon Mission. ... By Rev. Gustavus Hines. *Buffalo: Geo. H. Derby.* 1851. 12mo, pp. 437. Portrait. B., BA. 31953

And, in 1859, the publisher once more changed the title, omitting the words "Life on the Plains of the Pacific."

HINGELEY (E.) The Character and Greatness of Abraham Lincoln. A Discourse delivered April 23, 1865. By Rev. E. Hingeley, Pastor of the M. E. Church, Monongahela City, Pa. [n. p. n. d.] 8vo, pp. 15. 31954

HINGERLE (A.), *Soc. Jes.* De India ejusque gloriosa juventute sermones habiti a rhetoribus Viennensibus. *Viennæ.* 1726. 8vo.

"La dernière partie traite de l'Amérique, et contient trois planches dont un portrait d'un Canadien et un autre d'une Canadienne." Title and note from Tross' Catalogue.

HINGHAM, *Mass.* A Narrative. *See* [Thaxter (Thomas)].

Agricultural and Horticultural Society Transactions, 1858. *Boston.* 1858. 8vo. Continued. 31956

Report of the Committee on the Financial Affairs of the Town of Hingham, for the Year ending February 23, 1833. ... *Hingham.* 1833. 8vo. 31957

A Vindication of the Proceedings of the First Church and Parish in Hingham, in settling the Rev. Joseph Richardson as their Gospel Minister. *Newburyport.* 1805. 8vo, pp. 80. M. + Second Edition. *Boston: Printed by B. Parks.* 1807. 8vo, pp. 80.

HINGSTON (E. P.) The Genial Showman. Being Reminiscences of the Life of Artemus Ward, and Pictures of a Showman's Career in the Western World. By Edward P. Hingston. New Illustrated Edition. *London: John Camden Hotton.* [1870.] 12mo, pp. x, 519. 19 Plates. C. + [*Ibid.*] 2 vols., 8vo, pp. xii, 363, (1); vi, 395, (1). B. + *New York: Harper & Brothers.* 1870. 8vo, pp. 155. B., BA. 31959

HINCKS (E. W.) Synopsis of the Military Services of Brigadier General and Brevet Major General Edward W. Hincks ... [*Boston.* 1860.] 8vo, pp. 12. H. 31960

HINMAN (R. R.) Blue Laws. *See* Vol. II., No. 6010.

HINMAN. A Catalogue of the Names of the First Puritan Settlers of the Colony of Connecticut; with the Time of their Arrival in the Colony, and their Standing in Society, together with their Place of Residence, as far as can be discovered by the

Records. Collected from the State and Town Records, by R. R. Hinman. *Hartford: Printed by E. Gleason.* 1846. 8vo, pp. 367. B., H. 31961

The motto *caveat emptor* is specially applicable to this book. It was never completed. It was reissued as: "A Catalogue of the Names of the Early Puritan Settlers of the Colony of Connecticut; with the Time of their Arrival in the Country and Colony, their Standing in Society, Place of Residence, Condition in Life, where from, Business, &c., as far as is found on Record. Collected from Records by Royal R. Hinman, of Hartford." *Hartford: Press of Case, Tiffany & Co.* 1852. 8vo, pp. 801—and terminated with "Danielson;" then, in 1856, a sixth number was published, passing over the intermediate names, and relating to the E. Hinman family only. *Hartford: Case, Lockwood and Company.* 8vo, pp. 805–884. This last part was reprinted in 1872.

HINMAN. A Historical Collection, from Official Records, Files, &c., of the Part Sustained by Connecticut, during the War of the Revolution. With an Appendix, containing Important Letters, Depositions, &c., written during the War. Compiled by Royal R. Hinman ... . *Hartford: Printed by E. Gleason.* 1842. 8vo, pp. 643, (1). Portrait. B., BA., H. 31962

HINMAN. Letters from the English Kings and Queens, Charles II, James II, William and Mary, Anne, George II, &c. to the Governors of the Colony of Connecticut. Together with the Answers thereto, from 1635 to 1749. And other Original, Ancient, Literary and Curious Documents, compiled from Files and Records in the Office of the Secretary of the State of Connecticut. By R. R. Hinman. ... *Hartford: John B. Eldredge.* 1836. 12mo, pp. 372. B., BA., H. + [*Ibid.*] 1842. C. 31963

Some copies are entitled: "Antiquities of Connecticut."

HINMAN (S. D.) Journal of the Rev. S. D. Hinman, Missionary to the Santee Sioux Indians. And Taopi, By Bishop Whipple. ... *Philadelphia: McCalla & Stavely, Printers.* 1869. 12mo, pp. xviii, 87. B., H. 31964

Also: Dakota Indians, to the Friends of the Santee Indian Mission. ... [n. p. n. d.] 8vo, pp. 20. H.

HINRICHS (Gustavus). *See* Iowa.

HINTON (J. H.) The History and Topography of the United States of North America, from the Earliest Period to the Present Time, comprising Political and Biographical History; Geography, Geology, Mineralogy, Zoology and Botany; Agriculture, Manufactures and Commerce; Laws, Manners, Customs and Religion; with a Topographical Description of the Cities, Towns, Sea-Ports, Public Edifices, Canals, &c. &c. Including all the Information necessary for Emigrants of every class. Edited by John Howard Hinton, A.M. ... Illustrated with a Series of Views, ...

and Maps ... . *London: Jennings & Chaplin & J. T. Hinton.* 1830–1832. 2 vols., 4to, pp. (6), xvi, 476; viii, (2), 580. 99 Plates and Maps. BA., H. + [*Ibid.*] 1834. 2 vols., 4to, pp, xvi, (2), 520; viii, (2), 580. 99 Plates. H. + Third Edition. *London: J. Dowding.* 1842. 2 vols., 4to, pp. (2), xvi, (1), 501; viii, (2), 580. Maps and Plates. B., C. 31965

This once popular history, first published in monthly parts, is now sought for mainly on account of the fine steel engravings with which it is illustrated, and in this respect, the early editions are of course preferable. Some copies were issued with the plates on India paper, of which a few impressions were published in folio. It was reprinted as:

HINTON. The History and Topography of the United States of North America, ... the Cities, Towns, Sea-Ports, Public Edifices, Canals, &c. &c. By John Howard Hinton, A.M. ... With Additions and Corrections by Samuel L. Knapp, ... A New Edition. *Boston: Samuel Walker.* 1834. 2 vols., 4to, pp. (6), viii, 427; (4), viii, 507, (1). Map and 40 Plates B., C. + [*Ibid.*] 1835. + Second Edition. ... *Boston: Samuel Walker.* 1844. + [*Ibid.*] 1846. + [*Ibid.*] 1851. + Third Edition. [*Ibid.*] 1853. pp. viii, 427; viii, 507. + [*Ibid.*] 1855. 31966

The additions are confined to the letter-press. The plates are less numerous and much inferior to those in the English edition.

HINTON. Memoir of William Knibb, Missionary in Jamaica. By John Howard Hinton, M.A. *London: Houlston and Stoneman.* 1847. 8vo, pp. x, 562. Portrait. B., C., P. 31967

HINTON. The Test of Experience; or, the Voluntary Principle in the United States. By John Howard Hinton. 1857. 12mo, pp. 126. 31968

Relates to Church and State.

[HINTON (Richard J.)] Rebel Invasion of Missouri and Kansas, and the Campaign of the Army of the Border, against General Sterling Price, ... 1864. *Chicago: Church & Goodman.* 1865. 8vo, pp. (4), 351. Portraits. B. + Second Edition. [*Ibid.*] 8vo, pp. 351. 8 Plates. C. 31969

Hints addressed to Wise Men; concerning the dispute which ended Nov. 8, 1809, in the Dismission of Mr. Jackson, the British Minister to the United States. *Boston.* [n. d.] 8vo. W.

Hints for a Specific Plan for an Abolition of the Slave Trade, and for Relief of the Negroes in the West Indies. ... *London: J. Debrett.* 1788. 8vo. 31971

See "M. Rev.," LXXVIII. 429.

Hints for American Husbandmen; with Communications to the Pennsylvania Agricultural Society. *Philadelphia.* 1827. 8vo.

Hints for some new Regulations in the Sugar Trade; with Remarks on the State of Commerce in the French and British West India Islands. By an Impartial Man. *London: J. Symonds.* 1792. 8vo, pp. 31. 31973

Hints on a Cheap Mode of Purchasing the Liberty of a Slave Population. *New York: G. A. Neumann.* 1838. 12mo, pp. 21.

Hints on Banking, in a Letter to a Gentleman in Albany. By a New-Yorker. *New-York: Printed by Vanderpoel & Cole.* 1827. 8vo, pp. 43. B. 31975

Hints on the Case of Canada for the Consideration of Members of both Houses of Parliament. *London: John Murray.* 1838. 8vo. 31976

Hints on the Important Crisis of a New Reign and a New Parliament. *London.* 1761. 8vo, pp. 62. 31977

Hints on the Re-Organization of the Navy. [n. p.] 1845. 8vo. 31978

Hints on the State of the Country in this Momentous Crisis. *London.* 1812. 8vo. 31979

Hints to a Patriot Parliament. *London.* 1782. S. 31980

Hints to Both Parties; or Observations on the Proceedings in Parliament upon the Petitions against the Orders in Council, and on the Conduct of His Majesty's Ministers in granting licences to import the Staple Commodities of the Enemy. ... *London: J. M. Richardson.* 1808. 8vo, pp. 95. P. + *New York: E. Sargeant.* 1808. 8vo, pp. 92. C. 31981

Hints to Emigrants, addressed chiefly to Persons contemplating an Emigration to the United States of America ... . *Liverpool: Printed by W. Bethell.* 1817. 8vo, pp. 37. BA. 31982

Hints to Emigrants from Europe to the United States ... on Subjects Economical and Political, affecting their welfare. By the Shamrock Society of New York. *London.* 1817. 8vo, pp. 29.

Hints to Emigrants, on the Choice of Lands; particularly addressed to Farmers in the North-Eastern States. By Agricola. *Albany: Printed by J. Buell.* MDCCCXVII. 8vo, pp. 8. 31984

Hints to my Countrymen. *See* [Sedgwick (Theodore)].

Hints to People in Power on the Present Melancholy Situation of our Colonies in North America. *London.* 1783. 8vo.

Hints to the Farmers of Rhode Island. By a Freeman. *Providence.* 1829. 8vo, pp. 18. 31986

Relates to the controversy about the Act providing for the use of Broad-Rimmed Wheels.

Hints to Young Generals. By an Old Soldier. [General Armstrong.] *Kingston: J. Buel.* [1812.] 12mo, pp. 71.

HIPPISLEY (G.) A Narrative of the Expedition to the Rivers Orinoco and Apuré, in South America; which sailed from England in November 1817, and joined the Patriotic Forces in Venezuela and Caraccas. By G. Hippisley, Esq. ... *London: John Murray.* 1819. 8vo, pp. xix, (1), Errata, 1 slip, 653, (1). BA.

Lord Byron made use of this work to put himself to sleep. *See* Blackwood's "Magazine," January, 1834.

HIPPISLEY. Histoire de l'Expédition aux Rivières d'Orénoque et d'Apuré dans l'Amérique Méridionale, ... en Novembre 1817, ... par le Colonel Hippisley ... traduit de l'Anglais par M.... *Paris: Chez G. C. Hubert.* 1819. 8vo, pp. 164. H., S. 31989

Mr. Rich suggests that this translation is also an abridgment.

The Hireling and the Slave. Second Edition. *Charleston: John Russell.* 1855. 12mo, pp. 108. 31990

A pro-slavery poem.

Hireling Artifice Detected; Or, the Profit and Loss of Great-Britain, in the Present War with Spain, Set in its True Light; By laying before the Publick, as Full, Compleat, and Regular a List as can be had, of the British Ships taken since the Beginning of the War; with proper Remarks upon the List, and upon our Conduct both at Home and Abroad. With An Appendix, containing a List of the Ships taken since November 16. 1741. *London: T. Cooper.* 1742. 8vo, pp. (2), 76. 31991

HIRST (H. B.) The Coming of the Mammoth, the Funeral of Time, and other Poems. By Henry B. Hirst. *Boston: Phillips & Sampson.* MDCCCXLV. 12mo, pp. 168. C., H. 31992

HIRST (W. L.) Anniversary Discourse before the Philadelphia Forum, Nov. 4, 1826. By William L. Hirst. *Philadelphia.* 1826. 8vo, pp. 42. 31993

HISCOX (E. T.) The Baptist Church Directory. By E. T. Hiscox, D.D. *New York: Sheldon & Company.* 1859. 18mo, pp. 287. 31994

HISLOP (*Governor*). Account of Circumstances between Governor Hislop and Thomas Talboys, Missionary. *George Town, Demerara.* 1817. 8vo. 31995

Relates to the Island of Trinidad.

His Catholick Majesty. *See* [Philip V.]

His Jewels; or a Story of New England in War Time. Founded on Facts. *Boston.* 1868. 16mo, pp. 281. Plate.

His Majesty's Declaration of War against the King of Spain. *Edinburgh.* 1739. Folio, pp. 2. 31997

His Majestie's Letter to the Earle of Southampton and Council and Company of Virginia, commanding the setting up of Silkeworks, and planting of Vines in Virginia. As also a Treatise of the Art of making Silke, planting Vines, Olives, Oranges, &c. set forth for the benefit of the two renowned and most hopeful Sisters, Virginia and the Summer-Islands, by John Bonoeil. 1622. 4to. Portrait of James I. 31998

A volume of extreme rarity, which I have not seen. Title from one of Joseph Lilly's catalogues.

His Majesty's most gracious Speech to Parliament, on Tuesday, Nov. 13, 1770. Folio, pp. 4. 31999

Contains the first allusion from the Throne to the outbreak in Massachusetts Bay, where "very unwarrantable practices are still carried on."

His Majesty's Most Gracious Speech to both Houses of Parliament, on Wednesday, November 30, 1774. *London: Charles Eyre and William Strahan.* MDCCLXXIV. Folio, pp. 4. 32000

The King says "It gives me much concern to inform you that a most daring spirit of Resistance and Disobedience to the Law still unhappily prevails in the Province of the Massachusetts Bay, and has, in divers parts of it, broke forth in fresh Violence of a very criminal nature."

His Majesty's most gracious Speech to both Houses of Parliament on Thursday, October 26, 1775. *London: Printed by Charles Eyre and William Strahan.* 1775. Folio, pp. 4. + *Boston: Printed by John Howe.* [n. d.] Folio, pp. 4. 32001

"The rebellious war now levied is become more general, and is manifestly carried on for the purpose of establishing an independent Empire. I need not dwell on the fatal effects of the success of such a plan."—*Extract.*

His Majesty's Most Gracious Speech to both Houses of Parliament, on Friday, October 27, 1775. ... *Philadelphia: Printed by Hall and Sellers.* [1776.] 4to, pp. 1. P. 32002

His Majesties Propriety. *See* [Clavel (R.)], Vol. IV.

His Majesty's Ship Liverpool, ... 4to, pp. 1. P. 32003

Orders for crew to join, published Jan. 17th, 1778; *J. Humphreys, Philadelphia, Printer.*

Hispania, 1629. *See* [Laet (J. de)].

Hispania victrix. *See* [Gomara (F. L. de)], Vol. VII.

Hispanicarum Rerum Scriptores aliquot ex Bibliotheca Clarissimi Viri Domini Roberti Beli Angli, nunc accuratius emendatiusque recusi, cum Indice. *Francoforti.* 1579–81. 3 vols., folio.

An interesting and valuable work, containing productions of the most eminent Spanish historians, which relates in part to Mexico, Peru, Florida, etc. The third volume is very scarce and seldom found with the others.

Hispaniæ Illustratae, seu Rerum Urbiumque Hispaniæ, Lusitaniæ, Æthiopiæ, et Indiæ Scriptores Varii, partim editi nunc primum partim aucti atque emendati, operâ et studio doctorum hominum, edidit And. Schottus. *Frankoforti.* 1603. 2 vols., folio. 32005

In the second volume (pp. 1282–84) will be found the celebrated letter of Columbus "de Insulis nuper inventis."

Histoire abregée des Provinces-Unies des Pays-Bas, ou l'on voit leur Progrés, leur Conquêtes, leur Gouvernement, et celui de leurs Compagnies en Orient & en Occident comme aussi les Hommes Illustres dans les Armes & les Savans dans les Lettres. Enrichie d'un grand nombre de figures. *A Amsterdam, Chez Jean Malherbe Marchand Libraire sur le Vygendam* MDCCI. Folio, pp. (8), 109. 2 Maps and 4 folded Plates. J.C.B., S. 32006

Contains a brief history of the progress, conquests, and government of Holland, including the Companies of the East and West Indies; illustrated with thirty-seven plates, embracing nearly three hundred portraits and historical events from medals, etc.

Histoire de ce qvi s'est passé av Royavme dv Japon, es annees 1625. 1626. et 1627. Tiré des lettres adressées au R. Pere Mvtio Viteleschi, general de la Compagnie de Jesvs. Traduite d'italien en françois par vn Pere de la mesme Compagnie. *Paris: Sebastian Cramoisy.* 1633. 8vo, pp. (8), 485. 32007

The translator was P. Jean Vireau. Pp. 474–485 relate to Paraguay. *See* Carayon, No. 918.

Histoire de ce qui s'est passé en Éthiopie, Malabar, Brésil et les Indes Orientales. Tirée des lettres écrites ès annés 1620 jusqu'à 1624; adressées au R. P. Mutio Vitelleschi, général de la Compagnie de Jésus, traduite de l'italien en françois par un Père de la même Compagnie [le P. Jean Darde]. *Paris: Sebastian Cramoisy.* 1628. pp. (6), 451. A. 32008

Histoire de Kamschatka. *See* Kracheninnikof (Stephan).

Histoire de l'Administration. *See* [Hilliard d'Auberteuil].

Histoire de la Chine, avec un itinéraire du Nouveau-Monde et la découverte du Nouveau-Mexique, traduite de l'Espagnol par Lucas de la Porte. *Paris.* 1600. 8vo. 32009

Title from Ternaux, No. 1243.

Histoire de la Colonie Française. *See* [Faillon (*l'Abbé*)].

Histoire de la Conqueste de la Floride. *See* Florida, Vol. VI.

Histoire de la dernière conspiration de Lisbonne. Ouvrage traduit du portugais. *Francfort.* 1759. 8vo. 32010

Included in Martius' lithographed Catalogue of Books on America.

Histoire de la dernière Guerre. *See* Leboucher (Odet-Julien).

Histoire de la dernière guerre, commencée l'an 1756, et finie par la paix d'Hubertsbourg, le 15 Février, 1763. Nouvelle Édition. *Cologne.* 1769. 16mo, pp. 192. 2 Maps and Plate. C. + [*Ibid.*] 1770. 32011

See also [Boucher (M.)], Vol. II., Nos. 6840, 6841.

Histoire de l'expedition de ... vaisseaux. *See* [Behrens (C. F.)]

Histoire de la Fondation des Colonies des Anciennes Républiques, adaptée à la Dispute présente de la Grande Bretagne, avec ses Colonies Americaines. Traduite de l'anglais. A la quelle on a ajouté Trois Lettres intéressantes sur le même dispute & les articles de l'union d'Utrecht comparés aux articles de l'Union des Colonies de l'Amérique septentrionale. *Utrecht: J. van Schoonhoven.* MDCCLXXVIII. 8vo, pp. (8), 247, (1). B., C., H. 32012

The translator was Antonie Marie Cerisier

Histoire de la Guerre d'Amérique. Divisees par Années. Chacune terminée par une Table historique et chronologique des principaux Evénemens qui, pendant son cours, ont occupé la scêne du monde. *Londres.* 1783. 8vo, pp. xxxii, 151. J.C.B.

Histoire de la guerre, 1759. *See* [Poullin de Lumina].

Histoire de l'ile de Saint-Domingue. *See* [Malo (C.)], *and* Saint Domingo.

Histoire de la Jamaïque. *See* Jamaica, *and* [Raulin].

Histoire de la Navigation. *See* Churchill (J.), Vol. IV.

Histoire de la negociation de la France et de l'Angleterre depuis le 26 Mars ou 20 Septembre 1761. *Paris.* 1761. 32014

Title from Muller's Catalogue, No. 245. Relates to the disputes concerning American territory.

Histoire de la Paix entre les Roys de France et d'Espagne, avec le succez de plusieurs Navigations faictes aux Indes Orientales, Occidentales et Septentrionales. *Paris.* 1609. 8vo. 32015

Contains the voyage of M. Du Pont to Canada in 1604. It is not noticed by Faribault, Ternaux or Rich.

Histoire de la Persécution. *See* Cardenas, Vol. III., No. 10804.

Histoire | de la premiere | Descovverte et | Conqveste des Canaries. | Faite dés l'an 1402. par Messire Iean de | Bethencovrt, Chambellan | du Roy Charles VI. | Escrite du temps mesme par F. Pierre Boutier Religieux | de S. François, & Iean le Verrier Prestre, | domestiques dudit sieur de Bethencourt. | Et | Mise en lumiere par M. Galien de Bethencourt, Con- | seiller du Roy en sa Cour de Parlement de Rouën. | Plvs | vn Traicté de la Navi- | gation et des Voyages de | Descouuerte & Conqueste modernes, & principalement des François. | *A. Paris,* | *Chez Iean de Hevqveville, rüe sainct* | *Iacques, à la Paix.* | M. DC. XXX. | *Avec Privilege dv Roy.* | 8vo, pp. (20), 208, Table, 6 l., followed by Traicté, 6 l., 303. C. 32016

Stevens characterizes this as a curious and rare work, written with great fidelity. Priced, Tross, No. 2859, 1866, 200 francs. Introduced here because it was accidentally omitted under Boutier, after having been referred to him under Bethencourt.

Histoire de la Presse. *See* [Cucheval-Clarigny.]

Histoire de la Princesse Jaiven reine du Mexique. Traduite de l'Espagnol. Composé en françois par l'Abbé Cl.-Fr. Lambert. *A La Haye: Aux depens de la Société.* MDCCLI. 18mo, pp. 104, 104.

L'Histoire de la Terre Neue du Pérou, en l'Inde Occidentale, qui est la principale mine d'Or du Monde, naguères descouverte, et conquise et nommeè la Nouvelle Castille, traduite de l'italien

en Francois [par Jacq. Gohorry]. *On les vend à Paris au Palais, en la boutique de Vincent Sertenas.* 1545. 8vo. J.C.B. 32018

"Traduction de la troisième partie du No. 43 (Anghiera). Le traducteur français nous annonce, dans une note, page 3, que cette relation est un extrait d'Oviedo. Le traducteur italien, tout au contraire, la donne comme une relation particulière, ce qui est plus vraisemblable, puisque l'auteur parle comme témoin oculaire. Cette relation qui finit à la mort d'Atabaliba, est écrite d'un style naif et ne manque pas d'intérêt. Il doit y avoir à la fin une carte qui manque dans presque tous les exemplaires."—TERNAUX, No. 52. This should have followed *our* No. 1554.

Histoire de Moncade, dont les principales Aventures se sont passées au Méxique. Avec le Marquis de Leyva, Nouvelle Espagnole. *Paris.* 1736. 2 vols., 12mo. + *Amsterdam.* 1737.

Histoire de Nicolas I. Roy du Paraguai, et Empereur de Mamelus. *A Saint Paul.* 1756. 12mo, pp. 88. C. 32020

"The fabrication of some needy and ignorant impostor, who wrote, not for the purpose of injuring the Jesuits, but in the hope of making money by duping the curiosity of the public. He makes Roubioni a Spaniard by birth, a rogue by breeding, and a Jesuit by profession, who raises a rebellion among the Indians at Nova Colonia; proclaims himself King of Paraguay, deposes and murders the missionaries and takes the title of Emperor. This is set forth as true history."—SOUTHEY'S *History of Brazil,* Vol. III. 74.

Histoire der Boecaniers. *See* [Exquemelin], Vol. VI.

Histoire des Découvertes. *See* [Pallas (P.-S.)]

Histoire des Drogves. *See* Orto (Garcia).

Histoire des Isles Sandwich et de la Mission Américaine, depuis 1820. Traduit de l'Anglois. *Paris.* 1836. 18mo, pp. 288.

Histoire | des ioyavx, | et des principales | Richesses de l'Orient & | de l'Occident. | Tirée des diuerses Relations des plus | fameux Voyageurs de nôtre siecle. | Piece curieuse, | Et accompagnée de belles recherches pour | la connoissance de l'Uniuers, & | pour le Commerce. | Suiuie d'vne description exacte des | Regions & des lieux, dont il est | parlé dans cette Histoire. | *A Paris, Chez Guillaume de Luynes Marchand* | *Libraire au Palais, en la Gallerie des* | *Merciers, à la Iustice.* | M.DC.LXV. | 12mo, pp. (10), 182. 32022

"Petit opuscule rare, resté à ce qu'il parait inconnu aux bibliographes qui ont traité de l'Amérique."—TRÖMEL.

Histoire des navigations. *See* [Brosses (C. de)], Vol. II.

Histoire des Naufrages. *See* [Deperthes (M.)], Vol. V.

In addition to the imprints there enumerated, add *Paris: Cochet.* M DCC LXXXIX. 3 vols. 8vo.

Histoire des Ordres Monastiques. *See* [Helyot (*le Père*)].

Histoire des Osages. *See* [Vissier (Paul)].

Histoire des Plantes de l'Europe, et des plus usitées qui viennent d'Asie, d'Afrique, et d'Amerique. *Lyon.* 1653. 12mo. + *Lyon.* 1680. 32023

Title from a bookseller's catalogue.

Histoire des Plantes nouvellement trouvées en l'Isles Virgine et autres lieux, &c. Non encore veuës n'y imprimées par cy deuant. *Paris: Maceau.* 1620. 16mo. J.C.B. 32024

Of extreme rarity. Not mentioned by Rich or Ternaux.

Histoire des Pyramides. *See* [La Condamine (C. M.)]

Histoire des Sevarambes. *See* [Vairasse (*d'Alais* D.)]

Histoire des Tremblemens. *See* Individual, &c.

Histoire des Trembleurs. [*Paris.*] MDCCXXXIII. 12mo, pp. (2), 286, (16). 32025

A history of the Quakers, which, the anonymous author says, he gathered from the writings of George Fox, William Penn, and George Keith. Brunet says "this work is by P. Catrou, a Jesuit," and adds "les feuilles portent la signature: t. III. Cet ouvrage fait partie de l' 'Histoire du fanatisme dans la religion protestante,' publiée par le même auteur en 1707, 4to, et reimprimée en 1733, 3 vols., 12mo."

Histoire du commerce et de la navigation des peuples anciens et modernes. *Amsterdam.* 1758. 2 vols., 12mo. 32026

Histoire du grand royaume de la Chine. *See* [Mendoça (J. G.)]

Histoire | dv massacre | de plvsievrs religievx, | de S. Dominiqve, | de S. Francois, | et de la Compagnie de Iesvs, | et d'autres Chrestiens, aduenu en la rebellion de quel | ques Indois de l'Occident contre les Espagnols. | Item | diuerses Lettres escrites par aucuns de ladite | Compagnie, qui du Païs-bas ont esté enuoyez | aux Indes Occidentales en l'an 1615. | Et | Vne du P. Nicolas Trigavlt, enuoyée | depuis son retour aux Indes Orientales. | *A. Valencienne,* | *De l'Imprimerie de Iean Vervliet,* | *à la Bible d'or, l'an* M.DC.XX. 12mo. C. 32027

Collation: Title (2), Dedication (4); 2d Title, differing from the above, pp. 31, 80, 59, (2), 44. A volume of much rarity.

Histoire du Paraguay. *See* Paraguay.

Histoire | Du Pays nomme | Spitsberghe. | Monstrant comment qu'il est | trouvée, son naturel & ses animauls, | avecques | La triste racompte des maux, que noz Pecheurs, | tant Basques que Flamens, ont eu a souffrir des Angiois, | en l'esté passée l'An de grace,

1613. | Escrit par H[essel] G[erritz] A[ssum]. | Et en apres une Protestation contre les Angloys, | & annullation de touts leurs frivoles argumens, parquoy | ils pensent avoir droict, pour se faire Mai- | stre tout seul, dudict Pays. | *En Amsterdam, a l'ensiegne de la Carte nautiq.* | M. DC. XIII. | 4to, pp. 32. Maps and 2 Plates.

Fifty copies of this very rare pamphlet were reprinted in facsimile by Messrs. J. Enschedé and Sons at Haarlem, from the only known copy of the original in the Royal Library at the Hague. On the exceeding importance of this little book—which partly relates to Greenland—in a geographic and nautical point of view, *see* Tiele, Mémoire, pp. 197–198. It was reprinted with a different title: *A Amsterdam, chez Hessel Gerard A. a l'enseigne de la Carte Nautiq.* MD. C. XIII. An abridgment is included in Veer's Voyage to the North.

Histoire d'un pou françois ou l'Espion d'une nouvelle espece, tant en France et l'Angleterre. [Par Delauney.] *Paris.* 1779. 8vo. + [*Ibid.*] 1781. 32029

"A satire on the political affairs of the time; especially Franklin's Mission to France."

Histoire et Commerce. *See* [Butel-Dumont (G. M.)]

Histoire générale. *See* [Bois-Meslé (J.-B. T.)], Vol. II., No. 6158, [Gomara (F. L. de)], Vol. VII., *and* Prevôt d'Exiles.

Histoire Générale des divers États d'Europe et de l'Amérique, depuis 1848. *Bruxelles.* 1853. 8vo. 32030

Histoire ... de la Nouvelle Ecosse. *See* Nova Scotia.

Histoire Naturelle. *See* Pennsylvania, [Quélus (D.)], [Rochefort (C.)], *and* [Venegas (M.)]

Histoire Philosophique. *See* [Raynal (G. F.)]

Histoire ... Nova Francia, 1613. *See* [Lescarbot].

Histoire véritable. *See* [Boucher (P.)], Vol. II., No. 6843.

Historia de America. Noticia de un manuscrito muy interesante. [*Habona.* 1820?] 8vo, pp. 9. 32031

Historia Cristiana de la California. Obra traducida al español por G. Madrid y Ormaechea. *Mexico.* 1864. 8vo. 32032

Historia de conquista del Nuevo-Mundo. *Madrid.* 1829–33. 9 vols. 8vo. 32033

A general title to a series of reprints of Solis, Garcillaso de la Vega, etc.

Historia de la Revolucion de 1854. Por Aly Bey. *Lima.* 1861. 12mo. 32034

Historia de la Revolucion. *See* Mexico.

Historia de Portugal. Composta em Inglez por uma Sociedade de Literatos, transladada em Vulgar com as Notas da Edição Franceza, e do Traductor Portuguez, A. de Moraes da Silva; e continuada até os nossos Tempos: em nova Ediçaõ: por H. José da Costa. *Londres.* 1809. 3 vols., 12mo. 32035

Includes copious details of Brazilian History.

Historia de los tres niños de Flaxcaltecos, Christovalito, Antoñito y Juanito que murieron por la confesion de la fe catholica. *En el imperial collegio de Flatilulco.* 1601. 32036

"Je ne connais pas d'autre ouvrage sorti des presses du collège de Flatilulco, qui n'est pas, comme on pourrait le croire, une ville du Mexique, mais un couvent situé dans un des faubourgs de Mexico."—TERNAUX, No. 252.

Historia de un sumario. *Bogotá.* 8vo, pp. 28. 32037

Historia del establecimiento. *See* [Butel-Dumont], Vol. III.

Historia do Brazil desde seu descobrimento em 1500 ate' 1810, Vertida de Francz, e accrescentada de mutas notas do Traductor ... *Lisboa: Na Officina de J. F. M. de Campos.* 1817. 2 vols., 18mo, pp. xxiv, 316; 332, (1). 2 Plates. 32038

Historia Universal desde o tempos mais remotos até os nossos dias: relatando os acontecimentos mais notaveis em todas as épocas, e os feitos dos homens mais celebres de todas os povos. Composta sobre o plano de Gabriel Gottofredo Bredow, por um brasileiro. *Rio de Janeiro: Na Typ. Univ. de Laemmert.* 1846–1847. 5 vols., 8vo. 24 Plates. 32039

Historia dos descobrimentos, e conquistas dos Portugueses, no novo mundo. *Lisboa: na officina de Antonio Gomez.* MDCCLXXXVI. 4 vols., 16mo, pp. (2), xxxiv; 374; (2), 446; (2), 467; 487.

Historia general de las Indias. *See* [Gomara (F. L. de)].

Historia naturalis Brasilæ. *See* [Pison (G.)]

Historia navigationis in Brasiliam quæ et America dicitur. Qua describitur authoris navigatio quæque in mare vidit memoriæ prodenda: Villagagnonis in America gesta, Brasiliensium victus et mores a nostris admodum alieni cum eorum linguæ dialogo: Animalia etiam, arbores, atque herbæ, reliquaque singularia et nobis penitus incognita. *Genevæ.* 1594. 8vo. 32041

Title from one of Tross' catalogues, No. 489.

Historia Secreta. *Habana, imprenta del Aviso.* 1809. 8vo.

Historiadores primitivas de Indias. Coleccion dirigida é ilustrada por Don Enrique de Vedia. ... *Madrid: M. Rivadeneyra* 1858. 2 vols., 4to, pp. xxi, 599, (1); xxii, 574, (1). BA. 32043

Forms Vols. XXII. and XXVI. of the "Biblioteca de autores españoles," begun by Aribau; and is a reproduction of Barcia. *See* Vol. I., No. 3350.

The Historian's Guide, or England's Remembrancer; being a Summary Account of all the Actions, Exploits, Sieges, &c., and other Remarkable Passages, that hath happened in His Majesty's Dominions from 1600 until 1679. *London.* 1679. 12mo.

Reproduced as: The Historian's Guide, or Britain's Remembrancer. ... from 1600 to 1688. ... *London.* 1688. 12mo. C.

Las Historias del Origen de los Indios de esta Provincia de Guatemala. Traducidas de la Lengua Quiché al Castellaña para mas comodidad de los Ministros del S. Evangelio, por el R. P. F. Francisco Ximenez; publicado por la primera vez, por el Dr. C. Scherzer. *Vienna.* 1857. 8vo, pp. xvi, 216. 32045

Historic Certainties respecting the Early History of America, developed in a Critical Examination of the Book of the Chronicles of the Land of Ecnarf. *London.* 1851. 8vo. 32046

For Ecnarf read France.

Historical Details, having relation to the Campaign of the North-Western Army under General Harrison and Winchester, during the Winter of 1812–13; together with some Particulars relating to the Surrender of Fort Bower. Edited by Thomas Eastland. *Lexington, Ky.* 1818. 8vo. 32047

Historic Doubts relative to Napoleon Buonaparte [by R. Whately], and Historic Certainties respecting the Early History of America. *New-York: Robert Carter & Brother.* M. DCCC. LIII. 18mo, pp. 184. 32048

Historic Progress. *See* [Whipple (Oliver)].

Historical Account. *See* [Eaton (Asa)], [Henry (David)], [Hewatt (A.)], Jamaica, *and* [Smith (W.)]

Historical Account of Sturbridge and Bury Fairs, and of the most famous Fairs in Europe and America. *Cambridge.* [n. d.] 8vo. 32049

An Historical Account of the Circumnavigation of the Globe, and of the Progress of Discovery in the Pacific Ocean, from the Voyage of Magellan to the Death of Cook. ... *Edinburgh: Oliver and Boyd.* 1836. 12mo. + [*Ibid.*] 1840. + *London: T. Nelson & Son.* 1852. 12mo. + [*Ibid.*] 1854. + *New-York: Harper & Brothers.* 1837. + [*Ibid.*] 1839, 1840, and 1842. 16mo, pp. 366. 32050

The Edinburgh edition forms part of the Edinburgh Cabinet Edition; the New York edition is part of Harper's Family Library.

An Historical Account of the Discovery of the Island of Madeira, Abridged from the Portugueze Original. *London.* 1675. + To which is added An Account of the present State of the Island in a Letter to a Friend. *London: J. Payne, and J. Boquet,* M,DCC,L. 8vo, pp. (2), x, 88. J.C.B. 32051

Included in J. R. Bartlett's Catalogue of J. C. Brown's Library.

An Historical Account of the Interment of the Remains of the American Martyrs at the Wallabout, who perished on board the Jersey Prison Ship during the Revolutionary War; with the Oration of Benjamin De Witt on the Occasion. *New-York.* 1808. 12mo, pp. 96. C. 32052

Published by the Tammany Society; for another edition *see* Stiles (H. R.)

An Historical Account of the late Disturbance between the Inhabitants of the Back Settlements of the Province of Pennsylvania, and the Philadelphians, Impartially related. *Philadelphia.* [1764.] 8vo, pp. 8. N., P. 32053

A very rare pamphlet relative to the Paxton Boys.

An Historical Account of the many Signal Naval Achievements obtained by the English over the Spaniards from the year 1350 to the Present Time. Containing all the Voyages and Adventures of the following Admirals, Captains, and Commanders of the English Nation. Viz. Capt. Hawkins, Sir Francis Drake, Sir Walter Raleigh, Sir R. Grenville, Earl of Cumberland, Admiral Cavendish, Admiral Howard, Sir John Norris, Earl of Essex, Sir R. Levison, Sir William Monson, Admiral Blake, Admiral Benbow, Sir George Rooke, Sir John Leake, Sir Charles Wager, Admiral Byng, Lord Cobham, Sir John Jennings, Admiral Holmes, &c. To which is added some remarkable Speeches in Parliament on the Spanish Depredations. *London: J. Torbuck.* 1739. 8vo, pp. (8), 112, (2). J.C.B. 32054

An Historical Account of the Rise and Establishment of the People call'd Quakers, with a brief view of their religious Principles, and of their Tenets respecting civil Society. ... Extracted from Writers of the best Authority. By a Friend. *London: J. Newbery.* 1756. 8vo. 32055

An | Historical Account | of the | Rise and Growth of the | West-India | Collonies, | And of the great Advantages they | are to England, in respect | to Trade. | ... *London: Printed for Jo. Hindmarsh* ... 1690. 4to, pp. (6), 53. 32056

Reprinted in the "Harleian Tracts," Vol. IX.

Historical Account of the Washington Monument [at Richmond], with Biographical Sketches. *Richmond.* 1869. 16mo.

An Historical and Descriptive Account of Iceland, Greenland, and the Faroe Islands; with Illustrations of their Natural History. *Edinburgh: Oliver and Boyd.* 1840. 12mo. + *New-York: Harper & Brothers.* 1841. 18mo. + [*Ibid.*] 1842. 32058

Historical and Descriptive Lessons, embracing Sketches of the History, Character, and Customs of all Nations, ... *Brattleboro' [Vt.]: Holbrook & Fessenden.* 1828. 18mo, pp. 336. C. 32059

Historical and Genealogical Researches and Recorder of Passing Events of Merrimack Valley. Illustrated with Numerous Engravings. *Haverhill: Alfred Poor.* [n. d.] Small 4to. M.

Vol. I., Nos. I. and II., April, 1857, January, 1858. All published.

Historical ... Society. *See* Ohio, Pennsylvania, &c.

Historical and Physical Sketch of a Malignant Epidemic prevalent in Maryland and Neighboring States. *Baltimore.* 1815. 8vo. 32061

Historical and Political Reflections. *See* [Galloway (J.)]

Historical and Scientific Sketches of Michigan, comprising a Series of Discourses Delivered before the Historical Society of Michigan, and other Interesting Papers relative to the Territory. *Detroit: Stephen Wells and George L. Whitney.* 1834. 12mo, pp. 215. 32062

By Lewis Cass, Henry Whiting, John Biddle, and Henry R. Schoolcraft. Now very scarce. *See* "N. A. Rev.," XLIV. 60.

Historical and Statistical Sketches of Buffalo; with a Map of the Village and a View of the Harbor. *Buffalo.* 1825. 8vo.

Historical Anecdotes, Civil and Military: in a Series of Letters, written From America, in the years 1777 and 1778, to different Persons in England; containing Observations on the General Management of the War, and on the Conduct of our Principal Commanders, in the Revolted Colonies, During that Period. *London: J. Bew.* M.DCC.LXXIX. 8vo, pp. (6), 85.

Very scarce. Rice's copy sold for $14.00. *See* Rich, I. 274. "These letters seem to have been written by a zealous North British Loyalist; who chooses to demonstrate his aversion to the rebels and their cause, by bestowing, most liberally on both, the choicest flowers of scurrility."—*Monthly Review*, LX. 474.

Historical Collections. *See* under the names of the respective Societies, Towns, Cities or States.

Historical Description. *See* [Johnson (Robert)].

Historical Documents. *See* Lewis (A.)

Historical Essay. *See* [Ramsay (Allan)].

An Historical, Geographical, Political, and Natural History of North America, and of the British and other European Settlements. *London.* 1805. 2 vols., 12mo. 32065

Historical Journal. *See* Vol. V., No. 17020.

The Historical Magazine, and Notes and Queries concerning the Antiquities, History, and Biography of America. Vol. I. *Boston: C. Benjamin Richardson.* 1857. 4to, pp. iv, 380, xvi.

Vols. II., *et seq.*, were published at New York. It was edited by various hands, including J. Ward Dean, J. Gilmary Shea, and H. R. Stiles. Vol. X. concludes the first series. The New Series, edited by H. B. Dawson, bears the imprint *Morrisania, N. Y.*, and was commenced in 1867; it has appeared somewhat irregularly. Complete sets are scarce.

Historical Memorial, 1761. *See* Mémorial historique.

Historical Narrative, Explanation, and Vindication of the Course pursued by the Grand Lodge of the State of New-York, in relation to the Unmasonic and Unconstitutional Attempt of a portion of their body to revolutionize the organization thereof:— ... *New-York: Br. J. M. Marsh, Printer.* 1850. 8vo. 32067

Historical Miscellany of the Curiosities and Rarities in Nature and Art; in every part of the Habitable World. *London.* [n. d.] 3 vols., 8vo. Plates. 32068

Several pieces relate to America.

An Historical Miscellany. *London.* 1772. 12mo. + Second Edition. [*Ibid.*] 1772. 12mo. 32069

Notices Columbus; the Government, Civil Policy, Manners of the Americans, etc.

Historical Notes. [1825.] *See* [Griffith (William)], Vol. VII.

Historical Notes on Slavery and Colonization: with particular reference to the efforts which have been made in favor of African Colonization in New-Jersey. *Elizabeth-Town: Printed by E. Sanderson.* 1842. 8vo, pp. 53. 2 Plates. S. 32070

Historical Notes on the Canadian Colony of Detroit. *Montreal.* 1861. 12mo. S. 32071

Historical Notices of the First Congregational Church at Canterbury, Connecticut. *Northampton, Mass.* 1853. 8vo. 32072

Historical Notices. *See* Boston, *also* [Eliot (Ephraim)].

The Historical Reader, designed for the use of Schools and Families, on a new Plan. *Concord, N. H.* 1827. 16mo.

Historical Record of the First, or King's Regiment of Dragoon Guards. *London.* 1837. 8vo. 32074

There are also records of various other regiments who served in the American Revolution.

The Historical Register; containing an Impartial Relation of all Transactions, both Civil and Military, Foreign and Domestic, from July, 1714, to Jan. 1716–17. *London.* 1724. 2 vols., 8vo. + The Historical Register; containing an Impartial Relation of all Transactions, Foreign and Domestic. *London.* 1716–38. 23 vols., 8vo. S. 32075

Published by the Sun office, to save the expense of newspapers to their subscribers. The first volume having taken up the historical affairs of the year 1717, the next two volumes, published in 1724, took up the previous affairs from 1714 up to that date. With these introductory volumes the "Historical Register" forms a Chronicle of the affairs of Great Britain and other countries, and includes many pieces relative to the American Colonies, the Dutch West India Company, etc.

The Historical Register of the United States, from the Declaration of War in 1812 to Jan., 1815. Edited by Thomas H. Palmer. *Philadelphia.* 1814–16. 4 vols., 8vo. 32076

Historical Relics of the White Mountains, and a Concise White Mountain Guide. ... *Boston: N. Noyes.* 1853. 16mo, pp. 100. 32077

Historical Remarks, 1788. *See* [Meredith (W.)]

Historical Reminiscences of the City of Albany. [n. p. n. d.] 8vo, pp. 18. 32078

An Historical Review and Directory of North America, containing a Geographical, Political and Natural History of the British and other European Settlements, the United and Apocryphal States, etc; and an Account of the Indian Nations. By a Gentleman immediately returned from a Tour of the Continent. *Cork: W. Matthews.* 1801. 2 vols., 16mo, pp. xxviii, 268; ix, 377. 32079

Historical Review. *See* [Franklin (B.)], Vol. VII.

Historical Sketch or Sketches of Boston, containing a brief Account of its Settlement, Rise and Progress. *Boston.* 1861. 12mo, pp. 96. 32080

Historical Sketch, 1864. *See* Florida, Vol. VI.

Historical Sketch of St. Anthony and Minneapolis. With Statistics of Business and Capital, from their first settlement to November, 1855. *St. Anthony.* 1855. 4to, pp. 24. 32081

Historical Sketch of the Church and Missions of the United Brethren, commonly called Moravians. *Bethlehem, Pa.* 1848. 12mo, pp. 93. 32082

Historical Sketch of the College of William and Mary, in Virginia. *Richmond: Gary & Clemmitt, Printers.* 1866. 8vo, pp. 24. 32083

An Historical Sketch of the Convention of the Congregational Ministers in Massachusetts; with an Account of its Funds; its Connection with the Massachusetts Congregational Society; and its Rules and Regulations. *Cambridge: Printed by Hilliard and Metcalf.* 1821. 8vo, pp. 32. BA. 32084

An Historical Sketch of the Paper Money issued by Pennsylvania; together with a complete List of all the Dates, Issues, Amounts, Denominations, and Signers By a Member of the Numismatic Society of Philadelphia. *Philadelphia: ... A. C. Kline.* 1862. 8vo, pp. 40. 32085

Historical Sketch of the Rebellion. *Published at the Office of the U. S. Coast Survey.* 1864. 8vo. S. 32086

Historical Sketches of Politics and Public Men, for the Years 1812 and 1813. *London.* 1813–14. 2 vols., 8vo. N., P. 32087

Some of the sketches relate to the War of 1812.

Historical Sketches of the Principles and Maxims of American Jurisprudence in contrast with the English Laws on the subject of Crimes and Punishments. *Steubenville, Ohio.* 1819. 8vo.

Historical Society. *See* under the name of the State, County or City.

Historical Summary, 1812. *See* [Mitchell (S. L.)]

An Historical View of the Public Celebrations of the Washington Society, and those of the Young Republicans, from 1805 to 1822. *Boston: True and Greene.* 1823. Sm. 12mo. Portrait.

Historico-Dramatico Ambrosial Eclogues. By Hengist Hobnail. *New York.* 1820. 24mo, pp. 16. 32090

A satire on Governor Clinton and his friends. A manuscript key to the personages is usually found with it.

HISTORICUS, *pseudon.* The Sham-Patriot Unmasked, or an Exposition of the Fatally Successful Arts of Demagogues to exalt themselves, by Flattering and Swindling the People. By Historicus. *Haverhill.* 1805. 8vo, pp. 47. 32091

HISTORICUS, *pseudon.* *See* [Harcourt (W. G. G. V.)]

Historie der beroerten van Engelandt aengaende veelderley seeten, die aldaer in Kerche Jesu Christo zijn ontstaen. *Dordrecht: H. van Esch.* 1647. 8vo. 32092

Contains an account of the Brownists who finally emigrated to America.

Historie | der | Inquisitie | tot | Goa. | En in andere Gewesten van | Indien | Vyt het Frans vertaalt | *t'Amsterdam.* | *bij Pieter Mortier.* | MDCXCVII. | 12mo, pp. (12), 282, (18). 32093

"Les p. 224 à 235 de cet ouvrage sur l'Inquisition, dont nous ignorons l'auteur, traitent du Brésil."—TRÖMEL.

Historie der Martelaren, die om het getuygenisse der evangelischer waerheyt haer bloet gestort hebben van de tijden Christi af tot den jare 1655 toe. Niet alleen in dese Nederlanden, maer ook in Vranckrijck, Engelandt, Amerika, etc. etc. *Amsterdam.* 1658. Folio. + [*Ibid.*] 1671. 32094

This history includes American martyrs, and contains 150 plates.

Historie dell' Indie. *See* [Gomara (F. L. de)], Vol. VII.

Historie der Reisen oder Sammlung von Reisebeschreibungen. *Leipzig.* 1755–59. 21 vols., 4to. 32095

A large portion of these voyages are in America.

Historie der Sevarimbes. *See* [Vairasse (D.)]

Hedendaagsche Historie, of Tegenwoordige staat van Amerika, behelzende de historie der ontdeckingen, beschrijving, natuurlijke historie, enz. *Amsterdam.* 1766. 3 vols., 8vo. Plate and Map. + [*Ibid.*] 1769. 32096

Forms part of a collection entitled: "Hedendaagsche historie, of Tegenwoordige staat van alle volkeren, par Sanson, etc."

Hedendaagsche Historie, ... behelzende de historie der deensche, fransche, oostendensche en zweedsche Oostindische maatschappijen, benevens die van het zuydelijk vaste land. *Amsterdam.* 1781. 4to. 32097

Chapter v. relates to the voyages of Schouten, Le Maire, and van Noort.

Historie van een reyse ghedaen inden Lande van Brasilien, andersins ghenoemt America. *Amsterdam: Corn. Claesz.* 1596. 4to. 32098

Title from an English auctioneer's catalogue.

Historien der Königreiche Hispañien, Portugal vnd Aphrica. Teutsch durch A. Fürst. *München.* 1589. Folio. 32099

Partly relative to their American possessions.

Historique des événements qui se sont passés à la Basse-Terre ... depuis la révolution. *Guadeloupe, imp. de V. Bénard.* 1791. 8vo. 32100

Historisch-Geographische Beschreibung der in diesem Krieg von den Engländern eroberten französichen Antillischen Inseln, besonders von Guadaloupe und Martinique &c. ... *Stutgart bey Johann Benedict Mezler*, 1762. 8vo, pp. (8), 264. A., B., C.

Historisch-Geographische Beschreibung von America für Jünglinge. *Nürnberg: Johann Eberhard Zeh.* 1784. 12mo, pp. (8), 336, Index. 32102

This historical account of America is intended for juvenile readers.

Historisch-Statistische Notiz der Grozbrittannischen Colonien in America, mit politischen Anmerkungen, die gegenwärtigen Americanischen Unruhen betreffend. *Frankfurt und Leipzig.* 1776. 12mo, pp. 96. 32103

"It was upon information such as is contained in this rare book, that the Princes were induced to sell their Hessians to serve under Burgoyne and others in America in 1777."—STEVENS.

Historische Beschryving. *See* [Prevôt (*Abbé*)].

Historische und Geographische Beschreibung des an dem grossen Flusse Mississippi in Nord America gelegenen herrlichen Landes Louisiana; in welches die neu-aufgerichtete Frantzösische grosse Indianische Compagnie Colonien zu schicken angefangen; worbey zugleich einige Reflexionen über die weit-hinaus sehende Desseins gedachter Compagnie und des darüber entstandenen Actien-Handels eröffnet; auch über dieses noch einige curiose Beylagen so zu der Historie dieser Angelegenheit gehören mitgetheilet werden. *Leipziger Neu-Jahrs Messe.* 1720. 8vo, pp. (6), 84. Map of Louisiana, Portrait of J. Law. J.C.B. + Zweite Auflage. *Leipzig.* 1720. 8vo, pp. 102. Map and Portrait.

An historical and geographical description of Louisiana, "on the great river Mississippi," to which the newly organized, powerful "French Indian Company" had begun to send colonies. Together with sundry reflections on the far-reaching designs of that company and the stock-jobbing incidents thereto. It closes with a French squib in verse. Some copies contain an appendix: "Remarques über den Mississippischen Actien-Handel." *Frankfurt.* 1720. pp. 11.

Historische und geographische. *See* Nova Scotia.

Historische Betrachtungen der Englischen Amerikanischen Colonien. *Bonn.* 1779. 8vo. 32105

Historischer Abrisz der in Nord Amerika vorgefallenen Staats Veränderung. Vom Anfange des Jahrs 1774, bis den ersten Jenner 1778. Von M***, einem Amerikaner. Aus dem Französischen. *Bern, in der Hallerschen Buchhandlung.* 1779. 12mo, pp. xii, 351. 32106

Historischer Bericht von den sämmtlichen durch Engländer geschehenen Reisen um die Welt, und den neuesten, dabey gemachten Entdeckungen, in einem getreuen Auszuge aus der Seefahrer Tagebüchern. Aus dem Englischen. *Leipzig bey Junius.* 1775–80. 6 vols., 8vo. 32107

History and Description of Canada. *See* Vol. III., No. 10463.

History and Horrors of the Helderberg War, by a Continentaler. *Albany.* 1840. 8vo. B. 32108

The History and Lives of the most notorious Pirates and their crews, from Capt. Avery who first settled at Madagascar to Capt. John Gow and James Williams, his Lieutenant, who were hanged at Execution Dock, June 11, 1725, for Piracy & Murther, ... And in this edition continued to the present year 1720. Giving a more full and true account than any yet published, of all their Murthers, Piracies, Maroonings, Places of Refuge and Ways of

Living. The Third Edition. ... *London: Edward Midwinter.* 1729. 12mo, pp. (8), 132. J.C.B. + *London.* 1765. 12mo. + *London.* [n. d.] 12mo. 32109

The accounts of the proceedings of the Pirates in Newfoundland, Barbadoes, Jamaica, Virginia, the Bermudas, Guiney, Boston, Charlestown, Carolina, Philadelphia, Antigua, Florida, Havanna, New England, Rhode Island, and other parts of America, are curious and amusing.

History and Organization of the Catholic Institute in Cincinnati, O.—Geschichte und Organisation des Katholischen Instituts in Cincinnati, O. *Cincinnati, O.* 1860. 8vo. 32110

The | History and Philosophy | of | Earthquakes, | from the | Remotest to the Present Times: | collected | from the best Writers on the Subject. | With a particular account of | the Phænomena of the great one of November | the 1st, 1755, in Various Parts of the Globe. | By a Member of the Royal-Academy of Berlin. | *London* | *printed for J. Nourse.* | 1757. 8vo, pp. (4), 351. C. 32111

The History, Debates, and Proceedings of both Houses of Parliament, 1743 to 1774. [Followed by] Parliamentary Register, or History of the Proceedings and Debates of the House of Commons, 1774 to 1780. Together, 24 vols., 8vo. 32112

Contains the debates during the early period of the American war.

The History and Progress of the four Indian Kings to the Kingdom of England, etc. *London: Printed by A. Hinde.* 1710. pp. 8. 32113

Perhaps the same as our No. 25283, Vol. VI.

History, Articles of Faith, etc., of the Hanover Church. *Boston.* 1826. 12mo, pp. 24. 32114

The History, Manners and Customs, of the North American Indians. *Philadelphia: American Sunday School Union.* [n. d.] 24mo, pp. 245. 32115

The History of a Case of Discipline in the South Congregational Church, Brooklyn, L. I., with Result of Council. *New York.* 1854. 8vo. 32116

History of a Corporation of Servants, Discovered a few Years ago in the Interior Parts of South America, containing some very Surprising Events and Extraordinary Characters. *London: E. & C. Dilly.* MDCCLXV. 8vo, pp. 76. B. + *Glasgow.* 1765. 8vo. C.

The History of a Cotton Bale. *London: Griffith & Farran.* 186–. Square 16mo. 32118

History of a French Louse; or the Spy of a New Species, in France and England; Containing a Description of the most remarkable Personages in those Kingdoms, giving a Key to the chief Events of the Year 1779, and those which are to happen in 1780. Translated from the Fourth Edition of the Revised and Corrected Paris Copy. *London: T. Beckett.* MDCCLXXIX. 8vo, pp. iv, 123. J.C.B. 32119

See "M. Rev.," LXII. 81. See also chapter XIV. for a curious dialogue between Monsieur Benjamin le Frank and his neighbor concerning Doctor Franklin. This is a version of "Histoire d'un pou françois," our No. 32029.

History of a Long War. *See* [Mather (Cotton)].

History of Agricultural Societies on the Modern Berkshire System, from 1807 to 1820. *Albany.* 1820. 8vo. 32120

A History of all the Engagements by Sea and Land, that Happened in America and Europe, and the East and West Indies, during the American Revolution, betwixt the English Alone, against the American and French, and the Spanish and Dutch Nations from the Battle of Lexington, April 19, 1775, to the Treaty of Peace in 1783. *Manchester: T. Harper.* 1787. 8vo, pp. (4), 436. 32121

"The authenticity and importance of this publication cannot be disputed, as the Actions are copied from the accounts given by the Secretaries of State and the Admiralty Board."—*Preface.*

The History and Description of America in the Turkish Language. *Printed at Constantinople by Ibraham Effendi in the year of the Hegira* 1142 [about 1729]. 4to. 4 Maps, 13 Plates.

This is believed to be the earliest book printed in Turkey with wood-engravings. Ibraham Effendi was the reviver of printing in Turkey, and this appears to be the first book of a popular nature that was printed. The engravings are curious, and quite distinct from anything produced in Western Europe. A copy is in the British Museum.

History of America. *See* Everett (E.), [Morse (J.)]

The History of America. In Two Books. *Philadelphia.* 1795. 16mo. Maps. 32123

History of American Missions to the Heathen, from their Commencement to the Present Time. *Worcester.* 1840. 8vo, pp. 726. A., P., S. 32124

The History of American Taxation, from the Year 1763, to the end of the last Session. In which is introduced an account of the Official Abilities of the following Ministers, and how far they have been concerned either in pursuing or receding from the

present scheme of Governing America. The Rt. Hon. Charles Townshend; the Hon. Mr. Grenville; Lord Rockingham; and Lord Chatham. With an account of the Act asserting the entireness of British Legislative Authority, By Edmund Burke, Esq., ... and delivered by him in a Speech in the House of Commons. Third Edition. *Dublin: John Exshaw.* MDCCLXXV. 8vo, pp. 98. 32125

The History of an Expedition. *See* Vol. II., No. 7211.

The History of an old fringed Petticoat; a Fragment: translated from the original MS. Greek of Democritus. With an Epistle and Dedication to Lord N——. *London: Blythe, &c.* 12mo. 32126

Tells against the Americans. See "M. Rev.," LIV. 156.

History of Andover. From its First Settlement. *Andover: Flagg & Gould.* 1829. 12mo, pp. 204. 32127

History of Antietam National Cemetery, Including a Descriptive List of all the Loyal Soldiers Buried Therein; together with the Ceremonies and Address on the Occasion of the Dedication of the Grounds, Sept. 17, 1867. *Baltimore: John W. Woods, Printer.* 1869. 8vo, pp. 202. Plates. 32128

The History of Banks: to which is added, a Demonstration on the Advantages and Necessity of Free Competition in the Business of Banking. *Boston.* 1837. 12mo, pp. 142. 32129

Includes an account of John Law's scheme, the United States banks, etc.

The History of Boston from 1630 to 1857. *Boston: F. C. Moore & Co.* 1857. 18mo, pp. 246. 32130

See also Vol. II., No. 6522.

History of Broome County, N. Y., from 1806 to 1867. *Syracuse.* 1867. 8vo. 32131

History of Caledonia. *See* Darien, Vol. V., No. 18506.

The History of Commodore Anson's Voyage round the World, at the Commencement of the late Spanish War. Performed in three Years and nine Months, viz., from September 1740 to June 1744. By a Midshipman on board the Centurion. *London: M. Cooper.* MDCCLXVII. 8vo, pp. 192. Portrait. + *London: A. Manson.* [n. d.] 32132

History of Congress. *See* Vol. IV., No. 15532.

The History of Defection in New-England ... . To which is now added An Address to the People of New-England. [*New York.* 1832.] pp. 92, 85. 32133

A Methodist piece. The address was first printed in 1817.

History of De Kalb County, Ill. *Chicago.* 1868. 8vo. Portrait. 32134

History of Democracy in the United States. By the Author of the Republic of the United States of America. Nos. I.–IV. *Boston.* [1852.] 8vo. 32135

History of Earthquakes, including those of Lima and Callao, in Peru. *London.* 1748. 8vo. 32136

A History of every Attempt at Resistance to the Federal Government. *New York: William E. Chapin.* 1861. 8vo, pp. 32.

A History of French Influence in the United States; to which is added an Exposition of a Congressional Caucus. *London.* 1812. + *Philadelphia.* 1812. 8vo, pp. 69. B., N., S. 32138

History of Jamaica, 1774. *See* [Long (Edward)].

An History of Jamaica & Barbadoes, with an Authentic Account of the Lives Lost, and the Damage Sustained in each Island, by the late Hurricanes. To which is prefixed, a Sermon, preached on the Melancholy Occasion, at St. Clements, Lombard Street. *London: Frys, Couchman & Collier.* 1781. 4to, pp. 49.

The History of Jewels, and of the Principal Riches of the East and West. Taken from the Relations of divers of the most famous Travellers of our Age. ... *London: H. Kemp.* 1671. 24mo, pp. (16), 128. C., P. 32140

Contains numerous particulars of the American mines and pearl fisheries.

The History of John Smith's Picture. *Cambridge.* 1858. pp. 15. 32141

Six copies only printed.

The History of Kamschatka. *See* Kracheninnikof (Stephan).

History of Maritime Discovery. *See* [Cooley (W. D.)]

The History of Maryland, to which are added brief Biographies of distinguished Statesmen, Philanthropists, Theologians, etc. Prepared for the Schools of Maryland. *Philadelphia: E. H. Butler & Co.* 1866. 16mo, pp. 164. C. 32142

History of my Friend. Shewing how he was Deprived of his Military Commission, etc. merely because a Great Man thought my Friend called him a Nincompoop!! *New York.* 1816. 8vo.

History of New England, 1654. *See* [Johnson (E.)]

History of North America, from the Discovery thereof: by Silvanus Americanus: *New Jersey, anno* 1761. 32144

Title from Faribault, No. 859.

The History of North America. Containing An Exact Account of their first Settlements; Their Situation, Climate, Soil, Produce, Beasts, Birds, Fishes, Commodities, Manufactures, Commerce, Religion, Charters, Laws, Governments, Cities, Towns, Ports, Rivers, Lakes, Mountains, and Fortifications. With The present State of the different Colonies; and A large Introduction. ... *London: Sold by Millar, Thomson, Jones, Davidson, Wilson, and Gardiner.* MDCCLXXVI. 12mo, pp. (4), 284. Map.

A capital book. The singular speech on page 82 was composed by Dr. Franklin.

History of North America; comprising, A Geographical and Statistical View of the United States, and of the British Canadian Possessions; including a great variety of Important Information on the Subject of Emigrating to that Country. ... *Leeds: Printed by Davies and Co.* 1820. 2 vols., 8vo, pp. iv, 498; (2), 458. 3 Plates, Maps. 32146

The History of North and South America, containing, An Account of the first Discoveries of the New World, the Customs, Genius, and Persons of the original Inhabitants, and a particular Description of the Air, Soil, natural Productions, Manufactures and Commerce of each Settlement. Including a Geographical, Commercial, and Historical Survey of the British Settlements, From the earliest Times to the present Period. With an Account of the West Indies and the American Islands. To which is added, An impartial Enquiry into the present American Disputes. *London: J. Whitaker.* 1776. 2 vols., 12mo, pp. (18), including Frontispiece, 7–276; (14), including Frontispiece, 5–280. C. 32147

First published in 16 parts

History of Our Own Times. *See* [Campbell (T.)], Vol. III.

History of Pennsylvania Hall. *See* [Webb (S.)]

History of Pirates. *New York: Printed by W. Bradford.* 1724.

Title from Watson's Annals, p. 20.

The History of Pompey the Little, or, the Life and Adventures of a Lap-dog. *London: M. Cooper.* MDCCLI. 12mo, pp. viii, 272. Plate. + The Second Edition. [*Ibid.*] 32149

Relates to American topics.

The History of Prime Ministers and Favourites in England, from the Conquest down to the Present Time, with reflections on the fatal Consequences of their Misconduct, &c. *London: J. Kearsley.* 1763. 8vo, pp. (2), 163. 32150

The History of Prince Lee Boo. To which is added the Life of Paul Cuffee, a Man of Colour. *Dublin: Printed by M. Goodwin.* 1818. 18mo, pp. 180. + *London: Printed by Dean & Munday.* [n. d.] 16mo. + Also some account of John Sackhouse, the Esquimaux. *Dublin.* 1822. 24mo, pp. 180. S. 32151

A History of Shipwrecks and Disasters at Sea, from the most Authentic Sources. *London: Whitaker, Treacher & Co.* MDCCCXXXIII. 2 vols., 18mo, pp. viii, 343; iv, 316. Plates. 32152

This is a translation, without acknowledgment, of Deperthes. See our Nos. 19620, 19621. It was afterwards reissued in 4 vols. with some additions.

History of Silk, Cotton, Linen, and other Fibrous Substances; including Observations on Spinning, Dyeing, and Weaving. *New-York: Harper & Brothers.* 1845. 8vo, pp. xxxi, (1), 464.

History of Spain and Portugal. *See* [Busk (M. M.)]

History of Temperance in Saratoga County, New-York. *Saratoga Springs.* 1855. 8vo. C. 32154

History, Proceedings, and Debates of the Fifth Session of the House of Commons, Fourteenth Parliament, 1779. [*London.*] 1779. 8vo. M. 32155

Important for the debates on American topics.

The History of the American Revolution, including an Impartial Examination of the Causes which produced that Important Event; and Monthly Register of the United States, from the Date of their Independence to the Present Time. Vol. the First. *Charleston, S. C.: Printed ... by Gabriel Manigault Bountetheau,* ... 1806. 8vo, pp. (10), 384, Contents, vii; Vol. II., No. 1. pp. 24. C., S. 32156

No more published.

History of the American Revolution. *See* [Shepherd (T.)], [Snowden (R.)], [Wilson (S. T.)]

History of the American Troops during the Late War under Cols. Fenton and Campbell. 1829. 12mo. 32157

History of the American War of 1812, from the Commencement, until the Final Termination Thereof, on the Memorable Eighth of January, 1815, at New Orleans. ... Second Edition. *Philadelphia: Wm. McCarty.* 1816. 12mo, pp. 252. + [*Ibid.*] 1817. + Third Edition. [*Ibid.*] 12mo. 32158

History of the Old Second Division of the Army of the Cumberland. Commanders McCook, Till and Johnson. *Chicago: Church & Goodman.* 1864. 8vo. 32159

History of the Baptist Churches, composing the Sturbridge Association, from their Origin to 1843. *New York.* 1844. 24mo, pp. 54. 32160

History of the British Dominions in North America; from the First Discovery of that Vast Continent by Sebastian Cabot in 1497, to its present Glorious Establishment, as Confirmed by the Late Treaty of Peace in 1763. In Fourteen Books. *London: W. Strahan.* MDCCLXXIII. 4to, pp. (x), 297, 275. Map.

See "M. Rev.," XLVIII. 18. See also "Historical Magazine," I. 189, concerning the supposed authorship, where it is commended, but Mr. Rich calls it "a work of no great authority; probably a bookseller's speculation, in consequence of the interest which the affairs of America excited about this time." It was translated into German as:

Geschichte der Englischen Colonien in Nordamerika, von der ersten Entdeckung dieser Länder durch Sebastian Cabot, bis auf den Frieden 1763. Aus dem Englischen [von Anton Ernst Klausing]. *Leipzig: C. Fritsch.* 1775–76. 2 vols., 16mo, pp. (16), 452; (8), 424, (8). Map. B., C. 32162

History of the British Empire, from the Year 1765, to the end of 1783. Containing An Impartial History of the Origin, Progress, and Termination of the American Revolution. By a Society of Gentlemen. *Philadelphia: R. Campbell & Co.* M.DCC.-XCVIII. 2 vols., 8vo, pp. 475; 452, 59. Portraits of Washington and Franklin. C. + Second Edition. [*Ibid.*] 1803. 32163

These volumes contain a comprehensive history of the American Revolution. It was also issued as a "History of England, from the Revolution to the End of the American War and Peace of Versailles in 1783."

History of the Buccaneers. *See* [Exquemelin (J.)], Vol. VI.

The History of the Church of Malabar. With some Remarks upon ... the Christians of St. Thomas in the Indies ... Done out

of Portuguese into English, By Michael Geddes ... *London: S. Smith and B. Walford.* 1694. 8vo, pp. 443. 32164

The History of the Civil War. *See* [Hall (*Captain*)].

History of the Colonization. *See* [Barron (W.)], No. 3644*a*.

History of the Delaware and Iroquois Indians, Formerly inhabiting the Middle States. With Various Anecdotes illustrating their Manners and Customs. ... *Philadelphia: American Sunday School Union.* 1832. 8vo, pp. 153. Plate and Map. C.

History of the Discovery of America. *See* [Trumbull (H.)]

A History of the Division of the Presbyterian Church in the United States. By a Committee of the Synod of New York and New Jersey. *New York.* 1852. 12mo, pp. 278. P.

History of the Establishment and Progress of the Christian Religion in the Islands of the South Sea. With Preliminary Notices of the Islands, and of their Inhabitants. *Boston: Tappan & Dennett.* 1841. 16mo, pp. x, 387. Map. C. 32167

Included in Mr. Rich's "Bibliotheca Americana."

History of the Extra Session of Congress, convened in Washington, by Proclamation, on the Fourth of September and terminated on the Fourth of October, 1837. Embracing a faithful Abstract of the Important Currency Debates with which it was occupied, on the proposed measures of Financial Legislation: and an accurate table of the yeas and nays ... . *New York: L. Scott.* 1838. 8vo, pp. 105. C., S. 32168

History of the Federal and Democratic Parties in the United States, from their Origin to the Present Time. By a Citizen of Wayne County, Ind. *Richmond* [*Indiana*]. 1837. 8vo, pp. 56.

The History of the Garret, &c., &c. Translated from the Hieroglyphics of the Society: By a Member of the Order of the Blue-String. *Gotham* [*i. e. New York*]. 18mo, pp. 143. S.

A History of the Gift Book Business. *Boston.* 1859. 16mo, pp. 56. 32171

History of the Great Western Sanitary Fair (held at Cincinnati, December 23–31, 1863). *Cincinnati: C. F. Vent & Co.* [1864.] 8vo, pp. 578. Portrait. 32172

History of the Humane Society of Massachusetts; with List of Premiums. *Boston.* 1845. 8vo, pp. 95. 32173

History of the Indian Wars, 1812. *See* [Sanders (D. C.)]

A History of the Indian Wars with the First Settlers of the United States, to the Commencement of the Late War; together with an Appendix, not before added to this history, containing Interesting Accounts of the Battles Fought by Gen. Andrew Jackson. *Rochester (N. Y.): Printed by Edwin Scranton.* 1828. 12mo, pp. 196 [including Woodcut of King Philip]. C. 32174

History of the Islands of Cape Breton and St. Johns. *London.* 1670. 8vo. 32175

Title from a sale catalogue—probably incorrect.

History of ... Paper-Money. 8vo, pp. 20. *See* [Hart (A. M.)]

History of the Kingdoms and States of Asia, Africa and America. *London.* 1705. 8vo. 32176

The History of the late Minority, exhibiting the Conduct, Principles, and Views, of that Party dvring the Years 1762, 1763, 1764, and 1765. The Third Impression. *London: Printed in the Year* MDCCLXV; And Reprinted with some Additions in the Year MDCCLXVI. 8vo, pp. xii, 332. + The Fourth Impression. *London.* MDCCLXV. 8vo, pp. xii, 332. S. 32177

The first edition, which consisted of but twelve copies, was printed in 1765; the second, a very large one, in June, 1766; and the third, much larger, about the middle of the same month. The "Monthly Review," XXXIV. 482, calls it "An infammatory piece of party-work which hath engrossed a much greater share of public attention than it seems to have merited." The authors were John Almon and H. Cotes.

History of the Late Ecclesiastical Oppressions in New England and Vermont, &c. *Richmond.* 1799. 8vo. P., W. 32178

History of the Late War. *See* [McAfee (R. B.)], Rolt (*Mr.*)

The History of the Late War between the United States and Great Britain: containing a brief recapitulation of the events which led to the Declaration of War, its Progress, and an account of the various brilliant Land and Naval Victories, including the Battle of New Orleans. *Wheeling, Wis.* 1831. 18mo. + *New York.* 1832. 18mo. 32179

History of the Late War, or Annual Register of its Rise, Progress and Events in Europe, Asia, Africa and America. Illustrated with Heads, Plans, Maps and Charts. *Dublin.* 1774. 8vo. 32180

History of the Lives of the most notorious Pirates and their Crews. *J. Hodges on London Bridge.* 1740. 18mo. 32181

The History of the Lives and Bloody Exploits of the Most Noted Pirates, their Trials and Executions. *Hartford: S. Andrus.* 1835. 12mo. 32182

The History of the Little Frenchman and his Bank Notes. "Rags! Rags! Rags!" *Philadelphia: Edwad* [sic] *Earle.* 1815. 12mo, pp. 27. H. 32183

On the paper currency of the United States.

History of the Massacre at Indian Keys in Florida, by the Seminole Indians. *Philadelphia.* 1841. 8vo. 32184

The History of the Moravian Missions among the Indians in North-America, from its Commencement to the Present Time. With a Preliminary Account of the Indians. By a Member of the Brethren's Church. *London: T. Allman.* 1838. 16mo, pp. vi, 316. P. 32185

The History of the Nature of Excise Laws; with Some Account of the Excise on Snuff and Refined Sugar. *Philadelphia.* 1795. 8vo. P. 32186

History of the Negotiations in Reference to the Eastern and North Western Boundary of the United States in 1841. *New York.* 1841. 8vo. 32187

History of the New-England Emigrant Aid Company. With a Report on its future Operations. ... *Boston: Press of John Wilson and Son.* 1862. 8vo. 32188

A History of the New-York Kappa Lambda Conspiracy. *New-York.* MDCCCXXXIX. 8vo, pp. 32. N. 32189

A History of the New York National Guard; the Celebrated Seventh Regiment, from the day of its organization down to the present time ... . *New York: Dinsmore & Company.* M.D.CCCL.IX. Small 4to, pp. 68. 32190

One number only issued.

History of the Origin and Progress of the Late War from its Commencement. *London.* 1764. 2 vols., 8vo. 32191

This is perhaps the original edition of the following:

The History of the Origin, Rise and Progress of the War in America between Great Britain and her Colonies, from its Commencement in the Year 1764, to the Time of General Gage's Arrival at Boston in 1774. *London, Printed. Boston, in the State of Massachusetts: Reprinted by Thomas and John Fleet* ... M,DCC,LXXX. 8vo, pp. 90. [Continued as:] The History of the Rise

and Progress of the War in North-America, from the Time of General Gage's Arrival at Boston, in May, 1774. *London Printed. Boston, in the State of Massachusetts: Reprinted by Thomas and John Fleet* ... M,DCC,LXXX. 8vo, pp. 381, Appendix, 34. B.

"End of the first volume" are the last words in the book; whereas the previous volume of 90 pp. is in fact the first. The next title is a continuation.

The History of the War in America between Great Britain and her Colonies. Vol. II. *London Printed. Boston Re-printed by Thomas and John Fleet.* M,DCC,LXXX. 8vo, pp. 84, 4. B., BA.

This concludes the series, and is in fact Vol. III. A complete set is of extreme rarity. In this volume the history is continued to 1779.

The History of the New World, called America. *Dublin: R. Jackson.* [1776.] 24mo, pp. 180. C. 32194

The History of the Peace with France, and War with Holland, in the Year 1672 *et seq.* *London.* 1712. 8vo, pp. 71. M.

The History of the Pilgrims; or a Grandfather's Story of the First Settlers of New England. *Boston: Massachusetts Sabbath-School Union.* 1831. 16mo, pp. 142. Plate. C. 32196

History of the Pirates containing the Lives of those Noted Pirates, Misson, Bowen, Kidd, Tew, Halsey, White, and others, ... also, an Account of the Piracies and Cruelties of John Augur, Wm. Cunningham, Dennis Mackarthy, Wm. Dowling, and others, who were ... executed at Nassau, New Providence, December 10th, 1718; also a Correct Account of the Piracies in the West Indies and the Expedition of Commodore Porter. *Haverbill, Mass.* 1825. 12mo. + *Hartford: Silus Andrus.* 1834.

History of the Present War from its Commencement in 1756 to the End of the Campaign, 1760. *London.* 1761. 8vo.

Title from an English auction catalogue.

History of the Priesthood, from the Beginning of the World to the Present Time. [n. p. n. d.] 12mo, pp. 168. 32199

A Mormon work.

History of the Proceedings and Cruelties of the Court of Inquisition in Spain, Portugal, &c., with many remarkable Tryals and Sufferings. *London.* 1737. 12mo. Plates. 32200

Contains (pp. 199–236) an account of the examination of Louis Rame by the Inquisition of Mexico, for refusing to kneel to the host; after four years imprisonment he was sent in chains to Spain.

The History of the Raising of the first American Flag on the Capitol of Mexico. *Washington.* 1856. 32201

History of the Rebel Steam Ram "Atlanta," now on Exhibition in Philadelphia. [n. p.] 1863. 12mo. 32202

The History of the Reign of George the Third, King of Great-Britain &c. ... to which is prefixed, A Review of the late War. ... *London: For the Author.* MDCCLXX. 8vo, pp. (4), iv, 402, (1). B. 32203

History of the Revolution in Texas; particularly of the War of 1835 and 1836: together with the Latest Geographical, Statistical, and Topographical Accounts of the Country. *New York.* 1838. 12mo. C. 32204

History of the Revolution of the 18th Fructidor, Sept. 4th, 1797, and of the Deportations to Guiana in consequence of that Revolution, with Observations on that Colony and of the Negroes. *London.* 1800. 8vo. 32205

The History of the Rise and Fall of South Sea Stock, 1722.

History of the Rise, Progress and Destiny of the American Party. With a Review of the Letter of the Hon. Henry A. Wise against the Know Nothings. *Philadelphia.* 1855. 12mo.

History of the Rise, Progress, and Suppression of Rebellious Insurrections. 1780. 8vo. 32208

History of the Sandwich Islands: with an Account of the American Mission established there in 1820. *Philadelphia: American Sunday School Union.* 1831. 16mo, pp. 197. Map. C.

The History of the Second Ten Years of the Reign of George the Third, King of Great Britain, &c. From the Conclusion of the Third Session of the Thirteenth Parliament, in 1770, to the End of the Last Session of the Fourteenth Parliament of Great Britain, in 1780. *London: Evans.* 1782. 8vo, pp. 463.

"The most important part of this work is that which relates to the commencement and prosecution of the war with America. The author aims at impartiality, and no where discovers the zeal of a partizan. He is neither a determined Whig nor a pertinacious Tory, but seems to have made it a rule to steer a middle course. This volume is intended as a continuation to the history of the first ten years of the reign of George III., written apparently by a different author."—RICH, I. 303.

History of the Sioux or Dakota Indian Mission. *Boston: Massachusetts Sabbath School Society.* 1841. 18mo, pp. 94. Plate. C.

History of the 16th Regiment Pennsylvania Cavalry, for the Year ending October 31st, 1863. Commanded by Colonel John Irvin Gregg, of Centre Co., Pa. *Philadelphia: King & Baird.* 1864. 8vo, pp. 44. 32212

History of the Southern Iowa Soldiers' Fair, at Burlington, Iowa, from September 26 to October 1, 1864. *Burlington (Iowa): Hawke Eye Press.* 1865. 8vo, pp. 14. 32213

History of the Spirit Lake Massacre: 8th March 1857, and of Miss Abigail Gardiner's three Months Captivity among the Indians according to her own account, as given to L. P. Lee. *New Britain, Ct.* 1857. 8vo, pp. 48. 32214

A History of the Steamboat Case, lately discussed by Counsel before the Legislature of New Jersey, in a Letter to a Gentleman at Washington. *Trenton.* 1815. 8vo, pp. 52. N. 32215

History of the Strange Sounds, or Rappings, heard in Rochester and Western New York, and usually called, The Mysterious Noises, which are supposed by many to be Communications from the Spirit World. *Rochester.* 1850. 12mo, pp. 80. 32216

History of the Temperance Reform in America. *Albany.* 1833. 8vo. 32217

History of the United States, from their First Settlement as Colonies, to the Close of the War with Great Britain, in 1815. *New-York: C. Wiley.* 1825. 12mo, pp. (4), 337. C. + *London: John Miller.* 1826. 8vo, pp. (4), 467. 32218

History of the United States. *See* [Callender (J. T.)], [Fergus (H.)], [Hale (S.)], [Prentiss (C.)]

History of the United States, compiled from American and other sources. *London.* 1834. Imp. 8vo. 32219

History of the United States, and Biography of the Signers of the Declaration of Independence. To which will be added the History of the Southern Rebellion. *Boston: S. Walker.* [n. d.] 4to. Plates. 32220

This is Hinton's United States with a new title and some additions.

History of the United States. [n. p. n. d.] 64mo, pp. 160.

History of the United States from their First Settlement. For the Use of Schools. *New York.* 1838. 18mo. 32222

The History of the War between the United States and Great Britain, which commenced in June, 1812, and closed in February, 1815; containing Correspondence which passed between the two Governments, &c., compiled chiefly from Public Documents. With an Appendix, &c. *Hartford.* 1815. 12mo. + *New York.* 1815. 12mo. + Third Edition. *Philadelphia.* 1817. 12mo.

History of the War between the United States and Mexico. *Philadelphia: Zieber & Co.* 1847. 8vo, pp. 168. 8 Plates. C.

History of the War between the United States and Tripoli, and other Barbary Powers ... *Printed at the Salem Gazette Office.* 1806. 12mo, pp. 144. P., W. 32225

The | History | of the | War in America, | between | Great Britain | and | her Colonies, | from | Its Commencement to the end of the Year 1778. | In which its Origin, Progress, and Operations are | faithfully related, together with Anecdotes and Characters | of the different Commanders, and Accounts of such | Personages in Congress as have distinguished themselves | during the Contest. | To which is added, | A Collection of Interesting and Authentic Papers | tending to elucidate the History. | In Two Volumes. | *Dublin: Printed for the Company of Booksellers.* M,DCC,LXXIX. 3 vols., 8vo, pp. (1), vi, v, 399; Map and folded Table, 21¾ × 17¾; 427, (4). H. Vol. III. M,DCC,LXXXV. pp. (4). xii, 432. C.

"After part of the first chapter of Part II. of this work was printed, the author appears to have changed his mind, and commences anew with another chapter I. and a new paging, leaving the unfinished chapter, apparently to avoid the necessity of reprinting the sheet."—RICH, I. 273; but of this part there was a reissue radically different, and Horatio Rogers, of Providence, R. I., informs me that "in fact the reissue is not divided into parts at all. In it the whole of the first part is omitted bodily and chapter I. of the reissued volume is what is called chapter I. of Part II. of the old issue, save that the first three pages of chapter I. of Part II. are omitted and two new pages are substituted, both issues becoming alike in the third line from the bottom of page 2, the paging in the old issue having a page 2* as well as a page 2." The third volume, which continues the history to 1783, was a subsequent publication, and is seldom found with the other two. At page 267 begins an Appendix of State papers. The folded table, giving the names and rank of the killed, wounded, and missing of the British forces at the battles of Concord and Bunkerhill, is frequently wanting. Lowndes attributes the work to P. Gordon.

A History of the War with America, France, Spain and Holland. Begun in the Year 1775 and ended in 1783. *London.* 1787. 8vo. 32227

History of the Western World. *See* [Fergus (H.)], Vol. VI.

The History of the Works of the Learned. *London.* 1699. 4to. 32228

Contains a discussion, whether California be an island.

History of Witches and Wizards; giving a true account of all their Tryals in England, Scotland, Sweedland, France, and New England. *London.* [n. d.] 12mo. 32229

History, Resources, and Prospects of the Saginaw Valley ... . [*East Saginaw.* 1862.] 8vo, pp. 15. H. 32230

A Hit at Banking. By Banquo. *Richmond.* 1841. N. 32231

HITCHCOCK (A.) The Trial of Alpheus Hitchcock ... for the Murder of his Wife ... County of Madison [N. Y.], July, 1807. Reported by George Richards, Junior. *Utica: George Richards, Junior.* 1807. 8vo, pp. 50, (1). BA. 32232

HITCHCOCK (B. W.) Hitchcock's Chronological Record of the American Civil War ... from November 8th, 1860, to June 3d, 1865; also a Complete List of Vessels captured by the Confederate Navy. *New York: Benjamin W. Hitchcock.* 1866. 8vo, pp. 566. + [*Ibid.*] 1868. 8vo, pp. (2), 566. Portrait. B.

HITCHCOCK (C.) ... A Discourse ... before the Ancient and Honorable Artillery Company, June 7, 1841, being the CCIIId Anniversary. By Calvin Hitchcock ... . *Boston: Press of J. Howe.* 1841. 8vo, pp. 21. B., H., S. 32234

HITCHCOCK. A Sermon ... at the Funeral of Mrs. Joanna Strong ... Dec. 26, 1845. By Rev. Calvin Hitchcock, D.D. ... *Gilmanton: Printed by Alfred Prescott.* 1848. 8vo, pp. 15. H.

Also: ... A Sermon, ... Sharon, June 11, 1828, before the Norfolk County Education Society. ... *Boston: Printed by Crocker and Brewster.* 1828. 8vo, pp. 32. B., S.

HITCHCOCK (C. H.) *See* New Hampshire-Geology.

HITCHCOCK (D.) The Knight and Quack: or, a Looking-Glass for Impostors in Philosophy, Physic and Government, an Allegorical Poem. By David Hitchcock. *Hudson.* 1805. 4to, pp. 27. 32236

HITCHCOCK. Poems. By David Hitchcock. With a Sketch of the Author's Life. 1805. 12mo. 32237

HITCHCOCK. The Poetical Works of David Hitchcock ... . *Boston: Etheridge and Bliss.* 1806. 12mo, pp. 164. B., BA., H.

HITCHCOCK. The Social Monitor; or, a Series of Poems, on Some of the most Important and Interesting Subjects. By David Hitchcock ... . *Stockbridge.* 1812. 12mo. + Second Edition. *New York: Gould, Banks & Gould.* 1814. 12mo, pp. 204. BA.

Also: ... Address before the Great Barrington Branch of the Washington Benevolent Society, April 21, 1812. ... 8vo, pp. 15. N.—Poetical Dictionary; or, Popular Terms Illustrated in Rhyme, etc. ... *Lenox.* 1808. 12mo. N.—The Shade of Plato: or, a Defence of Religion, Morality & Government: a Poem, etc. ... *Hudson.* 1805. 12mo, pp. 107. BA., H., N.

HITCHCOCK (D. K.) Remarks of Hon. David K. Hitchcock, in the Massachusetts Senate, on the Pay of the Chaplains, March 19th, 1855. *Boston: Printed by Stacy & Richardson.* 1855. 12mo, pp. 11. BA., H., M. 32240

HITCHCOCK (E.) An Attempt to Discriminate and Describe the Animals that made the Fossil Footmarks of the United States, and especially of New England. By Edward Hitchcock. *Boston.* 1848. 4to. 24 Plates. 32241

Also forms "Memoirs of American Academy of Arts and Sciences," Vol. III., New Series.

HITCHCOCK. A Catalogue of Plants growing without Cultivation in the Vicinity of Amherst College. By Edward Hitchcock ... . *Amherst: J. S. and C. Adams, and Co., Printers.* 1829. 8vo, pp. 64. BA., H., W. 32242

HITCHCOCK. Catalogue of the Animals and Plants of Massachusetts. *Amherst: J. S. & C. Adams.* 1835. 8vo, pp. 142. A., C. + Second Edition. Corrected and Enlarged. *Amherst.* 1835. 8vo. W. 32243

Contents: Land and fresh water shells. From the second edition of the Report on the Geology, etc.

HITCHCOCK. Geology. *See* Massachusetts, *also* Vermont.

HITCHCOCK. Ichnology of New England. A Report on the Sandstone of the Connecticut Valley, especially its Fossil Footmarks, made to the Government of the Commonwealth of Massachusetts. By Edward Hitchcock ... . *Boston: William White, Printer.* 1858. 4to, pp. xii, 220. 60 Plates. B., BA. + Supplement ... 1863. *Boston: Wright & Potter, State Printers.* 1865. 4to, pp. 96. 20 Plates. C. 32244

Some copies have the imprint, *Boston: Phillips, Sampson & Co.* 1858.

HITCHCOCK. The Inseparable Trio. A Sermon, ... before His Excellency ... at the Annual Election ... January 2d, 1850. By Edward Hitchcock, D.D. ... *Boston: Dutton and Wentworth.* 1850. 8vo, pp. 45. BA., M. 32245

HITCHCOCK. Outline of the Geology of the Globe, and of the United States in Particular; with two Geological Maps, and

Sketches of Characteristic American Fossils. By Edward Hitchcock, D.D. ... *Boston.* 1853. 8vo. + *Amherst.* 1853. 12mo, pp. 136. 6 Plates. B. + Second Edition. *Boston: Phillips, Sampson & Company.* 1854. 8vo, pp. 136. 2 Maps, 6 Plates. P. + Third Edition. [*Ibid.*] 1856. H. 32246

HITCHCOCK. The Power of Christian Benevolence ... in the Life ... of Mary Lyon. Compiled by Edward Hitchcock, D.D. ... *Northampton: Hopkins, Bridgman, and Company.* 1851. 8vo, pp. viii, 486. Portrait. B., BA. + Second Edition. [*Ibid.*] H.

HITCHCOCK. Reminiscences of Amherst College, Historical, Scientific, Biographical, and Autobiographical: Also, of Other and Wider Life Experiences. With Four Plates and a Geological Map. By Edward Hitchcock ... . *Northampton: Bridgman & Childs.* 1863. 12mo, pp. vii, (1), 412. Portrait. B., H., C.

HITCHCOCK. Sketch of the Scenery of Massachusetts. From Geological Report of Prof. Hitchcock. *Northampton.* 1842. 4to.

HITCHCOCK. A Sketch of the Geology, Mineralogy and Topography of the Connecticut [River] ... By Rev. Edward Hitchcock ... . *New Haven: J. Converse.* 1823. 8vo, pp. iv, 154. Map, 2 Plates. H. 32250

Also: ... An Address ... before the Hampshire, Franklin & Hampden Agricultural Society. ... *Amherst: J. S. and C. Adams, Printers.* 1827. 8vo, pp. 24. B., W. — ... An Address ... before the Mechanical Association in Andover Theological Seminary, Sept. 21, 1830. ... *Amherst: J. S. and C. Adams.* 1831. 12mo, pp. 36. H., W. — Highest Use of Learning: An Address ... at his Inauguration to the Presidency of Amherst College. ... *Amherst: J. S. and C. Adams, Printers.* 1845. 8vo, pp. 51. — ... A Discourse ... Nov. 27, 1828, at the Funeral of Mrs. Fidelia Lord ... . *Amherst: J. S. & C. Adams, Printers.* 1829. 8vo, pp. 19. H. — ... A Discourse, ... before the Berkshire Medical Institution. ... *Pittsfield: Printed by Phinehas Allen.* 1823. 8vo, pp. 32. B. — Elementary Geology. ... *Amherst.* 1840. 12mo. + Eighth Edition. *New York: M. H. Newman & Co.* 1847. 12mo, pp. 361. 2 Maps. + [Another] Eighth Edition. *New York: Newman and Ivison.* 1853. 12mo, pp. 361. B. + Thirtieth Edition. *New York: Ivison & Phinney.* 1855. 12mo, pp. 424. 2 Maps. — An Essay on Temperance. Addressed particularly to Students, and the Young Men of America. ... *Amherst.* 1830. 18mo. + Second Edition. *Amherst: J. S. and C. Adams.* 1830. 18mo, pp. 36. H. — First Anniversary Address before the Association of American Geologists, at their Second Annual Meeting in Philadelphia, April 5, 1841. ... *New Haven: Printed by B. L. Hamlen.* 1841. 8vo, pp. 48. C. — History of a Zoological Temperance Convention. Held in Central Africa, in 1847. ... *Northampton.* 1850. 16mo. Plates + *Northampton: Hopkins, Bridgman & Co.* 1854. 16mo, pp. 160. Plates. B. + *Boston: N. Noyes.* 1855. 16mo, pp. 160. C. — Retrospection. A Sermon delivered in the Collegiate Institution, Amherst, May 13, 1823. *Northampton.* 1823. 8vo, pp. 24. — ... A Sermon ... at the Installation of Rev. Flavel Griswold ... December 3, 1828. ... *Amherst: J. S. and C. Adams, Printers.* 1829. 8vo, pp. 31. BA. — ... The Twelfth Anniversary Address before the Mount Holyoke Female Seminary, August First, MDCCCXLIX. ... *Amherst: J. S. & C. Adams, Printers.* 1849. 8vo, pp. 37. H.

HITCHCOCK (E.) A Discourse on the Causes of National Prosperity, illustrated by Ancient and modern History, exemplified in the late American Revolution. Addressed to the Society of the Cincinnati, in the State of Rhode-Island, at their Annual Meeting at East-Greenwich, July 4, 1786. By Enos Hitchcock, A.M. Of Providence. ... *Providence: Printed by Bennett Wheeler.* [1786.] 8vo, pp. 28. BA., H., M., W. 32251

HITCHCOCK. A Discourse delivered at the Dedication of the New Congregational Meetinghouse in Providence; and also, at the Westparish in Brookfield, November 10, 1795, on a like occasion. By Enos Hitchcock, D.D. ... *From the press of Rice & Waldo, Brookfield, Massachusetts:* 1795. 8vo, pp. 17. BA., W.

HITCHCOCK. A Discourse, on the Dignity and Excellence of the Human Character; Illustrated in the Life of General George Washington ... delivered February 22, 1800, ... in Providence ... By Enos Hitchcock, D.D. ... *Providence: Printed by John Carter, Jun.* 1800. 8vo, pp. 35. BA., H. 32253

HITCHCOCK. The Farmer's Friend, or the History of Mr. Charles Worthy, Who, from being a poor Orphan, rose, through Various Scenes of Distress and Misfortune, to Wealth, and Eminence, by Industry, Economy, and Good Conduct. Interspersed with many Useful and Entertaining Narratives. Suited to please the Fancy, improve the Understanding, and mend the Heart, By Enos Hitchcock, D.D. *Boston: I. Thomas and E. T. Andrews.* MDCCXCIII. 12mo, pp. 271. S., W. 32254

HITCHCOCK. Memoirs of the Bloomsgrove Family. In a Series of Letters to a respectable Citizen of Philadelphia. Containing Sentiments on a Mode of Domestic Education, suited to the present State of Society, Government, and Manners, in the United States of America: And on the Dignity and Importance of the Female Character, ... By Enos Hitchcock, D.D. *Boston: Printed by Thomas and Andrews.* MDCCXC. 2 vols., 12mo, pp. 299; 300. B., BA., H. 32255

HITCHCOCK. An Oration: Delivered July 4, 1788, at ... Providence, in Celebration of the Anniversary of American Independence, and of the Accession of Nine States to the Federal Constitution. By Enos Hitchcock, A.M. *Providence: Printed by Bennett Wheeler.* [n. d.] 8vo, pp. 24. B., H. 32256

HITCHCOCK. An Oration, in Commemoration of the Independence of the United States of America. ... Providence, July 4th, 1793. *Printed by J. Carter.* [1793.] 8vo, pp. 19. BA.

Also: A Discourse on Education: ... at ... Providence, November 16, 1785. ... *Providence: Printed by Bennett Wheeler.* [n. d.] 4to, pp. 16. H. — A Discourse ... at the Ordination of the Rev. Abel Flint to ... a Christian Church at Hartford, April 20th, 1791. ... *Hartford: Printed by Elisha Babcock.* M,DCC,XCI. 8vo, pp. 23. H. — A Discourse delivered at the Ordination of the Reverend Jonathan Gould, ... at Standish, September 18, 1793. ... *Portland: Printed by Benjamin Titcomb, Jun.* [1793.] 4to, pp. 22. BA. — A Funeral Sermon, occasioned by the Death of Mrs. Sarah Bowen, consort of the Hon. Jabez Bowen, Esq., who died March 17, 1800 ... . *Providence: Printed by John Carter, Jun.* 1800. 8vo, pp. 24. H. — A New-Year's Sermon; delivered at Providence, January 1, 1797. ... *Providence: Printed by Carter and Wilkinson.* 1797. 8vo, pp. 12. W. — A Sermon, delivered at Wrentham, at the Ordination of the Rev. Elisha Fisk, June the 12th, 1799. ... *Providence: Printed by Bennett Wheeler.* 1799. 8vo, pp. 28. H., N.

HITCHCOCK (G.) Natural Religion aided by Revelation and perfected in Christianity. A Discourse ... in the Chapel of the University at Cambridge, ... September 1, 1779. At the Lecture founded by the Hon. Paul Dudley, Esq. By Gad. Hitchcock ... . *Boston: Printed by T. & J. Fleet.* M,DCC,LXXIV. 8vo, pp. 32. BA., H. 32258

HITCHCOCK. A Sermon ... in the 2d Precinct in Pembroke, N. E. before a Company voluntarily formed, for the Revival of Military Skill, &c., October 10, 1757. *Boston: Printed by Edes and Gill.* M,DCC,LVII. 8vo, pp. 23. BA., H. 32259

HITCHCOCK. A Sermon ... before ... Thomas Gage, Esq; Governor ... of the Province of the Massachusetts-Bay in New-England, May 25th, 1774. ... *Boston: Printed by Edes and Gill.* M,DCC,LXXIV. 8vo, pp. 56. B., BA., H., M. 32260

HITCHCOCK. A Sermon ... at Plymouth December 22d, 1774. ... The Anniversary Thanksgiving, in Commemoration of the first Landing of our New-England Ancestors in that Place, Anno Dom. 1620. *Boston: Printed by Edes and Gill.* M,DCC,LXXV. 8vo, pp. 44. BA., W. 32261

Also: A Sermon, ... at the Ordination of the Reverend Mr. Enos Hitchcock ... in Beverly, ... May 1st, 1771. ... *Salem: Printed by Samuel Hall.* MDCCLXXI. 8vo, pp. 31.

HITCHCOCK (G.) Address delivered at Hanson, Mass., before the School Dames, their Pupils, &c., September, 1827. By Gad. Hitchcock, A.M. *Hingham.* 1828. 8vo, pp. 19. M. 32262

HITCHCOCK (H. L.) God acknowledged in the Nation's Bereavement. A Sermon delivered in Hudson, Ohio, on the day of the Obsequies of Abraham Lincoln, April 19, 1865. By Henry L. Hitchcock. *Cleveland: Fairbanks, Benedict & Co., Printers.* 1865. 8vo, pp. 23. 32263

Also: ... A Sermon ... at the Funeral of Rev. James Rowland. ... *Columbus.* 1854. 8vo, pp. 22. B.

HITCHCOCK (P.) Loyalty to the Government. Speech of Hon. Peter Hitchcock, of Geauga, in the Ohio Senate, March 4, 1863, on the Loyalty Resolutions of Mr. Welsh. [n. p. n. d.] 8vo, pp. 10. 32264

HITCHCOCK (R.) Funeral Oration on the Death of Mr. Elizur Belden, of Wethersfield, June 8, 1786. By Reuben Hitchcock. *New Haven.* 1786. 8vo, pp. 22. 32265

HITCHCOCK (R. D.) A Eulogy on Daniel Webster, delivered before the Students of Bowdoin College, ... Nov. 12th, 1852. By Roswell D. Hitchcock ... . *Brunswick: Printed by J. Griffin.* 1852. 8vo, pp. 44. B., BA. 32266

HITCHCOCK. Our National Sin: A Sermon, Preached on the Day of the National Fast, September 26, 1861, in ... New York City. By Rev. Roswell D. Hitchcock, D.D., ... *New York: Baker & Godwin, Printers.* 1861. 8vo, pp. 24. 32267

HITCHCOCK. A Sermon delivered at the Dedication of the New Chapel of Bowdoin College, Thursday, June 7, 1855. By Rev. Roswell D. Hitchcock ... . *Brunswick: George T. Barrett.* 1855. 8vo, pp. 24. H. 32268

HITCHCOCK. Thanksgiving for Victories. A Discourse delivered in Plymouth Church, Brooklyn, September 11, 1864. By Rev. Roswell D. Hitchcock. *New York: J. A. Gray & Green.* 1864. 8vo, pp. 7. 32269

Also: Chronological Record of the American Civil War. ... *New York.* 1866. — The Laws of Civilization. The Substance of an Address delivered on Several Occasions during ... 1860. ... *New-York: John A. Gray, Printer.* 1860. 8vo, pp. 24. — The Charge and Inaugural Address delivered on Occasion of the Induction of the Rev. Roswell D. Hitchcock, D.D. into the Washburn Professorship of Church Histoy, in the Union Theological Seminary, New York, ... May 6, 1856. ... *New York: J. F. Trow, Printer.* 1856. 8vo, pp. 48. B.

HITTELL (J. S.) Nineteenth Anniversary Oration before the Corporate Society of the California Pioneer Association. By Hon. John S. Hittell. *San Francisco.* 1869. 8vo. 32270

HITTELL. Mining in the Pacific States of North America. By John S. Hittell. *San Francisco: H. H. Bancroft and Company.* 1861. 12mo, pp. 224. BA. + 1862. C., S. 32271

HITTELL. The Resources of California: comprising Agriculture, Mining, Geography, Climate, Commerce, &c., and the Past and Future Development of the State. By John S. Hittell.

New York. 1863. 8vo. C. + Second Edition, with an Appendix on Oregon and Washington Territory. *San Francisco: A. Roman and Company.* 1866. 12mo, pp. xvi, 494. B., BA. + Third Edition. [*Ibid.*] 1867. 12mo, pp. xv, xvi, 462. C. + Fourth Revised Edition. *San Francisco and New York: A. Roman & Co.* 12mo. + Fifth Edition, with an Appendix on Oregon, Nevada, and Washington Territory. [*Ibid.*] 1869. 12mo, pp. xxiv, 504. C. 32272

[HITTELL.] The Resources of Vallejo: containing a Statement of the great Natural Advantages of the Place, showing that it is the most convenient Seaport, the safest Harbor, the natural Railway Centre, and the best Manufacturing Site, with a prospect of becoming the Commercial and Financial Metropolis of California. [*Vallejo:*] *Solano County Advertiser Office.* 1869. 8vo, pp. (2), 72. 2 Maps. C. 32273

HITTELL. Yosemite: its Wonders and its Beauties. By John S. Hittell. *San Francisco: H. H. Bancroft & Co.* 1868. 12mo, pp. 59. Map and 20 Photographic Plates. C. 32274

HITTELL (T. H.) The Adventures of James Capen Adams, Mountaineer and Grizzly Bear Hunter, of California. By Theodore H. Hittell. Illustrated. *Boston: Crosby, Nichols, Lee and Company.* 1860. 12mo, pp. 378. H. + [*Ibid.*] 1861. B., P.

HITTELL. The General Laws of the State of California, from 1850 to 1864 inclusive; being a Compilation of all Acts of a general nature now in force, with full references, etc. By Theodore H. Hittell. *San Francisco.* 1866. 2 vols., rl. 8vo, pp. 1186. 32276

The Hive ... March 11th, 1826. 8vo, pp. 96. 32277

The Hive; or a Collection of Thoughts on Civil, Moral, Sentimental and Religious Subjects. ... *Worcester: Press of Isaiah Thomas, Jun.* 1795. 12mo, pp. 252. B. + *Worcester: Press of Thomas, Son and Thomas.* MDCCXCVI. 12mo, pp. 227. H.

The Hive; a Collection of Thoughts from 100 Writers. *Philadelphia.* 1796. 12mo. 32279

HL (J. D.) *See* H[er]l[ein], No. 31495.

[HOADLEY (B.)] An Enquiry into the Reasons of the Conduct of Great Britain. With Relation to the present State of Affairs in Europe. *London.* 1727. 8vo, pp. 112. S. + Pub-

lished (here) for the Information of the Inhabitants of New-England. *Boston.* 1727. 8vo, pp. 103. B. 32280

Partly on the commerce with America. Also: A Defence of the Enquiry ... &c., occasioned by the paper ... in the Craftsman, Jan. 4, 1728–9. ... *London.* 1729. 8vo, pp. 40. S.

HOADLY (C. J.) *See* Connecticut, Vol. IV., *also* New Haven, *and* Historical Magazine, I. 191.

HOADLY (Loammi I.) An Address, delivered at the Union Celebration of Independence at Sutton, Mass. July 5, 1824. By L. Ives Hoadly ... *Worcester: William Manning, Printer.* [n. d.] 8vo, pp. 19. BA., W. 32281

HOAG (J.) Journal of the Life of Joseph Hoag, an eminent Minister of the Gospel, in the Society of Friends. *Auburn: Knapp and Peck, Printers.* 1861. 8vo, pp. 396. 32282

HOAG. Journal of the Life of Joseph Hoag, containing his Remarkable Vision. *London: A. W. Bennett.* 1862. Post 8vo, pp. xix, 381. 32283

A record of labors and wanderings, and a testimony against the doctrines propagated among the Quakers by Elias Hicks and Joseph John Gurney.

HOAGLAND (C. C.) Gleanings for the History of the Protestant Reformed Dutch Church, of Harlingen, New Jersey. By Christopher C. Hoagland. *Somerville, N. J.: S. L. B. Baldwin, Printer.* 1847. 8vo, pp. 15. B., S. 32284

HOAR (Ebenezer Rockwood). Charge to the Grand Jury, at the July Term of the Municipal Court, in Boston, 1854. By E. R. Hoar ... . *Boston: Little, Brown & Company.* 1854. 8vo, pp. 22. B., BA. 32285

HOAR (L.) The Sting of Death | and | Death Unstung | Delivered in two | Sermons | In which is shewed | the Misery of the Death of those that Dye in their Sins, & out | of Christ, and the Blessedness of theirs that Dye in the Lord. | Preached on the occasion of the Death of the truly noble and virtuous | The Lady Mildmay. | By Leonard Hoar, M.D. | Sometime Preacher of God's Word in Wansstead. | ... | *Boston: Printed by John Foster.* 1680. Sm. 4to, pp. (8), 24. 32286

A rare and very early Boston imprint. The Epistle Dedicatory is signed by Josiah Flint of Dorchester.

HOAR (Samuel). Remarks ... on the Resolutions [Abolition of Slavery in the District of Columbia,] Introduced by Mr.

Jarvis, ... and Mr. Wise, ... delivered ... January 21, 1836. *Washington.* 1836. 8vo, pp. 13. BA. 32287

Also: Address at Fitchburg, Mass. ... [n. p. n. d.] S. — Report, Resolves concerning the Treatment of Samuel Hoar by South-Carolina; Declaration. ... *Boston.* 1845. 8vo, pp. 53. S.

HOARE (P.) Memoirs of Granville Sharp, Esq. Composed from his own Manuscripts, and other Authentic Documents ... . By Prince Hoare. ... *London: Henry Colburn and Co.* 1820. 4to, pp. xxxii, 324, xxxiii. B. + Second Edition. *London.* 1828. 2 vols., 8vo. C. 32288

See "M. Rev.," XCIV. 51. Sharp was originally in the ordnance service, but resigned his place on account of the American War. He was intimate with most of the leading men of the day in America, with whom his correspondence is extensive. His exertions in behalf of the negro race are well known.

HOBART (A.) An Historical Sketch of Abington, Plymouth County, Massachusetts. With an Appendix. By Aaron Hobart. *Boston: Printed by Samuel N. Dickinson.* 1839. 8vo, pp. 176. A.

HOBART (B.) History of the Town of Abington, Plymouth County, Massachusetts, from its first Settlement. By Benjamin Hobart, A.M. *Boston: T. H. Carter and Son.* 1866. 12mo, pp. xix, (1), 453. Portrait and Plates. B. 32290

HOBART (B.) Oration at Abington [Mass.], July 4, 1805. By Benjamin Hobart. *Boston.* 1805. 8vo. 32291

HOBART (J.) A Confession of Faith and Covenant adopted by the Church of Christ in Berlin. *New Bedford.* 1810. 8vo, pp. 8. 32292

[HOBART (John Henry).] The Charter of the Corporation of Trinity Church defended against the Attacks of a late Pamphlet. Believed to be by Bishop Hobart. Reprinted from the original, published A. D. 1813. *New York: James A. Sparks.* 1846. 8vo, pp. 21. B., H. 32293

HOBART. Letter to the Vestry of Trinity Church, ... in Answer to a Pamphlet, entitled "A Solemn Appeal to the Church," by the Rev. Cave Jones. ... [With] Appendix, by ... Rev. T. Y. How. *New York: E. Sargeant.* 1811. 8vo, pp. (2), 113, 20. B., BA., H., M., N., W. 32294

HOBART. The Origin, the General Character, and the Present Situation of the Protestant Episcopal Church in the United States of America—A Sermon ... May 18th, A.D. 1814. ...

Opening of the General Convention ... and of the Consecration of ... Bishop Moore, of Virginia. *Philadelphia: Bradford and Inskeep.* 1814. 8vo, pp. 38. BA., N. + Second Edition. *New York.* 1814. 8vo, pp. 29. BA. 32295

HOBART. A Pastoral Letter to the Laity of the Protestant Episcopal Church in the State of New-York, on the Subject of Bible and Common Prayer Book Societies. *New-York: Printed by T. and J. Swords.* 1815. 8vo, pp. 24. BA. 32296

This Pastoral produced a controversy concerning such societies, which was carried on with some warmth. We content ourselves with enumerating: "Strictures on a Pastoral Letter ... on Bible ... Societies, of Bishop Hobart. By a Layman." *New-York: Van Winkle and Wiley.* 1815. 8vo, pp. 19. B., BA., S. — "An Answer to Bishop Hobart's Pastoral Letter on the subject of Bible and Common Prayer-Book Societies. By an Episcopalian." ... *New-York: Whiting & Watson.* 1815. 8vo, pp. 16. To which "Answer," Hobart replied in an anonymous tract entitled: "Reply to 'An Answer' ... By another Episcopalian." *New-York: Printed by T. and J. Swords.* 1815. 8vo, pp. 33. B., BA.

HOBART. The Posthumous Works of ... John Henry Hobart ... With a Memoir of his Life, by the Rev. William Berrian. ... *New-York: Swords, Stanford, and Co.* 1833–32. 3 vols., 8vo, pp. (4), 423, Portrait; viii, 521; viii, 502. H. 32297

[HOBART.] Remarks on the Hon. John Jay's Letter to the Rev. Cave Jones. [*New York.*] 1812. 8vo, pp. 24. 32298

HOBART. The Security of a Nation. A Sermon, Preached ... April 13, A.D. 1815; being the Day ... of Thanksgiving ... for ... Peace. By John Henry Hobart, D.D. ... *New-York: Printed by T. and J. Swords.* 1815. 8vo, pp. 21. B. 32299

HOBART. A Statement addressed to the Episcopalians, in the State of New-York, Relative to some Recent Events in the Protestant Episcopal Church in the Said State. *New York: Printed by T. and J. Swords.* 1812. 8vo, pp. (2), 99. N., W.

HOBART. The United States of America compared with some European Countries, particularly England: in a Discourse delivered ... October, 1825. By John Henry Hobart, D.D. ... *New York: Printed by T. and J. Swords.* 1825. 8vo, pp. 48. B., W. + *London: J. Miller.* 1826. 8vo, pp. 47. + Second Edition, with Additional Notes. *New York: Printed by T. and J. Swords.* 1826. 8vo, pp. 44. + *London: J. Miller.* 1828. 8vo, pp. 51.

Answered by "... A Review of Bishop Hobart's Sermon, entitled 'The United States of America compared with some European Countries, particularly England.'" ... *New-York: Printed by T. and J. Swords.* 1826. 8vo, pp. 32. B. — Also: Address to the

Committee acting under the Authority of the Meeting at Mechanic Hall. ... *New York.* 1812. 8vo, pp. 14.—Address delivered before the Auxiliary New-York Bible and Common Prayer Book Society. ... *New York: Printed by T. and J. Swords.* 1816. 8vo, pp. 36. BA., H.—Address to Episcopalians, on the Subject of the American Bible Society. ... *New York.* 1816. 12mo, pp. 12.—Address ... before the New-York Protestant Episcopal Missionary Society, ... 5th March, 1817. ... *New York.* 1817. 8vo, pp. 16. BA., H.—Address to the Vestry of Trinity Church, New York. ... 1811. 8vo.—An Address ... Annual Convention of the Protestant Episcopal Church in ... New-York: ... 1821. ... *New-York: Printed by T. and J. Swords.* 1821. 8vo, pp. 40. Also many other addresses at various conventions.—An Apology for Apostolic Order and its Advocates, occasioned by the Strictures and Denunciations of the Christian's Magazine. ... *New York: T. & J. Swords.* 1807. 8vo, pp. 273. + Second Edition. *New York.* MDCCCXLIV. 12mo, pp. 273. B.—A Brief Statement relative to the late Election of Wardens and Vestrymen in Trinity Church. ... *New York.* 1812. 8vo, pp. 4.—A Charge to the Clergy ... in the State of New York. ... *New York.* 1815. 8vo, pp. 52.—Charge to the Clergy ... at the ... Convention, October, 1817, and to the Clergy ... Connecticut, June, 1818. ... *New York.* 1818. 8vo, pp. 31. N.—The Christian Bishop ... A Sermon preached in ... October, A.D. 1827, at the Consecration of the Right Rev. Henry U. Onderdonk, D.D. ... *Philadelphia: Jesper Harding, Printer.* 1827. 8vo, pp. 36.—... A Sermon, ... at the Consecration of Trinity Church, Newark, New-Jersey, ... May 21, A.D. 1810. ... *New-York: Printed by T. and J. Swords.* 1810. 8vo, pp. (4), 41. B., M.—A Funeral Address ... at the Interment of Right Rev. Benjamin Moore; ... [with] Appendix ... *New York: Printed by George Long.* 1816. 8vo, pp. 72. The appendix occupies 54 clearly printed pages, and goes fully into this much controverted question. —... An Address ... at the Funeral of the Rt. Rev. Benjamin Moore, D.D. ... March 1, 1816 ... and a Dissertation on the Same Subject. ... *New York: Thomas N. Stanford.* 1857. 12mo, pp. 94. B.—An Introductory Address ... Opening of the General Theological Seminary of the Protestant Episcopal Church ... delivered ... 11th of March, 1822. ... *New-York: Printed by T. and J. Swords.* 1822. 8vo, pp. 40. B. —... A Sermon, preached at the Consecration of Trinity Church, in ... New-Haven, ... the 21st day of February, A.D. 1816. ... *New-Haven: Printed by Oliver Steele.* 1816. 8vo, pp. 29, Errata, 1 slip. BA.—Pastoral Letter relating to Measures for Theological Education. ... *New York.* 1820. 8vo, pp. 24.—A Pastoral Letter, addressed to the Clergy and Laity of the Protestant Episcopal Church in the State of New York. ... *New York: T. and J. Swords.* 1829. 8vo, pp. 23. BA.—... A Sermon ... at the Institution of the Rev. George Upfold, M.D. ... *New York: T. & J. Swords.* 1828. 8vo, pp. 28. H.—... A Sermon ... in Rochester ... August 29, 1830, at the Institution of the Rev. Henry J. Whitehouse, A.M. ... *New York: T. and J. Swords.* 1830. 8vo, pp. 22. H. Many of the sermons and charges by Bishop Hobart might be enumerated, but they relate chiefly, if not entirely, to church matters.

HOBART. Memorial of Bishop Hobart. A Collection of Sermons on the Death of the Right Reverend John Henry Hobart, D.D. Bishop of the Protestant Episcopal Church in the State of New York: with A Memoir of his Life and Writings. *New-York: T. and J. Swords.* MDCCCXXXI. 12mo, pp. 258. Portrait. W. 32302

The following also relate to Bishop Hobart:

A Declaration and Protest of the Wardens and Vestry of Christ Church, Cincinnati, against the Proceedings of Bishop Hobart. *Cincinnati.* 1823. 8vo, pp. 14. 32303

A Reply to a Letter to the Right Rev. Bishop Hobart, occasioned by the Strictures on Bible Societies, contained in his late Address to the Convention of New York. By a Chairman of the Diocese of New York, in a Letter to that Gentleman. By Corrector. *New York.* 1823. 8vo, pp. 98. B., N. 32304

A Vindication of the Pastoral Letter of the Right Rev. Bishop Hobart ... . *New York: T. and J. Swords.* 1829. 8vo, pp. 15, (1).

Also: A Word for the Church: consisting of "The Churchman," and "The High Churchman Vindicated;" Two Episcopal Charges by Rt. Rev. John Henry Hobart, D.D. with an Appendix of Authorities, and a Preliminary Notice. By George W. Doane ... . *Boston: Stimpson and Clapp.* 1832. 8vo, pp. 100. B., BA., H.

HOBART (N.) The Absence of the Comforter Described and Lamented, in a Discourse ... . By Nehemiah Hobart. *New-London: Printed by Timothy Green.* 1717. 8vo, pp. (2), x, 316.

HOBART (N.) An Attempt To illustrate and confirm The ecclesiastical Constitution of The Consociated Churches, In the Colony of Connecticut. Occasioned by a late "Explanation of the Saybrook Platform." By Noah Hobart, A.M. Pastor of a Church in Fairfield. ... *New-Haven: Printed by B. Mecom.* M,DCC,LXV. 8vo, pp. 44. 32307

HOBART. Civil Government the Foundation of Social Happiness. A Sermon preached before the ... Assembly of ... Connecticut, ... the Day of ... Election, May 10th, 1750. By Noah Hobart ... . *N. London: Printed by T. Green.* 1751. 18mo, pp. (4), 52. B., C., H. 32308

[HOBART.] A Congratulatory Letter from a Gentleman in the West, to his Friend in the East; upon the success of his Letter, entituled, "The Present State of the Colony of Connecticut considered." *New Haven: James Parker.* 1755. 4to, pp. 15. N. 32309

HOBART. A Serious Address to the Members of the Episcopal Separation in New-England, occasioned by Mr. Wetmore's Vindication of the Professors of the Church of England in Connecticut. ... By Noah Hobart, A.M. ... *Boston: Printed by J. Bushell and J. Green.* 1748. 16mo, pp. 139. BA., C. 32310

HOBART. A Second Address to the Members of the Episcopal Separation in New-England; occasioned By the Exceptions made to the former, by Dr. Johnson, Mr. Wetmore, Mr. Beach, and Mr. Caner. To which is Added, by way of Appendix, a Letter from Mr. Dickinson in Answer to some things Mr.

Wetmore has charged him with. By Noah Hobart. ... *Boston: Printed by D. Fowle.* 1751. 8vo, pp. 172, (2). B., BA., H., C.

"Perhaps more suggestive than any other one volume of the materials for the historian, who contemplates a history of the Establishment of Episcopacy, or the Church of England, in New England."—STEVENS. Also: Ministers of the Gospel considered as Fellow-Labourers. A Sermon ... at the Ordination Of ... Noah Welles, at Sanford, Dec. 31. 1746. ... *Boston: D. Henchman.* 1747. 12mo, pp. 34. B.—The Principles of Congregational Churches relating to the Constitution and Authority of Ecclesiastical Councils ... applied to the ... Ordination at Wallingford. ... *New-Haven: Printed by James Parker, and Company.* 1759. 8vo, pp. 40. BA.

HOBART (*Lord* Vere Henry). Political Essays. *London and Cambridge: Macmillan and Co.* 1866. 8vo, pp. (8), 152. BA., C.

Relates to intervention, maritime capture and blockade, etc.

HOBART COLLEGE. Catalogue of the Officers and Students of Hobart College, for ... 1829. 8vo. Continued. 32313

The title was afterwards changed to "Register of Hobart College, Geneva, N. Y." —Poem before the Students of Hobart College and the Citizens of Geneva, Feb. 22, 1862. ... *Geneva, N. Y.* 1862.

HOBBS (G.) Genealogy of the Hobbs Family of Massachusetts. Compiled by George Hobbs, Esq., Eastport, Me. *Boston: Dutton & Wentworth, Printers.* 1855. 8vo, pp. 16. 32314

HOBBY (W.) The Happiness of a People, having God for their Ally. Illustrated in A Sermon Preach'd at Reading, April 30. 1758, On Occasion of an Expedition design'd against Canada. In the Audience of Col. Nichols, and a Part of his Regiment. By William Hobby, A.M. *Boston: Printed by S. Kneeland.* 1758. 8vo, pp. (2), ii, 28. B., BA., H. 32315

HOBBY. An Inquiry into the Itinerancy, and the Conduct of the Rev. Mr. George Whitefield, an Itinerant Preacher: vindicating the former against the Charge of Unlawfulness and Inexpediency, and the latter against some Aspersions which have been frequently cast upon him. By William Hobby, ... *Boston: Printed by Rogers and Fowle.* 1745. 4to, pp. 28. BA., W. 32316

This elicited "A Twig for Billy's Breech. A Letter to the Rev. Mr. William Hobby. Being a Gentle and Necessary Correction of him, for his Folly and Wickedness lately published to the world, in a piece entitled 'A Defence of the Itinerancy and Conduct of Mr. Whitefield.' By J. C." *Boston, N. E.: T. Fleet.* 1745. 4to, pp. 13. W. Also, "A Letter to Mr. Hobby. By J. F." [*Boston.*] 1745. 4to, pp. (2), 9.

HOBBY. The Soldier caution'd and counsel'd. A Sermon ... to the ... Honourable Artillery-Company, at Boston: June 1, 1747, for their Election of Officers. *Boston, N. E.: D. Henchman and J. Edwards.* 1747. 8vo, pp. 38. BA., H., M. 32317

Also: Advice to his People from the Grave. ... 8vo, pp. 8. N.—The Faithful Minister the Glory of Christ. ... Sermon ... at the Ordination of the Reverend Daniel Emerson, ... Dunstable. ... *Boston: S. Eliot.* 1743. 8vo, pp. 39. BA., M.—Self-Examination ... Urged and Applied, in Sundry Sermons, delivered at Reading. ... *Boston: S. Kneeland & S. Green.* 1746. 16mo, pp. (2), vi, iv, 192. B., C.—A Vindication of the Protest against the Result of the Northampton-Council, in Answer to ... Reverend Messieurs Breck. ... *Boston: Printed by S. Kneeland.* [1751.] 4to, pp. (2), 17. BA., H.

HOBBY (W.) Exposition of a part of the Frauds, Corruptions and Improprieties committed in the Pay Department of the Army of the United States, since the year 1816. By William Hobby. Second Edition. *Washington.* 1830. 8vo, pp. 32. S. 32318

Hobomok. *See* [Child (L. M.)], Vol. IV., No. 12718.

HOBSON (J.) Prospectus of a Plan of Instruction for the Young of Both Sexes. ... By John Hobson ... . *Philadelphia: For the Author.* 1799. 8vo, pp. iv, 7–22. BA. 32319

Der Hoch-Deutsche Americanische Calender, 1739. *Germantown, Penn.* 1739. 4to. Continued. 32320

Hochelaga. *See* [Warburton (E.)]

HOCHHEIMER (H.) Fest und Fasting. Predigt am 1. Juni 1865, ... als an dem ... Busz- und Bettage, zum Gedächtnisse des ermordeten Präsidenten Abraham Lincoln. ... [*Baltimore:*] *Gedruckt bei Th. Krob.* [1865.] 12mo, pp. 10. 32321

HOCHHEIMER. Predigt, ... 19. April 1865, als am Tage des Leichenbegängnisses des Präsidenten der Ver. Staaten Abraham Lincoln's. Von H. Hochheimer, Rabbiner ... in Baltimore. ... [*Baltimore:*] *Gedruckt bei Th. Krob.* [n. d.] 12mo, pp. 9.

HOCK (C.) Die Finanzen und die Finanzgeschichte der Vereinigten Staaten von Amerika. Von Dr. Carl Freiherrn von Hock ... . *Stuttgart: J. G. Cotta.* 1867. 8vo, pp. xiv, 811, (1).

HODDER (E. M.) The Harbours and Ports of Lake Ontario, in a series of [20] Charts, accompanied by a Description of each; together with the Lighthouses, Harbour Lights, Depth of Water, &c. Compiled from Authentic Sources, Recent Surveys, and Personal Observations. By Edward M. Hodder, M.D., Commodore of the Royal Canadian Yacht Club. *Toronto.* 1857. 8vo.

HODGDON (M.) An Oration, pronounced at Dover, New Hampshire, ... Fourth of July, 1808. By Moses Hodgdon, Esq. *Dover: Printed by James K. Remich.* 1808. 8vo, pp. 18.

HODGE (A.) Trial of Arthur Hodge, Esq. late one of the Members of H.M. Council for the Virgin Islands at the Island of Tortola, for the Murder of his Negro Man Slave, named Prosper. Second Edition. *London.* 1811. 8vo, pp. 145.

This report is by R. Hetherington, Esq., President of the Virgin Islands.

HODGE. A Report of the Trial of Arthur Hodge, Esquire, ... Taken by A. M. Belisario ... *Middletown: Printed by Tertius Dunning.* 1812. 12mo, pp. 186. B., BA., H. 32327

HODGE (C.) The Constitutional History of the Presbyterian Church in the United States of America. (1705–1788.) By Charles Hodge ... Part I. 1705 to 1741. Part II. 1741 to 1788. *Philadelphia: William S. Martien.* 1839–40. 2 vols., 8vo, pp. 256; 516. BA. + [*Ibid.* 1851.] 2 vols., 8vo, pp. 215; 425. C.

[HODGE.] England and America. From the Princeton Review for January, 1862. ... *Philadelphia: William S. & Alfred Martien.* 1862. 8vo, pp. 31. H. + Second Edition. [*Ibid.*] B.

HODGE. The State of the Country. From the Princeton Review, January, 1861. [*Philadelphia?* 1861.] 8vo, pp. 32.

This elicited "Reply to Professor Hodge, on the 'State of the Country.'" [By W. J. Grayson.] *Charleston: Evans & Cogswell.* 1861. 8vo, pp. 32. B. Also: Articles from the Biblical Repertory for Jan., 1861, and Jan., 1862, relating to the Civil War. —A Brief Account of the Last Hours of Albert B. Dod. ... *Princeton, N. J.: Printed by John T. Robinson.* [1845.] 8vo, pp. 16.—Essays and Reviews. Selected from the Princeton Review. ... *New York: Robert Carter & Brothers.* 1857. 8vo, pp. (4), 633. —The Reunion of the Old and New School Presbyterian Churches. ... *New York: C. Scribner & Co.* 1867. 8vo, pp. 37.—What is Presbyterianism? An Address delivered before the Presbyterian Historic Society. ... 1855. 18mo.

HODGE (D. M.) The Highest Law. By Rev. D. Munson Hodge. Author's Edition. *New Haven: H. H. Peck.* 1870. 12mo, pp. 146. C. 32331

[HODGE (James T.)] Report. Ulster Mine at Glenville, Ulster County, New-York. [*New York:*] *D. Felt & Hosford.* 1852. 8vo, pp. 8. 32332

HODGE (M.), *Jun.* An Address to the Members of the Merrimack [Mass.] Humane Society, ... Sept. 6, 1808. By Michael Hodge, Jun. *Newburyport: Press of E. W. Allen.* 1808. 8vo, pp. 23. BA., W. 32333

HODGE. An Oration ... before ... St. Peter's Lodge, ... Newburyport, ... June 24th, 5802. By ... Michael Hodge, Jun. ... *Newburyport: Angier March.* 5802. 4to, pp. 15. C., W.

HODGE (W. L.) The Public Debt, the Currency, Specie Payments, and National Banks. By William L. Hodge. *Washington.* 1867. 8vo, pp. 30. H. 32335

Also: Disunion and its Results to the South. ... [*Washington.* 1861.] 8vo, pp. 23.

HODGES (A. D.) Genealogical Record of the Hodges Family in New England, containing the Names of over 1500 Persons, from 1633 to 1853, numbering Eight Generations. By Almon D. Hodges, ... *Boston: Printed by Dutton and Wentworth.* 1853. 8vo, pp. 71. B., BA., S. 32336

HODGES (A. G.) The Public Printing. Statements of John M. M'Calla and G. E. Russell, reflecting Certain Charges relative to the Division of the Profits of the Public Printing, preferred by A. G. Hodges. *Frankfort: Printed by Robinson & Adams.* 1840. 8vo, pp. 15. H. 32337

HODGES (C. E.) ... Disunion our Wisdom and our Duty. By Rev. Charles E. Hodges. [*New York: American Anti-Slavery Society.* n. d.] 16mo, pp. 12. B. 32338

HODGES (C. W.) Sermons. By Rev. C. W. Hodges. *Burlington.* 1850. 12mo. Portrait. 32339

[HODGES (James).] A | Just and Modest | Vindication | of the | Scots Design, | For the having Established a | Colony at Darien. | With | A Brief Display, how much it is | their Interest, to apply themselves | to Trade, and particularly to that | which is Foreign. | [*London?*] *Printed in the Year,* 1699. | 8vo, pp. (30), 214.

HODGES (J.) Report of the Trial of John Hodges, Esq. on a Charge of High Treason; ... in the Circuit Court ... for the Maryland District ... May Term, 1815. [n. p. n. d.] 8vo, pp. 35. BA., S. 32341

Hodges was arrested for assisting in the return of British prisoners to their army, during the attack on Washington and the surrounding country in 1814.

HODGES (J.) Construction of the Great Victoria Bridge in Canada. [Elaborately Illustrated by Views, Plans, Elevations, and Details of the Bridge; together with Designs of the Machinery and Contrivances used in the Construction ... .] By James Hodges, Engineer ... . *London: John Weale.* 1860. 4to, pp. (6), 104. Atlas of 45 Plates in folio. B. 32342

A most important and valuable engineering work.

HODGES (J.) A Tract for the Times. By Jubal Hodges. *Ogdensburg.* 1852. 32343

HODGES (R. M.) An Address ... at the Laying of the Corner-Stone of a House of Worship for the First Congregational Society in Somerville, September 28, 1844. By R. M. Hodges. *Cambridge: Metcalf and Company, Printers.* 1844. 8vo, pp. 19. M.

HODGES. ... A Sermon commemorative of The Rev. Edmund Quincy Sewall, Preached in Scituate and in Cohasset ... September 23d, 1866. By the Rev. R. M. Hodges. *Boston: Leonard C. Bowles.* 1866. 8vo, pp. 24. 32345

Also: An Address, delivered before the Bridgewater Society for the Promotion of Temperance, Jan. 4th, 1831. ... *Boston: Carter, Hendee and Babcock.* 1831. 8vo, pp. 15.—A Sermon delivered ... in West-Bridgewater, 27th February, 1831, ... after the Interment of ... Rev. John Reed, D.D. ... *Cambridge: E. W. Metcalf and Company.* 1831. 8vo, pp. 32.— ... A Sermon ... March, 1869, before the First Congregational Society in Somerville, in Commemoration of the Seventy-Fifth Anniversary ... *Boston: Little, Brown and Company.* 1869. 8vo, pp. 35. B.

HODGES (R.) Record of the Families in New England, of the name of Hodges; Collected ... by Rufus Hodges ... . *Cincinnati.* 1837. 12mo, pp. 22. 32346

HODGINS (J. G.) The Geography and History of British America, and of the other Colonies of the Empire; to which is added a Sketch of the various Indian Tribes of Canada, and brief biographical Notices of eminent Persons connected with the History of Canada. By J. George Hodgins ... . *Toronto.* 1857. 8vo, pp. 128. + Second Edition. [*Ibid.*] 1860. 32357

[HODGINS.] Progress of the Common School System of Upper Canada. *Toronto.* 1856. 8vo. S. 32348

HODGINS. A School History of Canada and of the other British North American Provinces. By J. George Hodgins, LL.B., F.R.G.S., ... *Montreal.* 1865. 12mo, pp. 282. 32349

Also: Memorandum of the Steps ... taken ... to establish a System of Meteorological Observations through Upper Canada. ... 8vo. Map.—A Summary of Canons and Resolutions adopted by the Synod of the Diocese of Toronto, from 1851 to 1864 inclusive. With an Index. ... *Toronto.* 1865. 8vo, pp. 79.

HODGINS (T.) The Canada Educational Directory, and Calendar for 1857–1858: containing an Account of the Schools, Colleges, and Universities; the Professions, Scientific and Literary Institutions; Decisions of the Courts on School Questions, &c., &c. Edited by Thomas Hodgins. *Toronto: Maclear & Co.* 1857. 8vo, pp. 144. H., S. 32350

Includes historical notices of the schools and other institutions enumerated. Also: The Educational Manual for Upper Canada: containing the Laws and Regulations relating to Common and Grammar Schools and the University of Toronto, with ... Notes ... *Toronto.* 1856. 8vo, pp. 167.

HODGKIN (T.) An Inquiry into the Merits of the American Colonization Society: and a Reply to the Charges brought against it. With an Account of the British African Colonization Society. By Thomas Hodgkin, M.D. ... *London: J. & A. Arch,* ... 1833. 8vo, pp. 62. Map. M. 32351

Also: A Letter on Negro Emancipation and American Colonization Society; in reply to the Accusations and Insinuations raised against that Benevolent and Important Institution. ... *London: J. and A. Arch* ... —On the British African Colonization Society. To which are added some Particulars respecting the American Colonization Society; and a Letter from Jeremiah Hubbard ... on the same Subject. ... *London.* 1834. 8vo. —On the Importance of studying and preserving the Languages spoken by Uncivilized Nations, with the view of elucidating the Physical History of Man. ... *London.* 1835. 8vo, pp. 12.

HODGKINSON (J.) A Narrative of his Connection with the Old American Company, from ... September, 1792, to ... March, 1797, By John Hodgkinson. *New-York: Printed by J. Oram.* 1797. 8vo, pp. 28, (1). BA., N., P. 32352

See Clapp's "Annals of the Boston Stage," pp. 14, 33, 52.

HODGMAN (E. R.) A Brief Memoir of Rev. Joseph Bancroft Hill ... June 16, 1864. By Rev. Edwin R. Hodgman. *Boston: Printed by A. Mudge & Son.* 1868. 12mo, pp. 126. 32353

HODGMAN (L.) A Memorial of the Golden Wedding of Leonard and Jenette Hodgman, at Stillwater, N. Y., Jan. 12, 1865. *Albany: J. Munsell.* 1865. 8vo, pp. 14. 32354

HODGMAN (S. A.) The Nation's Sin and Punishment; or the Hand of God in the Overthrow of Slavery. By S. A. Hodgman. *New York.* 1864. 12mo. 32355

HODGSON (A.) A Letter to M. Jean-Baptiste Say, on the Comparative Expense of Free and Slave Labour. By Adam Hodgson. The Second Edition. *Liverpool: Hatchard and Son.* 1823. 8vo, pp. (4), 55, Appendix, 17. B., BA., P. + *New-York: Reprinted for the Manumission Society, by Mahlon Day.* 1823. 8vo, pp. 50, 14. 32356

HODGSON. Letters | from | North America, | written | During a Tour | in the | United States and Canada. | By Adam Hodgson. | ... | *London: Hurst, Robinson, & Co.* 1824. 2 vols., 8vo, pp. (5), xv, 405, (1), Plate; (2), iv, 459, (2), Map. B., BA., C. 32357

The account of his visit to the Creek and Choctaw Indians, and the Appendix, contain interesting particulars relating to the aborigines and their antiquities, and on the traces of an Asiatic origin exhibited by the present race of Indians. Stevens' "Nuggets" gives the collation as pp. xv, 405, Errata, 1 slip; (4), iv, 472, Errata, 1 slip. 2 Plates.

HODGSON. Remarks | during a | Journey through North America | in the | Years 1819, 1820, and 1821, | in | a Series of Letters: | with | An Appendix, | Containing | an Account of Several of the Indian Tribes, | and the | Principal Missionary Stations, &c. | Also, | a Letter to M. Jean Baptiste Say, | on the | Comparative Expense | of | Free and Slave Labour. | By Adam Hodgson, Esq. of Liverpool, Eng. | Collected, Arranged, and Published by Samuel Whiting. | *New York* [*S. Whiting*]. 1823. 8vo, pp. 335. B., BA., C.

Mr. Hodgson's "book is creditable to his heart and his principles; we should be glad if as much could be said of his discretion and judgment."—*North American Review*, XVIII. 221. The edition described *supra* is probably more complete. *See also* "Edinburgh Review," XL. 427.

HODGSON (A.) A Lecture on Colonization and Emigration. Delivered at ... Wallsall, Staffordshire, ... March 20, 1849, By Arthur Hodgson, Esq. *London.* 1849. 8vo, pp. 30. 32359

HODGSON (F.) ... A Defence of the Methodist E. Church against the Calumnious Assaults of Rev. F. A. Ross and Rev. A. Converse, D.D. By Francis Hodgson, D.D. ... *Philadelphia: Thomas Stokes.* 1848. 8vo, pp. 113, (1). H. 32360

HODGSON (H.) Letters to Mrs. Kindersley. By the Rev. H. Hodgson. *London: J. Wilkie.* 18—. 8vo. 32361

"Relates to Mrs. Kindersley's notes on Brazil."—*Monthly Review*, LIX. 397.

HODGSON (J.) The Trial of William Wemms, James Hartegan, William M'Cauley, Hugh White, Mathew Killroy, William Warren, John Carrol, and Hugh Montgomery, Soldiers in his Majesty's 29th regiment of foot, for the Murder of Crispus Attucks, Samuel Gray, Samuel Maverick, James Caldwell, and Patrick Carr, on Monday Evening, the 5th of March, 1770, at the Superior Court of Judicature, Court of Assize, and General Gaol Delivery, held at Boston. The 27th Day of November, 1770, by Adjournment. Before the Hon. Benjamin Lynde, John Cushing, Peter Oliver, and Edmund Trowbridge, Esquires, Justices of said Court. ... Taken in Short Hand by John Hodgson. *Boston: Printed by J. Fleeming*, ... M,DCC,LXX. 8vo, pp. 217. + *London.* 1770. 8vo, pp. 216. 32362

Reprinted in 1807, 1824, and included in Chandler's "Criminal Trials," p. 302. "As the unfortunate accident which gave birth to these proceedings hath been taken up on party grounds, and the circumstances have been variously represented, those who are desirous of knowing the real state of the case, will here meet with satisfaction."—*Monthly Review*, XLIV. 338.

HODGSON (Robert). Some Account of the Mosquito Territory, contained in a Memoir written in 1757, while that country

was in possession of the British, and now first published from the original Manuscript of the late Col. Hodgson, Commander in Chief of the Mosquito Shore. *London.* 1822. 8vo. + Second Edition. *Edinburgh.* 1822. 8vo. S. 32363

HODGSON. The Defence of Robert Hodgson, Esq. Late Superintendent, Agent, and Commander in Chief of the Mosquito Shore. Humbly addressed to the Right Honourable the Lords of Trade and Plantations. In Answer to the Complaints against him from sundry Inhabitants of the British Settlement there. *London.* 1779. 8vo, pp. (4), 146, Appendix, 77, (1). H.

This and the following were privately printed for the parties concerned.

HODGSON. To the Right Honourable the Lords of Trade and Plantations. The Reply of H. M.'s Subjects, the principal Inhabitants of the Mosquito Shore, to the printed pamphlet, entitled, The Defence of Robert Hodgson, Esq. late Superintendent of the Mosquito Shore, &c. *London.* 1780. 8vo, pp. 744. 32365

HODGSON (S.) Truths from the West Indies, including a Sketch of Madeira in 1833. By Captain Studholme Hodgson, His Majesty's 19th Regiment of Foot. *London: William Ball.* 1838. Post 8vo, pp. xv, 372. Plate. 32366

"Furious attacks on the planters, enlivened with horrors to suit all appetites."—*Athenæum*, 1839, p. 131.

H[ODGSON (William).] The Divine Cosmographer, or a Brief Survey of the Whole World delineated. *Cambridge: Daniel.* 1640. Folio, Engraved Title, and Plate by W. Marshall.

HODGSON (W.) An Examination of the Memoirs and Writings of Joseph John Gurney. By William Hodgson, Jr. *Philadelphia: C. G. Henderson & Co.* 1856. 8vo, pp. 145. H.

HODGSON. A Few Remarks on the Peculiar Trials of our Day; in Reply to an Editorial in "the Friend ...". By William Hodgson, Jr. *Philadelphia: Wm. S. Young, Printer.* 1858. 8vo, pp. 18. H. 32369

HODGSON. Select Historical Memoirs of the Religious Society of Friends, commonly called Quakers. For the Information of Young Persons, and Inquirers after Divine Truth. By William Hodgson, Jr. ... *Philadelphia: ... the Author*, ... 1844. 12mo, pp. 420. C., H., P. 32370

HODGSON. Select Historical Memoirs of the Religious Society of Friends, commonly called Quakers; Being a Succinct Account of their Character and Course during the Seventeenth and Eighteenth Centuries. By William Hodgson. ... Second Edition. *Philadelphia: J. B. Lippincott & Co.* 1867. 8vo, pp. 412, (1).

Also: Selections from the Letters of Thomas B. Gould, a Minister of the Gospel in the Society of Friends; with Memoirs of his Life. ... *Philadelphia.* 1860. 12mo.—A Short Memoir of Lydia Ann Barclay. ... *Philadelphia.* 1855. 8vo.

HODGSON (W. B.) The Gospels, written in the Negro Patois of English, with Arabic Characters, by a Mandingo Slave in Georgia. By W. B. Hodgson. *New York.* 1857. 8vo, pp. 16.

HODGSON. Memoir on the Megatherium, and other Extinct Gigantic Quadrupeds of the Coast of Georgia, with Observations on its Geological Features. By William B. Hodgson. *New-York: Bartlett & Welford.* 1846. 8vo, pp. 47. Map and 2 Plates. BA. 32373

HODING (S.) A Land Log Book, a Cluster of Anecdotes from the Journal kept by the Author in the United States of America. By Sarah Hoding. *London: Simpkin & Co.* 1836. 8vo. 32374

HÖHNE (F.) Wahn und Ueberzeugung. Reise des Kupferschmiede-Meisters Friedrich Höhne in Weimar nach Nord-Amerika in 1839, 40 und 41. *Weimar: W. Hoffman.* 1844. 12mo, pp. 435. 32375

HOEKSTRA (Klaas). Dagverhaal van het verongelukken van het Galjootschip Harlingen in Straat-Davids. De Togt van de Equipagie met sloepen over en langs het ijs, en overwintering van dezelve in het Noordelijk gedeelte van Groenland. *Harlingen: Vander Plaats.* 1828. 8vo. Map. 32376

Journal of the shipwreck of the ship Harlingen in Davis' Straits.

[HÖEN (M. W.)] ... Beschreibung von der unglücklichen Reise derer jüngsthin aus Teutschland nach ... Carolina und Pensylvanien wallenden Pilgrim, ... dem ... Kochenthalerischen Bericht ... entgegen gesetzt. ... *Frankfurt und Leipzig:* [*Andreä.*] M DCC XI. 8vo, pp. (14), 127. H. + *Hamburg: Wierng.* 1712. 8vo, pp. 384, (2). 32377

HOËVELL (W. R. v.) Beschouwingen over de emancipatie der slaven in Nederlandsche Indië zoodanig als die is voorgesteld door Dr. W. R. van Hoëvell. *Nieuwediep.* 1849. 8vo.

HOËVELL. De emancipatie der slaven in Nederlandsche Indië. *Groningen.* 1841. 8vo. 32379

HOËVELL. Slaven en vrijen onder de Nederlandsche wet. *Zalt Bomm.* 1854. 2 vols., 8vo. 32380

HOFF (B.) Pestilence, the Judgment of God: A Sermon, preached on the Day of Fasting, Humiliation and Prayer, in the Ref. Protestant Dutch Church at Rhinebeck, August 3, 1849, By Rev. Brogun Hoff. ... *Rhinebeck: William Luff, Printer.* 1849. 8vo, pp. 20. 32381

HOFFER (Adrian). Nederduytsche Poemata. *Amsterdam: Broer Jansz.* 1635. 4to. 32382

With emblematical engravings. This interesting and scarce volume of Dutch poetry contains: Felicitation for the West-Indian fleet; On the victory of P. Heyn in 1628; Poem on the capture of the silver-fleet by P. Heyn; Epitaph of P. Heyn.

HOFFER (I.) Genealogy of Mathias Hoffer and his Descendants in the United States. By Isaac Hoffer. *Mount Joy (Pa.): J. R. Hoffer.* 1868. 16mo, pp. (4), 31. C. 32383

HOFFMAN (Charles Fenno). The Echo, or Borrowed Notes for Home Circulation. *Philadelphia.* 1844. 8vo. 32384

In answer to the "Foreign Quarterly Review."

HOFFMAN. Greyslaer: A Romance of the Mohawk. By C. F. Hoffman, Esq. *New York: Baker & Scribner.* 1842. + *London: Richard Bentley.* 1842. 3 vols., post 8vo, pp. vii, 303; (1), 315; (1), 326. + Fourth Edition. *New York: Baker & Scribner.* 1849. 12mo, pp. 540. C. + *London.* 1849. 32385

An interesting historical novel, founded on Indian and early Border Warfare.

HOFFMAN. Wild Scenes in the Forest. By C. F. Hoffman, Esq. ... *London: Richard Bentley.* 1839. 2 vols., post 8vo, pp. v, (1), 292; (4), 284. Plate. + Two Volumes in One. *London: Richard Bentley.* [n. d.] BA. 32386

"The Indian legends and stories narrated in these volumes, though tinged with the graceful romance, in which the imagination of the author's genius clothed his writings, are still truthful to the phases of aboriginal life which the author had witnessed."—FIELD. Reprinted as:

HOFFMAN. Wild Scenes in the Forest and Prairie. With Sketches of American Life. By C. F. Hoffman, Esq. ... *New York: William H. Colyer.* 1843. 12mo, pp. viii, 13–207; (4), 13–210. B. 32387

HOFFMAN. Wilde Scenen in Wald und Prairie, mit Skizzen Amerikanischen Lebens. 1845. 2 vols., 8vo. 32388

[HOFFMAN.] A Winter in the West. By a New-Yorker. ... *New York: Harper & Brothers.* 1835. 2 vols., 12mo, pp. (4), 337; (4), 346. C. + Second Edition. [*Ibid.*] 12mo, pp. (2), 282; 286. B. 32389

"The numerous incidents of personal intercouse with Indians of various western tribes, the interesting details which the author's ardent curiosity regarding them drew from persons familiar with their life and habits, and the voluminous notes appended to these volumes, extracted from works not easily accessible, entitle them to a high rank in aboriginal literature."—FIELD. Reprinted in London as:

HOFFMAN. A Winter in the Far West. By Charles Fenno Hoffman, Esq. *London: R. Bentley.* 1835. 2 vols., post 8vo, pp. xii, 282; xiii, 286. 32390

Also: Love's Calendar, Lays of the Hudson, and other Poems. ... *New-York.* 1858. 24mo, pp. 221. S.—The Pioneers of New-York. An Anniversary Discourse delivered before the St. Nicholas Society of Manhattan, December 6, 1847. ... *New-York: Stanford and Swords.* 1848. 8vo, pp. 55. N.—The Vigil of Faith, and Other Poems. ... *New-York: S. Colman.* M DCCC XLII. 12mo, pp. 84. + [*Ibid.*] MDCCCXLV. *See also* Sparks' "American Biography," Second Series, Vol. III.; "The Literary World," Vol. I., II., and the "Knickerbocker Magazine."

HOFFMAN (C.) Longevity: being an account of various Persons, who have lived to an Extraordinary Age, with Curious Particulars respecting their Lives. By Christian Hoffman. *New York: J. S. Mott.* 1798. 12mo, pp. 120. C. 32391

HOFFMAN (D.) Emigration to the United States, upon a new and practical Plan. By David Hoffman, LL.D. *London.* 1851. 8vo, pp. 52. S. 32392

HOFFMAN. The Fremont Estate: An Address to the British Public respecting Col. Fremont's leasing powers to the Author from June, 1850. December 20th, 1851. By David Hoffman, LL.D. *London: Charles Richards.* [n. d.] 8vo, pp. (1), 63.

HOFFMAN. Letter by an American Citizen ... addressed to British Capitalists, and ... to Gentlemen disposed to emigrate to the United States, each possessed of about £3000; ... By David Hoffman ... . *London: John Miller.* 1849. 8vo, pp. 31. H.

Also: Views on the Formation of a British & American Land and Emigration Company. ... *London: John Miller.* 1848. 8vo, pp. 36. H.

[HOFFMAN (David).] Miscellaneous Thoughts on Men, Manners, and Things. By Anthony Grumbler of Grumbleton Hall. ... *Boston: Charles C. Little & James Brown.* 1841. 12mo,

pp. 374. H. + Second Edition. *Baltimore: Plaskitt & Cugle.* 1841. 12mo, pp. 374. C., S. 32395

Also: Lecture delivered in the University of Maryland, on the Law of Personal Rights and Personal Remedies. ... *Baltimore.* 1825. 8vo, pp. 50. M.—Viator; or, a Peep into my Note Book. ... *Baltimore: Plaskitt & Cugle.* 1841. 12mo, pp. 355. + *Boston: Charles C. Little & James Brown.* MDCCCXLI. 12mo, pp. 355. BA., H.

HOFFMAN (E. A.) The Martyr President. A Sermon Preached in Grace Church, Brooklyn Heights, N. Y., By the Rev. Eugene Augs. Hoffman, D.D., Rector, on Thursday, 20 April, A.D. 1865, Being the Day of Mourning appointed by the Governor of the State after the Death of President Lincoln. ... *New York: C. A. Alvord, Printer.* 1865. 8vo, pp. 16. 32396

HOFFMAN. The System of Free Churches. A Sermon ... 5 March, 1854. By the Rev. Eugene Aug's Hoffman ... . *New-York: Pudney & Russell.* 1854. 8vo, pp. 23. H. 32397

Also: Parish Statistics of Christ Church, Elizabeth, N. J., and Third Annual Address ... 1856. ... *New York.* 1856. 8vo.—Fifth Annual Address ... . *New-York: Pudney & Russell, Printers.* 1858. 8vo, pp. 24. H.

HOFFMAN (J. T.) Hoffman and Beach: their Lives and Services; with Biographical Sketches of Oliver Bascom, David B. M'Neil and Edwin O. Perrin. *New York.* 1868. 12mo.

Also: Finances, Faith & Credit of the State. ... Speech ... August 17 ... [n. p. n. d.] 8vo, pp. 12. H.

HOFFMAN (J. O.) Oration delivered before the Society of Black Friars, in the City of New York, November 10, 1788. By Josiah Ogden Hoffman. *New York.* 1788. 8vo. N. 32399

HOFFMAN (M.) Laws relating to the City and County of New York. Digest of the Charters, Statutes, and Ordinances of and relating to the Corporation of the City of New York, the Organization of the County, and to other Bodies or Officers connected with the Government of such City or County, with Historical Notes, Judicial Decisions, Opinions of Counsel, Reports, Resolutions, etc. ... By Murray Hoffman. *New York: E. Jones & Co., Printers.* 1865. 2 vols., 8vo, pp. 861; 1087.

[HOFFMAN.] A Letter to the Clergy and Laity of the Protestant Episcopal Church in the Diocese of New-York, on the question "Who shall be our Provisional Bishop?" By Pacificator. *New-York.* 1850. 8vo, pp. 11. S. 32401

HOFFMAN. Notes upon the Penal Law of the Protestant Episcopal Church. With a Draft of a General Canon. ... *New-York.* 1853. 8vo, pp. 103, viii. S. 32402

HOFFMAN. Speech ... on the Proposition to Amend the Constitution of the United States, respecting the Election of President and Vice-President ... March 29, 1826. [*Washington.* 1826.] 12mo, pp. 44. B., H. 32403

HOFFMAN. A Treatise on the Law of the Protestant Episcopal Church in the United States, by Murray Hoffman. *New York.* 1850. 8vo. 32404

HOFFMAN. A Treatise upon the Estate and Rights of the Corporation of the City of New York, as Proprietors. By Murray Hoffman, Esq. *New York: McSpedon & Baker, Printers.* 1853. 8vo, pp. xi, 15–320, cxxiv. 2 Plates. H. 32405

Also: Address to the Graduating Class of the Law School of Columbia College, of May, 1861. ... *New York: John W. Amerman, Printer.* 1861. 8vo, pp. 27. B.—Ecclesiastical Law of the State of New York. ... *New York.* 1868. 8vo.

HOFFMAN (O.) An Address delivered before the ... Alumni of Columbia College, May 2, 1832. By Ogden Hoffman. ... *New York: G. & C. & H. Carvill.* M DCCC XXXII. 8vo, pp. 28.

Comprises a sketch of the history of Columbia College from 1754, and of its Presidents and Professors.

HOFFMAN. Oration of Ogden Hoffman, Jun., at the Celebration of the Obsequies of Henry Clay by the Citizens of San Francisco, California, August 10th, 1852. *New York.* 1852. 8vo, pp. 16. 32407

Also: Speech ... Feb. 12, 1840, on State Appropriations. ... [n. p. n. d.]

HOFFMAN (W.) The Monitor; or, Jottings of a New York Merchant during a Trip round the Globe. By William Hoffman. *New York: Carleton.* 1863. 12mo, pp. xiv, 448. Portrait and 8 Plates. C., S. 32408

HOFFMANN (F.) The Treasure of the Inca. From the German of Franz Hoffmann, by J. F. Smith. *Philadelphia: Lutheran Board of Publication.* 1870. 16mo, pp. 169. 2 Plates.

HOFFMANN (F. A.) Die Entdeckung von Amerika. Nach den neuesten Quellen der Jugend erzählt. Von Friedrich [August] Hoffmann. Columbus. ... *Wesel: J. Bagel.* 1846. 16mo, pp. viii, 328. Plates. + [*Ibid.*] 1847. pp. viii, 367. Plates. H.

HOFFMANN (W.) Abraham Lincoln, der Befreier der Neger-Sclaven. Eine Erzählung für die Jugend von Wilhelm Hoffmann. ... *Breslau: Verlag von Eduard Trewendt.* 1867. 32411

HOFFMEISTER (J. M.) ... Come to the Rescue! An Appeal to the People of the South. By Rev. J. M. Hoffmeister. *Raleigh.* 1863. 12mo, pp. 14. B. 32412

HOFLAND (*Mrs.* Barbara Wreaks Hoole). Matilda; or, the Barbadoes Girl. A Tale for Young People. By Mrs. Hofland. *Philadelphia.* 1817. 12mo. P. 32413

HOFMANN (Johann Jac.) ... Lexicon Vniversale, Historiam sacram et profanam ... chronologiam ... geographiam et veteris et novi orbis ... virorum ... celebrium Enarrationem ... explanans ... . *Lugduni Batavorum: apud Jacob Hackium* ... . MDCXCVIII. 4 vols., folio. BA., S. 32414

This, like all books of its class, includes many American topics.

HOFSTEDE (P.), *and others.* Over de voortplanting van het Evangelie in de Colonien van den Staat. [*Haarlem.* 1778.] 8vo.

HOFSTETTER (J. B.) Galerie des voyages pittoresques dans l'Asie, l'Afrique, l'Amérique ... . *Vienne: Muller.* 1840. 8vo.

In French and German.

The Hog. Composed by a Father for his Son. *Washington.* 1823. 4to. P. 32417

[HOGAN (Edmund).] The Pennsylvania State Trials; containing the Impeachment, Trial, and Acquittal of Francis Hopkinson, and John Nicholson, Esquires. The Former being Judge of the Court of Admiralty, and the Latter, the Comptroller-General of the Commonwealth of Pennsylvania. Vol. I. *Philadelphia: Printed by Francis Bailey.* M,DCC,XCIV. 8vo, pp. xii, 776. B., BA., C., H. 32418

No more published.

[HOGAN.] The Prospect of Philadelphia, and Check on the next Directory. Part I. ... *Philadelphia: Edmund Hogan.* M,DCC,XCVI. 8vo, pp. 180. C., H., P. 32419

[HOGAN (John).] Thoughts about the City of St. Louis, her Commerce, Manufactures, Railroads, &c. [Missouri Republican.] *St. Louis.* 1854. 8vo, pp. 80. S. 32420

HOGAN (John S.) Canada. An Essay: to which was awarded the First Prize by the Paris Exhibition Committee of Canada. By J. Sheridan Hogan. [Second Edition.] *Montreal: B. Dawson.* 1855. 8vo, pp. 86, (1). 2 Maps. 32421

Also in French as:

Hogan. Le Canada. Essai auquel le premier prix a été adjugé par le Comité canadien de l'Exposition de Paris. Par J. Shéridan Hogan. *Montréal: Imprimerie John Lovell.* 1855. 8vo, pp. 106. 2 Maps. 32422

Also: Review of the Proceedings of the Reform Convention, held in the St. Lawrence Hall, Toronto, 9th November, 1859. ... *Toronto.* 1859. 8vo, pp. 15.

Hogan (W.) Considerations on the Improvement of Northern New-York; ... By William Hogan. ... *New-York: H. Anstice.* 1842. 8vo, pp. 20. H. 32423

Hogan (W.) An Address to the Congregation of St. Mary's Church, Philadelphia. By the Rec. Wm. Hogan. *Philadelphia.* 1821. 8vo, pp. 28. 32424

[Hogan.] Sundry Documents, submitted to the Consideration of the Pewholders of St. Mary's Church. By the Trustees of that Church. *Philadelphia: Printed by Lydia R. Bailey.* 1812. 8vo, pp. 26. 32425

Hogan. The Trial of the Rev. William Hogan, Pastor of St. Mary's Church, for an Assault and Battery on Mary Connell. Tried ... in ... Philadelphia, ... April, 1822, ... Taken in Shorthand by Joseph A. Dowling ... . *Philadelphia: R. Desilver.* 1822. 8vo, pp. 272, 8, (2). BA., C. 32426

Also: An Address to the Congregation of St. Mary's Church, Philadelphia. ... [n. p. 1820.] 12mo, pp. 35. + Continuation. 1821. 12mo, pp. 36, and another continuation, pp. 31.—Auricular Confession and Popish Nunneries (in America). ... *Boston: Saxton & Kelt.* 1845. 12mo, pp. 214. + 1868. 12mo.—Hogan Exploded; or, an Unprejudiced Refutation of Hogan's Farewell Address. ... [n. p. n. d.] For a list of publications relative to Hogan, *see* Finotti's "Bibliog. Cath. Amer.," p. 140, etc.

Hoge (A. H.) Address ... by Mrs. Hoge ... at a Meeting of Ladies, ... at ... Brooklyn, L. I., March, 1865, in Aid of the ... Northwestern Fair. ... *New York: Sanford, Harroun & Co.* 1865. 8vo, pp. 22. 32427

Hoge. The Boys in Blue; or Heroes of the "Rank and File." Comprising Incidents and Reminiscences from Camp, Battle-Field, and Hospital, with Narratives of the Sacrifice Suffering, and Triumphs of the Soldiers of the Republic. By Mrs. A. H. Hoge ... . With an Introduction by Thomas M. Eddy, D.D. ... *New York: E. B. Treat & Co.* 1867. 8vo, pp. 477. 7 Plates. B., C., H. 32428

Hoge (J.) The Law of Love: a Missionary Sermon delivered in Chillicothe, Oct. 5, 1817, By the Rev. James Hoge. To

which is annexed the First Annual Report of the Synod of Ohio. *Chillicothe.* 1817. 8vo. 32429

Hoge (J. P.) Speech of Hon. Joseph P. Hoge, of Illinois, on the Oregon Question. Delivered ... January 30, 1846. *Washington: Blair & Rives.* 1846. 8vo, pp. 12. 32430

Hoge (M. C.) History of Margaretta C. Hoge. *Philadelphia.* [n. d.] 12mo. 32431

Hoge (M. D.) ... A Sermon Preached at the Funeral of Capt. Benjamin Sheppard ... Richmond, Va. By Rev. Moses D. Hoge. *Richmond: H. K. Ellyson.* 1855. 8vo, pp. 19.

[Hoge.] The Victory Won: a Memorial of the Rev. Wm. J. Hoge, D.D. ... *Richmond, Va.* 1864. 12mo, pp. 16. 32433

Hoge (W. J.) A Discourse delivered by the Rev. William J. Hoge, D.D., Collegiate Pastor of the Brick Presbyterian Church, New York, on the Resignation of his Charge, July 21, 1861. *New York.: Baker & Godwin, Printers.* 1861. 8vo, pp. 26.

Hoge. Installation Services of Rev. William J. Hoge, as Associate Pastor ... Sermon by Rev. Dr. Spring, Charge to the Pastor ... by Rev. Dr. Krebs, Charge to the People by Rev. Dr. Potts. *New-York.* 1859. 8vo, pp. 46. S. 32435

Hoge. Sketch of Dabney Carr Harnson, Minister of the Gospel and Captain in the Army of the Confederate States of America, By William J. Hoge, D.D. ... *Richmond: Presbyterian Committee of Publication of the Confederate States.* 1862. 18mo, pp. 55. 32436

Hogerwaart (W.) Afscheids-reden tot de Gemeinte op Batavia, daar nog by komt Prof. Hoornbeek's Sorg en raad, aang. de Evangelie-prediking in Oost- en West-Indien. Vert. en opgeheld. door H. Velse. *s' Gravenhage.* 1732. 4to, pp. 12, 103, 64.

Last sermon to the congregation at Batavia, to which is joined Prof. Hornbeek's solicitude and counsel concerning the preaching of the Gospel in the East and West Indies. Translated and elucidated by H. Velse, V.D.M. "The part by Prof. Hoornbeek is highly interesting for the history of the Dutch Reformed Church in New Netherland and Brazil, giving a full list of all the Dutch Ministers there, for instance, J. Michaelius, J. Megapolensis, and others, with short notices on their lives, and many particulars relating to them, by the translator and publisher."—F. Muller.

Hogg (J.) A New, Authentic, and Complete Collection of Voyages Round the World: Undertaken and Performed By Royal Authority. Containing a New, Authentic, Entertaining, Instructive, Full, and Complete Historical Account of Captain

Cook's ... Voyages, ... To which is added, Genuine Narratives of other Voyages of Discovery Round the World, &c. viz. those of Lord Byron, Capt. Wallis, and Capt. Carteret. Together with the Discoveries of other Voyagers and Circumnavigators: And including the Substance of all the most remarkable and important Travels and Journeys, which have been undertaken at various Times to the different Quarters of the World. The whole comprehending A full Account, from the Earliest Period, to the present Time, Of whatever is curious entertaining, and useful both by Sea and Land, in the various Countries of the known World; being the most elegant and perfect Work of the Kind. Illustrated with a vast Number of Copper Plates finely engraved by the most eminent Masters. ... By Capt. John Hogg, ... *London: Alex. Hogg.* [1785.] 5 vols., 8vo. 32438

Hoit (C. W.) Fraudulent Mexican Land Claims in California ... . A Lecture ... March 24th, and repeated ... July 28, 1869. By C. W. Hoit. *Sacramento: H. S. Crocker & Co.* 1869. 8vo, pp. 26. Diagram. H. 32439

Hoit (T. W.) The Right of American Slavery. ... By T. W. Hoit ... . Third Edition. *St. Louis: L. Bushnell.* 1860. 8vo, pp. 51. B., C. 32440

Holböll (G.) Ornitholog. Bidrag til den Grönlandske Fauna. *Kjøbenhavn.* 1843. 8vo. 32441

Holböll. Ornithologischer Beitrag zur Fauna Grönlands, übersetzt von J. H. Paulsen. *Leipzig.* 1854. 8vo. Plate.

Holböll. Ornithologische und klimatologische Notizen über Grönland. [n. p.] 1854. 8vo. 32443

[Holbrook (Charles W.)] Record of the Descendants of Silence Holbrook of Weymouth, Mass. *Worcester: Printed by Henry J. Howland.* [1851.] 8vo, pp. 19. B. 32444

Holbrook (D. N.) The Boston Committee in Canada. A Series of Eight Letters. By D. N. Holbrook. *Boston.* 1851. 8vo, pp. 43. M. 32445

[Holbrook (Geo. R.)] A Description of the Boston Water Works ... from Lake Cochituate to the City of Boston. With Maps and Illustrations. *Boston: Geo. H. Holbrook & Co.* 1848. 12mo, pp. 46. B. 32446

Also: Holbrook's New England Railroad Guide ... . *Boston: Geo. R. Holbrook.* [1849.] 32mo.

Holbrook (J.) Ten Years Among the Mail Bags: or, Notes from the Diary of a Special Agent of the Post Office Department, By J. Holbrook. ... *Philadelphia.* 1855. 12mo, pp. 432. H. + *Boston: Shepard, Clark & Co.* 1856. 12mo. B. 32447

Holbrook (J. C.) ... A Sermon preached before the Cortland County Bible Society, at its Semi-Centennial Anniversary, ... at Homer, Dec. 18, 1866. By Rev. J. C. Holbrook, D.D. *Homer.* 1867. 8vo. S. 32448

Holbrook. Discourses, Dedicatory and Historical. By John C. Holbrook. *Dubuque, Iowa.* 1860. 8vo, pp. 16. 32449

Holbrook. Prairie-Breaking; or, Scenes in the Work of a Western Pastor. By John C. Holbrook, ... *Boston: H. Hoyt.* 1865. 18mo, pp. 89. 32450

Holbrook. Sketch of the History of the Congregational Church in Homer, N. Y. By J. C. Holbrook. [n. p. n. d.] 8vo, pp. 9. 32451

Holbrook (J. E.) Ichthyology of South Carolina, By John Edwards Holbrook, M.D. *Charleston.* 1855–57. 4to. 27 colored Plates. A. 32452

Holbrook. North American Herpetology; or, a Description of the Reptiles inhabiting the United States. By John Edwards Holbrook, M.D. *Philadelphia: J. Dobson.* 1836–38. 3 vols., 4to.

No more of this edition published; these three volumes were afterwards reissued with two others, dated as below which circumstance will account for the fact that copies of Vols. I–III. are not uncommon, entire sets are rare.

Holbrook. North American Herpetology; or, a Description of the Reptiles inhabiting the United States. By John Edwards Holbrook, M.D. ... *Philadelphia: J. Dobson.* 1842–43. 5 vols., 4to, pp. 152; 142; (2), 128; 138; iii–vi, 3–118; Errata, 1 l. 157 Plates. B., BA., H. 32454

The first systematic work, on the Reptiles of the United States, ever attempted. The plates are beautifully colored; and the work is worthy of a place in the library of the naturalist by the side of Audubon and Wilson.

Holbrook. Southern Ichthyology: or, a Description of the Fishes Inhabiting the Waters of South Carolina, Georgia, and Florida. No. 2. *New York: Wiley & Putnam.* 1847. 4to, pp. 32. 4 colored Plates. C. 32455

Holbrook (M.) An Oration ... 24th June, A.L. 5811. Before Ancient Land Mark Lodge, and Mount Vernon Chapter.

By Br. Moses Holbrook ... . *Portland: Printed by F. McKown.* 1811. 8vo, pp. 23. BA. 32456

Holbrook (S. F.) Threescore Years: an Autobiography, containing Incidents of Voyages and Travels, including Six Years in a Man-of-War. Details of the War between the United States and the Algerine Government, ... Also, Two Years in California, ... By Samuel F. Holbrook. *Boston: James French and Company.* 1857. 8vo, pp. 504. B., C., H. 32457

Holbrook (T. W.) Address to the People of the United States. The Great Rebellion: Causes, Progress, and Remedy, By Timothy Washington Holbrook. ... *Rochester.* 1864. 8vo, pp. 52. 32458

Also: God's Way of Peace: War the Duty and Destiny of the Nation; and a "Proclamation," 1864, in which he nominates himself for President of the United States, and in so doing, proclaims himself a fool.

Holcomb (C. P.) Address ... before the Montgomery County, Maryland, Agricultural Society ... September 14, 1854: By Chauncey P. Holcomb ... . *Washington: Globe Office.* 1854. 8vo, pp. 14. H. 32459

Holcomb (E.) A Wonderful Providence, in Many Incidents at Sea: an Engagement with a Pirate, and a Mutiny at Sea, on Board Ship Ann, of Boston ... By Eliah Holcomb. ... Eighth Edition. *Boston: Damrell & Moore.* 1853. 8vo, pp. 36. B.

Holcomb (R.) Sermon at Sterling Mass., on the Fast, July 23, 1812. By Reuben Holcomb. *Worcester.* [n. d.] 8vo. W.

Holcombe (H.) The Advocate of Peace. By Henry Holcombe, D.D. ... *Philadelphia.* 1823. 12mo, pp. 60. 32462

Holcombe. A Sermon, Occasioned by The Death of Mr. Charles Bealer, Delivered at Euhaw [*sic*], By Henry Holcombe, ... *Charleston: Printed by Marbland & McIver.* MDCCXCIII. 8vo, pp. 12. 32463

Holcombe. A Sermon, Occasioned By the Death of Lieutenant-General George Washington ... . Delivered in ... Savannah, Georgia, January 19th, 1800. ... By Henry Holcombe, Minister of the Word of God in Savannah. ... [*Savannah: Printed by Seymour & Woolhopter.* [1800.] 4to, pp. 16, (2). BA.

Also: The First Fruits, in a Series of Letters. ... *Philadelphia: Ann Cochran.* 1812. 16mo, pp. 228. Portrait. C.—Letter to Thos. Gillison, Esq., of South Carolina, on the Silence of the Second Annual Report of the Baptist Board of Foreign Missions

relative to their Exchange of Vice Presidents. ... *Philadelphia.* 1816. 8vo.—Protest against the Proceedings of the Philadelphia Baptist Association by the First Baptist Church of Philadelphia, with prefatory and concluding Extracts and Remarks. ... *Philadelphia.* 1816. 8vo.—The Whole Truth relative to the Controversy betwixt the American Baptists. Part I. ... *Philadelphia.* 1820. 8vo. *See* Georgia, No. 27049.

Holcombe (H.) A History of the Rise and Progress of the Baptists in Alabama. With a Miniature History of the Denomination from the Apostolic Age down to the Present Time. By Hosea Holcombe. *Philadelphia: King & Baird.* 1840. 16mo, pp. 375. C. 32465

Holcombe (J. P.) The Election of a Black Republican President an Overt Act of Aggression on the Right of Property in Slaves: ... a Speech before the People of Albemarle, on the 2d ... January, 1860. By James P. Holcombe, ... *Richmond: Chas. H. Wynne, Printer.* 1860. 8vo, pp. 16. H. 32466

Holcombe. Sketches of the Political Issues and Controversies of the Revolution: A Discourse ... January 17, 1856. By James P. Holcombe ... . *Richmond: William H. Clemmitt.* 1856. 8vo, pp. 63. B., H. 32467

Also: An Address ... before the ... Alumni of the University of Virginia ... June 29th, 1853. ... *Richmond: Macfarlane & Fergusson.* 1853. 8vo, pp. 43. B., H.—An Address ... before ... Virginia State Agricultural Society, November 4th, 1858. ... *Richmond: Macfarlane & Fergusson.* 1858. 8vo, pp. 21.— ... Is Slavery Consistent with National Law? An Address ... before the Virginia State Agricultural Society ... 4th November, 1858. ... [*Richmond.*] 1858. 8vo, pp. 21.—Literature in Letters; Manners, Art, Criticism, Biography, History, and Morals, Illustrated in the Correspondence of Eminent Persons. ... *New York: D. Appleton and Company.* 1866. 8vo, pp. xvi, 520. B., C., H.

Holcombe (W. H.) The Alternative: A Separate Nationality, or the Africanization of the South. By William H. Holcombe. *New Orleans.* 1860. 8vo, pp. 15. B., H. 32468

Holcombe. Suggestions as to the Spiritual Philosophy of African Slavery. ... By William H. Holcombe, M.D. *New York: Mason Brothers.* 1861. 8vo, pp. 32. B. 32469

Also: Poems. ... *New-York: Mason Brothers.* 1860. 12mo, pp. 360.—Report on the Yellow Fever of 1867. ... *New Orleans: A. Eyrick.* 1869. 8vo, pp. 22. H.

Holden (A. W.) Early Voyages of Discovery—First Attempts to establish a Colony in Canada—Discovery of Northern New York, by Samuel de Champlain, in 1609—Battle between the Algonquins and Iroquois. *Albany: J. Munsell.* 1851. 8vo, pp. 8. 32470

Intended as a sample of a History of Warren County, N. Y.

Holden (C.) Doings of the First Editors and Publishers' Convention in Maine. Address of Hon. Charles Holden. *Portland: Printed by Brown Thurston.* 1864. 8vo, pp. 39. 32471

Holden (F. A.) Genealogy of the Descendants of Banfield Capron, from A.D. 1660 to A.D. 1859. By Frederic A. Holden. ... *Boston: Printed by Geo. C. Rand & Avery.* 1859. 12mo, pp. 263. Portraits. B., C., S. 32472

Holden (H.) A Narrative of the Shipwreck, Captivity and Sufferings of Horace Holden and Benj. H. Nute: who were cast away in the American Ship Mentor, on the Pelew Islands, in the Year 1832; and for Two Years afterwards were subjected to unheard of Sufferings among the Barbarous Inhabitants of Lord North's Island. *Boston: Russell, Shattuck & Co.* 1836. 12mo, pp. 133. B., BA., C. + Fourth Edition. [*Ibid.*] 1836. Plates. + *Cooperstown, N. Y.: H. & E. Phinney.* 1841. 12mo, pp. 120. 32473

Dedicated to John Pickering, Esq., who makes frequent reference to this narrative in his "Memoirs of Lord North's Island."

Holden (Nathaniel J.) ... Speech ... in the Massachusetts Senate ... June 9th, on ... the Boston, Hartford and Erie Rail Road ... . *Boston.* 1870. 8vo, pp. 8. H. 32474

[Holden (Oliver).] Sacred Dirges, Hymns, and Anthems, Commemorative of the Death of General George Washington, the Guardian of his Country, and the Friend of Man. ... An Original Composition. By a Citizen of Massachusetts. *Printed at Boston: by I. Thomas and E. T. Andrews.* [1800.] Oblong 4to, pp. 24. BA. 32475

Very rare. Also: American Harmony. ... *Boston: Printed by Isaiah Thomas, and Ebenezer T. Andrews.* MDCCXCII. Oblong 8vo, pp. 32. H., M.—Plain Psalmody, or Supplementary Music. ... [*Boston.* 1800.] 8vo. M.—The Union Harmony ... *Printed ... at Boston by Isaiah Thomas and Ebenezer Andrews.* 1793. 2 vols., oblong 4to, pp. 120; 175, (1). B., BA. + Second Edition ... [*Ibid.*] 1796. H.

Holden (W. S.) Confiscation; Emancipation. Speech of Hon. W. S. Holden, of Indiana, in House ... May 23, 1862. [n. p. n. d.] 8vo, pp. 8. 32476

Holden (W. W.) Oration delivered in the City of Raleigh, North-Carolina, July 4th, 1856. By William W. Holden, Esq. ... *Raleigh: Holden & Wilson.* 1856. 8vo, pp. 30. 32477

[Holden.] The President's Plan Considered. The Proposed Constitutional Amendment explained, and its Adoption urged. The Union the Paramount Good. [*Raleigh.* 1866.] 8vo, pp. 16.

Holden. Speeches of Gov. William W. Holden and Gen. Nelson A. Miles, in Raleigh, N. C., November 6, 1868, at the Grant and Colfax Celebration. *New York: C. A. Alvord.* 1869. 8vo, pp. 11. H. 32479

Holder (C.) The Faith and Testimony of the Martyrs, and Suffering Servants of Christ Jesus, persecuted in New England vindicated, against the lyes and slanders cast on them by Nathaniel Morton in his Book intituled, New England's Memorial. Written for the sake of the honest hearted, by a servant of the living God, who is a witness of the Resurrection of Christ Jesus, and of his appearance the second time without sin unto salvation, Christopher Holder. [n. p. about 1670.] 4to, pp. 12. 32480

A tract of extreme rarity—partly written by John Rous.

Holder (H. E.) A Short Essay on the Subject of Negro Slavery, with a Particular Reference to the Island of Barbadoes. By the Rev. H. E. Holder, of that Place. *London: Printed by Couchman and Fry.* M DCC LXXXVIII. 8vo, pp. 45. H. 32481

See "M. Rev.," LXXX. 350. Also: Discourses delivered in the Island of Barbadoes ... 1791. 2 vols.

Hold-Fast (S.), *pseudon.* Facts are Stubborn Things, or Nine plain Questions to the People of Connecticut, with a Brief Reply to Each. By Simon Hold-Fast. ... *Hartford: Printed by Hudson and Goodwin.* 1803. 8vo, pp. 23. BA. 32482

Holdich (J.) The Life of Wilbur Fisk, D.D., First President of the Wesleyan University. By Joseph Holdich. *New York.* 1842. 8vo. + *New-York: Harper & Brothers.* 1856. 8vo, pp. 455. B., C. 32483

Holdich. The Wesleyan Student; or Memoirs of Aaron Haynes Hurd, late a Member of the Wesleyan University, Middletown, Conn. By Joseph Holdich. *Middletown (Conn.): E. Hunt & Co.* 1839. 18mo, pp. 281. C. 32484

Also: ... A Sermon, preached to the Students of the Wesleyan University, on the Death of Mr. William F. Bailey, ... *Middletown, Con.: Wm. D. Starr, Printer.* 1836. 8vo, pp. 32. BA.—True Greatness: a Discourse on ... Rev. Willbur Fisk ... in ... Middletown, Conn., ... April 3d, 1839. ... *Middletown: E. Hunt & Co.* 1839. 8vo, pp. 36. B., H.

Holditch (R.) The Emigrant's Guide to the United States of America; ... the Latest Information concerning the Climate, Productions, Population, Manners, Prices of Land, Labour, and Provisions, ... By Robert Holditch, Esq. ... *London: William Hone.* 1818. 8vo, pp. iv, 123, (1). C., H. 32485

Holdredge (S. M.) State, Territorial, and Ocean Guide Book of the Pacific; ... and the interior, including California, Oregon, Nevada, Washington, Idaho, Utah, New Mexico, Arizona, British Columbia, Vancouver's Island, Central and South America, and Mexico. By Sterling M. Holdredge. *San Francisco.* 1865. 12mo. 32486

Holdsworth (E.) Muscipula: The Mouse-Trap, or the Battle of the Cambrians and Mice; a Poem by Edward Holdsworth, translated into English by R. Lewis. *Annapolis.* 1728. 8vo. 32487

Of great rarity. We are informed in the translator's dedication to Governor Calvert, that this is the

"First Essay
Of Latin Poetry, in English dress,
Which Maryland hath published from the press."

It has a Latin as well as an English title. The three lines in Greek letters in the Latin title are supplied with a pen, the printer probably not having any Greek type.

Hole in the Wall; or a Peep at the Creed-Worshippers. Embellished with Cuts by the Author. [n. p.] 1828. 8vo, pp. 36. 32488

Relates to the Hicksite (Quaker) controversy.

Holgate (J. B.) American Genealogy, being a History of some of the Early Settlers of North America and their Descendants, from their First Emigration to the Present Time, with their Intermarriages and Collateral Branches, including Notices of Prominent Families and Distinguished Individuals, with Anecdotes, Reminiscences, Traditions, Sketches of the Founding of Cities, Villages, Manors, and progressive Improvements of the Country, from its Wilderness State to the Present Era. Illustrated by Genealogical Tables. By Jerome B. Holgate ... *Albany: Printed by Joel Munsell.* 1848. 4to, pp. (6), 244, (1).

First issued in parts. Two hundred and fifty copies printed; now very scarce. Some copies have the imprint, *New York: George P. Putnam.* 1851.

Holgate. Atlas of American History, On a Novel Plan. Presenting, at one View, the most Important Events in the History of the Country, from its Discovery by Columbus down to the Present Time, 1842: Including the Spanish and English Navigators of the Fifteenth Century; Plantation of Colonies; Founding of Cities; Governors of the Colonies and of the Republic; Indian Wars; Sachems, Divines, First Printers, Statesmen, Orators, Warriors, Admirals, Commodores, Ministers Plenipotentiary, Secretaries, and Presidents; Battles, Sieges,

Earthquakes, and Remarkable Phenomena; Population at Different Periods, Literature, Slave Trade, and Ecclesiastical History: Arranged Contemporaneously with the Kings of England, France, and at Particular Times of Other Kingdoms. By James B. Holgate, ... Designed to be the Same to History that Maps are to Geography. ... *New York.* 1842. Folio, pp. 10. 6 Charts.

See "N. A. Rev.," Jan., 1843.

Holgate. Genealogical, Historical, Biographical, and Chronological Chart. By J. B. Holgate. *New-York.* 1838. Folio. + Key [to the same]. 8vo. A., P. 32491

Holguin (D. G.) Vocabulario de la Lengua general de todo el Peru llamada Quichua, o del Inca. Compvesta por el Padre Diego Gonzalez Holguin de la Compañia de Jesus Natural de Caceres. *En la Ciudad de los Reyes.* 1586. 8vo. J.C.B. 32492

A volume of extreme rarity. *See* Brunet, III. 262.

Holguin. Gramatica y | arte nveva dela | lengva general de todo el | Peru, llamada lengua Qquichua, o | lengua del Inca. | Añadida y cvmplida en todo lo qve le | faltaua de tiempos, y de la Grammatica, y recogido en forma de Arte | lo mas necessario enlos dos primeros libros. Con mas otros dos | libros postreros de addiciones al Arte para mas perficio- | narla, el vno para alcançar la copia de vocablos, | y el otro para la elegancia y ornato. | Compvesta por el Padre Diego Gonça- | lez Holguin dela Compañia de Iesus natural de Carçeres. | ... | *Impressa enla Ciudad de los Reyes del Peru por | Francisco del Canto impressor.* | *Año* M. DC. VII. | *Esta tassada esta Arte a vn real cada pliego en papel.* | *Y tiene* 37. *pliegos.* | 8vo, 4 l., Text, 143 l., (1). 32493

A volume of almost equal rarity with the preceding. *See* Ternaux, No. 307. It was reprinted as below:

Holguin. Gramática y arte nueva de la lengua general de todo el Peru llamada lengua Qquichua o lengua del Inca. ... Compuesta por el Padre Diego Gonzales Holguin. Nueva edicion revista y corregida. [*Genova: Pagano.*] MDCCCXLII. 8vo, pp. 320. A. 32494

Holguin. Vocabvlario | dela lengva gene- | ral de todo el Perv lla- | mada lengua Qquichua, o del Inca. | Corregido y renovado conforme ala | propriedad cortesana del Cuzco, Diuidido en dos libros, que son dos Vo- | cabularios enteros en que salen a luz de nueuo las cosas q̃ faltauan | al Vocabulario. Y la suma de las cosas que se aumentanse | vea enla hoja siguiente. Vanañadidos al fin los |

priuilegios concedidos alos Indios. | Compvesto por el Padre Diego Gon- | çalez Holguin de la Compañia de Iesus, natural de Caçeres. | Dedicado al Doctor Hernan- | do Arias de Vgarte del Consejo de su Magestad | Oydor de la Real Audiencia | de Lima. | ... | *Con Licencia.* | *Impresso enla Ciudad de los Reyes. Por Francisco del | Canto. Año* M. DC. VIII. | *Esta tassado este Vocabulario a vn Real cada pliego en papel.* | *Y tiene* 90. *pliegos.* | 8vo, pp. (8), 375, 332, (4). J.C.B.

Very scarce. *See* Ternaux, No. 314. "The 'Dictionary' of Molina, the most complete work on these languages," cites Holquin, "Vir sacrarum litterarum studio addictisimus, in quas multa commentatus est prælo digna."—Backer.

Holiday Exercises; or, the Christian A. B. C. consisting of Seven Alphabets, with a Text of Scripture affixed to every Letter. *Printed by Kline & Reynolds, and sold by Mr. Baley, Mr. Aitkin, Philadelphia, and Sam. Loudon, New York.* MDCCLXXXV. 8vo, pp. 32. N. 32496

Besides the alphabets, this very rare volume contains several pieces of American poetry. After Eliot's Harmony, and Aitkin's American Bible, this is one of the earliest specimens of printing parts of the Bible in English in America.

Holinski (A. J. J.) La Californie et les routes interocéaniques. Par Alexandre Jean Joachim Holinski. *Bruxelles: Meline, Cans et Cie.* 1853. 12mo, pp. 414. 32497

"Ouvrage prohibé en France."—Lorenz.

Holinski. L'Équateur, Scénes de la Vie Sud-Américaine. *Paris: Amyot.* 1861. 12mo. 32498

Holisso Holitopa. *See* Choctaw, Vol. IV., No. 12874.

Holland (E. C.) Odes, Naval Songs, and other Occasional Poems. By Edwin C. Holland. *Charleston, S. C.* 1813. 12mo.

Originally printed in "The Portfolio."

[Holland.] A Refutation of the Calumnies circulated against the Southern & Western States, respecting the Institution and Existence of Slavery among them. ... By a South-Carolinian. *Charleston: Printed by A. E. Miller.* 1822. 8vo, pp. 86, (1). BA.

Holland (Elihu G.) Essays: and a Drama in Five Acts. By E. G. Holland. *Boston: Phillips, Sampson and Company.* 1852. 12mo, pp. iv, (4), 400. Portrait. B. 32501

The drama is founded on Arnold's Treason.

Holland. Memoir of Rev. Joseph Badger. By E. G. Holland. Third Edition. *New York: C. S. Francis and Co.* 1854. 8vo, pp. 473. Portrait. + Fourth Edition. [*Ibid.*] B. 32502

Holland. Niagara and other Poems. By E. G. Holland. *New York: Rudd and Carleton.* MDCCCLXI. 18mo, pp. (8), 170.

Holland (F. W.) A Thanksgiving Discourse ... in Rochester ... November 26, 1846. By F. W. Holland. *Rochester: J. M. Patterson, Printer.* 1846. 8vo, pp. 22. H. 32504

H[olland] (Henry). Herωologia Anglica hoc est clarissimorvm et doctissimorvm aliqvot Anglorvm, qvi florverunt ab anno Christi M.D. vsq' ad presenten annum M. D. C. XX Viuæ Effigies Vitæ et elogia Duobus tomis Authore H. H. Anglo Britannoæ: *Impensis Crispini Passæi Chalcographus et Jansonii Bibliopolæ Arnhemiensis.* [1620.] Folio. H. 32505

Collation: Engraved Title, pp. (20), 240, (1). 64 Portraits, 2 Monuments. Rarely found complete; it is the first regular series of English portraits, and includes Richard Grenville, Thomas Candish, Sir M. Frobisher, Sir J. Hawkins, and Sir F. Drake, with memoirs. The "post prefatio" is often deficient. Hosmer's copy sold for £34 in 1861.

Holland (J.) Strictures upon the Letter of General Joseph Dickson. By James Holland. *Lincolnton.* 1800. 8vo. C.

Holland. Memoirs of the Life and Ministry of the Rev. John Summerfield, A.M., late a Preacher in Connexion with the Methodist Episcopal Church in America. By John Holland. With an Introductory Letter, by James Montgomery. *New York.* 1829. 8vo. + [*Ibid.* n. d.] + Fourth Edition. *New-York: Printed by William A. Mercein.* 1830. 12mo, pp. 360. Portrait. + Eighth Edition. *New-York.* 1846. 8vo. C. + With an Introductory Letter by James Montgomery. Abridged, with Additional Letters and Reminiscences. *New York: American Tract Society.* [1850.] 8vo, pp. 339. Portrait. B. 32507

Holland (J. C.) Speech of Col. John C. Holland at the Union Mass Meeting, Rockville, Montgomery Co., Maryland, Oct. 3, 1863. [n. p. n. d.] 8vo, pp. 8. 32508

Holland (Josiah Gilbert). The Bay-Path; a Tale of New England Colonial Life. By J. G. Holland. *New York: G. P. Putnam & Co.* 1857. 12mo, pp. 418. BA., H. + [*Ibid.*] 1862. 12mo. + *New York: Charles Scribner.* 1864. 8vo, pp. 418. B.

Holland. Eulogy on Abraham Lincoln, Late President of the United States, pronounced at ... Springfield, Mass., April 19, 1865. By J. G. Holland. *Springfield: Samuel Bowles & Co.* 1865. 8vo, pp. 18. B., H. 32510

Holland. History of Western Massachusetts. The Counties of Hampden, Hampshire, Franklin, and Berkshire. Embracing an Outline, or General History, of the Section, an Account of its Scientific Aspects and Leading Interests, and Separate Histories of its One Hundred Towns. By Josiah Gilbert Holland. ... *Springfield: Samuel Bowles and Company.* 1855. 2 vols., 12mo, pp. 520, Map; 619. B., BA., H. 32511

Holland. The Life of Abraham Lincoln. By J. G. Holland ... . *Springfield (Mass.): Gurdon Bell.* 1866. 8vo, pp. 544. Portrait, 3 Plates. B., BA. 32512

Also: [Address] at the Dedication of the New City Hall, Springfield, Mass., Jan. 1, 1856; with a Description of the Building. ... *Springfield.* 1856. 8vo, pp. 39.—Bitter-Sweet. A Poem ... *New York.* 1859. 12mo.—Gold Foil, hammered from Popular Proverbs. By Timothy Titcomb ... . *New York: Charles Scribner.* 1859. 12mo. pp. 358. + Seventh Edition. *New York.* 1859. 12mo. + [*Ibid.*] 1862. 12mo.—Letters to the Joneses. By Timothy Titcomb. *New York.* 1853. 12mo. + *New York: Charles Scribner.* 1863. 12mo, pp. 347. + Eleventh Edition. [*Ibid.*] 1864.—Miss Gilbert's Career. An American Story. ... *New York: Charles Scribner.* 1860. 12mo, pp. iv, 476. + *New York.* 1862. 12mo.—Plain Talks on Familiar Subjects. A Series of Popular Lectures. ... *New York: Charles Scribner & Co.* 1866. 12mo, pp. 335.—Timothy Titcomb's Letters to Young People, Single and Married. ... *New York: Charles Scribner.* 1858. 12mo, pp. 251. + [*Ibid.*] 1861. + [*Ibid.*] 1862.

[Holland (*Mrs.* Robert).] Channing, sa vie et ses œuvres, avec une nouvelle préface de M. Charles de Rémusat. Seconde édition. *Paris: Didier & Cie.* 1861. 12mo, pp. (4), xxxvi, 439.

Holland (S.) Charts of the Coasts and Harbors of New England. Surveyed under the Direction of the Lords of Trade, By Samuel Holland. *London.* 1776. Folio. 32514

Holland (W. M.) The Life and Political Opinions of Martin Van Buren, Vice-President of the United States. By William M. Holland. *Hartford: Belknap & Hamersley.* 1835. 12mo, pp. 364. Portrait. + Second Edition. [*Ibid.*] 1836. 12mo, pp. xvii, 13–372, Notices, 6 l. Portrait. C. 32515

Also: Address before the Hartford County Peace Society, May, 1831. ... *Hartford, Con.* 1831. 8vo.

Holland Land Company, *Erie County, N. Y.* Convention of Delegates on Title of Holland Land Company. Two Reports, and Appeal to the People of New-York. *Buffalo.* 1830. 8vo.

Holland Purchase [Baptist] Association. Minutes, 1821. *Batavia, N. Y.* 1821. 8vo. S. 32517

Holland's Alton City Directory for 1868–9. *Chicago: Western Publishing Company.* 1869. 8vo, pp. 168. 32518

Holland aan de Vereenigde Staten van Noord-Amerika, ten opzigte van de voldoening van derzelver schulden ten voorbeeld voorgesteld. *Amsterdam.* 1842. 8vo. S. 32519

In this piece Holland is represented to the United States as a model in discharging her debts.

De Hollanders in Iowa. Brieven uit Pella van een Gelderschman. *Arnhem.* 1858. 8vo. Plate. 32520

The Dutch in Iowa. Letters from Pella by a man from Gueldre.

Hollands Rijkdom, behelzende den oorsprong van den Koophandel en van de magt van dezen staat. Uit het Fransch vertaald, merkelijk veranderd en vermeerd, door E. Luzac. *Leyden.* 1781. 4 vols., 8vo. 32521

This "Holland's wealth, containing the origin of the commerce and the power of that state, translated from the French, considerably changed and augmented," forms a complete history of the Dutch commerce in all parts of the world. *See* Netscher's "Les Hollandais au Brésil." This book is partly a translation of the French work "La richesse de la Holland," by Accarias de Serionne, with many interesting additions. *See* F. Muller's Catalogue.

Het Hollants wijve-praetjen, tuschen drie gebueren Trijntje, Grietje, en Neeltje, noopende den tegenwoordighen Staet der Vrye Vereenichde Nederlanden, en het gepretendeerde Parlement van Engelandt. *Haarlem: Pt. Davidtsz* [*pseud.*] 1652. 4to, 12 l. 32522

Relates in part to the West-Indische Kompagnie.

Hollantse Mercurius historischwijs vervatende het voornaemste in Christenrijck voorgefallen van 1650. *Haerlem.* 1651. 4to.

This "Dutch Mercury" is a sort of Annual Register, and is continued to 1815, or later; the volumes which cover the period of the Dutch colonization in New-Netherland, and of the first period of the English government there, and the history of the War of Independence, are of much value to the student. The Dutch Colonies in Brazil, the Silver Fleet, Canada, Guiana, Cuba, etc., are also the subject of some of the articles. "This periodical publication, very similar to that of Wassenaer, contains some important materials for the History of New-Netherland."—Asher.

Hollemback (H.) The American Eclectic Materia Medica. containing One Hundred and Twenty-Five Illustrations, of Trees and Plants of the American Continent. By Henry Hollemback. *Philadelphia: For Sale by Henry Rittenhouse, M.D.* [1865.] 8vo, pp. 676. B. 32524

[Hollenberg (W. N.)] Die Deutschen in Amerika. Mittheilungen des Berliner Vereins für die ausgewanderten Deutschen der evangelischen Kirche in Westen Nordamerikas. *Berlin: Wiegandt und Grieben.* 1859. 8vo, pp. 40. 32525

Holley (A. L.) American and European Railway Practice. ... By Alexander L. Holley. *New York: D. Van Nostrand.* 1861. Folio, pp. 192. 77 Plates. B., BA. 32526

Also: Oration before the Theta Delta Chi Fraternity, June 1, 1855. ... *Providence.* 1855. 8vo.

Holley (H.) A Discourse occasioned by the Death of Col: James Morrison, delivered in ... Lexington, Kentucky, May 19th, 1823. By the Rev. Horace Holley ... *Lexington: Printed by John Bradford.* 1823. 8vo, pp. 37. B., H. 32527

Also: Address Washington Benevolent Society, 1815.—Pilgrims' Anniversary, 1817. *See also* our Vol. VI., No. 25167.

Holley (M. A.) Texas. Observations, Historical, Geographical and Descriptive, in a Series of Letters, written during a Visit to Austin's Colony, with a view to a permanent settlement in that country, in the Autumn of 1831. By Mrs. Mary Austin Holley. With an Appendix ... . *Baltimore: Armstrong & Plaskitt.* 1833. 12mo, pp. 167. Map. BA. + *Lexington, Ky.: J. Clarke & Co.* 1836. pp. viii, 410. Map. + *Baltimore.* 1838. 12mo.

See "N. A. Rev.," XLIII. 26.

Holley (M.) Address of the United States Anti-Masonic Convention, held in Philadelphia, September 11, 1830, to the People of the United States. Adopted upon the Report of the Committee, of which Myron Holley ... was Chairman. ... *John Clarke, Philadelphia:* ... 1830. 8vo, pp. 22. 32529

[Holley.] An Address to the People of the United States, on the Subject of the Anti-Masonic Excitement, or New Party. ... By a Citizen of New York. *Albany: Printed by J. B. Van Steenbergh.* 1830. 8vo, pp. 31. B. 32530

Holley. Oration ... 22d of February, 1812, being the Anniversary of the Birth-Day of Geo. Washington. By M. Holley, Esq. ... *Canandaigua: Printed by J. D. Bemis.* 1812. 8vo, pp. 16. B., BA. 32531

Also: An Initiatory Discourse ... at Geneva, 27th November, 1828, before ... the Domestic Horticultural Society. ... *Geneva: Printed by James Bogert.* 1828. 8vo, pp. 27. S.—Memorial of Myron Holley to the Legislature of New York. *Albany.* 1826. 8vo.—Speech, ... on the Canal Bill. ... *Albany.* 1821. 8vo.

Holley. History of the Erection of the Monument on the Grave of Myron Holley. [With Address of Gerrit Smith.] *Utica.* 1844. 12mo, pp. 20. 32532

Holley (Orville L.) A Description of the City of New York: with a brief account of the Cities, Towns, Villages, and

Places of Resort within Thirty Miles ... Edited by O. L. Holley. *New York: J. Disturnell.* 1847. 18mo, pp. 114. B., C. 32533

[Holley.] A Gazetteer of the State of New York, with the Census of 1840, and the Tables of Distances. *Albany: J. Disturnell.* 1842. 12mo, pp. 479. Map and Plate. C. + [*Ibid.*] 1848. 32534

Holley. The Life of Benjamin Franklin. By O. L. Holley. *Boston: Sanborn, Carter, Bazin & Co.* [1848.] 12mo, pp. (1), 468. Portrait and Illustrations. B. + *New York: George F. Cooledge & Brother.* [1848.] 12mo, pp. (1), 468. C. 32535

Holley. Life of General Israel Putnam. By O. L. Holley. *New York: George F. Cooledge & Brother.* [n. d.] 12mo, pp. 383.

Holley. New-York State Register, For 1843; ... with Political, Statistical, and other Information relating to the State of New-York and the United States. ... Contains a full list of U. States Government Officers, &c. Edited by O. L. Holley. *Albany: J. Disturnell.* 1843. 12mo, pp. 432. 32537

Continued to 1848, or later.

Holley. The Picturesque Tourist; being a Guide through the Northern and Eastern States and Canada; giving an accurate Description of Cities and Villages, celebrated Places of Resort, etc. ... Edited by O. L. Holley. *New York: J. Disturnell.* 1844. 18mo, pp. (6), 336. C. 32538

Also: ... An Address ... before the Mechanics of Troy ... on the 4th of July, 1825. ... *Troy: Printed by Tuttle and Richards.* 1825. 8vo, pp. 14.—An Address ... Mount Moriah Lodge at Palmyra, on the 24 of June, A.L. 5822 ... . *Palmyra, N. Y.: Printed by Br. T. C. Strong.* 5822. 8vo, pp. 13. H.

Holley (R.) Lecture on the Pilgrim Fathers; illustrative of the Government Prize Picture by Charles Lacy. By Robert Holley, D.D. *Manchester.* [n. d.] 4to. 32539

Holliday (F. C.) Life and Times of Rev. Allen Wiley; containing Sketches of Early Methodist Preachers in Indiana, &c. By F. C. Holliday. ... Edited by D. W. Clark. *Cincinnati.* 1853. 12mo. C. 32540

Holliday (J.) A Short Account of the ... Putrid Bilious Yellow Fever, vulgarly called the Black Vomit: Which appeared in the City of the Havanna ... in ... June, July, ... August, 1794. ... By Mr. John Holliday ... . *Boston: S. Hall, and C. Bingham.* 1796. 8vo, pp. 15. B., H. 32541

Hollingsworth (Robert J.) The Five Government Tests authorized by the Treasury Department of the United States, for Detecting Counterfeit Greenbacks and National Notes. [*Cincinnati: Author.* 1861.] 8vo, 2 l. c. 32542

[Hollingsworth (S.)] An Account of the Present State of Nova Scotia. *Edinburgh: William Creech.* M,DCC,LXXXVI. 8vo, pp. viii, 157. BA., C. 32543

[Hollingsworth.] The Present State of Nova Scotia: with a brief Account of Canada, and the British Islands on the Coast of North America. The Second Edition, corrected and enlarged. Illustrated with a Map. *Edinburgh: William Creech.* MDCCLXXXVII. 8vo, pp. xii, 221. Map. 32544

See "M. Rev.," LXXX. 82; Faribault, 918; "N. A. Rev.," XIX. 237. The following is a French translation:

[Hollingsworth.] Relation de l'État actuel de la Nouvelle Ecosse. Traduit de l'Anglois par F. Soulès. *Paris: Lagrange.* 1787. 8vo, pp. 139. 32545

Hollingsworth. A Dissertation on the Manners, Governments, and Spirit, of Africa. To which is added, Observations on the present Application to Parliament for Abolishing Negro Slavery in the British West Indies. By S. Hollingsworth. *Edinburgh: William Creech.* MDCCLXXXVIII. 8vo, pp. (6), 24. H.

See "M. Rev.," LXXVIII. 430. The following is a German translation:

[Hollingsworth.] Abhandlung von der Sitten der Regierungsart und dem Geist der Völker in Africa nebst dessen Anmerkungen über die Abschaffung des Sclavenhandels in dem Brittischen Westindien. *Halle: Johann Jacob Gebauer.* 1789. 12mo, pp. 116. 32547

Hollingsworth (Samuel L.) Memoir of Moreton Stillé, M.D. ... April 2, 1856. By S. L. Hollingsworth. *Philadelphia: T. K. and P. G. Collins.* 1856. 8vo, pp. 35. Portrait. H.

Hollinshead (W.) An Oration ... at the Orphan-House of Charleston ... October 18, 1797 ... . By the Rev. William Hollinshead, D.D. ... *Charleston: Printed by W. P. Young.* 1797. 8vo, pp. 22. H. 32549

Hollinshead. Sermon, Delivered March 21st, 1798, before the Incorporated Baptist Church, in Charleston, South Carolina. By Rev. William Hollinshead. *Charleston.* 1798. 8vo. 32550

Also: Dedication Sermon at Charleston, S. C. ... *Charleston.* 1787. 8vo. W. — Funeral Sermon preached at Dorchester, on the Death of Mrs. Eliza Adams. ... 1800.

Hollis (Thomas). Memoirs. *See* [Blackburne Francis)].

[Hollis (Thomas).] The Trve Sentiments of America: contained in a Collection of Letters sent from the Hovse of Representatives of the Province of Massachvsetts Bay to Several Persons of High Rank in this Kingdom: Together with Certain Papers relating to a svpposed Libel on the Governor of that Province, and a Dissertation [by John Adams] on the Canon and Fevdal Law. *London: J. Almon.* 1768. 8vo, pp. 158. B.

The collecting and publication of these important papers in England is due to Thomas Hollis, an ardent Friend of the Colonies in London. They include the celebrated letter written by Samuel Adams to Dennis De Berdt, Agent for the House of Representatives in England, dated January 12, 1768, adopted by the Colonial Legislature and signed by the Speaker. Until recently there were doubts as to the authorship of this document, but all uncertainty is now removed, Mr. Bancroft having in his possession the original draft in the handwriting of Mr. Adams. *See* "History of the United States," Vol. VI., pp. 120–125, *and* "M. Rev.," XXXIX. 87.

Hollis, *pseudon.* Facts [&c.] *See* Harvard College, *note.*

Hollister (G. H.) The History of Connecticut, from the First Settlement of the Colony. By G. H. Hollister. ... *New Haven: Durrie and Peck.* 1855. 2 vols., 8vo, pp. 508; 663. 17 Portraits. H. + Second Edition, Enlarged and Improved. *Hartford: Printed by Case, Tiffany & Co.* 1857. 2 vols., 8vo, pp. 613; 758. 17 Portraits. B., BA. 32552

See Putnam's Magazine, v. 549.

Hollister. Mount Hope; or, Philip, King of the Wampanoags: an Historical Romance. By G. H. Hollister ... . *New York: Harper and Brothers.* 1851. 12mo, pp. 280. H. 32553

"Fiction, tinged with a little fact."—Field. Also: Introductory Address ... April 9th, 1856, before the Litchfield County Historical and Antiquarian Society ... . *Hartford: Press of Case, Tiffany and Company.* M.DCCC.LVI. 8vo, pp. 24.—Oration at Litchfield, Con., July 4, 1842. ... *Hartford.* 1842. 8vo.—A Poem by G. H. Hollister, and the Valedictory Oration by C. F. Burnam. Pronounced before the Senior Class in Yale College, July 1, 1844. *New Haven.* 1844.

Hollister (H.) Contributions to the History of the Lackawanna Valley. By H. Hollister, M.D. *New York: W. H. Tinson, Printer.* 1857. 12mo, pp. 328. Portrait and Map. S.

Hollister (H.) Pawlet [Vt.] for One Hundred Years. By Hiel Hollister. *Albany: Printed by J. Munsell.* 1867. 12mo, pp. 272. B. 32555

Hollister (I.) Brief Narration of the Captivity of Isaac Hollister, who was taken by the Indians in 1763. *Suffield, Con.* 1803. 12mo. W. 32556

Hollister (O. J.) The Mines of Colorado; By Ovando J. Hollister ... . *Springfield, Mass.: Samuel Bowles & Company.* 1867. 8vo, pp. vii, 450. Map. C. 32557

Hollman (J.) Conflict of Jurisdiction between State and Federal Courts. Opinion in Case of Jos. Hollman *vs.* H. Fulton, on Habeas Corpus. *Keokuk.* 1869. 8vo. 32558

Holloway (J. N.) History of Kansas: from the First Exploration of the Mississippi Valley, to its Admission into the Union; embracing a Concise Sketch of Louisiana; American Slavery, and its Onward March; the Conflict of Free and Slave Labor in the Settlement of Kansas, and the Overthrow of the Latter, with all other Items of General Interest, ... By J. N. Holloway, A.M. *Lafayette, Ind.: James, Emmons & Co.* 1868. 8vo, pp. 584. B., H. 32559

Holloway (L. C.) The Ladies of the White House. By Laura Carter Halloway. *New York: United States Publishing Co.* 1870. 8vo, pp. (2), 658. 2 Plates, 13 Portraits. 32560

Holloway (W.) The Peasant's Fate: a Rural Poem. With Miscellaneous Poems. By William Holloway. ... *Wilmington, Del.: Printed by Bonsal and Niles.* 1803. 12mo, pp. x, (1), 128.

Holloway (W. R.) Indianapolis. A Historical and Statistical Sketch of the Railroad City, a Chronicle of its Social, Municipal, Commercial and Manufacturing Progress, with Full Statistical Tables. By W. R. Hallowav. *Indianapolis.* 1870. 8vo, pp. (2), vii, (1), 390. 24 Plates and Map. B., C. 32562

Hollowell, *Me.* Report of the Committee of the Massachusetts Legislature on the Hollowell and Augusta Bank. [n. p. 1816.] 8vo. W. 32563

Holly (I.) A Sermon preached at Suffield, the Sabbath after the news arrived that the People at Boston had destroyed a large quantity of Tea rather than submit to Parliament Act, &c., By Israel Holly. *Hartford.* 1774. 4to. 32564

Holly (J. T.) A Vindication of the Capacity of the Negro Race for Self-Government, and Civilized Progress, as demonstrated ... in the Haytian Revolution ... . *New Haven: William H. Stanley, Printer.* 1857. 8vo, pp. 48. Portrait. H. 32565

Holm (T. C.) *See* [Campanius (T.)], Vol., III., Nos. 10202–3.

Holman (J.) A Voyage Round the World, including Travels in Africa, Asia, Australia, America, etc. etc. from MDCCCXXVII to MDCCCXXXII. By James Holman, R.N. ... *London: Smith, Elder and Co.* 1834. 4 vols., 8vo, pp. (2), x, (2), 491; xiv, 492; xv, 473; viii, 519. 23 Plates, Maps, &c. BA. 32566

The author was the celebrated blind traveller. Reprinted 1834–5.

Holman. Travels in Brazil, Cape Colony, and part of Caffreland, Mauritius, Madagascar, &c. By James Holman. Second Edition. *London.* 1840. 8vo. C. 32567

One of the volumes of the preceding with a new title.

Holman (J. H.) The Spirit of '76: A Weekly Publication Devoted to Politics and Local Discussions in Kentucky during the Excitement caused by the Desha Murder and Beauchamp Tragedy. March 10 to July 14, 1826. *Frankfort, Ky.* [n. d.] 19 Nos. 32568

Holman (J. W.) ... A Sermon ... at the Dedication of the Free-Will Baptist Meeting-House, ... April 17, 1838. By J. W. Holman. *Boston: J. N. Bang, Printer.* 1838. 8vo, pp. 22.

Holman (N.) A Funeral Oration, delivered in ... Rhode Island College, ... June 29, 1796; Occasioned by the Death of Mr. Alva Spalding ... . By Nathan Holman. *Providence: Joseph Fry.* 1796. 8vo, pp. 14. 32570

Also: A Sermon ... at the Ordination of the Rev. David Holman ... in Douglas, October 19, 1808. ... *Sutton, Massachusetts: Printed by Sewall Goodridge.* MDCCCX. 8vo, pp. 34.—A Sermon ... February 17, 1811, occasioned by the Death of Deacon Amos Walton ... . *Taunton, Mass.: Printed by A. Danforth.* 1816. 8vo, pp. 20.—A Sermon ... in Easton, at the Interment of Mr. Isaac Lothrop ... May 11, 1815 ... . *Boston: Printed by Thomas Rowe.* 1817. 8vo, pp. 12. H.

Holman (W. S.) Right of Secession—the Impending Crisis. Speech of William S. Holman on the State of the Union ... January 16, 1861. *Washington: M'Gill & Witherow, Printers.* 1861. 8vo, pp. 15. H. 32571

Also: Frauds on the Treasury. Speech ... in the House ... April 29, 1862. *Washington: McGill & Witherow.* 1862. 8vo, pp. 16.

Holmberg (H. J.) Ethnographische Skizzen über die Völker des Russischen Amerika. Von H. J. Holmberg. ... *Helsingfors: Gedruckt bei H. C. Fries.* 1855. 4to, pp. (2), 141. A., B. 32572

Holme (B.) A Collection of the Epistles and Works of Benjamin Holme. To which is prefix'd, An Account of his Life and Travels in the Work of the Ministry, through several

Parts of Europe and America; Written by Himself. *London: Luke Hinde.* 1753. 8vo, pp. vii, 194. + [*Ibid.*] 1754. 32573

Chapters IV. and V. give an account of his travels in America from 1715 to 1720. He visited "scattering the truth and confounding the priests," various parts of New England, particularly Rhode Island and Connecticut, thence to Long Island, New York, New Jersey, Pennsylvania, Virginia, and Carolina.

Holme. An Epistle from Benjamin Holme, being a Salutation to Friends of Great Britain and Ireland. *London: Printed by the Assigns of J. Sowle.* 1718. 8vo, pp. 16. 32574

Written from the Bayside in Maryland, the 14th of the 4th month, 1717.

Holme. An Epistle to Friends and Tender-Minded People in America: ... By Benjamin Holme. *Printed by the Assigns of J. Sowle.* 1722. 8vo, pp. 16. 32575

Holmes (A.) American Annals; or A Chronological History of America from its Discovery in MCCCCXCII to MDCCCVI. ... By Abiel Holmes ... . *Cambridge: Printed by W. Hilliard.* 1805. 2 vols., 8vo, pp. iv, 484; 540, (1). B., BA., H., P., W. 32576

Holmes. American Annals: or, A Chronological History of America, from its Discovery in 1492 to 1806. By Abiel Holmes, D.D. ... With Additions and Corrections By the Author, and Maps ... *Cambridge (Mass.) Printed; London, Reprinted for Sherwood & Co.* 1813. 8vo, pp. (2), iv, 412; (2), 457. 2 Maps.

Holmes. The Annals of America, from the Discovery by Columbus in the Year 1492, to the Year 1826. By Abiel Holmes, D.D. ... Second Edition. *Cambridge: Hilliard and Brown.* 1829. 2 vols., 8vo, pp. xvi, 584; (4), 599. B., BA., H.

Best edition of "one of the best works of the kind ever published. Everything of importance relating to the History of America is related in a clear and concise manner; with copious and interesting notes and references to the original authorities: it is scarce."—Rich. *See* "N. A. Rev.," XXIX., "Quart. Rev.," II.

Holmes. The Counsel of Washington, Recommended in a Discourse, Delivered at Cambridge, February 22, 1800. By Abiel Holmes ... . *Printed by Samuel Hall ... Boston.* 1800. 8vo, pp. 23. BA., H. 32579

Very superior to many of the Washington orations, and very rare.

Holmes. A Discourse delivered before the Society for Propagating the Gospel among the Indians and Others in North America, at their Anniversary Meeting in Boston, November 3, 1808. By Abiel Holmes ... . *Boston: Farrand, Mallory and Co.* 1808. 8vo, pp. 68. B., BA., H. 32580

Includes historical notes on aboriginal affairs.

Holmes. The History of Cambridge. By Abiel Holmes, A.M. ... *Printed by Samuel Hall, Boston.* 1801. 8vo, pp. 67. B.

Reprinted in the "Mass. Hist. Soc. Collections," First Series, Vol. VII.

Holmes. The Life of Ezra Stiles, D.D. LL.D. A Fellow of the American Philosophical Society; of the American Academy of Arts and Sciences; of the Connecticut Society of Arts and Sciences; a Corresponding Member of the Massachusetts Historical Society; Professor of Ecclesiastical History; and President of Yale College. By Abiel Holmes, A.M. Pastor of the First Church in Cambridge. Published according to Act of Congress. *Boston: Printed by Thomas & Andrews ... May,* 1798. 8vo, pp. vi, 403, (1). Portrait of Dr. Stiles. B., BA., H. 32582

Dr. Stiles was for many years a minister in Newport.

Holmes. A Memoir of the French Protestants, who settled at Oxford, in Massachusetts, A.D. MDCLXXXVI.; with a Sketch of the Entire History of the Protestants of France. By Abiel Holmes, D.D. ... *Cambridge: Printed by Hilliard and Metcalf.* 1826. 8vo, pp. iv, 84. B., H. 32583

Also included in the "Mass. Hist. Soc. Collections," Third Series, Vol. II., and the "Worcester Magazine and Historical Journal."

Holmes. A Sermon on the Freedom and Happiness of America; preached at Cambridge, February 19. 1795. The day ... for a National Thanksgiving. By Abiel Holmes ... . *Printed by Samuel Hall, Boston.* 1795. 8vo, pp. 31. BA., W. 32584

Holmes. A Sermon Preached at Cambridge, ... after the Interment of His Excellency Increase Sumner, Esquire, Governor of ... Massachusetts, Who died June 7. 1799, Ætat. 53. By Abiel Holmes ... . *Boston: Printed by Manning & Loring.* [n. p. n. d.] 8vo, pp. 24. B., BA., M. 32585

Holmes. A Sermon, Preached at Cambridge, ... December 29, 1799, Occasioned by the Death of George Washington. ... By Abiel Holmes ... . [And Hymn.] *Printed by Samuel Hall, Boston.* 1800. 8vo, pp. 22, (1). BA., H. 32586

Holmes. Two Discourses, on the Completion of the Second Century from the Landing of the Forefathers of New England at Plymouth, 22 Dec. 1620. Delivered at Cambridge 24 Dec. 1820. By Abiel Holmes, D.D. ... *Cambridge: Printed by Hilliard and Metcalf.* 1821. 8vo, pp. 28. B., BA., H. M. 32587

Holmes. Two Sermons preached at Cambridge, 25 January, 1829, the XXXVIIth Anniversary of the Author's Installation. By

Abiel Holmes, D.D. ... *Cambridge: Printed by E. W. Metcalf.* 1829. 8vo, pp. 31. B., BA., H. 32588

Also: An Address, ... before the Washington Benevolent Society at Cambridge, 5 July, 1813. ... *Cambridge: Printed by Hilliard and Metcalf.* 1813. 8vo, pp. 28.—An Address ... before the American Antiquarian Society, ... Boston, on their Second Anniversary, October 22, 1814. ... *Boston: Isaiah Thomas, Jun.* 1814. 8vo, pp. 29, (1).—A Discourse, delivered at Plymouth, 22 December, 1806, at the Anniversary Commemoration of the First Landing of the Fathers, A.D. 1620. ... *Cambridge: Printed by William Hilliard.* 1806. 8vo, pp. 32.—A Discourse on the Validity of Presbyterian Ordination, delivered ... May 9, 1810, at the Anniversary Lecture founded by the Hon. Paul Dudley, Esq. ... *Cambridge: William Hilliard.* 1810. 8vo, pp. 44. B., H.—A Discourse ... at the Old South Church in Boston before the Society for Foreign Missions of Boston and the Vicinity, Jan 1, 1813. ... *Cambridge: Printed by Hilliard and Metcalf.* 1813. 8vo, pp. 36.—A Discourse delivered at the Opening of the New Almshouse in Cambridge, XVII. September, MDCCCXVIII. ... *Cambridge: Printed by Hilliard and Metcalf.* 1818. 8vo, pp. 40.—A Sermon ... at the Ordination of the Rev. Jonathan Whitaker, ... in Sharon, Massachusetts, February 27, 1799. ... *Dedham: Printed by Herman Mann.* 1799. 8vo, pp. 49.—A Sermon preached ... in Boston, and at Cambridge, April 25, 1799, the Day appointed ... for a National Fast. ... *Boston: Printed for Young and Minns.* 1799. 8vo, pp. 31.—A Sermon ... December 10, 1800, at the Ordination of the Reverend Otis Lane ... in Sturbridge. ... *Cambridge: Printed by William Hilliard.* 1801. 8vo, pp. 36.—A Sermon, preached at Cambridge, January 4, 1801, the First Lord's Day in the Nineteenth Century. ... *Cambridge: Printed by William Hilliard.* 1801. 8vo, pp. 27, (1).—A Sermon ... October 20, 1802, at the Ordination of the Rev. David Kendal ... in Hubbardston. ... *Worcester: Printed by Isaiah Thomas, Jun.* 1803. 8vo, pp. 36. BA.—A Sermon ... before the Massachusetts Missionary Society, ... in Boston, May 29, 1804. ... *Cambridge: Printed by William Hilliard.* 1804. 8vo, pp. 28.—A Sermon ... at Cambridge 30 September, 1804 ... after the Interment of the Rev. Joseph Willard, ... President of Harvard College ... . *Cambridge: Printed by William Hilliard.* MDCCCIV. 8vo, pp. 23. H. *See also* Lathorp (D.)—A Sermon, delivered at the Ordination of the Reverend William Bascom to the Pastoral Care of the First Church in Fitchburg, 16 October, 1805. ... *Cambridge: Printed by William Hilliard.* 1805. 8vo, pp. 31. H.—A Sermon, ... at Cambridge, April 6, 1809, the Day of Public Fast. .. *Cambridge: Printed by Hilliard & Metcalf.* 1809. 8vo, pp. 23.—A ... Sermon in Cambridge, December 25, 1809 ... . *Cambridge: Printed by Hilliard and Metcalf.* 1810. 8vo, pp. 24.—A Sermon ... at the Ordination of the Rev. John Bartlett, ... in Marblehead, 22 May, 1811. ... *Cambridge: Printed by Hilliard & Metcalf.* 1811. 8vo, pp. 46, (1).—A Sermon ... at the Inauguration of the Rev. Ebenezer Porter, A.M. ... at Andover, April 1, 1812. ... *Boston: Printed by Samuel T. Armstrong.* 1812. 8vo, pp. 31.—A Sermon ... at the Ordination of Rev. Thomas Brattle Gannett, ... Cambridgeport, Jan. 19, 1814. ... [With Memoir of Cambridgeport appended.] ... *Cambridge: Printed by Hilliard and Metcalf.* 1814. 8vo, pp. 36.—A Sermon ... before the Convention of Congregational Ministers of Massachusetts ... XXVII May MDCCCXIX. ... *Cambridge: Printed by Hilliard and Metcalf.* 1819. 8vo, pp. 36. B.—A Sermon ... at the Funeral of the Rev. David Osgood, D.D. ... who died 12 December, 1822. ... *Cambridge: Printed by Hilliard and Metcalf.* 1822. 8vo, pp. 24.—A Sermon ... at the Ordination of the Rev. Hosea Hildreth ... in Gloucester, August 3, 1825. ... *Cambridge: Hilliard and Metcalf.* 1825. 8vo, pp. 30. H. *See our* Vol. III., No. 10125, *also* "Mass. Hist. Soc. Collections," First Series, Vol. IX.; "Memoirs of the American Academy," &c., Vol. III., Part I.

Holmes. Proceedings of the Council at Ordination of Abiel Holmes, at New Haven, Sept. 13, 1785; with Memoir of the

Church at Medway, Ga., and Pastoral Letter. [n. p. n. d.] 8vo, pp. 16. M. 32589

Holmes (A.) An Address, ... before the ... Bar of the County of Bristol, Mass. at New-Bedford, June Term, 1834. By Abraham Holmes. *New Bedford: Press of Benjamin T. Congdon.* 1834. 8vo, pp. 24. BA. 32590

Also: Oration at Rochester [Mass.], July 4, 1801. ... *New Bedford.* 1801. 8vo.

Holmes (A.) Parties and their Principles: A Manual of Political Intelligence, exhibiting the Origin, Growth, and Character of National Parties. With An Appendix containing Valuable and General Statistical Information. By Arthur Holmes. *New York: D. Appleton & Company.* M.DCCC.LIX. 8vo, pp. 394.

Also: The Constitution and Personal Liberty. Speech ... March 9, 1859, ... [*Albany.* 1859.] 8vo, pp. 8. B.

Holmes (D.) Dialogues on Slavery, and Miscellaneous Subjects, Based on the Word of God, By Daniel Holmes. *Dayton.* 1854. 8vo, pp. 29. 32592

Poetical effusions.

Holmes (D.) The Wesley Offering; or, Wesley and his Times. By Rev. D. Holmes, A.M. ... *Auburn.* 1852. + *Boston: James P. Magee.* 1860. 12mo, pp. 308. B. 32593

Holmes (E.) A Letter to the Proprietors of Stock in the South-Sea Company. By Edward Holmes. *London.* 1853. 8vo, pp. 14. S. 32594

Holmes (E.) A Sermon, occasioned by the Death of the Rev. Peter S. Wynkoop, ... of Bloomingrove, ... preached in ... Hudson, November 3, 1848. By Edwin Holmes. *Albany: Printed by Joel Munsell.* 1849. 8vo, pp. 31. B. 32595

Holmes (E. B.) Speech of Mr. Elias B. Holmes, ... on the ... Mexican War, ... June 18, 1846. *Washington: Printed by J. & G. S. Gideon.* 1846. 8vo, pp. 15. Map. B., H. 32596

Also: Speech ... Aug. 7, 1848 [on the River and Harbor Bill. n. p. n. d.] 8vo, pp. 15. H., S.

[Holmes (Elizabeth Emra).] Scenes in our Parish. By a "Country Parson's" Daughter. To which is prefixed, a Memoir of the Author, by her Sister. *New York: Stanford & Swords.* 1851. 12mo, pp. xliv, 374. C. 32597

Holmes (Ezekiel). Report of an Exploration and Survey of the Territory on the Aroostook River, during ... 1838. By E. Holmes. *Augusta: Smith & Robinson.* 1839. 8vo, pp. 78, (1).

HOLMES (F. S.) Phosphate Rocks of South Carolina and the "Great Carolina Marl Bed." ... a Popular and Scientific View of their Origin, Geological Position and Age; also their Chemical Character and Agricultural Value; together with a History of their Discovery and Development. By Francis S. Holmes, A.M. ... *Charleston: S. C. Holmes' Book-House.* 1870. 8vo, pp. 87. 5 Plates. B., C. 32599

HOLMES. Post-Pliocene Fossils of South Carolina. By Francis S. Holmes, A.M. ... *Charleston: S. C. Russell & Jones.* 1858–60. 4to, pp. 118. 24 Plates. C. 32600

Also: The Horse not originally imported into America from the East. ... [*Charleston: James and Williams.* 1858.] 8vo, cover, pp. 16. *See* Tuomey (M.) *and* Holmes (F. S.)

HOLMES (G. F.) The Southern Fifth Reader. Prepared under the Supervision of Prof. Geo. F. Holmes. *New York: Richardson & Co.* 1867. 12mo, pp. 408. 32601

Also, a First, Second, Third, and Fourth Reader, all of which contain some historical facts.

HOLMES (I.) An Account of the United States of America, derived from Actual Observation, during a Residence of Four Years in that Republic: including Original Communications. By Isaac Holmes. *London: Caxton Press.* [1823.] 8vo, pp. (4), 476. Map and Table. C., H. 32602

See "M. Rev.," CI. 304.

HOLMES (I. E.) Speech of Mr. Isaac E. Holmes, of S. C., on the Civil and Diplomatic Appropriation Bill: ... June 28, 1848. ... [*Washington:*] *J. & G. S. Gideon, Printers.* 1848. 8vo, pp. 8. H. 32603

HOLMES (J. G.) James G. Holmes, Commissioner of the City Debt, to the Stockholders of the Debt, 1st October, 1857. *Charleston: Walker, Evans & Co.* 1857. 8vo, pp. 7, (1). H.

HOLMES (J.) An Address ... at Saco, on the 24th of June, A.L. 5818 ... before the Members of Saco Lodge. By Br. John Holmes. ... *Portland: Printed by Francis Douglas.* 1818. 8vo, pp. 46. BA. 32605

HOLMES (J.) Historical Sketches of the Missions of the United Brethren for Propagating the Gospel among the Heathen. By John Holmes ... . *Dublin: Printed by R. Napper.* 1818. 8vo, pp. v, (3), 472. H. 32606

HOLMES. Historical Sketches of the Missions of the United Brethren for Propagating the Gospel among the Heathen, from

their Commencement to the year 1817. By the Rev. John Holmes ... . Second Improved Edition. *London: Printed for the Author.* 1827. 8vo, pp. viii, 470, Errata, 1 l. 32607

The author was Minister of the Brethren's Congregation in Dublin, and gives an account of their missionary labors from their commencement to 1818. The Missions chiefly described are in Greenland, Labrador, among the Delaware and Iroquois Indians, the West Indies, South America, etc. Also: History of the Protestant Church of the United Brethren. ... *London.* 1825, 1830. 2 vols., 8vo,

HOLMES (J.) A Letter of Directions to his Father's Birthplace, By John Holmes. With Notes and a Genealogy by D. Williams Patterson. *New York: Printed for the U. Q. Club.* 1865. 8vo, pp. 76. 32608

HOLMES (J.) An Oration, pronounced at Alfred [Me.], ... 4th of July, 1815 ... By Hon. John Holmes. *Boston: Printed by Rowe and Hooper.* 1815. 8vo, pp. 23. B., BA., M. 32609

HOLMES. Speech of Mr. Holmes, of Maine, ... in the Senate ... February 18, 1830, in the Debate ... Relative to the Public Lands. *Washington.* 1830. 8vo, pp. 24. B., H., M. 32610

HOLMES. The Statesman, or Principles of Legislation and Law. By John Holmes. *Augusta.* 1840. 8vo, pp. 510. C., S.

Also: Speech, ... on the Subject of Internal Improvement ... in the Senate ... April 21–2, 1824. *Washington: Printed by Gales & Seaton.* 1824. 12mo, pp. 22. —Speech ... in the Senate ... on the Mission to Panama, March, 1826. [n. p. n. d.] 12mo, pp. 22.—Speech ... on the Nomination of J. J. Crittenden, 4th February, 1829. *Washington: Printed by Peter Force.* 1829. 8vo, pp. 16. H.—Speech ... calling upon the President of the United States for the Reasons of his Removing from Office, and Filling the Vacancies thus created, in the Recess of the Senate. *Washington.* 1830. 8vo, pp. 28. + [*Ibid.*] pp. 37.—Speech ... on the ... Appropriation Bill, ... April 9th, 10th, and 11th, 1832. [n. p. n. d.] 8vo, pp. 24. + [*Ibid.*] pp. 19. H.

HOLMES (J. McC.) The Crisis, and its Claims: A Sermon, ... October 19th, 1862, in ... Brooklyn, L. I., By ... Rev. John McClellan Holmes. *New York: Printed by Samuel Booth.* 1862. 8vo, pp. 16. 32612

HOLMES (J. M.) "The Pilgrim Temple-Builders," Sermon, Dec. 17, 1865, By John Milton Holmes. *New York.* [n. d.] 8vo. 32613

HOLMES (J. S.) An Oration delivered before the Municipal Authorities of the City of Boston, July 5, 1858, By John S. Holmes, together with the Speeches at the Dinner ... . *Boston: Geo. C. Rand and Avery.* 1858. 8vo, pp. 107. B. 32614

HOLMES (J. T.) Quincy in 1857. Or, Facts and Figures exhibiting its Advantages, Resources, Manufactures and Commerce. By Joseph T. Holmes. *Quincy (Ill.)* 1857. 16mo, pp. 69. C. 32615

HOLMES (M. J.) Ethelyn's Mistake; or, the Home in the West. A Novel. By Mrs. Mary J. Holmes. *New York: G. W. Carleton.* 1869. 12mo, pp. 380. 32616

HOLMES. Tempest and Sunshine; or, Life in Kentucky. By Mrs. Mary J. Holmes. *New York.* 1854. 12mo. + *London: J. Blackwood.* 1854. 12mo, pp. 178. 32617

Also: The English Orphans; or, a Home in the New World. ... *New York.* 1855. 12mo, pp. 329.—Homestead on the Hillside, Lena Rivers, Meadow Brook, Dora Deane. ... *New York.* 1858–60. 12mo.—Rose Mather; a Tale [of the War]. *New York: W. Carleton & Co.* 1868. 12mo, pp. 407.

HOLMES (*Lieut.-Gen.* Thomas H.) *See* Vol IV., No. 15367.

HOLMES (M.) A Soldier of the Cumberland: Memoir of Mead Holmes, Jr., Sergeant of Company K, 21st Regiment Wisconsin Volunteers. By his Father. With an Introduction by John S. Hart, LL.D. ... *Boston: American Tract Society.* [1864.] 16mo, pp. 240. BA. 32618

HOLMES (O.) The Harp and the Hickory Tree: Jackson and Liberty. An Address Delivered before the Baltimore Democratic Association. By Dr. Oliver Holmes. *Baltimore: Printed by Sherwood & Co.* 1853. 8vo, pp. 8. 32619

HOLMES (O. W.) The Benefactors of the Medical School of Harvard University; with a Biographical Sketch of the Late Dr. George Parkman ... November 7, 1850. By Oliver Wendell Holmes. *Boston: Ticknor, Reed, and Fields.* MDCCCL. 8vo, pp. 37. B., BA., H. 32620

HOLMES. Oration ... Boston, on the Fourth of July, 1863. By Oliver Wendell Holmes. *Boston: J. E. Farwell and Co.* 1863. 4to, pp. (8), 71. BA. + [*Ibid.*] 1863. 8vo, pp. 60. H. + *Philadelphia: Printed for Gratuitous Distribution.* 1863. 8vo, pp. 30. B., H. 32621

Of the 4to edition twelve copies only were printed for the author. Also: Astræa: ... A Poem ... before the Phi Beta Kappa Society of Yale College, ... 1850. ... *Boston: Ticknor, Reed, and Fields.* MDCCCL. 12mo, pp. 39.—The Autocrat of the Breakfast Table. ... Twenty-Second Thousand. *Boston.* 1859. 12mo. + *Boston: Ticknor and Fields.* MDCCCLX. 12mo, pp. viii, 373. Illustrations. + *London: Alexander Strahan.* 1865. 12mo, pp. xii, 329. B., H.—Boylston Prize Dissertations for 1836–37: on Indigenous Intermittent Fever, in New England; ... *Boston.* 1836. 8vo.—Humorous Poems. ... *Boston: Ticknor & Fields.* 1865. 12mo, pp. 100. Illustrations.—Oration ... before

the New England Society, in ... New York ... December 22, 1855. ... [n. p. n. d.] 8vo, pp. 46. H.—Poem ... at the Dedication of the Pittsfield Cemetery, September 9, 1850. ... [n. p. n. d.] 8vo, pp. 8.—Poems. ... *Boston: Otis, Broaders, and Company.* MDCCCXXXVI. 12mo, pp. xiv, (2), 163, (1). + *London: O. Rich & Sons.* MDCCCXLVI. 8vo, pp. xx, (4), 175, (1). BA. + New and Enlarged Edition. *Boston: William D. Ticknor & Company.* MDCCCXLIX. 12mo, pp. x, (2), 272. + *Boston: Ticknor, Reed and Fields.* MDCCCL. 12mo, pp. x, (1), 286. B. + [*Ibid.*] MDCCCLII. 16mo. + [*Ibid.*] 1862. 16mo, pp. xi, 410. + Seventh Edition. *Boston.* 1864. 24mo, pp. xi, 410.—The Professor at the Breakfast-Table; with the Story of Iris. ... *Boston: Ticknor and Fields.* MDCCCLX. 8vo, pp. (4), 410. B.—Songs in Many Keys. ... Fourth Edition. *Boston: Ticknor and Fields.* 1862. 12mo, pp. x, 308.—Soundings from the Atlantic. ... *Boston: Ticknor and Fields.* 1864. 12mo, pp. (6), 468. H.—Urania: a Rhymed Lesson ... before the Mercantile Library Association, October 14, 1846. ... *Boston: William D. Ticknor.* MDCCCXLVI. 8vo, pp. 31, (1). BA. + Second Edition. [*Ibid.*]

HOLMES (S.) ... A Sermon occasioned by the Death of Gen. Shepard Leach, delivered at Easton, Sept. 23, 1832. By S. Holmes. *Boston: Printed by Perkins & Marvin.* 1832. 8vo, pp. 29. B., BA. 32622

HOLMES (S. N.) Holmes' Patriotic Songs, For Coming Campaigns. By S. N. Holmes. *Syracuse, N. Y.* 1867. 16mo, pp. 59.

HOLMES (S. T.) The Verdict of the People—The Duty of Congress. Speech of Hon. Sidney T. Holmes ... January 3, 1867. [*Washington.* 1867.] 8vo, pp. 4. 32624

Also: Reconstruction. Speech ... March 10, 1866. [*Washington.* 1866.] 8vo, pp. 8. H.

HOLMES (S.), *Jr.* The Guerillas of the Osage: or the Price of Loyalty on the Border. By Stephen Holmes, Jr. *New York: American News Company.* 1864. 8vo, pp. 45. 32625

[HOLMES (Sylvester).] Official Papers [referring to S. Holmes and the North Congregational Church in New Bedford. *New Bedford.* 1843.] 8vo, pp. 8. 32626

HOLMES. A Sermon, ... at the Funeral of Mr. Shadrack Standish, November, 1837. Also, a Sermon, preached May, 1847, after the Death of Mrs. Averick Parker, ... By Sylvester Holmes ... . *New Bedford: Benjamin Lindsey, Printer.* 1847. 8vo, pp. 27. B. 32627

Also: ... A Sermon ... Day of Public Thanksgiving ... December 1st, 1814. ... *New-Bedford: Printed by Benjamin Lindsey.* 1815. 8vo, pp. 24. H.—A Sermon ... at the Ordination of Mr. Freeman P. Howland ... October 25, 1826. ... *Plymouth: Printed by Allen Danforth.* 1827. 8vo, pp. 24.—A Sermon ... at the Funeral of Hon. Laban Wheaton, at Norton, March 26, 1846. ... *Boston.* 1846. 8vo, pp. 24.—Report of the Doings of the Ecclesiastical Council convened May 14, 1850, to act upon the Dismission of the Rev. Sylvester Holmes, ... *New Bedford: Printed by E. Anthony.* 1850. 8vo, pp. 15.—A Statement concerning the Recent Assault upon the Character of the Rev. Sylvester Holmes, ... *Boston: Printed by Charles C. P. Moody.* 1851. 8vo, pp. 46. H.

HOLMES (W.) Prospect of the Times. By W. Holmes. *New Haven.* 1774. 8vo. 32628

HOLMES (W. H.) Free Cotton; How and Where to Grow it; with a Map of British Guiana, By Sir W. H. Holmes ... . *London: Chapman and Hall.* 1862. 8vo, pp. 43. B., BA., C.

HOLMESBY (J.) The Voyages, Travels, and Wonderful Discoveries of Capt. John Holmesby. Containing a Series of the most Surprising and Uncommon Events, which befel the Author in his Voyage to the Southern Ocean, in the year 1739. *London: F. & J. Noble.* [1739.] 12mo, pp. viii, 216. 32630

[HOLROYD (John Baker), *1st Earl of Sheffield.*] Observations on the Commerce of the American States with Europe and the West Indies; including the several articles of Import and Export; and on the Tendency of a Bill now depending in Parliament. *London: J. Debrett.* 1783. 8vo, pp. 75. 32631

HOLROYD. Observations on the Commerce of the American States. With an Appendix; containing An Account of all Rice, Indigo, Cochineal, Tobacco, Sugar, Molasses, and Rum imported into and exported from Great Britain the last ten Years. Of the Value of all Merchandize imported into and exported from England. Of the Imports and Exports of Philadelphia, New-York, &c. Also an Account of the Shipping employed in America previous to the War. The Second Edition. *London: J. Debrett.* MDCCLXXXIII. 8vo, pp. (4), 122, Tables I, iv. BA.

HOLROYD. Observations on the Commerce of the American States. By John Lord Sheffield. A New Edition, much enlarged. With an Appendix, Containing Tables of the Imports and Exports of Great Britain to and from all Parts. Also, the Exports of America, &c. With Remarks on those Tables, and on the late Proclamations, &c. *London: J. Debrett.* MDCCLXXXIV. 8vo, pp. (16), 288. 10 folded Tables; Tonage, etc., 1 page. BA. + The Sixth Edition, Enlarged. With a Complete Index to the whole. *London: J. Debrett.* M,DCC,LXXXIV. 8vo, pp. (4), xlvii, (1), 345, (24). 29 Tables. B. + *Dublin.* 1784. 8vo. 32633

HOLROYD. Observations on the Commerce of the American States with Europe and the West Indies; including the several articles of Import and Export. Also, an Essay on Canon and Feudal Law. By John Adams, Esquire Ambassador Plenipotentiary, from the United and Independent States of North America, to their High Mightinesses the States General of the

United Provinces of Holland. To which is annexed, the Political Character of the said John Adams, Esquire. By an American. *Philadelphia: Robert Bell.* MDCCLXXXIII. 8vo, pp. 62. + [Another Edition, with] Additional Notes, on the Commerce of the United States. *Philadelphia.* 1783. 8vo, pp. 77. H., N.

"The sale of his (Lord Sheffield's) Observations was diffusive and beneficial, and he proves by weight of fact and argument that the mother country may survive and flourish after the loss of America."—GIBBON's *Autobiography.* *See also* McCulloch's "Literature of Political Economy," p. 54. The author predicts the future greatness of America. It elicited several replies as below:

A Brief Examination of Lord Sheffield's Observations on the Commerce of the United States. In seven numbers. With two Supplementary Notes on American Manufactures. *Philadelphia: M. Carey.* 1791. 8vo, pp. 135. + *London: J. Phillips.* 1792. 8vo. 32635

A Free and Candid Review, of a Tract, intitled, "Observations on the Commerce of the 'American States;'" shewing The Pernicious Consequences, both to Great Britain, and to the British Sugar Islands, of the Systems Recommended in that Tract. *London: T. and W. Lowndes.* M.DCC.LXXXIV. 8vo, pp. 108. 32636

See "M. Rev.," LXX. 433.

Remarks on Lord Sheffield's Observations on the Commerce of the American States; by an American. *London: John Stockdale.* M.DCC.LXXXIV. 8vo, pp. (1), 51. C. 32637

An antagonist to Lord Sheffield, who inveighs against the climate, soil, and productions of Great Britain, and draws a comparison between Great Britain and France, to the disadvantage of the former. *See also* [Bingham (W.)], Vol. II., Nos. 5458 and 5459, and *add* to 5458, Second Edition. [*Ibid.*] + *Dublin.* 1784. 12mo; *also* [Champion (R.)], Vol. III., Nos. 11832 and 11833, and after Sheffield, in No. 11833, *add* entitled, "Observations on the Commerce of the American States;" shewing the Advantages, and urging the Necessity of relaxing the Act of Navigation in Favour of America, both in Great Britain and the West Indies. Interspersed with some Observations on the State of Canada, Nova Scotia, and the Fisheries; and with various Accounts necessary to shew the State of the Shipping and Trade of this Country and the United States; as well as of the Connection of the latter with the West Indies, previous to the War.

HOLROYD. Observations sur le commerce des États-Unis d'Amérique, par Jean Lord Sheffield. *Londres.* 1789. 8vo. + *Rouen.* 1789. 4to, pp. 237. S. 32638

HOLROYD. Observations on the Project for Abolishing the Slave Trade; and on the Reasonableness of attempting some practicable Mode of relieving the Negroes. By John Lord Sheffield. *London: J. Debrett.* 1789. 8vo, pp. 72. 32639

See "M. Rev.," Second Series, II. 232.

HOLROYD. The Orders in Council and the American Embargo Beneficial to the Political and Commercial Interests of Great Britain. By Lord Sheffield. *London: Printed by W. Bulmer and Co.* 1809. 8vo, pp. 51. BA., C. 32640

HOLROYD. Strictures on the Necessity of inviolably maintaining the Navigation and Colonial System of Great Britain. By John Lord Sheffield. *London: J. Debrett.* 1804. 8vo, pp. 65. + New Edition ... Enlarged with an Appendix, &c. ... *London.* 1806. 8vo. 32641

See "M. Rev.," New Series, XLIV. 215.

[HOLROYD.] A True and Candid Statement of Facts, relative to the late Affairs and Proceedings of the Government of Brown University. *New Haven, Conn.* 1826. 8vo, pp. 15. 32642

Relates to the removal of President Messer. *See* Bartlett's "Bibliography of Rhode Island." Also: An Oration ... before Mount Vernon Lodge, ... February 22d, A.L. 5811. ... *Providence: Office of the American.* 1811. 8vo, pp. 16. B.

HOLSTEIN (H. L. V. D.) Memoirs of Gilbert Motier La Fayette. By Gen. H. L. V. Ducoudray Holstein, Who contributed, under the fictitious name of Peter Feldmann, to his liberation from the Prisons of Olmutz. Translated from the French Manuscript. *New York: Charles Wiley.* 1824. 12mo, pp. (4), 305. W. + Second Edition ... . *Geneva: John Greves & Co.* 1835. 8vo, pp. 300. B. 32643

HOLSTEIN. Memoirs of Simon Bolivar, President Liberator of the Republic of Colombia, and of his principal Generals; Secret History of the Revolutions, and the Events which preceded it, from 1807 to the present time. By Gen. H. L. V. Ducoudray Holstein. With an Introduction containing an Account of the Statistics, and the present situation of said Republic; Education, Character, Manners and Customs of the Inhabitants. *Boston: S. G. Goodrich & Co.* 1829. 8vo, pp. 384. + [*Ibid.*] 1830. C., P. + *London: Henry Colburn and Richard Bentley.* 1830. 2 vols., post 8vo, pp. xii, 359; iv, 308. Map, Portrait.

HOLT (C.) A Short Account of the Yellow Fever, as it appeared in New London, in August, September, and October, 1798; with an accurate List of those who died of the disease; the donations, &c., &c., &c. By Charles Holt. *New London: Printed by C. Holt.* 1798. 8vo, pp. 24 32645

HOLT (E.) The Public and Domestic Life of his late most Gracious Majesty, George the Third; Comprising the most ...

Important Period in the Annals of British History. ... By Edward Holt, Esq. ... *London: Sherwood, Neely, and Jones.* 1820. 2 vols., 8vo, pp. xiv, (2), 462; xiii, 668. Portraits. B., BA., S. 32646

The American Revolution occupies a portion of the work.

HOLT (E.) Historical Sketch of the North Church, A Discourse delivered at the Re-opening and Dedication of the North Church in Portsmouth, Jan. 31, 1838. By Edwin Holt. *Portsmouth: C. W. Brewster, Printer.* 1838. 12mo, pp. 30. B., S.

Also: Sermon at the Installation of Andrew Rankin. ... *Portsmouth.* 1837. 8vo. — ... A Sermon ... at Portsmouth, on Thanksgiving Day, 25th of November, 1841. ... *Portsmouth: Printed by C. W. Brewster.* 1841. 8vo, pp. 19. H.

Holt's New-York Register, for 1804. *Hudson.* 1804–06. 2 vols., 18mo. S. 32648

HOLT (H.) Valedictory Poem and Oration ... before the Senior Class in Yale College ... June 25th, 1862. Class Poet, Henry Holt, Class Orator, D. Henry Chamberlain. ... *New Haven: Printed by Tuttle, Morehouse & Taylor.* 1862. 8vo, pp. 38, (1). H. 32649

HOLT (J.) An Address by the Hon. Joseph Holt, to the People of Kentucky, delivered at Louisville, July 13, 1861, also his Letter to J. F. Speed, Esq. *New York: James G. Gregory.* 1861. 12mo, pp. 31. 32650

Some copies are entitled: "The Fallacy of Neutrality. An Address by the Hon. Joseph Holt, to the People of Kentucky, Delivered at Louisville, July 13th, 1861; Also His Letter to J. F. Speed, Esq." *New York: James S. Gregory.* 1861. 12mo, pp. 31. + Address ... at Louisville, July 13th, 1861. [n. p. n. d.] 8vo, pp. 16.

HOLT. Letter from the Hon. Joseph Holt, upon the Policy of the General Government, the Pending Revolution, its Objects, its Probable Results if Successful, and the Duty of Kentucky in the Crisis. *Washington: Henry Polkinhorn, Printer.* 1861. 8vo, pp. 23. H. + Second Edition. [*Ibid.*] B. + *Louisville, Ky.: Printed by Bradley & Gilbert.* 1861. 8vo, pp. 15. H. 32651

HOLT. Report of the Judge Advocate General on the "Order of American Knights," or "Sons of Liberty." A Western Conspiracy in aid of The Southern Rebellion. *Washington: Government Printing Office.* 1864. 8vo, pp. 16. 32652

HOLT. Review by the Judge Advocate General of the Proceedings, Findings, and Sentence of a General Court Martial held in the City of Washington, for the Trial of Major General

Fitz John Porter, of the United States Volunteers. *Washington.* 1863. 8vo, pp. 31. B. 32653

For a reply to this, *see* Johnson (R.) Also: Address ... at Irving Hall, New York, Sept. 5, 1861. [*Baltimore: John W. Woods.* 1861.] 8vo, pp. 4.—A Magnificent Argument. The Union Forever. A Kentuckian Speech. [n. p. n. d.] 8vo, pp. 16.—Reply ... to Hon. Montgomery, Late Postmaster General, September 13, 1865. [n. p. n. d.] 8vo, pp. 12.—Report ... on the Case of T. C. A. Dexter. *New York.* 1867. 8vo.—Speech ... at Irving Hall, New York, September 3, 1861. ... *New York: G. P. Putnam.* 1861. 8vo, pp. 8.—Speech to the Troops of Indiana, and the Chamber of Commerce, New York. ... *Detroit: H. Barns & Co.* [n. d.] 8vo, pp. 8.—Speeches recently delivered in the Cities of Boston and New York, on the Present Crisis in the Affairs of the Republic. ... *Washington: H. Polkinhorn.* 1861. 8vo, pp. 20.—Treason and its Treatment. Remarks at a Dinner in Charleston, S. C., on the Evening of the 14th of April, 1865, after the Flag-Raising at Fort Sumter. ... *New York: Young Men's Republican Union.* 1865. 8vo, pp. 8. + *Washington, D. C.: Gibson Brothers, Printers.* 1865. 8vo, pp. 8.

HOLT. Vindication of Judge Advocate General Holt, from the Foul Slanders of Traitors ... acting in the Interest of Jefferson Davis. [*Washington.* 1866.] 8vo, pp. 9. H. 32654

HOLT, *and others.* Letters of the Hon. Joseph Holt, the Hon. Edward Everett, and Commodore Charles Stewart, on the Present Crisis. *Philadelphia: Wm. S. & Alfred Martien.* 1861. 8vo, pp. 45. B., H. 32655

HOLT (P.) Election Sermon, N. H., June 2, 1814. By Rev. Peter Holt. ... *Concord.* 1814. 8vo, pp. 30. 32656

HOLT (T.) A Sermon delivered at the Ordination of the Rev. Reed Paige to the Pastoral Care of the Church in Hancock, State of New Hampshire, September 21, 1791. By Thomas Holt. *Worcester, Mass.: Isaiah Thomas & Leonard Worcester.* 1792. 8vo. W. 32657

HOLTON (H. B.) Report of the Committee on Elections, in the Case of Hart B. Holton *vs.* Littleton Maclin, with accompanying Evidence. [n. p. n. d.] 8vo, pp. 31. 32658

HOLTON. Protest of Hart B. Holton against the taking of further Testimony in the Case of Holton *vs.* Maclin. [n. p. n. d.] 8vo, pp. 7. 32659

HOLTON. Minority Report of the Committee, in the Case of the Contested Seat of Holton *vs.* Maclin. [n. p. n. d.] 8vo, pp. 8. 32660

A Maryland piece, growing out of the Civil War of 1861–65. Maclin's seat was contested as he had given aid and comfort to the Confederates. *See also* Ridgely *and* Waters (L. L.)

HOLTON (I. F.) New Granada: Twenty Months in the Andes. By Isaac F. Holton .... With Maps and Illustrations. *New York: Harper & Brothers.* 1857. 8vo, pp. 605. 32661

HOLTON (W. C.) Cruise of the U. S. Flag-Ship Hartford, 1862–63: Being A Narrative of all her Operations since going into Commission, in 1862, until her Return to New York in 1863. From the Private Journal of William C. Holton. [Edited] By B. S. Osbon. *New York: L. W. Paine, Printer.* 1863. 12mo, pp. 84. B. 32662

HOLWELL (——). Holwell's Predictions, of Many Remarkable things, which may probably come to pass, from the year 1689 to 1700. *Cambridge, Mass.* 1690. 12mo. W. 32663

Holy Bible. *See* Vol. II., Nos. 5165–5182.

A Holy, Sacred and Divine Roll and Book; from the Lord God of Heaven, to the Inhabitants of Earth: revealed in the United Society at New Lebanon, County of Columbia, State of New-York, United States of America. *Printed in the United Society, Canterbury, N. H.* 1843. Parts I. and II. 12mo, pp. vii, 402, (3). 32664

This United Society is a "Shaker" institution, and this is one of their "*bibles.*"

[HOLYOAKE (G. J.)] The Life of Thomas Paine, By the Editor of the "National." 1847. 8vo. 32665

HOLYOKE (E.) The Doctrine of Life, | or of Mans | Redemtion, | by The Seed of Eve, the Seed of Abraham, the | Seed of David, &c. as it was taught in severall | Periods of Time, from Gen. 3. 15. till Christ came in the Flesh, | to fulfill all Typicall Prefigurations of him by his Death. | Wherein also | Sundry other Fundamentall Points are discussed and cleared | from some common mistakes. As Daniels Chronologie of Se- | venty Sevens, which is cleared from the uncertainty | which too many Expositors have unadvisedly cast upon it. | And about the Jewes calling; that it must not be understood | of any return to Canaan, or of their Restauration to a perspicuous | Common wealth any more, but of he calling of a Remnant of them | to the Faith, in the Countries where they live dispersed. | And with the true nature of our Lords Sufferings: with | sundry other such like Points, as may be seen in the Table. | Propounded by way of Question and Answer, with Annota- | tions thereunto annexed; Divided into three Parts. | By Edward Holyoke of New-England. | *London, Printed by T. R. for Nath. Ekins, and are to be | sold at his Shop at the Gun in St. Pauls Church-yard,* 1658. | 4to, pp. (18), 426, (18). B., H., J.C.B.

HOLYOKE (E.) The Duty of Ministers of the Gospel to guard against the Pharisaism and Sadducism, of the present Day. Sermon Preach'd to the Convention of Ministers of the Province of the Massachusetts-Bay, N. E. at Boston, on Thursday, May 28. 1741. By Edward Holyoke. ... *Boston: D. Henchman and J. Eliot.* 1741. 8vo, pp. 39. B., BA., H. 32667

HOLYOKE. An Ephemeris of the Cœlestial Motions, &c., for the Year 1709. *Boston.* 1709. 16mo. 32668

Continued to 1715, or later.

HOLYOKE. Integrity and Religion to be principally regarded, by such as design others to Stations of publick Trust. [An Election] Sermon, ... May 26. 1736. *Boston.* 1736. 8vo, pp. (4), 51. B., M. 32669

HOLYOKE. Reply to Mr. George Whitefield's Letter to him, respecting the College Testimony against Whitefield. *Boston.* 1748. 4to. 32670

Title from Thomas' "History of Printing," Second Edition.

HOLYOKE. ... A Sermon Preach'd before ... His Majesty's Council, and the Assembly of the Province of the Massachusetts-Bay in New-England, on the Anniversary for the Election of Counsellors ... May 26. 1736. By Edward Holyoke, M.A. ... *Boston, in New-England: J. Eliot.* 1736. 8vo, pp. (2), 51. BA.

HOLYOKE. ... Sermon Preach'd at the Ordination of the Reverend Mr. James Diman, ... over a Church of Christ in Salem; On the Eleventh Day of May, 1737. By Edward Holyoke ... . *Boston: Printed by Thomas Fleet.* 1737. 8vo, pp. (4), 47. B., BA., H. 32672

HOLYOKE (E. A.) An Ethical Essay. By Edward Augustus Holyoke. To which is added an Appendix, containing some Miscellaneous Papers. ... With a Biographical Memoir by John Brazer. *Salem.* 1830. 8vo, pp. xxviii, 183. B., C., H., 32673

See [Pierson (A. L.)]

HOLYOKE (S.) The Columbian Repository of Sacred Harmony, ... By Samuel Holyoke. *Exeter, N. H.: Press of Henry Raulet.* 4to, pp. xxiv, 471, (1). H. 32674

HOLYOKE. Harmonia Americana. Containing a concise Introduction to the Rounds of Music, with a variety of Airs suitable

for Divine Worship and the Use of Musical Societies, consisting of Three and Four Parts. *Boston: Thomas & Andrews.* 1791. Oblong 8vo. 32675

Also: Odes Set to Music. ... *Exeter.* 1800.

HOLYOKE, *Mass.* Local and Business Directory for 1869. ... *Holyoke: C. H. Lyman.* 1869. 8vo. 32676

[HOLYWOOD (John).] Sphera Volgare novamente tradotta con molte notande additioni di Geometria, Cosmographia, Arte Navigatoria, et Stereometria, Proportioni et Quantita delli Elementi, Distanze, Grandeze, et Novimenti di tutte li Corpi celesti, cose certamente rade et maravigliose. Auctore M. Mauro Fiorentino Phonasco et Philopanareto. *Venetiis, B. Zanetti,* 1537. 4to. 32677

"It is evident that a work originally written in the early part of the thirteenth century cannot contain anything on America; but the *De Sphera* of Sacro-Bosco (*i. e.* John Holywood, *Oxon.*) became to the mathematicians and geographers of the century following the re-discovery by Columbus, an inexhaustible source of commentaries, some of which certainly contain references to the oceanic discoveries, attributed, especially by the Italian commentators to Vespuccius. The above contains only a woodcut of a globe with America."—*Bib. Amer. Vet.*

[HOLYWOOD.] Trattato della Sfera, raccolto da Giovanni di Sacrobusto e da altri, per Antonio Brucioli. *In Venezia per Francesco Brucioli, e Frategli* 1543. 4to. 32678

[HOLYWOOD.] Sphera. *Antverpiæ: Apud Ioannem Richardson.* 1547. 32679

[HOLYWOOD.] Sphæra emendata. Eliæ Vineti Santonis Scholia in Sphærum, ab ipso Authore restituta. *Coloniæ.* 1566. 8vo. Woodcuts. 32680

[HOLYWOOD.] Sphæra emendata. Eliæ Vineti Santonis scholia in eandem Sphæram. Adiunximus compendium in Sphæram per Pierium Valerianum Bellunensem et Petri Nonii Salaciensis demonstrationem eorum quæ in extremo capite de climatibus Sacroboscius scribit de inæquali climatum latitudine, eodem Vineto interprete. *Paris: Apud Hier. de Marnef & G. Cauellat.* 1572. 8vo. 32681

Usually followed by: "Quaestiones Novae in Libellum de Sphera Ioannis de Sacro Bosco collectae ab Ariele Bicardo," etc. *Paris: G. Cauellat.* 1569. "Libellvs Ioannis Sacrobosco de anni ratione, sev vt vocatvr vvlgo compvtvs ecclesiasticvs." *Paris.* [1572.] 8vo.

[HOLYWOOD.] Liber Ioannis de | Sacrobvsto | de Sphæra. | Additi est præfatio in eundem librum | Philippi Mel. ad Simonem | Grineum. | [Colophon:] *Venetijs per Ioan. Anto. & Petrum Fratres*

de Nicolinis de Sabio. Sumptu & requisitione D. Melchioris Sessae. Anno Domini MDXLV. Small 8vo, 31 l. J.C.B. 32682

[HOLYWOOD.] La Sfera di Messer G. Sacrobosco tradotta emendata & distinta in Capitoli da Piervincentio Dante de Rinaldi con molte et utili Annotazioni del Medesimo Rivista da Frate Egratio Danti. *Fiorenza: Giunti.* 1571. 32683

There is also another Italian edition, *Venetia.* 1550.

[HOLYWOOD.] Tractado de la Sphera, que compuso Go de Sacrobosco, Con muchas addiciones. Agora nueuamente traduzido de Latin en lengua Castellana, por el Bachiller Hieronymo de Chaves. *Impresso en la muy noble y leal Ciudad de Sevilla, en casa de Juan de Leon.* 1545. 4to. 32684

On folio 27 there is a diagram in proof of the rotundity of the earth, which contains a small map of America, in which the southern continent is more clearly and better drawn than the northern, and exhibits the courses of the Orinoco and the Amazon. This is probably the work of Chaves, who prepared a large map of the New World, which has never yet been printed. The only reference in the text to the Western Hemisphere is on the reverse of folio 25, where the disappearance of stars in the heaven and the appearance of new ones is noted as meeting the observation of voyagers on the Western ocean, to Peru or to Magellan's Strait. "The Latinized form of the name of John Holywood is Sacro Bosco, who flourished at the beginning of the XIIIth century, and whose learned treatise, '*De Sphaera Mundi,*' the most famous book of the Middle Ages, was for centuries the subject of a host of commentators. He was named from Holywood, in Yorkshire, the place of his birth."—MAJOR's *Life of Prince Henry the Navigator,* p. 102. A work of great popularity in its day. The earliest edition mentioned by Brunet is that of *Ferrara,* 1472, 4to. Hain describes no less than twenty-six editions of this, with works of the same kind, as having appeared in the fifteenth century.

HOLZWARTH (J.) Petrus Claver, Sklave der Negersklaven. Bilder aus der Mission unter den Negern. *Tübingen: H. Laupp.* 1855. 16mo, pp. 16, (2), 282. C. 32685

HOMANN (J. B.) Catalogvs Mapparvm Astronomicarvm et Geographicarvm. [n. p.] 1792. 12mo, pp. 48. M. 32686

This author's various atlasses contain many references to America.

HOMANS (B.) Laws of the United States, in Relation to the Navy and Marine Corps, to the close of the Session of the 26th Congress, together with the Acts and Resolutions granting Medals, Swords, &c., from 1791 to 1840. Compiled by Benjamin Homans. *Washington: J. & G. S. Gideon.* 1841. 8vo, pp. xxviii, 223. C. 32687

HOMANS. Register of the Commissioned and Warrant Officers of the Navy of the United States ... to ... April, 1843 ... . By Benjamin Homans. *Baltimore: Printed by John Murphy.* 1843. 8vo, pp. iv, 65. B., BA. 32688

HOMANS. United States Register of the Officers of the Army of the United States, including the Cadets at West-Point: Corrected and Compiled by B. Homans, for 1843 and 1844. *Washington.* [n. d.] 12mo. S. 32689

See "Military and Naval Magazine."

HOMANS. The United States Railroad Directory, for 1856. Compiled by Benjamin Homans. ... *New-York: B. Homans.* 1856. 8vo, pp. iv, 211. BA., H., S. 32690

HOMANS (I. Smith). The Banker's Almanac, for 1851. ... *Boston: Phillips, Sampson & Co.* [1851.] 8vo, pp. xxviii, 458. Continued. B., BA. 32691

HOMANS. The Banker's Commonplace Book: ... *Boston: Phillips, Sampson & Co.* 1851. 12mo, pp. 137. C., H. 32692

[HOMANS (I. Smith), *Jr.*] The Commercial Laws of the States: ... *New York.* 1870. 8vo, pp. 328. B., C. 32693

HOMANS. The National Bank Act: an Act to provide a National Currency secured by a Pledge of United States Bonds, and to provide for the Circulation and Redemption thereof, 1864, and Amendments of 1865–70. ... *New York.* 1870. 8vo, pp. 100, 20, 63. C. 32694

HOMANS (J. S.) A Cyclopedia of Commerce and Commercial Navigation. Edited by J. Smith Homans ... and by J. Smith Homans, Jr. ... *New-York: Harper & Brother.* 1858. Rl. 8vo, pp. vi, 2007. + [*Ibid.*] 1859. 2 vols. B., BA. 32695

Based on McCulloch's Cyclopedia.

HOMANS. An Historical and Statistical Account of the Foreign Commerce of the United States, showing the Foreign Commerce of each State, with the aggregate Imports from, and Exports to, each Foreign Nation, from the Year 1820 to the Year 1856, and the Foreign Commerce of the United States with every Important Maritime Country in the World during the same Period; Including a Review of the Progress of American Commerce, and a Preliminary Sketch of the Trade of the American Colonies. Compiled by J. Smith Homans, Junior. *New-York: G. P. Putnam & Co.* 1857. 8vo, pp. vi, 190. B., C., H.

[HOMANS.] History of Boston, from 1630 to 1856. ... *Boston: F. C. Moore & Company.* 1856. 8vo. pp. (30), 246. BA. 32697

HOMANS. The Merchant's and Banker's Almanac for 1852. ... *Boston: Phillips, Sampson & Co.* [1852.] 8vo, pp. xxx, (1), 155.

Continued as "The Merchants' and Bankers' Register" for 1859.

[HOMANS.] Sketches of Boston, Past and Present, and of some Few Places in its Vicinity. ... *Boston: Phillips, Sampson, and Company.* 1851. 12mo, pp. viii, 246, 112. B., H. 32699

Also: A Few Plain Words to England and her Manufacturers. ... *New York:* 1862. 8vo, pp. 8.—United States Tariffs of 1846 and 1857, ... With an Introduction, showing the Changes that have been made in the United States Tariffs from the year 1789 to the year 1856, and the Tariff Act which passed Congress March 3d, 1857. *New-York.* 1857. 8vo. C.

HOMBERG (E.) Lettre adressée à M. le président de l'Assemblée nationale. Paris, ce 30 août 1791. [Signé E. Homberg le jeune.] Adresse des citoyens negociants et capitaines de navires du Havre à l'Assemblée nationale. [n. p. n. d.] 8vo, pp. 48.

Relates to the troubles at Saint Domingo.

HOMBRON (M.) Aventures les plus Curieuses des Voyageurs. Coup d'œil autour du monde, d'après les relations anciennes et modernes et des documents recueillis sur les lieux. *Paris: Belin-Leprieur.* 1846. 2 vols., 8vo. + *Paris.* 1847. C. 32701

HOME (Henry). Sketches of the History of Man. By Lord Kames. *Edinburgh.* 1774. 2 vols., 4to, pp. 531; 507. + *Philadelphia.* 1776. + Second Edition. *Edinburgh.* 1778. 4 vols., 8vo. + New Edition, Considerably enlarged. *Glasgow.* 1819. 3 vols., 12mo. 32702

Book II., Sketch XII., treats of the "Origin and Progress of American Nations"

HOME (John). The Unfortunate Englishman; or, A Narrative of John Cockburn. *Leith.* 1817. 8vo. 32703

Title from Allibone—probably an error as to the authorship. *See our* Nos. 14095–8.

The Home and Foreign Record ... being the Organ of the Boards of Missions, Education, Foreign Missions, and Publication. *Philadelphia.* 1850. 8vo. Continued. 32704

Home Ballads. *See* Carter (*Mrs.* A. A.), Vol. III.

Home and the World. By the Author of "Souvenirs of a Residence in Europe." *New York.* [n. d.] 12mo, pp. 408.

HOME ASSOCIATION. Constitution and Charter of Home Association ... . *Quincy: Geiger & Miller, Printers.* 1860. 8vo, pp. 15. H. 32706

Home Book of the Picturesque, or American Scenery, Art, and Literature; comprising a series of Essays by W. Irving, W. C. Bryant, F. Cooper, Miss Cooper, N. P. Willis, B. Taylor, H. T. Tuckerman, E. L. Magoon, Dr. Bethune, A. B. Street, Miss Field, etc. With Engravings ... from pictures by eminent artists. *New York: Geo. P. Putnam & Co.* 1852. 4to, pp. xii, 188. 13 Plates. 32707

Republished, without date, as "Home Authors and Home Artists." Proof copies of the plates of the original edition were published and sold separately.

Home Evangelization. A View of the Wants and Prospects of our Country, ... By one of the Secretaries of the American Tract Society. *New York: American Tract Society* [about 1850]. 18mo, pp. 174. B., BA., N. 32708

The Home in the West, A Poem, delivered at Dartmouth College, July 4, 1817. By a Member of the Junior Class. *Hanover: David Watson, Jun.* 1817. 12mo, pp. 19. BA.

HOME LEAGUE. Address of the Home League to the People of the United States. *New-York: James Van Norden & Co.* 1841. 8vo, pp. 16. BA. 32710

Also: Report of a Committee of the Home League on the Tariff Laws and their Effects. ... [*New York.* 1842.] 8vo, pp. 8. H.

The Home Missionary, and American Pastor's Journal. ... Vol. I. 1828. *New York: Printed by Alexander Ming, Jr.* 1829. 8vo. Continued. BA. 32711

The Home Monthly. Edited by Mrs. H. E. G. Arey and Mrs. C. H. Gildersleeve. *Buffalo, N. Y.* 1850. 2 vols., 8vo.

The Home of the Mutineers. [By T. B. Murray?] *Philadelphia: American Sunday School Union.* 1854. 16mo, pp. 342. 9 Plates. C. 32713

Home, The School, and The Church; or the Presbyterian Education Repository. Edited by C. Van Rensselaer ... . *Philadelphia.* 1850. 8vo. Continued. S. 32714

Home Views of the Picturesque and Beautiful. Sixty-eight "Home Views," engraved on steel by the best American artists. ... *Cincinnati: Poe & Hitchcock.* 1863. Imp. 8vo. 32715

Home Words for the Soldier. *Cincinnati.* 1862. 8vo, pp. 4.

HOMENS (Fr. Francisco da Mãe dos). Oração, que na real capella d'esta corte, celebrando-se as acções de graças pelas noticias do armisticio geral, no dia 17 de Junho de 1814, reciton, etc. *Rio de Janeiro, na Imp. Regia.* 1814. 4to, pp. 38. 32717

Homeri Ilias. Francisci Xaverii Alegrii Americani Veracrucensis Homeri Ilias Latino carmine expressa, cui accedit ejusdem Alexandrias, sive de expugnatio de Tyri ab Alexandro Macedone. *Bononiæ, Typis Ferdinandi Pisarri.* 1776. 2 vols., 4to. 32718

This Mexican translation of a Greek classic is introduced here because it contains an allusion to Mexico in the fourth book of the Alexandrias. *See* "Bib. Historica."

Homeri Ilias. Francisci Xaverii Alegre Mexicani Veracucensis Homeri Ilias Latino carmine expressa. Editio Romana Venustior. et emendatior. *Apud Salvionem, tipogr. Vaticanum.* 1788. 8vo. 32719

"Differs considerably from the first edition of 1776. On the title-page of this edition are medallion portraits of Homer and Alegre, and on the next leaf is a copperplate engraving representing the Mexican Arms over a preface headed Mexicana Civitas, and signed by Joannes à Malo de Villavicencio."—STEVENS' *Bibliotheca Historica.*

HOMER (Arthur). Proposals for Printing by Subscription a new Work for the benefit of a Public Institution, entitled Bibliotheca Universalis Americana, or an Universal American Library; containing a General Catalogue of Publications relating to America and the West Indies, from the first Discovery of those Countries by Columbus in 1492 to the end of the present Century. *Printed by S. Gosnell, Little Queen Street, London.* 1799. Folio, pp. 4.

"This promising project of a Grand Bibliotheca Americana in two quarto Volumes of 500 pages each, price £2 2s, or 10 dollars in America, was never carried out, although Mr. Homer prints the names of above 200 subscribers, a respectable list headed by Rufus King, the American Minister, and including Gov. Franklin, of New Jersey, Richard Penrose, etc."—STEVENS. If the reader will consult the preface to Stevens' "American Bibliographer" he will perhaps be inclined to run a parallel. The original MS. of this work is now at Harvard College. *See our* Vol. II., No. 5198.

HOMER (J. L.) An Address delivered before the Massachusetts Charitable Mechanic Association, at the ... Tenth Triennial Festival, October 6, 1836. By James Lloyd Homer. *Boston: For the Association.* 1836. 8vo, pp. 40. BA. 32721

[HOMER.] Notes on the Sea-Shore; or Random Sketches, ... of Hull, ... Boston [and other Places in Massachusetts]. *Boston: Redding & Co.* 1848. 8vo, pp. 54, (1). B., H. 32722

[HOMER.] Nahant, and other Places on the North-Shore; being a Continuation of Notes on the Sea-Shore ... . *Boston: Printed by William Chadwick.* 1848. 8vo, pp. vii, 48. B. 32723

[HOMER.] Short Inquiry into the Commercial Policy of the United States. By a Merchant of Boston. *Boston.* 1845. 8vo, pp. 22. B. 32724

HOMER (J.) A Brief Sketch of the Present State of the Province of Nova Scotia; With a Project offered for its Relief. By John Homer, M.P. for Barrington, N. S. *Halifax.* 1834. 8vo, pp. 31. 32725

HOMER (J.) The Character and Duties of a Christian Soldier, considered and applied in a Sermon ... before the ... Company of Artillery, ... June 7, 1790; Being the Anniversary of the Election of Officers. By Jonathan Homer. *Boston: Printed by Benjamin Russell.* 1790. 8vo, pp. 21. BA., H., M. 32726

HOMER. Description and History of Newton, in the County of Middlesex. By Jonathan Homer. [n. p. n. d.] 8vo, pp. 28.

HOMER. A Sermon, delivered in Newton, Oct. 13, 1816, upon ... the Decease of Mr. Samuel Hammond, of Brookline ... By Jonathan Homer. *Dedham: Abel D. Alleyne, Printer.* 1817. 8vo, pp. 26. H., M. 32728

Includes "Fragments of the History of Newton, Massachusetts."

HOMER. The Succession of Generations among Mankind, illustrated and improved in a Century Sermon, Preached at Newton, on Lord's Day, Dec. 25, 1791; Being the Commencement of a new Century, from the Incorporation of said Town. By Jonathan Homer ... . *Boston: Printed by Belknap and Young.* MDCCXCII. 8vo, pp. 26. BA. + pp. 27. B., H., W. 32729

Also: The Mourner's Friend, or, Consolation, and Advice offered to Christian Parents in the Death of their Little Children. ... Sermon ... at Newton, December 7, 1792. ... *Boston: Printed by S. Hall.* MDCCXCIII. 8vo, pp. 24.—A Sermon ... before the Massachusetts Society for promoting Christian Knowledge. ... May 29, 1828. ... *Boston: Printed by Crocker & Brewster.* 1828. 8vo, pp. 40. H.—The Way of God vindicated. ... Sermon ... September 16, 1804. After the Interment of his only Child ... . *Boston: Printed by Manning & Loring.* 1804. 8vo, pp. 32. BA., H., W.

HOMER (W. B.) Writings of William Bradford Homer, late Pastor of the Congregational Church in South Berwick, Maine. With an Introductory Essay and a Memoir by Edwards A. Park, Professor in Andover Theological Seminary. Second Edition. *Boston: T. R. Marvin.* 1849. 8vo, pp. lix, 13–395. H., M., S.

HOMERGUE (John D'). Essays on American Silk and the best means of rendering it a source of Individual and National Wealth; with Directions for raising Silk Worms. By J.

d'Homergue. *Philadelphia.* 1830. 12mo. P. + *Washington.* 1830. 8vo, pp. 88. 32731

HOMES (H. A.) Observations on the Design and Import of Medals. By Henry A. Homes. *Albany.* 1863. 8vo, pp. 8. S.

HOMES. Our Knowledge of California and the North-West Coast One Hundred Years Since. ... By Henry A. Homes. *Albany: Joel Munsell.* 1870. 8vo, pp. 20. BA. 32733

See also "Albany Institute Transactions," Vols. IV. and VI. Mr. Homes is also the compiler of the Catalogue of the New York State Library.

HOMES (J.) The Fighting Quaker's [Peter Bosse] Expedition in Pensilvania. By John Homes, a Baptist Teacher. 32734

"I can give no further particulars about this book, having searched in vain to find a copy."—SMITHS' *Cat. of Friends' Books*, Vol. I. 299.

HOMES (W.) A Brief and Plain Discourse, Wherein, The Doctrine of the Sabbath is explained. ... By William Homes. ... *Boston: Samuel Gerrish.* 1727. 8vo, pp. (2), vi, vii, 52. B., BA.

HOMES. The Good Government of Christian Families Recommended: to which is added, A Discourse on Secret Prayer. By the late Rev. William Homes, A.M. *Boston.* 1747. 12mo, pp. (2), 164. B. 32736

"The Preface," pp. 10, is biographical, and signed "Joseph Sewall. Thomas Prince." The "Discourse" has a separate title-page.

HOMES. Proposals of Some Things to be done in our administring Ecclesiastical Government: Whereby it may more effectually reach it's End in some Respects, than now it seems to do, *viz.* The Peace, Purity, and Edification Of our Churches: Humbly offered to Consideration, By William Homes, A.M., And Pastor of the Church of Christ in Chilmark. ... *Boston in New-England: Printed for B. Gray*, ... 1732. 8vo, pp. (4), iv, 36. B., W. + *Newburyport: Re-Printed by E. Lunt and H. W. Tinges.* MDCCLXXIV. 8vo, pp. 43. BA., H. 32737

Also: A Discourse concerning the Publick Reading of the Holy Scriptures, by the Lords People, in their Religious Assemblies: deliver'd at Tisbury. August 12, 1719. ... *Boston: Printed by B. Green.* 1720. 12mo, pp. iv, 34. BA., M., W.

HOMES (W.) Inaugural Address ... at the Opening of the Mercantile Library Hall, of St. Louis, Mo., October 17, 1854. *St. Louis: Published by the Association.* 1855. 8vo, pp. 47. B., S.

Also: Dedication Sermon ... Union Presbyterian Church of St. Louis, 1854. ... *St. Louis, Mo* 8vo, pp. 38.

Homes for All. Published by the North Missouri R. R. Co. *St. Louis.* 1869. 8vo. 32739

Homes of American Authors; comprising Anecdotical, Personal, and Descriptive Sketches, by Various Writers. Illustrated with Views of their Residences from Original Drawings, and a Facsimile of the MS. of each Author. *New York: G. P. Putnam & Co.* 1853. Square 8vo, pp. viii, 366. 19 Plates. B., H.

Homes of American Statesmen: with Anecdotical, Personal and Descriptive Sketches, by Various Writers. Illustrated with Engravings on Wood, from Drawings by Döpler, and Daguerreotypes: and Fac-similes of Autograph Letters. *New York: G. P. Putnam & Co.* M.DCCC.LIV. Square 8vo, pp. viii, 469. H. + *Hartford: C. D. Case & Co.* M.DCCC.LV. + *New York: Alfred U. Upham.* M.DCCC.LIX. 8vo, pp. viii, 484. 2 Plates. + [*Ibid.*] 1860. B. 32741

Homes of the West, and How they were Made Happy. By the author of "Johnny Wright," etc. *Philadelphia: Presbyterian Board of Publication.* [1864.] 18mo, pp. 288. Plate. 32742

Homesteads for Actual Settlers on the Public Domain. Act of Congress approved April 20, 1862. [n. p. n. d.] 8vo.

Homesteads for City Poor. ... *Boston.* [1854.] 8vo, pp. 16.

Homesteads, the Republicans and Settlers against Democracy and Monopoly. The Record. [n. p. n. d.] 8vo, pp. 16.

Les Hommes rouges de l'Amérique du nord. Rapport à M. le ministre de l'intérieur des États-Unis, par M. le chef du bureau des affaires indiennès. *Paris: imp. Dupont.* 1854. 8vo, pp. 26.

HOMO, *pseudon.* The Interim; or, Thoughts on the Traffic of West India Slaves, and on some other Slaves, not less worthy of Compassion; with an Address to Mr. Wilberforce. By Homo. *Printed at Newark: and sold by Gardner, & Co. in London.* 1792. 8vo, pp. 33. 32747

See "M. Rev.," New Series, VIII. 446.

HOMO, *pseudon.* The Financiers A, B, C, respecting Currency. By Homo. *Washington City: E. De Krafft.* 1819. 8vo, pp. 22. 32748

HOMO, *pseudon.* Signs of the Times: A Warning Voice; or, Clerical and Political Corruption Exposed. *Athens, Tenn.* 1840. 8vo. N. 32749

HONDIUS (J.) Historia Mundi: or Mercator's Atlas. Containing his Cosmographicall Description of the Fabricke and Figure of the World. ... By the studious industry Of Ivdocvs Hondy. Englished by W. S. ... *London: Michael Sparks.* 1635. Folio, 12 l., 930, (32). 32750

See Bertius, Vol. II., Nos. 5012–5014, *also* Mercator, and Spilbergen.

HONDIUS. Nova Italiæ Hodiernæ Descriptio. *Lugduni Batavorum.* 1627. Folio. 32751

Contains some particulars concerning Vespucius.

HONDURAS. Account of the British Settlement of Honduras, with Sketches of the Musquito Indians. *London.* 1811. 8vo. Map. 32752

Boletin Oficial del Gobierno Supremo de Honduras. *Comayagua.* 1851. 8vo, pp. 88. 32753

Carta dirigida por Don Francis Dias Zapata al Redactor, etc. [*Reprinted, Comayagua.* 1853.] 8vo, pp. 15. 32754

Charter of the Honduras Interoceanic Railway. Concluded, June 23, 1853. Accepted and Approved, July 28, 1853. Ratified and Proclaimed, April 28, 1854. [*New York: Phair & Co., Printers.* n. d.] Folio, pp. 12. H. 32755

Consideraciones sobre la Posibilidad de estableceo un Gno. Jeneral en Centro-América. [Colophon:] E. Hoyas, Juan J. Bonilla, Marcelo Agala. *Tegucigalpa.* 1852. 3 l. 32756

Constitucion politica del Estado de Honduras. [*Comayagua.* 1848.] 12mo, pp. 21. 32757

Correspondence relative to the Condition and Treatment of Slaves at Honduras; 1820–1823. *London.* 1823. Folio.

Cuadro estadistico del departamento de Gracias precedido de un compendio elemental de estadistica. Por Don Leon Alranado. *Paris.* 1857. 8vo, pp. vii, 38. Table. 32759

The Defence of the Settlers of Honduras against the Unjust and Unfounded Representations of Colonel George Arthur ... . Principally contained in his Correspondence relative to the Condition and Treatment of the Slaves at Honduras, 1820–1823, and printed by Order of the House of Commons, 16th June, 1823 Published by Order of the Inhabitants of Honduras ... . To which is added (by the Printer) An Account of the Descent of

the Spaniards on the Settlement in the year 1798. *Jamaica: Printed by Alex. Aikman, June,* 1824. Folio, pp. 101. + *London: Baldwin.* 1824. 8vo, pp. iv, 102. H. 32760

Defensa que el Clero de Honduras hace á se Prelada, contra los Ataques de la Gaceta de Gobierno Guardiola. *San Salvador.* 1861. 4to, pp. (8). 32761

Documentos Juslicativos de la Conducte Observado. Por el Spmo., G. de Honduras, en las negociaciones de paz con el de Guatemala. Habidas Ultimente Bajo la intervencion amistosa del Salvador. *Comayagua.* 1855. Folio, pp. (4), 39. 32762

Eisenbahn zur Verbindung des Atlantischen Oceans mit dem Stillen Meere. *Paris.* 1869. 8vo, pp. 37. Map. 32763

Esposicion del Presidente del Estado de Honduras á los Centro-Americanas. *Comayagua.* [1845.] 8vo, pp. 12. 32764

A Full Answer to the King of Spain's last Manifesto, respecting the Bay of Honduras, and the Mosquito Shore: in which All the Accusations ... against the Subjects of Great Britain ... in the Bay of Honduras ... are candidly stated and refuted: ... *London: T. Cadell.* M.DCC.LXXIX. 8vo, pp. 75. H. 32765

Honduras Almanack for 1829. *Belize.* 1829. 12mo, pp. 198.

Honduras Interoceanic Railway. Preliminary Report. By E. G. Squier. ... *New-York: Tubbs, Nesmith & Teall, Printers.* 1854. 8vo, pp. 63. 32767

See also Squier (E. G.)

Lijeras observaciones sobre la Entrega del Estado de Honduras, hesha por el Sénor D. Felipe Jauregui, al Encargado de Negocios del Gobierno Ingles, Mr. Frederico Chatfield. *Leon.* 1850. 6 l.

Manifestation de los Patriotas de Honduras contra los perturbadores de la paz Publico y los refractarios de la union. *Tegucigalpa.* 1853. Folio, 9 l. 32769

Memoria presentada al Saherano Cuerpo Lejislativo; por el Ministro jeneral Señor Don Francisco Alvarado. [*Comayagua.*] 1852. 8vo, pp. 16. 32770

Memoria Presentada por el Señor Ministro Jeneral Laenciado Da José Maria Rugama á las Cámaras, etc. [*Comayagua.*] 1851. pp. 10. 32771

El Presidente del Estado de Honduras á rus Conciudadanos. [*Comayagua, Marzo 2 de* 1852.] 12mo, pp. 6. 32772

Regulations ... Bay of Honduras. *See* Barnaby (W.)

See also Parliamentary Reports on Honduras, 1828, 1852, 1853, 1855, 1856, 1857. Folio.

La vérité sur le projet de chemin de fer interocéanique du Honduras; par un Franco-Américain. *Paris.* 1869. 8vo, pp. 24. Map. 32773

Also: América del Centro. Memoria dirigida por el Ministerio de estado á la Asambléa Constituegente. *Leon.* [1847.] pp. (2), 28.—[Carta de un Ciudadano de Centro-América á los] Editores del "Salvador Rejenerado." [*S. Salvador.* 1847.] pp. 21.—Contestacion al Comunicado sobre la Nacionalidad, inserto en la Gaceta Oficial de Guatemala. [*S. Salvador.* 1846.] 4 l.—Convenio celebredo entre SS. MM. los Reges de España é Inglaterra, etc., en Londres á 14 de Julio de 1786. *Comayagua.* 1846. 8vo, pp. 7.—Dictamen sobre los Pactos celebrados por la convencion de Nacaome. *Comayagua.* 1848. 8vo, pp. 23.—Por Disposicion del Gufierno Jeneral de Centro-América, etc. [*Leon.*] 1851. 8vo, pp. 7.

HONE (P.) An Address ... before the Mercantile Library Association ... in Boston, October 3, 1843. By Philip Hone. *Boston: William D. Ticknor.* 1843. 8vo, pp. 44; followed by a Poem, viz.: George Lunt, pp. 45–70. B., BA., H. 32774

The Honest Grief of a Tory, expressed in a Genuine Letter to the Monitor. *London: Angel.* 1759. 8vo. 32775

The Honest Man's Almanack, For the City of Pittsburgh, etc. No. I. 12mo. 32776

Honest Politician. Part I, Containing the First Eight Numbers; Together with a Publication under the Signature of Vindex ... *Baltimore: For the Author.* 1808. 8vo, pp. viii, 65. BA.

The honest | Welch-Cobler, | for her do scorne to call her | selfe the simple Welch-Cobler: | Although her thinkes in all her | Consciences, if her had as many as would stand | betweene Paules and Sharing-Crosse that her have | not so much wit as her Prother Cobler of A- | merica, yet her thinke her may have as much | knavery; and though her have not so much Creek, | which her holds to be Heathenish; nor Hebrew, | which her holds to be Shewish Language; nor | Latine, which is the Language of Rome, yet her | shall endever her selfe to teliver her selfe in as | cood Tialect as her can for her hart plood, for the | petter understanding of all her friends and kind- | red, whether Comro or Siss, wherein her shall | find variety of counsells, profitable instructions, seasonable cautions, to prevent tangers that may come | upon all

her countrymen here; Her also shall find some | truth, little honesty, some wit, and a creat teale of kna- | verie. | By Shinkin ap Shone, ap Griffith, ap Gearard, ap Shiles, ap | Shoseph, ap Lewis, ap Laurence, ap Richard, ap Tho- | mas, ap Sheffre, ap Sheames, ap Taffie, ap Harie, | All Shentleman in Wales. | [*London:*] *Printed by M. Shinkin, Printer to S. Taffie, and | are to be sold at the Signe of the Goat on the | Welch Mountaine.* 1647. | 4to, pp. 8. 32778

Published the same year as Nat. Ward's "Simple Cobler of Agaanwam," and included in Stevens' "American Nuggets," No. 2807.

HONESTUS, *pseudon.* *See* [Austin (B.)], *and* Baltimore, Vol. I.

HONESTUS, *pseudon.* Vindication of the Land Agent, and Refutation of Anonymous "Remarks," addressed to the Governor ... of Maine. By Honestus. *Portland: Thomas Todd, Printer.* 1828. 8vo, pp. 34. H. 32779

HONESTY (O.), *pseudon.* The Reverend Mr. Smith vindicated from the Imputation of Perjury, in a Letter to a Friend. ... Obadiah Honesty. (Price three Coppers.) Folio, pp. 2. P., S.

HONESTY. The Second Edition, with Additions, of, A Remonstrance, by Obadiah Honesty, in the Case of the Reverend Mr. Sm—th, with some Remarks on his being call'd before the House of A——y. ... Price 4d. Folio, pp. 4. P., S. 32781

Honesty Shewed to be True Policy; or, a General Impost Considered and Defended. By a Plain Politician. *New York: Printed by Francis Childs.* M,DCC,LXXXVI. 8vo, pp. 20. BA.

HONEYMAN (James). A Sermon preached at the King's Chapel in Boston, N. E. at a convention of Episcopal Ministers, in the year 1726. *Boston.* 1726. 12mo. 32783

H[ONEYWOOD] (S[t.] J[ohn].) Poem on reading President Washington's Address, declining a Re-Election to the Presidency. ... By S. J. H. Esquire ... . *Albany: Printed by Charles R. and George Webster.* [1796.] 8vo, pp. 8. B., N. 32784

[HONEYWOOD.] A Poem on the President's Farewell Address, with a Sketch of the Character of his Successor. *Philadelphia: John Ormrod.* [1800.] 8vo, pp. 8. 32785

HONEYWOOD. Poems by St. John Honeywood, A.M. With Some Pieces in Prose. *New York: Printed by T. & J. Swords.* 1801. 12mo, pp. viii, 159, (1). B., C., S. 32786

HONIG Jz (Jac.) De Hollanders in Braziliё, of lotgevallen van kapitein Alderick. Schetsen uit de 17de eeuw. *Amsterdam.* 1851. 2 vols., 8vo. 32787

The Dutch in Brazil, or adventures of Captain Alderik. Sketches from the seventeenth century.

HONORATO (M. da C.) Diccionario topografico, estadistico o historico da provincia de Pernambuco por Manoel da Costa Honorato. *Recife.* 1863. 8vo, pp. vi, 188. 32788

The Honor of the United States of America, under the Administration of Tyler, Webster and Co. *New York.* 1842. 8vo.

The Honour of Parliament and the Justice of the Nation Vindicated. In a Reply to Dr. Price's Observations on the Nature of Civil Liberty. *London: W. Davis.* MDCCLXXVI. 8vo, pp. 64. 32790

The defender exclaims without mercy against the Americans, and is sarcastic on Dr. Price's profession as a preacher.

The Honour of the Gout, or a Rational Discourse demonstrating that the Gout is one of the greatest blessings that can befall Mortal Man, &c. *London Printed. Reprinted by B. Franklin in Philadelphia.* 1732. 16mo, pp. 65–5. 32791

HONTAN (*le Baron de la*). *See* La Hontan.

HONTER (Joannis). Rudimentorum cosmographiae libri duo. Quorum prior Astronomiae, posterior Geographiae principia complectitur. [Colophon:] *Cracoviae, Mathias Scharfenbergius excudebat* MDXXXIIII. Sm. 8vo, 16 leaves. 32792

"Original edition of the highest rarity, unknown, as far as we could ascertain, to all bibliographers. The part relating to America will be found in the chapter: Nomina insularum Oceani et Maris: '... In occiduo Doreades, Hesperides, Fortunatae, *America, Parias, Isabella, Spagnola,* etc.' "—F. MULLER.

HONTER. Rudimenta Cosmographica. *Antverp. J. Richard* [about 1540]. 12mo. 13 Woodcut Maps. 32793

HONTER. Rvdimen- | ta Cosmogra- | phica. *Tigvri Apvd Froscho- | uerum. Anno,* M.D.XLVI. 12mo, 30 leaves. 13 Woodcut Maps. 32794

"This book is interesting for America, as the text (a poetical description of the world) is followed by an appendix of 14 leaves, containing an atlas of the world. This appendix has also been published separately."—MULLER.

HONTER. Rvdimen- | torum Cosmographico- | rum Ioan. Honteri Coronensis libri III cum | tabellis Geographicis elegantissimis.

| De uariarum rerum nomenclaturis per | classes, liber I. | *Tigvri apvd Froscho- | uerum. Anno* M.D.XLVIII. Sm. 8vo, 30 leaves, 2 blank leaves, 1 leaf for a title, 25 leaves for 13 Maps. S.L.M.B. + [*Ibid.*] M.D.XLIX. 8vo, 30 leaves; Second Part, 4 leaves, 14 Maps. 32795

See Harrisse, No. 287.

HONTER. Rvdimentorum Cosmographicorum Ioan Honteri Coronensis libri III. [IV.] cum tabellis Geographicis elegantissimis. De uariarum rerum nomenclaturis per classes, liber I. *Tigvri apvd Froschouerum. Anno* M.D.XLIX. 12mo, 29 leaves in verse, blank leaf for title, 25 leaves for 13 Maps. + [*Ibid.*] M.D.LII.

HONTER. Rvdimen- | torum Cosmogra- | phicorum Ioan Honteri Coronen- | sis libri III. cum tabellis | Geographicis elegan- | tissimis. | De uariarum rerum nomenclaturis per | classes, liber I. *Tigvri, apud Froschouerum. Anno* MDLXV. 12mo, 30 leaves. 13 Maps. 32797

On the first map America is laid down in a long narrow strip.

HONTER. Rvdimentorum cosmographicorum libri IIII. Cum tabellis geographicis. [n. p.] 1570. Sm. 8vo. + [n. p.] 1585.

HONTER. Rvdimentorum cosmographicorum libri IIII. Cum tabellis geographicis. [n. p. 1590?] Sm. 8vo. 32799

With exactly the same maps as in the preceding edition, but newly engraved, finer, and more correct. The signatures at the foot of pages b 2 and d 2, are correct in this edition; in the former they were by two different hands. *See also* Dionysius, Vol. v., Nos. 20209–20211, *and* Proclus.

HOOD (C.) Poem ... at the Dedication of the Dorchester High School, December 7th, 1852. By Charles Hood. *Boston: Wright & Hasty, Printers.* 1852. 8vo, pp. 12. H. 32800

HOOD (G.) A History of Music in New England, with Biographical Sketches of Reformers and Psalmists. By George Hood. *Boston: Wilkins, Carter & Co.* 1846. 12mo, pp. 252.

HOOD (Samuel). Letters [&c.] *See* Bernard (F.)

[HOOD (Samuel).] A Brief Account of the Society of the Friendly Sons of St. Patrick; with Biographical Notices of Members, and Extracts from Minutes. *Philadelphia: W. S. Young.* 1844. 12mo, pp. 112. Plate. C. 32802

HOOD (T. S.) Documentos relativos a la Mision del Hon. Sr. D. Tomas Samuel Hood, &c. *Buenos Aires.* 1846. Folio, pp. 51. 32803

HOOGERDUIN (D. E.) Echt historisch verhaal zo uit de mond als pen, van drie zeelieden met naame Harme Hendrick Kreuger, en deszelfs zoon, en Carsen Cuulce, wegens het verongelukken van het schip, de Wilhelmiena. Van de Helder als ook de nootlottige en droevige ongelukken van nog negen andere Scheepen, dewelke alle verongelukt zyn in Groenland, door de bezetting van het West-Ys, in den Jare 1777. *Amsterdam.* 1778. 4to, pp. 36.

HOOGHE, *or* HOOGE (Romain de). Les Indes Orientales et Occidentales, et autres lieux; représentés en très-belles figures, ... *Leide, P. van der Aa* [about 1700]. Oblong folio, pp. (2). 6 Maps, 41 Plates. C. 32805

These plates were probably cut as part of the illustrations to Van der Aa's great collection of voyages.

HOOK (W. F.) A Church Directory. By Walter Farquhar Hook, D.D. Sixth Edition. Revised and Adapted to the Protestant Episcopal Church in the United States of America by a Presbyter of said Church. *Philadelphia.* 1854. 8vo. 32806

HOOK. The Disestablished Church in the Republic of the United States of America. An Address ... . By W. F. Hook. With a Preface. *London: John Murray.* 1869. 8vo. 32807

HOOK (W. H.) Lecture on the Backward March of American Society. By W. H. Hook. *Madison, Wis.* 1869. 8vo.

HOOKE (W.) New-Englands Sence, | of | Old-England | and | Jrelands | Sorrowes. | A Sermon Preached upon a day of | generall Humiliation in the Churches of | New-England. | In the behalfe of Old-England and Jrelands | Sad condition. | By William Hooke, Minister of | Gods Word at Taunton in | Nevv-England. | ... *London, | Printed by John Rothwell at the Signe of the Sunne | in Pauls-Church-yard.* 1645. | Sm. 4to, pp. (2), 34. H., J.C.B.

HOOKE. New | Englands | Teares, | for Old Englands | Feares. | Preached in a Sermon on July 23. | 1640 being a day of Publike Humiliation, | appointed by the Churches in behalfe of our | native Countrey in time of | feared dangers. | By William Hooke, Minister of Gods | Word; sometimes of Axmouth in Devonshire, | now of Taunton in New England. | Sent over to a worthy Member of the honourable | House of Commons, who desires it may be for | publick good. | *London, | Printed by E. G. for Iohn Rothwell and Henry Overton, and | are to be sould at the Sunne in Pauls Church- | yard, and in Popes-head Alley.* 1641. | 4to, pp. (4), 23. 32810

"A Sermon preached to some in New-England for Old England's sake." The following edition differs only in the form of the title-page.

HOOKE. New | Englands | Teares, | for Old | Englands | Feares. | Preached in a Sermon on July 23. 1640. | being a day of Publike Humiliation, ap- | pointed by the Churches in behalfe of | our native Countrey in time | of feared dangers. | By William Hooke, Minister | of Gods Word; sometimes of Axmouth | in Devonshire, | now of Taunton in New England. | Sent over to a worthy Member of the honour- | able House of Commons, who desires | it may be for publick good. | *London, | Printed for T. P. by Iohn Rothwell and Henry Overton, | and are to be sould at the Sunne in Pauls Church- | yard, and in Popes-head Alley.* 1641. | 4to, pp. (4), 23. 32811

"How do they [in England] talke of New-England with delight; and when a New-England man returnes thither, how is he lookt upon; the ground he walks upon beloved for his sake, & the house held the better where he is; neither is any love held too much for such a man."—Page 21. Also: Discourse concerning the Witnesses, relating to the Time, Place and Manner of their being Slain. ... *London.* 1681. 4to. w.—The Priviledges of the Saints on Earth beyond those in Heaven. ... *London.* 1673. 8vo.

HOOKER (A.) ... A Sermon Preached on the Day of the General Election, at Hartford, in the State of Connecticut, May 9th, 1805. By Asahel Hooker, A.M. ... *Hartford: Printed by Hudson & Goodwin.* 1805. 8vo, pp. 41. B., BA., H., W. 32812

Also: ... Sermon ... at the Ordination of the Rev. James Beach ... January 1st, A.D. 1806. ... *Hartford: Printed by Lincoln and Gleason.* 1806. 8vo, pp. 27. BA., H., and other sermons.

HOOKER (E. C.) The Nation Responsible to God for the Punishment of Traitors. A Discourse ... in ... Newburyport ... June 27, 1862. By E. C. Hooker. *Newburyport: William H. Huse & Co., Printers.* 1862. 8vo, pp. 14. H. 32813

HOOKER (E. W.) The Life of Thomas Hooker. By Edward W. Hooker. ... *Boston.* 1849. 12mo, pp. 324. B., H.

"Lives of the Chief Fathers of New England," Vol. VI.

HOOKER. Memoir of Mrs. Sarah L. Huntington Smith, By Edward W. Hooker, D.D. ... *Boston: Perkins & Marvin.* 1839. 12mo, pp. 407. Portrait. + Second Edition. *Boston: T. R. Marvin.* 1844. 12mo, pp. 396. Portrait. B., BA. + Third Edition. *American Tract Society.* [1845.] B., H. 32815

[HOOKER.] Memorials of the Families of Mr. James Thompson, and of Dea. Augustus Thompson, of Goshen, Connecticut. *Hartford: Press of Case, Tiffany & Co.* 1854. 8vo, pp. 106.

Also: A Discourse on the Sabbath following the Funeral of Miss Elizabeth P. Hooker; ... By her Father. *Hartford: Case, Tiffany and Company.* 1850. 8vo, pp. 24. B.—A Sermon occasioned by the Catastrophe on Board the U. S. Ship of War Princeton: preached ... March 17, 1844. ... *Troy, N. Y.: Press of N. Tuttle.* 1844. 8vo, pp. 24. H.

HOOKER (H. E.) & Co. Catalogue of the Rochester Commercial Nurseries. *Rochester, N. Y.* 1856. 8vo, pp. 52.

[HOOKER (Herman).] An Appeal to the Christian Public, on the Evil and impolicy of the Church engaging in Merchandise ... and evil-working, of Charity Publication Societies. *Philadelphia: King & Baird, Printers.* 1849. 8vo, pp. 24. B., S. 32818

The author was an Episcopalian minister and bookseller

HOOKER (J.) ... A Sermon preached at the Funeral of the Rev. John Hunt, ... who died ... December 20th, 1775. By John Hooker, A.M. ... *Boston: Printed by Thomas and John Fleet.* 1776. 8vo, pp. 30. B., BA., M., W. 32819

Also: Sermon at the Ordination of Thomas Allen, Pittsfield, April 18, 1764. ... *Boston.* 1764. 8vo, pp. 46.

[HOOKER (J.)] New-England Loyal Publication Society. The following Letter, written by an eminent Lawyer of Connecticut [etc. n. p. n. d.] 8vo, pp. 8. B., H. 32820

Signed, John Hooker. Also: Letter to the Democratic Party on the Issues of the Day. [n. p. n. d.] 8vo.

HOOKER (Joseph). Chancellorsville and its Results; Maj.-Gen. Hooker in Command of the Army of the Potomac. [n. p. n. d.] 32821

HOOKER (J. D.) The Botany of the Antarctic Voyage of H.M. Discovery Ships *Erebus* and *Terror*, in the Years 1839–1843. Under the Command of Captain Sir James Clark Ross, ... R.N., F.R.S., &c. By Joseph Dalton Hooker, M.D., R.N., F.L.S., ... Botanist to the Expedition. *London: Reeve, Brothers.* 1847. 2 vols., 4to, pp. xii, (1), 208; (6), 209–574. 198 Plates. B., C. 32822

Known as the Flora Antarctica, and published with the plates, plain and colored. "The descriptions of the plants in this work are carefully drawn up, and much interesting matter, critical, explanatory, and historical, is added in the form of notes. The drawings of the plants are by Mr. Fitch; and we know of no botanical illustrations that are superior in faithful representation and botanical correctness."—*Athenæum.*

HOOKER. Victoria Regia. By J. D. Hooker. *London.* Folio. 4 colored Plates by Fitch. 32823

HOOKER (M. A.) Memoir of Mary Anne Hooker ... *Philadelphia: American Sunday-School Union.* [1840.] 8vo, pp. 177.

HOOKER (Nathanael). The Religious Improvement of the Harvest. A Sermon July 27, 1766. *Hartford.* 1766. 8vo, pp. 24. 32825

HOOKER. Six Discourses, on different subjects; preached by The Rev. Nathanael Hooker, A.M. And late Pastor of the fourth Church of Christ in Hartford. Being, A Posthumous Publication, from the Author's Original Manuscripts, At the Desire, and with the Advice of many judicious Persons, both of the Clergy and Laity. *Hartford: Printed ... by Ebenezer Watson,* ... 1771. 8vo, pp. (6), 99. 32826

Also: The Invalid Instructed: or God's Design in sending Sickness upon Men, and their Duty under it. ... *Hartford.* 1763. 4to, pp. 34.

HOOKER (S.) Connecticut Election Sermon May 10, 1677. By Samuel Hooker of Farmington, Conn. *Boston.* 1677. 4to, pp. 28. 32827

HOOKER (T.) The Application of Redemption, ... for the bringing home of lost Sinners to God. The first eight Books. ... By ... Thomas Hooker ... with ... an Epistle, By Thomas Goodwin, and Philip Nye. *London.* 1656. 8vo. + Second Edition. *London: Printed by Peter Cole.* 1659. 4to, pp. (22), 702, (30). B. 32828

HOOKER. The Application of Redemption by the effectual work of the Word and Spirit of Christ, for bringing home lost Sinners to God, the ninth and tenth Books made in New England, By Thomas Hooker. Published by T. Goodwin and P. Nye. *London.* 1659. 4to. B. 32829

The entire work is rarely found complete, the first volume, in 8vo, being almost unknown. The words "ninth and tenth books" in the second volume have been supposed to apply to the general collection of his works.

HOOKER. A Brief Exposition of the Lord's Prayer; Wherein the meaning is laid open to the understanding of weake Christians, ... *London: Moses Bell.* 1645. 4to, pp. 90. 32830

H[OOKER]. The | Christians | Tvvo Chiefe | Lessons, | viz. [Selfe Deniall, | and | Selfe Tryall. | As Also | the Priviledge of Adoption | And Triall thereof. | In three Treatises ... | By T. H. | *London,* | ... *P. Stephens and C. Meredith,* ... | 1640. | 4to, pp. (22), 303. H. 32831

HOOKER. A Comment upon Christ's last Prayer in the XVIIth of John, wherein is opened the Union Believers have with God and Christ, and the glorious priviledges thereof. By Thomas Hooker ... . With Preface by Thomas Goodwin and Philip Nye. *London.* 1656. 4to. + [*Ibid.*] 1657. 32832

HOOKER. The Covenant of Grace opened, wherein are handled what the Covenant of Grace is; What the Seales of the Covenant are; Who are the Subjects fit to receive these Seales; from which particulars Infants' Baptism is fully proved and vindicated: being severall Sermons preached at Hartford, in New England. By Thomas Hooker ... . *London: G. Dawson.* 1649. 4to. J.C.B. 32833

HOOKER. The Danger | of | Desertion: | or | a Farvvell Sermon | of Mr. Thomas Hooker, | Sometime Minister of God's Word at Chains- | ford in Essex; but now of New England. | Preached immediately before his departure | out of old England. | Together | with Ten Particvlar | rules to be practiced every day by | Converted Christians. | *London, | Printed by G. M. for George Edwards in the | Old Baily in Green-Arbour, at the signe | of the Angell.* 1641. 4to, pp. (4), 29. 32834

HOOKER. The Danger | of | Desertion: | or | a Farvvell Sermon | of Mr. Thomas Hooker, | Sometimes | Minister of Gods Word at Chainsford in Essex; | but now of New England. | Preached immediately before his Departure out | of Old England. | Together | with Ten Particv- | lar Rules to be practised every | day by converted Christians. | The Second Edition. | *London, | Printed by G. M. for George Edwards in the Old | Baily in Green-Arbour, at the Signe of | the Angell.* 1641. 4to, pp. (4), 28. B., H. 32835

Mr. Prince attributes the Rules to the Rev. E. Reyner. An interesting historical sermon.

H[OOKER]. The | Eqvall | Wayes of God: | Tending | to | the Rectifying | of the | Crooked | Wayes of Man. | The Passages whereof are briefly | and clearly drawne from the sacred | Scriptvres. | By T. H. | *London,* | ... *Iohn Clarke* ... | 1632. 4to, pp. (8), 40. 32836

HOOKER. The Faithful Covenanter. A Sermon preached at the Lecture in Dedham in Essex, by Mr. Tho. Hooker, late of Chelmsford; now in New England. *London, Christopher Meredith.* 1644. 4to. 32837

HOOKER. Fovre ... Treatises; Viz. The Carnall Hypocrite. The Churches Deliverances. The Deceitfulnesse of Sinne. The Benefit of Afflictions. By Th. Hooker. *London,* ... *Andrew Crooke* ... 1638. 12mo, pp. (4), 293. B. 32838

HOOKER. Heaven's Treasury Opened in a Fruitful Exposition of the Lord's Prayer, with a Treatise of the Principles of Religion. *London.* 1645. 4to. 32839

HOOKER. Heautonaparnumenos: Or a Treatise of Self-Denyall. Intended for the Pulpit; but now committed to the Presse for the Publike Benefit. By Thomas Hooker. *London, Printed by Wilson, for Richard Royston.* 1646. 32840

H[OOKER]. The | Immortality | of the | Soule: | The Excellencie of Christ | Jesvs, treated on. | Wherein the faithfull people of | God may finde comfort | for their Souls. | By T. H. | Published according to Order. | *London, | Printed in the yeer* 1646. | 4to, pp. (2), 21. 32841

HOOKER. A Letter from the Rev. Thomas Hooker of Hartford, in Answer to the Complaints of Gov. Winthrop, of Massachusetts, against Connecticut. ... *Hartford.* 1859. 8vo, pp. 18.

[HOOKER.] The Poore Dovting Christian drawne vnto Christ. ... *London, Printed in the yeare* 1629. 8vo. 32843

[HOOKER.] The | Poore | Doubting | Christian | Drawn to | Christ. | Wherein the main Lets and | Hinderances which keep men | from coming to Christ | are discovered. | With speciall Helps to re- | cover Gods favor. | The Sixth Edition. | *London, | Printed by I. Raworth, for Luke Fawne,* | ... 1641. | 12mo, pp. (2), 163.

HOOKER. The Poor Doubting Christian drawn to Christ. ... *London.* 1659. 12mo, pp. (2), 158 for 185. + *London.* 1667. 16mo. W. + The Twelfth Edition. *London.* 1700. 32845

HOOKER. The Poor Doubting Christian drawn to Christ. Wherein the main Hindrances, which keep men from coming to Christ, are discovered. With special Helps to recover God's favour. By Thomas Hooker, ... With an Abstract of the Author's Life [by Thomas Prince]. *Boston: D. Henchman.* 1743. 24mo, pp. (2), 14, 144. B., C., H. 32846

HOOKER. The Poor Doubting Christian. ... By Thomas Hooker. With Life and Introduction, by Edward W. Hooker, D.D. *Hartford.* 1845. 18mo. 32847

This, the earliest and most popular of Hooker's works, first appeared in a collection of sermons entitled "The Saints' Cordialls," attributed to Sibbs.

HOOKER. The | Saints | Dignitie, | and | Dutie. | Together with | The Danger of Ignorance | and Hardnesse. | Delivered in Severall Sermons: | By that Reverend Divine, | Thomas Hooker, | Late Preacher in New-England. | *London, | Printed by G. D. for Francis Eglesfield,* | ... 1651. pp. (6). [Second Title:] The Gift | of | Gifts: | Or, | The End why | Christ | Gave Himself. | By that Reverend Divine, | Thomas Hooker, | Late Preacher in New-England. | ... 4to, pp. (8), 248, 4. 32848

Consists of seven sermons, each with a separate title.

HOOKER. The Sovles Effectvall Calling to Christ. ... *London*, ... *Andrew Crooke* ... 1637. 4to, pp. 33–668. 32849

This should probably follow our No. 32856, *infra*.

H[OOKER]. The | Sovles | Exaltation. | A | Treatise | containing | The Soules Vnion with Christ, on 1 Cor. 6. 17. | The Soules Benefit from Vnion | with Christ, on 1 Cor. 1. 30. | The Soules Justification, on | 2 Cor. 5. 21. | By T. H. | *London*, | ... *Andrew Crooke*, ... 1638. | 4to, pp. (16), 311, *i. e.* 313. B. 32850

"The Soules Benefit," has a separate title-page.

[HOOKER.] The | Sovles | Hvmiliation. | *London*, | ... *Andrew Crooke*, ... 1637. 4to, pp. (2), 224. B. + The Second Edition. [*Ibid.*] 1638. 4to, pp. 223, (8). 32851

[HOOKER.] The | Sovles | Hvmiliation. | The Third Edition. *London*, | ... *Andrew Crooke*, ... 1640. 4to, pp. 223, (8). 32852

A reprint of the second edition.

[HOOKER.] The | Sovles | Hvmiliation. | *Amsterdam.* | *Printed for T. L. ... neare* | *unto the English Church*, | *Anno* 1638. | 16mo, pp. 302. 32853

[HOOKER.] The Soules | Implantation. | A Treatise | Containing, | The broken Heart, | ... | The Preparation of the Heart, | ... | The Soules ingrafting into Christ, | ... | Spirituall Love and Joy, | ... | *London*, | *Printed by R. Young*, ... | 1637. | 4to, pp. (2), 266.

The third treatise is entirely different from the "Sovles Ingrafting," described *infra*.

H[OOKER]. The Soules | Implantation | into | the Naturall Olive. | By T. H. | Carefully corrected, and much enlarged, with | a Table of the Contents prefixed. | *London*, | *Printed by R. Young*, ... 1640. | 4to, pp. (6), 320. 32855

H[OOKER]. The | Sovles | Ingrafting | into Christ. | By T. H. | *London*, | ... *Andrew Crooke*, ... | 1637. | 4to, pp. (2), 30. B.

This is usually followed by "The Broken Heart," pp. 320, but perhaps should be followed by the "Sovles Effectval Calling to Christ" as it is of the same date, the pagination is directly sequent, and the subject is more consonant.

[HOOKER.] The Sovles Preparation for Christ. Or, A Treatise of Contrition. Wherein is discovered hovv God breakes the heart, and wounds the Soule in the Conversion of a Sinner to Himselfe. *London, Robert Dawlman.* 1632. 4to.

The first edition of Hooker's first work, no doubt written in Holland.

[HOOKER.] The | Sovles | Preparation | for Christ. | Or, | A Treatise | of Contrition. | Wherein is discovered | Hovv God breakes the heart, | and wounds the Soule, in the con- | version of a Sinner to Himselfe. | The fourth Edition. | *London*, | *Printed by the Assignees of T. P. for T. Nickoles*, ... 1638. | 4to, pp. (6), 242. B. + The sixth Edition. *London*, ... *R. Dawlman.* 1643. 12mo, pp. (8), 386. + The Seventh Edition. *London*, ... *R. Dawlman*, ... 1658. 12mo, pp. (8), 386. 32858

H[OOKER]. The | Sovles | Vocation | or | Effectval | Calling to Christ. | By T. H. | *London*, | ... *Andrew Crooke*, | ... 1638. | 4to, pp. (24). [Second Title:] The | Sovles | Effectvall | Calling to Christ. | By T. H. | [*Ibid.*] 1637. 4to, pp. 33–668. B. 32859

HOOKER. A | Survey | of the Summe of | Church-Discipline. | Wherein, | the Way of the Churches of | New-England | is warranted out of the Word, | and all Exceptions of weight, which | are made against it, answered: Whereby | also it will appear to the Judicious Reader, | that something more must be said, then | yet hath been, before their Prin- | ciples can be shaken, or they | should be unsetled in | their practice. | By Tho. Hooker, late Pastor of the Church at | Hartford upon Connecticott in N.E. | *London*, | *Printed by A. M. for John Bellamy* ... M.DC.XLVIII. | 4to, pp. (36); Part I. pp. 139 and 185–296; Part II. pp. 90; Part III. pp. 46; Part IV. pp. 59. B., BA., C., H. 32860

The Epistle "To the Reader" is signed "Edward Hopkins, William Goodwin." Verses "In obitum Hookeri," are signed "Sam. Stone, Teaching Elder at Hartford," "On Mr. Thomas Hooker," "J. Cotton," "In sepulchrum Hookeri," "E. Rogers," and a "Preface" is signed "Tho. Goodwin."

HOOKER. A Survey of the Summe of Church Discipline, wherein the Way of the Congregational Churches of Christ in New England is warranted and cleared by Scripture and Argument, and all Exceptions of weight made against it by sundry learned Divines [Mr. Rutherford, Mr. Hudson, Mr. Baylie, The Author of Vindiciæ Clavium,] Answered. In two Books.

The First, { By Mr. Thomas Hooker, late Pastor of the Church at Hartford upon Connecticut. } in New England.
The Second, { By Mr. John Cotton, now Teacher of the Church at Boston. }

London: Printed by A. M. for John Bellamy, ... M.DC.XLVIII. 4to, pp. (38), 296, 90, 46, 59, (12), 104, 44. B. 32861

Each treatise has its separate title; for the second, *see* Cotton (J.), Vol. v., No. 17091. Cotton introduces many historical particulars into his argument with regard to the conversion of the Indians, the Hutchinson controversy, &c.

H[OOKER]. The | Vnbeleevers | Preparing for | Christ. | By T. H. | *London*, | ... *Andrew Crooke*, ... 1638. | 4to, pp. (4), 204, 4. Second Part, pp. 119, 4. 32862

The author was the first minister of Cambridge, Mass., and one of the founders of the colony of Connecticut. Mather characterized him as "a son of thunder." He appeared with such majesty in the pulpit, that it was pleasantly said of him "he could put a king into his pocket." He has been called the Luther of New England. *See* Cawdrey (D.), Vol. III., No. 11615.

HOOKER (W. J.) The Botany of Captain Beechey's Voyage: comprising an Account of the Plants collected by Messrs. Lay and Collie, and other Officers of the Expedition, during the Voyage to the Pacific and Behring's Strait, performed in His Majesty's Ship Blossom, under the Command of Captain F. W. Beechey, By Sir William Jackson Hooker, R.N. ... *London: Henry George Bohn.* MDCCCXLI. 4to, pp. (4), 485. 99 Plates. BA., H. 32863

HOOKER. Contributions towards a Flora of South America, and the Islands of the Pacific. *London?* 1841. 8vo. Plates. C.

HOOKER. Flora Boreali-Americana; or, the Botany of the Northern Parts of British America; compiled principally from the Plants collected by Dr. Richardson & Mr. Drummond on the late Northern Expeditions, under Command of Captain Sir John Franklin, R.N. To which are added (by Permission of the Horticultural Society of London,) those of Mr. Douglas ... and other Naturalists. By Sir William Jackson Hooker, LL.D. ... *London: Treuttel & Würtz.* MDCCCXXXIII–MDCCCXL. 4 vols. (2 of Text, 2 of Plates), rl. 4to, pp. vi, 48, 351; vi, 328; Vol. III. Map, 158 Plates; Vol. IV. 159–238 Plates. BA., C. + *London: Henry G. Bohn.* MDCCCXL. 2 vols., rl. 4to, pp. vi, v–vi, 335, Plates 118, Index 329–351, (1); (1), 270, Plates 119–238, Index 271–328.

HOOKER. Notes on the Botany of the Antarctic Voyage conducted by Captain James Clark Ross, R.N. ... in Her Majesty's Discovery Ships, Erebus and Terror. With Observations on the Tussac Grass of the Falkland Islands. By Sir W. J. Hooker ... *London.* 1843. 8vo, pp. 84. 2 colored Plates. 32866

Also: Filices Exoticæ; or, Coloured Figures and Descriptions of Exotic Ferns, chiefly of such as are cultivated in the Royal Gardens of Kew. The Drawings Executed by Mr. Fitch. ... *London: L. Reeve.* 1859. 4to, 3 p. l., 101 l. 100 colored Plates. C.

HOOKER (W.) ... Lessons from the History of Medical Delusions. By Worthington Hooker. *New York: Baker & Scribner.* MDCCCL. 12mo, pp. v, 105. B. 32867

Also: An Oration ... before the Norwich Lyceum and Mechanics' Institute, on the 5th of July, 1830. ... *Norwich: Printed by J. Dunham.* 1830. 8vo, pp. 20. BA

HOOLE (E.) The Year-Book of Missions for 1847. Containing a comprehensive Account of the several Missionary Societies, British, American, and Continental: a Description of the Countries, Cities, &c. in which their Missions are established; the particular Statistics of each Missionary Station throughout the World, arranged in geographical order; ... By E. Hoole. *London.* 1847. 8vo. 32868

Hoop Petticoats, Arraigned and Condemned by the Light of Nature and Law of God. *Boston: James Franklin.* [1726.]

HOOPER (E. J.) Hooper's Western Fruit-Book. A Compendious Collection of Facts, from the Notes and Experiences of Successful Fruit Culturists. Arranged for Practical Use in Orchard and Garden. Third Edition ... . *Cincinnati.* 1858. 12mo. 32870

Also: The Practical Farmer, Gardener, and Housewife. ... *Cincinnati.* 1840. 12mo.

HOOPER (J.) The Book of Evergreens. A Practical Treatise on the Coniferæ, or Cone-bearing Plants. By Josiah Hooper. *New York.* 1868. 12mo, pp. 435. 32871

HOOPER (L.) The Complete Poetical Works of the late Miss Lucy Hooper. *New York: D. Fanshaw.* 1855. 8vo, pp. 402, (2). 32872

HOOPER. Poetical Remains of the late Lucy Hooper, Collected and Arranged; with a Memoir, by John Keese. ... *New York: Samuel Colman.* 1842. 8vo, pp. 291. BA., C., H. 32873

[HOOPER (Samuel).] Banking Association and Uniform Currency Bill ... . [Submitted to Congress in December, 1861, and December, 1862. n. p. n. d.] 8vo, pp. 8. H. 32874

[HOOPER.] Currency or Money; its Nature and Uses, and the Effects of the Circulation of Bank-Notes for Currency. By a Merchant of Boston. *Boston: Little, Brown and Company.* 1855. 8vo, pp. 112. B., BA., C., H. 32875

HOOPER. A Defence of the Merchants of Boston. ... By Samuel Hooper. *Boston: Little, Brown, and Company.* 1866. 8vo, pp. 59. B., H. 32876

[HOOPER.] Specie Currency. The True Interests of the People. *Boston.* 1855. 8vo, pp. 6. B., H. 32877

Also: An Examination of the Theory and the Effect of Laws regulating the Amount of Specie in Banks. ... *Boston: Little, Brown, and Company.* 1860. 8vo, pp. 55. BA. — The National Finances. Speech ... on the Loan Bill, ... February 21, 1866.

Washington: McGill & Witherow, Printers. 1866. 8vo, pp. 14. B. — Necessity of resuming Specie Payments. Speech ... in the House of Representatives, February 5, 1869. *Washington: F. & J. Rives & Geo. A. Bailey.* 1869. 8vo, pp. 13. — Rede ... 3. Februar 1862. [Das Haus, im Comite des Ganzen, hatte den Finanz-Entwurf unter Berathung. n. p. n. d.] 8vo, pp. 7. — Speech ... on the Treasury Note Bill; .. February 3, 1862. [n. p. n. d.] 8vo, pp. 8. — Speech ... on the Finances. .. January 19, 1863. [n. p. n. d.] 8vo, pp. 8. — Speech ... on the Necessity of Regulating the Currency ... April 6, 1864. *Washington: L. Towers & Co., Printers.* 1864. 8vo, pp. 15. — Speech ... on the Bill to amend the National Banking Law; ... February 5, 1867. *Washington.* 1867. 8vo, pp. 15. + [Another Edition.] 8vo, pp. 22.

HOOPER (Thomas). In Memoriam. T. Hooper. [*Charlestown.*] 1868. 16mo, pp. 10. B. 32878

HOOPER (T. W.) An Oration ... before ... St. Peter's Lodge ... in Newburyport ... June 24, 5796. By ... Thomas W. Hooper, P.M. *Printed at Newburyport by Brothers Blunt and March.* 5796. 4to, pp. 16. BA. 32879

HOOPER (W.) The Apostles Neither Impostors nor Enthusiasts. A Sermon ... . Preached ... in Boston, September 1742. By William Hooper, A.M. ... *Boston*, ... *Rogers and Fowle* ... . 1742. 8vo, pp. 48. B., BA., H., M., W. 32880

Also: A Sermon ... at the Funeral of Thomas Greene, Esq; August 5. 1763. ... *Boston: Printed by Richard and Samuel Draper, and Thomas and John Fleet.* MDCCLXIII. 4to, pp. 34. B. — ... A Sermon ... Preached at the West Church in Boston, October 4th. 1741. ... *Boston: J. Edwards.* 1741. 8vo, pp. 28. H. — ... A Sermon ... in Boston, December 24. 1741. ... *Boston: J. Edwards and S. Eliot.* 1742. 8vo, pp. 22.

HOOPER (W.) Fifty Years Since: An Address, ... before the Alumni of the University of North-Carolina, on the 7th of June, 1859. ... By William Hooper ... . *Raleigh: Holden & Wilson.* 1859. 8vo, pp. 50. B., H. 32881

Also: The Sacredness of Human Life. An Address ... . *Raleigh.* 1857. 8vo.

HOOPER (W. H.) The Utah Bill. A Plea for Religious Liberty. Speech of Hon. W. H. Hooper, of Utah, Delivered ... March 23, 1870. 8vo, pp. 31. H. + Together with the Remonstrance of the Citizens of Salt Lake City, in Mass Meeting, held March 31, 1870, to the Senate of the United States. *Washington, D. C.: Gibson Brothers, Printers.* 1870. 8vo, pp. 40.

Also: Extension of Boundaries. Speech ... February 25, 1869. *Washington: F. & J. Rives & Geo. A. Bailey.* 1869. 8vo, pp. 14. H., W.

HOOPER (William Hulme). Ten Months among the Tents of the Tuski, with Incidents of an Arctic Boat Expedition in Search of Sir John Franklin, as far as the Mackenzie River and Cape Bathurst. By Lieut. W. H. Hooper, R.N. *London: John Murray.* 1853. 8vo, pp. xv, (1), 417, (1). Map, 6 Plates. BA.

HOORN (Jan ten). Oost- | en | West Indische | Warande. | Vervattende aldaar de | Leef- en genees-konst. | Met een verhaal van de Speceryen, | Boom- en Aard-gewassen, Dieren &c. | in Oost- en West Indien voorvallende. | Door | Jacobus Bontius, | Gulielmus Piso, | En | Georgius Markgraef, | Doctoren in de Medicijne. | Hier nevens is bygevoegt | De nieuw verbeterde Chirurgijns | Scheep-Kist [door J. Verbrugge]. *t'Amsterdam*, | *By Jan ten Hoorn, Boekverkooper tegen* | *over 't Oude Heere-Logement.* 1694. | 16mo, pp. (8), 304, (8), 96. 32884

This is a corrected title of *our* No. 6341. It was edited by Hoorn, and was intended for the use of medical men at the East and West Indies. *See* Bontekoe (W. Y.), Vol. II., Nos. 6337–6340.

HOORNBEEK (J.) Disputatio theologica | de | Conversione Indorum & | Gentilium. | Decima-nona. | Qvam, | Favente Deo Opt. Max. | Sub Præsidio | Clarissimi, Doctissimique Viri, | D. Johannis Hoornbeek, S. S. Theol. | Doct. ... | *Sumptibus Academiæ* | *Lugduni Batavorum*, | *Apud Viduam & Hæredes Johannis Elsevirii*, | *Academ Typograph.* | cIↃ IↃ c LXIII. | 4to, 6 l. 32885

HOORNBEEK. Johannis Hoornbeek, | S. Literarum in Ecclesia & Academia, primum Trajectina, | deinde Lugduno-Batava, Doctoris & Professoris. | De | Conversione | Indorum & Gentilium. | Libri Duo. | Accessit | Ejusdem Vita ab Amico edita. | *Amstelodami*, | *Apud Johannem Janssonium à Waesberge*, | *& Viduam Elizæi Weyerstraet, Anno* MDCLXIX. | 4to, pp. (55), 259, (13), (2); 260–265. Portrait. J.C.B. 32886

A posthumous publication. Prefixed is a life of the author, perhaps by the editor, D. Stuart. The large folded portrait of Hoornbeek, by Santvoort, is often wanting. The supplemental chapter XIV after the index, relates to the efforts of Mayhew, Eliot, Shepard, and others among the Indians in New England.

HOORNBEEK. De | Waare Deught | En | s'Christens Hoogste Goedt, | Voor Gestelt. | In een Leerreeden, over | Hebr. XII. 14. | Door Jacob Hoornbeek, | Ouderling der Neder-Duytse Gereformeerde gemeynte te Rochester, in | Ulster County, in de Provintie van Niew-York, in Noord-America. | ... *Niew-York:* | *Gedruckt en te koop by J. Parker and W. Weyman*, | *in de Niewe Druckery in de Bever Straat*, 1755. | 8vo, pp. 30. 32887

A piece of very great rarity; the Albany Institute has a copy.

THE HOOSAC TUNNEL. A Brief Report of the Hearing of the Troy and Greenfield Railroad Company, Petitioners for a Loan of $2,000,000, before the Legislature of Massachusetts. *Boston.* 1853. 8vo, pp. 78. 32888

The Memorial of the Western Railroad Corporation, relating to the Application of the Troy and Greenfield Railroad for a State Loan of Two Millions of Dollars. *Boston: Eastburn's Press.* 1853. 8vo, pp. 25. B. 32889

Remarks on the Present Position of Hoosac Tunnel Enterprise. [n. p. n. d.] 8vo, pp. 10. 32890

Also: Report of the Hearing before the Massachusetts Legislature, 1854. *See* Bird (F. W.) *and* [Harris (D. L.)]

HOOSICK FALLS. Celebration of Washington's Birth Day at Hoosick Falls, 1862. [n. p. n. d.] 8vo, pp. 6. 32891

HOOTON (C.) St. Louis' Isle, or Texiana; with additional Observations made in the United States and in Canada. By Charles Hooton, Esq., ... *London.* 1847. 8vo, pp. 217. Portrait. 32892

HOOTON (R. T.) Life and Frolics of Major Stevens, the Wonderful Dwarf ... his Numerous Adventures ... his Perils in Rhode Island by "Flood and Field" ... By Robert Treat Hooton. *Boston: The Author.* 1832. 8vo, pp. 28. B. 32893

HOOVER (D.) Memoir of David Hoover, a Pioneer of Indiana, with Facts pertaining to the Settlement of the Whitewater Valley. *Richmond, Ind.* 1857. 8vo. 32894

HOPE (A. J. B. B.) The American Disruption. 1. A Popular View of the American Civil War. 2. England, The North, and the South. 3. The Results of the American Disruption. In Three Lectures, delivered by Request ... before the Maidstone Literary & Mechanics Institute. By A. J. B. Beresford Hope, Esq. *London: James Ridgway.* 1862. 8vo, pp. 116. + Sixth Edition. [*Ibid.*] B., BA. 32895

HOPE. England, the North, and the South. By A. J. B. Beresford Hope. Third Edition. *London: James Ridgway.* 1862. 8vo, pp. 40. C., H., S. + Fourth Edition. [*Ibid.*] 1862.

HOPE. A Popular View of The American Civil War. By A. J. B. Beresford Hope. *London: James Ridgway.* 1861. 8vo, pp. 39. + pp. 28. H. + Third Edition. [*Ibid.*] 1862. C.

HOPE. The Results of the American Disruption: a Lecture ... in Continuation of a Popular View of the American Civil War, and England, The North and the South. By A. J. B. Beresford Hope. Third Edition. *London: James Ridgway.* 1862. 8vo, pp. 40. H. 32898

HOPE. The Social and Political Bearings of the American Disruption. By A. J. B. Beresford Hope. *London: William Ridgway.* 1863. 8vo, pp. 42. + Second Edition. [*Ibid.*] + Third Edition. [*Ibid.*] B., BA., H. 32899

HOPE (H.) Letters from Canada. By Henry Hope, LL.B. *London.* 1863. 8vo, pp. 83. 32900

HOPE (J. B.) An Elegiac Ode: recited by James Barron Hope, on the occasion of Completing the Monument erected by the Ladies of Warren County, N. C. over the Remains of Annie Carter Lee. *Richmond: Examiner Job Print.* 1866. 12mo, pp. 89. 32901

HOPE. A Poem: pronounced by James Barron Hope, on the Two Hundred and Fiftieth Anniversary of the English Settlement at Jamestown, May 13th, 1857. *Richmond: Chas. H. Wynne, Printer.* 1857. 8vo, pp. 16. H. 32902

[HOPE.] Chronicles of Yonkers. *Yonkers: Privately Printed.* 1864. 8vo, pp. 23. 32903

Hope Deferred. *See* Despard (G. P.), Vol. v., No. 19752.

HOPEDALE, *Mass.* Constitution, By-Laws and Regulations of Fraternal Community, No. 1. Located at Hopedale, Milford, Worcester County, Mass. ... *Hopedale, Milford, Mass.* 1846. 8vo, pp. 16. 32904

Also: Constitution, By-Laws, Rules and Regulations of the Hopedale Community: as revised and approved, July 10, 1850. *Hopedale: Printed by A. G. Spalding.* 1850. 8vo, pp. 28. H.

HOPKINS (A.) Proceedings at the Centennial Commemoration of the organization of the Berkshire Association of Congregational Ministers, held at Stockbridge, Mass., October 28, 1863. Historical Discourse by Prof. Albert Hopkins, LL.D. *Boston: J. E. Farwell and Company, Printers.* 1864. 8vo, pp. 56. 32905

HOPKINS. A Sermon Delivered at Williamstown, Mass., on the Day of the Annual State Fast, March 28, 1839. By Albert Hopkins, ... *Troy, N. Y.: Stevenson and M'Call, Printers.* 1839. 8vo, pp. 21. BA. 32906

Also: Address, at the Opening of the Observatory of Williams College, in 1838. ... *Pittsfield.* [1838.] 8vo.

HOPKINS (A. T.) The American Patriot. A Discourse, Thanksgiving. By A. T. Hopkins. *Buffalo.* 1843. 8vo. S.

Also: The Evils and Remedy of Lewdness. A Sermon ... . *Utica.* 1834. 8vo, pp. 36.

Hopkins (C.) A History of Boston, from its Origin to the Present Period; with some Account of the Environs. By Caleb Hopkins. *Boston: A. Bowen.* 1825. 8vo. + Second Edition. [*Ibid.*] 1828. 8vo. 32908

Hopkins (D.) A Sermon preached December 29, 1799, ... the Lord's Day after the Melancholy Tidings ... of the Death of General George Washington ... . By Daniel Hopkins, A.M. *Salem: Printed by Thomas C. Cushing.* [1800.] 8vo, pp. 28. C.

Also: Sermon, preached at the Dedication of the New South Meeting House, in Salem, Jan. 1, 1805. ... *Salem.* 1805. 8vo, pp. 24.

Hopkins (D. C.) The True Cause of all Contention, Strife and Civil War. By D. C. Hopkins. *New York.* 1862. 12mo.

Hopkins (E. A.) Historico-Political Memorial upon the Regions of the Rio De la Plata, and Conterminous Countries, ... By Edward A. Hopkins ... . *New-York: Pudney & Russell, Printers.* 1858. 8vo, pp. 63. Portrait. H. 32911

Hopkins. Memoria acompanando un proyecto de ley, proveyando los medios de disponer de las tierras publicas de la Confederacion Argentina, y otros objetos. Por Eduardo Augusto Hopkins. *Buenos-Aires.* 1859. 4to, pp. xiv, 222. 32912

Also: Proposals for Steam Navigation on the head Waters of the Rio de la Plata. ... *New-York.* 1851. s.

[Hopkins (Erastus).] The Objections to African Colonization Stated and Answered. ... *Philadelphia: Printed by Russell and Martien.* 1833. 8vo, pp. 24. 32913

Hopkins. Speeches ... on the Bill to incorporate the College of the Holy Cross, in ... Worcester; delivered in the House of Representatives, April 24th & 25th, 1849: ... *Northampton: Butler & Bridgman.* 1849. 8vo, pp. 44. B., H. 32914

Hopkins (F. W.) Eulogy at Norwich, Vt., Feb. 22, 1848, during the Obsequies of Truman B. Ransom, Col. 9th Regiment. By Gen. Frederick W. Hopkins. *Hanover, Vt.* 1848. 8vo. + Second Edition. *Troy.* 1849. 8vo. S. 32915

Hopkins (G. W.) Letter of George W. Hopkins ... to Col. James H. Piper ... [on Mr. Van Buren,] 1840. [*Washington.* n. d.] 8vo, pp. 32. BA., S. 32916

Hopkins (G. T.) A Mission to the Indians, from the Indian Committee of Baltimore Yearly Meeting, to Fort Wayne, in

1804. Written at the time, by Gerard T. Hopkins, with an Appendix, Compiled in 1862, by Martha E. Tyson. *Philadelphia: T. Elwood Zell.* 1862. 18mo, pp. 198. 32917

Not printed for sale, but presented to "Friends and others interested in Indian affairs." *See* Field's Essay, No. 716.

Hopkins (H. B.) Renunciation of Freemasonry. By Hiram B. Hopkins. *Boston: John Marsh & Co.* 1830. 12mo, pp. 12.

Hopkins (J.) Opinion of James Hopkins, Esq., on the Susquehanna Bridge Co. *Columbia.* 1813. 12mo. P. 32919

Hopkins (J. D.) An Address to the Members of the Cumberland Bar, delivered during the Sitting of the Court of Common Pleas, at Portland, June Term, 1833. By James D. Hopkins ... . *Portland: Printed by Charles Day and Co.* 1833. 8vo, pp. 79. BA. 32920

Contains a history of the Cumberland Bar, and notices of deceased members.

Hopkins. An Oration ... at the Consecration of Oriental Lodge, Bridgton, September 20th, A.L. 5804. By ... James D. Hopkins ... . *Portland: Printed by Jenks & Shirley.* [n. d.] 8vo, pp. 20. BA. 32921

Also. An Oration pronounced before the Inhabitants of Portland [Me.], July 4th, 1805. ... *Portland.* 1805. 8vo, pp. 25 B., BA., H., W.

Hopkins (J.) The Patriot's Manual; comprising various Standard and Miscellaneous Subjects, interesting to every American Citizen; ... By Jesse Hopkins. *Utica: Printed by William Williams.* 1828. 16mo, pp. 220. C. 32922

Hopkins (John). Notions. *See* John Hopkins.

Hopkins (J. B.) The Fall of the Confederacy. By John Baker Hopkins. *London: William Freeman.* [1867.] 12mo, pp. 96. B., BA. 32923

Hopkins. Introduction to the Hon. James Williams' "The South Vindicated," etc. *London.* 186–. 8vo, pp. xii, 40.

Hopkins. Peace or War? An Unbiassed View of the American Crisis. By John B. Hopkins. ... *London: Diprose and Bateman.* 1861. 8vo, pp. 15. H. 32925

Hopkins (J. H.) The American Citizen: his Rights and Duties, according to the Spirit of the Constitution of the United States. By John Henry Hopkins, D.D. *New York: Pudney & Russell.* 1857. 12mo, pp. 459. B., BA., C., S. 32926

Hopkins. Extract from the American Citizen, his Rights and Duties in Reference to Slavery. By John Henry Hopkins ... . *New-York: Pudney & Russell.* 1860. 12mo, pp. 121–144. H.

[Hopkins.] ... Bible View of Slavery. [n. p. 1863.] 8vo, pp. 16. [Handbook of the Democracy, Papers No. 8.] H.

This is a Letter to G. M. Wharton, etc., in reply to a Note from them, requesting the Bishop's Views on the Aspect of Slavery. It elicited several replies as: Bishop Hopkins' Letter on Slavery Ripped up, and his Misuse of the Sacred Scriptures Exposed. By a Clergyman of the Protestant Episcopal Church. *New York: John F. Trow, Printer.* 1863. 12mo, pp. 44.—Letter to the Right Rev. John H. Hopkins ... Bishop of Vermont on the Bible View of Slavery. *New York: Printed by W. F. Kost.* 1861. 8vo, pp. 12.—Protest of the Bishop and Clergy of the Diocese of Pennsylvania, against Bishop Hopkins' Letter on African Slavery, September, 1863. 4to, pp. 3.—Review of a "Letter from the Right Rev. John H. Hopkins, D.D., LL.D., Bishop of Vermont, on Bible View of Slavery," By a Vermonter. *Burlington.* 1861. 8vo, pp. 28. *See also* our Vol. II., Nos. 5189–5190, *also* Goodwin (D. R.), Vol. VII., No. 27936, [Lea (Henry Cary)], [Lundy (J. P.)], *and* [May (C.)]

Hopkins. The Bishop of Vermont's Protest, and Draft of a Pastoral Letter. [n. p. n. d.] 8vo, pp. 16. 32929

Hopkins. Letter to Rev. M. A. DeWolf Howe, D.D., 1863. [n. p. n. d.] 32930

See A Reply to the Letter of Bishop Hopkins, addressed to Dr. Howe in the, Print called "The Age," of December 8th, 1863. *Philadelphia.* 1864. 8vo, pp. 18.

Hopkins. The Novelties which Disturb our Peace: Letters addressed to the Bishops, Clergy and Laity of the Protestant Episcopal Church. By Rev. John Henry Hopkins ... . *Philadelphia: Herman Hooker.* 1844. 8vo, pp. 71. A Second Letter, pp. 80; a Third Letter, pp. 84; a Fourth Letter, pp. 71. H.

Another Edition published by *James M. Campbell & Co.* pp. 66; Letter II. pp. 73; Letter III. pp. 76; Letter IV. pp. 56.

Hopkins. A Scriptural, Ecclesiastical, and Historical View of Slavery, from the Days of the Patriarch Abraham, to the Nineteenth Century. Addressed to the Right Rev. Alonzo Potter, D.D. ... By John Henry Hopkins, D.D., LL.D. ... *New York: W. I. Pooley & Co.* [1864.] 12mo, pp. (2), vii, (1), 376.

Hopkins. Slavery: its Religious Sanction, its Political Dangers, and the Best Mode of doing it away. A Lecture delivered before the Young Mens' Associations of ... Buffalo, and Lockport ... . By John Henry Hopkins. ... . *Buffalo: Phinney & Co.* 1851. 8vo, pp. 32. B., BA. 32933

Also: An Address ... before the House of Convocation of Trinity College ... Hartford, July 26th, 1854. ... *Hartford: S. Hanmer & Co.* 1854. 8vo, pp. 30.—Address ... August 2, 1850, on the Death of General Zachary Taylor ... . *St. Albans: Printed*

by E. B. Whiting. 1850. 8vo, pp. 26.—Defence of the Convention of the Protestant Episcopal Church, in the State of Massachusetts, against ... 'the Banner of the Church.' ... *Boston: Stimpson & Clapp.* 1832. 8vo, pp. 44.—History of the Church, in Verse. Composed for the Use of Bible-Classes, ... in the Protestant Episcopal Church in the United States. ... *New York: W. I. Pooley.* 1867. 12mo, pp. 256.—Religion the Only Safeguard of National Prosperity. A Sermon ... Boston, December 1, 1831 ... the Day of Annual Thanksgiving. ... *Boston: Samuel H. Parker.* 1831. 8vo, pp. 24.— ... A Sermon ... at the Ordination of Ten Candidates for the Diaconate, in ... New York ... June 27th, 1841. ... *New-York: Dean & Trevelt.* 1841. 8vo, pp. 24.— ... Sermon before the General Convention of the Protestant Episcopal Church ... in ... New York ... October 6th, 1847. ... *New-York: Daniel Dana, Jr.* 1847. 8vo, pp. 24.— ... A Sermon ... in the Old South Church, Boston, Jan. 18, 1832, before the Howard Benevolent Society. ... *Boston: Perkins & Marvin.* 1832. 8vo, pp. 20. Duyckinck's Cylclopedia, Vol. II. 393, enumerates several other works by Bishop Hopkins.

Hopkins (J. H.), *Jr.* Poor Trinity. The Report of a Committee on the Condition of the Finances of Trinity Church, examined by John H. Hopkins, Jr. ... *New-York.* 1859. 8vo, pp. 29. B. 32934

This elicited: "Rich Trinity. A Layman's Answer to 'Poor Trinity,' examined by John H. Hopkins, Jr. ..." *New York.* 1859. 8vo, pp. 32. Also: The Faith and Order of the Protestant Episcopal Church in the United States. ... *New York.* [n. d.] 12mo, pp. 14.

[Hopkins (John).] Report of the Finance Committee of the Baltimore and Ohio Railroad Company ... December 8th, 1869 ... . *Baltimore.* 1869. 8vo, pp. 15. H. 32935

Hopkins (J. R.) Report of the Case of Trespass & Assault and Battery, wherein John Evans was Plaintiff, And Ellis Yarnall, ... and [others] ... were Defendants. Including an Interesting and Important Discussion respecting the Discipline of the Religious Society of Friends; and containing the valuable Speeches of the Counsel, Revised from the short-hand Notes of T. Lloyd. Tried at ... Philadelphia ... . By Joseph R. Hopkins. *Philadelphia: P. Byrne.* 1810. 8vo, pp. 150. 32936

Hopkins (M.) Baccalaureate Sermons and Occasional Discourses, by Mark Hopkins, D.D., President of Williams College. *Boston: T. R. Marvin & Son.* 1862. 8vo. 32937

The following are all Baccalaureate Sermons published separately: ... A ... Sermon, ... August 18, 1850. ... *Boston.* 1850. 8vo, pp. 28. + ... August 17, 1851. 8vo, pp. 27. + ... August 15, 1852. ... *Boston.* 1852. 8vo, pp. 24. + ... August 15, 1855. ... *Boston.* 1855. 8vo, pp. 24. + ... August 3, 1856. ... *Boston.* 1856. 8vo, pp. 24. + ... August 4, 1857. ... *Boston.* 1857. 8vo, pp. 20. + ... August 1, 1858. ... *Boston.* 1858. 8vo, pp. 24. + ... July 31, 1859. ... *Boston.* 1859. 8vo, pp. 26. + ... August 1, 1860. 8vo. + ... August 2, 1863. ... *Boston.* 1863. 8vo, pp. 24. + ... July 31, 1864. ... *Boston.* 1864. 8vo, pp. 24. + ... July 30, 1865. ... *Boston.* 1865. 8vo, pp. 26. + ... July 28, 1867. ... *Boston.* 1867. 8vo, pp. 25. + ... July 26, 1868. ... *Boston.* 1868. 8vo, pp. 22. + ... June 20, 1869. ... *Boston.* 1869. 8vo, pp. 23. + ... June 26, 1870. ... *Boston.* 1870. 8vo, pp. 24.

Hopkins. Colleges and Stability. A Discourse ... in Marietta, Ohio, Nov. 8, 1868, at the Quarter-Century Anniversary of the Society for the Promotion of Collegiate and Theological Education at the West. By Mark Hopkins, D.D. [*New York:*] *Reprinted from the Proceedings of the Society.* [1860.] 8vo, pp. (20).

Hopkins. A Discourse Commemorative of Amos Lawrence, delivered ... in the Chapel of Williams College, February 21, 1853. By Mark Hopkins ... , D.D. *Boston: Press of T. R. Marvin.* 1853. 8vo, pp. 36. B., BA., H. 32939

Hopkins. The Living House, on God's Method of Social Unity. A Baccalaureate Sermon, delivered at Williamstown, Mass., August 3, 1862. By Mark Hopkins, D.D. *Boston: T. R. Marvin & Son.* 1862. 8vo, pp. 26. 32940

Relates to the Rebellion in the South.

Hopkins. Miscellaneous Essays and Discourses. By Mark Hopkins, D.D. ... *Boston: T. R. Marvin.* 1847. 8vo, pp. 514.

Hopkins. A Sermon ... before ... Edward Everett, Governor, etc. ... on the Anniversary Election, January 2, 1839. By Mark Hopkins, D.D. *Boston: Dutton and Wentworth, Printers.* 1839. 8vo, pp. 40. B. 32942

Hopkins. The Temple of God. A Sermon ... at the Dedication of the South Congregational Church, Pittsfield, Mass., Nov. 13, 1850. By Mark Hopkins, D.D. *Boston: T. R. Marvin.* 1850. 8vo, pp. 22. B., H. 32943

Also: An Address, delivered at the Dedication of Williston Seminary, at East-Hampton, Mass., December 1, 1841. ... *Northampton: J. H. Butler.* 1841. 8vo, pp. 23.—An Address, delivered before the ... Alumni of Williams College, at the Celebration of the Semi-Centennial Anniversary, August 16, 1843. ... *Boston.* 1843. 8vo, pp. 41. + Second Edition. *Boston: Press of T. R. Marvin.* 1843. 8vo, pp. 40. BA.—An Address, ... before the Society for the Promotion of Collegiate and Theological Education at the West. ... *Boston: Press of T. R. Marvin.* 1852. 8vo, pp. 24. H.—The Central Principle. An Oration delivered before the New-England Society of New York, December 22, 1853. ... *New York: E. French.* 1854. 8vo, pp. 36.— ... A Discourse ... before the Congregational Library Association ... Boston, May 29, 1855. .. *Boston: Press of T. R. Marvin.* 1855. 8vo, pp. 36. B.—A Discourse [on] the Death of the Rev. Edward Dorr Griffin, D.D. ... November 26, 1837. ... *Troy: Tuttle, Belcher & Burton, Printers.* 1837. 8vo, pp. 20. B.—Fruit in Old Age. A Discourse, commemorative of Nathan Jackson ... May 17, 1863. ... *Boston: Press of T. R. Marvin & Son.* 1863. 8vo, pp. 26.—The Inaugural Discourse, delivered at Williams College, September 15, 1836. ... *Troy: N. Tuttle, Printer.* 1836. 8vo, pp. 31. B.—The Sabbath and Free Institutions. A Sermon, May, 1847. ... *Boston.* 1847. 8vo.—The Sabbath and Free Institutions. A Paper read before the National Sabbath Convention, Saratoga, Aug. 13, 1863. ... *New York: Printed by Edward O. Jenkins.* 1863. 8vo, pp. 20. B.—Science and Religion. A Sermon delivered in ... Albany, ... August 24, 1856. ... *Albany: Van Benthuysen, Printer.* 1856. 8vo, pp. 35. B.,

BA., H.—A Sermon ... at Plymouth, on the Twenty-Second of December, 1846. ... *Boston: Press of T. R. Marvin.* 1847. 8vo, pp. 32. B.—A Sermon ... before the Annual Convention of the Congregational Ministers of Massachusetts ... May 29, 1845 ... *Boston: Press of T. R. Marvin.* 1845 8vo, pp. 32.—A Sermon ... before the Pastoral Association of Massachusetts ... May 30, 1843. ... *Boston: Tappan and Dennet.* 1843. 8vo, pp. 31.—A Sermon [on] the Death of Prof. Ebenezer Kellogg ... Oct. 11, 1846. ... *Boston: Press of T. R. Marvin* 1846. 8vo, pp 28. B. *See also* Berkshire Jubilee, Vol. II, No 4893.

Hopkins, Woodward (S. B.), *and* Hoar (S.) Address to the People of Massachusetts, on the Present Condition and Claims of the Temperance Reformation. ... *Boston: Daniel Kimball, Printer.* 1846. 8vo, pp. 20. B., H. 32944

Hopkins (S.), *died* 1755. Historical Memoirs, Relating to the Housatunnuk Indians: or, An Account of the Methods used, and Pains taken, for the Propagation of the Gospel among that Heathenish-Tribe, and the Success thereof, under the Ministry of the late Reverend Mr. John Sergeant: Together, With the Character of that eminently worthy Missionary; and an Address to the People of this Country, representing the very great Importance of attaching the Indians to their Interest, not only by treating them justly and kindly, but by using proper Endeavours to settle Christianity among them By Samuel Hopkins, A.M. Pastor of a Church in Springfield. ... *Boston, N. E.* ... *S. Kneeland,* ... 1753. 4to, pp. (2), iv, 182. B., BA., C., H., P., S. 32945

Neatly executed. The preface is dated Nov. 14. 1752. Reprinted in part in 1757:

Hopkins. An Address to the People of New-England. Representing the very great Importance of attaching the Indians to their Interest; not only by treating them justly and kindly; but by using proper Endeavours to settle Christianity among them. By Samuel Hopkins, A.M. Pastor of a Church in Springfield. ... Printed in Boston, 1753. Being a Conclusion to the Historical Memoirs relating to the Housatunnuk Indians; with an account of the Methods used for the Propagation of the Gospel among the said Indians, by the late reverend Mr. John Sergeant. Now recommended to the serious Consideration of the Inhabitants of Pennsylvania, and the other Colonies. *Philadelphia: Reprinted by B. Franklin, and D. Hall.* 1757. 8vo, pp. 27. N., P. 32946

Hopkins. An | Abridgment | of | Mr. Hopkins' | Historical Memoirs, | relating to the | Housatunnuk, or Stockbridge Indians; | or, | A brief Account of the Methods used, and | Pains taken, for civilizing and propagating the | Gospel among that Heathenish Tribe, | and the Success thereof, under the Ministry of | the late Rev. Mr. John Sergeant. | *Philadelphia: Printed and Sold by B.*

Franklin and D. Hall. M,DCC,LVII. 8vo, pp. 40, Conrad Weiser's Letter, pp. 7. 32947

Mr. Hopkins' Memoir is one of the rarest of works relating to New England, as it is one of the most intrinsically valuable. This abridgment fails in the last quality by reason of its abbreviation, but is nearly as rare. The letter of Conrad Weiser narrates some remarkable incidents of his visit to the Onondagas not elsewhere preserved.

[Hopkins (Samuel)], *died* 1803. A Dialogue concerning the Slavery of the Africans, shewing it to be the Duty and Interest of the American States to Emancipate all their African Slaves. With an Address to the owners of Slaves. To which is prefixed, the Institution of the Society in New-York for promoting the Manumission of Slaves. ... *Norwich, Conn., J. P. Spooner.* 1776. S. + *New York, Reprinted, R. Hodge.* 1785. 16mo, pp. 72.

Hopkins. An Inquiry concerning the future State of those who die in their Sins ... and whether Endless Punishment be Consistent with Divine Justice, Wisdom, and Goodness: ... By Samuel Hopkins, D.D. .. *Newport, Rhode Island: Printed by Solomon Southwick.* 1783. 4to, pp. (4), vi, 194. B., BA., W. 32949

[Hopkins.] The Life ... of Mr. Jonathan Edwards. *See our* Vol. VI., No. 21948.

Hopkins. Memoirs of the Rev. Jonathan Edwards, A.M. ... Revised and Enlarged ... By John Hawksley. *London: James Black.* 1815. 12mo, pp. xii, 266. C., H. 32950

Hopkins. The Life and Character of Miss Susanna Anthony, who died, in Newport, (R. I.) June 23, MDCCXCI, in the Sixty-Fifth Year of her Age. Consisting chiefly in Extracts from her Writings, with some Brief Observations on them. Compiled by Samuel Hopkins, D.D. ... *Printed at Worcester, Massachusetts, By Leonard Worcester.* MDCCXCVI. 8vo. + *Hartford: Re-printed by Hudson and Goodwin.* 1799. 8vo, pp. 168. + Memoirs of Miss Susanna Anthony ... . A New Edition, with a recommendatory preface, By Dr. Ryland, Mr. Fuller, and Mr. Sutcliff. *Clipstone: J. W. Morris.* 1803. 8vo, pp. (4), 241. 32951

Also: The Life and Character of Miss Susanna Anthony. ... Second Edition. *Portland: Lyman, Hall & Co.* 1810. 12mo, pp. 187. Another American edition was printed in *Boston,* 1810. Miss Anthony was an eminently pious woman of Rhode Island, whose parents were Quakers. This volume consists chiefly of extracts from her writings.

Hopkins. Memoirs of the Life of Mrs. Sarah Osborn ... . By Samuel Hopkins, D.D. *Worcester: Printed by Leonard Worcester.* 1799. 12mo, pp. 380. B. + Second Edition. *Catskill: N. Elliot.* 1814. 12mo, pp. 359. 32952

Hopkins. Sketches of the Life of the Late Rev. Samuel Hopkins, ... Pastor of the First Congregational Church in Newport, written by Himself; interspersed with Marginal Notes, extracted from his Private Diary; to which is added a Dialogue, by the Same Hand, on the Nature and Extent of True Christian Submission; also, a Serious Address to Professing Christians: closed by Dr. Hart's Sermon at his Funeral; with an Introduction to the Whole, by the Editor. Published by Stephen West, D.D., Pastor of the Church in Stockbridge, Mass. *Hartford: Printed by Hudson & Goodwin.* 1805. 18mo, pp. 240. Portrait.

Hopkins. Timely Articles on Slavery. By Samuel Hopkins, D.D. ... *Boston: Congregational Board of Publication.* 1854. 8vo, pp. vi, (2), 549–624. B. 32954

Hopkins. The Works of Samuel Hopkins, D.D. *Boston.* 1854. 3 vols., 8vo, pp. viii, 266, (1), 534; viii, 770; vi, 3–798. Portrait. B., H. 32955

Edited by Prof. E. A. Park. Also: Animadversions on Mr. Hart's late Dialogue; In a Letter to a Friend. ... *New London: Printed by T. Green.* M,DCC.LXX. 8vo, pp. 31.—An Enquiry concerning The Promises of the Gospel. Whether any of them are made to the ... Unregenerate. ... Containing, Remarks on two sermons ... by Dr. Mayhew of Boston. ... Also, A brief enquiry into the Use of Means. ... *Boston, N. E.: Printed by W. M'Alpine and J. Fleeming.* M,DCC,LXV. 8vo, pp. (4), viii, 144. + pp. (2), viii, 145. BA.—An Inquiry into the Nature of True Holiness. With an Appendix; containing an Answer to the Rev. Mr. William Hart's Remarks on President Edwards's Dissertation on the Nature of True Virtue ... . *Newport, R. I.: Printed by Solomon Southwick.* M,DCC,LXXIII. 12mo, pp. vi, (2), 220. W. + *New York.* 1791.—Sermon ... at the South Church in Boston. ... *Boston.* 1768. 8vo, pp. 35.—A Treatise on the Millennium. ... *Boston: Printed by Isaiah Thomas and Ebenezer T. Andrews.* MDCCXCIII. 8vo, pp. 158. Dr. Hopkins originated the peculiar sect known as Hopkinsonians, and is the original of the Doctor in Mrs. Beecher Stowe's "Minister's Wooing."

Hopkins (S.) An Half Century Discourse, delivered in Hadley, March 3, 1805. By Samuel Hopkins, D.D. *Northampton: Thomas M. Pomroy.* 1805. 8vo, pp. 32. S. 32956

Hopkins (S.) The Puritans; or, the Church, Court, and Parliament of England during the reigns of Edward VI. and Queen Elizabeth. By Samuel Hopkins. *Boston: Gould and Lincoln.* 1859–61. 3 vols., 8vo, pp. xiv, 549; 539; 675. BA.

Hopkins. The Youth of the Old Dominion. By Samuel Hopkins. *Boston: John P. Jewett & Co.* 1856. 12mo, pp. viii, 473. B., BA., C., H. 32958

A romantic and picturesque sketch of the early History of Virginia, and the heroic adventures of Capt. John Smith and the early settlers.

HOPKINS (S.) ... A Sermon ... on Fast Day, April 18, 1839. By Samuel Hopkins ... . *Saco: S. L. Goodale.* 1839. 8vo, pp. 14.

HOPKINS. ... A Sermon ... Day of Public Thanksgiving, November 29, 1838. By Samuel Hopkins ... . *Saco: S. L. Goodale.* 1839. 8vo, pp. 15. B. 32960

[HOPKINS (Samuel Miles).] Letters concerning the General Health; with Notes and considerable Additions to the Numbers, as they lately appeared in the New York Gazette. By a House Holder. *New York: Lang and Turner.* 1805. 8vo, pp. 52.

HOPKINS. An Oration delivered before the Washington Benevolent Society, in the City of New-York, ... on the Twenty-Second of February, 1809. By Samuel M. Hopkins, Esq. *New-York: Printed by J. Seymour.* 1809. 8vo, pp. 20. N., S.

Also: Address, before the Agricultural Society of Genesee County. ... *Batavia.* 1819. 12mo.—Speech ... upon ... Taxing Bank Stock. *Albany.* 1822. 8vo, pp. 15.

HOPKINS (S. D.) Centennial Discourse, Oct. 15, 1865. By S. D. Hopkins. 1865. 8vo, pp. 16. 32963

[HOPKINS (Stephen).] A Copy of a Relation, &c., made Use of by Two Parties claiming Land in Nantucket. [n. p.] 1770. 4to, pp. 16. M. 32964

HOPKINS. Letter to the People of Rhode Island, giving "some public account of such parts of my conduct as have been most censured." *[Dated] Providence, March* 31, 1757. Folio, pp. 5. 32965

[HOPKINS.] The Rights of Colonies Examined. Published by Authority. *Providence: Printed by William Goddard.* M.DCC.-LXV. 4to, pp. 24. H. 32966

"A modest yet pathetic recital of the hardships laid on our American brethren by the stamp act," &c.—*Monthly Review*, XXXIII. 484. *See also* J. R. Bartlett's catalogue of J. C. Brown's library, where it is said to have been reprinted in Great Britain in the same year, which is, I think, an error. The original edition is extremely rare, and the following, which is a reprint, is far from common.

[HOPKINS.] The Grievances of the American Colonies Candidly Examined. ... Printed by Authority, at Providence, in Rhode-Island. *London: Reprinted for J. Almon.* MDCCLXVI. 8vo, pp. 47. B., BA., H., P. 32967

On page 38, of this edition, several paragraphs are omitted which appear in the original. It was also reprinted in the "Colonial Records of Rhode Island," VI. 416–427.

HOPKINS. A true Representation of the Plan formed at Albany, for uniting all the British Northern Colonies, in order

to their common safety and defence; containing abstracts of the authorities given by the several governments to their commissioners; and of several letters from the Secretaries of State, and Lords Commissioners for Trade and Plantations, concerning such Union. Together with a Representation of the state of the English and French Colonies in North America; and the said plan of Union, with the doings of the Commissioners thereon; and some remarks on the whole. *[Dated] Providence, March* 29, 1755. Folio, pp. 14 32968

The Commissioners from Rhode Island were Stephen Hopkins and Martin Howard. The Colonies represented were Massachusetts Bay, New Hampshire, Connecticut, Rhode Island, New York, New Jersey, Pennsylvania, Maryland, Virginia, North Carolina and South Carolina. *See our* Vol. II, No. 7889, "Mass. Hist. Soc. Collections," Second Series, Vol. IX., *and* Tudor's "Otis," Chap. XII.

HOPKINS (T.) An Appeal to the Tribunal of Public Justice; being a Concise Statement of the Facts which led to the Extraordinary Case, of Stockton *versus* Hopkins. By Thomas Hopkins. *Philadelphia: The Author.* 1808. 8vo, pp. iv, vi, (2), 48.

HOPKINS (T. M.) A Discourse, on the Death of Abraham Lincoln, Delivered in the 1st Presbyterian Church in Bloomington, Indiana, April 19th, 1865. By Rev. T. M. Hopkins. [n. p. n. d.] 8vo, pp. 7. B. 32970

HOPKINS. Reminiscences of Col. John Ketcham, of Monroe County, Indiana ... Rev. T. M. Hopkins ... . *Bloomington: Whitaker & Walker, Printers.* 1866. 8vo, pp. 22. H. 32971

HOPKINS (W.) Speech of Hon. William Hopkins ... on the ... State of the Country. Delivered in the Pennsylvania House of Representatives, April 9, 1863. [n. p. n. d.] 8vo, pp. 4.

HOPKINS (W. R.) Report on the New Town at the Foot of Lake Huron. By William R. Hopkins. *Geneva.* 1837. 8vo.

HOPKINS ACADEMY, *Hadley, Mass.* Catalogue, 1849. 8vo.

The Hopkinsian Magazine, 1824 and 1825. Rev. Otis Thompson, Editor. Volume I. *Providence: Carlile & Brown, Printers.* 1824. 8vo, pp. (4), 572. Continued to 4 volumes. B.

HOPKINSON (F.) An Account of the Impeachment and Trial of the Late Francis Hopkinson, Esq. Judge of the Court of Admiralty for the Commonwealth of Pennsylvania. *Philadelphia: Francis Bailey.* MDCCXCIV. 8vo, pp. 3, 62. 32976

Also included in the "Pennsylvania State Trials."

HOPKINSON. The Battle of the Kegs. By Francis Hopkinson. *Philadelphia: Oakwood Press.* 1866 8vo, pp. 30. 32977

Eighty-two copies privately printed on blue paper.

HOPKINSON. An Exercise, containing a Dialogue and an Ode, on the Accession of George the Third. By Francis Hopkinson. *Philadelphia.* 1762. 4to. P. 32978

HOPKINSON. The Miscellaneous Essays and Occasional Writings of Francis Hopkinson, Esq. *Philadelphia: T. Dobson.* M,DCC,XCII. 3 vols., 8vo, pp. vi, 384; iv, 422; vi, 215, 204. B.

[HOPKINSON.] A Pretty Story. Written in the Year of our Lord 1774. By Peter Grievous, Esq., A. B. C. D. E. *Philadelphia: John Dunlap.* M.DCC.LXXIV. 8vo, pp. 32. + Second Edition. *[Ibid.]* M. + *Williamsburgh.* 1774. C. 32980

See "Historical Magazine," I. 62. Reprinted with the following title:

HOPKINSON. The Old Farm and the New Farm; A Political Allegory. By Francis Hopkinson, a Member of the Continental Congress. With an Introduction and Historical Notes, by Benson J. Lossing ... . *New York: Dana and Co.* 1857. 12mo, pp. 76. + *New York: Anson D. F. Randolph.* 1864. 12mo, pp. 76.

HOPKINSON. Science. A Poem. By Francis Hopkinson, Esq. ... *Philadelphia: Printed by William Dunlap,* ... MDCCLXII. 4to, pp. 19. P. 32982

Another edition was published clandestinely the same year in 12mo. *See our* Vol. VI., No. 25279.

HOPKINSON (J.) Eulogium in Commemoration of the Hon. Bushrod Washington, ... By Joseph Hopkinson. *T. S. Manning, Printer, Philadelphia.* 1830. 8vo, pp. 32. 32983

HOPKINSON. Song [Hail Columbia], adapted to the President's March, sung at the Theatre by Mr. Fox at his benefit. *Philadelphia.* [n. d.] 8vo, pp. 6. 32984

[HOPKINSON.] What is our Situation? and what our Prospects? A few pages for Americans. By an American. [*Philadelphia.* 1799?] 8vo. 32985

Also: Annual Discourse, delivered before the Pennsylvania Academy of the Fine Arts, on the 13th of November, 1810. ... *Philadelphia: Bradford and Inskeep.* 1810. 8vo, pp. 36.—An Address delivered before the Law Academy of Philadelphia, at the Opening of the Session of 1826–7. ... *Philadelphia: Law Academy.* 1826. 8vo, pp. 21. B.—A Summary Statement of the Origin and Present State of the Washington Benevolent Society, with an Account of the Opening and Dedication of the Hall, and an Oration. ... *Philadelphia.* 1816. 8vo.

HOPKINSON *and* CHAUNCEY. Speeches of Joseph Hopkinson and Charles Chauncey on the Judicial Tenure, delivered in the Convention of Pennsylvania for Revising the Constitution. *Philadelphia: E. L. Carey & A. Hart.* 1838. 8vo, pp. 48. B.

[HOPKINSON (Thomas).] Liberty: An Elegiac Poem or Ode. *Philadelphia.* [n. d.] 8vo. 32987

Begins "Awake my soul 'tis fancy's magic hand," in four-line verses.

HOPKINSON (T.) Argument of Thomas Hopkinson, Esq., on behalf of the Petition of Horace P. Wakefield and others, for a Railroad from Salem to Lowell. *Boston.* 1848. 8vo, pp. 29.

HOPKINTON, *Mass.* The Result of an Ecclesiastical Council Publickly declared to the Church of Christ in Hopkinton, September 19th 1735. [n. p. n. d.] 8vo, pp. 8. B. 32989

HOPKINTON ASSOCIATION. *See* Vol. V., No. 19257.

HOPKIRK (J. G.) Second Edition. An Account of the Insurrection in St Domingo, begun in August 1791, taken from authentic sources, by J. G. Hopkirk, LL.B. *William Blackwood, Edinburgh;* MDCCCXXXIII. 8vo, pp. 59. 32990

HOPPE (Janus). Californiens Gegenwart und Zukunft. Nebst Beiträgen von A. Erman, über die Klimatologie von Californien, und über die geographische Verbreitung des Goldes. *Berlin: G. Reimer.* 1849. 8vo, pp. viii, 152. 2 Maps. 32991

HOPPE. Californien, dets Nutig og Fremtid. Af J. Hoppe og A. Erman, oversat af J. C. Smythe. *Kjöbenhavn: Steen & S.* 1850. 8vo. Map. 32992

HOPPER (E.) The Dutch Pilgrim Fathers and Other Poems, Humorous and Not Humorous. By Edward Hopper. *New York: Hurd and Houghton.* 1865. 16mo, pp. 216. BA. 32993

HOPPER. Republican Homes. An Address delivered before the Association of the Alumni of the University of the City of New-York, ... June 19th, 1861. By Rev. Edward Hopper ... *[New York:] University Press.* 1861. 8vo, pp. 27. H. 32994

Also: The Fire on the Hearth in Sleepy Hollow. ... *New York: Hurd & Houghton.* 1865. 16mo, pp. 105. C.—One Wife Too Many; or, Rip Van Bigham. A Tale of Tappan Zee. ... *New York: Hurd and Houghton.* 1867. 16mo, pp. 262. B.—Sermon ... Presbyterian Church, Sag Harbor. ... *New York.* 1855. 8vo.

[HOPPER (Isaac T.)] Narrative of the Life of Thomas Cooper. Fourth Edition. *New York: Isaac T. Hopper.* 1837. 24mo, pp. 35. H. 32995

[HOPPER.] Testimony of the New-York Association of Friends for the Relief of those held in Slavery, &c., concerning Charles Marriolt, deceased. ... *New-York: Piercy & Reed, Printers.* 1844. 24mo, pp. 15. H. 32996

HOPPIN (F. E.) Dedication of Lyceum Hall. Oration, by Francis E. Hoppin, and Poem, by Henry C. Whitaker ... November 19, 1858 ... . *Providence.* 1859. 8vo, pp. 53. 32997

HOPPIN. In Memory of Francis Edwin Hoppin, who died on the 20th Day of June, 1868. [n. p.] 1868. 8vo, pp. 27.

HOPPIN (N.) An Anniversary Sermon, in Christ Church, Cambridge, Mass., ... November 25, 1860. By the Rev. Nicholas Hoppin, D.D. ... *Boston: E. P. Dutton and Company.* M DCCC-LXI. 8vo, pp. 29. B., BA., H. 32999

HOPPIN. One Soweth and Another Reapeth. A Commemorative Sermon on the One Hundredth Anniversary of Christ Church, Cambridge, Mass., ... October 15, 1861. By the Rev. Nicholas Hoppin, D.D., Rector. ... *Cambridge: Miles and Dillingham.* M DCCC LXI. 8vo, pp. 36. B. 33000

HOPPIN. A Sermon on the Re-Opening of Christ Church, Cambridge, Mass., preached ... November 22, 1857; with a Historical Notice of the Church. By the Rev. Nicholas Hoppin, ... *Boston: Ide and Dutton.* MDCCC LVIII. 8vo, pp. 79. Plate.

HOPPIN (W. J.) Eulogy on the Life and Services of James S. Wadsworth Brigadier-General of Volunteers in the Army of the United States: Read at a Meeting of the Century Association, December 3, 1864. By William J. Hoppin. *New York: D. Van Nostrand.* M DCCC LXV. 8vo, pp. 32. H. 33002

HOPPIN (W. W.) Report of the Special Committee on the Memorial of certain Citizens of Providence, in relation to the Election of William W. Hoppin. *Providence: Sayles, Miller & Simons.* 1853. 8vo, pp. 14. 33003

HOPSON (P. T.) Treaty between Governor Peregrine Thomas Hopson, and the Mickmack Indians, 22 Nov. 1752. *Halifax: J. Bushell.* 1753. Folio. 33004

A rare piece relative to Nova Scotia, in French and English.

HORATIUS (Quintus Flaccus). The Lyric Works of Horace, Translated into English Verse: To which are added, A Number of Original Poems. By a Native of America. *Philadelphia:*

Printed by Eleazer Oswald, at the Coffee-House. M.DCC.LXXXVI. 8vo, pp. xli, 334, (16). Plate. C. 33005

The frontispiece was drawn by P. Markoe, engraved by J. P. Malcom. The author was Lt.-Col. John Parke. Most of the pieces are inscribed to public characters, and, though the pagination is continuous, there are separate title-pages to the "Carmen Seculare," the "Translations," etc., and "Virginia, a Pastoral Drama." Henry Stevens remarks: "This is perhaps the rarest and oddest of all the American Books of Poetry." *See* "Bibliotheca Historica," *and* Duyckinck's "Cyclopædia," I. 305.

Horace in New-York. *See* [Clason (Isaac Starr)], Vol. IV.

HORE (M. P.) Sketches, Miscellaneous, Descriptive and Statistical, of the Seat of the Federal Government, the States of Virginia, Maryland, Pennsylvania, Delaware, New Jersey, New York, New Hampshire, Connecticut, Vermont and Massachusetts, during a residence of Fifteen Years. By Maurice P. Hore. *Cork: Printed by F. Jackson.* MDCCCXXXII. 8vo, pp. 95.

Contains sketches of the leading Irishmen and the Catholic Religion in the United States.

HORER (*Mr.*) Speech of Mr. Horer, in defence of W. H. Harrison, and Sketch of his Life. *Baltimore.* 1836. 8vo.

HORLACHER (J.) Is Slavery Condemned by the Bible or Prohibited by the Constitution of the United States? By Dr. Jacob Horlacher. *Allentown, Pa.: Trexler, Horlacher & Weiser.* 1864. 12mo, pp. 32. 33008

HORLACHER. Ist Sclaverei verdammt in der Bibel? oder in der Constitution verboten? *Philadelphia.* 1862. 8vo, pp. 16.

HÖRMEYER (Joseph). Beschreibung der Provinz Rio Grande do Sul in Südbrasilien mit besonderer Rücksicht auf deren Kolonisation. Herausgegeben von Mich. Kröff. *Koblenz: [Hölscher].* 1854. 12mo, pp. 100. 33010

HÖRMEYER. Südbrasilien. Ein Handbuch ... für Auswanderer. *Hamburg: Würger.* 1857. 8vo, pp. xvi, 339. Map.

HORN (A.) The Confession of Adam Horn, alias And. Hellman—embodying particulars of his Life. Convicted Nov. 27, 1843, in Baltimore County Court, for the Murder of his Wife. *Baltimore.* 1843. 8vo, pp. 31. 33012

HORN (G.) Georgi Horni Arca Noe sive Historia Imperiorum et Regnorum, à Condito orbe ad nostra Tempora. *Lugduni Batavorum, Ex officina Hackiana.* 1666. 24mo, pp. (32), 548, (43). + *Francofurti et Lipsiae.* 1674. 16mo. + *[Ibid.]* 1675. + *Gorinchemi.* 1677. 12mo. 33013

Pages 455–545 contain "Occidentalis res Americae."

HORN. GeorgI HornI | De | Originibvs | Americanis | Libri Qvatvor. | ... *Hagæ Comitis,* | *Sumptibus Adriani Vlacq* | cIↃIↃCLII. | [Colophon:] *Lvgdvni Batavorvm,* | *Typis Philippi de Cro-y,* | *Arnhemo-Geldri,* 1652. | 8vo, pp. (20), 282. B., BA. 33014

HORN. [Engraved Title:] Georgii Hornii | de Originibus Americanis | Libri Quatuor. | *Hemipoli.* | *Sumptibus Ioannis Mülleri.* 1669. | [Printed Title:] GeorgI HornI | De | Originibvs | Americanis. | Libri Qvatvor. | *Hemipoli.* | *Sumptibus Joannis Mülleri Bibl.* | *Anno* 1669. | Sm. 12mo, pp. (24), 503. 33015

Written at the suggestion of De Laet, in answer to the "De Origine Gentium Americanorum" of Hugo Grotius, from whom it provoked an angry rejoinder, which was answered by a counter-treatise by J. de Laet. Whatever may be thought of Horn's theories concerning the original population of the Western continent, they are at least very curious and supported by an infinite wealth of learning; indeed, all of these essays display a high degree of erudition. Respecting the author, *see* the "Biographie Universelle," XX. 399; *see also* Ternaux, No. 725, Rich, No. 289.

[HORN.] Historia ecclesiastica et politica. *Lugduni Batavorum.* 1671. 12mo, pp. (34), 442, (26). + [n. p. n. d.] 12mo, pp. (34), 368, 72, (28). B. 33016

"Among ye N E Books, bec of his Great mistakes about N E Ppl & Principles."—T. PRINCE's *M.S. Catalogue.* The following is a Dutch translation:

HORN. Kerckelycke Historie ... tot 1666. Uit het Latyn in het Nederd. vert. en ... vervolgt tot 1633, door Balth. Bekker. *Amsterdam.* 1684. 8vo. Plates. 33017

Continuation to 1683, by B. Bekker. Contains notices of the Brownists and their settlement in New Netherland, New England, etc.

HORN. Historia Totius Orbis Antiquis cogniti Geographicis Tabulis accurate delineata opus sacræ et profanæ Doctrinæ necessarium. *Amstelodami.* 1658. Folio. A. 33018

Also: Orbis politicus imperiorum, regnorum, principatuum, rerum-publicarum. Ed. II. *Lipsiae.* 1685. 12mo.—Orbis imperans seu tractatus de XIII. orbis imperiis. *Francofurti.* 1693. 12mo.

HORN (G.) A Sermon preached before the University of Oxford ... February 21, 1781, being the day appointed by His Majesty's Proclamation, to be observed as a day of Fasting and Humiliation. [On account of the American War.] By George Horn, D.D. *Oxford.* MDCCLXXXI. 4to, pp. 28. 33019

HORN (H. J.) Strange Visitors: a series of original papers, embracing Philosophy, Science, Government ... . By the Spirits of Irving, Willis, Thackeray, ... and others now dwelling in the Spirit World. Dictated through a Clairvoyant while in a state of Trance. *New York: Carleton.* 1869. 12mo, pp. 250. C.

Instead of Irving, etc., read fools—perhaps the title ought to be omitted.

HORN (H. B.) Horn's Overland Guide, from the U. S. Indian Sub-Agency, Council Bluffs, on the Missouri River, to the City of Sacramento, in California; ... By Hosea B. Horn. *New York: J. H. Colton.* 1852. 12mo, pp. 83, (1). Map. BA.

HORN (J.) Some Considerations on the African Slave Trade, and the Use of West India Produce. By John Horn. *G. Cooke, Printer.* [1805.] Folio. 33022

HORN (*Mrs.*) An Authentic and Thrilling Narrative of the Captivity of Mrs. Horn and her two Children, with Mrs. Harris, by the Camanche Indians, and the Murder of their Husbands and Travelling Companions. *Cincinnati: The Author.* [n. d.] 8vo, pp. 32. 33023

HORN. A Narrative of the Captivity of Mrs. Horn, and her two Children, with Mrs. Harris; by the Camanche Indians, after they had Murdered their Husbands and Travelling Companions; with a brief account of the Manner and Customs of that Nation of Savages, of whom so little is Generally known. *St. Louis.* 1839. 12mo, pp. 60. 33024

HORN (*Professor*). Important Message to the People, and more so to the Jews. *Sacramento.* 1858. 8vo, pp. 36. 33025

HORN (W. O.), *pseudon.* *See* [Oertel (G. W. O.)]

HORNBECK (H. B.) St. Thomas dansk amerikansk O, optaget i 1835–39. *Kjöbenhavn.* 1846. 33026

HORNBLOWER [Josiah]. Letter from Mr. Hornblower to Mr. Kitchell, on the Subject of Schuyler's Copper Mine, in New-Jersey. April 18th, 1800. ... [n. p. n. d.] 8vo, pp. 4. BA.

HORNBLOWER (W. H.) The Duty of the General Assembly to all the Church under its care. A Vindication of the Minority in opposition to the Resolutions on the State of the Country. *Paterson: A. Mead.* 1861. 8vo, pp. 10. 33028

HORNBLOWER. Sermon on the Death of Abraham Lincoln, April 16, 1865. *Paterson, N. J.* 1865. 8vo. 33029

HORNBY (E.) Report of the Proceedings of the Mixed Commission on Private Claims established under the Convention between Great Britain and the United States of America, of the 8th February, 1853. Compiled from the Original by Edward Hornby. *London.* 1856. 8vo. 33030

Horne (H.) Essays concerning Iron and Steel; The First, containing Observations on American Sand-Iron. The Second, Observations founded on Experiments on Common Iron Ore, ... By Henry Horne. *London: T. Cadell.* M.DCC.LXXIII. 12mo, pp. (4), 223. 33031

The first Essay has a separate title: "Observations on American Sand-Iron. In a letter to the late Mr. John Ellicott, F.R.S. read at the Royal Society, March 3, 1763." pp. 31.

Horne (J.) The Trial (at large) of John Horne, Esq. Upon an Information filed ex officio by his Majesty's Attorney General for a Libel, on Friday, July 4th, 1777. Published by the Defendant. *London: G. Kearsley.* 1777. Folio, pp. 69. 33032

The libel for which Horne was convicted is as follows: "King's Arms Tavern, Cornhill, June 7, 1775. At a Special Meeting this day of several members of the Constitutional Society, during an adjournment, a gentleman proposed that a subscription should be immediately entered into by such members present who might approve the purpose for raising the sum of £100, to be applied to the relief of the widows, orphans, and aged parents of our beloved American fellow-subjects, who, faithful to the character of Englishmen preferring death to slavery, were for that reason only inhumanly murdered by the King's troops at or near Lexington and Concord, Mass. on the 19th of last April, which sum being immediately collected, it was thereupon resolved that Mr. Horne do pay to-morrow into the hands of Mess. Brownes and Collison, on the account of Dr Franklin, and that he be requested to apply the same to the above mentioned purpose." Another edition is entitled: "Case before the House of Lords between Rev. John Horne, Plaintiff, and King George III., Defendant," etc. *London.* 1778. Folio.

Horne (T. H.) An Introduction to the Study of Bibliography. To which is prefixed a Memoir on the Public Libraries of the Antients. By Thomas Hartwell Horne. Illustrated with Engravings. *London: T. Cadell & W. Davies.* 1814. 2 vols., 8vo, pp. xiv, xxv, 402; (4), 403–738, (2), clvi. 10 Plates.

On page 92, *et seq.*, is a chapter on Mexican and North American picture-writing. Fifty copies printed on large paper.

Hornell, *N. Y.* Annual Report of the Hornell Library Association, 1869. 8vo. S. 33034

Horner (Gustavus R. B.) Medical Topography of Brazil and Uruguay: with Incidental Remarks. By G. R. B. Horner, ... *Philadelphia: Lindsay & Blakiston.* 1845. 8vo, pp. 296. C.

Also: Observations on the Isthmus of Panama, and on the Hospitals of Havana. ... *Philadelphia.* 1859. 8vo. C.

Horner (J. M.) The Modern Emigrant; or, Lover of Liberty: being A Discourse, delivered in the City of New-York, by the Rev. J. M. Horner, ... *New-York: Printed by W. Mitchell.* 1832. 8vo, pp. 18. 33036

Horner (W. E.) Necrological Notice of Dr. Philip Syng Physick; delivered before the American Philosophical Society, May 4, 1838. By W. E. Horner, M.D. ... *Philadelphia: Haswell, Barrington, and Haswell.* 1838. 8vo, pp. 32. B. 33037

This elicited a pamphlet I have not seen, which was answered by "Examination of a Pamphlet ... on Dr. Horner's ... Notice of P. Syng Physick, M.D." ... *Philadelphia.* 1838. 8vo. S.

[Horner.] Observations on the Mineral Waters in the South Western Part of Virginia. In a Series of Letters. By a Physician of Philadelphia. ... *Philadelphia: Printed by J. Thompson.* 1834. 8vo, pp. 30. H. 33038

[Hornot (Ant.)] Anecdotes Américaines, ou Histoire Abrégée des principaux événements arrivés dans le Nouveau Monde, depuis sa découverte jusqu'à l'époque présente. *Paris: Vincent.* M DCC LXXVI. 12mo, pp. xv, 782. A., B., BA. 33039

Horrocks (J.) Upon the Peace. A Sermon. Preach'd at the Church of Petsworth ... August the 25th, ... By the Reverend James Horrocks, A.M. ... *Williamsburg: Printed by Joseph Royle.* MDCCLXIII. Sm. 4to, pp. 15. BA. 33040

The Horrors of the Negro Slavery existing in our West Indian Islands irrefragably demonstrated. *London.* 1805. 8vo. C.

Horrors of the Slave Trade. 1848. 8vo, pp. 16. 33042

Horry (E.) Address delivered in Charleston, before the Agricultural Society of South Carolina, 19th August, 1828. By Elias Horry. *Charleston.* 1828. 8vo, pp. 40. 33043

Horry (P.) Life of Gen. Francis Marion, a Celebrated Partizan Officer in the Revolutionary War, against the British and Tories in South-Carolina and Georgia. By Brig. Gen. P. Horry. Second Edition. *Baltimore: W. D. Bell & J. F. Cook.* 1814. 12mo, pp. 270. C. 33044

Afterwards reprinted as:

Horry. The Life of Gen. Francis Marion ... . By Brig. Gen. P. Horry, of Marion's Brigade and M. L. Weems. ... Fourth Edition ... . *Philadelphia: M. Carey.* 1816. 12mo, pp. 260. BA. + Sixth Edition. *Philadelphia: M. Carey & Son.* 1818. 12mo, pp. 251. + Seventh Edition. [*Ibid.*] 1821. + [*Ibid.*] 1822. + *Frankfort.* 1826. 12mo. + *Philadelphia: H. C. Carey & I. Lea.* 18 . 12mo, pp. 251. + *Philadelphia: Joseph Allen.* 1828. 12mo, pp. 252. Plate. C. + [*Ibid.*] 1829. + [*Ibid.*]

1833. + By Colonel Horry, of Marion's Brigade, and M. L. Wheems [*sic*], Chaplain to Washington. *New-York: P. M. Davis.* 1835. 12mo, pp. 252. + [*Ibid.*] 1837. + *Philadelphia: Joseph Allen.* 1841. 12mo, pp. 252. + [*Ibid.*] 1844. + [*Ibid.*] 1855. 33045

Horry. The Life of General Francis Marion, a Celebrated Partisan Officer in the Revolutionary War, against the British and Tories, in South Carolina and Georgia; abridged from Horry and Weem's Life of Marion. *Devon.* 1835. 18mo, pp. 324.

Title from Rich's "Bibliotheca Americana," Vol. II. 272.

Horsburgh (J.) The India Directory, or Directions for sailing to and from the East Indies, China, Japan, Australia, and the Interjacent Parts of Africa and South America. By James Horsburgh. Fifth Edition. *London.* 1841. 4to. C. + Eighth Edition. *London: Wm. H. Allen & Co.* 1864. 2 vols., 4to, pp. xii, xxv, (1), 848; vii, (3), 881. B. 33047

First published in 1826 with a title differing but slightly.

Horsey (J. R.) Ordinances of the City of Charleston, from the 14th September, 1854, to the 1st December, 1859: and the Acts of the General Assembly, relating to the City Council of Charleston, and the City of Charleston, during the same Period. Compiled by John R. Horsey. *Charleston: Walker, Evans & Co.* 1859. 8vo, pp. xv, 102, 46. C. 33049

Horsfield (T.) Experimental Dissertation on the Rhus-Vernix, Rhus-Radicans and Rhus-Glabrum; commonly known in Pennsylvania by the names of Poison-Ash, Poison-Vine and Common Sumach. By Thomas Horsfield. *Philadelphia.* 1798.

Horsford (E. N.) The Army Ration. How to Diminish its Weight and Bulk, Secure Economy in its Administration, Avoid Waste, and Increase the Comfort, Efficiency, and Mobility of Troops. By E. N. Horsford ... . *New York: D. Van Nostrand.* 1864. 12mo, pp. 42. B., H. 33050

Horsford. Report on Mystic Pond to the Boston Harbor Commission. By E. N. Horsford ... . *Boston: Geo. C. Rand & Avery, Printers.* 1861. 8vo, pp. 19. Chart. B., H. 33051

Horsford. Solidification of the Coral Reefs of Florida, and Source of Lime in the Growth of Corals. By E. N. Horsford, ... *Boston.* 1853. 8vo, pp. 11. B., H. 33052

Horsford (J.) A Voice from the West Indies; being a Review of the Character and Results of Missionary Efforts in the British and other Colonies in the Caribbean Sea: with some Remarks on the Usages, Prejudices, &c., of the Inhabitants. By Rev. John Horsford. *London: Heylin.* 1856. Post 8vo, pp. 492.

Horsford (J.) Speech ... In Favor of the Establishment of an Agricultural Bureau, June 24, 1852. *Washington.* 1852. 8vo, pp. 7. H. 33054

Horsford (M. G.) Indian Legends and other Poems. By Mary Gardiner Horsford. *New York: J. C. Derby.* 1855. 12mo, pp. 167. B., H. 33055

Horsley (S.) Remarks on the Observations made in the late Voyage to the North Pole, for determining the Acceleration of the Pendulum in latitude 79° 50′. By Samuel Horsley, L.L.D. Sec. R.S. In a Letter to the Hon. Constantine John Phipps. *London.* 1774. 4to. 33056

"This pamphlet ought to be annexed to every copy of Captain Phipps's book, and bound up with it."—*Monthly Review*, LI. 131. It is very rare.

Horsley (Samuel). Speech of the Bishop of Rochester in House of Peers on the Bill to Prohibit the Trading in Slaves on the Coast of Africa. *London.* 1799. 8vo. C. 33057

[Horsmanden (Daniel).] A | Journal | of the | Proceedings | in | The Detection of the Conspiracy | formed by | Some White People, in Conjunction with Negro and other Slaves, | for | Burning the City of New-York in America, | And Murdering the Inhabitants. | Which Conspiracy was partly put in Execution, by Burning His Majesty's House in | Fort George, within the said City, on Wednesday the Eighteenth of March, 1741, and | setting Fire to several Dwellings and other Houses there, within a few Days succeeding. | And by another Attempt made in Prosecution of the same infernal scheme, by putting | Fire between two other Dwelling Houses within the said City, on the Fifteenth Day of | February, 1742; which was accidentally and timely discovered and extinguished. | Containing. | I. A Narrative of the Trials, Condemnations, Executions, and Behaviour of the | several Criminals, at the Gallows and Stake, with their Speeches and Confessions; with | Notes, Observations and Reflections occasionally interspersed throughout the whole. | II. An Appendix, wherein is set forth some additional Evidence concerning the said | Conspiracy and Conspirators, which has come to Light since their Trials and | Executions. | III. Lists of the several Persons (Whites

and Blacks) committed on Account of the | Conspiracy; and of the several Criminals executed; and of those transported, with | the Places whereto. | By the Recorder of the City of New-York. | ... | *New York:* | *Printed by James Parker, at the New Printing-Office.* 1744. 4to, pp. (1), vi, 205, (1), Appendix, pp. 16. H.

An excessively rare work. The only copy sold in New York during many years was one damaged by water belonging to Mr. Bruce, at whose sale it was bought for Mr. Rice; it was resold with his collection for $140.00. Mr. Quaritch, in a recent catalogue, offers a copy for £45, and remarks "I know of no other copy sold in the London market." The work had become so scarce even in 1810, that the editor of the edition of that year intimates that he experienced the greatest difficulty in finding a copy. Parker (the printer of this volume) was an apprentice to Bradford, and succeeded to the business in 1742. The following are reprints:

[Horsmanden.] A Journal of the Proceedings in the Detection of the Conspiracy Formed by some White People, in conjunction with Negro and other Slaves, for burning the City of New-York in America and murdering the Inhabitants. ... By the Recorder of the City of New-York. ... *Printed at New-York: London, Reprinted and Sold by John Clarke.* 1747. 8vo, pp. viii, 425, (7). 33059

Almost as rare as the preceding.

Horsmanden. The New-York Conspiracy, or a History of the Negro Plot, with the Journal of the Proceedings against the Conspirators at New-York in the Years 1741–2. Together with several interesting Tables, ... By Daniel Horsmanden, Esq. *New York: Southwick & Pelsue.* 1810. 8vo, pp. 385, (7). BA., H.

For an account of this alleged Conspiracy and the Trial, *see* Chandler's "American Criminal Trials," Vol. I., p. 211.

[Horsmanden.] The Negro Conspiracy in the City of New York, in 1741. Edited by William B. Wedgwood. *New York.* 1851. 8vo, pp. 96. 33061

H[orsnell] (W[illiam].) The Ice-Bound Ship, and the Dream. By W. H. *Montreal.* 1860. 8vo, pp. 48. 33062

Horta (Garcia da). *See* Orta (Garcia de).

Hortensius, *pseudon.* *See* [Ramsay (D.)]

Horticosa (P.) Petrii di Horticosa Concilii Mexicani Decreta. *Mexico.* 1627. Folio. 33063

Title from Ternaux, No. 498.

Horticultural Register, and Gardiner's Magazine. ... Volume I. *Boston: George C. Barrett.* 1835. 8vo, pp. v, 479. Plates. Continued. B. 33064

Horticultural Society of the Valley of Genesee. Constitution, etc. 1848. + Officers, etc. 1852. 33065

The Horticulturist, and Journal of Rural Art and Rural Taste. ... Edited by A. J. Downing. Vol. I. July, 1846–June, 1847. *Albany: Luther Tucker.* [n. d.] 8vo, pp. vii, 576. Continued.

Afterwards by P. Barry and J. Jay Smith.

Hortigosa (Fran. Antonio). Sermon en Honras del P. Pedro Navarrette, Padre de todas las Provincias de esta Nueva-España, Islas adyacentes, y Philipinas. *Mexico: Imprenta de la Bibliotheca Mexicana.* 1756. 4to. 33067

Hortini (J. Roscii). Elogia Militaria. *Romæ, apud Ruffinellum.* 1596. 4to. 33068

A collection of poems celebrating the heroic deeds of Ferdinand Cortes, Sir John Hawkwood, and others.

Horton (F.) Poem at the Anniversary of the Brookfield Temperance Society, January, 1833. By Francis Horton. *Brookfield, Mass.* 1833. 12mo. 33069

Horton (G. M.) The Poetical Works of George M. Horton, the Colored Bard of North-Carolina, to which is prefixed the Life of the Author, written by Himself. *Hillsborough: Printed by D. Heartt.* 1845. 24mo, pp. 96. H. 33070

Horton (H. P.) A Digest of the Militia Law of the State of New-York, with copious Forms adapted to every case. *Albany: J. Munsell.* 1848. 8vo, pp. 40. S. 33071

Horton (N. S.) Acadia College. Address, with Appendix, containing A History of the College, etc. By N. S. Horton. *Halifax.* 1851. 8vo, pp. 52. 33072

Horton (R. W.) Exposition and Defence of Earl Bathurst's Administration of the Affairs of Canada, when Colonial Secretary, during the Years 1822 to 1827, inclusive. By ... Sir Robert Wilmot Horton, Bart., ... *London: John Murray.* MDCCCXXXVIII. 8vo, pp. 106. 33073

Horton. First Letter ... on Negro Slavery, being an Inquiry into the Claims of the West Indians for equitable Compensation. By the Right Hon. R. Wilmot Horton. *London: Edmund Lloyd.* 1830. 8vo, pp. 112. + Second Letter. [*Ibid.*] 8vo, pp. (4), 74.

Horton. Ireland and Canada; supported by Local Evidence. "Intended to prove the facility with which Sufferings in Ireland

may be converted into Comfort and Prosperity in British North America." By ... Sir R. W. Horton ... . *London.* 1839. 8vo, pp. 78. S. 33075

Also: Correspondence between ... Sir R. W. Horton, ... and J. B. Robinson, Esq., Chief Justice of Upper Canada, upon the Subject of a Pamphlet ... entitled "Ireland and Canada." *London: John Murray.* 1839. 8vo, pp. 32.

Horton. A Letter addressed to the Anonymous Author of "England and America." *Colombo.* 1834. 8vo, pp. 37, 29.

Privately printed and very scarce. Also: Speech ... 19th May, 1826, on a Motion touching the Condition of Slaves. *London.* 1826. 8vo, pp. 27.—Thoughts on the Present Crisis of the Canadas. ... *London.* 1839. 8vo.

Horton (Rushmore G.) The Life and Public Services of James Buchanan. Late Minister to England ... . Including the most Important of his State Papers, By R. G. Horton. ... *New York: Derby & Jackson.* 1856. 12mo, pp. 428. Portrait. H. + [*Ibid.*] 1860. C. 33077

Horton. A Youth's History of the Great Civil War in the United States, from 1861 to 1865. By R. G. Horton. *New York: Van Evrie, Horton & Co.* 1866. 16mo, pp. 384. B. + [*Ibid.*] 1868. 33078

See also Tammany Society, *and* "Manual of the Common Council of New York."

Horton (S. J.) ... A Sermon ... New Bedford, ... September 15th, 1850. By Sanford J. Horton, Rector. *Providence.* 1850. 8vo, pp. 16. 33079

With an Appendix, containing an Obituary Notice of Mrs. Anna E. Horton, wife of the rector.

Horton (V. B.) Speech of Hon. V. B. Horton, of Ohio, on the Treasury Note Bill. ... February 5, 1862. [n. p. n. d.] 8vo, pp. 8. H. 33080

Also: The Tariff. Speech ... in the House of Representatives, February 14 and 16, 1857. [*Washington.* n. d.] 8vo, pp. 8. H.

Hosack (A.) History of the Yellow Fever, as it appeared in the City of New York in 1795. By Alexander Hosack, Jun., M.D. ... *Philadelphia: J. Dodson.* 1797. 8vo, pp. 36. 33081

See "M. Rev.," XXV. 531. Also: An Inaugural Essay on the Yellow Fever, as it appeared in the City of New York in 1795. ... *New York.* 1797. 8vo.

Hosack (A. E.) History of the Case of the late John Kearny Rodgers, M.D. Addressed to the Profession. By Alexander E Hosack. *New York: Printed by S. W. Benedict.* 1851. 8vo, pp. 47. B., H. 33082

Hosack (D.) The American Medical and Philosophical Register, or Annals of Medicine, Natural History, Agriculture, and the Arts. Conducted by David Hosack and John W. Francis. *New York.* 1810–14. 4 vols., 8vo. 33083

Contains many historical articles and views of buildings now demolished.

Hosack. A Biographical Memoir of Hugh Williamson, M.D. ... Delivered on the First of November, 1819, at the Request of the New-York Historical Society. By David Hosack, M.D. ... *New-York: Printed by C. S. Van Winkle.* 1820. 8vo, pp. 91. + *New York: E. Bliss and E. White.* 1821. 8vo, pp. 78. C.

Also included in the "New York Hist. Soc. Collections," First Series, Vol. V., p. 3.

Hosack. A Catalogue of Plants contained in the Botanic Garden at Elgin, in the Vicinity of New-York, established in 1801. By David Hosack, M.D. ... *New-York: Printed by T. & J. Swords.* 1806. 16mo, pp. 29. B., BA., H., N., P. 33085

Hosack. Hortus Elginensis: or a Catalogue of Plants, Indigenous and Exotic, cultivated in the Elgin Botanic Garden, in the Vicinity of the City of New-York, established in 1801. By David Hosack, M.D. ... Second Edition, Enlarged. *New-York: Printed by T. & J. Swords.* 1811. 8vo, pp. x, (2), 65, (1). Plate.

Hosack. An Inaugural Address, delivered before the New-York Historical Society, ... February, 1820. By David Hosack, M.D. ... *New York: Printed by C. S. Van Winkle.* 1820. 8vo, pp. 14. B., BA. + *New York: Bliss & White.* 1821. 8vo. C.

Hosack. Memoir of DeWitt Clinton: with an Appendix, containing numerous Documents, Illustrative of the Principal Events of his Life. By David Hosack, M.D., F.R.S. *New York: Printed by J. Seymour.* 1829. 4to, pp. xxiv, 21–530. Portrait.

Hosack. A Statement of Facts Relative to the Establishment and Progress of the Elgin Botanic Garden, and the subsequent Disposal of the same to the State of New-York. By David Hosack, M.D. ... *New-York: Printed by C. S. Van Winkle.* 1811. 8vo, pp. 56. B., BA., H. 33089

Also: Address delivered at the First Anniversary of the New York City Temperance Society: ... May 11, 1830. [n. p. n. d.] 8vo, pp. 24.—Essays on Various Subjects of Medical Science. ... *New York: Printed by J. Seymour.* 1824–30. 3 vols., 8vo, pp. 380; iv, (2), 11–472; vi, 9–473. Plates. BA.—A Funeral Address ... on the Twenty-Sixth of May, 1818, at the Interment of Doctor James Tillary ... . *New York: Printed by C. S. Van Winkle.* 1818. 8vo, pp. 14.—An Inaugural Address ... before the Medical Society of the County of New-York on the 12th Day of July 1824. ... *New-York: Printed by J. Seymour.* 1824. 8vo, pp. 24. B.—An Inaugura

Discourse, delivered at the Opening of Rutgers Medical College, ... New York, ... the 6th Day of November, 1826. ... *New-York: Printed by J. Seymour.* 1826. 8vo, pp. 176. Plate.—An Inaugural Discourse ... before the New-York Horticultural Society, ... 31st of August, 1824. ... *New-York: Printed by J. Seymour.* 1824. 8vo, pp. 46. —An Inaugural Dissertation on Cholera Morbus, submitted to the Examination of the Rev. John Ewing ... the Trustees and Medical Professors of the University of Pennsylvania; ... on the Twelfth Day of May, ... 1791. [Dedicated to Richard Bayley, Nicholas Romayne, William Shippen, Adam Kuhn, and James Hutchinson.] ... *New York: Printed by Samuel Campbell.* M.DCC.XCI. 8vo, pp. 32.—An Introductory Discourse, ... and a Tribute to the Memory of the Late Dr. Benjamin Rush. ... *New-York: Printed by C. S. Van Winkle.* 1813. 8vo, pp. 35. B.—Introductory Lecture on Medical Education ... . *New York.* 1801. 8vo, pp. 48.—Observations on the Establishment of the College of Physicians and Surgeons in the City of New-York. ... *New York: Printed by C. S. Van Winkle.* 1811. 8vo, pp. 13.—Observations on Febrile Contagion, and on the Means of improving the Medical Police of the City of New-York. ... Introductory Discourse ... the Sixth of November, 1820. ... *New-York: Elam Bliss.* 1820. 8vo, pp. 79.—Syllabus of the Course of Lectures on Botany, ... in Columbia College. ... *New-York: Printed by John Child.* M,DCC,XCV. 12mo, pp. 22. + *New-York: Reprinted by Van Winkle and Wiley.* 1814. 8vo, pp. 20. B.—Tribute to the Memory of the late Caspar Wistar, M.D., ... By his Friend, David Hosack, M.D. ... delivered ... Jan. 26, 1818. *New York: Printed by C. S. Van Winkle.* 1818. 8vo, pp. 17. B., BA., N.

HOSACK (J.) The Rights of British and Neutral Commerce, as affected by Recent Royal Declarations and Orders in Council. By John Hosack. *London: Sweet.* 1854. 12mo. 33090

HOSFORD (B. F.) Discourse at the Re-Dedication of the Centre Church, Haverhill, Mass., January 27, 1860. By B. F. Hosford. *Boston: Press of T. R. Marvin & Son.* 1860. 8vo, pp. 39. H. 33091

Hosford's Calender. *Albany.* 1826. 12mo. Continued.

HOSKENS (J.) The Life and Spiritual Sufferings of that Faithful Servant of Christ, Jane Hoskens, a Public Preacher among the People called Quakers. Never before printed. *Philadelphia: ... William Evitt,* ... 1771. 8vo, pp. 16. + Second Edition. *Stanfield, Printed.* 1810. 12mo, pp. 54. 33093

Reprinted in Vol. I. of "The Friends' Library," *Philadelphia,* 1837, also reprinted *Manchester: John Harrison.* [n. d.] 12mo, pp. 36. + The Second Edition. [*Ibid.*]

HOSKINS (B. S.) A Few Thoughts on Volunteering. By Bradford S. Hoskins. *Quebec.* 1862. 8vo, pp. 24. 33094

HOSKINS (J.) The Pensilvania Bubble Bubbled by the Treasurer, or, An Account of his Admitting Purchasers for Shares, Lodging 8578*l* 12*s*., in the Bank of England, and the Sale of his Lands in Pensilvania to the Company. With An Estimate of how much of the Company's Money he plac'd to his own account, and of the loss the Company has sustained by

him, Together with the Judgment of the Seven Arbitrators in his Favour, and the Reasons of the Five other Arbitrators offered in Arrest of Judgment. With Remarks on the whole. *London: Printed for the Author.* 1726. 4to. 33095

An extraordinary book of personal gossip, aimed chiefly at Thomas Story.

HOSKINS (N.) A History of the State of Vermont, from its Discovery and Settlement to the Close of the Year MDCCCXXX. By Nathan Hoskins. ... *Vergennes: J. Shedd.* 1831. 12mo, pp. 316. B., C., H. 33096

HOSKINS. Notes upon the Western Country contained within the States of Ohio, Indiana, Illinois, and the Territory of Michigan, taken on a Tour through that Country in the Summer of 1832. By Nathan Hoskins, Jr. *Greenfield: Printed by James P. Fogg.* 1833. 12mo, pp. 108. 33097

HOSMER (C. L.) Aldermanic Wisdom, ... upon the Question of License and No-License. By C. Lawton Hosmer. ... *Boston: Bela Marsh.* 1849. 8vo, pp. 16. B., BA. 33098

HOSMER (G. W.) "A Leader and a Judge among the Pioneers." An Address delivered at the Funeral of Nathaniel Fillmore, Esq., of Aurora, Erie Co., N. Y., March 31, 1863. By George W. Hosmer, D.D. *Buffalo.* 1863. 8vo, pp. 14. 33099

HOSMER. Report of Delegates from the General Aid Society for the Army, at Buffalo, N. Y. To visit the Government Hospitals, and the Agencies of the United States Sanitary Commission. By Rev. G. W. Hosmer ... . *Buffalo.* 1862. 8vo, pp. 16.

Also: An Address ... at the Fair of the Erie County Agricultural Society ... at Buffalo ... September 25, 1863. ... *Buffalo: Wheeler, Matthews & Warren.* 1863. 8vo, pp. 7.— ... Inaugural Discourse ... in ... Antioch College, June 26, 1867. ... *Buffalo: Thomas, Howard & Johnson.* 1867. 8vo, pp. 16. H.—The Physiognomy of Buffalo: The Annual Address delivered before the Buffalo Historical Society, Jan. 13, 1864. ... [n. p. n. d.] 8vo, pp. 9. H.— ... A Sermon ... at the Installation of the Rev. William L. Stearns ... in Rowe, Mass. January 30, 1833. ... *Greenfield: James P. Fogg, Printer.* 1833. 8vo, pp. 17. *See also* our Vol. III., No. 9058.

[HOSMER (Harriet).] Boston and Boston People, in 1850. *Boston.* 1850. 12mo, pp. 45. B. 33101

Rather severe on some prominent Bostonians. Suppressed and very rare.

HOSMER (Hezekiah L.) Early History of the Maumee Valley. By H. L. Hosmer. *Toledo: Hosmer & Harris.* 1858. 8vo, Cover, pp. 9–70. BA., C. 33102

HOSMER (H. P.) Kate Klayton, the Indian Captive of Cherry Valley ... . By H. P. Hosmer. *Rochester, N. Y.* 1855. 12mo, pp. 90. S. 33103

HOSMER (J. B.) Genealogy of the Hosmer Family. By James B. Hosmer. *Hartford: Elihu Geer.* 1861. 8vo, pp. 16.

HOSMER (J. K.) The Color-Guard: being a Corporal's Notes of Military Service in the Nineteenth Army Corps. By James K. Hosmer ... . *Boston: Walker, Wise and Company.* 1864. 8vo, pp. xii, 9–244. B., BA., H. 33105

HOSMER. The Thinking Bayonet. By James K. Hosmer, ... *Boston: Walker, Fuller, and Company.* 1865. 16mo, pp. 326. + Second Edition. [*Ibid.*] H. 33106

HOSMER (M.) The Child Captives. A True Tale of Life among the Indians of the West. By Mrs. Margaret Hosmer. *Philadelphia: Presbyterian Board of Publication.* [1870.] 18mo, pp. 230. 3 Plates. 33107

[HOSMER.] You-Sing: the Chinaman in California. A True Story of the Sacramento Flood. ... *Philadelphia: Presbyterian Publication Society.* 1868. 18mo, pp. 150. 3 Plates. 33108

[HOSMER (Rufus).] A History of the Fight at Concord ... By Rev. Ezra Ripley ... History of the Battle at Lexington, By Elias Phinney. Centennial Address at Acton ... . By Josiah Adams, Esq. [n. p. n. d.] 8vo, pp. 6. H. 33109

HOSMER (S. D.) ... A Centennial Discourse ... October 15, 1865, in ... Nantucket. By S. D. Hosmer. *Nantucket: Hussey & Robinson, Printers.* 1865. 8vo, pp. 16. H. 33110

HOSMER (S.) Discourse at the Ordination of the Rev. Timothy Symmes, Millington, December 2, 1736. By Stephen Hosmer ... . *New London.* 1738. 8vo, pp. 26. N. 33111

HOSMER. ... A Sermon ... before the General Assembly, of the Colony of Connecticut, at Hartford, May 12th, 1720. By Stephen Hosmer ... . *New-London: Printed by Timothy Green.* 1720. 12mo, pp. 41. H. 33112

HOSMER (Titus). *See* [Barlow (J.)], Vol. I., No. 3419.

HOSMER (W.) The Higher Law, in its Relations to Civil Government: with Particular Reference to Slavery, and the

Fugitive Slave Law. By William Hosmer. *Auburn: Derby & Miller.* 1852. 12mo, pp. 204. C., H. 33113

HOSMER. Slavery and the Church. By William Hosmer. *Auburn.* 1853. 12mo. 33114

HOSMER (W. H. C.) The Pioneers of Western New York: A Poem pronounced at Geneva, N. Y., before the Literary Societies of Geneva College, August 1st, 1838. *Geneva, N. Y.: Ira Merrell.* 1838. 12mo. S. 33115

The Appendix contains notes respecting the Indians. Also: The Poetical Works of William H. C. Hosmer. ... *New York: Redfield.* 1854. 2 vols., 12mo, pp. ix, 374; 376, (1). B.

HOSMER. Yonnondio, or Warriors of the Genesee: A Tale of the Seventeenth Century. *New-York.* 1844. 12mo. S.

For a list of other works by this author, *see* Griswold's "Poets and Poetry of America."

Hospital Days. *See* [Woolsey (*Miss*)].

Hospital Life; being Incidents from the Prayer Meeting and Hospital. *New York: Board of Publication of the Reformed Protestant Dutch Church.* 1863. 18mo, pp. 180. 3 Plates. 33117

Hospital Transports. A Memoir of the Embarkation of the Sick and Wounded from the Peninsula of Virginia in the Summer of 1862. Compiled and Published at the Request of the Sanitary Commission. *Boston: Ticknor & Fields.* 1863. 16mo, pp. 167.

Hospitales. Resolucion de la Diputacion provincial de 9 de Diciembre de 1831, establaciendo un fondo comun de Hospitales. *Carácas.* 1834. 8vo, pp. 25. 33119

Hostilities with Creek Indians. Message ... of the President, February 14, 1837. [n. p. n. d.] 8vo, pp. 61. 33120

HOSTMANN (F. W.) Bedenkingen en opmerkingen ... de Aziatischen braakloop ... voor de plantaadje-bewoners der kolonie Suriname. *Paramaribo.* 1832. 8vo. 33121

HOSTMANN. Over de Beschaving van Negers in Amerika, door Kolonisatie met Europeanen, of beschouwingen omtrent de maatschappelijke vereeniging der Negers in Afrika, den staat, waarin zij door den zoogenaamden Slavenhandel komen, en later door Abolitie en Emancipatie overgaan. *Amsterdam: J. C. A. Sulpke.* 1850. 2 vols., 8vo, pp. lxvi, 346; 463. 33122

On the civilization of negroes in America by colonization with Europeans.

Hot Springs, Bath County, Virginia; with some Account of their Medicinal Properties ... . *Richmond: Gary, Clemmitt & Jones, Printers.* 1869. 12mo, pp. 92. Map. H. 33123

HOTALING (S.) The Questions in the Canvass. Considered by a Merchant of New York City. Speech of Samuel Hotaling, Esq. Before the Young Men's Republican Union, ... Oct. 29th, 1860. *New York: Baker & Godwin, Printers.* 1860. 8vo, pp. 12.

HOTCHKIN (J. H.) A History of the Purchase and Settlement of Western New York, and of the Rise, Progress, and Present State of the Presbyterian Church in that Section. By Rev. James H. Hotchkin. *New York: M. W. Dodd.* 1848. 8vo, pp. xvi, 600. Plate. B., BA., C., H., S. 33125

HOTCHKISS (F. W.) On National Greatness. A Thanksgiving Sermon ... in Say-brook, November 29th, 1792. By F. W. Hotchkiss. *New-Haven: Printed by Thomas and Samuel Green.* M,DCC,XCIII. 8vo, pp. 23. H. 33126

HOTCHKISS. An Oration at Saybrook, February 22, 1800, the Day set apart ... by ... Congress for the People ... to testify their grief for the Death of General George Washington, ... By Frederick W. Hotchkiss. *New London.* 1800. 8vo, pp. 32.

HOTCHKISS. A Retrospect on the Ministry and Church of Saybrook. A Half Century Sermon, preached on Lord's Day, September 22, 1833. By Frederick William Hotchkiss. *New Haven: Press of Whitmore & Buckingham.* 1833. 8vo, pp. 23. + *Hartford: J. B. Eldredge.* 1838. 8vo, pp. 23. N. 33128

HOTCHKISS. A Sermon before ... Free Masons in Lyme, Connecticut, October 7th, 1800. By Frederick W. Hotchkiss. ... *New London.* 1800. 8vo, pp. 35. 33129

Partly relates to George Washington. Also: Discourse at Saybrook [Conn.], Nov. 3, 1793, on the Death of Mrs. Deborah, Wife of Samuel Sanford. ... *New York.* 1795. 8vo.—Masonic Sermon at Haddam [Conn.], June 25, 1821. ... *Middletown.* [n. d.] 8vo. W.—Valedictory Address before the First Church and Congregation in Saybrook, Conn., January 7, 1838. ... *Hartford.* 1838. 8vo.

HOTCHKISS (Giles W.) Reward for the Capture of Booth. Report of Mr. Hotchkiss, from the Committee of Claims, on the Resolution instructing them to inquire into the Fairness and Propriety of the Distribution of the Rewards offered for the Arrest of Jefferson Davis and the Conspirators to murder President Lincoln, May 7, 1866. [n. p. n. d.] 8vo, pp. 12. 33130

39th Congress, 1st Session, House of Representatives, Report No. 99.

HOTCHKISS (J.), *and* ALLAN (W.) The Battle Fields of Virginia. Chancellorsville, Embracing the Operations of the Army of Northern Virginia, from the First Battle of Fredericksburg to the Death of Lieutenant-General Jackson. By Jed. Hotchkiss ... and William Allan ... . With 5 Maps, and Portrait of Lieut.-Gen. Jackson. *New York: D. Van Nostrand.* 1867. 8vo, pp. 152. B. 33131

HOTCHKISS (W. A.) Codification [etc.] *See* No. 27026.

The Hotel Folly. A Series of Letters in reference to the building of a Monster Hotel in the City of Philadelphia, by a Corporation. [n. p. n. d.] 4to, pp. 30. 33132

In opposition to the construction of what is now the Continental Hotel, Philadelphia.

HOUCKGEEST (E. v. B.) Voyage de l'Ambassade de la Compagnie des Indes Hollandais, vers l'Empereur de la Chine, dans les années 1794, 5, par E. Van Braam Houckgeest. *Philadelphia: Moreau de St. Mery.* 1798. 2 vols., 4to. Plates, Maps.

"One of the most valuable works on China, describing Districts never before traversed by Europeans." It is a curious fact that the Official Report of the Dutch East India Company's Embassy to China should first be published in this country. The Author and Head of the Embassy, M. Van Braam Houckgeest (a distinguished savant), fixed his residence in South Carolina, and this work was edited and published by M. Moreau de St. Mery, the celebrated French statesman, who for five years carried on the publishing business at Philadelphia, before he was recalled to France by Napoleon. The plates, &c., are very creditable specimens of American art. It is for this reason the work is allowed a place in this Dictionary.

HOUDIN (M. G.) Et sicut illud statutum est hominibus, ut semel moriantur, postea vero judicium. A Funeral Oration, on the Death of George Washington: Delivered in ... Albany, ... on the Twenty-Second of February, 1800. By Michael Gabriel Houdin, Major in the late Revolutionary Army of the United States. *Albany: Printed by Barber & Southwick.* [1800.] Sm. 4to, pp. 11. Portrait. B., BA. 33134

Also: Houdin's Last Respects to George Washington. *Albany.* 1800. 8vo, pp. 7. A very rare piece.

HOUGH (*Bishop*). A Sermon before the Society for the Propagation of the Gospel, By The Lord Bishop of Litchfield and Coventy. *London.* 1705. 8vo, pp. 28. 33135

HOUGH (F. Benjamin). Bibliographical List of Books and Pamphlets containing Eulogies, Orations, Poems, or other Papers, relating to the Death of General Washington, or to the Honors Paid to His Memory. By Franklin B. Hough. *Albany.* 1865. Imp. 8vo, pp. 59. 33136

Twenty-four copies printed separately from the work described No. 33154, *infra.*

HOUGH. Census of the State of New York for 1855, prepared under direction of the Secretary of State, by F. B. Hough, Superintendent of the Census, and including Tables of the Population of each Town, at each Census, since 1790; with Illustrative Diagrams. *Albany.* 1857. Folio, pp. 525. + For 1865. *Albany.* 1867. Folio, pp. (4), cxxvi, (2), 743. B. 33137

Also: Constitution of the State of New York, adopted in 1846. With ... Constitutional Provisions of other States ... . *Albany: Weed, Parsons & Company, Printers.* 1867. 4to, pp. 4, 239. B., H.

HOUGH. Diary of the Siege of Detroit in the War with Pontiac. Also a Narrative of the Principal Events of the Siege, by Major Rogers; A Plan for Conducting Indian Affairs, by Colonel Bradstreet; and other Authentick Documents, never before printed. Edited with Notes by Franklin B. Hough. *Albany, N. Y.: J. Munsell.* M.D.CCC.LX. 4to, Half Title, pp. xxiii; Second Half Title, pp. 304. BA. 33138

Ten copies printed on large paper. This interesting volume forms No. 4 of Munsell's "Historical Series."

HOUGH. History of Duryee's Brigade, during the Campaign in Virginia under Gen. Pope, and in Maryland under Gen. McClellan, in the Summer and Autumn of 1862. By Franklin B. Hough. *Albany: J. Munsell.* 1864. 8vo, pp. vi, 9–200. Portrait. B., BA., H. 33139

HOUGH. A History of Jefferson County in the State of New York, from the Earliest Period to the Present Time. By Franklin B. Hough ... . *Albany: Joel Munsell.* 1854. 8vo, pp. 601. Portraits and Plates. B., H. 33140

HOUGH. A History of St. Lawrence and Franklin Counties, New York, from the Earliest Period to the Present Time. By Franklin B. Hough ... . *Albany: Little & Co.* 1853. Rl. 8vo, pp. 719, (1). Portraits, Maps, and Plans. B., BA., H. 33141

Twenty-five copies were printed on fine paper with additional illustrations.

HOUGH. A History of Lewis County, in the State of New York, from the Beginning of its Settlement to the Present Time. By Franklin B. Hough ... . *Albany: Munsell & Rowland.* 1860. Rl. 8vo, pp. iv, 319. 21 Portraits. B., BA., H. 33142

Twenty-five copies were printed on fine paper, for private distribution.

HOUGH. The New York Civil List, containing the Names and Origin of the Civil Divisions, and the Names and Dates of Election or Appointment of the Principal State and County Officers, from the Revolution to the Present Time ... . By Franklin

B. Hough ... . *Albany: Weed, Parsons & Company.* 1860. 12mo, pp. (1), 472, (1). H. 33143

HOUGH. The Northern Invasion of October 1780 a Series of Papers relating to the Expeditions from Canada under Sir John Johnson and others against The Frontiers of New York which were supposed to have Connection with Arnold's Treason prepared from the Originals with an Introduction and Notes by Franklin B. Hough. *New York.* M DCCC LXVI. 8vo, pp. 224, (3). Map and Plate. BA. 33144

Forms No. VI. of the "Bradford Club Publications." Includes a narrative of the invasion of the Mohawk valley by Sir John Johnson, and his corps of Tories and Indians; with many illustrative documents.

HOUGH. Notices of Peter Penet and of His Operations among the Oneida Indians, including a Plan prepared by him for the Government of that Tribe ... . By Franklin B. Hough. *Lowville, N. Y.* 1866. 8vo, pp. 36. Map. S. 33145

Fifty copies only printed. Also included in Vol. V. of the "Transactions of the Albany Institute." Penet was a French adventurer, sometime employed as an agent by the Continental Congress, who absconded from Paris without accomplishing anything.

HOUGH. Papers Relating to Pemaquid and parts adjacent in the present State of Maine, known as Cornwall County, when under the Colony of New-York. Compiled from Official Records in the Office of the Secretary of State at Albany, N. Y. By Franklin B. Hough. *Albany: Weed, Parsons & Companie.* MDCCCLVI. 8vo, pp. vii, 136. B., BA., C. 33146

Also in the "Maine Historical Collections," Vol. V.

HOUGH. Papers Relating to the Island of Nantucket, with Documents relating to the Original Settlement of that Island, Martha's Vineyard, and other Islands adjacent, known as Duke's County, while under the Colony of New York. Compiled from Official Records ... . By Franklin B. Hough ... . *Albany:* [*J. Munsell.*] 1856. Sm. 4to, pp. xviii, 162, (1). Map. 33147

One hundred and fifty copies privately printed.

HOUGH. Proceedings of the Commissioners of Indian Affairs, Appointed by Law for the Extinguishment of Indian Titles in the State of New York. Published from the Original Manuscript in the Library of the Albany Institute. With an Introduction and Notes by Franklin B. Hough ... . *Albany: Joel Munsell.* M DCCC LXI. 2 vols., 4to, pp. 255; (4), 257–501. 3 Maps.

Ten copies printed on large paper. Forms Parts IX. and X. of Munsell's "Historical Series," and contains most of the documents, which record the extinguishment of the title of the Six Nations to a great portion of the State of New York in 1784. The same work was also issued in *one* volume on large paper by the Albany Institute. Indeed, the probabilities are that its introduction into Munsell's "Historical Series," was an afterthought.

HOUGH. Plan for seizing and carrying to New-York Coll. Wm. Goffe the Regicide, as set forth in the affidavit of John London, Apr. 20, 1678. Published from the Original in the Office of the Secretary of State of New-York. By Franklin B. Hough, M.D. With other documents on the same subject among the State Papers of Connecticut. ... *Albany: Weed, Parsons & Co.* M. DCCC. LV. Sm. 8vo, pp. 17. B., H. 33149

Fifty copies only printed.

HOUGH. Proceedings of a Convention. *See* Vol. II., No. 6543

[HOUGH.] Proclamations for Thanksgiving, issued by the Continental Congress, Pres't Washington, by the National and State Governments on the Peace of 1815, and by the Governors of New York since the Introduction of the Custom; with those of the Governors of the Several States in 1858. With an Historical Introduction and Notes. *Albany: Munsell & Rowland.* 1858. Rl. 8vo, pp. xvii, 183. B., BA. 33150

One hundred and fifty copies printed.

HOUGH. Results of a Series of Meteorological Observations made ... at Sundry Academies in the State of New-York, from 1826 to 1850, inclusive. ... Compiled ... By Franklin B. Hough. *Albany: Weed, Parsons and Company.* 1855. 4to, pp. xvi, 502. Map and 4 Plates. H. 33151

HOUGH. The Siege of Charleston, by the British Fleet and Army, under the Command of Admiral Arbuthnot and Sir Henry Clinton, which terminated with the Surrender of that Place, on the 12th of May, 1780. With Notes ... By Franklin B. Hough. *Albany: J. Munsell.* 1867. Sm. 4to, pp. 224. 2 Portraits. C.

HOUGH. The Siege of Savannah by the combined American and French Forces under the Command of Gen. Lincoln and the Count d'Estaing, ... in the Autumn of 1779. With Introduction, Notes, ... By Franklin B. Hough. *Albany: J. Munsell.* 1866. Sm. 4to, pp. 187. Portrait. 33153

HOUGH. Washingtoniana: or, Memorials of the Death of George Washington, giving an Account of the Funeral Honors paid to his Memory, with a List of Tracts and Volumes printed upon the Occasion, and a Catalogue of Medals commemorating

the Event. By Franklin B. Hough. *W. Elliot Woodward, Roxbury, Mass.* 1865. 2 vols., 8vo, pp. 272, Portrait, Map; pp. 304, Portrait. B., BA. 33154

Two hundred copies printed in imperial 8vo, eighty-one in crown 4to, and ten in royal 4to. Also: Address on the Early History of St. Lawrence County, Ogdensburgh, 1852.—Agricultural Statistics of the State of New York, by Counties, from the Census of 1865. With a Summary of Agricultural Statistics reported to the State Agricultural Society. ... *Albany: C. Van Benthuysen & Sons.* 1867. 8vo, pp. 187. C.—Biographical Notice of Dr. Sylvester D. Willard. ... *Albany.* 1866. 8vo.—Biographical Notice of Dr. Charles Milford Crandall. ... *Albany.* 1868. 8vo, pp. 6.—Census of the District of Columbia. Report ... [n. p. 1867?] 8vo, pp. 9–38.—Essay on the Climate of the State of New York. ... *Albany.* 1857. 8vo.—History of the Census in New York, and a Plan for the State Census of 1865. ... *Albany.* 1866. 8vo.—Prize Essay on Medical and Vital Statistics. ... *Albany: Van Benthuysen & Sons.* 1867. 8vo, pp. 37.—Statistics of Population of the City and County of New York as shown by the State Census of 1865 ... . *New York.* 1866. 8vo, pp. 81. *See also* Lowville, N. Y., *and* Papers relating to Hatfield, etc.

HOUGH (J.) A Sermon ... before the Vermont Colonization Society, at Montpelier, October 18, 1826. By John Hough ... *Montpelier: Printed by E. P. Walton.* 1826. 8vo, pp. 20. BA.

Also: Sermon at the Ordination of the Rev. Beriah Green, Pastor of the Congregational Church, Brandon, Vermont, April 16, 1823. ... 8vo. N.

HOUGH (L. S.) The Wanderer: a Poem. By Lewis S. Hough. *Cleveland.* 1847. 16mo. 33156

HOUGH (William J.) Speech of W. J. Hough, of New York, on the Bill for the Reduction of the Tariff. ... July 1, 1846. *Washington: Printed at the Office of Blair and Rives.* 1846. 8vo, pp. 8. H. 33157

HOUGHTON (A.) The Gentlemen's and Ladies' Diary, and Almanac ... for ... 1802 ... By Asa Houghton. *Keene (N. H.): John Prentiss.* 8vo. 33158

Also: Houghton's Genuine Almanac. The Gentlemen's and Ladies' Diary, and Almanac ... for ... 1804. ... *Keene, [N. H.]: John Prentiss.* 8vo. Continued. H.

HOUGHTON (D.) *See* Michigan—Geology.

HOUGHTON (E. B.) The Campaigns of the Seventeenth Maine. By Edwin B. Houghton, A Member of the Regiment. ... *Portland: Short & Loring.* 1866. 12mo, pp. x, (1), 333. B.

A few copies with rubricated title were privately printed on large paper.

HOUGHTON (G. F.) An Outline of the Controversy of the New Hampshire Grants; with a Sketch of the Life and Services of Col. Seth Warner. An Address delivered before the Legislature of the State of Vermont, in Montpelier, October 20, 1848,

By George Frederick Houghton ... . *Burlington.* 1849. 8vo, pp. 54. B., BA., H. 33160

See also Butler (J. D.), Vol. III., No. 9645.

HOUGHTON (G. H.) An Address delivered at the Opening of the Church of the Transfiguration, in the City of New-York, ... March 10th, 1850. By G. H. Houghton. *New York: Pudney & Russell, Printers.* 1851. 12mo, pp. 28. H., N. 33161

HOUGHTON (J.) Reply of Joab Houghton, late Chief Justice of the Supreme Court of the Temporary Civil Government of ... New Mexico, to the ... slanderous attack of R. H. Weightman ... . [*Washington.* 1852.] 8vo, pp. 16. H. 33162

HOUGHTON (T.) The | Alteration | of the | Coyn, | with a | Feasible Method | to do it, | Most Humbly Proposed to Both | Houses of Parliament. | To which is Annexed, | A Projection or Scheem | of Reasonable Terms, for Esta- | blishing a Firm and General | Peace in Europe. | By Thomas Houghton, of Lymestreet, Gent. | *London: Printed for the Author*, 1695. | pp. 50. Europe's Glory: | Or, | Peace & Plenty | to the | People thereof. | Being a Projection: Or, a Scheam of | Reasonable Terms ... . 4to, pp. 31. 33163

Contains interesting Notices of the Discoveries of Guinea and America, the Conquest of Mexico, Discovery of Peru, &c., &c.

HOUGHTON. Royal Institutions; being Proposals for Articles to Establish and Conform Laws, Liberties, and Customs of Silver and Gold Mines, ... in such parts of Africa and America which are now or shall be ... dependant on the Crown of England. With Methods of Mining ... By Thomas Houghton. *London: For the Author.* 1694. Sm. 8vo. C. 33164

It was reproduced as: The Golden Treasury, or the Compleat Minor, being Royal Institutions ... . *London.* 1699. Sm. 8vo.

HOUGHTON (W. A.) Our Fathers' Altar; a Centennial Sermon preached June 7, 1846, in commemoration of the Founding of the First Christian Church in Northborough, Mass. By Rev. William A. Houghton. *Worcester: H. J. Howland.* [1846.] 8vo. 33165

HOUGHTON. ... A Sermon ... at the Dedication of the Evangelical Congregational Meeting-House in Northborough; February 23, 1848. By Rev. William A. Houghton ... . *Worcester: Printed by Henry J. Howland.* [n. d.] 8vo, pp. 24. H. 33166

THE HOUGHTON ASSOCIATION. Constitution and Officers ... with the Proceedings of the ... Meeting ... in Worcester ... March 3, 1847. *New-York: Van Norden & Amerman, Printers.* 1847. 8vo, pp. 15. H. + Report of the Agent to England. *New York: Jared W. Bell, Printer.* 1848. 8vo, pp. 27. 33167

[HOUK (George W.)] Puritan. A Poem in Seven Cantos. *Cincinnati: Printed by Robert Clarke and Company.* MDCCCLXVIII. 8vo, pp. 94. B., H. 33168

The Houmas Land Claim. [A Collection of Documents relating to the Claim. n. p. 1860?] 8vo, pp. 4. H. 33169

Hours at Home: a Popular Monthly, devoted to Religious and Useful Literature. Edited by J. M. Sherwood. Vol. I. ... *New York: Charles Scribner & Co.* 1865. 8vo, pp. 576. Continued.

The volume for 1865 contains many articles on the Death of Abraham Lincoln by Carpenter, Drs. Gillette, N. McLeod, etc.

HOUSATONIC AGRICULTURAL SOCIETY. Transactions of the Housatonic Agricultural Society during ... 1854. *Pittsfield: Printed by Reed, Hull & Peirson.* 1855. 8vo, pp. 50. Continued.

HOUSATONIC CANAL COMPANY. Proposals, Reports, and Documents. 8vo. 33172

HOUSATONIC RAILROAD. Report of the Commissioners on the Housatonic Railroad to the General Assembly, May Session, 1843. *Hartford.* 1843. 8vo, pp. 8. M. 33173

Annual Report of the Board of Directors of the Housatonic Railroad Company, to the Stockholders, at their Annual Meeting, February 25, 1851. *Bridgeport: William S. Pomeroy, Printer.* 1851. 8vo. 33174

Also: Report of Directors of Housatonic Rail Road Company, to the Stockholders, 20th June, 1844. ... *New-York: Printed by H. Cogswell.* 1844. 8vo, pp. 16. B.

House Documents, and House List. *See* Congress, Vol. IV.

The House of Wisdom. *See* Touchstone (Geoffrey).

The House Old Nick Built. *Baltimore: Armstrong and Plaskitt.* 1834. 12mo, pp. 16. H. 33175

The House that Jeff Built. *New York.* 186–. 33176

The House that Tweed Built. *The American News Company.* [Colophon:] *Cambridge, Mass.* 1871. 8vo, pp. 40. 33177

HOUSER (H.) An Exact Model or Platform of Good Magistracy: or a Sermon ... before the Governour, Council, and Assembly ... in Jamaica, Feb. i. 1671. By Rev. Henry Houser. *London: Francis Tyton.* 1673. 4to, pp. (6), 19. H., M. 33178

Houses of Refuge and Schools of Reform. Proceedings of the First Convention of Managers and Superintendents ... in the United States ... held in the City of New York, May, 1857. *New York.* 1857. 8vo, pp. 147. B., H. + Second Convention. [*Ibid.*] 1860. 8vo, pp. 175, (1). B., H. 33179

HOUSEWORTH (T.) California Scenery. A Series of Stereoscopic Views of most of the Points of Interest on the Pacific Coast [of the United States]. *San Francisco: T. Houseworth & Co.* [1868.] 4to. 67 Photographs. C. 33180

HOUSTON (A. B.) Nineteenth Century: or, Glances at Home and Abroad. By A. B. Houston. *Springfield: Printed by Stephenson & Co.* 1852. 8vo, pp. 48. 33181

HOUSTON (G. S.) The Mexican Treaty. Speech of Hon. G. S. Houston, of Alabama, June 28, 1864. [n. p. n. d.] 8vo, pp. 8. 33182

HOUSTON. Speech ... on the Oregon Question ... February 6, 1846. *Washington.* 1846. 8vo, pp. 14. H. 33183

HOUSTON. Speech ... May 26, 1846. ... On the Civil and Diplomatic Appropriation Bill ... . [n. p. n. d.] 8vo, pp. 7.

Also: Speech ... Jan. 24, 1852, on Mexican Indemnity. [n. p. n. d.] 8vo.—Speech ... April 27, 1842, on Apportionment. *Washington.* 1842. 8vo.—Treaty of Peace with Mexico. Speech ... February 5, 1849 ... . [n. p. n. d.] 8vo, pp. 7. H.

HOUSTON (J. A.) An Address Explanatory of the Principles of the United Brothers of Temperance, Delivered at ... New York, Sept. 11th, 1844. By James Alexander Houston. *New York.* 1844. 8vo, pp. 10. 33185

HOUSTON. ... Proceedings and Debates of the United States Senate. First Session—Thirtieth Congress. By James A. Houston. *Washington, D. C.* MDCCCXLVIII. 4to, pp. 7, 1031, Appendix, 35. B., BA., C. 33186

HOUSTON (J. W.) Speech of John W. Houston, ... July 2, 1846, on the Tariff. *Washington.* 1846. 8vo. 33187

HOUSTON (M. H.) An Address ... before the Ohio County Medical Society, on the Evening of its Organization. July 5,

1847. By M. H. Houston, M.D. ... *Wheeling: Printed by William Ewing.* 1847. 8vo, pp. 20. H. 33188

HOUSTON (S.) Documents of Major Gen. Sam. Houston, ... to his Excellency David G. Burnet, President of the Republic of Texas; containing a Detailed Account of the Battle of San Jacinto. *New Orleans: John Cox & Co., Printers.* [1836.] 8vo, pp. 18, (1). BA. 33189

HOUSTON. Letter of General Sam. Houston to General Santa Anna. *Washington.* 1852. 8vo, pp. 8. 33190

HOUSTON. The Life of Sam Houston (of Texas). ... *New York: J. C. Derby.* 1855. 12mo, pp. 402. Plates. B., BA.

Perhaps by Charles Edwards Lester.

HOUSTON. Life of General Sam. Houston. [n. p. n. d.] 8vo, pp. 15. + Another Edition. [*Washington: Printed by J. T. Towers.* n. d.] 8vo, pp. 15. B., BA., H. 33192

HOUSTON. Nebraska Bill. Indian Tribes. Speech of Hon. Sam Houston of Texas delivered ... Feb. 14 and 15, 1854, in Favor of maintaining the Public Faith with the Indian Tribes. *Washington.* 1854. 8vo, pp. 15. B. 33193

HOUSTON. Speech of Hon. Sam. Houston ... Exposing the Malfeasance and Corruption of John Charles Watrous, Judge in Texas. *New York: Pudney & Russell, Printers.* 1860. 12mo, pp. 100. 33194

HOUSTON. Speeches of Sam Houston, of Texas, on the Subject of an Increase of the Army, and the Indian Policy of the Government, delivered in the Senate ... January 29 and 31, 1855. *Washington.* 1855. 8vo, pp. 20. BA., H. 33195

Also: The Compromise Measures. Speech ... in the Senate ... Dec. 22, 1851 ... . [*Washington.* n. d.] 8vo, pp. 8.—Debate in the Senate on the Protection of Property in the District of Columbia. From Houston's Senate Debates. ... April 20, 1848. [n. p. n. d.] 8vo, pp. 16.—A Lecture on the Trials and Dangers of Frontier Life, as exemplified in the History of Texas. ... January 28, 1851. [n. p. n. d.] 8vo, pp. 32.—Message of Gov. Houston, of Texas, on Secession. [n. p. n. d.] 8vo, pp. 8.—Message of Gov. Sam Houston, on the South Carolina Resolutions. By Authority. *Austin: Printed by John Marshall & Co.* 1860. 8vo, pp. 16.—Naval Retiring Board. Speech ... in the Senate ... April 23, 1856. [*Washington.* n. d.] 8vo, pp. 24. H.—Remarks on the Memorial of the New England Clergymen; United States Senate, March 14, 1854. [n. p. n. d.] 8vo.—Speech ... on the Massachusetts Claim. March 25, 1826. [n. p. n. d.] 12mo, pp. 23.—Speech ... on the Change of the Newspapers in which the Laws are directed to be printed. *Washington.* 1827. 8vo.—Speech ... on the Bill for the Relief of Yucatan. *Washington.* 1848. 8vo, pp. 14.—Speech ... on the Subject Compromise. In the Senate ... February 8, 1850. [*Washington.* n. d.] 8vo, pp. 16. B.—Speech ... in Reply to ... Articles ... in the

"Southern Press," September 9, 1850. [n. p. n. d.] 8vo, pp. 19.—Speech, United States Senate, on the Resolution reaffirming the Compromise Measures, 1851. [n. p. n. d.] 8vo, pp. 8.—Speech ... in the Senate ... July 15, 1854, on the Texan Navy—Commodore Moore. *Washington.* 1854. 8vo, pp. 15.—Speech ... on the Nebraska and Kansas Bill, ... March 3, 1854. [n. p. n. d.] 8vo, pp. 8.—Speech ... Aug. 1, 1854, on Texan Affairs. [n. p. n. d.] 8vo.

HOUSTOUN (G.) Reliquiæ Houstounianæ: seu Plantarum in America Meridionali a Gulielmo Houstoun ... Collectarum Icones manu propria ære incisæ; cum descriptionibus e schedis ejusdem In Bibliotheca Josephi Banks, ... *Londoni.* MDCCLXXXI. 4to, pp. 12. 26 Plates. B., H., J.C.B. + Editio in Germania Prima. *Norimbergæ: ex officina Raspeana.* MDCCXCIV. 8vo, pp. 24. 15 Plates. J.C.B. 33196

HOUSTOUN (J.) Memoirs of the Life and Travels of James Houstoun, M.D. (Formerly Physician and Surgeon-General to the Royal African Company's Settlements in Africa, and late Surgeon to the Royal Assiento Company's factories in America), From the Year 1690 to this Present Year 1747. Containing A great Variety of curious Observations that occurred during the Course of above Thirty Years Travels in divers Foreign Parts. Collected and Written by his Own Hand. *London: J. Robinson, J. Wood, and W. Owen.* MDCCXLVII. 8vo, pp. (8), 435. B.

This was originally published under the name of Jacob Bickerstaff. It was also put forth with the following title:

HOUSTOUN. Dr. Houstoun's Memoirs of his Own Life-time. Containing Among other Curious Particulars, during upwards of Thirty Years Travels. An Account of I. The Scotch Settlement at Darien. II. The great Advantages accruing to Great Britain from an Incorporated Union of the Whole Island. III. The Rise and Progress of Royal African and Assiento Companies. IV. The Rise and Fall of the grand South Sea Bubble, &c. in 1720. V. The Conduct of the Spaniards, and Manner of their Trade in the West Indies. VI. The secret Expedition thither in 1740. VII. Some Anecdotes of the Government of Jamaica with the Characteristicks of its Inhabitants. VIII. The Importance of Cape Breton to the British Nation. IX. An Essay on Genius and Education. Collected from the Author's Original Manuscripts, and Publish'd by Jacob Bickerstaff, M.A. *London: Lawton Gilliver.* 1747. 8vo, pp. (4), 435. 33198

A very curious book, by a Scotch adventurer, who was concerned in the Darien settlement. He was surgeon to the Assiento Company's factories in America, and passed most of his life trading and negotiating in Central America and the Spanish Main. The author gives much information on Colonial Affairs, Civil, Military and Naval. It was again reproduced with some additional introductory matter as:

HOUSTOUN. The Works of James Houstoun, M.D. Containing Memoirs of his Life and Travels in Asia, Africa, America, and most Parts of Europe. From the Year 1690, to the present Time. Giving a particular Account of the Scotch Expedition to Darien in America, the great Advantages accruing to Great Britain from the Union; the Rise, Progress, and Fall of the two great Trading African and South-Sea Companies; the late Expedition to the Spanish West-Indies; the Taking and Restitution of Cape-Breton. ... *London: For the Author.* 1753. 8vo, pp. xviii, 435. BA., C., H. 33199

HOUSTOUN (*Mrs.* M. C.) Hesperos, or Travels in the West. By Mrs. Houstoun. *London: J. W. Parker.* 1850. 2 vols., post 8vo, pp. vii, 293; 243. 33200

HOUSTOUN. A Yacht Voyage to Texas and the Gulf of Mexico. By Mrs. Houstoun. *London.* 1844. 2 vols., post 8vo, pp. 690. Plates. 33201

See "Quart. Rev.," LXXVI. 124. Reprinted as:

HOUSTOUN. Texas and The Gulf of Mexico; or, Yachting in the New World. By Mrs. Houstoun. *London.* 1844. 2 vols., post 8vo. + *Philadelphia: G. B. Zieber & Co.* 1845. 12mo, pp. 288. H. 33202

Also included in Smith's "Weekly Volume," *Philadelphia*, 1845. Folio.

HOVEY (A.) A Memoir of the Life and Times of the Rev. Isaac Backus, A.M. By Alvah Hovey, D.D. *Boston: Gould and Lincoln.* 1858. 12mo, pp. 369. B., H. + [*Ibid.*] 1859.

This volume contains much pertaining to the religious history of Rhode Island, and especially the Baptists.

HOVEY (C. F.) Tribute to the Memory of Charles F. Hovey, Esq. [From "The Liberator," May 6, 1859. n. p. n. d.] 12mo, pp. 24. BA. 33204

HOVEY (Charles M.) Address ... at the Dedication of the New Hall of the Massachusetts Horticultural Society ... September 16, 1865. By C. M. Hovey. *Boston: Henry W. Dutton & Son, Printers.* 1866. 8vo, pp. 31. B., H. 33205

HOVEY. The Fruits of America, containing Richly Colored Figures, and Full Descriptions of all the choicest Varieties cultivated in the United States. ... *Boston: Hovey and Co.* 1852. 2 vols., 4to, pp. viii, 100; iv, 96. 48 Plates, 2 Portraits. B., C. + *New York.* 1853. Imp. 8vo. A. 33206

First published in parts in 1847, *et seq.*, and the finest work of its kind in the United States.

HOVEY. The American Gardener's Magazine. ... Vol. I. 1835. Conducted by C. M. Hovey and P. B. Hovey, Jr. *Boston: Russell, Shattuck and Williams, and Hovey and Company.* 1835. 8vo, pp. vii, (1), 472. Continued. B., BA., H. 33207

HOVEY. Magazine of Horticulture, Botany, and all useful Discoveries and Improvements in Rural Affairs. By C. M. Hovey. *Boston.* 1835. 8vo. Continued. A. 33208

HOVEY (H. C.) Freedom's Banner. A Sermon preached to the Coldwater Light Artillery, and the Coldwater Zouave Cadets, April 28th, 1861. By Rev. Horace C. Hovey. *Republican Print, Coldwater.* 1861. 8vo, pp. 11. H. 33209

HOVEY. The National Fast. A Sermon, preached at Coldwater, Mich., January 4, 1861. By Rev. Horace C. Hovey. *Republican Print, Coldwater.* 1861. 8vo, pp. 12. H. 33210

Also: Loyalty. A Sermon preached in Northampton, February 22, 1863. ... *Northampton: Metcalf & Co., Printers.* 1863. 8vo, pp. 16.

HOVEY (I.) A Farewell Sermon. A Sermon, preached at Rochester, Oct. 15, 1769. By Ivory Hovey. *Boston.* 1770. 8vo, pp. 32. 33211

HOVEY. ... A Sermon occasioned by the Death of Lieut. John Hammond of Rochester; who was born at Sandwich, Nov. 22, 1663, and died April 19, 1749 ... By Ivory Hovey. *Printed by S. Kneeland, Boston.* 1749. 12mo, pp. (2), ii, 34. BA.

HOVEY. A Sermon Preached ... in Plymouth (Massachusetts), June 8, 1794. Occasioned by the sudden death of two young persons in the town, who died about the same hour of the day, May 31, 1794; and several aged persons, within a short space before. By Ivory Hovey, A.M. ... *Boston: Printed by Joseph Bumstead.* 1795. 8vo, pp. 34. BA. 33213

HOVEY (S.) Letters from the West Indies: Relating Especially to the Danish Island St. Croix, and to the British Islands Antigua, Barbadoes, and Jamaica. By Sylvester Hovey ... . *New York: Gould and Newman.* 1838. 12mo, pp. iv, 13–212.

[HOVEY (William).] A Remonstrance to the ... Senate ... of Massachusetts ... [on the State Lunatic Hospital. n. p. n. d.] 8vo, pp. 11. H. 33215

HOVEY (W. A.) Woman's Rights. An Essay ... at the Exhibition of the English High School ... July 16, 1860. By

William A. Hovey. ... *Boston: Yerrinton & Garrison, Printers.* 1860. 12mo, pp. 7. H. 33216

HOW (D.) Diary of David How, a Private in Colonel Paul Dudly Sargent's Regiment of the Massachusetts Line, in the Army of the American Revolution. From the Original Manuscript. With a Biographical Sketch of the Author by George Wingate Chase, and Illustrative Notes by Henry B. Dawson. *Morrisania, N. Y.* 1865. Rl. 8vo, pp. xv, 51. BA., H. 33217

Two hundred and fifty copies printed; forms No. IV. of Dawson's "Gleanings in the Harvest-Field of American History."

HOW (H.) The Mineralogy of Nova Scotia. A Report to the Provincial Government. By Henry How, D.C.L. ... *Halifax: Charles Annand.* 1869. 8vo, pp. vi, (1), 217. B., BA., H.

Also: Sketch of the Mineralogy of Nova Scotia as Illustrated by the Collection of Minerals sent to the Paris Exhibition. ... *Halifax.* 1867. 8vo.

HOW (H. R.) The Battle of Trenton. A Poem. By Henry R. How. *New Brunswick.* 1856. 8vo, pp. 15. 33219

HOW (N.) A Narrative of the Captivity of Nehemiah How, who was taken by the Indians at the Great-Meadow-Fort above Fort-Dummer, where he was an Inhabitant, October 11th, 1745. Giving an Account of what he met with in his travelling to Canada, and while he was in Prison there. Together with an Account of Mr. How's Death at Canada. ... *Boston N. E., Printed and Sold opposite to the Prison in Queen Street.* 1748. 16mo, pp. 22, (2). B., BA. 33220

HOW (S. B.) An Address, delivered by the Rev. S. B. How, at his Inauguration as Principal of Dickinson College, in Carlisle, Pa. ... March 30, 1830. *Carlisle, Pa.* 1830. 8vo, pp. 23. H.

HOW. A Sermon, preached at the Opening for Public Worship, of the Second Reformed Dutch Church, at Somerville, New Jersey, Feb. 18, 1835. By Samuel B. How. *Somerville: Baldwin & Hassey, Printers.* 1835. 8vo, pp. 12. BA. 33222

HOW. Slaveholding Not Sinful. An Argument before the General Synod of the Reformed Protestant Dutch Church, October, 1855. By Samuel B. How, D.D. ... *New-York: Printed by John A. Gray.* 1855. 8vo, pp. 32. B. + Second Edition. *New-Brunswick, N. J.: John Terhune.* 1856. 12mo, pp. 136.

This was followed by "An Answer to Slaveholding not Sinful." *New Brunswick.* 1856.

HOW (T. Y.) Letters addressed to the Rev. Samuel Miller, D.D. in Reply to his Letters concerning the Constitution and Order of the Christian Ministry. ... By Rev. Thomas Y. How. *Utica: Printed by Seward and Williams.* 1808. 8vo, pp. 124.

HOW. A Statement by the Rev. Mr. How, in reply to those parts of the Pamphlet of the Rev. Mr. Jones, which relate more particularly to himself. [*New York.* 1811.] 8vo, pp. 20. BA.

HOW. A Vindication of the Protestant Episcopal Church, in a Series of Letters addressed to the Rev. Samuel Miller, D.D. ... with Preliminary Remarks. By Thomas Y. How, D.D. *New York: Eastburn, Kirk & Co.* 1816. 8vo, pp. xxxvi, 492. B., C.

Also: An Address delivered before the Auxiliary New-York Bible and Common Prayer Book Society, in St. Paul's Chapel, in ... New-York, ... the 28th Day of January, ... 1817. ... *New York: Printed by T. & J. Swords.* 1817. 8vo, pp. xii, 5–52. B., BA., H.

... How Bull Rull Battle was lost. The Ball's Bluff Massacre. Department of the West. Fremont. *Tribune War Tracts.* 1861? 8vo, pp. 8. 33227

How can we best help our Camps and Hospitals. Woman's Central Association of Relief, March 27, 1863. [n. p. 1863.] 8vo, pp. 42. 33228

How our National Debt can be Paid. *Philadelphia.* 1865. 8vo.

How the South Rejected Compromise in the Peace Conference of 1861. Speech of Mr. Chase, of Ohio. *New York: W. C. Bryant & Co.* 1863. 8vo, pp. 11. 33230

Loyal Publication Society, No. 37.

How the War was Commenced. An Appeal to the Documents. Southern Documents especially quoted. From the Cincinnati Daily Commercial. *New York.* 1864. 8vo, pp. 16. C.

Loyal Publication Society, No. 46. Translated into German as:

Wie der Krieg angefangen wurde. [Uebersetzt von F. Schütz.] *New York.* 1864. 8vo, pp. 15. 33232

Loyal Publication Society, No. 53.

How to abolish Slavery in America, and to prevent a Cotton Famine in England: with Remarks upon Coolie and African Emigration. By a Slave Driver. *London: Alfred W. Bennett.* 1858. 8vo, pp. 16. 33233

How to get a Farm. *See* [Morris (Edmund)].

How to kill Three Birds with one Stone. Articles printed in the Charleston Courier. *Charleston, S. C.: Printed by A. E. Miller.* 1852. 8vo, pp. 12. H. 33234

How to Renew our National Strength. A Sermon preached in Christ Church, Savannah, On Friday, November 15th, 1861, Being the Day of Humiliation, Fasting, and Prayer, appointed by the President of the Confederate States. ... *Savannah.* 1861. 8vo, pp. 16. 33235

How to settle the Texas Question. Address to the Friends of Free Institutions. *Boston.* [n. d.] 12mo, pp. 10. 33236

HOWARD (——). Essays of Howard: or, Tales of the Prison. Originally printed in the New-York Columbian, and supposed to be written by a Debtor, who has been confined for Sixteen Years in the New-York Debtor's Jail. ... *New-York: C. S. Van Winkle, Printer.* 1811. 8vo, pp. 99. BA. 33237

HOWARD (B.) A Sermon ... at the Ordination of the Rev. Allen Pratt ... in Westmoreland, October 6, 1790. By Bezaleel Howard, D.D. *Keene* [*N. H.*]*: Printed by James D. Griffith.* [1790.] 8vo, pp. 26. H. 33238

HOWARD. A Sermon ... at the Ordination of the Rev. Benj. R. Woodbridge ... in Norwich, October 17th, 1799. By Bezaleel Howard, D.D. *Springfield: Printed by Timothy Ashley.* M,DCC. 8vo, pp. 15. H. 33239

HOWARD (B. C.) Report of the Decision of the Supreme Court of the United States, and the Opinions of the Judges thereof, in the Case of Dred Scott *versus* John F. A. Sandford. December Term, 1856. By Benjamin C. Howard. *Washington: Cornelius Wendell, Printer.* 1857. 8vo, pp. 239. + *New York: D. Appleton & Co.* 1857. 8vo, pp. 389–633. B. 33240

HOWARD. Reports of Cases argued and adjudged in the Supreme Court of the United States, January Term 1843, [to December Term 1860.] By Benjamin C. Howard. *Philadelphia, Boston, and Washington.* 1843–1861. 24 vols., 8vo.

These Reports follow Peters', and with those Reports, and Dallas, Cranch, and Wheaton's, comprise all the decisions of the highest Court known to American Law.

HOWARD (C.) Inquiries addressed to Parson Brownlow, relative to the Defense of Slavery ... By Charles Howard. *Alton, Illinois: Parks & Pinckard ... Printers.* 1864. 8vo, pp. 16. H.

HOWARD. Memorial [etc.] *See* Vol. I., No. 3042.

HOWARD (C. W.) Christian Benevolence, as illustrated in the Early History of Georgia. A Lecture ... before the Young Men's Christian Association, of Augusta, Ga. ... January 10, 1860. By Rev. C. W. Howard. *Augusta, Georgia.* 1860. 8vo, pp. 29. B. 33243

HOWARD. Life and Character of Oglethorpe. An Address ... before the Literary Societies of the University of Georgia ... August 2, 1860. By Rev. C. W. Howard. *Athens, Georgia.* 1860. 8vo, pp. 26. B. 33244

Also: A Sermon ... at the Re-Opening and Dedication of the French Protestant Church of Charleston, S. C. ... 11th ... of May 1845. ... *Charleston: Burges & James, Printers.* 1845. 8vo, pp. 24. B.—The Southern Gentleman: an Address ... before the Alpha Phi Delta & H.H.H. Societies ... July 11, 1860. ... *Augusta, Ga.* 1860. 8vo, pp. 22. B.

[HOWARD (Edward).] Sir Henry Morgan, the Buccaneer. *London.* 1842. 3 vols., post 8vo. + *Paris: Baudry's European Library.* 1842. 8vo, pp. (2), 351. 33245

[HOWARD.] The Buccaneer, Sir Henry Morgan. *London: Ward & Locke.* 1861. 12mo, pp. 330. 33246

[HOWARD (F. K.)] Fourteen Months in American Bastiles. *Baltimore: Printed by Kelly, Hedian & Piet.* 1863. 8vo, pp. 89. + *London: Henry F. Mackintosh.* MDCCCLXIII. 8vo, pp. 84. H.

Three or more editions were published.

HOWARD (George William Frederick), *Earl of Carlisle.* Two Lectures, On the Poetry of Pope, and on his own Travels in America. By the Right Honourable the Earl of Carlisle. Delivered to the Leeds Mechanics' Institution & Literary Society, December 5th and 6th, 1850. *Leeds: Printed by Edward Baines and Sons.* 1850. 4to, pp. 44. H. + *London.* 1850. 4to + [Another Edition.] *London.* 1851. 8vo. + Tenth Thousand. *London.* 1851. 33248

Reprinted as below:

[HOWARD.] Travels in America. The Poetry of Pope. Two Lectures delivered to the Leeds Mechanics' Institution and Literary Society, December 5th and 6th, 1850. By the Right Honorable the Earl of Carlisle (Lord Morpeth). *New-York: G. P. Putnam.* 1851. 12mo, pp. 135. H. 33249

HOWARD (H. R.) The History of Virgil A. Stewart, and his Adventure in Capturing and Exposing the Great "Western

Land Pirate" and his Gang, in Connexion with the Evidence. Also of the Trials, Confessions, and Execution of a Number of Murrell's Associates in the State of Mississippi during the Summer of 1835, and the Execution of Five Professional Gamblers by the Citizens of Vicksburg, on the 6th July, 1835. ... Compiled by H. R. Howard. *New York: Harper & Brothers.* 1836. 12mo, pp. 273. BA., C., H. 33250

[HOWARD.] The Life and Adventures of Joseph T. Hare, the Bold Robber and Highwayman ... . *New York: H. Long and Brother.* [n. d.] 8vo, pp. 107. BA. 33251

HOWARD (Jacob M.) Speech of Hon. J. M. Howard of Michigan on the Confiscation of Property ... in the Senate of the United States, April 18, 1862. [n. p.: *L. Towers & Co., Printers.* n. d.] 8vo, pp. 16. H. 33252

HOWARD. Speech ... on the Joint Resolution for the Recognition and Readmission to the Union of Louisiana. Delivered ... February 25, 1865. [n. p. n. d.] 8vo, pp. 15. H. 33253

Also: San Juan Island. Speech ... April 16, 1869 ... *Washington: F. & J. Rives & Geo. A. Bailey ... Printers.* 1870. 8vo, pp. 13.—Report ... on ... Memorial of Davis Hatch on San Domingo Affairs. *Washington.* 1869. 8vo.—Military Interference with Elections. Speech ... in the ... Senate, March 23 & 24, 1864. [*Washington.* n. d.] 8vo, pp. 32.—Speech, January, 1864, on the Motion to expel Mr. Davis of Kentucky, for offering a Series of Resolutions in the Senate, tending to incite Insurrection. [n. p. n. d.] 8vo, pp. 15.—Transcontinental, Memphis and El Paso Railroad. Speech ... in the Senate ... June 22 and 23, 1870. [n. p. n. d.] 8vo, pp. 16. H.

HOWARD, *and* BINNEY (James). Correspondence. [*Washington.* 1867.] 8vo, pp. 16. H. 33254

HOWARD (J. S.) A Statement of Facts relative to the Dismissal of James S. Howard, Esq. Late Postmaster of the City of Toronto, U. C. ... *Toronto: J. H. Lawrence, Printer.* 1839. 12mo, pp. 28. H. 33255

HOWARD (J.) Baily et al *v.* Poindexter's Ex'r. ... Note of Argument of John Howard for Appellants. [n. p.] 1857. 8vo, pp. 8. 33256

Relates to slavery.

HOWARD. Williamson et al *vs.* Coulter's Ex'rs et al. Note of Argument of John Howard for Appellants. [n. p. 1858.] 8vo, pp. 43. 33257

Concerning a bequest of slaves.

HOWARD (J. C.) A Discourse delivered before the Humane Society of ... Massachusetts, ... June 12, 1804. ... By John C. Howard. *Boston: Printed by Hosea Sprague.* 1804. 8vo, pp. 64.

HOWARD (J. E.) An Oration delivered before the Washington Society of Alexandria, Va., February 22, 1815, By Col. Eager Howard. *Alexandria: Printed by Allen and Hill.* [n. d.] 8vo, pp. 16. 33259

HOWARD (J. H.) The Laws of the British Colonies in the West Indies and other Parts of America, concerning Real and Personal Property, and Manumission of Slaves, with a View of the Constitution of each Colony. By John Henry Howard, Solicitor. *London.* 1827. 2 vols., rl. 8vo. C. 33260

[HOWARD (John S.)] Descendants of Samuel Hayward of Taunton, Mass. [Chelsea, Mass., October 1, 1863.] Folio, 1 l.

"I believe but one copy was printed."—WHITTEMORE.

HOWARD (Joseph P.) Howard's Gold Chart; showing at a glance all the fluctuations in the Price of Gold during 1862–3. *New York.* 1864. 8vo. 33262

HOWARD (L.) A Collection of Letters and State Papers, from the Original Manuscripts of many Princes, Great Personages, and Statesmen, together with some curious and scarce Tracts, and Pieces of Antiquity, Religious, Political, and Moral. By Leonard Howard, M.D. *London.* 1753–6. 2 parts making 1 vol., 4to.

Very scarce. Commences with a long letter concerning the Expedition of Penn and Venables against the Island of Hispaniola, during the Protectorship of Oliver Cromwell; also some interesting particulars relative to Virginia, St. Christopher's, Nova Francia, including Letters of Sir George Calvert and others. *See* "Retrospective Review," New Series, Vol. I.

HOWARD (Luke). Memoir of John Woolman, chiefly extracted from a Journal of his Life and Travels. *London: Printed by William and Samuel Graves.* 1815. 12mo, pp. 36. 33264

Frequently reprinted, as was also the following:

HOWARD. Memoir of Thomas Chalkley; chiefly extracted from a Journal of his Life, Travels and Christian Experiences. *London: Printed by William and Samuel Graves.* 1817. 12mo, pp. 72. 33265

HOWARD (M.) Trial of Mrs. Margaret Howard, for the Murder of Miss Mary Ellen Smith, her Husband's Paramour, in Cincinnati, on the 2d of February. *Cincinnati.* 1849. 8vo, pp. 64. C. + *Albany: J. Munsell.* 1849. 8vo, pp. 64. 33266

HOWARD (M.) Despotic Doctrines, declared by the United States Senate, Exposed; and Senator Dixon Unmasked. By Mark Howard. *Hartford: Case, Lockwood & Co.* 1863. 8vo, pp. 24. 33267

HOWARD (*Mr.*) Documents in relation to the Comparative Merits of Canals and Railroads, submitted by Mr. Howard, of Maryland, to the House of Representatives. *Washington.* 1832. 8vo. 33268

HOWARD. ... Kansas Affairs. Mr. Howard, from the Select Committee, made the following Report. ... [n. p. n. d.] 8vo, pp. 29. 33269

HOWARD (M. S.) ... A Sermon preached in South Dartmouth on the occasion of the Annual Thanksgiving, Nov. 27, 1862. By Rev. Martin S. Howard ... . *New Bedford: Edmund Anthony, Printer.* 1862. 8vo, pp. 23. 33270

HOWARD. Protection in the Family, in Society, and in the State. A Sermon ... in South Dartmouth, April 7, 1864. [n. p. n. d.] 8vo, pp. 8. 33271

Also: ... A Sermon occasioned by the Death of Deacon Samuel Staples; preached in South Dartmouth, March 9th, 1862. ... *New Bedford: E. Anthony, Printer.* 1862. 8vo, pp. 15.— ... A Sermon occasioned by the Death of Mrs. Betsy, wife of Deacon Matthews Thacher. ... South Dartmouth, Aug. 10th, 1862. ... *New Bedford: E. Anthony, Printer.* 1862. 8vo, pp. 16.

HOWARD (M.) The Conquest of Quebec: A Poem. By Middleton Howard ... . *Oxford: J. Fletcher.* MDCCLXVIII. 4to, pp. 12. 33272

An Oxford Prize Poem. Reprinted in the "Oxford Prize Poems." *Oxford.* 1810. 12mo. *See* "M. Rev.," XL. 139.

HOWARD (O. O.) Major General Howard's Address at the Second Anniversary of the U. S. Christian Commission. *Philadelphia: ... Press of C. Sherman, Son & Co.* 1864. 12mo, pp. 23.

Also: Report of Brevet Major General O. O. Howard, Commissioner Bureau of Refugees, Freedmen, and Abandoned Lands to the Secretary of War, October 20, 1869. *Washington.* 1869. 8vo, pp. 30.—Statement ... before the Committee on Education and Labor in Defense against the Charges presented by Hon. Fernando Wood; and Argument of Edgar Ketchum, Esq., of Counsel for Gen. Howard. ... *New York.* 1870. 8vo, pp. 55. *See also* Vol. VII., No. 27239.

HOWARD, *and* JOHNSON (E.) Addresses by Major-General O. O. Howard and Rev. Edwin Johnson, at the laying of the Corner-Stone of the First Congregational Church, Washington, D. C. *Boston: Theoph. G. Wadman.* 1867. 8vo, pp. 16. B.

Howard (P.) The Barbarities of the Rebels, as shown in their Cruelty to the Federal Wounded and Prisoners; in their Outrages upon Union Men; in the Murder of Negroes, and in their Unmanly Conduct throughout the Rebellion. By Colonel Percy Howard, Late of the Royal Horse Guards. *Providence, R. I.: The Author.* 1863. 8vo, pp. 40. H. 33275

Howard (R.) The Indian Queen. A Tragedy. By Sir Robert Howard. *London: H. Herrington.* 1665. Folio, pp. 141–212. J.C.B. 33276

Howard (Robert). Report of Hon. Mr. Howard, in the United States Senate, on Interference in Elections by Military and Naval Officers. *Philadelphia.* 1864. 8vo, pp. 32. 33277

Howard (S.) A | Sermon | preached | To the Ancient and Honorable | Artillery-Company, | in Boston, New-England, | June 7th, 1773. Being the Anniversary of their | Election of Officers. | By Simeon Howard, A.M. ... *Boston: Printed by John Boyles.* 1773. 8vo, pp. 43. BA., H. 33278

Reprinted in Thornton's "Pulpit of the Revolution."

Howard. A Sermon Preached before the Honorable Council ... of the State of Massachusetts-Bay, in New-England, May 31, 1780. Being the Anniversary for the Election of the Honorable Council. By Simeon Howard, A.M ... | *Boston,* ... *Printed by John Gill* ... MDCCLXXX. 8vo, pp. 48. B., BA., H. 33279

Also: ... A Discourse delivered May 16, 1779 [after the Death of Prof. J. Winthrop and others]. ... *Boston: Printed by J. Gill and T. and J. Fleet.* 1779. 8vo, pp. 35. — A Discourse ... [on] the Death of Mrs. Elizabeth Howard, ... Delivered the Lord's Day after her Decease. By her bereaved Consort. ... *Boston: Printed by T. & J. Fleet, and J. Gill.* MDCCLXXVII. 8vo, pp. 36. B., BA. — A Sermon on Brotherly Love, preached ... in Boston, December 28, 1778. Before the ... Society of Free- ... Masons ... *Boston: Printed by Brother Thomas Fleet.* [1778.] 8vo, pp. 27. H. — A Sermon ... in Boston, November 18, 1791; at the Ordination of the Rev. Thomas Adams, ... in the Town of Camden, in South-Carolina. ... *Boston: Printed by Joseph Belknap and Alexander Young.* MDCCXCI. 8vo, pp. 36. B., BA., H.

Howard (S. *and* C.) Abridged Statement of Differences with the Detroit and Milwaukee Railroad Company. [n. p. n. d.]

Howard (Volney E.) Speech ... on the Mexican Boundary Question. *Washington.* 1852. 8vo. 33281

Howard, *and* Hutchinson (A.) The Statutes of ... Mississippi ... with the Constitutions of the United States and of this State: and an Appendix containing Acts of Congress ... . By Volney E. Howard and A. Hutchinson. *New Orleans: E. Johns & Co.* 1840. 8vo, pp. xii, 885. H. 33282

Howard (W.) Report on the Survey of a Canal from the Potomac to Baltimore. By William Howard. *Baltimore.* 1828. 8vo. 33283

Howard (W.) Speech of Hon. William Howard ... on the Political Questions of the Day. ... in the House ... April 24, 1860. [n. p. n. d.] 8vo, pp. 8. H. 33284

Also: State of the Union. Speech ... January 30, 1861. [n. p. n. d.] 8vo, pp. 8.

Howard (W. A.) Kansas-Lecompton Constitution. Speech ... March 23, 1858. [*Washington.* 1858.] 8vo, pp. 8. B., H.

Howard, *pseudon.* A Disquisition on Imprisonment for Debt, as the Practice exists in the State of New-York. By Howard. ... *New York: Charles Wiley and Co.* 1818. 8vo, pp. 47. BA.

Howard Benevolent Society. *See* Boston, Norfolk, &c.

Howard University, *D. C.* Catalogue. *Washington.* 1870. 8vo. 33287

[Howe (*Dr.* Estes).] Irishmen! Hear the Voices of O'Connell and Emmett!! [On voting. n. p. n. d.] 8vo, pp. 4. H.

Howe. An Oration ... in Worcester (Massachusetts), on the Fourth of July, 1808. ... By Estes Howe. *Worcester: Printed by Henry Rogers.* 1808. 8vo, pp. 16. B., W. 33289

Howe (E. D.) Mormonism Unvailed; or, a Faithful Account of that Singular Imposition and Delusion, from its Rise to the Present Time. With Sketches of the Characters of its Propagators, and a Full Detail of the Manner in which the Famous Golden Bible was brought before the World; to which are added, Inquiries into the Probability that the Historical Part of the Said Bible was written by one Solomon Spalding, more than twenty Years ago, and by him intended to have been published as a Romance. By E. D. Howe. *Painesville: Printed and Published by the Author.* 1834. 12mo, pp. 290. Plate. BA.

Howe (E. P.) The Young Citizen's Catechism, explaining the Duties of District, Town, City, County, State, and United States Officers. Together with Rules for Parliamentary and Commercial Business. *New York: A. S. Barnes & Burr.* 1861. 16mo, pp. 189. C. 33291

Howe (G.) Early History of Presbyterianism in South Carolina. Sermon at Charleston, Nov. 15, 1854. By George Howe, D.D. *Columbia.* 1855. 8vo. 33292

Howe. Early Presbyterian Immigration into South Carolina. Discourse before the General Assembly, May 7th, 1858. By George Howe, D.D. *Columbia.* 1858. 8vo. 33293

Howe. Eulogy on the Rev. Joshua Bates, ... August 9, 1854. By G. Howe, D.D. *Boston: Press of T. R. Marvin.* 1855. 8vo, pp. 40. Portrait. B., H. 33294

Howe. History of the Presbyterian Church in South Carolina. By George Howe, D.D. ... Vol. I. *Columbia: Duffie & Chapman.* 1870. 8vo, pp. 709. B. 33295

Howe. The Scotch Irish, and their first Settlements on the Tyger River in South Carolina. A Centennial Discourse. By George Howe, D.D. *Columbia.* 1861. 8vo. 33296

Howe (H.) Adventures and Achievements of Americans; a Series of Narratives illustrating their Heroism, Self-reliance, Genius and Enterprise. By Henry Howe. Illustrated by F. O. C. Darley and others. *Cincinnati: F. A. Howe.* 1865. 8vo, pp. x, (1), 15–720. Illustrations. BA., C. 33297

Howe. The Great West: containing Narratives of the Most Important and Interesting Events in Western History—Remarkable Individual Adventures—Sketches of Frontier Life—Descriptions of Natural Curiosities—to which is appended Historical and Descriptive Sketches of Oregon, New Mexico, Texas, Minnesota, Utah, California, Washington, Nebraska, Kansas, etc., etc., etc. By Henry Howe. Enlarged Edition. *New York: G. F. Tuttle.* 1857. 8vo, pp. 576. + [*Ibid.*] 1859. 33298

A compilation of material, relating largely to adventures among the Indians, derived from seventy-five other printed works. For the first edition *see* No. 33300, *infra.*

Howe. Historical Collections of Ohio; Containing A Collection of the Most Interesting Facts, Traditions, Biographical Sketches, Anecdotes, etc. Relating to its General and Local History: with Descriptions of its Counties, Principal Towns and Villages. Illustrated by 177 Engravings. ... By Henry Howe. *Cincinnati: For the Author.* 1847. 8vo, pp. 581, (1). Map. BA., C., H. + *Cincinnati: Bradley & Anthony.* 1848. 8vo, pp. 599. Map. + [*Ibid.*] 1849. + [*Ibid.*] 1850. + Eighteenth Thousand. *Cincinnati: H. Howe.* 1857. 8vo, pp. 620. + A New Impression. *Cincinnati: Robert Clarke & Company.* 1869. 8vo, pp. (2), 599. B. 33299

Of this last edition one hundred copies were printed on tinted paper. "Fully one-half of this volume is devoted to descriptions of massacres by the Indians, tales of captivity among them, and biographical notes of the borderers who fought them.

Much of this material was derived from unpublished manuscripts and oral communication with the actors or their families."—Field.

Howe. Historical Collections of the Great West: containing Narratives of the most Important and Interesting Events in Western History—Remarkable Individual Adventures—Sketches of Frontier Life—Descriptions of Natural Curiosities: To which is appended Historical and Descriptive Sketches of Oregon, New Mexico, Texas, Minnesota, Utah and California. By Henry Howe ... Illustrated ... . *Cincinnati: Henry Howe.* 1851. 8vo, pp. (2), vi, (2), 33–440. B., C. + [*Ibid.*] 1852. + [*Ibid.*] 1853. + [Added] Washington, Nebraska, Kansas, etc., etc. *Cincinnati: Henry Howe.* 1854. 8vo, pp. 440. + *Greenville, Tenn.: James A. Roberts.* 1855. 8vo, pp. 448. Illustrations. BA. 33300

Howe. Historical Collections of Virginia; containing a Collection of the most Interesting Facts, Traditions, Biographical Sketches, Anecdotes, &c., relating to its History and Antiquities, together with Geographical and Statistical Descriptions. To which is appended, an Historical and Descriptive Sketch of the District of Columbia. Illustrated by over 100 Engravings ... . By Henry Howe. *Charleston: S. C. Babcock & Co.* 1845. 8vo, pp. (2), 544. Map. H. + [*Ibid.*] 1846. C. + *Charleston: W. R. Babcock.* 1847. + [*Ibid.*] 1849. + [*Ibid.*] 1852. 8vo, pp. (2), 544. B., BA. + [*Ibid.*] 1856. 8vo. 33301

Mostly scissors and paste, but very well done. The 'Account of the Battle of Point Pleasant,' 'The Captivity of the Moore Family,' and the 'Biographical Sketches of the Campbells,' are new and interesting.

Howe. Memoirs of the most Eminent American Mechanics: ... Together with a Collection of Anecdotes, Descriptions, ... relating to the Mechanic Arts. By Henry Howe. *New York: Harper & Brothers.* 1841. 12mo. BM. + [*Ibid.*] 1844. + [*Ibid.*] 1847. 12mo, pp. 482. B., C. + [*Ibid.*] 1852. 12mo. + [*Ibid.*] 1858. 12mo. 33302

Howe. The Times of the Rebellion in the West; a Collection of Miscellanies, showing the part taken in the War by each Western State. By Henry Howe. *Cincinnati: F. A. Howe.* 1867. 8vo, pp. 252. C. 33303

Howe. The Travels and Adventures of Celebrated Travelers in the principal Countries of the Globe. By Henry Howe. *Cincinnati.* 1853. 8vo. C. 33304

See Barber (J. W.), Vol. I., No. 3330–2. Also: Life and Death on the Ocean; a Collection of Extraordinary Adventures, in the form of Personal Narratives ... . *Cincinnati.* 1855. 8vo. + [*Ibid.*] 1856. + *New York and Cincinnati.* 1860. 8vo.

Howe (H.) Report on the Educational Policy of the State of New York ... in Auburn, August, 1848. By Henry Howe ... *Canandaigua.* 1849. 4to, pp. 12. B. 33305

Howe (J. B.) A Sermon ... before ... the ... Council and ... Legislature of ... New Hampshire, June 8, ... being the Anniversary Election. By Rev. James B. Howe ... *Concord: Printed by Hill and Moore.* 1820. 8vo, pp. 21. H. 33306

Howe (J. H.) Oration at North East, N. Y., July 4, 1845. By Rev. James H. Howe. *Poughkeepsie, N. Y.* 1845. 12mo.

Howe (Jemima). Genuine ... Account. *See* Gray (B.), Vol. VII., No. 28377, *see also* Hancock (John), Vol. VIII., No. 30178.

Howe (J.) Address occasioned by the Death of Aaron Bean, Esq. at ... Boston, April 18, A.L. 5820. By John Howe. ... *Boston: Printed by Joseph T. Buckingham.* 1820. 8vo, pp. 21, (1).

Also: An Address ... Washington Lodge ... December 6th, A.L. 5819. ... *Boston: Printed by Joseph T. Buckingham.* 1819. 8vo, pp. 31, (1). — Address ... in Brighton [Mass.], ... December 24, A.L. 5822. ... *Boston.* 1823. 8vo, pp. 15. — An Address ... at the Installation of the Officers of St. Paul's Royal Arch Chapter, Boston, January 25, A.L. 5821. ... *Boston: Henry Bowen, Printer.* 1821. 8vo, pp. 22. BA., M.

Howe (J.), *Jr.* Report of John Howe, Jr., relative to State Aid for Soldiers' Families in Vermont, September, 1863. [n. p. n. d.] 33310

[Howe (Joseph).] Letters to ... Lord John Russell, on the Government of British America. 1846. [n. p. 1846.] 8vo, pp. 41. H. 33311

[Howe.] ... Letters to the Right Honorable Lord John Russell ... on the Right of British Americans to be governed by the Principles of the British Constitution. ... *Halifax, N. S.* 1839. 8vo, pp. 48. H. 33312

Howe. The Reciprocity Treaty, its History, ... A Speech delivered By the Honorable Joseph Howe, of Nova Scotia, On the 14th ... July, 1865. At ... Detroit. ... *Hamilton: Printed by T. & R. White.* 1865. 8vo, pp. 15. B., H. 33313

Howe. Speech ... on the Importance and Value to Great Britain of her North American Colonies. ... *London.* 1851. 8vo, pp. 28. S. + *Halifax.* 1851. 8vo. 33314

Howe. The Speeches and Public Letters of the Hon. Joseph Howe. Edited by William Annand, M.P.P. *Boston: John P. Jewett & Company.* 1858. 2 vols., 8vo, pp. ix, 642; iv, 558. S.

Also: Address before the Halifax Mechanic's Institute. ... *Halifax.* 1834. 8vo, pp 23. — Confederation considered in relation to the Interests of the Empire. ... *London* 1866. — Lecture before St. John Early Closing Association. ... *St. John.* 1859. 8vo, pp. 17. — A Letter to the People of Nova Scotia against Irish Roman Catholics. ... [n. p. n. d.] 8vo, pp. 9. — Letter to Rt. Hon. W. E. Gladstone, being a Review of the Debate on the Foreign Enlistment Bill and our Relations with the United States. ... *London.* 1856. 8vo. — Letter to the Hon. Francis Hincks. Being a Review of his Reply to Mr. Howe's Speech on the Organization of the Empire. *Halifax.* 1855. 8vo, pp. 22. — Letter to the Rt. Hon. C, B. Adderley, M.P., on the Relations of England with her Colonies. ... *London.* 1863. 8vo, pp. 61. + *Hamilton.* 1863. — Letters on the recent Railway Riots, their Causes and Results; and the Political Position of the "Young Ireland Brigade." ... *Halifax.* 1857. — Letters to Earl Grey. ... *Halifax.* 1850. — The Organization of the Empire. ... *London.* 1866. 8vo, pp. 30. — The Practicability and Importance of connecting Halifax with all the Counties lying round the Basin of Mines by means of a Railroad to Windsor. ... *Halifax.* 1835. 8vo. — Speech ... on Inter-Colonial Railroads, and Colonization; Delivered at Halifax, Nova Scotia, May, 1851. *Halifax: Printed by Richard Nugent.* 1851. 8vo, pp. 24. M. — Speech at the International Commercial Convention at Detroit. *Hamilton and Montreal.* 1865. 8vo.

Howe (J.) Nova Scotia: Report on the Gold Fields. By J. Howe. *Halifax.* 1861. Folio. S. 33316

Howe (J. W.) Speech ... on the California Question. ... June 5, 1850. [n. p. n. d.] 8vo, pp. 8. BA. 33317

[Howe (Julia Ward).] Passion Flowers. *Boston: Ticknor, Reed and Fields.* MDCCCLIV. 12mo, pp. iv, 187. B., BA. 33318

Howe. A Trip to Cuba. By Mrs. Julia Ward Howe. *Boston: Ticknor and Fields.* M DCCC LX. 12mo, pp. iv, 251. BA.

Also: Words for the Hour. ... *Boston: Ticknor and Fields.* M DCCC LVII. 16mo, pp. 165. — The World's Own. ... *Boston: Ticknor and Fields.* M DCCC LVII. 16mo, pp. 141.

Howe (M. A. DeWolfe). ... A Discourse ... in ... Philadelphia, on Thanksgiving Day, November 24, 1844. By M. A. DeWolfe Howe. *Philadelphia: Crissy & Markley, Printers.* 1864. 8vo, pp. 21. H. 33320

Also: Loyalty in the American Republic, What is it? and What its Object? A Discourse delivered in ... Philadelphia, on ... November 26th, 1863, being the ... National Thanksgiving. ... *Philadelphia: J. S. McCalla, Printer.* 1863. 8vo, pp. 19. — ... An Oration ... before the Connecticut Beta of the Phi Beta Kappa Society ... Hartford, July 28th, 1852. ... *Hartford: S. Hanmer & Co.* 1852. 8vo, pp. 18. H. — Letter Relative to his Reply to Bishop Hopkins, 1863. — A Reply to the Letter of Bishop Hopkins, addressed to Dr. Howe in ... "The Age" ... . *Philadelphia: King & Baird, Printers.* 1864. 8vo, pp. 18. H.

Howe (M. A.) The Rival Volunteers; or, the Black Plume Rifles. By Mary A. Howe. *New York: J. Bradburn.* 1864. 12mo, pp. 377. B., C. 33321

Howe (N.) A Century Sermon delivered in Hopkinton on Lord's Day, December 24, 1815. By Nathanael Howe, A.M. ...

Andover: Flagg and Gould. 1816. 8vo, pp. 31. B., H. + Second Edition, Revised and Corrected. *Andover: Flagg & Gould.* 1817. 8vo, pp. 31. BA., C., H. + Third Edition, with Notes, Revised and Corrected. *Boston: Crocker & Brewster.* 1825. 8vo, pp. 32. + Fourth Edition, with a Memoir of the Author and Explanatory Notes. By Elias Nason, A.M. *Boston: John P. Jewett & Co.* 1851. 8vo, pp. 56. B., BA. 33322

For a readable notice of this original production *see* Stevens' "Bibliotheca Historica," No. 1443. The sermon was reviewed in the "North American Review" most favorably, and in a subsequent edition Mr. Howe noticed the reviewer.

Howe. An Oration pronounced at Paris, ... Maine, on the Fourth of July, 1805 ... . By Nathanael Howe, A.M. ... *Portland: From the Argus-Press* ... *By N. Willis, Jun.* 1805. 8vo, pp. 15. BA., M., W. 33323

Howe. A Sermon ... at Hopkinton ... Feb. 28, 1808. Occasioned by the Death of Three Persons ... . By Nathanael Howe, A.M. ... *Boston: Printed by Lincoln & Edmands.* 1808. 8vo, pp. 24. BA. 33324

[Howe (R. H.)] Appeal from a Countryman to the Union Men of the South. [n. p. n. d.] 8vo, pp. 4. H. 33325

Howe (Richard). Being appointed by the Vice-Admiral Viscount Howe ... 4to, pp. 1. P. 33326

Articles of agreement, etc., for the row-gallies on the Delaware; Feb., 1778. Forty-five copies, *printed by J. Humphreys.*

Howe. A Candid [&c.] *See our* Vol. III., No. 10658.

Howe. An Extract of a Letter to the Right Honorable Lord Viscount Howe on his Naval Conduct in the American War. *London.* 1781. 12mo, pp. 27. 33327

Howe. Letter to Viscount H——e. *See* [Galloway (Joseph)], Vol. VII., *see also* [Drayton (W. H.)], Vol. V.

Howe [Robert]. Proceedings | of a | General Court Martial, | held at Philadelphia, | in the State of | Pennsylvania, | By Order of His Excellency | General Washington, | Commander in Chief | of the Army of | the United States of America, | For the Trial of | Major General Howe, | December 7, 1781. | Major General Baron Steuben, President. | *Philadelphia: Printed by Hall and Sellers, in Market-Street.* M,DCC,LXXXII. Folio, pp. 31. BA., C. 33328

One of the Revolutionary State Trials, and extremely scarce.

Howe (S. Gridley). The Cretan Refugees and their American Helpers. ... By Samuel G. Howe. *Boston: Lee and Shepard.* 1868. 16mo, pp. 64. Plate and Map. B., BA., H. 33329

Howe. An Essay on Separate and Congregate Systems of Prison Discipline; being a Report made to the Boston Prison Discipline Society. By Samuel G. Howe. *Boston: William D. Ticknor and Company.* 1846. 8vo, pp. xi, 90. BA., H. 33330

Howe. Essai sur la discipline des prisons ou comparaison entre les systèmes de séparation et d'agrégation des prisonniers. Traduit de l'anglais de M. Howe. *Paris: Imprimerie Crapelet.* 1848. 8vo, pp. viii, 128. H. 33331

Howe. Dr. Howe's Report on the Case of Laura Bridgman, May 1, 1843. [*Boston.* 1843.] 8vo, pp. 15. H. 33332

Howe. The Refugees from Slavery in Canada West. Report to the Freedmen's Inquiry Commission. By Samuel G. Howe. *Boston: Wright & Potter, Printers.* 1864. 8vo, pp. iv, 110. C.

Also: Address ... at the Ceremony of laying the Corner-Stone of the New York State Institution for the Blind, at Batavia, September 6, 1866. ... *Boston: Walker, Fuller & Company.* 1866. 8vo, pp. 51. — Insanity in Massachusetts, ... [from "N. A. R."] *Boston: J. H. Eastburn, Printer.* 1843. 8vo, pp. 20. — A Letter on the Sanitary Condition of the Troops in the Neighborhood of Boston. ... *Washington.* 1861. 8vo, pp. 16. B. — A Letter to J. H. Wilkins, H. B. Rogers, and F. B. Fay, Commissioners of Massachusetts, for the State Reform School for Girls. ... *Boston: Ticknor and Fields.* M DCCC LIV. 8vo, pp. 36. — A Letter to Mrs. ——, and other Loyal Women, touching the Matter of Contributions for the Army, and other Matters connected with the War. ... *Boston: Ticknor & Fields.* 1862. 8vo, pp. 28. B. — A Letter to the Governor of Massachusetts, upon his Veto of a Bill ... for an Increase of State Beneficiaries at the School for Idiotic Children. ... *Boston: Ticknor & Fields.* 1857. 8vo, pp. 24. — List of Contributions received from Various Societies of Loyal Women ... for the Use of the ... Hospitals of the Army ... . [n. p. n. d.] 8vo, pp. 26. — Report ... to the Legislature of Massachusetts, upon Idiocy ... [1848,] 50; [with] The Causes and Prevention of Idiocy. *Boston.* 1848. 8vo, pp. 100, Table, pp. 46, (1). B., H.

Howe (Timothy O.) The Authority of the Nation Supreme and Absolute; that of the States Subordinate and Conditional. Speech of Hon. T. O. Howe ... in the Senate of the United States, January 10, 1866. *Washington, D. C.: Henry Polkinhorn & Son ... Printers.* 1866. 8vo, pp. 20. H. 33334

Howe. The Currency—Resumption without Contraction. Speech ... in the Senate ... January 24, 1870. *Washington: F. & J. Rives & Geo. A. Bailey.* 1870. 8vo, pp. 13. H. 33335

Howe. Impeachment of the President. Opinion of Mr. Howe, ... in the Senate ... May 11, 1868. [n. p. n. d.] 8vo, pp. 26. H. 33336

HOWE. Reconstruction. Speech ... in the Senate ... January 31, 1868. *Washington: F. & J. Rives & Geo. A. Bailey.* 1868. 8vo, pp. 15. H. 33337

Also: An Address before the American Iron Association, ... delivered in Chicago, May 24th, 1865. *Chicago: John A. Norton.* 1865. 8vo, pp. 18. H. + *Green Bay: Robinson Brothers.* 1865. 8vo, pp. 19.—An Address ... before the Wisconsin State Teachers' Association ... August 2d, 1865. ... *Madison: Printed by C. M. Campbell.* 1865. 8vo, pp. 20. H.—Speech ... Aug. 2, 1861, on Approving certain Acts of the President. [n. p. n. d.] 8vo.—Speech ... on the Issue of United States Notes; ... February 12, 1862. *Washington.* 1862. 8vo, pp. 14. H.—Speech ... on the Bill to Confiscate the Property and Free the Slaves of Rebels, delivered ... May 5, 1862. *Washington.* 1862. 8vo.—Speech on his Bill to aid in restoring Order and preserving the Public Peace, within the Insurrectionary Districts ... May 26, 1862. [n. p. n. d.] 8vo.—Speech ... April 4, 1864, on Amendment to the Constitution. [n. p. n. d.] 8vo.—Speech ... on Reconstruction; ... in the Senate ... June 5 and 6, 1866. *Washington.* 1866. 8vo, pp. 22.—Speech ... Jan. 14 and 15, 1869, on the Claims of Loyal Citizens of the South during the Rebellion. [n. p. n. d.] 8vo.—The State and the National Governments. Speech ... in the Assembly Chamber, March 29, 1860. [n. p. n. d.] 8vo, pp. 16

HOWE (W.) By His Excellency Sir William Howe, K.B. General and Commander in Chief, &c. &c. &c. Proclamation. ... *Philadelphia: Printed by James Humphreys, junr.* Folio, 1 l. P.

Dated near Germantown, Sept. 28. 1777; relates to protections, etc. The Philadelphia library has an extensive series of broadsides, issued by Howe during his occupation of Philadelphia, we note the following: Proclamation, dated Germantown, Oct. 1st, 1777: enjoining oath of allegiance, etc.—A Proclamation, *Printed by J. Humphreys*, offering land for military service, etc; dated Germantown, Oct. 8th, 1777.—Eine durch Seine Excellenz ... *Philadelphia, gedruckt bey Christoph Saur, jun. und Peter Saur.* A German translation of the preceding.—His Excellency the Commander in Chief, ... Robert Mackenzie, Secretary. Head-Quarters, Philadelphia, 4th December, 1777. Appoints port-wardens.—Proclamation, dated Philadelphia, Nov. 7th, 1777, denouncing depredations, etc. *Printed by James Humphreys.*—Proclamation, dated Phila. Nov. 24th, 1777, respecting liquors.—Proclamation appointing Jos. Galloway Superintendant of Exports and Imports, etc., dated Philadelphia, Dec. 4th, 1777.—Proclamation, dated Phila. 4th Dec. 1777, appointing Jos. Galloway, Superintendant General of Police. Fifty copies, *printed by J. Humphreys.*—Proclamation, issued Dec. 14th, 1777, forbidding unlicensed sale of spirits, etc. in less than ten gallons.—Proclamation, *printed by J. Humphreys*, dated Philadelphia, Dec. 18th, 1777, relative to commerce, etc.—Proclamation ordering lanthorns to be carried between tattoo and revellie; signed J. Galloway Sup.-Gen.; dated Philada. Jan. 9th, 1778. Proclamation, signed J. Galloway. Sup. Gen. Jan. 11th, 1778, forbidding felling wood, etc. *Printed by J. Humphreys, Philadelphia.*—Proclamation dated Philad'a, Jan. 12th, 1778, ordering returns of maritime stores. *Printed by J. Humphreys.*—Proclamation for returns of blankets, etc., issued Jany. 15th, 1778. *Printed by J. Humphreys, Philadelphia.*—Proclamation at Philad'a, Feb. 4. 1778, by Will: Erskine, Q. M. G.; and orders returns of carts, etc.—Proclamation for returns of forage, signed Dan. Wier, Commissary-General, Philad'a; Feb. 27th, 1778. *Printed by J. Humphreys.*—Proclamation, signed J. Galloway Sup'. Gen. dated at Philad'a, 23rd March, 1778; relates to street-cleaning; "*printed by Macdonald & Cameron, in Chesnut Street, a few Doors above the Barrack-Office.*"—Proclamation, dated Philad'a, 23rd March, 1778; signed J. Galloway, Sup'. Gen.: forbids plundering the King's friends; *printed by Macdomald & Cameron.*

HOWE. Campagnes Militaires du Lieutenant Général Sir William Howe, en Amérique: d'après le Compte rendu par lui-même dans un Committé de la Chambre des Communes le 29 Avril, 1779. Et d'après les Observations qu'il a publiées contre les Lettres à un Gentilhomme. *La Haye: Chez Van Cleef, Gosse, Detune.* MDCCLXXXI. 8vo, pp. viii, 70; Observations, pp. 116. B. + *Rotterdam: Beunet & Hake.* MDCCLXXXI. pp. viii, 70, 116.

This edition has an interesting preface of six pages not in the original, wherein the whole struggle is forcibly presented to the Dutch. "Twenty times," exclaims the translator, "have the English encouraged the idea and flattered themselves with it of putting a speedy termination to the war, yet after six years they are no farther advanced in the conquest or reconciliation than they were on the first day." This preface is dated, Amst. 25 Nov. 1780.

HOWE. A Full Vindication of the R. H. General's Conduct, against the Attacks of an Anonymous Libeller; who, in a Letter to the Printer of the London Chronicle, Jan. 28, 1779, stiles himself "a Friend to Great Britain." Ly a Friend to Truth. *London.* 1779. 8vo. 33340

General Howe's military operations in America are here ironically defended.

H[OWE]. A Letter to the People of America, lately printed at New York; now re-published by an American. With a Post-script, by the Editor. Addressed to Sir W****** H***. *London: T. Beckett.* MDCCLXXVIII. 8vo, pp. (2), 74. BA., J.C.B.

"The author earnestly admonishes and exhorts the revolted Americans to make it up with us; endeavoring to convince them, by every popular argument, that nothing but immediate reconciliation can save them from destruction."—*Monthly Review.*

HOWE. The Narrative of Lieut. Gen. Sir William Howe, in A Committee of the House of Commons, on the 29th of April, 1779, Relative to his Conduct, during his Late Command of the King's Troops in North America: To which are added, some Observations upon a Pamphlet, entitled, Letters to a Nobleman. *London: Printed by H. Baldwin.* M DCC LXXX. 4to, pp. (2), 110. + The Second Edition. [*Ibid.*] 4to, pp. (4), 110. B., H. + The Third Edition. [*Ibid.*] M DCC LXXXI. 4to, pp. (2), 110. BA.

"Sir William's vindication now appears; and candour must acknowledge that it is not a feeble attempt to rescue the general's reputation from the obloquy thrown upon it, not only by the author of the letters (to Joseph Galloway, esq.), but many other writers, who had joined in the cry against the noble commander."—*Monthly Review,* LXIII. 307. *See* [Galloway], Vol. VII., No. 26436.

HOWE. Observations upon the Conduct. *See* [Mauduit (I.)]

HOWE. Parliamentary Debates relative to the Conduct of Gen. Sir William Howe, 1779. [*London.* 1779.] 8vo. M.

HOWE. Remarks upon Howe's Account. *See* [Mauduit (I).]

HOWE. A Reply to Observations. *See* Vol. VII., No. 26443.

HOWE. Three Letters to Lord Howe. *See* [Mauduit (I.)]

[HOWE.] Two Letters from Agricola to Sir William Howe; to which are Annexed, by the same Author, Political Observations. *London: J. Millidge.* 1779. 8vo, pp. 63. 33344

Scarce. "The author is very severe on Sir William Howe, whom he charges with the most shameful indolence and languor, in the conduct of the American war, which he accuses him of protracting, to the utter distress and ignominy of his country, while possessed of every superiority and advantage for putting a speedy and glorious end to the contest."—*Monthly Review.* *See our* Vol. IV., No. 15960, *and* A View of the Evidence.

HOWE (W.) An Address ... before the Society for the Prevention of Pauperism, March 1, 1840. By William Howe. *Boston: Weeks, Jordan and Company.* 1840. 12mo, pp. 24. B.

HOWE (W. B. W.) ... A Sermon ... in ... Charleston, December 15th, 1861 ... after the Great Fire. By W. B. W. Howe. *Charleston: Press of Evans & Cogswell.* 1861. 8vo, pp. 15.

HOWELL (G. R.) The Early History of Southampton, L. I., New York. With Genealogies. By George Rogers Howell. *New York: J. N. Hallock.* 1866. 12mo, pp. 318. C. 33347

HOWEL *or* HOWELL (J.) Epistolæ-Ho-Elianæ. Familiar Letters Domestic and Forren ... . By James Howel. Fourth Edition. *London: Thomas Guy.* 1673. 8vo, pp. (16), 510, (24). BA., H. + Fifth Edition. [*Ibid.*] 1678. 8vo, pp. (14), 510, (20). H. + The Ninth Edition, very much Corrected. *London: J. Darby.* 1726. 8vo. + Eleventh Edition. *London: R. Ware* ... MDCCLIV. 8vo, pp. 518, (10). H. + *London.* 1779.

A letter dated March 28, 1618, pp. 5–7, relates to the return of Sir W. Raleigh from Guiana; another, dated May 5, 1645, pp. 368–373, defends the first against some objections. Also pp. 304, 306, 307, 355, 448, 475, 476, contain allusions to America. These letters, relating to one of the most interesting periods of English History, the reigns of James I. and Charles I., discover a variety of literature, and abound with much entertaining and useful information. Ant. à Wood informs us "they were written by the author when confined in the Fleet prison for debt." *See* "Retrospective Review," Part IV.

HOWELL (J. B.) Railroad Grants and Land Monopoly. Speech of Hon. James B. Howell ... March 1, 1870. *Washington: F. & J. Rives & Geo. A. Bailey ... Printers.* 1870. 8vo, pp. 8. H. 33349

HOWELL (J.) The Life and Adventures of Alexander Selkirk; containing the real Incidents upon which the Romance of Rob-

inson Crusoe is Founded: ... By John Howell ... . *Edinburgh: Oliver & Boyd.* 1829. 12mo, pp. (4), 196. BA., P. 33350

HOWELL (R.), *and others.* Report from Reading Howell, Frederick Antes, and William Dean, Commissioners, appointed to explore the Head Waters of the Rivers Delaware, Lehigh, Schuylkill and Susquehannah. Also, the Report of the Commissioners appointed to examine the Western Waters of the State of Pennsylvania. *Philadelphia.* 1791. 8vo. P. 33351

HOWELL (R. B. C.) The Early Baptists of Virginia. An Address, delivered in New York, before the American Baptist Historical Society, May 10, 1856, By Robert Boyle C. Howell, D.D. *Philadelphia: Press of the Society.* 1857. 8vo, pp. 113. C.

Also: An Address delivered before the University of Nashville, Tenn., Oct. 2, 1839. ... *Nashville.* 1839. 8vo, pp. 27. M.

HOWELL (W. T.) The Right of the General Government to Lease Mineral Lands within a State, and the Sovereign Right of Michigan to the Mines and Minerals within her Borders. By W. T. Howell. *Detroit.* [1846.] 8vo. 33353

HOWELLS (W. D.), *and* HAYES (John L.) Lives and Speeches of Abraham Lincoln and Hannibal Hamlin. *Columbus, O.: Follett, Foster & Co.* 1860. 8vo, pp. 406. 2 Portraits. H. + *New York.* 1860. 8vo. C. 33354

[HOWEN (*Mme*), *née* UITENHAGE DE MIST).] Voyage en Afrique et en Amérique. *Namur.* 1821. 8vo. 33355

HOWES (E.) Some Account of the Proceedings on board Ship Niagara of Boston, commanded by one Ebenezer Howes, Jr. during her passage from Liverpool to Boston in April and May, 1836. With Remarks on the Rights of Seamen. *Boston: Joseph S. Hart.* 1836. 8vo. 33356

HOWES (F.) An Address to the Essex Agricultural Society ... at Topsfield, Oct. 6, 1823. By Frederick Howes ... *Salem: For the Society.* 1824. 8vo, pp. 23. B. 33357

HOWES (R. A.) A Plan for a Funding Bill, and for ... the ... Resumption of Specie Payments. ... By Reuben W. Howes ... [*New York.* 1870.] 8vo, pp. 10. H. 33358

[HOWES (William B.)] Protection and Free Trade Compared, in their Influence on National Industry. ... *Salem.* 1846. 8vo, pp. 24. H., M. 33359

HOWGILL (F.) The Dawnings of the Gospel Day, and its Light and Glory Discovered, being a Collection of the Works of Francis Howgill. *London: E. Hooks.* 1676. Folio, pp. (32), 736, (6). 33360

Includes an account of the cruelties exercised in Virginia and Maryland; also, "The Heart of New-England Hardned," in answer to Norton's "The Heart of New-England Rent," "The Popish Inquisition Newly Erected in New-England," and other similar pieces.

HOWGILL. The | Deceiver | of the | Nations | Discovered: | And his | Cruelty | Made Manifest. | And | How he hath deceived the Nations, and wrought his | Works of Darkness, more hiddenly under the Mask of Higher | Power, and Holy Church; and so persecutes the Righteous | Seed, and makes them suffer under the Name of evil Doers, | in these latter daies. | More especially his cruel works of Darkness laid open and re- | proved in Maryland in Virginia, And the sad Sufferings of | the Servants of the Lord there, by his cruel Instruments. | Sent back unto them again, that they may view their Work a- | gain, and repent and be ashamed; lest the Wrath of God | sink them into the Pit, as it hath done many before them, | who have opposed the Lord. | By a Lover of Mercy and Truth, | Fra. Howgill. | *London: Printed for Thomas Simmons,* ... 1660. | 4to, pp. 27. 33361

A very rare tract relating to Maryland.

HOWGILL. The | Heart | of | New-England | Hardned | through | Wickedness: | In Answer to a Book, Entituled | The Heart of New-England Rent, | Published by John Norton appointed thereunto by the General Court. | The Doctrine of the Quakers Uindicated, his Arguments made void, his | Ignorance manifested, and his lying Doctrines brought to Light, | and Judged with the Word of Truth, and Truth cleared | from his Aspersions & Slanders. | By him that waits to See the Throne of Righteousness Exalted above all | Deceit. | Francis Howgill. | ... *London, Printed for Thomas Simmons, at the Bull and Mouth* | *near Aldersgate,* 1659. | 4to.

Partly by Edward Burroughs. Forms pp. 299–323 of his works, but has a separate title-page.

HOWGILL. The Popish | Inquisition. | Newly Erected in | New-England, | whereby | Their Church is manifested to be a | Daughter of Mysterie Babylon, which did drink the | blood of the Saints, who bears the express Image, | of her Mother, demonstrated by her fruits. | Also, | Their Rulers to be in the Beasts power | upon whom the Whore rideth, manifest by their | wicked compulsary [*sic*] Laws against the Lamb and his | Followers, and their cruel

and bloody practi- | ses against the dear Servants of the Lord, | who have deeply suffered by this hy- | pocritical generation. | Some of their miserable sufferings for the Testimony of | Jesus, declared as follows, and some of their unjust | and vvicked Lavvs set dovvn by vvhich they have made the un- | godly to reioyce, and the righteous to lament, that all who | fear the Lord, may come out of their foot-steps. | Published by a Lover of Mercy and Truth, and an Enemy to Envy | and Cruelty. Francis Howgill. | *London, Printed for Thomas Simmons, at the Bull and Mouth* | *near Aldersgate,* 1659. | 4to, pp. (4), 72. 33363

Another edition forms pp. 239–262 of his works, but is issued with an independent title-page, and is sometimes found separately.

[HOWGILL.] A Testimony concerning the Life, Death, Trials, Travels, and Labours of Edward Burroughs, that worthy Prophet of the Lord, who died a Prisoner, ... *London: ... William Warwick.* 1662. 4to, pp. 25. + *London, Printed in the Year* 1663. 4to. 33364

HOWICK (*Lord*). Corrected Report of the Speech of Viscount Howick in the House of Commons on Colonial Slavery, with Appendix, containing a Plan for the Abolition of Slavery. *London.* 1833. 8vo. 33365

Also: Speech for Abolition of Negro Apprenticeship. ... *London.* 1838. 8vo.

HOWISON (J.) Sketches of Upper Canada, Domestic, Local, and Characteristic; To which are added, Practical Details for the Information of Emigrants of every Class; and some Recollections of The United States of America. By John Howison, Esq. ... *Edinburgh: Oliver & Boyd.* 1821. 8vo, pp. (2), xvi, 339. B., H. + Second Edition. [*Ibid.*] 1822. 8vo, pp. 9–353. + Third Edition. [*Ibid.*] 1825. 8vo. C. 33366

"This volume affords a great portion of useful information for emigrants, but Mr. H. has unhappily a *cacoethes* for fine writing, in which he does not excel. In describing the Falls of the Niagara, he has out-Heroded Herod, and beaten *Bombastes Furioso* out of the field: he has copied the poet's advice, has made the 'sound to echo the sense,' and, like the cataract itself, his description of it is all splash, dash, roar, and foam."—*Monthly Review,* XCIX. 171. *See also* "Edinburgh Review," XXXVII. 249, Blackwood's "Magazine," X. 537.

HOWISON. Tales of the Colonies. By John Howison. *London.* 1830. 2 vols., post 8vo. C., P. 33367

The same author's "European Colonies, in various Parts of the World ..."—*London.* 1834. 2 vols., 8vo—does not include America.

HOWISON (N. M.), *Lieut. U. S. N.* Oregon. Report of ... an Examination in ... 1846, of the Territory of Oregon. [n. p. 1848.] 8vo, pp. 36. B: 33368

HOWISON. Report on the Soil, Climate, etc., of Oregon. *Washington.* 1844. 8vo. 33369

HOWISON (R. R.) A History of Virginia, from its Discovery and Settlement by Europeans to the Present Time. By Robert R. Howison. ... *Philadelphia: Carey & Hart.* 1846. 8vo, pp. 496; Vol. II. *Richmond: Drinker & Morris.* 1848. pp. 528. C.

HOWISON. Reports of Criminal Trials in the Circuit, State and United States Courts, held in Richmond, Virginia. By Robert R. Howison. *Richmond: Geo. M. West & Brother.* 1851. 8vo, pp. (4), 120. B., C. 33371

HOWITT (Emanuel). Selections from Letters written during a Tour through the United States, in the Summer and Autumn of 1819; Illustrative of the Character of the Native Indians, and of their Descent from the Lost Ten Tribes of Israel; As well as descriptive of the Present Situation and Sufferings of Emigrants, and of the Soil and State of Agriculture. By E. Howitt. ... *Nottingham: ... J. Dunn,* ... [1820.] 12mo, pp. xxi, (1), 230. B., H., P. 33372

HOWITT (M.) Our Cousins in Ohio. By Mary Howitt. With Four Illustrations ... from Original Designs by Anna Mary Howitt. *London.* 1848. Sq. 16mo, pp. 304. + *London.* 1849. 12mo. + *New-York: Collins & Brother.* 1849. 18mo. S. + Second Edition. *London: Darton.* 1857. 16mo, pp. 280. + *London: Alfred Bennett.* 1863. Sq. 16mo. 33373

A charming picture, scarcely sustained by facts however.

HOWITT. A Popular History of the United States of America; from the Discovery of the American Continent to the Present Time. By Mary Howitt. ... *London: Longman, Brown* ... . 1859. 2 vols., 12mo, pp. ix, 406; ix, (1), 405. B. + *New York: Harper & Brothers.* 1860. 2 vols., 12mo, pp. ix, 406; ix, (1), 387. B., BA. 33374

HOWITT. Vignettes of American History. By Mary Howitt. *London: S. W. Partridge & Co.* [1868.] 12mo, pp. (6), 138. 19 Plates. 33375

Also: Patience Welbeck. ... 16mo.

HOWITT (W.) Colonization and Christianity: a Popular History of the Treatment of the Natives by the Europeans in all their Colonies. By William Howitt. ... *London: Longman,* ... 1838. 8vo, pp. xi, 508. BA., C. 33376

HOWITT. George Fox and His First Disciples, or The Society of Friends as it was, and as it is. By William Howitt. *Philadelphia: Merrihew and Gunn, Printers.* 1837. 12mo, pp. 38.

HOWITT. The History of the Supernatural in all Ages and Nations and in all Churches Christian and Pagan demonstrating a Universal Faith. By William Howitt. *London.* 1863. 2 vols., 12mo. + *Philadelphia: J. B. Lippincott.* 1863. 2 vols., 12mo, pp. 519; 500. B., BA., H. 33378

HOWITT (W. *and* M.) The Desolation of Eyam, the Emigrant, a Tale of the American Woods, and other Poems. By William and Mary Howitt. *London.* 1827. Fcap 8vo. + Second Edition. *London: Wightman and Cramp.* 1828. Fcap 8vo. 33379

HOWLAND (C. H.) Remarks ... on ... "Equality of all Men before the Law" ... in Senate of Missouri, January 13, 1865. [n. p. n. d.] 8vo, pp. 3. H. 33380

HOWLAND (E.) Grant as a Soldier and Statesman; being a Succinct History of his Military and Civil Career. By Edward Howland. ... *Hartford: J. B. Burr & Company.* 1868. 8vo, pp. xi, (1), 11–631. B., C. 33381

A subscription book, some copies have an English imprint.

[HOWLAND (Henry J.)] The Heart of the Commonwealth: or, Worcester as it is; being a Correct Guide ... With many Engravings, and a New Map of the City. *Worcester, Massachusetts: Henry J. Howland.* 1856. Sm. 4to, pp. 31. BA. 33382

HOWLAND (J.) An Address ... before the Providence Association of Mechanics and Manufacturers, April 9, 1810. Being the Anniversary ... . By John Howland, Esq. Secretary ... . *Providence: From the Press of Jones & Wheeler.* 1810. 8vo, pp. 25. 33383

HOWLAND. A Lecture read at a Quarterly Meeting of the Providence Association of Mechanics and Manufacturers, January 4, 1799. By John Howland. *Providence: Bennett Wheeler.* 1799. 4to, pp. 14. W. 33384

Reprinted in Stone's "Sketch of the Association."

HOWLAND. Notices of the Military Services rendered by the Militia as well as by the Enlisted Troops of the State of Rhode

Island during the Revolutionary War. By John Howland. *Providence.* 1832. 12mo, pp. 11. 33385

Also: Address ... before the Providence Association of Mechanicks and Manufacturers, on ... Opening Mechanicks' Hall, January 10, A.D. 1825. ... *Providence: H. H. Brown.* 1830. 8vo, pp. 12.—Letter ... relative to the Rhode Island Regiment, commanded by Col. Christopher Lippitt, in the years 1776 and 1777. *Providence: H. H. Brown.* 1831. 12mo, pp. 11.—An Oration ... before the Providence Association of Mechanicks and Manufacturers, April 13, 1818 ... . *Providence: Printed by Miller and Hutchens.* 1818. 8vo, pp. 24.

HOWLAND (S. A.) Steamboat Disasters and Railroad Accidents in the United States. To which is appended, Accounts of Recent Shipwrecks, Fires at Sea, Thrilling Incidents, &c. By S. A. Howland. Second Edition. *Worcester.* 1840. 12mo.

HOWLETT (H.) Address ... against Immediate Emancipation. By Heman Howlett. *New-York.* 1834. s. 33387

HOWLETT (T. R.) The Dealings of God with the Nation. A Discourse delivered in Washington, D. C., on the Day of Humiliation and Prayer, June 1, 1865. By Rev. T. R. Howlett ... . *Washington: Gibson Brothers, Printers.* 1865. 8vo, pp. 7, Cover, 2 l. 33388

Relates to the death of Abraham Lincoln.

[HOWS (E.)] Of the Circumference of the Earth; or, A Treatise of the Northeast [northwest] Passage. *London.* 1632. 16mo, pp. 26. M. 33389

HOWS (J. A.) In the Woods with Bryant, Longfellow, and Halleck. Illustrated from Drawings, by John A. Hows. *New York.* 1866. Sq. 8vo, pp. 28. 33390

HOWS *and* STREET (A. B.) Forest Pictures in the Adirondacks. By John A. Hows. With Original Poems by Alfred B. Street. *New York: James G. Gregory.* 1865. Sm. 4to, pp. (4), 63. 16 Plates. C. 33391

HOWSE (J.) A Grammar of the Cree Language; with which is combined an Analysis of the Chippeway Dialect. By Joseph Howse, Esq. F.R.G.S. And Resident Twenty Years in Prince Rupert's Land, in the Service of the Hon. Hudson's Bay Company. *London: J. G. F. & J. Rivington.* 1844. 8vo, pp. xix, (1), 324. 33392

The language of the Indians who occupy the vast region from the Lakes to the Esquimaux country, and from the Rocky Mountains to Labrador. It is the most complete work on the language ever published, and exhibits a grammatical structure surprisingly elegant and elaborate.

HOWSON (Henry). American Jute. Paper read at ... the Franklin Institute, Philadelphia, October 16th, 1862. By H. Howson. *Philadelphia.* 1862. 8vo, pp. 8. H. 33393

HOXSE (J.) The Yankee Tar. An Authentic Narrative of the Voyages and Hardships of John Hoxse, and the Cruises of the U. S. Frigate Constellation, and her Engagements with the French Frigates Le Insurgente and Le Vengeance, in the latter of which the author loses his right arm. Written by Himself. *Northampton: John Metcalf.* 1848. 16mo, pp. 200. C. 33394

HOY (J.) Jani Hoyeri de religione Grönlandorum naturali dissertationes tres. *Hafniæ.* 1756. 4to. 33395

HOYLAND (J.) Poems. By the Rev. J. Hoyland. *London.* 1769. 12mo. 33396

The Rev. J. Hoyland was about to emigrate to South Carolina when this was printed.

HOYO (J.) Relacion Com-|pleta, y exacta del Av-|to Publico de Fe, qve se Ce-|lebro en esta Civdad de Lima|A 20. de Diziembre de 1694. Ad-|jvnto otro precedente del|Ano de 1693.|Con el Prelvdio Panegirico de|Catholicos Progressos, qve resve-|nan en los Numeros, y Clavsvlas de vn|Historico compendio encomiastico.|Dedicala.|Al Supremo|Consejo de la Santa|Inquisicion.|Y a las Sagradasaras del Exc^mo. S^or.|Don Diego Sarmiento de|Ualladres, Obispo de Plasencia,|Inqvisidor General de Espana. &c.|El Doct. D. Ioseph del Hoyo, Contador,|Abogado de los Presos, Secretario del Secreto,|y qve de Presente Sirve, Como en otras|ocasionis de Promotor Fiscal. *Del S. Oficio|Con Licencia; en Lima en la Imprenta Real|Por Joseph de Contreras, y Alvarado, Impressor del|Santo Officio. Año de* 1695.| 4to, 44 prel. leaves, Text, 58 folioed leaves, Svmario de Al-|gvnas Indvlgencias, etc., pp. 8. 33397

HOYT (A.) A. Hoyt's Acquittal from the Anonymous Charges of Rev. J. Emory and B. Waugh, Agents of the Methodist Book Concern, his Defence before the New-York Quarterly Conference. *New-York: S. Hoyt & Co.* 1831. 12mo, pp. 35. 33398

HOYT (A. H.) Necrology of New-England Colleges, for the Academic Year ending in 1868. Compiled by Albert Harrison Hoyt, A.M. ... . [n. p. n. d.] 8vo, pp. 12. BA. 33399

HOYT (C.) Memoirs of Dolly E. Hoyt, a Member of the Union Missionary Family ... Arkansas ... Osage Nation ... By Comfort Hoyt. *Danbury, Conn.* 1828. 18mo, pp. 107. S.

HOYT (D. W.) A Genealogical History of John Hoyt of Salisbury, and David Hoyt of Deerfield (Massachusetts), and their Descendants: with some Account of the Earlier Connecticut Hoyts, and an Appendix containing the Family Record of William Barnes of Salisbury, a List of the First Settlers of Salisbury and Amesbury, &c. By David W. Hoyt, Member of the New England Historical and Genealogical Society. *Boston: C. Benjamin Richardson.* 1857. 8vo, pp. 144. Portrait, 3 Plates.

HOYT (E.) Antiquarian Researches: comprising a History of the Indian Wars in the Country bordering Connecticut River and Parts Adjacent, and other Interesting Events, from the First Landing of the Pilgrims, to the Conquest of Canada by the English, in 1760: With Notices of Indian Depredations in the Neighboring Country: And of the First Planting and Progress of Settlements in New England, New York and Canada. By E. Hoyt, Esq. *Greenfield, Mass.: Printed by Ansel Phelps. Dec.* 1824. 8vo, pp. (2), xii, 312. BA., H. 33402

See "N. A. Rev.," XXI. 234–7.

HOYT (E.) Cavalry Discipline. A Treatise on the Military Art. By Epaphras Hoyt. *Brattleborough.* 1793. 33403

Also: Rules and Regulations for Drill, Sabre Exercise, Equitation, &c. ... Being a Second Edition of Cavalry Discipline. Revised. + Cavalry Exercises. Third Edition. *Greenfield, Mass.* 1816. 12mo.—Practical Instructions for Military Officers ... . *Greenfield, Mass.* 1811. 8vo. Plates.

HOYT (G. H.) Kansas and the Osage Swindle. By George H. Hoyt. ... *Washington: Gibson Brothers, Printers.* 1868. 8vo, pp. 15. H. 33404

HOYT (J.) God with the Nation. A Thanksgiving Sermon delivered November 27, 1862, in Orange, New Jersey. By James Hoyt. *Orange, N. J.: Edward Gardner.* 1862. 12mo, pp. 26. 33405

HOYT. "The Mountain Society:" a History of the First Presbyterian Church, Orange, N. J. By Rev. James Hoyt. *New York: C. M. Saxton, Barker & Co.* 1860. 12mo, pp. 281. 3 Plates. C. 33406

HOYT (J.) Letters from Jesse Hoyt, to the Secretary of the Treasury, explanatory of the Action of George Poindexter and his Colleagues, Commissioners for the Investigation of the Affairs of the Custom-House at New York. *New York: Evening Post.* [1842?] 8vo, pp. 139. + [n. p. 1842?] 4to, pp. (4), 47. BA.

HOYT (J. W.) Report on Education by John W. Hoyt, United States Commissioner. *Washington.* 1870. 8vo. 33408

Also: Address on University Progress ... at Trenton, N. J. ... *New York.* 1870. 8vo. S.

HOYT (J. G.) An Address at the Inauguration of Joseph G. Hoyt, LL.D., as Chancellor of Washington University, Saint Louis, ... October 4, 1859. ... *St. Louis: R. P. Studley and Co., Printers.* 1859. 8vo, pp. 84. H. 33409

HOYT. Miscellaneous Writings: Addresses, Lectures, and Reviews. By Joseph G. Hoyt, LL.D. *Boston: Crosby and Nichols.* 1863. 12mo, pp. viii, (1), 302. 33410

HOYT (——). The Horticultural Embellishment of School-House Grounds. An Essay ... By Mrs. Hoyt. *Madison.* 1860. 8vo. 33411

HOYT (R.) A Chaunt of Life and other Poems, with Sketches and Essays. In Six Parts. By Rev. Ralph Hoyt. Part I. *New York: Piercy & Reed.* 1844. 8vo, pp. (2), 32. Plate.

HOYT. Sketches of Life and Landscape. By Ralph Hoyt. *New-York.* 1849. 12mo. + *New York.* 1862. 12mo. + Fourth Edition, Enlarged. *New York.* 1866. 8vo. 33413

HUANTAJAYA. Description of the Silver Mines in Huantajaya, in Peru; with ... a project for reduction of their ... refuse ores ... the accumulation of a century and a half ... *London: Printed by Blades, East, and Blades.* 1864. 8vo, pp. 14. 33414

HUBARD. Catalogue of Subjects contained in the Hubard Gallery; with a brief Memoir of Master Hubard. *New York.* 1820. 16mo. 33415

HUBARD (E. W.) Speech of Edmund W. Hubard, of Virginia, on the United States Fiscal Bank Bill: ... August 4, 1841. *Washington: Printed by Blair and Rives.* 1841. 8vo, pp. 37.

Also: Speech ... on the Tariff; ... May 1, 1844. *Washington.* 1844. 8vo, pp. 15. H.—Speech ... June 25, 1846, on the Tariff. *Washington.* 1846. 8vo.

HUBBARD (A. C.) A Thanksgiving Sermon preached at the First Baptist Church, on November 27, 1862. By Rev. A. C. Hubbard. *Springfield: Bailhache & Baker.* 1862. 8vo, pp. 16.

HUBBARD (B.) The Climate of Detroit, Mich. An Essay. By Bela Hubbard. *Detroit.* [n. d.] 8vo. 33418

HUBBARD (D.) Letter of David Hubbard to the Voters of the Second Congressional District of the State of Alabama. *Washington.* 1840. 8vo. 33419

HUBBARD (E.) A Sermon ... in Marblehead ... June 12, 1796. Occasioned by the Death of the Hon. Azor Orne, Esq. ... By Rev. Ebenezer Hubbard. *Printed at Salem, by Thomas C. Cushing.* 1796. 8vo, pp. 31. B., BA., H., M., N. 33420

HUBBARD (E.) Concise Statement of the Proceedings of the Baptist Church at Leverett and Montague [Mass.], in their Labour with, and Exclusion of Elizabeth Hubbard. By a Member of the Church. *Wendell.* 1824. 8vo. W. 33421

HUBBARD (G. G.) Union of the Post-Office and Telegraph. Letter to the Postmaster General on the European and American Systems of Telegraph ... . By Gardiner G. Hubbard. *Boston: Wright & Potter, Printers.* 1868. 8vo, pp. 32. H. 33422

Also: Report on Postal Telegraph, 1869. ... *Washington.* 1869. 8vo.

HUBBARD (G. H.) Eulogium on Thomas C. Brinsmade, M.D. ... By Geo. H. Hubbard ... . February 2, 1869 ... . *Albany: Weed, Parsons & Co., Printers.* 1869. 8vo, pp. 238–46. H.

HUBBARD (Giles H.) Life and Dying Confession of John Van Alstine, executed March 19, 1819, for the Murder of William Huddleston, Esq. ... ... *Cooperstown: Printed by H. & E. Phinney.* 1819. 8vo, pp. 24. H. 33424

HUBBARD (H.) Oration at Pittsfield [Mass.], July 4, 1826. By H. Hubbard. *Pittsfield.* 1826. 8vo. 33425

HUBBARD (H. G.) A Historical Discourse, delivered on the Fiftieth Anniversary of the Organization of the First Baptist Church, In Bristol, R. I., By the Pastor, H. G. Hubbard. *Providence: A. Crawford Greene, Printer.* 1861. 8vo, pp. 18.

HUBBARD (Henry). Speech of Mr. Hubbard ... upon the Bill making further Provisions for the Persons engaged in the ... Revolutionary War ... February 29, 1832. *Washington: Printed by F. P. Blair.* 1832. 8vo, pp. 29. H. 33427

HUBBARD. Speech of Mr. Hubbard, of Virginia, on The Tariff, delivered in the House of Representatives, June 25, 1846. *Washington.* 1846. 8vo, pp. 14. 33428

Also: Speech ... on setting apart Surplus Revenue for the Defence of the Country. *Washington.* 1836. 8vo. S.—Speech ... March 7, 1836 [upon the ... Abolition of

Slavery in the District of Columbia ... . n. p. n. d.] 8vo, pp. 7.—Speech ... [February 18, 1840 ... on Assumption of the Debts of the States by the Federal Government. n. p. n. d.] 8vo, pp. 16.—Speech on ... the Issue of Treasury Notes ... March 30, 1840. [*Washington.*] 1840. 8vo.—Speech ... on the Bankrupt Bill. ... May 25, 1840. *Washington.* 1840. 8vo, pp. 15.—Speech ... on the Permanent Prospective Pre-emption Bill ... February 2, 1841. [*Washington.* 1841.] 8vo, pp. 16.

[HUBBARD (Jeremiah). Letter on African Colonization, dated Guilford County, North Carolina, 3d Month 4th, 1834. n. p. n. d.] 8vo, pp. 8. B. 33429

[HUBBARD (John).] The Benefactors of Yale College, a Poetical Attempt. *Boston.* 1733. 12mo. 33430

HUBBARD (J.) Letter From the Association of the County of New Haven, to the Rev. Elders in the Colonies of Rhode-Island and Massachusetts, who assisted in the Ordination of Rev. John Hubbard, at Meriden, June 22, 1769. *New Haven.* [1769.] 8vo, pp. 24. N. + With Remarks on the Confession of Faith and Examination of the said Mr. Hubbard. *New Haven.* [1770.] 12mo. 33431

For a reply *see* [Breck (Robert)], Vol. III., No. 7655.

HUBBARD. The Transactions of the Council called for the Ordination of the Rev. John Hubbard. *New Haven.* 1768. 12mo, pp. 22. W. 33432

HUBBARD (J.) The American Reader: containing a Selection of Narration, Harangues, Addresses, Orations, Dialogues, Odes, ... By John Hubbard. Fourth Edition. *Walpole.* 1808. W. + Fifth Edition. *Walpole (N. H.): Isaiah Thomas & Co.* 1811. 16mo, pp. 215. C. 33433

HUBBARD. Oration at Walpole, N. H., July 4, 1799. *Walpole.* [n. d.] 4to. W. 33434

HUBBARD. The Rudiments of Geography: a Concise Description of the various Kingdoms, States, Empires, Countries, and Islands in the World: [With] an enlarged Chronological Table of the most Important Events. By John Hubbard. *Walpole.* 1803. 12mo. + Second Edition, Revised and Corrected. *Walpole, N. H.: Geo. W. Nichols.* 1805. 12mo. + Sixth Edition. ... *Barnard (Vt.): Joseph Dix.* 1814. 18mo, pp. 219. C. 33435

HUBBARD (J. N.) Sketches of Border Adventures, in the Life and Times of Major Moses Van Campen, a Surviving Soldier of the Revolution. By his Grandson John N. Hubbard A.B. *Bath, N. Y.: R. L. Underhill & Co.* 1842. 8vo, pp. 310.

HUBBARD (John W.) Oration at Worcester, Mass., July 4, 1811. *Worcester.* [n. d.] 8vo. W. 33437

HUBBARD (S. G.) Catalogue of ... Autographs, Coins, Medals, etc., donated to the Great Western Sanitary Fair, to be sold ... for ... U. S. Sanitary Commission. ... *Cincinnati, O.: Robert Clarke & Co.* 1864. 8vo, pp. 39. H. 33438

HUBBARD (S[amuel] D.) Letter from S. D. Hubbard to his Constituents on the alarming Crisis in the Affairs of the Country. [*Washington, March* 13, 1846.] 8vo, pp. 8. H. 33439

HUBBARD. ... Mr. Hubbard's ... Report ... Petition of Hewing Wood, praying Indemnification for Losses by a Seizure ... for an alleged violation of laws regulating trade with the Indian Tribes ... [*Washington.* 1840.] 8vo, pp. 9. 33440

HUBBARD (S. M.) Speech of Prof. Samuel M. Hubbard, A.M., June 26th, 1862. Subject: the Ethics and Policy of the American Civil War; ... *Kalamazoo: Printed by Olney & Curtiss.* 1862. 8vo, pp. 29. H. 33441

HUBBARD (W.), *b.* 1621, *d.* 1704. The Benefit Of a Well-Ordered Conversation ... a Sermon ... June 24th, 1682. On a Day of publick Humiliation. As also A Funeral Discourse upon ... the Death of ... Major General Denison ... By William Hubbard ... . *Boston, Printed by Samuel Green.* 1684. 8vo, pp. (8), 218. B., M., H. 33442

An address "To the Serious Reader" is signed "J. Allin. Josh. Moodey," and is followed by a copy of Verses, signed "N. N." A very rare volume.

HUBBARD. A General History of New England, from the Discovery to MDCLXXX. By the Rev. William Hubbard, Minister of Ipswich, Mass. ... Published by the Massachusetts Historical Society. *Cambridge: Hilliard & Metcalf.* 1815. 8vo, pp. vi, (8), 676. B., BA. + Second Edition, Collated with the Original MS. ... *Boston: Charles C. Little and James Brown.* MDCCCXLVIII. 8vo, pp. vi, (14), 7–676. BA. 33443

This work by the author of the "Narrative of the Troubles with the Indians," 1677, was never before printed, although the MS. was known to, and made use of, by Mather, Prince, and Hutchinson. Hubbard derived the most important part of his early history from Gov. Winthrop's MS. Journal. *See* "N. A. Rev.," II. 221.

HUBBARD. The Happiness of a People|In the Wisdome of their Rulers|Directing|and in the Obedience of their Brethren|Attending|unto what Israel ougho [*sic*] to do:|Recommended in a|Sermon|Before the Honourable Governour and Council, and|

the Respected Deputies of the Mattachusets Colony|in New-England.|Preached at Boston, May. 3d. 1676. being the day of|Election there.|By William Hvbbard Minister of Ipswich.| *Boston, Printed by John Foster.* 1676.| 4to, pp. (8), 63. B., H.

Usually found bound up with the following:

HUBBARD. A|Narrative|of the Troubles with the|Indians|In New-England, from the first planting thereof in the|year 1607, to this present year 1677. But chiefly of the late|Troubles in the two last years, 1675 and 1676.|To which is added a Discourse about the Warre with the|Pequods|In the year 1637.|By W. Hubbard, Minister of Ipswich.|Published by Authority.|*Boston;|Printed by John Foster, in the year* 1677.| 4to.

Collation: 7 prel. leaves, viz.: Licence, signed "Simeon Bradstreet," etc.; Title; Dedication, pp. (4), signed "William Hubbard;" "An Advertisement," etc., pp. (2); "To the Reverend Mr. William Hubbard," etc., 1 p., signed "J. S.;" "Upon The elaborate Survey," etc., pp. (2), signed "B. T.;" "The Printer to the Reader," 1 p.; "A Map of New-England, Being the first that ever was here cut," etc.; "A Narrative," etc., pp. 132; "A Table," etc., pp. (7); "A Postscript," 1 p. & pp. [7–12]; "A Narrative of the Troubles With the Indians in New-England, From Pascataqua to Pemmaquid," pp. 88. A fine and perfect copy of this rare and valuable work, with the map which is often wanting, is one of the *desiderata* in an American collection. This book has been frequently reprinted, and will always remain an authority upon the subjects of which it treats. The Sermon, No. 33444, *supra*, which usually follows the "Narrative" is not a necessary part of the book, but we have never seen a copy of the "Narrative" in the original binding which did not contain it; our opinion is that the publisher, having many copies of the Sermon, bound it up with the "Narrative" to get rid of "The Happiness;" an unsalable tract. It possesses in itself high bibliographical interest, for, according to Thomas' "History of Printing," it is probably one of the first books printed in Boston, all the printing in the British Colonies, previous to 1676, having been done at Cambridge; that year the first press was set up at Boston. There are errors in the pagination in signature m, page 84, but the error is corrected on page 93. In some copies the errata on the last page fills 10 lines, whereas there are generally 12 lines. The money value of this work is great; Mr. Rice's copy sold in 1870 for $180. The buyer must be sure to get the right map, and concerning this he is referred to the note appended to the following reprint:

HUBBARD. The|Present State|of|New-England.|Being a|Narrative|Of the Troubles with the Indians|in|New-England, from the first planting|thereof in the year 1607, to this present year 1677:|But chiefly of the late Troubles in the two last|years 1675, and 1676.|To which is added a Discourse about the War|with the Peqvods in the year 1637.|By W. Hubbard Minister of Ipswich.|*London:|Printed for Tho. Parkhurst at the Bible and Three Crowns in Cheapside,|near Mercers-Chappel, and at the Bible on London-Bridg.* 1677.| 4to. 33446

Collation: 7 prel. leaves, viz.: Licence; Title; Dedication, pp. (4); An Advertisement, pp. (2); To the Reverend Mr. William Hubbard, pp. (2), signed "J. S.;" Vpon the elaborate Survey, etc., pp. (2), signed "B. T.;" "A Map of New-England, etc.;"

Text, pp. 131; "A Table," etc., pp. (7); "Postscript," pp. (6); "A Narrative," etc., pp. 88. It will be noticed that, while the collation of the preliminary leaves is identical with the Boston edition as to their numbers, their contents differ. "The Printer to the Reader," which is in fact errata, is omitted, while the poetical addresses occupy 2 leaves instead of 3 pages as in the Boston edition. The errata on page 88 of the "Narrative" is also omitted, in other respects its contents are precisely the same. Its mercantile value is less than that of the Boston edition, and for this reason the map, which really belongs to the London edition, is often inserted in the "Narrative." The proper map can readily be identified by the following differences: in the Boston edition the mound, which is delineated immediately below the title of the map, is properly designated "The White Hills"—in the London edition this mound is called "The Wine Hills." There are other differences in the map which are minutely pointed out in Field's "Essay," Nos. 431 and 432. Mr. Field remarks that "It has remained a matter of some doubt whether the London edition is not complete without the map," on which we remark that there is no doubt at all about it, each edition has its own proper map without which either are incomplete. Mr. Field's conjecture as to the London edition having been printed from MS., based on the date of the licence, is scarcely tenable; the licence to print proves nothing. Finally the map to each of these editions has been produced in exact facsimile by Henry Stevens in London, and the map to the Boston edition was reproduced by W. E. Woodward in Boston, so that the motto *caveat emptor* will be good advice.

HUBBARD. Narrative | of the | Indian Wars | in | New-England, | From the first Planting thereof in the Year 1607, to | the Year 1677. | Containing | A Relation of the Occasion, Rise and Progress | of the War with the Indians, in the Southern, Wes-| tern, Eastern and Northern Parts of said Country. | By William Hubbard, A.M. | Minister of Ipswich. | ... | *Boston: ... John Boyle ...* 1775. 12mo, pp. viii, 288. H. 33447

This second American edition is altered and abbreviated. "The whole country was the seat of war, and every man procured his bread in jeopardy of his life."—*Preface.* The following is the third edition:

HUBBARD. A Narrative of the Indian Wars in New England, From the first Planting thereof in the Year 1607, to the Year 1677, Containing A Relation of the Occasion Rise and Progress of the War with the Indians, in the Southern, Western, Eastern, and Northern Parts of the said Country. By William Hubbard, A.M. Minister of Ipswich. *Printed at Worcester, (Massachusetts) by Daniel Greenleaf, For Joseph Wilder.* 1801. 12mo, pp. 410. 33448

HUBBARD. A Narrative of the Indian Wars in New England, from the first Planting thereof in the year 1607, to the year 1677. Containing a Relation of the Occasion, Rise and Progress of the War with the Indians, in the Southern, Western, Eastern and Northern parts of said Country. By William Hubbard, A.M. Minister of Ipswich. *Norwich: Printed by John Trumbull.* [1802.] 12mo, pp. 228. 33449

HUBBARD. A | Narrative | of the | Indian Wars | in | New-England, | from the first planting thereof in the | Year 1607, to the Year 1677: | Containing | A Relation of the Occasion, Rise and | Progress of the War with the Indians, | in the Southern, Western, Eastern | and Northern parts of said Country. | By William Hubbard, A.M. | Minister of Ipswich. *Printed at Stockbridge, (Massachusetts) by | Heman Hilliard | May* 1803. 8vo, pp. 375, 6. 33450

HUBBARD. A | Narrative of the | Indian Wars | in New-England, | from the first Planting there- | of, in the year 1607, to | the year 1677. | Containing a Relation of | The Occasion, Rise and Progress | of the War with the Indians, | in the Southern, Western, | Eastern and Northern Parts | of said Country. | By William Hubbard, A.M. | ... | *Danbury: Printed by Stiles Nichols.* 1803. 12mo, pp. 274. 33451

HUBBARD. A Narrative of the Indian Wars in New-England, from the First Planting thereof in the year 1607, to the year 1677: containing ... the Occasions, Rise and Progress of the War with the Indians, ... By William Hubbard, A.M. ... Fourth Edition. *Brattleborough: William Fessenden.* 1814. 12mo, pp. 359. H. 33452

HUBBARD. The History of the Indian Wars in New England from the First Settlement to the Termination of the War with King Philip, in 1677. From the Original Work, by the Rev. William Hubbard. Carefully Revised, and Accompanied with an Historical Preface, Life and Pedigree of the Author, and Extensive Notes. By Samuel G. Drake. *Roxbury, Mass.: W. Elliot Woodward.* MDCCCLXV 2 vols., fcap 4to, pp. (2), xxxi, (1), 292, Map; 303. B., BA. 33453

Of this edition three hundred and fifty copies were printed, fifty in imp. 8vo, and fifty in 4to. Prefixed is a bibliographical Preface by the editor. It is a fine specimen of Munsell's typography, and forms Vols. III. and IV. of Woodward's "Historical Series."

HUBBARD (W. B.) Annual Address at the ... United States Agricultural Society ... . By William B. Hubbard ... . *Washington City: H. Polkinhorn, Printer.* 1862. 8vo, pp. 8. 33454

The Hubbard Silver Mine ... at Austin, Nevada ... . *Boston: Wright & Potter, Printers.* 1865. 8vo, pp. 22. 33455

HUBBARDSTON. School Report of the Town of Hubbardston. 1849–50. *Hubbardston.* 1850. 8vo. 33456

HUBBARDTON, *Vt.* Sketches of the History of the Town of Hubbardton, Vt., with Remarks on the Ancient Customs and Practices of the People and some Miscellaneous Articles. By an Old Man. ... *Rutland: Steam Press of G. A. Tuttle and Co.* 1855. 12mo, pp. (4), 64. 33457

The Advertisement is signed "Amos Churchill."

HUBBELL (H.) Arnold, or the Treason of West Point: a Tragedy, in Five Acts. By Horatio Hubbell. *Philadelphia.* 1847. 12mo, pp. 76. 33458

Also: Reply ... to a Circular of ... Members of the Faculty of Yale College, in 1855. ... [n. p. n. d.] 8vo, pp. 8. BA., H.

HUBBELL (J. H.) The National Legal Directory, embracing the Names of one or more of the Leading and most Reliable Attorneys in over Three Thousand Cities and Towns in the United States and Territories. ... *St. Louis: Hubbell & Craven.* 1870. 16mo, pp. 268. C. 33459

HUBBELL (L.) Oration delivered before the Young Men's Association of the City of Albany, ... July 4, 1835. By Levi Hubbell ... *Albany: Printed by Hoffman and White.* 1835. 8vo, pp. 19. B., BA. 33460

Also: Oration at Libertyville, N. Y., July 4, 1838. ... *Ithaca.* 1838. 12mo, pp. 14.

HUBBELL (L.) Trial and Impeachment of Levi Hubbell, Judge of the Second Judicial Circuit, by the Senate of the State of Wisconsin, June, 1853. Reported by T. C. Leland. *Madison.* 1853. 8vo. C. 33461

[HUBBELL (*Mrs.* Martha Stone).] The Shady Side; or, Life in a Country Parsonage. By a Pastor's Wife. *Boston.* 1853. 12mo. 33462

"As pretty a martyrdom as the world has now to show."—*Athenæum*, 1853, p. 616.

HUBBELL (S.) A Narrative of the Sufferings of Seth Hubbell & Family, in his Beginning a Settlement in the Town of Wolcott, in the State of Vermont. *Danville, Vt.: E. & W. Eaton, Printers.* 1826. 12mo, pp. 24. H. 33463

"In the latter part of February, 1789, I set out from the town of Norwalk in Connecticut, on my journey to Wolcott, to commence a Settlement," says the author, at which time also he commenced his troubles, adventures, etc.

HUBBELL (S.) A Discourse Commemorative of the Rev. Joseph Fish, for Fifty Years, from 1732 to 1781 Pastor ... in North Stonington ... By S. Hubbell. *Norwich.* 1863. 8vo, pp. 26. B. 33464

HUBBELL (W. W.) Reply ... to the Pamphlet headed "Bureau of Ordnance and Hydrography, ... Washington ... April, 1862," in relation to his Claim for Patent Explosive Shell and Fuse, used from the Great Guns of the Ships and Gun Boats ... *Washington, D. C.: Scammell & Co., Printers.* 1862. 8vo, pp. 8.

HUBBELL. Testimony and Brief of Facts, etc., on behalf of William Wheeler Hubbell, Esq., in support of his Claim on the Government ... for payment for the use of his Improvements in Explosive Shells and Fuses ... October, 1861. ... *Philadelphia: Printed by King & Baird.* 1861. 8vo, pp. 79, and Index. H.

HUBBELL. Views and Opinions of William Wheeler Hubbell on the Legal Tender Act of Congress of 1862. *Philadelphia.* [1870.] 8vo. S. 33467

HUBBELL. The Way to Secure Peace and Establish Unity as One Nation. By William Wheeler Hubbell. *Philadelphia.* 1863. 8vo, pp. 28. 33468

Also: Letter to the Chairman of the Naval Committee. ... Dec. 12, 1860. [n. p n. d.] 12mo, pp. 23.—Statement from the Bureau of Ordnance and Hydrography relative to the Claim ... for Remuneration for the use of an Explosive Shell, April, 1862. [n. p. n. d.] 12mo, pp. 23.

The Hubbell & Patton Gold and Silver Company, established in ... Philadelphia ... . *Philadelphia: E. C. Markley & Son, Printers.* 1867. 8vo, pp. 11. 33469

HUBBERT (*Prof.*) Catalogue of the Flowering Plants and Ferns indigenous to, or naturalized in Canada. To facilitate the exchanging of specimens, etc. By the Rev. Professor Hubbert, M.A. ... *Montreal.* 1867. 8vo, pp. 28. 33470

HUBER (B.) Aperçue Statistique de l'Ile de Cuba, précédé de quelques Lettres sur la Havane, et du tracé des côtes depuis la Havane jusqu'à Matanzas, et suivi de Tableaux Synoptiques d'une carte de l'Ile, etc. Par B. Huber, Attaché au Ministère des Affaires Étrangères ... . *Paris: Chez P. Dufart.* 1826. 8vo, pp. 331, (1). 6 Charts, Plate, Map. B., H., S. 33471

HUBER (V. A.) Sociale Fragen. II. Die Nord-Amerikanische Sclaverei. *Nordhausen.* 1864. 12mo. 33472

HUBLEY (B.) The History of the American Revolution, including the most Important Events and Resolutions of the Honourable Continental Congress during that Period and also, the most Interesting Letters and Orders of His Excellency

General George Washington, Commander in Chief of the American Forces. By Benrard Hubley. Vol. I. [All published.] *Northumberland, Pennsylvania: Printed for the Author, by Andrew Kennedy.* 1805. 8vo, pp. (4), 606, (1). H. 33473

A scarce and important history.

HUC *et* DE CHAZELLES. Martinique et Guadeloupe. Conseils coloniaux. Session de 1840. Rapports sur la question de l'émancipation. *Fort Royal, Martinique.* 1841. 8vo, pp. 96. 33474

[HUDDART (R. T.)] Appeal in Behalf of the Church in California. ... September, 1849. *New York: William Van Norden, Printer.* 1849. 12mo, pp. 8. H. 33475

HUDSON (C.) Valedictory Discourse, delivered before the Society of United Christian Friends, in the City of Norwich, (Con.) April 8, 1823. By Charles Hudson, Preacher of the Restoration. ... *New-London: Printed by Samuel Green.* [1823.] 8vo, pp. 23. 33476

HUDSON (C.) Doubts Concerning the Battle of Bunker's Hill. Addressed to the Christian Public. By Charles Hudson. *Boston and Cambridge: James Munroe and Company.* MDCCCLVII. 12mo, pp. (2), 41. Plate. B., C., H. 33477

HUDSON. History of the Town of Lexington, Middlesex County, Massachusetts, from its First Settlement to 1868, with a Genealogical Register of Lexington Families. By Charles Hudson ... . *Boston: Wiggin & Lunt.* 1868. 8vo, pp. 449, 296. Plates. B., BA. 33478

Twenty copies printed on tinted paper with portrait.

HUDSON. History of the Town of Marlborough, Middlesex County, Massachusetts, from its First Settlement in 1657 to 1861; with a Brief Sketch of the Town of Northborough, A Genealogy of the Families in Marlborough to 1800, and an Account of the Celebration of the Two Hundredth Anniversary of the Incorporation of the Town. By Charles Hudson ... . *Boston: Press of T. R. Marvin and Son.* 1862. 8vo, pp. xvi, 13–544, Note, (1). Portraits. B., BA., C., H. 33479

HUDSON. A History of the Town of Westminster, from its First Settlement to the Present Time. By Charles Hudson. *Mendon, Massachusetts.* 1832. 8vo, pp. 42. 33480

See also Westminster, Mass.

HUDSON. Non-Resistance. By Charles Hudson ... . *Boston: Wm. Crosby and H. P. Nichols.* 1848. 8vo, pp. 28. H. 33481

Relates to the Rebellion.

HUDSON. Report and Resolves in relation to the North-Eastern Boundary, March 1833. *Boston.* 1838. 8vo. Maps.

Also: An Address ... to the Citizens of the Fifth Congressional District, ... [Feb. 20, 1849.] *Washington.* [1849.] 8vo, pp. 14.—Character of Abraham Lincoln. [n. p. n. d.]—Speech ... on the Cost of the War and Finances of the Country. ... Feb. 15, 1848. *Washington: Printed by J. & G. S. Gideon.* 1848. 8vo, pp. 16. B. —Speech ... on the Subject of Discriminating Duties, ... Dec. 27 & 28, 1841. *Washington: Printed by Gales and Seaton.* 1842. 8vo, pp. 16.—Speech ... April 10, 1844.—Speech ... on the Annexation of Texas. ... Jan. 20, 1845. [*Washington.* 1845.] 8vo, pp. 15.—Speech ... on the Subject of the War with Mexico. Delivered ... May 14, 1846. [*Washington.*] 1846. 8vo, pp. 16.—Speech ... on the Wheat Trade of the Country, delivered ... February 26, 1846. *Washington: J. & G. S. Gideon, Printers.* 1846. 8vo, pp. 16. + *Boston: Eastburn's Press.* 1846. 8vo, pp. 16. —Speech ... on the Tariff Bills. ... July 8, 1842. [n. p. n. d.] 8vo, pp. 20. H. —Rep. No. 420. Tariff. April 10, 1844. ... [n. p. n. d.] 8vo, pp. 32.—Speech ... on the Tariff ... June 29, 1846. [*Washington.* 1846.] 8vo, pp. 16.—Speech ... on ... the Mexican War. ... Dec. 16, 1846. *Washington: Printed by J. & G. S. Gideon.* 1846. 8vo, pp. 16. + [n. p. n. d.] 8vo, pp. 8.—Speech ... on the Three Million Appropriation Bill. Delivered ... Feb. 13, 1847. [*Washington.* n. d.] 8vo, pp. 16.—Speech ... on the Constitutional Power of Congress over the Territories. ... June 20, 1848. *Washington: Printed by J. & G. S. Gideon.* 1848. 8vo, pp. 16. BA.

[HUDSON (*Rev.* Charles).] A Word for Trinity Church: From the American Church Monthly. *New-York.* 1857. 8vo, pp. 28. S. 33483

HUDSON (D.) History of Jemima Wilkinson, a Preacheress of the Eighteenth Century; containing an Authentic Narrative of her Life and Character, and of the Rise, Progress and Conclusion of her Ministry. ... By David Hudson. *Geneva (N. Y.): Printed by S. P. Hull.* 1821. 12mo, pp. 208, xx. B., H. 33484

Relates chiefly to the proceedings of Friends in Rhode Island. She insisted on the Shaker doctrine of celibacy, and the exercises of their religious meetings resembled those of that sect. Reprinted as:

HUDSON. Memoirs of Jemima Wilkinson, a Preacheress of the Eighteenth Century; containing an Authentic Narrative of her Life and Character. *Bath, N. Y.* 1844. 18mo. 33485

HUDSON (D.) Apuntes cronologicos para servir á la historia de la antigua Provincia de Cuyo. Por D. Hudson. *Mendoza.* 1852. 18mo, pp. 100. 33486

HUDSON (E. M.) Der Zweite Unabhängigkeits-Krieg in Amerika. Von E. M. Hudson ... . *Berlin: A. Charisius.* 1862. 8vo, pp. vii, (1), 99, (1). B., C. 33487

HUDSON. The Second War of Independence in America. By E. M. Hudson ... . Translated by the Author from the Second revised and enlarged German Edition. With an Introduction by Bolling A. Pope. *London: Longman, Green, Longman* ... 1863. 8vo, pp. l, 177. B., C. + Second Edition. [*Ibid.*] 8vo, pp. viii, 132. H. 33488

HUDSON (Henry). Beschryvinghe | Vander | Samoyeden Landt | in Tartarien. | Nieulijcks onder 't ghebiedt der Moscoviten ghebracht. | Wt de Russche tale overgheset, Anno 1609. | Met een verhael | Vande opsoeckingh ende ontdeckin- | ge vande nieuwe deurgang ofte straet int Noord- | westen na de Rijcken van China ende Cathay. | Ende | Een Memoriael gepresenteert aenden | Coningh van Spaengien, belanghende de ont- | deckinghe ende ghelegentheyt van 't Land ghe- | naemt Australia Incognita. | *t'Amsterdam, by Hessell Gerritsz. Boeckvercooper, opt | Water, inde Pascaert, Anno* 1612. | 4to, 20 leaves. 3 Maps. 33489

This rare work relates to the discovery of Hudson's Bay in 1611.

HUDSON. Descriptio ac delineatio Geographica Detectionis Freti. Sive, Transitvs ad Occasum, supra terras Americanas, in Chinam atq; Japonem ducturi, Recens investigati ab M. Henrico Hudsono Anglo. Item, Narratio Sermo. Regi Hispaniæ facta, super tractu, in quinta Orbis terrarum parte, cui Avstraliæ Incognitæ nomen est, recens detecto, per Capitaneum Petrum Ferdinandez de Quir. Vnà cum descriptione Terræ Samoiedarvm & Tingoesiorvm, in Tartaria ad Ortum Freti Waygats sitæ nuperq; Imperio Moscovitarum subactæ. *Amsterodami, Ex officina Hesselij Gerardi. Anno* 1612. 4to, 24 leaves. 3 Maps. J.C.B. 33490

See Brunet, III. 358, for a note as to the two editions. Concerning this extremely rare first edition *see* Asher's "Essay," Murphy's "Hudson in Holland," and Muller's "Essai," p. 103, Brunet's "Manuel," Leclerc's Catalogue, No. 742, and though last, not least, Tiele's "Essai." This and the following should perhaps have appeared under Gerritsz (Hessel).

HUDSON. Descriptio ac delineatio Geographica | Detectio- | nis Freti, | Sive, Transitus ad Occasum suprà | terras Americanas, in Chinam | atq; Iaponem ducturi. | Recens investigati ab M. Henrico Hudsono Anglo. | Item, | Exegesis Regi Hispaniæ facta super | tractu recens detecto, in quintâ Orbis parte, cui nomen, | Avstralis incognita. | Cum descriptione | Terrarum Samoiedarum, & Tingoesiorum, in | Tartarià ad Ortum Freti Waygats sitarum, nuperq; | sceptro Moscovitarum adscitarum. | *Amsterodami | Ex Officina Hesselij Gerardi. Anno* 1613. 4to, 24 leaves, one of which is blank. 5 Maps. J.C.B. 33491

The last leaf has "Veram effigiem Balenarum," with woodcut. After this there was

another issue with an appendix of 4 pages (signature G), or 52 pages in all. Mr. Muller of Amsterdam had the work reproduced in exact facsimile with the old types of the seventeenth century by Messrs. J. Enschedé and Sons at Haarlem, on old paper. An English translation of part of this will be found in Reed's "Hudson," pp. 191–195.

HUDSON. The Adventures of Henry Hudson, with copious Notes. *Philadelphia.* 1843. 18mo. View of New York. + *New York.* 1843. 33492

[HUDSON (Henry N.)] A Chaplain's Campaign with Gen. Butler. *New York: Printed for the Author.* 1865. 8vo, pp. 66.

Rather severe on the General. *See* [Butler (B. F.)], Vol. III., No. 9618. Also: Christian Patriotism. A Sermon preached in St. Clement's Church, New York, ... Jan. 4th, 1861. ... *New York: F. D. Harriman.* 1861. 12mo, pp. 27. H.

HUDSON [Isaac] & MENET [Albert]. Annual ... for 1870, containing a Full List of all Newspapers and Periodicals published in the United States and Canada ... . *New York: Hudson & Menet.* 1870. 8vo, pp. 216. B. 33494

HUDSON (S.) The | Essence | and | Unitie | of the | Church Catholike | Visible, | And the Prioritie thereof in regard | of Particular Churches | Discussed. | By Samuel Hudson Minister of the Gospel. | *London, | Printed by George Miller for Christopher Meredith at the | Signe of the Crane in Pauls Church- | yard.* 1645. | 4to, pp. (4), 52. 33495

In answer to Cotton and other New England divines.

HUDSON. A | Vindication | of the | Essence and Unity | of the | Chvrch Catholike Visible. | And | The Priority thereof in regard of | Particular Churches. | In answer to the Objections made against it, both | by Mr John Ellis junior, and by that Reverend and | worthy Divine Mr Hooker, in his Survey | of Church Discipline. | By Samuel Hudson Minister of the Gospel | at Capell in Suff. | *London, | Printed by A. M. for Christopher Meredith at the Signe of the | Crane in Pauls Church-yard.* 1650. | 4to, pp. (30), 265. B. 33496

Reissued with the date 1658, with the following:

HUDSON. An | Addition or Postscript | to the | Vindication | of the | Essence and Unity | or the | Church-Catholick visible, | And he Priority thereof in regard of | Particular Churches. | In answer to the Objections made against it, | both by Mr Stone, and some others. | By Samuel Hudson, Minister of the Gospel | at Capell in Suff. | *London, | Printed by J. B. for Andrew Kemble, and are to be sold | at his shop neer S. Margarets hill in Southwark and by Edward Brewster at the Crane in Paul's Church-yard, | and Thoma*

Basset under Dunstanes Church | Fleet-street, 1658. | 4to, pp. (4), 52. B. 33497

HUDSON (T. J.) Address of Hon. Thomas J. Hudson ... at the Agricultural Fair. ... November 9th, 1858. ... *Jackson: E. Barksdale, State Printer.* 1858. 8vo, pp. 14. H. 33498

HUDSON (T. B.) Our National Literature, its Character and Prospects. An Address by the Late Rev. Timothy B. Hudson, ... with a Biographical Notice. [n. p.] 1858. 8vo, pp. 49.

HUDSON & SMITH. Signal Book for Boston Harbor. By Hudson & Smith. ... *Boston: Eastburn's Press.* 1848. 12mo, pp. 77. H. 33500

HUDSON, *N. J.* Charter of the City of Hudson in the State of New Jersey. ... *Hoboken, N. J.* 1855. 8vo, pp. 37.

HUDSON, *N. Y.* Directory ... for 1851–52. By Parmenter & Van Antwerp. *Hudson.* 1852. 18mo, pp. 70. Continued.

The Hudson City and Columbia County Directory, for ... 1862–63, with ... a Record of the Soldiers ... . *Albany: J. Munsell.* 1862. 12mo, pp. 208. H. 33503

HUDSON FEMALE SEMINARY, *N. Y.* Catalogue, 1857. 8vo.

Also: Manual of the First Presbyterian Church of Hudson. ... *Hudson, N. Y.* 1852. 12mo. s. — Manual of the First Reformed Dutch Church. 1815. 12mo, pp. 15. s.

HUDSON, *O.* Proceedings of the Fifty-Sixth Anniversary of the Settlement of Hudson (O.); with Tables Showing the Longevity of the Pioneer Settlers. *Hudson: E. F. Chittenden & Bro.* 1856. 8vo, pp. 36. C. 33505

Western Reserve College Catalogue. *Hudson.* 1844. 8vo. Continued. 33506

Also: Catalogus eorum qui aliquovis gradu ornati fuerunt. [n. p.] 1845. 8vo.

Documents in relation to the application of the Hudson and Delaware Canal Company for Legislative Aid. *Albany.* 1829–. 1831. 8vo. 33507

Some Account of the Hudson and Mohawk Railroad in 1831, By C. De Witt Bloodgood, with some additional Notes. *Albany: J. Doolittle.* 1831. 16mo. 33508

HUDSON RIVER. Documents relative to the Construction of a Bridge across the Hudson River, at or near the City. *Albany.* 1814. 8vo. 33509

Guide to the Hudson River, by Rail Road and by Steam Boat. *Albany: J. Munsell.* 1866. 16mo, pp. 56. Colored Map.

The Hudson and Northern Routes from New York to Montreal. *New York: New York News Co.* 186–. 16mo, pp. 160.

The Hudson between Sandy Hook and Sandy Hill, with the Post Road between New York and Albany. *New York: A. T. Goodrich & Co.* 1820. 14 parts. 33512

The Hudson Illustrated with Pen and Pencil; comprising Sketches, Local and Legendary, of its several Places of Interest, together with the Route to Niagara Falls; forming a Companion for the Pleasure Tourist. *New York: T. W. Strong.* 1852. 4to, pp. 32. 33513

Hudson River and its Vicinity. *New York.* 1837. 16mo.

The Hudson River Guide; Containing a Description of all the Landings and Principal Places on the Hudson River as far as Navigable; ... Map. ... *New York: J. Disturnell.* M DCCC XXXV. 18mo, pp. 16. Plate. BA. 33515

Hudson River, and the Hudson River Railroad, ... *New York: Wm. C. Locke & Co.* [1851.] 8vo, pp. 50. Map. BA. 33516

Legends and Poetry of the Hudson. *New York: P. S. Wynkoop & Son.* 1866. Sq. 16mo, pp. 87, v. 33517

Letters about the Hudson River. *See* [Hunt (Freeman)].

Panorama of the Hudson River from New York to Albany. *New York: J. Disturnell.* 1846. 12mo, pp. 32. Map. BA.

Panoramic View of the Hudson River, from Jersey City ... to Albany, and down from Albany to New York, 13 feet long. *New York.* 1845. 33519

The Picturesque Beauties of the Hudson River and its Vicinity; illustrated in a Series of Views, from Original Drawings, taken expressly for this Work, and engraved on Steel, by Distinguished Artists. With Historical and Descriptive Illustrations, by Samuel L. Knapp, Esq. *New-York: J. Disturnell.* 1835. 4to.

Of this fine work Parts I. and II. only were issued. The panic of 1857 caused its discontinuance.

Proposition for an Anthracite Coal Steam Power Boat & Barge Company, for Passengers on the North River. pp. 12. 33521

Report of the Board of Commissioners to the Legislature of New York of a Plan for Improving the Navigation of the Hudson River. *Albany.* 1820. 8vo. 33522

A Report of the Committee appointed by the Directors of the Northern Inland Lock Navigation Company, in the State of New York, to examine Hudson's River. *From the Press of W. Durell, Albany.* 1792. 8vo. 33523

This important geographical paper is signed by Philip Schuyler, Abraham Ten Broeck, Jacobus Van Schonhoven, Stephen Van Rensselaer, and Henry Quackenbosh. Also: Report ... relative to the Construction of an Aqueduct over the Hudson River [near the Saratoga Dam]. Assembly, March 20, 1858. [n. p. n. d.] 8vo. Map.

Sketches of the North River. *New York: William H. Colyer.* 1838. 12mo, pp. 119. Map. C. 33524

Survey of Hudson River. Letter from the Secretary of War, transmitting Report of Colonel of Corps of Topographical Engineers, relative to the examination and survey of the Hudson River, &c. January 18, 1844. [n. p. n. d.] 8vo. 33525

Traveller's Steamboat and Railroad Guide to the Hudson River, describing the Cities, Towns, and Places of Interest along the Route, ... *New York: Gaylord Watson.* [1850.] 8vo, pp. 50.

Views on the Hudson. *London and New York: Nelson.* [n. d.] pp. 15. 12 Plates. 33527

Report of the Committee ... relative to a Bridge across the Hudson River at Albany. Senate, March 7, 1856. [n. p. n. d.] 8vo, pp. 19. 33528

Also: Document submitted to the Committee by the Opponents of the Bill in relation to a Bridge, &c. March 29, 1854. [n. p. n. d.] 8vo. [Sen. Doc., No. 98.] — Report of the Committee ... on the Petitions for and the Remonstrances against a Bridge across the Hudson River at Albany. April 2, 1841. [n. p. n. d.] 8vo, pp. 15, 105. — Report of the Minority of the Committee on ... a Bridge over the Hudson at Albany. April 16, 1841. [n. p. n. d.] 8vo, pp. 18. — Report of the Committee on Roads and Bridges, in relation to a Bridge across the Hudson at Albany. March 27, 1854. [n. p. n. d.] 8vo. [Sen. Doc., No. 97.] — Testimony taken before the Senate Committee in the matter of bridging the Hudson at Albany. In Senate, February 29, 1856. [n. p. n. d.] 8vo, pp. 303.

Wall's Hudson River Portfolio. Views from Drawings by W. G. Wall, engraved by J. Hill. *New York.* [1824]. Imp. oblong folio. 21 colored Plates. 33529

With letter-press. Appears never to have been finished. Scarce.

Wilson's Illustrated Guide to the Hudson River. Twelfth Edition. *New York: H. Wilson, March* 15, 1851. 18mo, pp. 61, 20. 33530

HUDSON RIVER BAPTIST ASSOCIATION. Anniversary ... 1815. *New York.* 1815. 8vo. Continued. 33531

Anniversary of the Hudson River Baptist Association North. 1851. 8vo. Continued. 33532

Second Annual Report of the Hudson River Industrial School Association, organized as a branch of the Children's Aid Society, March, 1856. *New-York: M. B. Wynkoop ... Printer.* 1856. 12mo, pp. 18, (2). Continued. H. 33533

HUDSON RIVER INSTITUTE, *Claverack, N. Y.* Catalogue for 1864–5. *New York.* 1865. 8vo. Continued. 33534

HUDSON RIVER RAILROAD. Address of the Directors and Commissioners ... To the Public ... etc. *New York*, 13 *Nov.*, 1846. 8vo, pp. 8. 33535

Annual Report of the Directors ... to the Stockholders. *New York.* 1848. 8vo. Continued. 33536

Communications from James Boorman to the Stockholders of the Hudson River R. R. Co., in Reply to Mr. A. C. Flagg. *New York.* 1849. 33537

... Statement, showing the ... Importance of the Proposed Railroad. *New York: E. B. Clayton and Sons.* 1846. 8vo, pp. 18 B. 33538

HUDSON'S BAY. Catechisme, Recueil de Prieres et Cantiques à l'usage des sauvages d'Albany, Baie d'Hudson. *Montreal: Louis Perrault.* 1854. 12mo, pp. 94. 33539

The Hudson's Bay Question, from the "Colonial Intelligencer." *London: W. Tweedie.* 1857. 8vo, pp. 28. 33540

Extent and Value of the Possessory Rights of the Hudson's Bay Company in Oregon, south of the Forty-Ninth Degree. [Legal Opinions,] 1848, 9. 8vo, pp. 51. S. 33541

A Few Words on the Hudson's Bay Company, with a Statement of the Native and Half-Caste Indians. *London.* [1846.] 8vo. 33542

First Report of Select Committee to ... receive Information as to the Rights of the Hudson's Bay Company, June 8, 1857. [A Canadian Legal Document.] 4to, pp. 24. S. 33543

The Hudson's Bay Company; What is it? *London.* 1864. 8vo. 33544

Notices on the Claims of the Hudson's Bay Company; to which is added a copy of their Royal Charter. *London: John Murray.* 1819. 8vo, pp. 69. 33545

Red River Settlement. *London.* 1849. Folio, pp. 118.

The running title of this document more clearly indicates its scope. "Correspondence relative to complaints of the inhabitants of the Red River Settlement." It is a great mass of testimony relative to the treatment of the Indians of that portion of British America by the imperial company who controlled them, and charges servants of that company with horrible cruelty.

Rapport du comité chargé de prendre et recueillir des informations relatives aux droits de la Compagnie de la Baie d'Hudson, en vertu de sa charte, &c. *Toronto.* 1857. 8vo, pp. 27. 33547

Report from the Committee appointed to enquire into the State and Condition of the Countries adjoining Hudson's Bay, and of the Trade carried on there. *Printed in the Year* 1749. Folio, pp. 60, Appendix, pp. xxxi. 33548

Contains a copy of the charter of the Hudson's Bay Company. It was reprinted in Vol. II. of the Reports from Committees of the House of Commons

Report from the Select Committee on the Hudson's Bay Company; together with the Proceedings of the Committee, Minutes of Evidence, Appendix and Index. Printed by Order of the House of Commons, July and August, 1857. *London.* 1857. Folio, pp. xviii, 547. 3 large Maps. S. 33549

Contains an enormous mass of evidence relative to the Hudson's Bay Company, their mode of dealing with the Indians, &c.

Report of the Committee appointed to receive and collect Evidence as to the Rights of the Hudson's Bay Company under their Charter, &c. *Toronto.* 1857. 8vo, pp. 25. 33550

Return to an Address of the ... Legislative Assembly for Copies of Charters, Leases, &c., under which the Hudson's Bay Company claim Title to the Hudson's Bay Territory; including a Memorandum by the Hon. J. Cauchon, Commissioner of Crown Lands, on the Subject of Territory, Boundary and Jurisdiction. *Toronto.* 1857. 8vo, pp. 75. 33551

A Short State of the Countries and Trade of North America. Claimed by the Hudson's Bay Company, Under Pretence of a Charter for Ever, of Lands without Bounds or Limits, and an exclusive Trade to those unbounded Seas and Countries; Shewing the Illegality of the said Grant, and the Abuse they have

made of it; and the Great Benefit Britain may obtain by settling those Countries, and extending the Trade amongst the Natives by civilizing and incorporating with them, and laying a Foundation for their becoming Christians and industrious Subjects of Great-Britain; and the Necessity there is of a Parliamentary Enquiry into the pretended Rights and exclusive Monopoly claimed by the said Company, and their Abuse of the Grant. That those Countries may be settled, either by fixing a Company under proper Regulations and Restrictions, or by laying open the Trade to all the British Merchants, and settling them at the Publick Expence, or by a moderate Tax upon that Trade. *London: J. Robinson.* M,DCC,XLIX. 8vo, pp. 44. BA., C., H. 33552

See the English Parliamentary Reports, 1842, &c., folio, *also* [Douglas (T.)], Vol. v., No. 20699, *and* Papers, Reasons, and Short Narratives.

HUEJUTLA. Coleccion de certámenes públicos de doctrina cristiana, ortologia, ortografía etc. que se han celebrado por los alumnos del establecimiento de educacion pública de la cabecera de Huejutla. 1828. *Mexico.* 1828. 4to, pp. 740, (2). 33553

HUELSTETT (——). Huelstett über die nordwestliche Durchfahrt. *Düsseldorf.* 1838. 4to. 33554

HUEN-DUBOURG (J.) Vie du Cardinal De Cheverus, Archevêque de Bordeaux, Par J. Huen-Dubourg ... . *Paris.* 1837. 8vo, pp. (4), iv, 425. Portrait. 33555

HUEN-DUBOURG. The Life of Cardinal Cheverus, Archbishop of Bordeaux, formerly Bishop of Massachusetts. By J. Huen-Dubourg, ... Translated ... by E. Stewart. *Boston: James Munroe and Company.* 1839. 12mo, pp. xxvii, 389. + Translated from the French by Robert M. Walsh. *Philadelphia: Hooker & Caxton.* 1841. 8vo, pp. 280. C. 33556

The real author is said to be the Rev. Mr. Hamon, a sulpitian. *See* Finotti's "Bibliotheca Catholica Americana," p. 44.

HUÉRFANOS. La Ciudad de los Huérfanos. Traduccion dedicada á los benévolos fundadores y sostenedores de la Casa de Beneficencio de Carácas. *Carácas.* 1869. Sm. 8vo, pp. 19.

HUERGO (P.) Cuestiones politicas y economicas. Por Palemon Huergo. *Buenos-Aires.* 1855. 8vo, pp. 184. 33558

HUERTA (A. de). Arte de la Lengua Quechua general de los Yndios de este Reyno del Piru. Compuesto por el Dr. Alonso de Huerta. *Impresso por Francisco del Canto, En los Reyes*, 1616. 4to, 8 l., 40 l. 33559

HUERTA. Contestacion al Discurso del Señor Huerta, pronunciado en la sesion secreta del 15. de Mayo de 1827. *Guadalajara.* 1827. 4to, pp. 56. 33560

HUERTA (Juan A.) Carta Pastoral por Juan A. Huerta, Obispo de Puno. *Lima.* 1865. 8vo, pp. 16. 33561

Also: Constituciones del primer Sinodo Diocesano Punense. *Puno.* 1868. 4to, pp. 100.

HUES (R.) Tractaet ofte handelinge van het gebruijck d. hemelscher ende aertscher Globe. Overghes. ende vermeerd. d. J. Hondius. *Amsterdam.* 1597. 4to. 33562

First edition of this treatise of the use of celestial and terrestrial globes. Pages 26–28 contain a description of America and Magellanica.

HUES. Traicté des Globes, traduict par D. Henrion. *Paris.* 1618.—L'Usage du Compas et Proportion, ... par Henrion. *Paris.* 1626.—Logocanon, ou Regle Proportionelle. *Paris.* 1626. 33563

Contains interesting notices of the early navigators, Vespucius, Corsali, Frobisher, Davis, etc.

HUESTIS. Adventures of Captain Huestis during his Banishment from Canada to Van Dieman's Land. *Boston.* 1848. 12mo.

HUESTIS (J. W.) Physical Observations and Medical Tracts and Researches on the Topography and Diseases of Louisiana. By Jabez W. Huestis. *New York.* 1817. 8vo, pp. 162.

HUESTIS (J.) Reply to the Letter of the Rev. Manassah M. York, against the Methodist Episcopal Church. By Jonathan Huestis. *Ithaca.* 1821. 8vo. 33566

HUET (P. D.) Tractatus de Situ Paradisi Terrestris, accedit ejusdem Commentarius de Navigationibus Salomonis. *London.* 1698. 8vo. 33567

America is the probable seat of the Eldorado and the land of Ophir.

HUET. A View of the Dutch Trade in all the States, Empires and Kingdoms of the World, showing its first Rise and amazing Progress ... From the French ... *London.* 1700. 12mo. + Second Edition. *London.* 1722. 12mo, pp. 232. 33568

HUFF (J. W.) The Government of the Methodist Episcopal Church. An Examination of Dr. Bond's Rejoinder to a Reply to his First Letter to Hon. Reverdy Johnson. ... By J. W. Huff. *Philadelphia: T. K. Collins, Jr.* 1852. 8vo, pp. 20. B.

HUFFINGTON (W.) Oration, in Dover, 4th July, 1827, on the Order of the Delaware Blues. By William Huffington. *Dover.* 1827. 8vo. C. 33570

See also Vol. v., No. 19384.

HUFFUMBOURGHAUSEN (*Baron*), *pseudon.* The Congress between the Beasts, under the Mediation of the Goat, for negotiating a Peace between the Fox, the Ass, wearing a Lion's Skin, the Horse, the Tigress, and other Quadrupeds at War: A Farce of two Acts, now in Rehearsal at a new grand Theatre in Germany. Written originally in High-Dutch, by the Baron Huffumbourghausen; and translated by J. J. H—D—G—R, Esq.; ... Second Edition. *Philadelphia.* 1748. 33571

HUGER (A.) Letter of Hon. Alfred Huger, in Answer to the Resolutions of a Meeting in St. Thomas' Parish. [n. p. 1832.] 8vo, pp. 8. BA., M. 33572

Includes a Letter by Langdon Cheves on State Rights.

HUGER. A Letter from the Hon. Alfred Huger, to the People of Spartanburgh District. *Charleston.* 1833. 8vo, pp. 8. H.

HUGGINS (E.) Case in Nevis, 1817, of Edward Huggins. *London.* 1817. C. 33574

Relates to slavery.

HUGGINS (J. R. D.) Hugginiana; or Huggins's Fantasy, being a Collection of the most esteemed Modern Literary Productions. Exposing the Art of making a Noise in the World, without beating a Drum or Crying Oysters; and showing how, like Whittington of old, who rose from nothing to be Lord Mayor of London, a mere Barber may become an Emperor, if he has but spirit enough to assume, and talents enough to support the title. By John Richard Desborus Huggins. *New York: Printed by H. C. Southwick, Wall street. Most Excellent Printer to his most Barbarous Majesty.* 1808. 12mo, pp. 288. 7 Plates.

Scarce and curious.

HUGHAN (W. J.) Masonic Sketches and Reprints. I. History of Freemasonry in New York. II. Unpublished Records of the Craft. With valuable Appendices. By William James Hughan. *New York.* 186–. 8vo, pp. 224. 33576

[HUGHES (B. F.)] Annapolis considered as a suitable situation for a Great Naval Depot and Arsenal of Marine Stores. *Annapolis.* 1818. 8vo, pp. 12. 33577

Hughes (B. F.) Eulogium on the Life and Character of William Wilberforce, Esq. Delivered and published at the Request of the People of Color of the City of New York, Twenty-second of October, 1833. By Benjamin F. Hughes, (a Man of Color.) *New-York: Printed at the Office of the Emancipator.* 1833. 8vo, pp. 16. B. 33578

Also: An Oration ... before the Boyer Lodge, 25th of June, 1827 ... . *New York: Printed by Mahlon Day.* 1827. 8vo, pp. 15. B.

Hughes (D. L.) A Sketch of the Life, Character, and Writings of the Rev. James Y. M'Ginnes, of Shade Gap, Pennsylvania. By Rev. D. L. Hughes. *Philadelphia.* 1854. 12mo, pp. 352. C. 33579

Hughes (E. B.) The New York Church Year Book for 1859–60. ... By Edward B. Hughes. *New York.* 1859. 12mo, pp. 113. 33580

Hughes (G. W.) Memoir Descriptive of the March of a Division of the United States Army under the Command of Gen. J. E. Wool, from San Antonio de Bexar in Texas to Saltillo in Mexico. By George W. Hughes, Lieut. Col. United States Engineers. [*Washington.* 1846.] 8vo, pp. 67. Plates. S.

Also: Letter ... in Answer to the Hon. J. M. Clayton, Secretary of State, on Intermarine Communication. *Washington.* 1850. 8vo. — Report in relation to the working of Copper Ores, 1844. [n. p. n. d.] 8vo. [Cong. Doc.] — Report on the Location and Survey of the Potomac and Annapolis Canal ... to the Governor of Maryland. ... *Annapolis.* 1837. 8vo. — Report ... on the Tioga Coal & Iron Mines. ... *Albany: Printed by John B. Van Steenbergh.* 1829. 8vo, pp. 8. B.

Hughes (G.) The Natural History of Barbados. In Ten Books. By the Reverend Mr. Griffith Hughes, A.M., Rector of St. Lucy's Parish, in the said Island. ... *London: Printed for the Author.* MDCCL. Folio, pp. (16), vii, (1), 314, (19). Map, 29 Plates. B., BA., H. 33582

Also on large paper. There is a well-written article on this work in the "Monthly Review," III. 197, which states that it is of no value to the naturalist. The book is handsomely printed, and the plates are finely executed from drawings by Ehret, and are colored only in large paper copies of the work.

Hughes (H.) A Report on the African Apprentice System, read at the Southern Commercial Convention, By Henry Hughes. Held at Vicksburg, May 10th, 1859. [*Vicksburg.* 1859.] 8vo, pp. 15. H. 33583

Hughes. State Liberties; or the Right to African Contract Labor, By Henry Hughes. *Port Gibson.* 1858. 12mo, pp. 53.

Hughes (H.) Memorials and Documents in the case of Col. Hugh Hughes, Deputy Quarter-Master General, during the War of Independence, 1802, &c. *Washington.* 1802. 8vo. 33585

Hughes (J.) Speech of the Hon. James Hughes ... on the Admission of Oregon, delivered ... February 10, 1859. *Washington: Lemuel Towers.* 1859. 8vo, pp. 15. 33586

Also: Speech ... in favor of the Kansas Policy of the Administration, at a Democratic Meeting, New York. *Washington.* 1858. 8vo, pp. 15. — The Baker-Cumback Correspondence. Speech ... in the Indiana Senate Chamber, ... January 15th, 1869. ... *Indianapolis.* 1869. 8vo, pp. 15. H.

Hughes (J.) Almanac for 1726. By John Hughes. 1726.

Hughes (J.) Biographical Sketch of the Most Rev. John Hughes, D.D., Archbishop of New York. *New York: Metropolitan Record Office.* 1864. 8vo, pp. 62. 33588

Hughes. The Catholic Chapter in the History of the United States. A Lecture ... March 8, 1852 ... By ... John Hughes ... *New-York: Edward Dunigan & Brother.* M.DCCC.LII. 8vo, pp. 38. B. 33589

Hughes. Complete Works of the Most Rev. John Hughes, D.D., Archbishop of New York. Comprising his Sermons, Letters, Lectures, Speeches, etc. Carefully Compiled from the best Sources, and edited by Lawrence Kehoe. *New York: Lawrence Kehoe.* 1865. 2 vols., 8vo, pp. 666; 5, xiv, 9–796. B. 33590

Hughes. A Letter on the Moral Causes that have produced the Evil Spirit of the Times; addressed to the Honorable James Harper, Mayor of New-York. Including a Vindication of the Author from the Infamous Charges made against him by Jas. Gordon Bennett, William L. Stone, and Others. By ... Rev. Dr. Hughes ... . *New-York.* [1844.] 8vo, pp. 23. BA. 33591

Hughes. The Life of Archbishop Hughes. ... *Philadelphia: T. B. Peterson & Brothers.* [1864.] 12mo, pp. 17–70. Portrait.

Hughes. A Sermon on the Civil War in America, delivered August 17, 1862, on his return to America from Europe. *Philadelphia: T. B. Peterson.* 1862. 8vo, pp. 4. 33593

Also: Archbishop Hughes in Reply to General Cass, and in Self-Vindication. *New York: Edward Dunigan & Brother.* M.DCCC.LIV. 8vo, pp. 34. — Brooksiana; or, the Controversy between Senator Brooks and Archbishop Hughes. ... *New York: Edward Dunigan & Brother.* 1850. 12mo. — The Church and the World. A Lecture ... January 31, 1850 ... . *New-York: Edward Dunigan & Brother.* 1850. 8vo, pp. 31. — Christianity, the only Source of Moral, Social and Political Regeneration. A Sermon: ... Hall of the House of Representatives ... Dec. 12, 1847. ... *New-York: Edward Dunigan.* MDCCCXLVIII. 8vo, pp. 32. — Kirwan Unmasked. A Review of Kirwan, in Six Letters ... . *New York: Edward Dunigan & Brother.* MDCCCXLVIII. 32mo, pp. 72. — A Lecture on the Importance of a Christian Basis for ... Political Economy ... . 17th and 18th January, 1844. ... *New-York.* [1844.] 8vo, pp. 27. — Letter to Bishop Lynch of South Carolina. *Baltimore.* — Pastoral Letters of the Right Rev. Dr. Hughes, Bishop of New York, to the Clergy and Laity of the Diocese of New York for Lent, 1847. *New York.* 1847. 8vo, pp. 16. — Reflections and Suggestions in regard to what is called the Catholic Press in the United States. *New-York.* 1856. 8vo, pp. 34. — Sermon at the Cathedral of St. Patrick ... . *New York.* 1863.

Hughes, *and* Breckinridge (J.) A Discussion of the Question, Is the Roman Catholic Religion Inimical to Civil or Religious Liberty, and is the Presbyterian Religion Inimical. *Baltimore.* 1856. 8vo. 33594

Hughes (J. T.) California; its History, Population, Climate, Soil, Productions and Harbors, from Sir George Simpson's "Overland Journey round the World." An Account of the Revolution in California, and Conquest of the Country by the United States. By John T. Hughes. *Cincinnati: J. A. & U. P. James.* 1849. 16mo, pp. 105. + [*Ibid.*] 1850. 33595

Hughes. Doniphan's Expedition; containing an account of the Conquest of New Mexico; General Kearney's Overland Expedition to California; Doniphan's Campaign against the Navajos; his unparalleled March upon Chihuahua and Durango; and the Operations of General Price at Santa Fé: With a Sketch of the Life of Col. Doniphan. ... By John T. Hughes, A.B., of the First Regiment of Missouri Cavalry. *Cincinnati: U. P. James.* [1847.] 8vo, pp. 144. Also in 12mo. + [*Ibid.*] 1848. 12mo, pp. 407. Map, 2 Portraits, and Plans. + [*Ibid.*] 1850.

Hughes (John W.) Trial and Execution of Dr. J. W. Hughes for the Murder of Miss Tamzen Parsons; with a Sketch of his Life, as related by himself. *Cleveland.* 1866. 8vo, pp. 57.

Hughes (L. B.) The Model Character George Washington. A Lecture ... September 8, 1863. By Rev. L. B. Hughes ... . *Philadelphia: Bryson & Son, Printers* ... 1863. 8vo, pp. 24. H.

Hughes. National Union. A Sermon ... in ... Bainbridge, Pennsylvania, on National Fast, January 4, 1861. By L. B. Hughes ... . *Lancaster: Pearsol & Geist, Printers.* 1861. 8vo, pp. 24. BA. 33599

Hughes (M.) A Sketch of the Life of Lieut. Mathew Hughes, late of the United States Army, serving on the Niagara Frontier during the late War between this Country and Great Britain. Written by a near Connection. To which is annexed Letters that he wrote to his Father and Mother after he marched from Winchester, Va. to the Frontier ... *Alexandria: Printed by J. Corse and N. Ronnsavell.* 1815. 8vo, pp. 56. 33600

Hughes (N.) A Solemn Warning to all the Dwellers upon Earth, given forth in obedience to the express command of the Lord God, in several extraordinary Visions, and Miraculous Revelations ... . By Nimrod Hughes, of Virginia. *Trenton.* 1811. 8vo. 33601

Hughes (S. R.) Hughes' Michigan General Shippers' Guide, and Railroad, Express and Steamboat Agent's Directory, 1868. By S. R. Hughes. *Detroit.* 1868. 8vo, pp. 127. C. 33602

Hughes (T.) The Cause of Freedom: Which is its Champion in America, the North or the South? By Thomas Hughes ... [*London: William Wisley.* 1863.] Post 8vo, pp. 16. B., BA.

Hughes (T. S.) The History of England, from the Accession of George III., 1760, to ... 1837. By Rev. T. S. Hughes. *London: George Bell.* 1855. 7 vols., 8vo, pp. xx, ix–xvi, 517, Portrait; xi, 424; viii, 460; viii, 451; xi, 475; xi, 507; viii, 615, (1). B., H., 33604

Includes copious details of the American Revolution.

Hughes (W.) The American Physitian; or, a Treatise of the Roots, Plants, Trees, Shrubs, Fruit, Herbs, &c. Growing in the English Plantations in America ... [with] A Discourse of the Cacao-Nut-Tree ... . By W. Hughes. ... *London: William Crook.* 1672. 24mo, pp. (24), 159. B., H., P., S. 33605

Hughes (W.) An Answer to the Rev. Mr. Harris's "Scriptural Researches on the Licitness of the Slave Trade." By the Rev. W. Hughes, M.A. *London: T. Cadell.* 1788. 8vo.

See "M. Rev.," LXXVIII. 269, 575, *and* "M. Rev.," LXXX. 68.

Hughes. A Discourse in favour of the Abolition of Slavery in the British West Indies. Preached in the Parish Church of Ware, Herts. By the Rev. W. Hughes, M.A. *London: T. Cadell.* 1788. 4to. 33607

Hughes (W.) The Geography of British History: Comprehending a Geographical Description of the British Islands and the Colonial Empire of Britain, treated historically, in successive periods, from the earliest times to the present day. By William Hughes. ... *London: Longman and Co.* 1861. 33608

Hughes, Denver *and* Peck. Argument in support of The Right of the United States to hold the Coin and Bullion claimed by the Bank of Virginia, the Farmers' Bank, and the Exchange Bank, all of Richmond, Va. By Hughes, Denver & Peck, Special Counsel. *Washington.* 1866. 8vo, pp. 22. H. 33609

Hughes, &c. Review of the Opinion of Charles O'Conor, Esq., on what he styles the "Treasury Agent System of Cotton Seizures at the South:" addressed to Hon. Hugh McCulloch, Secretary of the Treasury. By Hughes, Denver and Peck ... . *Washington.* 1866. 8vo, pp. 19. C., H. 33610

Hughs (Mary, *late* Robson). The Life of William Penn, abridged and adapted to the use of Young Persons. By Mary Hughs (late Robson). *London: William Darton.* 1822. 12mo, pp. 192. Portrait and Facsimile. C. 33611

Hughs (*Mrs.*) The Life of William Penn, Compiled from the Usual Authorities and also Many Original Manuscripts. By Mrs. Hughs ... . *Philadelphia: Carey, Lea & Carey* ... . 1828. 12mo, pp. 224. BA. 33612

Hugo (V.) Bug-Jargal o la rivolta dei negri di San Domingo. Claudio Gueux. *Milano.* 1855. 2 vols., 16mo. Plates.

Hugo. ... Bug-Jargal. Claude Gueux. ... *Paris: Librairie de L. Hachette et Cie.* 1858. 8vo, pp. (4), 446, (1). BA. + *New York.* 1856. B. 33614

Hugo. Bug Jargal, eller Negeropstanden paa St. Domingo. En Fortælling af Victor Hugo, oversat. *Kjøbenhavn.* 1830.

Hugo. John Brown. Par Victor Hugo. *Paris: Dusacq et Cie.* 1861. 8vo. Portrait. 33616

Hugo. John Brown, with a Photograph representing his Execution. By Victor Hugo. *Paris: E. Dentu.* 1861. 8vo, pp. 8. 33617

Hugo. Letters on American Slavery from Victor Hugo, De Tocqueville, Emile De Girardin, Carnot, Passy, Mazzini, Humboldt, Lafayette, etc. *Boston: American Anti-Slavery Society.* 1860. 12mo, pp. 24. 33618

Hugo. Les Miserables ... By Victor Hugo. A New Translation, Revised. *Richmond: West & Johnston.* 1863–64. 8vo.

"A few scattered sentences, reflecting on slavery ... it has been deemed advisable to strike out."—*Preface.*

Hugo. Victor Hugo's Letter on John Brown, with Mrs. Ann S. Stephens' Reply. *New York.* 1860. 12mo. 33620

Huguenots. *See* [Lee (H. F.)]

Hugues *et* Lebas. Rapport fait aux Citoyens Hugues et Lebas, sur la situation du Volcan de la Guadeloupe, et les effets de l'eruption qui a eu lieu dans la nuit, 7 au 8 du mois la vendemiaire. *Guadeloupe. An* VI [1798]. 4to. 33621

Hugues, Hughes, Hugon (Jean). *See* Linschoten.

Huhn (J. B.) Denckmahl göttlicher Güte und Vorsorge vor seine evangelische Kirche an dem Exempel der saltzburgischen Emigranten. *Gotha.* 1732. 4to. B. 33622

Hühn (W.) Mittheilungen betreffend die deutsche Kolonie Dona Francisca in der südbrasilianischen Provinz Santa Catharina. Herausgegeben von W. Hühn, ... *Hamburg, im November* 1852. *Druck von G. F. Thiele.* 8vo. 33623

A periodical. Five numbers were published.

Huidekoper (F.) A Letter from Professor Frederic Huidekoper ... on ... the Meadville Theological School. *New-York: John Westall & Co., Printers.* [1847.] 12mo, pp. 24. H., S.

[Huidekoper (H. J.)] Remarks on the late Proceedings of the Nicholson Commissioners ... in Relation to the Lands formerly of the Pennsylvania Population Company. [*Meadville.* 1842.] 8vo, pp. 16. H. 33625

Also: Obituary ... . [From the Christian Examiner for September, 1854.] *Boston: Crosby, Nichols, and Company.* 1854. 8vo, pp. 12. H.

Huish (R.) The Late Voyage of Captain Sir John Ross, R.N., to the Arctic Regions, for the Discovery of a North West Passage, performed in the Years 1829, 30, 31, 32, 33. From Authentic Information, and Original Documents, transmitted by William Light, Purser's Steward to the Expedition. By Robert Huish, ... *London.* 1835. 8vo, pp. 760. 33626

An unauthorized Narrative, wholly different from that by Capt. Ross. It was severely handled in the "Quarterly Review," LIV. 1.

Huish. Memoirs of the Late Wm. Cobbett, Esq., M.P. for Oldham; embracing all the Interesting Events of his Memorable Life, obtained from Private and Confidential Sources; Also A Critical Analysis of his Scientific and Elementary Writings. By Robert Huish. *London: J. Saunders.* 1836. 2 vols., 8vo, pp. x, 496; 474. 33627

Details his American experiences.

Huish. The Northwest Passage. A History of the Most Remarkable Voyages made in Search of the Northwest Passage, from the Earliest Periods. By Robert Huish. *London.* 1851. 8vo. 33628

Huish. Public and Private Life of George the Third: with a variety of Secret Anecdotes of his Majesty, the Royal Family, and other Distinguished Characters. Comprising also, an Historical Memoir of the House of Brunswick. Translated from the Latin work entitled Origines Guelphicæ. By Robert Huish. *London: Thomas Kelly.* 1821. 4to, pp. ii, viii, 724. 18 Plates.

Huit (E.) The whole | Prophecie | of | Daniel | explained, | By a Paraphrase, Analysis, | and briefe Comment: | Wherein the severall Visions shewed to the Prophet, are | clearly Interpreted, and the Application thereof vindi- | cated against dissenting Opinions. | By Ephraim Huit sometime Preacher at Roxall in Warwickshire, | now Pastor to the Church at Windsor in New-England. | Imprimatur, Jam: Cranford. | [*London:*] *Printed for Henry Overton, and are to be sold at his Shop,* | *entering into Popes-head Alley out of Lumbard* | *Street.* MDCXLIV. | 4to, pp. (6), 358, and 10 folded leaves. B., J.C.B. 33630

"The Epistle Dedicatorie," is signed "Simeon Ash, Samuel Clarke, Will. Overton."

Hulbert (C.) Museum Americanum; or Select Antiquities, Curiosities, and Beauties Of Nature and Art, in America; By Charles Hulbert, ... *Shrewsbury: C. Hulbert.* 1823. 18mo, pp. 346. Plate. 33631

Hulbert (D. P. M.) Education, Emigration, and Supremacy, theologically considered. By Daniel P. M. Hulbert. *London.* 1850. 12mo. C. 33632

Hulburd (C. T.) Address before the St. Lawrence County Agricultural Society ... Sept. 1857. By ... Calvin T. Hulburd. *Ogdensburgh: Hitchcock ... Printers.* 1857. 8vo, pp. 23. B.

Hulett (T. G.) Every Man his own Guide to the Falls of Niagara ... . To which is added a Chronological Table, containing the Principal Events of the Late War between the United States and Great Britain. By T. G. Hulett. ... Fourth Edition. *Buffalo: Printed by Faxon & Co.* 1844. 18mo, pp. 128. Plan and Plate. BA. 33634

Also: Every Stranger his own Guide to Niagara Falls. ... *Buffalo.* 1844. 12mo, pp. 32. Plate, Map. B. H.

Hull (A. G.) A Tribute to the Memory of James A. Powell, Union College, July 23, 1829. By A. Gerald Hull. *Privately printed.* 1829. 8vo, pp. 128. Portrait. S. 33635

Hull (I.) Minutes of Proceedings of the Court of Enquiry, into the Official Conduct of Capt. Isaac Hull, as Commandant of the United States' Navy-Yard, at Charlestown, in the State of Massachusetts, convened at the Navy-Yard, in said Charlestown, on the 12th Day of August, A.D. 1822 ... *Washington City: Davis and Force.* 1822. 8vo, pp. 244, Appendix, pp. 64.

Hull (J.) Diary of John Hull, with Memoir of the Author. Printed from the Original MS. *Boston.* 1857. 8vo. Facsimile.

Hull (J. S.) Remarks on the United States of America, drawn up from his own Observations, and from the Observations of other Travellers. By John Simpson Hull. *Dublin* [about 1796]. 8vo. 33638

Hull (L.) Annual Address ... before the Medical Society of the State of New York, February 6, 1839. By Laurens Hull ... . *Albany: Printed by J. Munsell.* 1839. 8vo, pp. 14. B.

Also: Annual Address ... Feb., 1840 ... *Albany: J. Munsell.* 1840. 8vo, pp. 15.

Hull (M. N. B.) Letters of Morris N. B. Hull, preceded by Remarks on Capital Punishment. *Utica.* 1821. 8vo.

Hull (W.) The Capitulation, or a History of the Expedition conducted by William Hull ... . By an Ohio Volunteer. ... *Chillicothe: Printed by James Barnes.* 1812. 12mo, pp. 78, iv, (2).

Hull. Defence of Brigadier General W. Hull. Delivered before the General Court Martial, of which Major General Dearborn was President, at Albany, March, 1814. With an Address to the Citizens of the United States. Written by Himself. Copied from the Original Manuscript, and published by his authority. To which are prefixed, The Charges against Brigadier General Hull, as Specified by the Government. *Boston: Wells and Lilly.* 1814. 12mo, pp. (2), xlvi, 215. BA., H.

Hull. Memoirs of the Campaign of The North Western Army of the United States, A.D. 1812. In a Series of Letters addressed to the Citizens of the United States. With an Appendix, Containing a Brief Sketch of the Revolutionary Services of the Author. By William Hull, Late Governour of the Territory of Michigan, and Brigadier General in the Service of the United States. *Boston: True & Greene.* 1824. 8vo, pp. 229, x.

See "N. A. Rev.," xx. 227.

HULL. [Proceedings of the Court Martial, in the Case of William Hull, Brigadier General in the Army of the United States. n. p. n. d.] 12mo, pp. 37. BA. 33644

HULL. Report of the Trial of Brig. General William Hull; Commanding the North-Western Army of the United States. By a Court Martial Held at Albany on Monday, 3d January, 1814, and succeeding days. Taken by Lieut. Col. Forbes ... . *New York: Eastburn, Kirk, and Co.* 1814. 8vo, pp. (4), 156, Appendix, 119, 29. C., H., P. 33645

HULL. Trial of Brig. Gen. William Hull, for Treason ... with the Sentence of the Court, and Remission thereof by the President of the United States. *Boston: Russell, Cutler & Co.* 1814. 8vo, pp. 28. H. 33646

Also: An Oration delivered to the Society of the Cincinnati in ... Massachusetts, July 4, 1788. ... *Boston: Printed by Benjamin Russell.* 1788. 4to, pp. 22. B., BA., S. *See* Clarke (J. F.), Vol. III., No. 10263.

HULL-GULL. The Wars of the Gulls. An Historical Romance in Three Chapters. Chapter I. Showing How and Why, and with Whom the Gulls went to War. II. How the Gulls made the Deep to Boil like a Pot. III. Showing how a Certain Doughty General of the Gulls goes forth to Play the Game of Hull-Gull in Upper Canada:

"And from the pinnacle of glory,
Falls headlong into purgatory."

After having quieted himself with the sagacious reflection—

"That when a fight becomes a chase,
Those win the day that win the race."

New York. 1812. 8vo, pp. 36. 33647

HULL, *Mass.* Notes on the Sea-shore, or Random Sketches in relation to the Ancient Town of Hull, Mass.; its Settlement and its Inhabitants, its Wrecks and Wreckers. Remarkable fish stories, fish and clam chowder, frog-fishing, clam-digging, lobster-catching and hog-killing, and two or three hundred other interesting subjects. By the Shade of "Alden." *Boston.* 1848. 8vo, pp. 56. 33648

The Table of Contents alludes to a frontispiece, but we are not certain whether one was ever engraved.

A Sketch of Hull, Mass. *Hingham.* 1830. 12mo.

HÜLSEMANN (J. G.) The Austro-Hungarian Question. Correspondence between Mr. Hülsemann, Austrian Chargé d'Affaires, and Mr. Webster, Secretary of State of the United States. *Washington: Printed by Gideon & Co.* 1851. 8vo, pp. 23. B., BA.

HÜLSEMANN. Geschichte der Democratie in den Vereinigten Staaten von Nord America. Von Johann Georg Hülsemann. *Göttingen.* 1823. 8vo, pp. xxii, (2), 388. B. 36651

A writer in the "North American Review," XXIII. 334, says that this "History of Democracy in the United States," is, to all appearance, a semi-official emanation of the Austrian Cabinet.

HULSE *or* HULSIUS (Levinus). Sammlung von Sechs und Zwanzig Schiffahrten in verschiedene fremde Länder durch Lev. Hulsium und einige andere, aus dem Holländischen ins Deutsche übersetzt und mit allerhand Anmerkungen versehen. *Nürnberg, Frankfurt, Oppenheim und Hanover.* 1598–1650. 26 vols., 4to.

This is a general title to this celebrated collection of voyages, which was doubtless suggested by the success that had attended the publications of the series by the brothers De Bry; it is in some respects an imitation of these series, in others it is superior. A complete set exceeds in rarity a set of De Bry, and as Stevens remarks "Who sets his heart on a perfect Hulsius, let him sit down and count the cost of 'time and treasure.'" As several of the parts do not relate to America, we content ourselves with an enumeration of the date and collation of a series, and give the titles of the books which relate to America in full.

I. Kurtze Warhafftige | Beschreibung der newen Reyse oder | Schiffahrt, ... in denn | Orientalischen Indien, ... | Durch | Levinum Hulsium. | ... | *Gedruckt zu Nürmberg bey Christoff Lochner, In verlegung L. Hulsii Anno* 1598. 4to, pp. 72. 12 Maps and Plates. + Secunda editio. *Gedruckt zu Nürnberg, In verlegung Levini Hulsij* 1599. 4to, Title, pp. (2), 76. 13 Maps and Plates. + Tertia Editio. *Nürnberg, In Verlegung Levini Hulsij.* 1602. 4to, Title, pp. (6), 76. 13 Maps and Plates. + Editio quarta. *Gedruckt zu Franckfurt am Mayn durch Wolffgang | Richtern, in Verlegung Leuini Hulsii Erben.* M. D. VI. 4to, Title, pp. 70. 13 Maps and Plates. + Editio Quinta. *Getruckt zu Franckfurt am Mayn durch Hartmann | Palthenium, in Verlegung der Hulsischen. | Anno* M.DC.XXV. 4to, pp. 67. 13 Maps and Plates. 33653

II. Ander Schiffart. | In die Orientalische | Indien, ... | Durch | Levinum Hulsium. | *Nürnberg, In verlegung Levini Hulsij,* 1602. 4to, pp. (2), 126. 2 Maps and 13 Plates. + Editio Secunda. *Franckfurt, In verlegung Levini Hulsii.* 1605. 4to, Title, pp. 118. 15 Maps and Plates. + Editio Tertia. [*Ibid.*] 1615. 4to.

III. Warhafftige Relation. | Der dreyen newen vner- | hörten, seltzamen Schiffart, so die Hol- | ländischen vnd Seeländischen Schiff gegen Mitternacht, | drey Jar nach einander, als Anno 1594, 1595, vnd 1596, verricht. | Wie sie Nortvvegen, Lappiam, Biarmiam, vnd Russiam, oder Mos- | coviam (vorhabens ins Königreich Cathay vnd China | zukommen) vmbsegelt haben. | Als auch wie sie das Fretum Nassoviæ, Waygats, No- | vum Semblam, vnd das Land vnter dem 80. Gradu latitud. So man ver- | meint das Groenland sey, gefunden: vnd was für gefahr, wegen der | erschröcklichen Bern, Meerwunder, vnd dem Eysz, sie auszgestanden. | Erstlich in Niderländischer sprach beschrieben, durch Gerhart de Ver. so selb- | sten die letzten zwo Reysen hat helffen verrichten, jetz aber ins Hochteutsch | gebracht, Durch. | Levinum Hulsium. *Noribergæ, Impensis L. Hulsij. Anno* M.D.XCVIII. 4to, pp. (16), 146. 34 Plates and Maps. + Secunda editio. *Nürnberg. Impensis Levini Hulsii.* M.DCII. 4to, pp. (18), 121. 34 Maps and Plates, slightly altered from the first edition. + Tertia editio. *Gedruckt zu Franckfurt am Mayn, bey Erasmo Kempffern. In Verlegung Leuini Hulsij Wittibe. Im Jahr* 1612. 4to, pp. (16), 95. 33 Maps and Plates. + Quarta Editio. *Gedruckt zu Franckfort am Mayn. In Verlegung Christoff le Blon. Im Jahr* 1660. 4to, pp. (16), 95. 32 Plates and Woodcut. 33655

IV. Vierte Schiffart. | Warhafftige Historien | Einer Wunderbaren | Schiffart, welche Ulrich Schmidel von Straubing, | von Anno 1534, bisz 1554 in American oder Newenwelt, | bey Brasilia vnd Rio della Plata gethan. Was er in diesen Neuntzehn | Jahren auszgestanden, vnd was für seltzame Wunderbare Länder vnd | Leut er gesehen: | durch ermelten Schmidel selbs beschrieben, An jetzt a- | ber an Tag geben mit Verbesserung vnd Corrigierung der Stätt, | Länder vnd Flüsz namen, deszgleichen mit einer nothwendi- | gen Landtaffel, Figuren, vnd anderer mehr | Erklerung, gezieret. | Durch. | Levinum Hvlsivm. | *Noribergae, | Impensis Levini Hulsij* 1599. 4to, pp. (9), 103. 17 Maps and Plates. + Editio Secvnda. *Noribergæ. Impensis Levini Hulsij. Anno* 1602. 4to, pp. (9), 103. 17 Maps and Plates. + Editio tertia. *Gedruckt zu Franckfurt am Mayn, bey Erasmo Kempffern, In Verlegung Leuini Hulsii Wittibe. Im Jahr* 1612. 4to, pp. 104. 17 Maps and Plates. 33656

The following is a Latin translation:

Vera historia, | Admirandæ cvivs- | dam nauigationis, quam Hul- | dericus Schmidel, Straubingensis, ab Anno 1534. usque ad annum 1554. in Americam vel nouum | Mundum, iuxta Brasiliam

& Rio della Plata, confecit. Quid | per hosce annos 19. sustinuerit, quam varias & quam mirandas | regiones ac homines viderit. Ab ipso Schmidelio Germanice, | descripta: Nunc vero, emendatis & correctis Vrbium, Regio- | num & Fluminum nominibus, Adiecta etiam tabula | Geographica, figuris & alijs notationi- | bus quibusdam in hanc for- | mam reducta. | *Noribergæ: Impensis Levina Hulsij.* 1599. 4to, pp. 101. 17 Maps and Plates. 33657

Brunet remarks that this translation is preferable to that which is given in the Seventh Part of the "Grands Voyages" of De Bry.

V. Kurtze Wunderbare Beschreibung. | Desz Goldreichen Konig- | reichs Guianæ in America, oder newen Welt, vnter der | Linea AEquinoctiali gelegen: So newlich Anno 1594, 1595, | vnnd 1596, von dem Wolgebornen Herrn, Hernn Walthero Ra- | legh einem Englischen Ritter, besucht worden: Erstlich ausz befehl seiner | Gnaden in zweyen Büchlein beschrieben, darausz Iodocus Hondius, ein | schöne Land Taffel, mit einer Niderländischen erklärung gemacht, | Jetzt aber ins Hochteutsch gebracht, vnd ausz vnter- | schietlichen Authoribus erkläret. | Durch | Levinum Hulsium. | *Noribergæ, impensis Levini Hvlsii,* MDXCIX. 4to, pp. (5), 16, (1). Map and 6 Plates. + [Second Edition.] *Noribergæ, Impensis Levini Hvlsii.* M.DCI. 4to, pp. (5), 17, (1). Map and 6 Plates. + [Third Edition.] *Noribergæ, Typis Christophori Lochneri, Impensis Levini Hulsii.* CIↃ IↃ CIII. 4to, pp. (5), 17, (1). 6 Plates. + [Fourth Edition.] *Gedruckt Franckfurt am Mayn, bey Erasmo Kempffern, In verlegung Leuini Hulsij Wittibe. Im Jahr* 1612. 4to, pp. (5), 17, (1). Map and 6 Plates. + [Fifth Edition. *Ibid.*] 33658

Asher calls our second edition the first, and Brunet makes our third the second—all are rare—the second and fifth especially so. The Lenox Library contains a copy of the second edition in which pp. 12 to 17 are evidently reprinted. The following is a Latin edition:

Brevis et admiranda descriptio | regni Guianæ, avri | abvndantissimi, in America, | seu Novo Orbe sub linea equinoctilia | siti: Quod nuper admodum, annis nimirum | 1594, 1595, & 1596. | Per Generosum Dominum, Dn. Gvalthurvm Ralegh eqvi- | tem Anglum, detectum est: paulò post jussu ejus | duobus libellis comprehensa: | Ex quibus Iodocvs Hondivs tabvlam geo- | graphicam adornavit, addita explicatione | Belgico sermone scripta: | Nunc verò in Latinum sermonem translata, & ex variis | authoribus hinc inde declarata. | *Noribergae, | Impensis Levini Hulsii* D.M.XCIX [*sic*]. 4to, pp. (6), 13. 5 Plates. 33659

VI. Sechste Theil, | Kurtze Warhafftige | Relation vnd beschreibung der Wun- | derbarsten vier Schiffarten, so jemals verricht | worden. Als nemlich: | Ferdinandi Magellani Portugalesers, mit Sebastiano de Cano. | Francisci Draconis Engeländers. | Thomæ Candisch Engeländers. | Oliuarij von Noort, Niderländers. | So alle vier vmb den gantzen Erdtkreisz gesegelt, auz vnterschte- | denen authoribus vnd sprachen zusamen getragen, vnd mit nötigen Landt | Charten feinen Figuren vnd nützlichen erklerungen geziert, | vnd verfertiget. Durch, | Levinum Hulsium. | *Noriberge, | Impensis collectoris,* M.DCIII. [Colophon, dated CIↃ IↃ CII.] 4to, pp. (6), 53. 5 Maps, 9 Plates. + [Second Edition.] *Francofvrti, Impensis Hvlsianis.* M.DCXVIII. 4to, pp. (6), 53. 5 Maps, 9 Plates. + [Third Edition.] *Getruckt zu Franckfurt bey Hartmanno Paltherus in Verlegung der Hulsischen Im Jahr* 1626. 4to, pp. (6), 53. 5 Maps, 9 Plates. 33660

VII. Siebende Schiffahrt | In das Goldreich Ko- | nigreich Guineam ... . An Tag geben durch | Levinvm Hvlsivm. | *Getruckt zu Franckfurt am Mayn, durch Wolffgang | Richtern, in Verlegung Levini Hulsii.* | *Im Jahr* M.DCIII. 4to, pp. (6), 228. Map and 18 Plates. + [Second Edition.] *Getruckt zu Franckfurt am Mayn, durch Wolffgang Richtern, in Verlegung Levini Hvlsii Erben, Im Jahr* M.DC.VI. 4to, pp. (6), 228. Map and 18 Plates. + [Third Edition.] *Gedruckt zu Franckfurt am Mayn, durch Egenolff Emmeln, in Verlegung Levini Hvlsii Erben, Im Jahr* M.DC.XXIV. 4to, pp. (2), 232. Map and 18 Plates. 33661

VIII. Achte Schiffart. | Kurtze Beschreibung, | was sich mit den Holländern vnd Seelän- | dern, ... zugetra- | gen, ... durch | Levinum Hvlsivm. | *Franckfurt bey Wolffgang Richtern, in Verlegung | desz Collectoris. Anno* M.DCV. 4to, pp. 58. 2 Maps and 5 Plates. + [Second Edition.] *Gedruckt zu Franckfurt am Mayn, durch Matthis Beckern: in Verlegung Leuini Hulsij Wittib, im Jahr* M.DC.VIII. 4to, pp. 56. 2 Maps, 5 Plates. + [Third Edition.] *Franckfurt am Mayn, In Verlegung Christophori le Blon.* M.DC.XI. 4to, pp. 56. 7 Maps, 5 Plates. 33662

IX. Neundte Schiffart, | Das is: | Gründtliche Erklärung, | ... | *Gedruckt zu Franckfurt am Mayn, bey Wolffgang Richtern, | in Verlegung Levini Hulsii seligen Witteben.* | M.DC.VI. 4to, pp. 51. Map and 4 Plates. + [Second Edition.] *Getruckt Franckfurt am Mayn, bey Erasmo Kempffern, In verlegung Levini Hvlsii, seligen Wittiben.* M. DC. XII. 4to, pp. 48. Map and 4 Plates. 33663

X. Zehende | Schiffahrt oder Reyse | ... | *Gedruckt zu Franckfurt am Mayn, durch Matthis | Beckern: in Verlegung Leuini Hulsij | Wittib, im Jahr.* | M.DC.VIII. 4to, pp. 52. Map and 4 Plates. + [Second Edition.] *Gedruckt zu Franckfurt am Mayn, durch Erasmo Kempffern: in Verlegung Leuini Hulsij Wittib, im Jahr.* M.DC.XIII. 4to, pp. 52. Map and 4 Plates. 33664

XI. Eylffte Schiffart, | Oder | Kurtze Beschreibung | einer Reyse, ... *Gedruckt zu Franckfurt am Mayn, bey Erasmo Kempffern, | In Verlegung Leuini Hulsii Wittibe. | Im Jahr* 1612. 4to, pp. 102. Map and 7 Plates. + [Second Edition.] *Gedruckt zu Franckfurt am Mayn, bey Hartmanno Palthenio, In Verlegung der Hulsischen. Anno* M. DC. XXIII. 4to, pp. 96. Map and 7 Plates. + Eylffter Schiffart ander Theil ... *Gedruckt zu Franckfurt am Mayn, bey Erasmo Kempfferr, In Verlegung Leuini Hvlsii seligen Wittiben.* | M. DC. XIII. 4to, pp. 67. 4 Plates. 33665

XII. Zwolffte Schiffahrt | oder | Kurtze Beschreibung | der Newen Schiffahrt gegen Nord Osten, | vber die Amerische Inseln in Chinam vnd Japponiam, | von einem Engellender Heinrich Hudson newlich erfunden, Bene- | ben einen Discursz an Ihr Kön. Maj. in Spanien, wegen desz fünfften | Theils der Welt, Terra Australis incognita genandt, Auch | kurtze Beschreibung der Länder der Samojeden vnd | Tingoesen in der Tartarey gelegen. | In Hochteutscher Sprach beschrieben durch | M. Gothardum Arthusen von Dantzig. | *Gedruckt zu Oppenheim, bey Hieronymo Gallern, | In Verlegung Levini Hulsii Wittib.* | M DCXIV. 4to, pp. (2), 67. [Followed by:] Folgen etliche | Mappen oder Land- | Taffeln, vnd Kupfferstück, darin die | Gelegenheit der Landtschafften, davon in dieser | obgesetzten Schiffart Meldung geschehen, eigentlich | abgebildet vnd für Augen gestellet | werden. | In Kupffer gestochen vnd an Tag gegeben. | Durch | Johann-Theodor de Bry. | [*Ibid.*] *Im Jahr* 1614. 3 Maps, 4 Plates. + [Second Edition. *Ibid.*] MDCXXVII. 4to, pp. (2), 67. 3 Maps, 4 Plates.

XIII. Dreysehente Schiffart. *See our* Vol. VIII., No. 30122.

Another edition was published the same year in which the first word is "Dreyzehende," in other respects there are trifling variations. De Bry's version does not include the three interesting letters with which this concludes.

XIV. Viertzehende Schiffart, | Oder | Gründliche vnd warhaffte | Beschreibung desz Neuwen Engellandts, | einer Landschafft in Nordt Indien, eines Theils in Ame- | rica, vnter dem Capitein Johann Schmidt, Rittern, Admiral | derselben Landtschafft, auch dem glücklichen Fortgang so er mit | Sechs Schiffen deren Orts

gehabt. | Beneben einem kurtzen Discursz, wie es jhme auff der | Reise ergangen, von den Frantzosen gefangen, vnd der Gefäng- | nusz erlediget, vnnd wie es jtzo daselbst beschaffen, alles | nechst abgelauffenen 1616 Jahrs. | Durch einen Liebhaber der Historien ausz dem Eng- | lischen in Hoch Teutsch versetzt. | *Gedruckt zu Franckfurt am Mayn. In verlegung der Hülsischen.* | *Im Jahr Christi* 1617. 4to, pp. (8), 62. Map and Plate. + [Second Edition.] *Gedruckt zu Franckfurt am Mayn, In Verlegung Leuini Hvlsii Erben. Im Jahr* 1628. 4to, pp. (8), 62. Map and Plate. 33667

XV. Fünffzehende Schiffart. | Warhafftiger vnd zu- | vor nie erhörter Bericht ... . *Gedruckt zu Hanaw in verlegung der Hulsischen.* | *Anno* M.DC.XVII. 4to, pp. 75. + [Second Edition.] *Gedruckt zu Franckfurt in verlegung Christophel le Blon. Anno* M. DC. XLVIII. 4to, pp. 75. 33668

XVI. Die sechtzehende Schifffahrt. | Journal, | oder Beschreibung der wun- | derbaren Reise Wilhelm Schouten ausz Hollandt, im Jahr 1615. | 16 vnd 17. | Darinnen er eine neuwe Durchfahrt neben dem | Freto Magellanico, welche biszhero noch vnbekannt | gewesen, in die Suyd See entdeckt. | Beneben erzehlung, was für Land, Insuln, Leut, allda | gefunden, vnd sich sonsten auff der Reise in der | Suyd See zugetragen. | Mit schönen Land Charten, vnd Kupfferstücken erklärt. | *Gedruckt zu Franckfurt am Mayn, durch Nicolaum | Hoffmann, sumptibus Hulsianis.* | *Im Jar* M.DC.XIX. 4to, pp. 90. 4 Maps and 5 Plates. 33669

XVII. Die Siebenzehende Schiffart. | Das ist: | Eigentliche vnnd war- | haftige beschreibung, der wunderbahrē | Reiz vnd Schiffart, so durch Herr Georgio | von Spilbergen glücklichen | volbracht. | Beneben Erzehlung, was für Land- | schafften, Insuln Völcker vnd Nationen all- | da gefunden, vnd sich sonsten auff der | Reisz denckwürdiges zu- | getragen. | Mit schönen Charten vnd Kupfferstücken | erklärt vnd für Augen gestelt. | *Gedruckt zu Franckfurt am Mayn, durch Johan | Hofern, sumptibus Hulsianis.* | *Im Jahr,* M.DC.XX. 4to, pp. 95. 8 Plates. 33670

XVIII. Achtzehender Theil der | Newen Welt, | Das ist: | Gründlicke volkommene Entdeckung aller der | West Indianischen Landschafften, Insuln vnd Königreichen, | Secusten, fliessenden vnd stehenden Wassern, Port vnd Anlendungen, Ge- | bürgen, Grentzen, vnd Ausztheilung der Provincien, sampt eygentlicher Beschreibung der Stät- | te Flecken vnd Dörffer, Herrschafft vnd Regierung, Bistummen, Stifft vnd Clöster, wie

starck | dieselben an Inwohnern, wie reich an Einkommen, was jedes Orts Gewerb, Handthierung vnd Bequemlichkeiten. Fruchtbarkeit vnd Nutzung, alles nach jetziger Gestalt vnd Be- | schaffenheit von newem entdecket vnd beschrieben. | Durch | Antonium de Herrera, Königlichē bestellten Historien schreiber der Reiche | Castilien vnd Indien, Ausz der Hispanischen Sprach in die Teutsche vbergesetzet. | etc. *Gedruckt zu Franckfurt am Mayn, durch Johann Friederich Weissen, | in Verlegung der Hulsischen. Anno* 1623. 4to, pp. (6), 256. 14 Maps. 33671

XIX. Die Neuntzehende Schiffarth, | Inhaltende, | Fünff Schiffarthen ... . *Gedruckt zu Franckfurt am Mayn, in verlegung der Hulsischen,* | *Bey Hartmanno Palthenio.* | *Anno Christi Iesu* M. DC.-XXVI. 4to, pp. 105. 7 Plates. 33672

XX. Zwantzigste Schifffahrt, | oder | Gründliche vnd sattsa- | me Beschreibung desz Newen En- | gellands: Wie auch | Auszführliche Erzehlung von Beschaf- | fenheit der Landtschafft Virginia, vnd der Insel Bar- | muda, deren man biszhero schlechte vnnd vnvollkommene | Wissenschafft gehabt, an jetzo aber durch dero | Landt erfahrne Leuht, völliglich an | Tag gegeben. | *Gedruckt zu Franckfurt am Mayn, bey Wolffgang | Hoffmann, In Verlegung der Hulsischen Erben. In Jar.* 1629. 4to, pp. 116. Map, 4 Plates.

XXI. Die ein vnd zwantzigste Schifffahrt, | oder Gründliche, vnd vmb- | ständliche fernere Beschreibung der voll- | kommesten Landtschafft Brasilien, Americæ, vnd | deroselben Innwohner vnd Sitten, mit sampt einem angehenck- | ten Verlauff, wie ein Engellendischer Capiteyn, Parcket genant, | S. Vincentem, vnd den Portum Bellum erobert. | Item: | Was Gestalt, der schöne Portus vnd Hafe Totos los Sanctos, | sampt der Statt Salvator in Anno 1624, von der Holländern ge- | wunnen, vnd hernach wider verlassen worden. | Item: | Ein Vollkömlicher Discurs, wie die Spanische Silber-Flotta in der In- | sul Cuba, in der Baia Matanca in Anno 1628, von dem Manhafften Peter Peters | Heyn, vnd Admiral Henrich Cornelius Loncq erobert vnd glück- | lich in Hollandt eingebracht worden. | *Getruckt zu Franckfurt am Mayn, bey Wolffgang Hoffmann,* | *in Verlegung der Hulsischen Erben* 1629. 4to, pp. 131. Map, 3 Plates and Portrait. 33674

XXII. Die Zwey vnd Zwäntzigste Schiffart | Das ist | Historische Eygentliche | Beschreibung der Gewaltigen, Mächtigen | Schiffahrt, so vnder dem Admiral Iacob l'Hermite Im | 1623, 1624, 1625 vnd 1626. Jahr vmb die | gantzen Welt beschehen. | Darinn | Auszführlichen von Adolph Deckern von Straszburg, | der dieser

Reysz eygner Person beygewohnt, Erzehlt wird, was sich bey | solcher von tag zu tag Merckwürdiges zugetragen vnd vorgangen. | Mit vnderschiedlichen Kupfferstücken | gezieret. | *Gedruckt zu Franckfurt am Mayn, In verlegung der | Hulsischen Erben.* | *Anno* M.DC.XXX. 4to, pp. 114 (pp. 8 to 17 are omitted). Map and 7 Plates. 33675

XXIII. Die drey vnd zwantzigste Schiffahrt, | ... *Gedruckt zu Franckfurt am Mayn, bey Wolffgang | Hoffmann. In Verlegung Friderici Hulsii.* | *Anno* 1632. 4to, pp. (8), 222. 8 Maps and Plates.

Reissued with a different title the same year.

XXIV. Die Vier vnd zwantzigste | Schiffahrt, | ... *Gedruckt zu Franckfurt am Mayn, bey Philippo Fivet,* | *Im Jahr* 1648. 4to, pp. (12), 81. Portrait of Bontekuhe and 9 Plates. 33677

XXV. Die fünff vnd zweyntzigste Schifffahrt, | Nach dem Königreich Chili in West-Indien, | Verrichtet durch Herrn Heinrich Brawern, | vnd Herrn Elias Herckemann, im Jahr | 1642 vnnd 1643. | Sambt einer Beschreibung der zweyen Insulen | Formosa vnd Japan. | Mit zugehörigen Kupffer-Taffeln. | *Franckfurt am Mayn,* | *In Verlegung Christophel Le Blon, im Jahr* | M.DC.XLIX. 4to, pp. (10), 62. 3 Maps and Plate. 33678

Die XXVI. Schiff-Fahrt: | Beschreibung einer | Hochst-mühseligen vnd gantz gefährlichen | Reyse, durch den See-verständigen Capitain, Herrn | Johann Müncken, inn Jahren 1619, vnd | 1620, verrichtet. | Nach dem er von Weyland dem Durchleuchtigsten | Fürsten vnd Herrn Herrn Christiano IV, König in Dennemark, Nor- | wegen, &c. befelcht worden mit zweyen Schiffen nach dem Freto oder der | Enge Hudsons zu segeln, vmb zu versuchen, ob nicht deren Gegend eine Enge, so Groenland von America abscheide, vnd also eine | Durchfahrt nach Ost-Indien zu | finden: | Sampt vorhergehender gar deutlichen Erläuterung desz Alten | vnd Newen Groenlands, zu gegenwärtiger Schiff-Fahrts-Beschrei- | bung insonderheit dienlich. | *Frcnkfurt am Mayn,* | *Bey Christophoro Le Blon.* | MDCL. 4to, pp. (2), 63. Map and 10 Plates. 33679

Humane Society. History of the Humane Society of Massachusetts. With ... List of Premiums ... . *Boston: Samuel N. Dickinson, Printer.* 1845. 8vo, pp. 95, (1), Appendix, 44. BA.

The Institution of the Humane Society of the Commonwealth of Massachusetts. With the Rules ... . *Boston.* 1788. 8vo, pp. 27. BA. + [Another Edition. n. d.] 12mo, pp. 15. 33681

Also: Order of Performances at the Anniversary, June 11, 1811. *Boston.* 1811. 8vo. Continued.—Proceedings, &c., 1805. [n. d.] 8vo.—A Statement of Premiums awarded by the Trustees ... from July 1817, to April 1829; Extracts from ... Correspondence ... . With an Appendix. *Boston: Freeman & Bolles, Print.* 1829. 8vo, pp. 60. B., BA., H.

Humanitas, *pseudon.* A New and Interesting View of Slavery. By Humanitas. ... *Baltimore.* 1820. 8vo, pp. 72. 33682

Humanitas. Reflections on Slavery; with Recent Evidence of its Inhumanity, Occasioned by the Melancholy Death of Romain, A French Negro. By Humanitas. *Philadelphia: Printed ... by R. Cochran.* 1803. 8vo, pp. 40. Plate. S. 33683

Humard (——). The True Way to Abolish Slavery. *London: W. & F. G. Cash.* [1855.] 8vo, pp. 8. 33684

Humason (W. L.) From the Atlantic Surf to the Golden Gate. First Trip on the Great Pacific Railroad. Two Days and Nights Among the Mormons, with Scenes and Incidents, By W. L. Humason. *Hartford: Press of Wm. C. Hutchings.* 1869. 8vo, pp. 56. B. 33685

Humble Address of the House of Lords, to the King, March 23, 1714–15. With His Majesty's most Gracious Answer. *Boston.* 1715. Folio, 1 l. 33686

The Humble Address of the People of Great Britain to His Majesty. *London.* 1763. 8vo. 33687

Included in J. R. Smith's Catalogue of Americana.

Humble Address. *See* Carolina, Vol. III., No. 10972.

The | Humble Address | of the | Publicans | of | New-England, | To which King you please. | With Some | Remarks | Upon it. | A Publican is a Creature that lives upon the | Common-wealth. | *London: Printed in the Year,* 1691. Sm. 4to, pp. 35. BA., M.

A pamphlet of extreme rarity. It is a parody on the "Humble Address of the Gentry."

The Humble Address of the Right Hon. the Lords Spiritual and Temporal, presented to His Majesty on Friday, October 27, 1775. With His Majesty's most gracious Answer. *London: Charles Eyre and William Strahan.* 1775. Folio, pp. 4. 33689

The Humble Address of the Right Honourable the Lords Spiritual and Temporal in Parliament assembled, presented to His Majesty, October 27, 1775. With His Majesty's most gracious Answer. *London: Charles Eyre.* 1775. Folio, pp. 18.

Relates to the disaffection in the American colonies.

An Humble Address to every Christian, of every Nation and Denomination of People under Heaven, showing an Effectual Means to Prevent Wars among all Nations of the Earth, and to maintain an Everlasting Union in Families, Societies, Churches, Towns, States, and in all the Kingdoms of this Lower World. *Newark, N. J.* MDCCXCIII. 8vo, pp. 68. 33691

An Humble Address to the King, concerning the Dearness of Provisions, and Emigrations; ... and some Proposals to Remedy the Same. *London: J. Wilkie.* 1775. 8vo. 33692

The Humble Address to the Right Hon. the Lords Spiritual and Temporal in Parliament assembled, presented to his Majesty December 1, 1774. With His Majesty's Most Gracious Answer. *London: Charles Eyre and William Strahan.* MDCCLXXIV. Folio, pp. 4. 33693

"We think it an indispensable Duty to declare, on this Occasion, an Abhorrence an' Detestation of the daring Spirit of Resistance and Disobedience to the Laws, which so strongly prevails in the Province of the Massachusetts Bay."—*Extract.*

An Humble Apology for the Quakers, Addressed to Great and Small. Occasioned By certain gross Abuses and Imperfect Vindications Of that People, relative to the late Public Fast. To which are added Observations on a New Pamphlet, intituled A Brief View of the Conduct of Pennsylvania For the Year 1755. So far as to shew the real Spirit and Design, of that Angry Writer. And also A much Fairer Method pointed out, Than That contained in the Brief State of Pennsylvania, to prevent the Incroachments of the French, and restore Quiet to the Province. *Stanley Crowder, and Henry Woodgate, London.* MDCCLVI. 12mo, pp. 38, (1). 33694

See "M. Rev.," XIV. 588.

A Humble Attempt. *See* [Franklin (W.)], No. 25637.

An Humble Enquiry. *See* [Zubly (J. J.)]

The Humble Petition and Address of the General Court sitting at Boston, New England, unto the High and Mighty Prince Charles The Second. *Cambridge: Printed by S. Green.* 1660. 4to, pp. 8. 33695

Extremely rare, if not unique.

The | Humble | Petition | and | Address | Of the General Court Sitting at | Boston in New-England, | unto | The High and Mighty | Prince | Charles | The Second. | And presented unto His Most-

Gracious | Majesty Feb. 11, 1660. | [*London:*] *Printed in the Year* 1660. Sm. 4to, pp. 8. J.C.B. 33696

A most rare book relating to the early history of New England. Signed "John Endecot Govr. In the Name, and with the Consent of the General Court." Reprinted in the Hutchinson "Collection of Papers," p. 325.

The Humble Petition of Proprietors of Plantations in Nevis and St. Christophers; ... *London.* 1706. Folio, 1 l. 33697

Relates to the devastations of the French; and the pitiable condition of the inhabitants.

The Humble Representation. *See* Darien, No. 18557.

The Humble Request of his Majesties Loyal Subjects, the Governour and the Company lately gone for New England, to the rest of the Brethren in, and of the Church of England for the obtaining of their prayers, and the Removal of Suspicions and Misconstructions of their Intentions. With the Letter of Thomas Dudley to the Countess of Lincoln, dated March 12, 1630, giving an account of the Settlement in Boston. [1659.] 16mo. M., W. 33698

An extremely rare piece.

The Humble Submission of several Kings, Princes, Generals, &c. to the Crown of England, lately presented to Sir Nath. Johnson, the present Governor of Carolina under her Majesty Queen Ann. *London.* 1707. Folio. BM. 33699

Humboldt (Friedrich H. A. von). Analyse raisonnée de la carte de l'ile de Cuba, par A. De Humboldt. ... [*Paris.* 1826?] 8vo, pp. 38. H. 33700

Humboldt. Alexander von Humboldt on two Attempts to Ascend the Chimborazo. Translated from the German by Dr. Barry. *London.* 1837. 8vo. 33701

Humboldt. Alexander von Humboldt's Ansichten der Natur, mit wissenschaftlichen Erläuterungen. Vol. I. *Tübingen: J. G. Cotta.* 1808. 16mo, pp. viii, 334. C. 33702

No more published.

Humboldt. Ansichten der Natur. Mit wissenschaftlichen Erläuterungen von Alexander von Humboldt. ... Dritte verbesserte und vermehrte Auflage. *Stuttgart: J. G. Cotta.* 1849. 2 vols., 8vo, pp. xviii, 362; (4), 407. BA., H. + *Stuttgart und Augsburg.* 1860. 2 vols., 8vo, pp. x, 262; (2), 294. B. 33703

Humboldt. Tableaux de la Nature, ou considérations sur les déserts, sur la physionomie des végétaux, sur les cataractes de l'Orénoque, sur la structure et l'action des volcans dans les différentes régions de la terre. Par A. de Humboldt, traduits de l'Allemand par J. B. B. Eyries. *Paris, Chez F. Schoell* ... 1808. 2 vols., 12mo, pp. (2), x, 240; (2), 240. H. + *Paris.* 1828. 2 vols., 8vo, pp. xvi, 270; (4), 250. H. + Dernière édition ... traduits par Ferd. Hoefer. *Paris: Firmin Didot Frères.* 1850. 2 vols., 8vo, pp. (4), iii, 312, (1); (4), 363, (1). Map. H.

See "M. Rev.," LIX. 473.

Humboldt. Tableaux de la nature, nouvelle édition avec changements et additions importantes, et accompagnée de notes de l'auteur; traduit sous sa direction par Ch. Galusky. *Paris.* 1852. 2 vols., 12mo. 7 Maps. 33705

Humboldt. Tableaux de la nature; traduction de M. Ch. Galuski, le seule approuvée et surveillée par Humboldt. Nouvelle édition, augmentée de notes biographiques et ornée de planches et de cartes. *Paris: Morgand.* 1865. 8vo. 33706

Humboldt. Aspects of Nature, in different Lands and different Climates; with Scientific Elucidations. By Alexander von Humboldt. Translated by Mrs. Sabine. *London: Longman.* 1849. 2 vols., post 8vo, pp. xv, (6), 301; (4), 347. BA. + *Philadelphia: Lea & Blanchard.* 1849. 12mo, pp. ix, 475. + [*Ibid.*] 1850. 33707

Humboldt. Views of Nature: or Contemplations on the Sublime Phenomena of Creation; with Scientific Illustrations. By Alexander von Humboldt. Translated from the German by E. C. Otté, and Henry G. Bohn. ... *London: Henry G. Bohn.* 1850. Post 8vo, pp. xxx, xi–xiv, (1), 452. Plate. B., BA., C.

Humboldt. Correspondance scientifique et littéraire; recueillie, publiée, et précédée d'une notice et d'une introduction, par M. de La Roquette; suivie de la biographie des correspondants de Humboldt, ... *Paris: E. Ducrocq.* 1865. 8vo, pp. xliv, 466, (4). 2 Plates. C. 33709

Humboldt. De Distributione Geographica Plantarum secundum cœli temperiem et altitudinem montium Prolegomena Auctore Alexandro de Humboldt. ... *Lutetiæ Parisiorum.* M. DCCC.-XVII. 16mo, pp. (6), 249, (4). Plate. A., B., P. 33710

Humboldt. Essai Géognostique sur le Gisement des Roches dans les deux Hémispheres, Par Alexandre de Humboldt. *Paris: Chez F. G. Levrault.* 1823. 8vo, pp. viii, 379. B., P. + *Paris.* 1826. 8vo. S. 33711

Humboldt. A Geognostical Essay on the Superposition of Rocks, in both Hemispheres. By Alexander de Humboldt. Translated from the original French. *London.* 1823. 8vo. C.

Humboldt. Essai Politique sur le Royaume de la Nouvelle-Espagne. Par Al. de Humboldt. *A Paris, Chez F. Schoell,* ... 1811. 5 vols., 8vo, pp. (10), 456; (4), 522, Tableau; (4), 419, (1); (4), 564, (1), Plate; (4), 350. Map. B. + Deuxième édition. *Paris: Renouard.* 1825–27. 4 vols., 8vo, pp. xviii, 471; 500; 479; 380. Map and Plan. + *Paris.* 1825. 4 vols., 8vo. 33713

See "Edinburgh Review," XVI. 62; XIX. 164. For an extensive notice of the work *see* "El Español," Tom. I., No. IV., 30 Julio, 1810, pp. 243–304.

Humboldt. Minerva. Ensayo politico sobre el reyno de Nueva-España, sacado del que publicó en Francés Alexandro de Humboldt. Por D. P[edro] M[aria] de O[live]. *Madrid: Por Ibarra, ... en la imprenta de Nuñez.* MDCCCXVIII. 2 vols., 8vo, pp. 448; 462, (2). B. 33714

Humboldt. Political Essay on the Kingdom of New Spain. Containing Researches relative to the Geography of Mexico, the Extent of its Surface and its political Divisions into Intendancies, the physical Aspect of the Country, the Population, the State of Agriculture and Manufacturing and Commercial Industry, the Canals projected between the South Sea and Atlantic Ocean, the Crown Revenues, the Quantity of the precious Metals which have flowed from Mexico into Europe and Asia, since the Discovery of the New Continent, and the Military Defence of New Spain. By Alexander de Humboldt. With Physical Sections and Maps, founded on Astronomical Observations, and Trigonometrical and Barometrical Measurements. Translated from the Original French, By John Black. *London: Longman & Co.* 1811. 4 vols., 8vo, pp. xvii, (2), cxlv, 289, (1); (2), 531, (1); (6), 493, (1); (2), 374, Index, (99). Atlas, 4to. + *New York: I. Riley.* 1811. 2 vols., 8vo, pp. xii, cxii, 221; 377 [no more published]. + Second Edition. *London.* 1814 4 vols., 8vo. Atlas. + Third Edition. [*Ibid.*] 1822. 33715

The London editions are all alike. *See* "M. Rev.," LXIX. 34.

Humboldt. An Abridgment of Humboldt's Statistical Essay on New Spain, being a Geographical, Philosophical, and Political Account of the Kingdom of Mexico, or the Vice-Royalty of Mexico, and the internal Provinces, subject to the Commandant, or Governor General, residing at Chihuahua. By a Citizen of Maryland. *Baltimore: Wane and O. Reilly.* 1813. 8vo, pp. 41.

Humboldt. Versuch über den politischen Zustand des Königreichs Neu-Spanien ... Von Friedrich Alexander von Humboldt. *Tübingen: J. G. Cotta.* 1809–1814. 5 vols., 8vo, pp. (8), clxviii, viii, 205; (2), 278; (2), 180; (2), 430; (2), 178, (1). 3 Maps. H. 33717

Humboldt. Ensayo Politico sobre ... la Nueva-España. Por Alej. de Humboldt; Traducido al Español por Don Vincente Gonzalez Arnao ... . *Paris: En casa de Rosa.* 1822. 5 vols., 8vo, pp. (8), 460; (4), 470; (4), 436, (1); (4), 415. 3 Plates, Map. B. + *Paris: J. Renouard.* 1827. 5 vols., 8vo. 6 Plates. + Tercia edicion. *Paris.* 1836. 5 vols., 8vo. Maps, and Plates. 33718

Humboldt. Essai Politique sur l'Ile de Cuba, par Alexandre de Humboldt. Avec une carte et un Supplément qui renferme des Considérations sur la Population, la richesse Territoriale et le Commerce de l'archipel des Antilles et de Colombia. *Paris: Gide fils.* 1826. 2 vols., 8vo, pp. xlvi, 364, Map; 408. A., H.

Humboldt. Ensayo Politico sobre la Isla de Cuba; por el Baron A. de Humboldt. Con un Mapa. Obra traducida al Castellano par D. J. B. de V. y M. *Paris: Jules Renouard.* 1827. 12mo, pp. (2), xxxii, 361, (2). Map. B., H. + Obra traducida al Castellano por D. José Lopéz de Bustamente. Nueva edicion. *Paris: Lecointe y Lasserre.* 1840. 8vo, pp. (2), xxxii, 361, (2). Map. 33720

Humboldt. The Island of Cuba. By Alexander von Humboldt. Translated from the Spanish, with Notes and a preliminary Essay by J. S. Thrasher. *New York: Derby & Jackson.* 1856. 12mo, pp. 397. Map. B., BA., S. 33721

Remarkable for having omitted Humboldt's Views on Slavery, of which the author publicly and deservedly complained.

Humboldt. Examen Critique de l'Histoire de la Géographie du Nouveau Continent et des Progrès de l'Astronomie Nautique aux quinzième et seizième siècles. Par Alexandre de Humboldt.

Paris: Librairie de Gide. 1836–39. 5 vols., 8vo, pp. xxvii, 362; 373; 407; 336; 263. 4 Maps. B., BA., H. 33722

A reprint of the text of the "Atlas Historique et Géographique" which accompanies Humboldt's Voyage, and all that was published in this form. "This noble work, which we consider the greatest monument ever erected to the early history of this continent, is, despite a few immaterial errors, a sure guide, which has proved to us an inexhaustible source of valuable suggestions. The bibliographical notes contained in the Examen are not, we confess, in keeping with the learned and profound dissertations which we can never cease to admire, but there is scarcely a page which does not throw a vivid light upon every question connected with the geography, discovery and history of America."—*Bibliotheca Americana Vetustissima.*

Humboldt. Histoire de la Géographie du Nouveau Continent et des Progrès de l'Astronomie Nautique aux quinzième et seizième siècles. *Paris.* [1839.] 2 vols., 8vo. 33723

Consists of the unsold sheets of the above, with a new title-page, and an introduction of four pages, but without the sections of the La Cosa chart, which, in this new issue, are replaced by two well-executed maps of this continent.

Humboldt. Kritische Untersuchungen über die historische Entwickelung der geographischen Kenntnisse von der neuen Welt, und die Fortschritte der nautischen Astronomie in dem 15ten und 16ten Jahrhundert. Von Alexander v. Humboldt. Aus dem Französischen übersetzt von Jul. Ludw. Ideler. *Berlin: Nicolai.* 1836–52. 3 vols., 8vo. C. + Neue mit einem vollständigen Namen- und Sachregister vermehrte Ausgabe. [*Ibid.*] 1852. 3 vols., 8vo, pp. 560, (2); 528; (2), 316. BA. 33724

One of the most important books of the famous author, giving a historical display of geographical knowledge in the New World, in the fifteenth and sixteenth centuries. This German translation has an index which is not in the original.

Humboldt. Kleinere Schriften. Von Alexander von Humboldt. Erster Band. Geognostische und physikalische Erinnerungen. Mit einem Atlas, enthaltend Umrisse von Vulkanen aus den Cordilleren von Quito und Mexico. *Stuttgart: J. G. Cotta.* 1853. 8vo, pp. (4), viii, 474, (1). 5 folded Plates. A., B., BA.

The Atlas forms a separate volume. Oblong folio. 12 Plates and 2 leaves.

Humboldt. Kosmos. Entwurf einer physischen Weltbeschreibung. Von Alexander von Humboldt. ... *Stuttgart: J. G. Cotta.* 1845–62. 5 vols., 8vo, pp. xvi, 493, (1); (2), 544, (1); (2), 644; (2), 649, (1); (2), 1297. BA., H. 33726

This, the greatest work of one of the greatest men of the nineteenth century, includes some articles on America. The editions in German, French, and English, are too numerous and too general for us to enumerate. For the Atlas to this work *see our* Vol. II., No. 8201. We content ourselves with remarking that it was stereotyped at *Philadelphia,* 1855, rl. 8vo; translated into Swedish, *Kjobenhavn,* 1847–48, 2 vols., 8vo; into Dutch, *Leiden,* 1846–58, 4 vols., 8vo; into Russian, by N. Froloff and M. Gussew,

Moscow, 1848–57, 4 vols., rl. 8vo; into Polish, by J. Baranowski, L. Zejszner, i H. Skrzynski, *Warszawa*, 1849–52, 2 vols., 8vo, Portrait; into Spanish, by Francisco Diaz Quintero, *Madrid*, 1851, 2 vols., 8vo; into Italian, by Giulio Vallini e V. Lazzari, *Venezia*, 1846–54. 8vo.

HUMBOLDT. Cosmos: Sketch of a Physical Description of the Universe. By Alexander von Humboldt. ... Translated under the superintendence of Col. Edward Sabine ... . *London: Longman* ... . 1846–1850. 4 vols., post 8vo: Vol. I. pp. (22), 357, cxxxviii; Vol. II. pp. vii, (1), 359, cxlii; Vol. III., Part I. pp. (4), ii, 214, (1), lxxviii; Vol. III., Part II. pp. (2), 215–457, lxxvii-clxii, xv; Vol. IV., Part I. pp. xiii, 516, clxxxiii, (1). BA.

Vol. IV. contains an article on the discovery of America by the Irish. It has been reprinted several times and in various forms. The translator was Mrs. Sabine, and it is claimed by the publishers that this was the only authorized translation.

HUMBOLDT. Κοσμος: a General Survey of the Physical Phenomena of the Universe. By Alexander von Humboldt. Translated by Augustin Prichard, M.D. ... *London: Hippolyte Baillière*. 1845–48. 2 vols., post 8vo, pp. xv, (4), 482; 534. BA. 33728

HUMBOLDT. Cosmos; a Sketch of a Physical Description of the Universe. By Alexander von Humboldt. Translated ... by E. C. Otté. ... *London: Henry G. Bohn*. 1849–58. 5 vols., post 8vo, pp. xvii, ix, 369, (3), 18; xxi, 370–742, (16); (6), 289, (8); xv, 291–601, 7, (1); viii, 500. BA. + *New-York: Harper & Brothers*. 1851–52. 5 vols., 12mo, pp. 375; 367; 219; 234; 462. B. 33729

In this edition the notes are placed beneath the text; Humboldt's analytical Summaries and the passages hitherto suppressed are included, and new and comprehensive indices are added. Mr. Bohn printed an elaborate notice of this edition, with some criticisms on Mrs. Sabine, in 12mo, pp. 16.

HUMBOLDT. Cosmos. Essai d'une description physique du monde; traduction de M. H. Faye ... et de M. Ch. Galuski ... . Édition mise dans un meilleur ordre, et augmentée d'une notice biographique sur Humboldt, avec des fragments inédits de sa correspondance. *Paris: Morgand*. 1864. 4 vols., 8vo, pp. lix, 2790. 33730

HUMBOLDT. Briefe über Alexander von Humboldt's Kosmos. Ein Commentar zu diesem Werke für gebildete Laien. ... Bearbeitet von Bernhard Cotta ... . *Leipzig*. 1848–60. 6 vols., 8vo. Supplement. + Dritte vermehrte Ausgabe. *Leipzig: T. O. Weigel*. 1855–59. 4 vols., 8vo, pp. xiv, 416, (2), Plates; (4), 482, Plates; viii, v, 468, 2 Maps, 2 Charts, 6 Plates; xiv, 419, (1), Plates. BA. 33731

HUMBOLDT. Life, Travels [etc.] *See* [Stoddard (R. H.)]

HUMBOLDT. Notes Statistiques, Physiques et Politiques sur l'Amérique Espagnole. [Extraites des Ouvrages du Baron de Humboldt et autres Voyageurs Modernes, sur ces Pays.] Traduit de Espagnole, par J. L. F. V. D. G. *Philadelphia*. 1812. 8vo. 33732

HUMBOLDT. Pétrifactions recueillies en Amérique par M. A. de Humboldt et Ch. de Genhardt, décrites par L. de Buch. *Berlin: Dümmler*. 1839. Folio. 2 Plates. 33733

HUMBOLDT. Pittoreske Ansichten der Cordilleren und Monumente americanischer Völker. *Tübingen*. 1810. Map.

HUMBOLDT. Prospect [zum] Tagebuch einer Reise vom Mississippi nach den Küsten der Südsee, von Baldwin Möllhausen. ... *Verlag von Hermann Mendelssohn in Leipzig*. 1857. 4to, pp. 11, (1). B. 33735

HUMBOLDT. Reis van Humboldt en Bonpland naar de Keerkringen, 1799–1804. Uittreksel uit hunne aanteeken van J. C. Delametherie. *Amsterdam*. 1805. 8vo. 33736

This Voyage to the Tropics is an abridged translation.

HUMBOLDT. Reis van Humboldt en Bonpland. Eerste gedeelte. Algemeene Natuurkunde en Historisch berigt der reis. Met Platen. *Te Haarlem, bij A. Loosjes*. 1808. 3 vols., 8vo. 33737

HUMBOLDT. Reise in die Aequinoctial-Gegenden des Neuen Continents, in den Jahren 1799, 1800, 1801, 1802, 1803 und 1804. Verfasst von Alexander von Humboldt und A. Bonplandt. Mit Kupfern. *Stuttgart und Tübingen: J. G. Cotta*. 1815–1829. 6 vols., 8vo. + Bearbeitet von G. A. Wimmer. *Wien: C. Gerold*. 1830. 4 vols., 16mo. C. + [*Ibid.*] 1844. + In deutscher Bearbeitung von Hermann Hauff. ... *Stuttgart: Cotta*. 1859–60. 4 vols., 8vo, pp. xiii, 403; (2), 416; (2), 403; (2), 444. Map. B. + *Stuttgart*. 1861 (?) 6 vols., 16mo, pp. xvi, 260; 300; 242; 293; 267; 396. Map. 33738

HUMBOLDT. Reise in die Aequinoctial-Gegenden des Neuen Continents und Reisen im Europäischen und Asiatischen Russland. Von H. Kletke. *Berlin*. 1858. 4 vols., 8vo. 33739

HUMBOLDT. Selections from the Works of the Baron von Humboldt, relating to the Climate, Inhabitants, Productions, and

Mines of Mexico. With Notes by John Taylor, Esq. *London: Longman*. 1824. 8vo, pp. (4), xxviii, (6), 310. Plate. A., C.

Some copies on fine paper.

HUMBOLDT. Tableau Statistique de l'Ile de Cuba, por les annees 1825 a 1829. Par M. Alexandre de Humboldt ... . *Paris: Gide fils*. 1831. 8vo, pp. 88. 4 Tables. 33741

HUMBOLDT. Tablas Estatisticas del Reyno de España en el año de 1803. 4to. 33742

HUMBOLDT. Tablas Geografico-politicas del Reyno de Nueva España, presentadas al Exmo Sñr Virrey de Mexico. 4to.

HUMBOLDT. The Travels and Researches of Alexander von Humboldt; being a condensed Narrative of his Journeys in the Equinoctial Regions of America, and in Asiatic Russia: together with Analyses of his more important Investigations. By W. Macgillivray, A.M. *Edinburgh: Oliver & Boyd*. 1833. Post 8vo, pp. 418. + *New-York: Harper & Brothers*. 1833. 18mo, pp. 367. + [*Ibid.*] 1835. + [*Ibid.*] 1837. + [*Ibid.*] 1840. + Enlarged Edition. *Edinburgh*. 1852. + [*Ibid.*] 1855. 33744

HUMBOLDT. Reisen und Forschungen. Eine gedrängte Erzählung seiner Wanderungen in den Aequinoctial-Gegenden Amerikas und im asiatischen Russland. Nebst einer Zusammenstellung seiner wichtigsten Untersuchungen, u.s.w. von Dr. W. Macgillivray. *Leipzig: Baumgärtner*. 1832. 16mo, pp. (2), xxiv, 430, (2). Map and 7 Plates. + [*Ibid.*] 1836. C. 33745

HUMBOLDT. Tribute to the Memory of Alexander von Humboldt, by the New York Geographical and Statistical Society. *New York*. 1859. 12mo. C. 33746

HUMBOLDT. Untersuchungen über die Geographie des neuen Continents, berechnet von Jabbo Oltmanns. *Paris*. 1810. 2 vols., 8vo. 33747

Extremely rare, nearly the whole edition having been destroyed at sea. *See* Stevens' Catalogue of Humboldt's Library, Lot 4595.

HUMBOLDT. Untersuchungen über Amerika's Bevölkerung aus dem alten Kontinente, dem Herrn Alexander von Humboldt gewidmet von Johann Severin Vater ... . *Leipzig*. 1810. 8vo, pp. 211. P. 33748

HUMBOLDT. Volcans des Cordillères de Quito et du Mexique par Alexandre de Humboldt. *Paris*. 1854. Oblong 4to, pp. 15.

12 Plates. + Pour servir aux Œuvres de Humboldt et spécialement aux Mélanges de géologie et de physique générale. Nouvelle édition. *Paris: Morgand*. 1864. Oblong 4to, pp. 15. 12 Plates. 33749

HUMBOLDT. Vues des Cordillères, et Monumens des Peuples Indigènes de l'Amérique. Par Al. de Humboldt. ... *Paris: Maze*. 1815. 2 vols., 8vo, pp. 392; 411, (2). 19 Plates. + *A Paris: A la Librairie grecque* ... 1816. 2 vols., 8vo. 33750

HUMBOLDT. Researches, concerning the Institutions & Monuments of the Ancient Inhabitants of America, with Descriptions & Views of some of the most Striking Scenes in the Cordilleras. Written in French by Alexander de Humboldt, & Translated into English by Helen Maria Williams. *London: Longman* ... . 1814. 2 vols., 8vo, pp. iv, 411; 324. 19 Plates. B., BA., H.

This translation of the text of the celebrated "Vues des Cordillères," is a valuable adjunct to the great folio of plates, for all students not familiar with the language of the original.

HUMBOLDT AND BONPLAND.

The following titles are arranged in the order in which a set is usually bound up. It will be noticed that some of the titles have already appeared, but the following list describes only such works as are usually found with the folio and 4to series.

Voyage aux régions Equinoxiales du Nouveau continent, fait en 1799, 1800, 1801, 1802, 1803 et 1804. Par Al. de Humboldt et A. Bonpland; rédigé, par Alexandre de Humboldt; avec deux atlas, qui renferment, l'un les Vues des Cordillères et les monumens des peuples Indigènes de l'Amerique, et l'autre des Cartes Géographiques et Physiques. *Paris: F. Schoell*. 1814–25. 3 vols., rl. 4to, pp. (10), 643; (4), 722; (8), 632. A., B., H. Atlas. *Paris: Librairie de Gide*. 1814–34. pp. (4), 3. 40 Plates.

This general title of "Voyages," etc., with some variations, precedes all the books described in this series. "This work has been justly called by a competent judge 'a work of gigantic extent and richness, to which the modern literature of Europe can hardly offer a parallel.'"—*Encyclopædia Americana*. A fourth volume was announced but never published.

Atlas Géographique et Physique des Régions Equinoxiales du Nouveau Continent. Examen critique de l'Histoire et de la Géographie du Nouveau Continent aux quinzième et seizième siècles. *Paris: G. Dufour et Cie*. 1814–34. Folio, pp. (6), vi, 562. 39 Maps. 33753

Vues des Cordillères et Monumens des Peuples Indigènes de l'Amerique. Par Al. de Humboldt. *Paris: Chez F. Schoell*. 1810. Folio, pp. (10), 350, (1). 69 Plates. + *Paris*. 1813. B.

Every class of Mexican or Aztec, and Peruvian Antiquities, receives in this work the clearest philosophical analysis. Many of the plates are beautifully colored; indeed, it is the most beautiful and generally interesting of Humboldt's works. Some copies have proof impressions of the plates. Many copies have been sold lacking pp. 272–350, and plates 50–69, and the collation in some copies is pp. xvi, 350; 69 Plates.

Recueil d'Observations de Zoologie et d'Anatomie comparée, faites dans l'Océan Atlantique, dans l'intérieur du Nouveau Continent et dans la Mer du Sud pendant les années 1799, 1800, 1801, 1802 et 1803. Par Al. de Humboldt et A. Bonpland. *Paris: Schoell*. 1811–33. 2 vols., 4to, pp. (4), viii, 368; (4), 352. 57 Plates. B., H. 33755

According to Rich, Vol. I. was published, *Paris: Schoell*. 1805. 4to, pp. 412. 30 colored Plates. It was reproduced, *Paris*, 1841.

Essai Politique sur le Royaume de la Nouvelle-Espagne. Par Alexandre de Humboldt. Avec un Atlas physique et géographique, fondé sur des observations astronomiques, des mesures trigonométriques et des nivellemens barométriques. ... *Paris: F. Schoell*. 1811. 2 vols., 4to, pp. (14), xcii, (2), iv, 350, (6); (8), 351–904, (1). Atlas, folio, pp. (iv), 4. 20 Plates. A., BA., S.

The maps are numbered 1–6, 9, 13–30, No. 19 being numbered twice, making in all twenty. The eleven pages of descriptive letter-press are sometimes deficient. The date varies in copies from 1811 to 1814. There are copies on large vellum paper. *See* "M. Rev.," LXIV. 353.

Recueil d'Observations Astronomiques. D'Operations Trigonométriques, et de Mesures Barométriques faites pendant le cours d'un Voyage aux Regions Équinoxiales du Nouveau Continent, depuis 1799 jusqu'en 1803. Par Alexandre de Humboldt; Rédigées calculées, d'après les Tables les plus exactes par Jabbo Oltmanns. ... *A Paris: F. Schoell*. 1810. 2 vols., 4to, pp. (4), lxxvi, 138, 33, (1), 382, (2); (4), 629. 2 Plates. A., B., BA.

Some copies are printed on vellum paper.

Physique générale et Géologie. *Paris*. 1807. 4to. 33758

Essai sur la Géographie des Plantes, accompagné d'un Tableau physique des Régions équinoxiales, fondé sur des mesures executées, depuis le dixième degrè de latitude ... australe ... par Al. de Humboldt et A. Bonpland. ... *Paris: Chez Fr. Schoell*. 1807. 4to, pp. (6), 155. Table. A., B., H. 33759

Plantes Équinoxiales, recueillies au Mexique, dans l'île de Cuba, dans les provinces de Caracas, de Cumana et de Barcelonne, aux Andes de la Nouvelle-Grenade, de Quito et du Pérou, et sur les bords du Rio-Negro, de l'Orénoque et de la rivière des Amazones. Par Al. de Humboldt et A. Bonpland. *Paris: Chez F. Schoell*. 1808–9. 2 vols., folio, pp. (2), 234, Portrait; (2), 191. 140 Plates. A., B., BA. + *Paris*. 1813. H. 33760

Some copies printed on vellum paper. It is perhaps one of the grandest works on American botany ever put forth.

Nova Genera et Species Plantarum quas in Peregrinatione ad Plagam Æquinoctialem orbis novi colligerunt, descripserunt, partem adumbraverunt Amat. Bonpland et Alex. de Humboldt. Ex schedis autographis A. Bonplandi in ordinem digessit Carol. Sigismund Kunth. Accedunt tabulæ æri incisæ, et Al. de Humboldt notationes ad geographium plantarum spectantes. *Lutetiæ Parisiorum*. 1815–25. 7 vols., folio, pp. (6), xlvi, (2), 302; (8), 323, (1); (8), 456; (8), 247; (6), 338; (6), 420, (2); (8), 399. 700 Plates. 33761

Complete sets are very scarce. It was issued with the plates plain, price 1,800 francs, vellum paper, 3,600 francs, plates colored, 5,500 francs. Some copies printed on large paper, colored plates, 7,200 francs.

Monographie des Melastomacées, comprenant Toutes les Plantes de cet ordre recueillies jusqu'à ce jour, et notamment au Mexique, dans l'île de Cuba, dans les provinces de Caracas, de Cumana, et de Barcelone, aux Andes de la Nouvelle-Grenade, de Quito et du Pérou, et sur les bords du Rio-Negro, de l'Orénoque et de la rivière des Amazones; par Al. de Humboldt et A. Bonpland. ... Melastomes. *Paris*. 1816. Folio, pp. (12), vi, 142, (4). 60 Plates. B. 33762

Monographie des Melastomacées ... . Rhexies. *Paris: Chez Gide Fils*. 1823. Folio, pp. (8), ii, 158, (2). 60 Plates. B., H.

Mimoses et autres Plantes légumineuses du Nouveau Continent recueillies par MM. de Humboldt et Bonpland, décrites et publiées par Charles-Sigismond Kunth, avec Figures coloriées. *Paris*. 1819. Folio, pp. (10), 223. 60 colored Plates. A., B. 33764

Distribution méthodique de la famille des Graminées par Charles-Sigismond Kunth ... . *Paris*. 1835. 2 vols., folio, pp. (8), 578, (2); (4), 220 Plates. B. 33765

Révision des Graminées, publiées dans les Nova Genera et Species Plantarum, de MM. Humboldt et Bonpland; précédée d'un travail général sur la famille des Graminées par C. S.

Kunth. Ouvrage accompagné de cent Planches coloriés. *Paris: Gide*. 1829–34. 3 vols., folio. 33766

Another edition was published in 1839, with 220 uncolored plates, in 2 vols., folio, at 264 francs.

Synopsis Plantarum, quas in itinere ad plagiam æquinoxialem Orbis Novi, collegerunt Al. de Humboldt et Am. Bonpland. Auctore Carolo Sigism. Kunth. *Parisiis: F. G. Levrault*. 1822–1825. 4 vols., 8vo, pp. (6), iv, 491; (6), 526; (4), 496; (6), 528.

Voyage au régions équinoxiales du Nouveau Continent, fait en 1799, 1800, 1801, 1802, 1803 et 1804, par A. de Humboldt et A. Bonpland. Rédigé par A. de Humboldt, avec un Atlas géographique. *Paris: Schoell, Dufour, Gide et Maze*. 1816–31. 13 vols., 8vo, pp. (4), 459, (1); (4), 381, Plate; (4), 381, (2); 331, (5), 69; (4), 318; (4), 396; (4), 455; 526, (2); (4), 527, (1); (4), 419; (4), 478; (4), 416; 407; (6), 166. 33768

Viage á las Regiones Equinocciales del Nuevo Continente hecho en 1799 hasta 1804 por Al. de Humboldt y A. Bonpland, redactado por A. de Humboldt; continuacion indespensable al Ensayo Politico sobre e Reino de la Nueva España. *Paris*. 1826. 5 vols., 8vo. Maps. + *Paris*. 1828. 33769

Personal Narrative of Travels to the Equinoctial Regions of the New Continent in 1799–1804. By Alexander de Humboldt, and Aimé Bonpland. Written in French by Alexander de Humboldt, and translated into English by Helen Maria Williams. *London: Longman*. 1814–26. 7 vols., 8vo, pp. xii, li, (2), 293; 294; 575; (4), 573; Vol. V., Part I. pp. (4), 502; Part II. pp. (2), 502–865; Vol. VI., Part I. pp. vii, 390; Part II. pp. iv, 391–845; (4), 482. 8 Maps. 33770

These seven volumes are usually bound in six. There are some variations in the date and collation of Vols. I. and II., which reached a third edition, 1822. Its republication was commenced in *Philadelphia: M. Carey*. 1815. 8vo, pp. 432, but did not proceed any farther. Concerning the work *see* "M. Rev.," LXXI. 1, LXXXVIII. 234, XC. 14. The following is another translation:

Personal Narrative of Travels to the Equinoctial Regions of America, ... during the years 1799–1804. By Alexander von Humboldt. Translated and Edited by Thomasina Ross. *London: Henry G. Bohn*. 1852. 3 vols., post 8vo, pp. xx, ii, 505, (1); vi, 521, (1); vi, 442. + *London*. 1818–29. 7 vols. in 8.

Reis naar de landen bij den Equator. Uit het Fransch vertaald. *Haarlem*. 1808–18. 6 vols., 8vo. Portrait and Plates. 33772

Voyage to the Equator. Translated from the French.

Beobachtungen aus der Zoologie und Vergleichungen. Anatomie, gesammelt auf einer Reise nach den Tropenländern des neuen Continents in den Jahren 1799–1804. *Tübingen*. 1806. 14 Plates. 33773

This concludes our long list of the works of this great *savant*. We cannot do less than quote the words of three distinguished reviewers: "No name stands higher than that of Humboldt, among the lovers of geographical and physical science. Zealous, active, vigorous; imbued with liberal knowledge, skillful in general physics, and particularly attached to chemistry and its kindred branches, possessing ample means of indulging his taste, he has directed his inquiries into every department of nature and society. The mass of curious information which he procured in those distant travels, and the superb collection which he was enabled to make, relative to different objects of science, far exceed anything that has heretofore been achieved by the exertions of an individual." —*Edinburgh Review*, XVI. 223–24. "Humboldt is the most illustrious traveller of his day. Nothing seems too vast, too varied, too wonderful, or too minute, for the keen eye, penetrating intellect, and unwearied exertions of this extraordinary man. A botanist, zoologist, statist and philosopher, the genius of this great writer seems to have been peculiarly fitted for surveying the varieties and immensity of the physical world; and he accordingly takes the foremost rank of all the travellers, dead or living."—DIBDIN. "To write a book upon America without referring to Baron Humboldt at almost every page, is nearly impossible. He was the first who applied the light of science to the New World."—WARD's *Mexico*. *See also* "M. Rev.," LXXIX. 16; "Quart. Rev.," XV. 440; "Edinb. Rev.," XVI. 223, XXIV. 133; "North Amer. Rev.," XVI. 1; Ghillany (F. W.), *our* Vol. VII., No. 27261.

HUMBOLDT (G.), *pseudon*. Poems and Letters to Don Brown, by Gay Humboldt alias Burr Lington, D.L.L. *Albany: E. H. Bender*. M DCCC LVII. 18mo, pp. x, (2), 252. H. 33774

Humbug: A Look at some Popular Impositions. *New York: S. F. French & Co*. 1859. 12mo, pp. 100. B. + [*Ibid.*] 1860. 12mo, pp. 96. 33775

HUME (G. H.) Canada, As It Is. Comprising Details Relating to the Domestic Policy, Commerce and Agriculture, of the Upper and Lower Provinces, ... for ... Settlers and Emigrants. By George Henry Hume. *New-York: William Stodart*. 1832. 18mo, pp. xxiv, 173. H. 33776

HUME (H.) The Life of Edward John Eyre, late Governor of Jamaica. By Hamilton Hume. *London: Richard Bentley*. 1867. 12mo, pp. xvi, 320. Portrait. B., BA., C. 33777

HUME (J.) Sermon before the Incorporated Society for the Propagation of the Gospel in Foreign Parts, February 19, 1762. By John, Bishop of Oxford. *London*. 1762. 8vo, pp. 91. N.

HUME (J.) The Celebrated Letter of Joseph Hume, M.P. to Wm. Lyon Mackenzie, Mayor of Toronto, declaratory of a

Design to "Free these Provinces from the baneful Domination of the Mother Country!" With the Comments of the Press of Upper Canada on the pernicious and treasonable tendency of that Letter, and the Speeches, Resolutions, and Amendments of the Common Council of this City, the result of a Motion to disavow all participation in the sentiments of Mr. Hume. *Toronto: G. P. Bull.* 1834. 8vo. 33779

Also: Debate on Sugar Duties. Speech ... in the House of Commons, on the 13th of May, 1841, on the Motion of Lord John Russell. [*London.* 1841.] 8vo, pp. 22.

H[UME] (S[ophia]). An | Exhortation | to the | Inhabitants | Of the Province of | South-Carolina, | To bring their Deeds to the Light of | Christ, in their own Consciences. | By S. H. | In which is inserted, | Some Account of the Author's Ex- | perience in the Important Business of | Religion. | ... *Philadelphia: Printed by William Bradford.* [1747.] 8vo, pp. 158. + *Philadelphia: Printed by B. Franklin and D. Hall.* MDCCXLVIII. 8vo, pp. 86. BA. + *Bristol: Printed by Samuel Farley.* M.DCC.L. 8vo, pp. 80. C. + [*Ibid.*] M,DCC,LI. 8vo, pp. 111, (1). H. + *London: ... Luke Hinde* ... 1752. 8vo, pp. 152. + *Leedes: Printed by James Lister.* 1752. 12mo, pp. 108. + *Dublin: Printed by Isaac Jackson.* MDCCLIV. 12mo, pp. 164. C. 33780

HUME. An Epistle to the Inhabitants of South-Carolina; Containing Sundry Observations proper to be consider'd by every Professor of Christianity in General. By Sophia Hume. ... *London: Printed by Luke Hinde.* 1754. 8vo, pp. 114. C., H., W.

HUMES (T. W.) Second Report to the East Tennessee Relief Association at Knoxville. By Thomas W. Humes ... . *Knoxville, Tenn.: Printed by Brownlow, Haws & Co.* 1866. 8vo, pp. 23. H. 33782

See also Knoxville, Tenn.

The Humming Bird; or, Morsels of Information, on the Subject of Slavery: with various Miscellaneous Articles. Vol. I. *Leicester: A. Cockshaw.* 1825. 8vo, pp. x, 364. 33783

Humours of Eutopia; a Tale of Colonial Times. By an Eutopian. *Philadelphia.* 1828. 12mo. 33784

HUMPHREY (Asa). Personal Satire: or Satirical Epistle. Written by a Schoolmaster in the Eastern Country. *Boston.* 1804. 12mo. W. 33785

HUMPHREY (E. P.) A Discourse on the Death of Gen. Zachary Taylor ... July 13, 1850. By Edward P. Humphrey ... *Louisville: Hulls and Shannon.* MDCCCL. 8vo, pp. 16. H.

Also: An Address ... on the Dedication of the Cave Hill Cemetery; near Louisville: July 25, 1848. ... *Louisville, Ky.* 1848. 8vo, pp. 32. BA.

HUMPHREY, *and* CLELAND (T. H.) Memoirs of Rev. Thos. Cleland. By E. P. Humphrey and T. H. Cleland. *Cincinnati.* 1859. 12mo. S. 33787

HUMPHREY (H.) An Address, ... at the Collegiate Institution in Amherst, Ms., By Heman Humphrey, D.D., On Occasion of his Inauguration to the Presidency of that Institution, Oct. 15, 1823. *Boston: Printed by Crocker and Brewster.* 1823. 8vo, pp. 40. B., BA., H., M., W. 33788

HUMPHREY. The Character and Sufferings of the Pilgrims. A Sermon ... at Pittsfield, (Mass.) December 22, 1820; ... By Heman Humphrey, D.D. *Pittsfield: Printed by Phinehas Allen.* 1821. 8vo, pp. 40. BA. 33789

HUMPHREY. Death of President Harrison. A Discourse delivered in ... Amherst, Mass. On ... the Annual State Fast, April 8, 1841. By Heman Humphrey, D.D. ... *Amherst: J. S. and C. Adams.* 1841. 8vo, pp. 24. Portrait. B. 33790

HUMPHREY. Indian Rights & our Duties. An Address delivered at Amherst, Hartford, etc. December, 1829. By Heman Humphrey, D.D. *Amherst: J. S. & C. Adams and Co.* 1830. 12mo, pp. 24. B., H. + *Albany.* 1831. P., W. + [*New York:*] *Stereotyped for the Association for diffusing information on the Subject of Indian Rights.* 1831. 12mo, pp. 24. BA. 33791

The effort of an earnest and learned man to arouse the people of the United States to a knowledge of the wrongs perpetrated on the Indians.

HUMPHREY. The Life and Labors of the Rev. T. H. Gallaudet, LL.D. By Rev. Heman Humphrey, D.D. *New York: Robert Carter & Brother.* 1857. 12mo, pp. 440. Portrait. S.

HUMPHREY. Memoir of Rev. Nathan W. Fiske, ... Amherst College; ... with ... Sermons and other Writings. By Heman Humphrey, D.D. *Amherst: J. S. and C. Adams.* 1850. 12mo, pp. 392. Portrait. 33793

HUMPHREY. Miscellaneous Discourses and Reviews: By Heman Humphrey, D.D. *Amherst: J. S. and C. Adams.* 1834. 12mo, pp. 415. BA. 33794

Also: An Address ... Opening of the Convention of Teachers and of the Friends of Education ... Hartford, November 10, 1830. ... *Hartford.* 1831. 8vo, pp. 19.—Charges against Slavery. Extracts from a Discourse delivered at Pittsfield, January 4, 1861. ... *Boston: American Tract Society.* 1861. 18mo, pp. 32.—A Discourse delivered before the Connecticut Alpha of Φ. B. K. at New Haven, August 14, 1838. ... *New Haven.* 1839. 8vo.— ... A Discourse ... at the Funeral of Mrs. D. W. V. Fiske, February 21, 1844. ... *Amherst: J. S. and C. Adams.* 1844. 12mo, pp. 48.—The Kingdom of Christ: a Sermon preached before the Annual Convention of the Congregational Ministers of Massachusetts, in Boston, May 29, 1830. ... *Boston: Peirce and Williams.* 8vo, pp. 36.—The Missouri Compromise: An Address delivered before the Citizens of Pittsfield ... Feb. 26, 1854. ... *Pittsfield: Reed, Hull & Peirson, Printers.* 1854. 8vo, pp. 32.—Our Nation. A Discourse ... at Pittsfield, Mass., January 4, 1861, on the Day of the National Fast. ... *Pittsfield, Mass.: Henry Chickering, Printer.* 1861. 8vo, pp. 37. H.—Parallel between Intemperance and the Slave Trade. An Address ... at Amherst College, July 4, 1828. ... *Amherst: J. S. and C. Adams, Printers.* 1828. 8vo, pp. 40.— ... A Sermon, delivered at Goshen [Conn.], at the Ordination of the Rev. Messrs. Hiram Bingham, & Asa Thurston, as Missionaries to the Sandwich Islands, Sept. 29, 1819. ... *Boston: Samuel T. Armstrong.* 1819. 8vo, pp. 40, xvi.—Revival Sketches and Manual. In Two Parts. ... *New York: American Tract Society.* [1859.] 12mo, pp. 476.— ... A Sermon ... at the Installation of the Rev. Horatio N. Brinsmade ... in Pittsfield, Mass. February 11, 1835. ... *Pittsfield: Printed by Phinehas Allen and Son.* [1835.] 8vo, pp. 20. H.—Sermon before the General Association of Connecticut, at New Haven, June 18, 1816. ... *New Haven.* 1816. 8vo, pp. 24.— ... A Sermon, ... at Pittsfield, (Mass.) on the Day of the Annual Fast, April 4th, 1818. ... *Pittsfield: Printed by Phinehas Allen.* 1818. 8vo, pp. 46.—Sermon at the Dedication of the College Chapel, Feb. 28, 1827. ... *Amherst.* 1827. 8vo, pp. 32.— ... A Sermon, Preached in the City of Boston before the Pastoral Association of Massachusetts. May 31, 1826. ... *Amherst: Mark H. Newman.* 1826. 8vo, pp. 32. B.—A Tribute to the Memory of Rev. Nathan W. Fiske, late Professor of Intellectual and Moral Philosophy in Amherst College. ... *Amherst: Press of J. S. & C. Adams.* MDCCCXLVIII. 8vo, pp. 29.—Valedictory Address, ... Amherst College. ... *Amherst: J. S. & C. Adams, Printers.* 1845. 8vo, pp. 23.—The Way to Bless and Save our Country: A Sermon ... May 23, 1831. ... *Philadelphia.* 1831. 12mo, pp. 24.

HUMPHREY (J.) Obituary Notices and Funeral Services of James Humphrey. *Brooklyn: For the Family.* 1866. 8vo, pp. (2), 97. Portrait. B. 33795

HUMPHREY (Z. M.) Funeral Sermon ... at the Obsequies of Colonel E. E. Ellsworth, ... Chicago, June 2, 1861. By Rev. Z. M. Humphrey. ... *Chicago.* 1861. 8vo, pp. 16. B.

HUMPHREYS (A. A.), *and* ABBOT (H. L.) Report upon the Physics and Hydraulics of the Mississippi River; upon the Protection of the Alluvial Region against Overflow; and upon the Deepening of the Mouths: based upon Surveys and Investigations made under the Acts of Congress directing the Topographical and Hydrographical Survey of the Delta of the Mississippi River, with such Investigations as might lead to determine the most Practicable Plan for securing it from Inundation, and the Best Mode of deepening the Channels at the Mouths of the

River. Submitted to the Bureau of Topographical Engineers, War Department, 1861. Prepared by Captain A. A. Humphreys and Lieut. H. L. Abbot ... . *Philadelphia: J. B. Lippincott & Co.* 1861. 4to, pp. xxiv, 17–456; Appendix, cxlvi. 20 Plates.

Also: A Reply to Certain Portions of the Minority Report of the Hon. Z. Kidwell ... upon the Pacific Railroad ... . December, 1856. [*Washington.* 1856.] 8vo, pp. 8.

[HUMPHREYS (C. A.)] A Sketch of the History of the first Half Century of the Third Congregational Society of Springfield, Mass. ... [With] Sermon upon ... Rev. William B. O. Peabody, D.D. With an Appendix. *Springfield: Samuel Bowles & Company, Printers.* 1869. 8vo, pp. 50. H. 33798

HUMPHREYS (D.) A Plain Attempt to hold up to View The Ancient Gospel ... . By Daniel Humphreys ... . *Portsmouth.* 1800. 12mo, pp. 35. B., BA. 33799

Also: The Compendious American Grammar; or, Grammatical Institutes in Verse. ... *Portsmouth, N. H.* 1792. 16mo, pp. 71. M.

HUMPHREYS (David). An Account of the Endeavours Used by the Society for the Propagation of the Gospel in Foreign Parts, To instruct the Negro Slaves in New York. Together with Two of Bp. Gibson's Letters on that subject. Being an Extract from Dr. Humphreys's Historical Account of the Incorporated Society for the Propagation of the Gospel in Foreign Parts, from its Foundation to the Year 1728. *Printed at London in* 1730. 8vo, pp. 45. 33800

HUMPHREYS. An Historical Account of the Incorporated Society for the Propagation of the Gospel in Foreign Parts. Containing their Foundation, Proceedings, and the Success of their Missionaries in the British Colonies, to the Year 1728. By David Humphreys, D.D. Secretary to the Honorable Society. *London: Joseph Downing.* M.DCC.XXX. 8vo, pp. xxxi, 356. 2 Maps by H. Moll. BA., H. + *New York.* 1853. 8vo, pp. 135.

The labors of the Society embraced the New England Colonies, New York, Pennsylvania, New Jersey, North and South Carolina, etc. This volume was compiled from papers transmitted to the Society by Governors of Colonies, or persons of note abroad, or from religious congregations and the missionaries. These original papers are still preserved in the archives of the Society in London. The New York edition is reprinted from the "Church Review" of 1851–52.

HUMPHREYS (D.) The Conduct of General Washington, respecting the Confinement of Capt. Asgill, placed in its True Point of Light. By David Humphreys. With a Preface and Appendix. *New York: Printed for the Holland Club.* 1859. 8vo, pp. 35.

A few copies only printed.

HUMPHREYS. Discours en Vers, adressé aux Officiers et aux Soldats des différentes Armées Américaines. Par M. David Humphreys, Colonel au service des États-Unis, & Aide-de-Camp de son Excellence le Général Washington. Imprimé pour la premiere fois, à New-Haven, dans le Connecticut. *A Paris: Chez Prault* ... 1786. 12mo, pp. 66. BA., H., S. 33803

Beautifully printed on fine paper. The translator was the Marquis de Chastellux. The English and French versions occupy opposite pages (the latter, by the way, is in prose).

HUMPHREYS. An | Essay | on the | Life | of the | Honorable Major-General | Israel Putnam: | Addressed to the State Society of the Cincinnati, | in Connecticut. | By Col. David Humphreys. | *Hartford:* | *Printed by Hudson & Goodwin.* | M.DCC.LXXXVIII. 12mo, pp. vi, 188. BA., H. + *Middletown: Printed by Moses H. Woodward.* M,DCC,XCIV. 12mo, pp. v, 7–168. H. + Third Edition. *Brattleborough: William Fessenden.* 1812. 18mo, pp. 144. C. + With an Address to the Armies of the United States, and a Poem on the Happiness of America. *Philadelphia: W. McCarty.* 1811. 16mo, pp. 285. Plate. C. 33804

HUMPHREYS. An Essay on the Life of the Honourable Major General Israel Putnam. Addressed to the State Society of the Cincinnati in Connecticut, And first published by their order. By Colonel David Humphreys. With Notes and Additions. With an Appendix, containing an Historical and Topographical Sketch of Bunker Hill Battle. By S. Swett. *Boston: Samuel Avery.* 1818. 12mo, pp. 276. B., BA. 33805

HUMPHREYS. The Life and Heroic Exploits of Israel Putnam ... By Col. David Humphreys. *New York: Ezra Strong.* 1834. 18mo, pp. 190. B. + [*Ibid.*] 1835. 12mo. + *Hartford.* 1847. 12mo, pp. 190. Portrait. + *Hartford.* 1851. B.

Early in the Revolutionary War Colonel Humphreys became attached to General Putnam's staff as Major, to whom he subsequently showed his gratitude by writing this essay on his life. It is a smooth and complimentary piece of biography, which certainly anticipates no modern doubts as to the bravery of "Old Put."

HUMPHREYS. Letters from the Hon. David Humphreys, ... to ... Sir Joseph Banks, ... Containing some Account of the Serpent of the Ocean, frequently seen in Gloucester Bay. *New-York: Kirk & Mercein.* 1817. 12mo, pp. 86. BA., P. 33807

"The ingenious and scientific Mr. Rafinesque concludes, there are, perhaps, not less than a hundred kinds of sea serpents."

HUMPHREYS. The Miscellaneous Works of Colonel Humphreys. *New-York: Printed by Hodge, Allen and Campbell;* ... M.DCC.XC. 8vo, pp. 348. B., BA., H., P., S. 33808

Contains his Essay on the Life of Major-General Putnam, and other imaginary tales.

HUMPHREYS. The Miscellaneous Works of David Humphreys, Late Minister Plenipotentiary from the United States of America to the Court of Madrid. *New York: Printed by T. and J. Swords.* 1804. 8vo, pp. xv, 394, (14). Portrait and Plate.

[HUMPHREYS.] A Poem, addressed to the Armies of the United States of America. By a Gentleman of the Army. ... *New-Haven: Printed by T. and S. Green.* M, DCC, LXXX. 8vo, pp. 16. BA. 33810

HUMPHREYS. A Poem, Addressed to the Armies of the United States of America. By David Humphreys, Esq; Colonel in the service of the United States: and Aid de Camp to His Excellency the Commander in Chief. ... *New-Haven: Printed by T. and S. Green,* 1784. *Paris, reprinted* 1785. 4to, pp. 28. BA., H. + [*Ibid.*] ... *London, in the same Year, for G. Kearsley* ... 4to, pp. 28. H. 33811

Printed Humphries in the London edition. *See* "M. Rev.," LXXII. 388.

HUMPHREYS. A Poem on the Happiness of America; Addressed to the Citizens of the United States. By David Humphreys, Esquire. [n. p. 1786.] 4to, pp. 53. BA., H. + *London, printed* 1786. *Hartford, Re-printed by Hudson and Goodwin.* 1786. 4to, pp. 51. + *Portsmouth, N. H.* 1790. 8vo, pp. 45. 33812

There is also an edition, no date [1799]. 4to, pp. 53.

HUMPHREYS. A Poem on Industry. Addressed to the Citizens of the United States ... . By Colonel David Humphreys ... *Philadelphia: Mathew Carey.* 1794. 8vo, pp. 22. BA., H.

HUMPHREYS. Poems by Col. David Humphreys, late Aid-de-Camp to his Excellency General Washington. Second Edition: —With Several Additions. *Philadelphia: Printed by Mathew Carey.* M,DCC,LXXXIX. 12mo, pp. (2), 90, (1). BA., H. 33814

HUMPHREYS. A Valedictory Discourse, delivered before the Cincinnati of Connecticut, in Hartford, July 4th, 1804, at the Dissolution of the Society. By David Humphreys ... . *Boston: Printed by Gilbert and Dean.* 1804. 8vo, pp. 60. B., BA., H.

With a frontispiece; a quaint woodcut of the Seal of the Society, "*printed by order of the Society,* John Chamberlayne, Secretary." Partly poetical, and with many valuable

historical notes. Also: A Discourse on the Agriculture of the State of Connecticut; ... delivered at New-Haven, ... 12th September, 1816. ... *New-Haven: Printed by T. G. Woodward.* 1816. 8vo, pp. 42, (2). BA., M. *See* Duyckink's "Cyclopædia of American Literature," Vol. I.

HUMPHREYS, *and others.* Anarchiad. *See* Vol. I., No. 1365.

HUMPHREYS (D[avid] C.) Address to the People of Alabama. By D. C. Humphreys. [*Huntsville, Ala.* 1864.] 8vo, pp. 8.

Also: The Campaign in the South. Speech ... June 1st, 1868. n. p. n. d.] 8vo, pp. 4. H.

HUMPHREYS (E[dward] R.) America, ... a Lecture. By E. R. Humphreys. ... *Newport, R. I.: Charles E. Hammett, Jun.* 1869. 8vo, pp. (2), 77. B., H. 33817

HUMPHREYS. The Dangers and Duties of the Present Time: ... Two Lectures ... 11th and 25th January, 1853. By E. R. Humphreys. *London: John W. Parker and Son.* MDCCCLIII. 8vo, pp. 64. H. 33818

HUMPHREYS. Education of Officers, Preparatory and Professional. By E. R. Humphreys. *Boston: Lee and Shepard.* 1862. 8vo, pp. 40. 33819

HUMPHREYS. Freemasonry, the Healer of the Nation's Wounds. An Address ... Newport, R. I., on St. John's Day, 1869, By E. R. Humphreys, LL.D. *Newport: Davis & Pitman, Printers.* 1870. 12mo, pp. 26. B., H. 33820

HUMPHREYS (F.) A Sermon preached December 13, 1776, being the Fast Day on account of the Troubles in America; at Hampstead. By Francis Humphreys. *London: T. Cadell.* 1777. 4to. 33821

See "M. Rev.," LVI. 160.

HUMPHREYS (H.) Address to the Alumni and Graduates of St. John's College, and to the Friends of Education in Maryland. By Hector Humphreys. *Annapolis.* 1835. 8vo. 33822

HUMPHREYS (W. H.) Some Suggestions on ... Monopolies & Special Charters. By W. H. Humphreys. *Nashville, Tenn.: E. G. Eastman & Co., Printers.* 1849. 8vo, pp. 14. H. 33823

Also: [Letter] To R. G. Payne, ... on the ... Usury Law. [n. p. n. d.] 8vo pp. 23. H.

HUMPHRYS (Alexander). Address to ... the Peers of Scotland by Alexander Earl of Stirling & Dovan, &c. ... to which is added a Particular Statement of his Case by T. C. Banks, Esq. ... *Edinburgh: William Tait.* MDCCCXXXI. 8vo, pp. 47. H.

HUMPHRYS. Two Letters addressed to the Right Honourable Thomas Lord Denman ... By the Earl of Stirling. *Paris: Printed by J. Smith.* 1845. 8vo, pp. 77. H. 33825

HUMPHRYS. Narrative of the Oppressive Law Proceedings, and other Measures, resorted to by the British Government and numerous Private Individuals, to overpower the Earl of Stirling, and subvert his Lawful Rights. Written by Himself. Also a Genealogical Account of the Family of Alexander, Earls of Stirling, etc. *Edinburgh.* 1836. 4to. 33826

HUMPHRYS. Report of the Trial of Alexander Humphrys or Alexander, claiming the Title of Earl of Stirling, before the High Court of Justiciary at Edinburgh, for the Crime of Forgery, With an Appendix, containing the whole documentary Evidence. By Archibald Swinton, Advocate. *Edinburgh: Thomas Clark.* M.DCCC.XXXIX. 8vo, pp. (2), xxiv, 356, cviii. 33827

HUMPHRYS. The Stirling Peerage. Trial of Alexander Humphrys or Alexander, styling himself Earl of Stirling, before the High Court of Justiciary, for Forgery, on 29th April, 1839, and four following days. ... Edited by William Turnbull, Esq. ... *William Blackwood and Sons, Edinburgh;* MDCCCXXXIX. 8vo, pp. (6), 48, cxxii, 289, Appendix, 28. H. 33828

Six copies printed on thick paper.

HUMPHRYS. Vindication of the Rights and Titles, Political and Territorial, Alexander, Earl of Stirling and Dovan, and Lord Prietor of Canada and Nova Scotia, also The Trial of Lord Stirling. *Washington.* 1853. 8vo. Facsimile, &c. 33829

Also: Remarks on the Trial of the Earl of Stirling, for Forgery, by an English Lawyer. *Edinburgh.* 1839. 8vo.

Der Hundertjährige Calender, auf das gegenwärtige Jahrhundert nach Christi Geburt, von 1800 bis 1899; ... Erste verbesserte amerikanische Auflage. *Harrisburg: J. Heilman.* 1849. 16mo, pp. 105. C. 33830

HUNDLEY (D. R.) Social Relations in Our Southern States. By D. R. Hundley, Esq. *New York: Henry B. Price.* 1860. 12mo, pp. 367. 33831

HUNFALVY (P.) A Dakota Nyelv. By P. Hunfalvy. *Pest.* 1856. 8vo, pp. 68. 33832

HUNGERFORD (J.) The Old Plantation, and what I gathered there in an Autumn Month. By James Hungerford, of Maryland. ... *New York: Harper & Brothers.* 1859. 12mo, pp. 369.

HUNGERFORD (Orville). Speech of Mr. Hungerford, of New York, on ... The Duty on Imports, ... June 29, 1846. *Washington: Union Office.* 1846. 8vo, pp. 7. 33834

[HUNN (John S.)] Observations on the Improvements of the City of New York south of Grand Street. *New York.* 1806. 8vo. 33835

HUNN (N.) ... A Sermon ... before the General Assembly of ... Connecticut ... on the ... Anniversary Election, May 14th, 1747. By Nathanael Hunn ... . *N. London: Printed by Timothy Green.* 1747. 12mo, pp. (4), 35. H. 33836

HUNNICUTT (J. W.) The Conspiracy Unveiled. The South Sacrificed; or, the Horrors of Secession. By Rev. James W. Hunnicutt ... . *Philadelphia: J. B. Lippincott & Co.* 1863. 12mo, pp. xiv, 13-454. Portrait. B., H. 33837

HUNT (B. F.) An Oration ... before the Washington Society, in Charleston ... 4th of July, 1839. By Benj. Faneuil Hunt. *Charleston: Printed by S. S. Miller.* 1839. 8vo, pp. 45. BA.

HUNT. Speech of Col. Benj. Faneuil Hunt ... in Reply to the Doctrines of Daniel Webster, on the Currency and a National Bank. [n. p. n. d.] 8vo, pp. 8. 33839

Also: An Address ... to the American Friendly Association ... 22d of February, 1825: ... *Charleston, S. C.: Printed by C. C. Sebring.* 1825. 8vo, pp. 14. H.—The Argument ... in the case of the arrest of the Person claiming to be a British Seaman, under the 3d Section of the State Act of Dec. 1822, in relation to Negroes, &c. ... [*Charleston: Printed by A. E. Miller.* 1823.] 8vo, pp. 22.—Speech ... December 18, 1850—On a Bill ... on the Questions of Federal Usurpations. [n. p. n. d.] 8vo, pp. 6. BA.

[HUNT (Benjamin S.)] Remarks on Hayti as a Place of Settlement for Afric-Americans; and on the Mulatto as a Race for the Tropics. *Philadelphia: T. B. Pugh.* 1860. 8vo, pp. 36.

HUNT (C. H.) Life of Edward Livingston. By Charles Havens Hunt. With an Introduction by George Bancroft. *New York: D. Appleton and Company.* 1864. Rl. 8vo, pp. xxiv, 448. 2 Portraits. B., BA. 33841

Seventy-five copies printed on large paper.

HUNT (C. E.) The Shenandoah; or the Last Confederate Cruiser. By Cornelius E. Hunt (one of her Officers). *New York: G. W. Carleton & Co.* MDCCCLXVII. 12mo, pp. 273. Plate.

HUNT (D.) History of Pomfret [Conn.]: A Discourse delivered on the Day of Annual Thanksgiving, in the First Church in

Pomfret, Nov. 19th, 1840. By Rev. Daniel Hunt ... . *Hartford: J. Holbrook, Printer.* 1841. 8vo, pp. 35. B., C. 33843

HUNT (E. B.) Union Foundations: A Study of American Nationality as A Fact of Science. By Capt. E. B. Hunt ... . *New York: D. Van Nostrand.* 1863. 8vo, pp. 61. BA. 33844

HUNT (E. M.) The War and Its Lessons, By Ezra M. Hunt ... . *New York: Printed by F. Somers.* 1862. 8vo, pp. 35.

HUNT. Words about the War; or, Plain Facts for Plain People. By Ezra M. Hunt. *New York: F. Somers.* 1861. 8vo, pp. 39. 33846

HUNT (F. W.) The Pantological System of History. ... By F. W. Hunt, M.D. *New-York.* 1853-55. 2 vols., folio. C.

[HUNT (Freeman).] American Anecdotes: Original and Select. By an American. ... *Boston: Putnam & Hunt.* MDCCCXXX. 2 vols., 12mo, pp. 300; 300. H. 33848

[HUNT.] Letters about the Hudson River. And its Vicinity. Written in 1835 & 1836. ... By a Citizen of New York. *New York: Freeman Hunt & Co.* 1836. 18mo, pp. 209. H. + Third Edition, with Additions and Engravings. [*Ibid.*] 1837. 18mo, pp. 252. 2 Maps, 2 Plates. 33849

HUNT. The Library of Commerce: Practical, Theoretical, and Historical. By Freeman Hunt ... . Volume I. *New York.* 1845. 12mo, pp. 342. B. 33850

HUNT. Lives of American Merchants. By Freeman Hunt, A.M. ... *New York.* 1856-58. 2 vols., 8vo, pp. xlvii, 33-576; 13-605. 19 Portraits. B., BA., H. 33851

HUNT. The Merchants' Magazine, and Commercial Review. *New York: Freeman Hunt.* MDCCCXXXIX. 8vo. Continued.

HUNT. Worth and Wealth: a Collection of Maxims, Morals and Miscellanies for Merchants and Men of Business. By Freeman Hunt ... *New York: Stringer & Townsend.* 1857. Cr. 8vo, pp. xx, 25-504. H. 33853

Also: A Comprehensive Index to the Merchants' Magazine ... embracing the first ten volumes ... . *New York.* 1846. 8vo, pp. 37.

HUNT (G. J.) The Late War between the United States and Great Britain, from June, 1812, to February, 1815; written

in the Ancient Historical Style: also, a Sketch of the late Algerine War. ... The Treaty with Great Britain, and the Treaty with the Creek Indians. By Gilbert J. Hunt. *New York: D. Longworth.* 1816. 12mo. Portraits. 33854

HUNT. The Historical Reader; containing "The Late War between the United States and Great Britain, from June, 1812, to February, 1815. Written in the Ancient Historical Style." Altered and adapted for the Use of Schools throughout the United States. By Gilbert J. Hunt, ... Third Edition. With Improvements by the Author. *New York: David Longworth.* 1819. 12mo, pp. 233. B., H. + *New York: Daniel D. Smith.* 1819. 12mo, pp. 233. 33855

HUNT. The Tour of General La Fayette through the United States, from his departure from France until his departure from America in 1825, with a Sketch of his Life. *New York.* 1825. 12mo, pp. 35. 33856

Also: An Elegy on the Death of Mrs. Magdalen Hunt, late wife of the Author. Also, The Falls of Passaic. ... *Newark, N. J.* 1823. 8vo, pp. 14, (1).

HUNT (H. K.) Glances and Glimpses; or Fifty Years Social, including Twenty Years Professial Life. By Harriot K. Hunt, M.D. ... *Boston: John P. Jewett and Company.* 1856. 12mo, pp. xii, 418. B. 33857

HUNT (H. J.) Report of Light Battery M, 2d Artillery U. S. A., under command of Major Henry J. Hunt, Battle of Bull Run, July 21, 1861. *Washington.* 1861. 8vo, pp. 4. 33858

HUNT (Hiram P.) Speech of Mr. Hunt, of New York, on the Fortification Bill. ... Tuesday, June 7, 1836. *Washington: Printed by Gales & Seaton.* 1836. 8vo, pp. 13. 33859

HUNT. Speech of Hon. Hiram P. Hunt, of New York, on the Subject of the Reception of Abolition Petitions and Papers, ... January 23, 1840. *Washington: Madisonian Office.* 1840. 8vo, pp. 15. S. 33860

Also: Speech ... on the Sub-Treasury Bill ... June 3, 1840. *Washington: Gales and Seaton.* 1840. 8vo, pp. 15.

HUNT (H.) A Digest of the Decisions of the Grand Lodge I. O. of O. F., of the State of New York. Compiled by H. Hunt. *New York: A. J. Townsend, Printer.* 1850. 12mo, pp. iv, (1), 119. B. 33861

HUNT (I.) The Case of Isaac Hunt, Esq; of Philadelphia. ... *London, December* 7, 1776. 4to, pp. 15. P. 33862

Apparently by himself. Isaac Hunt was the father of Leigh Hunt. He was carted out of Philadelphia by the Whig mob to the tune of Yankee Doodle.

HUNT. Discourse delivered at St. Paul's Church, Shadwell, for the Benefit of the West Indian Sufferers of the Islands of Jamaica and Barbadoes. By Rev. Isaac Hunt. With Substance of Discourse on the Death of Captain Farmer, of the Quebec. 1782. 4to. Plate by Benjamin West. 33863

HUNT. A Discourse ... With ... Remarks on the present miserable Situation of the (once happy) United States of America. The Third Edition. Preached ... August the 20th, 1786 ... By Isaac Hunt, A.M. ... [n. p. n. d.] 8vo, pp. 24. BA. 33864

HUNT. The Family Compact; or a Discourse pointing out the Advantages of an Union between Great Britain and her Colonies. By Isaac Hunt. *Philadelphia.* 1775. 8vo. 33865

HUNT. The Political Family: or a Discourse pointing out the Reciprocal Advantages, which flow from an uninterrupted Union between Great Britain and her American Colonies. By Isaac Hunt. Numb. I. ... *Philadelphia: Printed, By James Humphreys, Junior.* M DCC LXXV. 8vo, pp. 32. BA. 33866

Also: Rights of Englishmen; an Antidote to the Poison now vending by the transatlantic Republican Thomas Paine, in reply to his whimsical Attacks against the Constitution and Government of Great Britain. ... *London.* 1791. 8vo. S.

HUNT (I. H.) Astounding Disclosures! Three Years in a Mad House. By a Victim. Written by Himself. A true Account of the barbarous, inhuman and cruel treatment of Isaac H. Hunt, in the State of Maine Insane Hospital, in the Years 1844, '45, '46 and '47, by Drs. Isaac Ray, James Bates, ... [*Boston:*] *Isaac H. Hunt.* 1851. 8vo, pp. 84. B. + *Augusta.* 1851. 8vo. + [With] a Short Account of the Horrid Torture of Miss Elizabeth T. Stone, ... by Dr. Luther V. Bell, in the M'Lean Asylum ... Also ... the Burning of the Maine Asylum, Dec. 4th, 1850. ... Second Edition, ... with many ... Additions. [*Boston:*] *For the Author.* 1852. 8vo, pp. 96. B., H. 33867

HUNT (J.) On the Negro's Place in Nature. By Dr. James Hunt, F.R.S. [Read before the Anthropological Society of London, Nov. 17th, 1863.] *London: For the Anthropological Society* 1863. 8vo, pp. viii, 60. BA. + The Negro's Place in Nature. A Paper read before the London Anthropological Society, By

Dr. James Hunt, F.R.S., President of the Association. *New York: Van Evrie, Horton & Co.* 1864. 8vo, pp. 27. B. + *New York: Anti-Abolition Tracts, No.* 4. 1868. 8vo, pp. 27. H.

HUNT (J.) An Adventure on a Frozen Lake; a Tale of the Canadian Rebellion of 1837-8, By J. Hunt, Jr. Also, The Massacre at Owego; an Indian Tale. *Cincinnati.* 1853. 8vo.

[HUNT (J.)] The American Union shown to be the New Heaven and the New Earth, and its Predicted Restoration to Life within Four Years from its Death. *New York: J. Thompson.* 1865. 8vo, pp. 41. H. 33870

HUNT (J.) Victory ... . A Sermon ... January 31, 1730. ... Death of Thomas Hollis, Esq; By Jeremiah Hunt ... . *London: T. Cox.* 1731. 8vo, pp. (4), 32. BA. 33871

Also: A Sermon preach'd at Pinner's Hall, Jan. 4, 1735-36; occasioned by the Death of John Hollis, Esq. ... *London.* 1736. 8vo, pp. 30.

HUNT (J.) A Sermon Preached September 25th, 1771, By John Hunt, ... At his Ordination, and at the Instalment of the Rev. John Bacon, to the ... Charge of the South-Church in Boston. ... *Boston: Printed by Kneeland & Adams.* MDCCLXXII. 8vo, pp. 36. H. 33872

HUNT. A Sermon occasioned by the Death of Mrs. Sarah Gill, ... Preached ... in Boston ... . By John Hunt, M.A. ... *Boston: Printed by Edes & Gill.* MDCCLXXI. 8vo, pp. (4), 79. B.

HUNT (J.) A Bill in the Chancery of New-Jersey, at the suit of John Hunt; against William Earl of Stirling And Others, Proprietors of the Eastern Division of the Province of New-Jersey. *Philadelphia: Printed by William Goddard.* M.DCC.LXVII. Folio, pp. 21. 33874

HUNT (J.) Journal of the Life, Religious Exercises, and Labours in the Work of the Ministry of John Hunt. *Philadelphia.* 1837. 12mo. 33875

HUNT (J. D.) The Union Restored By Legal Authority. Its Past Errors, Its Present Restoration, and Its Bright Future. By J. Dickinson Hunt, M.D. ... *New York.* 1865. 8vo, pp. 63.

HUNT (J. G.) Address before the Natural History Club of Philadelphia, December 3, 1868. By Dr. J. G. Hunt. *Philadelphia.* 1868. 8vo. 33877

HUNT (J. W.) The Wisconsin Almanac and Annual Register, 1856. By John Warren Hunt. *Milwaukie.* [n. d.] 8vo, pp. 96. 33878

HUNT. Wisconsin Gazetteer, containing the Names, Location, and Advantages, of the Counties, Cities Towns, Villages, Post Offices, and Settlements, together with a description of the Lakes, Water Courses, Prairies, and Public Localities, in the State of Wisconsin. Alphabetical arranged. By John Warren Hunt. *Madison: Beriah Brown, Printer.* 1853. 8vo, pp. 255, (1). Map. B., C. H. 33879

HUNT (J.), *Jr.* Address before the Washington Benevolent Society. By Jonathan Hunt, Jun. *Brattleborough.* 1812. 8vo.

HUNT (M.) Address of Memucan Hunt to the People of Texas, Soliciting the payment of his claims against the State at the next regular Session of the Legislature. With a few of his public and private papers in behalf of what he deemed the best interests of Texas in 1836, until annexation; together with a Speech of the Hon. W. M. Williams, before the last regular Session of the Legislature, on behalf of said claims; with which Speech is a copy of a Letter from Ex-President Houston, in reference to Memucan Hunt in 1836. *Galveston.* 1851. 8vo, pp. 84.

HUNT. Gen. Hunt's Letter to Senator Sam Houston. [n. p. 1849.] 12mo, pp. 11. BA. 33882

[HUNT.] The Public Debt and Lands of Texas. ... [n. p. 1848.] 8vo, pp. 16. BA. 33883

HUNT (N.) Memoir of Nathan Hunt (From the *Annual Monitor*, No. 12, New Series for 1854, page 167). 1854. 12mo.

HUNT (N. H.) The End of Strife. A Thanksgiving Sermon, preached in Baltimore, Md., December 7, 1865. By Noah H. Hunt. *Baltimore: Wm. H. Boyle, Printer.* 1865. 8vo, pp. 16.

[HUNT (Randell).] To the Union Party of South Carolina. [n. p. n. d.] 8vo, pp. 11. BA. 33886

HUNT (Richard S.), *and* RANDEL (J. F.) A New Guide to Texas, consisting of a Brief Outline of the History of its Settlement, and the Colonization and Land Laws; and Several Views of the Country. ... *New York.* 1844. 12mo. Map. + [*Ibid.*] 1846. 12mo. Map. 33887

HUNT (R. M.) Designs for the Gateways of the Southern Entrances to the Central Park. By Richard M. Hunt ... With a Description of the Designs, ... *New York: D. Van Nostrand.* 1866. 4to, pp. 36. B., H. 33888

HUNT (R.) An Address to the Merchants of the Mercantile Navy of the United Kingdom on the Advantages of Maritime Volunteer Service. By Rowland Hunt. *Shrewsbury.* 1803. 8vo.

Contains allusions to Lord Hood in the West Indies.

HUNT (T. G.) Good Faith and Union. Speech of Hon. Theodore G. Hunt in the House of Representatives, March 23, 1854, on the ... Nebraska and Kansas Territories ... . [*Washington.* n. d.] 8vo, pp. 8. B., BA. 33890

HUNT (T. L.) Canada and South Australia. A Commentary on that part of the Earl of Durham's Report which relates to the Disposal of Waste Lands and Emigration. In Three Papers, ... By Thornton Leigh Hunt. *London: A. Gole & Co.* 1839. 8vo, pp. 95. 33891

For a Reply *see* Rolph (Thos.)

HUNT (T. S.) Canada: a Geographical, Agricultural, and Mineralogical Sketch. By T. Sterry Hunt ... . *Dublin: Printed for Distribution at the Dublin Exhibition.* 1853. 33892

HUNT. Geological Survey of Canada. ... Report of Dr. T. Sterry Hunt, F.R.S., on the Gold Region of Nova Scotia. ... *Ottawa.* 1868. 8vo, pp. 48. 33893

HUNT. ... On the Laurentian Limestones of North America. By T. Sterry Hunt ... . Reprinted with Additions from the Report of the Geological Survey of Canada for 1863-66. *Albany.* 186-. 8vo, pp. 54. 33894

See New Brunswick.

HUNT (T. P.) The Book of Wealth; in which is proved from the Bible, that it is the Duty of Every Man, to become rich. By Rev. Thomas P. Hunt. *New-York: Ezra Collier.* 1836. 12mo, pp. 119. 33895

Also: The Wedding Days of Former Times. ... *Philadelphia.* 1845. 24mo. Plate.

HUNT (Timothy D.) Address ... before the New England Society of San Francisco ... on the Twenty-Second ... of December, A.D. 1852. By Rev. T. Dwight Hunt ... . *San Francisco: Cooke, Kenny & Co.* 1853. 8vo, pp. 20. B., H. 33896

HUNT (W.) Remarks of Washington Hunt ... February 9, 1844, on ... Representatives ... elected by General Ticket are entitled to their Seats. [n. p. n. d.] 8vo, pp. 8. H. 33897

HUNT. Speech of Mr. Washington Hunt ... on the Naturalization Laws, and Frauds on the Ballot-Box ... December 29, 1845. ... [n. p. n. d.] 8vo, pp. 8. H. 33898

Also: Address of Ex-Gov. Hunt in Defence of the Union Electoral Ticket. [n. p. n. d.] 8vo, pp. 8. B.—No. 14. Papers from the Society for the Diffusion of Political Knowledge. ... Speech of Ex-Gov. Hunt, at Lockport. [n. p. n. d.] 8vo, pp. 8. B.—Report on Harbors and Rivers, with other Documents. ... [n. p. 1848.] 8vo.—Speech ... on Native Americanism, 1845. [n. p. n. d.] 8vo.—Speech ... on the Tariff, ... June 24, 1846. [n. p. n. d.] 8vo, pp. 15. H.

HUNT (W.) American Biographical Panorama. By William Hunt. ... *Albany: Printed by Joel Munsell.* 1849. 8vo, pp. 480. Chronology of Zadock Pratt, pp. 18. Portraits and Plates. B.

The portraits are not only original engravings, but original designs. They are imaginary likenesses. *See* Munsell's Catalogue of his publications. It was also issued as "The American Biographical Sketch Book."

HUNT. Hunt's Albany Commercial Directory, for 1848-9. Compiled ... by William Hunt ... . *Albany: Joel Munsell, Printer.* 1848. 18mo. 33900

Also: Leaves from the American Biographical Sketch Book. [Biography of Mrs. Emma Willard.] ... *Albany: J. Munsell.* 1848. 8vo, pp. 8.

HUNT (W.) The Cabinet of Nature and Philosophy. Book the First. The Cabinet of Shells. By William Hunt, M.D. *Boston: Munroe and Francis.* 1833. 8vo, pp. 16. 4 Plates. H.

HUNT (W.) Letters to the People from W. Hunt, D. D. Barnard, and Sam Houston, July, 1856. [n. p. n. d.] 8vo, pp. 16. 33902

HUNT (W. *and* N.) Memoirs of William and Nathan Hunt, taken chiefly from their Journal and Letters. *Philadelphia: Uriah Hunt & Son.* 1858. 16mo, pp. 320. 33903

HUNT (W. G.) An Address on the Character and Services of De Witt Clinton, delivered at Nashville, March 11, 1828, at the request of the Grand Chapter of Tennessee. By William Gibbes Hunt ... . *Nashville: Printed by John S. Simpson.* 1828. 8vo, pp. 20. B., BA., H. 33904

HUNT. An Appeal to the Public, in Consequence of an Attack by the Rev: Nathan H. Hall ... in an Anonymous Article signed Spectator. By William Gibbes Hunt. *Lexington.* 1824. 8vo, pp. 15. B., BA., H. 33905

Hunt. A Masonic Eulogy on ... the late Thomas Smith Webb, Esq. ... September 1st, 1819. By ... William Gibbes Hunt ... . *Lexington.* 1819. 8vo, pp. 16. BA. 33906

Hunt. An Oration in Honor of Gen. Lafayette; delivered in his Presence, Nashville, May 4, 1825, at the Request of the Grand Lodge of Tennessee. *Nashville.* 1825. 8vo, pp. 12.

Hunt (W. L. G.) Genealogy of the Name and Family of Hunt, exhibiting Pedigree of Ten Thousand Persons. With Historical Sketches, &c. By W. L. G. Hunt. *Boston.* 1862. 4to, pp. 414. 33908

[Hunter (Alfred).] An Alphabetical List of Patented Models ... . *Washington: Alfred Hunter.* 1859. 8vo, pp 66.

[Hunter.] A Popular Catalogue of the Extraordinary Curiosities in the National Institute ... . Second Edition. *Washington: Alfred Hunter.* 1857. 8vo, pp. 71. B. + [*Ibid.*] 1859. 8vo, pp. 38, (10). B. 33910

Hunter (C. G.) Authentic Account of the Fatal Duel fought on Sunday the 21st March, 1830, near Chester, Penn., between Mr. Charles G. Hunter and Mr. William Miller, Jr. ... *Washington: Jonathan Elliot.* 1830. 8vo, pp. 81. 33911

Hunter (D. J.) A Sketch of Chili, expressly prepared for the Use of Emigrants, from the United States and Europe ... . With a Map and ... Papers relating to the ... War between that Country and Spain, and the Position assumed by the United States ... . By Daniel J. Hunter. *New York: Printed by S. Hallet.* 1866. 8vo, pp. (2), iii, 53. BA., H. 33912

The Second Part is entitled: Chili, the United States and Spain: a Series of Lectures ... on the Position ... of Chili in the Pending War with Spain. ... *New York: Printed by S. Hallet.* 1866. 8vo, pp. (2), 128. BA., H.

Hunter (D.) Correspondence, Orders, etc., between Major General David Hunter, Major-General J. G. Foster, and Brigadier-General H. M. Naglee, and others, February and March, 1863. *Philadelphia: J. B. Lippincott & Co.* 1863. 8vo, pp. 60.

Hunter. Letter to Edwin M. Stanton, Secretary of War. *Boston: Emancipation League.* 1862. 8vo, pp. 4. 33914

On the Resolution of Mr. Wyckoff of Kentucky.

Hunter (E. P.) Funeral Eulogy and Prayer on the Death of M. W. Edmund P. Hunter, Grand Master of the Grand Lodge of Virginia. November 4, 1854. *Richmond.* 1854. 8vo, pp. 16. 33915

Hunter (F.) Western Border Life; or, What Fanny Hunter Saw and Heard in Kansas and Missouri. *New York: Derby & Jackson.* 1857. 12mo, pp. 408. H. 33916

Hunter (H. A.) A Narrative of the Captivity and Sufferings of Isaac Knight from Indian Barbarity. Giving an Account of the Cruel Treatment he received from the Savages while afflicted with the Small Pox: His Escape and Joyful Return after enduring the Hardships of an Indian Prisoner, during Two Years and Six Months. Communicated by Himself, And at his Request written by Hiram A. Hunter. *Evansville: Printed at the Journal Office.* 1829. 12mo, pp. 34. 33917

Hunter's narrative of captivity forms the first half of the volume, and anecdotes of Indians the remainder, both reprints of very common books, without addition.

Hunter (J.) Observations on the Diseases of the Army in Jamaica, and on the best Means of preserving the Health of Europeans in that Climate. ... By John Hunter, M.D. ... *London.* 1788. 8vo. + Second Edition. [*Ibid.*] 1796. 8vo. + Third Edition. *London: Payne.* 1808. 8vo, pp. 315. 33918

Hunter (J.) Remarks of John Hunter in the Senate of New York, in relation to the Legislative Power of Expulsion. [n. p.] 1836. Folio. S. 33919

Also: Speech ... on the Commercial Bank, 1836. [n. p. n. d.] 8vo. S.

Hunter (J. D.) Manners and Customs of several Indian Tribes located West of the Mississippi; including some Account of the Soil, Climate, and Vegetable Productions, and the Indian Materia Medica: to which is prefixed the History of the Author's Life during a Residence of several years among them. By John D. Hunter. *Philadelphia: Printed for the Author by J. Maxwell.* 1823. 8vo, pp. 402. BA., H., P. 33920

Reprinted with the following title:

Hunter. Memoirs of a Captivity among the Indians of North America, from Childhood to the age of Nineteen: With Anecdotes descriptive of their Manners and Customs. To which is added, some account of the Soil, Climate, and Vegetable Productions of the Territory Westward of the Mississippi. By John D. Hunter. A New Edition, with Portrait. *London: Longman,* .. 1823. 8vo, pp. ix, 447. BA., H. + The Third Edition, with Additions. [*Ibid.*] 1824. 8vo, pp. xi, 468. Portrait.

There having been some insinuations that the work was a fabrication, the author, in the third edition, addressed a note to his publishers, referring to Colonel Aspinwall and others, as certifying to the authenticity of the work. *See* "Quart. Rev.," XXXI. 76–111; "M. Rev.," New Series, CII. 243; "Blackwood's Magazine," XVI. 639, XVII. 56; "Literary Gazette" for 1823, p. 242, &c., "N. A. Rev.," XXII. 94 [by General Cass]. *See also* Norgate (E.) *and* Neale (J.)

Hunter. Der Gefangene unter den Wilden in Nord Amerika. Herausgegeben von W. A. Lindau. *Dresden.* 1824. 16mo. 33922

[Hunter.] Reflections on the Different States and Conditions of Society; with ... a Plan to ameliorate the Circumstances of the Indians of North Carolina. *London: Printed by J. R. Lake.* 1823. 8vo, pp. 20. H. 33923

Hunter (J. H.) A Sermon ... Death of Mrs. Susannah Hull ... Jan. 15, 1832. By ... Rev. John H. Hunter ... . *New Haven: Printed by S. Babcock.* 1832. 8vo, pp. 16. 33924

Hunter (J.) Collections concerning the Early History of the Founders of New Plymouth, the First Colonists of New-England. By Rev. Joseph Hunter ... . *London: J. Russell Smith.* 1849. 8vo, pp. (2), 70. B., BA., C., S. 33925

Reprinted in the "Mass. Hist. Soc. Collections," Vol. I., Fourth Series.

Hunter. Collections concerning the Church or Congregation of Protestant Separatists formed at Scrooby, in North Nottinghamshire, in the Time of King James I.: The Founders of New-Plymouth, the Parent-Colony of New-England. By Rev. Joseph Hunter ... *London: J. Russell Smith.* M.DCCC.LIV. 8vo, pp. xiv, (2), 205, Errata, 1 slip. B., BA., H. 33926

Some copies have "A View of the Archiepiscopal Palace at Scrooby, the residence of William Brewster, the Pilgrim Father."

Hunter (R. M. T.) Mr. Hunter's Oration. Opening Ode [by John R. Thompson] delivered at the Inauguration of the Equestrian Statue of Washington, Richmond, Virginia, 22 February, 1858. [*Richmond:*] *Macfarlane & Fergusson.* 1858. 8vo, pp. 24. + [n. p. n. d.] 8vo, pp. 24. 33927

Hunter. Observations on the History of Virginia. A Discourse ... before the Virginia Historical Society ... December 14, 1854. By R. M. T. Hunter. *Richmond: Clemmitt & Fore, Printers.* 1855. 12mo, pp. 48. BA., H. 33928

Hunter. Speech of R. M. T. Hunter, of Virginia, on the Bill Reducing the Duty on Imports, and for other Purposes. Delivered ... June 30, 1846. *Washington.* 1846. 8vo, pp. 13.

Also: Address ... before ... Virginia Military Institute, July 3, 1857. *Richmond: Macfarlane & Fergusson.* 1857. 8vo, pp. 59.—Speech ... on the Loan Bill: ... July 10, 1841. *Washington: Printed by Blair and Rives.* 1841. 8vo, pp. 16.—Speech ... July 4, 1842, on the Tariff. *Washington.* 1842. 8vo.—Speech ... on the Subject of the Retrocession of Alexandria to Virginia ... May 8, 1846. *Alexandria, D. C.* 1846. 8vo, pp. 12.—Speech ... on the Resolution of Notice to Great Britain to abrogate the Convention of Joint Occupancy relative to the Oregon Territory. ... January 10, 1848. [n. p. n. d.] 8vo, pp. 8. H.—Speech ... on the Ten Regiment Bill. ... February 7, 1848. [n. p. n. d.] 8vo, pp. 15.—Speech ... on the Oregon Territory Bill. ... July 11, 1848. *Towers, Printer, Washington.* 1848. 8vo, pp. 16.—Speech ... January 31, 1850. On suspending our Diplomatic Relation with Austria. [*Washington.* 1850.] 8vo, pp. 70.—Speech ... July 18, 1850, on the Admission of California. [n. p. n. d.] 8vo, pp. 16.—Speech ... February 17, 1852, on the Bill granting Land to the State of Iowa in Aid of constructing certain Railroads. [n. p. n. d.] 8vo, pp. 8.—Speech ... Feb. 24, 1854, on the Kansas and Nebraska Bill. *Washington.* 1854. 8vo.—Speech ... on the Resolutions of the Massachusetts Legislature concerning the Assaûlt on Mr. Sumner. ... June 24, 1856. *Washington.* 1856. 8vo, pp. 12.—Speech ... at the Democratic Demonstration at Poughkeepsie, N. Y. [n. p.] 1856. 8vo.—Speech ... Feb. 26, 1857, on the Tariff. *Washington.* [n. d.] 8vo, pp. 7.—Speech .. on the Admission of ... Kansas ... March 12, 1858. [*Washington:*] *Printed by Lemuel Towers.* [1858.] 8vo, pp. 16.—Speech ... Invasion of Virginia, delivered ... January 30, 1860. [n. p. n. d.] 8vo, pp. 16.—Speech ... on the Resolution proposing to retrocede the Forts, Dock-Yards, etc., to the State applying for the same. ... Jan. 11, 1861. [n. p. n. d.] 8vo, pp. 16.—The Ruling Passion Strong in Death Speech ... on the Bill for Arming the Slaves. *Manchester, England.* Folio, 1 l.

Hunter, *and others.* The Address of Southern Delegates in Congress, to their Constituents. [*Washington.* n. d.] 8vo, pp. 15. BA. 33930

Hunter (T.) An Historical Account of Earthquakes, extracted from the most Authentic Historians. And a Sermon preached at Weaverham, in Cheshire, on Friday, the 6th of February last [1756]. By Rev. Thomas Hunter. *Liverpool: R. Williamson.* 1756. 8vo, pp. (4), 159. C. 33931

Hunter (W.) National Calamities founded in National Dissension and Dissipation. Preached on the late General Fast. By William Hunter, A.M. ... *London: T. Cadell.* 1780. 4to.

Relates to Sir William Howe.

Hunter (W.) Oration Pronounced before the Citizens of Providence, on the Fourth of July, 1826, being the Fiftieth Anniversary of American Independence. By William Hunter ... . *Providence: Smith & Parmenter, Printers.* 1826. 8vo, pp. 46, (3). + Second Edition. [*Ibid.*] 1826. 8vo, pp. 46, (3). BA. 33933

Relates chiefly to the part taken by Rhode Island in the "splendid drama" of American Independence.

Hunter. Speech of the Hon. William Hunter ... Feb. 2d, 1813. On ... seizing ... East-Florida by the Troops of the U. States. *Newport, R. I.: Rousmaniere & Barber.* 1813. 8vo, pp. 39. BA. 33934

Also: Annual Address, delivered before the Rhode Island Society for the Encouragement of Domestic Industry, October 20, 1824. ... *Providence: Carlile & Brown.* 1826. 8vo, pp. 43.—An Oration; delivered in Trinity-Church, in Newport, on the Fourth of July, 1801. ... *Newport: Newport Mercury.* 1801. 8vo, pp. 32.—An Oration ... in Newport, July 4, A.D. 1795, On the Celebration of the Nineteenth Anniversary of American Independence. ... *Newport: Printed by Henry Barber.* 1795. 8vo, pp. 30.

Hunter (W.) Sovereignty, Allegiance and Secession; an Essay on the Constitution and Government of the United States. By William Hunter. *Memphis: Printed by James Dumars.* 1868. 8vo, pp. 43. H. 33935

Also: Charge ... to the Grand Jury of the Criminal Court of Memphis. ... June 11th, 1866. [n. p. n. d.] 8vo, pp. 8. H.

Hunter (W. S.), *Jr.* Eastern Township's Scenery, Canada East. By William S. Hunter, Jr. *Montreal.* 1860. 4to, pp. 36. Plates. S. 33936

Hunter. Hunter's Ottawa Scenery, in the Vicinity of Ottawa City, Canada. *Ottawa City.* 1855. 4to, pp. 19. 15 Engravings and Map. 33937

Hunter. Panoramic Guide from Niagara Falls to Quebec; with a folded Picture Map of the most Celebrated and Picturesque Points along the Rivers St. Lawrence and Niagara, and Lake Ontario. By William S. Hunter, Jr. *Montreal and Boston.* 1857. 8vo, pp. 66. B. + *Montreal.* 1866. + [*Ibid.*] 1867.

Also: Chisholm's Panoramic Guide from Niagara Falls to Quebec. ... *Montreal: C. R. Chisholm.* 1869. 12mo, pp. iii, 66. Large folded Plate. B.

Argument in the case of the Ship Hunter. *Washington.* 1824. 8vo. B. 33939

Also: Second Memorial in case of Ship Hunter. *New York.* 1823.

The Hunter's Guide and Trapper's Companion. A Complete Guide in all the various methods by which to capture all kinds of Game, Fur Animals, and how to Cure and Tan their Skins. *Hinsdale.* 1867. + New Edition. *Hinsdale, N. H.: Hunter & Co.* 1869. 16mo, pp. 60. + [*Ibid.*] 1871. 18mo, pp. 74.

The Hunters of Kentucky; or the Trials and Toils of Traders and Trappers during an Expedition to the Rocky Mountains, New Mexico, and California. [By B. Bilson.] *New York: W. H. Graham.* 1847. 8vo, pp. 100. 33941

"A reproduction of Pattie's narrative, which the penury of the thieving writer's imagination has not empowered him to clothe with new language, or interleave with new incidents."—T. W. Field.

Hunting (S[ylvan] S[tanley]). A Funeral Sermon occasioned by the Death of Frank A. Brown, preached ... Manchester, February 2, 1859. By S. S. Hunting. *Manchester, N. H.: Printed by Charles S. Livingstone.* 1859. 8vo, pp. 19.

Huntington (A.) A Discourse designed to comfort the Afflicted, delivered Feb. 28th, 1806, at the Interment of the Rev. Levi Frisbie, A.M. ... By Asahel Huntington ... . *Salem: Printed by Joshua Cushing.* 1806. 8vo, pp. 24. BA. 33943

Huntington. Reply to "the Alarming Developments" ... of the Rev. B. F. Clark ... in the Matter of the "Wrong Member of the Middlesex Bar convicted of Perjury," &c. By Asahel Huntington ... . *Lowell, Mass.: For the Author.* 1848. 8vo, pp. 22. BA., H. 33944

Huntington. A Sermon delivered at Topsfield, January 5, 1800. Occasioned by the Death of George Washington. ... Asahel Huntington, A.M. ... *Salem: Printed by Joshua Cushing.* 1800. 8vo, pp. 32. 33945

Very rare. Contains "An Historical Sketch" of General Washington.

Huntington (C. B.) Trial. *See* [Brady (J. T.)], No. 7314.

Huntington (D.) Address ... at the Consecration of the Union Cemetery, at ... North Bridgewater, Mass., May 21, 1849. By Daniel Huntington ... . [n. p. n. d.] 8vo, pp. 8. H.

Huntington. A Discourse in the North Meeting-House in Bridgewater, Dec. 22, 1820, being the Second Centurial Anniversary of the Landing of the Pilgrims at Plymouth. By Daniel Huntington ... . *Boston: Ezra Lincoln.* 1821. 8vo. W. 33947

Contains a History of the Township of Bridgewater, Mass.

Huntington. An intolerant Spirit, hostile to the interests of Society. A Sermon ... before ... John Brooks, Esq. Governor ... on the Anniversary Election, May 29, 1822. By Daniel Huntington ... . *Boston: B. Russell.* 1822. 8vo, pp. 20. B., BA.

Huntington. The Love of Jerusalem, the Prosperity of a People. A Sermon Preached at the Anniversary Election, Hartford, May 12, 1814. By Daniel Huntington ... . *Hartford: Printed by Hudson and Goodwin.* 1814. 8vo, pp. 40. H. 33949

[Huntington.] Memories, Counsels, and Reflections. By an Octogenary. Addressed to his Children and Descendants, and printed for their use. ... *Cambridge: Metcalf and Company.* 1857. 8vo, pp. (4), 119. H. 33950

Also: A Discourse ... at the Request of the Female Charitable Society, in ... Middletown, December 26th, 1809. ... *Middletown: Printed by T. Dunning.* 1810. 8vo, pp. 19.—A Discourse ... at Braintree [Mass.], ... April 9, 1818, at the Funeral of Mrs. Sarah Strong Storrs, Wife of the Rev. Richard S. Storrs; ... *Boston: Printed by Nathaniel Willis.* 1818. 8vo, pp. 24.—A Discourse ... at the Organization of the Trinitarian Congregational Church, in Taunton, Mass.—Aug. 16, 1821. ... *Boston: Printed by True, Green and Field.* 1821. 8vo, pp. 16.—Discourse ... at the Funeral of the Rev. Philip Colby ... March 3d, 1851. ... *New Bedford: Press of Benjamin Lindsay.* 1851. 8vo, pp. 18.—A Poem, on the Pleasures and Advantages of True Religion. Delivered before the United Brothers' Society, in Brown University, on their Anniversary, August 31, 1819. ... *Providence.* 1819. 8vo, pp. 23.—Sermon at Bridgewater [Mass.], May 12, 1812, at the Funeral of Alpheus Packard. ... *Boston.* 1812. 8vo.—A Sermon ... before the Massachusetts Society for Promoting Christian Knowledge, May 26, 1824. ... *Boston: Printed by Crocker and Brewster.* 1824. 8vo, pp. 32.

Huntington (E.) Discourse at the Freeman's Meeting, Killingworth, Conn., April 11, 1768. By Eliphalet Huntington. *Hartford.* 1768. 8vo, pp. 24. 33951

Huntington (E.) An Address on the Life ... of Elisha Bartlett, M.D. ... December 26, 1855. By Elisha Huntington, M.D. ... *Lowell: S. J. Varney.* 1856. 8vo, pp. 27. BA., H.

Huntington (E. A.) ... A Discourse ... Thanksgiving Day, November 20, 1856 ... By E. A. Huntington. *Auburn.* 1856. 8vo, pp. 24. H. 33953

Huntington (E. B.) A Genealogical Memoir of the Huntington Family in this Country; embracing ... Descendants of Simon and Margaret Huntington, who have retained the Family Name, and the First Generation of the Descendants of other Names. By Rev. E. B. Huntington, A.M. *Stamford, Conn.: The Author.* 1863. 8vo, pp. xii, 9–428. Portraits. B., BA., H.

Huntington. History of Stamford, Connecticut, from its Settlement in 1641, to the Present Time, including Darien, which was one of its Parishes until 1820. By Rev. E. B. Huntington, A.M. *Stamford: The Author.* 1868. 8vo, pp. (8), 492. Plates and Portraits. B., BA., H. 33955

Huntington. Soldiers' Memorial. By Rev. E. B. Huntington, A.M. *Stamford: The Author.* 1869. 8vo, pp. 165, (1).

Huntington (E.) A Discourse ... Death of the Honorable Jabez Hamlin, Esq. who departed this Life April 25th, 1791 ... By Enoch Huntington ... . *Middletown: Printed by M. H. Woodward.* M,DCC,XCI. 12mo, pp. 24. B. 33957

Huntington. The Happy Effects of Union, and the Fatal Tendency of Divisions. Shewn in a Sermon, Preached before the Freemen of the Town of Middletown, at their Annual Meeting, April 8, 1776. By Enoch Huntington ... . *Hartford: Printed by Eben. Watson.* MDCCLXXVI. 8vo, pp. 28. H., S.

Huntington. An Oration delivered at Middletown, in the State of Connecticut, February 22, A.D. 1800. By Enoch Huntington, A.M. ... *Middletown: Printed by Tertius Dunning.* 1800. 8vo, pp. 9. H. 33959

On the Death of General Washington.

Huntington. Political Wisdom. Or Honesty the best Policy. Sermon at Middletown, April 10, 1786. By Enoch Huntington ... . *Middletown.* 1786. 8vo. W. 33960

Huntington. A Sermon ... at Middletown, July 20th, A.D. 1775, The Day appointed by the Continental Congress ... as a Day of ... Fasting ... . By Enoch Huntington ... . *Hartford: Printed by Eben. Watson.* [1775.] 12mo, pp. 26. BA., M. 33961

Also: Sermon at East Haddam, Conn., Oct. 28, 1772, at the Ordination of Elijah Parsons. ... *New London.* 1773. 12mo, pp. 35.—Sermon at Middletown, occasioned by the Death of Mr. Hezekiah Hulbert. ... *Middletown.* 1800. 8vo, pp. 19.—A Sermon ... at Haddam, June 14, 1797, On the Day of the Execution of Thomas Starr, ... for ... Murder of ... Samuel Cornwell ... . *Middletown: Printed by Moses H. Woodward.* 1797. 8vo, pp. 24. BA., H.

Huntington (E. A.) ... A Sermon ... at the Dedication of the new House of Worship Erected by the Third Presbyterian Church, on Clinton Square, Albany, ... Dec. 3, 1845. By Rev. Ezra A. Huntington ... . *Albany: J. Munsell.* 1845. 8vo, pp. 46. 33962

Two hundred and fifty copies printed. Also: A Funeral Discourse on David Perkins Page, A.M., late Principal of the State Normal School, Albany, ... Jan. 9, 1848 ... . *Albany: E. H. Pease & Co.* 1848. 8vo, pp. 39.—A Sermon ... Death of William Gould ... January 25, 1846. ... [n. p.] 1846. 8vo, pp. 8.—Strife for Supremacy in the Church. A Sermon, ... at the Opening of the Synod of Albany, October 12, 1852. ... *Albany.* 1852. 8vo, pp. 36.

Huntington (F. D.) Christian Citizenship and Honest Legislation. A Sermon ... at the Annual Election ... Jan. 6, 1858. By Rev. Frederic D. Huntington, D.D. ... *Boston: Gould and Lincoln.* 1858. 8vo, pp. 44. H., M. 33963

HUNTINGTON. The Conclusion of a Ministry in ... Emanuel Church; A Sermon ... March 21, 1869. By ... F. D. Huntington ... . *Boston.* 1869. 8vo, pp. 24. B. 33964

Also: ... An Address ... before the Mass. Charitable Mechanic Association ... September 24, 1856. ... *Boston.* 1856. 8vo, pp. 35.— ... An Anniversary Sermon for Emanuel Church ... September 22, 1861. ... *Boston: E. P. Dutton and Company.* 1861. 8vo, pp. 34, (1).—The Character of Manlius Stimpson Clarke. A Discourse delivered ... May 1, 1853. ... *Boston: Crosby, Nichols, and Company.* 1853. 8vo, pp. 32.—A Discourse preached ... on the First Sunday in the Year ... *Boston: Leonard C. Bowles.* 1845. 8vo, pp. 24.—A Discourse in behalf of the Ministry at Large, ... delivered ... before the "Fraternity," April 16, 1854. ... *Boston: Printed by John Wilson & Son.* 1854. 8vo, pp. 27.—The Famine and the Sword. Brotherhood of Nations. A Sermon ... February 21, 1847. ... *Boston: Leonard C. Bowles.* 1847. 8vo, pp. 15.—The Great Conflict of the Day: A Discourse ... September 20, 1846. ... *Boston: Leonard C. Bowles.* 1846. 8vo, pp. 11.—Home and College. A Public Address delivered in the ... Massachusetts House of Representatives, March 8, 1860. ... *Boston: Crosby, Nichols* ... . 1860. 16mo, pp. 70. H.—Massachusetts a Field for Church Missions. A Sermon ... May 20, 1863. ... *Boston: E. P. Dutton and Company.* 1863. 12mo, pp. 42. B.—Our Duty, as Christian Citizens, to the Sailor. An Address ... May 28, 1862 ... . *Boston: Press of T. R. Marvin & Son.* 1862. 8vo, pp. 11, (1).—Peace, the Demand of Christianity. A Sermon ... December 28, 1845. ... *Boston: Leonard C. Bowles.* 1846. 8vo, pp. 24.—Personal Humiliation demanded by the National Danger. A Sermon ... April 24, 1864. ... *Boston: E. P. Dutton & Co.* 1864. 12mo, pp. 16.— ... A Sermon ... before the Howard Benevolent Society ... January 15, 1844. ... *Boston: William Crosby.* 1844. 8vo, pp. 26.— ... A Sermon delivered in behalf of the Warren Street Chapel at the Ninth Anniversary of the Opening of the Building, January 26, 1845. ... *Boston: Dutton and Wentworth.* 1845. 8vo, pp. 15. BA.—A Sermon ... on the Fiftieth Anniversary of the Boston Female Asylum, Sept. 20, 1850. ... *Boston: Printed by John Wilson.* 1850. 8vo, pp. 40.— ... A Sermon ... at the Installation of the Rev. E. E. Hale ... . *Boston: Leonard C. Bowles.* 1856. 8vo, pp. 63.—A Sermon on the Character and Death of Leonard Donham, ... of the Senior Class in Harvard ... . *Cambridge: Metcalf and Company.* 1857. 8vo, pp. 15. B.—A Sermon before the Society for the Relief of the Widows and Orphans of deceased Clergymen of the Protestant Episcopal Church ... March 13, 1864. ... *Boston: E. P. Dutton and Company.* 1864. 16mo, pp. 23, (1). B. *See also* Hadley, Mass.

HUNTINGTON (G.) The Guests of Brazil, or the Martyrdom of Frederick. A Tragedy. By Gurdon Huntington. *New York: Burgess, Stringer, & Co.* 1844. 12mo, pp. 70, (1). BA. 33965

HUNTINGTON. The Shadowy Land, and other Poems, including The Guests of Brazil. By Rev. Gurdon Huntington. *New York: D. Dana, Jr.* 1860. 8vo, pp. 506, (2). + *New York: J. Miller.* 1861. 8vo, pp. 506, (2). B., C., H. 33966

HUNTINGTON (Jabez W.) Speech of Mr. Huntington, of Connecticut, On the ... Removal of the Deposites. ... January, 1834. By J. W. Huntington. *Washington: Printed by Gales & Seaton.* 1834. 8vo, pp. 32. B. + [Another Edition.] 8vo, pp. 28. 33967

HUNTINGTON. Speech of Mr. Huntington, on the Bill to provide for the Removal of the Indians West of the Mississippi, Delivered in the House of Representatives, May 18, 1830. [n. p. n. d.] 8vo, pp. 28. 33968

Also: Speech ... on the Amendment to the Bill "to incorporate the Subscribers to the Fiscal Bank of the United States" ... . July 3, 1841. *Washington.* 1841. 8vo, pp. 15.—Speech ... on the Oregon Question: ... April 13, 1845. *Washington: Gales and Seaton, Printers.* 1846. 8vo, pp. 15.—Speech ... March 21, 1842, on the Resolutions of Mr. Clay. *Washington.* 1842. 8vo.—Speech ... May 31, 1842, on Apportionment. *Washington.* 1842. 8vo.

[HUNTINGTON (Jedediah Vincent).] Alban. A Tale of the New World. *New York: George P. Putnam.* M.DCCC.LI. 12mo, pp. 496. BA. 33969

Reprinted as: Alban. A Tale ... *London: Colburn & Co.* 1851. 3 vols., post 8vo. + Alban: or, the History of a Young Puritan. ... *Bedford, N. Y.* 1853. 2 vols., 12mo.

[HUNTINGTON.] The Forest. A Sequel to Alban. *New York.* 1852. 33970

Relates to an Indian hunting ground. Also: America Discovered: a Poem. ... *New York.* 1852. 8vo.—Poems. ... *New York.* 1843. 12mo.

END OF VOLUME EIGHT.

A DICTIONARY OF BOOKS

RELATING TO AMERICA.

UNTINGTON (J.) A Discourse adapted to the Present Day, on the Health and Happiness, or Misery and Ruin, of the Body Politic, In Similitude to that of the Natural Body, Preached at Coventry, April, 1781. By Joseph Huntington, D.D. *Hartford.* 1781. 8vo, pp. 24. 33971

HUNTINGTON. God ruling the Nations for the most glorious end. A Sermon in presence of his Excellency [Gov. Trumbull] and both Houses of Assembly, Hartford, May 15th, 1784. By Joseph Huntington, D.D. *Hartford: Printed by Hudson & Goodwin.* M.DCC.LXXXIV. 8vo, pp. 42. 33972

[HUNTINGTON.] A Plea before the Ecclesiastical Council at Stockbridge, in the Cause of Mrs. Fisk, ... delivered 6th and 7th of October, 1779. ... By a Gentleman of Connecticut. *Norwich: J. Trumbull.* 1780. 4to, pp. 32. + *Boston: Printed by N. Coverly and R. Hodge.* M.DCC.LXXXII. 12mo, pp. 44. BA. + [Another Edition.] pp. 46. BA. 33973

For a letter to the author *see* Impartialis, *pseudon.* Also: Discourse on the Vanity and Mischief of presuming on Things beyond our Measure. ... *Norwich.* 1774. 4to, pp. 30.—A Sermon ... at the Funeral of Mrs. Esther Strong ... October 21st, 1793. ... *Hartford: Printed by Hudson and Goodwin.* MDCCXCIII. 8vo, pp. 24. B.

HUNTINGTON (J.) Funeral Eulogy by General J. Huntington, and Oration by Lyman Law, delivered at New-London, January 11th, 1800. On the Death of General Washington. *New-London Jany* 20, 1800. 8vo, pp. 17. 33974

Not very scarce. Published without a title-page.

HUNTINGTON. Gropings after Truth: a Life Journey from New England Congregationalism to the One Catholic and Apostolic Church. By Joshua Huntington. *New York: Catholic Publication Society.* 1868. 16mo, pp. (2), 167. B., C., H. 33975

HUNTINGTON. Memoirs of the Life of Mrs. Abigail Waters; who died in Boston, November 22d, 1816, in the 96th year of her Age. By Joshua Huntington. ... Second Edition. *Boston.* 1817. 18mo, pp. 144. B. + *York.* 1829. 33976

HUNTINGTON (L. S.) The Independence of Canada. ... Address ... before the Agricultural Society of the County of Missisquoi at Bedford, Sept. 8, 1869. By the Hon. L. S. Huntington, Q.C., M.P. ... *Montreal.* 1869. 8vo, pp. 14. H. 33977

[HUNTINGTON (*Miss*).] Sea-Spray: A Long-Island Village. By Martha Wickham. *New-York.* 1857. 12mo, pp. 461. S.

HUNTINGTON (Susan). *See* [Wisner (Benjamin B.)]

HUNTINGTON (W. R.) American Catholicity. A Sermon ... before the Church Union of ... Massachusetts ... May 16, 1865. By Rev. William R. Huntington ... . *Boston.* 1865. 12mo, pp. 28, (2). B., H. 33979

Huntington and Broad Top Mountain Railroad and Coal Company. Annual Report of the President and Directors, for the year 1854. *Philadelphia.* 1854. 8vo. P. 33980

[HUNTLEY (*Sir* Henry V., R.N.)] California: its Gold and its Inhabitants. ... *London: Thomas Cautley Newby.* 1856. 2 vols., post 8vo, pp. iv, 303; (2), 286. BA., C. 33981

Also: Seven Years Service on the Slave Coast of Western Africa. ... *London.* 1850. 2 vols., post 8vo. P.

HUNTLEY (Lydia). *See* Sigourney (L. H.)

HUNTOON (B.) A Eulogy ... in Commemoration of Rev. and R. W. Thaddeus Mason Harris, D.D. and R. W. Brother Samuel Thaxter ... May 4th, 1842. By Benjamin Huntoon ... . *Boston: Benjamin H. Greene.* 1842. 8vo, pp. 15, (1). BA., H. 33982

HUNTOON. A Sermon, preached at the Re-opening and Dedication of the Church of the First Congregational Parish in Milton, December 9, 1835. By Benjamin Huntoon ... . *Boston: Russell, Shattuck & Co.* 1836. 8vo, pp. 24. M. 33983

Also: An Address at the Installation of the Officers of Mount Zion Royal Arch Chapter, Stoughton, 15 December, A.L. 5828. ... 8vo. + Second Edition. *Boston.*

1829. 8vo.—A Discourse ... before the ... Free ... Masons ... at Walpole [Mass.], ... June 24, 1823. ... *Boston: Charles Crocker, Printer.* 1823. 8vo, pp. 16. W.—An Address ... at New Haven, September 5, A.L. 5850, on ... Centennial Celebration of Hiram Lodge. ... *New Haven: Thomas J. Stafford, Printer.* 1850. 8vo, pp. 44.—A Sermon ... at the Dedication of the "Union Street Brick Church," Bangor, September 3d, 1829. ... *Bangor: Printed by Burton & Carter.* 1829. 8vo, pp. 24.—A Sermon ... May 18, 1831, at the Ordination of Mr. William Farmer ... . *Augusta: Eaton & Severance, Printers.* 1831. 8vo, pp. 23. BA., H.

HUNTT (H.) A Visit to the Red Sulphur Spring of Virginia, during the Summer of 1837: with Observations on the Waters. By Henry Huntt, M.D. With an Introduction, containing Notices of Routes, &c. By an Annual Visiter [Thomas H. Perkins]. *Boston: Dutton and Wentworth.* 1839. 8vo, pp. 40. Plate. BA.

HUNTTING (J. M.) A Sermon, containing a General History of the Parish of Westfield, N. J., Jan. 1, 1839. By James M. Huntting. *Elizabethtown.* 1840. 8vo. 33985

[HUOT (L. H.)] Le Rougisme en Canada. Par un Observateur. *Québec.* 1864. 12mo, pp. 79. 33986

HURD (I.) A Discourse delivered ... in Boston, ... June 11th, 1799, before the Humane Society ... of Massachusetts. By Rev. Isaac Hurd. *Boston: Printed by John & Thomas Fleet.* 1799. 4to, pp. 23. B., BA., H., M., W. 33987

HURD (J. C.) The Law of Freedom and Bondage in the United States. By John Codman Hurd, Counsellor at Law. *Boston: Little, Brown & Company.* M.DCCC.LVIII–M.DCCC.LXII. 2 vols., 8vo, pp. xlvii, (1), 617; xliii, (1), 800. BA., C. 33988

HURD. Topics of Jurisprudence connected with Conditions of Freedom and Bondage. By John C. Hurd ... . *New York: D. Van Nostrand.* M.DCCC.LVI. 8vo, pp. ix, 113. B., C. 33989

HURD (J. R.) A National Bank, or No Banks; an appeal to the Common Sense of the People of the United States: especially of the Laboring Classes. By John R. Hurd. ... *New York: W. E. Dean.* 1842. 8vo, pp. 104. BA., H. 33990

[HURD] (R.) A Sermon ... December 13. 1779 ... Fast Day on account of the Troubles in America, before the House of Lords ... By Richard, Lord Bishop of Litchfield ... *London: T. Cadell.* 1777. 33991

See "M. Rev.," LII. 78. Liberal in tone and spirit. Also: A Sermon ... before the ... Society for the Propagation of the Gospel in Foreign Parts ... February 16 1781. ... *London.* M DCC LXXXI. 4to, pp. 77, (1). M

HURD (R. C.) A Treatise on the Right of Personal Liberty, and on the Writ of Habeas Corpus, and the Practice connected with it: with a View of the Law of Extradition of Fugitives. By Rollin C. Hurd. *Albany: W. C. Little & Co.* 1858. Rl. 8vo, pp. xxvii, 677. B. 33992

Also: Speech ... in ... Mount Vernon ... October 10, 1863. [*Mount Vernon, Ohio.* n. d.] 8vo, pp. 12. H.

HURD (W.) A New Universal History of the Religious Rites, Ceremonies, and Customs of the Whole World. ... By William Hurd, D.D. *Blackburn: Printed by J. Hemingway.* 1799. 4to, pp. 930. Plate. + *London.* 1812. Plates. 33993

First published in folio. [n. p. n. d.] C.

HURLBURT (J. B.) Britain and her Colonies. By J. Beaufort Hurlburt ... . *London: Stanford.* 1865. 8vo, pp. xvi–271.

HURLBURT. The Forests of Canada. By J. Beaufort Hurlburt ... . *Montreal.* 1862. 33995

HURLBUT (E. P.) Civil Offices and Political Ethics; ... By E. P. Hurlbut. Third Edition. *New-York.* 1844. 12mo.

HURLBUT. Essays on Human Rights and their Political Guaranties. By E. P. Hurlbut. *New-York: Greeley & McElrath.* 1845. 12mo, pp. 219. H. + With a Preface by George Combe. *Edinburgh.* 1847. Rl. 8vo. 33997

HURLBUT. A Secular View of Religion in the State, and the Bible in the Public Schools. By E. P. Hurlbut ... . *Albany: Joel Munsell.* 1870. 8vo, pp. 55. B., H. 33998

Also: An Oration ... at Little Falls, N. Y., July 4th, 1856. ... *Little Falls.* 1856. 8vo, pp. 18. H.

[HURLBUT (Henry A.), *and others*).] A Narrative of some Recent Occurrences in the Church of the Puritans, New York; with Documents relating thereto. *New York: William S. Dorr, Printer.* 1857. 8vo, pp. 49. H. 33999

HURLBUT (H. H.) A Paper read at a Family Meeting of some of the Descendants (comprising Children, Grandchildren and Great-Grandchildren) of Samuel Hurlbut, born at Chatham, Conn., 1748, and his wife Jerusha (Higgins) Hurlbut, born at Haddam, Conn., 1750, held at Racine, Wis., September 20, 1860. By Henry Higgins Hurlbut. *Racine, Wis.: Printed for the Author.* 1861. 8vo, pp. 22. Table. H. 34000

HURLBUT (M. L.) Address ... before the ... New-England Society, in Charleston ... December 22d, 1821. By M. L. Hurlbut. *Charleston: Printed ... by A. E. Miller.* 1828. 8vo, pp. 16. BA., H. 34001

HURLBUT (S. A.) Oration ... at the Anniversary Celebration of the Independent Order of Odd Fellows, of ... South-Carolina, January 1, 1842. By S. A. Hurlbut. [n. p. 1842.] 8vo, pp. 19. H. 34002

The printed title differs.

[HURLBUT (William Henry).] Gan-Eden: or, Pictures of Cuba. ... *Boston: John P. Jewett and Company.* 1854. 12mo, pp. viii, (4), 235, (1). B., BA., H. 34003

Reprinted in England as:

HURLBUT. Pictures of Cuba. By William H. Hurlbut. *London: Longman & Co.* 1855. Post 8vo, pp. viii, 132. B.

Also: Wealth and Beauty. A Poem ... before the Phi Beta Kappa Society in Cambridge, July 19, 1855. ... *Cambridge: John Bartlett.* M DCCC LV. 12mo, pp. 31.

HURLBUT. General McClellan and the Conduct of the War. By William Henry Hurlbert [*sic*]. *New York: Sheldon and Company.* 1864. 12mo, pp. 312. 2 Maps. BA., C. 34005

HURN (H. F.) Sweet amidst the Bitter. A Thanksgiving Sermon, preached in Easton, Penn., Nov. 27, 1862, By Rev. H. F. Hurn. *Philadelphia: Perkinpine & Higgins.* 1862. 8vo, pp. 28. 34006

HURNARD (J.) The True Way to abolish Slavery. By James Hurnard. *London: W. & F. G. Cash.* [1855.] 8vo, pp. 8.

Le Huron. *See* V[oltaire] (*M.* de).

HURON, *Mich.* The Town of Huron at the foot of Lake Huron, St. Clair Co., Michigan. Circular addressed to Capitalists and those who design removing to the West. Published by the Proprietors. *New York: E. D. Clayton, Printer.* 1837. 8vo, pp. 32. Map. 34008

HURON COLLEGE. The Gospel in Canada, and its Relation to Huron College. In Addresses by the Lord Bishop of Huron; Right Rev. Dr. McIlvaine, Bishop of Ohio; Right Rev. G. F. Bedell, D.D., Assistant Bishop of Ohio; and the Opinions of the Canadian Bishops. With an Introduction, by the Rev. T. R. Birks, M.A. ... *London.* 1865. Post 8vo. 34009

Report of the Huron Fishing Company ... 1839. *London.* 1839. 8vo, pp. 15. 3 Plates. 34010

HURON MINING COMPANY. Report of the Directors ... of the Huron Mining Company, January 31, 1864. ... *Boston: Press of Geo. C. Rand & Avery.* 1864. 8vo, pp. 38. Map. H.

The Hurricane: a Poem. *See* [Burk (E.)], Vol. III.

HURRIN (J.) Confession and Declaration of John Hurrin and Alexander Buchan, who were executed at Easton, Penn., Jan. 1, 1774. *Philadelphia.* 1774. 34012

HURST (M. B.) History of the Fourteenth Regiment Alabama Vols. With a List of the Names of every Man that ever belonged to the Regiment. By M. B. Hurst, Chief Musician 14th Regiment Alabama Volunteers. *Richmond.* 1863. 12mo, pp. 48. B. 34013

HURST (S. H.) Journal-History of the Seventy-Third Ohio Volunteer Infantry. By Samuel H. Hurst. *Chillicothe, O.* 1866. 12mo, pp. 254. C. 34014

HURSTHOUSE (C.) Emigration: Where to go, and Who should go—New Zealand and Australia (as Emigration Fields) in contrast with Canada and the United States—Canterbury and the Diggins. By Charles Hursthouse, Jun. ... *London.* 1852. 12mo, pp. 130. P. 34015

HURT (J.) A Funeral Sermon on the Death of Mr. Daniel Kellogg ... 20th of August 1788. ... By ... John Hurt. *Augusta: Printed by John E. Smith.* MDCCLXXXVIII. Sm. 4to, pp. 12. BA.

HURT. The Love of our Country. A Sermon, preached before the Virginia Troops in New-Jersey. By John Hurt ... . *Philadelphia: Printed by Styner and Cist.* MDCCLXXVII. 8vo, pp. 23. BA., N., W. 34017

HURT-BINET (M. G.) Neuf Mois aux États-Unis de l'Amérique. Fragment des Mémoires de M. Marc-Gabriel Hurt-Binet. *Genève: Joël Cherbuliez.* 1862. 16mo, pp. 184. B., H. 34018

HURTADO DE MENDOZA. *See* Mendoza (H. de).

HURTADO (M.) Considérations sur l'Etat présent de l'Amérique du Sud, et sur l'arrivée à Paris de M. Hurtado ... . *Paris: Chez C. J. Trouvé.* 1824. 12mo, pp. 47. H. 34019

Hurtel (J. F.) Las Ilustres Americanas. Por Juan F. Hurtel. *Reimpresa en Filadelfia, Año* 1824. 12mo. 34020

Hurton (W.) The Doomed Ship; or, the Wreck of the Arctic Regions. By William Hurton. ... A New Edition. *London: Henry Lea.* [1856.] 8vo, pp. viii, 182. 16 Plates.

[Husband (Harmon).] An Impartial | Relation | of the | First Rise and Cause | of the | Recent Differences | in | Publick Affairs | In the Province of North-Ca- | rolina; and of the past Tu- | mults and Riots that lately | happened in that Province. | Containing most of the true and genuine | Copies of Letters, Messages and Remonstrances, | between the Parties contending! ——— By which | any impartial Man may easily gather and see the | true Ground and Reasons of the Dissatisfaction | that universally reigns all over said Province in | a more or less Degree. *Printed for the Compiler.* 1770. 18mo, pp. 104. J.C.B. 34022

A volume of great rarity, giving an account of the "Regulators" of North Carolina, for an account of whom *see* Bancroft's "History," VI. 284–291. The supposed author was a member of the North Carolina Legislature; his early education must have been neglected.

[Husband.] Some Remarks on Religion, with the Author's experience in pursuit thereof. For the consideration of all people; being the real truth of what happened. Simply delivered, without the help of Schools-Words, or Dress of Learning. *Philadelphia: Printed by William Bradford, for the Author.* M,DCC,-LXI. 8vo, pp. 38. P. 34023

Husband (J. L.) Our National Finances. By J. L. Husband. *Philadelphia.* [1864.] 8vo, pp. 8. H. 34024

Husbands (J. D.), *and* Lathrop (H.), *Jr.* Addresses delivered at the Thirty-Fifth Commencement of Hartwick Seminary, Otsego County, N. Y., August 27th and 28th, 1850. By Joseph D. Husbands and Horace Lathrop, Jr. *Albany: J. Munsell.* 1850. 8vo, pp. 37. 34025

Huse (J.) A Discourse, Occasioned by the Death of General George Washington ... delivered in Warren, (District of Maine.) on the 22d, of February, 1800, ... By Jonathan Huse, A.M., Pastor ... in Warren ... . *Wiscasset: Printed by Henry Hoskins.* 1800. 8vo, pp. 12. BA. 34026

One of the rarest of Washington orations.

[Huske (John).] The Present State of North America. I. The Discoveries, Rights and Possessions of Great Britain.

II. The Discoveries, Rights and Possessions of France. III. The Encroachments and Depredations of the French upon His Majesty's Territories in North America in Times when Peace subsisted in Europe between the Two Crowns, &c., &c. *London: Printed by R. & J. Dodsley.* MDCCLV. 4to. + The Second Edition, with Emendations. *[Ibid.]* 4to, pp. (4), 88. + *Boston, Reprinted.* 1755. 8vo, pp. 64. 34027

Principally taken from Dumont's "Histoire et Commerce des Colonies Angloises." *See* Reed's "Life of Reed," p. 33; "M. Rev.," XII. 484; "Gentleman's Magazine," XXV. 238; "Boston Gazette," Nov. 4, 1764; Bancroft's "History," IV. and V. 170.

Huskisson (W.) The Speeches of the Right Honourable ... William Huskisson. With a Biographical Memoir ... . *London: John Murray.* MDCCCXXXI. 3 vols., 8vo, pp. xxiv, 320, Portrait; viii, 574; viii, 688; 244. B. 34028

Huskisson. Select Speeches. With a Biographical Sketch. Edited by R. Walsh. *Philadelphia.* 1837. 8vo. 34029

Includes Speeches on the American Colonies, Slavery, etc.

Huskisson. Substance of Two Speeches ... in the House of Commons, on the 21st and 25th of March, 1825, by ... William Huskisson, respecting the Colonial Policy and Foreign Commerce of the Country. *London.* 1825. 8vo. S. + *Baltimore: F. Lucas, Jr.* 1826. 8vo, pp. 88. B. 34030

Also: Shipping Interest. Speech ... the 7th of May, 1827. ... With an Appendix, containing the Several Accounts referred to. *London: J. Hatchard & Son.* 1827. 8vo, pp. 93. S.

Husmann (G.) The Cultivation of the Native Grape and Manufacture of American Wine. By George Husmann. *New York: G. E. & F. W. Woodward.* 1866. 12mo, pp. 192.

Husnot (T.) Catalogue des cryptogames recueillis aux Antilles françaises en 1868, et essai sur leur distribution géographique dans ces îles. Par T. Husnot. *Caen: Le Blanc-Hardel.* 1870. 8vo, pp. 60. Map. 34032

Hussey (G.) Memorabilia Mundi; or, Choice Memoirs of the History and Description of the World. By G. Hussey. *London.* 1670. 12mo. 34033

Pages 14 to 18 relate to America.

Hussey (J.) An Oration ... before the Fraternity of Masons, ... Hanover, ... June the 24th, A.L. 5793. ... By Josiah Hussey, Esq. *Boston: Printed by Brother Benjamin Russell.* 5793. 8vo, pp. 12. BA., M., W. 34034

Hussey (S. F.) A Brief Examination of Asa Rand's Book, called a "Word in Season;" with a Refutation of some of his erroneous Statements and Charges against the People called "Quakers;" whereby his work will appear out of Season. By Samuel F. Hussey. *Salem: T. C. Cushing.* 1821. 12mo, pp. 238. C. 34035

Husted & Kroehl. Proposition ... to remove ... "Hell-Gate" presented to the Legislature of New York, January, 1855. [n. p. n. d.] 8vo, pp. 3. S. 34036

Huston (A.) Letter of Gen. Almanzon Huston in Reply to Gen. Wool's Letter dated at Troy, Dec. 31, 1860. *Washington.* 1861. 8vo. 34037

Huston (Charles). An Essay on the History and Nature of Original Titles to Land in the Province and State of Pennsylvania. *Philadelphia: T. & J. W. Johnson.* 1849. 8vo, pp. 484.

Huston (*Gen.* Felix). Address at Southern Convention. *Natchez.* 1850. 8vo. 34039

Huston (J.) Legendes canadiennes. Recueilles par J. Huston. *Paris: P. Jannet.* 1853. 12mo, pp. 303. 34040

Huston. Le répertoire national ou recueil de littérature canadienne. *Montréal: Lowell et Gibson.* 1848. 4 vols., 8vo, pp. viii, 368, (8); 376, (8); 384, (8); 404, (8). 34041

Huston (R. W.) *vs.* Dicks (J.) Trial ... Lancaster County, ... 1815; An Action of Trespass for levying a Fine ordered to be collected by Sentence of a Court Marshal, under an Act of the Legislature of Pennsylvania, which was alleged to be repugnant to the Constitution and Laws of the United States, with Arguments of Counsel and Decision of Judges. *Lancaster.* 1815.

Hutcheson (A.) Collection of Treatises relating to the National Debts and Funds. To which is added a Collection of Treatises relating to the South Sea Stock and Scheme. By Archibald Hutcheson, Esq. *London.* 1721. Folio. 34043

This scarce book gives a full detail of the various schemes which grew out of the explosion of the South Sea Scheme in 1820. *See* Hume's "Essay on Public Credit," *and* McCullock's "Literature of Political Economy," p. 319.

Hutcheson (C.) Southern Martyrs: a Poetical Tale of Patagonia. By Charles Hutcheson. *London: Hamilton, Adams & Co.* 1853. 12mo 34044

Hutchings (James M.) Scenes of Wonder and Curiosity in California. Illustrated with over One Hundred Engravings. A Tourist's Guide to the Yo-Semite Valley, the Big Tree Groves—the Natural Caves and Bridges—the Quicksilver Mines of New Almaden and Henriquita—Mount Shasta—The Farallone Islands, with their Sea Lions and Birds—the Geyser Springs—Lake Tahoe, and other Places of Interest. Also giving Outline Map of Routes to Yo-Semite and Big Tree Groves—Tables of Distances—Rates of Fare—Hotel Charges ... . By J. M. Hutchings. *New York and San Francisco.* 1860. C. + [*Ibid.*] 1862. + *London: Chapman & Hall.* 1865. 8vo, pp. viii–267. + *San Francisco: A. Roman & Company.* 1870. 8vo, pp. 292. 6 Plates and Map. B., BA., H. 34045

Also: Hutching's California Magazine ... 1858.—Hutchings' California Scenes. ... *San Francisco.* 1853–56. 4to, 14 l.

Hutchings (R. C.) The Usurpations of the Federal Government. The Dangers of Centralization. Speech of Hon. Robert C. Hutchings of New York, on the Governor's ... Message, ... February, 26th, 1863. *Albany.* 1863. 8vo, pp. 16.

Hutchins (J.) Freedom *vs.* Slavery. Speech of ... John Hutchins, of Ohio ... May 2, 1860. [n. p. n. d.] 8vo, pp. 8.

Also: Speech ... on the Bill for the Release of certain Persons held to Service or Labor in the District of Columbia. Delivered ... April 11, 1862. *Washington.* 1862. 8vo, pp. 7.—Speech ... May 19th, 1862, on Low and Uniform Postage. *New York: D. Appleton & Co.* 1862. 8vo, pp. 32. H.

Hutchins (J.) A Sermon Preached on the Opening of the Franklin College at Lancaster, July 17, 1787. By Joseph Hutchins, D.D. *Philadelphia.* 1806. P. 34048

Hutchins (J. N.) Hutchins' Improved: Being an Almanack and Ephemeris ... for 1760. By John Nathan Hutchins. *New-York.* [n. d.] 12mo. 34049

Continued under varying titles, as Hutchins' New-York, Vermont, Massachusetts and Connecticut Almanack. *Troy.* 1803. 12mo.—Hutchins' Revived Almanack. *New-York: Smith & Forman.* 1812. 12mo.—Hutchins' Improved, etc., to the present time.

Hutchins (L.) The Autobiography of Levi Hutchins: with a Preface, Notes, and Addenda, by his Youngest Son. ... *Cambridge: Printed at the Riverside Press.* M DCCC LXV. 16mo, pp. iv, 188. Portrait. B., H. 34050

[Hutchins (Samuel).] Benjamin Franklin: A Book for the Young and the Old: for All. ... *Cambridge: For the Author.* M DCCC LII. 16mo, pp. 36. BA. 34051

Hutchins (S. C.) Civil List of Forms of Government of the Colony and State of New York. Compiled from Official and Authentic Sources. By S. C. Hutchins. Published annually by Weed, Parsons & Co. *Albany.* [1866.] 12mo, pp. (2), vi, 587. Plates. B. 34052

Hutchins (T.) A Topographical Description of Virginia, Pennsylvania, Maryland, and North Carolina, comprehending the Rivers Ohio, Kenhawa, Sioto, Cherokee, Wabash, Illinois, Mississippi, &c. The Climate, Soil and Produce, whether Animal Vegetable, or Mineral; ... By Thomas Hutchins, Captain in the 60th Regiment of Foot. With a Plan of the Rapids of the Ohio, a Plan of the several Villages in the Illinois Country, ... and an Appendix, containing Mr. Patrick Kennedy's Journal up the Illinois River ... . *Boston: Printed by John Norman.* MDCC-LXXXVII. Sm. 8vo, pp. 30, (2). 2 Plans and Table. B., BA., H.

Very scarce. "The greater part," says Hutchins, "done from my own Surveys preceding and during the last war, and since in many reconnoitering tours between 1764 and 1775."

Hutchins. A | Topographical Description | of | Virginia, Pennsylvania, | Maryland, and North Carolina. | Comprehending the | Rivers Ohio, Kenhawa, Sioto, Cherokee, | Wabash, Illinois, Mississippi, &c. | The | Climate, Soil and Produce, | whether | Animal, Vegetable, or Mineral; | The | Mountains, Creeks, Roads, Distances, Lati- | tudes, &c. and of every Part, laid down in the an- | nexed Map. Published by Thomas Hutchins, | Captain in the 60th Regiment of Foot. | With a | Plan of the Rapids of the Ohio, a Plan of the several | Villages in the Illinois Country, a Table of the | Distances between Fort Pitt and the Mouth of the | Ohio, all Engraved upon Copper | And | an Appendix, containing Mr. Patrick Kennedy's | Journal up the Illinois River, and a correct List of the | different Nations and Tribes of Indians, with the | Number of Fighting Men, &c. *London: | Printed for the Author, and sold by J. Almon,* | ... | M DCC LXXVIII. 8vo, pp. (2), ii, 67, (1). 2 Maps and Table. H. 34054

Also included in the third edition of G. Imlay's "Western Territory, 1797."

Hutchins. Description Topographique de la Virginie, de la Pensylvanie, du Maryland et de la Caroline Septentrionale: contenant les Revieres d'Ohio, Kenhawa, Sioto, Cherokee, Wabash, des Illinois, du Mississipi, &c.; le Climat, le Sol, les Productions, tant Animales que Végétales ou Minérales; les Montagnes, les Rivieres, Chemins, Distances, Latitudes, et de Toutes les parties représentées dans les cartes ci-jointes. Publiée par Thomas

Hutchins, Capitaine du soixantieme Régiment d'Infanterie: Accompagnée d'un Plan des Sauts de l'Ohio, d'un autre de tous les Villages du Canton des Illinois; une Table des Distances en milles entre le Fort-Pitt & l'embouchure de l'Ohio dans le Missisipi; Plus, un Supplément, que contient le Journal de Patrice Kennedy's, sur la Riviere des Illinois, & un Etat véritable des différentes Nations & Tribus des Indiens, avec le nombre des Combattans. Traduit de l'Anglois. *A Paris, Chez Le Rouge.* M.DCC.LXXXI. 8vo, pp. 68, Table, 2 l., Map and Table folded.

Hutchins. An Historical Narrative and Topographical Description of Louisiana, and West-Florida, comprehending the River Mississippi with its Principal Branches and Settlements, and the Rivers Pearl, Pascagoula, Mobille, Perdido, Escambia, Chacta-Hatcha, etc.—The Climate, Soil and Produce, whether Animal, Vegetable or Mineral; with Directions for Sailing into all the Bays, ... on the North Side of the Gulf of Mexico, and for Navigating between the Islands situated along that Coast, and ascending the Mississippi River. By Thomas Hutchins, Geographer to the United States. *Philadelphia: For the Author.* M.DCC.LXXXIV. 8vo, pp. 94, Table, 1 l. BA., H. 34056

Reprinted in Imlay's third edition, pp. 388–458.

Hutchinson (A.) Valour for the Truth. In a Sermon ... at Newbury-Port, April 23d, 1767. By Aaron Hutchinson ... . *Boston: Printed by W. McAlpine.* MDCCLXVII. 8vo, pp. 26. B.

Hutchinson. A Reply to the Remarks of the Rev. Mr. John Tucker, ... on a Sermon Preached at Newbury-Port, April 23. 1767, intitled Valour for the Truth. By Aaron Hutchinson, ... *Boston: Printed by Thomas & John Fleet.* 1768. 8vo, pp. 54, (1).

Hutchinson. A Well Tempered Self-Love a rule of Conduct towards others. A Sermon preached at Windsor, July, 1777, before the Representatives of the Towns and Counties of Charlotte, Cumberland, and Gloucester, for the forming the State of Vermont. By Aaron Hutchinson ... . *Dresden: J. Padock & A. Spooner.* 1777. 8vo. C. 34059

Reprinted in "Vermont Hist. Soc. Collections," I. 67–101. Also: Iniquity purged by Mercy and Truth. A Sermon at Grafton, Oct. 23, 1768, after the Execution of Arthur, a Negro, at Worcester. ... *Boston.* 1769. 8vo, pp. 29.— ... Two Sermons, Grafton, Nov. 15, 1772; being the last delivered in publick there. ... *Boston.* 1773. 8vo, pp. 39. M., W.

Hutchinson (A.) *See* Mississippi Laws.

[Hutchinson (C. C.)] A Colony for an Indian Reserve in Kansas. Climate, Soil, Products, Timber, Water, Kind of Settlers Wanted, &c. ... *Lawrence.* 1863. 8vo, pp. 15. 34060

Narrates the steps by which the Ottawa Indians became citizens, and endeavored to induce the settlement of the remaining portion by industrious whites.

Hutchinson (——). Angleterre, Etats-Unis d'Amerique, et France. Seigneurs de Chatham, de Colston-Basset, de Cropwell-Bishop, ... propriétaires d'Arnold et de Tollerton, en l'Angleterre; ... Hawthorn-Hill, Beaver-Brook en Massachusetts; de Bunker-Hill et Washington à Singapore, dans la province de Malacca, aux Indes Orientales. ... Folio, pp. 9. 34061

"The journal from which this is taken is entitled 'Le Nobiliaire Universel de France.'" This title is from Whittemore's "American Genealogy."

[Hutchinson (E.)] "Young Sam" or Native American's Own Book! containing the Principles and Platform on which the Order stands; accompanied by an array of some of the most thrilling Facts ever published. By a Native American. *New York: American Family Publication Co.* 1855. 8vo, pp. (2), 119.

Hutchinson (F.) An Historical Essay concerning Witchcraft. With Observations upon Matters of Facts; tending to clear the Texts of the Sacred Scriptures, and confute the vulgar Errors about that Point. And also Two Sermons; One in Proof of the Christian Religion; The other concerning the Good and Evil Angels. By Francis Hutchinson ... . *London: R. Knaplock.* MDCCXVIII. 8vo, pp. xv, (4), 270. BA., H., C., S. + The Second Edition, with considerable Additions. *London: R. Knaplock.* MDCCXX. 8vo, pp. (29), (3), 336. B., H. 34063

Chapter v. gives an account of the witchcraft troubles at Salem, Boston, and Andover, in New England.

Hutchinson (J. W.) The Book of Brothers. (Second Series) being a History of the Adventures of John W. Hutchinson and his Family in the Camps of the Army of the Potomac. *Boston: S. Chism.* 1864. 12mo, pp. 24. 34064

Hutchinson. Hutchinson's Republican Songster, for ... 1860. Edited by John W. Hutchinson, of the Hutchinson Family of Singers. *New York: O. Hutchinson.* 1860. 12mo, pp. 72. B.

Hutchinson (K. M.) A Memoir of Abijah Hutchinson, A Soldier of the Revolution. By his Grandson K. M. Hutchinson. *Rochester: William Alling, Printer.* 1843. 12mo, pp. 22. 34066

Abijah Hutchinson was born in Lebanon, Conn., in 1756, he was a Connecticut privateer, lived half a century in Vermont, and settled in 1835 in Genesee, N. Y., where he died in 1843. His captivity among the Indians of Canada is detailed at length.

H[utchinson] (S[amuel].) A Declaration of a Future Glorious Estate of a Church to be here | upon Earth, at Christs Personal Appearance for the Restitu- | tion of all things, a Thousand | Year before the Ultimate Day | of the General Judgement. | Set forth by a Letter to a Friend. | As also further proved by divers Scriptures, together with | the Testimony of many Godly Divines, both | Ancient and Modern. | By S. H. of Boston in New-England. | *London: Printed in the year* 1667. 4to, pp. 36. 34067

"Samuel Hutchinson, the author of this extraordinary and rare compilation, was brother of William, the father of Anne Hutchinson, the strong-minded of New England 200 years ago. He was a Fifth-monarchy man, and has here not only set forth his own views both in prose and verse, but has collected the opinions of competent writers of the old world and the new upon the establishment of the Fifth Kingdom, that of Christ, the new Heaven and the new Earth. His principal paper is 'A Letter sent to a Friend in Old England concerning the Personal Monarchial Reign of Christ with the Saints here upon Earth, being an Answer to a Letter sent from *Old* England to *New* in 1659.'"—Stevens.

[Hutchinson (Thomas).] The Case of the Provinces of Massachusetts-Bay and New-York, respecting the Boundary Line between the two Provinces. *Boston ... Printed by Green and Russell* ... 1764. Folio, pp. xxx. Table. 34068

An extremely rare pamphlet.

[Hutchinson.] A Collection of Original Papers Relative to the History of the Colony of Massachusetts-Bay. *Boston: New-England: Printed by Thomas and John Fleet.* 1769. 8vo, pp. (2), ii, 576. B., BA., H. 34069

"This collection of papers was published by Lieut.-Gov. Hutchinson, 'to support and elucidate the principal facts related in the first part of the History of Massachusetts Bay, and may serve as an appendix to it.' 'The author of that History was possessed of many other ancient and very curious original papers, which are irrecoverably lost by an unfortunate event sufficiently known.' (This alludes to the destruction of his papers by a mob, at the time of the Riots in Boston on account of the Stamp Act, in 1765.)" —Rich. It is sometimes erroneously bound up and lettered as Vol. III. of the "History." It is a necessary adjunct to Hutchinson's "History of Massachusetts Bay." It was reprinted by the Prince Society as:

Hutchinson. The Hutchinson Papers. A New Edition. Collated with and Corrected from the Original Manuscript, and Edited, with Illustrative Notes. *Albany, N. Y.: Printed by Joel Munsell.* 1865. 2 vols., 4to, pp. xv, (1), ii, 324; vii, 354. B.

Edition, one hundred and sixty copies, of which ten copies are on large paper.

Hutchinson. Copy | of | Letters | Sent to Great Britain, by His Excellency | Thomas Hutchinson, the Hon. Andrew | Oliver, and several other Persons, born | and educated among us. | Which original Letters have been returned | to America, and laid before the honor-|able House of Representatives of this|Province.|In which (notwithstanding his Excellency's|Declaration to the House, that the Ten-|dency and Design of them was not to| subvert the Constitution, but rather to|preserve it entire) the judicious Reader|will discover the fatal Source of the|Confusion and Bloodshed in which this|Province especially has been involved, and which threatened total Destruction to the Liberties of all America.|*Boston: Printed by Edes and Gill,* ... 1773. 8vo, pp. 40. B., BA., H. + *Salem: Reprinted and sold by S. & E. Hall.* 1773. 8vo, pp. 30. 34071

These are the famous letters which found their way back to Boston, it is said, through Dr. Franklin, the publication of which, by order of the General Court, did more, perhaps, to bring revolutionary matters to a crisis than any previous publication; indeed, "nothing except the 'Tea Party' ever created a greater political sensation in Boston, or more speedy results than the publication, by authority of the General Court, of these letters." They were reprinted in England as:

HUTCHINSON. The Letters of Governor Hutchinson, and Lieut. Governor Oliver, &c. Printed at Boston. And Remarks thereon. With the Assembly's Address, and the Proceedings of the Lords Committee of Council. Together with the Substance of Mr. Wedderburn's Speech relating to those Letters. *London: J. Wilkie.* MDCCLXXIV. 8vo, pp. (2), 134. + [With] the Report of the Lords Committee to his Majesty in Council. The Second Edition. *London: J. Wilkie.* MDCCLXXIV. 8vo, pp. (4), 142. B., BA., H. 34072

"This edition was published, with remarks, in exculpation of Gov. Hutchinson, by his friend Israel Mauduit."—*Monthly Review*, L. 157. Also, *Reprinted* (with Benjamin Franklin before the Privy Council), *Philadelphia.* 1859. 8vo.

[HUTCHINSON.] Dissertation on the Currencies of the British Plantations in North America; and Observations on a Paper Currency. *Boston.* 1741. 8vo, pp. 62. + Postscript. [*Ibid.*]

[HUTCHINSON. Documents of the Senate and House of Representatives of the Commonwealth of Massachusetts; containing the correspondence and proceedings, relative to the controversy between that Commonwealth and the Massachusetts Historical Society respecting the ownership and possession of the "Hutchinson Papers" so called. *Boston.* 1868–71.] 2 vols., 8vo.

House Document, No. 150.

HUTCHINSON. The|History|of the|Colony|of|Massachusets-Bay,|from the|first Settlement thereof|in 1628.|Until its Incorporation|with the Colony of Plimouth, Province of Main, &c.|by the|Charter of King William and Queen Mary,|in

1691.|...|By Mr. Hutchinson,|Lieutenant-Governor of the Massachusets Province.|*Boston, New-England:*|*Printed by Thomas and John Fleet,* ... MDCCLXIV. 8vo, pp. vi, 566. BA. 34075

This is the first edition of what, in fact, forms Vol. I. of the work. It was reprinted in London as:

HUTCHINSON. The|History|of the|Colony|of|Massachusets-Bay,|from the|First Settlement thereof|in 1628,|until its Incorporation|with the|Colony of Plimouth, Province of Main, &c.|By the|Charter of King William and Queen Mary,|in 1691.|...|By Mr. Hutchinson,|Lieutenant-Governor of the Massachusets Province.|The Second Edition.|*London:*|*Printed for M. Richardson* ...|M DCC LX [*i.e.* M DCC LXV]. 8vo, pp. (6), iv, 566. 34076

The error in the date was not discovered until many copies had been sold, and the work is sometimes found with the original title and with the reprinted title, in which the date is corrected to read M DCC LXV. It is very probable that the V fell out of the printer's form in the first instance.

HUTCHINSON. The History of the Colony of Massachusetts Bay [as above]. By Mr. Hutchinson, Late Lieutenant Governor, and now Commander-in-Chief of the Massachusetts Province. The Third Edition. *Boston: Printed and sold by I. Thomas.* [1774.] 8vo, pp. 152. 34077

This edition appeared in the "Royal American Magazine," which is supposed to have terminated with the fifteenth number. It is an unfinished work, and is the rarest of the editions of this history.

HUTCHINSON. The|History|of the|Province|of|Massachusets-Bay,|from the|Charter of King William and Queen Mary,| in 1691,|Until the Year 1750.|By Mr. Hutchinson,|Lieutenant-Governor of the Province.|*Boston, New-England: Printed by Thomas & John Fleet,* ... MDCCLXVII. 8vo, pp. (4), iv, 539.

First edition of the second volume with an index to both volumes. It was reprinted the following year in England as:

HUTCHINSON. The|History|of the|Province|of|Massachusets-Bay,|from the|Charter of King William and Queen Mary,| in 1691,|Until the Year 1750.|By Mr. Hutchinson,|Lieutenant Governor of the Province.|Vol. II.|The Second Edition.| *London:*|*Printed by J. Smith .. for G. Kearsley* ... M DCC LXVIII. 8vo, pp. (4), iv, 539. H. 34079

Printed nearly page for page throughout from the Boston edition.

HUTCHINSON. The History of Massachusetts from the First Settlement Thereof in 1628, until the Year 1750. By Thomas Hutchinson, Esq. Late Governor of Massachusetts. ... The

Third Edition, with additional Notes and Corrections. Vol. I. *Printed at Salem: by Thomas C. Cushing, for Thomas and Andrews.* 1795. 8vo, pp. 478, (10). Vol. II. *Printed at Boston: by Manning and Loring, for Thomas and Andrews.* 1795. 8vo, pp. 452.

This edition has a few additional notes by the anonymous editor; in the matter of paper and type "it is the poorest of all."—CHARLES DEANE in the *Historical Magazine.* The following was a posthumous publication:

HUTCHINSON. The History of the Province of Massachusetts Bay, from the Year 1750 until June 1774. By Mr. Hutchinson, Late Governor of the Province. Vol. III. *London: John Murray.* MDCCCXXVIII. 8vo, pp. iv, 551. 34081

Five hundred copies were struck off with this title for the American market; but the exigencies of trade have induced some Boston bookseller, who bought up a number of copies, to reprint the title, omitting "Vol. III.," thus making it appear an entire work. Five hundred copies were also printed for sale in England with the following title:

HUTCHINSON. The|History of the Province|of|Massachusetts Bay|from 1749 to 1774,|comprising a Detailed Narrative of the|Origin and Early Stages|of the American Revolution.| By Thomas Hutchinson, Esq. LL.D.,|formerly Governor of the Province.|Edited from the Author's MS., by his Grandson,|the Rev. John Hutchinson, M.A.|*London: John Murray* ... M DCCCXXVIII. 8vo, pp. xx, 551. 34082

Contains a Dedication and Preface, 16 pages, which were omitted in the edition described *supra.* This volume concludes the "History;" the "Collection of Papers" should be added. It is a work of permanent value and is indispensable in any American Collection. Judge Davis remarks "The reputation of Governor Hutchinson's 'History' rests on the solid basis of utility and truth." Tudor observes "that he is more valuable for his facts than his style."—*Life of Otis*, Chap. XXVI.

[HUTCHINSON.] A Journal of the Proceedings of the Commissioners appointed for Managing a Treaty of Peace: To be begun and held at Falmouth in the County of York, the Twenty-seventh of September, Anno Domini One thousand seven hundred and forty-nine; Between Thomas Hutchinson, John Choate, Israel Williams and James Otis, Esqrs; Commissioned by the Honourable Spencer Phips, Esq; Lieutenant-Governour and Commander in Chief, in and over His Majesty's Province of the Massachusetts-Bay in New-England, on the one Part; and the Eastern Indians on the other Part. *Boston; New-England: Printed by John Draper, Printer to His Honour the Lieutenant-Governour and Council.* [n. d.] 4to, pp. 18. P., W. 34083

[HUTCHINSON.] The Proceedings of the Council, and of the House of Representatives of the Province of the Massachusetts-

Bay, Relative to the Convening, Holding and Keeping The General Assembly at Harvard College in Cambridge: And the several Messages which passed between His Honor the Lieutenant Governor and the two Houses, upon the Subject. ... *Boston: Printed by Edes and Gill, Printers to the Honorable House of Representatives.* 1770. 8vo, pp. 83; Continuation, pp. 66. 34084

HUTCHINSON. The Representations of Governor Hutchinson and others, contained in certain Letters Transmitted to England, And afterwards returned from thence, And laid before the General-Assembly of the Massachusetts-Bay. Together with the Resolves Of the two Houses thereon. *Boston: N. E. Printed and Sold by Edes and Gill,* ... 1773. 8vo, pp. (2), 94. BA., W.

HUTCHINSON. The|Speeches|of|His Excellency Governor Hutchinson,|to the|General Assembly|Of the Massachusetts-Bay.|At a Session begun and held on the Sixth|of January, 1773.|With|the Answers|of|His Majesty's Council|and the| House of Representatives respectively.| [Publish'd by Order of the House.] *Boston; New-England: Printed by Edes and Gill, Printers to the Honourable House of Representatives.* M,DCC,LXXIII. 8vo, pp. (2), 126. B., BA., H. 34086

[HUTCHINSON.] Strictures upon the Declaration of the Congress at Philadelphia. In a Letter to a Noble Lord, &c. *London: Printed in the Year* 1776. 8vo, pp. 32. C., S. 34087

"The author of these 'Strictures' gives, as his reason for writing them, that the noble Lord to whom they are written had observed that he was utterly at a loss to what facts many parts of the Declaration of Independence referred, that he might judge of the grievances of the colonies." In a volume of tracts which belonged to Sir James Wright, this piece is stated to have been written by Gov. Hutchinson.

HUTCHINSON. The Witchcraft Delusion of 1692. By Gov. Thomas Hutchinson, from an Unpublished Manuscript ... in the Massachusetts Archives. With Notes by William Frederick Poole. *Boston: Privately Printed.* 1870. 4to, pp. 43. B.

See also our Vol. IV., No. 15954, *and* Vol. VI., No. 23409.

HUTCHINSON (T. J.) Buenos Ayres and Argentine Gleanings: with extracts from a diary of Salado Exploration in 1862 and 1863. By Thomas J. Hutchinson ... . *London: Edward Stanford.* 1865. 8vo, pp. xxi, (1), 321, (1). Map and Plates. B.

HUTCHINSON. The Parana; with Incidents of the Paraguayan War, and South American Recollections, from 1861 to 1868. By Thomas J. Hutchinson ... . *London: Edward Stanford.* 1868. 8vo, pp. xxvii, 424. Map and 8 Plates. B., BA. 34090

HUTCHINSON (T.) An Oration delivered at the South Parish in Woodstock, Vermont, on the Fourth Day of July, A.D. 1806. By Titus Hutchinson. *Randolph, Vermont: Sereno Wright.* 1806. 8vo. 34091

Political and historical, with an Appendix containing an Ode on Science and Liberty, and an account of the celebration. Also: An Oration ... at Woodstock, July 4, 1809. ... [*Windsor: Oliver Farnsworth, Printer.* 1809.] Sm. 4to, pp. 8. BA.

HUTCHINSON (W.) Address at Oswego, Dec. 25, 1838, on Claims of Foreign Powers in the United States. By Rev. William Hutchinson. *Oswego.* 1839. 8vo. 34092

HUTCHINSON. The History of the Hutchinson Family. *New York.* 1852. 12mo, pp. 48. 34093

HUTCHINSON, KROHL & Co. in Support of their Right to the Possession of Property purchased of the Russian American Company in Alaska. [*Washington.* 1869.] 8vo, pp. 16. H. 34094

HUTTEN (Ulrich de). De Gvaiaci medicina et morbo gallico liber vnus. *Moguntæ: Joan Scheffer.* 1519. 4to. 34095

Relates to the American wood Guaiacum.

HUTTEN. Of the VVood|called Gvaiacvm,|that healeth|the Frenche|Pockes,|and also helpeth the goute in the|feete,|the stoone,|the|palsey, lepree,|dropsy,|fallynge euyll, and o-|ther dyseases.|...|*Londini in Aedibus*|*Tho. Bertheleti*|M.D.XXXVI. *Cvm Privilegio.*| 16mo, pp. (5), Text, 82 folioed leaves for 79.

HUTTEN. ... Of the|VVood cal-|led Gvaia-|cvm,|that healeth|the frenche pockes, and also|helpeth the goute in the feete,|the stone, palsey, lepre,|dropsy, fallynge|euyll, and o-|ther dis-|eses. Made in latyn by Ulrich Hutten|knyght, and translated in|to englysh by Tho-|mas Paynel.|...|*Londini.*|*Ex Officina Thomæ Bertheleti regii*|*impressoris. Cum priuilegio*|*ad imprimendum solum.*|*Anno.* M.D.XL.| 4to, pp. (4), Text, 58 folioed leaves.

HÜTTEN (U. von), *pseudon.* An Appeal to The Laity of Maryland, against the Divine Right of Episcopal Despotism, By Ulric von Hütten. *Washington: Printed by Jno. T. Towers.* 1850. 8vo, pp. 44. 34098

HÜTTEN. An Epistle congratulatory to the Rt. Rev. the Bishops of the Episcopal Court at Camden, N. J. From Ulric von Hütten. 1853. 8vo, pp. 74. S. 34099

[HUTTICH (J.)] Novvs Orbis Regio-|nvm ac Insvlarvm veteribvs incognitarvm,|unã cum tabula cosmographica, & aliquot alijs consimilis|argumenti libellis, quorum omnium catalogus| sequenti patebit pagina. |His accessit copiosus rerum memorabilium index.|...|*Basileae apvd Io. Hervagivm, Mense*|*Martio, Anno* M.D.XXXII.| Folio, 24 l., pp. 584. Register and Colophon, 1 l. Map, "Typvs Cosmographicvs Vniversalis." A., B. 34100

For a note, concerning the authorship of this collection, *see* Harrisse's "Bib. Am. Vet.," p. 292. It contains the voyages of Cadamosto, the three voyages of Columbus, Nino, Pinzon, Vespucius, Cabral, and part of the Fourth Decade of Peter Martyr, also many other pieces which do not relate to America. Notwithstanding the statement in Mr. Grenville's Catalogue respecting the frequent absence of the map, there is no doubt but that a map does belong to the work, and Mr. F. Muller has reproduced ten copies in exact facsimile. Harrisse remarks "Whether they were the maps really belonging to the work, and described by Munster, we are unable to say, as no two copies of this edition had the same. We have before us one, which is as follows: On one line: TYPVS COSMOGRAPHICVS VNIVERSALIS. Then a border, and two inscriptions, one beginning with the word INDIA, the other SCYTHARVM. The newly rediscovered world is represented on the north of a long strip of land, bearing the inscription *Terra de Cuba.* The southern part contains these words only: *Parias Canibali* AMERICA|TERRA NOVA|*Prisilia.* Then, in type, the word: ASIA. This we are inclined to consider as the genuine map. We have seen four or five copies of the 'Novus Orbis' of Basle, 1537, *infra*, each containing a map which is literally copied from the present, but with this only difference: the word Asia is printed in a kind of type somewhat different and smaller. The latter is also frequently seen in the 'Novus Orbis' of Basle, 1555. Another 'Novus Orbis' of Basle, 1532, contains a map bearing the following inscription: 'Tabula nouarum Insularum, quas diuersis respectibus Occidentales & Indianas uocant.' In this the word America is not to be found; we only read on the southern part of this continent: 'Nou orbis, Insula Atlantica quam uocant Brasil & Americam,' and 'Die Nüw|Welt.'] We think it belongs to some of the small folio *Ptolemies.*"—*Abridged and corrected from* HARRISSE. For a list of the contents *see* Trömel's "Bibliothèque Americaine," No. 4; consult also Ternaux, No. 38, *and* Rich, No. 7.

[HUTTICH.] Novvs Orbis Re-|gionvm ac Insvlarvm ve-|teribus incognitarum, unã cum tabula cosmographica, &|aliquot aliis consimilis argumenti libellis, quorum|omnium catalogus sequenti patebit pagina.|His accessit copiosus rerum memorabilium index.| Vogue la galee. *Parisiis apvd Galeotvm a'*|*Prato, in aula maiore Palatii regii ad primam columnam.*| [Colophon:] *Impressum Parisiis apud Antonium Augellerum, impensis Ioannis*|*Parui & Galeoti ã Prato. Anno* M.D.XXXII. VIII.|*Calen. Nouembris.*| Folio, 26 l. (including 19 of Index), pp. 507 [for 514], Register and Colophon, 1 l. Folded Map, "Nova, et Integra vniversi orbis descriptio."

The map, for a description of which *see* Harrisse's "Bib. Am. Vet.," p. 298, is by Orontius Fine, and has been reproduced in facsimile by Frederick Muller. Cancellieri says of this edition "più rara di tutte." So far as contents are concerned it is merely a reprint of *our* No. 34100. The preface is sometimes wanting, as it contains a passage offensive to the Inquisition, and some copies contain these passages struck out with a pen. The following is the same edition as this with another title-page, in which the only change is in the name of the publisher.

[HUTTICH.] Novvs Orbis Re-|gionvm ac Insvlarvm ve-|teribus incognitarum, unã cum tabula cosmographica, &|aliquot aliis consimilis argumenti libellis, quorum|omnium catalogus sequenti patebit pagina.|His accessit copiosus rerum memorabilium index.| [Jehan Petit's printer's mark.] *Parisiis apvd Ioannem*|*Paruum sub flore Lilio, uia ad sanctum Iacobum.*| [Colophon:] *Impressum Parisiis apud Antonium Augellerum, impensis Ioannis*|*Parui & Galeoti ã Prato. Anno* M.D.XXXII. VIII.|*Calen. Nouembris.*| Folio, 26 l., pp. 507 [for 514], Colophon, 1 l. Map, as in 34101. 34102

[HUTTICH.] Novvs Orbis Regio-|nvm ac Insvlarvm veteribvs incognitarvm|unã cum tabula cosmographica, & aliquot alijs consimilis|argumenti libellis, quorum omnium catalogus|sequenti patebit pagina.|His accessit copiosus rerum memorabilium index.| ... |Adiecta est hvic postremae Editioni|Nauigatio Caroli Cæsaris auspicio in comi-|tijs Augustanis instituta.|*Basileae apvd Io. Hervagivm Mense*|*Martio Anno* M. D. XXXVII.| [Colophon:] *Basileae per Io Hervagivm Mense Novembri.*| *Anno* M. D. XXXVI [*sic*].| Folio, 24 l., pp. 600, Printer's mark, 1 l. Map, entitled "Typvs Cosmographicvs Vniversalis." 34103

In addition to the contents of the earlier editions, this contains on pp. 585–600 the letter of Maximilian of Transylvania. The map is the same as that in the edition of *Basileae*, 1532. The preface and map are often lacking. *See* Trömel, No. 10.

[HUTTICH.] Novvs Orbis Re-|gionvm ac Insvlarvm vete-| ribvs incognitarvm vna cvm Tabvla Cos-|mographica, & aliquot alijs consimilis argumenti libellis, nunc no-|uis navigationibvs auctus, quorum omnium catalogus|sequenti patebit pagina.|His accessit copiosus rerum memorabilium index.| ... |Adiecta est hvic postremae Editioni|Nauigatio Caroli Cæsaris auspicio in comi-|tijs Augustanis instituta.|*Basileæ apvd Io Hervagivm,*| *Anno* M.D.LV.| Folio, 26 l., of which the 20th is blank, pp. 677, Printer's mark, 1 l. Map, "Typvs Cosmographicvs Vniversalis."

"This edition contains, besides the matter of the first, also four supplementary pieces, including the second and third letters of Cortes. The only variation between different copies of the Grynæus maps is that the letter-press portion (the names of the regions) was, in a second issue, set up in a partly altered type. This circumstance, observed in different copies of different editions, has caused some vague statements which catalogues constantly repeat, one from another, concerning the rarity of the map and the existence of counterfeits."—QUARITCH. "On en (de cette collection) recherche les exemplaires, et surtout ceux de l'édition de 1555 qui est la plus complète."—BRUNET.

[HUTTICH.] Novus Orbis.|id est,|Navigationes|Primæ in Americam:|quibus adjunximus|Gasparis Varrerii discvrsvm| super Ophyra Regione.|Elenchum Autorem [*sic*] versa pagina| Lector inveniet.|*Roterodami,*|*Apud Iohannem Leonardi Berewout*|

Anno CIↃ. IↃ. CXVI.| 8vo, 8 l., pp. 570. [Followed by:] Casparis|Varrerii Lvsitani|Commentarius|de Ophyra|Regione,|In sacris litteris Lib. III. Regum|& II. Paralipomenon.|*Roterodami,*| *Apud Ioannem Leonardi Berevvout,*|*Anno* 1616.| Title, 41 l. BA.

An Abridgment. Contents: Columbus (C.), Navigatio; Pinzon (V.), Navigatio; Vespucius (A.), Navigatio; Martyr (P.), De insulis nuper repertis; Cortes (F.), De suis peregrinationibus; Herborn (N.), De Indis convertendis; Varrerius (J. de), De Ophyra regione. "Ce recueil renferme la partie de la collection de Grynæus qui se rapporte à l'Amérique, et de plus la dissertation de Varrerius, vulgairement nommé *Caspar Barreiros*, neveu du célèbre Jean de Barros."—BRUNET. The preface is by Balthasar Lydius. The question whether or not the land of Ophyr was Peru is discussed by Varrerius in this curious and rare volume, which is not always found with the work, although called for by the title and contents.

[HUTTICH.] Die New|welt, der landschaf-|ten vnnd Insulen, so|bis hie her allen Altweltbeschrybern vnbekant,|Jungst aber von den Portugalesern vnnd Hispaniern jm|Nider-|genglichen Meer herfunden. Sambt den sitten vnnd gebreuchen der Inwonenden|völcker. Auch was Gütter oder Waren man bey jnen funden, vnd jnn|vnsere Landt bracht hab. Do bey findt man auch hie den vrsprung vnd|altherkummen der Fürnembsten Gwaltigsten Völcker der Alt-|bekanten Welt, als do seind die Tartern, Moscouiten,|Reussen, Preussen, Hungern, Sschlafen. etc.|nach anzeygung vnd jnnhalt diss vmb-|gewenten blats.| *Gedruckt zů Strasżburg durch Georgen Vlricher*|*von Andla, am viertzehenden tag des Mertzens.*| *An.* M. D. XXXIIII.| Folio, 6 leaves, Text, 242 [for 252] folioed leaves. C. 34106

A German translation by Michael Herr; it is less known and much rarer than the original. The version is somewhat broad, and is distinguished by a certain originality in expression. Although it has no map, it has, on the other hand, the merit of being augmented in the text. It contains a full translation of Peter Martyr's Decades, leaf 174–229, and also his three books "De Legatione Babylonica," 235–248, both wanting in all the different Latin editions. Besides, it contains all the pieces of the first Latin edition of 1532, except Munster's "Introductio in tabulam geograph.," to which the map belongs, and would, therefore, have been superfluous in this edition. The preface by Grynæus is omitted, but a new one by the translator, Michael Herr, is added. It is curious that none of these differences have been noted by Harrisse. *See* "Bibliotheca Americana Vetustissima," No. 188; Rich, No. 9; Ternaux, No. 45; "Bibliotheca Grenvilliana," p. 498.

[HUTTICH.] Die nieuvve vveerelt der Landt-|schappen ende Eylanden, die tot hier toe allen ouden|weerelt bescrijverẽ onbekent geweest sijn. Maer nv onlancx vandẽ Poor-|tugaloiseren eñ Hispanierẽ, inder nedergankelijke zee geuondẽ Midtsgaders den zee-|den, manieren, ghewoonten ende vsantien der inwoonenden volcken. Oock wat|goeden ende waeren, men by henlieden gheuonden, ende in onse landen|ghebracht heeft oft hebben, daer by vintmen oock den oorspronck|eñ ouder hercomen, der vermaersten, machtichsten, eñ ge-|weldichste volcken, der ouder bekender weerelt, ghe-|lijck daer sijn die Tartaren, Muscouitë, Ruys-|sen, Pruyssen, Hongeren, Slauen, etc. | Naet wt wijsen ende inhout des|omghekerden blats.|...|Met gratie ende Priuilegie voor den tijt van vj. iaren | *Gheprint Thantwerpen in die Cammerstrate inden Arent|tsegen Scarabeum by my Jan van der Loe.* | *Anno* M. D. LXIII.| Folio, pp. (8), dcccxviij [818]. 34107

A Dutch translation from the German version, with augmentations, so that it is the most complete of all editions of this valuable collection. It was made by the notary Cornelis Ablyn, who abridged the preface and added a dedication to William, Prince of Orange. The History of the newly discovered Islands of Canaria, on pp. 504–521, exists in no other edition. It is quite rare.

This large Collection of Voyages, compiled by J. Huttich, and edited by Simon Grynæus, with a Geographical Preface by Sebastian Munster, all of the old University of Basle, was printed at the expense of a Jo. Hervagius, a Basle publisher, and should find a place in every public library, inasmuch as the original editions of the Papers of which it is made up are now hardly to be found. Considering the date of the first edition of 1532, the reader should study some of the Voyages with both of his eyes open, the one to detect the mistranslations and the other the misconceptions of inland geographers, who misread the reports of the navigators. It is a grand old book of reference, containing, in a fair Latin version the Voyages, 1. of Cadamosto; 2. Columbus; 3. Alonzo Niño; 4. Vincent Pinzon; 5. Americus Vespucci; 6. Pedro Alvarez Cabral; 7. Joseph the Indian; 8. The Portuguese to India, described in a letter of Emanuel to Leo x.; 9. Varthema; 10. The Holy Land, by Brocard; 11. Marco Polo; 12. Haython's Tartars; 13. Sarmatia, by Matthew Miechow; 14. Muscovie, by Paulus Jovius; 15. Peter Martyr's New Islands; 16. Stella's Prussia; and 17. Maximilian of Transilvania, his Account of Magellan's Voyage. I have corrected the proof of this series of "Huttich's" in the warehouse of Mr. F. Muller, Bookseller of Amsterdam.

HUTTON (George). An Appeal to the Nation, on the subject of Mr. Gilbert Wakefield's Letter to William Wilberforce. To which are subjoined Four Sermons, ... 8vo, pp. 162. N. 34108

HUTTON (M.) Sermon ... before the ... Society for the Propagation of the Gospel in Foreign Parts ... . By Right Reverend ... Mathew, Lord Bishop of Bangor. *London: J. Roberts and A. Millar.* MDCCXLV. 8vo, pp. 74. M., S. 34109

HUTTON (W.) Canada, A Brief Outline of her Geographical Position, Productions, Climate, Capabilities, Educational and Municipal Institutions, &c. By William Hutton ... . Third Edition. *Quebec.* 1861. 8vo, pp. 64. 34110

HUTTON. Stanford's Emigrant's Guides. Canada; its Present Condition, Prospects and Resources, fully described for the Information of intending Emigrants. By William Hutton ... . *London.* [1854.] 16mo. C. + Second Edition. *London: Edward Stanford.* 1857. 16mo, pp. xxxii, 120. Map. B. 34111

Also: Caird's Erroneous View of Canada Answered and Refuted. ... *Toronto.* 1858.

HUXON (A. B.) Contributions to the Rhymes of the War—May, 1865. *Baltimore: J. D. Toy.* 1865. 12mo, pp. 25.

HUYGHUE (D. S.) The Nomades of the West; or Ellen Clayton. By Douglas S. Huyghue. *London: Richard Bentley.* 1850. 3 vols., post 8vo, pp. vi, 295; (1), 299; (1), 304.

Also: Argimon: an Indian Tale. The author was a native of St. John, N. B.

HYATT (T.) The Prayer of Thaddeus Hyatt to James Buchanan, President ... In Behalf of Kansas, asking for a Postponement of all the Land Sales in that Territory, and for other Relief: ... October 29, 1860. *Washington: Henry Polkinhorn, Printer.* 1860. 8vo, pp. 68, (4). B., C., H. 34114

HYDE (A.) Memoir of Rev. Alvan Hyde, D.D. of Lee, Mass. *Boston: Perkins, Marvin & Co.* 1835. 12mo, pp. vii, 13–408, Errata. Portrait. C. 34115

HYDE. The Nature and Danger of Heresy. A Sermon ... before the Convention of the Clergy of Massachusetts, May 29, 1817. By Alvan Hyde, D.D. *Boston: Samuel T. Armstrong.* 1817. 8vo, pp. 22. B., H. 34116

HYDE. Sketches of the Life, Ministry and Writings of the Rev. Stephen West ... . By Alvan Hyde ... . *Stockbridge: Printed by Charles Webster.* 1819. 8vo, pp. 18. BA. 34117

Also: A New-Year's Sermon, preached at Lee, Jan. 1st, 1804. ... *Stockbridge (Mass.): H. Willard.* 1804. 8vo, pp. 28. C.—A Sermon, delivered at the Funeral of Mr. Nathan Ball ... . *Printed at Lee Jan. 13th 1800 by Cyrus Yale.* 12mo, pp. 22. H. + *Albany.* 1802.—A Sermon ... at Lee ... December 20th, 1807 ... after the Interment of Mr. Jonathan Thacher ... and of Mrs. Mary Ingersoll ... . *Pittsfield: Printed by Seymour & Smith.* 1808. 8vo, pp. 23.—A Sermon ... at Lee, December 22nd, 1820; ... *Stockbridge: Printed by Charles Webster.* 1821. 8vo, pp. 31. BA.—Thanksgiving Sermon at Lee Dec. 13, 1796. ... *Stockbridge.* 1797. 12mo. + *Boston.* 1797. 8vo, pp. 24.

HYDE (A. M.) The American Boy's Life of Washington. By Mrs. Anna M. Hyde. ... *New York: James Miller.* 1868. 16mo, pp. 255. Portrait and Illustrations. B. 34118

HYDE (C.) A Sermon ... May 26, 1851. At the Funeral of Rev. Chauncey Booth ... . By Rev. Charles Hyde ... . *Hartford.* 1851. 8vo, pp. 15. H. 34119

HYDE (E.) A Sermon in which the Doctrine of the Lot is stated and applied to Lotteries, Gambling and Card Playing for

Amusement. By Eli Hyde, of Oxford, N. Y. *Oxford, N. Y.: J. B. Johnson.* 1812. 8vo. 34120

HYDE (E.) History of ... Winchendon, from the Grant of the Township ... in 1735, to the Present Time. By Ezra Hyde. *Worcester: Printed by Henry J. Howland.* [1849.] 12mo, pp. 136.

HYDE (Jabez B.) Kianasa nana Nonedowaga Neuwenuda. *Buffalo.* 1819. 16mo. 34122

Hymns in the Seneca language.

HYDE (J. F. C.) The Chinese Sugar-Cane; its History, Mode of Culture, Manufacture of the Sugar, &c., with Reports of its Success in Different Portions of the United States, and Letters from Distinguished Men. Written and Compiled by James F. C. Hyde ... . *New York.* 1857. 12mo, pp. 106. + *Boston: John P. Jewett & Company.* 1857. 12mo, pp. 106. Plates.

HYDE (J.), *Jr.* Mormonism: Its Leaders and Designs. By John Hyde, Jun., formerly a Mormon Elder and Resident of Salt Lake City. *New York: W. P. Fetridge & Company.* 1857. 12mo, pp. 335. B., BA. + Second Edition. [*Ibid.*] 34124

HYDE (N. M.) The Writings of Nancy Maria Hyde, Of Norwich, Conn. Connected with a Sketch of her Life. *Norwich: Printed by Russell Hubbard.* 1816. 12mo, pp. 252. BA.

HYDE (W.) An Address delivered at the Opening of the New Town Hall, Ware, Mass., March 31, 1847. Containing Sketches of the Early History of that Town, and its First Settlers. By William Hyde. *Brookfield.* 1847. 8vo, pp. 56. M. 34126

HYDE (W. L.) History of the One Hundred and Twelfth Regiment N. Y. Volunteers. By Wm. L. Hyde ... . *Fredonia, N. Y.: W. McKinstry & Co.* 1866. 8vo, pp. 214. Portraits.

HYDE PARK. First Annual Report of ... Expenditures of the Town of Hyde Park ... February 15, 1869. *Boston: Lyman Rhodes, Printer.* 1869. 8vo, pp. 40. H. 34128

HYENNE (R.) Un Bandit californien (Joaquin Murieta). Par Robert Hyenne. *Paris: Lécrivain et Toubon.* 1862. 4to.

Also: William Palmer, empoisonneur et faussaire; suivi de: Une Affaire d'or; épisode de la vie californienne. ... *Paris: Havard.* 1860. 4to.

HYLACOMYLUS. *See* Waldseemüller (Martin).

HYLKES (R.) Merkwaardig Verhaal van Reinier Hylkes, uitgevaren na Groenland en aldaar met 9 andere schepen verongelukt. *Amsterdam: Nic. Byl.* 1779. 4to. 34130

Curious Journal of R. Hylkes, shipwrecked in Greenland.

Hymen; an Accurate Description of the Ceremonies used in Marriage by every Nation in the Known World, showing the Oddity of some and Absurdity of others, the Drollery of many and the Real and Intended Piety of all. *London.* 1760. 12mo.

Of the twenty-three chapters, twelve relate to different tribes of American Indians.

Hymn for ... American Independence. *See* [Boker (G. H.)]

Hymne à la Liberté. *New York.* 1826. 8vo. 34132

Hymns and Odes. 1800. *See* [Sewall (J.)]

Hymns and Tunes for the Army and Navy. *New York: American Tract Society.* [n. d.] 12mo, pp. 128. B. 34133

Hymns for the Camp. ... Second Edition ... . [n. p. n. d.] 32mo, pp. 127. H. + Third Edition ... . [n. p. n. d.] 32mo, pp. 127. B. + *Raleigh: Biblical Recorder Print.* 1864. BA.

Hymns for the Nation, in 1782. *London: Printed by J. Paramore* ... . 1781. 12mo, pp. 24. P. 34135

Among the Hymns given in this scarce little volume are the following: "After the Defeat at the Chesapeak;" "For the Loyal Americans;" "A Prayer for Congress," four 8 line stanzas; "For the Conversion of the French;" "Thanksgiving for the Success of the Gospel in America," etc.

HYNDMAN (W.) History of a Cavalry Company. A Complete Record of Company "A," 4th Penn'a Cavalry ... . By Capt. William Hyndman. *Philadelphia: Jas. B. Rodgers Co., Printers.* 1870. 12mo, pp. v–343. H. 34136

HYNEMAN (Leon), *Editor.* The Universal Masonic Record: ... Containing the Name, Business, Profession and Residence of Subscribers; ... Containing also, a List of Masonic Lodges in America and Europe. *Philadelphia: L. Hyneman.* 1857. 8vo, pp. 234. C. 34137

HYNEMAN. Worlds Masonic Register; containing the Name, Number, Location, and Time of Meeting of every ... Chapter, Council, and Commandery in the United States and Canada; ... with the Statistics of each Masonic Jurisdiction; ... By Leon

Hyneman. *Philadelphia: Printed for the Author, by J. B. Lippincott & Co.* 1860. 8vo, pp. 566. 34138

Also: Masonic Library. ... *Philadelphia.* 1854, 1855. 8vo, pp. 768, 751.

HYNEMAN (R.) The Leper, and other Poems. By Mrs. Rebekah Hyneman. *Philadelphia: A. Hart.* 1853. 12mo, pp. 266. 34139

Hypocrisy Unmasked. *See* [Johnson (S.)]

The Hypocrite; or Sketches of American Society from a Residence of Forty Years. By Aesop. ... *New York: Thomas Fox & Co.* 1844. 8vo, pp. 120. Portrait. S. 34140

(H.) Histoire d'une jeune fille sauvage. Publiée par Madame H. I. *Paris.* 1755. 12mo. A. 34141

I. (J.) The Little Look Open‡ A Prophecy or, Prophetical Dissertation. Predicting and declaring the Coming of the expected Redeemer, in the Character of Lord and King: the setting up of a National Theocracy in the Calling of the Jesus, and Redemption of the Gentile Church. Part I. Consisting of an Astro-Théological Unfolding of certain formerly obscure, but highly-interesting and capital points of Doctrine. Adapted to the present Crisis of Affairs. By J— I—. ... *Philadelphia: Printed for the Author.* MDCCLXIII. 8vo, pp. 281. Astro-theological folded Plate. P.

I have never seen Part II. An ill-executed, wild book, printed with several sets of type and different sizes of paper.

I. (R.) *See* [Johnson (Robert)].

I. R. C. A Cóndensed History of the Independent Royster-ing Club. [n. p. n. d.] 8vo, pp. 174. 34143

Thirty-two copies only printed for the cadets at West Point.

IABOATAM (A. de S. M.) Orbe serafico novo Brasilico ... parte primeira da Chronica dos frades menores da mais Estreita e Regular Observancia da Provincia do Brasil, por Fr. Antonio de Santa Maria Iaboatam, &c. *Lisboa: Anton Vicente da Silva.* 1761. Folio. 34144

A rare piece; no more published, I believe.

I am a Soldier. [Advice. n. p. 1863.] 8vo, pp. 8. 34145

Ianthe-Guido, A Tale and other Poems. Sketches from History. *New York: G. & C. Carvill.* 1828. 12mo. 34146

Includes the "Lament of Columbus."

IARRICI (P.) *See* Jarrici (P.)

IBAGNEZ (P.) Jesuitisches Reich in Paraguay, durch Original-Documente der Gesellschaft Jesu bewiesen, von dem aus dem Jesuitenorden verstossenen Pater Ibagnez. Aus dem Italienischen übersetzt. *Cölln: Peter Marteau.* 1774. 12mo, pp. (8), 264. 34147

IBAÑEZ DE ECHAVARRIA (B). *See* Echavarry (I. de), Vol. VI.

IBANEZ DE SEGOVIA (Gaspar). Noticia y juicio de los mas Principales Historiadores de España ... *Madrid.* 1784. 12mo.

IBAR (F.) Muerte Politica de la Republica Mexicana, ó Cuadro Historico-Critico de los Sucesos Politicos, desde 1823 hasta 1829. Por Francisco Ibar. *Mexico.* 1829. 8vo. 34149

IBARRA (Miguel de). Alegacion de sus meritos por la Cathedra de decreto, etc., en que hace mencion de algunos Mexicanos. *Mexico.* 1650. Folio. 34150

Title from Ternaux, No. 690.

ICAZA (I.) Coleccion de las Antigüedades Mexicanas que ecsisten en el Museo nacional, y dan à luz Isidro Icaza é Isidro Condra. Litografiadas por Frederico Waldeck, é impresas por Pedro Robert. *Mexico.* 1827. Folio, pp. 8. 13 Plates.

ICAZBALCETA (J. G.) Apuntes para un Catálogo de Escritores en Lenguas Indígenas de América. Por Joaquin García Icazbalceta. *México. Se han impreso 60 ejemplares en la imprenta particular del autor.* 1866. 12mo, pp. xiii, 157. 34152

This little volume, which is very rare, is a valuable contribution to the Bibliography of Books in the Mexican Languages.

ICAZBALCETA. Coleccion de documentos para la Historia de México publicada por Joaquin García Icazbalceta. *México: Libreria de J. M. Andrade.* 1858–66. 2 vols., 4to, pp. cliii, 544, 2 Plates; lxvi, (1), 600, 15 facsimile signatures. BA. 34153

Each volume forms a separate and complete collection by itself. The first contains: "Historia de los Indios de Nueva España por Fr. Toribio de Motolinia," followed by several partly inedited documents; the second volume contains: "la Relacion de la Conquista de México por Andrés de Tapia," and other inedited pieces. Three hundred copies only printed. It is the most valuable modern work which has been published on the history of Mexico.

ICAZBALCETA. Documentos para la Historia de México. ... Vol. I.–II. *México: V. G. Torres.* 1852–53. 8vo. 34154

Contents: Vol. I.–II. Sumario de la residencia tomada à D. Fernando Cortes.

ICAZBALCETA. Documentos para la Historia de México. ... 4ª série. Vol. I.–VII. *México: V. G. Torres.* 1856–57. 8vo.

Contents: Vol. I. Continuacion de los materiales para la historia de Sonora; Vol. II. Sinaloa y Sonora (Materiales, etc.); Vol. III.–IV. Nueva-Vizgaya (Documentos, etc.); Vol. V. Establecimiento i progresos de las misiones de la Antigua California; Vol. VI.–VII. Noticias de la Nueva California por el R. P. Fr. F. Palou. Agresiones y hazañas de tres Apaches.

ICAZBALCETA. Documentos para la Historia de México. ... *México: J. M. Andrade.* 1858. 8vo, pp. cliii, 544. B., C., H.

Contents: Historia de los Indios de Nueva España, por Fr. Toribio Motolinia, pp. 1–277; Noticias de la vida y escritos de fray Toribio de Motolinia, por J. F. Ramirez, pp. cliii; Varios documentos del siglo XVI., pp. 279–537. The distinguished editor of these various works is thus spoken of by M. Harrisse; we need scarcely add, we cordially coincide with his remarks: "A scholar of methodical habits and clearness of perception, a critic of great acumen, and a disinterested, modest, persevering votary of science, Señor Icazbalceta deserves well of the student of American history."

Iceland, Greenland, and the Faroe Islands. *Edinburgh: Oliver & Boyd.* 1840. Post 8vo. 34157

Schedæ | Ara Prests | Froda | Vm Island. | *Prentadar i Skalhollte af Hendrick Kruse.* | *Anno* 1688. | 4to, pp. 14, Registur, 4 leaves.

Ich und die Evangelisch-Lutherische Synode von Pennsylvanien. Ein freimüthiges Wort an alle Deutsche. *Philadelphia.* 1841. 8vo. 34159

Icones | qvinqvaginta | virorvm | illustrium doctrina & erudi | tione præstantium ad vivum | effictæ, cum eorum vitis | descriptis | a | Ian. Iac. Boissardo Vesunti: | Omnia recens in æs artificiosé | incisa, | & demum foras data | per | Theodorum de Bry *Leodien* | *civem Francofurti.* | *Anno* MD.XCVII–XCIX. 4 vols., 4to, pp. (11), 288, (8); 300, (8); (6), 327, (8); (6), 335, (8). 200 Portraits. 34160

Perhaps the earliest collection of engraved portraits, including Columbus and other distinguished navigators, with biographies. This is a corrected title of *our* No. 6161, in Vol. II.

Ida Randolph, of Virginia. A Poem in Three Cantos. *Philadelphia: Willis P. Hazard.* 1860. 12mo, pp. 60. B. 34161

IDAHO. The Banditti of the Rocky Mountains, and Vigilance Committee in Idaho. An Authentic Record of Startling Adventures in the Gold Mines of Idaho. *New York: Wilson & Co.* 1865. 8vo, pp. 17–143. 34162

The Imperial Gold and Silver Tunnel Company ... . *Boston: Press of Geo. C. Rand & Avery.* 1866. 8vo, pp. 42. Plate. H.

Journal of the First Session of the Legislative Council of Idaho Territory. 1863–64. *Lewiston.* 1864. 8vo. Continued.

Journal of the Fourth Session of the Council of Idaho Territory. ... 1866 ... 1867. *Boise City.* 1867. 8vo, pp. 474. H.

Laws passed at the First Session of the Legislative Assembly of the Territory of Idaho, 1863–64, at Lewiston. Together with the Territorial Organic Act, Declaration of Independence, Federal Constitution, Pre-emption and Naturalization Laws. *Lewiston: A. Glascock, Territorial Printer.* 1864. 8vo. 34166

Laws, Memorials and Resolutions passed by the Fourth Legislative Assembly of the Territory of Idaho, 1866–67. Also, the Codified Revenue Law. *Boise City.* 1867. 8vo. 34167

Annual Message of Governor Lyon, of Idaho. Delivered November 16, A.D. 1864. *Lewiston: Frank Kenyon ... Printer.* 1864. 8vo, pp. 7. H. 34168

Also: Second Annual Message of Governor Lyon, of Idaho. *Boise City: Jas. S. Reynolds & Co. ... Printers.* 1865. 8vo, pp. 8. H.

Proceedings of the Grand Lodge of Idaho, A. F. & A. M., at First Annual Communication. 1867. *Portland.* 1868. 8vo.

IDE (G. B.) Battle Echoes, or, Lessons from the War. By George B. Ide, D.D. ... *Boston: Gould and Lincoln.* 1866. 12mo, pp. iii, 325. B., BA., C., H. 34170

IDE. The Freedmen of the War: A Discourse ... Annual Meeting of the American Baptist Home Mission Society, Philadelphia, May 19th, 1864. By George B. Ide, D.D. *Philadelphia.* 1864. 16mo, pp. 44. 34171

Also: Pious Men the Nation's Hope. ... *Boston: Gould and Lincoln.* 1863. 8vo, pp. 30. B.

IDE (J.) ... Intemperance. A Sermon, preached in Medway, December 14, 1817. By Jacob Ide, A.M. ... *Dedham: Abel D. Alleyne, Printer.* 1818. 8vo, pp. 31. 34172

IDE. The Office of the Christian Ministry: A Sermon, ... at the Ordination of Mr. Charles T. Torrey, ... March 22d, 1837. By Rev. Jacob Ide. ... *Providence: Published by John E. Brown.* 1837. 8vo, pp. 31. B. 34173

IDE. A Pastor's Review. A Discourse Preached in Medway, Mass., Nov. 2, 1864, on the Fiftieth Anniversary of the Author's Ordination and Settlement. By Jacob Ide, D.D. *Boston: Congregational Board of Publication.* 1865. 8vo, pp. 72.

IDE. A Sermon, delivered December 29, 1819, at the Ordination of the Rev. David Brigham, ... in Randolph. By Jacob Ide, A.M. ... *Boston: Printed by Lincoln and Edmands.* [n. d.] 8vo, pp. 28. B. 34175

Also: Discourse in Medway, West Parish, at the Installation of the Mount Lebanon Chapter, June 24, 1825. ... *Boston.* 1825. 8vo.—A Sermon ... May 12, 1816 ...

the Death of Mr. James Partridge ... . *Dedham: Abel D. Alleyne, Printer.* 1816. 8vo, pp. 22. B.—A Sermon delivered December 13, 1820, at the Ordination of the Rev. John M. Putnam as Pastor of the Church in Ashby. ... *Boston.* 1820. 8vo, pp. 28.— ... A Sermon ... at the Ordination of the Rev. Sewall Harding ... January 17, 1821. ... *Boston: Printed by True and Green.* 1821. 8vo, pp. 42.—A Sermon ... Sept. 12, 1821, at the Ordination of the Rev. George Fisher. ... *Peters and Biglow, Printers, Concord, Mass.* 1822. 8vo, pp. 31.—A Sermon ... Death of Mr. George W. Barber ... preached ... Dec. 14, 1823. ... *Dedham: H. & W. H. Mann, Printers.* 1824. 8vo, pp. 15.—Sermon occasioned by the Death of the late Mr. Edmund P. Sanford, Medway. ... *Boston.* 1826. 8vo, pp. 29.— ... A Sermon ... May 3, 1840 ... Death of Mrs. Hannah Miller ... . *Providence: Printed by B. T. Albro.* 1840. 8vo, pp. 29.—A Sermon ... at the Funeral of Deacon Daniel Wiley ... . *Boston: Press of T. R. Marvin.* 1847. 8vo, pp. 24. B.—A Sermon ... at the Funeral of Rev. David Long ... March 15, 1860. ... *Milford: Press of G. W. Stacy.* 1850. 8vo, pp. 19.—A Sermon ... at the Installation of Rev. Samuel Hunt ... *Boston: Printed by Charles C. P. Moody.* 1851. 8vo, pp. 44. H.

Idea Mercurial. *See* Zuarez (J.)

Ideas de un Comerciante sobre el modo de destruir el Contrabando por reformas del arancel vijente. *Vera Cruz.* 1850. 8vo, pp. 20. 34176

Ideas importantes acerca del Patronato. *Guadalajara.* 1825. 4to, pp. viii, 92. 34177

Ideas Necesarias a todo pueblo Americano independiente, que quiera ser libre. *Philadelphia: D. Huntington.* 1821. 12mo. + *Puebla, Mexico.* 1823. 12mo. 34178

Idée de la traite et du traitement des Nègres. [Par Clarkson et de Sartines.] *Philadelphie.* 1790. 8vo, pp. 108. 34179

Idees Sommaires, 1792. *See* [Gouy (L. M. de)], Vol. VII.

The Ides of March; or, Abraham Lincoln, Private Citizen. Being a Sequel to the End of the Irrepressible Conflict. By a Merchant of Philadelphia. *Philadelphia: King & Baird, Printers.* 1861. 8vo, pp. 29. B., H. 34180

The Idle Man. *See* [Dana (R. H.)], Vol. V., No. 18439.

The Idler. *London: J. Newberry.* MDCCLXI. 2 vols., 12mo, pp. (8), 294; (6), 285. 34181

Repeatedly reprinted. Contains an article on the Battle of Louisbourg, Speech of an Indian, &c.

An Idyl for The People. April 1, 1863. 12mo, 6 l. 34182

Iean de Vierde. *See* Joam IV.

Iets over de emancipatie der slaven door eenen voormaligen bewoner van de kolonie Suriname. 1856. *'s Hage.* 1857. 8vo.

Iets over de gevolgen van de afschaffing der slavernij in de Englisch West Indische Kolonien. *'s Hage.* 1859. 8vo.

IGLESIAS (A.) Relacion sencilla del funeral y Exequias del Illmo. y Rmo. Señor Marstro D. F. Antonio de San Miguel Iglesias, Obispo que fué de la santa iglesia catedral de Valladolid de Michoacan, etc. etc. Dispuesta por un Presbítero de la misma Ciudad. *Mexico.* 1805. 4to, pp. 13, 13, xxxix, 30. 34185

IGNACIA (M.) Apologia a favor do R. P. Ant. Vieyra da Comp. de Jesu da Provincia de Portugal, porque se desvanece, e convence o tratado, que com o nome de Crisis escrevue contra elle a Rev. Senhora Dona Joanna Igner da Crus, Religiosa de S. Jeronymo de Provincia de Mexico das Indias Occidentales. Escreveua Am. Sor Margarida Ignacia. *Lisboa Occidental, B. da Costa.* 1727. 4to. 34186

IGNACIO (J.) Contestacion de Mucio Valdovinos, á la defensa de D. José Maria Anzorena, escrita por su hijo D. José Ignacio. *Mexico.* 1850. 4to, pp. 55. 34187

IGNACIO. Defensa de D. José Maria de Ansorena, Intendente que fue de la antigua provincia de Valladolid, el año de 1810. Escrita por su hijo José Jgnacio, contra las criminales imputaciones que se le hacen en la "Historia de Mexico" de Lucas Alaman. *Mexico.* 1850. 4to, pp. 31. 34188

IGNACIO. Respuesta de José Mariano de Anzorena, à la Contestacion que dió D. Mucio Valdovinos á la Defensa de D. José Maria de Anzorena, escrita por su hijo D. José Ignacio. *Mexico.* 1850. 4to, pp. 54. 34189

IGNACIO (M.) Manifesto con otras Documentos para desengaño de los Incautos, por Manuel Ignacio, Obispo de Puebla. *Mexico.* 1812. 4to. 34190

IGNACIO (S.) Lecciones espirituales para las tandas de ejercicios de S. Ignacio, dadas á los Indios en el idioma mexicano. Compuestas por un sacerdote del Obispado de la Puebla de los Angeles. *Puebla.* 1841. 8vo, pp. 213. 34191

IGNACIO DE ARENA (T.) Relacion de los Estragos y Ruynas, que a padecido la Ciudad de Santiago de Guathemala, por terremotos, y fuego de sús Bolcanes en este año de 1717. Escrivela del Thomas Ignacio de Arena. *Guathemala, por el Alferes Antonio de Pineda Ybarræ.* 1717. Folio. 34192

IGNAZIO DE AZEVEDO (P.) Vita e martirio del venerabil P. Ignazio de Azevedo, ucciso dagli Eretici con altri trentanove della Campagnia di Gesù. *Venetia, Teverin.* [1744.] 12mo.

Ignace de Azevedo was a missionary in Brazil.

IKINS (A.) History, Topography, ... of Texas. By Arthur Ikins. *London: Sherwood & Co.* 1841. 18mo. 34194

Iles de France. Journal des îles de France et de Bourbon. 1786. 8vo. 34195

ILLESCAS (G. de). Historia Pontifical y Catholica, en la qual se contienen las vidas, y hechos notables de todos los Summos Pontifices Romanos. ... Con mas vna breve recapitvlacion de las cosas de España ... . Dende Halarico Primero, hasta Don Phelippe Segundo, nuestro Señor. Compuesta, y ordenada por el Doctor Gonçalo de Illescas ... . Por el mismo autor en muchos lugares añadida en la quinta Impression. ... Primera e Segunda Parte, 1306–1572. *Barcelona.* 1589. 2 vols., folio, pp. xvi, 620, xxviii; 812, xix. Tercera Parte, 1572–1592, por Luys de Bavia, 1609. pp. xii, 520, liv. Quarta Parte ... por F. Marco de Guadalajara y Xabierr, 1592–1605. *En Caragoça.* 1612. pp. xii, 732, xxxiii. S. + *Barcelona: Por Sebastian de Cormellas.* M.DC.XXII. 5 vols., folio, pp. (16), 278, (29). Segunda Parte, M.D.LXXXXV. pp. (2), 364, (20). Tercera Parte, 1621. pp. (16), 520, (54). Quarta Parte, M.DC.XXI. pp. (8), 432, (54). Quinta Parte, 1630. pp. (16), 584, (32). B. Sesta Parte, por J. Baños de Velasco. *Madrid.* 1678. Together 6 vols., folio.

A very interesting General History of the World, with copious particulars about the Spanish possessions in America, etc. Not mentioned by Salva. The two first volumes of this work appeared first in 1564. Brunet accounts for only five parts, though he names six. The parts have been published in several editions and in various places. "On trouve difficilement cet ouvrage complet."—BRUNET.

ILLINOIS. An Account of the ... Ilinois [*sic*] ... Land Companies. *See* [Smith (William)].

Address of the National Democratic State Central Committee of Illinois. [n. p. 1860.] 8vo, pp. 8. 34197

Agriculture. Transactions of the Illinois State Agricultural Society, with the Proceedings of the County Societies, and Kindred Associations. John A. Kennicott, Corresponding Secretary, ... Vol. I. 1853–4. *Springfield: Lanphier & Walker, Printers ...* 1855. 8vo, pp. viii, 612, Index, iv. B., BA., H. 34198

Continued to 9 vols. A New Series was commenced in 1871. Also: Report of the Annual Exhibition, 1850. *Springfield.* 1850. 8vo. Continued.—Transactions of the State Board of Agriculture, 1861. Continued.

Banks. General Banking Law. *Springfield.* [1851.] 8vo.

Report of the Bank Commissioners of the State of Illinois, for the year 1858. *Springfield: Bailhache & Baker, Printers.* 1859. 8vo, pp. 24. Plan. Continued. H. 34200

Reports of Joint Select Committee on the State Bank, 1840.

Canals. Report of the Canal Commissioners of Illinois, on Incorporating a Company to open a Canal to connect Lake Michigan and the Illinois River. *Vandalia.* 1825. 8vo. 34202

Report, in Congress, on the Memorial of the General Assembly of Illinois, relative to a Canal Communication between the Illinois River and Lake Michigan. *Washington.* 1825. 8vo.

Illinois and Michigan Canal. Documents relating to the Negotiation ... with the Foreign Creditors of Illinois ... . *Boston.* 1844. 8vo, pp. 44. H. 34204

The Illinois and Michigan Canal. January, 1852. *Boston.* 1852. 8vo, pp. 17. H. 34205

Memorial of the Legislature of Illinois to Congress on the Improvement of the Illinois and Michigan Canal. *Washington.* 1868. 8vo. 34206

Report of ... Trustees of the Illinois and Michigan Canal, for ... 1857 and 1858. *Springfield: Bailhache & Baker, Printers.* 1859. 8vo, pp. 135. B. 34207

Also: Rules, By-Laws, etc., of Trustees. *Chicago.* 1848. 8vo.—Report ... in reply to certain Charges which were preferred by Mr. Charles Oakley ... at a Meeting of Subscribers to the Loan of $1,600,000. ... *Washington.* 1847. 8vo. S.

Report of the Canal Commissioners to the Governor, Dec. 1, 1870. *Springfield.* 1871. 8vo. 34208

H. C. Chandler & Co.'s Railway Business Directory and Shippers' Guide, for the State of Illinois. *Indianapolis: H. C. Chandler & Co.* 1868. 8vo, pp. xxiv, 936, 190. Map. C. 34209

Churches. Abstract of the Proceedings of the Baptist Convention of Illinois, 1840–41. *Louisville, Ky.* 1841. 8vo, pp. 16.

Minutes of the Illinois Baptist Pastoral Union. Ninth Annual Meeting ... . *Chicago: Hays & Thompson, Printers.* 1854. 8vo, pp. 36, (4). Continued. H. 34211

Minutes of the Anniversary of the Baptist General Association of Illinois, and Pastoral Union, held in 1849. *Chicago.* 1849. 8vo. 34212

Minutes of the General Association of Illinois ... . 1852. *Peoria: Printed by B. Foster.* 1852. 8vo, pp. 15, (1). Continued

Illinois General Association. Report of Committee of Investigation on the Rights of Congregationalists in Knox College. *Chicago.* 1859. 8vo. 34214

Annual Minutes of the Illinois Conference of the Methodist Episcopal Church, 1854. *Springfield.* 1854. 8vo, pp. 32. Continued. 34215

Minutes of the Rock-River Conference of the Methodist-Episcopal Church, Chicago, September, 1853. *Chicago.* 1853. 12mo, pp. 22. 34216

Commissioners of Public Charities. First Biennial Report. *Springfield.* 1870. 8vo. Continued. 34217

Conventions. Constitution of the State of Illinois, adopted in Convention ... August 26, 1818. *Kaskaskia [Ill.]: Blackwell & Berry.* 1818. 8vo, pp. 24. C. 34218

Illinois Constitutional Convention. Constitution ... adopted by the Convention ... June 7, 1847 ... . *Springfield: Lanphier & Walker, Printers.* 1847. 8vo, pp. 39. H. 34219

New Constitution ... adopted March 24, 1862. *Springfield.* 1862. 8vo. 34220

Journal of the Constitutional Convention of Illinois, 1862. *Springfield.* 1862. 8vo. 34221

Debates and Proceedings of the Constitutional Convention. Convened at the City of Springfield, Dec. 13, 1869. *Springfield: E. L. Merritt & Brother.* 1870. 2 vols., 4to, pp. (8), 1076; (4), 1077–1896, 132. C. 34222

Journal of the Constitutional Convention, 1869. *Springfield.* 1870. 8vo, pp. 1022, (2), xi. C. 34223

Education. An Act to establish ... Free Schools ... February 15, 1855. *Springfield: Lanphier & Walker, Printers.* 1855. 8vo, pp. 43. H. 34224

Biennial Report of the Superintendent of Common Schools, 1846. 8vo. Continued. 34225

Second Biennial Report of the Superintendent of Public Instruction of the State of Illinois, 1857–58. *Springfield: Bailhache & Baker, Printers.* 1859. 8vo, pp. 423. Map. BA. 34226

An Appeal in behalf of the Illinois College, recently founded at Jacksonville, Illinois. *New York.* 1831. 8vo. W. 34227

Catalogue of the Officers and Students of Illinois College, 1832–33. [n. p. n. d.] 8vo, pp. 8. Continued. 34228

Historical Sketch of the Origin, Progress, and Wants, of Illinois College. June, MDCCCXXXII. *New York.* 1832. 8vo. + Second Edition. *John T. West, Printer, New-York.* 1832. 8vo, pp. 16. 34229

Illinois Asylum for the Education of the Deaf and Dumb. Second Biennial Report, for 1847, 48. Jan. 31, 1849. *Springfield.* 1849. 8vo. Continued. S. 34230

Seventh Biennial Report of the Trustees and Principal of the Illinois Institution for the Education of the Deaf and Dumb, for the years 1857 and 1858. *Alton, Ill.* 1858. 8vo, pp. 62. Continued. B., H. 34231

First Annual Report of the Directors of the Illinois Branch of the American Education Society ... August 14, 1832. *Jacksonville: Printed by James G. Edwards.* 1832. 8vo, pp. 17, (1).

First Annual Report of the Board of Trustees of the Illinois Industrial University ... March 12, 1867, to ... June 13, 1868. *Springfield: Baker, Bailhache & Co., Printers.* 1868. 8vo, pp. xii, 323. Continued. B., H. 34233

Annual Report of the Regent, 1870. *Champaign.* 1870. 8vo.

Circular and Catalogue of the ... Illinois Industrial University. 8vo. 34235

Laws relating to the Illinois Industrial University, together with the Minutes of the first Meeting of the Trustees. 8vo. S.

Also: Report of Committee on Courses of Study and Faculty for the ... University. ... *Springfield: Baker, Bailhache & Co., Printers.* 1867. 8vo, pp. 22, (1). H.

Illinois Institution for Feeble-Minded Children. Annual Report, for 1864. *Jacksonville.* 1864. 8vo. 34237

Illinois Institution for Feeble-Minded Children. First Report of Directors of the Experimental School. 1866. 34238

Illinois Soldiers' College. Catalogue and Circular, 1867. *Fulton, Ill.* 1867. 8vo. 34239

Illinois State College Association and Central College Association. Proceedings at Evanston, August, 1869. *Ann Arbor.* 1870. 8vo. 34240

Manual of Instruction: explanatory of the Common School Law of the State of Illinois. [By John P. Brooks.] *Rockford: Adams & Blackmer.* 1864. 8vo, pp. 280. Plate. 34241

Illinois Normal University. Catalogue for 1861–2. *Bloomington.* 1862. 8vo. 34242

Illinois Southern Normal University. Annual Report, for 1869. *Springfield.* 1870. 8vo. 34243

Illinois Teacher: Organ of the State Teachers Institute. *Peoria.* 1855. 8vo. Continued to 1869. H. 34244

Illinois Wesleyan University. Annual Catalogue of Officers and Students for 1856. *Bloomington.* 1856. 8vo. 34245

North-Illinois University, Henry, Ill. Report of the Board of Trustees, 1857–58. *Boston.* 1858. 8vo, pp. 7. 34246

School Law. An Act to establish ... Free Schools ... February 21, 1859. *Springfield: Bailhache & Baker, Printers.* 1859. 8vo, pp. 41, vi. H. + [*Ibid.*] 8vo, pp. 16. B. + 1861. 8vo, pp. 42, v. H. 34247

School Laws of Illinois, as Amended February 16th, 1865, with Official and Judicial Decisions in Relation to Common Schools. Prepared by Newton Bateman ... . *Springfield, Ill.: Johnson & Bradford, Printers.* 1865. 8vo, pp. 208. + Second Edition, Enlarged. [*Ibid.*] 1866. 8vo. 34248

Also: School Laws of Illinois—1869. An Act to establish and maintain a System of Free Schools, approved February 16, 1865; ... . *Springfield.* 1869. 8vo, pp. 55, Index, viii. B.

Synopsis of the Illinois School Law. By H. S. Cooley, 1849. 8vo. 34249

Finance. Biennial Reports of the Auditor of Public Accounts of the State of Illinois, to the Twenty-second General Assembly. *Springfield.* 1861. 8vo. 34250

Continued to 1868, after which they are annual.

Biennial Report of the Treasurer of the State of Illinois to the Twenty-Second General Assembly. *Springfield.* 1861. 8vo.

Annual in 1869.

Geology. Illinois Geological Survey. Abstract of a Report on Illinois Coal; with Descriptions and Analyses, and a General Notice of the Coal Fields. ... By J. G. Norwood, M.D. ... *Chicago.* 1857. 8vo, pp. 93, v. 2 Tables and Map. H. 34252

Geological Survey of Illinois. A. H. Worthen, Director. *Chicago.* 1866–76. 6 vols., imp. 8vo. C. 34253

Contents: Vol. I. Geology. Assistants: Prof. J. D. Whitney, Prof. Leo Lesquereux, Mr. Henry Engelmann. 1866. pp. xvi, 504, iii. 11 Maps and Plate. Vol. II. Palæontology. Descriptions of Vertebrates; By J. S. Newberry and A. H. Worthen. Descriptions of Invertebrates; By F. B. Meek and A. H. Worthen. Descriptions of Plants; By Leo Lesquereux. 1866. pp. xix, (2), v, 9–470, vi, (2). 50 Plates. Vol. III. Geology and Palæontology. Geology; By A. H. Worthen, and assistants, Henry Engelmann, H. C. Freeman, H. M. Bannister. Palæontology; By F. B. Meek and A. H. Worthen. 1868. pp. vii, 574, vii, (40). Map and 25 Plates. Vol. IV. Geology and Palæontology. Geology; By A. H. Worthen, and assistants. Palæontology; By J. S. Newberry, A. H. Worthen and L. Lesquereux. 1870. pp. viii, 508, v, (62). 32 Plates. Vol. V. Geology and Palæontology. Geology; By A. H. Worthen and J. Shaw. Palæontology; By F. B. Meek and A. H. Worthen. 1873. pp. vii, 620, v, (64). 33 Plates. Vol. VI. Geology and Palæontology. Geology; By A. H. Worthen, and assistants, G. C. Broadhead and E. T. Cox. Palæontology; By O. St. John, A. H. Worthen, and F. B. Meek. 1876. pp. viii, 532, vi, (68). 34 Plates and Map.

Hospitals. Annual Report of the Illinois State Hospital for the Insane. *Springfield.* 18—. 8vo. 34254

Fourth Biennial Report ... of the Illinois State Hospital for the Insane, at Jacksonville. December, 1852. Second Edition. *Chicago: Chas. Scott & Co., ... Printers.* 1858. 8vo, pp. 40. Continued. H. 34255

Reports of the Illinois State Hospital for the Insane. 1847–62. *Chicago: F. Fulton & Co., ... Printers.* 1863. 8vo, pp. 422. Continued. B., C., H. 34256

Report of the Investigating Committee on the Hospital for the Insane, made to the Governor of Illinois, 1867. *Springfield.* 1869. 8vo. 34257

Southern Insane Asylum. Report of Commissioners for 1869–70. 8vo. 34258

Illinois Institution for the Blind. First Biennial Report, for 1855 and 1856. *Springfield.* 1857. 8vo. 34259

Illinois in 1837; A Sketch descriptive of the Situation, Boundaries, Face of the Country, Prominent Districts, Prairies, Rivers, Minerals, Animals, Agricultural Productions, Public Lands, Plans of Internal Improvement, Manufactures, &c. of the State of Illinois: also, Suggestions to Emigrants, Sketches of the Counties, Cities, and Principal Towns in the State: together with a Letter on the Cultivation of the Prairies, By the Hon. H. L. Ellsworth. To which are annexed The Letters from a Rambler in the West. ... *Philadelphia: S. Augustus Mitchell.* 1837. 8vo, pp. 143. Map.

Reprinted as: "Illinois in 1837 and 1838." *Philadelphia: S. Augustus Mitchell.* 1838. 8vo. The publisher is probably the author. It was got up mainly to promote the sale of Illinois Lands then owned by John Grigg of Philadelphia.

The Illinois Monthly Magazine, conducted by James Hall. Vol. I. *Vandalia.* 1831. Vol. II. *Cincinnati.* 1832. 8vo. C.

Followed by the "Western Monthly Magazine."

Transactions of the Illinois Natural History Society. Edited by C. D. Wilber, Secretary. Vol. I. Series I. *Springfield, Ill.* 8vo, pp. 194. Plates. + Second Edition. [*Ibid.*] 1862. 8vo.

Illinois State Gazetteer and Business Directory, for the Years 1864–5, embracing Descriptive Sketches of all the Cities, Towns and Villages throughout the State ... . *Chicago: J. C. W. Bailey.* 1864. 8vo, pp. 820, lxvii. C. 34263

Illinois State House Commissioners. Report to the Governor, Dec. 30, 1868. *Springfield.* 1869. 8vo. 34264

Transactions of the Illinois State Medical Society for the Year 1854. *Chicago: J. F. Ballantyne.* 1855. 8vo, pp. 112. + For the Year 1855. *Peoria.* 1855. 8vo, pp. 88. H. 34265

Also: Ninth Annual Meeting of the Illinois State Medical Society, ... June 7 & 8. 1859. *Chicago: W. Cravens & Co., Printers.* 1859. 8vo, pp. 144. + Tenth Annual Meeting ... Paris, Ill., May 8th and 9th, 1860. *Chicago.* 1860. 8vo. Continued.

Illinois State Sanitary Bureau. Report of Transactions ... from its Organization December 18th, 1862, to September 12th, 1863. And also of the Illinois State Sanitary Commission, from September 12th, 1863, to January 1st, 1864. *Springfield: Press of Baker & Phillips.* 1864. 8vo, pp. 98. B. 34266

Impartial Appeal to the Reason, Interest and Patriotism of the People of Illinois on the Tyrannous Effects of Slave Labor. [n. p.] 1824. 12mo. 34267

The Impending Contest. The Issues of the Campaign. The Question for True Union Men. Shellabarger and Cox contrasted. *Springfield Republican.* [n. d.] 8vo, pp. 16. 34268

Inaugural Message to the General Assembly; delivered January 12, 1857. Continued. 34269

Inaugural Address of Richard Yates, Governor ... January 14, 1861. 8vo, pp. 24. 34270

Inaugural Address of Richard J. Oglesby, Governor ... January 16, 1865. *Springfield.* 1865. 8vo, pp. 24. 34271

Insurance. Annual Report of the Insurance Companies. 1868. *Springfield.* 1868. 8vo. 34272

Invitation serieuse aux habitans des Illinois. *Philadelphie.* 1772.

Journals of the Senate and House of Representatives of the Fourth General Assembly. *Vandalia.* 1824. 8vo. Continued.

Journal of the Senate of the First General Assemby, 1822–23. *Springfield.* 1823. 8vo. Continued. 34275

Journal of the House of Representatives of the Fifth General Assembly. *Vandalia.* 1826. 8vo. Continued. 34276

Rules and Joint Rules of the Senate and House ... of Illinois. ... January 11, 1867. *Springfield: Baker, Bailhache & Co., Printers.* 1867. 8vo, pp. 16. H. 34277

Laws. Amendments to the Internal Improvement Laws: passed by the General Assembly of Illinois ... . *Vandalia: William Walters ... Printers.* 1839. 8vo, pp. 13. H. 34278

Compilation of the Statutes of ... Illinois. ... By N. H. Purple. *Chicago.* 1856. 2 vols., 8vo. + Second Edition. [*Ibid.*] 1857. C. 34279

Election Laws of Illinois. *Springfield.* 1865. 8vo. 34280

Incorporation Laws, Passed by General Assembly at the Session of 1836–7. *Vandalia.* 1837. 8vo. 34281

Incorporation Laws of Illinois, 1838. *Vandalia: Public Printer.* 1839. 8vo, pp. 249, viii, (2). C. 34282

An Index to all the Laws of the State of Illinois, both Public and Private, which are not printed at large in Gross's Statutes of

1869, except Private Acts of 1868. 1818 to 1869. By Eugene L. Gross and William L. Gross. *Springfield: E. L. & W. L. Gross.* 1869. 8vo, pp. xii, 140. C. 34283

Laws passed by the [First] General Assembly of Illinois ... 1819. *Kaskaskia.* 1819. 8vo. C. 34284

Continued and published at Vandalia and Springfield.

The Public and General Statute Laws of the State of Illinois: containing all the Laws published in the "Revised Statutes" of 1833, except such as are repealed, together with all the Acts of a General and Public Nature, passed by the Ninth General Assembly, at their First Session, commencing December 1, 1834, and ending February 13, 1835; and at their Second Session, commencing December 7, 1835, and ending January 18, 1836; and those passed by the Tenth General Assembly, at their Session, commencing December 5, 1836, and ending March 6, 1837; and at their Special Session, commencing July 10, and ending July 22, 1837; which are not repealed; and also the Militia Law. ... *Chicago: Stephen F. Gale.* 1839. 8vo, pp. iv, 743. C., H. 34285

Revised Code of Laws of Illinois, enacted by the Fifth General Assembly, at their Session held at Vandalia, commencing on the 4th of December, 1826, and ending the 19th of February, 1827. *Vandalia.* 1827. 8vo. S. 34286

The Revised Code of Laws of Illinois, containing those ... passed by the Sixth General Assembly, ... December, 1828; and those enacted previous thereto. ... *Shawneetown.* 1829. 8vo, pp. 278. C., S. 34287

Some copies have the imprint *Cincinnati.* 1829.

The Revised Laws of Illinois, containing all Laws of a general and public nature passed by the Eighth General Assembly, at their session held at Vandalia, commencing on the third day of December, 1832, and ending the second day of March, 1833, together with all Laws required to be re-published by the said General Assembly. ... *Vandalia: Printed by Greiner & Sherman.* 1833. 8vo, pp. 677, (40). B. 34288

Revised Statutes of the State of Illinois, adopted by the General Assembly at the Session held 1844–5. ... Revised and prepared for Publication, with Notes, Index, &c., by M. Brayman. *Springfield.* 1845. 8vo, pp. 749. 34289

Statutes of Illinois ... in force ... 1857. With Marginal Notes ... By Samuel H. Treat, W. B. Scales, and R. S. Blackwell. *Chicago.* 1858. 2 vols., 8vo. 34290

Legislative Reports of the General Assembly of Illinois, 1839, etc. Continued. 34291

Manual of the House of Representatives for 1832–3. Continued. 34292

Map of the Military Bounty Lands in the Illinois and Missouri Territories ... With a Description of the Soil, Timber, &c., of each section. *Baltimore.* 1818. 8vo. Map. 34293

A very scarce pamphlet.

Memorial of the Illinois and Wabash Land Company. 13th January, 1797. Referred to Mr. Jeremiah Smith, Mr. Kittera, and Mr. Baldwin. Published by Order of the House of Representatives. *Philadelphia: Printed by Richard Folwell.* [n. d.] 12mo, pp. 8, 8, 7, 7, BA. 34294

Ludewig describes a tract with a similar title as pp. 26. Also: Report of the Committee [on] the Memorial of the Illinois and Wabash Land Company. 3d February, 1797 ... . [n. p. n. d.] 8vo, pp. 4. BA.

Memorial of the Ilinois [*sic*] and Ouabache Land Companies to the Honourable Congress of the United States, intended as a Full Recapitulation and Clear Statement of the Former Addresses, Petitions, Memorials ... presented at the Sessions, 1802. [n. p. 1802.] 8vo, pp. 20. BA. 34295

Memorial of the United Illinois and Wabash Land Companies to the Senate and House ... of the United States. *Baltimore: Printed by Joseph Robinson.* 1810. 8vo, pp. 44. BA. 34296

Memorial of the Illinois Association [at Quincy], completing a Quarter of a Century of its History, and an Historical Appendix, by Wm. Carter, Oct. 26, 1869. 8vo, pp. 98. 34297

Message of the Governor of Illinois [Yates] to the ... Assembly, at its Extraordinary Session, Convened April 23, 1861. *Springfield.* 1861. 8vo, pp. 8. + January 5, 1863. *Springfield.* 1863. 8vo, pp. 64. 34298

Military. Annual Report of the Adjutant General of the State of Illinois [for 1861–62]. *Springfield: Baker & Phillips, Printers.* 1863. 8vo, pp. 383. B., H. 34299

Report of the Adjutant General of the State of Illinois. Volume I. Containing Reports for the Years 1865 and 1866. ... *Springfield: Baker, Bailhache & Co., Printers.* 1867. 8vo, pp. vii, 694. Continued. B., H. 34300

A List of Officers of the Illinois Regiment, and of Crockett's Regiment. A List of Non-Commissioned Officers and Soldiers of the Illinois Regiment, and the Western Army. [n. p. n. d.] 4to. 34301

Official Register of the Officers of the Illinois Volunteers, 1846. *Alton, Ill.* 1846. 8vo. 34302

Report of the Proceedings ... of the Muster-In of the 86th Reg't of Illinois Infantry ... at Peoria ... Aug. 27th, 1866. ... *Peoria, Ill.* 1866. 8vo, pp. 11. H. 34303

State Sanitary Commissioner. Report on Condition of Troops, Hospitals, etc., 1864. 8vo. 34304

Sanitary Report of Colonel John Williams to Gov. Richard Yates, of Illinois. *Springfield.* 1862. 8vo, pp. 19. 34305

War Record of the State of Illinois to Oct. 1, 1863. Proclamation of Gov. Yates, and Report of Adj. Gen Fuller, Feb. 1, 1864. *Springfield.* 1864. 8vo. 34306

Odd Fellows. I. O. of O. F. Constitution and By-Laws of the Grand Lodge of the U. S. ... of Illinois ... of Subordinate Lodges. ... *Springfield, Ill.* 1847. 8vo, pp. 31. 34307

Prisons. Reports of the Superintendent of the Illinois State Penitentiary, made to the Twenty-First General Assembly, Jan. 5, 1859. *Springfield.* 1859. 8vo, pp. 29. 34308

Reports of the Illinois State Penitentiary, by the Commissioners, for the years 1859 and 1860. *Springfield.* 1861. 8vo, pp. 92. Plan. Continued. 34309

Proceedings of the Antiquarian and Historical Society of Illinois, at its First Session, in December 1827: With an Address ... *Edwardsville: Printed by Robert K. Fleming.* 1828. 12mo, pp. 22. H. 34310

Proceedings of the Board of Commissioners of Public Works of Illinois. *Vandalia.* 1837. 8vo. 34311

Proceedings of the First Convention of the Colored Citizens of the State of Illinois, convened at the City of Chicago, Thursday, Friday, and Saturday, October 6th, 7th, and 8th, 1853. *Chicago.* 1853. 8vo, pp. 18. 34312

... Proceedings of the Illinois Anti-Slavery Convention, October, 1837. *Alton: Parks and Breath.* 1838. 8vo, pp. 36. BA.

Proceedings of the Illinois Land Company, 1839. *New-York: H. Ludwig, Printer.* 1839. 8vo, pp. 64. H. 34314

Proceedings of the State Board of Equalization at Springfield, Oct. 5, 1869. *Springfield.* 1869. 8vo. 34315

Railroads. Great Western Railroad Company of Illinois. Minutes of the Meetings of Creditors and Bondholders, held Sept. 1st, 5th, and 19th, 1857; ... *New-York.* 1857. 8vo.

The Illinois Central Rail Road Company offer for sale over 2,400,000 Acres selected Prairie, Farm and Wood Lands, in tracts of any size, to suit purchasers, on Long Credits, and at Low Rates of Interest, situated on each side of their Rail Road, extending all the way from the extreme North to the South of the State of Illinois. *Salem.* 1854. 8vo, pp. 30. + *New-York: John W. Amerman, Printer.* 1855. 8vo, pp. 32. + Offers ... over 2,000,000 Acres. *New-York.* 1856. 8vo. S. + Offers ... over 1,500,000 Acres. *Boston: Geo. C. Rand & Avery, Printers.* 1857. 8vo, pp. 80. B., S. 34317

Also: Report to the Directors ... by a Committee ... on the Progress and Condition of the Work. ... *New-York.* 1853. 8vo. S.

Documents Relating to the Organization of the Illinois Central Rail-Road Company. *New-York: Geo. S. Roe.* 1851. 4to, pp. 141. Map. S. 34318

Letter on the Lands of the Illinois Central Railway Company. By James Caird, Esq., M.P. *London, January,* 1859. 8vo.

... Report of the Illinois Central Railroad Company, March 15, 1854. *New-York: Geo. Scott Roe.* 1854. 8vo, pp. 32, (12).

Remarks on the Retirement of Chief Justice Caton from the Bench of the Supreme Court of Illinois. ... *Chicago: Jones & Small ...* 1864. 8vo, pp. 11. 34321

Reports made to the Senate and House of Representatives of the State of Illinois, December 9, 1839. *Springfield.* 1840. 8vo.

Report from the Committee on Internal Improvement of the Senate of Illinois, January 28, 1840. *Springfield.* 1840. 8vo, pp. 14. M. 34323

Report of the Engineer-in-Chief [James B. Eads], of the Illinois and St. Louis Bridge Company. St. Louis, May, 1868. *St. Louis.* 1868. 8vo, pp. 77. Plate and 3 Maps. 34324

Sketches of Illinois, descriptive of its principal Geographical Features, ... Productions, ... and Public Lands. *Philadelphia: S. Augustus Mitchell.* 1838. 8vo, pp. 32. Map. 34325

This is part of *our* No. 34260 (Illinois in 1837), with another title-page.

Statistics. Annual Reports of Public Officers and State Institutions for 1851. Continued. 34326

See "N. A. Rev.," LI. 92, *also* Hunt's "Magazine," v. 427.

Ill-judged Bounties tend to Beggary on both sides; or, Observations on a paper intituled, Reasons for laying a Duty on French and Spanish Indico, and granting a Bounty on what is made in the British Plantations. *London: Printed for the Author.* 1748. 8vo, pp. 14. J.C.B. 34327

ILLOWY (B.) Oration ... for Jewish Widows & Orphans, January 12, 1862. By Rev. Dr. B. Illowy. *New Orleans: Clark & Brisbin, Printers.* 1862. 8vo, pp. 15. H. 34328

Illuminatio Britannicæ; or, A True and Faithful Narrative of what passed at a Conference held at the Admiralty Office, Whitehall, Jany 11, 1740–41. Between the Rt. Hon. Sir Charles Wager, First Lord of the Admiralty, and Capt. John Morke (a Dane) by express appointment of Sir Charles, &c. In a Letter from a Gentleman in Town to his Friend (an old Revolution Whig of Distinction), in the Country. *London: Printed for the Author.* 1742. 4to, pp. 91. J.C.B. 34329

Relates to the affairs of North America, with schemes for fortifying certain prominent points in the British colonies.

Illustrated Agriculturist's Almanac. Edited by G. W. Marshall. *New York: J. G. Reed.* 1852. 12mo. S. 34330

Illustrated Annual Register of Rural Affairs and Cultivator Almanac for 1855. By J. J. Thomas. *Albany, N. Y.: L. Tucker & Son.* 8vo, pp. 144. Continued. S. 34331

The Illustrated Catholic Family Almanac, for the United States, for ... 1870. ... *New York: Catholic Publication Society.* [1869.] 12mo, pp. 108. Continued. B. 34332

Illustrated Description of the Broadway Pneumatic Underground Railway ... . *New-York: S. W. Green, Printer.* 1870. 4to, pp. 20. H. 34333

The Illustrated Family Christian Almanac for the United States, for ... 1848. *New York: American Tract Society.* 12mo. Continued. 34334

The Illustrated Hand-Book, a new Guide for Travelers through the United States of America. *New York: Sherman & Smith.* 1846. 18mo, pp. 233. Map. C. 34335

The Illustrated Miners' Hand-Book, and Guide to Pike's Peak, with a new and reliable Map. Showing all the Routes, and the Gold Regions of Western Kansas, and Nebraska. Illustrated with Appropriate Engravings. *Parker & Huyett, Saint Louis.* 1859. 18mo, pp. 75. Maps. 34336

The Illustrated Mount Vernon Record, the Organ of the Mount Vernon Ladies' Association of the Union, Containing Important Official Matter of the Association, Appeals of Vice Regents and Lady Managers, Monthly Reports of the Secretary, List of all Contributions to the Fund; Together with a great variety of Valuable and Highly Interesting Matter relative to our Colonial and Revolutionary History. Vol. I. *Philadelphia: Devereaux and Company.* [1859.] 4to, pp. 184. 34337

The Illustrated Pilgrim Almanac, 1860. Published in Aid of the Monument Fund. *Boston: A. Williams & Co.* [1860.] Rl. 8vo, pp. 50. BA. 34338

Continued to 1863, or later.

The Illustrated Pilgrim Memorial. ... *Willard M. Harding, Boston.* 1863. Rl. 8vo, pp. 48. H. 34339

Issued as a companion to the above work.

Illustrations and Expositions of the Principles of the People's Co-Operative Equal Rights Party. [n. p. n. d.] 8vo. 34340

Illustrations of Southern Chivalry, as shown by Photographic Portraits of their Prisoners of War. Extracts from a Narrative of Privations and Sufferings of United States Officers and Soldiers while Prisoners of War in the hands of the Confederate Authorities. Being the Report of a Commission of Inquiry appointed by the U. S. Sanitary Commission. *London: Bennett.* 1865. 18mo, pp. 52. 34341

Illustrations of Masonry. *See* [Morgan (W.)]

Illustrious Men of the United States. 32mo, pp. 96. 34342

Thirty-one very short notices of famous characters, from Pocahontas and Cotton Mather to Red Jacket, Polk, and Tyler.

Illustrious Personages of the Nineteenth Century; with an Introduction, by Henry P. Tappan. *New York.* 1853. 8vo. C.

Illustrirte Familien-Bibliothek. ... *Leipzig: Payne.* 1855. 8vo. Continued. 34344

This collection contains translations of several works relating to America, so does the "Illustrirte Familien-Bibliothek," *Leipzig: Payne.* *See* Kayser's "Bücher-Lexicon."

Ilsley (C. P.) Forest and Shore; or, Legends of the Pine-Tree State. By Charles P. Ilsley. *Boston: J. P. Jewett & Co.* 1856. 12mo, pp. 426. C. 34345

Ilsley (F.) The West India Interest Considered. By F. Ilsley. *London.* 1810. 34346

Relates to the cost of sugar.

Ilustracion de el derecho que compece á la S. Iglesia Cathedral de Mexico, para la percepcion del diesmo, que causa el fruto del maguey, el que por medio de su fermentacion passa naturalmente á la especie de Pulque, de cuya bebida usan los Naturales de estos Reynos, y no pocos de los Españoles. *Mexico.* 1750. Folio, pp. 85. 34347

Ilustracion de las pinturas dei Arco de Triunfo que para la entrada publica y solemne de D. Joachin de Monserrat, Virrey de esta Nueva España, erigió esta Ciudad de Mexico el dia 25. de Enero de 1761. *Mexico.* 1761. 4to, 20 l. 34348

Ilustracion Hispano-Americana. *Paris.* 1857. Folio. Continued. 34349

La Ilustracion mexicana, publicada por I. Cumplido. *Mexico: I. Cumplido.* 1851–55. 5 vols., 4to. 34350

"Collection complète, très intéressante pour l'histoire américaine et spécialement mexicaine."—Andrade.

Dos Ilustres Sabios. *See* [Paz-Soldan].

An Imaginary Conversation between President Jackson and the Ghost of Jefferson [on Nullification]. *Columbia, S. C.* 1831. 12mo, pp. 22. 34351

Imbert (É.) Adresse á MM. de l'Assemblée nationale. [Signé Imbert.] Mémoire pour Éloy Imbert, citoyen actif du

Port-au-Prince ... banni de la colonie de Saint-Domingue par un arrêt du conseil supérieur du Port-au-Prince, et demandant justice contre la violation de tous droits qui a été commise en sa personne. [*Paris: imp. de Quillau.* n. d.] 4to, pp. 48 or less.

Imlay (G.) The Emigrants, &c., or the History of an Expatriated Family, being a delineation of English manners, drawn from real characters. Written in America, by G. Imlay, Esq. ... *London: A. Hamilton.* 1793. 3 vols., 12mo, pp. xii, 221; 222; 192. 34353

A philosophical novel, founded on facts, in the form of letters written chiefly from different parts of Pennsylvania. Several lively descriptions of American scenes are introduced. It is well spoken of in the "Monthly Review," XI. 468.

Imlay. A Topographical Description of the Western Territory of North America; containing a succinct account of its Climate, Natural History, Population, Agriculture, Manners and Customs; with an ample description of the several divisions into which that country is partitioned. And an accurate Statement of the various Tribes of Indians that inhabit the Frontier Country. To which is annexed, a delineation of the Laws and Government of the State of Kentucky. Tending to shew the probable rise and Grandeur of the American Empire. In a Series of Letters to a Friend in England. By G. Imlay, A Captain in the American Army during the late War, and a Commissioner for laying out Land in the Back Settlements. *London: J. Debrett.* 1792. 8vo, pp. (2), 247. H., S. 34354

See "M. Rev.," VIII. 390; XX. 265; XXIV. 230.

Imlay. A Topographical Description of the Western Territory of North America: Containing A Succinct Account of its Soil, Climate, Natural History, Population, Agriculture, Manners, and Customs. With an ample Description of the several Divisions into which that Country is partitioned; to which are added, the Discovery, Settlement, and Present State of Kentucky. And An Essay towards the Topography, and Natural History of that important Country. By John Filson. To which is added I. The Adventures of Col. Daniel Boon, one of the First Settlers, comprehending every important Occurrence in the Political History of that Province. II. The Minutes of the Piankashaw Council, held at Post St. Vincent's, April 15, 1784. III. An Account of the Indian Nations inhabiting within the Limits of the Thirteen United States; their Manners and Customs; and Reflections on their Origin. By George Imlay, A Captain in

the American Army during the War, and Commissioner for laying out Lands in the Back Settlements. Illustrated with correct Maps of the Western Territory of North America; of the State of Kentucky, as divided into Counties, from the latent [*sic*] Surveys; and a Plan of the Rapids of the Ohio. The Second Edition, with considerable Additions. *London: J. Debrett.* MDCCXCIII. 8vo, pp. (4), xvi, 433; Index, 19; Errata, 1 p. 2 Maps, Plan, and Table. B. 34355

Imlay. A Topographical Description of the Western Territory of North America; containing a succinct account of its Climate, Natural History, Population, Agriculture, Manners and Customs. With an ample Description of the several Divisions into which that Country is divided. And an accurate Statement of the various Tribes of Indians that inhabit the Frontier Country. To which is annexed a delineation of the Laws and Government of the State of Kentucky. Tending to shew the probable rise and grandeur of the American Empire. In a series of Letters to a Friend in England. By G. Imlay, A Captain in the American Army during the late War, and a Commissioner for laying out Land in the Back Settlements. *New York: Printed by Samuel Campbell.* M,DCC,XCIII. 2 vols., 12mo, pp. xxiii, 260; 204. 2 Maps and Plan. C., J.C.B., M. 34356

Imlay. A Description of the Western Territory of North America; containing a succinct account of its Climate, Natural History, Population, Agriculture, Manners and Customs, with an ample description of the several divisions into which that country is partitioned, And an accurate Statement of the various Tribes of Indians that inhabit the Frontier Country. To which is annexed. A Delineation of the Laws and Government of the State of Kentucky. Tending to shew the Probable Rise and Grandeur of the American Empire. In a Series of Letters to a Friend in England. By G. Imlay, A Captain in the American Army during the late War, and a Commissioner for laying out Land in the Back Settlements. *Dublin: William Jones.* 1793. 12mo, pp. (4), xx, 249. B. 34357

Imlay. A Topographical Description of the Western Territory of North America: containing a succinct Account of its Soil, Climate, Natural History, Population, Agriculture, Manners, and Customs. With an ample Description of the several Divisions into which that Country is partitioned. To which are added, I. The Discovery, Settlement, and present State of Ken-

tucky; with an Essay towards the Topography and Natural History of that important Country, by J. Filson. Also the Minutes of the Piankashaw Council, 1784. II. An Account of the Indian Nations inhabiting within the Limits of the XIII States; their Manners and Customs; and Reflections on their Origin. III. The Culture of Indian Corn, Hemp, Flax, Hops, Tobacco, Indigo, Cotton, Senega Root, Esquine, Madder, Jalap, Potatoes, Silkworms, Persimmon, various Kinds of Grapes, Berries, and Nuts, the Candleberry Myrtle, Sumach, Coffee, and other Particulars in the vegetable Kingdom. IV. Observations on the ancient Works, the native Inhabitants of the Western Country, &c. By Major Jonathan Heart. V. Historical Narrative and Topographical Description of Louisiana and West-Florida, containing a great Variety of interesting Particulars, by Mr. Thomas Hutchins. VI. Account of the Soil, growing Timber, and other Productions of several Lands, particularly the Genesee Tract, lately located, and now in the Progress of being settled. VII. Remarks for the Information of those who wish to become Settlers in America, by Dr. Franklin. VIII. Topographical Description of Virginia, Pennsylvania, Maryland, and North-Carolina, by Mr. Tho. Hutchins. IX. Mr. Patrick Kennedy's Journal up the Illinois River, &c. X. Description of the State of Tenasee, and of the South-western Territory, with the Constitution of Tenasee established 1796. XI. An Act for establishing Knoxville. XII. Treaty concluded between the United States of America and the Crown of Spain, for the free Navigation of the Mississippi. XIII Plan of Association of the North American Land Company, &c. By Gilbert Imlay, A Captain in the American Army during the War, and Commissioner for laying out Lands in the Back Settlements. Illustrated with correct Maps of the Western Territory of North America ... . The Third Edition, with great additions. *London: J. Debrett.* 1797. 8vo, pp. xii, 598, (28). 2 Maps and Plate.

In the enlarged shape, which the work took in the present and last edition, it comprises a most valuable mass of materials for the early history of the Western Country, embodying the entire works of Filson, Hutchins, and various other tracts and original narratives. The author's Christian name varies in the title-pages.

Imlay. Nachrichten von dem westlichen Lande der Nord-Amerikanischen Freistaaten, von dem Klima, den Naturproduction der Volksmenge, den Sitten und Gebräuchen desselben nebst einer Angabe der Indianischen Völkerstämme ... . Aus dem Englischen übersetzt von E. A. W. Zimmermann. *Berlin: Voss.* 1793. 8vo, pp. xv, 168. J.C.B. 34359

Another German version is included in J. G. Forster's "Magazin."

Imlay (J. H.) Address at the Federal Republican Meeting, at Freehold, August 22, 1808. By James H. Imlay. *Trenton.* 1808. 34360

Immaculatæ Virginis deiparæ S. Mariæ de Guadalupe Mexicanæ Patronæ principalis. Pro festo celebrando die propia 12 decembris etiam Romæ apud salesianas sanctimoniales ... hymnus. *Fayentiæ, A. Archii.* 1773. 1 l. 34361

Immediate Emancipation in Maryland. Proceedings of the Union State Central Committee, ... Baltimore, December 16, 1863. *Baltimore: Bull & Tuttle.* 1863. 8vo, pp. 20. 34362

Immediate, not Gradual Abolition; or, an Inquiry into the Shortest, Safest, and most Effectual Means of getting rid of West Indian Slavery. Third Edition. With an Appendix ... . *London: Hatchard and Son.* MDCCCXXIV. 8vo, pp. 32. H. + *Philadelphia.* 1824. 8vo, pp. 24. + *New York.* 1825. 8vo, pp. 24. + *Boston: Isaac Knapp.* 1838. 12mo, pp. 35. 34363

Immense Meeting in Favor of the Union. [*Philadelphia.* 1863.] 8vo, pp. 16. 34364

Immigrants' Friend Society. Proceedings of the Second Annual Meeting of the Immigrants' Friend Society for the Valley of the Mississippi, May 23, 1837. *Cincinnati.* [n. d.] 8vo, pp. 16. 34365

The Immigrants' Guide to Minnesota in 1856. By an Old Resident. *St. Anthony: W. W. Wales* ... 1856. 12mo, pp. 116. Map. H. 34366

Imminent Dangers. *See* [Morse (S. F. B.)]

The Immortals or the Heroes of the XVIIIth Century [in verse]. *Jamaica: Printed for the Author.* [n. d.] 4to. 34367

El Imparcial. Periódico politico, cientifico y literario. Nos. 1–45. *Mexico.* 1837. Folio. 34368

An Impartial Account. *See our* Vol. II., No. 7301.

An Impartial Account of the Civil War. *See our* No. 10463.

An Impartial Account Of ... Expedition. *See* [Oglethorpe].

An Impartial and Correct History. *See* [O'Conor (T.)]

Impartial Citizen. April, 1849. *Syracuse.* 4to. S. 34369

An Impartial Enquiry into the Right of the French King to The Territory West of the Great River Mississippi, in North America, not ceded by the Preliminaries, including a Summary Account of that River, and the Country adjacent; with a short Detail of the Advantages it possesses, it's Native Commodities, and how far they might be improved to the Advantage of the British Commerce. Comprehending a Vindication of the English Claim to that Whole Continent, from Authentic Records, and indisputable Historical Facts; and Particular Directions to Navigators for entering the several Mouths of that important River. *London: W. Nicoll.* [1762.] 8vo, pp. (2), 58. BA., C., H.

See "M. Rev.," XXVII. 460.

An Impartial Enquiry. *See* [Martyn (B.)]

Impartial Enquiry into the Transactions of the late Directors of the South-Sea Company. To which is added, the Secret History of the South Sea Directors. *London.* 1735. 8vo. C.

An Impartial History of Great Britain, Civil and Political, during the Last Two Years, from the Commencement of the Year 1779 to the Taking of St. Eustatia from the Dutch in 1781. *London.* 1781. 8vo, pp. 122. 34372

An Impartial History of the late Glorious War in Europe, Asia, Africa, and America, with an Account of the Places ceded to Great Britain. *Manchester.* 1767. 34373

An Impartial History of the late War, from 1749 to 1763 [in Canada, &c.] *London.* 1763. 12mo. Portraits and Plates.

Attributed to John Almon.

An Impartial History of the War in America, between Great Britain and Her Colonies, from Its Commencement to the end of the Year 1779. Exhibiting a circumstantial, connected, and complete Account of the real Causes, Rise, and Progress of the War, interspersed with Anecdotes and Characters of the different Commanders, and Accounts of such Personages in Congress as have distinguished themselves during the Contest. With an Appendix, containing A Collection of Interesting and Authentic Papers tending to elucidate the History. Illustrated with a Variety of beautiful Copper Plates, representing real and animated Likenesses of those celebrated Generals who have distinguished themselves in the important Contest. *London: R.*

Faulder. MDCCLXXX. 8vo, pp. xi, 608; Appendix, 44. Map and 13 Portraits. + [*Ibid.*] 8vo, pp. iv, 608; Appendix, 31. B.

The portraits of American and British Generals comprise those of Washington, Arnold, Wooster, Putnam, Charles Lee, Com. Hopkins, Samuel Adams, Hancock, Franklin, Gen. Howe, Admiral Howe, American Rifleman. Some copies have the imprint: *R. Faulder and J. Milliken*; others, *Carlisle*, 1780. "A work, far from being an *impartial* history."—*Monthly Review*, LXIII. 466. It is sought for mainly for the portraits which are usually extracted by the "illustrators." It was altered as to the text and title, and reprinted as:

An Impartial History of the War in America, between Great Britain and the United States, from Its Commencement to the End of the War: Exhibiting a circumstantial, connected, and complete Account of the real Causes, Rise, and Progress of the War, interspersed with Anecdotes and Characters of the different Commanders, and Accounts of such Personages in Congress as have distinguished themselves during the Contest. ... Illustrated with beautiful Copper Plates ... . *Boston: Printed by Nathaniel Coverly and Robert Hodge.* M.DCC.LXXXI. 3 vols., 8vo, pp. iv, 445; Vol. II. M.DCC.LXXXII. pp. 448; Vol. III. *Boston: Printed by Nathaniel Coverly.* M.DCC.LXXXIV. pp. 190. 12 Portraits and 2 Plans. H. 34376

"The so-called 'beautiful portraits' are exceedingly rude productions, without the slightest resemblance to the men they are intended to represent."—J. R. Bartlett. Sets are rare, the third volume particularly so. Some copies purport to be a second edition.

The Impartial Inquirer. *See* [Lowell (John)].

Impartial Narrative. 1798. *Cambridge* [*N. Y.*]: *Printed by Tennery & Stockwell.* [n. d.] 34377

Impartial Narrative of the Reduction of Belle Isle. *London.* 1761. 8vo. 34378

Impartial Observations, To be considered on by The King, His Ministers, and the People of Great Britain. [*London.* 1763.] 4to, pp. 27. C., S. 34379

Relates entirely to America. Signed "Impartiality, March 25, 1763."

Impartial Reflections on the Conduct of the late Administration and Opposition, and of the American Colonies; in which the Causes and Consequences of the destructive War between Great Britain and the Revolted Colonies are particularly considered, and an immediate Suspension of Hostilities is earnestly Recommended. *London: W. Nicoll.* [1782.] 8vo, pp. 84. J.C.B.

"The writer improves the many opportunities offered him of blaming the errors of all parties; of course, all parties will be even with him, and despise his censure.

He makes occasionally a number of pertinent observations, but, being desultory, they possess no aggregate force."—*Monthly Review*, LXVI. 468.

Impartial Reflections upon the Present State of Affairs. *London.* 1761. 8vo. P. 34381

An Impartial Relation. *See* [Husband (Harmon)], Vol. VIII.

An Impartial Relation of the Hail-Storm on the fifteenth of July and the Tornado on the second of August 1799. Which appeared in the Towns of Bozrah, Lebanon and Franklin in the State of Connecticut. To which is annexed an estimate of the Damages done by the Storm, made by a Committee from said Towns. The whole published under their direction for the information of the Public. *John Trumbull, Norwich.* 1799. 8vo, pp. 30. 34382

An Impartial Review of the Rise and Progress of the Controversy between the Parties known by the Names of the Federalists, & Republicans. Containing an Investigation of the Radical Cause of Division; and of some of the Subordinate or Auxiliary Causes which have been instrumental in Enlarging the Breach and inflaming the Minds of the Partizans. In a Series of Letters from A Partaker in the American Revolution to a Junior Citizen. *Philadelphia: Printed by John Ormrod.* 1800. 8vo, pp. 50.

An Impartial Sketch, of the Various Indulgences granted by Great-Britain to her Colonies, upon which They have founded their Presumption of soaring towards Independence. By an Officer. *London: W. Davenhill.* M.DCC.LXXVIII. 8vo, pp. (4), 43.

The author thinks "the New England men are more prone to sedition than the other colonists"—that during the long winter months "they have nothing to do but cabal with their neighbours, and instruct their children in reading, writing, and praying; for," adds he "you'll not meet a New England man but has the Bible by heart, and all the laws of his Province."—*Page* 31. *See* "M. Rev.," LVIII. 314.

An Impartial Statement of the Controversy respecting the Decision of the late Committee of Canvassers. Containing, the Opinions of Edmund Randolph, Esq., Attorney General of the United States, and several other eminent Law Characters. *New-York: Printed by Thomas Greenleaf.* M.DCC.XC.II. 8vo, pp. 46.

Relates to the Otsego County votes.

An Impartial View of the Conduct of the Ministry in regard to the War in America ... In answer to the many attacks of Pamphleteers. *London: J. Robinson.* 1756. 8vo, pp. 52.

Partly relates to Major-General Washington. *See* "M. Rev.," XV. 295.

IMPARTIALIS, *pseudon.* Letters of Gratitude, to the Connecticut Pleader, the Reverend Joseph Huntington, D.D. for his Letters of Friendship, to a Certain Class of Gentlemen, with Illustrations from Recent Examples, By Impartialis. ... *Hartford: Printed by Hudson and Goodwin.* M.DCC.LXXXI. 12mo, pp. 76.

Imperial and County Annual Register for the years 1809–10, containing a History of Great Britain, with an ample Collection of State Papers; the Public and Private Annals of the British Provinces. *London.* 1810–11. 8vo. N. 34388

Imperial and Provincial Acts, &c., for the Protection of the Fisheries of British North America. *Halifax, N. S.* 1852. 8vo.

The Impolicy and Injustice of Emancipating the Negro Slaves. *London.* 1824. 8vo. 34390

Impolicy of building Another Rail Road between Washington and New York. *Philadelphia: King and Baird, Printers.* MDCCCLXIV. 8vo, pp. 24. 34391

Importance of a Register Law to the Purity of the Elective Franchise. *Louisville.* 1840. 8vo, pp. 16. M. 34392

Importance of Canada. *See* [Lee (Charles)].

The Importance of Cape Breton consider'd. *See* No. 10731.

The Importance of Effectually Supporting the Royal African Company of England Impartially considered; shewing That a Free and Open Trade to Africa, and the Support and Preservation of the British Colonies and Plantations in America, depend upon Maintaining the Forts and Settlements, Rights and Privileges belonging to that Corporation, against the Encroachments of the French and all other Foreign Rivals in the Trade. *London: M. Cooper.* 1744. 4to, pp. 47. Map. + The Second Edition. With a New and more Correct Map than any hitherto published shewing the Situation of the several European Forts and Settlements in that Country. In a Letter to a Member of the House of Commons. *London: E. Say.* 1745. 4to, pp. (4), 47. Map. 34393

The money-getting earnestness of this book may well shock the sensibilities at the present day of the rich descendants of the Royal African Traders of last century. *See* Stevens' "Bibliotheca Historica."

The Import Duties Considered in relation to the Happiness of the People and Prosperity of the Union. By a Friend of the Administration. *Philadelphia, January* 14, 1832. 8vo, pp. 10

The Importance of Gaining. *See* [Kennedy (A.)]

The Importance of Jamaica. *See* Jamaica.

The Importance of the British Dominion in India, compared with that in America. *London: J. Almon.* MDCCLXX. 16mo, pp. 60. J.C.B. 34395

See "M. Rev.," XLII. 322.

The Importance of the British Plantations. *See* [Hall (F.)]

The Importance of the Colonies. *See* [Ray (Nicholas)].

The | Importance | of the | Sugar Colonies | to | Great-Britain | Stated, | and Some | Objections against the | Sugar Colony Bill answer'd. | In a Letter to a Member of the | House of Commons. | *London:* ... *J. Roberts.* 1731. 8vo, pp. 40. C., H. 34396

See "Gentleman's Magazine" for 1731, *and a* "Short Answer."

Importance of Usury Laws. *See* [Whipple (John)].

Importancia del restablecimiento de los Jesuitas para la publica educacion. *Mexico.* 1845. 4to, pp. vi, 98, 24. 34397

Important Documents. *See* [Paez (J. A.)]

Important Documents which accompanied the Message of the President of the United States at the Opening of the Second Session of the Eleventh Congress, November, 1809. *New-York: Prior and Dunning.* 1809. 8vo, pp. 88. B. 34398

The original edition starts "Documents ..." *Washington City: Printed by Roger C. Weightman.* 1809. 8vo, pp. 88, 7.

Important Documents presented to Congress, Nov. 29, 1809, containing the Correspondence between America, England and France. *Worcester, Mass.* 1809. 12mo. 34399

Important State Papers. ... Documents accompanying the President's Message to Congress, Nov. 29, 1809. [n. p. n. d.] 8vo, pp. 27. + No. 2. pp. 29–32. H. + *Boston.* 1809. 8vo, pp. 52. N. 34400

Important Extracts from recent Letters from the United States, by Emigrants. Second Series. *London.* 1818. 8vo. 34401

Important Facts ... proving ... that the Approaching Presidential Election is forever to decide the Question between Freedom and Slavery. [*Detroit.* 1856.] 8vo, pp. 32. B. 34402

Important Question Examined. [n. p. 1819.] 12mo, pp. 12.

Important Report of a Joint Committee on the Subject of the Foreign Relations of the United States. *New-York.* 1810. 8vo, pp. 16. S. 34404

Important to Tax-Payers. [n. p. 1852.] 8vo, pp. 6. H.

Draft of a Petition to the General Assembly of Pennsylvania for a New Licence Law for selling Liquor.

The Imposition of Inoculation as a Duty religiously considered. *Boston.* 1721. 12mo, pp. 18. 34406

The Impracticability of a North-West Passage for Ships Impartially Considered. *London.* 1824. 8vo, pp. 182. 34407

"Without a publisher's name, and no doubt printed for private circulation. The Preface is signed 'Scrutator.'"—RICH.

The Impress considered as the Cause why British Seamen desert from our Service to the Americans. With a Review of the Encouragement now held out by the Royal Navy, and the Means in our Power of abolishing the Impress. *London: Luffman.* 1810. 8vo, pp. 29. C. 34408

See "M. Rev.," LXV. 217.

All Impressments Unlawful and Inadmissible. [*Boston: William Pelham.* n. d.] 8vo, pp. 12. BA. + *Philadelphia.* [1810.] 8vo, pp. 18. C. 34409

Impressions of the West and South during a Six Weeks' Holiday. *Toronto: Armour & Co.* 1858. 8vo, pp. 83. C. 34410

The Improved New-England Primer. *See* New England.

Improved Railway Connections in Philadelphia. *Philadelphia: James H. Bryson, Printer.* M.D.CCC.LX.III. 8vo, pp. 15. H.

Impugnacion á la iniciativa del H. Congreso de Zacatecas, de 9 de junio de 1834, sobre reformas eclesiasticas. *Mexico.* 1834. 4to, pp. 39. 34412

Impugnacion á los Observaciones relativas á la Pacificacion de Yucatan. *Mejico.* 1831. 4to. 34413

Impugnacion al impreso que se publicó en S. Salvador con este titulo: "El Monstruo de dos Cabezas." *Guatemala: Imprenta Nueva.* [1831.] 4to, pp. 73. 34414

IMRAY *and* SON (James). Nautical Description of the Gulf of Mexico and Bay of Honduras, &c. From the Surveys made by order of the British, United States and Spanish Governments. Seventh Edition. *London.* 1856. 8vo. C. 34415

In Chancery. Breviate. John Penn, Thomas Penn, and Richard Penn, Esqrs; Plaintiffs. Charles Calvert Esq; Lord Baltimore in the Kingdom of Ireland, Defendant. For the Plaintiffs. Upon a Bill to compell a Specifick Execution of Articles of Agreement entred into between the Partys for setling the Boundarys of the Province of Pensilvania, the Three Lower Countys, and the Province of Maryland, and for perpetuating Testimony, &c. Mr. Attorney General Sir Dudley Ryder. Mr. Solicitor General Murray. Mr. King's Council Noell. Paris and Weston, Solicitors. [n. p. 1740?] Folio, 2 l., pp. 116; Plaintiff's Case, 13 l., printed on one side only, and Articles of Agreement, 7 l. 2 Maps. H. 34416

Rich conjectures the date to be 1742, and adds "This work being printed on large paper with a small type, each page contains as much matter as twelve common octavo pages. It contains everything that could be collected from records and books relating to the history and establishment of the three lower counties on Delaware,' now the State of Delaware, and was probably printed only for the use of the parties immediately concerned, and not for sale."

In Congress, Thursday, September 22. 1774. ... *Printed by W. and T. Bradford.* 12mo, pp. 1. P. 34417

Resolution asking a suspension of importations of English goods.

In Hoc Volumine. *See* [Lilio (Z.)]

In Memoriam H. L. A[bbott] Ob. May VI., A.D. MDCCCLXIV. ... *Boston: Printed for Private Distribution.* 1864. 8vo, pp. 31.

In the Court of Exchequer ... . The Attorney General *v.* Sillem and Others, claiming the Vessel "Alexandria," seized under the Foreign Enlistment Act ... . Report of the Arguments on the Application of the Attorney-General for leave to move for a new trial ... resulting in a Rule nisi to show cause why a new trial should not be had. And the Arguments thereon; together with the Judgment of the Court; and also an Appendix ... *London: Printed by George E. Eyre and William Spottiswoode* ... 1864. Rl. 8vo, pp. 571, xxvii. 34419

In the Tropics. By a Settler in Santo Domingo. With an Introductory Notice by Richard B. Kimball. *New York: Carleton.* 1863. 12mo, pp. 306. 34420

In Vinculis or the Prisoner of War. Being the Experience of a Rebel in Two Federal Pens, interspersed with Reminiscences of the late War; Anecdotes of Southern Generals, etc. By a Virginian Confederate. *Richmond, V.: Daily Index Office.* 1866. 12mo, pp. 216. 34421

INA, *pseudon.* Paragraphs on the subject of Judicial Reform in Maryland, showing the Evils of the present System, and Pointing out the only Remedy ... . By Ina. *Baltimore.* 1846. 8vo. BM. 34422

[INANA Y TORRE (José Isidro).] Carta de un Americano a un Diputado de las Cortes Extraordinarias de España. 1821. *Londres: Imprenta de Nichols.* [n. d.] 8vo, pp. 50. H. 34423

Signed "José Isidro Inana y Torre," and addressed to Don A. P. y M.

Inauguracion de la estatua del Libertador Simon Bolivar en la capital del Estado soberano de Guayana. *Ciudad Bolivar.* 1869. 8vo, pp. 88. 34424

Inauguration. *See* Perry, Warren, Webster, &c.

Inc'Wadi | Yokuqala Ka-Yowannes | Intloko Yokuqala | [Colophon:] *Ibishicilelwe* | *E-Chumie* | *Emaxoseni,* | 1832. | 8vo, pp. 16.

"Presumed to be in the Mohawk Indian language."—STEVENS.

Inchiquin's Letters. *See* [Ingersoll (C. J.)]

Incidents and Sketches connected with the Early History of and Settlement of the West. With numerous Illustrations. *Cincinnati: J. A. & U. P. James.* [1847.] 8vo, pp. 72. 9 Plates and Frontispiece. + [*Ibid.* 1853.] C. 34426

A collection from newspapers, and other equally authentic sources, of fragments of narratives of border life and Indian warfare. Worthless for historical purposes.

Incidents in Dixie: being Ten Months in the Military Prisons of Richmond, New Orleans and Salisbury. ... Published for the benefit of Maryland State Fair, for the Christian and Sanitary Commissions. *Baltimore: Printed by James Young.* 1864. 16mo, pp. 89. 34427

Incidents in the Life of a Slave Girl. *See* [Jacobs (Harriet)].

Incidents of a Trip, 1867. *See* [Seymour (Silas)].

Incidents of American Camp Life, being events which have actually taken place during the present Rebellion. *T. R. Dawley, New York.* 1862. 12mo, pp. 72. + Second Edition, Revised and Enlarged. [*Ibid.*] pp. 104. 34428

Incidents of Border Life. Comprising Narratives of Strange and Thrilling Adventure, Accounts of Battles, Skirmishes and Personal Encounters with the Indians, Descriptions of their Manners, Customs, Modes of Warfare, Treatment of Prisoners, &c., &c. Also the History of several Remarkable Captivities and Escapes, to which are added, Brief Historical Sketches of the War in the North-West, embracing the Expeditions under Gens. Harmer, St. Clair and Wayne. *Chambersburgh, Pa.* 1839. 12mo. 34429

Incidents of the Civil War in America. *New York: Frank Leslie.* 1862. 8vo, pp. 100. B. 34430

Incitativa de un español americano á todos los españoles ultramarinos residentes en la Península. *Imprenta Liberal.* 1820. 4to.

INCKEL (——). Mislukte reis naar Noord-Amerika. *Kampen: K. van Hulst.* 1849. 8vo. 34432

INCLÁN (L. G.) Recuerdos del Chamberin, o breve relacion de los hechos mas publicas y memorables de este noble caballo. *Mexico.* 1860. 8vo, pp. 63. 34433

The Income Record. *See* New York.

Increase of Piety, or the Revival of Religion in the United States of America; containing several interesting Letters not before published, together with three Remarkable Dreams, in succession, as related by a Female in the Northern Liberties of Philadelphia, to several Christian Friends, and handed to the Press by a respectable Minister of the Gospel. *Philadelphia.* 1802. 12mo. 34434

INDARTE (J. R.) Efemerides de los Deguellos. Asesinatos y Matanzas del Degollador Juan Manuel Rosas. Por Jose Rivera Indarte. *Montevideo: Imprenta del Nacional.* [1829.] 8vo, pp. 32. 34435

INDARTE. Poesias de Jose Rivera Indarte, con una biografia del autor, escrita por el coronel de artilleria D. Bartolome Mitre. *Buenos Aires.* 1853. 8vo, pp. lxxxviii, 406, (6). Portrait.

INDARTE. Rosas y Sus Opositores; por Jose Rivera Indarte, Editor del "Nacional" de Montevideo. [*Montevideo:*] *Imprenta del Nacional.* ... 1843. 8vo, pp. (4), 363, lxxii, 4. H. 34437

Should be followed by an "Appendice al Num. 26, del Archivo Americano. Contiene la Correspondencia entre el Exmo. Senor General D. Juan Manuel de Rosas, Gefe

supremo de la Confederacion Argentina, encargado de sus relaciones exteriores, General en gefe de sus ejercitos y el Exmo. Senor Ministro Plenipotenciario de su Majestad Britanica honorable caballero D. Henrique Southern, con motivo de las inauditas agresiones del Gobierno Brasilero." *Buenos Aires.* 1867. 8vo, pp. 130. Contains documentary materials of the greatest importance. Very rare. Also: La Battalia de Caa-Guazu Poema. *Montevideo.* 1834. 4to.

Indemnity for Expenses of War in Florida. [*Washington.* 1836.] 8vo, pp. 84. 34438

Indenture of Agreement 4th July, 1760, between Lord Baltimore and Thomas and Richard Penn, Esquires, Settling the Limits and Boundaries of Maryland, Pennsylvania, and the Three Lower Counties of Newcastle, Kent and Sussex, on Delaware. *Philadelphia: Printed by Kite and Walton.* 1851. Folio, pp. (2), 31. B. 34439

Seventy-eight copies privately printed, on writing paper, for E. D. Ingraham, of Philadelphia. *See also* our No. 34416.

This Indenture Witnesseth ... *Philadelphia: Printed and sold by Cornelia Bradford, at the Sign of the Bible in Front-Street;* ... Folio, 1 l. P. 34440

A redemptioner's indenture; printed about 1751. A rare imprint.

L'Indépendance absolue des Américains des Etats-Unis, prouvée par l'état actuel de leur Commerce avec les Nations Européennes. ... *Paris: Laran.* 1798. 8vo, pp. (2), 149, (1).

"Written by an American merchant" in answer to Fauchet (*see our* Vol. VI., No. 23919), who said that, "judging by the actual state of the commerce between the United States and Great Britain, one would think that the former were still a colony of the latter, or fear they might become so."—RICH, I. 412.

Independence Day; or, two modes of spending it. *Philadelphia.* 1852. 16mo. BM. 34442

... The Independence Guide. A Complete Guide for the Day. For Citizens and Strangers. ... *Boston: W. M. L. Kent & Co.* 1858. Sm. 16mo, pp. 16. H. 34443

Independence Hall. *See* Philadelphia.

Independence Programme for July 4, 1865. ... [n. p. 1865.] 12mo, pp. 12. H. 34444

Independencia de Mexico. Aniversario del primer Grito de independencia celebrado en la capital del Estado libre de Zacatecas el 16 de Setiembre de 1826. *Zacatecas.* 1826. 8vo, pp. 19.

La Independencia mexicana. Diario político, literario y comercial. *San Luis Potosi.* 1863. Folio. 34446

"Le tout publié de ce journal intéressant, No. 1–190."—ANDRADE.

Independency the Object of the Congress in America. Or, an Appeal to Facts. *London: John, Francis, and Charles Rivington.* MDCCLXXVI. 8vo, pp. (2), 70. BA., H. 34447

"We have seldom seen a performance which exhibits more equivocal marks of passion, prejudice, and antipathy, than the present."—*Monthly Review*, LV. 64. Samuel Adams is called "the would-be Cromwell of America"—"and as to his colleague John Hancock, that gentleman is, in the language of Hudibras,

'A very good and useful tool,
Which knaves do work with, called a Fool.'"

The Independent Citizen; or, The Majesty of the People asserted against the Usurpations of the Legislature of North Carolina, in several Acts of Assembly, passed in the years 1783, '85, '86 and '87. [n. p. n. d.] 4to, pp. 21. N. 34448

Independent Company of Cadets. The Constitution and By-Laws ... with Extracts from the Laws of the U. States, and the Militia Laws of Massachusetts. ... *Boston: Dickinson & Co., Printers.* 1845. 16mo, pp. 47. Continued. H. 34449

Independent Ledger, and Lyceum Weekly Journal. Vol. I. *Berwick, Columbia Co. (Penn.)* 1839. 4to. 34450

Independent Mechanic. *New York.* 1811–12. Folio. 34451

The Independent Reflector; or, Weekly Essays on Sundry Important Subjects; more particularly adapted to the Province of New York. [Colophon:] *New York: Printed by James Parker* ... . 1752–53. Folio, pp. 212, 16. N., S. 34452

See Sedgwick's "Life of W. Livingston," Chap. III. Fifty-two numbers form a set. It relates to Kings now Columbia College, Freedom of Government in New York, etc.

The Independent Whig. [Colophon:] *Printed and sold by Samuel Keimer, in Philadelphia.* [1720.] 4to, pp. (16), 227.

"The Independent Whig" consists of an Introduction of 16 pages and 53 numbers, generally of four pages each, reprinted from the London edition. "Written by Gordon and Trenchard, in order to oppose the High Church party."—LOWNDES, p. 1931. *See* Walpole's "Letters to Mann," Aug. 2, 1717.

The Index. A Weekly Journal ... devoted to the Exposition of the Mutual Interests, political and commercial, of Great Britain and the Confederate States of America. May 1, 1862, to May 1, 1864. *London.* 1862–64. 4 vols., folio. C. 34454

Index to the Documents of the House of Representatives, 18th–21st Congress. *Washington.* 1832. 8vo. B. 34455

Index to Executive Communications and Documents. *See* Vol. IV., Nos. 15539–40.

INDEX, *pseudon.* Queries about the "Sanitary Commission" by "Index." And the Reply of the New York Evening Post, March 30, 1864. [n. p. n. d.] 8vo, 1 l. H. 34456

The Indian Advocate. Vol. I., No. 3. *Louisville, Ky.: American Indian Mission Association.* 1846. 8vo. S. 34457

Indian Atrocities! Affecting and Thrilling Anecdotes respecting the Hardships and Sufferings of our Brave and Venerable Forefathers, in their Bloody and Heart-rending Skirmishes and Contests with the Ferocious Savages: containing numerous Engravings, illustrating the most General Traits of Indian Character, their Customs and Deeds of Cruelty, with Interesting Accounts of the Captivity, Sufferings and Heroic Conduct of many who have fallen into their hands. *Boston: A. J. Wright's Steam Press.* [1846.] 8vo, pp. 32. Frontispiece. H. 34458

Indian Back-Pay and Bounty Frauds! Indian Pensioners to the Front!! The Names of 480 Indians placed upon the Pension Rolls in a Lump, by Order of Secretary Harlan! White Widows and Orphans compelled to wait! ... [n. p. n. d.] 8vo, pp. 15. H. 34459

Indian Battles, Captivities, and Adventures. Illustrated. *New York: J. C. Derby.* 1855. 12mo, pp. 408. 34460

Indian Battles, Murders, Sieges, and Forays in the South-West. Narratives of Gen. Hall [and others]. *Nashville, Tenn.* [1853.] 8vo. + [*Ibid.*] 1853. 8vo, pp. 100. C., N. 34461

The Indian Converts, Tschoop and Shabasch. A Narrative of Facts. *Dublin.* 1830. 12mo, pp. 47. 34462

The Indian Council. *See* [Kip (L.)]

INDIAN CREEK. Prospectus of the Indian Creek and Jack's Knob Coal, Salt, Lead, Lumber, Oil and Manufacturing Company, with a Geological Report ... by Dr. J. S. Newberry ... . *Cincinnati: Wrightson & Co., Printers.* 1866. 8vo, pp. 20. H.

Indian Department (Canada) Return. [*London.* 1856.] Folio, pp. 42. Continued. 34464

The Indian Fairy Book. *See* [Mathews (Cornelius)].

The Indian Girl. Written for the Massachusetts Sabbath School Society. ... *Boston: Massachusetts Sabbath School Society.* [n. d.] 24mo, pp. 54. Frontispiece. 34465

Indian Massacre in Minnesota. *See* [Burleigh (W. A.)]

INDIAN MISSION ASSOCIATION. Proceedings of the First Annual Meeting, held at Louisville, Ky., October, 1843. *Louisville.* 1843. 8vo. 34466

INDIAN MISSIONS. The American Board and the American Missionary Association. (From the American Missionary.) [n. p. n. d.] 8vo, pp. 16. H. 34467

This tract contains a curious narration of the adoption of the slave code by the Cherokee Indians, themselves fugitives from the slave owners of Georgia.

The Indian Missions in the United States of America, under the care of the Missouri Province of the Society of Jesus. *Philadelphia: King and Baird, Printers.* 1841. 12mo, pp. 34.

Indian Narratives. Containing A Correct and Interesting History of The Indian Wars, from The Landing of our Pilgrim Fathers, 1620, to Gen. Wayne's Victory, 1794. To which is added A correct Account of the Capture and Sufferings of Mrs. Johnson, Zadock Steele, and others; and also a Thrilling Account of the Burning of Royalton. *Claremont, N. H.: Tracey and Brothers.* 1854. 12mo, pp. 276. 34469

Indian of New England. *See* [Tenesles (Nicola)].

Indian Portraits. Catalogue of One Hundred and Seventeen Indian Portraits, representing Eighteen Different Tribes, accompanied by a Few Brief Remarks on the Character, &c., of most of them. [n. p. n. d.] 8vo, pp. 24. H. 34470

Indian Primer; or, the First Book. By which Children may know truely how to read the Indian Language. And, Milk for Babes. In Massachusetts Indian and English. *Boston.* 1720. BM. + [*Ibid.*] 1722. 12mo, pp. 84, (165). + [*Ibid.*] 1747. 32mo.

The Indian Question. *Albany Argus Extra, Friday, June* 19, 1830. 8vo, pp. 7. 34472

Indian Reservation Sulphur Springs, near Buffalo, N. Y. With an account of its analysis. *Buffalo.* 1848. 18mo, pp. 30. + [*Ibid.*] 1859. 8vo, pp. 19. S. 34473

Indian Rights and our Duties. *Amherst.* 1830. 8vo. 34474

The Indian Scalp, or Canadian Tale; A Poem. *London: Folingsby.* 1778. 4to. 34475

Indian Songs of Peace, with a Proposal for erecting Indian Schools, and a Postscript introducing Yariza, an Indian Maid's Letter. *New York: J. Parker & W. Wayman.* 1752. 12mo, pp. 27. C. 34476

Indian Stories; containing among others an authentic Narrative of the Captivity of John Stover, among the Miami Indians. *New York, reprinted.* 1836. 8vo. 34477

The Indian Tale interpreted and told in English verse. *Printed by Benjamin Franklin.* 1734. 34478

Title from the "Historical Magazine," IV. 75.

Indian Trade. From the Detroit Gazette, 15 December, 1820. [n. p. n. d.] 8vo, pp. 13. + 22 December, 1820. 8vo, pp. 10. 34479

An Indian Tradition. No Fiction. The Tracditionary History of a Narrow and Providential Escape of some White Men from being Tomahawked, Scalped, and Robbed by a Party of Taro-way Indians. [n. p. n. d.] 8vo, pp. 4. 34480

Indian Treaties, and Laws and Regulations relating to Indian Affairs: to which is added an Appendix, Containing the Proceedings of the Old Congress, and Other Important State Papers in relation to Indian Affairs. Compiled and published under orders of the Department of War. ... *Washington City: Way & Gideon, Printers.* 1826. 8vo, pp. xix, (1), 529. H. 34481

Contains an abstract of almost all the treaty stipulations of the government with the Indians. Besides the more legal statement of the obligations, by which the savage tribes and the United States authorities mutually bound themselves, there is a vast mass of historical data, the names and numbers of the tribes, the names of the chiefs and their significations, and on page 485 is George Guess' (Sequoiyah's) alphabet of syllables of the Cherokee language. "A valuable compilation, judiciously executed, containing many important documents. This work serves as the text to a very interesting and well written article in the 'North American Review,' XXIV. 345, on the conduct of the Government of the United States towards the Indians within and bordering on their territories, compared with that of the English Government, in answer to an article in the 'London Quarterly Review,' No. 61. The writer (supposed to be Gov. Cass), says, 'We look with deep sympathy on the condition of this feeble remnant, who, like the autumnal foliage of their own forests, are scattered at every blast, but to whom no spring will bring renovation; and we regard with deep solicitude every effort for their preservation and melioration.' These sentiments do honor to the person who wrote them, and should be deeply impressed in the mind of every American. Our country, he should remember, was once theirs, and as we have risen up to greatness, their tribes have dwindled away and disappeared from off the face of the earth. He should recollect that but for us, they might now have been great and flourishing nations, happy in their native forests and hunting the deer, upon the very sites of our greatest cities. With a nature entirely different from that of Europeans, they have never been able to reconcile themselves to their customs and habits: what we call civilization has

been death to them. The experience of several generations having shewn that the character of the North American Indian can never assimilate with that of his white brethren, let us leave the small remnant of them unmolested in their wilderness. We, who boast of our Independence, should not surely interfere with theirs."—*North American Review*, XXIV. 346.

Indian Treaties to 1837. *See* Treaties.

Indian Tribes—Northwestern Frontier. Letter from the Secretary of War, transmitting the Information required by a Resolution of the House of Representatives, of the 12th inst. in relation to the hostile disposition of the Indian Tribes of the Northwestern Frontier, May 21st, 1828. ... *Washington: Printed by Gales and Seaton.* 1828. 8vo, pp. 19. 34482

INDIANA. Address to the Democracy of Indiana. [n. p. 1863.] 8vo, pp. 8. H. 34483

Appeal to the Democracy of Indiana, together with the Resolutions of the 66th, 93d and 34th Indiana Regiments, and a Speech of Alexander H. Stevens ... . *Indianapolis.* 1863. 8vo, pp. 8. H. 34484

By Alvin P. Hovey, and others.

An Appeal for the Rights of Conscience. ... *Richmond, Ind.* 1863. 12mo, pp. 12. H. 34485

Agriculture. Circular from the Indiana State Board of Agriculture. ... *Indianapolis: J. P. Chapman, State Printer.* 1851. 8vo, pp. 10. H. 34486

First Annual Report of the State Board of Agriculture ... 1852. *Indianapolis: J. P. Chapman, State Printer.* 1852. 8vo, pp. 322. Continued. H. 34487

Eleventh Annual Report of the Indiana State Board of Agriculture, and the Report of Prof. E. T. Cox, State Geologist. *Indianapolis: Alexander H. Conner, Printer.* 1869. 8vo, pp. iii, xlii, (3), 504. + Geological Survey. pp. 239, (2). H. 34488

Transactions of the State Board of Agriculture, 1851. *Indianapolis.* 1852. 8vo. 34489

Banks. Report of the State Bank, December, 1842. [*Indianapolis.* 1842.] 8vo, pp. 12. Table. H. 34490

Report of Mr. [N. B.] Palmer, Agent of the State ... to examine the ... Condition of the State Bank and Branches. *Indianapolis.* 1842. 8vo. 34491

Biographical Sketches of the Members of the Forty-First General Assembly of Indiana. *Indianapolis.* 1861. 8vo.

Brevier Legislative Reports: embracing Short-Hand Sketches of the Journals and Debates of the General Assembly. By Ariel and W. H. Drapier, Reporters. *South Bend.* 1863–71. 12 vols., 8vo. 34493

Canals. ... Report of the Indiana Canal Company, on the Improvement of the Falls of the Ohio. *Cincinnati: T. Wrightson & Co., Printers.* 1856. 8vo, pp. 23. H. 34494

Catalogue of the Indiana State Library for the year 1859. Compiled and arranged by J. R. Bryant, State Librarian. *Indianapolis: J. C. Walker.* 1859. 8vo, pp. 96. C. + Catalogue and Rules and Regulations of the Indiana State Library, arranged by M. G. McLain, State Librarian. *Indianapolis: Alexander H. Conner.* 1869. 8vo, pp. 91. B. 34495

Churches. General Association of Baptists in Indiana. Proceedings of the Seventh Anniversary, Delphi, October, 1849. *Indianapolis.* 1849. 8vo, pp. 20. Continued. 34496

The Discipline of the Society of Friends, of Indiana Yearly Meeting, reviewed ... 1854. *Cincinnati: A. Pugh, Printer.* 1854. 8vo, pp. 136. 34497

Extracts from the Minutes of Indiana Yearly Meeting, held at White-Water, ... 1826. *Richmond, I. A.: Printed by Buxton and Walling.* 1826. 8vo, pp. 12. Continued yearly. 34498

Also: Review of a Pamphlet, called "A Testimony, and Epistle of Advice," lately issued by ... "Indiana Yearly Meeting." *Philadelphia: Printed by Joseph Parker.* 1828. 8vo, pp. 16. B.—A Testimony and Epistle of Advice issued by Indiana Yearly Meeting. *Cincinnati: Morgan, Fisher, and L'Hommedieu.* 1827. 8vo, pp. 12.

Journal of the Proceedings of the Annual Convention of the Protestant Episcopal Church of ... Indiana. 1840. 8vo. Continued. 34499

Secession of a Large Body of Friends from the Yearly Meeting of Indiana, in Consequence of Antislavery Action. *Dublin, reprinted.* 1843. 12mo, pp. 28. 34500

Colonization. Report of the Secretary of the State Board of Colonization of ... Indiana, to the Governor. For ... 1853. *Indianapolis: Austin H. Brown.* 1853. 8vo, pp. 23. H. 34501

Also Annual Reports for 1834.—Report of the Agent of the Colonization Society, of the State of Indiana, in Reply to a Resolution of the Senate. ... *Indianapolis: Austin H. Brown, State Printer.* 1855. 8vo, pp. 15, (1). H.

Constitution of the State of Indiana, and the Address of the Constitutional Convention. *New Albany, Ia.: Kent & Norman, Printers.* 1851. 8vo, pp. 32. B., H. 34502

Documents of the Senate of Indiana. Twenty-fourth Session. *Indianapolis.* 1840. 8vo. 34503

Documents of the General Assembly of Indiana at the Thirty-third Session ... . *Indianapolis: John D. Defrees, State Printer.* 1850. Part I. 8vo, pp. 167. Tables. Part II. pp. 321. Table. Continued. H. 34504

Documents respecting the Claim of the Persons Therein Mentioned to a certain Tract of Land called Indiana. *Philadelphia.* Folio. P. 34505

Education. An Act to provide for a general System of Common Schools. *Indianapolis.* 1852. 8vo. + Approved March 6, 1865. *Indianapolis.* 1865. 8vo. S. 34506

Also: An Address to the Legislature of Indiana, December 6th, 1847. Upon Popular Education. By One of the People. *Indianapolis: Printed by John D. Defrees.* 1848. 12mo, pp. 45, (1). + [*Ibid.*] 1848.—Address to the Legislature of Indiana on Education. *Terre Haute.* 1849. 8vo. + *Indianapolis.* 1852. 8vo.—First Annual Meeting of the Association for the Improvement of Common Schools in Indiana. Read September 3, 1833. *Madison, Ia.: Printed by J. Lodge & E. Patrick.* 1833. 8vo, pp. 16. BA.

Report of the Superintendent of Common Schools ... of Indiana. *Indianapolis: J. P. Chapman, State Printer.* 1851. 8vo, pp. 30. BA. 34507

First Annual Report of the Superintendent of Public Instruction of Indiana ... . *Indianapolis: J. P. Chapman, State Printer.* 1852. 8vo, pp. 75. Continued. BA. 34508

Also: ... Annual Report of the Superintendent of Public Instruction ... January 19, 1855. *Indianapolis: Austin H. Brown, State Printer.* 1855. 8vo, pp. 87. Continued. H.— ... Annual Report of the Board of Education of Indiana. *Fort Wayne.* 1863. 8vo.

Documents and Annual Reports of the Officers of Public Institutions for 1864. *Indianapolis: J. J. Bingham.* 1865. 8vo, pp. 858. C. 34509

Indiana Institute for the Education of the Blind. First Annual Report of the Trustees ... . *Indianapolis.* 1847. 8vo. + Third Annual Report ... . *Indianapolis: John D. Defrees, State Printer.* 1849. 8vo, pp. 31. Continued. C., H. 34510

First Annual Report of the Trustees of the Indiana Asylum for the Education of the Deaf and Dumb ... . For the year 1844. *Indianapolis.* 1855 [*sic*]. 8vo, pp. 7. B., C. 34511

Also: Annual Report of the Indiana Institution for Deaf and Dumb, for 1853. *Indianapolis.* 1853. 8vo, pp. 54. Continued.

Third Annual Report of the Directors of the Indiana Branch of the Presbyterian Education Society, ... October 9, 1833. *Madison, Indiana: Printed by J. Lodge and E. Patrick.* 1833. 8vo, pp. 16. H. 34512

Indiana State Teachers' Association. Minutes of the First Annual Session. Indianapolis, Dec. 25, 1854. [*Indianapolis.*] 1855. 8vo. S. 34513

The Indiana School Journal, published on the 15th of each Month by the Indiana State Teachers' Association. ... Vol. I. ... *Indianapolis: Cameron & M'Neely, Book and Job Printers.* 1856. 8vo. Continued. H. 34514

Catalogue of the Officers and Students of the Indiana Asbury University ... 1852–3. *Indianapolis: Indiana State Journal Steam Press.* 1853. 8vo, pp. 28. Continued. H. 34515

INDIANA COLLEGE. Laws and Resolutions ... from 1827 to 1861. *Indianapolis: W. S. Cameron ... Printer.* 1862. 8vo, pp. 64. B. 34516

INDIANA UNIVERSITY. Address by a Committee of the Trustees to the People of Indiana. *Indianapolis.* 1840. 8vo, pp. 15. 34517

Also: Annual Report ... Including the Catalogue for the Academic Year MDCCCLVII–VIII. Bloomington. *Indianapolis: Joseph J. Bingham, State Printer.* 1858. 8vo, pp. 42, (1). Frontispiece. Continued. H.

Catalogue of the Trustees, Officers, and Students of Indiana University, 1842–3. *Bloomington: M. L. Deal, Pr.* 1843. 8vo, pp. 18. Continued. H. 34518

Also: Catalogue of the Officers and Students of Indiana University, 1840–41. *Indianapolis.* [1840.] 8vo, pp. 18.—Inauguration of the Fourth President of Indiana University. Address of Investiture by ... Ashbel P. Willard. Inaugural Address by President John H. Lathrop ... . *Indianapolis: Bingham, Doughty & Co., ... Printers.* 1861. 8vo, pp. 50. H.

School Laws of the State of Indiana, with Forms. 1844. 8vo, pp. 105. + School Law of ... Indiana, ... *Indianapolis: J. P. Chapman, State Printer.* 1853. 8vo, pp. 64. BA. 34519

The Revised School Law of the State of Indiana; approved March 5, 1855. ... *Indianapolis: Austin H. Brown, State Printer.* 1855. 8vo, pp. 52. H. 34520

School Laws of Indiana, as Amended in 1865 and 1867; with Opinions, Instructions, and Judicial Decisions relating to Common Schools, and to the Officers thereof. ... *Indianapolis: Alexander H. Conner.* 1867. 8vo, pp. 72. H. + As Amended in 1865, 1867, and 1869. [*Ibid.*] 1869. 8vo, pp. 96. B. 34521

Also: Suggestions on the Revision of the School Law. *Indianapolis.* 1859. 8vo.

Catalogue of the University of Notre Dame, Indiana. 1855–1857. 8vo. S. 34522

Facts for the People. The Address adopted by the Democratic State Convention, ... Indianapolis, March 15, 1866. 8vo.

Finance. Report of Fund Commissioner [N. Noble], to his Excellency, Samuel Bigger. [n. p. 1841.] 8vo, pp. 52. BA.

Report of Milton Stapp, Esq., late Fund Commissioner of Indiana, to the General Assembly, December, 1841. *Indianapolis.* 1841. 8vo, pp. 55. 34525

Report of W. H. H. Terrell, Financial Secretary, to the Governor, May, 1864. *Indianapolis: Joseph J. Bingham.* 1864. 8vo, pp. 25. 34526

Also: ... An Act to provide for the Funded Debt of ... Indiana, and for the Completion of the Wabash and Erie Canal to Evansville, passed 19th January, 1846, and an Act supplementary thereto, passed 27th January, 1847. *New-York: Van Norden & Amerman, Printers.* 1847. 8vo, pp. (2), 54. — ... Communication of the Agent of the Foreign Holders of Indiana State Bonds, to ... James Whitcomb, Governor of Indiana, December, 1845. *Indianapolis: J. P. Chapman, State Printer.* 1845. 8vo, pp. 22. — ... Annual Report of the Auditor of State of Indiana, for the Fiscal Year ending October 31, 1845. *Indianapolis: J. P. Chapman, State Printer.* 1845. 8vo, pp. 64, 5. Tables. Continued. — Memorial of Bondholders of the Indiana State Bank for 1844–1845. 8vo. — Report of Minority Committee on the sale of State Bonds. 1865. 8vo. — Report of the Treasurer of State, December, 1841. 8vo, pp. 15. Continued.

Geology. First Annual Report of the Geological Survey of Indiana, made during the Year 1869. By E. T. Cox, State Geologist, assisted by Prof. Frank H. Bradley, Dr. Rufus Haymond, and Dr. G. M. Levette. *Indianapolis: Alexander H. Conner, State Printer.* 1869. 8vo, pp. 239, (2). 3 Maps, 1 colored Section. BA. + pp. 239, (2). Frontispiece and Diagrams. + Second Report. *Indianapolis: R. J. Bright.* 1871. 8vo, pp. 304. 8 Plates, 3 Map. Continued. C. 34527

A Third and Fourth Report was published in 1872, with a volume of maps.

Report of a Geological Reconnoissance of ... Indiana; made in ... 1837 ... By David Dale Owen ... *Indianapolis.* 1838. 8vo, pp. 34. + [*Ibid.*] 1853. 8vo, pp. 33. + Second Report ... 1838 ... [*Ibid.*] 1839. 8vo, pp. 54. S. + *Indianapolis: John C. Walker.* 1859. Part First. 8vo, pp. 63. Part Second. pp. 69, (1). 34528

Report of a Geological Reconnoissance of Indiana made during the Years 1859 and 1860, under the Direction of the late David Dale Owen, M.D., State Geologist, by Richard Owen, M.D., Principal Assistant, now State Geologist. Also, Reports on the Analysis of the Soils, by R. Peter, M.D., Chemist; Survey of the Coal Fields, by Leo Lesquereux, Fossil Botanist; and Topographical Work, by Joseph Lesley, Topographical Geologist. Published by Authority of the Indiana Legislature. *H. B. Dodd & Co., Indianapolis.* 1863. 8vo, pp. xvi, 368. 34529

Governor's Message, delivered to both Houses of the General Assembly of the State of Indiana, ... 1837. *Indianapolis: Printed by Douglass and Noel.* 1837. 8vo. Continued. 34530

The Indiana Annual Register, and Pocket Manual, revised and corrected for the year 1845. ... By C. W. Cady. ... *Indianapolis: Printed by E. Chamberlain.* MDCCCXLIV. 16mo, pp. 208. + For 1846. *Indianapolis: Samuel Turner.* MDCCCXLVI. 16mo, pp. 261. C., H. 34531

Indiana Gazetteer, or Topographical Dictionary; containing a Description of the several Counties, Towns, Villages, Settlements, Roads, Lakes, Rivers, Creeks, and Springs, in the State of Indiana. *Indianapolis.* 1833. 12mo. 34532

The Indiana Gazetteer, or Topographical Dictionary of the State of Indiana. Third Edition ... *Indianapolis: E. Chamberlain.* 1849. 12mo, pp. 440. BA. 34533

Some copies are dated 1850.

Indiana Railway Gazetteer, Travellers' Guide, and Express and Shippers' Directory. By D. A. Redfield. *Indianapolis (Ind.)* 1865. 8vo. 34534

Second Edition of George W. Hawes' Indiana State Gazetteer and Business Directory, for 1860 and 1861. Number Two. ... Published Biennially. *George W. Hawes, Publisher and Compiler,* ... *Indianapolis, Ind.* [n. d.] 8vo, pp. xxxvi, 778. + For 1864 and 1865. [*Ibid.*] 1864. 8vo, pp. xxvi, 535. 34535

Hospitals. First Annual Report of the ... Hospital for the Insane, ... *Indianapolis: John D. Defrees, State Printer.* 1849. 8vo, pp. 85–130. + *Indianapolis: J. P. Chapman, State Printer.* 1851. 8vo, pp. 39. Continued. H. 34536

Indiana State Horticultural Society. First Annual Report ... *Indianapolis.* 1861. 8vo. Continued. 34537

Journal of the House of Representatives of the State of Indiana, during the First Session of the General Assembly ... Nov. 1816. *Corydon.* 1817. 8vo. Continued. W. 34538

Journal of the Senate of the State of Indiana, for the First Session of the Legislature ... Nov. 1816. *Corydon.* 1817. 8vo. Continued. W. 34539

Laws. Laws of Indiana Territory, comprising the Acts formerly in force and as revised by John Rice Jones and John Johnson ... Also the Original Acts passed at First Session of Second General Assembly. *Vincennes.* 1807. 8vo, pp. 540, Index, 28.

Laws passed at the First Session of the General Assembly. 1817. *Corydon.* 1818. 8vo. Continued. C. 34541

Laws of Indiana from Nov. 1816 to Jan. 22, 1820, with the Constitution of the State. *Corydon and Jeffersonville.* 1817–20. 8vo. 34542

Laws of a Local Nature passed at the Nineteenth and Twentieth Sessions of the General Assembly. *Indianapolis.* 1835. 8vo. Continued. 34543

Message from the President ... transmitting the Laws of the Indiana Territory ... from January, 1801, to February, 1802. [n. p. n. d.] 8vo, pp. 32. B. 34544

The Revised Laws of Indiana, adopted ... by the General Assembly at their Eighth Session. To which are prefixed ... sundry other Documents, connected with the Political History of the Territory and State of Indiana. *Corydon.* 1824. 8vo. 34545

The Revised Laws of Indiana, ... adopted and enacted by the General Assembly at their Fifteenth Session. To which are prefixed ... sundry ... Documents connected with the Political History of ... Indiana. *Indianapolis: Printed by Douglass and Maguire.* 1831. 8vo, pp. 596. B., C., S. 34546

The Revised Statutes of ... Indiana, adopted and enacted by the General Assembly at their Twenty-Second Session. ... *Indi-*

anapolis: Douglass & Noel, Printers. 1838. 8vo, pp. 667. C., S. + [*Ibid.*] 1843. 8vo. C. 34547

The Revised Statutes of ... Indiana, passed at the Twenty-seventh Session of the General Assembly. To which are prefixed the Constitutions of ... Indiana. [By Samuel Bigger and George H. Dunn.] *Indianapolis.* 1843. 8vo, pp. 1114. C., S.

The Revised Statutes of the State of Indiana, passed at the Thirty-sixth Session of the General Assembly; also, sundry Acts, Ordinances, and Public Documents directed to be printed along with the said Statutes: to which are prefixed the Constitution of the United States and of the State of Indiana. *Indianapolis.* 1852. 2 vols., 8vo, pp. 592; xv, 646. B. 34549

The Same, in the German language. *Indianapolis.* 1853. 2 vols., 8vo, pp. 650; 830. C.

Masonry. Constitution and By-Laws of the M. W. Grand Lodge of the State of Indiana, with Rules for the Government of Lodges under her Jurisdiction. *Indianapolis.* 1866. 8vo, pp. 318. 34550

Indiana Masonic State Directory and Masonic Advertiser. *Indianapolis.* 1866. 16mo. 34551

Proceedings of the Grand Council of Royal and Select Masters, of the State of Indiana, held at Richmond, May, 1859. ... *Indianapolis: Elder & Harkness.* 1858. 8vo, pp. 36. H. 34552

Proceedings of the Grand Lodge of the State of Indiana from 1817 to 1845 inclusive. *Shelbyville, Ind.* 1861. 8vo. 34553

Catalogue of the Trustees, Officers, and Students of the Indiana Medical College, Laporte, Ind., 1847–48. *La Porte.* 1848. 8vo, pp. 16. 34554

Memorial of the Citizens ... of the Indiana Territory, praying for the Interposition of Congress, to relieve them from certain Oppressions and Embarrassments. *Washington.* 1844. 8vo. BM.

Governor's Message delivered to the General Assembly of the State of Indiana. January 4, 1855. *Indianapolis: Austin H. Brown, State Printer.* 1855. 8vo, pp. 47. Continued. H.

Also: Message of the Governor of Indiana, to the General Assembly. January 9th, 1863. *Indianapolis: Berry R. Sulgrove, State Printer.* 1863. 8vo, pp. 32. + Message ... Jan. 6, 1865. [n. p. n. d.] 8vo, pp. 33. + Message ... Delivered January 11, 1867. [*Indianapolis.* 1867.] 8vo, pp. 31. + Message of ... Governor ... Special Session, ... Nov. 14, 1865. [n. p. n. d.] 8vo, pp. 26. H.

Military. Communication from W. H. H. Terrell, Adjutant General, to the General Assembly ... November, 1865. ... *Indianapolis: W. R. Holloway, State Printer.* 1865. 8vo, pp. 18. H.

Operations of the Indiana Legion and Minute Men, 1863–4. Documents presented to the General Assembly, Jan. 6, 1865. *Indianapolis.* 1865. 8vo. 34558

Proceedings and Resolutions of the Indiana Soldiers, in the "Department of the Cumberland." ... *Indianapolis: Indianapolis Journal Company, Printers.* 1863. 8vo, pp. 8. H. 34559

Proceedings of the Indiana Sanitary Convention, held in Indianapolis, Indiana, March 2, 1864. *Indianapolis: Indianapolis Journal Company, Printers.* 1864. 8vo, pp. 76. H. 34560

Prospectus of the Proposed Loan of the State of Indiana, for War Purposes. *New York.* 1861. 8vo, pp. 10. C. 34561

Report of the Adjutant General of Indiana, 1861–62. *Indianapolis: J. J. Bingham.* 1863. 8vo, pp. 339. + [*Ibid.*] 1863. 8vo, pp. 342, (1). B., BA. 34562

Also: Report of Laz. Noble, Adjutant General, from Jan. 1, 1863, to Nov. 12, 1864. 8vo, pp. 33.

Report of the Adjutant General [W. H. H. Terrell]. Containing Indiana in the War of the Rebellion, and Statistics and Documents. *Indianapolis.* 1865–9. 8 vols., 8vo. B. 34563

Report of the Allotment Commissioners on Transmission of Money for Soldiers of Indiana for 1865. [n. p. n. d.] 8vo, pp. 23. 34564

Also: Report of Pay Agents, December 31, 1862. [n. p. n. d.] 8vo, pp. 4. — Report of Special Agents, Pay Agents, et al., Visiting Troops, etc. *Indianapolis: Joseph J. Bingham.* 1863. 8vo, pp. 220. — Report of the State Paymaster of the Indiana Volunteer Militia, December 31, 1862. [n. p. n. d.] 8vo, pp. 7. — Report of Indiana Military Agencies, to the Governor. *Indianapolis: W. R. Holloway.* 1865. 8vo, pp. 76. — Report of J. P. Liddell, Draft Commissioner. [n. p. n. d.] 8vo, pp. 39.

Report of the Quartermaster General, May 1, 1862. *Indianapolis: Joseph J. Bingham.* 1863. 8vo, pp. 27. 34565

Also: Report of John C. New, Quartermaster General, Nov., 1862. *Indianapolis: J. J. Bingham.* 1863. 8vo, pp. 14. — Agent to purchase Arms for the State of Indiana. Report of Robert Dale Owen, September 4, 1865. *Indianapolis: Joseph J. Bingham.* 1863. 8vo, pp. 21. — Report of Ashel Stone, Quartermaster General, Jan. 1, 1865. *Indianapolis: W. R. Holloway.* 1865. 8vo, pp. 86.

Report of the Indiana Sanitary Commission, Jan. 2, 1865. *Indianapolis: W. R. Holloway.* 1865. 8vo, pp. 132. 34566

Rules and Regulations for the Government of the Militia of the State of Indiana. *Indianapolis.* 1853. 8vo. 34567

The Soldier of Indiana in the War. *See* [Merrill (Catherine)].

Prisons. Indiana State Prison. First Annual Report ... for ... 1845. ... *Indianapolis.* 1845. 8vo. Continued. 34568

Proceedings of the Grand Division of the Sons of Temperance of ... Indiana, ... April 17th, A.D. 1849. First Semi-Annual Session. *Indianapolis: Printed by John D. Defrees.* 1849. 8vo, pp. 44. H. 34569

Proceedings of the Indiana Convention to organize a State Anti-Slavery Society, at Milton, September 12, 1838. *Cincinnati: S. A. Alley.* 1838. 8vo, pp. 28. 34570

Railroads. Northern Indiana Railroad Company. Circular Statement, Sept. 1851. *New-York.* 1851. 8vo. + Opinion of Judge Bronson. *New-York.* 1851. 8vo. 34571

Registry Law, and an Act regulating general Elections, and prescribing the duties of Officers in relation thereto. *Indianapolis: A. H. Conner.* 1867. 8vo, pp. 20. C. 34572

Reports made to the House of Representatives, of the Legislature of Indiana. 24th Session, 1839. 8vo. Continued.

... Resolution of the General Assembly of Indiana, in favor of the Encouragement of Domestic Manufactures and Internal Improvements. ... *Washington: Printed by Duff Green.* 1828. 8vo, pp. 3. H. 34574

... Resolution of the General Assembly of the State of Indiana, in reference to Major General Lafayette.—February 15, 1825. ... *Washington: Printed by Gales & Seaton.* 1825. 8vo, pp. 5. H. 34575

Sheppard's Indiana State Gazetteer and Shipper's Guide, for 1866–7. *Cincinnati.* 1866. 8vo, pp. xv, 588. 34576

The State of Indiana Delineated: Geographical, Historical, Statistical, & Commercial, and a Brief View of the Internal Improvements, Geology, Education, Travelling Routes, &c., Prepared to accompany Colton's Map. *New York: J. H. Colton.* 1838. 18mo, pp. 92. Map. H. 34577

To the Democratic and Conservative Voters of the State of Indiana. [n. p. n. d.] 8vo, pp. 4. 34578

View of the Title to Indiana, a Tract of Country on the Ohio. [n. p. 1775.] 8vo, pp. 24. 34579

View of the Title to Indiana, a Tract of Country on the River Ohio. Containing Indian Conferences at Johnson-Hall, in May, 1765 --- the Deed of the Six Nations to the Proprietors of Indiana --- the Minutes of the Congress at Fort Stanwix, in October and November, 1768 --- the Deed of the Indians, settling the Boundary Line between the English and Indians Lands --- and the Opinion of Counsel on the Title of the Proprietors of Indiana. *Philadelphia: Printed by Styner and Cist* ... MDCCLXXVI. 8vo, pp. 46. BA., W. 34580

Very rare; perhaps by Samuel Wharton. *See* Sparks' "Franklin," IX. 78.

Indianapolis Directory, City Guide and Business Mirror; or, Indianapolis as it is in 1855. First Issue. *Indianapolis: Grooms & Smith.* 1855. 8vo, pp. 264. Map and Plates. 34581

Indianapolis City Directory for 1865. *Indianapolis: Hawes & Co.* [n. d.] 8vo, pp. 208, 75. + Edwards's Annual Director to the City of Indianapolis for 1865–6. *Indianapolis, Ind.* 1866. 8vo, pp. 73–436. + Edwards's Annual Directory ... for 1867. *Indianapolis: Edwards & Boyd.* 1867. 8vo, pp. 412, cxv. C. + Logans' Directory for 1867[–68. *Indianapolis:*] *Logan & Co.* 1867. 8vo, pp. xxiv, 357. + Logan's Indianapolis Directory for 1868. *Indianapolis: Logan & Co.* 1868. 8vo, pp. xiv, 280. + Logan's Indianapolis Directory for ... July 1, 1868. With a History of Indianapolis. By Ignatius Brown. *Indianapolis.* 1869. 8vo, pp. xiv, 250, 26, 100. + Edwards's Annual Director to Indianapolis, for 1869. *Indianapolis: Charless Publishing Company.* [n. d.] 8vo, pp. 415. 34582

A Memorial of the Board of Trade and Common Council of the City of Indianapolis, to Congress, in regard to the location of a Western National Armory. [n. p. n. d.] 8vo, pp. 4.

Proceedings of the Indianapolis Bar on the Death of Hon. Oliver H. Smith, March, 1859. ... *Indianapolis.* 1859. 8vo, pp. 21. BA. 34584

Proceedings of the Christian Convention, held at Indianapolis, ... November, 1859, with an Address, ... by Elder Jonas Hartzell ... Also the Constitution of the Christian Missionary Society. *Cincinnati.* 1859. 8vo, pp. 81. H. 34585

Report to the Board of Trade on the Manufacturing Advantages, Prospects, etc., of the City. *Indianapolis.* 1857. 8vo.

Indiane Primer. *See* Eliot (J.), Vol. VI., No. 22161.

INDIANIAN, *pseudon.* Is Slavery as it exists in the Southern States, Morally Wrong? *Brownstown, Ind.* 1865. 34587

Indianischer Religionstandt. *See* Friccius (V.), Vol. VII.

INDIANS.

In addition to the following list of *anonymous* books, relative to the Indians in general, the reader is referred to Conferences, Minutes, Treaties, the various names of the Indian Tribes, names of States, and other headings, which will be grouped in the Index to this Dictionary. For a list of the numerous United States documents, relating to the Indians, *see* the Catalogue of the Upper Hall of the Boston Public Library, p. 826, and Supplement, p. 650.

Additional Inquiries respecting the Indian Languages. [n. p. n. d.] 12mo, pp. 32. BA. 34588

Address from the Trustees and Treasurer of the Friendly Association for Preserving Peace with the Indians to William Denny, Esq., Governor of Pennsylvania. *Philadelphia.* 1757. 8vo. 34589

Address to the Ministers of England and Wales, on Propagation of the Gospel among the Indians, &c., in New England. 1649. Folio, 1 l. M. 34590

Address to the People of the United States, and to the Members of Congress in particular. On the Civilization and Christian Instruction of the Aborigines of our Country. By Indiana Yearly Meeting of Friends, ... 1838. *Cincinnati: A. Pugh, Printer.* 1838. 12mo, pp. 16. H. 34591

Adventures on the Prairie and Life among the Indians. *Glasgow.* [n. d.] 8vo. 34592

Aiamie Tipadjimo8in Masinaigan ka ojitogobanen kaiat ka niina8isi mekate8ikonaie8igobanen kanactageng 8ak8i ena8indibanen. *Moniang: John Lovell.* 1859. 12mo, pp. (2), 338.

Extracts from the Bible in the Algonquin language, usually followed by—"Ka tite tebeniminang Jezos, ondaje aking. ..." *Moniang: John Lovell.* 1861. pp. 396—the Life of Christ.

Alabama, or Here we Rest. An Indian Legend of Olden Times. *Cleveland, O.* 1863. 8vo. 34594

American Society for promoting the Civilization and General Improvement of the Indian Tribes within the United States. Constitution, List of Officers, &c *Washington.* 1822. 8vo, pp. 15. 34595

Abstracts from Reports and Epistles from America on Indian Civilization. 1823. 8vo. + *London: Printed by William Phillips.* 1824. 8vo, pp. 8. 34596

Account of a New Society for the Benefit of the Indians, organized at the City of Washington. 1822. 8vo. 34597

Account of a Plan. *See* C[rowley] (T[homas]), Vol. v.

Account of Conferences. *See* Conferences *and* Johnson (W.)

An Account of some late Attempts by the Correspondents of the Society for propagating Christian Knowledge, To Christianize the North American Indians. *Edinburgh.* M,DCC,LXIII. 8vo, pp. 12. H. 34598

Includes Letters from Mather, Chauncey, Bostwick, also Accounts of the Mohawks and Oneida Indians.

Account of the Behaviour and Sentiments of some well disposed Indians, mostly of the Minissing Tribe. *New York.* 1803. 12mo. 34599

An Account of the North American Indians, written for Maun-Gwu-Daus, a Chief of the Ojibway Indians, who has been travelling in England, France, Belgium, Ireland, and Scotland. ... *Leicester: Printed by T. Cook.* 1848. 8vo, pp. 24. H.

An Account of the Treaty Held at the City of Albany, in the Province of New-York, by His Excellency the Governor of that Province, and the Honourable the Commissioners for the Provinces of Massachusetts, Connecticut and Pennsylvania, with the Indians of the Six Nations, in October, 1745. *Philadelphia: Printed by B. Franklin, at the New-Printing-Office, near the Market.* M,DCC,XLVI. Folio, pp. 20. P. 34601

Accounts of some Proceedings of Committees of the Yearly Meetings of Friends of Philadelphia, New York, Baltimore and Ohio. For the Welfare and Civilization of the Indians of North America. *Dublin: Printed by Graisberry and Campbell.* 1817. 12mo, pp. 16. 34602

Accounts of Two Attempts towards the Civilization of some Indian Natives. *London: Phillips and Fardon, Printers* ... [1806.] 8vo, pp. (2), 48, 47. H. 34603

This is a reprint of the "Brief Account," No. 34617, *infra*, with a general title to the two.

Anecdotes of the American Indians, Illustrating their Eccentricities of Character. By the Author of "Evenings in Boston," ... [J. L. Blake.] *New York: A. V. Blake.* 1844. 16mo, pp. 252. C. + *Hartford: C. M. Welles.* 1850. + [*Ibid.*] 1852.

This is a correct title of our No. 5779.

Anichinabek Amisinahikaniwa, The Indian Book. *Detroit: Printed by Geo. L. Whitney.* 1830. 18mo, pp. 106. 34605

Annual Register. *See* McCoy (I.)

The First Annual Report of the American Society for promoting the Civilization and General Improvement of the Indian Tribes in the United States. ... *New Haven: Printed ... by S. Converse.* 1824. 8vo, pp. 74. B., BA., S. 34606

Annual Report of the Commissioner of Indian Affairs, transmitted with the Message of the President at the Opening of the 2d Session of the 24th Congress. *Washington.* 1836. 8vo, pp. 47. Continued. 34607

A complete series of these reports is very rarely found. They are of the highest value for the historical student.

First Annual Report of the Associated Executive Committee of Friends on Indian Affairs. Adopted at their Meeting Held at Mt. Pleasant, Ohio, Eighth Mo. ... 1870. *Philadelphia: Sherman & Co., Printers.* 1870. 8vo, pp. 12. 34608

Annual Report of the Board of Indian Commissioners to the President of the United States. 1868. *Washington.* 1868. 8vo.

Annual Report of the Select Committee of the Society for Propagating the Gospel among the Indians and others in North America. ... *Boston: Samuel N. Dickinson, Printer.* 1843. 8vo, pp. 20. Continued. H. 34610

After 1854 called "Reports," &c. *See also* our Vol. III., No. 10466.

Second Annual Report of the Joint Delegation appointed by the Committee on the Indian Concern of the Yearly Meetings of Ohio and Genesee ... . *Rochester, N. Y.* 1870. 12mo, pp. 48.

Second Annual Report of the Aborigines Protection Society ... *London: Printed for the Society, by P. White & Son.* 1839. 8vo; pp. 32. Continued. H. 34612

Answer to a Letter to the Freemen, etc. of the City of New York; wherein is fully shewn the True Causes of the Defection of the Six Nations, etc. *New York.* 1752. 8vo, pp. 18. N.

Apocalypse de Chiokvyhikoy. *See* Vol. IV., No. 12816.

Articles of Peace Between ... Charles II. ... And several Indian Kings and Queens, &c. Concluded the 25th day of May, 1677 ... *London: Printed by John Bill* ... 1677. 4to, pp. 18.

The Bible Boy taken Captive by the Indians. Written for the American Sunday-School Union, and revised by the Committee of Publication. *Philadelphia.* [n. d.] 18mo, pp. 35. H.

The Book of American Indians, containing Comprehensive Details of Indian Battles, Massacres, Border Warfare, Biographical Sketches of Distinguished Indians, etc. New Edition. *Dayton, Ohio: B. F. Ellis.* 1854. 12mo, pp. 384. 34616

Consists of Hunter's narrative of his captivity, and anecdotes of Indians, being reprints of two common books.

A Brief Account of the Proceedings of the Committee, appointed in the Year 1795, by the Yearly Meeting of Friends of Pennsylvania, New-Jersey, &c. for promoting the Improvement and Gradual Civilization of the Indian Natives. *Philadelphia: Printed ... by Kimber, Conrad & Co.* 1805. 8vo, pp. 45. + *London: Reprinted by Phillips and Fardon.* 1806. 8vo, pp. (2), 48.

A brief Account of the present State of the Society for propagating the Gospel among the Indians and others in North-America,—with a Sketch of the Manner in which they mean to pursue the Objects of their Institution. [n. p. 1790.] Folio, pp. 4. H. 34618

A brief Account of the present State, Income, Expenditures, &c. of the Society for propagating the Gospel among the Indians, and others in North-America. [*Boston.* 1795.] 4to, pp. 3. H.

Brief Account of the Society for propagating the Gospel among the Indians and others in North-America. [*Boston.* 1798.] 4to, pp. 7. H., M. 34620

Brief and True Account of the Persecution of the Church; The Beginning and Progress of the War with the Indians, etc. *London.* 1690. 4to. 34621

Title from an auctioneer's catalogue.

A Brief Sketch of the Efforts of Philadelphia Yearly Meeting of the Religious Society of Friends, to promote the Civilization and Improvement of the Indians; also, of the Present Condition of the Tribes in the State of New York. ... *Philadelphia.* 1866. 8vo, pp. 56. H. 34622

British Trade with North American Indians. [n. p. n. d.] 8vo. 34623

The Captive Children. ... *New York ... Church Book Society.* [n. d.] 16mo, pp. 35. 34624

Narrates the conduct of some captives among the Indians.

Catechism in the Indian Language. Translated by Rev. John Eliot. Printed at the Expense of the Corporation in England for propagating the Gospel amongst the Indians of New England. *Cambridge: Printed by S. Green.* 1653–4. 34625

No known perfect copy extant. Supposed to be the first book printed in New England in the Indian language. *See* "Proceedings of American Antiquarian Society, No. 61, p. 45. Report of J. Hammond Trumbull.

Catechisme Algonquin avec syllabaire et cantiques. Niina aiamie kak8edjindi8inimasinaigan ate gaie kekinoamagemagak masinaigan gaie aiamie nikamonan.—Kanactagerg. *Moniang: Tak8abikickote endate John Lovell.* 1865. 16mo, pp. 52. H.

Charlestown, May 27, 1789. To the Members of the Society for propagating the Gospel among the Indians, and others, in North-America [respecting John Alford's Legacies]. Incorporated by an Act of this Commonwealth. 4to, pp. 8, (1). H.

Signed "Richard Cary," and addressed to Oliver Wendell and members of the society.

Cherokee Indians. Letter from the Secretary of War. [*Washington.* 1840.] 8vo, pp. 64. 34628

The Cherokee Question. Report of the Commissioner of Indian Affairs to the President ... June 15, 1866 ... . *Washington.* 1866. 8vo, pp. 58. H. 34629

Chronicles of the North American Savages. [n. p.] 1835. 8vo, pp. 80. 34630

A periodical devoted to the history, traditions, language, etc. of the Indians—stopped at the fifth number. *See our* Vol. IV., No. 12966.

A Collection of Indian Anecdotes. *Concord, N. H.* 1837. 64mo, pp. 190. 34631

Comments on the Objections of Certain Cherokee Delegates to the Proposition of the Government to separate the Hostile Parties of the Cherokee Nation. *Washington.* 1866. 8vo, pp. 16.

Signed by "John R. Ridge" and four others.

Condition of the Indian Tribes. *See* [Doolittle (J. R.)]

The Conference with the Eastern Indians. *See our* Vol. IV., No. 15441, and *add* pp. 20, in No. 15442 strike out "or 31;" *see also* No. 15429, *and* Vol. II., No. 4391.

Considerations on the Present State of the Indians, and their Removal to the West of the Mississippi. From the North American Review, No. LXVI., for January, 1830. *Boston.* 1829. 8vo, pp. 61. 34633

By Gen. Lewis Cass.

Conversations. *See our* Vol. IV., No. 16205, *also* [Sanders (D. C.), *and* [Tuttle (S.)]

Conversion and Instruction of the Free Indians and Negroe Slaves in the Colonies. [*London.* n. d.] 34634

Copy of a Letter addressed to ... Daniel Webster, on the Colonization of the Indians. *New-York: Piercy & Reed, Printers.* 1838. 16mo, pp. 8. H. 34635

Correspondence, Addresses, &c., connected with the Subscriptions of various Indian Tribes in Upper Canada, in aid of the Funds for the Re-construction of Brock's Monument, on Queenstown Heights. *Toronto: Printed by Robert Stanton.* 1841. 8vo, pp. 32. 34636

During a short civil war in Canada the monument erected to Gen. Brock had been destroyed by one of the marauding parties. To exhibit their loyalty, various Indian tribes of Canada, to the number of fifteen, sent addresses and contributions. This book contains the speeches and letters of their chiefs.

Correspondence on the Subject of the Emigration of Indians, between The 30th November, 1831, and 27th December, 1833, with Abstracts of Expenditures by disbursing Agents in the removal and Subsistence of Indians, etc., etc. *Washington: Printed by Duff Green.* 1835. 8vo, pp. (2), 771. 34637

23d Cong., 1st Sess., Sen. Doc. 512.

Correspondence on the Subject of the Removal of Indians, between The 30th November, 1831, and 27th December, 1833, with Abstracts of Expenditures by disbursing Agents, in the Removal and Subsisting of Indians, etc. etc. Furnished in answer to a Resolution of the Senate of 27th December, 1833, by the Commissary General of Subsistence. *Washington: Printed by Duff Green.* 1834. Vol. I. 8vo, pp. 1179. Vol. II. pp. (2), 972.

Correspondence, etc., relating to Expeditions against the Indians. *Salem, Oregon.* 1855. 8vo. 34639

A Council held at Philadelphia, August, 1744, with the Deputies of the Delaware Indians. *Philadelphia.* Folio. P. 34640

Creek Indians. Message ... upon the ... claims of ... Georgia and the claim of the Creek Indians. *Washington.* 1829. 8vo, pp. 9. 34641

Disbursements to Indians. Letter from the Second Auditor of the Treasury, transmitting Accounts of Disbursement of Moneys, Goods, or Effects, for the benefit of Indians, from 1st October, 1837, to 30th September, 1838, &c. [*Washington.*] 1839. 8vo, pp. 118. 34642

Disbursements to the Indians. Letter from the Second Auditor of the Treasury, transmitting Copies of the Accounts of Persons charged with the Disbursement of Money, Goods, or Effects for the Indians, &c. [*Washington.*] 1847. 8vo, pp. 171.

Documents in relation to Difficulties existing in the Cherokee nation of Indians. *Washington.* 1846. 8vo, pp. 9. 34644

Documents relative to the Indian Trade. *Washington.* 1822. 8vo. 34645

Emigrating Indians. *See our* Vol. V., No. 17459, *add* pp. 11, and strike out the note.

Essay towards propagating the Gospel among the neighboring Nations of Indians. *New London.* 1750. 12mo, pp. 18. 34646

Essays on the ... Indians. *See* [Evarts (J.)], Vol. VI.

Estimates of Appropriations Necessary to comply, in Part, with the Treaty Stipulations made with certain Indian Tribes. *Richmond: Tyler, Wise, Allegre and Smith, Printers.* 1862. 8vo, pp. 15.

A Confederate publication—very rare.

Extract from the Annual Report of the Commissioner of Indian Affairs for the Year 1868. The Question of the Transfer of the Indian Bureau to the War Department. *Washington.* 1869. 8vo, pp. 21. H. 34648

Extracts from the Papers and Proceedings of the Aborigines Protection Society. Nos. I. and II. May and June, 1839. *London: William Ball, Arnold and Co.* 1839. 8vo, pp. 64. Continued. C., H. 34649

Extracts from Reports of Missions to the Cherokees, Creeks, etc., 1835. 8vo. 34650

The Four Indian Kings Speech. *See* Vol. VI., No. 25283.

Further Information respecting the Aborigines, Containing Extracts from the Proceedings of the Meeting for Sufferings in London, and of the Committee on Indian Affairs, of the yearly meetings of Philadelphia and Baltimore; together with some particulars relative to the Seminole War. Printed in pursuance of the direction of the yearly meeting. *London: Harvey and Darton.* 1839. 8vo, pp. 34. + Second Edition. *London: Edward Marsh.* 1843. 8vo, pp. (2), 34. 34651

Tracts relative to the Aborigines, No. 3.

Further Information respecting The Aborigines; Containing Reports of the Committee on Indian Affairs at Philadelphia, Extracts from the Proceedings of the yearly meeting of Philadelphia, New York, New England, Maryland Virginia, and Ohio. Together with some particulars relative to the Natives of New Zealand, New Holland, and Van Dieman's Land. Published by direction of the Aborigines Committee of the Meeting for Sufferings. *London: Edward Marsh.* 1842. 8vo, pp. 40. 34652

Tracts relative to the Aborigines, No. 8.

The General; or, Twelve Nights in the Hunters' Camp. A Narrative of Real Life. ... [By William Barrows.] *Boston: Lee and Shepard.* 1869. 16mo, pp. iv, 268. Frontispiece. 34653

George Town On Arrowsick Island Aug. 9th, 1717. Annoque Regni Regis Georgii Magnæ Brittaniæ, &c. Quarto. A Conference of His Excellency the Governour [Samuel Shute], with the Sachems and Chief Men of the Eastern Indians. *Boston: Printed by B. Green.* 1717. 4to, pp. 13. H., W. 34654

A very rare tract. This is a corrected title of our No. 15437, Vol. IV.

Georgia Lands occupied by the Cherokee Indians. Report of a Committee, and Resolutions of the Legislature of the State of Georgia, in Relation to Certain Lands occupied by the Cherokee Indians, belonging to the said State. January 28, 1828 ... *Washington: Printed by Gales and Seaton.* 1828. 8vo, pp. 13. 34655

The Good Indian Missionary. *See* Vol. VII., No. 27830.

Graphic Sketches. *See* [Wyth (John)].

The History, Manners and Customs. *See* Vol. VIII.

A History of the Indian Wars. *See* Vol. VIII., No. 32174.

History of the Indians. *See* [Goodrich (S. G.)], Vol. VII.

History of the Massacre. *See* Vol. VIII., No. 32184.

The Indians, 1790. *See* [Richardson (W.)]

Indians—Cherokees—May 26, 1840. [*Washington.* 1840.] 8vo, pp. 23. 34656

Petition of a delegation.

Indians—Cherokee Nation, West. Memorial ... April 1, 1840. [*Washington.* 1840.] 8vo, pp. 15. 34657

Indians—Choctaw Citizens of Mississippi. Memorial of the Choctaw Citizens of the State of Mississippi, To the Congress of the United States. December 15, 1841. ... *Washington.* 1841. 8vo, pp. 5. 34658

The Indians. Or Narratives of Massacres and Depredations on the frontiers in Wawasink and its Vicinity during The American Revolution By a descendant of the Huguenots. *Rondout, N. Y.* ... 1846. 8vo, pp. 79. 34659

Indians removed to West of the Mississippi from 1789. *Washington.* 1839. 8vo, pp. 10. 34660

Inquiries, respecting the History, Present Condition and Future Prospects of the Indian Tribes of the United States. [*Washington.* 1847.] 4to, pp. (2), 55, Circular, (1). BA., H. 34661

Journal of the General Council of the Indian Territory ... assembled in Council at Okmulgee, in the Indian Territory ... . *Laurence.* 1871. 8vo, pp. 64. Continued. H. 34662

Removal of Indians. ... Mr. Bell ... made the following Report: [*Washington.* 1830.] 8vo, pp. 32. B. 34663

Report, No. 227, 21st Cong., 1st Sess.

Report from the Secretary of War, ... relative to Indian Affairs, &c. &c. February 10, 1829. ... [*Washington.* n. d.] 8vo, pp. 118. 34664

Report from the Secretary of War, exhibiting ... the difficulties ... between the Government and the Cherokee people. [*Washington.* 1840.] 8vo, pp. 62. 34665

Report from the Secretary of War, showing ... Massacres ... by the hostile Indians in Florida. [*Washington.* 1840.] 8vo, pp. 3.

The Report of the Aborigines Committee of the Meeting for Sufferings, read at the yearly meeting, 1840, ... and some particulars calculated to give information and promote interest respecting the present state of Aboriginal Tribes. ... *London: Harvey & Darton.* 1840. 8vo, pp. 27. 34667

Tracts relative to the Aborigines, No. 5.

Report of the Commissioner of Indian Affairs. *Washington.* 1835. 8vo. Continued. 34668

"The reports of the Indian bureau, and of the Commissioner for Indian affairs, form a body of material relating to the Indians, almost unrivaled for its minuteness in any department of history. The names, numbers, and condition of the Indian tribes, are given with all the attention to details and correctness, which a multitude of agents more or less efficient, and sometimes conscientious, could be induced by interest and discipline to collect. To no other source can we look for the progressive steps, by which the savage tribes retreated before the overwhelming charge of the army of civilization. The reports cover the whole history of the dealings of the government with its Indian wards. A complete set is very rarely to be found."—Field.

Report of the Committee for the Gradual Civilization of the Indian Natives; made to Yearly Meeting of the Religious Society of Friends, held in Philadelphia, in the fourth Month 1838. *Philadelphia: Joseph and William Kite.* 1838. 8vo, pp. 26.

Report of the Committee on Indian Affairs relative to Excitements, on the part of British Subjects, of the Indians, to Commit Hostility against the United States, etc., June 13, 1812. *Washington.* 1812. 8vo. 34670

Report of Committee on Indian Affairs, May 20, 1834, in relation to the Western Territory, &c. [*Washington.* 1834.] 8vo, pp. 131. Map. BA. 34671

Report, No. 474, 23d Cong., 1st Sess.

Report of the Committee on Indian Concerns to the Yearly Meeting held at Baltimore, 9th mo. 8th, 1819. [n. p.] 1819. Folio, 1 l. + [The Same.] 1819. 8vo, 1 l. 34672

Report of the Committee on the Subject of Appropriations for the Indian Department. *Philadelphia.* 1800. 34673

The Report of the Meeting for Sufferings respecting the Aborigines, presented to the yearly meeting, 1841. *London.* 1841. 8vo, pp. 12. Continued. 34674

Tracts relative to the Aborigines, No. 7.

Report of the Parliamentary Select Committee on Aboriginal Tribes, (British Settlements.) Reprinted, with Comments, by the "Aborigines Protection Society." *London: William Ball.* 1837. 8vo, pp. xi, (1), 140. C., H. 34675

Report of the Proceedings of an Indian Council, at Cattaraugus, in the State of New-York; held 6th month, 1843. *Baltimore: Printed by William Wooddy.* 1843. 8vo, pp. 34. 34676

By a General Committee representing the Yearly Meetings of Genesee, New York, Philadelphia, and Baltimore.

... Report on the Management of the Indians in British North America, by the British Government. 1870. [By F. N. Blake. *Washington.* 1870.] 8vo, pp. 38. H. 34677

41st Cong., 2d Sess., Miss. Doc., No. 35.

Report on the Passage of a General Law concerning Indians. 1865. 34678

Reports to the yearly Meeting of Friends held in Philadelphia, from its Committee for Promoting the Improvement, and gradual Civilization of the Indian Natives, in 1818 and 1819. *London: Printed by William Phillips.* 1819. 8vo, pp. 15. 34679

U. S. Department of the Interior. Report of the Board of Indian Commissioners ... for 1809 ... . *Washington.* 1810. 8vo, pp. 166. Continued. BA. 34680

For other anonymous works, relative to the Indians, *see* under the first word in the title-page, articles omit, and read the note on page 86.

Indicacion de Algunos de los principales objetos di historia natural, es decir; Minerales, Vejetales, y Animales, que deberian solicitarse para la exhibicion industrial Venezolana que tendra lugar el 10 de Diciembre, de 1864, en Carácas. *Carácas.* 1864. 8vo, pp. 22. 34681

This exhibition never took place.

Indicaciones al Congreso Demonstrando las causas Fundamentales que demandan Imperiosamente Providencias Necesarias a la felicidad de la Nacion. *Huancayo.* 1839. 4to, pp. 8. 34682

Indictment and Tryal of Sir Richard Rum. A Person of Noble Birth and Extraction, well known both to the Rich and Poor throughout all America, who was accused of several Misdemeanors against his Majesty's Liege People. Fourth Edition. *Boston.* 1750. 34683

Los Indios del Andaqui. Memorias de un viajero [Albis]. Publicados por José Maria Vergara y Vergara i Evarista Delgado. *Popayan: imprenta de la Matricaria.* 1855. 12mo, pp. 29.

Individual y Verdadera. *See* [Lozano (Pedro)].

Indulgencias perpetuas concedidas á los Congregantes de la Congregacion del Alumbrado y Vela continua al Sant. Sacramento, fundada en la Parroquia de San Sebastian de esta Corte. *Mexico.* 1793. 4to, pp. 20. 34685

The Industrial and Financial Resources of the United States of America, as developed by Official Federal and State Returns; accompanied by a new Statistical Map. With an Appendix. *New York: Samuel Hallett, Banker.* 1864. 8vo, pp. vi, 312.

Industry & Frugality Proposed As the Surest Means to make us A Rich and Flourishing People; and The Linen Manufacture Recommended As tending to promote These among us. With Reflexions on Charity. ... *Boston: Printed by Thomas Fleet.* 1753. 8vo, pp. 15. B., BA. 34687

A scarce piece, relating principally to Massachusetts.

Ines de la Cruz. *See* Cruz (I. de la), Vol. v., Nos. 17733-5.

Our No. 17735 is slightly incorrect. There is also an edition, *Madrid*, 1725, with additions; of Vol. II. there is one with the same imprint as 17734, pp. (6), 438, (6), of this 17734 there is another edition, *Madrid*, 1700; of Vol. III. there is also an edition, *Barcelona: Raf. Figuera*, 1701.

Inexorable Logic. Congressional Sovereignty *vs.* Democratic Faith. *St. Louis.* 1860. 8vo. 34688

Inez; A Tale of the Alamo. *New York.* 1855. 12mo. C.

An Infallible Cure for Political Blindness, if administered to Patients possessing Sound Minds, Honest Hearts, and Independent Circumstances. [*Printed July*, 1798.] 12mo, pp. 38.

Infamous Sentiments. Read for Yourselves. [1862.] BA.

A broadside, relating to the civil war.

The Infantry Exercise of the United States Army, abridged, for the use of the militia of the United States. Third Edition ... *Poughkeepsie.* 1819. 12mo, pp. 156. Plates. + Fourth Edition. [*Ibid.*] 1820. 12mo. S. 34692

Infernal Conference: or, Dialogues of Devils, By the Listener. *Printed at Worcester, Massachusetts, by Leonard Worcester, For Isaiah Thomas.* MDCCXCV. 8vo. + *Leominster, Mass.* 1808. 12mo.

The Infidel. *See* [Bird (R. M.)], Vol. II., No. 5553.

Influence de la Révolution de l'Amérique sur l'Europe. *Amsterdam.* M.D.C.C.LXXXVI. 8vo, pp. 48, (1). B. 34694

Influence du despotisme. *See* Beaumarchais (P. A. C. de), and *add* pp. 145.

Relates to the politics and prospects of Carthagena and Canada, during the war between England and France.

De l'influence française dans l'Amérique du Sud, Rio de la Plata. *Paris.* 1851. 34695

Influence of Catholic ... Doctrines. *See* [Fitton (J.)], Vol. VI.

Influence of the Railroads of the United States in the Creation of its Commerce and Wealth. *New York.* 1869. 8vo, pp. 42.

Influence of Slavery upon the White Population. *New York Anti-Slavery Society.* [n. d.] 12mo. 34697

Influences of Democracy. *See* [Ames (F.)], Vol. I., No. 1299.

Informacion para la Historia del Sacro monte Llamado de Valparaiso y Antiguamente Illipulitano junto a Granadu, Primera Parte. 4to. 34698

Title from an English catalogue.

Information and Direction. *See* [Penn (William)].

Information concernant ... Darien. *See* Vol. v., No. 18558.

Information concerning the Slave-Trade, printed by order of a Committee acting under the direction of the Yearly Meeting of the Religious Society of Friends, to aid in promoting the Total Abolition of that iniquitous Traffic, Yearly Meeting, 1821. *Printed by Harvey, Darton & Co., London.* 1821. 8vo, pp. 54.

Information for Army Meetings, June, 1864. *Philadelphia: J. B. Rogers.* 1864. 12mo. Continued monthy. 34700

Information for Emigrants. By an Englishman. *London.* 1848. 12mo. 34701

No. I. North America viewed as to its eligibility for British Emigration. pp. 48. No. III. The Cape and Canada. pp. 52.

Information for Europeans who are disposed to migrate to the United States. *Philadelphia.* [1790.] 12mo, pp. 16. 34702

Information for Immigrants. *See* Boston, Vol. II., No. 6729.

Information in relation to the Geology and Topography of California, with Report of the Secretary of War. [*Washington.*] 1850. 8vo. 34703

Information published by His Majesty's Commissioners for Emigration, respecting the British Colonies in North America. *London.* 1832. 8vo. + Second Edition. *London.* 1842. 8vo.

Information respecting the Aborigines in the British Colonies. Circulated by Direction of the Meeting for Sufferings. Being principally Extracts from the Report presented to the House of Commons, by the Select Committee appointed on that Subject. *London: Darton and Harvey.* 1833. 8vo, pp. xii, 60. 34705

Tracts relating to the Aborigines, No. 1. *See also* Indians.

Information respecting ... Canada. *See* Vol. III., No. 10465.

Information to Emigrants. An Account of the Island of Prince Edward, with Practical Advice to those Intending to Emigrate; and Some Observations on ... Canada, and the Red River. To which are added, Sailing Directions ... . By a late Resident of that Colony. *London: James Asperne.* [n. d.] 8vo, pp. 31. Map. 34706

Information to Persons. *See* [Ellsworth (H.)], Vol. VI.

Information upon the subject of Aves Island. *Washington.* 1861. 8vo. 34707

Informations concerning the Province of North Carolina, addressed to Emigrants from the Highlands and Western Isles of Scotland. By an Impartial Hand. *Glasgow: James Knox.* MDCCLXXIII. 8vo, pp. 32. 34708

Signed "Scotus Americanus." Title from Stevens' "Nuggets," No. 1498.

Informe á la Nacion sobre los principales acontecimientos de Mazatlan, desde el 7 de Noviembre al 1. de Diciembre de 1844, á consecuencia del movimiento de sa guarnicion, secundando el de Jalisco. *Mexico.* 1845. 4to, pp. 38. 34709

Informe de el Pleyto, que Siguela Señora Doña M. Maria de Sandoval, y Cavellero, contra el Capitano D. Jos. Fernandez de Lara, y Consortes, Dueño de Haziendas de labor de reigo en la Provincia de Guexotzingo, sobre el agua de Rio de Quesalâm, en virtud de la merced, que en él se refiere, y expresa. *Mexico.* 1713. Folio. 34710

Informe de la Comision del Camino de Nuevitas. *Puerto Principe.* 1836. 4to. 34711

Informe de la comision del M. I. Cabildo de Puerto-Príncipe, impugnando el oficio del 15 de Setiembre, dirigido por el Excmo.

Sr. Gefe superior político de acuerdo con la Diputacion provincial de la Habana, y acuerdo del Cabildo de 19 de Octubre de 1821. *Puerto-Principe: imprenta patriótica de José Minuese.* 1821.

Informe de la Junta directiva de la empresa de los Caminos de hierro de Cárdenas y Júcaro, leido en Junta general ordinaria celebrada el dia 25 de Agosto de 1865. *Habana.* 1865. 8vo, pp. 46. 34713

Informe de la suprema Corte de Justicia al Sr. Vice-Presidente, sobre la ilegalidad con que algunos Alcades del Escmo. Ayuntamiento han condenado á varios reos á la pena de obras publicas. *Mexico.* 1830. 4to, pp. 42. 34714

Informe de una comision del M. I. A. de la Habana, sobre poblacion blanca. *Nueva Orleans.* 1847. 12mo, pp. 19.

Informe del Commisionado de la Sociedad del rio Bermejo, a los señores accionistas. *Buenos-Aires.* 1831. 4to. 34716

Informe del Secretario. *See* Costa Rica, Vol. v., No. 17017.

Informe del Visitador General. *See* [Galvez (J. de)].

Informe dirigido por el presidente de la Republica de Guatemala. ... *Guatemala.* [1851.] Folio, pp. (9). 34717

See also Vol. VII., pp. 480-483.

Informe elevado al Sr. Vice-gobernador de Chiapas en ejercicio del supremo poder por el Sr. Gobernador Constitucional y General en Gefe de las tropas del mismo Estado sobre sus operaciones militares contra los facciosos. *Veracruz.* 1850. 4to, pp. 14.

Informe en Derecho, y Memorial del Pleyto sobre denunciacion de la Mina de Demasias de Gonzalo Franquez, que denunciò Damian de Villavicensio, Vezino, y Minero de las Minas de Guanaxuato, por el denunciador. [*Mexico.* n. d.] Folio.

Informe en Derecho del que assiste ad M. Perez de Barreda, en el Pleyto con Diferentes Acreedores; a D. Pedro Perez de Barreda su Padre, sobre el Vinculo de unas Casas. *Mexico.* 1714. Folio. 34720

Informe general, &c. *See* Habana, Mexico, &c.

Informe Presentado. *See* Vol. v., No. 17780, and for Agricula read Agricultura.

Informes en Derecho. Libelo de la Suplicacion hecha á la Real Audiencia de esta Corte por D. Maria P. de Câtbrana y Fundamentos de hecho, y derecho, con que la instruye. *Mexico.* 1714. 34721

Inga (A.) West-Indische | Spieghel, | Waer inne men sien kan, | alle de Eylanden, | Provintien, Lantschappen, het | Machtige Ryck van Mexico, en't Gout | en Silver-rycke Landt van Peru. | 'Tsampt | De Coursen, Havenen, Klippen, | Koopmanschappen, etc. soo wel inde Noort als in | de Zuyt-zee. Als mede hoe die vande | Spanjaerden eerst geinvadeert syn. | Door | Althanasium Inga, | Peruaen, van Cusco. | [*Amsterdam: Broer Iansz en Iacob Pietersz Wachter.* 1624.] 4to, Engraved and Printed Titles, pp. (4), 435, (8). Maps and Plates. 34722

This is a "West Indian Mirror, wherein are to be seen all the islands, provinces, countries, the mighty empire of Mexico, the gold and silver land of Peru, with the courses, harbors," etc. *See* Trömel's "Bibliothèque Américaine," No. 114.

Los Ingenios. *See* Cuba, Vol. v., No. 17782.

Ingeröe (Julie). Et aar i Utah; eller, Mormonismens hemmeligheder. *Chicago: "Skandinavens" Office.* 1867. 12mo, pp. 62. C. 34723

[Ingersoll (Charles).] A Brief View of Constitutional Powers, showing that the Union Consists of Independent States United. *Philadelphia.* 1864. 8vo, pp. 76. C. 34724

[Ingersoll.] The Diplomatic Year: being A Review of Mr. Seward's Foreign Correspondence of 1862. By A Northern Man. *Philadelphia.* 1863. 8vo, pp. 68. + Second Edition, with a Postscript. *Philadelphia: John Campbell.* 1863. 8vo, pp. 68, or more. 34725

[Ingersoll.] A Letter to A Friend in a Slave State. By A Citizen of Pennsylvania. *Philadelphia: John Campbell.* 1862. 8vo, pp. 60. B., BA., C. 34726

Forty-nine copies printed on large paper in 4to. For a reply, *see* Thayer (M. R.)

[Ingersoll.] An Undelivered Speech on Executive Arrests. *Philadelphia.* 1862. 8vo, pp. vi, 98. 34727

Against arrests under the suspension of the Habeas Corpus. The author was himself arrested for this publication. Also: An Address ... before the Law Academy of Philadelphia. ... *Philadelphia: Printed by Thomas Kite & Co.* 1833. 8vo, pp. 15. BA. —Speech in Case of Kneedler *vs.* Lane—Conscription Case. [n. p. n. d.] 8vo.

Ingersoll (C. J.) A Communication on the Improvement of Government: read before the American Philosophical Society,

at a Meeting attended by General La Fayette, October 1st, 1824. By Charles Jared Ingersoll ... . *Philadelphia: Printed by Abraham Small.* 1824. 8vo, pp. 24. B. 34728

Ingersoll. A Discourse ... before the Society for the Commemoration of the Landing of William Penn, on the 24th of October, 1825. By C. J. Ingersoll, Esq. ... *Philadelphia: R. H. Small.* 1825. 8vo, pp. 36. B., BA., P. 34729

Ingersoll. A Discourse concerning the Influence of America on the Mind; being the Annual Oration delivered before the American Philosophical Society, ... 18th October, 1823. ... By C. J. Ingersoll ... . *Philadelphia: Abraham Small.* 1823. 8vo, pp. 67. B., BA. + With an Account of the English Settlements in the Illinois. By R. Flower. *London.* 1824. 8vo. 34730

Ingersoll. Historical Sketch of the Second War between the United States of America, and Great Britain, declared by Act of Congress, the 18th of June, 1812, and concluded by Peace, the 15th of February, 1815. By Charles J. Ingersoll. [Vol. I.] Embracing the Events of 1812-13. [Vol. II.] Embracing the Events of 1814. *Philadelphia: Lea and Blanchard.* 1845-49. 8vo, pp. vi, 13-515; viii, 17-317, in double columns. [Second Series, Vols. I. and II.] Embracing the Events of 1814 and 1818. *Philadelphia: Lippincott, Grambo & Co.* 1852. 8vo, pp. vi, 9-422; iv, 7-374. B. + [*Ibid.*] 1853. BA., C., S.

Complete sets are scarce. *See* "Westminster Review," New Series, IV.

[Ingersoll.] Inchiquin, The Jesuit's Letters, during a late residence in the United States of America; being a fragment of a Private Correspondence, accidentally discovered in Europe; Containing a favourable View of the manners, literature and state of society, of the United States, and a refutation of many of the aspersions cast upon this country, by former residents and tourists. By some Unknown Foreigner. ... *New York: I. Riley.* 1810. 8vo, pp. v, 165. B., BA. 34732

Contains notices of the then prominent authors, Marshall, Barlow, &c. *See* "Quart. Rev.," 1814, No. 21, Vol. x., p. 516, for a criticism on this work, which is the text for a violent diatribe against the United States. *See* Rich II. for an extended notice. For replies to the review, *see* [Dwight (T.)], No. 21555, *and* [Paulding (J. K.)]

[Ingersoll.] Julian: A Tragedy. *Philadelphia.* 1831. 8vo, pp. 87. 34733

[Ingersoll.] Sketch of James Madison. [n. p. n. d.] 8vo, pp. 12. B. 34734

INGERSOLL. A View of the Rights and Wrongs, Power and Policy, of the United States of America. ... By Charles Jared Ingersoll ... . *Philadelphia: C. & A. Conrad & Co.* 1808. 8vo, pp. 157. B., BA., C., P., W. 34735

In defense of Jefferson's Administration. Also: Edwy and Elgiva: a Tragedy. ... *Philadelphia.* 1801. 8vo. BM.—Improvement of Government. ... *Philadelphia.* 1824. 8vo. B.—An Oration ... July 4, 1812. ... *Philadelphia: Printed by John Binns.* 1812. 4to, pp. 8.—Oration delivered before The Philadelphia Association for celebrating the Fourth of July, without Distinction of Party. ... July 4, 1832. *Philadelphia.* 1832. 8vo, pp. 24.—Opinion of the United States Bank and the Question of Vested Rights. ... *Philadelphia.* 1836. 8vo.— ... Report on Currency and Corporations. [n. p. n. d.] 8vo, pp. 8. B.—Speech ... April 14, 1842, on the Appropriation Bill. *Washington.* 1842. 8vo.—Speech ... on Remedial Justice, 1812. [n. p. n. d.] 8vo.—Speech ... on the Right to Repeal Bank Charters. Delivered in the Convention of Pennsylvania. *Washington City.* 1839. 8vo, pp. 48.—Stricture on the Letter of Chas. J. Ingersoll, Esq. touching the Right of a Legislature to Repeal a Charter, with an Appendix. *Baltimore.* 1835. 8vo, pp. 104.—A View of River Rights. ... *Philadelphia: P. H. Nicklin & T. Johnson.* 1835. 8vo, pp. 33. *See* "Democratic Review," VI. 339, XVI. 221; "N. A. Rev.," XVIII. 157, XXII. 212.

INGERSOLL (C. M.) Speech of Mr. C. M. Ingersoll, of Connecticut, delivered in the House ... March 31, 1852, on The Democracy of Connecticut—The Slave Question. *Washington.* 1852. Rl. 8vo, pp. 7. 34736

INGERSOLL (E. C.) Reconstruction and Andrew Johnson. Speech of Hon. Ebon C. Ingersoll ... May 5, 1866. [*Washington.* 1866.] 8vo, pp. 16. BA. 34737

INGERSOLL (E.) Abridgment of the Acts of Congress now in force, excepting those of private and local application, with notes of decisions, giving construction to the same, in the Supreme Court of the United States. By Edward Ingersoll. *Philadelphia.* 1825. 8vo. 34738

INGERSOLL. A Digest of the Laws of the United States of America, from March 4th, 1789, to May 15th, 1820; including also the Constitution, and the Old Act of Confederation, and excluding all acts relating to the District of Columbia ... . By Edward Ingersoll. *Philadelphia.* 1821. 8vo. C., S. 34739

INGERSOLL. The History and Law of the Writ of Habeas Corpus; with an Essay on the Law of Grand Juries. By Edward Ingersoll. *Philadelphia.* 1849. 8vo, pp. (2), 67. 34740

[INGERSOLL.] Personal Liberty and Martial Law: A Review of Some Pamphlets of the Day. *Philadelphia, April,* 1862. 8vo, pp. 38. 34741

INGERSOLL (G. G.) A Discourse delivered before the Legislature of Vermont, on the Day of General Election, October 14, 1830. By Geo. G. Ingersoll. *Burlington: Chauncey Goodrich.* 1830. 8vo, pp. 46, (1). BA. 34742

Also: A Farewell Address to the ... Society, in Burlington, Vt. ... June 2, 1844. ... *Burlington: Printed by Stilman Fletcher.* 1844. 8vo, pp. 48.—A Sermon ... on Fast Day ... in Burlington, Vermont. ... *University Press.* ... *Burlington: Printed by Stilman Fletcher.* 1843. 8vo, pp. 22.—Home, A Thanksgiving Sermon ... at King's Chapel. ... *Boston: Wm. Crosby & H. P. Nichols.* 8vo, pp. 24.—Sermon at Burlington, Vt. April 12, 1826. ... *Burlington.* 1826. 8vo.—A Sermon ... on Thanksgiving Day. ... *Burlington: Chauncey Goodrich.* 1831. 8vo, pp. 24. BA.

INGERSOLL (G. S.) An Address delivered before the Literary Society of the University of Vermont, August 2, 1837. By George S. Ingersoll. *Burlington.* 1837. 8vo. 34743

INGERSOLL (Jared). Mr. Ingersoll's Letters relating to the Stamp-Act. *New-Haven: Printed ... by Samuel Green.* M,DCC,LXVI. 4to, pp. (2), iv, 68. BA., W. 34744

Jared Ingersoll accepted the appointment of Stamp Commissioner in Connecticut, and was therefore mobbed and maltreated until he resigned. These letters relate to his appointment and his persecutions, and are of much historical interest.

INGERSOLL (J.) Connecticut Election Sermon, May 14, 1761. By Jonathan Ingersoll. *New London.* 1761. 12mo, pp. 46. W.

INGERSOLL (J. R.) Eulogy on Gen. Zachary Taylor, late President of the United States, delivered October 2d, 1850, By Hon. Joseph R. Ingersoll. *Philadelphia: Crissy & Markley.* 1850. 8vo, pp. 57. P. 34746

INGERSOLL. Memoir of the late Samuel Breck, Vice-President of the Historical Society of Pennsylvania. Read before the Society, by Joseph R. Ingersoll, January 12th, 1863. *Philadelphia: King & Baird, Printers.* 1863. 8vo, pp. 40. B. + Second Edition. *Philadelphia: Printed ... by King & Baird.* 1863. 8vo, pp. 56. 34747

[INGERSOLL.] Secession: a Folly and a Crime. *Philadelphia: King & Baird, Printers.* 1861. 8vo, pp. 29. B. 34748

INGERSOLL. Separazione una Follia, ed un Diletto. Discorso del Lodevole J. R. Ingersoll di Filadelfia. Traduzione dall' Inglese di C. G. Moroni. *Philadelphia: King & Baird, Printers.* 1861. 8vo, pp. 31. 34749

[INGERSOLL.] Secession Resisted. *Philadelphia: King & Baird.* 1861. 8vo, pp. 38. B., H. 34750

Also: Address before the Literary Societies of the University of Georgia, Aug. 5, 1847. ... *Athens.* 1847. 8vo.—An Address ... before the Literary Societies of Lafayette College ... July 4, 1833. ... *Philadelphia.* 1833. 8vo, pp. 38.—Address, on the Annual Commencement of the College of New Jersey. ... *Princeton.* 1828. 8vo. + [*Ibid.*] 1829. 8vo.—An Address ... Opening of the Wills Hospital for the Indigent Blind and Lame. March 3, 1834. ... *Philadelphia: Printed by James Kay, Jun. & Co.* [n. d.] 8vo, pp. 28.—An Address delivered before the Phi Beta Kappa Society, Alpha of Maine, in Bowdoin College, Brunswick, September 7, 1837. ... *Brunswick: For the Society.* 1837. 8vo, pp. 40.—Address ... Pennsylvania Colonization Society. October 25, 1838. ... *Philadelphia: William Stavely.* 1838. 8vo, pp. 56.—Annual Discourse before the Philomathean Society of the University of Pennsylvania, July 25, 1827. ... *Philadelphia.* 1827. 8vo, pp. 32.—Obituary Notice of Henry D. Gilpin. Read before the American Philosophical Society ... September 21, 1860. [n. p. n. d.] 8vo, pp. 16.—An Oration delivered before the Washington Benevolent Society, July 5, 1813. ... *Philadelphia.* 1813. 8vo, pp. 24.—Report on the Massachusetts Resolutions, 28th Congress.—Speech ... on the Judiciary, delivered in the Convention of Pennsylvania, November 1, 1837. *Harrisburg.* 1837. 8vo, pp. 26.—Speech ... against the Proposed Tariff. ... July 2, 1846. *Washington.* 1846. 8vo.

INGERSOLL (L. D.) Iowa and the Rebellion. A History of the Troops furnished by the State of Iowa to the Volunteer Armies of the Union, which conquered the Great Southern Rebellion of 1861–5. By Lurton Dunham Ingersoll. *Philadelphia: J. B. Lippincott & Co.* 1866. 8vo, pp. 743. B., BA. + Third Edition. [*Ibid.*] 1867. C. 34751

INGERSOLL (R. J.) Speech of Ralph J. Ingersoll ... March 6, 1826, on the Proposition to amend the Constitution of the United States. [n. p. n. d.] 12mo. W. 34752

Also: Speech ... on the Reduction of the Tariff. *Washington.* 1833. 8vo.—Speech ... July 2, 1842, against the Proposed Tariff. *Washington.* 1842. 8vo.

INGERSOLL (S. B.) Sermon ... at Shrewsbury [Mass.], June 18, 1820, ... By the late Rev. Samuel B. Ingersoll ... *Worcester: Manning & Trumbull, Printers.* 1821. 8vo, pp. 30. BA., W.

Contains a memoir of the author.

[INGHAM (Samuel D.)] An Exposition of the Political Character and Principles of John Quincy Adams. ... *Washington: Printed by Duff Green.* 1827. 8vo, pp. 21. BA. 34754

INGHAM. Speech of Mr. Ingham of Pennsylvania, on the Mission to Panama, delivered in the House of Representatives, April 18, 1826. *Washington.* 1826. 8vo, pp. 23. 34755

Also: Observations on the Currency of the United States. ... *Trenton.* 1851. 8vo, pp. 12. BA.

INGHAM UNIVERSITY. Annual Synopsis. *Rochester.* 1857. 8vo. Continued. S. 34756

INGHERAMI (Tom. Fedra). Garcilasso Mendozę de la Vegha Serr: & Catholl: Re|gis & Regine Hispanię. VI. Pont.|Max. Oratori. T. Phedrus.| [n. p. 1497.] 12 l. 34757

Title from Harrisse, II. 5. *See* a passage on the *verso* of the 11th leaf.

INGLEFIELD (E. A.) A Summer Search for Sir John Franklin, with a Peep into the Polar Basin. By Commander E. A. Inglefield, R.N. With short notices, by Professor Dickie, on the Botany, and by Dr. Sutherland, on the Meteorology and Geology. And a new Chart of the Arctic Sea. *London.* 1853. 8vo. Colored Plates and Maps. C., P. 34758

[INGLESI (A.)] An Address to the Public of Philadelphia: containing a Vindication of the Character and Conduct of the Rev. Mr. Inglesi, from Charges ... by the Rev. Mr. Harold. Translated from the French ... *Philadelphia: Printed for the Author.* 1824. 8vo, pp. 36. 34759

INGLIS (C.) The Christian Soldier's Duty Briefly delineated: In a Sermon ... September 7, 1777, before The American Corps newly raised For His Majesty's Service. By Charles Inglis ... . *New-York: Printed by H. Gaine.* [1777.] 4to, pp. (4), 26. BA.

INGLIS. The Claim and Answer with the Subsequent Proceedings, in the Case of the Right Reverend Charles Inglis; under the Sixth Article of the Treaty ... between His ... Majesty and the United States ... . *Philadelphia: Printed by R. Aitken.* MDCCXCIX. 4to, pp. 110, (1). BA. 34761

[INGLIS.] Proceedings of the Board of Commissioners in the Case of the Right Reverend Charles Inglis against the United States, Philadelphia, 1799. [n. p. n. d.] 4to, pp. 40. BA.

INGLIS. Dr. Inglis's Defence of his Character against certain False and Malicious Charges contained in a Pamphlet entitled, A Reply to Remarks on a Vindication of Gov. Parr and his Council, &c. &c. *London: Printed in the Year* 1784. 8vo, pp. 15.

See "Notes and Queries," VI. 151. For a reply, *see* Viator (John).

[INGLIS.] Letters of Papinian: in which the Conduct, Present State and Prospects of the American Congress are Examined. *New York.* 1779. 8vo, pp. viii, 86. N. + *London: J. Wilkie.* MDCCLXXIX. 8vo, pp. vi, 86, (1). 34764

INGLIS. Steadfastness in Religion and Loyalty Recommended, in a Sermon Preached before the Legislature of His Majesty's

Province of Nova-Scotia, ... April 7, 1793. By the Right Reverend Charles, Bishop of Nova-Scotia. *Halifax: Printed by John Howe.* M DCC XCIII. 8vo, pp. 34. BA. 34765

[INGLIS.] A Vindication of The Bishop of Landaff's Sermon from The gross Misrepresentations, and Abusive Reflections, Contained In Mr. William Livingston's Letters To his Lordship; With Some Additional Observations On certain Passages in Dr. Chauncey's Remarks, &c. By a Son of Truth and Decency. *New York: J. Holt.* M,DCC,LXVIII. 8vo, pp. viii, 82.

Also: A Charge delivered to the Clergy of the Diocese of Nova Scotia, at the Primary Visitation, holden in the Town of Halifax ... June 1788. *Halifax.* 1789. 8vo, pp. 62. + Charge ... at the Triennial Visitation, ... Town of Halifax. *Halifax.* 1792. 4to. + [in] ... June and August, 1803. Second Edition. *Halifax.* 1804. 8vo, pp. 56.—A Farewell Sermon, preached at St. George's and St. Paul's Chapels, in the City of New York, October 20, 1783. ... *London.* 1784. 8vo.—Sermon ... occasioned by the Death of John Ogilvie, D.D. ... *New York.* 1774. 8vo, pp. 30.—Sermon occasioned by the Death of Rev. Dr. Samuel Auchmuty, March 9, 1777. ... *New York.* [1777.] 12mo.—Sermon preached before the Grand Lodge, New York. ... *New York.* 1783.—Sermon ... at Halifax, 25 April, 1794, the Day appointed ... for a General Fast and Humiliation in H. M. Province of Nova Scotia. ... *Halifax.* 1794. 8vo. The author was rector of Trinity Church, New York, but, being a loyalist, resigned his charge, removed to Nova Scotia, and for his loyalty was created a Bishop.

INGLIS (D.) Righteousness Exalteth a Nation: A Thanksgiving Sermon. By Rev. David Inglis. *Hamilton.* 1866. 8vo, pp. 14. 34767

INGLIS (J.) A Discourse delivered in ... Baltimore, ... October 2nd, 1814, before the ... First Regiment of Artillery, 3d B. M. M. By Rev. James Inglis, D.D. *Baltimore.* 1814. 8vo, pp. 22. 34768

[INGLIS (John).] Journal of Visitation in Nova Scotia, Cape Breton and along the Eastern Shore of New Brunswick; by the Lord Bishop of Nova Scotia, in the Summer and Autumn of 1843. *London.* 1844. 18mo, pp. 70. Map. 34769

[INGLIS.] Memoranda respecting King's College at Windsor, in Nova Scotia ... . By One of the Alumni. *London.* 1836. 8vo, pp. 31. 34770

INGLIS. A Sermon ... at Halifax; on Behalf of the Incorporated Society for the Propagation of the Gospel in Foreign Parts, on the 19th February, 1832. ... By the ... Reverend John Inglis, D.D. ... *Halifax: Printed by Edmund Ward.* 1832. 8vo, pp. 27. B. 34771

Also: A Pastoral Address. ... *Halifax.* 1838. 8vo, pp. 11.

[INGRAHAM (Edward D.)] A Sketch of the Events which preceded the Capture of Washington, by the British, on the Twenty-Fourth of August, 1814. ... *Philadelphia: Carey and Hart.* 1849. 8vo, pp. iv, 66. Map. B., BA., C. 34772

Privately printed. Also: An Address delivered before the Law Academy of Philadelphia, Session 1828–29. ... *Philadelphia.* 1828. 8vo, pp. 24.

[INGRAHAM (Joseph H.)] Burton; or, the Sieges. ... *New-York: Harper & Brothers.* 1838. 2 vols., 12mo, pp. v–261; 277.

[INGRAHAM.] Lafitte, the Pirate of the Gulf. *New York.* 1836. 2 vols., 12mo. + *New York: De Witt & Davenport* [about 1840]. 8vo, pp. 11–200. 34774

[INGRAHAM.] The South-West. By a Yankee. *New-York: Harper & Brothers.* 1835. 2 vols., 12mo, pp. xi, 294; xi, 276.

INGRAHAM. The Sunny South; or, the Southerner at Home, embracing five years' experience of a northern Governess in the Land of the Sugar and the Cotton. By Kate Conyngham. Edited by Professor J. H. Ingraham, of Mississippi. ... *Philadelphia: G. G. Evans.* 1860. 12mo, pp. 526. B. 34776

Also: The Avenging Brother; or, the Two Maidens. ... *New York: R. M. De Witt.* 1869. 16mo, pp. 100.—Bonfield: or, the Outlaw of the Bermudas. A Nautical Novel. ... *New York: H. L. Williams.* 1846. 8vo, pp. 98.—The Corsair of Casco Bay; or, the Pilot's Daughter. ... *Gardiner, Me.: G. M. Atwood.* 1844. 8vo, pp. 58.—The Dancing Feather; and its Sequel Morris Græme. ... *New York: Williams Brothers.* 1845–47. 8vo, pp. (2), 92. 2 Plates.—The Free-Trader: or, the Cruiser of Narragansett Bay. ... *New-York: Williams Brothers.* 1847. 8vo, pp. 96.—The Red Wing; or, Belmont, the Buccanneer of the Bay. ... *New York: R. M. De Witt.* 1869. 16mo, pp. 100. Plate.—The White Wing; or, the Pirate of the Rigolets. ... *New York: R. M. De Witt.* 1868. 16mo, pp. 100. Also, "Rivingstone," "Will. Teller," and others.

INGRAHAM (J. P. T.) A Sermon in Memory of Captain F. A. Root, and Lieutenant R. J. Chivas, ... By ... Revd. J. P. T. Ingraham ... December 20th, 1863. *Milwaukee.* 1864. 8vo, pp. 14. BA. 34777

INGRAHAM (J. W.) A Manual for the Use of Visiters to the Falls of Niagara. ... By Joseph Wentworth Ingraham. ... *Buffalo: For the Author.* 1834. 18mo, pp. 72. B., BA. 34778

INGRAM (D.) An Historical Account of the Several Plagues that have appeared in the World since the year 1346, etc. By Dale Ingram. *London: R. Baldwin.* M,DCC,LV. 8vo, pp. (4), iv, 208. A. 34779

Contains some reference to the plague in Barbadoes.

INGRAM (E. J.) Vindiciæ Lusitaniæ; or, An Answer to a Pamphlet entitled, The Causes and Consequences of the late Emigration to the Brazils. By Edward James Ingram. *London.* 1808. 8vo. 34780

INGRAM (R.) An Account [&c.] *See* Israel (Menasseh Ben).

INIGO (J.) Funeral gratitud del conventu de S. Franc. de la ciudad de la Puebla de los Angeles contr. a las solemnes exequias el Señ. D. Andreas de Arce. *Puebla de los Angeles.* 1774. 4to, pp. (28), 43. 34781

The Injurious Tendency of the Proposed Slave Registry Bill; referring to Evidence received by the House of Assembly, Jamaica. *London.* 1816. 8vo, pp. 24. 34782

INMAM (H.) Catalogue of Works by the late Henry Inman. ... with a Biographical Sketch ... . *New-York.* 1846. 8vo, pp. 20. 34783

INMAN (J.) The Sudden and Sharp Doom; a Tale of West India Piracy. By John Inman. [n. p. n. d.] 12mo. P. 34784

INNES (J.) Letter to Lord Glenelg, Secretary of State for the Colonies; containing a Report, from Personal Observation, on the Working of the New System in the British West India Colonies. By John Innes. *London.* 1835. 8vo, pp. 119. + Second Edition. [*Ibid.*] 34785

INNES. Letter to the Lord Glenelg ... on Negro Apprenticeship. *London.* 1838. 8vo, pp. 29. S. 34786

INNES. Thoughts on the Present State of the British West India Colonies. By John Innes. *London.* 1840. 8vo. 34787

[INNES (William).] Letter to the Members of Parliament who have presented Petitions for the Abolition of the Slave Trade; By a West India Merchant. *London.* 1792. 8vo. C.

[INNES.] Slave Trade Indispensable; in Answer to the Speech of William Wilberforce, on the 13 May, 1789; By a West India Merchant. *London.* 1790. 8vo. C. 34789

INNOCENT X. (*Pope*). Bref de N. S. P. le pape Innocent x, sur le differend d'entre l'Euesque d'Angelopolis, en la Nouvelle Espagne, dans les Indes-Occidentales et les PP. Jésuites. *Rome.* 1659. 4to. 34790

Relates to Mexico.

Inoculation. The Abuses and Scandals of some late Pamphlets in favor of Inoculation modestly obviated, and Inoculation further considered, in a Letter to A[lexander] S[tuart], M.D. and F.R.S. [By William Douglass, M.D.] *Boston.* 1730. 12mo.

An Account of the Success of Inoculation for the Small Pox, in England and America; ... *London.* 1759. 4to. P. 34792

Inoculation of the Small Pox as practised in Boston, considered in a Letter to A[lexander] S[tuart], M.D. ... [By William Douglass, M.D.] *Boston.* 1722. 12mo. 34793

See also [Douglass (W.)], Vol. V., No. 20720, &c. Also: Dissertation concerning Inoculation of the Small Pox. Giving some Account of the Rise, Progress, Success, Advantages, and Disadvantages of receiving the Small Pox by Incisions. Illustrated by sundry Cases of the Inoculated. *Boston.* 1730. 8vo.—A Letter from one in the Country to his Friend in the City; in Relation to the Distresses occasioned by Inoculation. *Boston.* 1721. 8vo.—A Letter to a Friend in the Country, attempting a Solution of the Objections against Inoculation. *Boston.* 1721. 8vo.

The Inquirer. Essays on Various Subjects, Notes and Queries, etc. *London: Longmans.* 1822–23. 2 vols., 8vo. 34794

Contains articles on slavery, America, and American poetry.

Inquiries of an Emigrant; being the Narrative of an English Farmer, from the year 1824 to 1830, during which period he traversed the United States and Canada. Fourth Edition. *London.* 1832. 12mo. 34795

Inquiries relating to Negro Emancipation. *London.* 1829. 8vo. S. 34796

Inquiries, respecting the ... Indians. *See* [Cass (L.)], Vol. III.

An Inquiry into the alleged Tendency of the Separation of Convicts, one from the other, to produce Disease and Derangement. By a Citizen of Pennsylvania. ... *Philadelphia: E. C. & J. Biddle.* 1849. 8vo, pp. 160. B., S. 34797

An Inquiry into the Causes and Cost of Corrupt State Legislation. By a Citizen of Philadelphia. *Philadelphia.* 1863. 8vo, pp. 32. 34798

An Inquiry into the Causes and Origin of Slavery in the United States, and a Plan suggested for its Extinction. By an American Citizen. ... *Philadelphia: William S. Young, Printer.* 1844. 8vo, pp. 8. BA. 34799

An Inquiry into the Causes of our Naval Miscarriages; with some Thoughts on the Interest of this Nation, as to a Naval

War, and of the only true way of manning the fleet. ... Second Edition. *London.* 1707. 4to, pp. 37. + Sixth Edition. *London.* 1714. 8vo, pp. 32. 34800

Reprinted in the "Harleian Miscellany," XI. Relates to the success and failure of the British fleets in various parts of America, &c.

Inquiry into the Causes. *See* Raguet (Condy), *and* St. Domingo.

An Inquiry into the Causes of the Public Distress. *New York.* 1834. 8vo, pp. 52. 34801

Inquiry into the Causes which have retarded the Accumulation of Wealth and Increase of Population in the Southern States. *Washington.* 1846. 8vo, pp. 27. 34802

Inquiry into the Commercial Policy of the United States; or the Right Principles of Revenue Laws and International Commerce. *Boston.* 1845. 8vo. 34803

An Inquiry into the Condition and Prospects of the African Race in the United States, and the means of bettering its Fortune. By an American. *Philadelphia.* 1839. 12mo, pp. 214.

Inquiry into the Conduct of Great Britain in the present Affairs of Europe. *London.* 1727. 8vo. + *Boston.* 1727. 8vo.

An Inquiry into the Constitutionality of Military Reserves within the Boundaries of the Several States. [n. p. n. d.] 8vo, pp. 35. 34806

An Inquiry into the Effects. *See* [Ramsay (J.)]

An Inquiry into the Fitness of Attending Parliament. *London.* 1739. 8vo. 34807

Partly relates to the free navigation of the American seas.

An Inquiry into the Natural Rights of Man, as regards the Exercise of Expatriation ... . *New York: Printed by Pelsue & Gould.* 1813. 8vo, pp. 20. B. 34808

An Inquiry into the Nature and Causes of the Present Disputes between the British Colonies in America and their Mother-Country; And their reciprocal Claims and just Rights impartially examined, and fairly stated. *London: J. Wilkie.* MDCCLXVIII. 8vo. + The Second Edition. [*Ibid.*] MDCCLXIX. 8vo, pp. (4), 76. 34809

Perhaps by Dr. Franklin. *See* Sparks' "Life of Franklin," IV. 281. *See also* "M. Rev.," XXXIX. 495.

An Inquiry into the Nature and Uses of Money; More especially of the Bills of Publick Credit, Old Tenor. Together with A Proposal of some proper Relief in the present Exigence. To which is added, A Reply to the Essay on Silver and Paper Currencies. *Boston: S. Kneeland & T. Green.* 1740. 8vo, pp. (2), 78. B. 34810

A learned and elaborate essay, discussing the question of bills of credit, or paper money, which at this period was emitted by the American colonies to a large amount *See* [Douglass (W.)], Vol. v., No. 20723.

An Inquiry into the Origin and Consequences of the Influence of the Crown over Parliament. Submitted to the Consideration of the Electors of Great Britain. *London: J. Dodsley.* 1780. 8vo. 34811

Incidentally American. *See* "M. Rev.," LXIV. 20.

An Inquiry into the Plans, Progress, and Policy of the American Mining Companies. *London: John Murray.* MDCCCXXV. 8vo, pp. 88. C. 34812

An Inquiry into the Policy of the Penal Laws, affecting the Popish Inhabitants of Ireland ... with some Hints respecting America. *London.* 1775. 8vo, pp. 151. S. 34813

An Inquiry into the Present State of the British Navy. Together with Reflections on the Late War with America; its Probable Consequences, &c. &c. &c. By an Englishman. ... *London: C. Chapple.* 1815. 8vo, pp. xv, (1), 166. BA. 34814

An Inquiry into the Present State of the Foreign Relations of the Union, as affected by the Late Measures of Administration. ... *Philadelphia: Samuel F. Bradford.* 1806. 8vo, pp. 183. BA.

An Inquiry into the right to change the Ecclesiastical Constitution of the Congregational Churches of Massachusetts. ... To which is prefixed, Dr. Morse's Report to the General Association of Massachusetts, from the Pamphlet of August, 1815. *Boston: Wells and Lilly.* 1816. 8vo, pp. 79, Notes, pp. viii. B.

Inquiry into the State of the Nation. *See* [Fox (H. R.)]

Nos Los Inquisidores Contra la Heretica Pravedad, y Apostasia, en esta Ciudad y Provincias de la Nueva-España: Nueva Gallicia, Guatemala, Nicaragua, Yucatan, Verapaz, Honduras, Ylas Philippinas, y sús districtos, y Jurisdicciones, por Authoridad Apostolica, etc. 1670. Folio. 34817

INSAURRALDE (J.) Ara poru aguiyey haba yaoca ymomocoinda: Conico: quatia ambuae poromboe marãngâtu ha, P. Joseph Insaurralde amyre Jesus Noõga reheguare rembiquatia cuera conumbuçu reta ųpe guarãma; ang ramò mbia reta memengatu Parana hae Uruguaí ĩgua upe yquaabeé mbi, Yyepia mongeta aguiyey hãguã, teco bay tetirõ hegui ynepihirõ haguama, hae teco marãngâtu rupitĩ haguamari, ymbopicopibo, Tupã gracia reromanõ hapebe. *Yquatia pirè Tabuçu Madrid è hápe, Joachin Ibarra quatia apo ucu hara rope* 1759–60. *Roì pìpe.* 2 vols., 8vo, pp. (24), 464; (12), 368. 34818

This rare and important work, on the good employment of time, is the most voluminous book printed entirely in the Guarani language. Father Insaurralde was superior of the missions to Parana and Uruguay.

Inside Out. *See* [Coffey (W. A.)], *and* Francis (S. W.)

Insigne victoria que el Señor Marquez de Guadalcazar, Vir-|rey en el Reyno del Pirû, ha alcançado en los puertos de Lima,| y Callao, contra vna armada poderosa de Olanda, despachada|por orden del Conde Mauricio. Dase cuenta de como el ene-|migo lleuaua intento de coger la prata de su Magestad: y el de-|sastrado fin que tuuo por mano de los Españoles. Auisase tam-|bien de vna declaracion que hizo vn soldado del enemigo, | Frances de nacion, y en su profession Catolico, llama-|do Iuan de Bulas, que huyô de su exer-|cito, ante el señor Virrey, a ocho | de Enero deste año | de 1625. [Colophon:] *Em Lisboa. Por Geraldo de Vinha.*| [1625.] Folio, 4 unnumbered pages. 34819

INSKIP (J. S.) Life of Rev. William Summers, a Blind Man. By Rev. John S. Inskip. *Baltimore.* [n. d.] 12mo. 34820

The Insolvent Register. Vol. I. *New York.* 1811–12. 4to.

Fifteen or more numbers published.

Inspection of the General Hospitals. Second Report. By H. G. Clark, M.D., January 21, 1863. *New York: United States Sanitary Commission.* 1863. 8vo, pp. 10. 34822

De Instellinge van de Generale Compagnie. *See* Brazil.

Instituta ordinis Beati Francisci. *Mexico.* 1567. 4to. 34823

A very early, rare Mexican imprint, which I have not seen. Not described by Señor Icazbalceta.

Institute of Reward for Orphans of Patriots. Journal. Vol. I. *New York.* 1864. 8vo. 34824

Also: Annual Report. 1861. Continued.

The Institution of the ... Cincinnati. *See* Vol. IV., 13121–7.

Institution and First Proceedings of the Society for the Encouragement of Arts, Manufactures, and Commerce established in Barbadoes, 1781. *Printed at Barbadoes.* [n. d.] 12mo. Folded Tables. 34825

Instituto historico geographico e ethnographico do Brasil, fundado no Rio de Janeiro. 8vo. 34826

Instruccion de los Comisionados de la Direccion General y Juzgado privativo de alcabalaj y pulques del Reyno. *Mexico.* 1783. Folio, pp. 30. 34827

"Pièce authentiquée."—ANDRADE.

Instruccion general. *See* Cuba, Vol. v., No. 17783.

Instruccion Nautica que acompaña à la carta de la Ria de Guayaquil, publicada por la Direccion Hidrografica, en 1825. *Madrid.* 1827. Sm. 4to, pp. 15. 34828

Instruccion para el gobierno de la Real Aduana de Mar de esta Plaza y demas de la Isla. *Habana: Imprenta del Gobierno.* 1831. Folio, pp. 58. 2 Tables. 34829

Instruccion para el gobierno interior y buen régimen de la Guarnicion del Presidio del Carmen. *Mexico.* 1774. Folio, pp. 23. 34830

Instruccion para los ayuntamientos constitucionales juntas provinciales y gefes politicos superiores. Decretado por las Cortes generales y extraordinarias en 23 de Junio de 1813. *Mexico.* 1820. Sm. 8vo, pp. 48. 34831

Instruccion para que se liquiden las cuentas generales y particulares de las temporalidades de Indias. *Buenos Aires.* Folio, pp. 24. 34832

Instruccion para reducir facilmente las pesas y medidos extrangeras designadas en el articulo 15 del Arancel de Aduanas Maritimas, decretado en 4 de Octubre de 1845, á las pesas y medidas Mexicanas. *Mexico.* 1846. 8vo, pp. 18. 34833

Instruccion sobre el cultivo del Nopal y cria de la Cochinilla de America. [n. p.] 1825. 4to. 34834

Instruccion y arte para regular el oficio divino. *Mexico.* 1579. 8vo. 34835

A rare Mexican imprint; not described by Señor Icazbalceta.

Instruccion y forma que se ha de tener, y guardar en la publicacion, predicacion ... de la Bula de la santa Cruzada ... le qual se ha de hazer en Arcobispado de Mexico, i Opispado de Mechoacan, i Guaxara, Tlaxcala, Nueva Galicia, Yucatan, Guatimala, Honduras, Chiapa, Verapaz, i Nicaragua, i en el Arcobispado de Santo Domingo, i Obispado de Puertorico, i de Cuba, i Abadia de Jamaica, etc. *Madrid.* 1648. Folio, 8 l. 34836

Instruccion y metodo con que se ha de establecer el Hospital para la Tropa de la Guarnicion de Presidio de Nuestra Señora del Carmen. *Mexico.* 1774. Folio, pp. 15. 34837

Instrucciones para la constitucion fundamental de la monarquia española, y su gobierno, de que se ha de tratarse en las próximas cortes generales de la nacion. Dadas por el M. I. Ayuntamiento de la M. N. Y. L. ciudad de Guatemala, á su diputado el Sr. D. Antonio de Larrazabal canónigo de esta iglesia metropolitana. Formadas por el Sr. D. José Maria Peinado, regidor perpetuo. *Cadiz: Imprenta de la junta superior.* 1811. Folio, pp. 63.

Instrucciones que los Virreyes de Nueva España dejaron a sus Sucesores. Añadense algunas que los mismos trajeron de la Corte y otros Documentos semejantes a las Instrucciones. *Mexico: Imprenta Imperial.* 1867. Folio, pp. 317. 34839

"These instructions are of importance to the student of Mexican History, as they give the judgment of various Vice Roys on the state of the country at the time of their leaving. This Collection was printed by order of the Emperor Maximilian. Nearly the whole impression was destroyed during the Siege of Mexico."

Instrucções para os Viajantes e Empregados nas colonias, sobre a maneira de colher, conservar e remetter os objectos de Historia Natural. Traduzida do original francez por ordem de Sua Magestade Fidelissima, augmentada ... e precedida de algumas reflexões sobre a Historia Natural do Brasil, e estabelecimento do Museu e Jardim Botanico em a côrte do Rio de Janeiro. *Rio de Janeiro, na Imp. Regia.* 1819. 4to, pp. lvi–77. 34840

Instruction for Heavy Artillery; Prepared by a Board of Officers for the use of the Army of the United States. *Richmond, Va.: West & Johnston.* 1862. 16mo, pp. xvi, 272. 39 Plates.

Instruction for Officers on Outposts and Patrol Duty *New York.* 1862. 12mo. + [*Ibid.*] 1863. 34842

Instruction Nautique. *See* Vol. v., No. 17784.

Instruction Nautique pour se rendre d'Europe à l'Embouchure du Mississippi ... et détails sur la navigation de ce fleuve, et sur celle du canal de Bahama. *Paris.* 8vo, pp. 58. S. 34843

Instruction pour les Colonies Françoises, contenant un projet de Constitution, presentée a l'Assemblée Nationale, au nom des comités de constitution, des colonies, de la marine, d'agriculture et de commerce. *A Paris, de l'imprimerie Nationale.* 1791. 8vo, pp. 74. P. 34844

Relates entirely to St. Domingo.

Instructions and Forms to be observed in applying for Army Pensions, under the Act of July 14, 1862. *Washington: Government Printing Office.* 1862. 8vo, pp. 13. 34845

Instructions by the Commissioners of his Majesty's Customs in America to Robert Trail, Esq., appointed Collector of the Customs at the Port of Piscataway, in America. [n. p. n. d.] 8vo, pp. 39. M. 34846

Signed by "Henry Hulton, J. Temple, William Burch, and John Robinson."

Instructions by the Commissioners of his Majesty's Customs, for the due Collection of his Majesty's Revenue of Customs in America. [*London.* n. d.] Folio, pp. 7. 34847

Instructions by the Commissioners of his Majesty's Customs in America. [n. p. 1767.] 8vo, pp. 35. 34848

Instructions| By the Commissioners of his Majesty's|Customs in America, to| |who is appointed| |of the Customs at the Port of| |in America.| [*Boston.* 1770?] 8vo, pp. 40.

Instructions concerning the Tax on Legacies, Distributive Shares, and Gifts and Assignments, April, 1863. [n. p. n. d.] 8vo, pp. 6. 34850

Instructions for the Agents for Collecting Subscriptions to the Produce Loan, Jan. 3, 1862. *Richmond.* 1862. 8vo, pp. 3. B.

Instructions for the Collectors and Comptrollers in America and the West Indies, respecting Remittances by Bills of Exchange. [*London.*] 1782. 4to, pp. 7. 34852

Instructions for the Commanders of Merchant Ships, having Letters of Marque and Reprisals for Private Men of War, against the French King, the King of Spain, and also against the Rebellious Colonies in America. *London.* 1778–81. Folio. 34853

Instructions for the Guidance of Her Majesty's Naval Officers employed in the Suppression of The Slave Trade. *London.* [1844.] Folio. 34854

Instructions for the Guidance of the Medical Officers of the Navy of the Confederate States. *Richmond: Macfarlane & Fergusson.* 1864. 12mo, pp. 40. 34855

Instructions for the Management. *See* Barbadoes, No. 3272.

Instructions for the Treatment of Negroes, &c. &c. *London: Shepperson and Reynolds.* 1788. 12mo. + [*Ibid.*] 1799. 34856

See "M. Rev.," LXXVIII. 161; Second Series, XXIV. 106.

Instructions for treating with the Indians, given to the Commissioners appointed for that Service. By the Hon. Spencer Phipps ... In the Year 1752. Now first printed from the Original Manuscript. *Boston: Samuel G. Drake.* 1865. 4to, pp. 8.

Fifty copies privately printed.

Instructions from the Inhabitants. *See* Orleans.

Instructions from the Prudential Committee of the American Board of Commissioners. [n. p. n. d.] 8vo, pp. xvi. 34858

Instructions given with a Commission for seizing the Ships, etc. belonging to the Inhabitants of the Rebellious Colonies. 1777. Folio. 34859

Instructions in Preparing Soldiers' Pay. *Washington.* 1862. 8vo. 34860

Instructions in reference to collecting Nests and Eggs of North American Birds. pp. 22. [Followed by:] Circular in reference to ... North American Grasshoppers. pp. 4. Circular in reference to collecting North American Shells. pp. 4. *Washington: Smithsonian Institute.* 1860. 34861

Instructions nautiques. *See* Guiana, Vol. VII., No. 29174.

Instructions nautiques, relatives aux cartes et plans du Pilote de Terre-Neuve, publié au Depôt général des cartes, plans, et journaux de la Marine, en 1784; pour l'usage des vaisseaux du Roi, et des batimens particuliers employés à la pêche. Extrait du Recueil des divers mémoires Anglois, intitulé: "Sailing Directions for the North American Pilot" ... . *Paris: Imprimerie royale.* 1784. 4to, pp. 80. Atlas. 34862

Instructions on the Erection of Four New Catholic Episcopal Sees in the United States, and the Consecration of their First Bishops, celebrated in Baltimore ... . *Baltimore: Bernard Dornin.* 1810. 12mo, pp. 43. BA. 34863

Instructions pour naviguer sur la côte méridionale de Terre-neuve. *Paris.* 1784. Folio. 34864

Instructions to Charles Cotesworth Pinckney, John Mashall and Elbridge Gerry, Envoys Extraordinary and Ministers Plenipotentiary to the French Republic, Referred to in the Message of the President ... . *Philadelphia: Way and Graff.* 1798. 8vo, pp. 20. C. 34865

... Instructions to and Dispatches from the Late and Present Ministers in China. *Washington.* 1860. 8vo. S. 34866

... Instructions to General Jessup and Letter from Gov. Schley, of Georgia, In relation to Hostilities of Creek Indians. [*Washington.* 1836.] 8vo, pp. 3. 34867

Instructions to Inspectors on Campaign Duties. *U. S. Sanitary Commission.* 186–. 8vo, pp. 4. 34868

Followed by "Camp Instruction Returns," with Forms, pp. 11, 26, 28.

Instructions to Mustering Officers and others, of Kindred Duties. *Washington.* 1863. 8vo. 34869

Instructions to the Envoys Extraordinary and Ministers Plenipotentiary from the United States of America, to the French Republic, their Letters of Credence and Full Powers, and the Despatches received from them relative to their Mission. Published by the Secretary of State in conformity with the resolution of Congress, June 22, 1798. *Philadelphia: W. Ross.* [1798.] 8vo, pp. 131. 34870

Instructions to the Surveyors General of Public Lands ... also, a Manual of Instructions to ... Deputy Surveyors ... . *Washington: A. O. P. Nicholson ... Printer.* 1855. 8vo, pp. vi, 35, Index, 56. 3 Diagrams. B. 34871

Instructive and Curious Epistles; from Catholic Clergymen of the Society of Jesus, in ... either America; being a Selection [from] the "Lettres Edifiantes." Translated by Thomas A. Power. *Dublin.* 1829. 12mo. C. 34872

The Instructor. *New York: [J. Parker and W. Weyman].* 1755. Sm. 4to, pp. 4. 34873

A weekly paper. "We shall begin with some Historical Remarks on the present state of Affairs on the Continent of North-America."

The Insurance Times. A Journal solely devoted to Life, Fire and Marine Insurance. [Monthly.] Stephen English, Editor. *New York: S. English.* [1868.] 4to. Continued. 34874

The Insurgents; An Historical Novel. *Philadelphia: Carey, Lea & Blanchard.* 1835. 2 vols., 12mo, pp. vii, 13–284; (2), 5–276. C. 34875

INTEGAR, *pseudon.* Letters to the High and Mighty United States of America. By Integar, Candidate for the Office of Accomptant-General to their Excellencies the Continental Congress. *New York.* 1777. 8vo, pp. (4), 80. + *London: B. Law.* [1777.] 8vo, pp. (4), 80. 34876

"A fellow of infinite jest; but we wish him a subject better adapted to the proper exertions of humor."—*Monthly Review*, LVII. 167.

Intelligence from the Moon, found on board the East Indiaman, captured by Commodore Johnstone. *Philadelphia.* pp. 16.

The Intercourse of Nations: being a Collection of Short, Correct and Easy Rules for reducing Thirteen different Coins and Currencies into each other, with a concise method of calculating Federal Money. ... *New York: G. Forman.* 1795. 8vo, pp. 126. 34878

Intereses sur-Americanos. ... *Bogota: Imprenta del Neo-Granadino.* 1855. 8vo, pp. 32. H. 34879

The Interest in Slavery of the Southern Non-Slaveholder. The Right of Peaceful Secession. Slavery in the Bible. *Charleston: Evans & Cogswell.* 1860. 8vo, pp. 30. 34880

The Interest of Great Britain, 1760. *See* [Jackson (Robert)].

The Interest of Great Britain in the approaching Congress considered. In a Letter from a newly elected Member to a Noble Minister of State. *London: Bristow.* 1761. 8vo.

See "M. Rev.," XXIV. 439.

The Interest of the Country In laying Duties: or a Discourse, shewing how Duties on some sorts of Merchandize may make the Province of New-York richer than it would be without them. *New-York* [about 1726]. 8vo, pp. 35. B. 34882

This elicited the following:

The Interest of the Country in laying no Duties *New York.* 1726. 12mo. 34883

The Two Interests reconciled. *New York.* 1726. 12mo.

The Interest of the Merchants and Manufacturers of Great Britain, in the Present Contest with the Colonies, Stated and Considered. *London: T. Cadell.* M,DCC,LXXIV. 8vo, pp. (2), 50. BA., C., H., S. + *London: Printed. Boston: Re-printed ... at Draper's.* [n. d.] Sm. 8vo, pp. 20. B., W. 34885

By "a ministerial writer, whose principal endeavor is to prevent any interference of the merchants and manufacturers of Great Britain in behalf of the people of America, by representing that the continuance of their trade to the colonies clearly and entirely depends upon the laws of England, having authority there."—*Monthly Review*, LI. 476.

The Interest of the Nation, as it respects all the Sugar Plantations Abroad, and Refining of Sugar at Home, truly stated. *London: Motte.* 1691. Sm. 4to. 34886

Interesting Account of the Early Voyages, made by the Portuguese Spaniards, &c. To Africa, East and West Indies. The Discovery of Numerous Islands; with Particulars of the Lives of those Eminent Navigators. Including the Life and Voyages of Columbus. To which is prefixed the Life of that Great Circumnavigator Captain Cook, with particulars of his Death. Extracted from Dr. Kipps's. *London: Printed for the Proprietors.* M,DCC,XC. 4to, pp. (24), 7–276. 7 Maps, and Plates. C.

An Interesting Account of the Plague, Yellow Fever, &c. as they have prevailed in Different Countries. ... *Boston: Printed by James Loring.* 1820. 8vo, pp. 24. B. 34888

Interesting Account of the Project of France respecting Louisiana. By a French Counsellor of State. *Martinsburg: Printed by John Alburtis.* 1803. 12mo, pp. 48. 34889

An Interesting Account of those Extraordinary People the Esquimaux Indians, &c. *Sheffield.* [n. d.] 12mo, pp. 36.

An Interesting Collection of Modern Lives; with Observations of the Characters and Writings, of the following Eminent Men, Jeffrey Lord Amherst, ... Dr. Benjamin Franklin, ... John Horne Tooke, Esq. And Mr. Thomas Paine ... . *London: G. Riebau.* 1792. 8vo. 34891

Interesting Description of the City of Buenos Ayres, on the River Plate. *London: Fairbairn.* 1806. Sm. 8vo. 34892

Interesting Detail. *See* E[aton] (W[illiam]), Vol. VI.

Interesting Extracts, Historical and Fictitious, Embracing Adventures of Soldiers, Robbers, Pirates, etc. *New York.* 1833. 12mo. 34893

Interesting Incidents in the History of several of the Converts to Christianity, under the Ministry of the Moravian Missionaries in Greenland; taken from the Journal of the Missionaries ... . *New York.* [n. d.] 18mo. 34894

An Interesting Narrative ... of the Sufferings of Mr. Joseph Barker and his Wife Martha, who were taken by a Scouting Party of British and Indians, and all their Property Destroyed, in the Year 1777. Embellished with one Engraving. Founded on Fact. Published for the benefit of Solomon Barker, Son of the late Joseph and Martha. *Rochester, N. Y.: W. E. Hutchins, Printer.* 1836. 8vo, pp. 16. Folded Woodcut. 34895

Undoubtedly founded on fact, especially the woodcut.

Interesting Narratives and Discoveries, including ... Maurice Griffiths' Discovery of a Nation of Welshmen in the Interior of America. *Shrewsbury.* 1817. 8vo. 34896

Interesting Narratives of Extraordinary Sufferings and Deliverances of the Crews and Passengers of Sundry Shipwrecked Vessels. ... *Philadelphia: Printed for Mathew Carey.* 1810. 12mo, pp. 70. BA. 34897

Interesting Official Documents relating to the United Provinces of Venezuela, viz. Preliminary Remarks, the Act of Independence, Proclamation, Manifesto to the World of the Causes which have impelled the said Provinces to separate from the Mother Country; together with the Constitution, framed for the Administration of their Government, In Spanish and English. *London: Longman.* 1812. 8vo, Engraved and Printed Title, pp. xxiv, 309.

Interesting Papers illustrative of the Riots in the City [of Baltimore]. *Baltimore.* 1812. 8vo. 34899

Interesting Political Discussion. *See* [Lowell (John)].

Interesting State Papers, from President Washington, M. Fauchet and M. Adet, the late and present Ambassadors from the French Convention to the United States of America. Likewise Conferences with George Hammond, Esq. Minister Plenipotentiary from his Britannic Majesty, as laid by the President

before the Legislature of the United States in their present session. Quoted by Edmund Randolph, late Secretary of State. And included in a Defence of his Resignation of that Office. *Philadelphia: Printed. London: Re-printed by J. Owen.* 1796. 8vo, pp. (2), 136. 34900

Interesting Facts on the Subject of Taxing the British Colonies in America. *London: J. Almon.* [v. d.] 34901

A publisher's title to a series of tracts described in this Dictionary under their respective titles. *See also* Jamaica.

The Interests Of the Several Princes and States of Europe Consider'd, with respect to the Succession of the Crown of Spain. And the Titles of the several Pretenders thereto, Examin'd. *London: Printed in the Year* MDCXCVIII. 8vo, pp. (2), 32.

Includes some reference to the West Indian Colonies.

Les Interêts des Colonies Hollandoises du sud d'Amerique. *A La Haye.* 1776. 8vo. 34903

The Interference of the British Legislature, in the Internal Concerns of the West India Islands, respecting their Slaves, Deprecated. By a Zealous Advocate for the Abolition of the Slave Trade. *London: J. Mawman.* 1816. 8vo, pp. (4), 58.

INTERIANO (P.) Ristretto | delle | Historie | Genovese | di Paulo Interiano. [Colophon:] *In Lvcca per Io Busdrago* | MDLI. 4to, Engraved Title, 233 leaves. 34905

This "History of Genoa" contains a brief notice of Columbus. *See* J. R. Bartlett's Catalogue of J. C. Brown's Library.

Interior Causes of the War: The Nation Demonized, and its President a Spirit-Rapper. By a Citizen of Ohio. ... *M. Doolady, New York.* 1863. 8vo, pp. 115. B. 34906

Internal Improvement. *See* [Carey (M.)], No. 10889, *note.*

Internal Improvements in the State of New York. Originally published in the Merchant's Magazine. [n. p. n. d.] 8vo, pp. 34. H. 34907

Internal Relations of the Cities, Towns, Villages, Counties, and States of the Union; or, the Municipalist: ... Second Edition. *New-York: Ross & Tousey* ... 1859. 24mo, pp. (2), vi, 5–302. Portrait. H. 34908

Internal Revenue. Act amendatory of the Internal Revenue Laws and for other Purposes. Approved, March 3, 1863. *Washington.* 1863. 8vo, pp. 23. 34909

An Act to reduce Internal Taxation, ... approved, June 30, 1864; and Acts amendatory thereof, approved, July 13, 1866. [*Washington.* 1866.] 8vo, pp. 75. 34910

... The Internal Revenue Law. Approved, July 13, 1866. An Act to reduce Internal Taxation ... . *New York: Baker, Voorhis & Co.* 1866. 8vo, pp. 81. B. 34911

Internal Revenue Law as it affects Savings Banks in California. *San Francisco.* 1870. 8vo. 34912

Internal Revenue—Report of the Commissioner of Internal Revenue on the Operations of the Internal Revenue System for the year ending June 30, 1863. *Washington: Government Printing Office.* 1864. 8vo, pp. 241. + For 1864. pp. 300. + For 1865. pp. 411. + For 1866. pp. xxiii, 349. + For 1867. pp. 40. 34913

Internal Revenue Statutes now in force; with Notes referring to all Decisions of the Courts and Departmental Rulings, Circulars, and Instructions, reported to October 1, 1870. Edited by Orlando F. Bump. *New York: Baker, Voorhis & Co.* 1870. 8vo, pp. xxi, 404. 34914

Laws of the United States relating to Internal Revenue, comprising the Act of June 30, 1864 ... including the Act of March 26, 1867. ... *Washington.* 1867. 8vo, pp. viii, 166. B. 34915

Report from the Committee of Ways and Means of the House of Representatives, on a Bill to provide, etc., 1862. *Washington.* 1862. 8vo. 34916

Report of the Select Committee on Internal Revenue Frauds, to the House of Representatives, February 25, 1867. *Washington: Government Printing Office.* 1867. 8vo, pp. 283.

The Internal Revenue Recorder and Excise Journal, July, 1865. Vol. I. *New York.* 1865. 4to, pp. 208. B. 34918

Continued as:

Internal Revenue Record and Customs Journal. Vol. II., No. 27. *New York.* 1865. 4to, pp. 208. B. 34919

Internal Tax Bill. A Draft of an Act to provide Internal Revenue, to support the Government ... with ... Remarks by Committee of Boston Board of Trade. *Washington: Henry Polkinhorn, Printer.* 1862. 8vo, pp. vii, 45. H. 34920

The International Art-Union Journal. ... *New-York: Goupil, Vibert & Co.* 1849. 8vo. 34921

International Bridge Company. Memorial to the Legislature of New York. [n. p.] 1858. Folio. S. 34922

International Coinage. I. Report of Senator Sherman. II. Report of Senator Morgan. III. Bill to establish a Uniform Coinage. IV. Report of S. B. Ruggles. [*Washington: Government Printing Office.* 1868.] 8vo, pp. 42. 34923

International Commercial Convention. Proceedings ... in the City of Portland, Me., August 4th and 5th, 1868. Reported by J. M. W. Yerrinton. *Portland: B. Thurston and Company, Printers.* 1868. 8vo, pp. 160. B., H. 34924

International Copyright Association. Meeting of Authors and Publishers ... April 9, 1868, and Organization of the ... Association. *New York: International Copyright Association.* 1868. 8vo, pp. 46. C. 34925

International Exchange. Joint Resolutions of the General Assembly of Florida, etc. *Tallahassee.* 1853. 8vo. 34926

International Exhibition, 1862. Catalogue of Canada Products, etc. With Account of the Eastern Townships of Lower Canada. *London.* 1862. 8vo. 34927

International Exhibition, 1862. Catalogue of the Nova Scotian Department. *Halifax, N. S.: Printed by Jas. Bowes & Sons.* 1862. 8vo, pp. 50. Map. 34928

International Law. War and Peace. *New York: Sinclair Tousey.* [n. d.] 8vo, pp. 10. 34929

International Literary Exchanges, with Documents relating thereto. *Augusta* [*Ga.*] 1857. 8vo, pp. 109. 34930

International Literary Exchanges. Proceedings of a Meeting of the Citizens of the United States in Paris, at the Athenee Royale, March 27, 1843, ... embracing an Address ... by Alexander Vattemare. *Paris.* 1843. 8vo. N. + Proceedings of a Meeting [at] Albany ... November 27, 1847, for ... promoting ... a plan proposed by M. A. Vattemare. *Albany: Printed by C. Van Benthuysen.* 1849. 8vo, pp. 19. B. 34931

The International Monthly Magazine of Literature, Science and Art. Edited by R. W. Griswold. *New York: Stringer and Townsend.* 1850–52. 5 vols., 8vo. N., P. 34932

International Policy. Essays on the Foreign Relations of England. *London: Chapman & Hall.* 1866. 8vo, pp. ix, 603.

International Statistical Congress. Programme of the Fourth Session ... July 16th, 1860 ... . *London: Printed by George Edward Eyre and William Spottiswoode.* 1861. 4to, pp. xix, (1), 548.

International Statistical Congress. Report of the Proceedings of the Fourth Session ... in London, July 16th, 1860 ... . *London.* 1860. 4to, pp. xii, 217. B. 34935

Also: International Statistical Congress at Berlin. VI. Session. ... September 11th, 1863. [S. B. Ruggles'] Report from the United States of America. [*Berlin: Printed by R. Decker.* 1863.] 4to, pp. 8. B.

International Topographical Rail Road Guide between the Atlantic Seaboard and Missouri River. ... *Niagara Falls.* 1856. 32mo, pp. 172. Map. B. 34936

International Tourist Guide ... Information regarding the Principal Routes East and West ... . *Rand, McNally & Co.* ... *Chicago.* [1870.] 18mo, pp. 91. B. 34937

Interoceanic Canal. The Atlantic-Pacific Canal for all Nations; Capital £2,500,000, Preliminary Statement. [n. p.] Folio, pp. (6), 16. 2 Maps. 34938

Delusions Dispelled in regard to Interoceanic Communication; being a Collection of Facts relating to the competing Plans submitted for Public Consideration; viz.: The Inter-Oceanic Canal for all Nations [the Humboldt Line, by the Atrato-Cupica Valleys]; ... *London.* 1854. 8vo, pp. 39. Map. 34939

Report of the Survey and Estimates of the cost of constructing the Inter-Oceanic Ship Canal, from the Harbor of San Juan del Norte, (Greytown,) on the Atlantic, to the Harbor of Brito, on the Pacific, in the State of Nicaragua, Central America, made for the American, Atlantic and Pacific Ship Canal Co., in the Years 1850–51–52. By Orville W. Childs, Chief Engineer. ... *New York: Wm. C. Bryant & Co., Printers.* 1852. 8vo, pp. (2), ii, 153. Maps. 34940

See also Vol. IV., No. 12738.

Inter-Oceanic Railways and Canals. Containing Descriptions and Maps of various proposed Railways and Ship Canals between the Atlantic and Pacific Oceans. *Washington.* 1866. 8vo, pp. 28. 13 Maps. 34941

Sen. Exec. Doc., No. 62, 39th Cong., 1st Sess.

Interposicion de la R. N. de C. A., para al pacifico deseulace de la cuesten politica que se ventila en Nicaragua, 1851. [*Leon.*] 1851. 6 l. 34942

Interrogatorien van Jos. Galloway, onlangs spreeker van de Vergadering van Pensylvanien voor het Lagerhuis, in eene commissie op de Americaansche Papieren. Uit het Engelsch. [*Amsterdam.*] 1781. 8vo, pp. 107. 34943

The first authentic piece in Dutch relating to American affairs, especially the campaigns of Sir William and Lord Howe, etc. *See our* Vol. VII., No. 26427–28.

Interrogatories on Naval Construction. [n. p. n. d.] pp. 3.

L'Intervention française au Mexique, accompagnée de documents inédits et d'un long mémoire adressé par l'empereur Maximilien à l'empereur Napoléon et remis à Paris par l'impératrice Charlotte; précédée d'une préface de Clément Duvernois. *Paris, imp. Labure; lib. Amyot.* [n. d.] 8vo, pp. xvi, 418. 34945

The Intolerants. A Drama. Three First Acts of Things amongst us; as performed at the * * * * with more pefect effect than applause. *Philadelphia: Printed and published for the Purchaser.* 34946

Relates to the celebrated George Fox.

Introduction à l'Histoire de l'Europe, de l'Amerique, l'Afrique, et l'Asie. *Chatelain.* 1735. 2 vols., 12mo. Maps of America.

This interesting work, although containing a body of information in its 930 pages, is a curious instance of a publisher's impudence. The second volume is garnished with a bookseller's catalogue of second-hand books (1700) extending to 140 pages.

Introduction and early Progress. *See* Cotton, No. 17154.

The Introduction of Paper Money involves the Abolishment of Taxation. [n. p. n. d.] 8vo. 34948

Introduction to the History of America. *Philadelphia: Young & M'Culloch.* 1787. 16mo, pp. 208. Map. C. 34949

Introduction to ... Observations. *See* Quebec.

Introduction to the Study of Philosophy, for the use of Pupils, by a Gentleman educated at Yale College. *New London: T. Green.* 1731. 12mo, pp. 31. 34950

Introduction to the Study of Philosophy, with a Catalogue of some of the most valuable Authors necessary to be read. *New London: T. Green.* 1743. 34951

Inventor's National Institute. National Convention. Call of a Convention of Inventors ... to be held in ... Baltimore ... March 6, 1849 ... . *Baltimore: Printed by Sherwood & Co.* 1849. 8vo, pp. 7. H. 34952

Inventory of Property for the Various Defensive Works, &c., &c., &c. [*Richmond.* 1862.] 8vo, pp. 20. 34953

A very scarce confederate document.

El Investigador Mexicano. Tomo I. Num. 1–16. Junio 18 de 1837–Agosto 2 de 1837. *Mexico.* Folio. 34954

No more published.

El Investigador del Peru. *Lima, Imprenta de los huerfanos: por D. Bernardino Ruiz.* 1814. 4to. 34955

Investigacion de los Medios mas opurtunos y Eficaces de estimular a los habitantes del Peru segun la situation social al trabajo mas Ordenado y provechoso *Lima.* 1867. 8vo. 34956

Investigaciones Politico-Ecclesiasticas Jurisdiccion Ecclesiastica. *Lima.* 1827. 34957

An Investigation and Exposure of the Management of the Home for Little Wanderers, and the Benevolent Operations of the Rev. Wm. C. Van Meter. [*New York.* 1862.] 8vo, pp. 16.

Investigation into the Fifteen Gallon Law of Massachusetts ... Jan. 29 and closed Feb. 20, 1839, upon the Memorial of Harrison Gray Otis and Others for the Repeal of the Law; with the Arguments of Franklin Dexter & B. F. Hallett ... . *Boston: Printed by J. H. Buckingham.* 1839. 8vo, pp. 111. B. 34959

Investigation of that False, Fabulous and Blasphemous Misrepresentation of Truth set forth by Thomas Paine ... By a Delaware Waggoner [*i. e.* D. Nelson?] 8vo, pp. 192. 34960

Investigation; or a Defence of the Order, Government & Economy of the United Society called Shakers, against sundry Charges & Legislative Proceedings. Addressed to the Political World. By the Society of Believers at Pleasant Hill, Ky. *Lexington: K. Smith & Palmer.* 1828. 12mo, pp. 47. 34961

Investigation, or a Defence of ... the Shakers. *Lexington, Ky.* 1846. 12mo, pp. 104. 34962

Investigation: or Monarchy and Republicanism Analyzed. A Poem. *London: J. Chapman.* 1794. 8vo, pp. 34. 34963

INVESTIGATOR, *pseudon.* The Rebellion: Its Consequences, and the Congressional Committee, denominated the Reconstruction Committee; with their Action. By Investigator. *New Orleans.* 1866. 8vo, pp. 231. B. + [*Ibid.*] pp. 248. Portrait.

Invitation Sérieuse aux Habitants des Illinois. [*Philadelphie.* 1772.] 8vo, pp. 15. P. 34965

A rare, curious, and valuable tract. Signed "H. des Kaskaskia."

INVISIBLE SAM, *pseudon.* Despotism; or the Last Days of the American Republic. By Invisible Sam. *New York: Hall & Wilson.* 1856. 12mo, pp. 463. 34966

Io Triumphe! A Poem upon Adm. Vernon. By an Undergraduate of Jesus College, Oxford. [n. p.] 1741. 4to. 34967

Relates to his victories in America.

Ioernael.|ofte.|Voyagie vande Groenlants-|Vaerders, Namelijck vande Seven Matrosz. die|Ghebleven waren op het Eylant genaemt Mau-|ritius om op het selfde Eylant te overwinteren, oock om|te besien hoe hem dit Lant toe soude draghen,|den gheheelen Winter.|Noch hebt ghy hier by, de Beschrivinghe van haer handel,| ende wandel, oock wat sy gehoort ende gesien hebben, als Beeren,|Wal-visschen ende meer andere Zeegedrochten, alles perfecktelijcken|Beschreven, tot de tijt hares Overlijdens toe.|*Tot Rotterdam.*|*By Abraham Nering, Boeckvercooper, by de Roode|Bruggbe, Op het Zeeusche Veer, in de Druckerije.*|*Anno* 1634.| 4to, pp. (2), 44. 34968

Concerning this rare piece *see* Tiele, p. 275.

IOOR (W.) The Battle of the Eutaw Springs, and Evacuation of Charleston; or the Glorious 14th of December, 1782. A National Drama, in Five Acts. By William Ioor ... . *Charleston: For the Author.* 1807. 8vo, pp. 59. BA. 34969

IOOR. Independence; or, Which do you like best, the Peer or the Farmer? A Comedy. By William Ioor. *Charleston.* 1805. 8vo. 34970

IOWA—*Agriculture.* Report of the ... Iowa State Agricultural Society, for 1853. *Des Moines.* 1854. Continued annually.

Also: Addresses ... at the Opening of the Agricultural College, March 17, 1869. *Davenport, Iowa.* 1869. 8vo, pp. 47.—Plan of Organization of the Iowa State Agricultural College ... October 21, 1868. ... *Des Moines.* 1868. 8vo, pp. 24.—Report and Proceedings of the State Agricultural Society at Fairfield, 1855.—Report of the Secretary of the Iowa State Horticultural Society for ... 1868. ... *Des Moines: F. M.*

Mills, State Printer. 1869. 8vo, pp. 134.—Report of the State Board of Agriculture. 1868. 8vo.—Report of the Secretary of the Iowa State Agricultural Society, for ... 1868. ... *Des Moines: F. M. Mills, State Printer.* 1869. 8vo, pp. 501. H.

The Annals of the State Historical Society of Iowa. Issued by the Committee of Publication, with the assistance of the Librarian. *Iowa City: Jerome & Duncan, Printers.* 1863. 8vo.

Continued as:

The Annals of Iowa: A Quarterly Publication by the State Historical Society, at Iowa City, July, 1864. Edited by the Corresponding Secretary. *Davenport, Iowa: Luse, Lane & Co.* [n. d.] 8vo. + October, 1864. Edited by Theodore S. Parvin. [*Ibid.* n. d.] Vols. I.–II. pp. 384; III.–V. pp. 385-972. Portraits. Continued. B. 34973

Also: Biennial Report of the Executive Committee, of the Iowa State Historical Society; to the Governor ... . *Des Moines, Iowa: John Teesdale, State Printer.* 1860. 8vo, pp. 14. Continued. H.

Biennial Message, delivered to the Iowa General Assembly ... by Governor S. J. Kirkwood, ... January 14, 1862. *Des Moines: F. W. Palmer, State Printer.* 1862. 8vo, pp. 19. Continued. H.

Biennial Report of the Iowa State Librarian ... January, 1860. *Des Moines, Iowa: John Teesdale, ... Printer.* 1860. 8vo, pp. 10.

Census. The Census Returns of the different Counties ... for 1856 ... *Iowa City: Crum & Boye, Printers.* 1857. 8vo, pp. 426. Tables. B. 34976

Also: The Census ... for 1859 ... *Des Moines: John Teesdale, ... Printer.* 1859. 8vo, pp. 95. Table. + For 1867. *Des Moines: F. W. Palmer, State Printer.* 1867. 8vo, pp. 250. + For 1869 ... *Des Moines: State Printer.* 1869. 8vo. C.

Choice Farming Lands 1,000,000 Acres, for Sale ... by the Iowa Railroad Land Company ... . *Cedar Rapids, Iowa.* 1870. 8vo, pp. 37. Map. H. 34977

Churches. Minutes of the General Association, June, 1855; with the Constitution. *Boston.* 1855. 8vo. S. + June, 1856. *Burlington, Iowa.* [n. d.] 8vo, pp. 18. Continued. H. 34978

Minutes of the Iowa Baptist State Convention, October 8–10, 1859. ... *Chicago: Church, Goodman & Cushing ... Printers.* 1860. 8vo, pp. 32. H. 34979

Minutes of the ... Annual Session of the Iowa Annual Conference of the Methodist Episcopal Church, ... 1843. [n. p. n. d.] 12mo. 34980

Constitution for the State of Iowa, Adopted in Convention, May 18, 1846. *Iowa City.* 1846. 8vo. 34981

The Debates of the Constitutional Convention, 1857. W. B. Lord, Reporter. *Davenport: Luse, Lane & Co.* 1857. 8vo, pp. ii, 1096, 103. C. 34982

Journal of the Constitutional Convention, 1857. *Muscatine: J. Mahin.* 1857. 12mo, pp. 406. C. 34983

A Description of Central Iowa, with especial reference to Polk County and Des Moines, the State Capital, together with Eight adjacent Counties. *Des Moines,* ... 1858. 8vo, pp. 32. S.

Education. Addresses and Discourse at the Inauguration of the Rev. George F. Magoun, ... as President of Iowa College, July 19, 1865. *Chicago: Horton & Leonard, Printers.* 1865. 8vo, pp. 60, (1). H. 34985

Also: Catalogue of the Officers and Students of Iowa College ... 1856–57. *Davenport: A. P. Luse & Co. ... Printers.* 1856. 12mo, pp. 21.—Second Annual Catalogue of the Officers and Students of Iowa Conference Seminary ... July 12, 1855. *Rock Island, Ill.* 1855. 8vo, pp. 16. H.

Educational Laws of ... Iowa passed by the Board of Education at its first and second sessions, and by the General Assembly, at its Eighth Regular Session. *Des Moines, Iowa: John Teesdale, State Printer.* 1860. 8vo, pp. 103. H. 34986

Journal of the Board of Education, December, 1858. *Des Moines.* 1858. 8vo. 34987

Report of the Commissioners of Revision of the School Laws, under the Act of the General Assembly, July 14, 1856. 8vo. S.

Report of the Secretary of the Board of Education ... to the Board ... and the ... General Assembly ... . *Des Moines.* 1860. 8vo, pp. 67. 34989

Also: Report ... at its Third Biennial Session ... December 2, 1861. *Des Moines: F. W. Palmer, ... Printer.* 1861. 8vo, pp. 77, Appendix, 119, (1). 2 Plates H.

Biennial Report ... of the Superintendent of Public Instruction. *Iowa City: Mahony & J. B. Dorr, State Printers.* 1854. 8vo, pp. 38. Continued. 34990

Also: Report of the State Commissioners on the Affairs of the Superintendent of Public Instruction. *Des Moines: John Teesdale, State Printer.* 1858. 8vo, pp. 43. H.

Iowa Institute of Science and Arts. Celebration of the Humboldt Centennial and Opening of the Iowa Institute of Science

and Arts, at Dubuque, September 14th, 1869. *Dubuque.* 1869. 8vo, pp. 56. H. 34991

Iowa Instructor and School Journal. *Des Moines.* 1858. 8vo. Continued. 34992

STATE UNIVERSITY OF IOWA. Plan of Organization and Course of Studies adopted ... June 28th, 1860. *Iowa City.* 1860. 8vo, pp. 28. H. 34993

Also: Catalogue of the State University of Iowa, for ... 1860–1. *Iowa City: Jerome & Duncan, Printers.* 1861. 8vo, pp. 25. Continued. H.—First Circular ... September 1, 1855. [*Iowa City:*] *Sylvester, Harrison & Brother, Printers.* [1855.] 8vo. H.—Report of Trustees for 1859. *Des Moines.* 1859. 8vo.

IOWA UNIVERSITY. Catalogue of the Officers and Students for 1856–7. *Des Moines.* 1857. 8vo. Continued. 34994

Also: First Annual Announcement of the Medical Department of the University of Iowa, Iowa City, I. *Andrew.* 1848. 16mo, pp. 8. Continued.

IOWA WESLEYAN UNIVERSITY. Addresses delivered upon the Installation of Rev. Lucien W. Berry, D.D., as President of the Iowa Wesleyan University, July 2, A.D. 1856. ... *Mount Pleasant: Elliott & Mehaffy ... Printers.* 1856. 8vo, pp. 37. H. 34995

Iowa Institution for the Education of the Blind. Fourth Biennial Report ... January 10, 1860. *Iowa City.* 1860. 8vo, pp. 16. Continued. H. 34996

Iowa Institution for the Education of the Deaf and Dumb. Fourth Biennial Report ... . *Iowa City.* 1861. 8vo, pp. 32. Continued. H. 34997

School Laws of Iowa: compiled by James D. Eads, Superintendent of Public Instruction. [n. p.] 1855. 8vo, pp. 96.

Also: School Law of Iowa. *Des Moines.* 1858. 8vo.

Finances. Report of the Auditor of the State to the ... General Assembly ... November 7, 1859. *Des Moines: John Teesdale, State Printer.* 1860. 8vo, pp. 54. Continued. H. 34999

Geology. Report on the Geological Survey of the State of Iowa: embracing the Results of Investigations made during Portions of the Years 1855, 56 & 57. By James Hall, State Geologist; J. D. Whitney, Chemist and Mineralogist. ... [n. p.] 1858. Vol. I., Part I.; Geology. 8vo, pp. xv, (1), 472, (1), Appendix, 4, Index, 4. 3 Maps. Part II.; Palæontology. pp. (2), 473–724, Index, 3. 29 Plates, Description of Plates, pp. 30. B.

State Geological Survey of Iowa. Preliminary Notice of New Genera and Species of Fossils. By Charles Abiathar White and Orestes Henry St. John. [*Iowa City.*] 1867. 8vo, pp. 3.

Geological Survey. First and Second Annual Report of Progress by the State Geologist [C. A. White], and the Assistant [O. H. St. John], and Chemist [G. Hinrichs], on the Geological Survey of the State of Iowa. Together with the Substance of Popular Letters contributed to the Newspapers of the State during the Years 1866 and 1867 ... . *Des Moines: F. W. Palmer, State Printer.* 1868. 8vo, pp. 284. B., C., H. 35002

Report on the Geological Survey of the State of Iowa, to the Thirteenth General Assembly, January, 1870, containing Results of Examinations and Observations made within the Years 1866, 1867, 1868, and 1869. By Charles A. White, M.D. Geological Corps: Charles A. White, State Geologist. Orestes H. St. John, Assistant. Rush Emery, Chemist. *Des Moines: Mills & Co.* 1870. 2 vols., 4to, pp. viii, 391; viii, 443. 17 Plates, 2 Maps. B., BA., H. 35003

Hollanders in Iowa. *See* Vol. VIII., No. 32520.

Inaugural Address, of Ralph P. Lowe ... to the Seventh General Assembly ... *Des Moines, Iowa: J. Teesdale, State Printer.* 1858. 8vo, pp. 14. H. 35004

Inaugural Address ... to the ... General Assembly ... by Governor S. J. Kirkwood, ... January 15, 1862. *Des Moines: F. W. Palmer, State Printer.* 1862. 8vo, pp. 12. H. 35005

Inaugural Address delivered to the Tenth General Assembly ... by Governor William M. Stone. *Des Moines: F. W. Palmer, State Printer.* 1864. 8vo, pp. 20. Continued. H. 35006

Insurance. First Annual Report of the Insurance Department. Fire Insurance: 1868–1869. *Des Moines: State Printer.* 1870. 8vo. Continued. C. 35007

Iowa Hospital for the Insane. First Biennial Report ... December, 1861. *Des Moines: F. W. Palmer, State Printer.* 1862. 8vo, pp. 62. Continued. B., H. 35008

Report of the Joint Committee, appointed ... to investigate the Affairs of the Iowa Hospital for the Insane. *Des Moines: John Teesdale, State Printer.* 1860. 8vo, pp. 52. Table. H.

Iowa Land Company; Brief Circular relating to the Counties of Clinton, Cedar and Linn ... *Chicago, Ill.* 1858. 8vo, pp. 18.

Iowa: The Home for Immigrants, being a Treatise on the Resources of Iowa, and giving useful Information with regard to the State, for the benefit of Immigrants and others. Published by order of the Iowa Board of Immigration. *Des Moines: Mills & Co.* 1870. 8vo, pp. 96. 35011

Also in the Netherlandish and German languages.

Journal of the House of Representatives, First Session of the General Assembly. 1848. *Kesauqua.* 1848. 8vo. Continued.

Journal of the Senate. First Session of the General Assembly. 1848. *Iowa City.* 1848. 8vo. Continued. 35013

Laws. Acts and Resolutions passed at the First Session of the General Assembly, convened at Iowa City, Nov. 30, 1846. *Iowa City.* 1847. 8vo. C. 35014

Continued as:

The Code of Iowa, passed at the Session of the General Assembly of 1850–51, and approved February 5, 1851. *Iowa City.* 1851. 8vo, pp. 685. C. 35015

The Code of Iowa. [Edited] by Darwin. 1857. 8vo.

Laws of the Territory of Iowa, 1838–39 [First Session of the Legislative Assembly], to 1841. *Burlington.* 1840–41. 8vo. Continued. C. 35017

Local Laws of the Territory of Iowa, 1842–43. *Iowa City.* 1843. 8vo. C. 35018

Revision of 1860, containing all the Statutes of a general nature, of the State of Iowa, which are now in force, or to be in force, as the result of the Legislation of the Eighth General Assembly. *Des Moines.* 1860. 8vo. 35019

Statute Laws of the Territory, enacted at the First Session of the Legislative Assembly, 1838–9. *Dubuque.* 1839. 8vo.

Legislative Documents compiled by order of the General Assembly, 1857. [Sen. Doc.], 1860. *Iowa City.* 1857. 8vo. Continued. 35021

Proceedings of the Grand Lodge of Iowa, ... of Free and Accepted Masons, ... A.L. 5844 to A.L. 5858, Inclusive. *Muscatine.* 1858. 2 vols., 8vo. Continued. 35022

Also: Constitution ... of the Grand Lodge of Iowa; also, the Ancient Constitution. *Muscatine, Iowa.* 1854. 8vo, pp. 6.—Transactions of the Grand Chapter of the State of Iowa, from its Organization, June 8, 1854, to ... October 17, 1867, Inclusive ... *Iowa.* 1868. 8vo, pp. 613, Index, v, Appendix, 27. Continued. BA.

Memorial of the Twelfth General Assembly of Iowa, to Congress, relative to Water Communication between the Atlantic and Mississippi. *Des Moines.* 1868. 8vo. 35023

Message of Governor Abram A. Hammond, January 11, 1861. 8vo, pp. 13. 35024

Also: Special Message of Governor Kirkwood, May 21, '61. 8vo, pp. 7.

Military. Report of the Adjutant General of the State of Iowa ... for the Year ending December 31, 1861. *Des Moines: F. W. Palmer, State Printer.* 1861. 8vo, pp. 494. Continued.

Report of the Adjutant General and Acting Quartermaster General of Iowa ... January 1, 1863. *Des Moines: F. W. Palmer, State Printer.* 1863. 2 vols., 8vo, pp. xxviii, 1080; (2), 910. + January 1, 1863, to January 11, 1864. [*Ibid.*] 1864. 8vo, pp. xliv, 799. + January 11, 1864, to January 1, 1865. [*Ibid.*] 1865. 8vo, pp. xx, 1502. H. + January 1, 1865, to January 1, 1866. [*Ibid.*] 1866. 8vo, pp. xx, 536. Continued. H. 35026

Report of the Commissioners ... to investigate the Several State Offices, for ... 1858 and 1859. *Des Moines: John Teesdale, State Printer.* 1860. 8vo, pp. 104. H. 35027

Report of Wm. C. Drake, Commissioner, of the Des Moines River Improvement, to the General Assembly of ... Iowa. *Des Moines, Iowa: John Teesdale, State Printer.* 1860. 8vo, pp. 8.

Northern Iowa. By a Pioneer. Containing Valuable Information for Emigrants. Published by the Dubuque Emigrant Association. *Dubuque: W. A. Adams, Printer.* 1858. 8vo, pp. 40. + Second Edition. [*Ibid.*] H. 35029

Orphans' Home of Industry, near Iowa City. *New-York.* 1858. 12mo. 35030

Also: General Report ... June 1st, 1861, to October 1, 1862. *New-York: John A. Gray, Printer.* [n. d.] 8vo, pp. 24.—Report of the Proceedings of the Second Annual Meeting of the Iowa Soldiers' Orphans Home ... 7th & 8th of June, 1865. *Des Moines.* 1865. 8vo, pp. 29. H.—Report of the Officers of the Iowa Soldiers Orphans Home, ... November 4, 1867. *Des Moines: F. W. Palmer, State Printer.* 1868. 8vo, pp. 35. B.

Railroads. Burlington and Mississippi Rail Road in Iowa. Exhibit of Condition. *New York.* 1856. 8vo. 35031

Report of the Register of the State Land Office, November 16, 1863. J. A. Harney, Register. *Des Moines: F. W. Palmer, ... Printer.* 1863. 8vo, pp. 106. Continued. H. 35032

Report of the Secretary of State, in Relation to the Criminal Returns, of ... Iowa. For the Years 1860–1. *Des Moines: F. W. Palmer, State Printer.* 1862. 8vo, pp. 58. Continued. H.

Report of the Treasurer of State ... November 7, 1859. *Des Moines, Iowa: John Teesdale, State Printer.* 1859. 8vo, pp. 14. Continued. H. 35034

Also: Biennial Report of the State Treasurer, Nov., 1867. *Des Moines.* 1867. 8vo.

Report of the Commissioners ... to investigate the Affairs of the Iowa Penitentiary. *Des Moines, Iowa: John Teesdale, State Printer.* 1859. 8vo, pp. 36. 2 Tables. H. 35035

Report of the Warden of the Iowa Penitentiary to the Legislature, Nov. 30, 1856. 8vo. S. 35036

Report of the Iowa Sanitary Commission from its Organization Oct. 13th, 1861, to the Close of its Service ... Dec. 1st, 1863. ... *Davenport: Luse, Lane & Co.* 1864. 8vo, pp. 35, (1). H.

Special Message delivered to the House of Representatives of the State of Iowa, by Governor S. J. Kirkwood ... February 6, 1862. *Des Moines: F. W. Palmer, State Printer.* 1862. 8vo, pp. 20. H. 35038

Special Message of the Governor of Iowa to the ... General Assembly, in Reference to the ... Improvements of the Fox and Wisconsin Rivers, February 9, 1870. *Des Moines: F. M. Mills, State Printer.* 1870. 8vo, pp. 8. Map. H. 35039

Original Hymns in the Iowa Language. 1843. 18mo, pp. 62.

IOWA CITY, *Iowa.* Charter and Laws of Iowa City, passed 1853–9, with List of Officers, etc. *Iowa City.* 1859. 8vo. S.

IOWA CO., *Wis.* Constitution of the Iowa County Agricultural Society, and List of Premiums for the Eighth Annual Fair, ... September 23d, 24th, and 25th, 1863. *Dodgeville: R. Crosby & Co., ... Printers.* 1863. 8vo, pp. 16. Continued. H. 35042

IPSWICH, *Mass.* Annual Report of the Receipts, Expenditures, &c. ... for ... 1868. *Salem.* [1868.] 8vo, pp. 19. Continued. H. 35043

Concise History of the First Church ... in Ipswich, from its Formation, A.D. 1634, to A.D. 1862. ... with the Rules of Order and of Discipline: ... *Boston: Wright & Potter, Printers.* 1862. 12mo, pp. 21. H. 35044

Ipswich Seminary for Female Teachers: Catalogue ... 1828. *Ipswich: Printed by John H. Harris, Jr.* 1828. 12mo, pp. 8. Continued. H., S. 35045

A Plain Narrative of the Proceedings which caused the Separation of a Number of aggrieved Brethren from the Second Church in Ipswich: or A Relation of the Cause which produced the Effects that are exhibited in the Reverend Mr. Pickering's late Print, Intitled, A bad Omen to the Churches. ... *Boston: Printed by Kneeland and Green.* 1747. 8vo, pp. 16. BA., W.

The pretended Plain Narrative convicted of Fraud and Partiality. Or, a Letter From the Second Church in Ipswich, to their separated Brethren, ... To which is prefixed a ... Letter of the late Rev. Mr. Pickering's ... Annexed the Result of an Ecclesiastical Council ... . *Boston: Printed by S. Kneeland and T. Green.* 1748. 4to, pp. 38. B., BA., H. 35047

The Chebacco Narrative Rescued. *See* Vol. IV., No. 13592, *also* Marcus, *pseudon*, Massachusetts, *and* [Parsons (Theophilus)].

Report of the School Committee ... for ... 1851. ... *J. F. Kimball, Printer, Lynn News Office.* 1851. 8vo, pp. 16. H.

IRARRAZABUL (M. A. B. de S.) Exposicion de mi dictamen en el compromiso y consulta legal que nos encargaron los SS. hijos del difunto S. D. Miguel Antonio Bravo de Saravia Irarrazabul sobre si debian reconocer como subsistente el mayorazgo de la casa de Bravo de Saravin que poseia el difunto y legal la posesion en que se halla el hijo primojenito. *Santiago.* 1835. 8vo. 35049

IRASUSTA Y URANGA (J. M. O.) ¿ Para que sirven los Frayles en el Mundo? Sermon panegirico que el dia 25 de Setiembre de 1814 dixo Fr. Jose Maria Orruño Irasusta y Uranga. *Mexico.* 1815. 4to, pp. 34. 35050

IRASUSTA Y URANGA. Sermon panegirico moral predicado en la Santa Iglesia Metropolitana de Mexico la Dominica cuarta de Adviento de Año de 1813, en la funcion anual que de orden del supremo consejo de castilla se celebra, para desagraviar a Jesu-

cristo Sacramentado de las injurias con que fue insultado por los Tropas Alemanas, por el R. P. Pred. Fr. Jose Maria Orruño Irasusta y Uranga. *Mexico.* 1814. 4to, pp. (10), 27. 35051

A very curious pamphlet.

IRASUSTA Y URANGA. Sermon panegirico moral, predicado en esta Santa metropolitana iglesia de México, el dia 2 de febrero de 1814, en la festividad de la Purificacion de la Santisima Virgen; por el R. P. F. Jose Maria Orruño Irasusta y Uranga. *Mexico: Imprente de D. José Maria de Benavente.* [n. d.] 4to, pp. 6, 25.

IREDELL (James). *See* North Carolina.

IRELAND (J.) A Funeral Panegyric on George Washington, 22 February, 1800, in the United Churches of St. Paul's and Christ Church, Baltimore. By Rev. John Ireland. *Baltimore.* 1802. 8vo. 35053

IRELAND. Record of Proceedings of a Board of Clergy Canonically constituted for trying the Truth of Certain Charges against the Rev. John Ireland, of Brooklyn. *New York.* 1810. 8vo. 35054

IRELAND. A Second Solemn Appeal to the Church: containing Remarks and Strictures on the late violent Proceedings of a Pretended Ecclesiastical Court against the author. By the Rev. John Ireland ... . *Brooklyn: Printed by Thomas Kirk.* 1811. 8vo, pp. 74. BA., H., M. 35055

IRELAND (J. B.) Wall-Street to Cashmere. A Journal of Five Years in Asia, Africa, and Europe; comprising Visits, during 1851, 2, 3, 4, 5, 6, ... By John B. Ireland. *New York: S. A. Rollo & Co.* 1859. 8vo, pp. xviii, 13–531. 73 Plates, Map.

[IRELAND (Joseph N.)] Fifty Years of a Play-goers Journal, or Annals of the New York Stage from A.D. 1798 to A.D. 1848. With Biographical Sketches of all the Principal Performers. *New York.* [n. d.] 3 parts, 12mo. 35057

All published, afterwards amplified into:

IRELAND. Records of the New York Stage, from 1750 to 1860. By Joseph N. Ireland. *New York: T. H. Morrell.* 1866. 2 vols., 8vo, pp. iv, 663; (2), 746. B. 35058

Two hundred copies printed in 8vo, sixty copies in 4to, and three on drawing paper in 4to.

Ireland and America; a Letter to the O'Donoghue, M.P. By an American Citizen. *New York: P. O'Shea.* 1862. 8vo, pp. 18. 35059

Ireland and America, via Galway. *London.* 1852. 8vo.

IRELAND. Address of Natives of Ireland to American Friends of Freedom on the Alien and Sedition Laws. [n. p.] 1800. 8vo.

Address of the Twelve United Colonies of North America, by their Representatives in Congress, to the People of Ireland. *Philadelphia: Printed by W. and T. Bradford.* 1775. 8vo, pp. 10. + *Norwich: Printed by Robertson and Trumbull.* 1775. 8vo.

See also Vol. I., No. 403.

Irenicvm; | or, an | Essay | Towards a Brotherly | Peace & Vnion, | Between those of the Congregational and Presbyterian Way; | Shewing out of the most Learned and Renowned Di- | vines of the Congregational Way, that their Positions | Concerning 1. Church Matters and Members. 2. Church Constitution and Form. 3. Church State. 4. Church Officers and Ordination. 5. Church Government and Censures. 6. Church Combinations and Synods. 7. Communion with and Separation from Churches. Are sufficient for the establishing a firme and lasting | Peace between them and the Presbyterians. | Drawn up and published by | Discipulus De Tempore Junior. | In pursuance of the good design begun at the Savoy, where it was agreed, and declared, That such Reforming Churches as | consist of Persons sound in the Faith, and of conversation be- | coming the Gospel, ought not to refuse the communion of each o- | ther, so far as may consist, With their own principles respe- | ctively, though they walk not in all things according to the same | Rules of Church Order, Canon 29. | *London, Printed for Nathanael Webb and William Grantham, | at the black Bear in Pauls Church-yard, near the little North-door.* 1659. | 4to, pp. (14), 75. 35063

The larger portion relates to the religious affairs and squabbles in New England; Baptism, &c. Mr. Cotton's, Mr. Hook's, and Mr. Shepard's books are frequently quoted.

[IRHOVEN VAN DAM (W. van).] Missive aan ... R. M. van Goens, betreffende den schryver van zeker Politiek Vertoog. *Rotterdam.* 1781. 8vo, pp. 58. + 1782. 8vo. 35064

A vehement pamphlet, by W. van Irhoven van Dam, against the political deduction.

IRIARTE (F.) Manifesto a los pueblos de la republica Mejicana. Por F. Iriarte. *Méjico.* 1829. 8vo, pp. 46. 35065

IRIARTE (F. S.) Defensa pronunciada ante el Gran Jurado el 21 de Marzo de 1850, por Francisco Suarez Iriarte, acusado en 8 de Agosto de 1848 por el Secretario de Relaciones en Aquella fecha, de los crimines de sedicion contra el Gobierno de Querétaro é infidentia contra la patría, en sus actos como Presidente de la Asamblea municipal de la ciudad y Distrito de Mexico. *Mexico.* 1850. 8vo, pp. 147. Map. 35066

IRIARTE (T.) Glorias Argentinas y Recuerdos historicos. 1818–1825. Por el General Tomas Iriarte. ... *Buenos Aires: Libreria de la Victoria.* 1858. 8vo, pp. (4), v, 243, (2). C., H.

IRIARTE. Memoria sobre immigracion y linea de fronteras sobre los Indios salvajes. Por el General Iriarte. *Buenos Aires.* 1852. 4to, pp. 36. 35068

IRIBARREN (Guillermo). Pensamientos sobre Caminos. *Carâcas.* 1847. 4to, pp. 142. 35069

IRION (L. F. B.) Indagaciones sobre las antiguedades mexicanas; pruebas de la civilizacion adelantada de los Mexicanos en el xv siglo. *Mexico.* 1841. 8vo, pp. 35. 35070

The Iris, or Literary Messenger. ... Volume I. *New-York.* M DCCC XL–XLI. 8vo. N. 35071

El Irís. Periódico critico y literario, por Linati, Galli y Heredia. *Mexico.* 1826. 2 vols., 8vo. 35072

"C'est tout ce qu'il a été publié de ce journal critique et littéraire."—ANDRADE.

El Iris. Periódico quincenal de literatura. Director: Agustin de Vedia. [Abril, 1864–Julio, 1865.] *Montevideo.* 1864–65. 4to, pp. 102. 35073

All published.

L'Iris Américaine. Feuille Hebdominaire. Quæ colliget, spargit. Tome premier. *Au Port-au-Prince: Chez Guillot. Imprimeur brêveté du Roi à l'exclusion de tous autres.* MDCCLXIX. 12mo, pp. 480. 35074

According to the advertisement this work was published weekly. The Epistle Dedicatory to Madame D* C* is signed D*** D***, ci-devant Officier d'Infantrie.

Iris de Nueva España. [n. p. n. d.] 35075

See Ternaux's "Bibliothèque Américaine," No. 443, *note.*

IRISARRI (A. J. de). Carta de Antonio Jose de Irisarri a los EE. del Mercurio de Valparaiso. *Santiago de Chile.* 1833. Sm. 4to, pp. 8. 35076

IRISARRI. Defensa de los Tratados de Paz de Pancarpata por Antonio Jose de Irisarri hecha en Arequipa. *Arequipa.* 1838. Sm. 4to. 35077

IRISARRI. Dialogos segundo, tercero quinto e sexto sobre la defensa del tratado de Pancarpata contestando al Arancon. N. 401, 402, 404, 405. *Arequipa.* 1838. Sm. 4to. 35078

IRISARRI. Emprestito de Chile por Antonio Jose de Irisarri. *Santiago de Chile.* 1833. Sm. 4to. 35079

These pieces elicited the following replies: Refutacion del Folleto escrito en Arequipa por Don Antonio Jose de Irisarri en defensa del tratado de Paz de Pancarpata. *Santiago de Chile.* 1838. 12mo.—Revista de los escritos publicados en Chile contra los Tratados de Paz de Pancarpata, por Antonio Jose de Irisarri. *Arequipa.* 1838. Sm. 4to.

IRISARRI. Historia critica del asesinato cometido en la persona del Gran Mariscall de Ayacucho. Por Antonio José de Irisarri. *Bogotá: Jose A. Gualla.* MDCCCXLVI. 8vo, pp. 367, Appendice, lxxx, Cuadro sinoptico, 1 l., Erratas, 1 l. + *Carâcas.* 1846. 8vo, pp. xlv, 266. 35080

Also: Impugnacion a los Articulos publicados en el Mercurio de Valparaiso sobre la Campagna del ejercito restaurador por Antonio Jose de Irisarri. *Arequipa.* 1838. Sm. 4to.

IRISARRI (F. de). Vida Admirable y Heroycas Virtudes del Ven. Padre Juan de Alloza, por Fermin de Irisarri. *Madrid.* 1715. 4to. 35081

This life of the celebrated Alloza, a native of Lima (1595), contains much information relative to the history of Peru.

IRISH (D.) Observations on a living and effectual Testimony against Slavery; introduced with some Remarks upon Excess and Superfluity, recommended to the Consideration of the Society of Friends. By David Irish. *New York: For the Author.* 1836. 12mo, pp. 30. 35082

Also: Self-Justification; Self-Condemnation. A Dialogue. ... *New York: For the Author.* 1836. 12mo, pp. 17.

Address of the Central Executive Committee of Irish Citizens, at Washington, D. C., to their Countrymen throughout the United States. *Washington, D. C.: McGill & Witherow, Printers.* 1866. 8vo, pp. 8. H. 35083

The Irish-Office-Hunter-oniad. By Blarney O'Democrat. *New York.* 1839. 12mo. 35084

A keen satire on the Irishmen in America.

The Irish Patriot. Daniel O'Connell's Legacy to Irish Americans. *Philadelphia.* [n. d.] 8vo, pp. 32. 35085

Irishmen! *See* [Howe (*Dr.* Estes)], Vol. VIII., No. 33288.

IRMINGER (C.) The Arctic Current around Greenland. *London.* 1856. 8vo. Map. 35086

Die Irokesische Jungfrau. Eine Erzählung aus der Kirchengeschichte. Nach dem Französischen bearbeitet von K. Deutschmann. *Aachen: Kneuertz.* 1846. 12mo. Plate. 35087

IRONY (S.), *pseudon.* Fashion, or the Art of making Breeches: an Heroi-Satiri Didactic Poem. By Solomon Irony. *Philadelphia.* 1800. 8vo, pp. 19. 35088

IRON (N. C.) Hearts Forever; or, The Old Dominion Battle-Grounds. A Tale of 1782. By N. C. Iron. *New York: Beadle & Co.* 1867. 12mo, pp. 100. 35089

IRON GRAY, *pseudon.* The Gospel of Slavery, etc. By "Iron Gray." *New York.* [n. d.] 35090

IRON. Address and Report upon the Practicability of Manufacturing Railroad Iron at or near Saint Louis, Missouri. ... *St. Louis: R. P. Studley and Co., Printers.* 1860. 8vo, pp. 34.

Also: Charter and By-Laws of the Great Western Iron Company; also, an Act to encourage the Manufacture of Iron in ... Pennsylvania. [n. p. n. d.] 8vo, pp. 16.

Iron Clad Ships. Letter from the Secretary of the Navy to the Committee on Naval Affairs, in relation to Iron-Clad Ships, Ordnance, etc. *Washington.* 1869. 8vo, pp. 6. 35092

House of Representatives, Miscellaneous Document, No 82, 37th Cong., 2d Sess.

Proceedings of the Iron Convention, ... at Pittsburgh, November 21st, 22d and 23d, 1849. *Pittsburgh.* 1849. 8vo, pp. 14, (1).

Iron Dike. Tracts concerning the Reclamation of Swamp and Marsh Lands, and Strengthening of River Levees, etc. *New York.* [n. d.] 8vo. 35094

Iron is King. Hollidaysburg a suitable site for the National Foundry and Armory, and for all kinds of Iron Manufacture. *Pittsburgh: W. S. Haven.* 1862. 8vo, pp. 8. 35095

Exhibit of the Conditions and Prospects of the Iron Mountain Railroad Company ... March, 1855. *Rochester.* 1855. 8vo. S.

Also: Annual Report, 1855. *Rochester.* 1856.—Memorial of the Directors ... to the Legislature of Michigan. *Rochester, N. Y.* 1857. S.

The Iron Platform. 9 Nos. *New York.* 1862–64. 4to. S.

The Iron Resources of Michigan, and General Statistics of Iron: Showing the Rise and Progress of its Manufactures, in the different countries in the world. ... *Detroit: Printed by H. Barns.* 1856. 8vo, pp. 24. H., S. 35098

Proceedings of a Convention of Iron Workers, held at Albany ... 12th ... Dec., 1849. *Albany: For the Convention.* 1849. 8vo, pp. 58, (2). BA., S. 35099

IRONSIDE (J.), *pseudon.* The Truth. No. I. By J. Ironside. *New Haven.* 1819. 8vo, pp. 16. W. 35100

IRONTON, *O.* Memorial to Congress for the establishment of a National Foundry and Gun-Boat Yard at Ironton, Ohio. *Washington: H. Polkinhorn.* 1862. 8vo, pp. 14. 35101

[IROQUOIS.] *See* Chiokvyhikoy, Vol. IV., No. 12816, and for imprint read, *A Philadelphie, Chez W. Roberdson, Imprimeur ordinaire des Colonies du Confedérées.* 1777. 8vo, pp. (2), iv, 111.

Another Tongue brought in, to confess the great Saviour of the World; or, Some Communications of Christianity, put into a Tongue used among the Iroquois Indians in America. And put into the hands of the English and Dutch Traders. To accommodate the Great Intention of communicating the Christian Religion unto the Salvages among whom they may find anything of this language to be intelligible. *Boston: Printed by T. Green.* 1707. 12mo, pp. 16. J.C.B., N. 35103

Sentences in relation to God, Jesus Christ and the Trinity, in the Iroquois, Latin, English and Dutch languages.

Catechisme en Iroquois. *Paris.* 1826. 12mo. 35104

Catechism Iroquois. *Poissy.* 1842. 8vo. 35105

Les deux Amis, Conte Iroquois. *Paris.* 1770. Sm. 8vo.

Curious Indian tale, describing scenery on the Ohio and St. Lawrence.

The Iroquois. *See* [Johnson (*Miss*)].

Iroquois Language. *See* Mohawk Language.

IRVIN (S. M.), *and* HAMILTON (W.) An Ioway Grammar, illustrating the Principles of the Language used by the Ioway, Otoe, and Missouri Indians. By the Rev. S. M. Irvin and William Hamilton. *Ioway and Sac Mission Press.* 1848. 18mo, pp. 152. 35107

Also: An Ioway Primer ... with English Explanations. *Ioway and Sac Mission Press.* 8vo, pp. 17–24.

Irvine (A.) Cause and Effects of Emigration from the Highlands. By A. Irvine. 1802. 35108

Noticed by Sidney Smith in the "Edinburgh Review," I. 61–63.

Irvine (Baptis). On the Commerce of Southern America. A Canal at Darien. By B. Irvine. *Philadelphia.* 1822. P.

Irvine. Strictures on a Voyage to South America, &c. By Baptis Irvine. *Baltimore.* 1820. 8vo. 35110

See Brackenridge (H. M.), Vol. II., No. 7179.

[Irvine.] Traits of Colonial Jurisprudence; or, a Peep at the Trading Inquisition of Curaçao. ... *Baltimore: For the Author.* 1824. 8vo, pp. vi, 6–50. BA. 35111

Also: Address in Support of Mr. Clinton's Election to the Presidency. ... [n. p. n. d.] 8vo. W. — Address to the Patrons of the Whig. 8vo. W.

Irvine. The Case of Baptis Irvine, in a Matter of Contempt of Court. ... By a Gentleman of the Bar. ... *Baltimore: Printed by S. Magill.* 1808. 8vo, pp. 57. BA. 35112

Irving (E.) Statement of the Causes which affect the decrease or increase of the Slave Population in the British Colonies. By Edward Irving. *London.* 1833. 8vo. 35113

[Irving (J. Treat)], *Jr.* The Attorney; or the Correspondence of John Quod. *New-York.* 1853. 12mo. S. 35114

Irving. Hawk Chief: A Tale of the Indian Country. By John T. Irving, Jr. *Philadelphia: Carey, Lea and Blanchard.* 1837. 2 vols., 12mo, pp. viii, 13–246; (2), 8–254. 35115

Irving. Indian Sketches, taken during an Expedition to the Pawnee Tribes. By John T. Irving, ... *Philadelphia: Carey, Lea and Blanchard.* 1835. 2 vols., 12mo, pp. (4), 9–272; 296.

Reprinted in England as:

Irving. Indian Sketches, taken during an Expedition to the Pawnee and other Tribes of American Indians. By John T. Irving, Junior. *London: John Murray.* MDCCCXXXV. 2 vols., post 8vo, pp. xl, 273, Portrait; viii, 301. 35117

This was a Government Expedition in charge of Mr. Elsworth as Commissioner, he was accompanied by Mr. Irving, who in this work gives us the result of his observations. Also: Address before the New York High School for Females, Jan. 21, 1826. .. *New York.* 1826. 8vo. — A Discourse on ... Classical Learning, with a Sketch ... of the Late William Samuel Johnson ... 5th May, 1830. ... *New York: G. & C. & H. Carvill.* 1830. 8vo, pp. 35. — Oration ... On the 4th of July, 1809, before the Tammany Society. ... *New York: Printed by Frank and White.* 1809. 8vo, pp. 23 Also, "Harry Harson," written under the *pseudonym* of John Quod.

Irving (P. M.) The Life and Letters of Washington Irving. By his Nephew, Pierre M. Irving. *New York: G. P. Putnam.* 1862–64. 4 vols., 12mo, pp. 463; 492; 9, 13–403; 450. 5 Portraits. B., BA., H. + [*Ibid.*] 1867. B. 35118

One hundred and ten copies printed on large paper. Reprinted in various editions in England, by Richard Bentley, H. G. Bohn, etc.

Irving (Ralph). Experiments on the Red and Quill Peruvian Bark. *Edinburgh.* 1785. 8vo. 35119

Irving (T.) The Conquest of Florida, by Hernando de Soto. By Theodore Irving ... . *Philadelphia: Carey, Lea & Blanchard.* 1835. 2 vols., 12mo, pp. 290; 302. + *New York: G. P. Putnam.* 1851. 12mo, pp. 457. + *New York: G. P. Putnam & Co.* 1857. 12mo. H. + [*Ibid.*] 1869. 12mo. 35120

A compilation from Garcilaso de la Vega, the English translation of the Portuguese work by a gentleman of Elvas, and Herrera. The English edition is entitled:

Irving. The Conquest of Florida, under Hernando de Soto. By Theodore Irving. ... *London: Edward Churton.* 1835. 2 vols., post 8vo, pp. xii, 296; (2), 315. + *London: Henry G. Bohn.* 1850. Post 8vo, pp. viii, 280. H. 35121

Irving (T.) Remarks upon the Evidence given by Thomas Irving, Esq. on the Slave Trade. *London.* 1791. 8vo. C.

Irving (T. P.) Funeral Discourse on the Death of Gov. Richard Dobbs Spaight ... in Newbern, N. C.; 1862. By Rev. T. P. Irving. *Baltimore: John W. Woods, Printer.* 1859. 12mo, pp. 8. B. 35123

[Irving (Washington).] A Word in Season, touching the Present Misunderstanding in the Episcopal Church. *New York.* 1811. 8vo, pp. 59. M. 35124

[Irving (Washington).] Adventures of Captain Bonneville; or, Scenes beyond the Rocky Mountains of the Far West. *London: Richard Bentley.* 1837. 3 vols., post 8vo. + [*Ibid.*] 1840. + New Edition. *London: George Routledge.* 1855. 12mo, pp. 272. 35125

This is the title to the English edition of *our* No. 35195, *infra*, which title was afterwards adopted, in part, by the American publishers, who finally issued it as:

Irving. The Adventures of Captain Bonneville in the Rocky Mountains and the Far West. Digested from the Journal of Captain B. L. E. Bonneville of the Army of the United States, and illustrated from various other sources, By Washington Irving.

New York. 1847. 2 vols., 12mo, pp. 248; 248. + *New York: G. P. Putnam.* 1849. 12mo, pp. (2), 428. 2 Plates. + [*Ibid.*] 1851. C. + [*Ibid.*] 1867. B. + [*Ibid.*] 1869. 16mo, pp. 496. 2 Plates. 35126

Irving. Abenteuer des Capitain Bonneville ... übertragen von Dr. Ed. Freisleben. *Leipzig: B. Tauchnitz, Jun.* 1837. 3 vols., 8vo. + ... von A. von Treskow. *Quedlinburg: Basse.* 1837. 2 vols., 8vo. 35127

Irving. Lotgevallen en ontmoetingen van Kapitein Bonneville, op zijne avontuurlijke togten aan gene zijde van het klipgebergte van Noord-Amerika. Naar het Engelsch. *Haarlem.* 1838. 2 vols., 8vo. 35128

Irving. Astoria or Anecdotes of an Enterprise beyond the Rocky Mountains. By Washington Irving. *Philadelphia: Carey, Lea, & Blanchard.* 1836. 2 vols., 8vo, pp. 285; 279. Map. BA., H., P. + *New York: G. P. Putnam.* 1849. 12mo, pp. viii, 519. 2 Plates. A. + [*Ibid.*] 1851. + [*Ibid.*] 1867. + [*Ibid.*] 1868. 12mo, pp. xxvi, 649. Plate. B. 35129

Reprinted in London with the following title:

Irving. Astoria; or, Enterprise beyond the Rocky Mountains. By Washington Irving. ... *London: Richard Bentley.* 1836. 3 vols., post 8vo, pp. xvi, 317; ix, 320; vii, 294. + [*Ibid.*] 1839. Fcp 8vo, pp. viii, 440. + *Paris: Galignani & Co.* 1846. 8vo. 35130

See "N. A. Rev.," XLIV. A narration of one of those attempts to found a viceroyalty, in a distant and unexplored territory, which smacks of the romance and chivalric enterprise of the old Spanish adventurers. It was translated into French, German, and Dutch, as follows:

Irving. Voyages dans les Contrées Désertes de l'Amérique du Nord, entrepris pour la fondation du comptoir d'Astoria sur la côte nord-ouest. Par Washington Irving. Traduit de l'Anglois, par P. N. Grolier. *Paris.* 1839. 2 vols., 8vo. + *Paris: Allouard.* 1843. 2 vols., 8vo. 35131

Irving. Astoria, oder die Unternehmung jenseits des Felsengebirges. Aus dem Englischen von A. von Treskow. *Quedlinburg: Basse.* 1837. 2 vols., 8vo. 35132

Irving. Astoria, oder Abenteuer in den Gebirgen und Wäldern von Canada. Aus dem Englischen von Dr. E Brinckmeier. *Braunschweig: G. E. Meyersen.* 1837. 12mo. 35133

Irving. Historia of avontuurlyke Reize naar en over het Klipgebergte van Noord Amerika door J. J. Astor. *Haarlem.* 1837. 2 vols., 12mo. 35134

Irving. Beauties of Washington Irving. With Illustrations by George Cruikshank. *London: Printed by C. Whittingham.* 1835. 12mo. + *London: William Tegg.* [n. d.] 35135

Irving. Biographie der jungen amerikanischen Dichterin Margarethe Miller Davidson. Aus dem Englischen. *Leipzig: F. A. Brockhaus.* 1843. 12mo. 35136

See Davidson (M. M.), Vol. v., No. 18735.

Irving. Biographies and Miscellanies. By Washington Irving. Edited by ... Pierre M. Irving. *New York: G. P. Putnam and Son.* 1869. 8vo, pp. 487. Portrait. B. 35137

[Irving.] A Book of the Hudson. Collected from the various works of Diedrich Knickerbocker. Edited by Geoffrey Crayon. *New York: George P. Putnam.* 1849. 16mo, pp. 115.

[Irving.] The Crayon Miscellany. ... No. I. A Tour on the Prairies. *Philadelphia: Carey, Lea, & Blanchard.* 1835. 12mo, pp. 274. BA. + [*Ibid.*] 1836. + *London.* 1836. 35139

See "N. A. Rev.," XII., 1–28. The two other volumes of this "Miscellany" do not relate to America.

Irving. The Crayon Miscellany, Author's Revised Edition, ... *New York: George P. Putnam.* 1849. 12mo, pp. 379. A. + *New York: Hurd & Houghton.* 1865. 16mo, pp. 441. + *New York: G. P. Putnam* ... . 1867. 12mo, pp. 379. B. + [*Ibid.*] 1869. 16mo, pp. (2), 441. Plates. B. 35140

Irving. Tour in the Prairies; and, Abbotsford and Newstead Abbey. By Washington Irving. New Edition. *London: G. Routledge & Co.* 1855. 12mo, pp. 248. 35141

Irving. Voyage dans les prairies à l'ouest des États-Unis. Traduit par A. Sobry. *Paris.* 1835. 8vo. 35142

Irving. Un Tour dans les prairies à l'ouest des États-Unis; traduit de l'anglais de Washington Irving par Ernest W. Nouvelle édition. *Tours: Mame et fils.* 1851. 12mo, pp. 239. + [*Ibid.* 1865.] 35143

Irving. Ausflug auf die Prairien zwischen dem Arkansas und Red-river. *Stuttgart und Tübingen: J. G. Cotta.* 1835. 12mo, pp. (4), 136. C. 35144

Also: ... Reise durch die Prairien. Aus dem Englischen. *Berlin: Veit und Comp.* 1835. 8vo. — ... Eine Wanderung in den Prairien. Aus dem Englischen von H. Roberts. *Braunschweig: Vieweg.* 1835. 16mo.

Irving. The Crayon Reading Book: comprising Selections from the various Writings of Washington Irving. ... *New York: G. P. Putnam.* 1849. 12mo, pp. 255. C. + *New-York: G. P. Putnam & Company.* 1855. 12mo, pp. 255. 35145

[Irving.] Fragment of a Journal of a Sentimental Philosopher, during his Residence in the City of New York. *New York.* 1809. 8vo. 35146

Irving. Esquisses morales et littéraires, ou Observations sur les mœurs, les usages et la littérature des Anglais et des Américains, par M. Washington Irving. Traduites de l'anglais sur la quatrième édition, par MM. Delpeux et Villetard. *Paris: Constant Letellier.* 1822. 2 vols., 8vo. 6 Lithographs. + Seconde édition. [*Ibid.*] 1827. 2 vols., 8vo. 35147

[Irving.] The Gentleman in Black, and Tales of other Days. With Illustrations by George Cruikshank and Others. *London: C. Daly.* 1840. 12mo, pp. (2), v, 392. 18 Plates. C.

The same as "Beauties of Irving," No. 35135, *supra.*

[Irving.] A History of New York, from the Beginning of the World to the End of the Dutch Dynasty. Containing among many Surprising and Curious Matters, the Unutterable Ponderings of Walter the Doubter, the Disastrous Projects of William the Testy, and the Chivalric Achievments of Peter the Headstrong, the three Dutch Governors of New Amsterdam; being the only Authentic History of the Times that ever hath been, or ever will be Published. By Diedrich Knickerbocker. ... *New York: Inskeep & Bradford.* 1809. 2 vols., 12mo, pp. xxiii, 268; (2), 258. Folded View of New Amsterdam. B., C., P. 35149

This is the title of the first edition of this admirable fiction. It is not difficult to elicit from its pages a fair proportion of legitimate history. Indeed, it will not be saying too much, to assert that a large portion of the readers of the present day owe their knowledge of the history of New York to the interest created by this unrivaled performance. It has been so repeatedly reprinted that we shall not be surprised to find that the following list of editions is far from complete. We purposely abridge their titles.

[Irving.] A History of New York ... . *London.* 1809. 2 vols., 12mo. 35150

[Irving.] A History of New-York ... . The Second Edition with Alterations. ... *New-York: Inskeep and Bradford,* ... 1812. 2 vols., 12mo, pp. 292; 248. Plate. + The Third Edition. ... *Philadelphia: M. Thomas.* 1819. 2 vols., 12mo, pp. 296; 265. 2 Frontispieces. H. 35151

[Irving.] A Humorous History of New York ... . *London: John Murray.* 1820. 8vo. C. 35152

[Irving.] A History of New York ... . New Edition. *London: John Murray.* 1821. 2 vols., post 8vo, pp. 341; (8), 282. 2 Plates. 35153

[Irving.] A Humorous History of New York ... . A New Edition. *London: W. Sharpe & Son.* 1821: Post 8vo, pp. xxxii, 372. 35154

[Irving.] History of New York ... . *Glasgow: John Wylie & Co.* 1821. 8vo. 35155

Six copies of this edition were printed on large paper.

[Irving.] A History of New York ... . Fourth American Edition. *New-York: Printed by C. S. Van Winkle.* 1824. 2 vols., 12mo, pp. xiii, 300; 268. BA. 35156

[Irving.] A History of New York ... . [Same title as the Second Edition.] *London: Wm. Charlton Wright.* 1824. 8vo, pp. xxiv, 312. Plate. + *Paris: Galignani & Co.* 1824. 2 vols., 12mo. 35157

[Irving.] Knickerbocker's History of New York. *London.* 1825. 12mo. 35158

Plate by Corbould. A very handsomely printed little edition.

[Irving.] A History of New York ... . Fifth Edition. *New York.* 1826. 2 vols., 12mo. + Sixth American Edition. *Philadelphia: Carey, Lea & Carey.* 1829. 2 vols., 12mo, pp. 276; 235. + [*Ibid.*] 1830. + [*Ibid.*] 1831. + Seventh Edition. [*Ibid.*] 1832. 2 vols., 12mo. 35159

[Irving.] Knickerbocker's History of New York. *London: John Murray.* MDCCCXXXV. Fcp 8vo, pp. xxxvi, 397. Plates by Cruikshank. + *London: Thomas Tegg and Son.* MDCCCXXXVI. Fcp 8vo, pp. xxvi, 397. Plates. BA. + [*Ibid.*] MDCCCXXXVIII. + [*Ibid.*] MDCCCXXXIX. 35160

This very pretty edition forms part of Murray's "Family Library," and has often been reprinted; the latest issues bear the name of *William Tegg & Co.* as publishers.

[Irving.] A History of New York ... . *New York: George P. Putnam.* 1848. 12mo, pp. xvi, 13–454. + [*Ibid.*] 1849. + [*Ibid.*] 1853. 35161

[Irving.] A History of New York, from the Beginning of the World to the End of the Dutch Dynasty. ... By Diedrich Knickerbocker. With Illustrations by F. O. C. Darley. Engraved by Eminent Artists. *New York: G. P. Putnam.* 1850. Sq. 8vo, pp. xvi, 13–459. 35162

Fifty copies printed on large and tinted paper. First issue of this fine edition. The same plates were used in the edition dated 1867.

[Irving.] Knickerbocker's History of New York. *London: W. S. Orr & Co.* 1854. Rl. 8vo, pp. 113. 35163

[Irving.] A History of New York ... The Author's Revised Edition. *New York: George P. Putnam.* 1859. 12mo, pp. 452. + *New York: G. P. Putnam's Sons.* [1864.] 12mo, pp. 528.

[Irving.] Knickerbocker's History of New York. With Designs by Darley. *New York: G. P. Putnam.* 1867. 8vo, pp. 459. + [*Ibid.*] 1867. 8vo, pp. 472. 2 Plates. B. 35165

Some copies were printed on large paper, imp. 8vo. The last edition is *New York: G. P. Putnam.* 1869. 16mo, pp. 528. Plates. B. It is scarcely necessary to say that it forms one volume of the various editions of Irving's Works issued in England, and sold separately. The following are foreign versions:

[Irving.] Histoire de New-York depuis le commencement du monde jusqu'à la fin de la domination hollandaise, contenant, entre autres choses curieuses et surprenantes, les innombrables hésitations de Walter-l'-Indécis, les plans désastreux de William-le-Bourru, et les exploits chevalbresques de Pierre-Forte-Tête, les trois Gouverneurs de New-Amsterdam; seule histoire authentique de ces temps qui ait jamais été ou puisse être jamais publiée, par Diedrick Knickerbocker ... traduit de l'Anglais. *Paris: A. Sautelet et Cie.* MDCCCXXVII. 2 vols., 8vo, pp. (4), 351; (2), 290.

[Irving.] Dietrich Knickerbocker's humoristische Geschichte von New-York, von Anbeginn der Gründung der Colonie durch Hendrick Hudson, bis zur Endschaft der holländischen Dynastie. *New-York und Philadelphia: Schäfer & Koradi.* 1851. 8vo.

Irving. New-York's Historia fran verldens begynnelse intill Holländska väldets slut. Af Washington Irving. ... *Stockholm: Bernh. Magn. Bredberg.* 1827. 8vo, pp. xxxix, 263, (1). H.

Irving. A History of the Life and Voyages of Christopher Columbus. By Washington Irving. *London: John Murray.* MDCCCXXVIII. 4 vols., 8vo, pp. xii, 473, (1); (8), 490, (1); viii, 413, (2); vii, 489, (1). Map. P. + *New York: G. & C. Carvill.* 1828. 3 vols., 8vo, pp. xvi, 399; 367; viii, 13–419, (1). Map.

See "Edinburgh Review," XLVIII. 1, *also* "N. A. Rev.," XXVIII. 103. I am unable to determine which of these two is the first edition; Murray's, however, is preferable for its paper and type. Murray's edition, dated 1851, is a reissue of Putnam's of that date. The author remarks that "It is the object of this work to relate the deeds and fortunes of the mariner, who first had the judgment to divine, and the intrepidity to brave, the mysteries of the perilous deep;" and he has in this work presented for the first time, in English, the result of his extensive researches while residing in Spain. *See* a long note in Rich's "Bib. Am.," II. 209.

Irving. The History of the Life and Voyages of Christopher Columbus. By Washington Irving. *Paris: Galignani & Co.* 1829. 4 vols., 18mo. A. 35170

Irving. History of the Life and Voyages of Christopher Columbus. By Washington Irving. ... *New-York: G. & C. & H. Carvill.* 1831. 2 vols., 8vo, pp. xii, 411; vii, 356. Map.

This edition also appeared with the imprint *Philadelphia: Carey, Lea & Blanchard,* 1835, and again as *Philadelphia: Carey & Lea,* 1840. Some copies of this edition, dated 1838, are so arranged as to form three volumes. Vol. III. starts with, what is in fact, page 82 of Vol. II.

Irving. The Life and Voyages of Christopher Columbus. Author's Revised Edition. *London.* 1850. 8vo. 35172

Irving. The Life and Voyages of Christopher Columbus; to which are added those of his Companions. By Washington Irving. Revised Edition. *New York: George P. Putnam.* 1848–1849. 3 vols., 12mo, pp. 437; 493; 492. 2 Plates. + [*Ibid.*] 1851. + [*Ibid.*] 1861. + *New York: G. P. Putnam and Son.* 1867. 3 vols., 12mo, pp. 461; 526; 494. 6 Plates. + [*Ibid.*] 1869. pp. xxx, 497; xii, 565; xi, 11–634. Portrait and Plates.

Some issues have the title "History of the Life and Voyages of Columbus." ... *New York: G. P. Putnam.* 1856, &c. 3 vols., 12mo. The following are translations:

Irving. Histoire de la Vie et des Voyages de Christophe Colomb. Par M. Washington Irving. Traduite de l'Anglais par M. C. A. Defauconpret. *Paris.* 1828. 4 vols., 8vo. 3 colored Maps. + Seconde édition, revue et corrigée. *Paris.* 1836. 4 vols., 8vo. 3 Maps. 35174

Irving. Vie et Voyages de Christophe Colomb; traduit de l'anglais par G. Renson. *Bruxelles: Lacroix, Verboeckhoven et Cie.* 1863–1864. 3 vols., 8vo. 35175

IRVING. Historia de la Vida y Viages de Cristobal Colon, por Washington Irving. Traducida al Castellano por D. José Garcia de Villalta. *Madrid.* 1833–34. 4 vols., sm. 8vo. + [*Ibid.*] 1852. 8vo. 35176

IRVING. Vida y Viajes de Cristobal Colon por Washington Yrving. *Mexico.* 1853. 2 vols., 8vo, pp. 380; 375. 35177

IRVING. Storia della vita e dei viaggi di Cristoforo Colombo. Prima versione italiana corredata di note adorna di carte geografiche e ritratto. *Geneva.* 1830. 4 vols., 8vo. 35178

IRVING. Storia della vita e viaggi di Cristoforo Colombo scritta da Washington Irving americano trad. dall' inglese. ... *Firenze: dalla tipografia Coen E. Comp.* 1829–30. 4 vols., 24mo, pp. 468; 480; 420; 440. B. 35179

IRVING. Die Geschichte des Lebens und der Reisen Christoph Columbus. Aus dem Englischen von Ph. A. G. von Meyer. *Frankfurt: Sauerlander.* 1828. 16mo. 2 Maps. 35180

Also: Die Geschichte [as before]. Im Auszug für die Jugend ... von Rud. Friedner. *Neustadt: Christmann.* 1829. 8vo. + ... von F. H. Ungewitter. *Frankfurt: Wesché.* 1829. 8vo. + *Stuttgart: Cotta.* 1833. 8vo.

IRVING. Het Leven en de Reizen van Christoffel Columbus. Uit het Engelsch. *Haarlem.* 1828–34. 5 vols., 8vo. Map and Portrait. 35181

The fifth volume contains the voyages of some of the companions of Columbus.

IRVING. The Life and Voyages of Christopher Columbus, By Washington Irving. (Abridged by the same.) ... *New York: G. & C. & H. Carvill.* 1829. 8vo, pp. 311. + *London: John Murray.* MDCCCXXX. Sm. fcp 8vo, pp. xi, 357. Portrait of Columbus, 2 Maps. H. + *Paris.* 1830. 12mo. + *New-York: G. & C. & H. Carvill.* 1831. 12mo, pp. 267. + *Leipzig: B. Tauchnitz.* 1832. 16mo. + *Leipzig: Baumgärtner.* 1832. 8vo. + A New Edition, with Additions and Improvements, by the Author. [*New York:*] *Printed by J. & J. Harper.* 1833. 18mo, pp. 267. + *Amsterdam: Schalekamp and van de Grampel.* 1836. 8vo. + Second Edition. *London: Thomas Tegg.* 1841. Fcp 8vo, pp. x, 356. + *Bath, N. Y.: R. L. Underhill & Co.* 1844. 18mo, pp. iv, 218. + *Leipzig: Renger.* 1846. 16mo. + *Leipzig: Baumgärtner.* 1846, '53, '57, '61, '66. 8vo, pp. xii, 308.

IRVING. The Life and Voyages of Christopher Columbus. Including the Author's Visit to Palos. *Boston: Marsh, Capen, Lyon & Webb.* 1839. 12mo, pp. xii, 9–325. Map and Portrait.

+ *Leipzig: B. Tauchnitz.* 1846. 16mo. + New Edition. *London: W. Tegg.* 1866. 18mo, pp. xvi, 367. + *Paris: imp. Cusset et Cie.* 1869. 18mo, pp. viii, 414. 35183

IRVING. The Life and Voyages of Christopher Columbus. By Washington Irving. Herausgegeben und mit einem ausführlichen Wörterbuche versehen von H. J. Lohmann. *Quedlinburg.* 1863. 8vo, pp. viii, 320. 35184

IRVING. Voyages et aventures de Christophe Colomb, traduits de l'anglais de Washington Irving, par Paul Merruau. *Tours.* 1843. 12mo. + Quatrième édition. *Tours: Chez Mame.* 1851. 12mo, pp. 240. + Sixième édition. *Tours: Mame et Cie.* 1857. 12mo, pp. 240. Plate. + Neuvième édition. *Tours: Mame et fils.* 1865. 12mo, pp. 239. 2 Plates. + Dixième édition. [*Ibid.*] 1869. 35185

IRVING. The Hudson Legends. Comprising the Legend of Sleepy Hollow and Rip Van Winkle. *New York: G. P. Putnam.* 1863. 4to, pp. 84. 35186

IRVING. Legend of Sleepy Hollow. From "The Sketch-Book" of Washington Irving. *New York: G. P. Putnam.* 1863. 4to, pp. 50. 35187

Also: Illustrations of the Legend of Sleepy Hollow designed and etched by Felix O. C. Darley .... [*New York.*] MDCCCXLIX. Obl. folio, pp. 16. 6 Plates. BA.

[IRVING.] Letters of Jonathan Oldstyle, Gent. By the author of The Sketch Book. With a Biographical Notice. *New-York: William H. Clayton.* 1824. 8vo, pp. x, 67. B. + *London: Effingham Wilson.* 1824. 8vo, pp. x, 67. 35188

IRVING. Life of George Washington. By Washington Irving. In three Volumes [*i. e.* 5]. *New York: G. P. Putnam & Co.* 1855–9. 5 vols., 8vo, pp. xvi, 504; xii, 518, and Erratum (1); xiv, 523; x, 518; xii, 456. 5 Portraits, 2 Plates of Facsimiles, 2 Maps. B., BA. 35189

Of this popular work there were many editions, and the same edition was issued in various sizes. The one described above being the first and so-called "Library Edition;" subsequently in 1856–59, to meet the wishes of the "Illustrators," one hundred and ten copies were put forth in royal 4to, with the addition of 102 Portraits and Views on India paper. In the years 1857–61, a "Subscription Edition" was issued in parts, in imperial 8vo, with later impressions of the plates used in the 4to edition; it was then issued in 12mo, uniform with Putnam's various editions of Irving's other works. We have characterized it as a popular work; being Irving's, it could not be otherwise. It was, however, almost an unnecessary book, it has added little to what was already known, and is, in fact, a publisher's book. It was reprinted, *London: H. G. Bohn.* 1855–59. 5 vols., post 8vo; *London: John Murray.* 1856–59. 5 vols., post 8vo; *Leipzig: Bernard Tauchnitz.* 1856–59. 5 vols., 16mo.

IRVING. Lebensgeschichte Georg Washington's. Aus dem Englischen von dem Uebersetzer der Werke Prescott's. *Leipzig. Brockhaus.* 1856–59. 5 vols., 8vo, pp. xvi, 423; xvi, 484; xvi, 471; xiii, 470; xv, 336. 35190

IRVING. Het Leven van George Washington. Een leesboek voor de Jeugd. Naar het Engelsch. *Haarlem.* 1838. 8vo.

IRVING. The Manuscript of Diedrich Knickerbocker, Jr. *New York.* 1824. 12mo. 35192

IRVING. Rip Van Winkle; a Posthumous Writing of Diedrich Knickerbocker. Illustrated with Six Etchings on Steel by Ch. Simons from Drawings by Darley. *London.* 1850. 4to.

See our Vol. v., No. 18582.

IRVING. Rip Van Winkle. A Legend of the Katskill Mountains. By Washington Irving. *New York: G. P. Putnam.* 18—. Imp. 8vo, pp. 32. Photographs. 35194

IRVING. The Rocky Mountains: or, Scenes, Incidents, and Adventures In the Far West; digested from the Journal of Captain B. L. E. Bonneville, of the Army of the United States, and illustrated from various other sources, By Washington Irving. ... *Philadelphia: Carey, Lea, & Blanchard.* 1837. 2 vols., 12mo, pp. 248; 248. 2 Maps. B., BA., H. + [*Ibid.*] 1843. •35195

Printed in London as: "Adventures of Captain Bonneville." *See* No. 35126, *supra.*

IRVING. Selections from the Works of Washington Irving. Illustrated by Henry Ritter and William Camphausen. ... *Leipzig: F. A. Brockhaus.* 1857. Imp. 8vo, pp. viii, 276. 35196

[IRVING.] The Sketch Book of Geoffrey Crayon, Gent. ... *New York: Printed by C. S. Van Winkle.* 1819–20. 2 vols., 8vo, pp. 443; 108, 120, 123. BA. 35197

This, the most widely known of the author's works, was first issued in seven parts, and is very scarce. It has been repeatedly reprinted, and will doubtless maintain its position as a classic in every age and nation.

[IRVING.] The Sketch-Book of Geoffrey Crayon, Gent. ... *London: John Miller.* 1820. 8vo, pp. vi, (2), 354. H. + *London: John Murray.* MDCCCXXI. 2 vols., fcp 8vo, pp. vi, (1), 296; (4), 316. 2 Plates. + [*Ibid.*] MDCCCXXVI. + [*Ibid.*] MDCCCXXXIV. + [*Ibid.*] MDCCCXXXVIII. + With a Life of the Author. *Paris.* 1830. 2 vols., 18mo. + *Philadelphia: Carey, Lea, & Blanchard.* 1834. 2 vols., 12mo, pp. 236; 264. + A

New Edition. [*Ibid.*] 1835. + *Bremen: Schünemann.* 1840. 8vo. + *Hamburg: Erie.* 18—. 2 vols., 12mo. + *Leipzig: Bernard Tauchnitz.* 1843. 12mo, pp. x, 361. Portrait. 35198

[IRVING.] The Sketch Book of Geoffrey Crayon, Gentn. Author's Revised Edition. With Original Designs by F. O. C. Darley. Engraved by Childs, Herrick, etc. *New York: G. P. Putnam.* 1848. 12mo, pp. 465. 2 Plates. 35199

Fifty copies printed on large tinted paper in 8vo. Reissued in 1867, 12mo.

[IRVING.] Sketch Book of Geoffrey Crayon, Gent. Artist's Edition. Illustrated with One Hundred and Twenty Engravings on Wood, from Original Designs. *New York: G. P. Putnam.* M.DCCC.LXIV. 4to, pp. 504. + [*Ibid.*] MDCCCLXV. 35200

One hundred copies printed on large paper.

[IRVING.] Schetsen en Portretten, in Engeland en Amerika. Uit het Engelsch. *Leeuwarden.* 1823. 2 vols., 8vo. 35201

IRVING. Spanish Papers and other Miscellanies, hitherto Unpublished or Uncollected. By Washington Irving. Arranged and Edited by Pierre M. Irving. ... *New York: G. P. Putnam; Hurd and Houghton.* 1866. 2 vols., 12mo, pp. xv, 466; 5–487. Portrait. B. + [*Ibid.*] 1868. + [*Ibid.*] 1869. 12mo, pp. xxiv; (2), 531. Portrait and Plate. B. 35202

The edition dated 1866, was also printed on large paper.

[IRVING.] Tales of a Traveller. By Geoffrey Crayon, Gent. ... *Philadelphia: H. C. Carey & I. Lea.* 1824. 4 parts, 8vo, pp. 165; 212; 135; 161. BA. + *London.* 1824. 2 vols., 8vo. + Second American Edition. *New York: Printed by C. S. Van Winkle.* 1825. 2 vols., 12mo, pp. xii, 300; 7–326. + Third American Edition. *Philadelphia: Carey, Lea & Blanchard.* 1835. 2 vols., 12mo, pp. 235; 247. + [*Ibid.*] 1837. + With a Life of the Author. 1844. 8vo. + *Paris: Galignani.* 1844. + Author's Revised Edition. *New York: George P. Putnam.* 1849. 12mo, pp. 456. A., H. 35203

[IRVING.] Tales of a Traveller. By Geoffrey Crayon, Gentn. With Illustrations by F. O. C. Darley. Engraved by Eminent Artists. *New York: G. P. Putnam.* 1850. Sq. 8vo, pp. (2), 477.

Fifty copies printed on large paper, with 17 Plates on India paper. Reprinted in 1867 and 1868, pp. (2), 530.

[IRVING.] A Tour on the Prairies. *See* No. 35139, *supra.*

IRVING. Voyages and Discoveries of the Companions of Columbus. By Washington Irving. *London: John Murray.* MDCCCXXXI. Fcp 8vo, pp. xviii, 337. 2 Plates and Map. BA. + *Philadelphia: Carey and Lea.* 1831. 8vo, pp. 350. H., P. + *Philadelphia: Carey, Lea, & Blanchard.* 1835. 8vo, pp. 350. + With a complete Vocabulary compiled by E. Amthor. Revised Edition. *Leipzig: Renger.* 1846. 16mo. 35205

IRVING. Voyages of the Companions of Columbus. *Paris: Galignani.* 1831. 12mo, pp. 360. A. 35206

Beautifully printed by Jules Didot, Sr. Superior to Murray's edition.

IRVING. Voyages and Discoveries of the Companions of Christopher Columbus. Being a Sequel to the Life of Columbus. *London: William Tegg.* 1866. 16mo, pp. xviii, 337.

This edition is a reproduction of No. 35182, and forms Vol. XXII. of "The Family Library."

IRVING. Voyages and Discoveries of the Companions of Columbus. Mit Noten zur Erklärung des Textes ... nebst einem Wörterbuche. *Leipzig: Baumgärtner.* 1835, '37, '40. 8vo. Map. 35208

IRVING. Histoire des voyages et découvertes des compagnons de Christophe Colomb, suivie de l'histoire de Fernand Cortez et de la conquête du Mexique, et de l'histoire de Pizarre et de la conquête de Pérou. Ouvrages traduites de l'anglais par A. J. B. et C. A. Defauconpret. *Paris.* 1823. 3 vols., 8vo. 3 Maps.

IRVING. Voyages et découvertes des compagnons de Colomb. Traduit de l'anglais de Washington Irving, par Henry Lebrun. ... Neuvième édition. *Tours: Mame et fils.* 1864. 12mo. + Dixième édition. *Paris.* 1866. 12mo, pp. 288. 4 Engravings. + Onzième édition. *Tours: Mame et fils.* 1868. 12mo, pp. 286.

First printed in 1840.

IRVING. Viajes y descubrimientos de los compañeros de Colon. *Madrid.* 1854. 35211

IRVING. Voyage d'un Américain à Londres; ou, esquisses sur les mœurs anglaises et américaines; traduit de l'Anglais de M. Irwin Washington. *Paris: Ponthieu.* 1822. 2 vols., 12mo, pp. (8), vii, 352; (4), 375. + [*Ibid.*] 1824. 8vo. C. 35212

IRVING. Wolfert's Roost and other Papers, now first Collected. By Washington Irving. *New York: G. P. Putnam & Co.* 1855. 12mo, pp. 383. Plate. BA., H. + [*Ibid.*] 1867.

12mo, pp. 383. 2 Plates. + *New York: G. P. Putnam and Son.* 1868. 12mo, pp. (4), 431. Plates. + *Leipzig: Bernard Tauchnitz.* 1855. Sq. 16mo. + *Göttingen: Wigand.* 185–. 16mo.

IRVING. Works of Washington Irving. With a Memoir of the Author. *Paris: Galignani.* 1834. Imp. 8vo. Portrait.

IRVING. The Works of Washington Irving. ... *Philadelphia: Lea and Blanchard.* [1840.] 2 vols., rl. 8vo, pp. viii, 534, Portrait; vii, 516. 35215

IRVING. The Works of Washington Irving. New Edition, Revised. *New York: G. P. Putnam & Co.* 1853–54. 23 vols., 12mo. 35216

Each volume has an independent title-page, and the dates vary.

IRVING. The Works of Washington Irving. New Edition, Revised. *London: Henry G. Bohn.* 1854. 10 vols., post 8vo.

IRVING. The Works of Washington Irving. New Edition, Revised. *New York: G. P. Putnam.* 1860–63. 23 vols., sq. 8vo. 35218

Of this revised edition one hundred copies were printed on slightly tinted and large paper, and this set, with P. M. Irving's "Life of Irving," forms together twenty-eight volumes. It is unnecessary to add that sets, as thus described, are rare. Of the collected editions of Irving's works, there are so many names given to the various forms, of what are, in fact, the same edition, that it is difficult to discriminate their differences. The one described above is undoubtedly the best. Next, in order of merit, is the "National Edition," in which the same steel and stereotype plates are used—the plates not being so fine; then we have a so-called "Sunnyside Edition;" a "Popular Edition;" and lastly the entire works are printed in a smaller (16mo) size, and are known as the "Knickerbocker Edition." Having given the collations of so many as relate to America, under their respective names, we omit a repetition.

IRVING GIFT. Choice Gems from Washington Irving. 12mo.

IRVING. Classic Grounds of American Authors. *New York, February.* 1864. Folio. 35220

IRVING MEMORIAL. Washington Irving. Mr. Bryant's Address on his Life and Genius. Addresses by Everett, Bancroft, Longfellow, Felton, Aspinwall, King, Francis, Greene. Mr. Allibone's Sketch of his Life and Works. With Eight Photographs. *New York.* 1860. Sq. 8vo, pp. 113, 63. 35221

[IRVING, *and others.*] Salmagundi; or, the Whim-Whams and Opinions of Launcelot Langstaff, Esq. and Others. ... *New-York: D. Longworth.* 1807. 2 vols., 18mo, pp. (2), 430. H. + [*Ibid.*] 1808. 2 vols., 18mo, pp. 424. P. + Reprinted from

the American Edition, with an Introductory Essay and Explanatory Notes, By John Lambert. *London: ... J. M. Richardson.* 1811. 2 vols., fcp 8vo. + *New-York.* 1814. 2 vols., 18mo. + Third Edition. *New-York: Thomas Longworth and Co.* 1820. 2 vols., 18mo, pp. 540. 3 Plates. + *London.* 1824. + *London: John Murray.* MDCCCXXX. Fcp. 8vo. + *London: Charles Daly.* [n. d.] Fcp 8vo. + *New York: G. P. Putnam & Co.* 1857. 16mo, Engraved Title, pp. 244. Plate. 35222

IRVING (W.), *and others.* Salmagundi; or, the Whim-Whams and Opinions of Launcelot Langstaff, Esq., and Others. By William Irving, James Kirke Paulding and Washington Irving. Printed from the Original Edition, with a Preface and Notes by Evert A. Duyckink. *New York: G. P. Putnam.* 1860. Sq. 8vo, pp. xiv, 13–412. 3 Plates. 35223

One hundred copies printed on large paper. Reprinted, *New York: G. P. Putnam and Son.* 1867. 16mo, pp. xiv, 13–412. 2 Plates. + [*Ibid.*] 1869. 16mo, pp. xix, 473. 2 Plates. B.

IRVING. ... Salmagundi. ... *New York: G. P. Putnam & Son.* 1867. 16mo, pp. 264. 35224

This "Railway Classics" edition was printed from Daly's English stereotype plates.

[IRVING.] Salmagundi. Second Series. By Launcelot Langstaff, Esq. Vol. III. *Holy and Thomas, New York* ... 1820. 12mo, pp. 321. + *London.* 1824. 12mo, pp. viii, 389. H.

IRVINGIANA. *See* [Duyckinck (E. A.)], Vol. VI., No. 21499.

IRWIN (T.) To the Public. ... Thomas Irwin. *Philadelphia, August* 1, 1771. Folio, pp. 2. P. 35226

Relates to the Wikoff affair. *See* Furman (M.), Vol. VII., No. 26224.

IRWIN (W.) A Sermon, Preached on Sabbath Morning, April 16, 1865, the Day after the Death of President Lincoln, By the Rev. William Irwin. [At Rondout, N. Y.] *New York: John A. Gray & Green, Printers.* 1865. 8vo, pp. 20. 35227

IRWIN (W. W.) Speech of Hon. William W. Irwin, on the Duty of Congress in the Present Crisis; ... August 12, 1842. *Washington.* 1842. 8vo, pp. 8. 35228

Also: Speech ... July 11, 1842, on the Tariff. *Washington.* 1842. 8vo.

Is a Member of the Legislature, or a Justice of the Supreme Court, eligible to the Office of United States Senator? *Geneva, N. Y.* 1867. 12mo. 35229

Is Cotton our King? From the Continental Monthly Magazine, March, 1862. [n. p. n. d.] 35230

Is it Calumny? or is it Truth? An Examination of a Pamphlet, entitled "Calumny refuted" ... *Philadelphia: John Penington.* 1846. 8vo, pp. 61. B., H. 35231

Relates to the Quakers. *See our* Vol. III., No. 10082.

Is it Expedient that a State Convention should be called to Remodel the Constitution? [of Massachusetts. n. p. n. d.] 12mo, pp. 14. H. 35232

Is our Prosperity a Delusion? Our National Debt and Currency (the age of Greenbacks). By a Boston Merchant. *Boston: A. Williams & Co.* 1864. 16mo, pp. 72. 35233

Is the Government of the State, a Republic or a Despotism?

"Is the North Right!" or, a Word about Slavery and the Colored Race. Addressed to the People of Massachusetts. By a Fellow Citizen. ... Written for the Boston Post. [1855.] 8vo, pp. 12. H. 35235

Is the South ready for Restoration? [n. p. n. d.] 8vo, pp. 20.

Is the System of Slavery sanctioned or condemned by Scripture? To which is subjoined an Appendix, containing two Essays upon the State of the Canaanite and Philistine Bondsmen. under the Jewish Theocracy. *London: John and Arthur Arch.* 1824. 8vo. 35237

ISABEL DE BORBON. Pompa Fvnebre y Exceqvias qve el excel. S. D. Pedro de Toledo y Leyba Marques de Mancera, Virrey destos Reynos hizon en la muerte de la Reyna nuestra Señora Doña Ysabel de Borbon. [*Lima.*] 1645. 4to. 35238

"A curious and rare volume, consisting of numerous and distinct pieces, separately paged." Title and note from an English catalogue.

ISAIAH. *See* Mohawk Language, *and* Wolf (N. G.)

ISABELLE (A.) Voyage a Buénos-Ayres et à Porto-Alègre, par la Banda-Oriental, les Missions d'Uruguay et la Province de Rio-Grande-do-Sul, (de 1830 a 1834;) Suivi de Considérations sur l'état du Commerce Français à l'extérieur, et principalement au Brésil et au Rio-de-la-Plata. ... Par Arsène Isabelle. *Havre: J. Morlent.* 1835. 8vo, pp. (2), 618, (4). Maps and Plates. H.

Isambert (François André). Manuel du Publiciste et de l'homme d'État ... . Par M. Isambert ... . *Paris: Brissot-Thivars et Ce.* 1826. 4 vols., 8vo, pp. (4), 432, xv; (4), 418, vi; (4), 476; (4), 486. BA. 35240

Contains numerous proclamations, conventions, decrees, etc., issued by or relating to the various states of North and South America.

[Isassi (J. D.)] Memorias de lo acontecido en Córdova en tiempo de la revolucion, para la historia de la independencia Megicana. *Jalapa.* 1827. 18mo. 35241

Isbell (T. M.) An Address ... before the Society of Alumni of Randolph Macon College ... 7th June, 1842. By Thomas M. Isbell ... . *Lynchburg: Toler, Townley & Statham, Printers.* 1842. 8vo, pp. 15. H. 35242

Isert (P. E.) Paul Erdmann Isert's, ehemal. königl. dänisch. Oberarzte an den Besitzungen in Afrika. Reise nach Guinea und den Caribäischen Inseln in Columbien, in Briefen an seine Freunde beschreiben. *Kopenhagen: T. F. Morthorst.* 1788. 8vo, pp. (16), 376, lxx, (7). Plate. H. 35243

Isert. Voyages en Guinée et dans les Îsles Caraïbes en Amérique, Par Paul Erdman Isert, Ci-devant Médicin-Inspecteur de S. M. Danoise, dans ses Possessions en Afrique; Tirés de sa correspondance avec ses Amis. Traduits de l'Allemand, avec Figures ... . *Paris: Maradan.* M. DCC. XCIII. 8vo, pp. viii, 343. 2 Plates. A., C., H., P. 35244

Isert. Reis na Guinea en de caribische eilanden in Columbien. ... Uit het Hoogduitsch. *Dordrecht ... De Leeuw en Krap.* 1790. 8vo, pp. (2), viii, 220. 2 Plates. BA., C. 35245

Isert. Reize van Koppenhagen naar Guinea, de West-Indien en de Caraïbische eilanden. *Amsterdam.* 1797. 8vo.

Isham (J.) An Oration commemorative of the Illustrious General Washington, delivered the 22d February, 1800, at the Meeting House of the West Society of Colchester, at the particular request of the Inhabitants. By Jirah Isham. *New London.* 1800. 8vo, pp. 16. 35247

One of the rarest of the Washington eulogies.

[Isherwood (B. F.)] To His Excellency Andrew Johnson, President of the United States: ... [n. p.] 1866. 8vo, pp. 12.

Isherwood. Facts in Relation to the Official Career of B. F. Isherwood, Chief of the Bureau of Steam Engineering of the Navy Department. *Philadelphia.* 1866. 8vo, pp. 57. H.

Also: The Official Reports on the Inefficiency of the U. S. S. Wampanoag, and Mr. Isherwood's Defence. Remarks on Mr. Isherwood's Defence. *New York: George Thompson & Co.* 1868. 8vo, pp. 43. H.

Isla (R. de). Tratado contra las bubas, sive Fruto de Todos Santos, o Antidoto eficaz contra el mal Frances hallado, y dispuestos en el Hospital de Todos Santos de Lisboa. Ad Joannem III. Portugalliæ Regum. Por el maestro Ruiz de Isla. *Hispali apud Dominicum Roberti.* 1542. Folio. 35250

Island Pond Copper Manufacturing Co. Island Pond, Brighton, Vermont. [n. p. n. d.] 8vo, pp. 16. H. 35251

Isle (Guil. Phil. Buache de L'). Atlas Nouveau, des Empires, Monarchies, Royaumes, Republiques, &c. 1733. 66 colored Maps. 35252

Also: Atlas Géographique et Universel. ... *Paris.* 1789. 2 vols., folio. 156 Maps

Isle (J. N. de L'). Explication de la Carte des Nouvelles Decouvertes au Nord de la Mer du Sud; Par M. De L'Isle, de l'Académie Royale des Sciences, & Professeur de Mathématiques au College Royal. *A Paris, Chez Desaint et Saillant* ... . MDCCLII. 4to, pp. 18. M., P. 35253

Isle. Nouvelles Cartes des découvertes de l'Amiral De Fonte, et autres Navigateurs Espagnols, Portugais, Anglois, Hollandois, François & Russes, dans les Mers Septentrionales, avec leur explication; qui comprend l'Histoire des Voyages, tant par Terre que par Mer, dans la partie Septentrionale de la Terre, les Routes de Navigation, les Extraits des Journaux de Marine; ... avec la description des Pays, l'histoire et les mœurs des habitans, etc. Par M. De L'Isle ... *Paris.* 1753. 4to, pp. 60. 4 Maps. + [*Ibid.*] 1754. A. 35254

An abridgment of this memoir, by Arthur Dobbs, is printed with the "Letter from a Russian Sea Officer," 1754, which see.

The Isle of | Pines, | or, | A late Discovery of a fourth Island in | Terra Australis, Incognita. | Being | A True Relation of certain English persons, | Who in the dayes of Queen Elizabeth, making a | Voyage to the East India, were cast away, and wrack- | ed upon the Island near to the Coast of Terra Austra- | lis Incognita, and all drowned, except one Man and | four Women, whereof one was a Negro. And now | lately Anno Dom. 1667. a Dutch ship

driven by foul | weather there by chance have found their Posterity | (speaking good English) to amount to ten or twelve | thousand persons, as they suppose. The whole Rela- | tion follows, written, and left by the Man himself a | little before his death, and declared to the Dutch by | his Grandchild. | Licensed June 27. 1668. | *London,* | *Printed by S. G. for Allen Banks and Charles Harper* | ... | 1668. | 4to, pp. (2), 9. + *Reprinted, London.* 1768. 12mo, pp. 19. B. 35255

This rare piece has been ascribed respectively to H. Neville, George Pine, and Cornelius Van Sloetten. The last named person is certainly the author of another piece on the same subject. This is probably by Neville.

Wahrhafftige Beschreibung der newen Insel Pines genannt. So 1667 von den Holländern erfunden worden. [n. p. n. d.]— Beschreibung des Eilandes Pines oder eine neue Entdeckung des vierten Eylandes in dem unbekannten Süder-Land. [n. p.] 1668. 4to, 4 l. 35256

Oprecht verhaal van 't Eiland van Pines, en deszelfs bevolking; of laatste ontdekking van een vierde Eiland in Terra Australis, Incognita. *Rotterdam* (*na de copye van London*), *J. Naeranus.* 1668. 4to, pp. 20. 35257

This "True account of the Island of Pines ... made after the copy printed at London," is a literary forgery; on the verso of the title is a warning against an edition printed in Amsterdam, as incomplete.

Informe sobre las propriedades higienico-medicinales de las Aguas y Temperatura de la Isla de Pinos. *Habana.* 1865. 8vo, pp. 44. 35258

Isle of Shoals. The Fifth Annual Report of the ... Society for promoting Religious Instruction in the Isle of Shoals. *Newburyport: I. W. Allen, Printer.* 1826. 8vo, pp. 7, (1). H. 35259

Isle Royale. Report of the Directors of the Isle Royale Mining Co. ... 17th of April, 1855. [n. p. n. d.] 8vo, pp. 8. Continued. H. 35260

Isnard (Achille Nicolas). Observations sur le principe qui a produit les Révolutions de France, de Genève et d'Amérique, dans les dix-huitième siècle. *Evreux: Veuve Malassis.* 1789. 8vo, pp. 80. 4 Maps. 35261

Isnardi (F.) Risposta di Felice Isnardi all' articolo ... del 13 Giugno 1838 intorno a Cristoforo Colombo ... . *Genova: De Fratelli Pagano.* 1838. 12mo, pp. 14. H. 35262

Isocrates, *pseudon.* The Question of the Bahama Jurisdiction over the Turk's Islands, discussed; ... By Isocrates. ... *London: F. Harding.* 1803. 8vo, pp. 91, (1). H. 35263

Isolanis (Isodorus de). In hoc volumine hec continentur. | De Imperio Militantis Ecclesiæ libri quattuor. | Primus est de dignitate eiusdem Imperii. | Secundus de Maiestate Romani Pontificis. | Tertius de Concilio Generali. | Quartus de uario temporum decursu a prædica | tione euangelii usq3 ad finem mundi. | Habes quoq3 lector ingenue suis locis ordinatas disputatiões phi | losophica: Iuris Pontifici Doctoribus ac Theologis perutiles: de | pdicatione euangelii apud Insulas magni maris Occeani: De | cōuersione Infideliū: ... [Colophon:] *Impressum Mediolani apud Gotardum Ponticum Anno ab ortu* | *fœlicissimo Christi Iesu Maximi Imperatoris cœli & terræ* | M.D.X.V.II. *Francischo secundo Regni Franchorum ac Mediolani Ducatus sceptra tenente* ... Folio, 129 l. Plates. 35264

This rare book, which treats of military and ecclesiastical history in general, relates incidentally to the conquest of America by the Spaniards.

Isonnonthouan. Memoirs of Isonnonthouan, a King of the Indian Nation called Roundheads. 2 vols., 8vo. 35265

Isqvierdo (P. S.) Alegato por el Obispo de la Puebla, en defensa de la jurisdiccion ecclesiastica y espiritual, con D. Pedro Saenz Isqvierdo, Alcade Mayor y Teniente de General de dicha Ciudad. [*Puebla.* 1657.] Folio, 10 l. 35266

Israel (M. B.) *See* Manasseh ben Israel.

Israel *and* Lundt. Journal of a Cruise in the U. S. Ship Delaware, 74, in the Mediterranean, in the years 1833 and 1834, with a Sketch of a Journey to Jerusalem, by Israel and Lundt. *Mahon, the Widow Serra & Son.* 1835. 12mo. 35267

Israel Vindicated; being a Refutation of the Calumnies propagated respecting the Jewish Nation; in which the Objects and Views of the American Society for Ameliorating the Condition of the Jews are Investigated. By an Israelite. *New York.* 1820. 8vo, pp. 110. N. 35268

Isselt (E. W. van Dam van). Hassar of de Negers. Dichtstuk. *Tiel.* 1829. 8vo. 35269

Hassar, or the Negroes. A poem.

The Issue Explained. [*New Orleans.* 1864.] 8vo, pp. 8. B.

Against the election of Mr. Hahn as Governor of Louisiana.

The Issue Fairly Presented. The Senate Bill for the Admission of Kansas as a State. Democracy, Law, Order, and the Will of the Majority of the whole People of the Territory, against Black Republicanism, Usurpation, Revolution, Anarchy, and the Will of a meagre Minority. ... *Washington: Printed at the Union Office.* 1856. 8vo, pp. 30. H. 35271

The Issues of the Hour. *See* [Codding (Milo Defonz)].

Isthmus of Panama. [*Edinburgh.* n. d.] 12mo, pp. 32.

From "Chamber's Miscellany."

István (P.) Xantus János levelei Ejeszakamerikából. Tizenkét, eredeti rajzok utaú hésült köes egynehány fametszettel. Kozli Prépost István. *Pesten,* ... [n. d.] 8vo, pp. 175, (1). 12 Plates. 35273

This Hungarian work relates to California, the Indians, etc. The title is correctly given, but we are not certain as to which of the two later names is the author's surname.

Itabayana (*Visconde de*). Exposição fiel sobre a negociação do emprestimo que o imperio do Brasil ha contrahido em Londres, e sobre as vantagens delle resultantes. *Londres: J. Barnard.* 1827. 8vo, pp. 90. 35274

Italian Mercury. *See* Mercurio Italico.

Items, on Travel, Anecdote and Popular Errors. By One in Retirement. *Quebec.* 1855. 8vo. + Second Edition. [*Ibid.*]

Ithaca, *N. Y.* Prospects of the Ithaca & Owego Rail Road Company. *Albany: Printed by Hosford and Wait.* [1833.] 8vo, pp. 14. B., S. 35276

Report of the Ithaca and Owego Railroad Company. *Ithaca.* 1833. 8vo. B., S. 35277

The Scenery of Ithaca, and the Head Waters of the Cayuga Lake, as portrayed by different Writers. *Ithaca.* 1856. 8vo, pp. 151. Plates. 35278

Statement of Facts in relation to the Claims of the Inhabitants of the County of Tompkins, for a Bank at Ithaca. *Albany.* 1829. 8vo. 35279

Views of Ithaca and its Environs. By an Impartial Observer. *Ithaca: D. & A. Spencer.* 1835. 8vo, pp. 44. S. 35280

See also Cornell University, Vol. IV.

Itier (J.) Mémoire sur la Guyane française. Par J. Itier. *Paris.* 1798. 12mo. 35281

Itier. Notes Statistiques sur la Guyane française; par M. Jules Itier, Inspr des Douanes. *Paris: Arthus Bertrand.* 1844. 8vo, pp. 110. 35282

Itinerariū Portugallēssiū. *See* Zorzi–Madrignano.

Itta y Parra (Bartholome Phelipe). Los Tres Gemidos del Aguila Mexicana: Sermon Panegyrico-Funeral, del Don Juan Vazquez de Acuña, Cavallero del Orden de Santiago, y de la Nueva España. *Madrid.* 1740. 4to. 35283

Itta y Parra. Oracion Funebre que en las Exequias del P. Juan Fogueras, Comissario Geñeral de la Nueva España. *Mexico.* 1748. 35284

Also other Sermons and Orations preached in Mexico on various State Occasions, Funerals, etc.

Itta y Para (Elizalde). Dia Festivo proprio para el Culto, y Rezo de S. San Joachin, por Elizalda Itta y Para, Rector de la Real Universidad de Mexico. *Mexico: F. H. Sanchez.* 1744. 4to. 35285

Itta y Para (J. M. G. de). La Sombra Imagen de la Grandeza del D. Joseph del Campillo y Cossio, Oracion Funebras. *Mexico.* 1744. 4to. 35286

[Iturbide (Augustin de).] Breve Diseño Critico de la Emancipation y Libertad de la Nacion Mexicana y de las causas que influyeron en sus mas ruidosos sucesos, acæcidos desde el grito de Iguala hasta la espantosa muerte del libertador en la villa de Padilla. *Mexico.* 1827. 12mo, pp. 16, xxviii, 205. 35287

Iturbide. Catastrophe de Don Aug. de Yturbide proclamé Empereur du Mexique, 18 Mai, 1822, ou Relation exacte des circumstances qui ont accompagné le Débarquement et la Mort de cet homme célèbre. 1825. 8vo. 35288

Iturbide. Denkwürdigkeiten aus dem öffentlichen Leben des Exkaisers von Mexico, Augustin de Iturbide, von ihm selbst geschrieben. Nach der Englischen Ausgabe übersetzt. *Leipzig: Brockhaus.* 1824. 8vo, pp. 117. 35289

Iturbide. Discurso Civico, en Elogio de Exmo. Sr. D. Agostin de Iturbide, Pronunciado en Morelia el 27 de Sept. de 1853. *Mexico.* [n. d.] 35290

Iturbide. Memoirs of Agustin de Iturbide, chiefly concerning the late Revolution in Mexico. Written by Himself. To which is added an Appendix of Documents, &c. *London: John Murray.* 1824. 8vo, pp. 96. 35291

Rich remarks "This pamphlet, with a few alterations, is the same as the 'Statement,' *infra*, but wants the Preface. Neither has the Appendix mentioned on the title." This latter remark is an error, *see* below.

Iturbide. Mémoires autographes de Don Augustin Iturbide, ex-Empereur du Mexique ... traduits de l'anglais de M. J. Quin, par J. T. Parisot ... . *Paris: Charles Gosselin.* 1824. 8vo, pp. (4), xxxviii, 209. C., H., S. 35292

Iturbide. Memoria que escribio en Liorna á 27 de Setiembre 1823 sobre su carrea militar y politica. *Mexico.* 1827. 4to, pp. 64. 35293

Iturbide. Proyecto del Ceremonial que para la Inauguracion y Coronacion de su Magestad el Emperador Augustin primero. *Mexico.* 1822. 4to. 35294

Iturbide. Representaciones que la viuda de Don Agustin de Iturbide ha dirigido al Supremo Poder legislativo de los Estados-Unidos-Mexicanos. *Mexico.* 1833. 4to, pp. 8. 35295

Iturbide. A Statement of Some of the Principal Events in the Public Life of Agustin de Iturbide. Written by Himself. With a Preface by the Translator, and an Appendix of Documents. *London: John Murray.* 1824. 8vo, pp. xxiii, 157.

Rich says, pp. xxiii, 95. For an autobiography of Iturbide *see* the "Pamphleteer," XXVIII. Also: Plan del Señor Coronal D. Aug. Iturbide. *Mexico.* 1821. 1 l.

Iturbide (M. J.) Solemnes Exequias de la Senora Doña Maria Josepha Aramburu de Iturbide, celebradas en la Parroquia de San Puebla. *Mexico.* 1822. 8vo. 35297

Iturri (F.) Carta Crítica sobre la historia de América del Señor D. Juan Bautista Muñoz. Escrita de Roma por D. Francisco Iturri. ... *Madrid: Año de* 1798. 12mo, pp. 120. B., H. + *Reimpreso en Buenos Aires.* 1818. Sm. 4to, pp. 111. + *Reimpreso en Puebla.* 1820. 4to, pp. 67. 35298

Iturrigaray (Don José de). Virrey que fue de Nueva Espana vindicado en forma legal contra las falsas imputaciones de

infidencia propuestas por el acuerdo de Mexico y apoyadas por D. J. Lopez Cancélada en sus dos manifiestos. *Cadiz.* 1812. Sm. 4to. 35299

Several pamphlets relative to D. José de Iturrigaray, who was viceroy of Mexico, were printed at Cadiz, Havana, and Mexico, between 1812 and 1823.

Ivernois (F. d'). Effets du Blocus Continental sur le Commerce, les Finances, le Crédit et la Prosperité des Iles Britanniques; par Sir Francis D'Ivernois. Seconde édition. *Londres.* 1809. 8vo, pp. 140. N. + [*Ibid.*] 1810. 8vo. C. 35300

Ivernois. Effects of the Continental Blockade upon the Commerce, Finances, ... of the British Islands. ... Translated from the third French Edition ... . By Sir Francis D'Ivernois. *London: Printed by Cox, Son, and Baylis.* 1810. 8vo, pp. 152, xxiii, (1). BA. 35301

Contains slight references to American commerce.

Ivernois. Historical and Political Survey of the Losses sustained by the French Nation, in Population, Agriculture, Colonies, Manufactures, and Commerce, in consequence of the Revolution ... . From the French of Sir Francis D'Ivernois. ... *London: J. Wright.* 1799. 8vo. 35302

See "M. Rev.," XXX. 92. Also: Réflexions sur la Guerre en Réponse a Réflexions sur la Paix. Avec Remarques, Citation, etc., par J. Adams, President des États-Unis. ... *Philadelphia.* 1798. 8vo, pp. 157.

Ives (A. E.) Victory turned into Mourning. A Discourse, on occasion of the death of Abraham Lincoln, late President ... Preached at Castine By Alfred E. Ives. ... *Bangor: Wheeler & Lynde, Printers.* 1865. 8vo, pp. 14. B. 35303

Ives (C.) Chips from the Workshop. Parnassus, The Outlaw's Bride [etc.], and other Poems. By Charles Ives. *New Haven: Hitchcock & Stafford.* 1843. 12mo, pp. 180. Plate. C.

Ives (C. G.) Discourses on his Fiftieth Anniversary as Deacon in the Congregational Church in Bristol, Conn., February 2, 1859. By Charles G. Ives. *Hartford.* 1859. 8vo. 35305

Ives (J. M.) New England Fruit Book. *Boston.* 35306

Title from Allibone's "Dictionary."

Ives (J. C.) Memoir to accompany a Military Map of the Peninsula of Florida, south of Tampa Bay, compiled by Lieut. J. C. Ives, ... April, 1856. War Department. *New York: [illegible] Wynkoop.* 1856. 8vo, pp. 42. Large Map. + Another Edition. *Washington.* 1856. 35307

IVES. Report upon the Colorado River of the West, Explored in 1857 and 1858 by Lieutenant Joseph C. Ives, Corps of Topographical Engineers, under the direction of the office of Explorations and Surveys, A. A. Humphreys, Captain Topographical Engineers, in Charge. ... *Washington.* 1861. 4to, pp. 131, 14, 154, 30, 6, 31, (1). 27 Plates and Map. C., H. 35308

This river, flowing between perpendicular walls a mile and a quarter in altitude is not the only development of this exploration which excites our interest. Lieutenant Ives was the first to give us the results of an intelligent observer of the celebrated yet almost mythical, fortified villages of the Moquis Indians. Contents: Part I. General Report. II. Hydrographic Report. III. Geological Report; by J. S. Newberry IV. Botany; by A. Gray, J. Torrey, G. Thurber, and G. Engelmann. V. Zoology (Birds); by S. F. Baird. Appendix. Astronomical Observations.

IVES (L. S.) Church and State Charities Compared: with Special Reference to ... New York State Charities: Two Lectures ... January 29th and February 26th, 1857. By L. Silliman Ives, LL.D. ... *New York: Edward Dunigan and Brother.* 1857. 8vo, pp. 68. H. 35309

IVES. The Introductory Address of the Historical Society of the University of North Carolina, delivered ... June 5th, 1844. By L. Silliman Ives ... . *Raleigh: Printed by T. Loring.* 1844. 8vo, pp. 18. H., M. 35310

IVES. A Sermon, Preached in St. Luke's Church, New-York, September 25, 1831, on Taking Leave of his Congregation. By Levi Silliman Ives ... . *New-York.* MDCCCXXXI. 8vo, pp. 15. H. 35311

Also: A Pastoral Letter to the Clergy and Laity of his Diocese. *New-York.* 1846. 12mo.—Sermon before the Convention, Oct. 2, 1844. ... *Philadelphia.* 1844. S.—A Sermon at the Opening of the First Convention after his entering on the Duties of his Episcopate: delivered ... Edenton, N. C. May, 1832 ... . *New-York.* 1832. 8vo, pp. 36.

IVES. Examination of the Doctrine declared and the Powers claimed by the Rt. Rev. Bishop Ives, in a Pastoral Letter to the Clergy and Laity of his Diocese. By a Lay Member of the Protestant Episcopal Church of North Carolina. *Philadelphia.* 1849. 8vo. S. 35312

IVES (M. B.) The Late Moses Brown Ives. Extracts from the Providence Journal, August 8, and August 12, 1857. Providence Tribune and Providence Post. Resolutions adopted by various public bodies at the time of Mr. Ives's Death, etc. *Providence: Privately printed.* 1857. 8vo, pp. 12. 35313

IVES (Robert). The Rhode Island Controversy. A short History of the Case of Ives *vs.* Hazard. From the Boston Law Reporter for June. *Boston: Geo. C. Rand & Avery.* 1859. 8vo, pp. 12. 35314

Also: "The Astonishing Development." Ives *vs.* Hazard. From the Republican Herald, Providence, June 4, 1859.—Supreme Court ... Robert Ives *vs.* Charles T. Hazard, Henry A. Middleton, Mumford Hazard. Opening Argument for Complainant. *Providence: Knowles, Anthony & Co.* 1855. 8vo, pp. 30. + Closing Argument for Complainant. [*Ibid.*] 1855. 8vo, pp. 19. + Arguments for Defendants. [*Ibid.*] 1855. 8vo, pp. 127.—A Lawyer's unbought Opinion, in the Ives and Hazard Case, addressed to the Honorable General Assembly of the State of Rhode Island. *January,* 1861. 8vo, pp. 7.—Report of the Special Committee on Equity Powers of Supreme Court. *Providence: Knowles, Anthony & Co.* 1859. 8vo, pp. 8.—Robert H. Ives *vs.* Charles T. Hazard and others. Deposition of Moses B. Ives. *Providence.* 1859. 8vo, pp. 6.—Report of the Case of Ives *vs.* Hazard and others, in the Supreme Court of Rhode Island, ... 1855. ... *Boston: Little, Brown & Co.* 1858. 8vo, pp. 15.

IVIMEY (J.) The Utter Extinction of Slavery an Object of Scripture Prophecy: A Lecture ... at ... Chelmsford ... the 17th of April, 1832: ... By Joseph Ivimey ... . *London: ... G. Wightman* ... . 1832. 8vo, pp. viii, 74. B., H. 35315

Ivison & Phinney's Quarterly Educational News. *New-York, August,* 1858. 8vo. S. 35316

IVNGERUTIT. *See* Eskimo, Vol. VI., No. 22859.

IVON (N. G.) Black-Hollow; or, the Dragoon's Bride. A Tale of the Ramapo in 1779. By N. C. Ivon ... . *New York: Beadle & Co.* [186-.] 16mo, pp. 100. 35317

IXTLILXUCHITL (F. de A.) Horribles Crueldades de los Conquistadores de Mexico, ... memoria escrita por D. Fernando de Alva Ixtlilxuchitl. Publicala por supplemento á la Historia del Padre Sahagun Carlos Maria de Bustamante. ... *Mexico: A. Valdes.* 1829. 8vo, pp. (2), xii, 118. 35318

Translated into French by Ternaux with the following title:

IXTLILXUCHITL. Cruautés horribles des Conquérants du Mexique et des Indiens qui les aidèrent à soumettre cet empire à la couronne d'Espagne, mémoire de don Fernando d'Alva Ixtlilxochitl; supplément à l'histoire du Père Sahagun, publié et dédié au gouvernement suprême de la confédération mexicaine par Charles-Marie de Bustamente. *Mexico.* 1829. 8vo, pp. (4), xlvii, 312. + *Paris: Arthus Bertrand, Editeur.* 1838. 35319

Forms Vol. VIII. of Ternaux's "Recueil." For an Italian version *see* Marmocchi Viaggi, Vol. V., Part II.

IXTLILXUCHITL. Histoire des Chichimèques ou des Anciens Rois de Tezcuco, par Don Fernando d'Alva Ixtlilxochitl, traduite sur le manuscript espagnole ... inédite. *Paris: Arthus Bertrand.* M DCCC XL. 2 vols., 8vo, pp. xvi, 380; (6), 357. B., H. 35320

Forms Vols. XII. and XIII. of Ternaux's "Recueil." *See also* Kingsborough's "Antiquities," IX., for the Spanish version, *and* Appendix to Prescott's "History of Mexico," for extracts. Bustamente calls the author the "Mexican Cicero," and Clavigero, himself an authority of the highest rank, speaks of the author as extremely conversant with the antiquities of his nation, and as having written the very learned and valuable works which bear his name at the request of the viceroy of Mexico.

IZARD (George). Official Correspondence with the Department of War, relative to the military operations of the American army under the command of Major General Izard, on the Northern Frontier of the United States. In the Years 1814 and 1815. *Philadelphia: Thomas Dobson.* 1816. 8vo, pp. vii, 152. B., P.

[IZARD (R.)] An Account of a Journey to Niagara, Montreal and Quebec, in 1765, or "Tis Eighty Years since." *New-York: Printed by Wm. Osborn.* 1846. 8vo, pp. 30. N., S.

IZARD. Correspondence of Mr. Ralph Izard, of South Carolina, from the Year 1774 to 1804; With a Short Memoir [by his Daughter, Mrs. Ann Izard Deas]. Vol. I. *New-York: Charles S. Francis & Co.* 1844. 12mo, pp. xiv, 389, (2). Portrait. A.

No more printed. *See* "Democratic Review," XIX. 40. The author was intimate with General Washington.

IZQUIERDO (S.) + | El Padre Sebastian Izquierdo, | Assistente en Roma por las Provincias de España, | mandò al Procurado General de Indias en esta Corte, | el año de 1673. dar à la estampa, este Papel. | [*Lima.* 1673?] Folio, 8 l. 35324

IZQUIERDO. Practica de los Exercicios Espirituales de Nuestro Padre S. Ignacio. *Mexico en la Imprenta de los Heredios del Lice. D. Jos. de Jautegui.* 1782. 8vo. 35325

This edition has twelve copperplates engraved by another Mexican artist, Pavia by name. They are the same designs as those engraved by Moreno.

J (A.) *See* J[ones] (A[bsalom]).

J. (C.) A Letter to the Rev. Dr. Auchmuty. [Signed C. J.] *America: Printed in the Year* M,DCC,LXXV. 8vo, pp. 8. BA.

To which is added a printed sheet: A Letter from Dr. Auchmuty to Capt. Montresson, Chief Engineer, at Boston, dated New York, April 19, 1775.

J. (G.) Bemoaning Letter of an ingenious Quaker, wherein the government of the Quakers among themselves, (as hath been exercised by George Fox, and others) is brought to light, &c. by G. J. *London.* 1700. 12mo. 35327

J. (J.) Candid Reflections on the Expedition to Martinico; with an Account of the taking of Guadaloupe by General Barrington. By J. J., a Lieutenant in the Navy. *London: A. Johnson.* 1759. 8vo, pp. 50. 35328

"Made up from the newspapers."—*Monthly Review.*, XXI. 85.

J. (J. G.) *See* [Johnson (J. G.)]

J. (S. L.) Life in the South, from the Commencement of the War. By a Blockaded British Subject. Being a Social History of those who took place in the Battles, from a personal Acquaintance with them in their own Homes. From the Spring of 1860 to August, 1862. By S. L. J. *London: Chapman & Hall.* 1863. 2 vols., post 8vo, pp. xvi, 427; viii, 404. C.

J. (T.) *See* J[efferson] (T[homas]).

J. (W.) *See* J[ordan] (W.)

J. (W.) A Remembrancer of Former Times for this Generation, and our Degeneracy lamented. By W. J. Part I. *Boston.* 1697. 16mo, pp. 32. M., W. 35330

J. (W.) W. J. against J. W. or three letters to the Rev. Mr. John Wesley, designed as an answer to a Pamphlet of his called "A Calm Address to the Inhabitants of England. By W. J. a Lover of King George and of every real Christian. [n. p.:] *Printed for the Author.* [1777.] 12mo, pp. 22. 35331

J. (W.) Extracts from a Journal kept during a Voyage from Philadelphia to Calcutta, by way of the Isle of France. By W. J. *Serampore.* 1812. 8vo. 35332

JABOATAM (A. de Sancta Maria). Discurso historico, geographico, genealogico, politico e encomiastico, recitado em a nova celebridade, que dedicaram os pardos de Pernambuco ao sancto da sua côr o B. Gonçalo Garcia. *Lisboa, por Pedro Ferreira.* 1751. 4to. 35333

JABOATAM. Novo orbe serafico Brasilico, ou chronica dos Frades Menores da provincia do Brasil. Impressa em Lisboa em 1761, e reimpressa por ordem do Instituto histor. e geogr. brasileiro. *Rio de Janeiro.* 1858. 2 vols., 8vo. + Parte segunda (inedita). [*Ibid.*] 1859–61. 2 vols., 8vo. 35334

See also Iaboatam (A. de S. M.), No. 34144; and for collation add, pp. xxxiv, 248, 283, 15. Engraving.

JACINTO DE CAXICA (P. Maestro Fray). Sermon ... San Felipe de Jesus. *Mexico.* 1639. 35335

JACK (C. J.) A Political Lecture upon the "Influence of Slavery on the Constitution and Union," delivered ... Brooklyn, by C. J. Jack, Esq., ... the 22d ... of June, 1860 ... . *Brooklyn: E. B. Spooner ... Printer.* 1860. 8vo, pp. 17. B., BA. 35336

Also: Review of the Opinion of Hon. Edward King. ... *Philadelphia.* 1846. 8vo.—Speech ... at the Meeting in favor of the Re-annexation of Texas to the United States, ... April 3, 1844. *Philadelphia.* 1844. 8vo, pp. 12.

JACK (*Colonel*). *See* [Defoe (D.)], Vol. V., No. 19279.

JACK HALLIARD, *pseudon.* Voyages and Adventures of Jack Halliard, in the Arctic Ocean. *Boston: Allen and Ticknor.* 1833. Sq. 16mo, pp. 130. 35337

The Jack Morgan Songster. Compiled by a Captain in Gen. Lee's Army. *Raleigh: Branson & Farrar.* 1864. 16mo, pp. 64. + [n. p. n. d.] 16mo, pp. 32. 35338

Jack Retort; or an Attempt at Scurrility. By W. T. Franklin. *Quilsylvania* (probably *Philadelphia*). 1765. 8vo, pp. 48. 35339

[JACKMAN (Benjamin).] A Refutation and Exposure of Clerical Misrepresentation made against the Late Thomas P. Beach. ... *Georgetown: Charles Nason, Printer.* 1848. 8vo, pp. 16. H.

JACKMAN (J.) *See* Goodridge (E. P.), Vol. VII., No. 27930.

JACKSON (A.) Official Report of the Trial of Hon. Albert Jackson, Judge of 15th Judicial Circuit of Missouri. By Thos. J. Henderson. *Jefferson.* 1859. 8vo. 35341

JACKSON (A.) Annual Messages, Veto Messages, Proclamation, &c., of Andrew Jackson, President of the United States, from 1829 to 1834. *Baltimore: E. J. Coale & Co.* 1835. 8vo, pp. 227. + Second Edition. [*Ibid.*] 8vo, pp. 272. 35342

JACKSON. Correspondence between Gen. Andrew Jackson and John C. Calhoun, President and Vice-President of the U. States, on the subject of the course of the latter, in the deliberations of the cabinet of Mr. Monroe, on the occurrences in the Seminole War. *Washington: Printed by Duff Green.* 1831. 8vo, pp. 52. B., BA., H. 35343

JACKSON. Correspondence between Major General Jackson, and Brevet Major General Scott, on the subject of an order, bearing date the 22d April, 1817; Published by the Former, to the Troops of his Division ... . [*Richmond.*] 1819. 8vo, pp. 16.

JACKSON. Correspondence between General Jackson and Mr. Monroe. As published in the National Intelligencer. *Washington: May,* 1824. 8vo, pp. 23. H. 35345

JACKSON. Gen. Andrew Jackson, and the Rev. Ezra Stiles Ely. ... [*New York: George H. Evans, Printer.* n. d.] 8vo, pp. 8.

JACKSON. Gen. Jackson's Farewell Address to the People of the United States, together with his Proclamation to South Carolina. *Harrisburg.* 1850. 8vo. P. + [*Ibid.*] 1851. 35347

Also: Farewell Address of Andrew Jackson, to the People of the United States. Delivered March 4, 1837. *Harrisburg.* 1864. 8vo, pp. 15.

JACKSON. Gen. Jackson's Letter to Carter Beverley, and Mr. Clay's Reply. Mr. Clay's Speech at the Lexington Dinner. Gen. Jackson's Reply to Mr. Clay ... Mr. Buchanan's Reply ... *Portsmouth: Printed by Miller and Brewster. Aug.* 21, 1827. 8vo, pp. 16. B., H. 35348

JACKSON. Memorial, presented to the Senate of the United States, by General Andrew Jackson, relative to the Seminole War. *Washington.* 1820. 8vo. 35349

JACKSON. Messages of Gen. Andrew Jackson: With a Short Sketch of his Life. *Concord, N. H.: John F. Brown and William White.* 1837. 12mo, pp. 430. Portrait. 35350

JACKSON. Opinions of General Andrew Jackson on the Annexation of Texas. [n. p. n. d.] 8vo, pp. 8. 35351

JACKSON. Proclamation, by Andrew Jackson, President of the United States. 1833. Folio, 1 l. 35352

The famous Proclamation of Nullification, December 10, 1833. A few copies were printed on satin, with ornamental border.

[JACKSON.] Proclamation of the President of the United States, against Nullification. *Louisville: Printed by S. Penn, Jr.* 1833. 12mo, pp. 24. + *New York.* 1833. 18mo. + *London: Richard Phillips.* [1833?] 8vo, pp. 25. 35353

JACKSON. Proclamation ... to the People of South Carolina. December 10th, 1832. *Harrisburg: A. Boyd Hamilton.* 1862. 8vo, pp. 17. + *Harrisburg: Singerly and Myers.* 1864. 8vo, pp. 16. + Another Edition. 8vo, pp. 20. 35354

Reprinted in the "Pulpit and Rostrum," New York.

JACKSON. Proklamation durch Andreas Jackson, ... Dezember 10, 1832. *Harrisburg.* 1862. 8vo, pp. 13. 35355

JACKSON. Protest of the President of the United States, against the Recent Unconstitutional Proceedings of the Senate of the United States. Read in Senate, April 17, 1834. *City of Washington: Printed by Francis Preston Blair.* 1834. 8vo, pp. 15.

JACKSON. Veto Message, returning the Bank Bill, with his Objections, &c. [n. p. n. d.] 8vo, pp. 16. + *New York.* 1832. 8vo. 35357

JACKSON. Veto-Botschaft des Präsidenten, 10ten Julius, 1832. [n. p. n. d.] 8vo, pp. 16. 35358

Review of the Veto. Containing an Examination of the Principles of the President's Message, and his objections to the bill to modify and continue the act of rechartering the Bank of the United States. *Philadelphia.* 1832. 8vo, pp. 60. 35359

Also: Review of the Veto. ... [*Printed at Washington, D. C.* 1832.] 8vo, pp. 32. + [Another Edition.] 8vo, pp. 24.

General Jackson is known by what he did, rather than by what he wrote. He has been the occasion of much writing, however, and the following list contains anonymous biographies, also military, political, and electioneering pieces relating to him.

Biographical Sketch of the Life of Andrew Jackson ... the Hero of New-Orleans. ... *Hudson, N. Y.: William E. Norman.* 1828. 18mo, pp. 65. Portrait. BA. + *Bristol, R. I.: J. Gladding & Co.* 1836. 18mo, pp. 65. Portrait. B. 35360

A Brief and Impartial History. *See* [Snelling (William J.)]

Brief Sketch of ... Jackson. *See* [Hill (Isaac)], No. 31831.

The Case of the Six Mutineers, whose Conviction and Sentence were approved of by General Jackson ... . *Albany: Printed by Webster & Wood.* 1828. 8vo, pp. 32. B. 35361

A Concise Narrative of General Jackson's First Invasion of Florida, and of his immortal Defence of New-Orleans: with Remarks. ... *New-York, February,* 1827. 8vo, pp. 48. B. + Second Edition—with Additions. By Aristides. ... *New-York: Printed by E. M. Murden & A. Ming, Jr.* 1827. 8vo, pp. 40. + Fifth Edition. *Albany.* 1828. 8vo, pp. 24. B. 35362

Civil and Military Life of Andrew Jackson, by an American Officer. *New York.* 1825. 8vo, pp. 359. 35363

A Dialogue between a Colonel of the Militia, and a Militiaman, in relation to the Execution of the Six Militia-men, Shot by order of General Jackson. [n. p. n. d.] 8vo. 35364

Facts and Official Documents, relative to the Fitness of General Jackson and Mr. Adams for the Office of President, and to the Conduct of the Parties supporting them. [n. p. n. d.] 8vo, pp. 16. 35365

A History of the Life and Public Services of Major General Andrew Jackson. Impartially compiled from the most authentic sources. [n. p.] 1828. 8vo, pp. 37. 35366

An Impartial and True History of the Life and Services of Major General Andrew Jackson. [n. p. 1828.] 8vo, pp. 36.

... An Impartial & True History of the Life & Services of Major-General Andrew Jackson. [n. p. n. d.] 8vo, pp. 16.

The Inauguration of Mill's Equestrian Statue of Andrew Jackson, at Washington, January 8, 1853. [n. p. n. d.] 8vo, pp. 8.

Contains an oration by Stephen A. Douglas.

Jackson Democratic Association. Proceedings at the Banquet, Jan. 8, 1852. *Washington.* 1852. 8vo, pp. 20. S. 35370

Jackson and New Orleans. An Authentic Narrative of the Memorable Achievements of the American Army, under Andrew Jackson, before New Orleans, in the Winter of 1814–15. *New York.* 1856. 12mo, pp. 411. 35371

The Jackson Offering; or, National Souvenir, illustrated with Portrait, Plates, and Map. *Philadelphia.* 1829. 8vo. 35372

The Jackson Wreath. *See* Walsh (Robert), Jr.

A Letter from the Jackson Committee Of Nashville, in answer to one from a similar Committee at Cincinnati, upon the subject of Gen. Jackson's Marriage ... . *Nashville: Printed by Hall & Fitzgerald.* 1827. 12mo, pp. 30. 35373

Letters of Gen. Adair and Gen. Jackson relative to the charge of Cowardice made by the latter against the Kentucky Troops at New Orleans, April 10, 1815. *Lexington, Ky.* 1816. 8vo.

Memoirs of General Andrew Jackson, and the Public Acts of General Andrew Jackson in Florida. *Bridgeton, N. J.* 1824. 8vo, pp. 40. 35375

Memoirs of Gen. Andrew Jackson, together with the Letter of Mr. Secretary Adams, in Vindication of the Execution of Arbuthnot and Ambrister, and the other Public Acts of Gen. Jackson in Florida. *New York.* 1824. 8vo, pp. 40. 35376

Memoirs of General Andrew Jackson, seventh President of the United States: ... To which is added The Eulogy of Hon. Geo. Bancroft, delivered at Washington, D. C. Compiled by a Citizen of Western New-York. *Auburn, N. Y.: James C. Derby & Co.* 1845. 8vo, pp. 270. 35377

Memoirs of Andrew Jackson. *See* [Smith (J. V. C.)]

[42] Message from the President of the United States, ... with the Documents relating to A Misunderstanding between Andrew Jackson ... and Elijius Fromentin ... . January 29, 1822. ... *Washington: Printed by Gales & Seaton.* 1822. 8vo, pp. 326.

Notice Biographique sur le Général Jackson ... . *Paris.* M.DCCC.XXIX. 8vo, pp. 31. BA. 35379

Obsequies in honor of Andrew Jackson. *See* Dallas (G. M.)

Pictorial Life of Andrew Jackson; containing Anecdotes, Illustrations of his Character: For Young People ... . *Philadelphia: Lindsay and Blakiston.* 1845. 12mo, pp. x, 183. 35380

Probably by John Frost, A.M. *See our* Vol. VII., No. 26054, *note.*

Plain Reasons of a Plain Man, for prefering Gen. Jackson to Mr. Adams, as President of the United States. *Baltimore: Printed by Benjamin Edes.* 1825. 8vo, pp. 16. BA. 35381

Plain Truth. ... Jackson and Burr. [n. p. n. d.] 8vo, pp. 15.

Published by the Ohio County (Va.) Committee of Vigilance.

The Political Mirror; or Review of Jacksonism. ... *New-York: J. P. Peaslee.* 1835. 12mo, pp. xvi, 316. BA. 35383

The Presidency. [n. p. n. d.] 8vo, pp. 45. B. 35384

By an old man. Against General Jackson.

Principles and Men considered in reference to the Election of President. By a Citizen of Rhode Island. *Providence.* 1823. 8vo. 35385

Relates to Andrew Jackson.

Reminiscences; or Extracts from the Catalogue of General Jackson's Juvenile Indiscretions, between the age of 22 and 60. [n. p. n. d.] 8vo, pp. 8. 35386

Reflections on the Character and Public Services of Andrew Jackson, with reference to his Qualifications for the Presidency. With General Remarks. By a Native American. *New York.* 1828. 8vo, pp. 48 B. 35387

Report and Documents, relative to the Fine imposed on General Andrew Jackson ... in 1815 ... . *New Orleans.* 1843. 8vo, pp. 31. 35388

Report of Committee on the Judiciary, on refunding the Fine heretofore imposed on Gen. Jackson. ... Jan. 31, 1843. 8vo, pp. 53. S. 35389

A Review of Gen. Jackson's Letters to Mr. Monroe. Dedicated, with great respect, to the Members of the House of Representatives of the United States. [n. p. 1825.] 8vo, pp. 8.

Some Account of General Jackson. *See* Vol. VI., No. 21732.

The Tennessee Farmer; or Farmer Jackson in New York. *New York.* 1821. 8vo, pp. 8. 35391

Also: Address and Proclamation of Andrew Jackson.—Address of the Republican General Committee of Young Men of the City ... of New-York, friendly to the Election of Gen. Andrew Jackson ... . To the Republican Electors of the State ... . *New-York: Alexander Irving, Jr., Printer.* 1828. 8vo, pp. 48. B.—Address to the People of the United States on the Subject of the Presidential Election, comprising a comparative View of the Character and Administration of Andrew Jackson. By a Freeman of the United States. *Washington.* 1832. 8vo.—Address, Resolutions, and other Proceedings of a Public Meeting at Columbus, Ohio, Nov. 17, 1827, by the Citizens of Franklin County, favorable to the Election of Andrew Jackson. *Columbus.* [n. d.] 8vo.—An Address, to the People of the United States, on the ... Presidential Election: with ... Reference to the Nomination of Andrew Jackson ... . [n. p.:] *For the Proprietor.* 1828. 8vo, pp. 48.—Addresses on the Presentation of the Sword of Gen. Andrew Jackson to the Congress of the United States, delivered in the Senate and House of Representatives February 26, 1855. *Washington.* 1855. 8vo, pp. 40. Portrait.—Addresses, delivered at the Celebration of the Thirteenth Anniversary of the Victory of New Orleans. ... *Philadelphia: Printed by William Stavely.* 1828. 8vo, pp. 16.—A Brief Account of General Jackson's Dealings in Negroes. [*New York.* 1828.] 8vo, pp. 18.—A Brief Inquiry into some of the Objections urged against the Election of Andrew Jackson, to the Office of President of the United States. [n. p. n. d.] 16mo, pp. 34.—The Claims of Andrew Jackson to the Office of President, impartially examined. *New-York: Printed by John M. Danforth.* 1832. 8vo, pp. 12. —Great Jackson Meeting in Baltimore. No. 1. *Boston.* 1829. 12mo.—Great Meeting of Irishmen at Philadelphia. ... August 6, 1832, ... to prevent the re-election of Andrew Jackson ... . [*Philadelphia.*] 1832. 8vo, pp. 23. BA.—Some Account of some of the [tyrannical] deeds of General Jackson. [*Franklin.* 1818.] Folio, 1 l. Also various broadsides, such as "Account of the Execution of the Six Militia-men, with the Approval of General Jackson, 21 Feb. 1815."

JACKSON (A.) Narrative and Writings of Andrew Jackson, of Kentucky; ... Narrated by Himself; Written by a Friend. *Syracuse.* 1847. 12mo, pp. 120. B. 35392

JACKSON. The Freedom's Songster; Containing a Choice Selection of Liberty Hymns, Songs, &c., with Several Pieces of Music. By Rev. Andrew Jackson. *Syracuse: Finney & Marsh.* 1847. 16mo, pp. 64. 35393

[JACKSON (Charles), *and others.*] Report on the Establishment of a Farm School. [*Boston.* 1832.] 8vo, pp. 8. BA. 35394

JACKSON (C.) An Oration, delivered before ... St. Peter's Lodge, ... Newburyport, ... June 25, 5798. By ... Charles Jackson, P.M. *Newburyport: Printed by Brother Angier March.* 5798. 4to, pp. 24. BA., H. 35395

[JACKSON (Charles David).] A Pastoral Letter, to the Parishioners of St. Peter's Church, [on] ... the proposed erection of a new Church Edifice. ... *New-York: Pudney & Russell, Printers.* 1851. 8vo, pp. 24. H. 35396

JACKSON (C. T.) An Address ... before the Plymouth County Agricultural Society, at ... Bridgewater, Sept. 25, 1850. By Charles T. Jackson, M.D., ... *Boston: Printed by Charles C. P. Moody.* 1850. 8vo, pp. 29. B., H. 35397

JACKSON. Geological Report of Lands belonging to the Ridgway Company, in ... Pennsylvania. By Dr. Charles T. Jackson, ... *Philadelphia: Parry & McMillan.* 1856. 8vo, pp. 19. H.

JACKSON. Report on the Geology of the Public Lands, belonging to the Two States of Massachusetts and Maine. By C. T. Jackson ... . *Boston.* 1833. 8vo, pp. xii, 93, (1). 35399

JACKSON. Second Annual Report on the Geology of the Public Lands, belonging to the Two States of Maine and Massachusetts. By C. T. Jackson ... . *Augusta: Luther Severance, Printer.* 1838. 8vo, pp. xi, 100, 9 Plates, xxxvii. H. + *Boston: Dutton and Wentworth,* ... *Printers.* 1838. 8vo, pp. xii, 93, (1).

[JACKSON.] Report on the Copper Mine of the North Carolina Copper Company, in Guilford Co., North Carolina. [*G. F. Nesbitt & Co., Printers, N. Y.* 1853.] 8vo, pp. 8. H. 35401

Also: Twenty-fourth Anniversary Address, before the American Institute, New York, ... on the 16th ... of October, 1851. ... *New York: D. Murphy & Son, Printers.* 1851. 8vo, pp. 23. B.—List of Mines and Minerals belonging to the Maine Mining Company, which have been Explored and Reported on. ... *London.* 1837. 8vo. N.—Report on the Albert Coal Mine [with Report on the Geological Relations, &c., of the Coal by J. G. Percival, A. A. Hayes, &c.] ... *New-York: George F. Nesbitt & Co.* 1851. 8vo, pp. 48. B.—Report on the Contoocook Valley Plumbago Mine. ... *Boston: Geo. C. Rand & Avery, Printers.* 1864. 8vo, pp. 19. B.— ... Report to the Trustees of Lake Superior Copper Company. November, 1845. *Boston: Printed by Beals and Greene.* 1845. 8vo, pp. 19. Plates. H. + Second Report. [*Ibid.*] 1845. 8vo, pp. 19.—Report upon the ... Black River Mines ... C. E. ... October 22, 1862. ... *Boston: Press of Geo. C. Rand & Avery.* 1862. 8vo, pp. 7, (1). Plan. + [*Ibid.*] 1863. 8vo, pp. 8. Plan.—Report upon the ... Oxford Plumbago Mining Company ... in ... Maine. ... *Boston: Press of Geo. C. Rand & Avery.* 1863. 8vo, pp. 11.—Reports upon ... St. Margaret's Copper Mine ... in St. Sylvester, C. E. ... *Boston: Press of Geo. C. Rand & Avery.* 1863. 8vo, pp. 7. 2 Diagrams. *See* Maine, Massachusetts, Michigan, New Hampshire, Rhode Island, and Wisconsin.

JACKSON, *and* ALGER (F.) Remarks on the Mineralogy and Geology of Nova Scotia, ... By Charles T. Jackson and Francis Alger. *Cambridge: E. W. Metcalf and Company.* 1832. 4to, pp. (4), 116. Map and 4 Plates. B., H. 35402

From the "Memoirs of the American Academy," New Series, Vol. I. Originally published in Vols. XIV. and XV. of Silliman's "American Journal," &c.; in which compare also at Vol. XXII., p. 167.

JACKSON. Full Exposure of the Conduct of Dr. Charles T. Jackson, leading to his Discharge from the Government Service, and Justice to Messrs. Foster and Whitney, U. S. Geologists. [n. p. 1849.] 8vo, pp. 32. H. 35403

JACKSON (D. T.) Petition of David T. Jackson to Congress, February 15, 1869. *New York.* 1869. 8vo. 35404

JACKSON (E.) Address ... before the Middlesex County Agricultural Society ... October 13th, 1842. By Hon. Ebenezer Jackson. *Middleton, Conn.: W. D. Starr, Printer.* 1842. 8vo, pp. 19. H. 35405

JACKSON (E.), *and* BOWDITCH (H. I.) Report of the Minority of the Committee of the Primary School Board, on the Caste

Schools of Boston. With Remarks on the City Solicitor's Opinion by W. Phillips. *Boston.* 1846. 8vo, pp. 36. B. 35406

[JACKSON (Edward).] A Council of Six Churches, conven'd at Woburn, upon the Request of the Rev. Mr. Jackson Pastor and the first Church in said Town, to hear ... upon the great and uncommon Difficulties among them, Dec. 24. 1746. ... . [*Woburn.* 1746.] 4to, pp. 8. BA. 35407

JACKSON (F.) A History of the Early Settlement of Newton, County of Middlesex, Massachusetts, from 1639 to 1800. With a Genealogical Register of its Inhabitants, prior to 1800. By Francis Jackson ... . *Boston: Printed by Stacy and Richardson.* 1854. 12mo, pp. 555, (1). Portrait and Map. B., C., H. 35408

JACKSON (F.) In Memoriam. Testimonials to the Life and Character of the late Francis Jackson ... [President of the Mass. Anti-Slavery Society.] *Boston: R. F. Wallcut.* 1861. 12mo, pp. 36. H. 35409

[JACKSON (Francis James).] Important State Papers. [Correspondence between the British Ministers and Mr. Smith. *Boston.* 1809.] 8vo, pp. 27. BA. 35410

See [Hanson (A. C.)], Vol. VIII., No. 30257.

JACKSON. [Ten] Hints. *See* [Lowell (John)].

JACKSON (Frederick). Il Recrutio, A Comic Opera, as originally produced by Members of the Forty-fourth Regiment, in Barracks at Newbern, N. O. [*Roxbury.* 1863.] 8vo, pp. 15.

[JACKSON (Hall).] Observations and Remarks on the Putrid Malignant Sore Throat, which has mortally raged for many years past [1784–1786]. By a Gentleman of the Faculty. *Portsmouth, N. H.* 1786. 8vo, pp. 28. N., S. 35412

JACKSON (H.) Civilization of the Indian Natives; or, A Brief View of the Friendly Conduct of William Penn towards them, in the early Settlement of Pennsylvania; the subsequent care of the Society of Friends in endeavoring to promote peace and friendship with them by pacific measures; and A concise narrative of the proceedings of the Yearly Meetings of Friends of Pennsylvania, New Jersey, and parts adjacent, since the year 1795, in promoting their improvement and Gradual Civilization. By Halliday Jackson. ... *Philadelphia: Marcus T. C. Gould.* 1830. 8vo, pp. 120. 35413

JACKSON (H.) An Account of the Churches in Rhode-Island. Presented at an adjourned session of the Twenty-eighth Annual Meeting of the Rhode-Island Baptist State Convention, Providence, November 8, 1853. By Henry Jackson ... . *Providence: George H. Whitney.* 1854. 8vo, pp. 134. Plate. B., C. 35414

JACKSON. Historical Discourse delivered at the 250th Anniversary of the First Baptist Church in America. By Henry Jackson ... . *Providence, R. I.* 1854. 8vo. 35415

JACKSON. An Historical Discourse, delivered in the Central Baptist Meeting House, Newport, R. I., January 8, 1854. By the Pastor, Henry Jackson. ... *Newport: Cranston & Norman.* 1854. 8vo, pp. 45. 35416

Also: A Discourse in Commemoration of the ... Anniversary of the Mite Society; and the ... Anniversary of the First Baptist Church in America. ... *Providence: John R. Stickney.* 1854. 8vo, pp. 32.—Discourse occasioned by the Death of the Rev. Zalmon Tobey, September 17, 1858. ... October 3, 1858. ... *Providence: Coggeshall & Stewart.* 1859. 8vo, pp. 32.—A Good Minister ... exemplified in the Life and Character of the Late Rev. Ebenezer Nelson. ... *Boston: Printed by George C. Rand.* 1852. 12mo, pp. 21. H.

JACKSON (H. R.) Eulogy upon the Life and Character of the Hon. Chas. J. McDonald, pronounced at Marietta, April 20, 1861. By Henry R. Jackson. *Atlanta, Ga.* 1861. 8vo, pp. 35.

McDonald was Solicitor-General, Senator, Governor of the State, Judge of the Supreme Court, &c.

JACKSON. The Crisis—What is Resistance? Letters from Henry R. Jackson to the Hon. Alex. H. Stephens. *Savannah: John M. Cooper & Co.* 1860. 8vo, pp. 31. 35418

JACKSON. Tullulah, and other Poems. By Henry R. Jackson. *Savannah: John M. Cooper.* 1850. 8vo, xv, 15–235. H.

JACKSON (H. W. R.) Historical Register, and Confederate's Assistant to National Independence. Containing ... Valuable Recipes, for the Soldier and the People in general, throughout the Confederate States of America. *Augusta, Ga.* 1862. 12mo, pp. 44. 35420

JACKSON. The Southern Women of the Second American Revolution, Our Naval Victories and Exploits of Confederate War Steamers, Capture of Yankee Gunboats, &c. By H. W R. Jackson. *Atlanta, Georgia.* 1863. 8vo, pp. 120, Index, 2.

A collection of articles from various newspapers, with comments by H. W. R. Jackson. The covers of this work contain the titles of three other works, neither of which I have seen, of which H. W. R. Jackson is the editor or compiler, viz.: Historical and Statistical Register ... . *Airen* [*i. e. Aiken*], *South Carolina.*—Poems of the Confederate States. ... *Aiken, South Carolina.*—The Confederate Monitor and Patriot's Friend.

JACKSON (I. R.) The Life of William Henry Harrison, (of Ohio,) the People's Candidate for the Presidency. With a History of the Wars with the British and Indians on our northwestern frontier. By Isaac R. Jackson. Fourth Edition. *Philadelphia: Marshall, Williams & Butler.* 1840. 24mo, pp. x, 15–222. B., C. + Fifth Edition. [*Ibid.*] 1840. P. 35422

JACKSON. Lebensgeschichte des Generals Harrison ... . Aus dem Englischen des I. R. Jackson. *Philadelphia: Marschall, Williams, und Butler.* 1840. 8vo, pp. 32. B., BA., H. 35423

JACKSON (J.) An Address, delivered at the Funeral of John Gorham, M.D. on the 31st ... of March, 1829. ... By James Jackson, M.D. *Boston: W. L. Lewis, Print.* 1829. 8vo, pp. 16.

JACKSON. An Eulogy on the Character of John Warren, M.D. ... Delivered at the request of the ... Massachusetts Medical Society. By James Jackson, M.D. ... *Boston: Printed by C. Stebbins.* 1815. 8vo, pp. 34. B., BA., C., H., N. 35425

JACKSON. A Memoir of James Jackson, Jr., M.D. with Extracts from his Letters to his Father; and Medical Cases ... . By James Jackson, M.D. ... *Boston: Printed by I. R. Butts.* 1835. 8vo, pp. (4), 444. B., BA., H. 35426

JACKSON. Memoir of James Jackson, Jr. M.D. written by his Father, with Extracts from his Letters, and Reminiscenses of him, by a Fellow Student. ... *Boston: Hilliard, Gray & Co.* 1836. 16mo, pp. xi, (4), 228. B., BA., H. 35427

JACKSON. Memoir on the Last Sickness of General Washington and its Treatment by the Attendant Physicians. By James Jackson, M.D. *Boston: Privately Printed.* 1860. 12mo, pp. 31. B., H. 35428

JACKSON. A Report ... on the ... Common Continued Fever of New-England ... 1821, to ... 1835 ... By James Jackson, M.D. ... . *Boston: Whipple & Damrell.* 1838. 8vo, pp. (2), 95.

JACKSON (J. C.) American Womanhood: its Peculiarities and Necessities. By James C. Jackson, M.D., Physician-in-Chief of "Our Home on the Hill-Side," Dansville, Livingston County, New York. *Dansville, New York.* 186–. 12mo, pp. 160. Portrait. 35430

JACKSON (J. W.) Life of James W. Jackson, the Alexandria Hero, the Slayer of Ellsworth, the first Martyr in the Cause of Southern Independence; containing A Full Account of the Circumstances of his Heroic Death, and the many Remarkable Incidents in his Eventful Life, constituting a True History, more like Romance than Reality. ... *Richmond: West & Johnston.* 1862. 8vo, pp. 48. B. 35431

JACKSON (J. W.) Speech by Jesse W. Jackson ... before the Georgia Legislature ... November 14th, 1866. *Madison, Ga.* 1867. 8vo, pp. 16. H. 35432

JACKSON (J.) A Faithful Account of the Massacre of the Family of Gerald Watson ... By John Jackson ... . *Boston: Printed for N. Coverly.* 1819. 8vo, pp. 24. H. 35433

JACKSON (J.) ... Lecture on British Colonial Slavery ... 4th January, 1833. By the Rev. John Jackson ... . *Newcastle: Printed ... by J. Blackwell and Co.* 1833. 12mo, pp. 11. H.

JACKSON (J.) Reflections on Peace and War. By John Jackson. *Philadelphia: T. E. Chapman.* 1846. 18mo, pp. (2), 78.

[JACKSON (J. C.)] Duties and Dignities of American Freemen. *Boston: New-England Anti-Slavery Tract Association.* 18—.

JACKSON (J. G.) Speech of John G. Jackson [on the Embargo], in the House ... February 6, 1809. [n. p. 1809.] 8vo, pp. 32. B., C. 35437

[JACKSON (John Mills).] A View of the Political Situation of the Province of Upper Canada, in North America. In which her Physical Capacity is stated; the Means of diminishing her Burden, increasing her Value, and securing her Connection to Great Britain, are fully considered. With Notes and Appendix. *London: W. Earle.* 1809. 8vo, pp. xi, (1), 79. H. 35438

See "M. Rev.," LXVIII. 369. This elicited "Letters from an American Loyalist in Upper Canada to his Friend in England, on a Pamphlet published by John Mills Jackson, entitled: A View of the Province of Upper Canada." [*Halifax.* 1810.] 8vo, pp. 104.

JACKSON (J. P.) A General Railroad System for New Jersey ... and a Main Trunk Double-Track Railway for the Nation ... being a Correspondence between Citizens of New Jersey and John P. Jackson ... . *Newark, N. J.: A. Stephen Holbrook, Printer.* 1860. 8vo, pp. 44. Maps. H. 35439

JACKSON (J. W.) The Union—The Constitution—Peace. A Thanksgiving Sermon, delivered in ... Harrisburg, Pa. By

Jno. Walker Jackson, ... August 6, 1863. ... *Harrisburg.* 1863. 8vo, pp. 33. H. 35440

Also: The Sentiments and Conduct proper to the present Crisis in our National Affairs. A Sermon ... at Philadelphia, April 21, 1861. ... *Philadelphia: Collins, Printer.* 1861. 8vo, pp. 13.

[JACKSON (Jonathan).] Thoughts upon the Political Situation of the United States ... in which that of Massachusetts Is more particularly considered. With some Observations on the Constitution for a Federal Government. Addressed to the People of the Union. By a Native of Boston. ... *Worcester: Printed by Isaiah Thomas.* MDCCLXXXVIII. 8vo, pp. 209. B., BA., H. 35441

This piece has also been attributed to G. R. Minot. Also: Report of the Secretary of the Treasury, on the Petition of Jonathan Jackson, &c. *Philadelphia.* 1798. P.

JACKSON (J. C.) The Relations of the American Lawyer to the State. An Oration ... September, 1859. By Joseph C. Jackson ... . *Cambridge: Welch, Bigelow and Company, Printers.* 1859. 8vo, pp. 26. B., H. 35442

JACKSON (J. H.) A Narrative of the Adventures and Experience of Joseph H. Jackson, in Nauvoo, disclosing the depths of Mormon Villany. *Warsaw, Illinois, August,* 1844. 8vo, pp. 32.

JACKSON (J. W.) The Union and State-Rights Parties of Georgia. Speech of Hon. Joseph W. Jackson ... March 16, 1852 ... . [n. p. n. d.] 8vo, pp. 7. H. 35444

JACKSON (L. E.) ... Church Directory for New York City. By Lewis E. Jackson. *New York: New York City Mission.* 1867. 16mo, pp. 96. 35445

JACKSON (M.) Extracts from Letters and other Pieces, written by Margaret Jackson, during her last Illness. *Philadelphia: Benjamin & Thomas Kite.* 1825. 16mo, pp. 95. H.

JACKSON (P.) Case of Potter Jackson. *London.* 1807. 8vo.

Relates to slavery. Also: Account of the most cruel Treatment he received from Captain Lively and his Chief Mate. ... *London.* 1806. 8vo. C.

[JACKSON (P. T.)] Boston Memorial on the Cotton Manufacture. To ... Congress ... . [n. p. 1846.] 8vo, pp. 11.

Signed by "P. T. Jackson" and many others.

[JACKSON.] Convention of the Friends of American Industry Report on the Production and Manufacture of Cotton. *Boston.* 1832. 35449

[JACKSON (Richard).] The Interest of Great Britain Considered, With Regard to her Colonies, And the Acquisitions of Canada and Guadaloupe. To which are added, Observations concerning the Increase of Mankind, Peopling of Countries, &c. *London: T. Becket.* M,DCC,LX. 8vo, pp. (2), 58. BA. + The Second Edition. [*Ibid.*] M DCC LXI. 8vo, pp. (2), 58. H. + *Dublin: P. Wilson.* 1760. 8vo, pp. 46. + *London, Printed: Philadelphia, Re-printed by William Bradford.* MDCCLX. 8vo, pp. 47. + *Boston: Reprinted by B. Mecom.* 1760. 8vo, pp. 59, (5).

The "heads of divisions are not in the author's original edition, but were subsequently added by another hand, and have since been retained."—SPARKS. Dr. Franklin considerably aided in this work, and it is sometimes found described under his name; indeed, the publisher of the Boston edition has plainly indicated that the work is by Dr. Franklin; it was, in fact, published by him when residing in London as Agent for Pennsylvania. *See* Bancroft, IV. 360; "M. Rev.," XXII. 432.

JACKSON (R.), *Jr., and* POTTER (E. R.) Address from the Hon. Richard Jackson, Jun., and Elisha R. Potter, Representatives in Congress from the State of Rhode Island, to their Constituents, March 16, 1812. [*Washington.* 1812.] 8vo, pp. 22.

JACKSON (R. E. S.) The Life of William Scoresby, M.A., ... Corresponding Member of the Institute of France, etc. By His Nephew, R. E. Scoresby-Jackson ... . *London: T. Nelson and Sons.* MDCCCLXI. Post 8vo, pp. 406. Portrait, 4 Plates, Map.

JACKSON (R. M. S.) The Mountain. By R. M. S. Jackson. *Philadelphia: J. B. Lippincott & Co.* 1858. 12mo, pp. 202, 15.

JACKSON (R.) An Outline of the History and Cure of Fever ... more expressly the ... Yellow Fever in the West Indies. ... By Robert Jackson, M.D. ... *Edinburgh: Mundell & Son.* 1798. 8vo, pp. xi, 396. H. 35454

JACKSON. Sketch of the History and Cure of Febrile Diseases; more especially as they appear in the West Indies among the Soldiers of the British Army. By Robert Jackson, M.D. ... Second Edition, with many Additions. *London.* 1820. 2 vols., 8vo. C. 35455

JACKSON. A Treatise on the Fevers of Jamaica, with some Observations on the Intermitting Fever of America, and an Appendix, containing some Hints on the means of preserving the Health of Soldiers in hot Climates. By Robert Jackson, M.D. ... *London: John Murray.* 1791. 8vo, pp. 440. S. + *Philadelphia: Robert T. Campbell.* 1795. 12mo, pp. xi, 276, 19. BA. 35456

JACKSON. Ueber die Fieber in Jamaika. Aus dem Englischen mit Anmerkungen von K. Sprengel. *Leipzig.* 1796. 8vo.

JACKSON (S.) An Account of the Yellow ... Fever, ... in ... Philadelphia in 1820. By Samuel Jackson, M.D. ... *Philadelphia: M. Carey & Sons.* 1821. 8vo, pp. 116. B., BA. 35458

[JACKSON.] Review of the Memorial of Dr. John Bell to the Trustees of the University. *Philadelphia.* 1850. 8vo. 35459

Also: The Annual Discourse before the Philadelphia County Medical Society, ... February 10, 1852. ... *Philadelphia: T. K. and P. G. Collins, Printers.* 1852. 8vo, pp. 23.—A Discourse commemorative of the late William E. Horner, M.D., ... October 10, 1853. ... *Philadelphia: T. K. and P. G. Collins, Printers.* 1853. 8vo, pp. 46.—A Discourse commemorative of Nathaniel Chapman, M.D. ... October 13, 1854. *Philadelphia: T. K. and P. G. Collins, Printers.* 1854. 8vo, pp. 28. H.—Memoir of Isaac Parrish, M.D. ... February 2, 1853. ... *Philadelphia: T. K. and P. G. Collins, Printers.* 1853. 8vo, pp. 27. Portrait.—Oration at Philadelphia, July 4, 1818. ... *Philadelphia.* 1818. 8vo.—Also, Biography [of] Benjamin Rush, 1745–1813. pp. 17–85 of American Medical Biography.

JACKSON, MEIGS (C. D.), *and* HARLAN (R.) Report of the Commission appointed to visit Canada, for the Investigation of the Epidemic Cholera. By Samuel Jackson, M.D., Charles D. Meigs, M.D., and Richard Harlan, M.D. *Philadelphia.* 1832. 8vo, pp. 37.

JACKSON (S. C.) Religious Principle—a Source of Public Prosperity. A Sermon ... at the Annual Election ... January 7, 1843. By Samuel C. Jackson ... . *Boston: Dutton and Wentworth, Printers.* 1843, 8vo, pp. 55. B., BA. 35461

JACKSON (Stonewall). *See* Jackson (Thomas J.)

JACKSON (T.) Authorities Cited Antagonistic to Horace Binney's Conclusions on the Writ of Habeas Corpus. By Tatlow Jackson. *Philadelphia: John Campbell.* 1862. 8vo, pp. 8. B.

Twenty copies printed on large paper, in 4to.

JACKSON. Martial Law: What is it? and Who can Declare it? By Tatlow Jackson. *Philadelphia: John Campbell.* 1862. 8vo, pp. 19. B., BA. 35463

Twenty copies printed on large paper, in 4to.

JACKSON (T.) The Centenary of Wesleyan Methodism. A Brief Sketch of the Rise, Progress, and Present State of the Wesleyan-Methodist Societies throughout the World. By Thomas Jackson ... . *London: John Mason.* 1839. 12mo, pp. viii, 388. 2 Portraits. B. 35464

Also: Lives of Early Methodists. Chiefly by themselves. *London.* 1849. 2 vols., 12mo.

JACKSON. Life of Rev. Charles Wesley; ... and Sketch of the Rise and Progress of Methodism. By Thomas Jackson. *London: John Mason.* 1841. 2 vols., 8vo. C. 35465

Describes "Wesley's Visit to America," Vol. I., pp. 38–79.

[JACKSON (Thomas J.)] Life and Military Career of "Stonewall" Jackson. *London: Bacon & Co.* [1863.] 8vo, pp. 15.

JACKSON. The Life of Lieut. Gen. T. J. Jackson. By an Ex-Cadet. *Richmond, Va.: James E. Goode.* 1863. 8vo, pp. 128.

Another edition, same imprint, 12mo, pp. 196.

JACKSON. The Life of Thomas J. Jackson. By an Ex-Cadet. Second Edition, Revised and Enlarged by the Author. *Richmond: James E. Goode.* 1864. 8vo, pp. 196. 35468

Many of the incidents related came under the immediate observation of the author, and the remainder are drawn from authentic sources.

JACKSON. The Life [etc.] *See* [Daniel (J. M.)], No. 18492.

JACKSON. "Stonewall" Jackson. A Biographical Sketch. By the Author of "Life in the South." *London: Chapman & Hall.* 1863. Post 8vo. 35469

JACKSON. Prospectus for a Statue to the late General Thos J. "Stonewall" Jackson. *London.* 1863. 4to. 35470

This statue was erected September, 1875. Also: Stonewall Jackson's Song Book. *Richmond.* 1864. 16mo.

[JACKSON (William).] Rise, Progress, and Present State of the Dispute between the People of America and the Administration. By the Bishop of Oxford. *London.* 1776. 8vo. C.

See also our Vol. IV., No. 16088.

JACKSON (W.) Eulogium, On the Character of General Washington, ... Pronounced before the Pennsylvania Society of the Cincinnati, On the Twenty-Second day of February, Eighteen Hundred ... At ... Philadelphia. By Major William Jackson, Aid-de-camp to the late President of the United States, ... *Philadelphia: Printed by John Ormrod.* 1800. 8vo, pp. 44. C.

It was reprinted, with the title slightly altered, as below:

JACKSON. Eulogium, ... Pronounced at the request of the Pennsylvania Society of the Cincinnati, before the President of the United States and the members of both houses of Congress; ... By Major William Jackson ... . New Edition. *Philadelphia: Printed by John Ormrod,* ... 1800. 8vo, pp. 44. 35473

This edition is usually found at the end of "Monuments of Patriotism." *Philadelphia.* 1800.

JACKSON. An Oration to Commemorate the Independence of the United States of North America, delivered ... in Philadelphia, July 4, 1786, By Major William Jackson, and Published at the Request of the Pennsylvania Society of the Cincinnati. *Philadelphia: Eleazar Oswald.* MDCCLXXXVI. 4to, pp. 29. P.

Also: Memorial on behalf of the Surviving Officers of the Revolutionary Army of the United States to the Congress of the United States. N.

[JACKSON (William).] A Brief Notice of the Settlement of ... Newton, prepared by a Committee who were charged with the Duty of Erecting a Monument to the Memory of its First Settlers, September, 1852. *Boston: Printed by C. C. P. Moody.* 1852. 8vo, pp. 38, (4). H. 35475

[JACKSON.] Letter to Marshall S. Rice. [n. p. 1849.] 8vo, pp. 7. H. 35476

Also: A Lecture on Railroads ... January 12th, 1829, Before the Massachusetts Charitable Mechanic Association. ... *Boston.* 1829. 8vo, pp. 32. + Second Edition. *Boston: Henry Bowen.* 1829. 8vo, pp. 36. B., BA., H., W.

JACKSON (W. A.) ... Address ... at Albany, February 22, 1858, by the late Col. William A. Jackson ... . [*Albany.* 1867.] 8vo, pp. 15. B., H. 35477

JACKSON. Documents relative to an Attack upon the Character of the late Col. Wm. A. Jackson. [*Albany.* 1863.] 8vo, pp. 16, (1). B., H. 35478

JACKSON. Memoir of William A. Jackson, a Member of the Albany Bar, and Colonel of the 18th Regiment, N. Y. Volunteers, who Died at ... Washington, November 11, 1861. ... *Albany: Joel Munsell.* 1862. 8vo, pp. 40. BA., S. 35479

JACKSON. An Oration, ... at Windham Centre, Greene County, N. Y., July 4, 1859. By the late Col. William A. Jackson ... . *Albany: C. Van Benthuysen, Printer.* 1863. 8vo, pp. 24. B., H., S. 35480

[JACKSON.] Review of a Tract entitled "Secret Societies in Colleges ..." Union College, Nov. 21, 1850. 8vo, pp. 4. S.

JACKSON (W. M.) The Christian Patriot's Duty, At the Present Crisis, A Sermon preached in ... Norfolk, Va., Aug. 18, 1850, By Rev. William M. Jackson. ... *Norfolk: Printed by T. G. Broughton & Son.* 1850. 8vo, pp. 12. 35482

JACKSON. Remains of the Rev. William Jackson, late rector of Paul's Church, Louisville, Ky. With a Brief Sketch of his

Life and Character. By the Rev. William M. Jackson. *New York.* 1847. 8vo. C., P. 35483

JACKSON (William S.) An Essay on the Rights of Government. *Wilmington, Del.* 1846. 8vo, pp. 19. 35484

JACKSON, *Michigan.* Jackson City Directory, for 1869–70, also including the villages of Grass Lake, Parma, Brooklyn, Napoleon, Concord, Leoni, and Norvell. Compiled and published by James M. Thomas. *Jackson (Mich.): J. M. Thomas.* 1869. 8vo, pp. (6), 295. C. 35485

JACKSONVILLE, *Florida.* Jacksonville City Directory, and Business Advertiser, for 1871. *Jacksonville (Fla.): Florida Union Job Office.* 1871. 12mo. C. 35486

[JACOB (Gérard).] Voyage Philosophique dans l'Amérique Méridionale. Rédigé par l'Éditeur de l'An 2440. *Paris.* 1829. 8vo. 35487

[JACOB (John J.)] A Biographical Sketch of the Life of the late Capt. Michael Cresap. *Cumberland, Md.: Printed for the Author by J. M. Buchanan.* 1826. 12mo, pp. 124. C. 35488

This original edition, which is very rare, is a defense of Col. Cresap, contradicting the statements made by Mr. Jefferson, in his "Notes on Virginia." For a gushing notice *see* Field's "Essay," No. 769. It was reprinted with notes and appendix as:

JACOB. A Biographical Sketch of the Life of the Late Captain Michael Cresap. By John J. Jacob. *Cincinnati: ... William Dodge.* 1860. 4to, pp. 158; Boyer's Journal, pp. 53. BA.

JACOB (J.) A Discourse concerning Faith and Fervency in Prayer, especially respecting the Glorious Visible Kingdom of our Lord Jesus Christ over all the Earth, with a Vindication of the only true Scriptural Mode of Standing in Singing. By Joseph Jacob. [*Boston, N. E.* 1710.] 8vo. 35490

With a long preface by Increase Mather.

JACOB (S.) A Poetical Essay, delivered at Bennington, on the Anniversary of the 16th of August, 1777. By Stephen Jacob, A.B. 1778. *Hartford: Printed by Watson and Goodwin.* M,DCC,-LXXIX. 8vo, pp. 8. B. 35491

JACOB (W.) An Historical Inquiry into the Production and Consumption of the Precious Metals. By William Jacob, Esq., F.R.S. *London: John Murray.* 1831. 2 vols., 8vo, pp. xvi, 380; xi, (1), 415. B., BA. + *Philadelphia.* 1832. 8vo. H. 35492

Relates in part to American mines. Also: Report on the Trade in Foreign Corn

and on the Agriculture of the North of Europe. ... *London.* 1826. 8vo. + Second Report ... . [*London.*] 1828. Folio, pp. (4), 199.—Tracts relating to the Corn Trade and Corn Laws: ... *London: John Murray.* MDCCCXXVIII. 8vo, pp. vi, (2), 293. BA.

JACOB OMNIUM, *pseudon.* A Second Letter to Lord John Russell, by Jacob Omnium. *London.* 1848. 8vo, pp. 64.

Relates to the sugar trade.

JACOBI (*Dr.* E.) Dictionnaire Mythologique Universel, ou Biographie Mythique des dieux et des personnages fabuleux de la Grèce, ... du Japon, ... de l'Amérique, de la Polynésie, etc. *Paris: Firman Didot.* 1846. 12mo. 35494

Jacobin Looking-Glass. By a Friend to Rational Liberty. *Printed at Worcester ... By Leonard Worcester.* MDCCXCV. 8vo, pp. 22. BA. 35495

JACOBS (B.) Memoir of Rev. Bela Jacobs, A.M. compiled chiefly from his Letters and Journals, By his Daughter. With a Sketch of his Character, By Barnas Sears ... . *Boston: Gould, Kendall & Lincoln.* 1837. 12mo, pp. 305. Portrait. B. 35496

JACOBS. A Voice from the West. Rev. Bela Jacobs' Report of his Tour in the Western States ... in ... 1833. ... *Boston: J. Howe, Printer.* 1833. 8vo, pp. 27, (1). H. 34597

Relates to Indian instruction, etc.

[JACOBS (Curtis M.)] The Free Negro Question in Maryland. *Baltimore: John W. Woods, Printer.* 1859. 8vo, pp. (2), 28.

JACOBS. Speech of Col. Curtis M. Jacobs, on the Free Colored Population of Maryland, Delivered in the House of Delegates, on the 17th of February, 1860. *Annapolis: Printed by Elihu S. Riley.* 1860. 8vo, pp. 32. H. 35498

JACOBS (J. A.) ... Opinion concerning the Rights of the City of Cambridge in and to the Waters of Fresh Pond. By Justin A. Jacobs, Esq. *Cambridge: Metcalf and Company* ... . 1856. 8vo, pp. 12. H. 35500

[JACOBS (Harriet).] Incidents in the Life of a Slave Girl. Written by Herself. ... Edited by L. Maria Child. *Boston: For the Author.* 1861. 12mo, pp. 306. B., H. 35501

JACOBS (M.) Notes on the Rebel Invasion of Maryland and Pennsylvania and the Battle of Gettysburg, July 1st, 2d, and 3d, 1863. Accompanied by an Explanatory Map. By M. Jacobs,

Professor of Mathematics and Chemistry in the Pennsylvania College, Gettysburg. *Philadelphia: J. B. Lippincott & Co.* 1864. 12mo, pp. 47. B., BA., H., S. 35502

JACOBS (P.) Journal of the Reverend Peter Jacobs, Indian Wesleyan Missionary, from Rice Lake to the Hudson's Bay Territory, and returning. Commencing May, 1852. With A Brief Account of his Life, and a Short History of the Wesleyan Mission in that Country. *Toronto.* 1853. 8vo, pp. 32. 35503

JACOBS (R. T.) Information in relation to the arrest of Col. Richard T. Jacobs, Lieut. Governor of Kentucky, and Col. Frank Wolford, one of the Presidential Electors of that State. Communicated to Congress by the President. *Washington.* 1865. 8vo, pp. 25. 35504

Sen. Exec. Doc., 16, 38th Cong., 1st Sess., 1865.

JACOBS (S. S.) Nonantum and Natick. By Sarah S. Jacobs. ... *Boston.* 1853. 12mo, pp. 336. Map. B., H. 35505

Narrative of the missions of Eliot among the Indians.

JACOBS (T. J.) Scenes, Incidents, and Adventures in the Pacific Ocean, or the Islands of the Australasian seas, during the cruise of the clipper Margaret Oakley, under Capt. Benjamin Morrell. ... By Thomas Jefferson Jacobs. ... *New York: Harper & Brothers.* 1844. 12mo, pp. 372. B., C., P. 35506

JACOBSEN (F.) Et aar i Groenland. *Kjöbenhavn.* 1862. 8vo. 2 Maps. 35507

JACOBUS (M. W.) A Discourse delivered on Occasion of the late National Fast. By Melancthon W. Jacobus. *Brooklyn.* 1841. 8vo, pp. 24. 35508

JACOBUS, *pseudon.* The Big Bull in a Court House. A Tale of Horror. By Jacobus, Jackson County, Georgia. *Athens, Ga.* 1855. 12mo, pp. 56. 35509

JACOMB (R.) A Sermon at Salter's Hall, for the Spreading of the Gospel among the Indians in North America. By the Rev. Robert Jacomb. *London.* 1776. 8vo. 35510

[JACQUEMARD.] Réflexions d'un cultivateur américain, sur le projet d'abolir l'esclavage et la traite des nègres. *Londres et Paris. Lagrange.* 1783. 12mo, pp. (2), 99. + [*Ibid.*] 1790. 35511

[JACQUEMART (Fr.)] Le Nouveau Mississippi, ou les Dangers d'habiter les Bords du Scioto. Par un Patriote Voyageur. *Paris: Jacob Sion.* 1790. 8vo, pp. (6), 44. J.C.B. 35512

The facts set forth in this tract purport to be the result of inquiries made by a committee, relative to lands on the river Scioto and communicated to M. Necker, of the French National Assembly. The Scioto Company had an agent in Paris for the purpose of selling their lands.

JACQUEMIN. Mémoire sur la Guiane française par le Citoyen Jacquemin qui a residé dans la Guiane française pendant vingt deux ans. *Paris, an* VII (1799). 12mo. 35513

JACQUEMIN. Mémoire sur la Louisiane, contenant la description du sol et des productions de cette colonie et les moyens de la rendre florissante en peu de temps; avec un vocabulaire et un abrégé de la grammaire de la langue des sauvages, par Jacquemin. *Paris: Eberhart.* 1803. 12mo, pp. 68. 35514

Pages 47-67 contain a vocabulary of the Huron and Algonquin languages.

JACQUEMONT (V.) Correspondance inédite de Victor Jacquemont avec sa famille et ses amis 1824–1832 ... . *Paris: Michel Lévy Frères.* 1867. 2 vols., 8vo, pp. (4), xvi, 390; (4), 384. B. + Correspondance ... 1828–1832. *Paris: Michel Lévy Frères.* 1869. 2 vols., 12mo, pp. (4), xxxv, 455; (4), 364. Map. H.

The author travelled in the United States.

JACQUES (A.) Excursion au Rio-Salado et dans le Chaco. *Paris.* 1857. 8vo, pp. 59. 35516

JACQUES (J. W.) Three Years' Campaign of the Ninth N. Y. S. M. during the Southern Rebellion. By John W. Jacques. *New York.* 1865. 12mo. 35517

JACQUES, *pseudon.* Theatrical Contribution of "Jacques," to the United States Gazette; being an Account of the Performances at the new Theatre, Philadelphia, in 1825–26. *Philadelphia.* 1826. 24mo, pp. 188. 35518

JACQUIN (Nicolas Joseph), *Baron.* Dreyhundert auserlesene Amerikanische Gewächse nach Linneischer Ordnung. *Nürnberg: Raspische Buchhandlung.* 1785–89. 300 colored Plates, in 3 vols., 8vo. 35519

Composed chiefly of reduced copies of the plates (264) of Jacquin's "Selectorum stirpium Americanarum historia," with explanations of the plates.

JACQUIN. Nicolai Josephi Jacquin | Enumeratio | systematica | Plantarum; | quas | In | Insulis Caribæis vicinaque Americes con-|

tinente detexit novas, aut jam | cognitas emendavit. | *Lugduni Batavorum: apud Theodorum Haak.* MDCCLX. 8vo, pp. (4), 41. J.C.B. + *Norimbergæ.* 1762. 8vo. 35520

JACQUIN. Nicolai Josephi Jacquin, Selectarum Stirpium Americanarum Historia in qua ad Linnæanum systema determinatæ descriptæque sistuntur plantæ illæ, quas in insulis Martinica, Jamaica, Domingo, aliisque, et in vicinæ continentis parte, observavit rariores; adjectis iconibus in solo natali delineatis. *Vindobonæ, ex officina Krausiana.* MDCCLXIII. Folio, Frontispiece, Title, &c., pp. (12), vii, Catalogue, (5), Text, 284, Index, (14). clxxxiii Plates. A., B., J.C.B. 35521

Copies with colored plates are very scarce. Graesse says, that only three are existing in that condition.

JACQUIN. Selectarum Stirpium Americanarum Historia in qua ad Linnæanum systema determinatæ, descriptæque sistuntur plantæ illæ, quas in insulis Martinica, Jamaica, S. Domingo, aliisque et in vicinæ continentis parte, observavit rariores, Nic. Jos. Jacquin; adjectis iconibus ab authoris archetypo pictis. *Vindobonæ* [about 1780]. Large folio, pp. 137. C. 35522

This splendid work consists of 264 colored drawings of plants, with printed descriptions. It is supposed that not more than twenty-five copies were executed; but it does not appear to be generally known that the whole of them were copied in a neat little work, published at Nürnberg in 1785, &c. *See our* No. 35519, *supra.*

JACQUIN. Nic. Josephi Jacquin Selectarum Stirpium Americanarum Historia in qua ad Linnaeanum Systema Determinatae Descriptaeque sistuntur Plantae illae, quas in Insulis Martinica, Jamaica, Domingo, Aliisque, et in Vicina Continentis Parte Observavit Rariores. Cum Approbatione Auctoris ad exemplar Majoris Operis Vindobonae Editi Recusum. *Manhemii In Bibliopolo Novo Aul. & Acad.* MDCCLXXXVIII. 8vo, pp. xv, 363. J.C.B.

JAEGER (*Dr.*) Der Amazonas und seine Confluenten. *Hamburg.* 1839. 4to, pp. 52. 35524

JAEGER (B.) Class Book of Zoology; with a List of the different Species found in the State of New York. By B. Jaeger. *New York.* 1849. 12mo, pp. 180. 35525

JAEGER. The Life of North American Insects ... . By Prof. B. Jaeger. Assisted by H. C. Preston, M.D. *New York: George Savage.* 1853. 8vo, pp. 264. + Published for the Author. *Providence: Sayles, Miller and Simons, Printers.* 1854. 8vo, pp. iv, 204. 6 Plates, Portrait. H. 35526

JAEGER. The Life of North American Insects. By B. Jaeger ... . With numerous Illustrations, from Specimens in the Cabinet of the Author. *New York: Harper & Brothers.* 1859. 12mo, pp. 319. B., BA. 35527

JAEGER (G. F.) Leben des Andreas Jackson. Aus dem Englischen übersetzt von G. F. Jackson. 1835. 35528

JAFFREY, *N. H.* The Invoice and Taxes of ... Jaffrey, for April 1st, 1869. *Peterboro'.* 1869. 8vo, pp. 24. H. 35529

Reports of the Selectmen, and the Superintending School Committee, ... of Jaffrey, for ... 1856. *Peterborough: C. Scott, Printer.* 1856. 8vo, pp. 19, (1). Continued. H. 35530

School and Financial Reports of ... Jaffrey, Rendered March 10th, 1868. *Winchendon: Frank W. Ward ... Printer.* 1868. 8vo, pp. 25. Continued. H. 35531

JAGGAR (W.) An Address to the Mechanics and Laborers of all Classes ... of New York. By William Jaggar. [n. p.:] *For the Author.* 1837. 8vo, pp. 23. BA. 35532

JAGGER (S. H.) A Centennial Discourse, Delivered June 3d, 1864; and A Quarter Century Discourse, Delivered June 26th, 1867; ... Marlborough, New-York, By the Rev. S. H. Jagger, Pastor. Also, The Anniversary Exercises at the Parsonage. *Newburgh: Ruttenber & Co., Printers.* 1867. 8vo. 35533

JAGGER (W.) ... Information acquired from the best Authority, with respect to the Institution of Slavery. By William Jagger. *New York: R. Craighead, Printer.* 1856. 8vo, pp. 28.

[JAGGER.] To the People of Suffolk. [Letter, December 20th, 1837. *New York.* n. d.] 8vo, pp. 8. BA. 35535

Also: To the People of Suffolk County. [June 27, 1837. *New York.* n. d.] 8vo, pp. 4. + [September 4th, 1837. *Ibid.*] 8vo, pp. 8. BA. + To the People of Suffolk, of all Parties. [*Ibid.*] 1838.

JAHNSENYKES (W.) Memoir [etc.] *See* Jenks (W.)

Jahrbuch für Romanische und Englische Literatur unter besonderer Mitwirkung von Ferdinand Wolf. Herausgegeben von Dr. Adolf Ebert ... . Erster Band. *Berlin: Ferd. Dümmler.* 1859. 8vo, pp. (4), 482. BA., H. 35536

In Vol. III. (pp. 177–195, 245–267,) is "Beiträge zur Geschichte der spanisch-americanischen Literatur. Von Don Juan Maria Gutierrez. Deutsch bearbeitet von Adolf Wolf."

The Jail Question. Prepared by a Member of the Committee. [*Portland.* 1855.] 8vo, pp. 40. H. 35537

JAILLOT (Charles Hubert Alexis). Atlas françois, contenant les cartes géographiques de l'Europe, de l'Asie, de l'Afrique et de l'Amérique. *Paris: Iaillot.* 1695. Folio, Engraved Title, pp. (2). 115 Maps and Tables. C. 35538

The preliminary or index leaf is an insertion, which bears the imprint, *Rotterdam: Reinier leers.* 1695.

JAIVEN (*Princesse*). Histoire [etc.] *See* Vol. VIII., No. 32017.

JALAPA. Documentos relativos a las conferencias en Jalapa entre el Ministro de relaciones exteriores Plenipotenciario de la republica y il Contra Almirante Plenipotenciario de Francia sobre el arreglo de las diferencias entre ambas Naciones. *Mexico.* 1838. 8vo. 35539

The following is a translation:

State Documents relating to the Conferences at Jalapa, between the Mexican Minister for Foreign Affairs, Plenipotentiary of the Republic, and Rear Admiral Baudin, Plenipotentiary of France, Concerning the Adjustment of the Differences between the two Nations. Translated from the Spanish By J. F. B. *London: Smith, Elder and Co.* 1839. 8vo, pp. (ii), 106. 35540

Reglamento para el Gobierno Interior del Congreso General. *Jalapa.* 1824. 8vo. 35541

Reglamento para el Colegio Nacional de la Ciudad de Jalapa. *Jalapa.* 1843. 8vo. 35542

JALISCO. Arancel para el cobro de derechos judiciales y de la Curia eclesiastica en el estado de Jalisco. *Guadalajara.* 1825. 4to, pp. 24. 35543

El Comandante, Gral del Estado de Jalisco a sus Conciudadanos. *Guadalajara.* 1856. Sm. 4to, pp. 23. 35544

Carta Pastoral. *See* Guadalajara, Vol. VII., No. 29019.

Contestacion del Cura de la aldea al de un pueblo de Jalisco. *San Luis Potosi.* 1858. 4to, pp. 81. 35545

Contestaciones habidas entre el supremo Gobierno del Estado de Jalisco y el Gobernador de la Mitra sobre Contribucion directa. *Guadalajara.* 1825. 8vo. 35546

Documentos oficiales de la Revolucion de Jalisco. *Guadalajara.* 1862. 4to, pp. 8. 35547

Diario de las sesiones del congreso del estado de Jalisco. *Guadalajara.* 1824–1825. 4 vols., 4to. 35548

Documentos oficiales de la Comandancia general del Estado de Jalisco, en Junio y Julio de 1834. *Guadalajara.* 1834. 4to, pp. 57. 35549

Esposicion que dirige al pueblo Jesus Lopez Portillo, Gobernador que fue del estado de Jalisco. *Mexico.* 1853. 8vo, pp. 12.

Esposicion dirigida a las Camaras del Congreso General por el Secretario de Estado y del Despacho de Guerra y Marina, acerca de los acontecimientos del estado de Jalisco en noviembre del año pasado. *Mexico.* 1832. Folio, pp. 21. 35551

Estadistico de Ialisco. *Guadalajara.* 1825. 12mo. 35552

Informe á la Nacion. *See* Vol. VIII., No. 34709.

Manifestacion que hace la Junta directiva de Estudios del Departamento de Ialisco á S. M. el Emperador, pidiendo la continuacion de los estudios profesionales en Guadalajara, cuando se publique el nuevo plan de enseñanza. *Guadalajara.* 1865. 4to, pp. 16. 35553

Memoria del Estado de Jalisco. *Guadalajara.* 1848. 35554

Patriotica iniciativa que la Ecsma Asamblea Departamental de Jalisco eleva á las Augustas Camaras, y otros Documentos de la misma importancia. *Guadalajara.* 1844. 4to, pp. 34. 35555

JAMAICA. Account of a Shooting Excursion (of Negroes) on the Mountains near Dromilly Estate, in the Parish of Trelawny, and Island of Jamaica; in the Month of October, 1824!!! *London: Harvey and Darton.* 1825. 8vo, pp. 15. 35556

An Account of Jamaica, and its Inhabitants. By a Gentleman, long Resident in the West Indies. *London: Longman ... .* 1808. 8vo, pp. xii, 305. H. + [*Ibid.*] 1809. P. + Second Edition. *Kingston, Jamaica.* 1809. 8vo, pp. 213. Plate. C.

An Account of the Island of Jamaica. *See* [Marsden (Peter)].

Account of the Interest and Conduct of the Jamaica Planters. 1754. 8vo. 35558

An uncertain title from an English catalogue.

Account | of the | Late Earthquake | in | Jamaica. | June the 7th. 1692. | Written by a Reverend Divine there to his | Friend in London. | With some Improvement thereof by another Hand. | ... *London,* | ... *Tho. Parkhurst: ... .* 1693. | 4to, pp. (8), 26. H.

For a Dutch translation *see* "Nauwkeurig Verhael," etc.

Account of the Proceedings. *See* [Edwards (B.)], Vol. VI., No. 21893; for collation read, pp. lxxxviii, 109.

The Acts and Monuments of our late Parliament; or, a Collection of the Acts, Orders, Votes, and Resolves that hath passed in the House, by J. Canne, Intelligencer Generall. *London: Printed according to Order.* 1659. Sm. folio. 35560

"June 8th. Ordered that Mr. Harrington be forthwith dispatched to Jamaica, that famous island, and forme his Commonwealth there, and that he hath all the golden mines for his paines."

Address of the Governor and Council of Jamaica to Queen Anne, respecting the Duties on Prize Goods brought into Jamaica. 1709–10. Folio. S. 35561

Address to the Inhabitants. *See* [Witherspoon (John)].

Addresses and Memorial to his Majesty, from the House of Assembly at Jamaica, voted in the years 1821 to 1826 inclusive: and which have been presented to his Majesty by the Island Agent. *Printed by Order of the House of Assembly of Jamaica.* [1828.] 8vo, pp. 39. + Second Edition. *London.* [1828.] 8vo, pp. 40. S. 35562

African Slave-trade in Jamaica, and Comparative Treatment of Slaves. Read before the Maryland Historical Society, October, 1854. *Baltimore: Printed for the Maryland Historical Society by John D. Toy.* [1854.] 8vo, pp. 14. B., M. 35563

Agricola's Letter. *See* [Whitehouse (W. F.)]

Almanac and Register for the Island of Jamaica, for ... 1750. 12mo. Continued. 35564

An Answer to a Calumny. *See our* Vol. I., No. 1653, and for imprint read, *London: Printed by W. Wilkins.* M.DCC.XXVIII.

An Answer to some False and Malicious Objections given out, to prevent the Duties on Prize Goods being remitted, with some Observations. *London.* 1709. Folio, pp. 2. 35565

See our Vol. VI., No. 24957.

Appendix to the Report of the Central Board of Health of Jamaica. ... Presented to the Legislature ... . *Spanish-Town: F. M. Wilson.* 1852. 8vo, pp. (6), 282. 35566

A brief Description of the Island of Jamaica, and a Relation of possessing the Town of St. Jago de la Viga, with the Routing of the Enemies from their Forts and Ordinance, and taking the said Island, May 10. 1655. 4to. 35567

The Case of the Free-Labour British Colonies ... . *London: James Madden.* 1852. 8vo, pp. xvi, 155. BA. 35568

Case of the Island of Jamaica, in relation to their Privateers, the high duties of Prize Goods in America. 1710. Folio, 1 l.

The Case of the Agent of Jamaica on behalf of the Legislature of that Island in opposition to the Principle, Preamble and Provisions of the Bill now pending in the House of Lords, intituled "An Act to provide for the Enactment of certain Laws in the Island of Jamaica." *London.* 1839. 8vo, pp. 43. 35570

Case of the Mariners and others of the ship Bristol, charging Captain Elliot with having sold the said Prize and Cargo at Jamaica, and converted the same to his own use. [1697.] Folio, 1 sheet. 35571

Catalogue of Plants. *See* [Dancer (T.)], Vol. V., No. 18460.

The Constitution of Jamaica: Political, Judicial, and Ecclesiastical. Including the Annual Laws of that Colony in force for 1844. *London.* 1844. Rl. 8vo, pp. 384. S. 35572

Correspondence respecting the Conduct of Military Officers during the late Disturbances. *London.* 1866. Folio. 35573

Correspondence respecting a Proposed Settlement of the Debt due by the Island of Jamaica. *London.* [n. d.] Folio. 35574

Courts of Jamaica. *London.* 1855. 8vo. 35575

Description de l'Isle de la Jamaïque. *See* [Bernard (J. F.)]

Description of the Island of Jamaica. *See* Blome (R.)

Dioddefiadau, etc. *Carmarthen.* [n. d.] 16mo. 35576

Sufferings of the Africans in Jamaica. In Welsh.

An Exposition of the System. *See our* Vol. VI., No. 23463.

Facts and Documents connected with the Late Insurrection in Jamaica and the Violations of Civil and Religious Liberty arising out of it. *London.* [n. d.] 8vo, pp. 24. S. 35577

The Fall of the Sugar-Planters of Jamaica; with Remarks on their Agricultural Management and on the Labour Question in that Island. *London: N. Trübner & Co.* 1869. 35578

Farewell Addresses presented to H. E. Sir C. T. Metcalfe, on the occasion of his Resignation of the Government of, and Departure from this Island. With His Excellency's Replies. *Kingston.* 1842. 8vo, pp. 65. S. 35579

The following Address. *See* Vol. VI., No. 24957.

Form of Prayer for a Perpetual Fast to be observed in the Island of Jamaica on the seventh of June, being the Anniversary of the Dreadful Earthquake in the year 1690. *Jamaica.* [n. d.] Sm. 4to, pp. 18. + [Another Edition.] *James Fannin, Montego Bay.* 1790. 8vo. 35580

Forms of Prayer to be used in the Island of Jamaica, on the seventh day of June, being the Anniversary of the Dreadful Earthquake. And on the 28th day of August, being the Anniversary of the Dreadful and Surprising Hurricane. *London: J. Davidson.* [1748.] 8vo, 7 l. 35581

Freedom in Jamaica: or, The First of August, 1838. [*London: J. Haddon, Printer.* 1838.] 8vo, pp. 23. B. 35582

Further Proceedings of the ... House of Assembly of Jamaica, Relative to a Bill, Introduced into the House of Commons, for Effectually preventing the unlawful Importation of Slaves, and holding Free Persons in Slavery, in the British Colonies. To which are annexed Examinations taken upon Oath before a Committee of the House, for the Purpose of Disproving the Allegations of the said Bill. *Jamaica: Printed by Alex. Aikman, Jun.* 1816. Folio, pp. 108. 35583

Geology. Memoirs of the Geological Survey. Reports on the Geology of Jamaica; or, Part II. of the West Indian Survey. By James G. Sawkins, with Contributions from G. P. Wall, Lucas Barrett, Arthur Lennox, and C. B. Brown. And an Appendix by Robert Etheridge. Published by Order of the Lords Commissioners of Her Majesty's Treasury. *London: Longmans ... .* 1869. 8vo, pp. vi, 339. 10 Plates and Map. C.

Contents: Analyses and Assays; by L. Barrett. pp. 292–302. Appendix v. to the

Geological Survey of Jamaica, Area and Summary of the Palæontology of the Caribbean Sea; by R. Etheridge. pp. 306–339. Geological Report on the Island of Jamaica; by J. G. Sawkins. pp. 1–262. Outline of the Flora of Jamaica; by N. Wilson. pp. 263–291.

Great News from Jamaica. *See* Vol. VII., No. 28456.

The Groans of Jamaica. *See* Vol. VII., No. 28914.

Histoire de la Jamaïque, traduit de l'Anglois par M * * *, ancien Officier de Dragons. Premiere et Seconde Partie. *A Londres: Chez Nourse.* MDCCLI. 2 vols., 12mo, pp. (4), 285; 248. 6 Plates. J.C.B. 35585

A translation by M. Raulin of "A New History of Jamaica," published in 1740. *See* Boucher de la Richarderie, Vol. VI., p. 186, for a long note respecting this work, which was probably printed at *Paris.*

An Historical Account of the Sessions of Assembly, for the Island of Jamaica: Which began on Tuesday the 23d of Sept. 1755, Being the Second Sessions of that Assembly. Containing a Vindication of his Excellency Charles Knowles, Esq; Then Governor of that Island; Against several groundless Accusations that have been brought against him, particularly from those contain'd in a Petition, which has been presented to his Majesty, by several Persons who called themselves Members of that Assembly, the Matter of which Petition is now depending. *London: Printed in the Year* MDCCLVII. 8vo, pp. 76. J.C.B. 35586

History of Jamaica. *See* [Long (Edward)].

History of Jamaica & Barbadoes. *See* Vol. VIII., No. 32139.

The Humble Petition and Memorial of the Assembly of Jamaica. *Philadelphia.* 1775. 8vo, pp. 8. 35587

The Importance of Jamaica to Great-Britain, consider'd. With some Account of that Island, from its Discovery in 1492 to this Time: and a List of the Governors and Presidents, with an Account of their Towns, Harbours, Bays, Buildings, Inhabitants, Whites and Negroes, &c. The Country and People cleared from Misrepresentations; the Misbehaviour of Spanish Governors by entertaining Pirates, and plundering the Inhabitants and Merchants of Jamaica, and the Rise of the Pirates among them. An Account of their Fruits, Drugs, Timber and Dying-Woods, and of the Uses they are apply'd to there: With a Description of Exotick Plants, preserved in the Gardens of the Curious in England; ... Also of their Beasts, Birds, Fishes, and

Insects; with their Eatables and Potables, Distempers and Remedies. With an Account of their Trade and Produce; with the Advantages they are of to Great-Britain, Ireland, and the Colonies in North-America, and the Commodities they take in Return from them, with the Danger they are in from the French at Hispaniola, and their other Islands and Settlements on the Continent, by the Encouragements they have over the British Planters. ... In a Letter to a Gentleman. In which is Added, A Postscript, of the Benefits which may arise by keeping of Carthagena, to Great-Britain and our American Colonies; ... *London: A. Dodd,* [about 1744.] 8vo, pp. (2), 81, (1). H. 35588

Published while Admiral Vernon was attacking Carthagena.

Index to the Second-Twelfth [each] Volume of Journals of Assembly of Jamaica. *Jamaica.* 1805–17. Folio. 35589

An Inquiry Concerning the Trade, Commerce, and Policy of Jamaica, Relative to the Scarcity of Money, and the Causes and bad Effects of such Scarcity, peculiar to that Island. ... With an Appendix ... *Printed at St. Jago de Cuba.* 1757. 4to. + *Jamaica, Printed: London, Re-printed for T. Kinnersly.* MDCCLIX. 4to, pp. (4), 92. H. 35590

See "M. Rev.," XIX. 131.

Interesting Tracts, relating to the Island of Jamaica, consisting of State Papers, Councils of War, Letters, Petitions, Narratives, &c., &c., which throw great light on the History of that Island, from its Conquest [by the English, 1655], down to the year 1702. *St. Jago de la Vega: Lewis, Lunan & Jones.* 1800. 4to, pp. vi, 300. C., M. 35591

A very rare volume.

Jamaica. A Poem, in three Parts. Written in that Island, in the Year MDCCLXXVI. To which is annexed, A Poetical Epistle from the Author in that Island to a Friend in England. *London: W. Nicoll.* MDCCLXXVII. 4to, pp. 43. 35592

See "M. Rev.," LVIII. 142.

Jamaica Almanac for 1816. *Kingston.* 1816. 12mo. Continued. 35593

Contains the names of all the proprietors of lands, the number of slaves, stock, &c.

Jamaica as it Was, as it Is, and as it May be: ... also an Authentic Narrative of the Negro Insurrection in 1831; ... By a Retired Military Officer. ... *London: T. Hurst.* 1835. 12mo, pp. vii, 313, (2). Plate. BA., C. 35594

The Jamaica Association Develop'd. *Jamaica: Printed in the Year* 1755. 8vo. + *London: Re-printed* 1757. 8vo, pp. 26.

Jamaica, Enslaved and Free. *London: Religious Tract Society.* 1846. 18mo, pp. 192. 35596

Jamaica. From the Liverpool Saturday's Advertiser, February 10, 1827. Jamaica Papers. [*Liverpool: Printed by G. Cruickshank.* n. d.] Folio, pp. (2). BA. 35597

The Jamaica Magazine; or, Repository of Entertainment and Knowledge. Vol. I. *St. Jago de la Vega.* 1804. 8vo. Continued.

The Jamaica Magistrate's and Vestryman's Assistant, Containing a Digest of all the Laws of the Island alphabetically arranged, from 33 Charles II. to 8 George IV. *Jamaica: Office of the St. Jago de la Vega Gazette.* 1828. 8vo, pp. (4), 320, (2). 35599

The Jamaica Movement, for promoting the Enforcement of the Slave-Trade Treaties, and the Suppression of the Slave-Trade; With Statements of Fact, Convention, and Law: Prepared at the request of the Kingston Committee. ... *London: Charles Gilpin.* 1850. 8vo, pp. (4), 430. B., C., H. 35600

The Jamaica Physical Journal. Edited by James Paul, M.D. and William Arnold, M.D. *Kingston, Jamaica.* 1834. 8vo, pp. (4), 392. C. 35601

The Jamaica Question: Papers relative to the Condition of the Labouring Population of the West Indies. ... From the Edinburgh Review, July, 1839. ... *Lindfield.* 1839. 8vo, pp. 28.

Jamaica. Respondents Case. The Merchants, Factors and Agents, residing at Kingston in the said Island, Complainants against The Inhabitants of Spanish-Town ... and ... the Members of the honourable Assembly ... at Saint Jago de la Vega ... Respondents. *London.* 1754. 4to, pp. viii, (2), 72. H. 35603

Jamaica under the Apprenticeship System. By a Proprietor. *London: Andrews.* 1838. 8vo. 35604

Jamaica under the New Form of Government. With an Appendix, containing an Abstract of the last Official Report of Sir J. P. Grant. A Series of Letters (Reprinted from the European Mail). By a West Indian. *London: Field and Tuer.* 1869. 8vo, pp. 32. 35605

Jamaica; Who is to Blame? By a Thirty Years' Resident. With Introduction and Notes by the Editor of the "Eclectic Review." *London: E. Wilson.* 186–. 8vo, pp. 106. 35606

The Jamaica Lady: Or, The Life of Bavia. Containing an Account of her Intrigues, Cheats, Amours in England, Jamaica, and the Royal Navy. ... Relation of the Amours of the Officers of a Fourth Rate Man of War, with their Female Passengers, in a Voyage from Jamaica ... *London: T. Bickerton.* 1720.

Journals of the Assembly of Jamaica. Vol. I. From January the 20th, 1663–4, ... To April the 20th, 1709 ... *Jamaica: By Alexander Aikman.* M.DCCC.XI. Folio, pp. (2), 470, Appendix, (4), 53, Index, (2), 54. Continued. B. 35608

Laws. Abridgment of the Laws in Force in Jamaica. 1704.

An Abridgment of the Laws of Jamaica, in manner of an Index. [With] a Table of the General and Marginal Titles, under which the subject-matter of each Act and Clause is properly Digested. *London: C. Brett.* 1756. Folio, pp. (4), 43. C.

An Abridgment of the Laws of Jamaica, being an Alphabetical Digest of all the Public Acts of Assembly now in Force. *St. Jago de la Vega.* 1802. 4to. A. + Second Edition. [*Ibid.*] 1802. 4to, pp. ix, 240. 35611

Abstract of the Slave Laws of Jamaica (from 33 Car. II. to 59 Geo. III.), with Abstracts of Acts of Parliament on the Abolition of the Slave Trade. By W. Lunan. *St. Jago de la Vega.* 1819. 4to. 35612

An Act to oblige the several Inhabitants of this Island to provide themselves with a sufficient number of White Men, &c. &c. *Saint Jago de la Vega: Printed by Alexander Aikman.* M,DCC,XCII. 4to, pp. 31. H. 35613

Acts of Assembly, Passed in the Island of Jamaica; From 1681, to 1737, inclusive. *London.* 1737. Folio, pp. xxii, 388. S. + *London: Printed by John Baskett* ... MDCCXXXVIII. Folio, pp. (2), xxii, 387, (1). B., C. + With Abridgment, etc. *London.* 1740. Folio. N. 35614

Also on large paper; both editions are probably the same.

Acts of Assembly, passed in the Island of Jamaica; From 1681, to 1754, inclusive. *London: Curtis Brett and Compy.* MDCCLVI. Folio, pp. (4), 27, 358, (2). [Followed by:] An Abridgment of the Laws of Jamaica, etc. pp. (4), 43. C., H.

Acts of Assembly, passed in the Island of Jamaica; From the year 1681 to the year 1768 inclusive. *St. Jago de la Vega, Jamaica.* 1769–71. 2 vols., folio. H. 35616

Acts of Assembly Passed in the Island of Jamaica, From 1770, to 1783, inclusive. *Kingston,* ... *Jamaica: Printed for James Jones, Esq. by Lewis and Eberall.* M,DCC,LXXXVI. 4to, pp. (6), 31, 3–424, Abridgment, pp. 40. H. 35617

Contains a list of the principal inhabitants on the island at the time.

The Acts of Assembly of the Island of Jamaica ... commonly called the Consolidated Act ... passed ... 19th ... December 1787 ... By Stephen Fuller, Esq. ... *London: B. White, and Son.* M.DCC.LXXXVIII. 4to, pp. (4), 34. H. 35618

Act for the Subsistence, Clothing, and the better Regulation and Government of Slaves. *Jamaica.* 1817. 8vo. C. 35619

Also: Act for the Government of Slaves, February 19, 1830. *St. Jago de la Vega.* 1831.—An Act to Alter and Amend the Slave Laws of this Island. [n. p. n. d.] 8vo, pp. 47. B.

The Consolidated Slave Law, Passed the 22d December, 1826 ... Second Edition ... [n. p.] 1827. 8vo, pp. xiv, 47.

Copies of Acts passed by the Legislature of Jamaica for building, repairing, and regulating Gaols, Houses of Correction, &c.; of the Resolutions of the Meetings of Planters, &c. on 12th April, 10th May, and 4th June; and of the Memorials of the Association of Jamaica Proprietors ... 30th May. Ordered to be printed 25th June, 1830. [*London.* 1830.] Folio, pp. 28. S.

The Laws of Jamaica, Passed by the Assembly, and confirmed by his Majesty in Council, February 23, 1683. To which is added, A short Account of the Island and Government ... *London: Printed by H. Hills for Charles Harper.* 1683. 8vo, pp. (64), 218, (1). Map. B., C. 35622

The Laws of Jamaica, passed by the Assembly, and confirmed by his Majesty in Council, April 17, 1684. To which is added the State of Jamaica, as it is now, under the Government of Sir Thomas Lynch. *London.* 1684. Folio. Map. N. 35623

The Laws of Jamaica, Pass'd by the Governours, Council and Assembly in that Island, and confirm'd by the Crown. *London: Printed by W. Wilkins.* 1716. 8vo, pp. xxx, (6), 457, (1). BA.

Appended as part of the book is: Mr. Francis Hanson's Account of the Island and Government of Jamaica, written about 1682.

The Laws of Jamaica: comprehending All the Acts in Force, Passed between the Thirty-Second Year of the Reign of King Charles the Second, And the Thirty-Third Year of the Reign of King George the Third. To which is prefixed, a Table of the Titles of the Public and Private Acts passed during that Time. ... *St. Jago de la Vega, Jamaica: Printed by Alexander Aikman.* M.DCC.XCII. 3 vols., 4to, pp. viii, (136), lxxix, 426; (2), 660, (4); Vol. III. M.DCC.XCIII. pp. (12), 281, (3). B. + [to] the 57th of George III. *St. Jago de la Vega.* 1802–17. 6 vols., 4to. 35625

The New Act of the Assembly of the Island of Jamaica, ... commonly called the New Consolidated Act, which was passed by the Assembly on the 5th of November ... 1788, being the present Code Noir of that Island. Published ... by Stephen Fuller, Agent for Jamaica. *London: B. White and Son.* M.DCC.LXXXIX. 4to, pp. vii, 17. S. 35626

New Code of Laws for the Government of the Negro Slaves in the Island of Jamaica, passed on Dec. 6, 1788. By Stephen Fuller. *London.* 1789. 4to. 35627

The Revised Statutes of Jamaica, as to Crimes and Misdemeanors: Analytically and Alphabetically arranged, down to the Session 6th of Victoria, Anno 1842–3, inclusive. *London: J. Haddon.* 1844. 8vo, pp. viii, 376. S. 35628

Slave Law of Jamaica; with Proceedings and Documents relative thereto. *London: James Ridgway.* 1828. 8vo, pp. xiii, (1), 263, Errata, 1 l. C., S. 35629

With Gov. Metcalfe's Speech to the Legislature, 1840.

A Letter concerning the Privileges of the Assembly of Jamaica. ... *Kingston, Jamaica: Printed by Weatherby, Allen & M'Cann.* [1765.] Sm. 4to, pp. 28. C. + The Second Edition. [*Ibid.*] 4to, pp. x, 28, (xii). P. 35630

The appendix contains, *inter alia*, "an historical account of the establishment of the Colony of Jamaica." This tract relates to a serious quarrel on the question of privilege.

The Local Government of Jamaica and British Guiana. *London.* 1848. 8vo, pp. 20. 35631

Memorial and Petition of the Council and Assembly of Jamaica to the King. 4to, pp. 8. N. 35632

A | Narrative | of | Affairs | Lately received from his Majesties | Island of Jamaica: | viz. | I. His Excellency the Governour Sir

Thomas Linch's | Speech to the Assembly met Sept. 21. 1682. | II. Samuel Bernard, Esq; Speaker of the said Assembly, his | Speech to the Governour. | III. An humble Address from his Majesties Council, and | the Gentlemen of the Assembly, to his most Sacred Majesty. | IV. The Governour's Speech at the Prorouging the As- | sembly. | *London:* | *Printed for Randal Taylor* ... 1683. Folio, pp. (2), 6. 35633

Narrative of certain Events connected with the late Disturbances in Jamaica, and the Charges preferred against the Baptist Missionaries. *London.* 1832. 8vo. 35634

Neu Jahrs Geschenk aus Jamaika in West Indien für ein Kind in Europa. *Göttingen: in der Bandenhölschen Buchhandlung.* 1780. 12mo, pp. 48. J.C.B. 35635

New and Exact Account. *See* [Leslie (Charles)].

A New History of Jamaica, from the Earliest Accounts, to the Taking of Porto Bello by Vice Admiral Vernon. In Thirteen Letters from a Gentleman to his Friend. ... In which are ... interspersed, The Characters of its Governors and Lieutenant-Governors; viz. Colonel D'Oyley [and twenty-four others]. With Two Maps, one of the Island and the other of the circumjacent Islands and Territories belonging to France, Spain, &c. *London: Printed by J. Hodges.* 1740. 8vo, pp. iv, 340. 2 Maps. + The Second Edition. [*Ibid.*] + *Dublin.* 1741. 8vo.

"Contains a great deal relating to Morgan and the Buccaneers."—RICH, I. 59. The title-page is unusually long, and is, in fact, a Table of Contents. For a French translation *see* No. 35585, *supra.*

The New Jamaica Almanack, and Register, Calculated to the Meridian of the Island for the Year of our Lord 1798. Being the Second after Bissextile or Leap Year. [Second Edition—Carefully Corrected.] *Kingston: Printed by Stevenson and Aikman.* [1798.] 12mo, pp. 157, 15. Map. Continued. 35637

The New Jamaica Magazine from Jan. 1798 to May 1799. *St. Iago de la Vega.* 1798–99. 3 vols. 35638

For a continuation *see* "Jamaica Magazine."

The New Slave Laws of Jamaica and St. Christopher's examined: with an especial reference to the Eulogies recently pronounced upon them in Parliament. *London.* 1828. 8vo, pp. 24.

Notes on the Two Reports from the Committee of the Honourable House of Assembly of Jamaica, appointed To examine

into, and report, the allegations and charges against the several petitions which have been presented to the British House of Commons on the subject of the Slave Trade, and the Treatment of the Negroes ... By a Jamaica Planter. *London: James Phillips.* M.DCC.LXXXIX. 8vo, pp. (2), 62. P. + *Philadelphia.* 1794. 8vo. 35640

Observations on, and Reasons against Vacating the Bonds taken by her Majesty's Collector at Jamaica. [n. p. n. d.] Folio, 1 l.

Observations on the System by which Estates have been and are still Managed in Jamaica; and on the Apprenticeship introduced by the recent Abolition Act By a Proprietor. *Edinburgh: Maclachland and Stewart.* MDCCCXXXVI. 8vo, pp. 27. 35642

Occasional Papers. *See* [Wood (W.)]

Papers laid before the Royal Commission of Inquiry by Governor Eyre. ... *London: Printed by George Edward Eyre and William Spottiswoode.* 1866. 8vo, pp. (2), 483, (1). Map. B., BA.

Papers relative to the Affairs of Jamaica. ... *London: Printed by George Edward Eyre and William Spottiswoode.* 1866. Folio, pp. iv, 279, (1). B., BA. 35644

Papers relating to the Disturbances in Jamaica. Part I. ... *London: Printed by Harrison and Sons.* 1866. Folio, pp. iv, (1), 262. + Further Papers ... Part II. ... [*Ibid.*] 1866. Folio, pp. (4), 45. B., BA. 35645

Petition and Memorial of the Assembly of Jamaica to the King, Dec. 28, 1774. *Philadelphia.* 1775. 8vo. N., P. 35646

The Political Constitution of Jamaica, including the Judicial and Ecclesiastical Establishments of that Colony, and its Annual Laws in force for 1844. *London.* 1844. 8vo, pp. iv, about 300.

The Politicks and Patriots of Jamaica. A Poem. *London: T. Warner.* MDCCXVIII. 8vo, pp. 19. J.C.B. 35648

The | Present State | of | Jamaica. | With the | Life | Of the Great Columbus | The first Discoverer: | To which is Added | An Exact Account of Sir Hen. Morgan's | Voyage to, and famous Siege and ta- | king of Panama from the Spaniards. | *London,* | *Printed by Fr. Clark for Tho. Malthus* | ... 1683. | 12mo, pp. (10), 54. Title. Morgan's Voyage, pp. 57–117. 35649

This is probably one of the books containing the libel upon Sir Henry Morgan, for which he recovered the sum of £200, in an action against the publisher, T. Malthus. *See* "London Gazette," June 8, 1685. Rich's Catalogue, No. 401, says, "this work was published in order to make a favorable impression as to Morgan."

The Privileges of the Island of Jamaica Vindicated; with an Impartial Narrative of the late dispute between the Governor and House of Representatives, upon the case of Mr. Olyphant, A Member of that House. [With an Appendix, giving an Historical Account of the Establishment of the Colony, its Constitution and form of Government.] *Jamaica Printed: London, Reprinted for J. Williams.* 1766. 8vo, pp. xx, 67; Appendix, pp. xxviii. BA., C., H. 35650

See "M. Rev.," XXXV. 473.

Proceedings of the Hon. House of Assembly of Jamaica, on the Sugar and Slave-Trade, In a Session which began the 23d of October, 1792. ... *St. Jago de la Vega: Printed by Alexander Aikman.* M.DCC.XCII. 4to, pp. (2), 23, Appendix, (34). BA. 35651

Proceedings of the Court-Martial held upon Ensign Cullen and Assistant-Surgeon Morris. *London.* 1867. 35652

Proceedings of the ... Assembly. *See* Vol. VI., No. 21908.

Proceedings of the Honourable House of Assembly of Jamaica, in Relation to those which took place in the British House of Commons, on the 15th of May last, in consequence of Mr. Buxton's Motion for the Gradual Abolition of Slavery throughout these Colonies. ... *Jamaica: Printed by Alex. Aikman, Jun.* 1823. 8vo, pp. 22. BA. 35653

Reasons for temporarily suspending the Constitution of Jamaica. *London.* 1839. 8vo, pp. 16. S. 35654

Report from the Committee of the ... House of Assembly, Appointed to Inquire into the State of the Colony, as to Trade, Navigation, and Culture, &c. &c. Since ... November, 1792. ... *St. Jago de la Vega: Printed by Alexander Aikman.* 1800. Folio, pp. (4), 48. BA. 35655

A Report of a Committee of the ... House of Assembly of Jamaica, ... 1817, Relative to the Present State of the Island, with respect to its Population, Agriculture and Commerce, Dec. 10, 1817. *London: J. Darling.* 1818. 8vo, pp. (2), 55.

Report of the Jamaica Royal Commission, 1866. Part I. ... *London: Printed by George Edward Eyre and William Spottiswoode.* 1866. Folio, pp. 41, (1). Map. + Part II. [*Ibid.*] 1866. Folio, pp. ix, 1162. B., BA. 35657

Report of Committee of the Assembly on the Slave Trade, Nov. 23, 1804. 4to, pp. 40. S. 35658

Report, Resolutions, and Remonstrance of the Council and Assembly of Jamaica on the Slave Trade, October 20, 1790. Published by Stephen Fuller. *London.* 1790. 4to. 35659

The Representation and Memorial of the Council of the Island of Jamaica, To the Right Honourable The Lords Commissioners for Trade and Plantations. Together with the Addresses of the Governour and Council, and Town of Kingston; and Association of the Principal Inhabitants. With a Preface, by Mr. Wood. *London: W. Wilkins.* 1716. 8vo, pp. (2), viii, 46. 35660

A Short Account of the Interest and Conduct of the Jamaica Planters. In an Address to the Merchants, Traders and Liverymen of the City of London. *London: M. Cooper.* MDCCLIV. 8vo, pp. (2), 21. 35661

Some Modern Observations. *See* [Wharton (Philip), *Duke of*].

State of Society and Slavery in Jamaica: a Reply to an article in the Edinburgh Review, No. LXXV. *London: Ridgway.* 1824. 8vo, pp. 23. 35662

The State of The Island of Jamaica. Chiefly in Relation to its Commerce, and the Conduct of the Spaniards in the West-Indies. Address'd to a Member of Parliament. By a Person who resided several Years at Jamaica. *London: H. Whitridge.* 1726. 8vo, pp. 79. H. 35663

To the King's most Excellent Majesty In Council, The Humble Petition and Memorial Of The Assembly of Jamaica. [Voted in Assembly, on the 28th of December, 1774.] *Philadelphia: Printed by William and Thomas Bradford* ... M.DCC.LXXV. 8vo, pp. 8. P. 35664

In favor of the Americans.

A Trip to Jamaica. *See* [Ward (E.)]

A True Account of the late Pyracies. *See* [Wagstaffe (A.)]

The Truest and Largest | Account | of the | Late Earthquake | in | Jamaica, | June the 7th, 1692. | Written by a Reverend Divine there to his | Friend in London. | With some Improvement thereof by another Hand. | *London, Printed, and are to be Sold by J. Buttler ... at | Worcester*, 1693. | 4to, pp. (8), 26. C. 35665

The same as our No. 35559, with a different title-page.

Two Reports ... from the Committee of the Honourable House of Assembly, Appointed To Enquire into, and report to the House, the Allegations and Charges contained in the several Petitions which have been presented to the British House of Commons, on the Subject of the Slave-Trade, and the Treatment of the Negroes, etc. ... *Saint Jago de la Vega: David Douglass.* I,DCC,LXXXVIII. 4to, pp. 37. BA. 35666

Reprinted with the following title:

Two Reports (one presented the 16th of October, the other on the 12th of November, 1788,) from the Committee of the Honourable House of Assembly of Jamaica, Appointed to Examine into and report to the House the Allegations and Charges contained in the several Petitions which have been presented to the British House of Commons on the Subject of the Slave-Trade, and the Treatment of Negroes, &c. &c. Published by order of the ... Assembly by Stephen Fuller, Esq. ... *London: B. White and Son* ... . M.DCC.LXXXIX. 4to, pp. (2), 35. H., P., S. 35667

See "M. Rev.," LXXX. 450.

A View of the Proceedings of the Assemblies of Jamaica, For some Years past. With some Considerations on the Present State of that Island; In Several Occasional Papers. Earnestly Recommended to the Planters, Traders, and Free-holders of Jamaica. *London: Printed in the Year* M.DCC.XVI. 8vo, pp. vi, 42.

A Vindication Of the Late Governor and Council of Jamaica. Occasion'd by A Letter in St. James's Post of the 23d of July last, as from Bath. In a Letter to——. *London: W. Wilkins.* 1716. 8vo, pp. 32. 35669

A Vindication of the Proceedings of the House of Assembly of Jamaica, On a Late occasion, by an Impartial Hand. *Printed, Anno* 1765. 4to, pp. 24. P. 35670

Votes of the Honourable Assembly of the Island of Jamaica, 1753. [n. p. n. d.] Folio, pp. 96. Continued. 35671

Votes of the Honorable House of Assembly of Jamaica; in a Session, begun Oct. 31st, and ended December 22d, 1775. ... *Saint Jago de la Vega, Jamaica.* M,DCC,LXXVI. Folio, pp. (2), 116. Continued. H. 35672

JAMAICA, *N. Y.* Address: To the Parents and Guardians of the Children of Public School No. 1, of the Village of Jamaica. [*Jamaica.* 1854.] 8vo, pp. 6. H. 35673

First Annual Report of the Board of Education, of the Village of Jamaica. August 8, 1854. *Jamaica, L. I.: James J. Brenton, Printer.* 1854. 8vo, pp. 12. Continued. H. 35674

JAMES I. *of England.* A Covnterblaste to Tobacco. *Imprinted at London by R. B. Anno* 1604. + Republished by T. H. *London.* 1672. 4to. 35675

Reprinted in Arber's English Reprints, Vol. VIII.

JAMES I. Letter to the Governor of Virginia on Cultivating the Silkworm. *London.* 1622. 35676

Title from Ternaux, No. 451. *See* Raleigh (Sir W.)

JAMES II. Commission of King James the Second to Sir Edmund Andros. June 3, 1686. *Washington: Peter Force.* 1846. 8vo, pp. 14. 35677

JAMES (Benjamin). *See* South Carolina.

JAMES (C. P.) Address delivered at Camp McRae before the Citizens' Guards of Cincinnati. By Charles P. James. *Cincinnati.* 1842. 8vo, pp. 24. 35678

JAMES. Oration and Poem, delivered before the Cincinnati Literary Club, July 4th, 1853. Oration by Charles P. James. Poem by C. A. L. Richards. *Cincinnati: Truman & Spofford.* 1853. 8vo, pp. 46. B. 35679

JAMES (C. T.) Letters on the Culture and Manufacture of Cotton. ... in reply to the Communications of A. A. Lawrence, Esq., ... By Charles T. James. *New York: G. W. Wood.* 1850. 8vo, pp. 35. N. 35680

Also: Speech of Hon. C. T. James, ... on the Collins Line of Steamers. Delivered ... May 6, 1852. *Washington: Printed by John T. Towers.* 1852. 8vo.—Charles T. James *vs.* the Atlantic DeLaine Company, *et al.* The Bill in Equity. T. A. Jenckes for Complainant. R. W. Greene, A. Payne, Jas. B. Parsons, for Respondents. *Providence: Knowles, Anthony & Co.* 1859. 8vo, pp. 211.

JAMES (E. M.) Annals of Virtue, a Selection of the most interesting Anecdotes, of the most Virtuous Acts in the Histories of America, Japan, Spain, Portugal and China, By Miss E. M. James. *Bath.* 1794. 8vo. 35681

JAMES (E.) Account of an Expedition from Pittsburgh to the Rocky Mountains, Performed in the Years 1819 and '20, By Order of the Hon. J. C. Calhoun, Sec'y of War: under the Command of Major Stephen H. Long. From the Notes of Major Long, Mr. T. Say, and other Gentlemen of the Explor-

ing Party. Compiled by Edwin James, Botanist and Geologist for the Expedition. *Philadelphia: H. C. Carey and J. Lea.* 1823. 2 vols., 8vo, pp. (4), 5, (2), 503; (6), 442, xcviii, and Atlas of 10 Maps in 4to, dated 1822. BA. 35682

Known as "Long's First Expedition." *See* Keating (W. H.)

JAMES. Account of an Expedition from Pittsburgh to the Rocky Mountains, performed In the Years 1819, 1820. ... Compiled from the Notes of Major Long, Mr. T. Say, and other Gentlemen of the Party. By Edwin James, Botanist and Geologist to the Expedition. ... *London: Longman.* 1823. 3 vols., 8vo, pp. vii, 344; vii, 356; vii, 347. Map and colored Plates.

A valuable contribution to geographical and ethnographical literature. *See* "N. A. Rev.," XVI. 242–269; XXII. 61.

JAMES. A Narrative of the Captivity and Adventures of John Tanner, (U. S. Interpreter at the Saut de Ste. Marie,) during Thirty Years Residence among the Indians in the Interior of North America. Prepared for the Press By Edwin James, M.D. ... *New York: G. & C. & H. Carvill.* 1830. 8vo, pp. 426. Portrait. B. + *London.* 1830. 8vo. 35684

The narrative was related *viva voce* by Tanner to Dr. James. Field remarks that "His relation of his life among the Northern Indians, is probably the most minute, if not authentic detail of their habits, modes of living, and social customs, ever printed." Schoolcraft does not believe in the narrative.

JAMES. John Tanner's Denkwürdigkeiten über seinen dreissigjährigen Aufenthalt unter den Indianern Nord-Amerika's. Aus dem Englischen übersetzt von Karl Andree. *Leipzig: Engelmann.* 1840. 8vo, pp. 344. 35685

JAMES. Memoires de John Tanner, ou Trente Années dans les deserts de l'Amérique du Nord. *Paris.* 1855. 2 vols., 8vo.

JAMES. Outline of the Paradigma of a Chippeway Vocabulary ... *Albany.* [n. d.] Folio. 35687

Also: Chippeway First Lessons in Spelling and Reading. Published by order of the Baptist Board of Missions.—Essay on the Chippeway Language. Read before the American Lyceum, at the Third Annual Meeting, in the City of New York, May 3d, 1833. 8vo, pp. 73–80 of No. v. of "The North American Savages," September, 1835. For the New Testament in Chippeway *see our* Vol. IV., No. 12833.

JAMES (E.) The Bankrupt Law of the United States. 1867. With Notes, and a Collection of American and English Decisions upon ... the Law of Bankruptcy. ... By Edwin James ... *New-York: Harper & Brothers.* 1867. 8vo, pp. 325. B.

JAMES. A Letter to the Artisans and Operatives of the City of New York. By Edwin James. *New York: Baker & Godwin.* 1863. 8vo. 35689

JAMES. Oration delivered before the Young Men's Association of Brooklyn, N. Y., on the Fourth of July, 1863. By Edwin James. *New York: Baker & Godwin, Printers.* 1863. 8vo, pp. 23. 35690

JAMES. Suggestions for an Act to Establish a Uniform System of Bankruptcy Law throughout the United States. By Edwin James. *New York: Baker & Godwin.* 1864. 8vo, pp. 32.

James, formerly an M.P., was debarred in England, came hither, was for a time an enthusiastic American citizen, failed to impress the American people with his greatness, returned to England, and became a peripatetic reviler of America and the Americans.

JAMES (E. P.) A Catalogue of Plants collected in a Journey to and from the Rocky Mountains. By E. P. James. *Philadelphia.* 1820. 4to. P. 35692

JAMES. Remarks on the Sandstone and Floetz Formations of the Valley of the Mississippi. By E. P. James. *Philadelphia.* 1821. 4to. P. 35693

JAMES (E.) An Address ... before the Scituate Auxiliary Society for the Suppression of Intemperance: ... January 15, 1833. By Elisha James, Jr. *Hingham: J. Farmer, Printer.* 1833. 8vo, pp. 28. B. 35694

JAMES (George Payne Rainsford). A Brief History of the United States Boundary Question. Drawn up from Official Papers, By G. P. R. James, Esq. *London: Saunders and Otley.* 1839. 8vo, pp. 32. C. 35695

JAMES. The Old Dominion. A Novel. By G. P. R. James, Esq., ... *London: Thomas Cautley Newby.* 1856. 3 vols., post 8vo, pp. (2), 300; (2), 321; (2), 348. 35696

Reprinted in New York as: The Old Dominion; or, the Southampton Massacre. ... *New York: Harper & Brothers.* 1856. 8vo, pp. (2), 152. B., C.

JAMES. Ticonderoga; or, the Black Eagle: a Tale of Times not long past. By G. P. R. James, Esq. *London: Thomas C. Newby.* 1854. 3 vols., post 8vo, pp. 900. 35697

Reprinted as: Ticonderoga, or the Black Eagle; a Romance of Days not far Distant. ... *New York: Harper & Brothers.* 1854. 8vo, pp. 138. B. The following contain some matter relating to American topics: Lives of the most Eminent Foreign Statesmen. ... *London: Longman.* 1832–38. 5 vols., 12mo.—Memoirs of Great Commanders. ... *London.* 1835. 2 vols., 12mo. + *Philadelphia.* 1835. 2 vols., 12mo.

JAMES (H.) The Social Significance of Our Institutions: An Oration ... at Newport, R. I., July 4th, 1861. By Henry James. *Boston: Ticknor and Fields.* 1861. 8vo, pp. 47. B., BA. 35698

JAMES. What constitutes the State? A Lecture ... Albany. By Henry James. *New York: John Allen.* 1846. 8vo, pp. 59.

Also: Speech ... March 20, 1856, on the Tariff. [n. p. n. d.] 8vo.

JAMES (H. F.) Abolition Unveiled; or its Origin, Progress, and Pernicious Tendency fully Developed. By Henry F. James. *Cincinnati.* 1856. 8vo. S. 35700

JAMES (H.) Annual Report of the Superintendent of Negro Affairs in North Carolina, 1864. With an Appendix, containing the History and Management of the Freedmen up to June 1, 1865. By Horace James, Superintendent. *Boston: W. F. Brown & Co.* 1865. 8vo, pp. 64. 35701

JAMES. The Two Great Wars of America. An Oration delivered in Newbern, North Carolina, before the Twenty-Fifth Regiment Massachusetts Volunteers, July 4, 1862. By Horace James, Chaplain. *Boston: Printed by W. F. Brown & Co.* 1862. 8vo, pp. 30. B. 35702

Also: Address of the Rev. Horace James, of Worcester, Mass., at the Anniversary of the American Home Missionary Society, New York, May 7, 1856 ... [n. p. n. d.] 8vo, pp. 7.—The Captain of our Salvation. ... [n. p.] 1862. 8vo, pp. 8.—The Christian Patriot. A Sermon. ... *Worcester.* 1861. 8vo, pp. 7.—A Sermon, in behalf of the American Education Society, ... May 29, 1854. ... *Boston: Press of T. R. Marvin.* 1854. 8vo, pp. 17. B., S.

JAMES (I.) Lives of the Signers of Declaration of Independence by I. James. *New York.* 1829. 12mo. Portraits.

JAMES (I.) Providence Displayed: or, the Remarkable Adventures of Alexander Selkirk, of Largo, in Scotland, who lived 4 years and 4 months on the Island of Juan Fernandez.—An Account of others left there, particularly William, a Mosquito Indian, &c. By Isaac James. *Bristol.* 1800. 12mo. Map.

See "M. Rev.," New Series, XXXIV. 221.

JAMES (John Angell). Ueber die grosse Erweckung in Amerika. Ein Vortrag. [Aus dem Englischen.] *Hamburg: Oncken.* 1859. 16mo, pp. 32. 35705

JAMES (J.) The Two Epistles. The Angels' Address, or the Glorious Message, Commanded to be sent to Abraham Lincoln, July 21, 1864. By James James. [*Albany.* 1864.] 8vo, pp. 8. 35706

JAMES (J. H.), *Jr.* On Military Commissions for the Trial of Citizens. By John H. James, Jr. *Cincinnati.* 1869. 8vo, pp. 16. 35707

JAMES (J. W.) Eulogy on Thomas Jefferson, Delivered at the Columbian College, D. C. on the Fourth of October, 1826. By John W. James. ... *Washington.* 1826. 8vo, pp. (2), 8.

JAMES. Second Edition. An Oration ... on the Occasion of the Inauguration of Andrew Jackson as President of the United States, 4th March, 1829 ... . By John Warren James. *Boston: Press of True and Greene.* 1829. 8vo, pp. 30. 35709

JAMES (J.), *and* MOORE (D.) A System of Exchange with almost all parts of the World ... . By Joseph James and Daniel Moore. *New York: J. Furman.* 1800. 16mo, pp. 180. C.

JAMES (T.) The | Strange | and Dange- | rovs Voyage of Captaine Thomas Iames, in | his intended Discouery of the Northwest | Passage into the South Sea. | Wherein The Miseries indvred both | Going, Wintering, Returning; and the Rarities | obserued, both Philosophicall and Mathematical, | are related in this Iournall of it. | Published by His Maiesties | command. | To which are added, A Plat or Card for the | Sayling in those Seas. | Diuers little Tables of the Author's, of the Va- | riation of the Compasse, &c. | With | An Appendix concerning Longitude, | by Master | Henry Gellibrand Astronomy Reader | of Gresham Colledge in London. | And | An Aduise concerning the Philosophy of these late | Discoueryes, By W. W. | *London,* | *Printed by Iohn Legatt, for Iohn Partridge.* | 1633. | 4to, pp. (6), 120, (22). Map. C. 35711

The map is often wanting. Captain James was a native of Bristol, and undertook this voyage with the sanction of King Charles I. at the solicitation and expense of the merchants of that city. It contains some remarkable physical observations respecting the intensity of the cold, and the accumulation of ice in northern latitude; the relations interspersed throughout, with the descriptions of various parts of North America he visited are very interesting. This book is rare in any condition, with the map containing in the upper left corner a portrait of Captain James, especially so; its place is often supplied by a facsimile. The gallant explorer has been censured for the lack of geographical information contained in his book, but the map is assuredly free from any such blame, for it contains a singularly correct delineation of the high latitudes in which Hudson, Baffin, James, and Fox pursued their search for the North-west passage.

JAMES. The Dangerous Voyage of Capt. Thomas James, In his intended Discovery of a North West Passage into the South Sea: Wherein The Miseries indured, both Going, Wintering and Returning, and the Rarities observ'd Philosophical, Mathematical and Natural are related in this Journal of it, publish'd by the Special Command of King Charles I. To which is added, A Map for Sailing in those Seas: Also divers Tables of the Author's of the Variation of the Compass, &c. With an Appendix concerning the Longitude, by Master Gellibrand, Astronomy Reader at Gresham College. The Second Edition, Revised and Corrected. *London: Printed in* 1633, *and now Reprinted for O. Payne*, MDCCXL. 8vo, pp. (10), 142. Map. C. 35712

Rreprinted in Mavor's "Voyages," Vol. I. *See also* Churchill, Vol. II.

JAMES (T. P.) An Obituary Notice of Dr. William Darlington, read before the American Philosophical Society, Feb. 19, 1864. By T. P. James. [n. p. n. d.] 8vo, pp. 12. B. 35713

JAMES (Uriah P.) James's Travelers' Companion: being a complete Guide through the West and South, to the Gulf of Mexico and the Pacific, with historical Notes [etc.] *Cincinnati: J. A. & U. P. James.* 1853. 18mo, pp. 193. C. 35714

JAMES. James's Rail Road and Route Book for the Western and Southern States. [Compiled by J. Griswold.] *Cincinnati: J. A. & U. P. James.* 1853. 16mo, pp. xii, 11–69. C. 35715

This is the correct title of *our* No. 28885.

JAMES. James's River Guide: containing Descriptions of all the Cities, Towns, and principal objects of Interest on the Navigable Waters of the Mississippi Valley. *Cincinnati.* 1856. 8vo.

JAMES (W.) A Full and Correct Account of the Chief Naval Occurrences of the late War between Great Britain and the United States of America; preceded by a Cursory Examination of the American Accounts of their Naval Actions fought Previous to that Period: to which is added an Appendix; with Plates. By William James. ... *London: T. Egerton.* 1817. 8vo, pp. xv, (1), 528, ccxvi, (16). Plates. BA., C. 35717

See "M. Rev.," LXXXV. 311.

JAMES. A Full and Correct Account of the Military Occurrences of the late War between Great Britain and the United States of America; With an Appendix, and Plates. By William James. ... *London: Printed for the Author.* 1818. 2 vols., 8vo, pp. xxxii, 476; (2), 582, (16). 4 Maps. B., BA., C. 35718

See also "M. Rev.," LXXXVIII. 164.

JAMES. An Inquiry into the Merits of the Principal Naval Actions, between Great-Britain and the United States; comprising an Account of all British and American ships of War,

Reciprocally Captured and Destroyed, since the 18th of June 1812. By William James. ... *Halifax, N. S.: Printed for the Author.* 1816. 8vo, pp. vi, 102. 3 Tables. B., BA., C. 35719

This author considered that little credit for naval or other exploits was due to the statesmen; and evinced great disgust at the American idea that "they are an intelligent, active and enlightened people, beyond all former example."

JAMES. The Naval History of Great Britain, from the Declaration of War by France, in February, 1793; to the Accession of George IV. in January, 1820; with an Account of the Origin and Progressive Increase of the British Navy; illustrated, from the Commencement of the Year 1793, by a Series of Tabular Abstracts contained in a separate quarto volume. By William James .... *London.* 1822. 4 vols., 8vo. Tables. P. 35720

JAMES. The Naval History of Great Britain, from the Declaration of War by France in 1793, to the Accession of George IV. By William James. A New Edition, with Additions ... . [Edited] By Captain Chamier ... *London: Richard Bentley.* 1837. 6 vols., 8vo, pp. xii, xxxii, 404; vii, 396; viii, 376; vi, (1), 375, (1); vii, (1), 404; viii, 567, (1). 6 Portraits, 28 Tables. B. + [*Ibid.*] 1859. 6 vols., post 8vo. 35721

Includes accounts of the actions in the West Indies, and in the War of 1812–13. "A work of which it is not too high praise to assert that it approaches as nearly to perfection, in its own line, as any historical work perhaps ever did."—*Edinburgh Review.* Also: James' Reply to a Brief Statement on his Naval History, 1824.

JAMES. Warden Refuted; being a Defence of the British Navy Against the Misrepresentations of a Work recently published at Edinburgh, entitled "A Statistical, Political, and Historical Account of the United States ... by D. B. Warden ... ." In a Letter to the Author of that Work; by William James ... . *London: J. M. Richardson.* 1819. 8vo, pp. 48, Errata, 3 lines. Table. 35722

JAMES (W. D.) A Sketch of the Life of Brig.-Gen. Francis Marion, and A History of his Brigade, from its Rise in June, 1780, until Disbanded in December, 1782; with Descriptions of Characters and Scenes not heretofore published. Containing also, an Appendix, with Copies of Letters which passed between several of the leading Characters of that day; principally from Gen. Greene to Gen. Marion. By William Dobein James, A.M., during that period one of Marion's Militia, at present one of the Associate Judges in Equity, South Carolina. *Charleston, S. C.: Printed by Gould and Riley.* 1821. 8vo, pp. 182, 39. 35723

JAMES RIVER. Annual Report of the James River and Kanawha Company. *Richmond.* 1836. 8vo. Continued. 35724

Collection of all Acts and parts of Acts of the General Assembly of Virginia, from October, 1784, down to the Session of 1829–30, inclusive, relating to the James River Company. *Richmond.* 1830. 8vo. 35725

Report of the Joint Committee on the Affairs of the James River & Kanawha Co. 1853–54. 8vo, pp. 35. 35726

Statement of James River Company. *Richmond.* 1805. 8vo.

Also: Reports of the United States Engineers on the Survey of the James River and Kanawha Canal, and on the Advantages of the Central Water Line as a National Work. *Richmond.* 1871. 8vo, pp. 104.

JAMESON [Anna]. Sketches in Canada, and Rambles among the Red Men. By Mrs. Jameson. *London: Longman.* 1852. 8vo. + New Edition. [*Ibid.*] 1862. Post 8vo, pp. (4), 314.

This very entertaining book which is an abridgment of No. 35731, *infra*, also forms Vol. XII. of the "Traveller's Library."

JAMESON. Visits and Sketches at Home and Abroad. By Mrs. Jameson. *London: Saunders and Otley.* 1834. 2 vols., post 8vo, pp. vii, 307; iv, 323. + Third Edition. [*Ibid.*] 1839.

JAMESON. Visits and Sketches at Home and Abroad. With Tales and Miscellanies now first collected ... By Mrs. Jameson. *New-York: Harper & Brothers.* 1834. 2 vols., 12mo, pp. 304; (4), 271. 35730

JAMESON. Winter Studies and Summer Rambles in Canada. By Mrs. Jameson. ... *London: Saunders & Otley.* 1838. 3 vols., post 8vo, pp. xi, vi, 315; vi, 341; vi, 356. B. + *New-York: Wiley and Putnam.* 1839. 2 vols., 12mo, pp. viii, 341; iv, 339.

Includes sketches of Indian life, personal appearance and biographical notes of such Indians as she met, and such narrations of their traditions and religious sentiments, as a woman would be permitted to hear or report.

JAMESON. Winterstudien und Sommerstreifereien in Canada. Ein Tagebuch von Mrs. Jameson. Aus dem Englischen übersetzt von A. W. *Braunschweig: F. Vieweg & Sohn.* 1839. 3 vols., 12mo. C. 35732

JAMESON (J. A.) The Constitutional Convention; Its History, Powers, and Modes of Proceeding. By John Alexander Jameson ... . *New York: Charles Scribner and Company.* 1866.

8vo, pp. xix, 561. + Second Edition. [*Ibid.*] 1867. + Third Edition. *Chicago: Callaghan & Co.* 1873. 8vo. C. 35733

Also: Responsibilities of American Merchants for the Conversion of the World to Christ. ... *New York: I. W. Brinckerhoff.* 1855. 12mo, pp. 47. B.

JAMESON (Robert), *Joint Author. See* Murray (H.)

JAMESON (William H.), *Jr.*, *and* FERGUSON (George). Table of Pay of the Commissioned Officers of the [U. S.] Army, under the Law of the 39th Congress. [*Washington.* 1867.] 4to.

JAMESTOWN, *N. Y.* Catalogue of the Jamestown Academy. 1857–58. 8vo. S. 35735

The Fiftieth Anniversary of the Organization of the First Congregational Church, of Jamestown, N. Y.—Sermon, Historical Sketch, Addresses, &c. *Democrat Book & Job Office.* 1866. 8vo, pp. 72. S. 35736

Sermon by T. H. Rouse; Historical Sketch and an Address by A. Hazeltine. The contents of this pamphlet are printed on the cover.

JAMESTOWN, *Va.* Celebration of the Two Hundred and Fiftieth Anniversary of the English Settlement of Jamestown, Va., May 18, 1857. *Washington.* 1857. 8vo, pp. 32. B. 35737

First Celebration of the Anniversary of the Settlement at Jamestown, Va., on the 13th of May, 1607. Hon. George W. Summers, Orator. *New York: Pudney & Russell, Printers.* 1860. 8vo, pp. 109. BA. 35738

Report of the Proceedings of the late Jubilee at Jamestown, in Commemoration of the 13th of May, the Second Centesimal Anniversary of the Settlement of Virginia; ... Reported by the Select Committee. *Petersburg.* 1807. 8vo. C. 35739

JAMIESON (J.) The Sorrows of Slavery, a Poem; containing a faithful Statement of Facts respecting the African Slave Trade. By the Rev. J. Jamieson. *London: John Murray.* 1789. 12mo, pp. 80. 35740

JAMIESON (M.) Journal and Notes of a Campaign in Mexico: containing a History of Co. C. of the Second Regiment of Ohio Volunteers. By Milton Jamieson. *Cincinnati: Ben Franklin Printing House.* 1849. 8vo, pp. 105. C. 35741

JAMIESON (*Mrs.*) Popular Voyages and Travels throughout the Continents and Islands of Asia, Africa, and America. ... By

Mrs. Jamieson. *London: G. B. Whitaker & Co.* 1820. 2 vols., post 8vo. 35742

Written for young people. *See* "M. Rev.," XCIII. 448.

JAMISON (D. F.) The Life and Times of Bertrand du Guesclin: A History of the Fourteenth Century. By D. F. Jamison, of South Carolina. *Charleston: John Russell.* MDCCCLXIV. 2 vols., 8vo, pp. xvi, 287, Portrait; viii, 314. 35743

The author was president of the convention in Charleston, S. C., which passed the ordinance of secession. It was really printed in London, and does not relate to America, although often included in catalogues under such a heading.

JANES (E. L.) Wesley his own Historian. Illustrations of his Character, Labors, and Achievments. ... By Rev. Edwin L. Janes. *New York: Carlton & Lanahan.* 1870. 12mo, pp. 464.

JANES (F.) The Janes Family. ... With ... Notice of Bishop Edmund S. Janes ... By the Rev. Frederic Janes. ... *New York: John H. Dingman.* 1868. 8vo, pp. 419. 4 Portraits. B. 35745

JANES (W.) Masonic Poem at Mansfield [Conn.], with an Address on the Death of Austin Stowell, at Pomfret, Feb. 22, 1814, and also an Address June 30, 1819, at the Interment of Stephen Lewis. By Walter Janes. *Brookfield, Mass.* 1819. 8vo.

Also: The Harmonic Minstrelsy; containing a New Collection of Sacred Music. ... *Dedham, Mass.* 1807. Ob. 8vo, pp. 103. S.

JANES, FOWLER, KIRTLAND & Co. Memorial to Congress, concerning Work on the Dome of the Capitol. [n. p. n. d.] 8vo.

JANESVILLE, *Wis.* First Annual Report of the Board of School Commissioners. *Janesville.* 1857. 8vo. Continued. S.

Janesville: its Business, Manufactories, Water Power, etc. From the Janesville Democrat, 1866. 8vo. 35749

JANEWAY (J. James). A Historical Discourse prepared for the Semi-Centenary Sabbath, and delivered on that day ... in New-Brunswick; ... By Jacob J. Janeway, D.D. *New-Brunswick: John Terhune's Press.* 1840. 8vo, pp. 28. B., S. 35750

JANEWAY. Hope for my Country: showing the Divinity of Jesus Christ, and His Care over his Church, as exhibited in the past History of our Country. ... By J. J. Janeway, D.D. *New-Brunswick, N. J.: Press of J. Terhune.* 1856. 8vo, pp. 64.

Also: The Duty of the Presbyterian Church. A Discourse, ... before the General Assembly, of the Presbyterian Church, ... in 1819. ... *New-Brunswick: Printed by Terhune & Letson.* 1836. 8vo, pp. 39. BA., S.

JANEWAY (J.) Mr. James Janeway's | Legacy | to his | Friends, | Containing Twenty Seven Fa- | mous Instances of God's Providen- | ces in and about Sea Dangers and | Deliverances, with the Names of Se- | veral that were Eye-witnesses to many | of them. | Whereunto is Added a Sermon on the | same Subject. | *London, Printed for Dorman Newman, at | the Kings Armes in the Poultry*, 1674. | 16mo, pp. (8), 134. 35752

"A great part of this book relates to New England, and other parts of America."—STEVENS.

JANEWAY. A seasonable and earnest Address to the Citizens of London, Soon after the Dreadful Fire ... in ... 1666. By ... Mr. James Janeway. To which is added, Dr. Smollett's Account of the said Conflagration. Together with a particular Relation of the Great Fire of Boston, in New-England; March 20, 1760. *Boston: Sold by Benjamin Mecom.* [1760.] 16mo, pp. 55. B., BA. 35753

JANEWAY. A Token for Children. ... To which is added, A Token for the Children of New-England, or Some Examples of Children, in whom the Fear of God was remarkably Budding before they died, in several Parts of New-England, Preserved and Published for the Encouragement of Piety in other Children. *Boston.* 1728. 12mo, pp. xii, 117. B. + *Boston:* Z. *Fowle.* 1771. 12mo, pp. 156. C., M. 35754

JANEWAY. A Token for Mariners, containing many Famous and Wonderful Instances of God's Providence in Sea Dangers and Deliverances ... . *Printed on London-Bridge for T. Norris.* 1721. 12mo. Plate. 35755

Relates principally to the Coasts of America and the West Indies.

JANEWAY (J. L.) *See* Lincoln (Abraham).

JANEWAY (T. L.) Memoir of the Rev. Jacob J[ones] Janeway, D.D. By Thomas Leiper Janeway, D.D. *Philadelphia: Presbyterian Board of Publication.* 1861. 12mo, pp. 304. Portrait.

JANEY (J.) Histoire du royaume de Chili, par Jean Janey [en hollandais]. *Amsterdam.* 1619. 4to. 35757

Title from Boucher de la Richarderie, Vol. VI., p. 341—probably incorrect.

JANIN (A.) Fulton Georges et Robert Stephenson ou les bateaux a vapeur et les chemins de fer. Par André Janin ... . *Paris: Grassart.* 1861. 12mo, pp. (4), 448. B. 35758

JANISCH (J.) Washington. Historisch-epische Dichtung in vier Gesängen. Nebst geschichtlichen Erläuterungen. Von Joseph Janisch. ... *Leipzig: Moritz Schäfer.* ... 1870. 4to, pp. 176. B., C. 35759

JANNEY (S. M.) History of the Religious Society of Friends, from its Rise to ... 1828. By Samuel M. Janney ... . Second Edition. *Philadelphia: Hayes & Zell.* 1860–1867. 4 vols., 8vo, pp. xvi, 19–483; 456; 504; 347. B. 35760

JANNEY. The Life of George Fox; with Dissertations on his Views concerning the Doctrines, Testimonies, and Discipline of the Christian Church. By Samuel M. Janney ... . *Philadelphia: Lippincott, Grambo & Co.* 1853. 8vo, pp. 499. Plate. B.

JANNEY. The Life of William Penn: with Selections from his Correspondence and Autobiography. By Samuel M. Janney. *Philadelphia.* 1852. 8vo, pp. 576. Portrait. C. + Second Edition Revised. *Philadelphia: Lippincott, Grambo & Co.* 1852. 8vo, pp. 576. 2 Portraits. B. + [*Ibid.*] 1853. + [*Ibid.*] 1856. 8vo, pp. 592. Portrait. 35762

Also: ... The Last of the Lenapé, and other Poems. ... *Philadelphia: H. Perkins.* 1839. 12mo, pp. 180. C.

JANNEY (T.) An | Epistle | from Thomas Janney, | to | Friends of Cheshire, | And by them desired to be made Publick. | [Signed:] Thomas Janney. | From my House near the | Falls of Delaware in | the County of Bucks in | Pensylvania, the 16th | day of the 10th. | Month, 1693. | [Colophon:] *London, | Printed ... by T. Sowle* ... 1694. | 4to, pp. 8. 35763

JANOS (X.) Utazás Kalifornia deli Részeeben. Irta Xántus Janos, ... *Pesten: Kiadjáh Lauffes és Stolp.* 1860. Rl. 8vo, pp. (10), 191. 8 Plates and Map. 35764

JANS (A.) Anneke Jans and Trinity Church. *New York.* 1857. 8vo. 35765

JANS. Account of Anneke Janse and of her Family, with her Will in Dutch and English. *Albany.* 1870. 12mo. 35766

JANSEN (Jacob). Verhaal der merkwaardige reize met het schip de Vrouw Maria Elisabeth, den zevenden April des jaars 1769, van Hamburg naar Groenland ter walvischvangst uitgezeild; tot den twintigsten November in het Ys bezet geweest; den een en twintigsten dier maand daaruit geraakt; en den der-

tienden December deszelfden jaars gelukkig weder te Hamburg aangekomen. Uit het Hoogduitsch vertaald. *Haarlem: J. Enschede.* 1770. 4to, pp. 24. Plate. 35767

Account of the curious voyage of J. Jansen, from Hamburg to Greenland.

JANSEN (Martin). Kort, doch echt verhaal wegens het verongelukken van zyn schip genaamd het Witte Paard, en nog negen andere scheepen, dewelke alle verongelukt zyn, in Groenland, door de bezetting van 't West Ys, ten jaare 1777. Waar by nog copia, van een brief van Comm. Hidde Dirks Kat, aan zyn huisvrouw, geschreven uit Straat-Davids, behelzende meede haare ongelukken en rampen op reis geleeden. *Leeuwarden.* 1778. 4to, pp. (4), 23. + *Amsterdam.* 1778. 4to, pp. (4), 18.

Account of the shipwreck of Maarten Jansen in Greenland. The Amsterdam edition does not contain the letter written from Davids Straits by H. D. Kat to his wife.

JANSEN (M. H.) Een brug over den Oceaan. Stromvaart op Amerika. Goedkooper brood en meer werk. *Delft: J. Waltmann, Jr.* 1869. 8vo, pp. 8, 311. Map. 35769

Relates to steam navigation between Holland and America.

JANSON (C. W.) The Stranger in America: Containing Observations made during a Long Residence in that Country, on the Genius, Manners and Customs of the People of the United States; with Biographical Particulars of Public Characters; Hints and Facts relative to the Arts, Sciences, Commerce, Agriculture, Manufactures, Emigration, and the Slave Trade. By Charles William Janson, Esq. Late of the State of Rhode Island, Counsellor at Law. Illustrated by Engravings. *Albion Press: Printed for James Cundee. London.* 1807. 4to, pp. 22, 499, (1). 10 Plates. B., BA., C. 35770

"This large and most ill-arranged volum contains, apparently, whatever Mr. Janson could recollect of America, aiding his memory by a few notes and memorandums. He went to America with high expectations, engaged in several speculations, all of which failed, and after thirteen years' absence, returned to England, where, as many others have done since, he vented his spleen in writing a book."—*Monthly Review*, LIII. 443.

[JANSON (Forbin), *Evêque de Nancy.*] Souvenir de retraite, ou mémorial abrégé de ce qui s'est dit ou fait, jour par jour, pendant la retraite commencée à Montreal le 13 Décembre 1840 et terminée le 21 Janvier 1841. *Montreal.* 1841. 8vo, pp. 76.

JANSSEN (Carl Emil). Kalatdlit Inuvdluar-Kugamigit 1857. *Nungme.* 1858. 8vo, pp. 27. 35772

Printed at Godthaab on the first printing-press sent to Greenland, in the summer of 1857. Also: Skoleundervüsningen og den deraf fremgaaede almindelige Folkeplysning i Grönland, in "Ugeskrift f. d. evang. Kirke i Denmark," XI. 16–23.

JANSSON (Juan). Novus Atlas, sive Theatrum Orbis Terrarum. *Amstelodami.* 1640–50. 6 vols., rl. folio. Frontispieces and 466 large colored Maps. 35773

The text of this great Atlas is the same as that of Blaeu's, which appeared some ten years later, but the maps are all different, and not always inferior. They are, in fact, the same as those in Mercator's Atlas, with the addition of many more, including some of America.

JANSSON. Nuevo Atlas; o, Teatro de todo el Mundo. *Amsterdam.* 1653. 4 vols., folio. C. 35774

The same as the foregoing, with the text in Spanish.

JANSZ (Bernard). *See* [Potgieter (B. J.)]

JANSZOON (W.) Het licht der zee-vaert ... Custen ende havenen vande westersche, noordsche ende middellandsche zee'n. Ook van ... Guinea, Brasilien, Oost- ende West-Indiën, enz. *Amsterdam: W. Janszoon.* 1620. 2 vols., folio. 35775

"Le 2e vol. intitulé: 'Tweede boeck enz. ... havenen ende eylanden v. de noordsche ende oostersche zeeën ... Laplandt ende Muscovien.' L'Auteur était le père de fameux géographe J. J. Blaeu." Title and note from Martinus Nijhoff's Catalogue.

JANUS, *pseudon.* The Critical Moment on which the Salvation or Destruction of the British Empire depends. Containing the Rise, Progress, Present State, and Natural Consequences of our American Disputes. By Janus. *London: H. Setchell.* MDCCLXXVI. 8vo, pp. 121. 35776

"This author shows a more comprehensive knowledge of his subject than is common to the pamphleteers of the times. ... His zeal for the colonies, and the acrimony with which he speaks of the administration at home, lead to the suspicion that he is a native of America."—*Monthly Review*, LIV. 230.

JANVIER (F. De Haes). Patriotic Poems. By Francis De Haes Janvier ... . *Philadelphia: J. B. Lippincott & Co.* 1866. 12mo, pp. 88. B., C. 35777

JANVIER. The Sleeping Sentinel. By Francis De Haes Janvier. *Philadelphia: T. B. Peterson.* 1863. 12mo, pp. 19.

Relates to William Scott, a soldier from Vermont, who, while on duty as a sentinel, fell asleep, and was condemned to die.

Japanese Treaties concluded at Jeddo in 1858 with the Netherlands, Russia, Great Britain, the United States and France. Facsimile of the Japanese Text, with Preface. Published by J. Hoffmann. *The Hague.* 1862. 4to. Lithographed. 35779

Japanicæ Epistolæ de Multorum Gentilium in variis Insulis ad Christi Fidem per Societatis nominis Jesu Theologos Conver-

sione: in quibus etiam Mores, Leges, Locorumque Situs, luculenter describuntur. *Lovanii.* 1569. 2 vols., 8vo. 35780

"These letters from Japan, Brazil, the Molucca Isles, and various parts of Asia, comprise ample details of the manners and customs of the people, their laws and religious creed, from 1542 to the date of publication."—THORP's *Catalogue*, No. 10438.

JAQUES (G.) Transactions of the Worcester County Horticultural Society, from its formation to the commencement of the year 1847. ... By George Jaques. ... *Boston: Eastburn's Press.* 1847. 8vo, pp. 84. B. 35781

JAQUES (J. W.) Three Years' Campaign of the Ninth, N. Y. S. M., during the Southern Rebellion. By John W. Jaques, formerly of Company D. *New York: Hilton & Co.* 1865. 12mo, pp. 199, (2), 47, (1). B. 35782

JAQUES (M.) Case of Contempt; or, Proceedings of the House of Assembly of the State of New York, against Moses Jaques and Levi D. Slamm, charged with Contempt of the Authority of that Body. Together with the Protest and Defence of the Accused. *New York.* 1837. 8vo, pp. 18. N. 35783

JARDIN (D.) Criminal Trials supplying Copious Illustrations of the Important Periods of English History during the Reigns of Queen Elizabeth and James I. ... With Historical Prefaces and Notes. By David Jardin. *London.* [n. d.] 2 vols., fcap 8vo. 35784

Includes Sir Walter Raleigh's Imprisonment, Voyage to Guinea, and Execution.

JARDIN (G. de). *See* Orta (Garcia de).

JARDINE (L. J.) A Letter from Pennsylvania to a Friend in England: containing Valuable Information with respect to America. By L. J. Jardine, M.D. *Bath, R. Cruttwell;* MDCCXCV. 8vo, pp. (4), 31. C., W. 35785

"Consists of comparative views of the several plans which offer themselves to a new settler in America for the choice of a situation, and an account of the expenses of living in some parts of Pennsylvania, which State Dr. Jardine recommends above all others."—*Monthly Review*, XVIII. 102.

JARMAN (R.) A Journal of a Voyage to the South Seas, in the Japan, employed in the Sperm Whale Fishery, under the Command of Captain John May. By Robert Jarman. *London.* 1839. 12mo. 35786

JARNAGIN (S.) Speech of Spencer Jarnagin on the Treaty for the Annexation of Texas, delivered ... June 6, 1844. [*Washington.* 1844.] 8vo. 35787

JARNETTE (D. C.) The Monroe Doctrine. Speech of Hon. D. C. Jarnette, of Virginia, in the Confederate House of Representatives, January 30th, 1865, pending Negotiations for Peace. [*Richmond?* 1865.] 8vo, pp. 20. BA. 35788

JARRATT (D.) The Life of the Reverend Devereux Jarratt, ... Written by Himself, in a Series of Letters Addressed to the Rev. John Coleman ... . *Baltimore: Printed by Warner & Hanna.* 1806. 12mo, pp. (2), iv, (2), 5–223. B. 35789

Also: Addresses to the Right Rev. the Bishops, the Rev. the Clergy, and Lay Members of the Protestant Episcopal Church in the State of Virginia. ... *Richmond.* 1792. 8vo, pp. 31.—A Sermon ... before the Convention of the Protestant Episcopal Church, in Virginia. At Richmond, May 3, 1792. ... *Richmond (Virginia): Printed. New-London: Reprinted by T. Green and Son.* M,DCC,XCII. 8vo, pp. 31. BA. + *Bristol, R. I.: Reprinted.* 1808. 8vo, pp. 28. + Third Edition. *New Haven.* 1809. 8vo, pp. 24.

JARRIC (Pierre du). Histoire des choses plus memorables advenues tant ez Indes Orientales, que autres pais de la descouverte des Portugais. *Bourdeaux.* 1608–14. 3 vols., 4to.

Only three complete copies of this interesting, elaborate, and valuable work appear to have occurred for sale, one of which was in the curious collection of the late Robert Lang, Esq., who had written in it, "The third volume of this work is very scarce, and although the two first volumes are found amongst collections of scarce voyages, I never saw or heard of but one other copy of the third volume, which is in the library of Lord Bute at Luton." Sold in Mr. Lang's sale for £8, 8s.

JARRIC. R. P. Petri Jarrici Tholosani Societ. Jesu Thesaurus Rerum Indicarum. In quo Christianæ ac Catholicæ Religionis tam in India Orientali quam alijs Regionibus Lusitanorum opera nuper detectis Ortus, Progressus, Incrementa, & maxime quæ à P. P. Soc. Jesu ibidem in dictæ Fidei plantatione ac propagatione ad Annum usq3 MDC. gesta atq3 exantlata sunt, non minus vere quàm eleganter recensentur. Additæ sunt passim Earundem Regionum & eorum quæ ad eas pertinent tam Chorographicæ quàm Historicæ Descriptiones. Opus nunc primum à M. Matthia Martinez e gallico in latinum sermonem translatum. Permissu Superiorum. *Coloniæ Agrippinæ. Sumptibus Petri Henningij. Anno* MDCXV–XVI. 4 vols., small 8vo, pp. 794; 808; 653; 621. C. 35791

Contains a full account of the Jesuit Mission to Brazil, St. Thomas, etc., with chorographical and historical descriptions of those countries. *See* "Bibliotheca Grenvilliana."

JARRIGE (P.) Les Jesuites mis sur l'Eschafaut pour plusieurs crimes capitaux par eux commis dans la Province de Guienne avec la Response aux calomnies de Jaques Beaufé, par Pierre Jarrige. [*Leiden.*] 1649. 8vo. + *Jouxte la copie impr. a Leiden.* 1676. 8vo. 35792

JARRIGE. Jesuita in ferali pigmate ob nefanda crimina in provincia Guienna perpetrata. *Lugduni Batavorum.* 1665. 8vo.

JARRIGE. Nachricht von den vielen Lastern, welche die Jesuiten in der Provinz Gvienne begangen haben, nebst einer Verantwortung auf die Verläumdungen des Jacob Beaufes. Aus dem Französischen und Lateinischen übersetzt. [n. p.] 1761. 8vo. 35794

JARVES (J. J.) The Art Idea: Part Second of Confessions of an Inquirer. By James Jackson Jarves. *New York: Hurd and Houghton.* 1864. Fcap 8vo, pp. xlvi, 381. 35795

Contains notices of the progress of art in the United States, criticisms on American artists, etc.

JARVES. History of the Hawaiian or Sandwich Islands, embracing their Antiquities, Mythology, Legends, Discovery by Europeans in the Sixteenth Century, Re-discovery by Cook, with their Civil, Religious, and Political History, from the Earliest Traditionary Period to the Present Time. By James Jackson Jarves ... . *Boston: Tappan and Dennet.* 1843. 8vo, pp. xx, 407. Plates and Map. BA., C. + *London: Edward Moxon.* 1843. Post 8vo, pp. 377. + Third Edition. *Honolulu: Charles Edwin Hitchcock.* 1847. 8vo, pp. 240. B., BA. 35796

JARVES. Italian Sights and Papal Principles, seen through American Spectacles. By James Jackson Jarves ... . *New York: Harper & Brothers.* 1856. 12mo, pp. 382. Illustrations. BA.

[JARVES.] Parisian Sights and French Principles, seen through American Spectacles. ... *New York: Harper & Brothers.* 1852. 12mo, pp. 264. + Second Series. [*Ibid.*] 1855. 12mo, pp. 277.

JARVES. Kiana: A Tradition of Hawaii. By James J. Jarves ... *Boston and Cambridge: James Munroe and Company.* M DCCCLVII. 12mo, pp. 277. Plates, 2 Portraits. BA. 35799

JARVES. Scenes and Scenery in the Sandwich Islands, and a Trip through Central America, during the years 1837–42. By James Jackson Jarves ... . *Boston: James Munroe & Co.* 1844. 12mo, pp. 341. Map and Plates. C. + New Edition. [*Ibid.*]

JARVIS (Abraham). Bishop Jarvis's Charge to the Clergy of his Diocese. Delivered Immediately after his Consecration, ... October 18, 1797. Together with the Address ... . And the Bishop's Answer. *Printed at Newfield, By Lazarus Beach.* 1798. 8vo, pp. 29. BA. 35801

Also: Discourse at New Haven [Conn.], before a Special Convention of the Episcopal Church, May 5, 1796. ... *New Haven.* [n. d.] 8vo.—Discourse, ... Death of R't Rev. S. Seabury. *New Haven.* 1796. 8vo. S.

JARVIS (E.) Insanity among the Coloured Population of the Free States. By Edward Jarvis ... . *Philadelphia: T. K. & P. G. Collins, Printers.* 1844. 8vo, pp. 15. BA. 35802

[JARVIS.] Interest of the State in the Health and Longevity of the People. Memorial of the Boston Sanitary Association to the Legislature of Massachusetts, asking for the Establishment of a Board of Health and Vital Statistics. *Boston.* 1861. 8vo, pp. 31. H. 35803

JARVIS. The Law of Insanity, and Hospitals for the Insane in Massachusetts. By Edward Jarvis, M.D. ... *Boston: Press of Geo. C. Rand & Avery.* 1859. 8vo, pp. 24. BA. 35804

JARVIS. Memoir of the Life and Character of George Cheyne Shattuck, M.D. ... By Edward Jarvis, M.D. [n. p. n. d.] 8vo, pp. 16. B. 35805

Also: Address, delivered at the Laying of the Corner Stone of the Insane Hospital, at Northampton, Massachusetts. ... *Northampton: Printed by J. & L. Metcalf.* 1856. 8vo, pp. 39.—Insanity and Insane Asylums: ... *Louisville, Ky.: Prentice and Weissinger.* 1841. 8vo, pp. (4), 40.—On the Supposed Increase of Insanity. From the American Journal of Insanity. ... [n. p. n. d.] 8vo, pp. 36.—What shall we do with the Insane of the Western Country? ... [*Louisville.* 1842.] 8vo, pp. 45. BA.

[JARVIS (Edward), *and others.*] The Sixth Census of the United States. [As published in the Merchant's Magazine, for February, 1845.] Memorial to the Honorable the Senate and House of Representatives in Congress assembled: [n. p. n. d.] 8vo, pp. 15. B. 35806

JARVIS (J. B.) Report relative to the Survey of the proposed Caughnawaga Canal, by J. B. Jarvis; with Documents relative to the Survey and Improvement of the Rapids of the River St. Lawrence, by MM. Maillefert and Raasloff. *Quebec.* 1855. 8vo, pp. 76. Plans. 35807

JARVIS (Leonard). Speech of Mr. Jarvis, of Maine, on the Navy Appropriation Bill, in House of Representatives, April 4, 1836. *Washington: Blair and Rives,* ... 1836. 8vo, pp. 14. N.

[JARVIS (Russell).] A Biographical Notice of Com. Jesse D. Elliott; Containing a Review of the Controversy between him and the late Commodore Perry; and a History of the Figure-Head of the U. S. Frigate Constitution. ... By a Citizen of

New York. *Philadelphia: Printed for the Author.* 1835. 12mo, pp. 480. B., C. 35809

[JARVIS.] Facts and Arguments against the Election of General Cass, Respectfully addressed to the Whigs and Democrats of all the Free States. By an Anti-Abolitionist. *New York: Printed by R. Craighead.* 1848. 8vo, pp. 64. B., S. 35810

JARVIS. An Oration, delivered before the Republicans of Boston, on the Fourth of July, 1823. By Russell Jarvis. *Boston: Press of True and Greene.* 1823. 8vo, pp. 27. B., BA. 35811

JARVIS (S. F.) A Discourse on the Religion of the Indian Tribes of North America. Delivered before the New-York Historical Society, December 20, 1819. By Samuel Farmar Jarvis. ... *New York: C. Wiley & Co.* 1820. 8vo, pp. 111. C.

JARVIS. A Narrative of Events connected with the Acceptance, and Resignation of the Rectorship of the St. Paul's Church. *Boston.* [1825.] 8vo, pp. 108. B., BA., S. 35813

JARVIS. ... A Sermon ... in ... Hartford ... May 30, 1847. ... At the Admission to the Order of Priests of The Rev. A. Jackson ... . By the Rev. Samuel Farmar Jarvis, D.D. ... *Hartford: N. S. Parsons.* 1847. 8vo, pp. 32. B. 35814

JARVIS. A Voice from Connecticut; occasioned by The Late Pastoral Letter of the Bishop of North Carolina to the Clergy and Laity of his Diocese. By the Rev. Samuel Farmar Jarvis, ... *Hartford: A. C. Goodman & Co.* MDCCCXLIX. 8vo, pp. 100 or more. 35815

JARVIS. Want of Patronage the Principal Cause of the Slow Progress of American Literature. An Oration, delivered before the Society of Phi Beta Kappa ... December 5th, 1806. By Samuel F. Jarvis. ... *New-Haven: Printed by Oliver Steele & Co.* 1806. 8vo, pp. 22. BA. 35816

Also: An Address ... on the Birthday of Linnæus, May 26, 1836, in behalf of the Natural History Society of Connecticut. ... *Hartford.* 1836.—No Union with Rome. An Address to the Members of the Protestant Episcopal Church, in ... America ... . *Hartford: H. Huntington.* 1843. 12mo, pp. 44.—Office of Institution of the Rev. Samuel Farmar Jarvis, D.D. as Rector of St. Paul's Church, Boston ... the 7th of July, 1820. *Boston: Printed by Munroe and Francis.* [1820.] 8vo, pp. 22.— ... A Sermon ... at Saybrook, ... Connecticut ... April 9th, 1815, at the Funeral of Mrs. Jannette Hart. ... *New-York: Eastburn, Kirk & Co.* 1815. 8vo, pp. 25.— ... A Sermon ... Oct. 1, 1816, ... Annual Convention of the Protestant Episcopal Church ... . *New-York: David Longworth.* 1816. 8vo, pp. 37.—A Sermon preached before the Auxiliary Education Society of the Young Men of Boston, January 23, 1822. ... *Boston: Printed by*

Joseph W. Ingraham. 1822. 8vo, pp. 24.— ... A Sermon, Preached ... June 20, 1821, before the Annual Convention of the Protestant Episcopal Church, in the State of Massachusetts. With Notes, and an Appendix ... . *Boston: Joseph W. Ingraham.* 1822. 8vo, pp. 76.—Sermon, Christian Unity, Board of Missions. ... *New-York.* 1837. 8vo, pp. 50.—Thanksgiving Sermon, Bloomingdale, April, 1815. For Peace .. *New York.* 1815. 8vo, pp. 16.

JARVIS (S. M.) The Great Divorce Case: A Full and Impartial History of the Trial of the Petition of Mrs. Sarah M. Jarvis, for a Divorce from her Husband, the Rev. Samuel F. Jarvis, D.D. ... before a Committee of the Legislature of ... Connecticut. ... *New-York.* 1839. 8vo, pp. 60. B. 35817

Also: Report of the Proceedings, on the Petition of Mrs. Sarah M. Jarvis, for a Divorce from her husband, Rev. Samuel F. Jarvis, D.D., LL.D. before a Committee of the Legislature of Connecticut. *Hartford, May,* 1839. 8vo, pp. 116. B.

JARVIS (W. C.) An Oration, delivered at Pittsfield, before the Washington Benevolent Society of the County of Berkshire, on the 4th July, 1812. By William C. Jarvis, Esq. A.M. ... *Pittsfield: Printed by Milo Smith & Co.* 1812. 8vo, pp. 22. BA.

JARVIS. The Republican; or, a Series of Essays on the Principles and Policy of Free States. Having a particular reference to the United States of America and the Individual States. By William C. Jarvis, Esq. *Pittsfield: Printed by Phinehas Allen.* 1820. 12mo, pp. 368, (1). B., BA., C., S. 35819

Also: Speech, ... Favor of Religious Freedom. ... *Boston: Printed by True and Greene.* 1823. 8vo, pp. 15. B., BA.

JASKI (F. C.) Aanteekeningen op mijne reis om de wereld in 1851 en 52. *Amsterdam.* 1855. 8vo. 35820

JAUREGUI (A. de). Cartel del certamen Templo del Honor y la virtud. En el plausible triunfal recibimiento del Exmo S^{or}. Don Augustin de Jauregui y Aldecoa, Gobernador y Capitan General de estos Reynos de Peru y Chile. En la real Universidad de San Marcos de esta Ciudad de Lima Corte del Peru. [*Lima.* 1783.] 4to, pp. 243, (104), Eulogio, por J. B. Baquijano, 82. Portrait.

JAUREGUI (F.) Justificacion que el Lié D. Felipe Jauregui hau de su conduct puiblica ... . *Leon.* 1850. Folio, pp. (2), 9.

Also: Parte oficial que el Jeneral Dom Santos Guardiola da la Exmo, Señor Don Felipe Jauregui ... . *Comayagua.* 1850. Folio, 5 l.

JAUREGUI (J. T. de). Memoria sobre proporcionar arbitrios para la construccion de Caminos, en esta jurisdiccion, por D. Juan Tomás de Jáuregui para consul del Real tribunal del Consulado de esta ciudad é Isla. *Havana, Estevan, Boloña.* 1795. Folio, pp. (2), 12. 35823

JAURET (Georges). Le Mexique devant les Chambres. *Paris: E. Dentu.* 1866. 8vo. 35824

JAY (Antoine). Le Glaneur, ou Essais de Nicolas Freeman, recueillis et publiés par M. A. Jay. ... *Paris: Cérioux jeune.* 1812. 8vo, pp. xv, 416. S. 35825

A fiction in which literature, criticism, and discussion of life in America, are blended.

JAY (J.) Dissertatio Medica Inauguralis, de Fluore Albo, ... eruditorum examini subjicit Jacobus Jay, Novi Eboracensis. *Edinburgi: Hamilton, Balfour, et Neill.* M,DCC,LIII. 4to, pp. (4), 28.

JAY (J.) A Letter to the Governors of the College of New York; Respecting the Collection That was made in this Kingdom in 1762 and 1763, For the Colleges of Philadelphia and New York. To which are added, Explanatory Notes; and An Appendix, containing the Letters Which passed between Mr. Alderman Trecothick and the Author. By Sir James Jay, Knt. M.D. *London: Printed for G. Kearsly* ... . 1771. 8vo, pp. vi, 42.

The governors had drawn on Sir James for a larger amount than he had collected, and on the protest of the bills, commenced suit against him. Hence this publication.

JAY. A Letter to the Universities of Oxford and Cambridge, &c. In respect to the Collection that was made for the Colleges of New York and Philadelphia. By Sir James Jay, Knt. M.D. Being A Vindication of the Author, occasioned by the groundless Insinuations, and very illiberal Behaviour of Mr. Alderman Trecothick, with authentic Evidence. *London: ... G. Kearsly* ... . M,DCC,LXXIV. 8vo, pp. (2), 20. S. 35828

See "M. Rev.," XLIV. 422.

JAY (J.) Memorial of Sir James Jay to the Senate and House of Representatives in Congress. [n. p.] 1813. 8vo, pp. 16. N.

[JAY (John).] An Address to the People of the State of New-York, on the subject of the Constitution, agreed upon at Philadelphia, the 17th of September, 1787. *New-York: Printed by Samuel and John Loudon, Printers to the State.* [1787.] Small 4to, pp. 19. S. 35830

Signed "A Citizen of New York."

JAY. The Charge delivered by the Hon. John Jay, Chief Justice of the State of New York, to the Grand Jury at the Supreme Court held at Kingston, in Ulster County, September 9, 1777. *Kingston: Printed by John Holt, Printer to the State of New York.* 1777. 8vo, pp. 12. N. 35831

Jay. A Charge, delivered by the Hon. John Jay, Esq., Chief Justice of the United States, to the Grand Jury of the United States Court, Virginia. *Richmond.* 1793. 4to, pp. 12. 35832

Jay. Letters, being the Whole of the Correspondence between The Hon. John Jay, Esquire, and Mr. Lewis Littlepage. A Young Man whom Mr. Jay, when in Spain, Patronized and took into his Family. *New-York: Printed ... by Francis Childs ...* M.DCC.LXXXVI. 4to, pp. 76. BA. + With an Appendix. *New York.* 1786. 4to, pp. 102. C. + A New and Correct Edition, to which is added an Appendix, not before published. *New-York: Printed by Eleazer Oswald.* M.DCC.LXXXVI. 4to, pp. 54. N.

This elicited: "An Answer to a Pamphlet, containing the Correspondence of the Hon. John Jay, and Lewis Littlepage. *New-York.* [n. d.] 4to, pp. 29. + *Philadelphia.* [n. d.] P.

Jay. Lettre circulaire du Congrès des États-Unis de l'Amérique, adressée à leurs commettans, dans le tems où le discrédit de leur papier-monnoie leur faisoit craindre la chûte de leur révolution, qui jusqu'alors avoit triomphé de tous les efforts de l'Angleterre. Traduit de l'Anglois .... *Paris: Pougin, An* IIIe. [1795.] 8vo, pp. 23. 35834

[Jay.] The Objections to the Taxation of Our American Colonies, by the Legislature of Great Britain, Briefly Considered. *London: J. Wilkie.* 1765. 4to, pp. 20. + Second Edition. [*Ibid.*] 1765. pp. 23. 35835

"On exactly opposite principles to Mr. Otis, being an attempt to prove not only the right of the Legislature of Great Britain, to impose taxes on her colonies, but the expediency, and even the necessity of exercising that right in the present conjuncture." —*Monthly Review*, XXXII. 327. *See also* Rich's "Bibliotheca Americana," I. 149.

Jay (J.) America Free, or America Slave. An Address on the State of the Country. Delivered by John Jay, Esq., at Bedford, Westchester County, New York, October 8th, 1856. ... [*New York.* 1856.] 8vo, pp. 20. B., H. 35836

Jay. The American Church and the African Slave Trade. Mr. Jay's Speech in the New York Diocesan Convention of the Protestant Episcopal Church, September 27, 1860; with a Note of the Proceedings had in that Council on the Subject. *New York: Roe Lockwood & Sons.* 1860. 8vo, pp. 30. 35837

Jay. The American Rebellion: its History, its Aims, and the Reasons why it must be Suppressed. An Address, delivered at Mt. Kisco, New York, on the 4th of July, 1861, the 85th Anniversary of American Independence. By John Jay, Esq. *London: Trübner & Company.* ... 12mo, pp. 50. B., BA. 35838

[Jay.] Caste and Slavery in the American Church. By a Churchman. ... *New-York and London: Wiley and Putnam.* 1843. 8vo, pp. 51. B., N. 35839

Jay. The Church and the Rebellion. Mr. Jay's Letter to the Rector and Vestry of St. Matthew's Church, Bedford, with a Preface in Reply to the Rector's Speech from the Chancel, ... June 21, 1863, touching the recent visit of a clergyman of doubtful loyalty. *Bedford (Westchester Co., N. Y.)* 1863. 8vo, pp. 37.

Jay. Correspondence between John Jay and Henry B. Dawson, and between James A. Hamilton and Henry B. Dawson, concerning the Fœderalist. *New York: Printed by J. M. Bradstreet & Son.* 1864. 8vo, pp. (4), 48. B. 35841

Some copies printed on large paper in 4to. Also: Dawson's "Federalist." Letter from Mr. Jay. [*New York.* 1864.] 8vo, pp. 8. B.

Jay. Facts connected with the Presentment of Bishop Onderdonk: A Reply to Parts of the Bishop's Statement. By John Jay .... *New-York: Stanford and Swords.* 1845. 8vo, pp. 23.

This elicited the following: "Jay's Pamphlet reviewed, being a Brief Answer to ... Parts of the Bishop's Statement, by John Jay .... By a Looker On ...." *New-York: Henry M. Onderdonk.* 1845. 8vo, pp. 12. B.

Jay. The Great Conspiracy. An Address delivered at Mt. Kisco, ... 4th of July, 1861, the Eighty-fifth Anniversary of American Independence. By John Jay, Esq. *New-York: Roe Lockwood & Son* ... 1861. 8vo, pp. 50. B. + *New York: James G. Gregory.* 1861. 8vo, pp. 50. BA. + Second Edition. *New York: A. D. F. Randolph.* 1863. 8vo, pp. 50. 35843

Jay. New Plottings in Aid of the Rebel Doctrine of State Sovereignty. Mr. Jay's Second Letter on Dawson's Introduction to the Federalist. Exposing its Falsification of the History of the Constitution; ... *New York: American News Company.* 1864. 8vo, pp. 54, viii. B. 35844

Suppressed, and very scarce. First printed with the imprint, *New York: A. D. F. Randolph.* 1864.

Jay. New Plottings to Aid the Rebellion. *New York: James G. Gregory. London: Sampson Low* ... 1864. 8vo, pp. 50. H.

Also suppressed, and very scarce.

Jay. The Progress and Results of Emancipation in the English West Indies. A Lecture ... By John Jay .... *New-York: Wiley and Putnam.* 1842. 8vo, pp. 39. B., BA., N. 35846

[Jay.] A Review of a Pamphlet by the Hon. John C. Spencer, entitled Report to the Vestry of St. Peter's Church, Albany, of the Lay Delegates appointed by them who attended the Diocesan Convention held at New-York, September 23–30, 1845. *New-York.* 1846. 8vo, pp. 38. 35847

Jay. Thoughts on the Duty of the Episcopal Church, in relation to Slavery: ... Speech ... February 12, 1839. By John Jay. *New-York: Piercy & Reed, Printers.* 1839. 12mo, pp. 11.

[Jay.] Union League Club of New York. Address of the President June 23, 1866. [Colophon:] *Paris: Printed by E. Brière.* [1866.] 8vo, pp. 66. 35849

Also: The Constitutional Principles of the Abolitionists, and their Endorsement by the American People. A Letter to the American Anti-Slavery Society ... December, 1833. ... *New York.* 1864. 8vo, pp. 12.—The Great Issue. An Address delivered before the Union Campaign Club, of East Brooklyn, New York, ... Oct. 25, 1864. ... *New York: Baker & Godwin, Printers.* 1864. 8vo, pp. 32.—Mr. Jay's Argument in the Du Lux Case. Nov. 27th, 1857. [*New York.* 1857.] 8vo, pp. 88. H.—Judge Jay's Portrait at White Plains. Correspondence in reference to Its Original Acceptance by the County of Westchester, and the Recent Attempt to Remove it from the Court House. *New York: James G. Gregory.* 1863. 8vo, pp. 24.—Letter on the recent Relinquishment of the Monroe Doctrine, [New York, March 30, 1863.] ... [n. p. n. d.] 8vo, pp. 8. H.—A Letter to the Trustees of the Building Fund of the New York Historical Society. ... *New York.* 1851. 8vo, pp. 21. N.—The Narrowness of the Call for the Baltimore Convention. A Letter to the Hon. Edwin D. Morgan, Chairman of the Republican Committee, appointed at Chicago in 1860, on the Call for Presidential Convention at Baltimore, on the 7th June, 1864. ... *New York: Baker & Godwin.* 1864. 8vo, pp. 13.—"The New York Election and the State of the Country." ... Address to the Citizens of Westchester County, on the Approaching State Election. ... Morrisania, N. Y., Oct. 30, 1862. *New York: John F. Trow, Printer.* 1862. 8vo, pp. 24.—Our Duty to the Freedmen. Remarks at the Inaugural Meeting of the American Freedmen's Aid Union, at the Cooper Institute, ... May 9, 1865. ... [n. p. n. d.] 8vo, pp. 7.—Our Triumph and our Duties. Mr. Jay's Remarks at the Celebration Dinner of the East Brooklyn Union Campaign Club. ... December 22, 1864. [n. p. 1864.] 8vo, pp. 6.—The Presidential Election—What it Means for America and Europe. An Address before the Grant and Colfax Club of Katonah, New York, October 21, 1868. ... *New York.* 1869. 8vo, pp. 68.—The Proxy Bill and the Tract Society. ... *New York.* 1859. 8vo, pp. 31.—Remarks on the Clarendon-Johnson Treaty for adjusting the Alabama Claims. ... *New York: Charles Scribner & Co.* 1869. 12mo, pp. 16.—Report [to the Governor of New York] on Antietam Cemetery. With a Communication in Reply to a Letter written Gov. Fenton by Hon. John Covode. ... [*Albany.*] 1868. 8vo, pp. 48.—The Rise and Fall of the Pro-Slavery Democracy, and the Rise and Duties of the Republican Party. Address to the Citizens of Westchester County, New York. Delivered at Bedford, November 5, 1860. ... *New York: Roe Lockwood & Co.* 1861. 8vo, pp. 45.—Rome in America. An Address before the Bible Society at Mount Kisco, New York, September 21, 1868. ... *New York.* 1869. 8vo, pp. 26.—[Speech] at the American Thanksgiving Dinner at Vienna on ... 18th Nov., 1869 ... in presenting the First Toast ... [*Vienna: F. B. Geitler.* 1869.] 8vo, pp. 9.—A Statistical View of American Agriculture, Its Home Resources and Foreign Markets, with Suggestions for the Schedules of the Federal Census in 1860. An Address delivered at New York, before the American Geographical and Statistical Society ... . *New York: D. Appleton & Company.* M.DCCC.LIX. 12mo,

pp. 81.—Union League Club of New-York. Its Memories of the Past. The President's Address ... March 26, 1868. [*New York:*] *Club-House* ... 1868. 8vo, pp. 24.

Jay (J. C.) A Catalogue of Recent Shells, with Descriptions of New or Rare Species in the Collection of John C. Jay. *New York.* 1835. 8vo. S. + Second Edition. [*Ibid.*] 1836. 8vo, pp. 80, (8). 4 colored Plates. C. 35850

Jay. A Catalogue of the Shells, arranged according to the Lamarckian System; together with Descriptions of New or Rare Species, contained in the Collection of John C. Jay. Third Edition. *New-York: Wiley and Putnam.* 1839. 4to, pp. 126. 10 colored Plates. A., C., N. 35851

Jay. A Catalogue of the Shells, arranged according to the Lamarckian System. With their Authorities, Synonyms, References to Works where figured and described, together with a Supplement contained in the Collection of John C. Jay. Fourth Edition. *New York.* 1852. 4to. 35852

Jay (P. A.) An Oration delivered before the Washington Benevolent Society, in the City of New-York, on the Twenty-Second of February, 1810. By Peter Augustus Jay, Esq. ... *New-York: Printed by C. S. Van Winkle.* 1810. 8vo, pp. 23.

Jay. A Report of a Committee of the Humane Society, appointed to inquire into the number of Tavern Licenses. ... *New York.* 1810. 8vo, pp. 15. N. 35854

Also: An Appeal to the Christians in America, in behalf of the American Bible Society. ... *New York.* 1816. 8vo, pp. 54.

Jay (W.) An Address delivered before the American Peace Society, ... May 26, 1845. By William Jay. ... *Boston: American Peace Society.* 1845. 8vo, pp. 31. B., M. 35855

[Jay.] The Creole Case, and Mr. Webster's Dispatch; with the Comments of the New York American. *New York.* 1842. 8vo, pp. 39. 35856

Jay. An Inquiry into the Character and Tendency of the American Colonization and American Anti-Slavery Societies. By William Jay. *New-York: Leavitt, Lord & Co.* 1835. 12mo, pp. (2), 202. B. + Second Edition. [*Ibid.*] 1835. 12mo, pp. 206. BA. + Third Edition. [*Ibid.*] + Sixth Edition. *New York: American Anti-Slavery Society.* 1838. 12mo, pp. 206. + Tenth Edition. [*Ibid.*] 1840. 12mo, pp. 206. B. 35857

For a reply *see* Reese.

[Jay.] A Letter to ... Bishop Hobart, occasioned by the Strictures on Bible Societies, contained in His Late Charge to the Convention of New-York. By a Churchman .... *New-York: John P. Haven.* 1823. 8vo, pp. 80. B., BA. 35858

Also: A Letter to the Right Rev. Bishop Hobart, in reply to the Pamphlet Addressed by him to the Author, under the signature of Corrector. ... *New York: John P. Haven.* 1823. 8vo, pp. 33. B., BA.

Jay. A Letter to the Right Rev. L. Silliman Ives, Bishop of ... North Carolina; Occasioned by his late Address to the Convention of his Diocese. By William Jay. *Washington, D. C.: Buell & Blanchard, Printers.* [1846.] 8vo, pp. 15. + *New York: William Harned.* 1848. 12mo, pp. 32. + Third Edition. [*Ibid.*] 1848. 8vo, pp. (4), 32. B., H., S. 35859

Jay. Letter respecting the American Board of Commission for Foreign Missions, and the American Tract Society. By William Jay. ... *New York: Lewis J. Bates.* 1853. 8vo, pp. 16.

Relates to slavery.

[Jay.] Letter to ... Samuel A. Eliot. *See* Hancock, 30195.

Jay. The Life of John Jay: with Selections from his Correspondence and Miscellaneous Papers. By his Son William Jay. ... *New-York: ... J. & J. Harper.* 1833. 2 vols., 8vo, pp. viii, 520; (4), 502. Portrait. B., BA. 35861

See "N. A. Rev.," XXXVII. 340.

Jay. Miscellaneous Writings on Slavery. By William Jay. *Boston: John P. Jewett & Company.* 1853. 12mo, pp. 670. Portrait. B., C., S. 35862

Jay. Remarks on ... Jay's Letter. *See* [Hobart (J. H.)]

Jay. Reply to Remarks of Rev. Moses Stuart, ... on Hon. John Jay, and an Examination of ... "Conscience and the Constitution." By William Jay. *New-York: Printed by John A. Gray.* 1850. 8vo, pp. 22. B., BA. 35863

Jay. A Review of The Causes and Consequences of The Mexican War. By William Jay. *Boston: Benjamin B. Mussey & Co.* 1849. 12mo, pp. 333. BA. + Fourteenth Thousand. [*Ibid.*] + Second Edition. [*Ibid.*] + Third Edition. [*Ibid.*] B. + Fourth Edition. [*Ibid.*] 1849. 12mo, pp. 333. B. 35864

Jay. Slavery in America; or, an Inquiry into the Character and Tendency of the American Colonization, and the American

Anti-Slavery Societies. With an Introduction by S. H. Cox. *London: F. Westley & A. H. Davis.* 1835. 12mo, pp. xxiv, 198.

Jay. A View of the Action of the Federal Government, in Behalf of Slavery. By William Jay. ... *New York: J. S. Taylor.* 1839. 12mo, pp. viii, 13–217. BA. + Second Edition. *New York: American Anti-Slavery Society.* 1839. 12mo, pp. 240. B. + *Utica: James C. Jackson.* 1844. 12mo, pp. 112. H. 35866

Jay. War and Peace: the Evils of the First, and a Plan for Preserving the Last. By William Jay. ... *New York: Wiley and Putnam.* 1842. 12mo, pp. 101. BA. + *London: Thomas Ward and Co.* 1842. 8vo, pp. 48. B., H. 35867

Also: Address to the Inhabitants of Westchester County. ... *New York.* 1834. 8vo.—The Character and Tendency of Colonization, and Anti-Slavery. ... *New York.* 1835. 12mo.—An Examination of the Mosaic Laws of Servitude. ... *New-York: M. W. Dodd.* 1854. 8vo, pp. 56.—The Kossuth Excitement ... . *Boston: American Peace Society.* 1852. 8vo, pp. 8. B., H.—Letter ... to Hon. Theodore Frelinghuysen, on Slavery. *New York.* 1844. 8vo, pp. 8.—Letter to Hon. William Nelson, M.C., on Mr. Webster's Speech, ... [of March, 1850]. *New-York: William Harned.* 1850 12mo, pp. 12.—Letter to Hon. William Nelson, M.C., on Mr. Clay's Compromise. .. *New York: William Harned.* 1850. 12mo, pp. 22.—Letter on the Reasons assigned by the American Tract Society, for its Silence in regard to American Slavery. ... [n. p.] 1853. 12mo, pp. 90. + Second Editon. [*Ibid.*]—A Letter to the Rev. William Berrian, D.D., on the Resources, Present Position, and Duties of Trinity Church ... . *New-York: Anson D. F. Randolph.* 1856. 8vo, pp. 20.—A Letter to the Committee chosen by the American Tract Society, to inquire into the Proceedings of its Executive Committee, in relation to Slavery. ... [n. p. 1857.] 8vo, pp. 38. B.—A Reply to a Second Letter to the Author; from the Right Rev. Bishop Hobart, with Remarks on his Hostility to Bible Societies, ... and ... his Vindication of the Reverend Mr. Norris's Late Pamphlet. ... *New-York: John P. Haven.* 1823. 8vo, pp. 32.—A Reply to Webster, in a Letter from Hon. William Jay to Hon. Wm. Nelson, M.C. *Boston: Wm. Crosby and H. P. Nichols.* 1850. 8vo, pp. 12. BA.

Jay (William), *and others.* Address to the Inhabitants of New Mexico and California, on ... the Social and Political Evils of Slavery. *New-York.* 1849. 12mo, pp. 56. BA., S. 35868

Jay (W.) Remarks on the Character and Narrative of the Rev. John Clark. By Rev. William Jay. Interspersed with Brief Sketches from the Narrative, by Way of Illustration, by Another Hand. *Boston: Cummings and Hilliard.* 1821. 8vo, pp. viii, 91. BA. 35869

Jayme (M.) Sermon patriotico en la funcion publica, con el ayuntamiento constitucional de la noble ciudad de Tepic. *Guadalajara.* 1821. 4to, pp. (22). 35870

Jayne (Ebenezer). Letter to Ephraim Green. *Byram.* 1811.

Jayne (P.) The Substance of a Sermon preached at Lynn ... on the First Day of December, 1803; being the day of Publick Thanksgiving .... By P. Jayne .... *Salem: Printed by William Carlton.* 1804. 8vo, pp. 13. BA., W. 35872

Jeaffreson (John Cordy). The Life of Robert Stephenson ... By J. C. Jeaffreson .... With descriptive chapters on ... his ... important professional works, by William Pole .... *London: Longman, Green* ... 1864. 2 vols., 8vo, pp. xv, (1), 363; ix, (2), 335. 2 Portraits, 5 Plates. B., BA. 35873

Includes notices of his travels and operations in America.

Jeanne (G.) Histoire des États-Unis. Par Grégoire Jeanne. *Paris: F. Chamerot.* 1856–59. 4 vols., 12mo, pp. 176, (4); 231; 247; 218. H. 35874

Jeannette: A Poem, with Three Portraits. By Æsculapius non Vinetus. *New York.* 1857. 8vo, pp. 92, (2). 35875

Jedema, *pseudon.* Briev van Broeder Jedema aan zyn vriend Will. Penn Sec., waarby gevoegd zyn de twee memorien ... door den Ridder Yorke ... gepresenteert, op rym gebragt en in keurig muzyc gezet door Hans Ours. *Gedruckt in Groenland by de Witte Beer.* [1780.] 8vo, pp. 16. 2 Plates of Music. 35876

Letter of Brother Jedema to his friend William Penn, Secretary, to which are added the two memorials of the Chevallier Yorke, rendered in verse and set to music by Hans Ours.

Jefferds (C. M.) Trial of Charles M. Jefferds for Murder, at New York, December, 1861. Charles E. Wilbour, Reporter. *New York: Ross & Tousey.* 1862. 8vo, pp. 233. 35877

Jefferds (Chester Daniel). A Sermon ... at the Funeral of Rev. Nathan S. Haseltine ... January 24, 1860. By Rev. C. D. Jefferds .... *Windsor.* 1860. 8vo, pp. 16. H. 35878

Jefferson (T.) The Address of Thomas Jefferson, to the Senate, ... on the 4th ... of March, 1801 .... *Baltimore: Printed by W. Pechin.* 1801. 8vo, pp. 8. B. 35879

Jefferson. An | Appendix | to the | Notes on Virginia | Relative to the Murder of Logan's Family. | By Thomas Jefferson. | *Philadelphia:* | *Printed by Samuel H. Smith.* | M.D.CCC. 8vo, pp. 51.

Very rare. In this pamphlet Jefferson presents in a very logical form the evidence on which he charged Cresap and his party with the murder of Logan's family and other peaceable Indians.

Jefferson. Authentic Copies of the Correspondence of Thomas Jefferson, Esq. Secretary of State to the United States of America, and George Hammond, Esq. Minister Plenipotentiary of Great-Britain, on the Non-Execution of Existing Treaties, the delivering the Frontier Posts, and on the Propriety of a Commercial Intercourse between Great-Britain and the United States. *Philadelphia, Printed; London: Reprinted J. Debrett.* 1794. 2 parts, 8vo, pp. (2), 89; (2), 11, 59. M. 35881

"These papers comprehend everything necessary to afford complete information with respect to the grounds of the disputes which arose between Great Britain and the United States."—*Monthly Review*, XIV. 459.

[Jefferson.] Book I. Autobiography, with Appendix. [*Washington.* 1853.] 8vo, pp. (2), 178. Portrait and Facsimiles.

Jefferson. Correspondence between ... Thomas Jefferson, President of the United States, and James Monroe, Esq. ... *Boston: Printed by B. Parks.* 1808. 4to, pp. 8. BA. 35883

Jefferson. Correspondence of Thomas Jefferson, with his Address in the Senate Chamber, 1801, on taking the Oath of Office as President. *Baltimore.* 1801. 8vo. 35884

Jefferson. A Dialogue [etc.] *See* Vol. v., No. 19933.

Jefferson. Inaugural Address of Thomas Jefferson, third President of the United States, Delivered March 4th, 1801. *Philadelphia: B. Franklin Jackson.* 1861. 8vo, pp. 8. 35885

This was reprinted at New York, and was also issued in French, Italian, and German.

Jefferson. The Inaugural Speeches and Messages of Thomas Jefferson, Esq. Late President of the United States. Together with the Inaugural Speech of James Madison, Esq. his Successor in Office. *Boston: Printed by S. G. Snelling.* 1809. 16mo, pp. 126.

Jefferson. A Manual of Parliamentary Practice, for the use of the Senate of the United States. By Thomas Jefferson. *Washington City.* MDCCC. 12mo. + *Washington City: Printed by Samuel Harrison Smith.* MDCCCI. 12mo, pp. 188, (4). + Another Edition. pp. (199). H. + Second Edition, with the last Additions of the Author. *Georgetown.* 1812. 24mo, pp. 188. + *Washington.* 1812. 12mo. C. + Third Edition. *Lancaster, Pennsylvania: Printed by William Dickson.* 1813. 12mo, pp. 166, 29–46. B., P. + To which is added, The Rules and Orders of the Senate and House of Representatives ... and Joint Rules of the Two Houses. *Washington City: Printed by Davis & Force.*

1820. 16mo, pp. 220. H. + To which are added, The Rules and Orders of both Houses of Congress. *Concord: George Hough & Jacob B. Moore.* 1823. 16mo, pp. 188. B., BA., C. + *Washington.* 1828. 12mo. C. + *Philadelphia: Hogan & Thompson.* 1834. 18mo, pp. 191. + [*Ibid.*] 1837. + [*Ibid.*] 1840. 18mo, pp. 204. + With all the Amendments ... . *Columbus, Ohio: ... Jonathan Phillips.* 1842. 18mo, pp. 222, (1). + *Philadelphia: Hogan and Thompson.* 1850. 16mo, pp. vi, iv, (2), 13–196. H. + *New-York: Clark, Austin & Smith.* 1858. 35887

JEFFERSON. Manuel du droit parlementaire, ou précis des règles suivies dans le Parlement d'Angleterre et dans le Congrès des États-Unis, pour l'introduction, la discussion et la décision des affaires; traduit de l'anglais par L. A. Pichon. *Paris: Nicolle.* 1814. 8vo, pp. 233. S. 35888

JEFFERSON. Manual del derecho parlamentario. *Paris.* 1837. 12mo. 35889

JEFFERSON. Mélanges Politiques et Philosophiques Extraits des Mémoires et de la Correspondance de Thomas Jefferson, précédés d'un Essai sur les Principes de l'École Américaine et d'une Traduction de la Constitution des États-Unis, avec un Commentaire tiré, pour la plus grande partie, de l'ouvrage publié, sur cette Constitution, par William Rawle, LL.D. Par L. P. Conseil. *Paris: Paulin.* MDCCCXXXIII. 2 vols., 8vo, pp. (4), 468; (4), 475, (2). B. 35890

See "N. A. Rev.," XXXIX. 467; XL. 170, *also* "Ed. Rev.," II.

JEFFERSON. Memoir, Correspondence, and Miscellanies, from the Papers of Thomas Jefferson. Edited by Thomas Jefferson Randolph. *Charlottesville: F. Carr, and Co.* 1829. 4 vols., 8vo, pp. viii, (2), 466; (4), 500; (4), 519; (4), 532. Portrait, and 4 Facsimiles. B. + Second Edition. *Boston: Gray and Bowen.* 1830. 4 vols., 8vo, pp. viii, 464; (4), 500; (4), 519; (2), 532. Portrait. B., BA., H. 35891

"These volumes begin with a short fragment concerning (Jefferson) himself, drawn up at the age of seventy-seven: and close with a still shorter journal kept by him while Secretary of State during Washington's administration. The rest consists exclusively of a voluminous correspondence, ranging from 1775, after blood had been spilt at Boston, to June, 1826, ten days only before his death, so appropriately fixed for the fiftieth anniversary of American Independence."—*Edinburgh Review.* The contents of these volumes are not embraced in the congressional publications. Reprinted in England as:

JEFFERSON. Memoirs, Correspondence, and Private Papers of Thomas Jefferson, late President of the United States. ...

Edited by Thomas Jefferson Randolph. *London: Henry Colburn and Richard Bentley.* 1829. 4 vols., 8vo, pp. x, 464; 496; 521; 552. C., P. 35892

The type and paper of the English edition are very superior to the American editions.

JEFFERSON Discorsi (Messaggio) del Sig. Tommaso Jefferson Presidente. Fatti tradurri dall' Sig. Giacomo Leandro Cathcart. *Livorno.* 1804. 16mo. C. 35893

For other Messages by Jefferson *see* Messages, Vol. XI.

[JEFFERSON.] Notes on the State of Virginia; written in the Year 1781, somewhat corrected and enlarged in the winter of 1782, for the use of a Foreigner of distinction, in answer to certain queries proposed by him respecting 1. Its Boundaries. 2. Rivers. 3. Sea ports. 4. Mountains, &c. [*Paris.*] MDCCLXXXII. 8vo, pp. (2), 391. 35894

Two hundred copies printed, some of which have a "Draught of a Fundamental Constitution ... of Virginia." pp. 14. "This edition of Mr. Jefferson's celebrated 'Notes' was evidently printed in Paris; but as Mr. Jefferson did not reach France until the year 1784, the date on the title probably is not that of the year in which it was printed, but of the year in which the manuscript was completed. A copy presented to M. Malesherbe had the following note, in Mr. Jefferson's handwriting: 'Mr. Jefferson having had a few copies of these notes printed to present to some of his friends, and to some estimable characters beyond that line, takes the liberty of presenting a copy to M. de Malesherbe, as a testimony of his respect to his character. Unwilling to expose them to the public eye, he begs the favour of M. de M. to put them into the hands of no person on whose care and fidelity he cannot rely, to guard them against publication.'" RICH, I. 301. The proof-sheets of this work, with corrections in the handwriting of the author, are in the New York State Library at Albany.

J[EFFERSON]. Observations sur la Virginie, Par M. J***. Traduites de l'Anglois. *A Paris: Chez Barrois.* 1786. 8vo, pp. (4), viii, 290 [should read 390], (1). Map and Table. H.

This French translation was made by the Abbé Morellet. According to Tucker's "Life of Jefferson," Vol. I. pp. 155, 173, it was a bookseller's translation, and is a tissue of blunders, although in part revised by the author. The fine map engraved by Neele first appeared in this edition.

JEFFERSON. Notes on the State of Virginia. Written by Thomas Jefferson. Illustrated with A Map, including the States of Virginia, Maryland, Delaware, and Pennsylvania. *London: John Stockdale.* M.DCC.LXXXVII. 8vo, pp. (4), 382. Map. BA.

Rich, Vol. I., p. 340, speaks of this edition as a "reprint from an American edition, printed in the same year," which is an error; it is a reproduction of the edition described No. 35894, *supra*, put forth with Mr. Jefferson's approval, and contains the map which first appeared in the French translation, No. 35895, *supra*. *See* Sparks' "Franklin," X. 315, *and* "M. Rev.," LXXVIII. 377, 450.

JEFFERSON. Notes on the State of Virginia. Written by Thomas Jefferson. *Philadelphia: Printed ... by Prichard and Hall,* ... M.DCC.LXXXVIII. 8vo, pp. (ii), 204. Folded Sheet.

This is the first American edition. Mr. Charles Thomson, Secretary to Congress, furnished the Appendix. *See* Tucker's "Jefferson," Vol. I. Dr. O'Callaghan ("Hist. Mag.," Vol. I., p. 52), describes a "Second American Edition:" *Philadelphia.* 1788. pp. ii, 336; and another "Second American Edition:" *Philadelphia.* 1792. pp. ii, 336; neither of which have I seen.

JEFFERSON. Notes on the State of Virginia. By Thomas Jefferson. Second American Edition. *Philadelphia: Mathew Carey.* 1794. 8vo, pp. (4), 336. Map and Table. H. 35898

JEFFERSON'S Notes, on the State of Virginia; with the Appendixes complete. *Baltimore: Printed by W. Pechin.* 1800. 8vo, pp. 194, Appendix, 52. B. 35899

JEFFERSON'S Notes on the State of Virginia; with the Appendixes complete. To which is subjoined a Sublime and Argumentative Dissertation on Mr. Jefferson's Religious Principles. *Baltimore: W. Pechin.* 1800. 8vo, pp. 194, Appendix, 53, A Vindication, 21. Table. 35900

JEFFERSON. Notes on the State of Virginia. With an Appendix. By Thomas Jefferson. Third American Edition. *New York: M. T. & W. A. Davis.* 1801. 8vo, pp. 392. Map and Portrait. 35901

JEFFERSON. Notes on the State of Virginia. ... *Newark: Printed by Pennington & Gould.* 1801. 8vo, pp. 392. Map and Portrait. 35902

Precisely the same as the preceding.

JEFFERSON. Notes on the State of Virginia. By Thomas Jefferson. First Hot-Pressed Edition. *Philadelphia: R. T. Rawle, June,* 1801. 8vo, pp. (4), 436, Appendix, 56. Map, Portrait of Jefferson, and View of the Natural Bridge. C., H.

"This appears to be the best edition of this work, having the appendix relating to the murder of Logan's family, printed separately in 1800, and other pieces not in the preceding editions."—RICH, II. 1.

JEFFERSON. Notes on the State of Virginia. With an Appendix. By Thomas Jefferson. Eighth American Edition. *Boston: Thomas & Andrews* ... 1801. 8vo, pp. 364. Map, Plan, and Portrait. B. + Ninth American Edition. *Boston: Printed by H. Sprague.* 1802. 18mo, pp. 368. Map, Portrait, and Table.

JEFFERSON. Notes on the State of Virginia. With an Appendix relative to the Murder of Logan's Family. By Thomas Jefferson. *Trenton: Printed by Wilson & Blackwell, July* 12, 1803. 12mo, pp. 363. C. 35905

The first edition in which the appendix relating to the murder of Logan's family, by Captain Cresap, was announced on the title-page.

JEFFERSON. Notes on ... Virginia. ... By Thomas Jefferson *New York.* 1804. 8vo, pp. 392. 35906

"Best edition," so says Dr. O'Callaghan in the "Hist. Mag.," Vol. I., p. 52. I have not seen it.

JEFFERSON. Notes on the State of Virginia. With an Appendix ... . By Thomas Jefferson. *Philadelphia.* 1812. 12mo. Portrait. + *Trenton.* 1812. 12mo. Portrait. + *Philadelphia: Hogan and Thompson.* 1815. 12mo. + *Philadelphia: H. C. Carey & I. Lea.* 1825. 12mo, pp. 344. + *Boston: Wells and Lilly.* 1829. 12mo, pp. (4), 280. B., BA. + *Boston: Lilly and Wait.* 1832. 12mo, pp. (4), 280. C. 35907

JEFFERSON. Notes on the State of Virginia. By Thomas Jefferson: Illustrated with a Map, including the States of Virginia, Maryland, Delaware and Pennsylvania. A New Edition, prepared by the Author, containing Notes and Plates never before published. *Richmond: J. W. Randolph.* 1853. 8vo, pp. iv, (4), 275. Map, 2 Plates, and Folded Sheet. 35908

Printed from President Jefferson's own copy of Stockdale's edition, containing many additions and corrections, and a map and plates. Also: Letters from Gen. Dearborn and Judge Gibson relating to the Murder of Logan; a Topographical Analysis of Virginia for 1790; and Translations of all Jefferson's Notes in Foreign Languages by Prof. Schele de Vere. This completes our list of the various editions of this remarkable work. It elicited: "Observations upon certain passages in Mr. Jefferson's Notes on Virginia, which appear to have a tendency to Subvert Religion, and establish A False Philosophy." *New-York.* 1804. 8vo, pp. 32. BA. Jacob's Cresap, etc.

JEFFERSON. Beschreibung von Virginien. ... *Leipzig.* 1789.

JEFFERSON. Notes on the Establishment of a Money Unit. By Thomas Jefferson. *Annapolis.* 1784. 8vo. 35910

[JEFFERSON.] Papers relative to Great Britain. [Beginning with a letter of November 29th, 1791, and ending with ... September 25th, 1793. n. p. 1793.] 8vo, pp. 159, (1), B. 35911

A collection of papers prepared by Jefferson as Secretary of State, containing his correspondence with George Hammond, British Minister Plenipotentiary, etc.

JEFFERSON. The Proceedings of the Government of the United States, in maintaining the Public Right to the Beach of

the Missisipi [*sic*], Adjacent to New-Orleans, against the Intrusion of Edward Livingston. Prepared for the Use of Counsel, by Thomas Jefferson. *New-York: Ezra Sargeant.* 1812. 8vo, pp. 80. Map. B., BA., S. + Republished with Corrections and Additional Notes by the Author. [n. p. n. d.] 8vo, pp. 299. 3 Plans. 35912

[JEFFERSON.] Proposals of Oliver Fairplay for publishing the Private and Public Life of the First Consul. *Philadelphia.* 1804. 8vo. Folded. C. 35913

JEFFERSON. Republican Notes on Religion; And An Act Establishing Religious Freedom, passed in the Assembly of Virginia, in the Year 1786. By Thomas Jefferson, Esquire, President of the United States. *Danbury: Printed by Thomas Row.* 1803. 8vo, pp. 11. 35914

JEFFERSON'S Selbstbiographie. Aus dem Englischen von W. Kapp. *Philadelphia.* 1853. 8vo. Portrait. 35915

JEFFERSON. Speech of Thomas Jefferson, President of the United States, delivered at his Instalment, March 4, 1801. *Philadelphia.* 1801. 12mo. C. 35916

Also issued as a broadside, and translated into French, Italian, and Dutch. 8vo, pp. 16.

JEFFERSON. Speech of Thomas Jefferson, the newly elected President, to the Senate of the United States. With a few Remarks by an Englishman. *London.* 1801. 8vo. C. 35917

[JEFFERSON.] A Summary View of the Rights of British America. Set forth in some Resolutions intended for the Inspection of the present Delegates of the People of Virginia, Now in Convention. By a Native, and Member of the House of Burgesses. *Williamsburg: Printed by Clementina Rind.* [1774.] 12mo, pp. 23. C., N., P. + *Williamsburg, Printed; Philadelphia: Re-Printed by John Dunlap.* M,DCC,LXXIV. 8vo, pp. 23. W. + The Second Edition. *Williamsburg, Printed by Clementina Rind. London: Re-printed for G. Kearsly.* 1774. 8vo, pp. xvi, 44. H.

The title of the first edition is printed in Roman capitals. "This summary was intended to convey to the late convention of the delegates of Virginia the sentiments of one of their members who was prevented from attending." The Dedication to the King is signed "Tribunus." *See* Tucker's "Jefferson," I. 58, *also* "M. Rev.," LI. 393. The Library of Congress has a copy with manuscript notes by the author.

JEFFERSON. The Writings of Thomas Jefferson: Being his Autobiography, Correspondence, Reports, Messages, Addresses,

and other Writings, Official and Private. Published by the Order of the Joint Committee of Congress on the Library, from the Original Manuscripts, deposited in the Department of State. With Explanatory Notes, Tables of Contents, and a Copious Index to each Volume, as well as a General Index to the Whole, By the Editor H. A. Washington. *Taylor & Maury, Washington, D. C.* 1853–54. 9 vols., 8vo, pp. viii, (2), 615, Portrait; vi, (2), 598; vi, 599; vii, 597; ix, 612; vi, 611; viii, 658; vii, 607; vii, 589. BA., H. + *Philadelphia: J. B. Lippincott & Co.* 1864.

The following are some of the works which relate to Jefferson:

Address to the People of the United States; with an Epitome and Vindication of the Public Life and Character of Thomas Jefferson. By Americanus. *Philadelphia: Printed by James Carey.* 1800. 8vo, pp. 32. + Second Edition. *Worcester, Massachusetts: Printed by Sewall Goodridge.* MDCCCII. 8vo, pp. 32.

An Appendix to Aristides's Vindication of the Vice-President of the United States, by a Gentleman of North Carolina, proving that General Hamilton at the last Presidential Election exerted all his Influence to support Mr. Jefferson in opposition to Mr. Burr. *Virginia Printed, and for sale by the Booksellers in this State.* 1804. 8vo, pp. 20. 35921

Celebration of Jefferson's Birth Day in Washington, April 13, 1859. *Washington.* 1859. 8vo, pp. 14. 35922

The Claims of Thomas Jefferson to the Presidency Examined at the Bar of Christianity. By a Layman. *Philadelphia.* 1800. 8vo, pp. 54. 35923

Attributed to William Brown, *see* Vol. II., No. 8573, also to Asbury Dickins.

Comparison of the Principles of the Washington and Jefferson Administrations. *Boston.* 1810. 8vo. 35924

Concise Account of the Life of Thomas Jefferson, with his Inaugural Speech. *Philadelphia.* 1801. 12mo. + [*Ibid.*] 1804.

Cursory Reflections on the Consequences which may ensue, should Mr. Jefferson & Mr. Burr have Equal Votes both from the Electors and States. *New-York: Printed by Furman and Loudon.* 1801. 12mo, pp. 25. H. 35926

Defence of the Character of Thomas Jefferson, against a Writer in the New York Review ... . By a Virginian. *New-York: Printed by W. Osborn.* 1838. 8vo, pp. 46. S. 35927

Imaginary Conversation between Presidents Jefferson and Jackson [on Nullification. n. p. n. d.] 8vo. 35928

Impartial Address of the Federal Committee of Albany; or the Thirty-five Anti-Federal Objections refuted. *Albany.* 1787. 16mo. 35929

Relates to Jefferson.

Jefferson against Madison's War, being an Exhibition of President Jefferson's Opinions on the Impolicy, and Folly of All Wars ... together with some Remarks on the Present War, and the Propriety of Choosing Electors who will vote for a Peace President. By a True Republican. [n. p. 1812.] 8vo, pp. 20.

This is an address to the republicans of Massachusetts in favor of De Witt Clinton.

... The Life of Thomas Jefferson. With a Portrait, and a Parallel, (Washington and Jefferson Compared,) ... *Philadelphia: J. G. Russell.* 1844. 12mo, pp. 189–389, (1). H. 35931

Serious Facts, opposed to Serious Confederations: or, the Voice of Warning to Religious Republicans. *New York.* 1800. 8vo, pp. 16. 35932

A Solemn Address. *See* [Wortman (Tunis)].

Strictures upon the Letter Imputed to Mr. Jefferson, Addressed to Mr. Mazzei. *Printed, June,* 1800. 12mo, pp. 12. 35933

Signed "Greene."

Test of the Religious Principles of Thomas Jefferson, extracted from his Writings. *Easton.* 1800. 8vo. C. + *Philadelphia: J Bioren.* 1800. 8vo, pp. ii, 10. 35934

Vindication of the Public Life and Character of Thomas Jefferson. *Richmond, Va.* 1800. 8vo. W. + *Philadelphia.* 1800.

A Vindication of the Religion of Mr. Jefferson, and a Statement of his Services in the Cause of Religious Liberty. By a Friend to Real Religion. *Baltimore: W. Pechin.* [n. d.] 8vo, pp. 21. 35936

See also our Vol. I., No. 4037; Vol. III., No. 11004; Vol. IV., Nos. 13724, 14312; Vol. V., Nos. 17426, 18070; Vol. VI., Nos. 23186, 23365; Vol. VIII., No. 29986, *and* Johnson, Junius, Nichols, Sidney (A), Smith (W. L.), and Veritas.

JEFFERSON, *and* CABELL (J. C.) Early History of the University of Virginia, as contained in the Letters of Thomas Jefferson and Joseph C. Cabell. Hitherto Unpublished; with an Appendix, consisting of Mr. Jefferson's Bill for a Complete System of Education, and other Illustrative Documents; and an

Introduction, comprising A Brief Historical Sketch of the University, and a Biographical Notice of Joseph C. Cabell. *Richmond: J. W. Randolph.* 1856. 8vo, pp. xxxvi, 528. B., BA.

JEFFERSON, *pseudon.* Examination of the Charleston Memorial.—No. 1. ... [On the Tariff. n. p. n. d.] 8vo, pp. 22. B.

JEFFERSON COLLEGE, *Canonsburgh, Pa.* Catalogue of the Members, and Library, of the Philo Literary Society of Jefferson College, Canonsburgh, Pa.—from its Formation, August 23, 1797, to July 4, 1840. *Pittsburgh: Printed by A. Jaynes.* 1840. 8vo, pp. 32. H. 35939

Catalogue of the Officers and Students of Jefferson College, Canonsburg. July, 1833. *Pittsburgh: Printed by D. and M. Maclean.* [n. d.] 8vo, pp. (23). Continued. BA. 35940

Also: Catalogue of Members of the Philo Literary Society of Jefferson College, Canonsburgh, Pa. ... . *Pittsburgh: Printed by A. Jaynes.* 1844. 8vo, pp. 34. H.—General Catalogue of Jefferson College ... from the time it was chartered in 1802, to 1856. ... *Pittsburgh: I. T. Shryock ... Printer.* 1857. 8vo, pp. 58. H.—Catalogue of Jefferson College, Canonsburg, Pa. [n. p.] 1850.—Triennial Catalogue of the Franklin Literary Society of Jefferson College, containing the Names of Members from 1797 to 1856. *Pittsburgh.* [n. d.] *See also* Washington College.

JEFFERSON COLLEGE, *Washington, Miss.* The Charter and Statutes of Jefferson College, with a Historical Sketch of the Institution ... . [With] a Catalogue of its Library, Apparatus, &c. ... *Natchez: The Book and Job Office.* 1840. 8vo, pp. 90.

JEFFERSON COUNTY, *Mo.* A Description of its Productions, Resources, &c. *Hillsboro.* 1867. 8vo. 35942

JEFFERSON COUNTY, *N. Y.* Gazetteer and Directory of Jefferson County, N. Y., for 1866–7. Compiled by Hamilton Child. *Watertown, N. Y.: L. Ingalls & Co., Printers.* 1867. 8vo. + For 1868–9. *Watertown: G. Moss & Co.* 1869. 8vo, pp. 356. Continued. 35943

Journal of the Proceedings of the Board of Supervisors of the County of Jefferson, for 1859. *Watertown.* 1859. 8vo. Continued. 35944

Proceedings of the First Cattle Show and Fair, of the Agricultural Society of Jefferson County, September, 1818. *Watertown: For the Society.* [1818.] 8vo, pp. 24. Continued. BA.

Also: Proceedings of the Jefferson County [N. Y.] Agricultural Society, for the Year 1858. [*Watertown.*] 1858. 8vo, pp. 16, 4.—Transactions of Jefferson County Agricultural Society ... for 1867. *Watertown, N. Y.* 1867. 8vo, pp. (2), 83. Continued. H.

JEFFERSON MEDICAL COLLEGE. Catalogue of the Graduates of the Jefferson Medical College of Philadelphia, from ... 1826 to ... 1856 inclusive. With the ... Session of 1856–57. *Philadelphia: T. K. and P. G. Collins, Printers.* 1856. 8vo, pp. 32.

Also: Catalogue of the Trustees, Faculty, and Students of Jefferson Medical College ... for ... 1841–2. *Philadelphia: Printed by Merrihew and Thompson.* 1842. 8vo, pp. 8. Continued. H.

The Jefferson Monument Magazine. Conducted by the Students of the University of Virginia. *Charlottesville, Va.: James Alexander.* 1849. Vol. II.—No. 3, December, 1850. 2 or more vols., 8vo. 35947

Addresses delivered before the Young Men's Jefferson Society, on the Fourth of July, Year of Independence 56. [*New York:*] *R. Stevenson and R. Holstead, Printers.* [1832.] 8vo, pp. 13.

The Jeffersonian Weekly. H. Greeley, Editor. Vol. I., Feb. 1838–Jan. 1839. *Albany.* 1838. 4to, pp. 408. S. 35949

JEFFERSONVILLE ASSOCIATION. Engineer's Report to the Jeffersonville Association, September, 1836. [H. L. Barnum.] *Cincinnati.* 1836. 12mo, pp. 10. 35950

JEFFERSONVILLE AND NEW-ALBANY CANAL COMPANY. An Act to incorporate the Jeffersonville and New-Albany Canal Company; with Report of Engineer. [n. p.] 1838. 8vo, pp. 16.

JEFFERY (R.) The Mission of Abraham Lincoln. A Sermon ... Philadelphia ... June 1st, 1865. By R. Jeffery, D.D. *Philadelphia: Bryson & Son, Printers.* 1865. 8vo, pp. 28. B.

JEFFERYS (T.) The American Atlas: Or, A Geographical Description of the Whole Continent of America: wherein are delineated at large, its Several Regions, Countries, States, and Islands; and chiefly The British Colonies, Composed from numerous Surveys, several of which were made by Order of Government. By Major Holland, Lewis Evans, William Scull, Henry Mouzon, Lieut. Ross, J. Cook, Michael Lane, Joseph Gilbert, Gardner, Hillock, &c. &c. Engraved on Forty-Nine Copper-Plates. By The Late Mr. Thomas Jefferys, Geographer to the King, and Others. *London: R. Sayer.* MDCCLXXVI. Folio, pp. (4). 30 Maps on 49 Plates. H. 35953

This very useful and valuable collection is composed of separate maps, on a large scale, mostly executed by the surveyors of the various colonies between the years 1762–1776. Copies differ in respect to their contents. The following have come under my notice: The American Atlas: ... Engraved on Forty-Eight Copper-Plates. ... *London:*

Printed by R. Sayer and J. Bennett. MDCCLXXV. Folio, pp. (4). 29 Maps on 48 Plates. + [*Ibid.*] MDCCLXXVIII. Folio, pp. (4). 30 Maps on 49 Plates. B., BA. + [*Ibid.*] MDCCLXXXII. There is an edition dated 1775, which I have not seen.

[JEFFERYS.] Atlas Ameriquain Septentrional contenant les details des differentes provinces de ce vaste Continent. Traduit des cartes levées par ordre du Gouvernement Brittanique. Par le Major Holland, Evans, Scull, Mouzon, Ross, Cook, Lane, Gilbert, Gardner, Hillock, &c. &c. *Paris: Chez le Rouge.* 1778. Folio. 26 Maps and Plate. 35954

[JEFFERYS.] Atlante dell' America contenente le migliore carte geografiche, e topografiche dell principale città, laghi, fiumi, e fortezze dell Nuovo Mondo con una succinta Relazione dei diversi Stabilimenti Europei in quella parte di Globo, e principalmente dei Luoghi, che servono adesso di Teatro alla presente Guerra fra i Coloni Inglesi, e la Madre Patria. *Livorno: Tommaso Masi.* 1777. Folio, pp. 15. 43 Maps and Plans. 35955

JEFFERYS. A Complete Pilot for the West-Indies, ... done from Actual Surveys ... By Thomas Jefferys ... *London: Robert Sayer.* [1788.] Folio, pp. (2). 26 Maps. + A New Edition ... Engraved on Twenty-Nine Plates. ... *London: Robert Laurie and James Whittle.* [n. d.] pp. (2). 27 Maps. H. 35956

[JEFFERYS.] The Conduct of the French, With Regard to Nova Scotia; From its first Settlement to the present Time. In which are exposed the Falsehood and Absurdity of their Arguments made use of to elude the Force of the Treaty of Utrecht, and support their unjust Proceedings. In a Letter to a Member of Parliament. *London: T. Jefferys.* MDCCLIV. 8vo, pp. (2), 77.

"Our author has given a regular, and, as it appears to us, an authentic account of the several proprietors of these countries, from their first settlement by Europeans, as well as of the treaties that have been concluded relative thereto. Both the quantity and quality prove its coming from the hand of no common catch-penny writer."—*Monthly Review,* XI. 472.

[JEFFERYS.] Conduite des François, par rapport à la Nouvelle Ecosse, depuis le premier établissement de cette colonie jusqu'à nos jours. Ouvrage ou l'on expose la faiblesse des argumens dont ils se servent pour éluder la force du Traité d'Utrecht & pour justifier leurs procédés illégitimes, dans une lettre à un membre du parlement. Traduite de l'Anglois, avec des notes d'un François, dans lesquelles il disculpe sa nation des imputations dont on la charge, etc. *A Londres: Chez les Frères Vaillant.* 1755. 12mo, pp. XV, 281. 35958

See Faribault, p. 67. Barbier says the notes were written by Butel-Dumont.

JEFFERYS. A Description of the Spanish Islands and Settlements On the Coast of the West Indies, Compiled from authentic Memoirs, Revised by Gentlemen who have resided many Years in the Spanish Settlements; and Illustrated With Thirty-two Maps and Plans, Chiefly from original Drawings taken from the Spaniards in the last War, And Engraved by Thomas Jefferys, Geographer to His Majesty. *London: T. Jefferys.* 1762. 4to, pp. (6), xxiv, 106, (2). 32 Maps and Plans. A., BA., C., S.

See "M. Rev.," XXVII. 386.

JEFFERYS. A Description [etc.] ... By the late Thomas Jefferys. The Second Edition. *London: Printed for Faden and Jefferys.* 1774. 4to, pp. (4), xxiv, 106, (2). 32 Maps and Plans.

JEFFERYS. Directions for Navigating the Gulf and River of St. Lawrence; With a particular account of the Bays, &c. Founded on accurate observations and experiments made by the officers of H. M.'s Fleet. By order of Charles Saunders, Esq., Vice Admiral of the Blue, and Commander in Chief of the British Naval Forces in the Expedition against Quebec in 1759. By Thomas Jefferys. *London: T. Jefferys.* 1760. 4to, pp. 31.

JEFFERYS. A General Topography of North America and the West Indies. Being a Collection of all the Maps, Charts, Plans, and Particular Surveys, That have been published, of that Part of the World, Either in Europe or America. Engraved by Tho. Jefferys ... . *London: Printed for Robert Sayer, ... and Thomas Jefferys.* MDCCLXVIII. Folio, pp. 4. 93 Maps. 35962

Duplicate title and contents in the French language. This is the first issue of what is generally known as Jeffery's Atlas. The maps and plates are clear, distinct, brilliant, and very superior to those of later date, described No. 35953, *supra,* in which many of the plans in this edition are not included.

JEFFERYS. The Great Probability. *See* Vol. VII., No. 28460.

[JEFFERYS.] Explanation for the New Map of Nova Scotia and cape Britain [*sic*], With the Adjacent Parts of New England and Canada. *London: T. Jefferys.* MDCCLV. 4to, pp. 22. BA.

JEFFERYS. The Natural and Civil History of the French Dominions in North and South America. Giving a particular Account of the Climate, Soil, Minerals, Animals, Vegetables, Manufactures, Trade, Commerce and Languages, together with The Religion, Government, Genius, Character, Manners and Customs of the Indians and other Inhabitants. Illustrated by Maps and Plans of the principal Places, Collected from the best

Authorities, and engraved by T. Jefferys ... Part I. Containing A Description of Canada and Louisiana. Part II. Containing Part of the Islands of St. Domingo and St. Martin, The Islands of St. Bartholomew, Guadaloupe, Martinico, La Grenade, and The Island and Colony of Cayenne. *London: Printed for Thomas Jefferys.* MDCCLX. Part I. Folio, pp. (8), 168. Part II. pp. (2), 246. 18 Maps and Plans. A., B., BA., C., H., P. 35964

For an extended notice of this work *see* "M. Rev.," XXII. 81, *also* Faribault, p. 67.

JEFFERYS. Neptune Occidental. The Western Neptune, or Pilot for America; comprehending the British Channel, ... and the Atlantic Ocean, with the Island and Bank of Newfoundland, the Great Bay of Chesapeake, also the Gulf of Florida at large, etc. From Actual Surveys by Mr. Thomas Jefferys. *London.* 1778. Folio. 16 Plates. 35965

JEFFERYS. The North American Pilot for Newfoundland, Labradore, the Gulf and River of St. Lawrence; being a Collection of sixty accurate Charts and Plans, drawn from Original Surveys taken by J. Cook, M. Lane, and J. Gilbert, and others. Engraved by Thomas Jefferys on 36 large Copper-Plates. Part Second: The North American Pilot for New England, New York, Pennsylvania, Maryland, and Virginia, the two Carolinas, and Florida. Drawn from Original Surveys taken by J. Gascoigne, J. Fisher, J. Blarney, and others. *London: Sayer and Bennett.* MDCCLXXV. 2 vols., folio. 53 Maps. 35966

Reissued as:

JEFFERYS. The First Part of the North American Pilot: for Newfoundland, Labradore ... . New Edition. *London: R. Laurie & J. Whittle.* 1806. Folio, pp. (6). 25 Charts. C.

JEFFERYS. A New Edition, Enlarged, of the Second Part of the North American Pilot ... . *London: R. Laurie & J. Whittle.* 1800. Folio, pp. (2). 20 Charts. C. 35968

JEFFERYS. Pilote Americaine Septentrionale pour les côtes de Labrador, Nouvelle Ecosse, Nouvelle Angleterre, New York, Pensilvanie, Maryland, Virginie, les deux Carolines et Florides. Par Jefferys, Lane, Morris, Chevalier des Barres, Smith, Blaskowitz et Scull. Publié à Londres en 1776. Traduit de l'Anglois. *A Paris: Chez Le Rouge. Ing. Géographe du Roi.* 1778. Folio. Engraved Frontispiece and Table. 44 Charts. 35969

JEFFERYS. Voyage from Asia to America. *See* Muller (S.)

JEFFERYS. The West-India Atlas: or, A Compendious Description of the West-Indies: Illustrated with Forty Correct Charts and Maps. Together with An Historical Account of the Several Countries and Islands which compose that part of the World. By the late Thomas Jefferys. *London: Robert Sayer and John Bennett.* M.DCC.LXXV. Folio, pp. (2), 27. 40 Maps. + [*Ibid.*] 1780. S. + *London: Robert Sayer.* 1794. Folio, pp. (5), 28, (1). 61 Maps. BA. + *London: Robert Laurie and James Whittle.* 1799. Folio, pp. (6), 28. 61 Charts, Maps and Plans.

Rich, Vol. I., p. 251, quotes an edition, 1777, and J. R. Smith describes one with 61 maps, 1783. I have not seen either.

JEFFERYS. The West-India Islands: from Actual Surveys and Observations. In Seventeen Correct Maps. ... By The Late Thomas Jefferys ... . *London: R. Sayer and J. Bennett.* MDCCLXXV. Folio, pp. (2). 17 Maps. BA. 35971

JEFFRIES (J. C.) In Memoriam. James Culbertson Jeffries. *Columbus, O.: R. Nevis, Printer.* 8vo, pp. 8. 35972

JEFFRIES (C.) Wabash Captives; or the Awful Sentence: Thrilling Narrative of Crime and Death, and Wonderful Adventures of James Brady and others, among the Indians on the Wabash, 60 years ago, near the spot where La Fayette now stands; Founded on Facts, by C. Jeffries ... . *La Fayette: The Author.* 1846. 12mo, pp. 16. 35973

Also: "The Suffering Army" and "Hull's Surrender."

JEFFRIES (J.) An Account of the Last Illness of the Late Hon. Daniel Webster ... . By John Jeffries, M.D. ... *Philadelphia: T. K. and P. G. Collins, Printers.* 1853. 8vo, pp. 13. B.

Also: An Address ... before the Suffolk District Medical Society ... April 27, 1850. ... *Boston: Printed by David Clapp.* 1850. 8vo, pp. 49, (1). B., BA., H.

JEFFRIES (J. P.) The Natural History of the Human Races, with their primitive Form and Origin, Primeval Distribution, Distinguishing Peculiarities; Antiquity, Works of Art ... . Also, an Account of the Construction of the Globe, Changes of its Surface, ... with other Interesting Matter. By John P. Jeffries. *New York: W. O. Jenkins.* 1869. 8vo, pp. 380. 4 Plates. C.

[JEFFRIES (Thomas Fayette).] "Crippled Fayette," of Rockingham, ... Made helpless by the Rheumatism since the 20th of October, 1847. ... *Mountain Valley, Va.: Printed at the Office of Joseph Funk & Sons.* 1857. 18mo, pp. 187, (1). BA. 35976

JEHAN (L. F.) Dictionnaire de Linguistique et de Philologie comparée. ... Par L. F. Jehan (de St. Clavien) ... *Paris: J. P. Migne.* 1858. 8vo, pp. 724. 35977

Includes notices of many American languages. Dr. Shea, in the "Historical Magazine," Vol. III., p. 64, gives it a mixed character.

JEKYLL (N.) The Vindication of N. Jekyll, late Capt. of the 43rd Regt., with the Proceedings of the General Court Martial held on Colonel Stewart, of the same Regiment; and Memorials, &c., to the Commander-in-Chief, with their Answers. *London.* 1805. 8vo, Introduction, pp. 44; Vindication, 170.

Jekyll served in Canada.

JELLY (T.) A Brief Inquiry into the Condition of Jamaica: with a view to ascertain if any and what steps might be taken to relieve that Island from her perilous state of Political, Financial, and Agricultural Embarrassment. By Thomas Jelly. *London.* 1847. 8vo, pp. 78. P. 35979

JEMISON (M.) *See* Seaver (J. E.), *also* Wright (A.)

JENCKES (T. A.) A Bill to establish a Uniform System of Bankruptcy throughout the United States. Reported by the Hon. Thomas A. Jenckes ... . February 15, 1864. *New York: Printed by Dodge & Grattan.* 1864. 8vo, pp. 29. 35980

JENCKES. The Bankrupt Law. Speech of Thomas A. Jenckes, of Rhode Island. Delivered in the House of Representatives, June 1, 1864. *Washington, D. C.: M'Gill & Witherow, Printers.* 1864. 8vo, pp. 16. H. 35981

JENCKES. The Civil Service of the United States of America. Report of Mr. Jenckes, ... May 14, 1868. *Washington.* 1868. 8vo, pp. vii, 219, 14, 16. 35982

Also: Speech ... on the Bill to regulate the Civil Service of the United States and to promote the Efficiency thereof; delivered ... January 29, 1867. *Washington.* 1867. 8vo, pp. 14. + Speech [on the same bill] ... May 14, 1868. *Washington: F. & J. Rives & Geo. A. Bailey ... Printers.* 1868. 8vo, pp. 15.—Speech ... on Reconstruction; ... January 17, 1868. *Washington: F. & J. Rives & Geo. A. Bailey ... Printers.* 1868. 8vo, pp. 8.—Civil Service. Speech ... April 5, 1869. *Washington: F. & J. Rives & Geo. A. Bailey ... Printers.* 1869. 8vo, pp. 15. H.

JENIFER [Daniel]. Speech of Mr. Jenifer, of Maryland, on the bill making Appropriations for ... Fortifications: ... May 24, 1836. *Washington.* 1836. 8vo, pp. 14. 35983

Also: Remarks ... at the Opening of the Convention of Tobacco Planters of the United States ... at Washington City, December 15, 1840. *Washington.* 1840. 8vo, pp. 16.—Speech ... on the Proposition to print the Testimony in Relation to the New

Jersey contested Election. Delivered during the Morning Hour, March 11, 12, 13, 14, and 17, 1840. *Washington: Printed by Gales and Seaton.* 1840. 8vo, pp. 32. H.

JENINGS (E.) The Candour of Henry Laurens, Esq.; Manifested by his Behaviour to Mr. Edmund Jenings. [*London.*] *July,* 1783. 4to, pp. 38. M. 35984

JENINGS. A Full Manifestation of what Mr. Henry Laurens falsely denominates Candour in himself, and Tricks in Mr. Edmund Jenings. *London: Printed in the year* 1783. 4to, pp. (4), 80. 35985

An answer to the pamphlet entitled "State of the Case by which his Candour to Mr. Edmund Jenings is manifested, and the Tricks of Mr. Jenings detected," by Henry Laurens. This, together with the preceding No. and Laurens' "State of the Case," comprise a complete series of the publications relating to the *Pitiful Quarrel* between Messrs. Jenings and Laurens. *See* Laurens (Henry).

[JENINGS.] A Plan for Settling the Unhappy Dispute between Great Britain and her Colonies. ... [n. p.: *Privately Printed.*] MDCCLXXVI. Sm. 8vo, pp. 26. J.C.B. 35986

[JENINGS.] A Translation of the Memorial to the Sovereigns of Europe upon the Present State of Affairs, between the Old and the New World, into Common Sense and intelligible English. *London: J. Stockdale.* M.DCC.LXXXI. 8vo, pp. (2), 45.

The memorial referred to was written by Governor Pownall. The author of the present work says the original is said to be by Governor P——l, but that it contains "so many quaint words, and dark expressions, intermixed with so many good thoughts and with so much knowledge of America, that it seems worth translating." Governor Pownall says his ideas have been entirely misrepresented in this work.

JENKINS (C.) England's Triumph: or, Spanish Cowardice expos'd. Being a Compleat History of the many Signal Victories gain'd by the Royal Navy and Merchants Ships of Great Britain, for the Term of Four Hundred Years past, over the insulting and haughty Spaniards. Wherein is particularly related A true and genuine Account of all the Expeditions, Voyages, Adventures, &c. of all the British Admirals from the Time above-mention'd whose Successes have already filled all Europe with Amazement. By Capt. Charles Jenkins, who has too sensibly felt the effects of Spanish Tyranny. *London: Printed in the Year* MDCCXXXIX. 12mo, pp. 300. 2 Plates, 1 Table. C.

Originally issued in twenty-four numbers. A large part of this scarce volume pertains directly or indirectly to America, containing accounts of the various expeditions of Hawkins, Drake, Raleigh, and many others, from 1567 to 1730.

JENKINS. Eulogy on the Life and Services of Henry Clay, delivered ... in Augusta, Ga., Nov. 4, 1852. By Charles J. Jenkins. *Augusta, Georgia.* 1853. 8vo, pp. 19. 35989

[JENKINS (Edward).] The Coolie, his Rights and Wrongs. Notes of a Journey to British Guiana, with a Review of the System and of the recent Commission of Inquiry. ... *London: Strahan & Co.* 1871. 8vo, pp. xii, 446. C. 35990

JENKINS *vs.* VAN RENSSELAER. Assault and Battery. Report of the Trials of the Causes of Elisha Jenkins *vs.* Solomon Van Rensselaer. Solomon Van Rensselaer *vs.* John Taylor. The same *vs.* Chas. D. Cooper, and the same *vs.* Francis Bloodgood. Before Arbitrators, at Albany, August 16th, 17th, and 18th, 1808. *Albany: Croswell & Tracy.* 1808. 8vo, pp. 80. Plate. N.

JENKINS (G.), *pseudon.* Legislative Sketches from a Reporter's Note Book. By Geoffrey Jenkins. *Albany: Weed, Parsons & Co.* 1866. 16mo, pp. 93. C. 35992

JENKINS (H. M.) Our Democratic Republic: Its Form—Its Faults—Its Strength—Its Need. Three Articles on the Suffrage Question. By Howard M. Jenkins. *Wilmington, Del.: Press of Jenkins & Atkinson.* 1868. 8vo, pp. 32. H. 35993

Also: The Republican Form: A Constitutional Inquiry. ... *Wilmington, Del.:* ... *Press of Jenkins & Atkinson.* 1867. 8vo, pp. 12. H.

[JENKINS (James).] Naval Achievements of Great Britain, from the years 1793 to 1817. *London.* 1817. Folio. C. 35994

JENKINS (J.) Canada's Thanksgiving ... . A Sermon by Rev. John Jenkins, D.D. *Montreal.* 1865. 8vo, pp. 21. 35995

JENKINS. ... A Fast Day Discourse ... in Philadelphia ... September 26th, 1861, by the Rev. John Jenkins, D.D. *Philadelphia: C. Sherman and Son, Printers.* 1861. 8vo, pp. 32.

JENKINS. The National Fast. Why it should be kept, and how. A Sermon, by the Rev. John Jenkins, D.D. ... *Philadelphia: C. Sherman, Son & Co., Printers.* 1863. 8vo, pp. 27.

JENKINS. The Truthful Minister; A Life of the Rev. William Squire. By Rev. John Jenkins, D.D. *Montreal.* 1853. 12mo, pp. 120. 35998

Also: Pauperism in Great Cities. ... *Philadelphia.* 1854.—Thoughts for the Crisis. ... *Philadelphia: J. B. Lippincott & Co.* 1861. 12mo, pp. 24. B.

JENKINS (J. F.) Relations of War to Medical Science. The Annual Address before the Westchester County (N. Y.) Medical Society, June 19, 1863. By J. Foster Jenkins. *New York: Baillière Brothers.* 1863. 8vo, pp. 16. 35999

Jenkins (J. J.) Ho! Our Country, to the Rescue!! By John J. Jenkins. *New York.* 1859. 36000

Jenkins (J. S.) Daring Deeds of American Generals. By John S. Jenkins ... . *New York.* 1857. 12mo. 36001

Jenkins. The Generals of the Last War with Great Britain. By John S. Jenkins ... . *Auburn.* 1849. 12mo, pp. 407. s.

Jenkins. History of Political Parties in the State of New-York, From the Acknowledgment of the Independence of the United States to the Close of the Presidential Election in Eighteen Hundred Forty-Four. ... By John S. Jenkins ... . *Auburn, N. Y.: Alden & Markham.* 1846. 12mo, pp. vii, 17–528. Portraits. A. + Second Edition. *Auburn: Alden & Parsons.* 1849. 12mo, pp. 580. c. 36003

Jenkins. History of the War between the United States and Mexico, from the Commencement of Hostilities to the Ratification of the Treaty of Peace. By John S. Jenkins ... . *Auburn: Derby, Miller, & Company.* 1848. 12mo, pp. 506. + [*Ibid.*] 1849. 12mo, pp. 514. Portraits and Plates. + [*Ibid.*] 1851.

Jenkins. Jackson and the Generals of the War of 1812. By John S. Jenkins ... . *Philadelphia.* 1854. 12mo. 36005

Jacob Brown, Edmund Pendleton Gaines, W. H. Harrison, Alex. Macomb, Zebulon Montgomery Pike, and Winfield Scott, are the other generals.

Jenkins. James Knox Polk, and a History of his Administration ... . By John S. Jenkins ... . *Auburn and Buffalo: John E. Beardsley.* [1850.] 12mo, pp. iii, 395. Portrait. BA. 36006

The title was afterwards changed to read: The Life of James Knox Polk. ... *Auburn: James M. Alden.* 1850. 12mo.

Jenkins. Life and Public Services of Gen. Andrew Jackson, with the Eulogy by Hon. Geo. Bancroft. *New York.* 1858. 12mo. 36007

The same as the following with a change in the title-page.

Jenkins. The Life of General Andrew Jackson, seventh President of the United States. With an Appendix, containing the most important of his State Papers. Third Edition. *Auburn, N. Y.* 1847. 12mo. c. + To which is added, the Eulogy of Hon. George Bancroft. [*Ibid.*] 1845. 12mo. + *Buffalo.* 1852. 12mo. 36008

Jenkins. The Life of John Caldwell Calhoun. By John S. Jenkins ... . *Auburn: James M. Alden.* 1850. 12mo, pp. 454. Portrait. A., BA. 36009

Jenkins. The Life of Silas Wright, late Governor of the State of New York. With an Appendix, containing a selection from his speeches ... . By John S. Jenkins ... . *Auburn, N. Y.: Alden & Markham.* 1847. 12mo, pp. 384. + [*Ibid.*] 1850. + *Auburn and Buffalo: John E. Beardsley.* [1847.] 12mo, pp. 378.

Jenkins. The Lives of the Governors of the State of New York. By John S. Jenkins ... . *Auburn: Derby and Miller.* 1851. 8vo, pp. 826. 14 Portraits. c. 36011

This elicited a severe review—printed, but not published—*Cherry Valley.* 1853. 8vo, pp. 23. Signed Jabez D. Hammond.

Jenkins. The Lives of Patriots and Heroes, distinguished in the Battles for American Freedom. By John S. Jenkins ... . *Auburn: J. C. Derby & Co.* 1847. 18mo, pp. 293. s. 36012

Jenkins. Recent Exploring Expeditions to the Pacific, and the South Seas, under the American, English, and French Governments. By John S. Jenkins ... . *London: T. Nelson & Sons.* 1853. Post 8vo, pp. viii, 508. Plate. c. 36013

Jenkins. Voyage of the United States Exploring Expedition, under Captain Charles Wilkes, in 1838–42, together with Explorations and Discoveries made by Admiral d'Urville, Capt. Ross, and an Account of the Expedition to the Dead Sea, under Lieut. Lynch. By John S. Jenkins ... . *Auburn: James M. Alden.* 1850. 8vo, pp. 517. 36014

Mr. Jenkins was an industrious literary hack, and these works possess as much merit as most books of their class.

Jenkins (J. W.) Speech of John W. Jenkins, Esq. ... on the Political Issues of the Day. ... Winchester, Virginia May 23, 1867. *Winchester.* 1867. 8vo, pp. 14. H. 36015

Jenkins (J.) An Address delivered before the Massachusetts Charitable Mechanick Association, December 17, 1818 ... . By Joseph Jenkins, G.M. *Boston: Printed by Munroe & Francis.* 1819. 8vo, pp. 24. BA., H. 36016

Also: An Address delivered before the Grand Lodge of Massachusetts ... December 28, 1829. ... *Boston: Peirce and Williams.* 1830. 8vo, pp. 24. H. + Second Edition. [*Ibid.*] MDCCCXXX. 8vo, pp. 24. H.—An Oration ... at Barre, Massachusetts, before Mount Zion, Harris, and Thompson Lodges, June 24, A.L. 5820; ... *Boston: Printed by J. T. Buckingham.* [1820.] 8vo, pp. 24. BA.

Jenkins (O.) Remarks upon the Defence of the Reverend Mr. Hemphill's Observations ... . By Obadiah Jenkins. ... *Philadelphia: Andrew Bradford.* M,DCC,XXXV. 12mo, pp. (2), 22.

Jenkins (T. A.) Paper read by Commodore Thornton A. Jenkins, U. S. Navy ... January 21, 1868, in reply to Rear Admiral Goldsborough's claim to be continued on the active list of the Navy. *Washington, D. C.: McGill & Witherow, Printers.* [n. d.] 8vo, pp. 38. H. 36018

[Jenkins.] Rear Admiral Goldsborough and the Retiring Laws of the Navy. No. 2. *Washington: Mohun & Bestor.* 1868. 8vo, pp. 19. H. 36019

Jenkins (T.) Speech of Timothy Jenkins ... in Congress, on the Wilmot Proviso. Delivered ... February 13, 1847. *Washington: ... Blair and Rives.* 1847. 8vo, pp. 16. BA.

Also: Speech ... June 30, 1846, ... on the Tariff. *Washington.* 1846. 8vo, pp. 12. H.—Speech ... on the Contested Election Case from New Jersey. Delivered ... March 4, 1846. *Washington: Printed [by] Blair and Rives.* 1846. 8vo, pp. 7.— ... Speech ... on the Mexican Treaty ... February 17, 1849. [*Washington.*] 1849. 8vo, pp. 16.—Speech ... April 14, 1852, against giving away the Public Lands. [*Washington.* 1852.] 8vo, pp. 8. H.

Jenkins (W.) The Ohio Gazetteer, and Travelers' Guide; containing a Description of the several Towns, Townships and Counties, with their Water Courses, Roads, Improvements, Mineral Productions, &c. &c. Together with an Appendix, or General Register; embracing Tables of Roads and Distances; of Post Offices, their Location and Distance from the Capital of the State and of the United States; of Works of Internal Improvement; of the several Officers of State, their Residence, &c.; of the Colleges and their Officers; of Banks, their Officers and Capital, &c. &c. First Revised Edition. By Warren Jenkins. *Columbus: Isaac N. Whiting.* [1837.] 12mo, pp. xxiv, 51–546. Map. H. + Revised Edition, with a Second Appendix, containing the Census of the State for 1840. ... [*Ibid.*] 1841. 12mo, pp. xxiv, 52–578. Map. A., B., C. 36021

"As far as we are able to form a judgment of its merits, this seems to be an extremely well composed and valuable manual."—*North American Review, January,* 1840.

Jenkins (W.) Q. M. D.; or, Book of Reference for Quartermasters. By Capt. Walworth Jenkins, Asst. Quartermaster U. S. A. *Louisville, Ky.: John P. Morton & Co.* 186–. 12mo, pp. 303. 36022

[Jenkinson (Charles).] A Discourse on the Conduct of the Government of Great-Britain, in respect to Neutral Nations, during the Present War. By Charles Lord Hawkesbury. *London: R. Griffiths.* M.DCC.LVIII. 4to, pp. (2), 84. BA. + Second

Edition. [*Ibid.*] M.DCC.LIX. 8vo. + [*Ibid.*] M.DCC.LXXXV. 8vo. + A New Edition. ... *London: J. Debrett.* 1794. 8vo, pp. 96. BA. + A New Edition. *London: T. Cadell, Jun. and W. Davies.* 1801. 8vo, pp. (2), xlix, 108. BA., H. + Second Edition. *Edinburgh.* 1837. 12mo. 36023

See our Vol. IV., Nos. 14372, 15202, and 15203.

Jenkinson (I.) The Peace Party and its Policy. (Ft. Wayne, Ind., March 16, 1863.) By Isaac Jenkinson. *Ft. Wayne: Ruyheuser, Printer.* 1863. 8vo, pp. 16. 36024

[Jenkinson (Robert B.)] The Speech of Lord Liverpool in The House of Lords, ... the 26th of May, 1820, ... on ... The Foreign Trade of the Country. With an Appendix ... . *London: John Hatchard and Son.* 1820. 8vo, pp. (2), 56, (4).

[Jenkinson.] Substance of the Speech delivered in the House of Lords, on the 15th of March, 1824, by the Earl of Liverpool, on the Marquess of Lansdown's Motion for the Recognition of the Independence of the late Spanish Colonies in South America, by the British Government. *London: John Murray.* 1824. 8vo, pp. 44. c. 36026

Jenkinson (W. C.) An Answer to Vamp Overreach's Letter to the Right Hon. W. C. Jenkinson. Written in the Christmas Holidays, By Mr. Jenkinson's Porter. *London: Smith.* 1782. 4to. 36027

See "M. Rev.," LXVI. 142.

Jenks (G. E.) The Statesman. Statistical Almanac, and Political Manual for ... New Hampshire. 1866 ... Compiled by George E. Jenks. *Concord: McFarland and Jenks.* [1866.] 12mo, pp. 176. H. 36028

See also New Hampshire.

Jenks (S. H.) An Address ... at Nantucket, before Urbanity Lodge of Free and Accepted Masons; Oct. 3, A.L. 5822. By Samuel H. Jenks. ... *Nantucket: Printed by Joseph C. Melcher.* 1822. 8vo, pp. 21. B. 36029

Jenks (W.) An Address ... American Antiquarian Society, ... Boston, on their First Anniversary, October 23, 1813. By William Jenks, A.M. ... *Boston: Isaiah Thomas, Jun.* 1813. 8vo, pp. 28. H. 36030

Jenks. An Eulogy, illustrative of the life, and commemorative of the beneficence of ... Hon. James Bowdoin, Esquire,

with Notices of his Family; Pronounced in Brunswick (Maine), ... September 2d, 1812. By William Jenks, A.M. ... *Boston: Printed by John Eliot, Jun.* 1812. 4to, pp. 40. BA., C. 36031

Jenks. The Jenks Family. Copy of a Letter to Alonzo Lewis, Esq. [*Boston.* 1855.] 8vo, pp. 6. M. 36032

[Jenks.] Memoir of the Northern Kingdom, written, A. D. 1872 [*sic*], in Six Letters to his Son. By the late Rev. Williamson Jahnsenykes, LL.D. ... *Quebeck, now first published,* 1901 [*sic*]. 8vo, pp. 48. B., BA. 36033

The real imprint should read *Boston.* 1808.

Jenks. A Memoir of the Rev. Louis Dwight ... By William Jenks, D.D. ... *Boston: Press of T. R. Marvin.* 1856. 8vo, pp. 41. B., BA., H., M. 36034

Jenks. A Sermon ... before His Excellency John Brooks, Esq. Governor ... on the Annual Election, May 31, 1820. By William Jenks, A.M. ... [*Boston:*] *Benjamin Russell.* 1820. 8vo, pp. 24. B., BA., H. 36035

Also: An Address ... New England Historic-Genealogical Society, ... March 1st, 1852 ... *Boston: Thomas Prince, Printer.* 1852. 8vo, pp. 18, (2).—Constitution of the Marine Bible Society ... and an Address on the Formation of the Society. *Boston: Printed by True and Weston.* 1820. 8vo, pp. 12.—A Discourse ... in Freeport (Maine) Feb. 10, 1809, at the Funeral of Rev. Samuel Veazie, A.M. ... *Portland: Printed by Weeks & M'Kown.* [1809.] 8vo, pp. 20.—A Discourse ... June 24th, 1870, before the ... Solar and United Lodges of Free and Accepted Masons, ... at Bath (Maine); ... *Portland: Printed by F. M'Kown.* [1807.] 8vo, pp. 26. M.—A Discourse ... on the Festival of Saint John the Baptist, June 24th, 1807, ... at Bath (Maine). ... *Portland: Printed by F. M'Kown.* [1807.] 8vo, pp 26.—An Eulogy, pronounced in Brunswick (Maine), July 18th, 1807, at the Funeral of the late Rev. Joseph M'Keen, D.D. ... *Portland: Printed by Thomas B. Wait & Co.* 1807. 8vo, pp. 15–38. B., H.—Report of the Committee ... of Harvard College, appointed to visit the Library, ... in 1850. ... *Boston: Printed by John Wilson and Son.* 1851. 8vo, pp. 11. B., H.—A Sermon ... before the Massachusetts Society for promoting Christian Knowledge ... May 25, 1825. ... *Boston: Crocker & Brewster.* 1825. 8vo, pp. 36. BA.—A Sermon, delivered before the Massachusetts Society for the Suppression of Intemperance ... June 1, 1821. With the Annual Report. ... *Boston: Printed by Phelps and Farnham.* 1821. 8vo, pp. 31, (1). M.—The true Spirit of Missions. A Sermon ... before the Maine Missionary Society ... in Northyarmouth [*sic*] (Maine), July 5, 1809. ... *Hallowell: Printed by N. Cheever.* 1809. 8vo, pp. 28. H.

Jenner (T.) Descendants of Rev. Thomas Jenner. [By William S. Appleton. *Boston.* 1865.] 8vo, pp. 3. 36036

[Jennings (Clotilda).] The White Rose in Acadia; and Autumn in Nova Scotia, A Prize Tale and Poem. By "Maude." *Halifax.* 1855. 8vo, pp. 36. 36037

Also: Linden Rhymes. ... *Halifax.* 1854. 8vo, pp. 152.

Jennings (D.) An Abridgment of the Life Of the late Reverend and Learned Dr. Cotton Mather, of Boston in New-England. Taken from the Account of him published by his Son, the Reverend Mr. Samuel Mather. Proposed as a Pattern to all Christians, who desire to excel in Holiness and Usefulness, and especially to Younger Ministers. By David Jennings. ... *London: J. Oswald.* 1744. 12mo, pp. xii, (4), 143. BA., H. + *Leeds.* 1802. 18mo. + A New Edition. *Edinburgh: Waugh and Innes.* 1822. 12mo, pp. 242. 36038

Also: The Life of ... Dr. Cotton Mather, of Boston (New England). ... *Philadelphia: American Sunday School Union.* [n. d.] Sm. 12mo, pp. 107. B.

Jennings (E.) A Sermon ... in Dalton [Mass.], March 4, 1808; at the Funeral of the Hon. William Williams, Esq. ... By Ebenezer Jennings. *Pittsfield: Printed by Seymour & Smith.* 1808. 8vo, pp. 31. H., W. 36039

Also: Address delivered at Plainfield, Mass., on the Fourth of July, 1836. ... *Northampton.* 1836. 8vo, pp. 16. M.

Jennings (H. S.) Address of Henry S. Jennings, delivered before the Order on St. John's Day, June 24, 1857. *Dubuque, Iowa.* 1857. 8vo, pp. 16. 36040

Jennings (I.) Memorials of a Century. ... The Early History of Bennington, Vt. and its First Church. By Isaac Jennings ... . *Boston: Gould and Lincoln.* 1869. 8vo, pp. 408. 2 Plates. BA., H., S. 36041

Jennings (J.) A Practical Treatise on the History, Medical Properties, and Cultivation of Tobacco. By James Jennings, Esq. *London: Sherwood Gilbert and Piper.* 1830. 12mo, pp. vi, (2), 159. 36042

Also: The Prospects of Africa, with other Poems. ... *London: T. Lester.* 1814. 8vo, pp. (6), 136.

Jennings (L. J.) Eighty Years of Republican Government in the United States. By Louis J. Jennings. *London: John Murray.* 1868. 12mo, pp. xv, 288. BA., C. + Second Edition. [*Ibid.*] 1868. + First American from the Second London Edition. *New York: Charles Scribner & Co.* 1868. 12mo, pp. xv, 288. H. 36043

The so-called American edition is probably Murray's with a new title-page.

Jennings (O.) Debate on Campbellism; held at Nashville, Tennessee. In which the Principles of Alexander Campbell are confuted, and his Conduct examined. By Obadiah Jennings,

D.D. To which is prefixed, a Memoir of the Author, by Rev. M. Brown, D.D. *Pittsburgh: D. & M. Maclean.* 1832. 12mo, pp. 252. S. 36044

An account of the debate and of Campbell by one of the debaters.

Jennings (P.) A Colored Man's Reminiscences of James Madison. By Paul Jennings. *Brooklyn: George C. Beadle.* 1865. 4to, pp. 21. Facsimile. BA., C. 36045

Seventy-five copies privately printed for Dr. J. G. Shea. Forms No. II. of the "Bladensburg Series."

Jennings (R.) Report of the Trials of the Murderers of Richard Jennings, at ... Goshen, ... February 23rd, 1819. With Arguments of Counsel. ... *Newburgh: Printed by Benjamin F. Lewis, and Co.* ... 1819. 8vo, pp. 132. BA., S. 36046

Jennings (R. D.) The Case of Richard Downing Jennings, an English Subject, who Resided at Saint Eustatius, as a Merchant, When that Island was captured by Lord Rodney and General Vaughan In the Year 1781. ... *London: Printed by J. W. Galabin.* M.DCC.XC. 8vo, pp. 62. C., H., J.C.B., M. 36047

Jennings (S.) The | State of the Case, | Briefly but Impartially given betwixt the | People called | Quakers, | in | Pensilvania, &c. in America, who re- | main in Unity; And | George Keith. | With some few Seduced by him into a Separa- | tion from them. As also a Just Vindication | of my Self from the Reproaches and Abuses | of those Backsliders. | By Samuel Jennings. | ... | *London: Printed and Sold by T. Sowle,* ... | 1694. | 12mo, pp. (6), 80.

In Thomas' "History of Printing," Vol. II., this is quoted as having been printed in *Philadelphia,* 1693. I am unable to find any further evidence on this subject.

[Jennings (Samuel K.), *M.D.*] An Exposition of the late Controversy in the Methodist Episcopal Church, ... by which Reformers were Expelled in Baltimore, Cincinnati, and other places; ... to which are appended remarks on an article entitled Asbury's Life ... . By a Layman. *Baltimore.* 1831. 8vo, pp. viii, 247. 36049

Jenny Ambrose; or, Life in the Eastern States. By the Author of "Lights and Shadows of Factory Life." *Philadelphia: T. B. Peterson & Brothers.* 1866. 8vo, pp. 116. 36050

Jenny Wade, of Gettysburg. *Philadelphia: J. B. Lippincott & Co.* 1864. 12mo, pp. 33. 36051

Contrary to the legend of the poem the heroine is said to have been a rebel sympathizer, who baked bread for the Federal army under compulsion.

Jennyns (J. C.) Address of J. Clayton Jennyns to the Planters and Merchants of the United Colony of Demerara and Essequebo, on the Relative Duties of Master and Slave. *London.* 1816. 8vo. C. 36052

Also: ... On the Unconstitutional Continuance of Foreign Laws in the Colonies, ceded to Great Britain. *London.* 1828. 8vo.

Jenyns (L.) *See* Darwin, Vol. v., No. 18694.

[Jenyns (Soame).] The Objections to the Taxation of our American Colonies, by the Legislature of Great Britain, Briefly Consider'd. *London: J. Wilkie.* 1765. 8vo, pp. 20. + The Second Edition. [*Ibid.*] 1765. 8vo, pp. 23. H. 36053

Also included in his works, *London: Cadell.* 1793. 4 vols., 12mo. For a reply *see our* Vol. IV., No. 15949.

J[E]PH[SO]N (R[al]ph). The Expounder Expounded: or, Annotations upon a short Account of God's Dealing with the Rev. Mr. G——e W—f—d. By R—ph J—ph—n of the Inner Temple. *London: W. & T. Payne.* 1740. 16mo, pp. 82. C.

Relates to George Whitfred.

Jequitinhonna. Reflexoes sobre as finanças do Brasil operaçoes de credito do thesouro e o emprestimo contrahido em Londres de cinco milhoes de libras esterlinas no corrente anno, por Visconde de Jequitinhonna. *Rio de Janeiro.* 1865. 8vo, pp. 86.

Jeremie (J.) Four Essays on Colonial Slavery, by John Jeremie, Esq., President of the Royal Court of St. Lucia. *London.* 1831. 8vo. S. 36056

Jeremie. Remarks on Mr. Jeremie's Conduct as President of the Royal Court of St. Lucia. By an Inhabitant of that Island. *London: Privately Printed.* 1832. 8vo. 36057

Also: Reply to Mr. Jeremie's Pamphlet, by an Inhabitant of St. Lucia. *London.* 1832. 8vo. C.

Jerman (John). The American Almanack for 1749. *Philadelphia: A. Bradford.* 1749. Continued to 1760 or later.

Jermon (J. W.) Abram Lincoln and South Carolina. By J. Wagner Jermon, Esq. *Philadelphia: D. E. Thompson, Printer.* 1861. 8vo, pp. 15. H. 36059

Jerningham (Edward). The Fall of Mexico. A Poem. By Mr. Jerningham. *London: J. Robson.* 1775. 4to, pp. 59.

See "M. Rev.," LIV. 165.

[JERNINGHAM.] Yarico to Inkle, an Epistle. *London.* 1766.

The last twenty-seven lines are reproduced in Isaac Story's "Epistle from Yarico to Inkle." Another piece with the same title was printed at *Hartford*, 1792.

JERNOTT (W.) Trial of William Jernott, for Piracy in the Island of Cuba. *London.* 1812. 36062

JEROME (C.) History of the American Clock Business for the past sixty years, and Life of Chauncey Jerome, written by himself. Barnum's Connection with the Yankee Clock Business. *New Haven: F. C. Dayton, Jr.* 1860. 12mo, pp. 144. Portrait.

JEROME (C. W. J.) Projet de Colonisation dans les deux Amériques. Par C. W. J. Jerome. *Paris: Imp. de Herhan.* 1827. 4to. 36064

JERROLD (W. B.) The Old Woman who Lived in a Shoe; being Conversations with Britannia on her Colonial Shoes; with an Essay on Colonial Government. By W. Blanchard Jerrold. *London.* 1849. 8vo, pp. 108. 36065

JERSEY CITY, *N. J.* Charters of and Acts relating to Jersey City, and the Ordinances thereof; together with some Statistical Information, &c. *Jersey City: Southard & Post, Printers.* 1844. 8vo, pp. 80. 36066

Combined Directories of Jersey City, Hoboken and Hudson, for 1854–55: with an Appendix, containing various Statistical and Historical Information and a Map. *Jersey City.* 1854. 12mo.

Continued annually.

Directory of Jersey City & Hoboken for 1856–7 ... . Compiled and published by James & William Gopsill. *New York: John W. Oliver, ... Printer.* 1856. 12mo, pp. 29–36, 203, (1). BA.

Jersey City, Harsimus, and Pavonia Directory, for 1849–'50. *Jersey City.* 1849. 12mo. Continued. 36069

Ordinances of Jersey City. 12mo, pp. 81–92. 36070

JERVIS (J. B.) Description of the Croton Aqueduct; By John B. Jervis, Chief Engineer. *New-York: Slamm and Guion.* 1842. 8vo, pp. 31. H. 36071

[JERVIS.] Letters addressed to the Friends of Freedom and the Union, by "Hampden." Originally published in the New York "Evening Post." *New York: Wm. C. Bryant & Co., Printers.* 1856. 8vo, pp. 20. H. 36072

Also: Hudson River Railroad. Report on the Location of t Line between Fishkill and Albany; ... January 12th, 1848. *New York: Wm. C. Bryant & Co., Printers.* [n. d.] 8vo, pp. 38.—Report on the Hudson River Railroad. ... *New York.* 1846. 8vo. Map.—Report ... in relation to the Railroad Bridge over the Mississippi River, at Rock Island. *New York: Wm. C. Bryant & Co., Printers.* 1857. 8vo, pp. 15. H.

JERVOIS [W. F. D.] Letter to the Secretary of State for War with reference to the Defence of Canada. By Lieutenant-Colonel Jervois ... . *London: Printed by George Edward Eyre and William Spottiswoode.* 1865. Folio, pp. 7, (1). B. 36073

JESSE, *pseudon.* Chronicles of the Farmers' and Merchants' Bank of Memphis. By Jesse, the "Scribe." *Memphis.* 1847. 12mo, pp. 79. H. 36074

JESSE (J. H.) Memoirs of the Life and Reign of King George the Third. By J. Heneage Jesse ... . *London: Tinsley Brothers.* 1867. 3 vols., 8vo, pp. x, 601; x, 562; ix, 616. BA. 36075

JESSUP (E.) Sermon in Memory of Thomas T. Guion. By Edward Jessup. *New York.* 1862. 36076

JESSUP (J.) Report of a Cause, John Jessup *vs.* John Ifirth, Esq. For a Libel, Tried at Woodbury, ... 1807, ... New Jersey. *Trenton: Printed by Wilson & Halsey.* 1807. 8vo, pp. 56.

JESSUP (W.) Address before the New-York State Agricultural Society, at the Fair, Watertown, October 3, 1856. By William Jessup. *Albany.* 1856. 8vo. S. 36078

JESU (*Fray* Antonio de). Oracion Funebre del F. Pedro Juan de Molina, 16 Oct. 1777. *Mexico.* 1792. 8vo. 36079

JESUITS. Algemeyne Oprekeninge van de huyzen, collegien, seminarien ende missien der Jesuiten in alle landen. *Aelst: J. d' Herdt.* [1700.] 8vo, pp. 34. 36080

This general enumeration of the houses of the Jesuits includes the establishments in America, and is scarce.

Berichten over Asie, Afrika, en Amerika, Getrokken uit de Stigtelyke Brieven, en Reisbeschryvingen der Jesuiten, etc. *Harlingen.* 1769. 3 vols. 36081

Epistolæ Indicæ et Japanicæ de multarum gentium ad Christi fidem per Soc. Jesu conversione, item de Tartarorum potentia moribus et totius penè Asiæ religione. *Lovanii.* 1570. 8vo.

"This third edition has the advantage of an index, and rarely occurs; it contains much more than the second."—*Bibliotheca Grenvilliana.* *See* Vol. VI., No. 22704, for previous editions.

Los Jesuitas juzgadas por los padres de Familia y la prensa liberal y religiosa, o sea contestacion a los nuevos ataques de sus adversarios en Mexico. *Mexico.* 1855. 12mo, pp. 43. 36083

Los Jesuitas en Mexico, o memorias para servir a la historia del restablecimiento, destruccion y otros sucesos relativos a la compañia de Jesus, en la república mexicana, desde 1816 hasta la fecha. *Mexico.* 1850. 4to. 36084

Les Jesuites, marchands, usuriers, usurpateurs, et leurs cruautés dans l'ancien et le nouveau continent. *La Haye: Vaillant.* 1759. 12mo, pp. viii, 382, (2). C., S. 36085

Jesuita Mexicana. Memorial al rey Nuestro senor por la Provincia de la Compania de Jesus de la Nueva Espana. *Madrid.* 1652. 4to. 36086

See also Letters, Litteræ, Mémoire, Narrative, Nouvelles, Paraguay, Recueil, Relations, Travels, and other anonymous headings.

JESI (Giorgini da). *See our* Vol. VII., No. 27473, and correct the collation to read 153 leaves instead of 153 pages.

JESUS (José Manual de). Sermon Fúnebre en las Honras, que el dia 26 de Oct. 1825, hizo en sú Iglesia de México la Provincia de Carmelitas Descalzos de S. Alberto al Ill. Señor D. Fr. Bernardo del Espiritu Santo. *Mexico.* 1821. 8vo. 36087

JESUS (Raphaèl de). Castrioto Lusitano; Parte I. Enterpreza e restauração de Pernambuco, e das capitanias confinantes, varios e bellicosos successos entre portuguezes e belgas, acontecidos pelo discurso de 24 annos, e tirados de noticias, relações e memorias certas, offerecidos a João Fernandes Vieira, Castrioto Lusitano. *Lisboa, por Antonio Craesbeck de Mello.* 1679. Folio. 36088

JESUS. Castrioto Lusitano, ou historia da guerra entre o Brasil e a Hollanda, durante os annos de 1624 a 1654, terminada pela gloriosa restauração de Pernambuco e das capitanias confinantes. Obra em que se descrevem os heroicos feitos de illustre Jose Fernando Vieira. Por Fr. Raphaèl de Jesus. Nova edição, segundo a de 1679, dedicada a S. M. I. o senhor D. Pedro II, imperador do Brasil. Ornada com o retrato de João Fernandes Vieira, e duas estampas historicas. *Paris: ... João Pedro Aillaud.* 1844. 8vo, pp. xxxii, 605. 36089

JESUS MARIA (Felix de). Vida, virtudes y dones sobrenaturales de la ven. sierva de dios Sor. Maria de Jesus, Religiosa Professa en el monasterio de la Immaculada Concepcion de la Puebla

de los Angeles en las Indias Occidentales. *Roma.* 1756. 4to. + *Mexico.* 1807. 4to. 36090

JESUS MARIA (Nicolas de). El Moral mas bien enxerto, Memorias Honorificas Funebres, con que la Gratitud Religiosa de Carmelo Americano, sino desahoga sú obligacion, si manifesta sú agradecimiento â sú Benefactor Fundador en la Ciudad de Theoacan, el Señor Sacerdote D. Juan del Moral. *En la Puebla.* 1743. 8vo. 36091

JESUS MUNGUIA (C.) Sermon de Ntra Sra. de Guadalupe predicado en su insigne y nacional colegiata el 12 de Marzo de 1859, en la funcion que anualmante le hace por su turno la diocesis de Michoacan, por el illmo. Sr. Dr. Don Clemente de Jesus Munguia, obispo de Michoacan. *Mexico.* 1866. 8vo, pp. 82.

JET, *pseudon.* *See* [Tuel (J. E.)]

JETER (J. B.) A Memoir of Mrs. Henrietta Shuck, the first American Female Missionary to China. By Jeremiah B. Jeter, D.D. *Boston: Gould, Kendall & Lincoln.* 1846. 16mo, pp. 251. Portrait. C. 36093

Also: Campbellism Examined. ... *New York.* 1855. 12mo.—Campbellism Re-Examined. ... *New York.* 1856. 12mo. C.

JETER (——). The Mirror; or, a Delineation of Different Classes of Christians, [etc.] With an Introduction, by A. M. Poindexter. *Charleston (S. C.): Southern Baptist Publication Society.* 1855. 16mo, pp. 246. C. 36094

Jeu de cartes de la géographie. *Paris.* 1644. Folio. 52 Plates of Cards and a Map of the World. 36095

Thirteen of these cards relate to America.

Le Jeune voyageur. *See* [Blocquel], Vol. II., No. 5947.

JEUNESSE (A.) Géographie de l'Amérique. Par Auguste Jeunesse. *Paris: Philippart.* 1861. 16mo. 36096

JEVER (J.) Verzeichniss Allerhand Pietistischer Intriguen und Unordnungen, in Litthauen, vielen Städten Teutschlandes, Hungarn, und America: Durch Jo. Jeverum, Wiburgensem. A. C. MDCCXXIX. 8vo, pp. (2), 173. 36097

JEVONS (W. S.) A Serious Fall in the Value of Gold ascertained, and its Social Effects set forth. With Two Diagrams. By W. Stanley Jevons ... . *London: Edward Stanford.* 1863. 8vo, pp. (4), 73. B., BA., H. 36098

JEWELL (F. S.) School Government: a Practical Treatise, presenting a thorough Discussion of its Facts, Principles, and their Applications. By F. S. Jewell, A.M. *New York: A. S. Barnes & Co.* 1866. 12mo, pp. 308. 36099

JEWELL (H.) ... Opinion of Hon. Harvey Jewell ... on the Question of Order regarding Money Bills. April 21, 1868. *Boston: Wright & Potter, Printers.* 1868. 8vo, pp. 28. H.

JEWELL (J.) The Bowery Tragedy. Trial of Joseph Jewell for the Murder of Luciese Louis Leuba, with the Speeches of the Counsel, etc. *New York: R. H. Elton.* 1836. Sm. 4to, pp. 16. C. 36101

JEWELL (W.) Historical Sketches of Quarantine. ... By Wilson Jewell, M.D. *Philadelphia: T. K. and P. G. Collins, Printers.* 1857. 8vo, pp. 32. 36102

JEWELL. Sanitary, Meteorological and Mortuary Report of the Philadelphia County Medical Society, for 1855, ... accompanied with a Geological Chart ... . By Wilson Jewell, M.D. *Philadelphia: T. K. and P. G. Collins.* 1856. 8vo, pp. 64.

JEWELL. Yellow or Malignant Bilious Fever, in ... Philadelphia, 1853. ... With an Appendix. By Wilson Jewell, M.D. ... *Philadelphia: T. K. and P. G. Collins, Printers.* 1853. 8vo, pp. 40. Diagram. H. 36104

The Jewell Register, containing a List of the Descendants of Thomas Jewell of Braintree, near Boston, Mass. *Hartford: Case, Lockwood & Co.* 1860. 8vo, pp. 104. 36105

JEWETT (C.) Speeches, Poems, and Miscellaneous Writings, on Subjects connected with Temperance ... . By Charles Jewett, M.D. *Boston: John P. Jewett.* 1849. 12mo, pp. 204. Portrait.

JEWETT (C. Coffin). ... Notices of Public Libraries in the United States of America. By Charles C. Jewett. ... Appendix to the Fourth Annual Report of the Board of Regents of the Smithsonian Institution. *Washington, D. C.: For the House of Representatives.* 1851. 8vo, pp. (2), 207. B., BA., H. 36107

JEWETT. Smithsonian Report: On the Construction of Catalogues of Libraries, ... and their Publication by Means of Separate, Stereotyped Titles. With Rules and Examples. By Charles C. Jewett ... . *Washington: Smithsonian Institution.* 1852. 8vo,

pp. vi, (2), 78. + Second Edition. *Washington.* 1853. Rl. 8vo, pp. xii, 96. B., BA., C. 36108

A well written summary of all that has been done towards solving this difficult subject. Librarians and private collectors will find in it many valuable practical hints. Also: Facts and Considerations relative to Duties on Books ... . *Providence: John F. Moore, Printer.* 1843. 8vo, pp. 24. H., P. *See our* Vol. II., No. 8605.

JEWETT. In Memoriam. Charles C. Jewett. [By Reuben A. Guild.] *Providence.* 1868. 8vo. 36109

JEWETT (D. T.) A Guide to National Improvement. ... By Dyar Throop Jewett. *New London: Printed by Samuel Green.* 1833. 8vo, pp. 201, (3). 36110

JEWETT (E.) A Sketch, of the Life of Miss Ellen Jewett, who was Murdered in ... New York, ... April 9, 1836. ... *New York.* 1836. 12mo. + *Boston: For the Publisher.* 1836. 12mo, pp. 24. Portrait. 36111

JEWETT (H. O.) Biographical Sketch of the late A. B. Shipman, M.D., of Syracuse, N. Y., by ... H. O. Jewett, M.D. ... *Albany, N. Y.* 1869. 8vo, pp. 12. 36112

JEWETT (I. A.) Memorial of Samuel Appleton, of Ipswich, Massachusetts; with Genealogical Notices of some of his Descendants. Compiled by Isaac Appleton Jewett. *Boston.* MDCCCL. 8vo, pp. 183. Plates and Tables. B., BA., H. 36113

JEWETT (J.) The Necessity of Good Works | the Fruit and Evidence of Faith. | A | Sermon | Delivered at Portsmouth, in the Province of New-Hamp- | shire, December 10, 1741. | By Jedediah Jewett, A.M. | *Boston.* 1742. 8vo, pp. 27. N. 36114

Also: A Sermon ... at Newbury, ... April 18th, 1774. At the Ordination of The Reverend Mr. David Toppan ... *Newbury-Port: Printed by E. Lunt and W. H. Tinges.* MDCCLXXIV. 8vo, pp. 29, (1).—Sermon Nov. 17, 1773, at the Ordination of Jonathan Searl, at Salisbury, N. H. ... *Newbury-Port.* 1772. 8vo, pp. 31.—Sermon on the Death of Mr. George Whitefield. ... *Portsmouth, N. H.* 1771. 8vo.

JEWETT (J. L.) Franklin—his Genius, Life, and Character. An Oration delivered before the N. Y. Typographical Society ... January 17, 1849. By John L. Jewett. ... *New York: Harper & Brothers.* M.DCCC.XLIX. 8vo, pp. 37. H. 36115

JEWETT (P.) The New-England Farrier; or, a Compendium of Farriery, in Four Parts: ... By Paul Jewett ... *Newburyport: Printed by William Barrett.* MDCCXCV. 18mo, pp. 46, (2). S. + The Second Edition. *Salem: Printed by Joshua Cushing.* 1807. 18mo, pp. 45, (2). B. 36116

JEWETT (W. C.) An Appeal to the Governors and People of the Northern States of America, and Representative Vallandigham. By William Cornell Jewett; Urging an Independent State Move to restore the Constitutional Liberties of the People and State Rights, usurped by the Federal Government, and to secure a just Tribunal-Peace. [*London.* 1863.] 8vo, pp. 8. H.

JEWETT. Mediation in America. By William Cornell Jewett. [*London.* 1863.] 8vo, pp. 16. H. 36118

[JEWETT.] Mediation Position of France in connection with A Congress of Nations. [*London.* 1863.] 8vo, pp. 32. H.

Also: The Friendly American Mediation Move, of the Emperor of France, in connection with the Independent National European Visit of William Cornell Jewett, of Colorado Territory, U. S. *Portland Advertiser Print.* 1862. 8vo, pp. 7.—His Majesty Leopold I. King of the Belgians, at an audience with ... Mr. William Cornell Jewett, upon "Mediation." With Mr. Jewett's Personal Appeal. ... [n. p. n. d.] 8vo, pp. 11.—Mediation Address to England ... Containing a Communication from Count Rechberg, and Mr. Jewett's Appeals to President Lincoln and His Imperial Majesty Napoleon III. ... [*London.* 1863.] 8vo, pp. 7. H.—National Appeal, in connection with The Independent Peace Mission of William Cornell Jewett ... . [*London.* 1863.] 8vo, pp. 8.—Position of the Friendly Mediation Move of France, in connexion with the ... Mission of William Cornell Jewett to Europe. *London: Savill & Edwards.* 1863. 8vo, pp. 8.

The Jewish Chronicle. Published under the direction of the Society for meliorating the Condition of the Jews, and Edited by John Lillie. ... *New York.* 1845. Continued. S. 36120

The Jewish Intelligencer. By J. S. C. Frey. *New York.* 1837. Continued. 36121

JEWITT (J. R.) A Journal kept at Nootka Sound, by John R. Jewitt One of the surviving crew of the ship Boston of Boston, John Salter, Commander, who was massacred on 22d, March, 1803. Interspersed with some account of the Natives, their Manners and Customs. *Boston: For the Author.* 1807. 12mo, pp. 48. H. + *New York.* 1812. 16mo. W. 36122

JEWITT. Narrative of the Adventures and Sufferings, of John R. Jewitt only survivor of the crew of the Ship Boston, during a captivity of nearly three years among the Savages of Nootka Sound: with an account of the Manners, Mode of Living, and Religious Opinions of the Natives. ... *New York.* [n. d.] Plates. + *Middletown: Printed by Seth Richards.* 1815. 12mo, pp. 204. Plate. BA. + *Middletown: Printed by Loomis & Richards.* 1815. 12mo, pp. 203. 2 Plates. + [*Ibid.*] 1816. 12mo, pp. 208. 2 Plates. B. + *New York: Daniel Fanshaw.* 1816. 12mo, pp.

208. Plate. + *Wakefield* [*England*]. 1816. 12mo. + *New York.* [1816.] 12mo, pp. 166. + *Middletown.* 1820. 12mo, pp. 208. 2 Plates. + *America Printed; Edinburgh: Re-Printed.* 1824. 12mo. + *Ithaca, N. Y.* 1840. 8vo. + [*Ibid.*] 1849. 12mo, pp. 165. + [*Ibid.*] 1851. 12mo. + *New York: Printed for the Publisher.* [n. d.] 16mo. 36123

A popular book, compiled from Jewitt's "Oral Relations," by Richard Alsop. Another edition edited by S. G. Goodrich, "Peter Parley." 12mo, pp. 259. It affords us many particulars concerning the life and habits of the aborigines. A vocabulary of the Nootka language occupies four pages. A German version is included in Hulswit's "Tagebuch." *Munster.* 1828. 12mo. *See* "Hist. Mag.," III. 125, *also* Greenhow's "Oregon," p. 268, *note.*

JEWITT (L.) Grave-Mounds and their Contents: A Manual of Archaeology, as exemplified in the Burials of the Celtic, the Romano-British, and the Anglo-Saxon Periods. By Llewellynn Jewitt ... . With nearly Five Hundred Illustrations. *London: Groombridge and Sons.* 1870. 12mo, pp. xxiv. 306 Plates. BA.

[JEWSBURY (Geraldine Endsor).] The Aristocrat: an American Tale. By the Author of "Zoe," etc. *Philadelphia: Key & Biddle.* 1833. 2 vols., 16mo, pp. 260; 224. C. 36125

JEX-BLAKE (S.) A Visit to some American Schools and Colleges. By Sophia Jex-Blake. *London: Macmillan.* 1867. 12mo, pp. xii, 250. 36126

Jim Gambol; or how he went to Rondout. Done into Rhyme by one of "Em." [n. p.:] *Privately Printed.* 1858. 8vo.

JIMENEZ (J. J.) Tratado de violencias judiciales y enormidad de ministros. No. I. Por el Bachiller D. Juan Justo Jimenez. *Habana: Imprenta de Arazoza y Soler.* 1820. 4to. 36128

JIMENEZ (M. M.) Apologia de la conducto militar del General Santa-Anna en la accion de Cerro Gordo. *Mexico.* 1847. 4to, pp. 8. 36129

JIMESON (A. A.) ... A Funeral Discourse, occasioned by the Death of Sir Knight Joseph Foster. By Rev. A. A. Jimeson, M.D. ... *Covington.* 1854. 8vo, pp. 14. 36130

JINGLE (Bob), *pseudon.* *See* Vol. I., No. 2238.

JOAM IV. Andere Declaratie | Van | Iean de Vierde, | Koninck van Portugael. | Aen alle Koninghen, Potentaten en Natien des Christen- | rijcx, over haere subijte veranderinghen, in staet | van regeeringhe. | Nae de rechte Originale Copye, uyt den Portugeesch. | t'*Amsterdam, gedruckt voor Chrispijn van de Pas.* | *Anno* 1641. | *En men vintse te koop by Ian van Hilten, ende Broer Jansz.* | 4to, 9 l. 36131

Translated from the Portuguese. The original was printed at *Lisbon*, 1641.

JOAN BAPTISTA (*Fray*). Confessionario | En Lengua Mexicana y Caste | llana. ¶ Con muchas aduertencias muy necessarias | para los Confessores. ¶ Compuesto por el Padre Fray Ioan Baptista | de la orden del Seraphico Padre Sanct Francis- | co, lector de Theologia en esta prouincia del san- | cto Euangelio, y guardian del conuento de Sanc | tiago Tlatilulco. | Con priuiligio. ¶ *En Sanctiago Tlatilulco, Por Melchior | Ocharte. Año de.* 1599. 12mo, 16 p. l., 112 l., and Table. J.C.B. 36132

JOAN BAPTISTA. A Iesu Christo S. N. ofrece este Sermonario en lengua Mexicana. ¶ Su indigno sieruo Fr̃. Ioan Baptista ... . Primera Parte. ... *En Mexico, con licencia.* ¶ *En casa de Diego Lopez Daualos: y a su costa. Año* 1606. ... 4to, pp. (52), 710. 24 l. of Tables, dated 1607. Engraving. 36133

No more of this very rare work was ever published.

JOAN BAPTISTA. Libro de la Miseria y breuedad de la vida del hombre: y de sus quatro postrimerias, en lengua Mexicana. Compuesto por el Padre fray Ioã Baptista ... . Dedicado al Doctor Sanctiago del Riego, del consejo del Rey N. S. y su Oydor en esta Real Audiencia de Mexico. *En Mexico. En la emprenta de Diego Lopez Daualos, y à su costa. Año de* 1604. 8vo, 4 p. l., 2–152, 20 l. 36134

JOANNE (A.) Voyage illustré dans les cinq parties du monde, en 1846, 1847, 1848, 1849. *Paris: Aux Bureaux de l'Illustration.* 1849–50. Sm. folio. 36135

JOBSON (D. W.) The Allen Trials, viz.: Allen *versus* Hunter, Warner *versus* Griffen, Jobson *versus* Allen, and Jobson against Daniel E. Sickles. With an Appendix illustrative of Mr. Daniel E. Sickles' professional Morality. By D. Wemyss Jobson. *New York.* 1857. 8vo, pp. 58. 36136

JOBSON (F. J.) America, and American Methodism. By the Rev. Frederick J. Jobson. With a Prefatory Letter by the Rev. John Hannah, D.D. ... *London: J. S. Virtue.* 1857. Post 8vo, pp. xvi, 399. Illustrations. B., BA., C., H. 36137

JOCELIN (S.) Chorister's Companion; containing the Rules of Psalmody, and a Collection of Psalm Tunes. By Simeon Jocelin. Second Edition. *New Haven.* 1788. 8vo. + Supplement. [*Ibid.*] 1792. 36138

JOCELYN (G. B.) An Address ... before the Grand Lodge of Iowa ... June 9, 1859, By Rev. Bro. Geo. B. Jocelyn ... . 1859. 8vo, pp. 19. 36139

JOCELYN. Manual of the Templars of Honor and Temperance, By Rev. G. B. Jocelyn, D.D. With a History of the Order, by J. Wadsworth, M.D., etc. *New York: J. N. Stearns.* 1869. 12mo, pp. 286. 36140

JOCKEY CLUB. *New York.* 1793. *See* [Pigot (Charles)].

JOERG (E.) Briefe aus den Vereinigten Staaten von Nord-Amerika. Von ***. *Leipzig.* 1853. 2 vols., 16mo. 36141

Joernael. *See* Ioernael, No. 34968.

JOGUES (I.) Narrative of a Captivity among The Mohawk Indians, a description of New Netherland in 1642–3, and other Papers. By Father Isaac Jogues, of the Society of Jesus. With a Memoir of the Author, by John Gilmary Shea. *New York: Edward Dunigan & Brother.* 1856. 8vo, pp. 69. + [*Ibid.*] 1857.

Some copies have the imprint: *New York: Press of the Historical Society*, 1856. "A most astonishing relation of the persistent cruelties of a savage race. They afford us the most intimate, as they do the most authentic account of the character of the Mohawks, of which we are now cognizant."—FIELD.

JOGUES. Novum Belgium, Description de Nieuw Netherland et Notice sur René Goupil. Par le R. P. Isaac Jogues, de la Compagnie de Jésus. *A New York, dans l'Ancien Nieuw Netherland, Presse Cramoisy de J. M. Shea.* 1862. 8vo, pp. 5–44. Map.

Of this and the following one hundred copies only were printed. Also on large paper. Forms No. XVI. of Shea's "Cramoisy Series."

JOGUES. Novum Belgium: An Account of New Netherland in 1643–4. By Rev. Father Isaac Jogues ... . With a Facsimile of his Original Manuscript his Portrait a Map and Notes, by John Gilmary Shea. *New York: Privately Printed.* 1862. 4to, pp. (2), 53, (1). 4 leaves of Facsimile, 2 Portraits, Map and View. B., H. 36144

Edited, for the first time, from the Jesuit manuscript narrative dated 1646. Dr. Shea regards this as the only account of so early a date, which is erroneous; *see* Michaelius (J.)

John Beedle's Sleigh-Ride, Courtship and Marriage. *New York.* 1844. 12mo. 36145

Attributed to Captain Maclintoch, but probably by J. Neal.

John Bull in America. *See* [Paulding (J. K.)]

John Hopkins' Notions on Political Economy. *Boston.* 1833. 8vo. 36146

John Smith's Letters, with 'Picters' to Match. Containing Reasons why John Smith should not change his Name; Miss Derby Smith's Juvenile Spirit; together with the only Authentic History extant of the late War in our Disputed Territory. *New-York: Samuel Colman.* 1839. 12mo, pp. 139. 36147

John the Painter. *See* Hill (James), Vol. VIII., Nos. 31833–41.

John, the Traitor; or, the Force of Accident. A Plain Story. By one who has Whistled at the Plough. *New York.* 1843. 8vo.

Relates to John Tyler.

JOHNES (A. J.) Philological Proofs of the Original Unity and Recent Origin of the Human Race, derived from a Comparison of the Languages of Asia, Europe, Africa, and America ... . By Arthur James Johnes, Esq. *London: Samuel Clarke.* 1843. 8vo, pp. lx, 172, 105. C., P. 36149

Printed at the suggestion of Dr. Prichard, to whose work it will be found a useful supplement. Reproduced with a new title-page only.

JOHNS (E.) ... Sermon ... at Long Meadows, on the 13th of April, 1815, the day appointed for a National Thanksgiving. By Evan Johns ... . *Springfield.* 1815. 8vo. N. 36150

JOHNS. ... A Thanksgiving Sermon, Preached ... the 24th of November 1803. By Evan Johns ... . *Hartford: Printed by Hudson and Goodwin.* 1804. 8vo, pp. 15. BA. 36151

Also: A Sermon ... at Northampton ... March 31, 1812. ... *Northampton, Mass.* 1812. 8vo, pp. 22. M.

JOHNS (H. T.) Life with the Forty-Ninth Massachusetts Volunteers. By Henry T. Johns ... . *Pittsfield, Mass.: For the Author.* 1864. 12mo, pp. 391. 14 Plates. BA., C. 36152

JOHNS (H. V. D.) ... Sermon ... before The New-York Bible Society, ... May 6th, 1855 ... . By Rev. H. V. D. Johns, D.D. ... *New-York: Collins, Bowne & Co.* 1855. 8vo, pp. 21.

JOHNS (J.) A Narrative of the Life and Sufferings of Mrs. Jane Johns, who was barbarously Wounded and Scalped by Seminole Indians, in East Florida. ... *Charleston: Printed by Burke & Giles.* 1837. 8vo, pp. 29, and cover. + *Baltimore: Lucas & Deaver.* 1837. 8vo, pp. 24. C. 36154

[JOHNS (John).] Address of the Board of Trustees of the Protestant Episcopal Theological Seminary of Maryland, to The Members of the Church in This Diocess. *Georgetown, D. C.: James C. Dunn, Printer.* 1822. 8vo, pp. 25. 36155

JOHNS. An Address delivered in St. Paul's Church, Richmond, on the Fourth of January 1848, on the Occasion of the Funeral of Mrs. Sarah Coles Stevenson ... . By the Right Rev. J. Johns, D.D. *Richmond: Printed by Shepherd and Colin.* 1848. 8vo, pp. 20. H. 36156

JOHNS. A Memorial of the Life of the Right Rev. William Meade, D.D., Bishop of Virginia. By the Right Rev. J. Johns, D.D. With a Memorial Sermon by Rev. W. Sparrow, D.D. *Baltimore: Innes & Co.* 1867. 12mo, pp. vi, 537. 2 Portraits.

Also: An Address delivered before the American Whig and Cliosophic Societies of the College of New Jersey, September 29, 1840. ... *Princeton: Printed by John Bogart.* 1840. 8vo, pp. 26.—Address ... Richmond, on the Occasion of the Funeral of ... Rev. William Meade, D.D., March 17th, 1862. *Baltimore: Entz & Bash.* 1862. 8vo, pp. 14. + *Richmond: Macfarlane & Fergusson, Printers.* 1862. 8vo, pp. 8. H.—A Valedictory Discourse: ... Baltimore, October 3, 1842. ... *Baltimore: N. Hickman.* 1842. 8vo, pp. 26. S.

JOHNS (K.) Speech of Kensley Johns, Jr., of Delaware, on the Indian Bill, in the House ... May, 1830. *Washington.* 1830. 8vo, pp. 19. 36158

JOHNSON (A. B.) The Advanced Value of Gold, Suspended Specie Payments, Legal-Tender Notes, Taxation, and National Debt, investigated impartially: By A. B. Johnson. *Utica, N. Y.: Curtiss & White.* 1862. 8vo, pp. 32. B., H., S. 36159

JOHNSON. A Guide to the Right Understanding of our American Union: or Political, Economical, and Literary Miscellanies. By A. B. Johnson ... . *New York: Derby & Jackson.* 1857. 12mo, pp. 407. B. 36160

JOHNSON. The Philosophical Emperor: a Political Experiment; or the Progress of a False Position, dedicated to the Whigs, Conservatives, Democrats and Locofocos. By A. B. Johnson. *New-York.* 1841. 18mo. S. 36161

JOHNSON. A Treatise on Banking. The Duties of a Banker, and his Personal Requisites therefor: By A. B. Johnson. ... *Utica: Seward & Thurber.* 1850. 8vo, pp. 44. H. 36162

Treats incidentally and considerably of New York banks. Also: An Address to the Utica Forum ... December 9, 1824. ... *Utica: Printed by William Williams.* 1824. 8vo, pp. 16.—Address to the Utica Temperance Society, delivered July 29, 1829. ... *Utica.* [1829.] 8vo, pp. 16.— ... Address ... before the Utica Lyceum on the Fifth Day of February, 1824. ... *Utica: Printed by H. Gray.* 1824. 8vo, pp. 13. B.—An Address to the Utica Lyceum, ... February 17, 1825. ... *Utica: Printed by Merrell & Hastings.* 1825. 8vo, pp. 16.—The Approaching Presidential Election. ... Respectfully inscribed to the Chicago Convention. Utica, August 18, 1864. [n. p. n. d.] 8vo, pp. 9. H.—An Inquiry into the Nature of Value and of Capital, and into the Operation of Government Loans, Banking Institutions, and Private Credit. ... *New-York: For the Author.* 1813. 8vo, pp. (8), 117.—An Oration, Commemorative of American Independence, ... at Utica, July 5, 1824. ... *Utica: Printed by William Williams.* 1824. 8vo, pp. 16.—Our Monetary Condition. ... [n. p. 186–.] 8vo, pp. 21.—Speech before an Auxiliary of the American Colonization Society. Utica January 13, 1834. ... *Utica: Press of William Williams.* [n. d.] 8vo, pp. 16. H.—On the Political Contest, 1834.—Speech on United States Bank. ... *Utica.* 1834.—Thoughts on ... the approaching State Convention. ... *Utica.* 1846. 12mo. S.

JOHNSON. Obituary Notices of Alexander Bryan Johnson, who was Born in England, May 29, 1786, and Died at his Home in Utica, Sept. 9, 1867. *Utica.* 1868. 8vo. S. 36163

JOHNSON (A.) A Sermon ... at New Gloucester, February 10th, 1802, at the Ordination of Elisha Mosely ... . By Alfred Johnson ... . *Portland: E. A. Jenks.* 1802. 8vo, pp. 39. BA.

JOHNSON (A.) Eulogy at Belfast, Me., on John Adams and Thomas Jefferson, Aug. 10, 1826. By Alfred Johnson, Jr. *Belfast.* [n. d.] 8vo. W. 36165

Also: ... An Address ... before the Washingtonian Societies of Belfast. February 22, 1843. ... *Belfast: Charles Giles ... Printer.* 1843. 8vo, pp. 16. B., H.

JOHNSON (A. G.) A Chapter of History, or the Progress of Judicial Usurpation. By A. G. Johnson. *Troy, N. Y.* 1863. 8vo, pp. 63. H., S. 36166

[JOHNSON.] Special Report on the Present State of Education in the United States and other Countries, and on Compulsory Instruction. By V. M. Rice. *Albany: Van Benthuysen & Sons.* 1867. 8vo, pp. 253. C. 36167

The preface states distinctly that Johnson is the compiler of the Report.

JOHNSON (A.) Mensaje del Presidente Andres Johnson al Congreso de los Estados Unidos. *Buenos Aires: Imprenta del Siglo, Victoria.* 1866. 8vo, pp. 32. B. 36168

See also Message of the President.

JOHNSON. Speech of Hon. Andrew Johnson, of Tennessee, on the Proposed Expulsion of Mr. Bright; ... in the Senate ... January 31, 1862. *Washington.* 1862. 8vo, pp. 15. B. 36169

JOHNSON. Speeches of Andrew Johnson, President of the United States. With a Biographical Introduction. By Frank Moore. *Boston: Little, Brown, and Company.* 1865. 12mo, pp. xlviii, 494. Portrait. B., BA., H. 36170

Also: The Constitutionality and Rightfulness of Secession. Speech ... in the Senate ... December 18 and 19, 1860. ... [n. p. n. d.] 8vo, pp. 23.—Invasion of Harper's Ferry. Speech ... in the Senate ... December 12, 1859 ... . [*Washington.* n. d.] 8vo, pp. 16.—Speech ... April 29, 1852, on the Homestead Bill. ... [n. p. n. d.] 8vo.—Speech ... on the State of the Union; ... In the Senate of the United States, February 5, and 6, 1861. *Washington.* 1861. 8vo, pp. 28.—Speech ... in Reply to Senator Lane, of Oregon, March 2, 1861. *Washington.* 1861. 8vo, pp. 8.—Speech ... on the War for the Union: ... In the Senate ... July 27, 1861. *Washington.* 1861. 8vo, pp. 20. B., H.

The following pieces relate to Johnson:

Congress and the President; or, who has hindered Reconstruction? December, 1867. [n. p. 1867.] 8vo, pp. 8. H. 36171

The Great Impeachment and Trial of Andrew Johnson, President of the United States. With the Whole of the Preliminary Proceedings in the House of Representatives, and in the Senate of the United States. Together with the Eleven Articles of Impeachment, and the Whole of the Proceedings in the Court of Impeachment ... . *Philadelphia: T. B. Peterson & Brothers.* 1868. 8vo, pp. 9–289. B. 36172

Also: The Impeachment of Andrew Johnson. His Suspension from Office while on Trial. Gen. Grant to succeed, &c., &c. [n. p. n. d.] 8vo, pp. 8.—Impeachment and Trial of Andrew Johnson. *Philadelphia: Barclay & Co.* [n. d.] 8vo, pp. 122.

Life and Speeches of Andrew Johnson, President of the United States. Edited by Frank Moore. *Boston: Little, Brown & Co.* 1865. 12mo, pp. xlviii, 493. 36173

Life and Speeches of President Andrew Johnson. Embracing his Early History, Political Career, Speeches, Proclamations, etc. With a Sketch of the Secession Movement, and his Course in relation thereto; also his Policy as President of the United States. By C. Bacon. *London: Bacon & Co.* [1865?] 12mo, pp. v, 137. Portrait. 36174

Life, Speeches and Services of Andrew Johnson, Seventeenth President of the United States. ... *Philadelphia: T. B. Peterson & Brothers.* [1865.] 12mo, pp. 15–214. Portrait. BA. 36175

Life and Times of Andrew Johnson, Seventeenth President of the United States. Written from a National Stand-point By a National Man. ... *New York: D. Appleton and Company.* 1866. 12mo, pp. xii, 363. B. 36176

The President [Johnson]: His Assailants, and his Policy. 1867. [*Baltimore.* 1867.] 8vo, pp. 4. 36177

Proceedings in the Trial of Andrew Johnson, President of the United States, before the United States Senate, on Articles of Impeachment exhibited by the House of Representatives; with an Appendix. *Washington: F. & J. Rives & George A. Bailey.* 1868. 8vo, pp. 1090, 50, xxviii. 36178

Supplement to the Congressional Globe: containing the Proceedings of the Senate sitting for the Trial of Andrew Johnson, President of the United States. ... *Washington City: F. & J. Rives & George A. Bailey.* 1868. 4to, pp. xiv, 526. B. 36179

Testimony taken ... in the Investigation of the Charges against Andrew Johnson. *Washington.* 1867. 8vo. S. 36180

39th Cong., 2d Sess., and 40th Cong., 1st Sess., 1867.

Trial of Andrew Johnson, President of the United States, before the Senate of the United States, on Impeachment by the House of Representatives, for High Crimes and Misdemeanors. Published by order of the Senate. ... *Washington.* 1868. 3 vols., 8vo, pp. (2), xxii, 741; (2), xxii, 498; (2), xxii, 401. B. 36181

Also: Mass Meeting of Citizens of New York to approve the Principles announced in the Message of Andrew Johnson. *New York.* 1866. 8vo.—Moses; or, The Man who Supposes himself to be Moses, no Moses at All. *New York.* 1866. 8vo. *See* [Isherwood (B. F.)], Proceedings of a Called Meeting, *and* sundry Speeches and Documents issued by the National Johnson Club, 1865, etc.

JOHNSON'S New Illustrated Family Atlas ... with Descriptions Geographical, Statistical, and Historical. ... Text by Richard Swainson Fisher, M.D. ... Compiled, drawn, and engraved under the supervision of J. H. Colton and A. J. Johnson. *New York.* 1862. Folio. C. + *New York.* 1864. Folio. + *New York: A. J. Johnson.* 1866. Folio, pp. (2), 134, (1). Maps. 36182

[JOHNSON (Anna C.)] The Iroquois; or, the Bright Side of Indian Character. By Minnie Myrtle. *New York: D. Appleton and Company.* 1855. 12mo, pp. 317. 8 Plates. H. 36183

Legendary, historical, and biographical. The author lived among the Senecas for several months. Some copies have the name of *Mason Brothers* as publishers.

JOHNSON (B. P.) Report of Benjamin P. Johnson, as Agent of the State of New-York, to attend the Exhibition of the Industry of all Nations, 1851. *Albany.* 1852. 8vo. A., S.

See also Windham Centre.

JOHNSON (B. R.) Speech of Hon. B. R. Johnson, on the Personal Liberty Bill. In Assembly, March 14, 1860. [n. p. n. d.] 8vo, pp. 4. H. 36185

Also: Remarks ... on ... "An Act for the Trial of certain Offenders," Feb. 28, 1859. ... [n. p. n. d.] 8vo, pp. 4.—Memorials of Benjamin P. Johnson and Herman Ten Eyck Foster. *Albany.* 1870. 8vo.

JOHNSON (C.) Oration on the late Treaty with France. By which Louisiana was Acquired: Delivered in Staunton on the Third of March, 1804. By Chapman Johnson, Esq. ... *Staunton: Printed by Ira Woodruff.* [n. d.] 16mo, pp. 20. 36186

JOHNSON (C.) A General History of the Robberies and Murders Of the most notorious Pyrates, and also Their Policies, Discipline, and Government, From their first Rise and Settlement in the Island of Providence, in 1717, to the present Year 1724. With The remarkable Actions and Adventures of the two Female Pyrates, Mary Read and Anne Bonny. To which is prefix'd An Account of the famous Captain Avery and his Companions; with the Manner of his Death in England. The Whole digested into the following Chapters; Chap. I. Of Captain Avery. II. The Rise of Pyrates. III. Of Captain Martel. IV. Of Captain Bonnet. V. Of Captain Thatch. VI. Of Captain Vane. VII. Of Captain Rackam. VIII. Of Captain England. IX. Of Captain Davis. X. Of Captain Roberts. XI. Of Captain Worley. XII. Of Captain Lowther. XIII. Of Captain Low. XIV. Of Captain Evans. And their several Crews. To which is added, A short Abstract of the Statute and Civil Law, in Relation to Pyracy. By Captain Charles Johnson. *London: Ch. Rivington.* 1724. 8vo, pp. (22), 17–320. 3 Plates. J.C.B.

An appropriate sequel to Exquemelin's "History of the Buccaniers." Thomas' "History of Printing," quotes an edition, *New York: Printed by Wm. Bradford.* 1723. + Second Edition. [*Ibid.*] 1724.

JOHNSON. A General History of the Pyrates, from their first Rise and Settlement in the Island of Providence, to the present Time. With the remarkable Actions and Adventures of the two Female Pyrates Mary Read and Anne Bonney; Contained in the following chapters. Introduction. I. Of Capt. Avery. II. Of Capt. Martel. III. Of Capt. Teach. IV. Of Capt. Bonnet. V. Of Capt. England. VI. Of Capt. Vane. VII. Of Capt.

Rackam. VIII. Of Capt. Davis. IX. Of Capt. Roberts. X. Of Capt. Anstis. XI. Of Capt. Worley. XII. Of Capt. Lowther. XIII. Of Capt. Low. XIV. Of Capt. Evans. XV. Of Capt. Phillips. XVI. Of Capt. Spriggs. And their several Crews. To which is added a short Abstract on the Statute and Civil Law in Relation to Pyracy. The Second Edition, with considerable Additions. By Captain Charles Johnson. *London: T. Warner.* 1724. 8vo, pp. (20), 17–427. 3 Plates. C. + Third Edition. [*Ibid.*] 1725. 8vo. 36188

This rare work embodies many items relating to the Colonial History of British America, nowhere else extant, as, the Adventures of Blackbeard, and his Capture by Lieut. Maynard in the James River, Va., Life and Career of Captain Kyd, &c.

JOHNSON. A General History of the Pyrates [nearly the same title as the foregoing]. *Dublin: J. Walt.* MDCCXXV. 12mo, pp. (8), 248. 36189

JOHNSON. A General History of the Pyrates ... The Fourth Edition. With the remarkable Actions and Adventures of the two Female Pyrates Mary Read and Anne Bonny; to which is added a short Abstract of the Statute and Civil Law, in Relation to Pyracy. *London: T. Woodward.* 1726. 2 vols., 8vo, pp. 438; 413. + [*Ibid.*] 1727. 36190

JOHNSON. The History of the Pirates, containing the Lives of Those Noted Pirate Captains, Misson, Bowen, Kidd ... who were ... executed at Nassau, New-Providence ... the 12th of October, 1718. ... By Captain Charles Johnson. ... *London, Printed. Norwich: Re-Printed by R. Hubbard.* 1814. 12mo, pp. 288. B.

JOHNSON. Histoire des Pirates Anglois depuis leur Établissement dans l'Ile de la Providence jusqu'à présent, contenant toutes leurs Avantures, Pirateries, Meurtres, Cruautéz et Excès, avec la Vie & les Avantures des deux Femmes Pirates Marie Read et Anne Bonny. Et un Extrait des Loix et des Ordonnances concernant la Piraterie. Traduite de l'Anglois du Capitaine Charles Johnson. *Utrecht: Jaques Broedelet.* 1725. 12mo, pp. 315. + *Londres: J. Walter.* 1726. 12mo, pp. lvj, 382, (2). + *Trévoux: par la Compagnie.* 1744. 16mo, pp. lvi, 360, (8). C. 36192

This last also forms Vol. IV. of Exquemelin's "Histoire des avanturiers filibustiers."

JOHNSON. Historie der Engelsche Zee-Roovers beginnende met de geschiedenisse van Capit. Avery in 1692, waar by gevoegd is het leeven van Mary Read en Anne Bonny, twee zeeroovende vrouwen. Uit het Engelsch overgezet d. R. Hennebo. *Amsterdam: H. Uytwerf.* 1725. 2 vols., 8vo. Plates. 36193

JOHNSON. A General History of the Lives and Adventures of the most famous Highwaymen, Murderers, Street Robbers, &c.; To which is added, A Genuine Account of the Voyages and Plunders of the most Notorious Pyrates. Interspersed with several diverting Tales, and pleasant Songs, And Adorned with the Heads of the most remarkable Villains ... . By Capt. Charles Johnson. ... *London: Printed by J. Janeway.* M.DCC.XXXIV. Folio, pp. (2), 484, (2). 17 Plates. C., H. 36194

Very scarce, and is seldom found in good condition. Interesting to the American collector, as some of their exploits were in this country. The following is the same edition with a new title-page and some additional plates:

JOHNSON. A General History of the Lives and Adventures of the most famous Highwaymen, Murderers, Street Robbers, &c. From the famous Sir John Falstaff in the Reign of King Henry IV. 1399 to 1733: To which is added a Genuine Account of the Voyages and Plunders of the most notorious Pyrates. Interspersed with diverting Tales, and pleasant Songs. And adorned with six and twenty large Copper Plates, engraved by the best Masters. By Capt. Charles Johnson. *London: Olive Payne.* MDCCXXXVI. Rl. Folio, pp. (2), 484, (2). 26 Plates.

[JOHNSON.] A History of the Lives and Exploits of the most remarkable Pirates, Highwaymen, Murderers, Street Robbers, &c. Interspersed with several Tales and pleasant Songs. Adorned with Effigies of the most notorious Offenders curiously engraven on Copper. *Birmingham: T. Aris.* 1742. Folio, pp. (2), 373, (2).

Contains the Lives of the Filibusters and Pirates. This edition is abridged, and without the author's name.

JOHNSON. Lives and Actions of the most famous Highwaymen, Street-Robbers, and the Voyages and Plunders of the most noted Pirates. *Edinburgh.* 1814. Post 8vo. + *Norwich.* 1814. 12mo, pp. 288. 36197

JOHNSON (C. B.) Letters from the British Settlement in Pennsylvania, To which are added, the Constitutions of the United States, and of Pennsylvania; and Extracts from the Laws respecting Aliens and Naturalized Citizens. By C. B. Johnson, M.D. *Philadelphia: H. Hall* ... 1819. 18mo, pp. xii, 25–192. Map. BA. + A New Edition. ... *London: John Souter.* 1820. 18mo, pp. 175. Map. 36198

Rich, Vol. II., p. 119, says "Written by Dr. Rose."

JOHNSON. Letters from North America ... By C. B. Johnson, M.D. A New Edition. *Philadelphia.* 1821. 12mo, pp. xii, 185.

This is a reissue of the edition of 1819 with a new title-page.

JOHNSON (C. P.) ... Speech of Charles P. Johnson ... upon the Bill to provide for the Calling of a Convention, delivered December 15th, 1863 ... . [n. p. n. d.] 8vo, pp. 24. 36200

JOHNSON (C. W.) The Farmer's Encyclopædia, and Dictionary of Rural Affairs; ... By Cuthbert W. Johnson ... . Adapted to the United States. *Philadelphia: Carey and Hart.* 1844. 8vo, pp. vii, 1165. 17 Plates. + Adapted ... by Governor Emerson. *Philadelphia.* 1851. 8vo. B., BA., C. 36201

JOHNSON (E.) Short Account of a North West Voyage made in 1796–7–8. By Ebenezer Johnson. 1798. 8vo. W. 36202

[JOHNSON (Edward).] A | History | of | New-England. | From the English planting in the Yeere | 1628. untill the Yeere 1652. | Declaring the form of their Government, | Civill, Military, and Ecclesiastique. Their Wars with | the Indians, their Troubles with the Gortonists, | and other Heretiques. Their manner of gathering | of Churches, the commodities of the Country, | and description of the principall Towns | and Havens, with the great encou- | ragements to increase Trade | betwixt them and Old | England. | With the names of all their Gouvernours, Magistrates, | and eminent Ministers. | *London,* | *Printed for Nath: Brooke at the Angel* | *in Corn-hill.* 1654. | 4to, pp. (4), 236, (4). BA., C., H.

Better known by its running title of "Wonder-working Providence." There are copies with a different title-page, entitled by "T. H.," and the dedication to all copies is so signed. It is a very rare, curious, and highly interesting volume. It was regarded so very good that it was stolen bodily by one of the "Gorges," and forms a part of "America Painted to the Life" by that enterprising firm. The author had "a most intolerable itch for versifying, celebrating many of his characters in quaint metre." The following is in honor of Gov. Endecot:

"Strong, valiant John, wilt thou march on, and take up station first,
Christ call'd hath thee, his souldier be, and fail not of thy trust;
Wilderness wants, Christ's Grace supplants, then plant his churches pure,
With tongues gifted, and graces led, help thou to his procure;"

and a lot more in the same Tupperian strain. It appeared at the same time with the title changed as below:

[JOHNSON.] Historical Relation of the first planting of the English in New-England in the year 1628 to the year 1653, and all the materiall passages happening there Exactly performed. ... By T. H. [*London:*] *Printed for Nathaniel Brooke, and sold at his Shop at the Angel in Cornhill.* 1654. 4to, pp. (4), 236, (4).

It was reprinted in the "Mass. Hist. Soc. Coll.," Second Series, Vols. II., III., IV., VII., VIII.; and again reprinted as below:

JOHNSON. Wonder-Working Providence of Sions Saviour in New England. ... [Second title: A History of New-England

From the English planting in the Yeere 1628. untill the Yeere 1652. ... *London: Nath: Brooke.* 1654. Reprinted] with an Historical Introduction and an Index by William Frederick Poole ... . *Andover: Warren F. Draper.* 1867. Sm. 4to, pp. (8), cliv, (6), 265. Facsimile. B., BA. 36205

Of this edition two hundred and fifty copies were printed, fifty of which were on large paper.

JOHNSON (E. F.) The Navigation of the Lakes and Navigable Communications therefrom to the Seaboard and to the Mississippi River ... . By Edwin F. Johnson ... . *Hartford: Press of Case, Lockwood & Company.* 1866. 8vo, pp. 48. B., H. 36206

JOHNSON. Railroad to the Pacific. Northern Route. Its General Character, Relative Merits, &c. By Edwin F. Johnson, C.E. Second Edition. *New York.* 1854. 8vo, pp. 166. 3 Maps. B., C., H. 36207

See Northern Pacific Railroad Company.

JOHNSON (E. M.) Toleration: A Discourse ... in ... Brooklyn, on Thanksgiving day, December 10, 1835. By Evan M. Johnson ... . *New-York.* M DCCC XXXV. 8vo, pp. 16. 36208

JOHNSON. ... A Discourse delivered in St. John's Church, Brooklyn, February 24th, 1839 ... . With Explanatory Notes. By Evan M. Johnson, Rector. *New-York: Louis Sherman.* 1839. 8vo, pp. 32. 36209

JOHNSON (E. R.) Emancipation Oration, By Dr. Ezra R. Johnson, and Poem, By James M. Whitfield, ... January 1, 1867 ... Fourth Anniversary of President Lincoln's Proclamation of Emancipation. 1864. *San Francisco: Elevator Office.* 1867. 8vo, pp. 32. C., H. 36210

JOHNSON (F.) Speech [on J. Q. Adams' Administration. n. p. n. d.] 8vo, pp. 32. B. 36211

Also: Speech ... on the change of the Newspapers in which the Laws are directed to be published. ... *Washington.* 1827. 8vo.

JOHNSON (F. H.) Every Man his own Guide at Niagara Falls ... By F. H. Johnson ... . *Buffalo: Phinney & Co.* [1852.] 18mo, pp. 142. Map. + *Rochester: D. M. Dewey.* [1852.] 18mo, pp. 144. Map. B., BA. 36212

JOHNSON. Guide to Niagara Falls and its Scenery, including all the points of Interest both on the American and Canadian Side. Geology and Recession of the Falls, by Sir Charles Lyell. ... By F. H. Johnson ... . [n. p. 1868.] 18mo, pp. 80.

JOHNSON. Statistics of Niagara Falls, and Vicinity. By F. H. Johnson ... . *Buffalo: E. A. Maynard & Co., Printers.* 1848. 12mo, pp. 21, (2). BA. 36214

JOHNSON (G. W.) Maple Leaves. By George Washington Johnson. *Hamilton, U. C.* 1864. 12mo, pp. 204. 36215

JOHNSON (H. C. R.) A Long Vacation in the Argentine Alps; or where to settle in the River Plate States. By H. C. Ross Johnson. *London: Richard Bentley.* 1868. Map. 36216

JOHNSON (H. Margaret). Poems. By Helen M. Johnson. ... *Boston: J. V. Hines.* 1855. 12mo, pp. 249. H. 36217

Some of the poems are on Canadian subjects.

JOHNSON (H.) The Banners of a Free People set up in the name of their God. A Thanksgiving Sermon ... Nov. 24, 1864. By Rev. Herrick Johnson. *Pittsburgh: W. S. Haven.* 1864. 8vo, pp. 34. 36218

JOHNSON. "God's Ways Unsearchable." A Discourse, on the Death of President Lincoln, ... Pittsburgh, Pa. ... April 23d, 1865. By Rev. Herrick Johnson ... . *Pittsburgh: W. G. Johnston & Co., Printers.* [1865.] 8vo, pp. 11. B. 36219

Also: The Nation's Duty: A Thanksgiving Sermon, preached in the Third Presbyterian Church, Pittsburgh, ... November 27, 1862. ... *Pittsburgh: W. S. Haven.* 1862. 8vo, pp. 26. H.—The Shaking of the Nations. A Sermon preached ... September 11th, 1864. *Pittsburgh: W. S. Haven.* 1864. 8vo, pp. 27.

JOHNSON (H.) Sergeant Slasher; or the Border Feud. A Romance of the Tennessee Mountains. By Herrick Johnson. *New York: American News Company.* 1865. 8vo, pp. 41.

JOHNSON (H. S.) A Discourse ... Funeral of ... Silas Wright, Late Governor ... . By Rev. H. S. Johnson. *Albany: Printed by Charles Van Benthuysen.* 1848. 8vo, pp. 24. 36220a

JOHNSON (H. V.) The War with Mexico. Speech ... Senate, 1848. [n. p. 1848.] 8vo, pp. 16. S. 36221

JOHNSON (J.) Sermon at the Funeral of Col. Christopher Avery, of Groton, Conn. *New London.* 1767. 12mo, pp. 36.

[JOHNSON] (J.) A Sermon ... before the Incorporated Society for the Propagation of the Gospel in Foreign Parts; at their Anniversary ... February 24, 1758. By ... James, Lord Bishop of Glocester. *London: A. Millar.* MDCCLVIII. 4to, pp. 77. N.

JOHNSON (J.) The Influence of Tropical Climates on European Constitutions. To which is added Tropical Hygiene; or

the Preservation of Health in all Hot Climates ... . By James Johnson ... . Second Edition ... . *London: For the Author.* 1818. 8vo, pp. viii, 464. 36224

JOHNSON. The Influence of Tropical Climates ... on European Constitutions; [being a treatise on the principal diseases incidental to Europeans in the East and West Indies] ... . By James Johnson, M.D. ... *London: J. Callow.* 1815. 8vo, pp. xv, (1), 534. B. + From the Third London Edition. *Philadelphia.* 1824. 2 vols., 12mo. S. + Greatly enlarged. *New-York: Evert Duyckinck.* 1826. 8vo, pp. 416. + Fifth Edition. *London.* 1836. 8vo. C. 36225

JOHNSON. De invloed der keerkrings-luchtstreken op Europesche gestellen. Met aanteek. en aanhangsel van J. M. Daum. *Amsterdam.* 1824. 2 vols., 8vo. S. 36226

Vol. II. relates to the West Indies.

JOHNSON (J.) Warden's Report of the Trial of James Johnson ... for the Murder of Lewis Robinson; also of John Sinclair, for the Murder of David Hill. *New York.* 1811. 8vo, pp. 36.

JOHNSON (J.) Documents in relation to The Claim of James Johnson for transportation on the Missouri and Mississippi Rivers. March 1, 1821. ... *Washington: Printed by Gales & Seaton.* 1821. 8vo, pp. 293. 36228

JOHNSON (J.) Oration ... on the Centennial Anniversary of George Washington's Birth. By James Johnson. *Baltimore: Printed by Richard J. Matchett.* 1835. 8vo, pp. 11. BA. 36229

JOHNSON (James). *See* [Livermore (George)].

JOHNSON (J. A.) Chinese Immigration. Speech of Hon. James A. Johnson ... January 25, 1870. [n. p. n. d.] 8vo, pp. 8. H. 36230

JOHNSON (J. E.) An Analytical Abridgment of Kent's Commentaries on American Law. With a full Series of Questions ... By J. E. Johnson. *New York.* 1839. 8vo. 36231

JOHNSON (Jesse Z.) The Young Student: or, Literary Remains of J. Zimmerman Johnson, with a Brief Sketch of his Life, by his Father. Edited by J. Newton Brown, D.D. *Philadelphia: J. A. Wagenseller.* 1865. 16mo, pp. 192. Portrait. C.

JOHNSON (J.) A Short Account of Ann Rogers, By John Johnson. *Philadelphia.* 1794. P. 36233

JOHNSON (J.) The Rape of Bethesda; or the Georgian Orphan House Destroyed. A Poem, By John Johnson. *Charleston, S. C.* MDCCXCII. 12mo, pp. 16. W. 36234

JOHNSON (J.) An Interesting Correspondence between the Rev. John Johnson ... and Miss Elizabeth Jones ... . Second Edition. *Philadelphia.* 1817. 8vo, pp. 41. + *New-York: Printed by Charles N. Baldwin.* 1817. 8vo, pp. 43. BA., H. 36235

JOHNSON (J.) The Life and Confession of John Johnson, the Murderer of James Murray, with some Particulars of his Family. *New York: Brown & Tyrell.* 1824. 8vo, pp. 26. 36236

JOHNSON (J.) A Defence of Republicanism. By John Johnson ... . An Address ... before the Kansas City Republican Club on the 15th ... of September, 1860. ... [*Kansas City, Mo.* n. d.] 8vo, pp. 15. H. 36237

JOHNSON (J. B.) The Dealings of God with Israel and America. A Discourse delivered on the 4th July, 1798. By John B. Johnson. *Albany.* 1798. 8vo, pp. 21. N. 36238

JOHNSON. Eulogy on General George Washington. A Sermon, delivered February 22d, 1800, in ... Albany, before the Legislature of the State of New-York ... . By John B. Johnson, One of the Chaplains of the House of Assembly ... . *Albany: Printed by L. Andrews* ... 1800. 8vo, pp. 22. BA. 36239

JOHNSON. A Farewell Sermon, delivered September 26th, 1802, in the North Dutch Church, Albany By John B. Johnson ... . *Albany: Printed by Charles R. and George Webster.* 1802. 8vo, pp. 96. BA., H. 36240

JOHNSON. An Oration on Union, delivered ... on the Twelfth of May, 1794. The Anniversary of the Tammany Society, or Columbian Order. By John B. Johnson. ... *New-York: Printed by John Buel.* MDCCXCIV. 8vo, pp. 24. N. 36241

[JOHNSON (J. G.)] A Criticism of Mr. Wm. B. Reed's Aspersions on the Character of Dr. Benjamin Rush, with an Incidental Consideration of General Joseph Reed's Character. By a Member of the Philadelphia Bar. ... *Philadelphia: Collins, Printer.* 1867. 8vo, pp. 61. H. 36242

JOHNSON (J. H.) A Funeral Sermon on Mrs. Clark. By John H. Johnson. *Cobourg.* 1853. 36243

Also: Inaugural Address as Principal of the Belleville Seminary. ... *Hamilton.* 1857.

JOHNSON (J. I.) Reflections on Political Society, Oration before the Tammany Society. By John I. Johnson. *New York.* 1797. 12mo. 36244

JOHNSON (J.) Traditions and Reminiscences chiefly of the American Revolution in the South: including Biographical Sketches, Incidents and Anecdotes, few of which have been published, Particularly of Residents in the Upper Country. By Joseph Johnson, M.D., of Charleston, S. C. *Charleston, S. C.: Walker & James.* 1851. 8vo, pp. viii, 592. Map and Plans. B.

A highly interesting and rather scarce book. Also: Address to the Literary and Philosophical Society of South-Carolina. ... *Charleston.* 1822. 4to.—An Oration ... before the Medical Society of South Carolina ... Dec. 24th, 1807. ... *Charleston: Marchant, Willington and Co.* 1808. 8vo, pp. 24. 2 Diagrams. BA.

JOHNSON (J. B.) Fears and Hopes for the Nation. A Sermon ... February 22, 1863. By Rev. Joseph B. Johnson. ... *Boston: Wright & Potter, Printers.* 1863. 8vo, pp. 24. B.

Also: Minority Report of the Committee on Elections on the Petition of J. P. Johnson, "claiming the Seat of A. H. Garland." [n. p. n. d.] 8vo, pp. 4. B.

JOHNSON (L.) Botanical Teacher for North America: in which are described the Indigenous ... Plants, growing north of the Gulf of Mexico. By Laura Johnson: ... *Albany: Oliver Steele.* 1834. 12mo, pp. 268. H. 36247

JOHNSON (L.) An Elementary Arithmetic. ... By L. Johnson, A.M. ... *Raleigh: Branson & Farrar.* 1864. 16mo, pp. 154.

Specimen brick: "If 1 Confederate soldier can whip 7 Yankees, how many soldiers can whip 49 Yankees?" Also: Common School Arithmetic.

[JOHNSON (Lorenzo D.)] A Boston Merchant of 1745; or, Incidents in the Life of James Gibson, a Gentleman Volunteer at the Expedition to Louisburg; with a Journal of that Siege, never before published in this Country. By One of his Descendants. *Boston: Redding and Company.* 1847. 12mo, pp. 102.

JOHNSON. Chaplains of the General Government, with Objections to their Employment Considered. Also, a List of all the Chaplains to Congress, in the Army and in the Navy, from the formation of the Government to this Time. By Lorenzo D. Johnson. ... *New-York: Sheldon, Blakeman & Co.* 1856. 8vo, pp. 82. C., H. 36250

JOHNSON. The Churches and Pastors of Washington, D. C.; together with five hundred topics of Sermons, delivered in 1855 '6. To which is added, a list of all the church-edifices, and their localities. By Lorenzo D. Johnson ... . *New York: M. W. Dodd.* 1857. 12mo, pp. v, 171. C., H. 36251

JOHNSON. Martha Washingtonianism, or A History of the Ladies' Temperance Benevolent Societies. By Lorenzo D. Johnson. *New York: Saxton & Miles.* 1843. 18mo, pp. 88.

JOHNSON. Memoir of Mrs. Thomazin Johnson, of Braintree, Mass. with an account of her Pious Lineage, from John Alden, the first Pilgrim Father who placed foot on Plymouth Rock. By her Son, Lorenzo D. Johnson. *Boston: J. Loring.* 1835. 24mo, pp. 117. C. 36253

JOHNSON. The Spirit of Roger Williams, with a Portrait of One of his Descendants. ... By Lorenzo D. Johnson. *Boston: Cassady and March.* 1839. 8vo, pp. 94. BA., H. 36254

JOHNSON (L.) Every Lady her own Flower Gardener. By Louisa Johnson. Containing ... Directions for cultivating Plants ... in the Northern and Southern States. ... *Charleston: S. Babcock & Co.* 1842. 12mo, pp. 142. B. 36255

JOHNSON (L. H.) Sin of Slavery. A Discourse ... in ... Rockford, Ill., July 15th, 1860. By ... Lyman H. Johnson. ... *New York: John P. Prall, Printer.* 1860. 8vo, pp. 24. H.

JOHNSON (*Mrs.*) *See* Johnson (Susannah).

JOHNSON & CASEY. Reports on the Bear Mountain Rail Road, by Johnson & Casey, Civil Engineers; and on the Coal and Iron Ores of the Bear Valley Coal Basin, by James Hall ... *New York: Privately Printed.* 1845. 8vo, pp. 88. Maps.

JOHNSON (O.) An Address ... in Middlebury, by Request of the Vermont Anti-Slavery Society ... February 18, 1835. By Oliver Johnson. *Montpelier: Knapp and Jewett, Printers.* 1835. 8vo, pp. 32. B. 36258

JOHNSON. Correspondence between Oliver Johnson and George F. White. With an Appendix. *New York: Oliver Johnson.* 1841. 12mo, pp. 48. 36259

JOHNSON (O.), *and* WINTER (W. H.) Route across the Rocky Mountains, with a Description of Oregon and California. By Overton Johnson and William H. Winter. *Lafayette (Ind.): J. B. Semans.* 1846. 8vo, pp. 152. C. 36260

JOHNSON (R.) An Argument to establish the illegality of Military Commissions in the United States, and especially of the one organized for the Trial of the Parties charged with Conspiring to Assassinate the Late President, and others, presented ... 19th of June, 1865, ... by Reverdy Johnson, one of the Counsel of Mrs. Surratt. *Baltimore: Printed by John Murphy & Co.* 1865. 8vo, pp. 31. H. 36261

JOHNSON. A Brave Soldier, ... defended ... . Reply of Hon. Reverdy Johnson, to the Paper which Judge-Advocate Holt furnished to the President, urging General Porter's Condemnation. [n. p. n. d.] 8vo, pp. 56. B., H. 36262

In "Hand-Book of the Democracy," 1863–64, No. 13.

[JOHNSON.] The Dangerous Condition of the Country, the Causes which have led to it, and the Duty of the People. By a Marylander. *Baltimore.* 1867. 8vo, pp. 24. B., H. 36263

In some copies the title reads *lead* instead of led.

[JOHNSON.] A Further Consideration of The Dangerous Condition of the Country, the Causes which have lead [*sic*] to it ... . *Baltimore.* 1867. 8vo, pp. 21. 36264

JOHNSON. The Memorial of Reverdy Johnson to the Legislature of Maryland, praying indemnity for the destruction of his property in the City of Baltimore, by a Mob, in August, 1835. [n. p. n. d.] 8vo, pp. 19. + *Annapolis: William McMeir, Printer.* 1836. 8vo, pp. 18. + With an Appendix. *Baltimore.* 1840. 8vo, pp. 20, 46. 36265

[JOHNSON.] Remarks on Popular Sovereignty, as maintained and denied respectively by Judge Douglass, and Attorney General Black. By a Southern Citizen. *Baltimore: Murphy & Co.* 1855. 8vo, pp. 48. + [Another Edition. *Ibid.*] 8vo, pp. 40. 36266

JOHNSON. A Reply to the Review of Judge Advocate General Holt, of the Proceedings, Findings and Sentence, of the General Court Martial, in the case of Major General Fitz John Porter, and a Vindication of that Officer, By Reverdy Johnson. *Baltimore: Printed by John Murphy & Co.* 1863. 8vo, pp. 88. + Second Revised Edition. [*Ibid.*] 1863. 8vo, pp. 88. BA.

Included in the "Hand-Book of the Democracy," 1863–64. It elicited the following: "A Reply to the Hon. Reverdy Johnson's Attack on the Administration in the case of Fitz John Porter, convicted of shameful Misbehaviour before the Enemy." *Baltimore: Sherwood & Co.* 1863. 8vo, pp. 19.

JOHNSON. Report of Reverdy Johnson, as Commissioner of the United States, in New Orleans; transmitted by the President of the United States to the Senate, under a Resolution of December 15, 1862. [n. p. n. d.] 8vo, pp. 64. 36268

37th Cong., 3d Sess., Exec. Doc., No. 16.

[JOHNSON.] Riparian Rights on the Potomac.

Also: Defence of Capt. W. K. Latimer ... before Court of Enquiry, No. 3. *Washington.* 1857. 12mo.—Opinion ... on the Rights ... of the Union Pacific R. R. Co. 1868. [n. p. 1868.] 8vo.—Opinion ... on the ... Capitation Tax on the Washington Branch Road of the Baltimore and Ohio Railroad Company. *Baltimore.* 1870. 8vo, pp. 10. H.—Opinion ... on the Question of the Constitutionality of the State Tax on Passengers over the Washington Branch Road of the Baltimore & Ohio Railroad. *Baltimore.* [1870.] 8vo, pp. 12.—Railroads in New Jersey. ... Speech ... January 19, 1865; ... [*Washington, D. C.: Gibson Brothers, Printers.* n. d.] 8vo, pp. 16. H.—Remarks ... in the Case of the Heirs of Gen. Thadeus Kosciusko, and Major G. Tochman, April, 1848. *Washington.* 1848. 8vo, pp. (2), 8. C.—Speech ... on the Tariff. Delivered in the Senate ... July 25, 1846. *Washington: Printed by John T. Towers.* 1846. 8vo, pp. 24. H.—Speech ... on ... the Three Million Bill. ... In the Senate ... February 6, 1847. [n. p. n. d.] 8vo, pp. 16.—Speech ... April 10, 13, 1848, on Extent of Executive Power. [n. p. n. d.] 8vo, pp. 16.—Speech ... on the Abolition of Slavery. *Washington.* 1840. 8vo.—Speech ... in the Senate ... July 10, 1848. ... [On] the bill to establish a Territorial Government in Oregon ... . [n. p. n. d.] 8vo, pp. 16.—Speech ... on the Proposed Compromise Bill. ... In the Senate ... July 17, 1848. *Washington: Printed by John T. Towers.* 1848. 8vo, pp. 14.—Speech ... on the Ten Regiment Bill. Delivered in the Senate ... January 10, and 11, 1848. [n. p. n. d.] 8vo, pp. 16. BA.—Speech ... before the Political Friends of Hon. Stephen A. Douglas, ... in ... Boston ... June 7, 1860. *Baltimore: Printed by John Murphy & Co.* 1860. 8vo, pp. 16.—Speech ... in Support of the Resolution to Amend the Constitution so far as to Abolish Slavery. Delivered in the Senate ... April 5, 1864. [*Washington.* 1864.] 8vo, pp. 24. + [*Ibid.*] 8vo, pp. 22. B.—Abänderung der Constitution in Hinblick auf die Abschaffung der Sklaverei. Rede des ... Reverdy Johnson ... Im Senate ... 5 April 1864. [*Washington.* n. d.] 8vo, pp. 8.—Speech ... in Reply to the Speech of Senator Drake ... to censure the President; ... December 12, 1867. *Washington.* 1867. 8vo, pp. 16. H.—Speech ... before the Brooklyn McLellan Central Association, October 21, 1864. [n. p. n. d.] 8vo, pp. 15.—Speech ... on Organization of Provisional Governments within the States whose People were lately in Rebellion against the United States; ... in the Senate ... January 11, 1866. *Washington.* 1866. 8vo, pp. 15.—Speech ... on the Questions connected with the Condition of the Country, ... at Towsontown, ... November 3d, 1866. *Baltimore.* 1866. 8vo, pp. 32.—Speeches ... on the Military Reconstruction Bill. ... In the Senate ... February 20 and March 2, 1867. *Washington.* 1867. 8vo, pp. 10. B.

JOHNSON *and* GILLETTE (R. H.) Review of the Proceedings of the Court of Enquiry on Colonel S. D. Miles' Case. By Reverdy Johnson and R. H. Gillette. [n. p. n. d.] 8vo, pp. 62.

[JOHNSON *and* GLENN (John).] Reply to a Pamphlet entitled, "A Brief Exposition of Matters relating to the Bank of Maryland," with an Examination into some of the Causes of the Bankruptcy of that Institution. *Baltimore: Printed by Jas. Lucas & E. K. Deaver.* 1834. 8vo, pp. 54, Correspondence, 51. B.

[JOHNSON *and* GLENN.] A Final Reply to the Libels of E. Poulteney, late President of the Bank of Maryland, and a further Examination of the Causes of the failure of that Institution [with an Appendix of Letters]. *Baltimore.* 1835. 8vo, pp. 27.

JOHNSON. Letter to Hon. Reverdy Johnson, on the Proceedings of the Meeting held at the Maryland Institute, January 10, 1861. [n. p. n. d.] 8vo. 36273

JOHNSON (R. Mentor.) Authentic Biography of Col. Richard M. Johnson, of Kentucky. *New York: Henry Mason.* 1833. 12mo, pp. 107. + *Boston: For the Proprietor.* 1834. 12mo, pp. 93. BA. 36274

JOHNSON. A Biographical Sketch of Col. Richard M. Johnson, of Kentucky. By a Kentuckian. *New York: Saxton & Miles.* 1843. 8vo, pp. 46. 36275

This gentleman has the credit (?) of having killed Tecumseh. This book tells the story, also that of the Battle of Tippecanoe. Asahel Langworthy is the supposed author.

JOHNSON. Liberia as it Is. R. M. Johnson, to the Colored Citizens of the American Republic. *Philadelphia: Brown.* 1853. 8vo, pp. 16. 36276

[JOHNSON.] Report on Stopping the United States Mail, and closing the Post-offices on Sundays, January 19, 1829. [n. p. n. d.] 8vo, pp. 4. 36277

20th Cong., 2d Sess., Sen. Doc., No. 46.

JOHNSON. Review of a Report of the Committee, to whom was referred the several Petitions on the subject of Mails on the Sabbath, ... January, 16, 1829, By the Hon. Mr. Johnson, of Kentucky. ... [*Boston.*] 1829. 8vo, pp. 27. 36278

Also: The Logic and Law of Col. Johnson's Report on Sabbath Mails, 1829. [n. p. n. d.] 8vo.—Speech ... on the Bank Bill, Jan. 22, 1811. [n. p. n. d.] 8vo, pp. 14.—Speech ... on a Proposition to Abolish Imprisonment for Debt. ... January 14, 1823. *Boston.* 1823. 8vo, pp. 23, (1).—Speech ... on the Public Lands, March 30, 1830. *Washington.* 1830. 8vo.—Speech ... on California. [n. p. n. d.] 8vo.—Sunday Mails. Mr. Johnson's Report on the Transportation of the Mail on Sunday. *Boston: Henry Bowen.* 1829. 24mo, pp. 12. BA.

JOHNSON (——). Dangers and Duties. Reconstruction and Suffrage. Speech in the House of Representatives, Indianapolis, Ind., November 17, 1865. *Cincinnati: Gazette Office.* 1865. 8vo, pp. 16. 36279

JOHNSON. Suffrage in the District of Columbia. Speech in the House of Representatives, January 16, 1865. [n. p. 1865.] 8vo, pp. 8. 36280

JOHNSON (R. G.) An Historical Account of the First Settlement of Salem, in West Jersey, by John Fenwick, Esq. ... With many of the important events ... down to the present generation, embracing a period of one hundred and fifty years. By R. G. Johnson. *Philadelphia: Orwin Rogers.* 1839. 18mo, pp. 173.

[JOHNSON (Robert).] Historicall Description of the most famous Kingdomes and Commonweales in the worlde, translated into Englishe, with an addition of the relation of Saxony, Geneva, Hungary, and Spaine. *London: John Jaggard.* 1603. Sq. 8vo.

Reprinted in 1608, with one chapter on America.

[JOHNSON.] Relations,|of the most Fa-|movs Kingdoms and| Common-Weales tho-|rovgh the World. Discoursing of their Scituations, Man-|ners, Customes, Strengthes|and Policies. Translated into English ... . *London: Iohn Iaggard.* 1610. 4to, pp. (4), 437. + [*Ibid.*] 1611. 4to, pp. (4), 437. C. + Enlarged according to moderne Observation. [*Ibid.*] 1616. 4to. + *Reprinted, London.* 1630. 36283

There are very considerable alterations and additions in the edition of 1616, including an article of fourteen pages on America, which is not in the edition of 1603. In describing Virginia, it says, "Tobacco now begins to be so base and low prized that it is scarcely worth the costs and labour of bringing." This book is commonly ascribed to Johnson, but it appears to be due to some foreign author.

[JOHNSON.] Nova Britannia.|Offring Most|Excellent fruites by Planting in|Virginia.|Exciting all such as be well affected|to further the same.|*London*|*Printed for Samvel Macham, and are to be sold at*|*his Shop in Pauls Church-yard, at the*|*Signe of the Bul-head.* 1609. 4to, 18 l. 36284

A very scarce book. I have seen a copy in which the third word in the title-page is spelt "Offering." Reprinted with a prefatory note, by Dr. F. L. Hawks, under the following title:

[JOHNSON.] Nova Britannia. Offering most excellent Fruits by Planting in Virginia. Exciting all such as be well affected to further the same. *New York: J. Sabin.* 1867. 4to, 2 p. l., 18 l.

[JOHNSON.] The New Life of Virginea: declaring the former Svccesse and present Estate of that Plantation, being the Second Part of Noua Britannia. Published by the Authoritie of his Maiesties Counsell of Virginia. *London: W. Welby.* 1612. 4to, 27 l.

[JOHNSON.] The Traveller's Breviat, or an Historical Description of the most Famous Kingdomes in the World, relating their Situation, Manners, Customes, and Civil Government, and other Memorable Matters. *London.* 1601. 4to. 36287

This first edition of *our* No. 36282, *supra*, is not mentioned by Lowndes.

JOHNSON (Robert W.) Address to Citizens of Arkansas, Jan. 29, 1850. *Washington.* 1850. 8vo. 36288

JOHNSON. Speech of Mr. Johnson of Arkansas, in the C. S. Senate, February 9th, 1864, on the Bill to limit and define the Terms of Office of the ... Heads of Departments. *Richmond: James E. Goode, Printer.* 1864. 8vo, pp. 19. BA. 36289

JOHNSON (R. V.) Poems, by Rosa Vertuer Johnson. *Boston: Ticknor & Fields.* 1847. 12mo, pp. 334. 36290

[JOHNSON (Samuel).] Elementa Philosophica:|Containing chiefly,|Noetica,|Or Things relating to the|Mind or Understanding:|and|Ethica,|Or Things relating to the|Moral Behaviour.| *Philadelphia:*|*Printed by B. Franklin, and D. Hall, at the*|*New-Printing-Office, near the Market.* 1752.| 8vo, pp. (2), xxiv, 103; vii, (1), 103. Table and Errata, 2 l. H. 36291

This is the general title-page to "Noetica" and "Ethica," which were also issued separately as below:

[JOHNSON.] Noetica:|Or the First Principles of|Human Knowledge.|Being a|Logick,|Including both|Metaphysics and Dialectic,|Or the Art of Reasoning.|With a brief Pathology, and an Account of the|gradual Progress of the Human Mind, from|the first Dawnings of Sense to the highest|Perfection, both Intellectual and Moral, of|which it is capable.|To which is prefixed,|A Short Introduction|To the|Study of the Sciences.|...|*Philadelphia:*| *Printed by B. Franklin, and D. Hall,* ... 1752.| 8vo, pp. xxiv, 103.

[JOHNSON.] Ethica:|Or the First Principles of|Moral Philosophy;|And especially that Part which is called|Ethics.|In a Chain of necessary Consequences|from certain Facts.|... The Second Edition.|*Philadelphia:*|*Printed by B. Franklin, and D. Hall,* ... 1752.| 8vo, pp. vii, (1), 103. H. 36293

The first edition appeared at *New Haven,* 1744.

[JOHNSON.] Ethices Elementa. Or the First Principles of Moral Philosophy. And Especially That Part of it which is called Ethics. ... By Aristocles. *Boston: Printed by Rogers and Fowle.* MDCCXLVI. 4to, pp. 70. BA. 36294

JOHNSON. A Sermon concerning The Obligations We are under to Love and Delight in the Public Worship of God. Preached in Christ's-Church at Stratford ... on the opening of that Church, July the 8th 1744. ... By Samuel Johnson ... . *Boston: Printed by Rogers and Fowle.* 1746. 8vo, pp. 46. BA.

For other works by this author *see* Stevens' "Nuggets," Nos. 1553–55.

[JOHNSON (Samuel), *LL.D.*] Aningait & Ajutt: a Greenland Tale. Inscribed to Samuel Johnson, A.M. Taken from the Fourth Volume of his Rambler. Versified by a Lady. *London: Dodsley.* 1760. 4to. 36295*a*

See "M. Rev.," XXIV. 315.

[JOHNSON.] The False Alarm. *London: T. Cadell.* MDCCLXX. 8vo, pp. 53. BA. + Second Edition. [*Ibid.*] pp. 53. H.

This elicited the following: "The Constitution defended, and Pensioner exposed; in Remarks on the False Alarm." ... *London: E. and C. Dilly ... and J. Ridley.* M.DCC.LXX. 8vo, pp. (2), 31. Also: A Letter to Samuel Johnson, LL.D. ... [*London:*] *J. Almon.* 1770. 8vo, pp. 54—this latter is a severe refutation of the "ministerial rhapsody."

[JOHNSON.] Hypocrisy Unmasked; Or, A Short Inquiry into the Religious Complaints of our American Colonies. To which is added, A Word on the Laws against Popery in Great Britain and Ireland. *London: W. Nicoll.* MDCCLXXVI. 12mo, pp. 24. + Second Edition. [*Ibid.*] + Third Edition. [*Ibid.*] 36297

The object of the author seems to be to defend the Quebec Bill, which protects the Canadians in the exercise of the Roman Catholic religion. The American Colonies classed this bill among their grievances. The author of the tract in question shows that many of the colonies extended the same rights to Roman Catholics that the Quebec Bill did to the Canadians.

[JOHNSON.] The Life of Mr. Richard Savage ... . The Fourth Edition. To which are added, The Lives of Sir Francis Drake, and Admiral Blake. ... *London: Printed for F. Newberry.* M.DCC.LXIX. 12mo, pp. ii, 298, (2). 36298

[JOHNSON.] Miscellaneous and Fugitive Pieces. *London: T. Davies.* MDCCLXXIV. 3 vols., 12mo. 36299

[JOHNSON.] Papers Relative to the Late Negotiation with Spain; and the Taking of Falkland's Islands From the English. *London: J. Almon.* M DCC LXXVII. 4to, pp. 34; 5–48. H. + Second Edition. [*Ibid.*] 4to, pp. 34; 5–48. 36300

See "M. Rev.," XLIV. 261.

[JOHNSON.] The Patriot. Addressed to the Electors of Great Britain. ... *London: T. Cadell.* MDCCLXXIV. 8vo, pp. (2), 33. BA. + The Second Edition. [*Ibid.*] + The Third Edition. [*Ibid.*] MDCCLXXV. H. + *Dublin: E. Lynch.* MDCCLXXV. 8vo, pp. 17. 36301

See "M. Rev.," LI. 298. This elicited: "Remarks on the Patriot. Including some hints respecting the Americans: with an Address to the Electors of Great Britain." *London: Richardson and Urquhart.* MDCCLXXV. 8vo, pp. (2), 46.

[JOHNSON.] Political Tracts. Containing, The False Alarm,

Falkland's Islands, The Patriot; and Taxation no Tyranny. *London: W. Strahan.* MDCCLXXVI. 8vo, pp. 264. 36302

See "M. Rev.," LV. 73. Also forms Vol. XII. of Johnson's Works, edited by Murphy —*London.* 1823. 12 vols., 8vo—and is usually found in other collected editions of his works.

[JOHNSON.] Taxation no Tyranny; an Answer to the Resolutions and Address of the American Congress. *London: T. Cadell.* MDCCLXXV. 8vo, pp. (2), 91. + The Second Edition. [*Ibid.*] + The Third Edition. [*Ibid.*] pp. (4), 91. B., BA., H. + The Fourth Edition. [*Ibid.*] pp. (4), 91. C. 36303

"This tract claims its importance from the celebrity of its author. It was written in the sixty-sixth year of his age, when he was at the meridian of his fame. Bancroft describes it at length as an exemplification of the tone of public sentiment then prevailing in England. It called forth several replies, each of which is aimed at pointing out the fallacy that lurks in its title as well as in all its reasonings."—J. R. BARTLETT. *See* "M. Rev.," LII. 446, 548; LIII. 574, *also* McCulloch's "Literature of Political Economy," p. 89.

The following are some of the replies:

An Appendix to a Letter to Dr. Shebbeare. To which are added some Observations on a Pamphlet intitled, "Taxation no Tyranny;" in which the Sophistry of that Author's Reasoning is detected. By a Doctor of Law. *London: J. Donaldson.* 1775. 8vo. 36304

A Letter to Dr. Samuel Johnson, occasioned by his late Political Publications, with an Appendix, containing some Observations on a Pamphlet lately published by Dr. Shebbeare. *London: Towers.* 1775. 8vo. N., P. 36305

See "M. Rev.," LII. 184.

The Pamphlet, entitled, "Taxation no Tyranny," candidly considered, and it's Arguments, and Pernicious Doctrines, Exposed and Refuted. *London: W. Davis and T. Evans.* [1775.] 8vo, pp. (2), 131. BA., H. 36306

Resistance No Rebellion: in Answer to Dr. Johnson's "Taxation no Tyranny." *London: J. Bell.* MDCCLXXV. 8vo, pp. (4), 35. 36307

"This reply, 'by way of parody,' appears to be in general well conducted, and capable of affording much entertainment, with some information."—*Monthly Review*, LII. 450.

Taxation, Tyranny. Addressed to Samuel Johnson, LL.D. *London: J. Bew.* 1775. 8vo, pp. 80. 36308

"The style and argument of this performance deserves commendation, but in some cases the author appears not to be well acquainted with facts in regard to the dispute."—*Monthly Review*, LII. 449.

Tyranny Unmasked. An Answer to a Late Pamphlet, entitled Taxation no Tyranny. ... *London: For the Author.* MDCCLXXV. 8vo, pp. (2), 90. B., BA., H., M., P. 36309

"This pamphlet contains many very harsh, and some very just strictures on the doctrines and tenets advanced by Dr. Johnson, whose pamphlet has been honoured with unmerited notice."—*Monthly Review*, LII. 448. *See also* our Vol. I., No. 1657; Vol. V., No. 19254, *and* "Plain English."

[JOHNSON.] Thoughts | on the | Late Transactions | respecting | Falkland's Islands. *London: T. Cadell.* MDCCLXXI. 8vo, pp. (4), 75. + The Second Edition. [*Ibid.*] BA. + *New York: Hugh Gaine.* 1771. 8vo, pp. 48. + *Dublin.* 1771. 8vo, pp. 42. + *London.* 1814. 8vo. 36310

See "M. Rev.," XLIV. 330.

[JOHNSON.] Pensées sur les transactions touchant les isles de Falkland. Traduit de l'Anglais d'après la seconde édition. *Amsterdam.* 1771. 8vo. 36311

This piece was answered by:

A Refutation Of a Pamphlet, called Thoughts on the late Transactions respecting Falkland's Islands; in a Letter Addressed to the Author, and dedicated to Dr. Samuel Johnson. *London: T. Evans.* M.DC.LXXI [*sic*]. 8vo, pp. (4), 22. H.

The date should read M.DCC.LXXI. *See* "M. Rev.," XLIV. 416.

JOHNSON (S.) The Crisis of Freedom. A Sermon ... at ... Lynn ... June 11, 1854. By Samuel Johnson. ... *Boston: Crosby, Nichols & Co.* 1854. 8vo, pp. 21. B. 36313

JOHNSON. A Discourse preached on the Day of the National Funeral of President Lincoln, ... April 19, 1865. By Samuel Johnson ... . [n. p. n. d.] 8vo. 36314

Printed on one side of the paper only. Not published.

JOHNSON (S. B.) Letters from Chili. By Samuel B. Johnson, Lieutenant U. S. Navy. 1810. 36315

Title from Allibone.

JOHNSON (S. M.) The Dual Revolutions. Anti-Slavery and Pro-Slavery. By S. M. Johnson. *Baltimore: Printed by W. M. Innes.* 1863. 8vo, pp. 48. 36316

JOHNSON. Free Government in England and America: containing the Great Charter, ... the Federal Constitution. By S. M. Johnson. *New York: Carleton.* MDCCCLXIV. 8vo, pp. 576.

[JOHNSON.] A Letter to the President about the title to Yerba-Buena Island, Bay of San Francisco ... . *Washington City: M'Gill & Witherow, Printers.* 1870. 8vo, pp. 10, 4. 36318

[JOHNSON.] The "Southern Rights," and "Union" Parties in Maryland Contrasted. *Baltimore: Printed by W. M. Innes.* 1863. 8vo, pp. 30. 36319

JOHNSON (S. R.) California: A Sermon ... in ... Brooklyn, N. Y. ... February 11, 1849. By Samuel Roosevelt Johnson, D.D. ... *New-York: Stanford and Swords.* 1849. 8vo, pp. 19, (1).

JOHNSON. A Memorial Discourse on The Life, Character and Services of General Jeremiah Johnson, of Brooklyn, The First President of the St. Nicholas Society of Nassau Island ... . By Samuel Roosevelt Johnson, D.D. ... *Brooklyn: I. Van Anden's Press.* 1854. 8vo, pp. 34. Portrait. B., H. 36321

Also: ... A Sermon ... in ... New Albany, Indiana; at the Ordination of the Rev. Andrew Wylie, D.D., President of Indiana University ... 1841. ... *Lafayette: Printed by John B. Semans.* 1842. 8vo, pp. 14. B.—A Sermon ... at the Funeral of Jasper Bradley ... May 11th, 1847 ... . *Lafayette: John Rosser, Printer.* 1847. 12mo, pp. 13.—A Sermon ... in ... Brooklyn, New York, on Thanksgiving Day ... Nov. 25, 1844. ... *Brooklyn: Printed by L. Van Anden.* 1847. 8vo, pp. 10.—A Sermon ... In Memory of Mrs. Adaline Haskins ... A.D. 1848 ... . [n. p. n. d.] 8vo, pp. 21–32. — ... The Sermon at the Consecration of St. John's Church, Lafayette, Indiana. ... July 29, 1858. ... *Lafayette, Indiana: Luse & Wilson, Printers.* 1858. 8vo, pp. 19.—A Sermon commemorative of the Life ... of the Rev. Samuel H. Turner, D.D. ... New York, October 8th, 1862. ... *New York: Printed by Edward O. Jenkins.* 1863. 8vo, pp. 40. H.

JOHNSON (S.) ... A Sermon, Preached before the General Assembly of the Colony of Connecticut, at Hartford, on the Day of their Anniversary Election, May 10th, 1770. By Stephen Johnson, A.M. ... *New-London: Printed by Timothy Green*, ... M,DCC,LXX. 4to, pp. 39. 36322

[JOHNSON.] Some Important Observations occasioned by, and adapted to the Publick Fast, Dec. 18, 1765. Sermon at Newport, R. I. *Newport.* 1766. 4to, pp. 61. 36323

JOHNSON (Susannah). A Narrative of the Captivity of Mrs. Johnson Containing An Account of her Sufferings during Four Years with the Indians and French. Published according to Act of Congress. *Printed at Walpole, Newhampshire, by David Carlisle, Jun.* 1796. 18mo, pp. 144. C., W. 36324

JOHNSON. The Captive American, or a Narrative of the Sufferings of Mrs. Johnson during Four Years Captivity with the Indians and French. Written by herself. ... *Newcastle: M. Angus.* 1797. 18mo, pp. 72. 36325

JOHNSON. The Captive American; containing an Account of the Sufferings of M^rs^. Johnson, during four years with the Indians and French. The author, Mrs. Johnson, now Mrs. Hastings, is still living in Charlestown, Newhampshire, and first published her Narrative at Walpole in Newhampshire, in the year 1796.—The sufferings she met with during her captivity, she bore with a degree of magnanimity that will astonish the reader while he peruses the following pages. *Air: Printed by J. and P. Wilson.* 1802. 12mo, pp. 24. C. 36326

JOHNSON. A Narrative of the Captivity of Mrs. Johnson. Containing An Account of her Sufferings, during Four Years, with the Indians and French. ... Second Edition, Corrected and Enlarged. *Windsor (Vt.): Printed by Alden Spooner.* 1807. 12mo, pp. 144. + Together with an Appendix; containing the Sermons preached at her Funeral, ... with sundry other Interesting Articles. Third Edition Corrected, and Considerably Enlarged. *Windsor (Vt.): Thomas M. Pomroy.* 1814. 12mo, pp. 178. C. + Fourth Edition. *Lowell: Daniel Bixby.* MDCCCXXXIV. 18mo, pp. 150. BA., C. + *New York.* 1841. 18mo. S. 36327

One of the most interesting of all the Indian captivities. She was captured at Charlestown, New Hampshire, in 1754, carried through what is now Vermont to Canada where she resided several years, and returned to New Hampshire by the way of England and New York. Included in Farmer and Moore's "Collection," Vol. I.

JOHNSON (T. T.) Sights in the Gold Region, and Scenes by the Way. By Theodore T. Johnson. *New York: Baker & Scribner.* 1849. 12mo, pp. xii, 278. + Second Edition, Revised and Enlarged. [*Ibid.*] 1850. 12mo, pp. 324. C. 36328

JOHNSON. California and Oregon; or, Sights in the Gold Region, and Scenes by the Way. By Theodore T. Johnson. ... Fourth Edition. ... *Philadelphia: Lippincott, Grambo & Co.* 1851. 12mo, pp. xii, 348. B. 36329

It was reproduced as: "California and Oregon, ... with an Appendix containing full Instructions to Emigrants by the Overland Route to Oregon, by Hon. Samuel R. Thurston." *Philadelphia.* 1857. 12mo. The latest edition has the same title as No. 36329, with the imprint, *Philadelphia: J. B. Lippincott & Co.* 1865. It relates to the massacre of the Oregon party of white men by Indians, and the horrible revenge taken by the miners upon a tribe entirely innocent of the offense.

JOHNSON (T. C.) Cotton Lands the Best Permanent Investment for Capital, and Alabama one of the best ... . By Thos. C. Johnson ... . *Montgomery, Ala.* 1865. 8vo, pp. 15. Map. H.

JOHNSON (T. W.) A Brief History of ... the Temperance Reform; with Historical Facts ... . By T. W. Johnson. *Glen's Falls: M. & T. J. Strong.* 1845. 8vo, pp. 56. 36331

JOHNSON (W. Rogers). The Coal Trade of British America, with Researches on the Characters and Practical Values of American and Foreign Coals. By Walter R. Johnson ... . *Washington: Taylor & Maury; Philadelphia: A. Hart.* 1850. 8vo, pp. 179.

JOHNSON. A Memoir of the late Lewis David von Schweinitz, P.D. With a Sketch of his Scientific Labours. ... By Walter R. Johnson. ... *Philadelphia: Printed by William P. Gibbons.* 1835. 8vo, pp. 38, (1). Portrait. B. 36333

JOHNSON. A Report to the Navy Department of the United States, on American Coals, applicable to Steam Navigation, and to Other Purposes. By Walter R. Johnson. *Washington: Printed by Gales & Seaton.* 1844. 8vo, pp. v, 607. 3 Plates. B. + *Washington: Blair and Rives, Printers.* 1844. 8vo, pp. xii, iv, 607. 3 Plates. BA. 36334

Also: Address ... on laying the Corner Stone of the Academy of Natural Sciences of Philadelphia; May 25th, 1839. ... *Philadelphia: ... T. K. & P. G. Collins.* 1839. 8vo, pp. 8.—Analysis of some of the ... Iron Ores found on the Head Waters of Beaver Creek, in the Counties of Luzerne, Northampton and Schuylkill, Pa. ... [n. p. n. d.] 8vo, pp. 10.—Comparison of Experiments on American and Foreign Building Stones to determine their Relative Strength and Durability. ... *New Haven: Printed by B. L. Hamlen.* 1850. 8vo, pp. 19.—Examination of "Remarks," on a Second College in Connecticut. ... 1825. 8vo.—Examination of some of the Anthracites found in Sugar Loaf Township, Luzerne County, Pennsylvania. ... [n. p. n. d.] 8vo, pp. 5.—A Lecture on the Mechanical Industry and the Inventive Genuis of America ... . *Baltimore: Printed by Sands and Mills.* 1849. 8vo, pp. 23.—Observations on the Improvement of Seminaries of Learning in the United States; with Suggestions for its Accomplishment. ... *Philadelphia: E. Littell.* 1825. 8vo, pp. 28.—An Oration ... at Germantown, Pennsylvania, on the 20th July, 1826 ... to commemorate ... Thomas Jefferson and John Adams. ... *Philadelphia: Robert H. Small.* 1826. 8vo, pp. 25.—Report ... of the Mines, Iron Works ... Clearfield Coke and Iron Company ... . *Philadelphia: Lydia R. Bailey, Printer.* 1839. 8vo, pp. 22. Plan.—Report on the Coal Lands of the Deep River Mining and Transportation Company in North Carolina. ... *Albany.* 1851. 8vo.—Report of a Survey ... of Coal and Ore Lands, belonging to the Allegheny Coal Company, in Somerset County, Pennsylvania, accompanied by Maps, Profiles, and Sections. ... *Philadelphia: Printed by Joseph & William Kite.* 1841. 8vo, pp. 64. Maps. H.—Report of ... the Bear Valley Coal District, in Dauphin County, Pennsylvania. ... *Philadelphia: Printed by Joseph & William Kite.* 1841. 8vo, pp. 36.

JOHNSON (W.) Sermon and Narrative of the Dangers and Deliverances at Sea, with the Name of the Master and those that suffered, also the Owners of the Ship. By William Johnson. *London.* 1664. 8vo. + *London.* 1672. 12mo. 36335

Reprinted as:

JOHNSON. Deus Nobiscum. A Narrative of a great Deliverance at Sea. With the Name of the Master, Ship, and those that suffered. Sixth Edition. *London: G. Keith.* 1769. 12mo, pp. viii, 46. 36336

This scarce volume which was unknown to Lowndes, contains an account of the

voyage and wreck of the ship William and John, of Ipswich, belonging to W. Blithe and John Smythe, merchants of that port, which sailed from Harwich, September 29th, 1648.

JOHNSON (W.) An Account of Conferences held, and Treaties made, Between Major-general Sir William Johnson, Bart. and The chief Sachems and Warriours of the Mohawks, Oneidas, Onondagas, Cayugas, Senekas, Tuskaroras, Skaniadaradighronos, Chugnuts, Mahickanders, Shawanese, Kanuskagos, Toderighronos, and Oghquagoes, Indian Nations in North America, At their Meetings, on different Occasions at Fort Johnson in the County of Albany, in the Colony of New York, in the Years 1755 and 1756. With A Letter from the Rev. Mr. Hawley to Sir William Johnson, written at the Desire of the Delaware Indians. And a Preface, Giving a short Account of the Six Nations, some Anecdotes of the Life of Sir William, and Notes illustrating the Whole; Also an Appendix Containing an Account of Conferences between several Quakers in Philadelphia, and some of the Heads of the Six Nations, in April 1756. *London: A. Millar.* M.DCC.LVI. 8vo, pp. (4), xii, 77. BA., H. 36337

Very scarce. *See* "M. Rev.," XV. 196.

JOHNSON. Letter dated Camp at Lake George, Sept. 9, 1755, to the Governours of the several Colonies who raised the Troops on the present Expedition; giving an Account of the Action of the preceding Day. [n. p. 1755?] Folio, pp. 3. 36338

JOHNSON. Proceedings and Treaty with the Shawanese, Nanticokes, and Mohikander Indians, living at Otsiningo; negotiated at Fort Johnson [April, 1757]. *New York.* 1757. Folio, pp. 14.

JOHNSON (W.) Eulogy on Thomas Jefferson, Delivered August 3d, 1826, ... By The Hon. William Johnson ... . *Charleston: Printed by C. C. Sebring.* 1826. 8vo, pp. 38. Portrait. BA.

JOHNSON. Nugæ Georgicæ; An Essay, delivered to the Literary and Philosophical Society of Charleston, South-Carolina, October 14, 1815. By the Honorable William Johnson ... . *Charleston, S. C.* 1815. 4to, pp. 40. B., BA., C. 36341

JOHNSON. The Opinion of the Hon. William Johnson, delivered on the 7th August, 1823, in the case of the arrest of the British Seaman under the 3d section of the State Act ... . [*Charleston:*] *Printed by C. C. Sebring.* [1823.] 8vo, pp. 15.

[JOHNSON.] Remarks, Critical and Historical, on an Article in the Forty-Seventh Number of the North American Review,

Relating to Count Pulaski. Addressed to the Readers of the North American Review, by the Author of the Sketches of the Life of Greene. *Charleston: Printed by C. C. Sebring.* 1825. 8vo, pp. 37. S. 36343

See "N. A. Rev.," XXIII. 414.

JOHNSON. Sketches of the Life and Correspondence of Nathanael Greene, Major General of the Armies of the United States, In the War of the Revolution. Compiled chiefly from Original Materials. By William Johnson, of Charleston, South-Carolina. *Charleston: Printed for the Author, by A. E. Miller*, ... 1822. 2 vols., 4to, pp. xi, 515, (1); (2), 476, (1), 11. Portrait, 7 Plans, and Map. B., BA. 36344

The Appendix, pp. 11, was subsequently printed, and is not in all copies. *See* [Bentalou (P.)], Vol. II., No. 4758, *and* "Blackwood's Magazine," XVII. 68.

JOHNSON (W.) An Address on the Aspect of National Affairs and the Right of Secession, March 16, 1861. By William Johnson. *Cincinnati: Rickey & Carroll.* 1861. 8vo, pp. 42. 36345

Also: Speech ... on the Bill to Provide Homesteads on the Forfeited and Confiscated Lands of Rebels. House of Representatives, May 4, 1864. [n. p. n. d.] 8vo, pp. 8.

JOHNSON (W. C.) Speech of Mr. Wm. Cost Johnson, of Maryland, on the Bill to appropriate the Proceeds of the Sales of the Public Lands, and to grant Pre-emption Rights. ... June 25 and 29, 1841. *Washington.* 1841. 8vo, pp. 21. M. 36346

JOHNSON. Speech ... on the ... Rejection of Petitions for the Abolition of Slavery: ... January 25, 27, and 28, 1840. *Washington: Printed by Gales and Seaton.* 1840. 8vo, pp. 63. B., BA.

Also: Speech ... on the Sub-Treasury Bill ... in the House of Representatives, October 12, 1837. *Washington.* [n. d.] 8vo, pp. 22. B.

JOHNSON (W. D.) Lincoln University; or, the Nation's First Pledge of Emancipation. By William D. Johnson ... . *Philadelphia: For the Author.* 1867. 8vo, pp. 32. Plate. 36348

JOHNSON (W. L.) ... A Sermon ... December 10, 1829; being the Day ... observed as a Day of Thanksgiving ... . By William L. Johnson, A.M. ... *Trenton: Printed by A. W. Phillips.* 1829. 8vo, pp. 22. 36349

JOHNSON (W. M.) Our Martyred President. A Discourse on the Death of President Lincoln, preached at Stillwater, N. Y., April 16, 1865. By Rev. William M. Johnson. *Troy, N. Y.: Daily Times Office.* 1865. 8vo, pp. 14. 36350

[JOHNSON (William Samuel).] Governor and Company of Connecticut, and Moheagan Indians, by their Guardians. Certified Copy of Book of Proceedings before Commissioners of Review, MDCCXLIII. *London: Printed by W. and J. Richardson.* MDCCLXIX. 4to, pp. (1), xxi, 283. Facsimiles H. 36351

JOHNSTON (A. K.) Dictionary of Geography, Descriptive, Physical, Statistical, and Historical, forming a complete General Gazetteer of the World. By Alex. Keith Johnston ... . *London: Longman* ... MDCCCL. 8vo, pp. viii, 1432. BA. + New Edition, Revised to February, 1862. [*Ibid.*] 1862. 8vo, pp. 1360.

JOHNSTON. The National Atlas of Historical, Commercial, and Political Geography, Constructed from the most recent and authentic Sources, with a copious Index compiled from the Maps By Alex. Keith Johnston ... . *Edinburgh.* [1844.] Folio. + [*Ibid.*] 1850. Folio. C. 36353

JOHNSTON. The Physical Atlas of Natural Phenomena. By Alexander Keith Johnston ... . *Edinburgh & London: William Blackwood & Sons.* MDCCCXLVIII. Folio. + A New and Enlarged Edition. [*Ibid.*] MDCCCLVI. Folio, pp. (6), 137. 35 Plates. B.

Reprinted at *Philadelphia*, 1850.

JOHNSTON (C.) A Narrative of the Incidents attending the Capture, Detention, and Ransom of Charles Johnston, of Botetourt County, Virginia, who was made Prisoner by the Indians, on the River Ohio, in the year 1790; Together with an Interesting Account of the Fate of His Companions, Five in number, One of whom suffered at the Stake. To which are added, Sketches of Indian Character and Manners, with Illustrative Anecdotes. *New-York: J. & J. Harper.* 1827. 12mo, pp. 264.

JOHNSTON (D. C.) American Comic Annual. Edited by Henry J. Finn. With Numerous Comic Illustrations by D. C. Johnston. *Boston.* 1831. 12mo. 36356

[JOHNSTON.] Outlines Illustrative of the Journal of F**** A*** K*****. *Boston: D. C. Johnston.* 1835. 8vo. 8 Plates.

The journal is that of Fanny A. Kemble.

JOHNSTON. Scraps ... Designed, Etched, & Published, by D. C. Johnston. *Boston.* 1830–49. 9 parts, obl. 4to. 36358

This series includes "Trollopania"—"Fiddle—D. D. being a series of Illustrations to Observations on the United States and Canada by the Rev. Isaac Fidler."

JOHNSTON (E. S.) Sermon delivered ... June 1st, 1865. ... in consequence of the Assassination of Abraham Lincoln; at ... Harrisburg, Pa. By Rev. E. S. Johnston. [*Harrisburg:*] *Theo. F. Scheffer, Printer.* 1865. 8vo, pp. 11, cover, 2 l. B. 36359

JOHNSTON (F.) Proceedings in the case of Francis Johnston, Esq., late Receiver-General of the Land Office, prosecuted for Delinquencies in the said Office. *Lancaster: Francis and Robert Bailey.* 1799. 8vo, pp. 27. P. 36360

[JOHNSTON (F.), *and* HAMILTON (W.), *Editors.*] The Washingtoniana; Containing A Sketch of the Life and Death of the Late Gen. George Washington; with a Collection of Elegant Eulogies, Orations, Poems, &c., Sacred to his Memory. Also, an Appendix, Comprising all his Most Valuable Public Papers, and his Last Will and Testament. *Lancaster: William Hamilton.* 1802. 8vo, pp. 411. B. 36361

See "Hist. Mag.," II., April, 1858.

JOHNSTON (F.) A Poem, by Frank Johnston, and a Valedictory Oration by Joseph Fenton, July 1, 1835. [n. p.] 1835. 8vo.

JOHNSTON (G. P.) Oration ... before the Society of California Pioneers, at ... the Fifth Anniversary of the Admission of ... California into the Union. By Geo. Pen Johnston. Ode: By Edmond Pillet. San Francisco, September 10th, 1855. *San Francisco.* 1855. 8vo, pp. 15, (2). 36363

JOHNSTON (I. N.) Four Months in Libby, and the Campaign against Atlanta. By Captain I. N. Johnston. *Cincinnati: For the Author.* 1864. 16mo, pp. 191. C. 36364

JOHNSTON (J.) A History of the haunted Caverns of Magdelama, An Indian Queen of South America ... Written by Dr. James Johnston. During a Captivity of three years, being taken up as a Spy by the above Queen ... . With the Rise and Progress of the Indian Tribes, and that of the White Inhabitants of South America. ... *Philadelphia: James Sharon.* 1821. 12mo, pp. 206. Plates. C. 36365

"If after having been stuck full of light wood splinters, set on fire and dying for several days, and then being burnt out in the tremendous fire at Savannah, the author does not win the sympathy of his reader, I cannot conceive what amount of dying will do it."—FIELD.

JOHNSTON (J. D.) The Contemplated Secession from The Federal Republic of North America, by the Southern States.

By John Dale Johnston. Detroit, December 9, 1860. [n. p. n. d.] 8vo, pp. 7. 36366

See also Detroit, Vol. v., No. 19786.

JOHNSTON (J. D.) China and Japan: Being a Narrative of the Cruise of the U. S. Steam-Frigate Powhatan, in the Years 1857, '58, '59, and '60. Including an Account of the Japanese Embassy to the United States. ... By Lieut. James D. Johnston, U. S. N. ... . *Philadelphia: Charles Desilver.* 1861. 12mo, pp. 448. 8 colored Plates, and Map. B., C. 36367

[JOHNSTON (James F.)] The Suspending Power and The Writ of Habeas Corpus. *Philadelphia: John Campbell.* 1862. 8vo, pp. 48. B., BA., C. 36368

JOHNSTON (J. F. W.) Notes on North America, Agricultural, Economical, and Social. By James F. W. Johnston ... . *William Blackwood & Sons, Edinburgh.* M.DCCCLI. 2 vols., post 8vo, pp. xvi, 415; xii, 512. + *Boston: Charles C. Little and James Brown.* MDCCCLI. 2 vols., 12mo, pp. xvi, 415, Map; xii, 512. B.

See "Edin. Rev.," XCIV. 46; "Blackwood's Magazine," LXX. 699; "N. A. Rev.," LXXIII. 210.

JOHNSTON. Report on the Agricultural Capabilities of the Province of New Brunswick. By J. F. W. Johnston ... . *Fredericton: J. Simpson, Printer.* 1850. 8vo, pp. (2), 262. BA. + Second Edition. *Fredericton.* 1850. 8vo. B., C. 36370

JOHNSTON (J. H.) Address of Rev. James H. Johnston, at the Inauguration of Rev. Joseph F. Tuttle, D.D. as President of Wabash College; and the Inaugural Discourse of the President ... July 24th, 1862. *New York: W. S. Dorr ... Printer.* 1862. 8vo, pp. 31. B. 36371

JOHNSTON. A Ministry of Forty Years in Indiana. A Historical Discourse, ... respecting the Progress of Presbyterianism in the State, during that Period, delivered ... February 5, 1865. By Rev. James H. Johnston. *Indianapolis: Holloway, Douglass & Co., Printers.* 1865. 8vo, pp. 30. 36372

JOHNSTON (J. R.) Discourse ... Dedication of Presbyterian Church, Hamptonburgh, Feb. 26, 1845. By James R. Johnston. *Goshen.* 1845. 8vo. 36373

JOHNSTON (J.) ... An Address ... before the Middlesex County Agricultural Society ... October 9th, 1846. By John Johnston ... . *Middletown, Conn.: Charles H. Pelton, Printer.* 1846. 8vo, pp. 18. B. 36374

JOHNSTON (J.) The Autobiography and Ministerial Life of Rev. John Johnston, D.D. Edited and Compiled by the Rev. James Carnahan, D.D. Together with an Appendix. *New York: M. W. Dodd.* 1856. 12mo, pp. 225. 2 Portraits, 1 Plate. C.

JOHNSTON (J. Eggleston). Report of General Joseph E. Johnston, of his Operations in the Department of Mississippi and East Louisiana, together with Lieut. General Pemberton's Report of the Battles of Port Gibson, Baker's Creek, and the Siege of Vicksburg. Published by order of Congress. *Richmond: R. M. Smith, Public Printer.* 1864. 8vo, pp. 213. B.

See our Vol. IV., No. 15264.

JOHNSTON, *and others.* Reports of the Secretary of War, with Reconnoissances of Routes from San Antonio to El Paso, by Brevet Lt. Col. J. E. Johnston; Lieut. W. F. Smith; Lieut. E. T. Bryan; Lieut. N. H. Michler, and Capt. S. G. French of Q'rmaster's Dep't. Also, the Report of Capt. R. B. Marcy's Route, from Fort Smith to Sante Fé; and the Report of Lieut. J. H. Simpson, of an Expedition into the Navajo Country; and the Report of Lieut. H. C. Whiting's Reconnoissances of the Western Frontier of Texas, July 24, 1850. *Washington: Union Office.* 1850. 8vo, pp. 250. 2 Maps and 71 Plates. 36377

There is much interesting matter in the reports relating to Indian tribes, then first visited, and the plates are principally illustrative of Indian life or aboriginal antiquities.

JOHNSTON (Josiah S.) Letter ... to the Secretary of the Treasury ... relative to the Culture of the Sugar Cane. *Washington: Printed by Gales & Seaton.* 1831. 8vo, pp. 21. B., W.

JOHNSTON. Letter ... to a Gentleman in New York ... [relative to] the Duty on Sugar. ... *Washington.* 1831. 8vo, pp. 8.

JOHNSTON. Remarks of Mr. Johnston, of Louisiana, relative to certain charges against The Bank of the United States, in Reply to Mr. Benton. [n. p. n. d.] 8vo, pp. 10. B. 36380

Also: Speech ... on the Mission to Panama. March, 1826. *Washington City: Printed by Gales & Seaton.* 1826. 8vo, pp. 24. + [n. p. n. d.] 12mo, pp. 25.—Speech ... on the Bill to regulate The Commercial Intercourse between the United States and the British Colonies: ... February 23, 1827. *Washington: Printed by Gales & Seaton.* 1827. 8vo, pp. 32.—Speech ... on the Public Debt. ... March 3, 1828. *Washington: Printed by Gales & Seaton.* 1828. 8vo, pp. 16.—Speech ... The Resolution of Mr. Foot ... relative to the Public Lands ... . Delivered ... March 30, 1830. *Washington: Printed by Gales & Seaton.* 1830. 8vo, pp. 20.—Speech ... respecting the Powers of the Vice President. ... February 14, 1828. *Washington: Printed by Gales & Seaton.* 1828. 8vo, pp. 16.—Speech ... at a public dinner given to him and ... E. D. White, in ... New Orleans, on the 8th of June, 1831. [*New Orleans.* 1831.] 8vo, pp. 8. B.

JOHNSTON (J. W.) Speech ... by ... Hon. J. W. Johnston ... 19th March, 1850, on ... the Self-government of Nova Scotia in her Local Affairs: ... *Halifax, Nova Scotia.* 1850. 8vo, pp. 15.

[JOHNSTON (Richard M.)] Georgia Sketches; containing Mr. Israel Meadows and his School, Judge Mike and his Court, How Bill Williams took the Responsibility. From Recollections of an Old Man, by Philemon Perch. ... [*Augusta:*] *Stockton & Co.* 1864. 8vo, pp. 114. 36382

JOHNSTON (R.) Four Letters to the Reverend James Caughey ... on the participation of the American Methodist Episcopal Church in the Sin of American Slavery: three from Robert Johnston ... and one from Richard Allen ... . *Dublin: Samuel J. Machen.* 1841. 12mo, pp. 28. BA. 36383

JOHNSTON (R.) A Sermon delivered on Thanksgiving Day: in ... Peoria, Illinois, ... November 27th, 1862. By Rev. Robert Johnston ... . *Peoria, Illinois: Benj. Foster.* 1862. 8vo, pp. 19. B. 36384

JOHNSTON (Samuel B.) Letters written during a Residence of Three Years in Chili, with an Account of the Revolutionary Struggle of that Province. *Erie (Pa.): R. J. Curtis.* 1816. 12mo, pp. (4), 13–205. C., S. 36385

JOHNSTON (T.) Travels through Lower Canada, interspersed with Canadian Tales & Anecdotes, and Interesting Information to intending Emigrants. By Thomas Johnston. *Edinburgh: J. Glass.* 1827. 12mo, pp. 96. Frontispiece. 36386

JOHNSTON (W.) An Address on the Life and Public Services of Hon. Edwin M. Stanton. By William Johnston ... . *Cincinnati: R. W. Carroll & Co.* 1870. 8vo, pp. 16. B. 36387

JOHNSTON. Argument of William Johnston, in the case of The State *vs.* Ames, before the Criminal Court of Cincinnati. *Cincinnati: Marshall & Langtry, Printers.* 1853. 8vo. 36388

JOHNSTON (W. J.) Sketches of the History of Stephenson County, Ill., and Incidents connected with the early settlement of the North West. ... by William J. Johnston. *Freeport, Illinois: ... J. O. P. Burnside* ... 1854. 12mo, pp. 102. 36389

JOHNSTONE (A.) The Address of Abraham Johnstone, a Black Man, who was hanged at Woodbury, in ... New Jersey

... the 8th Day of July ... to the People of Colour. ... *Philadelphia: For the Purchasers.* 1797. 8vo, pp. 47. BA., H. 36390

[JOHNSTONE (Charles).] Chrysal: or, the Adventures of a Guinea. ... in America, England, Holland, Germany, and Portugal. By an Adept. ... *London.* 1760. 2 vols., 12mo. + *London: T. Cadell.* MDCCXCIV. 4 vols., 12mo, pp. 271; 292; 227; 228. H. 36391

The imprint in Vols. II. and IV. reads *T. Cavell.* Other editions: *London,* 1762, 1763, 1767, 1768, 1771, 1775, 1783; *Baltimore,* 1810; *Baltimore: F. Lucas, Jun. & Joseph Cushing.* 1816. 2 vols., 12mo, pp. xi, 153, 119; xvii, 287; *London,* 1822. It is a masterly and caustic satire. Reprinted in "Ballantyne's "Novelists' Library." A key to the characters is in Davis' "Olio," p. 13–21. *See* "M. Rev.," XXIII. 137.

[JOHNSTONE (*Chevalier de*).] The Campaign of Louisbourg; 1750–'58. [*Quebec.* 1867.] 8vo, pp. 28. 36392

Edited by Mr. J. M. Le Moine. Pages 27 and 28 form a memoir of Johnstone.

[JOHNSTONE.] Manuscripts relating to the Early History of Canada. The Invasion of Canada in 1775. A Journal by Col. H. Caldwell. *Quebec.* 1866. 8vo, pp. 55. 36393

See also Vol. III., No. 9903.

JOHNSTONE. Memoirs of the Rebellion in 1745 and 1746. By The Chevalier de Johnstone ... . Containing a Narrative of the Progress of the Rebellion, from its Commencement to the Battle of Culloden: the Characters of the Principal Persons engaged in it, and Anecdotes respecting them; ... with an Account of the Sufferings and Privations experienced by the Author ... before he effected his Escape to the Continent, &c. &c. Translated from a French MS. originally deposited in the Scots College at Paris ... . *London: Longman.* 1820. 8vo, pp. xlix, (1), 348. 2 Portraits. + Second Edition. [*Ibid.*] 1821. 4to, pp. xlix, (1), 348. 2 Portraits. + Third Edition with Additional Notes, &c. [*Ibid.*] 1822. 8vo, pp. lxxii, 456. 2 Portraits and Plan.

"A very interesting work, written under the influence of disappointment and ill humour. Some of the stories are altogether fictitious."—LOWNDES. Includes the author's adventures in Cape Breton, Canada, etc.

JOHNSTONE (*Admiral* George). Remarks on Com. Johnstone's Account of his Engagement with a French Squadron, under the Command of Mons. de Suffrein, on April 16, 1781 in Fort Praya Road, in the Island of St. Jago. *London: J. Debrett.* M DCC-LXXXI. 8vo, pp. (2), 22. 36395

See "M. Rev.," LXV. 156. This is by Admiral Blake. The title takes the place of the note to *our* Vol. II., No. 5792.

JOHNSTONE. Observations and Closer Remarks on Commodore Johnstone's Letter to the Earl of Hillsborough, Dated at Port Praya, In the Island of St. Jago. By a Seaman. *London: J. Stockdale.* 1782. 8vo, pp. 48. 36396

JOHNSTONE (G.) An Appeal to the Public, in behalf of George Johnstone, Esq: Governor of West Florida. In Answer to the North-Britain Extraordinary. *London: Morgan.* 1763. 8vo.

See "M. Rev.," XXVIII. 391.

JOHNSTONE. Governor Johnstone's Speech, on the Question of Recommitting the address declaring the Colony of Massachusetts Bay in Rebellion. To which is added The two most Masterly Letters of Junius, To the people of England in favour of the Americans. *London: G. Allen.* [1776.] 8vo, pp. 32. BA.

JOHNSTONE. Gov. Johnstone's Speech on American Affairs, on the Address in Answer to the King's Speech. ... *Edinburgh: John Wood.* M,DCC,LXXVI. 12mo, pp. (2), 16. H. 36399

Governor Johnstone charges the government with having drawn all its knowledge of colonial affairs from Governor Hutchinson. "The civil war in America," he says, "seems step by step to have been carried on by his advice. Whoever reads his letters lately published, sees every measure pursued by the administration to have been antecedently pointed out by him, until his sentiments seem dictated at last more by revenge and disappointment than any other principle."

JOHNSTONE. Remarks [etc]. *See* [Reed (Joseph)].

JOHNSTONE (W.) A Series of Letters descriptive of Prince Edward Island, in the Gulph of St. Laurence, addressed to the Rev. John Wightman ... By Walter Johnstone ... The Author of these Letters went out for the express purpose of surveying Prince Edward Island, and collecting information on the subject of Emigration. During two Summers, and one Winter, he was ... engaged in the prosecution of this object; and the small Volume ... will be found to contain a full and particular Account of the Climate, Soil, Natural Productions, and Mode of Husbandry adopted in the Island; together with Sketches of Scenery, Manners of the Inhabitants, &c. &c.; the whole being intended for the guidance of future Emigrants, particularly as to what Implements and Necessaries it may be proper to provide themselves with before crossing the Atlantic. *Dumfries: J. Swan.* 1822. 12mo, pp. 72. 36400

JOHNSTONE. Travels in Prince Edward Island, Gulf of St. Lawrence, North-America, In the Years 1820–21. Undertaken with a Design to Establish Sabbath Schools, And Investigate the

Religious State of the Country: Wherein is given a Short Account of the Different Denominations of Christians, their Former History and Present Condition, interspersed with Notes relative to the various Clergymen that have officiated on the Island. By Walter Johnstone ... . *Edinburgh: David Brown.* 1823. 12mo, pp. 132. Map. + [With] Nine Letters Descriptive of the Agricultural State of that Island. ... *Edinburgh: James Robertson & Co.* 1824. 12mo, pp. 132. Map. B. 36401

JOHNSTOWN, *N. Y.* Catalogue of Johnstown Academy. For the year 1855-6. *Johnstown, N. Y.* 1856. 8vo, pp. 12. Cont'd.

Also: Catalogue of the Students, and the Rules, etc.

JOHNSTOWN, *Pa.* *See* Cambria Iron Company, No. 10109.

JOHONNOT (J.) The Remarkable Adventures of Jackson Johonnot, of Massachusetts, who Served as a Soldier in the Western Army, in the Expedition under Gen. Harmar and Gen. St. Clair. Containing an Account of his Captivity, Sufferings, and Escape from the Kickappo Indians. Written by Himself, and Published at the Earnest Request and Importunity of his Friends for the Benefit of American Youth. *Printed at Walpole, Newhampshire By I. Thomas and D. Carlisle, Jun.* MDCCXCV. 12mo, pp. 12. H. + *Greenfield, Mass: Printed by Ansel Phelps.* 1816. 12mo, pp. 24. 36403

Both editions are scarce. It is included in Metcalf's "Narratives."

JOHONNOT (James). Country School-Houses; containing Elevations, Plans and Specifications ... with numerous [70] Designs, by S. E. Hewes. *New York.* 1859. 8vo, pp. 220. S. 36404

Joint Address. *See* Canada, Vol. IV., No. 10472.

Joint Letter from the most considerable Proprietors of the Island of Barbadoes to Colonel Richard Scot, Colonel Robert Stewart, Richard Bate, Patrick Mein, and Thomas Fullerton, touching the African trade. [n. p.] 1709. Folio, 1 l. 36405

[JOINVILLE (*Le Prince de*).] Campagne de l'Armée du Potomac [mars–juillet 1862]. Par A. Trognon. *New York: F. W. Christern.* 1862. 8vo, pp. 64. Map. B., BA. 36406

JOINVILLE. ... The Army of the Potomac: its Organization, its Commander, and its Campaign. By the Prince de Joinville, Translated from the French, with Notes, By William Henry Hurlbert. *New York: Anson D. F. Randolph.* 1862. 8vo, pp. 118. Map. B., BA. 36407

[JOINVILLE.] Guerre d'Amérique. Campagne du Potomac. Mars–Juillet, 1862. *Paris: Michel Levy Frères.* 1863. 8vo, pp. 211. Map. C. 36408

JOLIET, *Ill.* Progress, Resources and Prospects of the City of Joliet, Will County, Ill. With the evidences of the enterprise of her Citizens. *Joliet: Snoed & Logan.* 1856. 8vo, pp. 40. 2 Plans. BA. 36409

[JOLINE (John K.)] An Heroic Address for the 4th July, 1813, etc. [n. p. n. d.] 8vo. N. 36410

JOLIS (D. G.) Saggio sulla Storia Naturale della Provincia del Gran Chaco e sulle pratiche, e su' costumi dei Popoli che l'abitano insieme con tre giornali di altrettanti viaggi, fatti alle interne contrade di que Barbari. Composta dal Signor Abate D. Giuseppe Jolis. Tomo I. *Faenza: Lodovico Genestri.* 1789. 8vo, pp. 601. Map. 36411

Intended to form four volumes, one only appeared. The author was one of the Spanish Jesuits who were expelled from South America. It is chiefly devoted to the natural history of the Gran Chaco in Paraguay. It also contains accounts of various Indian tribes.

JOLLIFFE (J.) Belle Scott; or, Liberty overthrown; A Tale for the Crisis. By John Jolliffe. *Cincinnati.* 1856. 12mo. C.

JOLLIFFE. Chattanooga. ... *Cincinnati: Wrightson & Company, Printers.* 1858. 12mo. C. + 1863. 8vo, pp. 400. 36413

Our No. 27973, in Vol. VII., was prepared by John Jolliffe.

JOLLIVET [Adolphe]. Les Colonies Françaises devant la Chambre des Pairs. Analyse de la discussion générale du projet de loi sur le régime colonial. Par M. Jollivet ... . *Paris.* 1845. 8vo, pp. 112. P. 36414

JOLLIVET. Documents américains. Annexion du Texas; Émancipation des Noirs; Politique de l'Angleterre. [La dépêche de M. Calhoun à M. King, à Paris; la lettre de Hammond, etc.] Par M. Jollivet ... . *Paris: Bruneau.* 1845. 8vo, pp. 40. C.

JOLLIVET. Documents américains. Troisième série. Les États-Unis d'Amérique et l'Angleterre. Annexion du Texas, l'Orégon. Par M. Jollivet ... . *Paris: Bruneau.* 1845. 8vo, pp. 74. C., P. 36416

[JOLLIVET.] A Los Habitantes de la Isla de Cuba. *Paris.* 1844. 8vo, pp. 20. 36417

JOLLIVET. Observations sur un projet d'ordonnance relatif au pécule et au rachat des Noirs dans les Colonies Françaises. Par M. Jollivet ... . *Paris.* [1845.] 8vo, pp. 23. P. 36418

JOLLIVET. Parallèle entre les Colonies Françaises et les Colonies Anglaises. Par M. Jollivet ... . *Paris.* 1842. 8vo, pp. 40.

JOLLIVET. Des Pétitions de quelques ouvriers et ouvrières de Paris pour l'abolition immédiate de l'esclavage. Véritable situation des Noirs dans les Colonies Françaises. Par M. Jollivet ... *Paris.* 1844. 8vo, pp. 20. 36420

JOLLIVET. Plan de Colonization [au Texas]. ... *Paris.* 1842. 8vo, pp. 32. 36421

JOLLIVET. Question des Sucres en Angleterre. Du Travail Libre et du Travail Esclave. Par M. Jollivet ... . *Paris: De l'Imprimerie de Bruneau.* 1845. 8vo, pp. 23. B., P. 36422

Also: L'Émancipation Anglaise jugée par ses Résultats. ... *Paris.* 1842.

JOLY (J.) Memorie voor Jean Joly, cum suis, alle Coloniers wonende in de Colonie de Berbice, en eigenaars van Plantagien geleegen in dezelve Colonie: dienende zoo tot appui als justificatie van de verzoeken, door dezelve by Requeste aan Haar Hoog Mogenden gedaan. [n. p. 1776?] Folio, pp. 93, 67. Tables.

JOLY (J. C.) *See* Crétineau-Joly, Vol. v., No. 17491.

JOLY (*M. de.*) Adresse des Citoyens de couleur des Isles et Colonies Françoises; à l'Assemblée générale des representans de la commune de Paris. Prononcée le premier Février 1790. *Paris.* 1790. 8vo, pp. 15. 36424

JOLY DE ST. VALIER (*Le Sieur*). Exposé ou Examen des Operations des Ministres en Angleterre depuis Le Commencement de la Guerre contre les Americains jusqu'ici. Par Le Sieur Joly de St. Valier ... . *A Londres, Ches* [sic] *M. Boissiere* ... [n. d.] 4to, pp. (4), 59. + [*Ibid.*] M.D.CC.LX.XXI. 12mo, pp. 82. H.

JOLY DE ST. VALIER. Exposé ou Examen des Opérations des Ministres d'Angleterre depuis Le Commencement de la Guerre contre les Américains jusqu'aujourd'hui, comparées avec les opérations qui auraient convenu aux interêts de la Grande Bretagne. Par M. Joly de St. Valier, Lieut.-Col. d'Infanterie. II. Partie. On trouvera dans cette seconde partie les vrais motifs qui ont porté les Ministres d'Angleterre à ordonner les actes d'hostilité contre les Provinces Unies; motifs d'autant plus intéressants à connoître qu'il parait que personne jusqu'ici ne les a pas même soupçonné. *Amsterdam: B. Haw.* MDCCLXXXI. 8vo, pp. x, 52. 36426

No printer or publisher in London would have anything to do with this second part, therefore the author was obliged to have it printed in Holland.

JOLY DE ST. VALIER. An Exposure, or Examination of the Operations of the British Ministers, From the Commencement of the War against the Americans, till the present Time; Contrasted with the Operations that were most suitable to the Interests of Great-Britain. By Mr. Joly de St. Valier, Lieutenant Colonel of Infantry. ... *London.* 1781. 8vo, pp. 7, 111. H.

Very rare. The lower part of the title with the imprint is usually cut off. "It has lately been seen that the booksellers, dreading the keenness of the Ministry's resentment, refused to vend the English translation of the 'Exposure,' &c., which has laid the author under the necessity of vending it at his own lodgings," &c. "From a printed letter from the same person to Mr. Pitt dated Bridewell, December, 1784, it appears that his pamphlet had got him into difficulties, that he had been imprisoned, and had been released on condition of his leaving England; that the 'Chevalier Yorke' had had something to do with it, for which he felt himself aggrieved, and in consequence returned to England, and sent him a challenge, for which he was again condemned to a year's imprisonment in Bridewell."—RICH.

JOLY DE ST. VALIER. Histoire Raisonnée des Opérations Militaires et Politiques de la Dernière Guerre, suivie d'Observations sur La Révolution qui est arrivée dans les Mœurs sur celle qui est sur le point d'arriver dans la Constitution d'Angleterre. Par M. Joly de St. Valier ... . *Liège.* M DCC LXXXIII. 8vo, pp. xii, 235, (1). BA. 36428

See Rich's "Bib. Am.," p. 299.

JOLY DE ST. VALIER. Lettre à William Pitt, Prémier Ministre de la Grande Bretagne au Lord Sidney Secrétaire d'État, &c., &c. [n. p. n. d.] 8vo, pp. 22. 36429

JOLY DE ST. VALIER. Mémoire du Sieur Joly de St. Valier ... ou, Exposé de sa Conduite avant et depuis qu'il a quitté la France pour venir offrir ses Services a sa Majesté le Roy d'Angleterre. ... *A Londres, Chès M. Boissiere.* [n. d.] 4to, pp. (3), 67. + Seconde édition. *Londres.* 1780. 8vo, pp. 93. M. 36430

JOLY (S. J. Ducœur). *See* Ducœur Joly (S. J.), Vol. v.

JOMARD (Edme-François). Les Antiquités Américaines au Point de Vue des Progrès de la Géographie. Par M. Jomard ... *Paris.* [n. d.] 8vo, pp. 12. 36431

From the "Bulletin de la Société de Géographie," December, 1847.

JOMARD. Les Monuments de la Géographie, ou recueil d'anciennes cartes Européennes et Orientales, accompagnées de Sphères Terrestres et Célestes, de Mappemondes et Tables Cosmographiques, d'Astrolabes, ... depuis les temps les plus reculés jusqu'à l'époque d'Ortelius et de Girard Mercator. ... *Paris: Chez Mm. Duprat.* 1855–62. Imp. folio. 36432

This magnificent work, most important for the history of cartography, contains 82 plates in facsimile in the size of the originals. Brunet calls it an "Ouvrage remarquable sous tous les rapports." Some copies have no date.

[JOMARD.] Note sur les Botecudos, accompagnée d'un vocabulaire de leur langue et de quelques remarques. *Paris.* 1846. 8vo, pp. 13. 36433

Extracted from the "Bulletin de la Société de Géographie, 1846.

JOMARD. Rapport sur le Concours relatif à la Géographie et aux Antiquités de l'Amérique Centrale. Par M. Jomard ... . *Paris: P. Renouard.* 1836. 8vo, pp. 47. 36434

[JOMARD.] Seconde Note sur une Pierre Gravée, trouvée dans un ancien Tumulus Américain. Et, a cette occasion, sur l'Idiome Libyen. ... *Paris: Benjamin Duprat.* [1845.] 8vo, pp. 30. Plate. BA. 36435

Also: Monument à Christophe Colomb. *Hanley.* [n. d.] 8vo, pp. 13. Portrait. *See also* "Revue Contemporaine," I. 575; II. 73; VI. 282.

JOMINI [Henri, *Baron de*]. A Hand-Book for the Practice of War, for the use of Military Men of all Ages and Countries. By Gen. Jomini. Translated ... . *Richmond: West & Johnston.* 1863. 18mo. 36436

[JONAMA, *de.*] Cartas al abate de Pradt, traducidas del francés al castellano por J. D. Diaz. Dado de nuevo á luz. *Madrid.* 1829. 4to. 36437

"Ces sont des lettres sur les rapports des colonies américaines du midi avec l'Espagne."—ANDRADE.

JONAMA (S.) De la prueba por Jurados, o sea consejo de hombres buenos por Don Santiago Jonama. *Mexico.* 1824. 12mo, pp. xii, 136. 36438

JONATHAN, *pseudon.* Brieven uit en over de V..eenigde Staaten van Noord-Amerika. Door Jonathan. Uitgegeven door Dr. E. B. Swalue. *Schoonhoven: S. E. Van Nooten.* 1853. 8vo, pp. xiv, 304. 5 Plates and Map. C. 36439

Letters from and on the United States.

JONATHAN BULL *and* MARY BULL. *See* Madison (James).

[JONES (——).] Life and Adventure in the South Pacific. By a Roving Printer. *New York: Harper & Brothers.* 1861. 12mo, pp. 361, including 22 Plates. C. 36440

JONES (A. D.) Memoir of Elder Abner Jones. By his Son, A. D. Jones. ... *Boston: William Crosby & Company.* 1842. 12mo, pp. 207. Portrait. B., BA. 36441

J[ONES] (A[bsalom]), *and* A[LLEN] (R[ichard]). A Narrative of the Proceedings of the Black People, during the late Awful Calamity in Philadelphia, in the Year 1793; and A Refutation of Some Censures, Thrown upon them in some late Publications. By A. J. and R. A. *Philadelphia: William W. Woodward.* 1794. 12mo, pp. 28. M., P. 36442

Also: Thanksgiving Sermon—Abolition of Slave-Trade. ... *Philadelphia.* 1808.

JONES (A.) The Revenue Book: containing The New Tariff of 1846, together with The Tariff of 1842 ... . By A. Jones. *New-York: Geo. H. Bell.* 1853. 8vo, pp. 67. + [*Ibid.*] 1854.

JONES (A.) Cuba in 1851; containing Authentic Statistics of the Population, Agriculture, and Commerce of the Island for a series of Years; with Official and other Documents in relation to the Revolutionary Movement of 1850 and 1851. By Alexander Jones. *New York: Stringer & Townsend.* 1851. 8vo, pp. 80. 36444

JONES. The Cymry of '76; or, Welshmen and their Descendants of the American Revolution. ... By Alexander Jones, M.D. ... To which is added a Letter on Eminent Welshmen. By Samuel Jenkins, Esq. and a Brief Sketch of the St. David's Benevolent Society. *New York: Sheldon, Lamport & Co.* 1855. 8vo, pp. (4), 132. Errata, 4 lines. B. 36445

JONES. Historical Sketch of the Electric Telegraph: including its Rise and Progress in the United States. By Alexander Jones. ... *New-York: George P. Putnam.* M.DCCC.LII. 8vo, pp. xiii, 3–194. B., C. 36446

JONES (A. A.) Copies of Several Letters ... from A. A. Jones, Surveyor's Department ... relating to the Number of Clerks ... in the Custom-House Departments of ... New-York; ... *New-York: G. F. Hopkins and Son Printers.* 1836. 8vo, pp. 21. BA. 36447

JONES' Digest. Being a particular and detailed Account of the Duties performed by the various Officers belonging to the Custom-House Departments of the United States, but more especially of those attached to the District of New York. [With] a Tariff of Duties on Merchandise. By A. A. Jones. *New York.* 1835. 8vo, pp. 370. C. 36448

JONES (A. D.) Illinois and the West. With a Township Map, containing the latest Surveys and Improvements. By A. D. Jones. *Boston: Weeks, Jordan and Company.* 1838. 18mo, pp. v, 255, (1). Map. 36449

JONES. The Illustrated American Biography; containing Correct Portraits and Brief Notices of the Principal Actors in American History; embracing Distinguished Women, Naval and Military Heroes, Statesmen, Civilians, Jurists, Divines, Authors, and Artists; together with Celebrated Indian Chiefs. ... Complete in Six Volumes. ... By A. D. Jones. Volume I. *New York: J. Milton Emerson and Company.* MDCCCLIII. Rl. 8vo, pp. 264, (1). Illustrations. BA. 36450

A mere vehicle for advertisements, which occur on alternate pages. Three volumes only appeared, and then it was made up into one volume with the following title:

JONES. The American Portrait Gallery; containing Correct Portraits and Brief Notices of the Principal Actors in American History; ... By A. D. Jones. *New York.* MDCCCLIII–LV. Imp. 8vo, pp. 768. + *New York.* 1867. 8vo. + *New York: Henry Miller.* 1869. Imp. 8vo, pp. 768. B. 36451

The portraits are of equal merit with the text, which is not very high praise.

JONES (A. H.) Reconstruction of Mississippi. Speech of Hon. Alexander H. Jones ... in the House of Representatives, April 1, 1869 ... . [*Washington.* n. d.] 8vo, pp. 4. 36452

JONES (A. T.) Poems. By Amanda T. Jones. *New York: Hurd & Houghton.* 1867. 12mo, pp. 203. 36453

JONES (A.) Letters relating to the History of Annexation. By Anson Jones ... . *Galveston.* 1848. 12mo, pp. 30. + *Philadelphia.* 1852. 12mo, pp. 30. 36454

JONES. Memoranda and Official Correspondence relating to the Republic of Texas: its History and Annexation. Including a brief Autobiography of the Author. By Anson Jones, Late President of the Republic of Texas. *New York: D. Appleton & Co.* 1859. 8vo, pp. 648. C. 36455

JONES (A. T.) A Horse Story, by an Old Gray Horse, continued by Arthur T. Jones, including a Narrative of all the Proceedings in the case of the Impeachment of John Orser, High Sheriff of ... New-York, with the Decision of the Governor ... and the Trial and Conviction of Deputy Thomas Carlin. *New-York: George F. Nesbitt & Co., Printers.* 1856. 8vo, pp. (8), 337.

JONES (B.) A Letter from Benjamin Jones in Alexandria in Virginia, to John Jones, in Pennsylvania. Taken from a late Newspaper. *Reprinted* 1754. 12mo, pp. 7. P. 36457

Dated July 17th, 1754, and relates to the French aggressions at Fort du Quesne.

JONES (B.) Speech of Benjamin Jones of East Tennessee ... November 20, 1863. [n. p. n. d.] 12mo, pp. 16. 36458

JONES (B. M.) Railroads considered in regard to their effects on the Value of Land, in Increasing Production, Cheapening Transportation, Preventing Emigration, and as Investments for Capital, By B. M. Jones. *Richmond.* 1860. 8vo. 36459

JONES (C.) A Description of Wier's Cave, in Augusta County, Virginia. In a Letter from General Calvin Jones, to Mr. ******* in North-Carolina; ... *Albany: Printed by Henry C. Southwick.* 1815. 8vo, pp. 8. B., BA., S. 36460

JONES (*Captain*). Legend of. *See* [Lloyd (David)].

JONES (Cave). Dr. Hobart's System of Intolerance exemplified in the Late Proceedings against his Colleague, the Author. *New York: For the Author.* 1811. 8vo, pp. 82. 36461

JONES. Documents relative to the Submission to Arbitration between Cave Jones and the Corporation of Trinity Church. *New York.* 1813. 4to, pp. 59. N. 36462

[JONES.] Serious Thoughts on a late Administration of Episcopal Orders. *New York.* 1812. 8vo, pp. 80. 36463

JONES. A Solemn Appeal to the Church: being a Plain Statement of Facts in the Matters pending between Dr. Hobart with others, and the Author. By the Rev. Cave Jones, A.M. ... Together with an Appendix ... . *New-York: For the Author.* 1811. 8vo, pp. (4), 104. BA., M., S., W. 36464

JONES. Testimony in the Case of the Rev. Mr. Jones and the Vestry of Trinity Church. [n. p. n. d.] 8vo, pp. 172.

See Davis (M. L.), Hobart (J. H.), Jay (J.), Protestant Episcopal Church, Vindex, *and* [Wilkins (Isaac.)

[JONES (Charles).] A Candid Examination, into the Origin of the Difference of Colour, in the Human Family ... . *Philadelphia: For the Author.* 1812. 12mo, pp. 36. B., P. 36466

JONES (C.) A Sermon on Foundation Principles. By Rev. Charles Jones, of ... Cambridgeport, Mass. Together with the Action of the Church on the subjects of Temperance and Slavery. *Cambridge: John Ford.* 1855. 12mo, pp. 23. 36467

JONES (Charles A.) The Outlaw, and other Poems. *Cincinnati.* 1835. 36468

"Privately Printed," says Allibone. I have not seen the book.

JONES (C. Colcock). Historical Address, delivered to The Liberty Independent Troop, upon its Anniversary, February 22, 1856. By Rev. Charles C. Jones. ... *Savannah: Press of John M. Cooper & Co.* 1856. 8vo, pp. 63. 36469

The appendix to this pamphlet gives a list of its members from 1794 to 1856, and other interesting matter. The subject of the address is on the "Early Use of Cavalry in this Country."

JONES. The Religious Instruction of the Negroes In the United States. By Charles C. Jones. *Savannah: Thomas Purse.* 1842. 12mo, pp. xiii, 277. B. + [*Ibid.*] 1855. 18mo, pp. 132.

JONES. Suggestions on the Religious Instruction of the Negroes in the Southern States; ... By Charles Colcock Jones, D.D. *Philadelphia: Presbyterian Board of Publication.* 1847. 8vo, pp. 56.

Also: Sketch of the Life ... of Miss Anne Clay: delivered ... in ... Georgia ... January, 1843. ... *Boston: Press of Crocker and Brewster.* 1844. 8vo, pp. 23. B.

JONES (C. C.) Ancient Tumuli on the Savannah River. By Charles C. Jones, Jr. [*New York.* 1868.] 8vo, pp. 14. Map.

Fifteen copies privately printed.

JONES. Ancient Tumuli in Georgia ... By Charles C. Jones, Jr. *Worcester: Printed by Charles Hamilton.* 1869. 8vo, pp. 29.

JONES. Antiquities of the Southern Indians, particularly of the Georgia Tribes. By Charles C. Jones, Jr. *New York: D. Appleton and Company.* 1873. 8vo, pp. xvi, 532. 30 Plates.

One of the most scholarly works of its class.

JONES. Chatham Artillery of Savannah. Celebration of the Seventy-Fifth Anniversary, May 1, 1861. Oration by Charles C. Jones, Jr. *Savannah.* 1861. 8vo, pp. 65. 36475

The oration contains an account of the part taken by this corps in the sepulture of Gen. Nathaniel Greene, in June, 1786, also biographical sketches of the different commanders, and a roll of its members.

JONES. Historical Sketch of The Chatham Artillery during The Confederate Struggle for Independence. By Charles C. Jones, Jr. Late Lieut. Colonel of Artillery, C. S. A. ... *Albany, N. Y.: Joel Munsell.* 1867. 8vo, pp. 240. Map. B., BA.

Fifty copies printed on large paper. A very interesting and graphically written monograph, by an author who understands his subject.

JONES. Historical Sketch of Tomo-Chi-Chi, Mico of the Yamacraws. By Charles C. Jones, Jr. ... *Albany, N. Y.: Joel Munsell.* 1868. 8vo, pp. 133. B., BA. 36477

"The large-minded and heroic Indian chief, who welcomed Oglethorpe to the lands of his nation, and fed and protected the infant colony during those early years, when disease and the Spaniard threatened its existence, well deserved a biography. Mr. Jones has done full justice to his subject, by fortifying the facts of his biography with undoubted authorities."—FIELD.

JONES. Indian Remains in Southern Georgia. Address ... before the Georgia Historical Society ... . By Charles C. Jones, Jr. *Savannah: Press of John M. Cooper & Co.* 1859. 8vo, pp. 25.

JONES. Monumental Remains of Georgia: By Charles C. Jones, Jr. Part First. *Savannah: John M. Cooper and Company.* 1861. 8vo, pp. 119. Map. B., BA. 36479

The result of a personal examination of the aboriginal monuments of Georgia, aided by such fortuitous circumstances as seldom fall to the lot of the explorer.

JONES. Reminiscences of the Last Days, Death and Burial of General Henry Lee. By Charles C. Jones, Jr. *Albany, N. Y.: Joel Munsell.* 1870. 4to, pp. 43. Portrait. H. 36480

JONES. Siege of Savannah in 1779. By Charles C. Jones, Jr. *Albany: Joel Munsell.* 1870. 4to. Map. 36481

Also: The Siege of Savannah in December, 1864, and the Confederate Operations in Georgia and South Carolina during Sherman's March. ... *Albany.* 1874. 4to.

JONES (C. L.) Supplemental Memorial of Charles Lee Jones, in Reply to the Counter Memorial from Jalapa, in Mexico, under the Signature of certain of the Volunteers there in Garrison, in relation to Capt. George W. Hughes, there exercising the Command of a Colonel. *Washington.* 1848. 8vo, pp. 13. H.

JONES (C. L. S.) American Lyrics: comprising The Discovery, a Poem; Sapphic, Pindaric and Common Odes; Songs and Tales of American and Patriotic Subjects. ... By Charles L. S. Jones. *Mobile: Pollard & Dade.* 1834. 12mo, pp. 306. C.

JONES (C. J.) The Providence and Purpose of God in our National History. A Thanksgiving Sermon preached at Staten

Island, November 26, 1863. By Rev. Charles J. Jones. *New York: J. A. Gray & Green.* 1863. 8vo, pp. 23. 36484

Also: A Hopeful View of National Affairs. A Thanksgiving Sermon ... at Staten Island, September 11, 1864. ... *New York: Printed by Edward O. Jenkins.* 1864. 18mo, pp. 23.

JONES (D.) Letter from the Secretary of the Treasury, accompanying his Reports on the Memorial of David Jones, and the Petitions of Obadiah Scott ... 25th March, 1800. ... [*Washington.* 1800.] 8vo, pp. 13. B. 36485

JONES (D.) Defensive War in a just cause sinless. A Sermon, preach'd on the day of the Continental Fast, at Tredyffryn, in Chester County, by the Rev[d] David Jones, A.M. ... *Philadelphia: Printed by Henry Miller.* 1775. 8vo, pp. 27. P. 36486

JONES. A Journal of Two Visits made to Some Nations of Indians on the West Side of the River Ohio, In the Years 1772 and 1773. By the Rev. David Jones, Minister of the Gospel at Freehold, in New Jersey. *Burlington: Printed and Sold by Isaac Collins.* M.DCCLXXIV. 8vo, pp. iv, 95. 36487

This original edition is rare. It is an interesting account of the manners and customs among some Indian tribes now nearly extinct. Reprinted as below:

JONES. A Journal of Two Visits made to some Nations of Indians on the West Side of the River Ohio, in the Years 1772 and 1773. By the Rev. David Jones, Minister of the Gospel at Freehold, in New Jersey. With a Biographical Notice of the Author, by Horatio Gates Jones, A.M. ... *New York: Reprinted for Joseph Sabin.* 1865. 8vo, pp. xi, 5–127. B., BA. 36488

Fifty copies printed on large paper, imperial octavo.

JONES (D. S.) Memorial [etc.] *See* [Jones (W. A.)]

JONES (E. C.) The Harp of Sylva. By Edward C. Jones. *Philadelphia: R. S. George.* 1841. 12mo, pp. 218. C. 36489

JONES (E. F.) Stockbridge, Past and Present; or, Records of An Old Mission Station. By Miss Electa F. Jones. *Springfield: Samuel Bowles & Company.* 1854. 12mo, pp. 275. B., C.

JONES (E.) Review of Facts and Observations made by Naturalists and Travellers in America on the Properties and Productions of the Sugar-Maple Tree ... *London: Privately Printed.* 1832. 8vo, pp. 72. S. 36491

JONES (E.) Address delivered at the Fifth Anniversary of the Peace Society of Minot, November 5, 1828. By Rev. Elijah Jones. *Portland: Shirley and Hyde, Printers.* 1828. 8vo, pp. 28.

Also: Sermon delivered in Hallowell, June 24, 1840, before the Maine Missionary Society .... *Portland.* 1840. 8vo, pp. 46.

JONES (E.) Memoir of Elizabeth Jones, a little Indian Girl, who lived at the River-Credit Mission, Upper Canada. *New York: Carlton & Porter.* [n. d.] 18mo, pp. 36. Plate. 36493

JONES (E. C.) A Collection of Poems on different Subjects. By Elizabeth C. Jones. *Providence.* 1819. 36494

JONES (E.) Oration on the American Rebellion, delivered at Rochdale, ... March 7, 1864. By Ernest Jones. *Rochdale: G. Howarth.* 1863. 8vo, pp. 16. 36495

JONES. The Slaveholder's War. A Lecture .... By Ernest Jones, Esq. ... November 16th, 1863. ... [*Manchester. John Heywood, Printer.* n. d.] 16mo, pp. 44. 36496

JONES (Frederick). History [of the World] from 1831 to 1840. [*Philadelphia.* 1841.] 8vo. 36497

JONES [George]. Speech ... on the Removal of the Deposites. Delivered in the House of Representatives, U. S., January, 1834. [n. p. n. d.] 8vo, pp. 32. B. 36498

JONES (G.) Excursions to Cairo, Jerusalem, Damascus and Balbec, from the United States Ship Delaware .... By George Jones, A.M. ... *New-York: Van Nostrand and Dwight.* 1836. 12mo, pp. (4), 388. BA., C., S. 36499

JONES (G.) Oration on the National Independence, Richmond, Va., July 4, 1840, before the Franklin Society, at the City Hall. Written and Pronounced by George Jones, Tragedian .... *Richmond.* 1840. 8vo, pp. 43. 36500

JONES. An Original History of Ancient America, Founded upon the Ruins of Antiquity; the Identity of the Aborigines with the People of Tyrus and Israel; and the Introduction of Christianity by the Apostle St. Thomas. By George Jones ... *London, New York, Berlin, and Paris.* 1843. Rl. 8vo, pp. (20), 461, (1).

The author was afterwards known as the Count Johannes. The work is entirely speculative in its character, and grandiloquent in style. It was commended by Sir R. Meyrick; *see* "Athenæum," July 1, 1843, for an adverse notice. The title above given is engraved; the printed title reads:

JONES. The History of Ancient America, anterior to the time of Columbus; proving the Identity of the Aborigines with the Tyrians and Israelites; and the Introduction of Christianity into

the Western Hemisphere by the Apostle St. Thomas. By George Jones ... The Tyrian Æra. Second Edition. *London: Longman.* 1843. Rl. 8vo, pp. (20), 461, (1). + Third Edition. [*Ibid.*]

JONES. Tecumseh and the Prophet of the West; An Historical, Israel-Indian Tragedy; in Five Acts: with Historical Notes, Original Letters, &c.—The Life and History of General Harrison, late President of the United States, inclusive to the Treaty of Washington of August 9, 1842: with Original Letters, &c. ... By George Jones .... *London: Longmans.* 1844. 8vo, pp. (20), 242. 36503

JONES (G[eorge] W.) Speech of Hon. G. W. Jones ... on ... Harbors and Rivers, Delivered in the House of Representatives ... March 11, 1846. *Washington: Printed at the Office of Blair and Rives.* 1864. 8vo, pp. 7. H. 36504

Also: Letter ... to the Democratic State Central Committee. Expenditures of Government from 1843, to July, 1858. ... [n. p. n. d.] 8vo, pp. 24. H.—Speech ... on ... the better Organization of the Treasury ... April 1, 1846. *Washington: Printed at the Office of Blair and Rives.* 1846. 8vo, pp. 15. H.

[JONES (G. Wymberley).] Observations on Doctor Stevens's History of Georgia. *Savannah.* MDCCCXLIX. 8vo, pp. 28. A.

A severe and able criticism. Privately printed at Philadelphia. One hundred copies on fine and five on large paper. Intended to be added to the Wormsloe publications.

JONES (H.) Strange Phenomena of New England: in the Seventeenth Century: including the "Salem Witchcraft," "1692." From the Writings of "The Rev. Cotton Mather, D.D. ..." By Henry Jones .... *New-York: Piercy & Reed.* 1846. 8vo, pp. 54.

JONES (H. W. F.) Sermon ... Funeral of Capt. Simeon A. Mellick. By Henry W. F. Jones. *Bergen Point, N. J.* 1862.

[JONES (H. G.)] The Bradford Prayer Book. 1710. ... [*Philadelphia:*] *Privately Printed for Horatio Gates Jones.* 1870. 8vo, pp. 10. 36508

JONES. The Levering Family; or, a Genealogical Account of Wigard Levering and Gerhard Levering, Two of the Pioneer Settlers of Roxborough Township, Philadelphia County, (Pennsylvania,) and their Descendants; and an Appendix, containing brief Sketches of Roxborough and Manayunk. By Horatio Gates Jones .... *Philadelphia: Printed by King and Baird.* 1858. 8vo, pp. (4), iv, 193. 7 Plates. 36509

JONES. Report of the Committee of the Historical Society of Pennsylvania, on their Visit to New York, May 20, 1863, at the Celebration of the Two Hundredth Birth-Day of William Bradford, who Introduced the Art of Printing into the Middle Colonies of British America. Read June 8, 1863. With the Resolutions then adopted. By Horatio Gates Jones .... *Philadelphia: King & Baird.* 1863. 8vo, pp. 14. C. 36510

Also: ["Andrew Bradford, Founder of the Newspaper Press in the Middle States of America."] An Address ... at the Annual Meeting of the Historical Society of Pennsylvania, February 9th, 1869. ... *Philadelphia: King & Baird, Printers.* 1869. 8vo, pp. 36. Facsimile. B.

JONES (H.) The | Present State | of | Virginia. | Giving | A particular and short Account of the In- | dian, English, and Negroe Inhabitants of that | Colony. | Shewing their Religion, Manners, Government, | Trade, Way of Living, &c. with a Description of | the Country. | From whence is inferred a short View of | Maryland and North Carolina. | To which are added, | Schemes and Propositions for the better Promotion of | Learning, Religion, Inventions, Manufactures, and Trade in | Virginia, and the other Plantations. | For the Information of the Curious, and for the Service of such | as are engaged in the Propagation of the Gospel and Advancement | of Learning, and for the Use of all Persons concerned in the | Virginia Trade and Plantation. | ... | By Hvgh Jones, A.M. Chaplain to | the Honourable Assembly, and lately Minister of | James-Town, &c. in Virginia. | *London:* | *Printed for J. Clarke, at the Bible, under the Royal-* | *Exchange.* M DCC XXIV. | 8vo, pp. (4), viii, 151, (1). B., P., S. 36511

Contains an account of the Tramontane Order, the state of the Church, and many other valuable particulars of the then existing order of affairs in Virginia. "This is one of the scarcest works relating to Virginia published in this century. The author thinks that the settlement of America by the Europeans is a fulfillment of the scriptural text on his title-page, *Japheth* being the English, *Shem* the Indians, and *Canaan* the Negroes."—RICH, I. Mr. Rich rather overstates its rarity. Reprinted as:

JONES. The Present State of Virginia. By Hugh Jones, A.M. *New York: ... Joseph Sabin.* 1865. 8vo, pp. (8), viii, 151. BA.

Fifty copies printed on large paper. Forms No. v. of Sabin's Reprints. Also: A Protest against Popery, &c. ... *Annapolis, Md.* 1745. 8vo. S.

[JONES (Ignatius).] Random Recollections of Albany, from 1800 to 1808: with some Additional Matter. Second Edition. *Albany: Charles Van Benthuysen.* 1850. 8vo, pp. 90. 36513

JONES (I.) The Mandate of God for Israel's Advancement: A Sermon delivered in Trinity Church, Milton, and St. Michael, Litchfield, Nov. 5, 1845; being one hundred years since the

formation of the Episcopal Church in ... Litchfield, Conn. By Isaac Jones, A.M., Rector. *Litchfield: Printed at the Enquirer Office.* 1846. 8vo, pp. 62. N. 36514

JONES (I. D.) Remarks of I. D. Jones, June 16, 1842, on the Apportionment Bill. *Washington.* 1842. 8vo. 36515

[JONES (J.)] The Flying Artillerist; or, the Child of the Battle-Field. A Tale of Mexican Treachery. By Harry Hazel. *New York.* 1853. 8vo. 36516

[JONES.] Yankee Jack; or, the Perils of a Privateersman. By Harry Hazel. *New York.* 1852. 8vo. 36517

JONES (J. A.) A Biographical Memoir of the late Ichabod Norton, Esq., of Edgartown, Mass. By J. Athearn Jones. Printed for Private Distribution. *Boston: Coolidge & Wiley, Printers.* 1848. 8vo, pp. 26. 36518

JONES. Haverhill; or, Memoirs of an Officer in the Army of Wolfe. By James Athearn Jones. ... *New-York: J. & J. Harper.* 1831. 2 vols., 12mo, pp. (4), 228; (2), 263. + *London: T. & W. Boone.* 1831. 3 vols., post 8vo, pp. viii, 314; (4), 335, (1); (2), 350. BA. 36519

JONES. A Letter to an English Gentleman, on the Libels and Calumnies on America, by British Writers and Reviewers. By James Athearn Jones. *Philadelphia.* 1826. 8vo, pp. 43. C.

JONES. Traditions of the North American Indians: being a second and revised edition of "Tales of an Indian Camp." By James Athearn Jones. *London: Henry Colburn and Richard Bentley.* 1830. 3 vols., post 8vo, pp. xxviii, 312; (2), iv, 336; iv, 341. 6 Plates. BA. 36521

A curious and rather apocryphal performance. The copious and numerous notes upon Indian history and customs, scattered through the volumes, have an authenticity which entitle them to respect. *See* Field's "Essay." I have seen copies of this work in which the date is expressed as MDCCCXXX, and in which there are xxxiii additional pages.

[JONES.] Sagen der nordamerikanischen Indianer. [Aus dem Englischen]. *Altenburg: J. Helbig.* 1837. 16mo, pp. (2), 346. Plate. C. 36522

JONES (J. C.) Speech of Hon. James C. Jones ... on ... the Fugitive Slave Law ... In the Senate ... June 26, 1854. *Washington.* 1854. 8vo, pp. 11. B. 36523

Also: Speech ... on Non-Intervention, delivered in the United States Senate, March 18, 1852. *Washington.* 1852. 8vo, pp. 16. N.

JONES (J.) Plain Concise Practical Remarks, on the Treatment of Wounds and Fractures: To which is Added, An Appendix, on Camp and Military Hospitals; Principally Designed, for the Use of young Military and Naval Surgeons, in North-America. By John Jones, M.D. Professor of Surgery, in King's College, New York. *New York.* 1775. 8vo, pp. 92. + *Philadelphia: Robert Bell.* MDCCLXXVI. 8vo, pp. 114. P. 36524

JONES (J.) The Tower of Babel; or, Essays on the Confusion of Tongues, from a ground-work of the late Mr. Le Brigant, with comparisons between the Languages of the Old and New World, and a defence of those rights which Ancient Britons derive from the first European Settlement formed in America by a Prince of Wales. By John Jones. *London: Theodore Page.* [1800?] 8vo, pp. 92. 36525

An essay to establish the existence of a tribe of Welsh Indians and the discovery of America by their ancestors. "We feel bold to refer unbelievers to original papers in possession of Lady Juliana Penn, we mean the good and great William Penn's M.S. Journals, where the Welsh Indians are frequently mentioned without the least doubt of their existence."—*Page* 77.

JONES (J.) *See* Vol. IV., Nos. 12832–33.

JONES (J.) The Black Laws of Illinois, and a few reasons why they should be repealed. By John Jones. ... *Chicago.* 1864. 8vo, pp. 16. B. 36526

JONES (John B.) Adventures of Col. Gracchus Vanderbomb, of Sloughcreek, in Pursuit of the Presidency; Also, the Exploits of ... his Secretary, Mr. Numerius Plutarch Kipps. By J. B. Jones .... *Philadelphia: A. Hart.* 1852. 12mo, pp. viii, 19–202.

JONES. Life and Adventures of a Country Merchant; a Narrative of his Exploits at Home, during his Travels, and in the Cities. Designed to Amuse and Instruct. By J. B. Jones .... *Philadelphia.* 1854. P. 36528

JONES. Major Jones's Sketches of Travel, comprising the Scenes, Incidents, and Adventures in his Tour from Georgia to Canada. ... *Philadelphia: Carey & Hart.* 1848. 12mo, pp. 192. 8 Plates. + *Philadelphia: A. Hart.* 1853. 12mo. S. 36529

Also: Major Jones's Courtship, pp. 216; Chronicles of Pineville; embracing Sketches of Georgia Scenes, Incidents and Characters, Yankee Hill, etc., pp. 186.

JONES. The Monarchist; an Historical Novel. By J. B. Jones *Philadelphia* 1852 12mo. C. 36530

JONES. A Rebel War Clerk's Diary at the Confederate States Capital. By J. B. Jones, Clerk in the War Department of the Confederate States Government .... *Philadelphia: J. B. Lippincott & Co.* 1866. 2 vols., cr. 8vo, pp. 392; 480. B., BA. 36531

JONES. The Rival Belles; or, Life in Washington. By J. B. Jones .... *Philadelphia: T. B. Peterson & Brothers.* 1864. 12mo, pp. 13–270. 36532

JONES. The War-Path: a Narrative of Adventures in the Wilderness, with minute Details of the Captivity of sundry Persons, ... fearful Battles with the Indians .... By J. B. Jones .... *Philadelphia.* 1858. 12mo, pp. 335. C. 36533

JONES. Wild Southern Scenes. A Tale of Disunion! and Border War! By J. B. Jones, Esq. ... *Philadelphia: T. B. Peterson & Brothers.* [1859.] 12mo, pp. iv, 502. Plate. C., H.

[JONES.] Wild Western Scenes; a Narrative of Adventures in the Western Wilderness, forty years ago; wherein the Conduct of Daniel Boone, the great American Pioneer, is particularly described .... By a Squatter. *Philadelphia: E. Ferrett & Co.* 1845. 8vo, pp. 247. + [*Ibid.*] 1851. 12mo. + *Philadelphia.* 1865. 12mo. + *Philadelphia.* 1869. 12mo. + Second Series. *Philadelphia: J. B. Lippincott & Co.* 1867. 12mo, pp. 335.

This second series is also published as the "War Path," No. 36533, *supra.*

JONES. Wild Western Scenes; or, the White Spirit of the Wilderness. Being a Narrative of Adventures, embracing the same Characters portrayed in the Original "Wild Western Scenes," over one Hundred Editions of which have been sold in Europe and America. By J. B. Jones .... *Richmond: M. A. Malsby.* 1863. 12mo, pp. iv, 123, (1). B., BA. 36536

Printed on confederate paper with brown ink.

[JONES.] The Winkles; or, the Merry Monomaniacs. An American Picture with Portraits of the Natives. ... *New York: D. Appleton and Company.* 1855. 12mo, pp. xii, 424. P. 36537

Also: The Spanglers and Tinglers; or the Rival Belles. A Tale unveiling some of the Mysteries of Society and Politics as they exist at the present time in the United States. ... *Philadelphia.* 1852. 8vo.—Thoughts on the Literary Prospects of America. ... *Baltimore.* 1839. 8vo, pp. 16.

JONES (J. E.) The Young Abolitionists; or Conversations on Slavery. By J. Elizabeth Jones. *Boston: Anti-Slavery Office.* 1848. 24mo, pp. 131. B. 36538

JONES (J. F.) Story of Jack Halyard, the Sailor Boy, designed for American Children .... By John Franklin Jones. *New-York: E. Bliss and E. White.* 1824. 18mo. 36539

JONES (J. G.) An Oration, delivered ... the twenty-ninth of November, 1796, At the Great Room, in Brewer Street [London], On the Resignation of General Washington, including A short Review of his Life, Character and Conduct. By John Gale Jones. *London: T. C. Jones.* [1796.] 8vo, pp. 33. P. + Second Edition. *London.* 1825. 8vo, pp. 20. S. 36540

JONES (J. G.) Concise History of the Introduction of Protestantism into Mississippi and the Southwest. By Rev. John G. Jones. *St. Louis: P. M. Pinckard.* 1866. 12mo, pp. 257. C.

JONES (J. G.) Speech of Hon. J. Glancy Jones, of Penn'a, on the Tariff. ... in the House of Representatives, December 13, 1852. [*Washington.* n. d.] 8vo, pp. 8. H. 36542

Also: Reply ... to Henry M. Fuller's attack on the political Opinions of Mr. Buchanan. [n. p.] 1856. 8vo.

JONES (J. H.) The Trial of John H. Jones, First Lieutenant of the Privateer Schooner Revenge, on a Charge of Piracy; Including the Argument of the Counsel, and Charge of Judge Washington. Reported by one of the Counsel concerned in the Cause. *Philadelphia.* 1813. 8vo, pp. 63. 36543

JONES (J. M.) The Naturalist in Bermuda; a Sketch of the Geology, Zoology, and Botany, of that remarkable Group of Islands, together with Meteorological Observations. By John Matthew Jones, Esq. ... Assisted by Major J. W. Wedderburn ... and J. L. Hurdis, Esq. ... *London: Reeves & Turner.* 1859. Post 8vo, pp. xii, (2), 200. Map. B., BA. 36544

Also: Contributions to the Ichthyology of Nova Scotia. ... *Halifax.* 1863. 8vo.—Contributions to the Natural History of Nova Scotia. ... Insecta Coleoptera.—Part I. *Halifax, Nova Scotia: Printed by James Bowes & Sons.* 1870. 8vo, pp. 15.—Contributions to the Natural History of Nova Scotia. Reptilia. ... *Halifax.* 1865. 8vo, pp. 15.—Contributions to the Natural History of the Bermudas. Part I. Mollusca. .. *Halifax.* 1864. 8vo, pp. 13.

JONES (J. R.) An Address delivered at a Town-Meeting of the Anti-Masonic Citizens of Philadelphia, October 5th, 1830. By John R. Jones. *Philadelphia: Printed by John Clarke.* 1830. 8vo, pp. 15. B. 36545

JONES ([John] P.) The Interesting Life, Travels, Voyages, and Daring Engagements, of that celebrated and justly notorious

Pirate, Paul Jones: Containing Numerous Anecdotes of Undaunted Courage, in the prosecution of his nefarious undertakings. ... *New York: George Sinclair.* 1807. 12mo, pp. 36. N. + *New York.* 1809. 12mo. 36546

JONES. The Interesting Life, Travels, Voyages, and daring Engagements, of the celebrated Paul Jones: Commodore in the American Navy during the late Revolutionary War: containing Numerous Anecdotes of Undaunted Courage, in the prosecution of his Undertaking. *Hudson: William E. Norman* ... 1809. 18mo, pp. 46. 36547

JONES. The Interesting Life, Travels, Voyages, and Daring Engagements of that Celebrated and Justly Renowned Commander Paul Jones. Containing Numerous Anecdotes of Undaunted Courage, in the Prosecution of his various Enterprises. Written by Himself. [The first Philadelphia from the fourth London Edition.] *Philadelphia: William M'Carty.* 1812. 8vo, pp. 36. + [*Ibid.*] 1817. 36548

JONES. The Life and Adventures of Paul Jones. *New York: W. H. Graham.* 1846. 8vo, pp. 64. + [*Ibid.*] 1848. 8vo. + [*Ibid.*] 1869. 36549

JONES. The Life and Character of John Paul Jones during the Revolutionary War. *New York.* 1851. 8vo. Portrait.

JONES. Life and Correspondence of John Paul Jones, including his Narrative of the Campaign of the Liman. From Original Letters and Manuscripts, in the Possession of Miss Janette Taylor. ... *New York.* 1830. 8vo, pp. 555, (1). Portrait. BA.

JONES. The Life and Exploits of the celebrated Pirate, Paul Jones. *London.* 1803. 8vo. Frontispiece. 36552

JONES. The Life and History of Paul Jones, the English Corsair: giving an account of the Wonderful and Extraordinary Perils, Escapes, & Voyages of that bold and determinate Pirate & Smuggler. *London: J. Lee.* [n. d.] 12mo, pp. 34. Plate.

JONES. The Life of Paul Jones, from Original Documents in the possession of John Henry Sherburne, Esq. Register of the Navy of the United States. *London: John Murray.* MDCCCXXV. Post 8vo, pp. xii, 320. 36554

JONES. The Life, Travels, Voyages, and daring Engagements of Paul Jones: containing Numerous Anecdotes of Undaunted

Courage. To which is prefixed the Life and Adventures of Peter Williamson, Who was kidnapped, when an Infant, from his Native Place, Aberdeen, and sold for a Slave in America. *Albany: Printed by H. C. Southwick.* 1813. 18mo, pp. 108.

There is another edition with a similar title, *Albany*, 1809.

JONES. The Life, Travels, Voyages, and Daring Engagements of Paul Jones. *Boston: N. Coverley.* [n. d.] 12mo. 36556

JONES. Life of Rear-Admiral John Paul Jones, ... Compiled from his Original Journals and Correspondence: including an Account of his Services in the American Revolution ... . *Philadelphia: Walker & Gillis.* 1845. 12mo, pp. 399. C. + [*Ibid.*] 1847. 12mo. + [*Ibid.*] 1853. 12mo. + *Philadelphia: J. B. Lippincott & Co.* 1858. 12mo, pp. 399. H. + *Philadelphia.* 1869.

Edited by B. Walker.

JONES. Memoirs of Rear-Admiral Paul Jones. ... Now First Compiled from his Original Journals and Correspondence: including an Account of his Services under Prince Potemkin, prepared for Publication by Himself. *Edinburgh: Oliver & Boyd.* MDCCCXXX. 2 vols., 12mo, pp. xii, 331; (4), 341. BA., H. + *London: Re-published by H. Washbourn.* MDCCCXLIII. 2 vols., 12mo, pp. xii, 331; (4), 341. 36558

JONES. Mémoires de Paul Jones, Ou il expose ses principaux services, et rappelle ce qui lui est arrivé de plus remarquable pendant le cours de la révolution américaine, particulièrement en Europe. écrits par lui-même en anglais, et traduits sous ses yeux par le citoyen André. ... *Paris: Louis. An* VI. 1798. 12mo, pp. (4), xix, 244. Portrait. B., C., J.C.B. 36559

JONES. A Narrative of the Unparalleled and Celebrated Commodore, Paul Jones. Translated from a Manuscript written by Himself. [n. p. n. d.] 12mo, pp. 23. 36560

See Fanning (N.), Vol. VI., No. 23782. The following pieces relate to John Paul Jones:

Bill for the Relief of the Heirs of John Paul Jones. [n. p. n. d.] 8vo. 36561

Missive van Z. Hoogheid omtrent de 2 Engelsche pryscheepen, onder P. Jones Texel binnengekomen, 22 Dec. 1779. Folio. 36562

Dispatch of His Highness on the English ships which have entered the Texel under Paul Jones.

Nader Aanteekening van Dordrecht, Rotterdam en Schiedam omtrent de resolutie van 17 Nov. 1779 in de saak van Paul Jones. 22 Dec. 1779. Folio. 36563

Further notes of Dordrecht, Rotterdam, and Schiedam, on the resolution of November 17, 1779, in the affair of Paul Jones.

Een Nieuw Lied op de groote held Paul Jonas: "Hier komt Paul Jones aan | Het is soon aardig ventje." [1779.] Folio, pp. (2), 4. 36564

This new song on the great hero Paul Jones, was composed in honor of his arrival in the Texel with two vessels captured from the English in 1779. Particulars about this and other poems on the same subject may be found in the "Navorscher," III. 38-40. The song itself has often been reprinted in Dutch collections of songs.

Paul Jonas. [*Amsterdam.* 1780?] Sm. 8vo, pp. 94. 36565

A chap-book of popular songs. "Of the utmost rarity."—F. MULLER.

Paul Jones, or the Fife Coast Garland; a Heroical Poem ... . [*Privately Printed*] *Edinburgh.* 1779. 4to, pp. 37. 36566

A poetical satire.

Paul-Jones, ou Prophéties sur l'Amérique, l'Angleterre, la France, l'Espagne, la Hollande, &c. Par Paul-Jones Corsaire, Prophète & Sorcier comme il n'en fût jamais. Y joint Le Rêve d'un Suisse sur La Révolution de l'Amérique, Dédié à Son Excellence M[gneur] l'Ambassadeur Franklin, & à leurs Nobles & Hautes Puissances Messeigneurs du Congrès. De l'Ere de l'Independance de l'Amérique l'An V. [*Basle.* 1781.] 8vo, pp. 120. B.

A very amusing *jeu d'esprit*, the author of which shows himself to be no false prophet. The date is doubtful; J. R. Bartlett makes it 1781, Stevens says 1797.

Paul Jones der Kühne Seemann und Gründer der Amerikanischen Marine. Aus dem Englischen. *Leipzig.* 1826.

Resolutie op de Memorie van d. Groot-Brittan. Ambass. raakende het geval van twee schepen door P. Jones genomen, leggende op de Rheede van Texel, 21 Oct. 1779. Folio, pp. 10.

Resolution on the memorial of the English ambassador, relating to the ships captured by Paul Jones.

Resolutie ... 17 Nov. 1779. Folio, pp. 4. 36570

On the arrival of Paul Jones in the harbor of Texel.

JONES (J. P.) An Eulogium upon Antony Laussat. By John Pringle Jones. *Philadelphia.* 1834. 8vo. P. 36571

JONES (J. R.) Slavery Sanctioned by the Bible. The first part of a General Treatise on the Slavery Question. By John

Richter Jones. *Philadelphia: J. B. Lippincott & Co.* 1861. 8vo, pp. 34. B., H. 36572

JONES [John W.] Speech of Mr. Jones ... on the Loan Bill; ... in the House of Representatives, July 12, 1841. *Washington: Printed by Blair and Rives.* 1841. 8vo, pp. 16. BA. 36573

Also: Speech ... May 16, 1838, on the Bill to authorize the issuing of Treasury Notes to meet the Current Expenses of the Government. [n. p. n. d.] 8vo, pp. 16.

JONES (J. W.), *and* MORRIS (T. B.) Hanes y gwrthryfel mawr yn y Talaethan Vnedig; yn nghyd a byr grybwyllion ain y prif ddigwyddiadau o ddarganfyddiad America hyd adferiad heddwch, yn 1865; at yr hyn yr ychwanegir bywyd ae arlywydiaeth Abraham Lincoln, gyd ag amryw ddarluniau prydferth. *Utica (N. Y.): J. M. Jones.* 1866. 8vo, pp. 631. 5 Portraits.

JONES (J.) Agricultural Resources of Georgia. Address before the Cotton Planters' Convention of Georgia, at Macon, December 13, 1860. By Joseph Jones, M.D. ... *Augusta, Ga.* 1861. 8vo, pp. 13. 36575

JONES. First Report to the Cotton Planters' Convention of Georgia, on the Agricultural Resources of Georgia. By Joseph Jones, M.D. ... *Augusta, Ga.* 1860. 8vo, pp. xv, 312, (8). BA.

JONES. Researches, Chemical and Physiological, concerning certain North American Vertebrata. By Joseph Jones, M.D. ... *Washington.* 1856. 4to, pp. 150. 36577

Included in the "Smithsonian Contributions," Vol. VIII.

JONES (*Major* Joseph), *pseudon.* *See* [Thompson (W. T.)]

JONES (J. H.) Outline of a Work of Grace in the Presbyterian Congregation at New Brunswick, N. J., during the year 1837. By Joseph H. Jones ... . *Philadelphia: Henry Perkins.* 1839. 12mo, pp. 148. B., H. 36578

Also: A Discourse on the Death of Helen Elizabeth Lawson. ... *Philadelphia.* 1853. 24mo, pp. 46. H. *See* Green (A.), Vol. VII., No. 28503.

JONES (J. S.) A Defence of the Revolutionary History of the State of North Carolina from the Aspersions of Mr. Jefferson. By Jo. Seawell Jones, of Shocco, North Carolina. ... *Boston: Charles Bowen.* ... 1834. 12mo, pp. xii, 343. BA., C. 36579

JONES. Memorials of North Carolina. By J. Seawell Jones, of Shocco. *New-York: Scatcherd & Adams.* 1838. 8vo, pp. 87.

JONES (J.) Virginia Graham, the Spy of the Grand Army. By Justin Jones. *Boston: A. K. Loring.* 1869. 12mo, pp. 165.

JONES (L. A.) The Bold Scalp-Hunter; or, The Mysterious Being of the Cave. By L. Augustus Jones. *New York: Geo. Munro & Co.* 1865. 16mo, pp. 7-100. 36582

Also: The Indian Queen's Revenge. A Tale of the Mohawk Valley in Revolutionary Times. ... *New York: Geo. Munro & Co.* [n. d.] 16mo, pp. 100.—Slim Jim; or, The Indian Maid's Last Arrow. ... *New York: G. Munro & Co.* 1867. 18mo, pp. 100.—Sly Sam, the Quaker Spy; or, The Foundling of the Prairie. ... *New York: Geo. Munro & Co.* [n. d.] 16mo, pp. 97.

JONES (L.) A Discourse, delivered on the Twenty-Fifth Anniversary of The Church of the Epiphany, ... January 10, 1858. By ... Rev. Lot Jones, A.M. ... *New York: Anson D. F. Randolph.* 1858. 8vo, pp. 23, (1). H. 36583

JONES. Memoir of Mrs. Sarah Louisa Taylor, or an illustration of the work of the Holy Spirit, in awakening, renewing, and sanctifying the heart. By Lot Jones, A.M. ... *New-York: J. S. Taylor.* 1838. 12mo, Engraved Title, pp. 324. Portrait. C., S. + Fifth Edition. [*Ibid.*] 1847. 12mo. Portrait. H. 36584

JONES (*Mrs.*) Account of the Loss of the Wesleyan Missionaries in the "Maria" Mail Boat off the Island of Antigua, By Mrs. Jones, the only Survivor. *London.* 1826. 8vo.

[JONES (Morris Charles).] Notes respecting the Family of Waldo. Printed for private circulation only. *Press of Ballantyne & Co., Edinburgh.* 1863. 8vo, pp. 35. 36586

This English genealogy includes some of the American branches of that name.

JONES (N. W.) No. I. Indian Bulletin for 1867. Containing a brief Account of the North American Indians, and the Interpretation of Many Indian Names. By Rev. N. W. Jones. *New York: Printed by C. A. Alvord.* 1867. 8vo, pp. 16. B., H. + (No. II.) for 1868; containing an Account of Chinese Voyages to the N. W. Coast of America, and the Interpretation of two hundred Indian Names. *New York.* 1869. 8vo. 36587

JONES (P.) My Uncle Hobson and I; or, Slashes at Life with a free Broad-Axe. By Pascal Jones. *New-York: D. Appleton & Co.* MDCCCXLV. 12mo, pp. 268. C., H. 36588

JONES (Paul). *See* Jones (John P.)

JONES (P.) A Collection of Chippeway and English Hymns, for the use of the native Indians. Translated by Peter Jones,

Indian Missionary. To which are added a Few Hymns translated by the Rev. James Evans and George Henry. ... *New-York: Lane and Tippett.* 1847. 24mo, pp. vi, 289. BA. + *New York.* 1853. 24mo. 36589

JONES. History of the Ojebway Indians; with especial reference to their Conversion to Christianity. By Rev. Peter Jones, (Kahkewaquonaby) ... . With a brief Memoir of the Writer; and Introductory Notice by the Rev. G. Osborn, D.D. ... *London: A. W. Bennett.* 1861. Post 8vo, pp. vi, (2), 278. 16 Plates. B.

Reissued without a date.

JONES. Life and Journals of Peter Jones. *Toronto.* 1860. 12mo, pp. 424. 36591

JONES. Ojebway Spelling Book, Translated. 1828. 36592

JONES. Netum Ewh Oomahzenahegun owh Moses, Genesis aszhenekahdaig. Kahahnekahnootah moobeung owh kahkewaquonaby, ahneshenahba Makadawekoonahya. *Toronto: Auxiliary Bible Society.* 1835. 12mo. 36593

The Book of Genesis in Chippewa, by Peter Jones. *See also* Ojebwa, *and* Vol. IV., No. 12832. Also: Additional Hymns, Translated a short time before his death. *Brantford.* 1861.

JONES (Philip). Instructions for Gentlemen, Merchants, Students, Souldiers, Marriners, &c., employed in the Servises abroad. *London: Printed by John Wolfe.* 1589. 4to. 36594

Dedicated to Sir Francis Drake, the ornament of his country, etc. Rare.

JONES (*Dr.* Pleasant), *pseudon.* The Slaveholder Abroad; or, Billy Buck's Visit, with his Master, to England. A Series of Letters from Dr. Pleasant Jones to Major Joseph Jones, of Georgia. *Philadelphia: J. B. Lippincott & Co.* 1860. 12mo, pp. 512. 7 Plates. C. 36595

JONES (P.) Annals and Recollections of Oneida County. ... By Pomroy Jones. *Rome: The Author.* 1851. 8vo, pp. xvi, 893.

JONES (R.) Memorials of Rebecca Jones (of Philadelphia). Compiled by W. J. Allison. *Philadelphia.* 1849. 8vo. 36597

JONES (R.) Panama in 1855. By R. Jones. *New York.* 1856. 12mo. 36598

JONES (R. D.) Opening Address before the N. Y. State Teachers' Association, at Utica, ... August 1, 1855. By R. D. Jones, Esq. *Albany.* 1855. 8vo, pp. 12. B. 36599

JONES (S.) A Century Sermon: Delivered in Philadelphia, at the Opening of the Philadelphia Baptist Association, October 6th, 1807. By Samuel Jones, D.D. ... *Philadelphia: Thomas Dobson.* 1807. 8vo, pp. 26, (2), H. 36600

JONES. Resignation, a Funeral Sermon, occasioned by the Death of the Rev. Isaac Eaton, A.M. late Minister of the Baptist Church, at Hopewell, in New Jersey; preached at Hopewell, by Samuel Jones, A.M. ... *Philadelphia: James Humphreys.* 1772.

JONES. A Treatise of Church Discipline, and a Directory. By appointment of the Philadelphia Baptist Association. By Samuel Jones, D.D. *Philadelphia: S. C. Ustick.* 1798. 16mo, pp. 38. C. 36602

Also: Sermon Preached at Pennepeck in Pennsylvania, ... 1783. ... *Philadelphia.* 1783. 12mo.

JONES (Samuel). Pittsburgh in the Year Eighteen Hundred and Twenty-Six, containing Sketches Topographical, Historical and Statistical; together with a Directory of the City, and A View of its various Manufactures, Population, Improvements, &c. ... By S. Jones. *Pittsburgh: Johnston & Stockton.* 1826. 12mo, pp. 153. Plates. C. 36603

This is the second directory of Pittsburgh; the first was published in 1820.

JONES (S.) A Treatise on the Right of Suffrage, With an Appendix. By Samuel Jones. ... *Boston: Otis, Broadus and Company.* 1842. 12mo, pp. 274. BA., C. 36604

JONES (S. B.) Discourses at the Inauguration of William H. Green, as Professor ... at Princeton ... By Rev. S. B. Jones ... and W. H. Green. *Philadelphia.* 1857. 8vo, pp. 51. S. 36605

JONES (S. W.) Memoir of the Hon. James Duane, Judge of the District Court of the United States for New York. By Samuel W. Jones. *New York.* 1852. 8vo, pp. 51. N. 36606

[JONES (*Miss* Sarah L.)] Life in the South. *See* J. (S. L.), No. 35329, and for the word "place" in the third line *read* part.

JONES (S.) Speech of Mr. Seaborn Jones, of Georgia, on The Bill Reducing the Duty on Imports, ... delivered ... June 18, 1846. *Washington.* 1846. 8vo, pp. 7. H. 36607

Also: Speech ... on The Oregon Question. ... January 15, 1846. *Washington: Blair & Rives.* 1846. 8vo, pp. 7. H.

JONES (T. A.) The Old Trapper's Pride. By T. Augustus Jones. *New York: G. Munro & Co.* [n. d.] 16mo, pp. 98.

JONES (T.) American Insurance Manual for 1855 ... . *New York: T. Jones, Jun. & Co.* 1855. 36609

JONES (T.) Dedication Sermon, delivered at the New Brick Meeting-House, of the Second Society of Universalists in Boston, October 16th, 1817. By Thomas Jones ... . *Boston: Printed by Thomas G. Bangs.* 1817. 8vo, pp. 16. BA., H. 36610

Also: An Address delivered on the Gun-House Square, at Gloucester, July 30, 1807, Before the Field Officers of the Regiment ... . *Salem.* 1807. 8vo, pp. 8.—A Sermon, delivered at the General Convention of Universalists, ... in September, ... 1813, at Winchester, New Hampshire. ... *Boston: Printed by Joseph T. Buckingham.* 1813. 8vo, pp. 20.—A Sermon ... June 22, 1825, at the Ordination of Rev. Calvin Gardner ... in Charlestown, Mass. ... *Boston: Howe & Norton, Printers.* 1825. 8vo, pp. 30, (1).

JONES (T.) The Experience of Thomas Jones, who was a Slave for Forty-Three Years. Written by a Friend, as given to him by Brother Jones. *Boston: Printed by Daniel Laing, Jr.* 1850. 8vo, pp. 47. BA. + *Springfield.* 1854. 12mo, pp. 48. + *Worcester: Printed by Henry J. Howland.* 1857. 8vo, pp. 48.

Reproduced as: "Experience and Personal Narrative of Uncle Tom Jones: ... Also the Surprising Adventures of Wild Tom, of the Island Retreat, a Fugitive Negro from South Carolina." *Boston.* 1855. 8vo, pp. 54. H.

JONES (T. G.) Recreations of a Southern Barrister. With an Introduction, by Rev. T. G. Jones. *Philadelphia: J. B. Lippincott & Co.* 1859. 12mo, pp. (6), 212, (1). B. 36612

JONES (T. A. C.) ... Proceedings of a Court-Martial on Commodore Thomas Ap. Catesby Jones, and certain Correspondence between the Secretary of the Navy and Commodore Jones. *Washington.* 1851. 8vo, pp. 400. W. 36613

31st Cong., 2d Sess., Ex. Doc., No. 45.

JONES (T. L.) Impeachment of the President. Speech of Hon. Thomas Laurens Jones ... February 24, 1868. *Washington: F. & J. Rives & Geo. A. Bailey* ... 1868. 8vo, pp. 8. H.

JONES. Reply of Hon. Thos. L. Jones to Governor Stevenson, of Kentucky. *Washington, D. C.: McGill & Witherow, Printers.* [1870.] 8vo, pp. 40. H. 36615

Also: Amnesty. Remarks ... December 19, 21, and 22, 1870. [*Washington.* n. d.] 8vo, pp. 4.—Washington Family Relics. Speech ... March 3, 1869. *Washington: F. & J. Rives & Geo. A. Bailey ... Printers.* 1869. 8vo, pp. 7. H.

JONES (T. P.) An Address on the Progress of Manufactures ... in the United States; and ... the Employment of Slaves in the manufacturing of Cotton and other Goods. ... November 6, 1827. By Thomas P. Jones, M.D. *Philadelphia: Judah Dobson.* 1827. 8vo, pp. 18. BA. 36616

JONES (T. G.) An Address before the ... Alumni of William & Mary College, ... By Rev. Tiberius Gracchus Jones, of Norfolk, Va. *Richmond: H. K. Ellyson, Printer.* 1856. 8vo, pp. 36.

JONES (U. J.) History of the Early Settlement of the Juniata Valley: embracing an Account of the Early Pioneers, and the Trials and Privations incident to the Settlement of the Valley, Predatory Incursions, Massacres, and Abductions by the Indians during the French and Indian Wars, and the War of the Revolution, &c. By U. J. Jones. *Philadelphia: Henry B. Ashmead.* 1856. 8vo, pp. 380. C. 36618

JONES (W.) The Case of the Battalion Stated, with an Exposition of the Grounds upon which Chas. Lee Jones, Esq., expected to have the Command of the Battalion consisting of Three Companies raised by Himself, ... conferred upon him, ... as Lieutenant Colonel: by Walter Jones. *Washington: Printed by J. & G. S. Gideon.* 1847. 8vo, pp. 32. BA. 36619

Relates to the Mexican War.

JONES (W.) Oration at Concord [Mass.], July 4, 1794. By William Jones. *Concord.* 1794. 8vo. W. 36620

JONES. True Account of all the Presbyterian and Congregational Ministers that were settled or preached for a year or more from Kennebec to St. George's Fort, for seventy and seven years past. By William Jones. [n. p.:] *Printed for the Author.* 1808. 8vo. 36621

[JONES (William).] Reflections upon the Perils and Difficulties of the Winter Navigation of the Delaware. *Philadelphia.* 1822. 8vo, pp. 15. 36622

JONES. Remarks on the Proposed Breakwater at Cape Henlopen. ... By William Jones ... . To which are added, the Report and ... Memorial ... . *Philadelphia: Printed by Order of the Chamber of Commerce of Philadelphia.* 1825. 8vo, pp. 31. B. + Second Edition. [*Ibid.*] 1826. 8vo, pp. 34. B. + Third Edition. [*Ibid.*] 1828. 8vo, pp. 24. B. 36623

Also: Report of a Survey of a Route for the Genesee Valley Canal. ... [n. p.] 1826. 8vo.

JONES (William A.) Characters and Criticisms. By W. Alfred Jones, A.M. *New York: I. Y. Westervelt.* 1857. 2 vols., 12mo, pp. viii, 289; iv, 268. B., C. 36624

Jones. Columbia College Library. ... With Alterations and Additions. By William A. Jones, A.M., Librarian. *New York.* 1861. 8vo, pp. 32. H. 36625

Also: Report of the Librarian to the Library Committee. May 14, 1862. *New York.* 1862. 8vo, pp. 24.

Jones. Long Island. By W. Alfred Jones. ... *New York: Baker & Godwin, Printers.* 1863. 8vo, pp. 23. H. 36626

[Jones.] Memorial of the Late Honorable David S. Jones. With an Appendix, Containing Notices of the Jones Family, of Queen's County. *New-York: Stanford and Swords.* 1849. Sq. 8vo, pp. 99. B. 36627

Also: The Analyst: a Collection of Miscellaneous Papers. ... *New York: Wiley & Putnam.* 1840. 12mo, pp. 174. — Essays upon Authors and Books. ... *New York: Stanford and Swords.* 1849. 12mo, pp. 236. — The First Century of Columbia College. Columbia College, 1754–1854. ... *New York: Privately Printed.* 1863. 8vo, pp. 12. s. — Literary Studies: a Collection of Miscellaneous Essays. ... *New York: Edward Walker.* 1847. 2 vols., 12mo, pp. 295.

Jones (W. B.) Wonderful Curiosity; or, a Correct Narrative of the Celebrated Mammoth Cave of Kentucky. By William Basil Jones. *Russellville.* 1844. 16mo. 36628

Jones (W. C.) ... Report on the subject of Land Titles in California .... By William Carey Jones .... *Washington: Gideon & Co., Printers.* 1850. 8vo, pp. 60. + *Washington.* 1851. 8vo.

Also: Review of Attorney-General Black's Report on Land Titles in California. ... *San Francisco.* 1860. 8vo. — "Pueblo Question" solved in a plain Statement of Facts and Law. ... *San Francisco.* 1860. 8vo.

Jones (W. D.) Mirror of Modern Democracy: a History of the Democratic Party, from its organization in 1825, to ... 1861. ... prefixed a Sketch of The Old Federal and Republican Parties. By William D. Jones. *New-York: J. C. Derby & N. C. Miller.* 1864. 8vo, pp. 270. BA. 36630

Jones' Falls, *Md.* Report of the Joint Standing Committee on Jones' Falls, to the ... City Council of Baltimore, October 7, 1870. ... *Baltimore.* 1870. 8vo, pp. 186. 4 Maps. C. 36631

Jonesville, *N. Y.* Catalogue of Jonesville Academy, Saratoga Co., N. Y. For the year 1858–59. 8vo. S. 36632

Jong (Cornelius de). Reize naar de Caribische Eilanden in de Jaren 1780 en 1781. *Haarlem.* 1807. 8vo. C. 36633

Jong (D. de), Kobel (H.), *and* Salieth (M.) Nieuwe Beschryving der Walvisvangst en Haringvisschery. Met veele byzonderheden daar toe betreklyk. Met xxi. fraaye Kaarten en Plaaten vercierd, door D. de Jong, H. Kobel en M. Salieth. *Amsteldam: J. Ross.* 1791. 4 vols., 4to. C. 36634

Jonge (J. C. de). Geschiedenis van het Nederlandsch Zeewezen. *'sGravenhage.* 1833–48. 6 vols., 8vo. + *Haarlem.* 1858–62. 5 vols., rl. 8vo. Plates and Portraits. 36635

"The second edition is much enlarged by the authentic papers added by J. K. J. de Jonge, the son of the author. It is the most authentic history of the Dutch navy, founded entirely on documents in the royal archives. Its value for the American collector needs not to be specified, as it contains very ample material for the history of the West-India-Company, the early expeditions to America, the wars with the Spaniards and Portuguese there, and the transmarine."—Muller.

Jonge (J. K. J. de). De opkomst van het Nederlandsch gezag in Oost-Indie, ... 1595–1647. *Amsterdam.* 1862–1870. 5 vols., 8vo. 36636

This account of the "rise of the Dutch power in the East Indies" contains some pieces relating to America, as: Account of a voyage to Guiana and Trinidad in 1597–98, by A. Cabeliau; Resolutions of the States General on the navigation to India by the Straits of Magellan; unedited journals of Dutch navigators to the Indies, etc.

Jonnès (A. Moreau de). *See* Moreau de Jonnès.

Jonae *or* Jonssön (Arngrimi). Grönlandia, eller Historie om Grönland, af Islandske Haand-Srevne Histori-Böger og Aar-Registere. Af det Latinske Manuscript paa det Islandske Sprog udsat ved E. Ejolfssön, og trijkt i 1688; nu paa Dansk fortolket af A. B[ussaeus]. *Kjöbenhavn.* 1738. 8vo. 36637

Jonveaux (E.) L'Amérique actuelle. Par Émile Jonveaux. Précédé d'une introduction par Édouard Laboulaye ... . *Paris: Charpentier.* 1869. 12mo, pp. (4), xvi, 339, (1). B. 36638

Joor (W.) *See* Ioor (W.), No. 34970, and *add* pp. 70.

[Joosten Tolck (Joseph).] De groote wonderlijcke wereldt. Beschrijvinghe des gantsche aert-bodem als Europa, Asia, Africa en America also ick se doorgereyst hebbe, namentlyck Hungaryen, Poolen, Ruslandt ... Bresilien, etc. Nog vergroot met de Turckse Grammatica. *Amsterdam.* 1659. 4to, pp 12, 76. Map.

This account of the "great marvellous world" contains a description of Brazil, the more interesting as the author was seven years in that country, during the government of Prince John Maurice. The first edition is very rare.

[Joosten.] De Kleyne wonderlijke werelt ... Bresilien, etc. *Amsterdam: D. Uittenbroek.* 1649. 4to, pp. 16, 80. 36640

"The description of Brazil is exactly the same as in the 'Groote wonderlijcke Wereldt.'"—F. Muller. Other editions: *Amsterdam.* 1694. 4to; *Utrecht.* 1709. 4to; *Amsterdam: J. Kannewet.* [n. d.] 4to; *Amsterdam: G. de Groot Keur.* 1739. 4to; *Amsterdam: J. Kannewet.* [1740.] 4to, pp. 72; *Zwolle: S. Clement.* [1760?] 4to, pp. 72. In these two last editions the account of Brazil is much abridged.

Jordan (C. J. M.) Corinth and Other Poems of the War. By Cornelia J. M. Jordan. ... *Lynchburg: Johnson & Schaffter, Printers.* 1865. 12mo. C. 36641

Most of the copies were accidentally burnt.

Jordan. Richmond: Her Glory and Her Graves. A Poem. ... By Cornelia J. M. Jordan. ... *Richmond, Va.* 1867. 8vo, pp. xxxix. C. 36642

Also: Flowers of Hope and Memory. Poems ... . *Richmond.* 1861. 12mo.

Jordan (E.) An Interesting Trial of Edward Jordan, and Margaret his Wife ... At Halifax, N.S. Nov. 15th, 1809, for ... Piracy and Murder ... . *Boston.* [n. d.] 12mo, pp. 36. H. 36643

Jordan (E. S.) Death of Abraham Lincoln. A Discourse delivered on the Day of the National Fast, June 1, 1865, at ... Cumberland Centre, Me. By Rev. E. S. Jordan. ... *Portland: Printed by David Tucker.* 1865. 8vo, pp. 18. 36644

Jordan (G.) Great Cave of Dry Fork of Cheat River, Virginia. By George Jordan. *Baltimore.* 1855. 8vo. C. 36645

Jordan (G. W.) The Claims of the British West Indian Colonists to the Right of obtaining Necessary Supplies from America, and of employing ... under a limited and duly regulated Intercourse, Stated and Vindicated, in Answer to Lord Sheffield's Strictures. By G. W. Jordan, Esq. ... Colonial Agent for Barbados. *London: T. Cadell.* 1804. 8vo, pp. (2), 119. H. 36646

See "M. Rev.," xlvii. 389.

Jordan. An Examination of the Principles of the Slave Registry Bill, and of the Means of Emancipation, proposed by the Authors of the Bill. By G. W. Jordan, Esq. ... *London: T. Cadell and W. Davies.* 1816. 8vo, pp. (4), 147. BA. 36647

Jordan. Papers ... Relating to the British Colonies in The West Indies. By ... G. W. Jordan, Esq. ... *London: Printed by W. Reynolds.* [1819.] 8vo, pp. (4), 71. H. 36648

Also: An Account of the Management of certain Estates in the Island of Barbados. *London.* 1824. 8vo, pp. 16. — Queries on the Silver and Copper Coins in Barbados; and answer, recommending measures necessary, &c. ... *London.* 1816. 8vo, pp. 30.

Jordan (J.) Serious Actual Dangers of Foreigners and Foreign Commerce, in the Mexican States: ... By John Jordan. ... *Philadelphia: Printed by P. M. Lafourcade.* 1826. 8vo, pp. 52.

Jordan (R.) A Biographical Memoir of Richard Jordan, a Minister ... in the Society of Friends; ... . Second Edition. *Philadelphia: Benjamin & Thomas Kite.* 1827. 8vo, pp. 38. BA.

Jordan. A Journal of the Life and Religious Labours of Richard Jordan ... Late of ... New Jersey. ... *Philadelphia: Thomas Kite.* 1829. 8vo, pp. 172. H. + *London.* 1829. 8vo.

Included in the "Friends' Library," Vol. xiii.

Jordan (S.) The Restorer of the Union of the United States to its Original Purity ... . By Samuel Jordan ... . *Augusta, Georgia.* 1866. 8vo, pp. 171. H. 36652

Also: Ensign of Liberty, and the Wicked One Revealed. ... *Frazersville (S. C.)* 1849. 8vo.

Jordan (T.) The South; its Products, Commerce, and Resources. By Colonel Thomas Jordan, Adjutant-General to Major-General Beauregard, 1st Corps (Confederate) Army of the Potomac. *William Blackwood and Sons, Edinburgh.* MDCCCLXI. 8vo, pp. 23. 36653

Jordan *and* Pryor (J. P.) The Campaigns of Lieut.-Gen. N. B. Forrest, and of Forrest's Cavalry, with Portraits, Maps, and Illustrations. ... By General Thomas Jordan and J. P. Pryor. *New-Orleans, La., Memphis, Tenn., and New-York: Blelock & Company.* 1868. 8vo, pp. iii, 704. H. 36654

Jordan (W.) Geschichte der Insel Hayti und ihres Negerstaats. Von Wilhelm Jordan. *Leipzig.* 1846–49. 8vo, pp. vi, 414, 158. C. 36655

J[ordan] (W.) *See* J. (W.), No. 35332.

Jorgensen (A.) The Emigration from Europe during the Present Century; its Causes and Effects. Translated from Norwegian Statistics and Reports, and from extracts of "Historique de l'Emigration Européene, Asiatique et Africaine, au xix Siècle." By A. Jorgensen. *Quebec.* 1865. 8vo, pp. 23.

Jorio (M. de). Storia del Commercio e della Navigazione. *Napoli.* 1778–83. 4 vols., sm. 4to. 36657

Jornada dos vassalos da Coroa de Portugal, pera se recuperar a Cidade do Salvador na Bahya de todos os Santos, 1624–5. *Lisboa.* 1825. 4to. Large Plate. 36658

Jornel (*General*). Tejas y los Estados Unidos de America en sus relaciones con la Republica Mexicana. *Mexico.* 1837. 8vo. 36659

Jörres (Ludwig). Die Freymaurerey; oder Offenbarung aller Geheimnisse, Ceremonien, Eides-Formeln, Handgriffe und Sinnbilder der drey ersten Grade. Nach Morgan und andern Schriftstellern. Nebst einer genauen Beschreibung von der Entführung des William Morgan, und seiner wahrscheinlichen Ermordung durch die Freymaurer. Mit einem Anhange [etc]. *Pennsylvanien: Verfasser.* 1829. 12mo, pp. viii, 164. C. 36660

Josef (*Don*). Nuevo Sistema de Gobierno Economico, para la America. *Madrid.* 1789. 8vo. 36661

Joseph (E. L.) History of Trinidad, By E. L. Joseph. *Trinidad: Henry James Mills.* [1838.] 12mo, pp. (10), 272. Map.

Joseph (H.), *and* Otis (A.) The Trial of Henry Joseph and Amos Otis, for the Murder of James Crosby ... in the Circuit Court of the United States. ... *Boston: Light & Horton.* 1834. 8vo, pp. 44. H. 36663

Joseph, *pseudon.* New York Aristocracy; or, Gems of Japonicadom. By "Joseph." *New York: C. B. Norton.* 1851. 12mo, pp. 152. 12 Plates. C. 36664

Joseph | and | Benjamin. | A | Conversation. | Translated from a French | Manuscript. | *London:* | ... *J. Murray,* ... | MDCCLXXXVII. | 8vo, pp. (4), xv, 238. Portrait of Franklin. 36665

The *Joseph* here named is Joseph, Emperor of Austria; *Benjamin,* is Benjamin Franklin. The conversation relates chiefly to American affairs.

Josephus (F.) The ... Works of Flavius Josephus ... . To which is added ... a Continuation of the History of the Jews ... to the present Time ... By George Henry Maynard ... . *New-York: Printed ... by William Durell ... near the Fly-Market.* M.DCC.XCII. Folio, pp. 723, (3). 58 Plates, 2 Maps. B. 36666

Worthy of notice for the specimens of early engraving in the United States. The following are the artists: 17 by C. Tibout; 14 by A. Doolittle; 4, and 2 Maps, by Dr. Anderson; 7 by Robinson; 3 by J. Allen; 3 by Benjamin Turner, and 12 are anonymous.

Josephus, *Jr., pseudon.* The Annals of Harper's Ferry, from the Establishment of the National Armory in 1794 to the Present Time, 1869. With Anecdotes of Harper's-Ferrians [by Joseph Barry]. *Hagerstown (Md.): Dechert & Co.* 1869. 8vo, pp. 64. + Second Edition. *Martinsburg, W. Va.* 1872. 8vo. C.

Josh Billings, *pseudon.* *See* [Shaw (H. W.)]

Joslin (B. F.) A Discourse ... delivered before the New-York Alpha of the Phi Beta Kappa Society, July 23, 1833. By Benjamin F. Joslin, M.D. ... *Schenectady: Printed by S. S. Riggs.* 1833. 8vo, pp. 28. B., H. 36668

Joslin. Meteorological Observations and Essays ... . By B. F. Joslin. *Albany: Printed by Packard and Van Benthuysen.* 1836. 8vo, pp. (2), 69. B. 36669

Joslin (L. K.) War; the Great Crime of our Civilization. ... [*Providence.* n. d.] 8vo, pp. 4. H. 36670

Joss (N.) Reise nach dem Staat Ohio in Nordamerika. *Bern.* 1833. + Nachtrag ... [*Ibid.*] 1833. 36671

There were two other editions.

Josselyn (J.) An | Account | Of Two | Voyages | to | New-England. | Wherein you have the setting out of a Ship, | with the charges; The prices of all necessaries for | furnishing a Planter and his Family at his first com- | ing; A Description of the Countrey, Natives and | Creatures, with their Merchantil and Physical Use; The Government of the Countrey as it is now pos- | sessed by the English, &c. A large Chronological Ta- | ble of the most remarkable passages, from the first dis- | covering of the Continent of America, to the year | 1673. | By John Josselyn Gent. | ... | *London, Printed for Giles Widdows, at the Green-Dragon* | *in St. Paul's-Church-yard,* 1674. | Sm. 8vo, pp. (8), 279, 3. BA. + Second Edition. *London: G. Widdowes.* 1675. Sm. 8vo. H.

The second edition is the first, with a new title-page only. Both are rare. "The relation is curious and faithful—when the author makes his own remarks they are in the oddest, most uncouth expressions imaginable."—Locke. It was reprinted in the "Mass. Hist. Soc. Coll.," Vol. iii., 3d Series; and again reprinted with numerous annotations as below:

Josselyn. An Account of Two Voyages to New-England, Made during the years 1638, 1663. By John Josselyn, Gent. *Boston: William Veazie.* MDCCCLXV. 4to, pp. vii, (4), 211. BA.

Seventy-five copies printed in medium 4to, and twenty-five on large paper.

Josselyn. New-Englands | Rarities | Discovered: | in | Birds, Beasts, Fishes, Serpents, | and Plants of that Country. | Together with | The Physical and Chyrurgical Remedies | wherewith the Natives constantly use to | Cure their Distempers, Wounds | and Sores. | Also | A Perfect Description of an Indian Sqva, | in all her Bravery; with a Poem not | improperly conferr'd upon her. | Lastly | A Chronological Table | of the most remarkable Passages in that | Country amongst the English. | Illustrated with Cvts. | By John Josselyn, Gent. | *London, Printed for G. Widdowes at the* | *Green Dragon in St. Pauls Church-yard.* 1672. | Sm. 8vo, pp. (4), 114, (2). Winged Dragon; and folded Plate at page 54. B., H.

Rare. "The earliest work on the Natural History of New England."—Rich. The description of the "Indian Sqva, in all her Bravery," together with the "Poem not improperly confer'd upon her," occupy pp. 99 to 102. The description of Indian medicaments, and the use made of various herbs by the natives, occupy much of the remainder of the work. The winged dragon is the printer's device. The following reprint is rendered valuable by the numerous additions by the editor:

Josselyn. New-England's Rarities discovered in Birds, Beasts, Fishes, Serpents, and Plants of that Country. By John Josselyn, Gent. With an Introduction and Notes, By Edward Tuckerman, M.A. *Boston: William Veazie.* MDCCCLXV. 4to, pp. viii, 169. BA. 36675

Seventy-five copies printed on medium and twenty-five on large paper.

[Josselyn (Lewis).] Appeal to the People. Proof of an Alliance between American Whigs and British Tories. ... *Boston.* 1840. 8vo, pp. 14. BA. 36676

Jottrand (——). La nouvelle constitution de New-York pour 1847, avec un commentaire. *Bruxelles.* 1847. 12mo, pp. 35. S. 36677

Joubert (P. Ch.) Manuels Roret. Nouveau manuel complet du fabricant et de l'amateur de tabacs, contenant son histoire, sa culture et sa fabrication. *Paris: Roret.* 1844. 18mo. Plate.

Jouet (C.) A Letter, addressed to the Rev. Doctor Beech, on his and the Rev. Richard Moor's Illiberal Treatment of the Author. By the Rev. Cavalier Jouet, D.D. *United States: Printed for the Author.* 1795. 4to, pp. 12, (1). N. 36679

Jouffroy (*le marquis* Achille de). Des Bateaux à Vapeur. ... *Paris.* 1816. 8vo. + *Paris: Mathias.* 1841. 8vo. 2 Plates.

Written to prove the priority of his invention over that of Robert Fulton. Also: Le Droit des gens maritime universel. ... *Berlin: Umlang.* 1806. 8vo, pp. 400.

Jourdain (P.) Cosmographie et Pélerinage du Monde Universel. *Paris.* 1669. 8vo, pp. 316. S. 36681

[Jourdan (S.)] *See our* Vol. iii., No. 9759, and add to the note, "Reprinted in Vol. v. of Hakluyt's Voyages, New Edition."

Jourdan (de la Haute-Vienne). Rapports fait sur les moyens de rétablir l'ordre à Sainte Domingue. Séance du 16 prairial an v. *Paris: De l'imprimerie nationale an* v. [1797.] 8vo, pp. 6.

Jourdanet (D[enis]). Le Mexique et l'Amérique tropicale, climats, hygiène et maladies; par D. Jourdanet ... . *Paris.* 1864. 8vo, pp. 400. 36683

Journael. *See* Brazil, No. 7593, Brouwer (H.), Bry (T. de), Hermite (J. l'), Noordt (O. v.), Prins (T.), Raven (A.), Ruyter (M. de), Segerez van der Brugge, *and* Weert (S. de).

Journael, | uyt 't Schip de Prins te Paert, | Van wegen het Gepasseerde | Op 't | Eylandt | Martenique, | Voorgevallen op den 20 Iuly 1674. | *'tAmsterdam,* | *Gedruckt by Alexander Lintman,* 1674. | 4to, pp. 7, 1 l. 36684

Contains an account of the naval battle between the Dutch and French at Martinique, in 1674.

Journal, Acts, &c. *See* Vol. iv., Nos. 15541–15557.

Journal d'un déporté. *See* [Barbé-Marbois], Vol. i., No. 3308.

Journal d'un officier. *See* [Estaing (C. H.)], Vol. vi.

Journal d'un Voyage sur les Costes d'Afrique et aux Indes d'Espagne. Avec une Description Particulière de la Rivière de la Plata, de Buenosayres, & autres lieux; commencé en 1702. & fini en 1706. *Amsterdam: Paul Marret.* 1723. 12mo, pp. (2), 372. Map. + *Amsterdam: Aux dépens de la Compagnie.* 1730. 12mo, pp. (2), 372. + *Paris: Chez P. Bauche.* M. DCC. XXXVII. 12mo, pp. (2), 372. H. 36685

Evidently these three editions are all alike.

Journal d'un Voyage. *See* [Anburey (T.)] *and* [Valette Laudun (M. de)].

Journal de la Campagne. *See* Gautier du Tronchoy, Vol. vii.

Journal de l'Expédition sur le Fleuve Saint-Laurent, contenant un rapport détaillé des mouvements de la flotte et de l'armée anglaise, depuis le moment de son embarquement, à Louisbourg,

jusqu'à la reddition de Québec, en 1759. ... [*Québec.* 1855.] 8vo, pp. 16. s. 36686
Extracted from the New York "Mercury," December 31, 1759.

Journal de la femme d'un missionaire dans les prairies de l'ouest aux États-Unis. Traduit de l'anglais par Mlle. Rilliet de Constant. *Génève.* 1867. 8vo. 36687

Journal de la Guerre du Micissippi contre les Chicachas, En 1739 et finie en 1740, le Ier d'Avril. Par un Officier de l'Armée de M. de Nouaille. *Nouvelle York, Isle de Manate: De la Presse Cramoisy de Jean-Marie Shea.* M.DCCC.LIX. Sm. 8vo, pp. 92.
Also on large paper. Forms No. x. of Shea's "Cramoisy Series."

Journal de l'Instruction. *See* Chauveau (P. J. O.), *note.*

Journal de tout ce qui s'est passé à la prise des forts de Bocachica et au siège de Carthagène aux Indes Occidentales, tiré des relations de S. de Eslaba. [n. p.] 1741. 4to, pp. 14. 36689
A rare piece on the defeat of the English fleet. *See* Vol. III., Nos. 11128–37.

Journal du Cultivateur. *See* Canada, Vol. III., No. 10346.

Journal historique de l'établissement des Français a la Louisiane. *Nouvelle-Orléans: A.-L. Boimre. Paris: Hector Bossange.* 1831. 8vo, pp. (4), 412. BA. 36690

Journal of a Convention, held for the Promotion of Agriculture and Manufacture. *Harrisburg.* 1827. 8vo. 36691

Journal of a Convention of Delegates from several States at Baltimore, to nominate a Candidate for Vice-President, May, 1832. *Albany, N. Y.* 1832. 8vo. W. 36692

Journal of a Convention. *See* Protestant Episcopal Church.

Journal of a March. *See* [Latrobe (J. H. B.)]

Journal of a Tour in North and South America during the Year 1850. *London.* 1852. 12mo. 36693

Journal of a Tour, of a Detachment of Cadets, from the A. L. S. & M. Academy, Middletown, to the City of Washington, in December, 1826. *Middletown, Conn.: W. D. Starr.* 1827. 12mo, pp. 100. s. 36694

Journal of a Tour. *See* [Harris (N. S.)], Vol. VIII., No. 30491.

Journal of a Traveller to Florida. *See* Vol. VI., No. 24869.

Journal of a Visitation. *See* Church in the Colonies, Vol. IV.

Journal of a Voyage from London to Madeira, and thence to New Providence, and back again to London, ... Charles Burton, Commander. *London: J. Robinson.* [n. d.] 8vo. 36695
See "M. Rev.," L. 326.

Journal of a Voyage. *See* Cook (J.), Vol. IV., No. 16242, and add, *Dublin.* 1772. 12mo.

Journal of a Voyage of Discovery, to the Arctic Regions, performed between the 4th of April and the 18th of November, 1818, in His Majesty's Ship Alexander, Wm. Edward Parry, Esq., Lieut. and Commander. By an Officer of the Alexander. *London: Richard Phillips.* [1819.] 8vo, pp. viii, 104. Map.
Forms No. I., Vol. I. of Phillips' "Collection of Voyages." *See* "M. Rev.," LXXXIX. 337, *and* Parry (W. E.)

Journal of a Voyage of Discovery from Okkak in Labrador, to Ungava Bay. [n. p. n. d.] 36697

Journal of a Wanderer, being a Residence in India and Six Weeks in North America. *Edinburgh.* 1844. Fcap 8vo, pp. 268.

A Journal, of a Young Man. *See* [Waterhouse (Benjamin)].

Journal of Agriculture ... J. S. Skinner, Editor. *New York.* 1845. 8vo. Continued. 36699

The Journal of Agriculture. Edited by William S. King. Vol. I. *Boston.* 1851. 8vo. Continued. s. 36700

A Journal of An Excursion Made by the Corps of Cadets, of the American Literary, Scientific and Military Academy, under Capt. Alden Partridge, June, 1822. *Concord: Printed by Hill and Moore.* 1822. 12mo, pp. 38. + *Windsor, Vt.: Printed by Simeon Ide.* 1824. 12mo, pp. 48. H. 36701

Journal of an Excursion to the United States and Canada, in the year 1834, with Hints to Emigrants; and a fair and impartial Exposition of the Advantages and Disadvantages attending Emigration. By a Citizen of Edinburgh. *Edinburgh.* 1835. 16mo, pp. 165. 36702

Journal | of an | Expedition | Performed by the Forces of | Our Soveraign Lady Anne. | ... Queen, ... &c. | Under the Command of the Honourable | Francis Nicholson, | General and Commander in Chief, in the Year 1710. | for the | Reduction of Port Royal in

Nova Scotia, or | any other Place in those Parts in America, then in | Possession of the French. | *London: | Printed for R. S. and Sold by J. Morphew.* MDCCXI. 4to, pp. 24. 36703
A very rare pamphlet; the only copy we have seen belongs to Mr. Lewis of Boston.

Journal of an Officer during the Siege of Fort Detroit, in the War with Pontiac as Leader of the North American Tribes against the English after the Conquest of Canada, 1763–4. Now first printed. *London.* 1858. Fcap 8vo. 36704

The Journal of an Unfortunate Prisoner [Charles Calvert Egerton] on board the British Prison Ship Loyalist. *Baltimore.* 1813. 8vo. 36705

Journal of Both Sessions of the Convention at Little Rock, Arkansas, 1861. *Little Rock.* 1861. 8vo. 36706
A Confederate publication; very rare.

Journal of Captain Cook's last Voyage to the Pacific Ocean, on Discovery; performed in the Years 1776, 1777, 1778, 1779. Illustrated ... . *London: E. Newberry.* MDCCLXXI. 8vo, pp. iv, xlvi, 388. 6 Plates. 36707
See also our Vol. IV., Nos. 16242 and 16247.

The Journal of Education for Lower Canada. Edited by P. J. O. Chauveau ... . *Montreal.* [1857.] 4to. Continued.

The Journal of Education for Ontario, edited ... by J. George Hodgins ... Volume XXI.—For the Year 1868. *Toronto.* 1868. 4to, pp. iv, 188. Continued. H. 36709

Journal of Education. *See* Canada, Vol. III., No. 10423.

The Journal of Education, Province of Quebec. ... *Quebec.* [1856.] 4to. Continued. 36710

A Journal of Incidents connected with the Travels of the Twenty-Second Regiment Connecticut Volunteers, for Nine Months. In Verse. By an Orderly Sergeant. *Hartford: Williams, Wiley & Waterman.* 1863. 8vo, pp. 28. 36711

The Journal of Law. Conducted by an Association of Members of the Bar. ... *Philadelphia: S. C. Atkinson.* 1833. 8vo, pp. (2), 384. H. 36712

Journal of Proceedings of the Commercial Convention of the Southern and Western States, held in ... Charleston, South-Carolina, during the week commencing on Monday 10 April, 1854. *Charleston.* 1854. 8vo, pp. 159, Appendix, xxi. 36713

Journal of Social Science: containing the Transactions of the American Association. No. 1. June, 1869. *New York: Leypoldt & Holt.* [1869.] 8vo, pp. (4), 200, (2). Continued. BA.

The Journal of the American Baptist Anti-Slavery Convention. *Worcester, Mass.* 1841. 8vo. 36715

Journal of the American Institute ... devoted to ... Agriculture, Commerce, Manufactures and the Arts ... . Vol. I. *New-York: T. B. Wakeman.* 1836. 8vo, pp. xi, 664. Continued.

Journal of the American Silk Society and Rural Economist. *Baltimore.* 1840. 2 vols., 8vo. 36717

Journal | of the | Congress | of the Four | Southern Governors, | and the | Superintendent of that District, | with the | Five Nations of Indians, | At Augusta, 1763. | *South-Carolina. | Charles-Town: Printed by Peter Timothy,* MDCCLXIV. 4to, pp. 45. 36718
An extremely rare and very interesting pamphlet.

Journal of the Congress of the United States of America. *Philadelphia: William and Thomas Bradford.* MDCCLXXVI. 8vo, pp. (4), 218. Continued. 36719
The Journal described is from September 5, 1775 to December 30, and seems to be in continuation of *our* No. 15543, Vol. IV.

Journal of the Council of Censors, convened at Philadelphia on Monday the tenth day of November, one thousand seven hundred and eighty-three. *Philadelphia: Printed by Hall & Sellers.* 1783. Folio, pp. 168. P. 36720

Journal of the Ethnological Society of London. Vol. I. *London.* 1848. 8vo. Continued. 36721
Contains articles on American topics.

Journal of the Executive Proceedings. *See* No. 15553.

A Journal of the Expedition. *See* [Wentworth (*Gen.*)]

Journal of the Expedition to La Guira and Porto Cavallos in the West-Indies, Under the Command of Commodore Knowles. In a Letter from an Officer on board the Burford to his Friend at London. *London: J. Robinson.* 1744. 8vo, pp. 63. BA., H.

A Journal of the Expedition up the River St. Lawrence, from the Embarkation at Louisbourg 'til after the Surrender of Quebeck. By the Sergeant Major of Gen. Hopson's Grenadiers. *Boston: Fowle & Draper.* 1759. 16mo, pp. 24. C.

Journal of the First Congress. *See* Nos. 15541 and 15551.

Journal of the Free Trade Convention held in Philadelphia, from September 30 to October 7, 1831; and their Address to the People of the United States: to which is added, a Sketch of the Debates in the Convention. *Philadelphia.* 1831. C., P. 36724

Journal of the House of Representatives. *See* No. 15554.
In our note we have stated that the "Journal was continued to 1796 in folio"—this is erroneous—some others of an earlier date were in 8vo.

Journal of the House of Representatives of the United States, being the First Session of the First Congress, begun and held at the City of New York, March 4, 1789. ... Volume I. Reprinted by order of the House of Representatives. *Washington: Printed by Gales & Seaton.* 1826. 8vo, pp. 839. 36725
This is the correct title of Vol. I. of *our* No. 15555 in Vol. IV. The title there given is the title for the series.

Journal of the Internal Improvement Convention, which assembled in ... Baltimore, on the 8th Day of December, 1834. *Baltimore: Printed by Sands & Neilson.* 1835. 8vo, pp. 93, (1). Map. H. 36726

A Journal of the Landing of His Majesty's Forces on the Island of Cape-Breton, and of the Siege and Surrender of Louisbourg. Extracted from Major General Amherst's and Admiral Boscawen's Letter to the R. H. Mr. Secretary Pitt. The Third Edition. *Boston, N. E.* [1758.] 8vo, pp. 22. C., M. 36727

Journal of the March of a Party of Provincials from Carlisle to Boston, and from thence to Quebec; begun the 13th of July, and ended the 31st of December, 1775. To which is added an Account of the Attack and Engagement at Quebec the 31st of December, 1775. *Glasgow: R. Chapman.* MDCCLXXV. 12mo, pp. 36. 36728
A very rare piece. It is a journal of a company of riflemen under Captains William Hendricks and John Chambers, sent from a gentleman in Quebec to his friend in Glasgow. The Americans under General Montgomery were defeated and made prisoners. The account of the engagement at Quebec, is not by the American officer who wrote the journal, but by the gentleman who sent it to Glasgow.

Journal of the National Republican Convention ... in ... Baltimore, Dec. 13[–16], 1831, for the Nomination of Candidates to fill the offices of President and Vice-President. ... *Washington.* [n. d.] 8vo, pp. 32. H. 36729

Journal of the Pilgrims at Plymouth. *See* [Mourt (G.)]

Journal of the Principal Occurrences. *See* Shortt (W. T. P.)

A Journal of the Proceedings. *See* [Horsmanden (Daniel)].

A Journal of the Proceedings at Two Conferences Begun to be held at Falmouth in Casco-Bay, in the County of York, within the Province of the Massachusetts-Bay in New-England, on the Twenty-Eighth Day of June, 1754, Between His Excellency William Shirley, Esq; Captain-General, Governour and Commander in Chief, in and over the Province aforesaid, and the Chiefs of the Norridgwalk Indians; And on the Fifth Day of July following, Between His said Excellency and the Chiefs of the Penobscot Indians. *Boston in New-England: Printed by John Draper, Printer to His Excellency the Governour and Council.* 1754. Folio, pp. 27. C., M., P. 36730
A very rare pamphlet; I cannot record the sale of a copy.

A Journal | of the Proceedings in the late | Expedition | To Port-Royal, On board Their Majesties Ship, the Six Friends, | The Honourable S[r] William Phipps Knight, | Commander in Chief &c. | A True Copy, Attested by Joshua Natstock Clerk, | *Boston in New-England, Printed for Benjamin Harris at the London-Coffee-House. Anno Domini.* MDCXC. 4to, pp. 16. 36731

Journal of the Proceedings of a Convention, composed of Delegates from the Thirteen Original United States, held in Independence Hall ... July 5, 6, 1852, for the purpose of considering the propriety of erecting one or more Monuments in Independence Square, Philadelphia, in commemoration of the Declaration of Independence, July 4, 1776, &c. *Philadelphia.* 1853. 8vo, pp. 46. S. 36732

Journal of the Proceedings of a Meeting of the Board of Trustees from the Old Thirteen States, held in ... Philadelphia, June 12, 1860, in furtherance of the recommendation of a Convention of Delegates from those States, to erect a Monument in Independence Square, to commemorate the Declaration of Independence .... *Philadelphia: Crissy & Markley.* 1860. 8vo, pp. 15.

Journal of the Proceedings of a Convention of Literary and Scientific Gentlemen, held in ... New York, October, 1830. *New York: Jonathan Leavitt and G. & C. & H. Carvill.* 1831. 8vo, pp. 286, (1). 36734

Journal of the Proceedings of Delegates assembled at Brunswick, September, 1816, on the subject of Separation from Massachusetts; with the Debates taken by Gamaliel E. Smith. To which is affixed the decision of the Legislature of Massachusetts thereon. ... *Kennebunk: Printed by James K. Remick.* 1817. Sm. 8vo, pp. 80. W. 36735

A Journal of the Proceedings of Jacob Wendell, Samuel Watts, Thomas Hubbard, and Chambers Russel, Esq[rs:] Commissioners appointed by the Honourable Spencer Phips, Esq; Lieutenant-Governour and Commander in Chief, in and over His Majesty's Province of the Massachusetts-Bay in New-England, to Treat with the several Tribes of Eastern Indians in order to Renew and Confirm a general Peace. *Boston in New-England: Printed by John Draper, Printer to the Honourable the Lieutenant-Governour and Council.* 1752. 4to, pp. 16. M., P. 36736

Journal of the Proceedings of the Commissioners appointed by his Excellency Governor Shirley to treat with several Tribes of the Eastern Indians. *Boston.* 1753. 4to, pp. 26. 36737
Title from Thomas' "History of Printing."

A Journal of the Proceedings. *See* [Hutchinson (T.)]

Journal of the Proceedings of the Commissaries of the Colony of New York, at a Congress with the Commissaries of the Massachusetts Bay, relating to the Establishment of a Partition Line of Jurisdiction between the two Provinces. *New York.* [1767.] 4to, pp. 20. M., N. 36738

Journal of the Proceedings. *See our* Vol. IV., No. 15542.
There is another edition with the same imprint, pp. (4), 132; also an edition printed at *New York.* To *our* No. 15543 add *Wilmington: J. Adams.* 1776. 8vo, and to No. 15547 add pp. 202.

The Journals of the Proceedings of Congress. Held at Philadelphia, from January to May, 1776. *Philadelphia: Printed by R. Aitken.* MDCCLXXVI. 8vo, pp. 93, 237. 36739

Journal of the Proceedings of the Forces under General Maclean, &c., when besieged by 3500 Rebels at Penobscot, with the various Proclamations, &c. *London.* 178–. 8vo. Map.

Journal of the Proceedings of the National Republican Convention, held at Worcester, Oct. 11, 1832. *Boston.* 1832. 8vo, pp. 75. W. 36741

Journal of the Proceedings of the Provincial Synod of the United Church of England and Ireland in Canada. Fourth Session ... . *Quebec.* 1868. 8vo, pp. viii, 132. 36742

Journal of the Resolution's Voyage. *See* Cook (J.), Vol. IV.

Journal of the Route from New York to Real del Monte by way of Tampico. [1847.] 4to. 36743

Journal of the Senate of the United States, in Cases of Impeachments. *Washington.* 1805. 8vo. C. 36744
Including the Trials of William Blount, John Pickering, and Samuel Chase. *See also* Vol. IV., Nos. 15551–52.

Journal of the Stated Preacher. *See* [Ely (E. S.)], Vol. VI.

The Journal of the Telegraph. J. D. Reid, Editor. Vol. I. *New York.* 1867–68. 4to. Continued. 36745

Journal of the Times — Politics, History, and Biography. Vol. I. [*Baltimore.* 1818–19.] 8vo, pp. 416. B. 36746

Journal of the United States Agricultural Society for 1855. *Boston.* 1856. 8vo. Continued. M. 36747

Journal of the Voyage of the Sloop Mary, from Quebeck, Together with an Account of her Wreck off Montauk Point, L. I., Anno 1701. With Introduction and Notes by E. B. O'Callaghan. *Albany, N. Y.: J. Munsell.* 1866. Sm. 4to, pp. xvii, (2), 50. B. 36748
One hundred copies only printed.

Journal of Travels over the Rocky Mountains to the Columbia River. *Cincinnati.* 1847. 12mo. + Second Edition. 1852.
This very doubtful title is from Taylor's "Bibliography of California."

Journal of Travels through Several Towns in the Country, and to Boston again, in the Winter Past; containing many strange and remarkable Occurrences. In the method of Mr. Whitefield's Journal, but vastly more entertaining. *Boston.* 1745.

Journal of Useful Knowledge. January, 1854. 36751

Journal of Visitation. *See* [Inglis (John)], No. 34769.

Journal van de Reise naar Grönland. *Amsterdam.* 1787. 4to.

Journals of Congress from the First Meeting to the Adoption of the Constitution. *Boston.* 1821. 4 vols., 8vo. 36753
See also Congress, Vol. IV., No. 15550, etc.

Journals of the First Legislative Assembly of the Territory of Arizona, 1864. *Prescott.* 1865. 8vo. 36754

Journals of the House of Commons from Nov. 8th, 1547 to 1854. Reprinted by Order ... *London.* [v. d.] 111 vols., folio.

It is scarcely necessary to say that these "Journals" include many topics of American interest. The indexes to 1839 form seven volumes, folio.

Journals of the House of Lords, beginning anno primo Henrici Octavi 1509, with the Rolls of Parliament prefixed to supply the deficiencies in the Journals 1509–1854. *London.* [v. d.] 86 vols., folio. A. 36756

Indexes to 1832, 4 vols., folio. A "Calendar of the Journals of the House of Lords, 1509–1826"—*London.* 1810–30. 2 vols., folio—is a useful appendix.

Journals and Appendices of the Legislative Assembly of Canada. 1852. Rl. 8vo. Continued. 36757

La | Journée | du | Chrétien | sanctifiée | par la priere | et la | méditation | ... | Nouvelle édition | ... | *Baltimore: De l'imprimerie de William Pechin.* | MDCCXCVI. | 24mo, pp. 284. 36758

The first French Catholic prayer-book printed in the United States.

The Journeymen Cabinet and Chair-Makers, Philadelphia Book of Prices. Second Edition, Corrected and Enlarged. *Philadelphia.* MDCCXCV. 8vo. 36759

JOUTEL (*M.*) Journal historique du Dernier Voyage que feu M. de la Sale fit dans le Golfe de Mexique, pour trouver l'embouchure, & le cours de la Rivière de Missicipi, nommée à présent la Rivière de Saint Loüis, qui traverse la Louisiane. Où l'on voit l'Histoire tragique de sa mort, & plusieurs choses curieuses du nouveau monde. Par Monsieur Jovtel, l'un des Compagnons de ce Voyage, redigé & mis en ordre par Monsieur De Michel. *A Paris: Estienne Robinot.* MDCCXIII. 12mo, pp. xxxix, 386. Map. B., BA., C., H., J.C.B. 36760

JOUTEL. Diario Historico del ultimo viaje que hizo M. de la Sale para descubrir el Desembocadero y Curso del Missicipi. Contiene la Historia tragica de su Muerte y muchas cosas curiosas del Nuevo Mundo. Escrito en idioma Frances por M. T. Joutel, uno de los compañeros de M. La Sale en el Viaje. Traducido al Español por el Coronel Jose Maria Tornel, Ministro de Mexico en los Estados Unidos. *Nueva York: José Desnoues.* 1831. 12mo. 36761

With a preface and some valuable notes by the translator. This edition, though printed in New York, was put forth for the Mexican market.

JOUTEL. A | Journal | Of the Last | Voyage | Perform'd by | Monsr. de la Sale, | To the | Gulph of Mexico, | To find out the | Mouth of the Missisipi [*sic*] River; | Containing, | An Account of the Settlements he endeavour'd to | make on the Coast of the aforesaid Bay, his | unfortunate Death, and the Travels of his | Companions for the Space of Eight Hundred | Leagues across that Inland Country of America, | now call'd Louisiana, (and given by the King of | France to M. Crozat,) till they came into Canada. | Written in French by Monsieur Joutel, | A Commander in that Expedition; | And Translated from the Edition just publish'd at Paris. | With an exact Map of that vast Country, and a Copy of the | Letters Patents granted by the K. of France to M. Crozat. | *London: Printed for A. Bell.* 1714. 8vo, pp. (2), xxi, (9), 205, (5). Map. B., BA., H. 36762

Reprinted in 1719 with the following different title:

JOUTEL. Mr. Joutel's | Journal | of his | Voyage | to | Mexico: | His Travels Eight hundred | Leagues through Forty Nations | of Indians in Lovisiania | to Canada. | His Account of the great | River Missasipi. | To which is Added | A Map of that Country; | with a De- | scription of the great Water-Falls in the | River Misouris. | Translated from the French publish'd at Paris. | *London:* | *Printed for Bernard Lintot.* | 1719. 8vo, pp. (2), xxi, (9), 205, (5). Map. B., C. 36763

This curious relation was the last which the public received of the unfortunate expedition in which La Sale was assassinated by some of his men, March 19, 1687. It was written by one of the companions of that celebrated traveler, who seems to have been the only one on whom La Sale could rely. Charlevoix speaks highly of Joutel, and of the services he rendered to La Sale. Mr. Parkman remarks, "Of the three narratives of this journey, those of Joutel, Cavelier and Douay, the first is by far the best. That of Cavelier seems the work of a man of confused brain and indifferent memory. Joutel's account is of a very different character, and seems to be the work of an honest and intelligent man. Douay's account is brief, but it agrees with that of Joutel in most essential points."—*France and England in North America*, Part III., p. 356. *See also* B. F. French's "Hist. Coll.," I.

JOUVENCY (J.) Canadicæ Missionis Relatio Ab anno 1611 usque ad annum 1613, cum statu ejusdem missionis, annis 1703 & 1710. Auctore Josepho Juvencio, Societatis Jesu, Sacerdote. *Romæ: Ex Typographia Georgii Plachi.* M. D. CC. X. 8vo. + [*Albany: Munsell.* 1871.] 8vo, pp. (2), v, (1), 38. 36764

JOUVENCY. Historiæ Societatis Jesu pars quinta, Tomus posterior ab anno Christi 1591. ad annum 1616. Autore Josepho Juvencio, Societatis ejusdem Sacerdote. *Romæ.* 1710. Folio.

Said by Charveloix ("Hist. Nouv. France," Liste des Auteurs) to contain an account of the Jesuits in Acadia in 1611, etc. *See* Carayon (A.), Nos. 173, 2005, and 3261.

JOUVENCY. De Regione et Moribus Canadensium seu barbarorum Novæ Franciæ. Auctore Josepho Juvencio, Societatis Sacerdote. ... *Romæ: Ex Typographia Georgii Plachi.* M. D. CC. X. 8vo. + [*Albany: Munsell.* 1871.] 8vo, pp. 54, (1). 36766

JOUVENCY. Recueil de pieces touchant l'histoire de la Compagnie de Jesus. Par Joseph Jouvency. *Liege.* 1716. 12mo.

JOUY (Victor Joseph Étienne de). Fernand Cortez, ou la Conquète du Mexique, Opéra en trois actes, Paroles de Jouy et Esménard ... . *Paris.* 1809. 8vo. + *Paris.* 1821. 8vo.

JOUY. L'Hermite de la Guiane, ou Observations sur les mœurs et les usages français au commencement du XIXe siècle. Par M. de Jouy. Troisième édition. *Paris.* 1816. 3 vols., 12mo. Copper-plates. + *Paris.* 1817. + *Paris: Pillet aîné.* 1818. 2 vols., 12mo, pp. (2), iv, 364; (2), 336. 2 Plates. A.

Also included in his "Œuvres complètes."

JOVET (*Le Sieur*). L'Histoire des Religions de tous les Royumes du Monde. Par le Sieur Jovet, Chanoine de Laon ... . *Paris.* 1686. 3 vols., 12mo. Plates. 36770

JOVET. Storia | delle | Religioni | di tutti i Regni | del Mondo. | Riveduta, corretta, accresciuta, | e posta in ordine migliore, | in questa Edizione | Napoletana. | Del Sig. Jovet | ... | Tradotta dal Francese. | ... | *In Napoli*, MDCCLXIII. | *A spese di Antonio Cervone.* | *Presso Vincenzo Manfredi.* | 3 vols., 12mo. 36771

A translation of the previous work.

Jovial Songster. Containing a Collection of the best Humorous and Entertaining Songs. *New York: J. Tiebout.* 1805. 16mo, pp. 80. 36772

Containing Hunting, Miscellaneous, and Masonic Songs.

JOVIUS (Paulus). Elogia virorum bellica virtute illustrium. *Basileae.* 1561. 8vo. + *Basileae: P. Perna.* 1575. Sm. folio. + *Basileae.* 1596. Folio. 36773

The first book contains, pp. 190–194, a biography of Christopher Columbus with his portrait. There are other editions.

[JOVIUS.] Icones herovm bellica virtvte maxime illvstrivm. Elogiis illvstratae a V. Thilone. *Basileae.* 1589. 4to. 36774

JOVIUS. Historia General de todas las cosas succedidas en el mundo en estos cincuenta años de nuestro tiempo. Traducido en castellano por G. d. Baeça. *Salamanca.* 1562. 2 vols., folio.

"Livre important pour l'histoire de l'Amérique."—ANDRADE.

JOVIUS. Warhafftige Beschreibunge aller Chronickwirdiger namhafftiger Historien und Geschichten vom Jahre 1494 bis auff 1547 zugetragen. *Frankfort.* 1570. 3 vols., folio. 36776

"Cette chronique traite aussi de l'histoire de l'Amérique."—WEIGEL.

JOY (B.) Statement of Facts relative to the Conduct of Mr. Benjamin Joy, Executor of the ... Will ... of ... Joseph Barrell, Esq. ... . August, 1816. [*Boston.* 1816.] 8vo, pp. 20. B., BA.

[JOY.] A True Statement of Facts, in Reply to a Pamphlet lately published by Messrs. Charles Barrell ... . *Boston: Printed by John Eliot.* 1816. 8vo, pp. 17. BA., M., W. 36778

[JOY (George).] American Question. A Letter from a Calm Observer, to a Noble Lord ... relative to the Orders in Council. *London: Printed by A. J. Valpy.* 1812. 8vo, pp. 16. BA. 36779

JOY (James F.) Messrs. Wade & Chandler. The Senator ship. *Detroit, January* 5, 1863. 8vo, pp. 13. 36780

JOY. The Testimony of Gen. Hitchcock and the Peninsular Campaign. *Detroit, February* 4, 1863. 8vo, pp. 14. 36781

JOYCE (J.) Confession of John Joyce, alias Davis, who was executed ... 14th March, 1808. For the Murder of Mrs. Sarah Cross ... . *Philadelphia.* 1808. 12mo, pp. 18. B., H. 36782

JOYNES (E. S.) Education after the War. A Letter addressed to a Member of the Southern Educational Convention, Columbia, S. C. 28th April, 1863. ... By Prof. Edward S. Joynes. *Richmond: Macfarlane & Fergusson, Printers.* 1863. 12mo, pp. 16.

JUAN (*Don*). Triunfo Sosaya, Informe de Paucartambo Andes grandes del Cuzco. *Lima.* 1663. Folio, pp. 21. 36784

A doubtful title, from an American bookseller's catalogue.

JUAN BAPTISTA (*Fray*). Compendio en las Excelsias, de la Bulla de la Sancta Cruzada, en lengua Mexicana. *Mexico, à costa de Christoval de la Paz, Alguazil de la Sancta Cruzada. En la Imprenta de Enrico Martinez, Interprete del Sancto Officio de la Inquisicion Año* 1599. 8vo. 36785

JUAN BAPTISTA. Hvehvetlahtolli. [*Mexico.* 1599.] Small 8vo, 96 l. J.C.B. 36786

The title "Hvehvetlahtolli" (which means "old words" or "ancient sayings"), runs through the whole book on the top of each page, misprinted "Hvehvetlatholli" on the recto of 38, 48, and 56th leaves. The work contains a number of those allocutions in

the Mexican or Nahuatl languages, which Indian parents or civil authorities used to deliver at certain solemn occasions such as births, marriages, deaths, etc. The preface says that they contain excellent moral doctrines. *See* Sahagun, Book VI., Chapter 19, *see also our* Vol. I., Nos. 3242, 3997–98, and Vol. IX., Nos. 36132–34.

JUAN DIAZ FREILE. Summario compendioso de las quentas de plata y ora, que en los reynos del Peru, son necessarias a los mercaderes. *Mexico.* 1556. 4to. 36787

Title from Ternaux, No. 73; accidentally omitted in its proper place.

JUAN DE ALVARADO (*Fray*). Lagrimas gustosas que en las Exequias celebradas en la Iglesia de N. P. Santo Domingo de Mexico el dia 19 de enero del año proximo passado de 1731, en la muerte de N. SS. P. Benedicto XIII. predico el M. R. P. M. Fr. Juan de Alvarado, Hijo de la Provincia de Santiago de Predicadores de Nueva España, etc. *Mexico.* 1732. 4to, pp. (14), 29.

JUAN DE ANGLIARA. Viagio ed paese de lisola de loro trouato p Juan de angliara capitanio di re di Spagna cũ tuto il viuer et costumi p^{t}. incipit cũ lo adiunto del clementissimo et definit de laltra isola caret. *impsioẽ ẽ ĩ* 4° *et prosa toscana. Costo en ferrara medio quatrin a* 4 *di de mayo de* 1521. *y el ducado val.* 378 *quatriẽs.*

JUAN DE AVILA (*Fray*). Sermon de el Glorioso Martyr San Felipe de Jesus. *Mexico.* 1681. 36790

JUAN DE DIOS ARIAS (C.) Reseña historica de la formacion y operaciones del cuerpo de Ejército del Norte durante la Intervencion francesa, sitio de Queretaro y noticias oficiales sobre la captura de Maximiliano, su proceso integro y su muerte, escrita por el C. Juan de Dios Arias. *Mexico.* 1867. 8vo, pp. 725. Portraits and Plans. 36791

A republican report on the late war in Mexico, with official documents from the Juarez government. The plans of battles are drawn on the indications of the republican generals, chiefly of Escobedo.

JUAN DE SAN BERNARDO. Devocion, y novena de la esclarecida virgen, y martyr S. Barbara. *Mexico, Uiuda de F. R. Lupercio.* 1695. 18mo, pp. (6), 21. C. 36792

JUAN DE SAN MIGUEL. Sermon de las lagrimas de el principe de los Apostoles San Pedro en la ciudad Zacatecas. Por Juan de S. Miguel ... . *Mexico: M. de Ribera.* 1703. 4to, 17 l. 36793

JUAN DE VARGAS. Les aventures de Don Juan de Vargas, racontées par lui-même, traduites de l'espagñol sur le Mss. inédit par Ch. Navarin. *Paris.* 1853. 12mo. 36794

Relates to voyages to Mexico and Peru in the sixteenth century.

JUAN DE LA ANUNCIACION. Aq̃ Secõ tiene un Sermon para publicar la Sancta Bulla, q̃ por Mandamiento del yllusérissimo Señor D. Pedro Moya de Contreras, Arçobispo de Mexico. En Lengua Mexicana y Castellana. [*Mexico.* 1577.] 4to, 9 l.

An excessively rare tract.

JUAN DE LA ANUNCIACION. Doctrina Christia | na mvy cvmplida, donde se con- | tiene la exposicion de todo lo necessario para Do- | ctrinar alos Yndios ... | ... Compuesta en lengua | Castellana y Mexicana por elmuy Re | uerendo padre Fray Iuan de la Anun- | ciacion ... | *En Mexico,* | *en casa de Pedro Balli.* 1575. 4to, pp. (12), 275, (14). 36796

This excessively rare Mexican book is printed in double columns, in Spanish and Mexican. It is not cited by Ternaux or Brunet.

JUAN DE LA ANUNCIACION. La Inocencia vindicada. Respuesta à un papel anonymo contra el libro de la Vida Interior, que de si escribió el ... D. Juan de Palafox y Mendoza, Obispo de la Puebla de los Angeles. *Madrid.* [n. d.] 4to, pp. 390, (16).

An English catalogue quotes an edition, *Sevilla*, 1694, which may be an error.

JUAN DE LA ANUNCIACION. Sermonario en lengua Mexicana, donde se contiene (por el orden del Missal Nuevo Romano) dos Sermones en todas las Dominicas y Festividades principales de todo el año: y otro en las Fiestas de los Sanctos, con sus vidas y Comunes. Con un Cathecismo en lengua Mexicana y Española, con el Calendario. Compuesto por el reuerendo padre Fray Iuan de la Anunciacion ... *En Mexico, por Antonio Ricardo.* M.D.LXXVII. ... 4to, 8 p. l., 272 l. 36798

A volume of extreme rarity and value.

JUAN DE LA CONCEPCION (*Fr.* Recoleto Augustino Descalzo). Historia General de Philipinas. Conquistas espirituales y temporales de estos Españoles Dominos, establecimientos, progresos, y decadencias, comprehende los Imperios Reinos y Provincias de Islas y Continentes con quienes há havido communicacion, y Comercio por immediatas coincidencias. Con Noticias universales geographicas, hidrographicas de Historia Natural, de Politica, de Costumbres, y de Religiones ... . *En Man*[*ila*] *en la Impr. del Seminar, Conciliar y Real de S. Carlos, por Augustin de la Rosa y Balagtas.* 1788–92. 14 vols., 4to, pp. (54), 434, (62); 502, (58); 439, (56); 487, (62); 478, (70); 439, (70); 364, (52); 391, (56); 424, (64); 410, (50); 420, (48); 419, (38); 464, (34); 381, (32). 10 Maps. 36799

Brunet says of this rare work "Cet ouvrage, le plus volumineux, peut-être, qui

ait paru aux Philippines, rarement se trouve complet." The sixth and the following volumes have the imprint, *En el Conv. de Nra. Sra. de Loreto del Pueblo de Sampaloc, por el Hermano Balthasar Mariano. Donado Franciscano, Año de* 1788. The best and most complete work on the Philippine Islands; it is highly important in reference to the Spanish possessions in that country and incidentally to their Spanish-American territory.

JUAN DE LA CRUZ. Bonilla, Ozaeta y Aguirre, Segundo 15 de Enero de la corte Mexicana: Solemnes Fiestas que a la canonizacion del Mystico Dr. S. Juan de la Cruz, celebrò la Provincia de San Alberto. *Mexico.* 1730. 4to. 36800

Also on large paper.

JUAN Y SANTACILIA (Jorge). Compendio de Navegacion para el uso de los Cavalleros Guardias-Marinas. *Cadiz.* 1757. Sq. 8vo. 12 Plates. 36801

JUAN *and* ULLOA (A. de). Dissertacion Historica y Geographica sobre el meridiano de demarcacion entre los Dominios de España y Portugal, y los parages por donde passa en la America Meridional, conforme a los Tratados, y derechos de cada Estado, y las mas seguras y modernas observaciones. Por Don Jorge Juan, ... y Don Antonio de Ulloa ... . *En Madrid, en la Imprenta de Antonio Marin.* 1749. 12mo, pp. 175. 36802

The boundary line between the Spanish and Portuguese possessions in America was a subject of discussion from the time of the infallible decision of Pope Alexander VI. until they became independent States. This important treatise on the subject was prepared by two of the most learned men in Spain."—RICH, I. 95. It was translated into French as below:

JUAN. Dissertation Historique et Géographique Sur le Méridien de Demarcation entre les Domaines d'Espagne et de Portugal. Por Don Georges Juan ... Don Antoine de Ulloa ... . Traduit de l'Espagnol. *Paris: Chez Ant. Boudet* ... . M.DCC.LXXVI. 12mo, pp. viii, 205. Map. H. 36803

JUAN. Historische Reisbeschryving van geheel Zuid-America; gedaan op bevel des Konings van Spanje, door Don George Juan, .. Bevelhebber van de Compagnie der Edele Opzieneren over de Scheepsvaart; en door Don Antonio de Ulloa, Luitenant van dezelfde Compagnie; Beiden, Opperbevelhebberen der Spaansche Zeemagt; ... Versierd met zeer fraaije Afbeeldingen, Platte Gronden en Kaarten, door voorname Meesters gegraveerd, ... *Te Goes, By Jacobus Huysman,* M.DCC.LXXI. [Colophon:] *In's Gravenhage, Jacobus van Karnebeek,* 1771. 2 vols., 4to, pp. (8), xxiv, 428. Vol. II. M.DCC.LXXII. [Colophon:] 1773. pp. viii, iv, 407. 25 Plates. C. 36804

JUAN. Mémoires philosophiques, historiques, physiques, concernant la découverte de l'Amérique, ses anciens habitans, leurs mœurs, leurs usages, etc. Avec des observations et additions sur toutes les matières. Traduit par M*** [Le Febvre de Villebrune]. *Paris: Buisson.* 1787. 2 vols., 8vo, pp. viij, 376, xv; (2), 499, xv. P. 36805

See also Carli (J. R.), Vol. III., No. 10912.

JUAN. Noticias Americanas: entretenimientos fisico-históricos sobre la América Meridional, y la Septentrional oriental: Comparacion general de los territorios, climas y producciones en las tres especies vegetal, animal y mineral; con una relacion particular de los Indios ... *Madrid: Imprenta Real.* 1792. 4to, pp. (14), 342.

JUAN. Noticias Secretas de America, sobre el estado naval, militar, y politico de los reynos del Peru y provincias de Quito, costas de Nueva Granada y Chile: gobierno y regimen particular de los Pueblos de Indios: cruel opresion y extorsiones de sus Corregidores y Curas: abusos escandalosos introducidos entre estos habitantes por los Misioneros: causas de su origen y motivos de su continuacion por el espacio de tres siglos. Escritas fielmente segun las Instrucciones del Excelentisimo Señor Marques de la Ensenada, primer Secretario de Estado, y presentadas en informe secreto à S. M. C. el Señor don Fernando VI. Por Don Jorge Juan y Don Antonio de Ulloa. ... Sacadas a luz para el verdadero conocimiento del gobierno de los Españoles en la America Meridional, por Don David Barry. En dos partes. *Londres: En la Imprenta de R. Taylor.* 1826. Folio, pp. (4), xiii, 707, (1). 2 Portraits. BA., C. 36807

"These secret memoirs, in which everything concerning the manners, government, and state of defence of that portion of America which once belonged to Spain, is accurately described, are written with that truth, impartiality and good judgment which distinguished the informants."—SALVA, No. 4121. The benevolent and virtuous Las Casas has been accused of exaggeration and falsehood in his account of the cruelties of the Spaniards to the Indians, but these revelations, which have lain in the archives of Madrid for over half a century, exhibit so monstrous a system that it is difficult to realize that the revelations are true. There are copies on large paper with portraits on India paper.

JUAN. Observaciones Astronomicas, y Phisicas Hechas de Orden de S. Mag. en los Reynos del Peru. Por D. Jorge Juan ... y D. Antonio de Ulloa ... . De las Quales Se Deduce La Figura, y Magnitud De La Tierra, y se aplica À La Navegacion. *Madrid: Por Antonio Marin.* M.D.CC.XL.VIII. Folio, pp. (16), xxviii, 396, (14). 8 Plates. A. C., H. 36808

Some copies have the imprint, *Madrid: Por Juan de Zuñiga.* Usually found with the "Relacion," No. 36811, *infra.*

JUAN. Observaciones Astronomicas, y Phisicas, Hechas de Orden de S. M. en los Reynos del Peru. Por D. Jorge Juan, ... y D. Antonio de Ulloa ... . De las Quales se Deduce La Figura, y Magnitud de la Tierra, y se aplica à la Navegacion. Corregidas y emendadas por el Autor. *Madrid: En la Imprenta Real de la Gazeta.* 1773. Folio, pp. (72), xxviii, 396, (12). Portrait, Plates, and Maps. H. 36809

This second edition contains a memoir of the author. The historical relation was written by Ulloa, the astronomical part by Juan. The expedition to which it relates was the one to which La Condamine and Bouguer were sent by the French Academy of Sciences, for the purpose of determining the figure of the Earth at the Equator. There are copies on large paper.

JUAN. Reise nach Süd-America. *Leipzig: Arkstée & Merkus.* 1751. 4to, pp. (20), 656, (28). 17 Maps, 21 Plates. 36810

Forms Vol. IX. of the "Allgemeine Historie der Reisen."

JUAN. Relacion Historica del Viage à la America Meridional hecho de Orden de S. Mag. Para Medir Algunos Grados De Meridiano Terrestre, y venir por ellos en conocimiento de la verdadera Figura, y Magnitud de la Tierra, con otras varias Observaciones Astronomicas, y Phisicas: Por Don Jorge Juan, ... y Don Antonio de Ulloa ... . *En Madrid: Por Antonio Marin y Juan de Zuñiga, año de* M.DCC.XLVIII. 4 vols., folio, Frontispiece, pp. (24), 404; (4), 405–682; (12), 379; (4), 381–603. 34 Plates. A., BA., C., H. 36811

"The voyage of Ulloa arose out of the desire of the French government to send certain members of the Academy of Sciences to measure a degree in the equinoctial countries of Peru. This request was not only accorded in the most courteous manner, but the King of Spain conceived the idea of sharing the honor of a scheme devoted to the advancement of knowledge, and sent two of the most scientific officers of the Spanish navy to accompany the expedition. The party carried on a series of operations of unexampled difficulty, and encountered hardships and sufferings which demanded the strength of the strongest constitutions and the energy of minds stimulated by a love of science. Much information was collected and published, which for the want of later, has been reproduced in other works on South America." The work has been many times reprinted. There are copies on large paper.

JUAN. Voyage Historique de l'Amerique meridionale fait par ordre du roi d'Espagne Par Don George Juan ... et Par Don Antoine de Ulloa ... Ouvrage orné des figures, plans et cartes necessaires. Et qui contient une Histoire des Yncas du Perou, [extrait de la traduction de Garcilasso de la Vega par Richelet,] Et les Observations astronomiques & physiques, faites pour déterminer la Figure & la Grandeur de la Terre. *A Amsterdam et à Leipzig: Arkstée & Merkus.* M DCCLII. 2 vols., 4to, Frontispiece,

pp. (22), 554; (2), 316, (6); Astronomical Observations, (6), 309, (3). 45 Maps and Plates. B., BA. 36812

Some copies of this French translation have the imprint, *Paris: Charles Antoine Jombert.* M DCCLII; this has given rise to the idea that an edition was printed there, which is not the case; there is merely a change in the title. The translator was M. de Mauvillon.

JUAN. A Voyage to South-America: Describing at Large The Spanish Cities, Towns, Provinces, &c., on that extensive Continent. Interspersed Throughout With Reflections on the Genius, Customs, Manners, and Trade of the Inhabitants; Together with The Natural History of the Country. And An Account of their Gold and Silver Mines. Undertaken by Command of his Majesty the King of Spain, By Don George Juan, and Don Antonio de Ulloa, Both Captains of the Spanish Navy, ... Translated from the Original Spanish. Illustrated with Copper Plates. ... *London: L. Davis and C. Reymers.* MDCCLVIII. vols., 8vo, pp. xvi, (8), 509; (6), 420, (18). 7 Plates. B., C. + *Dublin: William Williamson.* MDCCLVIII. 2 vols., 8vo, pp. 378; (4), 9–365. 5 Plates. A., B. + The Second Edition, revised and corrected. *London: L. Davis and C. Reymers.* MDCCLX. 2 vols., 8vo, pp. xx, (4), 498; (4), 410, (18). 7 Plates. + The Second Edition. *Dublin: Alexander Ewing.* 1765. 2 vols., 8vo. + *Dublin.* 1767. 2 vols., 8vo. + *Dublin.* 1770. 2 vols., 8vo. + The Third Edition: To which are added, By Mr. John Adams, of Waltham-Abbey, who resided several Years in those Parts, Occasional Notes and Observations; an Account of some Parts of the Brazils, hitherto unknown to the English Nation; and a Map of South America corrected. *London: Lockyer Davis.* MDCCLXXII. 2 vols., 8vo, pp. xxiv, 479; (4), 419, (14). 7 Plates. + The Fourth Edition. Illustrated with Plates. *London: John Stockdale.* 1806. 2 vols., 8vo, pp. xxvii, 479; (4), 419, (14). 7 Plates. BA., C. + The Fifth Edition. Illustrated with Plates. *London: John Stockdale.* 1807. 2 vols., 8vo, pp. xxvii, 479; iv, 419, (14). Map and 7 Folded Plates. 36813

This translation is somewhat mutilated and abridged. "Juan and Ulloa's Travels may be selected as the most entertaining and satisfactory work of its kind; they are the acknowledged source of much that has been published in other forms."—*Retrospective Review.* Either from ignorance or design, John Adams, Esq., who merely furnished the account of the Brazils, is made to appear to be the translator of the two last editions of the work. *See* Knox's "New Collection of Voyages," I., *also* Mavor's "Voyages," II.

JUANA INES DE LA CRUZ. Fama, y Obras Posthumas de Fenix de Mexico, Decima Musa, Poetisa Americana, sor Juana Ines De La Cruz ... . *Madrid: Manuel Ruiz de Murga.* 1700. Sm. 4to, pp. (142), 210, (5). B. 36814

JUANA INES DE LA CRUZ. Poemas de la Unica Poetisa Americana; Musa Dezima, Soror Juana Inez De La Cruz ... . *Con Licencia: En Zaragoza, Por Manuel Roman ... . Año de* M.DC.LXXXII–1725. 3 vols., sm. 4to, pp. (20), 336, (8); (8), 470, (5); (20), 352, 3. B. 36815

The third volume consists of verses by Spanish-American writers in her praise. The first volume contains pieces in Mexican, in Negro-Spanish, in Basque, and in Latin mixed up with the Spanish poems. The works of this accomplished lady are so rare, and so generally unknown, that it will be difficult to find a reference to them in bibliographical hand-books. "Bouterwek places her on a level with Lope de Vega for facility of invention and versification, and considers some of the dramatic pieces of the Mexican nun (especially that entitled 'El Divino Narcisso') as surpassing in merit all the similar writings of the Spanish poet." For other editions of her works *see* Vol. V., Nos. 17733–35.

JUAREZ (Benito), *Gobernador.* Esposicion al Soberano Congreso al abrir sus sesiones el 2 de Julio de 1848. *Oaxaca.* 1848. Folio, pp. 35, (72). 36816

JUARROS (D.) Compendio de la historia de la Ciudad de Guatemala. Escrito por el Br. D. Domingo Juarros, presbítero secular de este Arzobisbado, que comprende los preliminares de la dicha historia. *Guatemala: Por Don Ignatio Beteta.* 1808–18. 2 vols., 8vo, pp. (6), 385; xv, 361. C. + Edicion del Museo Guatemalteco. *Guatemala: Imprenta de Luna.* 1857. 2 vols., 8vo, pp. 374, (2); 384. 36817

The first edition is rare. The author was a native of Guatemala. It is mostly taken from a manuscript history by Fuentes y Guzman. The following translation is somewhat abridged:

JUARROS. A Statistical and Commercial History of the Kingdom of Guatemala, in Spanish America; Containing Important Particulars relative to its Productions, Manufactures, Customs, &c. ... With an Account of its Conquest by the Spaniards, and a Narrative of the Principal Events down to the Present Time. By Don Domingo Juarros ... . Translated by J. Baily ... . *London: John Hearne.* 1823. 8vo, pp. viii, 520. B., BA., C., H., P.

See "N. A. Rev.," XXVI. 127, *and* Rich, II.

JUBA, *pseudon.* "United We Stand; Divided We Fall." A Poem. By "Juba." *New York.* 1812. 12mo. 36819

JUBILEE COLLEGE, *Ill.* An Account of the Landed Estate, Houses, and other Property of Jubilee College. *Robin's Nest.* 1842. 8vo. 36820

A Plea for Jubilee College, established by Bishop Chase, in Peoria County, Illinois, for the Education of Ministers of Christ,

and Youth of both Sexes, in the Primitive Faith and Worship. *Savannah, Ga.* 1840. 8vo. 36821

A Statement in behalf of Jubilee College, Ill. E. B. Kellogg, Agent. *Jubilee College.* 1853. 8vo, pp. 7. M. 36822

The Jubilee at Mount St. Mary's, October 6, 1858. Published by the President of Mount Saint Mary's College, Emmettsburg, Md. *New York: Edward Dunigan & Brother.* 1859. 12mo, pp. 288. 36823

Jubilos de Lima, y Glorias del Peru: Comicos aplausos, y Reverentes Cultos con que los Gremios de Abastos, celebran la felize Exaltacion de Nuestro Invictisimo Monarca el S^r. D^n. Carlos IV. (que Dios prospere) en el trono de rey de las Españas, y Emperador de las Indias; los que pone a los pies de tan augusto Soberano, Don Antonio Enderica. Escribiala D. S. P. D. L. E. *Lima: En la Imprenta Real.* [n. d.] 4to, 22 l. 36824

Relates to the festivities which took place at Lima upon the celebration of the ascension to the throne of King Charles IV. of Spain.

[JUCHEREAU DE ST. IGNACE, *La Mère* Françoise.] Histoire de l'Hôtel-Dieu de Québec. *Montauban: Chez Jerosme Legier.* [1751.] 12mo, pp. (16), 556. + *Paris: L'Hérissant.* 1751. 12mo. 36825

JUDÆIS (Cornelii de). Speculum Orbis Terrarum. *Antverpiæ: A. Coninckx.* 1593. Folio. 36826

The maps of the World, spherical and Mercator's projection, are curious as giving America, with land reaching both to the North and South Pole, of which Polar regions also separate maps are given. Of America, one map is devoted to Brazil and Peru, including Mexico, Yucatan, and the West Indies; another to North America, from the Gulf of Mexico to the North Pole, in which California, Florida, Virginia, Labrador, Nova Francia, exhibit the names of the Indian tribes then inhabiting those countries, with costumes of the natives of Virginia, the present United States. The letter-press which accompanies the maps gives an outline description of each territory.

[JUDAH (Samuel B. H.)] Gotham and the Gothamites, a Medley. *New York.* 1823. 18mo, pp. lvi, 93, (1). S. 36827

This was suppressed, and the author and publisher were both imprisoned and fined. It is a satire on the New Yorkers. John Allan's copy sold for $5.25.

JUDAH. Odofriede, the Outcast; a Dramatic Poem. By Samuel B. H. Judah. *New York.* 1822. 8vo. 36828

[JUDAH.] A Tale of Lexington: a National Comedy, founded on the Opening of the Revolution. *New York.* 1823. 36829

"The Buccaneers," *our* No. 8838, is by this author. It was rigidly suppressed, and all known copies are imperfect in the introduction, a libellous sentence being abstracted.

[JUDAH (Theodore D.)] Report of the Chief Engineer on the ... Cost of Construction of the Central Pacific Railroad, of California, across the Sierra Nevada Mountains ... . *Sacramento, October 1,* 1861. 8vo, pp. 36. H. 36830

JUDD (A. B.) "Union for the sake of the Union." Speech on the State of the Country, in the Legislature of Connecticut, July 9, 1862. By A. B. Judd. *Hartford: O. F. Jackson.* 1862. 8vo, pp. 24. 36831

JUDD (D. W.) The Story of the Thirty-Third N. Y. S. Vols: or Two Years Campaigning in Virginia and Maryland. By David W. Judd ... . *Rochester: Benton & Andrews.* 1864. 12mo, pp. (2), iv, 349, 76. Portrait. B., BA., C. 36832

JUDD (G. N.) History of the Division of the Presbyterian Church in the United States of America: by a Committee of the Synod of New York and New Jersey. *New York.* 1852. 12mo.

JUDD. A Sermon ... at Bloomfield, N. J., Dec. 13th, 1827, ... a day of Public Thanksgiving. By Gideon N. Judd, A.M. *Newark.* 1828. 8vo, pp. 21. 36834

JUDD. ... A Sermon ... in Catskill, Jan. 10, 1851, at the interment of the Rev. David Porter ... By Gideon N. Judd ... . *New York: Printed by Edward O. Jenkins.* 1851. 8vo, pp. 16.

JUDD (H. O.) Look within for Fact and Fiction consisting of Instructing Sketches, and Thrilling Narratives. By H. O. Judd. *Macon, Ga.: For the Author.* 1864. 12mo, pp. 204. BA.

JUDD (Jonathan). A Sermon at Southampton, May 28, 1758, to a number of Soldiers. 8vo, pp. 24. 36837

Imperfect title from Thomas' "History of Printing."

JUDD (N. B.) Speech of Hon. Norman B. Judd ... on the Rights of American Citizens abroad; ... December 2, 1867. *Washington.* 1867. 8vo, pp. 8. H. 36838

Also: Apportionment of Representation. Speech ... January 17, 1870. [*Washington.* 1870.] 8vo, pp. 7. H.—Rights of American Citizens. Speech ... February 4 and 5, 1868. [n. p. n. d.] 8vo, pp. 8. H.

JUDD (O.) Wesleyan University, Middletown, Conn. Alumni Records, 1833 to 1869. Compiled by Orange Judd, A.M. ... *New-York: Orange Judd & Company.* 1869. 8vo, pp. 264. B.

[JUDD (S.)] Margaret. A Tale of the Real and Ideal, Blight and Bloom. ... *Boston: Phillips, Sampson, and Company.* 1845.

12mo. + [*Ibid.*] 1851. 2 vols., 12mo, pp. viii, 321; (4), 304. + Revised Edition. *Boston.* 1857. 2 vols., 12mo. H. 36840

"Seeks to preserve some reminiscences of the age of our immediate fathers."—*Preface. See* Darley (F. O. C.)

JUDD. A Moral Review of the Revolutionary War ... . A Discourse ... at ... Augusta ... March 13th, 1842. ... By Rev. Sylvester Judd. ... *Hallowell: Glazier, Masters & Smith, Printers.* 1842. 8vo, pp. 48. B., BA. 36841

[JUDD.] Richard Edney and The Governor's Family. A Rus-Urban Tale ... . *Boston: Phillips, Sampson & Company.* 1850. 12mo, pp. iii, 468. B., BA., H. 36842

Relates to the career of a young man in the rural districts of New England. Also: Philo: An Evangeliad. ... *Boston: Phillips, Sampson, and Company.* 1850. 12mo, pp. 244. H.—The Birthright Church: A Discourse ... Jan. 6, 1853. ... *Boston: Crosby, Nichols, & Company.* 1853. 8vo, pp. 49. + *Augusta: William H. Simpson, Printer.* 1854. 8vo, pp. 44. B.—The True Dignity of Politics; A Sermon ... Augusta, Me., May 26, 1850; ... Printed by Request of the Legislature of Maine. *See* Hall (A.), Vol. VII., No. 29717.

JUDD (S.) History of Hadley, including the Early History of Hatfield, South Hadley, Amherst and Granby, Massachusetts. By Sylvester Judd. With Family Genealogies, By Lucius M. Boltwood. *Northampton: Printed by Metcalf & Company.* 1863. 8vo, pp. 636. B., BA., H. 36843

JUDD. Thomas Judd and his Descendants. By Sylvester Judd ... . *Northampton: Printed by J. & L. Metcalf.* 1856. 8vo, pp. 112. B. 36844

JUDD (T.) An Essay on the Improvement in the Manufacture of Sugar adapted for Louisiana. By Thomas Judd. *Boston.* 1836. 8vo, pp. 36. 36845

JUDD (W.) William Judd's Address To the People of ... Connecticut on the ... removal of himself and four other Justices from Office, by the General Assembly of said State, ... For declaring ... their opinion that the people of this State are ... without ... Civil Government. [*New Haven:*] *From Sidney's Press.* 1804. 8vo, pp. 23, (1). BA., N., W. 36846

A Jeffersonian campaign document.

JUDD. Judd *vs.* Trumbull; or, Plain Truths. Addressed to the real Friends of ... Connecticut, of every Sect, Denomination, and Party, whatever. By Judd. ... *New-Haven: Printed by J. Barber.* 1820. 8vo, pp. 20. H. 36847

JUDD (W.) The Memoirs and Remains of Rev. Willard Judd, Embracing A Review of Professor Stuart ... Miscellanies, and A Biographical Sketch, by Orrin B. Judd, With an Introductory Essay by Spencer H. Cone. ... *New York: Lewis Colby.* 1845. 12mo, pp. xxviii, 452. B., C., H. 36848

JUDGE (J. J.) The Southern Orator: being a Collection of Pieces in Prose, Poetry, and Dialogue. By Jonathan J. Judge. *Montgomery* [*Ala.*]: *Brittan & De Wolf.* 1853. 8vo, pp. 400.

The Judgment, a Vision. By the Author of "Percy's Masque." *New York: James Eastburn.* 1821. 8vo, pp. 46.

The Judgment Of Several Eminent Divines of the Congregational VVay. Concerning A Pastors Power Occasionally to Exert Ministerial Acts in another Church besides that which is His Own Particular Flock. *Boston: Printed by Benjamin Harris, and are to be Sold by Richard Wilkins.* 1693. 8vo, pp. (2), 13.

Perhaps by Increase Mather. Prefixed is a recommendation signed "James Allen Samuel Willard. Michael Wigglesworth. Cotton Mather. Nehemiah Walker."

Judgment of Whole Kingdoms. *See* [Defoe (D.)], Vol. V.

Judgments of God upon the Nations. *New York.* 1855. 12mo, pp. 134. 36852

The Judicial Chronicle. *See* [Gibbs (George M.)], Vol. VII.

Judith, Esther, and other Poems. By a Lover of the Fine Arts [Maria Brooks]. *Boston: Cummings & Hilliard.* 1820 18mo, pp. 112. 36853

JUDSON (A.) A Sermon ... in ... Plymouth, December 22, 1802, in Memory of the Landing of our Ancestors, December 22, 1620. By Adoniram Judson, A.M. ... . *Boston: Printed by David Carlisle.* 1803. 8vo, pp. 23. B., BA., H. 36854

JUDSON (A. T.) An Address delivered at South Coventry, Connecticut, at the request of the Hale Monument Association, Nov. 25, 1836. By Andrew T. Judson. *Norwich.* 1837. 8vo.

[JUDSON.] Comments on the Trial of Dr. Siah Fuller. [n. p. n. d.] 8vo, pp. 10. B. 36856

JUDSON *and* NEWELL. A Correction of erroneous statements concerning the embarkation of the Rev. Messrs. Judson and Newell, at Salem, February 18, 1812. ... *Boston: Press of T. R. Marvin.* 1849. 8vo, pp. 24. B. 36857

JUDSON (A. M.) History of the Eighty-Third Regiment Pennsylvania Volunteers. By A. M. Judson ... . *Erie, Pa.: B. F. H. Lynn.* [n. d.] 8vo, pp. 9–139, (1). B. 36858

JUDSON (D.) Timely Warning against Surfeiting and Drunkenness. Discourse at New-Town, Connecticut, Jan. 12, 1752. By David Judson. *New York.* 1752. 4to, pp. 29. 36859

Also: Sermons on Church Government; in Reply to a discourse on that subject ... by Mr. Ross. ... *New Haven.* [1774.] 8vo.

[JUDSON (Edward Z. C.)] Cruisings, Afloat and Ashore, from the Private Log of Ned Buntline. Sketches of Land and Sea ... *New York: Robert Craighead.* 1848. 8vo, pp. 102. Plate. H.

[JUDSON.] Life in the Saddle; or, The Cavalry Scout. *New York: F. A. Brady.* 1864. 8vo, pp. 81. 36861

[JUDSON.] The Mysteries and Miseries of New-York. ... By Ned Buntline. *New-York.* 1848. 8vo, pp. 116. S. 36862

With a glossary of "Flash Terms" used in the work. Also: Life, Career and Character of Ned Buntline. *New York.* 1849. 8vo.—Sadia: A Heroine of the Rebellion. ... *New York: F. A. Brady.* [1864.] 8vo, pp. 92.

JUDSON (E.) Alderbrook. A Collection of Fanny Forester's Village Sketches, Poems, etc. By Miss Emily Chubbuck. *Boston: William D. Ticknor & Company.* MDCCCXLVII. 2 vols., 12mo, pp. 276; 263. Portrait. B. + Eleventh Edition. Revised with Additions. *Boston: Ticknor & Fields.* 1856. 2 vols., 12mo, pp. 285; 285. C. 36863

JUDSON (E.) ... A Sermon ... at the Ordination of the Reverend Jonathan Strong ... in Braintree, January 28, 1789. By Ephraim Judson, A.M. ... *Providence: Printed by Bennett Wheeler.* 1789. 8vo, pp. 43. BA. 36864

Also: Sermon at the Ordination of the Rev. Ebenezer Fitch, President of Williams College, Williamstown, June 17, 1795. ... *Stockbridge.* 1796. 8vo.—Sermon at the Ordination of the Rev. Holland Weeks, Waterbury, November 20, 1799. ... *Stockbridge.* 1801. 8vo. N.—Sermon delivered in Durham, at the Ordination of the Rev. David Smith, 1799. ... *Middletown.* 1800. 8vo.

JUDSON (L. C.) A Biography of the Signers of the Declaration of Independence, and of Washington and Patrick Henry. With an Appendix, containing the Constitution of the United States and other Documents. By L. Carroll Judson ... . *Philadelphia: J. Dobson, and Thomas Cowperthwait & Co.* 1839. 8vo, pp. ix, 9–354. C. 36865

JUDSON. The Probe, or one hundred and two essays on The Nature of Men and Things. By L. Carroll Judson … . With an Appendix … . Third Edition. *Philadelphia: For the Author.* [1846.] 12mo, pp. 272, 48. Portrait. H. 36866

JUDSON. The Sages and Heroes of the American Revolution. In Two Parts. Including the Signers of the Declaration of Independence. … By L. Carroll Judson … . *Philadelphia.* 1851. 8vo. + Revised Stereotype Edition. *Philadelphia: The Author.* 1852. 8vo, pp. 480. Portraits and Facsimile. B., S. + [*Ibid.*] 1853. + [*Ibid.*] 1854. 36867

De Juffer in schyn, of zeldzame levensgevallen van Graaf B***, neevens van een Fransche Juffer … Vorstinne der Huronnen … *'s Gravenhage.* 1739. 2 vols., 8vo. Plates. 36868

"The lady in appearance, or curious adventures of Count B***, and of a French lady, Princess of the Hurons, and the piracies of the American buccaneers." Very rare.

JUGE (M. A.) The American Planter: or the Bound Labor Interest in the United States. By M. A. Juge. *New York: Long and Brother.* 1854. 8vo, pp. 42, (1). B., BA., H. 36869

JUGEMANN (Bernhard Severin). Kunnuk og Maja elter Grõn lænderne. En Fortælling. *Kjöbenhavn.* 1842. 36870

JUGLAR (Clément). Des Crises commerciales et de leur retour périodique en France, en Angleterre et aux États-Unis. Par le docteur Clément Juglar. *Paris: Guillaumin et Cie.* 1862. 8vo, pp. xvi, 262. 36871

Juicio de imprenta. Documentos relativos al promovido por D. Eustaquio Barron contra Benito Gomez Fariaz. *Mexico.* 1856. 4to, pp. 56. 36872

Juicio historico-canonico-politico de la autoridad de las naciones en los bienes eclesiasticos. *Oaxaca.* 1847. 4to, pp. 45. 36873

Juicio Imparcial sobre los Acontecimientos de Mexico, en 1828 y 1829. *New-York: C. S. Van Winkle.* 1830. 8vo, pp. 48. B. + *Reimpreso en Mexico.* 1830. 4to, pp. 32. 36874

Juicio posesorio de los terrenos del Cenicero. *Onerida.* 1869. 8vo, pp. 35. 36875

JUJAT (*Abbé*). Mission de l'Orégon. Notice sur les Travaux Apostoliques de Mgr Demers … . Rédigée par M. l'abbé Jujat … *Paris: Typographie de Vrayet de Surcy et Cie.* 1851. 12mo, pp. (2), 16. H. 36876

JUKES (J. B.) Excursions in and about Newfoundland, during the Years 1839 and 1840. By J. B. Jukes, … late Geological Surveyor of Newfoundland. *London: John Murray.* 1842. 2 vols., post 8vo, pp. x, 322; iv, 354. Map. B., BA., H. 36877

JUKES. General Report of the Geological Survey of Newfoundland … during the Years 1839 and 1840. By J. B. Jukes … *London: John Murray.* 1843. 8vo, pp. (2), 160. 2 Geological Maps. BA. 36878

JUKES. Forbes, Playfair, W. W. Smith, Percy and Hunt: Lectures on Gold, for the Instruction of Emigrants … to California. By J. B. Jukes … . *London.* 1852. 12mo. S. 36879

JULAP (G.) The Glosser. A Poem. By Giles Julap, of Chotauk, Va. [*Virginia.*] 1802. 12mo. 36880

A poetical squib against Jefferson.

JULIÁN (Antonio). Historia del Rio Grande y de la Magdalena. *Madrid.* 3 vols., 8vo. 36881

JULIÁN. La Perla de la America, Provincia de Santa Marta, reconocida, observada, y expuesta en discursos historicos por el Sacerdote Don Antonio Julian, á mayor bien de la Católica Monarquia, fomento del comercio de España, y de todo el Nuevo Reyno de Granada, é incremento de la Christiana Religion entre las naciones barbaras, que subsisten todavia rebeldes en la Provincia. *Madrid.* MDCCLXXXVII. *Don Antonio de Sancha.* 4to, pp. (2), xxx, 280. P. + [*Ibid.*] 1788. H. 36882

Contains articles on the gold and silver mines, pearls and pearl fisheries of this province, and on the Indians, its original inhabitants, defending the treatment they received from the Spaniards. The second part relates to the Indian nations (Indios Tayronas, Arnacos, Tupes, Chimilas, Motilones, Guagiros, &c.) Chapter XIV. is entirely on the language of the Guagiros.

JULIÁN. Trasformazione dell' America o sia Trionfo della S. Chiesa Su la Rovina della Monarchìa del Demonio in America dopo la Conquista fattane da' Monarchi delle Spagne: Con Riflessioni Apologetiche, E coll' aggiunta di una Dissertazione Critico-Espositiva, nella quale spiegandosi le parole di S. Pietro Epi. I. c. 3. Qui increduli fuerant in diebus Noe, cum fabricaretur Arca. vv. 18. 19. 20. Dimostrasi con valide ragioni, essere tutto ciò accaduto nell' America. Opera del Sacerdote Antonio Juliàn Stato per molti anni Missionario in quelle parti. *In Roma.* MDCCXC. 8vo, pp. xii, 286. Plate. B., S. 36883

JULIAN (G. W.) The Cause and Cure of our National Troubles. Speech of Hon. George W. Julian … in the House of Representatives … January 14, 1862. *Washington, D. C.: Scammell & Co., Printers.* 1862. 8vo, pp. 15, (1). H. 36884

JULIAN. The Rebellion—the Mistakes of the Past—the Duty of the Present. Speech of Hon. George W. Julian … February 18th, 1863. [n. p. n. d.] 8vo, pp. 8. H. 36885

Also: Confiscation and Liberation. Speech … in the House of Representatives, … May 23, 1862. *Washington, D. C.: Scammell & Co., Printers.* 1862. 8vo, pp. 8.—Dangers and Duties. Reconstruction and Suffrage. Speech … in … Indianapolis, Ind. … November 17, 1865 … . *Cincinnati.* 1865. 8vo, pp. 16.—Homesteads for Soldiers—Who are their Friends? Speech … May 12, 1864. [n. p.: *Printed by Lemuel Towers.* 1864.] 8vo, pp. 8. H.—Homesteads for Soldiers on the Lands of Rebels. Speech … March 18, 1864. [n. p. n. d.] 8vo, pp. 8. H.—How to Resume Specie Payments. Speech … February 5, 1869. [*Washington.* n. d.] 8vo, pp. 8.—Our Land Policy—Its Evils and their Remedy. Speech … March 6, 1868 … . *Washington.* 1868. 8vo, pp. 16.—The Public Lands. Speech … January 29, 1851 … . [*Washington.* n. d.] 8vo, pp. 7. H.—Radicalism and Conservatism—the Truth of History Vindicated. Speech … February 7, 1865. [n. p. n. d.] 8vo, pp. 7.—Radicalism the Nation's Hope. Speech … June 16, 1866. [*Washington.* n. d.] 8vo, pp. 8. H.—Regeneration before Reconstruction. Speech … January 28, 1867. *Washington.* 1867. 8vo, pp. 8.—Sale of Mineral Lands. Speech … February 9, 1865. [n. p.: *Printed by L. Towers.* 1865.] 8vo, pp. 8.—The Slavery Question. Speech … May 14, 1850 … on the President's Message transmitting the Constitution of California. [*Washington: Printed by Buell & Blanchard.* 1850.] 8vo, pp. 16.—Southern Land Grants. Speech … January 22 and 28, 1868 … . [*Washington.* n. d.] 8vo, pp. 8.—Southern Land Grants. Speech … February 4, 1868. *Washington: F. & J. Rives & Geo. A. Bailey.* 1868. 8vo, pp. 8.—Speech … on the Slavery Question, delivered in the House of Representatives, May 14, 1850. *Washington.* 1850. 8vo, pp. 15.—Speech … on Amending the Constitution; … January 29, 1866. *Washington.* 1866. 8vo, pp. 8. H.—Spoliation of the Public Domain—The Saving Remedy. Speech … March 6, 1868. *Washington: F. & J. Rives & Geo. A. Bailey.* 1868. 8vo, pp. 14.—Suffrage in the District of Columbia. Speech … January 16, 1866. [*Washington.* 1866.] 8vo, pp. 8. B.

JULIAN, *and others.* The Rights of Pre-emptors on the Public Lands of the Government Threatened—The Conspiracy Exposed. Remarks of G. W. Julian and Others … July 5, 1866. [*Washington.* n. d.] 8vo, pp. 24. H. 36886

JULIAN (I. H.) Memoir of Isaac H. Julian, a Pioneer of Indiana: a Settler of Indiana. *Richmond, Ind.* 1857. 8vo, pp. 44.

JULIUS (J. M.) Hoboken, and other Poems. By Julia Matilda Julius. *New York.* 1866. 12mo. 36888

JULIUS (N. H.) Die Amerikanischen Besserungs-Systeme. … Von Dr. Julius. *Leipzig: F. A. Brockhaus.* 1837. 8vo, pp. x, 50.

JULIUS. Catalogus Bibliothecæ per XL annos … in Europa et America collectæ … . *Berolini.* 1850. 8vo, pp. (8), 182. B., S.

JULIUS. Nordamerikas sittliche Zustände. Nach eigenen Anschauungen in den Jahren 1834, 1835, und 1836, von Dr. N. H. Julius. Boden und Geschichte Religiöses Erziehung und Unterricht. Armuth und Mildthätigkeit. Volk und Gesellschaft. Mit einer von Nordamerika und zwei Musikbeilagen. *Leipzig: F. A. Brockhaus.* 1839. 2 vols., 8vo, pp. xxviii, 514; xii, 502, (2). Map, 67 folded Tables, and 13 Plates. A. 36891

On the moral, political, and religious condition of the people; civilization of the Indians; schools; slavery, etc., music of negro songs, and plans of prisons.

JULIUS. Du Système pénitentiaire américain en 1836, suivi de quelques observations, traduit de l'allemand par M. Victor Foucher. *Paris: Joubert, Pouchin.* 1837. 8vo. 36892

JULIUS, *pseudon.* A Geographic Narrative, containing a Concise Description of the Several States and Provinces of the American Continent … . *Hanover (N. H.): Printed by Moses Davis.* 1805. 8vo, pp. 19. BA., BM. 36893

JULIUS, *pseudon.* John Randolph Abroad and at Home. … By Julius. Third Edition. *Washington: Peter Force.* 1829. 8vo, pp. 31. 36894

JULIUS, *pseudon.* *See* [Rush (R.)]

JUMEL (E. B.) Obituary of Madame Eliza B. Jumel. In the New York Times of July 18th, 1865. *New York.* 1865. 4to.

Thirty copies only privately reprinted.

JUMPERTS (H.) Career, Tragedy, and Trial of Henry Jumperts, at Chicago, for Murder. *Chicago.* 1850. 12mo. 36896

Junction of the Atlantic and Pacific Oceans by a Navigation across the Isthmus of Darien without Locks. *London.* 1853. 8vo, pp. 15, (1). 2 Maps. 36897

Perhaps by Sir Charles Fox. *See also* [Sampson (M. B.)]

Jungerutit. *See* Greenland, Vol. VII., No. 28651.

JUNIATA, *Pa.* Report, in the Legislature, on the Juniata and Conemaugh Canal. *Harrisburg.* 1824. 8vo. 36898

JUNIENT (Manuel de). Amaty y Reglamento para el gobierno de la aduana de Lima y metodo delos reales derechos de Almoxarifazgo y Alcabala del reyno del Peru en virtud de reales ordenes de S. M. con adaptacion de los que se formaron para el Reyno de Mexico y Provincia de Goatemala. *Lima.* 1773. 4to. 36899

The Juniper Hill Cemetery, in Bristol, R. I. … [A Poem. n. p. n. d.] 12mo, pp. 16. H. 36900

Don Junípero.—Periódico satirico-jocoso con Abundancia de caricaturas, dirigido por D. Victor Patricio de Landaluze. Octubre 5, 1862, to Abril 24, 1864. *Habana.* 4to, pp. 418, 240.

Eighty-two numbers—all published.

JUNIUS, *pseudon.* Conduct of a Commander. *See* No. 15197.

[JUNIUS.] An Enqviry into the Condvct of a late Right Honovrable Commoner. *London: J. Almon.* [n. d.] 8vo, pp. 72.

This scarce pamphlet relates to William Pitt, afterwards Earl of Chatham.

[JUNIUS.] A | Letter | To an Honourable | Brigadier General, | Commander in Chief of His Majesty's Forces | in Canada. | *London: J. Burd.* 1760. 8vo, pp. (2), 31, (1). 36903

The brigadier-general is Lord George Townshend, against whom the writer makes serious charges for incompetency in the campaigns in Canada. Written by "Junius" six years before the publication of his celebrated Letters, and unknown to all the editors. *See* Britton on the Author of "Junius." It elicited the following:

A | Refutation | of the | Letter | to an | Honble Brigadier-General, | Commander of His Majesty's Forces in Canada. | By an Officer. | … *London: R. Stevens.* MDCCLX. 8vo, pp. (2), 52. + The Second Edition. [*Ibid.*] + The Fourth Edition. [*Ibid.*] 36904

See Walpole's "George III.," I. 21, Sparks' "Life of Charles Lee," p. 15, *and* "Notes and Queries," Third Series, III., 122. The "Refutation" is probably by Lord Thurlow. Both of these pamphlets were reproduced with the following title:

JUNIUS. "A Letter to an Honourable Brigadier General, Commander in Chief of His Majesty's Forces in Canada." London, 1760. Now First Ascribed to Junius. To which is added, "A Refutation of the Letter, Etc., By an Officer." With incidental Notices of Lords Townshend and Sackville, Sir Philip Francis, and others. Edited by N. W. Simons, of the British Museum. *London: William Pickering.* 1841. Fcap 8vo, pp. (4), xxiv, 110. B., BA. 36905

These pieces are all, of course, included in the various and multitudinous editions of "Junius;" we content ourselves with recording a few only of the editions of that "great unknown" political writer.

JUNIUS. … *London: Printed for Henry Sampson Woodfall* … . MDCCLXXII. 2 vols., 12mo, Engraved Titles, pp. vii, xxxii, 208; 356, Index, 19 l. 36906

The original edition—some copies have no date.

JUNIUS. … *London: Printed by T. Bensley.* 1797. 2 vols., 8vo, pp. xxx, 274; v, 318. 36907

A beautiful edition, with portraits, head and tail-pieces.

JUNIUS. … Illustrated by Mr. Edward Bocquet, Historical Engraver, from Original Paintings. *London.* 1812. 4to. 12 Portraits. 36908

Among the portraits are Lord Chatham, John Wilkes, &c.

JUNIUS. The Letters of Junius complete … with Notes Biographical and Explanatory; also, A Prefatory Inquiry respecting the real author. By John Almon. *London.* 1806. 2 vols., 12mo. 36909

JUNIUS, including Letters by the Same Writer, under other Signatures (Now first collected), to which are added, his Confidential Correspondence with Mr. Wilkes, and his Private Letters addressed to Mr. H. S. Woodfall. With a Preliminary Essay, Notes, Facsimiles, &c. *London: Printed by G. Woodfall.* 1812. 3 vols., 8vo, pp. xii, 336, 248; xi, 516; xiii, 511, (1). + Second Edition. [*Ibid.*] 1814. 3 vols., 8vo. + A New … Edition, by John Wade. *London: Henry G. Bohn.* 1850. 2 vols., post 8vo. 36910

Repeatedly reprinted. Several of the letters relate to American questions. Woodfall's edition is generally regarded as the best. There are numerous American editions; the first is *Philadelphia,* 1795. 12mo. Woodfall's edition was reprinted in *Philadelphia,* 1813 and 1836; of this last some copies were printed on writing paper for the late E. D. Ingraham. In Bohn's edition of Lowndes' "Bibliographer's Manual," is a list of the various editions of "Junius," as well as of the many controversial books and pamphlets relating to the authorship of these remarkable letters. Respecting the authorship of "Junius" *see* Allibone's "Dictionary."

[JUNIUS.] The Political Contest; Containing, a Series of Letters, between Junius and Sir William Draper: Also the whole of Junius' Letters to his Grace the D*** of G***** Brought into one point of view. *London: F. Newbery.* [n. d.] 8vo, pp. (4), 55; Part II. pp. (2), 38. + The Second Edition. [*Ibid.*]

JUNIUS. The Posthumous Writings of Junius. To which is prefixed, an Inquiry respecting the Author, also a Sketch of the Life of John Horne Tooke. *New York: G. & C. & H. Carvill.* 1829. 8vo, pp. 428. Portrait and Facsimile. 36912

JUNIUS. A Serious Letter to the Public, on the late Transaction between Lord North and the Duke of Gordon. By Junius. … *London: Hooper and Davis.* MDCCLXXVIII. 8vo, pp. 24.

JUNIUS Unmasked: or, Thomas Paine the author of the Letters of Junius, and the Declaration of Independence. *Washington, D. C.: John Gray & Co.* 1872. 12mo, pp. 322. H. 36914

The date of this title is later than that of books usually included in this "Dictionary;" its audacity is our apology for letting it appear.

JUNIUS and his Letters. Affairs of Great Britain and America, 1763–85. *Boston.* 1831. 8vo. 36915

JUNIUS. The King's Answer to Junius. *Philadelphia.* 1771.

JUNIUS, *pseudon.* … A Letter to Daniel Webster, … in Reply to his Legal Opinion to Baring, Brothers & Co. upon the Illegality and Unconstitutionality of State Bonds, and Loans of State Credit. By Junius. *New York.* 1840. 8vo, pp. (2), 79. H.

JUNIUS, *pseudon.* The Letters of Junius; exposing to The Public, for their Benefit, the Mal-Practices in the Administration of the Law, the Corruption in the Offices in the State House Row, in … Philadelphia … . By an Experienced Member of the Philada. Bar. *Philadelphia.* 1848. 8vo, pp. 48. B. 36918

JUNIUS, *pseudon.* *See* [Colton (Calvin)], Vol. IV., No. 14768.

JUNIUS, *Junior, pseudon.* The Spirit of Liberty: or, Junius's Loyal Address. Being a Key to the English Cabinet: … By Junius, Junior. To which is added, A Polemical Tale; or, the Christians Winter Piece: … [n. p.] 1770. 8vo, pp. (2), v, 232. + *Boston.* 1772. 8vo. 36919

In a MS. note in one copy this book is ascribed to J. Allen.

JUNIUS, *Jr., pseudon.* The Vision of Judgment; or, A Present for the Whigs of '76 & '37. … By Junius, Jr. … *New-York: H. R. Robinson.* 1838. 8vo, pp. 32. 36920

JUNIUS, *pseudon.* A Statement of Reasons against the assumption and exercise of Executive … Powers by the Supreme Judicial Court: … against the Sale of Spiritual Liquors; … . *Boston: William Chadwick, Printer.* 1849. 12mo, pp. 40. H.

JUNIUS (J.), *pseudon.* The Philadelphia Pursuits of Literature, a Satirical Poem. By Juvenal Junius, of New Jersey, with Notes by Robert Heron, Jr. Second Edition. *Philadelphia.* 1805. 12mo, pp. 16. 36922

JUNIUS (R.) Of the Conversion of 5900 East-Indians. With a Post-script of the Gospels good Success also amongst the West-

Indians, in New-England. *London: John Hamond.* 1656. 4to, pp. (8), 38, (1). 36923

A pamphlet of extreme rarity, probably collected from John Eliot's Tracts.

JUNIUS AMERICANUS, *pseudon.* *See* [Lee (Arthur)].

JUNIUS AMERICANUS, *pseudon.* A Review of "A Discourse occasioned by the Death of Daniel Webster, preached at the Melodeon on Sunday, October 31, 1852, by Theodore Parker, Minister of the Twenty-Eighth Congregational Society in Boston." By "Junius Americanus." *Boston and Cambridge: James Munroe and Company.* 1853. 8vo, pp. 89. BA., C. 36924

JUNIUS BRUTUS, *pseudon.* Verzameling van stukken tot de dertien Vereenigde Staaten van Noord-America betrekkelijk. Door Junius Brutus. *Leyden: L. Herdingh.* 1781. 8vo, pp. xlij, 300. C. 36925

Contents: Voorreede, door Junius Brutus. Brief van zijne excellentie Jonathan Trumbull, gouverneur [etc.] van Connecticut, æn jr. Johan Derk van der Capellen. Artikelen van regeering, gemaakt in 1638. Eenige getuigschriften van de mishandelingen der Engelschen.

JUNIUS PHILÆNUS, *pseudon.* A Letter to Thomas Jefferson, President of the United States. By Junius Philænus. *New York: P. R. Johnson.* 1802. 8vo, pp. 64. 36926

JUNIUS REDIVIVUS, *pseudon.* A Tale of Tucuman, with Digressions, English and American, By Junius Redivivus. *London.* 1831. 12mo. 36927

JUNIUS SECUNDUS, *pseudon.* *See* [Kelsall (C.)]

JUNKIN (D. X.) The Christian Statesman: a Discourse occasioned by the Death of the Hon. James McDowell, Late Governor of Virginia; … Washington City, … September 14, 1851, By Rev. D. X. Junkin, D.D. … *James Nourse,* … *Washington.* [1851.] 8vo, pp. 20. H. 36928

JUNKIN. The Oath a Divine Ordinance, and an Element of of the Social Constitution: its Origin, Nature, Ends, Efficacy, Lawfulness, Obligations, Interpretation, Form, and Abuses. By D. X. Junkin … . *New-York: Wiley and Putnam.* 1845. 12mo, pp. x, 233. B. 36929

JUNKIN. The Rev. George Junkin, D.D., LL.D. A Historical Biography. By D. X. Junkin, D.D. *Philadelphia.* 18—. Cr. 8vo, pp. 609. 36930

Also: Address … at the Funeral of Sophia, Wife of Major Gen. Towson … . [*New-York: Angell, Engel & Hewitt, Printers.* 1852.] 8vo, pp. 20. H.

Junkin (G.) The Integrity of our National Union, *vs.* Abolitionism: An Argument from the Bible. ... By Rev. George Junkin, D.D. ... *Cincinnati: Printed by R. P. Donogh.* 1843. 8vo, pp. 79. B., BA. 36931

Junkin. Political Fallacies: an Examination of the False Assumptions, and Refutation of the Sophistical Reasonings, which have brought on this Civil War. By George Junkin, D.D. ... *New York: Charles Scribner.* 1863. 12mo, pp. 332. Portrait. B.

Junkin. A Review of the Rev. Dr. Junkin's Synodical Speech, in Defence of American Slavery; Delivered September 19th and 20th .... *Cincinnati.* 1844. 8vo, pp. 136. H. 36933

Junkin. The Vindication, containing A History of the Trial of the Rev. Albert Barnes, by the Second Presbytery, and by the Synod .... By Rev. George Junkin, D.D. *Philadelphia: Printed by Wm. S. Martien.* 1836. 12mo, pp. iv, xxvi, 159. B., BA., S.

Also: An Apology for Collegiate Education: being the Baccalaureate Address ... June 18th, 1851. ... *Lexington, Va., July,* 1851. 8vo, pp. 26.—Civil Government an Ordinance of God. A Lecture for the Times, ... in Philadelphia, October 27 1861. ... *Philadelphia: I. B. Chandler.* 1861. 8vo, pp. 22.— ... The Baccalaureate in Miami University ... August 11th, 1842. ... *Rossville: J. M. Christy, Printer.* 1842. 8vo, pp. 21. + August 10th, A.D. 1843. [*Ibid.*] 1843. 8vo, pp. 23. + August 8th, A.D. 1844. [*Ibid.*] 1844. 8vo, pp. 32.—A Plea for North-Eastern Pennsylvania. The Tenth Baccalaureate ... . *Easton, Pa.: J. P. Hetrich, Printer.* 1845. 8vo, pp. 24.—Sabbatismos. A Discussion and Defence of the Lord's Day of Sacred Rest. ... *Philadelphia.* 1866. 12mo.

La Junta Superior de Cadiz á la America Española, Pueblos de America. [n. p. n. d.] 8vo. 36935

The Junto, or the Interior Cabinet laid open. A State Farce, now acting upon the most capital Stage in Europe. *London: S. Bladon.* 1778. 8vo. 36936

"Low, scurrilous stuff, about the evil politics and misconduct of 'The Thane, Lord Jefferies, Lord Boreas, Lord Mindon,'" etc.—*Monthly Review*, LX. 64.

Jurado (J.) Representaciones del Sr. D. Juan Jurado, Fiscal de la Excma. Audiencia territorial presentadas á S. E. á consecuencia de los mas atroces y repetidos atentados perpetrados en la desgraciada ciudad de Puerto-Príncipe por el Alcalde 1°. y Ayuntamiento de diha ciudad. *Imprenta filantrópica á cargo de D. Pedro Pascual Arias.* 1823. 8vo. 36937

Jurado celebre. *Veracruz.* 1843. 8vo, pp. 56. 36938

Juras Reales (*Baron de*). *See* [Moxa (Benito Maria de)].

Jürgensen (Christian August). Breve fra Grönland.

In Rönne's "Dansk Religionsblad," Vol. II., 1826, III., V., VI., VII., 1831.

Jürgensen (Jörgen). Efterretning om Engellænderne og Nordamerikanernes Fart og Handel paa Sydhavet. *Kjöbenhavn.* 1807. 36939

Jurisconsult, *pseudon.* *See* [Boyd (S. S.)], *and* [Madison (J.)]

Jurisconsultus, *pseudon.* Observations on the Reform of the Court of Chancery of New York. By Jurisconsultus. *Albany.* 1809. 8vo. 36940

Juris Consultus, *pseudon.* *See* Vol. VII., No. 30925.

Jusselain (A.) Un Déporté à Cayenne; Souvenirs de la Guyane. Par Armand Jusselain. *Paris: Michel Lévy frères.* 1865. 18mo, pp. 330. 36941

Jussieu (L.) Simão de Nantua ou o Mercador de Feiras. Seguido das suas obras posthumas por Lourenço de Jussieu. Obra premiada pela sociedade de instrucção elementar. Nova edição. *Maranhão.* 1867. Sm. 8vo, pp. 252, iv. Portrait.

A Just and Modest Vindication. *See* [Hodges (J.)], Vol. VIII.

Justa repulsa contra las horribles calumnias con que se ha procurado disfamar la casa de Iriarte y Laza de la Habana en varios libelos impresos últimamente en esta ciudad, con motivo del litis instaurado por dicha casa en Junio de 1806 contra D. Francisco Gomez ... [*Habana:*] *Imprenta de Arazoza y Soler.* 1813. Folio.

[Justel (Henri).] Recueil de divers Voyages faits en Afrique et en l'Amerique qui n'ont point esté encore publiez; Contenant l'Origine, les Mœurs les Coûtumes & le Commerce des habitans de ces deux Parties du Monde. Avec des Traitez curieux touchant la Haut Ethyopie, le debordement du Nil, la mer rouge & le Prete-Jean. Le tout enrichi de Figures, & de Cartes geographiques, qui servent à l'intelligence des choses contenuës en ce volume. *Paris: Chez Louis Billaine.* M.DC.LXXIV. 4to, pp. (16), 262, 35, 23, 49, 81. 13 Plates and Map. 36944

It was reprinted in 1684, with merely a new title-page.

Justia, *pseudon.* Our World; or, the Democrat's Rule. By Justia, a Know-Nothing. [F. Colburn Adams.] *London: S. Low, Son & Co.* 1855. 12mo, pp. viii, 398. 4 Plates. C.

J[ustice] (A[lexander].) A General Treatise of the Dominion of the Sea: And a Compleat Body of the Sea-Laws: Containing What is most Valuable on that Subject in antient and Modern Authors; ... and Adjudg'd Cases in several Courts concerning Trade and Navigation. By A. J. Second Edition .... *London.* 1705. 4to. + The Third Edition, with large Additions, and Improvements. And a New Appendix ... *London: For the Executors of J. Nicholson;* ... . [1707.] 4to, pp. (26), 684, 107. 2 Plates. B., C. 36946

The Justice and Necessity of Taxing the American Colonies, Demonstrated. Together with a Vindication of the Authority of Parliament. *London: J. Almon.* 1766. 8vo, pp. 36. B., BA.

"This is, in truth, a most fiery politician, and his pamphlet a mere firebrand. In reply to the objections of the colonists to a standing army, he says that they have need of the *gentlemen of the blade*, to polish and refine their manners, to rub off the rust of puritanism," etc.—*Monthly Review*, XXXIV. 71.

The Justice and Necessity of the War with our American Colonies Considered. [n. p. 1775.] 8vo, Half Title, pp. 50.

The writer lays the whole blame for the disputes between Great Britain and her colonies to the latter. "After the most violent outrage on private property," he says, "the most haughty refusal of satisfaction when demanded, and the most daring resistance to the execution of the laws, they have resorted to open rebellion to justify their conduct. ... Liberty was but a pretence, for they were always free; independence was their aim."

Justice and Policy. An Essay on the increasing Growth and Enormities of our Great Cities. ... Also a descant on the present State of the Nation in regard to America, &c. &c. ... *London: C. Dilly.* 1774. 8vo. 36949

See "M. Rev.," LII. 88.

The Justice and Policy of a War with Spain Demonstrated. *London: J. Hatchard.* 1804. 8vo, pp. 46. 36950

On the restitution of the Spanish silver-ships. *See* "M. Rev.," XLVI. 94.

Justice and Policy. *See* [Knox (William)].

The Justice of the Present War against the French. Sermon to the Soldiers, Sept. 22, 1755. By J[onathan] E[llis]. *Newport.* [n. d.] 4to, pp. 24. 36951

Justificacion de los Assientos de Averia, Almojaribazzos y Alcavalas, en satisfacion de las respuestas de los fiscales del consejo real de las Indias y de la audiencia de Lima. ... [*Lima?*] 1726. Folio, pp. 86. 36952

Justification de la résistance des Colonies américaines aux oppressions du Gouvernement britannique, dans une lettre écrite de la Hollande à M*** à Londres. *Leide: Chez Haak et Comp.* MDCCLXXVI. 8vo, pp. 30. 36953

"A sensible advocate for the colonies, and apparently one well acquainted with the principal objects of the American controversy."—*Monthly Review*, LV. 241.

A Justification of the Conduct of the Ministry relative to Falkland's Islands. In a Letter to both Houses of Parliament. *London.* 1771. 8vo. 36954

Justification of the Present War. *See* [Stubbes (Henry)].

Justification, 1660. *See* Schulenburgh (J.)

Justin (J. P.) Discourse delivered at the New Edifice of the Baptist Church, May 8, 1845. *Providence.* 1845. 12mo.

Justin (P.) Histoire politique et statistique de l'Ile de Hayti, Saint-Domingue; écrite sur les Documents Officiels et des Notes communiquées Par Sir James Barskett, Agent du Gouvernement Britannique dans les Antilles. Par M. Placide-Justin. ... *Paris: Brière.* 1826. 8vo, pp. (8), 547. Map and Table. H. 36956

Probably the same as *our* No. 3885, Vol. I., with a different title.

Justin. Politische und statistische Geschichte der Insel Hayti (St. Domingo), entworfen nach amtlichen Berichten ... des Sir James Berskett. Nach dem Französischen bearbeitet von C. G. Hennig. *Ronneburg: F. Schumann.* 1827. 8vo, pp. xvi, 503.

Justinian, *pseudon.* Remarks on the Report of the Secretary of the Treasury. ... By Justinian. *Wilmington (Del.): R. Porter.* 1820. 8vo, pp. 40. 36958

Justinian, *pseudon.* Sovereign Rights of the States. By Justinian. *Washington.* [n. d.] 8vo. 36959

Justinian, *pseudon.* The Currency of the Future. *Brooklyn, E. D.: L. Darbee & Son, Printers.* 1868. 8vo, pp. 12. H.

Justitius, *pseudon.* Remarks on the Organization and Constitutional Powers of the Council of Appointment of the State of New York. By Justitius. *Albany.* 1799. 4to, pp. 15. 36961

Justiz (F. J.) Manifestacion que hace á este ilustrado público el director subinspector interino del cuerpo nacional de ingenieros de esta plaza D. Francisco José Justiz en contestacion al papel

impreso en la oficina de Palmer ... . [*Habana:*] *Oficina de Arazoza y Soler.* 1820. 4to, pp. 47. 36962

Justos reclamos por el modo con que se trata a los buques mejicanos en las islas de Cuba y Puerto Rico: Se indica el remedio de este mal, y Se proponen con tal motivo varias providencias importantes, de conformidad con los tratados vigentes, para proteger la marina mercante de la Republica, todo por los EE. del Globo y Estandarte Mejicano. *Mexico.* 1849. 12mo, pp. 60. 36963

Juvencio (J.) *See* Jouvencey (J.)

Juvenile Anti-Slavery Series [of Tracts]. *Leeds.* 1856. 12mo.

Juvenile Biography. *Worcester: Isaiah Thomas.* [n. d.] 32mo.

Juvenile Miscellany, including some Natural History, for the use of Children. *Philadelphia: Jacob Johnson.* 1808. 24mo.

Ornamented with 18 engravings.

Juvenile Poems, for the use of Free American Children of every complexion. *Boston: Garrison & Knapp.* 1835. 18mo, pp. 72. 36967

G. C. An Authentic Exposition of the Origin, Objects, and Secret Work of the Organization known as the Knights of the Golden Circle. *U. S. National, U. C., February,* 1862. 8vo, pp. 16. H. 36968

Also: A Full Exposure of the Southern Traitors; the Knights of the Golden Circle. ... *Boston: E. H. Bullard & Co.* [1861.] 8vo, pp. 8. H.

K. (J. M.) *See* [Oglethorpe (J.)]

K. (L.) *See* Whitefield (George).

K. (O.) *See* K[eye] (O[tto]).

K. (W.) *See* Kingsford (William).

Ka Titc Tebeniminang Jezos ondaje aking-Oom masinaigan ki ojitogoban ka ojitogabanen. Aianrie tipadjimo8in masinaigan 8ak8l ena8indibanen Monniang. [*Montreal:*] *Ate Mekate8ikonaie8ikomikong kanactageng.* 1861. 12mo, pp. 396. 36969

The "Life of Jesus" in the Algonquin language, translated by the Rev. Mr. Cuoq.

Kaap *or* Kap-Breton. *See* [Bollan (Wm.)] *and* Cape Breton.

Kachline (A.) State of the Accounts of Andrew Kachline, Esq. Sub-Lieutenant of Bucks County, From April 1777, to March 1780. ... *Philadelphia: Printed by F. Bailey* ... M. DCC.-LXXXV. 8vo, pp. 24. P. 36970

Also: ... Accounts ... from ... March 1780, until ... 1781. ... *Philadelphia: Printed by Robert Aitken* ... M, DCC, LXXXIII. 8vo, pp. 14. P.

Kagige debwe winan, kaginag ge-takwendang katolik enamiad. *Cincinnati.* 1855. 12mo. 36971

"Eternal Truths," translated into Mandan.

Kah-ge-ga-gah-bouh, die Ojibway-Eroberung. Sage aus dem Nordwesten-Amerikas. Aus dem Englischen übersetzt von N. Adler. *Frankfurt am Main: Brönner.* 1851. 12mo, pp. xx, 70.

A translation from George Copway; *see our* Vol. IV., No. 16716-27.

Ka nu thi Kithi masi naikan ka ya si disdemin mena aski disdamen kidiho yo thikemeva mena ki bi ma thiyoi mena thi sas kayis ... *London: British and Foreign Bible Society.* 1861. 8vo, pp. 851, 292. 36973

A Bible in the Cree language.

Kahl (August). Reisen durch Chile und die westlichen Provinzen Argentiniens. Natur- und Sittenschilderungen, mit besonderer Bezugnahme auf das volkswirthschaftliche Leben jener Nationen. *Berlin: Gärtner.* 1866. 8vo, pp. viii, 394. 36974

Kaiatonsera Ionterennaienlak8a ne Teieiasontha Taiakos8ateten tsi iakori8iioston kahna8ake tiakoshon—Tsiatak nihonon8entsiake onk8e on8e akoiatonsera. *Tiohtiaki: John Lovell.* 1852. 12mo.

Prayer-book in Iroquois, printed at Montreal.

Kailaz, ou Les Jeunes Sauvages: Drame. [*Londres?*] 1770. 8vo. S. 36976

Kaladlit Assilialiait, Gronlandske træsuit. *Godthaab. Trykt i inspektoratets, bogtrykkeri, af L: Moller og R. Berthelsen.* 1860. 4to, 27 l. Folded colored Plate. 36977

A Greenlander has in this work attempted to give representations of the traditions, manners, weapons, and habits of his own race. This is the correct title of *our* No. 22860, Vol. VI.

Kaladlit okalluktualliait. kalâdlisut kablunâtudlo. *Noungme: Nunnap nalegata nakitteriviane nakittat L: Mollermit, irsigirsoralugo R: Berthelsen.* 1859-61. 3 vols., 8vo, pp. (4), 136, 8 pp. of music; (6), 111; (6), 136, (1). B., BA., C., H. 36978

A collection of popular songs, legends, etc., of the Esquimaux

Kalamazoo Co., *Mich.* Catalogue of the Theological Seminary and College, 1855-6. *Kalamazoo.* 1856. 8vo. 36979

Catalogue of the Officers and Students of Kalamazoo College ... 1865-6. *Detroit.* 1866. 8vo, pp. 28. Frontispiece. H.

Kalendarium Pennsilvaniense, Or America's Messinger, being and [*sic*] Almanac for the Year of Grace 1686, By Samuel Atkins, Student in Mathematicks and Astrology. *Printed and sold by William Bradford in Pennsilvanie.* 1685. 36981

Supposed to be the first thing printed by him.—*Wallace's Commemorative Address.* Title from the "N. E. Historical Register," VIII. 20.

Kalifornien. *See* California, Vol. III., Nos. 10015-17.

Kalisch (I.) Lecture on the Source of all Civilization, and the Means of Preserving our Civil and Religious Liberty. ... By Rev. Isidor Kalisch, D.D. ... Second Edition. *Indianapolis.* 1864. 8vo, pp. 16. B., H. 36982

The Kaleidoscope. An Intermittent Periodical. Edited by the Brothers Triplex. *New York.* 1869. 8vo, pp. 32. B.

[Kalkoen (Joh.)] Brief | van de | wel Erwarde Classis van Amsterdam, | aan de E. Heeren | Predikanten en Onderlingen in de | Provincien van Nieuw-York en Nieuw-Jersie | die zig de | Coetus Noemen. | *Gedrukt te Nieuw-York, by John Holt, Boekdrukker en Verkoper by de Royel Exchange.* 1765. 8vo, pp. 15. S.

Signed by "Joh. Kalkoen and Wilh. Van Den Broek," of Amsterdam.

Kalloch (I. S.) Memorial Sermons: being Two Discourses preached in Tremont Temple, May 27th, 1860. By Rev. I. S. Kalloch. I. The Tremont Temple Enterprise. II. Farewell Words. *Boston.* 1860. 8vo, pp. 40. H. 36985

Kalm (P.) En Resa til Norra America, på Kongl. Swenska Wetenstaps Academiens befallning, och publici kostnad, förrättad af Pehr Kalm, Professor i Abo. *Stockholm: Lars Salvii.* 1753-1761. 3 vols., sm. 8vo. A., C. 36986

A work of high character, especially for its natural history, for which the author was immortalized by Linnæus, in the beautiful Genus *Kalmia*, so common in the United States. It contains some interesting notices of the Swedish colonies in Pennsylvania, Delaware, and New Jersey; *see* pages 59-77 of Vol. III. It is still referred to by writers as presenting a truthful account of the countries visited by the author. The following are translations:

Kalm. Des Herrn Peter Kalms Beschreibung der Reise die er nach dem Nördlichen Amerika auf den Befehl gedachter Akademie und öffentliche Kosten unternommen hat. *Göttingen: Abm. Vandenhoek.* 1754-64. 3 vols., 8vo, pp. (18), 568; 592; 648. 9 Plates. C. 36987

"The translators of this edition were Jo. Philippo and Jo. Andrea Murray."—Meusel. Some copies have the imprint *Leipzig*; others *Stockholm*.

Kalm. Reis door Noord Amerika, gedaan door den Heer Pieter Kalm ... . Vercierd met kopern Platen. *Te Utrecht, By J. van Schoonhoven en Comp.* MDCCLXXII. 2 vols., 4to, Engraved Title, pp. (16), 233; (12), 240, (8). Map and 4 Plates. C.

Also on large paper. "Far superior to the Swedish or English editions."—Stevens.

Kalm. Travels into North America; containing Its Natural History, and A circumstantial Account of its Plantations and Agriculture in general, with the Civil, Ecclesiastical and Commercial State of the Country, The Manners of the Inhabitants, and several curious and Important Remarks on various Subjects. By Peter Kalm .... Translated into English By John Reinhold Forster, F.A.S. Enriched with a Map, several Cuts for the Illustration of Natural History, and some additional Notes. *Warrington: Printed by William Eyres.* MDCCLXX. 8vo, pp. xvi, (8), 400. 2 Plates. Vol. II. *London: The Editor, and T. Lowndes.*

MDCCLXXI. pp. 352. 3 Plates. Vol. III. [*Ibid.*] pp. viii, 310, (14), List of Subscribers, 8 pp. B., BA., C. + The Second Edition. *London: T. Lowndes.* 1772. 2 vols., 8vo, pp. iv, iii–xii, 414; iv, 423, (8). Map and 6 Plates. 36989

See Bartram's "Observations," Boucher de la Richarderie, "M. Rev.," XLV. 209, *and* Pinkerton's "Voyages," XIII.

KALM. Enfaldiga tankar om nyttans om England kan hafva af Sina Nybyggen i Norra America. *Åbo.* 1763. 4to, pp. 22.

[KALM *et* MITTELBERGER.] Histoire naturelle et politique de la Pensylvanie, et de l'établissement des Quakers dans cette contrée. Traduite de l'Allemand. P[ar]. M. D[e]. S[urgy]. ... *Paris: Ganeau.* 1768. 16mo, pp. xx, 372 (4). Map. C. 36991

KAMES (*Lord*). *See* Home (Henry), Vol. VIII., No. 32702.

KAMPEN (N. G. van). Geschiedenis der Nederlanders buiten Europa, of Verhaal van de togten, ontdekkingen ... der Nederlanders in Aziën, ... Amerika ... van het laatste der 16ᵉ eeuw. *Haarlem.* 1832. 4 vols., 8vo. + ... van het laatst des zestien de eeuw tot op dezen tijd. 3ᵉ dl. 2ᵉ (laatste) stuk, van 1800–1830. *Haarlem: Erven F. Bohn.* 1844. 8vo. 36992

This "History of the Dutch abroad" contains discoveries, etc., of the Dutch in America, etc., from the end of the sixteenth century.

[KAMPEN.] Levens van beroemde Nederlanders sedert het midden van den 16ᵉ eeuw. *Haarlem.* 1838–40. 2 vols., 8vo.

Contains the biographies of J. H. von Linschoten, John Maurice of Nassau, called the American (or Brazilian), etc. *See also* "Magazijn voor Wetenshappen," 1829.

KAMPNER (P.) *vs.* HAWKINS (M.) Report of a Case decided on ... the 16th of November, 1793, in the General Court of Virginia; wherein Peter Kampner, was Plaintiff, against Mary Hawkins, Defendant; ... touching the Constitutionality of an Act of Assembly ... . By a Gentleman of the Bar. *Philadelphia: A. M'Kenzie, & Co.* 1794. 8vo, pp. 104. H. 36994

KANAWHA CO., *Va.* [Memorial of Citizens to the Legislature on Inequality of Representation. *Smith & Sheppard, Print.* 1841.] 8vo, pp. 20. B. 36995

... Memorial of the Manufacturers of Salt, in the County of Kanawha, Virginia, against the Repeal of the Duty on Imported Salt. Jan. 21, 1828. Printed by Order of the Senate of the United States. *Washington: Printed by Duff Green.* 1828. 8vo, pp. 21. Table. H. 36996

20th Cong., 1st Sess., Doc. 47.

Memorial of the Manufacturers of Salt in Kanawha County, Virginia: praying for A Restoration of the Duty on Imported Salt. Addressed to the Senate and House of Representatives of the United States. *Kanawha C. H., Virginia.* 1830. 8vo, pp. 19, Appendix, 7. B., S. 36997

KANE (E. K.) The U. S. Grinnell Expedition in Search of Sir John Franklin. A Personal Narrative. By Elisha Kent Kane ... . *New York: Harper & Brothers.* 1853. 8vo, pp. 552. Plates. + [*Ibid.*] 1854. 8vo, pp. 552. 3 Maps, 12 Plates. + New Edition. *Philadelphia: Childs & Peterson.* 1856. 8vo, pp. xix, 552. Portrait. + [*Ibid.*] 1857. 8vo, pp. xix, 13–552.

These new editions contain a sketch of the Life of Sir John Franklin by S. A. Allibone. They also appeared with Boston and London imprints. The following are translations:

KANE. Kane, der Nordpolfahrer. Arktische Fahrten und Entdeckungen der zweiten Grinnell-Expedition zur Aufsuchung Sir J. Franklin's in den Jahren 1853, 1854, und 1855. [Nach dem Englischen von F. Kiesewetter.] *Leipzig: O. Spamer.* 1858. 12mo, pp. xii, 288. Map, 10 Plates. + Zweite Auflage. [*Ibid.*] 1859. Map, 8 Plates. + [*Ibid.*] 1861. 37999

Also: Dr. Kane's Arctic Voyage; explanatory of a Pictorial Illustration of the Second Grinnell Expedition. *New York: Barton & Son, Printers.* 1857. 8vo, pp. 26.

KANE. Zwei Nord-Polar-Reisen zur Aufsuchung Sir John Franklin's. [Aus dem Englischen] Deutsch bearbeitet von Julius Seybt. *Leipzig: Karl B. Lorck.* 1857. 12mo, pp. (2), xxviii, 298. 2 Maps. C. 37000

KANE. Arctic Explorations: The Second Grinnell Expedition in Search of Sir John Franklin, 1853, '54, '55. By Elisha Kent Kane, M.D., U.S.N. Illustrated by upwards of Three Hundred Engravings, From Sketches by the Author. ... *Philadelphia: Childs & Peterson.* 1856. 2 vols., 8vo, pp. (2), 464; (2), 467. Map, 2 Portraits, and Chart. + [*Ibid.*] 1857. + *London and New York: Nelson & Sons.* 1868. Post 8vo. 37001

A great part of these volumes is occupied with descriptions of the Esquimaux.

KANE. The Far North: Explorations in the Arctic Regions. By Elisha Kent Kane ... . *Edinburgh: William Nimmo.* 186–. Fcap 8vo, pp. 228. B. 37002

KANE. ... Tidal Observations in the Arctic Seas. By Elisha Kent Kane ... . Made during the Second Grinnell Expedition in Search of Sir John Franklin, in 1853, 1854, '55 ... Reduced and

discussed by Charles A. Schott ... . [*Washington.* MDCCCLXIII.] 4to, pp. (6), 82, (1). 4 Plates. B. 37003

Included in the "Smithsonian Contributions," XIII. Vols. x. and XI. of the "Contributions" have scientific papers relative to this expedition. Also: ... Access to an open Polar Sea in connection with the search after Sir John Franklin. ... *New York: Baker, Godwin & Co., Printers.* 1853. 8vo, pp. 24. Map. B.

KANE. Report of the Joint Committee appointed to receive the Remains and conduct the Obsequies of the late Elisha Kent Kane ... . *Philadelphia.* 1857. 8vo, pp. 94. S. 37004

Also: Funeral Obsequies of the late Dr. Kane, in the Senate Chamber, Columbus, Ohio, March 8, 1857. [n. p. n. d.] 8vo.

Act of Incorporation ... and By-Laws of the Kane Monument Association. *New York: Baker & Godwin, Printers.* 1859. 12mo, pp. 16. H. 37005

See also our Vol. VI., No. 25573.

[KANE (John Kent).] Notes on Some of the Questions decided by the Board of Commissioners under the Convention with France, of the 4th July, 1831. *Philadelphia: Printed by James Kay, Jun. & Brother.* 1836. 8vo, pp. 108. 37006

Relative to the French spoliations on American commerce. Also: Address on the Patent Laws ... before the Franklin Institute ... October, 1849. ... *Washington: Buell & Blanchard, Printers.* 1849. 8vo, pp. 16.—A Discourse ... Law Academy of Philadelphia. ... *Philadelphia.* 1831. 8vo.

KANE (P.) Wanderings of an Artist among the Indians of North America from Canada to Vancouver's Island and Oregon through the Hudson's Bay Company's Territory and back again. By Paul Kane. *London: Longman.* 1859. 8vo, pp. xvii, (1), 455, (8). Map and 8 Plates. B., BA. 37007

The author, a Canadian painter, traversed, almost alone, the territories of the Red River Settlement; the valley of the Saskatchewan; across the Rocky Mountains, down the Columbia River; the shores of Puget Sound, and Vancouver's Island. It is an interesting collection of the incidents of life and travel, among the Indian tribes inhabiting the regions over which he passed. He is also the author of several pieces on the Indians in the "Canadian Journal" for 1855–57.

KANE. Wanderungen ... unter den Indianern Nordamerika's ... Aus dem Englischen übersetzt von Luise Hauthal. *Leipzig: Matthes.* 1862. 8vo, pp. xii, 225. 4 colored Plates. 37008

[KANE.] Les Indiens de la Baie d'Hudson. Promenades d'un artiste parmi les Indiens de l'Amérique du Nord, depuis le Canada jusqu'à l'île de Vancouver et l'Orégon ... . Imité de l'anglais par E. Delessert. *Paris: Amyot.* 1861. 18mo, pp. vii, 273. 37009

KANE (T. L.) Alaska and the Polar Regions. Lecture of Gen. Thomas L. Kane, ... May 7, 1868. *New York.* 1868. 8vo, pp. 32. H. 37010

KANE. The Mormons. A Discourse delivered before the Historical Society of Pennsylvania: March 26, 1850. By Thomas L. Kane. *Philadelphia: King & Baird, Printers.* 1850. 8vo, pp. 92. + Second Edition. [*Ibid.*] B., BA., C., H. 37011

KANE (W.) Speech of William Kane, of Illinois, upon the arrangement of the Colonial Trade with Great Britain ... in the Senate ... April 8, 1832. *Washington.* 1832. 8vo. S. 37012

Kane County Gazetteer. With Directories of Cities (Aurora City, Batavia, Dundee, Elgin City, Geneva, St. Charles), Kane County Business Directory, etc. By John C. W. Bailey. *Chicago: The Author.* 186–. 8vo, pp. 347, xv. 37013

KANOUSE (P.) An Historical Sermon discussed as a Memorial to the Inhabitants of Wantage, Sussex County, N. J. ... Preached January 7, 1844. By Peter Kanouse. *New York: M. W. Dodd.* 1844. 12mo, pp. 16. 37014

Also: An Observance of the Precepts of Christianity, the ... source of National ... Prosperity. An Address ... Deckertown School ... 4th of July, 1839. ... *Newton, N. J.: John H. Hall.* 1839. 8vo, pp. 15.

KANSAS. Address to the People of the United States (of Members of Congress who opposed the passage of the bill to organize the Territories of Nebraska and Kansas), June, 1854. [n. p. n. d.] 8vo, pp. 4. S. 37015

An Address to the People of the United States, and of Kansas Territory, by the Free State Topeka Convention, held March 10, 1857. *Leavenworth City.* 1857. 8vo, pp. 18. H. 37016

Agriculture. Transactions of the Kansas State Board of Agriculture ... . *Topeka, Kansas: S. S. Prouty, Public Printer.* 1873. 8vo, pp. 432, and Report of Horticultural Society, pp. 206, (1).

American Slavery and the Kansas Question, from the "Edinburgh Review." *London: Longman.* 1856. 8vo. 37018

Auditor's Report, for ... 1863. [n. p. n. d.] 8vo, pp. 59. Continued. B. 37019

The Border Ruffian Code in Kansas. [*New York.* 1856.] 8vo, pp. 15, (1). H., S. 37020

Extracts. Constitution, Chap. 151, Slaves, etc.

First Census Instructions of Kansas. *Topeka.* 1865. 8vo.

Circular issued by the Surveyor General of Kansas and Nebraska ... . *Leavenworth, Kansas.* 1861. 8vo, pp. (8). H. 37022

A Colony for an Indian Reserve. *See* [Hutchinson (C. C.)]

Message of the President [James Buchanan] ... transmitting ... The Constitution of Kansas. February 2, 1858. *Washington: William A. Harris, Printer.* 1858. 8vo, pp. 15. 37023

Constitution of Kansas. *See* Douglas (Stephen A.), *note.*

Constitution of the State of Kansas, adopted at Wyandot, July 29th, 1859. [*Wyandot.* 1859?] 8vo, pp. 16. H. 37024

Also issued as a broadside.

Constitution and By-Laws of the Kansas Emancipation League. *Leavenworth, Kansas.* 1862. 24mo, pp. 8. H. 37025

A Description of Kansas. *Boston.* 1854. 12mo, pp. 28.

Education. An Act for the Organization, ... of Common Schools. [n. p. n. d.] 8vo, pp. 26. H. 37027

Annual Report of the Superintendent of Public Instruction of ... Kansas. Topeka, Dec. 31, 1863. *Lawrence: John Speer ... Printer.* 1864. 8vo, pp. 68. Continued. B. 37028

Catalogue of the University of Kansas, with Officers and Students and a General Description of the University. *Lawrence, Kansas: John Speer.* 1866. 8vo, pp. 18. Continued. 37029

Also: Annual Report of the Board of Regents of the University of Kansas. [*Lawrence, Kansas.* 1871.] 8vo, pp. 4. H.

Common School Law of Kansas Territory. An Act to provide for the Organization ... of Common Schools. Approved, February 12, 1858. *Leavenworth City.* [n. d.] 8vo, pp. 16. H.

The Kansas Educational Journal. The Organ of the State Teachers' Association. Rev. P. McVicar, Editor. *Topeka.* 1866. 8vo. Continued. H. 37031

Also: Report of the Territorial Superintendent of Common Schools. Kansas, 1859. [*Leavenworth City.* 1859.] 8vo, pp. 51. H.

Geology. First Annual Report on the Geology of Kansas. By B. F. Mudge, A.M., Professor of Geology ... and State Geologist for 1864. *Lawrence (Kansas): John Speer, Printer ...* 1866. 8vo, pp. 56, (1). B. 37023

Preliminary Report of the Geological Survey of Kansas, By G. C. Swallow, State Geologist. *Lawrence: John Speer, Printer ...* 1866. 8vo, pp. 198, (1). B., H. 37033

Governor's Message; ... January 10, 1861. [*Topeka.* 1861.] 8vo, pp. 8. Continued. 37034

Veto Message of Governor Medary, on the Bill prohibiting Slavery in Kansas. [n. p. 1860.] 8vo, pp. 16. H. 37035

Hand-book of the Kansas State Agricultural College, Manhattan, Kansas. *Manhattan, Kansas.* 1874. Sm. 4to, pp. 124.

Hand-book of the Kansas Pacific Railway. *St. Louis.* 1870. 8vo. 37037

House ... Memorial of the Senators and Representatives, and the Constitution of the State of Kansas; also, the Majority and Minority Reports of the Committee on Territories on the said Constitution. *Washington: Cornelius Wendell, Printer.* 1856. 8vo, pp. 59. H. 37038

In Perils by mine own Countrymen. Three Years on the Kansas Border. By a Clergyman of the Episcopal Church. *New York and Auburn: Miller, Orton & Mulligan.* 1856. 12mo, pp. 240. B., H., S. 37039

... In the Senate of the United States. August 11, 1856. ... Report [of] the Committee on Territories, to whom was referred a Bill from the House of Representatives for "An Act to reorganize the Territory of Kansas, and for other Purposes" ... [By Mr. Douglas. *Washington.* 1856.] 8vo, pp. 16. H. 37040

34th Cong., 1st Sess., Sen. Rep. Com., No. 282. *See also* Nebraska.

In the Senate ... . February 18, 1858. ... Mr. Green made the following Report. [of] The Committee on Territories [on] a Constitution for Kansas as a State, adopted by the Convention which met at Lecompton ... 4th of September, 1857 ... . [n. p. n. d.] 8vo, pp. 88. B. 37041

35th Cong., 1st Sess., Rep. Com., No. 82.

Inaugural Address of Governor J. W. Geary; delivered at Lecompton, September 11, 1856. 8vo. 37042

Inaugural Address of R. J. Walker, Governor of Kansas Territory ... Lecompton, K. T., May 27, 1857. *Lecompton.* 1857. 8vo. pp. 24. H. 37043

Information in regard to Kansas, from the Voltenburgh Kansas Association. *Boston.* 1857. 8vo, pp. 8. 37044

The Issue fairly Presented. *See* No. 35271.

Journal of the House of Representatives of the Territory of Kansas, at the First Session of the First Territorial Assembly ... held at ... Pawnee, on ... the 2d Day of July, ... One Thousand Eight Hundred and Fifty-five. *Shawnee, M. L. S.: John T. Brady, Public Printer.* 1855. 8vo, pp. 382, Appendix, 69. H.

Journal of the Council of the Territory of Kansas, at their First Session, 1855. *Shawnee, M. L. S.* 1855. 8vo. Cont'd.

Journal of the Territorial Council of Kansas ... at Lecompton ... January 3d, A.D., 1859, and adjourned to ... Lawrence, January 7th, A.D., 1859. ... *Lawrence: J. K. Goodin, Printer.* 1859. 8vo, pp. 26. H. 37047

House Journal of the Legislative Assembly of the State of Kansas, begun and held at Topeka, on Tuesday, January 14th, 1868. *Lawrence (Kansas): John Speer.* 1868. 8vo, pp. 1066.

Kansas Aid Societies. Report of the Proceedings of a Convention of Delegates ... held at Cleveland, Ohio, ... June 1856, and ... at Buffalo ... New York, ... July 1856. [n. p. n. d.] 8vo, pp. 21. H., S. 37049

Kansas and Nebraska—The Nebraska Question comprising the Speeches on the Subject in the United States Senate; together with the History of the Missouri Compromise—Daniel Webster's Memorial in regard to it—History of the Annexation of Texas. The Organization of the Oregon Territory and the Compromise of 1850. *Redfield, New York.* 1856. 8vo. 37050

Kansas and the Constitution. *See* [Fisher (E. E.)], Vol. VI.

The Kansas Annual Register for the Year 1864. ... Andrew Stark, Editor. *Leavenworth.* 1864. 8vo, pp. 265. Map and 6 Portraits. B., H. 37051

Kansas Asylum for the Deaf and Dumb, Olathe. Annual Report for 1865. *Topeka.* 1865. 8vo. Continued. 37052

Kansas Contested Election. ... Report of Mr. Hickman, from the Committee of Elections [of the House of Representatives, in the Kansas Contested Election Case, Made March 5, 1856. n. p. n. d.] 8vo, pp. 26. B., H. + Another Edition. pp. 8, 31.

34th Cong., 1st Sess Rep. No. 3.

Kansas Emigrant Aid Company. Organization, Objects, ... of the Emigrant Aid Company: also A Description of Kansas. ... *Boston: Printed by Alfred Mudge & Son.* 1854. 8vo, pp. 22. + Second Edition ... . [*Ibid.*] 8vo, pp. 24. B., BA. 37054

Kansas Herald of Freedom. *Lawrence: G. W. Brown & Co.* 1855. 2 vols., folio. 37055

Kansas in 1856. An Authentic Account of the Outrages in Kansas, since the appointment of the Kansas Investigating Committee, and not embraced in their Report to the House of Representatives. ... By an Officer of the Commission. [*Washington.* 1856.] 8vo, pp. 15. 37056

Kansas Lands. [n. p. n. d.] 8vo, pp. iii, 15. H. 37057

Kansas Pacific Railway. Report of Surveys across the Continent, in 1867–'68 ... for a Route extending the Kansas Pacific Railway to the Pacific Ocean ... . By Gen. Wm. J. Palmer, December 1st, 1868. *Philadelphia: W. B. Selheimer, Printer.* 1869. 8vo, pp. 250. B. 37058

Kansas State Penitentiary. Report of the Directors ... for ... 1863. *Lawrence.* 1864. 8vo, pp. 11. Continued. B. 37059

Kansas State Rights. An Appeal to the Democracy of The South, By A Southern State-Rights Democrat. *Washington: Henry Polkinhorn, Printer.* 1857. 8vo, pp. 39. B., H. 37060

The Kansas Struggle of 1856, in Congress, and in the Presidential Campaign; with Suggestions for the Future. *New York: American Abolition Society.* 1859. 8vo, pp. 80. S. 37061

The Kansas War, or the Conquest of Chivalry in the ... XIX Century. A Heroic Poem. *New York: Mason and Brother.* 1856. 12mo pp. 184. 37062

Laws. An Act to punish Offences against Slave Property. Passed ... August 14, 1855. ... *Shawnee: John T. Brady ... Printer.* 1855. 8vo, pp. 4. B. 37063

Laws of the Territory of Kansas, passed at the Second, Third and Fourth Sessions of the Legislative Assembly, held during the years of 1857, 1858; ... *Lecompton.* 1857–58. 2 vols., 8vo.

The Statutes of the Territory of Kansas; passed at the First Session of the Legislative Assembly, 1855; ... the Acts of Congress organizing said Territory and other Acts of Congress, having immediate relation thereto ... . *Shawnee.* 1855. 8vo. C.

General Laws of the State of Kansas, passed at the First Session of the Legislature, 1861. *Lawrence.* 1861. 8vo. Continued. 37066

General Laws of the State of Kansas, in force at the close of the Session of the Legislature ending March 6, 1862. Published by Authority. *Topeka.* 1862. 8vo. 37067

The General Statutes of the State of Kansas: revised by John M. Price, Samuel A. Riggs, and James McCahn, Commissioners ... *Lawrence: Printed ... by John Speer.* 1868. 8vo, pp. xi, 1270.

Kansas Emigrants. Lays of the Emigrants, as sung By the Second Party for Kansas, on their departure from Boston, ... August 29th, 1854. *Boston.* 1854. 16mo, pp. (3). B. 37069

Also: Lays of the Emigrants, as sung by the Parties for Kansas, ... during the Spring of 1855. *Boston.* 1855. 12mo, pp. 4. B.

Memorial of the Senators and Representatives, and the Constitution of the State of Kansas: Also the Majority and Minority Reports of the Committee on Territories on the said Constitution. *Washington.* 1856. 8vo, pp. 59. S. 37070

Message of the President [Buchanan], communicating Correspondence between the Executive Department and the present Governor of Kansas, and between the Executive and any other Governor of Kansas, or other Officer of the Government there. [n. p. 1857.] 8vo, pp. 134. 37071

35th Cong., 1st Sess., Sen. Exec. Doc., No. 8.

Minutes of the General Association of Congregational Ministers & Churches in Kansas, at ... Topeka, April 25–27, 1857. *Ogden, K. T.* [n. d.] 8vo, pp. 10. H. 37072

Minutes of the First Kansas Baptist Convention: ... June 6th, 7th and 8th, 1860. *Leavenworth.* 1860. 8vo, pp. 11, (2). H.

Office of the Western Kansas Immigration Society. [Inviting Immigration]. *Salina, Kansas, August* 20, 1867. Folio, 1 l.

Organization of the Free State Government in Kansas, with the Inaugural Speech and Message of Governor Robinson. *Washington, D. C.: Buell & Blanchard, Printers.* 1856. 8vo, pp. 13. H. 37075

Another edition differs in the title-page.

Papers transmitted to the United States Senate on the Sale of Shawnee Indian Lands in Kansas. *Washington.* 1870. 8vo.

Proceedings of the Territorial Delegate Convention, held at Big Springs, on the 5–6th of Sept., 1855. *Herald of Freedom Print, Lawrence, K. T.* [n. d.] 8vo, pp. 16. H. 37077

Public Documents of ... Kansas for ... 1862. ... *Lawrence, Kansas.* 1862. 8vo, pp. 79. B. 37078

Protestant Episcopal Church, Diocese of Kansas. Journal of the Annual Convention, held in 1859. *Philadelphia.* 1859. 8vo.

The Reign of Terror in Kansas: as encouraged by President Pierce, and carried out by the Southern Slave Power ... . *Boston: Charles W. Briggs.* 1856. 8vo, pp. 34. BA. 37080

Report of Edward Hoogland ... Commissioner of Claims, under Act of Feb. 7, 1859. ... [n. p. n. d.] 8vo, pp. 27. H.

Report of the Adjutant General of ... Kansas. Volume I.—1861–1865. *Leavenworth, Kansas.* 1867. 8vo, pp. (8), v, xlviii, (2), 1109, vii. Continued. B., H. 37082

Report of the Congressional Committee, presented in the House of Representatives, July 1, 1856. [n. p. n. d.] 8vo, pp. 30. 37083

Report of the Home Committee appointed to visit the Cherokee Neutral Lands, 1870. *Topeka, Kansas: S. S. Prouty ... Printer.* 1870. 8vo, pp. 164. B. 37084

Report of the Minority of the Committee of the Senate, on the Kansas Resolutions. [In Senate, March 17, 1858. n. p. n. d.] 8vo, pp. 8. B. 37085

Report of the Secretary of State of Kansas, 1865. [n. p. n. d.] 8vo. 37086

Report of the Special Committee appointed to investigate the Troubles in Kansas; with the Views of the Minority of said Committee. July 2, 1856. *Washington: Cornelius Wendell, Jr. Printer.* 1856. 8vo, pp. vii, 132, 1206. + [*Washington.* 1856.] 8vo, pp. 67. BA. 37087

34th Cong., 1st Sess., H. of R., Rep. No. 200.

Report of the Special Committee on "Claim Bonds." [n. p. 1861.] 8vo, pp. 37, (1). H. 37088

Reports of the Comptroller and Treasurer of Kansas Territory, December 31, 1858. *Lecompton, Kansas.* [n. d.] 8vo, pp. 15. H. 37089

Rules of the Senate and House of Representatives ... for ... 1861 ... . *Topeka, Kansas: Edmund G. Ross, Printer.* 1861. 8vo, pp. 43, (3). H. 37090

Senate Journal of the Legislative Assembly of the State of Kansas, begun and held at Topeka, on Tuesday, January 14th, 1868. *Lawrence, (Kansas): J. Speer.* 1868. 8vo, pp. 680. C.

Six Months in Kansas. *See* [Ropes (H. A.)]

Subduing Freedom in Kansas. Report of the Congressional Committee, presented in the House of Representatives, On ... July 1, 1856. [n. p. n. d.] 8vo, pp. 31. H. 37092

KANSAS CITY, *Mo.* First Annual Announcement of the Kansas City College of Physicians and Surgeons ... Kansas City, Mo. Session of 1869–70. (Preliminary). [n. p. n. d.] 8vo, pp. (4). B., H. 37093

KAPP (F.) Geschichte der deutschen Einwanderung in Amerika. Von Friedrich Kapp. Vol. I. Die Deutschen im Staate New York bis zum Anfange des neunzehnten Jahrhunderts. *New York: E. Steiger.* 1867. 8vo, pp. vii, 411. Map. B., C. + *Leipzig.* 1868. 37094

KAPP. Geschichte der Sklaverei in den Vereinigten Staaten von Amerika. Von Friedrich Kapp. *New York: L. Hauser.* [1860.] 8vo, pp. x, 516. Map. B., BA. + *Hamburg.* 1861.

KAPP. Leben des amerikanischen Generals Johann Kalb. Von Friedrich Kapp. ... *Stuttgart: Cotta.* 1862. 8vo, pp. xiv, 306. Portrait. B., C. 37096

KAPP. Leben des amerikanischen Generals Friedrich Wilhelm von Steuben. Von Friedrich Kapp. *Berlin.* 1858. 8vo. Portrait. 37097

KAPP. The Life of Frederick William von Steuben, Major General in the Revolutionary Army. By Frederick Kapp. With an Introduction by George Bancroft. *New York: Mason Brothers.* 1859. 8vo. BA. + Second Edition. [*Ibid.*] 1859. 8vo, pp. xvi–735. Portrait. B., C., H. 37098

KAPP. Immigration, and the Commissioners of Emigration of the State of New York. By Friedrich Kapp ... . *New York: The Nation Press.* 1870. 8vo, pp. (2), iii, (1), 5–241. 6 Plates, Portrait. B., BA., C., H. 37099

KAPP. Die Sklavenfrage in den Vereinigten Staaten. Von Friedrich Kapp. *Göttingen.* 1854. 16mo, pp. vi, 185. Plate.

KAPP. Der Soldatenhandel deutscher Fürsten nach Amerika (1775 bis 1783) von Friedrich Kapp. *Berlin: Franz Duncker.* 1864. 8vo, pp. (4), xix, 299, (1). B., BA. 37101

Also: European Immigration to the United States. ... *New York.* 1869. 8vo, pp. 29.—Friedrich der Grosse und die Vereinigten Staaten von Amerika. Mit einem Anhang: die Vereinigten Staaten und das Seekriegsrecht. ... *Leipzig: Quandt & Händel.* 1871. 8vo, pp. iv, 202, xxx.—Report ... to the ... Commissioners of Emigration, on the Condition of the Emigrant-Ship Leibnitz ... . *New York: Stone & Barron ... Printers.* 1868. 8vo, pp. 14. H.

KAPPLER (A.) Sechs Jahre in Surinam, oder Bilder aus dem militärischen Leben dieser Colonie, und Skizzen zur Kenntniss seiner socialen und naturwissenschaftlichen Verhältnisse. *Stuttgart.* 1854. 8vo. + *Utrecht.* 1854. 2 vols., 8vo. 37102

KARIGAL (H. I.) A Sermon ... at ... Newport, Rhode-Island, On the Day of Pentecost, ... May 28, 1773. ... By ... Haijm Isaac Karigal ... . *Newport, Rhode-Island: Printed ... by S. Southwick.* 1773. 8vo, pp. 19. B., BA., N., W. 37103

KARSTEN (H.) Florae Columbiae terrarumque adiacentium specimina selecta in peregrinatione duodecim annorum observata delineavit et descripsit H. Karsten. Vol. I. *Berolini: apud Ferdinandi Duemmleri successores.* MDCCCLVIII–LXI. Folio, pp. (5), 200. 100 colored Plates. Vol. II. MDCCCLXII–LXIX. pp. (3), 188. 100 colored Plates. H. 37104

KARSTEN. Die geognostischen Verhältnisse Neu-Granada's. *Berlin: F. Schneider.* 1858. 4to, pp. 41. 37105

From the "Verhandlungen der Versammlungen deutscher Naturforscher" in Wien.

KARSTEN. Die medicinischen Chinarinden Neu-Granada's. *Berlin: F. Schneider.* 1858. 8vo, pp. 71. 2 Plates. 37106

KARSTEN. Über die Vulkane der Anden. Vortrag, gehalten im Verein für wissenschaftliche Vorträge am 14. Februar 1857. *Berlin: Decker.* 1857. 8vo, pp. 26. 37107

KARSTEN (L. G.) Tablas Mineralogicas Dispuestas segun los Discubrimientos mas recientes e ilustradas con notas, traducida por D. And. M. Del Rio. *Mexico.* 1804. Folio. 37108

KARTHAUS (P. A.) ... A Statement Of various commercial transactions, by Peter Arnold Karthaus ... which occurred since the embargo ... in 1809 ... . [*Baltimore: Printed by J. T. Hanzsche.* 1837.] 12mo, pp. 12. BA. 37109

KASSON (J. A.) Speech of John A. Kasson, of Iowa, on the Amendment to the Constitution, ... January 10, 1865. [n. p. n. d.] 8vo, pp. 16. 37110

KAT (Hidde Dirks). Dagboek eener reize ter walvisch- en robbenvangst gedaan in de jaren 1777 en 1778, met eene kaart van Groenland. *Haarlem: de wed. A. Loosjes.* 1818. 8vo, pp. (2), viii, 76. Map and Portrait. C. 37111

Journal of a voyage to the whalefishery.

KATCHENOVSKY (D.) Amérique et ses hommes d'État. Daniel Webster, sa vie et ses œuvres. Aperçu de l'histoire des États-Unis. *Bruxelles: F. Claassen.* 1858. 8vo. 37112

KATHMAN (J. C.) Information for Immigrants into the State of Louisiana. Published Officially by J. C. Kathman ... . *New Orleans: Republican Office Print.* 1868. 8vo, pp. 55. 37113

Katholische Erzählungen ... . *Shaffhausen: Hurter.* 8vo.

Vol. v. is "Der Menschenhändler ... Characterische Bilder aus dem republikanischen, sogenannt glücklichen Amerika. Von Ed. von Ambach." 1852. 8vo, pp. xiv, 186.

Katolik. Enamiad o Nanagatawenda mowinan. ... *Wawhatanono (Detroit): Jabez Fox.* 12mo, pp. iv, 712, (2). 37115

Die Katholische Kirche in den Vereinigten Staaten von Nordamerika, dargestellt von einheimischen Schriftstellern. Deutsch von den Benediktinern zu St. Meinrad, im Indiana-Staat. *Regensburg: Manz.* 1864. 8vo, pp. xvi, 518. 37116

KAUFMAN (D. S.) The Texas Boundary. Speech of David S. Kaufman in the House of Representatives, June 5, 1848. [*Washington.* 1848.] 8vo, pp. 15. H. 37117

Also: Speech ... June 29, 1846, on the Tariff. *Washington.* 1846. 8vo.—Speech ... on the Territorial Relations between the United States and Texas. ... July 27, 1848. *Washington.* 1848. 8vo, pp. 12. H.

KAUFMANN (Peter). Die Ermordung Abraham Lincoln's, und die Geschichte der grossen Verschwörung. ... Nach dem Englischen. *Cincinnati, Ohio: J. R. Hawley & Co.* 1865. 8vo, pp. 84. 37118

KAUTZ (A. V.) Customs of Service for Non-commissioned Officers and Soldiers as derived from Law and Regulations and practised in the Army of the United States. Being a Hand-book for the Rank and File of the Army ... . By August V. Kautz ... . *Philadelphia: J. B. Lippincott & Co.* 1864. 18mo, pp. 303. C.

KAUTZ. Customs of Service for Officers of the Army, as derived from Law and Regulations, and practised in the United States Army. Being a Hand-book of Military Organization for Officers of the Line ... . By August V. Kautz ... . *Philadelphia: J. B. Lippincott & Co.* 1866. 24mo, pp. 389. 37120

Kawanio Che Keeteru: A True Relation of a Bloody Battle Fought between George and Lewis, In the Year 1755. [*Philadelphia:*] *Printed in the Year* 1756. 8vo, pp. 16. P. + Second Edition. *Philadelphia.* 1756. 37121

In hudibrastic metre; alludes to parts taken by French, English, and colonists in the American war. The signification of the Indian words at the head of the title-page is "Expression of a Hero relying on God to bless his Endeavours in protecting what he has put under his Care."

KAY (Alex. M.) Die westliche Welt. Reise durch die Ver einsstaaten von Amerika. Aus dem Englischen übersetzt von M. Heine. Nebst Einleitung und Illustrationen von W. Heine. *Leipzig.* 1861. 2 vols., 8vo. 37122

KAYE (J. W.) The Life and Correspondence of Charles Lord Metcalfe, late ... Governor of Jamaica, and Governor-General of Canada, from unpublished Letters and Journals preserved by Himself, his Family, and Friends. By John William Kaye. ... *London: Richard Bentley.* MDCCCLIV. 2 vols., 8vo, pp. (2), xvi, 516; vii, (1), 654. B., BA. + A New and Revised Edition. *London: Smith, Elder and Co.* M.DCCC.LVIII. 2 vols., rl. 16mo, pp. xxiv, 454, Portrait; viii, 480. H. 37123

The new edition, published in 1858, is contracted as to the earlier, and expanded as to the latter part of the life. *See* "Blackwood's Magazine," LXXVII., "Fraser's Magazine," L., *and* "Edinburgh Review," CII.

KAYSER (J. C.) Commercial Directory. *Philadelphia.* 1823. 4to. S. 37124

[KAUKEL (Johann).] *See* Reesa Book.

K[EACH] (B[enjamin].) War with the Devil, or, the Young Man's Conflict with the Powers of Darkness ... . By B. K. ... The Twelfth Edition. [n. p. n. d.] 12mo, pp. (6), 177.

Printed in New York by William Bradford, not earlier than 1715. A poem in "Commemoration of these Poems" is signed "W. B.," and is bad enough poetry to be the work of Bradford himself.

KEACH (H. A.) Rhode Island Library. Burrillville; As it Was, And As it Is. By Horace A. Keach. *Providence: Knowles, Anthony & Co., Printers.* 1856. 12mo, pp. x, 170. BA.

KEACH (I.) Address at Bennington, August 15, 1829, on the Fifty-second Anniversary of the Bennington Battle. By Rev. Israel Keach. *Bennington.* 1829. 37127

KEAN (P.) Report of Evidence. *See* Vol. IV., No. 15370.

KEAN (P.) An Oration ... at Elizabethtown (N. J.) ... July 4, 1812. By Peter Kean, Esq. ... *Morris-town: Printed by Henry B. Russell, July,* 1812. 12mo, pp. 16. 37128

Also: Oration ... at Connecticut Farms, on the Fourth of July, 1818. ... *Elizabethtown, N. J.* 1818. 8vo.

KEARNEY [Philip]. Official Reports of General Kearney and General Birney of the Battle of Seven Pines, May 31, 1862. *Philadelphia.* 1863. 8vo, pp. 16. 37129

KEARSAGE. ... Correspondence arising out of the Conflict between The "Kearsage" and the "Alabama," ... May 19, 1865. *London: Printed by Harrison and Sons.* [1865.] Folio, pp. (2), 15.

KEARSAGE. ... Informations and Depositions ... against certain Persons for having enlisted on board the United States Ship of War "Kearsage" ... . [*London.* 1864.] Folio, pp. 7, (2). BA.

Also: ... Correspondence respecting the Enlistment of British Seamen at Queenstown on Board the ... "Kearsage." ... 1864. *London: Printed by Harrison and Sons.* [1864.] Folio, pp. (2), 10, (2). + Further Correspondence. ... 1864. [*Ibid.* 1864.] Folio, pp. (2), 7, (1). B., BA.

KEARSAGE. Report of the Special Committee of the Chamber of Commerce on Testimonials to Captain, Officers, and Crew of the United States Sloop of War "Kearsage." *New York.* 1865. 8vo. 37132

[KEARSLEY (G.)] An Abridgment of Captain Cook's last Voyage, ... 1776 ... 1780, ... Extracted from the Quarto Edition. ... The Fifth Edition. ... *London: G. Kearsley.* MDCCLXXXVII. 12mo, pp. xxiv, 442, (16). Plates and Map. 37133

The same publisher issued an abridgment of the first and second voyages, which I have not seen.

KEARSLEY (J.) A Narrative, of many Facts, relating to the late disputed Will of Samuel Flower, Esq; Published with a view to defend an Injured Reputation, and to remove Ill-Grounded Prejudices. By Dr. John Kearsley, Junr. ... *Philadelphia: Printed by J. Crukshank, and I. Collins* ... M,DCC,LXX. 4to, pp. 16.

Dated "Phila. Feb. 21, 1770." A piece of local scandal.

KEATH (*Sir* W.) *See* Keith (*Sir* W.)

KEATING (M.) The Genuine Narrative Of the Life and Transactions of Major Maurice Keating, The noted Pirate and Murderer, Who was executed on Monday the 27th of December, 1784, at Cuckold's-Point, near Port-Royal, in the Island of Jamaica. ... To which is added, A True and Faithful Account of the Loss of the Brigantine Tyrrell, And the uncommon Hardships suffered by the Crew. *London: Printed by J. Miller* ... . [1784.] 8vo, pp. 16. 37135

For the whole of the long title *see* Stevens' "Nuggets," No. 1587.

KEATING (W[illiam] H.) Considerations upon The Art of Mining. To which are added, Reflections on its Actual State in Europe, and the advantages which would result from An Introduction of this Art into the United States. By W. H. Keating, A.M. ... *Philadelphia: M. Carey and Sons.* 1821. 8vo, pp. 87.

KEATING. Narrative of an Expedition to the Source of St. Peter's River, Lake Winnepeek, Lake of the Woods, &c. &c. Performed in the year 1823, by order of the Hon. J. C. Calhoun, Secretary of War, under the Command of Stephen H. Long, Major U. S. T. E. Compiled from the Notes of Major Long, Messrs. Say, Keating, and Calhoun, by William H. Keating, A.M. &c. ... *Philadelphia: H. C. Carey & J. Lea.* 1824. 2 vols., 8vo, pp. xii, (2), 9–439; (6), 5–459. 15 Plates and Map. + *London: Geo. B. Whittaker.* 1825. 2 vols., 8vo, pp. xiii, (3), 458; vi, 248, Appendix, clvi. 3 folded Sheets, 8 Plates, and Map. B., BA., H.

Known as "Long's Second Expedition;" for an account of the first *see* James (E.), No. 35682. Almost a cyclopædia of material, relating to the Indians of the explored territory. Nothing escaped the attention or record of the gentlemen who accompanied the expedition; and their statements respecting the Sioux and Chippeway tribes are among the most valuable we have. Vol. II. contains a vocabulary. *See* "N. A. Rev.," XXI. 178., *and* "M. Rev.," CVIII. 113.

KEATINGE (G.) The Maryland Ahiman Rezon of the Free ... Masons, containing the History of Masonry ... . Compiled by Brother G. Keatinge. *Baltimore.* 1797. 8vo. 37138

KEBER (M.) Die Kolonisations-Gesellschaft in Königsberg zur Gründung einer deutschen Kolonie auf Müskito in Mittelamerika. *Königsberg: Voigt.* 1846. 16mo. Map. 37139

KECHT (J. Sm.) Der verbesserte praktische Weinbau in Gärten, und vorzüglich auf Weinbergen. Den amerikanischen Weinbauern gewidmet von H. B. Saer. *Reading: H. B. Sage.* 1828. 16mo, pp. vi, 84 l. 2 Plates. C. 37140

Keckley (E.) Behind the Scenes. By Elizabeth Keckley, formerly a Slave, but more recently modiste, and friend to Mrs. Abraham Lincoln. Or Thirty Years a Slave, and Four Years in the White House. *New York: G. W. Carleton & Co.* M DCCC-LXVIII. 12mo, pp. v, 371. Portrait. B., C., H. 37141

Kedar (O.) A Vision. The Cause and Progress of the Present War, and its Final Termination foretold By Obed Kedar, July 4, 1861. *Columbus, Ohio.* 1862. 8vo, pp. 13. 37142

Kedar. Visions concerning the Present War ... Seen by Obed Kedar. *Columbus, Ohio.* 1863. 8vo, pp. 45. 37143

Keefer (J.) Slavery: its Sin, Moral Effects, and certain Death. ... By Justus Keefer. *Baltimore.* 1864. 8vo. 37144

Keefer (T. C[oltrin]). Essai Couronné. De l'Avenir et de l'Influence des Canaux du Canada: ... Par Thos. C. Keefer ... . *Toronto: Chez Andrew H. Armour et Cie.* 1850. 8vo, pp. (2), 120.

Keefer. Prize Essay. The Canals of Canada: their Prospects and Influence. ... By Thos. C. Keefer ... . *Toronto: Andrew H. Armour and Co.* 1850. 8vo, pp. 111. BA., C. 37146

Also: "Montreal" and "the Ottawa:" two Lectures ... . *Montreal.* 1854. 8vo, pp. 73.—Report ... of Survey of Georgian Bay Canal Route to Lake Ontario, by Way of Lake Scugog, ... with Maps, &c. ... *Whitby, C. W.: W. H. Higgirs, Printer.* 1863. 12mo, pp. 20. H.—Report on a Survey for the Railway Bridge Over the St. Lawrence at Montreal, Surveyed in 1851–'52. ... *Montreal: Printed by John Lovell.* 1853. 8vo, pp. (2), 53, (2). Map. S. *See also* Morgan's "Bibliotheca Canadensis," p. 209, No. 1.

Keehan (H. M.) Liberty or Death, or the Mother's Sacrifice. By Hattia M. Keehan. *Indianapolis.* 1859. 37147

Keeler (J.) The South Sea Islanders, with a ... Sketch of Captain Morrell's Voyage. ... By John Keeler ... . *New York: Printed by Snowden.* 1831. 12mo, pp. 34. B., BA. 37148

Keeler (R.) Vagabond Adventures. By Ralph Keeler. *Boston: Fields, Osgood, & Co.* 1870. 12mo, pp. 274. B. 37149

Keeler [W. J.] Notes to accompany Keeler's Map of the U. S. Territory, from the Mississippi River to the Pacific Ocean ... *Washington.* 1868. 8vo, pp. 30. H. 37150

Keeling (R. J.) The Death of Moses. A Sermon preached ... April 23, 1865, By Rev. R. J. Keeling, Rector, as a Tribute of Respect to the Memory of Abraham Lincoln, ... Assassinated

... Washington, ... April 14, 1865. *Washington, D. D.:* [sic] *W. H. & O. H. Morrison.* 1865. 8vo, pp. 16. B. 37151

Keely (P. C.) Specifications of the Work and Materials necessary in building the Church of ... the Immaculate Conception, Boston. ... *Boston.* 1857. 8vo, pp. 20. H. 37152

Keen (M. W.) Life and Confessions of Moses W. Keen, who was hung for the Murder of his Wife. *Maysville, Ky.* 1842. 12mo, pp. 24. 37153

[Keene] (E.) Sermon before the Society for Propagation of the Gospel in Foreign Parts, 1757. By the Right Rev. Edmund, Bishop of Chester. *London.* 1757. 4to, pp. 83. M. 37154

Keene (R. R.) A Letter from Richard Raynal Keene, To Luther Martin, Esq., Attorney General of Maryland; upon the subject of his 'Modern Gratitude.' *Baltimore: Printed by Prentiss & Cole.* 1802. 8vo, pp. 53. BA., N. 37155

Keene. A Letter of Vindication to His Excellency Colonel Monroe, President of the United States. By Richard Raynal Keene ... . [*Philadelphia.* 1824.] 8vo, pp. 47. BA. 37156

"Keene studied law in Baltimore under Luther Martin, whose daughter he married—was accused of being interested in Burr's conspiracy. This pamphlet is a sketch of his Life." It was also printed in London as:

Keene. A Letter of Vindication to Colonel Munroe, President of the United States: By Richard Raynal Keene ... . *London: Printed by Ambrose Cuddon.* 1824. 8vo, pp. 86. 37157

See Martin (Luther).

Keene. An Appendix, intended to illustrate the Merits and Objects of a Letter of Vindication, ... to the President of the United States. By Richard Raynal Keene ... . *Washington: Printed by E. De Krafft.* 1825. 8vo, pp. 11. H. 37158

Keene, *N. H.* Keene Directory and Register. *Keene.* 1831. 12mo. Continued. 37159

Report of the ... School Committee of Keene, N. H. ... March, 1847. ... *Keene: Printed by J. W. Prentiss & Co.* 1847. 8vo, pp. 24. Continued. H. 37160

Keep (J.) An Address ... December 22, 1837 ... in Lockport, N. Y. Commemorative of the Martyrdom of Rev. E. P. Lovejoy, who was killed by The Mob ... November 7, 1837. By John Keep ... . *Lockport: Printed by George Reese.* 1838. 12mo, pp. 22. BA. 37161

[Keep.] Sketches of the Religious Life and Faith of Mrs. Lydia Hale Keep of Oberlin. By her Husband. ... *Oberlin.* 1866. 24mo, pp. 20. H. 37162

Also: Congregationalism and Church-Action: with the Principles of Christian Union, etc. ... *New York: S. W. Benedict & Co.* 1845. 18mo, pp. 143.—A Narrative of the Origin and Progress of the Congregational Church in Homer, N. Y.; with Remarks. ... *Homer.* 1833. 8vo, pp. 16.— ... A Sermon, Delivered in Northampton, August 24, 1815. Before the Hampshire Missionary Society. ... *Printed at Northampton, W. W. Clapp.* 1815. 8vo, pp. 40.— ... A Sermon ... Oct. 21, 1818, before the ... Domestic Missionary Society of Massachusetts ... in Northampton. ... *Northampton: Printed by Thomas W. Shepard & Co.* 1818. 8vo, pp. 24.— ... A Sermon ... October 25, 1838, at the installation of the Rev. D. N. Merritt ... in Riga ... N. Y. ... *Rochester: Printed by Shepard, Strong & Dawson.* 1839. 8vo, pp. 30. H.

Keese (J.), *Editor.* The Poets of America. Illustrated by One of her Painters. ... Edited by John Keese. *New York: S. Colman.* 1840. 12mo, pp. 284. BA., H. + Fourth Edition. *New York.* 1841. + Sixth Edition. *Boston.* 1841. 12mo. + Second Series. *New York.* 1842. 12mo, pp. 320. C. 37163

Edited by the late John Keese, the facetious and well-known book-auctioneer, and illustrated by J. G. Chapman. Contains the gems of the best American authors, including Drake's "Culprit Fay," etc.

Keferstein (Horst). Geschichts-Repetition. Für Schulen und zum Privatgebrauch. Ethnographisch und mit ausführlicher Berücksichtigung des culturgeschichtlichen Stoffes. *Dresden.* 1861. 5 parts, 8vo. 37164

Part 1. has "Amerika und Australien." pp. 64.

Keferstein (W.) Ueber neue und wenig bekannte Batrachier aus Australien und Amerika. Von Wilh. Keferstein ... . *Berlin: Nicolai.* 1868. 8vo, pp. (2), 48. 5 Tables. B. 37165

Kehukee, *N. C.* Minutes of the Kehukee Baptist Association, held at Whitfield's Meeting House, Pitt County, North Carolina, 1789. *Edenton, North Carolina: Printed by Hodge and Wills.* 1789. 4to. Continued. 37166

These minutes contain an account of the spread of the Baptist faith in North Carolina, etc.

Keiler Vouchers. Petition of the Adams Express Company to the Secretary of War, praying the reversal of the Decision of the United States Commission, at St. Louis, on the "Keiler" Vouchers, held by the Company for certain parties in Cincinnati. *New York: G. F. Nesbitt & Co.* 1862. 8vo, pp. 11. 37167

Relates to clothing furnished for the soldiers by Mr. Keiler, a contractor.

[Keiley (A. M.)] In Vinculis; or, the Prisoner of War. Being, the Experience of a Rebel in Two Federal Pens, interspersed with Reminiscences of the Late War; Anecdotes of Southern Generals, etc. By a Virginia Confederate. *New York: Blelock & Co.* 1866. 12mo, pp. (2), 216. H. 37168

Some copies have the imprint, *Petersburg, Va.*, 1866, and others have the author's name on the title-page. A well-written, interesting, and amusing narrative.

[Keiley.] Prisoner of War, or Five Months among the Yankees. Being a Narrative of the Losses, Calamities, and Consolations of a Petersburg Militiaman during an enforced Residence North. By A. Rifleman, Esq., Gent. ... *Richmond, Va.: West & Johnston.* 1865. 8vo, pp. 120. C. 37169

Keily's Brief Description and Statistical Sketch of Georgia. 1849. 8vo. Map of Irwin County. 37170

Title from J. R. Smith's Catalogue.

Keim (De B[enneville] R.) San Domingo. Pen Pictures and Leaves of Travel, Romance and History. From the Portfolio of a Correspondent in the American Tropics. By De B. Randolph Keim ... . *Philadelphia: Claxton, Remsen & Haffelfinger.* 1870. 12mo, pp. 336. B., BA. 37171

Keim. Sheridan's Troopers on the Borders: A Winter Campaign on the Plains. By De B. Randolph Keim ... . *Philadelphia: Claxton, Remsen & Haffelfinger.* 1870. 8vo, pp. 308. Portrait, 7 Plates. B., BA. 37172

The author narrates the incidents of a campaign against the Indians of the Plains.

Keim (William H.) Speech ... on the Revision of the Tariff, ... February 10, 1859. [n. p. n. d.] 8vo. 37173

[Keimer (Samuel).] Caribbeana. Containing Letters and Dissertations, together with Poetical Essays, on various Subjects and Occasions; chiefly wrote by several Hands in the West-Indies, and some of them to Gentlemen residing there. Now collected together in Two Volumes. Wherein are also comprised, divers Papers relating to Trade, Government, and Laws in general; but more especially, to those of the British Sugar-Colonies, and of Barbados in particular: As likewise the Characters of the most eminent Men that have died, of late years, in that Island. To which are added in an Appendix, Some Pieces never before Published. ... *London: T. Osborne and W. Smith.* M.DCC.XLI. 2 vols., 4to, pp. x, 404, (9); xvi, 358, (7). C.

Made up from the "Barbados Gazette," edited by Samuel Keimer, a printer, formerly of Philadelphia. Contains many curious epigrams, satirical poems, and love songs,

and also historical notices relating to New England and other States. Arranged in a stiff imitation of the "Tatler." *See* Duyckinck's "Cyclopædia of American Literature."

Keimer. The Independent Whig, 1721. Published in numbers, price one penny. *Philadelphia.* 1721. Dedication, pp. (16), 227. 37175

Keimer. A Touch of the Times ... . *Philadelphia: Printed by S. Keimer.* 1729. 37176

Keimer was the original publisher of "The Universal Instructor in all Arts and Sciences," and the "Pennsylvania Gazette."

Keith (George). Account of a National Church and the Clergy, &c. Humbly presented to the Bishop of London. With some Queries concerning the Sacrament. *Philadelphia. Reynier Jansen.* 1701. 4to, pp. 8. 37177

A very rare imprint.

Keith. An Account of the Great Divisions, Amongst the Quakers in Pensilvania, &c. As appears by their own Book, here following, Printed 1692. and lately came from thence, intituled, viz. The Plea of the Innocent, against the False Judgment of the Guilty, Being a Vindication of George Keith and his Friends, who are joyned with him in this present Testimony, from the False Judgment, Calumnies, false Informations and Defamations of Samuel Jenings, John Simcock, Thomas Lloyd, and others, joyned with them, being in Number Twenty Eight. Directed, by way of Epistle, to Faithful Friends of Truth, in Pensilvania, East and West-Jersey, and else-where, as occasion requireth. ... *London: ... John Gwillim ...* 1692. 4to, pp. 26. 37178

Signed by "George Keith" and "Thomas Budd." It is a reprint of "The Plea of the Innocent," No. 37205, *infra.* The errata at the foot of page 26 is not in some copies.

Keith. An | Answer | to | Mr. Samuell Willard | (One of the Ministers at Boston in New-England) | his | Reply | To my Printed Sheet, called, A Dangerous and | hurtful Opinion maintained by him, viz. | That the Fall of Adam, and all the Sins of Men necessarily | come to pass by virtue of Gods Decree and his Determin- | ing both of the Will of Adam, and of all other Men to | Sin. | By George Keith, M.A. | *Printed and Sold by William Bradford at the Sign of the Bible | in New-York,* 1704. | 4to, pp. (4), 41. N.

Dedicated "To his Excellency Edward Viscount Cornbury Captain General and Governour in Chief in and over Her Majesties Provinces of New-York, and New-Jersey," etc. Very rare.

Keith. The Anti-Christs and Sadducees detected Among a Sort of Quakers; or, Caleb Pusie, of Pensilvania, and John

Pennington; with his Brethren ... Proved Anti-Christs and Sadducees, out of a Printed Book lately published by them, Falsly called a Modest Account of the principal Difficulties betwixt George Keith, and ... Quakers in Pensilvania, etc. ... By George Keith. *London: The Author.* [n. d.] 4to, pp. 44.

Like all people of his kind Mr. Keith is an intemperate pamphleteer. Having twice been a Quaker he became an Episcopalian and in the long title to this tract refers to his late co-workers as "A gang and sort of Quakrs" [*sic*].

[Keith.] An Appeal from the Twenty-eight Judges To The Spirit of Truth & true Judgment In all Faithful Friends, called Quakers, that meet at this Yearly Meeting at Burlington, the 7 month, 1692. [*Philadelphia: William Bradford.* 1692.] Sm. 4to, pp. 8. 37181

Extremely rare. Signed by "George Keith," "Thomas Budd," and four others. For place, printer, and date of publication, *see* "Books to be sold by William Bradford in Philadelphia, 1692." at the end of "A True Copy of Three Judgements," No. 37223, *infra.* For printing this book Bradford was imprisoned, upon the charge of "uttering and spreading a malicious and seditious paper." His tools and type were taken away from him, and this was the beginning of the persecution which afterwards drove him, with his printing-press, from Philadelphia to New York, in 1693. For an account of his arrest and committal to prison, evidently written by himself, *see* the postscript at the end of this tract. Smith says "*Reprinted at New York*"?

Keith. The Causeless Ground of Surmises, Jealousies and unjust Offences remov'd, in a full Clearing of Faithfull Friends, and a sober Vindication of my Innocency, and the Friends concerned with me, in relation to the late Religious Differences and Breaches among some of the People called Quakers in America. By Geo. Keith. *London, Printed for R. Levis.* 1694. 4to, pp. 16.

Keith. A Challenge to Caleb Pusey, and a Check to his Lyes and Forgeries, &c. With a Postscript by Daniel Leeds. [*Printed by Wm. Bradford, at New York.*] 1693. 4to, pp. 4. W.

Keith. George Keith's Challenge to William Pen and Geor. Whitehead: two Eminent Quakers. *London.* 1696. 16mo, pp. 8.

[Keith.] The | Christian Faith | of the People of God, called in Scorn, | Quakers | in Rhode-Island (who are in Unity with all faithfull Brethren | of the same Profession in all parts of the World) | Vindicated | From the Calumnies of Christian Lodewick, that formerly | was of that Profession, but is lately fallen therefrom. | As also from the base Forgeries, and wicked Slanders of | Cotton Mather, called a Minister at Boston, who hath greatly | commended the said Christian Lodewick, and approved his false | Charges against us, and hath added thereunto many gross | impu-

dent and vile Calumnies against us and our Brethren, in his | late Address, so called, to some in New-England, in which in | due time may receive a more full answer, to discover his Igno- | rance, Prejudice and Perversion against our Friends in gene- | ral and G. K. in particular, whom he hath most unworthily | abused. | To which is added some Testimonies of our Antient | Friends to the | true Christ of God; | &c. ... | *Printed and Sold by William Bradford at Philadelphia in Pennsyl- | vania, in the Year* 1692. Sm. 4to, pp. 16. 37185

Extremely rare. Signed by "George Keith," and twelve others. The "Testimonies," which fill eight pages, are signed by "Will. Bradford." Unnoticed in Smith's "Catalogue of Friends' Books."

Keith. The | Christian Quaker; | or, | George Keith's Eyes opened. | Good News from Pensilvania. | Containing a Testimony against that False and Absurd | Opinion which some hold, viz. | That all true Be- | lievers and Saints, immediately after the Bodily Death at- | tain to all the Resurrection they Expect, and enter into the | fullest Enjoyment of Happiness, | And also, That the Wicked, immediately after Death, are | raised up to receive all the Punishment they are to Expect. | Together with a Scriptural Account of the Resurrection of | the Dead, Day of Judgment, and Christ's last Coming | and Appearance without us. | Also, Where, and What these Heavens are into which the | Man Christ is gone, and entered into. | By George Keith. | *Printed in Pensilvania, and Reprinted in London for Benjamin* [should be *Elias*] *Keach* ... . 1693. 4to, pp. 12. C. 37186

An exact reprint of "A Testimony," etc., No. 37221, *infra*, except the title.

Keith. A Chronological Account of the Several Ages of the World from Adam to Christ, and from thence to the end of the World. [n. p. 1694.] 4to, pp. 32. 37187

Keith. A Counter Testimonial, Signed by Seventy-eight persons, disavowing all those concerned in the denial of George Keith. Written by George Keith A.D. 1692. *Philadelphia: Printed by William Bradford.* 1692. 4to. 37188

Keith. A Dangerous and Hurtful Opinion maintained by Samuell Willard. By Geo. Keith, M.A. *New York: Printed by William Bradford* [*about* 1704]. 4to. 37189

Keith. The | Doctrine | of the Holy | Apostles & Prophets the Foundation | of the Church of Christ, | As it was Delivered in a | Sermon | At Her Majesties Chappel, at | Boston in New-England, the | 14th. of June 1702. | By George Keith, M.A. |

Boston: | Printed for Samuel Phillips at the Brick Shop. 1702. 4to, pp. (2), 17. B. 37190

Keith. An Exact Narrative Of the Proceedings At Turners Hall, The 11th of ... June, 1696. Together with the Disputes and Speeches There, Between G. Keith and other Quakers, Differing from Him in Some Religious Principles. ... By George Keith. ... *London: B. Aylmer and J. Dunton.* 1696. 4to, pp. 62.

Also: A Second Narrative Of the Proceedings At Turners-Hall, The 29th of ... April, 1697. ... *London: B. Aylmer.* 1697. 4to, pp. 36.—A Third Narrative Of the Proceedings At Turners-Hall, The Twenty First Day of April 1698. ... *London: C. Brome.* 1698. 4to, pp. (4), 68.—George Keith's Fourth Narrative, Of his Proceedings at Turners-Hall. ... *London: Brabazon Aylmer.* 1700. 4to, pp. (6), 116.—George Keith's Fifth Narrative, Of his Proceedings at Turners-Hall; ... The 4th. of June, 1701. ... *London: B. Aylmer, and C. Brome.* 1701. 4to, pp. (4), 68. BA.

Keith. Some Seasonable Reflections upon the Quakers Solemn Protestation against George Keith's Proceedings at Turner's Hall, 29th April, 1697. By an Impartial Hand. ... *London: C. Browne.* 1697. 4to. P. 37192

[Keith.] An Exhortation & Caution to Friends concerning buying or keeping of Negroes. [*Philadelphia: Printed by William Bradford.* 1693.] 4to, pp. 6. 37193

"Given forth by our Monethly Meeting in Philadelphia, the 13th day of the 8th Moneth, 1693, and recommended to all our Friends and Brethren, who are one with us in our Testimony for the Lord Jesus Christ, and to all others professing Christianity."

Keith. The False Judgment of a Yearly Meeting of Quakers in Maryland, condemned by George Keith, Thomas Budd, and other Quakers. To which is added a Discovery of this Mystery of Iniquity. By George Keith. [*Printed by William Bradford*] *New York.* 1692. 4to, pp. 24. 37194

[Keith.] False Judgements Reprehended: And A Just Reproof to Tho. Everndon, And his Associates and Fellow-Travellers, For the false and rash Judgement T. E. gave against G. K. and his faithful Friends and Brethren, at the public Meeting at Philadelphia the 27. of 10. Mon. 1692. ... *Printed* [*by William Bradford at Philadelphia*] *in the Year* 1692. Sm. 4to, pp. 8, 4.

Signed "George Keith, Thomas Budd."

[Keith.] A Further Account. *See* Vol. vi., No. 23894.

[Keith.] A Further | Discovery | Of the Spirit of | Falsehood & Persecution | in | Sam. Jennings, | And his Party that joyned with him in Pen- | silvania; and some Abettors that cloak and de- | fend him here in England: In Answer to his | scandalous

Book, called, The State of the Case. | [Colophon:] *London: R. Levis.* 1694. 4to, pp. 52. C. 37196

Signed "George Keith." This Jennings was the man who whipped his servant maid in bed; of which, and other mal-practices Keith makes mention, and gives some interesting particulars respecting William Bradford and his printing-press at Philadelphia in 1692.

KEITH. The great Necessity & Use | of the | Holy Sacraments | of | Baptism & the Lords Supper, | Delivered In A | Sermon | preached at | Trinity-Church in New-York, | The 28th of November, 1703. | By George Keith, M.A. | *Printed and Sold by William Bradford at the Sign of the Bible* | *in New-York.* 1704. 4to, pp. 24. 37197

Of great rarity; I have only seen three copies.

KEITH. Gross Errours and Hypocrisie Detected in George Whitehead, and Some of his Brethren; As both appear from the disingenuous and hypocritical Answer he and some others have given to some Queries sent to the last Yearly Meeting of the People called Quakers, in the Third Month, 1695, by comparing the said Answer with the Printed Books, of the said George Whitehead, William Penn, and John Whitehead, Leading Men in the said Meeting; wherein the great Inconsistency and Contradiction of their present late Answers to the Express Words and Sentiments of their Printed Books, is discovered; With a further Account of their vile and pernicious Errours. By George Keith. *London: Printed for Walter Kettilby,* ... 1695. 4to, pp. (14), 23, 3. 37198

[KEITH.] The Heresie and Hatred. *See* Delavall (J.), Vol. v.

KEITH. A | Journal | Of | Travels | From | New-Hampshire | To | Caratuck, | On the Continent of | North-America. | By George Keith, A.M. | Late Missionary from the Society for the Pro- | pagation of the Gospel in Foreign Parts; and | now Rector of Edburton in Sussex. | *London:* | *Printed by Joseph Downing, for Brab. Aylmer, at the Three-Pigeons* | *over-against the Royal-Exchange in Cornhill.* 1706. 4to, pp. (4), 92. B., BA., C., H., P. 37199

Page 89 contains an "Account of the several Treatises" written and published "in print, in North America," by George Keith, "within the time of his abode there, in the years 1702 and 1703 to 1704." The "Journal" contains few facts interesting to an historian, but a regular notice of his disputes with the Quakers, and the texts from which he preached. The "Journal" was reprinted in Vol. I. of the "Historical Collections of the Protestant Episcopal Church."

KEITH. The Judgment given by Twenty Eight Quakers against George Keith and his Friends; With Answers to the

said Judgment, Declaring those Twenty Eight Quakers to be No Christians: As also an Appeal (for which several were imprisoned. &c.) by the said George Keith, &c. to the Yearly Meeting. Sept. 1692. With a full Account of the said Yearly Meeting. Signed by 70 Quakers. ... [*Philadelphia: Printed by William Bradford.*] 1693. 4to, pp. 24. BM. 37200

In the British Museum Catalogue this is dated 1694, but Thomas puts it under date 1693. It was reprinted in *London.* 1694. 4to, pp. 22. *See* Smith's Catalogue, II. 28.

KEITH. A Modest Account of the Principal Differences in Doctrine, betwixt George Keith and the Quakers in Pensilvania. *For the Author.* [1696.] 4to. 37201

KEITH. More | Divisions | amongst the | Quakers: | As appears by the following Books | of their own Writing. | viz. | I. The Christian Faith of New-England | Quakers condemn'd by a Meeting of Pen- | silvanian Quakers. | II. The false Judgment of a Yearly Meeting of | Quakers in Maryland, condemn'd by George Keith, Thomas Budd, &c. | all Quakers. | To which is added, | A Discovery of this Mystery of Iniquity. | By George Keith. | *First Printed beyond Sea* [*at Philadelphia*], *and now Reprinted, and are to be* | *Sold by Richard Baldwin near the Oxford-Arms in* | *Warwick Lane.* 1693. 4to, pp. (2), 22. C. 37202

A reprint of "The Christian Faith," No. 37185, *supra.*

[KEITH.] New-England's Spirit of Persecution | Transmitted To | Pennsilvania, | And the Pretended Quaker found Persecuting the True | Christian-Quaker, | In the | Tryal | Of | Peter Boss, George Keith, Thomas Budd, | and William Bradford, | At the Sessions held at Philadelphia the Nineth, Tenth and | Twelfth Days of December, 1692. Giving an Account | of the most Arbitrary Proceedure of that Court. | [*Philadelphia:*] *Printed* [*by William Bradford*] *in the Year* 1693. 4to, pp. (2), 38. 37203

Of extreme rarity. Doubts have been entertained whether this volume was really printed at Philadelphia, on the ground that the printer having suffered imprisonment for printing and publishing "An Appeal" would not likely have ventured to issue a work of this character there, and thus subject himself to a probable recurrence of farther difficulty with the authorities. It has been surmised that the tract might have been printed at New York, but in that case Bradford could have had no possible reason for withholding his name from the title-page. On the other hand, our printer, having been discharged from arrest and had his press restored to him by Gov. Fletcher on the sole ground of his having been imprisoned for "a religious difference," could not have had any misgivings whatever respecting the publication of a bare recital of the trial and its attendant circumstances, with its present imprint. Nor was one of his resolute character, smarting under what he conceived to be an outrage and a wrong, likely to suspend its publication during the five months which elapsed between the termination of his trial and his settlement at New York. It is of much historical interest in con-

nection with the earliest efforts to establish the press in the middle colonies, and gives a very curious and interesting insight into the social economy and manners of the early Quaker settlers in Pennsylvania as well as some account of printers and printing at the time. It was reprinted as "Tryals," etc., No. 37226, *infra*, and is of almost equal rarity.

KEITH. The Notes of the | True Church | With the Application of them to the | Church of England, | And the great Sin of Seperation from Her. | Delivered in A | Sermon | Preached at | Trinity Church in New-York, | Before the Administration of the holy Sacrament | of the Lords Supper. | The 7th of November, 1703. | By George Keith, M.A. | *Printed and Sold by William Bradford at the Sign of the Bible* | *in New-York.* 1704. 4to, pp. (7), 20.

Exceedingly rare.

[KEITH.] The Plea of The Innocent Against the False Judgment of the Guilty. Being a Vindication of George Keith and his Friends, who are joyned with him in this present Testimony, from the False Judgment, Calumnies, False Informations and Defamations of Samuell Jenings, John Simcock, Thomas Lloyd, and others joyned with them, being in Number Twenty-Eight. Directed by way of Epistle to faithful Friends of Truth in Pennsilvania, East and West-Jarsey, and else-where, as Occasion requireth. [*Philadelphia: William Bradford.* 1692.] 4to, pp. 24. 37205

Signed by "George Keith," and "Thomas Budd." For imprint *see* list of "Books," etc., at the end of "Some of the Fundamental Truths," etc. For a reprint *see* "An Account," etc., No. 37178, *supra.*

KEITH. The | Power | of the | Gospel, | in the | Conversion of Sinners | in a | Sermon | Preach'd at | Annapolis In Maryland, | By George Keith, M.A. | July the 4th | *Printed and are to Sold by Thomas Reading,* | *at the Sign of tho* [sic] *George, Anno Domini* MDCCIII. 4to, pp. (1), 19. 37206

Very rare. There was no press at Annapolis until 1726. Before that time printing for the colony was done at Philadelphia and New York by William Bradford. *See* Thomas' "History of Printing," II. 127.

KEITH. The | Presbyterian and Independent | Visible Churches | in | New-England | And else-where, | Brought to the Test, and examined accor- | ding to the Doctrine of the holy Scriptures, | in their Doctrine, Ministry, Worship, Consti- | tution, Government, Sacraments and Sabbath | Day, and found to be No True Church of | Christ. | More particularly directed to these in New-Eng- | land, and more generally to those in Old- | England, Scotland, Ireland, &c. | With | a Call and Warning from the Lord to the People | of Boston and New-England, to Repent, &c. And two | Letters to

the Preachers in Boston; and an Answer to the | Gross Abuses, Lyes and Slanders of Increase Mather and | Samuel Norton, &c. | By George Keith. | *Philadelphia, Printed and Sold by Will. Bradford,* | *Anno* 1689. Sm. 8vo, pp. (12), 232. B. 37207

Exceedingly rare. One of the earliest issues of Bradford's press.

KEITH. The | Presbyterian and Independent | visible | Churches | in | New-England | And else-where, | Brought to the Test, and examined according to the | Doctrin of the holy Scriptures, in their Doctrin, | Ministry, Worship, Constitution, Government, Sacraments, | and Sabbath Day. | More particularly directed to those in New-England, and | more generally to those in Old-England, Scotland, | Ireland, &c. | With | A Call and Warning from the Lord to the People of | Boston and New-England, to Repent, &c. And two | Letters to the Preachers in Boston; and an Answer to | the gross Abuses, Lies and Slanders, of Increase Mather | and Nath. Morton, &c. | By George Keith. | *London:* | *Printed for Thomas Northcott, in George-Yard* | *in Lombard-street,* 1691. Sm. 8vo, pp. (10), 230. 37208

KEITH. The Pretended | Antidote | Proved Poyson: | Or, The true Principles of the Christian | & Protestant Religion Defended, | And the Four Counterfit Defenders | thereof Detected and Discovered; | the | Names of which are James Allen, Joshua | Moodey, Samuel Willard, and Cotton Mather, | who call themselves Ministers of the Gospel | in Boston, in their pretended Answer to my | Book, called the Presbyterian & Independent | Visible Churches in New-England, and else- | where, brought to the Test, &c. And G. K. | cleared not to be guilty of any Calumnies | against these so called Teachers of New-Eng- | land &c. | By George Keith. | With an Appendix by John Delavall, by | way of Animadversion on some Passages in a | Discourse of Cotton Mathers before the ge- | neral Court of Massachusets, the 28th of the | Third Moneth 1690. | *Philadelphia, Printed by Will. Bradford.* 1690. Sm. 8vo, pp. (2), 224. B. 37209

A most rare volume; Menzies' copy sold for $24.00. It was written in reply to James Allen and others. *See our* Vol. I., No. 828.

KEITH. The Pretended Yearly Meeting of the Quakers, their Nameless Bill of Excommunication given forth against George Keith, ... With a brief Answer to the same, ... reproving the evil and wicked Practices of them in Pensilvania, ... particularly their Persecution of G. Keith and some of his Friends. ... *Printed for R. Levis.* 1695. 4to, pp. 12. W. 37210

KEITH. A | Refutation | of | A dangerous & hurtful Opinion maintained | by Mr. Samuell Willard, an Independent Minister at Boston, & President at the Commencement in Cambridge | in New-England, July 1, 1702. ... | Sent to him in Latin soon after the Commencement, and since translated into English. | By George Keith, M.A. | [*New York: Printed by William Bradford.* 1702.] Sm. 4to, pp. 7. 37211

Very rare; Menzies' copy sold for $13.00.

KEITH. A Refutation of the Three Opposers of Truth by Plain Evidence of the Holy Scriptures, viz. I. Of Pardon Tillinghast, who pleadeth for water Baptism, its being a Gospel Precept, and Opposeth Christ within as a false Christ. To which is added something concerning the Spirit, &c. II. Of B. Keech in his Book called a Tutor for Children, where he disputeth against the sufficiency of the Light within, in order to Salvation; and calleth Christ in the Heart a false Christ in the secret Chamber. III. Of Cotton Mather, who in his Appendix to his Book called Memorable Providences relating to Witchcraft, &c., doth so weakly defend his Father Increase Mather from being justly chargeable with abusing the honest People called Quakers, that he doth the more lay open his Father's Nakedness; and besides the Abuses and Injuries that his Father had cast upon that People, C. Mather the son addeth New abuses of his own. And a few words of a Letter to John Cotton called a Minister at Plymouth in New-England. *Philadelphia: Printed and Sold by William Bradford.* 1690. 4to, pp. 74. W. 37212

KEITH. A | Reply to Mr. Increase Mather's | Printed Remarks | on a | Sermon | Preached by G. K. at Her Majesty's Chappel | in Boston, the 14th of June, 1702. | In Vindication of the Six good Rules in | Divinity there delivered. | Which he hath attempted (though very Feebly and Unsuc- | cessfully) to Refute. | By George Keith, M.A. | *Printed and Sold by William Bradford at the Bible in* | *New York.* 1703. 4to, pp. 35. 37213

KEITH. A Seasonable Information and Caveat Against a Scandalous Book of Thomas Elwood, called An Epistle to Friends, &c. By George Keith. *London: R. Levis.* 1694. 4to, pp. 40. 37214

KEITH. A | Serious Appeal | to all the more Sober, Impartial & Judicious People | in | Nevv-England | to whose Hands this may come, | Whether Cotton Mather in his late Address, &c. hath not | extreamly failed in proving the People call'd Quakers guilty |

of manifold Heresies, Blasphemies and strong Delusions, | and whether he hath not much rather proved himself ex- | treamly Ignorant and greatly possessed with a Spirit of | Perversion, Error, Prejudice and envious Zeal against them | in general, and G. K. in particular, in his most uncharit- | able and rash Judgment against him, | Together with a Vindication of our | Christian Faith | In those Things Sincerely Believed by us, especially respect- | ing the Fundamental Doctrines and Principles of | Christian Religion. | By George Keith. | *Printed and Sold by William Bradford at Philadelphia in Pennsyl-* | *vania, in the year* 1692. 4to, pp. (4), 67.

In answer to Cotton Mather. An exceedingly rare piece.

[KEITH.] Some brief Remarks upon a late Book en- | tituled "George Keith once more brought to | the Test," &c., having the Name of Caleb | Pusey at the end of the Preface, and C. P. | at the end of the Book. | [*New York: William Bradford.* 1704.] Sm. 4to, pp. 20. 37216

Dated "March 2, 1704," and signed by "George Keith." At the end of the tract is a certificate signed by "William Bradford," respecting the manner of his discharge from arrest by Gov. Fletcher. A great part of the volume is occupied with that subject.

KEITH. Some of the Fundamental Truths of Christianity. Briefly hinted at, by Way of Question and Answer. With a Postscript by the Author G. K. The Third Edition. [*Philadelphia: William Bradford.* 1692.] Sm. 4to, pp. 15, (1). 37217

At the end of this very rare tract is a list of "Books lately Printed and to be Sold by William Bradford in Philadelphia, 1692."

[KEITH.] Some of the many false, scandalous, blasphemous, & self-contradictory Assertions of William Davis, faithfully collected out of his Book, printed Anno 1700. entituled, Jesus the Crucified Man, the Eternal Son of God, &c. in exact quotations word for word, without adding or diminishing. [*New York: William Bradford.* 1703.] Sm. 4to, pp. 12. 37218

Dated "Philadelphia, the 26th of March, 1703." Signed by "George Keith," and "Evan Evans." This rare tract is Keith's account of 'his public recantation from, and denouncement of Quakerism, under the patronage and protection of the Rev. Evan Evans, the then Minister of Christ Church and Rector of Philadelphia. The proceedings became so turbulent that Keith and his newly acquired friends were turned out of the meeting-house, in which they were assembled, into the street; while the Quaker Mayor, William Shippen, fearing a breach of the peace, sent "the constable," also a Quaker, "with his constables staff" to disperse them, which he did; an act that caused much animadversion.

[KEITH.] Some Reasons and Causes of the Late Seperation that hath come to pass at Philadelphia betwixt us, called by some the Seperate Meeting, and Others that meet apart from us. More particularly opened to Vindicate and Clear us and our

Testimony in that respect, viz: That the Seperation lyeth at their Door, and They (and not We) are justly chargeable with it. With An Account of our Sincere Christian Faith. [*Philadelphia: Printed by William Bradford.* 1692.] Sm. 4to, pp. 36. 37219

For imprint *see* list of "Books," etc., at the end of "Some Fundamental Truths."

KEITH. The | Spirit | of | Railing Shimei | and of | Baal's Four Hundred Lying Prophets | Entered into | Caleb Pusey | and his | Quaker-Brethren in Pennsilvania, | who Approve him. Containing an Answer to his and their Book, falsly | called, Proteus Ecclesiasticus, Detecting many of their gross | Falshoods, Lyes, Calumnies, Perversions and Abuses, as well | as his and their gross Ignorance and Infidelity contained in | their said Book. | By George Keith, A.M. | *Printed and Sold by William Bradford at the Sign of the Bible* | *in New York.* 1703. 4to, pp. (6), 61. 37220

Very rare. Dedicated "To His Excellency Coll. Francis Nicholson, Her Majesties Lieut. and Governour General of the Dominion of Virginia."

KEITH. A Testimony against That False and Absurd Opinion Which some hold, viz: That all True Believers and Saints immediately after the Bodily Death attain to all the Resurrection they expect, and enter into the fullest Enjoyment of Happiness. And also That the Wicked, immediately after Death, are raised up to receive all the Punishment they are to expect. By George Keith. [*Philadelphia: William Bradford.* 1692.] 4to, pp. 12.

For place, printer, and date, *see* "Truth and Innocency," No. 37225, *infra.* For another edition *see* "The Christian Quaker," No. 37186, *supra.*

KEITH. The True Copy of a Paper Given in to the Yearly Meeting of the People called Quakers, ... 1695. By George Keith ... Together with a short List of some of the vile and gross Errors of George Whitehead, John Whitehead, William Penn, their chief Ministers, and now having the greatest sway among them (being of the same sort and nature with the gross Errors charged on some in Pensilvania) ... And a Proposition to VVilliam Penn, to prove his charge, That G. K. is an Apostate. *London: Printed for R. Levis.* 1695. 4to, pp. 32. 37222

[KEITH.] A True Copy of three Judgements given forth by a Party of Men, called Quakers at Philadelphia, against George Keith and his Friends. With two Answers to the said Judgements. [Also:] An Expostulation with Samuell Jenings, Thomas Lloyd and the rest of the twenty-eight Unjust Judges &c. ... [*Philadelphia: William Bradford.* 1692.] Sm. 4to, pp. 9, 7, (1).

Very rare. At the end of this tract is a list of "Books to be Sold by William Bradford in Philadelphia. 1692." in which nearly all the untitled and undated books printed

by Bradford, and described in this "Dictionary," will be found. In addition to the interesting book-list with its prices ranging from 4d. to 9d. per volume, there is the following curious note concluding the final page: "And whereas it is reported, That the Printer, being a favourer of G. K. he will not print for any other, which is the reason that the other Party appear not in print as well as G. K. These are to signifie, that the Printer hath not yet refused to print any thing for either Party, and also signifies that he doth not refuse, but is willing and ready to print any thing for the future that G. K.'s Opposers shall bring to him." Signed "Thomas Budd, William Bradford," and five others. Smith says it was reprinted at *New York*, 1693.

KEITH. Truth advanced in the Correction of many gross and hurtful Errors; wherein is occasionally opened and explained many great and peculiar Mysteries and Doctrines of the Christian Religion. With a Chronological Treatise of the several Ages of the World. By George Keith. [*Philadelphia:*] *Printed in the Year* 1694. 4to, pp. 216. W. 37224

Contains an elaborate statement of the author's altered opinions.

KEITH. Truth and Innocency, Defended against Calumny and Defamation, in a late Report spread abroad Concerning the Revolution of Humane Souls, With a further Clearing of the Truth, by a plain Explication of my Sence, &c. By George Keith. [*Philadelphia: William Bradford.* 1692.] 4to, pp. 20.

For place, printer's name, and date, *see* "Books lately Printed, by William Bradford, 1692." at the end of "Some of the Fundamental Truths," etc., No. 37217, *supra.*

[KEITH.] The | Tryals | of | Peter Boss, George Keith, | Thomas Budd, and William Bradford, | Quakers, | For several Great Misdemeanours | (As was pretended by their Adversaries) | before | A Court of Quakers: | At the Sessions held at Philadelphia, in | Pensylvania, the Ninth Tenth and | Twelfth Days of December, 1692. | Giving also an Account of the most Arbitrary Pro- | ceedure of that Court. | *Printed first Beyond-Sea, and now Reprinted in London for* | *Richard Baldwin.* 1693. 4to, pp. 34.

KEITH. Two Sermons delivered in Trinity Church, New York, on the Holy Sacraments, and the true Church. *New York: Printed by William Bradford.* 1704. 4to, pp. 48. 37227

[KEITH.] A Vision concerning the mischievous Seperation among Friends in Old England. *Printed and sold by Will. Bradford, at Philadelphia.* 1692. 4to, pp. 8. 37228

"George Keith was originally a member of the Society of Friends. In 1682 he emigrated to East Jersey, where he became Surveyor-General. After being extensively engaged in writing and travelling in the cause of the Quakers, he deserted that sect, joined the Episcopalians in England, and was consecrated as a Missionary, in which capacity he preached both in Boston and New York. Returning to England, he became Rector at Edburton, in Sussex, where he died. His publications were numerous, but almost exclusively of a controversial character." For a further list *see* Smith's "Catalogue of Friends' Books," Vol. II.

Keith (G. B.) An Offering to the Republican Democracy in support of the United States Constitution, until it may be changed in Sovereign Convention. By George B. Keith ... . *Dedham: Printed for the Author.* 1863. 8vo, pp. 28. 37229

Keith (G. M.) A Voyage to South America and the Cape of Good Hope, in His Majesty's Brig Protector. By Sir George Mouat Keith ... . *London: Printed for the Author.* 1819. 4to, pp. xxx, (2), 119. A., C., H. + *London: Richard Phillips.* 1819. 8vo, pp. 43. 37230

Also included in Phillips' "Collection of Voyages," XI.

Keith (I. S.) National Affliction, and National Consolation! A Sermon, on the Death of General George Washington, ... delivered on the Twelfth of January, One Thousand Eight Hundred, ... in Charleston, South-Carolina. By Isaac Stockton Keith, D.D. ... *Charleston: Printed by W. P. Young.* M.DCCC. 8vo, pp. (2), 30. H. 37231

Keith. Sermons, Addresses, and Letters. Selected from the Writings of the late Rev. Isaac Stockton Keith, D.D. ... . To which are prefixed ... A Brief Sketch of his Life, and the Sermon preached on ... his Death. By Rev. Andrew Flinn, D.D. ... *Charlestown: Printed by S. Etheridge, Jr.* 1816. 8vo, pp. 448.

Also: Charge at the Ordination of the Rev. James Adams, May 8th, 1799, Dorchester. ... [n. p. n. d.] 8vo, pp. 38.—Friendly Influence of Religion and Virtue on the Prosperity of a Nation. Sermon at Charleston, S. C. June 14, 1789. ... *Charleston.* 1789. 8vo.— ... Sermon, Preached, with Some Special Reference to the State of the Public Mind, in the Prospect of War; in ... Charleston, South-Carolina, July 12, 1807. ... *Charleston: ... W. P. Young* ... 1807. 8vo, pp. 29. N.

Keith (Israel). Masonic Charge at Boston, Dec. 27, 1780. *Boston.* 1780. 4to. 37233

Keith (J.) Bridgewater's Monitor. Two Sermons, Preached to a New Assembly of Christians at Bridgewater; On 14 d. vi. m. 1717. A day of Prayer kept by them, at their entering Into the New Edifice, Erected for the Worship of God among them. The first by James Keith, and the second by Samuel Danforth. With a Preface of Dr. Increase Mather, and Dr. Cotton Mather. *Boston.* 1717. 12mo, pp. iv, 32, 39. W. 37234

Keith. Bridgwater's Monitor. A Sermon Preached ... at Bridgwater; On 14 d. vi. m. 1717. ... By James Keith ... . .. The Second Edition, to which is added another Preface. *Boston: Printed ... by William M'Alpine* ... 1768. 8vo, pp. (2), v, 26.

Keith (O. B.) An Address delivered at the Funeral Solemnities of the late President Lincoln, at ... Jenkintown, ... April 19, 1865. By Rev. O. B. Keith ... . *Philadelphia: King & Baird, Printers.* 1865. 8vo, pp. 8. 37236

Keith (T.) Struggles of Capt. Thomas Keith, in America. Including the Manner in which he, his Wife and Child, were Decoyed by the Indians; their Temporary Captivity, and Happy Deliverance; which befell them after their Departure, to the time of their Redemption. Interspersed with occasional descriptions of the United States, Soil, Productions, &c. *London: Thomas Tegg.* [n. d.] 8vo, pp. 28. Folded Plate. 37237

See also Smith (S.)

Keith (W.) A Collection of Papers and other Tracts, Written occasionally on Various Subjects. To which is prefixed, By Way of Preface, An Essay On the Nature of a Publick Spirit. By Sir William Keith, Bart. *London: Printed by and for J. Mechell.* MDCCXL. 12mo, pp. xxiv, 228. C., P.

Reproduced with the following title:

Keith. A Collection of Papers and other Tracts, Written occasionally; containing, I. An Essay on the Nature of a Publick Spirit. II. The Citizen. Containing Twenty-five Discourses on Trade, with other Practical and Moral Subjects, tending to encourage and promote both publick and Private Virtue. III. A Dissertation on the Liberty of the Subject in Great-Britain. IV. An Essay on the Education of a Young British Nobleman. V. Observations on the Office of an Ambassador. VI. A Discourse on the present State of the British Plantations in America, with Respect to the Interest of Great-Britain. VII. A Report to the Right Hon. the Lords Commissioners of Trade and Plantations in the Year 1718. VIII. A Discourse on the Medium of Commerce. IX. Some useful Observations on the Consequences of the War with Spain, 1740. By Sir William Keath, Bart. The Second Edition. *London: Jacob Loyseau.* MDCCXLIX. 12mo, pp. xxiv, 228. C., S. 37239

In this volume, which contains much on America, is "The Citizen," which seems to have been a weekly paper, published from Feb. 9 to July 27, 1739. At page 168 is a discourse on the present state of the colonies in America with respect to the interest of Great Britain, and another on the medium of commerce, wherein the necessity of a paper currency to carry on business between Great Britain and some of her plantations in America is particulary explained.

Keith. The | History | of the | British Plantations in America. | With | A Chronological Account of the most remarkable | Things which happen'd to the first Adventurers | in their several Discov-

eries of that New World. | Part I. | Containing the History of Virginia; with Remarks on the | Trade and Commerce of that Colony. | By Sir William Keith, Bart. | *London: | Printed at the Expence of the Society for the Encouragement of Learning, by S. Richardson;* ... M.DCC.XXXVIII. 4to, pp. (8), 187. 2 Maps. BA.

One of the maps is America, with a curious plate of the cod-fishery, and the other, representing Virginia, is inscribed to Thomas, Lord Fairfax. "The first of an intended series of colonial histories, which was not continued." The author was Governor of Pennsylvania from 1717 to 1726, and had previously been Surveyor of the Customs. He died in 1749, aged eighty years. Jefferson, in his "Notes on Virginia," says it is "agreeable enough," but passes over points of importance. *See* Bancroft's "History of the United States," III. 58.

Keith. A Letter from Sir William Keith, Bart. Governour of Pennsylvania, to Mr. James Logan, Secretary to the Proprietorship of the said Province, On Occasion of Mr. Logan's having sent to Sir William a Copy of his Printed Paper, called the Antidote. *Philadelphia: Printed and Sold by Andrew Bradford.* 1725. 12mo, pp. 16. P. 37241

Dated "Phila. Dec. 13th, 1725." It contains Sir William's views of the question as to the powers of the Governor, etc.

[Keith.] Some useful Observations on the Consequences of the Present War with Spain. *London: J. Mechell.* [1739.] 8vo, pp. 28. 37242

Keith. A Just and Plain Vindication of Sir William Keith, Bart. late Governor of Pennsylvania, from the Untruths, &c. in a Paper printed at London under the title of "The Case of the Heir at Law, and Executrix of the late Proprietor of Pensilvania," &c. *Philadelphia.* 1726. P. 37243

Also: A More Just Vindication of the Honourable Sir William Keith against the Unparalleled Abuse put upon him. Folio, pp. 4. Speech of Sir William Keith, 1724.

[Keith, *and others.*] Two Papers, on the Subject of Taxing the British Colonies in America. ... *London: J. Almon.* 1767. 8vo, pp. 22. H. 37244

Keitt (L. M.) Speech of Hon. Lawrence M. Keitt, ... on Slavery, and the Resources of the South; ... January 15, 1857. *Washington.* 1857. 8vo, pp. 14. H. 37245

Also: Politics of the Country. Speech ... April 7, 1856. [n. p. n. d.] 8vo, pp. 7.

Kekitchemanitomenahn. *See* Vol. IV., No. 12833.

Keler (*P.*) Vida y virtudes de los PP. Keler y Provincial Mateo Ansaldo, de la Compañia de Jesus. *En Megico.* [n. d.] 4to. 37246

Kell (E.) A Discourse Delivered at The Unitarian Chapel, Newport, Isle of Wight, On Occasion of the Death of the Rev. William Ellery Channing, D.D. ... By Edmund Kell, A.M. *London: John Green, and John Mardon.* 1842. 8vo, pp. 20.

Kelland (*Prof.*) Transatlantic Sketches. By Professor Kelland ... . *Edinburgh: Adam and Charles Black.* MDCCCLVIII. 16mo, pp. viii, 77. B. 37248

Keller (F. A. E.) Canal de Nicaragua. Notice sur la Navigation Transatlantique ... sur les routes de plus court trajet D'Europe a Saint-Jean de Nicaracua [*sic*] et retour ... . Par F.-A.-E. Keller ... . *Paris: Chez Dalmont et Dunod.* 1859. 8vo, pp. 221. 2 Maps. B. 37249

Keller (G.) A Trip across the Plains, and Life in California; embracing a Description of the Overland Route; its Natural Curiosities; the Gold Mines of California; its Climate, ... By George Keller. *Massillon (O.): White's Press.* [n. d.] 16mo, pp. 58. C. 37250

Keller (M.) Requiem to the Memory of A. Lincoln. A Song. B. 37251

Kellet (A.) The Mental Novelist, and amusing companion; a collection of Histories, Essays, & Novels; containing Historical Description of the Indians in North America. ... Unheard of Sufferings of David Menzies amongst the Cherokees and his Surprising Deliverance. ... With many other Literary Productions of Alexander Kellet, Esq. *London: W. Lane.* 1783. 12mo, pp. (4), 283. 37252

The accurate local references indicate this to be a true relation.

Kellet. A | Packet | of | Prose and Verse : | being a | Selection | from the | Literary Productions | of | Alexander Kellet, Esq. | *Bath: Printed by R. Crutwell.* | M DCC LXXVIII. 18mo, pp. (4), 283.

The first thirty-three pages treat of the North American Indians.

Kellett (T. P.) The History of the War Debt of England; the History of the War Debt of the United States, and the two Compared. *New York.* [n. d.] 8vo, pp. 16. 37254

Kelley (D. G.) What I Saw and Suffered in Rebel Prisons. By Daniel G. Kelley. With an Introduction by Anson G. Chester. *Buffalo: Matthews & Warren.* 1866. 12mo, pp. 86.

Kelley (F.) Projet d'un canal maritime sans écluses entre l'Océan atlantique et l'Océan pacifique à l'aide des rivières Atrato et Truando. ... Précédée d'une Introduction ... par M. V. A. Malte-Brun, et suivi d'une lettre de M. le Baron Alexandre de Humboldt. *Paris.* 1857. 8vo, pp. 80. Map. 37256

Kelley (F. M.) On the Junction of the Atlantic and Pacific Oceans ... . Edited by Charles Manby ... . *London.* 1856. 4to, pp. 8. Map. H. 37257

Kelley. The Union of the Oceans by Ship-Canal without Locks, via the Atrato Valley. By Frederick M. Kelley. *New York: Harper & Brothers.* 1859. 8vo, pp. 114. Map. B., BA.

Kelley (H. J.) Discoveries, Purchases of Lands, &c. on the North West Coast, being a Part of an Investigation of the American Title to the Oregon Territory. By Hall J. Kelley. [n. p. 183–.] 8vo, pp. 16. BA. 37259

Kelley. A General Circular to all Persons of Good Character, who wish to emigrate to the Oregon Territory, embracing some account of the Character and Advantages of the Country. ... By Hall J. Kelley. By order of the American Society for encouraging the Settlement of the Oregon Territory, ... *Charlestown, Mass.: Wheldon.* 1831. 8vo, pp. 28. W. 37260

See "N. A. Rev.," L. 120.

Kelley. A Geographical Sketch of that Part of North America, called Oregon: containing An Account of the Indian Title:— ... Discoveries;—Climate ... Mountains ... Rivers ... Soil ... Animals ... [with] a New Map of the Country. By Hall J. Kelley, A.M. *Boston: J. Howe.* 1830. 8vo, pp. 80. Map. + Second Edition, Enlarged ... . *Boston.* [1830.] 8vo.

Kelley. A History of the Settlement of Oregon and the Interior of Upper California; and of Persecutions ... endured by the Author, Hall J. Kelley, A.M. *Springfield, Mass.* 1868. 8vo, pp. xv, (2), 128. H. 37262

Kelley. A Narrative of Events and Difficulties in the Colonization of Oregon, and the Settlement of California; ... By ... Hall J. Kelley. *Boston: Printed by Thurston, Torry & Emerson.* 1852. 8vo, pp. 92. H. 37263

Also: History of the Colonization of the Oregon Territory. ... *Worcester: For the Author.* 1850. 8vo, pp. 12. H.—Memorial ... praying for a Donation of Land, and Testimonials, concerning the Colonization of the Oregon Territory. [n. p. n. d.] 8vo, pp. 18. + pp. 12. H

[Kelley (J. Filmore).] History of the New Bedford Churches. *New Bedford: Printed by E. Anthony.* 1854. 8vo, pp. 74. + *New Bedford: E. Anthony & Sons, Printers.* 1869. 12mo, pp. 148, (1). B. 37264

[Kelley.] New Bedford Traders in Rhyme. *New Bedford: Printed by Benj. Lindsey.* 1860. 12mo, pp. 23. 37265

[Kelley.] Sketches of the Members of the Municipal Government, New Bedford, for the year 1861. *New Bedford.* 1861. 12mo, pp. 24. 37266

Kelley (W. D.) An Address delivered at the Democratic Town Meeting, in the State House Yard, July Fourth, 1841. By William D. Kelley. [n. p.] 1841. 8vo, pp. 16. 37267

Kelley. Oration delivered by Hon. William D. Kelley, at the Celebration of the laying of the Atlantic Cable, held at Philadelphia, September 1, 1858. [n. p. n. d.] 8vo, pp. 12. H.

Kelley. ... The Practice of Justice our only Security for the Future. Remarks of Hon. William D. Kelley ... in Support of his Proposed Amendment to the Bill "To Guarantee to Certain States, whose Governments have been usurped or overthrown, a Republican Form of Government;" Delivered in the House of Representatives, January 16, 1865. *Washington.* 1865. 8vo, pp. 23. + *New York: [Loyal Publication Society, No.* 82.] 1865. 8vo, pp. 61. B. 37269

Kelley. The Recognition of Hayti and Liberia. Speech ... June 3, 1862. [*Washington, D. C.* 1862.] 8vo, pp. 8. BA.

Another edition differs in the title-page.

Kelley. Replies of Hon. William D. Kelley ... to George Northrop, Esq., in the Joint Debate ... . *Philadelphia: Collins, Printer.* 1864. 8vo, pp. 89. BA., H. 37271

Also: Reply ... to George Northrop, Esq. ... September 23, 1864. [n. p. n. d.] 8vo, pp. 8.—Speech ... September 26, 1864. [n. p. n. d.] 8vo.—Speech ... September 28, 1864. [n. p. n. d.] 8vo, pp. 12.—Speech ... October 3, 1864. [n. p. n. d.] 8vo.—Speech ... October 4, 1864. [n. p. n. d.] 8vo, pp. 12.—Reply ... October 6, 1864. [n. p. n. d.] 8vo, pp. 11.—Closing Speech ... October 7, 1864. [n. p. n. d.] 8vo, pp. 11. *See* Northrop (G.)

Kelley. United States *vs.* William Smith. Piracy. Speech of Hon. William D. Kelley. [*King & Baird, Printers, Philadelphia.*] 8vo, pp. 13. BA., H. 37272

Also: Address delivered at the Colored Department of the House of Refuge ... December 31st, 1849. ... *Philadelphia: T. K. and P. G. Collins* ... 1850. 8vo, pp. 24. —An Address ... Philadelphia, on September 9th, 1856. ... *Philadelphia.* [1856.]

8vo, pp. 16.—Characteristics of the Age: An Address ... Sept. 18th, 1850. ... *Gettysburg: Printed by H. C. Neinstedt.* 1850. 8vo, pp. 16. BA.—Contraction the Road to Bankruptcy—Not to Resumption. Speech ... January 18, 1868. *Washington: F. & J. Rives & Geo. A. Bailey.* 1868. 8vo, pp. 16.—Conversation with Horatio Seymour, on the National Debt and Taxes. Speech ... September 8th, 1868. [*King & Baird, Printers, Philadelphia.* 1868.] 8vo, pp. 16.—The Dangers and Duties of the Hour; An Address ... at Philadelphia, March 15, 1866. *Washington.* 1866. 8vo, pp. 12. —Farmers, Mechanics, and Laborers need Protection ... Speech ... March 25, 1870. *Washington: F. & J. Rives & Geo. A. Bailey.* 1870. 8vo, pp. 30.—Have Faith in God and the People. Speech ... June 15, 1864. [n. p. n. d.] 8vo, pp. 8.—How and when our War Debt can be paid. Speech ... January 3, 1867. *Washington.* 1867. 8vo, pp. 22.—Internal Revenue. Speech ... June 1, 1868. *Washington: F. & J. Rives & Geo. A. Bailey.* 1868. 8vo, pp. 8.—International Coinage. Speech ... April 13, 1870. *Washington: F. & J. Rives & Geo. A. Bailey.* 1870. 8vo, pp. 8. —Judge Kelley's Views on the Chinese Question ... . [n. p. n. d.] 8vo, pp. 8.—Mr. Wells's Report. Speech ... January 11, 1870. *Washington: F. & J. Rives & Geo. A. Bailey.* 1870. 8vo, pp. 16. H.—The Policy of the Administration. Speech ... January 31, 1862. [*Washington, D. C.: Scammell & Co., Printers.* 1862.] 8vo, pp. 7. —Remarks ... In Reply to the Opponents of the Conscription Bill. Delivered ... February 24th, 1863. [n. p. n. d.] 8vo, pp. 7.—Remarks ... in Opposition to the Employment of Slaves in Navy-Yards, Arsenals, Dock-Yards, etc., and in Favor of the Pacific Railroad. [*Washington.* 1862.] 8vo, pp. 8.—Report of Special Commissioner of the Revenue. Remarks ... February 4, 1869. *Washington: F. & J. Rives & Geo. A. Bailey.* 1869. 8vo, pp. 14. H.—The Safeguards of Personal Liberty. An Address ... June 22, 1865. ... *Philadelphia: Merrihew & Son, Printers.* 1865. 8vo, pp. 16. H.—The South—Its Resources and Wants. ... embracing his Address to the Citizens of New Orleans ... . *Washington, D. C.* [n. d.] 8vo, pp. 20. H.—Speech ... June 15, 1864, on Slavery. [n. p. n. d.] 8vo.—Speech ... September 16, 1856. *Philadelphia: King & Baird, Printers.* 1856. 8vo, pp. 16.—Speech ... on Freedmen's Affairs. ... Feb. 23, 1864. [n. p. n. d.] 8vo, pp. 8.—Speech ... at Spring Garden Institute, September 29, 1864. [n. p. n. d.] 8vo, pp. 11.—Speech ... on Protection to American Labor; ... in the House of Representatives, January 31, 1866. *Washington.* 1866. 8vo, pp. 31. + *Philadelphia: E. C. Markley & Son.* 1866. 8vo, pp. 32.—Speech ... [on] the Bill "To guarantee to Certain States, whose Governments have been usurped or overthrown, a Republican Form of Government;" ... January 16, 1865. [n. p. n. d.] 8vo, pp. 24.—Suffrage in the District of Columbia. Speech ... January 10, 1866. [*Washington.* 1866.] 8vo, pp. 8. H.—Trade with British America. Speech ... March 7, 1866. [*Washington.* 1866.] 8vo, pp. 8. H.—The Trent Case, and the Means of Averting Foreign War. Speech ... January 7, 1862. *Washington.* 1862. 8vo, pp. 7.—The Way to Attain and Secure Peace. Speech ... December 19, 1862. [n. p. n. d.] 8vo, pp. 8. *See also* our Vol. IV., No. 15909, and Vol. VI., No. 22713.

Kelley, *and others.* Opinions of Our National Banks ... . *Washington.* 1868. 8vo, pp. 24. H. 37273

Kelley. A Reply to the Minority Report of Messrs. Kelley and Moorehead, on Sites for Navy Yards; with a brief Comment on the Testimony before the Naval Committee. *New London: D. S. Ruddock.* 1864. 8vo, pp. 86. Map. 37274

Kelley. Report from the Select Committee to investigate the Assault upon the Hon. W. D. Kelley, by A. P. Field, a Citizen of Louisiana. [n. p. 1865.] 8vo, pp. 33. 37275

38th Cong., 2d Sess., House Report, No. 10.

Kello (J.) A Sermon preached December 13, 1776, being the Fast Day on account of the Troubles in America, to a Congregation ... at Bethnal-Green. By John Kello. *London: J. Buckland.* 1777. 8vo. 37276

See "M. Rev.," LVI. 79.

Kellogg (A. S.) Memorials of Elder John White, one of The First Settlers of Hartford, Conn., and of His Descendants. By Allyn S. Kellogg. *Hartford: Printed for the Family.* 1860. 8vo, pp. xviii, 13–321, (1). B., BA., H., S. 37277

Kellogg (B.) Oration by Prof. Brainerd Kellogg, and Poem by Mrs. J. C. R. Dorr ... at the Pioneer Centennial Celebration, Middlebury, Vermont, July 4th, 1866. *Middlebury.* 1866. 8vo, pp. 40. H. 37278

Kellogg (C.) Family Meeting of the Descendants of Charles Kellogg, of Kelloggsville, N. Y., with some Genealogical Items of the Kellogg Family. ... *Boston: Henry W. Dutton & Son, Printers.* MDCCCLVIII. 8vo, pp. 8. 37279

Kellogg (C. D.) The Duties of the Hour. A Discourse preached at Wilmington, Delaware, on the occasion of the National Thanksgiving, August 6, 1863. By Rev. Charles D. Kellogg. *Wilmington: Henry Eckel.* 1863. 8vo, pp. 16.

Kellogg (D.) ... A Sermon Preached before the Middlesex Lodge ... Framingham, on the Twenty-Fourth Day of June, 1796. By David Kellogg ... . *Boston: Printed by Thomas Fleet, jun.* MDCCXCVI. 8vo, pp. 23. BA., M., W. 37281

Kellogg (D. O.) The City of Troy [N. Y.]: its Commerce, Manufactures, and Resources. By D. O. Kellogg. *Troy, N. Y.: Young and Hartt.* 1847. 18mo, pp. 48. B. 37282

Kellogg. Genealogical Items of the Kellogg Family. No. II. By D. O. Kellogg ... . *Boston: H. W. Dutton & Son.* 1860. 8vo, pp. 88. 37283

[Kellogg (Edward).] Currency: the Evil and the Remedy. Sixth Edition. *New York.* 1846. 8vo. N. 37284

Kellogg. Labor and other Capital: The Rights of each secured and the Wrongs of both eradicated. ... By Edward Kellogg ... . *New-York: The Author.* 1849. 8vo, pp. 298. BA.

Kellogg. A New Monetary System: ... By Edward Kellogg. ... Edited by Mary Kellogg Putnam *New York: Rudd*

& Carleton. *London: Sampson Low, Son & Co.* MDCCCLXI. 12mo, pp. 366. H. + Third Edition. *New York: Kiggins, Tooker & Co.* 1868. 12mo, pp. 366. C., H. 37286

[KELLOGG.] Remarks upon Usury and its Effects. ... By Whitehook. *New-York: Printed by Harper & Brothers.* 1841. 12mo, pp. 69. B. 37287

Also several Juvenile Stories founded on American topics.

KELLOGG (E.) An Oration ... on the 29th of May, 1795; at the Enterment [*sic*] of the Rev. Thomas Smith, A.M. ... By Elijah Kellogg ... . *Printed at Portland, by Thomas Baker Wait.* 1795. 8vo, pp. 19. H., W. 37288

Also: Oration pronounced at Portland, July 4, 1795. ... *Newburyport.* [1795.] 8vo, pp. 28.—Thanksgiving Sermon at Portland, Nov. 30, 1797. ... *Portland.* 1797.

KELLOGG (E. H.) Address delivered before the Association of the Manufacturers of Berkshire County, Feb. 22, 1855, By Hon. Ensign H. Kellogg; with an Account of the Introduction of Woolen Manufactures into the County, by Thaddeus Clapp, 3d. *Pittsfield.* 1855. 8vo, pp. 34. M. 37289

[KELLOGG.] The Johnson Protocol and International Good Neighborhood: Two Letters to Gen. Grant. By Pontoosuc. *Pittsfield: Chickering & Axtell, Printers.* 1869. 8vo, pp. 24.

Also: Cable Interview between the President and the Queen. ... *Springfield, Mass: Samuel Bowles & Company.* 1870. 12mo, pp. 47. H.—Oration ... before the Social Union Society of Amherst College. ... *Amherst.* 1836.

KELLOGG (E. B.) War Contrary to the Gospel. A Sermon, preached before the Peace Society of Windham County, February 4, 1830. By Ezra B. Kellogg ... . *Providence: H. H. Brown, Printer.* 1830. 8vo, pp. 32. BA., H. 37291

KELLOGG (F. W.) Reciprocity Treaty. Speech of Hon. F. W. Kellogg, of Michigan, in the House of Representatives, May 25, 1864. [n. p. n. d.] 8vo, pp. 8. 37292

KELLOGG (G. B.) An Oration ... July 4, 1829, before the Anti-Slavery Society of Williams College. By Giles B. Kellogg. *Williamstown: Printed by Ridley Bannister.* 1829. 8vo, pp. 22. H. 37293

KELLOGG (L.) A Sketch of the History of Whitehall, Civil and Religious. A Discourse delivered 27th June, 1847. By Lewis Kellogg. *Whitehall.* 1847. 8vo, pp. 16. N., S. 37294

[KELLOGG (Martin).] A Statement in Behalf of the College of California. 1860. [n. p. 1860.] 8vo, pp. 23. H. 37295

Dated "Vernon, Conn., July, 1860."

KELLOGG (M. K.) Fine Arts in the United States. A Paper read ... at Washington, D. C., December 27th, 1869. By Miner K. Kellogg. *Washington: Joseph L. Pearson, Printer.* 1870. 8vo, pp. 11. H. 37296

[KELLOGG.] Justice to Hiram Powers. Addressed to the Citizens of New Orleans. 1848. [*Cincinnati.* n. d.] Sm. 8vo, pp. 14. B. 37297

Also: Mr. Miner K. Kellogg to his Friends. *Paris.* 1858. Sm. 8vo, pp. 24.

KELLOGG (O.) Speech of Hon. Orlando Kellogg ... on the Measures Necessary to put down the Rebellion ... May 31, 1864. [*Printed by Lemuel Towers, Washington.* 1864.] 8vo, pp. 8. H.

KELLOGG. Obituary Addresses on the Death of the Hon. Orlando Kellogg. *Washington.* 1865. 8vo. S. 37299

KELLOGG (R. H.) Life and Death in Rebel Prisons: giving a Complete History of the Inhuman and Barbarous Treatment of our Brave Soldiers by Rebel Authorities, inflicting Terrible Suffering and Frightful Mortality, principally at Andersonville, Ga., and Florence, S. C., describing Plans of Escape, Arrival of Prisoners, with numerous and varied Incidents and Anecdotes of Prison Life. By Robert H. Kellogg, Sergeant-Major 16th Regiment Connecticut Volunteers. Prepared from his Daily Journal. To which is added as Full Sketches of other Prisons as can be given without Repetition of the Above, by Parties who have been confined therein. ... Illustrated. Sold by Agents only. *Hartford, Conn.: L. Stebbins.* 1865. 12mo, pp. viii, 11–399. B., BA. + To which is added, an Account of the Capture of Davis, and Life, Trial, and Execution of Wirz. ... [*Ibid.*] 1866. 8vo.

KELLOGG (T. D.) Kellogg's United States Mercantile Register, for ... 1867–8. In Two Parts. Part I. A Compendium of Information with Reference to the Wants of Merchants and Business Men. Part II. Business Directories of the Principal Commercial Cities of the United States. *New York: Kellogg, Johnston & Co.* 1868. 8vo, pp. 470, xxx; 471–1043. 37301

KELLOGG (W.) Confiscation of Rebel Property. Speech of Hon. William Kellogg ... in the House of Representatives, May

24, 1862. *Washington, D. C.: Scammell & Co., Printers.* 1862. 8vo, pp. 16. H. 37302

Also: Speech ... on the Treasury Note Bill ... February 6, 1862. [n. p. n. d.] 8vo, pp. 8.

KELLY (A.) Report of Alfred Kelly, on the Subject of a Canal at the Falls of Ohio. *Columbus.* 1824. 8vo. 37303

KELLY (C.) A New ... Universal Geography; ... of the Whole World, ... By Christopher Kelly, Esq. ... *London: Thomas Kelly.* [1816–17.] 2 vols., 4to, pp. (4), xx, 774; (2), 1105. 82 Maps and Plates. 37304

KELLY (E.) Five Letters upon Different Moral Subjects, including other interesting miscellaneous matter. Composed by Edmond Kelly. *Philadelphia.* 1856. 8vo, pp. 24. 37305

Also: Appeal to the Colored People of the United States. ... *Philadelphia.* 1855. 8vo.

KELLY (E. B.) Ebenezer Beriah Kelly, an Auto-Biography. *Norwich, Conn.: J. W. Stedman.* 1856. 12mo, pp. 100. C.

Kelly was an American sailor who was impressed into the British service.

KELLY (G.) A Sermon preached December 13, 1776, being the Fast day on account of the Troubles in America. By the Rev. George Kelly, Jun. ... *London: J. Bew.* 1777. 4to

See "M. Rev.," LVI. 238.

KELLY (G. F.) Eight Months in Washington, or Scenes behind the Curtain. Corruption in High Places ... . By George F. Kelly. [n. p.] 1863. 8vo, pp. 38. 37308

KELLY (J. W.) First Directory of Nevada Territory, containing: The Names of Residents ... A Historical Sketch ... Description of all the Quartz Mills; ... By J. Wells Kelly. *San Francisco: Valentine & Co.* 1862. 8vo, pp. 264. B. 37309

KELLY (J.) The American Catalogue of Books (Original and Reprints), published in the United States from Jan., 1861, to Jan., 1866, with Date of Publication, Size, Price, and Publisher's Name. With Supplement containing Pamphlets, Sermons, and Addresses on the Civil War in the United States, 1861–1866; and Appendix, containing Names of Learned Societies and other Literary Associations, with a List of their Publications, 1861–1866. Compiled and arranged by James Kelly. *New York: John Wiley & Son.* 1866. 8vo, pp. (4), 303. + Vol. II. [*Ibid.*] 1871. 8vo, pp. (4), 488. B., H. 37310

Intended as a continuation of Roorbach's "Bibliotheca Americana." Pages 241–

303 of Vol. I. contain a list of pamphlets, sermons, and addresses on the civil war in the United States.

KELLY (J.), *and* MCCLURE (A. W.) The School Question. A Correspondence between Rev. J. Kelly ... and Rev. A. W. McClure ... . *New-York: C. Scribner.* 1853. 12mo, pp. 47. B.

KELLY (J.) A Sermon ... at the Funeral of Doct. William Cogswell, of Atkinson (N. H.), January 3, 1831. By John Kelly ... . *Boston: Printed by Crocker & Brewster.* [1831.] 8vo, pp. 16. B., W. 37312

KELLY (J.) Homestead Bill. Speech of Hon. John Kelly ... May 25, 1858. [n. p. n. d.] 8vo, pp. 16. H. 37313

KELLY (J.) Life and Adventures of John Kelly. *St. Louis.* 1853. 8vo, pp. 52. 37314

[KELLY (Jonathan F.)] Dan Marble; a Biographical Sketch ... By Falconbridge ... . *New York: Dewitt & Davenport.* [1851.] 12mo, pp. xvi, vii, 13–205. Plate. B. 37315

KELLY (P[atrick]). The Universal Cambist and Commercial Instructor; being a Full and Accurate Treatise on the Exchanges, Monies, Weights, and Measures, Of all Trading Nations and their Colonies; ... By P. Kelly, LL.D. ... *London.* 1821. 2 vols., 4to. C. + *London: For the Author.* 1826. 2 vols., 4to, pp. xl, (2), 409, (1); xxiv, 380. 2 Maps. BA. + The Second Edition ... [*Ibid.*] 1835. 2 vols., 4to, xl, (2), 409, (1); xxiv, 380. 2 Maps. A., B., H. 37316

KELLY (R.) An Address on the Character ... of the late Daniel Seymour ... January, 1851. By Robert Kelly. ... *New York: William C. Bryant & Co., Printers.* 1851. 8vo, pp. 23.

KELLY. Life and Character of the late Prof. Edward C. Ross, LL.D. An Address ... July 22d, 1851. By Robert Kelly. ... *New York: Wm. C. Bryant & Co.*, ... 1851. 8vo, pp. 35. B.

KELLY (T. W.) Menana; A Romance of the Red Indians; ... and Two other Poems of the American Woods. By T. W. Kelly. *London: The Author.* MDCCCLXI. 8vo, pp. (6), Errata, 1 slip, pp. 198. C. 37319

KELLY (W.) Across the Rocky Mountains, from New-York to California; with a Visit to the Mormon Colony at the Great Salt Lake. By William Kelly. *London.* 1852. 16mo. C.

KELLY. An Excursion to California over the Prairie, Rocky Mountains, and Great Sierra Nevada. With a Stroll through the Diggings and Ranches of that Country. By William Kelly, J.P. ... *London: Chapman and Hall.* M DCCC LI. 2 vols., post 8vo, pp. x, 342; viii, 334. C. 37321

KELLY (W.) Address ... New York State Agricultural Society, Albany, Feb. 15, 1855. By William Kelly. *Albany.* 1855. 8vo. S. 37322

Kelroy, a Novel. By a Lady of Pennsylvania. *Philadelphia.* 1812. 12mo, pp. 301. 37323

[KELSALL (Charles).] Constantine and Eugene, or, An Evening at Mount Vernon. A Political Dialogue. By Junius Secundus. *Printed for the Author, Brussels, by P. J. de Mat, Printer to the Academy.* M.DCC.XVIII. 12mo, pp. (4), 252 Plate. B., C.

KELSEY (J.) Lives and Reminiscences of the Pioneers of Rochester and Western New York. By John Kelsey. *Rochester.* 1854. 8vo. 37325

KELSEY (W[illiam] H.) Impeachment of the President. Remarks of Hon. W. H. Kelsey ... and Hon. George S. Boutwell ... February, 1868. *Washington: F. & J. Rives & Geo. A. Bailey.* 1868. 8vo, pp. 8. H. 37326

KELSO (I.) The Stars and Bars; or, the Reign of Terror in Missouri. By Isaac Kelso, of Platte City, Mo. ... *Boston: A. Williams & Co.* 1863. 12mo, pp. 324. BA., S. 37327

KELTY (Mary Ann). Early Days in the Society of Friends, exemplifying the Obedience of Faith in some of its First Members. *London: Harvey & Darton.* 1840. 12mo, pp. 471. + Memoirs of the Lives and Persecutions of the Primitive Quakers ... Second Edition. [*Ibid.*] 1844. 12mo, pp. xx, 471. 37328

Gives an account of the Quakers in America.

KEMBLE (F. A.) Journal of a Residence on a Georgian Plantation in 1838–1839. By Frances Anne Kemble. ... *London: Longman* ... . 1863. Post 8vo, pp. (6), 434. BA., C. + *New York: Harper & Brothers.* 1863. 12mo, pp. 337. B., H. 37329

KEMBLE. The Views of Judge Woodward and Bishop Hopkins on Negro Slavery at the South, illustrated from the Journal of a Residence on a Georgian Plantation, By Mrs. Frances Anne Kemble, (late Butler.) ... *Philadelphia.* 1863. 8vo, pp. 32, cover, pp. 4. BA., H. 37330

KEMBLE. What Became of the Slaves on a Georgia Plantation? Great Auction Sale of Slaves, at Savannah, Georgia, March 2d & 3d, 1859. A Sequel to Mrs. Kemble's Journal. [n. p.] 1863. 8vo, pp. 20. H. 37331

KEMBLE. Fanny Kemble in America: or the Journal of an Actress Reviewed. With Remarks on the State of Society in America and England. By an English Lady, Four Years Resident in the United States. *Boston: Light & Horton.* 1835. 8vo, pp. 48. C., H., S. 37332

See also Butler (F. A. K.), Vol. III., Nos. 9632–33.

KEMEYS (J. G.) Free and Candid Reflections Occasioned by the late Additional Duties on Sugars and on Rum; Submitted to the Consideration of the British Ministry, The Members of both Houses of Parliament, and The Proprietors of Sugar Estates in The West-India Colonies. By John Gardner Kemeys, Esq; Of ... Jamaica. *London: The Author.* MDCCLXXXIII. 8vo, pp. 13, 152. H. + *Dublin: Printed by P. Byrne.* M,DCC,LXXXV. 8vo, pp. 127. 37333

KEMP (A. Ferrie). Digest of the Minutes of the Synod of the Presbyterian Church of Canada, with a Historical Introduction, and an Appendix of Forms and Proceedings. By Rev. Alexander F. Kemp. *Montreal.* 1861. 16mo, pp. xx, 474.

Also several articles in the "Canadian Naturalist."

KEMP (F. A. van der). Lofrede op George Washington to Oldenbarneveld, den 22sten van Sprokkelmaand 1800, in Oneida District, Staat van New York, in de Engelsche taale uitgelsprooken, door Franc. Adr. van der Kemp. *Amsterdam: Gerrit Warnars.* 1800. 8vo, pp. 30. 37335

KEMP (——). Father Kemp and his Old Folks. A History of the Old Folks' Concerts, comprising an Autobiography of the Author ... *Boston: The Author.* 1868. 12mo, pp. 254. Portrait.

KEMP (J.) A Pastoral Letter Addressed to the Members of the Protestant Episcopal Church in the Diocese of Maryland. By James Kemp, D.D. ... *Baltimore: Printed by J. Robinson.* 1822. 8vo, pp. 28. H. 37337

KEMP. A Sermon, Delivered in ... Cambridge, in Maryland; On the Twenty-Second of February, 1800, Being the Day of Mourning appointed by Congress for the Death of General George Washington. ... By James Kemp, A.M., Rector of Great

Choptank Parish. *Easton: Printed by James Cowan.* [1800.] 8vo, pp. 15, Hymn, 1 l. BA., C. 37338

Also: Address at the Commencement of the General Theological Seminary ... July 29, 1825. ... *New York.* 1825. 8vo.—Charge to the Clergy in the Dioce**s**s of Maryland ... June 5, 1822. ... [n. p. n. d.] 8vo.—Letter in defence of the Clergy of the District of Columbia, 1822. ... [n. p. n. d.] 8vo.—Sermon delivered before the Convention of the Protestant Episcopal Church of Maryland in Baltimore, 2 June, 1803. ... [n. p. n. d.] 8vo.

KEMPER COLLEGE, *Mo.* Annual Circular of the Medical Department of Kemper College; with an Address ... by John S. Moore, M.D. *St. Louis.* 1842. 8vo, pp. 19. M. 37339

Catalogue ... for the Academical Year, 1842–3. *Saint Louis.* 1843. 8vo, pp. 24. H. 37340

Catalogue of the Officers and [Medical] Students ... for ... 1842–43. *St. Louis: Printed by Ustick & Davies.* 1843. 12mo, pp. 12. H. 37341

The Laws of Kemper College ... March, 1840. *St. Louis: Churchill & Harris, Printers.* 1840. 8vo, pp. 12, (1). H. 37342

KEMPIS (T. à). The Christian Pattern, or the Imitation of Jesus Christ, being an abridgement of the Works of Thomas à Kempis. By a female hand. ... *Germantown: Re-printed, by Christophor Sowr.* 1749. 8vo, pp. 278. P. 37343

Scarce, as most of the books printed at Germantown were used for cartridges during the revolution.

KEMPSHALL (E.) A Thanksgiving Sermon, delivered by Rev. Everard Kempshall, ... Elizabeth, N. J. November 26th, 1863. *New York.* 1863. 8vo, pp. 20. 37344

KENDAL (S.) ... A Sermon ... before ... Caleb Strong, Esq., Governor ... May 30, 1804, the Day of General Election. By Samuel Kendal, A.M. ... *Boston: Young & Minns.* 1804. 8vo, pp. 34. B., BA., H., M. 37345

KENDAL. A Sermon, ... National Thanksgiving, February 19, 1795. By Samuel Kendal, ... *Printed by Samuel Hall, Boston.* 1795. 8vo, pp. 31. B., BA., H. 37346

KENDAL. A Sermon, delivered at Weston, January 12, 1813, on the Termination of a Century since the Incorporation of the Town. By Samuel Kendal, D.D. ... *Cambridge: Printed by Hilliard and Metcalf.* 1813. 8vo, pp. 60. B., BA., H., W. 37347

Also: A Discourse, delivered at Mendon, June 14, 1810, at the Interment of the Honourable Samuel Dexter. ... *Boston: Press of John Eliot, Jun.* 1810. 8vo, pp. 24.

—A Discourse ... at Ellsworth, ... Maine, September 9, 1812, at the ... Ordination of the Rev. Peter Nurse. ... *Boston: Printed by John Eliot, Jun.* 1812. 8vo, pp. 23, (1). BA.— ... A Sermon, ... October 23, 1793, at the Ordination of Mr. Thaddeus Mason Harris, ... Dorchester. ... *Boston: Printed by Belknap and Hall.* 1794. 8vo, pp. 48.—A Sermon ... March 14, 1804, at the Ordination of the Rev. Isaac Allen. ... *Cambridge: Printed by William Hilliard.* 1804. 8vo, pp. 25.— ... A Sermon, ... at the Ordination of the Rev. Avery Williams, ... Lexington, December 30, 1807. ... *Boston: Printed by Munroe, Francis, & Parker.* 1808. 8vo, pp. 42, (1). BA.

KENDALL [Amos]. Mr. Kendall's Address to the People of the United States. [n. p. n. d.] 8vo, pp. 7. H. 37348

[KENDALL.] British Telegraph Monopoly. A Grand Scheme ... under the names of the Atlantic Telegraph Company ,.. and the American Telegraph Company. [n. p. 1858.] 8vo, pp. 39.

KENDALL. A Letter to the Hon. George E. Badger, in Relation to the Claim of A. & J. E. Kendall against the United States, for certain Wrongs done them, with an Appendix. By Amos Kendall. *Washington, D. C.: Buell & Blanchard, Printers.* 1852. Rl. 8vo, pp. 27. H. 37350

Relates to an affair with the Western Cherokees.

KENDALL. Letters to John Quincy Adams, relative to the Fisheries and the Mississippi; first published in the Argus of Western America, revised and enlarged. *Lexington, Ky.: Will. Tanner.* 1823. 8vo, pp. 102. 37351

KENDALL. Life of Andrew Jackson, Private, Military, and Civil. With Illustrations. *New York: Harper & Brothers.* 1843–4. 7 Nos., 8vo, pp. 288. B. 37352

KENDALL. Morse's Patent. Full Exposure of Dr. Chas. T. Jackson's Pretensions to the Invention of the American Electro-Magnetic Telegraph. By Hon. Amos Kendall ... . *Washington: Printed by Jno. T. Towers.* 1852. 8vo, pp. 64. H. 37353

Also: Morse's Telegraph and the O'Reilly Contract: the Violations of the Contract Exposed and the Conduct of the Patentees Vindicated. ... *Louisville.* 1848. 8vo, pp. 35.

KENDALL. Secession. Letters of Amos Kendall; also, his Letters to Colonel Orr and President Buchanan. ... *Washington: Printed by Henry Polkinhorn.* 1861. 8vo, pp. 50. H. 37354

Also: Address ... on Indian Affairs ... in Relation to the Claim of Amos and John E. Kendall. *Washington: Printed by William Greer.* 1854. 8vo, pp. 23.—[Circular to the Stockholders of the American Telegraph Company. Dated New York, August 27th, 1860.] 8vo, pp. 13. H.

[KENDALL.] In Memoriam. *Gibson Bros., Printers, Washington.* [1870.] 12mo, pp. 40. H. 37355

[Kendall (B. F.)] The Doleful Tragedy of the raising of Jo. Burnham, or the "Cat let out of the Bag." In five Acts, illustrated with engravings. By Timothy Tickle, Esq. *Woodstock, Vt.: W. W. Prescott.* 1832. 16mo. 37356

"With five Vermont woodcuts which are difficult to match as is some of the dialogue as well as the poetry. We could give the key to the *dramatis personæ* of this tragedy, but as the persons are confined to Woodstock, South Woodstock, Reading, Randolph, Cavendish and Windsor, and they are not all quite dead yet we prefer to wait a while." —H. Stevens.

Kendall (Edward A.) Argument for Construing Largely the Right of an Appellee of Murder to insist on Trial by Battle, and also for Abolishing Appeals in the British North American Colonies, &c. *London.* 1818. 8vo. Frontispiece. 37357

Kendall. Travels through the Northern Parts of the United States, in the years 1807 and 1808. By Edward Augustus Kendall, Esq. ... *New-York: I. Riley.* 1809. 3 vols., 8vo, pp. xi, (1), 330; vi, 309; vi, 312. B., BA., H., P. 37358

The author visited various tribes of Indians and obtained much interesting information.

K[endall] (E. D.) Master and Pupil; or, School Life at the Old Baldwin. A Story for older Boys and Girls. By E. D. K. *Boston: D. Lothrop & Co.* 1869. 16mo, pp. 351. 4 Plates.

Kendall (G. W.) Narrative of the Texan Santa Fé Expedition, comprising a Description of a Tour through Texas, and across the Great Southwestern Prairies, the Camanche and Caygüa Hunting-grounds, with an Account of the Sufferings from Want of Food, Losses from Hostile Indians, and final Capture of the Texans, and their March, as Prisoners, to the City of Mexico. With Illustrations and a Map. By George Wilkins Kendall. *New York: Harper & Brothers.* 1844. 2 vols., 12mo, pp. (2), 405; xii, 11–406. Map and Plates. H., P. + Sixth Edition. [*Ibid.*] 1847. 2 vols., 12mo, pp. (2), 405; xii, 11–406. Map and Plates. BA. + A New Edition. *London: Henry Washbourne.* 1847. Fcap 8vo, pp. iv, 599. 37360

A romantic narrative of adventure, describing the terrible disasters which befell the expedition from the attacks of the hostile Indians, and the author's subsequent captivity in Mexican prisons. The sixth edition was reissued with the dates 1850, 1855, etc. *See* "N. A. Rev.," IX. 205.

Kendall. A Sketch of the History of the Ohio Mechanic's Institute; and A Statement of its Present Condition. ... By Geo. W. Kendall. *Cincinnati: Printed by Achilles Pugh.* 1853. 8vo, pp. 32. H. 37361

Kendall. The War between the United States and Mexico Illustrated, embracing Pictorial Drawings of all the Principal Conflicts, by Carl Nebel, ... with a Description of each Battle, by Geo. Wilkins Kendall, ... *New York: D. Appleton & Company.* 1851. Folio, pp. iv, 52. 12 colored Plates. A., BA., C. 37362

Among the battles represented are those of Buena Vista, Cherubusco, Cerro Gordo, Palo Alto, Chapultepec, etc. The book was manufactured in Paris, and is scarce.

Kendall's Expositor. Vol. I. *Washington.* 1841. 8vo. C.

Kendall (J.) A Discourse, Delivered at Plymouth, February 22d, 1800. At the Request of the Inhabitants, ... as a Testimony of Grief for the Death of George Washington, ... who Died Dec. 14, 1799. By James Kendall, A.M. ... *Boston: Printed by John Russell.* 1800. 8vo, pp. 24. BA., H., W. 37364

Kendall. A Discourse delivered January 1, 1850, upon the Fiftieth Anniversary of his Ordination ... in Plymouth. By James Kendall. *Plymouth: James Thurber, Printer.* 1850. 8vo, pp. 24. B., BA., H., M. 37365

Kendall. A Sermon, delivered before the Society for Propagating the Gospel among the Indians and Others in North America, at their Anniversary, November 7, 1811. By James Kendall, A.M. ... *Boston: Printed by John Eliot, Jun.* 1812. 8vo, pp. 44. B., BA., C., H., M. 37366

Also: A Discourse in King's Chapel, Boston, before the Humane Society of Massachusetts, ... June 8, 1813. ... *Boston: Printed by John Eliot.* 1813. 8vo, pp. 31. B., H., N.—A Discourse ... February 9, 1823, on the Danger and Remedy of Evil Habit. ... *Plymouth.* 1823. 8vo, pp. 15.— ... Sermon at Plymouth, Sept. 21, 1800, on the Death of the Widow Jane Robbins ... . *Boston.* 1800. 8vo. W.— ... Sermon Artillery ... Election ... Boston, June 2, 1806. ... *Boston: Printed by Munroe & Francis.* 1806. 8vo, pp. 29. H.—A Sermon, delivered at Plymouth, September 4, 1803. Occasioned by the Death of the Rev. David Tappan, D.D. ... *Boston: Printed by Gilbert and Dean.* 1803. 8vo, pp. 22.—A Sermon ... at the Ordination of Rev. James Augustus Kendall ... in Medfield, Mass. Nov. 10, 1830. ... *Boston: Leonard C. Bowles.* 1831. 8vo, pp. 24.—A Sermon ... at the Ordination of Oliver Hayward ... in Barnstable, Nov. 8, 1815. ... *Boston: Printed by Samuel T. Armstrong.* 1816. 8vo, pp. 23.—A Sermon ... at Dennis, January 2, 1805, at the Ordination of the Rev. Caleb Holmes ... . *Boston: Printed by Gilbert & Dean.* 1805. 8vo, pp. 40.— ... Sermon ... at Plymouth ... after the Interment of Deacon Ephraim Spooner, who died March 22d, 1818 ... . *Boston: Printed by Lincoln & Edmands.* [1818.] 8vo, pp. 24. BA.—A Sermon ... at the Ordination of Hersey Bradford Goodwin, as Colleague Pastor with Ezra Ripley, D.D. ... Concord, ... Feb. 17, 1830. ... *Concord.* MDCCCXXX. 8vo, pp. 38, (1).— ... A Funeral Sermon ... at Plymouth [Mass.], December 14, 1800. Occasioned by the Death of Col. George Watson, who died December 3d ... . *Boston: Printed by Samuel Hall.* 1801. 8vo, pp. 29. BA.—A Sermon ... February 14, 1836, occasioned by the Loss of the Brig Regulator, of Boston, in Plymouth Harbor. ... *Plymouth.* [1836.] 8vo, pp. 16. H.

Kendall (John). The Life of Thomas Story, carefully abridged: in which the Principal Occurrences and the most Interesting Remarks and Observations are Retained. *London: Printed ... by James Phillips* ... 1786. 8vo, pp. 387. 37367

Story labored abundantly in various parts of New England.

Kendall (J.) An Address ... Washington Benevolent Society of Leominster and Fitchburg at ... their Annual Meeting. By Jonas Kendall. *Jaffray, N. H.* 1814. 8vo. BM. 37368

Kendall (J. B.) ... A ... Report of the Discussion at Brunswick, Rensselaer County, N. Y., ... between Revs. John B. Kendall and C. F. Le Fevre ... [and] Letter to Henry J. Grew. By Rev. John B. Kendall. *Troy: N. Tuttle, Printer.* 1834. 8vo, pp. 16. BA., S. 37369

Kendall (R. C.) Cotton and Common Sense. A Treatise on Perennial Cotton; ... Its Commercial Value as Compared with Herbaceous Cotton—the Feasibility of its Culture in Northern Latitudes, etc., etc. By R. C. Kendall, Esq. ... *New York: Mapes & Lockwood.* 1862. 8vo, pp. 32. 37370

Kendrick (A.) Sketches of the Life and Times of Eld. Ariel Kendrick. Written by Himself. Third Edition. *Windsor, Vt.: P. Merrifield.* 1850. 24mo, pp. 120. B., BA. 37371

Kendrick (A. C.) ... A Discourse ... in Hamilton, N. Y. ... August 14, 1850, at the Funeral of the Reverend Abel Woods. By Asahel C. Kendrick, D.D. ... *Boston: Ticknor, Reed, and Fields.* MDCCCL. 8vo, pp. 28. B. 37372

Kendrick. The Life and Letters of Mrs. Emily C. Judson. By A. C. Kendrick ... . *New York: Sheldon & Company.* ... 1860. 12mo, pp. 426. Portrait. BA., H. 37373

Kendrick (B.) Rhodes Railroad and Steamboat Directory; ... By Burton Kendrick. ... *Philadelphia, Pa.: Charles C. Rhodes.* [1857.] 8vo, pp. 182. H. 37374

Kendrick (C.) A Sermon ... on the Day of General Election, at Montpelier, October 8, 1818 ... . By Clark Kendrick ... *Montpelier, Vt.: Printed by E. P. Walton.* 1818. 8vo, pp. 38.

Keninon (J.) Case between John Keninon, Esq., and others, respecting a Cargo of 525 Slaves, which were purchased on the

Coast of Africa, and shipped to America, and sold for £31,542 6s 8d. *Privately Printed.* 1773. Folio. 37376

Keninon was a slave dealer. Title from Hotten's Catalogue—doubtful of course.

Kenly (J. R.) Our Republic, a Lecture delivered before the Eagle Artillery, February 22d, 1844. By John R. Kenly, Esq. *Baltimore: John Murphy.* [1844.] 8vo, pp. 32. 37377

Kennard (J.) Selections from the Writings of James Kennard, Jr., with a Sketch of his Life and Character. *Boston: William D. Ticknor & Company.* M DCCC XLIX. 12mo, pp. xxxix, 307. B., H. 37378

Kennard (T. W.) The Atlantic and Great Western Railway. Banquet to Thos. W. Kennard, Esq., ... at ... London, 12th May, 1865. *London: Printed by John King & Co.* 1865. 4to, pp. 40. H. 37379

Kennaway (J. H.) On Sherman's Track; or, the South after the War. By John H. Kennaway ... . *London: Seeley, Jackson and Halliday.* MDCCCLXVII. Post 8vo, pp. x, 320. C.

Kennebeck Bridge. Report of the Committee appointed to inquire into the Conduct of the Proprietors of the Kennebeck Bridge. *Boston.* 1818. 8vo. W. 37381

Kennebec Co., *Me.* Catalogue of the ... Teachers' Institute, for the County of Kennebec ... November, 1850. *Augusta: Wheeler & Simpson, Printers.* 1850. 12mo, pp. 12. H. 37382

Minutes of the Kennebec Conference of Churches, Clinton, September 18 & 19, 1833. *Winthrop: William Noyes & Co., Printers.* 1833. 8vo, pp. 18, (2). H. 37383

Also: [Minutes of the Conference held in Vassalborough, Sept. 14 & 15, 1825. n. p. 1825.] 8vo, pp. 8. H.

Statement of the Kennebeck Claims, by the Committee ... of the General Court of the 28th of October, A.D. 1783. ... *Boston: Printed by Adams and Nourse.* M,DCC,LXXXVI. 4to, pp. 29.

Kennebec Locks & Canals Company. Report of Colonel William Boardman, Engineer, ... November 1, 1837. *Augusta.* 1837. 8vo. S. 37385

Proprietors of the Kennebec Purchase. A Schedule of Lands, &c., to be Sold at Auction January 22, 1816. [n. p. n. d.] 8vo, pp. 18. M. 37386

See Plymouth Company.

Kennebec River. Survey of Kennebec River. Letter from the Secretary of War, transmitting a Report of a Survey of Kennebec River, in ... Maine. January 26, 1827. ... *Washington: Printed by Gales & Seaton.* 1827. 8vo, pp. 6. BA. 37387

19th Cong., 2d Sess., House Doc. No. 103.

Letter from the Secretary of War, transmitting a Report of the Surveys of the Kennebeck River, and of Contemplated Routes for Canals, connected with the Waters of said River, February 22, 1828. *Concord.* 1828. 8vo. N. 37388

Kennedy [Andrew]. Speech of Mr. Kennedy, of Indiana, on the Resolution authorizing the Committee on the Rhode Island Controversy to send for Persons and Papers. Delivered ... March 13, 1844. *Washington: Globe Office.* 1844. 8vo, pp. 7.

Also: Remarks on the Bankrupt Law; delivered ... Dec. 28, 1842. ... *Washington.* 1842. 8vo.—Speech ... March 18, 1842, on the Loan Bill. *Washington.* 1842. 8vo.—Speech ... on the Oregon Question. ... January 10, 1846. *Washington.* 1846. 8vo, pp. 8. H.

Kennedy (A[ndrew] J[ames]). La Plata, Brazil, and Paraguay, during the Present War. By Commander A. J. Kennedy, R.N. *London: Edward Stanford.* 1869. 12mo, pp. viii, 273. Map. B., C. 37390

Kennedy (A.) Speech of the Hon. Anthony Kennedy ... on the Cuba Bill ... February, 1859. *Baltimore: Printed by John Murphy & Co.* 1859. 8vo, pp. 16. H. 37391

[Kennedy (Archibald).] The Importance of Gaining and Preserving the Friendship of the Indians to the British Interest, Considered. *New-York: ... James Parker,* ... 1751. 8vo, pp. 31. BA., P. + *London: E. Cave.* M.DCC.LII. 8vo, pp. (2), 46.

The author recommends a confederacy among the American colonies for their mutual support, and for contributing towards the expenses of building forts and cultivating the friendship of the Six Nations. A congress, or convention, of the Northern Colonies was held at Albany, N. Y., in 1754, with a view to accomplish the purpose here recommended. *See also* "Gent's Mag.," XXI. 46; Hopkins (Stephen), Vol. VIII., No. 32968; "M. Rev.," VI. 150, XL. 16, *and* Rich's "Bibliotheca Americana," I. 100.

[Kennedy.] Observations on the Importance of the Northern Colonies under Proper Regulations. *New-York: Printed by James Parker.* 1750. 8vo, pp. (4), 36. H., P. 37393

Kennedy. Serious Considerations on the Present State of the Affairs of the Northern Colonies. By Archibald Kennedy, Esq., ... *New-York: Printed by James Parker.* 1754. 8vo, pp.

24. BA. + ... *London, Reprinted for R. Griffiths.* [1754.] 8vo, pp. 24. BA. 37394

The author was a royalist and Receiver General of the Colony of New York. Thomas quotes a Philadelphia edition—an error probably.

Kennedy (D.) An Address on Occasion of the Funeral of John T. McCoun ... Troy, April 30, 1861. By D. Kennedy, D.D. ... *Troy, N. Y.: A. W. Scribner and Co., Printers.* 1861. 8vo, pp. 40. B. 37395

Kennedy. A Sermon ... May 6, 1849, in ... Albany, on ... the ... Death of the Rev. William J. Pohlman, ... By Duncan Kennedy, D.D. ... *Albany: Printed by Joel Munsell.* 1849. 8vo, pp. 46. B., S. 37396

Also: A Discourse ... October 1, 1851, on Occasion of the Inauguration of the Rev. W. H. Campbell, D.D., as Professor ... in ... New Brunswick, N. J. ... *Albany: Gray, Sprague & Co.* 1851. 8vo, pp. 48.—Speech ... in behalf of the University of Albany. *Albany.* 1852. 8vo.

Kennedy (J.) Oration at Charleston, S. C., on the 4th of July, 1801. By James Kennedy. *Charleston.* 1801. 8vo. C.

Kennedy (J.) Essays Ethnological and Linguistic by the late James Kennedy, Esq. Edited by C. M. Kennedy ... . *London: Williams & Norgate.* 1861. 8vo, pp. vi, (1), 230. 37398

Kennedy. Ethnological and Philological Essays. By James Kennedy, Esq. ... I. Probable Origin of the American Indians. II. Question of the supposed Lost Tribes of Israel. ... *London: Hall and Virtue.* 1855. 8vo, pp. 42, 57, 30. 37399

One hundred copies only printed. First issued as:

Kennedy. Probable Origin of the American Indians with particular reference to that of the Caribs. ... By James Kennedy, Esq. ... *London: E. Lumley.* 1854. 8vo, pp. (2), 42. 37400

Kennedy (J.) Hebrew Servitude and American Slavery: an Attempt to prove that the Mosaic Law furnishes neither a Basis nor an Apology for American Slavery. By the Rev. John Kennedy ... . *London: Jackson, Walford, & Hodder.* 1863. 12mo, pp. (4), 60. B., BA., C. 37401

Kennedy (J.) A History of the Civil War in the United States, from its Commencement in 1861, to January, 1862. By John Kennedy. *Philadelphia: Kennedy & Co.* 1861. 12mo, pp. (4), 308. 8 Plates. C. 37402

Kennedy (John H.) Discourse. Sympathy, its Foundation and Legitimate Exercise Considered, in Special Relation to Africa. ... *Philadelphia.* 1828. 37403

Kennedy [John Pendleton]. African Colonization—Slave Trade—Commerce. Report of Mr. Kennedy, from the Committee on Commerce on he Memorial of the Friends of African Colonization; with Papers on African Colonization, ... and the Diplomatic Correspondence between the United States and Great Britain on the African Slave Trade. *Washington.* 1843. 8vo. Map of Liberia. 37404

27th Cong., 3d Sess., House Rep. No. 283.

[Kennedy.] The Blackwater Chronicle: A Narrative of an Expedition into the Land of Canaan, in Randolph County, Virginia ... in ... 1851. By "The Clerke of Oxenforde." With Illustrations from Life, by Strother. *Redfield, New York.* 1853. 12mo, pp. (2), 223. C., H. S. 37405

[Kennedy.] The Border States; Their Power and Duty in the Present Disordered Condition of the Country. [*Baltimore.* 1861.] 8vo, pp. 46. H. 37406

This first edition was anonymous. Reprinted as:

Kennedy. The Border States: ... By Hon. John P. Kennedy. *Philadelphia: J. B. Lippincott & Co.* 1861. 8vo, pp. 47.

[Kennedy.] Defence of the Whigs. By a Member of the Twenty-Seventh Congress. *New York: Harper & Brothers.* 1844. 12mo, pp. 152. B., BA., H. 37408

Kennedy. Discourse on the Life and Character of George Calvert, the first Lord Baltimore: made by John P. Kennedy, before the Maryland Historical Society, December 9, 1845. ... *Baltimore: Printed for the Society by J. Murphy.* MDCCCXLV. 8vo, pp. 50. B., BA., C., H., N. 37409

No. 5 of the Society's Publications. It elicited a "Review of the Hon. John P. Kennedy's Discourse On the Life and Character of George Calvert ... ." [By B. U. Campbell.] *Baltimore: Printed by John Murphy.* MDCCCXLVI. 8vo, pp. 32; and this in its turn produced:

Kennedy. Reply of J. P. Kennedy to the Review of his Discourse on the Life and Character of [George] Calvert, published in the United States Catholic Magazine, April, 1846. *Baltimore: Printed by John Murphy.* MDCCCXLVI. 8vo, pp. 32.

Kennedy. Remarks of the United States Catholic Magazine on the Discussion between John P. Kennedy and his Reviewer. [*Baltimore.* 1846.] 8vo, pp. 8. N. 37411

Kennedy. A Discourse on the Life ... of William Wirt ... at ... Baltimore, on the 20th of May, 1834. By John P. Kennedy. *Baltimore: William & Joseph Neal.* 1834. 8vo, pp. (2), v, 4–63. B., BA., H. 37412

[Kennedy.] Horse Shoe Robinson; a Tale of the Tory Ascendency. ... *Philadelphia: Carey, Lea & Blanchard.* 1835. 2 vols., 12mo, pp. iv, (1), 13–325; 298. BA. + [*Ibid.*] 1836. + Revised Edition. *New-York: George P. Putnam.* 1852. 12mo, pp. xiv, 9–598. B., C. + *Philadelphia.* 1860. 12mo. H. + *Philadelphia: J. B. Lippincott & Co.* 1865. 12mo, pp. xiv, 9–598. Portrait. B. 37413

[Kennedy.] Letters of A Man of the Times, to the Citizens of Baltimore. *Baltimore: Sands & Neilson.* 1836. 8vo, pp. 24.

Kennedy. Memoirs of the Life of William Wirt, Attorney General of the United States. By John P. Kennedy. ... *Philadelphia: Lea & Blanchard.* 1849. 2 vols., 8vo, pp. 417; 450, (1). Portrait and Facsimile. B., H., C., P. + A New and Revised Edition. [*Ibid.*] 1850. 2 vols., 12mo. + New Edition. [*Ibid.*] 1852. 2 vols., 12mo. B. + [*Ibid.*] 1853. + [*Ibid.*] 1856. 2 vols., 12mo, pp. 368; v, 391. Portrait and Facsimile. H. + *Philadelphia: J. B. Lippincott & Co.* 1860. 2 vols., 12mo, pp. 368; v, 391. Portrait and Facsimile. H. 37415

Kennedy. Mr. Ambrose's Letters on the Rebellion. By John P. Kennedy. *New York: Hurd and Houghton.* 1865. 16mo, pp. vii, 246. B., BA., H. 37416

[Kennedy.] Quodlibet: containing some Annals thereof. ... By Solomon Secondthoughts. ... *Philadelphia: Lea & Blanchard.* 1840. 12mo, pp. 350. H. + Second Edition. *Philadelphia: J. B. Lippincott & Co.* 1860. 12mo, pp. 268. B., BA. 37417

[Kennedy.] A Review of Mr. Cambreleng's Report from the Committee of Commerce. ... By Mephistopheles. ... *Baltimore: Printed by Wm. Ogden Niles.* 1830. 8vo, pp. 72. 37418

[Kennedy.] Rob of the Bowl: a Legend of St. Inigoe's. ... *Philadelphia: Lea & Blanchard.* 1838. 2 vols., 12mo, pp. (4) 13–270; 275. + Revised Edition. *New York: G. P. Putnam*

& Co. 1854. 12mo, pp. 432. + *Philadelphia: J. B. Lippincott & Co.* 1860. 12mo, pp. 432. Portrait. BA. + *New York: Hurd and Houghton.* 1860. 12mo, pp. 432. + *New York.* 1866.

[KENNEDY.] Slavery the Mere Pretext for the Rebellion; not its Cause. ... Picture of the Conspiracy Drawn in 1863, by a Southern Man. *Philadelphia: C. Sherman, Son & Co., Printers.* 1863. 8vo, pp. 16. H. 37420

[KENNEDY.] Swallow Barn, or a Sojourn in the Old Dominion. ... *Philadelphia: Carey & Lea.* 1832. 2 vols., 12mo, pp. x, 312; iv, 320. B., H., P. + Revised Editon. *New-York: George P. Putnam.* 1851. 12mo, pp. 506. B. + Second Revised Edition. [*Ibid.*] 1852. 12mo, pp. 506. + *Philadelphia: J. B. Lippincott & Co.* 1860. 12mo, pp. 505, (1). + [*Ibid.*] 1861.

[KENNEDY.] To the Mechanics, Manufactures, and Working Men of ... Baltimore. *Baltimore: Printed by Samuel Sands.* 1845. 8vo, pp. 16. BA. 37422

KENNEDY. The Works of J. P. Kennedy, Esq. *New York: George P. Putnam.* 1854. 3 vols., 12mo, pp. 598; 506; 432.

A general title to "Horse Shoe Robinson," "Rob of the Bowl," and "Swallow Barn." Also: Address ... on the ... Opening of the Collegiate Department of the University of Maryland, on the 3d of January, 1831. ... *Baltimore: Printed by John D. Toy.* 1831. 8vo, pp. 26.—Address ... Horticultural Society of Maryland, June 12, 1833. ... *Baltimore.* 1833. 8vo, pp. 33.—An Address ... before the American Institute ... Oct. 17th, 1833. ... *New York: D. K. Minor.* MDCCCXXXIII. 8vo, pp. 24.—Address ... before the Maryland Institute ... of the Mechanic Arts ... on the 21st October, 1851. ... *Baltimore: Printed by John Murphy & Co.* 1851. 8vo, pp. 36. 2 Plates.—The Great Drama; An Appeal to Maryland. ... *Baltimore: John D. Toy, Printer.* [1861.] 8vo, pp. 16.—Letter ... to his Constituents ... on ... the Protective System. [*Baltimore?* 1842.] 8vo, pp. 32.—Report from the Committee on Commerce ... May 28, 1862. [n. p. n. d.] 8vo, pp. 63.—Some Passages in the Life of William Thom: A Lecture, ... February 4, 1846 ... . [*Ashbury.*] 1846. 12mo, pp. 24.—Speech ... 22d and 23d June, 1838 ... on the Sub Treasury Bill. *Baltimore: Printed by John D. Toy.* 1838. 8vo, pp. 32.—Speech ... on the Annexation of Texas. ... January 11, 1845. [*Washington:*] *J. & G. S. Gideon, Printers.* [1845.] 8vo, pp. 16. BA.

KENNEDY. Tributes to the Memory of Hon. John Pendleton Kennedy. *Reprinted from the Proceedings of the Massachusetts Historical Society* [*Boston.* 1870?] 8vo, pp. 16. B., H. 37424

See Vol. I., No. 2467, *and* Peabody Institute.

KENNEDY (J. C. G.) Agriculture of the United States in 1860. Compiled from the Original Returns of the Eighth Census .... By Joseph C. G. Kennedy .... *Washington.* 1864. 4to, pp. clxxii, 292. 37425

KENNEDY. History and Statistics of the State of Maryland, according to the returns of the Seventh Census of the United States, 1850. ... By Jos. C. G. Kennedy .... *Washington: Printed by Gideon & Co.* 1852. Folio, pp. (2), iii, 104, Errata, 1 slip. C.

KENNEDY. Population of the United States in 1860; Compiled from the Original Returns of the Eighth Census, under the Direction of the Secretary of the Interior. By Joseph C. G. Kennedy .... *Washington: Government Press.* 1864 [1865]. 4to, pp. cvii, 694. H. 37427

KENNEDY. Preliminary Report on The Eighth Census. 1860. By Jos. C. G. Kennedy, Superintendent. *Washington: Government Printing Office.* 1862. 8vo, pp. xvi, 294. 37428

KENNEDY. The Progress of the Republic, ... a Full and Comprehensive Review of the Progress ... Commercial, Railroad, Manufacturing and Industrial Resources of the American Confederacy. ... Illustrated ... Edited by Hon. J. C. G. Kennedy ... Geographical and Historical Description of each State and Territory ... By Richard Swainson Fisher ... *Washington: Wm. M. Morrison & Co.* [1856.] Rl. 8vo, pp. (8), 414. B. 37429

[KENNEDY.] Review of the Report ... on the Returns of the Seventh Census. *Washington: Gideon and Co., Printers.* 1852. 8vo, pp. 27. H. 37430

KENNEDY. The Seventh Census. Report of Jos. C. G. Kennedy, late Superintendent of the Census for December 1, 1852; to which is appended the Report for December 1, 1851. *Washington: Robert Armstrong, Printer.* 1853. 4to. N. 37431

This is the correct title of *our* No. 11670.

[KENNEDY.] Statement of the Differences ... in the Census Law of 1850 and the House Bill No. 424. ... [n. p. n. d.] 8vo, pp. 9. H. 37432

KENNEDY. Statistics of American Railroads. Prepared by J. C. G. Kennedy. *Washington.* 1852. 8vo. 37433

Also: Catalogue of the Newspapers and Periodicals published in the United States ... compiled from the Census of 1850. ... *New York.* 1852. 8vo, pp. 56.—Progress of Statistics; read before the American Geographical & Statistical Society ... in New York, Dec. 1, 1859. ... *New York: J. F. Trow, Printer.* 1861. 8vo, pp. (2), 29.

KENNEDY (J. P.) Case of the Mississippi Territory against Joseph Pulaski Kennedy for Barratry. *New Orleans.* 1807. 8vo.

KENNEDY. Joseph Pulaski Kennedy to the World. A Vindication. *Mississippi Territory.* 1807. 8vo. C. 37435

KENNEDY (L. H.) An Official Report of the Trials of Sundry Negroes, charged with an Attempt to raise an Insurrection in the State of South-Carolina: preceded by an Introduction and Narrative; and in an Appendix, a Report of the Trials of Four White Persons, on Indictments for attempting to Excite the Slaves to Insurrection. Prepared and Published at the Request of the Court. By Lionel H. Kennedy & Thomas Parker. ... *Charleston: Printed by James R. Schenck.* 1822. 8vo, pp. (2), 188, Appendix, x, 4. B., H. 37436

KENNEDY (P.) An Answer to Mr. Paine's Letter to Gen. Washington: or Mad Tom Convicted of the Blackest Ingratitude. Including Some Pages of Gratuitous Counsel to the Author [Mr. Erskine] of the "Cause and Consequences," &c. ... By P. Kennedy, Esq. *London: For the Author.* 1797. 8vo, pp. (2), 55. + Third Edition. [*Ibid.*] + *Philadelphia: Republished by William Cobbett. Jan.* 1798. 8vo, pp. (2), 42. P.

KENNEDY (R.) Fast Day Sermon at Greencastle, July, 1812. By Robert Kennedy. *Hagerstown* [*Md.*] 1812. 12mo, pp. 34.

KENNEDY (T.) Songs of Love and Liberty .... By Thomas Kennedy. *Washington City.* 1817. 12mo, pp. 98. S. 37439

Also: Poems. ... *Washington, D. C.* 1816. 16mo.

KENNEDY (W.) Texas: the Rise, Progress, and Prospects of the Republic of Texas. ... By William Kennedy, Esq. ... *London: R. Hastings.* 1841. 2 vols., 8vo, pp. lii, 378; iv, 548. 2 Maps. + Second Edition. [*Ibid.*] B., C. 37440

Reprinted in an abridged form as:

KENNEDY. Texas: its Geography, Natural History, and Topography. By William Kennedy, Esq. *New York: Benjamin and Young.* 1844. 8vo, pp. 118. BA. 37441

KENNEDY. Geographie, Naturgeschichte und Topographie von Texas. Aus dem Englischen von Otto von Czarnowsky. *Frankfurt am Main: J. D. Sauerländer.* 1845. 8vo, pp. 212. Map. 37442

KENNEDY (W.) A Short Narrative of the Second Voyage of the Prince Albert, in Search of Sir John Franklin. By William Kennedy, Commander. *London: W. H. Dalton.* 1853. Post 8vo, pp. xiv, 202. Map and 4 Plates. C., P., S. 37443

KENNEDY (W.) Proceedings of the Democratic Republican ... Committee of the City of New York, relative to the Death of Col. Wm. Kennedy. [n. p. n. d.] 8vo, pp. 6. 37444

KENNEDY (W. M.) The Privilege of the Writ of Habeas Corpus under the Constitution of the United States. ... By William M. Kennedy. *Philadelphia.* 1862. 8vo, pp. 16. B. 37445

KENNEDY (W. S.) The Plan of Union; or, A History of the Presbyterian and Congregational Churches of the Western Reserve, with Biographical Sketches of the Early Missionaries. By William S. Kennedy. *Hudson, Ohio.* 1856. 12mo, pp. 262.

[KENNETT (White).] Bibliothecæ Americanæ Primordia. | An Attempt | Towards laying the Foundation of an | American Library, | In several | Books, Papers, and Writings, | Humbly given to the | Society | for | Propagation of the Gospel in | Foreign Parts, | For the Perpetual Use and Benefit of their Members, | their Missionaries, Friends, Correspon- | dents, and Others concern'd in the Good Design of | Planting and Promoting Christianity within Her | Majesties Colonies and Plantations in the West- | Indies. | By a Member of the said Society. | *London: | Printed for J. Churchill* ... 1713. | 4to, pp. (2), iii, xvi, 3–275, (224). B., H. 37447

There are copies on large paper. "In this short catalogue will be found about twenty original tracts relating to Newfoundland; above fifty concerning Virginia; a hundred or more of New-England; and so on in proportion to the colonies."—*Preface.* "This, as far as it goes, is the best Catalogue of Books relating to America extant, the titles being copied at full length with the greatest exactness, together with name of the printer, and the number of pages in each volume. It unfortunately contains only the books given to the society by White Kennett, Bishop of Peterborough. It is rich in English tracts relating to New England."—RICH. The collection to which it refers has disappeared—some scattered and neglected remains were found a few years since among the archives of the society at Lambeth. Pinelo excepted, this is the first printed catalogue of books relating to America. The copious Index was made by the Rev. Robert Watts. Dr. Dibdin says this catalogue was reprinted in 1791, which is a mistake, *see* [Homer (Arthur)], Vol. VIII., No. 32720.

KENNETT. ... Sermon ... before the Society for the Propagation of the Gospel in Foreign Parts, ... on ... the 15th of February, 17 1/2. With some ... Matters of Fact. And an Abstract of the Proceedings ... within the Year last past. By White Kennett, D.D. ... *London: Printed by Joseph Downing.* 1712. 8vo, pp. 48. BA. 37448

KENNETT. The Life of the late Lord Bishop of Peterborough, with several Original Letters ... . *London.* 1730. 8vo, pp. 308.

Includes an Account of the Society for the Propagation of the Gospel in America.

KENNEY (J.) Historical Sketches of the Baptist Church in Sturbridge, Mass., from 1740 to 1843. By Rev. Joel Kenney. *New York.* 1844. 12mo, pp. 54. 37450

[KENNEY (Lucy).] A Letter addressed to Martin Van Buren, President of the United States, in answer to the late Attack upon the Navy, by the Official Organ of the Government. [n. p. 1838.] 8vo, pp. 8. 37451

Also: A Pamphlet addressed to Martin Van Buren, how easily the Wand of a Magician may be broken by a Woman. ... [n. p. 1837.] 8vo.

KENNICOTT (E. D.) Lethe, and other Poems. By E. D. Kennicott. *Rochester.* 1837. 8vo, pp. 64. 37452

KENNION (J. W.) The Architects' and Builders' Guide. An Elaborate Description of all the [noteworthy] Buildings already Constructed, and about to be Erected in New York and its Environs. By John W. Kennion. *New York: Fitzpatrick & Hunter.* 1868. 8vo, pp. xxxi, 318, vii. 5 Plates. C. 37453

KENNISTON (L.) *and* (L.) Report of the Evidence at the Trial of Levi & Laban Kenniston ... for the Robbery of Major Elijah P. Goodridge, December 19, 1816. ... *Salem: Printed by T. C. Cushing.* 1817. 8vo, pp. 32. BA., H., M. 37454

KENNISTON. Report of the Evidence & Arguments of Counsel at the Trial of Levi and Laban Kenniston ... for ... Robbery ... December, 1816. ... *Boston: Printed by J. T. Buckingham.* 1817. 8vo, pp. 63. BA., H., M. 37455

KENNON (B.) Message from the President [James Monroe] of the United States, transmitting a Report of the Secretary of the Navy, accompanied with the Proceedings of a Court Martial ... for the Trial of Lieut. Beverly Kennon, May 18, 1824. Rendered in obedience to a Resolution of the House of Representatives, of the 25th April, 1824. ... *Washington.* 1824. 8vo, pp. 94, Appendix, 53. B., C. 37456

KENNY (D. J.) The American Newspaper Directory and Record of the Press. Containing an accurate list of all the Newspapers, Magazines, Reviews, Periodicals, etc. in the United States & British Provinces ... By Daniel J. Kenny. *New York: Watson & Co.* 1861. 12mo, pp. 123. C. 37457

KENNY (W.) Argument in Defense of W. Kenny, before a Naval General Court Martial. *Philadelphia.* 1863. 8vo, pp. 18.

KENOSHA, *Wis.* Inaugural Address of the Mayor, April 17, 1854. *Kenosha.* 1854. 8vo. 37459

Revised Charter and Ordinances of the City of Kenosha. *Kenosha.* 1858. 8vo. 37460

KENRICK (J.) Horrors of Slavery. By John Kenrick. In Two Parts. ... *Cambridge: Printed by Hilliard and Metcalf.* 1817. 12mo, pp. 59. BA., W. 37461

KENRICK (W.) The American Silk Grower's Guide; or the Art of raising the Mulberry and Silk, and the System of Successive Crops in each Season. By William Kenrick. *Boston: George C. Barrett* ... 1835. 16mo, pp. 111. + Second Edition Enlarged and Improved. *Boston: Weeks, Jordan & Co.* 1839. 16mo, pp. 167. B., C., H. 37462

KENRICK. The New American Orchardist, or, an Account of the most Valuable Varieties of Fruit, ... adapted to Cultivation in the Climate of the United States, from the Latitude of 25° to 54°. Also, a Brief Description of the most ornamental Forest Trees, Shrubs, Flowers, &c. *Boston: Carter, Hendee & Co.* 1833. 12mo, pp. xxxvi, 25–423. C. + Second Edition ... *Boston: Russell, Odiorne, and Metcalf.* 1835. 12mo, pp. 418. H. + Third Edition, Enlarged ... . *Boston.* 1841. 12mo. 37463

Also: 1835 and 1836. Nursery of William Kenrick, ... Annual Catalogue ... . *Boston: Press of John Putnam.* 1835. 12mo, pp. 42, 4. Continued. B.

KENRICK (W.) Notes on Ogdensburg; its Position, its Rivers and Lakes, and Proposed Rail-Road. By William Kenrick. *Boston: Dutton and Wentworth* ... 1846. 8vo, pp. 16. H.

KENSINGTON. Correspondence relative to the Corvette Kensington which was dismasted with the Russian Minister Plenipotentiary. *New York.* 1830. 8vo. 37465

"Opuscule fort rare qui n'était pas dans le commerce." Title and note from a Parisian catalogue. It would be interesting to know how the Russian Minister felt after he was dismasted.

Kensington District. *See* Philadelphia, Pa.

[KENT (Aratus).] Address and Discourse at the Inauguration of the Rev. Aaron L. Chapin, M.A. as President of Beloit College, July 24, 1850. *Milwaukee.* 1850. 8vo, pp. 52. 37466

[KENT (Benjamin).] A Sermon in Marlborough, July 9. 1734. ... Per Amicum. *Boston.* 1734. 8vo, pp. (2), 24. B. 37467

KENT (B.) Address delivered at the Funeral of the Hon. George Partridge, July 9, 1828; and a Sermon preached ... on the next Sabbath. By Benjamin Kent. ... *Boston: Press of Isaac R. Butts and Co.* 1828. 8vo, pp. 36. B., BA., H. 37468

KENT (E. N.) Instructions for Collecting, Testing, Melting and Assaying Gold, ... for the Use of Persons who are about to visit the Gold Region of California. By Edward N. Kent ... . *New-York: Van Norden & Amerman, Printers.* 1848. 8vo, pp. 39.

KENT (G.) The Characteristics and Claims of the Age in which we live: an Oration ... August 23, 1832, before the New Hampshire Alpha of the Phi Beta Kappa Society. By George Kent. ... *Concord: Moses G. Atwood.* 1832. 8vo, pp. 42. BA.

KENT (H. O.) Report of Henry O. Kent, Commissioned on the part of New Hampshire, to Ascertain, Survey, and Mark the Eastern Boundary of said State, from the Town of Fryeburg to the Canada Line, A.D. 1859. *Concord: Geo. G. Fogg, ... Printer.* 1859. 8vo, pp. 24. 37471

KENT (J.) An Anniversary Discourse, delivered before the New-York Historical Society, December 6, 1828. By James Kent ... . *New-York: G. & C. Carvill.* 1829. 8vo, pp. 40. C.

Reprinted in "New York Hist. Soc Coll.," v. 9–36. *See* "N. A. Rev.," LIV. 306–7.

KENT (J.) Commentaries on American Law. By James Kent ... . *New-York: O. Halsted.* 1826–30. 4 vols., 8vo, pp. vi, (2), 508; viii, 528; viii, 413; viii, 550. BA. + Second Edition. *New-York.* 1832. 4 vols., 8vo. + Third Edition. [*Ibid.*] 1836. + Fourth Edition. [*Ibid.*] 1840. + Fifth Edition. [*Ibid.*] 1844. + Sixth Edition. [*Ibid.*] 1848. 4 vols., 8vo, pp. 560; 646; 514; 586. + Seventh Edition. [Edited by William Kent.] *New-York: William Kent.* MDCCCLI. 4 vols., 8vo. B. + Eighth Edition. [*Ibid.*] 1854. + Ninth Edition. *Boston: Little, Brown and Company.* 1858. 4 vols., 8vo, pp. xxxvi, 687; lxxii, 877; lv, 662; xlvii, 709. + Tenth Edition. [*Ibid.*] M.DCCC.LX. 4 vols., 8vo, pp. xxxiv, (2), 692; lxxvi, 901; lix, 682; lii, 733. B. + Eleventh Edition, Edited by George F. Comstock. [*Ibid.*] 1866. 4 vols., 8vo, pp. xxxv, 668; lxxxi, 864; lxii, 651; liv, (2), 713. BA. 37473

See "N. A. Rev.," XXIV. 345, *also* "Am. Quart. Rev.," I. 162.

KENT. Dissertations: being the Preliminary Part of a Course

of Law Lectures. By James Kent ... . *New-York: Printed by G. Forman.* 1795. 8vo, pp. 87. BA. 37474

Includes "The History of the American Union."

KENT. The Opinions of Chancellor Kent and Mr. Justice Radcliffe, on the Question of Blockade, in the Cause of Andrew Voss and John Boonen Graves, *vs.* the United Insurance Company, in the City of New York. *Albany.* 1801. 8vo. 37475

Also: An Address delivered at New Haven, before the Phi Beta Kappa Society, September 13, 1831. ... *New Haven: Printed by Hezekiah Howe.* 1831. 8vo, pp. 48. —An Address delivered before the Law Association of the City of New-York, October 21st, 1836. ... *New-York: G. & C. Carvill & Co.* 1836. 8vo, pp. (2), 39. BA.

KENT. Proceedings of the Bar of the City of New-York, on the ... Death of Chancellor Kent, December 14, 1847. *New-York: Van Norden & King.* 1847. 8vo, pp. 18. S. 37476

KENT (J.) Speech of Joseph Kent ... on the Removal of the Public Deposits. *Washington.* 1834. 8vo. 37477

KENT. Speech of Joseph Kent, of Maryland, in support of an Amendment to the Constitution to restrain the Veto Power of the President ... delivered in the Senate ... Feb. 20, 1835. *Washington.* 1835. 8vo. P., S. 37478

Also another Speech in the House of Representatives on the same subject [*Washington*, 1834].

KENT, *and others.* An Address to the People of Maryland ... in the Late National Republican Convention: ... *Baltimore: Printed by Sands & Neilson.* 1832. 8vo, pp. 62. B. 37479

KENT (R.) Anti-Ministerial Objections Considered, or The Unreasonable Pleas Made by some against their Duty to Their Ministers, With Respect to their Maintenance Answered. ... In a Letter to Richard Kent, Esq. ... *Boston, N. E.: Printed by B. Green, Jun. for Samuel Gerrish.* 1725. 8vo, pp. (2), 45. B., W.

KENT (W.) Recollections of Albany. An Address ... February 7th, 1854. By William Kent. *New-York: Van Norden & Amerman, Printers.* 1854. 8vo, pp. 23. B. 37481

Also: An Address ... before the Phi Beta Kappa Society of Union College ... July 27th, 1841. ... *New York: Printed by James Van Norden & Co.* MDCCCXLI. 8vo, pp. 30.

KENT ACADEMY. Catalogue ... 1839–40. *Providence: Printed by Knowles and Vose.* 1840. 12mo, pp. 8. H. 37482

KENT COUNTY, *Del.* Statement of the Number of Paupers and of the Expenditures ... of Kent County, for ... 1844 ... . *Dover, Delaware: S. Kimmey, Printer.* 1845. 8vo, pp. 14. H.

KENT COUNTY, *R. I.* Memorial of the Farmers ... of the County of Kent ... for ... Protection to Domestic Manufactures. January 14, 1828. ... *Washington: Printed by Gales & Seaton.* 1828. 8vo, pp. 4. H. 37484

20th Cong., 1st Sess., House Doc. No. 64.

The Kentuckian in New York. *See* [Caruthers (W.)]

KENTUCKY. Account of the extraordinary Revival of Religion, in a Letter from Lexington, Kentucky, 16 Aug. 1801. 8vo. 37485

Account of some of the Proceedings of the Legislatures of the States of Kentucky and New-Hampshire,—1828 &c.—In Relation to the People called Shakers. *Reprinted—New-York.* 1846. 18mo, pp. 84, 19. 37486

An Address to the Presbyterians of Kentucky, Proposing a Plan for the Instruction and Emancipation of their Slaves. ... *Cincinnati.* 1835. 8vo, pp. 64. + *Newburyport: Charles Whipple.* 1836. 12mo, pp. 36. 37487

Agriculture. First Report of the Kentucky State Agricultural Society, 1856 and 1857. *Frankfort.* 1857. 8vo. Continued.

Also: ... Awards, 1857; Address of L. W. Powell. *Frankfort.* 1857. 8vo. s.

Asylums. ... Report of the Managers of the Eastern Lunatic Asylum, for the Years 1852 and 1853. [n. p. n. d.] 8vo, pp. 24. Continued. B., C. 37489

Annual Report of the Directors and Physician of the Kentucky Lunatic Asylum, December, 1845. *Frankfort, Ky.* 1846. 8vo, pp. 30. Continued. 37490

Annual Report of the Trustees of the Kentucky Institution for the Deaf and Dumb, January 1, 1846. [n. p. n. d.] 8vo, pp. 6.

Also: Report of the Joint Committee appointed to visit the Deaf and Dumb Asylum at Danville, ... February 1, 1840. [n. p.] 1840. 8vo, pp. 7.—Report of the Managers of the Lunatic Asylum for 1841. [n. p. n. d.] 8vo, pp. 17. M.

Banks. Charter of the Bank of Kentucky. [n. p. 1834.] 8vo, pp. 8. BA. 37492

Also: An Act granting certain powers to the Bank of Kentucky [with Subsequent Resolves of the Bank. n. p. 1842.] 12mo, pp. 11. BA.

A List of the Present Holders of the Original Stock in the Bank of Kentucky ... . *Louisville: Printed by Morton & Griswold.* 1841. 8vo, pp. (2), 28. BA. 37493

Also: Memorial of the President and Directors of the Bank of Kentucky, in Relation to the Report of the Joint Committee on Banks. *Frankfort, Ky.: A. G. Hodges, State Printer.* 1841. 8vo, pp. 12. BA.—Report of the President and Directors of the Bank of Kentucky, January, 1837. [n. p. n. d.] 8vo, pp. 19. + January, 1841. 8vo.—Response of the Bank of Kentucky and Branches, to the Interrogatories propounded by the Joint Committee on Banks. ... [n. p. 1840.] 8vo, pp. 87. BA.

Farmers' Bank of Kentucky, October, 1850. *New York.* 1850. 12mo, pp. 11. 37494

Report of the Joint Committee on Banks, 1837. [n. p. n. d.] 8vo. Continued. 37495

See our Vol. I., No. 3174.

A Brief History of the Proceedings in the Synod of Kentucky relative to the Cumberland Presbyterians. *Lexington.* 1823.

Christian Almanac for Kentucky, for 1838 and 1840. *Louisville.* 8vo. 37497

The Catholic Question in Politics: ... a Series of Letters ... By a Kentucky Catholic. *Louisville, Ky.: Webb, Gill & Levering.* 1856. 12mo, pp. 120. B. 37498

The Constitution ... of Kentucky [in 1799. n. p. n. d.] 8vo, pp. 19. H. 37499

Report of the Debates and Proceedings of the Convention for the Revision of the Constitution of the State of Kentucky. 1849. ... *Frankfort, Kentucky: Printed [by] ... A. G. Hodges & Co.* 1849. 8vo, pp. 1129. C., H. 37500

New Constitution of Kentucky, 1850. C. 37501

Conversations on some matters to be acted on in the General Assembly of Kentucky. *Louisville.* 1824. 8vo. 37502

Declaration of Independence and Constitution of the Provisional Government of ... Kentucky; ... with the Message of the Governor. *Bowling Green, Ky.: W. N. Haldeman, State Printer.* 1861. 8vo, pp. 16. H. 37503

A Description of Kentucky. *See* [Toulmin (Harry)].

Education. Annual Report of the Superintendent of Public Instruction of the State of Kentucky. *Frankfort.* [1839.] 8vo. Continued. 37504

Also: Annual Report of the Board of Education [January, 1842. n. p. 1842.] 8vo, pp. 11. BA.

Common School Laws of the State of Kentucky. 1856. [*Frankfort.* 1856.] 8vo, pp. 23. 37505

Kentucky Institution for Feeble-Minded Children. Report of Commissioners for 1864–5. *Frankfort.* 1866. 8vo. 37506

Report of the Commissioners appointed ... to ... prepare and report a System of Common Schools. ... *Frankfort: Printed by Kendall and Russell.* 1822. 8vo, pp. 64. H. 37507

Also: Report of the Committee on Education, of the House of Representatives, ... on so much of the Governor's Message as relates to Schools ... . Second Edition. ... *Lexington, Kentucky: Printed by Joseph G. Norwood.* 1830. 8vo, pp. 52.—Statutes of the Centre College of Kentucky, in Danville, enacted February, 1823. *Danville.* 1823. 8vo, pp. 16.

First Annual Announcement of Kentucky University, 1859, Harrodsburg, Kentucky. *Louisville, Ky.: Morton & Griswold, Printers.* 1859. 8vo, pp. 33. Continued. H. 37508

A Few Reflections of a Cool-minded Man on the Present Judiciary Question of Kentucky. [n. p.] 1825. 8vo, pp. 12.

Finance. Report of the Committee on the Sinking Fund, ... 1838. [*Frankfort.* 1838.] 8vo. Continued. 37510

Also: Annual Report of the Commissioners of the Sinking Fund ... January 2, 1840. *Frankfort.* 1840. 8vo. Continued. M.

Annual Report of the Auditor of Public Accounts, for ... 1834. *Frankfort: Printed by A. G. Hodges* ... 1834. 8vo, pp. 14. Table. Continued. 37511

Also: Report of the Second Auditor for the Year ending October 10, 1840. *Frankfort, Ky.* 1840. 8vo.—Report of the Select Committee, to whom was referred the Response of the Treasurer. [*Frankfort.* 1840.] 8vo.

Geology. Memorial from the Kentucky Historical Society, in Relation to a Geological Survey of Kentucky. [January 9, 1847.] 8vo, pp. 13. H. 37512

Report of the Geological Survey in Kentucky, made during the Years 1854 and 1855, by David Dale Owen, ... Assisted by Robert Peter, Chemical Assistant; Sidney S. Lyon, Topographical Assistant. *Frankfort, Kentucky: A. G. Hodges, State Printer.* 1856. 4to, pp. 416. Maps and Plates. H. + Second Report. [*Ibid.*] 1857. 4to, pp. 391. + Third Report. [*Ibid.*] 1857. 4to, pp. 589. BA. + Fourth Report. [*Ibid.*] 1861. 37513

George W. Hawes' State Gazetteer and Business Directory, for 1859 and 1860. No. I. *Louisville.* [n. d.] 8vo, pp. 527.

Guide des Emigrants. *See* Vol. VII., No. 29204.

Hunters of Kentucky. *See* Vol. VIII., No. 33941.

Insurance Bureau. Annual Report for 1870. *Frankfort.* 1870. 8vo. Continued. 37515

Journal of the House of Representatives of the Commonwealth of Kentucky, ... December 5, 1814. *Frankfort.* 1814. 8vo. Continued. 37516

Journal of the Senate of the Commonwealth of Kentucky, December Session, 1805. *Frankfort.* [n. d.] 8vo. 37517

Kentucky; A Tale. *See* [Haliburton (T. C.)], Vol. VII.

Notices of the Press concerning the Kentucky Coal Mining Company. ... *Philadelphia: Barnard & Jones.* 1855. 8vo, pp. 20.

Also: Act of Incorporation ... of the Kentucky Coal Mining Company, with General View of the Coal Fields of Kentucky. *Philadelphia.* 1855. 8vo.

Kentucky Colonization Society. Fifth Annual Report; with Address by Hon. James T. Morehead. *Frankfort, Ky.* 1834. 8vo, pp. 32. Continued. 37519

Kentucky Farmer's Almanack. *Lexington.* 1846. 12mo.

Act of Incorporation, and Constitution and By-Laws of the Kentucky Historical Society, organized March, 1838, at Louisville, Kentucky. *Louisville: Prentice and Weissinger, Printers.* 1838. 8vo, pp. 12. BA., M. 37521

First Annual Report of the Kentucky Improvement Co. ... December 31, 1866. *New York: Cooper & Sheridan.* 1867. 8vo, pp. 52. H. 37522

Report of the Second ... Exhibition of Kentucky Mechanics' Institute, Louisville, 1854. ... *Louisville.* 1854. 8vo, pp. 94.

KENTUCKY MINING AND MANUFACTURING CO. ... Charter ... granted ... February 28, 1854. [n. p. n. d.] 8vo, pp. 9.

Transactions of the First Annual Meeting of the Kentucky State Medical Society ... in ... Frankfort, ... October, 1851. *Frankfort, Kentucky: A. G. Hodges & Co., Printers.* 1851. 8vo, pp. 30. Continued. B. 37525

Kentucky State Register, ... Edited by T. P. Shaffner. *Louisville.* 1847. 12mo. 37526

Laws. Acts passed at the First Session of the Seventh General Assembly, 1798. *Frankfort.* 1799. 8vo. Continued.

Acts of a Local or Private Nature, passed at the Second Session of the Sixth General Assembly, for the Commonwealth of Kentucky, 1798. *Frankfort.* [n. d.] 8vo, pp. 87. Continued.

Acts passed by the Commonwealth of Kentucky, from 1812 to 1816. *Frankfort.* 1813–16. 8vo, pp. 688. 37529

... Acts ... relating to the Existing War ... 1861. *Frankfort, Ky.: Jno. B. Major, State Printer.* 1861. 8vo, pp. 16. H.

Code of Practice in Civil and Criminal Cases for the State of Kentucky. Prepared by M. C. Johnson, James Harlan, and J. W. Stevenson, Commissioners. ... *Frankfort, Ky.* 1854. 8vo.

The Code of Practice in Civil and Criminal Cases for the State of Kentucky. With all Amendments made prior to January 1, 1867. With Notes ... . Edited by Harvey Myers. *Cincinnati.* 1867. 8vo, pp. 822. 37532

A Collection of all the Public and Permanent Acts of the General Assembly of Kentucky which are now in force; together with Acts of Virginia relating to Land Titles, ... Encouragement of Learning ... . By Harry Toulmin. *Frankfort.* 1802. 12mo.

A Digest of the Statute Law of Kentucky: being a Collection of all the Acts of the General Assembly of a public and permanent Nature, from the Commencement of the Government to May Session, 1822. ... By William Littell and Jacob Swigert. *Frankfort.* 1822. 2 vols., 8vo. C. 37534

A Digest of the Statute Laws of Kentucky, ... from the Commencement of the Government to the Session of the Legislature, ending on the 24th February, 1834. With References to Judicial Decisions. ... By C. S. Morehead and Mason Brown. *Frankfort, Ky.: Printed by Albert G. Hodges.* 1834. 2 vols., 8vo, pp. viii, 792; iv, 793–1648. + Digest ... since 1834. ... By Preston S. Loughborough. *Frankfort.* 1842. 8vo. C. 37535

Digest of the General Laws of Kentucky, enacted by the Legislature, between the Fourth of December, 1859, and the Fourth of June, 1865. With Notes of the Decisions of the Court of Appeals of Kentucky, and an Appendix containing the Laws of 1865–66. By Harvey Myers. *Cincinnati.* 1866. 8vo.

Laws of Kentucky; comprehending those of a General Nature, now in force, and which have been acted on by the Legislature thereof. Together with A Copious Index and a list of Local or Private Acts, With the Dates of the Sessions at which they were passed. To which is prefixed the Constitution of the United States, with the Amendments, The Act of Separation from the State of Virginia, And the Constitution of Kentucky. *Lexington: Printed by John Bradford.* 1799. 8vo, pp. lxxxvii, 514. 37537

The Revised Statutes of Kentucky, by C. A. Wickliffe, S. Turner, and S. S. Nicholas; in force from July 1, 1852. Approved and adopted by the General Assembly, 1851 and 1852. *Frankfort.* 1852. 8vo, pp. 796. C. 37538

Revised Statutes of Kentucky, approved and adopted by the General Assembly, 1851 and 1852, and in force from July 1, 1852; with all the Amendments subsequently enacted, and Notes of the Decisions of the Court of Appeals of Kentucky, and an Appendix containing all the Enactments of the Legislature passed during the Session of 1859 and 1860. By Richard H. Stanton. *Cincinnati.* 1860. 2 vols., 8vo. C. 37539

The Statute Law of Kentucky, with Notes, Praelections, and Observations on the Public Acts. Comprehending also, the Laws of Virginia and Acts of Parliament in Force in this Commonwealth: The Charter of Virginia, The Federal and State Constitutions, and so much of the King of England's Proclamation of 1763 as relates to the Titles to Land in Kentucky. ... By William Littell. *Frankfort.* 1809–14. 4 vols., 8vo. C.

Legislative Documents and Journals of the Senate and House of Representatives for 1853–4. *Frankfort.* 1854. 3 vols., 8vo.

Masonry. Proceedings of the Grand Lodge of Kentucky. *Lexington.* 1804. 12mo. Continued. 37542

Proceedings of the Grand Royal Arch Chapter of Kentucky, ... May, A.D. 1818 ... . *Lexington, K.: Printed by T. T. Skillman.* 1818. 8vo, pp. 16. Continued. BA. 37543

The Kentucky Freemason; An Organ of Ancient Craft Masonry. ... Edited by Rob. Morris, K.T. ... *Louisville, Ky.* 1853. Rl. 8vo. 37544

Closed with the eighth number, and Vol. II. commenced as the "American Freemason," which was discontinued.

Kentucky Freemason. ... A Masonic Monthly Journal, Devoted to the Interests of the Craft. *Frankfort, Ky.: A. G. Hodges.* 1868. 4to. Continued. 37545

Memorial and Protest of Union Men of Kentucky, in Regard to Removal of Political Disabilities and Enforcement of Article XIV, Amendment to the Constitution. [n. p. n. d.] 8vo, pp. 4.

Message of the Acting Governor, to the House of Representatives, Communicating the Correspondence between the Kentucky and Tennessee Commissioners on the Boundary Line, with the Reports of the Kentucky Commissioners. *Frankfort: Kendall & Russell.* 1820. 8vo, pp. 40. 37547

Governor's [Desha] Message, in relation to the Resolutions adopted in the House of Representatives on the Motion of Mr. Breckinridge. [n. p.] 1825. 8vo, pp. 44. 37548

Message of the Lieutenant and Acting Governor of Kentucky to Both Branches of the Legislature, December Session, 1839. *Frankfort, Ky.: A. G. Hodges, State Printer.* 1839. 8vo, pp. 16. Continued. 37549

Military. An Act [relating to] the Militia. [n. p.] 1817. 12mo, pp. 9. 37550

Adjutant General's Report, 1862. [n. p. n. d.] 8vo, pp. 199.

Annual Report of the Adjutant General of the State of Kentucky, for the year 1863. *Frankfort: W. E. Hughes.* 1864. 8vo, pp. 232. 37552

Report of the Adjutant General, 1861–66. *Frankfort: T. H. Harney.* 1866–67. 2 vols., 4to, pp. vii, 985; 981, 178. 37553

Annual Report of the Quartermaster General for 1863–64. *Frankfort.* 1865. 8vo, pp. 42. 37554

Catalogue of the Officers and Cadets of the Kentucky Military Institute, 1853–54. *Frankfort.* 1854. 8vo, pp. 29. Cont'd.

Response of the Adjutant General of Kentucky in regard to the Federal Enrollments in the State, March 1, 1865. *Frankfort: G. D. Prentice.* 1865. 8vo, pp. 20. 37556

Minority Report of the Committee on the proposed Amendment of the United States Constitution, February 14, 1865. [n. p. n. d.] 8vo, pp. 8. 37557

Minutes of the General Association of Baptists in Kentucky, October 20, 1837. *Louisville.* 1837. 8vo, pp. 19. 37558

Also: Minutes of the First Annual Meeting of the General Association of Baptists in Kentucky, October, 1838. *Louisville.* 1839. 8vo, pp. 40. Cont[illegible] of the General Association of Baptists in Kentucky, of the Kentucky and Foreign Bible Society, and of the Roberts' Fund and China Mission Society. *Louisville.* 1840. 8vo, pp. 60.

Minutes of the Kentucky Baptist Anniversaries for ... 1843; with ... Tables of all the ... Associations, Churches and Ministers in Kentucky. *Louisville.* 1844. 12mo, pp. 48. Continued.

Preamble and Resolutions of the Legislature ... in relation to the late decision of the Court of Appeals on the Replevin and Endorsement Laws ... . [n. p. 1823.] 8vo, pp. 28. BA. 37560

The Opinion of the Court of Appeals, for ... Kentucky; in the Case of the Commonwealth, *vs.* James Morrison [President of the Bank of the United States]. Delivered by Judge Rowan. *Frankfort, Ky.: Printed by J. H. and W. B. Holeman.* 1819. 8vo, pp. 27. BA. 37561

Origine et Progrès de la Mission du Kentucky, par un Temoin Oculaire. *Paris: Adrien Le Clerc.* 1821. 8vo, pp. 32. 37562

Overthrow of the Ballot. A Complete History of the Election in ... Kentucky. August 3, 1862. [*Richmond.* 1863.] 8vo, pp. 21. BA. 37563

Papers, Acts, and Resolutions, of the Kentucky Legislature, relating to the Existing War, Session of 1861. *Frankfort, Ky.: Jno. B. Major, State Printer.* 1861. 8vo, pp. 28, (1). H. 37564

Presbyterian Church in Kentucky. Proceedings of the Convention at Versailles, Ky., March 17 [1840. n. p. 1840.] 8vo, pp. 21. 37565

Proceedings of the Kentucky Anti-Slavery Society at its First Meeting, in Danville, Ky., March 19, 1835. [n. p. n. d.] 8vo, pp. 8. 37566

Proceedings of the State Convention of Colored Men, held at Lexington, Kentucky ... November 26th, 27th, and 28th, 1867. ... *Frankfort, Ky.: Frankfort Commonwealth Print.* 1867. 8vo. pp. 13. H. 37567

Theological Seminary of the Protestant-Episcopal Church in Kentucky. Charter, Regulations, Course of Study ... . *Lexington, Ky.* 1834. 8vo, pp. 19. + [*Ibid.*] 1837. 8vo, pp. 16. H.

Journal of the Proceedings of the Fourth Convention of the Protestant-Episcopal Church in Kentucky, June, 1832. *Danville, Ky.* 1832. 8vo, pp. 19. Continued. 37569

Report of the ... Keeper of the Penitentiary. [n. p. 1837.] 8vo, pp. 4. Continued. H. 37570

... First Annual Report ... relating to the Registry ... of Births, Marriages, and Deaths, from January 1, 1852, to December 31, 1852. *Frankfort, Kentucky: A. G. Hodges, State Printer.* 1853. 8vo, pp. 112. Continued. B. 37571

Report of the Board of Internal Improvement of the State of Kentucky [1838. *Frankfort.* 1838.] 8vo, pp. 176. Table. Continued. H. 37572

Afterwards entitled the "Annual Report," etc. Also: Report of the Board of Internal Improvement, in Answer to Resolutions, ... January, 1841. [n. p. 1841.] 8vo, pp. 6.

Report of the Commissioners for the Erection of the State Capitol, made to the Legislature, October 1, 1857. *Frankfort.* 1857. 8vo. 37573

Report of the Committee on Religion ... praying a Repeal of the Laws authorizing the Sale of Spirituous Liquors. [n. p. n. d.] 8vo, pp. 4. BA. 37574

Report of the Committee on the Coal-trade and Iron Interests of Kentucky. [n. p. n. d.] 8vo, pp. 20. 37575

Report of the Committee on the Official Conduct of the Judges of the Court of Appeals. [n. p. 1824.] 8vo, pp. 21.

Report of the Excursion made by the Executive and Legislatures of ... Kentucky and Tennessee ... on the 26th, 27th, & 28th Jan., 1860; ... *Robert Clarke & Co., Cincinnati.* 1860. 8vo, pp. 139. H. 37577

Report of the Kentucky Commissioners to the late Peace Conference ... at Washington City .... *Frankfort, Ky.: Jno. B. Major, State Printer.* 1861. 8vo, pp. 88. H. 37578

Reports communicated to both Branches of the Legislature of Kentucky, at the December Session, 1843. *Frankfort: A. G. Hodges, State Printer.* 1843. 8vo, pp. 558. Continued. C.

Resolutions of the General Assembly of Kentucky, upon the American System, and in answer to certain Proceedings of the Legislatures of South Carolina and other States, concerning the Powers of the General Government. *Frankfort.* 1830. 8vo.

Response of the Judges of the Court of Appeals to the Preamble, Resolutions, and Address. 1824. [n. p. 1824.] 8vo, pp. 38. 37581

KENYON (A.) The Object and Principles of Civil Government, and the Duty of Christians thereto. Being a Discourse preached before the West Baptist Church and Society, August 14, 1842. By Archibald Kenyon. *Providence: B. T. Albro.* 1842. 8vo, pp. 11. 37582

KENYON (H. B.) Backus and Kenyon on Secret Societies: being a Discourse delivered by Rev. J. S. Backus, of Auburn, and a Reply to the same by Rev. H. B. Kenyon, of Ira, Cayuga County, N. Y. *Albany: J. Munsell.* 1850. 12mo, pp. 44, 52, xiv. 37583

KENYON COLLEGE, *Ohio.* By-Laws of Kenyon College and Grammar School. *Gambier, O.* 1831. 12mo, pp. 16. 37584

Catalogue of the Officers and Students of Kenyon College. 1830. 8vo. Continued. 37585

Catalogue of the Library, and Names of Members, of the Philomathesian Society of Kenyon College, from its Formation in 1827 to 1840. *Gambier, Ohio: Printed by Thomas R. Raymond.* 1840. 8vo, pp. 44. B. 37586

Also: Catalogue of the Theological Seminary ... . Kenyon College. ... *Gambier: George W. Myers, Printer.* 1835. 8vo, pp. 20. Continued. H.

Laws of Kenyon College and Theological Seminary of Ohio. *Gambier, Ohio: George W. Myers, Printer.* 1833. 8vo, pp. 16.

Letter to the Right Hon. Lord Kenyon on the Applications now making in Behalf of Various Institutions connected with the Protestant Episcopal Church in the United States. [*London.* 1824.] 8vo, pp. 15, (1). H. 37588

A Memento of the Donors and Founders of the Theological Seminary of the Protestant Episcopal Church in the Diocese of Ohio, and Kenyon College; Being the Report of a Committee of the Board of Trustees, Presented Sept. 27, 1860. *Cincinnati: Moore, Wilstach, Keys & Co., Printers.* 1860. 8vo, pp. 79. 3 Plates. BA. 37589

Reply of Trustees of Kenyon College ... to the Statement of D. B. Douglass .... *Philadelphia: Stavely and McCalla.* 1844. 8vo, pp. 48. H. 37590

Three Letters addressed to Bishop Chase in the matter of the present Indebtedness of Kenyon College, Introduced by a Letter from Bishop Chase to Bishop McIlvaine. *Peoria.* 1843. 8vo, pp. 27. 37591

KEOGH (J.) Catholic Principles of Civil Government. A Lecture by Rev. James Keogh ... *Cincinnati.* 1862. 8vo, pp. 20.

KEOKUK. In the Supreme Court of the State of Kansas, January Term, 1870. Albert Wiley, Plaintiff, *vs.* Keokuk, Chief of the Sac and Fox Indians, Defendant. ss. On Petition in Error. Argument and Brief for the Defendant [by James Christian. n. p. 1870.] 8vo, pp. 41. H. 37593

Keokuk General Directory ... for 1866–7. *Keokuk: Rees, Printer.* 8vo, pp. 139. Continued. B. 37594

Keokuk in 1856. *See* Clemens (O.), Vol. IV., No. 13622.

KEOKUK LIBRARY ASSOCIATION. Catalogue of Books ... with a Historical Sketch. ... *Keokuk, Iowa.* 1866. 12mo, pp. (4), 166. H. 37595

KEPPEL (F.) A Sermon ... before the ... Society for the Propagation of the Gospel in Foreign Parts; ... February 16, 1770. By the Rt. Rev. Frederic the Bishop of Exeter. *London: Printed by E. Owen and T. Harrison.* MDCCLXX. 4to, pp. 62.

KEPPEL (T.) The Life of Augustus Viscount Keppel ... . By the Hon[ble] & Rev[d] Thomas Keppel ... . *London: Henry Colburn.* 1842. 2 vols., 8vo, pp. xvi, 446, Portrait and Genealogical Record; (2), vi, 438. B. 37597

Relates to his services in North America, capture of the island of Cuba, etc. Also: Description of the Gold Box presented with the Freedom of the City of London to Admiral Keppel on his taking the Havannah, Conquest of Cuba ... . *London.* [n. d.] 4to. Plates.

[KEPPEL (William Coutts)], *Viscount Bury.* Exodus of the Western Nations. By Viscount Bury, M.P. ... *London: Richard Bentley.* 1865. 2 vols., 8vo, pp. xii, 483, (1); viii, 494. BA.

KER (H.) Travels through The Western Interior of the United States, from the Year 1808 up to the Year 1816. With a particular Description of a great part of Mexico, or New-Spain. Containing, a particular account of thirteen different tribes of Indians through which the author passed; describing their Manners, Customs, &c.; with some account of a tribe whose customs are similar to those of the ancient Welch. Interspersed with Valuable Historical Information, drawn from the Latest Authorities. By Henry Ker. *Elizabethtown, N. J.: Printed for the Author.* 1816. 8vo, pp. 372. B., BA. 37599

A performance of doubtful authenticity.

KER (J.) The Memoirs of John Ker, of Kersland in North Britain Esq; containing His Secret Transactions and Negotiations in ... Foreign Parts. ... *London: Printed in the Year* M.DCC.XXVI. 8vo, pp. xi, iv, 180, (4). + Part II. ... pp. (2), vii, 184, (6). + Part III[d] and Last. To which is added, A Copy of the Information exhibited by the Attorney-General against the First Part of these Memoirs. ... pp. (2), 221, 157, (2), 16. + Second Edition. [*Ibid.*] + The Third Edition. *London: Printed in the Year* M.DCC.XXVII. 3 parts in 2 vols., 8vo. Part I. pp. (16), 180, (4). Part II. M.DCC.XXVI. pp. (2), viii, 184, (6). Part III. and Last. pp. (4), vi, 221. Remarks, &c. 1727. pp. 160. Appendix, 16. Map of Louisiana. 37600

Vol. II. contains curious details respecting Louisiana and the French Dominions in America. Although the notorious Curll was afraid to put his name as printer, he has bound a full list of his publications at the end—and a curious one it is. For publishing this work Curll was pilloried. *See* Allibone on the subject; *see also* W. George's Catalogue, No. 13.

KER. Mémoires de Jean Ker ... contenant ses Négociations secrètes ... Avec une relation de la Compagnie d'Ostende, des particularités intéressantes sur la puissances des Français dans l'Ile d'Hispaniola et sur leurs établissemens dans Mississippi, etc. Traduit de l'Anglais. *Rotterdam.* 1726–28. 3 vols., 8vo, pp. 302; 228; 308. Map of Louisiana. 37601

KER. Memorien ... behelzende zijne geheime verhandelingen ... nevens verhaal van de Oostendische Maatschappij. *Rotterdam.* 1727. 3 vols., 8vo. Portrait and Map. 37602

KER (L.) Slavery Consistent with Christianity. By the Rev. Leander Ker. *Jefferson City: Printed by W. Lusk and Son.* 1842. 8vo, pp. 32. BA. + Second Edition ... *Baltimore.* 1845. 8vo, pp. 31. + *Weston, Md.* 1853. 12mo, pp. 36. 37603

KÉRATRY (*le comte* É. de). La Contre-guérilla française au Mexique. ... Par le comte Émile de Kératry. Seconde édition. *Paris: Librairie Internationale.* 1869. 16mo, pp. (4), 313. C.

KÉRATRY. La Créance Jecker, les indemnités françaises, et les emprunts mexicains. Par le comte Émile de Kératry. *Paris: Librairie Internationale.* 1868. 8vo, pp. 158, (2). C. 37605

KÉRATRY. L'Élévation et la chute de l'empereur Maximilien. Intervention française au Mexique 1861–1867. Par le comte Émile de Kératry. *Paris.* 1867. 8vo, pp. xx, 372. H. 37606

KÉRATRY. L'empereur Maximilien, son élévation et sa chute. D'après des documents inédits par le comte Émile de Kératry. *Leipzig: Duncker et Humblot.* 1867. 12mo, pp. (4), 323, (1).

KÉRATRY. Kaiser Maximilians Erhebung und Fall. Originalcorrespondenzen und Documente in geschichtlichem Zusammenhange dargestellt. Von Emil Grafen Kératry. *Leipzig: Duncker und Humblot.* 1867. 8vo, pp. vi, 328. B. 37608

KÉRATRY. The Rise and Fall of the Emperor Maximilian. A Narrative of the Mexican Empire, 1861–7. From Authentic Documents. With the Imperial Correspondence. By Count Émile de Kératry. Translated ... by G. H. Venables. *London: Sampson Low, Son and Marston.* 1868. 12mo, pp. viii, 312. Plate.

KÉRAUDREN (P. F.) De la fièvre jaune observée aux Antilles et sur les vaisseaux du roi, considérée principalement sous la rapport de sa transmission. Par P. F. Kéraudren. *Paris: Imprimerie royale.* 1823. 8vo. 37610

KERCHEVAL (S.) A History of the Valley of Virginia. By Samuel Kercheval. *Winchester: Samuel H. Davis.* 1833. 12mo, pp. (2), 486. B. + Second Edition: Revised and Extended by the Author. *Woodstock, Va.: John Gatewood, Printer.* 1850. 8vo, pp. 447. 37611

The title to the second edition is scarcely honest. The relation of Mannheim's captivity, and the chapter on slavery is omitted. Brantz Mayer mildly remarks "Some liberties have been taken with Mr. Doddridge's 'Notes on the Indian Wars,' in this reprint of it by way of transposition," which is a delicate way of saying that this is a piratical reprint of Doddridge. T. W. Field refers to a second volume, which does not exist.

[KERFOOT (John B.)] The Bishop's Address and Charge to the ... Diocese of Pittsburgh ... June 14th, 1870. *Pittsburgh: Printed by Ballwell & Marthens.* 1870. 8vo, pp. 28. B. 37612

[KERFOOT.] Some Facts touching the Kohne Legacy to the General Theological Seminary. [n. p. 1862.] 8vo, pp. 16. H.

Also: ... The Inaugural Address ... before ... Trinity College ... June 28, 1865. ... *Hartford: Press of Case, Lockwood and Company.* 1865. 8vo, pp. 27. B.

KERFOOT (S. H.) Bishop [Henry J.] Whitehouse and the Diocese of Illinois. By Sam'l H. Kerfoot .... *Chicago: Thompson and Day ... Printers.* 1860. 8vo, pp. 55, (1). H. 37614

KERGUÉLEN-TRÉMAREC (Y. J. de). Relation des combats et des évènements de la guerre maritime de 1778 entre la France et

l'Angleterre, ... et terminée par un précis de la guerre présente ... Par Y. J. de Kerguélen .... *Paris.* 1796. 8vo, pp. 403. 37615

KERGUÉLEN-TRÉMAREC. Relation d'un Voyage dans le Mer du Nord, aux côtes d'Islande, du Groenland, de Ferro, ... Fait en 1767 & 1768. ... *Paris: Prault.* M.DCC.LXXI. 4to, pp. viii, (3), 220. 17 Maps and Plates by Eisen. + *Amsterdam et Leipzig: Arkstée et Merkus.* 1772. 4to, pp. vii, 220. 17 Maps and Plates.

KERGUÉLEN-TRÉMAREC. Des Herrn de Kerguelen-Tremarec Beschreibung seiner Reise nach der Nordsee, die er in den Jahren 1767 und 1768 an die Küsten von Island, Grönland [etc.] gethan. Aus dem Französischen übersetzt. *Leipzig.* 1772. 8vo. Maps.

An English translation is included in J. Pinkerton's "Voyages," Vol. I.

KERGUÉLEN-TRÉMAREC. Relation de deux Voyages dans les Mers Australes & des Indes, faits en 1771, 1772, 1773 & 1774. Par M. de Kerguélen, Commandant les vaisseaux du Roi le Berrier, la Fortune, etc. Ou extrait du Journal de sa navigation pour la découverte des terres Australes, etc. *Paris: Knapen & Fils.* 1782. 8vo, pp. viii, 244. S. 37618

An account of the discovery of "Kerguelen's Land," in the Southern Hemisphere. It is said that most of the edition was seized and destroyed by the French government on account of its dedication "A la Patrie." Pages, who wrote an account of the same voyage, accompanied Kerguelen.

KERHALLET (C. P. de). Considérations générales sur l'océan Atlantique. Suivies des prescriptions nautiques pour échapper aux ouragans, et d'un mémoire sur les courants de l'océan Atlantique. Par Charles Philippe de Kerhallet. Troisième édition. *Paris.* 1854. 8vo. + Quatrième édition. *Paris: Ledoyen; Bossange et fils.* 1860. 8vo, pp. xvi, 226. 37619

First published in 1851.

KERHALLET. Considérations générales sur l'océan Pacifique, pour faire suite à celles sur l'océan Atlantique et sur l'océan Indien. Par Charles Philippe de Kerhallet. Seconde édition, augmentée. *Paris: Ledoyen.* 1856. 8vo, pp. 236. 3 Maps.

First published in 1852.

KERHALLET. General Examination of the Pacific Ocean, followed by Nautical Directions for avoiding Hurricanes. Translated from the Second French Edition ... . *New York: E. & G. W. Blunt.* 1861. 8vo, pp. xv, 212. 3 Charts. C. + Translated from the Third French Edition by R. H. Wyman. *Washington: Government Printing Office.* 1870. 8vo, pp. xiii, 217. 5 Maps.

KERHALLET. ... Manuel de la Navigation dans la Mer des Antilles et dans le Golfe du Mexique. Par Charles Philippe de Kerhallet. *Paris: Firmin Didot frères.* 1853. 2 vols., 8vo, pp. vi, 595, 3 Maps; vi, 644. (Atlas) Vues des côtes. 1854. 4to. 48 Plates. + Seconde édition, revue et corrigée. *Paris: Firmin Didot.* 1862. 2 vols., 8vo, pp. xxiii, 914. 3 Maps. + Troisième partie, seconde édition, entièrement revue et corrigée. *Paris: Bossange.* 1864. 8vo, pp. xxvii, 502. 5 Maps. 37622

KERL (S.) The Alamo, and other Poems Original and Collected. By Simon Kerl. *New York: The Author.* 1868. 12mo, pp. 359. C. 37623

KERN (R. H.) A Practicable Route for the Pacific Railroad. Letter from Richard H. Kern ... to Hon. W. M. Gwin, ... read in the Senate ... January 18, 1853. [n. p. n. d.] 8vo, pp. 9. B.

KERNEY (M. J.) Catechism of the History of the United States: with a Chronological Table of American History, From its Discovery in 1492, to ... 1850. ... By M. J. Kerney, Esq. ... *Baltimore: John Murphy & Co.* 1850. 16mo. + To ... 1854. ... Third ... Revised Edition. [*Ibid.*] 1856. 16mo, pp. 125. H.

Kernwood. *See* [French (L. V.)], Vol. VII, No. 25877.

KERR (Henry T.) Remarks before the Committee of Ways and Means, on the subject of the Tariff on Silk Manufactures, March 3, 1864. [n. p. n. d.] 8vo, pp. 20. 37626

KERR (H.) A Poetical Description of Texas, and Narrative of Many Interesting Events in that Country, a Period of several years, Interspersed with Moral and Political Impressions; also, an Appeal to those who oppose the Union of Texas with the United States, and the Anticipation of that Event. To which is added, The Texas Heroes, Nos. 1 and 2. By Hugh Kerr. *New York: The Author.* 1838. 12mo, pp. 122. C. 37627

KERR (J.) The Several Trials of the Rev. David Barclay, Before the Presbytery of New-Brunswick, with their Judgment at Oxford. An Appeal to the Synod of New York, and New Jersey: ... and a vote of Censure on Jacob Kerr one of the Complainants. By Jacob Kerr. ... *Elizabeth-Town: The Author.* 1814. 12mo, pp. (2), 404. H. 37628

KERR (L.) Exposition of the Criminal Laws of the Territory of Orleans ... By Lewis Kerr. *New-Orleans.* 1806. 8vo.

KERR (M. C.) Power of Congress to equalize Civil Rights amongst Citizens of the States. Speech of Hon. Michael C. Kerr ... March 8, 1866. *Washington, D. C.* 1866. 8vo, pp. 11.

Also: Speech ... Feb. 18, 1871, on the McGarrahan Claim. [n. p. n. d.] 8vo.

KERR (Orpheus C.), *pseudon.* *See* [Newell (Robert H.)]

KERR (R.) A General History and Collection of Voyages and Travels, arranged in systematic order: forming a Complete History of the Origin and Progress of Navigation, Discovery and Commerce, by Sea and Land, from the Earliest Ages to the Present Time. By Robert Kerr. Illustrated by Maps and Charts. *Edinburgh: William Blackwood.* 1811–1816–MDCCCXXIV. 18 vols., 8vo, pp. xvi, 512; iv, 524; vii, 503; vii, 512; viii, 512; viii, 506; viii, 520; viii, 518; viii, 562; vi, 513; vi, 534; viii, 503; vi, 508; vi, 507; viii, 514; xiii, 503; x, 529; viii, 654. A., C., P. 37631

For Vol. XVIII. *see* Stevenson (W.) The distinguishing feature of this collection is that it is devoted to voyages and travels of discovery, wherein the boundaries of geographical knowledge were enlarged. It consequently contains all the early expeditions to America and the Pacific *in extenso.* The eighteenth volume is a history of the progress of maritime and inland discovery, with a bibliographical catalogue of voyages and travels, by William Stevenson; which is a work of great value, and being published at a later time is frequently wanted.

KERR (T.) A Practical Treatise on the Cultivation of the Sugar Cane, and the Manufacture of Sugar. By Thomas Kerr. *London.* 1851. Post 8vo, pp. 146. B., C. 37632

KERR (W. C.) *See* North Carolina—Geology.

KERR [William Schomberg Robert]. The Confederate Secession. By the Marquess of Lothian. *William Blackwood and Sons, Edinburgh.* MDCCCLXIV. Post 8vo, pp. vi, (2), 226. BA.

KERR. La Question Américaine. Par le Marquis de Lothian. *Paris: Faure.* 1865. 8vo, pp. xi, 398. B., P. 37634

KERSEY (J.) A Narrative of the Early Life, Travels, and Gospel Labours of Jesse Kersey, late of Chester County, Pennsylvania. *Philadelphia.* 1852. 12mo. 37635

KERSEY. A Treatise on Fundamental Doctrines of the Christian Religion: in which are illustrated the Profession ... of the Society of Friends. By Jesse Kersey. *America Printed: London Reprinted.* 1815. 12mo, pp. vii, (4), 107. + *Concord: Daniel Cooledge.* 1818. 12mo, pp. 142, (2). B., H. 37636

Also: Memorial concerning several Ministers and others. ... *New York.* 1816. 8vo.

Een Kersfeest in Californie. Kerstboek voor Kinderen. *Amsterdam: H. de Hoogh en C^o^.* 1871. 8vo, pp. 8. 37637

[Kershaw (Philip G.)] Reflections on Itinerary Parliaments. By Marcullus. *Montreal.* 1856. 12mo, pp. 33. 37638

Kershaw, *S. C.* Memorial of the Citizens of Kershaw District, South Carolina, adverse to the Proposed Tariff on Woollens. March 21, 1828. ... *Washington: Printed by Duff Green.* 1828. 8vo, pp. 10. H. 37639

20th Cong., 1st Sess., No. 153.

Kerst (S. Gottfried). Die Länder am Uruguay. Vortrag gehalten in der Sitzung des Berliner Vereins zur Centralisation deutscher Auswanderung und Colonisation. ... *Berlin.* 1851. 8vo, pp. 16. Map. 37640

Kerst. Die Plata-Staaten und die Wichtigkeit der Provinz Otuquis und des Rio Bermejo seit der Annahme des Princips der freien Schifffahrt auf den Zuflüssen des Rio de la Plata. *Berlin.* 1854. 8vo, pp. (4), 139. Map. C. 37641

J. R. Smith refers to two other tracts by the same author, relating to the Brazils and La Plata, which I have not seen.

Kerversau *et* Leborgne. Rapport fait au Gouvernement, sur les troubles du Sud de St. Domingue, au mois du fructidor an 4; sur les opérations militaires dirigées dans cette partie, et la trâhison du General Rigaud. [*Paris.* 1797.] 8vo, pp. iv, 88.

Ketchum (E. B.) Letters, Affidavits, and other Documents upon which is based the Application for the Pardon of Edward B. Ketchum. *New York.* 1866. 8vo, pp. 72. 37643

Ketchum (H.) Connecticut Aroused! Great Demonstration at New Haven. Speech of Hon. Hiram Ketchum. [n. p. n. d.] 8vo, pp. 15. 37644

Ketchum. A Eulogy on the late Daniel Webster, ... before ... Yale College, January 18, 1853. By Hiram Ketchum, Esq. ... *New Haven: Printed by J. H. Benham.* 1853. 8vo, pp. 40.

Ketchum. General M'Clellan's Peninsula Campaign. Review of the Report of the Committee on the Conduct of the War relative to the Peninsula Campaign. By Hiram Ketchum, ... [n. p.] 1864. 8vo, pp. 72. B. 37646

Also: Oration delivered at New Haven, July 4, 1861. ... *New Haven: T. J. Stafford.* 1861. 8vo, pp. 30.—Speech ... before a Committee of the Senate of the State of New York, in relation to the Public Schools of the City of New York ... . *New*

York. 1841. 8vo, pp. 16. M.—Speech ... at New Haven, 1856, on Fillmore and Fremont. *New York.* [n. d.] 8vo, pp. 15.

Ketchum (S.) A Sermon ... in Wardsboro', Vt., ... Sept. 24, 1865; ... being a Farewell Discourse. By Silas Ketchum, ... *Brattleboro: Printed by D. B. Stedman.* 1866. 24mo, pp. 12.

Ketchum (W.) An Authentic and Comprehensive History of Buffalo, with some Account of its Early Inhabitants, both Savage and Civilized, comprising Historic Notices of the Six Nations or Iroquois Indians, including a Sketch of the Life of Sir William Johnson, and of other Prominent White Men, long Resident among the Senecas. Arranged in Chronological Order. By William Ketchum. ... *Buffalo, N. Y.: Rockwell, Baker & Hill, Printers.* 1864–5. 2 vols., 8vo, pp. xvi, 432; v, (2), 443. 2 Maps. BA., C. 37648

Keteltas (A.) God arising and Pleading his Peo-|ple's Cause; or the American|War in Favor of Liberty, against|the Measures and Arms of Great|Britain, shewn to be the Cause|of God:|In a Sermon ... October 5th, 1777 ... . By Abraham Keteltas, A.M.|*Newbury-Port: Edmund Sawyer.* MDCCLXXVII. 8vo, pp. 32. BA., M. 37649

Keteltas. Reflections on Extortion, Enforced in a Sermon preached at Newbury-Port ... February 15th, 1778, By Abraham Keteltas, A.M. *Newbury-Port: Printed by J. Mycall.* 1778. 8vo, pp. 38. BA., H. 37650

This discourse is remarkable for the revolutionary spirit which it breathes. *See* pages 35 and 36. Also: Charity Sermon, in the French Protestant Church, in New York, December 27, 1773. ... *New York.* 1774. 8vo.—The Religious Soldier; or, The Military Character of King David. Sermon to Officers and Soldiers, Elizabethtown, March 8, 1759. ... *New York.* 1759. 8vo, pp. 18.

Keteltas (William). The Crisis: an Appeal to a Candid World, on the War entered into by the United States ... against Great Britain and her Dependencies; ... By Wm. Keteltas ... . *Poughkeepsie.* 1812. 8vo, pp. 14. BA. 37651

For another edition *see our* Vol. IV., No. 14897.

Kettelas (W.) Political Hipocrites Unmasked and Exposed. ... By William Kettelas, Esq. ... *New-York: Printed for the Good of the People.* 1808. 8vo, pp. 20. BA. 37652

Kettell (G. F.) A Sermon on the Duty of Citizens with respect to the Fugitive Slave Law. By G. F. Kettell. *White Plains.* 1851. 8vo, pp. 20. N. 37653

[Kettell (Samuel).] Quozziana: or Letters from Great Goslington, Mass. giving an Account of the Quoz Dinner ... By Sampson Short-and-Fat. ... *Boston: William White & H. P. Lewis.* 1842. 12mo, pp. 68. H. 37654

A satire on the dinner given in Boston to Charles Dickens.

Kettell. Specimens of American Poetry, with Critical and Biographical Notices. By Samuel Kettell. *Boston: S. G. Goodrich and Co.* MDCCCXXIX. 3 vols., 12mo, pp. xlviii, 353; x, 408; x, 406. B. 37655

This collection embraces specimens of 188 American poets, beginning with Cotton Mather and ending with J. G. Whittier. The third volume contains a Bibliographical and Chronological List of American Poets. *See* Vol. IV., No. 14898.

Kettell (T. P[rentice]). Constitutional Reform: in a Series of Articles ... upon Constitutional Guarantees in political Government; ... added, two Letters of the Hon. M. Hoffman ... Also, the Correspondence of T. Jefferson on Constitutional Reform. Edited by Thomas P. Kettell. *New York.* 1846. 8vo.

With so much that is consti utional on the title this should be a healthy book.

Kettell. History of the Great Rebellion, from its Commencement to its Close, giving an Account of its Origin, the Secession of the Southern States, and the Formation of the Confederate Government, the Concentration of the Military and Financial Resources of the Federal Government, the Development of its Vast Power ... . By Thomas P. Kettell ... . Vol. I. *Worcester: Stebbins.* 1862. 8vo, pp. 407. + *Hartford, Conn.: L. Stebbins.* 1866. 8vo, pp. 778, (4). Plates and Maps. BA.

Kettell. Southern Wealth and Northern Profits, as exhibited in Statistical Facts and Official Figures: showing the Necessity of Union to the Future Prosperity and Welfare of the Republic. By Thomas Prentice Kettell ... . *New York: George W. & John A. Wood.* 1860. 8vo, pp. 173. B., C. 37658

This elicited: "Notes on 'Southern Wealth and Northern Profits.'" *Philadelphia: C. Sherman & Son.* 1861. 8vo, pp. 31.

Keulen (G. van). Curaçao, from the Dutch Originals of Gerard van Keulen. 1775. 37659

Ke-wa-ze-zhig. An Address, delivered in ... Boston, February 26th, 1861, before a Convention ... to ... improve the condition of the Indians in the United States. By Ke-wa-ze-zhig, a Son of the Chief of the Chippeways. With a Report of the

Proceedings of the Convention; and a Poem, by a Friend. *Boston: Published by the Author.* 1861. 12mo, pp. 27. H. 37660

Keweenaw. Report of Survey and Estimates of the Keweenaw and Cliff Railroad and Lac La Belle Harbor Improvement. By J. N. Greene ... . *Boston: Wright & Potter.* 1864. 8vo, pp. 10. H. 37661

Kewen (E. J. C.), *and* Soule (F.) Oration and Poem before the Society of California Pioneers, at their Celebration of the Anniversary of the Admission of ... California into the Union, San Francisco, September 9th, 1854. By E. J. C. Kewen, Esq., and Hon. Frank Soule ... . *San Francisco: O'Meara & Painter, Printers.* 1854. 8vo, pp. 24. BA., C., P. 37662

[Kewley (John).] An Enquiry into the Validity of Methodist Episcopacy, with an Appendix. By an Episcopalian of ... Maryland. *Wilmington.* 1807. 8vo, pp. 68. N. 37663

Kewley. Masonry on Christian Principles. A Discourse ... at the Institution of Warren Lodge, at East Hampton ... 25th Sept. 1811, A.L. 5811. By John Kewley, M.D. [*sic*] ... *Hartford: Peter B. Gleason and Co., Printers.* 1812. 8vo, pp. 15.

Also: A Sermon, preached at the Institution of the Rev. Henry Whitlock. ... *New Haven,* Aug. 29, 1811. ... *New Haven: Printed ... by Walter and Steele.* 1811. 8vo, pp. 20. B.

Key (A. C.) A Narrative of the Recovery of H. M. S. Gorgon (Charles Hotham, Esq. Captain), stranded in the Bay of Monte Video, May 10, 1844. By Astley Cooper Key, Commander, R.N. late Lieut. of H. M. S. Gorgon. *London.* 1847. 8vo, pp. 114. Map, 17 Plates. A., P. 37665

Key (F. S.) Oration, in the Capitol of the United States, on the 4th of July, 1831, By Francis S. Key. *Washington.* 1831. 8vo. C. 37666

Key. Poems of the Late Francis S. Key, Esq., ... With an Introductory Letter, by Chief Justice Taney. *New York: Robert Carter & Brothers.* 1857. 12mo, pp. 203. B., C. 37667

Key. The Star Spangled Banner: Illustrated from Drawings by F. O. C. Darley. *New York: James G. Gregory.* 1863. 4to.

Also: ... An Oration, delivered at Bristol College, July 23, 1834, before the Philologian Society. ... *Bristol.* 1834. 8vo, pp. 19.

Key (*Col.*) The Report of Col. Key relative to the Exchange of Prisoners. [n. p. n. d.] pp. 3. 37669

Key to Canada. *See* Vol. III., No. 10473.

A Key to the Church-Catechism ... . *London: Printed for the Author* ... 1719. 8vo, pp. viii, 314. P. 37670

Prepared for the use of the colonies, and dedicated "To Mr. William Trent, Merchant in Philadelphia," who gave its name to Trenton, N. J.

A Key to the Orders in Council. *London: John Murray.* 1812. 8vo, pp. (2), 19. 37671

The Key. *Frederick Town: John D. Cary.* 1798. 37672

The earliest periodical issued in Maryland. Twenty-seven numbers published. *See* "Hist. Mag.," I. 317.

K[eye] (O[tto]). Het Waere Onderscheyt|tusschen|Koude en Warme|Landen,|aengewesen|In de Nootsakelyckheden die daer vereyscht worden,|Ten I om beyde die Landen te konnen bewoonen.|Ten II Tot de Kulture van die selve Landen. Ende|Ten III In de ongemeene groote voordeelen, dewelcke de warme|Landen, door middel van hare Vruchten, boven de koude|Landen, opbrengen.|Voorgestelt en vergeleken met Nieu-Nederlant,|als synde een koudt Landt en Guajana synde een warm Landt, en|beyde gelegen in America, doch onder een besonder Climaet, en dat|by gelegenheyt van de bevolckinge dewelcke tegenwoordig in bey-|de die gewesten wort gedaen. Op dat, daer door alle Patroonen|mogen onderregt worden in wat Landen sy hare Colonijnien|met de minste onkosten, ende de spoedichste en grootste|profyten konnen leggen:|Als mede op dat alle Luyden dewelcke haer, ofte uyt noot, ofte op hope van|groote winsten te doen met'er woon na alsulcke Nieuwe Landen willen begeven|daer uyt mogen bekennen, in welcke van beyde Landen, het voor haer het ghe-mackelijkste sal syn te leven, en waer inne zy de spoedigste, grootste en verseec-kerste profijten sullen konnen doen. Door O. K.| ... |*In 's Graven-Hage, gedruct voor den Autheur, by Henricus Hondius, in de nieuwe Konst-en-Boeck-druckery, in de Hof-Straet.* [1659.] 4to, pp. (20), 178. 37673

This "True Difference between Cold and Warm Countries" is written in disparagement of New-Netherland and in Praise of Guiana. It was reprinted with the following title:

[Keye.] Beschryvinge van het Heerlijcke ende Gezegende Landt Guajana, waer inne gelegen is de seer voorname Lantstrecke genaemt Serrenamme, die jegenwoordigh beseten wort by den Staet van de Vereenigde Nederlantsche Provintien. Mits-

gaders Aenwysinge vande groote vermaeckelijckheden ... *'s Gravenhage: Henricus Hondius.* [1660.] 4to, pp. (12), 178, (4).

Concerning this rare book *see* Asher's "Essay," No. 10. This second issue is very uncommon. For an appendix to this narration *see* Gerbier, Vol. VII., No. 27125. The following is a German translation:

Keye. Otto Keyens|kurtzer Entwurff|von|Neu-Niederland|Vnd|Guajana|Einander entgegen gesetzt,|Vmb den Vnterscheid zwischen warmen und|kalten Landen herauss zu bringen,|Und zu weisen|Welche von beyden am füglichsten zu bewohnen,|am behendesten an zu bauen und den besten Nutzen|geben mögen.|Denen Patronen, so da Colonien an zu legen|gesonnen, als auch denen Personen und Familien, die|ihr Vaterland zu vergessen sich bey dergleichen Bevölckerung|nach fremden Küsten und Reichen gebrauchen|lassen wollen.|Auss dem Holländischen ins Hochteutsche|versetzt|durch|T. R. C. S. C. S.|*Leipzig|Im Ritzschischen Buchladen.*|M. DC. LXXII.| 4to, pp. (20), 144, (7). C., S. 37675

A volume of much rarity and va.ue.

Keyes (B. F.) Historical ... and Genealogical Register of ... West Boylston, Massachusetts, from its Early Settlement to 1858; ... By Benjamin F. Keyes. *Worcester.* 1861. 12mo, pp. (2), 4, (2), 84. B. 37676

[Keyes (Edward L.)] ... Free Soil, Free Democracy, Free Ideas. Sketches with a Free Pen. [n. p. 1845.] 8vo, pp. 11.

[Keyes.] Report and Resolutions ... upon the Subject of the Mexican War and Slavery. [*Boston.* 1847.] 8vo, pp. 35.

Mass. House of Reps., No. 187.

Keyes (E. W.) Argument in the Matter of the Arbitration between the United States and the Green Bay and Mississippi Canal Company, held at Madison, Wis. By Elisha W. Keyes. [n. p. n. d.] 12mo. 37679

Keyes. (E. W.) A History of Savings Banks in the State of New York from 1819 to 1869. To accompany the Annual Report of the Superintendent relative to Savings Banks. By Emerson W. Keyes. *Albany: Argus Company, Printers.* 1870. 8vo, pp. 334. 37680

Keyes. State of New York. Special Report on Savings Banks, made by Emerson W. Keyes, Deputy Superintendent of the Bank Department ... . *Albany: Van Benthuysen & Sons.* 1868. 8vo, pp. 173, 412. BA. 37681

Also: Address before the Cortland County, N. Y., Teachers' Institute, Oct. 25, 1858. ... *Homer.* 1859. 8vo.—The Educational System of the State of New-York. An Address at Lockport, Aug. 5, 1858. ... *Albany.* 1858. 8vo.—Opinion of the Attorney General of the U. S. on the Conversion of National Banks to State Banks, with a Review of the same ... *Albany.* 1870. 8vo, pp. 21.—Review of the Opinion of the Attorney General of the U. S., concerning the Dissolution of National Banks, and their Reorganization under the Laws of this State. ... *Albany.* [1870.] 8vo. S.

Keyes (F. J.) A Life-Poem, and other Poems. By Frederick J. Keyes. *Boston: Phillips, Sampson & Co.* 1855. 12mo, pp. 118, (2). B. 37682

Contains "Mount Auburn" and "My Native Land."

Keyes (J. S.) Letter of John S. Keyes to ... John G. Palfrey, with Mr. Palfrey's reply ... also The Letter of Hon. Benjamin Thompson ... . [n. p. 1848.] 8vo, pp. 4. H. 37683

Keyes (W.) History of Quincy, Ill., and Lecture delivered before the New England Society, December 22, 1862. "Early Reminiscences of Quincy." By William Keyes. [n. p. n. d.] 8vo, pp. 105. 37684

Keymersant (Mich.) Guineische und westindische Reisebeschreibung de Anno 1639–45, zum neuen übersehen und zum andermal aufgelegt. 8vo. 37685

An uncertain title, from an American auctioneer's catalogue.

Keymis (L.) A Relation of the|second Voyage to|Guiana.| Performed and written in the yeare 1596. By Lawrence Keymis, Gent.|*Imprinted at London by Thomas Dawson,|dwelling at the three Cranes in the Vinetree,|and are there to be solde.*|1596. Sm. 4to, Title; Dedication to Sir W. Raleigh, pp. 3; to the reader, pp. 4; Poems, pp. 7; Text, 24 l. C., H. 37686

An extremely rare and interesting volume. The voyage was made by direction of Sir Walter Raleigh. It is included in the collection of Hakluyt. *See* Rich, No. 900.

Keymis. Waerachtighe ende grondighe beschryvinge van|het groot en Goudt-rijck Coninckrijck van Guiana, gheleghen zijnde in America, by noorden de|groote Riviere Orelliana, vanden vijfden graed by zuyden, totten vijfden graed by noorden de Middellinie, in welcke be-|schryvinghe de rechte gheleghentheyt vande groote ende rijcke Hoofdstadt Manoa, Macureguarai, ende andere steden des selvighen Coninck-|rijcks, ende van het groot Souten Meyr Parime, (zijnde ontrent 200. spaensche mylen lanck) verclaert wordt: Insghelijcks|wat voor rijcke Waren daer te lande eñ daer ontrent vallen; als namelick groote overvloet van Gout, costelick|ghesteente, ghenaemt Piedras Hijadas, Peerlen,

Balsem-olie, lanck Peper, Gineber, Suijcker,|Wieroock, verscheyden Medicinale wortelen, Droogheryen, ende Gummen.| Item Zyde, Cottoen ende Brasilie houdt.|Midtsgaders de beschryvinge vande omliggende rijcke Landtschappen Emeria, Arromaia, Amapaia eñ Topago; in welck laetste de Krijghs-vrouwen|(Amazones genoẽt) woonen: mette.beschryvinge van 53. groote Rivieren, onder welcke Oronoque de voornaemste is, welcke spruijt ontrent 500 duytsche mylen te lande-|waert in, niet verre van Quito, een vermaerde hoofstadt in Peru. Alles met groote neerstigheyt ontdeckt eñ beschreven in den jaere 1595. eñ 1596.| Door den E. Heere Walter Ralegh, Ridder eñ Capiteijn over de Guarde van de Majesteyt van Enghelandt,|ende den vermaerden Zeevaerder Capiteyn Laurens Keymis.|*t'Amstelredam by Cornelis Claesz. opt Water, int Schrijf-boeck, A^o^.* M. D. XCVIII. Oblong 4to, pp. (60). 37687

Reproduced with a new title as below:

Keymis. Waerachtighe ende grondighe beschryvinghe|vande tweede Zeevaert der Engelschen nae Guiana, eñ de omliggende Landtschappen:|Waer inne seer bescheydelick beschreven worden alle de Zee-custen met de Eylanden, Hoofden, Voorghe-|berghten, Inwijcken, Havenen, Reeden, Diepten, Ondiepten, Clippen, verscheyde Opdoeningen van Lan-|den, de ghestaltenisse van winden, streomen ende tyden des jaers. Met verclaringe vande rechte ghelegent-|heyt van 53. Rivieren, die aldaer in de Zee vloeyen, met benaminghe der steden daer op ghebouwet, van wat|volcken die worden bewoont, wat voor zeden die selvighe hebben; hoedanighe Cassiken ofte Vorsten daer te|lande regieren, ende hoe menigherley costelijcke waren aldaer vallen.|Alles met groote neerstigheyt ontdeckt, ende beschreven inden jaere 1596. Door den cloeck-|moedighen ende vermaerden Zee-vaerder Capiteijn Laurentium Keymis.|*t'Amstelredam, by Cornelis Claesz. opt Water, int Schrif-boeck. A^o^.* 1598.| Oblong 4to, pp. (viii), Text, (94). 37688

Keymis. Warachtighe ende grondighe beschryvinghe van| het ... Coningrijck van Guiana ... .|*t'Amstelredam, by Cornelis Claesz, opt Water, int Schrijf-boeck. Anno* 1605. Oblong 4to. pp. (viii), Text, (94). 37689

Keymis. Warachtighe ende grondige beschryvinghe van|het ... Coningrijck van Guiana ... . *Tot Amsterdam, By Michiel Colijn, Boeck-vercooper op t' Water, aende oude Brugge int Huys-boeck,* 1617.| Oblong 4to, 50 l. 37690

The edition of 1605 is the same as that of 1598: that of 1617 only differs slightly.

KEYMIS. Grondige ende waerachtige beschrijvinge van | het ... Koninckrijck van Guiana ... daer omtrent vallen. | Mitsgaders | Vande omlegghende rijcke Landtschappen ... . *Gedruckt in 't Jaer onses Heeren* 1644. | Oblong 4to, pp. (2), (96). 37691

This last issue forms part of Commelin's "Collection." For other editions *see* Raleigh (W.) A Latin version was made by Gotthardt Arthus: "Itinerarium Indicum." *Francofurti.* 1599. Folio. *See also* Wood's "Athenæ Oxonienses," edited by Bliss, II. 230.

KEYMOLEN (L.) Manifeste faisant suite sur le procés dit de Calinas. *Mexico.* 1855. 8vo, pp. 72. 37692

Key-Notes of American Liberty; comprising the most important Speeches, Proclamations, and Acts of Congress, from the Foundation of the Government to the Present Time. With a History of the Flag, by a distinguished Historian. *New York: E. B. Treat & Co.* 1866. 12mo, pp. 273. 2 Plates. + [*Ibid.*] 1867. 12mo, pp. 673. C. 37693

KEYNTON (J.) A Discourse upon The Life and Character of Stephen A. Douglas, delivered ... June 13th, 1861, By John Keynton, Esq. *New York: John J. Bloomfield.* 1861. 8vo, pp. 24. 37694

[KEYSER (Charles S.)] Fairmount Park. Sketches of its Scenery, Waters, and History. *Philadelphia: Claxton, Remsen & Haffelfinger.* 1871. 12mo, pp. 144. Plate. 37695

The author's name appeared in the fifth edition, or sooner.

[KEYSER.] Lemon Hill, in its Connection with the Efforts of our Citizens ... to obtain a Public Park. ... *Philadelphia: Crissy & Markley, Printers.* 1856. 8vo, pp. 28. H. 37696

KEYSER (R.) The Religion of the Northmen; by Rudolph Keyser ... Translated by Barclay Pennock. *New York: Charles B. Norton.* 1854. 12mo, pp. 346, (1). B. 37697

The third chapter is "The Discovery of America by the Northmen."

Keystone Agricultural Almanac, for 1840; ... *Philadelphia: William W. Walker.* [1840.] Sm. 4to, pp. 34. H. 37698

Memorial of the Keystone Publishing and Manufacturing Company, of Philadelphia, to the Senate ... of the United States. [*Philadelphia.* 1870.] 8vo, pp. 7. H. 37699

KIDD (A.) The Huron Chief, and other Poems. By Adam Kidd. *Montreal.* 1830. 8vo, pp. 216. C. 37700

KIDD (W.) The Arraignment, Tryal and Condemnation of Capt. William Kidd, for Murther and Piracy upon six several indictments at the ... Old Bailey, ... May 1701. ... To which are added Capt. Kidd's two Commissions; one under the Great Seal of England, the other under the Great Seal of the Admiralty. *London: J. Nutt.* 1701. Folio, pp. 60. J.C.B. 37701

KIDD. The Arraignment, Tryal and Condemnation of Captain William Kidd, for Murther and Piracy upon six several indictments, at the Admiralty-Sessions, at the Old-Bailey. ... May, 1701. *London: Jonathan Robinson.* 1703. Sm. 8vo, pp. (27). 37702

Extracted from "An Exact Abridgement of all the Tryals ... relating to High Treasons, Piracies," etc.

KIDD. A Full | Account | of the | Proceedings | In Relation to | Capt. Kidd. | In two Letters. | Written by a Person of Quality to a | Kinsman of the Earl of Bellomont | in Ireland. | *London,* | *Printed and Sold by the Booksellers of London and* | *Westminster.* MDCCI. | Sm. 4to, pp. (8), 51. B., BA. + The Second Edition. [*Ibid.*] 1701. 8vo, pp. 40, (1). 37703

The following is probably a reprint:

KIDD. A Full Account of the Actions of the Late Famous Pyrate, Capt. Kidd. With the Proceedings against Him, and a Vindication of the Right Honourable Richard Earl of Bellomont, Lord Coloony, late Governor of New-England, and other Honourable Persons, from the Unjust Reflections cast upon them. By a Person of Quality. *Dublin: Re-printed for Mathew Gunn.* 1701. 4to, pp. 42. 37704

Reprinted in W. W. Campbell's "Robin Hood and Captain Kidd," *New York*, 1853, where Mr. Campbell shows good cause to suppose Kidd's prosecution was but a step in that of Lord Somers, and that he was far from being the wretch popular opinion supposes him to have been. Mr. Campbell intimates a notion that this work was by Lord Somers or Lord Halifax; but this is very improbable.

KIDD. The Proceedings of the Kings Commission of the Peace ... held for the Tryal of Captain William Kidd and Nine of his Men ... May 1701. [n. p. n. d.] Folio, pp. 4. 37705

Also: Account of some of the Traditions and Experiments respecting Captain Kidd's Piratical Vessel. *New York.* 1844. 8vo.

Captain Kidd was employed by the Earl of Bellmont—who was suspected, in popular opinion, to be implicated with Captain Kidd—to act against the pirates who infested the North American coast in 1696, but turned pirate himself. He was afterwards taken at Boston, sent to England, tried, and hung with several others. "No unimportant man has caused more fear, speculation, and gold-digging, than Captain Kidd."—C. W. ELLIOTT'S *New-England History.* There are many traditional stories of Kidd extant in New England, and a ballad, containing his last words and dying speech, commencing

"My name was Captain Kidd,
As I sail'd," etc.

was to be had of the peddlers in New England not many years ago. *See our* Vol. IV., No. 16654, Cooper's "Naval History," p. 58, *and* Watson's "Annals," II. 212.

KIDDER (D. P.) Mormonism and the Mormons. A Historical View of the Rise and Progress of the Sect, Self-styled Latter-Day-Saints. By Daniel P. Kidder. *New-York: G. Lane & P. P. Sandford.* 1842. 18mo, pp. 342. C. + [*Ibid.*] 1845. + *New-York: Lane & Scott.* 1852. 18mo, pp. 342. B. 37706

KIDDER. Recollections of William Theophilus, a Pilgrim of Fourscore. Edited by D. P. Kidder. *New-York: Lane & Scott.* 1852. 18mo, pp. 152. C. 37707

KIDDER. Sketches of Residence and Travels in Brazil, Embracing Historical and Geographical Notices of the Empire and its several Provinces. By Daniel P. Kidder. ... *Philadelphia: Sorin & Ball.* 1845. 2 vols., 12mo, pp. (3), viii, 369; 404. 10 Plates, Map. 37708

Allibone says it "is embodied in one of the Blue Books of Parliament." Also: ... A Discourse in Memory of Melvin A. Pingree. Delivered ... September 9th, 1866. *Chicago: Charles Philbrick, Printer.* 1866. 8vo, pp. 24. B.

KIDDER *and* FLETCHER (J. C.) Brazil and the Brazilians, portrayed in Historical and Descriptive Sketches. By Rev. D. P. Kidder, D.D., and Rev. J. C. Fletcher. Illustrated by One Hundred and Fifty Engravings. *Philadelphia: Childs & Peterson.* 1857. 8vo, pp. 630. Map. BA. 37709

The sixth edition appeared under the name of Fletcher (J. C.), *and* Kidder (D. P.), *see our* Vol. VI., No. 24723. *See also* "N. A. Rev.," LXXXV. 533.

KIDDER (F.) The Abenaki Indians; their Treaties of 1713 & 1717, and a Vocabulary: with a Historical Introduction By Frederic Kidder of Boston. *Boston: Printed by Brown Thurston.* 1859. 8vo, pp. 25 [*i. e.* 35]. B. 37710

Also forms part of Vol. VI. of the "Maine Hist. Soc. Coll."

KIDDER. The Expeditions of Capt. John Lovewell, and His Encounters with the Indians; including a Particular Account of the Pequauket Battle, with a History of that Tribe; and a Reprint of Rev. Thomas Symmes's Sermon. By Frederic Kidder. *Boston: Bartlett and Halliday.* 1865. 4to, pp. 138, (1). Map.

Two hundred copies printed; twenty-five on large, and ten on drawing paper. *See* Symmes (T.)

KIDDER. History of the Boston Massacre, March 5, 1770 ... containing Unpublished Documents of John Adams ... By Frederic Kidder. *Albany, N. Y.: Joel Munsell.* 1870. 8vo, pp. (4), 291. Map and Plate. H. 37712

Contains reprints of the official narrative of the trial of the British soldiers, and some memoranda by John Adams.

KIDDER. History of the First New Hampshire Regiment in the War of the Revolution. By Frederic Kidder. *Albany: Joel Munsell.* 1868. 8vo, pp. vi, (2), 184. B. 37713

The first history of a revolutionary regiment that has been written.

[KIDDER.] History of New Ipswich. *See* [Gould (A. A.)]

[KIDDER.] The Kidder Family in England and America. [*Boston.* 1852.] 8vo, pp. 21. 37714

KIDDER. Military Operations in Eastern Maine and Nova Scotia during the Revolution, chiefly compiled from the Journals and Letters of Colonel John Allan, with Notes and a Memoir of Col. John Allan. By Frederic Kidder. *Albany: Joel Munsell.* 1867. Rl. 8vo, pp. x, (2), 5–336. Map. BA. 37715

Chiefly relates to a seven years' residence among the Micmacs, Maracheets, Passamaquody, and Penobscot Indians.

KIDDER. The Swedes on the Delaware and their Intercourse with New England. By Frederic Kidder. *Boston: David Clapp & Son, Printers.* 1874. Rl. 8vo, pp. 13. Facsimiles. 37716

KIDDER *and* UNDERWOOD (A. B.) Report on the Sudbury Fight. April 1676. [*Boston.* 1866.] 8vo, pp. 12. 37717

Showing that the date on the Sudbury Monument is false.

KIDERLEN (William L. J.) Geschichte der Vereinigten Staaten von Nord-Amerika, vom Jahre 1497–1837. Aus dem Englischen übersetzt und herausgegeben. *Philadelphia: Kiderlen & Stollmeyer.* 1838. 12mo, pp. viii, 447. C. 37718

The Kidnapped Clergyman; or Experience the Best Teacher. *Boston: Dow and Jackson.* 1839. 12mo, pp. 123. + *Boston: G. N. Thomson.* 1840. 12mo. 37719

The Kid-napper Trapan'd; or, the Treacherous Husband Caught in his Own Trap, being a Pleasant Relation of a Man that would have sold his Wife to Virginia, how he Bargain'd with the Master of a Ship, who finding that She was His Wife, released Her, and carried off the Husband. *London.* 1675. 4to.

KIDNEY (J. S.) Catawba River, and other Poems. By John Steinfort Kidney. *New York: Baker and Scribner.* 1847. 12mo, pp. (8), 119. B., C. 37721

KIDNEY. The Conflicts of the Age, a Poem delivered before the House of Convocation of Trinity College. By John Steinfort Kidney. *Hartford.* 1856. 8vo. 37722

KIEHL (E. J.) Ons verdrag met Amerika. Tractaat van vriendschap en commercie tusschen de Staten-Generaal der Vereenigden Nederlanden en de Vereenigden Staten van Amerika, dd. 8 Oct. 1782. *'s Hage.* 1864. 8vo. 37723

"Treaty of friendship and commerce between the United Netherlands and the United States."

KIERSTED (C. C.) Opinion of the Supreme Court in the Case of C. C. Kiersted *vs.* the People of the State, the Rector, &c. of Trinity Church and others: April 9. *New-York.* 1855. 8vo, pp. 32. 37724

KIERZKOWSKI (A.) The Question of the Seignorial Tenure of Canada, reduced to a Question of Landed Credit. By A. Kierzkowski. *Montreal.* 1852. 8vo. S. 37725

KIESEWETTER (*Dr.* Fr.) *See* Kane (E. K.), No. 36999.

KIESSELBACH (Wilhelm). Der amerikanische Federalist. Politische Studien für die deutsche Gegenwart. ... *Bremen: Kühtmann & Co.* 1864. Rl. 8vo, pp. xii, 896. + [*Ibid.*] 1868.

KIEWITCH (T. J.) Theodor jan Kiewitch de Miriewo, Sravnitel niy Slovar ... *St. Petersburg.* 1790–1791. 4 vols., 4to.

This is a comparative vocabulary of all the languages and dialects in Russian. "Pallas having published, in 1786 and 1789, the first part of the "Vocabularium Catharinæum" (a comparative vocabulary of 286 words in the languages of Europe and Asia), the material contained therein was published in the above edition in another form, and words of American languages added. The book did not come up to the expectations of the Government, and was therefore not published, so that but few copies can be found." —LUDEWIG.

KILBOURN (B.) Review of the Report of the Court convened for the Trial of Levi Hubbell. By Byron Kilbourn. *Milwaukee.* 1858. 8vo. 37728

See also Vol. VII., No. 33461.

KILBOURN (H.) Have the People of the District of Columbia any rights that Congress is bound to respect? Speech of Hallet Kilbourn ... . *Washington City: M'Gill & Witherow, Printers.* 1870. 8vo, pp. 16. H. 37729

KILBOURN (J.) The Ohio Gazetteer: or Topographical Dictionary, containing a Description of the Several Counties, Towns, Villages, Settlements, ... in the State of Ohio; alphabetically arranged. By John Kilbourn ... . *Columbus: P. H. Olmsted & Co.* 1816. 18mo, pp. 166. C. + Second Edition, Improved. *Columbus: J. Kilbourn.* 1816. 8vo, pp. 114. + Third Edition, Improved. *Columbus and Baltimore.* 1817. 12mo, pp. 180. 2 Plans. + *Albany: Joshua Fisk.* 1817. 16mo, pp. 180. + Fifth Edition. *Columbus: J. Kilbourn.* 1818. 12mo, pp. 144. + Sixth Edition. [*Ibid.*] 1819. 12mo, pp. 176. + Seventh Edition, Carefully Revised and Corrected. [*Ibid.*] 1821. 12mo, pp. 204. 2 Maps. + Eighth Edition ... . [*Ibid.*] 1826. 12mo, pp. 231. + Ninth Edition ... . [*Ibid.*] 1829. 12mo, pp. 280. Map. + Tenth Edition. [*Ibid.*] 1831. 16mo, pp. 336. Map. + Eleventh Edition. Revised and Enlarged by a Citizen of Columbus. *Columbus: Scott & Wright.* 1833. 18mo, pp. xlviii, 65–512. Map. + Revised Edition. By W. Jenkins. *Columbus.* 1839. 12mo. 37730

For other editions *see* Jenkins (W.), No. 36021.

KILBOURN. Public Documents concerning the Ohio Canals, which are to connect Lake Erie with the Ohio River, comprising a Complete Official History of these Great Works of Internal Improvement from their Commencement to 1832. Compiled by J. Kilbourn. *Columbus: I. N. Whiting.* 1832–33. 8vo, pp. 452, 28, 55. 37731

KILBOURN. Proceedings of the Kilbourn Historical and Genealogical Society. [n. p.] 1854. 8vo, pp. 16. 37732

Relates to the Kilbourn family only.

KILBOURNE (P. K.) A Biographical History of the County of Litchfield, Connecticut; comprising Biographical Sketches of distinguished Natives and Residents of the County; together with complete lists of the Judges, ... Sheriffs, Senators, ... from the Organization of the County to the Present Time. By Payne Kenyon Kilbourne. *New York: Clark, Austin & Co.* MDCCCLI. 12mo, pp. 413. 4 Plates. H. 37733

KILBOURNE. The Family Memorial. A History and Genealogy of the Kilbourn Family, in the United States and Canada, from ... 1635 to the Present Time. Including Extracts from Ancient Records, Copies of Old Wills, Biographical Sketches, Epitaphs, Anecdotes ... . By Payne Kenyon Kilbourne ... . *Hartford: Brown & Parsons.* 1845. 12mo, pp. 150, (2). 37734

KILBOURNE. The History and Antiquities of the Name and Family of Kilbourn ... . By Payne Kenyon Kilbourne, A.M. ... *New Haven: Durrie & Peck.* MDCCCLVI. 8vo, pp. 444, (8), pp. 33–72 repeated. Plates, 2 Portraits. B. 37735

KILBOURNE. Sketches and Chronicles of the Town of Litchfield, Connecticut, Historical Biographical and Statistical; together with a complete official register of the town. By Payne Kenyon Kilbourne, M.A. *Hartford: Press of Case, Lockwood and Company.* 1859. 8vo, pp. vii, 17–264. Map, 11 Plates. S.

Also: The Skeptic and other Poems. ... *Hartford.* 1843. 12mo.

KILBURN (J.) ... A Sermon ... at the Interment of Mrs. Priscilla Elvira Bascom ... 8th of April 1801; By Joseph Kilburn, A.M. ... *Northampton (Massachusetts): Printed by William Butler.* 1810. 8vo, pp. 21–47. B. 37737

KILBY BANK. [Mass.] Senate, No. 34. Report relating to Kilby Bank. [n. p. 1838.] 8vo, pp. 17. B. 37738

Also: [Mass.] Senate, No. 58. Report of the Committee on the Kilby Bank. [n.p. 1837.] 8vo, pp. 8.

KILGORE (D. Y.) The Dangers which Threaten the Republic. Oration, ... July 4, 1869, in ... Philadelphia. By Damon Y. Kilgore ... . *Philadelphia: Blood Brothers.* 1869. 8vo, pp. 36. H. 37739

KILGORE. The Questions of To-day ... . An Oration ... at Wilbraham, Mass., June 29, 1870. By Damon Y. Kilgore ... . *New York: Hurd and Houghton.* 1870. 8vo, pp. 35. H. 37740

Also: Closing Argument in Case of the Commonwealth of Pennsylvania, *vs.* Rev. S. M. Landis. ... *Philadelphia.* 1870. 8vo.

KILHAM (A.) An Affectionate Address to the Members of the Methodist Societies, in which some notice is taken of the False Accusations of Alexander Kilham. [n. p. n. d.] 8vo, pp. 19. N. 37741

Killdare, The Black Scout. *New York: T. R. Dawley.* 1865. 18mo, pp. 106. 37742

KILPATRICK [Judson]. Great Speech of Maj.-Gen. Kilpatrick, at Salem ... Oct. 27, 1868, in Opposition to the Re-Election of Gen. Butler to Congress. [n. p. n. d.] 8vo, pp. 24.

KILPATRICK. Kilpatrick and our Cavalry, with a Sketch of the Life of Gen. Kilpatrick. *New York.* 1865. Cr. 8vo. Portraits. 37744

KILTY (J.) The Land-Holders' Assistant, and Land-Office Guide; being an Exposition of Original Titles, as derived from the Proprietary Government, and more recently from the State, of Maryland: ... Containing A brief Historical account of the grant and settlement of the province of Maryland; ... By John Kilty ... . *Baltimore: Printed by G. Dobbin and Murphy.* 1808. 8vo, pp. 497, Appendix, xliv, Index, vi, (1). H., N. 37745

KILTY (W.) *See* Maryland—Laws.

KIMAYER (Thomas). Neu Eröffnetes Raritäten-Cabinet Ost-West-Indianischer und ausländischer Sachen. Darinnen allerhand rare Denk und Seltsahme Merckwürdigkeiten so sich in China, Japan, Choromandel, Peru, Guiana, &c. Tartarien und andern Ländern finden. Darinnen auch nicht weniger die Heyraths Ceremonien, Leichen Begängnissen, Fischen und Jägereyen, auch andere Sitten und Gewohnheiten etlicher dieser Heydnischen Länder und Völcker enthalten. *Hamburg verlegts Christian Liebezeit.* 1705. 12mo, pp. (16), 256. 37746

This description of "Rare Things in the East and West Indies" is quite scarce.

KIMBALL (C. O.) An Address ... Feb. 7, 1830, ... the Second Anniversary of the Society for the Promotion of Temperance in Haverhill ... . By Charles Otis Kimball. ... *Haverhill: Printed by A. W. Thayer.* 1830. 12mo, pp. 20. BA.

Also: Masonic Address at Lowell, Aug. 31, 1826. ... *Boston.* 1827. 8vo. W.

KIMBALL (D.) An Address ... before the Needham Temperance Society ... July 5, 1830. By Daniel Kimball ... . *Dedham: H. & W. H. Mann, Printers.* 1830. 8vo, pp. 16. H.

KIMBALL. An Address ... before the Massachusetts Temperance Union ... May 26, 1846. By Daniel Kimball ... *Boston.* 1846. 8vo, pp. 28. B., W. 37749

KIMBALL (D. T[enney]). The Fruits of Congregationalism. A Centennial Discourse, ... before The First Church ... in Ipswich, August 10, 1834. By David T. Kimball. ... *Boston: Printed by Leonard W. Kimball.* 1834. 8vo, pp. 32. B. 37750

KIMBALL. The Pastor's Jubilee. A Discourse delivered in Ipswich, October 8, 1856, By David Tenney Kimball, ... on the Fiftieth Anniversary of his Ordination. With an Appendix. ... *Boston: Press of John B. Chisholm.* 1857. 8vo, pp. 96. Portrait.

KIMBALL. A Sketch of the Ecclesiastical History of Ipswich. The Substance of a Discourse, in two parts, ... December 1820. By David T. Kimball ... . *Haverhill, Mass.: Gazette ... Office.* 1823. 8vo, pp. 44. BA. 37752

Also: ... A Discourse ... December 31, 1858, at the Funeral of the Rev. Isaac Braman ... . *Boston.* 1859. 8vo, pp. 24. — ... The First Sermon preached in the New Meeting-House of the First Parish, in Ipswich, ... February 4, 1847. ... *Boston: Daniel Kimball, Printer.* 1847. 8vo, pp. 26. B. — The Last Sermon preached in the Ancient Meeting House of the First Parish in Ipswich, February 22, 1846. ... *Boston: Daniel Kimball, Printer.* 1846. 8vo, pp. 32. — A Sermon, ... at Needham, December 12, 1821, at the Installation of the Rev. William Ritchie ... . *Dedham: Printed by H. & W. H. Mann.* 1822. 8vo, pp. 38. — Sermon on the Utility of a Permanent Ministry. ... *Ipswich.* 1839. 8vo, pp. 24.

[KIMBALL (Edmund).] Reflections upon The Law of Libel, ... By a Citizen. *Boston: Wells and Lilly.* 1823. 8vo, pp. 55.

KIMBALL (G. F.) A Sketch of the Kimball Gathering, at G. F. Kimball's, in Norway Village, November 25, 1852. ... *New Haven.* 1859. 24mo, pp. 21. H. 37754

KIMBALL (H.) ... A Sermon preached in ... Sandwich, November 21, 1861. By Rev. Henry Kimball. *Boston: Printed by Geo. C. Rand & Avery.* 1861. 8vo, pp. 16. B. 37755

KIMBALL (Horace). *See our* Vol. I., No. 1165.

KIMBALL (J.), *Jun.* The Essex Harmony ... By Jacob Kimball, Jun. *Exeter: T. C. Cushing and B. B. Macaulay.* 1800. 4to, pp. 111, (1). H. 37756

Also: The Rural Harmony. ... *Printed ... at Boston, by Isaiah Thomas and Ebenezer T. Andrews.* 1793. 4to, pp. 111, (1). H.

KIMBALL (J. B.) An Oration, delivered before the Municipal Authorities of the City of Providence ... July 4, 1856. By Jerome Bonaparte Kimball, and a Poem ... by William M. Rodman. *Providence: Knowles, Anthony & Co., City Printers.* 1856. 8vo, pp. 52. H. 37757

KIMBALL (John F.) & Co. Eastern, Western, and Southern Business Directory; ... Second Annual Issue. *New York: J. F. Kimball & Co.* 1846. 8vo, pp. vii, 604. C. 37758

KIMBALL. Kimball's Ohio, Kentucky, and Indiana State Register. Containing the Names of County Officers, Merchants ... . With Statistical Information in regard to Works of Internal Improvement ... . *New York: J. F. Kimball & Co.* 1846. 8vo, pp. 194. C. 37759

KIMBALL & DODGE. The Farmer's Guide. A Description of the Business of Nashua and Nashville. By Kimball & Dodge. *Nashua: Printed by the Publisher.* 1851. 12mo, pp. 64. H.

KIMBALL & JAMES. Kimball & James' Business Directory, for the Mississippi Valley: 1844. ... With a brief Notice of the Discovery and Occupation of the Mississippi Valley, and a Historical and Statistical Sketch of the principal Cities ... . *Cincinnati: Printed by Kendall & Barnard.* 1844. 8vo, pp. viii, 546. 2 Plates. C. 37761

KIMBALL *and* KNOX. Report on the Dismal Swamp Canal, ... a History of its Construction, Cost ... . By John Kimball and Jno. Jay Knox. *Washington.* 1867. 8vo, pp. 17. H. 37762

KIMBALL (J.) Thanksgiving Sermon. By Rev. Joseph Kimball. *New York.* 1864. 8vo. 37763

KIMBALL (M. G.) Discourse at Free Masons' Hall, St. Louis, March 21, 1869. By M. G. Kimball. *St. Louis.* 1869. 12mo.

KIMBALL (M[oses]). A Discourse Commemorative of Major Charles Jarvis, of the Ninth Vermont Volunteers. ... Delivered at his Funeral ... at Weathersfield Bow, Vt., December 13, 1863. By Rev. M. Kimball. *New York: Edward O. Jenkins, Printer.* 1864. 8vo, pp. 24. B. 37765

[KIMBALL (Richard Burleigh).] Cuba, and the Cubans; Comprising a History of the Island of Cuba, its Present Social, Political, and Domestic Condition; also, its Relation to England and the United States. By the Author of "Letters from Cuba." With an Appendix, containing Important Statistics, and a Reply to Senor Saco on Annexation, translated from the Spanish. *New York: Samuel Hueston.* 1850. 12mo, pp. iv, 7–255. Map. B.

KIMBALL. In the Tropics. *See* No. 34420.

KIMBALL. The Prince of Kashna; A West Indian Story. ... With an Editorial Introduction by Richard B. Kimball. *New York: Carleton.* MDCCCLXVI. 12mo, pp. xii, 7–450. 37767

Also: Saint Leger, or The Threads of Life. ... Third Edition. *New York: G. P. Putnam.* 1850. 12mo, pp. 384. + Seventh Edition. [*Ibid.*] 1853. 12mo. + *Leipsig: Bernard Tauchnitz.* 1853. 12mo, pp. vi, 408. B. — To-Day. A Romance. ... *New York: Carleton.* M.DCCC.LXX. 12mo, pp. 480. — Under-Currents of Wall-Street. A Romance of Business. ... *New York: G. P. Putnam.* 1862. 12mo, pp. 428. BA. His "Letters from Cuba," which appeared in Vols. XXIV., XXV., and XXVI. of "The Knickerbocker" (*New York.* 1844-45), were probably never published in a separate volume.

KIMBALL (S. C.) Poems. By Sullivan C. Kimball. *Albany.* 1858. 16mo. C. 37768

KIMBALL (T. J.) Emancipation in India. Published by the Anti-Slavery Society. 12mo. 37769

This incomplete title is from Allibone's "Dictionary."

KIMBALL UNION ACADEMY, *Meriden Village, N. H.* A Catalogue ... for the Year ending May 11, 1831. [*Windsor, Vt.: Simeon Ide, Printer.* 1831.] 12mo, pp. 12. Continued. H.

[KIMBER (S.), *Jun.*] A New "Sartor Resartus": being a Critical Analysis of a Pamphlet entitled "A Review of Mr. Seward's Diplomacy." By Dr. Syntax, Jr. [n. p.] 1862. 8vo, pp. 23. 37771

[KIMYSER (Arnold).] Ontdekking van 't Geheel ... Deel des Aardkloots America, Spaansche, Engelsche, Fransche, Hollandsche, Deensche Bezittingen, en Factorie der Hamburgers te St. Thomas; Ligging, Voorthrenging, Comercie des Vaste Lands, met Eilanden, Caribbee, Leewaardsche, of Antilles, naar en van Europa, Africa en Asia Generaal, &c. In 't Byzonder de Staten van de dertien Provincien thans benoemd Vereenigde Onafhanglyke Staten van America, eerste Ontdekkers, Situatie, Charteren, ... Splitzing, Bouwen, ... Producten, Negotie, Regtspleging van 't Admiraliteits-Hof in Boston, ... opgebragt in Salem, en Articulen van Associatie in Virginie 1777, met onze Colonien 1778, ... *Dordrecht: Johannis de Bruin.* 1782. 8vo, pp. (16), 198, (18).

This is a description of America, especially the United States.

KINDELAN (S.) Cuba y Marzo 15 de 1811. Carta de Sebastian Kindelan á D. Luis del Monte sobre los acontecimientos con el Sr. Arzobispo. *Puerto Príncipe: Imprenta de la Audiencia Territorial.* 4to, pp. 11. 37773

KINDER (T.) The Case of Thomas Kinder, as regards the Parras Estates [Mexico]. *London.* 1837. 8vo. 37774

KINDERHOOK, *N. Y.* Catalogue of ... Kinderhook Academy, for ... 1841. *Kinderhook: P. Van Schaack.* 1841. 12mo, pp. 16. Continued. B. 37775

Also: Constitution and By-Laws of the Kinderhook Division ... of the Sons of Temperance. *Kinderhook.* 1851. 16mo.

KINDERMANN (F. C.) Chile mit Berücksichtigung der Provinz Valdavia. *Berlin.* 1849. 8vo. 37776

KINDERSLEY [Nathaniel E.] Letters from the Island of Teneriffe, Brazil, the Cape of Good Hope, and the East Indies. By Mrs. Kindersley. *London: J. Nourse.* 1777. 12mo, pp. 301, Errata. Plate. C. 37777

See "M. Rev.," LVII. 243.

KINDERSLEY. Briefe von der Insel Teneriffa, Brasilien, dem Vorgebirge der Guten Hoffnung und Ostindien. Aus dem Englischen der Mistress Kindersley. *Leipzig: Weidmann's Erben und Reich.* 1777. 12mo, pp. 286. Plate. C. 37778

KING (A.) Memoir of George Dana Boardman, late Missionary to Burmah. ... By Rev. Alonzo King. *Boston: Gould, Kendall & Lincoln.* 1835. 12mo, pp. 320. Portrait. + [*Ibid.*] 1836. 12mo, pp. xxxv, 319. Portrait. + *Boston: Gould and Lincoln.* 1852. 12mo, pp. 8, xxxv, 9–319, (1). Plate. H. 37779

Also: An Address ... at Portland before the Cumber. County Temperance Society, February 9, 1832. ... *Portland.* 1832. 12mo, pp. (2), 18. H.

KING (A.) ... A Sermon preached at the Opening of the Synod of the Presbyterian Church of the Lower Provinces. By Rev. Andrew King, A.M. *Halifax.* 1861. 8vo, pp. 16.

Also: Inaugural Lecture at the Opening of the First Session of the Free Church College. ... *Halifax.* 1848. 8vo. — The Papacy: a Conspiracy against Civil and Religious Liberty. First Lecture before the Protestant Alliance of Nova Scotia. ... *Halifax.* 1859. 8vo, pp. 30.

KING (A.) British Sympathies in the American Crisis. A Letter on the Address of the Protestant Pastors of France to the Christian Ministers of all Denominations in Great Britain and Ireland. By A. King. *Dublin: Porteus & Gibbs.* 1863. 8vo, pp. 15. 37781

KING (B.) Fortieth Anniversary Sermon. A Sermon ... at Rockaway ... December 31, 1848. By Rev. Barnabas King ... *New York: J. M. Sherwood.* 1849. 8vo, pp. 23. B. 37782

KING (Charles). The British Merchant: a collection of papers ... by Sir Theodore Janssen, Bart. Sir Charles Cooke, ... and others. The Second Edition. *London: Charles Marsh and Thomas Davies.* MDCCXLIII. 3 vols., 12mo, pp. xxiv, 343; iv, 383; vi, 324, 27. 37783

Contains an account of the Assiento Contract, the Newfoundland Fishery, Brazil Mines, etc. It first appeared in weekly numbers, and was issued in a collected form, *London.* 1721. 3 vols., 8vo. *See* a long note, relative to the work, in McCulloch's "Literature of Political Economy," pp. 142–4.

KING (C.) The Charter and By-Laws, with a History of the Chamber of Commerce of the State of New York. By Charles King ... . *New York.* 1855. 8vo. 37784

[KING.] The Late Samuel Ward. [*J. P. Wright, Printer, New York.* n. d.] 12mo, pp. 16. H. 37785

KING. A Lecture on the History of the State of New Jersey. By Charles King, Esq., of Elizabethtown. 1842. 8vo. 37786

Title from Ludewig, p. 109. *See also* "New Jersey Hist. Soc. Proceedings," Vol. I.

KING. A Memoir of the Construction, Cost, and Capacity of the Croton Aqueduct, compiled from Official Documents: together with an Account of the Civic Celebration on the Fourteenth October, 1842, on Occasion of the Completion of the Great Work; preceded by a Preliminary Essay on Ancient and Modern Aqueducts. By Charles King. *New York: Printed by Charles King.* 1843. 4to, pp. vii, (1), 308. Plate. BA. 37787

Printed for private distribution. The title is evidently intended to be alliterative.

KING. Memoir of the Life of James Gore King. By Charles King ... . *New York.* 1854. 8vo. C. 37788

KING. Progress of the City of New-York, During the Last Fifty Years; with Notices of the Principal Changes and Important Events. A Lecture ... 29th December, 1851. By Charles King, LL.D. ... *New-York: D. Appleton & Company.* 1852. 8vo, pp. 80. H. 37789

Also: Address before the Queens County Agricultural Society, at Flushing, L. I., September 29th, 1852. ... *Jamaica.* 1852. 8vo. — Eulogy upon John Quincy Adams ... at ... the Borough of Elizabeth ... April 5th, 1848. ... *Elizabethtown, N. J.: Printed by E. Sanderson.* 1848. 8vo, pp. 35. BA. *See also* our Vol. IV., No. 14804, *and* Letter addressed to Charles King.

KING (Clarence). *See* Hague *and* King, Vol. VII., No. 29523.

KING (D.) The Life and Times of Thomas Wilson Dorr, with Outlines of the Political History of Rhode Island. By Dan King. *Boston: The Author.* 1859. 12mo, pp. 368. Portrait.

Also: Tobacco; What it Is, and What it Does. ... *New York.* 1861. 16mo. C.

KING (D. P.) An Address, Commemorative of Seven Young Men of Danvers, who were slain in the Battle of Lexington: delivered ... in Danvers, on the Sixtieth Anniversary of the Battle. With Notes. By Daniel P. King. *Salem: W. & S. B. Ives.* 1835. 8vo, pp. 32. B., M., S., W. 37791

Also: An Address to the Essex Agricultural Society, at Danvers, September 30, 1835 ... *Salem.* 1836. 8vo, pp. 22. — The California Question, and the Ordinance of '87.

Speech ... May 21, 1850. ... [*Washington.* 1850.] 8vo, pp. 8. B. — Eulogy, at the Funeral of General Gideon Foster, ... Danvers, November 3d, 1845. ... With Notes. *Danvers: G. R. Carlton.* 1846. 8vo, pp. 32. — Speech ... on the General Appropriation Bill and the Mexican War. ... Feb. 4, 1847. *Washington: Printed by J. & G. S. Gideon.* 1847. 8vo, pp. 16. B.

[KING, *and others.*] Answer of the Whig Members of the Legislature of Massachusetts, ... to the Address [of the Governor] delivered in the Convention of the Two Houses, January 22, 1840. *Boston: Printed by Perkins & Marvin.* 1840. 8vo, pp. 36. H. 37792

KING. Obituary Addresses delivered on the Occasion of the Death of the Hon. Daniel Putnam King, ... July 27, 1850. *Washington.* 1850. 8vo, pp. 7. BA., M. 37793

KING (D.) An Historical Sketch of the Redwood Library and Athenæum, in Newport, Rhode Island ... . By David King, M.D. *Boston: John Wilson and Son.* 1860. 8vo, pp. liii. B., S.

KING (D.) The State and Prospects of Jamaica. By the Rev. David King, LL.D. *Glasgow: Theobald.* 1850. 37795

KING (D. S.) Fireside Poetical Readings, Illustrative of American Scenery, Rural Life, and Historical Incidents, and also of Religious Feelings. ... Collected and Published by Dexter S. King. *Boston: D. S. King.* 1843. 12mo, pp. ii, 313. Plates.

KING (*Dr.*) The Franklin Expedition from First to Last. By Dr King, M.D. *London: John Churchill.* 1855. Post 8vo, pp. xxxviii, 224. 37797

KING (Edward). Remarks concerning Stones said to have Fallen from the Clouds, both in these Days and in Ancient Times, ... also of a Wonderful Storm at Detroit in America, in 1762, &c. *London.* 1796. 4to. Plate. 37798

Title from one of Thomas Thorp's Catalogues, No. 767.

KING (E.) Letter from Edward King and T. J. Wharton, accompanied with a Communication from the Agent of the Auburn Prison of the State of New York. *Harrisburgh.* 1829. 8vo, pp. 30. 37799

[KING (Edward).] Antiquities of Mexico: comprising Fac-Similes of Ancient Mexican Paintings and Hieroglyphics, preserved in the Royal Libraries of Paris, Berlin, and Dresden; in the Imperial Library of Vienna; in the Vatican Library; in the

Borgian Museum at Rome; in the Library of the Institute of Bologna; and in the Bodleian Library at Oxford. Together with the Monuments of New Spain, By M. Dupaix: with their respective scales of measurement and accompanying descriptions. The whole illustrated by many valuable Inedited Manuscripts, By Lord Kingsborough. The Drawings, on Stone, by A. Aglio. In even Volumes. *London: Robert Havell.* M.DCCC.XXXI. Folio.

Collation: Vol. I. 5 l., 261 Plates, 6 l.; II. 3 l., 304 Plates, 5 l.; III. 3 l., 290 Plates, 4 l.; IV. 3 l., 146 Plates, 8 l.; V. Title, 1 l., Aglio's Dedication, pp. v–vii, (1), 493; VI. Title, 1 l., pp. 540; VII. Title, 1 l., vi, (2 l.), pp. 464. Vol. VIII. *London: Henry G. Bohn.* MDCCCXLVIII. Title, 1 l., pp. 268, Supplement, 424; IX. Title, 1 l., pp. 468 [Vol. x.] 60.

Vol. IX. closes abruptly on page 468, with an unfinished relation by Don Alva Ixtlilxochitl; followed by pp. 1–60 of another work, on the rites and customs of the Indians of New Spain, at the end of which is printed "End of Vol. IX. Which concludes the work," but a closer examination will show that these pages have the signatures of Vol. X., of which no more was printed. Mr. Bohn reprinted the last leaf with the statement we have quoted, in order, we presume, to make the buyer satisfied; the work is, in fact, a valuable but unfinished production. Vols. VIII. and IX. were not published till seventeen years after the others. Ten copies were printed on large paper, 26 by 19 inches, entirely for presents, and two copies were printed on vellum, one of which was presented to the Bodleian Library, the other to the British Museum. An intending purchaser should secure a set with the plates colored, as the coloring is, in fact, an important feature in explanation of the text; the plates in Vol. IV., however, are never found colored. The story of this magnificent work is at once interesting and pathetic. Mr. Rich remarks that the noble author's "penchant for Mexican Antiquities was produced by a sight of the original Mexican manuscript described by Purchas ('Pilgrimes,' III.), preserved in the Bodleian Library, where his lordship was a student. From the time he first saw it, he appears to have devoted his mind to it, and to have thought of nothing else. Augustin Aglio, an excellent and well-known Italian painter, was employed by him to visit Rome, Vienna, Dresden, and other places, to search for, and to make copies of Mexican manuscripts, and after his return, to make drawings of them on stone. I visited Spain for him in 1830, and again in 1832. ... After having expended upwards of thirty thousand pounds upon this work, he got into difficulties with some of the persons with whom he dealt, particularly with a celebrated paper manufacturer. He was arrested in Dublin, and from obstinacy or unwillingness to pay a demand which he thought unjust, was thrown into prison. He was there seized with a typhus fever, which ended fatally in a few days." Had he lived a few months longer, he would have inherited the title of Earl of Kingston, with an estate of forty thousand pounds a year; and Mexican topics would doubtless have absorbed a large portion of his time and money. This sad story, although often related, is worthy of repetition wherever learning is honored, or devotion to literature esteemed. He seems to have become early imbued with that zeal bordering on infatuation which had allured so many scholars before him; the desire to prove that the American Indians were descendants of the Jews, and in this respect he has raised a monument which will at least preserve these unsolved symbols from destruction. We cannot do less than quote the remarks in the "Athenæum" that "This work in its magnificence recalls to mind the patronage of crowned heads, and the splendor of the princely patrons of literature. It has no taint about it of author or bookseller—it comes in the astounding form of *nine* volumes, imperial folio! and the cost of producing the whole will exceed fifty or perhaps sixty thousand pounds." The "Times" of Dec. 8, 1868 contains an eloquent tribute to the work, which is reproduced in Mr. Quaritch's Catalogue. *See also* Brunet's "Manuel," "N. A. Rev.," LI. 396, *and* Rich's "Bibl. Amer.," II.

[KING.] ... Catalogue of the Rare and Valuable Library of the late Rt. Hon. Edward Lord Viscount Kingsborough, comprising His Collection of Printed Books and Manuscripts in various languages of Europe and Asia, Drawings of Mexican Antiquities, etc. ... *Dublin.* CIↃ IↃ CCCXLII. 8vo, pp. (8), 110.

KING (E. T.) Memoir of Elizabeth T. King. With Extracts from her Letters and Journal. *Baltimore: Armstrong & Berry.* 1859. 12mo, pp. 128. C. 37802

KING (H. F.) The Rebellion; an Historical Poem. By Henry F. King. *Portland: Printed by Cyrus S. King.* 1865. 12mo, pp. 21. H. 37803

Fifty copies printed for distribution among the author's friends.

KING (H.) Early History of Ithaca; a Lecture delivered at Ithaca, April 5, 1847. By Horace King. *Ithaca.* 1847. 8vo.

KING (H.) Letter from Hon. Horatio King. To the ... Committee on Naval Affairs. [n. p. 1870.] 8vo, pp. 8. H.

KING (J.) A Sermon Preached before the Honourable Trustees For establishing the Colony of Georgia, in America, ... at their Anniversary Meeting, March 17, 1742–3. at ... London. By James King, D.D. ... *London: John Clarke.* M.DCC.XLIII. 4to, pp. 22. 37806

KING (J.) Introductory Address delivered to the Students of Washington College, May 14, 1850. By James King. *Washington, Pa.* 1850. 8vo. 37807

KING (J.) A True and Minute History of the Assassination of James King of Wm. at San Francisco, Cal. ... *San Francisco: Whitton, Towne & Co., Printers.* 1856. 8vo, pp. 26. B. 37808

KING (J. G.) Speech of James G. King, of New Jersey, ... on the Branch Mints. [n. p.] 1851. 8vo. S. 37809

KING (J.) Disclosures relating to the "A. B. C." Affair of Capt. Jeb King. 37810

I have seen only proof-sheets of this unpublished but suppressed pamphlet.

[KING] (J.) Sermon at Paule's Crosse, on behalfe of Paule's Churche, March 26, 1620. By John, Bishop of London. *London: E. Griffin.* 1620. 4to. 37811

"Your English Colonie in Virginia, (I named hir the little sister that had no breasts), hath drawne from the breasts of this Citty and Diœcesse a thousand pounds towards her church."—*Page* 48.

KING (J.) Thoughts on the Difficulties and Distresses in which the Peace of 1783, has involved the People of England; on the Present Disposition of the English, Scots and Irish, to Emigrate to America; and on the Hazard they run (without certain Precautions) of rendering their Condition more Deplorable. ... By John King, Esq. The Second Edition. *London: J. Fielding.* 1783. 8vo, pp. (1), 48. + With an Appendix. The Sixth Edition. *London: T. Davies.* 1783. 8vo, pp. 71. 37812

The appendix contains an account of Col. Edmund Fanning, the notorious Long Island Tory. Concerning this bitter invective *see* "M. Rev.," LXVIII. 371, *also* Rich, I. 314.

KING (J.) The American Dispensatory. By John King, M.D. ... Eighth Edition ... . *Cincinnati: Wilstach, Baldwin & Co.* 1870. 8vo, pp. 1439. B. 37813

KING (John A.) Twenty-Four Years in The Argentine Republic; embracing its Civil and Military History, and an Account of its Political Condition, before and during the Administration of Governor Rosas ... . By Col. J. Anthony King, an Officer in the Army of the Republic, and Twenty-Four Years a Resident of the Country. *New York: D. Appleton & Company.* M DCCC XLVI. 12mo, pp. 324. BA., C. 37814

Edited by T. R. Whitney. Chapter VII. contains a curious account of the Chirrione tribe of Indians. Reprinted in London as:

KING. Twenty-Four Years in the Argentine Republic; embracing the Author's Personal Adventures, with the Civil and Military History of the Country, and an Account of its Political Condition before and during the Administration of Governor Rosas ... . By Colonel J. Anthony King ... . *London: Longman.* 1846. 8vo, pp. xii, 442. B., P. 37815

KING (J. A.) Speech of Mr. John A. King ... on the Admission of California; ... June 4, 1850. *Washington: Gideon & Co., Printers.* 1850. 8vo, pp. 15. H., M. 37816

Also: Address ... at the ... N. York State Agricultural Society ... in ... Albany. ... January 17, 1850. *Albany: Weed, Parsons & Co. ... Printers.* 1850. 8vo, pp. 13. — A Letter ... to his Constituents ... . *Jamaica, L. I.* 1851. 8vo, pp. 15. — Union League Club of New York. Proceedings in Reference to the Death of Hon. John A. King, July 11th, 1867. [*New York.*] 1867. 12mo, pp. 26. B.

KING (J. B.) An Address ... in Behalf of the ... American Union ... By John B. King, Esq. *Ironton, Ohio.* 1869. 8vo, pp. 26. H. 37817

KING [John P.] Speech of Mr. King ... On the Memorial of the Society of Friends ... praying for the Abolition of Slavery

in the District of Columbia ... February 29, 1836. [n. p. n. d.] 8vo, pp. 6. H. 37818

Also: Speech ... on the Public Deposits, 1834. [n. p. n. d.] 8vo. — Speech ... on the Land Bill. ... 31st of January, 1837. [*Washington.* 1837.] 8vo, pp. 15. — Speech ... on the Bill imposing Additional Duties, as Depositaries ... on Public Officers; ... September 23, 1837. *Washington: Printed by Gales and Seaton.* 1837. 8vo, pp. 15. BA. — Speech ... September 23d, 1837, upon the "Sub-Treasury Bill." [n. p. n. d.] 8vo, pp. 24. — Speech ... March 18, 1840. *Washington.* 1840. 8vo. — To the Voters of Richmond County. [*Augusta, Ga.* 1865.] 8vo, pp. (2), 9. H.

KING (J. W.) Federalism: or The Question of Exclusive Power, the True Issue in the Present Monetary and Political Discussions in the United States. ... By John W. King, M.D. ... *Cincinnati: U. P. James.* 1840. 8vo, pp. 68. H. + *Cincinnati: Shepard & Stearns.* 1840. 8vo, pp. 24. B. 37819

KING (J.) Report ... May 1820, to the Female Domestic Missionary Society of Charleston ... . By ... Jonas King. ... . *Charleston: Printed by A. E. Miller.* 1820. 8vo, pp. 22, (1). H.

KING (J.) Petitions, &c. for the Appointment of Joseph King, Jr., to the Office of Surveyor of 22d Ward. *Philadelphia.* 1854. P. 37821

KING (J. W.) The Silent Dead, or Roll of Honor of Muskingum, Ohio. *Zanesville.* 1866. 8vo. 37822

KING (M. M.) Social Evils: their Causes and Cure. Being a brief Discussion of the Social Status, with reference to Methods of Reform. By Mrs. Maria M. King. *Boston: W. White & Co.* 1870. 8vo, pp. 55. C. 37823

KING (M.) A Discourse on the Qualifications and Duties of an Historian; delivered before the Georgia Historical Society on ... its fourth Anniversary ... 1843. By the Hon. Mitchell King. *Savannah.* 1843. 8vo, pp. 23. H., P. 37824

Also: Centennial Address, delivered before the St. Andrew's Society of the City of Charleston, 30th November, 1829. ... *Charleston, S. C.* 1829. 8vo, pp. 58. M.

KING [Peter]. The Life of John Locke, with Extracts from his Correspondence, Journals, and Common-Place Books. By Lord King. ... *London: Henry Colburn.* 1829. 4to, pp. xi, (1), 407, (1). Facsimile, Portrait. + New Edition. *London: Henry Colburn and Richard Bentley.* 1830. 2 vols., 8vo, pp. viii, 447, Facsimile, Portrait; iv, 375. BA. 37825

[KING (Philip Parker), *and others.*] Narrative of the Surveying Voyages of His Majesty's Ships Adventure and Beagle,

between the Years 1826 and 1836, describing their Examination of the Southern Shores of South America, and the Beagle's Circumnavigation of the Globe. ... *London: Henry Colburn.* 1839. 3 vols., 8vo, pp. xxviii, (4), 597; xiv, (1), 694, (1); xiv, 615; Appendix, viii, 352. 48 Plates, 8 Maps. BA. 37826

The first volume, by Capt. P. P. King, relates to the expedition under his command, with an Appendix, by Major Sabine; the second, by Capt. Rob. Fitzroy, relates to the second voyage, and the third, by Charles Darwin, is an account of his discoveries in Natural History. *See* "Blackwood's Magazine," IV. 286, V. 152; *see also* our Vol. V., Nos. 18645–50.

KING. Sailing Directions for the Coasts of Eastern and Western Patagonia, from Port St. Elena on the eastside, to Cape Tres Montes on the westside, including the Strait of Magalhaens, and the Sea Coast of Tierra del Fuego. *London.* 1832. 8vo.

[KING.] Instructions nautiques sur les côtes de la Patagonie, depuis les terres des États à l'est jusqu'au cap Tres-Montes à l'ouest, compris le détroit de Magellan el la côte du large de la Terre-de-Feu. Traduit de l'anglais par P. Martin. *Paris: Au dépôt de la marine.* 1864. 8vo. 37828

Also: Sailing Directions for South America. ... *London: J. D. Potter.* 1850. 8vo.

KING (P.) The Rights of the People of Kansas. Speech of Preston King ... March 16th, 1858 ... . [*Washington.* 1858.] 8vo, pp. 7, (1). B. 37829

KING. The Wilmot Proviso. Bill and Explanation of Preston King ... January 4 & 5, 1847. *Washington: Printed ... by Blair and Rives.* 1847. 8vo, pp. 8. H. 37830

Also: Minority Report of Committee on Public Printing. [*Washington.*] 1860. 8vo, pp. 8. — Remarks on the Compromise Measures. ... *Washington.* 1852. 8vo, pp. 8.

KING (R.) Narrative of a Journey to the Shores of the Arctic Ocean, in 1833, 1834, and 1835; under the Command of Capt. Back, R.N. By Richard King ... *London: Richard Bentley.* 1836. 2 vols., post 8vo, pp. xv, 312, (1); viii, 321, (1). 7 Plates.

Contains details of Indian life, as it was presented to the members of Captain Back's Expedition. The author charges Captain Back with appropriating his researches.

KING (R.) An Address delivered before the Washington Chapter, ... O. of U. A. By Robert King, Jr., ... June 18, 1846. *New York.* 1846. 8vo, pp. 13. 37832

KING (R.) Speech of the Hon. Rufus King, on the American Navigation Act, delivered in the Senate ... *New York: Kirk & Mercein.* 1818. 8vo, pp. 49. BA., H. 37833

KING. Speech ... on the Navigation Laws of the United States. *London.* 1819. 8vo. 37834

KING. Substance of two Speeches ... in the Senate of the United States, on the Subject of the Missouri Bill. By Rufus King ... . *New York: Kirk and Mercein.* 1819. 8vo, pp. 32. B.

Also: Letter to the Secretary of State, from London, 1796. S. — Speech ... March 18, 1824 ... respecting the election of the President of the U. States, be ... postponed. *Washington: Printed by Gales & Seaton.* 1824. 12mo, pp. 12. For Considerations in favor of Rufus King *see* [Van Buren (M.)]

KING (S. W.) An Exposition of the Course pursued by the School Committee ... of Lynn, in relation to Samuel W. King ... with Memoir ... . *Lynn: W. W. Kellogg, Printer.* 1857. 8vo, pp. 48. H. 37836

KING (T. B.) California: The Wonder of the Age. ... Being the Report of Thomas Butler King ... . *New York: William Gowans.* 1850. 8vo, pp. 34. B. 37837

An unauthorized edition of Mr. King's report. It is due to Mr. King to state that this title was not written by him.

KING. A Letter to the Right Hon. Lord John Russell. By the Hon. T. Butler King, Commissioner from the State of Georgia. *London: J. Morse.* 1861. 8vo, pp. 20. 37838

This was reprinted at *Mobile*, 1862, with a cover-title "Commercial Relations between the Confederate States and England."

KING. Lettre a S. Exc. M. le Ministre du Commerce par T. Butler King ... . *Paris: Dubuisson et Cᵉ.* 1861. 8vo, pp. 48.

KING. Report of Hon. T. Butler King, on California. *Washington: Printed by Gideon and Co.* 1850. 8vo, pp. 72. B.

Also: Address ... to the Voters of the First District of Georgia. [n. p. 1844.] 8vo, pp. 16. — Home Squadron ... July 7, 1841. ... Report ... . [n. p. n. d.] 8vo, pp. 22. B. — Speech ... on the "Bill additional to the act on the subject of Treasury Notes." ... March 18, 1840. [n. p. n. d.] 8vo, pp. 16. — Speech ... on the Oregon Question: ... February 9, 1846. *Washington.* 1846. 8vo, pp. 20. — Speech ... July 19, 1848, on Naval Affairs. [n. p. n. d.] 8vo.

KING *and* BROWNE (J. V.) Correspondence on ... Appraisements, &c. between T. Butler King, Collector, and J. Vincent Browne, Appraiser ... *Washington.* 1852. 8vo, pp. 30. H.

KING (T. F.) Oration, before the Tammany Society ... on the Fourth of July, 1821. By Thomas F. King. *New York.* 1821. 12mo. 37842

KING (T. K.) An Oration, delivered before the Kentish Artillery and Citizens of Apponaug, R. I. ... July 4, 1854. By Thomas K. King. *Providence: George H. Whitney.* 1854. 8vo, pp. 29. 37843

KING (T. S.) The Death of Mr. Webster: A Sermon ... Sunday, Oct. 31, 1852. By Thomas Starr King ... . *Boston: Benjamin H. Greene.* 1852. 8vo, pp. 40. B. + Second Edition. [*Ibid.*] 1852. 8vo, pp. 23. BA. 37844

KING. A Discourse ... before the Ancient and Honorable Artillery Company, on their CCXIII Anniversary. By Thomas Starr King ... . *Boston: A. Tompkins.* 1851. 8vo, pp. 24. B.

KING. Patriotism, and other Papers. By Thos. Starr King. With a Biographical Sketch, by Hon. Richard Frothingham. *Boston: Tompkins and Company.* 1864. 12mo, pp. 359. C.

KING. The Railroad Jubilee: two Discourses ... Sept. 21, 1851. By Thomas Starr King ... . *Boston: Benjamin H. Greene.* 1851. 8vo, pp. 54. BA., N. 37847

KING. The White Hills; their Legends, Landscape, and Poetry. By Thomas Starr King. With Sixty Illustrations ... . *Boston: Crosby, Nichols, Lee and Company.* 1860. 8vo, pp. xv, (2), 403. Map. + [*Ibid.*] 1863 and 1866. BA. 37848

Also: An Address in behalf of Rev. Charles Spear ... . [*Boston.* n. d.] 8vo, pp. 8. — Address in memory of Miss Sarah Paul, ... June 26, 1859. ... *Boston: Press of Geo. C. Rand & Avery.* 1860. 18mo, pp. 14. B. — ... American Nationality. An Oration ... in San Francisco. *San Francisco: Printed by R. C. Moore.* 1863. 8vo, pp. 8. — A Sermon ... at the Installation of Caleb D. Bradlee ... in Cambridge, Dec. 11, 1854. ... *Boston: Benjamin H. Greene.* 1855. 8vo, pp. 42. — The Losses and Gains of a Church: a Sermon, September 19, 1852, on ... the Death of Mr. Daniel Weld. ... *Boston: Printed by John Wilson & Son.* 1852. 8vo, pp. 29. — An Oration ... Apponaug, R. I. ... July 4, 1854. ... *Providence: George H. Whitney.* 1854. 8vo, pp. 31. B. — Oration ... before the Grand Lodge of ... Masons of California. ... May, A.L. 5863. *San Francisco: Frank Eastman, Printer.* 1863. 8vo, pp. 10. B.

KING. In Memoriam. Thomas Starr King. For the Benefit of the Sanitary Commission. [*New York.* 1864.] 8vo, pp. 22.

KING (W.) A Discourse Delivered in Chelsea, in the City of Norwich, Jan. 5, 1800, As a Token of Humiliation before God, on Account of the Death of Gen. George Washington ... . By Walter King ... . *Norwich: Printed by Thomas Hubbard.* 1800. 8vo, pp. (4), 22. 37850

KING. A Farewell Discourse ... to the ... Congregational Church ... of Chelsea ... August 18, 1811. ... with an Ap-

pendix, giving some Account of the Ground of Difficulty between the Pastor and Society: ... By Walter King ... . *Norwich, Conn.* 1811. 8vo. + *New York: Printed by J. Seymour.* 1811. 8vo, pp. 38. B. 37851

KING. ... Sermon ... at Chelsea in Norwich, December 24th, 1795. Being the Day of Public Thanksgiving, and Dedication of a House of Worship ... . By Walter King, A.M. ... *Norwich: Printed by Thomas Hubbard.* M,DCC,XCVI. 8vo, pp. 26.

Also: ... A Sermon delivered at the Ordination of the Rev. Daniel Hall, ... Sag-Harbor, Long Island, Sept. 21, 1797. With Appendix. ... *Printed at Norwich by Thomas Hubbard.* 1798. 8vo, pp. 31.

[KING (*Gen.* William).] The Disclosure — No. I. Documents relating to Violations and Evasions of the Laws during the Commercial Restrictions and Late War with Great Britain, &c. Part First. *Baltimore: For the People.* 1824. 8vo, pp. 32.

KING. Letter from the Secretary of War [J. C. Calhoun], transmitting a Copy of the Proceedings of a Court Martial, for the Trial of Colonel William King, May 3, 1820. *Washington: Gales & Seaton.* 1820. 8vo, pp. 128. C. 37854

KING. Letters to James Monroe, President of the United States, From William King, Late Colonel of the United States Army, 1820. [n. p. n. d.] 8vo, pp. 36, Errata, 8 l. BA. 37855

KING *and* HILL (M. L.) Remarks upon a Pamphlet published at Bath, Me. Relating to Alledged Infractions of the Laws during the Embargo, Non-Intercourse, and War. By William King and Mark L. Hill. *Bath: Printed by Thomas Eaton.* 1825. 8vo, pp. 25. B., W. 37856

KING (W. R.) The Sportsman and Naturalist in Canada, or Notes on the Natural History of the Game, Game Birds, and Fish of that Country. By Major W. Ross King ... *London: Hurst and Blackett.* 1866. Rl. 8vo, pp. xv, (2), 334, Errata, 4 l.

KING (W. R.) Obituary Addresses on ... the Death of the Hon. William R. King, of Alabama, Vice President of the United States ... in the Senate and in the House of Representatives ... Eighth of December, 1853. *Washington: Printed by Beverley Tucker.* 1854. 8vo, pp. 77. Portrait. + [*Ibid.*] 1854. pp. 63.

[KING (William S.)] Alphabetical List of Senators and Representatives, with their Residences in Washington. ... [*Washington.* 186–.] 8vo, pp. 7. + [*Ibid.* 1863.] 8vo, pp. 8. 37859

Also: Address ... before the New Hampshire Agricultural Society ... Oct. 7, 1852. ... With the Remarks of Hon. Franklin Pierce. *Boston: Bazin & Chandler, Printers.* 1853. 8vo, pp. 40. — ... An Address before the Hampshire, Franklin, and Hampden Agricultural Society ... October 12, 1853. ... *Boston: Bazin & Chandler, Printers.* 1854. 8vo, pp. 32. *See also* Journal of Agriculture, No. 36700.

King-Caucus, or "Secrets worth Knowing." Disclosed in Official Communications between the Prime Minister at Washington, and the Ambassador at Albany. [n. p. n. d.] 12mo, pp. 20. H. 37860

The King of Angelo, a Tragico Comico; or, Melo-Dramatico Burlesco, by the Louisville Literary Brass Band. [n. p. n. d.]

The King of Denmark's Ordinance relative to the Slave Trade, March 16, 1792. C. 37862

King of Spain's Declaration of War against Great Britain, done at Buen Retiro. Spanish and English. 1739. 8vo.

This and the following title are from J. R. Smith's Catalogue:

The King of Spain's Reasons for not paying the £95,000, stipulated in the Convention signed at the Pardo, 14 Jan. 1739, Examined. 1739. 8vo. 37864

The King of the Hurons. *See* [Paulding (J. K.)]

KINGDOM (W). America and the British Colonies. An Abstract of all the most Useful Information relative to The United States of America, and The British Colonies ... Exhibiting at one view the comparative advantages and disadvantages Each Country offers for Emigration. Collected from the most Valuable and Recent Publications. To which are added, A few Notes and Observations. ... By William Kingdom, Junr. *London: G. and W. B. Whittaker.* 1820. 8vo, pp. vii, (1), 359, (1). + Second Edition. [*Ibid.*] 1820. A., H. 37865

"A compilation from other works ... . Its principal object is to recommend to emigrants the British Colonies in preference to the United States." — *Monthly Review*, XCI. 332.

The Kingdom and Glory of the Branch, and Testament of The West. *Baltimore: William Wooddy, Printer.* 1833. 12mo, pp. 341. 37866

KINGMAN (B.) History of North Bridgewater, Plymouth County, Massachusetts, from its First Settlement to the Present Time, with Family Registers. By Bradford Kingman ... *Boston: The Author.* 1866. 8vo, pp. (2), xii, 696. 36 Plates and Map.

KINGMAN (J.) Letters written while on a Tour to Illinois and Wisconsin, in the Summer of 1838, by John Kingman. *Hingham.* 1842. 8vo, pp. 48. 37868

[KINGMAN (John), *and others.*] An Exposition of the Causes which Led to the Secession from the Methodist Episcopal Church, in Charleston, S. C. ... *Charleston: Printed by E. J. Van Brunt.* 1834. 8vo, pp. 31. BA. 37869

KINGOS (J. C.) Kreool A B C Buk. *S. Croix.* 1770. 8vo.

The King's Answer. *See* [Junius], No. 36916.

KING'S COLLEGE. The Alumni of King's College, Windsor, Established 1846. Incorporated, 1847 ... . *Halifax, N. S.: Printed by James Bowes & Son.* 1847. 8vo, pp. 16, (1). Cont'd.

The Calendar of King's College, Windsor, Nova Scotia. For ... 1855. ... *Halifax: Printed by James Bowes and Sons.* 1855. 8vo, pp. 31. Continued. H. 37872

Statutes Rules and Ordinances of ... King's College Windsor, N. S. ... Act of 1853. *Halifax, N. S.: Printed by James Bowes and Son.* 1854. 8vo, pp. 19. H. 37873

See Vol. III., No. 10428, *also* [Inglis (John)], No. 34770.

KINGS CO., *N. Y.* Minutes of the Board of Supervisors of the County of Kings, for 1865. *Brooklyn.* 1865. 8vo. 37874

Proceedings of the Board of Supervisors of the County of Kings, for ... 1860. Part First. ... Part Second ... [n. p. n. d.] 8vo, pp. (4), 495, (1). B. 37875

See also our Vol. II., No. 8316. Also: Report of the Committee on Accounts of the Superintendents of the Poor. ... *Brooklyn.* 1856–57. 8vo.

Inebriates' Home for Kings County. Superintendent's Report. *Brooklyn, April.* 1868. 12mo, pp. 24. H. 37876

Also: Report of the President of the Inebriates' Home for Kings County. *Brooklyn.* 1869. 8vo.

Annual Report of the ... Kings County Lunatic Asylum ... July 31st, 1860. *Brooklyn.* 1860. 8vo, pp. 12, (1). Plate. Continued. H. 37877

Annual Report of Superintendents of the Poor. 1854. *Williamsburgh.* 1854. 8vo. 37878

King's Mountain. *See* Vol. III., No. 11652.

KINGSBOROUGH (*Lord* Edward). *See* [King (Edward)].

KINGSBURY (A.) The Memorial Day. A Sermon ... Jan. 1, 1860. By A. Kingsbury. *Cincinnati.* 1860. 8vo, pp. 30.

KINGSBURY (A. A.) The Hero of Medfield; Containing the Journals ... of Allen Alonzo Kingsbury ... also, Notice of ... Three Soldiers belonging to the same Company ... . *Boston: John M. Hewes, Printer.* 1862. 12mo, pp. 144. Portrait. B. 37880

KINGSBURY (H.) The Immigrant's Good Samaritan. By Harmon Kingsbury ... . [*New York:*] *Daniel Fanshaw.* 1848. 16mo, pp. 117. H. 37881

KINGSBURY. Law and Government: The Origin, Nature, Extent, and Necessity of Divine and Human Government, and of Religious Liberty. By Harmon Kingsbury ... . *New York: C. M. Saxton.* 1849. 12mo, pp. viii, 13–236. B. 37882

Also: The Slavery Question Settled. Man-Stealing, Legitimate Servitude ... . *New York: John A. Gray, Printer.* 1862. 12mo, pp. 36.—Thoughts on the Fugitive Slave Law and Nebraska Bill. ... *New York.* 1855. 12mo, pp. 24.

KINGSFORD (E.) Claims of Abolitionism on the Church of Christ. By Ed. Kingsford. *Harrisburg.* 1838. 8vo. 37883

KINGSFORD (W.) The Canadian Canals, their History and their Cost, with an Inquiry into the Policy necessary to advance the well-being of the Province. By William Kingsford, C.E. *Toronto.* 1865. 12mo, pp. 191. 37884

KINGSFORD. The History, Structure, and Statistics of Plank Roads, in the United States and Canada. By W. Kingsford. With Remarks ... by F. G. Skinner; and a Letter ... by the Hon. Charles E. Clarke. *Philadelphia: A. Hart.* 1851. 8vo, pp. 40. C., H. 37885

K[INGSFORD]. Impressions of the West and South ... . Letters which "first appeared in a Toronto Newspaper." By W. K. *Toronto.* 1858. 8vo. 37886

KINGSLEY (C.) Round the World: a Series of Letters. By Calvin Kingsley, D.D. *Cincinnati: Hitchcock & Walden.* 1870. 2 vols., 16mo, pp. 344; 325. Portrait. C. 37887

KINGSLEY (C.) Sir Walter Raleigh and his Time, with other Papers. By Charles Kingsley. *Boston: Ticknor and Fields.* MD CCC LIX. 12mo, pp. (4), 461. BA. 37888

KINGSLEY. Westward Ho! or, the Voyages and Adventures of Sir Amyas Leigh, Knight ... . By Charles Kingsley. *Cambridge: Macmillan & Co.* 1855. 3 vols., 12mo, pp. viii, 303; vi, 356; vi, 373. BA. + *Leipzig: Bernard Tauchnitz.* 1855. 2 vols., 12mo, pp. (6), 370, (1); (6), 365, (1). + *Boston: Ticknor and Fields.* M DCCC LV. 12mo, pp. vi, 588. B., P. 37889

KINGSLEY (H.) Tales of Old Travel. Re-narrated. By Henry Kingsley ... . *London: Macmillan & Co.* 1869. 12mo, pp. (8), 368. Plates. BA. 37890

Contains a notice of Alvaro Nunez, etc.

KINGSLEY (J. L[uce]). A Historical Discourse, delivered ... before the Citizens of New Haven, April 25, 1838, The Two Hundredth Anniversary of The First Settlement of the Town and Colony. By James L. Kingsley. *New Haven: B. & W. Noyes.* 1838. 8vo, pp. 115. B., P. 37891

With valuable notes and biographical notices. *See* "N. A. Rev.," XLVII. 480; XLVIII. 432.

KINGSLEY. A Sketch of the History of Yale College, in Connecticut. Prepared by Professor Kingsley ... . *Boston: Printed by Perkins, Marvin & Co.* 1835. 8vo, pp. 48. BA. 37892

Also: An Eulogy on Alexander Metcalf Fisher, A.M. Professor ... in Yale College, who perished in the ... Albion, April 22nd, 1822. Delivered ... June 26, 1822. ... *New-Haven.* 1822. 8vo, pp. 23. BA.—Review of Webster's American Dictionary. From "N. A. Rev.," Vol. XXVIII. ... [n. p. n. d.] 8vo, pp. 40. *See* Sparks' "Amer. Biog.," XVI.

KINGSLEY (V. W.) French Intervention in America; or, a Review of La France, Le Mexique, et Les États-Confédérés. By Vine Wright Kingsley. *New York: C. B. Richardson.* 1863. 8vo, pp. 22. B. 37893

[KINGSLEY.] Reconstruction in America. By a Member of the New York Bar. *New York.* 1865. 8vo. 37894

[KINGSLEY (Z.)] A Treatise on the Patriarchal System of Society ... in some ... Colonies in America, and in the United States, under the Name of Slavery ... . By an Inhabitant of Florida. Third Edition, with an Appendix. [n. p.] 1833. 8vo, pp. 22. B. 37895

KINGSMILL (*Colonel*). The Greenwood Tragedy. Three Addresses delivered to the Prisoners in Toronto Gaol soon after the Suicide of William Greenwood, and having reference to that

event; to which is added an Appeal to the Ladies of Canada. By Colonel Kingsmill. *Guelph.* 1864. 8vo, pp. 35. 37896

KINGSMILL (J.) Missions and Missionaries, historically viewed from their Commencement. By Joseph Kingsmill. *London.* 1853. 8vo. C. 37897

KINGSTON (G. T.) Abstract of Magnetical Observations made at the Magnetical Observatory, Toronto, Canada West, during the years 1856 to 1862, inclusive, and during parts of the years 1853, 1854, and 1855. By G. T. Kingston ... . *Toronto.*

Also many contributions on kindred subjects in the "Canadian Journal."

KINGSTON (J.) The Life of General George Washington. By John Kingston. *Baltimore: J. Kingston.* 1817. 18mo, pp. 228. Portrait. 37899

This is Condie's "Life" with a new title-page only.

KINGSTON. The New American Biographic Dictionary; or, Memoirs of Many of the Most Eminent Persons that have ever lived in this or any other Nation ... . By J. Kingston. ... *Baltimore: John Kingston.* 1810. 18mo, pp. 303. Portrait of Washington. 37900

KINGSTON. The New Pocket Biographical Dictionary: ... Ancient and Modern. ... Embellished with Portraits. By John Kingston. Second Edition ... . *Baltimore: J. Kingston.* 1811. 18mo, pp. 308, (4). H. 37901

The previous work with a new title-page.

KINGSTON (W. H. G.) Adventures of Dick Onslow among the Red Skins. A Book for Boys. By William H. G. Kingston. *Boston: J. E. Tilton & Co.* 1864. 16mo, pp. vii, 336. C.

KINGSTON. How to Emigrate; or, the British Colonist: with an Appendix ... . By William H. G. Kingston. Second Edition, Revised. *London: Groombridge.* 1852. 18mo, pp. 296. + Third Edition. [*Ibid.*] 1855. 18mo, pp. 332. 37903

KINGSTON. Manco, the Peruvian Chief; or, an Englishman's Adventures in the Country of the Incas. By William H. G. Kingston, Esq. ... *London.* 1852. Fcap 8vo, pp. 448. + Third Edition. *London.* [1870.] Fcap 8vo. B. 37904

KINGSTON. Peter the Whaler; his Early Life and Adventures in the Arctic Regions and other Parts of the World. By

William H. G. Kingston. *New York.* 1852. 12mo, pp. 389. + *New York.* 1855. 16mo. 37905

KINGSTON. Some Suggestions for the formation of a System of General Emigration, and for the Disposal of Convicts in the Colonies. By William H. G. Kingston, Esq. *London.* ——. 12mo, pp. 24. 37906

KINGSTON. Western Wanderings; or, a Pleasure Tour in the Canadas. By William H. G. Kingston. ... *London: Chapman and Hall.* MDCCCLVI. 2 vols., 12mo, pp. xvi, 343; viii, 324. 2 Plates. BA., C. 37907

Also: At the South Pole, or the Adventures of Richard Pengelley. ... *London.* [n. d.] 8vo.—The Log House by the Lake; A Tale of Canada. ... *London.* [1864.] 18mo.

KINGSTON, *C. W.* A Directory of the City of Kingston, and the Villages of Waterloo, Portsmouth, Williamsville and Barriefield. *Kingston: John Duff.* 1855. 8vo, pp. 80. 37908

Directory of the City of Kingston, for 1857–1858; with Statistical and General Information respecting the United Counties of Frontenac, Lennox, and Addington, and Descriptive Notices of the Towns and Villages therein. Compiled by Thomas Flynn ... . *Kingston, C. W.: T. W. Robinson.* 1857. 8vo, pp. 288. Map. 37909

KINGSTON, *Mass.* Report of the Selectmen of ... Kingston ... March 1, 1862. *Boston: Press of Geo. C. Rand & Avery.* 1862. 8vo, pp. 32. Continued. H. 37910

Report of the School Committee of Kingston. Read April 1, 1839. *Plymouth: Printed by James Thurber.* 1839. 8vo, pp. 8. Continued. H. 37911

KINGSTON, *N. H.* Report of the Selectmen of ... Kingston ... March 6, 1856. *Haverhill: E. G. Frothingham, Printer.* 1856. 8vo, pp. 7, (1). H. 37912

KINGSTON, *R. I.* Catalogue of ... Kingston Academy; ... from 1819 to ... April 26, 1832. *Kingston: J. J. Brenton, Printer.* 1832. 8vo, pp. 14. H. 37913

A Statement of Facts, relating to the Funds of Kingston Academy. *Providence: Printed by E. A. Marshall.* MDCCCXXXVI. 8vo, pp. 15. H. 37914

KINGSTON, *W. I.* Ordinances of the Common Council of the City and Parish of Kingston, in Jamaica, from 1803 to 1810. *Jamaica.* 1803–10. 4to. 37915

Contains twenty-eight original ordinances, with autograph signature of the town clerk to each.

Proceedings relative to the Establishment of a Presbyterian Place of Worship in Kingston. *Kingston Chronicle Office.* 1814. 4to. 37916

Kingston and Rondout Directory; containing the Names of the Residents of Kingston, Rondout, Wiltwyck, and North-Haven. ... Also, an Historical Sketch of the Town of Kingston, 1857. *W. H. Boyd, ... New York.* 18mo. Continued. S.

To the Public. [Account of the Competition with the Transportation Company. n. p. 1838.] 8vo, pp. 8. BA. 37918

KINGSVILLE, *Ohio.* Twenty-First Annual Catalogue of ... Kingsville Academy; 1854–5. ... *Cleveland, Ohio: Cowles, Pinkerton & Co., Printers.* 1855. 8vo, pp. 19. H. 37919

KINKER (J.) Treurzang, bij het plechtig vieren der Nagedachtenis van Washington, in de Maatschappij van Verdiensten Felix Meritis, den 21. Maart 1800. Uitgesproken door Mr. Johannes Kinker, ... *Te Amsterdam, bij J. ten Brinck Gerritsz* ... 1800. 8vo, 18 l. Engraved Frontispiece. 37920

This "Solemn Celebration of the Memory of Washington in the Society Felix Meritis" is dedicated to John Adams.

KINKEAD (J. B.) Address ... Grand Lodge of Kentucky, at Lexington ... August 31, 1865. By Joseph B. Kinkead. 8vo, pp. 12. 37921

[KINLOCH (Francis).] Eulogy on George Washington, Esq. deceased, Late Commander in Chief of the American Armies, and sometime President of the United States. ... *Georgetown, S. C.: Printed by John Burd.* M.D.CCC. 8vo, pp. 19. 37922

Sixty copies reprinted with the following title:

KINLOCH. Eulogy on George Washington. By Francis Kinloch Of Georgetown, S. C. *New York: Privately Printed.* 1867. Rl. 8vo, pp. (4), 19. 37923

KINMONT (A.) Twelve Lectures on the Natural History of Man, and the Rise and Progress of Philosophy. By Alexander

Kinmont. With a Biographical Sketch of the Author. ... *Cincinnati: U. P. James.* 1839. 8vo, pp. viii, 355. H., W. 37924

Also: Discourse on the Ends and Uses of a Liberal Education; delivered before the Union Literary Society of South-Hanover College, Indiana. ... *Cincinnati.* 1836. 8vo pp. 26.

KINNE (A.) Alamoth. An Address delivered to the Singing Schools, in the First and Second Societies in Groton. By Rev. Aaron Kinne, A.M. *New London,* 1798. 8vo, pp. 16. 37925

Also: A New Year's Gift; presented especially to the Young People in the First Society of Groton, Jan. 1, 1788. ... *New London.* 1788. 8vo, pp. 16.

KINNE (A.) The most Important Parts of Kent's Commentaries, reduced to Questions and Answers. By Asa Kinne. *New York.* 1839. 8vo. 37926

KINNEAR (J. R.) History of the 86th Regiment Illinois Volunteer Infantry. By J. R. Kinnear. *Chicago.* 1866. 12mo.

KINNERSLEY (E.) A Course of Experiments, in that Curious and Entertaining Branch of Natural Philosophy, called Electricity; accompanied with Explanatory Lectures: In which Electricity and Lightning will be proved to be the same Thing. By Ebenezer Kinnersley, M.A. ... [*Philadelphia:*] *Printed by A. Armbruster.* MDCCLXIV. 12mo, pp. 8. P. 37928

A rare imprint, and curious as foretelling, in some respects, the science of telegraphy.

KINNERSLEY. A Letter to the Reverend the Ministers of the Baptist Congregations, in Pennsylvania, and the New Jerseys; containing some Remarks on their Answers to certain Queries, proposed to them, at their Annual Association in Philadelphia, September 24. 1746. By Ebenezer Kinnersley. ... *Philadelphia: Printed by W. Bradford* ... [1746.] 12mo, pp. 24. P. 37929

Thomas' "History of Printing" gives the titles of three works by this writer, which I have not seen.

KINNERSLEY (T.) A Selection of Sepulchral Curiosities, with a Biographical Sketch on Human Longevity: containing the most Sublime, Singular, and Authentic Epitaphs that were ever before Collected. Taken from Monuments and Grave Stones in the United Kingdoms ... and in the United States of America. By T. Kinnersley. *New York: T. Kinnersley.* 1823. 8vo, pp. viii, 352, (1). 37930

KINNEY (C.) Keeuka, and other Poems. By Coates Kinney. *Cincinnati.* 1855. 16mo. C. 37931

KINNEY (H.) A Review of the Principal Events of the last ten years in the life of Mrs. Hannah Kinney: together with some Comments upon the late Trial. Written by Herself. *Boston: J. N. Bradley & Co.* 1841. 12mo, pp. 87. BA., C. 37932

Also: Trial of Mrs. Hannah Kinney, for the ... Murder of her Husband ... . By a Member of the Bar. *Boston.* 1840. 8vo, pp. 62. H.

KINNEY (J. F.) Speech of Hon. John F. Kinney ... upon the Territories and the Settlement of Utah. ... March 17, 1864. *Washington: H. Polkinhorn, Printer.* 1864. 8vo, pp. 16. H.

[KINNICUTT (Thomas).] House No. 37. Commonwealth of Massachusetts. [Report on the Burning of the Ursuline Convent. n. p. 1835.] 8vo, pp. 24. H. 37934

KINNICUTT. Notice of the Life and Character of Hon. John Davis, read before the American Antiquarian Society ... 26th of April, 1854. By Hon. Thomas Kinnicutt. *Boston: Printed by John Wilson & Son.* 1854. 8vo, pp. 26. B. 37935

Also: An Oration ... before the Society of United Brothers, of Brown University, September 1, 1840. ... *Providence: Knowles and Vose, Printers.* 1840. 8vo, pp. 32.

KINO (*P. E. F.*) Exposicion | Astronomica | de el Cometa, | Que el Año de 1680 por los meses de | Noviembre, y Diziembre, y este Año de 1681 por los meses | de Enero y Febrero, se ha visto en todo el mundo, | y le ha observado en la Ciudad de Cadiz, | El P. Eusebio Francisco Kino | De la Compañia de Jesvs. | *Con Licencia, en Mexico por Francisco Rodriguez Lupercio.* 1681. 4to, pp. (16), 28 l. Chart. 37936

KINSMAN (H. W.) An Oration, pronounced before the Inhabitants of Boston, July the Fourth, 1836. By Henry W. Kinsman. ... *Boston: John H. Eastburn, City Printer.* 1836. 8vo, pp. 25. B., W. 37937

KINSMAN (J. B.) The Vermont Townsman: a Compilation of the Laws of Vermont in relation to the Powers, Duties, and Liabilities of Town Officers and Towns, ... By J. Burnham Kinsman ... . *Boston: Brown, Taggard, and Chase.* 1857. 12mo, pp. xxxiv, 425. H. 37938

Also: Circular Order No. 1. ... *Fort Monroe, Virginia, January 1st,* 1864. 12mo, pp. 3.—Freedmen at Fortress Monroe. Report of the General-Sup't of Negro Affairs, June 1, 1864. [n. p. n. d.] 8vo, pp. 20. H.

KINSMAN (N. S.) First Annual Report ... of Orphans and Destitute Children ... Sept. 1, 1847. By Mrs. N. S. Kinsman. *Boston: Press of Coolidge and Wiley.* 1847. 12mo, pp. 36. H.

[KINZIE (*Mrs.* J. H.)] Narrative of the Massacre at Chicago, August 15, 1812, and of some Preceding Events. *Chicago, Ill.: Printed by Ellis & Fergus.* 1844. 8vo, pp. 34. Plate. 37940

KINZIE. Wau-Bun, the "Early Day" in the North-West. By Mrs. John H. Kinzie, of Chicago. ... *New York: Derby & Jackson.* 1856. 8vo, pp. 498. Plates. + Second Edition. ... *Chicago: D. B. Cooke & Co.* 1857. 8vo, pp. 498. Plates. H.

This picture of the early days of the Northwest, drawn from the lips of an aged pioneer, is replete with authentic details of aboriginal manners. The so-called second edition has a new title-page only.

KIP (F. M.) A Discourse ... on the 12th of September, 1866, ... the 150th Anniversary of the First Reformed Dutch Church, Fishkill, N. Y. With an Appendix, furnishing a Brief Historical Sketch of the Associated Churches of Hopewell ... . By Francis M. Kip, D.D. *New York: Press of Wynkoop & Hallenbeck.* 1866. 8vo, pp. 64. Plate. BA. 37942

KIP. Memoirs of an Old Disciple and his Descendants: Christian Miller, Sarah S. Miller, Isaac L. H. Miller, Rev. John E. Miller. ... By Francis M. Kip ... . With an Introductory Chapter, by Thomas De Witt, D.D. *New York: R. Carter.* 1848. 16mo, pp. 309. S. 37943

KIP (L.) Army Life on the Pacific; a Journal of the Expedition against the Northern Indians, the Tribes of the Cœur d'Alenes, Spokans, and Pelouzes, in the Summer of 1858. By Lawrence Kip, Second Lieutenant ... . *Redfield, New York.* 1859. 12mo, pp. 144. H. 37944

[KIP.] The Indian Council in the Valley of the Walla-Walla. 1855. *San Francisco: Whitton, Towne & Co., Printers.* 1855. 8vo, pp. 32. H. 37945

Printed, not published. "The expansion of a journal, kept while with the escort from the fourth infantry at the Indian council."—*Preface.*

KIP (L.) California Sketches, with Recollections of the Gold Mines. By Leonard Kip. *Albany: J. Munsell.* 1850. 12mo.

[KIP.] The Volcano Diggings; a Tale of California Law. By a Member of the Bar. *New-York.* 1851. 12mo. S. 37947

KIP (W. I.) Address ... at Hombourg-les-Bains, Germany, on the First Day of June, 1865, ... the Day appointed by the President of the United States, as a Day of Humiliation and

Prayer. By William Ingraham Kip, D.D. *Frankfort-on-the-Main.* 1865. 8vo, pp. 11. H. 37948

Relates to the assassination of Abraham Lincoln.

Kip. The Early Jesuit Missions in North America; Compiled and Translated from the Letters of the French Jesuits, with Notes. By the Rev. William Ingraham Kip, M.A. *New York: Wiley and Putnam.* 1846. 12mo, pp. xiv, (4), 321. Map. B. + [*Ibid.*] 1847. + *Albany, N. Y.: Pease & Prentice.* 1866. 12mo, pp. xiv, (2), 325. Map. H. 37949

This edition has an index. The Wanderings and Death of Father Rawle; Catherine, the Iroquois Saint; Montcalm's Expedition to Fort George; Father Marest's Journey through Illinois and Michigan; Voyage up the Mississippi, etc., form the bulk of the work.

[Kip.] A Few Days at Nashotah. *Albany: Printed by J. Munsell.* 1849. 8vo, pp. 31. BA. 37950

Also: Address before the ... Convention of the Protestant Episcopal Church, ... California, May, 1862. ... *San Francisco: Towne & Bacon.* 1862. 8vo, pp. 22. — ... A Sermon, preached in ... Albany ... MDCCCXL ... after the Consecration of the Edifice ... *Albany: Printed by J. Munsell.* 1840. 8vo, pp. 24. B. — Our National Sins: A Sermon, preached in ... Albany ... MDCCCXL. ... *Albany: Printed by J. Munsell.* 1840. 8vo, pp. 21. — Two Pastoral Letters addressed to the Congregation of St. Paul's Church, Albany, by their absent Rector. *Albany: J. Munsell.* 1845. 12mo, pp. 12.

Kip. Prospectus of the Kip & Buell Gold Co. Colorado. ... *New York: Bogert, Bourne & Auten ... Printers.* 1864. 8vo, pp. 10. H. 37951

[Kippis (Andrew).] Account of the Early Voyages made by the Spaniards to Africa, East and West Indies, with Lives of eminent Navigators, including the Life and Voyages of Columbus. *London.* 1790. 4to. Maps and Plates. 37952

Title from an English auctioneer's catalogue.

[Kippis.] Considerations on the Provisional Treaty with America, and the preliminary Articles of Peace with France and Spain. *London: T. Cadell.* M.DCC.LXXXIII. 8vo, pp. (4), 164. + The Second Edition Corrected. [*Ibid.*] 8vo, pp. (2), 94.

"The author appears to have been a person of some note, well acquainted with the secrets of the British Cabinet. He enters into an examination of the several articles of the treaty, and vindicates them from the mistakes and misrepresentations of those who had not well weighed them, or were interested in decrying them. He observes, that 'we had not a moment to lose, and if we had lost the opportunity of reconciliation with America, it would in all probability never have returned till England was totally undone.'"—*Monthly Review,* LXVIII. 367. Concerning the authorship, *see* a note in Rich's "Bibl. Amer.," I. 314

Kippis. The Life of Captain James Cook. ... By Andrew Kippis, D.D. ... *London: J. Nicol.* M.DCC.LXXXVIII. 4to, pp. xvi, 527. Portrait. + *Dublin.* 1788. 8vo. + *Basil: Printed by J. J. Tourneisen.* M DCC LXXXVIII. 2 vols., 8vo, pp. xii, (2), 302; (4), 326. H. 37954

Kippis. Vie du Capitaine Cook, Traduite de l'Anglois du Docteur Kippis. ... Par M. Castera. *Paris.* M.DCC.LXXXIX. 2 vols., 8vo, pp. (4), xl, 387, (1); (4), 419, (1). + [*Ibid.*] 4to, pp. 546. 37955

Kippis. Leben des Capitäns James Cook, von Andr. Kippis. Aus dem Englischen [von A. Wittenberg]. *Hamburg: B. G. Hofmann.* 1789. 2 vols., 8vo, pp. 284; 301. Portrait of Cook.

Kippis. A Narrative of the Voyages round the World, performed by Captain James Cook. With an Account of His Life, during the previous and intervening periods. By A. Kippis ... . *Boston: Published by N. H. Whitaker.* 1832. 2 vols., 18mo, pp. 205; 211. + *New-York: Harper & Brothers.* [184-?] 18mo, pp. ix, 445. BA. + *Philadelphia: J. B. Lippincott & Co.* 1863. 12mo, pp. 424. B. 37957

[Kippis.] Voyages round the World, from the Death of Cook to the Present Time ... . *New York: Harper & Brothers.* 1865. 16mo, pp. 401. + *London: T. Nelson and Sons.* MDCCCLVII. 12mo, pp. 517. B. 37958

Also: An Address, delivered at the Interment of the ... Rev. Dr. Richard Price ... April, 1791. ... *London: T. Cadell and J. Johnson.* M. DCC. XCI. 8vo, pp. 27. BA. — Sermon ... on the Spread of the Gospel among the Heathen. ... *London.* 1777. 8vo. *See* "M. Rev.," LXXIX. 394.

Kirby (E.) Address, before the Jefferson County Agricultural Society, 1831. By Edmund Kirby. [n. p. n. d.] 8vo.

Kirby (James). *See* British Almanack, Vol. II., No. 8116.

Kirby (J.) A Sermon ... January 3, 1816, at the Dedication of the Church in the Third Parish, Newbury. By John Kirby. *Newburyport: Printed by William B. Allen & Co.* 1816. 8vo, pp. 20. H. 37960

Kirby (R. S.) Wonderful and Eccentric Museum; or Magazine of Remarkable Characters, including all the Curiosities of Nature and Art, from the remotest period to the present time. *London: R. S. Kirby.* 1820. 6 vols., 8vo. 124 Plates. 37961

Some of the articles relate to America.

Kirby (W.) The U. E. A Tale of Upper Canada. By William Kirby. *Niagara, U. C.* [n. d.] 16mo, pp. 175.

"The most thoroughly distinctive Canadian Poem we possess."—Morgan.

Kirby (W.) Entomologia Boreali Americana, or Natural History of the Insects of North America, more especially the Provinces under the Dominion of Great Britain, containing Descriptions of the Objects collected in the late Northern Expeditions under the Command of Captain Sir John Franklin; completed by an Enumeration of all those taken in the Arctic Regions by Captains Parry, Sir John Ross, and Back; as well as those described by Otho Fabricius, in his "Fauna Grœnlandica." By the Rev. William Kirby. *Norwich.* 1837. 4to, pp. xxxix, 325. 8 colored Plates. 37963

Forms Part IV. of the "Fauna Boreali Americana," *see* Richardson (John).

Kirby (W. W.) Hymns and Prayers: For the Private Devotions of the Slave Indians of McKenzies River. By Rev. W. W. Kirby. *New York: Rennie, Shea & Lindsay.* 1862. 12mo, pp. 16. 37964

Kirchen-Agende der Evangelisch-Lutherischen Vereinigten Gemeinen in North America. *Philadelphia: Gedruckt bey Melchior Steiner in der Rees-strasse.* 1786. 8vo, pp. (2), 58. 37965

A Liturgy for the United Evangelical Lutheran Congregations in North America, revised and enlarged in accordance with a vote of the Synod held in Philadelphia, in May, 1785.

Kircher (Athanasius). Iter Extaticum Terrestre. *Romæ.* 1657. 4to. 37966

Contains information respecting America.

Kircher. Mundus Subterraneus, quo divinum subterrestris mundi opificium, ... demonstratur. In hac editione tertia emendata. *Amstelodami.* 1665. 2 vols., folio. Maps and Plates. + [*Ibid.*] 1678. 37967

Several articles relate to America.

Kircher. D'onder-aardse wereld. Uit het Latin vertaalt. *Amsterdam: Waasberge.* 1682. Folio. 37968

Contains "America hoedanige waterholen daar zijn; America heeft veel baden; Rievieren in America in haar oorsprong beschreven; America heeft veel goud; Quikmijnen in America," etc.

Kirk (C. D.) Wooing and Warring in the Wilderness; a Story of Canetucky. By Charles D. Kirk. *New York.* 1860. 12mo, pp. 288. C. 37969

Kirk (E. N.) The Church Essential to the Republic. A Sermon in behalf of the American Home Missionary Society. Preached in ... New-York and Brooklyn, May, 1848. By Edward Norris Kirk ... . *New-York.* 1848. 8vo, pp. 23. 37970

Kirk. Great Men are God's Gift. A Discourse on the Death of the Hon. Daniel Webster. Delivered ... Oct. 31, 1852. By Edward N. Kirk ... . *Boston: Tappan & Whittemore.* 1852. 8vo, pp. 24. BA. 37971

Kirk. Memorial of the Rev. John Chester, D.D.; ... By Edward N. Kirk. *Albany: Printed by George Galpin.* 1829. 8vo, pp. 22, (1). B. 37972

Kirk. The Murderer. A Discourse occasioned by the Trial and Execution of John W. Webster. By Edward N. Kirk ... . *Boston: Tappan, Whittemore & Mason.* 1850. 8vo, pp. 26. H.

Kirk. Mustered Out. The Country's Welcome to its Heroes and Defenders ... By Rev. E. N. Kirk, D.D. *Boston.* [n. d.] 16mo, pp. 34. H. 37974

Kirk. Oration of the Rev. Edward N. Kirk, ... July 4, 1836, at the request of the Committees of the Common Council Civic Societies, Military Associations, &c. *Albany: Printed by L. G. Hoffman.* 1836. 8vo, pp. 47. B. 37975

Kirk. Sermons on Different Subjects ... By Rev. Edward Norris Kirk. With an Introduction, by Samuel Hanson Cox, D.D. ... *New York: Printed by John F. Trow.* 1840. 12mo, pp. viii, 316. B. + Second Edition. *New York: Gould, Newman & Saxton.* 1840. 12mo, pp. 367. C. 37976

Also: Address at the Anniversary of the Society for the Relief of Orphan and Destitute Children. ... *Albany.* 1831. 8vo. — ... An Address delivered at the Seventh Anniversary of the Mount Holyoke Female Seminary, South Hadley, Mass. August 1, 1844. ... *Boston: Press of T. R. Marvin.* 1844. 8vo, pp. 27. — Address to the Convention of Sunday School Teachers, Pittsfield, June 24, 1863. ... *Boston: Moses H. Sargent.* [1863.] 8vo, pp. 32. B. — Address to the Ladies' Grande Ligne Missionary Society of Boston ... Nov. 12, 1844. ... *Boston: John B. Hall, Printer.* 1844. 8vo, pp. 12. — The Church and the College. An Address before the Society for the Promotion of Collegiate ... Education at the West ... October 30, 1851. ... *Boston: Press of T. R. Marvin.* 1851. 8vo, pp. 22. + [*Ibid.*] 1856. 8vo, pp. 30. — The Love of Pleasure. A Discourse [on] the Opening of a New Theatre in Boston. ... September 10, 1854. ... *Boston: John P. Jewett & Company.* 1854. 8vo, pp. 26. H. — An Oration on the Occasion of the National Fast; ... May 14, 1841. ... *New York: John S. Taylor & Co.* 1841. 8vo, pp. 27. — "Our Duty in Perilous Times." A Sermon ... Boston ... June 1, 1856. ... *Boston: S. K. Whipple & Co.* 1856. 8vo, pp. 15. — A Plea for the Poor. A Sermon ... December 20, 1842. ... *Boston: Tappan & Dennet.* 1843. 16mo, pp. 63, (1). — ... Public Worship a Universal Duty. A Discourse ... in ... [Paris], September 6, 1857. ... *Paris: Napoléon Chaix et Cie.* 1857.

8vo, pp. 24. — Remarks ... at the Funeral of Jonas H. Lane, M.D. [n. p. n. d.] 8vo, pp. (3). — A Sermon on the Traffic in Intoxicating Liquors. ... *Albany.* [n. d.] 12mo, pp. 24. H. + *London.* 1838. — ... A Sermon ... November 13, 1839, at the Ordination of Samuel Wolcott, as a Foreign Missionary. ... *Boston: Printed by Perkins & Marvin.* 1839. 8vo, pp. 32. — Sermon and Speeches at the Settlement of Rev. Wm. C. Whitcomb, January 3, 1856, ... in ... Southbridge, Ms. ... *Boston: Charles C. P. Moody, Printer.* [n. d.] 8vo, pp. 50. — Sermon ... at the Ordination of Rev. William L. Gaylord, ... September 14, 1860. ... *Keene.* 1860. 8vo, pp. 31. — ... A Sermon ... at the Dedication of the Church [of] the Mount Vernon Congregational Society. ... *Boston: Tappan & Dennet.* 1844. 8vo, pp. 34. — A Valedictory Sermon, ... in ... Albany, April 2, 1837. ... *Albany: Packard & Van Benthuysen, Printers.* 1837. 8vo, pp. 38. + *Albany: Printed by A. J. Bready.* 1837. 12mo, pp. 48.

Kirk (G.) Supplement to New York Legal Observer, containing Report of the Case in the matter of George Kirk, a Fugitive Slave, heard before the Hon. J. W. Edmonds, Circuit Judge. Also, the Argument of John Jay, of Counsel for the Slave. *New York.* 1847. N., H. 37977

Kirk (T.) Sermon at the Ordination of the Rev. John Willard, at Stafford, Conn., March 23, 1757. By Thomas Kirk. [n. p. n. d.] 8vo. N. 37978

Kirkbride (J.) State of the Accounts of Joseph Kirkbride, Esquire, Lieutenant of Bucks County; and of Samuel Smith, Esq. Sub-Lieutenant of said County, to March 1780. ... *Philadelphia: Printed by Robert Aitken,* ... M,DCC,LXXXV. 8vo, pp. 16.

Kirkbride (Stacy B.), *Jr. See* New Jersey.

[Kirkbride (T. S.)] An Appeal to the Citizens of Pennsylvania for ... Additional Accommodations for the Insane. *Philadelphia: T. K. and P. G. Collins, Printers.* 1854. 24mo, pp. 19. B. 37980

Kirkbride. On the Construction, Organization and General Arrangements of Hospitals for the Insane. By T. S. Kirkbride. *Philadelphia.* 1854. 8vo, pp. (2), ii, 80. Plate. H. 37981

Also: Letter to the Regents of the South Carolina Hospital for the Insane. ... *Philadelphia.* 1854. 8vo. — Remarks on the Construction and Arrangements of Hospitals for the Insane. ... *Philadelphia: Printed by T. K. and P. G. Collins.* 1847. 8vo, pp. 19. *See also* Pennsylvania Hospital.

Kirkby (R.) An Account of the Arraignments and Tryals of Col. Richard Kirkby, Capt. John Constable, Capt. Cooper Wadé, Capt. Samuel Vincent, and Capt. Christopher Fogg, on A Complaint exhibited by the Judge-Advocate on behalf of Her Majesty, at a Court-Martial held on Board the Ship Breda in Port-Royal Harbour in Jamaica in America, the 8th, 9th, 10th, and 12th Days of October, 1702. For Cowardice, Neglect of

Duty, Breach of Orders, and Other Crimes, Committed by them in a Fight at Sea, commenced the 19th of August 1702, off of St. Martha, in the Latitude of Ten Degrees North, near the Main-Land of America, Between the Honourable John Benbow Esq; and Admiral Du Casse with Four French Ships of War. For which Col. Kirkby and Capt. Wade were Sentenc'd to be Shot to Death. Transmitted from Two Eminent Merchants at Port-Royal in Jamaica, to a Person of Quality in the City of London. *London: John Gellibrand.* [1703.] Folio, pp. (2), 10.

Another edition reads:

Kirkby. [As before.] Which said Sentence was executed upon them at Plymouth, on board the British Man of War. With a particular Relation of the said Engagement; and Death and Character of Admiral Benbow. *London: Crowder & Co.* [n. d.] Folio. 37983

Republished on occasion of the execution of Admiral Byng. *See* "M. Rev.," XVI. 360.

Kirke (Edmund), *pseudon. See* [Gilmore (J. R.)]

Kirkland (Caroline M. Stansbury). Autumn Hours and Fireside Reading. By Mrs. C. M. Kirkland. *New York.* 186-. 12mo. 37984

Kirkland. The Book of Home Beauty. By Mrs. Kirkland. With Twelve Portraits of American Ladies, from Drawings by Charles Martin, Esq. Engraved on Steel by Eminent Artists. ... *New York: G. P. Putnam.* MDCCCLII. 4to. 37985

Also issued with the plates colored.

[Kirkland.] The Emigrant's Home; or, Real Life in the West. By Mrs. Mary Clavers, an Actual Settler. *London: William Tegg.* 1848. 32mo, pp. 276. 37986

This is an English reprint of "Forest Life;" another edition is entitled "Emigrant's Home; or, Life in the Far West." *London: Knight.* 1852. 18mo.

Kirkland. The Evening Book; or, Fireside Talk on Morals and Manners, with Sketches of Western Life. By Mrs. C. M. Kirkland. *New York: Charles Scribner.* 1852. 8vo, Engraved Title, pp. 312. 7 Plates. 37987

A selection from Mrs. Kirkland's other works, issued in 12mo and 8vo.

[Kirkland.] Forest Life. ... *New York: C. S. Francis & Co.* 1842. 2 vols., 12mo, pp. 250; 234. + *London: Longman,* ... 1842. 12mo, pp. xv, 302; (4), 320. BA. 37988

Also reprinted in England as the "Emigrant's Home," etc.

Kirkland. The Helping Hand: ... an Account of The Home for Discharged Female Convicts. ... By Mrs. C. M. Kirkland. *New York: Charles Scribner.* 1853. 4to, pp. 141. Plate. 37989

Kirkland. Memoirs of Washington. By Mrs. C. M. Kirkland. With Illustrations. *New York: D. Appleton & Co.* 1857. 12mo, pp. xii, 516. B. 37990

The same edition was issued as a school book without plates.

[Kirkland.] A New Home, Who'll Follow? or Glimpses of Western Life. By Mrs. Mary Clavers, an Actual Settler. *New York.* 1839. 12mo, pp. 317. + Second Edition. [*Ibid.*] 1840. 2 vols., 12mo. + Third Edition. [*Ibid.*] 1841. 12mo, pp. 298. + *London.* 1844. 24mo. + Fourth Edition. *New York.* 1850. 12mo. + Fifth Edition. [*Ibid.*] 1855. 12mo.

The second edition was republished in England under the title of "Montacute, or the New Home: who'll follow?" *London: E. Churton.* 1840. 2 vols., post 8vo.

Kirkland. Patriotic Eloquence: being Selections from One Hundred Years' National Literature. Compiled ... By Mrs. C. M. Kirkland. *New York: Charles Scribner & Co.* 1866. 12mo, pp. xii, 334. 37992

Kirkland. Western Clearings. By Mrs. C. M. Kirkland. ... *New York: Wiley and Putnam.* 1845. 12mo, pp. viii, (2), 238. + [*Ibid.*] 1846. + *New York: John Wiley.* 1848. 12mo. H.

[Kirkland (Charles P.)] The Coming Contraband; a Reason against the Emancipation Proclamation, not given by Mr. Justice Curtis, to whom it is addressed, by an Officer in the Field. *New York: G. P. Putnam.* 1862. 12mo, pp. 21.

This is also attributed to C. G. Nott.

Kirkland. The Destiny of our Country. By Charles P. Kirkland. *New York: Anson D. F. Randolph.* 1864. 8vo, pp. 7-71. BA. 37995

Kirkland. A Letter to the Hon. Benjamin R. Curtis, late Judge ... in Review of his recently published pamphlet on the "Emancipation Proclamation" of the President. By Charles P. Kirkland ... . *New York: Latimer Bros. & Seymour.* 1862. 8vo, pp. 21. + Second Edition. *New York: Anson D. F. Randolph.* 1863. 8vo, pp. 20. BA. 37996

Kirkland. A Letter to Peter Cooper, on "The Treatment to be extended to the Rebels individually," ... With a Letter

from President Lincoln. By Charles P. Kirkland. *New York: Anson D. F. Randolph.* 1865. 8vo, pp. 46, 20. + Second Edition. [*Ibid.*] pp. 54, (2), 20. H. 37997

Also: Address to the Graduating Class of the Law School of Columbia College ... May 16, 1866. ... *New York: Anson D. F. Randolph.* 1866. 8vo, pp. 24. — Liability of the Government of Great Britain for the Depredations of Rebel Privateers on the Commerce of the United States, Considered. ... *New-York: Anson D. F. Randolph.* 1863. 8vo, pp. 37. H.

Kirkland (F.) Cyclopædia of Commercial and Business Anecdotes. ... By Frazar Kirkland. *New York: D. Appleton and Company.* 1864. 2 vols., 8vo, pp. xxviii, (2), 387; xii, (2), 391-779. Portraits and Plates. H. + [*Ibid.*] 1868. 37998

Kirkland. The Pictorial Book of Anecdotes and Incidents of the War of the Rebellion ... . By Frazar Kirkland. *Hartford: Hartford Publishing Co.* 1867. 8vo, pp. 705. 9 Plates.

A subscription book, with a long title-page full of promises, as is customary in such books.

Kirkland [Hugh]. "Patriarch." Narrative of Scenes and Events which occurred lately in Cincinnati, entitled Freedom of Speech Vindicated, Defended, and Maintained. With Engravings ... . *Cincinnati.* 1853. 8vo, pp. 36. 38000

Kirkland (J. T.) A Discourse occasioned by the Death of General George Washington. Delivered Dec. 29, 1799. By John Thornton Kirkland. ... To which is added the Valedictory Address of the late President, to the People of the United States. *Printed at Boston, by I. Thomas and E. T. Andrews.* 1800. 8vo, pp. 22, Valedictory, 22. BA. + Second Edition. [*Ibid.*] 1800.

Kirkland. A Discourse ... before ... Caleb Strong, Esq. Governor ... May 29, 1816, Being the Anniversary Election. By John Thornton Kirkland, D.D. *Boston: Benjamin Russell.* 1816. 8vo, pp. 27. BA., C. 38002

Relates to the situation of the government at the close of the war.

Kirkland. The Life of Commodore Edward Preble. [n. p. n. d.] 8vo, pp. (2), 30. Portrait. H. 38003

[Kirkland.] Notices of the Life of Major General Benjamin Lincoln. [*Boston.* 1815.] 8vo, pp. 23. H. 38004

See "Mass. Hist. Soc. Coll.," III., 2d Series.

[Kirkland.] To the ... Senate ... of Massachusetts in behalf of the Corporation ... of [Harvard College. n. p. 1812.] 8vo, pp. 8. B. 38005

Also: An Address ... at the Request of the Massachusetts Charitable Fire Society ... May 29, 1801. ... *Boston: Printed by Russell and Cutler.* 1801. 8vo, pp. 14, (1). — A Discourse delivered ... after the Interment of the Hon. George Cabot, who died April 18th, 1823. ... *Boston: Wells and Lilly.* 1823. 8vo, pp. (2), 26. — An Oration, Delivered, at the Request of the Society of Φ B K, ... Harvard College, ... July 19, 1798. ... *Boston: Printed by John Russell.* 1798. 8vo, pp. 24. — A Sermon ... before the Ancient and Honorable Artillery Company, In Boston, June 1, 1795 ... . *Boston: Printed by Joseph Belknap.* MDCCXCV. 8vo, pp. 35. — A Sermon, ... on the 9th of May, 1798. Being the Day of a National Fast ... . *Boston: Printed by John Russell.* 1798. 8vo, pp. 23. BA. — A Sermon, delivered at the Interment of the Rev. Jeremy Belknap, D.D. ... Boston, June 22, 1798. ... *Boston: Printed by Manning and Loring.* [1798.] 8vo, pp. 27. — A Sermon ... at Taunton, January 15, 1800; at the Ordination of Rev. John Pipon. ... *Cambridge (Mass.): Printed by William Hilliard.* 1800. 8vo, pp. 33. — A Sermon ... before the Massachusetts Society for the Suppression of Intemperance, ... in Boston, May 27, 1814 ... . *Boston: Printed by John Eliot.* 1814. 8vo, pp. 14, iii. *See also* our Vol. II., No. 6593.

Kirkpatrick (C.) Poems for the Times. By Mrs. Cynthia Kirkpatrick ... . *Parkersburg, W. V.: Blair & Gibbens ... Printers.* 1865. 12mo, pp. 28, (1). B. 38006

Kirkpatrick (J.) The Kirkpatrick Memorial; or, Biographical Sketches of Father and Son, and a Selection from the Sermons of the Rev. Jacob Kirkpatrick, Jr. The Sketches by Rev. George Hale. Edited by W. M. Blackburn. *Philadelphia: Westcott & Thomson.* 1867. 12mo, pp. 312. C., S. 38007

Kirkpatrick (J.) The Sea Piece. A Narrative, philosophical and descriptive Poem. By Dr. J. Kirkpatrick. *London.* 1750. 8vo. 38008

The author was for many years a resident in Carolina, and appended at the end of this volume a poetical description of the "Rainbow Bird of Carolina."

Kirkpatrick (J.) The Light of other Days: Sketches of the Past, and other Selections from the Writings of Mrs. Jane Kirkpatrick. *New-Brunswick, N. J.: Press of J. Terhune.* 1856. 8vo, pp. 80. C. 38009

Kirkpatrick (S. A.) Memorial of ... her Beloved Husband, who Died ... August 15, 1859 ... By Sophia A. Kirkpatrick. *New-Brunswick, N. J.: Press of J. Terhune.* 1859. 8vo, pp. 7.

Kirkwood (A.) A Short Treatise on the Milk-Weed, or Silk-Weed, and the Canadian Nettle, Viewed as Industrial Resources. By Alexander Kirkwood. *Ottawa.* 1867. 8vo, pp. 25.

Kirsten (A.) Skizzen aus den Vereinigten Staaten von Nordamerika, von A. Kirsten. *Leipzig: Brockhaus.* 1849. 12mo, pp. xxii, 347. + *Leipzig.* 1851. 12mo. C. 38012

Kirwan (R.) An Estimate of the Temperature of Different Latitudes. By Richard Kirwan. *London: P. Elmsly.* M.DCC.-LXXXVII. 8vo, pp. viii, 114. BA., S. 38013

Includes North America, West Indies, etc.

Kirwan. Estimation de la Température des differens degrés de latitude. Traduit de l'Anglois par M. Adet. *Paris.* 1789. 8vo, pp. 183. S. 38014

[Kirwan (Thomas).] Soldiering in North Carolina; ... By "One of the Seventeenth." ... *Boston: Thomas Kirwan.* 1864. 12mo, pp. 126. BA. 38015

Kirwan, *pseudon.* *See* [Murray (Nicholas)].

Kissam (S.) Memorials. By Rev. Samuel Kissam. *New York: D. Dana, Jr.* 1859. 12mo, pp. viii, 448. 38016

Kissingen and Brocket. Brief Account of the Mineral Waters of Frankfort, Ky. 1842. 12mo. 38017

Kist (N. C.) John Robinson, Prediker der Leidsche Brownisten-gemeente, en grondlegster der kolonie Plymouth in Noord-Amerika. *Leiden.* 1846. 8vo. 38018

Kitchel (H. D.) An Appeal to the People for the Suppression of the Liquor Traffic: A Prize Essay. *New-York: Oliver & Brother.* 1848. 12mo, pp. 48. + *New York.* 1850. 12mo.

Also issued as "Suppression of the Liquor Traffic. A Prize Essay." ... *New York.* 1870. 12mo, pp. 48. B. Also: ... A Sermon ... at the ordination of Rev. Joel L. Dickinson, Northfield, Conn., February 28, 1844. ... *Hartford: John Paine.* 1844. 8vo, pp. 16. — A Thanksgiving Sermon: ... in ... Chicago ... December 7, 1865. ... *Chicago.* 1865. 8vo, pp. 15. B.

Kitchell (W.) Geology of Cape May County, New Jersey. By William Kitchell. *Trenton.* 1857. Rl. 8vo. 38020

See also New Jersey—*Geology.*

Kitchin (T.) A General Atlas, describing the whole Universe; being an Improvement on the Maps of D'Anville and Robert, containing Maps of the whole Continent of America. By Thomas Kitchin. *London.* 1773. Folio. 38021

Kitchin, *and others.* New Universal Atlas, exhibiting all the Empires, Kingdoms, States, Republics, &c. &c. of the whole World, corrected with the greatest care and augmented from the last Edition of D'Anville and Robert, with Improvements by Major J. Rennell, and others, including all the Tracts and Di-

coveries of the British Circumnavigators, Biron, Wallis, Carteret, Cook, &c. &c. By Thos. Kitchin, and others. *London.* 1796. Imp. folio. C. 38022

[Kite (John L.)] Separations from the Religious Society of Friends. [*Philadelphia.* 1859.] 8vo, pp. 8. H. 38023

Kittlitz (F. H. von). Denkwürdigkeiten einer Reise nach dem russischen Amerika, nach Mikronesien und durch Kamtschatka. Von F. H. v. Kittlitz. *Gotha: Justus Perthes.* 1858. 2 vols., 8vo, pp. xvi, 383, (1); (4), 463, (1). Plates. B. 38024

Kittlitz. Twenty-four Views of the Vegetation of the Coasts and Islands of the Pacific; with Explanatory Descriptions taken during the Exploring Voyage of the Russian Corvette "Senjawin." Translated from the German, and edited by Berthold Seeman. *London: Longman* ... 1861. 4to. C. 38025

Contains some of the most interesting representations ever published of the unusual forms of exotic vegetation. The author, with artistic skill of a very high order, made most careful drawings of the many remarkable scenes visited from Chili to Kamtschatka by Lütke's expedition to the Pacific Ocean; and afterwards, on his return etched them in a singularly bold style, unsurpassed for freedom and truth, accompanying the plates with full explanatory letter-press.

Kittlitz. Über einige Vögel von Chili. 1830. 16 colored Plates. 38026

Kittredge (J.) An Address, ... before the Temperance Society of Plymouth, N. H. July 4, 1829. By Jonathan Kittredge. *Boston: Peirce and Williams.* 1830. 12mo, pp. 24. H.

Also: An Address, ... Temperance Society of Bath, N. H. July 4, 1828. Also, an Address, ... before the American Temperance Society ... Boston, Jan. 28, 1829. ... *Boston: Perkins & Marvin.* 1829. 12mo, pp. 20. H. — [Address, ... at the Annual Meeting of the American Temperance Society in Boston—1829. *Albany.* n. d.] 8vo, pp. 16. — ... An Address upon the Effects of Ardent Spirits. ... Lyme, N. H. January 8, 1827. ... *New-York: Printed by D. Fanshaw.* 1828. 12mo, pp. 24. + Intemperance. Extracts from an Address ... in ... Lime, [*sic*] N. H. ... [n. p. n. d.] 12mo, pp. 12.

Klachte | Der | West-Indische Compagnie | Tegen de | Oost-Indische Compagnie | Deser Vereenighde Nederlanden. | Voorgevallen in een Dialogue tusschen een Hollander | Engelsman en Fransman. | *Tot Middelburgh* | *By Paulus Klaessen. Anno* 1664. 4to, pp. 8. 38028

Complaint of the West India Company against the East India Company of these lands, in a dialogue between a Hollander, an Englishman, and a Frenchman.

Klaer Licht, | ofte | Vertoogh van 'sLants wel- | vaeren, | aengaende | De Combinatie van de Oost en | West-Indische Compagnien. | [n. p. 1644.] 4to, pp. 12. C. 38029

Clear light concerning the combination of the East and West India Companies.

Klaer Vertooch | van de schadelijcke Directie der Bewinthebbe- | ren der vereenichde Oost-Indische Com- | paignie in vier Jaren, nae dat het ac- | coort met d'Engelsche Compaig- | nie ghemaeckt is gheweest. | Int Jaer onses Heeren M. DC. XX IIII | *Tot Rees.* | *Bij Pieter Gerritsz. Anno* 1624. 4to, pp. 16. 38030

A clear demonstration on the mal-administration of the directors of the United East India Company.

Klagh-Vervolgh | Vanden | Deenschen Koninck | En desselfs Minister, | Aen de | Heeren Staten, | Over de pretense violentie, door de Neder- | lantsche West-Indische, op de Deensche | Africaensche Compagnie gepleecht. | Naer de Copye 1662. | *Voor Isaack Isaacxsen tot Delft.* | 4to, pp. 8. 38031

Second Complaint of the Danish King and his Minister ... on the pretended violence exercised by the Dutch West India Company.

Klagte over de bedorvene zeden der Voorgangeren, zoo in 't kerk- als burger-bestuur, in eene zeer vrugtbare ende eerst opluikende Colonie, voorgestelt in eene behandelinge, gepleegt aan een predikant, aan 't Eerw. Classis van Amtserdam [*sic*]. [By J. G. Kals. *Amsterdam.* 1733.] 4to, pp. 63. 38032

On the corrupted manners of the leaders in the church in Surinam. Represented in the treatment of a minister. *See* Wolbers' "Geschied. van Suriname," p. 195.

Klaproth (Heinrich Julius). Recherches sur le Pays de Fou Sang, mentionné dans les Livres Chinois, et pris mal à propos pour une partie de l'Amérique. Par M. J. Klaproth. *Paris.* [n. d.] 8vo, pp. 16. 38033

Klare Aenwijsinge. | Dat de Vereenighde Nederlanden, gheen Treves | met den Vyandt dienen te maecken. | Sijnde het | Derden Deel | Van't | Tractaet | tegens | Pays, Treves ende Onderhande- | linghe met den Vyandt. | *In 's Gravenhage,* | *By Aert Meuris, Boeckverkooper in de Papestraet* | *In den Bybel, Anno* 1630. | 4to, pp. 12.

Clear demonstration that the United Netherlands should make no truce with the enemy, etc.

Klare Besgryving van Cabo de Bona Esperanca; med de bygelegen Kust naar Angola toe, van Cabo Negro af. *Amsterdam: Jod. Hondius.* 1652. 4to. Map, 3 Plates. 38035

Klare und Gewisse Wahrheit. ... Betreffend den eigendlichen Zustand, so wohl [*sic*] der Wahren Friedliebenden Christen und Gottesfürchtigen, als auch der Verfallnen, Streit oder Kriegs-Süchtigen, zusammt ihrer beyder Hoffnung und Ausgang. Schrifftmässig dargelegt von einem Teutschen Geringen Handwercks Mann. *Gedruckt in Germantown bey Christoph Saur.* 1747.

Klauke (——). On North Western American Emigration; with a Supplement. 1867. 12mo, pp. 22, 22. 38037

Title from Morgan's "Bibliotheca Canadensis."

Klein (Hermann J.) An den Nordpol. Schilderung der arktischen Gegenden und der Nordpolfahrten von den ältesten Zeiten bis zur Gegenwart. *Kreuznach: Voigtländer.* [1870?] 8vo, pp. iv, 140. 5 Plates. 38038

Kleine Cosmographia, oder Summarische Beschreibung der Gantzen Welt, von vier Theilen der Erden, Asia, Europa, Africa, und America. [n. p. n. d.] 8vo. 38039

Kleinknecht (C. D.) Nachricht von der Durch das Blut des erwurgten Lammes Theur erkaufften Schwartzen Schaaf und Lämmer Heerde Das ist Neu bekehrten Malabarischen Christen in Ost-Indien. *Ulm.* 1738. 8vo. 38040

Contains some particulars relative to America.

Kleinknecht. Zuverlässige Nachricht von der ... schwarzen Schaaf- und Lämmer-Heerde, oder von den neubekehrten Malabarischen Christen in Ost-Indien. ... Deme noch beygefügt: Nachrichten von den Englischen Colonisten Georgiens zu Eben-Ezer in America. *Augspurg: Lotters Erben.* 1749. 8vo. Plate.

Very rare. Contains interesting details of the Saltzburg emigrants. *See* Part I., pp. 172–179; Part II., pp. 214–240.

Kleinschmidt (S.) Grammatik der Grönländischen Sprache mit theilweisem Einschluss des Labrador Dialects. Von Samuel Kleinschmidt. *Berlin: G. Reimer.* 1851. 8vo, pp. x, 182. B.

Klemm (G.) Die Staaten von Anahuac und das alte Aegypten. *Leipzig.* 1846. 8vo. 8 Plates. 38043

This is Vol. v. of his "Allgemeine Cultur-Geschichte."

Klencke (H.) Alexander von Humboldt's Leben und Wirken, Reisen und Wissen. Sechste illustrirte Ausgabe, erweitert und umgearbeitet von H. Th. Kühne. *Leipzig: Spamer.* 1870. 8vo, pp. viii, 432. 2 Maps, Portrait, and 8 colored Plates. B.

Klencke (P. F. H.) Alexander von Humboldt. Ein biographisches Denkmal. Von P. F. Hermann Klencke. *Leipzig: Otto Spamer.* 1851. 8vo, pp. x, (2), 252. Map, Portrait. B.

Klencke. Alexander von Humboldt: A Biographical Monument. By Prof. Klencke. Translated from the German, by J. Bauer. *New York.* 1853. 12mo. 38046

Klencke *and* Schlesier (G.) Lives of the Brothers Humboldt, Alexander and William. Translated and Arranged from the German of Klencke & Schlesier. By Juliette Bauer. *London: Ingram, Cooke, & Co.* MDCCCLII. 12mo, pp. (2), vi, (2), 431, (1). Portraits. BA. + *New York: Harper & Brothers.* 1853. 12mo, pp. 398. Portraits. P., H. 38047

The paging is continuous, but each of Klencke's and Schlesier's lives has its own title-page.

Klerk (J. de). Van den oorspronk en de kracht der Vooroordeelen, Door J. T. Als mede een koort Uyttreksel Uyt de Aanteykeninge van de Baron de Lahontan, rakende de Zeden, 't Geloof, en't verstant van de Wilden tot Canada, en de lof der hedendaagse Eeuw, in vergelykinge, van de voorgaande Eeuwen. En dat er zoo veele Atheisten niet zyn als men doorgaans gelooft, Door J. de Klerk. *Amsterdam: Jan Blom.* 1710. 12mo.

Kletke (H.) Alexander von Humboldt's Reisen in Amerika und Asien. Eine Darstellung seiner wichtigsten Forschungen. *Berlin: Hasselberg.* 1854–56. 4 vols., 8vo. 38049

Vols. I. and II.—pp. viii, 367; viii, 368—contain "Reisen in die Aequinoctial Gegenden Amerika's;" Vols. III. and IV. consist of "Reisen im europäischen und asiatischen Russland." For a later edition *see our* Vol. VIII., No. 33739.

Kletke. Reise Seiner Königlichen Hoheit des Prinzen Adalbert von Preussen nach Brasilien. Nach dem Tagebuche Sr. ... Hoheit ... . *Berlin: Hasselberg.* 1857. 8vo, pp. (4), 749. Portrait. 38050

De Kleyne ... werelt. *See* [Joosten (T. J.)], No. 36640.

Kleynhovii (C. F.) Ode ad Joh. Kinkerum, quum magni Washingtonis, pie defuncti, memoriam sociis collegii: Felix Meritis dicti, funerale carmine commendaret. *Amstelredami.* 1800. 4to, pp. 8. 38051

Relates to the death of Washington.

Klinckhardt (C. G.) *See* Temper (C. S.)

Kline (A. C.) The Stamp Collector's Manual. Being a Complete Guide to the Collectors of American and Foreign Postage Stamps ... . Compiled by A. C. Kline. ... *Philadelphia: A. C. Kline.* 1862. 16mo, pp. 48. H. 38052

Klinkowström (A.) Bref om de Förente Staterna författade under en resa till America. Aren 1818, 1819, 1820 af Friherre Axel Klinkowström. *Stockholm.* 1824. 2 vols. 38053

Letters on the United States, written during a journey through America in 1818–20.

Klippart (J. H.) The Wheat Plant: its Origin, Culture, Growth, Development, Composition, Varieties, Diseases, &c. &c. Together with a few Remarks on Indian Corn, its Culture, &c. By John H. Klippart. ... *Cincinnati: Moore, Wilstach, Keys & Co.* 1859. 8vo, pp. 706. + [*Ibid.*] 1860. 8vo. B.

Also: Address before the Ohio Agricultural Convention, Jan. 3, 1866. ... *Columbus.* 1866. 8vo.

Klöden (G. A. von). Handbuch der Länder- und Staatenkunde von Asien, Australien, Afrika und Amerika von Gustav Adolph von Klöden ... . *Berlin: Weidmannsche Buchhandlung.* 1862. 8vo, pp. xii, 895. 38055

With a second title-page, "Handbuch der Erdkunde ... . Dritter Theil."

Kloos (J. H.) Minnesota in zijne hulpbronnen, ontwikkeling ... *Amsterdam.* 1867. 8vo. 38056

Klunzinger (Karl). Antheil der Deutschen an der Entdeckung von Südamerika; oder, Abentheuer des Ambrosius Dalfinger und des Nicolaus Federmann, beider von Ulm, des Georg Hohemut von Speier, und des fränkischen Ritters Philipp von Hutten unter der Herrschaft der Welser von Augsburg in Venezuela. Nach den Hauptquellen dargestellt. *Stuttgart: C. A. Sonnewald.* 1857. 12mo, pp. (8), 116. Map. 38057

Knapp (A. L.) ... Speech of Hon. Anthony L. Knapp ... on the Policy ... of the War; ... June 5, 1862. [*Washington.* 1862.] 8vo, pp. 16. H. 38058

Knapp (C. L.) Assault on Senator Sumner. Speech of Hon. Chauncey L. Knapp ... July 12, 1856. [*Washington.* 1856.] 8vo, pp. 8. H. 38059

Knapp (F. N.) A Discourse ... at the Funeral of Rev. John Pierce, D.D. ... Brookline ... August 27, 1849. By Rev. Frederic N. Knapp. *Boston: Wm. Crosby & H. P. Nichols.* 1849. 16mo, pp. 63. BA. 38060

Knapp. ... Report concerning the Aid and Comfort given by the Sanitary Commission to Sick Soldiers found at the Railroad Station. By Frederic N. Knapp. ... September 23, 1861. [*Washington.* 1861.] 8vo, pp. 13. B. 38061

Also: Two Reports ... September 23, 1861 [October 21, 1861. *Washington.* 1861.] 8vo, pp. 23. + Third Report ... March 21, 1862. ... [*Washington.* 1862.] 8vo, pp. 29. + Fourth Report ... Dec. 15th, 1862. ... [*Washington.* 1862.] 8vo, pp. 22, (1). + Supplement to Fourth Report ... pp. 14. + Second Edition. [*Ibid.*] + Fifth

Report ... Oct. 1, 1863. [*Washington.* 1863.] 8vo, pp. 63. 2 Plans. B. + Report ... for the Quarter ending June 30, 1865. ... [*Washington.* 1865.] 8vo, pp. 47. B.

Knapp (H. S.) A History of the Pioneer and Modern Times of Ashland County, from the Earliest to the Present Date. By H. S. Knapp. *Philadelphia: J. B. Lippincott & Co.* 1863. 8vo, pp. 550. Plate. H. 38062

Knapp (I.) A Sermon ... at Westfield November 18th 1817; at the Funeral of Maj. Gen. William Shepard ... . By Isaac Knapp. *Springfield, Ms.: Printed by Thomas Dickman.* 1818. 8vo, pp. 16. H. 38063

Also: ... A Sermon ... at Northampton, before the Hampshire Missionary Society ... August 27, 1812. ... [n. p.:] *William Butler, Printer.* 1812. 8vo, pp. 32. H.

Knapp (J.) Autobiography of Elder Jacob Knapp. With an Introductory Essay by R. Jeffery. *New York: Sheldon and Company.* 1868. 12mo, pp. iv, 9, xxvi, 11–341. Portrait. 38064

Also: Conduct pursued by the Rev. J. Knapp in Relation to the Death and Funeral of his Father-in-Law. *Hamilton.* 1846. 8vo. B. *See our* Vol. III., No. 9200. — ... Farewell Sermon ... in ... Boston, March 19, 1842 ... . *Boston.* 1842. 32mo, pp. 94. Portrait. H.

Knapp (J. F.) An Authentic Account of the Last Hours of John Francis Knapp. ... *Milford, Mass.: Ballou & Stacy, Printers.* 1831. 8vo, pp. 15. BA. 38065

Knapp. Report of the Evidence and Points of Law, arising on the Trial of John Francis Knapp, for the Murder of Joseph White, Esquire. ... *Salem: W. & S. B. Ives.* 1830. 8vo, pp. (6), 74. + [*Ibid.*] pp. (6), 72. H. + An Appendix to the ... Trial of John Francis Knapp ... containing the New Evidence ... on the Second Trial. *Salem.* 1830. 8vo, pp. 72. H. 38066

Also: Trial of John Francis Knapp ... for the Murder of Capt. Joseph White ... July 20, 1830. ... *Boston: Dutton & Wentworth.* 1830. 8vo, pp. 60. + Second Trial ... August 14, 1830. ... [*Ibid.*] 1830. 8vo, pp. 28. — The Trial and Conviction of John Francis Knapp for the Murder of Joseph White, Esq. of Salem, on the Sixth of April, 1830. *Boston: Charles Ellms.* 1830. 8vo, pp. 35, (1). H.

Knapp (M.) Human Liberty against Ultra-Temperance Intolerance; or, Battle between Innkeepers and Ecclesiastics. By Martin Knapp ... . *New York.* 1853. 8vo, pp. 93. 38067

Knapp (M. L.) An Address ... at the Opening of the Rock-Island Medical School, Nov. 7, 1848. By Moses L. Knapp ... *Chicago: Campbell & Fuller, Printers.* 1849. 8vo, pp. 20. H.

Also: Address ... to the Graduating Class of the Indiana Medical College ... Feb. 18, 1847 ... . *Chicago.* 1847. 8vo, pp. 22, (1). B.

Knapp (S. L[orenzo]). American Biography, ... of Distinguished Americans. By Samuel L. Knapp. *New York: Conner & Cooke.* 1833. 12mo, pp. (2), 412. + *New York: C. C. Childs.* 1850. 12mo, pp. (2), 412. B. 38069

Forms Vol. III. of the American edition of Maunder's "Treasury of Knowledge." "American History and Literature" forms part of the same work.

Knapp. Biographical Sketches of Eminent Lawyers, Statesmen, and Men of Letters. ... By Samuel L. Knapp. *Boston: Richardson and Lord.* 1821. 8vo, pp. 360. BA., W. 38070

[Knapp.] Extracts from a Journal of Travels in North America, consisting of an account of Boston and its Vicinity. By Ali Bey, &c. ... *Boston: Printed by Thomas Badger, Jun.* 1818. 12mo, pp. 124. B. 38071

[Knapp.] Extracts from the Journal of Marshal Soult ... . *Newburyport: William B. Allen & Co.* 1817. 12mo, pp. 143. H.

Includes sketches of men, etc., in Massachusetts.

Knapp. Female Biography; containing Notices of Distinguished Women, in Different Nations and Ages. By Samuel L. Knapp. *New York.* MDCCCXXXIV. 12mo, pp. 360. + *Philadelphia: Thomas Wardle.* 1836. 12mo, pp. 501, (3). B. + [*Ibid.*] 1843. + [*Ibid.*] 1846. + *Philadelphia: Leary & Getz.* [n. d.] 12mo, pp. 503, (1). 38073

Knapp. The Genius of Masonry, or a Defence of the Order, containing some Remarks on the Origin and History, ... with some Notices of other Secret Societies in the United States. ... By Samuel L. Knapp. *Providence: Cranston & Marshall, Printers.* 1828. 12mo, pp. 107. C., H. 38074

Knapp. Lectures on American Literature, with Remarks on some Passages of American History. By Samuel L. Knapp. [*New York:*] *Elam Bliss.* 1829. 8vo, pp. 300. B., S. 38075

[Knapp.] Letters of Shahcoolen, a Hindu Philosopher, residing in Philadelphia, to his Friend El Hassan, an Inhabitant of Delhi. *Boston.* 1802. 12mo, pp. 152. 38076

First published in the New York "Commercial Advertiser." Letters II.–V. are on the Rights of Woman.

Knapp. The Life of Aaron Burr. By Samuel L. Knapp. ... *New-York: Wiley & Long.* 1835. 12mo, pp. 290. B. 38077

See "N. A. Rev.," LXXIX. 297.

Knapp. Life of Timothy Dexter; Embracing Sketches of the Eccentric Characters that Composed his Associates. By Samuel L. Knapp. ... *Boston: G. N. Thomson.* 1838. 18mo, pp. 105. Plate. C. 38078

Knapp. Life of Lord Timothy Dexter; ... including "Dexter's Pickle for the Knowing Ones." By Samuel L. Knapp. *Newburyport: John G. Tilton.* 1848. 18mo, pp. 107, (1), 36. + [With] An Introduction by "Cymon." *Boston: J. E. Tilton & Co.* 1858. 16mo, pp. 157. C. 38079

Knapp. The Life of Thomas Eddy; Comprising an Extensive Correspondence with many of the most Distinguished Philosophers and Philanthropists of this and Other Countries. By Samuel L. Knapp. ... *New York: Conner & Cooke.* 1834. 8vo, pp. 394. Portrait. + *London: Edmund Fry and Son.* 1836. 8vo, pp. 264. B. 38080

Knapp. A Memoir of the Life of Daniel Webster. By Samuel L. Knapp. *Boston: Stimpson and Clapp.* 1831. 12mo, pp. (2), 234. Portrait. + Second Edition. *New York: J. S. Redfield.* 1835. 12mo, pp. 108. BA. 38081

See "N. A. Rev.," July, 1835.

[Knapp.] James Munroe. [n. p. n. d.] 8vo, pp. 10. Portrait. B. 38082

[Knapp.] Memoirs of General Lafayette. With an Account of his Visit to America ... from his Arrival, August 15th, to the Celebration at Yorktown, October 19th, 1824. *Boston: E. G. House.* 1824. 12mo, pp. 264. Portrait. BA. 38083

[Knapp.] Sketches of Public Characters. Drawn from the Living and the Dead. With Notices of other Matters. By Ignatius Loyola Robertson, L.L.D. ... *New-York: E. Bliss.* 1830. 12mo, pp. viii, 5–259, (1). B., C. 38084

Webster, Calhoun, Everett, Livingston, Randolph, Dwight, etc., are the characters. Also: An Address ... before the Young Men of Boston, August 2, 1826, in Commemoration of the Death of Adams and Jefferson. ... *Boston: Ingraham and Hewes, Printers.* 1826. 8vo, pp. 31.—Advice in the Pursuits of Literature, containing Historical, Biographical, and Critical Remarks. ... *Middletown, N. J.* 1827. 12mo. + Second Edition. *New-York: J. K. Porter.* 1832. 12mo, pp. x, 7–296. + *New York.* 1841.—The Bachelors, and other Tales, founded on American Incidents, and Character. .. *New-York: J. and W. Sandford.* MDCCCXXXVI. 12mo, pp. 216.—A Discourse on the Life and Character of De Witt Clinton, ... March, 1828. ... *Washington: Printed by William Greer.* 1828. 8vo, pp. 36.—Eulogy ... in ... Boston, ... June 8, 1819, on the Character of ... Shubael Bell, Esq. ... *Boston: Printed by J. T. Buckingham.* 1819. 8vo, pp. 19. H.—An Oration ... at Dedham, June 24, A.D. 1820 ... . *Dedham.* 1820.

8vo, pp. 18.—An Oration ... before the Merrimack Humane Society ... September 3, 1811. ... *Newburyport: Press of E. W. Allen.* 1811. 8vo, pp. 22, (1).—An Oration ... at Newburyport, on the Fourth of July 1810. ... *Newburyport.* [1810.] 8vo, pp. 16.—An Oration ... before "The Associated Disciples of Washington," on the 22d of February, 1812. ... *Newburyport: Press of E. W. Allen.* 1812. 8vo, pp. 23. BA. —An Oration, ... before the Society of Phi Beta Kappa, at Dartmouth College, August 19, 1824. ... *Boston.* 1824. 8vo, pp. 32.—Oration ... at Newburyport, June 24, 1811. ... *Newburyport.* 1811. 8vo.—Tales of the Garden of Kosciusko. ... *New York: West & Trow.* 1834. 12mo, pp. 216. + Second Edition. *New York: Levison & Brother.* 1839. 12mo. *See* Hinton (J. H.), Vol. VIII., No. 31966, *also* Hudson River, No. 33520.

Knapp (W[illiam] H.) A Discourse of Demand and Supply in Church and State. By W. H. Knapp. *Boston: William V. Spencer.* 1869. 12mo, pp. 17. H. 38085

Knapp. Resistance to Evil: A Discourse delivered to the Barton-Square Society at Salem, Sept. 6, 1863. By W. H. Knapp. *Boston: Printed by John Wilson and Son.* 1863. 12mo, pp. 13. B. 38086

Kneas (H. R.) In the Matter of the Contested Election of District Attorney: Reed *vs.* Kneas. *Philadelphia.* 1851. 8vo.

Kneas. Proceedings of the Celebration of the Anniversary of the Glorious Battle of New-Orleans, by "The Personal and Political Friends" of George Mifflin Dallas. By Horn R. Kneas, Esq. *Philadelphia: Daily Keystone Office.* 1846. 8vo, pp. 25.

Kneedler *vs.* David M. Lane & others. 8vo, pp. 21.

Concerning the draft in Pennsylvania.

Kneeland (A.) National Hymns, original and selected; for the use of those who are "Slaves to no Sect." By Abner Kneeland. *Boston.* 1832. 16mo, pp. iv, 104. H. + [*Ibid.*] 1834.

Kneeland. Report of the Arguments of the Attorney of the Commonwealth, at the Trials of Abner Kneeland, for Blasphemy, in the Municipal and Supreme Courts, in Boston, January and May, 1834. ... [*Boston:*] *Printed by Beals, Homer & Co.* 1834. 8vo, pp. 93. B., C. 38091

Also: An Appeal to Common Sense ... occasioned by the Late Trial of Rev. Abner Kneeland ... . *Boston.* 1834. 8vo, pp. 14.—Introduction to the Defence of Rev. Abner Kneeland ... . *Boston.* 1834. 8vo. H.—A Review of the Prosecution against Abner Kneeland, for Blasphemy. By a Cosmopolite. *Boston.* 1835. 8vo, pp. 32.—A Review of the Trial, Conviction and final Imprisonment of Abner Kneeland for Blasphemy. ... *Boston.* 1838. 12mo, pp. 132.—Speech ... in his own Defence ... for Blasphemy. November Term, 1834. *Boston: J. Q. Adams.* 1834. 8vo, pp. (4), 32. —Speech ... in his own Defence, ... March 8, 1836. *Boston.* 1836. 8vo, pp. 44.

Knelb (P. H.) Narratives of an Old Traveller. ... *Philadelphia.* 1856. 8vo. 38092

Knelb. Perilous Incidents in the Lives of Sailors and Travellers. *Philadelphia: Willis P. Hazard.* 1854. 8vo. 38093

Knibb (W.) Colonial Slavery. Defence of the Baptist Missionaries from the Charge of Inciting the Late Rebellion in Jamaica; in a Discussion between the Rev. William Knibb and Mr. P. Borthwick ... December 15, 1832. ... Second Edition. *London.* [n. d.] 8vo, pp. (2), 30. B. 38094

Knickerbocker, *pseudon.* The Wreckmaster. By Knickerbocker, Jr. *Philadelphia: Daughaday & Becker.* 1870. 16mo, pp. 307. 6 Plates. 38095

Knickerbocker (Diedrich). *See* [Irving (W.)]

The Knickerbocker: or, New York Monthly Magazine. Vol. I. *New York: Peabody & Co.* M DCCC XXXIII. 8vo, pp. iv, 390. Plate. Continued. BA. 38096

Knickerbocker Almacac for 1848. *New York.* 8vo. 38097

The Knickerbocker Gallery; a Testimonial to the Editor of the Knickerbocker Magazine, from its Contributors. *New York.* 1855. 8vo. 48 Portraits. C., P. 38098

The Knickerbocker Sketch-Book: a library of Select Literature. Edited by Lewis Gaylord Clark ... . *New-York: Burgess, Stringer and Company.* [n. d.] 12mo, pp. 243. 38099

The Knickerbocker and Nevada Silver Mining Company. ... *New York: Wm. C. Bryant & Co., Printers.* 1865. 8vo, pp. 20. Map. H. 38100

Knight (A. C.) A Year in Canada; and other Poems. By Ann Cuthbert Knight. *Edinburgh.* 1816. 12mo. 38101

See "M. Rev.," LXXIX. 433.

Knight (A. R.) Recollections of a Mute. A Brief Sketch of Events ... within my Knowledge. By Miss A. R. Knight ... *Jackson, Jackson Co., Mich.* 1858. 12mo, pp. 15. H.

Knight (C.) Cyclopædia of the Industry of all Nations. By Charles Knight. *London.* 1851. 8vo. C. + *New York.* 1851. 8vo, pp. xxiv, 1810. 36 Plates. B. 38103

Knight. Geography of the British Empire, a Gazetteer of the United Kingdom and its Colonies. By Charles Knight. *London: Bradbury & Evans.* 1853. 2 vols., rl. 8vo, pp. 1359; 1519. 38104

Knight. The Popular History of England: ... from the Earliest Period to our Own Times. By Charles Knight. ... *London: Bradbury and Evans.* 1856–62. 8 vols., 8vo, pp. xi, (1), viii, 492; xii, 500; xi, 499, (1); xi, 499; xii, 483; x, 472, (2); xvi, 582; xvi, 672. Plates. BA. 38105

A so-called *Boston* edition is really printed in *London.* Covers the period of the American Revolution, upon which subject the details are copious and tolerably impartial. The "English Cyclopedia," conducted by Charles Knight, contains of course very much matter relative to America.

Knight (C. F.) ... A Sermon ... at the Opening of St. Mark's Church, Boston ... 1859. By C. F. Knight ... . *Boston: Damrell & Moore, Printers.* 1859. 8vo, pp. 15. H. 38106

Knight (D.) An Oration ... at Charlton, ... Anniversary of American Independence. By Daniel Knight. ... *Worcester.* 1819. 8vo, pp. 20. M. 38107

Knight (D. M.) A Proposal for Peace between Great Britain and North America; upon a New Plan. In a Letter to Lord North. By D. M. Knight. *Birmingham: Printed for the Author* [*by J. Baskerville*]. 1779. 8vo. 38108

"Mr. Knight proposes that the Americans should be acknowledged a free and independent people, and that George Prince of Wales should be received by them as their sovereign lord and chief."—*Monthly Review,* LX. 157.

Knight (*Dr.*) Narrative of a late Expedition against the Indians, with an Account of the Barbarous Execution of Col. Crawford and the Wonderful Escape of Dr. Knight and John Slover from Captivity in 1782. *Philadelphia: Printed by Francis Bailey.* M.DCC.LXXXIII. 16mo, pp. 38. + To which is added A Narrative of the Captivity and Escape of Mrs. Frances Scott, An inhabitant of Washington County Virginia. *Andover: Printed by Ames & Parker.* [n. d.] Sm. 12mo, pp. 46. 38109

Knight. A Remarkable Narrative of an Expedition against the Indians with an account of the Barbarous Execution of Col. Crawford, and Dr. Knight's Escape from Captivity. [n. p.:] *Printed for Chapman Whitcomb.* [n. d.] 12mo, pp. 24. 38110

Knight. Indian Atrocities. Narratives of the Perils and Sufferings of Dr. Knight and John Slover among the Indians, during the Revolutionary War. With short memoirs of Col. Crawford & John Slover. And a letter from H. Brackinridge, on the Rights of the Indians, etc. *Nashville.* 1843. 12mo, pp. 96. + *Cincinnati: U. P. James.* 1867. 12mo, pp. 72. 38111

Of this last edition five hundred copies were printed, seventy-five of which are on thick paper.

Knight (F.) An Oration ... Marblehead ... the Fourth of July, 1834. By Franklin Knight. *Boston.* 1834. 8vo, pp. 23.

[Knight (Frederick).] Twilight; A Poem ... at Litchfield, July 4th, 1812. By a Student at Law. ... *New-York: Printed by Collins and Co.* 1813. 12mo, pp. 48. BA. 38113

Knight. Thorn Cottage, or the Poet's Home. A Memorial of Frederick Knight, Esq. ... *Boston: Press of Crocker and Brewster.* 1855. 12mo, pp. 108. B. 38114

Knight (H. C.) Lady Huntington and her Friends; or, the Revival ... in the Days of Wesley, Whitefield, ... Compiled by Mrs. Helen C. Knight. *New York.* [1853.] 12mo, pp. 292. Portraits. 38115

[Knight (Henry Cogswell).] Letters from the South and West; By Arthur Singleton, Esq. *Boston: Richardson and Lord.* 1824. 8vo, pp. 158. H. 38116

Also: The Broken Harp. Poems. ... *Philadelphia.* 1815. 12mo.

Knight (J.) Important Extracts from ... Letters: written by Englishmen, in the United States ... to their Friends in England. ... By J. Knight ... . *Manchester.* 1818. 8vo, pp. 48.

Knight (J.) Report upon the Plan of Construction of several of the Principal Rail Roads in the ... Middle States, ... By J. Knight, ... and Benj. H. Lathrobe ... . *Baltimore: Printed by Lucas & Deaver.* 1838. 8vo, pp. 79. 13 Plans. + Sequel to the Report of the 8th of January, 1838 ... . [*Ibid.*] 1838. 8vo, pp. 36, (8). BA. 38118

Knight (J[onathan]). An Eulogium on Nathan Smith, M.D. ... pronounced at his Funeral ... By J. Knight, M.D. ... *New Haven.* 1829. 8vo, pp. 28. B. 38119

Also: Addresses at the Funeral of Timothy Phelps Beers, M.D. .. in New Haven, September 24, 1858. ... *New Haven: W. H. Stanley.* 1858. 8vo, pp. 18. H.

Knight (J.) A Sermon ... at the Interment of Mrs. Betsey Bartlett ... . By Joseph Knight ... . *Hartford: Printed by Goodwin & Co.* 1825. 8vo, pp. 18. H. 38120

Also: A Sermon ... at the Funeral of Deacon Cyrus Stowell, of Peru, February 17, 1859. ... *Pittsfield, Mass.: Henry Chickering, Printer.* 1859. 8vo, pp. 16. H.

[Knight (Nehemiah R.), *and others.*] Address. To the People of the United States. [*Providence.* 1844.] 12mo, pp. 15.

Knight (R.) History of the General or Six Principle Baptists, in Europe and America; In Two Parts. ... By Richard Knight. *Providence: Smith and Parmenter, Printers.* 1827. 8vo, pp. 367, (1). H. 38122

Knight (S.) Memoir of Sarah Knight. *Philadelphia.* 1829. 18mo. 38123

Knight [Sarah Kemble]. The Journals of Madam Knight, and Rev. Mr. Buckingham. From the Original Manuscripts, Written in 1704 & 1710. *New-York: Wilder & Campbell.* 1825. Sm. 8vo, pp. 129. BA. 38124

Madam Knight's journal consists of an account of a journey from Boston to New York in the year 1704. That of the Rev. Mr. Buckingham of the expedition against Canada in 1710 and 1711.

Knight. The Private Journal of a Journey from Boston to New York, in the Year 1704. Kept by Madam Knight. *Albany: Frank H. Little.* 1865. 4to, pp. 92. B. 38125

Three hundred copies printed, and fifty on large paper. *See* "Hist. Mag.," II. 253, *also* Littell's "Living Age," June, 1858.

Knight (T. F.) The American War: with some Suggestions towards effecting an Honorable Peace. By Thomas Frederick Knight. *Halifax.* 1864. 8vo, pp. 16. 38126

Knight. Descriptive Catalogue of the Fishes of Nova Scotia. By Thomas Frederick Knight. *Halifax.* 1866. 8vo, pp. (2), 54.

Knight. Nova Scotia and her Resources: A Prize Essay. By Thomas Frederick Knight. *Halifax & London.* 1862. 8vo, pp. 87. 38128

Knight. Shore and Deep Sea Fisheries of Nova Scotia. By Thomas Frederick Knight. *Halifax.* 1867. 8vo, pp. viii, 113.

Knight (T.) Elegy exhibiting a brief History of the Life, Labours, and Glorious Death of Rev. George Whitefield. By Titus Knight. *Halifax: The Author.* 1771. 8vo. 38130

Knight (W[illiam] H.) Hand-Book Almanac for the Pacific States: an Official Register and Year-Book of Facts, For the Year 1862. Edited by Wm. H. Knight. *San Francisco: H. H. Bancroft and Company.* 1862. 12mo, pp. 191. H. 38131

Continued to 1864 or later. The volume for 1864 contains a Business Directory of the States and Territories.

Knights. An Authentic Exposition of the "K. G. C." "Knights of the Golden Circle;" or, a History of Secession from 1834 to 1861. ... *Indianapolis, Ind.: C. O. Perrine.* 1861. 8vo, pp. 88. BA. 38132

See also No. 36968.

The Grand Encampment of Knights Templar ... of Massachusetts and Rhode Island. Its History ... . *Boston: Printed by John Wilson and Son.* 1864. 8vo, pp. 67. Continued. 38133

Also: Proceedings ... for the year 1864. *Boston: J. Wilson & Son.* 1864. 8vo Continued.—Abstract of the Proceedings ... for the year ending October, 1865. *Boston.* 1865. 8vo. Continued.

Proceedings of the General Grand Encampment of the Knights Templar of the United States of America. From its Formation, ... 1816 to 1856. *New Orleans.* 1860. 8vo, pp. (2), 361, xxvii.

The Knights of the Frozen Sea. A Narrative of Arctic Discovery and Adventure. ... *New York.* 1867. 16mo, pp. viii, 360.

Knoepfel. An Account of Knoepfel's Schoharie Cave, Schoharie County, New-York: With the History of its Discovery, Subterranean Lake, Minerals, and Natural Curiosities. Illustrated with Engravings. *New-York: Printed by W. E. & J. Sibell.* 1853. 8vo, pp. 16. 2 Plates. BA. 38136

Knole. Biographical Sketches of Eminent Persons, whose Portraits form part of the Duke of Dorset's Collection at Knole in Kent. 1795. 8vo. Plates. 38137

Among the celebrated persons whose portraits are in this collection, and of whom a short biographical account is given, are Sir Francis Drake, Admiral Blake, and others.

Knopf (D. C.) De Ornata Oris, nasi et aurium apud populos Americanos. *Gottingae.* 1832. 8vo. 7 Plates. 38138

Knot (G. C. P.) The Slave Trade. *London.* 1791. 8vo.

Title from Allibone's "Dictionary."

The Know-Nothing Almanac and True American's Manual for 1856. Edited by W. S. Tisdale. *New York.* [n. d.] 12mo, pp. 68. S. 38140

Know Nothing; A Poem for Natives and Aliens. *Boston: John P. Jewett & Company.* 1854. 12mo, pp. 36. S. 38141

The Know Nothing. (?) *Boston: John P. Jewett & Company.* 1855. 12mo, pp. 347. B. 38142

Know Nothing Platform: ... the Necessity of the Order ... . *Philadelphia.* [1854.] 8vo, pp. 100. P. 38143

To those Born on the Soil who Know Nothing but the Advancement of their Country's Good. Written by Nobody Knows Who, and dedicated (by Permission,) to all who like it. *Brooklyn.* 1854. 8vo, pp. 8. 38144

The Know Nothings Cause and Effect. [n. p. n. d.] 12mo, pp. 12. 38145

Startling Facts for Native Americans. *New York.* 1855. 8vo.

United States Senatorial Question. Speeches ... in ... New-York, by the Honorables Messrs. C. C. Leigh, ... and others, in Exposition of the Oaths ... of the Know-Nothings ... February ... 1855. *Albany: Weed, Parsons & Company, Printers.* 1855. 8vo, pp. 58. B. 38147

Know Nothingism. A Reply to Henry A. Wise. *Snow Hill, Md.* [n. d.] 8vo. 38148

See also our Vol. VI., No. 23431.

KNOWLAN (J.) Sermon ... at the Funeral of the late Mrs. Abigail Newton, ... of Liverpool, Nova Scotia ... . By James Knowlan. *Halifax.* 1819. 8vo. 38149

KNOWLES [Charles]. The Conduct of Admiral Knowles on the late Expedition set in a True Light. *London.* 1758. 8vo. Folded Plate. 38150

KNOWLES. Journal of the Expedition. *See* No. 36721.

KNOWLES. Minutes of the Proceedings at the Trial of Admiral Knowles. By Charles Fearne. *London.* 1750. 8vo.

KNOWLES. Refutation of the Charge brought against Admiral Knowles, in a Pamphlet, entitled "The Conduct and Treatment of John Crookshanks, Esq." *London: Millar.* 1759. 8vo. C.

Wrangham's Catalogue, page 316, describes briefly a tract relating to the Vindication of Admiral Knowles, *London*, 1757, which I have not seen.

KNOWLES (J. D.) Life of Mrs. Ann H. Judson, late Missionary to Burmah; with an Account of the American Baptist Mission to that Empire. By Rev. James Davis Knowles. *Philadelphia: American Sunday School Union.* [1830.] 18mo, pp. 266. Plates, Portrait. H. 38153

Also: Memoir of Mrs. Ann H. Judson ... . Second Edition. *Boston: Lincoln & Edmands.* 1829. 12mo, pp. 324. Map, Portrait. + Third Edition. [*Ibid.*] 1829. Sm. 8vo, pp. 324. Map. B. + Fourth Edition. [*Ibid.*] 1831. Sm. 8vo, pp. 408. Map, Portrait. + *Boston: Gould, Kendall and Lincoln.* 1847. 12mo, pp. 354. Map, Portrait. H.

KNOWLES. Memoir of Roger Williams, the Founder of the State of Rhode Island. By James D. Knowles ... . *Boston: Lincoln, Edmands and Co.* 1834. 12mo, pp. 437. Facsimile. C.

KNOWLES. Oration ... at the Columbian College, ... July 4, 1823; By James D. Knowles ... . *Washington City: John S. Meehan.* 1823. 8vo, pp. 20. H. 38155

KNOWLES. Perils and Safeguards of American Liberty: Address ... July 4, 1828. ... By James D. Knowles ... . *Boston: Printed by Lincoln & Edmands.* [n. d.] 8vo, pp. 27, (1). 38156

Also: Importance of Theological Institutions. An Address, ... November 14, 1832. ... *Boston: Lincoln & Edmands.* 1832. 8vo, pp. 28. BA.—Spirituous Liquors ... An Address ... in ... Boston, April 9, 1829, the Day of the Annual Fast. ... *Boston: Printed by Lincoln & Edmands.* 1829. 12mo, pp. 24. H.

KNOWLES (W[illiam] J.) Features of Inauguration of the Franklin Statue in Boston, September 17th, 1856. By W. J. Knowles. *Boston: For the Author.* 1856. 8vo, pp. 12. 38157

KNOWLTON (Charles). History of the Recent Excitement in Ashfield [Mass.] Part I. [n. p. 1834.] 8vo. W. 38158

KNOWLTON (J. M.) Our Hardy Grapes; What to Plant; How to Plant, Train, and Manage them. By J. M. Knowlton, Tarrytown, N. Y. *New York: Contant & Baker.* 1864. 16mo, pp. 82. 38159

KNOWLTON. Report of the Directors ... of the Knowlton Mining Company for ... 1869. *New-York: T. W. Roe & Co., Printers.* 1869. 8vo, pp. 9. H. 38160

[KNOX (Henry), *Major-General.*] A Plan for the General Arrangement of the Militia of the United States. ... [n. p. 1786.] 8vo, pp. 34. + *Philadelphia.* 1786. 8vo. + *New York: Printed by Francis Childs and John Swayne.* 1790. Folio, pp. 26.

KNOX (H.) The Dignity and Importance of the Gospel Ministry. A Sermon at his own Ordination, before the Presbytery of New York. By Rev. Hugh Knox. *New York.* 1755. 8vo, pp. 24. M. 38162

Also: Dr. Knox's New Year's Discourse of St. Christopher. [n. p.] 1768. 8vo. —Sermon on the Death of Johannes Theodorus Wilhelmus Maas. ... *New York.* 1775. 8vo, pp. 30.

[KNOX (John).] A New Collection of Voyages, Discoveries and Travels: Containing Whatever is worthy of Notice, in Europe, Asia, Africa and America: In respect to The Situation and Extent of Empires, Kingdoms, and Provinces; their Climates, Soil, Produce, &c. With the Manners and Customs of the several Inhabitants; their Government, Religion, Arts, Sciences, Manufactures, and Commerce. The whole consisting of such English and Foreign Authors as are in most Esteem; including the Descriptions and Remarks of some late celebrated Travellers, not to be found in any other Collection. ... *London: Printed for J. Knox.* MDCCLXVII. 7 vols., 8vo, pp. xiii, (3), 515, (1); (4), 496; (4), 520; (4), 464; (4), 472; (4), 543; (4), 528. 49 Maps and Plates. A., B., C. 38163

A capital compendium. Contains well-digested narratives of the voyages and discoveries of Columbus, Ulloa, Dampier, Kolben, Rogers, Drake, Pocock, Nieuhof, etc. *See* "M. Rev.," XXXVII. 54, LXIV. 515.

KNOX (J.) An Historical Journal of the Campaigns in North-America, for the Years 1757, 1758, 1759, and 1760: Containing The Most Remarkable Occurrences of that Period; Particularly The Two Sieges of Quebec, &c. &c. the Orders of the Admirals and General Officers; Descriptions of the Countries where the Author has served, with their Forts and Garrisons; their Climates, Soil, Produce; and A Regular Diary of the Weather. As Also Several Manifesto's, a Mandate of the late Bishop of Canada, The French Orders and Disposition for the Defence of the Colony, ... By Captain John Knox. ... *London: For the Author.* MDCCLXIX. 2 vols., 4to, pp. ix, (6), 405, (2); (2), 465, (2). Map and 2 Portraits. BA. 38164

"A very valuable collection of materials towards a history of our late war, and conquests in America, as well as for a description and natural history of the country, in which this attentive and industrious author personally served; and the best original authority for the death of Wolfe and the conquest of Canada."—*Monthly Review*, XLI. 395. The "North American Review" calls this "two heavy tedious volumes."

KNOX (J.) ... A Sermon on the Occasion of the Death of Lt. Col. Alexander Ramsay Thompson, of the U. S. Army,

who was killed in Battle with the Indians, at Okee-Cho-Bee, Florida, December 25, 1837, Delivered ... February 11, 1838. By the Rev. John Knox, D.D. ... *New-York: Printed by William Osborn.* 1838. 8vo, pp. 27. C. 38165

Also: ... Discourse ... on the ... Opening of the Reformed ... Church, ... Lafayette Place, May 9, 1839. ... *New York: Robert Carter.* 1839. 8vo, pp. 8.—Sermon, ... Death of Rev. Gerardus A. Kuypers. ... *New York.* 1833. 8vo.

KNOX. Memorial of the Rev. John Knox, D.D., containing Notice of Death and Funeral Services. Sermon by Thomas De Witt, D.D. ... *New York.* [1859.] 8vo, pp. 124, (1). Portrait.

KNOX (J.), *pseudon.* A Sermon for the Times. ... Preached in Aid of the "Jacobins in Maryland." By Rev. John Knox, L.M. *Baltimore: For the Author.* 1864. 8vo, pp. 8. B. 38167

A hit at Mr. Blair and the Maryland conservatives. The author's name is assumed.

KNOX (J. J.) The Fiftieth Anniversary of the Marriage of John J. and Sarah A. Knox, October 7, 1863. For Private Circulation. *New York: Anson D. F. Randolph.* [1863.] 8vo, pp. 41. Plate. B. 38168

KNOX (J. P.) A Brief History of the Protestant Reformed Dutch Church in Nassau. Preached Jan. 10, 1841. By John P. Knox. *Albany: Printed by J. Munsell.* 1841. 8vo, pp. 31.

KNOX. A Historical Account of St. Thomas, W. I., with its Rise and Progress in Commerce; Missions and Churches; Climate and its adaption to Invalids; Geological Structure; Natural History, and Botany; and incidental notices of St. Croix and St. Johns; Slave Insurrections in these Islands; Emancipation and Present Condition of Laboring Classes. By John P. Knox ... . *New York: Charles Scribner.* 1852. 8vo, pp. 271. Map, Plate.

KNOX (L. L.) ... A Funeral Discourse, for Rev. Daniel H. Mansfield ... Bangor, June 26th, 1855 ... . By Rev. Loren L. Knox ... . *Bangor: Wheeler & Lynde.* 1855. 8vo, pp. 16. H.

KNOX (R.) The Races of Men: a Fragment. By Robert Knox ... . *London: Henry Renshaw.* MDCCCL. 8vo, pp. viii, 479. + *Philadelphia: Lea & Blanchard.* 1850. 12mo, pp. 323. BA. + *London: Henry Renshaw.* MDCCCLXII. 8vo, pp. viii, 600. B.

KNOX (S.) A Discourse delivered ... Baltimore on the 14th January, 1815, ... a day of National Fasting, Humiliation and Prayer. By Samuel Knox ... . *Baltimore.* 1815. 12mo, pp. 40.

KNOX. A Funeral Oration commemorative of the Illustrious Virtues of the late Great and Good General Washington. Delivered in Fredericktown, 22d February, 1800. By Rev. Samuel Knox. *Fredericktown (Md.): M. Bartgis.* 1800. 8vo, pp. (2), 25.

Extremely rare. Also: A Discourse on the Present State of Education in Maryland ... before the ... General Assembly ... 31st of December, 1807. ... *Baltimore: Printed by Warner & Hanna.* 1808. 8vo, pp. 28. W.

KNOX [Thomas]. A Letter from Mr. Knox, of Bristol, to ... William Nelson, Esq; of Virginia. *Bristol: Printed by E. Ward.* 1759. 8vo, pp. 16. BA. 38175

KNOX (T. P.) Startling Revelations from the Department of South Carolina, and Expose of ... National Freedmen's Relief Association. By Thomas P. Knox ... . *Boston: William M. Kendall, Printer.* 1864. 8vo, pp. 16. H. 38176

KNOX (T. W.) Camp-Fire and Cotton-Field: Southern Adventure in Time of War. Life with the Union Armies, and Residence on a Louisiana Plantation. By Thomas W. Knox ... *New York: Blelock and Company.* 1865. 8vo, pp. 524. Plates.

[KNOX (William).] The Claim of the Colonies to an Exemption from Internal Taxes imposed by Authority of Parliament, Examined; In a letter from a Gentleman in London, to his Friend in America. *London: W. Johnston.* MDCCLXV. 8vo, pp. (2), 46. B., BA., H. 38178

"The author defends the scheme of the government for imposing stamp duties on the colonies, and undertakes to show the impropriety of the measures taken by the colonies to oppose the Stamp Act."—*Monthly Review*, XXXII. 227.

[KNOX.] Considerations on the Present State of the Nation. Addressed to ... Two Houses of Parliament, associated for the Preservation of the Constitution and Promoting the Prosperity of the British Empire. By a Late Under Secretary of State. *London: J. Debrett.* M.DCC.LXXXIX. 8vo, pp. xii, 68. BA.

[KNOX.] The Controversy between Great Britain and her Colonies Reviewed; The Several Pleas of the Colonies, In Support of their Right to all the Liberties and Privileges of British Subjects, and to Exemption from the Legislative Authority of Parliament, Stated and Considered; And The Nature of their Connection with, and Dependence on, Great Britain, shewn, upon the Evidence of Historical Facts and Authentic Records. *London: J. Almon.* MDCCLXIX. 8vo, pp. (2), 207, Appendix, lv.

BA., C. + *Boston: Printed by Mein and Fleeming* ... M DCC LXIX. 8vo, pp. 100. C. + *Dublin.* 1769. 8vo, pp. 207, 55. P. 38180

Written by William Knox, Under Secretary of State for American Affairs. "A very close and shrewd examination of the charter, constitution, government, past conduct and present pretensions of the British Colonies."—*Monthly Review*, XL. 103. It has also been ascribed to Mr. Whately, M.P., and John Mein. A manuscript note in Mr. J. C. Brown's copy says that "the writer was Mr. Mein, a Scotchman and bookseller in Boston, afterwards a bankrupt, and put in the Fleet prison in London. Mr. Hancock, on account of publishing this and other pieces, bought up his English debts, and making a sudden demand upon honest Mein, with which he could not instantly comply, brought on his ruin." Pages 66 to 86 are by George Grenville. *See* "Extra Official Papers," Appendix to Part II. 15, *also* Bancroft's "History of the United States," IV. 223, VI. 106.

[KNOX.] Extra Official State Papers. Addressed to The Right Hon. Lord Rawdon, and the other Members of the Two Houses of Parliament, associated for the Preservation of the Constitution and Promoting the Prosperity of the British Empire. By a Late Under Secretary of State. *London: J. Debrett.* M.DCC.LXXXIX. 2 vols., 8vo, pp. (4), 55, Appendix, 49, (2), 14, (2), 174, (1); 63, Appendix, 84. BA. + *Dublin: Reprinted.* MDCCLXXXIX. 8vo, pp. 308. A. 38181

"Dr. Knox, the author of this work, was deputy Secretary of State for the American department. He gives in these State papers some anecdotes relative to the American war, and to the great revolution which it produced; a scheme for establishing Episcopacy in Nova Scotia, and various plans relative to public matters."—*Monthly Review.*

[KNOX.] The Justice and Policy of the late Act of Parliament for Making more Effectual Provision for the Government of the Province of Quebec, Asserted and Proved; and the Conduct of Administration respecting that Province, Stated and Vindicated. *London: Printed in the Year* 1774. 8vo, pp. 32. BA. + *London: J. Wilkie.* MDCCLXXIV. 8vo, pp. 90. H. 38182

[KNOX.] Observations upon the Liturgy, with Proposals for its Reform, by a Layman of the Church of England, late an under Secretary of State, to which is added the Journals of the American Convention to form a Liturgy for the Episcopal Churches in the United States. *London.* 1789. 8vo. 38183

KNOX (W.) Three Tracts on the Conversion and Instruction of the Indians and Negroe Slaves. 1785. 38184

KNOX (W. E.) A Sermon ... at the Dedication of the Chapel of the N. Y. State Lunatic Asylum, October 27th, 1858. By Rev. W. E. Knox. *Utica, N. Y.: Curtiss & White, Printers.* 1858. 8vo, pp. 20. H. 38185

Also: Semi-Centennial Sermon, First Presbyterian Church, Rome, N. Y., Sept. 1850. ... *Rome.* 1851. 8vo. S.

KNOX (W. J.) On the best Means of bringing Water from the head of the Lachine Rapids to St. Pierre River and from thence to connect with the Harbour of Montreal. *Montreal.* 1867. 8vo. 38186

KNOX COLLEGE, *Ill.* Catalogue of ... Officers and Students of Knox Manual Labor College, Galesburg ... Ill. ... July 10, 1844. *Peoria: S. H. Davis, Printer.* 1844. 12mo, pp. 12. H.

Rights of Congregationalists in Knox College; being the Report of a Committee ... with an Appendix. *Chicago: Church, Goodman & Cushing, Pr's.* 1859. 12mo, pp. 93. BA. 38188

Also: Knoxiana. Published by the Knoxiana Publication Society of Knox College. *Galesburg, Ill.* 1851–1853. 3 vols., 8vo. S.

KNOX CO., *Ill.* Dewey's County Directory. [With an Historical Sketch of the Townships. By J. J. Dewey. *Galesburg, (Ill.): Liberal Book and Job Office.* 1868. 8vo, pp. 257. Map, 4 Plates. C. 38189

KNOXVILLE, *Tenn.* The Half-Century of Knoxville, containing the Address and Proceedings of the Semi-Centennial Anniversary of the Town, February 10, 1842. To which is added an Appendix containing a number of Historical Documents. *Knoxville: Printed at the Register Office.* 1852. 8vo, pp. 106.

See also Humes (T. W.), Vol. VIII., No. 33782.

KOB (K. F.) Wegweiser für Ansiedler im Territorium Kansas ... Von Dr. Karl Friedrich Kob. ... *New-York: G. B. Teubner.* 1857. 8vo, pp. 42, 43–48 Advertisements. 38191

KOBBE (Peter Ludwig Christian von). Darstellung der Geschichte des Freiheitskampfes im Spanischen und Portugiesischen America. ... *Hannover.* 1832. 8vo. 38192

KOCH (A. Charles). Description of the Hydrarchos Harlani: (Koch,) ... Sillimanii ... a Gigantic Fossil Reptile; lately discovered by the author, in the State of Alabama, March, 1845 ... By Doctor Albert C. Koch. ... *New-York.* 1845. 8vo, pp. 16. + Second Edition. [*Ibid.*] 8vo, pp. 24. H. 38193

KOCH. Description of the Missourium, or Missouri Leviathan; ... By Albert Koch. *St. Louis: Printed by Chas. Keemle.* 1841. 8vo, pp. 16. H. + Second Edition, Enlarged (on cover). *Louisville, Ky: Prentice and Weissinger, Printers.* 1841. 8vo, pp. 20. + With ... a Catalogue of the whole Fossil Collection. ... *London: E. Fisher.* 1841. 8vo, pp. 24. B. 38194

KOCH. Description of the Missourium Theristocaulodon (Koch), or Missouri Leviathan, (Leviathan Missouriensis,) together with its Supposed Habits, and Indian Traditions. ... By Albert Koch. Fifth Edition, Enlarged. *Dublin: Printed by C. Crookes.* 1843. 8vo, pp. 28. H., S. 38195

The German version was entitled:

KOCH. Beschreibung des Missourium Theristocaulon ... die ... Lebensart desselben und indianische Traditionen über den Ort wo es ausgegraben wurde ... . Nach der vierten Ausgabe des englischen Originals ... . *Magdeburg: Baensch.* 1844. 8vo. Plate.

KOCH. Kurze Bemerkungen ... der Hydrarchen ... . Mit ... Kampfscenen der Indianer mit den weissen Ansiedlern Amerika's. Von Dr. Albert C. Koch. *Dresden: C. C. Meinhold und Söhne.* [1845?] 8vo, pp. 32. H. 38197

KOCH. Die Riesenthiere der Urwelt oder das neuentdeckte Missourium Theristocaulon (Stichelzahn ...) ... . *Berlin: A. Duncker.* 1845. 8vo. 8 Plates. 38199

KOCH. A Short Description of the Fossil Remains found in the State of Missouri. By Albert Koch. *St. Louis.* 1840. 8vo, pp. 8. 38200

KOCH (Albrecht C.) Reise durch einen Theil der Vereinigten Staaten von Nordamerika in den Jahren 1844–46. ... *Dresden: Arnold.* 1847. 8vo, pp. 162. 2 Plates. C. 38198

KOCH (Christophe Guillaume). Abrégé de l'Histoire des Traités de Paix entre les Puissances de l'Europe depuis la Paix de Westphalie. ... *Basle.* 1796–97. 4 vols., 8vo. S. + *Basle.* 1802. 2 vols., 8vo, pp. 530; 498. C. + Ouvrage entièrement refondu, augmenté, et continué jusqu'au Congrès de Vienne et aux Traités de Paris de 1815. Par M. F. Schoell. *Paris.* 1817–1818. 15 vols., 8vo. A., B. 38201

KOCH (F. C. L.) Die deutschen Colonien in der Nähe des Saginaw-Flusses. ... *Braunschweig.* 1851. 8vo. Map and Plate.

KOCH. Die Mineral-Regionen der obern Halbinsel Michigan's (N. A.) am Lake Superior und die Isle Royale. ... *Göttingen: Dieterich.* 1852. 8vo, pp. 248. Map. C. 38203

KOCH (J. G. F.) Versuch eines Kriegs-Rechts der Negern in Afrika und der Indianer in Amerika. ... Von J. G. F. Koch, ... *Tübingen: Johann Georg Cotta.* 1781. 8vo, pp. 86. H. + *Tübingen.* 1786. 8vo, pp. 86. 38204

KOELER (Hermann). Einige Beobachtungen über die Temperatur der See-Oberfläche im Nord-Atlantischen Meere von H. Koeler. *Göttingen: Dieterich.* 1848. 8vo, pp. iv, 81. 38205

KOENEN (H. J.) Pavonia. Eene bijdrage tot de kennis der voormalige Nederlandsche Koloniën. ... *Arnhem.* 1846. 8vo, pp. 19. 38206

This colony in New-Netherland was founded by Mich. Pauw, in 1628. This is, we believe, the only special Dutch paper on the subject.

KOENIG (——). Surinam und seine Bewohner ... *Erfurt.* 1805. 8vo. 38207

KOERTEN (J.) Gedichten op de overheerlijke papiere snijkunst van J. Koerten huisvrouwe van A. Blok. Gedrukt na het origineel stamboek; benevens eene korte schets van haar leven. *Amsterdam.* 1735. 8vo. Portrait. + *Amsterdam.* 1736. 4to. Portrait. 38208

Contains a poem by Gualth. de Bois, kerkleeraar in Nieu-Nederlandt.

KOFFLER (J. F.) A Letter from a Tradesman in Lancaster to the Merchants of the Cities of Philadelphia, New-York and Boston, respecting the Loan of Money to the Government, with some Remarks upon the Consequences of the Refusal by John Frederick Koffler. [*Philadelphia:*] *Printed in the Year* 1760. 8vo, pp. (iii), 14. P. 38209

KOHL (J. G.) Aelteste Geschichte der Entdeckung und Erforschung des Golfs von Mexico und der ihn umgebenen Küsten durch die Spanier von 1492 bis 1543. Von J. G. Kohl. 8vo, pp. 40, 169–194. H. 38210

From the "Zeitschrift für allgemeine Erdkunde," Neue Folge, Band xv.

KOHL. Die beiden ältesten General-Karten von. Amerika. Ausgeführt in den Jahren 1527 und 1529, auf Befehl Kaiser Karl's v. Im Besitz der Grossherzoglichen Bibliothek zu Weimar. Erläutert von J. G. Kohl. *Weimar.* 1860. Folio, pp. x, 185, (1). 2 Maps. BA. 38211

KOHL. A Descriptive Catalogue of those Maps, Charts and Surveys relating to America, which are mentioned in Vol. III. of Hakluyt's Great Work. By J. G. Kohl. *Washington: Henry Polkinhorn, Printer.* 1857. 8vo, pp. 86. B. 38212

KOHL. Geschichte der Entdeckung Amerika's von Columbus bis Franklin. ... *Bremen: Strack.* 1861. 8vo, pp. v, 454.

KOHL. Kitschi-Gami oder Erzählungen vom Obern-See. Ein Beitrag zur Charakteristik der amerikanischen Indianer. ... *Bremen: Schünemann.* 1859. 2 vols., 8vo, pp. viii, 600. 38214

KOHL. Kitchi-Gami. Wanderings round Lake Superior. By J. G. Kohl. ... *London: Chapman and Hall.* 1860. 8vo, pp. xii, 428. BA. 38215

One of the most exhaustive and valuable treatises on Indian life ever written.

KOHL. A Popular History of the Discovery of America, from Columbus to Franklin. By J. G. Kohl. Translated from the German by Major R. R. Noel. *London: Chapman and Hall.* 1862. 2 vols., post 8vo, pp. ix, 275; vi, 284. Errata. B.

For the German version *see* No. 38213.

KOHL. Reisen in Canada, und durch die Staaten von New-York und Pennsylvanien. ... *Stuttgart.* 1856. 8vo, pp. 576.

KOHL. Reisen im Nordwesten der Vereinigten Staaten. ... *New-York: Appleton & Co.* 1857. 8vo. S. + Zweite Auflage. *St. Louis: Witter.* 1859. 8vo, pp. vi, 534. Map, 11 Plates.

KOHL. Travels in Canada, and through the States of New York and Pennsylvania. By J. G. Kohl ... Translated by Mrs. Percy Sinnett. Revised by the Author. ... *London: George Manwaring.* MDCCCLXI. 2 vols., post 8vo, pp. x, 345, (1); iv, 357, (1). B. 38219

See also "Maine Hist. Soc. Collections."

KÖHLER (Carl). Briefe aus America. Ein lehrreicher Wegweiser für deutsche Auswanderer. ... Zweite Auflage. *Darmstadt: G. G. Lange.* 1854. 12mo, pp. viii, 288. 6 Plates. C.

KÖHLER (Friedrich). Wörterbuch der Americanismen. Eigenheiten der englischen Sprache in Nordamerika. ... Nach J. Russell Bartlett's "Dictionary of Americanism," Dritte Ausgabe, *Boston,* 1860, bearbeitet. *Leipzig: Ph. Reclam, jun.* 1866. 8vo, pp. iv, 183. 38221

This is the work to which we have referred in *our* note to No. 3739, Vol. I.

KÖHLER (F. G.) Reis naar de IJszee, en naar de Kusten van Groenland en Spitsbergen, 1801. Benevens eene beschrijvinge des walvischvangst. Naar het Hoogduitsch. *Amsterdam.* 1820. 8vo. 38222

Voyage to the Ice-Sea and the coast of Greenland and Spitzbergen, with a description of the whale-fishery. We have not seen the German original.

KÖHLER (J. T.) Sammlung neuer Reisebeschreibungen aus fremden Sprachen besonders der Englischen ... von Johann Tobias Köhler ... Erster Band ... *Göttingen und Gotha: Johann Christian Dieterich.* 1767–69. 2 parts, 8vo, pp. 327, 5 l.; 329–668, (1). H. 38223

Vol. II. appears not to have been published.

KÖHLER (O.) Die deutschen Ackerbau-Kolonien in Santa Catharina (Brasilien). Ihre Lage und ihre Zukunft, dargestellt in den Berichten des Kaiserl. Brasilianischen Staatsrathes Luiz Pedreira do Coutto Ferraz. Ins Deutsche übertragen ... von Otto Köhler. *Hamburg: G. W. Niemeyer.* 1859. 8vo, pp. xv, 100. 38224

This should have appeared under Ferraz (L. P. do C.)

KOHLMEISTER (B.) Journal of a Voyage from Okkak, on the Coast of Labrador, to Ungava Bay; westward of Cape Chudleigh; undertaken To explore the Coast, and visit the Esquimaux in that unknown Region. By Benjamin Kohlmeister, and George Kmoch, Missionaries of the Church of Unitas Fratrum .... *London.* 1814. 8vo, pp. 83. Map. H.

[KOLB (Johann Ernst).] Erzählungen von ... der Negersklaven. ... *Bern.* 1789. 12mo, pp. xxiv, 288. H. 38226

KOLLOCK (H.) ... A Sermon ... before the General Assembly of the Presbyterian Church in the United States of America; ... May 23, 1803. ... By Henry Kollock, A.M. ... *Philadelphia: Printed by Jane Aitken.* 1803. 8vo, pp. 35. M. 38227

KOLLOCK (Shepard K.) Pastoral Reminiscences ... with an Introduction by A. Alexander. *New York.* 1849. 12mo. C.

KOLLONITZ (P.) The Court of Mexico. By the Countess Paula Kollonitz ... Translated by J. E. Ollivant. Third Edition. *London: Saunders, Otley & Co.* 1868. 8vo, pp. xix, 303.

KOLLONITZ. Eine Reise nach Mexico im Jahre 1864. Von Gräfin Paula Kollonitz. Zweite, revidirte Auflage. *Wien: Carl Gerold's Sohn.* 1867. 12mo, pp. (12), 247. BA. 38230

KOLONIEN. Abhandlungen über die Kolonien überhaupt, und die amerikanischen besonders. *Bern: Walthard.* 1779. 8vo, pp. 152. 38231

The author predicted that in one hundred years the seat of the English government would be in America!

De Kolonist, Tijdschrift toegewijd aan de welvaart van Suriname. *Paramaribo.* 1838–39. 8vo. 38232

KONINGSMARKE. *See* [Paulding (J. K.)]

KONSCHAK *or* KONSAG (Ferdinand). Carta de la Vida del P. Fernando Konsag. *Mexico.* 1764. 38233

KONSCHAK. Vida y muerte del P. Antonio Tempis, Jesuita Misionero de Californias. *Mégico.* 1748. 4to. 38234

Konschak also wrote a "Diario de Californias," appended to a "Historia de Californias," *Paris,* 1767–8; also contained in the "Apostolicos afanes," *our* No. 1768.

KOOCH [Jeremiah]. Extracts from the Manuscript of Kooch's Blue Book for the County of Philadelphia. [*Philadelphia.* 1834.] 8vo, pp. 28. 38235

Relates to local improvements.

KOONTZ (W. H.), *and* RAUM (G. B.) Impeachment of the President. Speeches of Hon. William H. Koontz ... and Hon. Green B. Raum ... March 2, 1868. *Washington: F. & J. Rives & Geo. A. Bailey ... Printers.* 1868. 8vo, pp. 8. H. 38236

KOPPE (F. W.) Briefe in die Heimath zwischen October 1829 und Mai 1830 während einer Reise über Frankreich, England und die Vereinigten Staaten von Nord America nach Mexico. *Stuttgart.* 1835. 8vo. 38237

KOPPE. Mexicanische Zustände aus den Jahren 1830–1832. *Stuttgart.* 1837. 8vo. 38238

KÖRBER (Philipp). Dampier's Leben und Reise um die Welt. Für die Jugend .... *Nürnberg: Lotzbeck.* 1848. 16mo, pp. 184. Plate. 38239

KÖRBER. Vie et Voyages de William Dampier. Ouvrage dédié aux enfants, par J. Paroz, instituteur. D'après l'allemand de P. Koerber. *Berne.* 1856. 8vo, pp. 231. 38240

KÖRBER. De IJsze, of de togt ter walvischvangst. Eene vertelling voor de jeugd. [Uit het Hoogduitsch.] *Amsterdam: Koopman en Schreuder.* 1845. 8vo. 2 Plates. 38241

Also: Die Ansiedler David Cover und seine Söhne. ... Erzählung nach Cooper für die Jugend .... *Nürnberg: Lotzbeck.* 1847. 16mo, pp. 126. Plate. — Christoph Columbus der Entdecker der neuen Welt. Historische Erzählung. Für die Jugend .... *Nürnberg: Lotzbeck.* 1848. 8vo, pp. viii, 240. Plate. — Die Eroberung von Mexiko durch Ferdinand Cortez. Historische Erzählung. Für die Jugend .... *Nürnberg: Lotzbeck.* 1848. 8vo, pp. 228. Plate. — El-Dorado. Schilderung einer Reise nach Californien's Goldminen im Jahre 1848. *Nürnberg: Lotzbeck.* 1852. 16mo, pp. 192. 3 Plates

— Die Familie Wharton. Erzählung aus dem amerikanischen Befreiungskriege unter Washington. Für die Jugend .... *Nürnberg: Lotzbeck.* 1852. 8vo, pp. 143. 3 Plates. — Alexander von Humboldt's Reisen in Amerika. Reise in New-Andalusien. Zur Belehrung ... für die Jugend. *Nurnberg: Lotzbeck.* 1847. 16mo, pp. 194. Plate. — Jakob und Edward Jefferson's Reise nach Californien. *Nurnberg: Lotzbeck.* 1852. 16mo. 3 Plates. — Capitain John Ross's zweite Nordpolexpedition in den Jahren 1829 bis 1833. Für die Jugend .... *Nurnberg: Lotzbeck.* 1852. 16mo, pp. 120. 3 Plates. — Dr. von Spix und Dr. von Martius Reise in Brazilien. Zur Belehrung und Unterhaltung für die Jugend. *Nurnberg: Lotzbeck.* 1847. 16mo, pp. 142. Plate.

KÖRNER (Friedrich). Eine Polarfahrt. Geographische Skizzen und Scenen aus dem Seemanns- und Jägerleben. ... *Leipzig: B. Schlicke.* 1858. 8vo, pp. (4), 105. Plate. C. 38242

The Koromantyn Slaves; or West-Indian Sketches. *London: Hatchard.* 1823. 18mo, pp. 280. S. 38243

Kort Berättelse om Wäst Indien eller America, som elliest kallas Nya Werlden. [*Wysingsborg.*] 1675. 4to, pp. (2), 42.

One of the scarcest of the Swedish typographical productions of the seventeenth century on America. The larger part of it is devoted to South America (pp. 12–42); of North America particular notice has been taken only of Virginia; its description fills (pp. 7–11). Although the book bears no printer's name, it is, no doubt, printed by John Kankel of Wysingsborg, as it forms part of the second edition of Hemmersam's voyage and other works on Asia.

Kort discours, | ofte naardere verklaringe van de onderstaende | V. Poincten, | 1 Aengaende de verlichtinghe die desen staat heeft ghenooten, | door de oprechtinghe en Oorloghen van de West-Indische | Compagnie. | 2 Dat men deselve Compagnie, met die van de Oost, of hare bey-|de Octroyen, vereenigende, nu ongelijck meerder verlichtin-|ge, jae in korten het eynde van dese lastighe en ghevaerlicke | Oorlogen, sal konnen erlangen. | 3 Dat sonder dese Combinatie den Staat van de voorsz. West-| Indische Compagnie, niet alleen gene verlichtinge meer en | heeft te verwachten: | 4 Maer in plaetse haer sal moeten beswaren met de Subsidien van | eenige tonnen Gouts gereet, en jaerlijcx tot de subsistentie van | de selve Compagnie. | 5 Ende daer en boven de Oorlochs lasten hier te lande, jaarlijcx | noch vele tonnen Gouts sullen aanwassen, om dat den Ko-| ninck van Spanien gheen aensoeck hebbende van de voorsz. | Compagnie, zijne retouren uyt West-Indien met de minder | kosten thuys bekomen, en sulcx te meerder macht tegen desen | Staat, ter Zee, en te Lande, sal konnen brengen. | *Gedruckt voor een Lief-hebber van 't Vaderlant,* 1644. | 4to, 18 l. C. 38245

See Asher's "Bibliographical Essay," No. 194. These Five Points all relate to America, and the commerce of the Dutch in the West Indies.

Kort en Bondigh Verhael, | Van 't geene in den | Oorlogh, | Tusschen den Koning van Engelant, &c. en | de Ho: Mo: Heeren Staten der Vrije Vereenighde Nederlanden, | en den Bisschop van Munster is voorgevallen. | Beginnende in den Jare 1664, en eyndigende met het sluiten van de Vrede | tot Breda, | in 't Jaar 1667. Waer in de voornaemste Geschiedenissen, | in denzelven Oorlogh voorgevallen, beschreven worden. | Met een korte Inleydingh, vervattende de ballinghschap en herstellingh | van de tegenwoordigen Koning van Engelandt. | Met verscheyde kopere Figuren verciert. | *t'Amsterdam, voor Jacob Benjamin, Boeckverkoper op 't Wa-| ter,* 1667. | 4to, pp. 256. Map and Plate. 38246

This short and concise account of what occurred in the war between the King of England, etc., the States General of the free United Netherlands, and the Bishop of Munster, contains an account of the conquest of New-Netherland by the English.

Kort en Bondigh Verhael, | van 't geene in den Oorlogh, | Tusschen den Koning van Engelant etc. de H: M: Heeren | Staten der vrye Vereenigde Nederlanden, en den Bis-| schop van Munster is voorgevallen. | Beginnende in den Jare 1664 en eyndigende met het sluyten van de Vrede | tot Breda, in 't Jaer 1667. Waer in de voornaemste Geschiedenissen, | in denselben Oorlogh voorgevallen, beschreven worden. | Met een korte Inleydingh, vervattende de ballingschap en herstelling van | den tegenwoordigen Koningh van Engelandt. | Met verscheyde Kopere Figuren verciert. | *t'Amsterdam, voor Marcus Willemsz. Doornick, op den Vygendam, in 't Kan-| toor Incktvat. Anno* 1667. | 4to, pp. 256. 2 Plates.

A different impression of the preceding book, without the map and a large engraving, representing the conclusion of the peace of Breda, which will be found in the other edition. This rare work may be considered as the most complete and authentic contemporary account of the war between Holland and England, the consequence of which was the final loss of New-Netherland, by the peace of Breda, 1667.

Een kort en bondigh Vertoogh van de considerable Colonie, die de Edele | Groot Mog. Heeren Staten van Hollandt ende West-Vrieslandt, naer lange en rype deliberatien, nae hare ghewoonelijcke hooge wijsheydt hebben | goedt-gevonden ende geresolveert (tot maintenu ende accressement van de Negotie ende Navigatie, ende welvaert van den Staet en Kercke Godes, en | van alle goede Ingezetenen deser Landen) uyt te setten op de vaste Kuste van America, vervattende het fundament tot beter establissement, bevolc-| kinghe en bescherminge van dien; de favorable conditien, by haer Edele Groot Mog. toe-gestaen aen de gene die haer op de selve als Principalen of | Hooft-Geinteresseerdens eerst sullen inteeckenen tot hondert toe in getal; de schoone en uytnemende ghelegentheden van die Landen, ende groote | winsten en profijten

die men daer in korten tijdt onder Godts genade en zegen uyt een geringh Capitael, of sonder Capitael door haer eygen neerstig-| heydt en vigilantie kan komen te genieten, met een korte trouhertighe aenmaninge aen de Koopluyden, Burgers en Landtluyden, die Lief-hebbers | zijn van de eere en Kercke Godes, de welvaert van haer eygen Vaderlandt, haer eygen selven en haer Familien. Die nu een bysondere gelegentheyt | hebben aen een yder van dien goede en aengename diensten te konnen toe-brengen, dat sy die niet versuymen, of haer laten verleyden door ydele | ongefondeerde schijn-reden, door eenige onwetende of quaedtwillige Menschen voorgewent, tot verhinderinge van soo een heylsaem werck, met een | nodige waerschouwinge ende onderrichtinge, hoe men die quade aerdt en intentien van sulcke malignanten sal ontdecken, ende haer schijn-redenen | op-lossen. | *In 's Graven-Hage, By Jacobus Scheltus, Ordinaris Drucker van de Edele Groot Mog. Heeren Staten van Hollandt ende West-Vrieslandt, Anno* 1676. | Folio, 1 l.

An official report, intended to demonstrate the great advantages to emigrants in settling in Guiana, and in the formation of a new colony on the Wiapoca, a branch of the Orinoco, by Joh. Price Apricius, English Minister at the Hague. Intended to be posted on walls as a placard.

Kort dog waarachtig Verhael van de Rebellie en Opstand der Negers in de Colonie de Berbice, en de ysselijcke wreedheden aan deszelfs Inwoonders gepleegt .... *Middelburg en Amsterdam.* 1763. 4to, pp. 15. 38249

A relation of the rebellion of the negroes in the colony of Berbice, and of the frightful cruelties committed on the inhabitants thereof, February 21 to June 14, 1763.

Kort historisch Verhaal van den eersten aanleg, lotgevallen en voortgang der particuliere colonie Berbice gelegen in het landschap Guiana in Zuid-America; in het bijzonder behandelende het onderwerp der privaate eigendomme der Societeit van Participanten in die colonie, en wel allerbijzonderst de zoogenaamde akkergelden. Met eene openlegging van het singulier en contrasteerend gedrag van den heere Abraham Jacob van Imbyze van Batenburg, als civil gouverneur der colonie. Door en colonist in Augustus 1805. *Amsterdam: C. Sepp Jansz.* 1807. 8vo, pp. xvi, 319. 38250

History of the colony of Berbice, including the question of the private possessions of the society of the shareholders and the conduct of Governor Batenburg.

Kort | Onderricht | Der | Participanten rechtveerdighe klachten over de | Bewinthebbers | van de | Oost-Indische | Compagnie. | [n. p. n. d.] 4to, 4 l. 38251

Kort overzigt. *See our* Vol. I., No. 1732.

Kort verhael van eenige merkwaardige geschiedenissen van Holland. *Amsterdam.* 1744. 8vo. 38252

This short account of some marvellous events of Holland, contains a history of the Greenland whale-fishery.

Kort Verhael | Van Nieuw | Nederlants Gelegentheit, Deughden, Natuerlyke Voorrechten, en by-| zondere bequaemheidt ter bevolkingh: Mitsgaders eenige | Requesten, Vertoogen, Deductien, enz. ten dien einden door | eenige Liefhebbers ten verscheide tijden omtrent 't laetst | van 't jaer 1661. gepresenteert aen de A. A. Heeren Bur-| germeesteren dezer Stede, of derzelver E. E. Hee-| ren Gecommitteerde, enz. | Ziet breeder achter de Voor-Rede den Korten Inhout, mitsga-| ders de Waerschouwingh aen de Boekverkoopers, staende | hier vervolgens op d'anderof tegenzyde. | [*Amsterdam?*] *Gedrukt in 't jaer* 1662. 4to, pp. (8), 84.

A short account of New-Netherland's situation, virtues, natural privileges and peculiar fitness for population. "One of the most interesting and scarcest of all books on New-Netherland. I found only three copies in the course of twenty years, and sold my last at 200 florins."—F. MULLER. *See* Asher, No. 13, Brodhead, v. 199, *and* O'Callaghan, II. 969.

Korte Aenwysinghe van de bysondere nuttighden ... van de Colonie Suriname. 4to. 38254

"Very rare."—F. MULLER'S *Catalogue, No.* 995, $10.00.

Korte | Aenwysin-| ghe | Der | Bewinthebbers Regieringe. | [n. p. 1622.] 4to, 8 l. 38255

A short account of the Government of Directors. *See* Asher, No. 87.

Korte | Antvvoort, | Tegens'T | Manifest ende Remonstrantie, | Overgelevert door d'Portugesche Natie, en In-| woonderen van Pharnambuco, wegens 't aen-nemen der Wa-| penen tegens de West-Indische Compagnie. ... *Gedruckt int Iaer ons Heeren,* 1647. | 4to, pp. 12. 38256

Short answer to the manifest and remonstrance delivered by the Portuguese Nation and the inhabitants of Pernambuco on the taking up of arms against the West India Company.

Korte en wonderlycke Beschryvinge van de seltsame wanschepsels van menschen, die gevonden worden in het coninckrijck Guianae, aen het Meyr Parime. Alsmede van de Satyrs, en van de Vrouwen die Amazoonen genoemt worden. *Amsterdam: G. J. Saeghman.* [1663.] 4to, pp. 16. Plates. 38257

Short and curious description of the monstrous men who are found in the Kingdom Guiana, near the lake Parime; also of the Satyrs, and women called Amazones. This is by far the rarest of all the parts of Saeghman's Collection of Voyages, of which it forms the last part.

Een Korte Handleiding voor een onwedergeboren Sondaar, om tot Christus te koomen opgostelt door een Liefhebber der Waarheid. *Nieuw-York, gedrukt by J. Peter Zenger.* 1740. 12mo, pp. 23. P. 38258

Korte Memorie van de Redenen, om|de welcke de Geoctroyeerde West-Indische Com-|pagnie deser Landen, van de betalinge van de 100000|Rycxdaelders, aen de Kroon van Sweeden, in meerder|Somme, tot redemptie van der selver Africaensche|Prætensien, door den Staet by het laatste Tractaet be-|looft, behoorde te werden geexcuseert; ten minsten|de voorsz. 100000 Rycxdaelders by den Staet betaelt,|op Reeckeninge van haer onbetaelde subsidien; ofte|wel verschoten, ten tydt ende wylen ingekomen sul-|len zyn de gelden, die de Kroone van Portugal by|het laetste Tractaet, tot Redemptie van de Prætensien|van de Compagnie op Brasil ende andere Conque-|sten, schuldigh is.| [n. p. n. d.] 4to, pp. 24. 38259

Short memoir of the reasons by which the West India Company should be delivered from the payment of 100,000 rix dollars to the crown of Sweden, promised by the State in the last treaty.

Korte observatien. *See our* Vol. II., No. 7595.

Korte|Onderrichtinghe ende ver-|maeninghe aen alle liefhebbers des Vader-|landts, om liberalijcken te teeckenen|in de West-Indische Compagnie.|In de welcke|Kortelijck wort aenghewesen, de nootsaeckelykheijt, doenlijckheyt ende nuttickeyt van de selve.|Door een liefhebber des Vaderlants inghestelt, ende|tot ghemeyne onderrichtinghe in druck|vervoordert.| *Tot Leyden|In de Druckerye van Isaak Elzevier, Boeck-drucker|vande Universiteijt, Anno* 1662.|*Men vintse te Koop tot Rotterdam, by Jan van Waes-|berghe op 't Marct velt.*| 4to, pp. 20. 38260

Short instruction and admonition to all the lovers of their country, to subscribe liberally to the West India Company. "An important pamphlet."—TIELE.

Korte opmerkingen, omtrent de suikercultuur met vrijen arbeid in de kolonie Suriname. [n. p. n. d.] 8vo. 38261

Korte Verklaringe van verscheidene Actiën, tusschen de Engelsche en Fransche Vlooten, geduurende den laatsten Oorlog in de West-Indiën voorgevallen. *Amsterdam.* 1791. 4to. 21 Maps.

Kortbondige beschryvinge. *See* Berbice, No. 4811.

KORTÜM (Fr.) Geschichte der Nordamerikanischen Revolution, oder des zweiten Englischen Bürgerkrieges. *Zürich: Gesner.* 1829. 8vo. 38263

Vol. III. of his "Entstehungsgeschichte der freistädtischen Bünde," with a second title-page.

KOSCIUSKO [Thaddeus]. Report of the Secretary of the Treasury ... relative to the Claim of General Kosciusko against the United States. House of Representatives, Dec. 28, 1797. ... *Philadelphia: Printed by Joseph Gales.* [1797.] 8vo, pp. 8. B.

See Tochman (G.), *also* Wanikowicz (L.)

KOSSUTH [Lajos]. Authentic Life of his Excellency Louis Kossuth ... To which is added, his Address to the People of the United States ... . *London: Bradbury and Evans.* 1851. 8vo, pp. 136. Facsimile. BA. 38265

KOSSUTH. Kossuth in New England: a full account of the Hungarian Governor's visit to Massachusetts; with his Speeches, ... *Boston: John P. Jewett & Co.* 1852. 8vo, pp. vii, 343. Portrait. H. 38266

KOSSUTH. Report of the Special Committee, appointed by the Common Council of the City of New York, to make arrangements for the reception of Governor Louis Kossuth. *New York.* 1852. 8vo, pp. 756. N. 38267

KOSSUTH. Select Speeches of Kossuth. Condensed and abridged with Kossuth's Express Sanction, by Francis W. Newman. *New-York: C. S. Francis & Co.* M.DCCC.LIV. 12mo, pp. 445. Portrait. B. 38268

KOSSUTH. Sketch of the Life of Louis Kossuth ... Kossuth's Address to the People of the United States; all his Great Speeches in England; and the Letter of Daniel Webster to Chevalier Hulsemann. *New York: Stringer & Townsend.* 1851. 8vo, pp. 96. BA. 38269

Also: Deutsche Kossuth-Versammlung in Boston. [n. p. n. d.] 8vo, pp. 8.—The Future of Nations: ... A Lecture ... June 21, 1852. ... *New-York.* [1852.] 8vo, pp. viii, 5-44.—Kossuth Coppered, or the Banquet of the Capitol of Laputa, containing Gulliver's Great Speech. *New York.* 1852. 8vo.—Life and Public American Speeches of Louis Kossuth. *New York.* 1852. 8vo.—Proceedings, Speeches, &c., at the Dinner ... Washington, Jan. 7, 1852. [*Washington.* 1852.] 8vo, pp. 16. B.

KOSSUTH. A Letter to Kossuth [on Slavery. n. p. n. d.] 8vo, pp. 80. 38270

KOST KA (B. S.) Relacion de la|Salvd Milagrosa, qve dio| el Bienaventurado Stanislao Kost Ka, Novicio|de la Compañia de Iesu, à otro Novicio de|la misma Compañia, en la Casa de Provacion|de San Antonio Abad de la Ciudad de|Lima, el dia 13. de Noviembre de|el año de 1673.|Y consta de la Processo,| que se hizo por orden de el señor Doctor Don|Ioseph Davila Falcon. Provisor, y Vicario|General de el Arçobispado de Lima en Sede-|vacante ... .|Con licencia en *Madrid: Año de* 1674.| 4to, 6 folioed leaves. 38271

KOSTER (H.) Travels in Brazil. By Henry Koster. *London: Longman* ... 1816. 4to, pp. ix, (3), 501, (1). 10 Plates and Maps. H. + Second Edition. [*Ibid.*] 1817. 2 vols., 8vo, pp. xii, 406; ix, 380. 10 Plates. + *Philadelphia: M. Carey & Son.* 1817. 2 vols., 8vo, pp. 340; 323. B., C. 38272

See "M. Rev.," LXXXVII. 112. Highly esteemed in Brazil, where the author is called Enrique da Costa.

KOSTER. Voyages dans la partie septentrionale du Brésil, depuis 1809 jusqu'en 1815, comprenant les provinces de Pernambuco, Seara, Paraïba, Maragnan, etc. Traduits de l'anglais par M. A. Jay. *Paris: Delaunay.* 1818. 2 vols., 8vo, pp. xlix, (2), 376; 512. 8 Plates. S. 38273

A few copies were printed on "papier vélin, avec trois états des planches: noires, coloriées et teintées."—LECLERC.

KOSTER. Reisen in Brasilien. Von Heinrich Koster. Aus dem Englischen. ... *Weimar.* 1817. 8vo, pp. x, 624. 2 Maps.

[KOSTER (T.)] Observations on the pending Question of Additional Duties on Cotton imported from the United States of America. By a Merchant. *London.* 1813. 8vo. 38275

KOTTE (C. F.) Brasilien und seine Bedeutung für die deutsche Auswanderung. Mit besonderer Rücksicht auf die Mucury-Colonie in der Provinz Minas Geraës. *Leipzig: Voigt und Günther.* 1855. 8vo, pp. viii, 88. 38276

KOTTENKAMP (F.) Geschichte der Colonisation Amerika's. ... Von Dr. Franz Kottenkamp. ... *Frankfurt a. M.* 1850. 2 vols., 8vo, pp. viii, 606; (4), 459. BA., C. 38277

KOTTENKAMP. Der Unabhängigkeitskampf der spanisch amerikanischen Colonien. ... *Stuttgart.* 1838. 2 vols., 8vo.

This is a supplementary volume to Ernst Münch's "Allgemeine Geschichte der neueren Zeit."

KOTZEBUE (A. von). False Shame: or The American Orphan in Germany, A Comedy ... From the German of Augustus Von Kotzebue. *Charleston: W. P. Young.* 1800. 12mo, pp. 76. + *Newark: Charles Smith.* 1801. 12mo, pp. 63. B. 38279

This rare play is founded on the storming of Charleston by the British, in the Revolutionary War.

KOTZEBUE. La Peyrouse: A Comedy. ... Translated from the German of Kotzebue. By Charles Smith. *New-York: Charles Smith and S. Stephens.* 1800. 8vo, pp. 40. B., P. 38280

Also: La Peyrouse: ... Translated from the German by Anne Plumptre. *London: Phillips.* 1797. 8vo.—La Perouse: ... from the German ... . By Benjamin Thomson ... *London: Vernor.* 1799. 8vo, pp. 40.—The Negro Slaves; a Dramatic Historical Piece. Translated from the German. *London: Cadell & Davies.* 1796. 8vo, pp. v, 142.

KOTZEBUE. Pizarro; a Tragedy in Five Acts as performed at the Theatre Royal in Drury-Lane. Taken from the German Drama of Kotzebue; and adapted to the English Stage. By Richrad [*sic*] Brinsley Sheridan. *London: J. Ridgway.* 1799. 8vo. + *Dublin.* 1799. + *Philadelphia.* 1799. P. + *New-York: Charles Smith and Stephen Stephens.* 1800. 8vo, pp. (2), 62. B. + Twenty-Seventh Edition. *London.* 1804. 8vo, pp. iv, 78. + *Boston.* 1809. + *Philadelphia: Turner & Son.* 1823. 24mo, pp. 56, (3). B. 38281

Pizarro ran through fifteen editions in one year. Part of the twenty-seventh edition is on fine paper, with portrait of Kemble as *Rolla.* *See* Dr. Beardsley's "Remains," *also* "M. Rev.," XXIX. 341, XXXIII. 430, 445. There were other translations as below:

KOTZEBUE. The Spaniards in Peru; or, the Death of Rolla, A Tragedy, in Five Acts: By Augustus Von Kotzebue. Translated ... By Anne Plumptre. *London: J. Phillips* ... 1799. 8vo, pp. 93. + Adapted to the English Stage, and enriched By R. B. Sheridan; translated into German By Constantin Geisweiler. *London: Robinson.* 1800. 8vo. 38282

KOTZEBUE. Rolla: or, the Peruvian Hero; a Tragedy. Translated from the German, by M. G. Lewis. *London.* 1799. 8vo. 38283

Also: The Virgin of the Sun, a Play, in Five Acts; translated from the German ... . By James Lawrence, Esq. *London.* 1799. 8vo. + *New York: Printed for Charles Smith and S. Stephens.* 1800. 8vo, pp. 96. B.

KOTZEBUE (Otto von). Entdeckungs-Reise in die Süd-See und nach der Berings-Strasse zur Erforschung einer nordöstlichen Durchfahrt. Unternommen in den Jahren 1815, 1816, 1817 und 1818. *Weimar: Hoffmann.* 1821. 3 vols., 4to. 6 Maps and 20 Plates. + Für die Jugend bearbeitet von Christoph Hilde-

brandt. *Hannover: Hahn.* 1821. 2 vols., 8vo. Plates. + *Wien.* 1825. 3 vols., 8vo. Maps. 38284

There are copies on fine paper. This voyage was undertaken at the expense of Count Romanzoff. Vol. III. is especially interesting for the notices on natural history and on the languages, with a comparative vocabulary, by A. von Chamisso.

KOTZEBUE. Ontdekkingsreis in de Zuid-Zee en naar de Berings-Straat, in de Jaren 1815, 1816, 1817 en 1818. Uit het Hoogduitsch. *Amsterdam.* 1822. 3 vols., 8vo. Maps, Plates.

A Dutch translation of the preceding work.

KOTZEBUE. Neue Reise um die Welt in den Jahren 1823, 24, 25 und 26. *Weimar: Hoffmann.* 1830. 2 vols., 8vo. Plates and Maps. + *Saint-Pétersbourg.* 1830. 2 vols., 8vo. Plates and 8 Maps. 38286

KOTZEBUE. Nieuwe Ontdekkingsreize rondom de Wereld in de Jaren 1823–26. Uit het Hoogduitsch. *Haarlem.* 1830. 2 vols., 8vo. C. 38287

KOTZEBUE. A New Voyage round the World in the Years 1823, 24, 25, and 26. By Otto Von Kotzebue, Post Captain in the Russian ... Navy. *London: Henry Colburn and Richard Bentley.* 1830. 2 vols., 8vo, pp. (8), 341, 3 Maps, Plate; (6), 362, Portrait. A., BA., P. 38288

Contains Explorations of the Navigators' and Radack Islands; California and the New Russian Settlements, etc., with Zoological Appendix by Prof. Eschscholtz.

KOTZEBUE. Poutechestvie v ioujenoï okéan. Voyage dans l'océan du sud et au détroit de Béring, entrepris en 1815, 1816, 1817 et 1818 sur le vaisseau Rurick pour chercher le passage nord-est. *Saint-Pétersbourg: Gretsch.* 1821–23. 3 vols., 4to. Atlas in folio. 38289

KOTZEBUE. Poutechestvie vokroug svéta. Voyage autour du monde ... sur le sloop de guerre Predprüatü. *Saint-Pétersbourg.* 1828. 8vo. 38290

KOTZEBUE. A Voyage of Discovery, into the South Sea, and Beerings Straits, for the Purpose of Exploring a North-East Passage, undertaken in the Years 1815–1818, at the Expense of his Highness the Chancellor of the Empire, Count Romanzoff, in the Ship Rurick, under the Command of the Lieutenant in the Russian Imperial Navy, Otto Von Kotzebue. Illustrated with Numerous Maps and Plates. ... *London: Longman* ... 1821. 3 vols., 8vo, pp. xv, (1), 358; (2), 433, (1); (2), 442. 15 Plates and Maps. B., BA., H. 38291

KOTZEBUE. A Voyage of Discovery in the South Sea and to Behring's Straits in search of a N. E. Passage, undertaken in the Years 1815, 16, 17, and 18, in the Ship Rurick. By Otto Von Kotzebue. *London: J. Phillips.* 1821. 8vo, pp. 220. 19 Maps and Plates. 38292

Also forms Parts I. and II. of the "Pamphleteer," VI.

KRACHENINNIKOW. *See* KRASCHENINNIKOFF.

Krachteloose Donder van de Helschen Hond ... waer in vertoont wort ... wat in 60 jaren ghepasseert is in desen staet en wat te verwachten staet in Duytschlandt ... Hongaryen, Moscovien, jae in Oost ende West-Indien selfs. [n. p. 1615?] 4to, pp. 8.

Powerless thunder of the hellish dog ... showing what happened in the last sixty years in this land and what may be expected in ... the East and West Indies. This violent pamphlet is directed against the Jesuits.

KRAFFT (M.) The American Distiller, ... according to the Latest Discoveries ... . By Michael Krafft ... . *Philadelphia: Thomas Dobson.* 1804. 8vo, pp. (4), 219. BA. 38294

One of the earliest works of its class.

KRAGH (P.) Okallòutit Sabbátinne akkudleesiksaet Evangeliumit sukuiàutèjt okiokun attuaegéksaet kattersórsimarsut káladlidlo okáuzeenut nuktérsimarsut. Pellesimit P. Kraghmit. *Kjöbenhavnime.* 1833. 8vo, pp. 464. 38295

Tales for the Sabbath, in the Esquimaux language.

KRAGH. Okalluktuàutit sajmâubingmik annékbingmiglo Jesuse-Kristusikut makpérsaekknnit Kablunâit adlaedlo okáuzeenne agléksimarsunnit kattersórsimarsut kaládlidlo okáuzeenut nuktérsimarsut. Pellesimit Pet. Kraghmit. *Kjöbenhavnime: F. de Tengnagel.* 1830. 18mo, pp. (8), 292. C. 38296

Christian tales in the Esquimaux language. *See also* our Vol. VI., Nos. 22851, 22871; Vol. VII., Nos. 28657–58.

[KRAITSIR (Charles V.)] The Poles in the United States of America, preceded by the Earliest History of the Slavonians, and by the History of Poland. *Philadelphia: Kiderlen and Stollmeyer.* 1837. 16mo, pp. (4), iv, 196. H., S. 38297

KRAMER (J. T.) The Slave-Auction. By Dr. John Theophilus Kramer ... *Boston: Robert F. Wallcut.* 1859. 18mo, pp. 48.

KRANTZII (Alb.) Regnorum Aquilonarium, Daniae, Sueciae, Norvagiae Chronica. Acced. ... Jac. Ziegleri Schondia. *Francof. a. M.* 1583. Folio. 38299

Pages 473–497 contain a reprint of the treatise "Schondia." *See* Ziegler (J.)

[KRASCHENINNIKOFF (Stephan Petrovich).] Aardrijks- en natuurkundige beschrijving van Kamtschatka en de Kurilsche eilanden, met een gedeelte van de kust van Amerika. Uit het Russ. *Amsterdam.* 1770. 8vo. 3 Plates. 38300

[KRASCHENINNIKOFF.] The History of Kamtschatka and the Kurilski Islands, with the Countries Adjacent; illustrated with Maps and Cuts. Published at Petersburg in the Russian Language, by Order of Her Imperial Majesty, And translated into English by James Grieve, M.D. *Glocester: T. Jefferys.* M.DCC.LXIV. 4to, pp. (8), 280, (8). 2 Maps, Plates. BA. 38301

An abridged translation.

[KRASCHENINNIKOFF.] Beschreibung des Landes Kamtschatka. Mit Landkarten und Kupferbildern, herausgegeben von T. Jefferys. In das Deutsche übersetzet und mit Anmerkungen erläutert, von J. Köhler. *Lemgo: Meyer.* 1766. 4to, pp. xvi, 344. 3 Plates, 4 Maps. C. 38302

See Chappe d'Auteroche's "Voyage en Sibérie."

[KRASCHENINNIKOFF.] Histoire de Kamtschatka, des Isles Kurilski, et des Contrées Voisines Publiée a Petersbourg, en Langue Russienne, par ordre de Sa Majesté Impériale. On y a joint deux Cartes, l'une de Kamtschatka, & l'autre des isles Kurilski. Traduite par M. E***. *A Lyon: Benoit Duplain.* M.DCC.LXVII. 2 vols., 12mo, pp. xv, (1), 327; (8), 359. 2 Maps.

"Traduction très-abrégée et bien moins complète que celle de Saint-Pié; voy. 'Histoire du Kamtschatka.'"—BRUNET. Traduite par M. A. Eidous, sur la traduction angloise faite par James Grieve.

[KRASCHENINNIKOFF.] Histoire et Description du Kamtschatka. Traduite du Russe. *Amsterdam.* 1770. 2 vols., 8vo.

This translation is made directly after the Russian original, and differs from the edition of 1767. The original Russian has not come under my notice.

[KRASKOWSKI (Thomas).] The Jewish Pride, revealed to M. S. Isaacs, Esq. *New Orleans, April* 28, 1864. 8vo, pp. 8. H.

KRATZ (A.) La Guerre d'Amérique. Résumé des Opérations Militaires et Maritimes. Par Arthur Kratz ... . *Paris: Arthus Bertrand.* 1866. 8vo, pp. (4), 116. 3 Maps. BA.

Extrait de la "Revue maritime et coloniale."

KRAUSE (W. E. F.) America or the Hope of Mankind. By William E. F. Krause. *San Francisco: Printed by Joseph Winterburn & Company.* 1869. 8vo, pp. 20. H. 38307

KRAUSE. Four Poems: By William E. F. Krause. ... *San Francisco: Printed by Joseph Winterburn and Company.* 1868. 8vo, pp. 16. H. 38308

The third poem is "The Advance of the United States." Also: American Interests in Borneo. ... Second Edition, with an Appendix ... . *San Francisco: H. H. Bancroft and Company.* 1867. 8vo, pp. 44.—The Influence of the United States Abroad. ... *San Francisco: Joseph Winterburn & Co.* 1868. 8vo, pp. 16.

KRAUTH (C. Porterfield). ... A Discourse ... Pittsburgh, Pa. on Thanksgiving Day, Nov. 26, 1857. By Charles P. Krauth. *Pittsburgh: Printed by W. S. Haven.* MDCCCLVII. 8vo, pp. 35.

KRAUTH. The Two Pageants. A Discourse ... Pittsburgh, Pa. ... June 1st, 1865. By Charles P. Krauth, D.D. ... *Pittsburgh: Printed by W. S. Haven.* 1865. 8vo, pp. 23. B. 38310

Relates to the assassination of Abraham Lincoln. Also: ... A Baccalaureate Address ... September 15, 1850 ... . *Gettysburg: Printed by H. C. Neinstedt.* 1850. 8vo, pp. 19.—A Discourse on the Life ... of Hon. Henry Clay ... at ... Gettysburg ... July 9th, 1852. ... *Gettysburg: Printed by H. C. Neinstedt.* 1852. 8vo, pp. 16.—Popular Amusements: A Discourse ... Winchester, Va. ... June 8th, 1851. ... *Winchester.* 1851. 8vo, pp. 42. Krauth has written other pieces. *See* Allibone's "Dictionary."

KREBS (E. H.) Rede zum Andenken an Abraham Lincoln, ... Ermordet am Charfreitage, April 14, 1865, A.D. ... Gehalten am 19 April 1865 ... von Ernst Hugo Krebs ... . [n. p. n. d.] 8vo, pp. 7. 38311

KREBS. A Sermon in Memory of Abraham Lincoln ... . Assassinated ... April 14, 1865. ... From the German of the Rev. Dr. Hugo Krebs. Translated by a Lady Hearer. [n. p. n. d.] 8vo, pp. 8. B. 38312

[KREBS (Henry J.)] The West Indian Marine Shells, with some Remarks. *Copenhagen: W. Laub.* 1864. 12mo, pp. (6), 137. C. 38313

KREBS (J. M.) The American Citizen. A Discourse ... New York, on Thanksgiving Day, December 12, 1850. ... By John M. Krebs, D.D. *New York: Charles Scribner.* 1851. 8vo, pp. 40. H. 38314

KREBS. ... A Sermon, preached December 20, 1835, on occasion of the Destructive Fire in ... the City of New York, on the night of December 16–17 previous. By John M. Krebs. *New York: Leavitt, Lord & Co.* 1838. 8vo, pp. 24. 38315

Also: A Discourse: on the Death of Zachary Taylor ... President of the United States. ... July 14, 1850. ... *New York: John Westall, Printer.* 1850. 8vo, pp. 27.—Education and Progress. An Address ... Lafayette College ... September 14, 1847.

Easton, Pa.: For the College. 1847. 8vo, pp. 43.—A Funeral Discourse ... September 18th, 1842. On Occasion of the Death of the Reverend Robert Birch ... . *New-Brunswick, N. J.: J. Terhune's Press.* 1842. 8vo, pp. 22.—The Leader Fallen. A Sermon ... in ... New-York ... April 11th, 1841, on ... the Death of William Henry Harrison ... . *New-York: Harper & Brothers.* 1841. 8vo, pp. 44.—Merciful Rebukes. A Sermon ... New-York ... May 14, 1841, on ... the National Fast. ... *New-York: Jonathan Leavitt.* 1841. 8vo, pp. 48. H.

KRETZSCHMAR (W.) Das Deutsche Colonisirungs-Projekt an der Mosquito-Küste, von W. Kretzschmar. *Königsberg.* 1845. 8vo, pp. 36. Map. 38316

[KRIDER (John).] Sporting Anecdotes, illustrative of the Habits of certain varieties of American Game. Edited by H. Milnor Klapp. *Philadelphia.* 1853. 8vo, pp. 292. C. 38317

KRIEGE (Hermann). Die Väter unsrer Republik in ihrem Leben und Wirken. *New York.* 1847. 8vo. 38318

Includes Dr. Benjamin Franklin and Thomas Paine.

KRIEGK (G. L.) Das Land Otuquis in Bolivia. Nach einem Originalberichte des Herrn Moritz Bach ... mit Beziehung auf allgemeine Südamerikanische Verhältnisse beschrieben von Dr. Georg Ludwig Kriegk. ... *Frankfurt am Main: Siegmund Schmerber.* 1838. 8vo, pp. ix, 54. Map. C., H. 38319

KROEGER (A. E.) Our Form of Government and The Problems of the Future. By A. E. Kroeger. [*St. Louis.* n. d.] 8vo, pp. 30. H. 38320

KRÖYER (H.) Grönlands Amfipoder Beskrevne af Henrik (Niels) Kröyer. ... *Kjöbenhavn.* 1838. 4to, pp. 98. 4 Plates. H.

Vom Kriege: Einfache Worte an einfache Leute von einem einfachen Manne. *Philadelphia.* 1863. 8vo, pp. 16. 38322

KRUGER (F. J.) Wohin soll der Deutsche auswandern? Entwurf einer deutschen Kolonial-Politik. ... *Hamburg: F. Schuberth.* 1857. 16mo, pp. 75. C. 38323

KRUGER (F.) The First Discovery of America, and its Early Civilization. Translated and enlarged from the German of Dr. F. Kruger, by W. L. Wagener ... . *New York: Sheldon & Co.* 1863. 12mo, pp. 134. C. 38324

KRULL (W.) Dichtgedachten by ... eere-grav van W. Krull, Schout by Nacht, gesneuveld by St. Eustatius, 1781. 8vo, pp. 2.

Poetical thoughts at the grave of W. Krull, Rear-Admiral, killed at St. Eustatius

KRUSEMAN (J. D.) Beschouwing der Kontrakten in 1840 door het Department van Kolonien gesloten met de Nederlandsche Handel-maatschappij. ... *'Hage.* 1840. 8vo. 38326

KRUSENSTERN (Adam Johann von). Poutechestvie vokroug svéta. Voyage autour du monde, entrepris en 1803, 1804, 1805 et 1806, sur les vaisseaux Nadéjéda et Neva. *Saint-Pétersbourg.* 1809–13. 3 vols., 8vo. Atlas in folio. 38327

KRUSENSTERN. Reise um die Welt in den Jahren 1803, 1804, 1805 und 1806, auf Befehl seiner kaiserlichen Majestät Alexander I. auf den Schiffen Nadeshda und Newa. *St. Petersburg.* 1810–12. 3 vols., 4to. Atlas in folio. 38328

"Relation intéressante d'un voyage dont le but principal était d'établir une communication entre les provinces occidentales et orientales de l'empire de Russie par le moyen de l'Ocean."—BRUNET.

KRUSENSTERN. Recueil de Mémoires Hydrographiques pour servir d'analyse et d'explication à l'Atlas de l'Océan Pacifique. Par A. J. Von Krusenstern. *Saint-Pétersbourg.* 1824–7. 2 vols., 4to, and Atlas of 34 Maps in folio. 38329

The two volumes of text contain not only copious hydrographical notes upon all the numerous islands and lands in the Pacific, but give also the history of geographical discovery in that region. The Atlas is scarce.

KRUSENSTERN. Reize om de Wereld gedaan in de Jaren 1803–1806. Uit het Hoogduitsch vertaalt. *Haarlem.* 1811–15. 4 vols., 8vo. Plates and Map. 38330

KRUSENSTERN. Voyage round the World, in the Years 1803, 1804, 1805, & 1806, by Order of His Imperial Majesty Alexander the First, on Board the Ships Nadeshda and Neva, under the Command of Captain A. J. von Krusenstern, of the Imperial Navy. ... Translated from the Original German By Richard Belgrave Hoppner, Esq. *London: John Murray.* 1813. 2 vols., 4to, pp. vii, xxxii, 314; (10), 404. Map, 2 Plates. A., B., BA.

"Capt. Krusenstern complained of the great number of defects in this English translation of his voyage, arising from the want of nautical information in the translator; hardly a single scientific or technical term has been properly translated, so that in some cases, the author's meaning can hardly be guessed at."—*North American Review*, XXV. 1. *See also* "M. Rev.," LXXIV. 113, 275.

KRUSENSTERN. Voyage autour du monde, fait dans les années 1803, 1804, 1805 et 1806, par les ordres de Sa Majestie Impériale Alexandre Ier, empereur de Russie, sur les vaisseaux la Nadiejeda et la Neva ... . Traduit .. avec des additions de l'auteur; la traduction revue par M. J.-B.-B. Eyriès ... . *Paris.*

Gide fils. 1821. 2 vols., 8vo, pp. xii, 418; (4), 531. Atlas in folio, pp. (4), 27 Plates, 3 Maps. A., H. 38332

See "N. A. Rev.," XXV. 1, *also* "Quart. Rev.," XXII. 109; XXVI. 346; XXVIII. 467; XXX. 163, 265.

KRUSENSTERN. Wörtersammlungen aus den Sprachen einiger Völker des östlichen Asiens und der Nordwestküste von Amerika. *St. Petersburg.* 1813. 4to, pp. xi, 68. A. 38333

Also on thick paper.

KUCHLER (J.) Valles de Sabinas y Salinas, por D. Jacobo Kuchler. *Mexico.* 1866. 8vo. 38334

KUFAHL (Ludwig). Die Geschichte der Vereinigten Staaten von Nordamerika, von der Entdeckung des Landes bis auf die neueste Zeit. ... *Berlin.* 1832–34. 3 vols., 8vo. 38335

KUGLER (J. B.) Our National Sins. Sermon, Dec. 30, 1860. By Rev. John B. Kugler. *Strasburg, Pa.* 1860. 8vo. 38336

KUHN (A.) Biographical Sketch of Adam Kuhn. *Philadelphia.* 1818. 8vo. 38337

KUHN (F. A.) Beschouwing van den toestand der Surinaamsche Plantagieslaven. *Amsterdam.* 1828. 8vo. 3 Plates.

On the condition of the slaves in Surinam.

KÜHN (J. M.) Merckwürdige Lebens- und Reise-Beschreibung, dessen Schiffahrten nach Grönland und Spitzbergen, Strat Davis, den canarischen Insuln ... . *Gotha.* 1741. 8vo. 38339

KUHN (W.) Speech pronounced by William Kuhn, on the occasion of his Graduation at Mount St. Mary's College, Emmetsburg. *Baltimore.* 1837. 8vo. 38340

KU-KLUX-KLAN. Horrible Disclosures. A Full and Authentic Exposé of the Ku-Klux-Klan. ... *Cincinnati: For the Compiler, by Padrick & Co.* 1868. 8vo, pp. ix–109. B. 38341

The Masked Lady of the White House; or the Ku-Klux-Klan. A most startling Exposure of doings of this Extensive Secret Band ... . *Philadelphia: C. W. Alexander.* [1868.] 8vo, pp. 19–62. 3834[illegible]

The Oaths, Signs, Ceremonies and Objects of the Ku-Klux-Klan. A Full Exposé. By a late Member. ... *Cleveland.* 186[illegible]. 12mo, pp. 30. H. 383[illegible]

KUIPERS (K. J.) Lotgevallen op zijne gedane zee- en landreizen van 1790–1818. *Groningen.* 1844. 8vo. 383[illegible]

KUNITZ (J. D.) Surinam und seine Bewohner oder Nachrichten ... Von J. D. Kunitz ... . *Erfurt.* 1805. 12mo, pp. viii, 352. 38345

KUNKEL (J. C.) Kansas contested Election. Speech of Hon. J. C. Kunkel ... March 10, 1856 ... on the ... Contested Election Case from the Territory of Kansas. [n. p. n. d.] 8vo, pp. 7. 38346

KUNSTMANN (F.) Die Entdeckung Amerikas. Nach den ältesten Quellen geschichtlich dargestellt von Friedrich Kunstmann. Mit einem Atlas alter bisher ungedruckter Karten. *München: A. Asher & Cie.* 1859. 4to, pp. (4), 151. B. 38347

The second title-page reads: "Monumenta sæcularia. Herausgegeben von der Königlich Bayerischen Akademie der Wissenschaften zur Feier ihres hundertjährigen Bestehens am 28 Mars 1859: III Classe." The text gives the history of the discovery according to the most authentic early documents, and the log-book of the third expedition of Francis Drake (1595–96), published in English for the first time. The Atlas is entitled:

KUNSTMANN. Atlas zur Entdeckungs-Geschichte Amerikas ... Herausgegeben von Friedrich Kunstmann. *München.* [1859.] Folio, pp. (4). 13 Maps. 38348

The maps published here for the first time elucidate many points hitherto obscure in the history of the discovery of America. As specimens of art, and perfect facsimiles, the maps are also extremely interesting; they were drawn from sources inaccessible to ordinary research. The maps numbered 6 and 12 are from a manuscript executed about 1540, and contain very full details of the Californian coast. The fourteenth map was made by an Englishman named Thomas Hood in 1592, and exhibits the coasts of Florida, Virginia, and Upper North America. The others are chiefly charts of the American coasts done by Portuguese and Spaniards at the beginning of the sixteenth century.

KUNTH (C. S.) *See* Vol. VIII., No. 33767.

KUNZE (G.) Filices a Leiboldo in Mexico lectae. [n. p. n. d.] 8vo. 38349

KUNZE (J. C.) Eine Aufforderung an das Volk Gottes in Amerika zum frohen Jauchzen und Danken. ... Von Johann Christoph Kunze ... *Philadelphia: Melchior Steiner.* 1784. 12mo, pp. 101. H. 38350

KUNZE. Sermon at the Dedication of the English Lutheran Church called Zion, in the City of New York, 11 October, 1801. By John C. Kunze. *New York.* 1801. 8vo. 38351

Also: Ein Wort für den Verstand und das Herz, vom rechten und gebahnten Lebenswege. ... *Philadelphia.* 1781. 8vo, pp. 243.

KÜRNBERGER (F.) Der Amerika-Müde. Amerikanisches Culturbild. *Frankfurt a. M.: Meidinger Sohn u. Co.* 1855. 8vo, pp. (4), 504. 38352

KURTZ (B.) Sendschreiben des Ehrw. Benjamin Kurtz ... zum Besten des theologischen Seminars, errichtet durch die General-Synode der evangelisch-lutherischen Kirche in den Vereinigten Staaten von Nordamerika. *Gettysburg.* 1827. 8vo.

[KURTZE (F.)] Copies of Documents relating to the Atlantic and Pacific Railroad to Costa Rica. *London: Wetherby & Co.* 1870. 8vo, pp. 69. 38354

Kurtze Nachricht von der Republique, so von denen R. R. P. P. der Gesellschaft Jesu der Portugiessisch- und Spanischen Provinzen in den über Meer gelegenen diesen zweyen Mächten gehörigen Königreichen aufgerichtet worden. Und von dem Krieg welchen gemelde Patres Jesuiten wider Spanien und Portugall geführet und ausgehalten haben. *Lissabon.* MDCCLX. 4to, pp. 67. 38355

Short account of the Republic as established by the Jesuits of the Portuguese and Spanish provinces across the ocean, and of the war which was waged by the Jesuit fathers against Spain and Portugal.

Kurtze Remarqves über den ietziger Zeit Welt-beruffenen Missisippischen Actien-Handel in Paris, und andere grosse Unternehmungen des Herrn Laws, Welche derselbe zum Profit seiner neu-errichteten Indianischen Compagnie, Vornehmlich aber zu Verbesserung der Königl. Financien und des Frantzösischen Commercii, biss hierher ziemlich fortgeführet; Wobey zugleich von der Natur der Actien insgemein und was es mit solchen in dergleichen grossen Compagnien vor eine Bewandniss habe, auch welches die festen Länder, Insuln, Festungen und See-Porten seyn, welche in America Septentrionali der Frantzösischen neuen Ost-Indischen Compagnie zu ihrem Handels-Gebrauch und Nutzen zugeeignet worden, gehandelt wird, entworfen von P. J. M. Cum Censura. *Leipzig, im Durchgange des Rathhauses.* 1720. 4to, 4 l. 38356

"Extrêmement rare, probablement le seul exemplaire qui en existe."

Ein Kurtzen Discours von der Schiff Fahrt bey dem Nord Pol nach Japan, China und so weiter. Aus dem Englischen ins Hochdeutsche übersetzt. *Hamburg.* 1676. 4to. Map. 38357

Title from J. R. Smith's Catalogue.

Kurze Beschreibung der dreizehn unabhängigen Nordamerikanischen Staaten; aus den englischen Quellen. *Köln.* 1783. 8vo.

Kurze Beschreibung des Geneserdistrikts in Nordamerika. *Bremen.* 1792. 8vo. 38359

Kurze Beschreibung der Staaten Michigan ... . *New York: T. Uhl, Printer.* 1845. 12mo, pp. 9. Map. 38360

Kurze Geschichte der politischen Parteien in den Vereinigten Staaten bis zum Jahre 1846. *New York.* 1851. 8vo. 38361

Kurze Nachricht. *See* South Carolina.

Kurze Schilderung der Grosbrittannischen Kolonien in Nord-America. *Göttingen.* 1777. Broad sheet 29 × 17. 38362

Ein kurzer Abriss. *See* Vol. III., No. 10376.

Kurzgefasste Geschichte der drey ersten Entdecker von Amerika. *Frankfurt: Eichenb. Erben.* 1781. 8vo, pp. 154. 38363

A short history of the first three discoverers of America.

Kurzgefasste historisch-geographische Nachrichten von den Englischen Kolonien in Nord Amerika bis auf jetzige Zeiten. *Hamburg, in der Möllerischen Buchhandlung.* 1778. 12mo, pp. 31.

Kurz gefasste Nachricht von dem Etablissement derer [der] Salzburgischen Emigranten zu Ebenezer, in der Provinz Georgien in Nordamerica, wie solche auf Verlangen von dem Hrn. Regierungsrath von Reck zu Ranzau mitgetheilet worden. *Hamburg, bey Ritter.* 1777. 8vo, pp. 44. 38365

Kurzgefasste naturliche und bürgerliche Geschichte des Königreichs Chile, aus dem italienischen durch Jagemann. *Hamburg.* 1782. 8vo. 38366

This is a German translation of *our* No. 12756, Vol. IV., which *see* for a note.

Kurzgefasste Neger-Englische Grammatik. *Bautzen.* 1854. 8vo, pp. 68. 38367

A concise grammar of the Negro-English language.

KÜSTEL (G.) Nevada and California Processes of Silver and Gold Extraction for general use, and especially for the Mining Public of California and Nevada ... . By Guido Küstel ... . *San Francisco: Frank D. Carlton.* 1863. 8vo, pp. 327. 11 Plates. B. + [*Ibid.*] 1868. 8vo, pp. 327. 11 Plates. C. 38368

This valuable work contains everything necessary for the practical workman to know in connection with the extraction of gold and silver, assaying, etc. It has also tables showing the amount of fine metal per ton of ore, and the value of gold and silver per ounce at different degrees of fineness.

KUTSCHER (F. J.) America, nach seiner ehemaligen und jetzigen Verfassung dargestellt nach den besten Geschichts- und Reisebeschreibungen. Ein Beytrag zur Geographie, Natur- und Völkergeschichte von Westindien; ... Von Franz Jacob Kutscher ... . *Schleswig: Johann Gottlob Rohss.* 1803–04. 3 vols., 8vo, pp. x, (2), 532; vi, 398, (4); (2), 246. H. 38369

KUTSCHER. Amerika, i sin forhen voerende og nu voerende Forfatning, uddraget af de bedste Historie en Reisebeskrivelser. Et Bidrag til Vestindiens Geographie- Natur- og Folkehistorie, oversat af C. B. Hallager. *Kiöbenhavn: M. J. Sebbelow.* 1804. 16mo, pp. x, 446. C. 38370

KUTZ (M. J.) Wab-ah-see, the White Swan; a Legend of the Sleeping Dew: and other Poems. By Mrs. M. Jennie Kutz. *Grand Rapids (Mich.): Dygert, Hart & Co.* 1870. 16mo, pp. 60.

KUYKENDALL (A. J.) Capital and Labor. Speech of Hon. A. J. Kuykendall ... January 18, 1867. *Washington, D. C.: McGill & Witherow, Printers.* 1867. 8vo, pp. 16. H. 38372

KYNASTON (H.) The Life and Adventures of Humphrey Kynaston, with the Surprising Adventures of Capt. Redmond O. Hanlon, a Celebrated Robber. *New York.* 1828. 8vo. 38373

L. (A.) A Reply to a Pamphlet entitled the "Answer of the Friend in the West to a Letter on the Present State of Connecticut." By A. L. [n. p.] 1775. 4to, pp. 63.

L. (B. v.) Die Glaubwürdigkeit von Maldonados nordwestlicher Schiffahrt. Untersucht von B. v. L. *Gotha.* 1712. 8vo, pp. 52. 38375

L. (B. K.) A Trip from Boston to New Hampshire and through the Notch of the White Mountains. By B. K. L. *Washington: Gideon, Jr.* 1836. 12mo, pp. 30. C. 38376

L. (C.) La República en el Perú y la Cuestion Peruano-Espanola, por C. L. *Lima.* 1865. 4to, pp. 136. 38377

L. (D.) Notice sur Haiti. [Signé D. L.] *Paris: imp de Vinchon.* 1837. 8vo. 38378

L. (D.) *See* L[eeds] (D[aniel]).

L. (Em. C.) L'impératrice du Mexique à Paris. *Paris: Chambéry.* 1866. 8vo, pp. 16. 38379

L. (E. N.) *See* L[ockerby] (E[lizabeth] N.)

L. (E.) Leisure Hours or Desultory Pieces in Prose and Verse. A private edition, inscribed to America by one of her Absent Daughters. By E. L. *Calcutta.* 1846. 12mo. 38380

L. (F.) Noticias de la Provincia de Californias en tres Cartas de un Sacerdote Religioso hijo del real convento de Predicadores de Valencia a un amigo suyo. *Valencia: Por los Hermanos de Orga.* 1794. 18mo, pp. 104, 96, 104. 38381

The author, who was a missionary, gives an apparently truthful account of California, wherein he attempts to correct some of the errors in which Venegas has fallen.

L*** (F.) Etudes historiques sur le Mexique au point de vue politique et social. Par F. L***, ancien consul. *Paris: imp. Chaix.* 1859. 8vo, pp. 93. P. 38382

L. (G.) L'Amérique et l'Europe en 1846, ou Congrès de Panama. Par Mr. G. L. *Bruxelles.* 1826. 8vo, pp. 84.

L. (H.) The ... Earthquake. *See* Jamaica, No. 35665.

L. (J.) *See* L[ogan] (J[ames]).

L. (J. D. H.) Beschryvinge van de Volk-Plantinge Zuriname, voortoonende het opkomst derselven Colonie, de amborewen bewertinge der zuiken, plantagien, neffens de art der eigene naturalische inwooners of Indianen. Door J. D. H. L. *Leeuwarden.* 1717. 4to. + Tweede Druck. [*Ibid.*] 1718. 4to. + *'s Hage.* 1727. 4to. 38384

L. (J. F.) *See* L[izardi] (J. F.)

L. (J. J.) Analisis Estadistico de la Provincia de Michuacan en 1822. Por J. J. L. *Mexico.* 1824. Sm. 4to. 38385

L. (J. N.) Ocho dias a Dios ó sea una semana de ejercicios en la profesa. Por J. N. L. *Mexico.* 1841. 8vo, pp. 66.

L. (J. P.) Bresil. A Constituiçao de Portugal. Por J. P. L. *Rio de Janeiro.* 1824. 4to. 38387

L. (L.) The Proselyte. By Mrs. L. L. *New York.* 1829. 8vo, pp. 71. 38388

L. (M. de). Histoire impartiale des Evénemens Militaires et Politiques dans la Derniere Guerre dans les quatre parties du Monde. Par M. de L. *A Paris: Chez la Veuve Duchesne.* 1785. 3 vols., 12mo, pp. 558, (1); 523; (2), 620. 38389

L. (M. de). *See* L[ongchamps] (Pierre de).

L. (R.) *See* L[ingard] (R.)

L. (T. D.) A Peep at the Western World; being an Account of a Visit to Nova Scotia, New Brunswick, Canada, and the United States. By T. D. L. *London: J. R. Smith.* 1863. Crown 8vo, pp. v, 126. 38390

L. (T.) *See* L[etchworth] (T.)

The L... Family. *See* [Watterston (George)].

Laactshures on various Subjects, by Paranamartagh, formerly Professor of Belles Lettres in the University on the Blue Ridge, on the tip top of the Allegheny Mountains. *Philadelphia.* 1847. 8vo. 38391

De laatste geldkrisissen in de Vereenigde Staten van Noord-Amerika en de Amerikaansche waarde. *'s Gravenhage: M. M. Couvée.* 1871. 8vo, pp. 16. 38392

La America. Cronica hispano-americana; dirigida por Eduardo Asquerino. Vol. I. *Madrid.* 1858. Folio. Continued.

Labanoff de Rostoff (A.) Catalogue des Cartes Géographiques, Topographiques & Marines, de la Bibliothèque du Prince Alexandre Labanoff de Rostoff, a Saint-Pétersbourg. Suivi d'une Notice de Manuscrits. *Paris: Typographie de Didot.* 1823. 8vo, pp. (4), viii, 495. A. 38394

Three hundred and forty copies printed, not for sale, thirty of them on large paper.

La Bar (G.) Reminiscences of George La Bar, the Centenarian of Monroe County, Pa.; with Incidents in the Early Settlement of the Pennsylvania side of the River Valley, from Easton to Buskirk. *Philadelphia.* [n. d.] 12mo. 38395

[La Barbinais (Le G. de).] Dissertation sur la Caffé ... . Par M. Gentil. *Paris: l'auteur.* M.DCC.LXXXVII. 8vo, pp. 177, (6). Plate. 38396

[La Barbinais.] Nouveau Voyage autour Du Monde. Par M. Le Gentil. Enrichi de plusieurs Plans, Vûës & Perspectives des principales Villes & Ports du Pérou, Chily, Bresil, & de la Chine. ... *Paris.* 1725. 3 vols., 12mo. + *A Amsterdam, Chez Pierre Mortier.* M. DCCXXVIII. 3 vols., 12mo, pp. (6), 314, (10); (12), 227; (2), 192, (24). Plans. H. + *A Paris: Chez Briasson.* 1728. 3 vols., 12mo, pp. 451; 313; 325, (26). S. 38397

The collation varies in some copies of the *Amsterdam* edition. Admiral Burney expresses a doubt whether this voyage was really made by Le Gentil. "The account is full of obscurity, which may have proceeded from the ignorance of the writer on maritime subjects, and from his general want of judgment. M. de Brosses has allowed credit to the narration as being genuine, observing at the same time that it was one of small importance to the history of navigation or commerce. It is given in the form of letters addressed to some unnamed correspondent between 1714 and 1718."—Burney, IV. 508. There are also editions dated 1727 and 1731.

[La Barbinais.] Le Gentils Reisen in den indischen Meeren in den Jahren 1761 bis 1769 und Chappe d'Auteroche Reise nach Mexico und Californien im Jahre 1769 aus dem Französischen nebst Karl Millers Nachricht von Sumatra und F. Mason's Beschreibung der Insel St. Miguel aus dem Englischen. *Hamburg: bey Carl Ernst Bohn.* 1781. 8vo, pp. 521. Plate. 38398

La Bárcena (Manuel de). Manifesto al Mundo la Justicia y la Necesidad de la Independencia de la Nueva España. *Impresso en Puebla y en Mexico.* 1821. 4to. + *Vera Cruz.* 1821. 4to, pp. 16. 38399

Labaree (Benjamin). Historical Address at the Dedication of a Monument in Charlestown, N. H. By B. Labaree. *Boston: ... T. R. Marvin & Son.* 1870. 8vo, pp. 28. H. 38400

Labaree. A Sermon on the Death of General Harrison, ... in Middlebury, Vermont ... . By Rev. Benjamin Labaree. *Middlebury: Printed by E. Maxham.* 1841. 8vo, pp. 35. H. 38401

Also: ... A Baccalaureate Discourse ... at Middlebury, Vermont, August 6, 1865. ... *Boston: Press of T. R. Marvin & Son.* 1865. 8vo, pp. 28. H.

La Barra (Justo de). Los dos Robinsones ó aventuras de Carlos y Fanny dos niños ingleses abandonados en una isla de América. Relacion imitada del inglés. Segunda edicion. *Madrid: Marin.* 1792–97. 3 vols., 18mo. 38402

La Barre (Le F. de). Description de la France Équinoctiale, cy-devant appellée Gvyanne, et par les Espagnols El Dorado, nouuellement remise sous l'obéissance du Roy, par le Sievr Le Febvre de la Barre, son Lieutenant Général dans ce Pais. Avec la carte d'icelvy, et un discovrs très-vtile et necessaire pour ceux qui voudront établir des colonies en ces contrées, qui les détrompera des impostures dont tous ceux qui en ont parlé ont remply leur écrits. *Paris: Iean Ribov.* 1666. 4to, pp. 52. Map.

"The author, founder of a colony in Guiana in 1664, wrote this work in order to excite a more general interest, especially to gain the protection of the King himself, for his colony, giving at the same time an account of his enterprises and results, and explaining the favorable prospects of the new colony. But his hopes were not fulfilled, the colony was taken by the English in the following war, and nearly all its new inhabitants were murdered or imprisoned."—Muller.

La Barrera y Troncoso (M. de). Elogio al coronel Jos. Joaq. Marquez Donallo. *Mexico.* 1818. 4to, 38 l. 38404

La Barreyrie (F. de). Révélations sur l'intervention française au Mexique De 1866 à 1867. Par F. De La Barreyrie ... . [n. p.:] *Weil et Bloch.* 1868. 8vo, pp. viii, 115, (2). B. 38405

Labarthe (C. de). Documents inédits sur l'Empire des Incas. Par Charles de Labarthe. *Paris.* 1861. 8vo, pp. 23.

Labarthe. De l'état social et politique du Mexique avant l'arrivée des Espagnols Par Charles de Labarthe ... . *Paris: l'auteur.* 1865. 8vo, pp. 25. 38407

Republished from the "Revue américaine," Seconde Série, No. 3.

La Bastide (M. de). Mémoire sur un nouveau passage de la mer du nord à la mer du sud. Par M. Martin de La Bastide.

Paris: l'Imprimerie de Didot fils âiné. M.DCC.XCI. 8vo, pp. (4), 70. Map. H., S. 38408

Relates to the formation of a canal or passage across the Isthmus of Darien.

[Labat (Jean Baptiste).] Nouveau Voyage aux Isles de l'Amerique, contenant l'Histoire Naturelle de ces Pays, l'Origine, les Mœurs, la Religion & le Gouvernement des Habitans anciens & modernes. Les Guerres & les Evenemens singuliers qui y sont arrivez pendant le long sejour que l'Auteur y a fait. Le Commerce & les Manufactures qui y sont établies, & les moyens de les augmenter. Avec une Description exacte & curieuse de toutes ces Isles. Ouvrage enrichi de plus de cent Cartes, Plans & Figures en Tailles-douces. *A Paris: ... Chez Pierre-François Giffart* ... M. DCC. XXII. 6 vols., 12mo, pp. xxxvi, (10), 525; (6), 598; iv, 549 [547]; vi, 558; vi, 524; vi, 514, (14). Map, 91 Plates. B., BA., H. 38409

The name of the author is affixed to the dedication to the Duc de Montmorency. Some copies of this edition have the imprint, *Paris: Theodore Le Gras,* M.DCC.XXII; others, *A Paris: ... Chez Guillaume Cavelier.* M.DCC.XXII. There are slight variations in the collation of these editions.

[Labat.] Nouveau Voyage aux Isles de l'Amerique. Contenant l'Histoire Naturelle de ces Pays, l'Origine, les Mœurs, la Religion & le Gouvernement des Habitans anciens & modernes: Les Guerres & les Evenemens singuliers qui y sont arrivez pendant le long séjour que l'Auteur y a fait. Le Commerce et les Manufactures qui sont établies, & les moyens de les augmenter. Avec une Description exacte & curieuse de toutes ces Isles. Ouvrage enrichi d'un grand nombre de Cartes, Plans, & Figures en Taille-douce. *A La Haye: Chez P. Husson, E. Johnson,* ... M.DCC.XXIV. 6 vols., 12mo, pp. (30), 504; (8), 576; (6), 528; (8), 539; (8), 504; (6), 514, 58. Map, 91 Plates. 38410

[Labat.] Nouveau Voyage aux Isles de l'Amerique. Contenant l'Histoire Naturelle de ces Pays, l'Origine, les Mœurs, la Religion & le Gouvernement des Habitans anciens & modernes: Les Guerres & les Evenemens singuliers qui y sont arrivez pendant le long séjour que l'Auteur y a fait: Le Commerce et les Manufactures qui y sont établies, & les moyens de les augmenter. Ouvrage enrichi d'un grand nombre de Cartes, Plans, & Figures en Taille-douce. *A La Haye: Chez P. Husson, E. Johnson,* ... M.DCC.XXIV. 2 vols., 4to, pp. (8), viii, (4), 360, Table, (4); (8), 520, (20). Map, 68 Plates. + *Paris.* 1724. 2 vols., 4to. B.

A reprint of the first edition, without any alteration except in the form. The collation varies in some copies. Faribault quotes an edition, *La Haye,* 1738, 2 vols., 4to, which is probably a mistake. The only quarto edition I have seen is dated 1724.

Labat. Nouveau Voyage aux Isles de l'Amerique, contenant l'Histoire Naturelle de ces Pays, l'Origine, les Mœurs, la Religion & le Gouvernement des Habitans anciens & modernes. Les Guerres & les Evenemens singuliers qui y sont arrivez pendant le séjour que l'Auteur y a fait. Par le R. P. Labat, de l'Ordre des Freres Prêcheurs. Nouvelle Edition augmentée considérablement, & enrichie de Figures en Tailles-douces. *A Paris: ... Chez Theodore Le Gras.* M. DCC. XLII. 8 vols., 12mo, pp. xxxvi, (14), 472; (6), 444; (6), 475; (4), 533; (5), 418; (4), 502; (6), 516; (5), 437, (7). 103 Plates. H. 38412

This edition is greatly augmented. Some copies have the imprint, *A Paris: Ch. J. B. Delespine,* M.DCC.XLII; others, *A Paris: ... Chez Guillaume Cavelier,* M.DCC.XLII, and *Paris: J. de Nully.* 1742. "A very pleasant and instructive work in many respects."—Chalmers. The most copious that we possess on the Antilles; very full on the Natural History and productions of those Islands. *See* Boucher de la Richarderie, VI. 195.

Labat. Voyage aux Isles Françaises de l'Amerique. Par le R. P. Labat. Nouvelle edition, conforme a celle de 1722. *Paris.* 1831. 8vo, pp. 268. 38413

This is in fact an abridgment, although not so called.

Labat. Voyage du Chevalier des Marchais en Guinée, Isles voisines, et à Cayenne, Fait en 1725, 1726 & 1727 ... . *Paris: Prault.* 1730. 4 vols., 12mo, pp. xxiv, (2), 381; (2), 364; (4), 350; (2), 681, (36). 31 Plates and Maps. + *Amsterdam: Aux dépens de la Compagnie.* M.DCC.XXXI. 4 vols., 12mo, pp. (4), xxii, (4), 335; (8), 292; (4), 330, 24; (4), 392. Plates, 3 Maps. B.

Some copies have the imprint, *Paris: Osmont.* 1730. Vols. III. and IV. relate almost entirely to the French possessions in South America, and are illustrated with D'Anville's maps.

Labat. Nieuwe Reizen naar de Franse Eilanden van America. Behelzende de Natuurlyke Historie van die Landen, derzelver Oorspronk, Zeden, Godsdienst, Regeering der oude en tegenwoordige Inwoonders; als ook die der zwarte Slaaven: Beneffens de Oorlogen en voornaamste Gevallen, die in het lang verblyf van den Auteur in dat Land zyn voorgevallen. Als ook een naauwkeurige Verhandeling van het maken der Suiker, Indigo, Cochenille, Cacao, en andere nuttigheden, tot den Koophandel dienende. Door den Heer P. Labat. En in't Nederduitsch in't ligt gebragt door W. C. Duyks. *Te Amsterdam: By Balthasar Lakeman.* 1725. 4 vols., 4to, pp. (4), 350; 404; 254; 200, 167, (32). 10 Maps, 76 Plates. 38415

Also on large paper.

Labat. Des Pater Labats, aus dem Orden der Prediger-Mönche, Reisen nach Westindien, oder den im amerikanischen Meere liegenden Inseln. Nach der neuesten Pariser Ausgabe übersetzet, auch mit nöthigen Anmerkungen und vollständigen Registern versehen, von Georg Friedrich Casimir Schad. ... *Nürnberg: Gabriel Nicolaus Raspe.* 1782–3. 3 vols., 12mo, pp. (10), 458; 500; (12), 525. Map, 24 Plates. 38416

The seventh and last volume appeared in 1788.

La Baume (Jules). *See* Regnault (É.)

Labbe (Jacobi Josephi). Selenopolitani Dissertatio Ludicro-Seria num possit aliqui extra Italiam natus bene latine scribere contra quam Robertus pronuntiat? 1778. 8vo. 38417

A satirical work relating to Mexico.

La Beaumelle (V. L. S. M. A. de). *See* Angliviel de la Beaumelle, Vol. I., No. 1570.

La Bédollière (É. Gigault de). Histoire de la guerre du Mexique. Mexico. Par Émile de La Bédollière. Illustrée par nos meilleurs artistes, avec une carte coloriée, dressée par A. H. Dufour. *Paris: G. Barba.* 1863. 4to. + [*Ibid.*] 1865. 4to, pp. 80. 38418

Labelle (M. F.) Biographie et oraison funebre du Rév. M. F. Labelle, et autre documents relatifs à sa mémoire, ainsi qu'à la visite de P. A. De Gaspé, écuier, au Collége de l'Assomption. *Montréal.* 1865. 8vo, pp. 85. 38419

Labillardière (Jacques Julien Houton de). Relation du Voyage à la Recherche de La Pérouse fait par ordre de l'assemblée constituante, Pendant les années 1791, 1792, et pendant la 1ère et la 2de. année de la République Françoise. Par le Cen Labillardière ... l'un des naturalistes de l'expedition. *Paris: H. J. Janssen ... An VIII. de la République Françoise.* [1799–1800.] 2 vols., 4to, pp. xvi, 442; 332, 113, (1). Atlas in folio. A., H. + [*Ibid.* 1799.] 2 vols., 8vo. Atlas. + [*Ibid.* 1800–11.] 2 vols., 4to, pp. xvi, 442; 332; 113, (1). Atlas in folio. B. + *Paris.* 1811. 2 vols., 8vo. P. 38420

See "M. Rev.," XXXI. 527; XXXII. 292.

Labillardière. Voyage in Search of La Pérouse, performed by order of The Constituent Assembly, during the Years 1791, 1792, 1793, and 1794 and drawn up by M. Labillardiere ... . Translated from the French. Illustrated with Forty-Six Plates.

London: John Stockdale. 1800. 4to, pp. xviii, (2), 17–476, 65. Map, 46 Plates. C., H. 38421

Labillardière. Voyage in Search of La Pérouse ... during the Years 1791, 1792, 1793, and 1794 ... . Translated from the French, by John Stockdale. *London: John Stockdale.* 1800. 2 vols., 8vo, pp. xxxii, 487; 344, Appendix, 105. 46 Plates. C.

Labillardière. An Account of a Voyage in Search of La Pérouse, undertaken by order of the Constituent Assembly of France, and performed In the Years 1791, 1792, and 1793, in the Recherche and Espérance, Ships of War, under the Command of Rear-Admiral Bruni D'Entrecasteaux. Translated from the French ... . *London: J. Debrett.* 1800. 2 vols., 8vo, pp. lxii, (2), 464; vii, (1), 423, Tables, pp. 43, (2). BA. + Second Edition. *London: B. Uphill.* 1802. 2 vols., 8vo, pp. lxii, (2), 464; vii, (1), 423, 43, (2). Atlas of 69 Plates. B. 38423

La Blanchardière (*l'abbé* Courte de). *See* Courte de La Blanchardière, Vol. V., No. 17176–77.

La Boissière. *See* Tanguy de la Boissière.

The Labor Question. Extracts, Magazine Articles, and Observations relating to Social Science & Political Economy ... in Europe, ... and America. *Chicago.* 1867. 12mo, pp. 144.

Labor Reform League of New England. ... An Address to the Members ... at their Late Convention in Boston. By one of the Members. *Boston: The Author.* 1847. 8vo, pp. 32. B.

La Borde (Jean Benjamin de). Histoire Abrégée de la Mer du Sud, ornée de plusieurs cartes; Dédiée au Roi, et composée pour l'éducation de Mgr Le Dauphin. Par M. De La Borde ... . *Paris: Chez P. Didot l'aîné.* M. DCC. XCI. 3 vols., 8vo, pp. (6), 11, lxxi, 415, 30, (2); (4), 412, (4), 70, (2), 5–15; (4), 472, 31. 7 Maps and 3 Plates. B. 38426

"Eleven charts are done up separately, and seldom found with the work."—Rich. At the end of the second volume, with a separate title and paging, is the following:

La Borde. Mémoire sur la prétendu Découverte, faite en 1783 par les Anglois, d'un continent qui n'est autre chose que la terres des Arsacides, découverte en 1768 par M. de Bougainville ... et en 1769 par M. de Surville ... suivi d'un projet de souscription pour un armement destiné à la recherche de M. de la Pérouse qu'on croit avoir fait naufrage sur quelque côte de la mer

du sud. On propose que cet armement soit commandé ou au moins dirigé par M. de Bougainville. [n. p.] 1791. 8vo, pp. 15.

La Borde (M.) History of the South Carolina College, from its Incorporation December 19, 1801, to Nov. 25, 1857, including Sketches of its Presidents and Professors. With an Appendix. By M. La Borde, M.D. ... *Columbia, S. C.: Peter B. Glass.* 1859. 8vo, pp. 463, (1). H. 38428

Laboria (——). De la Guyane Française et de ses Colonisations: par Laboria, Capitaine d'Artillerie de Marine ... . *Paris: Corréard.* 1843. 8vo, pp. 296. 38429

Laborie (P. J.) The Coffee Planter of Saint Domingo; with An Appendix, Containing a View of the Constitution, Government, Laws and State of that Colony, previous to the Year 1789. To which are added, some hints on the present state of the Island, under the British Government. By P. J. Laborie, LL.D. Planter in the North of St. Domingo, and Member of the Superior Council. *London: T. Cadell ...* M.DCC.XCVIII. 8vo, pp. xii, 198, Appendix, 145, (4). 22 Plates. H. 38430

"A curious, and in some respects a valuable performance. The author's knowledge of the French colonial system, under the ancient government, is accurate and profound. In no other book is so clear, exact, and perfect an account of the laws and constitution of St. Domingo, before the revolution, to be found."—*Monthly Review,* XXVIII. 355. Also: Extracts from the Coffee Planter of St. Domingo. ... *Nassau.* 1801. 4to.

Laborie. Cultivo del cafeto ó árbol que produce el café y modo de beneficiar este fruto, escrito en francés é inglés por M. T. Laborie, hacendado de la Colonia de Sto. Domingo. Traducido al castellano por D. P[ablo] B[oloña]. *Habana: imprenta del Gobierno.* 1809. 4to, pp. 108. 38431

Laborie. Réflexions sommaires adressées à la France et à la colonie de S.-Domingue. [*Paris:*] *imp. de Chardon.* [1789?] 8vo, pp. 48, or less. 38432

Laboulaye (É.) De la Constitution Américaine et de l'Utilité de son Étude, Discours prononcé le 4 décembre 1849 à l'ouverture du cours de législation comparée. Par Édouard Laboulaye. *Paris: Hennuyer et Cie.* 1850. 8vo, pp. 27. H.

Extracted from the "Revue de législation et de jurisprudence," Décembre, 1849.

Laboulaye. Correspondance de Benjamin Franklin traduite de l'anglais et annotée par Édouard Laboulaye ... . *Paris: Hachette et Cie.* 1870. 3 vols., 12mo, pp. (4), x, 352; (4), 284; (4), 355. B. 38434

This should have appeared under Franklin.

LABOULAYE. Estudios sobre la constitution de los Estados-Unidas. Por D. Eduardo Laboulaye. Traduccion de D. Manuel R. Garcia. *Paris: F. Brachet.* 1866. 12mo. 38435

LABOULAYE. L'État et ses limites, suivi d'essais politiques ... par Édouard Laboulaye ... Deuxième édition. *Paris: Charpentier.* 1863. 8vo, pp. vi, 391, (1). BA. 38436

"La France en Amérique; Les États-Unis et la France; Pourquoi le Nord ne peut pas accepter la séparation," occupy pp. 307–391.

LABOULAYE. Les États-Unis et La France. Par Édouard Laboulaye ... *Paris: E. Dentu.* 1862. 8vo, pp. 72. BA., H.

LABOULAYE. Histoire Politique des États-Unis depuis les premiers essais de colonisation jusqu'à l'Adoption de la Constitution Fédérale 1620–1789. Par Édouard Laboulaye ... *Paris: A. Durand.* 1855–66. 3 vols., 8vo, (4), xxiv, 532; xi, 448; xii, 574, (1). BA. + Deuxième édition. *Paris: Charpentier.* 1866. 3 vols., 18mo, pp. (4), xix, 470; xi, 448; xii, 574, (1). H. + [*Ibid.*] 1867. + Troisième édition. *Paris: Bourdier.* 1868. 3 vols., 18mo, pp. xlii, 1414. + Quatrième édition. *Paris: Visville et Capiomont.* 1870. 3 vols., 18mo, pp. xlii, 1498. 38438

[LABOULAYE.] Paris en Amérique. Par le Docteur René Lefebvre ... *Paris: Charpentier.* 1863. 12mo. + Quatrième édition. [*Ibid.*] 1863. 12mo, pp. (4), 450. BA. 38439

"Souvent réimprimé. Les dernières éditions portent le nom de M. Laboulaye à côté du pseudonyme."—LORENZ.

[LABOULAYE.] Paris in America. By Dr. René Lefebvre ... Translated by Mary L. Booth ... *New York: Charles Scribner.* 1863. 12mo, pp. 373. B., C. 38440

[LABOULAYE.] Parys in Amerika. Vry naar het Fransch, door Falkland. *Rotterdam.* 1865. 8vo. 38441

LABOULAYE. Pourquoi le Nord ne peut pas accepter la séparation. Par Édouard Laboulaye ... *New York.* 1863. 8vo, pp. 9. 38442

LABOULAYE. El Principio-Perro de Aguas, escrito en Francés por Eduardo Laboulaye, traducido libremente al español en Buenos Aires por Juan Maria Gutierrez. *Buenos Aires.* 1868. 8vo, pp. 258. 38443

LABOULAYE. The United States and France. By Edward Laboulaye ... Translated for the Boston Daily Advertiser. *Boston.* 1862. 8vo pp. 14. H. 38444

LABOULAYE. Upon Whom Rests the Guilt of the War? Separation: War Without End. By M. Edouard Laboulaye ... *New-York: W. C. Bryant & Co.* 1863. 8vo, pp. 19. + *Edinburgh: Murray & Gibb.* 1863. 12mo, pp. 14. + *New York: Loyal Publication Society, No.* 8. 1864. 8vo, pp. 19. B. 38445

LABOULAYE. Why the North Cannot Accept of Separation. By Edouard Laboulaye ... *New York: Charles B. Richardson.* 1863. 8vo, pp. 16. C. 38446

Also: Discours populaires. . Franklin. ... Horace Mann. ... *Paris.* 1870. 12mo. —Locke, Legislateur de la Caroline. . *Paris.* 1850. 8vo. C.—On the Presidential Election, 1864. ... [n. p. n. d.] 8vo.

LABOURIEU (T.) Les Carrières d'Amérique; par Théodore Labourieu. ... *Paris: Vanier.* 1869. 18mo, pp. 236. 3844-

El labrador argentino. *See* Vol. III., No. 9018.

LABREE (L.) Rebels and Tories; or, the Blood of the Mohawk! A Tale of the American Revolution. By Lawrence Labree. *New York: Dewitt & Davenport.* [1851.] 8vo, pp. 202.

LABRIE (J.) Les premiers rudiments de la Constitution Britannique, traduits de l'Anglais de M. Brooke, précédés d'un précis historique, et suivis d'observations sur la Constitution du Bas-Canada. Par Jacques Labrie, M.D. *Montréal.* 1827. 8vo.

LA CALLE (J. D. de). *See* Diez de la Calle, Vol. v.

LA CARRIÈRES (A. C. de). Voyage aux pays aurifères. Afrique, Mexique, Californie, Pérou, Chili, Nouvelle Calédonie, Australie, Russie. Par A. C. de La Carrières. *Paris: Courcier.* [1855.] 8vo. C. 38450

LACASA (P.) Biografia del Brigadier Argentino Don Miguel Estanisla Soler. Escrita por Pedro Lacasa. *Buenos Aires.* 1854. 8vo, pp. 64. 38451

LACASA. Vida militar y politica del General Don Juan Lavalle. Escrita por Pedro Lacasa. *Buenos Aires.* 1858. 4to, pp. 124.

LACERDA WERNECK (L. P. de). Estudos sobre o credito rural e hypothecario seguidos de leis, estatutos e outros documentos. *Rio de Janeiro.* 1857. 8vo. 38453

LACERDA WERNECK. Idéas sobre colonisação precedidas de uma succinta exposição dos principios geraes que regem a população. *Rio de Janeiro.* 1855. 8vo. 38454

LA CERNA (D. Jacinto). Sermon on San Felipe de Jesus. *Mexico.* 1652. 38455

This imperfect title is from an English catalogue, and is doubtless incorrect.

LACEY (J.) State of the Accounts of John Lacy, Junior, and George Wall, Esquires, Late Sub-Lieutenants of the County of Bucks ... from March 1777 to March 1780 ... *Philadelphia: Printed by Robert Aitken.* M,DCC,LXXXIII. 8vo, pp. 20. P.

LACEY [William B.] Notes on the Sayings and Doings of Dr. Lacey and his Three Friends ... By Philo Cor-Rector, Esq. *Albany.* 1830. 8vo, pp. 58. S. 38457

Also: The Utility of Apprentices' Libraries: A Sermon ... in ... Albany, 22d February, 1822. ... *Albany: Printed by Websters* ... 1822. 8vo, pp. 16. B.

LA CHAISE. Letter from Father La Chaise, Confessor to the French King, to Father Peters, Confessor to the King of England; in which is contained the Project and Designe of that Faction to introduce the Prince of Wales. Also a Letter from William Penn to Father La Chaise. *Printed in the City of Philadelphia, in the Land of Promise, by order of Father Penn.* 1688. 4to.

Title from J. R. Smith's Catalogue. If the imprint is to be trusted, this piece would range among the earliest books printed in Philadelphia. William Bradford's press was established this year in Philadelphia.

LACHAPELLE (A. de). Le Compte de Raousset-Boulbon et l'expédition de la Sonore. Correspondance souvenirs et œuvres inédites. *Paris.* 1859. 8vo. 38459

LACHARTIÈRE (A.) A. S. A. R. le Prince de Joinville. Le Tremblement de terre de la Guadeloupe. Par M. André de Lachartière. *Paris.* 1843. 8vo, pp. 32. 38460

LA CHEVALERIE (M. Bacon de). Observations, presentées a l'Assemblée de MM. les Electeurs de la Partie du Nord de Saint Domingue, le 27 Janvier, 1789, au Cap François. [n. p.:] *Quillau.* 1789. 4to, pp. 7. J.C.B. 38461

LACHLAN (R.) Narrative of the Failure of an Attempt to establish a great National Institution, for the reception of Orphan Children of Officers of the British Army; but so constituted, as to form, at the same time, a Seminary for the Education of Officers' Sons and Daughters in general; By Major Lachlan. *Montreal.* 1854. 8vo, pp. 45. 38462

LACHLAN. A Paper and Resolutions in Advocacy of the establishment of a Uniform System of Meteorological Observa-

tions throughout the whole American Continent. By Major R. Lachlan. *Cincinnati, O.* 1859. 8vo, pp. 14. H., S. 38463

Also: A Discourse ... Western District Literary ... Association ... *Sandwich, U. C.* 1842. 12mo, pp. 17.—How Patriotic Services are Rewarded in Canada, exemplified in the Case of Major Lachlan, late of Montreal. *Cincinnati.* 1856. 8vo, pp. 16.—A Retrospective Glance at the progressive state of the Natural History Society of Montreal. ... *Montreal.* 1852. 8vo, pp. 24.—Remarks on the state of Education in the Province of Canada, by "L." Reprinted from the British American Journal. *Montreal.* 1848. 8vo, pp. 72. + Renewed Remarks. *Montreal.* 1849. 8vo, pp. 48. Also several articles in the "Canadian Journal."

LACKLAND (T.) Homespun; or, Five and Twenty Years ago. By Thomas Lackland. ... *New York: Hurd and Houghton.* 1867. 16mo, pp. 346. BA., C. 38464

LACKAWANNA. Address by the Lackawanna Coal Mine and Navigation Company, relative to the proposed Canal from the Hudson to the Lackawaxen River. *New York.* 1824. 8vo.

Lackawanna & Lanesboro' Railroad: Extracts from the Report on the Survey by J. C. Trautwine ... *Philadelphia.* 1856. 8vo.

LACKEY (J.) The Trial of James Lackey, Isaac Evertson, and others for Kidnapping Capt. William Morgan; ... Canandaigua, Aug. 22, 1827. *New York.* 1827. 8vo, pp. 24. M.

LA CLÈDE (—— de). Histoire générale de Portugal. [Jusqu'à 1713.] *Paris: P. F. Giffart.* 1735. 2 vols., 4to, pp. (32), 783; (36), 844. 2 Maps. C. 38468

LA CLÈDE. Historia general de Portugal. Traduzida e illustrada com muitas notas historicas, geographicas e criticas ... *Lisboa.* 1781–85. 8 vols., 8vo. 38469

Vols. VII. and VIII. contain many particulars relative to the discovery of the West Indies, and the state of affairs there.

LACO, *pseudon.* *See* [Higginson (Stephen)], Nos. 31748–49.

[LACOCK (Abner.)] Great National Object. Proposed Connection of the Eastern and Western Waters, by a Communication through the Potomac County. [*Washington.* 1822.] 8vo, pp. 38.

A rare tract on the subject, sometimes followed by a "Report of the Commissioners appointed to Survey the River Potomac." 8vo, pp. 92.

LACOCK. Report. Mr. Lacock ... Reported. [*Washington.* 1818.] 8vo, pp. 40. 38471

Relates to the Seminole War, and the execution of Arbuthnot and Ambruster, etc. It elicited: "Strictures on Mr. Lacock's Report ... on the Seminole War." [*Washington?* 1819.] 12mo, pp. 21. BA.

LACOMBE (H. M. de). Le Mexique et les États Unis. Par H. Mercier de Lacombe. *Paris: E. Dentu.* 1863. 8vo, pp. 162.

Intended to prove that Mexico would be in a much better position if under the dominion of France.

LACOMBE. Observations sur le projet de loi concernant l'état des personnes libres aux Antilles Françaises. *Paris.* [n. d.] 8vo.

LACON (W. S.) Loss of the Orion, the Amazon, and the Birkenhead. A Letter to the President of the Board of Trade, on the Management of Ships' Boats. By William Stirling Lacon. Second Edition. *London.* 1852. 8vo. + Third Edition. [*Ibid.*]

LACON, *pseudon.* The Devil in America: a Dramatic Satire. By Lacon. *Mobile: J. K. Randall.* 1867. 12mo, pp. 225. C.

LACON, *Ill.* Proceedings of a Pacific Railroad Convention, at Lacon, Illinois; with the Address of Col. Samuel R. Curtis. *Cincinnati: Printed by John D. Thorpe.* 1853. 8vo, pp. 16. B.

LA CONCEPCION (D.) Oracion panegyrica en la muerte de Fr. Melchior Lopez de Jesu, trinitario. Por Diego de La Concepcion. *Mexico.* 1700. 4to. 38477

[LA CONDAMINE (Charles Marie de).] Histoire des Pyramides de Quito, élevées par les Académiciens Envoyés sous l'Équateur par Ordre du Roi. ... [*Paris.*] MDCCLI. 4to, pp. (2), 53. Plate.

In a London catalogue this work is stated to be very rare, from having been suppressed. This is probably a mistake, as the same work is reprinted with the "Journal du Voyage." It was printed separately merely for private distribution, hence its rarity.

LA CONDAMINE. Journal du Voyage fait par Ordre du Roi, a l'Équateur, Servant d'Introduction Historique a la Mesure des Trois Premiers Degrés du Méridien. Par M. de La Condamine. ... *Paris: De l'Imprimerie Royale.* M. DCCLI. 4to, pp. (2), xxxvi, 280, Table, xv. 6 Maps and Plates. B., BA., H. 38479

See Boucher de la Richardérie, VI. 310; VII. 329.

LA CONDAMINE. Geschichte der zehnjährigen Reisen nach Peru, 1735–45. *Erfurt.* 1763. 38480

LA CONDAMINE. Lettre à Madame * * * sur l'Emeute Populaire excite'e En la Ville de Cuenca au Perou, le 29. d'Août 1739. Contre les Acade'miciens des Sciences, Envoyés pour la mesure de la Terre. ... [*Paris.*] M. DCC. XLVI. 8vo, pp. (2), 108. Plate.

In this riot, which took place in the arena prepared for a bull-fight, Sieur Seniergues, Chirurgeon of the King, was killed. This letter is also published with La Condamine's account of his voyage.

L[A] C[ONDAMINE]. Lettre de M. D. L. C. à M * * *, sur le sort des astronomes qui ont eu part aux dernières mesures de la terre depuis 1735.—Lettre de M. Godin et l'aventure de Mme Godin dans son voyage de la Province de Quito à Cayenne par la fleuve des Amazones. [n. p. about 1773.] 8vo, pp. 30.

Godin's Letter fills pp. 7–30. Usually found with La Condamine's "Relation."

LA CONDAMINE. Mesure des Trois Premiers Degre's du Me'ridien dans He'misphere Austral, Tiree des Observations de Mrs de l'Académie Royale des Sciences, Envoyés par le Roi sous l'Équateur; Par M. de La Condamine ... *Paris: De l'Imprimerie Royale.* M. DCCLI. 4to, pp. (12), 266, x. 3 Plates. B., H. 38483

The official account of the great French Scientific Expedition to South America, for measuring an arc of the meridian at the Equator for more accurately determining the dimensions and figure of the Earth.

LA CONDAMINE. Relation abrégée d'un Voyage fait dans l'Interieur de l'Amérique Méridionale. Depuis la Côte de la mer du sud, jusqu'aux Côtes du Brésil & de la Guiane, en descendant La Riviere des Amazones; Lüe à l'Assemblée publique de l'Académie des Sciences, le 28. Avril 1745. Par M. De La Condamine, de la même Académie. Avec une Carte de Maragnon ou de la Rivière des Amazones, levée par le même. *Paris: Chez la Veuve Pissot.* M. DCC. XLV. 8vo, pp. (4), xvi, 216. Map. B., BA., C., H., S. 38484

Some copies are printed on thick paper.

LA CONDAMINE. Relation abrégée [as before]. Nouvelle Edition Augmentée de la Relation de l'Emeute populaire de Cuença au Pérou, Et d'une Lettre de M. Godin des Odonais, contenant la Relation du Voyage de Madame Godin, son Epouse, &c. *A Maestricht, Chez Jean-Edme Dufour & Philippe Roux.* M. DCC. LXXVIII. 8vo, pp. (4), xvi, 379. Map and Plate. + *A Francfort au Mein: J. J. Kessler.* M.DCC.LXXIX. 8vo, pp. (2), xvi, 379, (2). Map and Plate. H. 38485

LA CONDAMINE. Extracto del Diario de Observaciones Hechas en el Viage de ... Quito al Para, por el Rio de las Amazonas; Y del Para a Cayana, Surinam y Amsterdam. Destinado para ser leydo en la Assemblea publica de la Academia Real de las Ciencias de Paris. Por Monsr. de La Condamine, Uno de los tres Embiados de la misma Academia à la Linea Equinoccial, para la medida de los Grados terrestres. Traducida del Francès al Castellano. *Amsterdam: Joan Catuffe.* MDCCXLV. 8vo, pp. (6), 121. H. 38486

La Condamine was detained more than two months after his arrival in Holland, waiting for passports to enable him to proceed to Paris. In this interval he employed himself in translating his journal into Spanish, to send to his friends in America; for which purpose he caused the necessary number of copies to be printed, and no more.

LA CONDAMINE. Bekort Verhaal van een Reyze gedaan in 't binnelands gedeelte van Zuyd America, van de Zuyd Zee tot aan de Kusten van Brazil en Guiane, der Rivier der Amazoone afzakkende. Uyt 't Frans vertaald. *Amsterdam.* 1746. 8vo. Map. 38487

Also: Verhaal van een reize in Zuid-America, en van 't oproer van Cuenca. ... *Amsterdam.* 1746. 8vo. Map and Plate.

LA CONDAMINE. A Succinct | Abridgment | of a | Voyage | Made within the | Inland Parts | of | South-America; | from the | Coasts of the South-Sea, to the Coasts of Brazil | and Guiana, down the River of Amazons: | As it was read in the Public Assembly of the | Academy of Sciences at Paris, April 28, 1745. | By Mons. De La Condamine, of that Academy. | To which is annexed, | A Map of the Maranon, or River of Amazons, | drawn by the same. | *London: E. Withers.* MDCCXLVII. 8vo, pp. xii, 108. Map. C., H. 38488

A German version is included in "Hamburg Magazin," VI. 5–70 and 227–288.

[LA CONDAMINE.] Naufrage d'Isabelle de Grand Maison et Bruno, épouse de M. Godin des Odonais, et de sa famille sur les bords du fleuve des Amazones. *Paris: l'Imprimerie de Delalain.* 1827. 8vo, pp. 16. 38489

"This relation is an abridgment of the letter of M. Godin, printed with the letter of M. D. L. C. (de La Condamine) 'sur le sort des Astronomes.'"

LA CONDAMINE. Supplément au Journal historique du voyage à l'Equateur, et au livre de la mesure de trois premiers degrés du meridien: servant de réponse à quelques objections. Par M. de la Condamine. *Paris.* M. DCC. LII. 4to, pp. (1), viij, 52, (1). H. + Seconde Partie. ... *Paris: Durand* ... M.DCC.LIV. 4to, pp. (4), (4), 222, xxviii, (2). A., B., C. 38490

This supplement was intended principally to answer the objections which had been made by M. Bouguer, in his "Justification," 1752.

LA CONDAMINE. Voyage de la Rivière des Amazones. Par M. de La Condamine. Lû à l'Assemblée publique de l'Académie des Sciences le 28. Avril 1740. *Paris.* 1749. 4to, pp. 104. 2 Maps. 38491

See Bouguer (P.), Vol. II., No. 6876. *See also* Pinkerton's "Voyages," XIV.

LACONIA. *See* [Scribner (J. P.)]

LA CORNE (St.-L. de). Journal du Voyage de M. St-Luc de La Corne, dans le Navire l'Auguste, en 1761; avec le détail des circonstances de son naufrage, des routes difficiles qu'il a tenues pour se rendre en sa patrie [Canada], et des peines et traverses qu'il a essuyées dans cette catastrophe affligeante. *Montréal.* 1778. 12mo. + Seconde édition. [*Ibid.*] 1863. 8vo, pp. 23. + *Quebec: A Coté et Cie.* 1863. 8vo, pp. 28. 38492

LA CORNILLÈRE (*le comte de*). De la Martinique en 1842. Intérêts coloniaux, souvenirs de voyage. *Paris: Gidé.* 1843. 8vo. 38493

LACOUR (L.), *editor.* Mémoire dv voiage en Russie fait en 1586 par Jehan Savvage, suivi de l'expédition de Fr. Drake en Amérique, à la même époque. Publiés pour la première fois d'après les manuscrits de la Bibliothèque impériale, par Lovis Lacovr ... *Paris: A. Avbry.* 1855. 16mo, pp. x, 30. C.

LACOUTURE (É.) Mémoire a sa Majesté l'Empereur Napoléon III. La Vérité sur la Guerre d'Amérique. Par Édouard Lacouture, Membre honoraire de la Chambre de commerce de Norfolk. *Paris: E. Dentu.* 1862. 8vo, pp. 16. BA. 38495

A violent appeal to France to sustain the South.

LA CRENNE. *See* Verdun de la Crenne.

LACROIX (François J. P. de). Mémoires pour servir à l'Histoire de la Révolution de Saint-Domingue. Par le Lieutenant-Général Baron Pamphile de Lacroix. Avec une carte nouvelle de l'île et un plan topographique de la Crête-à-Pierrot. ... *Paris: Chez Pillet aîné.* 1819. 2 vols., 8vo, pp. xv, 416; (2), 350, (1). 2 Maps. + Seconde édition ... [*Ibid.*] 1820. 2 vols., 8vo, pp. (2), xv, 416, Plan; (4), 350, (1), folded leaf. Map. B., C.

END OF VOLUME NINE.

A Dictionary of Books

RELATING TO AMERICA.

LACROIX (F.) Possessions Anglaises dans l'Amérique du Nord, Canada, Nouveau Brunswick, Nouvelle Ecosse, Acadie. Par Frédéric Lacroix. *Paris: Firmin Didot Frères.* 1849. 8vo, pp. 158. B. 38497

See Vols. III., IV., and V. of "l'Univers Pittoresque," Famin (C.), Vol. VII., No. 23767, Larenaudière (P. de), *and* Regnault (É.)

LACROIX (H.) Opuscule sur le Présent et l'Avenir du Canada. Par Henri Lacroix. [n. p.] 1867. 8vo, pp. 32. 38498

LACROIX (Irenée A. de). Military and Political Hints, By Col. Ir. Amelot De Lacroix, humbly submitted to ... Congress and the General Officers of the ... United States. ... Translated by Samuel Mackay, A.M. ... *Boston: Etheridge and Bliss.* 1808. 12mo, pp. 121. BA. 38499

LA CROIX (Jacques Vincent de). Constitutions des Principaux États de l'Europe et des États-Unis de l'Amérique, par M. de La Croix ... . *Paris.* 1791. 3 vols., 8vo. B. + Seconde édition. *Paris: Chez Buisson.* 1791–1801. 4 vols., 8vo, pp. (4), lx, 484; (4), 408; (4), xii, 428; (4), 387. + *Paris.* 1791–1802. 6 vols., 8vo. C. 38500

LA CROIX. A Review of the Constitutions of the principal States of Europe, and of the United States of America. ... By M. de La Croix ... . Translated from the French, with notes, by the Translator ... . *London: G. G. J. and J. Robinson.* MDCCXCII. 2 vols., 8vo, pp. (2), lviii, (2), 499; (4), 553. BA., C., P. 38501

The translator was Eliza Ryves. *See* "M. Rev.," VI. 481; VII. 512; IX. 48; XXXVIII. 481.

[LA CROIX.] Mémoires d'un Américain, avec une description de la Prusse & de l'Isle de Saint Domingue. Par l'Auteur des Lettres d'Affi à Zurac & de celles d'un Philosophe sensible. *Lausanne: Et se trouve a Paris: V. Regnard.* MDCCLXXI. 2 vols., 12mo, pp. xxiv, 240; 191. + *Amsterdam.* 1772. 2 vols., 8vo.

LA CROIX. Peinture des Mœurs du Siècles, ou Lettres et Discours sur differens Sujets, par M. de la Croix. *Amsterdam.* 1777. 2 vols., 12mo. 38503

Contains "Lettres d'un Américain sur les Nègres," etc.

LA CROIX (A. Phérotée de). [Engraved Title:] Algemeene | Wereldt-Beschryving | door | A. P. De La Croix. | ... | *T' Amsterdam | Gedrukt by François Halma*, 1705. [Printed Title:] Algemeene | Weereld-Beschryving. | Nae de rechte verdeeling der Landschappen, Plaetsen ... | Geographisch, Politisch, Historisch, | Chronologisch en Genealogisch. | Op een gantsch nieuwe, zeer klaere ordre in 't Fransch | beschreeven, door den Heer | A. Pher. De La Croix, | ... | Nu vertaeld nae den tweeden Druk; met veel' aenmerkens waerdige | Byvoegzelen opgehelderd, uit de beroemste zoo oude als nieuwe | Aerdryks- en Reisbeschryvingen bynae een derde | deel vermeerdert door | S. De Vries. | Met naaukeurige Landkaarten van den Heere N. Sanson, en | Afbeeldingen der voormame Steden verrijks. | ... | *T' Amsterdam, | Gedrukt by François Halma, Boekverkoper*, | M D CCV. | 3 vols., 4to, 2 Titles each, pp. xxxii, 436, lxxx; iv, 612, lxxii; iv, 480, lxxiv. Maps and Plates.

This General Description of the World contains a statement as to the foundation of New-Amsterdam. There are copies on thick large paper, with the maps and plates exquisitely executed in colors and gold; very rare in this state. Vol. III., pp. 320–480, gives a description of America, with fifteen maps and a view of Mexico. This book is one of paramount merit. Created by the successive labors of eminent men of three different countries, it forms a most admirable resumé of the geographical science at the end of the seventeenth and at the beginning of the eighteenth century. *See* G. Asher's "Essay on New-Netherland," pp. 27–28.

LA CROIX. Nouvelle Méthode de la Géographie Universelle, enrichie de Cartes, Armoiries, Figures des Nations, &c. *À Lyon.* 1705. 5 vols., 12mo. Plates. 38505

Several of the plates portray the aborigines of the New World.

[LA CROIX DE CHEVRIÈRES DE SAINT VALLIER (Jean Baptiste de).] Estat Present de l'Église et de la Colonie Françoise, dans la Nouvelle France. Par M. l'Evêque de Quebec. *A Paris: Robert Pepie.* M.DC.LXXXVIII. 8vo, pp. (2), 267. BA. + [Seconde édition.] *Québec: A. Coté & Cie.* 1856. 8vo, pp. ix, 102. Portrait. C. 38506

See Faribault, No. 194, *also* Charlevoix.

LA CROSSE, *Wis.* ... La Crosse Directory, for 1866–7. With a Business Directory. Compiled by A. Bailey and J. M. Wolfe. *La Crosse: A. Bailey.* 1867. 8vo, pp. 138. 38507

LA CROSSE AND MILWAUKEE RAIL ROAD COMPANY. Annual Report of the Directors ... 1853. *Milwaukee.* 1853. 8vo. Continued. 38508

Also: A Compilation of the several Acts of the Legislature of Wisconsin affecting the La Crosse and Milwaukee Rail Road Company ... . By Moses M. Strong. *Milwaukee.* 1856. 8vo, pp. 105. + [*Ibid.*] pp. 107.—Annual Report of the Receiver ... *Milwaukee.* 1861. 8vo. Continued.—State of the Affairs of the La Crosse and Milwaukee Rail Road Company, July 23, 1857. ... *New-York.* 1857. 8vo. Continued.

LA CROSSE VALLEY BAPTIST ASSOCIATION. Minutes of Meetings ... held in 1859. *Sparta.* 1859. 8vo. Continued.

LA CROZE (M. V. de). Histoire du Christianisme des Indes. Par Mathurin Veyssière de La Croze. *La Haye.* 1724. 8vo. + *La Haye.* 1758. 2 vols., 12mo, pp. (24), 423; (4), 498. Map and Plate. C. 38510

LA CRUZ (J. de). Cautelas Espirituales, contra el Demonio, Mundo y Carne, por J. de La Cruz. *Puebla de los Angelos.* 1692. 8vo. 38511

LACUNZA (J. M. de). Discursos Históricos, leidos en la Academia del Colegio de S. Juan de Letran. *Mexico.* 1845. 4to. 38512

LACY (B.) Miscellaneous Poems compos'd at Newfoundland, on board His Majesty's Ship the Kinsale. By B. Lacy, A.M. then Chaplain to the said ship. *London: Printed for the Author.* MDCCXXIX. 8vo, pp. vi, 128. 38513

The poems are sad stuff. The book opens with a description of Newfoundland, commencing in this wise:

"The Ship Kinsale was by the King's Command
Ordered to sail forthwith to Newfoundland."

LACY (D.) A Thanksgiving Discourse ... in ... Raleigh, N. C., ... 27th November, 1851. By Rev. Drury Lacy ... . *Raleigh, N. C.* 1851. 8vo, pp. 18. H. 38514

LACY (E. S.) The Schools demanded by the Present Age. A Sermon ... in ... San Francisco. ... May 11, 1856. By Rev. E. S. Lacy ... . *San Francisco: Whitton ... Printers.* 1856. 8vo, pp. 15. H. 38515

LACY (L.) Notas historicas del plan del Excmo. Sr. D. Luis Lacy. *Habana: Imprenta Fraternal.* 38516

LACY (M.) The Female Shipwright, or Life and Extraordinary Adventures of Mary Lacy, giving an account of her leaving her parents, disguised as a man, with the means which led to a Discovery of her Sex. Written by Herself. *New York.* 1807. 12mo. 38517

[LADD (Joseph).] The Poems of Arouet. *Charleston.* 1786. 12mo, pp. xvi, 128. B. 38518

Kettell ascribes them to William Ladd.

LADD (J. B.) The Literary Remains of Joseph Brown Ladd, M.D., collected by his Sister, Mrs. Elizabeth Haskins ... . To which is prefixed, a Sketch of the Author's Life, by W. B. Chittenden. ... *New York: H. C. Sleight.* 1832. 8vo, pp. xxiv, 13–228. B., C., S. 38519

LADD (L. C.) Life of Luther C. Ladd, the First Martyr ... in the City of Baltimore, on the 19th of April, 1861 ... Also, ... Naval Engagement at Port Royal. By a Citizen of Alexandria. ... *Concord: P. B. Cogswell, Printer.* 1862. 8vo, pp. 40. B.

LADD (*Mrs.*) Banks of the Ohio: A Poem. By Mrs. Ladd. *Albany.* 1823. 8vo. 38521

[LADD (William).] A Brief Illustration of the Principles of War and Peace ... By Philanthropos. ... *Albany: Printed by Packard* ... 1831. 12mo, pp. 112. B. 38522

[LADD.] A Dissertation on a Congress of Nations. By Philanthropos. ... [*Boston:*] *Press of James Loring.* 1832. 8vo, pp. 28. H. 38523

[LADD.] ... The Duty of Women to promote the Cause of Peace. By Philanthropos. ... *Boston.* [n. d.] 8vo, pp. 39. H.

LADD. An Essay on a Congress of Nations, for the Adjustment of International Disputes without resort to Arms. Containing the substance of the Rejected Essays on that Subject. With original Thoughts and a copious Appendix. By William Ladd. *Boston: Whipple & Damrell.* 1840. 8vo, pp. xviii, 192. + [*Ibid.*] 1840. 8vo, pp. iv, 513–700. H. + Fifth Thousand. *London: Thomas Ward* ... 1840. 8vo, pp. 32. H. 38525

[LADD.] The Essays of Philanthropos on Peace & War. Which first appeared in the Christian Mirror, ... Portland, Maine. *Portland: Printed by Shirley* ... 1825. 12mo, pp. (2), 160. B., H.

+ Second Edition. *Exeter, N. H.: John T. Burnham.* 1827. 12mo, pp. 173, (2). + New Series. ... Revised ... by the Author. [*Ibid.*] 1827. 12mo, pp. 279, (4). B. 38526

[LADD.] On the Duty of Females to promote the Cause of Peace. By Philanthropos. ... *Boston.* 1836. 8vo, pp. 48. H.

[LADD.] ... A Solemn Appeal to Christians of all Denominations in Favor of the Cause of Permanent and Universal Peace. By Philanthropos. Stereotype Edition. *Boston.* 1836. 8vo, pp. (2), 38. H. 38528

Also: Address delivered at the Tenth Anniversary of the Massachusetts Peace Society, December 25, 1825. ... *Boston.* 1826. 8vo, pp. 27. H.—An Address ... at Portland, February 6, 1824, before the Peace Society of Maine. ... *Portland: Printed ... by A. Shirley.* 1824. 8vo, pp. 15. Also edited the "Harbinger of Peace."

LADD *and* BECKWITH (George C.) Prize Essays on a Congress of Nations for the Adjustment of International Disputes, without resort to Arms. *Boston.* 1840. 8vo. C. 38529

LADE (R.) Voyages du Capitaine Robert Lade en differentes parties de l'Afrique, de l'Asie et de l'Amerique: contenant l'Histoire de sa fortune, & ses Observations sur les Colonies ... des Espagnols, des Anglois, des Hollandois, &c. ... *Paris: Didot.* M.DCC.XLIV. 2 vols., 12mo, pp. (2), xvi, 370; (2), 360. Maps. + *Paris: Leblanc.* 1810. 8vo, pp. (4), xii, 599. Maps. H.

Ladies' Anti-Slavery Association. [*Liverpool: Printed by George Smith.* 1827.] 8vo, pp. 7. H. 38531

Ladies' Christian Commission: Auxiliary to the U. S. Christian Commission. *Philadelphia: C. Sherman, Son & Co., Printers.* 1864. 12mo, pp. 24. B. 38532

The Ladies' Companion. A Monthly Magazine. *New York.* 1834–44. 20 vols., 8vo. 38533

Continued as the "Ladies' Companion and Literary Expositor."

Ladies Depository ... for supplying work. Nineteenth Report, 1852. *New York.* 8vo. 38534

Report of the Ladies' Industrial Aid Association, of Union Hall, from July, 1861, to January, 1862. *Boston: J. H. Eastburn's Press.* 1862. 8vo, pp. 16, (1). H. 38535

The Ladies' Literary Cabinet, Edited by S. Woodworth. *New-York.* 1819–21. 4 vols., 4to. 38536

This was the harbinger of the "New-York Mirror."

The First Annual Report of the Ladies' London Emancipation Society. January 1864. *London: Emily Faithfull.* 1864. 12mo, pp. 15, (1). H. 38537

The Ladies' Magazine. *Savannah, Ga.* 1819. 8vo. 38538

Ladies' Memorandum Book; or Daily Pocket Journal for 1775. *Philadelphia.* 38539

Ladies' Mount Vernon Association. *See* [Cunningham (P. A.)]

Ladies' National Army Relief Association. *New York: T. R. Dawley, Printer.* [186–.] 12mo, pp. 11, (1). BA. 38540

The Ladies' Repository, and Gatherings of the West: A Monthly Periodical devoted to Literature and Religion. *Cincinnati.* 1842. 8vo. Continued. C. 38541

Edited by the Rev. L. L. Hamline.

First Annual Report of the Ladies' Society for the Promotion of Education in the West. *Boston.* 1847. 8vo. 38542

Also: History of the Formation of the Ladies' Society ... . *Boston.* 1846. 8vo.

The First Annual Report of the Ladies' Society for promoting the ... Education ... of the Children of Negroes ... in the British West Indies; ... Established 1825. *London: Printed by W. Marchant.* 1826. 12mo, pp. 35, (1). Continued. B. 38543

LADOR (J. A.) In Memoriam. An Address. *Cahawba, Alabama.* 1861. 8vo. 38544

LADRON DE GUEVARA (Baltasar). Manifesto que el real convento de religiosas de Jesus Maria de Mexico hace ... de las razones que le assisten, para que se digne de declararser la que siguen vida comun y conforme á su regla. *Mexico: F. de Zuñiga y Ontiveros.* 1771. Folio, pp. (2), 207. Portrait. 38545

See also Guevara, Vol. VII., No. 29144–45.

[LADUE (P. A.)] An Argument in Favor of a Land Grant to the Tebo and Neosho Railroad Company. [*Washington.* 1867.] 8vo, pp. 8. H. 38546

The Lady and the Dressmaker. *See* [Fenety (George E.)]

LADY HOBART. Account of the Loss of the Lady Hobart Packet on an Island of Ice in the Atlantic Ocean. *London.* [n. d.] 12mo. Plate. 38547

The Lady's Almanac, for the year 1854. By Damrell & Moore & G. Coolidge. *Boston: John P. Jewett & Co.* [1854.] 32mo, pp. 125, (3). Continued. B. 38548

The Lady's Book. A Magazine ... *Philadelphia.* 1830. 8vo.

After 1839 it was continued as "Godey's Lady's Book."

The Lady's Friend. Edited by Mrs. Henry Peterson. ... 1864. *Philadelphia.* [1864.] 8vo. Continued. 38550

The Lady's Magazine and Repository of Entertaining Knowledge. Vol. I. for 1792. *Philadelphia: W. Gibbons.* [n. d.] 8vo, pp. (2), 305. 38551

LAEMMERT (E.) Almanach administrativo, mercantil e industrial da Côrte e provincia do Rio de Janeiro, coordenado e redigido por Eduardo Laemmert. *Rio de Janeiro: E. & H. Laemmert.* 1844. 8vo. Continued. 38552

LA ENCINA (L. G. de). Edicto Pastoral Formado con el objeto de procurar la Pacificacion y Bien Espiritual y Temporal de su Diócesis, de Todo el Perú, de Toda la America ... . Por Louis Gonzaga de La Encina ... . *Lima.* 1815. 4to, pp. 67.

LAET (J. de). Nieuwe Wereldt | ofte | Beschrijvinghe | van | West-Indien, | wt veelerhande Schriften ende Aen-teekeningen | van verscheyden Natien by een versamelt | Door | Ioannes de Laet, | Ende met | Noodighe kaerten en Tafels voorsien. *Tot Leyden, | In de Druckerye van Isaack Elzevier.* | *Anno* 1625. | Met Privilegie der Ho. Mo. Heeren Staten Generael, voor 12 Jaren. | Folio, pp. (2), xxii, 526. Maps. A., S. 38554

See Asher's "Essay," No. 1. This invaluable work was much improved in the subsequent editions and translations by the author, but the maps were unchanged.

LAET. Beschrijvinghe | van | West-Indien | door | Ioannes de Laet | Tweede druk: | In ontallijcke plaetsen ver- | betert, vermeerdert, met eenige | nieuwe Caerten, beelden van | verscheyden dieren ende | planten verciert. | *Tot Leyden, bij de Elzeviers. A°.* 1630. | Folio. Maps. B. 38555

Collation: 14 p. l., including half-title, engraved title, and register of maps (of which there are 14), on the reverse Errata; text, pp. 622; "Register," 9 l. This second edition is corrected and augmented. Quaritch marks a copy £8. 8s.

LAET. Historie | Ofte | Iaerlijck Verhael | Van de | Verrichtinghen der Geoctroyeerde | West-Indische Compagnie, | Zedert haer Begin tot het eynde van 't jaer | sesthien-hondert ses-en-dertich; | Begrepen in Derthien Boecken, | Ende met verscheyden koperen

Platen verciert: | Beschreven door | Ioannes de Laet | Bewint- | hebber der selver Compagnie. | *Tot Leyden, | By Bonaventuer ende Abraham Elsevier, Anno* 1644. | Met Privilegie. | Folio, pp. (32), 544, Kort verhael, pp. 31, (12). 12 Maps and Plans. BA. 38556

Concerning this *see* Asher, No. 22, Ternaux, No. 636, and Trömel, No. 198. "At the end of the work we find: 'A short account of the services and advantages which the W. I. C. has rendered to the State,' giving very remarkable details on the state of finances, the captured booty, the equipment of the vessels, etc. of the Company."—MULLER. Quaritch quotes an edition, *Leyden, Elsevier*, 1636.

LAET. Novvs Orbis | seu | Descriptionis | Indiæ Occidentalis | Libri XVIII. | Authore | Ioanne de Laet Antverp. | Novis Tabulis Geographicis et variis | Animantium, Plantarum, Fructuumque | Iconibus illustrati. | Cvm Privilegio. | *Lvgd. Batav. apud Elzevirios. A°.* 1633. | Folio. Maps. BA., H. 38557

Collation: 16 p. l., including the half-title, engraved title, and list of maps (of which there are 14), text, pp. 690; index, (17). Chapters VII. to XII., pp. 101–110 contain a description of New-Netherland. "Opus egregium, maximeque rarum et infrequens."—MEUSELIUS.

LAET. L'histoire | dv | Nouveau Monde | ou | description | des Indes | Occidentales, | Contenant dix-huict Liures, | Par le Sieur Iean de Laet, d'Anuers; | Enrichi de nouuelles Tables Geographiques, & Figures des | Animaux, Plantes, & Fruicts. | *A Leyde,* | *Chez Bonauenture & Abraham Elseuiers, Imprimeurs | ordinaires de l'Vniuersité.* | cIɔ Iɔcxl. | Folio, pp. (28), 632, (xii). 14 Maps.

This French translation of Laet contains many materials not to be found in the original Dutch, chiefly vocabularies of Indian tribes. Dr. Asher was not able to procure a copy of this rare work; *see* his "Essay," p. 2. Charlevoix says: "This work is full of the most excellent and curious details of the natural history, and the character, manners, and customs of the American aborigines, derived from the reports of the European mission establishments in America. It contains many documents upon American philology, taken for the most part from the collection of Ramusio." *See* Faribault, p. 71.

LAET. Compendium historiæ universalis ... tam Romanorum quam Protest., ab Augusto ad ann. Christi J. 1640. *Lugd. Batav.* 1643. Sm. 8vo, pp. 768. 38559

This work, by the historiographer of New-Netherland, contains ample notices of the facts relating to the history of America and the part taken by his countrymen therein.

[LAET.] Hispania | sive | de Regis Hispa | niæ-regnis | et opibus | Commentarius. | *Lvgd. Batav.* | *Ex officina | Elzeveriana.* | *A°.* cIɔ Iɔcxxix. 24mo, pp. (16), 498, (1). 38560

Includes Nova Hispania.

LAET. Ioannis | de | Laet | Antuerpiani | Notæ | ad | dissertationem | Hvgonis Grotii | De Origine Gentium Americanarum: | et observationes aliqvot | ad meliorem indaginem difficil- | limæ illius

Quæstionis. | *Parisiis,* | *Apud Viduam Gvilielmi Pelé,* | *viâ Iacobæâ sub signo Crucis aureæ.* | M. DC. XLIII. | Sm. 8vo, pp. 223. 38561

This is Laet's first refutation of Grotius. It contains, pp. 139–151, comparative vocabularies of the Irish, Gaelic, Icelandish, Huron, Souriquois, and Mexican languages. Some copies have the imprint, *Amstelodami, Apvd Lvdovicvm Elzivirivm.* cIↄ Iↄcxliii.

LAET. Ioannis de Laet Antwerpiani Responsio ad Dissertationem Secundam Hvgonis Grotii, de Origine Gentium Americanarum. Cum Indice ad utrumque libellum. *Amstelrodami, Apud Ludovicum Elsevirium.* cIↄ Iↄcxliv. 8vo, pp. (4), 116, (8). Map. BA. 38562

A response to the second dissertation of Grotius. Extracts from Laet, relating to New-Netherland, are translated (in "N. Y. Hist. Coll.," v. 282–316), by George Folsom. *See also* O'Callaghan's "New-Netherland."

LA FARELLE (F. de). Coup d'Oeil sur le Régime Répressif, et Pénitentiaire des Principaux États de l'Ancien et du Nouveau Monde. Par M. F. de La Farelle ... . Extrait des Rapports et documents officiels fournis par le gouvernement à la commission pour la loi des prisons. *Paris: Paul Dupont.* 1844. 8vo, pp. (2), 92, (1). H., S. 38563

Pages 68–74 contain chapters on prisons in the United States.

LAFARGUE (É. de). Histoire Géographique de la Nouvelle Ecosse, Contenant le détail de sa situation, de son étendue & de ses limites; ... par Étienne de La Fargue, avocat. *Londres.* 1749. 16mo, pp. 164. + [*Ibid.*] M. DCC. LV. pp. vi, viii, 164.

LAFARGUE. Oeuvres Mêlées de M. de Lafargue ... . *Paris: Duchesne.* M. DCC. LXV. 2 vols., 8vo, pp. xix, 324; 359. H.

Vol. II., pp. 157–350, contain "Histoire géographique de la Nouvelle Ecosse."

LAFASSE (——). Avis sur les Maladies de St. Domingue. *Paris.* 1787. 8vo. 38566

LA FAYE BRÉHIER (J. de). Les Portugais d'Amérique. Souvenirs historiques de la guerre du Brésil en 1635. *Paris.* 1847. 8vo. Plates. 38567

LAFAYETTE (Marie-Paul-Joseph Roch-Ives-Gilbert de Motier, *Marquis de*). An Authentic Biography of General La Fayette. In which many Errors and Deficiencies existing in the Memoirs heretofore Published, are Corrected and Supplied. *Philadelphia: A. Sherman.* 1824. 12mo, pp. 152. Portrait. B. + *Wheeling.* 1825. 12mo. 38568

Also: Biographical Notice of General Lafayette. Translated from Notice Biographique ... Paris, 1818. ... and the Original work in French. *Philadelphia: Benjamin Tanner.* 1824. 8vo, pp. 23. BA.—Biographical Sketch of the ... Marquis de La

Fayette ... with ... his ... Reception in the United States. ... *Exeter: Printed by Gerrish* ... 1824. 12mo, pp. 24.—Life of General Lafayette. *Boston.* 1825. 8vo, pp. 64.—The Life and Services of Major-General the Marquis de Lafayette. ... *New York: Beadle and Company.* [1861.] 12mo, pp. 91. B.

LAFAYETTE. Complete History of the Marquis de La Fayette, Major-General in the Army of the United States of America in the War of the Revolution; embracing an account of his late Tour through the United States; By an Officer in the late Army. *New York.* 1826. 8vo. + *Hartford.* 1845. 8vo. + [*Ibid.*] 1849. 12mo. + [*Ibid.*] 1851. 12mo. B. 38569

LAFAYETTE. Epistle from the Marquis de Lafayette to General Washington. ... *Edinburgh: Mundell & Son.* 1800. 8vo, pp. (2), 32. 38570

This exceedingly rare poetical piece was written during the lifetime of General Washington, but was not printed until after his death.

LAFAYETTE. Historical Sketches illustrative of the Life of M. de Lafayette and the leading Events of the American Revolution. By an American. *New York.* 1824. 12mo, pp. 227.

LAFAYETTE. Letter ... supposed to be written by General Lafayette, to his adopted Countrymen, on the President's Message ... of ... 1832. *New-York: Peabody & Co.* M DCCC XXXIII. 18mo, pp. 18. H. 38572

LAFAYETTE. Life of Lafayette, including an Account of the Memorable Revolution of the Three Days of 1830. *Boston: Light & Horton.* 1835. 12mo, pp. viii, 274. 38573

See "N. A. Rev.," April, 1835.

LAFAYETTE. The Marquis de La Fayette's Statement of his own Conduct and Principles. Containing also a Comparative View of the French and American Revolutions, &c. &c. Translated from the Original French, and most respectfully inscribed to the Whig Club. *London: J. Deighton.* MDCCXCIII. 8vo, pp. 90. 38574

Partly relates to Washington and the American Revolution. *See* "M. Rev.," XII. 229.

LAFAYETTE. Mémoires, Correspondance et Manuscrits du Général La Fayette, publiés par sa Famille. *Paris: H. Fournier aîné.* M DCCC XXXVII–VIII. 6 vols., 8vo, pp. (4), viii, 495; (4), 504; (4), 520; (4), ii, 448, (1); (4), 544, (1); (4), 814. B., H. + *Bruxelles: Société Belge de Librairie, etc.* 1837. 6 vols., 18mo. + *Bruxelles.* 1837. 2 vols., imp. 8vo. 38575

Edited by his son George Washington Lafayette. Vols. I. II. and III. were translated

and published in London, but the work was not completed. The correspondence includes unpublished letters of all the distinguished Americans for more than half a century.

LAFAYETTE. Memoirs Correspondence and Manuscripts of General Lafayette. Published by his Family. *London: Saunders and Otley.* MDCCCXXXVII. 3 vols., 8vo, pp. xi, iv, 468, (1), Portrait; vii, 479, (1); viii, 497. BA., C. 38576

LAFAYETTE. Memoirs [as before. Edited by William A. Duer.] Vol. I. *New York: Saunders and Otley.* MDCCCXXXVII. 8vo, pp. (8), xiv, (1), 552. Portrait. BA., C. 38577

Of this reprint no more was published.

LAFAYETTE. Mémoires historiques, et pièces authentiques sur M. de Lafayette, pour servir à l'histoire des Révolutions. *Paris: Le Tellier an* II [1794]. 8vo, pp. xvi, 303. J.C.B. 38578

"A collection of papers and extracts relating to La Fayette."—RICH, I. 389.

LAFAYETTE. Memoirs of General La Fayette. Embracing Details of Public and Private Life, Sketches of the American Revolution, ... with Biographical Notices of Individuals, who have been Distinguished Actors in these Events. *Hartford: Barber & Robinson.* 1825. 12mo, pp. 455. + *New York.* 1825. 12mo. Portrait. + *New York.* 1825. 8vo. 38579

See also [Knapp (S. L.)], *our* No. 38083 Memoirs of Gen. Lafayette; with an Account of his Tour through the United States, 1824–25. *Boston.* 1825. 8vo, pp. 24.—Memoirs of the Military Career of the Marquis de La Fayette, During the Revolutionary War, down to the present time ... . *Boston: Allen and Watts.* 1824. 8vo, pp. 56. H.

LAFAYETTE. Outlines of the Life of General Lafayette ... . *Tappan, N. Y.: Wm. Broadwell and Co.* 1830. 18mo, pp. iv, 3–258. 38580

See also [Ticknor (G.)] Also: Pictorial Life of General Lafayette. ... *Philadelphia.* 1867. 16mo.—A Short Biography of the Illustrious Citizen, Marquis De Lafayette, the Hero, the Statesman, the Philanthropist, the Early and Constant Friend of America, and the Champion of the Equal Rights of Mankind. By a Citizen of Washington, D. C. *Washington.* 1824. 8vo, pp. 34.—Sketch of the Life and Military Services of Gen. La Fayette, during the American Revolution. *New York.* 1824. 8vo, pp. 24. C.—A Sketch of the Life of General Lafayette. Translated from the French by James P. Cobbett. *London.* 1830. 18mo, pp. vii, 86.

LAFAYETTE. Visit of General La Fayette to Louisiana, containing the Speeches addressed to him, with his Answers. ... preceded by a Biographical Notice, and a handsome Engraving of the Triumphal Arch erected in honor of the Hero of York-Town. By a Citizen of New Orleans. *New Orleans: M. Cruzat.* 1825. 12mo, pp. 86. 38581

LAFAYETTE. Visite du Général de La Fayette à La Louisiane, ... *Nouvelle Orleans.* 1825. 12mo. Plate. 38582

LAFAYETTE. Voyage du Général Lafayette aux Etats-Unis d'Amérique en 1824 et 1825. *Paris.* 1824–25. 3 parts, 8vo. Portrait. 38583

The following pieces relate to Lafayette: An Account of the Visit of General Lafayette to the United States, from his Arrival in August, 1824, to his Return to France. *Philadelphia.* 1827. 8vo.—Address to General Lafayette on his Course in relation to the Politics of France. By a North American. [n. p.] 1831. 8vo.—Description of the Book presented to General La Fayette, by the Common Council of New-York. *New-York.* 1825. 12mo.—A Description of the Grand Fête given at Washington Hall, by the Citizens of France, to Gen. Lafayette. *New York.* 1824. 8vo, pp. 16.—Expostulation to Lafayette.—Fayette in Prison; or, Misfortunes of the Great, a Modern Tragedy ... By a Lady of Massachusetts. *Worcester.* 1802. 8vo.—Le Général Lafayette a ses Collègues de la Chambre des Députés. *Paris: Paulin.* 1832. 8vo, pp. (4), 68.—Impeachment of Mr. La Fayette; ... with A Supplement, Containing the Letters, and other Authentic Pieces relating thereto. Translated from the French, By William Cobbett. *Philadelphia: Printed by John Parker.* M,DCC,XCIII. 8vo, pp. 104.—Itinéraire du Général Lafayette de Grenoble à Lyon; précédée d'une Notice Historique sur cet Illustre Citoyen. *Lyon.* 1829. 8vo.—La Fayette en Amérique. Poëme. *Paris.* 1825. 8vo.—Lafayette, or the Castle of Olmutz; a Drama. *New York.* 1824. 18mo.—The Lay of Gratitude; consisting of Poems occasioned by the recent Visit of Lafayette to the United States ... . *Philadelphia.* 1826. 8vo.—Lafayette Music. Consisting of a Dirge, Requiem and Ode, as performed in Faneuil Hall, Boston, on the occasion of the delivery of an Eulogy on the Character of Lafayette, by Edward Everett, September 6, 1834. Poetry by Grenville Mellen, and Isaac McLellan, Jr. Music by Lowell Mason and G. J. Webb. [n. p. n. d.] 4to.—The Order of Exercises in the Chapel of Transylvania University, a collection of original pieces in honour of the arrival of Gen. Lafayette. *Lexington, Kentucky.* 1825. 8vo.—Particulars of the Funeral Honours to the Memory of General La Fayette, with the Eulogium delivered by General James Tallmadge, June 26, 1834. [*New York.* 1834.] 8vo, pp. 56. + 12mo, pp. 128.—Report of a Committee on the Death of Gen. Lafayette; with Memoir. *Boston.* 1834. 8vo, pp. 8.—[Letter] To General Lafayette [from a North American]. United States, August 10, 1831. [n. p. n. d.] 8vo, pp. 14.—Visit to the Lafayette Female Academy, at Lexington, Ky., May 16th, 1825, and the Exercises in Honor of the Nation's Guest. *Lexington.* 1825. 8vo, pp. 30.

LAFAYETTE. Edwards' Annual Director to the Inhabitants, etc. of Lafayette. 1867. *Chicago: Edwards, Greenough & Deved.* 1867. 8vo, pp. 315. Continued. 38584

LAFAYETTE, *La.* Memorial of the City of Lafayette, Louisiana. [*Washington:*] *Towers, Printer.* [1846.] 8vo, pp. 10. BA.

LAFAYETTE COLLEGE, *Pa.* Inaugural Charge by J. M. Porter, Esq. ... and Inaugural Address of the Rev. George Junkin, D.D. President of Lafayette College. Delivered at the Installation of the Faculty, ... at Easton, Pa. May 1, 1834. [n. p.] *J. P. Hetrich, Printer.* [n. d.] 8vo, pp. 16. BA. 38586

Also: The Act of Incorporation of Lafayette College ... . *Easton, Pa.: Printed by*

J. P. Hetrich. 1854. 8vo, pp. 12.—Catalogue of ... Lafayette College, for ... 1844–5. *Easton.* 1845. 8vo, pp. 22. Continued. H.

LAFAYETTE, *Wis.* Minutes of the Meeting of the Baptist Association, held in 1852. *Lancaster.* 1852. 8vo. Continued.

LAFERRIÈRE (E.) Les Constitutions d'Europe et d'Amérique recueillies par M. E. Laferrière ... . *Paris: Cotillon.* 1869. 8vo, pp. vii, cxliv, 654. B., C., H. 38588

LAFFAURIS (——). Outre Mer, ou les intérèts coloniaux envisagés dans leur rapport avec la civilisation et nos industries. *Paris.* 1839. 8vo. 38589

[LAFFITTE (J.) & Co.] Note explicative sur l'Emprunt de Trente Sept Millions de Francs (Sept Millions de Dollars) émis par le Gouvernement du Texas. *Paris.* 1841. 8vo, pp. 8.

See Fournel (Henri), Vol. VI., No. 25288.

LAFITAU (J. F.) Histoire des Découvertes et Conquestes des Portugais dans le Nouveau Monde, Avec des Figures en taille-douce. Par le R. P. Joseph François Lafitau ... . *A Paris: Saugrain, & Jean-Baptiste Coignard.* MDCCXXXIII. 2 vols., 4to, pp. (6), xxiv, 616, (48); (2), 693, (89). Map, 15 Plates. BA.

Some copies of this and the next edition have the imprint, *A Paris: Chez Saugrain Père.*

LAFITAU. Histoire des Découvertes [as before]. *A Paris: Saugrain, & Jean-Baptiste Coignard.* MDCCXXXIII–IV. 4 vols., 12mo, pp. (6), xl, 432; (2), 381, (79); (2), 512; (2), 388, (149). Map, 15 Plates. B., H. + [*Ibid.*] MDCCXXXVI. 4 vols., 12mo.

"The title of this work is not very appropriate, as it relates almost entirely to the discoveries and conquests made by the Portuguese in Asia and Africa. It is, however, an esteemed and well-written work."—RICH. *See also* "Biographie Universelle."

[LAFITAU.] Historia dos descobrimentos, e conquistas dos Portuguezes, no novo mundo. *Lisboa: na officina de Antonio Gomez.* MDCCLXXXVI–VII. 4 vols., 16mo, pp. (2), xxxiv, 374; (2), 446; (2), 467; 487. 38594

[LAFITAU.] Algemeine Geschichte der Länder und Völcker von America. Nebst einer Vorrede Siegmund Jacob Baumgartens der h. Schrift Doctors und öffentl. Lehrers ... . Mit vielen Kupfern. *Halle, bey Johann Justinus Gebauer.* 1752. 2 vols., 4to, pp. (46), 688; (22), 905, Register, 63. 8 Maps, 60 Plates.

LAFITAU. Mémoire présenté à son altesse royale M. le Duc d'Orleans, regent du royaume de France: concernant la precieuse

plante du Ginseng de Tartarie, découverte en Canada, par le P. Joseph François Lafitau ... missionaire des Iroquois du Sault Saint Louis. *Paris.* 1718. 12mo. 38595

See a long note in Faribault, No. 352.

LAFITAU. Mœurs | des Sauvages | Ameriquains, | Compare'es aux Mœurs | des premiers temps. | Par le P. Lafitau, ... | Ouvrage enrichi de Figures en taille-douce. | *A Paris: Chez Saugrain l'aîné,* ... MDCCXXIV. 2 vols., 4to, pp. (22), 610, (1); (12), 490, (40). 41 Plates. A., B., BA., C., H. 38596

Gives very extended and very exact details of the customs, manners, and religion of the savages of America, though principally of the Indians of Canada. Charlevoix says, "We have nothing so exact upon the subject of which he treats. His parallel of ancient nations with the American Indians is very ingenious, and exhibits as great familiarity with the nations of antiquity in the old world, as with the aborigines of the new." *See* "Biographie Universelle."

LAFITAU. Mœurs des Sauvages Ameriquains [as before]. *Paris: Saugrain l'aîné.* MDCCXXIV. 4 vols., 12mo, pp. (24), 256; (8), 296; (4), 248; (8), 196, (66). 41 Plates. H. + *Amsterdam.* 1730. 4 vols., 12mo. 38597

This *Amsterdam* edition I have not seen; it is described in Trübner's Catalogue. Charlevoix and Faribault refer to an edition, badly reprinted at *Rouen,* 1724, which is probably the *Paris* edition of 1724. I have seen copies in which the collation differs slightly.

LAFITAU. De Zeden der Wilden van Amerika. Zynde Een nieuwe uitvoerige en zeer kurieuse Beschryving van derzelver Oorsprong, Godsdienst, manier van Oorlogen, Huwelyken, Opvoeding, Oeffeningen, Feesten, Danzeryen, Begravenisten, en andere zeldzame gewoonten; Tegen Der Zeden der oudste Volkeren vergeleken, en met getuigenissen uit de oudste Grieksche en andere Schryveren getoetst en bevestigt. Door den zeer geleerden J. F. La Fiteau ... . *In's Gravenhage, by Gerard Vander Poel, Boekverkoper.* MDCCXXXI. Folio, pp. (4), 36, (18), 555. 41 Plates. 38598

A Dutch translation of the former work, with fine copperplate engravings.

Lafitte: or the Greek Slave. By a Soldier. *Selma, Ala.* 1864. 8vo. 38599

Lafitte: the Pirate of the Gulf. *See* [Ingraham (J. H.)], No. 34774, *add* for collation, 2 vols., 12mo, pp. 213; 216.

LAFLÈCHE (L.) Quelques Considérations sur les Rapports de la Société Civile avec la religion et la famille. Par Rt. Rév. Louis Laflèche. *Montréal.* 1866. 12mo, pp. 268. 38600

LAFLÈCHE. Rapports sur les Missions du Diocèse de Québec. *Québec.* 1855. 12mo, pp. 122. 38601

[LAFOND DE LURCY (Gabriel).] Études sur l'Amérique espagnole, sous le rapport du commerce maritime de France. De l'Équateur. *Paris.* 1848. 8vo. 38602

[LAFOND DE LURCY.] Des Isles Marquises et des Colonies de la France. *Paris: Madame Dondey Dupré.* 1843. 8vo, pp. 48.

[LAFOND DE LURCY.] Un mot sur l'Émancipation de l'Esclavage et sur le Commerce maritime de la France. [n. p. n. d.] 8vo. 38604

LAFOND [DE LURCY]. Quinze ans de Voyages autour du Monde; par le Capitaine Gabriel Lafond. *Paris: Brockhaus et Avenarius.* 1840. 2 vols., 8vo, pp. 346; (4), 380. 4 Plates.

The author was born in 1802, and commenced his voyages in 1818.

LAFOND [DE LURCY.] Vogages autour du Monde et Naufrages Célèbres. Voyages dans les Amériques [Vol. III.], Mers du Sud ... [Vol. VI.], Naufrages Célèbres. *Paris.* 1842–45. 7 vols., rl. 8vo, pp. (2), 422; (2), 432; (2), 430; (2), 423; (2), 433; (2), 423; (2), 415. Plates. 38606

First published in 256 parts. Also: Notice sur le Golfe dans l'État de Costa-Rica, et sur un nouveau passage entre les deux océans. ... *Paris: Fontaine.* 1857. 8vo. *See also* Marmocchi, *and* Viaggi.

LAFONT (C.) *and* DESNOYERS (C. L. F.) Le tremblement de terre de la Martinique, drame en cinq actes, de MM. Charles Lafont et Desnoyers. *Paris: Mifliez; Tresse.* 1840. 8vo.

LA FONTAINE (Jean de). Les Bambous. Fables de Lafontaine, travesties en patois créole, par un vieux Commandeur [Bourdillon]. *Fort-Royal (Martinique): E. Ruelle et Ch. Arnaud.* 1846. 8vo, pp. ii, 140. + Nouvelle édition. *Port de France.* 1869. 8vo, pp. 144. 38608

LA FONTAINE (L. H.) Analyse de l'Ordonnance du Conseil spécial sur les Bureaux d'Hypothèques, suivie du texte anglais et français de l'ordonnance; des lois relatives à la création des ci-devant bureaux de comtés; et de la loi des lettres de ratification. *Montréal.* 1842. 8vo, pp. 244. 38609

Laforest, Citoyen de Couleur, Député de Saint-Domingue, a son collègue Gouly, Député de l'isle de France. *A Paris, de l'imprimerie de l'Union ... . An* III*e* *de la Republique.* 8vo, pp. 7.

LAFOSSE (J. F.) Avis aux habitants des colonies, particulièrement à ceux de l'Isle Saint-Domingue, sur les principales causes des maladies qu'on y éprouve le plus communément, et sur les moyens de les prévenir. Par J. F. Lafosse ... . *Paris: Royez.* 1787. 8vo. A. 38611

[LAFRAGUA (J. M.)] Historia de la revolucion de Mexico contra la dictadura del General Santa-Anna, 1853–1855. *México.* 1856. 4to. Maps and Plates. 38612

There are copies on vellum paper.

LAFRAGUA. Memoria de la primera Secretaria de Estado y del Despacho de Relaciones Interiores y Esteriores de los Estados-Unidos Mexicanos, leida al soberano Congreso Constituyente en los dias 14, 15, y 16 Diciembre de 1846. *Mexico.* 1847. Folio.

LAFRAGUA. Memorandum de los negocios pendientes entre Mexico y España, presentado al Exmo. Sr. Ministro de Estado por el Representante de la Republica, el dia 28 de Julio de 1857. *Poissy: Tipografia de Arbien.* 1857. 8vo, pp. 347. 38614

LA FRUSTON (F. de). Constitution et Organisation de l'Armée de Terre des États-Unis de l'Amérique Septentrionale. Par F. de La Fruston. *Paris: Corréard.* 1863. 8vo, pp. (4), 293. 41 Plates. BA. 38615

LA FUENTE (Ant. Gutierrez de). Manifiesto que di en Trujillo en 1824, sobre los motivos que me obligaron á deponer a D. Jose de la Riva-Aguero, y conducta que observé en ese acontecimiento. *Lima: Jose Masias.* 1829. Folio, pp. 29, xxviii, (2).

LA GARZA (L. de) Carta pastoral que el Illmo. Señor Arzobispo de Mexico Doctor D. Lazaro de la Garza dirigé á los Sres. Curas de su Diócesis sobre el contenido de la Enciclica de Ntro. Santisimo Padre El Señor Pio IX. *Mexico.* 1858. 8vo, pp. 32.

See also Vol. VII., Nos. 26719–21.

LA GASCA (M.) Genera et Species Plantarum, qua aut nova sunt, aut nondum recté cognoscuntur. *Madrid.* 1816. 4to.

Includes many American species.

La | Gloire | de S. Vrsvle | divisee en devx parties. | La premiere contient l'Histoire & Martyre des onze | mille Vierges, avec quelques considerations la | dessus. | La deuxieme et vn abrégé de la vie d'aucunes filles | de S. Vrsvle, Signalées en sainteté. | Recueillie par un Pere de la Compagnie de Jesus, | *A Valentiennes,* |

De l'imprimerie de Iean Bovcher au nom de Jesvs | M.DC.LVI. 4to, pp. (16), 367, (3). 38619

Lago (A. B. P. do). Carta da costa da provincia do Maranhão, levantada por observações astronomicas e trigonometricas, acompanhada de um Roteiro e descripção hydrographica da mesma costa. Por Antonio Bernardino Pereira do Lago. *Lisboa: na Typ. da Acad. R. das Sc.* [1823.] 38620

Lago. Estatistica historica-geographica da provincia do Maranhão, offerecida ao Soberano Congresso das Cortes ... . *Lisboa: na Typ. da Acad. R. das Sc.* 1822. 4to, pp. 91. 17 Maps.

[Lagrange de Checieux (G. A. F. Simon de).] La Conduite des François justifiée, ou observations sur un écrit anglois, intitulé: "Conduite des François à l'égard de la Nouvelle Ecosse," depuis son premier établissement jusqu'à nos jours. Par le Sieur D. L. G. D. C. Avocat en Parlement. *Utrecht.* 1756. 12mo, pp. viii, 256. A. 38622

See Jefferys (T.), Vol. ix., 35958, *also* Vol. iv., No. 15205, for a translation, *and* Faribault's Catalogue, p. 52.

La Grange, *Ala.* Catalogue of ... La Grange College, North Alabama. Session 1842–'43. *Tuscumbia: Printed by Messenger* ... 1843. 12mo, pp. (12). Continued. H. 38623

Lagrymas de la Paz, vertidas en las Exequias del Señor D. Fernando de Borbon, por Excellencia el Justo, vi. Monarcha, ... celebradas en el Augusto Metropolitano Templo de esta Imperial corte de Mexico: y despuestas por los Señores Diputados, Lic. D. Domingo Balcarcel y Formento, y Lic. D. Feliz Venancio Malo. *En Mexico, en la Imprenta de Real, y mas antiguo Colegio de San Ildefonso. Año de* 1762. 4to, pp. (4), 98, xxii. 38624

A copious collection of poems on the death of Ferdinand vi. of Spain, illustrated with many copperplates. The appendix consists of "Laudatio funebris Ferdinandi vi. Hispaniarum, et Indiarum Regis. Habita Mexici ... Ad. Ludovico Antonio de Torres."

La Guaira. Estado general que presenta al ministerio de fomento la direccion cesante de la Junta de fomento de La Guaira, comprendiendo todas sus operaciones desde su instalacion 1° de Febrero, 1864, hasta 6 de Diciembre, 1866, fecha en que terminó su administracion. *La Guaira.* 1867. 4to, pp. 39. 38625

Laguna (Francisco Gonzalez). El Zelo Sacerdotal. Para con los Niños No-Nacidos. *Lima.* 1781. Sm. 8vo. 38626

Lagunas (J. B. de). Arte y Dictionario: con otras Obras, en lengua Michuacana. Cõpuesto por el muy. R. P. Fray Iuan Baptista de Lagunas ... . *En Mexico, en casa de Pedro Balli.* 1574. 8vo, pp. (28), 174, 190. 38627

A volume of extreme rarity.

Lagunas y Castilla (P. J. B. de). Coleccion legal de Cartas, Dictámenes, y otros Papeles en Derecho, ... Escribiolus el Sr. Dr. D. Pedro Bravo de Lagunas y Castilla ... . *Impreso en Lima con las debidas licencias en la Oficina de los Huerfanos. Año de* 1761. 4to. 38628

Includes a defense of the royal jurisdiction.

Lagunas y Castilla. Discurso Historico-Juridico del Origen, Fundacion, Redificacion, Derechos, y Extenciones del Hospital de San Lazaro de Lima. Dedicado a la real audencia de los Reyes. *Lima. en la Oficina de los Huerphanos.* 1761. 4to, pp. (30), 272. 38629

Lagunas y Castilla. Voto Consultivo que ofrece al Excelentissimo Señor D. Joseph Antonio Manso de Velasco, virrey Governador y Capitàn General de los Reynos del Perù, el D. D. Pedro, Joseph Bravo de Lagunas y Castilla, Ministro Honor. del Supremo Consejo de las Indias Oydor de Lima. Sobre si se han de prefirir en la venta los trigos del distrito de Lima a los que se conducen por mar de Chile ... *Lima, en la calle del Tigre.* 1755. Sm. 4to, pp. (18), 247, (6). c. + Nueva edicion corregida, y aumentada. *Lima, en la Oficinas de los Huerphanos.* 1761. 4to, pp. (30), 310. 38630

[La Harpe (Bénard de).] Journal historique de l'établissement des Français à la Louisiane. *Nouvelle-Orléans: A. L. Boimare.* 1831. 8vo, pp. (4), 412. BA. 38631

Printed at *Paris* by Paul Renouard, and signed "Bénard de la Harpe," who resided in Louisiana from 1818 to 1823, at which period the journal ends.

La Harpe (Jean François de). Abrégé de l'Histoire Générale des Voyages, contenant ce qu'il y a de plus remarquable, de plus utile et de mieux avéré, dans les pays où les voyageurs ont pénétré, les mœurs des habitans, la religion, les usages, sciences et arts, commerce et manufactures; Par J.-F. Laharpe. *Paris.* 1780–1804. 44 vols., 8vo, Atlas in 4to. A. + *Paris: Chez Ledoux.* 1816. 24 vols., 8vo, Atlas in folio. + *Paris.* 1820. 24 vols., 8vo, Atlas in folio. + Nouvelle édition, ornée de soixante vignettes et d'un atlas in-4°. *Paris: Achille Jourdan.* 1822. 30 vols., 8vo. + *Paris.* 1825. 30 vols., 8vo, Atlas in folio. +

Nouvelle édition, augmentée d'un extrait des voyages récents, par M. de Roujoux et par M. Denaix ... . *Lyon: Rusand.* 1829–30. 30 vols., 8vo. Maps. 38632

A work that has met with greater success than any other of the same kind; the fidelity of the narration, the striking details of adventure, and the lively pictures of manners, etc., it presents, will always give it a peculiar and lasting merit. Contains all the early voyages to America.

La Hontan (N. *le Baron de*). Dialogues De Monsieur le Baron de La Honton Et d'un Sauvage, Dans l'Amerique. Contenant une description exacte des mœurs & des coutumes de ces Peuples Sauvages. ... *A Amsterdam, Chez la Veuve de Boeteman* ... M.DCCIV. 12mo, pp. (16), 103. Plate. A., B. 38633

The traits of the savages are doubtless fairly illustrated, but the work was used by the author as a medium to proclaim his deistical theories, and is of no historical importance. *See* "Hist. Mag.," i. 280; ii. 208. In some copies the title reads as below:

La Hontan. Dialogues De Monsieur le Baron de La Hontan Et d'un Sauvage, Dans l'Amerique. Contenant une description exacte des mœurs & des coutumes de ces Peuples Sauvages. Avec les Voyages du même en Portugal & en Danemarc, dans lesquels on trouve des particularitez très curieuses, & qu'on n'avoit point encore remarquées. Le tout enrichi de Cartes & de Figures. *A Amsterdam, Chez la Veuve de Boeteman* ... M.DCCIV. 12mo, pp. (16), 222. 4 Plates and Map. 38634

The "Dialogues" end at page 103.

La Hontan. Nouveaux Voyages de Mr. Le Baron de Lahontan, dans l'Amerique Septentrionale, Qui contiennent une Rélation des différens Peuples qui y habitent; la nature de leur Gouvernement; leur Commerce, leurs Coutumes, leur Religion, & leur maniére de faire la Guerre. L'intérêt des François & des Anglois dans le Commerce qu'ils font avec ces Nations; l'avantage que l'Angleterre peut retirer de ce Païs, étant en Guerre avec la France. Le tout enrichi de Cartes & de Figures. Tome Premier. *A la Haye, Chez les Fréres l'Honoré,* ... M.DCCIII. 12mo, pp. (22), 279. 15 Maps and Plates. BA. 38635

Mr. Muller says, there are two issues of this work, one has a plate of a sphere, the other a motto, "Honoratus," etc., on the title-page. We have one, *sub visu*, with both these features. Some copies have a sheet inserted—"L'Autheur au Lecteur, A Londres ce 26 Novembre. V. Stile.—12 pp., nearly three of which are errata, and the author does not spare his publisher. This matter is recast as the preface to the "Suite" or Vol. ii., and this sheet must have appeared before the "Suite." The title to Vol. ii. reads:

La Hontan. Memoires de l'Amerique Septentrionale, ou la suite des Voyages de Mr. Le Baron de Lahontan. Qui contiennent la Description d'une grande étenduë de Païs de ce Con-

tinent, l'intérêt des François & des Anglois, leurs Commerces, leurs Navigations, les Mœurs & les Coutumes des Sauvages, &c. Avec un petit Dictionaire de la Langue du Païs. Le tout enrichi de Cartes & de Figures. Tome Seconde. *A La Haye, Chez les Fréres l'Honoré,* ... M.DCCIII. 12mo, pp. 220, Table, (16). Map and 13 Plates. B., BA. 38636

See Nos. 38641–42, *infra*, for the second edition. The third volume, really by Nicolas Gueudeville, is entitled:

La Hontan. Supplement aux Voyages du Baron La Hontan, ou l'on trouve des dialogues curieux entre l'auteur et un sauvage de bons sens qui à voyagé. L'on y voit aussi plusieurs observations faites par le même auteur, dans ses voyages en Portugal, en Espagne, en Hollande, et en Danemarc, &c. Avec Figures. *A La Haye, Chez les Fréres l'Honoré* ... M.DCCIII. 12mo, pp. (14), 332. 4 Plates, 2 Maps. B. 38637

These three preceding numbers are the titles of the original edition of the work, which, in fact, consists of three volumes; *our* Nos. 38638–40, *infra*, describe other editions. Much of La Hontan's matter is evidently drawn from authentic sources, but his pretended discovery of Long River is wholly fictitious. The work has not received the amount of credit to which it is really entitled, although written by a man of more than ordinary learning and intelligence. Had he written no other work than the "New Voyages," it is probable that it would have experienced no lack of esteem, but his Relations, even when scrupulously exact, have felt the influence of the skepticism which he infused into his subsequent work. *See* "Biographie Universelle," Charlevoix, *and* Faribault, No. 357. In enumerating the succeeding editions I do it with some diffidence, for there are some variations which are not very clear; for example, in the edition of 1742, the "Suite" reads as Vol. ii., and the "Memoires" as Vol. iii. Some editions include the "Dialogues," others do not. To be quite sure about these details, one ought to have them all under the eye at the same time, and that has not been possible. Dr. Shea thinks there were editions in 1709 and 1731.

La Hontan. Nouveaux Voyages ... dans l'Amerique Septentrionale ... . *A La Haye, Chez les Fréres l'Honoré.* 1703. 2 vols., 12mo, pp. (24), 279; 220, (17). 25 Maps and Plates.

There is another edition, same title, date, and publisher, with 11 p. l. only. Although this bears the same imprint, a comparison shows them to be different editions. The text of the latter is, page for page, like that of the former; the type, however, is smaller, and all the capitals and ornaments are different; the epistle, prologue, and contents differ. The engravings in the latter are very inferior, and were evidently got up expressly for this edition, which is probably spurious. The Maps and Plates are reversed.

La Hontan. Nouveaux Voyages ... dans l'Amerique Septentrionale ... . *A La Haye, Chez les Fréres l'Honoré.* 1704. 2 vols., 12mo, pp. (16), 280; 222, (18). 25 Maps and Plates. + [*Ibid.*] 1709. + *Amsterdam, l'Honoré.* 1728. 2 vols., 12mo.

La Hontan. Nouveaux Voyages ... dans l'Amerique Septentrionale ... . *La Haye, Chez les Fréres l'Honoré.* MDCCXXXI. 2 vols., 12mo, pp. (8), 188, (4); (4), 220. 14 Plates and Maps.

La Hontan. Voyages du Baron de La Hontan dans l'Amerique Septentrionale, Qui contiennent une Rélation des différens Peuples qui y habitent; la nature de leur Gouvernement; leur Commerce, leurs Coûtumes, leur Religion, & leur maniére de faire la Guerre: L'Intérêt des François & des Anglois dans le Commerce qu'ils font avec ces Nations; l'avantage que l'Angleterre peut retirer de ce Païs, étant en Guerre avec la France. Le tout enrichi de Cartes & de Figures. Tome Premier, Seconde Edition, revuë, corrigée & augmentée. *A Amsterdam, Chez François l'Honoré,* ... MDCCV. 12mo, pp. (20), 376. 2 Maps, 11 Plates. + *A La Haye, Chez Jonas l'Honoré.* MDCCV. 12mo, pp. (20), 376. 2 Maps, 11 Plates. + *A La Haye, Charles Delo.* MDCCVI. 12mo, pp. (22), 376. 13 Maps and Plates. + *A Amsterdam, Chez François l'Honoré.* MDCCXXI. 12mo. Maps and Plates. + [*Ibid.*] M.DCC.XXVIII. 12mo, pp. (16), 408. 13 Maps and Plates. BA. + [*Ibid.*] MDCCXXXXI. 12mo, (8), 188, (4). Maps and Plates. C. 38641

Other editions, 1707 and 1715. Some copies of l'Honoré's edition have a preface of sixteen pages. After noticing the censure of the style it says: "All the Letters have been almost recast, and it is believed that the style will appear more pure, concise and simple, and with a little more *finesse* in the wit. ... There has been no scruple in probability where it lacked ... The best of the 'Dialogues' have been taken, and they have been adapted to the new style of the Voyages." The alteration is mainly in the "Dialogues" which are rewritten; the Voyages to Portugal and Denmark are omitted, and the whole work is thus brought into two volumes. Vol. ii. has the following title:

La Hontan. Memoires de l'Amerique Septentrionale, ou la suite des Voyages de Mr. Le Baron de La Hontan: Qui contiennant la Description d'une grande étenduë de Païs de ce Continent, l'intérêt des François & des Anglois, leurs Commerces, leurs Navigations, les Mœurs & les Coutumes des Sauvages, &c. Avec un petit Dictionaire de la Langue du Païs. Le tout enrichi de Cartes & de Figures. Tome Seconde. Seconde Edition, augmentée des Conversations de l'Auteur avec un Sauvage distingué. *A Amsterdam, Chez Francois l'Honoré & Compagnie.* MDCCV. 12mo, pp. (2), 5–376, Table, 2. Map, 9 Plates. + *A La Haye, Chez Jonas l'Honoré.* MDCCV. 12mo, pp. (2), 5–336, Table, 2. Map, 9 Plates. + *A La Haye, Charles Delo.* MDCCVI. 12mo, pp. 3–336, (2). 14 Maps and Plates. + *A Amsterdam, Chez François l'Honoré.* MDCCXXI. 12mo. Maps and Plates. + [*Ibid.*] M.DCC.XXVIII. 12mo, pp. (2), 238. 9 Maps and Plates. BA. + [*Ibid.*] MDCCXXXXI. 12mo, pp. (4), 220. Maps and Plates.

Other editions, 1707 and 1715. The difference in the number of plates is really in favor of the edition of 1705, as that has a small Carte générale, which is not in the second. The latter have a fresh frontispiece and a figure of a sphere in addition. The augmentations are merely imaginary dialogues between the author and an Indian chief,

in which questions of high morality and political economy are discussed. The third or supplementary volume, issued by another printer, bears the following title:

La Hontan. Suite Du Voyage, De l'Amerique, Ou Dialogues De Monsieur le Baron de La Hontan Et d'un Sauvage, Dans l'Amerique. Contenant une description exacte des mœurs & des coutumes de ces Peuples Sauvages. Avec les Voiages du même en Portugal & en Danemarc, ... Le tout enrichi de Cartes & de Figures. *A Amsterdam, Chez la Veuve de Boeteman* ... M. DCCIV. 12mo, pp. (16), 222. 6 Maps and Plates. + [*Ibid.*] M.DCC.XXVIII. 12mo, pp. (12), 257. 6 Maps and Plates. BA.

This is by Nicolas Gueudeville. *See our* Vol. vii., No. 29142, where the title is slightly incorrect.

La Hontan. New Voyages to North-America. Containing An Account of the several Nations of that vast Continent; their Customs, Commerce, and Way of Navigation upon the Lakes and Rivers; the several Attempts of the English and French to dispossess one another; with the Reasons of the Miscarriage of the former; and the various Adventures between the French, and the Iroquese Confederates of England, from 1683 to 1694. A Geographical Description of Canada, and a Natural History of the Country, with Remarks upon their Government, and the Interest of the English and French in their Commerce. Also a Dialogue between the Author and a General of the Savages, giving a full View of the Religion and strange Opinions of those People: With an Account of the Author's Retreat to Portugal and Denmark, and his Remarks on those Courts. To which is added, A Dictionary of the Algonkine Language, which is generally spoke in North-America. Illustrated with Twenty Three Mapps and Cutts. Written in French By the Baron Lahontan, Lord Lievtenant of the French Colony at Placentia in Newfoundland, now in England. Done into English. ... A great part of which never Printed in the Original. *London: ... H. Bonwicke* ... 1703. 2 vols., 8vo, pp. (24), 280; 302, (13). Maps and Plates. 38644

The engravings are by H. Moll: including the frontispiece to Vol. ii. there are twenty-four in number, viz.: thirteen in Vol. i., and eleven in Vol. ii. That designed for Vol. i., p. 89, is generally to be found in Vol. ii., p. 89. The map of Newfoundland, added by the author to this edition, is the twenty-fourth. In the preface he says the plates of the Holland edition were miserably done. This edition was published under his own eye. "La Hontan was a freethinker, and consequently had but little respect for the clergy; it is not therefore to be wondered at that he was persecuted in France, and his work traduced. The character given of the author and of the work by the Jesuits has been adopted by later writers, who ought to have known better. A writer in the 'North American Review' observes, that the Baron seems to have been an ardent and enterprising character, with more wit than discretion, but that his accounts

bear every mark of authenticity, and are quite confirmed by cotemporary as well as subsequent writers on the same country."—Rich, i. 4. Mr. Rich's remarks need a little qualification—Charlevoix is the only Jesuit who discusses La Hontan.

La Hontan. New Voyages to North-America. Containing An Account of the several Nations of that vast Continent; their Customs, Commerce, and the Way of Navigation upon the Lakes and Rivers; the several Attempts of the English and French to dispossess one another; with the Reasons of the Miscarriage of the former; and the various Adventures between the French, and the Iroquese Confederates of England, from 1683 to 1694. ... Illustrated with Twenty-Three Mapps and Cuts. Written in French By the Baron Lahontan, Lord Lieutenant of the French Colony at Placentia in Newfoundland, at that Time in England. Done into English. The Second Edition. ... *London: John Brindley.* M,DCC,XXXV. 8vo, pp. (24), 280. 10 Maps and Plates. BA. 38645

Some copies have the imprint, *London: J. and J. Bonwicke,* others, *J. Osborn.* It is the same as the edition of 1703. Vol. ii. has the following title:

La Hontan. New Voyages to North-America. Giving a full Account of the Customs, Commerce, Religion, and strange Opinions of the Savages of that Country. With Political Remarks upon the Courts of Portugal and Denmark, and the Present State of the Commerce of those Countries. The Second Edition. Written By the Baron Lahontan, Lord-Lieutenant of the French Colony at Placentia in Newfoundland: Now in England. *London: John Brindley.* M,DCC,XXXV. 8vo, pp. 304. 10 Plates.

Some copies have the imprint, *London: J. Waltboe.* 1735. Murray remarks "Becoming intimate with the Indians, La Hontan formed the plan of an expedition to the eastern regions beyond the Mississippi, *and was the first person* to make known, by communication from the Indians, the existence of the Rocky Mountains, the Columbia River, and the Ocean or 'Great Salt Lake.'" Dr. J. G. Shea says this is all fictitious. It was translated under the inspection of the author, from the French original. The vocabulary is reprinted on pp. 214–219 in Hadr. Relandi's "Dissertationes Miscellanæ." *Trajecti ad Rhenum.* 1706–7. 8vo. *See also* Pinkerton's "Voyages," Vol. xiii.

La Hontan. Des berühmten Herrn Baron La Hontan Neueste Reisen nach Nord-Indien, oder dem mitternächtischen America, mit vielen besondern und bey keinem Scribenten befindlichen Curiositæten. Aus dem Frantzösischen übersetzet von M. Vischer. *Hamburg und Leipzig: Im Reumannischen Verlag.* MDCCIX. 2 vols., 12mo, pp. (8), 459; (19), 753. Map. + *Hamburg.* MDCCXI. [*Ibid.*] 38647

La Hontan. Reizen van den Baron van La Hontan in het Noordelyk Amerika, Vervattende een Verhaal van verscheide

Volkeren die het bewoonen; den aart hunner Regeering, hun Koophandel, hun Gewoontens, hun Godsdienst, en hun wys van Oorloogen ... Vertaalt door Gerard Westerwyk ... . *In's Gravenhage, By Isaac Beauregard.* 1739. 2 vols., 16mo, pp. (12), 582; (2), 552. 2 Maps, 9 Plates. 38648

This Dutch edition, which is rare, contains many historical and geographical notes, and is in many respects better than either the English or French editions.

La Hontan. Den Oorspronk. *See* Klerk (J. de), No. 38048, and *add*, *Gedrukt in 't Jaar* 1723. 12mo, pp. 39.

La Hure (Baril, *Comte de*). *See* Baril, Vol. i., Nos. 3380–82.

Laicus, *pseudon.* Remarks on Religious Association. By Laicus. *Boston.* [n. d.] 8vo, pp. 16. 38650

Laicus. The Trial Tried; or, the Bishop and the Court at the Bar of Public Opinion. By Laicus. *New-York: D. Appleton & Company.* 1845. 8vo, pp. 24. B. 38651

Relates to Bishop Onderdonk.

[Laing (David).] Catalogue of a Portion of the Rare and Curious Library of an Eminent Collector in Edinburgh, particularly rich in Works relating to America. [n. p.] 1856. 8vo.

Laing (J.) An Account of a Voyage to Spitzbergen, containing a full Description of that Country and the Zoology of the North, and of the Shetland Isles, with an Account of the Whale Fishery. By John Laing, Surgeon. With an Appendix ... By a Gentleman of the Navy. *London: J. Mawman.* 1815. 8vo, pp. (6), 171, (2). + Second Edition, corrected and enlarged. *Edinburgh: Black; London: Underwood.* 1818. 12mo, pp. 165. + Third Edition. *Edinburgh: Tait.* 1820. 12mo, pp. 165.

Relates to the American whale-fishery. *See* "M. Rev.," lxxviii. 131, lxxxv. 410.

Laird (M.) The Effect of an Alteration of the Sugar Duties on the Condition of the People of England and the Negro Race considered. By Macgregor Laird, Esq. *London.* 1844. 8vo. 38654

Lake (W.) The Parnassian Pilgrim; or, the Posthumous Works of the late Mr. William Lake. With a Sketch of his Life. *Hudson.* 1807. 8vo, pp. 184. 38655

Lake Champlain. Lake Champlain and Connecticut River Rail Road ... Remarks ... of the Route and its Importance to the Trade of Boston. *Boston.* 1845. 8vo, pp. 16. BA. 38656

LAKE ERIE. The Battle of Lake Erie. [n. p. n. d.] 8vo, pp. 24. Plates. 38657

Charter of the Lake Erie and Mad-River Railroad Company. Report of the U. S. Civil Engineer employed in the Survey of the Route. *Springfield.* 1833. 8vo. 38658

See also our Vol. I., No. 2330; to the imprint of No. 3967 add, *Printed by Henry D. Cooke & Company;* Vol. VI., Nos. 22740; 22758; 22759; 22765, *and* U. S. Department of War, Bureau of Topographical Engineers.

LAKE GEORGE. Lake George and Lake Champlain; a Series of Oil-Colour Views. With descriptive Letter-Press. *London: Nelson.* [n. d.] 18mo, pp. 48. 38659

Noticia Verdadeira da Guerra da America entre os Francezes, e Inglezes, com a tomada do Forte de Sam Jorze ganhado pelos Francezes .... [n. p. n. d.] 4to, pp. 7. J.C.B. 38660

An extremely rare piece. The only copy we know belongs to the library of Mr. J. Carter Brown.

Relaciõ de huma batalha, succedida no campo de Lake Giorge na America Septemtrional, entre as Tropas Inglezas commandadas pelo Coronel Guilhelmo, e as Francezas das quaes era Commandante o General Baraõ Dieskau, aos 30 de Junho do prezente anno de 1757. Traduzida no Idioma Portuguez. Extrahida de huma Carta escrita pelo mesmo Coronel, logo despois do successo, ao General Wenswort, Governador da Nova Hamsphire [*sic*] e mandada inclusa em outra escrita em Postmante Capital da mesma Provincia. *Lisboa, Anno* MDCCLVIII. 4to, pp. 7. 38661

These Portuguese tracts relate to the contests between the British and French forces near Lake George, and are translations from the English. *See also* Vol. I., No. 2046, *and* New England.

LAKE FOREST, *Ill.* Catalogue of the Lake Forest Academy for 1869–70. *Lake Forest.* 1870. 8vo. 38662

LAKE HURON. Report of the Geological Survey of Canada, on the North Shore of Lake Huron. *Montreal.* 1849. 8vo. 2 Maps. 38663

LAKE MEMPHREMAGOG. A Hand-Book with Route List. With numerous appropriate Views. *Boston.* 1864. Sq. 12mo.

LAKE MICHIGAN. Report on a Ship Canal between Lake Michigan and the Mississippi River, for War Purposes. [n. p. 1862.] 8vo, pp. 13. 38665

House of Reps., Report No. 37, 37th Cong., 2d Sess.

LAKE ONTARIO. A Statement of the Lake Ontario and Hudson River Railroad ... 1857. *New-York.* 1857. 4to. Map.

LAKE INSURANCE. Proceedings of a Convention of Lake Underwriters, Buffalo, Jan. 8, 1856. *Buffalo.* 1856. 8vo, pp. 60.

The Lake Shore; or the Slave, the Serf and the Apprentice. [n. p. n. d.] 8vo. 38668

LAKE SUPERIOR. A Brief Account of the Lake Superior Copper Company by an Original Shareholder. June, 1845. *Boston.* 1845. 8vo, pp. 30. 2 Maps. H. 38669

[American Exploring, Mining and Manufacturing Company.] Copper Mines of Lake Superior. [n. p.] 1847. 8vo, pp. 14.

Exhibit of the Lake Superior Iron Company, March, 1853. *Rochester, N. Y.* 1853. 8vo, pp. 32. 38671

Geography, Topography and Geology of the Shores of Lake Superior. *Detroit.* 1846. 8vo. Map. 38672

Papers relative to the Exploration of Lake Superior and the Red River Settlements. [n. p.] 1859. Folio. 4 colored Maps.

An English Parliamentary Report.

The Second Annual Report of the Trustees of the Lake Superior Copper Company, Oct. 6, 1845; with Dr. Jackson's Statement .... *Boston.* 1845. 8vo, pp. 19. 38674

Report from a Committe of the U. S. Senate, April 3, 1844, in relation to a Ship Canal at St. Mary's Falls. *Washington.* 1844. 8vo. 38675

Reports of Wm. A. Burt and Bela Hubbard, Esqs, on the Geography, Topography and Geology, of the U. S. Surveys of the Mineral Region of the South Shore of Lake Superior, for 1845; Accompanied by a List of working and Organized Mining Companies; A List of Mineral Locations, by whom made, and a correct Map ... and ... a Chart of Lake Superior ... . By J. Houghton, Jr., and F. W. Bristol. *Detroit: Charles Willcox.* 1846. 12mo, pp. (6), 109. Map. 38676

This is the correct title of *our* No. 9486, Vol. III. *See also* Drake (M. L.), Vol. V., No. 20863, *and* Foster (J. W.), Vol. VI., No. 25249.

LA LANDE (J. J. de). Du Passage de Vênus sur le Soleil qui s'observera en 1769. *Amsterdam.* 1769. 4to. A. 38677

LALLEATÉGUI (J. D.) Description botanique du Chirantha dendron, arbre du Mexique, nouvellement connu; traduit par Lescallier. *Paris.* 1805. 4to. Plates. 38678

LALLEMANT (C.) Copie de Trois Lettres Escrittes ès années 1625. et 1626. Par le P. Charles Lallemant, Superieur des Missions de la Compagnie de Iesvs en la Novvelle France. *Albanie: De l'Imprimerie de J. Munsell.* M.DCCC.LXX. 8vo, pp. 14.

LALLEMANT. Lettre | dv Pere | Charles | l'Allemant, | Svperievr de la Mis- | sion de Canadas; de la Com- | pagnie de Iesus. | Enuoyee au Pere Hierosme l'Allemant | son frere, de la mesme Compagnie. | Où sont contenus les mœurs & façons de vi- | ure des Sauuages habitants de ce païs là; | & comme ils se comportent auec | les Chrestiens François qui y | demeurent. | Ensemble la description des villes de ceste contree. | *A Paris,* | *Par Iean Bovcher,* ... | 1627. | 8vo, pp. (2), 16. + [*Albany: Joel Munsell.* 1870.]

See "Mercure Français," Vol. XIII. p. 1, 1626, [Harrisse's] "Notes," No. 41, *and* Faribault, No. 361.

LALLEMANT. Lettre du Reuerend Pere l'Allemant, Superieur de la Mission des Peres Iesuites en la Nouuelle France. Envoyée de Bordeaux au R. P. Superieur du College des Iesuites à Paris, et datée du 22 Nouembre, 1629. ... *A Paris.* M.DC.XXXII. 8vo, pp. 15, (1). + [*Albany: Joel Munsell.* 1870.] BA. 38681

LALLEMANT. Relation de ce qui s'est passé en la Nouvelle France en l'année M.DC.XXVI. ... *Paris: Estienne Richer.* M.DC.XXIX. 12mo, pp. iv, 59. + [*Albany: Joel Munsell.* 1870]. BA.

LALLEMANT (H.) Lettres | envoiées | de la | Novvelle France | Au R. P. Iacqves Renavlt | Prouincial de la Compagnie de | Iesvs en la Prouince de la France, | Par le R. P. Hier. Lallemant Superieur des Missions de la dite Com- | pagnie en ce nouueau Monde. | *A Paris,* | *chez Sebastien Cramoisy,* | ... | M.DC.LX. | Auec Priuilege du Roy. | Sm. 8vo, pp. (2), 3-49, (3). 38683

Of extreme rarity. *See* [Harrisse's] "Notes," No. 113. A few copies only were reprinted by Joel Munsell for Mr. James Lenox, of New York, all for presents.

[LALLEMANT.] Relation | de ce qvi s'est passé | de plvs remarqvable | ès Missions des Peres de la | Compagnie de Iesvs, | en la | Novvelle France, | ès années 1645. & 1646. | Enuoyée au R. P. Prouincial de la Prouince | de France. | Par le Superieur des Missions de la mesme | Compagnie. | *A Paris,* | *chez Sebastien Cramoisy,* |

... | M.DC.XLVII. | Avec Privilege dv Roy. | 8vo, pp. (6), 184; (2), 3-128. S. 38684

The second piece is by Paul Ragueneau. *See* [Harrisse's] "Notes," No. 86, *and* Crayon, No. 1275.

[LALLEMANT.] Relation | de ce qvi s'est passé | de plvs remarqvable | ès Missions des Peres de la | Compagnie de Iesvs, | en la | Novvelle France, | svr le grand flevve | de S. Lavrens en l'année 1647. | Enuoyée au R. P. Prouincial de la Prouince | de France. | Par le Superieur des Missions de la mesme Compagnie. | *A Paris,* | *chez Sebastien Cramoisy,* | ... | M.DC.XLVIII. | Avec Privilege dv Roy. | Sm. 8vo, pp. (8), 276. S. 38685

This relates the tragical death of Father Jogues.

[LALLEMANT.] Relation | de ce qvi s'est passé | de plvs remarqvable | ès Missions des Pères de la | Compagnie de Iesvs, | en la | Novvelle France, | ès années 1647. & 1648. | Enuoyée au R. P. Prouincial de la Prouince | de France. | Par le Superieur des Missions de la mesme | Compagnie. | *A Paris,* | *chez Sebastien Cramoisy,* | ... | M.DC.XLIX. | Avec Privilege dv Roy. | 8vo, pp. (8), 158; (4), 3-135. 38686

[LALLEMANT.] Relation | de ce qvi s'est passé | de plvs remarqvable | avx Missions des Peres | de la Compagnie de Iesvs, | en la | Novvelle France, | ès années 1661. & 1662. | Enuoyée au R. P. André Castillon, Pro- | uincial de la Prouince de France. | *A Paris,* | *chez Sebastien, et Sebast.* | *Mabre-Cramoisy,* ... M.DC.LXIII. | Avec Privilege dv Roy. | 8vo, pp. (8), 118. 38687

[LALLEMANT.] Relation | de ce qvi s'est passé | de plvs remarqvable | avx Missions des Peres | de la Compagnie de Iesvs, | en la | Novvelle France, | ès années 1662. & 1663. | Enuoyée au R. P. Castillon, Pro- | uincial de la Prouince de France. | *A Paris,* | *chez Sebastien Cramoisy, et Sebast.* | *Mabre-Cramoisy,* | ... | M.DC.LXIV. | ... Sm. 8vo, pp. (16), 169. S. 38688

[LALLEMANT.] Relation | de ce qvi s'est passé | de plvs remarqvable | avx Missions des Péres | de la Compagnie de Iesvs, | en la | Novvelle France, | ès années 1663. & 1664. | Enuoyée au R. P. Prouincial de la Prouince | de France. | *A Paris,* | *chez Sebastien Cramoisy, & Sebast.* | *Mabre-Cramoisy,* ... M.DC.LXV. | ... | 8vo, pp. (16), 176. S. 38689

See also Vol. IV., No. 16676, Le Jeune (P.), Relation, *and* Vimont (B.)

LALLEMANT (Roberto Ave). Observações ácerca da epidemia da febre amarella de 1850 no Rio de Janeiro, colligidas nos hospitaes e na polyclinica. *Rio de Janeiro.* 1851. 8vo. 38690

LALLEMENT (Guillaume). Histoire de la Colombie. Par M. Lallement. *Paris: A. Eymery.* 1826. 8vo, pp. viii, 320. Map. + [*Ibid.*] 1827. 32mo. C., S. 38691

"Ouvrage remarquable pour le style et pour l'exactitude, et le premier qui ait paru sur cette vaste republique."—QUERARD.

LALLEMENT. Historia de la Colombia. Por M. Lallement. *Paris: Imp. de Pinard.* 1827. 8vo, pp. 318. 38692

A Spanish translation of the previous work.

LALLI (——). Fragments sur l'Inde, sur le General Lalli, et sur le Comte de Morangies. 1773. 12mo. 38693

LALLY-TOLENDAL (T. G.) Defense des émigrés français, adressée au peuple français. *Paris.* 1797. 38694

LALOR (John). England among the Nations. *London: Chapman & Hall.* 1864. 12mo, pp. (4), 124. C. 38695

LALOURCÉ (M.) Mémoire pour M. François Bigot, ci-devant Intendant de Justice, Police, Finance et Marine en Canada, Accusé; contre M. le Procureur Général du Roi, en la Commission, Accusateur. Partie 1re. contenant l'Histoire de l'Administration du Sieur Bigot dans la Colonie, et des réflexions générales sur cette Administration. Partie 2e. contenant la discussion et le détail des Chefs d'Accusation. *Paris: le Prieur.* 1763. 4to.

LA LUZERNE (*Comte de*). Dépêches de M. le comte de La Luzerne, ministre de la marine, aux administrateurs de Saint-Domingue [29 Sept. 1789. *Imprimé par ordre de l'Assemblée provinciale de la partie du nord de Saint-Domingue.* 1789.] 8vo, pp. 48, or less. 38697

LA LUZERNE. Supplément à la "Dénonciation de M. de La Luzerne" ... ou réponse par des pièces justificatives sans réplique au pretendu Mémoire justificatif qu'il a publié en juin 1790; par les députés de Saint-Domingue à l'Assemblée nationale. [n. p. n. d.] 8vo, pp. 48, or less. 38698

LAM (I. D.) Waerachtich verhael | Van de gantsche reyse ghedaen by den | eersamen | Ian Dircksz Lam, als | Admirael van een Vloot Schepen | uyt de vereenichde Nederlanden: | Ende voorts vande nederlaghe aent Kasteel de Myna, | ob de kust van Guinea voorghevallen. | Alles ghestelt by een loof-waerdich Persoon die selfs alles ghesien, | ende met nauwe oplettinghe beschreven heeft. |

Tot Amsterdam, | *Voor Ian van Hilten, inde Beurs-straet inde twee* | *vergulde Wapen-ringhen.* | *Anno* 1626. | 4to, 8 l. 38699

Concerning this voyage *see* Asher, No. 108, Netscher, p. 20, *and* Trömel, No. 120.

LA MADELÈNE (H. de). Le Comte Gaston de Raousset-Boulbon, sa vie et ses aventures (d'après ses papiers et sa correspondance). Par Henry de La Madelène. *Alençon.* 1856. 12mo, pp. 162. + Seconde édition. *Paris: Poulet-Malassis.* 1859.

Relates to Mexico.

LAMADRID (G. A. de). Observaciones sobre las memorias postumas del Brigadier-General D. José M. Paz, por el General D. Gregorio Araoz de Lamadrid y otros gefes contemporaneos. *Buenos Aires.* 1855. 8vo, pp. 408. 38701

LA-MAR (J. de). Narracion biografica del Gran-Mariscal D. José de La-Mar, y de la translacion de sus restos mortales de la republica de Centro-America a la del Perú. Escribela por Manuel Vicense Villaran. *Lima.* 1847. 4to, pp. 184. 38702

LAMAR (L. Q. C.) Compilation of the Laws of Georgia, passed since 1810, to the year 1819, inclusive. By Lucius Q. C. Lamar. *Augusta.* 1821. 4to. C. 38703

LAMAR (M. B.) Letter of Gen. Mirabeau B. Lamar, Ex-President of Texas, on the Subject of Annexation, addressed to several Citizens of Macon, Geo. *Savannah: Printed by Thomas Purse.* 1844. 8vo, pp. 48. 38704

Also: Verse Memorials. ... *New York.* 1854. 8vo, pp. 224. + [*Ibid.*] 1857. C.

LAMAR. A Sketch of its Position, Advantages and Prospects, with a Map of the Adjacent Country. *New-York: Van Norden ... Printers.* 1853. 8vo, pp. 11. Map. BA. 38705

LAMARTINE (Alphonse de). Christophe Colomb. Par A. de Lamartine. (1436–1506). *Paris: L. Hachette et Cie.* 1853. 12mo, pp. (4), 149. B. + *Bruxelles.* 1853. 12mo. + *Paris: L. Hachette et Cie.* 1862. 12mo. + *Paris: Lévy frères.* 1864. 12mo. + *Paris: Labure.* 1867. 18mo, pp. 139. + Nouvelle édition. *Paris: Michel Lévy frères.* 1869. 18mo, pp. 311.

LAMARTINE. Life of Christopher Columbus. By Alphonse Lamartine. *New York: Delisser and Proctor.* [1859.] 18mo, pp. 236. B. 38707

LAMARTINE. Christophe Colomb (Cristobal Colon). Par A. de Lamartine. Traduccion española por don Pascual Hernandez,

con el texto frances y notas. *Paris: L. Hachette et Cie.* 1865. 12mo, pp. 216. 38708

LAMARTINE. Memoirs of Celebrated Characters. By Alphonse de Lamartine. ... *New York: Harper & Brothers.* 1854–1856. 3 vols., 12mo, pp. 437; 406; 323. + Second Edition. *London: Richard Bentley.* 1854–1858. 3 vols., post 8vo. C. + Third Edition. [*Ibid.*] 1858. 3 vols., post 8vo, pp. xxi, 430; 459; 386. 38709

Includes Christopher Columbus.

LAMARTINE. Toussaint Louverture; poème dramatique de l'émancipation des esclaves. Par A. de Lamartine. *Paris: Lévy frères.* 1850. 8vo. + [*Ibid.*] 1854. 12mo. + [*Ibid.*] 1857. 12mo. + *Paris.* 1865. A., P. 38710

LA MARTINIÈRE. *See* Bruzen de La Martinière, Vol. III.

There is another edition, *Amsterdam,* MDCCXXXV; also *Amsterdam: Zacharie Chatelain* MDCCXXXVIII. 2 vols., 12mo, pp. (16), 504, (2); 426, (2). 6 Maps. The author's introduction to the "Histoire générale de l'Univers, par M. de Grace," contains a history of the Discovery and Conquest of America by the French.

LA MARTINIÈRE (Pierre Martin de). [Engraved Title:] Voyage | Des Païs | Septentrionavx | Par le Sr. D. L. M. | *A Paris* | *Chez Louis Vandosme proche* | *Monseig*r. *le Premier President.* | *G. Ladame.* [Printed Title:] Voyage | des Pays | Septentrionavx. | Dans lequel se void les mœurs, maniere de vivre, & superstitions des Norwegiuens, Lap- | pons, Kiloppes, Borandiens, | Syberiens, Samojedes, Zem- | bliens, Islandois. | Par le sieur de La Martiniere. | *A Paris,* | *Chez Louis Vendosme* ... 1671. | Avec Privilege dv Roi. | 12mo, pp. (16), 201. + Seconde Edition, revuë & augmentée | de nouveau. [*Ibid.*] 1676. 12mo, pp. (12), 322, (2). + *Paris.* 1682. 12mo. 38711

LA MARTINIÈRE. De | Noordsche Weereld; | Vertoond | In twee nieuwe, aenmercklijcke, derwaerts gedaene Reysen: | D'eene, van de Heer | Martiniere, | Door Noorweegen, Lapland, Boranday, Siberien, Samojessie, Ys-land, Groen- | land en Nova-Zembla: Met de Beschrijvingh van der Inwoonderen | Seden, Gewoonten, Overgeloven, Gestalte, Dragten, en | Huysen: De Koophandel, met haer gedreven: En dwa- | lingh der Weereld-beschrijvers, soo in de plaetsingh | als uytstreckingh van Groenland en Zembla. | D'andere, van de Hamburger | Frederick Martens, | Verright nae Spitsbergen, of Groenland, in't Jaer 1671. Met nauwkeurige | Aenteeckeningh van de gelegenheyd deses Lands, en desselven uy- | terste Deelen: Van de Zee; 't Ys; de Lught, de daer was-

sende | Kruyden; de sigh daer onthoudende Voge- | len, Dieren, Visschen, Walvisschen en Zee-qualmen. | Vertaeld, en doorgaens met toe-doeningen verrijckt, | Door | S. de Vries. | Met een goed getal nae't leven afgeteeckende Figueren. | *t'Amsteldam,* | *By Aert Dircksz.Ooszaen, Boeckverkoper op* | *den Dam.* M. DC. LXXXV. | 4to, two Titles, one of which is engraved, pp. (12), 334, (18). A.

[LA MARTINIÈRE.] A New | Voyage | into the | Northern Countries | Being a Discription [*sic*] of the Manners, | Customs, Superstition, Buildings, | and Habits of the Norwegians, La- | ponians, Kilops, Borandians, Sib- | erians, Samojedes, Zemblans and Islanders. | With Reflexions upon an Error in | our Geographers about the scitua- | tion and extent of Greenland and | Nova Zembla. | *London* | *Printed for John Starkey, at the Miter* | *in Fleetstreet near Temple-* | *Bar.* 1674. | 12mo, pp. (10), 153. 38713

[LA MARTINIÈRE.] A New Voyage to the North: containing a full account of Norway, the Laplands, both Danish, Swedish, and Muscovite; of Borandia, Siberia, Samogedia, Zembla, and Iseland. To which is added, a particular relation of the Court of the Czar; of the Religion and Customs of the Muscovites; and a short History of Muscovy, as it was taken by a French Gentleman who resided there many years. Now done into English. *London: T. Hodgson.* 1706. 12mo, pp. (14), 258. Plate.

[LA MARTINIÈRE.] Neue Reise in die nordischen Landschafften. Das ist: eine Beschreibung der Sitten, Gebräuche, Aberglauben, Gebäuden, und Kleidung der Norweger, Lapländer, Killopen, Borandianer, Siberianer, Samojeden, Zemblaner und Eisländer, sampt einem Bedencken über den Irrthum unser Erdbeschreiber, wo nemlich Grönland und Nova Zembla liegen, und wie weit sie sich erstrecken. Aus dem Englischen ins Deutsche übersetzet durch I. Langen. *Hamburg: Nauman & Wolff.* 1675. 4to, pp. (8), 80. + *Leipzig.* 1718. 38715

LA MARTINIÈRE. Nouveau Voyage vers le Septentrion. Où l'on représente le naturel, les coutumes, et la religion des Norwegiens, des Lapons, des Kiloppes, des Russiens, des Bourandiens, des Syberiens, des Zembliens, des Samoiedes ... . *A Amsterdam. Aux dépens d'Estienne Roger* ... MDCCVIII. 12mo, pp. 321, (14). 16 Plates. 38716

The last chapter contains some reflections upon the mistake of the geographers relative to the position of Nova Zembla, Greenland, etc.

LAMAS (A.) Andrés Lamas a sus compatriotas. [n. p.] 1855. 8vo, pp. 138. 38717

LAMAS. Colleccion de Memorias y Documentos para la Historia y la Jeografia de los Pueblos del Rio de la Plata, por Andrés Lamas. Tomo primero. *Montevideo.* 1849. 4to, pp. 670.

No more published—of much rarity.

LAMAS. Negocíaciones entre la República Oriental del Uruguay y el Imperio del Brasil sobre máterias de comercio y de navegacion 1856–1858. Documentos publicados, con autorizacion de su gobierno por D. Andrés Lamas ... . *Rio de Janeiro.* 1858. 4to, pp. 280. 38719

Also: Documentos Diplomáticos relativos a la Detencion del Pagnete Argentino "Salto" en las aguas de la República Oriental del Uruguay por el vopor de Guerra Nacional Villa del Salto. ... *Montevideo.* 1863. 8vo, pp. 124.—Documentos oficiales, relativos a los incidentes ocurridos del 28 de Agosta al 1 de Setiembre ultimos, con motivo de la presencia de la Escuadras de la Confederacion Argentina y de la Provincia de Buenos Aires, en el Puerto de Montevideo. ... *Montevideo.* 1859. 8vo, pp. 50.—Notice sur la République Orientale de l'Uruguay. Documents de statistique concernant sa population indigène et exotique et le développement de sa richesse; accompagnés de quelques considérations relatives aux questions politiques et internationales qui s'agitent au Rio de la Plata. Traduite de l'espagnol. *Paris: Guillaumin.* 1851. 8vo, pp. xxx, 60.—Tentativas para la pacificacion de la República Oriental del Uruguay, 1863–1865. ... *Buenos Aires.* 1865. 8vo, pp. 68.

LAMB (D.) Complete List of Congregational Ministers and Churches in Madison Co., Vt. By Rev. Dana Lamb. *Boston.* 1839. 8vo. 38720

LAMB (E. E.) Sermon on the Death of President Lincoln, preached in ... Rootstown, By Rev. E. E. Lamb. ... April 23, 1865. [n. p. n. d.] 8vo, pp. 14. 38721

LAMB (F.) Astroscepium; or, Two Hemispheres. *London.* 1573. 38722

LAMB (R.) Memoir of His Own Life, by R. Lamb; formerly a Serjeant in the Royal Welch Fuzileers ... . *Dublin: Printed by J. Jones.* 1811. 8vo, pp. 296. B. 38723

Gives an account of American affairs during the Revolutionary War.

LAMB. An Original and Authentic Journal of Occurrences during the late American War, from its Commencement to the year 1783. By R. Lamb, late Serjeant in the Royal Welch Fuzileers. *Dublin: Wilkinson & Courtney.* 1809. 8vo, pp. iv, xxiv, 5–438. B. 38724

Originally published in eleven parts. The author went to America in 1776, a non-commissioned officer in the ninth regiment of foot, and served until the peace, when he returned to his native country, Ireland, and became a schoolmaster. He undertook this work because he had seen no "impartial detail of the more minute, but no less important occurrences of the war, which, as secret springs, actuated the public movements, and which were never any further disclosed to the world, but as comprised in the general result."

LAMBARDO (F. M.) Memoria de Hacienda durante el Tiempo en que F. M. Lambardo. *Mexico.* 1840. 4to. 38725

LAMBERT (A. B.) A Description of the Genus Pinus, with directions relative to the Cultivation, and remarks on the uses of the several Species: also description of many other new Species of the Family of Coniferæ. By Aylmer Bourke Lambert, ... *London: Messrs. Weddell.* 1832. 2 vols., 8vo, pp. viii, (2), 75, 44 Plates and Portrait; (2), 107, (77–183), (4), 33 Plates. C.

LAMBERT. A Description of the Genus Pinus, illustrated with Figures; Directions relative to the Cultivation, ... By Aylmer Bourke Lambert, ... *London: George White.* 1837–38. 3 vols., folio. 112 Plates. A. 38727

This edition was enlarged by Don. Many of the species described are American.

LAMBERT. An Illustration of the Genus Cinchona; comprising Descriptions of all the Officinal Peruvian Barks, including several New Species. Baron De Humboldt's Account of the Cinchona Forests of South America: and Lambert's Memoir on the Different Species of Quinquina. To which are added, several Dissertations of Don Hippolito Ruiz, on various Medicinal Plants of South America. With Several Plates. And a short account of the Spikenard of the Ancients, with a Plate. By Aylmer Bourke Lambert, Esq. ... *London: John Searle.* 1821. 4to, pp. ix, (1), 185. 5 Plates. 38728

[LAMBERT (Claude François).] A Collection of Curious Observations on the Manners, Customs, Usages, Languages, Ceremonies, Religion, Medicine, Physics, Natural History, Commerce, &c., Of the several Nations of Asia, Africa, and America, Translated from the French, first printed at Paris in 1749, By John Dunn. *London: Printed for the Translator.* M DCC L. 2 vols., 8vo, pp. vi, 411; (2), 404, (16). C. 38729

A somewhat scarce and very interesting privately printed book, chiefly relating to the aboriginal inhabitants of America.

LAMBERT. Curious Observations upon the Manners, Customs, Usages, different Languages, Government, Mythology, Chronology, Antient and Modern Geography, Ceremonies, Religion, Mechanics, Astronomy, Medicine, Physics, Natural History, Commerce, Arts and Sciences, of the several Nations of Asia, Africa and America. Translated from the French of M. L'Abbé Lambert. *London: G. Woodfall.* [1751.] 2 vols., 8vo, pp. (2), iv, 411; (2), vi, 404, (16). + *London: Lockyer Davis.* 1755. 2 vols., 8vo, pp. xii, (4), 260; (2), 251, (18). + [*Ibid.*] 1760. 2 vols., 8vo. 38730

LAMBERT. Histoire Générale, Civile, Naturelle, Politique, et Religieuse de tous les Peuples du Monde ... . *Paris.* 1750. 14 vols., 12mo. S. 38731

LAMBERT (E. R.) History of the Colony of New Haven, before and after the Union with Connecticut. Containing a particular description of the towns which composed that Government, viz., New Haven, Milford, Guilford, Branford, Stamford, & Southold, L. I. With a Notice of the towns which have been set off from "The Original Six." Illustrated by Fifty Engravings. By Edward R. Lambert. *New Haven: Hitchcock & Stafford.* 1838. 12mo, pp. 216. Map. B. 38732

LAMBERT (Gillaume). Voyage dans l'Amérique du Nord, en 1853 et 1854, avec notes sur les expositions universelles de Dublin et de New York. *Bruxelles.* 1855. 2 vols., rl. 8vo, and Atlas of Maps. 38733

LAMBERT (J.) Travels through Lower Canada, and the United States of North America, in the Years 1806, 1807, and 1808. To which are added, Biographical Notices and Anecdotes of some of the leading Characters in the United States; and of those who have, at various Periods, borne a conspicuous Part in the Politics of that Country, By John Lambert. With Engravings. *London: Richard Phillips.* 1810. 3 vols., 8vo, pp. xxiv, 496; ix, (1), 494; (2), 506. 18 Plates and Map. B. + Second Edition. *London.* 1813. 2 vols., 8vo. C. + Third Edition, Corrected and Improved. *London: Baldwin, Cradock, and Joy.* 1816. 2 vols., 8vo, pp. xxxiv, (1), 544; viii, 532. 18 Plates.

See "M. Rev.," New Series, LXXIV. 238.

LAMBERT (M.) Letter from M. Lambert, Comptroller General of the French Finances, to Mr. Jefferson, Minister Plenipotentiary for the United States of America at the Court of Versailles; with an arret of the King's Council of State, for the encouragement of the Commerce of France with the United States of America. Both dated Dec. 29, 1787, and published by authority in France. *London: J. Johnson.* 1788. 4to, pp. 4, 8.

LAMBERT (N.) A Sermon before Isaac Tichenor, Governor, the Council, etc. of Vermont, October 8, 1801, at Newbury, it being General Election. By Rev. Nathaniel Lambert. *Windsor: Alden Spooner.* 1801. 8vo. 38736

LAMBERT (T. R.) Discourse delivered on The National Fast Day, January 4, 1861, in St. John's Church, Charlestown, By

the Rev. Thomas R. Lambert, M.A. *Charlestown: William H. D' Costa, Printer.* 1861. 8vo, pp. 16. 38737

LAMBERT (W.) Abstracts of Calculations, to ascertain the Longitude of the Capitol, in the City of Washington, from Greenwich Observatory, in England. By William Lambert. *Washington City: Printed by Edward de Krafft.* 1817. 4to, pp. 20.

LAMBERT. A Collection of Precedents, consisting of Proceedings and Decisions on Questions of Order and Appeals in the House of Representatives ... By William Lambert. *Washington City.* 1811. 8vo. C., N. 38739

Also: Message from the President ... transmitting a Report of William Lambert, on ... the Longitude of the Capitol of the United States, January 9, 1822. ... *Washington: Printed by Gales* ... . 1822. 8vo, pp. 81. B.

LAMBERT LILLY, *pseudon.* The History of New England, illustrated by Tales, Sketches and Anecdotes. *Philadelphia: Key, Mielke and Biddle.* 1831. 24mo, pp. 184. 38740

See also [Hawks (F. L.)], Vol. VIII., No. 30964.

LAMBERTIE (C. de). Voyage pittoresque en Californie et au Chili. Par Charles de Lambertie. *Paris.* 1854. 8vo. 38741

LAMBERTY (L. B. T. de). Memoires pour Servir a l'Histoire du xviii Siècle, Contenant les Negociations, Traitez, Resolutions, et Autres Documens Authentiques Concernant les Affairs d'Etat; liez par une narration historique. Par L. B. T. de Lamberty. *La Haye et Amsterdam.* 1724–40. 14 vols., 4to. S. + Seconde Edition. *A La Haye: Henri Scheurleer.* MDCCXXXI–M.DCC.XL. 14 vols., 4to. + *Amsterdam et Leipzig.* 1740–57. 14 vols., 4to.

Highly praised by Lord Mahon. It includes many articles concerning the diplomatic relations of America.

LAMBIRTH (T. H. B.) Life of T. H. Bowden Lambirth (native of Boston), one of the largest men in the World. [n. p. 1822.] 8vo. 38743

LAMBLY (*Capt.* John). Sailing Directions for the River St. Lawrence, from Cape Chat to the Island of Bic ... *Quebec.* 1808.

LAMBRECHTSEN (N. C.) Korte Beschrijving van de ondekking en der verdere lotgevallen van Nieuw-Nederland, weleer eene volkplanting van het gemeenebest der vereenigde Nederlanden in America, door Mr. N. C. Lambrechtsen van Ritthem, ... *Te Middelburg, bij S. Van Benthem.* MDCCCXVIII. 8vo, pp. (4), 102. Map. 38745

The object of this work is to give a concise account of the discovery and subsequent history of the colony of New-Netherlands, until its final cession to Great Britain in 1674. A map from Montanus is annexed, with the original Indian and Dutch names inserted. There are copies on thick writing paper. *See* "N. A. Rev.," XX. 77, *also* "N. Y. Hist. Soc. Coll.," Second Series, I.

[LAMBTON (J. G.)] Report on the Affairs of British North America, from the Earl of Durham, Her Majesty's High Commissioner, &c. &c. &c. (Officially communicated to both Houses of the Imperial Parliament, on the 11th of February, 1839.) *Montreal.* 1839. 8vo, pp. 126, (1). B. + *Toronto: Printed by Robert Stanton.* MDCCCXXXIX. 8vo, pp. 142, iv. B. 38746

[LAMBTON.] Report on the Affairs of British North America, from the Earl of Durham, Her Majesty's High Commissioner, &c. &c. &c. (Presented by Her Majesty's Command.) Ordered by the House of Commons to be Printed, 11 February, 1839. *London.* 1839. Folio, pp. 119, Appendix A, pp. 62, Appendix B, pp. 218. 38747

[LAMBTON.] The Report and Despatches of the Earl of Durham, Her Majesty's High Commissioner and Governor-General of British North America. *London: Ridgway.* MDCCCXXXIX. 8vo, pp. xvi, 423. B. + *Montreal.* 1839. 8vo.

[LAMBTON.] Rapport de Lord Durham, Haut-Commissaire de Sa Majesté, etc. sur les affaires de l'Amérique Septentrionale Britannique. *Québec.* 1840. 8vo, pp. 78. 38749

[LAMBTON.] Facts versus Lord Durham. Remarks upon that portion of Durham's Report, relating to Prince Edward's Island, showing the fallacy of the statements contained therein. To which is added, a tabular view of the British Provinces in North America, shewing their Territorial Extent, the Acres under Cultivation, and their comparative Population. By a Proprietor. *London.* 1839. 8vo, pp. 21, (1). 38750

[LAMBTON.] Report from the Select Committee, of the Legislative Council of Upper Canada: on the Report of the Right Honourable the Earl of Durham, Her Majesty's late Governor-in-Chief of British North America. ... [*Toronto:*] *R. Stanton, Printer.* MDCCCXXXIX. 8vo, pp. 25. 38751

Also: Canadian Crisis and Lord Durham's Mission to the North American Colonies. *London.* 1838. 8vo.—Letter to Viscount Melbourne on the Ordinance of the Earl of Durham. By a Commoner. *London.* 1839. 8vo, pp. 32. *See* [Haliburton (T. C.)], Vol. VII., No. 29693.

LAME (J. S.) Maryland Slavery and Maryland Chivalry, containing the letters of "Junius" originally published in Zion's Herald. By Rev. J. S. Lame. *Philadelphia: Collins.* 1858. 8vo, pp. 59. 38752

Lamentacion de Puben, escrita y dedicada en Quito en 1820 a una sensible y respetable quitena por un puberiano o popayanez. *Bogotá.* 1822. 4to, pp. 20. 38753

Lamentacion juridica, que la Provincia de Carmeritas Descalzos de Indias hace al Capitulo General de la misma Religion por mano de los dos Procuradores de dicha Provincia. [n. p. n. d.] Folio, pp. 96. 38754

The Lamentations of a Sow, on a late Thanksgiving-Day, at Danbury, in Connecticut. [A Poem. n. p.] 1778. P. 38755

LAMERCIER (N. L.) Christophe Colomb, Comedie Historique, par N. Louis Lamercier. *Paris.* 1809. 8vo. 38756

L'Americana Ramminga cioe Memorie di Donna Innez di Quebrada scritta da lei stessa. *Venezia.* 1763. 2 vols., 8vo.

L'Amérique, d'après les voyageurs les plus célèbres. Par un homme de lettres. Deuxième édition. *Lille: L. Lefort.* 1852. 12mo, pp. 190, (1). 38758

L'Amérique Délivrée. Esquisse d'un Poēme sur l'Independance de l'Amérique. *Amsterdam: Chez J. A. Crajenschot.* 1783. 8vo, pp. xxiv, 292. 38759

The dedication to John Adams is signed "L. C. D. L. A."

L'Amériquiade. Poème. *Philadelphia.* [*Amsterdam?*] 1780. 8vo, pp. 22. 38760

Poetical description of the American war; very rare. Unknown to Barbier. Signed R****, and probably printed in Holland.

LAMIRANDE (Ernest Sureau). Return Respecting the Extradition of Lamirande from Canada. *Ottawa: Hunter, Rose & Co.* 1868. 8vo, pp. 164. C. 38761

LAMIRAL (M.) M. Lamiral, Réfuté par lui-même, ou Réponse aux opinions de cet auteur, sur l'Abolition de la Traité des Noirs. *Paris.* 1790. 8vo. C., P. 38762

LAMMENS (——). Intérêts des Colonies hollandaises du Sud de l'Amérique. Relativement aux troubles actuels des Colonies de l'Amérique septentrionale. *La Haye.* 1776. 8vo. 38763

Also: Sterfte der Slaven in Suriname. ... [n. p.] 1818. 8vo.

LAMON (Ward H.) Marshal of the District of Columbia. [*Washington.* 1862.] 8vo, pp. 18. 38764

LAMONT (*Mrs.* Eneas). Poems and Tales in Verse. *New York.* 1819. 8vo. 38765

LAMONT (G. D.) Oration delivered by George D. Lamont, at the City of Lockport, July 4th, 1865. *Lockport, N. Y.: Henry Shaft, Printer.* 1865. 8vo, pp. 25. 38766

LAMONT. Report of Mr. Lamont in relation to the Personal Liberty Bill. [n. p.] 1859. 8vo, pp. 18. 38767

LAMONT (J.) Seasons with the Sea-Horses; or, Sporting Adventures in the Northern Seas. By James Lamont, Esq. *New York.* 1861. 8vo, pp. 282. Map and Plates. + *London: Hurst* ... 1861. 8vo, pp. xii, (2), 312. Map and Plates. BA.

LA MORANDIÈRE. *See* Turmeau de la Morandière.

LAMOTHE (G.) Investigation of the Police Committee of the City Council of Montreal into the Charges preferred by Councillor B. Devlin against Guillaume Lamothe, Esq., Chief of Police, and the Proceedings of the Council in reference thereto. *Montreal.* 1864. 8vo. 38769

The Lamplighter. *See* [Cummins (Maria S.)], No. 17935.

LAMPORT (W.) Cursory Remarks on the Importance of Agriculture in its connection with Manufactures and Commerce. By William Lamport. *London.* 1784. 8vo. 38770

Refers to the cultivation of land, and increase of trade with America.

LAMPREDI (——). Du Commerce des Neutres en temps de guerre. Traduite de l'italien, par J. Peuchet. *Paris.* 1802. 8vo, pp. 527. 38771

LAMSON (A.) Congregationalism. A Discourse ... before the Massachusetts Convention of Congregational Ministers, Boston, May 28, 1846. By Alvan Lamson, D.D. *Boston: Wm. Crosby* ... . 1846. 8vo, pp. 30. B. 38772

LAMSON. A History of the First Church and Parish in Dedham, In Three Discourses, ... delivered ... November 18, 1838 ... . By Alvin Lamson, D.D. *Dedham: Printed by Herman Mann.* 1839. 8vo, pp. 104. B., S. 38773

LAMSON. A Sermon preached October 31, 1858, the Sunday after the Fortieth Anniversary of his Ordination. By Alvan Lamson, D.D. *Boston: Crosby* ... . 1859. 8vo, pp. 63. 38774

LAMSON. Sermons. By Alvan Lamson, D.D. *Boston: Crosby, Nichols and Company.* 1857. 12mo, pp. vii, 424. BA. 38775

[LAMSON.] A Statement of the Proceedings in the First Church and Parish in Dedham, respecting the Settlement of a Minister, 1818. *Cambridge: Hilliard & Metcalf.* 1819. 8vo, pp. 102. C. 38776

Also: Agricultural Life in some of its intellectual Aspects. An Address ... before the Norfolk Agricultural Society, at Dedham, September 30, 1857. ... *Boston: J. M. Hewes, Printer.* 1857. 8vo, pp. 20.—A Discourse ... at the Dedication of the Bethlehem Church, ... Augusta, Maine, October 18, 1827. ... *Augusta: Printed by Eaton* ... 1827. 12mo, pp. 32.—A Discourse ... at Dedham, May 14, 1841 ... National Fast, on Occasion of the Death of William Henry Harrison ... . *Dedham: H. Mann ... Printer.* 1841. 8vo, pp. 23.—A Discourse ... in Dedham, October 20, 1850 ... after the Funeral of Mrs. Mary Dean ... . *Boston: Printed by Damrell* ... . 1851. 8vo, pp. 15. BA.—A Discourse ... at Dedham, June 14, 1857 ... after the Funeral of Mary Elizabeth Fisher. ... *Boston: Crosby* ... . 1857. 8vo, pp. 21. BA.—A Discourse ... at Dedham, July 19, 1857 ... after the Funeral of Annie Rebecca Farrington. ... *Dedham: Printed by Cox* ... . 1857. 8vo, pp. 16.—A Discourse ... at West Dedham, February 4, 1852, at the Funeral of the Rev. John White ... . *Boston: Crosby* ... . 1851. 8vo, pp. 23.—A Discourse ... February 8th, 1857, after the Funeral of Hon. John Endicott. ... *Boston: Crosby* ... . 1857. 8vo, pp. 24.—A Discourse on the Life and Character of Hon. James Richardson, delivered ... in Dedham, June 27, 1858. ... *Boston: Crosby* ... . 1858. 8vo, pp. 29. B.—A Discourse ... October 28, 1860, on Resigning the Pastoral Charge of the First ... Parish in Dedham ... . *Boston: Walker* ... 1860. 8vo, pp. 30.—A Sermon ... in Dedham, January 10, 1847 ... after the death of Ebenezer Fisher, Jr. ... *Boston: Printed by ... Coolidge.* 1847. 8vo, pp. 19.—... A Sermon, at the Ordination of the Rev. Charles C. Sewall, ... in Danvers, April 11, 1827. ... Second Edition. *Boston: Bowles and Dearborn.* 1827. 12mo, pp. 36. BA.—The Memory of John Robinson: A Discourse ... at Dedham ... Dec. 21, 1851. ... *Boston: Crosby* ... . 1852. 8vo, pp. 40.—The Validity of Congregational Ordination. ... Dudleian Lecture, May 14, 1834. ... [n. p. n. d.] 8vo, pp. 26. BA.

LAMSON (David R.) Two Years' Experience among the Shakers, being a Description of the Manners and Customs of that People, the Nature and Policy of their Government ... . *West Boylston: ... the author.* 1848. 12mo, pp. 212. Plates. C.

LAMSON (W.) A Centennial Discourse delivered on the One Hundredth Anniversary of the Formation of the Baptist Church, Newton, N. H., October 18, 1855. By William Lamson ... . *Portsmouth: C. W. Brewster & Son,* ... 1856. 16mo, pp. 62.

LAMSON. God Hiding Himself in Times of Trouble. A Sermon preached in Brookline, Mass., April 2, 1863. By Rev. William Lamson. *Boston: Gould & Lincoln.* 1863. 8vo, pp. 26.

Lamson. Portsmouth: its Advantages and Needs. A Thanksgiving Sermon, preached November 30, 1854. By William Lamson. *Portsmouth.* 1855. 8vo, pp. 23. 38780

Lamzweerde (St. à). Mare undique apertum, vel terra in omni parte circumnavigabilis. *Tielae.* 1756. 8vo. 38781

A La Nacion Española el Pensador del Peru. *Lima.* 1814. 4to. 38782

On the first attempts at emancipation in South America.

Lancaster (D.) The History of Gilmanton, embracing the Proprietary, Civil, Literary, Ecclesiastical, Biographical Genealogical, and Miscellaneous History, from the First Settlement to the Present Time; including what is now Gilford, to the time it was Disannexed. By Daniel Lancaster. *Gilmanton: Printed by Alfred Prescott.* 1845. 8vo, pp. viii, 13–304. Map.

Lancaster. A Sermon ... April 21, 1850, at the Funeral of Rev. William Cogswell, D.D. ... By Rev. Daniel Lancaster ... *Concord: Printed by McFarland* ... . [n. d.] 8vo, pp. 20. B.

Lancaster (Joseph). The British System of Education ... [and] Report of the Lancaster School, Georgetown. *Washington.* 1812. 16mo. 38785

Lancaster. Epitome of ... the Chief Events ... in the Life of Joseph Lancaster ... written by Himself ... . *New-Haven: For the Author.* 1833. 8vo, pp. 56. B. 38786

Lancaster. Letters on National Subjects, auxiliary to Universal Education ... addressed to ... Henry Clay ... and James Munroe ... . By Joseph Lancaster ... . *Washington City: For the Author.* 1820. 8vo, pp. (4), 60. BA. 38787

Lancaster, *Mass.* Account of the Proceedings at the Inauguration of the State Industrial School for Girls, Lancaster, Aug. 27, 1856. *Boston.* 1856. 8vo, pp. 63. M. 38788

An Address commemorative of the Two Hundredth Anniversary of the Incorporation of Lancaster, Massachusetts. With an Appendix. *Boston: Printed by John Wilson & Son.* 1853. 8vo, pp. viii, 230. 38789

Addresses ... at the Dedication of Lancaster Memorial Hall. *Boston.* 1868. 8vo. s. 38790

Catalogue of Lancaster Town Library. *Clinton [Mass.]: W. J. Coulter.* 1868. 16mo, pp. (4), 108, 31. c. 38791

The Lancaster Almanack; for ... 1776. By Anthony Sharp. *Lancaster: Francis Bailey.* [n. d.] 12mo, 18 l. 38792

The Almanac was first published in 1744.

Lancaster, *Pa.* At a Meeting of the Committee of Inspection, Observation and Correspondence, of the County of Lancaster. ... Committee-Chamber, Lancaster, June 5th, 1775. Folio, 1 l. 38793

Call for a union of the minor committees of the county.

Directory of the City of Lancaster, with Business Directory. 1868–9. *New York: Webb & Fitzgerald.* 1868. 8vo, pp. 144, 24.

Freyheits Brief der Deutschen Hohen Schule (College) in der Stadt Lancaster, im Staate Pennsylvaniën. *Philadelphia.* 1787. 8vo. P. 38795

Lancaster, Harrisburg, Lebanon, and York Directory for 1863–64. *Jersey City: James Gopsill.* 1864. 12mo, pp. 379.

Lancaster Co., *Pa.* Boyd's Lancaster County Business Directory. 1859–60. Compiled by William H. Boyd. *Lancaster (Penn.): Sprenger & Westhaeffer.* [1859.] 12mo, pp. (40), 41–316. Continued. 38797

Also: Directory of Lancaster County: ... 1869–70. *Lancaster (Pa.): Barnes & Pearsol.* 1869. 8vo. Continued.

Lancaster County, to wit: To the Electors of the Borough and County of Lancaster. ... Frederick Stone, Sheriff. January 8th, 1773. *Lancaster: Printed by Francis Bailey.* [n. d.] Folio, 1 l.

Neuer Lancästerscher Calender. *Lancaster, Pa.* 1796. 4to. Continued. s. 38799

Narrative of the ... Massacre. *See* [Franklin (B.)], Vol. VII.

The so-called Lancaster Massacre is one in which the Indians were massacred by the white population. It elicited a heated controversy in the shape of about ten pamphlets, which are in this Dictionary described under various headings, all being anonymous. *See* Cloven Foot, Conduct of the Paxton-Men, [Franklin (B.)], Plain Dealer, Positive, *pseudon.*, Quakerism Unmasked, Quakers Vindicated, Remonstrance, *and* Serious Address.

Report of the Managers of the Lancaster and Schuylkill Bridge Company ... March 3, 1814. *Philadelphia.* 1814. 8vo, pp. 15. Plate. P. 38800

State of the Accounts of the late Lieutenant and Sub-Lieutenants of Lancaster County, ... 1777, to ... 1780. ... *Philadelphia: Printed by John Dunlap.* M,DCC,LXXXIII. 8vo, pp. 77.

Also: State of the Accounts of Adam Orth, Esq. late Sub-Lieutenant ... Aug. 1778, to March 1780 ... . *Philadelphia: Printed by F. Bailey.* M,DCC,LXXXIV. 8vo, pp. 23.—State of the Accounts ... to the 20th of March 1780. ... *Philadelphia: Printed by Robert Aitken.* M,DCC,LXXXV. 8vo, pp. 7.—State of the Accounts of the Lieutenant and Sub-Lieutenants ... 1780 to ... 1781. ... *Philadelphia: Printed by Robert Aitken.* M,DCC,LXXXV. 8vo, pp. 46.—State of the Accounts of the Lieutenant and Sub-Lieutenants ... 1783. ... *Philadelphia: Printed by Robert Aitken.* M,DCC,LXXXV. 8vo, pp. 48.—State of the Accounts of James Ross, Esquire, Lieutenant ... to ... 1785. ... *Philadelphia: Printed by Robert Aitken.* M,DCC,LXXXV. 8vo, pp. 4.—State of the Accounts of Joshua Elder, Esquire ... . *Philadelphia: Printed by Robert Aitken.* M,DCC,LXXXV. 8vo, pp. 12. P.—State of the Accounts of Adam Hubley, Esquire ... . *Philadelphia: Printed by Robert Aitken.* M.DCC.LXXXVI. 8vo, pp. 3. P.

State of the Accounts of the Collectors of Excise, for Lancaster County ... . *Philadelphia: Printed by Hall and Sellers.* M,DCC,LXXXIII. 8vo, pp. 11. P. 38802

Also: State of the Accounts of William Hay, Esq. Collector of Excise ... 1782, to ... 1783. ... *Philadelphia: Printed by F. Bailey.* MDCCLXXXIV [for 1784]. 8vo, pp. 11.—State of the Accounts of George Graff, Esq. Collector of Excise, ... to the 2d of August, 1784. *Philadelphia: Printed by John Steele.* M,DCC,LXXXV. 8vo, pp. 6. + From the 2d of August 1784, to the 6th of August 1785. *Philadelphia: Printed by Robert Aitken.* M,DCC,LXXXVI. 8vo, pp. 9.—State of the Accounts of Samuel Turbett, Esquire, ... 1786. *Philadelphia: Printed by Robert Aitken.* M.DCC.LXXXVI. 8vo, pp. 4. + From 25th February, till 21st Sept. 1786. [*Ibid.*] 8vo, pp. 9. P.

The Voice of Lancaster County upon the subject of a National Foundry. *Lancaster.* 1839. 8vo. P. 38803

Lancaster, *Wis.* First Annual Catalogue of the Lancaster Institute, 1859. *Lancaster.* 1859. 8vo. 38804

Lance (W.) An Eulogium on ... Hon. Theodore Gaillard, ... of South Carolina, delivered, ... May 19, 1829. By William Lance. *Charleston: Printed by W. Riley.* 1829. 8vo, pp. 26.

Lance. Georgii Washingtonis Vita. Cura W. Lance. [1[a] pars, ad 1777.] *Carolopoli, in Carolina Australi: D. J. Dowling.* 1836. 12mo, pp. xi, 75. Portrait. c. 38806

Also: An Oration ... on the Fourth of July, 1820 ... . *Charleston: Printed by A. E. Miller.* 1820. 8vo, pp. 26. BA.

Lance (W.) Indian, Colonial, and United States Securities—Statement of Accounts. By W. Lance. *London.* 1857.

La Lanceta. Diario satirico-burlesco. *Buenos Aires.* 1853.

Each number has four pages.

Lancey (S. H.) The Native Poets of Maine. By S. Herbert Lancey. ... *Bangor: David Bugbee & Co.* 1854. 8vo, pp. xii, 324. 38809

Lanciego y Eguilaz (Joseph de, *Arçobispo de Mexico*). Carta pastoral que escribe â sus amadas hijas las religiossas de toda su filiacion. *Mexico, herederos de la viuda de M. de Ribera.* 1716. 18mo, 1 p. l., 46 l. c. 38810

Lanciego y Eguilaz. Oraciones Funerales en Exequias del Dr. Fr. Jos. de Lanciego y Eguilaz, 1 y 2, de Marzo 1728. *Mexico.* 1728. 4to. 38811

Lanctot (Mederic). Indépendance pacifique du Canada. *Montréal.* 1867. 8vo. 38812

[Lancy (J. de).] *See* [De Lancy (J.)], Vol. v., No. 19346.

Land (T.) Letter to the Rev. Mr. Whitefield designed to correct his mistaken Account of Regeneration, or the New Birth, written before his departure from London, and now published to prevent his doing mischief among the Common People upon his return to Georgia. *London.* 1739. 8vo. 38813

Land. Bounty Lands to the Surviving Officers of the late War, the Second of Independence, and to the Widows and Children of those who were killed in action or who died in service or subsequent to the War. *New York: W. Grattan.* 1826. 12mo.

Land Claims, &c. under Choctaw Treaty. pp. 54. Report, on the location of the Choctaw Claims. pp. 20. Choctaw Treaty claiming Babbit Creek, with Letters and Documents. pp. 179. *Washington.* 1841. 8vo. 38815

Land and Labor; their Relations in Nature, how violated by Monopoly. *Washington.* [n. d.] 8vo. + *New York.* [n. d.]

Land Laws of the United States. *Washington.* 1810. 8vo.

Land-Office ... communicating the Annual Report of the Commissioner of the General Land-Office, Dec. 13, 1847. [n. p. n. d.] 8vo, pp. 230. s. 38818

With surveys in Indiana, Northern Michigan, Iowa, Wisconsin, Arkansas, Tennessee, Louisiana, Alabama, and map of Florida.

Report ... Appropriations of Public Land for the Purposes of Education. [n. p.] 1821. 8vo. s. 38819

Report of the Commissioner of the General Land Office for the year 1851. *Washington.* 1852. 8vo. Continued. 38819*a*

These reports include a vast amount of valuable information relative to the agricultural, mineral, and other resources of the United States. First issued about 1828.

Resolutions of Congress under the Confederation, Treaties, Proclamations, and other Documents having operation and respect to the Public Lands, collected, digested and arranged ... 1817. [n. p. n. d.] 8vo. 38820

The Land we Love. Edited by General D. H. Hill. *Charlotte, N. C.* 1867–68. 8vo. 38821

The Land Owner. A Journal of Real Estate. Devoted to landed Interests, Building and Improvement. [Monthly.] *Chicago: J. M. Wing & Co.* [1870.] 4to. 38822

The Land of Powhatan. By a Virginian. [A Poem.] *Baltimore: F. Lucas, Jr.* 1821. 18mo, pp. 120. 38823

Landa (Ambrosius Cerdan de). Tratado General sobre las aguas que fertilizan los valles de Lima publicado en el Mercurio Peruano. *Lima, en la Imprenta Real.* 1793. 4to, pp. 224. + *Reimpreso en el Callao: Estevan Dañino.* 1852. 4to, pp. 138.

Landa (C. de). Sobre el Sistema Prohibitivo Como Contrario al Interes Nacional bien entendido ó sea Refutacion de las Ideas del Siglo Diez y Neuve, Por Carlos de Landa. *Mexico.* 1843. 3 parts, 8vo, pp. 46. B. 38825

Landa (D. de). Relation des choses de Yucatan de Diego de Landa. Texte espagnol et traduction française en regard comprenant les signes du calendrier et de l'alphabet hiéroglyphique de la langue Maya accompagné de documents divers ... avec une Grammaire et un Vocabulaire abrégés Français-Maya ... Par ... Brasseur de Bourbourg ... . *Paris: Auguste Durand.* 1864. Rl. 8vo, pp. (4), cxii, 516. B. 38826

This volume, published from the manuscript preserved in the archives of the "Academia de la Historia," is one of the most important publications relating to America. The author was one of the first missionaries to Yucatan, became Bishop of Merida in 1573, and died in 1579. Forms Vol. III. of Brasseur de Bourbourg's "Coleccion." Three hundred copies printed. *See* Field, No. 175, *and* Leclerc's Catalogue, No. 205.

Landais (P.) Memorial, to justify Peter Landai's Conduct during the Late War. *Boston: Printed by Peter Edes.* M,DCC,-LXXXIV. 4to, pp. 115. BA. 38827

Landais. The Second Part of the Memorial to Justify Peter Landai's Conduct, during the Late War. *New-York: Printed by Samuel Loudon.* [1787?] 4to, pp. 52. BA. 38828

The author, a native of France, was appointed by Congress captain of the frigate Alliance, the finest vessel then in its service. He was with Paul Jones in the memorable action between the Serapis and the Bon Homme Richard, was dismissed from the service for questionable conduct in that affair, and wrote these answers to the following piece: "Charges and Proofs respecting the conduct of Peter Landais." He continued to press his claim for restoration to rank for nearly forty years.

Landais. Charges and Proofs respecting the Conduct of Peter Landais. *New-York: Printed by Francis Childs.* [1787.] 4to, pp. 18. BA. 38829

Lander (F. W.) Remarks on the Construction of a First-class Double-tract Railway to the Pacific. *Washington.* 1854. 8vo, pp. 14. 38830

Lander (F. W.) Biographical Sketch of Mrs. F. W. Lander. *Philadelphia.* 1867. 8vo. 38831

Lander (M. M.) Carta al Ciudadano Antonio Guzman Blanco. *Carácas.* 1865. 8vo, pp. 52. 38832

Lander (S.) Our own School Arithmetic. By S. Lander, A.M. *Greensboro, N. C.: Sterling, Campbell & Albright.* 1863. 12mo, pp. 282. 38833

This is a Confederate publication with some curious propositions.

Lander (Tomas). Los Tribunales de Commercio y la Constitucion. *Carácas.* 1837. 8vo, pp. 18. 38834

Landers (A.) Remarks on the Impolicy and Injustice of laying a Duty on Timber, imported from British America, or taking off the Baltic Duty. By Anthony Landers. *London.* 1821. 8vo. 38835

The Landing of the French Atlantic Cable at Duxbury, Mass., July, 1869. *Boston: Alfred Mudge & Son.* 1869. 8vo, pp. 57. Plates. 38836

Landis (R. W.) Bethlehem Church and its Pastor; a Narrative of Proceedings of the Rev. Messrs. Albert Barnes and H. W. Hunt, Senr., relative to the Pastor of this Church. *New York.* 1851. 8vo, pp. 216. 38837

Landis. Liberty's Triumph. A Poem. By Robert W. Landis. ... *New York: John Wiley.* 1849. 8vo, pp. xvii, 544.

Also: A Letter to the Rev. George Junkin, D.D., touching the Requirements of the Ninth Commandment. ... *Wilmington: Henry Eckel, Printer.* 1867. 8vo.

Landivar (Raphaele). Rusticatio Mexicana, seu rariora quædam ex agris mexicanis decerpta atque in libros decem distributa a R. Landivar. *Mutinæ, apud Societatem Typographicam.* 1781. 8vo, pp. 133, (2). + Editio altera auctior et emendatior. *Bononiæ, ex typographia S. Thomæ Aquinatis.* 1782. 8vo, pp. xxviii, 209. 2 Plates. 38839

Landolphe (J. F.) Mémoires du Capitaine Landolphe, contenant l'Histoire de ses Voyages pendant trente-six ans, aux côtes d'Afrique et aux deux Amériques; Rédigés sur son manuscrit, Par J. S. Quesné ... . *Paris: Arthus Bertrand.* 1823. 2 vols., 8vo, pp. 350; 500. Map and 2 Plates. BA. 38840

Landon (G.) An Address delivered before The Literary Societies of the Wesleyan Academy, June 28, 1842. By Rev. George Landon, A.B. *Boston: Printed by D. H. Ela.* 1842. 8vo, pp. 31. B. 38841

Landon (S.) Fifty Years in the Itinerant Ministry. By S. Landon. *New York: N. Tibbals & Co.* 1868. 16mo, pp. 48.

Landor (H.) The Best Way to Stop the Slave Trade. By Henry Landor, Esq. *Norwich.* 1850. 8vo, pp. 24. 38843

Landor (H.) The Fearful Condition of the Church of England in the Diocese of Huron, as shown in the Speeches of the Bishop of Huron. *Hamilton.* 1866. 8vo. 38844

Landor (W. S.) Imaginary Conversations of Literary Men and Statesmen. By Walter Savage Landor. *London.* 1824 2 vols., 8vo. c. + Second Edition ... . *London: Henry Colburn.* 1826. 3 vols., 8vo, pp. xvi, 512; xii, 632; xvi, 546, (2). BA. + Second Series. *London: James Duncan.* MDCCCXXIX. 2 vols., 8vo, pp. (4), xxxii, (2), 527; vii, (2), 548. c. 38845

One of the conversations is between Washington and Franklin. Frequently reprinted.

Landreth's [David] Rural Register and Almanac 1868. ... *Phil'a: M'Calla & Stavely, Prs.* [1868.] 12mo, pp. 64. B.

Landreth (D. & C.) The Floral Magazine and Botanical Repository. By D. & C. Landreth. 8vo. 38847

Describes some plants peculiar to the United States.

A Landscape Book. By American Artists and American Authors. *New York: G. P. Putnam & Son.* 1867. Sm. 4to, pp. 108.

This is "Homes of American Authors," *our* No. 32740, with a new title-page.

Landverhuizing naar de Vereenigde Staten van Noord-Amerika. *Bergen-op-Zoom.* 1853. 8vo. 38849

Lane (E.) The Fugitives; or, a Trip to Canada. By Edward Lane. *London.* 1830. 12mo. 38850

[Lane (E.)] An Imperfect List of Descendants from Job Lane, Wm. Lane of Dorchester, and William Lane of Boston. With Notices of some Others of the same Name. [*Chicago.* 1856.] 4to, pp. 6. 38851

Also: Memoranda relating to the Lane, Reyner and Whipple Families, Yorkshire and Massachusetts. From "New Engl. Hist. and Geneal. Reg." *Boston.* 1857. 8vo.

Lane (E. H.) The Soldiers' Record of Jericho, Vermont. Prepared by E. H. Lane. ... *Burlington: R. S. Styles ... Printer.* 1868. 8vo, pp. 47. B. 38852

Lane (G. C.) Poems of G. C. Lane, with a Biographical Sketch. Edited by B. D. Ames. *Burlington, Vt.* 1860. 8vo.

Lane (H. L.) Speech of Hon. H. L. Lane, of Indiana, on the Resolution to expel Hon. Jesse D. Bright from his seat in that Body. ... January 21, 1862. [n. p. n. d.] 8vo, pp. 8.

Also: Remarks ... March 28, 1842, on the Loan Bill. *Washington.* 1842. 8vo. —Speech ... on the Discharge of State Prisoners. Senate, December 18, 1862. [n. p. n. d.] 8vo, pp. 16.—Speech ... February 8, 1866, on Reconstruction. [n. p. n. d.]

Lane (J. C.) Atlantic and Pacific Canal Company. Report of the Survey of the Rivers Atrato, Pato, and Baudo, made by James C. Lane, Esq., Civil Engineer. Showing the Practicability of constructing a Ship Canal connecting the Atlantic and Pacific Oceans. ... *New York: R. Craighead, Printer.* 1854. 8vo, pp. 44.

Lane (J. H.) Vindication of the Policy of the Administration. Speech of Hon. J. H. Lane, ... February 16, 1864, on the ... Bill ... to set apart a Portion of ... Texas for the Use of Persons of African Descent. *Washington, D. C.: Gibson Brothers, Printers.* 1864. 8vo, pp. 16. B. 38856

Also: Speech ... Waterbury, Conn., December 28, 1863. [n. p. n. d.] 8vo, pp. 8.

Lane (J.) A Memorial and Tear of Lamentation; with the Improvement of the Death of Pious Friends, Hampton Falls, July 17, 1766. By Jeremiah Lane. *Portsmouth, N. H.* 1766. 8vo, pp. 16. N. 38857

Lane (J.) Speech of the Hon. Joseph Lane, of Oregon, in Reply to Senator Johnson, in the Senate ... December 19, 1860. [n. p. n. d.] 8vo, pp. 8. 38858

Lane (L.) The Narrative of Lunsford Lane, formerly of Raleigh, N. C. Embracing an Account of his Early Life, the Redemption, by Purchase of Himself and Family from Slavery, and his Banishment from the Place of his Birth for the Crime of wearing a Colored Skin. Published by Himself. Third Edition. *Boston: Hewes and Watson.* 1845. 18mo, pp. iv, 54. + Fourth Edition. [*Ibid.*] 1848. 18mo, pp. 54. B. 38859

[Lane (William C.)] A Sketch of ... the Rev. Michael Eyster, late Pastor of ... Greensburg and Adamsburg ... Penn'a. *Pittsburgh: Printed by W. S. Haven.* 1853. 8vo, pp. 24. B.

Lane Seminary. History of the Foundation and Endowment of the Lane Theological Seminary. *Cincinnati.* 1848. 8vo, pp. 18. 38861

Also: Debate at the Lane Seminary, Cincinnati. Speech of James A. Thome ... May 6, 1834. Letter of the Rev. Dr. Samuel H. Cox ... . *Boston: Garrison & Knapp.* 1834. 8vo, pp. 16—Financial History and Condition of Lane Seminary, April, 1858. *Cincinnati.* [n. d.] 8vo, pp. 12.—Lane Theological Seminary, its History, Condition, and Claims ... . *Cincinnati.* 1870. 18mo, pp. 16.—Annual Report of the Trustees, with a Catalogue ... January, 1830. *Cincinnati.* 1830. 8vo. Continued.—A Statement of the Reasons which induced the Students of Lane Seminary, to dissolve their Connection with that Institution. *Cincinnati.* 1834. 8vo, pp. 28.

La Nevfville (L. de). Histoire Générale de Portugal. Par M^r^. Legeuen de la Nevfville. *A Paris, Chez Anisson.* M.DCC. 2 vols., 4to, pp. (14), 626, Table, (22); (2), 608, Table, (14).

La Neuville (M. J.) Elegie sur la Mort de Washington. *Philadelphia.* 1800. 8vo, pp. 8. 38863

Lang (Carl). Haushaltung oder Gallerie von Darstellungen der merkwürdigsten menschlichen Wohnplätze, Gebräuche, Arbeiten und Sitten der Chinesen, Patagonen ... . *Leipzig.* [n. d.] 8vo. Plates. 38864

Lang (J. D.) The Moral and Religious Aspect of the Future America of the Southern Hemisphere; or, A Letter to the Members of the Presbyterian Churches, ... in the United States of America. By John Dunmore Lang, D.D. ... *New-York: James Van Norden, Printer.* 1840. 8vo, pp. 27. 38865

Lang. Religion and Education in America; with Notices of the State and Prospects of American Unitarianism, Popery and African Colonization. By John Dunmore Lang, D.D. ... *London: Ward & Co.* 1840. Post 8vo, pp. viii, 474. 38866

Lang. View of the Origin and Migrations of the Polynesian Nations; demonstrating their ancient Discovery and progressive Settlement of the Continent of America. By John Dunmore Lang, D.D. *London: Cochrane.* 1834. Post 8vo, pp. vii, 256.

Lang *and* Taylor (S.) Report of a Visit to some of the Tribes of Indians, located West of the Mississippi River, By John D. Lang, and Samuel Taylor, Jun. *New-York: Press of M. Day & Co.* 1843. 8vo, pp. 34. + *Providence: Knowles and Vose.* 1843. 8vo. 38868

Lang (W. B.) Views, with Ground Plans, of the Highland Cottages at Roxbury, (near Boston,) designed and erected by Wm. Bailey Lang. *Boston: Printed by L. H. Bridgham and H. E. Felch.* MDCCCXLV. 4to, 19 l. C. 38869

Langdon (C.) An Oration on the Virtues and Death of General George Washington, ... delivered at Castleton, February 22d, 1800. ... By Chauncy Langdon. ... *Rutland: Printed by W. Fay.* [1800.] 8vo, pp. 24. BA. 38870

Also: Oration ... at Poultney, July 4th, 1804. ... *Salem.* 1804. 8vo.—Oration ... at Poultney, July 4, 1808 ... . *Rutland, Vt.* 1808. 8vo.—Oration ... in Castleton, Vt., on the Fourth of July, 1812. ... *Middlebury.* 1812. 8vo. S.

Langdon (J.) Some Account of Portsmouth, N. H. By John Langdon. [n. p.] 1840. 8vo, pp. 34. 38871

Langdon [John]. The Speech of ... Governor Langdon to the Legislature of New Hampshire, the Answer ... and the Protest ... June Session, 1811. [n. p. 1811.] 8vo, pp. 22. BA.

Langdon (Mary). *See* [Pike (*Mrs.* M. H.)]

Langdon (S.) Government ... A Sermon ... Before the ... Congress Of the Colony Of the Massachusetts-Bay ... Assembled at Watertown, ... 31st Day of May, 1775. Being the Anniversary ... For the Election of Counsellors. By Samuel Langdon, D.D. ... *Watertown: Printed by Benjamin Edes.* MDCCLXXV. 8vo, pp. 29. B. 38872

This sermon, in which the author animadverts severely on the tyranny of the mother country, was preached while the Congress was in involuntary session at Watertown. It is lso included in J. W. Thornton's "Pulpit of the American Revolution."

Langdon. Joy and Gratitude to God for the Long Life of a Good King, and the Conquest of Quebec. Thanksgiving Sermon, ... Portsmouth, N. H., Nov. 10, 1759. By Samuel Langdon. *Portsmouth.* 1760. 8vo, pp. 47. M., W. 38874

Langdon. ... A Sermon ... at the Ordination of the Reverend Mr. Samuel McClintock, ... Nov. 3, 1756. By Samuel Langdon ... . *Portsmouth, in New Hampshire: Printed by Daniel Fowle.* 1756. 8vo, pp. 47. 38875

The first printing-press in New Hampshire was established at Portsmouth, by Daniel Fowle, in 1756. *See* Thomas' "History of Printing." Also: A Correction of some Great Mistakes committed by the Rev. John Cosens Ogden ... in his Late Letters Published at Boston. ... *Portsmouth: Printed by John Melcher.* M,DCC,XCII. 8vo, pp. 5–22.—A Discourse ... before the Piscataqua Association of Ministers, Portsmouth, Oct. 12, 1791. ... *Exeter: B. Parket.* 1792. 8vo, pp. 30.— ... Sermon ... at Windham, ... at the Ordination of ... Reverend Mr. Peter Thacher Smith, ... September 22, 1762. ... *Portsmouth, N. H.: Printed by Daniel Fowle.* 1763. 8vo, pp. 40.— ... A Sermon at the Annual Lecture instituted ... by the ... Will ... of the Honorable Paul Dudley, Esq; ... November 1, 1775. ... *Boston: Printed by Samuel Hall.* 1776. 8vo, pp. 26.—Sermon ... at the Ordination of Edward Sprague, ... in Dublin, ... N. H., November 12, 1777. ... *Boston: Printed by Thomas & John Fleet.* 1778. 8vo, pp. 38.— ... Sermon ... after the Interment of the Hon John Winthrop, ... Professor ... in Harvard College ... Who departed this Life, May the 3d, 1779. ... *Boston, N. E.: Printed by Thomas and John Fleet.* 1779. 8vo, pp. 23.— ... A Sermon ... at Concord, ... New-Hampshire, Election, June 5, 1788. ... *Exeter: Printed by Lamson* ... M,DCC,-LXXXVIII. 8vo, pp. 48. BA. Also many other polemical and religious pieces.

Langdon (T.) Sermon at Danbury, Nov. 8, 1789, at the Execution of Anthony, a Free Negro, for Rape. By Timothy Langdon. *Danbury.* 1798. 8vo, pp. 23. 38876

Also: Sermon on the Pleasure and Advantages of Church Music. ... *Danbury.* 1797. 8vo.

Lange (G.) *See* Godard-Lange, Vol. VII., No. 27630.

Lange (H.) *See* Andree (K.), Vol. I., No. 1461–4.

Lange (M.) Abraham Lincoln der Wiederhersteller der Nordamerikanischen Union, und der grosse Kampf der Nord- und Südstaaten während der Jahre 1861–1865. Herausgegeben von D^r^. Max Lange. Mit 70 in den Text gedruckter Illustrationen. *Leipzig: Otto Spamer.* 1866. 8vo, pp. ix, 260. Map.

[Langeac (N. de l'Espinasse, *le Chevalier de*).] Anecdotes Anglaises et Américaines. Années 1776 à 1783. ... *Paris: Delaunay, Libraire.* 1813. 2 vols., 12mo, pp. (4), 298; (4), 324.

Langeac. Colomb dans les Fers, à Ferdinand et Isabelle, après la découverte de l'Amérique; Épitre qui à remporté le prix de l'Académie de Marseille, Précédée d'un Précis historique sur Colomb. Par M. le Chevalier de Langeac. *Londres, et se trouve à Paris, Chez Alexandre Jombert.* MDCCLXXXII. 8vo, pp. 150. S.

The poem which gives the title to this book occupies fourteen pages. A memoir of Columbus fills up the rest of the volume. It is very handsomely printed, and ornamented by a frontispiece and two vignettes, beautifully executed.

[Langenes (Barent).] Caert-thresoor, inhoudende de tafelen des gantschen werelts landen, met beschryvingen verlicht. *Amsterdam: Cornelius Claez.* 1598. Oblong 4to. 38880

First edition; very rare. The part relating to America contains fourteen maps and thirty-eight pages of text.

[Langenes.] Hand-boeck; of cort begryp der caerten ende beschrijvinghen van alle landen des werelds. Van nieuws oversien ende vermeerdert (door Jac. Viverius). *Amsterdam: Cornelius Claesz.* 1609. Oblong 8vo. 38881

Thirteen maps relate to America.

Langevin (E.) Notice historique sur la Mission de Ste. Croix de Tadoussac. ... *Québec.* 1864. 12mo, pp. 40. 38882

Langevin (Hector L.) Le Canada, ses institutions, ressources, produits ... . *Québec.* 1855. 8vo, pp. 186. 38883

Langevin (J.) L'Histoire du Canada en Tableaux ... par M. Jean Langevin. *Québec: St. Michel et Darveaux, Imprimeurs.* 1860. 8vo, pp. 8. + Seconde édition. [*Ibid.*] 1865. 38884

Langevin. Notes sur les Archives de Notre Dame de Beauport. ... *Québec.* 1860. 8vo, pp. 138, xxxvi. 38885

Langford (J.) A just and cleere Refutation of a false and scandalous Pamphlet, Entituled, Babylons fall in Maryland, &c. And, A true Discovery of certaine strange and inhumane proceedings of some ungratefull people in Maryland, towards those who formerly preserved them in time of their greatest distresse. To which is added a Law in Maryland concerning Religion, and a Declaration concerning the same. By John Langford Gentleman, Servant to the Lord Baltemore. ... *London, Printed for the Author.* 1655. 4to, pp. 35. BA. 38886

An extremely rare pamphlet.

Langford (J.) Murray's Tourist's Guide to the City of Montreal by John Langford. *Montreal.* 1866. 16mo, pp. 96. + Second Edition ... . *Montreal: Printed by John Lovell.* 1866. 12mo, pp. 96. 38887

Langford. The Stranger's Illustrated Guide to ... Montreal ... By John Langford. *Montreal: D. Ross.* 1865. 12mo, pp. 56.

Langford (J. A.) Prison Books and their Authors. By John Alfred Langford ... . *London: William Tegg.* 1861. Post 8vo, pp. ix, (1), 357. 4 Portraits. 38889

Contains some particulars concerning Sir Walter Raleigh.

[Langford (Jonas).] A Brief Account of the Sufferings of the Servants of the Lord, called Quakers: from their first Arrival in the Island of Antegoa, under the several Governours; from the Year 1660, to 1695. *London: T. Sowle.* 1706. 4to, pp. 28.

Langford (W.) Sermon at Salter's Hall, before the correspondent Board in London, of the Society in Scotland, for Propagating Christian Knowledge in the Highlands and Islands, and for spreading the Gospel among the Indians in America. *London.* 1774. 8vo. 38891

Langford & Chase. Augusta, Hallowell, and Gardiner Directory, for ... 1867–68. By Langford & Chase. *Augusta, (Me.): Pierce Bros.* 1867. 12mo, pp. 182, 32. 38892

Langley (H. G.) The Pacific Coast Business Directory for 1867: Compiled by Henry G. Langley ... . *San Francisco: Henry G. Langley.* 1867. 8vo, pp. 568. B. 38893

Langley (John). An Essay toward forming A More Complete Representation of the Commons of Great Britain. *London.* MDCCXCV. 8vo, pp. 59. 38894

Partly relates to American affairs.

Langman (C.), *and others.* *See* Deane (J.), Vol. V., 19029.

Langsdorff (Georg Heinrich von). Bemerkungen auf einer Reise um die Welt in den Jahren 1803 bis 1807. *Frankfurt am Main.* 1812. 3 vols., 4to. Atlas of 27 and 16 Plates. B.

Langsdorff. Voyages and Travels in Various Parts of the World, during the Years 1803, 1804, 1805, 1806, and 1807. By G. H. von Langsdorff, Aulic Counsellor to ... the Emperor of Russia, ... Illustrated by Engravings from Original Drawings. *London: Henry Colburn.* 1813–14. 2 vols., 4to, pp. xxi, (2), 362, (6); (8), 386, (6). Map, 21 Plates. B. + *Carlisle* [*Pa.*]: *Printed by George Philips* ... 1817. 8vo, pp. xvi, 617, Index, (15). Plate.

Langsdorff was naturalist to Krusenstern's expedition, which he quitted at Kamschatka, and explored the Aleutian Isles, the Northwest Coast, California, etc., and returned overland through Siberia. His work contains a fuller account of Sitka, the Settlement of St. Francisco, etc., than any other. *See* "M. Rev.," lxxvi. 240; lxxvii. 124.

Langsdorff. Mémoire sur le Brésil; pour servir de Guide à ceux qui desirent s'y établir. Par M. le Chevalier G. D. Langsdorff, Consul General de Russie au Brésil. *Paris.* 1820. 4to, pp. 32, or less. 38897

Langsdorff. Bemerkungen über Brasilien, mit gewissenhafter Belehrung für auswandernde Deutsche. ... *Heidelberg.* 1821. 8vo. 38898

Langstedt (F. L.) Reisen nach Südamerika, Asien und Afrika. ... Mit Kupfern. *Hildesheim.* 1789. 8vo, pp. 476.

[Langston (Lawrence)], *pseudon.* Bastiles of the North [By Reverdy Johnson]. *Baltimore.* 1863. 8vo. 38900

Langton (J.) Address before the Literary and Historical Society of Quebec at the Opening of the Session of 1862–63. By John Langton. *Quebec.* 1863. 8vo, pp. 20. + Session of 1863–64. [*Ibid.*] 1864. 8vo, pp. 34. 38901

Also several other papers in the "Transactions of the Literary and Historical Society of Quebec."

[Langworthy (Asahel).] *See* Vol. IX., No. 36274.

[Langworthy (Edward).] Anecdotes of the late Charles Lee Esq. ... Second Edition. With an Appendix of Additional Papers and Letters. *London: J. S. Jordan.* 1797. 8vo, pp. xii, 446. 38902

This is the "Memoirs" described No. 38903, *infra*, with a new title-page.

[Langworthy.] Memoirs of the Life of the late Charles Lee, Esq. ... Second in Command in the Service of the United States of America during the Revolution: to which are added his Political and Military Essays; also, Letters to, and from Many Distinguished Characters, both in Europe and America. *London: J. S. Jordan.* M,DCC,XCII. 8vo, pp. xii, 439. + *New York: Printed by T. Allen.* 1792. 12mo, pp. viii, 284. + Second American Edition. [*Ibid.*] 1793. 12mo. + *Dublin: Printed for Messrs. P. Byrne.* 1792. 8vo, pp. xii, 439. BA. 38903

Reproduced as: "The Life and Memoirs of Major General Charles Lee, Second in Command to General Washington, during the American Revolution." *New York.* 1795. 12mo. + *New York: R. Scott.* 1813. 12mo, pp. 352; also as "Political and Military Essays; ... With Memoirs of his Life ... . Second Edition. With an Appendix" ... . *London: Printed for J. S. Jordan.* 1797. 8vo, pp. xii, 446. BA. Contains many curious particulars relating to the war between Great Britain and the Colonies. Published under the direction of Edward Langworthy, Esq., M.C. from Georgia. The dates on the letters are often erroneous. The letter on page 305 was addressed to Lady Blake, not to Miss Macaulay; that on page 427, to Miss Frank of Philadelphia.

Langworthy (F.) Scenery of the Plains, Mountains, and Mines; or, a Diary kept upon the Overland Route to California, by way of the Great Salt Lake; embracing the Return by the

Pacific Ocean and Central America, in the years 1850, 51, '52, and '53. By Franklin Langworthy. *Ogdensburgh.* 1855. 12mo.

Langworthy (I. P.) A Historical Discourse, delivered at Chelsea, Mass., Sept. 20, 1866, at the Twenty-Fifth Anniversary of the Winnisimmet Congregational Church, by Isaac P. Langworthy ... . *Chelsea.* 1866. 8vo, pp. 47. 38905

Also: Farewell Sermon preached to the Winnisimmet Congregational Church, Chelsea, Mass., May 2, 1858. ... *Boston.* 1858. 8vo.—Sermon on the Liquor Law of Massachusetts, July 18, 1852. ... *Boston.* 1852. 8vo.

Langworthy (L. H.) Dubuque; its History, Mines, Indian Legends, etc. By Lucius H. Langworthy. *Dubuque: Literary Institute.* 1855. 8vo, pp. 82. C. 38906

Lanier (J. F. D.) The Financial Condition and Resources of the United States. By J. F. D. Lanier. *New York.* 1865.

[Lanigan (G. F.)] National Ballads of Canada, Imitated and Translated from the Originals, by "Allid." *Montreal.* 1865. 12mo, pp. 15. 38908

Lanjuinais (J. D.) Christophe Colomb, ou Notice d'un Livre Italien concernant cet Illustre Navigateur. Par J. D. Lanjuinais, Membre de l'Institut ... . *Paris: Chez Maradan.* 1819. 8vo, pp. (2), 17. Facsimile. B. 38909

For a refutation see [Brignoles (*Marquis de*)], Vol. I., No. 7920.

Lanjuinais. Études biographiques et littéraires sur Ant. Arnauld, P. Nicole et J. Necker, avec une notice sur Christophe Colomb. *Paris.* 1823. 8vo. 38910

Lanjuinais. Notice de l'ouvrage de M. l'Evêque et Sénateur Grégoire, intitulé: De la Littérature des Nègres. Par J. D. Lanjuinais. *Paris: Maradan.* 1808. 8vo, pp. 24. 38911

Lanman (C.) Adventures in the Wilds of North America. By Charles Lanman, edited by Charles Richard Weld. *London: Longman* ... 1854. Post 8vo, pp. 300. + [*Ibid.*] 1863.

Mostly abstracted from the following:

Lanman. Adventures in the Wilds of the United States and British American Provinces. By Charles Lanman ... . With an Appendix by Lieut. Campbell Hardy. *Philadelphia: John W. Moore.* 1856. 2 vols., 8vo, pp. xi, (4), 514; ii, 517, (2). Plates. B. + *London.* 1856. 2 vols., 8vo. + Second Edition. [*Ibid.*] 1859. 2 vols., 8vo. 38913

A republication of four of the following works, with three new pieces.

Lanman. Adventures in the Wilds of North America. By Charles Lanman. Sketches in Canada and Rambles among the Red Men. By Mrs. Jameson. *London: Longman* ... 1862. Square 8vo. 38914

Forms Vol. XII. of the "Traveller's Library."

Lanman. Adventures of an Angler in Canada, Nova Scotia and the United States. By Charles Lanman. *London: Richard Bentley.* 1848. Post 8vo, pp. xii, 322. Portrait. 38915

Lanman. A Canoe Voyage up the Mississippi and around Lake Superior. By Charles Lanman. *New York.* 1847. 12mo.

This is *our* No. 38925, *infra*, with a new title-page.

Lanman. Dictionary of the United States Congress, containing Biographical Sketches of its Members from the Foundation of the Government; with an Appendix, compiled as a manual of reference for the Legislator and Statesman. By Charles Lanman. *Philadelphia: ... J. B. Lippincott & Co.* 1859. 8vo, pp. 534, (1), Appendix, 159. + [*Washington:*] *Government Printing Office.* 1864. 8vo, pp. 556. C. + Third Edition revised and brought down to July 28, 1866. [*Ibid.*] 1866. 8vo, pp. (8), 602. + Fifth Edition; Revised and brought down to include the Fortieth Congress. *Hartford: T. Belknap and H. E. Goodwin.* 1868. 8vo, pp. 628. B. + Sixth Edition. [*Ibid.*] 8vo. C. 38917

Lanman. Essays for Summer Hours. By Charles Lanman. *Boston: Hilliard, Gray & Company.* 1841. 12mo, pp. (8), 175. + Second Edition. [*Ibid.*] 1842. 12mo, pp. vi, (1), 250. Plate. + Third Edition. *New York.* 1853. 12mo. 38918

Lanman. Haw-Ho-Noo; or, Records of a Tourist. By Charles Lanman. *Philadelphia: Lippincott, Grambo & Co.* 1850. 12mo, pp. (8), 13–266. C. 38919

Reproduced as "The Sugar Camp and other Sketches."

[Lanman.] Letters from a Landscape Painter. ... *Boston: J. Munroe & Co.* 1845. 12mo, pp. (4), 265. C., P. 38920

Part of this is reprinted in the previous work, No. 38919.

Lanman. Letters from the Allegheny Mountains. By Charles Lanman ... . *New-York: Geo. P. Putnam.* 1848. 12mo, pp. 198. A. + [*Ibid.*] 1849. B. 38921

Lanman. Life of William Woodbridge. By Charles Lanman. *Washington: Blanchard & Mohun.* 1867. 8vo, pp. 226. Portrait. 38922

[Lanman.] Life on the Lakes: ... a Trip to ... Lake Superior. ... *New-York: George Dearborn.* 1836. 2 vols., 12mo, pp. (4), 270; (4), 275. 2 Plates. BA. 38923

Lanman. The Private Life of Daniel Webster. By Charles Lanman ... . *New York: Harper & Brothers.* 1852. 12mo, pp. iii, 205. 3 Portraits, 2 Plates. B., C. + *London: Longman ...* 1853. Post 8vo, pp. 300. 38924

Lanman. A Summer in the Wilderness; embracing a Canoe Voyage up the Mississippi and around Lake Superior. By Charles Lanman ... . *New-York: D. Appleton & Company.* MDCCCXLVII. 12mo, pp. 5–208. C. 38925

Lanman. A Tour to the River Saguenay, in Lower Canada. By Charles Lanman ... . *Philadelphia: Carey and Hart.* 1848. 12mo, pp. viii, 17–231. C. 38926

Reprinted as: "Adventures of an Angler in Canada." *London: R. Bentley.* 1848. Post 8vo. *See also* Ely (A.), Vol. VI., No. 22378.

Lanman (J.) Oration at Norwich, Connecticut, 4th July, 1798. By James Lanman. *Norwich.* 1798. 12mo. 38927

Lanman (J. H.) History of Michigan, Civil and Topographical, in a Compendious Form: with a View of the Surrounding Lakes. By James H. Lanman. *New York: E. French.* 1839. 8vo, pp. xvi, 398. Map. 38928

Includes a minute narration of the early dealings of the whites with the aborigines of the territory, the Jesuit missions, and border wars.

Lanman. History of Michigan, from its Earliest Colonization to the Present Time. By James H. Lanman. *New-York: Harper & Brothers.* [1841.] 18mo, pp. vii, 269. BA. + [*Ibid.*] 1842. 18mo, pp. 269. + [*Ibid.*] 1843. 18mo. 38929

Lann (Adolf). Washington Irving. Ein Lebens- und Charakterbild. ... *Berlin: Oppenheim.* 1870. 2 vols., 8vo, pp. xiv, 245; iv, 292. 38930

Lanoye (Ferdinand Tugnot de). La Mer Polaire, voyage de "l'Erèbe" et de la "Terreur" et expéditions à la recherche de Franklin. *Paris: Hachette et Cie.* 1863. 12mo. 26 Plates, Maps and Plans. + Second Edition. [*Ibid.*] 1865. 38931

See also Hervé (É. A.) et Lanoye (F. de), Vol. VIII., No. 31601.

Lans (W. H.) Bijdrage tot de Kennis der Kolonie Suriname. *'s Gravenhage: Maatschappij van schoone Kunsten.* 1842. 8vo.

Contributions to the knowledge of Surinam.

Lans. De oorzaken van verval en middelen tot herstel der Surinaamsche plantaadjen. *'s Gravenhage.* 1829. 8vo. 38933

Relates to the plantations in Surinam.

[Lans.] Schets van een ontwerp tot behoud van Suriname. *'Gravenhage.* 1847. 8vo. 38934

Lansberge (Henrique van). Venezuela pintoresca, ó vistas de las principales ciudades, pueblos, rios, lagos y móntes de la República de Venezuela. *Carácas.* 1853. 8vo, pp. 28. Map, 6 Plates. 38935

Two numbers only published.

Lansdowne (*Marquis of*). Speech by the Marquis of Lansdowne, on a Motion for the Recognition of the Independence of the Spanish Colonies. *London.* 1824. 8vo. 38936

[Lansing (Abraham).] Brief Remarks ... March 11, 1837, ... touching the Nomination of a Candidate for the Boston Collectorship. ... *Boston.* 1837. 8vo, pp. 16. H. 38937

Lansing (D. C.) A Sermon ... March 6, 1817, at the Dedication of the New Presbyterian Church, in ... Auburn; By the Rev. Dirck C. Lansing. ... *Auburn: Printed by H. C. Southwick.* 1817. 8vo, pp. 16. 38938

Lansing (D. C.) A Sermon; Preached at the Dedication of The Clinton Avenue Congregational Church, Brooklyn, December 16th, 1855, By D. C. Lansing, D.D. ... *New-York.* 1856. 8vo, pp. 25. S. 38939

Lansing (R. R.) Exposition concerning the Mineral Coal of Michigan. By R. R. Lansing. March, 1854. *Detroit.* 1854. 8vo, pp. 18. 38940

Lansing (W. E.) Confiscation and Emancipation. Speech of Hon. W. E. Lansing, of New York, May 21, 1862. [n. p. 1862.] 8vo, pp. 8. 38941

Lanson (H.) The Life and Adventures of Henry Lanson the only Son of a Wealthy Planter in the West Indies who went on his Voyage to England was put on Shore on an uninhabited Island where on his perambulation up the Country he discovers the Ruins of an Ancient Temple; ... which contained an Immense and Inestimable Collection of precious Indian Curiosities. ... *London.* [1801.] 12mo, pp. 42. Frontispiece. 38942

Mr Field pronounces this "A wretched fiction."

Lanson (——). Précis histoire de la dernière expédition de St. Domingue. *Paris.* [n. d.] 8vo. 38943

The Lantern. *New York.* 1852. 4to. 38944

Twenty-three or more numbers published.

Lanterne Magique of Toverlantaern, O soo Moi! Fraai Curieus! vertoonende de wonderlyke zaaken van dezen tijd. [*Amsterdam.*] 1782–83. 20 parts, 8vo. 38945

This satirical journal contains numerous allusions to and remarks on the differences between England and its colonies, with special reference to the part the Dutch had in them.

Lanús (A.) Cuestion Papel Moneda, serie de articulos publicados en la "Nacion Argentina," escritos por Anacarsis Lanús. *Buenos Aires.* 1864. 8vo, pp. 52. 38946

[Lanusse (A.)] Les Cennelles. Choix des Poesies indigènes. *Nouvelle Orleans.* 1845. 12mo. 38947

The introduction and dedication are signed "Armand Lanusse."

Lanz (*Gen.*) Parte al supremo gobierno sobre la sorpresa, que el General Lanz con una seccion de cavalleria de los invasores intento darle en Tehuacan la madrugada del 13 de Enero de 1848. *Orizava.* 1848. 4to, pp. 7. 38948

Lanuza (V. Blasco de). Historias Ecclesiasticas y Seculares de Aragon, en que se continuan los annales de Çurita, y tiempos de Carlos V. con historias ecclesiasticas antiquas y modernas. *Çaragoça.* 1622. 2 vols., folio. 38949

"This rare work, a supplement to Curita down to 1618, contains, Vol. I., pp. 70–74, a Narrative of the discovery of America, by Columbus; pp. 163–67, a Narrative of the voyages of Hernando de Magallanes," etc.—Muller. *See also* [Harrisse], "Bib. Am. Vet.," p. 205.

Lanzi (L.) El devoto instruido en la santo Sacrificio de la Misa; por el P. Luiz Lanzi ... . Traduccion libre al idioma Yucateca, con unos afectos Por el P. Fr. Joaquim Ruz. ... *Merida de Yucatan: Impreso por José Antonio Pino.* 1835. 4to, 9 l.

Laon (L. de). Relation | dv Voyage | des Francois | fait av Cap de Nord | en Ameriqve: | Par ses soings de la Compagnie establie à | Paris, & sous la conduite de Monsieur | de Royville leur General; | auec une ample description du Pays, des | Mœurs & facon de viure des Sauuages, | & l'obseruation des hauteurs. | ... | Par L. de Laon Sieur Daigremont; Ingenieur du Roy, & Capitaine des

Troupes | de France Equinoxialle. | *A Paris, | chéz Pierre David Pépingué,* ... | M.D.CLIV. Sm. 8vo, pp. (8), 200. Map. 38951

This is an account of an expedition sent out under De Roiville, in 1651. The greater part of the colonists, seven hundred or eight hundred in number, perished in the space of fifteen months, from hunger and the fury of the Indians.

Laosipas (Ulises). De la colonizacion de la Baja California. *México.* 1859. 8vo. 38952

Lapa (Ludgero da Rocha Ferreira). Archivo medico brasileiro: gazeta mensal de medicina, cirurgia e sciencias accessorias. *Rio de Janeiro: Typ. Imparcial de Francisco de Paula Brito.* 1844–1847. 4 vols., 4to, pp. 292; 288; 288; 288. 38953

La Parra (J. de). Vida de Santa Rosa del Peru, por Fr. Jacinto de la Parra. *Dominico.* 1668. 4to. 38954

La Paz (*Marquis de*). Letters of the Marquis de la Paz and Col. Stanhope on the West Indies and the Dispute with Spain. *London.* 1720. 4to. 38955

La Peña (D. M. de). Manual de Nueva York ... . *Nueva York: Imprenta de S. W. Benedict.* 1851. 18mo, pp. 140. Map and Plates. B. 38956

La Peña (F. J. de). Breve Noticia de la Biblioteca Hispano-Americana Septentrional, y Apología de su Autor al Señ. D. J. M Berestain, por el Ciudadano F. Javier de la Peña. *Mexico.* 1842. Sm. 4to. 38957

La Pérouse (Jean François Galaup de). Découvertes dans la Mer du Sud; Nouvelles de la Peyrouse jusqu'en 1794; traces de son passage trouvées en diverses Iles et Terres de l'Océan Pacifique. *Paris.* [n. d.] 8vo. 38958

La Pérouse. Relation abrégée du Voyage de La Pérouse, pendant les années 1785, 1786, 1787 et 1788. ... *A Leipsick.* 1799. 8vo, pp. xxxvi, 562. Map and Portrait. 38959

La Pérouse. Voyage de La Pérouse autour du Monde, publié conformément au décret du 22 Avril 1791, et rédigé par M. L. A. Milet-Mureau, Général de Brigade dans le Corps du Génie, Directeur des Fortifications ... . *Paris: de l'Imprimerie de la République. An* V. [1797.] 4 vols., 8vo, pp. (4), lxxij, 346, Portrait; (4), 398; (4), 422; (4), 309. Atlas of 69 Plates in folio. A., B. + *Paris.* 1798. 4 vols., 8vo. Atlas of 70 Plates in folio.

Also on large paper in 4to. The able geographical disquisition, prefixed to the original, is said to have been drawn up by the unfortunate Louis XVI.

La Pérouse. Voyage de La Pérouse autour du Monde, publié conformément au décret du 22 avril 1791, et rédigé par M. L. A. Milet-Mureau, Général de Brigade dans le Corps du Génie ... *London: A. Hamilton.* 1799. 2 vols., 4to, pp lii, 539, Portrait; viii, 522; Index, (18). Maps and Plates. 38961

La Pérouse. A Voyage round the World, performed In the Years 1785, 1786, 1787, and 1788, by the Boussole, and Astrolabe, under the Command of J. F. G. de la Pérouse: published by order of the National Assembly under the Superintendence of L. A. Milet-Mureau ... . Translated from the French. *London: G. G. and J. Robinson.* 1799. 2 vols., 4to. Atlas in folio. + *London: A. Hamilton.* 1799. 2 vols., 4to, pp. (4), lvi, 538, Portrait; viii, 531, Index, (14). Atlas of 69 Plates in folio. 38962

The narrative of the enterprising but ill-fated Pérouse, is full of interest in all portions, but his relations of the peculiarities he observed in the natives of the northwest coast of North America, are especially valuable. The mysterious fate of this distinguished navigator has never been satisfactorily cleared up. The above account was transmitted from Botany Bay, after leaving this place the expedition was never heard of again.

La Pérouse. A Voyage round the World, in the Years 1785, 1786, 1787, and 1788. By J. F. G. de La Pérouse: published conformably to the decree of the National Assembly, on the 22d of April, 1791, and edited by M. L. A. Milet-Mureau ... Translated from the French. *London: J. Johnson.* 1798. 3 vols., 8vo, pp. x, (2), 532, Portrait; x, 498; viii, 446, Tables, 60. 42 Plates and Maps. + Second Edition. [*Ibid.*] 1799. 3 vols., 8vo, pp. x, (2), 532; x, 548; viii, 446, Tables, 60. 45 Plates and Maps. + [Another Edition. *Ibid.*] 1798. 2 vols., 8vo, pp. (8), cxc, 290; viii, 442, 56, 119. Atlas of Maps and Plates in folio. 1799. P. + [*Ibid.*] 1807. 3 vols., 8vo. 38963

La Pérouse. The Voyage of M. de La Pérouse round the World, in the Years 1785, 1786, 1787 and 1788. Arranged by M. L. A. Milet-Mureau. To which is prefixed the Voyage from Manilla to St. Blaise, and Travels over the Continent, with the Despatches of La Pérouse, by M. de Lesseps. Translated from the French. *London.* 1798. 2 vols., 8vo. 51 Plates and Maps.

La Pérouse. Voyage de la Pérouse, rédigé d'après ses manuscrits originaux, suivi d'un appendice renfermant tout ce que l'on a découvert depuis le naufrage jusqu'à nos jours, et enrichi de notes, par M. de Lesseps, seul débris vivant de l'expédition dont il était interprète. *Paris: Arthus Bertrand.* 1831. 8vo. Map, Portrait, and Facsimile. 38965

La Pérouse. A Voyage round the World, performed in the Years 1785, 1786, 1787, 1788, by M. de la Peyrouse: ... To which are added, a Voyage from Manilla to California, by Don Antonio Maurelle: and an Abstract of the Voyage and Discoveries of the late Capt. G. Vancouver. *Boston: Joseph Bumstead.* 1801. 12mo, pp. 333. B., S. 38966

La Pérouse. Sketch of a Voyage of Discovery, undertaken by Mons. de la Pérouse, under the Auspices of the French Government. Drawn from the Original, lately published at Paris. *London: Allen.* 1798. 8vo. + *Edinburgh.* 1798. 8vo. Plates.

See "M. Rev.," XXVII. 107, 291, 399.

La Pérouse. The Story of La Peyrouse; with Engravings. *London.* [n. d.] 12mo, pp. 282. 38968

La Pérouse. Ontdekkingen in de Zuidzee, en berichten aangaande de La Pérouse en zijne tochtgenooten ... . *Haarlem.* 1799. 8vo. 38969

See also Blanchard (Victor), Vol. I., No. 5838, Labillardière (J. J. H. de), Nos. 38420–23, *and* Pelham (Cavendish). For a German translation *see* "Magazin der merkwürdigen Reisebeschreibungen;" also translated into Swedish by Samoedham, *Stockholm.* 1799. 8vo.

[La Peyrère (Isaac de).] Relation dv Groenland. *A Paris, Chez Avgvstin Covrbé,* ... M. DC. XLVII. ... 8vo, pp. xvi, 278, (4). Map and Plate. + *Paris: Lovis Billaine.* 1663. 8vo. 38970

This valuable book was prepared from the most authentic sources during a residence in Denmark.

[La Peyrère.] Relation dv Groenland. *Paris: Thomas Iolly.* 1663. 8vo, pp. (40), 108, (2). Map and Plate. 38971

The same as the edition of 1647, with a new title-page. There are copies on large paper. Ternaux quotes an edition, *Paris.* 1651. 8vo. "Remarkable not only for its curious facts, but for the philosophical spirit, so rare in that age, which it displays."—*Bibl. des Voyages.*

[La Peyrère.] Bericht | Von | Gröhnland, | Gezogen aus zwo Chroniken: Einer alten Ihs- | landischen, und einer neuen Dänischen; übergesand | in Frantzösischer Sprahche | An | Herren von der Bote den Wayer von einem | unbenandten Meister, und gedruckt zu | Parihs bey Augustin Kürbe in 8. | Anno 1647. | Jetzo aber Deutsch gegäben, und, um desto färtiger ihn | zu gebrauchen, unterschihdlich eingetheihlet | Von | Henrich Sivers. | *Hamburg, | In Verlägung Johan Naumans und Jurgen Wolfs.* | *Gedruckt im Jahr Christi* | 1674. | 4to, pp. (6), 70, (2). Map and 3 Plates. C. 38972

This translation of Peyrère's "Relation du Groenland" is even more scarce than the original. *See* Ternaux, No. 915.

[La Peyrère.] Nauwkeurige Beschrijving | van | Groenland | Aen Heer De la Mothe le Vayer; | Verdeelt in twee Boecken, | 't Eerste van 't | Oud (nu verloorne) Groenlandt, | ... 't Tweede van 't | Nieuw (door 't soecken van 't Oud' gevondene) Groenland, | ... Nevens 't kort begrijp der seldsaeme Reysen, gedaen om | Oud-Groenland weer te vinden door M. Forbeissser uyt Engelland, | in 't Jaer 1577. Door Gotzke Lindenauw uyt Deenemarcken, in de Jae- | ren 1605. en 1606. Door Karsten Richards, in 't 1601. Door | 't Groenlandsch Geselschap te Koppenhagen, in 't Jaer 1636. | Met aenhangingh van 't Daghverhael der wonderlijke Be- | jegeningen des Deenschen Hoofdams Johan Munck, in | 't soecken van een wegh tusschen Groenland en America nae Oost-Indien: | Gelijck oock van den korten Inhoud en seldsaeme gevallen der Hol- | landsche en Zeeuwsche Scheeps-uytrustingh nae Nova Zembla, | gedaen ten selven eynde: Der ontmoetingen van seven per- | soonen, noch seven, en noch andere seven, gebleven op | Spitsbergen, om aldaer 't overwinteren, e. s. v. | Vertaeld, en met veerlerley Historische Byvoeghselen doorgaens vergroot, door | S[imon] de V[ries]. | *t'Amsterdam, by Jan Claesz. ten Hoorn, Boeckverkooper* | *tegen over 't Oude Heeren Logement.* 1678 | 4to, Engraved Title, pp. (8), 128. 2 Maps. C.

Concerning this accurate description of Greenland, and voyages by Frobisher, etc., *see* Tiele, No. 257.

[La Peyrère.] Ausführliche | Beschreibung | des | theils bewohnt- theils unbewohnt- so genannten | Grönlands, | in zwey Theile abgetheilt: | Deren erster handelt | von des | Alt- (nunmehro verlohrnen) Grönlands Gelegenheit, Er- | findung, Inwohnern, Fruchtbarkeit, Gewächsen, | Thieren und Meerwundern. | Der andere: | von dem | Neuen (durch Suchung des alten, gefundenen) Grönland, | Eigenschafft der Wilden, und viel andern merck- | würdigen Dingen mehr. | Nebenst | Einem kurtzem Begriff der seltsamen Reisen, so M. Forbeisser, Gotzke | Lindenau, Christian Richard, und die Koppenhagen-Grönländische Gesell- | schafft, alt Grönland wieder zu finden, in unterschiedlichen Jahren gethan. | Mit | Anfügung des Tagbuchs eines die Durchfahrt zwischen Grönland und | Amerika suchenden Dänischen Schiffes: wie auch des kurtzen Inhalts und | seltsamen Zufälle der Holl- und Seeländischen Schiffsausrüstung nach Nova | Zembla zu eben dem Ende vorgenommen: | Samt Erzehlung der wunderbaren Zufälle, so dreymal Sieben Personen, | welche den Winter über auf den Spitzbergen und der Mauritiusbay sich aufgehalten, | begegnet, und wie elendiglich sie umkommen sind. | Beschrieben, und mit verschiedenen Historischen Anhängen | durchgehends erklärt und

erweitert | durch | S[imon] von V[ries]. | *Nürnberg, in Verlegung Christof Riegels,* 1679. | 4to, two Titles, one of which is engraved, pp. (8), 131. 2 Maps. 38974

[La Peyrère.] Relation de l'Islande. *A Amsterdam, Chez Jean Frederic Bernard.* MDCCXV. 8vo, pp. 187. Map. 38975

The "Relation du Groenland" fills pp. 87–187. An English version is included in Churchill's "Voyages," Vol. II.

Lapham (Increase A.) ... The Antiquities of Wisconsin, as surveyed and described. By I. A. Lapham, Civil Engineer ... . [*Washington: Smithsonian Institute.* 1855.] 4to, pp. xii, 95. Map and 55 Plates. 38976

Some copies have the imprint, *New York: G. P. Putnam & Co.* 1855.

Lapham. A Catalogue of Plants, found in the Vicinity of Milwaukee, Wisconsin Territory. By I. A. Lapham. *Milwaukee.* 1838. 18mo, pp. 15. B. 38977

Lapham. A Documentary History of the Milwaukee and Rock River Canal. ... By I. A. Lapham. *Milwaukee.* 1840. 8vo, pp. 154. 38978

Lapham. A Geographical and Topographical Description of Wisconsin; with Brief Sketches of its History, Geology, Mineralogy, Natural History, Population, Soil, Productions, Government, Antiquities, &c. &c. By I. A. Lapham. *Milwaukee, Wisconsin: P. C. Hale.* 1844. 18mo, pp. 255, (1). Map. + Second Edition, Greatly Improved. *Milwaukee: I. A. Hopkins.* 1846. 12mo, pp. 208. C. 38979

Also: Communication to Gov. N. Dewey, on the subject of a State Penitentiary. ... [n. p.] 1848. 8vo.—Addresses of Hon. I. A. Lapham, LL.D., and Hon. Edward Salomon, ... [before] the State Historical Society of Wisconsin, ... January 24, 1866. ... *Madison, Wis.: W. J. Park ... Printer.* 1866. 8vo, pp. 31, (1).—A Paper on the ... Removal of the Indians of Wisconsin ... . By Lapham, Blossom and Dousman. With an Appendix on the Chronology of Wisconsin. *Milwaukee.* 1870. 8vo.—Report on the Disastrous Effects of the Destruction of Forest Trees, now going on so rapidly in the State of Wisconsin. ... By I. A. Lapham, J. G. Knapp and H. Crocker ... . *Madison, Wis.: Atwood & Rublee ... Printers.* 1867. 8vo, pp. 104. B., H., S.

Lapham Institute, *North Scituate, R. I.* Catalogue of the Officers and Students ... 1867 ... 1868. *Providence: A. Crawford Greene, Printer.* 1868. 8vo, pp. 20. H. 38980

Lapi (Michel Angelo). Vita del servo di Dio D. Torivio Alfonso Mogrovejo. *Roma, Nicolangelo Tinassi.* 1656. 4to, Engraved Title, pp. (8), 315, (10). 38981

Lapie (Pierre). Mémoire sur les voyages exécutés dans l'océan glacial arctique, au nord de l'Amérique septentrionale. [*Paris.*] 1821. 8vo, pp. 52. Map. 38982

Extracted from "Nouvelles annales des voyages," Vol. xi.

Laplace (Cyrille Pierre Théodore). Campagne de Circumnavigation de la Frégate l'Artemise, pendant les années 1837, 1838, 1839 et 1840, sous le Commandement de M. Laplace, Capitaine de Vaisseau; publiée par ordre du Gouvernement. *Paris: Arthus Bertrand.* 1840–53. 6 vols., 8vo. P. 38983

First published in twelve parts. The following is an extract:

Laplace. Observations sur l'émancipation des Noirs, extraites d'un ouvrage de M. le Contre-Amiral Laplace, avec notes de M. Jollivet. *Paris: Imprimerie Bruneau.* 1844. 8vo. P. 38984

Laplace. Voyage autour du Monde par les Mers de l'Inde et de la Chine; exécuté sur la Corvette de l'État la Favorite, pendant les années 1830, 1831 et 1832, sous le Commandement de M. La Place .... Avec Atlas hydrographique et Album historique. *Paris: Imprimerie Royale.* 1833–39. 5 vols., 8vo, and Atlas in 2 vols., folio. C. 38985

This valuable work, full of important scientific information, was published by order of the French Government. It is accompanied by an "Album Historique," or Atlas of Views, etc., seventy-two beautiful plates, proof impressions on India paper, which are perhaps the finest series of plates to any of the picturesque voyages, etc.

La Plata. An Account, Historical. *See* [Nuñez (Ignacio).]

Affaire de la Plata. Protestation. 1841. *Paris: impr. de Brière.* 1841. 8vo, pp. 28. 38986

Affaires de la Plata. Petition et Documens. *Paris.* 1844. 8vo, pp. 104. 38987

For other articles having the "Affaires," *see* [Bellemare (A. G.)], Vol. ii.

Anexos a la Memoria del Ministerio de Relaciones Exteriores. *Montevideo.* 1863–64. 4to. 38988

An Appeal on behalf of the British Subjects residing in and connected with the River Plate, against any further violent intervention by the British and French Governments in the Affairs of that Country. *London: Norris & Son.* 1846. 8vo, pp. 43. 38989

Apuntes historicos sobre la Banda Oriental del Rio de la Plata, desde el descubrimiento de este territoria hasta el ano de 1818, formado en Montevideo. *Montevideo.* 4to, pp. 56. 38990

Archivo Americano y espiritu de la prensa del mundo. Nueva Serie. *Buenos Aires.* 1847–1851. 7 vols., 4to. 38991

A bi-monthly political review issued in three languages; every article being published in English, in Spanish, and in French. Continued up to No. 28. It is one of the most important collections of documents relating to the politics of the La Plata States. The motto imprinted on every number—"Viva la Confederacion Argentina! Mueran las Salvajes asquerosos unitarios. Muera el loco traidor Salvaje unitaris Urquiza!"—will sufficiently characterize the tendency of the publication. It was the official organ and literary standard-bearer of the notorious Dictator Rosas, and contains all his proclamations and manifestos. It was published in three languages with the evident design of putting the Dictator's policy in a favorable light before the European readers. *See our* Vol. i., No. 1915.

Arjiropolis o la capital de las estados confederados del Rio de la Plata. Solucion de las dificultades que embarazan la pacificacion permanente del Rio de la Plata. *Santiago.* 1850. 8vo, pp. 161.

Articulos Reales para el gobierno ... de milicias en las provencias de la Plata. *Madrid.* 1801. 8vo, pp. 40. 11 Tables. S.

Coleccion de los documentos relativos a la Navegacion fluvial del Rio de la Plata .... *Carácas.* 1857. 8vo. 38994

Coleccion de Obras. *See* Angelis (P. de), Vol. i., No. 1537.

Constitucion de las provincias unidas del Rio de la Plata. Mandada observar en todo el territorio de la Nacion por convencion nacional convocada en la ciudad de Santa Fé en Setiembre de 1860. *Buenos Aires.* 1860. 4to, pp. 34. 38995

Les Dissensions. *See our* No. 20279; the collation should be 8vo, pp. 87, (1). Map.

Exposicion dirigida a las Provincias Unidas del Rio de La Plata por el ciudadano Dn. Manuel Moreno, Enviado Extraordinario y Ministro Plenipotenciario de Aquella Republica. En Respuesta a las Difamaciones del Tiempo y el Pampero. *Londres: impreso por R. Greenlaw.* 1829. 8vo, pp. 75. 38996

La Guerre dans la Plata en 1865 .... *Paris: Franck.* 1865. 8vo, pp. 36. 38997

Noticia y justificacion del titulo y buena fe conque se fundo la nueva colonia del Sacramento en las tierras de la capitania de S. Vicente en el sitio llamados S. Gabriel, a la ribera del rio de la Plata. [n. p.] 1680. Folio. 38998

Notes on the-Vice Royalty of La Plata, in South America, with a Sketch of the Manners and Characters of the Inhabitants, col-

lected during a Residence in the City of Monte Video, by a Gentleman recently returned from it. To which is added, a History of the Operations of the British Troops in that Country, and Biographical Military Anecdotes of the Principal Officers employed in the different Expeditions. *London: John Stockdale.* 1808. 8vo, pp. 300. Map, Portrait, and Plans. C. 38999

Observations Topographiques faites dans le Rio de la Plata. *Paris.* 1842. 8vo. 39000

Prospectus of the Rio de la Plata Agricultural Association. *London.* 1825. 8vo. Map. S. 39001

River Plate. Further Correspondence. *London: Printed by Harrison and Son.* 1867. Imp. 8vo. 39002

One of the English Parliamentary Blue Books

The River Plate as a Field for Emigration: Its Geography, Climate, Agricultural Capabilities, and the Facilities Afforded for Permanent Settlement. *London.* 186–. 8vo. 39003

War in the River Plate in 1865. *London: R. Hardwicke.* 1865. 8vo. Map. 39004

See Argentine Republic, *also* Demergoy, p. 379, "N. A. Rev.," xxiv. 295, *and* Hunt's "Magazine," xxi. 80.

La Poëpe (Claude de). L'ouverture de l'Amazone, et ses conséquences politiques et commerciales. *Paris: E. Dentu.* 1867. 8vo, pp. 60. C. 39005

La Poëpe. La Politique du Paraguay identité de cette politique avec celle de la France et de la Grande-Bretagne dans le Rio de La Plata. Par Claude De La Poëpe .... *Paris: E. Dentu.* 1869. 8vo, pp. (6), 348 [for 358]. + Deuxième édition. [*Ibid.*]

La Poix Fréminville (M. J. de). Nouvelle Relation du Voyage a la récherche de La Perouse executé en 1791, 1792, 1793 et 1794, par d'Entrecasteaux. Par le Chevalier de Fréminville. *Brest.* 1838. 8vo. 39007

At the end of the volume is a biographical notice of D'Entrecasteaux. *See also* McKeevor (T.)

La Politica Brasilera. *See* Vol. ii., No. 7614.

La Popelliniere (Lancelot Voisin de). Les|Trois|Mondes,| Par le Seignevr|de la Popellinière.|*A Paris, a l'Oliuier de Pierre l'Huillier*|...|1582.|...| 4to, 28 p. l., premier livre, 55 l., second livre, 56 l., troisiesme livre, 50 l., (1 l.) Map. J.C.B., S. 39008

"This curious work is divided into three books, two of which relate entirely to America. The author gives his motives for publishing the work in this manner: 'Quant au but de mon dessein, je ne me suis proposé autre fin, que de faire entendre à nos Riere—neveux les merveilles des jugemens de Dieu en la descouverte des Indes Orientales et Occidentales par le plus estrange effects que la nature produit jamais et avec la tout louable gaillardise des Italiens, Portugais et Espagnols si curieusement hardis de s'exposer á tant de mors: la pauvre pauvre—te du François, qui n'a jusques icy osé tenté si louable ny pareille entreprise.'"—Rich's *Catalogue*, No. 66. "Ce qui donne aujourd'hui du prix à cet ouvrage c'est que l'histoire et la description de l'Amérique en occupent la plus grande partie."—Brunet. "L'extrait du privilège donné le 6 avril 1582, porte: 'Acheué d'imprimer pour la seconde édition en Septembre 1582.'"—Leclerc. *See also* Catalogue of J. C. Brown's library, Vol. i.

Laporte (F. L. de; *comte* de Castelneau). *See* Castleneau.

La Porte (*l'Abbé*). *See* Delaporte (M.), Vol. v., 19359–61.

Laporte, *Ill.* Holland's Laporte City Directory for 1867–8. With a Business Directory. *Chicago: Western Publishing Company.* 1867. 8vo, pp. 163. 39009

La Potherie (B. de). *See* Bacqueville de La Potherie.

Laprade (V. de). Aux Canadiens français soldats de Pie ix [vers]; par Victor de Laprade. *Lyon: imp. de Vingtrinier.* 1868. 8vo, pp. 4. 39010

Laprado (A. E.) La seda en Guatemala, por Mr. A. E. Laprado. *Guatemala: imprenta en Lima.* 1862. 4to. 39011

Lapsley (J. W.) Prospectus of a Combined System of Railways ... and the Nearest and Best Harbor on the Gulf of Mexico. By J. W. Lapsley .... *New-York: S. W. Green, Printer.* 1870. 8vo, pp. 35. Map. H. 39012

Lapuente (L.) Republicanas, por Laurindo Lapuente. *Buenos Aires.* 1865. 8vo, pp. 110. 39013

La Pylaie (B. de). *See* Bachelot de La Pylaie (A. J. M.)

Lara Fernandes (A. F.) *See* Fernandez (A. F. de L.)

Lara Galan (Joseph de). Relacion cierta, y avtencica de vn milagro, qve la Divina Magestad de Dios se digno de obrar con el Capitan D. Pedro de Tapia, y Peralta, vezino de la Ciudad del Cuzco, mudo y Paralitico por tiempo de mas de dos años por la intercession de la Fantissima Virgen, y por la impetracion y Patrocinio de la milagrosa Imagen de N. Señora de la Purificacion, ó Candelaria del Pueblo de Characato. *Lima.* 1692. 4to, 11 l.

Lara (Joseph M. de). Memoria sobre el estado de la Hacienda de la Republica Boliviana en fin del año de 1832, presen-

tada al Congreso Constitucional por el Ministro J. M. de Lara. *Paz de Ayacucho* ... 1833. Folio. 39015

Lara (J. J. F. de). Retrato de los Jesuitas. Por el Cura de Tepeyanco D. Juan José Fernandez de Lara. *Puebla.* 1822. 4to, pp. 15. 39016

Lara (Mariano Aniceto de). Resumen historico de los hechos notables de los partidos Yorkino, Escoces y Santanista, desde la independencia hasta la toma de Mexico por los Norte-americanos, [poema]. *Mexico: S. Perez.* 1852. 18mo, pp. 70. C. 39017

Larchevesque-Thibaud. Extrait du Mémoire justificatif du citoyen Larchevesque-Thibaud .... [*Paris, 4 septembre,* 1793.] 8vo, pp. 40, or less. 39018

Larchevesque-Thibaud. Lettre du citoyen Larchevesque-Thibaud ... aux comités de marine et des colonies de la Convention nationale réunis. [17 septembre, 1793. *Paris:*] *imp. de Testu.* [n. d.] 8vo, pp. 82. 39019

On the affairs of St. Domingo.

Larchevesque-Thibaud. Notes sur les troubles de Saint-Domingue, présentées à la Convention nationale, par le citoyen Larchevesque-Thibaud, ancien procureur de la commune du Cap-Français. [14 mai 1793. *Paris:*] *Testu.* [n. d.]. 8vo, pp. 40, or less. 39020

[Larcom (*Capt.* Henry).] Distressing Narrative of the loss of the Ship Margaret of Salem. [*Beverly, Aug.* 2, 1810.] 12mo, pp. 12. H. 39021

Lard (*Mrs.*) The Banks of the Ohio: a Poem. By Mrs. Lard. *Albany.* 1823. 39022

Lardner (D.) Railway Economy: ... in the United Kingdom, on the Continent, and in America. By Dionysius Lardner. *London: Taylor* ... 1850. Post 8vo, pp. xxiii, (2), 528. + *New York: Harper & Brothers.* 1850. 12mo, pp. 442. B. + [*Ibid.*] 1856. 12mo. 39023

Also: Investigation of the Causes of the Explosion of the Locomotive Engine Richmond, near Reading, Pa. ... *New-York.* 1844. 8vo.

Larea (B. de). Cronica de la orden de N. S. padre S. Francisco de la provincia de S. Pedro y S. Pablo de Mechoacan, compuesta por Fr Bernardo de Larea. *Mexico, viuda de Calderon.* 1643. 4to. 39024

Title from Ternaux, No. 624.

La Reguera (J. D. G. de). Fama Postuma del D. Juan Domingo Gonzalez de La Reguera ... Oracion Funebre. *Lima.* 1805. 4to. Portrait and Plate. 39025

[La Reintrie (Henry Ray de).] A Petition to the Congress of the United States. [*Washington, December 1st,* 1860.] 8vo, pp. 15. H. 39026

Larenaudière (Philippe François de). Historia de Méjico. Por M. De Larenaudière ... Traducida por una sociedad literaria. *Barcelona.* 1844. 8vo, pp. 252, (8). Maps and Plates. B., C.

[Larenaudière.] Historia de Guatemala y del Perú. Traducida por una sociedad literaria. *Barcelona: Imprenta del Imparcial.* 1844. 8vo, pp. 127. Plates. B. 39028

Larenaudière. Notice sur le royaume de Mexico, d'après les derniers ouvrages publiés; suivie d'un coup d'œil historique sur les événemens qui s'y sont succédés depuis 1810. *Paris: J. Smith.* 1824. 8vo, pp. 64. 39029

Larenaudière *and* Lacroix (F.) Mexique et Guatemala, par M. de Larenaudière. Pérou, par M. [Frederic] Lacroix. *Paris: Firmin Didot Frères.* M DCCC XLIII. 8vo, pp. (4), 525, (2). 3 Maps, 78 Plates. BA., C. + [*Ibid.*] M DCCC XLVII. 8vo, pp. (4), 525, (2). Maps and Plates. 39030

Forms Vol. iv. of "l'Univers Pittoresque." *See also* Campe, Vol. iii., No. 10296.

Large Additions to Common Sense. *See* [Paine (Thomas)].

The Larger [and Shorter] Catechism, Agreed upon by the Assembly of Divines at Westminster .... *Philadelphia: Printed by B. Franklin* ... MDCCXLV. 8vo. 39031

This book has ten separate title-pages, but the paging is consecutive throughout. The "Larger Catechism" fills pp. 166–366.

[The Larger] Catechism, agreed upon by the Assembly of Divines at Westminster. Revised by A. McLeod, D.D. *New-York: Whiting & Watson.* 1813. 12mo. S. 39032

The first book stereotyped in America.

Larimer (S. L.) The Capture and Escape; or, Life among the Sioux. By Mrs. Sarah L. Larimer. ... *Philadelphia: Claxton, Remsen & Haffelfinger.* 1870. 12mo, pp. 252. Portrait, 2 Plates.

A vivid and apparently candid narrative of the terrible experience of a woman, the survivor of the massacre.

Larimore (J. W.) An Evening with the Chaplain. By J. W. Larimore. ... *Boston: American Tract Society.* [n. d.] 18mo, pp. 46. + *New York.* [n. d.] 18mo, pp. 46. B. 39034

Larios (H.) Arte de la Lengua Mame, por Fr. Hieronymo Larios. *Mexico.* 1697. 39035

The language of Guatemala. Barcia and Ternaux, No. 306, date this book 1607; but Ludewig, p. 105, gives the date as above.

La Riva Aguero (J.) *See* Aguero (J.), Vol. i., No. 523.

La Rivas (Manuel Joseph de). Grammatica construccion de los Hymnos Ecclesiasticos, dividida en siete libros, por el orden del Braviario Romano. Explicacion y medida de sus versos. *En Mexico, en la Imprenta de D. Francisco Xavier Sanchez.* 1738. 8vo, pp (16), 164. 39036

Larke (J. K.) General Grant and his Campaigns. By Julian K. Larke. Illustrated .... *New York: J. C. Derby & N. C. Miller.* 1864. 12mo, pp. 469, 40. Portrait. C. 39037

Larke. The Life of Gen. P. H. Sheridan. By Julian K. Larke. *New York: T. R. Dawley.* 1864. 12mo, pp. 108.

Larkin (E. *and* S.) Catalogue of Books, for Sale by E. and S. Larkin, No. 47, Cornhill, Boston ... *Boston.* [n. d.] 12mo, pp. 92. 39039

One of the earliest American catalogues.

Larkin (S.) The Nightingale. A Collection of ... Popular, Ancient, and Modern Songs: Set to Music. Selected by Samuel Larkin. ... *Portsmouth: William and Daniel Treadwell.* 1804. 12mo, pp. 288. H. 39040

Larned (Edwin C.) The Great Conflict, What has been gained, and What remains to be done. Oration ... by E. C. Larned, Esq., at Aurora, ... 4th of July, 1865. ... *Chicago: Printed by H. A. Newcombe & Co.* MDCCCLXV. 8vo, pp. 23. H.

Also: The New Fugitive Slave Law. Speech ... in ... Chicago, Oct. 25th, 1850, in Reply to Hon. S. A. Douglas ... *Chicago: Democrat Office.* 1850. 8vo, pp. 16. B.

Larned (*Mrs.* L.) The American Nun; or the Effects of Romance. By Mrs. L. Larned. *Boston: Otis, Broaders & Co.* 1836. 16mo, pp. vi, 142. 39042

La Rocha (P. F.) Revista Politica sobre la historia de la revolucion de Nicaragua en defensa de la administracion del ex

director D. I. S. Sandoval. *Granada: Imprenta de la Concepcion.* 1847. 4to, pp. 72. 39043

La Roche (A.) *and* Richardson (J.) Island of Anticosti. Scientific Reports made by A. La Roche and James Richardson. *New York.* 1865. 8vo, pp. 92. 39044

Laroche (Benjamin). Histoire de l'abolition de l'esclavage dans les colonies françaises. 1re partie: Ile de la Reunion. Administration du commissaire général de la république, M. Sarda Garriga, du 13 octobre 1848 au 8 mars 1850. *Paris: Victor Lecou.* 1851. 8vo. 39045

La Roche (——). Letter from Quebeck, in Canada, to M. L'Maine, containing an Account of the Designs of the French upon the English in North America, and the defenceless condition of the English Colonies. *Boston.* 1754. 8vo, pp. 8. 39046

La Roche (R.) Pneumonia: its supposed Connection, Pathological and Etiological, with Autumnal Fevers; including an Inquiry into the Existence and Morbid Agency of Malaria. By R. La Roche, M.D. ... *Philadelphia: Blanchard and Lea.* 1854. 8vo, pp. xx, 33–502. B. 39047

La Roche. Yellow Fever, considered in its Historical, Pathological, Etiological, and Therapeutical Relations. Including a Sketch of the Disease as it has occurred in Philadelphia from 1699 to 1854 .... By R. La Roche, M.D. ... *Philadelphia: Blanchard and Lea.* 1855. 2 vols., 8vo, pp. lxi, (2), 17–615; viii, 17–813. B. 39048

Also: An Oration ... before the Philadelphia Medical Society ... February 3, 1827. ... *Philadelphia: Mifflin and Parry, Printers.* 1827. 8vo, pp. (6), 31. B.

[Laroche-Catineau.] Communication Officielle de trois Lettres de Catineau-Laroche ... [n. p. 1816.] 4to, pp. 32. B.

See also Catineau-Laroche, Vol. iii., Nos. 11525–26.

La Roche Gallichon (F. C. de). Sendschreiben, betreffend die Wiederfindung des alten Grönlands, und der unzertrennlich damit verknüpften sogenannten Nordwestlichen Durchfahrt. *Kopenhagen: Gedruckt ... bey C. F. Holm.* 1787. 8vo, pp. 102.

La Roche-Héron (C. de). *See* [De Courcy (H.)], Vol. v.

La Roche-Tilhac (*M.* de). *See* Almanac Americain.

La Rochefoucauld-Liancourt (François Alexandre Frédéric, *Duke* de). A Comparative View of Mild and Sanguinary Laws; and the Good Effects of the former, Exhibited in the Present Economy of the Prisons of Philadelphia. *Philadelphia.* 1796. 12mo. + Second Edition. *London: Darton and Harvey.* 1796. 8vo, pp. 48. 39051

La Rochefoucauld-Liancourt. Opinion de M. de La Rochefoucault-Liancourt, Député du Département de l'Oise, Sur la Question des Colonies. *Paris: Du Pont.* 1791. 8vo, pp. 26.

[La Rochefoucauld-Liancourt.] Des Prisons de Philadelphie. Par un Européen. *Paris: Chez Du Pont. An* IV [1796]. 8vo, pp. 63. + Seconde Edition. *Amsterdam: W. Holtrop.* 1799. 8vo, pp. 97. + *Paris.* 1800. 8vo. + Fourth Edition. *Paris.* 1819. 8vo. 39053

[La Rochefoucauld-Liancourt.] On the Prisons of Philadelphia. By an European. *Philadelphia.* 1796. 8vo, pp. 46.

[La Rochefoucauld-Liancourt.] Over de gevangenhuizen van Philadelphia. Uit het Fransch. *Amsterdam.* 1796. 8vo. 39055

La Rochefoucauld-Liancourt. Voyage | dans | les Etats-Unis | d'Amérique, | fait en 1795, 1796 et 1797. | Par La Rochefoucauld-Liancourt. | *A Paris* | *Chez Du Pont, Buisson, Charles Pougens,* | *L'an* VII *de la République.* [1799.] 8 vols., 8vo, pp. xxiv, 365; (2), iv, 349; (2), iv, 384; (2), iii, 349; (2), iv, 400; (2), iii, 336; (2), iv, 366; (4), 244. 3 Maps and Plates. B., BA. + *Paris.* 1800. 8 vols., 8vo. Maps and Plates. 39056

See Faribault's Catalogue, No. 371.

La Rochefoucauld-Liancourt. Travels through The United States of North America, the Country of the Iroquois, and Upper Canada, in the Years 1795, 1796, and 1797; with an Authentic Account of Lower Canada. By the Duke de La Rochefoucault Liancourt. [Translated from the French by H. Neuman.] *London: ... R. Phillips ...* 1799. 2 vols., 4to, pp. xxiii, (1), 642, (12); (2), 686, (9). 3 Maps. BA., C. + Second Edition. *London: ... R. Phillips ...* 1800. 4 vols., 8vo, pp. xxiii, 591, (16); (2), 523, (16); (2), 717, (22); (2), 610, (8). 3 Maps, 5 Tables. C. + *London.* 1803. 4 vols., 8vo. 39057

The observations of this distinguished author, made during a three years residence, extend to the political constitution of the country, the manners, etc., of the inhabitants, its physical state and natural history. "The translator appears to have executed his

task faithfully, and to be well acquainted with the country described. His notes frequently increase the information, and sometimes correct the errors of the original. A copy of this work which formerly belonged to the late Robert Barclay, has the following note, apparently in his own handwriting: 'These travels are to be read throughout under the general belief of their being composed to please the French nation, with a view to the author's return from exile. Many of his statements, etc., are much questioned; and, above all, that degree of attachment he represents to exist among the Americans to France.'"—Rich, I. 415. *See also* Field's "Essay," No. 930, "M. Rev.," XXX. 1, 201; XXXV. 9, 113, Priestley (Joseph), Tuckerman's "America and her Commentators," p. 94, *also* included in part, in Mavor's "Voyages," Vol. XXIV.

La Rochefoucauld-Liancourt. Reisen in den Jahren 1795, 1796 und 1797 durch alle an der See belegenen Staaten der Nordamerikanischen Republik; imgleichen Ober-Canada und das Land der Irokesen. Aus der Französischen Handschrift übersetzt. *Hamburg: Benj. Gottlob Hoffmann.* 1799. 3 vols., 8vo, pp. viii, 774; vi, 588; xx, 629. 39058

La Rocque (C.) Notice biographique de Mgr. Lartique, premier évêque de Montreal. Suivie de son oraison funèbre par M. C. LaRocque, curé de l'Acadie. *Montréal.* 1841. 8vo, pp. 23. 39059

La Rocque *or* La Roque (*M.* de). Mémoire analytique: où l'on déduit par une grande réunion de faits les principes à l'aide desquels ou pourra faire prospérer de Nouvelles Colonies, plus rapidement que n'ont été élevées les établissemens aujourd'hui anciens, et dans lesquels le temps seul pouvoit fixer les methodes. Suivi de l'examen de questions relatives aux effets que les progrès de la population et des cultures du Nouveau Monde produiront sur l'Europe, avec un tableau de la population, et des produits de l'Archipel de l'Amérique. Par M. de la Rocque, ci-devant valet-de-chambre de la Reine ... . *Londres.* 1796. 8vo. C. 39060

Only two hundred and fifty copies printed. Dedicated to the King of Spain. *See* Rich, I. 399, *also* Literary and Historical Society of Quebec.

La Roquette (Jean Baptiste Marie Alexandre Dezos de). Notice biographique sur l'Amiral Sir John Franklin, par M. de La Roquette. [*Paris: Société de Géographie.* 1857?] 4to, pp. 67, (12). Facsimiles, 2 Maps, and Portrait. C. 39061

La Roquette. Notice sur la vie et les travaux de M. le Baron A. de Humboldt. Par M. de La Roquette. *Paris: Imprimerie Martinet.* 1860. 4to. 2 Portraits and Facsimile.

See also Humboldt (F. H. A. von), Vol. VIII., No. 33709.

La Rosa (Hipolito Buena de). Causa Medico Criminal que, en este real protomedicato del Peru, han seguido los Profesores de

la Facultad Mèdica contra los Cirujanos, Pharmaceuticos Phlebotómos, &c. Sobre contenerlos en los terminos de sus respectivos Professiones. [*Lima.* 1764.] 4to, 7 l. J.C.B. 39063

La Rosa (L. de). Comunicacion oficial al Ministro de relaciones, D. Luis de la Rosa, con motivo de su circular de 17 Enero ultimo sobre los ultimos sucesos de San Luis Potosi. *Orizava.* 1848. 4to, pp. 10. 39064

La Rosa. Impresiones de un Viage de Mexico á Washington en Octubre y Noviembre de 1848. Por D. Luis de la Rosa. *Nueva York.* 1849. 8vo, pp. 54. 39065

La Rosa Toro (A. de). Biblioteca de instruccion primaria superior por Agustin de La Rosa Toro. *Lima.* 1865–66. 13 parts in 15 vols., 12mo. 39066

Vol. VI. Mineralogia, pp. 58; VII. Botanica, pp. 64; VIII. Geografia politica universal comparada, pp. 154; XIB. Geografica fisica, fisografica y politica del Peru, pp. 18; XIIA. Historia de America, pp. 126; XIIB. Historia del Peru, pp. 158.

La Rosa Toro. Zoologia ó estudio de los animales ... por Agustin de la Rosa Toro. *Lima.* 1865. 12mo, pp. 106.

[Larpent (*Sir* George).] On Protection to West India Sugar. *London.* 1823. 8vo, pp. 71. S. 39068

A second edition contains a reply to Joseph Marryat's "Reply."

Larrabee (C.) Thoughts on Peace and War; the Result of Twenty odd Years Reflection. By Charles Larrabee. ... *Hartford: Press of Case, Tiffany ...* 1845. 8vo, pp. 63. 39069

[Larrabee.] To the Editors of the Albany Register, N. Y.; ... [*Groton Heights, Conn., July 17th,* 1854.] 8vo, pp. 12. B.

Also: ... An Appeal from our Present Divided Times, to the Counsels of Washington. ... *New London: Printed by Starr and Farnham.* 1854. 12mo, pp. 12. B. — A Report of the Condition of our Wounded Fellow-Citizens, ... with a brief Sketch of our Political Condition. ... *New Haven.* 1836. 12mo, pp. 72. B. — Speech December 17, 1859, on Organization of the House. [n. p. n. d.] 8vo.

Larrabee (W. C.) Asbury and his Coadjutors. By William C. Larrabee. Edited by D. W. Clark. *Cincinnati.* 1853. 2 vols., 16mo. C. 39071

Larrabee. Rosabower: a Collection of Essays and Miscellanies. By W. C. Larrabee. *Cincinnati: R. P. Thompson, Printer.* 1855. 12mo, pp. 281. 39072

Contains sketches of American, especially New-England scenery and character, also "The Poets of the West" and "The Backwoods Expedition."

Larrabee. Wesley and his Coadjutors. By Rev. Wm. C. Larrabee, A.M. Edited by Rev. B. F. Tefft, D.D. *Cincinnati: Swormstedt & Power.* 1851. 2 vols., 12mo, pp. 392; 280. Portrait. C. 39073

Also: Inaugural Address as Principal of Oneida Conference Seminary, November 10, 1831. ... *Cazenovia, N. Y.* 1831. 12mo.

Larragoiti (J. N.) Informe por la jurisdicion eclesiastica del Obispado de Valladolid de Michoacan. *Mexico.* 1782. Folio, pp. 127, 36. 39074

Larrain (J. F. de). Defensa de la Viuda. *See* No. 12764.

Larrainzar (Federico). Carta sobre los ultimos sucesos de Centro-America. *Mexico.* 1864. 4to, pp. 66. 39075

Larrainzar (M.) Algunas Ideas sobre la Historia y Manera de escribir la de Mexico, especialmente la contemporanea, desde la declaration de independencia en 1821, hasta nuestros dias. Memoria escrita y presentada a la Sociedad Mexicana de Geografia y Estadistica por su socio de numero el Sr. Lic. D. Manuel Larrainzar. *México: I. Cumplido.* 1865. Folio, pp. v, 105.

Contains "Catalogo de los principales historiadores de México, y otros autores que han escrito sobra las cosas de America."

Larrainzar. Biografia de Don Fray Bartolomé de Las Casas, Obispo de Chiapa. *Mejico.* 1837. 8vo. 39077

Larrainzar. Dictamen presentado à la Sociedad de geografia y estadistica de Mexico por el Sr. Lic. D. Manuel Larrainzar, sobre la obra del Sr. abate E. Carlos Brasseur de Bourboug, cuyo titulo es el siguiente: "Si ecsiste el origen de la historia primitive de Mexico ... ." *México: Imprenta de Ignacio Cumplido.* 1865. 4to, pp. 25. 39078

Larrainzar. Noticia Historica de Soconusco, y su incorporacion à la República Mexicana. Escrita por Manuel Larrainzar. *México: J. M. Lara.* 1843. 12mo, pp. viii, (4), 194.

Larrainzar. Voto particular del Sr. Senador Lic. D. Manuel Larrainzar, sobre el acuerdo de la Cámara de Diputados, relativo a la reforma de Aranceles que presentó en la Sesion del dia 20 de Marzo de 1849, como individuo de la comision especial a cuyo examen, ... pasò este negocio. *México.* 1849. 8vo, pp. 127.

Larrainzar (M.) Carta Edificante de la Vida del P. Martin Larrainzar, Natural de la Ciudad, y Puerto de Vera Cruz. *México.* 1763. 8vo. 39081

Larrañaga (B. F.) La America Socorrida en el Gobierno del Excelentisimo Señor Don Bernardo de Galvez Conde de Galvez ... . Egloga ... por Don Bruno Francisco Larrañaga. *Mexico.* 1786. 4to, pp. 25. 39082

Closely follows in form and words the first Egloga of Virgil's Bucolics, only that for its contents Mexican topics are substituted.

Larrañaga. Prospecto de una Eneida Apostólica, ô Epopeya, que celebra la predicacion del V. Apóstol del Occidente P. Fr. Antonio Margil de Jesus: Intitulada Margileida. Escrita con puros versos de P. Virgilio Maron, y traducida a verso Castellano: La que se propone al público de esta America septentrional por Subsripcion: Para que colectados anticipadamente los gastos necesarios, se proceda inmediatamente â su impresion. Su Autor Don Bruno Francisco Larrañaga. *Impresa en Mexico en la Imprenta nueva Madrileña de los Herederos del Lic. D. Joseph de Jauregui. Calle de S. Bernardo. Año de* 1788. 4to, pp. (4), 28.

The whole work has never been published. Immediately after its publication, this prospectus was so severely attacked by Alzate, the éditor of the "Gaceta de Literatura de Mexico," that Larrañaga was obliged to write in its defence: "Apologia de la Margileida y su prospecto y satisfacion a las notas de la Gaceta de Literatura." *Mexico.* 1789. 4to. M. Octave Delepierre, in his "Revue analytique des ouvrages ecrits en centons"—*London.* 1868. 16mo—gives a full description of this prospectus, which he considers to be very rare. *See also* Beristain de Souza's "Bibl. Hisp.-Amer. Sept."

Larrañaga (B. J. de). Poema heroyco, en celebridad de la colocacion de la estatua colosal de bronce de Carlos IV. rey de España, y emperador de las Indias. [*Mexico.*] 1804. 4to.

There are copies on thick paper.

Larrazabal (A.) Memoria documentada que al Illmo Sr. Arzobispo Coadjutor de esta santa Iglesia, Dr. Francisco Garcia Pelaez, presenta el Dr. Antonio Larrazabal, canonigo penitentiario, ... [*Guatemala.*] *Año de* 1864. 4to, pp. (6), 10, 13, 4, 6, 9.

See also Vol. IX., No. 34838.

Larrazabal. Informe documentado, que, con ocasion de la provision hecha de las dignidades y pretendas de este S. I. M. produce en su M. I. y V. Cabildo, como Presidente que ha sido de el y Dean que es hoy, el Ilmõ. Sr. Dr. Don Antonio Larrazabal, ... *Guatemala: Imprenta de Luna. Año de* 1848. 4to, pp. 49, (2).

Also: Relacion de las exequias que se hicieron en la S. iglesia catedr. de Guatemala al exmo. D. Fr. Ramon Casaus y Torres, arzobispo. *Guatemala.* 1846. 4to, 30 l.

Larrazábal (*Dr.* Felipe). Coleccion de Articulos sobre la Cuestion Arzobispo de Carácas y Venezuela, publicados en "El Patriota." *Carácas.* 1852. 4to, pp. 31. 39087

Larrazábal. Correspondencia General. *See* Bolivar, Vol. II., No. 6186, *add* Vol. II., pp. 579.

Larrazábal. Historia de los Seminarios Clericales. *Carácas.* 1856. 8vo, pp. 130. 39088

Larrazábal. Memorias contemporaneas. Apuntamientos sobre la vida pública del ciudadano Antonio Leocadio Guzman, para servir á la imparcial historia de Colombia y Venezuela. *Carácas.* 1846. 8vo, pp. 79. 39089

Larrazábal. The Life of Simon Bolivar, Liberator of Columbia and Peru, Father and Founder of Bolivia: Carefully written from Authentic and Unpublished Documents. By Dr. Felipe Larrazábal. Vol. I. *New York: American News Company.* 1866. 8vo, pp. viii, 410. 39090

No more of this translation published.

Larreátegui (J. D.) Descripciones de Plantas. Discurso que en la abertura del estudio de Botánica de 1 de Junio de 95. pronunció en el Real Jardin de México el Br. D. Joseph Dionisio Larreátegui ... . [*Mexico.*] 1795. 4to, pp. 48. H. 39091

With a description and colored plate of the newly discovered and beautiful Chironthodendron.

Larreátegui. Description Botanique du Chironthodendron, Arbre de Mexique, de l'Espagnol de Don J. D. Larreátegui, par M. Lescallier. *Paris.* 1805. 4to. 2 colored Plates. 39092

Larrey (P. J. de). Missive van zyn Hoogheid met een Reglement omtrent den Vaart en Handel op Essequibo en Demerary. *Gravenhage den 5 December* 1770. Folio, pp. 5.

Larreynaga (M.) Memoria sobre el Fuego de los Volcanes, escrita por Miguel Larreynaga, natural de Centro America. *Guatemala.* 1843. 8vo, pp. (8), 75, (1). 39094

Larreynaga. Noticia Biographica del distinguido Literato D. Miguel Larreynaga. Escrita por varios Gualtemaltecos. *Guatemala.* 1847. Imp. 8vo, pp. 10. 39095

Larrinaga (José Pastor). Cartas Historicas á un Amigo. *Lima.* 1812. 4to. 39096

Larriva (José Joay de). Elogio del exemo e illmo Señor D. D. Bart, Maria de las Heras pronunciado en la Universidad de san Marcos. *Lima.* 1815. 12mo. 39097

Larriva. Panegírico de la Concepcion de María. *Lima.* 1816. 4to, pp. 30. 39098

Larriva y Ruiz (J. J.) Sermon de Accion de Gracias por el Recibimiento del Excel. Señor D. J. de la Pezuela y Sanchez, Virey del Perú. *Lima.* 1816. 4to. 39099

Larroque (L.) Informe sobre los Depósitos de Guano de Mejillones presentado al Señor Ministro de Hacienda, por Don Luis Larroque (Injeniero de minas), comisado al efecto por el Gobierno. *Santiago.* 1863. 8vo, pp. 187. 4 Plates. 39100

Larroque (Patrice). De l'Esclavage chez les Nations Chrétiennes. *Bruxelles.* 1859. 12mo. + *Paris.* 1860. 12mo, pp. 212, (1). B. + Seconde édition. *Paris: Librairie Internationale.* 1864. 12mo. + Troisième édition. *Paris: Michel Lévy.* 1869. 12mo. 39101

Larsen (J. M.) América ante-colombiana ó sea noticias sobre algunas interesantes ruinas y sobre los viages en América anteriores á Colon. Por Juan Mariano Larsen. *Buenos-Aires: imprenta de Mayo.* 1865. 12mo, pp. (8), 262. C. + [*Ibid.*] 1866.

Lartigue (Joseph). Description de la Côte du Pérou, entre 19° et 16° 20′ de Latitude Sud; et Renseignemens sur la Navigation des Côtes Occidentales d'Amérique, depuis le Cap Horn jusqu'à Lima; ... Par M. Lartigue ... *Paris.* 1827. 8vo, pp. 42.

Lartigue. Instruction nautique sur les côtes de la Guiane Française, rédigée d'après les Ordres du Ministre de la Marine et des Colonies, par M. Lartigue ... . *Paris.* 1827. 8vo, pp. 100. Map. + Seconde édition. *Paris: Au dépot de la marine.* 1860. 8vo. Map, 2 Tables. 39104

Lartigue (J. J.) Mandement contre l'insurrection partielle du Bas Canada. Par J. J. Lartigue. *Montréal.* 1837. 8vo.

Lartigue. Mémoire sur l'inamovibilité des curés en Canada, suivi de remarques sur les notes de M. Lafontaine, avocat, relativement à l'inamovibilité des curés dans le Bas Canada. Par J. J. Lartigue. *Montréal.* 1837. 8vo. 39106

See also La Rocque (C.), No. 39059.

Larue (*Chevalier* de). Histoire du 18 fructidor, ou Mémoires contenant la vérité sur divers événements qui se rattachent à cette conjuration, précédés du Tableau des factions qui déchirent la France, et terminés par quelques détails sur la Guyane considérée

comme colonie, par le Chevalier de Larue, l'un des députés déportés à Sinnamary au 18 fructidor. *Paris.* 1821. 8vo.

LaRue (F. A. H.) Élogé funèbre de M. l'Abbé L. J. Casault, premier recteur de l'Université Laval. ... *Québec.* 1863. 18mo, pp. 29. 39108

Larzelere (J.) A Discourse on the Death of General George Washington, delivered in the Township of Northampton, Bucks County, Pennsylvania, February 22, 1800. By the Rev. Jacob Larzelere. *Mount Holly.* 1800. 8vo, pp. 18. N., W.

Very rare.

La Sagra. *See* Ramon de la Sagra.

La Sale *or* La Salle (*M.* de). *See* Cavelier (Jean), Vol. III., 11597, Joutel (*M.*), Vol. IX., 36760–63, *and* Tonti (*Chevalier*).

[La Salle (Antoine de).] La Salade nou | uellemēt Imprimee | a Paris Laquelle fait | mention de tous les pays du monde et du pays de | la belle sibille. Auec la figure pour aller aumont | de la dicte sibille. Et aussi la figure de la mer et de | la terre auec plusieurs belles remonstrances. | *Et se vendent a paris par Philippe le Noir* | *Relieur iure en luniversite de Paris demourant en la grãt rue Sainct Jacques a lẽseigne de la Roze* | *blanche couronnee.* | [1527.] 4to, pp. lx, (4). 39110

Concerning this rare piece, which contains a reference to Greenland, *see* Brunet's "Manuel" *and* [Harrisse's] "Bibl. Amer. Vet.," No. 140, and Vol. II., No. 80.

La Salle (A. de). Relation du Voyage autour du Monde, exécuté sur la Corvette la Bonite, commandée par Vaillant. *Paris.* 1845–52. 3 vols., 8vo. A. 39111

La Salle (A. N.) Tableau de la vie militaire d'Adrien Nicolas La Salle, Marechal de Camp le 1er Avril 1791, depuis Commandant de la Province de Saint Domingue, et deux fois Gouverneur général par interim, des Isles sous le vent. [*Paris.* 1793.] 8vo, pp. 50. 39112

La Salle, *Texas.* A Statement indicating some of the Advantages of the Proposed City of La Salle, on the Bay of Matagorda, in Texas. Together with the Manner in which the Title of the Property embracing its site is vested in the Trustees. *New Orleans.* 1848. 8vo, pp. 35. Map. 39113

Las Casas. *See* Casas (B. de las), Vol. III., Nos. 11229–89.

The following are additional titles and corrections.

Las Casas. Breve relacion de la destruccion de las Indias Occidentales. ... *Mexico.* 1822. 12mo, pp. 164. 39114

Las Casas. Tratado cõpro. *See our* No. 11231.

There are two editions of this tract; one, probably the first, is complete in 80 leaves, and the colophon differs.

Las Casas. Aqui se contiene | vna disputa, o controuersia: entre el | Obispo don fray Bartholome de las | Casas, o Casaus, Obispo que fue de la | Ciudad Real de Chiapa que es en- | las Indias, parte de la nueua Espa- | ña, y el doctor Gines de Sepulueda | Coronista del Emperador nuestro Se- | ñor, sobre q el doctor cõtendia, que las | conquistas de las Indias contra los | Indios eran licitas, y el Obispo por | el contrario defendio y affirmo auer si | do y ser impossible no serlo: tyranicas | injustas & iniquas. La qual question | se ventilo & disputo en presẽcia de mu- | chos letrados theologos & juristas, | en vna congregacion que mãdo su ma- | gestad juntar el año de mil y quiniẽtos | y cincuẽta en la villa de Vallad. Año. | 1552. | [Colophon:] *A loor y gloria de nuestro | señor Jesu Christo y de la sacratissima virgen sancta | Maria su madre. Fue impressa la presẽte obra | en la muy noble & muy leal ciudad de Se- | uilla, en casa de Sebastiã Trugillo im- | pressor de libros, frõtero de nue- | stra señora de gracia. Acabo- | sse a. x. dias del mes de Se- | tiembre Año de mil & | quiniẽtos & cincuẽtos | y dos Años.* | 4to, 62 leaves. 39115

This is another edition of *our* No. 11234.

Las Casas. Breve Relacion de la Destruccion de las Indias Occidentales, Presentada a Felipe II siendo Principe de Asturias por D. Fr. Bartolomé de las Casas, Del Orden de Predicadores, Obispo de Chiapa. *Impresa en Sevilla en* 1552. *Reimpresa en Londres Por Schulze y Dean.* 1812. 12mo, pp. (4), 140. 39116

This is a corrected title of *our* No. 11236.

Las Casas. Entre los remedios. *See our* No. 11229, and for collation *read* 54 leaves, the last leaf blank.

Las Casas. Le Mirror. *See our* No. 11270, and for collation *say* Engraved Title and 68 leaves.

Las Casas. La decouverte des Indies Occidentales, par les Espagnols et les moyens dont ils se sont servis pour s'en rendre Maitres. Ecrite par Dom Balthazar de Las Casas, Eveque de Chiapa. ... *A Paris, Chez Florentin & Pierre Delanlue,* ... M DCCI. Small 8vo, Engraved Title, pp. (10), 382, (2). 39117

This is a variation of *our* No. 11275.

Las Casas. Relation des Voyages. *See our* No. 11274, but for collation *read* pp. (12), 402, Plate, and for "curiceuse," *read* curieuse.

Las Casas. D. Bartholo- | mæi de las Casas, | Episcopi Chiapensis, viri | in omni Doctrinarvm Genere | exercitatissimi, erudita & elegans explicatio Quæstionis | Vtrùm Reges vel Principes iure aliquo vel titulo, & salua con- | scientia, Ciues ac Subditos à Regia Corona alineare, & alterius | Domini particularis ditioni subijcere possint? Ante hac | nunquam ab vllo Doctorum ita lucu- | lenter tractata. | Edita cura & studio Vuolffgangi Griestetteri. [Woodcut.] Cum gratia & priuilegio Casareæ Maiestatis. | *Francofvrti ad Mœnvm,* M. D. LXXI. [Colophon:] *Impressvm Francofvrti ad Mœnum apvd Georgivm Corvinum, Impensis Hieronymi Feyerabend,* M. D. LXXI. 4to, pp. (8), 67. 39118

A corrected title of *our* No. 11237. "This piece of Las Casas' was not included in his Spanish works, first issued in 1552–53, and has never been printed in Spain.—Stevens. It is even more rare than the other pieces of Las Casas which are so seldom reunited. Its only relation to America consists in the general question involved in the title.

Las Casas. The Spanish Colonie. *See our* No. 11287.

Add for a note: This is a translation from Migrode's French version of the Spanish originals, and not as Lowndes quotes "Englished from the Spanish by M. M. S."

Las Casas. A | Relation | Of the First | Voyages and Discoveries | Made by the Spaniards in America. | With | An Account of their unparallel'd Cruelties | on the Indians, in the destruction of a- | bove Forty Millions of People. | Together with the Propositions offer'd to the | King of Spain, to prevent the further Ruin | of the West-Indies. | By Don Bartholomew de las Casas, Bishop of Chiapa, | who was an Eye-witness of their Cruelties. | Illustrated with Cuts. | To which is added, | The Art of Travelling, shewing how a Man may | dispose his Travels to the best advantage. | *London: Printed for Daniel Brown at the Black Swan and Bible | without Temple-Bar, and Andrew Bell at the Cross | keys and Bible in Cornhil, near Stocks-market,* 1699. 8vo, pp. (8), 248, 40, 4. 2 folded Plates. B. 39119

The same as *our* No. 11289, with a different title-page.

[Las Casas.] Popery and Slavery Display'd Containing The Character of Popery, and a Relation of Popish Cruelties. Including the Spanish Butcheries on the Native Indians ... The Fourth Edition. *London: C. Corbett.* 1745. 8vo, pp. (4), 76. 39120

The dedication to George II. is signed "Thos. Harris." It is abridged and served up from Las Casas. This is a corrected title of *our* No. 30525, Vol. IX.

Las Casas. Relacion muy lastimosa de ciertas ruinas y casos notables succedidos en la ciudad de Arequipa y otros lugares, en el año de 1605. [n. p. 1605.] Folio. 39121

"This book is mentioned by Barcia, yet Alcedo, who gives the list of the bishops of Cuzco in his dictionary, has not said anything about the name of Las Casas."—Ternaux, No. 286.

Las Casas. Cancionero Spiritual, en que se contienen obras muy provechosas y edificantes, en particular unas coplas muy devotas en loor de nuestro Señor Jesucristo y de la sacratisima Virgen Maria, su madre; con una farsa intitulada, &c.; compuesto por el reverendo padre Las Casas, indigno religioso, &c.; dedicado al Illmo. Señor D. Fr. de Çumarraga, primero obispo de la gran cibdad de Temixtitlan. *Mexico, por Juan Pablos Lombardo,* 1546. 39122

Our No. 14667 is partly by Las Casas. *See* "Old England for Ever," Purchas' "Pilgrims," Vol. IV., p. 1569, *also* Marmocchi's "Viaggi," Vol. V.

Las Casas (L. de). Elogios fúnebres del excmo. señor D. Luis de Las Casas y Aragoni, teniente general de los R[les]. exércitos. Hechos y publicados por la Real sociedad económica de la Havana ... *Havana: Imprenta de la capitania general.* 1802. 4to, 10 l.

Las Cases (Emmanuel Dieudonné Marie Joseph, *Comte* de). Atlas Historique Généalogique Chronologique et Géographique de A. Lesage. *Paris: Leclère.* 1825–26. Folio, pp. (8). 41 Maps.

Las Cases. A Complete Genealogical, Historical, Chronological, and Geographical Atlas. ... From the Last London Edition, Improved by C. Gros ... and J. Aspin ... First American Edition ... *Philadelphia: M. Carey and Son.* 1820. Folio, pp. (10). 71 Maps. + Second American Edition ... [*Ibid.*] 1820. Folio, pp. (10). 70 Maps. B. + Third American Edition ... [*Ibid.*] 1821. Folio, pp. (8). 71 Maps. BA., C. 39125

Lascaux (Paul de). Benjamin Franklin, sa vie, ses ouvrages, ses découvertes. *Mirecourt: Humbert.* 1864. 16mo. 39126

Lascelles (A. R. W.) Treatise on the Nature and Cultivation of Coffee, with some Remarks on the Management and Purchase of Coffee Estates. By Arthur R. W. Lascelles. *London: S. Low, Son & Marston.* 1865. 12mo, pp. vi, (2), 74. C. 39127

Lasell Seminary. [First Annual Catalogue of the] Lasell Female Seminary, at Auburndale, ... Mass. for 1852–3. *Boston: Printed by Alfred Mudge.* 1853. 8vo, pp. 16. Continued.

Also: Annual Circular ... 1859–60. *Boston.* 1860. 8vo. Continued

La Serre (Barbier, *Chev.* de). Essais historiques et critiques sur la Marine de France de 1661 à 1789, et des principaux objets qui y sont relatifs, par le Chevalier De la Serre, Ancien officier ... *Paris.* 1814. 8vo, pp. viii, 377. S. 39129

Contains some references to the American Revolution.

A Lash for Petty Tyrants, or Government of Laws, Not Despotism. Being an Account of Outrages committed by some of the Police Officers of New-York. In English and Spanish. ... *New-York: Printed for the Translator.* 1827. 8vo, pp. 13.

Laso (B.) Discurso a la Convencion Nacional. [n. p.] 1834. 8vo. 39131

Also: Informe el Consejo de Gobierno sobre su Decreto de 6 de Junio. ... [n. p.] 1834. 8vo. Also other pieces.

Laso de la Vega (A. de C.) + | Por | D. Antonio de Cordova | Laso de la Vega, Capitan de las Guardas | de el Governador, y Teniente Gene- | ral de la Cavalleria del Reyno | de Chile. | Con | El Señor Fiscal del | Consejo de Indias, y el Promotor Fiscal | de Cobranças de él. | [*Lima.* 1620?] Folio, 4 l. 39132

Lasor a Varea (A.) Universus Terrarum Orbis Scriptorum calamo delineatus, hoc est Auctorum fere omnium, Qui de Europæ, Asiæ, Africæ, & Americæ Regnis, Provinciis, Populis, Civitatibus, Oppidis, Arcibus, Maribus, Insulis, Montibus, Fluminibus, Fodinis, Balneis, publicis Hortis, & de Aliis tam super, quàm subtus Terram Locis; de illorum varia Appellatione, Situ, Distantia, Terminis; de Gentium quoque Moribus, Religione, Legibus, Medendi Usu, Habitu, Idiomate, & reliquis permultis ad dicta Loca Spectantibus Quovis Tempore, & Qualibet Lingua Scripserunt, cvm anno, loco, et forma editionis eorum uberrimus Elenchus Varias, & plurimas exhibens Scriptorum Bibliothecas, Ac totam Veterem, & Novam Geographiam Ordine Litterarum Dispositam, Tabulis etiam, & Figuris plerunque ob Oculos Positam, Sub Alphabeto Latino-Vernaculo, & Vernaculo-Latino, Summatim Continens. Studio, et labore Alphonsi Lasor a Varea. *Patavii, ex Typogr. olim Frambotti, nunc Conzatti.* 1713. 2 vols., folio, pp. (80), 536; (4), 688. Plates and 56 Tables. 39133

Concerning this *see* Petzholdt's "Bibliotheca Bibliographica," p. 774.

La Sota (J. Manuel de). Catecismo geografico, politico e historico de la Republica Oriental de Uruguay. *Montevideo.* 1815. 18mo. S. 39134

Lassaga (J. L.) *and* Velasquez de Leon (J.) Representacion que a nombre de la Mineria de esta Nueva España hacen al Rey N. S. los Apoderados, de ella D. Juan Lucas de Lassaga, y D. Joaquin Velasquez de Leon. *Mexico.* 1774. Folio, pp. 98, 12. 39135

Lasselle (N. P.) Annie Grayson; or, Life in Washington. By Mrs. N. P. Lasselle. *Washington.* 1853. 12mo. 39136

Also: The Belle of Washington. ... *Philadelphia: T. B. Peterson and Brothers.* [1858.] 16mo, pp. x, 5–345. H.

Lassépas (U. U.) Historia de la colonizacion de la Baja California y decreto de 10 de marzo de 1857. *Mexico.* 1859. Sm. folio, pp. 249. 39137

Lasso de la Vega (G.) Elogios | en loor de | los Tres Famosos Varo- | nes Don Iayme Rey de Aragon, Don Fernan- | do Cortes Marques del Valle, y Don | Aluaro de Baçan Marques de | Santacruz. | Cõpuestos por Gabriel Lasso dela Vega Cõtino del R. N. S. | Dirigidos a Don Gaspar Galçaran de Castro y Pi- | nos, Cõde de Guimaran, Vizcõde de Ebol, &c. | Año 1601. | Con priuilegio, *En Caragoça, por Alonzo Rodriguez.* | 16mo, pp. (16), 144 folioed leaves. 39138

"C'est un recueil de passages de tous les poètes espagnoles où il est fait mention de ces hommes illustres."—Ternaux, No. 251.

Lasso de la Vega. Primera Parte | De Cortés valeroso, | y Mexicana, | De Gabriel Lasso de la Vega, criado del | Rey nuestro señor, natural de | Madrid. | Dirigida a Don | Fernando Cortés, nieto de don Fernando | Cortés, Marques del Valle, descubridor y | conquistador del Nueuo Mundo. | Con priuilegio: *En Madrid, En casa de Pedro Madrigal,* | *Año* M.D.LXXXVIII. | 4to, 6 p. l., Text, 193 l., Table, &c., 7 l. Portraits of Cortes and Lasso de la Vega. J.C.B., H. 39139

This first edition, of well known rarity (Heber's copy sold for £6), contains nothing but the two first cantos of this poem.

Lasso de la Vega. La Mexicana [Poema] de Gabriel Lasso de la Vega, emendada y añadida por su mismo autor ... *Madrid, Sanchez.* 1594. Sm. 8vo. 39140

Second edition, enlarged by three cantos. At the end is found: "Apologia en defensa del ingenio y fortalez de los Indios de la Nueva España conquistada por D. Fernando Cortez, marquez del Valle, por el licenciado Geronimo Ramirez."

[Lasso de la Vega (Luis).] Huey tlamahuiçoltica omonexiti in ilhuicac Tlatóca Çihuapilli Santa Maria Totlaçonantzin Guadalupe in nican huei altepenahuac Mexico itocayòcan Tepeyacac.

Impresso con licencia en Mexico: en la imprenta de Iuan Ruyz. Año de 1649. 4to, 3 p. l., 17 l., (1 l.) Plate. 39141

This is "With great wonder appeared the celestial queen and lady Holy Mary, our beloved Mother of Guadalupe, here in this great city of Mexico, where they call it Tapeyacac." On the authorship, *see* Bartolache, "Manifiesto," pp. 3–8. Lasso de la Vega signs the dedication. It is extremely rare and curious.

The Last Appeal. [*Philadelphia.* 1860.] 8vo, pp. 8. 39142

Against the election of A. G. Curtin as governor of Pennsylvania.

The Last Campaign of the Twenty-Second Regiment, N. G., S. N. Y. June and July, 1863. *New York: C. S. Westcott & Co., Printers.* 1864. 8vo, pp. 47. 39143

The Last Day's Debate on the Tariff, in the Senate of the United States. Address to the People of South Carolina. *Charleston.* 1832. 8vo, pp. 24. 39144

The Last Will and Testament of Wm. Turpin, formerly of Charleston, late of New-York. *New-York.* 1835. 8vo, pp. 31.

The Last | East-Indian | Voyage. | Containing Mvch | varietie of the State of the seuerall | kingdomes where they haue traded: | with the Letters of three seuerall Kings | to the Kings Maiestie of England, | begun by one of the Voyage: since continued | out of the faithfull obseruations of | them that are come home. | *At London,* | *Printed by T. P. for Walter Burre.* | 1606. | 4to, pp. (4), 40 l.

Title from Stevens' "Nuggets," No. 1656. What it has to do with America is not apparent in the title-page.

Lastarria (J. V.) La America por J. V. Lastarria. ... Segunda Edicion de Primera Parte. *Gante: Imprenta de Eng. Vanderhaeghen.* 1867. 8vo. 39147

Lastarria. Bosquejo histórico de la constitucion del gobierno de Chile durante el primer período de la revolucion, desde 1810 hasta 1814. *Chile.* 1847. 8vo, pp. 212. 39148

Lastarria. Discursos Academicos de J. V. Lastarria ... . *Santiago: Imprenta del Siglo.* 1844. 8vo, pp. (4), 176. B. 39149

Lastarria. Historia constitucional del Medio Siglo. Revista de los progresos del sistema representativo en Europa i America durante los primeros cincuenta anos del siglo XIX. Por J. V. Lastarria. ... Primera Parte. Desde 1800 A 1825. *Valparaiso: S. Tornero i C[a].* 1853. 8vo, pp. xiii, (2), 560. B. + Segunda edicion. *Gante.* 1866. 8vo, pp. xii, 420. 39150

Also: Discurso inaugural pronunciado en la reinstalacion del Circulo de Amigos de las letras en Santiago, el 23 de Mayo de 1869. ... *Santiago.* 1869. 4to, pp. 11.

Lastarria, *and others.* Historia jeneral de la República de Chile, desde su independencia hasta nuestras dias. Por los Señores J. V. Lastarria, M. A. Tocornal, Santa Maria, Barros Arana, Coucha i Toro ... . El editor, J. S. Valenzuela. ... Corregida por B. Vicuña Mackenna. *Santiago de Chile.* 1866–68. 4 vols., 8vo, pp. xxvi, 478; ; 756; 402. Portraits. 39151

Lasteirie (C. P.) Tratado sobre el Ganado Lanar de Espana su cria Viages, Trasquila, Lavado, y Comercio de las Lanas traducida de Francès al Castellano de orden del Supremo Gobierno, para fomento de este Ramo en la Republica Mexicana. [n. p. 1831. 4to. 39152

Lasteyrie (Ferdinand, *Comte* de). Esquisses Américaines. Souvenir d'un Séjour Chez les Planteurs du Sud. [*Paris: A. Lainé et J. Harvard.* 1865.] 8vo, pp. 16. H. 39153

Extracted from the "Revue française."

Lastri (M.) L'Elogio di Amerigo Vespucci composto dal proposto Marco Lastri Fiorentino. [Colophon:] *Finito l'Elogio di Amerigo Vespucci composto dal Proposto M. Lastri: Impresso in Firenze in numero di C. copie per Francesco Moücke fiorentino nel* MDCCLXXXVII. *a di xxiv. Settembre. Laus Deo.* 4to, 19 l., 7 l. H.

Only one hundred copies printed.

The Late King of Spain's Will and the Treaty for the Partition of the Kingdom of Spain, Recited and Consider'd ... With Animadversions upon Both, tending to Prove, That it is the Interest of all Europe, to Adhere inviolably to the Partition of the Spanish Monarchy; and more particularly conducing to the Welfare of England. *London: Printed for J. Nutt, near Stationers-Hall.* 1701. 4to, pp. (2), 19. 39155

Includes some reference to the Spanish-American, the West India colonies, etc.

The Late Occurrences in North America, and Policy of Great Britain, Considered. ... *London: Printed for J. Almon.* M.DCC.LXVI. 8vo, pp. (2), 42. BA., C. 39156

"The writer is in favor of conciliatory measures with the colonies, and rather severe on those who would let slip the dogs of war on their American brethren."—*Monthly Review,* XXXIV. 69.

The Late Regulations. *See* [Dickinson (J.)], Vol. V., 20043.

The Late Religious Commotions. *See* [Chauncy (C.)]

Later Years. *See* [Prime (W. C.)]

[La Terrière (Pierre De Salles).] A Political and Historical Account of Lower Canada; with Remarks on the Present Situation of the People, as regards their Manners, Character, Religion, &c. &c. By a Canadian. *London: William Marsh & Alfred Miller.* 1830. 8vo, pp. xvi, 275, (1). B., C. 39157

The preface states that this work was originally written in French, and that the author had it translated in hopes that thereby it might be more generally read.

Latham (A.) A Sermon on the Death of Rev. Charles T. Torrey. By Rev. A. Latham. *Taunton.* 1846. 8vo, pp. 16.

Latham (G. R.) Speech of Hon. George R. Latham, of West Virginia, on Reconstruction ... in the House ... January 8, 1866. *Washington.* 1866. 8vo, pp. 8. H. 39159

Latham (Henry). Coloni ab Anglia ad Americæ oram missi. *Oxford?* 1812. 8vo, pp. 8. M. 39160

An Oxford prize poem; privately printed.

Latham (H.) Black and White. A Journal of a Three Months' Tour in the United States. By Henry Latham. *London: Macmillan & Co.* 1867. 8vo, pp. xii, 304. BA. 39161

[Latham (Marcus).] Report of Labors among the Irish Population of Boston, &c. [*Boston.* 1852.] 8vo, pp. 4. M.

Also: Third Report of M. Latham's Mission on Fort Hill, for the Improvement of the Irish Population. [*Boston.* 1857.] 8vo, pp. 4. H.

Latham (M. S.) Defense of the Union. Speech ... in the Senate, July 20th, 1861. [*Washington.* n. d.] 8vo, pp. 16. B.

Also: Civil Fund of California. Speech ... May 9, 1854. *Washington: Printed by A. O. P. Nicholson.* 1854. 8vo, pp. 16.—Speech ... June 14, 1854, on the Rights of Neutrals—Cuba. *Washington.* 1854. 8vo.—Speech ... January 9, 1855, on the Establishment of Mail Steamships between California and China. [n. p. n. d.] 8vo.—Speech ... February 1, 1861, on the President's Message—"The Mission of Peace from Virginia." *Washington: Printed by Henry Polkinborn.* 1861. 8vo, pp. 15. B.—... Speeches ... on Steamship Line from California to China ... April 10th, 1862 ... . *Washington: McGill, Witherow & Co., Printers.* 1862. 8vo, pp. 31. B.

Latham (R. G.) The Ethnology of the British Colonies and Dependencies. By R. G. Latham. *London: John Van Voorst.* MDCCCLI. Post 8vo, pp. vi, 264. 39164

Latham. Man and his Migrations. By R. G. Latham. *London: John Van Voorst.* MDCCCLI. Fcap 8vo, pp. vi, 250. + *New York: Charles B. Norton.* 1852. 8vo, pp. 261. H. 39165

LATHAM. The Natural History of the Varieties of Man. By Robert Gordon Latham. ... *London: John Van Voorst.* M.D.CCCL. 8vo, pp. xxviii, 574. B. 39166

Concerning the North American Indians, *see* pp. 287–459.

LATHAM. Opuscula. Essays chiefly Philological and Ethnographical by Robert Gordon Latham .... *Williams & Norgate ... London.* 1860. 8vo, pp. vi, 418. H. 39167

Over one hundred pages are devoted to American languages. Also: Report on the Present State and Recent Progress of Ethnographical Philology. ... From the Report of the British Association for the Advance of Science, for 1847. *London.* 1848. 8vo.

LATHAM (W.) The States of the River Plate: their Industries and Commerce. Sheep-Farming, Sheep-Breeding, Cattle-Feeding, and Meat-Preserving; Employment of Capital; Land and Stock, and their Values; Labour and its Remuneration. By Wilfred Latham .... *London: Longmans* ... 1866. 8vo, pp. vi, (2), 200. + Second Edition. [*Ibid.*] 1868. 8vo, pp. x, 381. Map. B. 39168

See "Sat. Rev.," Jan. 5, 1867; XXIII. 28.

LATHROP (A. C.) Memoir of Asahel Grant, M.D. By A. C. Lathrop. *New York.* 1847. 18mo. S. 39169

LATHROP (C. C.) (Confidential) Answer to the Allegations made against the Appointment of Charles C. Lathrop, as Collector of the Port of New Orleans, with Biographical Sketch, ... *Philadelphia: William F. Geddes.* 1862. 8vo, pp. xiv, 11.

[LATHROP (D. W.)] An Argument ... for ... Christian Education in Southern Illinois, through the Establishment of Du Quoine Female Seminary ... . *New York: Printed by James D. Torrey.* 1856. 8vo, pp. 32. Plan and Plate. B. 39171

LATHROP. The Case of The General Assembly of the Presbyterian Church in the United States ... before the Supreme Court of ... Pennsylvania. Impartially reported ... with the Charge of Judge Rogers, ... By the Rev. D. W. Lathrop. *Philadelphia: A. M'Elroy.* 1839. 8vo, pp. 628. A., S. 39172

LATHROP (D.) The History of the Fifty-ninth Regiment Illinois Volunteers. By David Lathrop. *Indianapolis: Hall & Hutchinson.* 1865. 12mo, pp. 243. 3 Plates. C. 39173

LATHROP (E.) Metropolitan Influence, Cities in their Relation to the World's Evangelization. A Discourse ... at the

Opening of the Tabernacle Baptist Church, New York, Dec. 22, 1850. *New York.* 1851. 8vo. 39174

LATHROP (G.) Dark and Terrible Deeds of George Lathrop; Trial for the Murder of his Father. *New Orleans.* 1848. 8vo.

LATHROP (H.), *Jun.* Address, at the Thirty-fifth Commencement of Hartwick Seminary, N. Y. By Horace Lathrop, Jun. *Albany.* 1850. 8vo. 39176

LATHROP (J.) ... A Discourse before the Society for "Propagating the Gospel among the Indians, and others, in North-America." Delivered on the 19th of January, 1804. By John Lathrop, D.D. ... *Boston: Printed by Manning & Loring.* [1804.] 8vo, pp. 44. BA., S. 39177

LATHROP. A Discourse Preached, December 15th 1774. Being the day recommended By the Provincial Congress, To be Observed In thanksgiving to God for the Blessings enjoyed; and humiliation on account of public Calamities. By John Lathrop, A.M. ... *Boston: Printed by D. Kneeland;* ... 1774. 8vo, pp. 39.

With notes on the political situation.

LATHROP. A Discourse on the Peace; Preached on the Day of Public Thanksgiving, November 25, 1784. By John Lathrop, ... *Boston: Printed by Peter Edes.* MDCCLXXXIV. 8vo, pp. 35.

LATHROP. A Discourse, preached on March the Fifth, 1778. By John Lathrop, A.M. ... *Boston: Printed by Draper & Folsom.* M,DCC,LXXVIII. 8vo, pp. 24. BA., W. 39180

LATHROP. A Discourse, ... Preached at the Commencement of the Nineteenth Century. By John Lathrop ... . *Boston: ... John West.* 1801. 8vo, pp. 40. BA. 39181

LATHROP. A Discourse, delivered in Boston, April 13, 1815, The Day of Thanksgiving ... In Consequence of the Peace. By John Lathrop ... *Boston: J. W. Burditt.* 1815. 8vo, pp. 28.

LATHROP. God our Protector ... A Discourse, delivered at the Public Lecture in Boston, ... March 16, 1797. By John Lathrop, D.D. With an Appendix, Containing an Account of several daring Attempts to set Fire to the Town and rob the Inhabitants; ... *Boston: Printed by Manning & Loring.* 1797. 8vo, pp. 30. BA., M., W. 39183

LATHROP. Innocent Blood Crying To God From The Streets of Boston. A Sermon occasioned by the Horrid Murder of Mes-

sieurs Samuel Gray, Samuel Maverick, James Caldwell, and Crispus Attucks, with Patrick Carr, since dead, and Christopher Monk, judged irrecoverable, and several others badly wounded, by a Party of Troops under the Command of Captain Preston: on the Fifth of March, 1770, and preached the Lord's-Day Following: By John Lathrop, A.M. ... *London: E. and C. Dilly.* M.DCC.LXX. 4to, pp. 22. + *London, Printed. Boston: Re-printed by Edes and Gill.* M,DCC,LXXI. 8vo, pp. 21. BA., W. 39184

A rare piece, relating to the Boston Massacre. *See* "M. Rev.," XLII. 415.

LATHROP. The Present War Unexpected, Unnecessary, and Ruinous. Two Discourses delivered in Boston. The First on the 23d. of July, 1812, the Fast appointed By the Governor of Massachusetts: The Second on the 20th of August, the Fast appointed by the President of the United States, in Consequence of the Present War. By John Lathrop, D.D ... *Boston: J. W. Burditt, & Co.* 1812. 8vo, pp. 42. BA. 39185

LATHROP. A Sermon Preached to the Ancient and Honorable Artillery-Company in Boston, New-England, June 6th 1774. Being the Anniversary of their Election of Officers. By John Lathrop, A.M. ... *Boston: Printed by Kneeland and Davis.* 1774. 8vo, pp. 39. BA. 39186

LATHROP. The Speech of Caunonicus; or an Indian Tradition: A Poem, with Explanatory Notes. By John Lathrop, A.M. ... *Calcutta: Printed by Thomas Hollingbery* ... 1802. 4to, pp. 40. N. + With Notes. *Boston: Printed by David Carlisle.* 1803. 8vo, pp. 40. BA., M. 39187

Also: Biographical Memoir of Rev. John Lothropp. ... *Boston: Printed by John Eliot.* 1813. 8vo, pp. 18.— ... A Discourse Occasioned by the Death of Mrs. Mary Lathrop ... 24th September, 1778. ... *Boston: Printed by White and Adams.* 1779. 8vo, pp. 24— ... A Discourse, occasioned by the Death of Mrs. Elizabeth Lathrop ... 28 January, 1809 ... . *Boston: Munroe* ... 1809. 8vo, pp. 27.—A Discourse, before the Humane Society, in Boston: ... June, 1787. ... *Boston: Printed by E. Russell.* 1787. 8vo, pp. 34, Appendix, xiii.—A Discourse before the Massachusetts Charitable Fire Society, ... in Boston, May 27, 1796. ... *Boston: Printed by Samuel Etheridge.* 1796. 8vo, pp. 19.—A Discourse ... before the ... Boston Female Asylum, September 21, 1804 ... . *Boston: Printed by Russell and Cutler.* 1804. 8vo, pp. 22, (1).—A Discourse ... at Milton, October 3d, 1804, the Day on which the Pastoral Relation of The Rev. Joseph M'Kean to the Church ... in that Town was publickly dissolved. ... *Boston: Printed by Manning & Loring.* 1804. 8vo, pp. 20, (4).—A Discourse ... April 13, 1808. At the Interment of the Rev. Samuel West, D.D. ... *Boston: Printed by Belcher and Armstrong.* 1808. 8vo, pp. 21.—A Discourse ... on the Lord's Day, 17 May, 1812. ... [*Boston:*] *J. W. Burditt & Co.* 1812. 8vo, pp. 24.—A Discourse on the Law of Retaliation, delivered February 6, 1814. ... *Boston: James W. Burditt.* 1814. 8vo, pp. 20.— ... A Discourse, preached at ... Boston ... February 21, 1813, occasioned by the Death of Rev. John Eliot, D.D. ... *Boston: Printed by Watson & Bangs.* 1813. 8vo, pp. 28. + Second Edition. *Boston: Thomas Wells.* 1813. 8vo,

pp. 27, (1).—Funeral Sermon of Mrs. Lydia Whitney. ... *Brattleborough.* 1800. 12mo, pp. 13.—Patriotism and Religion. A Sermon ... on the 25th of April, 1799, the Day ... [of] a National Fast. ... *Boston: Printed by John Russell.* 1799. 8vo, pp. 30.—Peace and War. In relation to the United States of America. A Discourse, delivered in Boston, on the Day of Public Thanksgiving ... November 21, 1811. ... *Boston.* 1811. 8vo, pp. 18.—Prayer by ... Dr. Lathrop, and Eulogy by Professor Webber, at the Funeral of the Rev. Joseph Willard ... with a Sermon, the next Lord's Day, by the Rev. Mr. [Abiel] Holmes. *Cambridge: Printed by William Hilliard.* MDCCCIV. 8vo, pp. 41. B.—Sermon to a Religious Society of Young Men in Medford [Mass.], March 20, 1771. ... *Boston.* 1771. 12mo.—A Sermon ... at the Ordination of William Bentley ... in Salem, September 24, 1783. ... *Salem: Printed by Samuel Hall.* MDCCLXXXIII. 8vo, pp. 34.—A Sermon Preached ... in ... Boston, ... September 27, 1798. A Day religiously observed on Account of The Epidemic now prevailing in this Town, and Several other Seaports in America. ... *Boston: Printed by Benjamin Edes.* 1798. 8vo, pp. 24, Appendix, iv.—A Sermon ... at the Interment of the Rev. Joseph Eckley, D.D. ... Boston ... April 30, 1811 ... *Boston: Press of John Eliot, Jun.* 1811. 8vo, pp. 20.—A Sermon ... at the Dedication of the New South Meeting-House in Dorchester, Oct. 6, 1813. ... *Boston: Watson & Bangs* ... 1813. 8vo, pp. 20. B.—A Sermon ... at ... Weymouth [Mass.], October 29, 1814, at the Interment of Miss Mary P. Bicknell ... . *Boston: Printed by J. Belcher.* 1814. 8vo, pp. 15.—We Rejoice with Trembling. A Discourse, ... on the Day of Publick Thanksgiving, in the State of Massachusetts, Dec. 1, 1808. ... *Boston: Munroe* ... 1808. 8vo, pp. 20. BA., W.

LATHROP (J.), *Jun.* A Monody, Sacred to the Memory of the Rev. John Lovejoy Abbott ... who died October 17, 1814 ... By John Lathrop, Jun. *Boston: Munroe* ... 1815. 8vo, pp. 16.

LATHROP. An Oration written at the Request of the Officers of the Boston Regiment ... October 20, 1794. ... By John Lathrop, Jun. *Boston: Printed by E. W. Weld* ... 1795. 8vo, pp. 16.

LATHROP. An Oration, pronounced on the 4th Day of July, 1798, at ... Dedham ... . By John Lathrop, Jun. *Dedham: Minerva Press.* 1798. 8vo, pp. 19. BA. 39190

See Duyckinck's "Cyclopædia," Vol. I. 612. Also: An Address, delivered before the Associated Instructers of Youth, in Boston and its Vicinity, ... August 19, 1813. ... *Boston: Printed by John Eliot.* 1813. 8vo, pp. 20.—An Address, delivered before King Solomon's Lodge, Charlestown, ... June 24, A.L. 5811. ... *Boston: Russell and Cutler.* 5811. 8vo, pp. 23.—The Gentleman's Pocket Register, and Free-Mason's Annual Anthology, for the Year ... 1813. ... *Boston: Charles Williams.* [1813.] 16mo, pp. 252. Folded Plate. H.—An Oration, ... July 4, 1796, at ... Boston ... . *Boston: Printed by Benjamin Edes.* 1796. 8vo, pp. 23. BA., H., W.

[LATHROP (John H.)] An Address ... on the ... Anti-Masonic Excitement ... . By a Citizen of New-York. *Albany: Printed by J. B. Van Steenbergh.* 1830. 8vo, pp. 31. B. 39191

[LATHROP.] Wisconsin. [n. p. 1852.] 8vo, pp. 16.

This rare piece was published by Gustav van Heenrick, late commissioner of emigration, New York; the author was chancellor of the Wisconsin University. Also: Address, before the ... General Assembly of ... Missouri: delivered at ... Jefferson. ... December 22, 1842. *Columbia: Printed by Switzler & Williams.* 1843. 8vo, pp. 17.—Address before the State Agricultural Society of Wisconsin, October, 1851. ... *Mil-*

waukee. 1851. 8vo.—Eulogy on the Death of Henry Clay, at Madison, July 19, 1852. ... *Madison.* 1852. 8vo.—A Few Brief Remarks touching Mr. C. O. Shepard. ... [n. p. 1837.] 8vo.—Topographical Description of Wisconsin, for the use of the State Emigration Agency. ... *Madison.* 1852. 8vo.

LATHROP (J.) An Aged Minister commending his People to God; a Half Century Sermon, delivered at West-Springfield, August 26, 1806. By Joseph Lathrop, D.D. ... *Springfield: Printed by Henry Brewer.* [1806.] 8vo. 39193

LATHROP. The Constancy and Uniformity of the Divine Government ... . A Sermon ... in Springfield, April 7, 1803, ... a day of Public Fasting ... . By Joseph Lathrop ... . *Springfield: Printed by Henry Brewer.* [1803.] 8vo, pp. 21. BA., W. 39194

LATHROP. A Discourse ... at Springfield, October 30, 1805. On occasion of the Completion and Opening of The Great Bridge over Connecticut River, Between the towns of Springfield and West-Springfield. By Joseph Lathrop, D.D. ... *Springfield: [H. Brewer, Printer.* 1805.] 8vo, pp. 16. BA. + Second Edition. *Springfield.* [n. d.] 8vo. W. 39195

"Who among us," exclaims the preacher, "twenty years ago, expected to see the two banks of the Connecticut river united at Springfield by a bridge?"

LATHROP. The Happiness of A Free Government, and the Means of Preserving it: ... a Sermon ... on July 4th, 1794, in Commemoration of American Independence! By Joseph Lathrop ... . *Springfield: Printed by James R. Hutchins.* MDCCXCIV. 8vo, pp. 23. BA., W. 39196

Political and historical.

LATHROP. Sermons delivered on Various Occasions. By Joseph Lathrop, D.D. ... *Boston: Isaiah Thomas.* 1812. 8vo, pp. 392. C. 39197

LATHROP. Stedfastness in Religion ... Sermon ... in West-Springfield ... 25th day of August, ... 1796. By Joseph Lathrop, ... *West-Springfield: Printed by Edward Gray.* M,DCC,XCVII. 12mo, pp. 34. + To which is added, An Aged Minister commending his People to God; a Half Century Sermon, ... August 26, 1806. ... *Springfield: Printed by Henry Brewer.* [1806.] 8vo, pp. 43. BA., W. 39198

LATHROP. The Works of God in relation to the Church in general, and our own land in particular, especially in the last Century, considered in a Sermon, Delivered in West-Springfield, on the 1st day of the Nineteenth Century. By Joseph Lathrop,

... *Springfield: Printed by Ashley & Brewer.* M,DCCC,I. 8vo, pp. 26, (1). BA. 39199

A good local history. Also: Christ's Rebuke ... . A Sermon, ... in Boston, May 10, 1812. ... *Boston: J. W. Burditt, & Co.* 1812. 8vo, pp. 20.—Christ's Warning to the Churches, ... illustrated in Two Discourses. ... *Springfield.* 1789. 8vo. + Second Edition, with an Appendix ... . *Springfield: Printed by Ezra Waldo Weld.* M. DCC. XCI. 8vo, pp. 54. + Third Edition. *Springfield.* 1792. 8vo. + The Sixth Edition. With an Appendix and other Enlargements. *Boston: Printed by Samuel Hall.* MDCCXCIII. 8vo, pp. 63. + *Amherst, N. H.: Printed by Joseph Cushing.* 1804. 12mo, pp. 60. + Eleventh Edition, revised, corrected, and much enlarged. *Boston: Isaiah Thomas, Jun.* 1811. 12mo, pp. 117. + Twelfth Edition. *Boston.* 1823. 12mo, pp. 56. + With an Introductory Notice by the Rev. J. M. Wainwright. *New York.* 1844. 12mo.—A Church of God described, the Qualifications for Membership stated, and Christian Fellowship illustrated, in Two Discourses. *Hartford: Re-Printed by Hudson and Goodwin.* MDCCXCII. 8vo, pp. 48. + Third Edition. *Charlestown: Printed by S. Etheridge.* 1804. 12mo, pp. 56. + Fourth Edition. *Charlestown.* 1809. 12mo, pp. 88. B.—A Discourse delivered at the Funeral of the Rev. Robert Breck ... Springfield; who departed this Life, April 23, 1784. ... *Springfield: Printed by Brooks and Russell.* M,DCC,LXXXIV. 8vo, pp. 23.—A Funeral Sermon ... March 10, 1796, at the Interment of Rev. Ebenezer Gay, D.D. ... in Suffield. ... *Hartford: Printed by Hudson & Goodwin.* [1796.] 8vo, pp. 24.—A Funeral Sermon ... October 25, 1796, at the Interment of Mrs. Mary Gay ... in Suffield. ... *Suffield.* 1797. 8vo, pp. 23.—A Funeral Sermon ... January 28th, 1802, at the Interment of Rev. Noah Atwater, A.M. ... *Springfield: Printed by Ashley.* ... [n. d.] 8vo, pp. 14.—God's challenge ... A Sermon ... in West-Springfield, May 4, 1797 ... General Fast. ... *West-Springfield: Printed by Edward Gray.* [1797.] 12mo, pp. 36. + Second Edition. *Cambridge: Printed by William Hilliard.* 1803. 8vo, pp. 28. + Third Edition. *Cambridge.* 1805. 8vo, pp. 24.—The Infirmities and Comforts of Old Age. A Sermon to Aged People. ... *Springfield.* [n. d.] 8vo, pp. 14. + Second Edition. *Springfield, Mass.: [Henry Brewer.* 1802.] 12mo, pp. 14.— ... Last Sermon in the Old Meetinghouse at West Springfield, June 20, 1802. ... *Springfield.* [n. d.] 8vo.—National Happiness. Thanksgiving Sermon ... West-Springfield, February 19, 1795. ... *Springfield.* 1795 8vo.—The Presence of Christ, the Glory of the Temple, a Sermon ... in West-Springfield, June 24, 1802, which day completed one hundred years from the erection of the First Church. ... *Springfield: Ashley and Brewer.* [1802.] 8vo.—A Sermon ... in West-Springfield, December 14, MDCCLXXXVI, Being the Day ... for a Publick Thanksgiving. ... *Springfield: Printed by John Russell.* MDCCLXXXVII. 8vo, pp. 24.—A Sermon on the Dangers of the Times, from Infidelity and Immorality; and especially from a lately discovered Conspiracy against Religion and Government. ... *Springfield: Printed by Francis Stebbins.* 1798. 8vo, pp. 24.—A Sermon ... at Westfield, January 1, 1800. At the Dedication of the Academy ... . *Suffield: Printed by Edward Gray.* M,DCCC. 8vo, pp. 15.—A Sermon preached to the Hampshire Missionary Society, at their Annual Meeting, ... August, 1802, in Northampton. ... *Northampton: Printed by William Butler.* 1802. 8vo, pp. 22.—Sermon ... at Putney [Vt.], June 25, 1807, at the Ordination of Elisha D. Andrews. ... *Brattleborough.* 1807. 8vo.—Sermon ... at the Ordination of Rev. Heman Ball, Feb. 1, 1797. ... *Rutland (Vt.)* 1797. 12mo, pp. 34.—Sermon ... at the Ordination of Sylvester Burt. ... *Springfield.* 1806. 8vo.— ... A Sermon ... at Harvard, June 3, 1801; at the Ordination of the Rev. Stephen Bemis ... . *Harvard: Printed by Luther Parker.* 1801. 8vo, pp. 34.—A Sermon ... at the Ordination of the Rev. Jesse Fisher, ... in Windham, Connecticut, May 22d, 1811. ... *Windham: Printed by J. Byrne and Son.* 1811. 8vo, pp. 24.—A Sermon containing Reflections on the Solar Eclipse, which appeared on June 16, 1806. ... *Springfield.* [1806.] 8vo. + Second Edition. *Springfield, Mass.: Henry Brewer, Printer.* [n. d.] 8vo, pp. 20.— ... A Sermon ... at the Public Fast, in West-Springfield, April 7, 1808. ... *Springfield: Printed by Henry Brewer.* [n. d.] 8vo, pp. 16.— ... A Sermon ... in North

Wilbraham, June 15, 1808. At the Ordination of Rev. Thaddeus Osgood .. *Springfield.* [n. d.] 8vo, pp. 16. + *Boston: Printed by Greenough* ... 1811. 8vo, pp. 24. + *Brookfield: Printed by E. Merriam and Co.* 1821. 8vo, pp. 16.— ... A Sermon in Springfield, April 21st, 1812. ... for ... Foreign Missions. ... *Springfield: Printed by Thomas Dickman.* [n. d.] 12mo, pp. 23.—A Sermon ... in Springfield, before the Bible Society ... of Hampden ... August 31, 1814. ... *Springfield: Printed by Thomas Dickman.* 1814. 8vo, pp. 20.— ... Two Discourses ... on a Publick Fast, April 11, 1811. ... *Springfield, (Mass.): Printed by Thomas Dickman.* 1811. 8vo, pp. 32.—Two Sermons, on the Christian Sabbath, for Distribution in the New Settlements of the United States. ... *Northampton, (Massachusetts.) Printed by William Butler* ... 1803. 8vo, pp. 28. BA. + *Walpole, N. H.* 1813. 8vo.—Two Sermons, on the Atrocity of Suicide, and on the Causes which lead to it. Preached at Suffield ... Feb. 24, 1805. ... *Suffield.* 1805. 8vo, pp. 24. + Second Edition. *Springfield, Mas.: [Henry Brewer, Printer.* 1805.] 8vo, pp. 36.—Two Sermons ... at Southwick, July 23, 1809. On ... the Death of Four Young Women ... . *Springfield: Printed by Thomas Dickman.* 1809. 8vo, pp. 28. ... Two Sermons ... in ... West-Springfield, ... August 25, 1816. Being the Day which concluded the Sixtieth Year of his Ministry. *Springfield: Printed by Thomas Dickman.* 1816. 8vo, pp. 23. BA.

LATHROP. Sermons by the late Joseph Lathrop, D.D., Pastor ... in West Springfield, Mass. New Series. With a Memoir of the Author's Life, written by himself. *Springfield: A. G. Tannatt & Co.* 1821. 8vo, pp. lxx, 327. H. 39200

LATHROP (L. E.) A Discourse ... at Auburn, on ... Thanksgiving, December 12, 1850. By L. E. Lathrop, D.D. *Auburn, N. Y.: Derby and Miller.* 1850. 8vo, pp. 19. 39201

Also: Discourse ... Death of John Quincy Adams, 1848. [n. p. n. d.] 8vo.—A Valedictory Discourse ... 30th of October, 1836, ... in Salisbury, Conn. ... *Hartford: Hudson and Skinner, Printers.* 1836. 8vo, pp. 24. H.

LATHROP (N.) The Shepherd Boy of Minnesota; a Narrative of the Life of George Melvin Kelsey. By Rev. Noah Lathrop. *New York: Carlton & Porter.* 1866. 18mo, pp. 63. Plate. C. 39202

LATHROP (S. K.) A Sermon delivered before His Excellency Emory Washburn, Governor, ... The Honorable Council, and the Legislature of Massachusetts, at the Annual Election, ... January 3, 1855. By S. K. Lathrop, D.D. *Boston: William White.* 1855. 8vo, pp. 37. 39203

See our Vol. II., No. 6652.

Lathrop Family Tree. Descendants of Rev. John Lathrop, from 1634 to 1867. *Buffalo, N. Y.* 1867. 4to. S. 39204

LATIMER (E.) Life and Thought: or Cherished Memorials of the late Julia A. Parker Dyson. Edited by Miss E. Latimer. *Boston: Whittemore, Niles, and Hall.* 1856. 12mo, pp. xiii, (2), 314. Portrait. C. 39205

LATIMER (G.) ... The Joint Special Committee [C. F. Adams, Chairman, on] ... the Petition of George Latimer and more than sixty-five thousand citizens of Massachusetts ... report. [*Boston.* 1843.] 8vo, pp. 37. 39206

Mass. House Doc. 41. *See* Norfolk, *Va.*

LATIMER (W. K.) Defence of Capt. W. K. Latimer, U. S. Navy, read before a Court of Inquiry, held in the Bay of Naples, 1849–50. *Boston: White & Potter.* 1851. 8vo, pp. 66. C.

LATIMER. An Article on the Latimer Case. From the ... Law Reports. *Boston.* 1843. 8vo. 39208

A Latin Grammar for the use of the University and Academy of Pennsylvania in Philadelphia. *Exeter, Pa.* 1794. 12mo.

LATO-MONTE (L.) Catecismo de la independencia en siete declaraciones, por Ludovici de Lato-Monte. *Mexico.* 1821. 12mo, pp. 71. 39210

LATO-MONTE. Fabulas politicas y militares de Ludovico Lato-Monte. [In verse.] *Puebla.* 1821. Sm. 8vo, pp. 48.

LA TORRE (Jose Maria de). Compendio de geografia fisica, politica, estadistica y comparada de la isla de Cuba. ... *Habana: M. Soler.* 1854. 4to, pp. xi, (4), 128. 39212

LA TORRE *and* O'NEIL (J. T.) The Spanish West Indies. Cuba and Porto Rico: Geographical, Political, and Industrial. Cuba: From the Spanish of Don J. M. de La Torre. Porto Rico: By J. T. O'Neil, Esq. Edited by Richard S. Fisher, M.D. ... *New York: J. H. Colton and Company.* 1855. 8vo, pp. 190. Map. + [*Ibid.*] 1861. 8vo. 39213

LATOUANNE (*Vicomte* de). *See* Vol. II., No. 6874.

LATOUR (A. L.) Historical Memoir of the War in West Florida and Louisiana in 1814–15. With an Atlas. By Major A. Lacarriere Latour, Principal Engineer in the Seventh Military District United States' Army. Written Originally in French, and translated for the Author, by H. P. Nugent, Esq. *Philadelphia: John Conrad and Co. J. Maxwell, Printer.* 1816. 8vo, pp. xx, 264, Appendix, CXC. 7 colored Maps and Plans. B., H.

"Major Latour's narrative of the military events is minute and interesting, and the appendix contains an invaluable collection of state papers."—*North American Review,* III. 232–266. The atlas is often bound in a separate volume.

Latour. Proyecto de empedrado que presentaron al excmo. Ayuntamiento D. Francisco Javier Troncoso, D. Arsenio Lacarrier Latour y D. Juan Luis de Grudon. [n. p.:] *Imprenta de Diaz de Castro.* 1823. Folio, pp. 14. 39215

La Tour (*l'Abbé* Bertrand de). Mémoire sur la Vie de M. de Laval, premier Evêque de Québec. ... *Cologne: Motiens.* 1761. 2 vols., 12mo. + *Paris.* 1762. 4to. 39216

Of this last edition Volume 1. only was published. *See* Faribault, No. 378.

Latour (L. A. Huguet). Annuaire de la Ville-Marie, origine, utilité et progrès des institutions catholiques de Montreal. ... *Montreal.* 1861. 8vo, pp. 192. 39217

Also: Annales de la Tempérance. ... *Montréal.* 1854. 8vo, pp. 80.

La Tourette (J.) Sermon ... Fast Day. By Rev. James La Tourette, A.M. *Potsdam.* 1864. 8vo. 39218

Latrobe (B. H.) Remarks on the Address of the Committee of the Delaware and Schuylkill Canal Company to the Committee of the Senate and House of Representatives, as far as it notices the "View of the Practicability and Means of Supplying the City of Philadelphia with wholesome Water." By B. Henry Latrobe, Engineer ... . *Philadelphia: Printed by Zachariah Poulson, Junior.* 1799. 8vo, pp. 18. P. 39219

Also: View of the Practicability and Means of Supplying the City of Philadelphia with Wholesome Water. ... December 29th, 1798. ... *Philadelphia: Printed by Zachariah Poulson, Junior.* 1799. 8vo, pp. 20. P.

[Latrobe.] Report upon the Surveys ... of the Baltimore and Ohio Rail Road ... . *Baltimore: Printed by Lucas & Deaver.* 1838. 8vo, pp. (2), iii, 138, Appendix, (186). Table. H.

Corrected title of a note to *our* No. 2992, Vol. I. Also: Anniversary Oration ... before the Society of Artists of the United States ... on the eighth of May, 1811. ... *Philadelphia.* [1811.] 8vo, pp. 32.—Information respecting American Copper Mines. [n. p. n. d.] 12mo, pp. 8.—Letter from the Surveyor of the Public Buildings at ... Washington ... accompanying a Bill, making an appropriation for completing the South Wing of the Capitol. *Washington.* 1804. 8vo.—Letters ... and other papers relative to the Chesapeake and Delaware Canal Company. *Philadelphia.* 1809. 8vo. P.—A Private Letter to the ... Members of Congress, on the ... Public Buildings of the United States at Washington ... . *Washington City: Printed by Samuel H. Smith.* 1806. 8vo, pp. 32. Table.—Report ... on the Expediency of filling up the Basin of Baltimore. *Baltimore: McCoull & Slater.* 1838. 8vo, pp. 26.

Latrobe (C. J.) The Rambler in Mexico: MDCCCXXXIV. By Charles Joseph Latrobe ... . *R. B. Seeley and W. Burnside, London.* MDCCCXXXVI. Post 8vo, pp. viii, 309. Map. BA. + *New York: Harper & Brothers.* 1836. 12mo, pp. 228. B.

See Prescott's "Mexico," Vol. I., *also* Westminster and Eclectic Reviews.

Latrobe. The Rambler in North America: MDCCCXXXII.–MDCCCXXXIII. By Charles Joseph Latrobe ... . *R. B. Seeley & W. Burnside ... London.* MDCCCXXXV. 2 vols., post 8vo, pp. xi, 321; viii, 336. Map. + Second Edition. [*Ibid.*] MDCCCXXXVI. + *New York: Harper & Brothers.* 1835. 2 vols., 12mo, pp. vii, 14–243; iv, 9–242. 39222

The author accompanied Washington Irving in his tour on the prairies, and a large part of the work is occupied with observations of Indian life. It contains many satirical yet good-humored pictures of public life and social usages. *See also* "Quarterly Review," LIV. 392.

Latrobe (J. H. B.) The History of Mason and Dixon's Line; contained in an Address, delivered by John H. B. Latrobe, of Maryland, before the Historical Society of Pennsylvania, November 8, 1854. [*Philadelphia:*] *Press of the Society.* 1855. 8vo, pp. 52. BA., C. 39223

[Latrobe.] Journal of a March performed by the Corps of Cadets of the United States Military Academy in the Year Eighteen Hundred and Twenty-one. *Printed by Ward M. Gazlay, Newburgh.* 1822. 16mo, pp. 36. 39224

Latrobe. Memoir of Benjamin Banneker, read before the Maryland Historical Society, ... May 1, 1845, By John H. B. Latrobe, Esq. ... *Baltimore: Printed by John D. Toy.* 1845. 8vo, pp. 16. B. 39225

[Latrobe.] Three Great Battles. *Baltimore: Printed* [*not published*] *by John D. Toy.* [1863.] 8vo, pp. 35. H. 39226

Contains accounts of the Battle of Buena Vista, the Seven Days' Battle on the Peninsula, June 26 to July 2, 1862, and the Battle of Gettysburg. Also: ... Address on ... Manual Labor School. ... *Baltimore: Printed by John D. Toy.* 1840. 8vo, pp. 20.—Address ... at the laying of the Corner-Stone of the New Masonic Temple, in ... Baltimore, ... November 20th, 1866. ... [n. p.:] *Cushings & Medairy.* [n. d.] 8vo, pp. 15.—Address ... before the Reading Room of St. Mary's College, Baltimore, at the Annual Commencement, July 18, 1843. ... *Baltimore.* [n. d.] 8vo, pp. 23.—Address ... before the Cumberland County Agricultural Society ... October 14, 1869. ... *Carlisle, Pa.: Weakley & Wallace, Printers.* 1870. 8vo, pp. 23.—Address ... at the Laying of the Corner Stone of the City Hall, in ... Baltimore, ... October 18th, 1867, [n. p.:] *Cox's Monumental Printing Office.* [1867.] 8vo, pp. 22.—African Colonization. An Address ... at the Anniversary Meeting of the Massachusetts Colonization Society held in ... Boston, May 25, 1853. *Baltimore: Printed by John D. Toy.* 1853. 8vo, pp. 26. B.—African Colonization—Its Principles and Aims. Oration ... . *New-York: John A. Gray, Printer.* 1859. 8vo, pp. 16.—African Colonization. An Address ... at the Anniversary ... of the American Colonization Society, ... Washington, ... January 21, 1862. *Washington: Printed by H. S. Bowen.* 1862. 8vo, pp. 16.—American Colonization Society. Addresses ... in Washington, D. C. By John H. B. Latrobe, Esq., and Rev. Phinehas D. Gurley, D.D. *New York: T. R. Dawley, Printer.* 1864. 8vo, pp. 16.—Colonization. A Notice of Victor Hugo's Views of Slavery in the United States ... . *Baltimore: Printed by John D. Toy.* 1851. 8vo, pp. 48. BA.—

Colonization and Abolition. An Address ... at the Anniversary Meeting of the New York State Colonization Society ... May 13th, 1852. *Baltimore: Printed by John D. Toy.* 1852. 8vo, pp. 46.—Letters on Colonization, to Thomas Suffern. *Baltimore.* 1851. 8vo, pp. 48.

Latta (J. E.) A Sermon ... at New Castle, (Del.) on the Thirteenth Day of April, 1815. A day ... of Public Thanksgiving ... . By the Rev. John E. Latta, A.M. ... *Wilmington: Printed by Robert Porter.* 1815. 8vo, pp. 23. BA. 39227

Also: A Sermon ... on the 9th of September, 1813. ... A Day of Humiliation and Prayer. ... *Wilmington: Printed by Robert Porter.* 1813. 12mo, pp. 24.—A Sermon ... on the Twelfth of January, 1815. A Day ... of ... Fasting, and Prayer. ... *Wilmington: Printed by Robert Porter.* 1815. 8vo, pp. 24. BA.

Latta (S. A.) The Cholera in Cincinnati: or a Connected View of the Controversy between the Homeopathists and the Methodist Expositor; ... By S. A. Latta, M.D. *Cincinnati: Morgan ... Printers.* 1850. 8vo, pp. 40. 39228

The Latter Day Luminary, by a Committee of the Baptist Board of Foreign Missions for the United States. ... *Philadelphia: For the Board.* 1818. 8vo, pp. 528. + New Series; ... *Washington City: Anderson and Meehan.* 1822. 8vo. 39229

Contains valuable accounts of the Indians on the western border.

The Latter-Day Saints Millennial Star, Volume I. ... *Manchester: Printed by W. Shackleton & Son.* MDCCCXLI. 8vo, pp. iv, 312. Continued. H. 39230

Lattimore (S. S.) The Conspiracy. *See* [Newton (A.)]

Lattre (Ph.-A. de). Campagnes des Français a Saint-Domingue, et Réfutation des reproches faits au Capitaine-Général Rochambeau; Par Ph.-Albert de Lattre, Propriétaire, ex-Liquidateur des dépenses de la guerre à Saint-Domingue. ... *Paris: Locard. An* XIII [1805]. 8vo, pp. (4), 285, iii, (1). Folded Sheet.

Lauanha (Jo. Bap.) Regimento Nautico ... *En Lisboa: S. Lopez.* 1595. 4to. 39232

Laubyan y Vieyra (E. R. del Rio). Imago Sacris Coloribus Adumbrata Animosi Philippi V. ... Laudatio Funebris, Pro-Regis, Regalis Cancellariæ et celeberrimæ Mexicanæ urbis nomine in Templo ejusdem Maximo die 6 Feb. anni 1747. *Mexico.* 1748.

[Laudun (*M.* de V.)] *See* [Vallette Laudun (*M.* de)].

Laudonnière (René Goulaine de). L'histoire | notable de la Flo-|ride sitvee es Indes| Occidentales, contenant les trois voya-|

ges faits en icelles par certains Capitaines | & Pilotes François, descrits par le Capi-|taine Laudonnière, qui y a commandé | l'espace d'vn an trois mois: à laquelle a | esté adiousté vn quatriesme voyage fait | par le Capitaine Gourges. | Mise en lumiere par M. Basanier, | ... | *A Paris,* | *Chez Guillaume Auuray* ... | ... | M. D. LXXXVI. | ... | 8vo, (8), 123, (1) ll. C. 39234

Except the "Relaçam," *our* No. 24895, this is perhaps the rarest book relating to Florida; unless the first edition of Cabeça de Vaca may be reckoned as equally rare. Its accounts of the Indians in Florida are highly interesting, and its relation of the atrocities and massacre of the French by Menendez are appalling. Tross priced an uncut copy at 1,200 francs. The following reprint is also scarce:

Laudonnière. L'Histoire Notable de la Floride situee es Indes Occidentales Contenant les trois voyages faits en icelle par certains Capitaines et Pilotes françois, descrits par le capitaine Laudonnière, qui y a commandé l'espace d'un an trois moys: á laquelle a esté adiousté un quatriesme voyage fait par le capitaine Gourgues. Mise en lumiere par M. Basanier ... . *A Paris, Chez P. Jannet.* 1853. F'cap 8vo, pp. (4), xvi, 228. B., BA. 39235

Of this reprint one hundred copies only were issued.

Laudonnière. A Notable Historie | Containing foure voyages made by | Certayne French Captaynes vnto Florida: | Wherein the great riches and fruitfulnes | of the Countrey with the maners of the people, hitherto con-|cealed, are brought to light, written all, sauing the last, | by Monsieur Laudonniere, who remained there | himself, as the French Kings Lieuetenant | a yere and a quarter: | Newly translated out of French into English, by R. H. | In the end is added a large table for the | better finding out the principall matters contayned | in this worke. | *At London,* | *Imprinted by Thomas Dawson* 1587. | 4to, 64 l. Table. 39236

This translation of one of the most interesting of all the early volumes of travel, contains the voyages of Laudonniere, Ribault, and Gorgues, who visited Florida in 1561–67, to which Hakluyt has added much interesting matter. It is the rarest of Hakluyt's publications; the only copy in the United States is in the Lenox Library. *See also* Faribault, No. 39; French's "Hist. Coll.," Part VI.; "Hakluyt's Collection" (*London,* 1810, 4to), Vol. III. 367; Lowndes, No. 1319, *and* Ternaux, No. 171. For a Latin version *see* Bry (T. de), and for a Dutch translation *see* "Verscheyde Scheeps-Togten."

[Laugel (Auguste).] Les Causes et Caractères de la Guerre Civile aux États-Unis. (Extrait de La Revue des Deux Mondes livraison du 1er Novembre 1861.) [*Paris: J. Claye.* 1861.] 8vo, pp. 24. H. 39237

Laugel. Les États-Unis pendant la Guerre (1861–1865). Par Auguste Laugel. *Paris: Germer Baillière.* 1866. 8vo, pp. xvi, 363, (1). B. 39238

Laugel. La Guerre Civile aux États-Unis 1861–1863. ... Par M. Auguste Laugel. Extrait de La Revue des Deux Mondes livraison du 15 Octobre 1863. *Paris: J. Claye.* 1863. 8vo, pp. 28. H. 39239

Laugel. The United States During the War. By Auguste Laugel. *New York: Baillière Brothers.* 1866. 8vo, pp. xiii, (2), 313. B. 39240

Den langh-verwachten | Donder-Slach. | Voorsien en voorseijt in den Oost-Indischen Eclipsis. | Een swaer luydende discours, teghen de ontrouwe Be-| winthebbers, ende ongherechteghe ghewinhebbers van de Indische Compagnie. | Wt ghegheven uyt duyster wolcken, door den gheest | van den onbekenden | Ymant Adamsen. | *Tot Eev-Stadt* | *In de Landts-trouwe, naest de wel-bekende waerheydt.* | *Anno-o-*[1622.] 4to, pp. 10. 39241

[Laughan (*Dr.*)] Five Letters addressed to the Yeomanry of the United States; Containing some Observations on the dangerous scheme of Governor Duer and Mr. Secretary Hamilton, to establish National Manufactories. By a Farmer. *Philadelphia: Printed by Eleazer Oswald.* M,DCC,XCII. 8vo, pp 28. S.

[Laughan.] Letters addressed to the Yeomanry of the United States; Shewing the necessity of confining the Public Revenue to a fixed proportion of the net produce of the Land; and the bad policy and injustice of every species of Indirect Taxation and Commercial Regulations. By a Farmer. *Philadelphia: Printed by Eleazer Oswald.* M,DCC,XCI. 8vo, pp. 47. W. 39243

Laujon (A. de). Souvenirs de Trente Années de Voyages à Saint-Domingue, dans plusieurs Colonies étrangères, et au Continent d'Amérique. Par A. de Laujon. *Paris: Schwartz et Gagnot.* 1835. 2 vols., 8vo. 39244

Laujon (A. P. M.) Précis Historique de la dernière expédition de Saint-Domingue, Depuis le départ de l'Armée des Côtes de France, jusqu'à l'évacuation de la Colonie; suivi des moyens de rétablissement de cette Colonie. En Deux Parties. Par A. P. M. Laujon, ancien conseiller à Saint-Domingue. *Paris: Delafolie.* [1805.] 8vo, pp. iv, 257. A., BA., S. 39245

Launay de Valéry (Cordier de). Tableau Topographique et Politique de la Sibérie, ... et du Nord de l'Amérique. *Berlin.* 1806. 4to. 39246

L'Aunay (Mosneron de). Discours sur les Colonies et la traite des Noirs, prononcé le 26 Fevrier 1790, à la Société des amis de Constitution. *Paris.* 1790. 8vo, pp. 14. J.C.B. 39247

Launay (—— de). Le Français chez les Hurons, ou la vertu de la baguette; drame. ... *Amsterdam et La Haye.* 1783. 8vo, pp. 32. 39248

Laur (P.) De la Production des métaux précieux en Californie. ... *Paris: Dunod.* 1862. 8vo. 39249

Laura (M. de). Parte Tercera de las revoluciones periódicas de la Havana. Escribíala Miseno de Laura, con licencia de la verdad, de la razon, y de la justicia. En la Havana á 4 de Diciembre del año de 1795. *Havana: Imprenta de la Capitania general.* 1796. 4to, pp. (4), 31, (8). 39250

"Les licences indiquent el licdo. D. Pabo Estevez, comme étant l'auteur de cet opuscule qui est écrit en forme de dialogues. Nous ignorons si la première et la seconde partie ont été imprimées."—Leclerc, No. 856.

Lauraguais (*Comte* de). Mémoire sur la Compagnie des Indes, précédé d'un discours sur le commerce en général. *Paris: Lacombe.* 1769. 4to, pp. 82. 17 Tables. 39251

Laure (J.) Considérations pratiques sur les maladies de la Guyane et des pays marécageux situés entre les tropiques, par le docteur Jules Laure ... *Paris: V. Masson.* 1859. 8vo, pp. viii, 80.

[Laureau (M.)] L'Amérique découverte, en Six Livres. *Autun: Chez P. Ph. Dejussieu.* 1782. 12mo, pp. (4), 174.

"A Poem in prose by M. Laureau."—Barbier.

The Laurel: a Gift for all Seasons; being a Collection of Poems by American Authors. *Boston.* 1836. 16mo. 39254

Laurel Hill, *Pa.* Guide to Laurel Hill Cemetery, near Philadelphia. With numerous Illustrations ... . *Philadelphia.* 1844. Imp. 8vo, pp. 160. 12 Plates. 39255

Also: Regulations of the Laurel Hill Cemetery, ... and a Catalogue of the Proprietors of Lots. *Philadelphia.* 1837. 8vo, pp. 16. + *Philadelphia: Printed by John C. Clark.* 1840. 8vo, pp. 23. + [*Ibid.*] 1846. 8vo. *See* Smith (R. A.)

[Laurence (Isaac).] Shadows of the Metropolis. *New York.* 1859. 8vo, pp. 8. 39256

Laurens (E. R.) A Letter to the Hon. Whitemarsh B. Seabrook ... in ... Defence of "An Act to amend the Law in Relation to Slaves and Free Persons of Color." By Edward R. Laurens ... . *Charleston.* 1835. 8vo, pp. 24. H. 39257

Laurens (H.) Mr. Laurens' True State of the Case. By which his Candor to Mr. Edmund Jenings is manifested, and the Tricks of Mr. Jenings are detected. [*London: Privately Printed.*] 1783. 4to, pp. 77. C. 39258

Laurens. A South Carolina Protest against Slavery: being a Letter from Henry Laurens, ... August 14th, 1776. ... *New York: G. P. Putnam.* 1861. 8vo, pp. 3–6, 17–34. BA. 39259

See Jenings (E.), Vol. IX., Nos. 35984–85, "S. C. Hist. Soc. Trans.," Vol. I., *and our* Vol. VI., No. 23532.

Laurens (J.) The Army Correspondence of Colonel John Laurens in the Years 1777–8 now first published from Original Letters addressed to his Father Henry Laurens President of Congress With a Memoir by Wm Gilmore Sims. *New York,* M DCCC LXVII. Rl. 8vo, pp. 150. 39260

Bradford Club Series, No. 7. Seventy-five copies printed for subscribers, and seventy-five for the Club.

Laurens (J. W.) The Crisis; or, the Enemies of America Unmasked. By J. Wayne Laurens. *Philadelphia.* 1855. 12mo.

Laurent (*M.*) Zoophytologie. *See* (Vaillant (*M.*)

Laurent (P. M.) La Guerre du Mexique de 1862 A 1866. Journal de Marche du 3e Chasseur d'Afrique ... . Par Paul Marie Laurent. *Paris: Amyot.* 1867. 16mo, pp. (6), 352. B. 39262

Laurie (T.) Government is of God. A Sermon preached in Dedham and West Roxbury, May 12, 1861. By Rev. Thomas Laurie ... . *Boston: Press of S. O. Thayer.* 1861. 12mo, pp. 27.

Laurie. Three Discourses, preached in The South Evangelical Church, West Roxbury, Mass., April 13th, 19th, and 23d, 1865. By Thomas Laurie ... . *Dedham, Mass.: Printed by John Cox, Jr.* 1865. 8vo, pp. 40. B. 39264

Relative to the assassination of Abraham Lincoln. Also: An Historical Discourse ... to the South Evangelical Church, West Roxbury, June 10, 1860. ... *Boston: Printed by S. O. Thayer.* 1861. 8vo, pp. 24.—Magistrates Ministers of God to punish Evil-Doers. A Discourse ... in ... West Roxbury ... . *Boston: Press of H. Mason.* 1852. 8vo, pp. 12.—A Memorial of Dea. Isaac Newton Beach. ... *Providence.* 1870. 12mo, pp. 18.

Laurin, Le Chansonnier Canadien, ou Nouveau Recueil de Chansons. *Québec.* 1843. 16mo. 39265

Most of these songs are of Canadian origin, with a few Parisian pieces interspersed. They comprise some very spirited and racy compositions, and form a strong contrast to the elegant feebleness of most modern French poetry.

Laurnaga (P. de). Oracion panegirica, que en el dia deseado de la dedicacion y estreno del nuevo templo ... dixo el doctor D. Pablo de Laurnaga. *Lima, officina de la Calle de San Jacinto.* 1771. pp. lxxxviii. 39266

Laussat (A.) Address on the Death of Charles Carroll, of Carrollton. By Anthony Laussat. *Philadelphia.* 1832. 8vo.

Also: An Essay on Equity in Pennsylvania. ... *Philadelphia: For the Institution.* 1826. 8vo, pp. 157, (2). BA.

Lauts (G.) Beoefening der Nederlandsche geschiedenis in Noord-Amerika of de Generaal J. Watts de Peyster; door G. Lauts. [n. p. n. d.] 8vo, pp. 37. 39268

The study of Dutch history in North America, or General J. Watts de Peyster.

Lauts. Gedachten over de emancipatie der Negerslaven. *'s Gravenhage.* 1840. 8vo. Plate. 39269

Thoughts on the emancipation of the Negroes.

Lauts. Kalifornia. *Amsterdam.* 1849. 8vo, pp. 40.

Also many other articles relative to America in Dutch periodicals.

Lauzun (*Duc* de). Mémoires du Duc de Lauzun (1747–1783) publiés entièrement conformes au manuscrit avec une étude sur la vie de l'auteur. *Paris.* 1822. 8vo. + Seconde Edition sans suppressions et augmentée d'une preface et de notes nouvelles par Louis Lacour. *Paris: Poulet-Malassis et de Broise.* 1858. 8vo, pp. lxiii, 410, Table, 1 l. 39271

Lauzun. Memoirs of the Duke de Lauzun. Written by Himself. Second Edition. *London.* 1822. 12mo, pp. ix, 211.

The Duc de Lauzun accompanied Count Rochambeau in the French expedition to America. His Memoirs comprise many curious particulars of the conduct of the War, General Washington, etc.

Lauwerkrans voor Washington gevlochten door nederlandsche dichters ... Vooraf de levensbeschrijvinge ... . *Haarlem.* 1800. 8vo. 39273

Lava (A. de). Carta de Edificacion del P. M. Alvarez de Lava, y Noticia, que dà de sus Virtvdes à la Provincia de Nueva España ... . *Mexico.* 1742. 4to. 39274

Lavagnino (*Dr.*) Extracts from a Journal of Dr. Lavagnino describing the Federal Republic of Central-America. [n. p. 1825.] 8vo, pp. 16. 39275

Laval [Antoine Jean de]. Voyage de la Louisiane, fait par Ordre du Roy en l'année mil sept cent vingt: Dans lequel sont traitées diverses matières de Physique, Astronomie, Géographie & Marine. L'on y a joint les Observations sur la Refraction, faites à Marseille, avec des Reflexions sur ces Observations; Divers Voyages faits pour la correction de la Carte de la Côte de Provence; Et des Reflexions sur quelques points du Sisteme de M. Newton. Par le P. Laval de la Compagnie de Jesus. *Paris: Jean Mariette.* M.DCC.XXVIII. 4to, pp. xxiv, 304, 15 Maps and Tables; Observations, pp. 96, 4 Tables; Recueil, pp. 191, (9), 5 Tables. BA., C., H., S. 39276

Principally occupied with mathematical and astronomical details. A valuable and scientific book of travels, which enters very fully into the Physical Geography, &c., of the French Dominions in Louisiana and the Valley of the Mississippi. There are copies on large paper.

Laval (B.) The Voice of Episcopacy in the Wilderness. Its Succession unbroken. ... Edited by J. Belin Laval, ... *New-York: Alfred Cobb.* 1868. 8vo, pp. 24. 39277

Laval (F. P. de). *See* Pyrard de Laval (F.)

[Laval de Montmorency (François de).] Av Roy | et a Nosseigneurs de son Conseil. | Sire. | Supplient humblement les Habitants du Pais de Canada, | dit la Nouvelle France; Durant, que Monsieur de Petrée estant venu en la Province. Demandant que les lettres patentes de confirmation du mois d'Avril 1663 seront rapportées ... [n. p. 1677.] 4to, pp. 7. 39278

Laval de Montmorency (X. de). Esquisse de la vie et des travaux apostolique de Mgr. Xavier de Laval de Montmorency, premier Evèque de Québec suivie de l'éloge funèbre du prelate. *Québec.* 1845. 8vo, pp. 145. 39279

See also Quebec, *and* Université Laval.

Lavalle (J. A. de). Don Pablo de Olavide. Apuntes sobre su vida y sus obras por J. A. de Lavalle. *Lima.* 1859. 8vo, pp. viii, 128. Portrait and Facsimile. 39280

[La Vallée (*Abbé*).] Le nègre comme il y a peu de blancs. *Madras et Paris: Buisson.* 1789. 3 vols., 12mo. 39281

The following is a translation:

[La Vallée.] The Negro equalled by few Europeans. Translated from the French. To which are added, Poems on various Subjects, moral and entertaining; By Phillis Wheatley,

Negro Servant to Mr. John Wheatley, of Boston, in New-England. ... *Philadelphia: William W. Woodward.* 1801. 2 vols., 12mo, pp. 259; 244. C., H. 39282

Lavastida (A. de). Carta pastoral acompañada de la protesta que hizo contra varios articulos de la Constitucion Mejicana del 5. Febrero de 1856. *Paris.* 1857. 8vo, pp. 30. 39283

Lavastida. Sexta carta pastoral escrita desde Roma á todos sus diocesanos con motivo de la alocucíon de Pio IX. sobre el estado de los asuntos eclesiasticos la Republica Mejicana. Con documentos. *Paris.* 1857. 8vo, pp. 106. 39284

Also: Octava carta pastoral que dirige á sús diocesanos del D. P. A. de Lavastida y Davalos. *Habana.* 1858. 8vo.

Lavaux (C.) Discours prononcé par C. Lavaux, Député de Saint Domingue, le troisième jour complémentaire an V. *Paris: De l'imprimerie nationale, an* VI [1798]. 8vo, pp. 12. 39285

Lavaux. Réponse aux calomnies coloniales de Saint-Domingue. L'épouse du républicain Lavaux, gouverneur général (par intérim) des îsles françaises sous le vent, à ses concitoyens. [*Paris: imp. de Pain.* n. d.] 4to, pp. 40, or less. 39286

Lavaysse (J. J. Dauxion). *See* Dauxion-Lavaysse, Vol. V.

Add to *our* No. 18673, pp. (4), xxvi, 414; (4), 482, (1).

Lavayssière (P.) Les Émigrants en Amérique. Voyages, aventures, etc., d'une famille allemande. Par Lavayssière. *Paris: Martial Ardant frères.* 1865. 12mo, pp. 192. Plates. 39287

Lavayssière. Les Pionniers allemands en Amérique. Par Lavayssière. *Limoges: Ardant frères.* 1863. 12mo. Plates. + Seconde édition. *Limoges et Isle: E. Ardant et Thibaut.* 1870. 12mo, pp. 144. Plates. 39288

Also: Une Mission au Canada de 1751 à 1769. ... *Limoges: Ardant frères.* 1858. 12mo. Plates.—Un Missionnaire en Californie. ... *Limoges: Ardant frères.* 1863. 12mo. Plates.

Laveaux (E.) Réponse D'Etienne Laveaux Général de Division ex-gouverneur de San Domingue. Aux calomnies que le citoyen Vienot Vaublanc, colon de St. Domingue et membre du Conseil des Cinq Cents, s'est permis de mettre dans son discours prononcé dans la séance du 10. Prairial dernier. *Paris: J. F. Sorby, an* V [1797]. 8vo, pp. 28. 39289

Lavedan (A.) Tratado de los Usos y Abusos del propriedades y virtudes del Tobacco, Café, Té y Chocolate, extractado de los mejores autores que han Tratado de esta Materia. *Madrid.* 1796. 8vo, pp. (10), 237, (1). 39290

Lavega (Antonio de). Sermon funebre que en las Exequias á la Tierra, y Amable Memoria del Sr. D. Miguel Antonio Gutierrez, Coronel Alberto, 10 Noviembre, 1769. *Mexico.* 1770. 4to, pp. 23. 39291

La Vega (B.) Relacion de las grandezas del Peru, Mexico y los Angeles, por Bernardo de La Vega. *Mexico, Melchor de La Vega.* 1601. 12mo. 39292

All that Antonio tells us about this author, is that he came from Madrid and was Canon of Tucuman.

La Vega (Garcilasso de). *See* Vega (G. de la).

[La Vega (Gonzales de).] Review of the Report of the Committee on Foreign Affairs, of the Senate of the United States, relative to the Tehuantepec Matters. [n. p.] 1852. 8vo, pp. 106. 39293

La Vega (M. de). Historia del Descubrimiento de la América Septentrional por Cristobal Colón, Escrita por el R. P. Fr. Manuel de La Vega ... Dala a luz Con varias notas para mayor inteligencia de la historia de las Conquistas de Hernán Cortés que puso en mexicano Chimalpain, y para instruccion de la juventud mexicana Carlos Maria de Bustamente. *Mexico: Ortiveros.* 1826. 4to, pp. (11), 237. C. 39294

La Vega (R. de). Informe los Arquitectos de Ciudad ... *Mexico.* 1859. 4to. 39295

Laverdière *et* Casgrain (*les Abbés*). Découverte du Tombeau de Champlain. Par MM. les abbés Laverdière et Casgrain. *Québec.* 1866. 8vo, pp. (2), 19. 3 Plates. BA., S. 39296

Lavicomterie (L.) République sans Impôt. 1792. 8vo. 39297

Chapter IX. relates to America.

Lavin (G.) Contestacion al papel del Dr. D. Tomas Gutierrez de Piñeres sobre el reglamento de la Milicia nacional y su distrito, por D. Manuel García Lavin. *Imprenta del Gobierno.* 1821. 39298

Lavicos. *See* Larios (H.), No. 39035.

L'Avocat pour et contre, ou resumé historique et philosophique de tout ce qu'on a écrit sur la liberté du commerce des munitions navales. *Bruxelles.* 1779. 8vo. 39299

This question on the commerce of naval munitions was the principal complaint of England against Holland. Special reference is made to America on pp. 16-28.

Lavoisne (C. V.) *See* Las Cases (E. D. M. J., *Comte* de).

Lavollé (Charles Hubert). Voyage en Chine. Ténériffe. Rio-Janeiro. Le Cap. Ile-Bourbon. Malacca. Singapore. Manille. Macao. Canton. Ports chinois. Cochinchine. Java. *Paris: Just Rouvier, A Ledoyen.* 1852. 8vo, pp. (4), 466. 39300

Lavollée (M. P.) ... Notes sur les Cultures et la Production de la Martinique et de la Guadeloupe. Par M. P. Lavollée, ... *Paris: Arthus Bertrand.* 1841. 4to, pp. 151, (1). + *Paris: Imprimerie Royale.* 1841. 8vo, pp. vii, 151, (1). H. 39301

Rich places the title under 1839 and 1841.

Law (A.) A Collection of Hymns for Social Worship, with Hymn Tunes from the most modern and approv'd Authors. By Andrew Law, A.B. *Cheshire (Conn.): Printed by William Law.* [1782.] Square 12mo, pp. 36. 39302

Also other pieces. For an interesting account of the author *see* Allibone's "Dictionary," *and* Hood's "History of Music."

[Law (Edmund).] A Sermon ... before the Incorporated Society for the Propagation of the Gospel in Foreign Parts; ... February 18, 1774. By the Right Reverend Edmund Lord Bishop of Carlisle. *London: Printed by T. Harrison and S. Brooke.* M DCC LXXIV. 8vo, pp. xxiii, 70, (1). B. 39303

Law (G.) Reasons for repudiating Fillmore and Donelson. By George Law. *New York.* 1856. 8vo, pp. 8. 39304

Law. A Sketch of Events in the Life of George Law, published in advance of his Biography. Also, Extracts from the Public Journals. *New York: J. C. Derby.* 1855. 12mo, pp. 96. Portrait. B., C., S. 39305

This piece exhibits some phases of the "Know Nothing" party.

Law (J.) Address ... before the New York State Agricultural Society, at Albany ... February 9th, 1870. By ... James Law ... *Albany: For the Society.* 1870. 8vo, pp. 25. 39306

Law (J.) Aanmerkingen over den Koophandel en het Geldt; Door den Hr. Law, ... Als meede: Historische en Geographi-

sche beschryvinge van Louisiana; Geleegen in Noordt-America, aan de moudt van de Groote Rivier Mississippi. ... Door P. J. M. *t'Amsterdam, By Steenhouwer et Uetwerf* ... 1721. 12mo, pp. (12), 320. Portrait and Map. C. 39307

Notes on commerce and money. With an historical and geographical description of Louisiana, and an account of the new French Indian company.

Law. Curieuse Anmerckungen über den Staat von Frankreich, welchen Ludewig der XIV. fest gegründet, und nunmehro der Regente durch die listigen Rathschläge des Mr. Laws zu allgemeiner Bewunderung glücklich verbessert. [*Leipzig.*] 1720. 16mo, pp. (22), 136. 39308

Law. A Full and Impartial Account. *See* Vol. VII., 26144.

Law. Leven en character van J. Law, gewezene Controlleur-Generaal der Financien van Lodewijk XV. Uit authentische gedenkschriften zamengesteld door C. P. *Amsterdam.* 1722. 8vo. Frontispiece. 39309

This is the life and character of J. Law, the financial manager of Louis XV. Interesting in relation to his financial stock-jobbing schemes.

Law. A Letter to Mr. Law, upon his Arrival in Great Britain. The Fourth Edition. *London: J. Roberts.* [1721.] 8vo, pp. 23. BA. 39310

Relates to the Mississippi scheme, Mr. Law's design of planting a colony in North America, etc. Also: The Case of Mr. Law Truly Stated, in Answer. *London.* 1721. 8vo.

Law. The Memoirs, Life, and Character of the Great Mr. Law and his Brother at Paris. ... With an Accurate and Particular Account of the Establishment of the Mississippi [*sic*] Company in France, ... Written by a Scots Gentleman. *London: Sam. Briscoe.* 1721. 8vo, pp. (16), 44. 39311

Law. Memoirs of John Law of Lauriston, with an Account of the Rise and Termination of the Mississippi Scheme. *Edinburgh.* 1824. 8vo. Portrait. 39312

Law. Money and Trade considered; with a Proposal for supplying the Nation with Money. By John Law, Director to the Missisipi [*sic*] Territory. *Glasgow: R. and A. Foulis.* 1750. 12mo. + *Glasgow.* 1760. 12mo. 39313

First published at *Edinburgh.* 1705. Sm. 8vo, pp. 226.

Law. Œuvres de J. Law, ... contenant les principes sur le numéraire, le commerce, le crédit et les banques. Traduit de l'Anglois, avec des notes, par M. de Sénovert. *Paris.* 1790. 8vo

Law. Proposals and Reasons for constituting a Council of Trade in Scotland, by the celebrated John Law, Esq. afterwards Comptroller of the Finances in France. *Glasgow: R. and A. Foulis.* 1751. 12mo. M. 39315

These schemes, by this prince of schemers, were first proposed in Edinburgh in the year 1700, partly to rope in the Indian and African Company trading at Darien, and to recuperate Scotland that "it may be put in a hopeful way of regaining its losses by the union of the crowns."—Stevens.

Law (John). Address delivered before the Vincennes Historical and Antiquarian Society, February 22, 1839. By Judge Law. *Louisville, Ky.: Prentice and Weissinger.* 1839. 8vo, pp. 48. Map. C. 39316

Subject, "The Early Settlement, Rise and Progress of Vincennes." The following is an expanded edition:

Law. The Colonial History of Vincennes, (Indiana) under the French, British and American Governments, from its First Settlement down to the Territorial Administration of General William Henry Harrison, being an Address ... before the Vincennes Historical and Antiquarian Society, February 22d, 1839, with Additional Notes and Illustrations. *Vincennes: Harvey, Mason & Co.* 1858. 8vo, pp. viii, 156, (1). BA., S. 39317

Also: Jesuit Missionaries in the North West; Lecture at Cincinnati, January, 1855. ... [n. p. n. d.] 8vo.—Speech ... on the Bill "Emancipating Slaves of Rebels," and the Bill "Confiscating the Property of Rebels" ... May 23, 1862. [n. p. n. d.] 8vo, pp. 8.—Speech ... delivered in the House of Representatives, July 1, 1864. [n. p. n. d.] 8vo, pp. 16. *See also* "Virginia Historical Register," VI.

Law (Jonathan). *See* [Church (B.)], Vol. IV., No. 12984.

Law (Lyman). *See* Huntington (J.), Vol. IX., No. 33974.

Law (S. A.) Oration ... at Stamford, Delaware Co., July 3, 1858. By Samuel A. Law. *Albany.* 1858. 8vo. S. 39318

Law (S. D.) Copyright and Patent Laws of the United States, 1790 to 1866. With Notes of Judicial Decisions thereunder, and Forms and Indexes. By Stephen D. Law. *New York: The Author.* 1867. 12mo, pp. 264. 39319

Law. Digest of American Cases relating to Patents for Inventions and Copyrights from 1789 to 1862 ... . By Stephen D. Law. *New York.* 1862. 8vo. C. 39320

Law. The Jurisdiction and Powers of the United States Courts ... . By Stephen D. Law. *Albany.* 1852. 8vo, pp. 845.

[Law (Thomas).] An Address to the Columbian Institute, on ... "What ought to be the Circulating Medium of a Nation?" ... *Washington: Printed by Gales & Seaton.* 1830. 8vo, pp. 39.

Law. Considerations tending to render the Policy Questionable of Plans for Liquidating, within the next Four Years, the Six per Cent. Stocks of the United States; ... By ... Thomas Law. ... *Washington: S. A. Elliott, Printer.* 1826. 8vo, pp. 22.

[Law.] Remarks. *See* Justinian, *pseudon.*, Vol. IX., 36958.

Also: An Address ... before the Columbian Institute, December 17, 1825. ... *Washington: Printed by Gales & Seaton.* 1825. 8vo, pp. 40. BA.—An Address to the Columbian Institute, on a Moneyed System. ... *Washington: Printed by Gales & Seaton.* 1828. 8vo, pp. 95.—Plans for a National Circulating Medium. ... *Washington.* [n. d.] 8vo.—Proposition for creating means for commencing the Chesapeake and Ohio Canal. ... [n. p. n. d.] 8vo.—A Reply to Certain Insinuations Published as an Article, in the ... Quarterly Review. ... *Washington.* 1824. 8vo, pp. 26.—Synopsis of a Plan for a National Currency. ... *Washington.* 1833. 8vo. C.

Law (W.) An | Extract | from a | Treatise | By William Law, M.A. | Called, | The Spirit of Prayer; | or, | The Soul rising out of the Vanity of | Time, into the Riches of Eternity. | Discovering the true Way of turning to God, | and of finding the Kingdom of Heaven | the Riches of Eternity in our Souls. | *Philadelphia:* | *Printed by B. Franklin, and D. Hall.* 1760. 8vo, pp. 47.

Law. An Extract from a Treatise by William Law, M.A. ... With some thoughts on the nature of War, and its repugnancy to the Christian Life, &c. &c. *Philadelphia: Printed by Henry Miller* ... MDCCLXVI. 12mo, pp. 48. P. 39325

See also [Benezet (A.)], Vol. I., No. 4673.

Law. An Humble, Earnest and Affectionate Address to the Clergy, ... to which is prefixed a Short Account of his Life and Character. *Philadelphia: Joseph Cruikshank.* 1786. 8vo. + *Hartford.* 1796. 12mo. + *Exeter, N. H.: Printed by B. H. Meder.* 1831. 12mo, pp. 192. 39326

Law (W.) A Discourse delivered before the Georgia Historical Society [at their First Anniversary], ... February 12, 1840 [on the Early Settlements and History of Georgia]. By William Law. *Savannah.* MDCCCXL. 8vo, pp. 43. 39327

The first address before the Society, afterwards republished in the Georgia Historical Society's "Collections," Vol. I.

The Law Almanac for the Year 1870. ... *New York: Hurd and Houghton.* 1870. 8vo, pp. 201. 39328

Law and Lawyers; or, Sketches and Illustrations of Legal History and Biography. *London.* 1840. 2 vols., post 8vo. C. + *Philadelphia.* 1841. 2 vols., 12mo. 39329

The Law and the Facts, Submitted to the Consideration of the Militia of the United States. [n. p. 1827.] 8vo, pp. 24.

Relates to General Andrew Jackson.

The Law and the Testimony concerning Slavery. [n. p.:] *American Reform Tract Society.* [n. d.] 12mo, pp. 24. 39331

Law Given ... . *See* [Dawes (Thomas)], Vol. V., No. 18921.

Law Journal, No. 1. *New Orleans.* 1841. 39332

Contains the history of Louisiana jurisprudence, reminiscences of Judge Marshall, etc

The Law of Libels. *London.* 1765. 8vo, pp. 304. 39333

Contains the trial of John Peter Zenger.

The Law of Maine and the Law of God. Also a Review of Lovejoy's Lecture on ... Intoxicating Drinks. By a Massachusetts Clergyman. ... *Boston: Press of J. B. Chisholm.* 1852. 8vo, pp. 31. H. 39334

The Law of Slavery in the United States. *Boston.* 1863. 12mo. 39335

The Law of the Territories. *Philadelphia: Printed by C. Sherman & Son.* 1859. 12mo, pp. 127. B., C. 39336

The Law Papers ... relating to the Management of the Old, or Fulton Ferry. *Brooklyn.* 1822. 8vo, pp. 80. H. 39337

Law Reform Tracts: Compiled by a Member of the Ohio Bar. *Columbus.* 1849. 8vo. 39338

Law Reform Tracts. Published under the Superintendence of the Law Reform Association. *New York.* 1852. 8vo.

Law Case [of Pascal B. Smith]. Exhibiting the most Extraordinary Developments, arising from Mesmeric Clairvoyance, as Related by a Mormon Prophet. *Cincinnati.* 1848. 8vo.

Chief Justice Chase was engaged in this singular trial.

The Lawfulness, Excellency, and Advantage of Instrumental Musick in the Publick Worship of God ... . By a Presbyterian. ... *Philadelphia: Printed by William Dunlap.* M,DCC,LXIII. 8vo, pp. (2), 38. BA. 39341

This was followed by a satirical piece entitled:

A Second Edition [with necessary Improvements, which now render the Sense entirely plain] of the Lawfulness, Excellency, and Advantage of the Instrumental Musick in the Publick Worship of God, but chiefly of Organs. *Philadelphia: A. Steuart.* 1763. 16mo, pp. 16. M. 39342

LAWRENCE (A.) Letter to Abbott Lawrence, dated Boston, Feb. 4, 1846. [*Boston.* 1846.] 8vo, pp. 7. B. 39343

LAWRENCE. Letters from the Hon. Abbott Lawrence to the Hon. William C. Rives of Virginia. *Boston.* 1846. 8vo, pp. 35.

On the resources of Virginia, the tariff, and the cotton manufacture. Also: Correspondence with the Hon. Daniel Webster, on cheap Ocean Postage. ... [n. p.] 1851. 8vo, pp. 4.—Facts and Arguments. Letters from the Hon. Abbott Lawrence, on the Tariff.—Addressed to Hon. Wm. C. Rives. [*Boston.* 1846.] 8vo, pp. 8.—Institut des archives historiques. Abbott Lawrence. *Paris.* 1850. 4to, pp. 3.—Letter ... to a Committee of the Citizens of Boston, on the Subject of the Currency ... . *Boston: John H. Eastburn, Printer.* 1837. 8vo, pp. 12.—Remarks ... on the Duty of Congress to continue by Discriminating and Specific Duties, the Protection of American Labor, at the Convention of the Shoe and Leather Dealers, ... Boston, March 2, 1842. *Boston: Samuel N. Dickinson, Printer.* 1842. 8vo, pp. 8. B.

[LAWRENCE (Amos A.)] The Condition and Prospects of American Cotton Manufactures, in 1849–50. ... From Hunt's Merchants' Magazine. [n. p. 1849.] 8vo, pp. 29. 39345

LAWRENCE. Extracts ... . *See* Lawrence (W. R.)

LAWRENCE (A. B.) *See* Texas in 1840.

LAWRENCE (A. G.) Fort Fisher. [A Poem.] By Lt. Col. A. Gallatin Lawrence. *Providence: The Author.* 1865. 8vo, pp. 11. 39346

LAWRENCE (C. W.) The American Prints Works, *vs.* Cornelius W. Lawrence. Proceedings at the Trial of above ... Cause, ... 1852. ... *New-York: Collins, Bowne & Co.* 1852. 8vo, pp. 332. 39347

An action brought against the Mayor of New York for ordering the destruction of buildings, at the great fire of 1835, by exploding gunpowder therein.

LAWRENCE (E. A.) A Discourse, on the Death of Hon. Daniel Webster, delivered Oct. 31, 1852. By Edward A. Lawrence ... . *Boston: Press of T. R. Marvin.* 1852. 8vo, pp. 29.

Also: ... A Discourse ... at Marblehead, December, 1846, on the Disasters at Sea, Sept. 19, 1846. ... *Marblehead.* 1848. 8vo, pp. 19.—A Discourse ... at the Funeral of Rev. Leonard Woods, D.D. ... August 28, 1854. ... *Boston: S. K. Whipple ...* 1854. 8vo, pp. 38. Portrait.— ... An Inaugural Discourse ... July 20th, 1854. ... *Hartford: Press of Case ...* . 1854. 8vo, pp. 40.—The Mission of the Church; or Systematic Beneficence. ... *New York.* [n. d.] 24mo.

LAWRENCE (E. A.) Speech ... New York City Railroads. By E. A. Lawrence. [n. p. 1859.] 8vo, pp. 4. S. 39349

LAWRENCE (G.) An Oration on the Abolition of the Slave Trade ... the First Day of January, 1813 ... . By George Lawrence. ... *New-York: Printed by Hardcastle ...* 1813. 8vo, pp. 16.

[LAWRENCE (George Alfred).] Border and Bastile. By the Author of "Guy Livingstone." *London: J. Tinsley Brothers & Co.* 1863. 8vo, pp. xii, 277. + Second Edition. [*Ibid.*] 1863. 8vo. + New Edition. [*Ibid.*] 1864. 8vo. + *New York: W. J. Pooley & Co.* [1863.] 12mo, pp. xii, 291. BA. + *Leipzig: Bernhard Tauchnitz.* 1863. 12mo, pp. x, (4), 266. B. 39351

The author was captured by the United States authorities on his way to join the Confederate army.

LAWRENCE (G. G.) Three Months in America, in the Summer of 1863. Two Lectures. ... By Rev. G. G. Lawrence. *Huddersfield: Hardy & Coates, Printers.* [1863.] 12mo, pp. 63. B., C. 39352

LAWRENCE. Tour in the Southern States of America in the Summer of 1866. A Lecture. ... By Rev. G. G. Lawrence. *Huddersfield.* 1866. Crown 8vo. 39353

LAWRENCE (I.) Genealogy of the Ancestry and Posterity of Isaac Lawrence, and Centennial Meeting of his Descendants, November 27, 1851. *Albany: Joel Munsell.* 1853. 8vo, pp. 76.

LAWRENCE (James). An Account of the Funeral Honours bestowed on the Remains of Capt. Lawrence and Lieut. Ludlow, with the Eulogy pronounced at Salem, on the occasion, by Hon. Joseph Story. ... An Account of the Engagement between the Chesapeake and Shannon, with Documents relative to the Same, and Biographical and Poetical Notices. ... *Boston: Printed by Joshua Belcher.* 1813. 8vo, pp. 64. B. 39355

LAWRENCE. Biography of James Lawrence, Esq., late a Captain in the Navy of the United States: together with a Collection of the most Interesting Papers, relative to the Action between the Chesapeake and Shannon ... . *New Brunswick: L. Deare.* 1813. 18mo, pp. 244. Portrait. B. 39356

LAWRENCE (J.) The History of the Church of the United Brethren in Christ. ... By John Lawrence. Vol. I. *Dayton, Ohio.* 1860. 16mo, pp. 461. 39357

LAWRENCE (J.) A Genealogical Memoir of the Family of John Lawrence, of Watertown, 1636; with Brief Notices of Others of the Name in England and America. ... [*Boston.*] 1847. 8vo, pp. 64. B. 39358

LAWRENCE. The Genealogy of the Family of John Lawrence, of Wisset, in Suffolk, England, and of Watertown and Groton, Massachusetts. ... *Boston: S. K. Whipple and Company.* 1857. 8vo, pp. (8), 191. + Third Edition ... . *Boston: Nichols & Noyes.* 1869. 8vo, pp. 332. 39359

LAWRENCE (J. *Jr.*) A Selection from the Writings of the Late Jonathan Lawrence, Junior. *New York: Sleight & Van Norden.* 1833. 12mo, pp. vi, 172. C. 39360

Includes the Mission to Panama.

LAWRENCE (L.) No. 2 of a Series of Letters by Levin Lawrence ... to Nicholas Biddle, Esq. ... upon ... Moneytary Capital ... . [n. p. 1839.] 8vo, pp. 15. B. 39361

LAWRENCE (M. W.) Light on the Dark River; or, Memorials of Mrs. Henrietta A. L. Hamlin, Missionary in Turkey. By Margarette Woods Lawrence. Third Edition. *Boston: Ticknor and Fields.* MDCCCLIV. 12mo, pp. 321. Portrait. + Eighth Edition. [*Ibid.*] 1865. 12mo, pp. 321. Portrait.

LAWRENCE (*Mr.*) A Narrative of certain Facts, related by Mr. Lawrence, of the Bear Inn, Devizes, respecting his several Conferences with the Author of the late Fires at Portsmouth and Bristol. *London.* 1777. 4to. 39363

Relates to the case of James Hill, or John the Painter. *See* Vol. VIII., 31834–41.

LAWRENCE (M.) Address of Hon. Myron Lawrence ... with other Proceedings of a Meeting of Vermonters, held in Boston, in Behalf of Middlebury College. *Boston: Press of T. R. Marvin.* 1851. 8vo, pp. 16. M., S. 39364

LAWRENCE. Speech of Hon. Myron Lawrence ... in the Senate of Massachusetts, on the Amendment ... to the Lowell Rail-Road Bill. February 18, 1836. *Boston: Printed by J. T. Buckingham.* 1836. 8vo, pp. 22. BA. 39365

Also: Address ... before the Hampshire, Franklin and Hampden Agricultural Society, Northampton, Oct. 24, 1832. *Northampton.* 1832. 8vo.—An Oration ... at Springfield ... July 4, 1836. ... *Springfield: Geo. and Chas. Merriam.* 1836. 8vo, pp. 31.

LAWRENCE (R.) Remarkable Trial of Richard Lawrence for an attempt to Assassinate the President of the United States Containing also an Engraving of the eastern portico of the Capitol, Description of what took place on that memorable occasion with several particulars connected with the Event not before known to the Public. By a Washington Reporter. *New York* 1835. 8vo, pp. 16. C. 39366

LAWRENCE (R. F.) The New Hampshire Churches; comprising Histories of the Congregational and Presbyterian Churches in the State, with Notices of other Denominations; also containing many interesting Incidents connected with the First Settlement of Towns. ... By Robert F. Lawrence ... . *Published for the Author, Claremont.* 1856. 8vo, pp. 624. Plate. B., C. 39367

LAWRENCE (S.) The Gold Hunter: A Story of the Present Time. By Samuel Lawrence, Esq. *Marietta, Georgia.* 1855. 12mo, pp. 54. 39368

LAWRENCE (S. A.) Petition of Samuel A. Lawrence, with others, for Confirmation of their Title to Lands in East Florida. [n. p.] 1824. 8vo. 39369

LAWRENCE (S.) Slavery in the Territories. Speech of Hon. Sidney Lawrence ... . [n. p.] 1848. 8vo, pp. 16. 39370

LAWRENCE (T.) Historical Genealogy of the Lawrence Family, from ... A.D. 1635, to ... July 4th, 1858. By Thomas Lawrence. *New York: Printed by Edward O. Jenkins.* 1858. 8vo, pp. 240. Folded Table. 39371

[LAWRENCE (T. B.) Memorials of] T. Bigelow Lawrence. [*Boston.* 1869.] 16mo, pp. 43. Portrait. BA. 39372

Also: An Exposition of the Difficulties between T. B. Lawrence and his Wife Sallie Ward Lawrence which led to their Divorce. ... *Boston: Little and Co.* [1851.] 8vo.

LAWRENCE (W.) A Sermon ... at the Ordination of the Reverend Stephen Farrar ... in New-Ipswich ... New-Hampshire: October 22d, 1760. By Rev. William Lawrence, A.M. *Boston: Printed by S. Kneeland.* M,DCC,LXI. 8vo, pp. (2), 22. BA.

LAWRENCE (W.) The Will of William Lawrence, born in Groton, 1783, died in Boston 1848, to which are prefixed the wills of William Bordman Senior [and others]. *Boston.* 1860 Folio, pp. 48. 39374

Six copies printed for the use of the trustees.

LAWRENCE (William). New York Election Frauds. ... Mr. W. Lawrence, of Ohio, from the Select Committee on ... New York Election Frauds ... . [*Washington.* 1869.] 8vo, pp. 185. Portrait. + [With] Testimony. [*Ibid.*] 8vo, pp. 185, 892, (1).

LAWRENCE. Speech of William Lawrence ... December 22, 1869, on the Reconstruction of Georgia. [n. p. n. d.] 8vo.

Also: Admission of Georgia. Speech ... March 5, 1870. [n. p. n. d.] 8vo, pp. 8.—A Brief of the Authorities upon the Law of Impeachable Crimes ... prepared by Hon. Wm. Lawrence ... revised by B. F. Butler ... on the Impeachment of the President. *Washington.* 1868. 8vo, pp. 27.—Impeachment of the President. Speech ... December 13, 1867. [*Washington.* 1867.] 8vo, pp. 8.—National Expenditures ... Speech ... February 25, 1868. [n. p. n. d.] 8vo, pp. 8.—National Politics. ... Speech ... August 15, 1866. [n. p. n. d.] 8vo, pp. 16.—Reconstruction ... Speech ... February 17, 1866. [*Washington.* 1866.] 8vo, pp. 12. H.

LAWRENCE (William Beach). Circuit Court of the United States, Massachusetts District. In Equity, W. B. Lawrence *versus* R. H. Dana, Junr. *et al.* Bill Answers, Evidence Exhibits. *Boston: Alfred Mudge ...* 1866. 8vo, pp. 5–98. + [*Ibid.*] 1867. 8vo, pp. vii, 5–563, (1). B. + [*Ibid.*] 1868. + Reply ... [*Ibid.*] 1869. 8vo, pp. 98. B. 39377

Relative to the copyright in Wheaton's "International Law."

LAWRENCE. The Colonization and subsequent History of New-Jersey: Discourse pronounced before the Young Men's Association of New-Brunswick on the 1st of December, 1842. By William Beach Lawrence. *Somerville, N. J.: S. L. Baldwin, Printer.* 1843. 8vo, pp. 31. B. 39378

LAWRENCE. Discourses and Reviews, principally upon Subjects of Political Economy. By William Beach Lawrence. *New York.* 1834. 8vo. S. 39379

LAWRENCE. History of the Negotiations in reference to the Eastern and North-Eastern Boundaries of the United States. By William Beach Lawrence. [n. p.] 1841. 8vo. 39380

Originally published in the "New York Review," VIII. 195–260. Title and note from Allibone's "Dictionary."

LAWRENCE. L'Industrie Française et l'Esclavage des Nègres aux États-Unis. Lettre ... par William Beach Lawrence ... . *Paris: E. Dentu.* 1860. 8vo, pp. 16. B. 39381

This essay awakened much interest in Europe, and was translated for, and published in, the "London Morning Chronicle," under the following title:

LAWRENCE. French Commerce and Manufactures, and Negro Slavery in the United States. ... By William Beach Lawrence

... *Paris: E. Dentu.* 1860. 8vo, pp. 16. + From the National Quarterly Review, Isaac Lawrence, Editor, June 1st, 1860. [n. p. n. d.] 8vo, pp. 16. H. 39382

LAWRENCE. Visitation and Search; or, an Historical Sketch of the British Claim to Exercise a Maritime Police over the Vessels of all Nations, in Peace as well as in War, with an Inquiry into the Expediency of terminating the Eighth Article of the Ashburton Treaty. By William Beach Lawrence. *Boston: Little, Brown & Co.* 1858. 8vo, pp. ix, (2), 218. C. 39383

See Allibone's "Dictionary," Vol. II. Also: Address ... before the American Academy of Fine Arts. ... *New-York: James V. Seaman.* 1825. 8vo, pp. 44. + Second Edition, with Notes. *New-York: G. & C. Carvill.* 1826. 8vo, pp. 62.— ... Address ... before the Newport Democratic Union Club ... October 16th, 1856. [n. p. n. d.] 8vo, pp. 11. B.—The Bank of the United States; an article reprinted from the North American Review, for April, 1831. ... *Boston.* 1831. 8vo.—Biographical Memoirs of Albert Gallatin. ... [n. p.] 1843. 8vo.—An Inquiry into the Causes of the Public Distress. Reprinted, with Corrections, from the American Quarterly Review. ... *New York: G. & C. & H. Carvill.* M,DCCC,XXXIV. 8vo, pp. 51, (1).—The Origin and Nature of the Representative and Federative Institutions of the United States ... Discourse ... before the New-York Historical Society ... 19th of April, 1832. ... *New-York: G. & C. & H. Carvill.* M DCCC XXXII. 8vo, pp. 44.—Two Lectures on Political Economy ... December, 1831. ... *New York: G. & C. & H. Carvill.* M.DCCC.XXXII. 8vo, pp. (2), 72.—Lives of Reuben H. Walcot and Charles O'Conor. ... [n. p.] 1848. 8vo.—No North No South. An Address. ... *Newport.* 1856. 8vo.—Maine Law. Speech of Lieutenant Governor Lawrence, ... February 10, 1852. *Providence.* 1852. 8vo, pp. 12. BA.

LAWRENCE (W. R.) Extracts from the Diary and Correspondence of the late Amos Lawrence; With a brief Account of some Incidents in his Life. Edited by his Son, William R. Lawrence, M.D. *Boston: Printed by John Wilson & Son.* 1855. 8vo, pp. xii, 307. Plate, 2 Portraits. + *Boston: Gould & Lincoln.* 1856. 8vo, pp. 369. Portrait. H. + [*Ibid.*] 1857. 8vo, pp. (4), 369. 39384

[LAWRENCE.] A History of the Boston Dispensary. Compiled by one of the Board of Managers. ... *Boston: Printed by John Wilson & Son.* 1859. 8vo, pp. (2), xiii, (2), 244. Plates.

Lawrence & Lemay's North Carolina Almanack, for ... 1831; ... *Raleigh: Printed by Lawrence & Lemay.* [1831.] 8vo, pp. 36.

LAWRENCE, *Iowa.* Description of ... Lawrence, Van Buren County ... Iowa: ... *Keokuk: J. B. Howell & Company, Printers.* 1856. 8vo, pp. 10. H. 39387

LAWRENCE ACADEMY, *Mass.* Catalogue of the Library of Lawrence Academy, Groton, Mass. *Lowell: Printed by S. J. Varney.* 1850. 8vo, pp. 206, (1). Plate. BA. 39388

Also: Catalogue of the Officers and Students of Lawrence Academy, from the time of its Incorporation. *Groton.* 1848. 8vo, pp. 84. Continued.—Catalogue of the Trustees, Teachers, and Students, 1836. *Groton.* 1836. 12mo. + *New Ipswich.* 1836. 12mo, pp. 8. Continued.—Annual Exhibition of the Lawrence Academy, July 20, 1858. [n. p. n. d.] 12mo, pp. 4. Continued.

The Jubilee of Lawrence Academy, at Groton, Mass., July 12, 1854. *New-York: Maigne & Hall.* 1855. 8vo, pp. 76, 108. 2 Plates, 3 Portraits. BA., C., S. 39389

Also: Memorial soliciting Aid in rebuilding Lawrence Academy ... . 1868. *Groton: John H. Turner, Printer.* [1868.] 8vo, pp. 6. H.

LAWRENCE MANUFACTURING COMPANY. Statistics of the Lawrence Manufacturing Company, of Lowell, from 1831 to 1867. *Boston: Prentiss & Deland, Printers.* 1867. 8vo, pp. 35.

LAWRENCE, *Mass.* The Act of Incorporation of the Franklin Library Association, at Lawrence, Mass. ... *Lawrence: J. F. C. Hayes:* 1847. 8vo, pp. 11, (1). H. 39391

An Authentic History of the Lawrence Calamity, embracing a Description of the Pemberton Mill, a Detailed Account of the Catastrophe ... . *Boston: John J. Dyer & Co.* 1860. 8vo, pp. 96.

Also: Report of Treasurer of Committee of Relief for Sufferers of the Pemberton Mill. *Lawrence.* 1860. 8vo, pp. 51. + Final Report ... *Lawrence.* 1861. 8vo, pp. 23.

Catalogue of the Pacific Mills Library, Lawrence, Mass. Opened August 21, 1854. *Boston: Printed by Damrell ...* . 1855. 8vo, pp. 84. B. 39393

The Directory of ... Lawrence ... 1848. Published by William Filmer. *Lawrence: Hayes, Printer.* 1848. 18mo, pp. 76. + For 1857 ... . By George Adams ... . *Lawrence: John C. Dow.* 1857. 18mo, pp. 192. Continued. BA. 39394

The Municipal Register: ... of the City of Lawrence. *Lawrence.* 1853. 8vo, pp. 132. Continued. H. 39395

Annual Report of the Public Schools for 1846. *Lawrence.* 1846. 8vo. Continued. 39396

Also: Annual Report of the School Committee of ... Lawrence, 1847–8. *Lawrence: Harding & Co., Printers.* MDCCCXLVIII. 8vo, pp. 16.—Rules and Regulations, of the School Committee, of ... Lawrence, 1858. *Lawrence: Sargent & Merrill.* 1858. 8vo, pp. 26. H.

Report of the Committee ... of the Lawrence Machine Shop ... with the Report of the Treasurer ... October 18, 1854. *Boston: Printed by Dutton ...* 1854. 8vo, pp. 16. 39397

... Report of ... Receipts and Expenditures of Lawrence ... . *Lawrence: J. F. C. Hayes, Printer.* 1855. 8vo, pp. 27, (1). Continued. H. 39398

Sanitary Survey of the Town of Lawrence. By the Chairman of the Commissioners ... of the State. ... *Boston: Printed by Dutton ...* 1850. 8vo, pp. 23. Map, 4 Plans. BA. 39399

Also: Annual Report of the Lawrence City Mission ... 1865. *Lawrence, Mass.: Geo. S. Merrill, Printer.* 1865. 8vo, pp. 20.— ... Report, of the Financial Affairs, for ... 1849. *Lawrence: Hayes, Printer.* 1849. 8vo, pp. 24. H.

LAWRENCE UNIVERSITY, *Wis.* Annual Catalogue of the Library of Lawrence University, Appleton, Wis., for 1853. [n. p. n. d.] 8vo. Continued. 39400

Catalogue of the Library of Lawrence University. *Menasha: B. S. Heath ... Printer.* 1859. 8vo, pp. 48. H. + [*Ibid.*] 1870.

Also: Catalogue of the Appleton Library of Lawrence University. *Chicago.* 1869. 8vo.—Circular of Endowment Agent, ... 1864–5. *Milwaukee: Jermain & Brightman, Printers.* [n. d.] 8vo, pp. 8. Plate. H.

LAWRENCE, *Wis.* Lawrence Directory for 1864. *Lawrence, Wis.* 1864. 18mo. S. 39402

LAWRIE (A.) Lawrie's History of Freemasonry, with Additions, Notes, Critical and Historical. Also, an Historical Sketch of the Masonic Institution in America. By Charles W. Moore. *Boston: Printed by Moore & Sevey.* 1829. 16mo, pp. 256. B.

LAWS (S. S.) An Address, by S. S. Laws, in Behalf of Westminster College, ... at Fulton, Mo. ... *St. Louis, Mo.: Sherman Spencer, Printer.* 1857. 8vo, pp. 40. H. 39404

Laws and Decrees of the State of Coahuila and Texas, in Spanish and English. Also the Colonization Law of the State of Tamaulipas, and Naturalization Law of the General Congress, 1824 to 1835. *Houston.* 1839. 8vo. C. 39405

Laws and Information relating to Claims Against the Government of the United States. *Washington, D. C.: McGill & Witherow, Printers.* 1866. 8vo, pp. 32. H. 39406

Laws and Resolutions relating to the Direct and Excise Taxes. *Washington.* 1863. 8vo, pp. 151. 39407

Laws for the Army and Navy. *See* Vol. IV., No. 15279.

The Laws in force on the 14th of March, 1842, in the Bahama Islands ... By the Hon. George Campbell Anderson, Her Majesty's Attorney-General for the Bahamas ... To which is added a ninth part, containing the Acts of Assembly of the sixth year of Her Majesty's Reign. *Nassau.* 1843. Rl. 8vo, pp. 500.

Laws in Indian and English. The Hatchets to Hew down the Tree of Sin. *Boston.* 1705. 16mo. 39409

Laws Made, Manufactures Set up, and Trade Carried on in America, 1733–4. [n. p.] 1749. Folio. 39410

Laws of a Public and General Nature of the District of Louisiana, of the Territory of Louisiana, of the Territory of Missouri, and of the State of Missouri, to 1836. *Jefferson City.* 1842. 2 vols., 8vo. c. 39411

The Laws of Race, as connected with Slavery. ... *Philadelphia: Willis P. Hazard.* 1860. 8vo, pp. 70. B. 39412

Laws of the Cherokee Nation: adopted by the Council at various periods. ... *Cherokee Advocate Office, Tahlequah, C. N.* 1852. 12mo, pp. 179. 39413

Interesting as the laws of a civilized nation of Indians, printed by native hands, in the language of the government to which they acknowledge fealty. *See also* our Vol. III., No. 12463.

Laws of the Colonial and State Governments, relating to Indians and Indian Affairs from 1633 to 1831, inclusive. With An Appendix, containing the Proceedings of the Congress of the Confederation; and the Laws of Congress, from 1800 to 1830, on the same subject. *Washington City.* 1832. 8vo, pp. xv, 9–250, 72. C., N. 39414

Laws of the Government of New-Castle, Kent and Sussex, upon Delaware. ... Vol. II. *Wilmington: Printed by James Adams.* 1763. Folio. 39415

The first book printed in Delaware. For Vol. I. *see our* Vol. v., No. 19391.

The Laws of the Island of Antigua; consisting of the Laws of the Leeward Islands, commencing 8th of November, 1690, ending 13th of June, 1817; and the Acts of Antigua, commencing 10th of April, 1668, ending 7th of May, 1804. ... *London: S. Bagster.* 1805–18. 3 vols., 4to, pp. lxvii, 584; xx, 636; . + From August 15, 1817, to April 4, 1845. *London: J. B. Bateman.* 1846. 4 vols., 4to. 39416

Laws of the Legislature of the State of New York in force against Loyalists, and affecting the Trade of Great Britain, and British Merchants, and others having Property in that State. *London: J. Debrett.* MDCCLXXXVI. 8vo, pp. xv, 186. C. 39417

Some copies have the imprint, *H. Reynell.* *See* "M. Rev.," LXXV. 310.

Laws passed in the Territory of the United States Northwest of the Ohio River. *Philadelphia.* 1794. 12mo. + Laws of the Territory ... Northwest of the Ohio. 1795. 12mo. + Laws of the Territory ... Northwest of the Ohio. *Cincinnati.* 1796. 12mo. + Laws of the Territory ... Northwest of the River Ohio. *Cincinnati.* 1798. 12mo. 39418

Laws of the Territory of the United States Northwest of the Ohio River: with Laws enacted by the Governor and Judges of the Territory, and an Appendix. *Cincinnati.* 1800. 8vo.

Laws of the Northwest Territory, passed at the Second Session of the General Assembly, at Chillicothe, in the year 1800. *Chillicothe.* 1801. 8vo. 39420

Laws of the United States of America; ... With a Copious Index. Volume I. ... *Philadelphia: Printed by Andrew Brown.* M,DCC,XCI. 8vo, pp. (4), 490, (24). C. + *New York.* [1791.] + *Boston.* 1795. Folio, pp. 519. 39421

Laws of the United States of America, Passed at a Congress ... held at the City of New York, 1789. *Hartford.* 1791. 8vo.

Laws of the United States of America; comprising the Acts of the Second Session of the First Congress, and the Treaties. America. *Exeter (N. H.)* 1792. 8vo, pp. 700. 39423

Laws of the United States of America. Vol. I. *New-York: Childs and Swaine.* || In Three Volumes. Vols. II–III. *Philadelphia: Printed by Richard Folwell.* 1796. 4 vols., 8vo, pp. 494, (1); 576; 477, (130); Vol. IV. 1799. pp. 561, 26, v, (48).

The second title of Vol. IV. reads: "Acts ... of the Fifth Congress," etc. *See also* our Vol. IV., No. 15558.

Laws of the United States of America, arranged and published under the authority of an Act of Congress, 1789, to March 3, 1845. *Washington City.* 1815–1845. 10 vols., 8vo. C. 39425

Vols. I. to V. edited by John Bioren, W. John Duane, and R. C. Weightman; Vols. VI. and VII. by William A. Davis and P. Force; Vols. VIII., IX. and X. compiled by the Clerk of the House of Representatives.

Laws of the United States relative to Direct Taxes and Internal Duties. [*Boston.*] 1813. 12mo, pp. 69. + *Salem.* 1813. 12mo.

Laws of the United States relative to Naturalization. *Washington.* 1816. 8vo, pp. 12. + *New York.* 1841. 8vo, pp. 51.

Laws of the United States relating to Internal Revenue. *See* Vol. IX., No. 34915, and *add, New York: Baker, Voorhis & Co.* 1867. 8vo, pp. viii, 166.

Laws of the United States relating to the Military Establishments, in Force 1808. *Washington.* 1808. 16mo, pp. 30. C. + *Washington.* 1812. 16mo, pp. 106. 39428

Laws of the United States relating to Patents and the Patent Office. By the Commissioner. *Washington.* 1848. 8vo. P.

Laws of the United States, Resolutions of Congress under the Confederation, Treaties, Proclamations, and other Documents, having operation and respect to the Public Lands. ... *Washington: E. de Krafft.* 1817. 8vo, pp. 306, 72. S. 39430

Laws of the United States, Resolutions of Congress under the Confederation, Treaties, Proclamations, Spanish Regulations, and other Documents respecting the Public Lands. ... *Washington: Printed by Gales & Seaton.* 1828. 8vo, pp. xiii, 9–1095. S.

Laws of the United States, Treaties, Regulations and other Documents respecting the Public Lands, with the Opinions of the Courts of the United States in relation thereto, to March, 1833. ... *Washington.* 1836. 2 vols., 8vo. S. 39432

See also our Vol. IV., No. 15559.

Laws of War, and Martial Law: comprising a few Extracts from General Halleck's work on International Law, and their application to passing Events. *Boston: A. Williams & Co.* 1863. 12mo, pp. 15. B. 39433

Laws relative to the Embargo. 1807, 1808. 8vo. C. 39434

Laws relative to the Wabash and Erie Canal, and the State Bank of Indiana. *Indianapolis.* 1834. 8vo. 39435

Laws relating to the Direct and Excise Taxes, passed during ... the Thirty-Seventh Congress. ... *Washington.* 1862. 8vo, pp. 115. 39436

Laws relating to the Navy and Marine Corps, and the Naval Department. 1 July, 1865. *Washington.* 1865. 8vo. 39437

Laws relating to Pensions, Military and Naval Bounty, and Back Pay and Bounty Lands; in force at the close of the Second Session of the Thirty-Seventh Congress ... *Washington.* 1862. 8vo, pp. x, 84. 39438

Laws to encourage Immigration, to regulate the Carrying of Passengers, &c. [n. p. 1865.] 8vo. 39439

Laws which authorize the Traffic in Ardent Spirit as a Drink, morally wrong. *Boston.* 1833. 8vo. 39440

LAWSON (A.) Discourse at the Dedication of the Bethlehem Church, By Allan Lawson. *Augusta.* 1827. 8vo. 39441

LAWSON (D.) A Brief and True Narrative of some remarkable Passages relating to sundry Persons afflicted by Witchcraft, at Salem Village in New England, from 19th March to 5th April, 1692, Collected by Deodat Lawson. *Boston.* 1692. 4to, pp. 10.

An extremely rare piece.

LAWSON. Christ's Fidelity The only Shield against Satan's Malignity. Asserted in a Sermon Deliver'd at Salem-Village, the 24th of March, 1692. Being Lecture-day there, and a time of Publick Examination, of some Suspected for Witchcraft. By Deodat Lawson, Minister of the Gospel. *Boston Printed, by B. Harris, & Sold by Nicholas Buttolph, next to Guttridgs Coffee-House.* 1693. 8vo, pp. (16), 79. B. + The Second Edition. *Printed at Boston, in New-England, and Reprinted in London by R. Tookey for the Author;* ... 1704. 12mo, pp. (12), 120. B. 39443

Pages 93–120 of the second edition contain "Some Brief Account of those Amazing things which occasioned that Discourse."

LAWSON. The Duty & Property of a Religious Householder Opened in A Sermon ... at Charlestown ... December. 25. 1692. By Deodat Lawson ... *Boston in New-England. Printed by Bartholomew Green,* ... 1693. 4to, pp. (8), 64. B., BA. 39444

LAWSON (G.) The Royal Water Lily of South America and the Water Lilies of Our Own Land, their History and Cultivation. By George Lawson. *Edinburgh.* 18—. 12mo, pp. 108.

LAWSON (George C.) Sherman's Campaign through the Carolinas. [n. p. 1865?] 1 sheet folio, 22 verses. C. 39446

[LAWSON (James).] Liddesdale: or the Border Chief. A Tragedy. [*New York: Printed not Published.* 1861.] Rl. 8vo, pp. 114. 39447

One hundred copies privately printed.

[LAWSON.] Ontwa, the Son of the Forest. A Poem. *New York: Wiley & Halstead.* 1822. 12mo, pp. 136. C. 39448

[LAWSON.] Poems: Gleanings from Spare Hours of a Business Life. *New York.* 1857. 8vo, pp. 156. 39449

A few copies only privately printed for presentation. Also: Giordano. A Tragedy. *Yonkers: Printed, not Published.* 1867. Imp. 8vo, pp. 98. Forty copies only privately printed.

LAWSON (J.) Private Case before the House of Lords, between James Lawson and Jno. Tait, relative to Estates in the Province of Maryland, and to tracts of Land on the Potomack and Occoquan in Virginia, held by John Sempill, with full descriptions of the Estates which were purchased of Col. Ewell. *London: Privately Printed.* 1779. Folio, pp. 40. 39450

Title from J. Camden Hotten's Catalogue.

LAWSON (J.) A New | Voyage | to | Carolina; | Containing the | Exact Description and Natural History | of that | Country: | Together with the Present State thereof. | And | A Journal | Of a Thousand Miles, Travel'd thro' several | Nations of Indians. | Giving a particular Account of their Customs, | Manners, &c. | By John Lawson, Gent. Surveyor- | General of North-Carolina. | *London: | Printed in the Year* 1709. 4to, pp. (6), 258, (1). Map and Plate. 39451

I have seen two copies on large paper.

LAWSON. The | History | of | Carolina; | containing the | Exact Description and Natural History | of that | Country: | Together with the Present State thereof. | And | A Journal | Of a Thousand Miles, Travel'd thro' several | Nations of Indians. | Giving a particular Account of their Customs, | Manners, &c. | By John Lawson, Gent. Surveyor-General | of North-Carolina. | *London: | Printed for W. Taylor at the Ship, and J. Baker at the Black- | Boy, in Pater-noster-Row.* 1714. 4to, pp. (6), 258, (1). Map and Plate. + *London: Printed for T. Warner* ... 1718. 4to, pp. (6), 258, (1). Map and Plate. BA., H. + ... *Raleigh, N. C.: Printed by Strother & Marcom.* 1860. 12mo, pp. 390. B. 39452

Lowndes quotes an edition, *Dublin,* 1738, which is doubtless intended for Brickell's plagiarism from Lawson. The reader will not fail to discover that, except the one reprinted at *Raleigh,* these editions are, in fact, all alike; the changes in the title-pages are simply those made by the then publishers. It was first issued as a part of Stevens' "Collection of Voyages." It is "the relation of a man of acute habits of observation, some intelligence, and entire veracity. ... Lawson was a land surveyor in the employment of the government, and was the unhappy cause of the exile of the Tuscarora tribe to New York, and its consequent incorporation into the Iroquois Confederacy, by which its name was changed to the Six Nations."—FIELD. The following is a German translation:

[LAWSON.] Allerneueste Beschreibung der Provintz Carolina in West-Indien. Samt einem Reise-Journal von mehr als Tausend Meilen unter allerhand Indianischen Nationen. Auch einer Accuraten Land-Carte und andere Kupfer-Stichen. Aus dem Englischen übersetzet durch M. Vischer. *Hamburg,* ... *Thomas von Wierings Erben* ... *Anno* 1712. 12mo, pp. (14), 365, (3). Map and Plate. C., H. 39453

LAWSON (J.) The Maniac, with other Poems. By John Lawson. *Philadelphia: Hellings & Aitken.* 1811. 16mo, pp. xv, 101. C., S. 39454

LAWSON (J.) Letter on Prince Edward Island. By John Lawson. *Charlottetown.* [n. d.] 8vo, pp. 76. 39455

LAWSON. Meteorological Register for the Years 1826, 1827, 1828, 1829, and 1830; from Observations made by the Surgeons of the Army and Others at the Military Posts of the United States. Prepared under the Direction of Thomas Lawson, M.D., Surgeon-General ... To which is appended, the Meteorological Register for ... 1822, 1823, 1824, and 1825; Compiled under the Direction of Joseph Lovell, M.D., late Surgeon-General ... *Philadelphia: Haswell, Barrington and Haswell.* 1840. 8vo, pp. 161. Map. B. 39456

LAWSON. Meteorological Register for Twelve Years, from 1831 to 1842 inclusive: Compiled from Observations made by the Officers of the Medical Department of the Army at the Military Posts of the United States. Prepared under the Direction of Thomas Lawson ... *Washington: C. Alexander.* 1851. 8vo, pp. 324. + From 1843 to 1854. *Washington: A. O. P. Nicholson ... Printer.* 1855. 4to, pp. xi, 763, (3). Charts. B.

LAWSON. Statistical Report on the Sickness and Mortality in the Army of the United States; Compiled from the Records of the Surgeon-General's and Adjutant-General's Offices; embracing a Period of Twenty Years, from January, 1819, to January, 1839. Prepared under the Direction of Thomas Lawson, M.D. *Washington.* 1840. 8vo, pp. 346. Map. + From January, 1839, to January, 1855. Prepared under the Direction of Brevet Brigadier-General Thomas Lawson ... By Richard H. Coolidge, M.D. ... *Washington.* 1856. 4to, pp. 703. Maps. + From January, 1855, to January, 1860. *Washington.* 1861. 4to.

LAWTON (J.) The Power of Faith exemplified in the extraordinary case of Ashnah Lawton, who was remarkably healed ...

1821. By John Lawton. Third Edition. *Hamilton, N. Y.* 1851. 12mo, pp. 21. 39459

LAWTON (J.) Oration on the Importance of Scientific Knowledge, ... before the Providence Association of Mechanics and Manufactures, ... April 10, 1826. By Josiah Lawton. *Providence: Miller & Grattan, Printers.* 1826. 8vo, pp. 18. B.

LAWYER (J. O.) Our Country; its Peace, Prosperity and Perpetuity. A Sermon preached in Coeymans, New York, November 27, 1862. By Rev. John O. Lawyer. *Albany (N. Y.): S. R. Gray.* 1863. 8vo, pp. 24. 39461

Lawyers and Legislators; or, Notes on the American Mining Companies. *London.* 1825. 8vo. C. 39462

The Lawyers' Diary for ... 1850; ... *New York.* 1850. 18mo, pp. 50. S. 39463

Contains a list of lawyers in the City of New York.

The Lawyer's Magazine. *Dublin.* 1792. 2 vols., 8vo.

Contains some interesting decisions as to the effect of the American Confiscation Acts, etc.

LAY (B.) All Slave-Keepers that keep the Innocent in Bondage, Apostates pretending to lay Claim to the Pure & Holy Christian Religion; of what Congregation so ever; but especially in their Ministers, by whose example the filthy Leprosy and Apostacy is spread far and near; it is a notorious Sin, which many of the true Friends of Christ, and his pure Truth, called Quakers, has been for many Years and still are concern'd to write and bear Testimony against; as a Practice so gross & hurtful to Religion, and destructive to Government, beyond what Words can set forth, or can be declared of by Men or Angels, and yet lived in by Ministers and Magistrates in America. ... Written for a General Service, by him that truly and sincerely desires the present and eternal Welfare and Happiness of all Mankind, all the World over, of all Colours, and Nations, as his own Soul; Benjamin Lay. *Philadelphia: Printed for the Author.* 1737. 12mo, pp. 271, vi. P. 39465

Respecting this, *see* Joseph Smith's "Friends' Books," II. 93, *and* Vaux (R.) *See also* [Child (L. M.)], Vol. IV., No. 12722.

LAY (H. C.) ... A Sermon ... in ... New York, on the ... Consecration of the Rev. Charles Franklin Robertson ... as Bishop of Missouri. By Henry Champlain Lay, D.D. ... *New York: Pott & Amery.* 1868. 8vo, pp. 20. B. 39466

Also: A Sermon at the Consecration of the Church of the Nativity, Huntsville, Alabama, 1860. ... *Huntsville.* MDCCCLX. 8vo, pp. 24.

LAY (W.) A Narrative of the Mutiny, on Board the Ship Globe, of Nantucket, in the Pacific Ocean, Jan. 1824 and the Journal of a Residence of Two Years on the Mulgrave Islands; with Observations on the Manners and Customs of the Inhabitants. By William Lay and Cyrus M. Hussey. *New-London: Wm. Lay, and C. M. Hussey.* 1828. 8vo, pp. 168. B. 39467

The Lay of the Last Pilgrim. By the Author of "The Pilgrimage of Osmond." *Charleston, S. C.* 1832. 12mo, pp. 48.

The Lay of the Last Republican: or African Minstrels. Sung at the Concert Hall, Albany, April 14, 1866. *New York.* 1866. 12mo, pp. 16. 39469

The Lay Preacher. *See* [Dennie (J.)], Vol. v., No. 19585.

Lay of the Scottish Fiddle. *See* [Paulding (J. K.)]

LAYA (A.) France et Amérique, ou Des Institutions républicaines. Par M. Alexandre Laya ... *Paris: Pagnerre.* 1850. 8vo.

LAYMAN (*Capt.*) Plan for the Better Defence of the British West Indies. By Captain Layman. *London.* 1807. 8vo.

A Layman. Claims of Thos. Jefferson. *See* Vol. IX., 35923.

The Layman's Answer to Dr. Trapp; or, Mr. Whitefield and the Modern Enthusiast Vindicated. By an Unletter'd Laick. *London.* [n. d.] 8vo, pp. 104. 39472

LAYNEZ (J. de A.) Relacion de las fiestas de Lima en el octavario de los 23 martyres del Japon, por Fray Juan de Ayllon Laynez. *Lima.* 1623. 4to. 39473

Title from Ternaux, No. 459; perhaps the same as our No. 2515, Vol. I.

LAYRES (A.) A Defense of the Reconstruction Acts of Congress ... By ... Augustus Layres. *San Francisco: John Stratman.* 1868. 8vo, pp. 16. H. 39474

Lays of Liberty; or, Verses for the Times. ... *Boston: Bela Marsh.* 1854. 12mo, pp. 54. B. 39475

Lays of the Emigrants. *See* Vol. IX., No. 37069.

Lays of the Western World. *See* Mapleson (T. W. Gwilt).

Lázaro de la Garza (D.) Informe general de la visita diocesana practicada en las Vicarias foraneas de Zacualtipan, Huejutla y Pánuco, de orden ... del S. Arzobispo de Mexico, D. Lázaro de la Garza y Ballesteros, años de 1855 y 1856. [n. p. n. d.] 4to. 39476

Also: Carta Pastoral que el Illmo. Señor Arzobispo de Mexico Doctor D. Lazaro de la Garza dirigé à los Sres. Curas de su Diócesis sobre el contenido de la Enciclica de Ntro. Santisimo Padre el Señor Pio ix. *Mexico.* 1858. 8vo, pp. 32.—Pastoral que el Illmo. Arzobispo Doctor D. Lazaro de la Garza dirige a los fieles de su Diócesis, comunicandoles haber condenado S. S. el Señor Pio ix. la obra que se impresa. *Mexico.* 1852. 4to, pp. 8. *See also* Garza y Ballesteros, Vol. vii., No. 26719.

Lazarus (E.) Poems and Translations, written between the Ages of Fourteen and Seventeen. By Emma Lazarus. *New York: Hurd & Houghton.* 1867. 12mo, pp. viii, 297. 39477

Lazcano (F. X.) Exemplo, que segun la costumbre de los sabados de quaresma. ... *Mexico.* 1756. 4to, pp. 18. 39478

Lazcano. Honras Funerales de Francisco Xavier Lazcano, de la Sagrada Compañia de Jesus, y Cathedratico del Eximio en la Real y Pontificia Universidad de Mexico 19 y 20 de Julio de 1762. *Mexico.* 1762. 8vo. 39479

Lazcano. Vida exemplar, y virtudes heroicas del venerable Padre Juan Antonio de Oviedo, de la Compañia de Jesus. Escrita por el Padre Francisco Xavier Lazcano ... . Con Licencia. *En Mexico, en la imprenta del Real, y Mas-Antiguo Colegio de S. Ildefonso, año de* 1760. 4to, pp. (12), 582, (6). 2 Portraits.

The padre, whose exemplary but rather dull life among the poor degenerated natives of Mexico is here recorded, was born at Santa Fé de Bogota. Also: Vida del P. Francisco Xavier Lazcano. *Mexico.* 1763. 4to.

Lazo (F.) El Arguinaldo Coleccion de Recriminaciones, Ultrajes y denuesto, Inferidos al Peru ... por D. F. Lazo. *Lima.* 1867. 4to, pp. 38. 39481

Lea (A. M.) Notes on Wisconsin Territory. With a Map. By Lieutenant Albert M. Lea. *Philadelphia: Henry S. Tanner.* 1836. 12mo, pp. 53. Map. 39482

The cover-title reads: "Notes on the Wisconsin Territory, particularly with reference to the Iowa District, or Black Hawk Purchase."

[Lea (Henry C.)] Bible View of Polygamy. To the Reverend John Henry Hopkins, Bishop of ... Vermont. Signed, Mizpah. [n. p. n. d.] 8vo, pp. 4. H. 39483

Lea (H. C.) Catalogue of the Tertiary Testacea of the United States ... By Henry C. Lea. *Philadelphia.* 1848. 8vo.

Lea. Description of some new Fossil Shells from the Tertiary of Petersburg, Va. ... By Henry C. Lea. *Philadelphia.* [1843?] 4to, pp. 48. 4 Plates. P. 39485

Lea (I.) Contributions to Geology. By Isaac Lea. *Philadelphia: Carey, Lea and Blanchard.* 1833. 8vo, pp. 227. 6 Plates.

Contents: Tertiary formation of Alabama. New tertiary fossil shells from Maryland and New Jersey. New genus of fossil (foraminiferous) shells from New Jersey. Tufaceous lacustrine formation of Syracuse, N. Y.

Lea. Description of a New Genus of the Family Melaniana, and of many New Species of the Genus Melania, chiefly collected by Hugh Cuming, Esq., and now first described by Isaac Lea and Henry C. Lea. Also Descriptions of Five New Species of Anodontæ, collected by H. Cuming, By Isaac Lea. *Philadelphia.* 1851. 8vo. 39487

Lea. Fossil Foot-Marks in the Red Sandstone of Pottsville, Pa. By Isaac Lea, LL.D. ... *Philadelphia: Printed by T. K. and P. G. Collins.* 1855. Folio, pp. 16. Colored Plate. H. 39488

Lea. Observations on the Genus Unio, together with Descriptions of New Genera and Species in the Families Naiades, Conchæ, Colimacea, Lymneana, Melaniana, and Peristomeana, By Isaac Lea. *Philadelphia.* 1827–74. 13 vols., 4to. 39489

Vols. i. iii. and v. have no title-pages, and consist merely of papers detached from the "Transactions of the American Philosophical Society."

Lea. Index to Vol. i. to xi. of Observations on the Genus Unio, ... with Description of New Species of the Family Unionidæ ... By Isaac Lea, LL.D. ... *Philadelphia: For the Author.* 1867. 4to, pp. 62, (1). BA. 39490

Lea. Rectification of Mr. T. A. Conrad's "Synopsis of the Family of Naiades of North America." ... February, 1853. By Isaac Lea ... . *Philadelphia: Merrihew and Thompson, Printers.* 1854. 8vo, pp. 16. H. 39491

Lea. Rectification of a New Mollusk from the Red Sandstone, near Pottsville, Pa. ... May 12, 1855. By Isaac Lea ... . *Philadelphia.* 1855. 8vo. 39492

Lea. Remarks on the Number of Unionidæ. ... By Isaac Lea ... . *Philadelphia.* 1862. 8vo, pp. 48, (1). H. 39493

Lea. Sketch of the History of Mineralogy. By Isaac Lea. *Philadelphia.* 1823. 8vo. 39494

Lea. A Synopsis of the Family of Naiades. By Isaac Lea, ... *Philadelphia.* 1836. 8vo. + Second Edition, Enlarged. *Philadelphia.* 1838. 8vo. + Third Edition, Greatly Enlarged and Improved. *Philadelphia: Blanchard and Lea.* 1852. 4to, pp. xx, 17–88. B., H. 39495

Lea. A Synopsis of the Family Unionidæ. By Isaac Lea, LL.D. ... Fourth Edition, very greatly Enlarged and Improved. *Philadelphia: Henry C. Lea.* 1870. 4to, pp. xxx, (2), 25–184.

Also: Check List of Shells of North America. ... [*Washington, D. C.* 1860.] 8vo pp. 7.—Description of a New Genus ... of the Family Melanidæ, and of Forty-five New Species. ... *Philadelphia: Merrihew & Thompson, Printers.* 1862. 8vo, pp. 29.—Descriptions of Four New Species of Exotic Uniones. ... *Philadelphia: Merrihew & Thompson, Printers.* 1857. 8vo, pp. 24.—Description of a New Mollusk from the Red Sandstone, near Pottsville, Pa. ... *Philadelphia: Merrihew and Thompson, Printers.* 1855. 8vo, pp. 4. Plate.—Descriptions of New Species of Shells. ... *Philadelphia.* 1862. 8vo.—Descriptions of Eight New Species of Unionidæ, from Georgia, Mississippi and Texas. ... *Philadelphia: Merrihew & Thompson, Printers.* 1860. 8vo, pp. 24. H.—Descriptions of Twelve New Species of Unionidæ from South America. ... *Philadelphia: Merrihew and Son.* 1868. 8vo, pp. 32.—Descriptions of Twenty-Seven New Species of Uniones, from Georgia. ... *Philadelphia: Merrihew & Thompson.* 1859. 8vo, pp. 26.—Description of Six New Species of the Genus Unio, read before the American Philosophical Society, November 2nd, 1827; with Anatomical Observations on the Genus. ... *Philadelphia.* 1827. 8vo.—On Leaia Leidyi-Cypricardia Leidyi. Descriptions ... . *Philadelphia: Merrihew & Son, Printers.* 1866. 8vo, pp. 32.—On the Genus Acostæa of D'Orbigny, a fresh-water Lamellibranchia. ... *Philadelphia.* [n. d.] 8vo.—On the Fossil Foot-Marks in the Red Sandstone of Pottsville. ... *Philadelphia: For the Author.* 1852. 4to, pp. 13. 3 Plates.—On a Fossil Saurian of the New Red Sandstone Formation of Pennsylvania, with some Account of that Formation. Also: on some New Fossil Molluscs. ... *Philadelphia: Merrihew & Thompson, Printers.* 1852. 4to, pp. 28. 4 Plates.—On the New Red Sandstone Formation of Pennsylvania. Description of a New Sub-Genus of Naiades. Description of a New Species of Triquetra. ... New Fresh Water Shells from California. Description of Twenty-Five New Species of Exotic Uniones. ... *Philadelphia: Merrihew & Thompson, Printers.* 1856. 8vo, pp. 8.—Papers on Fossils, June, 1857–December, 1858. ... *Philadelphia.* 1859. 8vo, pp. 26.—Publications of Isaac Lea on Recent Conchology. January 1, 1861. [n. p. n. d.] 8vo. Mr. Lea has recenty printed a list of his numerous contributions to Natural History, many of which we do not name. *See* Allibone's "Dictionary" for the names of the journals, etc., in which most of these articles first appeared

Lea (J.) Cholera, with Reference to the Geological Theory: ... By John Lea. ... *Cincinnati: Printed by Wright* ... 1850. 8vo, pp. 25. H. 39497

Lea (M. C.) Photographic Mosaics. Edited by M. Carey Lea and Edward L. Wilson. *Philadelphia: Benerman & Wilson.* 1866. 12mo, pp. 144. 39498

[Lea (Pryor).] Circular. To the Voters of the Second Congressional District of Tennessee. [n. p. 1827.] 8vo, pp. 12.

Lea. Circular Concerning the Arkansas Road Company, by Pryor Lea, President; with an Exposition, by Albert M. Lea, Engineer. *New Orleans.* 1858. 8vo, pp. 22. 39500

Lea. Speech of Mr. Pryor Lea, of Tennessee, on the Bill proposing to construct a National Road from Buffalo to New Orleans. Delivered ... April, 1830. *Washington.* 1830. 8vo, pp. 15. 39501

Lea (R.) Fourth of July Sermon, delivered in Lawrenceville Presbyterian Church, By Rev. Richard Lea, Pastor. *Pittsburgh: Printed by J. T. Shryock.* 1859. 8vo, pp. 15. 39502

Lea (T. G.) Catalogue of Plants, Native and Naturalized, collected in the Vicinity of Cincinnati, Ohio, during the Years 1834–1844. By Thomas G. Lea. *Philadelphia: Printed by T. K. & P. G. Collins.* 1849. 8vo, pp. (4), 77. H., P. 39503

Leach (E.) A Short Supply or Amendment to the Propositions for the New Representative, for the Perpetual Peace and Quiet of this Nation, &c. which were lately published by Will. Leach of the Middle-Temple, Gent. and now published at the request of divers of this Nation, written and proposed by Edmund Leach of New-England, Merchant. *London.* 1651. Sm. 4to.

Leach (G.) Psalms of Freedom, for the American Christian Patriot. Selected, Arranged, and Composed, By George Leach. ... *New York.* 1861. 12mo, pp. 16. 39505

Leach [James Edward] *and* Goodwin [John A.] ... Mr. Leach's Oration, and Mr. Goodwin's Poem, before the Bridgewater Normal Association, August 15, 1849. To which is appended, a Memoir of the late Mr. Leach. *Providence: Printed by Joseph Knowles.* 1850. 12mo, pp. 36. H. 39506

Leach (J.) Rough Sketches of the Life of an Old Soldier: during a service in the West-Indies; ... By Lieut.-Colonel J. Leach, C.B. ... *London: Longman* ... M.DCCC.XXXI. 8vo, pp. xxix, 411. 39507

Leach (J.) Journal of John Leach, kept during his Confinement in Boston Gaol, in 1775. [n. p. n. d.] 8vo. 39508

Leach (J. M.) State of the Union. Speech of J. M. Leach, of North Carolina, in the House ... February 7, 1861. [n. p. n. d.] 8vo, pp. 8. 39509

Leach (W.) First a Bitt and a Knock for Vnder-Sheriffs, Serjeants, Bayliffs, Setters, and such Vermin, Catterpillars, and Varlets; or Catchpoles fallen from twenty to one.—Secondly, a Preservative against fraudulent Executors, &c.—Thirdly, for Honest Executors, &c.—Fourthly, for Preservation of Shiping from Wilfull Destruction by deceitful persons to defraud creditors of Ships, &c.—Written by William Leach of the Middle-Temple, and explained by Edmund Leach of New-England, Merchant. *London: Printed by E. Cotes, in the Year* 1652. 4to.

Leach (W. T.) Sermon ... Celebration of the Third Semi-Centennial Jubilee of the Society for the Propagation of the Gospel in Foreign Parts. By Archdeacon Leach. *Montreal.* 1851. 8vo, pp. 20. 39511

[Leacock (John).] The Fall of British Tyranny: Or, American Liberty Triumphant. The First Campaign. A Tragi-Comedy of Five Acts, as lately planned at the Royal Theatrum Pandemonium, At St. James's. The Principal Place of Action in America. Publish'd according to Act of Parliament. ... *Philadelphia: Printed by Styner & Cist* ... M DCC LXXVI. 8vo, pp. viii, 66. BA., S. + *Philadelphia, Printed: New-England, Boston: Re-Printed by John Gill, and Powers and Willis* ... [1777.] 8vo, pp. viii, 71. W. 39512

For selections from this rare pamphlet *see* Duyckinck's "Cyclopedia," i. 445. *See also* a large copperplate caricature in the same vein entitled: "Liberty Triumphant," *and* Robin's "New Travels," p. 18. Also: The Medley: or Harlequin have at all. ... Acted at Covent Garden, 1778. *See* Wilson's "Philadelphia," i. 104.

Lead Mines. Letter ... in Relation to the Lead Mines of the United States. *Washington: Printed by Gales & Seaton.* 1828. 8vo, pp. 10. 39513

Leaders of the Old Bar. *See* [Binney (H.)], No. 5478.

A Leaf for the People. Absolute Submission to a Rebel Conspiracy, or War. [n. p. n. d.] 8vo, pp. 4. 39514

Leaflets of Memory: an Illuminated Annual for 1846. Edited by Reynell Coates, M.D. *Philadelphia: E. H. Butler & Co.* 1846. 8vo. Continued. 39515

League Island. Advantages of League Island for a Naval Station. *Philadelphia.* 1866. 8vo. 39516

Reply to a Pamphlet entitled "Advantages of League Island for a Naval Station." *New London.* 1866. 8vo. 39517

Report of the Naval Commission to Examine League Island. *Philadelphia.* 1863. 8vo, pp. 31. 39518

Report of the Minority of the Naval Committee in favor of Accepting League Island, ... for a Station for the Construction, Cleansing and Repair of Iron and Armed Vessels. *Philadelphia.* 1864. 8vo, pp. 40. 39519

Also: Reports of the Secretary of the Navy, and the Commission by him appointed, on the proposed New Iron Navy Yard at League Island. *Philadelphia: Collins, Printer.* 1863. 8vo, pp. 56.—Letter of the Secretary of the Navy communicating Report on the Navy Yard at League Island. [*Washington.* 1862.] 8vo, pp. 29.—Statements relating to a Navy Yard in the Delaware, for the Construction and Equipment of Iron Clad Steamships of War, proposed to be established at League Island. *Philadelphia: Collins, Printer.* 1862. 8vo, pp. 27.

The League of United Southerners of ... Montgomery to the People of the Southern States. [n. p. n. d.] 8vo, pp. 8.

Leake (I. Q.) Memoir of the Life and Times of General John Lamb, an Officer of the Revolution, who Commanded the Post at West Point at the Time of Arnold's Defection, and his Correspondence with Washington, Clinton, Patrick Henry, and other Distinguished Men of his Time. By Isaac Q. Leake. *Albany: Joel Munsell.* 1850. 8vo, pp. x, 431. Portrait and Plans. + [*Ibid.*] 1857. 8vo, pp. x, 431. Portrait and Plans.

Narrates the proceedings of the "Sons of Liberty," prior to and during the Revolutionary War. Some copies were printed on fine paper.

Leake (S. M.) Life of Admiral Sir John Leake. By Stephen Martin Leake. *London.* 1750. 8vo. Map. 39522

Only fifty copies privately printed for the friends of the family. Bindley's copy sold for £4. Contains an account of the destruction of the French settlements in Newfoundland, etc.

[Leal (F.).] Coleccion de varios documentos oficiales extraidos de las Memorias del Ministerio de Relaciones exteriores del Brasil, y que, formando una interesante página de la diplomacia de la América del Sur, sirven para definir la política del Gobierno brasilero hácia un Estado vecino y amigo. Traducidos por un Sur Americano. *Carácas.* 1857. 8vo, pp. 232, v. 39523

Leal (R.) Guatemalensis Ecclesiæ Monumenta; collegit, digessit, concinnavit atque in lucem edidit Fr. Raimundus Leal, Ordinis Prædicatorum. *Madrid. Anno* MDCCXLIV. 4to, pp. (18), 58. 39524

Lealtad Peruana, ó Coleccion de papeles publicados en aquel reyno, con motivo de las circunstancias del dia. *Mexico, en la oficina de Arizpe.* 1809. 4to, pp. 40. 39525

Concerning this *see* Leclerc's Catalogue, No. 859.

Leaman (J.) A Tribute to the Memory of Mrs. Catharine M. Jenkins, of Lancaster County, Pa. By Rev. John Leaman, M.D. *Philadelphia.* 1857. 12mo, pp. 69. 39526

Leaming (A.) *and* Spicer (J.) The Grants, Concessions, And Original Constitutions Of the Province of New-Jersey. The Acts Passed during the Proprietary Governments, and other material Transactions before the Surrender thereof to Queen Anne. The Instrument of Surrender, and Her formal Acceptance thereof. Lord Cornbury's Commission and Instructions consequent thereon. Collected by some Gentlemen employed by the General Assembly. And Afterwards Published by Virtue of an Act of the Legislature of the said Province. With proper Tables alphabetically digested, containing the principal Matters in the Book. By Aaron Leaming and Jacob Spicer. *Philadelphia: Printed by W. Bradford, Printer to the King's Most Excellent Majesty for the Province of New-Jersey.* [1752.] Folio, pp. (6), 763. 39527

On page 593 is a certificate dated January 17, 1752, from which we infer the date.

Leaming (J. R.) Memoir of George P. Cammann, M.D. ... October 21st, 1863. By James R. Leaming, M.D. *Boston: E. P. Dutton and Company.* 1864. 12mo, pp. 38. 39528

Leaming (J.) The Address of the Episcopal Clergy of Connecticut to the Right Rev. Bishop Seabury, with the Bishop's Answer, and a Sermon before the Convention at Middletown, Aug. 3, 1785. By Jeremiah Leaming. Also Bishop Seabury's First Charge to the Clergy of his Diocese. ... *New Haven.* 1785. 8vo, pp. 45. W. 39529

Leaming. A Defence of the Episcopal Government of the Church: containing Remarks on two late, noted Sermons on Presbyterian Ordination. By Jeremiah Leaming, A.M. ... *New-York: Printed by John Holt.* M,DCCLXVI. 8vo, pp. 73. 39530

Leaming. A Second Defence, of the Episcopal Government, of the Church, ... On the Objections advanced by Mr. Noah Welles ... . By Jeremiah Leaming ... . *New-York: Printed by John Holt.* M,DCC,LXX. 8vo, pp. (2), iii, 81. H. 39531

Also: Dissertations upon various Subjects ... . *New-Haven; Printed by Thomas ... Green.* MDCCLXXXVIII. 8vo, pp. 68. + [*Ibid.*] M,DCC,LXXXIX.—The True Christian's Support under Affliction. A Sermon at Christ's Church in Stratford, Jan. 9, 1772, at the Funeral of Rev. Samuel Johnson, D.D. *New Haven.* 1772. 4to, pp. 18.

Leão (José da Rocha), *Jr.* Os libertinos e tartufos do Rio de Janeiro: polygraphia por Leo Junius. *Rio de Janeiro: Typ. de F. de Paula Brito.* 1860. 12mo, pp. 131. 39532

[Lear (Tobias).] Observations on the River Potomack, ... and the City of Washington. *New-York: Printed by Loudon and Brower.* 1794. 12mo, pp. 30. 39533

Also: Letter from the Secretary of State, enclosing his Report on the Memorial of Tobias Lear ... 25th January, 1803. ... *Washington City: Printed by William Duane & Son.* 1803. 8vo, pp. 16. H.

Learned (E.) How to pay it; or, a Method for Discharging the National Debt ... . By Edward Learned. *New-York: John W. Amerman, Printer.* 1869. 8vo, pp. 19. H. 39534

Learned (E.) ... A Sermon ... July 4th, 1800, at the Dedication of the New Meeting House in ... Charlton. By Erastus Learned ... . *Worcester: Printed by Isaiah Thomas, Jun.* 1800. 8vo, pp. 21. BA. 39535

Also: ... A Sermon ... at North-Woodstock, January 19th, 1815, at the Ordination of the Rev. Samuel Backus. ... *Windham: Printed by J. Byrne.* 1815. 8vo, pp. 34.—Sermon at the Ordination of the Rev. Cornelius Adams, Windham, December 5, 1805. ... *Windham.* 1806. 8vo, pp. 25.— ... A Sermon ... at Southbridge, Mass. December 18, 1816, at the Ordination of the Rev. Jason Park. ... *Worcester: Printed by William Manning.* 1817. 8vo, pp. 32. H.

Learned (J. C.) A Discourse ... at the Funeral of Rev. Levi W. Leonard, D.D. ... January 5, 1865. By Rev. J. C. Learned. ... *Exeter, N. H.: Printed by Thomas J. Whittem.* 1865. 8vo, pp. 16. B. 39536

Learned (J. D.) Report of the Trial of Col. Jos. D. Learned, of the 34th U. S. Reg't. Infantry, before a General Court-Martial, convened at Portland, District of Maine, on the 14th Day of November, A.D. 1814. *Portland: Printed by A. & J. Shirley.* 1815. 8vo, pp. 72. C. 39537

Learned. A View of the Policy of Permitting Slaves in the States West of the Mississippi: ... By Joseph D. Learned, Esq. *Baltimore: Printed by Joseph Robinson.* 1820. 8vo, pp. 47. H.

[Learned (Robert C.)] Historical Notices of the First Congregational Church in Canterbury, Conn., with Catalogues ... from ... 1711, to ... 1853 ... . *Northampton, Mass.: Hopkins ...* 1853. 12mo, pp. 42. H. 39539

LEARNED (W. L.) The Duty of Americans to preserve Civil and Religious Liberty: An Oration ... Newburgh, July 4, 1855. By Wm. L. Learned, Esq. ... *Newburgh.* 1855. 8vo, pp. 24.

LEARY (C. L. L.) Remarks of Hon. C. L. L. Leary & F. Thomas ... on the Indemnification Bill. ... February 18, 1863. [*Washington.* 1863.] 8vo, pp. 16. H. 39541

LEATHAM (W. H.) Montezuma, a Ballad of Mexico; ... By William Henry Leatham. *London: Longman* ... MDCCCXLV. 8vo, pp. 32. 39542

Leather Stocking and Silk; or, Hunter John Myers and his Times: a Story of the Valley of Virginia. *New York.* 1854. 12mo, pp. 408. + *London: S. Low* ... 1854. Post 8vo, pp. 267.

LEATON (J.) Slavery, Biblical and American. By Rev. James Leaton ... . *Chicago: Charles Philbrick, Printer.* 1864. 8vo, pp. 26. B. 39544

LÉAUMONT (L. M. de). A. M. de Mirbeck ... . Par M. Laurent-Marie de Léaumont, député de la paroisse de Torbec à l'assemblée coloniale de la partie française de St.-Domingue. Au Cap-Français, le 29 février 1792. [n. p. n. d.] 4to, pp. 40, or less. 39545

Leaven for Doughfaces; or Threescore and Ten Parables touching Slavery. By A former Resident of the South. *Cincinnati: Bangs and Company.* 1856. 12mo, pp. 332. 39546

LEAVENWORTH (M.) Charity Illustrated and recommended. A Sermon Delivered before the General Assembly of the Colony of Connecticut, at Hartford, on the Day of their Anniversary Election, May 14, 1772. By Mark Leavenworth, A.M. ... *New-London: Printed by T. Green* ... [1772.] 8vo, pp. 52. M.

Also: ... Sermon ... in Waterbury, January 20. 1754. Occasioned by the ... Death of Daniel Southmayd, Esq; Who departed this Life the 12th of the same Month ... *Boston: J. & T. Leverett.* 1754. 8vo, pp. (4), iv, 9–38. H.

LEAVENWORTH, *Kansas.* Collins' City Directory of Leavenworth, June, 1866. By Charles Collins. *Leavenworth.* 1866. 12mo, pp. 260. 39548

Collins' Business and Resident Directory of Leavenworth. January, 1868. *Leavenworth: C. Collins.* [1868.] 8vo, pp. 188. Map. 39549

Leaves about the War. [*New Haven.* 1864.] 12mo, pp. 28.

Leaves from a Trooper's Diary. With an Account of the Mutiny in the Anderson Cavalry. *Philadelphia.* 1869. 16mo.

Leaves from the Backwoods. *Montreal.* 1861. 12mo.

Leaves from the Note-Book of a New York Detective. The Private Record of J. B. *New York: Dick & Fitzgerald.* 1865. 8vo, pp. 186. 39553

LEAVITT (D.) Statement of David Leavitt, Receiver of the North American Trust & Banking Company, in reply to the Letter of John Rankin ... . [*New York.* 1844.] 8vo, pp. 27.

LEAVITT (D.) The Scholar's Almanack, and Farmer's Daily Register; for ... 1809. ... By Dudley Leavitt ... . *Exeter: Printed by Norris* ... [1809.] 12mo, pp. (23). Continued. H.

Also: Leavitt's Genuine Improved New-England Almanack and Agricultural Register, 1817. *Exeter.* [1817.] 8vo. Continued.—Leavitt's Improved New-England Farmer's Almanack, for ... 1827. ... *Concord: Jacob B. Moore.* [1827.] 12mo, pp. (24). B.

LEAVITT (Eli). Report of New Buildings erected in New York, 1844. [n. p. n. d.] 8vo. 39556

LEAVITT (F.) Sermon at the Ordination of the Rev. Mr. Jonathan Leavitt, Walpole, May 27, 1761. By Freegrace Leavitt. *New Haven.* [n. d.] 8vo, pp. viii, 40. 39557

LEAVITT (J.) A Genealogical Table of the Family and Descendants from Mr. Jacob Leavitt of Turner, Maine. *Lewiston: Wm. H. Waldron.* 1853. 18mo, pp. 16. 39558

LEAVITT (J.) A Summary of the Laws of Massachusetts, Relative to the Settlement, Support, Employment and Removal of Paupers. By Jonathan Leavitt, Esq. ... *Greenfield: Printed by John Denio.* 1810. 8vo, pp. 64. B., W. 39559

LEAVITT. Memoir of Jonathan Leavitt, ... a Member of the Junior Class in Yale College, who died at New Haven, the 10th of May, 1821. ... By a Sister. *New Haven: S. Converse.* 1822. 24mo, pp. 283. Plate. C. 39560

LEAVITT (J.) An Essay on the Best Way of developing improved Political and Commercial Relations between Great Britain and the United States ... . By Joshua Leavitt, D.D. ... *London: Macmillan and Co.* 1869. 8vo, pp. 44. H. 39561

LEAVITT (J.) The Great Duellist [Henry Clay. n. p. 1844.] 8vo, pp. 16. S. 39562

Also: Address at the Funeral of Rev. John R. M'Dowall. ... *New York.* 1837.

LEAVITT (J.) Cheap Postage. Remarks and Statistics on ... Cheap Postage and Postal Reform in Great Britain and the United States. By Joshua Leavitt. ... *Boston: Otis Clapp.* 1848. 8vo, pp. 72. B. 39563

LEAVITT. The Monroe Doctrine. By Joshua Leavitt. *New-York: Sinclair Tousey.* 1863. 8vo, pp. 50. H. 39564

Also: The Finance of Cheap Postage. ... From Hunt's Merchant's Magazine, for October, 1849. *New York: Printed by George W. Wood.* 1849. 8vo, pp. 7. B.—Memorial on the Tariff Laws. ... *Washington.* 1842. 8vo, pp. 160.—The Moral and Social Benefits of Cheap Postage. ... From Hunt's ... Magazine for December, 1849. *New York: Geo. W. Wood, Printer.* 1849. 8vo, pp. 12.—The Practical Working of Cheap Postage. ... From Hunt's Merchant's Magazine for January, 1850. *New York: Printed by G. W. Wood.* [n. d.] 8vo, pp. 12. B.

LEAVITT, *Judge.* Decision of Judge Leavitt, of Ohio, in the Vallandigham Habeas Corpus Case. *Philadelphia.* 1863. 8vo, pp. 16. 39565

LEAVITT (O. S.) Strictures on the New School Laws of Ohio and Michigan; with some general Observations on the Systems of other States. By O. S. Leavitt. *Cincinnati: Isaac Hefley & Co., Printers.* 1839. 8vo, pp. 31. B. 39566

LEAVITT (T. H.) Facts about Peat as an Article of Fuel. With Remarks upon its Origin and Composition; the Localities in which it is found; the Methods of Preparation and Manufacture ... . Compiled by T. H. Leavitt. *Boston: Leavitt & Hunnewell.* 1865. 8vo, pp. (2), 120. + Second Edition. [*Ibid.*] 1866. 8vo, pp. iii, iv, 168. Plate. B. + Third Edition, Revised and Enlarged. *Boston: Lee & Shepard.* 1867. 12mo, pp. 316. C.

LEAVITT (W. S.) A Farewell Sermon ... in the Eliot Church, Newton, Ms. November 13, 1853. By Rev. W. S. Leavitt ... *Boston: Press of J. Howe.* 1854. 8vo, pp. 22. H. 39568

LEAVITT. God the Protector and Hope of the Nation. A Sermon ... on Thanksgiving Day, November 27, 1862. By Rev. W. S. Leavitt ... . *Hudson: Bryan & Webb, Printers.* 1862. 8vo, pp. 18. H. 39569

LEAVITT. God's Law Unchangeable in its Claims. A Sermon ... Newton Ms. on the Anniversary of the Landing of the

Pilgrims, Dec. 22, 1850. By Rev. W. S. Leavitt ... . *Boston: Press of J. Howe.* 1851. 8vo, pp. 24. B. 39570

Also: A Sermon preached April 9, 1865, the Sunday after the Capture of Richmond. ... *Hudson: Bryan & Webb.* 1865. 8vo, pp. 18.

LEAVITT, STREBEIGH & CO. Catalogue of a Choice Collection of Valuable Books, chiefly relating to American Local History, Genealogy and Biography, ... Sold ... By Leavitt, Strebeigh & Co., ... April 23d, 1866 ... . *New York: J. M. Bradstreet & Son.* 1866. 8vo, pp. 45. 39571

Many other catalogues of Americana were issued by this house and its successors, G. A. Leavitt & Co.

LE B. (*Sieur*). Le Voyagevr cvrievx qvi fait le tovr dv monde. Avec ses matières d'entretièn qvi composent l'histoire cvrievse. *Paris: F. Clovsier.* 1664. Sm. 4to, pp. (16), 424, 360. 39572

LEBANON, *Conn.* *See* Wheelock (Eleazar).

LEBANON, *N. H.* The Centennial Celebration at Lebanon, N. H., July Fourth, 1867. *Boston: J. H. Farwell & Company, Printers.* 1862. 8vo, Cover, pp. 100. 39573

LEBANON, Lancaster County ... pp. 1. 39574

Blank form of balance found on settlements between the United States and their creditors. Pennsylvania about 1780.

LEBANON, *O.* Annual Catalogue of the Teachers and Students of the National Normal School. ... Lebanon, Warren County, Ohio. *Cincinnati.* 1856. 8vo. Continued. 39575

Catalogue of the Officers and Students of the Southwestern Normal School, Lebanon, Ohio. 18mo. 39576

Lebanon Springs Railroad. Prospectus. *New York.* 1852. 8vo. 39577

LEBARDIN (*l'Abbé*). Le Départ pour la Californie; comédie en trois actes, à l'usage des colléges, petits séminaires, sociétés de persévérance ... . *Lyon: Girard et Josserand.* 1853. 12mo.

[LE BARNES (John W.)] Memorial to the Massachusetts Constitutional Convention, presented May 12, 1853. [*Boston.* 1853.] 8vo, pp. 11. 39579

LEBASSU D'HELF (Joséphine). Colomb, ou la Terre promise. *Limoges: Barbou frères.* 1862. 12mo, pp. 102. 39580

LEBAUDY (A.) Deux Lettres sur les Desastres de la Guadeloupe, et le moyen d'y remédier, par A. Lebaudy, l'un des gerans de la maison Lafitte et Cie. *Paris.* 1843. 8vo, pp. 16. 39581

LE BEAU (C.) Avantures du Sr. C. Le Beau, Avocat en Parlement, ou Voyage Curieux et Nouveau, Parmi les Sauvages de l'Amérique Septentrionale. Dans le quel on trouvera une Description du Canada, avec une Relation très particulière des anciennes Coutumes, Mœurs & Façons de vivre des Barbares qui l'habitent & de la manière dont ils se comportent aujourd'hui. Ouvrage enrichi d'une Carte & des Figures necessaires. *Amsterdam: Herman Uytwerf.* MDCCXXXVIII. 2 vols., 12mo, pp. (14), 370, (6); (2), 430, (6). Map and 6 Plates. BA. 39582

A pleasant gossiping book, evidencing considerable acquaintance with the subjects described. It contains a description of the manners and customs of the Iroquois, the Hurons, the Algonquins, and other Indian tribes, derived from the author's personal experiences; although the style in which the work is written is rather that of a romance than of a true narrative. "This work is highly praised by La Richarderie (in his "Bib. des Voyages," Vol. VI.), upon whose judgment, however, very little reliance can be placed."—RICH.

LE BEAU. Geschichte des Herrn C. Le Beau, oder Merckwürdige und neue Reise zu denen Wilden des Nordlichen Theils von America. Worinnen man eine Beschreibung von Canada, nebst einem gantz besondern Bericht von denen alten Gebräuchen, Sitten, und Lebens-Arten dererjenigen Wilden, die darinnen wohnen, antrifft. Aus dem Frantzösischen übersetzt von W. E. Burkhard Roslern. *Erfurt: Joh. David Jungnicol.* 1752. 2 vols., 12mo. Map and Plates. 39583

LE BEAU. ... Reise unter die Wilden in Nord-America; ... übersetzt von Johann Bernhard Nack. *Frankfurt: ... Gebrüdern von Duren.* 1752. 2 vols., sm. 8vo, pp. (4), 415; (2), 504. 3 Plates. 39584

LE BEAU. Begebenheiten und Reisen zu den amerikanischen Wilden. Aus dem Französischen. *Leipzig: Meygand.* 1793. 8vo. 39585

Leben und Tapffere Thaten. *See* B[os], Vol. II., No. 6441.

Lebensbeschreibungen sämtlicher Unterzeichner der Unabhängigkeits-Erklärung der Vereinigten Staaten von Nord-Amerika. Nebst einer fasslichen Darstellung der merkwürdigsten Begebenheiten, welche die Trennung der Colonien von dem Mutterlande zur Folge hatten. Nach den besten englischen Hülfsquellen, mit besonderer Berücksichtigung des Werkes von C. A. Goodrich

bearbeitet. *Sumnytaun.* 1849. 8vo, pp. 528. 30 Portraits, 4 Facsimiles. 39586

Lebensbeschreibung von Gualtero Bodano, Prediger in Amsterdam. Als auch ein Brief geschrieben aus Pensylvanien in Amerika. *Creveld.* 1738. 8vo. 39587

The "curious letter written from Pennsylvania" contains a discourse, pp. 25–34, between a wild man and an English taylor on the habits of the Indians, their religion, etc.

LE BER (*Mlle.*) L'Héroine Chrétienne du Canada, ou vie de Mlle. Le Ber. *Villemarie.* 1860. 8vo, pp. xxviii, 404. 39588

LE BISSONNAIS (——). Constitution des États-Unis d'Amérique, traduite en Français, suivie d'un coup d'œil géographique et politique sur cette République; par Le Bissonnais. *New-York: F. G. Berteau.* 1840. 8vo, pp. 32. B. 39589

LE BLANC (V.) Les | voyages | famevx | dv sievr | Vincent Le Blanc | Marseillos, | Qu'il a faits depuis l'aage de douze ans iusques à soixante, | aux quatre parties du Monde; | a scavoir | Aux Indes Orientales & Occidentales, en Perse & Pegu. Aux Roy- | aumes de Fez, de Maroc & de Guinée, & dans toute l'Afrique | interieure, depuis le Cap de bonne Esperance iusques en | Alexandrie, par les terres de Monomotapa, du Preste Iean & de | l'Egypte. Aux Isles de la Mediterranée, & aux principales Prouin- | ces de l'Europe, &c. | Redigez fidellement sur ses Memoires & Registres, tirez de la Bibliotheque | de Monsieur de Peiresc Conseiller au Parlement de Prouence, | & enrichis de tres-curieuses obseruations. | Par Pierre Bergeron, Parisien. | *A Paris,* | *Chez Gervais Clovsier au Palais, sur les degrez de la Saincte Chappelle.* | M.DC.XLIX. | *Avec privilege dv Roy.* | 4to, pp. (8), 276, (4), 179, (4), 136 [*i. e.* 150], (4.) C. 39590

First edition. A portion of Part III. is devoted to America. Some copies are dated 1648.

LE BLANC. Les voyages famevx du Sievr Vincent Le Blanc Marseillois [as before]. Redigez fidellement sur ses mémoires, par Pierre Bergeron, et nouuellement reuue corrigé et augmenté par le Sr. Covlon. *A Troyes, par Nicolas Oudot, et se vendent a Paris, chez Gervais Clovsier.* 1658. 4to, pp. 202, (6), 147, (4), 109, (2.) 39591

LE BLANC. De Vermaarde | Reizen | Van de Heer | Vincent le Blanc | Van Marsilien, | Die hy sedert d'ouderdom van veertien jaren, tot aan | die van zestig, in de vier delen des Werrelts gedaan heeft; | Te weten | In Oost- en Westindien, in Persien, Arabien,

Pegu, en in meest alle de | Landen van Oostindien; in de Koninkrijken van Fez en Marokko, in Guinea, | en in't geheel innerlijk deel van Afrika, van de Kaap de Bone Esperance | af, tot in Alexandria, deur de Landen van Monomotapa, Abissyna, | en Egypten; in Spanjen, Frankrijk, Italien en Nederlant, | en in veel vermaarde Eilanden van de Werrelt. | Nieuwelijks door J. H. Glazemaker utt de Fransche in de Neder- | lantsche taal vertaalt, en met treffelijke kopere Platen verciert. | *t'Amsterdam,* | *door Ian Hendriksz. en Ian Rieuwertsz.* | *Boekverkopers.* 1654. | 4to, two Titles, one of which is engraved, pp. (4), 152, 116. 39592

LE BLANC. The World Surveyed: Or, The Famous Voyages & Travailes of Vincent le Blanc, or White, of Marseilles; Who from the Age of Fourteen Years, to Threescore and Eighteen, Travelled through most parts of the World, viz. The East and West Indies, Persia, Pegu ... Containing a more exact Description of several parts of the World, than hath hitherto been done by any other Author. The whole work enriched, with many Authentick Histories. Originally written in French, and faith fully rendered into English by F. B. Gent. *London, Printed for John Starkey* 1660. Folio, pp. (12), 407, Table, (12). 39593

The translator was Francis Brooke.

LE BLANC (*M.*) L'Incendie du Village, ou les Représailles Militaires, Mélodrame en trois Actes, de M. Le Blanc. *Paris.* 1815. 8vo, pp. 51. 39594

"La scène se passe pendant la dernière guerre entre les États-Unis et l'Angleterre, à Ellenbourg, sur le territoire du Canada, pres des frontières des États-Unis."

LE BLANC. Manco-Capac, Premier Inca du Pérou, Tragédie ... Par M. Le Blanc. ... *Paris: Chez Belin.* M.DCC.LXXXII. 12mo, pp. 92, (1). BA. 39595

LEBLANC (*M.*) Manifeste sur l'Infamie, la Trahison et la Perfidie employées par le Contre-Amiral Français M[r]. Leblanc, et Par les autres Agens de la France résidant à Montévideo, pour attaquer et soumettre a la tyrannie du rebelle Fructuoso Rivera l'État Oriental de l'Uruguay, qui, par sa Constitution était placé sous la Présidence légale du Brigadier Général D. Manuel Oribe. *Buenos-Ayres: Imprimerie de l'État.* 1839. 8vo, pp. 88. 39596

LEBLOIS (L.) Leduard Leblois, au Calomniateur Therou, et á ses complices, tous colons blancs, ennemis nés de la liberté et de l'egalité. ... [*Paris:*] *De l'imprimerie de Pain* ... [n. d.] 8vo, pp. 15. 39597

Relates to St. Domingo affairs.

LE BLOND (F. C.) Reconstruction. Speech of Hon. Frank C. Le Blond ... April 7, 1866. *Washington, D. C.* 1866. 8vo, pp. 8. H. 39598

LE BLOND (F. F.) Études spéciales sur les fleurs de la Guyane Française, de leurs rapports hygiéniques et de leur influence malfaisante sur la santé de l'homme. Par M. F. F. Le Blond. *Bordeaux: Lafargue.* 1855. 8vo, pp. 68. 39599

LE BLOND. Études sur les fruits de la Guyane Française, de leurs rapports hygiéniques et de leur influence malfaisante sur la santé de l'homme. Nouvelle édition, revue, corrigée et considérablement augmentée. Par M. F. F. Le Blond. *Bordeaux: Coderc, Decréteau et Poujol.* 1859. 8vo, pp. xii, 124. 39600

[LE BLOND.] L'Oréide, poëme de la Comté (Guyane Française); avec des notes explicatives des principales particularités contenues dans l'ouvrage. *Bordeaux: Coderc, Decréteau et Poujol.* 1862. 8vo, pp. 40. 39601

LE BLOND. Projet d'une Colonization agricole et industrielle à fonder à la Guyane Française, comme moyen d'affranchissement progressif. Par M. F. F. Leblond. *Paris: imp. de Vichon.* 1843. 8vo, pp. 16. 39602

LEBLOND (Jean Baptiste). Description abrégée de la Guyane Française, ou Tableau des Productions naturelles et commerciales de cette Colonie, expliqué au moyen d'une Carte géologico-topographique dessinée par M. Poirson ... Par M. Leblond ... *Paris: Alexis Eymery.* 1814. 8vo, pp. 91. Map. A., H., S. 39603

LEBLOND. Description de la Guyane Française; [as before]. Par feu M. Leblond. Deuxième édition, augmentée. *Paris.* 1824. 8vo, pp. 102. Map. 39604

LEBLOND. Mémoire sur la culture du cotonnier dans les terres basses, dites palétuviers, à la Guyane Française. Imprimé par ordre du C[en] Victor Hugues. *Cayenne: Imprimerie de la République, an* X. 4to, pp. (6), 21. 39605

"Pièce fort rare avec envoi autographe à la Societé libre d'agriculture de la Seine, et signé par l'auteur avec la date de *Cayenne le 28 vendemiaire an 10e de la Rèpublique française.*" Also: Observations sur la Fièvre jaune, et sur les maladies des tropiques. ... *Paris. An* XIII. [1805.] 8vo.

LEBLOND. Voyage aux Antilles et à l'Amérique méridionale, commencé en 1767, et fini en 1802, contenant un précis historique des révoltes et des guerres dont l'auteur a été témoin, et de nouveaux détails sur les mœurs et les usages des nations sauvages ou policées qu'il a visitées, la statistique des Antilles et de l'Amérique méridionale, et l'influence des diverses températures sur les hommes, les plantes et les animaux. Par J. B. Leblond. *Paris.* 1813. 2 vols., 8vo. Map and Plate. 39606

Only the first volume has been published; the journey of the author in Guiana is not contained in it. Eleven hundred copies printed. *See* "M. Rev.," LXXIV. 481.

LEBLOND. J. B. Le Blond's Reise nach den Antillen und nach Südamerika ... 1767 ... 1802, nebst geologischen ... Urzustand des Erdbodens ... Nach dem Französischen herausgegeben ... von C. A. W. von Zimmermann. *Hamburg: Bohn.* 1815. 8vo, pp. xxxx, 464. H. 39607

LEBON (H.) Vies de sainte Rose de Lima [etc]. Par Hubert Lebon. *Tours: Mame et fils.* 1865. 18mo, pp. 36. Plates.

LE BORGNE (J. F.) Abrégé de la Requeste presentée au Roy | Par Jeanne François, veuve du Sieur Emanuel Le Borgne, vivant chevalier de Saint Michel, | & leurs enfans, Seigneurs, & propriétaires de la meilleure partie de Laccadie & forts en dependans. [n. p. about 1670.] Folio, 1 l. 39609

LEBORGNE DE BOIGNE (Claude Pierre Joseph). Essai de Conciliation de l'Amérique et de la necessité de l'union de cette partie du monde avec l'Europe, considerée dans ses rapports politiques et commerciaux et dans ceux de leur prosperité et tranquilité respective. Par M. Leborgne de Boigne. *Paris.* 1818. 8vo, pp. 152. 39610

LEBORGNE DE BOIGNE. Nouveau Système de la colonisation pour St. Domingue. ... *Paris.* 1817. 8vo. 39611

Also: P. J. Leborgne, Ci-devant Commissaire de la Martinique aux Isles du Vent de l'Amérique, à Janvier Little, homme de Couleur, Deputé de la Martinique, sur la système de diffamation employé par la faction anglaise contre les patriotes. *Paris: Pain.* 1795. 8vo, pp. 15.—Compte Rendu sur la situation actuelle de la colonie de Saint Domingue. ... *Paris: de l'imprimerie nationelle, an VI.* [1798.] 8vo, pp. 30.

LE BOSQUET (John). The Congregational Manual: or a Concise Exposition of the Belief, Government and Usages of the Congregational Churches. With an Introduction by Rev. Benj. P. Stone. *Boston.* 1841. 18mo, pp. 127. 39612

[LE BOUCHER (Odet-Julien).] Histoire de la dernière Guerre, entre la Grande-Bretagne, et les États-Unis de l'Amérique, la France, l'Espagne et la Holland, depuis son commencement en 1775, jusqu'à sa fin en 1783. Ornée de Cartes géographiques & marines. ... *A Paris, Chez Brocas ...* M.DCC.LXXXVII. 4to, pp. xxxiv, (ii), 357, (3). 7 Maps. P. + [*Ibid.*] 1788. 2 vols., 4to.

LEBOUCHER. Histoire de la Guerre de l'Indépendance des États-Unis. Par Odet Julien Leboucher. Nouvelle édition, ... accompagnée d'un Atlas; publiée Par Emile Leboucher ... . *Paris: Anselin.* 1830. 2 vols., 8vo, pp. lxix, 326, Portrait; (4), 336, Atlas and Facsimile Letter of Washington. H. 39614

LE BRASSEUR (*Intendant Gal. de la Marine*). De l'état actuel de la marine et des colonies. *Paris: Couret.* 1792. 8vo, pp. 48.

LE BRETON (R.) *See* Raymond le Breton (R.)

LE BROCQ (P.) A Sermon ... December 13, 1776 ... the Fast Day on account of the Troubles in America, At Ealing, Hants. By the Rev. Philip Le Brocq. *London: Beescroft.* 1778. 4to. 39616

"The preacher's loyalty is manifested by his keen invective against the Americans."—*Monthly Review*, LVI. 160.

LEBROKE (A. G.) ... An Address ... before the Maine Board of Agriculture ... in Dover ... August 31, 1870. *Augusta.* 1870. 8vo, pp. 23. B. 39617

LE BRUN (——). Histoire Politique et Philosophique de la Revolution de l'Amerique Septentrionale. *Paris. An* IX. [1801.] 8vo. 39618

LEBRUN (*Mme* C.), *pseudon.* Trois mois à la Louisiane; par Mme Camille Lebrun. *Tours: Mame.* 1857. 12mo, pp. 191.

LEBRUN (H.) Abrégé de tous les Voyages au pôle du Nord, depuis Nicolo Zeno jusqu'au capitaine Ross (1380–1833), par Henri Lebrun. *Tours: Mame.* 1837. 12mo. + [*Ibid.*] 1840. 12mo. Plates. + Depuis les Frères Zeno jusqu'à trehouard (1380–1836). *Tours: Mame et Cie.* 1852. 12mo, pp. 284.

LEBRUN. Aventures et Conquêtes de Fernand Cortez au Mexique; par Henri Lebrun. *Tours: Mame.* 1839. 12mo. + Quatrième édition. [*Ibid.*] 1843. 12mo. + Onzième édition. *Tours: Mame et fils.* 1864. 12mo. + Douzième édition. [*Ibid.*] 1866. 12mo, pp. 288. Plates. + Treizième édition. [*Ibid.*] 1867. 12mo, pp. 287. 2 Plates. 39621

See also Irving (W.), Vol. VIII., No. 35210.

LEBRUN. Le Pôle Nord, ou Voyages et découvertes dans les régions arctiques aux XVIIIe et XIXe siècles; par Henri Lebrun. *Tours: Mame et Cie.* 1857. 12mo, pp. 192. 39622

LEBRUN. Voyages et aventures du Capitaine Cook; par Henri Lebrun. Nouvelle édition, revue. *Tours: Mame.* 1852. 12mo, pp. 240, or less. 39623

LEBRUN (Isidore Frédéric Thomas). Tableau statistique et politique des deux Canadas. Par M. Isidore Lebrun. *Paris: Treuttel et Würtz.* 1833. 8vo, pp. (2), 538, (2). C. 39624

LE BRUN (N.) Virgilius Christianus, auctore Laur. Le Brun, Armorico Nannetensi. *Augustæ Vindelicorum, Jo. Bencard.* [n. d.] 8vo. 39625

Contains "De ponto occidentali sive de Barbarie Canadensi Franciados libri duo," "De Nova Gallia," etc.

LE BRUN (P.) Theodore, or the Peruvians. Translated from the French. *New York.* 1825. 18mo. 39626

LE CAT (C. N.) Traité de la Couleur de la Peau Humaine en Général, de Celles de Negres en particulier, et de la Métamorphose d'une de ces couleurs en l'autre, soit de naissance, soit accidentellement; Ouvrage divisé en trois Parties. Par M. Le Cat ... . *Amsterdam.* MDCCLXV. 8vo, pp. (2), xiv, 191. BA., C.

Lecciones Espirituales para las tandas de Ejercicios de S. Ignacio, dadas á los Indios en el idioma Mexicano. Compuestas por un Sacerdote del Obispado de la Puebla de los Angeles. Quien las dedica á la Luz increada, bajo el poderosísimo amparo de la Madre Santísima de ella. *Puebla: Imprenta Antigua en el Portal de las floras.* 1841. 8vo, pp. 213. 39628

A rare work in the Mexican language.

LECESNE (L. C.) *and* ESCOFFERY (J.) Report on the Debate in the House of Commons, respecting the Deportation of Messrs. L. C. Lecesne and J. Escoffery, two persons of colour, from Jamaica—Letter, etc. (to Mr. Courtenay), with Appendix. *London.* [n. d.] 8vo, pp. 374. 39629

[LE CHALLEUX (Nicolas).] Brief discovrs et | histoire d'vn | voyage de quelques François en | la Floride: & du massacre autant | iniustement que barbarement exe- | cuté sur eux, par les Hespagnols, l'an mil cinq cens soixante cinq. | Par ci devant redige | au vray par ceux qui s'en retirerent: & maintenant | reuue & augmentée de noueau, par M. Vrbain Chavveton. Ensemble | vne requeste presen- | tee au Roy Charles neufiesme, en forme de | complainte, par les femmes vefues & enfans | orphelins, parens &

amis de ses suiets, qui | furent tuez audit pays de la Floride. | [n. p.] M.D.LXXIX. 12mo, pp. 104. J.C.B. 39630

The second portion, or "requeste," mentioned in the title, is not in the work. The work is extracted from G. Benzoni.

[LE CHALLEUX.] Discovrs De L'Histoire de la Floride, contenant la trahison des Espagnols, contre les subiets du Roy, en l'an mil cinq cens soixante cinq. Redigé au vray par ceux qui en sont restez. Chose autant lamentable à ouir, qu'elle a est é proditoirement & cruellement executee par lesdits Espagnols: Contre l'authorité du Roy nostre Sire, à la perte & dommage de tout ce Royaume. *A Dieppe, Pour lessé le Sellier.* 1566. 12mo, pp. 54 [for 52, (2)]. H. 39631

[LE CHALLEUX.] Discovrs | De L'Histoi- | re de la Floride, con- | tenant la cruauté des Espagnols contre | les subiets du Roy en l'an mil cinq cens | soixante-cinq. | Rédigé au vray | par ceux qui en sont restez. Chose autant la- | mentable á ouir, qu'elle a esté proditoirement & cruelle- | ment exécutée par lesdits Espagnols: Contre l'authorité du | Roy nostre Sire, à la perte & dommage de tout ce Royaume. Item vne reqvêste av | Roy, faite en forme de complainte par les fem- | mes vefues, petits enfans orphelins et autres | les leurs amis, parents et alliez de ceux qui ont esté | cruellement envahis par les Espagnols, en la | France anthartique, dite la Floride. | *De Dieppe, ce 22 de May* 1566. 12mo, pp. 62.

[LE CHALLEUX.] Discovrs de l'Histoire de la Floride ... . [n. p.] 1566. 12mo, pp. 22. 39633

"Dans cette deuxième édition on a ajouté (p. 48) une 'petite épître faite par l'auteur,' en 21 vers de huit syllabes."—TERNAUX, No. 101.

[LE CHALLEUX.] Histoire | Memorable | du Dernier | Voyage aux Indes, lieu appelé la Floride, fait par le Capitaine Iean Ribaut, et entrepris par le commandement du Roy en l'an M.D.LXV. | *A Lyon.* | *Par Jean Saugrain*, | M.D.LXVI. | Auec priuilege. | [Colophon:] *Fin de la Floride, acheuee d'imprimer le 25 d'Aoust* 1566. 12mo, pp. 71. J.C.B. 39634

"An edition unknown to bibliographers. Brunet describes an edition of the same year, and by the same printer, under Ribaut, and again under Le Challeux, who, in reality, was the writer of the work. Brunet says: 'Après le titre se lit une Epistre de l'auteur à un sien amy, signée M. le Challeux;' and that at page 9 commences 'La Floride,' etc., p. 56. Chauveton, in his Latin version of Benzoni, first printed in *Geneva* in 1578, 8vo, has given at the end of the volume a Latin translation of the relation of Le Challeux; and the original French text is reprinted at the end of Chauveton's French version of Benzoni, *Geneva*, 1579, 8vo. De Bry in the sixth part of the 'Grands Voyages,' 2d appendix, 'Expeditio in Floridam,' and at the end of Chap. I. and in Chap. II., pages 87 *et seq.*, has given an exact copy of Chauveton's Latin version of this little tract of Le Challeux.'—J. R. BARTLETT. The following is a translation:

[LE CHALLEUX.] A true and perfect de- | scription, of the last vo- | yage or Nauigation, attempted by | Capitaine Iohn Ribaut, deputie | and general for the Frenchmen, into | Terra Florida, this yeare past, 1565. | Truely sette forth by those that re- | turned from thence, wherein | are contayned things as la- | mentable to heare as they | haue bene cruelly | executed. | *Imprinted* | *at London by Henry Denham*, | *for Thomas Hacket, and* | *are to be solde at his Shop* | *in Lumbart* | *streate.* | [1566.] 12mo, 4 p. l., 24 l. J.C.B.

A volume of excessive rarity. We know of but two copies, one in Mr. Brown's library and one in the British Museum.

[LECHEVALIER (Jules).] Études et avant-projet d'une institution financière, ayant pour but de développer le commerce maritime et de faciliter la réorganisation des colonies françaises. ... *Paris: imp. de Bailly.* 1841. Folio. 39636

[LECHEVALIER.] Note sur la fondation d'une nouvelle colonie dans la Guyane Française, ou premier aperçu d'un nouveau mode de population et de culture, pour l'exploitation des régions tropicales, suivie de plusieurs pièces et documents ... . *Paris.* 1844. 8vo. 39637

LECHEVALIER. Rapport sur les Questions Coloniales, adressé a M. le Duc de Broglie, Président de la Commission Coloniale, a la suite d'un voyage fait aux Antilles et aux Guyanes, pendant les années 1838 et 1839. Par M. Jules Lechevalier ... . Publé par ordre de S. Exc. l'Amiral Baron de Mackau ... . Documents et pièces justificatives. Tome I. Première Partie. Pièces écrites et recueillies pendant le Voyage.—Enquêtes. *Paris: Imprimerie Royale.* M DCCC XLIV. Folio, pp. xl, 786. 2 Tables. Tome II. Deuxième Partie. Étude de l'Émancipation dans les Colonies Anglaises depuis l'année 1833 jusqu'au 3 Décembre 1842. *Paris: Imprimerie Royale.* M DCCC XLIII. Folio, pp. x, (2), 1280. C., H.

Beautifully printed, and not intended for sale.

LECHEVALIER (T.) Abolition de l'Esclavage dans les Colonies françaises. Proposition de M. Passy prise en considération par la Chambre de Deputés. Extrait du Journal de Paris. *Paris.* 1838. 8vo. A. 39639

LECHFORD (T.) Plain Dealing: | Or, | Nevves | from | New-England. | A short view of New-Englands | present Governmen, both Ecclesiasticall and Civil, | compared with the anciently received and esta- | blished Government of England, in | some materiall points; fit for the gravest | consideration in these times. |

By Thomas Lechford of Clements Inne, | in the County of Middlesex, Gent. | *London*, | *Printed by W. E. and I. G. for Nath: Butter, at the signe* | *of the pyde Bull neere S. Austins gate.* 1642. | 4to, pp. (8), 80. H. 39640

This first edition is of much rarity and value. For an account of the work and its author, *see* Hutchinson's "Hist. of Mass. Bay," I. 451. It was reproduced with a new title-page only as:

[LECHFORD.] New-Englands Advice to Old-England, or, Some Observations upon New-Englands Government, compared with the Ancient Government of Old-England: Not unfitting to be taken into serious consideration in these miserable distracted times. Written by one that hath lived there, and seene the division and danger that followeth upon the obtruding a different Government to that of Old England. ... [*London:*] *Printed in the Yeere*, MDCXLIV. 4to, pp. (8), 80. 39641

It was also included in "Mass. Hist. Soc. Coll.," III., 3d Series, and finally reprinted as below:

LECHFORD. Plain Dealing or News from New England. By Thomas Lechford. With an Introduction and Notes by J. Hammond Trumbull. *Boston: J. K. Wiggin & Wm. Parsons Lunt.* M DCCC LXVII. 4to, pp. xl, 211. BA. 39642

LECHLER (J.) The Confession and Dying Words of John Lechler who Murdered his Wife and the Wife of Mr. Haag, and was condemned to die on the Gallows. *Lancaster.* 1822. 8vo, pp. 16. 39643

LECK (——). The Family of Leck, of Bedlington, in the County of Durham, and the Charity of John George Leake, in New York, U. S. [*Newcastle.* 1855.] 8vo, pp. 14. 39644

LECKIE (G. F.) An Historical Survey of the Foreign Affairs of Great Britain, for ... 1808, 1809, 1810; with a view to explain the Causes of the Disasters of the ... Wars. By Gould Francis Leckie, Esq. *London: Printed by D. N. Shury.* 1810. 8vo, pp. xviii, (2), 607. Table. BA., C. 39645

Contains much material relative to the United States.

[LECLAIR (A.)] Levensgeschiedenis van Ma-Ka-Tai-Me-She-Kia-Kiak of Zwarte Havik, opperhoofd van den stam der Sac-Indianen in N. Amerika, met een berigt van de godsdienstige denkwijze, zeden en gebruiken van dien stam volgens zijne eigene opgaven ... uit het engelsch met aanmerkingen door R. Posthumus. *Leeuwarden.* 1847. 8vo. 39646

LECLERC (C.) Bibliotheca Americana Catalogue Raisonné d'une très-précieuse collection de livres anciens et modernes sur l'Amérique et les Philippines Classés par ordre alphabétique de noms d'Auteurs. Rédigé par Ch. Leclerc. *Paris Maisonneuve & Ce* M.D.CCC.LXVII. Rl. 8vo, pp. viii, 407. B. 39647

Describes one thousand six hundred and forty-five works; it includes a careful collation of each book, and in many instances analyses and important notes. It was followed by "Bibliotheca Historica; Catalogue raisonné d'une collection de livres sur l'Histoire de l'Europe et de l'Amérique." *Paris.* 1868. 8vo, pp. 193.

LE CLERCQ (C.) Dictionnaire caraïbe-français, par le Père Leclercq. *Rennes.* 1665. 39648

Title from Ternaux, No. 830.

LE CLERCQ. Nouvelle | Relation | de la | Gaspesie, | qui contient | Les Mœurs & la Religion des Sau- | vages Gaspesiens Porte-Croix, | adorateurs du Soleil, & d'autres | Peuples de l'Amerique Septen- | trionale, dite le Canada. | Dedie'e à Madame la | Princesse d'Epinoy, | Par le Pere Chrestien Le Clercq, Missionnaire Recollet de la Province de | Saint Antoine de Pade en Artois, & | Gardien du Convent de Lens. | *A Paris,* | *Chez Amable Auroy, ruë Saint* | *Jacques, à l'Image S. Jerôme, attenant* | *la Fontaine S. Severin.* | M.DC.XCI. | Avec Privilege du Roy. | 12mo, pp. (28), 572. BA., C. 39649

Important for its information relative to Northeastern Canada and the Province of New Brunswick. It contains a remarkable record of the labors of converting the Gaspé Indians. He not only records the results of his own missionary life among the savages inhabiting the shores of the St. Lawrence, but he has left us an account of their peculiar traits of character, religious rites, and mode of life, before these had been modified by contact with civilization. *See* Boucher de la Richarderie, VI. 21, Faribault, p. 82, Field's "Essay," No. 903, *and* [Harrisse's] "Notes," No. 170.

LE CLERCQ. Premier Etablissement | de la Foy | dans la Nouvelle France, | contenant la Publication | de l'Evangile, l'Histoire des Colonies Françoises, & les fameuses découvertes depuis | le Fleuve de Saint Laurent, la Loüisiane | & le fleuve Colbert jusqu'au Golphe | Mexique, achevées sous la conduite de | feu Monsieur de la Salle. | Par Ordre du Roy. | Avec les victoires | remportées en Canada par les armes de Sa Majesté sur les Anglois & les Iroqvois | en 1690. | Dédié à Monsieur le Comte de Frontenac, | Gouverneur & Lieutenant General de la | Nouvelle France. | Par le Pere Chrestien Le Clercq, Missionnaire | Recollet de la Province de Saint Antoine de Pade | en Arthois, Gardien des Recollets de Lens. | *A Paris,* | *Chez Amable Auroy rüe Saint Jacques,* | *attenant la Fontaine S. Severin à l'Image* | *Saint Jerôme.* | M.DC.XCI. |

Avec Privilege du Roy. | 2 vols., 12mo, pp. (28), 559; 458 [for 454], (8), Catalogue, (20). 39650

An extremely rare work. Soon after its publication it was suppressed by the French Government, and very few copies were circulated. It is peculiarly valuable as containing the first original account of the discoveries of La Salle by two missionaries who accompanied him. From this book also Hennepin drew the account of his pretended discovery of the Mississippi River. "Cet ouvrage que celui de Charlevoix sur le même sujet avait fait oublier, est exact et assez bien écrit. On le recherche beaucoup au Canada, et, comme il est peu commun."—BRUNET. *See* [Harrisse's] "Notes," No. 169. The work was reproduced in 1692, without the author's name, as:

[LE CLERCQ.] Histoire des Colonies Françaises et les fameuses découvertes ... de la Louisiane, Sous la conduite du feu M. de la Salle. *Paris et Lyon, Chez Thomas Amauroy.* 1692. 2 vols., 12mo, pp. 559; 458. 39651

This is identical with the former edition, except that the dedication to Count Frontenac is omitted. Charlevoix asserts that Frontenac was, in fact, the author of a large part of the work. The student of Canadian history will find it difficult to determine as to the relative credence to be given to Le Clercq and Charlevoix; he should read both and strike a balance, and in order to do so intelligently he will do well to consult Dr. Shea's translation of Charlevoix, from which T. W. Field has drawn largely in his "Essay." *See also* [Harrisse's] "Notes," No. 169. Joutel and Hennepin may also be consulted.

LECLERC (Frédéric.) Le Texas et sa révolution. ... *Paris: H. Fournier et Cie.* 1840. 8vo, pp. 104. Map. S. 39652

LECOMPTE (E. A.) A Discourse commemorative of John W. Crafts ... in ... Boston ... April 29, 1866. By Rev. E. A. Lecompte ... *Boston: Press of Geo. C. Rand ...* 1866. 8vo, pp. 14.

The Lecompton Constitution in the House of Representatives, March 10, 1858. [n. p. n. d.] 8vo, pp. 16. 39654

Also: The Lecompton Constitution, 1859. [n. p. n. d.] 8vo. S.

The Lecompton Question. Governor Wise's Tammany, Philadelphia and Illinois Letters, together with Letter to Charles W. Russell, Esqr. By a Virginia Democrat. [n. p. 1857.] 8vo, pp. 67. 39655

See also "Democratic Protests," Vol. V., No. 19513, *and* "Private and Confidential."

LECOINTE-PUIRAVEAU (——). Corps Législatif, Conseil des Cinq-Cents. Rapport fait par Lecointe-Puiraveau, au nom de la Commission des Colonies occidentales, sur les déportés et réfugiés du Saint-Domingue, soit en France, soit en Continent [illegible]caine. Séance du 4 Germinal, An V. ... [*Paris:*] *De* [illegible]*merie Nationale. Prairial, An* V. 39[illegible]

LECOMTE (F.) Campagnes de Virginie et de Maryland en 1862; documents officiels soumies au congrès, traduits de l'Anglais, avec introduction et annotations, par Ferdinand Lecomte. *Paris: Tenera.* 1863. 8vo. 2 Maps. B., C. 39657

Lecomte. Guerre de la Sécession. Esquisse de Evénements Militaires et Politiques des États-Unis de 1861 a 1865. Par Ferdinand Lecomte. *Lausanne: Ch. Tanera.* 1866–67. 3 vols., 8vo, pp. (4), 288; (4), 390; 312. 7 Maps. BA. 39658

Lecomte. De la Guerre Actuelle des États-Unis d'Amérique. Rapport ... au Département Militaire Suisse ... le 18 Aout 1862. Par Ferdinand Lecomte ... . *Lausanne: Imprimerie Pache.* 1862. 8vo, pp. (2), 216. 2 Maps. H. 39659

Lecomte. Guerre des États-Unis d'Amérique. Rapport au Département Militaire Suisse Précédé d'un Discours a la Société Militaire fedérale réunie a Berne le 18 Aout 1862 Par Ferdinand Lecomte ... . *Paris: Ch. Tanera.* 1863. 8vo, pp. 216. 2 Maps.

Lecomte. The War in the United States. Report to the Swiss Military Department; Preceded by a Discourse to the Federal Military Society assembled at Berne, Aug. 18, 1862. By Ferdinand Lecomte ... . Translated from the French. *New York: D. Van Nostrand.* 1863. 12mo, pp. 148. BA. 39661

Le Conte (J. L.) Classification of the Coleoptera of North America. Prepared for the Smithsonian Institution, by John L. Le Conte, M.D. *Washington, May,* 1861–62. 2 parts 8vo, pp. xxiv, 278; C. 39662

Le Conte. The Coleoptera of Kansas and New Mexico. By John L. Le Conte, M.D. *Washington.* 1858. 4to, pp. 58. Map and 2 Plates. 39663

Le Conte. The Coleoptera of Kansas and Eastern New Mexico. By John L. Le Conte, M.D. *Washington, December,* 1859. 4to, pp. 66. 3 Plates. 39664

Le Conte. List of the Coleoptera of North America. ... By John L. Le Conte, M.D. Part I. *Washington.* 1863–1866. 8vo, pp. 4, 77. C. 39665

Le Conte. New Species of North American Coleoptera. ... By John L. Le Conte, M.D. Part I. *Washington.* 1863–1866. 8vo, pp. 2, 177. S. 39666

Also: An Attempt to Classify the Longicorn Coleoptera of the part of America North of Mexico. ... *Philadelphia.* 1850. 4to. 2 Plates.—Description of New Species of Coleoptera from California. ... *New York.* 1851. 8vo.—Descriptions of some New

and Interesting Insects inhabiting the United States. ... *New York.* 1844. 8vo. Plate.—Fragmenta Entomologica. ... *Boston.* 1848. 4to, pp. 24.—General Remarks upon the Coleoptera of Lake Superior. ... *New York.* 1852. 8vo.—On the Pselphidæ of the United States. ... *New York.* 1848. 8vo.—Synopsis of the Coleopterous Insects of the Group Æridæ, which inhabit the United States ... . *New York.* [n. d.] 8vo, pp. 30.—Synopsis of the Species of Donacia (Fabr.) inhabiting the United States ... *New York.* 1852. 8vo. *See* Smithsonian Institution, Reports of Explorations and Surveys, Vol. XII., Part II., *and* "Amer. Phil. Soc. Trans.," New Series, Vol. X.

Lecraw (J. B.) A Sketch of the Life, Works and Sufferings of a Reformed Man; showing the Misery to which Intemperance brought him ... . Written by Himself. *Pawtucket: B. W. Pearce.* 1844. 12mo, pp. 36. 39667

The Lectures delivered before the American Institute of Instruction, ... 1831; including the Journal of Proceedings, and a List of the Officers. Published under the direction of the Board of Censors. *Boston.* 1832. Rl. 8vo. Continued annually.

Lectures before the Middlesex County Lyceum, on Taxation, Judicial Investigation [etc]. , *Charlestown.* 1833. 12mo. 39669

Lectures Historical, Expository, and Practical, on the Communion Office of the Protestant Episcopal Church in the United States. By a Presbyter of the Church. *Philadelphia: J. B. Lippincott & Co.* 1865. 12mo, pp. xiv, 13–273. B., C. 39670

Lectures on Popular Subjects, delivered in the Musical Fund Hall, To Aid in Rebuilding the Southwark Church. ... *Philadelphia: T. K. Collins, Jr.* 1851. 8vo, pp. 48. BA. 39671

Lectures on Slavery. Delivered in the North Presbyterian Church, Chicago. With an Appendix, containing a Discussion with Rev. Mr. Wolcott. *Chicago, Ill.* 1860. 8vo, pp. 100.

Ledderhose (Carl Friedrich). Christliche Biographien. ... *Heidelberg: K. Winter.* 1852–62. 7 vols., 8vo. 39673

The second volume contains, "Die Mission unter den freien Buschnegern in Surinam. Ein Bild aus der Missionsgeschichte der Brüdergemeine ... . Zweite stark vermehrte Auflage." *Heidelberg.* 1854. 8vo, pp. iv, 112.

Lede (Ch. van). De la Colonisation du Brésil. Mémoire sur la province de Sainte-Cathérine ... . Par Ch. van Lede. *Bruxelles.* 1843. Rl. 8vo. Map. 39674

Lede. De la Colonisation du Brésil. Rapport ... dans l'assemblée générale ... 1844 et 1845. Par Ch. van Lede ... . *Bruxelles.* 1846. 8vo, pp. (4), 216. B. 39675

Lederer (J.) The | Discoveries | of | John Lederer, | In three several Marches from | Virginia, | To the West of | Carolina, | And other parts of the Continent: | Begun in March 1669, and ended in September 1670. | Together with | A General Map of the whole Territory | which he traversed. | Collected and Translated out of Latine from his Discourse | and Writings, | By Sir William Talbot Baronet. | *London, Printed by J. C. for Samuel Heyrick, at Grays- | Inne-gate in Holborn.* 1672. | 4to, pp. (6), 27. Map. H. 39676

A very rare book; Griswold's copy sold for $315. Lederer appears to have been regarded by the Virginians with no little jealousy, but, in the face of some misgivings, he seems to have won the good opinions of his patron and translator, Sir W. Talbot, who states that he found him to be "a modest ingenious person, and a pretty scholar." It is dedicated to Anthony Lord Ashley, Baron Ashley of Wimborn St. Giles, etc., one of the proprietors of Carolina. *See* Pennington's "New Albion," *and* Rich's Catalogue, No. 358. I have seen a copy with the Licence, one leaf, preceding the title.

Ledesma (B. A.) ... De Septem novæ legis Sacramentis Summarium. *Mexico.* 1568. 4to. 39677

"Probably the first book printed in the roman letter in Mexico." This brief title and note are from Rich's "Catalogue," No. 46. Rich in his "Bib. Am. Vet," No. 46, quotes an edition dated 1566.

Ledesma (C. de). Compendio | del Despertador | de Noticias | de los Santos Sacramentos, | Que sacó a luz, y en este succinta (para | los que se han de presentar de | Confessores) dedicandole | a | Jesvs, Mariá, y Joseph. | El M. R. P. Fray Clemente de | Ledesma ... *En Mexico, por Doña Maria de Bena- | vides. Viuda de Juan de Ribera. Año de* 1695. 12mo, pp. (24), 368, 34, (8).

Ledesma (J. de). Vida y virtudes del P. Juan de Ledesma que murio en Mexico el anno de 1636. *Mexico.* 1636. 4to.

Ledesma (Ph. Rod. de). Sermon de la soledad de Maria Santissima N. Señ. en la Yglesia cathedral de la Ciudad de los Angeles. *Mexico, herederos de M. de Ribera Calderon.* 1718. 4to, pp. (16), 16. 39680

Title printed in red and black.

Ledesma (V.) Outlines of the Geography of Peru, by Don Valentine Ledesma. Communicated and translated by W. Ballaert, Esq. F.R.G.S. [n. p. n. d.] 8vo, pp. 19. 39681

Ledesme (*P.*) Doctrine Chrestienne du R. P. Ledesme de la Compagnie de Jèsus. Traduite en Langage Canadois, pour la Conversion des habitans dudit pays. Par un Père de la mesme Compagnie. *Rouen, Richard l'Allement.* 1630. 12mo, pp. 26.

"Petit volume rare, contenant le texte français et la traduction canadienne sur 2 col."—Brunet. Reprinted in Champlain's "Voyages" in 1632.

Lediard (T.) The Naval History of England, ... from 1066. ... to the Conclusion of 1734. Collected from the most Approved Historians, ... With many Facts and Observations, never before made Publick. By Thomas Lediard ... . *London: John Wilcox.* M DCC XXXV. Folio, pp. iv, (4), xii, (20), 933. C.

Contains notices on the life, actions and discoveries of Columbus, J. and S. Cabot, Ramusius, A. Jenkinson, Hawkins, H. Gilbert, Drake, Sir W. Raleigh, and others, accounts of the British colonies in America, etc.

Lednum (J.) A History of the Rise of Methodism in America ... 1736–1785. By John Lednum. *Philadelphia.* 1859. 12mo. Portrait. 39684

Ledo (O. M.) Exposicion que Octaviano Muñoz Ledo dirige á sus conciudadanos sobra la conducta politica que observó en el gobierno del estado de Guanajuato durante la ultima Revolucion. *Mexico.* 1853. 4to, pp. 84, 34. 39685

Ledoux (L. P.) ... A Discourse ... January 15, 1862, in ... Syracuse, N. Y., on the ... Installation of the Rev. L. H. Reid. By Rev. L. P. Ledoux. ... *Newburgh: E. M. Ruttenber, Printer.* 1862. 8vo, pp. 16. H. 39686

Ledru (André-Pierre). Voyage aux Iles de Ténériffe, la Trinité, Saint-Thomas, Saint-Croix, et Porto-Ricco, exécuté par ordre du Gouvernement Français, Depuis le 30 Septembre 1796 jusqu'au 7 Juin 1798, sous la Direction du Capitaine Baudin, pour faire des Recherches et des Collections relatives a' l'Histoire Naturelle; contenant Des Observations sur le Climat, le Sol, la Population, l'Agriculture, les Productions de ces Iles, la Caractere, les Moeurs et le Commerce de leurs Habitans. Par André-Pierre Ledru, l'un des Naturalistes de l'Expédition ... . Ouvrage Accompagné de Notes et d'Additions, Par M. Sonnini, ... *Paris: Arthus Bertrand.* 1810. 2 vols., 8vo, pp. (2), xlvii, 315, (1); (2), 324, (1). Map. A., H. 39687

See "M. Rev.," LXIV. 485.

Ledru. Reise nach den Inseln Teneriffa, Trinidad, St. Thomas, St. Cruz, und Porto-Rico, 1796–98, unter der Leitung des Capitain Baudin. Aus dem Französischen, mit Bemerkungen über Colonialwaaren von E. A. W. Zimmermann. *Leipzig.* 1811–12. 2 vols., 8vo. 39688

Le Duc (W. G.) The Minnesota Year Book for 1851. By W. G. Le Duc. *St. Paul, Minnesota Territory: W. G. Le Duc.* [1851.] 12mo, pp. 51. Map. B. + For 1852. [*Ibid.*] 1852. 12mo, pp. 98. C. 39689

Ledyard (I.) An Oration, Delivered on the 22d of February 1800, at Newtown, ... on account of the Death of George Washington, by the appointment of the different Congregations of that place ... . By Dr. Isaac Ledyard. *Brooklyn: Printed by Thomas Kirk.* 1800. 8vo, pp. 16. 39690

This rare piece is not mentioned in Hough's "List of Washingtoniana."

Ledyard (J.) A Journal of Capt. Cook's last Voyage to the Pacific Ocean, and in quest of a North-West Passage between Asia and America; performed in the Years 1776, 1777, 1778 and 1779. Illustrated with a Chart shewing the tracks of the Ships employed in this Expedition. Faithfully narrated from the original MS. of Mr. John Ledyard. *Hartford: Nathaniel Patten.* MDCCLXXXIII. 12mo, pp. 208. Map. N., W. 39691

Very rare. Ledyard accompanied Captain Cook in his last memorable voyage. The author's narrative is distinguished by its simplicity and evident authenticity. It includes a detailed account of the circumstances attending the death of Captain Cook. *See* Greenhow's "Oregon," pp. 149, 162, 163. Republished in England with the following title:

Ledyard. Travels and Adventures of John Ledyard; comprising his Voyage with Captain Cook's Third and last Expedition; his Journey on foot 1300 miles round the Gulf of Bothnia to St. Petersburgh; his Adventures and Residence in Siberia; and his Exploratory Mission to Africa. Second Edition. *London: Henry Colburn.* 1828. 8vo, pp. 428. + [*Ibid.*] 1834.

This is, in fact, Jared Sparks' compilation, with a careful omission of his name; *see* Sparks (J.)

Lee (A.) The Christian Citizen's Duty in the Present Crisis. A Discourse delivered in Wilmington, Delaware, April 21, 1861. By Alfred Lee, Bishop of ... Delaware. *Wilmington: Henry Eckle.* 1861. 18mo, pp. 16. 39693

Lee. A Few Words in Vindication of the Action of the Court of Bishops, convened at Camden, N. J., September, 1853. By Alfred Lee ... . *Philadelphia: H. Hooker.* 1854. 8vo, pp. 22.

Also: God to be Glorified in the Fires. Thanksgiving Discourse delivered in St. Andrew's Church, Wilmington, Nov. 27, 1862. ... *Wilmington: Henry Eckle.* 1862. 12mo, pp. 16.—The Great National Deliverance. ... A Sermon ... Thanksgiving, December 7, 1865, in ... Wilmington, Del. ... *Wilmington: Henry Eckel, Printer.* 1865. 8vo, pp. 20.— ... A Memoir of Susan Allibone. ... *Philadelphia: J. B. Lippincott & Co.* 1856. 8vo, pp. xii, 15–592.— ... A Sermon ... in ... Richmond ... October 13th, A.D. 1859, at the consecration of The Rt. Rev. William H. Odenheimer ... and ... Rev. Gregory Thurston Bedell ... . *Cincinnati.* 1859. 8vo, pp. 19. H.—A Sermon ... May 28, 1843; at the Consecration of St. Luke's Church, and Ordination of Mr. John Long to the order of deacons. ... *Wilmington: Wilson & Heald.* 1843. 8vo, pp. 17.— ... A Sermon ... in ... Wilmington, on ... March 8, 1846, on the ...

Decease of his Excellency, Thomas Stockton, Governor of ... Delaware. ... *Wilmington: Wilson & Heald.* 1846. 8vo, pp. 16.—Sermon ... Convention of the Diocese of Delaware ... May 25, 1842. ... *Wilmington: H. H. Cannon & Co., Printers.* 1842. 8vo, pp. 16.— ... A Sermon ... at the Convention ... May 31st, 1848. ... *Wilmington, Del.: Wilson & Heald.* 1848. 8vo, pp. 19.—The Sermon ... at the Opening of the General Convention of the Protestant Episcopal Church ... Oct. 7th, 1868. ... *New York.* [n. d.] 8vo, pp. 32. B.

Lee (A.) A Half-Century Sermon, preached at Hanover, the North Society in Lisbon, Oct. 25, 1818. By Andrew Lee, D.D. *Windham, Conn.* 1819. 8vo, pp. 20. S. 39695

Lee. The origin and ends of Civil Government. A Sermon, Preached ... at Hartford, on the Day of the Anniversary Election, May 14, 1795. By Andrew Lee, A.M. ... *Hartford: Printed by Hudson and Goodwin.* M DCC XCV. 8vo, pp. 38. BA. 39696

Also: ... A Discourse ... at the Ordination of the Rev. Jonathan Ellis ... at Topsham, Massachusetts, September 16th, A.D. 1789. ... *Portland.* 1790. 8vo, pp. 32.—Sermons on Various Important Subjects: written partly on sundry of the more Difficult Passages in the Sacred Volume. ... *Printed at Worcester: By Isaiah Thomas, Jun.* 1803. 18mo, pp. 403. BA.

Lee (Ann). *See* [Wells (S. Y.)]

[Lee (Arthur).] An Appeal to the Justice and Interests of the People of Great Britain, in the Present Disputes with America. By an Old Member of Parliament. *London: J. Almon.* MDCCLXXIV. 8vo, pp. (4), 63. + The Second Edition, [*Ibid.*] M DCC LXXV. 8vo, pp. 68. + The Third Edition. [*Ibid.*]

Lee. An Appeal [etc.] By Arthur Lee. The Fourth Edition. *New-York: Printed by James Rivington.* MDCCLXXV. 8vo, pp. 32. BA., C. 39698

The first three editions were published anonymously, but this fourth was published under Dr. Lee's name.

[Lee.] Considerations [etc.] *See our* Vol. IV., No. 15966.

Lee. Extracts from a Letter written to the President of Congress, by the Hon. Arthur Lee, Esq., in Answer to a Libel published in the Pennsylvania Gazette on the Fifth of December 1778, by Silas Deane, Esquire. *Williamsburg: J. Dixon and T. Nicolson.* 1779. 12mo, pp. 31. M. 39699

Lee. Extracts from a Letter written to the President of Congress, by the Honorable Arthur Lee, Esquire. In Answer to a Libel published in the Pennsylvania Gazette of the Fifth of December, 1778, by Silas Deane, Esquire. In which every Charge or Insinuation against him in that Libel, is fully and clearly

refuted. *Philadelphia: Printed by Francis Bailey.* M.DCC.LXXX. Sm. 4to, pp. 74. BA., H. 39700

A tract not only of great rarity but of much historical interest; which, together with "Deane's Address," and the "Paris Papers," afford material for an instructive and interesting episode in the history of the Revolution, in which Franklin, Jonathan Williams, Paul Jones, and Deane, may, possibly, be brought to occupy the same niche.

[Lee.] Monitor's Letter to the Inhabitants of the British Colonies. *Williamsburg.* 1769. 8vo. C. 39701

Lee. Observations on Certain Commercial Transactions in France, laid before Congress. By Arthur Lee, Esquire. *Philadelphia: Printed by F. Bailey.* M,DCC,LXXX. 4to, pp. 51. H.

Very rare. An exposition of the extravagant and wasteful expenditure of the public money by Franklin, and his nephew Jonathan Williams, during their official residence at Paris. Crisp and pungent. Williams charged Mr. Lee with "the delight of glutting his soul with the carnage of his (Williams') character," etc.

[Lee.] The Political Detection; or, the Treachery and Tyranny of Administration, both at Home and Abroad; displayed in a Series of Letters, signed Junius Americanus. *London: Printed by J. and W. Oliver.* M DCC LX[illegible]. 8vo, pp. (2), 151. H.

Addressed to the Earl of Hillsborough, Sir Francis Bernard, and the people of England. "To be continued" says the writer; but the continuation did not appear. "Although there is something illiberal in the manner, and malignant in the spirit, of this American *Junius*, yet there are in his letters many animadversions on the conduct of administration, particularly with respect to the colonies, which are worthy of public attention and enquiry."—*Monthly Review.*

[Lee.] A Second Appeal to the Justice and Interests of the People, on the measures respecting America. By the Author of the First. *London: J. Almon.* 1775. 8vo, pp. 90. BA. 39704

See "M. Rev.," LIV. 149.

[Lee.] A Speech intended to have been delivered in the House of Commons, in support of the Petition from the General Congress at Philadelphia. ... *London: J. Almon.* MDCCLXXV. 8vo, pp. (2), 67. C. 39705

"A very able and spirited exposition of the grievances alleged in the petition from the Congress, together with a review of the causes and progress of the American contest, and a vindication of the several measures pursued by the colonies."—*Monthly Review.* *See also* Jefferson's "Notes on Virginia," II. 22. Some copies have the imprint, *London: C. Dilly.* For a tract with a title very much like this, *see* Shipley (J.)

[Lee.] True State of Proceedings on the Part of Great Britain and the Province of Massachusetts Bay relative to giving and granting money of that Province. *London.* 1774. 39706

Reprinted with Franklin's name in Almon's Prior Documents, 1777. "Chiefly drawn up by Arthur Lee from materials furnished by Dr. Franklin."—Jared Sparks.

Lee (C.) Anecdotes of the late Charles Lee, Esq. *See* [Langworthy (Edward)], No. 38902.

[Lee.] The Importance of Canada Considered. In Two Letters to a Noble Lord. *London: R. and J. Dodsley.* M DCCLXI. 8vo, pp. (4), 38. C. 39707

See "M. Rev.," XXX. 233, *and* Faribault, No. 856.

Lee. A Letter from General Lee to General Burgoyne, printed from the New York Gazetteer, of July 6. To which is added General Burgoyne's Answer, and a Copy of a Letter from General Lee, declining an Interview proposed by General Burgoyne. *Boston: Draper's Printing Office.* 1775. 8vo, pp. 19. J.C.B. + *New York: J. Anderson.* 1775. 8vo. 39708

The first letter is dated Philadelphia, June 6, 1775, and is addressed to General Burgoyne on his arrival at Boston. Lee "sincerely laments the infatuation of the times when men of such a stamp as Mr. Burgoyne and Mr. Howe can be seduced into so impious and nefarious a service, by the artifice of a wicked, and insiduous court and cabinet." Both writers discuss the right of the British Government to tax the colonies.

Lee. Briefe bey Gelegenheit der Ankunft des General Burgoyne's in Boston. *Braunschweig: F. Waisenhaus.* 1777. 8vo, pp. 8. 39709

In Julius August Remer's "Amerikanisches Archiv, Vol. I.

Lee. Letters of Major General Lee, to the Right Honourable Earl Percy, and Major General John Burgoyne. With the Answers. *New-York: Printed by J. Rivington.* M,DCC,LXXV. 8vo, pp. 8, 4. BA., C., P. 39710

Lee. Memoirs. *See* [Langworthy (E.)], No. 38903, *and* note.

Lee. Proceedings | of a | General Court Martial, | Held at Brunswick, | in the State of New-Jersey, | by Order of | His Excellency | General Washington, | Commander in Chief | Of the Army of | The United States of America, | For the Trial of | Major General Lee. | July 4th, 1778. | Major General Lord Stirling, President. | *Philadelphia: | Printed by John Dunlap, in Market- | Street.* MDCCLXXVIII. | Folio, pp. 62. BA., P. 39711

Of this original edition a few copies only were printed. Menzies' copy sold for $50.

Lee. Proceedings of a General Court Martial, held at Brunswick, in the State of New-Jersey, by Order of His Excellency General Washington ... for the Trial of Major General Lee, July 4th, 1778. Major General Lord Stirling, President. *Cooperstown (N. Y.): Printed for the Publisher, by J. H. Prentiss.* 1823. 8vo, pp. 134. B., S. 39712

Of this reprint but few copies were published.

LEE. Proceedings of a General Court-Martial, ... for the Trial of Major-General Lee. July 4th, 1778. ... *New York: Privately Reprinted.* 1864. Rl. 8vo, pp. 239. BA. 39713

Of this elegant reprint one hundred copies were printed in 8vo, and twenty in 4to.

[LEE.] Strictures on a Pamphlet, entitled "A Friendly Address to All Reasonable Americans, on the Subject of our Political Confusions." Addressed to the People of America. *Philadelphia: Printed.* 1774. 8vo, pp. 15. + [*Ibid.*] 12mo. + *New York.* 1774. 8vo. + *Newport: S. Southwick.* 1775. 8vo, pp. 15. + *America: Boston: Re-printed and sold at Greenleaf's Printing-Office, opposite the Conduit, near the Market.* M,DCC,LXX,V. 8vo, pp. 20. — Another Edition. *Philadelphia.* 1775. 8vo, pp. 25. + *New-York, Printed; Boston, Re-printed, by I. Thomas.* MDCCLXXV. 12mo, pp. 12. + The Second Edition ... . *Philadelphia, Printed; New-London: Re-printed by T. Green.* M,DCC,-LXXV. 8vo, pp. 16. H. 39714

See [Barry (H.)], Vol. I., No. 3684, [Cooper (Myles)], *and* Chandler, No. 11881.

LEE (C. A.) A Catalogue of the Medicinal Plants, Indigenous and Exotic, growing in the State of New-York. With a brief account of their Composition and Medical Properties. By Charles A. Lee, M.D. ... *New-York: I. and H. G. Langley.* 1848. 8vo, pp. iv, 64. BA. 39715

LEE. The Elements of Geology, for Popular Use; Containing a Description of the Geological Formations and Mineral Resources of the United States. By Charles A. Lee ... . *New York: Harper & Brothers.* 1846. 12mo, pp. viii, viii, 375, (9).

Also: An Introductory Discourse on Medical Education, delivered to the Students of Geneva Medical College, October 1, 1844. ... *Geneva: Ira Merrell, Printer.* 1844. 8vo, pp. 40. — Addresses to the Graduates of Geneva Medical College ... January 26, 1847. ... *New York: S. W. Benedict.* 1847. 8vo, pp. 23. — Address to the Graduating Class of Geneva Medical College ... June 22, 1852. ... *Geneva: S. H. Parker, Printer.* 1852. 8vo, pp. 24. — On Provision for the Insane Poor of ... New York ... . *Albany.* 1866. 8vo, pp. 32. — Review ... of Dr. Charles A. Lee, and Others, of the Testimony of Drs. Salisbury and Swinburne, on the Trial of John Hendrickson, Jr., for the Murder of his Wife ... . *New York.* 1855. 8vo, pp. 41, (3). B.

LEE (C. C.) Virginia Georgics. By Charles Carter Lee. *Richmond: J. Woodhouse & Co.* 1858. 8vo, pp. 122, (4). C.

LEE (C. H.) The Judge Advocate's Vade Mecum: embracing a General View of Military Law, and the Practice before Courts Martial, with an Epitome of the Law of Evidence, as applicable to Military Trials. By C. H. Lee. *Richmond: West*

and Johnston. 1863. 8vo, pp. 251. + Second Edition, Revised and Enlarged. [*Ibid.*] 1864. 8vo, pp. 308. B. 39718

LEE (C.) The American Accomptant. ... By Chauncey Lee, A.M. *Lansingburgh.* M,DCC,XCVII. 12mo, pp. 297, (16). 39719

LEE. The Government of God ... . A Sermon preached on the day of the General Election, at Hartford, in the State of Connecticut, May 13th, 1813. By Chauncey Lee ... . *Hartford: Printed by Hudson and Goodwin.* 1813. 8vo, pp. 56. BA. 39720

Appended is a List of Election Sermons. Also: ... A Farewell Sermon ... in Colebrook ... February, 1828. ... *Hartford: Printed by Philemon Canfield.* 1828. 8vo, pp. 16. H. — A Sermon ... at the Funeral of Mr. Cyrus Babcock ... March 6, 1817 ... . *Hartford: George Goodwin and Sons, Printers.* 1817. 12mo, pp. 16. — ... A Sermon ... at the Funeral of the Rev. Ammi Ruhamah Robbins, ... in Norfolk ... October 31, 1813. ... *Hartford: Peter B. Gleason ... Printers.* 1814. 8vo, pp. 43. — Sermons. ... *Middletown, Conn.* 1824. 12mo. — The Tree of Knowledge of Political Good and Evil. A Discourse ... in Colebrook ... July 4th, 1800. ... *Hartford: Printed by Hudson and Goodwin.* 1800. 8vo, pp. 31. BA.

LEE (D.) Treatise on Peruvian Guano. By Daniel Lee, M.D. *Washington.* 1854. 8vo. 39721

LEE (D. K.) Summerfield; or Life on a Farm. By Day Kellogg Lee. *Auburn: Derby & Miller.* 1852. 12mo, pp. xv, 246. C. 39722

Also: The Master Builder; or, Life at a Trade. ... *New York.* 1852. 12mo. — Merrimack or Life at the Loom. A Tale. ... *New York: Redfield.* 1854. 12mo, pp. 353. C.

LEE (D.) On the Conduct of Gen. Putnam at the Battle of Bunker Hill. *Boston.* 1819. 8vo. 39723

LEE (D.) Ten Years in Oregon. By D. Lee and J. H. Frost, late of the Oregon Mission of the Methodist Episcopal Church. *New-York: The Authors.* 1844. 8vo, pp. 344. Map.

A minute journal of incidents among the Northwestern Indians, with vocabularies of their dialects.

LEE (E. F.) Notes on the Mammoth Cave. By Edmund F. Lee. *Cincinnati.* 1835. 48mo, pp. 30. Map. 39725

LEE (E.) The Dissolution of Earthly Monarchies ... A Sermon ... in Ridgfield, March 1st, 1794. By Elias Lee. *Danbury.* 1794. 8vo, pp. 28. 39726

LEE (E.) An Oration delivered at Lenox, the 4th July 1793, the Anniversary of American Independence: By Elisha Lee, Esq. *Stockbridge: Printed by Loring Andrews.* M,D,CCXCIII. 4to, pp. 15

LEE. An Oration, delivered in Sheffield, February the 22d, 1800, in ... Memory of Gen. George Washington, ... By Elisha Lee, Esq. *Stockbridge: Printed by ... H. Willard.* [1800.] 4to, pp. 10. BA., M. 39728

LEE (E. B.) Memoirs of Rev. Joseph Buckminster, D.D. and of his son, Rev. Joseph Stevens Buckminster. By Eliza Buckminster Lee. *Boston: Wm. Crosby ...* 1849. 12mo, pp. x, (2), 486. Portrait. + Second Edition. *Boston: Ticknor, Reed, and Fields.* MDCCCLI. 12mo, pp. ix, (1), 492. Portrait. 39729

LEE. Naomi; or, Boston Two Hundred Years Ago. By Eliza Buckminster Lee. *Boston: Wm. Crosby & H. P. Nichols.* 1848. 12mo, pp. iv, 324. BA. + Second Edition. [*Ibid.*] + [Another Edition. *Ibid.*] 1848. 12mo, pp. vii, 448. B. 39730

[LEE.] Sketches of a New-England Village, in the Last Century. *Boston: James Munroe ...* 1838. 12mo, pp. (2), 110.

Also: Florence, the Parish Orphan; and a Sketch of the Village in the last Century. *Boston: Ticknor, Reed and Fields.* MDCCCLII. 12mo, pp. (4), 176. B.

LEE (F. A.) Speech ... on the Aims ... of the existing Political Parties. *Cooperstown, N. Y.* 1856. 8vo, pp. 16. 39732

LEE (F. D.) Historical Record of the City of Savannah. By F. D. Lee and J. L. Agnew. *Savannah: J. H. Estill.* 1869. 12mo, pp. xii, 200. 3 Maps, 3 Plates. B. 39733

LEE (F.) Legends of New England. By Frances Lee. *New York.* 1864. 16mo. 39734

[LEE (Hannah F.)] The Huguenots in France and America. ... *Cambridge: John Owen.* 1843. 2 vols., 12mo, pp. xx, 336; vi, 302. H. + Second Edition. [*Ibid.*] 1843. 2 vols., 12mo.

[LEE.] The Log Cabin; or, the World before you. ... *Philadelphia.* 1844. 12mo. + *London: J. S. Pratt.* 1844. 24mo, pp. 448. Plate. 39736

[LEE.] Memoir of Pierre Toussaint, born a Slave in St. Domingo. ... *Boston: Crosby, Nichols, ...* 1854. 12mo, pp. (2), 154. Portrait. + Second Edition. [*Ibid.*] 1854. 12mo, pp. (2), 124. Portrait. + Third Edition. [*Ibid.*] H. 39737

[LEE.] Rosanna; or Scenes in Boston. A Story. ... *Cambridge: John Owen.* 1839. 12mo, pp. 134. BA. 39738

Also: Sketches and Stories from Life, for the Young. ... *Boston.* 1850. 12mo. — Tales ... *Boston: Hilliard, Gray & Co.* 1842. 12mo, pp. viii, 337.

LEE (H.). *General.* ... Champe's Adventure. By General Henry Lee. *New York: Rebellion Record Office.* 1864. 16mo, pp. 18. BA. 39739

[LEE.] A Cursory Sketch of the Motives and Proceedings of the Party which sways the Affairs of the Union; with some Remarks on the Nature of the Present Crisis. *Philadelphia.* 1809. 8vo. C., P. 39740

LEE. Memoirs of the War in the Southern Department of the United States. By Henry Lee, Lieutenant Colonel Commandant of the Partisan Legion during the American War. ... *Philadelphia: Bradford and Inskeep.* 1812. 2 vols., 8vo, pp. (2), 423; (2), 486. 2 Portraits. BA., H., P. + [*Ibid.*] 1819.

LEE. Memoirs of the War in the Southern Department of the United States. By Henry Lee, Lieutenant Colonel Commandant of the Partisan Legion, during the American War. ... A New Edition, with Corrections left by the Author, and with Notes and Additions by H. Lee, the Author of the Campaign of '81. *Washington: Printed by Peter Force.* 1827. 8vo, pp. 466.

LEE. Memoirs of the War in the Southern Department of the United States. By Henry Lee ... . A New Edition, with Revisions, and a Biography of the Author, By Robert E. Lee. *New York: University Publishing Company.* 1869. 8vo, pp. 620. 3 Plans, 3 Portraits. B. + [*Ibid.*] 1870. 8vo. 39743

"Lee's memoirs are very interesting and as fascinating as a romance, though they undoubtedly contain true history."—*Chancellor* KENT. *See also* W. B. Reed's "Life of Reed," I. 307; II. 55, 185, 395, 419.

[LEE.] Funeral Oration. [n. p. n. d.] 8vo, pp. 17. 39744

This is the original official edition of one of the ablest of the numerous orations on the death of George Washington. The following are reprints:

LEE. A Funeral Oration, In Honour of the Memory of George Washington, Late General of the Armies of the U. States; Prepared and Delivered at the Request of Congress, at the German Lutheran Church, Philadelphia, on Thursday, the 26th of December. By Major Gen. Henry Lee; One of the Representatives from the State of Virginia. *Brooklyn: Printed by Thomas Kirk.* 1800. 8vo, pp. 16. + Second Edition. [*Ibid.*]

Probably the first book printed in Brooklyn, L. I., where the press was first introduced by Thomas Kirk, in June, 1799. *See* Stiles' "History of Brooklyn," III. 927.

LEE. [Another Edition; same Title.] *Edinburgh: Printed by J. & A. Denman.* 1800. 8vo, pp. 16. 39746

LEE. Funeral Oration on the Death of General Washington. Delivered, at the Request of Congress, by Major-General Henry Lee, Member of Congress from Virginia. *Boston: ... Joseph Nancrede ...* [1800]. 8vo, pp. 15. BA. + *Stockbridge.* [1800.] 4to, pp. 10. M. + *Philadelphia.* 1800. 8vo. 39747

LEE. The National Eulogy of the Illustrious George Washington, pronounced at the Request of the United States, in Congress Assembled. By Major Gen. Henry Lee, at Philadelphia, in the German Lutheran Church, December 26th, 1799. *Portsmouth, (New-Hampshire,) Printed at the United States' Oracle-Office by Charles Peirce, January,* 1800. 8vo, pp. 16. H. 39748

LEE. A Funeral Oration On the Death of George Washington, late President & Commander in Chief ... . Delivered at the Request of Congress, By Major-General Henry Lee ... . To which is subjoined, An Eulogy, By Judge Minot. *London: Button.* 1800. 8vo, pp. (4), 28. + *Bristol: J. Cottle.* 1800. 8vo. 39749

Included in F. Moore's "American Eloquence," Vol. I. Of the three hundred and fifty (more or less) orations on the death of Washington, this is considered to be the most meritorious.

LEE (Henry), *Major.* The Campaign of 1781 in the Carolinas; with Remarks Historical and Critical on Johnson's Life of Greene. To which is added an Appendix of Original Documents, relating to the History of the Revolution. By H. Lee. *Philadelphia: E. Little.* 1824. 8vo, pp. (2), 511, xlvii. B., H.

LEE. Observations on the Writings of Thomas Jefferson, with particular reference to the attack they contain on the Memory of the Late Gen. Henry Lee. In a Series of Letters. By H. Lee, of Virginia. *New-York: Charles DeBehr.* M DCCC-XXXII. 8vo, pp. 237. BA. + Second Edition, with an Introduction and Notes, by Charles Carter Lee. *Philadelphia: J. Dobson.* 1839. 8vo, pp. (2), xix, 5–262. C., H. 39751

The first edition has become rare, mainly on account of its having been rigidly suppressed, and as far as possible destroyed.

LEE. A Vindication of the Character ... of Andrew Jackson; ... Originally published in the Nashville Republican, and attributed to Major Henry Lee ... : *Boston: True and Greene, Printers.* 1828. 8vo, pp. 51. BA. 39752

LEE (H.) An Exposition of Evidence in Support of the Memorial to Congress "setting forth the Evils of the existing

Tariff ..." Prepared ... By Henry Lee, of Massachusetts ... . *Boston.* 1832. 8vo, No. IV., pp. (2), 14; No. V., pp. 32; No. VI., pp. 37; No. VII., pp. 17; No. VIII., pp. 19; No. IX., pp. 22; No. X., pp. 6; No. XI., pp. 42. B., BA. 39753

Evidently some of these numbers were reprinted, as I have met with a variation of the collation. *See* Carey (Mathew).

[LEE.] An Exposition of Facts ... in Support of a Memorial ... by Citizens of Boston ... in favor of a Bank of Ten Millions. *Boston: Dutton and Wentworth ... Printers.* 1836. 8vo, pp. 67. + Second Edition. [*Ibid.*] 1836. 8vo, pp. 67. B. 39754

Senate Document, No. 30.

[LEE.] Letters to the Cotton Manufacturers of Massachusetts. [n. p. n. d.] 8vo. 39755

[LEE.] Report of a Committee of the Citizens of Boston and Vicinity, opposed to ... Increase of Duties on Importations. *Boston: Press of Nathan Hale.* 1827. 8vo, pp. 196. BA., H. + *Philadelphia: Reprinted by S. Parker.* 1828. 8vo, pp. 180.

For a reply *see our* No. 23363 [by Redwood Fisher]. Also: Strictures on Mr. Lee's Exposition of Evidence on the Sugar Duty, in behalf of the Committee of the Free-Trade Convention. [n. p. n. d.] 8vo, pp. 18.

[LEE (Henry), *Jr.*] The Militia of the United States. What it has been. What it should be. *Boston: Press of T. R. Marvin & Son.* 1864. 8vo, pp. 130, (1). B., S. 39757

LEE (H. T.) Address Commemorative of the Services of the Alumni and Former Students of Lafayette College in the War for the Union, ... by Major H. T. Lee, together with the Roll of Honor, and Obituaries of the Dead. *Easton, Pa.* 1867. 8vo, pp. 40. H. 39758

LEE (H. W.) ... A Sermon ... in ... Greenfield, Massachusetts, ... June 17, 1855 ... after the Death of the Rev. Titus Strong, D.D. ... By the Rt. Rev. Henry W. Lee ... . *Boston: Printed by William A. Hall.* 1855. 8vo, pp. 22. B. 39759

LEE. ... A Sermon ... in ... Davenport, Iowa, on Thanksgiving Day, November 26, 1857. By the Rt. Rev. Henry W. Lee ... . *Davenport: Luse, Lane & Co.* 1857. 8vo, pp. 22, (2).

LEE. A Sketch of the Life ... of the Right Rev. Alexander Viets Griswold, D.D. ... Ob. Feb. 15, 1843 ... . A Sermon by Rev. Henry W. Lee ... . *Springfield: Wood and Rupp, Printers.* 1843. 8vo, pp. 26. B. 39761

Also: The Great Deliverance. A Sermon ... in ... Davenport, on ... Thanksgiving ... December 7, 1865 ... . *Davenport: Luse and Griggs.* 1865. 8vo, pp. 20. H. — ... The Primary Charge to the Clergy of the Protestant Episcopal Church ... Iowa. ... May 27, 1857. ... *Davenport.* 1857. 8vo, pp. 31. — ... The Sermon ... in ... Iowa ... December 15, 1864, at the Consecration of the Rev. Thomas Hubbard Vail, D.D. ... as Bishop of ... Kansas. ... *Davenport: Luse, Lane & Co.* 1865. 8vo, pp. 26, iii, (1). H. — The Stranger at Home: or, an Address to Members of the United Church of England and Ireland, who have emigrated to the United States of America. ... *Boston.* 1849. 12mo, pp. 18. H.

[LEE (James), *Jr.*] To the Proprietors ... of Trinity Church, Boston, Mass. [*Boston.* n. d.] 8vo, pp. 14. H. 39762

LEE (J.) Life and Religious Experience of Jarena Lee. *Cincinnati.* 1839. 8vo. 39763

LEE (J.) A Short Account of the Life ... of Rev. John Lee. By Jesse Lee. *Baltimore: J. W. Butler.* 1805. 24mo, pp. 179.

LEE. A Short History of the Methodists in the United States of America; beginning in 1766, and continued till 1809. To which is prefixed a brief Account of their Rise in England, in the Year 1729 ... . *Baltimore: Magill & Cline.* 1810. 16mo, pp. 366, (10). C. 39765

See also Lee (L. M.), *and* Thrift (Minton).

LEE (J. K.) The Volunteer's Hand Book: ... By Capt. J. K. Lee ... Virginia Volunteers. Third Thousand. *Richmond: West & Johnston.* 1860. 16mo, pp. 111. + Twenty-fifth Edition. [*Ibid.*] 1861. 16mo, pp. (2), ii, 5–96. H. 39766

LEE (J.) A Letter to the President of the United States ... proposing a method whereby the merits of the Conflicting Claims of the United States and Great Britain on the Disputed Frontier may be ... determined ... . By John Lee ... . *Cambridge: Metcalf,* ... 1839. 8vo, pp. 22. Plate. B. 39767

Also: A Letter ... discovering and correcting the Errors of Blackstone and his Editors, on the Theory of Human Genealogy and Kindred ... . *Cambridge: Metcalf, Torry ...* 1840. 8vo, pp. 32.

LEE (J. H.) The Origin and Progress of the American Party in Politics: embracing a complete History of the Philadelphia Riots in May and July, 1844, ... and a refutation of the arguments founded on the charges of Religious Proscription and Secret Combinations. By John Hancock Lee. *Philadelphia: Elliott & Gihon.* 1855. 12mo, pp. 264. BA., C. 39768

LEE (J.) Sermon at the Ordination of Joel Bordwell, in Kent, Oct. 18, 1758. By Rev. Jonathan Lee. *New Haven.* 1759. 8vo, pp. 23. 39769

LEE. Sermon ... before the General Assembly of the Colony of Connecticut at Hartford on the Day of the Anniversary Election, May 8, 1766. By Rev. Jonathan Lee. *New London: Timothy Green.* 1766. 4to, pp. 27. M. 39770

LEE (J.) ... An Address ... presented to a Mutual Council, called for the Dismission of a Pastor from his Charge. By Jonathan Lee ... . *Middlebury: Printed by Elam R. Jewett.* 1837. 8vo, pp. 23. H. 39771

LEE (J.) A Half Century Discourse delivered ... Oct. 19, 1818, in Royalston, Mass., being the Fiftieth Anniversary of his Ordination. With an Appendix. By Joseph Lee, A.M. *Worcester.* 1819. 8vo, pp. 27. W. 39772

LEE. ... A Sermon ... October 30, 1805, at the Ordination of the Reverend William B. Wesson to the Pastoral Office over the Church and Society in Hardwick. By Joseph Lee ... *Northampton: Andrew Wright.* 1806. 8vo, pp. 16. H. 39773

Also: Funeral Sermon on Rev. Benj. Brigham, June 14, 1790. ... *Brookfield, Mass* 1800. 8vo.

LEE (L. M.) The Life and Times of the Rev. Jesse Lee. By Leroy M. Lee, D.D. ... *Richmond (Va.): J. Early.* 1848. 8vo, pp. 517. B. + *Louisville, Ky.: John Early.* 1848. 8vo, pp. 517. 39774

LEE (L. P.) *See* History of the ... Massacre, No. 32214.

LEE (L.) The Nation's Peril. Oration of Rev. Luther Lee, delivered in the City Hall, Syracuse, July 4, 1854. *Syracuse, N. Y.* 1854. Rl. 8vo, pp. 12. 39775

LEE. ... A Sermon, preached at the ordination of the Rev. Miss Antoinette L. Brown, at South Butler, Wayne County, N. Y., Sept. 15, 1853. By Rev. Luther Lee. *Syracuse, N. Y.: The Author.* 1853. 8vo, pp. 22. B. 39776

Also: Ecclesiastical Manual, or Scriptural Church Government Stated and Defended. ... *New York.* 1850. 12mo, pp. 264. — Slavery: A Sin Against God. ... *Syracuse.* 1853. 12mo, pp. 23. — Slavery Examined in the Light of the Bible. ... *Syracuse.* 1855. 12mo. — Wesleyan Manual: a Defence of the Organization of the Wesleyan Methodist Connection. ... *Syracuse.* 1862. 12mo.

LEE (M. E.) Poetical Remains of Mary Elizabeth Lee. With a Biographical Memoir by S. Gilman. *Charleston: Walker & Richards.* 1851. 16mo, pp. xl, 224. Plate. 39777

Also: Social Evenings: or Historical Tales for Youth. ... *Boston: Marsh, Capen, Lyon & Webb.* 1840. 18mo, pp. 260.

Lee (N.) Three Years among the Camanches, the Narrative of Nelson Lee, the Texan Ranger, containing a detailed account of his Captivity among the Indians, his singular escape Through the Instrumentality of his Watch, and fully illustrating Indian Life as it is on the War Path and in the Camp. *Albany: Baker Taylor.* 1859. 12mo, pp. 224. Portrait. + *Troy, N. Y.* 1871. 12mo, pp. 240. 39778

Lee (P.) Private History and Confession of Pamela Lee, who was convicted at Pittsburgh, Pa., Dec. 19, 1851, for the ... Murder of her Husband ... Written at ... her dictation by the Rev. Augustus Dimick. *Pittsburgh.* 1852. 12mo. 39779

Lee (R. B.) An Oration, delivered by Richard Bland Lee, Esq. at the request of the Washington Society, on the 22d February last. *Alexandria: Printed by S. Snowden.* 1811. 8vo, pp. 19, (1). H. 39780

Lee. An Oration ... July 5, 1819, in the ... House of Representatives. By Richard Bland Lee, Esq. ... [n. p. 1819.] 12mo, pp. 15. BA. 39781

Lee (Richard E.) Letter ... relative to the Conduct of Dr. John K. Read. *Richmond.* 1800. 8vo. C. 39782

[Lee (Richard Henry).] ... Additional ... Letters ... to the Republican; Leading to a Fair Examination of the System of Government, proposed by the late Convention; ... [n. p.:] *Printed in the Year* M,DCC,LXXXVIII. 8vo, pp. 41–181. BA.

This is a corrected title of our No. 383, and is a continuation of the following:

[Lee.] Observations leading to a Fair Examination of the System of Government, proposed by the late Convention; ... In a number of Letters from the Federal Farmer to the Republican. [n. p.:] *Printed in the Year* M,DCCLXXVII. 8vo, pp. 40. 39784

Lee (R. H.) Life of Arthur Lee, LL.D. Joint Commissioner of the United States to the Court of France, and Sole Commissioner to the Courts of Spain and Prussia, during the Revolutionary War. With his Political and Literary Correspondence and his Papers on Diplomatic and Political Subjects, and the affairs of the United States during the same period. By Richard Henry Lee, A.M. ... *Boston: Wells and Lilly.* 1829. 2 vols., 8vo, pp. 431; 399. B. 39785

See a criticism by Edward Everett in the "North American Review," XXII. 373–400, *also* "American Quarterly Review," December, 1829, p. 438.

Lee. Memoir of the Life of Harriet Preble, containing portions of her ... writings ... . By Richard Henry Lee ... . *New York: G. P. Putnam & Co.* 1856. 12mo, pp. 409. Portrait.

Lee. Memoir of the Life of Richard Henry Lee, and his Correspondence with the most Distinguished Men in America and Europe, Illustrative of their Characters, and of the Events of the American Revolution. By his Grandson Richard H. Lee, of Leesburg, Virginia. *Philadelphia: H. C. Carey* ... 1825. 2 vols., 8vo, pp. 299; (2), 238. Portrait. BA., H. 39787

See "N. A. Rev.," XXII. 224.

Lee. Oration by Richard Henry Lee, A.M., of Virginia. *Carlisle, Pa.* 1826. 8vo. 39788

Lee (R. H.) Letter of Rev. Richard H. Lee on the Protest of the Philadelphia Clergy against Bishop Hopkins' Views on Slavery [n. p.] 1863. 8vo. 39789

[Lee (Robert E.)] Reports of the Operations of the Army of Northern Virginia from June, 1862, to and including the Battle at Fredericksburg, Dec. 13, 1862. *Richmond: R. M. Smith, Public Printer.* 1864. 2 vols., 8vo, pp. 626, (1); 602.

Contains reports of the Battles of Port Republic, Cross Keys, Battles around Richmond, Cedar Run, Summer Campaign from Cedar Run to and including Sharpsburg, and Battle of Fredericksburg. Perhaps the most important of all the Confederate reports, and as rare as it is valuable. *See also* our Nos. 15364–65.

Lee. Tableau No. 6. The Praises of Lee and Jackson. ... [n. p. n. d.] 8vo, pp. 8. BA. 39791

Lee. Robert E. Lee. In Memoriam. A Tribute of Respect offered by the Citizens of Louisville. *Louisville: Printed by John P. Morton and Company.* 1870. 4to, pp. 45. S. 39792

Lee (S.) Contemplations on Mortality. ... By Samuel Lee, M.A. ... *Boston. Re-printed by B. Green, and J. Allen, for Samuel Phillips.* 1690. 8vo, pp. 100. + *Boston in N. E., Samuel Phillips.* 1698. 18mo, pp. (10), 149. 39793

Samuel Lee was an ejected non-conformist, who emigrated to America about 1686, and settled in Bristol, Rhode Island.

[Lee.] Ἐλεοθρίαμβος: Or The Triumph of Mercy in the Chariot of Praise. A Treatise of Preventing secret & unexpected Mercies, with some mixt Reflexions. ... *Boston: Printed by B. Green for Benj. Eliot* ... 1718. 18mo, pp. (8), 194 [for 158.]

Lee. The Great Day of Judgment; with A Preface by Cotton Mather. ... *Boston: Printed by B. Green for N. Buttolph.* 1672. 16mo. 39795

Lee. ... The Joy of Faith, or A Treatise Opening the true Nature of Faith ... . By Samuel Lee, A.M. *Boston: Printed by Samuel Green.* 1687. 8vo, pp. (18), 247, (1). B. 39796

The printer Samuel Green was a good friend to John Dunton. Green's wife was so good a woman that she sat for Dunton's picture of the "Best of Wives," which occupies six pages in his "Life." Green settled in New England in 1686, and the above is the first work known to have been printed by him.

Lee. The Library of The Late Reverend and Learned Mr. Samuel Lee. ... Exposed ... to Sale, By Duncan Cambell ... . *Boston: Duncan Cambell.* 1693. 4to, pp. (2), 16. B. 39797

In Mr. Prince's hand: "Mr B Green sais—This was prin[d] by his broth Samuel's Letter [type] in Boston." Perhaps the oldest work of its kind printed in the British colonies.

Lee (S.) A Historic Discourse: ... at the Centennial Celebration of the First Congregational Church in New Ipswich, October 22, 1860. By Samuel Lee ... . *Manchester, N. H.* 1861. 8vo, pp. 88. H. 39798

Lee. ... A Sermon ... at the Dedication of the Congregational Meeting-House, at New Ipswich, Feb. 5, 1852. By Samuel Lee ... . *Concord.* 1852. 8vo, pp. 15. B. 39799

Lee (Samuel Phillips). Report and Charts of the Cruise of the U. S. Brig Dolphin, made under direction of the Navy Department, By Lieut. S. P. Lee, United States Navy. *Washington: Beverley Tucker, Printer.* 1854. 8vo, pp. (2), vii, (1), 331, (2), Errata, 2. 15 Charts. BA. 39800

Lee (S.) An Oration ... at Wiscasset ... on the Fourth of July, 1799. By Silas Lee. ... *Wiscasset: Printed by Henry Hoskins.* 1799. 8vo, pp. 25. BA. 39801

Lee (T. H.) The Origin and Progress of the American Party in Politics. By Thomas Hancock Lee. *Philadelphia.* 1855. 12mo. 39802

[Lee (William).] Les États-Unis et l'Angleterre, ou Souvenirs et Réflexions d'un Citoyen Américain. Essais traduits sur le Manuscrit de l'Auteur. ... *A Bordeaux: Chez P. Coudert.* 1814. 8vo, pp. 346, (4). BA., H., C. 39803

By Mr. Lee, American Consul at Bordeaux. Edited by M. Jay. Relates to the War of 1812. *See* "Notes and Queries," February, 1869, p. 169.

Lee (W.) Missive van G. Fagel ... over 't geene voorgevallen is bij occasie van de communicatie van zekere onderschepte Missive van d'Avaux ... en ... over het gedrag d. regeering van Amsterdam ... in haare onbetamelijke onderhandelingen met den Americaansche commissaris William Lee. [n. p.] 1782. 8vo.

Lee (W.) The True and Interesting Travels of W. Lee, through the Back Settlements of America. [n. p. n. d.] Frontispiece. 39805

Lee (William), *Reporter. See* Cushing (T. H.), Vol. v., 18123.

Lee (W. B.) A Farewell Doctrinal Discourse. ... Fair Haven, Conn. March 18th, 1860. By W. B. Lee. *New-York: Geo. F. Nesbitt & Co. ... Printers.* 1860. 8vo, pp. 39. H.

Lee (Z. C.) The Age of Washington: An Address ... St. Mary's College. By Z. Collins Lee, Esq. ... July 17th, 1849. *Baltimore: Printed by John Murphy & Co.* 1849. 8vo, pp. 66.

Lee. Oration ... at the ... Commemoration of the Landing of the Pilgrims of Maryland, celebrated May 15, 1849. ... By Z. Collins Lee, Esq. ... *Baltimore: Printed by John Murphy & Co.* 1849. 8vo, pp. 39. 39808

Also: Address before the Chester Co., Penn., Horticultural Society, June, 1858. ... *West Chester.* 1858. 8vo.

... Lee & Walker's Musical Almanac for 1869. For the use of Seminaries, Professors of Music, and the Musical Public. ... *Philadelphia: Lee & Walker.* [1868.] 12mo, pp. 144. Cont'd.

Lee Academy. Catalogue of the Officers and Students of Lee Academy, Lee, Mass., for ... 1846. *Pittsfield: Press of C. Montague.* [n. d.] 12mo, pp. 12. H. 39810

Leech (D. D. T.) The Postal Laws, classified by Subjects ... Compiled by D. D. T. Leech. *New York: J. H. Colton* ... 1856. 8vo, pp. 36. BA. 39811

See also Post-Office, *infra.*

Leech (S.) Thirty Years from Home, or A Voice from the Main Deck being the Experience of Samuel Leech, who was for Six Years in the British and American Navies: was captured in the British Frigate Macedonian: afterwards entered the American Navy, and was taken in the United States Brig Syren, by the British Ship Medway. ... *Boston: Tappan & Dennet.* 1843. 18mo, pp. 305. + *Boston: John M. Whittemore.* 1847. 18mo, pp. 305. + *Boston.* [n. d.] 18mo. 39812

The Leech. Blood Iago, Blood. *Union College.* 1864. 4to.

Leechman (W.) ... A Sermon ... before The Society in Scotland for propagating Christian Knowledge ... in ... Edinburgh ... June 5. 1767. By Dr. William Leechman ... . *Edinburgh: Printed by Balfour* ... M,DCC,LXVIII. 8vo, pp. (4), 75. H.

Contains some particulars relative to America.

Leeds (D.) An Almanack For the Year of Christian Account 1687. Particularly respecting the Meridian and Latitude of Burlington, but may indifferently serve all places adjacent By Daniel Leeds, Student in Agriculture. *Printed and Sold by William Bradford, near Philadelphia in Pennsylvania, pro Anno* 1687. Folio. 39815

The first piece printed in Pennsylvania. It was reprinted about 1860. Bradford continued to print this almanac yearly, with varying titles and sizes. It is, perhaps, unnecessary to add, they are all rare. On Bradford's removal to New York, the title was changed as below:

Leeds. The American Almanack for 1700. By Daniel Leeds. *Printed by Will. Bradford in New York.* 1700. 12mo.

Continued to 1714, or later.

[Leeds.] The Great Mistery of Fox-Craft Discovered. And the Quaker Plainness & Sincerity Demonstrated ... . Introduced with two Letter [*sic*] written by G. Fox to Coll. Lewis Morris, deceased, exactly Spell'd and Printed as in the Originals, which are now to be seen in the Library at Burlington in New Jersey, and will be proved (by the likeness of the Hand, &c.) to be the Hand-Writing of the Quaker's Learned Fox, if denyed. To which is Added, A Postscript, with some Remarks on the Quaker-Almanack for this year 1705. [*New York: William Bradford.* 1705.] Sm. 4to, pp. 16. 39817

Exceedingly rare. Contains curious illustrations of the illiteracy of the great Quaker leader George Fox. *See also* Fox (G.), Vol. vi.

Leeds. News of a Trumpet Sounding in the Wilderness; or the Quakers Antient Testimony Revived, Examined, and Compared with their New Doctrine. Whereby the Ignorant may learn Wisdom, and the Wise advance in Understanding. By Daniel Leeds. *Printed and Sold by William Bradford, ... in New York.* 1697. Sm. 8vo, pp. 151. 39818

Of so much rarity that I have never seen a copy.

Leeds. The Rebuker | Rebuked | in a Brief | Answer | To Caleb Pusey his | Scurrilous Pamphet [*sic*], | Entituled, | A Rebuke ... Daniel Leeds, &c. | Wherein William Penn his Sandy Foun-

dation is fairly | quoted, showing that he calls Christ, The Finite | Impotent Creature. | By Daniel Leeds. | *Printed and Sold by William Bradford at the Bible in | New York,* 1703. Sm. 4to, pp, 11.

L[eeds]. The | Temple of Wisdom | For the | Little World, | In Two Parts. | The First Philosophically Divine, treating of | The Being of all Beeings, | And whence everything hath its original, as | Heaven, Hell, Angels, Men and Devils, Earth, | Stars and Elements. | And particularly of all Mysteries concerning the Soul; and | of Adam before and after the Fall. | Also, a Treatise of the four Complexions, with | the Causes of spiritual Sadness &c. | To which is added, A Postscript to all Students in | Arts and Sciences. | The Second Part, Morally divine, Contains | First. Abuses Stript and Whipt, by Geo. Wither, with his | discription [*sic*] of Fair Virtue. | Secondly. A Collection of Divine Poems from Fr. Quarles. | Lastly. Essayes and Religious Meditations of Sir Francis | Bacon Knight. | Collected, Published and intended for a general Good, | By D. L. | *Printed and Sold by William Bradford in Philadelphia, | Anno.* 1688. 12mo. 39820

Collation: Title, 1 leaf; Preface, pp. 3; To the Doctors, pp. 3; Text, pp. 125, (1), 1 blank leaf; Second Title, with imprint as above, pp. 1, 48; Third Title, "*Printed in the Year* 1688." pp. 1, 50–86, Errata, 1.

The first book printed South of Massachusetts. Concerning this probably unique volume, *see* Bacon's Works, Montague's Edition, Vol. XVI., Note No. 31, in which Mr. Montague observes "it is a fact not unworthy of notice, that the first book published in Philadelphia, consists partly of Lord Bacon's 'Essays.' It is entitled 'The Temple of Wisdom,' printed by William Bradford, Philadelphia, 1688." It is one of the rarest among rare American books. The first part is from Jacob Behm. *See also* "Hist. Mag.," Vol. III., No. 6, p. 173.

Leeds. A Trumpet Sounded out of the Wilderness of America; which may serve as a Warning to the Government and People of England, to Beware of Quakerisme. Wherein is shewed the Great Contradictions of the Quakers, both in their former and later writings. Also, how they deny Jesus of Nazareth to be the Christ. And how in Pensilvania, and thereaway, where they have the Government in their own Hands, they hire and encourage Men to fight; and how they Persecute, Fine, and Imprison, and take away Goods for Conscience sake. ... By Daniel Leeds. *Printed by William Bradford, at the Bible in New York; and are to be sold by B. Aylmer at the Three Pidgeons in Cornhill* ... 1699. Sm. 8vo, pp. 158. 39821

See Duyckink, I. 101, *also* Fisher's "Early Poets of Pennsylvania."

Leeds (F.) Almanack. By Felix Leeds. *Philadelphia.* 1727. 8vo. Continued. 39822

Some copies have the imprint *New York.*

Leeds (G.) A Commemorative Sermon upon the ... Death of the Rev. Charles Mason, D.D. ... April 13, 1862. By George Leeds, D.D. ... *Boston: David Clapp, Printer.* 1862. 8vo, pp. 20.

Also: A Sermon ... in ... Philadelphia, as a Memorial of ... Reverend Benjamin Dorr, D.D. ... October 31, 1869. ... *Philadelphia: Collins, Printer.* 1869. 8vo, pp. 31.

Leeds (J.) An Address ... before the Dorchester Temperance Society ... December 4, 1830. ... By Joseph Leeds. ... *Boston: T. R. Marvin, Printer.* 1831. 12mo, pp. 36. 39824

Leeds (S. P.) Address at the Funeral of Capt. Lorenzo D. Gove, slain by Rebels in Virginia, Delivered ... at Dartmouth College. By S. P. Leeds, Pastor. *Hanover, N. H.* 1863. 8vo, pp. 12. B. 39825

Also: ... A Discourse delivered on the National Fast, Sept. 26, 1861, in the Congregational Church at Dartmouth College. ... *Windsor, Vt.: Press of Bishop & Tracy.* 1861. 8vo, pp. 31. B.—Remarks made by the Pastor, March 9, 1862, after the President's Emancipation Message. [n. p. n. d.] 8vo, pp. 31.

Leeds (T.) The American Almanack for the year 1714. By Titan Leeds. *Philadelphia: A. Bradford.* [1714.] 12mo.

Continued to 1770, or later. Some copies have the imprint of *N. Boone* with variations in the title.

Leeds. The American Almanack for the Year ... 1731. ... By Titan Leeds, Philomat. *Printed and Sold by William Bradford in New York, and Andrew Bradford in Philadelphia.* [1731.] 12mo. 39827

In the almanac for 1739, in May, is found the often quoted entry, "the printer born the 20th, 1663," which, notwithstanding the inscription (1660) upon his tomb-stone, is now generally admitted to have been the date of his birth.

Leeds. First Annual Report of the Leeds Antislavery Association ... with a List of its Members and Officers. ... *Leeds: Printed by H. W. Walker.* 1854. 8vo, pp. 21. Continued. H.

Also: Leeds Anti-Slavery Tracts. *London.* 1853. Fcap 8vo.— ... A Few Facts ... regarding the Religious Bodies of America in the Matter of Slavery; ... a Report of an Anti-Slavery Meeting ... in ... Leeds, December 10th, 1855. ... *Leeds: Printed by Edward Baines & Sons.* 1855. 12mo, pp. 20. BA.

Leeds. Reports ... of the Leeds Copper Mining ... Company ... . *Boston: Wright & Potter, Printers.* 1864. 8vo, pp. 45. 2 Plans. H. 39829

Leemans (C.) Beredeneerde Beschrijving der Asiatische en Amerikaansche Monumenten van het Museum van Oudheden te Leyden. *Leyden: H. W. Hazenberg en C°.* 1842. 8vo.

Description of the Asiatic and American monuments of the Museum of Antiquities at Leyden.

Leeming (J.) Lecture on the Early Closing Movement. By John Leeming. *Montreal.* 1851. 8vo. 39831

Lees (H. A.) ... Historical Sketches of the Churches of the City of Brooklyn. H. A. Lees, Compiler, Badeau & Bro., Artists. *Brooklyn: Lees & Foulkes.* [n. d.] 8vo, pp. 24. 4 Plates.

No. 1. only published.

Lees (T. J.) The Musing of Carol: Containing an Essay on Liberty. The Desperado: A Tale of the Ocean, and other Original Poems. By Thomas J. Lees. *Wheeling, Va.* 1831. 12mo. 39833

Leese (J. P.) Historical Outline of Lower California, compiled by Jacob P. Leese. ... *New York: E. S. Dodge & Co., Printers.* 1865. 8vo, pp. 46. B. 39834

Leeser (I.) Commemoration of the Life and Death of ... William H. Harrison, being a Funeral Address ... April 10th, 1841, ... By Isaac Leeser. *Philadelphia: C. Sherman & Co.* 5601. 8vo, pp. 15. 39835

Also: The Claims of the Jews to an Equality of Rights. ... *Philadelphia.* 5601.

Leete (——). Remarks of Mr. Leete ... in the House of Representatives, on the Bill to establish a Uniform Rate of Interest. [n. p. n. d.] 8vo, pp. 4. H. 39836

Leeven en Daaden. *See* B[os] (V. D.), Vol. II., No. 6440.

Le Febvre de la Barre. *See* La Barre (L. F. de).

Lefebvre (R.) Paris in America. *See* [Laboulaye (E.)]

Le Fevre (C. F.) The Lexington Calamity. A Sermon ... in ... Bleecker-St. ... Church ... Feb. 9th ... Feb. 16, 1840. By C. F. Le Fevre. Second Edition. *New York.* 1840. 12mo, pp. 23. H. 39837

Lefêvre (E.) Documents Officiels ... de Maximilien. Histoire de l'intervention française au Mexique. Par E. Lefêvre ... *Bruxelles.* 1869. 2 vols., sm. 8vo, pp. (4), iv, 468; (4), 462. B.

Lefêvre. Le Mexique et l'intervention européenne. Par E. Lefêvre. *Mexico.* 1862. 4to, pp. 480. 39839

Lefevre (F. B.) The Hero of No Fiction: or, Memoirs of Francis Barnett Lefevre of "No Fiction;" and a Review of that

Work. With Letters and Authentic Documents. *Boston: C. Ewer and T. Bedlington.* 1823. 2 vols., 18mo, pp. 384; 360. B.
"No Fiction" was by Rev. Andrew Reed; he represented Lefevre as coming to Canada, and drew some very fanciful pictures of that country.

LEFÉVRE (P. F. A.) Zuma: Tragédie. *Paris.* 1777. 8vo.

LEFEVRE (Pierre Paul). Katolik Enamiad. *See* No. 37115.

LEFFINGWELL, CLARK & Co. Southern Missouri, its Resources ... together with the Essay of G. C. Swallow. *Springfield, Ohio.* 1858. 8vo, pp. 16. 39842

LEFROY (John Henry). Magnetical and Meteorological Observations at Lake Athabasca and Fort Simpson, By Captain J. H. Lefroy, ... and at Fort Confidence, in Great Bear Lake, By Sir John Richardson, C.B. ... *London: For her Majesty's Stationery Office.* 1855. 8vo, pp. xiv, (2), 391. Diagram. B. 39843
Edited by E. Sabine. Also: On the Probable Number of the Native Indian Population of British America. From the Proceedings of the Canadian Institute ... . *Toronto: Printed by Hugh Scobie.* [1853.] 8vo, pp. 19. B. *See* Sabine (Edward).

LEFTWICH (W. M.) Martyrdom in Missouri. A History of Religious Proscription, the Seizure of Churches, and the Persecution of Ministers of the Gospel in the State of Missouri during the Late Civil War and under the "Test Oath" of the New Constitution. By W. M. Leftwich, D.D. *Saint Louis: For the Author.* 1870. 2 vols., 12mo, pp. 436; 445. Portrait.

Legacion de Buenos Aires en Montevideo. Documentos relativos a los reclamos de la legacion de Buenos Aires en Montevideo, con motivo de las invasiones alli preparadas y de las resoluciones dictadas por aquel Gobierno y demas incidentes de esta referencia. Publicacion oficial. *Buenos Aires.* 1856. 4to, pp. 44.
A correct title of our No. 9018.

LE GAL (E.) School of the Guides; ... for the Use of The Militia of the United States. By Col. Eugene Le Gal ... . *New York: D. Van Nostrand.* 1862. 16mo, pp. (2), 60, (1). H.

LEGAL (G.) Dernier Vœu de la Justice, de l'Humanité, et de la Sainte Politique; en faveur des Colons de Saint-Domingue, et sur la nécessité et les moyens de rendre à cette Colonie sa prospérité. Par G. Legal ... . *A Paris, Chez Desenne, libraire ... An* v [1797]. 8vo, pp. 44. 39847

[LEGAL.] Observations sur tout ce qui concerne les colonies d'Amérique; notamment celle de Saint-Domingue. [n. p. 1798.] 8vo, pp. 36. H. 39848
Not mentioned by Quérard in the list of Legal's writings.

The Legal Bearings in the Louisiana Case. By a Member of the Louisiana Bar. [n. p. n. d.] 8vo, pp. 21. 39849

The Legal Claim of the British Sugar Colonies to enjoy an Exclusive Right of Supplying this Kingdom with Sugar. [*London: Privately Printed.*] 1792. 8vo, pp. 17. C. 39850

Legal Effects of Secession Troubles on the Commercial Relations of the Country. [*New York: Privately Printed.*] 1861. 8vo. 39851

LEGAL TENDER. Opinions delivered by the Judges of the [N. Y. State] Court of Appeals ... declaring Treasury Notes a Legal Tender ... . *Albany: Weed, Parsons ... Printers.* 1863. 8vo, pp. 162. BA. 39852
Also: ... Decision of the Supreme Court, of the State of New York, sustaining the Constitutionality of Legal Tender Notes, delivered at Rochester, April 4, 1863. *Rochester: A Strong & Co.* 1863. 8vo, pp. 42.

LEGARE (H. S.) Arbitrament of National Disputes. June 13, 1838. ... Mr. Legare ... made the ... Report. ... [n. p. n. d.] 8vo, pp. 11. H. 39853
25th Cong., 2d Sess., House of Reps., Report, No. 979.

LEGARE. Letter from the Hon. Hugh S. Legare, on the Probable Effects of the Sub-Treasury Policy with the Specie Clause, to his Excellency Pierce Butler ... . *Washington.* 1838. 8vo, pp. 37. BA. 39854

LEGARE. Writings of Hugh Swinton Legaré, late Attorney General and Acting Secretary of State of the United States; consisting of a Diary of Brussels, and Journal of the Rhine; Extracts from his Private and Diplomatic Correspondence; Orations and Speeches; and contributions to the New-York and Southern Reviews: prefaced by a Memoir of his Life. ... Edited by his Sister. *Charleston, S. C.: Burges & James.* 1846. 2 vols., 8vo, pp. lxxii, 558; 598. Portrait. BA. 39855
Also: An Oration ... Fourth of July, 1823 ... . *Charleston: Printed by A. E. Miller.* 1823. 8vo, pp. 30. B.—Third Edition. Speech ... on the Bill imposing Additional Duties as Depositaries, in certain Cases, on Public Officers. ... *Washington.* 1837. 8vo, pp. 16. B. + [*Ibid.*] 8vo, pp. 32.—Speeches ... on the Recognition of Hayti; in Favor of a Southern Naval Depot; ... December 18, 1838, and January 11 and 15, 1839. *Washington.* 1839. 8vo, pp. 24. H.

LEGARÉ (J. M.) Orta-Undis, and other Poems. By J. M. Legaré. *Boston: William D. Ticknor & Company.* M DCCC XLVIII. 8vo, pp. viii, (2), 102. B. 39856

Legend of the Manitou Rock. *Buffalo.* 1843. 18mo.

The Legendary. *See* Willis (N. P.)

La Legende Latine de S. Brandaines, avec une traduction inédite en prose et en poesie romane; publiée par Achille Jubinal, d'après les MSS. de la Bibliothèque du Roi, remontant au 11e, 12e et 13e siècles. *Paris: Techener.* 1836. 8vo, pp. 188. 39858
This is the famous Legend of the Sacred Isles of the West, current in the middle ages, before the discovery of America. One hundred copies only printed.

Legends and Poetry of the Hudson. *See* Vol. IX., 33517.

Legends of a Log-Cabin. By a Western Man. *New-York: George Dearborn.* 1835. 12mo, pp. (4), 277. C. 39859

LE GENTIL (*M.*) *See* La Barbinais (Le G. de), Nos. 38396–9.

LEGGE (C.) A Glance at the Victoria Bridge, and the Men who Built it. By Charles Legge ... . *Montreal: John Lovell.* 1860. 12mo, pp. 153. H. 39860

LEGGETT (A.) The Narrative of Major Abraham Leggett, of the Army of the Revolution, Now first Printed from the Original Manuscript. Written by Himself, with An Introduction and Notes, by Charles I. Bushnell. *New York: Privately Printed.* 1865. 8vo, pp. (2), 71. Portrait. 39861
Included in Bushnell's "Crumbs for Antiquarians," Vol. II.

LEGGETT (S.) An Explanation and Vindication of Samuel Leggett, late President of the Franklin Bank in the City of New York. *New York.* 1831. 8vo, pp. 87. 39862

LEGGETT (W.) A Collection of the Political Writings of William Leggett, selected and arranged, with a Preface, by Theodore Sedgwick, Jr. *New-York: Taylor & Dodd.* 1840. 2 vols., 12mo, pp. 312; 336. A., B. 39863

[LEGGETT.] Leisure Hours at Sea: being a few Miscellaneous Poems. By a Midshipman of the United States Navy. *New York.* 1825. 12mo. 39864

LEGGETT. Naval Stories. By William Leggett. ... *New-York: G. & C. & H. Carvill.* 1834. 18mo, pp. 179. B. + Second Edition. [*Ibid.*] 1835. 18mo. 39865

[LEGGETT.] Tales and Sketches. By a Country School Master. ... *New-York: Printed by J. & J. Harper.* 1829. 12mo, pp. 9–248. Portrait. B. 39866
See also "The Critic," Vol. v., No. 17548, *and* "The Plain Dealer."

The Legion of Liberty! and Force of Truth, Containing the thoughts, words, and deeds, of some prominent Apostles, Champions and Martyrs. ... Second Edition. ... *New-York.* 1843. 12mo. + Tenth Editon. ... [*Ibid.*] 1847. 12mo, pp. (356). B. + [*Ibid.*] 1857. 12mo, pp. 336. B. 39867

The Legion of Liberty. Remonstrance of some Free Men, States, and Presses, to the Texas Rebellion, against the Laws of Nature and of Nations. ... *Albany.* 1843. 12mo, pp. (64). H.

Der Legitime und die Republikaner; eine Geschichte aus dem letzten Amerikanisch-Englischen Kriege. *Zürich: Orell, Füssli u. Comp.* 1833. 3 vols., 8vo, pp. 796. 39869

LEGOYT (A.) L'Émigration Européenne, son Importance, ses Causes, ses Effets ... . Par Alfred Legoyt. *Paris: Guillaumin et Cie.* 1861. 8vo, pp. (6), lv, 333. B. 39870

LE GRAND (J. B. B.) Jean-Baptiste-Bernard Le Grand, Secretaire-Garde des Archives de la Commission de Sainte-Domingue. A la Convention Nationale. ... [*Paris:*] *De l'imprimerie de Laurens Jeune.* [n. d.] 8vo, pp. 7. 39871
Dated from the prison of the Luxembourg, 8 Fructidor, An II.

[LEGRAND (John C.)] Letter to Reverdy Johnson, on the Proceedings at the Meeting held at Maryland Institute, January 10, 1861. [*Baltimore: John Murphy & Co., Printers.* 1861.] 8vo, pp. 8. 39872
Also: An Oration delivered in the Senate Chamber of Maryland ... 4th July, 1842. ... *Annapolis: Wm. Johnston.* 1842. 8vo, pp. 31.—Oration on the Landing of the Pilgrims of Maryland, May 10, 1843. ... *Baltimore.* 1843. 8vo.

LEGRAND. Obituary Addresses on the Death of Hon. John C. Legrand, delivered in the Court of Appeals and Superior Court. *Annapolis.* 1862. 8vo, pp. 22. 39873

LEGRAND (L.) The Life of Maj.-Gen. Geo. B. McClellan ... By Louis Legrand, M.D. *New York: Beadle and Company.* 1862. 12mo, pp. 5–98. B. 39874

LEGRAND. The Military Hand-Book, and Soldier's Manual of Information. ... By Louis Legrand, M.D. *New York: Beadle and Company.* [1862.] 12mo, pp. 125. H. 39875

LEGRAS (A.) Phares des côtes orientales de l'Amérique anglaises et des États-Unis, corrigés en avril 1864. Par M. A. Legras, Capitaine de Frégate. *Paris: impr. P. Dupont.* 1864. 8vo, pp. 82. + [*Ibid.*] 1868. 8vo, pp. 93. + [*Ibid.*] 1870. 8vo, pp. 98. 39876
Also: Phares de la mer des Antilles et du golfe du Mexique, corrigés en janvier 1865. ... *Paris: impr. P. Dupont.* 1865. 8vo, pp. 37. + [*Ibid.*] 1868. 8vo, pp. 38.—Phares du grand Océan, îles eparses et côtes occidentales d'Amérique, corrigés en janvier 1868 ... . *Paris: P. Dupont.* 1868. 8vo, pp. 15.

LE GUEN (Lewis). Le Guen *vs.* Gouverneur S. Kemble. [*New York.* 1798.] 8vo, pp. 135. 39877
Report of an important law case in New York. Also: Special Verdict, in the Case of Lewis Le Guen and Isaac Gouverneur & Peter Kemble, in the Supreme Court of the State of New-York. 1797. *New-York: Printed at the Argus Office.* 1797. 8vo, pp. 61. B.

L'HERMITE (J.) *See* Hermite (J. l'), Vol. VIII., 31501–10.

LEHIGH. A History of the Lehigh Coal and Navigation Company. *Philadelphia: William S. Young.* 1840. 8vo, pp. 68.
Also: Defence of the Lehigh Coal and Navigation Company, from the Assaults made upon its Interests by X. *Philadelphia: Jesper Harding, Printer.* 1840. 8vo, pp. 66. Map. H.

Facts Illustrative of the Character of the ... Lehigh Coal, found in the Great Mines at Mauch Chunk ... . *Philadelphia: Printed by Solomon W. Conrad.* 1827. 12mo, pp. 20, (1). BA.

... History of the Lehigh Valley ... . *Bixler & Corwin, Easton, Pa.* 1859. No. 1. 8vo, pp. 80. 39880
No more published.

Report of the Board of Managers of the Lehigh Coal ... Company, ... January 12th, 1829. *Philadelphia: Printed by Solomon W. Conrad.* [n. d.] 8vo, pp. 15. Continued. BA.
These reports were published as early as 1822, or perhaps earlier.

The Lehigh and Susquehanna Coal Company. ... *New York: Wm. C. Bryant & Co., Printers.* 1864. 8vo, pp. 16. H. 39882

LEHIGH RIVER. Incidents of the Freshet on the Lehigh River, Sixth Month 4th and 5th, 1862. *Philadelphia.* 1863. 12mo, pp. 56. 39883

LEHIGH UNIVERSITY, *South Bethlehem, Pa.* Register of the Officers and Students of Lehigh University [for 1866–67]. ... *Bethlehem, Penn.* 1866. 8vo, pp. 40. Continued. H. 39884

LEHRE [Thomas]. Opinion of the Court ... at the Meeting ... of the Judges at Charleston ... in ... 1811 ... on a Motion for a New Trial, on Behalf of Colonel Lehre ... . By a Member of the Bar. [*Charleston.* 1811?] 8vo, pp. 32. 39885

LEIB (C.) Nine Months in the Quartermaster's Department; or, The Chances for Making a Million. By Charles Leib ... . *Cincinnati: Moore, ... Printers.* 1862. 12mo, pp. 200. Portraits.

LEIB (J. R.) Thoughts of The Elective Franchise, By James R. Leib. ... *Philadelphia: Printed by John C. Clark.* 1839. 8vo, pp. 20. BA. 39887
Also: Lecture on Scientific Education. ... December 18, 1830, before the ... Franklin Institute. ... *Philadelphia: Clark & Raser, Printers.* 1830. 8vo, pp. 16. BA. + [*Ibid.*] 1831. 8vo, pp. 16. H.

[LEIB (Michael).] Address of the State Committee of Correspondence to the Citizens of Pennsylvania. [n. p. n. d.] 8vo, pp. 10. 39888
Dated Philadelphia, July 25, 1808. Relates to the presidential election.

LEIB. Long Talk, delivered before The Tammany Society, ... May 13, 1816. By Dr. Michael Leib. *Philadelphia: Order of the Society.* 1816. 8vo, pp. 20. B. 39889
Also: Conduct of Dr. Lee in the Certificate Business. [n. p.] 1800. 4to. C.—Rascality Recorded; or a Monument of Infamy to Dr. Leib, respecting the Certificate. [n. p. n. d.] 8vo.

LEIB. Six Letters on the Intrigues, Apostacy, and Ambition of Dr. Michael Leib; Originally published in "The Democratic Press." By Veritas. *Philadelphia.* 1827. 8vo, pp. 24. C.

LEIBA (Diego de). Relacion de la Exemplar, y Religiosa Vida del Padre Nicolas de Guadalaxara, ... Provincia de Nueva-España. *Mexico.* 1684. 4to. 39891

LEIBA. Vida de el Venerable Padre Jr. Diego Romero. [*Mexico*], *por Juan de Ribera.* 1684. 4to. 39892

LEIBNITZ (Gottfried Wilhelm). Codex Juris Gentium Diplomaticus. Acced. Mantissa. *Hanoveræ.* 1693–1700. 2 vols., folio. + *Guelferbyti.* 1747. 2 vols., folio. C. 39893
Vol. I., pp. 472–474, contains, "Alexandri Bulla, qua Ferdinando et Elisabethae regi et reginae Castellae et Arragoniae *concedit jus in novum orbem a Colombo detectum.*" In the "Prodromus," p. 23: "Literae a Fernando, rege Siciliae, ad Ludovicum XI., Galliae regem, missae, quibus queritur, quod *Christ. Columbus* triremes suas depraedatus sit postulatque sibi ablata restitui [illegible] Ludovici XI."

LEIBNITZ. Novissima Sinica Historiam nostri temporis illustratura, edente Leibnitio. *Ultrajecti.* 1699. 8vo. Portrait.
Contains, among other very interesting matter, Increase Mather's letter to Leusden, relative to his mission among the Indians in New England, 1688, entitled: "De Successu Evangelii apud Indos Occidentales in Novâ Angliâ, Epistola. A Cresentio Mathero apud Bostonienses V. D. M."

[LEICESTER (Fitzgerald Charles).] The Earl of Harrington on the Maine-Law ... . *Derby: Printed by W. Bemrose and Sons.* MDCCCLVIII. 8vo, pp. (2), 38. B. 39895

LEICESTER, *Mass.* The Annual Report of the Selectmen of Leicester. March 3, 1851. ... *Worcester: Printed by Henry J. Howland.* [n. d.] 8vo, pp. 18. Continued. H. 39896

Articles of Faith and Form of Covenant, adopted by the Congregational Church in Leicester, in 1805. *Boston.* [n. d.] 12mo.

History of Leicester, Mass. [n. p.] 1826. 8vo, pp. 66.

Order of Consecration of Christ Church at Leicester, Mass., May 26, 1824. [n. p.] 1824. 8vo. W. 39899

Report of the School Committee of ... Leicester for 1849–'50: ... with a Historical Sketch of the District Schools ... . *Worcester.* 1850. 8vo, pp. 34. Continued. B. 39900
Also: Reports of the Town Officers ... of Leicester, for ... 1866. *Worcester: Tyler & Seagrave ... Printers.* [n. d.] 8vo, pp. 28. Continued. H.

Valuation, State, County ... Taxes, ... of Leicester, 1858. *Worcester: Printed by Chas. Hamilton.* [n. d.] 8vo, pp. 48. H.

LEICESTER ACADEMY. Festival at Leicester Academy, on the Seventy-First Anniversary, August 7, 1855; with the Address, by Rev. Alonzo Hill, D.D., and the Poem by Isaac F. Shepard, A.M. *Worcester: Printed by Fiske & Reynolds.* 1855. 8vo, pp. 72. Plate. 39902
Also: Catalogue of the Trustees ... Students of Leicester Academy, Massachusetts, for ... 1838. *Worcester: Press of J. M. Earle.* 1838. 12mo, pp. 12. Continued.

LEIDY (J.) The Ancient Fauna of Nebraska; or, a Description of Remains of Extinct Mammalia and Chelonia from the Mauvaises Terres of Nebraska. By Joseph Leidy, M.D. ... *Washington.* 1853. 4to, pp. 124. 25 Plates. C. 39903
From "Smithsonian Contributions," Vol. VI.

LEIDY. Cretaceous Reptiles of the United States. By Joseph Leidy, M.D. ... *Washington.* 1865. 4to, pp. 6, 135. 20 Plates.

LEIDY. The Extinct Mammalian Fauna of Dakota and Nebraska. Including an account of some allied forms from other localities, together with a Synopsis of the Mammalian Remains of North America. By Joseph Leidy, M.D. ... Preceded with an Introduction on the Geology of the Tertiary Formations of Dakota and Nebraska. By F. V. Hayden, M.D. *Philadelphia.* 1869. 4to, pp. 472. Map and 30 Plates. C. 39905

LEIDY. A Flora and Fauna within Living Animals. By Joseph Leidy, M.D. ... *Washington.* 1853. 4to, pp. 68. 10 Plates.
Also included in "Smithsonian Contributions," Vol. V.

LEIDY. Memoir upon the Extinct Species of Fossil Ox. By Joseph Leidy, M.D. ... *Washington.* 1852. 4to, pp. 20. 5 Plates.

LEIDY. A Memoir on the Extinct Sloth Tribe of North America. By Joseph Leidy, M.D. ... *Washington.* 1855. 4to, pp. 70. 16 Plates. C. 39908
From "Smithsonian Contributions," Vol. VI. Also: Report to the Councils of Philadelphia on Insects Injurious to our Shade-Trees. ... *Philadelphia.* 1862. 8vo. Also many other articles on Natural History in the "Journal of Natural Sciences," "Smithsonian Reports," etc.

LEIDY (P.) Speech of Hon. Paul Leidy ... on the Admission of Kansas. ... March 30, 1858. [n. p. n. d.] 8vo, pp. 16. H.

LEIG (Ch.) Zee-togt na Gujana anno 1604. *Leyden.* 1706. Map and Plates. 39910
Forms part of P. van der Aa's "Collection."

[LEIGH (Benjamin Watkins).] Address to the People of New-England, by Algernon Sydney. *Washington.* 1808. 12mo.

[LEIGH.] Letters of Algernon Sydney in defence of Civil Liberty ... Written by an Eminent Citizen of Virginia, ... 1818–19 ... Added ... The Remarks of Mr. Ritchie ... With an Introduction by the present publisher. *Richmond: T. W. White.* [1830.] 8vo, pp. viii, 65. 39912

LEIGH. Speech of Mr. Leigh, of Virginia, on the motion That the President's Protest against the Proceedings of the Senate should not be received and entered on the journal. Delivered ... April 18, 1834. *Washington: Printed by Gales and Seaton.* 1834. 8vo, pp. 16. 39913

LEIGH. Speech of Mr. Leigh, of Virginia, on Mr. Benton's Motion to expunge ... the Resolution of March 28, 1834

Delivered ... on the 4th and 5th April, 1836. *Washington: Printed by Gales & Seaton.* 1836. 8vo, pp. 30. BA. 39914

LEIGH. Speech of Mr. Leigh, of Virginia, on the Question to abolish Slavery within the District of Columbia. ... the 19th of January, 1836. [n. p. n. d.] 8vo, pp. 8. H. 39915

LEIGH. Speeches of Mr. Leigh, of Virginia, on The Removal of the Deposits, and on the bill to extend the charter of the Bank of the United States. Delivered ... March 12, & 18, 1834. *Washington: Printed by Gales & Seaton.* 1834. 8vo, pp. 16.

Also: Letter ... to the General Assembly of Virginia, March 2, 1836. [n. p. n. d.] 8vo. — Speech ... on the Expunging Resolution ... April 4, 1836. *Washington City.* 1836. 8vo, pp. 35.

LEIGH (C. C.) The Maine Law. Remarks ... in the Assembly of ... New York, on the ... Suppression of Intemperance ... 1854. *Albany.* [n. d.] 8vo, pp. 8. H. 39917

[LEIGH.] United States Senatorial Question. Speeches ... in the Assembly of ... New York, by ... C. C. L. and 12 others ... in Exposition of the Oaths ... of the Know-Nothings ... February ... 1855. *Albany: Weed, Parsons ... Printers.* 1855. 8vo, pp. 58. B. 39918

Also: Speech ... Feb. 13, 1855, on the Temperance Bill. [n. p. n. d.] 8vo.

LEIGH. The Freedmen in America. Speech of Charles C. Leigh, delivered in London, June 9, 1865. ... *London: Printed by W. H. Collingridge.* [n. d.] 24mo, pp. 19. H. 39919

LEIGH. Die befreiten Sclaven in Amerika. Auszug einer Aussprache des ... Chs. C. Leigh ... . *Frankfurt a/M.: C. Naumann.* 1865. 24mo, pp. 21. + *Bremen.* 1865. 12mo, pp. 12.

LEIGH. De vrijgemaakte Slaven van Noord-Amerika. ... *Amsterdam.* 1865. 8vo. 39921

LEIGH (E.) Bird's-Eye Views of Slavery in Missouri. By Edwin Leigh. *Saint Louis.* 1862. 8vo, pp. 3. 6 Maps. B.

[LEIGH (*Sir* Egerton).] Considerations on certain Political Transactions of the Province of South Carolina: containing a View of the Colony Legislatures (Under the Description of That of Carolina in Particular). With Observations, Shewing their Resemblance to the British Model. *London: T. Cadell.* M DCCLXXIV. 8vo, pp. (4), 83. BA. 39923

This shrewd and dispassionate examination of the internal disputes of the colony of

South Carolina, contains a detail of curious and interesting transactions. *See* "M. Rev.," L. 208, 426. It elicited the following:

[LEIGH.] An Answer to Considerations on certain Political Transactions of the Province of South Carolina. ... *London: J. Almon.* M DCC LXXIV. 8vo, pp. (4), 140. C., P. 39924

"From a most coarse and virulent antagonist, who defeats whatever advantages argument might afford him, by the gross illiberality of his language. He describes the author of the 'Considerations' 'as a wretch, whom his vices only have raised to a title.'"—*Monthly Review*, L. 486.

[LEIGH.] Extracts from the Proceedings of the Court of Vice-Admiralty in Charles-Town, South-Carolina; In the Cause, George Roupell, Esq; v. the ship Ann and Good: With a few Explanatory Remarks. To which is subjoined, some General Observations on American Custom-House Officers, and Courts of Vice-Admiralty. ... *America: Printed, Anno Domini* M,DCCLXVIII. 4to, pp. iv, 20. P. 39925

LEIGH. Extracts from the Proceedings of the High Court of Vice-Admiralty, in Charlestown, South Carolina, upon Six several Informations, adjudged by The Honourable Egerton Leigh, Esq; Sole Judge of that Court, and His Majesty's Attorney-General in the said Province, In the Years 1767 and 1768. With explanatory Remarks, &c. ... To which are subjoined, Recapitulation, reflexions arising from a retrospect of a late Case, and some General Observations on American Custom-House Officers ... . The Second Edition, with an Appendix. *Charlestown: Printed by David Bruce.* MDCCLXIX. Folio, pp. iv, 64. 39926

LEIGH. The Man Unmasked: or, the World Undeceived, In the Author of a Late Pamphlet, intitled, "Extracts from the Proceedings of the High Court of Vice-Admiralty in Charlestown, South-Carolina," &c. With Suitable Remarks on that Masterly Performance. By Egerton Leigh. ... *Charles-Town: Printed by Peter Timothy.* M,DCC,LXIX. 8vo, pp. 154, Appendix, 44, Postscript, 16, (1). BA., P. 39927

Leigh here declares that Laurens wrote the "Extracts."

LEIGH (J.) Illustrations of the Fulfilment of the Prediction of Merlin,—occasioned by the late Attack of the British Ship of War the Leopard, on the American Frigate Chesapeake ... . By Joseph Leigh. *Portsmouth.* 1807. 12mo. + Second Edition. [*Ibid.*] 1807. 12mo, pp. 22, (2). + Third Edition. [*Ibid.*] BA.

LEIGH (*Mr.*) Substitute Proposed by Mr. Leigh, of Dinwiddie, to the . Resolutions on the subject of the Right of the

State Legislatures to Instruct their Senators in ... Congress ... . [*Richmond.* 1811.] 8vo, pp. 16. BA. 39929

LEIGH (W.) Substitute Intended to be Offered to ... the Citizens of Richmond, on the subject of A Convention, In Lieu of the Report of the Committee. By Watkins Leigh. *Richmond: Printed by Shepherd & Pollard.* 1824. 8vo, pp. 25.

LEIGH (W.) An Oration in Commemoration of the Founders of William and Mary College, delivered on the Anniversary of its Foundation, August 15, 1771. By William Leigh, Student. *Williamsburg: Printed by William Rind.* MDCCLXXI. 4to, pp. 8.

LEIGH (W.) Address of William Leigh before the Military and Citizens of Martinsburg, Va., Feb. 22d, 1860. [n. p. n. d.] 8vo, pp. 16. H. 39932

LEIGHTON (W. B.) A Narrative of the Life and Sufferings of William B. Leighton. *Boston.* 1840. 18mo. Plate. 39933

LEINSULA (Franciscus). The Kingdom's Divisions Anatomized, together with a Vindication of the Armies Proceedings. *London.* 1649. 4to. 39934

The author observes, at pages 1 and 9, an expression made by John Cotton, of New England, "that God would pour his wrath on the Court of England," etc.; and at page 12 the author refers to Mr. Wheelwright being banished to New England, etc.

LEIRIS (*Mme*). L'Histoire des États-Unis, racontée aux enfants. Traduit librement de l'anglais par Mme Leiris. *Paris: Lelièvre.* 1844. 16mo. 39935

The author of the English work is unknown.

LEISLER (J.) Remarks on the Tragedy of Jacob Leisler. *New York.* 1848. 8vo. 39936

Also: Captain Leisler's Case. — Reasons for the Reversal of Leisler's Attainder. — Answer to the Reasons. — Reasons against the Reversing the Attainder of Captain Jacob Leisler. 1688–90. Four very curious papers relating to New York. On the arrival of the news of the landing of the Prince of Orange in England, Captain Nicholson, the Deputy Governor of New England and New York, in the absence of the Governor, Sir Edmond Andros, refused to declare for the Prince; upon which the military seized the fort, and the Assembly chose Capt. Leisler captain of the fort and commander-in-chief, and by letter from the Earl of Nottingham, he was appointed Deputy Governor, which position he held for thirteen months. Upon the arrival of Captain Ingoldsby, the new Governor, he refused to surrender until the arrival of Col. Slaughter, when he was tried and executed. The above papers detail the whole affair; but, whether printed or manuscript I am not certain. They are described in No. 1703, of one of Thomas Thorpe's Catalogues.

LEISTE (C.) Beschreibung des Brittischen Amerika zur Ersparung der englischen Karten. Nebst einer Special-Karte der

mittleren Brittischen Colonien. Von Christian Leiste, Conrector an der Herzoglichen grossen Schule zu Wolfenbüttel. *Daselbst gedruckt mit Bindseilschen Schriften.* 1778. 12mo, pp. 571. Map. BA. + *Braunschweig: in der Fürstl. Waysenhaus-Buchhandlung.* 1778. 12mo, pp. 571. Map. 39937

Both editions are the same book, *see* Cudena (P.), Vol v., 17830.

Leisure Hours A Monthly Magazine. Devoted to History, Biography, Prose, Poetry, Wit, Romance, Reality and Useful Information. *Pittsburgh, Pa.: O'Dwyer & Co.* 186–. 8vo.

Leisure Hours at Sea. *See* [Leggett (W.)], No. 39864.

LEITÃO (Antonio José Osorio de Pina). Elegia na morte do Senerissimo Senhor D. José Principe do Brasil. *Lisboa: na Off. de Antonio Gomes.* 1788. 4to, pp. 15. 39939

LEITÃO (Francisco de Andrade). Discurso politico sobre o se haver de largar á coroa de Portugal Angola, S. Thome, e Maranhão, exclamado aos Altos Estados de Hollanda. *Lisboa, por Antonio Alvares.* 1642. 4to. 39940

LEITCH (William). A Christian Amendment of the Constitution proposed. Addresses ... . [n. p. 186–.] 4to, pp. 3. H.

LEITH (*Lieut.-Gen.*) Memoirs and Services of Lieut. Gen. Leith in the West Indies ... . *London.* 1818. 8vo. 39942

LEITHOLD (T. von). Meine Ausflucht nach Brasilien, oder Reise von Berlin nach Rio de Janeiro, und von dort zurück ... . Von Theodor von Leithold. *Berlin: Maurersche Buchhandlung.* 1820. 8vo. 39943

LEITHOLD. Mijn uitstap naar Brazilie, of Reize van Berlijn naar Rio de Janeiro, en van daar terug, enz. 'Uit he Hoogduitsch. *Amsterdam: J. C. Van Kesteren.* 1821. 8vo, pp. iv, 228.

L[EJARZA] (J[uan] J[osé Martinez de]). Análisis Estadístico de la Provincia de Michuacan, en 1822. Por J. J. L. *México: Imprenta Nacional.* 1824. 4to, pp. (4), ix, 281. 9 Tables. C.

LE JEUNE (P.) Brieve | Relation | dv Voyage | de la | Novvelle France, | fait au mois d'Auril dernier par le | P. Paul le Ieune de la Compagnie | de Iesvs. | Enuoyée au R. P. Bartelemy Iacquinet | Prouincial de la mesme Compagnie en la Prouince de France. | *A Paris,* | *chez Sebastien Cramoisy,* | ... | M.DC.XXXII. | Auec Priuilege dv Roy. | 8vo, pp. 68, (2). 39946

LE JEUNE. Relation | de ce qvi s'est passé en | la Novvelle France | en l'année 1633. | Enuoyée | av R. P. Barth. Iacqvinot | Prouincial de la Compagnie de | Iesvs en la prouince de | France. | ar [*sic*] le P. Paul le Ieune de la mesme Compa- | gnie, Superieur de la residence de Kebec. | *A Paris,* | *chez Sebastien Cramoisy,* | ... | M.DC.XXXIV. | Avec Privilege dv Roy. | 8vo, pp. 216. 39947

LE JEUNE. Relation | de ce qvi s'est passé | en la | Novvelle France | en l'année 1633. | Enuoyée au R. P. Barth. Iacqvinot | Prouincial de la Compagnie de | Iesvs en la Prouince de | de [*sic*] France. | Par le P. Paul le Ieune de la mesme Compagnie, | Superieur de la residence de Kebec. | *A Paris.* | *Chez Sebastien Cramoisy,* ... | M.DC.XXXIV. | Avec Privilege dv Roy. | 8vo, pp. 216. 39948

The same work as the preceding, with a different arrangement in the title-page.

LE JEUNE. Relation | de ce qvi s'est passé | en la | Novvelle France, | en l'année 1634. | Enuoyée au | R. Pere Provincial | de la Compagnie de Iesvs | en la Prouince de France. | Par le P. Paul le Ieune de la mesme Compagnie, | Superieur de la residence de Kebec. | *A Paris,* | *chez Sebastien Cramoisy, Imprimeur* | *ordinaire du Roy,* ... | M.DC.XXXV. | Avec Privilege dv Roy. | 8vo, pp. (4), 342 [*i. e.* 344]. + [Another Edition. *Ibid.*] 8vo, pp. (2), 342, (2).

LE JEUNE. Relation | de ce qvi s'est passé | en la | Novvelle France | en l'année 1635. | Enuoyée au | R. Pere Provincial | de la Compagnie de Iesus | en la Prouince de France. | Par le P. Paul le Ieune, de la mesme Compagnie, | Superieur de la residence de Kebec. | *A Paris.* | *Chez Sebastien Cramoisy, Imprimeur* | *ordinaire du Roy,* ... | M.DC.XXXVI. | Avec Privilege dv Roy. | 8vo, pp. (4), 246, (2). 39950

LE JEUNE. Relation | de ce qvi s'est passé | en la Nouuelle France | en l'année 1634. | Enuoyée au R. Père Provincial de la Compagnie de Icsvs en la | Prouince de France | Par le Pere le Ievne de la Compagnie, Superieur de la | Residence de Kebec. | *En Avignon* | *de l'Imprimerie de Iaqves Bramereav,* | *Imprimeur de sa Sainctetê, de la Ville &* | *Vniversitê. Auec permission des Superieurs.* | M.DC.XXXVI. | 8vo, pp. (10), 416. 39951

The first part corresponds with Le Jeune's "Relation" of 1634 (*Paris,* 1635); the second part is a reprint of the "Relation" of 1635 (*Paris,* 1636).

LE JEUNE. Relation | de ce qvi s'est passé | en la | Novvelle France | en l'année 1636. | Enuoyée au | R. Pere Provincial | de la Compagnie de Iesvs | en la Prouince de France. | Par le P. Paul le Ieune de la mesme Compagnie, | Superieur de la Residence de

Kebec. | *A Paris,* | *chez Sebastien Cramoisy Imprimeur* | *ordinaire du Roy,* ... | M.DC.XXXVII. | Avec Privilege dv Roy. | 8vo, pp. (8), 172; Relation ... des Hvrons ... [par Jean de Brébeuf], pp. 223. + [Another Edition. *Ibid.*] 8vo, pp. (6), 199, (1). 39952

LE JEUNE. Relation | de ce qvi s'est passé | en la | Novvelle France | en l'année 1637. | Envoyée au | R. Pere Provincial de la Compagnie de Iesvs | en la Prouince de France. | Par le P. Paul le Ieune de la mesme Compagnie, | Superieur de la Residence de Kebec. | *A Rouen,* | *chez Iean le Bovllenger, prés le* | *College des PP. Jesuites.* | M.DC.XXXVIII. | Avec Privilege dv Roy. | 8vo, pp. (10), 336; Relation ... des Hvrons ... [par F. J. Le Mercier], pp. 256. + [Another Edition.] *A Roven,* | *chez Iean le Bovlenger. Et se vendent à Paris,* | *Chez Pierre de Bresche,* ... | M.DC.XXXVIII. | ... | 8vo, pp. (10), 336; 256. 39953

LE JEUNE. Relation | de ce qvi s'est passé | en la | Novvelle France | en l'année 1638, | Enuoyée au | R. Pere Provincial | de la Compagnie de Iesvs en | la Prouince de France. | Par le P. Pavle [*sic*] le Ieune de la mesme Compagnie, | Superieur de la Residence de Kébec. | *A Paris,* | *chez Sebastien Cramoisy, Imprimeur* | *ordinaire du Roy,* ... | M.DC.XXXVIII. | Avec Priuilege dv Roy. | 8vo, pp. (4), 78; Relation ... des Hvrons ... [par F. J. Le Mercier], pp. (2), 76 [*i. e.* 67]. 39954

LE JEUNE. Relation | de ce qvi s'est passé | en la | Novvelle France | en l'année 1638. | ... | Par le P. Pavl le Ieune ... | *A Paris,* | *chez Sebastien Cramoisy,* ... | M.DC.XXXVIII. | ... | 8vo, pp. 78; 67.

LE JEUNE. Relation | de ce qvi s'est passé | en la | Novvelle France | en l'Année 1639. | Enuoyée au | R. Pere Provincial | de la Compagnie de Iesvs | en la Prouince de France. | Par le P. Paul le Ieune, de la mesme Compagnie, | Superieur de la Residence de Kébec. | *A Paris,* | *chez Sebastien Cramoisy, Imprimeur* | *ordinaire du Roy,* ... | M.DC.XL. | Avec Privilege dv Roy. | 8vo, pp. (8), 166; Relation ... des Hvrons ... [par Hierosme Lalemant], pp. (2), 174. + [Another Edition. *Ibid.*] 8vo, pp. 116 [*i. e.* 166]; 174.

[LE JEUNE.] Relation | de ce qvi s'est passé | de plvs remarqvable | avx Missions des Peres | de la Compagnie de Iesvs, en la | Novvelle France, | ès années mil six cens cinquante six | & mil six cens cinquante-sept. | *A Paris,* | *Sebastien Cramoisy,* | *Imprimeur ordinaire du* | *Roy & de la Reyne.* | *Et* | *Gabriel Cramoisy.* | ... | M.DC.LVIII. | Avec Privilege dv Roy. | 8vo, pp. (12), 211. 39957

This "Relation" comprises, in addition to the letters of P. Paul Le Jeune, some by P. Le Mercier, and P. Paul Ragueneau.

[LE JEUNE.] Relation | de ce qvi s'est passé | de plvs remarqvable | avx Missions des Peres | de la Compagnie de Iesvs, | en la | Novvelle France, | ès années 1660. & 1661. | Enuoyée au R. P. Prouincial de la Prouince de France. | *A Paris,* | *chez Sebastien Cramoisy, Imprimeur* | *ordinaire du Roy, & de la Reine,* | ... | M.DC.LXII. | Auec Priuilege du Roy. | 8vo, pp. (8), 213, (3). 39958

A complete set of these "Relations" is of the highest rarity; they are all, however, reprinted in the "Relations des Jésuites," *Quebec.* 1858. 3 vols., imp. 8vo. The "Relations of the Jesuits" as to their Canada mission, including Biard's, 1616, and Lallemant's, 1627, with one in Latin, includes fifty-five volumes, nine being contemporaneous reprints. Intended to excite interest in their missionary work, these volumes have proved of high historical value as accounts of Indian tribes, their manners, language, etc., as well as records of events in the colony. Sulpitian authors state that the publication after 1672 was prevented by the French Government, but Harrisse could not find in the archives the documents cited by Faillon. Subsequent "Relations," prepared for publication after 1672, have been printed by James Lenox, J. G. Shea, and F. Felix Martin. To form a complete collection of the "Relations" of the Jesuit missionaries in Canada, on the borders, and in the great North West, from about 1630 to 1680, has been the laudable ambition of many American collectors, but few, if any, have succeeded. A perfect set is the *pons asinorum* of the American collector. The historical and geographical importance of these volumes cannot well be overstated. *See* [Harrisse's] "Notes," Nos. 49, 55, 56, 60, 63, 70, 74, 75, 110, 117.

[LELAND (Aaron W.)] A Letter, to the Citizens of Charleston, embracing Strictures, &c. &c. By Expositor. *Charleston, (S. C.)* 1818. 8vo, pp. 10. BA. 39959

LELAND. The Fatal Error, a Tragedy. By Aaron W. Leland ... . Exhibited at Williams College, March 25, 1807. *Pittsfield: Printed by Seymour & Smith.* 1807. 12mo, pp. 27. H.

LELAND. A Sermon ... July 13, 1823, at the Organization of the Third Presbyterian Church, in ... Charleston ... . By Aaron W. Leland ... . *Charleston: H. C. M'Leod.* 1823. 8vo, pp. 32. BA. 39961

Also: Discourse delivered in the Circular Church, Charleston, South Carolina, on the 4th of July, 1826. ... *Charleston.* 1826. 8vo. — A Discourse ... in ... Charleston, On the 27th December, 1815, before the Grand Lodge of South-Carolina. ... *Charleston, S. C.: For the Grand Lodge of South Carolina.* 1816. 8vo, pp. 19.

[LELAND (C. G.)] Ye Book of Copperheads. *Philadelphia: Frederick Leypoldt.* 1863. 8vo, pp. (2), 24, (6). BA. 39962

LELAND. Centralization or "States Rights," By Charles G. Leland. *New York: C. T. Evans.* 1863. 8vo, pp. 14.

Also: Hans Breitmann's Ballads. ... *Philadelphia: T. B. Peterson & Brothers.* [1869.] 12mo, pp. 118. + *London: Trübner & Co.* 1870. 12mo, pp. 68, (2). B. — Hans Breitmann's Christmas. With other Ballads. ... *London: Trübner & Co.* 1869. 12mo, pp. 80. — Hans Breitmann in Church. With Other New Ballads. ... Third Series o

the Breitmann Ballads. *Philadelphia: T. B. Peterson & Brothers.* [1870.] 12mo, pp. 8, 107–154. C. + *London: Trübner & Co.* 1870. 12mo, pp. (2), 79. — Hans Breitmann's Party. With other Ballads. ... *Philadelphia: T. B. Peterson & Brothers.* 1868. 8vo, pp. 32. + New and Enlarged Edition. [*Ibid.*] 12mo, pp. 48. — Hans Breitmann as a Politician. ... *London: Trübner & Co.* 1869. 12mo, pp. 72. — Hans Breitmann in Politics. ... *Philadelphia: J. B. Lippincott and Co.* 1869. 8vo, pp. 13. Plate. — Hans Breitmann and his Philosopede. ... *New York: Haney & Co.* 1869. 16mo, pp. 22. — Hans Breitmann about Town. And Other New Ballads. ... Second Series of the Breitmann Ballads. *Philadelphia: T. B. Peterson & Brothers.* [1869.] 8vo, pp. 62. B.

LELAND. The Union Pacific Railway, Eastern Division, or, Three Thousand Miles in a Railway Car, By Charles Godfrey Leland. ... *Philadelphia: Ringwalt & Brown.* 1867. 8vo, pp. 95. 39964

LELAND (H. P.) Americans in Rome. By Henry P. Leland. *New York: Charles T. Evans.* 1863. 12mo, pp. 311. 39965

LELAND. The Grey-Bay Mare, and other Humorous American Sketches. By Henry P. Leland. *Philadelphia: J. B. Lippincott & Co.* 1856. 12mo, pp. 314. H. 39966

LELAND (J.) A Blow at the Root, being a fashionable Fast-Day Sermon ... at Cheshire ... April 9, 1801. By John Leland. ... *New-London: Charles Holt.* 1801. 8vo, pp. 32. BA. 39967

LELAND. An Elective Judiciary ... Speech ... at Cheshire, July 4, 1805. By John Leland. ... *Pittsfield: Printed by Phinehas Allen.* 1805. 8vo, pp. 23. BA. 39968

LELAND. The Connecticut Dissenters' Strong Box: No. 1. Containing, The high-flying Churchman stript of his legal Robe, &c. By the rev. John Leland, Pastor of the Baptist Church in Cheshire, Mass. The Dissenter's Petition. Connecticut Ecclesiastical Laws. American Constitutions (Extracts from). Sixteen of which recognise the Rights of Conscience—and Three the doctrine of Church and State. Some remarks. Compiled by a Dissenter. *Printed by Charles Holt, New-London.* 1802. 8vo, pp. 40. 39969

LELAND. The Rights of Conscience inalienable, And therefore Religious Opinions not cognizable by Law: Or, The high-flying Church-man Stript of his legal Robe, appears a Yaho. By John Leland. ... *New-London: Printed by T. Green & Son.* M,DCC,XCI. 8vo, pp. 29. BA. + Second Edition. *Richmond, Va.* 1793. 12mo. W. 39970

LELAND. The Virginia Chronicle ... Dated Orange County, Virginia, March 1789. [*Norfolk.* 1789.] 12mo, pp. 7. 39971

A chronicle of the first settlement of Virginia, in fifty verses, after the style of scriptural history. Also: Oration at the Interment of Mrs. Lydia, wife of Stephen Northrop, of Cheshire, who died April 26, 1794. ... *Portsmouth, N. H.* 1794. 8vo, pp. 12.—Oration delivered at Cheshire, 5 July, 1802. ... *Pittsfield, Mass.* [1802.] 8vo, pp. 16. + Second Edition. *Hudson, N. Y.* 1802. 8vo.—A Stroke at the Branch, containing Remarks on Men and Things. ... *Hartford.* 1801. 8vo. C.

LELAND. Some Events in the Life of John Leland. Written by Himself. *Pittsfield.* 1838. 8vo, pp. 44. 39972

LELAND (P. W.) Is the North Right? a Word about Slavery. [n. p. n. d.] 8vo. 39973

LELAND (S.) The Leland Magazine, or a Genealogical Record of Henry Leland, and his Descendants, containing an account of nine thousand six hundred and twenty-four persons, in Ten Generations, and embracing nearly every Person of the name of Leland in America, from 1653 to 1850. By Sherman Leland. *Boston: Printed by Wier & White.* 1850. 8vo, pp. (2), 278, (1). H. 39974

LELAND (T.) A Sermon Preached before the University of Dublin, On Friday the 13th of December, 1776, being the Day Appointed by Authority for a General Fast and Humiliation. By Thomas Leland, D.D. ... *London: E. Johnston.* 1777. 4to, pp. 20.

The Fast was on account of the American Revolution. *See* "M. Rev.," LVI. 159.

LELAND SEMINARY, *Vt.* Catalogue of ... Leland Seminary, Townshend, Vt., for ... 1847-8. *Hanover.* 1848. 12mo, pp. 16.

LELEWEL (J.) Die Entdeckungen der Carthager und Griechen auf dem Atlantischen Ocean von Joachim Lelewel. ... Mit einem Vorworte von Professor Ritter ... . *Berlin.* 1831. 8vo, pp. xiv, 145. 2 Maps. B. 39977

LELEWEL. Géographie du Moyen Age, étudiée par Joachim Lelewel. *Bruxelles.* 1852-57. 4 vols., 8vo. Atlas of 50 Plates.

A work of great learning and research, embracing the whole subject of the early maritime discoveries, maps, etc., including the oriental geographies, Martin Behaim, Bianco, the Zeni, etc., with facsimiles of ancient maps, etc.

LE LONG (I.) Godts wonderen met zijne kerke vertoont in een verhaal van meest Boheemsche en Moravische Broeders die het Pausdom ontweken zynde. Tweede druk verbeetert. *Amsterdam.* 1738. 8vo, pp. 720. Plate. 39979

The wonders of the Lord in his church, exposed by an account of the Bohemian and

Moravian brethren. Contains (Vol. I., pp. 472-545,) the account of a voyage of a potter and carpenter to St. Thomas; (pp. 546-616,) a voyage to Greenland, etc.

LE LONG (J.) L'alliance du Brésil et des républiques de la Plata contre le gouvernement du Paraguay. Par John Le Long. *Paris: imprimerie Schiller.* 1866. 8vo, pp. 80. 39980

LE LONG. Intervention de la France dans le Rio de la Plata. Par John Le Long. *Paris: Imprimerie Lacombe.* 1849. 8vo.

LE LONG. Le Paraguay. La dynastie des Lopez avant et pendant la guerre actuelle; par John Le Long. ... *Paris: Dubuisson et Cie.* 1868. 8vo, pp. 31. 39982

LE LONG. Renseignment sur les Affaires de la Plata depuis la signature du Traité de Buénos-Ayres. Par John Le Long. *Paris.* 1842. 4to, pp. 48. 39983

LE LONG. Révélations à la France. Les Négociations au Rio-de-la-Plata. Par John Le Long. *Paris: Mme de Lacombe.* [n. d.] 8vo, pp. 107. 39984

Also: Appel aux populations laborieuses de France et d'Allemagne, pour la colonisation de la riche province de Corrientes [Confédération Argentine]. *Paris: Borrani et Droz.* 1856. 8vo. Map.—Mémoire; Rédigé par John Le Long. *Paris.* 1852. 8vo, pp. 23.

LE MAGE (G.) La Pléiade Rouge, par Gaspard Le Mage. *Quebec.* 1854-5. 8vo, pp. 22. 39985

LEMAIRE (H.) Beautés de l'histoire des voyages le plus fameux autour du monde et dans les deux hémisphères, ou tableau des découvertes, entreprises, aventures, naufrages, captivités, malheurs et succès des plus célèbres voyageurs ... . Par Henri Lemaire. Troisième édition. *Paris: Eymery, Fruger & Cie.* 1827. 2 vols., 16mo, pp. (4), viii, 370; (4), 368. 12 Plates.

LE MAIRE (J.) *See* Maire (J. le).

LE MASCRIER (*l'Abbé* J. B.) *See* Butel-Dumont, III. 9605.

LEMAY (L. P.) Essais Poétiques. Par Léon Pamphile Lemay. [Avec l'Évangeline de Longfellow, traduite en vers français.] *Québec: G. E. Desbarats.* 1865. 8vo, pp. xi, (1), 320.

A Canadian reviewer remarks that the version of "Evangeline" loses in the French the rhythm some metre in which Longfellow wrote it.

LEMBEYE (J.) Aves de la isla de Cuba. Por Juan Lembeye. *Habana: Imp. del Tiempo.* 1850. 8vo, pp. 137. 20 Plates. C.

LEMERCIER (*le Comte* Anatole). Discours prononcés dans la discussion de l'adresse. Politique intérieure. Question des États-Unis. Corps législatif. Session de 1863. *Paris: Dentu.* 1863. 8vo. 39988

LE MERCIER (A.) A Treatise against Detraction. In Ten Sections. By the Rev. Mr. Andrew Le Mercier ... . *Boston: Daniel Henchman.* 1733. 8vo, pp. (2), v, (9), vii, (1), 303. H.

[LE MERCIER (François).] Copie de devx | Lettres | envoiées de la | Novvelle France, | Au Pere Procureur des Missions | de la Compagnie de Iesvs | en ces contrées. | *A Paris* | *chez* | *Sebastien Cramoisy,* | *Imprimeur ordinaire du Roy* | *et Gabriel Cramoisy.* | ... | M.DC.LVI. | Auec Priuilege du Roy. | 8vo, pp. 28. + [*New York: Privately Reprinted by James Lenox.* 1854.] 8vo, pp. 28, (1). H.

[LE MERCIER.] Relation | de ce qvi s'est passé | en la Mission des Pères | de la Compagnie de Iesvs, | av pays de la | Novvelle France, | Depuis l'Eté de l'Année 1652. | iusques à l'Eté de l'Année 1653. | Enuoyée au R. P. Prouincial de la | Prouince de France. | Par le Superieur des Missions de la mesme | Compagnie. | *A Paris,* | *chez Sebastien Cramoisy, Imprimeur* | *ordinaire du Roy & de la Reyne,* | *et Gabriel Cramoisy,* ... | M.DC.LIV. | Avec Privilege dv Roy. | 8vo, pp. (4), 184. 39992

LE MERCIER. Relation | de ce qvi s'est passée | en la Mission des Pères | de la Compagnie de Iesvs, | en la | Novvelle France, | és années 1653. & 1654. | Enuoyée au R. P. Nicolas Royon, | Prouincial de la Prouince de France. | Par le R. P. François Le Mercier, | Superieur des Missions de la mesme | Compagnie. | *A Paris,* | *chez Sebastien Cramoisy,* | *Imprimeur ordinaire du Roy,* | *& de la Reyne,* | *et Gabriel Cramoisy.* | M.DC.LV. | Auec Priuilege du Roy. | 8vo, pp. (4), 176. H., S. 39993

[LE MERCIER.] Relation | de ce | qvi s'est passé | en la | Novvelle France, | és années 1664. & 1665. | Enuoyée au R. P. Provincial de la Province | de France. | *A Paris,* | *chez Sebastien Cramoisy,* | *& Sebast.* | *Mabre-Cramoisy,* | *Imprimeurs ordinaires* | *du Roy,* ... | M.DC.LXVI. | Avec Privilege dv Roy. | 8vo, pp. (12), 128. Map.

[LE MERCIER.] Relation | de ce qvi s'est passé | de plvs remarqvable | avx Missions des Pères | de la Compagnie de Iesvs, | en la | Novvelle France, | aux années mil six cent soixante cinq, | & mil six cent soixante six. | Enuoyée au R. P. Iacqves Bordier | Provincial de la Province de France. | *A Paris* | *chez Sebastien Cra-*

& Sebastien Mabre-Cramoisy, Imprimeurs ordinai- | *res du Roy,* ... | M.DC.LXVII. | Avec Privilege du Roy. | 8vo, pp. (8), 47. 39995

[LE MERCIER.] Relation | de ce qvi s'est passé | de plvs remarqvable | avx Missions des Peres | de la Compagnie de Iesvs. | En la | Novvelle France, | les années mil six cens soixante six, | & mil six cens soixante sept. | Enuoyée au R. P. Iacqves Bordier | Provincial de la Province de France. | *A Paris,* | *Chez Sebastien Cramoisy,* | *et Sebast. Mabre-Cramoisy,* | *Imprimeurs ordinaires du Roy,* ... | M.DC.LXVIII. | Auec Priuilege du Roy. | 8vo, pp. (8), 160. S. 39996

[LE MERCIER.] Relation | de ce qvi s'est passé | de plvs remarqvable | aux Missions des Peres | de la Compagnie de Iesvs, | en la | Novvelle France, | aux années mil six cens soixante sept. | & mil six cens soixante huit. | Enuoyée au R. P. Estienne Dechamps | Provincial de la Province de France. | *A Paris,* | *chez Sebastien Mabre-Cramoisy,* | *Imprimeur du Roy,* | ... | M.DC.LXIX. | Avec Privilege de sa Majesté. | 8vo, pp. (8), 219. H., S. 39997

[LE MERCIER.] Relation | de ce qvi s'est passé | de plvs remarqvable | avx Missions des Peres | de la Compagnie de Iesvs. | En la | Novvelle France, | les années 1669. & 1670. | Enuoyée au R. P. Estienne Dechamps | Provincial de la Province de France. | *A Paris,* | *chez Sebast. Mabre-Cramoisy,* | *Imprimeur du Roy,* ... | M.DC.LXXI. | Avec Privilege de sa Majesté. | 8vo, pp. (10), 3-318; Relation des Missions aux Ovtaovaks, pp. 102. S. 39998

Concerning these "Relations," it is sufficient to remark that they are rare, and important for the history of "Nouvelle France." *See* [Harrisse's] "Notes," Nos. 101, 103, 108, 124, 126-128, 135; *also* Le Jeune, Nos. 39954-55, 39957.

LEMERCIER (N. L.) L'Atlantiade; ou la Théogonie Newtonienne: Poëme en six chants. *Paris.* 1812. 8vo, pp. 80, Chants, 267. S. 39999

LEMERLE (E.) Loisirs d'un aveugle; poésies. Par E. Lemerle. *Paris: E. Maillet.* 1865. 18mo, pp. 248. 40000

"M. Lemerle chante une foule de pays, contenis: les Antilles, Cuba, Panama, le Niagara."—VAPEREAU.

[LEMESLE (Charles).] Réflexions d'un Vieillard du pays de Médoc, sur l'Arrêt du Conseil du 30 Août dernier, qui permet l'admission des Étrangers dans nos Colonies. 1785. [*Bourdeaux.*] 4to, pp. (4), 52. Table. H. 40001

Relates to the affairs of the French colonies, and was probably privately printed.

LE MIRE (Aubert). De statv religionis Christianæ, per Europam, Asiam, Africam, et orbem novum, libri iv. *Helmestadii, H. Mülleri.* 1670. 16mo, pp. (18), 456. C. 40002

LEMMON (J.) New York Court of Appeals. Report of the Lemmon Slave Case: containing Points and Arguments of Counsel on both Sides, and Opinions of all the Judges. *New York: Horace Greeley & Co.* 1860. 8vo, pp. 146. H. 40003

LE MOINE (J. M.) The Legendary Lore of the Lower St. Lawrence, by J. M. Le Moine. *Quebec.* 1862. 18mo, pp. 33.

LE MOINE. Maple Leaves: a Budget of Legendary, Historical, Critical, and Sporting Intelligence. By J. M. Le Moine, Esq. ... *Quebec: For the Author.* 1863. 8vo, pp. vii, (1), 104. + Second Series. [*Ibid.*] 1864. pp. (4), 224. + Third Series, "Canadian History and Quebec Scenery." [*Ibid.*] 1865. pp. (2), iv, 137. 2 Plates. B. 40005

A most interesting collection of facts, narratives, and incidents, connected with colonial history, biography, natural history, etc.

LE MOINE. Le Massacre au Fort George. La Mémoire de Montcalm Vengée: Documents Historiques recueillis par J. M. Le Moine, Ecr. *Quebec: J. N. Duguet & Cie., Editeurs.* 1864. 12mo, pp. 91. 40006

The details of this massacre by the Indians under Montcalm, are given by an eye-witness, and go far to prove Montcalm innocent of a guilty knowledge. *See* "Lettres Edifiantes," Vol. VI., *also* Kip's "Early Jesuit Missions in America," where it is attributed to Father Roubaud.

LE MOINE. Ornithologie du Canada. Quelques Groups d'après la nomenclature du Smithsonian Institution ... . Par J. M. Le Moine ... . *Québec: l'Auteur.* 1860-61. 2 parts, 12mo, pp. 398. C. + Seconde édition, 1e Partie. [*Ibid.*] 1861. 40007

LE MOINE. Les Pecheries du Canada. Par J. M. Le Moine, ... *Quebec.* 1863. 12mo, pp. 146, 2, iii. H. 40008

Also: Étude sur les Explorations arctiques de McClure, de McClintock, et de Kane. ... *Quebec.* [n. d.] 12mo.—The Sword of General Richard Montgomery. A Memoir. ... *Quebec.* 1870. 12mo. Also many contributions to Canadian periodicals.

LEMOINE (S. P.) Oration, delivered on the 17th of March, 1819, ... before the Shamrock Friendly Association, by Stephen P. Lemoine, Esq. *New York: Printed by Gatten and Banks.* 1819. 8vo, pp. 27. 40009

Lemon Hill. *See* [Keyser (Charles S.)], Vol. IX., No. 37696.

LE MONNIER (Pierre Charles). Mémoires concernant diverses Questions d'Astronomie (de Navigation) et de Physique. Lûs et communiqués à l'Académie royale des Sciences ... . Par M. Le Monnier, de la même académie. *A Paris.* 1781-88. 4 parts, 4to, pp. xxiv, 34; xvi, 32; viii, 50; xxiii, 48. S. 40010

Included by D. B. Warden in his "Bibliotheca Americana," No. 70.

LEMONNIER-DELAFOSSE (*M.*) Seconde Campagne de Saint-Domingue du 1er Décembre 1803 au 15 Juillet 1809; précédée de Souvenirs historiques & succincts De la Première Campagne. Expédition du Général en chef Leclerc, du 14 Décembre 1801 au 1er Décember 1803, par M. Lemonnier-Delafosse ... . *Havre: Imprimerie de H. Brindeau & Compie.* 1846. 8vo, pp. viii, 301. Map. 40011

LEMOS (*Conde* de). Relacion de | los Socorros, | que ha | remitido à Tierra-Firme el Excelentissi- | mo señor Conde de Lemos, Virrey, Go- | vernador, y Capitan General de los Rey- | nos, y Provincias del Perù, para la restau- | racion del Castillo de Chagre, y | Ciudad de Panamà, de que se | apoderò el Enemigo | Inglés. | [n. p. 1671.] Folio, pp. (4). 40012

LEMOS Y ANDRADA (*Conde* de). Descripcion de la Provincia de los Quixos. *Madrid.* 1608. 4to. Map. 40013

"Petit traité de 16 feuillets et de la plus grand rareté."—TERNAUX, No. 311. A privately printed book, without title or preliminaries, commencing with a dedication, from the Condé de Lemos to his father. Quixos is a province of Audiencia of Quito. *See* Rich's Catalogue, No. 107.

LEMOS FARIA E CASTRO (D. A. de). Historia geral de Portugal e suas conquistas. *Lisboa.* 1786-1804. 20 vols., sm. 8vo.

Includes particulars concerning Brazil and other colonial possessions of Portugal.

LEMOYNE DE MORGUES (J.) *See* Bry (T. de), Vol. III., p. 30.

LEMPRIERE (C.) The American Crisis Considered. By Charles Lempriere, D.C.L. ... *London: Longman* ... 1861. Post 8vo, pp. vi, (2), 296. BA. 40015

LEMPRIERE. Mexico in 1861 and 1862. Being a Survey of the Actual Condition of that Country, Politically and Socially Considered. By C. Lempriere, D.C.L. ... *London: Longman* ... 1862. 8vo, pp. (6), 480. Map and 11 Woodcuts. 40016

LEMPRIERE [John]. Lempriere's Biographical Dictionary, or, Sketches of ... Celebrated Characters in Every Age and Nation ... containing Sketches of ... John Adams and Thomas

Jefferson. *Richmond, Virginia: N. White.* 1826. 8vo, pp. 450. Plate. H. 40017

LEMPRIERE. Universal Biography; ... By John Lempriere. *New-York: Ezra Sargeant.* 1810. 2 vols., 8vo. + Together with ... original articles of American Biography. By Eleazar Lord. *New-York: R. Lockwood.* 1825. 2 vols., 8vo, pp. 784; 852, (8). B., C. 40018

LEMPRIERE (W.) Practical Observations on the Diseases of the Army in Jamaica, as they occurred between the Years 1792 and 1797; on the Situation, Climate, and Diseases of that Island; and on the most probable Means of lessening Mortality among the Troops, and among Europeans in Tropical Climates. By William Lempriere ... . *London: T. N. Longman.* 1799. 2 vols., 8vo, pp. xix, (1), 291; vii, 361, (1). Tables. H. 40019

LEMUS (D. de). Vida, Virtudes, Trabajos ... de la Ven. M. Sor Maria de Jesus, Angelopolitana Religiosa, en el insigne Convento de la limpia Concepcion de la Ciudad de los Angeles, en la Nueva España, y natural de ella. Dedicada a la Soberana Emperatriz del Cielo Maria Madre de Dios. Por el lic. Diego de Lemus. *En Leon, a costa de Anisson y Posuel.* MDCCLXXXIII. 4to, pp. (16), 533. 40020

LENDERMAN, *pseudon.* Lenderman's Adventures among the Spiritualists and Freelovers, explaining how the "Rappings," ... are done, and where the Spirit Communications come from. *Cincinnati: M. A. Arnold.* 1860. 12mo, pp. 305. 8 Plates. C.

LENDRICK (W. E.) Sugar Trade and Slave Trade: the West India Question Considered. By William E. Lendrick. *London.* 1853. 8vo, pp. 136. 40022

LENDRUM (J.) A Concise and Impartial History of the American Revolution. To which is prefixed, A General History of North and South America. Together with An Account of the Discovery and Settlement of North America, and a View of the Progress, Character, and Political State of the Colonies previous to the Revolution. From the Best Authorities. By John Lendrum. *Printed at Boston, by I. Thomas and E. T. Andrews.* 1795. 2 vols., 12mo, pp. (8), 13-339, (8), 13 411. BA., C., P. + *Boston: Printed. Trenton: Re-Printed and Published by James Oram.* 1811. 2 vols., 12mo, pp. (2), 315; viii, 228. 2 Maps. + *Exeter.* 1836. 2 vols., 32mo. 40023

[LENDRUM.] The History of America, in Two Books. ... Extracted from The American Edition of The Encyclopædia. The Second Edition. *Philadelphia: Printed by Thomas Dobson.* M.DCC.XCV. 12mo, pp. viii, 356. Map. B. 40024

[LENG] (J.) A Sermon Preached before the ... Society for the Propagation of the Gospel in Foreign Parts; ... 17th of February, 1726. ... By the Right Reverend ... John, Lord Bishop of Norwich. *London: Printed by J. Downing.* M.DCC.XXVII. 8vo, pp. 65, (3). BA., S. 40025

Contains reports from the American colonies, with the names of the society's missionaries.

LENG (W. C.) The American War: The Aims, Antecedents, and Principles of the Belligerents. A Lecture, delivered on the 10th December, 1862, in Castle Street Church. By William C. Leng. *Dundee.* MDCCCLXIII. 8vo, pp. 38. H. 40026

LENGLET DU FRESNOY (N.) Méthode pour Etudier la Géographie. ... Avec ... un Catalogue des Cartes Géographiques, des Relations, Voyages, & Descriptions les plus nécessaires pour la Géographie. Par Lenglet Dufresnoy. *Paris: Rollin fils & De Bure l'aîné.* M.DCC.XXXVI. 5 vols., 12mo, pp. xviii, clxviii, 338; x, 396; viii, 462; x, 504; xxviii, 367, (2), 236. Maps.

See Petzholdt, p. 789, *also* our Vol. V., No. 21149, and for imprint read: *Paris: Hocbereau.* 1716. 4 vols., 12mo.

LENGLET DU FRESNOY. Méthode pour Etudier l'Histoire, avec Un Catalogue des Principaux Historiens, & des Remarques sur la bonté de leurs Ouvrages, & sur le choix des meilleures Editions. Par Lenglet du Fresnoy. *Paris.* 1713. 2 vols., 12mo. + Augmenté par J. B. Mencke ... . *A Leipsic.* 1714. 2 vols., 12mo, pp. 580; 446, and Indexes. + *Paris.* 1729. 4 vols., 4to. Maps, &c. + Nouvelle Edition, Augmentée ... . *Paris: Pierre Gandouin.* M.DCC.XXXV. [Avec] Supplément de la Méthode pour Etudier l'Histoire. ... *Paris: Rollin fils & De Bure l'aîné.* M.DCC.XL. 6 vols., 4to, pp. xxii, (2), 504, Maps and Plates; (6), 498, Maps and Plates; (10), 336; (6), 452; xvi, 402; viii, 403-588, 279, (1). B. + Nouvelle Edition, Corrigée et Augmentée par Drouet. *Paris.* 1772. 15 vols., 12mo. 40028

A most valuable and comprehensive work, and the master-key to all the locked-up treasures of ancient and modern history, and to the more secret stores of the obscure memorialists of every nation. *See* Petzholdt, pp. 816, 817.

LENGLET DU FRESNOY. A New Method of Studying History ... . By Richard Rawlinson, LL.D. ... *London.* M.DCC.XXVIII.

2 vols., 8vo. + *London: Cha. Davis.* M.DCC.XXX. 2 vols., 8vo, pp. (2), 360, (8); (2), 550, (50). H. 40029

LENNARD (C. E. B.) Travels in British Columbia, with the Narrative of a Yacht Voyage round Vancouver's Island. By Capt. C. E. Barrett Lennard. *London: Hurst and Blackett.* 1862. 8vo, pp. xii, 307. Plate. BA. 40030

LENNEP COSTER (G. van). Aanteekeningen, gehouden gedurende mijn verblijf in de West-Indiën, in de Jaren 1837–1840. *Amsterdam: J. F. Schleijer.* 1842. 8vo, pp. vii, 359. 3 Plates.

A journal kept in the West Indies.

LENNEP COSTER. Herinneringen mijner Reizen naar onderscheidene Werelddeelen. *Amsterdam: J. F. Schleijer.* 1836. 2 vols., 8vo, pp. xii, 324; (2), viii, 320. 6 Plates. C. 40032

These memoirs of voyages to various parts of the world, contain the author's voyage to the West Indies.

LENNEP (J. van). Een Droom van Californië. Kluchtspel met Zang. *Amsterdam: P. Meijer Warnars.* 1849. 8vo.

This farce is a dream of California.

LENNEP. De voornaamste Geschiedenissen van Noord-Nederland, door Mr. Jacob van Lennep aan zijne Kinderen verhaald. *Amsterdam: P. Meijer Warnars.* 1848–53. 12 vols., 16mo. C.

LENNEP (J. H. van). Het Boek voor den Zeeman ... . *Haarlem: J. J. Weeveringh.* [1861–62.] 4 vols., 4to. Maps.

The seaman's book. Reproduces the original text, in modern orthography, of the voyages of Bontekoe and Raven to Greenland, and G. de Veer's relation of the three voyages to the North.

LENNOX (M.) Ante Bellum: Southern Life as it Was. By Mary Lennox. *Philadelphia: J. B. Lippincott & Co.* 1868. 12mo, pp. 322. B. 40036

LENNOXVILLE, *Canada East.* Geological Surveys ... of the Lennoxville Mining ... Company ... Canada East ... with ... Prospects of the Company. *Boston: Cutter, Tower & Co., Printers.* 1864. 8vo, pp. 22. Plan. H. 40037

LENOIR (A.) Antiquités Mexicaines. Relation des Trois Expéditions du Capitaine Dupaix, Ordonnés en 1805, 1806 et 1807, pour la Recherche des Antiquités du Pays, notamment celles de Mitla et de Palenque; Accompagnée des dessins de Castaneda, et d'une Carte du Pays exploré; suivie d'un parallèle de ces monuments avec ceux de l'Egypte, de l'Indostan et du reste de

l'ancien Monde, par M. Alexandre Lenoir; d'une dissertation sur l'origine de l'ancienne population des deux Amériques, et sur les Antiquités de ce Continent par M. D. B. Warden: avec un discours préliminaire, par M. Charles Farcy, et des notes explicatives et autres documents par MM. Baradère, de Saint-Priest et plusieurs voyageurs qui ont parcouru l'Amérique. *Paris: Imprimerie de Jules Didot l'âine.* 1833–34. 2 vols., folio, pp. xx, 20, 88, 56, 40, Recherches, 224, (4), Parallèle, 82, viii; Vol. II. (3), 166 Plates. S. 40038

Also on large paper. This was issued with the plates both plain and colored. It is almost an indispensable supplement to Humboldt's "Voyage dans l'Amérique," as it contains many interesting discoveries not in the latter work. *See also* [King (Edward)].

LENOIR DU PARE (*l'Abbé*). Nouveau recueil de plaidoyers français sur la ville de Lima. *Paris.* 1786. 12mo. 40039

Le Normand, Ode sur la conquête de l'Amérique, d'après le traité d'alliance avec les 13 États-Unis présentée au Roi, lors de son arrivée à Rouen le 25 Jùin 1786. [n. p. n. d.] 40040

[LENOX (James). Account of the] Letter of Columbus to Luis de Santangel, 1493. *Privately Printed.* [n. d.] 8vo, pp. 12.

Includes a facsimile of the Spanish letter of Columbus, published in 1493, from the only known copy in the Ambrosian Library, Milan. Mr. Lenox's collection of books relating to America is probably the most valuable library of its kind ever formed in this or any other country. By his generosity it has now become the property of the citizens of New York, and is now known as the Lenox Library.

LENOX ACADEMY, *Mass.* Catalogue of the Lenox Academy, January, 1828. [n. p. n. d.] 8vo. Continued. 40042

LEO (A.) The American Colony in Paris in 1867. From the French of Andre Leo. *Boston: Loring.* 1868. 8vo, pp. 12.

LEO AFRICANUS (J.) Historiale | Description de | l'Afrique, | tierce partie | du Monde; | Contenant ses Royaumes, Regions, Viles, Cités, | Chateaux et fortresses: les Ani- | maux, tant aquatiques, que terrestres; coutu- | mes, loix, religion, et façon de faire des habitãs | auec pourtraits de leurs habits, ensembles, autre | choses memorables, et singulieres nouueautes. | Escrite de nostre temps par Iean Leon, | African premierement en langue | Arabesque, puis en Toscane, et à | present mise en François, | Plus Cinq Nauigations au païs des Noirs, avec les discours sur icelles. | *A Lyon, par Iean Temporal.* 1556. 2 vols., folio, pp. (20), 495, Table, (22); (6), 160, Table, (8), Part III., (2), 282, Table, (14).

Includes the letters of Americus Vespucius; followed by a "summary" showing "how he was led astray from the correct path, and how he found it again by means of

astrology. How he discovered a country which began on the equinoctial line eight degrees from the Antarctic Pole, navigating along which he passed beyond the tropical line by seventeen degrees and a half." It is mostly a translation from Ramusio.

LEO. Historiale | Description | de l'Afriqve, Tier- | ce partie dv | Monde, | Contenant ses Royaumes, Regions, Viles, Citez, | Chateaus & forteresses: Iles, Fleuues, Ani- | maus, tant aquatiques, que terrestres: cou- | tumes, loix, religion & façon de faire des habitãs, | auec pourtraits de leurs habis: ensemble autre | choses memorables, & singulieres nouueautez: | Escrite de nôtre temps par Iean Leon, African, | premierement en langue Arabesque, puis en Tos- | cane, & à present mise en François. | *En Anvers.* | *Ches Iean Bellere.* | 1556. | 8vo, 16 p. l., 412 folioed leaves, Indice, etc., pp. 48. + [Another Edition.] *Paris.* 1830. 4 vols., 8vo.

Of the *Paris* reprint two hundred and fifty copies were printed, and nearly all distributed among the public libraries in France.

LEO. Ioannis Le- | onis Africani | de totivs Africae | descriptione li- | bri IX. Quibvs non solum Afri- | cæ regionem, insularum, & appidorem situs, lo- | corumque interualla accurate' complexus est, | sed Regum familias, bellorum causas & euentus | resq̃; in ea memorabilis, tam à seipso diligenti ob- | servatione indagatas, quam in veris Maurorum | Annalibus memoriæ traditas, copiose descripsit; | recens in Latinum linguam conuersi Io- | anne Floria- | no Interprete. Arabicè primum scripsit Author: deinde Italico sermo- | ne reddidit: Ioannes Floriannus | ex Italico Latinum fecit. His recens accedit | Hannonis Carthaginensium ducis Nauigatio, | qua Libycam oram vltra Herculis columnas lu- | strauit, Conrado Gesne- | ro interprete, cum | Scholijs. | *Tigvri per Andream Gesnervm F. Anno* M.D.LIX. | 8vo, pp. (28), 517, Hannonis Carthaginensi, 21. + *Lugduni Batavorum: Elzevir.* 1632. 8vo.

LEO. A Geographical Historie of Africa; Written in Arabicke and Italian by Iohn Leo, a More, borne in Granada, and brought vp in Barbarie. Wherein he hath at large described, not onely the Qualities, Situations, and true Distances of the Regions, Cities, Towns, Mountains, Rivers, and other places throughout all the Northe and Principall Partes of Africa, but also of the Descents and Families of their Kinges, the Causes and Euents of their Warres, with their Manners, Customes, Religions, and ciuile Gouernment, and many other memorable Matters: gathered partly out of his owne diligent Observations, and partly out of the ancient Records and Chronicles of the Arabians and Mores. Before which, out of the best ancient and moderne Writers, is prefixed, a generall Description of Africa; and also a

particular Treatise of all the maine Lands and Isles, vndescribed by Iohn Leo. ... Translated and collected by Iohn Pory, lately of Goneuill and Caius College in Cambridge. *Londini: Impensis Georgii Bishop.* 1600. Folio, pp. (8), 420. Map. 40047

LEOLIN, *pseudon.* Letter to Harrison Gray Otis on Resistance to the Laws of the United States. By Leolin. *Boston.* 1811. 8vo. C. 40048

LEOMINSTER, *Mass.* Annual Report of the School Committee of ... Leominster, for ... 1852–3. *Boston: Printed by Damrell & Moore.* 1853. 8vo, pp. 12. Continued. H. 40049

LEON PINELO (A. de). Autos, acuerdos y decretos de gobierno del real y supremo consejo de las Indias, juntolos et licenciado D Antonio de Leon Pinelo. *Madrid, Diaz de la Carrera.* 1658. Folio. 40050

LEON. Discurso sobre la importancia, y disposicion de leyes de las Indias. *Madrid.* 1623. Folio. 40051

Title from Ternaux, No. 460.

LEON. Epitome | de la | Biblioteca | Oriental i Occidental, Nautica | i Geografica. | ... | Por el Licenciado Antonio de Leon | Relator del Supremo i Real | Consejo de las Indias. | Con Priuilegio. | *En Madrid, Por Iuan Gonzalez.* | *Año de* M.DCXXIX. | 4to, Engraved Title, pp. (86), 186, Appendice, xii, Colophon, 1 l.

The author of this work, probably the first which contains a catalogue of books on America, afterwards took the surname of Pinelo. *See* Trübner's "Bibliographical Guide to American Literature," p. viii, *also* [Harrisse's] "Bib. Am. Vet." The following enlarged edition by Barcia is so clumsily thrown together that it is quite a relief to refer from it to this neat and well-arranged little manual.

LEON. Epitome de la Bibliotheca Oriental, y Occidental, Nautica, y Geografica, de Don Antonio de Leon Pinelo, del Consejo de Su Mag. en la Casa de la Contratacion de Sevilla, y Coronista maior de las Indias, Añadido, y enmendado nuevamente, en que se contienen los Escritores de las Indias Orientales, y Occidentales, y Reinos convecinos China, Tartaria, Japon, Persia, Armenia, Etiopia, y otros partes. ... *En Madrid, Por Francisco Martinez Abad.* MDCCXXXVII–VIII. 3 vols., folio, pp. (40), 561, (4), Catalogo, (94), (8); (2), 561–1192; (2), 1200–1729, Catalogo, 133. 40053

Notwithstanding the confusion and prolixity of this work, the notices it contains are very interesting, and their critical revision would be a useful and meritorious undertaking. Rich remarks that it is "The most complete general bibliography of geographical works, travels, missionary reports, etc. The second volume contains the works relating to

America, and its greatest value consists in the notices it gives of the Spanish manuscripts on the subjects, most of which are still existing in Spain." The author has had the bad taste, however, to translate all the titles into Spanish. *See also* Charlevoix, Vol. I., [Harrisse's] "Bib. Am. Vet.," *and* Trübner's "Bibliographical Guide to American Literature," p. ix.

LEON. Politica | de las Grandezas | y Govierno del Svpremo | y Real Consejo de | las Indias. | ... | Por el Licenciado Antonio de Leon. | [*Lima.* 1658?] 4to, Title, 20 folioed leaves. 40054

LEON. Relacion de las fiestas de la congregacion de Lima a la limpia concepcion de N. S. [*Lima.*] 1618. 4to. 40055

LEON. Relacion sobre la pacificacion y poblacion de las provincias del Manche, i Lacandon. *Madrid.* 1639. Folio.

LEON. Tratado de Confirmaciones Reales de Encomiendas, oficios i casos, en que se requieren para las Indias Occidentales. ... Por el Lic. Antonio de Leon. ... *Madrid, Juan Gonzalez.* 1630. 4to, Title engraved by I. de Courbes, 16 p. l., 173 and 17 leaves. 40057

This important work was compiled from original documents. "Relates principally to the new laws for the Indies, made in 1542, but neither this author, nor Herrera appear to have had any knowledge of their having been printed in 1543."—RICH'S *Catalogue*, No. 194.

LEON. [Printed Title:] Vida | del Ilvstr. i Reverend. | Don Toribio | Alfonso Mogrovejo | Arzobispo de Lima. | [Engraved Title:] Vida | del Ilvstrissimo | i Reverendissimo D. Toribio | Alfonso Mogrovejo. | Arcobispo de la Civdad | de los Reyes Lima | Cabeza de las Provincias del Piru. | ... | Por el Licenciado Antonio | de Leon Pinelo, Relator del Consejo Supre- | mo de las Indias, y del de la | Camara dellas. | [*Lima.*] 1653. 4to, Engraved Title, pp. (48), 421. Portrait of Toribius Alfonsus Mogrovejo.

LEON Y GAMA (A. de). Descripcion Histórica y Cronológica de las dos Piedras que con ocasion del nuevo Empedrado que se está formando en la Plaza Principal de México, se hallaron en ella el Año de 1799. Explícase el sistema de los Calendarios de los Indios, el método que tenian de dividir el tiempo, y la correccion que hacian de él para igualar el año civil, de que usaban, con el año solar trópico. Noticia muy necesaria para la perfecta inteligencia de la segunda piedra: á que se añaden otras curiosas é instructivas sobre la Mitología de los Mexicanos, sobre su Astronomía, y sobre los ritos y ceremonias que acostumbrahan en tiempo de su Gentilidad. Por Don Antonio de Leon y Gama.

México. En la Imprenta de Don Felipe de Zuñiga y Ontiveros Año de M.DCC.XCII. 4to, pp. (6), 116, (2). 3 Plates. C. 40059

An historical and chronological account of the carved stones discovered in 1790, upon removing the pavement on the great plaza in the city of Mexico. These two stones, one an idol, and the other the Aztec calendar, were buried by the Mexicans on the approach of the Spaniards in 1521, and remained within eighteen inches of the surface for two hundred and seventy years. The *Calendario* weighs about fifty tons and has sculptured upon it the symbols of their astronomical system, which had previously been found described in manuscripts. The other stone was a colossal idol. This work is accompanied by an essay upon the astronomical system of the ancient Mexicans, and to the student of Mexican archæology will be especially interesting. Prescott eulogizes the author, but Don José Antonio Alzate y Ramirez, in the "Gazeta de Literatura" of Mexico, of the 15th and 31st July, 1792, criticises this work rather severely, denying the conclusions drawn by Sr. Gama from the appearance of these curious antiquities.

LEON. Descripcion Histórica y Cronológica de las dos Piedras ... Por Don Antonio de Leon y Gama; dàla á luz, con notas, biografia de su autor y aumentada con la segunda parte que estaba inédita, y bajo la proteccion del Gobierno general de la Union: por Carlos Maria de Bustamente. Segunda edicion. *México, Al. Valdès.* 1832. Sm. 4to, pp. (2), viii, 114; Segunda parte, pp. 148, 5 Plans. 40060

The second part first appeared in this edition.

LEON. Descripcion orthographica universal del eclipse de sol del dia 24 de Junio de 1778. Por D. Antonio de Leon y Gama. *México, Felipe de Zuñiga.* 1778. 4to, pp. (12), 24. Map.

LEON. Disertacion Fisica sobre la Materia y Formacion de las Auroras Boreales, que con ocasion de la que aparecio en Mexico y otros Sugares de la Nueva España el dia 14 de Noviembre de 1789. Escribió D. Antonio de Leon y Gama. ... *Mexico: Por D. Felipe de Zuñiga y Ontiveros, ... año de* 1790. 4to, pp. (2), 37. 40062

LEON. Observaciones Critico-Apologeticas sobre la Respuesta Satisfactoria de Antonio de Leon y Gama. *Mexico.* 1783. 4to.

LEON. Respuesta satisfactoria a la Carta apologetica, que escribieron el Lic. D. Manuel Antonion Moreno, y el B. D Alejo Ramon Sanchez: y defensa contra la censura, que en ella se hace, de algunas proposiciones contenidas en la Instruccion sobre el remedio de las Lagartijas, que escribió D. Antonio de Leon y Gama. *Mexico.* 1783. 4to, pp. (8), 32. 40064

LEON. Saggio dell' Astronomia, Cronologia e Mitologia Degli Antichi Messicani, Opera Di D. Antonio Leon E [*sic*] Gama Tradotta dallo Spagnuolo ... [da P. G. Marquez]. *Roma, Presso il Salomoni.* 1804. 8vo, pp. (2), xiii, (1), 184. 2 folded Plates.

LEON (Antonio de), *General.* Contestacion al articulo del Cosmopolita del 16 de Enero ultimo, de D. Ignacio Guerra Manzanares, con ocasion de su fuga de esta Capital. *Belen de Oaxaca.* 1841. 4to, pp. 107. 40066

LEON. Esposicion que dirije al Congreso del Estado el General de Brigada Antonio de Leon, como depositario del Poder ejecutivo. *Oajaca.* 1834. 4to, pp. 34. 40067

LEON DE LARA. Sitio de S. Phelipe de Portovelo. [n. p. 1697.] Folio. 40068

LEON PINELO (Didacus de). Hypomnema apologeticvm pro regali Academia Limensi in Lipsianam periodvm. Accedvnt dissertativncvlæ gymnasticæ palæstricæ, canonico-legales, aut promiscuæ: partim ex temporaneæ, expolitæ, et vtiles; ceu res ipsa ostendet. *Limæ, Jvliani de los Santos & Saldaña.* 1648. 4to, 14 p. l., 155 and 19 leaves. Frontispiece. 40069

LEON PINELO (Diego de). Celebridad y Fiestas con que la Insigne y Nobilissima Ciudad de los Reyes ... . *En Lima.* 1670. 4to. 40070

LEON (E. de). La Vérité sur les États Confédérés d'Amérique. Par Edwin De Leon ... . *Paris: E. Dentu.* 1862. 8vo, pp. 32. Portrait. BA. 40071

Written with a strong Southern bias; the author makes Jefferson Davis a second Washington.

LEON (Francisco Ponce de). *See* Ponce de Leon (F.)

LEON (Francisco Ruiz de). *See* Ruiz de Leon (F.)

LEON (G. de). Compendio del Origen de la Esclarecida y Milagrosa Imagen ... . Sacado de la Historia, que compuso ... Antonio de la Colancha, de la Orden de N. P. S. Agustin, de la Provincia del Perù. Por ... Gabriel de Leon; ... *Madrid.* 1663. 16mo. H. 40072

LEON (J. A.) On Sugar Cultivation in Louisiana, Cuba, &c., and the British Possessions. *London.* 1848. 4 parts in 1 vol. 8vo.

LEON (J. A. de). Oracion ufnebre [*sic*] del ... D. Diego de Parada, Obispo de nuestra Señora de la Paz, y Arzobispo de la Iglesia Metropolitana de Lima. Predicada en sus exequias en esta Cathedral de los Reyes, el dia 11 de Mayo del año de 1779. Por el Doct. D. Joseph Antonio de Leon ... . *Lima: En la Imprenta de los Niños Huerfanos.* 1781. 4to, pp. (16), 87. 40074

LEON (J. R. de). Relacion de las provincias de Tipuane, Chunchos y Paititi, por Juan Recio de Leon. [n. p.] 1624. Folio. 40075

These three provinces are situated in Peru, and have almost always maintained their independence. The chief of the Chunchos Indians claims that he is a descendant of the Inca of Peru. *See* Ternaux, No. 470.

LEON (J. V. de). La Estirpe Vespasiana: Idea Alegorica de las Pinturas y Aparatos Festivos del Arco Triunfal para la entra publica de D. Matias de Galvez, Virrey de esta N. España erigió la Ciudad de Mexico el dia 8 de Febrero de 1784, por J. Velazquez de Leon. *Mexico.* 1784. 4to. 40076

LEON. Explicacion de los Adornos Simbolicos y Poeticas del Arco de Triunfo, que para la Entrada Publica y Solemne de Joachin de Monserrat, Virrey de esta Nueva España, erigió esta Ciudad de Mexico el dia 25 de Enero de 1761, por D. J. Velasquez de Leon. *Imprenta de la Bibliotheca Mexicana.* 1761. 4to.

LEON. Explicacion de los Adornos Simbolicos y Poeticas del Arco de Triunfo, que para la entrada publica y solemne de D. Ant. Maria de Bucareli y Ursua, Virrei de esta Nueva España, erigio esta Ciudad de Mexico el dia 31 de Octubre de 1771, por J. Velasquez de Leon. *Mexico.* 1771. 4to, pp. 22. 40078

LEON (L de). Proceso del P. M. Fray Luis de Leon, doctor teologo del Claustro y gremio de la Universidad de Salamanca. Ensayo histórico por el lic. Don Alejandro Arango y Escandor. *Mexico.* 1856. 8vo, pp. 117. Portrait. 40079

LEON (M. de). Camino del Cielo en lengua Mexicana, con todos los requisitos necessarios para conseguir este fin, cõ todo lo que vn Xp̃iano deue creer, saber, y obrar, desde el punto que tiene vso de rason, hasta que muere. Cõpuesto, por el P. F. Martin de Leõ, de la ordẽ de Predicadores. Dirigido al Excelentissimo Señor Don Fray Garcia Guerra de la ordẽ de nr̃o padre S. Domingo, Arçobispo de Mexico, y Virrey desta Nueua España. *En Mexico. En la Emprenta de Diego Lopez daualos. Y a costa de Diego Perez de los Rios. Año. De.* 1611. 4to, 12 p. l., 160 l., 6 l.

Sold by Puttick and Simpson, in 1868, for £13, 5s. This extremely scarce volume contains "Catechismo en Lengua Mexicano," "Symbola de la Fé de S. Athanasio," "Calendario Mexicano," "Confessario en Lengua Mexicano y Castellana," "Testamento Enforma," "Arte de Bien Morir," etc. It is not mentioned by Brockhaus, Brunet, Rich, Salva, Stevens, or any other bibliographer, except Ternaux, who probably never saw the work.

LEON. Manual breve y forma de administrar los Santos Sacramentos à los Yndios. Recopilado por el Padre fray Martin de Leon, de la Orden de los Predicadores. Y agora nueuamente corregido, y añadidas algunas cosas. Dirigido à nro M. R. P. Fr. Gaspar de Ledesma, Prior Prouincial desta Prouincia de Sanctiago de Predicadores. Por el Conuento de Nra. S. de la Piedad. *En Mexico, Por el Bachiller Ioan de Alcaçar, junto à la Inquisicion, Año de* 1617. 8vo, 55 leaves. + *En Mexico, en la imprenta de Francesco Robledo.* 1640. 8vo. 40081

LEON. Manual Breve, y forma de administrar los Santos Sacramẽtos à los Yndios. Por el Padre Fr. Martin de Leon, de la Orden de Predicadores. Y agora nuevamẽte sacado à luz, y añidido [*sic*] por el P. Lector Fr. Diego Cortezero, Cathedratico de lègua Mexicana en el Convento Real de N. Padre Santo Domingo desta Ciudad de Mexico. Con licencia: *Impresso en Mexico. Por Francisco Rodriguez Lupercio.* 1669. 8vo, 5 p. l., 85 l., Table, 1 l. 40082

Extremely rare. Not mentioned by Brunet or Rich.

LEON. Modo de enseñar la doctrina christiana a los Indios. 1604. 40083

Title from Ternaux, No. 273.

LEON. Primera Parte del Sermonario del tiempo de todo el año, duplicado, en lengua Mexicana. Compuesto por el R. P. F. Martin de Leon, de la Orden de Predicadores de N. P. sancto Domingo. Dirigido a nuestro muy R. P. Maestro fr. Hernando Baçan Cathedratico jubilado de la Vniuersidad Real, y Prouincial de esta Prouincia de Sanctiago de Mexico. *En Mexico, con licencia. En la Emprenta de la Viuda de Diego Lopez Daualos. Por C. Adriano Cesar. Año* M.DC.XIIII. 4to, 8 p. l., 330 l., 1 l. 40084

Rare. Not mentioned by Brunet, Rich, or Stevens.

LEON. Relacion de las Exequias que D. Juan de Mendoza, Virrey del Peru, hizo en la muerte de la reyna Margarita. *Lima.* 1612. 4to. 40085

[LEON (P. de).] Essai historique sur la colonie de Surinam, sa fondation, ses révolutions, ses progrès, depuis son origine jusqu'à nos jours, ainsi que les causes qui depuis quelques années ont arreté le cours de sa prospérité; avec la description & état actuel de la Colonie, de même que ses révenus annuels, les charges & impots qu'on y paye, comme aussi plusieurs autres objects civils et politiques; ainsi qu'un tableau des mœurs de ses habitans en

général. Avec l'histoire de la Nation Juive, Portugaise & Allemande y Etablie, leur privilèges immunités et franchises. Le tout redigé sur des pièces authentiques y jointes & mis en ordre par les Régens & Réprésentans de ladite Nation Juive Portugaise. *Paramaribo.* 1788. 2 parts, 8vo, pp. xxxviii, 192; 197.

[LEON.] Geschiedenis der Kolonie van Suriname. Behelzende derzelver opkomst, voortgang, burgerlyke en staatkundige gesteldheid, tegenwoordigen staat koophandel, en eene volledige en naawkeurige beschryving van het land, de zeden en gebruiken der ingezetenen. Geheel op nieuw samengesteld door een gezelschap van geleerde joodsche mannen aldaar. *Te Amsterdam: by Allart en van der Plaats.* MDCCXCI. 2 vols., 8vo, pp. 203; 160.

A history of the colony of Surinam, compiled by a society of Portuguese Jews, M. P. de Leon, S. H. de la Parre, D. C. Nassy, and S. W. Brandon, resident there. It was reproduced with a new title as:

[LEON.] Geschied- en handel-kundig Tafereel van de Bat. West-Indische Colonien. *Amsterdam.* 1802. 8vo. 40088

LEON (R. de). Panegyrico Augusto Castellano Latino, con Prosa de Lengua propria, Versos de las Estraña ... Por Rodriguez de Leon, Canonigo de la Catedral de Tlaxcala. *Mexico, por B. Calderon.* 1639. 4to. 40089

LEON, *Mexico.* Constituciones del seminario de la Madre Santissima de la Luz, establecido en la Ciudad de Leon. *Mexico.* 1847. 12mo, pp. 16. 40090

LEONARD (A.) A Prayer, composed For the Benefit of the Soldiery, in The American Army, ... By Abiel Leonard, A.M. Chaplain to General Putnam's Regiment ... . *Cambridge: S. & E. Hall.* 1775. 12mo, pp. 7. 40091

LEONARD. A Sermon ... in Clermont ... February 19, 1772. At the Ordination of the Rev'd. Mr. George Wheaton ... . By Abiel Leonard ... . *Portsmouth, New Hampshire: Printed by Daniel and Robert Fowle.* 1772. 8vo, pp. 23. H. 40092

Also: Thanksgiving Sermon at Woodstock [Conn.], Nov. 19, 1767. ... *Providence, R. I.* 1768. 4to.

LEONARD (A. S.) An Oration ... occasioned by the death of Robert Kelly, LL.D., ... Nov. 25th, 1856, by the Rev. Alexander S. Leonard, A.M. *New York: Sheldon, Blakeman & Co.* 1857. 8vo, pp. 31. 40093

LEONARD (B. G.) An Introductory Discourse ... before the Chillicothe Lyceum and Mechanics' Institute. On the 1st of

November, 1833. By Benjamin G. Leonard ... . *Chillicothe.* 1834. 8vo, pp. 61. BA. 40094

[LEONARD (Charles C.)] History of Pithole: by "Crocus." *Pithole City, Pa.: Morton, Longwell & Co.* 1867. 16mo, pp. 106.

LEONARD (C. H.) ... A Sermon ... at the Installation of Rev. N. M. Gaylord ... in Boston ... March 14, 1855. By C. H. Leonard. *Boston: Abel Tompkins.* 1855. 8vo, pp. 19. H.

[LEONARD (Daniel).] Massachusettensis. [*Boston.* 1775.] 8vo, pp. 118. 40097

These political essays, in the form of seventeen letters, first appeared anonymously in the Boston newspapers. They were then supposed to be from the pen of Jonathan Sewall, Attorney-General of the Province of Massachusetts. They took the side of the government against the colonies, and are written with great ingenuity. Tudor, in his "Life of Otis," Chap. XXIX., pp. 170, 203, characterizes them as "The most able papers on the Government side during the dispute." John Adams wrote, "On my return from Congress in November, 1774, I found the Massachusetts Gazette teeming with political speculations, and Massachusettensis shining like to the moon among the lesser stars. I instantly knew him to be my friend Sewall, and was told he excited great exultation among the Tories, and many gloomy apprehensions among the Whigs." Adams wrote a series of articles in reply under the signature of "Novanglus," *see our* Vol. I., Nos. 243, 244, and 263, *also* "Adams' Works," II. 405, IV. 410, "N. A. Rev.," IX. 376, and for September, 1819, p. 409, "M. Rev.," LIV. 410, *and* Rich's "Bib. Amer.," I. 232. Trumbull, in his "McFingall," paid his respects to the author without gloves, as one who

"Scrawled every moment he could spare
From cards, and barber, and the fair."

Eight of the seventeen letters were reprinted in New York as:

[LEONARD.] The Present Political State of the Province of Massachusetts-Bay in General, and the Town of Boston, in Particular, Exhibiting the Rise and Progress of the disordered State of that Country, in a Series of Letters, published weekly, at Boston, and now first collected. By a Native of New-England. *New-York: ... James Rivington.* MDCCLXXV. 8vo, pp. 86.

Closes thus: "In the Press, and shortly will be published a Continuation of this Work"—this continuation I have not seen. Rivington reissued this tract, naming "Massachusettensis" as the author, with a second title-page as below:

[LEONARD.] The Origin of the American Contest with Great-Britain, or, The present political State of the Massachusetts-Bay in general, and The Town of Boston in particular. Exhibiting the Rise and Progress of the disordered State of that Country, in a series of weekly Essays, published at Boston, under the Signature of Massachusettensis, A Native of New-England. *New-York: Printed by James Rivington.* 1775. 8vo, pp. (2), 86.

All the letters were reprinted in England with the following title:

[LEONARD.] Massachusettensis: Or a Series of Letters containing a faithful state of many important and striking facts, which laid the foundation of the present Troubles in the Province of the Massachusetts-Bay; interspersed with Animadversions and Reflections, originally Addressed to the People of that Province, and worthy the Consideration of the True Patriots of this Country. By a Person of Honor upon the Spot. ... *Boston printed: London reprinted for J. Matthews.* MDCCLXXVI. 8vo, pp. viii, 118. + The Second Edition. [*Ibid.*] BA. + The Third Edition. [*Ibid.*] + The Fourth Edition. [*Ibid.*] 40100

[LEONARD.] Strictures & Observations upon the three Executive Departments of the Government of the United States; Calculated to show the necessity of some change therein, that the public may derive that able and impartial execution of the powers delegated, upon which alone their happiness at home, and their respectability abroad, must materially depend. By Massachusettensis. *Printed in the United States of America.* MDCCXCII. 8vo, pp. 32. N., P., S. 40101

Part of the debate on adopting the Constitution.

LEONARD (D.) A Funeral Sermon ... at Holme's Harbour, Martha's Vineyard, Nov. 1st, 1795, occasioned by the Death of Mr. John Holmes. By David Leonard. *Boston.* 1795. 8vo, pp. 23. 40102

Also: Masonic Oration at Nantucket [Mass.], 1796. ... *New Bedford.* 1797. 8vo.

LEONARD (D. A.) An Oration occasioned by the Death of Gen. George Washington. Pronounced ... in the City of New York, on February, 22, 1800. ... By David A. Leonard, A.B. *New York.* 1800. 8vo, pp. 22. N. 40103

One of the scarcest of the eulogies on Washington. Also: Oration at Dighton [Mass.], July 4, 1803. ... *New Bedford.* 1803. 8vo.

LÉONARD (F.) Recueil de Traités de Paix, de Trève, de Neutralité, de Conféderation, d'Alliance et de Commerce, faits par les Rois de France avec tous les Princes et Potentats de l'Europe, et autres, depuis près de trois siècles: assemblés, mis en ordre et imprimés par Fréderic Léonard. *Paris.* 1693–1719. 8 vols., 4to. B. 40104

Includes the treaties relative to America. The last two volumes have no general title, and consist of twenty-nine treaties, etc., with separate title-pages dated from 1697 to 1719.

LEONARD (G.) Memorial of the Honorable George Leonard, ate of Boston, in New England, to Revive the Association of the

Loyalists of North America, and make that respectable body useful to the Public Service. [n. p. 177–.] Folio, pp. 6.

Leonard was a man of large fortune, and fitted out eleven ships of war, carrying three hundred and ninety-eight men, to defend various parts of New England against the attacks of the rebels. He mentions the various ships, stores, ports, etc., belonging to the rebels, which he destroyed.

LEONARD (G.) A Sermon ... at Windsor ... July 4, 1819. By Rev. George Leonard, A.M. ... *Windsor: Printed by Ide & Aldrich.* 1819. 8vo, pp. 21. BA. 40106

LEONARD. ... A Sermon ... Oct. 28, 1855 ... after the Death of his Daughter. By George Leonard ... . *Boston: Benjamin H. Greene.* 1855. 8vo, pp. 16. B. 40107

Also: Sermons on various Subjects. ... *Portland.* 1832. 12mo.

[LEONARD (Henry C.)] A Discourse ... in ... Orono, Me., at the Funeral of Mary E. Crane ... March 20, 1853 ... *Bangor.* 1853. 8vo, pp. 14. H. 40108

LEONARD (J. W.) A Masonic Register for 5855, containing a List of all Lodges, Chapters, Councils and Encampments, with the Membership of Each, in the State of New York. Compiled by Jno. W. Leonard, K.T. *New York: Jno. W. Leonard & Co.* 1855. 16mo, pp. (2), 366. H. 40109

LEONARD (Joseph). Catalogue of American Historical ... Works. Sold February, 1845. *Boston.* 1845. 8vo, pp. 49.

Also: Catalogue of ... Choice and Rare Books on America. Sold June, 1845. *Boston.* 1845. 8vo, pp. 50. Also other catalogues of Americana, many of which are distinguished by more than ordinary bibliographical accuracy.

LEONARD (J.) A Discourse ... 24 June, 1802, at Cazenova; Before the Masonic Lodge. By Joshua Leonard, A.M. *Utica.* 1802. 12mo, pp. 22. 40111

LEONARD (L. W.) A Discourse, delivered in Dublin, N. H., September 7, 1845. It being the Sabbath after the Twenty-Fifth Anniversary of his Ordination. By Levi W. Leonard ... *Keene: Printed by J. & J. W. Prentiss.* 1846. 8vo, pp. 28. B. 40112

LEONARD. Genealogy of the Family of William Smith of Peterborough, N. H. By Levi W. Leonard and Samuel Abbot Smith. *Keene: Printed by Horatio Kimball.* 1852. 8vo, pp. 24.

[LEONARD.] The History of Dublin, N. H., containing the Address by Charles Mason, and the Proceedings at the Centennial

Celebration, June 17, 1852; With a Register of Families. *Boston: Printed by John Wilson and Son.* 1855. 8vo, pp. vi, (2), 433. Map, 25 Portraits. H. 40114

LEONE (C.) Walk through the Fifth Avenue. By Carli Leone. *New York.* 1853. 12mo. 40115

LEONHART (R.) Nord und Süd im Krieg und Frieden oder Scenen aus der jüngsten Rebellion. *Pittsburgh, Pa.* [n. d.] 8vo, pp. 583. 40116

LEONIDAS, *pseudon.* A Reply to Lucius Junius Brutus' Examination of the President's Answer to the New-Haven Remonstrance: With an Appendix, containing the Number of Collectors, Naval Officers, Surveyors, ... District Attornies and Marshals in the United States, shewing how many incumbents are Republicans, and how many are Federalists. By Leonidas. *New York: Printed by Denniston and Cheetham.* 1801. 8vo, pp. 62, (3). C.

S. LEOPOLDO (*O Visconde* de). Annaes da Provincia de S.-Pedro. *Paris.* [n. d.] 8vo. 40118

LÉOTAUD (Antoine). Oiseaux de l'ile de la Trinidad (Antilles). Par A. Léotaud ... . *Port d'Espagne (Trinidad): Chronicle Publishing Office.* 1866. 8vo, pp. (4), xx, (2), 560, (2), viii, iv.

LEOYD (O.) Het | Gezigt | Van den | Panther. | In zes Hoofdstukken verdeeld, | Zo als het op den 28. van Wintermaand des Jaars 1653. in | den Morgenstond op het aanbreeken van den dag, ver- | toond wierdt aan | Owen Leoyd, | Die in den Jaare 1643 in Virginia woonde, en aldaar | zyn bezit en middelen verloor. | Zynde 't zelve in Engeland gedrukt in 't Jaar 1662. | Waar by nu gevoegd is zyne Brief aan John Rogers, | Prediker onder de Vyfde Monarchy-luyden: waar in | hy zyn gevoelen daar over te kennen geeft. | Nooit te vooren aldus gemeen gemaakt, maar nu ten | proeve aan een yder voorgesteld. | Uyt het Engelsch Vertaald. | *Gedrukt in 't Jaar* 1688. | 4to, pp. 18. 40120

Probably unique. The English original of this highly rare and curious tract is as yet undiscovered. It purports to be an account of a vision which appeared to Owen Lloyd, who was living in Virginia in 1643, and who had there lost his fortune. It concludes with an epistle to John Rogers, one of the Fifth-monarchy men, dated from the Flying Post, in White Friars, March 7, 1654.

LE PAGE (J.) The Island Minstrel. ... By John Le Page. *Charlottetown.* 1860. 12mo, pp. 274. 40121

LE PAGE DU PRATZ (*M.*) Histoire de la Louisiane, Contenant la Découverte de ce vaste Pays; sa Description géographique; un Voyage dans les Terres; l'Histoire Naturelle; les Mœurs, Coûtumes & Religion des Naturels, avec leurs Origines; deux Voyages dans le Nord du nouveau Mexique, dont un jusqu'à la Mer du Sud; ornée de deux Cartes & de 40 Planches en Taille douce. Par M. Le Page du Pratz. *A Paris, chez De Bure* ... M.DCC.LVIII. 3 vols., 12mo, pp. (4), xvj, 358, (1); (4), 441; (4), 451, (4). 2 Maps, 40 Plates. BA. 40122

Important as showing the French claims to the Southern territory now occupied by several states, but claimed also by the English under the name of "Carolana." The author resided in Louisiana fifteen years, and it is from his relation that most of the details of the life of the Natchez and other Mississippi tribes of Indians have been derived. Later historians have availed themselves of his materials. The plates are barbarous; indeeed, the "Monthly Review," XIX. 296, remarks, "they remind one of the cuts in the old 'Hortus Sanitatis.' The author appears to have been a very sensible and a very worthy man, but with very little talent as a writer. His stile is unequal and diffuse, and his work wants method." *See also* Boucher de la Richarderie's "Bib. des Voyages," Vol. VII., Faribault's Catalogue, p. 84, *and* Leclerc's Catalogue, No. 877.

LE PAGE DU PRATZ. The History of Louisiana, or of The Western Parts of Virginia and Carolina: Containing A Description of the Countries that lye on both Sides of the River Missisipi: [*sic*] With An Account of the Settlements, Inhabitants, Soil, Climate, and Products. Translated from the French, (lately published,) By M. Le Page Du Pratz; with Some Notes and Observations relating to our Colonies. ... *London: T. Becket and P. A. De Hondt.* MDCCLXIII. 2 vols., 12mo, pp. (4), l, vii, 368; (8), 272. 2 Maps. A., N. 40123

The long preface is the work of the English editor, who informs us that he "has left out many things that appeared to be trifling, and abridged some parts of it." It will also be perceived, on comparison of the titles, that he has even constructed one for the work to suit himself. *See* Field's "Essay," *and* "M. Rev.," XXIX. 444. This translation was reprinted in 1774, with the following title:

LE PAGE DU PRATZ. The History of Louisiana, or of the Western Parts of Virginia and Carolina: Containing a Description of the Countries that lie on both Sides of the River Missisippi: [*sic*] With an Account of the Settlements, Inhabitants, Soil, Climate, and Products. Translated from the French Of M. Le Page Du Pratz; With some Notes and Observations relating to our Colonies. A New Edition. *London: T. Becket.* M.DCC.LXXIV. 8vo, pp. (8), xxxvi, 387. 2 Maps. BA. 40124

Some copies have only pp. (2), xxxvi, 387. 2 Maps.

LE PAGE DU PRATZ. An Account of Louisiana, exhibiting a Compendious Sketch of its Political and Natural History and

Topography, with a Copious Appendix containing several Important Documents. *Newbern: Franklin & Garrow.* 1804. 18mo, pp. (4), 272, cxviii, (2). C. 40125

LE PAYS (M.) Demeslé de l'Esprit et du Jugement. *Paris.* 1688. 8vo. 40126

Contains the "Elogue du Tabac en Fumée," "Eloge du Tabac en Poudre," in prose and verse, and "à Monseigneur le Controlleur General en partant pour l'Amérique."

LEPELLETIER DE SAINT-REMY (R.) Les Colonies françaises depuis l'abolition de l'esclavage. Le travail, l'immigration ... la production, la propriété. Par M. Lepelletier de Saint-Remy ... . *Paris: P. Dupont.* 1858. 8vo, pp. 45. + Nouvelle édition. *Paris: Guillaumin et Cie.* 1859. 8vo, pp. v, 67. 40127

Reprinted from the "Revue des Deux Mondes," January, 1858. In the "Nouvelle édition" the name is spelled "Saint-Remi."

LEPELLETIER DE SAINT-REMY. Le Drawback du Sucre indigène et la détaxe du Sucre colonial. Par M. R. Lepelletier de Saint-Remy ... . *Paris: Guillaumin et Cie.* 1863. 8vo.

LEPELLETIER DE SAINT-REMY. Saint-Domingue. Étude et Solution Nouvelle de la Question Haïtienne. Par M. R. Lepelletier de Saint-Remy ... . *Paris: Arthus Bertrand.* 1846. 2 vols., 8vo, pp. xii, lxxxiii, 394; (4), 554. B., C. 40129

Also: Les Antilles françaises.—Quéstion monétaire.—Entrepôts réels.—Paquebots transatlantiques. ... *Paris: Guillaumin et Cie.* 1859. 8vo, pp. viii, 161. Plates.—Révision des constitutions coloniales. ... *Paris: P. Dupont.* 1862. 8vo.—Saint-Domingue et les nouveaux intérets maritimes de l'Espagne. ... *Paris: Guillaumin et Cie.* 1861. 8vo.

LE PERS (J.-B.) *See* Charlevoix (F. X. de).

[LE PICQUIER (——).] Observations sur la prise du navire Américain la Juliana; ... faite en mer par la corsaire l'Espérance ... [*Au Havre, de l'Imprimerie de Le Picquier.* 1797.] 4to, pp. 40.

LEPOUZÉ (C.) Poësies diverses, par Constant Lepouzé. *Nouvelle Orleans.* 1838. 8vo. 40131

LEPROHON (Rosanna Eleanor). Antoinette de Mirecourt; ... A Canadian Tale. *Montreal.* 1864. 8vo, pp. 369. 40132

This was translated into French by J. A. Genand, *Montreal,* 1865, 12mo, pp. 342.

LE RAY DE CHAUMONT (J.) *See* Chaumont (J. Le R. de).

LERCH (*Surgeon*). Unnersòutiksak ernisuksiortunnut kaládlit nunáen nêtunnut. Underretning for Jordemödre i Grönland.

Pellesimit Peter Kraghmit. *Kjobenhavnime: F. F. de Tengnagel.* 1829. 16mo, pp. (8), 63. c. 40133

This is in Danish and Esquimaux.

Lercher (L.) Ein neüwe zeitung ı wie des | Künigs auss Portugals Schiffleüt einen | grossen mann haben zu wegen bracht ı heisst Christian gross | India ı wie er sich vermähelt hat ı mit einer Yunckfrawen die | Christenheit Europa genannt ı würdt sein leib mit seinen gli- | dern im anfang schimpfflich beschriben ı aber zuletst Christen- | lich aussgelegt ı Auch wie die Yunckfraw die Christenheit | Europa jm werde kinder geberen ı vnd in einer | kurtzen zeit auff wachssen ı vnd jm helf- | fen kriegen wider den Türcken | vnd alle vngleübigen. | ... | Dises grossen mañs vnd seines gemahels bedesittung ı | würt Christenlich aussgelegt ı durch Laux Lerchern | von Riedlingen. | [n. p. Colophon:] *Getruckt vnd volendt auff das tausent fünff hun- | dert vnd sechs vnd viertzigst jar ı auff den | andern tag des Jenners.* | 4to, 7 l. 40134

A curious parody; "It strictly belongs, however, to a 'Bibliotheca Africana.'"—*Bibliotheca Americana Vetustissima, No.* 269. The only known copy in America belongs to Mr. S. L. M. Barlow.

Lerdo de Tejado (Fran). Exposicion sobre el juicio á que le sujetó, como encargado de la administracion de la aduana Maritima de Mazatlán ... . *Mexico.* 1849. 8vo. 40135

Lerdo (Ignacio Maria). Exposicion contra las observaciones del Pensador Mexicano. ... *Mexico.* 1826. 4to, pp. 110.

Lerdo de Texada (J.) Discurso en profesion de cuarto voto hecha p. J. M. Castaniga y Pedro Canton. ... *Mexico.* 1816. 4to, 18 l. 40137

Lerdo de Tejada (M. M.) Apuntes Historicos de la Heróica Ciudad de Vera-Cruz, precedidos de una Noticia de los descubrimientos hechos en las Islas y en el Continente Americano, y de las Providencias dictadas por los Reyes de España para el Gobierno de sus Nuevas Posesiones, desde el primer Viage de Don Cristobal Colon, hasta que se emprendió la Conquista de Mexico. ... *Mexico: Ign. Cumplido.* 1850–58. 3 vols., 8vo. Map and Plates. 40138

Lerdo de Tejada. Comercio esterior de México, desde la Conquista hasta hoy [1519–1853], por Miguel Lerda de Tejada. *México: R. Rafael.* 1853. 4to, pp. 63, 111 l. 2 Tables. c.

Lerdo de Tejada. Memoria presentada al Exmo. Sr. Presidente Sustituto de la Republica, por el C. Miguel Lerdo de

Tejado dando cuenta de la marcha que han seguido los Negocios de la Hacienda Publica, en el Tiempo que turo a su cargo la Secretaria de este Ramo. *Mexico: [Imprenta de V. G. Torres.]* 1857. Sm. folio, pp. 733. 40140

Lerio *or* Lerius (J. de). *See* Lery (J. de).

Le Rouge (*le Sieur*). Atlas Ameriquain Septentrional Contenant les Details des Differentes Provinces, de ce Vaste Continent. ... *A Paris: Chez le Rouge* ... 1778. Folio. 31 Maps.

Le Rouge. Introduction à la Géographie. ... *Paris.* 1748. Sm. 4to, pp. 36. 91 Maps. 40142

Le Rouge. Recueil des Plans de l'Amérique Septentrionale. ... *Paris.* 1755. Folio. 15 Plates. 40143

Lerow (G. L.) The Politician's Manual, containing the Declaration of ... Independence, the Constitution of the United States and of New York; ... together with ... Tables, Political and Statistical. By Geo. L. Lerow, A.M. Second Edition. *Poughkeepsie: William Wilson.* 1840. 16mo, pp. 175, (4). B.

Le Roy (P. L.) Relation des Aventures arrivées à quatre Matelots Russes, jettés par une tempête près de l'Isle deserte d'Ost-Spitzbergen sur laquelle ils ont passé six ans & trois mois. [n. p.] MDCCLXVI. 12mo, pp. 70. 40145

This shipwreck occurred in the Arctic Sea, near Spitzbergen, in 1750. The following is a Dutch version:

Le Roy. Kort, nauwkeurig en echt relaas van vier Russische Zeelieden, welke op het onbewoond Eiland Oost-Spitzbergen, 6 jaren ... hebben doorgebragt. Uit het Fransch vertaald. *Amsterdam.* 1768. Sm. 8vo. 40146

For an English version *see* Stæhlin (J. von), *and* Pinkerton.

Leroy, *N. Y.* Inaugural Services; on ... inducting the first president of the Ingham Collegiate Institute of Leroy, New York; ... including Inauguration and ... Inaugural Address of the President, Reverend Samuel Hanson Cox ... June 25, 1856. ... *New York: John F. Trow, Printer.* 1856. 8vo, pp. 71. B.

Lery (J. de). Histoire | d'vn Voyage | fait en la terre | dv Bresil, avtre- | ment dite Ame- | rique. | Contenant la nauigation, & choses remar- | quables, veuës sur mer par l'aucteur: Le compor | tement de Villegagnon, en ce païs là. Les meurs | & façons de viure estranges des Sauuages A- | meriquains: auec vn colloque de leur langage. | Ensemble la description de plusieurs Animaux, |

Arbres, Herbes, & autres choses singulieres, | & du tout inconues p r deça, dont ont verra les | sommaires des chapitres au comm ncement du | liure. | Non encores mis en lumiere, pour les causes | contenues en la preface. | Le tout recueilli sur les lieux par Iean de | Lery natif de la Margelle, terre | de sainct Sene au Duché de | Burgongne. | Seigneur, ie te celebreray entre les peu- | ples, & te diray Pseaumes entre les na- | tions. Pseav. CVIII. *A la Rochelle, Pour Antoine Chuppin.* M.D.LXXVIII. Sm. 8vo, pp. (48), 424, (13). B., BA., H. 40148

This first edition is very rare, especially when bearing the imprint *La Rochelle.* Some copies of this edition have no place named on the title-page. Ternaux cites an edition printed at *Rouen*, in 1578, perhaps an error, *Rochelle* being meant.

Lery. Histoire | d'vn Voyage | faict en la terre dv | Bresil, avtrement | dite Amerique. | Contenant la navigation, | & choses remarquables, veuës sur mer par l'aucteur: Le com- | portement de Villegagnon en ce pays- | la. Les mœurs & façons | de viure estranges des Sauuages Ameriquains: auec vn collo- | que de leur langage. Ensemble la description de plusieurs A- | nimaux, Arbres, Herbes, & autres choses singulieres, & du | tout incõnues par deçà: dont on verra les sommaires des cha- | pitres au commencement du liure. | Reveve, corrigee, et bien | augmentee en ceste seconde Edition, tant de fi- | gures, qu'autres choses notables sur le | suiet de l'auteur. Le tout recueilli sur les lieux par Iean de | Lery, natif de la Margelle, terre | de sainct Sene, au Duché de | Bourgogne. | *A Geneve. Pour Antoine Chuppin.* M. D. LXXX. Sm. 8vo, pp. (44), 382, (11). 40149

There are copies of this edition, [n. p.:] *Antoine Chuppin.* M. D. LXXX. 8vo, pp. (44), 382, (13).

Lery. Histoire d'vn Voyage faict en la terre dv Bresil, avtrement dite Amerique. ... Les mœurs & façons de viure estranges des Sauuages Brasiliens; auec vn colloque de leur langage. ... Avec les figures reueue, corrigée & bien augmentée de discours notables, en ceste troisième édition. Le tout recueilli sur les lieux par Iean de Lery ... . *Geneve. Pour Antoine Chuppin.* MDLXXXV. Sm. 8vo, pp. (67), 427, (15). Map. 40150

There are copies of this edition without the place of publication on the title, and Ternaux, No. 163, cites an edition, *La Rochelle*, 1585.

Lery. Histoire d'vn Voyage fait en la terre dv Bresil, autrement dite Amerique. ... Les mœurs & façons de viure estranges des Sauuages Ameriquains ... . Troisieme edition. ... par Iean de Lery ... . [*Geneve*] *Pour les Heritiers d'Eustache Vignon.* M. D.-XCIIII. Sm. 8vo, pp. (44), 382, (12). + [*Ibid.*] 1599. Sm. 8vo.

Lery. Histoire d'vn Voyage fait en la Terre dv Bresil, dite Amerique. ... Qvatrieme edition, ... Le tout recueilli sur les lieux, par Iean de Lery ... [*Geneve*] *Povr les Heritiers d'Evstache Vignon.* 1600. Sm. 8vo. + *Paris.* 1600. Sm. 8vo. + [*Geneve*] *Povr les Heritiers d'Evstache Vignon.* 1604. Sm. 8vo. + Cinqvieme edition, Dediee à la ... Princesse d'Orange ... . *Geneve, Povr Iean Vignon.* M. DC. XI. 8vo, pp. (80), 489, (15). H. + *Geneva.* 1642. Sm. 8vo. 40152

The editions, *Geneve*, 1599 and 1642, are cited here on the authority of Mr. J. R. Bartlett.

Lery. Historia | Navigationis | in Brasiliam, | quæ et America | dicitvr. | Qva describitvr avtoris | nauigatio, quæque in mari vidit memoriæ pro- | denda: Villagagnonis in America gesta: Brasi- | liensium victus & mores, à nostris admodum a- | lieni, cum eorum linguæ dialogo: animalia etiam, | arbores, atque herbæ, reliquáque singularia & no- | bis penitùs incognita. | A Ioanne Lerio Bvrgvndo | Gallicè scripta. Nunc verò primum Latinitate | donata, & variis figuris illustrata. | [*Genevæ*] *Excvdebat* | *Evstathivs Vignon.* | *Anno* CIↃ IↃ LXXXVI. | 8vo, pp. (62), 341, (17). 3 Plates. H. 40153

Brunet says there is another Latin translation under the title "De Sacro-Cæsaris quod Sancerrum vocant obsidione, fame, ditione historia," *Heidelbergae*, 1576, 8vo. The folded plate, page 170, represents the battle of the Tououpinambaults with the Margaiats. The author was a Protestant minister who went out to Brazil to establish a colony of Huguenots, under the protection of Admiral Coligny; but, the scheme not succeeding, he returned to France and published the work. This Latin version is, in reality, more valuable than the original, as it contains passages that were suppressed in the French. Among other things, the author gives musical notes to show the intonation of the Caraibs, etc., a fact totally unknown to Fétis. Even the preface is most interesting, as in it is to be found the letter written to Calvin by Villegagnon, so celebrated for deceiving the English squadron, by unexpectedly circumnavigating Scotland and conveying from its west coast Mary, Queen of Scotland, safely into Brittany. In chapter XX. is a dialogue in Brazilian and Latin. The entire work bears internal evidence of truth, and such only as an eye-witness of the events could have composed. One of its objects was to introduce the Protestant faith into South America, especially among the Aborigines. Brunet remarks, "Edition recherchée plus rare que l'original français." Another version also forms pp. 137–296 of Bry's "Voyages," Part III. *See also* Benzoni (H.)

Lery. Historia | Navigationis | in Brasiliam | quæ et America | dicitvr. | Qva describitvr avthoris | nauigatio, quæque in mari vidit memoriæ prodenda: Villa- | gagnonis in America gesta: Brasiliensium victus & mores, à | nostris admodum alieni, cum eorum linguæ dialogo: ani- | malia etiam, arbores, atque herbæ, reliquáque singularia & | nobis penitus incognita. | A Joanne Lerio Bvrgundo | Gallicè scripta. Nunc verò primùm Latinitate | donata, & varijs figuris illustrata. | Secvnda Editio. | *Genevæ.* | *Apud hæredes Eustathij Vignon.* | CIↃ IↃ XCIIII. | 8vo, pp. (58), 340, (16). Folded Plate.

Reprint of the preceding edition with some slight alterations.

Lery. Historie van een Reyse ghe- | daen inden Lande van Bresillien, andersins ghenoemt | America. Inhoudende de Schipvaer ende gedenck-weerdichste dingen by den | Autheur op-ter Zee gesien. Hoe hem Villegagnon in den zelven Lan- | de heeft ged agen. Het wesen ende die wonderlicke ma- | niere van leven der Wilde Americanen. | Met een Vocabulaer ofte t' zamensprekinghe in haer- | lieder Tale: Mitsgaders de beschryvinghe van veelderley Ghedierten, Boomen, | Cruyden, ende andere by-sonderste dinghen van dien Lande, her- | waerts over heel vreemt ende onbekent. | Alles beschreven door Ian de Lery, Bourgoignon, die inden | zelven Lande ghewoont ende verkeert heeft. Nu overgeset wt het Franchoys | te Geneve ghedruckt. Ende verchiert met verscheyden schoone | Figueren, ghemaeckt nae het leven. | ... *t'Amstelredam By Cornelis Claesz. opt Water.* 1597. | 4to, 111 l.

"This is, without question, the scarcest of all editions of Lery. It is the only Dutch translation, and so rare, even in Holland, that I have only met with two copies and never heard of another nor found it cited; it has remained unknown to Brunet, Rich, Trömel, Stevens," etc.—Muller. The plates are copied from those of the French original. Chapter XX., page 20, contains the dialogues in Brazilian and Dutch. I have met with not less than two foreign catalogues which quote a Dutch translation, *Amsterdam: Cornelis Claesz.* 1596. 4to. Another Dutch version is included in Aa's "Collection," in folio and 8vo. *See* Tiele, p. 291.

Lery. Des Herrn Johann von Lery Reise in Brasilien. Nach der von dem Herrn Verfasser selbst veranstalteten verbesserten und vermehrten lateinischen Ausgabe übersetzt. Mit Anmerkungen und Erläuterungen. *Münster, im Verlag der Platvoetischen Buchhandlung.* 1794. 8vo, pp. (8), 415, (2). c. 40156

The value of this German translation is considerably enhanced by many historical notes and bibliographical references. *See* Bartlett's Catalogue of J. C. Brown's Library, Boucher de la Richarderie, IV. 27, Brunet's "Manuel," Camus' "Memoirs," p. 61, Demarsy, p. 288, Leclerc, No. 282, Purchas, IV. 1325, Rich's Catalogue, Nos. 89, 178, Tiele, No. 275, *and* Trömel, No. 39.

Le Sage [Alain René]. Les avantures de M. Robert Chevalier, dit de Beauchêne, capitaine de filibustiers dans la Nouvelle-France, rédigées par Monsieur Le Sage. *Amsterdam, aux depens de la Compagnie.* 1733. 2 vols., 12mo, pp. (8), 199; (6), 187. + [*Ibid.*] 1793. 40157

For other editions *see* Beauchêne, Vol. I., No. 4163.

Le Sage. The Adventures of Robert Chevalier, call'd De Beauchene, Captain of a Privateer in New-France. By Monsieur Le Sage ... . *London: T. Gardner.* M,DCC,XLV. 2 vols., 12mo, pp. (8), 307; (8), 287. 40158

Contains an account of his residence among the Indians of North America, and his being sold as a slave in New England, and is said by the author to be a veritable narra-

tive. The plot of the French play "Les Mariages de Canada," first produced in 1734, is taken from M. de Mouneville's story in "Mémoires de Beauchêne."

Le Sage. Le Bachelier de Salamanque ... . *Paris: G. Havard.* 1857. 4to, pp. 71. 40159

Le Sage. The Bachelor of Salamanca. Translated ... . By James Townsend. *London.* 1828. 2 vols., 12mo. + *Philadelphia: Thomas W. Hartley.* 1868. 2 vols., 12mo. 40160

"It is evident that the second volume was written by some person conversant with Mexico under the vice-regal government. His statements bear the authentic ring of genuine revelations. The romance is entitled to respect as a delineation of manners and habits of that distant period in that distant locality."—*The Nation*, Nov. 5, 1868.

Le Sage (A.) Historisch-Genealogisch-Geographischer Atlas, aus dem Französischen ins Deutsche übertragen ... von Al. v. Dusch und Eiselein ... . *Carlsruhe: Velten.* 1826–27. Folio. 35 Plates. 40161

This atlas contains chronological tables recording the history of the various regions of the world. For other editions *see* Las Cases (E. D. M. J. de), Nos. 39124–25.

Le Saint (L.) Guerre du Mexique 1861–1867. Par L. Le Saint. *Lille: J. Lefort.* 1867. 8vo, pp. 224. Engravings.

Lescallier (Daniel). Exposé des Moyens de mettre en valeur et d'administrer La Guiane, Par D. Lascallier ... . *Paris: Buisson.* 1791. 8vo, pp. xxiv, 216. 2 Maps. + Nouvelle édition. *Paris: Chez Du Pont. An* VI [1798]. 8vo, pp. xxiv, 237. Map. H. 40163

Lescallier. Fragment sur la Géologie de la Guadeloupe ... Par M. Lescallier ... . [*Paris.* 1808.] 4to, pp. 15. Map. B.

Lescallier. Notions sur la culture des Terres Basses dans la Guiane. Et sur la cessation de l'Esclavage dans ces Contrées; Par le Citoyen Lescallier. [*Paris.* 1798.] 8vo, pp. 106. H.

See also Larreategui (J. D.), No. 39092.

Lescarbot (M.) Adiev à la France par Marc Lescarbot. *La Rochelle.* 1606. 40166

[Lescarbot]. La | Conversion | des Savvages | qvi ont esté ba- | tizés en la Novvelle | France, cette année 1610. | Avec vn bref recit | du voyage du Sieur de | Povtrincovrt. | *A Paris,* | *chez Jean Millot, tenant son boutique sur les degrez de la grand'salle du Palais.* | [n. d.] Avec Priuilege du Roy. | Sm. 8vo, pp. (4), 44, (2). 40167

Probably the rarest of Lescarbot's works.

[Lescarbot.] La Defaite | des Savvages Armov- | chiqvois par le Sagamos | Membertou & ses alliez sauuages, en | la Nouvelle France, au mois de Juillet | dernier, 1607. | Où se peuvent recognoistre les ruses de guerre | desdits Sauvages, leurs actes funebres, | les noms de plusieurs d'entre eux, | & la maniere de guerir | leurs blessez: | *A Paris,* | *chez Jeremie Perier, tenant sa boutique* | *sur les petits degrez de la grand'Salle du Palais.* | [n. d.] Avec Permission. | Sm. 8vo, Title, 12 l. 40168

Lescarbot. Histoire | de la Novvelle | France | Contenant les navigations, découvertes, & habi- | tations faites par les François ès Indes Occiden- | tales & Nouvelle-France souz l'avoeu & autho- | rité de noz Rois Tres-Chrétiens, & les diverses | fortunes d'iceux en l'execution de ces choses, | depuis cent ans jusques à hui. | En quoy est comprise l'Histoire Morale, Naturele, & Geo- | graphique de ladite province: Avec les Tables & | Figures d'icelle. | Par Marc Lescarbot Advocat en Parlement, | Témoin oculaire d'vne partie des choses ici recitées. | ... | *A Paris* | *chez Iean Milot, tenant sa boutique sur les degrez* | *de la grand'salle du Palais.* | M.DC.IX. | Avec Privilege dv Roy. | Sm. 8vo, pp. (48), 888. 3 Maps.

Followed by "Les Muses," described *infra.* "The first edition of a very important work in regard to the history of Canada, and the northern parts of America."—Rich. Charlevoix characterizes the author as "a man of sense and learning, but a little addicted to the marvellous;" but relieves the author of the suspicion conveyed in this remark by high praise of his care in relating the discoveries of the French in Canada. *See* [Harrisse's] "Notes," Nos. 16, 23, 25 and 31. Bolton Corney's copy sold in 1872 for £27.

Lescarbot. Histoire | de la Novvelle- | France | Contenant les navigations, découvertes et habi- | tations faites par les François és Indes Occiden- | tales et Nouvelle-France souz l'avœu et autho- | rité de noz Roys Très-Chrétiens, et les diverses | fortunes d'iceux en l'execution de ces choses, | depuis cent ans jusques à hui. | En quoy est comprise l'Histoire Morale, Naturele et Geo- | graphique de ladite province; avec les Tables | et Figures d'icelles. | Par Marc Lescarbot, Advocat en Parlement, | Temoin oculaire d'vne partie des choses ici recitées. | ... | *A Paris* | *Chez Iean Millot, devant St. Barthelemi aux trois* | *Couronnes: Et en sa boutique sur les degrez de la* | *grand'Salle du Palais.* | M.DC.XI. | Avec privilege. | Sm. 8vo, pp. (20), 877, (28). 3 or 4 Maps. 40170

In some copies of this and the following edition all the forty-eight unnumbered pages precede the text. We are unable to determine positively as to the number of maps. The author refers to three only in the text, but copies have been found with four maps, the last being that of Port Royal.

Lescarbot. Histoire | de la Novvelle- | France | Contenant les navigations, decouvertes et habi- | tations faites par les François és Indes Occiden- | tales & Nouvelle-France souz l'avœu &

autho- | rité de noz Roys Tres-Chrétiens, et les diverses | fortunes d'iceux en l'execution de ces choses, | depuis cent ans jusques à hui. | En quoy est comprise l'Histoire Morale, Naturele & Geo- | graphique de ladite province: avec les Tables | & Figures d'icelle. | Par Marc Lescarbot, Advocat en Parlement. | Témoin oculaire d'vne partie ces choses ici recitées. | ... | Seconde Edition, reveuë, corrigée, & augmentée par l'Autheur. | *A Paris* | *Chez Iean Millot, devant S. Barthelemi aux trois* | *Coronnes: Et en sa boutique sur les degrez de la grand'salle du Palais.* | M.DC.XII. | Avec privilege du Roy. | Sm. 8vo, pp. (20), 877, (28). 3 or 4 Maps. 40171

This edition differs from the former only in the matter of the errata, which in this issue is corrected. As to the number of maps, *see our* note to No. 40170. Leclerc's Catalogue, No. 887, cites "La troisième édition est de 1617, on croit cependant que sauf le titre, la nôtre est la même." We have never met with a copy with this date and infer that it is the second edition with a new title-page only. The following is a reprint:

Lescarbot. Histoire de la Nouvelle-France par Marc Lescarbot suivie des Muses de la Nouvelle-France. Nouvelle Édition publiée par Edwin Tross avec quatre cartes géographiques. *Paris: Librairie Tross.* 1866. 3 vols., 8vo, pp. (12), xviii, (2), 287; (6), 291–586; (6), 591–851, (28), 83, (1). 4 Maps. B., BA. 40172

Of this elegant reprint some copies are on "papier de Hollande." It is difficult to understand why the publisher should have reproduced this second edition which is a mere reprint of the first. A reprint of the first would have been quite natural in a bibliographical sense; while a reprint of the third would have given us the author's latest words. Mr. Tross' sketch of the author's life is very unsatisfactory, and his bibliography of Lescarbot's works is unworthy of so well-informed a man as Mr. Tross was.

Lescarbot. Histoire | de la Novvelle- | France. | Contenant les navigations, découvertes, & ha- | bitations faites par les François és Indes Occi- | dentales & Nouvelle-France, par commission | de nos Roys Tres-Chrétiens, & les diverses | fortunes d'iceux en l'execution de ces choses | depuis cent ans jusques à hui. | En quoy est comprise l'histoire Morale, Naturelle, & | Geographique des provinces cy décrites: avec | les Tables & Figures necessaires. | Par Marc Lescarbot Advocat en Parlement | Témoin oculaire d'vne partie des choses ici recitées. | *A Paris,* | *Chez Adrian Perier, ruë saint* | *Iacques, au Compas d'or.* | M.DC.XVIII. | Sm. 8vo, pp. (55), 970, Errata, 1 l. 4 Maps. 40173

This edition differs from all the preceding; the arrangement is altered, and there are many additions; it may, therefore, be considered the best. All of these editions are usually followed by "Les Muses de la Nouvelle France," described below:

[Lescarbot.] Les Muses | de la Novvelle | France. | A Monseigneur | le Chancellier. | ... | *A Paris* | *Chez Iean Millot, sur le.*

degrez de | la grand'salle du Palais. | M.DC.IX. | Avec privilege du Roy. | Sm. 8vo, pp. (6), 66. + Les Mvses | ... | *A Paris | Chez Iean Millot, devant S. Barthelemy, aux trois | Coronnes: Et en sa boutique sur les degrez de la | grand'salle du Palais.* | M.DC.XII. | Avec privilege dv Roy. | Sm. 8vo, pp. (4), 77. + Muses | ... | *A Paris | Chez Adrian Perier, ruë saint | Iacques, au Compas d'or.* | M.DC.XVIII. | Sm. 8vo, pp. 76. 40174

This is included in Mr. Tross' reprint of the "Histoire," and forty copies were issued separately; also six copies on Whatman's drawing paper. T. W. Field remarks, in language peculiar to himself, that this is sometimes found "unnited to the 'Histoire,'" on which we remark that we have never met with a copy of the "Histoire," in the original binding, in which it was not included.

[Lescarbot.] Nova Francia: | Or the | Description | of that part of | New France, | which is one continent with | Virginia. | Described in the three late Voyages and Plantation made by | Monsieur de Monts, Monsieur du Pont-Graué, and | Monsieur de Poutrincourt, into the countries | called by the Frenchmen La Cadie, | lying to the Southwest of | Cape Breton. | Together with an excellent seuerall Treatie of all the commodities | of the said countries, and maners of the naturall | inhabitants of the same. | Translated out of French into English by | P. E[rondelle]. | *Londini, | impensis Georgii Bishop.* | 1609. | 4to, pp. (12), 307. Map. 40175

This is a translation of the fourth and sixth books only. The author states in his preface that "The whole volume of the navigations of the French nation into the West Indies (comprised in three bookes) was brought to mee, to be translated by M. Richard Hakluyt, ... and by him this part was selected from the whole work, to the end, that comparing the goodnesse of the lands with that of Virginia," etc. "Which translation is but a part of a greater volume." The following is the same work with a new title-page:

[Lescarbot.] Nova Francia | Or the | Description | of that part of | Nevv France, | which is one continent with | Virginia. | Described in the three late Voyages and Plantation | made by Monsieur de Monts, Monsieur du Pont-Graué, and | Monsieur de Poutrincourt, into the countries called | by the French-men La Cadie, ly- | ing to the Southwest of | Cape Breton. | Together with an excellent seuerall Treatie of all the commodities | of the said countries, and maners of the naturall | inhabitants of the same. | Translated out of French into English by | P. E[rondelle]. | *London, Printed for Andrew Hebb, and are to be sold at the signe | of the Bell in Paul's Church-yard.* | [n. d.] 4to, pp. (12), 307. Map. 40176

[Lescarbot.] Noua Francia. | Gründliche History | Von Erfundung | der grossen Landschafft Noua | Francia, oder New

Franckreich ge- | nannt, auch von Sitten vnd Beschaffenheit | derselben wilden Völcker. | Ausz einem zu Parisz gedruck- | ten Französischen Buch summarischer | weisz ins Teutsch gebracht. | Anno M.DC.XIII. *Gedruckt zu Augspurg bey Chryso- | stomo Dabertzhofer.* 4to, 4 p. l., 86 l. c. 40177

This German version is a very brief summary of the "Histoire de la Nouvelle France," compiled apparently by Dabertzhofer.

Lescarbot. Relation | derniere | de ce qvi s'est | passé av voyage | du Sievr de Povtrincovrt | en la Nouuelle-France | depuis 20 mois ença. | Par Marc Lescarbot Aduocat | en Parlement. | *A Paris | chez Iean Millot, deuant | S. Barthelemy aux trois Couronnes.* | M.DC.XII. | Avec privilege dv Roy. | 18mo, pp. 39. 40178

A piece of very great rarity. Reprinted in the "Archives curieuses de l'Histoire de France," Vol. xv., First Series.

Lescarbot. Le tableau de la Suisse et autres alliez de la France és hautes Allemagnes. ... *Paris, A. Periere.* 1618. 4to.

"Ces poësies ne contiennent pas un seul mot concernant l'Amérique; nous plaçons le volume dans cette série à cause du nomme de l'auteur."—Tross.

Leschenault de la Tour (*M.*) Voyage à Surinam, par M. Leschenault de la Tour, en mission dans les Colonies de l'Ouest, à la fin de 1823 et au commencement de 1824. *Cayenne.* 1824. 4to. 40180

Les Citoyens François, habitans des États-Unis de l'Amérique Septentrionale, à leur patrie à ses Réprésentans. [n. p. 1791?] 8vo, pp. 8. 40181

Lesdernier (E. P.) Voices of Life: By Mrs. Emily P. Lesdernier. Published for the Author. *New York.* 1853. 12mo, pp. 38. Plate. 40182

Lesguillon (J.) Washington. Drame historique, par J. Lesguillon. *Paris: Librairie dramatique.* 1866. 12mo, pp. (6), 168. c. 40183

Lesieur (S.) Journal d'Observations faite pendant le Voyage de M. Santiago Lesieur, à New York, en France, et en Italie, dans les années 1838, 1839, et 1840. *Paris.* 1840. 8vo, pp. 24.

Lesley (J. P.) An Address to the Suffolk North Association of Congregational Ministers. By J. P. Lesley ... . With Sermons ... . *Boston: Wm. Crosby and H. P. Nichols.* 1849. 12mo, pp. 130. BA. 40185

Lesley (Joseph Peter). Report of a Reconnoissance made in April, 1865, of the Coal Property of the Catawissa R. R. Co. By J. P. Lesley. *Philadelphia.* 1865. 8vo. 40186

Lesley. The Iron Manufacturer's Guide to the Furnaces, Forges and Rolling Mills of the United States with Discussions of Iron as a Chemical Element, an American Ore, and a Manufactured Article, in Commerce and in History. By J. P. Lesley ... *New York: John Wiley.* 1859. 8vo, pp. (2), xxxiv, 772. 5 Maps and Plate. BA. + [*Ibid.*] 1866. 40187

Lesley. Manual of Coal and its Topography. Illustrated by Original Drawings, chiefly of Facts in the Geology of the Appalachian Region of the United States of North America. By J. P. Lesley. *Philadelphia.* 1856. 8vo, pp. 224. 40188

Lesley. A Few Facts regarding the Geological Survey of Pennsylvania, exposing the Erroneous Statements ... of J. P. Lesley ... . *Philadelphia: Collins, Printer.* 1859. 8vo, pp. 22.

[Leslie (Charles).] A New and Exact Account of Jamaica, wherein The Antient and Present State of that Colony, its Importance to Great Britain, Laws, Trade, Manners and Religion, together with the most remarkable and curious Animals, Plants, Trees, &c. are described: With a particular Account of the Sacrifices, Libations, &c. at this Day in Use among the Negroes. *Edinburgh: R. Fleming.* MDCCXXXIX. 8vo, pp. 358. + The Third Edition. To which is added, An Appendix, containing an Account of Admiral Vernon's Success at Porto Bello and Chagre. [*Ibid.*] MDCCXL. 8vo, pp. (6), ii, 376. 40190

Mr. John Russell Smith describes an edition, *Edinburgh*, 1737, which I have not seen.

[Leslie.] The Religion of Jesus Christ the only True Religion, or, A Short and Easie Method with the Deists, Wherein the Certainty of the Christian Religion Is demonstrated by Infallible Proof from Four Rules, which are Incompatible to any Imposture that ever yet has been, or that can possibly be. In a Letter to a Friend. The Seventh Edition. *Boston: Printed by T. Fleet, and are to be Sold by John Checkley, at the Sign of the Crown and Blue Gate over against the West End of the Town-House.* 1719. Sm. 8vo, pp. (2), xii, 51, (7). B., BA. 40191

First American edition. The only relation this book has to America consists in the fact that its publication created a litigation concerning the liberty of the press in America. The first edition was published in *London* in 1699. Mr. Checkley prefixed to this edition a preface of his own, consisting of twelve pages not in the following. Thomas, in his "History of Printing," Vol. II., p. 428, remarks, "Whether he

[Checkley] was a regular bookseller or not, I am not prepared to say; I have seen no book printed for him in America," which clearly indicates the scarcity of the book over fifty years ago. It was reprinted with the following title:

[Leslie.] A Short and Easie Method with the Deists. Wherein the Certainty of the Christian Religion Is demonstrated, by infallible Proof from Four Rules, which are incompatible to any Imposture that ever yet has been, or that can possibly be. In a Letter to a Friend. The Eighth Edition. *London: Printed by J. Applebee, and Sold by John Checkley, at the Sign of the Crown and Blue-Gate, over against the West-End of the Town-House in Boston.* 1723. 8vo, pp. 132. B., BA., H. 40192

In its original binding this work is always followed by "The Speech of Mr. John Checkley" ... as described in our No. 12365, of which speech there is a second edition: *London: J. Applebee.* 1738. 8vo, pp. (2), 40, and "A Specimen of a True Dissenting Catechism upon Right True-Blue Dissenting Principles" ... 8vo, 1 l. For the titles at length, *see our* Vol. III., No. 12365, *and* Stevens, "Nuggets," Nos. 536 and 537.

[Leslie.] A Short and Easie Method ... . The Fifth Edition. *Printed and Sold by William Parks, at his Printing-Offices, in Williamsburg, and Annapolis.* 1733. 8vo, pp. 90. 40193

This is one of the first books printed in Maryland. There are several other English and American editions; we note only the following:

[Leslie.] A Short and Easy Method ... . *Philadelphia: Reprinted ... by Robert Aitken.* M.DCC.LXXXIII. 12mo, pp. 36. BA. + *William Hilliard, Cambridge.* 1805. 12mo, pp. 60. BA. + A New American Edition. *Greenfield: Printed by John Denio.* 1809. 8vo, pp. 40. H. + *Windsor, Vt.* 1812. 12mo, pp. 168. + *Andover: Mark Newman.* 1826. 12mo, pp. 47. B. + *New York.* 1830. 12mo, pp. 40. H. 40194

[Leslie.] The Snake in the Grass: or, Satan Transform'd into An Angel of Light, Discovering The Deep and Unsuspected Subtility which is Couched under the Pretended Simplicity, of many of the Principal Leaders of those People call'd Quakers. *London: Printed for Charles Brome* ... 1696. 8vo. + The Second Edition, with Additions. [*Ibid.*] 1697. 8vo, pp. (2), xlv, (10), 381, (2). + The Third Edition. ... [*Ibid.*] 1698. 8vo, pp. (2), xliv, (8), 370. BA., P. 40195

It gives a long account of the "Fourth or New Quakers who reside mostly in Long Island and East Jersey, in America," one of whom was Mary Ross, who went to meeting stark naked, carrying a fiddle.

[Leslie.] A Defence of a Book Intituled, The Snake in the Grass. In Reply To Several Answers put out to it by George Whithead, Joseph Wyeth, &c. *London: Printed by M. Bennet, for C. Brome* ... 1700. 8vo, pp. (16), 184, 209 [for 241], 93.

[Leslie.] A Reply To a Book Entitul'd Anguis Flagellatus, or, A Switch for the Snake. ... Being A Second Defence, or, The Third and Last Part of The Snake in the Grass. Shewing That the Quakers are plainly Self-Condemn'd ... . *London: C. Brome* ... 1702. 8vo, pp. (8), 381. BA. 40197

Leslie (C. R.) Autobiographical Recollections. By the late Charles Robert Leslie. ... *London.* 1860. 2 vols., 8vo. c. + *Boston: Ticknor and Fields.* MDCCCLX. 12mo, pp. lviii, 363. BA.

Includes letters from and to Washington Irving.

Leslie (F.) Frank Leslie's Pictorial History of the American Civil War. Edited by the Hon. E. G. Squier. *New York: Frank Leslie.* 1862. Folio, pp xvi, 400. 40199

Leslie. Paris Universal Exposition, 1867. Reports of the United States Commissioners. Report on the Fine Arts. By Frank Leslie ... . *Washington: Government Printing Office.* 1868. Folio, pp. 43. B. 40200

Another issue is called the Author's Edition. *Washington.* 1868. 4to, pp. 43. 31 Plates. This was really written by E. G. Squier.

Leslie [*Sir* John]. Narrative of Discovery and Adventure in the Polar Seas and Regions; with illustrations of their Climate, Geology, and Natural History; and an account of The Whale Fishery. By Professor Leslie, Professor Jameson, and Hugh Murray, Esq. F.R.S.E. *Edinburgh: Oliver & Boyd.* 1830. Post 8vo. Map and Plate. + *New-York: Printed by J. & J. Harper.* 1831. 12mo, pp. (2), 373. + [*Ibid.*] 1833. + *New York: Harper & Brothers.* 1836. + [*Ibid.*] 1840, 1844, &c.

Leslie. The Polar Seas and Regions. ... With a Narrative of the recent Expeditions in Search of Sir John Franklin. By Sir John Leslie, Robert Jameson, and Hugh Murray. *New York.* 1860. 18mo, pp. 605. 40202

Includes notices of the voyages of Ross and Parry, Belcher, Franklin's Expedition, Searching Expeditions of 1850, 1851, and 1852, &c.

Leslie (*Miss*). Pencil Sketches; or Outlines of Character and Manners. *Philadelphia: Carey, Lea & Blanchard.* 1833–37. 3 vols., 12mo. c. 40203

[Lespade (A.)] Buenos Aires et le Peuple Basque: ou Précis Historique sur ce Peuple. Avec un rapide Analyse de sa merveilleuse Langue. *Buenos Aires.* 1859. 8vo. 40204

Lesperut (A.) Abraham Lincoln. Par A. Lesperut. *Paris: Dentu.* 1865. 8vo, pp. 16. Portrait. 40205

Lesquereux (L.) The Fossil Plants of the Coal Measures of the United States ... . By Leo Lesquereux ... . *Pottsville: Printed by Benj. Bannan.* 1858. 8vo, pp. 24. 2 Plates. H.

See also "Amer. Philos. Soc. Trans.," New Series, Vol. XIII.

Lesquereux. Lettres écrites de l'Amérique, destinées aux Émigrants. De M. Léo Lesquereux. *Neuchatel: H. Wolfrath.* 1849–50. 8vo, pp. 116. H. 40207

Extracted from the "Revue Suisse," 1849.

Lesseps [Jean Baptiste Barthélemy, *Baron* de]. Journal Historique du Voyage de M. De Lesseps ... employé dans l'expédition de M. le comte de la Pérouse ... . Depuis l'instant où il a quitté les frégattes Françoises au port Saint-Pierre & Saint-Paul du Kamtschatka, jusqu'à son arrivé en France, le 17 octobre 1788. *A Paris, de l'Imprimerie Royale.* M.DCCXC. 2 vols., 8vo, pp. (6), vii, (1), 280; (4), 380, vi, (4). 2 Maps and Plate. B.

"Ouvrage estimé, et dont les exmplaires ne sont pas communs."—Brunet.

Lesseps. Travels in Kamtschatka, during the years 1787 and 1788. Translated from the French of M. De Lesseps ... Interpreter to the Count de la Perouse, now engaged in a Voyage round the World, by Command of his most Christian Majesty. ... *London: J. Johnson.* 1790. 2 vols., 8vo, pp. xvi, 283, Map; viii, 408. BA., H. 40209

The author was interpreter to the expedition of La Pérouse, which he left at Kamtschatka to convey dispatches overland to France. *See also* our Nos. 38964–65.

Leslie (G.) ... Discourse at Newburyport, Aug. 12, 1779. By Rev. George Leslie. *Newburyport.* 1779. 8vo, pp. 31.

Lessman (F.) Album fotógraphico di Carácas. 12 Plates.

Lessman. Carácas ... hácia el Norte. *Carácas.* 1857. 8vo.

Lessoffsky (*Admiral*). Complimentary Banquet, given by the City Council of Boston to Rear-Admiral Lessoffsky, and the Officers of the Russian Fleet, ... June 7, 1864. *Boston.* 1864. 8vo. 40213

Lesson of St. Domingo. *See* [Wright (E.)]

Lesson (René Primevère). Voyage autour du Monde entrepris par ordre du gouvernement, sur la Corvette La Coquille;

Par P. Lesson ... . *Paris: P. Pourrat Frères.* 1839. 2 vols., 8vo, pp. (4), 510, (1); (4), 547, (2). 41 Plates. H. 40214

Lesson. Voyage Medical autour du Monde, exécute sur la Corvette du Roi la Coquille, commandée par M. L. J. Duperrey, pendant les années 1822, 1823, 1824, et 1825; ou rapport sur l'état sanitaire de l'équipage pendant la durée de la campagne, ... suivies d'un Memoire sur les races humaines répandues dans l'Océanie, la Malaisie ... . Par R. P. Lesson. *Paris: Roret.* 1829. 8vo, pp. 252. P. 40215

See also Dumont d'Urville, Vol. v., No. 21201, *and* Duperrey (L. J.), Vol. VI., No. 21353. Also: Histoire naturelle des Oiseaux-Mouches. ... *Paris.* 1829. Histoire naturelle des Colibris, suivie d'un supplement à l'histoire naturelle des Oiseaux-Mouches. ... *Paris.* 1831. Histoire naturelle des Oiseaux de Paradis. ... *Paris.* 1835. 3 vols., 8vo. 194 colored Plates.

Lessons from Biography, for Young Men. *Philadelphia: American Sunday School Union.* 1865. 18mo, pp. 191. 40216

Lessons of Piety and Patriotism, from Harrison and Washington. *Boston.* 1841. 12mo. 40217

Lessons to a Young Prince. *See* [Williams (D.)]

Lester (C. E.) The Artists of America: a Series of Biographical Sketches of American Artists; ... By Charles Edwards Lester. *New York: Baker & Scribner.* 1846. 8vo, pp. vi, 257. 5 Portraits. 40218

Washington Allston, H. Inman, B. West, G. C. Stuart, J. Trumbull, J. de Veaux, R. Peale, and T. Crawford, are the artists.

[Lester.] The Condition and Fate of England. ... *New-York: J. & H. G. Langley.* MDCCCXLIII. 2 vols., 12mo, pp. (2), 278; (2), 307. B. + Second Edition. [*Ibid.*] 1845. 40219

Lester. A Farewell Discourse, delivered before the Congregation of St. Peter's Church, in Spencertown ... May 5th, 1838. By Rev. Charles Lester. *New York.* 1838. 8vo. 40220

Lester. The Gallery of Illustrious Americans, Containing the Portraits and Biographical Sketches of Twenty-Four of the most Eminent Citizens of the American Republic, since the Death of Washington. From Daguerreotypes by Brady—Engraved by D'Avignon. C. Edwards Lester -- Editor. *New York: Brady, D'Avignon & Co.* MDCCCL. 4to, pp. (6), 26, (2). 24 Plates.

No. 1. ends with Taylor. Finished in 1856.

[Lester.] Glances at the Metropolis. A Hundred Illustrated Gems. *New York.* 1854. 4to. c. 40222

Contains a hundred plates from the London Art Journal, interspersed with notices of mercantile establishments in New York.

Lester. The Glory and the Shame of England. ... By C. Edwards Lester. *New-York: Harper & Brothers.* 1841. 2 vols., 12mo. + [*Ibid.*] 1842. 2 vols., 12mo, pp. 253; (2), 293. Plate. + *New York.* 1850. 2 vols., 12mo. c. + *New York: Bartram & Lester.* 1866. 2 vols., 8vo, pp. 304; (4), 307–601. 40223

For a reply, *see* Libertas, *pseudon.*

Lester. The Life and Voyages of Americus Vespucius; With Illustrations concerning the Navigator, and the Discovery of the New World. ... By C. Edwards Lester, and Andrew Foster. *New York: Baker & Scribner.* 1846. 8vo, pp. 431. B. + *New Haven.* 1853. 8vo. Plates and Portrait. + [*Ibid.*] 1854. 8vo. + Tenth Edition. *New Haven: H. Mansfield.* 1867. 8vo, pp. 470, vii. 12 Plates and Portrait. c. 40224

Contains also an account of the discoveries of Vasco de Gama beyond the Cape of Good Hope, Letters of Paolo Toscannelli to Columbus, Marco Polo and his travels, etc.

[Lester.] The Light and Dark of the Rebellion. ... *Philadelphia: George W. Childs.* 1863. 12mo, pp. 303. B. 40225

Lester. The Mountain Wild Flower: or, Memoirs of Mrs. Mary Ann Bise, A Lady who died at the Age of Twenty-three, in the Valley of the Green River. By Charles Lester. *New York: E. French.* 1838. 12mo, pp. xii, 243. c. 40226

Lester. My Consulship. By C. Edwards Lester. *New York: Cornish, Lamport & Co.* 1853. 2 vols., 12mo, pp. 312; 312. c. 40227

Lester. Passages from the History of the United States. By C. Edwards Lester. *New York.* 1866. 8vo. Plates.

Lester. Sam Houston and his Republic. By C. Edwards Lester. ... *New York: Burgess, Stringer & Co.* 1846. 8vo, pp. 208. Portrait. H. 40229

Also: The Social Life and National Spirit of America; an Oration ... at Great Barrington, July 4, 1849. ... *Great Barrington, Mass.: Cushing & Bryan, Printers.* 1849. 8vo, pp. (2), 18. H. *See also* Vol. v., No. 19495. We believe that Charles Lester and Charles Edwards Lester are the same person.

Lester (W. W.) Decisions of the Interior Department in Public Land Cases, and Land Laws passed by the Congress of the United States. Together with the Regulations of the General Land Office. ... *Philadelphia*. 1860. 8vo. c. 40230

See also our Vol. IV., No. 15266.

L'ESTRANGE (H.) Americans no Iewes, | or | Improbabilities that the | Americans are of that race. | ... | By Hamon L'Estrange, K! | *London*, | *Printed by W. W. for Henry Seile over against* | *St. Dunstans Church in Fleetstreet* 1652. | Sm. 4to, pp. (4), 80. H.

A rejoinder to Thorowgood (Thos.), *see infra*.

LESUEUR (P.) Memorials of the Quebec Conference, edited by Peter LeSueur ... . *Quebec: Printed for the Editor by Hunter, Rose & Co.* 1863. 8vo, pp. 107. 40232

LE SUIRE (Robert Mart.) Le Nouveau Monde. Poème. Par M. Le Suire, de l'Académie des Sciences. ... *Eleuthéropolis, et se trouvé à Paris.* 1781. 2 vols., 16mo, pp. xxxii, 149; 210. + Nouvelle Édition, entièrement refondue et corrigée. ... *Paris: l'Auteur, An* VIII [1800]. 2 vols., 8vo, pp. xxviii, 143; (4), 147.

LESUR (C. L.) Annuaire historique universel [politique et littéraire], pour 1818–1857. Avec un Appendice contenant les actes publiés, traités ... une chronique ... Par Charles Louis Lesur. *Paris.* 1819–58. 39 vols., 8vo. s. 40234

Continued after 1832 by M. Tencé and later by MM. Fouquier et Desprez.

"Let my People go." Originally published in Norfolk Co: Journal of December 14th, 1861. ... *Boston.* 1862. 8vo, pp. 8.

Let not the Faith, nor the Laws of the Commonwealth, be Violated. [n. p. n. d.] 8vo, pp. 30, (2). 40236

On lotteries in Pennsylvania.

Let us Unite. *See* [Waterman (J. A.)]

LETCHER (J.) To the People of Virginia! John Letcher and his antecedents. ... *Richmond.* 1859. 8vo, pp. 29, (1). H.

LETCHER. Wisconsin Railroad Grant. Speech of Hon. John Letcher ... March 1, 1854 ... . [n. p. n. d.] 8vo, pp. 8.

Also: Speech ... May 18, 1854, on the Tariff. [n. p. n. d.] 8vo.—Speech ... March 13, 1856, on Kansas Contested Election. [n. p. n. d.] 8vo.

LETCHER (M. E.) Message of Governor Letcher to the Legislature of Kentucky. December Session, 1840. *Frankfort, Ky.: A. G. Hodges ... Printer.* 1840. 8vo, pp. 14. H. 40239

LETCHER. Wonderful Discovery! Being an account of a recent exploration of the celebrated Mammoth Cave, in ... Kentucky, by Dr. Rowan, Professor Simmons and others, of Louisville, to its termination in an Inhabited Region, in the Interior of the Earth! ... a Letter from Montgomery E. Letcher, Esq. one of the exploring party ... . *New-York: R. H. Elton.* 1839. 12mo, pp. 24. 40240

L[ETCHWORTH] (T[homas]). A | Morning and Evening's | Meditation, | or, a | Descant | on the | Times. | A | Poem. | By T. L. | *London: Printed.* | *Philadelphia: Re-printed and Sold by B. Franklin and D. Hall.* 1766. Sm. 8vo, pp. 58. 40241

A very rare Franklin imprint.

LE TELLIER (*M.*) Le Mercure Indien, ou le Tresor des Indes. Par M. Le Tellier. *Paris.* 1668. 4to. 40242

Contains an account of the mines of Potosi, etc. Not mentioned by Ternaux.

LE TELLIER DE COURTANVAUX (F. C.) Catalogue de la bibliothèque de F. C. Le Tellier de Courtanvaux. *Paris: Nyon.* 1783. 8vo. 40243

Includes many rare books on Nouvelle France, which sold for about one fiftieth of the sum they would now bring.

Letera de la | nobil cipta: nouamente ritrouata alle In- | die con li costumi & modi del suo Re & | soi populi: Li modi del suo adorare con la | bella vsanza de le donne loro: & de la dua | persone ermafrodite donate da quel Re al | capitano de larmata. | [Colophon:] *El. V. S. V: Al Suo. D. L. S.* | *Data in Peru adi. xxv. de Nouembre.* | *Del* MDXXXIIII. | 4to, 4 l. 40244

A remarkable account of a city which the author calls Zhaval, but so obscurely written, that it is difficult to tell in what part of America it is situated. Harrisse suggests that it may be "Zavalita, a settlement of the province of Antioquia, in the Nuevo Regno de Granada." It is a piece of extreme rarity. Twenty-five copies were reprinted at *Milan*, 1830. *See* Ternaux, No. 42, and for other editions *see* "Lettera."

[LETHERBURY, PEREGRINE, *and others.*] Address to the Citizens of Kent, on the Approaching Election. [*Wilmington: Printed by James Wilson.* 1800.] 8vo, pp. 14. BA. 40245

Leti u Celich Evangelu Jesu Cristo, hebix San Lucas. *Londres.* 1865. 12mo, pp. 90. 40246

St. Luke; translated by Father Reiz into the Maya language.

Leti u Ebanhelio Hezu Crizto, Hebix Huan. *London.* 1869. 16mo, pp. 83. 40247

In the Maya language.

LETI (G.) Theatro belgico, ò verò ritratti historici, chronologici, politici e geografici delle Provincie Unite, scritto da Gregorio Leti. *Amsterdamo, Guglielmo de Jonge.* 1690. 2 vols., 4to. Plates, Portraits, and Plans. 40248

Contains an account of the Dutch war in Brazil.

LETI. Vita del Catolico Re Filippo II. Monarcha delle Spagne. *Coligni.* 1689. 2 vols., 4to. 40249

LETONA (Barth. de). Perfecta Religiosa, contiene tres libros. I. De la Vida de la Madre Geronima de la Afunçion, Fundadora de las Descalças de Manila en Philipinas. II. De la Oracion y Exercicios ... y un breve Catalogo de Indulgencias. III. De la Regla, y Constituciones ... y Documentos Singulares para la Confession. *Puebla [Mexico], por Juan de Borja.* 1662. 4to.

Letras Anvas | de la Compania | de Iesvs | de la Provincia | del Nvevo. Reyno | de Granada. | Desde el Ano de Mil y Seys cientos | y treinta y ocho, | hasta el Ano de Mil y Seys cientos | y quaranta y tres. | *En Zaragoza Año de* 1645. | *Impresas con licencia delos Superiores.* | 4to, pp. 239. 40251

LETTER.

See also under the names of persons to whom letters are addressed, names of states, cities, towns, etc., also pseudonyms, and the most obvious subjects.

Letter about a Good Management under the Distemper of the Measles, at this time spreading the Country. *Boston.* 1739.

A Letter about the Present State of Christianity among the Christianized Indians of New England. *Boston.* 1705. 12mo.

A very rare pamphlet.

Letter ... accompanying ... *See* Post-Office.

Letter addressed to a Congressman. Union and Liberty. Power of Congress in relation to the Slaves; with a Form of Enactment in conformity thereto. [n. p. n. d.] 8vo, pp. 8.

A Letter addressed to a Republican Member of the House of Representatives of the State of Massachusetts on the Subject of a petition for ... "A College of Physicians." *Boston: Printed by John Eliot, Jun.* 1812. 8vo, pp. 20. BA. 40255

A Letter addressed to Charles King, ... in Answer to his Defense of Bishop Doane. By a Lay Member of the Diocesan Convention of New-Jersey. [n. p.:] *Printed for the Publisher.* 1852. 8vo, pp. 15. B. 40256

A Letter addressed to Mercator in reply to his Letters on the Abolition of the Slave Trade. By a Planter. *London.* 1807. 8vo. 40257

Letter Addressed to Parents and Heads of Families, particularly those residing in the Country Towns and Villages in America. *Boston.* 1827. 8vo. 40258

A Letter addressed to the Hon. James Madison ... . *Printed in America.* 1808. 8vo, pp. (2), 35. + *Philadelphia.* 1808. 8vo, pp. 35. P. 40259

Letter, addressed to the Legislators of the several States, comprising the Federal Union; Recommending an Uniform Continental Currency ... . *New-York: For the Author.* ... [1795.] 8vo, pp. 23, (1). BA. 40260

A Letter addressed to the Members of the Legislature of Pennsylvania. By a Meeting of Pennsylvania Freeholders; Held at Philadelphia, on the 15th of March, 1817. ... [*Philadelphia.* 1817.] 8vo, pp. 8. BA. 40261

Letter addressed to the President of the United States on Slavery, considered in relation to the Constitutional Principles of Government, in Great Britain and in the United States. By an American Citizen. ... *Boston: Redding and Company.* 1855. 8vo, pp. (2), 91. H. 40262

A Letter Addressed to Two Great Men, on the Prospect of Peace; And on the Terms necessary to be insisted upon in the Negociation. *London: A. Millar,* MDCCLX. 8vo, pp. (2), 56. + The Second Edition, corrected. [*Ibid.*] + *Boston: Re-printed by Fowle and Draper.* M.DCC.LX. 8vo, pp. 43. + *Boston: Reprinted by B. Mecom.* 1760. 8vo, pp. 55. + Fourth Edition, enlarged. *Dublin.* 1760. 8vo, pp. 42. 40263

This tract, relating to the Treaty of Utrecht and the French Canadian question, has been attributed to Junius, also to William Pulteney, Earl of Bath, but with more probability to John Douglas, *see* No. 20684, Vol. V. The "Two Great Men" were Wm. Pitt and the Duke of Newcastle. The writer urges upon the government, in making peace with France, to require from her the relinquishment of all Canada, Guadaloupe, and Senegal. *See* Franklin's Works, 3 vols., 4to, *London*, Vol. III., p. 89, "Remarks," *and* [Jackson (R.)], Vol. IX., No. 35450.

Letter and Proposals of the International Steamship Company to his Excellency President Grant, relative to Iron Ship-building Yards. [*Washington.* 1870.] 8vo, pp. 10. H. 40264

The Letter-Bag. *See* [Haliburton (T. C.)], Vol. VII., 29689.

A Letter Commercial. *See* [Currie (*Dr.*)], Vol. V. 17977.

A Letter concerning. *See* Chandler (T. B.), Vol. III. 11876.

Letter concerning Libels. *See* [Wilkes (John)].

Letter concerning the Consequence. *See* Vol. V., No. 18559.

Letter concerning the General Health. *See* New York.

A Letter concerning the Naval Store Bill, with Observations on the Plantation Trade. *London.* 1721. 8vo, pp. 44. 40265

A Letter concerning ... Jamaica. *See* Vol. IX., No. 35630.

A | Letter | concerning the | Union, | With Relation to | Trade, | from several Scots Gentlemen, | Merchants in England, to their Country-Men, Merchants | in Scotland. | *London*, | *Printed for B. Bragg* ... . 1707. | 8vo, pp. 16. 40266

Relates to Darien. *See our* Vol. V., Nos. 18544–75.

A Letter, containing Some Candid Observations on Mankind, and the Republican Administrations of Jefferson & Madison. By a Farmer. *Morris-Town: Printed by Henry P. Russell, Sept.,* 1810. 12mo, pp. 37. 40267

A Letter descriptive of the different Settlements in the Province of Upper Canada. *London: J. Egerton.* 1795. 12mo.

"This pamphlet gives a very advantageous account of the country of Upper Canada, and of the settlers there, subjects to the British Government; it also contains some particulars relative to the American Indians."—*Monthly Review*, XX. 479.

Letter from a Chancellor out of Office to a King in Power on the War with America, a Solemn Appeal to the Political Wisdom of George III. *London.* [n. d.] 8vo, pp. 160. 40269

"Belongs to the Tom Paine's series of works." Title and note forms No. 212 of one of J. C. Hotten's catalogues.

A Letter from a Churchman to his Friend in New-Haven, containing a Few Strictures on a Pamphlet signed J. R. O. *New-Haven: Printed by Oliver Steele and Co.* 1808. 8vo, pp. 30. s.

A Letter from a Citizen of Port-Royal in Jamaica, to a Citizen of New-York. Relating to some Extraordinary Measures, lately set on Foot in that Island. *Dublin: Printed. London, Reprinted for J. Scott* ... M,DCC,LVI. 8vo, pp. 20. B. 40271

See "M. Rev.," XIV. 586.

A Letter from a Cobler to the People of England on Affairs of Importance. *London.* 1756. 12mo, pp. 17. 40272

Letter from a Congregationalist to a Friend, on the subject of joining the New Episcopalian Church. *Boston: Printed by Wells and Lilly.* 1820. 8vo, pp. 32. BA. 40273

A Letter from a Country Gentleman at Boston, To his Friends in the Country. [n. p. n. d.] Sm. 8vo, pp. 12. BA. 40274

Dated, June 10, 1740. On the subject of a land bank in the city of Boston.

Letter from a Farmer in the County of Rockingham to his Brother in the County of Merrimack, in New-Hampshire. [n. p. n. p.] 8vo, pp. 8. H. 40275

A Letter from a Farmer to his Friend. *Philadelphia.* [n. d.] 12mo, pp. 18. P. 40276

Letter from a Freeman of South Carolina to the Deputies of North America, assembled in High Court of Congress, at Philadelphia. *Charleston: Printed by Peter Timothy.* 1774. 8vo, pp. 47.

Letter from a Friend in the North to a Friend in the South, on the Effects of Disunion upon Slavery. *Philadelphia.* 1856. 8vo.

A Letter from a Friend [Timothy Davis] to some of his Intimate Friends, on the Subject of paying Taxes ... . *Watertown: Printed and Sold by B. Edes near the Bridge.* 1776. 8vo, pp. 8.

Purports to be written by a Quaker, in defense of supporting the American cause. *See also* our Vol. V., No. 18893.

A Letter from a Gentleman at Barbados. *See* [Baxter (T.)]

A Letter from [W. P.] a Gentleman at Elizabeth-Town to his Friend in New-York. *Philadelphia: Printed by Andrew Steuart.* MDCCLXIV. Sm. 8vo, pp. 8. C. 40280

A Letter from a Gentleman at Halifax, to his Friend in Rhode-Island, containing Remarks upon a Pamphlet, entitled "The Rights of Colonies Examined." *Newport: Printed by S. Hall.* M.DCC.LXV. 8vo, pp. 22. BA., P. 40281

For "A Defence" *see our* Nos. 19249, and 29702, *also* "Vindication," Hopkins (Stephen), Vol. VIII., Nos. 32966–67, *and* Bancroft's "Hist. of the U. S.," Vol. V.

A | Letter | From a Gentleman, | Containing some Remarks | upon the Several Answers | given unto Mr. Colman's | Entituled, The Distressed | State of the Town of Boston. | *Boston: Printed by S. Kneeland.* 1720. 8vo, pp. 15. 40282

Said to have been written by Dr. Noyes.

"We boast of Families, and make a mighty doe
Of Lords whose Fathers were, the Lord knows who."

A Letter from a Gentleman in Boston to his Friend in Connecticut. *Boston.* 1744. 4to, pp. 15. 40283

On paper currency.

A Letter from a Gentleman in Boston. *See* [Chauncy (C.)]

Letter from a Gentleman in Connecticut, relative to a Paper Currency. *Boston.* 1766. 8vo. 40284

Letter from a Gentleman in England to his Friend in Philadelphia; giving him his Opinion of the College in that City. *Philadelphia.* 1762. 8vo. 40285

Letter from a Gentleman in Halifax to his Friend in Boston. *Boston.* 1757. 8vo. 40286

On political affairs.

Letter from a Gentleman in London, to his Friend in Pennsylvania; with a Satire, containing some Characteristical Strokes upon the Manners and Principles of the Quakers. *London: J. Scott.* 1756. 8vo, pp. 23. J.C.B. 40287

A Letter from a Gentleman in Mount Hope to his Friend in Treamount. [n. p. 1721.] Sm. 8vo, pp. 7. 40288

A Letter from a Gentleman in New-York, to his Friend in Brunswick. [n. p.] 1750. 8vo. 40289

See "Reply" and "Some Observations."

A Letter from a Gentleman in Scotland to his Friend in New-England, containing an account of Mr. Whitefields Reception and Conduct in Scotland. *Boston: T. Fleet.* 1743. 8vo, pp. 16.

Letter from a Gentleman in Virginia to a Merchant in Philadelphia, July 22, 1768. *Philadelphia.* 1768. Folio, 1 l. P.

A Letter from a Gentleman in Virginia, to the Merchants of Great Britain Trading to that Colony. *London: Printed in the Year* MDCCLIV. 8vo, pp. 36. BA. 40292

Relative to a dispute with the Governor for taking a fee on signing patents for lands.

A Letter from a Gentleman. *See* Vol. III., No. 10504.

Letter from a Gentleman ... on Persecution. *See* [Penn (Wm.)]

A Letter from a Gentleman in the Country to his Friend in Town, on his Perusal of a Pamphlet addressed to Two Great Men. *London: J. Davis.* 8vo. 40293

See No. 40263, [Douglas (John)], Vol. V., No. 20684 *and* "M. Rev.," XXII. 166.

Letter from a Gentleman in the Country. *See* Crookshanks (J.), Vol. V., No. 17610, *note.*

A Letter from a Gentleman in the Country to S—— W——. *London.* 1729. 8vo, pp. 27. s. 40294

A Letter from a Gentleman of Baltimore. *See* [Sheed (J. J.)]

A Letter From A Gentleman of the City of New-York, To Another, Concerning the Troubles which happen'd in That Province in the Time of the late Happy Revolution. *New-York: Printed by William Bradford.* 1698. 4to, pp. 24. H.

A piece of the greatest rarity. Only one perfect copy is known to exist.

A Letter from a Gentleman to his Friend in New York. *Philadelphia.* 1764. 12mo. P. 40296

A Letter from a Gentleman travelling through Bucks County, to his Friend in Town. [*Philadelphia.* 1770.] Folio, pp. 4. P.

Letter from a Long-Island Farmer to his Friend in New York. [*New York.*] 1793. 8vo. 40298

A Letter from a Meeting of the Brethren called Quakers, to the Authors of the Pamphlet called Considerations on the German War, and of the several Pamphlets in answer to it. ... *Boston, N. E. reprinted* ... *by B. Mecom* ... 1761. 8vo, pp. 8. P.

Letter from a Member of Parliament to his Grace the Duke of ***** upon the Present Situation of Affairs. *London.* 1755. 8vo. 40300

Letter from a Member of Parliament in Town to his Friend in the Country, upon the three great objects of present attention, Place, Parties, and Resignations. *London: Burnet.* 1763. 8vo.

On American affairs. *See* "M. Rev.," XXVII. 50.

Letter from a Member of St. Paul's shewing the Source of the present Wranglings in that Congregation. *Philadelphia.* 1764. 8vo, pp. 8. 40302

Relative to the Lancaster massacre. *See our* Vol. III., No. 12358, for a refutation.

Letter From a Member of the Parliament. *See* Vol. V., 18560.

Letter from a Member of the last Parliament concerning the Conduct of the War with Spain. *London.* 1742. 8vo. 40303

A | Letter | from a | Merchant at Jamaica | to a | Member of Parliament in London, Touching the African Trade. | To which is added, | A Speech made by a Black | of Guardaloupe, at the Funeral of | a Fellow-Negro. | *London*, | ... *A. Baldwin.* MDCCIX. Sm. 8vo, pp. 31. C. 40304

A Letter from a Merchant in Amsterdam to a Friend in London about the South Sea Trade. *London: John Baker.* 1712. 8vo, pp. 24. J.C.B. 40305

A Letter from a Merchant in Halifax, to a Merchant in Boston, trading to Halifax, dated 17th of January 1757. [n. p. n. d.] 8vo, pp. 24. BA., W. 40306

Letter from a Merchant in London. *See* [Tucker (Josiah)].

A Letter from a Merchant of the City of London, to the R---t H----ble W---- P----, Esq; upon the Affairs and Commerce of North America, and the West-Indies; Our African Trade; the Destination of Our Squadrons and Convoys; New Taxes, and the Schemes proposed for raising the extraordinary Supplies for the current Year. ... *London: J. Scott.* 1757. 8vo, pp. 98. BA., N. 40307

See "M. Rev.," XVI. 174, *and* Pitt (William).

A Letter from a Merchant to a Farmer and Planter, on the Abuses and Advantages of Banks. [*Baltimore.* 1826.] 8vo, pp. 16. BA. 40308

Letter from a Merchant who has left off Trade, to a Member of Parliament. *London.* 1753. 8vo. 40309

Included in J. R. Smith's Catalogue of Americana.

Letter from a Minister. *See* [Wetmore (James)].

A Letter from a Patriot in Retirement to the Rt. Hon. Mr. William Pitt, upon the Resigning of his Employment. *London.* 1761. 8vo, pp. 78. Portrait. 40310

On American affairs. *See also* Pitt (William).

A Letter From a Residing Member of the Society For Promoting Christian Knowledge in London, to a Corresponding Member in the Country. The Second Edition, with considerable Additions. *London: J. Downing.* 1714. 12mo, pp. 54. B. + The Third Edition. *London.* 1723. 12mo, pp. 74. 40311

Letter from a Romish Priest in Canada. *See* [Seguinot].

A Letter from a Russian Sea-Officer, to a Person of Distinction at the Court of St. Petersburgh: Containing His Remarks

upon Mr. de l'Isle's Chart and Memoir, relative to the New Discoveries Northward and Eastward from Kamtschatka. Together with Some Observations on that Letter. By Arthur Dobbs, Esq; Governor of North-Carolina. To which is added, Mr. de l'Isle's Explanatory Memoir on his Chart Published at Paris, and now Translated from the Original French. *London: A. Linde.* 1754. 8vo, pp. (2), 83. J.C.B., H., S. 40312

"This pamphlet relates chiefly to the attempts that have been so worthily made by Mr. Dobbs, and other gentlemen, associated for the patriotic purpose of discovering a North-West passage to the South Sea."—*Monthly Review*, x. 320.

A Letter from ********, in London, to his Friend in America, on the ... Slave-Trade; together with Some Extracts ... Confirming the Principles ... in said Letter. ... *New-York: Printed by Samuel Loudon.* M,DCC,LXXXIV. 8vo, pp. 28. BA., C.

An Affectionate Letter from a solicitous Mother to her only Son, both living in New England. *Boston.* 1746. 8vo. + *Boston, Reprinted.* 1764. 8vo. 40314

Letter from a Tradesman, recently arrived from America, to his Brethren in Trade. *London.* 1835. 8vo, pp. 23. C. 40315

A Letter from a Veteran, to the Officers of the Army Encamped at Boston. *America: Printed in the Year*, 1774. 8vo, pp. 19, (1). BA. 40316

Extremely scarce. Remarkably well written. Attributed to the British General Prescott. *See* Tudor's "Life of Otis."

A Letter from a Virginian, to the Members of the Congress to be held At Philadelphia, on The First of September, 1774. *Printed in the Year* 1774. 8vo, pp. (2), 29. H. + *Boston: Reprinted by Mills and Hicks.* 1774. 8vo, pp. 31. BA. + [Another Edition.] *Boston.* 1774. 8vo, pp. 24. + *Boston.* 1774. 8vo, pp. 50. + *Boston, printed: London, reprinted; J. Wilkie.* 1774. 8vo, pp. (6), 60. 40317

The first-mentioned edition was probably printed at *Philadelphia*. "The writer points out the duties of Congress, and endeavors to dissuade the members of that body from adopting the non-importation and non-exportation agreements."—*Monthly Review*, LI 479. The author did not succeed in convincing the members.

A Letter from a Weaver to the Rev. Mr. Sherman, occasioned by a publication of his in the Fairfield Gazette, for the purpose of pinching the Episcopalian Clergy with the Truth. [n. p. n. d.] 8vo, pp. 20. 40318

A Letter from a West-India Merchant to a Gentleman at Tunbridg, concerning that part of the French Proposals, which

relates to North America, and particularly to Newfoundland. With some Thoughts on their Offers about our Trade to Spain and the West-Indies: And an Abstract of the Assiento. *London: Printed in the Year* 1712. 8vo, pp. 34. 40319

A Letter from Albemarle Street to the Cocoa-Tree, on some late Transactions. *London.* 1764. 4to. + Second Edition. *London.* 1764. 4to, pp. 40. N. 40320

A Letter from an American. *See* [Bingham (W.)], No. 5458, and *add:* Second Edition. [*Ibid.*] + *Dublin.* 1784. 12mo. + *Dublin: Re-printed by James Potts.* MDCCLXXXIV. 8vo, pp. 23.

Letter from an American Woman. *See* [Cutler (H. M. T.)]

A Letter from an Aged and a Retired Citizen of Boston ... on Coercive Measures in Aid of Temperance. *Boston.* 1848. 8vo. + Second Edition. *Boston: Eastburn's Press.* 1848. 8vo, pp. 11.

A Letter from An Elder in an Old School Presbyterian Church to His Son at College. ... [on secession]. *New York.* 1863. 8vo, pp. 24. H. 40323

A Letter from an Officer at New-York to a Friend in London. *London: W. Nicoll.* M.DCC.LXXVII. 8vo, pp. (2), 81. BA. 40324

Gives a sad account of the sufferings of the people in New York. "Many good families whom the army have ruined, have come in shivering to us for protection. Many of the ladies have scarce a petticoat to cover them, being stripped of furniture, apparel, and everything that could make a Yankee soldier either a shirt or a pair of breeches." "For *New York* read Grub-street."—*Monthly Review*, LVI. 395.

A Letter from an Officer Retired, to his Son in Parliament. ... *London: T. Cadell.* MDCCLXXVI. 8vo, pp. (4), 38. H. + A New Edition. *Edinburgh: Charles Elliot.* M,DCC,LXXVI. 12mo, pp. (iv), 29, (1). 40325

The writer, who has served in the army, urges more vigorous measures, and believes the safety of Great Britain depends upon her subduing her American colonies. *See* "M. Rev.," LIV. 232.

A Letter from an Old Whig. *See our* Vol. III., No. 10505.

Letter from Britannia to the King. *London: J. Fielding.* 1781. 8vo, pp. 61. J.C.B. 40326

Relates wholly to the war in America.

A Letter from Candor to the Public Advertiser. Third Edition. *London.* 1770. 8vo. S. 40327

Letter from Citizens. *See* Webster (D.)

Letter from Cocoa Tree, to the Country Gentleman. Third Edition. *London.* 1763. 4to. 40328

A Letter from Common Honesty, to Common Sense: ... *Boston: Printed by Thomas Fleet.* [1749.] 12mo, pp. 12. BA.

"He called me all the Rascals he could think of; said I was one of those concerned in mobbing his Master about the 'Excise Bill,' and shut the door in my face."

A Letter from Freeman. *See* Freeman, *pseudon*, Vol. VII.

Letter from Legion to his Grace the Duke of Richmond, ... containing an Exposure of the Character of the Evidence on the Colonial Side produced before the Committee. *London: Samuel Bagster.* 1832. 8vo, pp. 196. 40330

On the question of slavery in the British colonies.

Letter from New-England. *See* [Oliphant (A.)], *and* W. (J.)

A Letter from New Jersey in America, giving some Account and Description of that Province. By a Gentleman late of Christ's College, Cambridge. *London.* 1756. 8vo, pp. 26.

Belongs to the "catchpenny class."—*Monthly Review*, XV. 427. It is as rare as it is worthless; but would sell for a good price. The author's initials are T. T.

A Letter, From One in Boston, To his Friend in the Country. In Answer to a Letter directed to John Burril, Esqr. Speaker to the House of Representatives, for the Province of the Massachusetts-Bay in New-England. [*Boston.*] 1714. 8vo, pp. (2), 37.

Signed F---l. B---t. Relates to a banking project.

A Letter from One in the Country. *See* [Wigglesworth (E.)]

A Letter From one in the Country, to his Friend in the City; In Relation to their Distresses occasioned by ... Inoculation ... . *Boston: Nicolas Boone.* 1721. 8vo, pp. 8. H. 40333

A Letter From one of the Leeward Islands, Tending to show the immediate Necessity of a further Inspection into the State of the British Sugar Colonies and Trade. [*London.* 1734.] 8vo, pp. 15. H. 40334

A Letter from One of the Society of Friends, relative to the Conscientious Scrupulousness of its Members to bear Arms. [n. p.] 1795. 8vo, pp. 18. BA. 40335

Letter from (P. P.) in New-York, to his Friend in London. [*London.*] 1733. Sm. 4to, pp. 4. 40336

A Letter from some Aged Non-conforming Ministers, to their Christian Friends, Touching the Reasons of their Practice. August 24. 1701. The Fourth Edition, Corrected and Enlarged ... *Boston: Reprinted for Samuel Gerrish.* 1712. 8vo, pp. (2), iv, 72.

Preface by Increase Mather.

A Letter from South Carolina. *See* South Carolina.

Letter from the Acting Secretary of the Treasury communicating the Report of the Superintendent of the Coast Survey, showing the progress of that work. Dec. 15, 1847. *Washington.* 1847. 8vo, pp. 88. 40338

See also our Vol. IV., No. 13821.

Letter from the Assistant Postmaster-General. *See* Post-Office.

Letter from the Attorney-General, accompanying his Report on the Resolution of 8th ultimo, relative to the Contract between the United States and John Cleves Symmes. *Philadelphia.* 1796. 8vo, pp. 6. Report [on the same subject], 1797. 8vo, pp. 10.

Letter from the Chairman of the Committee of Ways and Means to the Secretary of the Treasury, Relative to the Public Revenue; with the Answer thereto. *Alexandria.* 1812. 8vo, pp. 16. + *Washington.* 1815. 8vo. 40340

Letter from the Commission. *See* Vol. V., No. 18561.

Letter from the Commissioner for Indian Affairs to Colonel Benton. *Washington: Printed at the Union Office.* 1855. 8vo, pp. 15. 40341

Letter from the Comptroller. *See* Treasury Department.

A Letter from the Country to a Gentleman in Philadelphia ... *Fairview, Nov.* 27. 1773. Folio, 1 l. P. 40342

Signed "Rusticus." In defense of the tea-tax.

Letter from the French Minister, and Proceedings of the Legislature of South Carolina. *Philadelphia.* 1794. P. 40343

A Letter from the General Assembly to the Churches. *Philadelphia.* 1810. 40344

A Letter from the Minister Plenipotentiary of the United States to Lord Mulgrave ... . [*London.* 1805.] 8vo, pp. 17.

Letter from the Postmaster-General. *See* Post-Office.

Letter from the Secretary of State. *See* Secretary of State.

Letter from the Secretary of the Navy. *See* Navy.

Letter from the Secretary of the Treasury. *See* Treasury.

Letter from the Secretary of War. *See* War Department.

Letter from the Superintendent of Indian Trade, to the Chairman of the Committee on Indian Affairs, communicating a Report in relation to Indian Trade. December 13, 1820. *Washington: Gales & Seaton.* 1820. 8vo, pp. 8. 40346

Letter from the Surgeon-General to the Secretary of War. Draft of Powers asked for. Order the Commission. Approval of the President. 40347

A Letter from the Town of Boston, to C. Lucas, Esq; .. Including A Short Narrative of the Massacre Perpetrated there, In the Evening of the Fifth Day of March, 1770, by Soldiers of the XXIXth Regiment, Quartered in the Town; with some Observations on the State of Things prior to that Catastrophe. *Dublin: Reprinted by Tho. Ewing.* [n. d.] 8vo, pp. 56. 40348

An extremely rare contemporary account of the Boston massacre.

Letter from ... Neighbouring Associations. *See* Whitefield (G.)

A Letter from W. A., a Minister in Virginia to his Friend T. B., Merchant, of Gracious-street, London, declaring the Advantages to those minded to Transport themselves thither. *London.* 1623. 4to, pp. 8. 40349

A pamphlet of much rarity; I have not seen it. Its title is taken from A. R. Smith's Catalogue, where it is priced £4, 4s.

Letter of a Citizen of Indiana to the Hon. John J. Crittenden, on the Anti-slavery Policy of President Lincoln, and the Duty of the National Democracy. *Fort Wayne, Ind.* 186–. 8vo.

The Letter of Aegles, addressed to Hon. Jno. C. Spencer, Chairman of the Bank Committee. *Baltimore.* 1819. 8vo, pp. 64. 40351

The Letter of Appomatox to the People of Virginia: ... on the ... Abolition of Slavery; ... . *Richmond: Thomas W. White, Printer.* 1832. 8vo, pp. 47. B. 40352

A Letter of Congratulation from Britannia to the King, ... on the Change of Ministry. *London: Debrett.* 1782. 8vo, pp. 32.

See "M. Rev.," LXVII. 150.

A Letter of Inquiry to Ministers of the Gospel on Slavery. By a Northern Presbyter. *Boston: W. P Fetridge & Co.* 1854. 8vo, pp. 32. 40354

A Letter of | Many Ministers | in Old | England, | Requesting | The judgement of their Reverend | Brethren in New England con- | cerning Nine Positions. | Written Anno Dom. 1637. | Together with their Answer thereunto returned, | Anno 1639. | And the Reply made unto the said Answer, and sent over | unto them, Anno 1640. | Now published ... | upon the desire of many | godly and faithfull Ministers in and about the City | of London, who love and seeke | the truth. | By Simeon Ash, and William Rathband. | ... | *London*, | *Printed for Thomas Underhill, at the signe of the Bible in* | *great Woodstreet.* 1643. | Sm. 4to, pp. (12), 90. C., H.

A Letter of Thanks. *See* South Sea.

Letter of the Commissioner of Agriculture, transmitting the Report of the Commission appointed ... 1863, for Investigations to test the Practicability of cultivating and preparing Flax or Hemp as a Substitute for Cotton. [*Washington.*] 1865. 8vo, pp. 96. 40356

Letter of the Freedmen's Aid Society to President Lincoln. *Washington: McGill & Witherow.* 1863. 8vo, pp. 15. 40357

Letter of the Justices. *See* [Dana (Francis)], Vol. V.

Letter on a Pamphlet [viz:] "The West India Question, practically considered." *London.* 1826. 8vo, pp. 16. 40358

A Letter on American History. *Philadelphia.* 1847. 8vo, pp. 39. M. 40359

A rare, privately printed pamphlet. Perhaps by William B. Reed.

Letter on Canada in 1806 and 1817. *London: Privately Printed.* 1853. 12mo. 40360

A Letter on Currency Matters; to the People of the United States. By One of the People. *New York.* 1841. 8vo, pp. 36.

Letter on Mr. Floyd's Report on the Indians. [n. p. n. d.] 8vo. 40362

Letter on the American War. By a Northern Sympathiser. *London: Henry Wayland.* 1863. Post 8vo, pp. 24. B. 40363

Letter on the Causes of the Rapid and Progressive Depreciation of West India Property. *London.* [n. d.] 8vo. 40364

Letter on the Election of a President. *Charleston.* 1808. 8vo.

A Letter on the Genius. *See* [Walsh (R.)]

Letter on the Importance. *See* Sugar Colonies.

Letter on the Ill-Treatment of the People of Color in the United States. *Boston.* [n. d.] 8vo. 40366

"New-England Anti-Slavery Tract Association," Tract No. 10.

Letter on the Presbyterian Doctrines of Election and Reprobation. *New London: T. Green.* 1724. 12mo, pp. 24. 40367

An early Connecticut imprint.

A Letter on the Present Crisis; containing Reflections on a Late Resignation. *London.* [n. d.] 8vo, pp. 48. 40368

Refers to the resignation of William Pitt.

A Letter on the Present State of the Spanish West Indies, to P. H. [by J. N.] *London: J. Applebee.* 1739. Sm. 4to, pp. 7.

Usually found with *our* No. 19726, Vol. V.

Letter on the President's Message, supposed to be written by General Lafayette ... on the Opening of the Second Session of the Twenty-Second Congress, December 4th, 1832. *New-York: Peabody & Co.* M DCCC XXXIII. 16mo, pp. 18. B. 40370

Letter on the Rebellion. *See* [Rush (Benjamin)].

Letter on the relation. *See* [Mitchell (James)].

Letter on the Relations of the States and General Government. December, 1832. [n. p. 1832.] 8vo, pp. 8. BA.

A Letter on the Subject of Paying Taxes. *Watertown.* 1776. 8vo. P. 40372

Letter on the Use and Abuse of Incorporations, addressed to the Delegation ... of New-York ... By one of their Constituents. *New-York: G. & C. Carvill.* 1827. 8vo, pp. 59. H.

Letter on Toleration. By a Gentleman. *Wilmington, Del.* 1764. 8vo. 40374

A Letter Relating to a Medium of Trade, In the Province of Massachusetts-Bay. *Boston.* MDCCXL. 8vo, pp. 16. BA. 40375

Signed "Philopolites." A very scarce pamphlet.

A Letter relating. *See* [Prescott (B.)]

A Letter strongly opposed to Emancipation. [n. p. n. d.] 8vo.
Signed "A. B."

Letter to a Bristol Merchant, concerning the petition of S—— T—— Esq. for the Exclusive Trade of the River Senegal. [n. p. 1762.] 8vo. 40377
Relates to the slave-trade.

Letter to a certain ... British Sailor. *See* [Vernon (*Admiral*)].

A Letter to a Certain Gentleman desiring a particular Account may be given of a Wonderful Meteor that appeared in New England on Dec. 11, 1719 .... *Boston: Printed by James Franklin.* 1719. 18mo, pp. 8. 40378

A Letter to a Clergyman, in the Colony of Connecticut, from his Friend. In which, the true Notion of Orthodoxy is enquired into; and some Thoughts are suggested concerning publick Tests of Orthodoxy, and the mischievous Effects of setting up false Tests thereof. *New-Haven: Printed by James Parker, and Company.* MDCCLVII. 8vo, pp. 24. 40379
Signed "Catholicus."

Letter to a Federalist. *See* [Elwyn (Thomas)], VI. 22375.

A Letter to a Friend at Boston. *London.* 1793. 8vo. 40380

A Letter to a Friend, concerning the Proposals for the Payment of the Nation's Debts. *London.* 1720. 8vo. 40381
Relates to the South Sea scheme.

A | Letter | To a Friend; | Giving a Concise, but just, Account, According to | the Advices hitherto received, | Of the Ohio-Defeat; | And | Pointing out also the many good Ends, this inglo-| rious Event is naturally adapted to promote: | Or, | Shewing wherein it is fitted to advance the Interest | of all the American British Colonies. | To which is added, | Some general Account of the New-England Forces, | with what they have already done, counter-ballancing the above | Loss. *Boston: ... Edes and Gill.* M,DCC,LV. 4to, pp. 15. + *Bristol: re-printed by Edward Ward on the Tolzey.* 1755. 8vo, pp. 30. + *London: J. Nunn.* 1755.
Corrected title of *our* No. 12320, Vol. III., which *see* for a note.

A Letter to a Friend. *See* [Chauncey (C.)], Vol. III. 12321.

A Letter to A Friend in a Slave State. *See* [Ingersoll (C.)]

Letter to a Friend in Ireland; containing a Relation of some sorrowful Instances of the sad Effects of Intemperance, as a

Warning to young People. *Philadelphia: Printed by S. Keimer.* 1723. 8vo. 40383
Introduced for the imprint, which is uncommon.

A Letter to a Friend in the Country, upon the News of the Town. *London.* [n. d.] 8vo. 40384
Upon the war with France and Canadian affairs.

Letter to a Friend in the Country. *See* [Dummer (J.)], Vol. V., No. 21199, [Franklin (B.)], Vol. VII., No. 25527, *and* Vol. IX., No. 34793, *note.*

A Letter to a Friend [on Canadian Affairs] dated Philadelphia, November 26, 1838. [n. p. n. d.] 8vo, pp. 8. BA. 40385

A Letter to a Friend; in which some Account is given of the Brethren's Society for the Furtherance of the Gospel among the Heathen. *London: Printed in the Year* MDCCLXIX. 8vo, pp. 12.
An extremely rare Moravian tract, relative to the Indians.

Letter to a Gentleman. *See* Maryland, *also* Massachusetts.

A Letter to a Gentleman; containing a Plea for the Rights of Liberty of Conscience. By a Dissenting Protestant. *Boston: S. Kneeland.* 1753. 8vo. W. 40387

A Letter to a Gentleman in London, from Virginia. *Williamsburg: Printed by William Hunter.* MDCCLIX. 8vo, pp. 28.

A Letter to a Gentleman of Maryland, on the Slave Trade. Fourth Edition. *London.* 1806. 8vo. 40389

A Letter to a Gentleman, relating to the Office of Ruling Elders in the Churches. [*Boston.* 1731.] 8vo, pp. 7. 40390
See "Some brief Remarks" *and* "Reply."

A Letter to A Great Character. *See* [Cunningham (Wm.)]

A Letter to a Great M---------r, on the Prospect of a Peace; Wherein the Demolition of the Fortifications of Louisbourg is shewn to be absurd; The Importance of Canada fully refuted; The proper Barrier pointed out in North America; and the Reasonableness and Necessity of retaining the French Sugar Islands. Containing Remarks on some preceding Pamphlets that have treated of the Subject, and a succint View of the whole Terms that ought to be insisted on from France at a future Negociation. By an unprejudiced Observer. *London: G. Kearsley.* MDCCLXI. 8vo, pp. (2), 148. 40391
See "M. Rev.," XXIV. 437.

Letter to a Lady in France, on the supposed Failure of a National Bank, the supposed Delinquency of the National Government, the Debts of the several States, and Repudiation. With Answers to Enquiries concerning the Book of Captain Marryatt and Mr. Dickens. *Boston.* 1843. 8vo. N. 40392

Letter to a Landholder, on the subject of Repudiation. *Baltimore.* 1842. 8vo. 40393

Letter to a Member of Congress in relation to Indian Civilization. By the Domestic Secretary of the United Foreign Missionary Society. *New York: Printed by Daniel Fanshaw.* 1822. 8vo, pp. 15. 40394

A Letter to a Member of Congress, on the subject of a British War ... *Providence: Printed by John Carter.* 1812. 8vo, pp. 32.

A Letter to a Member of Parliament. *London.* 1803. 8vo, pp. 48. 40396
Partly relates to America. *See also* B. (J.), Vol. I., No. 2555.

A Letter to a Member of Parliament, concerning the Importance of our Sugar Colonies. By a Gentleman who resided many years in Jamaica. *London.* 1745. 8vo, pp. 30. 40397

A Letter to a Member of Parliament, concerning the Naval Store Bill, brought in Last Session, with Observations on the Plantation Trade .... *London.* 1720. 8vo. 40398

A Letter to a Member of Parliament. Concerning the present State of Affairs at Home and Abroad. By a true Lover of the People. *London: T. Cooper.* 1740. 8vo, pp. 60. H. 40399
A portion relates to the West Indies.

A Letter to a Member of Parliament, occasion'd by the South-Sea Company's Scheme for Reducing Public Debts. *London: Printed by J. Roberts.* 1720. 8vo, pp. 35. + Second Edition. [*Ibid.*] 1720. 8vo. N. 40400

A Letter to a Member of Parliament, On the Importance of the American Colonies, and the Best Means of Making them most Useful to the Mother Country. *London: J. Scott.* M.DCC.-LVII. 8vo, pp. 24. BA. 40401

A Letter to a Member of Parliament on the Present Unhappy Dispute between Great-Britain and her Colonies. Wherein the Supremacy of the Former is Asserted and Proved; and the Necessity of Compelling the Latter to pay due Obedience to the

Sovereign State, is Enforced, upon Principles of Sound Policy, Reason, and Justice. *London: J. Walter.* MDCCLXXIV. 8vo, pp. (2), 47. H. 40402
"An advocate for the measures of government, whose opinion is that it is safer to enforce a doubtful, or even a pernicious measure, than tamely to yield a point."—*Monthly Review*, LI. 475.

A Letter to a Member of Parliament on the Regulation of the Plantation Trade. *Printed in the Year* 1701. 4to. 40403
A very rare tract, signed "J. B.," the same as *our* No. 2555, Vol. I. The writer complains "That several of our American Colonies, as Rhode Island, Conecticut, East and West Jersie, Pensilvania, etc., are like so many Independent Sovereignties, having the Election of Governors, either amongst themselves annually, as Rhode Island, and Conecticut; or depending on some persons in England." *See* Stevens' "Bibliotheca Historica," No. 1030.

A Letter to a Member of Parliament on the Settling a Trade to the South-Sea of America, dat. 3d of May, 1711. With Reasons to encourage a Trade from Great-Britain to the Country scituate in the South Seas of America. [*London:*] *J. Phillips.* [1711.] 12mo, pp. 14. J.C.B. 40404

A Letter to a Member of Parliament, setting forth the value of the St. Christophers Land. *London.* 1730. 8vo. 40405

A Letter to a Member of Parliament, Wherein the Power of the British Legislature, and the Case of the Colonists, are briefly and impartially Considered. *London: W. Flexney.* 1765. 8vo, pp. (2), 30. B., BA., H. 40406
"The sensible writer of this letter endeavours to prove that, in point of law, the colonists are bound to pay obedience to every act of the Parliament of Great Britain, wherein they are expressly named. At the same time he condemns the Stamp Act, as one of the worst measures of the ministry."—*Monthly Review*, XXXIII. 484.

A Letter to a Member of the British Parliament, on Events Civil and Military, of the past and present year in Mexico, to the period of the Banishment of Gen. Bravo, ex-Vice-President of the Mexican Republic. By an Impartial Observer. *Mexico.* 1828. 8vo, pp. 131. S. 40407

A Letter to a Member of the Congress of the United States of America from an English Clergyman; including a Republication, with Additions, of the Tract entitled, "Every Man his own Property." *London.* 1835. 8vo, pp. 30. 40408

Letter to a Member of the General Assembly of North Carolina, on the Navigation of the Roanoke. *Richmond, Va.* 1811. 8vo. 40409

Letter to a Member of the General Assembly of Virginia, on the ... Late Conspiracy of the Slaves; with a Proposal for their Colonization. *Baltimore: Printed by Bonsal & Niles.* 1801. 8vo, pp. 23. BA. 40410

A Letter to a Member of the Honourable House of Commons, on the Present Important Crisis of National Affairs. *London.* [n. d.] 8vo. 40411
Chiefly relating to America.

A Letter to a Member of the ... House of Representatives, On the present State of the Bills of Credit. ... *Boston: Printed in the Year*, MDCCXXXVI. 8vo, pp. (2), 9. B. 40412
Signed "Philopatriæ." Relates to Massachusetts.

A Letter to a Member of the Lower House. *See* [Gale (B.)]

A Letter to a Member of the House of Representatives of the Colony of Connecticut, in Vindication of Yale College against a Pamphlet, intituled, A Letter to a Member of the Lower House .... [*New Haven.*] 1759. 4to, pp. 18. C., M.
Corrected title of *our* No. 28222, Vol. VII.

A Letter to a Merchant at Bristol, concerning a Petition of S—— T——, Esq., to the King for an Exclusive Grant of the Trade to the River Senegal. *London.* 1760. 8vo. 40414
Relates to the slave-trade.

Letter to a Merchant in Boston in answer to one Received Respecting the Excise Bill. By a True Friend of Liberty. *Boston.* 1754. 8vo. 40415

A Letter to —— ——, Merchant in London, Concerning a Late Combination in the Province of the Massachusetts-Bay, in New England, to Impose or Force a Private-Currency called Land-Bank-Money. [*Boston:*] *Printed for the publick Good.* 1741. 8vo, pp. 14. B., BA. 40416
A pamphlet of much rarity. *See* "Letter to the Merchant," No. 40500.

A Letter to a New-Hampshire Land Owner, upon the Constitutionality of granting the Power of taking Private Property to Railroad Corporations. [n. p.:] *For the Publishers.* 1840. 8vo, pp. 8. H. 40417

Letter to a New-Jersey Farmer. [*New York: John W. Oliver ... Printer.* 1856.] 8vo, pp. 3. Map. H. 40418

A Letter to a Noble Lord. *See* Vol. III., No. 10507.

A Letter to a Noble Lord, wherein is demonstrated that all the great and mighty Difficulties in obtaining an honourable and lasting Peace, &c. are for the most part Chimerical and Imaginary. By an Englishman. *London.* 1760. 8vo. 40419
On Canada. *See* "N. Y. Hist. Soc. Coll.," III. 349. Smith or Livingston wrote it and Alexander had it printed in London.

A Letter to a Noble Peer, relating to the Bill in favour of the Sugar Planters. [*London.*] 1733. 8vo, pp. 22. C. 40420

Letter to a Parishioner, which J. Mott Pretended to answer in a Pamphlet entitled The Great Work of Christ's Spirit, &c. *New York: Printed by John Peter Zenger.* 1730? Sm. 8vo.
All of Zenger's imprints are scarce; this is especially so.

Letter to a Representative. *See* Western Railroad Corporation.

A Letter to a Republican Member of the House of Representatives of Massachusetts. *Boston.* 1812. 8vo, pp. 20.

Letter to a Whig Neighbor, on the approaching State Election, by an Old Conservative. Second Edition. *Boston: Crosby, Nichols, and Company.* 1855. 8vo, pp. 27. BA. 40423

A Letter to a Young Man who has just entered College, from an Older One who has been through. ... *Boston: Wm. Crosby and H. P. Nichols.* 1849. 8vo, pp. 39. H. 40424

Letter to a Young Officer. *See* [Drewe (E.)], Vol. V., 20938.

A Letter to an American Planter, from his Friend in London. *London: H. Reynell.* MDCCLXXXI. 12mo, pp. 24. 40425
Relates to negro slavery and the introduction of christianity among the negroes.

A Letter to An Eminent Clergy-Man in the Massachusett's Bay. Containing some Just Remarks, and necessary Cautions, relating to Publick Affairs in that Province. ... [*Boston:*] *Printed in the Year* 1720. 16mo, pp. 13. B., BA. 40426

A Letter to an English Friend on the American War. *New York: Anson D. F. Randolph.* 1863. 8vo, pp. 24. 40427

Letter to an English Friend, on the Rebellion in the United States, and on British Policy. *Boston: Ticknor & Fields.* 1862. 8vo, pp. 28. 40428

A Letter to an English Gentleman on the Libels and Calumnies on America by British Writers and Reviewers. *Philadelphia.* 1826. 8vo, pp. 43. 40429
Probably by Robert Walsh. *See* Walsh (R.)

A Letter to an Ex-President of the United States. [Hon. John Adams.] ... *Leominster, Mass.: Printed by Salmon Wilder.* 1812. 8vo, pp. 25. BA. 40430

A Letter to an Honourable Brigadier General. *See* [Junius].

A Letter to an Honorable Gentleman. *See* Yale College.

Letter to Benjamin Franklin. *See* Vol. VI., No. 25612.

A Letter to Bryan Edwards, Esq. *See* [Preston (William)].

A Letter to Caleb D'Anvers, Esq.: occasioned by the Depredations committed by the Spaniards in the West Indies. With some Observations on the Trade carried on from Jamaica to the Spanish Coast. *London: H. Whittridge.* 1729. 8vo, pp. 32.

A Letter to certain Bank Directors from a Merchant. *Philadelphia.* 1796. 8vo. P. 40432

Letter to Chas. Jas. Fox. *See* Vol. VII., No. 29176.

Letter to Charles Sumner, a Senator from Massachusetts; by John Bunyan. *Washington.* 1866. 8vo, pp. 8. B. 40433

A Letter to Cicero. *See* [Galloway (J.)], Vol. VII. 26434.

Letter to Citizens of South Carolina on the approaching Presidential Election. *Charleston.* 1808. 8vo. C. 40434

Letter to Dr. Samuel Johnson. *See* Vol. IX. 36296 & 36305.

A Letter to Dr. Tucker. *See* Tucker (Josiah).

A Letter to Dr. Wilson, Prebendary of Westminster, and Rev. Mr. Horne, ... on their Political Conduct. *London: Brough.* 1770. 8vo, pp. (2), 33. 40435

A Letter to Edmund Burke. *See* [Cartwright (J.)], Vol. III.

A Letter to Edward Baines, Esq. *See* Vol. III., No. 10508.

A Letter to Edward Livingston. *See* Livingston (E.)

Letter to G. G. *See* G[renville] (G[eorge]), Vol. VII. 28766.

Letter to Governor Wright of Indiana upon the Connection of the Methodist Episcopal Church with the Subject of Slavery. [n. p. n. d.] 8vo, pp. 13. 40436

Letter to Granville Sharp. *See* Sharp (G.)

A Letter to Gulian C. Verplanck. *See* Verplanck (G. C.)

Letter to Her Majesty's Under Secretary of State, respecting a Plan for a General Union of the British Provinces, and on the Proposed Union of the Two Canadas. *London.* 1824. 8vo, pp. 27. 40437

Letter to Her R——l H——s the P——s D-w-g-r of W—— On the approaching Peace .... *London: S. Williams.* 1762. 8vo. + The Third Edition. [*Ibid.*] 1762. 8vo, pp. 63. 40438
Relates in part to the settlement of the colonies.

Letter to his Excellency William H. Seward. *See* [Gray (W. F.)], Vol. VII., No. 28415, *and* Tompkins (D.)

A Letter to His Grace the Duke of Grafton, on the Present Situation of Public Affairs .... [By Richard Grenville.] *London: J. Almon.* [1768.] 8vo, pp. (2), 30. 40439

A Letter to His Grace the D—— of N——e, on the Duty he owes Himself, his King, his Country and his God, at this important Moment. *London.* 1757. 8vo, pp. 47. S. 40440

A Letter to His Grace the Duke of N********, on the Present Crisis in the Affairs of Great Britain. Containing Reflections on a late great Resignation. *London: R. Griffiths.* 1761. 8vo. 40441
Partly on America. *See* "M. Rev.," XXV. 316.

A Letter to Hon. Josiah Quincy, Judge of the Municipal Court, Boston, on the Law of Libel [Commonwealth *vs.* Buckingham]. *Boston.* 1823. 8vo, pp. 62. 40442

A Letter to John Barrow. *See* Barrow (J.), Vol. I. 3671.

A Letter to Lieut. Gen. Burgoyne. *See* Vol. III. 9263–64.

A Letter to Lord Brougham on the subject of American Slavery. By an American. *London.* 1836. 8vo. P. 40443

A Letter to ... Lord Camden. *See* [Bernard (T.)], Vol. II.

Letter to Lord Castlereagh. *See* Vol. III., No. 10511.

A Letter to Lord Chatham, concerning the present War of Great Britain against America; reviewing, candidly and impartially, its unhappy Cause and Consequence; and wherein the Doctrine of Sir William Blackstone, as explained in his Commentaries on the Laws of England, is opposed to Ministerial Tyranny, and held up in Favour of America. With some Thoughts on Government. By a Gentleman of the Inner Temple [Matthew Dawes]. *London: J. Kearsley.* 1776. 8vo, pp. 60. 40444

"This spirited writer is warm for liberty, and for the claims of America, as connected with what he apprehends to be the real interest of this country, as well as with the common rights inseparable from the very idea of a free community."—*Monthly Review*, LVI. 65. This is a corrected title of *our* No. 18919, Vol. v.

A Letter to Lord Geo. Germaine. *See* Vol. VII., No. 27143.

A Letter to Lord Melbourne on the Executions in Canada, with Remarks on Capital Punishment. By a Modern Moralist. *London.* 1839. 8vo, pp. 36. 40445

A Letter to Major-General Hamilton containing Observations on his Letter, concerning the Public Conduct and Character of John Adams, Esq. President of the United States. By a Citizen of these States. *New York: Printed by G. F. Hopkins.* 1800. 8vo, pp. 32. 40446

See also our Vol. III., No. 9863, Vol. IV., No. 13135, *and* Vol. VIII., Nos. 29959-61.

Letter to Members of Congress, on the Pay of Clerks in Government Offices. [n. p.] 1851. 8vo. 40447

A Letter to ... Mr. Calhoun. *See* Vol. IV., No. 9951, *also* [Hammond (J. D.)], Vol. VIII., No. 30095.

Letter to Mr. G——r, in Philadelphia. [n. p.] 1766. 8vo, pp. 8. C., P. 40448

Letter to Mr. Powys on the Independency of America. By a Man of Candor, who is totally divested of Party Prejudices. *London: Hooper and Davis.* MDCCLXXVIII. 8vo, pp. 44. 40449

"Were we so weak," says the writer, "to surrender the dependency of our American Colonies, we would destroy trade, ruin navigation, and every species of national industry. It would weaken our national consequence and endanger our safety.—We should lose our valuable possessions, until, at last, we become a prey to our enemies, and a province of France."

A Letter to Mr. Roger B. Taney. By a Faithful Federalist. [n. p. n. d.] 8vo, pp. 8. 40450

Letter to Philo Africanus upon Slavery; in answer to his, of the 22d November ... *Newport, R. I.* 1788. 8vo. + *London: Brown.* 1788. 8vo. C. 40451

See "Philo Africanus," *and* "M. Rev.," LXXVIII. 255.

A Letter to Mrs. P-------s. In which some Facts in her Number are rescued from the false Light she has put them and some others which she has omitted, are supply'd. *London. H. Carpenter.* M.DCC.XLIX. 8vo, pp. (2), 21. 40452

Relates to Mrs. Phillips' voyage to Jamaica.

Letter to one of the Members of the late General Assembly of New York. *New York.* 1736. Folio, 1 l. 40453

Letter to President Lincoln, August 5, 1862. [n. p. n. d.] 8vo, pp. 8. 40454

Relative to the great loss of life during the Peninsular Campaign.

Letter to Reverdy Johnson. *See* [Legrand (J. C.)], No. 39872.

Letter to the American Peace Society. *See* [Gibbs (G. M.)]

Letter to the Archbishop of Canterbury from eighteen Presbyterian Ministers in America. *New York.* 1767. 12mo, pp. 16. + *Philadelphia.* 1767. 12mo. 40455

Letter to the Author of Lucubrations during a Short Recess. *London.* 1782. 8vo. 40456

A Letter to the Author of the Halifax Letter, occasioned by his book, entitled A Defence of that Letter. *Printed for the Author.* 1765. 8vo, pp. 8. 40457

Letter to the Author. *See* Vol. II. 7656, *also* Vol. VIII. 30136.

A Letter to the Belfast ... Volunteers. By a Member of Parliament. *Belfast: Printed by Henry and Robert Jay and Co.* M,DCC,LXXXII. 8vo, pp. 30. BA. + Third Edition. *London.* 1783. 8vo. S. 40458

Relates incidentally to the American Revolution.

Letter to the Catholic Clergy. *See* Vol. III., No. 10425.

A Letter to the Christian Laity of the United States. ... *New-York: John A. Gray, Printer.* 1860. 8vo, pp. 35. H. 40459

A Letter to the Clergy. *See* Vol. IV., No. 15817.

Letter to the Commissioner of Indian Affairs. *See* Vol. III., No. 12464, *also* North Carolina.

Letter to the Committee of Ways and Means of the House of Representatives, on the Tariff on Lumber. *Washington.* 1870. 8vo. 40460

A Letter to the Common Council of London, on their late very extraordinary Address to His Majesty. *London.* 1765. 8vo. + Second Edition. *London.* 1765. 8vo, pp. 42. S.

A Letter to the Congregations of the Eighteen Presbyterian (or New Light) Ministers. With Remarks. *Philadelphia.* 1761. 16mo, pp. 28. 40462

A Letter to the Corporation. *See* Harvard College, Vol. VIII.

Letter to the Duke of Wellington, on ... West India Slavery, by a Jamaica Proprietor. ... *London: James Ridgway.* MDCCCXXIX. 8vo, pp. (4), 23. BA. 40463

A Letter to the Earl of Bute, on the Preliminaries of Peace. *London.* 1762. 8vo. 40464

A Letter to The Earl of B---, relative to the Late Changes that have happened in the Administration. *London: Richardson and Urquhart.* MDCCLXV. 4to, pp. (4), 15. 40465

A Letter to the Earl of Bute. *London: J. Almon.* 1771. 8vo, pp. 67. S. 40466

Letter to the Earl of Chatham, concerning his Speech and Motion in the House of Lords, on the memorable 30th of May; With some Observations on the Speeches of Lord Gower, the Duke of Grafton, Lord Lyttelton, Lord Camden, Lord Weymouth, The Archbishop of York, Lord Shelburne, and Lord Mansfield. To which are subjoined Reflections on his Majesty's ... Speech from the Throne, and an Index to Peace with America. *London: T. Evans.* MDCCLXXVII. 8vo, pp. 54. C. 40467

"A spirited, but not very elaborate declamation against Great Britain, in respect to her quarrel with the colonies; and a prophetic denunciation of the most melancholy consequences to the mother country."—*Monthly Review*, LVII. 165. "As to the American contest," says the writer, "I can hardly see a ray of hope of accommodation; for, as to conquest, I am convinced, that, in the common course of human events, it is impossible."

A Letter to the Earl of Chatham on the Quebec Bill. *London: T. Cadell.* MDCCLXXIV. 8vo, pp. (2), 36. + Second Edition, Corrected. [*Ibid.*] 8vo. + The Third Edition, Corrected. [*Ibid.*] 8vo. + The Fourth Edition. [*Ibid.*] 8vo. + Fifth Edition. [*Ibid.*] 8vo. 40468

Usually attributed to Thomas, Lord Lyttelton; but more probably by Sir William Meredith.

Letter to the Earl of Shelburne on the Peace. *London: J. Debrett.* MDCCLXXXIII. 8vo, pp. 40. + Third Edition. [*Ibid.*]

Signed "Portius, Feb. 5, 1783." "Anti-ministerial, and consequently anti-pacific." —*Monthly Review*, LXVIII. 178.

A Letter to the Editors of the Louisville Journal, May, 1840. *Louisville.* 1840. 8vo, pp. 4. 40470

Letter to the Electors of President and Vice-President of the United States. By a Citizen of New York. Accompanied with an extract of the secret debates of the Federal Convention, ... 1787, taken by Chief Justice Yates. *New-York: Printed by Henry C. Southwick.* 1808. 8vo, pp. 22. BA. 40471

A Letter to the English Nation, on the Present War with America; with a Review of our Military Operations in that Country; and a Series of Facts never before published, From which the absolute Impossibility of reducing the Colonies will sufficiently appear, and the Folly of continuing the Contest demonstrated. With a Prefatory Address to Sir George Saville, Bart. By an Officer returned from that Service. ... *London: G. Corrall.* MDCCLXXVII. 8vo, pp. iv, 59. H. 40472

"According to this mutinous officer, nothing remains for us to do but, in the first place, to desist from an attempt in which it is impossible for us to succeed, and in the next place, to bring the authors of all this mischief to condign punishment."—*Monthly Review*, LVII. 156.

Letter to the Evangelical ... Church. *See* [Farwell (W.)], Vol. VI., No. 23902.

A Letter to the Freeholders and other Inhabitants of the Massachusetts-Bay, relating to their approaching Election of Representatives. ... [n. p.:] *Printed in the Year*, 1739. 8vo, pp. (2), 12. + *Boston: Printed by Rogers and Fowle.* [1749?] 8vo, pp. 8. BA. 40473

The 1739 edition is signed "Americanus," the other "L. Quincius Cincinnatus."

A Letter to the Freeholders and other Inhabitants of this Province qualified to vote for Representatives. [*Boston.* 1742.] 8vo, pp. 8. 40474

A Letter to the Freeholders and Qualified Voters, Relating to the Ensuing Election. By a New-England-Man. *Boston: Printed by Rogers and Fowle.* MDCCXLIX. 4to, pp. 12. BA., C.

Letter to the Freeholders of the Town of Boston. *Boston.* 1750. 40476

A Letter to the Freemen and Freeholders of the City of New York, relating to the approaching Election of their Representatives. Wherein the several Papers that have lately appeared on the Subject of Politicks, are briefly considered; the Conduct of the Authors exposed and the Controversy represented in its true ——. *New York: I. Parker.* 1752. 12mo, pp. 24. 40477

An extremely scarce pamphlet.

A Letter to the Gentlemen of the Committee of London Merchants, Trading to North America: Shewing In what Manner, it is apprehended, that the Trade and Manufactures of Britain may be affected by some late Restrictions on the American Commerce, and by the Operation of the Act for the Stamp Duty in America; as also how far the Freedom and Liberty of the Subjects residing in Britain, are supposed to be interested in the Preservation of the Rights of the Provinces, and in what Manner those Rights appear to be abridged by that Statute. *London: W. Richardson & L. Urquart.* M DCC LXVI. 8vo, pp. 30. H. 40478

"The writer denies the virtual representation, and offers several arguments in favor of the colonies, in common with their other advocates."—*Monthly Review*, XXXIV. 157.

Letter to the Governor of Massachusetts. *See* [Cabot (J. E.)]

A Letter to the Great Man, occasioned by the Letter to two Great Men. In which many of that Writer's Absurdities, Inconsistencies, and Contradictions are detected, and the fatal Tendency of his Propositions exposed. By a Citizen of London, ... *London: Bristow.* 1760. 8vo. 40479

Letter to the Hon. Abbott Lawrence. *See* [Clapp (O.)]

A Letter to the Honorable A—r M—re, Coffiner of Trade and Plantation. *London: James Roberts* ... 1714. 8vo, pp. 39.

Letter to the Hon. Harrison Gray Otis. *See* [Bradford (G.)]

Letter to the Hon. James F. Simmons. By a Rhode Island Conservative. *Providence, April 1*, 1845. 8vo, pp. 8. 40481

A Letter to the Hon. John Quincey [*sic*] Adams, occasioned by his Letter to Mr. Otis. By Alfred. ... *Printed in America.* 1808. 8vo, pp. 43. B. 40482

Letter to the Hon John Randolph [by Numa. n. p. 1808.] 8vo. S. 40483

Letter to the Honorable Mr. Hawes, ... on the Graduates of the Military Academy. By a Graduate ... . *New-York: Wiley and Long.* 1836. 8vo, pp. 34. B. 40484

Signed "Justitia."

Letter to the Hon. S. A. Eliot, on the Fugitive Slave Bill *Boston.* 1851. 8vo. 40485

Letter to the Independent Reflector. *New York.* 1753. 4to, pp. 31. 40486

A Letter to the Inhabitants of ... the Massachusetts-Bay. By a New-England Man. *Boston.* 1751. 8vo, pp. 8. BA. 40487

Letter to the Inhabitants of the City and State of New York, on the Commerce of the Western States. By Agricola. *New York.* 1807. 16mo. 40488

A Letter to the Inhabitants of the Province of Quebec. Extract from the Minutes of Congress. *Philadelphia: Printed by William and Thomas Bradford, October*, 1774. 8vo, pp. (2), 37–50

An official letter from the Colonial Congress, inciting the Canadians to join the thirteen United Colonies in their opposition to Great Britain.

Letter to the Jurors of Great-Britain occasioned by an Opinion of the Court of King's Bench, read by Lord Chief Justice Mansfield in the case of the King and Woodfall; &c. *London: Pearch.* 1771. 8vo, pp. (2), x, 67. 40490

A Letter to the King of ***** *London.* 1756. 8vo.

Relates to Canada, etc.

Letter to the Legislature of Massachusetts, on the Repeal of the License Laws. [*Boston.* 1838.] 8vo, pp. 7. BA. 40492

Letter to the Legislative Authority of Connecticut, on Imprisonment for Debt. [n. p.] 1770. 8vo, pp. 16. 40493

Letter to the Liverpool Society for the Abolition of Slavery. *London.* 1824. 8vo, pp. 15. 40494

A Letter to the Lord Bishop of London. *See* [Gibson (E.)]

A Letter to the Lord Chancellor, on the Abolition of Slavery. By a West-Indian. *London.* 1833. 8vo, pp. 16. S. 40495

A Letter to the ... Lord Mayor. *See* [Heathcote (G.)]

Letter to the Lords Commissioners of Trade. *See* [Coade (G.)]

A Letter to the Members of the Associate-Reformed Church, In North-America, relative to A Theological Seminary. *New-York: Printed by Hopkins and Seymour.* 1805. 8vo, pp. 16.

A Letter to the Members of the Imperial Parliament, referring to the evidence of ... Jamaica, and shewing the injurious ... tendency of the proposed Slave Registry Bill. By a Colonist. *London: J. M. Richardson.* 1816. 8vo, pp. (2), 24. BA. 40497

Letter to the Members of the Pennsylvania Legislature on the Subject of the State Debt. *Philadelphia.* 1844. 8vo, pp. 24.

A Letter to the Merchant in London, To whom is Directed A Printed Letter relating to the Manufactory Undertaking, Dated New England, Boston February 21st 1740, 1. [n. p.:] *Printed for the Public Good.* 1741. 8vo, pp. 28. BA., H. 40499

Letter to the Merchants of Great Britain and the West India Planters, recommending an Increase on Freight of Sugars, &c., and the prevention of such rogues escaping Justice as have heretofore done by going to Jamaica ... . *London: Griffin.* 1769. 8vo.

A Letter to the Most Honorable the Marquis of Chandos. By a West India Planter. ... *London: James Ridgway.* MDCCCXXX. 8vo, pp. (8), 5–90. B. 40501

A Letter to the Most Noble the Marquis of Chandos, Chairman of the Body of West India Proprietors, Merchants, &c., on the Affairs of the West Indies. *London: Printed by Richard Clay.* 1830. 8vo, pp. 16. 40502

Signed "C. Barrow." This is the correct title of *our* No. 3653, Vol. I.

A Letter to the New Parliament; with Hints on some Regulations which the Nation hopes and expects ... *London: John, Francis, and Charles Rivington.* MDCCLXXX. 8vo, pp. (2), 59.

A Letter to the Negroes Lately Converted ... in America. And Particularly to Those ... at Mr. Jonathan Bryan's in South Carolina. ... By a Friend ... in England. ... *London: Printed by J. Hart.* MDCCXLIII. 8vo, pp. 32. B., N. 40504

A Letter to the Noblemen, Gentlemen, &c. who have addressed His Majesty on the Subject of the American Rebellion. *London: T. Cadell.* MDCCLXXVI. 8vo, pp. 37. 40505

Much ability is evinced in this tract which favors the reduction of the colonies. The writer calls upon the people "to join, not only in vindicating the supremacy of the Legislature, on which the very existence of government depends, but in maintaining the

freedom and preserving the possession of the American provinces."—Page 36. *See* "M. Rev.," LIV. 327.

Letter to the North American. *See* [Dickinson (J.)], Vol. v.

A Letter to the People of America, lately Printed at New York; now re-published by an American. With a Postscript, by the Editor, Addressed to Sir W****** H***. *London: T. Becket.* MDCCLXXVIII. 8vo, pp. (4), 74. 40506

"The author earnestly admonishes and exhorts the revolted Americans to make it up with us; endeavoring to convince them, by every popular argument, that nothing but immediate reconciliation can save them from destruction."—*Monthly Review*, LIX. 471. Probably by Joseph Galloway.

A Letter to the People of England, on the Necessity of putting an Immediate End to the War; and The Means of obtaining an Advantageous Peace. ... *London: R. Griffiths.* MDCCLX. 8vo, pp. (2), 54. BA. 40507

See "M. Rev.," XXII. 235, *also* [Shebbeare (John)].

Letter to the People of Great Britain from the Delegates of the American Congress in Philadelphia. [*Philadelphia.* 1774.] 8vo, pp. 16. 40508

A Letter to the People of Great-Britain, in Answer to that published by the American Congress. *London: F. Newbery.* MDCCLXXV. 8vo, pp. 59. 40509

"This letter-writer was it seems determined, *fas aut nefas*, to controvert every allegation of the Congress, in their letter to the people of Great Britain; and in doing this, we think we often see him offending against the truth."—*Monthly Review*, LII. 175. *See also* Bartlett's Catalogue of J. C. Brown's Library.

A Letter To the People of Pennsylvania; Occasioned by the Assembly's passing that Important Act for Constituting the Judges of the Supream Court and Common-Pleas, During Good Behaviour. ... *Philadelphia: Printed in* MDCCLX. 8vo, pp. 39. P. + Second Edition. [*Ibid.*] 40510

A Letter to the President of the Town of Catskill. January 10, 1838. *New-York: Printed by G. Mitchell.* 1838. 8vo, pp. 15.

Letter to the President of the United States, July 21, 1862. [n. p. n. d.] 8vo, pp. 8. N. 40512

See also [Barnard (F. A. P.)], No. 3458, *and* [Eliot (S. A.)], No. 22173.

Letter to the Representatives of Chester, Bucks and Philadelphia, from a great Number of their Constituents. May 9, 1774. [*Philadelphia.* 1774.] Folio, 1 l. P. 40513

A Letter to the Reverend Author. *See* [Webster (S.)]

A Letter to the Rev. Dr. Cooper, on the Origin of Civil Government; in Answer to his Sermon, preached before the University of Oxford, on the day appointed for a general Fast. *London: J. Almon.* 1777. 8vo, pp. 53. 40514

"A poignant antidote to the poison contained in Dr. Cooper's high-flying Tory Sermon."—*Monthly Review*, LVI. 473. *See also* our Vol. IV., No. 16589.

Letter to the Rev. Dr. Price. *See* Price (R.), *and* [Stewart (J.)]

A Letter to the Rev. Dr. Richard Watson, King's Professor of Divinity in the University of Cambridge. *London.* 1780. 8vo, pp. 45. 40515

An attack on Watson's notion respecting American affairs.

Letter to the Rev. James C. Richmond. By a South Carolinian. *New York.* 1845. 8vo. 40516

A Letter to the Rev. Jedediah Morse, author of the American Universal Geography. By a Citizen of Williamsburg. *Richmond: Thomas Nicolson.* 1795. 8vo, pp. 16. C. 40517

A defense of Williamsburg, Va.

Letter to the Rev. Mr. John Wesley. *See* [Evans (Caleb)], Vol. VI., No. 23138, *and* Wesley (John).

Letter to the Rev. Thomas Hinton on the Emigration of the Indians. *Washington.* 1828. 8vo, pp. 28. 40518

Letter to the Right Honourable Author of a Letter to a Citizen, with Animadversions on the Answer thereto, and on the Behaviour of the Corporation of the City of London. *London.* 1761. 8vo. 40519

Relates in part to America.

A Letter to the Right Honourable Charles Jenkinson. The Second Edition. *London: J. Debrett.* MDCCLXXXI. 4to, pp. 51. + The Third Edition. [*Ibid.*] + The Fourth Edition. [*Ibid.*]

Relates chiefly to American affairs, and is signed "An Independent Whig." A trenchant exposure of the evil influence of Jenkinson upon the King and the administration of the fleets and armies in America, being a scorching historical and critical review of the mal-administration of political and military arrangements from the Boston tea party to the surrender of Cornwallis, and interesting personal gossip respecting Burgoyne, Howe, Clinton, Franklin, Washington, Young, Lawrence, etc., especially in New York and the South. Also: A Second Letter to the Right Honourable Charles Jenkinson. *London: Murray.* 1781. 8vo. *See* "M. Rev.," LXVI. 70 and 141.

A Letter to the Right Honourable Ch----- T-----nd, Esq; *London: W. Nicoll.* MDCCLXIII. 8vo, pp. 24. S. + Second Edition. [*Ibid.*] + *London.* 1764. 8vo, pp. 43. 40521

A Letter to the Right Honourable Earl Grey, on ... Emigration, as connected with ... Railway Communication between the Atlantic and Pacific. *London: W. P. Metchim.* MDCCCL. 8vo pp. 27. 40522

Letter to the Right Hon. G. Grenville. *See* Vol. VII. 28767.

A Letter to the Right Honourable Lord M*****, on The Affairs of America. From a Member of Parliament. *London: J. Almon.* MDCCLXXV. 8vo, pp. 38. 40523

See "M. Rev.," LII. 85.

Letter to the Right Hon[ble] Lord North. To which is added a Petition to the King in favour of the Colonies. *London: J. Henderson.* [1776.] 8vo, pp. 28. 40524

A Letter to the Right Hon. Lord Rodney, K.B., on the St. Eustatius Prize Money. By a Navy Officer. *London.* 1788. 8vo. 40525

See "M. Rev.," LXXIX. 378.

A Letter to the Right Hon. W. Bertie. *See* [Linde (J.)]

Letter to the Right Hon. L—d Th—w, L—d H—h C—r of E——d, &c. *London.* 1780. 8vo. 40526

Partly on American affairs. Thurlow was the Lord Chancellor.

A Letter To the Right Honourable The Earl of B***, on A late important Resignation [viz., of Mr. Pitt] and its probable Consequences. *London: J. Coote.* MDCCLXI. 8vo, pp. (2), 75. + The Third Edition. [*Ibid.*] 1761. 8vo. + A Second Letter ... [*Ibid.*] 1761. 8vo, pp. 73. + A Third Letter ... in which the Causes and Consequences of the War between Great Britain and Spain, are fully considered. *London.* 1767. 8vo.

Partly relative to Canada, and believed to be written by Stuart. It elicited "An Answer To a Letter to the Right Honourable The Earl of B***, In which the false Reasoning, and absurd Conclusions, in that Pamphlet, are fully detected and refuted. Addressed to the Right Hon. Earl T–mple." *London: J. Wilkie.* 1761. 8vo, pp. 43.

A Letter to the Right Hon. the Earl of H——x, concerning a Parliamentary Peace. *London: A. Henderson.* 1783. 8vo.

See "M. Rev.," XXVII. 383.

A Letter to the Right Honourable The Earl of H—b—h. *See* Vol. VII., No. 28757, *also* Vol. VIII., No. 31912.

A Letter to the Right Honourable the Earl of Sandwich, on the present Situation of Affairs. By a Sailor. *London: J. Wilkie.* 1779. 8vo. 40529

See "M. Rev.," LXII. 84.

A Letter to the Right Honourable the Earl of Shelburne, on the Motives of his Political Conduct, and the Principles which have actuated the Opposition to the Measures of the Administration in respect to America. *London: William Davis.* MDCCLXXVI. 8vo, pp. 28. 40530

"The writer, who is very severe on Lord Shelburne, thus commences his attack: 'By a series of industrious chicane, which is never the effect of real genius, you have risen to a degree of consequence in this country. Nature designed you for some of those middling employments, where great industry, much artifice, void of real principle, an apparent ardor for religion would have gradually led to the fortune of a Jew."—*Monthly Review*, LV. 65.

Letter to the Right Hon. the Earls of Egremont and Halifax, on the Seizure of Papers. *London.* 1763. 8vo. 40531

A Letter To the Right Honourable The Lords Commissioners of Trade & Plantations: Or, A short Essay on the Principal Branches of the Trade of New-England, with the Difficulties they labour under; and Some Methods of Improvement. [By Thomas Banister.] *London.* 1715. 8vo, pp. (4), 19. 40532

Our No. 3170, Vol. I., is not correct.

A Letter to the Right Honourable Viscount H—e. *See* [Galloway (J.)], Vol. VII., No. 26435.

A Letter to the Right Honourable William Pitt, Esq; from an Officer at Fort Frontenac. *London: J. Fleming.* MDCCLIX. 8vo, pp. (4), 38. 40533

"Fort Frontenac was a French fort at the entrance to the St. Lawrence from Lake Ontario, on the site of the present town of Kingston. The writer gives a description of the fort and its surroundings, which he considers one of the most important positions in Canada. He recommends that it be fortified in the best manner possible, and that frigates be built to cruise upon the lake." *See* "M. Rev.," XX. 185.

A Letter to the Right Hon. William Pitt, Esq; on the present Negociations for a Peace with France and Spain. *London: J. Coote.* [n. d.] 8vo. 40534

See "M. Rev.," XXVII. 383.

A Letter to the Right Honourable W—— P—. By a Citizen. *London.* 1761. 8vo. 40535

Letter to ... Wills, Earl of Hillsborough. *See* [Canning (G.)]

Letter to the Right Hon. Sir R—— W——, &c., upon the present Position of Affairs, wherein, amongst other things, the Convention will be set in a clear light. *London.* 1739. 8vo.

Robert Walpole was the recipient of this epistle.

A Letter to the Right Reverend Father in God The Lord-B---p of L----n. Occasioned by a Letter of his Lordships' to the L—ds of Trade, on the Subject of the Act of Assembly passed in the Year 1758, intituled, An Act to enable the Inhabitants of the Colony to discharge their publick Dues, &c. in Money for the ensuing Year. From Virginia. [n. p. n. d.] 8vo, pp. 56, (2). 40537

Rich says, "Apparently first printed in Virginia." *See also* Gibson (E.), Vol. VII., Nos. 27310–13.

A Letter to the Rt. Rev. Beilby, Lord Bishop of London, on the Abolition of Slavery. *London: Longman.* 1788. 8vo.

Porteus was the Bishop. *See* "M. Rev.," LXXX. 93.

A Letter to the Roman Catholics of Philadelphia and the United States of America. By a Friend to the Civil and Religious Liberties of Man. *Philadelphia: Robert Desilver.* 1822. 8vo, pp. 82. 40539

Relates to the Rev. William Hogan, and church affairs in Philadelphia.

Letter to the Secretary of a Certain Board, with Verses to Admiral V[ernon]. *London.* 1744. 8vo. 40540

Letter to the Secretary of a Certain Board; a Supplement to the Original Papers relating to the Expedition to Carthagena, Cuba, and Panama. *London.* 1744. 8vo. C. 40541

Letter to the Secretary of the Treasury. Dated Boston, January 16, 1869. [n. p. n. d.] 8vo, pp. 8. H. 40542

For others *see* Treasury, *infra.*

Letter to the Secretary of War, or, Review of the Controversy on a Question of Rank between Generals Scott and Gaines. *New York.* 1826. 8vo, pp. 88. 40543

See also Secretary of War.

A Letter to the Senate and House of Representatives of the United States upon the Expediency of an Uniform System of Bankruptcy. ... *Boston.* 1821. 8vo, pp. 31. H. 40544

A Letter to the Wardens and Vestry of Christ Church, Cincinnati; in reply to their Declaration and Protest against the Proceedings of Bishop Hobart ... in relation to the Mission of Bishop Chase to England. By a Presbyter of the Diocese of New York. *New York.* 1824. 8vo, pp. 74. 40545

A Letter to the West India Merchants, in Answer to their Petition now before the ... House of Commons, praying for a Prohibition of the Trade carried on from the Northern Colonies, to the French and Dutch West India Settlements. By a Fisherman. *London: H. Whitridge.* 1751. 8vo, pp. 27. 40546

A Letter to the Whigs. *London: J. Almon.* MDCCLXXIX. 8vo, pp. 38. BA. 40547

On the Revolutionary War, etc.

A Letter to the Whigs, occasion'd by the letter to the Tories, ... Second Edition. *London: M. Cooper.* MDCCXLVIII. 8vo, pp. 40. S. 40548

Also: A Second and Third Letter to the Whigs. By the Author of the First. ... *London: M. Cooper.* MDCCXLVIII. 8vo, pp. (2), 92. H.

Letter to the Whigs with some Remarks on a Letter to the Tories. *London.* 1762. 4to, pp. 16. 40549

Letter to the Women of England, on Slavery, as it exists in the Southern States of America. *London.* 1863. 12mo. 40550

A Letter to those Ladies whose Husbands possess a Seat in either House of Parliament. ... *London:* ... *J. Almon* ... 1775. 4to, pp. 11. P. 40551

A Letter To Us, from One of Ourselves. ... The Second Edition. *London: G. Kearsley.* MDCCLXXVII. 8vo, pp. (4), 67.

Letter to W. Manning, Esq. M.P. on the Progressive Depreciation of West India Property. *London.* 1807. 8vo. 40553

Letter to William Meade Addison, of Baltimore, upon Religious Toleration in America. *Washington.* 1854. 8vo, pp. 13.

A Letter to Wm. E. Channing, D.D. ... on the Abuse of the Flag of the United States in ... Cuba, for Promoting the Slave Trade. By a Calm Observer. *Boston: William D. Ticknor.* 1840. 8vo, pp. 36. BA. 40555

A Letter to William Pitt. *See* [Randolph (Francis)].

A Letter to William Wilberforce [on Slavery]. 1807. 8vo.

The Letter Writer, or the Art of Polite Correspondence. ... [illegible] Edition. *Richmond: J. W. Randolph.* 1864. 16mo, 40557

[illegible]erate publication with some historical allusions.

Lettera de | La nobil Citta nuouamente | ritrouata alle Indie con li | suoi costumi & modi del | suo Re & soi popoli | Li modi del suo adorare con la | bella vsanza delle donne loro. | Et de le dua persone ermafrodite | donate da quel Real Capi- | tano della Armata. | [Colophon:] *Data in Zhaual. Adi. xxv. di Settembre.* M.D.XXXV. 4to, 4 leaves. 40558

The only known copy of the original edition is in the British Museum. A few copies have been reprinted.

Lettera dela | Nobil Citta nuouamēte ritrouata alle In- | die conli suoi costumi & modi del suo Re & soi popoli. | Li modi del suo adorare con la bella vsanza delle donne loro. | Et delle dua persone Ermafrodite donate da quel | Re al Capitano della Armata. | [n. p. n. d.] 4to, 2 l. 40559

Dated "xxx di Settembre M.D.XXXIX." *See also* Brunet's "Manuel," Vol. III., "Bib. Gren.," p. 822, and Part II., p. 445, *and* [Harrisse's] "Bib. Am. Vet.," Nos. 191, 206, and 227. For another edition *see* "Letera," No. 40244.

Lettera Apologetica dell' Esercitato Accademico della crusca contenente la Difesa del Libro Intitolato Lettere d'una Peruana per rispetto alla supposizione de Quipu scritta alla Duchessa di S****e dalla medesima fatta pubblicare. *In Napoli.* MDCCL. Folio, pp. (14), 320. 3 colored Plates of the Quipus. 40560

This letter from a learned academician of the *Della Crusca*, contains a defense of Madame de Grafigny, "Letters from a Peruvian Princess," published in 1747, wherein the author speaks of the extensive use of the *quipus* by the Peruvians. For a particular account of the *quipus* see Acosta, lib. VI., cap. 8; and Prescott's "Conquest of Peru," Vol. I., p. 118.

Lettere Americane. *See* [Carli], Vol. III., No. 10911.

Lettere annue d'Etiopia, Malabar, Brasil e Goa. *Roma: Corbelletti.* 1627. 12mo. 40561

Title from Ternaux, No. 493.

Lettere annve d'Ethiopia, Malabar, Brasil e Goa.—Histoire de ce qvi s'est passé en Éthiopie, Malabar, Brasil, et és Indes orientales. Tirée des lettres escrites és années 1620, iusques à 1624. Addressée au R. P. Mvtio Vitelleschi, Général de la Compagnie de Iesvs. Traduite de l'Italien en François, par un père de la mesme Compagnie [Iean Darde]. *A Paris, Chez Sebastien Cramoisy* ... MDCXXVIII. 16mo, pp. (4), 451. C. 40562

Lettere d'una Peruviana. *See* [Graffigny (F. d'l d'H. de)].

Lettere di Principi Libro primo. *Venetia.* 1564. 4to.

Contains a letter from Gonzalo Hernandes de Ovideo to Cardinal Bembo respecting Pizarro, the river Amazon, El Dorado, etc., and forms an interesting contemporary

account of the progress and successes of the Spaniards in Peru. Two sequent volumes were published in 1575 and 1581, and all three were reproduced in 1581 as:

Lettere di Principi, le quali o si scrivono da Principi, o sa Principi, o ragionano di Principi. *Venetia: F. Ziletti.* 1581. 3 vols., 4to. 40564

LETTERMAN (J.) Medical Recollections of the Army of the Potomac. By Jonathan Letterman, M.D. ... *New York: D. Appleton and Company.* 1866. 8vo, pp. 194. BA. 40565

Letters about the Hudson River. *See* [Hunt (Freeman)].

Letters addressed to C. Strong. *See* [Whelpley (Samuel)].

Letters addressed to John Sergeant [and others], Authors of An Address To The People of Pennsylvania, Adopted at a Meeting of the Friends to the Election of John Quincy Adams, held in Philadelphia, July 7, 1828; containing Strictures on their Address by The Committee of Correspondence of Philadelphia. *Philadelphia: Printed by William Staveley.* 1828. 8vo, pp. 88. P.

Letters addressed to Lord Liverpool and the Parliament on the Preliminaries of Peace. By Calvus. *London: H. Colburn.* 1814. 8vo, pp. (2), 100. C. 40567

Letters addressed to W. L. Stone, and to Benjamin Cowell, Esq., of Rhode Island, on Masonry and Anti-Masonry. To which is added a Portrait of Masonry by J. C. Spencer. *Providence.* 1833. 12mo, pp. 24. 40568

Letters addressed to the Army of the United States in the Year 1783; with a brief Exposition, etc. *Printed by J. Buel, Kingston, State of New York.* 1805. 8vo, pp. 19. 40569

Perhaps by General John Armstrong.

Letters addressed to the Editor of "A Collection of Essays on the subject of Episcopacy, which originally appeared in the Albany Centinel." *Albany.* 1806. 8vo. 40570

The "Collection of Essays" is *our* No. 14375, Vol. IV.

Letters addressed to the People of the Canadas and British North America, on Elective Institutions. By an East Anglian. *Cobourg.* 1858. 12mo. 40571

Letters Addressed to the People of the United States, by a Native of Virginia, on the subject of Illegal, and Improper Disbursements of the Public Money ... . *Baltimore.* 1822. 8vo, pp. 59. + Part First. *Boston.* 1822. 8vo. W. + *Cincinnati.* 1822.

Letters addressed to the Rev. Messrs. John Cree [and others], Members of the Associate Presbytery of Pennsylvania, in answer to their Pamphlet, entitled, Evils of the work now prevailing in the United States of America, under the name of a Revival of Religion ... and the work Vindicated as being agreeable to the Word of God. ... *Washington (Penn.): Printed for the Author.* 1805. 8vo, pp. 61. S. 40573

Signed "A Presbyterian."

Letters addressed to the Right Honourable Lord M——, on the late Expeditions to the Spanish Main; and on the Expediency of a gradual and systematical Emancipation of Spanish America; including a Sketch of a Plan for effecting it in a manner beneficial to Great Britain, and that Country. By a Native of Spanish America. *London: T. Cadell.* 1807. 8vo, pp. 95. 40574

Letters addressed to the Yeomanry. *See* [Laughan (*Dr.*)]

It has also been ascribed to George Logan.

Letters and Conversations. *See* [Tuttle (*Miss* Sarah)], *also our* Vol. III., No. 12465.

Letters and Dissertations. *See* [Crowley (T.)], Vol. V. 17704.

Letters and Documents of Distinguished Citizens of Tennessee, on the Buying and Selling of Human Beings. *New York.* 1828. 8vo, pp. 16. M. 40575

Letters and Memorials which have lately passed between the Ministers of Great Britain, France, and Spain. *London.* 1727. 8vo, pp. 48. W. 40576

Contains several letters relative to Admiral Hosier's squadron in the West Indies.

Letters and Papers on Agriculture. *See* Vol. VII., No. 29703.

Letters and Papers. *See* [Balch (T.)], Vol. I., No. 2871.

Letters between Theophilus and Eugenio. *See* [Franklin (B.)]

Letters by a South Carolinian. Sketches of some Virginians. *Norfolk: C. Bonsal.* 1827. 18mo, pp. 89. C. 40577

Letters concerning the Complaints of the People of Boston ... [n. p. n. d.] 16mo. 40578

Letters concerning the General Health. *See* [Hopkins (S. M.)]

Letters concerning the Present State of England. *London.* 1772. 8vo. C. 40579

Letters descriptive of the Virginia Springs. *See* [Nicklin (P. H.)]

Letters developing ... Hartford Convention. *See* [Otis (H. G.)]

Letters entitled, The American Commercial Claims, showing the Responsibility of the United States to such of her Citizens as have suffered by the French Spoliations. By a Gentleman of Baltimore. *Baltimore.* 1802. 8vo. 40580

Letters explanatory of the Difficulties. *See* Salisbury, *N. H.*

Letters for the People, on the Present Crisis. [n. p. n. d.] 8vo, pp. 52. 40581

Signed "Lynceus." On Slavery, the Indians, Nebraska, etc.

Letters from a Country Clergyman, to a Member of Parliament, on the Present State of the Nation. Third Edition. *London.* 1784. 8vo, pp. 72. 40582

Letters from a Farmer in Pennsylvania. *See* [Dickinson (J.)]

Letters from a Federal Farmer to the Republican, on the System of Government proposed by the Convention. [n. p.] 1788. 12mo, pp. 40. W. 40583

Letters from a General Officer to his Son, on his entering the Army; containing elegant Instructions for the Gentleman and Soldier. *Salem: Cushing & Appleton.* [n. d.] 2 vols., 12mo.

Letters from a Landscape Painter. *See* [Lanman (C.)]

Letters from a Maryland Mail Bag. [n. p. n. d.] 16mo, pp. 19. 40585

Poetry on the war; probably printed at Baltimore, 1863.

Letters from a Spaniard in London to his Friend at Madrid. *London.* 1739. 8vo. 40586

Letters from an Adopted Citizen. *See* [Treviranus, *pseudon*].

Letters from an American Loyalist. *See* Jackson (J. M.), *note.*

Letters from an Egyptian in New York to his Friend in Cairo, translated by Mathew Markwell. *New York.* 1848. 8vo, pp. 180

Letters from America to a Friend in England. *London.* 1795. 8vo. Map. 40588

A doubtful title from an auctioneer's catalogue.

Letters from Buenos Ayres and Chili. *See* [Davie (J.)]

Letters from Canada, with Numerous Illustrations. ... *London: Frederic Algar.* 1863. 8vo, pp. 83. B. 40589

Letters from Europe touching the American Contest, and acknowledging the Receipt, from Citizens of New York, of Presentation Sets of the "Rebellion Record" ... . *New York.* 1864. 8vo, pp. 27. BA. 40590

Letters from Nahant. *See* [Wheildon (W. W.)]

Letters from Naval Officers in relation to the Marine Corps. *Washington, D. C.: Frank Taylor.* 1864. 8vo, pp. 39. 40591

Letters from Nova Scotia and New Brunswick, illustrative of their Moral, Religious and Physical Circumstances, during the Years 1826, 1827, and 1828. *Edinburgh.* 1829. Post 8vo.

Letters from Settlers in the British Colonies. *London.* 1851. 18mo. 40593

Letters from Sussex Emigrants who sailed from Portsmouth in 1832, for Upper Canada, with Information for Emigrants; and a Gazetteer of the Places named in the Letters. *Petworth.* 1833. 8vo, pp. 107. 40594

Letters from Virginia, Translated from the French. ... *Baltimore: Fielding Lucas, Jr.* 1816. 24mo, pp. 220. B., P. 40595

The Philadelphia Library catalogue says "By W. Maxwell." They were, in fact, written in English by Professor Tucker.

Letters from Washington. *See* [Watterston (George)].

Letters from the Army of the Potomac. May, 1864. [*New York.* 1864.] 8vo, pp. 10. 40596

Letters from the Bahama Islands. *See* Vol. VIII., No. 30639.

Letters from the Commercial Correspondent of an Association of Cotton Manufacturers. ... *Boston: Press of Geo. C. Rand & Avery.* 1865. 8vo, pp. 16. H. 40597

Letters from the Comptroller. *See* Treasury Department.

Letters from the English Kings. *See* Hinman (R. R.)

Letters from the First Church in Glocester. *See* No. 27584.

Letters from the Havana. *See* Vol. VIII., No. 29439.

Letters from the Old World. *See* [Haight (*Mrs.* R. K.)]

Letters from the Prisons and Prison-Ships of the Revolution. With Notes by Henry R. Stiles, M.D. *New York: Privately Printed.* 1865. 8vo, pp. 49. 40598

Thirty-five copies printed on large paper. *See also* Wallabout.

Letters from the Secretary of State. *See* Secretary of State.

Letters from the South. By a Northern Man. *New-York.* 1835. 2 vols., 12mo. + New Edition. [*Ibid.*] 1835. 40599

See also Criswell (R.), Vol. v., [Knight (H. C.)], Vol. IX., *and* [Paulding (J. K.)]

Letters from the United States of America, exhibiting the workings of Democracy therein for the last Twenty Years. By an Anglo-American of several years' residence. *London.* 1844. 8vo, pp. 59. 40600

Letters from the Virgin Islands; illustrating Life and Manners in the West Indies. ... *London: John Van Voorst.* MDCCCXLIII. 8vo, pp. x, 286. Map. B., C. 40601

Letters ... inscribed to ... Doctor Samuel Cooper ... . *Boston.* MDCCLXXV. 8vo, pp. (2), 127. H. 40602

Letters lately published in the Diary, on the Subject of the present Dispute with Spain. Under the Signature of Verus. *London: G. Kearsley.* 1790. 8vo, pp. viii, 101. 40603

Attributed to J. Bland Burgess, Under-Secretary of State.

Letters of a Man of the Times. *See* [Kennedy (J. P.)]

Letters of a Nova Scotian, and of Scævola on Canadian Politics. *Quebec: T. Cary & Co.* 1828. 8vo, pp. (2), 106. C., H.

Letters of a South Carolina Planter on the Capture of American Vessels, by British Cruisers. *Philadelphia.* 1799. 8vo. 40605

Letters of an American, mainly on Russia and Revolution. Edited by Walter Savage Landor. *London.* 1854. 16mo.

Letters of an English Traveller. *See* [Dewey (O.)], Vol. VI.

Letters of Agricola on the Principles of Vegetation and Tillage. Written for Nova Scotia, and published first in the Acadian Recorder. *Halifax.* 1822. 8vo. 40607

The Letters of Common Sense respecting the State Bank and Paper Currency. *Raleigh: Printed by Thomas Henderson, jr.* [1811.] 8vo, pp. 48. BA. 40608

Letters of Decius to the Legislature, Delegate to Congress, and Governor of Indiana Territory; addressed to J. Madison. *Louisville (Ky.)* 1805. 16mo. 40609

See also [Courtenay (T. P.)], Vol. v., "Decius," Vol. v., *and* [Montgomery (*Dr.*)]

Letters of Friendship To those Clergymen who have lately renounced Communion with the Ministers and Churches of Christ in general. With Illustrations from recent Examples. ... *Printed by Hudson and Goodwin, Hartford.* M.DCC.LXXX. 8vo, pp. 134. BA. 40610

"Pious, ecclesiastical, biographical and valuable."—STEVENS.

Letters of Gen. Adair and Gen. Jackson. *See* No. 35374.

Part I. Letters of Loyal Soldiers. What General Grant says of the Administration. What General Dix says of the Rebellion. What General Sickels says of Peace. What General Hooker says of the Election. Part II. How General Sherman proclaimed Peace at Atlanta. How General McCall pronounced for Peace in Pennsylvania. Part III. How Douglas Democrats will Vote. Letters of General Wool & Logan. Part IV. Letter of General Dix ... . *New York: Loyal Publication Society.* 1864. 8vo, 4 pp. each. 40611

Letters of Loyal Soldiers upon McClellan and the Chicago Platform. 1864. [n. p. n. d.] 8vo. 40612

Letters of the British Spy. *See* [Wirt (Wm.)]

Letters of the Southern Spy. *See* [Umbaugh (W. A.)]

Letters on a National Currency in the United States. *Washington.* 1817. 8vo, pp. 37. 40613

Letters on American Affairs. [n. p. 1769.] 8vo, pp. 48.

Letters on Banks and Banking. *See* Silex, *pseudon.*

Letters on Emigration. By a Gentleman, lately returned from America. *London: C. and G. Kearsley.* MDCCXCIV. 8vo, pp. 276. BA. 40615

This gentleman is no friend to emigration. *See* "M. Rev.," XVIII. 331, Rich, I. 389.

Letters on Florida. [n. p. n. d.] 8vo, pp. 19. 40616

Letters on Interesting Subjects. *Philadelphia.* 1776. 8vo.

Letters on Political Liberty. [*See* Williams (David)].

Letters on Religious Subjects of Divers Friends Deceased. *London.* 1805. 12mo. 40618

Includes letters of Woolman, Sophia Hume, Anthony Benezet, Catherine Paton, etc.

Letters on the Boundary Line, first published in the City Gazette. *Saint John (New Brunswick): Alex. M'Leod.* 1828. 8vo, pp. 30. 40619

Letters on the Chickasaw ... Missions. *See* [Tuttle (Sarah)].

Letters on the Comparative Merits of the Pennsylvania and New York Systems of Penitentiary Discipline. By a Massachusetts Man. *Boston: Printed by Perkins & Marvin.* 1836. 8vo, pp. 48. H. 40620

Letters on the Condition of the African Race in the United States. By a Southern Lady. *Philadelphia: T. K. and P. G. Collins.* 1852. 8vo, pp. 34. 40621

Letters on the Eastern States. *See* [Tudor (Wm.)]

Letters on ... Barbadoes. *See* Vol. I., No. 3277.

Letters on the Late War between the United States and Great Britain, &c. *New York.* 1815. 8vo. 40622

Letters on the Mission. *See* [Tuttle (Sarah)].

Letters on the Missionary Organization of the Protestant Episcopal Church, addressed to the Right Rev. B. T. Onderdonk, D.D. ... of New York ... . By a Presbyter. [n. p.] 1841. 8vo, pp. 22. H. 40623

Letters on the Necessity of a Prompt Extinction of British Colonial Slavery. *London.* 1826. 8vo, pp. 100. 40624

Letters on the Necessity of Cheapening Transport between the West and the Ocean ... . By "A Western Trader." *Milwaukee: Jermain & Brightman ... Printers.* 1868. 8vo, pp. 16. 40625

Letters on the New Theatre. [*Boston.* 1827.] 8vo, pp. 15, (1).

Letters on the Pennsylvania System. *See* [Yard (Joseph)].

Letters on the Present Disturbances. *See* [Ramsay (Allan)].

Letters on the Present State and Probable Results of Theological Speculations in Connecticut. By an Edwardean. [n. p.] 1832. 8vo, pp. 44. 40627

Letters on the Present State of England and America; containing a Review of Several Interesting Particulars respecting the Laws, Policy, Trade, and Commerce, Agriculture, Manufactures, Churchill Institute, &c. &c. By the Author of the "Political Crisis." *London.* 1794. 8vo, pp. (4), 139. C. 40628

Letters on the Presidency, by a Kentucky Democrat, republished from the Louisville Journal. [n. p. 1840.] 8vo, pp. 28.

Letters on the Presidency. *Louisville, Ky.* [186–.] 8vo, pp. 56. 40630

Letters on the Relation. *See* [Mitchell (James)].

Letters on the Richmond Party. By a Virginian. *Washington.* 1823. 8vo. 40631

Letters on the Spirit of Patriotism. *See* [St. John (Henry)].

Letters on the Subject of a Line of Rail-Roads, from Boston to the Mississippi. *Boston.* 1839. 8vo, pp. 12. BA. 40632

Letters on the Subject. *See* [Croker (T. W.)], v. 17595.

Letters Respecting A Book dropped from the Catalogue of the American Sunday School Union in Compliance with the Dictation of the Slave Power. *New York: Wm. Harned.* 1848. 8vo, pp. 36. 40633

Letters, etc. [n. p. 1804.] 8vo. N. 40634

Respecting the eastern boundary of Louisiana.

Letters to a Friend, on Ecclesiastical Councils, Discipline and Fellowship; Comprizing a History of the late Dissentions in North Yarmouth (Maine). *Portland: Mirror Office.* 1824. 8vo, pp 80. 40635

The questions involved in this ecclesiastical trial are curious and of general interest outside the local quarrel.

Letters to a Member of the Present Parliament, upon the extraordinary and unprecedented Transactions in the last House of Commons. *London: J. Debrett.* 1784. 8vo, pp. 57. S.

Letters to a Nobleman. *See* [Galloway], Vol. VII. 26436.

Letters to a Student in the University of Cambridge, Massachusetts. *Boston.* 1796. 8vo. 40637

Letters to a Young Planter. *See* [Turnbull (Gordon)].

Letters to an Officer, stationed at an Interior Post [Michilimackinack] in North America; including many interesting Events. *London: Leacross.* 1773. 12mo. 40638

Letters to Chas. O'Conor. The Destruction of the Union is Emancipation. The Status of Slavery. The Rights of the States and Territories. [n. p. n. d.] 8vo, pp. 38. 40639

Letters to Congress. *See* Vol. IV., No. 15580.

Letters to Ladies, on the formation of a Martha Washington Society. *New York.* 1860. 8vo. 40640

Letters to Lord ***** on A Caveat. *See* [Smith (W.)]

Letters to ... Lord John Russell. *See* [Howe (Joseph)].

Letters to Sir Wm. Meredith. *See* [Meredith (W.)]

Letters to the British Legislature on American Independence. *Boston.* 1774. 8vo. 40641

Probably a reprint of [Cartwright (G.)], Vol. III., No. 11152.

Letters to the Contractors. *See* Vol. IV., No. 14597.

Letters to the Convention of Ministers and Representatives of the Evangelical Branches in the Church in Brooklyn. *New York.* 1866. 8vo, pp. 24. 40642

Letters to the Cotton Manufacturers. *See* [Lee (Henry)].

Letters to the Earl of Liverpool, on the State of the Colonies. Letter I. By a Member of Parliament. ... *London.* [1821.] 8vo, pp. 70. H. 40643

Letters to the Electors and People of England. By a Constitutionalist. *London: J. Almon.* 1780. 8vo. 40644

Letters to the Hon. Daniel Webster, on the Causes of the Destruction of the Steamer Lexington, as discovered in the Testimony before the Coroner's Jury in New York. By a Traveller. *Boston.* 1840. 8vo, pp. 46. 40645

Letters to the Hon. Harrison Gray Otis, by a Citizen of Massachusetts. Occasioned by the Petition of himself and others for a Repeal of the License Law of 1838. (First published in the Mercantile Journal.) *Boston: Whipple and Damrell.* 1839. 12mo, pp. 36. BA. 40646

Letters to the Honourable Levi Woodbury, Secretary of the Treasury ... . *New-York: E. B. Clayton, Printer.* 1837. 8vo, pp. 24. 40647

Letters to the King, from an Old Patriotic Quaker, lately deceased. *London: R. Baldwin.* MDCCLXXVIII. 8vo, pp. xv, 206

"The writer discusses wars in general, and dilates on the impolitic manner in which the war with the Colonies has been conducted. He thinks it improbable that the rebel Americans will be subjugated, and urges the necessity of an immediate accommodation."—*Monthly Review,* LVIII. 238.

Letters to the Laity of the Protestant Episcopal Church. By a Protestant Episcopalian. *Philadelphia.* 1843. 8vo, pp. 34. S.

Letters to the London "Times." *See* [Childe (E. V.)], Vol. IV., No. 12729, and *add* another edition: *Boston: Bazin & Chandler.* 1857. 12mo, pp. 259. Map. C. 40650

It is also attributed to George Lunt.

Letters to the Members. *See* [Bliss (Seth)], Vol. II. 5935.

Letters to the People. *See* [Lincoln (Levi)].

Letters to the People of England, on the Present Situation and Conduct of National Affairs. *London.* 1755. 8vo. 40651

Includes an account of General Braddock's march to Fort Duquesne on the Ohio River to dislodge the French, with comparative estimate of Virginia and Pennsylvania.

Letters to the People of New Jersey. *See* [Carey (H. C.)]

Letters to the People of the Northern States. [n. p. n. d.] 8vo, pp. 48. B. 40652

On the Kansas-Nebraska bill, and on slavery. Signed "A. P."

Letters to the President of the United States, by a Refugee. *New York: C. S. Westcott.* 1863. 8vo, pp. 32. 40653

Letters to the Right Honourable Lord Stanley ... shewing that the Proposed Repeal of the Union existing between the Island of Cape Breton and Nova-Scotia, would be Unconstitutional; ... *Halifax, N. S.: Printed by Richard Nugent.* 1842. 8vo, pp. 14.

See [Howe (J.)], Vol. VIII., Nos. 33311–12, *and* [Pitt (William)].

Letters to two Great Men. The first to the Earl of E——; The second to the Earl of B——. ... *London: A. Henderson.* 177–. 8vo. 40655

See "M. Rev.," XXVII. 156.

Letters under the signatures of "Senex," and of "A Farmer," comprehending an Examination of the Conduct of our Executive towards France and Great Britain, out of which the Present Crisis has arisen. Originally published in the North American. *Baltimore.* 1809. 8vo, pp. 108. 40656

Letters upon the Annexation of Texas, addressed to Hon. John Quincy Adams, ... in the Boston Atlas under the signature of Lisle. *Boston: White, Lewis & Potter, Printers.* 1845. 8vo, pp. 47. B. 40657

Letters written by a Peruvian Princess. *See* [Grafigny], 28195

Letters written during the late Voyage of Discovery in the Western Arctic Sea. By an Officer of the Expedition. *London: Sir Richard Phillips and Co.* 1821. 8vo, pp. iv, 124. 4 Plates.

Letters written from Colombia. *See* Vol. IV., No. 14598.

Letters Written in London by an American Spy. From the Year 1764 to the Year 1785. *London: J. Bew.* MDCCLXXXVI. Sm. 8vo, pp. xxi, 167. 40659

"These letters are said to be the correspondence of a Quaker with his friends in Philadelphia; and, while they display the honest bluntness of a sect, are animated by a warm philanthropy, true religion, and sound sense."—*Critical Review*, LXII. 155–156.

Lettre à l'Auteur de la reponse au Patriote Hollandois. [n. p.] 1740. 4to. 40660

Principally relating to America. An answer to "Sentiment d'un Patriote Hollandois."

Lettre à l'Auteur du Mercure Politique, par les auteurs de Traité intitulé: De la France et des États-Unis. *Bouillon.* 1787. 12mo, pp. 30. 40661

Lettre à Madame ***. *See* La Condamine (C. M. de).

Lettre a Napoléon III. sur l'Esclavage aux États du Sud. Par un Créole de la Louisiane [E. M.] *Paris: Dentu.* 1862. 8vo, pp. vii, 160. BA. 40662

Lettre A Sa Majesté l'Empereur Napoléon III. sur l'Influence Française en Amérique à propos du Message de M. Buchanan. Par Un Homme de la Race Latine. *Paris: Ledoyen.* 1858. 8vo, pp. 32. B. 40663

Lettre addressée aux Habitans de la province de Quebec, Ci-devant le Canada. De la part du Congrés Général de l'Amérique Septentrionale, tenu à Philadelphie. *Imprimé & publié par Ordre du Congrès, a Philadelphie, De l'Imprimerie de Fleury Mesplet.* M.DCC.-LXXIV. 8vo, pp. 18. P., W. 40664

This address is signed by Henry Middleton, President.

Lettre Addressée aux Habitans Opprimés de la Province de Quebec. De la part du Congrés Général de l'Amérique Septentrionale, tenu à Philadelphie. [*Philadelphie*, 29 *May* 1775.] 8vo, pp. 7. P. 40665

Lettre au Docteur Maty. *See* [Coyer (G. F.)], Vol. V. 17316.

Lettre au Espagnols-Américains. *See* [Viscardo y Guzman].

Lettre aux Philantropes, sur les malheurs, les droits et les réclamations des Gens de Couleur de Iles Françoises de l'Amérique. *Nancy.* 1790. 8vo. 40666

Lettre de Guillaume-le-Disputeur. *See* Vol. VII., No. 29230.

Lettre de M****, au sujet des écrits Anglois, sur les limites, de l'Amérique. [n. p.] 1755. 12mo, pp. 8. 40667

Lettre de MM. de la Municipalité de Brest à MM. les Membres de l'Assemblée Générale de Saint-Domingue à Paris. Brest, le 27 Septembre. 1790. ... Réponse de l'Assemblée Générale de la partie françoise de Saint-Domingue à MM. le Maire et Officiers de la Municipalité de Brest. *Paris, le* 2 *Octobre* 1790. 8vo, pp. 8. P. 40668

Lettre de l'Assemblée Générale de la Partie Françoise de Saint-Domingue aux Chambres du Commerce et Manufactures du Royaume. ... [*Paris:*] *De l'Imprimerie de Didot Fils aîné* ... [13 *Sept.* 1790]. 8vo, pp. 11. P. 40669

Lettre de M***** à Mr. S. B. *See* [Pinto (M. de)].

Lettre d'un Anglois a son Ami a La Haye, contenant une Relation Authentique de ce qui s'est passé entre les Cours de Londres et de Versailles, au commencement des Troubles Presents, Tirée des Piéces Originales. *A La Haye: Pierre de Hondt.* MDCCLVI. 8vo, pp. iv, 56. H. 40670

Lettre d'un habitant de Louisbourg, contenant une relation exacte de la prise de l'Ile Royale par les Anglais. *Québec.* 1745. 12mo. 40671

Lettre d'un Négociant sur le Crédit de la Grande-Bretagne et de l'Amérique Septentrionale Unie. Traduit du Hollandois. [n. p. 1781.] 8vo, pp. 16. 40672

Lettre d'un Officier de la Marine Russienne à un Seigneur de la Cour concernant la carte des nouvelles découvertes au Nord de

la mer du Sud, et la mémoire qui y sert d'explication publié par M. de Lisle a Paris en 1752. Traduit de l'original Russe. *Berlin: Haude et Spener.* [1752.] 4to, pp. 60. 40673

Translated into English in the following year; *see our* No. 40312, *ante.*

Lettre des Citoyens de Couleur, des Isles et Colonies Françoises, a MM. les Membres du Comité de Vérification de l'Assemblée Nationale. Du 23 Novembre 1789. *Paris: Lottin.* 1789. 8vo, pp. 14. J.C.B. 40674

Lettre des Commerçants et Fabricants d'Amiens à MM. les Colons français réunis à l'hôtel de Massiac [Dec. 10]. *Paris: imprimerie des affiches.* [n. d.] 8vo. 40675

Lettre des Commissaires de la Société d'Agriculture, des Arts & du Commerce de Nantes, aux Commissaires de l'Assemblée Coloniale de la Partie Françoise de Saint-Domingue. Nantes le 16 novembre 1792. ... Réponse des Citoyens Commissaires de Saint-Domingue. *Paris*, 26 *novembre* 1792. 8vo, pp. 11. P.

Lettre du Cap, au 18 Juillet 1791, écrite par un Créole blanc et propriétaire de St. Domingue; sur les manœuvres employées pour empêcher l'exécution du décret du 15 Mai. ... [*Paris:*] *De l'Imprimerie du Patriote François*, ... [n. d.] 8vo, pp. 16. P.

Lettre du Congrès Général de Philadelphie aux habitans des Colonies Américaines et au Peuple de la Grande-Bretagne, suivie de l'extrait de leurs résolutions. Traduit de l'Anglois. *London.* 1775. 8vo. 40678

Lettre du Délégué. *See* Vol. VII., No. 28798.

Lettre du Landgrave de Hesse, au Commandant de ses Troupes en Amérique. [n. p. n. d.] 8vo, pp. 8. N. 40679

Lettre du Parlement de Bordeaux au Roi, au sujet de l'arrêt du Conseil du 30 Août 1784, concernant le commerce étranger dans les Isles Françoises de l'Amérique. *À Paris.* 1785. 16mo, pp. 60.

Lettre du Parlement de Rouen au Roi, au sujet de l'arrêt du Conseil du 30 Août 1784, concernant le commerce étranger dans les Isles Françoises de l'Amérique. *À Paris.* 1785. 8vo, pp. 54.

Lettre missi-|ve, tovchant la|conversion et bap-|tesme du grand Sagamos de|la nouuelle Frãce, qui estoit|auparavant l'arriuée des Fran-|çois le chef & souuerain.|Contenant sa promesse d'amener ses subiets|à la mesme Conuersion, ou les y contrain-|

dre par la force des armes.|Enuoyée du Port Royal de la nouuelle France au Sr. de la Tronchaie, dattée|du 28 Juin 1610.|*A Paris,*| *chez Iean Regnovl*, ...|1610.|Auec permission.| 8vo, pp. 6.

Signed "Bertrand." Our title to [Bertrand], No. 5025, is not quite correct. It is a piece of unusual rarity.

Lettre Pastorale. *See* [Gibson (E.)], Vol. VII., No. 27311.

Lettres a M. de Jean, Docteur-Regent de la Faculté de Medecine, en l'Université de Paris. I. Sur les Maladies de St. Domingue. II. Sur les Plantes de la même isle. III. Sur la Remora & les Halcyons. Par M. Chevalier.... *A Paris: chez Durand* ... M.DCC.LII. 12mo, pp. (ii), 224, (2). P. 40683

Lettres à M. l'Abbé de Pradt, par un Indigène de l'Amérique du Sud. ... *Paris: Chez Rodriguez.* 1818. 8vo, pp. vii, 223.

A refutation of Pradt's "Des Colonies et de la révolution naturelle de l'Amérique."

Lettres à un Amériquain. *See* [Lignac (*l'Abbé*)].

Lettres Cherakeesiennes. *See* [Maubert (J. H.)]

Lettres Curieuses sur l'Amérique Septentrionale [Canada]. *Paris: imp. de Gros.* 1845. 12mo, pp. 288. 40685

Lettres d'Attache sur la Patente d'union des Missions des Freres Prescheurs establies dans les Isles Françoises de l'Amérique, à la Province de Toulouse. Données à Paris au mois de Septembre 1721. ... *A Paris: Chez Louis Denis Delatour & Pierre Simon* ... 1721. 4to, pp. 4. 40686

The patent itself, June 22, 1721, is also given.

Lettres d'un Citoyen des États-Unis à un de ses Amis d'Europe. *Paris.* 1828. 18mo. 40687

Lettres d'un Citoyen des États-Unis à un François, sur les affaires présentes. Par M. le Marquis de C*** [*i. e.* Condorcet]. *A Philadelphie.* 1788. 8vo, pp. 28. 40688

Should have appeared in Vol. IV. as 15191*a*

Lettres d'un Citoyen. *See* [Saintard].

Lettres d'un cultivateur américain. *See* [Crevecour (St. J. de)].

Lettres d'un fermier de Pensylvanie. *See* [Dickinson (J.)]

Lettres d'un fils à son père au sujet du voyage de Surinam. [n. p.] 1739 8vo. 40689

Lettres d'un François à un Hollandois. *See* [Moreau (M.)]

Lettre du Secrétaire d'État des États-Unis de l'Amérique au Général Charles C. Pinckney, Ministre Plénipotentiaire des dits États-Unis prés la République Française; en reponse aux différentes plaintes faites contre le gouvernement des États-Unis, par le Ministre Français, dans ses notes officielles de 27 Octobre et 15 Novembre 1796, adressées au Secrétaire d'État. *Paris.* 1797. 8vo, pp. 62. 40690

Citizen Fauchet, in his "Coup d'œil" *our* Vol. VI., No. 23919, refers to this letter, which he says was translated and circulated with profusion by the agents of Mr. Pickering, then Secretary in Paris.

Lettres de provision|de la charge de Viceroy, & Lieutenant gene-|ral pour le Roy, representant sa personne dans|tous les ports, haures, isles, costes, riuieres|& terres fermes de l'Amerique, données à|Monsieur le Duc Dampuille, verifiées en|Parlement le 27 [*sic pro* 21] Januier 1658.|*Donné à La Fère au mois de Juillet, l'an de grace* 1655. 4to, pp. 14. 40691

Lettres d'un Membre du Congrès. *See* Vincent (M.)

Lettres d'une Péruvienne. *A Paris: Duchesne.* M.DCC.LXXXVI. 8vo, pp. 455, (1). BA. 40692

This has also a title-page and the text, on opposite pages, in Italian, translated by G. L. Deodati. The author is Fr. d'Issembourg d'Happoncourt, dame de Grafigny. The Abbé G. L. Calabre Pérau had a considerable part in the composition of these letters.

Lettres d'une Péruvienne augmentées et suivies de celles d'Aza, tirées d'un Manuscrit Espagnol et traduites de l'Anglais par P. Durand. [Second Title:] Letters of a Peruvian Princess, Translated from the French, with the Sequel, taken from a Spanish Manuscript. *Paris: Durand.* 1802. 2 vols., 8vo, pp. 347; 399.

For other editions *see our* Vol. VII., Nos. 28192–98.

Lettres des diverses Sociétés des amis de la Constitution, qui reclament les droits de citoyen actif en faveur des hommes de couleurs des colonies. [n. p.] 1791. 8vo. 40694

Lettres du Japon et du Brésil envoyées au général de Jésuites. *Paris.* 1598. 8vo. 40695

"Nous n'avons pas pu vérifier ce titre dont la rédaction indique une traduction."—CARAYON. *See also* Ternaux, No. 227.

Lettres|Ecrites à la|Loge L'Aménité|No. 73,|À L'Occasion de l'Oraison Funébre|du F.·. George Washington.|Imprimé par Ordre de la Loge.|*A Philadelphie: Chez Thomas & William Bradford.* 1801. 8vo, pp. 16. 40696

Very rare. Contains correspondence relative to Chaudron's Oration, embracing letters from Theodore Sedgwick, John Adams, Thomas Jefferson, and others. *See our* Vol. III., Nos. 12288–91.

Lettres écrites de Cayenne. *See* Vol. III., No. 11619.

Lettres Édifiantes et Curieuses, Écrites des Missions Étrangères par quelques Missionaires de la Compagnie de Jesus. *Paris: Le Clerc.* 1702–1776. 34 vols., 12mo. S. 40697

"A set comprising the first edition of each volume is of uncommon rarity. Brunet and Carayon give the date of the first volume of this famous collection as 1717, which is certainly an error. Father le Gobien, editor of the early volumes, died in 1708. The first volume is approved by the Provincial of the Society of Jesus in May, 1702, and by the King, Aug. 23, 1702; this corresponds with the title given by Charlevoix: 'Lettres de quelques Missionaires de la Compagnie de Jesus, écrite de la Chine et des Indes Orientales.' *Paris.* 1702. 12mo. Charlevoix adds, "Ce premier recueil fut suivi peu après d'un second, sous ce titre: 'Lettres Édifiantes et Curieuses écrites des Missions Étrangères par quelques Missionnaires de la Compagnie de Jesus.'" He says, moreover, that these two collections, reprinted in 1717, were the first of the collection of "Lettres Édifiantes et Curieuses." "The second volume was approved Oct. 30, 1702, and the third in 1703. The publication undoubtedly followed shortly after the date of approval. Volume VII. was approved Feb. 20, 1707, and published in that year; volume VIII., approved Nov. 30, 1707, was published in 1708. Volumes I., II., and III. were certainly in print before 1707, when an English translation of the three appeared in one volume; *see* 'Edifying and Curious Letters,' *our* No. 21853; and a volume in 1713, from which 'The Travels of Certain Learned Missioners,' *London*, 1714, was translated, described *infra*. The publication was continued till 1758, when volume XXVIII. appeared; then the troubles of the order in France arrested the work, and its absolute suppression by the parliament of Paris, Aug. 6, 1762, made any further publication by them impossible. As, however, many valuable letters had been collected and the work enjoyed a popularity, a new volume (XXIX.) appeared in 1773, the very year when Pope Clement XIV. suppressed the order. Another volume also appeared in 1773, two in 1774, and two in 1776; the last bearing on the title the name of the Abbé Patouillet, who, according to Feller, had edited volumes XXVII. and XXVIII." The foregoing note is furnished to me by Dr. J. G. Shea, than whom there is no better authority. There are evidently two or more editions of the early volumes. Of the great value of these "Lettres," as illustrating the early history and settlement, not only of Canada, but of Central New York, Ohio, Michigan, Illinois, and Wisconsin, it is unnecessary to speak. These "Lettres" were collected by the Fathers Le Gobien, Du Halde, Ingoult, De Neuville, and Patouillet. For the missions among the American Indians, Charlevoix refers to volumes X., XI., XII., XIII., XVII., XX., and XXIII.; *see* his notice in "Liste des Auteurs." *See also* Shea's "Charlevoix," Sabin's "American Bibliopolist," *and* a very full history of the "Lettres Édifiantes" in Backer's "Bibliothek de la Comp. de Jesus," octavo edition, Vol. II., appendice, and in the folio edition, 1857–60, Vol. III., cols. 1737–53, Backer gives in detail the contents of the edition of 1838; and in cols. 1753–1860, he gives the contents of the German version and extension of the "Lettres."

Lettres Édifiantes et Curieuses .... Nouvelle édition augmentée [par l'abbé Y. M. M. de Querbeuf]. *Paris: J. G. Merigot.* MDCCLXXX–LXXXIII. 26 vols., 12mo. Maps. 40698

Volumes VI. to IX. inclusive, relate to America. J. R. Bartlett's Catalogue of J. C. Brown's Library gives a copious list of the contents of each volume. This edition is generally preferred to the original, because it has the advantage of being systematically arranged. "Fontenelle said 'that he had never read a work which answered better to its title.' Of the accuracy of those 'Lettres,' and the works of Du Halde and Gaubit, the author has often heard the late Sir G. Staunton speak in the highest terms."—CHARLES BUTLER.

Lettres Édifiantes et Curieuses .... Nouvelle édition. *A Toulouse, Chez Noel-Étienne Sens* ... 1810–11. 26 vols., 12mo. Atlas in 8vo. BA. 40699

Volumes VI. to IX. relate to America.

Lettres Édifiantes et Curieuses .... Nouvelle édition, ornée de cinquante belles gravures. *Lyon.* 1819. 14 vols., 8vo. S.

Lettres Edifiantes, écrites des Missions Étrangères, précédé de tableaux géographiques, historiques, politiques, religieux et littéraires, des pays de mission. Seconde édition, augmentée d'une notice historique sur les missions étrangères, avec les actes des rois de France concernant les missions, de nouvelles lettres édifiantes et autres morceaux choisis. *Paris.* 1824–26. 8 vols., 8vo.

Volumes VI. and VII. relate to America.

Lettres Édifiantes et Curieuses concernant l'Asie, l'Afrique et l'Amérique, avec Quelques Relations Nouvelles des Missions, et des Notes Géographiques et Historiques. Publiées sous la direction de M. L. Aimé-Martin [par Ernest G.....]. ... *Paris: Auguste Desrez.* M DCCC XXXVIII–XLIII. 4 vols., 4to, pp. xii, 820; (4), 806, (1); (4), 844; (4), 723. BA. + *Paris.* 1861. 3 vols., 8vo. + *Paris.* 1875–77. 4 vols., 8vo. 40702

Volumes I. and II. include the letters concerning America.

Lettres Édifiantes écrites par quelques Missionaires de la Compagnie de Jesus. De l'Amérique Septentrionale. *Bruxelles: G. Panwels.* 1771. 12mo, pp. 152. 40703

This is a selection from the "Lettres Édifiantes et Curieuses."

Choix des Lettres Édifiantes. *See* [Montmignon (J. B.)]

Nouvelles Lettres Édifiantes des Missions de la Chine et des Indes Orientales. *Paris: Adrien Le Clere.* 1818–23. 8 vols., 12mo, pp. (4), xxviii, 486, (1); (4), 560; (4), 503, (1); (4), 567, (1); viii, 603; (4), 511, (1); (4), 419; (4), 448. B., S.

Cartas Edificantes, y Curiosas, escritas de las Missiones Estrangeras, por algunos Missioneros de la Compañia de Jesus: Traducidas del Idioma Frances: por el Padre Diego Davin, de la Compañia de Jesus. *En Madrid: En la Oficina de la Viuda de Manuel Fernandez.* ... *Año* MDCCLIII–LVII. 16 vols., 4to. C.

This is a Spanish translation of the "Lettres Édifiantes." For a German version *see* Stoecklein (Joseph). The following is an Italian version:

Lettere Edificanti scritte dalle Missioni Straniere .... *Milano.* 1825–29. 6 vols., 8vo. 40706

The following are English versions:

The|Travels|Of several|Learned Missioners|of the|Society of Jesus,|into Divers Parts|of the|Archipelago,|India, China, and America.|Containing a general Description of the most remarkable|Towns; with a particular Account of the Customs,| Manners and Religion of those several Nations, the|whole interspers'd with Philosophical Observations and|other curious Remarks.|Translated from the French Original publish'd at Paris| in the Year 1713.|*London:*| ... *R. Gosling* ... M DCC XIV. 8vo, pp. (16), 336, Index, (12), Books, (4). 2 Plates. P. 40707

This volume contains twenty-two letters, the nineteenth relating to the Moxos, in South America, the twentieth being Marest's Account of Affairs at Hudson's Bay, and the twenty-first, Extract of an Account of the Country of Accadie in North America, etc., written by a French gentleman, and sent to a Missioner of the Society of Jesus. Now Charlevoix, in his "Liste des Auteurs" (Shea's "Charlevoix," I. 88), mentions this letter of Marest as in the tenth volume of the "Lettres Édifiantes," printed at Paris by Jean Barbou. In some copies the collation is pp. (16), 333, (17). *See also* our Vol. IV., No. 21853, *and* Kip (W. J.), Vol. IX., No. 37949. Dr. Shea informs me that there is another series by Dr. Kip, Junior.

Travels of the Jesuits, into Various Parts of the World: Compiled from their Letters. Now first attempted in English. Intermixed with an Account of the Manners, Government, ... of the several Nations visited by those Fathers. With Extracts from other Travellers, and Miscellaneous Notes. By Mr. Lockman. *London: John Noon.* 1743. 2 vols., 8vo, pp. 487; 508, (19). P. 40708

This is an excellent abridgment of the first ten volumes of the "Lettres Édifiantes;" it contains particulars of the Jesuit missions in Peru, by Ricolo and Nyel, Mexico, California, Hudson's Bay, Barrera's Abode among the Moxos and Chiriguanos of South America. Mr. Lockman proposed to have given the other fifteen which had then been published, but they never appeared.

Travels of the Jesuits, into Various Parts of the World: Particularly China and the East-Indies. Intermix'd with an Account of the Manners, Government, Civil and Religious Ceremonies, Natural History, and Curiosities, of the several Nations visited by those Fathers. Translated from the celebrated Lettres édifiantes & curieuses ... A Work so entertaining and curious, that it has already been translated into most of the European Languages. This Work is illustrated with Maps and Sculptures, engraved by the best Masters. To which is now prefixed, An Account of the Spanish Settlements in America, with a general Index to the whole Work. By Mr. Lockman. Second Edition, corrected. [*London:*] *T. Piety* ... 1762. 2 vols., 8vo, pp. (32), 488; (10), 508, (19), (24). C. + *London: David Steel.* M.DCC.LXVII. 2 vols., 8vo. 40709

Nouvelles des Missions d'Amérique, extraites des Lettres Édifiantes et Curieuses. *Paris: Librairie Martial Ardant Frères.* [1833.] 12mo, pp. (2), 288. Plate. 40710

This selection, from "Lettres Édifiantes," of relations of the Jesuit missionaries among the Indians, contains the narrative written by Father Rasles one year before he was massacred. All the letters are minutely descriptive of missionary life with the Indians.

Lettres et Memoires. *See* [Pichon (Thomas)].

Lettres Iroquoises. *See* [Maubert (J. H.)]

Lettres Patentes de Concession de l'Isle de Saint Jean, et de celles De Miscon, situées dans le Golfe de S. Laurent pour M. le Compte de S. Pierre. *Paris: Chez la Veuve Saugrain.* 1719. 4to, pp. 12. 40711

Lettres Patentes d'Octroy accordées par Sa Majesté Impériale pour le terme de trent années à la Compagnie générale à établir dans les Pays-Bas Autrichiens pour le commerce et la navigation aux Indes. *Bruxelles.* 1723. 4to. 40712

Includes the West Indies.

Lettres Patentes du Roy, Portant authorisation des Status & Reglemens faits par la Compagnie Royale de Saint Domingue. Données à Paris au mois de Juillet 1716. *Euregistrées au Parlement le deuxième Septembre* 1716. 4to, pp. 3. 40713

Lettres Patentes du Roy, portant confirmation du contrat d'Inféodation de la Terre de Belle-Isle, au profit de la Compagnie des Indes. Du troisième May 1720. *Paris: Saugrain et Pierre Prault.* 1720. 4to, pp. 8. 40714

Lettres-Patentes du Roy qui accordent à la ville de Dunkerque le privilége de faire le commerce aux Isles Françoises de l'Amérique. *Paris.* 1721. Sm. 4to, pp. 8. + *Dunkerque.* 1753.

Lettres Patentes en forme d'Edit, Portant Establissement d'une Compagnie de Commerce, sous le nom de Compagnie d'Occident. Donné à Paris au mois d'Aoust 1717. Registrées en Parlement. *A Paris, De l'Imprimerie Royale.* M.DCC.XVII. 4to, pp. 19.

The charter of John Law's famous Mississippi Company. Royal Arms on title. Du Pratz characterizes it as "A very scarce pamphlet."

Lettres Patentes por Compagnie d'Occident, ... 1717. *Paris, Aug.* 1717. 4to, pp. 19. 40717

Lettres Patentes portant révocation de la Compagnie de Saint Domingue. *Paris, Avril,* 1720. 4to. 40718

Lettres Patentes pour l'Établissement de la Compagnie Royale de Saint Domingue. *Paris.* 1720. 4to. 40719

Lettres Patentes sur arrest concernant le Commerce de la Nouvelle Colonie de la Louisianne donne à Paris le 26 Aout 1718. *Paris.* 1718. 4to. 40720

Lettres sur les États-Unis d'Amérique écrite en 1832 et 1833 et addressée à M. le Comte O'Mahony. Par J. M. B. de ***** [Bins de Saint-Victor]. *Lyon et Paris: Périsse Frères.* 1835. 2 vols., 8vo. P. 40721

Letts (J. M.) California Illustrated; including a Description of the Panama and Nicaragua Routes. By J. M. Letts. With Forty-Eight Illustrations. ... *New York: R. T. Young.* 1852. 8vo, pp. 224. + [*Ibid.*] 1853. B. 40722

Reproduced as:

[Letts.] Pictorial View of California; ... With Information and Advice Interesting to all, Particularly those who Intend to Visit the Golden Region. By a Returned Californian. *New York: R. T. Young.* 1853. 8vo, pp. 224. 48 Plates. 40723

Lettsom (J. C.) Some Account of the late John Fothergill, M.D. ... Member of the American Philosophical Society at Philadelphia. By John Coakley Lettsom. *London: C. Dilly.* 1783. 8vo, pp. (10), cxciii, (iii). 40724

Reprinted with the following title:

Lettsom. Memoirs of John Fothergill, M.D. &c. By John Coakley Lettsom. The Fourth Edition. *London: C. Dilly.* 1786. 8vo, pp. (2), v, (2), 280, (8). 6 Portraits. B. 40725

The best edition. Also issued on large paper, rl. 8vo. Dr. Fothergill was a distinguished physician in London, of Quaker parentage and principles, who thrice visited America. Before Franklin left for America, in 1774, he held a conference with a distinguished nobleman and Dr. Fothergill for the purpose of agreeing upon some conciliatory plan for the reconciliation of Great Britain and her American colonies. These gentlemen, although they held two conferences, were unable to agree upon a plan, when Dr. Franklin left. The propositions submitted at these conferences are given in this volume. *See also* Carver (J.) "Travels."

Leubel (A. G.) El Peru en 1860 ó sea Anuario nacional por Alfredo G. Leubel. Politica—Comercio—Estadistica—Literatura—Industria—Agricultura. Primer Ano. *Lima.* 1861. 8vo, pp. viii, 312. 40726

Leubelfing (J. von). Ein schön lustig Reiszbuch vorniemals in Truck kommen; darinnen begriffen, in was Gestalt die Unirten Niderl. Provincien ein Armada zugericht und auff dem Meer die

Insulen in Hispanien und West Indien besuchen lassen. *Ulm.* 1612. Small square 8vo. 40727

Leubelfing went out with the expedition under Prince Maurice of Nassau. This rare book consists of his journal. The object of this expedition was to visit the West India and other ports, partly with a view of seeking out suitable places for Dutch colonies. The American interest is chiefly confined to the title.

Leuli (J.) Des Émigrés français, ou réponse à M. de Lally-Tolendal, par J. Leuli ... *Paris.* 1797. 8vo. 40728

See Lally-Tolendal, No. 38694.

Leutze (Emanuel). Exhibition of Leutze's ... Picture of Washington crossing the Delaware ... *New York.* [1852.] 8vo, pp. 16. S. 40729

Levacher (Michel Gabriel). Guide médical des Antilles ou Études sur les maladies des colonies et particulièrement sur celle de la race noire. Par G. Levacher ... *Paris.* 1834. 8vo, pp. 252. + Guide ... des Antilles et des régions intertropicales ... Troisième édition. *Paris: Just Rouvier.* 1847. 8vo, pp. 480.

Le Vaillant (F.) Histoire Naturelle d'une partie d'Oiseaux nouveaux et rares de l'Amérique et des Indes. Par François Le Vaillant. Vol. I. *Paris.* 1801. 4to. 49 Plates. 40731

This beautiful work was never completed. It was also issued on large paper in folio, with the plates both plain and colored. Le Vaillant was an enthusiastic traveler, and a most accurate observer of nature. The plates to his works were made from the drawings of Barraband, the best ornithological painter France has ever produced. The author's "Histoire Naturelle des Oiseaux de Paradis et des Rolliers, suivie de celle des Toucans et des Barbus," *Paris,* 1806, 3 vols., folio, and "Perroquets," *Paris,* 1806, 2 vols., folio, include some American birds.

Levanto (L.) Catecismo de la Doctrina Christiana en Lengua Zaapoteca. Dispuesto por el M. R. P. Mrô. Fr. Leonardo Levanto, Provincial que fué dos veces de la Provincia de S. Hypolito Martyr de Oaxaca, y una de la de S. Miguel, y Santos Angeles de la Puebla ... *Impreso con las Licencias necesarias en la Puebla por la Viuda de Miguel de Ortega: y por su Original en la Oficina Palafoxiana de dicha Ciudad, año de* 1776. 4to, pp. (10), 32.

"Las aprobaciones y licencias son de 1732, cuya fecha debe ser la de la primera edicion."—Icazbalceta, No. 125. The language of Oajaca, Mexico. Very rare; not mentioned by Brunet, Ternaux, Rich, or Stevens.

Levanto. Crisis Americana, sobre el Canonicato reglar de Ste. Domingo de Guzman, en la Santa Iglesia Cathedral de Osma. Asserto Historial Apologetico, contra el Doctor Arguleta, y Maestro Noriega. Por Fr. Leonardo Levanto, Ex-Provincial de

las Provincias de San Hypolito Martyr de Oaxaca ... . *Madrid.* 1741. Folio, pp. (32), 484. 40733

A rare and interesting volume. Not mentioned by Brunet, Leclerc, Salva, Ternaux, or other bibliographers.

Levasseur (A.) Lafayette en Amérique en 1824 et 1825; ou Journal d'un Voyage aux États-Unis: Par A. Levasseur, secrétaire du Général Lafayette ... . *Paris: Baudouin.* 1829. 2 vols., 8vo, pp. (4), iv, 509; (4), 632. 10 Plates and Map. B.

Levasseur. Lafayette in America in 1824 and 1825; or, Journal of a Voyage to the United States: By A. Levasseur, Secretary to General Lafayette during his journey. Translated by John D. Godman, M.D. *Philadelphia: Carey and Lea.* 1829. 2 vols., 12mo, pp. vi, 9–227; iv, 9–265. B., BA. + *New York: White.* 1829. 2 vols., 12mo, pp. 227, (2); 284, (2). 40735

Levasseur. General Lafayette in Amerika, oder dessen letzte Reise durch Amerika in den Jahren 1824 und 1825. Aus dem Französischen übersetzt von A. Levasseur, geb. Zeis. *Naumburg: Wild.* 1829. 8vo, pp. 870, (2). C., S. 40736

Levasseur. Reis door de Vereenigde Staten van Noord-Amerika, in de Jaren 1824 en 1825. Naar het Fransch van zijnen Secretaris A. Levasseur. *Zutphen.* 1831. 2 vols., 8vo.

Levasseur (E.) Le Question de l'Or. Les Mines de Californie et d'Australie ... . Par Émile Levasseur ... . *Paris: Guillaumin et Ce.* 1858. 8vo, pp. vii, 357. BA. 40738

Levasseur. Recherches Historiques sur la Système de John Law. Par Émile Levasseur ... . *Paris: Guillaumin et Ce.* 1854. 8vo, pp. 424. C. 40739

Le Vasseur (L.) Analyse et Rapprochement des Opérations de l'Assemblée Coloniale de Cayenne. Par Léon Le Vasseur. *Paris.* 1792. 8vo. 40740

Levasseur (V.) La Tierra. Descripcion geográfica y pintoresca de las cinco partes del mundo, tomada de su libro y aumentada por A. F. de los Rios. *Madrid.* 1849. 8vo. + Adornada con 300 grabados. *Madrid.* 1849. 8vo. 40741

Level (F.) L'esclavage en Amérique. Lettre à M. Havin, directeur politique du siècle. Par Miss Fanny Level, vice-présidente du comité abolitioniste de Charleston. *Paris: Imprimerie Noblet.* 1865. 8vo, pp. 16. 40742

L[evel] (A[ndres] E.) Informe sobre el estado actual de los distritos de reduccion de indíjenas Alto-Orinoco, Central y Bajo Orinoco, y medidas que reclaman, Presentado á Su Excelencia el Poder Ejecutivo por el visitador nombrado al efecto A. E. L. *Carâcas.* 1850. 4to, pp. 98. 2 Tables. 40743

The Level of Europe and North America: or the Observer's Guide. *Philadelphia.* 1795. 4to. P. 40744

A periodical, in English and French.

Levendich | Discovrs | Vant ghemeyne Lants wel-|vaert | voor desen de Oost | ende nu oock de | West-Indische generale Compai-|gnie aenghevanghen | seer no-|tabel om lesen. | Door een Lief-Hebber des Vaderlandts. | *Ghedruckt by Broer Iansz. int Iaer ons | Heeren* 1622. | 4to, 12 l. 40745

This is a lively discourse on the welfare of the country, formerly by the East, now also by the West India Company.

Levens van beroemde Nederlanders. *See* [Kampen (N. G.)]

Leveret (S.) A Lacrymatory, designed for the Tears let fall at the Funeral of Mrs. Sarah Leveret, who died 2d 11mo. 1704, 5. *Boston: Samuel Phillips.* 1705. 18mo, pp. 4. 40746

Title from Kettell, who adds, "With a Funeral Sermon."

[Leverett (Charles Edward).] A Memoir, Biographical and Genealogical, of Sir John Leverett, Knt., Governor of Massachusetts, 1673–9; of Hon. John Leverett, F.R.S., Judge of the Supreme Court, and President of Harvard College; and of the Family generally. ... *Boston: Crosby, Nichols and Company.* 1856. 8vo, pp. 203. Portraits and Table. B., C. 40747

Leverett (J.) A Defence of the Title of the late John Leverett, Esq. to a Tract of Land in the Eastern Parts of the Province of the Massachusetts Bay ... [n. p.] 1736. Folio.

Perhaps by S. Waldo. *See also* [Willard (Samuel)].

Levering (R. E. H.) ... The Kingdom of Slavery: or the Ark of Liberty in the ... Hands of Two Hundred and Fifty Thousand Slaveholders: also an Appeal to the American Churches ... . By Robert E. H. Levering. ... *Circleville, Ohio.* 1844. 8vo, pp. 16. BA. 40749

Le Vert (O. W.) Souvenirs of Travel. By Madame Octavia Walton Le Vert. *New York: S. H. Goetzel and Company.* 1857. 2 vols., 12mo, pp. xvi, 348; viii, 348. B. + *New York.* 1859. 2 vols., 12mo. + [*Ibid.*] 1866. 2 vols., 12mo. 40750

Levett (C.) A | Voyage | Into New | England | Begun in 1623. and ended | in 1624. | Performed by Christopher Levett, | his Maiesties Woodward of Somersetshire, and | one of the Councell of New England. | ... *Printed at London, by William Iones, | and are to be sold by Edward Brewster, at the signe | of the Bible in Paules Church Yard.* | 1628. | 4to, pp. (6), 38. J.C.B., N. 40751

A tract of the greatest rarity; we have met with only two copies. It is reprinted in the "Mass. Hist. Soc. Coll.," Third Series, Vol. VIII., pp. 159–190, and in the "Maine Hist. Soc. Coll.," Vol. II., p. 36.

Levi (L.) Annals of British Legislation; being a Classified and Analysed Summary of Public Bills, Statutes, Accounts and Papers, Reports of Committees and of Commissioners, and of Sessional Papers generally, of the Houses of Lords and Commons: together with Accounts of Commercial Legislations, Tariffs, & Facts Relating to Foreign Countries: Edited by Leone Levi. *London: Smith, Elder and Co.* 1856–68. 18 vols., rl. 8vo. B., H. 40752

Levi. Commercial Law, its Principles and Administration; or, the Mercantile Law of Great Britain compared with the Codes and Laws of Commerce of the Following Mercantile Countries: ... *London.* MDCCCL–LI. 2 vols., 4to, pp. (4), xvii, 175; xxxii, 177–368, (1). B. 40753

Levi. International Code of Commerce, in connection with the Law of Nature and Nations: A Lecture. By Leone Levi, Esq.; ... *London: Simpkin, Marshall, & Co.;* MDCCCLI. 8vo, pp. 22, (2). H. 40754

Levien (D. A.) Debates on the Trinity Church Bill, in the Senate. By Douglas A. Levien. *Albany.* 1857. 8vo, pp. 98.

Levin (L[ewis] C.) Speech of Mr. L. C. Levin ... on the ... Naturalization Laws. ... December 18, 1845. [n. p. n. d.] 8vo, pp. 15. H. 40756

Also: Speech ... on the Oregon Question. ... January 9, 1846 ... . [n. p. n. d.] 8vo, pp. 8.—Speech ... on the Bill to raise a Regiment of Mounted Riflemen. ... April 7, 1846. *Washington: J. & G. S. Gideon, Printers.* 1846. 8vo, pp. 16.—Speech ... on ... the Naval Appropriation Bill ... June 13. *Washington.* 1846. 8vo, pp. 7.—Speech ... on the Proposed Mission to Rome, delivered ... March 2, 1848. ... [n. p. n. d.] 8vo, pp. 16. H.

Levinge (R. G. A.) Echoes from the Backwoods; or, Sketches of Transatlantic Life. By Captain R. G. A. Levinge. *London.* 1846. 2 vols., post 8vo. + *London: George Routledge and Sons.* 1860. 12mo. P. 40757

Levington (W.) Address, before the Female Benezet Philanthropic Society. By William Levington. *Albany.* 1822. 8vo.

Levinus (Apolonius). *See* Apolonius (Levinus), Vol. I. 1761.

There are copies of this edition dated M.D.LXVII. Ternaux, No. 158, describes an edition, *Basilæ,* 1583, folio.

Levins (T. C.) A Discourse delivered on the 17 March, 1828, in St. Patrick's Cathedral, New York. By Thomas C. Levins. *New York.* 1828. 8vo, pp. 47. 40759

Levis (Jeremy). *See* [Osborne (I aughton)].

Levis (T.) State of the Accounts of Thomas Levis, a Sub-Lieutenant of Chester County, from March 1777 to March 1780. ... *Philadelphia: Printed by Robert Aitken* ... M.DCC.LXXXIII. 8vo, pp. 11. P. 40760

Le Voici, of pourtrait en byzonderheeden aangaande den Politiek-Vertoog-Schryver, R. M. van Goens. [n. p.] 1782. 8vo.

Portrait and particulars concerning the author of the Politic Deduction. *See also* [Goens (R. M. van)], Vol. VII., No. 27683.

Levy [David]. Speech of Mr. Levy, of Florida, on the Tenth Article of the Treaty of Washington, and Certain Fugitive Criminals from Florida. Delivered ... March 5, 1844. *Washington: Printed by Blair and Rives.* 1844. 8vo, pp. 31. H.

Also: Speech ... on the Army Appropriation Bill. ... June 12, 1842. *Washington.* 1842. 8vo.

Levy (J. P.) Defence of Captain Jonas P. Levy, against the Report of the Hon. Elisha Whittlesey, First Comptroller of the United States Treasury. [n. p. n. d.] 8vo, pp. 24. H. 40763

Also: Memorial ... in Relation to his Claims on Mexico ... Feb. 2, 1848. [n. p. n. d.] 8vo, pp. 4.—Memorial ... [n. p. 1856.] 8vo, pp. 8. + [n. p. 1859.] 8vo, pp. 10.

Lévy (P.) Le Nicaragua, légendes et notes. Lettre à M. Michel Chevalier ... par Paul Lévy. *Paris: Imprimerie Martinet.* 1870. 8vo, pp. 15. 40764

Republished from the "Bulletin de la Société de Géographie," Mars 1870.

Levy (U[riah] P.) Manual of Internal Rules and Regulations for Men-of-War. By Capt. U. P. Levy ... . *New York: D. Van Nostrand.* 1861. 12mo, pp. 70. H. 40765

Levy. Memorial ... to the Congress ... complaining of the Action of the Board of Naval Officers, February 28, 1855 ... . *New York: Baker & Goodwin, Printers.* 1855. 8vo, pp. 30. H.

Lewe van Aduard (O. A.) De juris controversia Magnam Britanniam inter et dissidentes ab ea, seculo superiore, colonias Americanas. *Lugduni Batavorum.* 1835. 8vo. 40767

There are copies on thick paper.

Lewellin (J. L.) Account of Prince Edward Island, Addressed to Intending Emigrants. By J. L. Lewellin. *Charlotte-Town.* 1832. 8vo, pp. 29. + *London.* 1832. 12mo. 40768

Lewellin. Emigration. Prince Edward Island: a Brief but Faithful Account of this Fine Colony; ... By J. L. Lewellin. *London: W. M. Knight and Co.* 1833. 8vo, pp. 34. 40769

Lewenstein (M.) Intrée-predikatie gehouden te Paramaribo, 22 jan. 1858. *'s Hage.* 1858. 8vo. 40770

Lewes (C. L.) Comic Sketches; or, the Comedian his own Manager. Written and selected for the benefit of Performers in England, Ireland, Scotland, and America. ... By Charles Lee Lewes. *London: H. D. Symonds.* 1804. 16mo, pp. xxxv, 194. Portrait. C. 40771

Lewes (D.) The Good Minister. A Sermon preach'd at Stonington, Connecticut; December 27th, 1732. When the Rev. Mr. Joseph Fish was Ordained Pastor of a Church there. By Daniel Lewes, V.D.M. ... *New London: T. Green.* 1733. 12mo, pp. 39. 40772

Lewes. Of Taking Heed to, and Fulfilling the Ministry; ... A Sermon Preached ... in Plymouth, November 2. 1720. Being ... the Ordination of the Reverend Joseph Stacey ... . By Rev. Daniel Lewes ... . *Boston: D. Henchman.* 1720. 8vo, pp. (2), iv, 32. BA. 40773

Also: The Joy of Children walking in Truth. A Sermon, at the Boston-Lecture, August 15. 1723. ... *Boston: D. Henchman.* MDCCXXIII. 8vo, pp. (4), 28.—The Sins of Youth, Remembred with Bitterness. ... A Sermon At a Private Meeting of a Society of Young Men for Religious Exercise, ... Feb. 14. 1724, 5. ... *Boston: Printed by S. Kneeland.* MDCCXXV. 8vo, pp. (4), ii, 22. B. The author's name is sometimes spelt Lewis.

[Lewes (*Mrs.* Marian G. Evans).] Silas Marner, The Weaver of Raveloe. By the Author of "Adam Bede" ... . *Mobile: S. H. Goetzel.* 1863. 12mo, pp. 276. BA. 40774

A Confederate publication. The covers are printed on wall-paper.

Lewin (R.) The Life of a Soldier: a Narrative of Twenty-seven Years' Service in various parts of the World. [1793–1820.]

By Major Ross Lewin. Second Edition. *London: R. Bentley.* 1834. 3 vols., post 8vo. s. 40775

Republished in 1836 as "The Life of a Soldier: a Narrative of Twenty-seven Years' Service in various parts of the World. By a Field Officer." *London: R. Bentley.* 1836. 3 vols., post 8vo.

Lewis xv., *pseudon.* Letter from Lewis xv. to G——l M——t. *London: J. Pottinger.* MDCCLVII. 8vo, pp. 23.

General Mordaunt is the person to whom the letter is addressed. It is a sharp hit against William Pitt, Fox, and others; an account of the recent failures of the British arms, designed to arouse Great Britain, and make known the probable designs of the French.

Lewis (A.) Speech of Hon. Abner Lewis ... July 1, 1846. ... on ... the Tariff Law of 1842. [n. p. n. d.] 8vo, pp. 8. H.

Lewis (A. N.) Argument on the Liabilities of Bankers and Brokers under the Internal Revenue Laws, prepared by Alexander N. Lewis ... . [*New York:*] *Printed by Willard Felt & Co.* 1869. 8vo, pp. 46. H. 40778

Lewis (A.) A Guide through Nahant ... with an Account of the First Inhabitants ... . By Alonzo Lewis. *Lynn.* 1851. 8vo, pp. 14. 40779

Lewis. The History of Lynn. By Alonzo Lewis. ... *Boston: Press of J. H. Eastburn.* 1829. 8vo, pp. 260. 4 Plates.

Lewis. The History of Lynn, including Nahant. By Alonzo Lewis,—the Lynn Bard. ... Second Edition. *Boston: Printed by Samuel N. Dickinson.* 1844. 8vo, pp. 278. 2 Plates. BA.

Contains many particulars of Indian history.

Lewis. History of Lynn, Essex County, Massachusetts, including Lynnfield, Saugus, Swampscot, and Nahant. By Alonzo Lewis and James R. Newhall. *Boston: John L. Shorey.* 1865. 8vo, pp. 620. H. 40782

Lewis. The Picture of Nahant. By Alonzo Lewis. *Lynn: Printed by J. B. Tolman.* 1845. 12mo, pp. 14. B. + [*Ibid.*] 1848. 8vo, pp. 14. 40783

Also: Love, Forest Flowers and Sea Shells. ... *Boston: The Author.* 1845. 24mo, pp. 128.—Poems. ... *Portsmouth.* 1823. 12mo. + *Boston: John H. Eastburn.* 1831. 12mo, pp. (2), 208. Portrait. B.

Lewis (A.) The Covenant-Interest, of the Children of Believers, ... a solid Foundation for Infant Baptism. By Amzi Lewis, A.M. *Chatham* [*N. Y.*] 1783. 8vo, pp. 64. 40784

We have never seen another book with this imprint.

Lewis (A.) The Orderly Book of that Portion of the American Army stationed at or near Williamsburg, Va., under the command of General Andrew Lewis, from March 18th, 1776, to August 28th, 1786. Printed from the Original Manuscript, with [Preface by Th. H. Wynne, and] Notes and Introduction. By Charles Campbell ... . *Richmond, Va.: Privately Printed.* 1860. 4to, pp. (4), xi, 100. B., C. 40785

Ten copies printed on large paper. The book was printed by Joel Munsell of Albany, and was No. 1. of a projected series of "Historical Documents from the Old Dominion," which was discontinued on the breaking out of the Rebellion.

[Lewis (Archelaus, *and others*]. An Address to the People of Maine, on ... Separation. ... August 1, 1816. ... [n. p. n. d.] 8vo, pp. 24. BA. 40786

Lewis (C.) Narrative of Some of the Proceedings of the Mormons; giving an Account of their Iniquities, with Particulars concerning the Training of the Indians by them, Description of the Mode of Endowment, Plurality of Wives, &c. &c. By Catherine Lewis. *Lynn: The Author.* 1848. 8vo, pp. 24. + [*Ibid.*] 1853. 8vo, pp. 16. 40787

Lewis (C. T.) ... A Sermon ... on the National Fast ... April 30, 1863. ... Rev. Charlton T. Lewis ... . *Cincinnati.* 1863. 8vo, pp. 23. BA. 40788

Lewis (D.) Good Rulers the Fathers of their People ... . A Sermon Preach'd at Boston: In the Audience of His Excellency William Shirley, Esq; Governour ... Of the Province of the Massachusetts-Bay in New-England: On the Day of Electing His Majesty's Council, May 25. 1748. By Daniel Lewis, A.M. ... *Boston: Printed by John Draper for Daniel Gookin.* 1748. 12mo, pp. 29. BA. 40789

Lewis (D. W.) An Oration on the Death of Mr. Eli Kelsey. A Senior in Yale College. By D. W. Lewis. *New Haven.* 1788. 8vo, pp. 11. 40790

Lewis (D.) Catalogue ... of Dr. Dio Lewis's Family School for Young Ladies, Lexington, Mass. 1865. *Boston: Press of John Wilson and Son.* 1865. 8vo, pp. 23. H. 40791

Lewis (Dixon H.) Speech ... in the Senate ... July 13, 1846. On the ... Tariff ... of 1842 ... . [*Washington.* 1846.] 8vo, pp. 8. H. 40792

Lewis (E.) A Sermon preached December 13, 1776, being the Fast day on account of the troubles in America. ... To which is added a letter from a late Judge, concerning the Right of Great Britain to tax her Colonies. With an Appendix. By Edward Lewis. *Oxford.* 1776. 4to. 40793

The "Letter from a Judge" is said to have been written in 1763 by the late Sir Joseph Yeates to Christopher Griffith. *See* "M. Rev.," LVI. 237.

Lewis (E.) How Edmonia Lewis became an Artist. [n. p. 186–.] 64mo, pp. (7). 40794

Lewis (E.) An Eulogy, on the Life and Character of His Excellency George Washington, Esqr. ... Delivered at Lenox, February 22, 1800. By Eldad Lewis Esquire. ... *Pittsfield* (*Mass.*), *March*, 1800. 12mo, pp. 20. 40795

A very rare poetical piece.

Lewis (E. J.) The American Sportsman: containing Hints to Sportsmen, Notes on Shooting, and the Habits of the Game Birds, and Wild Fowl of America. By Elisha J. Lewis. *Philadelphia: Lippincott* ... 1855. 8vo, pp. (2), 494. + [*Ibid.*] 1857.

This is really an enlarged edition of the following:

Lewis. Hints to Sportsmen: containing Notes on Shooting; the Habits of the Game Birds and Wild Fowl of America; the Dog, the Gun, the Field, and the Kitchen. By Elisha J. Lewis. *Philadelphia.* 1851. 12mo. 40797

Lewis (E.) An Abridgment of the Criminal Law of the United States, containing the important Penal Acts of Congress of the United States, and of the principal States of the Union. ... By Ellis Lewis. *Philadelphia.* 1848. 8vo. 40798

Lewis (E.) Observations on a pamphlet, entitled, "Brief Examination of Scripture Testimony on the Institution of Slavery." By Enoch Lewis. [n. p. n. d.] 8vo. 40799

Lewis. Observations on the Militia System; addressed to the ... Citizens of Pennsylvania ... . By Enoch Lewis. *Philadelphia: Printed by Joseph Rakestraw.* 1845. 12mo, pp. 44. H.

Lewis. Vindication of the Society of Friends; being a Reply to a Review of Cox on Quakerism ... . By Enoch Lewis. *Philadelphia: Nathan Kite.* 1834. 8vo, pp. 73. B. 40801

Also: The African Observer. ... *Philadelphia.* 1826. 8vo.—A Dissertation on Oaths. ... [*Philadelphia.*] 1838. 12mo, pp. 100. BA.—Observations on Legal and Judicial Oaths. ... *Philadelphia.* 1846. 8vo, pp. 28. + [*Ibid.*] 1859. 8vo, pp. 16.

—A Brief Review of the Causes and Course of the Division in the Yearly Meeting of Ohio. ... *Philadelphia.* 1855. 8vo. *See also* "Friends' Library," Vol. v.

Lewis (E.) An Address to Christians of all Denominations, on the Inconsistency of admitting Slave-Holders to Communion and Church Membership. By Evan Lewis. *Philadelphia: S. C. Atkinson.* 1831. 16mo, pp. 19. 40802

Also: A Review of the Testimony ... against Elias Hicks. ... *New York: Printed by A. Ming, Jun.* 1829. 8vo, pp. 96, or less.

Lewis (G.) Impressions of America and the American Churches, from Journal of the Rev. G. Lewis, one of the Deputation of the Free Church of Scotland to the United States. *Edinburgh: W. P. Kennedy.* MDCCXLV. Post 8vo, pp. viii, 432. 40803

Lewis (G. C.) An Essay on the Government of Dependencies. By George Cornewall Lewis, Esq. *London: John Murray.* MDCCCXLI. 8vo, pp. xii, 382, (2). B. 40804

"A learned and valuable work."—McCulloch, p. 95.

Lewis (G.) An Appeal to those Members of the Society of Friends who stand aloof from the Antislavery Enterprise. By Graceanna Lewis. [n. p. n. d.] 12mo, pp. 8. 40805

Lewis (H.) Valley of the Mississippi, and Customs of the Indians. By H. Lewis. *Philadelphia.* 1858. 4to. 80 Views.

Title from the English Catalogue, *London*, 1864; we have not seen the book.

Lewis. Das Illustrirte Mississippithal, dargestellt in 80 nach der Natur aufgenommenen Ansichten vom Wasserfalle zu St. Anthony an bis zum Golf von Mexico, (eine Entfernung von ungefähr 2300 englischen Meilen) von H. Lewis ... . Nebst einer historischen und geographischen Beschreibung der den Fluss begränzenden Länder, mit besonderer Rücksicht auf die verschiedenen den obern Mississippi bewohnenden Indianerstämme. Nach dem engl. Original-Text von H. Lewis deutsch bearbeitet von George B. Douglas. ... *Düsseldorf: Arnz & Comp.* ... [1858.] 8vo, pp. 431. 24 Plates. 40807

Lewis (H.) Narrative of the Captivity and Sufferings of Mrs. Hannah Lewis and her three children, who were taken Prisoners by the Indians, near St. Louis on the 25th May, 1815, ... Second Edition. *Boston: Printed by H. Trumbull.* 1817. 12mo, pp. 24. + [*Ibid.*] 1818. 40808

Lewis (I.) A Discourse ... at Bristol, on the Public Thanksgiving, November 26, A.D. 1812. By Isaac Lewis ... . *Warren, R. I.: Printed by John F. Phillips.* 1812. 8vo, pp. 18. 40809

Lewis. The Political Advantages of Godliness. A Sermon Preached ... at Hartford on the Anniversary Election, May 11, 1797. By Isaac Lewis, D.D. ... *Hartford: Printed by Hudson & Goodwin.* 1797. 8vo, pp. 31. BA., W. 40810

Also: Sermon preached at Stamford, Oct. 11, 1796, before the Consecration of the Western District in Fairfield County. ... *New Haven.* 1796. 8vo.—A Sermon delivered in New-Haven, at the Ordination of the Rev. Jeremiah Day, A.M. President of Yale-College, July 23, 1817. ... *New-Haven.* 1817. 8vo, pp. 27. H.—A Sermon ... in West Greenwich, Connecticut, at the Installation of the Rev. Isaac Lewis, A.M. December 1, 1818. ... *New-York: Printed by J. Seymour.* 1818. 8vo, pp. 32. BA.

Lewis (I. W. P.) Cape Cod Harbor. Sailing Directions, by I. W. P. Lewis. *Boston.* 1841. 8vo, pp. 16. 40811

Lewis (J. O.) The Aboriginal Port-folio. *Philadelphia: J. O. Lewis.* 1835. Folio. 72 Portraits of Indians. 40812

Published in twelve numbers, each of which has a page commencing "Advertisement to the First—(and Second)—number of the Aboriginal Portfolio." No. 1. is dated "Phil. July 20th, 1835." The portraits are each lettered with the name and rank of the Indian personage represented.

Lewis. Catalogue of the Indian Gallery, painted by J. O. Lewis. *New-York: J. O. Lewis.* 1850. 8vo, pp. 23. 40813

Lewis (J.) Narrative of the Captivity and Providential Escape of Mrs. Jane Lewis, Wife of James Lewis, Who, with a son and daughter, ... and an infant babe were made prisoners, within a few miles of Indian Creek, by a party of Indians of the tribes of Sacs and Foxes, commanded by Black Hawk ... [*New York.*] 1833. 8vo, pp. 24. Plate. 40814

Lewis (J.) Narrative of the Life of John Lewis, who was executed at Chester, Sept. 21, 1750, together with his last Speech, Confession, and Solemn Declaration. *Philadelphia.* 1760. 8vo. + *New Haven. Reprinted.* 1760. 40815

Lewis (J.) A Brief Account of the School for the Liberal Education of Boys at Covington, Ky. By John Lewis. [n. p.] 1831. 8vo, pp. 8. M. 40816

Lewis (J. T.) A Lecture before the Brockville Library Association and Mechanic's Institute, introductory to the course. By Rt. Rev. John Travers Lewis ... . *Brockville.* 1855. 8vo, pp. 18. 40817

Lewis (J. W.) The Life, Labors, and Travels of Elder Charles Bowles, of the Free Will Baptist Denomination, by Eld. John W. Lewis. Together with an Essay on the Character and Condition of the African Race by the same. Also an Essay on the Fugitive Law of the U. S. Congress of 1850, by Rev. Arthur Dearing. *Watertown* [*N. Y.*]: *Ingalls & Stowell.* 1852. 12mo, pp. 285, (2). C. 40818

[Lewis (Joseph C.)] Letter to Hon. Schuyler Colfax ... *Washington: H. Polkinhorn & Son, Printers.* 1860. 8vo, pp. 4.

Lewis (J. J.) Letter to a Member of Congress, on the National Currency. By Joseph J. Lewis, Commissioner of Internal Revenue. *Philadelphia: King & Baird.* 1865. 8vo, pp. 15.

Lewis (M. G.) Journal of a West India Proprietor, kept during a Residence in the Island of Jamaica. By the late Matthew Gregory Lewis, Esq. M.P. ... *London: John Murray.* MDCCCXXXIV. 8vo, pp. (6), 408. BA., H. 40821

Reproduced in Waldie's "Circulating Library," Vol. III., and republished as:

Lewis. Journal of a Residence among the Negroes in the West Indies. By the late Matthew Gregory Lewis, Esq. ... *London: John Murray.* 1845. Post 8vo, pp. viii, 184. B.

S. T. Coleridge characterizes this work as "Almost the only unaffected book of travels I have read of late years." The "Life and Correspondence of M. G. Lewis ... With many pieces in Prose and Verse, never before published"...—*London.* 1839. 2 vols., 8vo, pp 392; 288. Portrait—includes some notes of his West Indian experiences.

Lewis (Merriwether). Documents accompanying a Bill making compensation to Messieurs Lewis and Clarke, and their companions, presented the 23d January 1807. *Washington: A. & G. Way.* 1807. 8vo, pp. 8. C. 40823

I have, for obvious reasons, made the following list of editions of Lewis and Clarke's Expedition, chronological.

Lewis. Message of the President of the United States communicating Discoveries made in Exploring the Missouri, Red River, and Washita, by Captains Lewis and Clark, Doctor Sibley, and Mr. Dunbar; with a Statistical Account of the Countries adjacent. Read in Congress February 19, 1806. *City of Washington: A. & G. Way, Printers.* 1806. 8vo, pp. 180, (8). Map. + *New York: G. F. Hopkins.* 1806. 8vo, pp. 178, and folded leaf. + *New York: Hopkins & Seymour.* 1806. 8vo, pp. 178. Folded Table. 40824

Another *Washington* edition, 1806, has pp. 171, (6). Between pages 24 and 25 are a few unnumbered pages consisting of tables. This "Message" forms the first published

account of the explorations of Lewis and Clarke, and contains vocabularies of the Sioux and Dakota languages. *See* "M. Rev.," LXXVIII. The following is a reprint:

Lewis. Discoveries made in Exploring the Missouri, Red River, and Washita, by Captains Lewis & Clark, Doctor Sibley and William Dunbar, Esq.; with a Statistical Account of the Countries adjacent. With an Appendix by Mr. Dunbar. *Natchez: Printed by Andrew Marshal.* 1806. 8vo, pp. 174.

It was reprinted in part in the "Political Cabinet," an appendix to the "Monthly Anthology," *Boston*, 1807, and afterwards collected under the title of "American State Papers," *Boston*, 1808, pp. 39–92.

Lewis. Travels in the Interior Parts of America; communicating Discoveries made in exploring the Missouri, Red River and Washita, by Captains Lewis and Clark, Doctor Sibley, and Mr. Dunbar; with A Statistical Account of the Countries adjacent. As laid before the Senate, by the President of the United States. In February, 1806, and never before published in Great Britain. *London: Richard Phillips.* 1807. 8vo, pp. 116, and folded Table. 40826

Almost an exact copy of the "Message."

Lewis. The Travels of Capts. Lewis & Clarke, from St. Louis, by way of the Missouri and Columbia Rivers, to the Pacific Ocean; performed in the years 1804, 1805, & 1806, by Order of the Government of the United States. Containing delineations of the Manners, Customs, Religion, &c. Of the Indians, compiled from Various Authentic Sources, and Original Documents, and a Summary of the Statistical View of the Indian Nations, from the Official Communications of Merriwether Lewis. Illustrated with a Map of the Country, inhabited by the Western Tribes of Indians. *London: Longman, Hurst, Rees & Orme.* 1809. 8vo, pp. ix, 309. Map. H. 40827

Almost a reproduction of the "Message," but Dr. Sibley's account of the Red River is omitted. It contains some documents not published in any other edition, including "Observations on the Voyage of William Dunbar and Dr. Hunter, extracted from their Journals." The article on the "Origin of the American Indian Population," pp. 211–237, is in fact a reprint from Carver's "Travels," Chap. 1.

Lewis. History of the Expedition under the Command of Captains Lewis and Clark, to the Sources of the Missouri, thence across the Rocky Mountains and down the River Columbia to the Pacific Ocean. Performed during the Years 1804–5–6. By Order of the Government of the United States. Prepared for the Press by Paul Allen, Esquire. *Philadelphia: Bradford and Inskeep.* 1814. 2 vols., 8vo, pp. xxviii, 470; ix, 522. 3 Maps.

Best edition of this valuable work, which the "Critical Review" says, "Exhibits not only some valuable geographical notices, but very copious and amusing details respecting

the manners, habits, and diversions of the North American tribes." It is to-day the best work we have on the countries described, and its republication would be an acceptable service. Mr. Allen has paraded his name as the editor of this edition, when, in fact, the work was done by Mr. Nicholas Biddle from the material left by Captain Lewis, who in a fit of insanity committed suicide. *See* "N. A. Rev.," I. 96.

Lewis. Travels to the Source of the Missouri River and across the American Continent to the Pacific Ocean. Performed by Order of the Government of the United States, in the Years 1804, 1805, and 1806. By Captains Lewis and Clarke. Published from the Official Report and Illustrated by a Map of the Route and other Maps. *London: Longman, Hurst, Rees, Orme, and Brown.* 1814. 4to, pp. xxiv, 663. 3 Maps. C. 40829

A reprint of the foregoing, omitting the appendix and the Life of Lewis. The preface is by Dr. Thomas Rees. *See* "M. Rev.," LXXVII. 225, 337.

Lewis. Travels to the Source of the Missouri River [same Title as the preceding]. A New Edition. ... *London: Longman* ... 1815. 3 vols., 8vo, pp. xxvi, (2), 411; xii, 434; xii, 394. 6 Maps. + [*Ibid.*] 1817. 40830

This edition was edited by Thomas Rees. It is a reproduction, in larger type and on better paper, of the *Philadelphia* edition of 1814, omitting the "Observations on the Government of the Indians," by Captain Lewis, and the eight meteorological tables. Another edition was printed in Dublin with the same title with the addition:

Lewis. Travels ... With the Life of Captain Lewis, by T. Jefferson, President of the United States of America. ... *Dublin: J. Christie.* 1817. 2 vols., 8vo, pp. xxvii, (12), 588; (2), xii, 643.

Lewis. The Journal of Lewis and Clarke to the Mouth of the Columbia River beyond the Rocky Mountains. In the Years 1804–5, & 6. Giving a faithful description of the River Missouri and its source—of the various Tribes of Indians through which they passed—manners and customs—soil—climate—commerce—gold and silvermines—animal and vegetable productions, &c. New Edition, with Notes, Revised, Corrected, and Illustrated ... . To which is added a Complete Dictionary of the Indian Tongue. *Dayton, O.: B. F. Ells.* 1840. 12mo, pp. 240. + *Dayton: Ells, Claflin & Co.* 1851. 12mo, pp. 240. 40832

This is the "Message" over again with verbal variations; got up to sell. The following is an abridgment:

Lewis. History of the Expedition [Title as in No. 40828]. Revised, and abridged by the Omission of unimportant details, With an Introduction and Notes. By Archibald McVickar ... . *New-York: Harper and Brothers.* 1842. 2 vols., 12mo, pp. vi, 371; x, 9–395. 4 Maps. BA. 40833

Reprinted with new title-pages 1843, 44, 45, 47, 1850, 51, 55, 58, 1860, 68, 1871, 72, 74, and 75.

Lewis. Account of the Expedition of Captains Lewis and Clark across the Rocky Mountains, and to the Mouth of the Columbia River. Prepared from the original edition, with an Introduction and Notes, containing Notices of recent Travellers, and a View of the present Condition of Oregon Territory. By Archibald M'Vickar. [*London.*] 1842. 2 vols., 12mo. 40834

This is doubtless Harper's Edition, with a new title to suit the English demand growing out of the Oregonian fever in 1842. For other accounts of this expedition, *see* Fisher (William), *and* Gass (Patrick). The following are translations:

Lewis. Tagebuch einer Entdeckungs-Reise durch Nord-America von der Mündung des Missuri an bis zum Einfluss des Columbia in den stillen Ocean in den Jahren 1804, 5–6. Von Capitains Lewis und Clark. Uebersetzt aus dem Englischen von P. C. Weyland. *Weimar.* 1814. 8vo. Map. 40835

This is Vol. II. of "Neue Bibliothek der wichtigsten Reisebeschreibungen."

Lewis. Reize naar de Bronnen van den Missouri, en door de vaste land van America naar de Zuidzee. Gedaan op last van de Regering der Vereenigde Staten van America, in de jaren 1804, 1805 en 1806. Door de Capitains Lewis en Clarke ... . Uit het Engelsch vertaald door N. G. Van Kampen. ... *Te Dordrecht, By A. Blussé & Zoon.* 1816–18. 3 vols., 8vo, pp. xxxii, 308; viii, 390; vii, 335. Map. 40836

[Lewis (——).] The Process for Extracting and Refining Salt-Petre. According to the Method practised at the Provincial Works in Philadelphia. Published by Order of the Committee of Safety. *Philadelphia: Printed by William and Thomas Bradford* ... M, DCC, LXXVI. 8vo, pp. 34. P. 40837

First printed in 1767.

Lewis (M.) Celebration of the Centennial Anniversary of the Birth of George Washington, New-York, February 22, 1832. With An Oration delivered ... before the Common Council and Citizens ... . By Maj. Gen. Morgan Lewis. ... *New-York: G. F. Hopkins & Son.* 1832. 8vo, pp. 11, 32. C., N. 40838

Lewis. A Concise Account of the Rise, Progress, and Final Dissolution of the late General Committee, friendly to the Re-Election of his Excellency, Morgan Lewis. *New York.* 1807. 8vo. N., S. 40839

Lewis. ... Expediency and the Means of establishing A University in ... New-York. ... *New-York: Grattan, Printer.* 1830. 8vo, pp. 29. B. 40840

For a tract relative to Governor Lewis, *see* Politicus, *pseudon.*

Lewis (O.) An Oration ... in ... Middletown ... September 30th, A.D. 1783. Before A General Convention Of several Lodges, ... of Free and Accepted Masons In ... Connecticut. By Oliver Lewis, A.M. ... *Hartford: Printed by Hudson and Goodwin.* [1783.] 8vo, pp. 16. BA. 40841

Lewis (O.) History of the One Hundred and Thirty-Eighth Regiment, Pennsylvania Volunteer Infantry. By Osceola Lewis. *Norristown: Wills, Iredell & Jenkins.* 1866. 12mo, pp. 198. Plate. B. 40842

Lewis (*Rev.* ——) of Thurenstein, Deacon according to the Order and Decorum of the Ancient Moravian Church. Every Man's Right to Live. A Sermon on Ezek. xxxiii, 2. Why will ye die? Preached in Philadelphia. Translated from German into English. *Philadelphia: Printed by B. Franklin.* 1743.

Title from Thomas' "History of Printing;" I have not seen this book.

Lewis (R. B.) Light and Truth, from Ancient and Sacred History. By Robert Benjamin Lewis. *Portland: D. C. Colesworthy, Printer.* 1836. 12mo, pp. 176. H. 40844

Lewis. Light and Truth, Collected from the Holy Bible, and Ancient and Modern History, containing the Universal History of the Colored and the Indian People ... . *Augusta.* 1843. 12mo, pp. 96. + *Boston.* 1844. 12mo. W. 40845

Lewis (R. W.) Christian Thanksgiving Perpetual. A Sermon ... by Rev. Robert W. Lewis, ... Sheldon, Vermont, November 28th, 1861. *Burlington: W. H. & C. A. Hoyt & Co., Printers.* 1861. 8vo, pp. 14. 40846

Lewis (R. W.) An Oration, delivered before the Washington Benevolent Society, ... New-York, on the Twenty-Second of February, 1812. By Roswell W. Lewis, Esq. ... *New-York: Printed by J. Seymour.* 1812. 8vo, pp. 20. S. 40847

Lewis (S.) Oration, before the Tammany Society, in Poughkeepsie. By Sabin Lewis. [n. p.] 1816. 8vo. 40848

Lewis (S.) Abolitionism Reviewed, being a Further Exposure of the False ... Doctrines ... of the Abolitionists. By Seth Lewis ... . [n. p. n. d.] 12mo, pp. (2), 76. B. 40849

Also: A Review of Abolitionism, or the Question of Slavery, as it exists in the United States, Considered. ... [n. p. n. d.] 12mo, pp. 18. B. — Strictures on Dr. Livingston's System of Penal Laws ... for ... Louisiana. ... *New-Orleans: Printed by Wm. Bloomfield & Co.* 1825. 8vo, pp. 67. BA.

[Lewis (S. J.)] Showing The Manner in which they do Things in the Presbyterian Church in the Nineteenth Century. ... *Morris-Town, N. J.: The Author.* 1837. 12mo, pp. 28.

Contains an account of the expulsion of S. J. Lewis from the Presbyterian church.

Lewis (T.) A Discourse on the True Idea of the State as a Religious Institution, together with the Family and the Church, ordained of God. Delivered Sept. 5, 1843, ... Andover, Mass. By Tayler Lewis. *Andover: Allen, Morrill* ... 1843. 8vo, pp. 56.

Lewis. An Essay on the Ground and Reason of Punishment, with special reference to the Penalty of Death. By Tayler Lewis. And a Defence of Capital Punishment. By Rev. George Cheever. *New York.* 1846. 12mo. 40852

Lewis. The Heroic Periods in a Nation's History. An Appeal to the Soldiers of the American Armies. By Tayler Lewis, ... *New York: Baker & Godwin, Printers.* 1866. 12mo, pp. 58.

Lewis. State Rights: a Photograph from the Ruins of Ancient Greece, with appended dissertations on the ideas of nationality, of sovereignty, and the right of revolution. By Prof. Tayler Lewis ... . *Albany: J. Munsell.* 1864. 8vo, pp. 96. + *Albany: Weed, Parsons & Company.* 1864. 8vo, pp. 47. BA. + [*Ibid.*] 1865. 8vo, pp. 96. B. 40854

Lewis (T.) Case of Thos. Lewis, Elizabeth Jorden, Owen Griffith, Elizabeth Mackay, and Thos. Joy, and others. *London.* [1709.] Folio, 1 l. 40855

Respecting the non-payment of money for service in Newfoundland in Captain Moody's Company.

Lewis (W.) A Discourse, delivered on a Special Occasion at Weymouth, South Parish, January 10, 1841. By Rev. Wales Lewis. *Boston: Printed by S. N. Dickinson.* 1841. 8vo, pp. 26, Appendix, two leaves numbered xxvii, xxviii. B. 40856

Lewis (W.) Experiments and Observations on American Potashes. With An easy Method of determining their respective Qualities. By W. Lewis ... . Made at the Request of the Society for the Encouragement of Arts, ... in consequence of an Application from the House of Representatives of Massachusetts Bay. *London. Printed by order of the Society.* M DCC LXVII. 8vo, pp. (2), 34. C., H. 40857

Lewis (W. D.) A Brief Account of the Efforts of Senator [James] Cooper ... to prevent the Confirmation of William D.

Lewis, Collector of the Customs for ... Philadelphia ... . [n. p. 1851.] 8vo, pp. 77, (2). BA. 40858

Lewis (W. H.) A Farewell Sermon ... in ... Brooklyn, L. I., February 26, 1860. By the Rev. Wm. H. Lewis, D.D. *New-York: Rev. F. D. Harriman.* 1860. 8vo, pp. 23. B. 40859

Lewis. Position of the Protestant Episcopal Church with reference to Other Protestant Denominations. By the Rev. William H. Lewis, D.D. ... *New York: Stanford & Swords.* M.DCCC.LII. 12mo, pp. 23, (1). B. 40860

Lewis. A Sermon, preached before the Annual Convention of the Protestant Episcopal Church, in the Eastern Diocese, ... September 27, 1837. By William H. Lewis ... . *Boston: Torrey & Blair, printers.* 1837. 8vo, pp. 21. B. 40861

Also: Considerations addressed to the Laity of the Protestant Episcopal Church, with Thoughts on the Daily Service. ... *New-York: Stanford and Swords.* 1853. 8vo, pp. 52. B.

Lewis (W. G. W.) Biography of Samuel Lewis, First Superintendent of Common Schools of the State of Ohio. By William G. W. Lewis. *Cincinnati.* 1857. 12mo. Portrait. C.

Lewis (W.) An Address ... before the New England Historic-Genealogical Society, ... January 1, 1862. By Winslow Lewis, M.D. ... *Boston: The Society.* 1862. 8vo, pp. 12. B.

Also: An Address [before the same Society]. ... January 7, 1863. ... *Boston: The Society.* 1863. 8vo, pp. 17, (1). + January 6th, 1864. ... *Albany, N. Y.: J. Munsell.* 1864. 8vo, pp. 9. + Jan. 4, 1865. ... *Boston: The Society.* 1865. 8vo, pp. 20.

Lewis. Address of Dr. Winslow Lewis, on resigning the Presidency of the Boston Numismatic Society, January 5, 1865. *New York.* 1866. 4to, pp. 13. H. 40864

[Lewis.] A Review of the Report of I. W. P. Lewis, on the State of the Light Houses on the Coasts of Maine and Massachusetts ... . *Boston: Printed by Tuttle and Dennett.* 1843. 8vo, pp. 60. BA. 40865

Lewis. Valedictory Address on retiring from the Office of President of the New England Historic-Genealogical Society. Delivered ... February 7, 1866. By Winslow Lewis, M.D. *Boston: The Society.* 1866. 8vo, pp. 23. B. 40866

Lewis (Z.) An Oration, on the Apparent, and the Real Political Situation of the United States, pronounced before the Connecticut Society of Cincinnati ... July the 4th, 1799. By

Zechariah Lewis ... . *New-Haven: Printed by Thomas Green and Son.* 1799. 8vo, pp. 27. BA., H. 40867

Lewis County, *N. Y.* By-Laws and Bill of Prices of the Lewis County Medical Society; adopted ... December 24, 1867. *Lowville.* 1867. 8vo. 40868

Proceedings of the Board of Supervisors of the County of Lewis, for 1857. *Lowville.* 1857. 8vo. Continued. S. 40869

Lewisburg, *Pa.* Catalogue of the Officers and Students of the University at Lewisburg. 1851–52. *Lewisburg, Union Co., Pa.: For the University.* 1852. 8vo, pp. 24. Plate. Continued.

Lewiston, *Me.* Catalogue of Manufacturers' and Mechanics' Library Association of Lewiston, with the Charter, Constitution and By-Laws. ... Incorporated 1861. *Lewiston.* 1861. 8vo, pp. 68. 40871

The Annual Report of the ... School Committee of ... Lewiston, for ... 1867. *Lewiston.* 1867. 8vo, pp. 52. Continued.

The Annual Reports of the Board of Selectmen ... of Lewiston for ... 1862. *Lewiston.* 1862. 8vo, pp. 38. Continued. B.

The First Annual Report of the ... Expenditures of the City of Lewiston, for ... 1864 ... . *Lewiston, Maine: Geo. A. Callahan ... Printer.* 1864. 8vo, pp. 144, (4). Continued. B. 40874

Lewiston and Auburn [N. Y.] Directory; together with a History of Lewiston and Auburn. *Lewiston: W. F. Stanwood.* 186–. 12mo, pp. 179. 40875

Lewiston Falls, *Me.* A Catalogue of the Officers ... of Lewiston Falls Academy, Me. for ... 1850. *Cambridge: John Bartlett.* 1850. 12mo, pp. 12. Continued. H. 40876

[Le Wright (J.)] Two Proposals Becoming England At this Juncture to Undertake. One, for Securing a Colony in the West Indies ... . And the other, for advancing Merchandize, And the Crown-Revenue To at least 40000 l. p. An. *Printed in the Year* 1706. 4to, pp. (4), 8. H. 40877

This is a project for a new settlement at Darien, in which the projector, referring to the failure of the Scots company, says, "We are now addressing to the English, between whom and the Scots we allow no comparison in point of trade." The caption reads, "Reasons by Capt. Le Wright, shewing why her Majesty ought to enter upon Her Propriety, now on the Continent of America."

Lex, *pseudon.* Condition of the Rebel States. [n. p. 1867.] 8vo, pp. 4. H. 40878

Lexicon Geographicvm; ... Edidit Philippvs Ferrarivs ... . *Parisiis: Apud Franciscum Muguel.* MDCLXX. Folio, pp. (12), 483, (19). 40879

Includes many American topics. *See also* Ferrari (F.), Vol. IV., No. 24163.

Lexington. A Poem. *See* [Wetmore (P. M.)]

Lexington, *Ky.* Address to the People of the United States, with the Proclamation and Resolutions of the Pro-Slavery Convention at Lexington. *St. Louis.* 1855. 8vo. 40880

A Catalogue of Books of the Lexington Library Company. With its Charter, Laws, and Regulations. *Lexington (Ky.): T. Smith.* 1821. 12mo, pp. xvi, 172. + Additions to the Catalogue ... from 1821 to the Present ... . *Lexington (Ky.): A. W. Elder.* 1852. 8vo, pp. 113. C. 40881

Directory of the City of Lexington and of the County of Fayette, for 1838 and '39. Containing an epitomized history of the city and its present condition. By Julius P. Bolivar MacCabe. *Lexington: J. C. Noble.* 1838. 16mo, pp. 136. 40882

Lexington City Directory for 1864–5. To which is appended a United States Post Office Directory. *Cincinnati: Williams & Co.* 1864. 8vo, pp. 122–106. Continued. 40883

Memorial of the Mechanics and Manufacturers of Lexington to Congress, Jan. 22, 1811. [n. p. 1811.] 8vo, pp. 14.

Report of the President of the Lexington and Ohio Railroad, to the Senate of Kentucky ... [*Frankfort.* 1840.] 8vo. 40885

See also Kentucky and Transylvania University.

School Exercises of the Lafayette Female Academy; including Triumphs of Genius, a Poem, by Caroline Clifford Nephew, ... *Lexington, Ky.: T. Smith, Printer.* [1826.] 8vo, pp. 75.

See also Lafayette, No. 38583, last note.

Lexington, *Mass.* Auditor's Report of the Receipts and Expenditures of the Town of Lexington, 1855–56. *Charlestown.* 1856. 8vo, pp. 24. Continued. 40887

Battle of Lexington—Bloody Butchery by the British Troops; or, The Runaway Fight of the Regulars. Broadside. M. 40888

This rare piece was reprinted without date. *See also* our Vol. VII., No. 26318.

Prospectus of the Lexington Manual Labor Seminary. *Boston: Russell, Odiorne & Co.* MDCCCXXXIII. 12mo, pp. 8. H. 40889

Report of a Committee appointed ... to investigate the Ministerial Fund of Lexington. *Concord: Herman Atwill.* 1832. 8vo, pp. 36. BA. 40890

Report of the School Committee of ... Lexington, for ... 1848–9. *Boston: Dutton and Wentworth, Printers.* 1849. 8vo, pp. 19. Continued. H. 40891

Selectmen's Report of the Expenditures of the Town of Lexington, for ... 1862–3 ... . *Boston: Press of T. R. Marvin & Son.* 1863. 8vo, pp. 19. Continued. H. 40892

Shall we have a Public Library in Lexington? [By Robert M. Copeland, and others. n. p. 1857.] 8vo, pp. 8. H. 40893

Lexington, *Mo.* The Book of Chronicles of the City of Lexington, and Fragments of the Book of Hadborim and Maazim. Translated out of the Original Tongue, and with the Original Manuscripts diligently compared and revised. *Lexington: Missouri Union Office.* MDCCCLXIII. 8vo, pp. 41, 7.

Lexington, *Va.* *See* Virginia.

Lexington, *Steamer.* Burning of the Lexington in Long Island Sound, with an Account of many other sad Catastrophes of the Disastrous Year 1839. *Boston.* 1840. 8vo. 40895

A Full and Particular Account of ... the Loss of the Steamboat Lexington, in Long-Island Sound, ... January 13, 1840; ... A portion of the profits of this work will be appropriated to the benefit of the destitute families of those who were lost. ... *Providence: H. H. Brown and A. H. Stillwell.* 1840. 8vo, pp. 32.

See also [Wheeler (J. B.)], for the Coroner's Inquest.

Ley del fondo piadoso de Californias. *Mejico.* 1833. 8vo.

Ley fundamental de instruccion publica y ejercicio de professiones en el estado. *San Luis Potosi.* 1863. Sm. 8vo, pp. 48.

Ley orgánica de la Milicia nacional y Decreto ejecutivo que la reglementa, derogando los de 16 de Junio de 1854 sobre la materia. Edicion oficial. *Carácas.* [1860.] 8vo, pp. 72.

See also Colombia, Mexico, Nicaragua, Peru, Santo Domingo.

Leyba (D. de). Vida de el Venerable Padre Fr. Diego Romero de la Regular Observancia de N. S. P., Francisco. Por Fr. Diego de Leyba, Predicador de la Provincia de Santa Evangelio de Mexico. *Mexico: J. de Riberra.* 1684. 4to. 40900

Leydt (Johannes). *See* [Ritzema (Joannes)].

Leyendecker *and* Schleiden (Em.) Observaciones que acera de algunas medidas encamin. al fomento de la republica, y particular. en Angangueo. *Morelia.* 1848. 8vo. 40901

Leyes de la recompilacion de Indias. *See* [Galvez (J. de)].

Leyes Dominicanos. *See* Vol. v., No. 20576.

Leyes relativas. *See* Mexico.

Leyes y ordenancas nueuamẽte hechas | por su Magestad ‸ pa la gouernacion de las Indias y buen trata | miento y conseruacion delos Indios: que se han de guardar en el | consejo y audiẽcias reales q̃ en ellas residen: y por todos los otros | gouernadores ‸ juezes y personas particulare dellas. | Con priuilegio imperial. | [Colophon:] *Las presentes leyes, y nuevas | ordenanzas y declaracion dellas | para la gouernacion de las In- | dias, y buen tratamiento de los | naturales dellas. Fueron im- | presas por mandado de | los señores: presidẽte, y del consejo de las In- | dias: en la villa | de Alcala | de | Henares: en casa de Joan | de Brocar ã ocho dias del | mes de Julio del año | de nr̃o saluador | Jesu cris- | to |* M.D.XLIII. | Folio, Title and 13 leaves. 40902

So rare that we can only refer to two copies in America, one in the Lenox Library, and one belonging to Samuel L. M. Barlow. These laws were issued by Charles V., and consist of two ordinances limiting the partitions of lands among the *conquistadores*, which were subsequently omitted. The British Museum (Grenville Library), has a copy printed on vellum which is unique. Ternaux No. 49, and Rich, No. 13, convey an erroneous impression as to their nature, which [Harrisse's] "Bib. Am. Vet.," No. 247, corrects; he says, "They were issued especially for the better treatment of the Indians, and, we believe, for limiting the partitions of lands among the conquerors. Leon Pinelo states, on the authority of Juan de Grivalja, that these laws 'tan odiosas,' were prompted by the publication of the manuscript tract 'Dies i seis remedios contra la peste que destruye las Indias.' They were issued at Barcelona, November 20th, 1542, completed at Valladolid, July 4th, 1543, and ordered to be printed, and enforced immediately throughout the Indies." So long ago as 1830 Mr. Rich priced the work at £21. For further particulars consult Rich's "Bib. Am.," II. 355, Brunet's "Manuel du Libraire," III., col. 1042, and especially [Harrisse's] "Bib. Am. Vet.," No. 247, for an elaborate article on the "Leyes" in general. A second edition was published with the following title, according to Pinelo-Barcia, Vol. II., col. 828:

Leyes, y Ordenanças nuevas, hechas por su Magestad, para la Governacion de las Indias, i buen tratamiento de los Indios, que se han de guardar en el Consejo, e i por todos los otros Governadores, Jueces, i Personas Particulares de ella. *En Madrid, en Casa de Francisco Sanchez.* 1585. Folio. 40903

A third, and perhaps the last edition, has the following title:

Leyes y | Ordenanças Nueva- | mente hechas por su Mages- | tad, para la gouernació de las Indias, y buen tratamiento | y conservacion de los Indios: que se han de guardar en | el Consejo y Audiencias Reales que en ellas | residen: y por todos los otros Gouerna- | dores, juezes y personas parti- | culares dellas. | *En Valladolid.* | *En la Imprenta del Licenciado Varez de Castro.* | *Año de* M.DCIII. | Folio, Title, 13 leaves, and 1 blank leaf. 40904

Leyes de los Reynos de Indias. Quinta edicion, notablemente aumentada y declarada oficial por la Regencia provisional del Reyno en Real orden de 16 de Diciembre 1840. *Madrid.* 1841. 4 vols., folio. 40905

"This celebrated collection of the Spanish Laws for the government of the Indies, as the Spanish Americas are usually called, had become so rare, that a copy could not be had in Spain at any price. The first edition was printed in 1681, the second in 1756, the third in 1774, and the fourth in 1791."—RICH, II. 355. *See* Encinas (Diego de), *our* No. 22550, Vol. IV., [Puga], *also* "Recopilacion," *and* "Sumario."

LEYPOLDT (Frederick). The American Catalogue of Books for 1869. ... *New York: Leypoldt & Holt.* 1870. 8vo, pp. xxi, 5–103. B. 40906

Mr. Leypoldt was formerly a bookseller; he possesses unusual intelligence, and is now engaged in making a catalogue of all books published in America, in print at this time, which promises to be a work of great value to the collector of American books, as distinguished from those which relate to America. He is also the editor of "The Publishers' Weekly."

LEYSLER (J.) A Modest and Impartial | Narrative | Of several Grievances and | Great Oppressions | That the Peaceable and most Considerable Inhabitants | of | Their Majesties Province | of | New-York | in | America | Lie Under, | By the Extravagant and Arbitrary Pro- | ceedings of Jacob Leysler and his | Accomplices. | [*New York.* 1690.] 4to, pp. 42. M. 40907

A piece of the greatest rarity; we know of no other copy. Probably printed by William Bradford. *See also* Leisler (J.), who is the same person.

LEZAMA (J. de). Exhortacion de Paz que descubierta la infame revolucion de Tierra dentro, predicó el Lic. Don José de Lezama ... 12 de Enero, de 1811. *Mexico.* 1811. 4to, pp. (2), 20. 40908

One of the numerous anathemas pronounced by the Mexican clergy against the insurrection of Hidalgo.

LEZAMIS (Jose de). Breve relacion de la vida y muerte del doctor D. Francisco de Aguiar, y Seyxas, arçobispo de Mexico. *Mexico.* 1699. 4to. 40909

"Livre fort rare resté inconnu."—ANDRADE.

LEZAMIS. Vida del Apostol Santiago, el mayor uno de los tres mas amados, y familiares de Jesu-Christo unico, y singular Patron de España con algunas antiguedes y excelencias de España, especialmente de Viscaya. *Mexico: por Dona Maria de Benavides.* 1699. 4to. 40910

Extremely scarce and curious. The first one hundred and four pages are occupied by a biography of D. Francisco Aguiar y Seyxas, one of the most beneficent prelates of Mexico. Pages 280–426 contain a treatise on the antiquities and language of the Vascongadi Province, with some specimens of prose and poetry in that language.

LEZAY (A.) Qu'est-ce que la constitution de 93? Constitution de Massachusetts. Par Adrien Lezay. *Paris: Chez Migneret. An* III *de la République.* 8vo, pp. xii, 84. BA. 40911

LEZAY-MARNEZIA (Cl. Fr. Ad. de). Lettres écrites des Rives de l'Ohio, Par Cl. Fr. Ad. de Lezay-Marnezia, Citoyen de Pensylvanie. *Au Fort-Pitt, Et se trouvent A Paris, Chez Prault, Imprimeur rue Taranne,* Nº 749, *a l'Immortalité. An* IX *de la République.* 8vo, pp. viii, 144. H. 40912

A very scarce pamphlet; we have seen only two copies. "Ces lettres ayant été arrêtées par la police sont très rares."—QUERARD.

LH......... (L. F.) Le Champ-D'Asile, Tableau Topographique et Historique Du Texas, Contenant des Détails sur le Sol, le Climat et les Productions de cette contrée; des Documens authentiques sur l'organisation de la Colonie des Réfugiés français; des Notices sur ses principaux fondateurs; des Extraits de leurs proclamations et autres actes publics: suivi de Lettres écrites par des Colons à quelque-uns de leurs compatriotes. ... Par L. F. LH......... (de l'Ain), l'un des Auteurs des Fastes de la Gloire. *Paris, Ladvocat, Libraire* ... 1819. 8vo, pp. xvi, 247. + Seconde édition augmentée d'une Description du Tombechbe ... . *Paris.* 1819. 8vo. 40913

Published for the benefit of the emigrants to Texas.

LHOYD (H[umfrey]). The historie of Cambria, | now called Wales: | A part of the most fa- | mous Yland of Brytaine, | written in the Brytish lan- | guage aboue two hundreth | yeares past; translated into | English by H. Lhoyd | Gentleman: Corrected, augmented, | and continued out of Re- | cords and best approued | Authors, by Dauid Powel | Doctor in Diui- | nitie, Cum Privilegio. | [Colophon:] *Imprinted at London by Rafe Newberie and Henrie Denham.* 1584. Sm. 4to, pp. (8), 22, 401. 40914

First and rarest of all the editions. A special interest in this work for the American collector consists in its relation of the most ancient "Voyage and Discovery of the West Indies, performed by Madoc, the sonne of Owen Guined, prince of North Wales, anno 1170." *See* Hakluyt, Vol. III., p. 1; Herbert's "Travels," p. 355; Pinkerton's

"Travels," Vol. XII., p. 156; Southey's "Madoc," and the notes thereto. Consult also Beattie's "Journal," David Jones' "Journal," and Williams' "Enquiry." It has been frequently reprinted. An edition, augmented by William Wynne, was published in *London,* 1697, 8vo, and again in 1702, 8vo. Improved and enlarged, *London,* 1774, 8vo. Corrected, augmented, &c., by David Powell, *London,* 1811, 4to. Revised and corrected, ... by Richard Lloyd, *Shrewsbury,* 1832, 8vo, pp. 289 and 330.

LIAIS (E.) Explorations scientifiques au Brésil. Hydrographie du haut San-Francisco et du Rio das Velhas, ou Résultat au point de vue hydrographique d'un voyage effectué dans la province de Minas-Geraes. Par Emmanuel Liais. Ouvrage accompagné de cartes levées par l'auteur ... . *Paris: Garnier frères.* 1865. Folio, pp. 33. 20 Plates. 40915

LIBBEY (H. W.) The Indian Hygieina. A complete Guide to Invalids ... . By H. W. Libbey. Third Number. *Cleveland.* [1865.] 12mo, pp. 96. 19 Plates. 40916

El Liberal. Historia de un Sumario. *Bogota.* [n. d.] 8vo.

Twelve or more numbers published.

The Liberal American. A Novel. By A Lady. *London: Lane.* 1785. 2 vols., 12mo. 40918

See "M. Rev.," LXXIII. 466.

The Liberal Preacher; a Monthly Publication of Sermons by Living Ministers. Edited by T. R. Sullivan. ... . *John Prentiss, Keene, N. H.* 1828. 8vo, pp. (4), 202. BA. 40919

Continued to 1838 or later.

El Liberalismo y sus efectos en la Republica Mexicana. *Mexico.* 1858. 4to. 40920

The Liberator. William Lloyd Garrison, Editor. ... *Boston.* 1831. Folio. 40921

A celebrated anti-slavery journal. Discontinued at the close of 1865.

LIBERIA. Constitution and Laws of Maryland in Liberia. With an Appendix of Precedents. *Baltimore.* 1837. 8vo, pp. 168. 40922

Also: Constitution, Government and Laws of Liberia, 1825. ... [n. p. n. d.] 8vo.

First Annual Report of the Trustees of Donations for Education in Liberia, ... January 15, 1851. *Boston: Press of T. R. Marvin.* 1851. 8vo, pp. 32. Map. Continued. H. 40923

Tenth Annual Report of ... the Ladies' Liberia School Association. ... November 1st, 1842. *Philadelphia: Printed by Lydia R. Bailey.* 1842. 8vo, pp. 11. H. 40924

The Independent Republic of Liberia; its Constitution, and Declaration of Independence; Address of the Colonists to the Free People of Color in the United States. ... *Philadelphia.* 1848. Folio. 40925

Drawn up by S. Greenleaf.

Liberia. The Land of Promise to Free Colored Men. *Washington: H. S. Bowen.* 1861. 8vo, pp. 31. 40926

Liberian Colonization: ... By an Abolitionist and Colonizationist. *New-York.* 1857. 12mo, pp. 31. 40927

Message of the President [D. B. Warner] of the Republic of Liberia to the Two Houses of Congress, December 11th, 1865. *New-York: John A. Gray & Green, Printers.* 1866. 12mo, pp. 12.

Treats of the relations of Liberia to the United States.

Tables showing the Number of Emigrants and Recaptured Africans sent to ... Liberia by the ... United States ... . *Washington.* 1845. 8vo, pp. (2), 299–414. Map, 2 Tables. 40929

LIBERTAS, *pseudon.* *See* [Brown (Peter)], Vol. II., No. 8543, Curtis (B. R.), Vol. V., No. 18028, *and* [Lester C. E.)]

Liberté, égalité, fraternité. A la Convention nationale. [n. p. n. d.] 8vo, pp. 48, or less. 40930

Signed "Clausson, F. A. Millet, commissaires des colons de St.-Domingue près la Convention nationale, 20 Thermidor an II."

"Liberty." *See* [Ames (Julius R.)], Vol. I., No. 1306.

Liberty. A Pindaric Ode. *Philadelphia: Printed ... by Robert Aitken.* M.DCC.LXXXIII. 4to, pp. 16. P. 40931

Liberty, a Poem; on the Independence of America. ... *Richmond: Printed by Aug. Davis.* M,DCC,LXXXVIII. Folio, pp. 20.

Liberty, A Poem, lately found in a bundle of papers, said to be written by A Hermit in New-Jersey. ... *Philadelphia: Printed by William Goddard* ... MDCCLXIX. 4to, pp. 12. BA., P. 40933

The Liberty Almanac. ... 1845 ... By J. N. T. Tucker. ... *Syracuse, N. Y.: Tucker & Kinney.* [1845.] 12mo, pp. 35, (1). Continued. H. 40934

Liberty: An Elegiac Poem. *See* [Hopkinson (Thomas)].

Liberty and Equality before the Law. Proceedings of the Convention of the Colored People of Va., held in ... Alexandria,

Aug. 2, 3, 4, 5, 1865. *Alexandria, Va.: Cowing & Gillis.* 1865. 8vo, pp. 24. 40935

Liberty and Patriotism; a Miscellaneous Ode; with Explanatory Notes, and Anecdotes. *London: Fielding and Walker.* 1778. 4to. 40936

Includes some reference to America. *See* "M. Rev.," LVIII. 307.

The Liberty and Property of British Subjects Asserted: In a Letter from an Assembly-Man in Carolina, To his Friend in London. *London: Printed for J. Roberts in Warwick-lane.* M.DCC.XXVI. 8vo, pp. 39. 40937

This letter is signed "J---- N----, Carolina, Charleston, January 15, 1725." It is understood to justify the people of Carolina in their complaints of the proprietary governments under which the Colony was then held. The preface, which was written in London, is nearly as long as the letter, and contains a general history of the Colony.

Liberty and Property Vindicated, and the St**pm*n burnt. A Discourse occasionally made on burning the Effigy of the St**pm*n in New London, Conn. [*New London.*] 1765. 4to, pp. 11. + *Boston.* 1765. 8vo, pp. 15. 40938

See also [Church (B.)], Vol. IV., No. 12981, for an edition dated 1766.

Liberty and Property without Oppression, as set forth in Sundry Letters, directed to the Public of the County of Monmouth, in the Province of New Jersey. [n. p. n. d.] 8vo, pp. 23.

Liberty and Union! Speeches ... at the ... Republican Festival, in commemoration of the birth of Washington, ... New York, February 22, 1860. ... *New York: Baker & Godwin, Printers.* 1860. 8vo, pp. 40. H. 40940

Liberty and Union, One and Inseparable. Speeches ... at the Republican Union Festival, in commemoration of the birth of Washington; ... Feb. 22, 1862 ... . *New York: G. P. Putnam.* 1862. Imp. 8vo, pp. 27. H. 40941

The Liberty Bell. By Friends of Freedom. ... *Boston: For the Massachusetts Anti-Slavery Fair.* M DCCC XXXIX. 8vo, pp. viii, 104. Plate. Continued. BA. 40942

Liberty Chimes. *Providence.* 1845. 12mo. 40943

LIBERTY COUNTY, *Ga.* Annual Report of the Missionary to the Negroes in Liberty County, Georgia. *Charleston.* 1834. 8vo. + Second Edition. [*Ibid.*] 1834. 8vo, pp. 15. Continued.

LIBERTY, *N. Y.* Circular of Liberty Normal Institute, Liberty, Sullivan Co., N. Y. [n. p. n. d.] 8vo, pp. 2. 40945

Liberty is the Birthright of All. Five Hundred Thousand Strokes for Freedom. *London.* 1853. 8vo. 40946

A series of anti-slavery tracts; edited by Wilson Armistead.

Liberty or Slavery. *See* [Thurston (E. B.)]

The Liberty Papers. No. 1. No. 2. Liberty, a Divine Inalienable Right. No. 3. Liberty; all Hail. No. 4. Liberty, a Power among the Nations. *New York.* 1861. 4 sheets, folio.

The Liberty Preacher, edited by Rev. Geo. W. Bassett. *Milwaukee.* 1851. 8vo. H. 40948

Vol. I., No. 1., June, 1851.

Liberty Saved, or The Warning of an old Kentuckian ... on the Danger of electing Partisans of the old Court of Appeals ... *Louisville.* 1825. 8vo, pp. 28. P. 40949

Liberty Tracts. *Boston.* [n. d.] 12mo. 40950

A series of seven or more tracts on slavery.

LIBORIUS (C. L. de). Defensa de las Señoras Carolina Litchfield de Liborius y Carolina Liborius de Olavarria en la causa que siguen con Chartier y Olavarria sobre nulidad de un contrato. *Valencia.* 1864. 8vo, pp. 40. 40951

Library Company of Philadelphia. *See* Philadelphia.

Library of American History. Intended to give the reader a full view of American History, from the earliest discovery to the present time, abounding with copious Notes, Biographical Sketches, and miscellaneous matter. Edited by Samuel L. Knapp. *New York.* 1837–39. 2 vols., 4to. 40952

Frequently reprinted. Includes reprints of Belknap's, Robertson's, Graham's, and Ramsay's Histories, Stiles' Judges, etc.

Library of American History, containing Biographical Sketches, ... Revolutionary Anecdotes ... . *Cincinnati.* [n. d.] Rl. 8vo, pp. 640. 40953

Library of Congress. *See* Congress, Vol. IV., No. 15560–79.

The Library Reporter and Book-Buyer's Guide: a Quarterly Record ... Jan. 1854, No. 1. *Boston.* 1854. 8vo. S. 40954

Libretto De Tutta La Nauigation De Re De Spagna De Le Isole Et | Terreni Nouamente Trouati. [Colophon:] *Finisse el libretto de tutta la nauigatiõe del Re de Spagna de le isole &* | *terreni nouamẽte trouati. Stampado in Venesia per Albertino Vercelle* | *se da Lisona a di. x. de aprile.* M. CCCCC. IIII | *Con Gratia et Privilegio.* | 4to, 14 leaves. 40955

Concerning this rare piece *see* [Harrisse's] "Bib. Am. Vet.," Vol. I., No. 32, and Vol. II., No. 16.

LIBRI (*M.*) Réponse de M. Libri au Rapport de M. Boucly publié dans le Moniteur Universel du 19 Mars, 1848. *Paris: Pancoucke.* 1849. 8vo. 40956

The following is the report alluded to: "Rapport adressé a M. le garde des sceaux Hébert par M. le procureur du Roi Boucly, suivi du procès intenté par M. Libri contre le gérant du Moniteur Universel à l'occasion de la publication de ce rapport et contre le gérant du National en raison d'un article inséré dans le nº du 5 Avril, 1848. *Paris: Pancoucke.* 1850. 8vo.

Libro de la Vida de el Ven. Padre Bernardino Alvarez, Patriarcha y Fundador de la Sagrada Religion de la Charidad en este Nueva-España. Compuesto por D. Juan de Arca, D.D. Mexicano. *Mexico.* 1762. 4to. 40957

Libro de las constituciones del r. orden terzero de penitencia de N. S. P. Francisco, modificadas por el dicho orden en Mexico. *Mexico.* 1796. 4to, pp. 44. 40958

Libro en q̄ estã copiladas algunas bullas de nr̄o muy sancto padre cõcedidas en fauor de la jurisdi- | cion real de sus altezas & todas las pragmaticas q estan fechas para la buena gouernaciõ del reyno | imprimido por mãdado de Juan ramirez escriuano del cõsejo del rey & de la reyna nuestros senores: | el qual fue tassado par sus altezas & por los senores del su consejo a vn castellano de oro cada volu- | men con priuilegio que sus altezas dierõ por su carta real q por tiempo de cinco años cõtados desde | primero dia de deziembre deste presente año de mill & quinientos & tres fasta ser complidos ningu- | no otro sin su poder lo pueda imprimir en el reyno ni fuera del ni vẽderlo so pena de cinquenta mill | mr̄s: la mitad para la camera: & la otra mitad para el dicho Juan ramirez & de perder lo q̄ ouire im- | primido o vẽdido o imprimiere o vẽdiere o trouiere p̃a vẽder cõ otro tãto p̃a el dicho Juã ramirez. | [Colophon:] *Fue impressa esta obra en la villa de Alcala de henarez por Lanzalao Polono imprimidor de libros a costa de Johan Ramirez escribano del Consejo del Rey e de la Reyna nuestros Señores a quien sus Altezas mandaron tener cayo de la imprimir: acabosse a*

diez e seis dias del mes de Noviembre de mill e quinientos e tres años. Folio, Title, 7 leaves, ccxlviii leaves, 1 leaf. J.C.BT. 40959

Concerning this rare volume *see* [Harrisse's] "Bib. Am. Vet.," II., No. 10. The only copy in the United States contains the autograph signature of Ferdinand II.

Con priuilegio imperial ... Libro llamado Thesoro de virtu- | des vtil & copioso. Copilado por vn religioso portugues. | de la ordẽ d'l serafico padre sãt frãcisco Dirigido al muy nuestro | señor Francisco pessoa: tesorero d'l muy esclarecido & inu ... . | [Colophon:] *A gloria: y alabanza de* | *dios todopoderoso y de su Bendita Madre* | *la virgen sancta Maria. Fue impressa* | *la presente obra, llamada Tesoro de virtu-* | *des, en la villa de Medina del cã-* | *po, por Pedro de Castro im-* | *presor de libros. Acabose a* | *veyente dias d' Otubre.* | *Año.* M . D . xliij. | 4to, Title, 20 leaves, 1 leaf blank, Text, 64 unnumbered leaves, and leaves numbered lxv–cxxxv, Colophon, 1 leaf. 40960

"This anonymous compilation by a Portuguese monk of the Franciscan order, interests us only on account of two letters: one from Martin de Valencia forwarded to the bishop of Mexico to the general chapter of the Franciscans held at Toledo; the other, addressed to the said de Valencia by the friars of the Franciscan Convent of Talmanaco, dated June 12th, 1531. These two letters have also been inserted in the Latin 'Cortez' of 1532 and in the 'Novus Orbus' of 1555."—[HARRISSE'S] *Bib. Am. Vet.* I., No. 243. The only known copy is in the possession of Señor J. G. Icazbalceta of Mexico.

Libro Primo de Provisiones. *See* Encinas (D. de), Vol. VI., No. 22550, and *add* "Libro Primo De" before "Provisiones."

Libro Primo della Historia. *See* Anghiera Vol. I., No. 1565.

LIÇANA (B. de). Devocionario de Nuestra Señora de Itzmal; historia y conquistada Espiritual de Yucatan, por Fr. Bernardo de Liçana. [n. p.] 1633. 8vo. 40961

LICEAGA (José Maria de). Adiciones y Rectificaciones a la Historia de Mexico que escribió D. Lucas Alaman. *Guanajuato.* 1868. 4to. 40962

The License Question, April, 1852, and the Liquor Traffic. [*Boston: Printed by John Wilson and Son.* 1852.] 16mo, pp. 35.

See also Massachusetts, *and* [Phillips (J.)]

Report and Bill concerning Licensed Houses, and the Sale of Intoxicating Liquors. [*Boston.* 1837.] 8vo, pp. 28. H. 40964

Mass. House of Representatives, No. 62.

Licentiousness Unmasked; or Liberty Explained. *London: J. Bew.* 1776. 8vo. S. 40965

"Of all the numerous answers which have appeared to Dr. Price's late publication, this seems to be the most unconnected, superficial, and unworthy."—*Monthly Review*, LV. 153. *See* Price (Richard).

El Liceo Mexicano. *Mexico: J. M. Lara.* 1844. 2 vols., 8vo, pp. 434, (6), 38 Plates; 264, 22 Plates. C. 40966

Esteemed for the biographies of the Viceroys of Spain who governed Mexico under the Spanish rule. Vol. II. was not completed.

LICHFIELD (Richard, *Lord Bishop of*). A Sermon preached before the ... House of Lords in the Abbey Church of Westminster, ... Dec. 13, 1776; being the day appointed by Authority for a General Fast, on Account of the American Rebellion. *London: T. Cadell.* MDCCLXXVII. 4to, pp. 16. 40967

See also Cornwallis (F.), Vol. IV., No. 16817, *and* Smallbroke (*Dr.*)

LICHTENSTEIN (H.) Beschreibung von Brasilien ... . *Berlin.* 1818. 4to. 12 Plates. 40968

Also many papers on American topics in the Transaction of the Berlin Academy.

LICKING COUNTY PIONEER SOCIETY. Pioneer Pamphlets, Nos. 1–7. *Newark, Ohio.* 1869. 8vo. Continued. 40969

LICKING COUNTY, OHIO, PIONEERS. Celebration at Clay, Licking Co., July 4, 1869; with an Address by Dr. Coulter, and Historical Sketches of Licking, Bowling Green, Franklin, Hopewell, &c., by Isaac Smacker. *Newark.* 1869. 8vo.

Liddesdale. *See* [Lawson (James)], No. 39447.

LIDDON (J.) A Sermon on Slavery. By Rev. John Liddon. *London.* 1792. 8vo. 40971

LIDENIUS (J. A.) The Lawfulness of Defensive War. A Sermon preached before the Members of the Church, at Chiechester, in the County of Chester, and Province of Pennsylvania, upon their Association for Defence, February 14, 1756. By John Abr. Lidenius, Itin. Miss. to the Swede Congregations. ... *Philadelphia: Printed ... by James Chattin*; ... 1756. 4to, pp. 16.

LIDSTONE (J. T. S.) The Bostoniad: ... a ... description of the Principal Establishments, ... and Substantial Business Men, in the Athens of America. By the Hon. James Torrington Spencer Lidstone. ... *Boston.* 1853. 8vo, pp. 110. BA. 40973

LIEBER (F.) On Civil Liberty and Self-Government. By Francis Lieber, LL.D. ... *Philadelphia: Lippincott* ... MDCCCLIII.

2 vols., 12mo, pp. xvii, (2), 25–355; (4), 13–371, (1). + *London: Richard Bentley.* 185–. 8vo, pp. 552. + Enlarged Edition, ... *Philadelphia: J. B. Lippincott and Co.* MDCCCLIX. 8vo, pp. 629. BA. + Third Edition. Edited by T. D. Woolsey. [*Ibid.*] 1874. 8vo, pp. 622. 40974

LIEBER. A Constitution and Plan of Education for Girard College for Orphans, with an Introductory Report, laid before the Board of Trustees, By Francis Lieber. ... *Philadelphia: Carey, Lea and Blanchard.* 1834. 8vo, pp. 227, (1). B. 40975

LIEBER. Essays on Property and Labour ... By Francis Lieber. *New York: Harper & Brothers.* [1841.] 12mo, pp. xx, (2), 225. + [*Ibid.*] 1842. + [*Ibid.*] 1843. + [*Ibid.*] 1859.

LIEBER. Legal and Political Hermeneutics, or Principles of Interpretation and Construction in Law and Politics, with Remarks on Precedents and Authorities. Enlarged Edition. By Francis Lieber. *Boston: Charles C. Little and James Brown.* MDCCCXXXIX. 8vo, pp. 240. BA., C. 40977

LIEBER. Letters to a Gentleman in Germany, written after a trip from Philadelphia to Niagara. Edited by Francis Lieber. *Philadelphia: Carey, Lea & Blanchard.* 1834. 8vo, pp. 356. C.

LIEBER. Lincoln oder McClellan? Aufruf an die Deutschen in Amerika. Von Franz Lieber. [*New-York: H. Ludwig.* 1864.] 8vo, pp. 4. BA. 40979

Translated as: ... Lincoln or McClellan. Appeal to the Germans in America. ... Translated from the German by T. C. [*New York.* 1864.] 8vo, pp. 8.— ... Lincoln of McClellan? Oproep aan die Hollanders in Amerika. [*New York.* 1863.] 8vo, pp. 4.

LIEBER. Manual of Political Ethics ... . By Francis Lieber. *Boston: Charles C. Little and James Brown.* MDCCCXXXVIII–IX. 2 vols., 8vo, pp. xiv, 443; xvi, 668. BA. + Second Edition. *Boston.* 1839–47. 2 vols., 8vo, pp. xiii, 428; xvi, 668. B. + *London: William Smith.* MDCCCXXXIX. 2 vols., 8vo, pp. xv, 413; xvi, 668. H. 40980

[LIEBER.] The Martyr's Monument. Being the Patriotism and Political Wisdom of Abraham Lincoln, as exhibited in his Speeches, Messages, Orders, and Proclamations from the Presidential Canvass of 1860 until his Assassination, April 14, 1865. ... *New York.* [1865.] 12mo, pp. iv, 297. BA. 40981

LIEBER. Notes on Fallacies peculiar to American Protectionists, or chiefly resorted to in America. By Francis Lieber ... . *New York: American Free Trade League.* 1869. 8vo, pp. 39. B. + Fourth Edition. [*Ibid.* 1870.] 8vo, pp. 48. H. 40982

LIEBER. Reflections on the Changes which may seem necessary in the Present Constitution of the State of New York, ... By Francis Lieber, LL.D. ... *New York.* 1867. 8vo, pp. 50.

LIEBER. The Stranger in America; or, Letters to a Gentleman in Germany: comprising Sketches of the Manners, Society, and National Peculiarities of the United States. By Francis Lieber. *Philadelphia: Carey, Lea & Blanchard.* 1835. 8vo, pp. 5–356. + *London: Richard Bentley.* 1835. 2 vols., 12mo, pp. viii, 301; v, 310. B. 40984

See "Quart. Rev.," LIII. 290, *and* "N. A. Rev.," October, 1835.

[LIEBER.] Washington and Napoleon. A Fragment. ... *New York.* 1864. Sm. 4to, pp. 12. H. 40985

Also: Abstraction of Moneys from the Public Treasury for Sectarian Uses. Over $500,000, from the City of New York alone, in 1869! [n. p. n. d.] 4to, pp. 4.— ... An Address on Secession. Delivered in South Carolina in ... 1851. ... *New York.* 1861. 8vo. + [*Ibid.*] 1865. 8vo, pp. 12.—Amendments of the Constitution, submitted to the Consideration of the American People. ... *New York.* 1865. 8vo, pp. 39.—The Ancient and the Modern Teacher of Politics. An Introductory Discourse ... on the State. ... 10th of October, 1859. ... *New York.* MDCCCLX. 8vo, pp. 35. BA.—The Arguments of Secessionists. A Letter to the Union Meeting, Held in New York, September 30, 1863. ... *New York: Holman, Printer.* 1863. 8vo, pp. 7. B.—The Character of the Gentleman: An Address to the Students of Miami University, ... August, 1846. ... *Cincinnati: J. A. James.* MDCCCXLVI. 8vo, pp. 31. + Second and Enlarged Edition. *Columbia and Charleston, S. C.: Allen, McCarter & Co.* MDCCCXLVII. 8vo, pp. 110. + Third and much Enlarged Edition. *Philadelphia: J. B. Lippincott & Co.* 1864. 16mo, pp. 121.—A Code for the Government of Armies in the Field, as authorized by the Laws and Usages of War on Land. ... February, 1863. *New York.* 1863. 8vo, pp. 25. H.—Dr. Francis Lieber's English Version of his German Address at the Humboldt Celebration in ... New York, September 14, 1869. ... [n. p. n. d.] 8vo, pp. 8. H.—Fragments of Political Science on Nationalism and Inter-Nationalism. ... *New York: Charles Scribner & Co.* 1868. 8vo, pp. 23.—Fragmentos de ciencia politica sobre nacionalismo e internacionalismo. Traducido del Ingles y precedido de una breve noticia acerca del autor. *New York: M. M. Zarzamendi.* 1870. 8vo, pp. 24. B.—Guerrilla Parties considered with reference to the Laws and Usages of War. ... August, 1862. *New York: D. Van Nostrand.* 1862. 12mo, pp. 22.—History and Political Science, necessary Studies in Free Countries. An Inaugural Address ... on the Seventeenth of February, 1858. ... *New York.* MDCCCLVIII. 8vo, pp. 62.—Introduction to a Treatise on Civil Liberty and Self-Government. ... *Philadelphia.* 1853. 12mo, pp. x.— ... Instructions for the Government of Armies of the United States, in the Field. ... *New York: D. Van Nostrand.* 1863. 12mo, pp. 36.— ... A Lecture on the History and Uses of Athenaeums, delivered at the ... Columbia Athenaeum, on the Seventeenth of March, 1836. ... *Columbia, S. C.* MDCCCLVI. 8vo, pp. 6, 5–32.—A Lecture on the Origin and Development of the First Constituents of Civilisation. ... *Columbia, S. C.: I. C. Morgan.* 1845. 8vo, pp. 18.—Letter on the Relation between Education and Crime, in a Letter to the Right Rev. William

White, D.D. ... *Philadelphia.* 1835. 8vo, pp. 24.—Letter to His Excellency Patrick Noble ... on the Penitentiary System. ... [n. p. 1839.] 8vo, pp. 33–62. BA.— ... A Letter to Hon. E. D. Morgan ... on the Amendment of the Constitution ... abolishing Slavery. ... *New York.* 1865. 8vo, pp. 4.—Memorial from Francis Lieber [to Congress] relative to Proposals for a Work on the Statistics of the United States. April 18, 1836. [n. p.] 1836. 8vo, pp. 17. H.—Nationalism. A Fragment of Political Science. ... [*New York.* 1868.] 8vo, pp. 6.—No Party now, but all for our Country. ... *Philadelphia: Crissy & Markley, Printers.* 1863. 8vo, pp. 12. + *New York: C. S. Westcott & Co., Printers.* 1863. 8vo, pp. 8.—On History and Political Economy, as Necessary Branches of ... Education in Free States. An Inaugural Address ... in South Carolina College ... 7th of December, 1835. ... *Columbia, S. C.: Printed by A. S. Johnston.* 1836. 8vo, pp. 26.—On International Copyright, in a Letter to the Hon. William C. Preston ... . *New-York: Wiley and Putnam.* MDCCCXL. 8vo, pp. 67. C.—Plantations for Slave Labor the Death of the Yeomanry. ... *New York.* 1863. 8vo, pp. 8.—A Popular Essay on Subjects of Penal Law ... . *Philadelphia.* 1838. 8vo, pp. 94.—Remarks on the Final Adjournment of the Loyal Publication Society [February 15, 1866.] ... [n. p. n. d.] 8vo, pp. 3.—Remarks on the Relation between Education and Crime ... To which are added, Some Observations by N. H. Julius, M.D. of Hamburg ... . *Philadelphia.* 1835. 8vo, pp. 24. BA.—Slavery Plantations and the Yeomanry. ... *New York: C. S. Westcott & Co., Printers.* 1863. 8vo, pp. 8. BA.—A Song on our Country and her Flag. Written after the Raising of the Flag on Columbia College ... . [n. p.:] *Printed by the Students.* [n. d.] 8vo, pp. 2.—The West, a Metrical Epistle. ... *New York.* 1848. 16mo, pp. 31.—What is our Constitution, League, Pact, or Government? Two Lectures on the Constitution of the United States ... to which is appended an Address on Secession written in the Year 1851. ... *New York.* 1861. 8vo, pp. 48. B. *See also* "Encyclopædia Americana," Vol. VI.

LIEBER (O. M.) The Assayer's Guide; or, ... Directions to Assayers, Miners, and Smelters ... . By Oscar M. Lieber. *Philadelphia: Henry Carey Baird.* 1852. 12mo, pp. 117.

LIEBER. Vocabulary of the Catawba Language. By Oscar M. Lieber. *Charleston, S. C.* 1858. 8vo. C. 40987

See also South Carolina—*Geology.*

LIEBERGEN (Arnout van). Apologiæ, | Ofte vvaerachtighe verantvvoordinghe | Van | Arnout van Liebergen. | Over de Enorme ende noyt gehoorde Proce-|dueren, tegens zijnen persoon gebruyckt, by de ge-|wesene Hooge Raden van Brasil, wegen eenige|gedeclareerde verraders, als Gabriel Soaris|ende Franciscus Vas,cum Socis, ende het | vervolg van dien; dienende tot een | Claer-lichtende Fackel: | VVaerin, als in eenen klaren Spiegel gesien kan wor-|den, 'tgeene in Brasil gepasseert is, soo weghen de boven-|genoemde verraders, als de onwettige Procedueren | tegens hem Liebergen gehouden. | Al doet de loogen wat zy mach, | De waerheyt brenght het aen den dach. | *t' Amsterdam,* | *Ghedruyckt voor den Autheur, woonende op het Rockin, aldaer-* | *naest de vergulde Leeuw, Anno* 1643. | 4to, pp. (32), 182. 40988

This is a defense of A. van Liebergen in respect of the incredible severities exercised towards him by the Superior Council of Brazil, upon charges of treason. The dedica-

tory preface is addressed to the Prince of Orange, who had then just succeeded in wresting the Brazilian provinces from the Portuguese. It is one of the most important books on the interior administration of the Dutch in Brazil, and is very scarce.

LIEBERKUHN (S.) The History of our Lord and Saviour Jesus Christ: comprehending all that the Four Evangelists have recorded concerning him; all their relations being brought together in one narration, so that no circumstance is omitted, but that inestimable history is continued in one series, in the very words of Scripture. By the Rev. Samuel Lieberkuhn, M.A. Translated into the Delaware Indian Language. By the Rev. David Zeisberger, Missionary of the United Brethren. *New-York: Printed by Daniel Fanshaw.* 1821. 12mo, pp. viii, 222.

LIEBMANN (F. M.) Mexicos Bregner, en System. Critisk Undersögelse. *Kjöbenhavn.* 1849. 4to. 40990

LIEBMANN. Mexicos Halvgræs. Philetæria, en ny Slægt af Polemoniacurnes Familie. *Kjöbenhavn.* 1850. 4to. 40991

Both from the "K. danske Videnskabernes Selskabs Skrifter." Also other pieces on Mexican and Central American affairs in the same journal.

LIEGEL (T. A.) Kaiser Maximilian I. von Mexiko. Erinnerungen ... . *Hamburg: W. Oncken.* 1868. 8vo, pp. vi, 178. Portrait. 40992

LIENAU (J. F. von). Darstellung meines Schicksals in Brasilien, und der von mir gemachten Erfahrungen über die Behandlung der durch den Major Schäffer dahin beförderten Europäischen Auswanderer. *Schleswig.* 1826. 8vo. 40993

LIÉS (E.) The Preludes. A Collection of Poems. By Eugene Liés. *New York.* 1846. 12mo, pp. 58. 40994

LIÉVANO (P. I.) Informe sobre el Canino carretero de Bogotá al Rio Magdalena, por la ruta de siete vueltas segun el trazado del Senor Poncet Indalecio Liévano. *Bogotá.* 1866. 4to, pp. 58.

Life Among the Mormons, and a March to their Zion: to which is added a Chapter on the Indians of the Plains and Mountains of the West. By An Officer of the U. S. Army. *New York: Moorhead Simpson, & Bond.* 1868. 12mo, pp. xv, 219.

Life and Adventure. *See* [Jones [——)], Vol. IX. 36440.

Life and Adventures of Colonel Daniel Boon. ... *Brooklyn.* 1823. 8vo, pp. 26. 40997

This is a variation of *our* No. 6370, Vol. II.

Life and Adventures of Duncan Cameron. Third Edition. *Philadelphia.* 1756. 8vo. 40998

The subject of this memoir was a soldier in Sir Peter Halket's regiment.

Life and Adventures of the accomplished Forger and Swindler, Colonel Monroe Edwards. *Philadelphia: T. B. Peterson* ... . [1848.] 8vo, pp. 152. B. 40999

The Life and Character of a Strange He-Monster, Lately Arriv'd in London from an English Colony in America. ... *London. An.* M DCC XXVI. 8vo, pp. 21. H. 41000

Life and Confession of Thomas D. Carr, who was hung at St. Clairsville, Ohio, March 24, 1870. *St. Clairsville: J. H. Heaton & Co.* 1870. 8vo, pp. 46. 41001

Life and Death of Alice Gilbert of Antigua. *London.* 1776. 12mo. 41002

The Life and Death of Old Father Janus, the vile author of the late wicked Courant. A Satyr. *Boston: Printed by J. Franklin, and by Benjamin for his Brother James.* 1726. 8vo, pp. 7.

"Old Father Janus" is the signature of a club who contributed to the New England Courant.

The Life and Death of Sam, in Virginia. By [Gardner] a Virginian. ... *Richmond: For the Author. A. Morris.* 1856. 12mo, pp. (6), 13–308. H. 41004

The Life and Death of that deservedly famous man of God, M. John Cotton, late Teacher of the Church of Christ of Boston in New-England. *London.* 1658. 4to. 41005

The Life and Glorious Reign | of | Queen Elizabeth: | Containing | Her Great Victories by Land and Sea; | And her other Successes against the Enemies of the | Protestant Religion. | Likewise, | An Account of Sir Francis Drake's | Voyage round the World. | Also, an Account of the Destruction of the great Fleet, | call'd the Spanish Armado. | With the Life and Death of the Earl of Essex, | Q. Elizabeth's Great Favourite. | *London: Printed and Sold by J. Bradford, at the Bible in* | *Fetter-Lane.* 1708. | 8vo, pp. 16. 41006

Life and its Aims. Ideal Life. Actual Life. *Philadelphia.* 1854. 12mo. 41007

Life and Manners in the United States, By a Traveler. *New Haven.* 1836. 12mo. 41008

The Life and Times of Christopher Carson, the Rocky Mountain Scout and Guide. With Reminiscences of Fremont's Exploring Expedition, and Notes of Life in New Mexico. *New York and London: Beadle and Co.* [n. d.] 12mo, pp. 94.

Includes incidents of border warfare, and encounters with the savage tribes of the great plains and the Rocky Mountains.

The Life and Times of Daniel Boone, the Hunter of Kentucky; with Sketches ... . *New York.* 1860. 16mo. 41010

See also our Vol II., Nos. 6373–74.

The Life and Times of Sam, written by Himself ***. *Claremont, N. H.* 1855. 8vo, pp. 32. S. 41011

Life in a Man-of-War, or Scenes in "Old Ironsides." Cruise in the Pacific. By a Fore-Top-Man. *Philadelphia: Privately Printed.* 1841. 8vo, pp. 267. 41012

Life in a Whale Ship: or, The Sports and Adventures of a Leading Oarsman. ... based upon the Cruise of an American Whale Ship ... during the Years 1836–7–8: ... *Boston: J. N. Bradley & Co.* [n. d.] 8vo. 41013

Life in America. *See* [Simms (W. G.)]

Life in California. *See* [Robinson (Alfred)].

Life in New York. By the Author of "The Old White Meeting-House." *New York: Robert Carter.* 1847. 18mo, pp. 240. + Second Edition. [*Ibid.*] 1851. 12mo. 41014

Life in New York, In Doors and Out of Doors. *New York: Bunce & Brother.* 1851. 8vo, 48 leaves. C. 41015

Life in Town, or the Boston Spy. Being a Series of Sketches ... of Whims and Women in the 'Athens of America.' By an Athenian. ... *Boston: Redding and Company.* 1844. 8vo, pp. 56. Plates. B. 41016

Life in the Itinerancy in its relation to the Circuit and Station, and the Minister's Home and Family. *Auburn.* 1856. 12mo.

Life in the New World; or Sketches of American Society. *New York: J. Wiley.* 1845. 12mo. 40918

Life in the South. *See* J. (S. L.), Vol. IX., No. 35328.

Life in the Union Army; or, Notings and Reminiscences of a Two Years' Volunteer. A Rhythmical History of the Fif-

teenth N. Y. Volunteer Engineers, ... During its ... Campaign in and about Washington, and ... Virginia. By Don Pedro Quærendo Reminisco, a Private in the Ranks. [*New York:*] *H. Dexter, Hamilton & Co.* [n. d.] 8vo, pp. 147. 41019

Life in the West. Backwood Leaves, and Prairie Flowers, Rough Sketches on the borders of the Picturesque, the Sublime and the Ridiculous. Extracts from the Note-book of Morleigh in search of an Estate. Second Edition. *London: T. C. Newby.* 1843. Cr. 8vo, pp. 376. 41020

The Life of a Backwoodsman, or Particulars of the Emigrant's Situation in settling in the Wild Lands of Canada. By a Settler at Stratford, Huron District, Canada West. *London.* 1843. 8vo.

The Life of a Planter in Jamaica, comprehending Characteristic Sketches of Society in the West Indies. *London.* 1828. 8vo.

"Drawn with truth and spirit by an actual observer of and actor in the scenes which he paints."—*Literary Gazette.*

Life of a Political Trickster; or the Duplicity and Treachery of J——, A. N——, of Milwaukee, Exposed. *Milwaukee.* 1857. 8vo. 41023

The Life of Benjamin Franklin. Illustrated by Tales, Sketches and Anecdotes. *New-York: Collins & Hannay.* 1832. 18mo, pp. 180. C. 41024

This is the work referred to in the note to *our* Vol. VII., No. 27907.

The Life of Captain James Cook. *Dublin: Printed by John Jones.* 1824. 16mo, pp. 179. 41025

The Life of Christopher Columbus. *New York: Collins & Hannay.* 1832. 18mo, pp. 187. C. 41026

Endorsed "Parley's Columbus," but disclaimed by S. G. Goodrich.

Life of Gen. Jacob Brown; with Short Memoirs of Generals Ripley and Z. Pike. *New York.* 1847. 24mo. 41027

The Life of Jeroboam O. Beauchamp, who was hung at Frankfort, Kentucky, for the Murder of Col. Solomon P. Sharp; comprising, a full and complete history of his intercourse and marriage with ... Miss Anna Cooke, ... *Frankfort, Ky.: O'Neill & D'Unger.* 1850. 8vo, pp. 28. 41028

The Life of Slavery, or the Life of the Nation? Mass Meeting of the Citizens of New York, at the Cooper Institute,

March 6, 1862. *New York: G. P. Putnam.* 1862. Imp. 8vo, pp. 11. 41029

From the "Rebellion Record."

Life on the Lakes. *See* [Ossoli (Margaret, *Countess*)].

Life on the Plains; or, Scenes and Adventures in an Overland Journey to California. *New York.* 18—. 12mo. 41030

Life Sketches of Executive Officers and Members of the Legislature of the State of New York, for 1863. *Albany.* 1863. 8vo, pp. 366. Continued annually. 41031

Life Sketches and Characters of Curious and Odd Characters. *Boston: G. Clarke.* 1833. 16mo, pp. 192. Plate. 41032

The Life, Voyages, and Discoveries of Christopher Columbus. The Third Edition. *London: John W. Parker.* M.DCCCXLIV. 18mo, pp. viii, 232. Plate. 41033

The Life, Voyages, and Discoveries of Captain James Cook. New Edition. *London: Longman ... & Co.* 1864. 16mo.

The Life, Voyages, and Sea Battles of that celebrated Pirate Commodore Paul Jones ... . *London: T. & J. Allman.* 1829. 12mo, pp. 5–28. Folded colored Plate. 41035

The Life-Wake or The Fine Arkansas Gentleman who died before his Time. *Washington: Franklin Philp.* 1859. 8vo, pp. 54

Liggins (J.) A Refutation of the Calumnies ... against the West India Planters. By Joseph Liggins. *London: Effingham Wilson.* 1833. 8vo, pp. 47. B. 41037

Light (G. W.) Keep Cool, Go Ahead, and a Few Other Poems. By George W. Light. ... *Boston: The Author.* 1851. 12mo, pp. 35. + Second Stereotype Edition. [*Ibid.*] 1853. H.

Also: The Young American's Magazine of Self-Improvement. *Boston.* 1847. 12mo. Plate.

Light (J.) Dialogue between Self and the Soul. By Johann Light. *New York: Hugh Gaine.* 1755. 12mo. 41039

The author was a minister of the Dutch church at New Brunswick.

Light and Dark of the Rebellion. *See* [Lester (C. E.)]

Light and Darkness; or, the Shadow of Fate: a Story of American Life. *London: J. Willoughby.* 1855. Cr. 8vo, pp. 326. 41040

Light and Truth of Slavery. Aaron's History. *Worcester.* 1827. 8vo, pp. 48. 41041

The Light Appearing. *See* [Whitfield (Henry)].

Light for Young America; a Series of Sketches. *New York.* 1852. 12mo, pp. 12. B. 41042

Light in Darkness. *See* [Mather (Cotton)].

The Light of Truth and Pleasure of Light. *Milledgeville.* 1827. 12mo, pp. 292. 41043

Light-Houses. Annual Report of the Light-House Board to the Secretary of the Treasury for the year 1868. *Washington.* 1868. 8vo, pp. 90. Continued. 41044

The Light-Houses, Beacons, and Floating Lights of the United States, for 1838. *Washington.* 1838. 8vo. Continued annually.

Afterwards issued as: "List of Light-Houses," etc.

List of Light-Houses, Lighted Beacons, and Floating Lights of the Atlantic, Gulf, and Pacific Coasts of the United States. ... *Washington.* 1866. 8vo. 41046

Papers on the comparative Merits of the Catoptric and Dioptric or Catadioptric Systems of Light-House Illumination, and other Subjects relating to Aids to Navigation; compiled from British, French, and United States Reports and Authorities. *Washington.* 1861. 8vo. 41047

Report of the Officers constituting the Light-House Board, convened under Instructions from the Secretary of the Treasury, to inquire into the Condition of the Light-House Establishment of the United States. *Washington.* 1852. 8vo, pp. 760. Plates.

Lightfoot (S.) An Account of the Religious Experience and some of the Trials, of ... Susanna Lightfoot, ... compiled from the Testimony given by Friends in America ... . *Manchester: Printed by John Harrison* ... 1844. 12mo, pp. 24.

[Lightfoote (William).] The Complaint of England, Wherein it is clearely prooued that the practises of Traitrous Papists against the state of this Realme, and the person of her Maiestie, are in Diuinitie vnlawfull, odious in Nature, and ridiculous in pollicie. In the which they are reproued in wilfull blindnes, in that they see not the filthines of the Romish gouernment; and conuinced of desperate madnesse; in that they

feare not the mischiefe of Spanish inuasion; The former whereof is exemplified by the Popes practises both here in England, and abroad in other countries; the later by the Spaniards outrages, in his exertions raised upon Naples, and his tyrannies execvted in the Indies. Lastly the necessitie, equitie, and benefits of the late proceeding in justice are set downe; with a friendly warning to seditious Papists for their amendment; and an effectuall consolation to faithfull subiectes for their incouragement. ... Scene and allowd. *London: Printed by Iohn Wolfe* ... 1587. 4to, 34 l. c.

This very curious pamphlet, relative to the Spanish invasion and interspersed with poetry, is dedicated to Sir George Burne, Lord Mayor of London. Lowndes gives the running title only, but does not refer to the sale of any copy; on sheets G and H is recorded the cruelty of the Spaniards at Cuba, Hispaniola, Mexico, etc.

The Lightning Columne, or Sea Mirrour, containing the Sea-coasts of the Northern, Eastern, and Western Navigation, as also the Situation of the Northerly Countries, as Islands, the Strate Davids, the Isle of Gan Mayen, Bear's Island, Old Greenland, Spitzbergen, and Nova Zembla; Adorneth with many Sea-cards and Discoveries. *Amsterdam.* 1693. Imp. folio. Maps. 41051

Title from a bookseller's catalogue; probably a free translation of a Dutch title.

Lighton (W. B.) Narrative of the Life and Sufferings of the Rev. William Beebey Lighton, containing an Interesting and Faithful Account of his early Life, and enlistment into the British Army; ... his subsequent sufferings, and final escape from Captivity and Settlement in the United States. Written by Himself. *Boston.* 1840. 12mo. + New and Revised Edition. *Boston: S. N. Dickinson.* 1843. 16mo, pp. 258. 10 Plates. + *Albany.* 1854. 12mo. + [*Ibid.*] 1855. 41052

Lights and Shadows of New York Picture Galleries. Forty Photographs, by A. A. Turner. Selected and described by William Young. *New York: D. Appleton & Co.* 1864. Folio.

[Lignac (Joseph-Adrien le Large, *Abbé* de).] Lettres á | un Américquain | sur l'histoire naturelle, générale et par- | ticuliere de monsieur de Buffon. | troisiéme partie. | *à Hamburg* | 1.7.5.1. Sm. 8vo, pp. (2), 31, 96, 69. + *Hamburg.* 1756. 9 vols., 16mo.

Lignano (J. da). Incomenza il libro de la prima navigatione ... Por Jacobo da Lignano. *Milano.* 1508. 4to. 41055

Title from Ternaux, No. 12.

La Ligne de Démarcation, ... dans l'approvisionnement des Isles françoises de l'Amérique & dans le commerce avec elles. [n. p. 178–.] 4to, pp. 12. BA., C. 41056

Ligon (R.) A Trve & Exact | History | Of the Island of | Barbados. | Illustrated with a Mapp of the Island, as | also the Principall Trees and Plants there, set forth | in their due Proportions and Shapes, drawne out by | their severall and respective Scales. | Together with the Ingenio that makes the Sugar, with | the Plots of the severall Houses, Roomes, and other places, that | are used in the whole processe of Sugar-making; viz. the Grinding- | room, the Boyling-room, the Filling-room, the Curing- | house, Still-house, and Furnaces; | All cut in Copper. | By Richard Ligon Gent. | *London,* | *Printed for Humphrey Moseley, at the Prince's Armes* | *in St. Paul's Church-yard:* 1657. | Folio, pp. (10), 122, Table, (3). Folded Plan and 9 Plates. BA., W. 41057

Reproduced with a new title-page as below:

Ligon. A True & Exact | History | Of the Island of | Barbadoes. | Illustrated with a Map of the Island, as also the | Principal Trees and Plants there, set forth in | their due Proportions and Shapes, drawn out by their several and respective Scales. | Together with the Ingenio that makes the Sugar, with | the Plots of the several Houses, Rooms, and other places, that | are used in the whole process of Sugar-making; viz. the Grinding- | room, the Boyling-room, the Filling-room, the Curing- | house, Still-house, and Furnaces; | All cut in Copper. | By Richard Ligon, Gent. | *London,* | *Printed and are to be sold by Peter Parker, ... and Thomas Guy* ... 1673. | Folio, pp. (10), 122, Table, (3). 6 Plates and 3 Plans. C., P. 41058

This volume, with its plates, has relation to the early modes of sugar-making in the West Indies. Lowndes speaks of it as "a curious, and, in general, accurate account." Contains, on page 55, the original of the story of Inkle and Yarico. "The book is amusing, and with the exception of a fib or two, as 'sauce piquante,' is a very accurate account of Barbadoes."—*Retrospective Review,* XIV. 226–256. A French translation is included in "Recueil de divers voyages," *Paris,* 1674, 4to, pp. 262. I have seen it described as a separate work, *Paris,* 1669 [*Paris,* 1657], and *Paris,* 1684; but incline to believe that all of them are a part of the "Recueil." *See* Kennett, p. 109, Rich's Catalogue, p. 307, *and* Ternaux, No. 907.

Ligon (T. W.) Public Debt and Internal Improvements. Speech of Hon. T. W. Ligon ... in the House of Representatives, February 8, 1848. [n. p. n. d.] 8vo, pp. 8. H. 41059

Het Lijkfeest. *See* [Uylenbrook (P. J.)]

Lijst van de Hollandsche, Hamburger en Bremer Groenlands-vaarders in 1721 ... . [n. p. n. d.] 8vo. 41060

Continued to 1784, or later. This is an annual list of the departure of ships to and return from the Greenland whale-fishery, with the quantity of oil procured, etc.

Lijst in welcke jaaren de meeste en weinigste visschen uit Groenland en de Straat Davids zijn aangebragt, 1669–1792. [n. p. n. d.] Folio, 1 sheet. 41061

List of the largest and the smallest quantities of fish taken in Greenland and Davis' Straits, from 1669 to 1792.

Lijst van Stukken betrefende Niew Nederland verschenen in Amerikaansche Mengelwerken. [n. p. n. d.] 8vo, pp. 12.

"A list of documents relating to New Netherland which have been published in different works; furnished by the Netherland Literary Society at Leyden, which is engaged in publishing a catalogue of everything that has been written on the subject of the Netherlands and its Colonies."—H. C. Murphy.

Lil (H. van). Het Leven, de Gevoelens en Lotgevallen van William Penn, Beroemd Kwaker, en Stichter van Pennsylvanien; uit echte bronnen verzameld door Herman van Lil ... . *Amsterdam: J. C. Sepp en Zoon.* 1820–25. 8vo, pp. iv, 287; (2), 443.

The life and adventures of William Penn, founder of Pennsylvania.

Lilbridge (G. R.) Report of the Conspiracy Trial of the Wayne County Circuit Court of Michigan, on Five Indictments for a Conspiracy for Burning the Freight Depot of the Michigan Central Railroad Company. By G. R. Lilbridge. *Detroit.* 1851. 8vo, pp. 395. 41064

Lilias and her Cousins: or a Tale of Planter Life in the Old Dominion. By the Author of "Thomas Jackson." *New York: General Protestant Episcopal Sunday-School Union.* 1860. 18mo, pp. 367. Plate. C. 41065

Lilius (Z.) Zachariae Lilii | vicentini | canonici | regvla- | ris or- | bis bre- | viarvm | fide | com- | pendio | or- | dineq; cap- | tv ac memo- | ratv facillimvm | foelix et gratvs legito. | [Colophon:] *Impressit* | *Florentie Antonius Miscominus* | *Anno Salutis* .M.CCCC-LXXXXIII. | *Nonis Iuniis.* | Sm. 4to, 130 leaves. H. 41066

This, of course, does not relate to America, but it exhibits the state of geographical knowledge just previous to Columbus' first voyage.

Lilius. In hoc volvmine con- | tinentvr hi libri. Primus liber De origine & laudibus scientiarum. | Secundus liber. Contra Antipodes | Tertius liber De miseria hominis & contemptu | mundi. | Quartus liber De generibus uentorum | Quintus liber Vita Caroli Magni. | [Colophon:] *Finis* | *Florentiae* | *Impressvm* | *Per Ser Francisci Bonaccursium* | *Impensa uero & sumptibus Ser* | *Petri Pacini de*

Piscia. Anno Salutis | M. CCCC. LXXXXVI | *Septimo idus Aprilis.* | 4to, 72 unnumbered leaves. BM. 41067

Extremely rare. Folio II contains an allusion to the recent discovery of the New World, and the verso of leaf 40 reads as follows: "De navigatione oceani maris – sed res postulare videtur ut quo tempore navigatus fit oceanus, paucis exponam: ne quisquam novum aut inusitatum credat, quod Rex hispaniæ, ut ferunt, in dies ad exploranda nova littora naves mittat. Nam temporibus Trajani, ut Plinius refert ..."

Lilius. Breve Descriptione del Mondo tradotta par M. Francesco Baldelli. Con l'additione de' nomi moderni. *Vinegia: Gabriel Giolito de Ferrari.* 1551. 8vo. 41068

"The object of this curious and learned geographical work, originally written just before the discovery of the new Continent, seems to have been to post up into one little book all the knowledge and all the ignorance respecting our globe that could be collected from the ancients, as well as mediæval writers, so as to start fair with the new light to be let in by Columbus. It is a sort of alphabetical dictionary of geography, with a good index. The works of Lilius are in Ortelius's famous list of geographical authorities published in 1570."—Stevens.

Lilius. Orbis Breviarivm, fide compendio ordineq; captv: ac memoratv facilimvm: Felix et Gratus legito. Veneunt in Gormōtiana libraria e regione Colegii Coquerettici ad insigne geminarum cipparum. *Paris: Jehan Gourmont.* 1515. 4to.

Lillie (A.) Canada: its Growth and Prospects. ... Two Lectures. By the Rev. Adam Lillie. *Brockville.* 1852. 8vo, pp. 47. + Second Edition ... . *Toronto: Thomas Maclear.* 1852. 8vo, pp. 47. B. + Fourth Edition. *Edinburgh.* 1852. 18mo.

Lillie. Canada: Physical, Economical, and Social. By A. Lillie, D.D. *Toronto.* 1855. 12mo, pp. 295. Map. 41071

Lillingston (L.) Reflections on Mr. Burchett's Memoirs. Or, Remarks on his Account of Captain Wilmot's Expedition to the West-Indies. By Coll. Luke Lillingston, Commander in Chief of the Land Forces in that Expedition. *London: Printed by John Nutt.* MDCCIV. 8vo, pp. (8), 171. B., H. 41072

See also Burchett (J.), Vol. III., Nos. 9205–9207.

Lilly (Lambert, *pseudon.*) The History of the Middle States, New York, New Jersey, Pennsylvania, Delaware, and Maryland. Illustrated by Tales, Sketches and Anecdotes. ... By Lambert Lilly, Schoolmaster. *Boston: Allen & Ticknor.* 1833. 16mo, pp. 156. + *Boston: William D. Ticknor & Co.* MDCCCXLIV. 18mo, pp. 167. H. + [*Ibid.*] 1852. 41073

Lilly. The History of the Western States, illustrated by Tales, Sketches and Anecdotes. ... By Lambert Lilly ... *Boston.* 1844. 16mo. + [*Ibid.*] 1847. + [*Ibid.*] 1852. 16mo, pp. 167.

Lilly. The Story of the American Revolution. Illustrated by Tales, Sketches, and Anecdotes. By Lambert Lilly. ... *Boston.* [n. d.] 18mo, pp. 204. 41075

See also [Hawks (F. L.)], Vol. VIII., No. 30964, *and* Vol. X., No. 38740.

Lillywhite (F.) The English Cricketers' Trip to Canada and the United States. By Fred. Lillywhite. *London.* 1860. 12mo, pp. 68. Map and Plates. + Second Edition. [*Ibid.*] 1861.

Lima, *Peru.* Aanmerkingen op de sware Aardbevinge geweest den 18 Sept. neffens een verhaal van de aardbevingen, die er nu in 25 jaren herwaarts gevoelt zijn. *Utregt.* 1692. 4to, pp. 20.

Remarks on the earthquake of September 18, with an account of the earthquakes twenty-five years ago (at Lima, Jamaica, etc.)

Actuaciones literarias de la Vacuna en la Real Universidad de San Marcos de Lima. [*Lima:*] *Impressas en la real casa de niños expósitos.* 1807. 4to, pp. (8), Tabla, Text, pp. 39. 41078

Alegatio que conforme a las constituciones de esta Real Universidad empezo a decir el D. D. Pedro Vasquez de Noboa, Cathedratico de Visperas de Leyes, despues de concluida su Leccion de oposition á la de Prima de Sagrados Canones ... . [*Lima:*] *En la Imprenta de la Plazuela de S. Christoval.* 1761. 4to, 15 l.

Anotaciones al Informe de la Comision de la Municipalidad encargada de Visitar los Establecimentos de Beneficial. *Lima.* 1828. 4to, pp. 35. 41080

Anti-Piti-Lista de los Toros ... . *Lima.* 1814. 4to, pp. 4.

Calendario y Guia de Forasteros de Lima, por D. Jose Greg. Parades. [*Lima:*] *Imprenta del Estado.* 1822. 12mo, pp. (2), 51.

Continued by various editors.

Casos Notables sucedidos en las Costas de la Ciudad de Lima, en las Indias, y Como el Armada Olandesa. *Sevilla.* [n. d.] Folio, pp. 4. 41082

Certamen Panegyrico historial poetico por la reedificacion de la ciudad de los Reyes. *Lima.* 1673. 4to. 41083

Chronica politica y literaria de Lima. *Lima.* 1827. Cont'd.

Compendio de algunas razones en que se funda la prudente resolucion que se ha tomado de cortar la guerra de Chile haciendo la defensiva, señalando raia, y el poco fundamento que tiene la

opinion contraria de seguir la como hasta aqui. *Lima.* 1611. Folio. 41085

Title from Ternaux, No. 337. This very rare book should have appeared under Chili or Compendio.

Concilium Limense celebratum anno 1583 ... . *Madrid: P. Madrigal.* 1591. 4to. 41086

Title from Ternaux, No. 187.

Concilivm Limense. Celebratum Anno 1583 sub Gregorio XIII. Sum. Pont. auctoritate Sixti Quinti Pont. Max. approbatum. Jussu Catholici Regis Hispaniarum, atq; Indiarum. Philippi Secundi, editum. *Madriti: Joannis Sanchez.* 1614. 4to, 4 leaves, Text, 92 and 4 leaves. 41087

Ternaux, No. 360, gives the title differently. *See also* Leclerc, No. 381, *and* Rich, No. 139.

Concilivm Limense. Svmario del Concilio Provincial, qve se celebro en la civdad de los Reyes, el año de 1567. Fecho y sacado por orden y con auctoridad del vltimo Concilio Prouincial, que se celebrô en la dicha Ciudad, este año de 1583. *En Seuilla, por Matias Clauijo.* 1614. 4to, pp. (8), 231. 41088

"Traduction espagnole du second et troisième concile de Lima. C'est un livre de toute rareté non cité par Pinelo. ... D'après les licences qui sont en tête du volume, on voit que ce livre a été imprimé à la requête de l'évêque de Cuzco ... . Du second concile de Lima, on ne connaît aucune édition imprimée. ..." Title and note from Leclerc, No. 382.

Consilia Limana, Constitutiones Synodales et alia utilia Monumenta. *Romæ.* 1684. 41089

Title from an English auctioneer's catalogue. *See also* our Vol. IV., No. 16605, etc.

El Conocimiento de los Tiempos Ephemeride de Año de 1725. ... *Lima.* [n. d.] 12mo, pp. (49). Continued. BA. 41090

Contistvciones [*sic*] y Ordenanças de la Vniversidad, y stvdio general de la ciudad de los Reyes del Piru. *Impresso en la Civdad de los Reyes con licencia del señor Visore y Don Luis de Velasco, por Antonio Ricardo, natural de Turin.* 1602. Folio, 8 and 2 leaves, Text, 46 and 18 leaves. 41091

"Édition précieuse et originale des Constitutions de la célèbre université de S. Marc de Lima. Elle est restée inconnue à Pinelo et à Ternaux."—Leclerc.

Constitvciones añadidas por los virreyes, marques de Montesclaros, y principe de Esqvilache, a las qve hizo el virrey don Fr. de Toledo para la Real Vniversidad, y estvdio general de San Marcos de la ciudad de los reyes del Pirv. Confirmadas, y declaradas por don Felipe IV, en su Consejo Real de las Indias. *Madrid, Imprenta Real.* 1624. Folio, 1 leaf, 11 leaves, 1 leaf.

Constitvciones y Ordenanzas antiguas, añadidas, y modernas de la real Vniversidad, y estudio general de San Marcos de la Ciudad de los Reyes del Perù. Reimpressas, y recogidas de mandato del marquez de Castelfverte ... por D. Alonso Eduardo de Salazar y Zevallos, rector de la dicha Universidad. *En la misma Ciudad de los Reyes, en la Imprenta Real, por Felix de Saldaña y Flores.* 1735. Folio, 33 leaves, Text, 83, 24 and 16 leaves.

"Cette nouvelle édition des constitutions de l'université de Lima a été augmentée des décrets royaux relatifs aux universitées, des chapitres de visite, prérogatives, etc., depuis sa fondation jusqu'en 1735."—LECLERC.

Cuestion Diplomatica con motivo del caso del "Emilio Rondanini." *Lima.* 1869. 8vo. 41094

Privately printed at the Peruvian Foreign Office.

Cuestion promovida al Ilmo Metropolitano sobre la publicacion del Jubileo Santo en 1866. *Lima.* 1866. 8vo. 41095

Descripcion del cementerio general mandado erigir en la ciudad de Lima. *Lima.* 1808. 4to. + *Habana, reimpresa por E. Boloña.* 1809. 4to, pp. 11. 41096

Descripcion fiel de la Demonstracion de Armas en Lima a los 23. de Enoro, de 1628. *Lima.* 1628. Folio, pp. 6. 41097

Desolacion de la Ciudad de Lima, y Dilubio del Puerto del Callao Cerrose esta Relacion en seis de quarenta y seis, y sigue la Calamidad, que darà matheria à mas larga explicacion de los venideros sucessos. *Lima.* [1746.] 4to. 41098

El Dia de Lima. *See* Llano Zaputa.

Diario de las noticias de Lima, en que se hace saber de una tragedia lastimosa que sobrevino del cielo de año de 1687. [*Lima.*] 1688. Folio. 41099

Diario de Lima. *Lima, con Privilegio de esta Real y superior Gobierno.* 1790. 4to. Continued. 41100

The first periodical publication in South America; the "Mercurio" was the second.

Dictamenes Theologico-Legales de Niños Expositos .... *Lima.* 1811. 4to. 41101

Relates to the Orphan Asylum at Lima.

Discurso Doctrinal sobre la Obediencia, y lealtad debida al Soberano, y á sus Magistrados, Compuesto por un cura de este

Arzobispado de Lima. *Lima: En la Casa Real de los Niños Expositos.* 1785. 12mo. 41102

Discursos Pronunciados en la Real Universidad de San Marcos en Ocasion del Acto Literario Dedicado por esta a los Ilustres Militares que defendieron la Plaza y puerto del Callao en las Invasiones de la Esquadra Insurgente de Chile. *Lima: Imprenta de Ruiz.* 1819. 4to, pp. 32. 41103

Edicto Pastoral con Motivo de la Presente Guerra. Por Jorge Arzobispo de Lima. *Lima.* 1837. 4to, pp. 8. 41104

Exequias de la reyna D. Maria de Austria celebradas en Lima. *Lima.* 1697. 4to. 41105

Title from Ternaux, No. 1092.

Explicacion Previa de los Carros y Mascara con que la nacion Indica de esta Capital de Lima y sus Pueblos cormacanos celébra la feliz Exaltacion al Trono de Nuestra Augusto Monarca el Señor Don Carlos IV. (que Dios garde) Bajo del Gobierno del Señor Subdelegado del Partido de Santiago del Cercado, y su Jurisdiccion Don Manuel del Valle y Portillo, Agente Asesor de este Superior Gobierno. [*Lima?* n. d.] 4to, 12 leaves. J.C.B.

Exposicion que el Illmo Fr. Arzobispo de Lima, ha dirijido al supremo Gobierno sobre la Ley de Redencion de Censos y Capellanias. *Lima.* 1865. 4to, pp. 20. 41107

Ferrol-Carril Central Trasandino. Seccion del Callao y Lima a la Oroya. *Lima.* 1869. 8vo, pp. 46. 41108

Fiestas de la Ciudad de Lima en la canonization de S. Pedro Nolasco. *Lima.* 1632. 4to. 41109

Title from Ternaux, No. 534.

Gazeta de Lima desde primero de Diciembre de 1743 hasta Mayo 1763. *Lima: Antonio Gutierrez de Zavallos.* 1743–63. 4to.

Guia de Forasteros de Lima, correjida para el año de 1822, por D. Jose Greg. Paredes. *Lima: Imprenta del Estado.* [1821?] 12mo, pp. 95. 41111

Histoire des Tremblements. *See* [Lozano (Pedro)].

Informe del Cabildo Eclesiastico de Lima sobre el Proyecto de Ley para la Division del Arzobispado. *Lima.* 1832. 8vo, pp. 160.

Informe del Cabildo Eclesiastico de Lima, sobre el Proyecto de Ley presentado por algunos señores Disputados del Departamento de Junin ... *Lima.* 1832. 8vo. 41113

Instruccion del metodo con que repartirse à los Indios de los partidos comprehendidos en el distrito de la deputacion provincial de Lima, las tierras y de lo acordado en junta ... propriedad para una moderada quota. *Lima.* 1814. 8vo. 41114

Jubileo del Año Santo. Conceido por N. M. S. P. y Señor Benedicti XIV. Para todo el Orbe Christiano, por Antonio de Barroetta y Angel, Arzobispo de Lima. *Lima.* 1652. 4to.

A curious proclamation addressed to the clergy, etc. It is an extremely rare piece; not quoted by Ternaux.

Lima contra el Espejo de mi Tierra. *Lima.* 1840. 8vo.

Lima por Dentro y Fuera en consejos economicos, saludables, politicos y morales que dá un amigo á otro con motivo de querir dexar la Ciudad de Mexico por pasar á la de Lima. Obra jocosa y divertida, en que con salados conceptos se describen, ademas de otras cosas, las costumbres, usos y mañas de las madamites de allí, de acá y de otras partes. *Cerca de la tablada de Lurip, S. Ayanque.* 1797. 18mo, pp. 188. C. + *Madrid: Imprenta de Villalpando.* 1798. 18mo, pp. (24), 192. 41117

For other editions *see* Vol. I., Nos. 2503–4. It was also reprinted, *Madrid,* 1836, 18mo; *Lima,* 1854, 12mo, and *Paris,* 1854; this last edition being illustrated, and with notes by Ignacio Merino. Mr. Bollaert says it is "A severe satire upon Lima and its people by Taraia or Taralla."

Manifiesto Imparcial de los acontecimientos de la capital del Peru. *Lima.* 1823. 4to. 41118

Manifiesto y Esclamacion. *See* [Rubio de Ribas (Alonzo)].

Memorial por el Tribunal del Consulado de Lima. *Lima.* 1683. Folio. 41119

Narracion circumstanciado de la Deplorable Catastrofe sufrida en la Ciudad de Lima e Inundacion del Puerto del Callao. *Lima.* [1863.] 8vo, pp. (2), 25, vi. 41120

The cover-title differs. A second edition was published in the same year.

Noticia de las cosas notables succedidas a los Olandeses en la ciudad de Lima y como dexo burlados a los Olandeses la armada de Lima. *Lima.* 1615. Folio. 41121

Title from Ternaux, No. 375.

Oraciones Panegyricas que en el Solemne Recibimiento, que hizo la Real Universidad de San Marcos de esta Ciudad de Lima ... al Ilust. Señor D. Jos. de Cevallos ... Sacalas a Luz A. Ventura Calderon y Cevallos. *Lima.* 1743. 4to. 41122

Por la Provincia de Lima. *See* [Ulloa (Nicolas)].

Reflecsiones sobre un Informe del Cabildo Eclesiastico de Lima. *Lima.* 1831. 4to. 41123

Regla, y Ordenanzas de las Religiosas y Canònigas Reglares del Monasterio de la Encarnacion de esta Ciudad de los Reyes. *Lima. Año* 1770. 4to. 41124

Reglamento para la Sociedad de Beneficiencia. *Lima.* 1836. 8vo, pp. 11. 41125

Relacion de las cosas notables succedidas en la ciudad de Lima y como dexo burlados a los navios Olandeses, la armada de España. *Lima.* 1625. Folio. 41126

Relacion de las Fiestas de Lima a levantar estandartes por el rey N. S. Felipe IV. *Lima.* 1622. 4to. 41127

Title from Ternaux, No. 445.

Relacion de las fiestas que el Comercio, Consulado de los Mercaderes de Lima. *Lima.* 1632. Folio, pp. 7. 41128

Relation. | Del Espantoso Terre- | moto que padecio esta Ciudad de los Reyes | Lima, y sus contornos el dia 14. de Iulio de | este presente año de 1699. sus lastimosos | efectos, de muertes, y ruynas. | [n. p. n. d.] 4to, pp. (7). 41129

Probably a privately printed account for officials only.

Relacion | del Exemplar Castigo qve | embiò Dios a la Ciudad de Lima Cabeza- del Perù, | y su Costa de Barlouento con los espantosos | Temblores del dia 20. de Octubre | del Año de 1687. | [Colophon:] *Con Licencia En Lima,* | *Por Ioseph de Contreras. Año de* 1687. | Folio, pp. (8). 41130

Relacion del tierremoto que succedio en Lima el 11 de noviembre de 1687. *Lima: J. de Contreras.* 1687. 4to. 41131

Title from Ternaux, No. 1017.

La Revista de Lima. Publicacion quincenal. *Lima.* 1859–1863. 6 vols., 8vo, pp. 858; 752; 522; 996; 480; 406.

Solemna Proclamacion que 5 Oct. 1701 hizo la Ciudad de los Reyes Lima .... *Lima.* 1701. 4to. 41133

A True and Particular Relation. *See* [Lozano (Pedro)].

Verdad aclarada y defensa politica con que la parte del Tribunal del Consulado de Lima desvanece las imposturas de un papel

impresso con el titulo de Manifiesto y Esclamacion, 1737. *Lima.* 1736–37. Folio. 41134

The squabble between the Spaniards and the Peruvian Chamber of Commerce, although not of very wide interest, nevertheless involves the history of the foundation and administration of the Board of Trade for the Indies, and the bases of the fiscal settlement of the new territories. It also foreshadows the break between Spaniards and Creoles which led to the separation of the two countries.

LIMA, *N. Y.* Catalogue of ... Genesee Wesleyan Seminary, ... 1846. *Lockport: Press of Harrison & Luckey.* 1846. 8vo, pp. 32. B. 41135

LIMAGO (Gaspard). *See* [Tache (J. C.)]

LIMANTOUR (*M.*) Représentation adressée à M. le ministre de France à propos de la vente faite à M. Limantour. *Mexico.* 1863. 8vo. 41136

The Limits of Nova Scotia, or Acadia. *See* Nova Scotia.

LIMON (J. G.) Sermon en la exaltacion al trono de Señ. Carlos Quarto predicó en la catedr. de Valladolid de Mechoacán. *Mexico.* 1791. 4to, 20 leaves. 41137

LIMONADE (*le Comte* de). Le Machiavelisme du Cabinet Français. Par le Comte de Limonade ... . [*Cap-Henry: Chez P. Roux.* 1814.] 8vo, pp. 35, (1). B. 41138

Relates to Hayti.

LIMONADE. Relation des Glorieux Événemens qui ont porté leurs Majestés Royales sur le Trône d'Hayti ... . Par le Comte de Limonade ... . *Au Cap Henry.* 1811. 8vo. + *Londres: De L'Imprimerie de Schulze et Dean.* 1814. 8vo, pp. xxviii, 218. B.

LIMONADE. Royaume d'Hayti. Le comte de Limonade ... A ses Concitoyens des Parties de l'Ouest et du Sud. [*Cap-Henry, chez P. Roux.* 181–.] 4to, pp. 12. BA. 41140

LINAGE (J. Veita de). *See* Veita Linage (J. de).

LIÑAN Y CISNEROS (Melchor de), *Arzobispo de Lima.* Carta pastoral à sus amadas Obejas, los Fieles de su Rebaño, a causa del lamentable sucesso, en la destruccion de los lugares Riobamba, Ambato, y la Tacunga, del Reyno de Quito, con la rebentazon de vn volcan que los destruyo. [*Lima.* 1699.] 4to, 88 leaves.

"Pièce de toute rareté et très-intéressante. Chapitre IV. traite: 'De la impiedad de los Negros esclavos.'"—TROSS.

LINÁRES (N. G.) A mis conciudadanos. *Carácas.* 1859. 4to, pp. 4. 41142

LINATI (C.) Costumes et Mœurs de Mexique. Par Linati. Une collection de trente-trois planches. *Londres: Engelmann, Graf, Coindet, & Cie.* M.DCCC.XXX. 4to, pp. (36). H. 41143

LINATI. Costumes civils, militaires et religieux du Méxique, dessinés d'après nature par C. Linati. *Bruxelles.* [n. d.] 4to. 48 colored Plates. 41144

LINCH (T.) A Description of ... Jamaica. *See* Blome (R.)

Blome's name does not appear in some copies.

LINCLAEN (L.) Guide to the Geology of New York and the State Geological Cabinet. By Ledyard Linclaen. *Albany.* [n. d.] 8vo. S. 41145

[LINCOLN (Abraham).] The Common Understanding of the Effect, and Consequence, of an Ordinance of Secession, upon a State of the United States, by which the same is adopted. [n. p. 1866.] 8vo, pp. 13. H. 41146

[LINCOLN.] The Common Understanding of the Reason why a State forfeits State Rights by its Hostility to the United States, as evidenced by the Adoption of an Ordinance of Secession. [n. p. 1867.] 8vo, pp. 8. H. 41147

LINCOLN. Douglas an Enemy to the North. Reasons why the North should Oppose Judge Douglas. Speech of Hon. Abraham Lincoln, of Illinois, delivered at Cincinnati, September 19, 1859. [*Washington.* 1859.] 8vo, pp. 8. 41148

LINCOLN. Gems from Abraham Lincoln. Born February 11th, 1809, in Hardin County, Ky. Died April 15th, 1865, at Washington, D. C. *Trent, Filmer & Co., New York.* [1865.] Sq. 8vo, 16 leaves. Portrait. 41149

LINCOLN. Letter of President Lincoln to the Missouri Radicals, and Speech of S. T. Glover ... in Jefferson City, Mo., ... October 17th, 1863. [n. p. n. d.] 8vo, pp. 18. H. 41150

Also: Letter of the President to the Union Convention at Springfield, Ills., Aug. 16, 1863. [n. p. n. d.] 8vo.—Letter to Erastus Corning and others on the Vallandigham Habeas Corpus Case. [n. p.] 1863. 8vo.

LINCOLN. The Letters of President Lincoln on Questions of National Policy. *New York: H. H. Lloyd & Co.* 1863. 8vo, pp. 22. + *Boston: Benj. B. Russell.* 1863. 8vo, pp. 22. 41151

Also: Lincoln's Anecdotes: A Complete Collection of the Anecdotes, Stories, and Pithy Sayings of Abraham Lincoln. ... *New York: American News Company.* [1867.] Sq. 12mo, pp. 63.

LINCOLN. Message. *See* Message of the President.

LINCOLN. On the Arrest of C. L. Vallandigham, June 12, 1863. *Cincinnati.* 1863. 8vo, pp. 8. 41152

LINCOLN. Reply to the Committee of Ohio Democrats, June 29, 1863. [n. p. n. d.] 8vo. 41153

LINCOLN. Erwiederung in Bezug auf die Verhaftung Vallandigham's. *Cincinnati.* 1863. 8vo, pp. 12. 41154

A German translation of the two previous tracts.

LINCOLN. The Opinions of Abraham Lincoln upon Slavery, and its Issues; indicated by his Speeches, Letters, Messages and Proclamations. *Washington.* [n. d.] 8vo, pp. 16. 41155

LINCOLN. Political Debates between Hon. Abraham Lincoln and Hon. Stephen A. Douglas, in the Celebrated Campaign of 1858, in Illinois; Including the preceding Speeches of each, at Chicago, Springfield, etc.; Also, the Two Great Speeches of Mr. Lincoln in Ohio, in 1859, ... *Columbus: Follett, Foster and Company.* 1860. 8vo, pp. (4), 268. BA. 41156

Some copies are dated 1859.

LINCOLN. President Lincoln and General Grant on Peace and War. [*August* 16,] 1864. 4to, 1 l. 41157

LINCOLN. President Lincoln on Vallandigham and "Arbitrary Arrest." [n. p. 1863.] 8vo, pp. 4. 41158

LINCOLN. President Lincoln's Views. The Truth from an Honest Man. ... An Important Letter on the Principles involved in the Vallandigham Case ... . *Philadelphia: King & Baird, Printers.* 1863. 8vo, pp. 16. H. 41159

Also: The President to General McClellan. [*Washington, April* 9, 1862.] 4to, 1 l.—The President's Appeal to the Border States. [n. p. n. d.] 8vo, pp. 15.

LINCOLN. The President's Words. *See* [Hale (E. E.)], VII.

LINCOLN. The Republican Party Vindicated— ... Speech of Hon. Abraham Lincoln, ... New York City, February 27, 1860. [*New York.* 1860.] 8vo, pp. 8. B. 41160

Also issued as: "National Politics. Speech of Abraham Lincoln ... Delivered .. February 27, 1860." [n. p. n. d.] 8vo, pp. 15. C.

LINCOLN. Republican Principles. Speech ... at Springfield, Illinois, June 16, 1858. [*Albany.* 1861.] 8vo, pp. 6. 41161

LINCOLN. Speech of Mr. Lincoln ... on the ... President's Message ... . January 14, 1848. *Washington: J. & G. S. Gideon, Printers.* 1848. 8vo, pp. 14. H. 41162

Also: Address ... at Bloody Brook, Aug. 31, 1838. ... [n. p. n. d.] 8vo.—The Address of the Hon. Abraham Lincoln, ... at Cooper Institute, February 27th, 1860 ... *New-York: George F. Nesbitt & Co., Printers.* 1860. 8vo, pp. 32. B.—Amnesty Proclamation, and Third Annual Message of Abraham Lincoln. Read in Congress, Dec. 9, 1863. [*Philadelphia.* n. d.] 8vo, pp. 20.—The Argument of the Secessionists. A Letter to the Union Meeting held in New York, September 30, 1863. [n. p.] 1863. 8vo, pp. 7.—Speech ... on the Civil and Diplomatic Appropriation Bill; ... in the House of Representatives ... June 20, 1848. *Washington: Printed by J. & G. S. Gideon.* 1848. 8vo, pp. 14.—Speech ... on the Presidential Question. ... July 21, 1848. [*Washington:*] *J. & G. S. Gideon, Printers.* [n. d.] 8vo, pp. 8.—A Speech ... in Reply to Judge Douglas. Delivered in ... Springfield, Illinois, June 26th, 1857. [n. p. n. d.] 8vo, pp. 7. H.

The following works relate to Abraham Lincoln. For other biographies, orations, etc., on his death, *see* under the names of the respective authors; *see also* under names of cities and towns for proceedings relative to his memory.

LINCOLN. Abraham Africanus I. His Secret Life, as Revealed under the Mesmeric Influence, and Mysteries of the White House. *New York: J. F. Feeks.* [1864.] 12mo, pp. 57.

Abraham Lincoln. [n. p. n. d.] 8vo, pp. 12. 41164

No. 17 of Union League Tracts. This is a Preamble and Resolution of the Union League of Philadelphia, signed "George H. Boker, Secretary."

Abraham Lincoln. A Study. *Liverpool: McKown and Finglass.* 1865. 12mo, pp. 32. 41165

Abraham Lincoln. A Threnody. *St. Louis: Privately printed.* 1866. 8vo, pp. 26. H. 41166

Abraham Lincoln, Foully Assassinated April 14, 1865. A Poem with an Illustration, from the London Punch, For May 6, 1865. With an Introduction by A. Boyd. *Albany: J. Munsell.* 1868. 4to, 13 leaves. Plate. 41167

Abraham Lincoln, Late President ... Demonstrated to be the Gog of the Bible, as foretold by the prophet Ezekiel ... . The thirteen Confederate States shown to be the Mountains of Israel, and all the Predictions contained in the Prophecy concerning them literally fulfilled in the late War between the North and South. ... [n. p.] 1868. 8vo, pp. 56. B. 41168

Abraham Lincoln. Sein Leben, Wirken und Sterben, von F. Bungener. *Bern: Verlag von Carl H. Mann.* 1866. 12mo, pp. 171. 41169

See also our Vol. III., No. 9164-6. Also: Abraham Lincoln. A Memoir. Appended, a Sketch on Slavery in the United States. *London.* 1861. 16mo. B.

Abraham Lincoln and Ulysses S. Grant: their Character and Constitution scientifically explained, with Engravings. *San Francisco: A. F. Köllner.* 1864. 8vo, pp. 15. B. 41170

Abraham Lincoln's Character. *See* [Broom (W. W.)], II.

Abramo Lincoln Presidente della Rupublica Stati-Uniti d'America. *Italia. Dalla tipografia di Diuseppe Chiantore-Pinevolo.* 1862. 8vo, pp. 16. 41171

Abramo Lincoln com' ei visse, qual' opera compiè qual fu la sua morte. *Firenze: Tipografia Claudiana.* 1866. 12mo, pp. 88.

The Assassination and History of the Conspiracy, ... Sketches of the Principal Characters, Reports of the Obsequies ... . *Cincinnati: J. R. Hawley & Co.* 1865. 8vo, pp. (2), xi, 21–163.

For a German translation *see* Kaufmann (P.), Vol. IX., No. 37118.

... The Assassination of Abraham Lincoln, late President of the United States of America, and the Attempted Assassination of William H. Seward, Secretary of State, and Frederick W. Seward, Assistant Secretary, on the Evening of the 14th of April, 1865. Expressions of Condolence and Sympathy inspired by these Events. *Washington: Government Printing Office.* 1866. 8vo, pp. xxxiv, 717. BA. + [*Ibid.*] 1867. 4to, pp. (2), xxx, 930. Portrait. H. 41174

Assassination of Lincoln. Report [of] the Committtee on the Judiciary to ... the House of Representatives ... into the nature of the evidence implicating Jefferson Davis and others in the Assassination of President Lincoln; ... [n. p. *July*, 1866.] 8vo, pp. 41. B. 41175

39th Cong., 1st Sess., House of Representatives, Report, No. 104.

Bibliographia Lincolniana: An Account of the Publications occasioned by the Death of Abraham Lincoln, ... With Notes and an Introduction by Charles Henry Hart ... . *Albany: Joel Munsell.* 1870. Imp. 8vo, pp. 86. 41176

Includes most of the titles contained in Andrew Boyd's work on the same subject.

Burlesque Life of Abraham Lincoln. *New York.* [n. d.] 18mo. 41177

Celebration of the Colored People's Educational Monument Association in Memory of Abraham Lincoln, on the Fourth of July, 1865, in ... Washington. ... *Washington, D. C.: McGill & Witherow.* 1865. 8vo, pp. 33. 41178

Character of Abraham Lincoln, and the Constitutionality of his Emancipation Policy. [By Charles Hudson. *Boston.* 1863.] 8vo, pp. 16. 41179

Commemorative Proceedings. *See* New York Athenæum Club

Complete and Unabridged Edition.—Containing the whole of the Suppressed Evidence. The Trial of the ... Assassins and Conspirators at Washington City, D. C., May and June, 1865. For the Murder of President Abraham Lincoln. ... Being a full and verbatim Report. *Philadelphia: T. B. Peterson & Brothers.* [1865.] 8vo, pp. 13–210. 41180

The Conspiracy Trial for the Murder of the President, and the Attempt to overthrow the Government by the Assassination of its Principal Officers. Edited, with an Introduction, by Ben. Perley Poore. *Boston: J. E. Tilton & Co.* 1865–66. 2 vols., 12mo, pp. 480; 582. 41181

Three volumes were announced; I have seen two only.

Conspiracy Trial. Assassination of President Lincoln, and the Trial of the Conspirators, David E. Herold, Mary E. Surratt, Lewis Payne, George A. Atzerodt, Edward Spangler, Samuel A. Mudd, Samuel Arnold, Michael O'Laughlin. Compiled and Arranged by Benn Pitman. *Cincinnati.* 1865. 8vo. 41182

Constitution of the Educational Monument Association, to the Memory of Abraham Lincoln ... . *Washington.* 1863. 12mo, pp. 9. 41183

Correspondence in Relation to the Public Meeting at Albany, N. Y. (Erastus Corning and others.) [n. p. n. d.] 8vo, pp. 9.

Corruptions and Frauds of Lincoln's Administration. [n. p. n. d.] 8vo, pp. 8. B. 41185

Campaign Document, No. 14.

Death of Lincoln. Proceedings in the Supreme Court of Illinois. Presentation of the Bar Resolutions in regard to Mr. Lincoln's Decease. *Chicago: J. W. Middleton & Co.* 1865. 8vo, pp. 17. 41186

Discourses. Memorial of Abraham Lincoln, ... delivered in Flemington, N. J., by the Pastors of the different Churches, ... April 19, 1865. ... *Lambertville, N. J.: Clark Pierson, Printer.* 1865. 8vo. 41187

Contains sermons by Rev. Thomas Swain, pp. 22; by the Rev. J. L. Janeway, pp. 16, and by Rev. J. P. Dailey, pp. 13. Also: Funeral March to the Memory of Abraham Lincoln. *Boston.* 1865. 4to, pp. 5. B.

Funeral Observances ... by German, English and American Ministers at Berlin [Prussia]. With Speeches on the Occasion. *Berlin.* 1865. 8vo, pp. 31. 41188

See also our Vol. III., No. 10138, *and* New London, Conn.

God Bless Abraham Lincoln! A Solemn Discourse by a Local Preacher. Dedicated to the Faithful. ... [n. p. n. d.] 8vo, pp. 16. B. 41189

The sentiments of this pamphlet are directly the reverse from what might be inferred from its title.

History and Evidence of the Passage of Abraham Lincoln from Harrisburg, Pa., to Washington, D. C., on the 22d and 23d of February, 1861. *Chicago.* 1868. 8vo, pp. 18. 41190

Illustrated Life, Services, Martyrdom, and Funeral of Abraham Lincoln ... . *Philadelphia: T. B. Peterson & Brothers.* 1866. 12mo, pp. 328. 41191

In Memoriam. Abraham Lincoln, assassinated At Washington, April 14, 1865: Being a Brief Account of the Proceedings of Meetings, Action of Authorities and Societies, Speeches, Sermons, Addresses, and other Expressions of Public Feeling on reception of the News, and at the Funeral Obsequies of the President, at Buffalo, N. Y. *Buffalo: Printing House of Matthews & Warren.* 1865. 8vo, pp. 64, Note and Poem, 1 l.

Edited by Henry W. Box of Buffalo.

In Memoriam. *New York.* 1865. Cr. 8vo, 14 l. H. 41193

See also "Gems from Abraham Lincoln," No. 41149, *and* [Morgan (William F.)]

Das Leben von Abraham Lincoln. Herausgegeben von der Young Men's Republican Union, ... New York. [*New York.* n. d.] 8vo, pp. 16. H. 41194

Leben, Wirken und Reden von Abraham Lincoln. *New York.* 1860. 12mo. 41195

Legacy of Fun; with Sketch of the Life of Abraham Lincoln. *London: Farrah.* 1866. 12mo. 41196

Legislative Honors. *See* New York State.

The Life, and Martyrdom of Abraham Lincoln ... . *Philadelphia: T. B. Peterson & Brothers.* 1865. 12mo, pp. (2), 203. Portrait. B. 41197

The Life and Public Services of Hon. Abraham Lincoln, of Illinois, and Hon. Hannibal Hamlin, of Maine. *Boston: Thayer & Eldridge.* 1860. 12mo, pp. 320. 41198

Life and Public Services of Abraham Lincoln ... . *Philadelphia: T. B. Peterson & Brothers.* [1864.] 8vo, pp. (2), 17–187. Port.

... The Life, Speeches, and Public Services of Abraham Lincoln, Together with a Sketch of the Life of Hannibal Hamlin ... *New York: Rudd & Carleton.* MDCCCLX. 12mo, pp. 117. Port.

Some copies are entitled "The Wigwam Edition." Also: The Life of Abraham Lincoln. [n. p. 1860.] 8vo, pp. 32. + *New York.* 1860. 8vo.

The Lincoln and Hamlin Songster, or, the Continental Melodist ... . *Philadelphia: Fisher and Brother.* [n. d.] 18mo, pp. 72.

Also: Lincoln and Johnson. An Earnest Appeal to the Patriotism and Good Sense of the Citizens of Missouri, by a Veteran Radical. [n. p. n. d.] 8vo, pp. 14.—Lincoln and Johnson Campaign Song Book ... . *New York: American News Company.* 1864. 12mo, pp. 38.—Lincoln and Johnson Club's Union Campaign Songster. *Philadelphia.* [n. d.] 12mo, pp. 12.

The Lincoln and Johnson Union Campaign Songster. *Philadelphia: A. Winch.* [1864.] 12mo, pp. 54. H. 41202

Lincoln and Liberty!!! Tract, No. 2. New York, June 26th, 1860. [*New York: Isaac J. Oliver.* n. d.] 8vo, pp. 4.

The Lincoln Catechism wherein the Eccentricities & Beauties of Despotism are fully set forth. A Guide to the Presidential Election of 1864. *J. F. Feeks, N. Y.* [1864.] 12mo, pp. 46.

Strongly opposed to the election of Abraham Lincoln

Der Lincoln Katechismus, worin die Schönheiten und Excentritäten des Despotismus vollständig dargestellt sind. ... *New York: J. F. Feeks.* [1864.] 12mo, pp. 46. 41205

The Lincoln Memorial: a Record of the Life, Assassination, and Obsequies of the Martyred President. *New York: Bunce & Huntington.* 1865. 8vo, pp. (2), 288. Portrait. B. 41206

Edited by John Gilmary Shea, LL.D.

Lincolniana; or the Humors of Uncle Abe. Second Joe Miller. By Andrew Adderup, Springfield, Ill. *New York: J. F. Feeks.* 1864. 12mo, pp. 91. 41207

Lincolniana. In Memoriam. *Boston: William V. Spencer.* 1865. 4to, pp. vi, (2), 346. H. 41208

Two hundred and fifty copies printed. Consists of memorial sermons and discourses, speeches, eulogies and letters, on the death of President Lincoln; with appendix, by Elias Nason.

Lincoln's Abolitionism. A Searching Analysis ... . *St. Louis.* 1860. 12mo. 41209

Also: Lincoln's Treatment of Gen. Grant. Lincoln's Treatment of General McClellan. [*New York.* 1864.] 8vo, pp. 8. B.

Majority and Minority Reports to the House of Representatives, on the Assassination of Lincoln, with Vindication of Judge-Advocate-General Holt. *Washington.* 1866. 8vo.

The Martyr President. [n. p. n. d.] 12mo, pp. 43. 41211

The Martyr President. *See* [Newell (R. H.)]

The Martyr's Monument. *See* [Lieber (F.)], No. 40981.

A Memoir of Abraham Lincoln ... his Opinion on Secession, Extracts from the United States Constitution, &c. to which is appended an Historical Sketch on Slavery, reprinted by permission, from "The Times." *London: Sampson Low ...* 1861. 8vo, pp. 126. Portrait. B. 41212

A Memorial of Abraham Lincoln, late President of the United States. *Boston: Printed by Order of the City Council.* MDCCCLXV. Imp. 8vo, pp. 153. BA. 41213

Another edition: *Boston: Ticknor & Fields.* 1865. 4to, pp. 153. Only two hundred and fifty copies of this last-named edition were printed.

A Memorial Lincoln Bibliography. Being an Account of Books, Eulogies, Sermons, Portraits, Engravings, Medals, &c., published upon Abraham Lincoln. By Andrew Boyd. *Albany: J. Munsell.* 1870. Rl. 8vo. 41214

Only a few copies printed.

Memorial Proceedings in Honor of ... Abraham Lincoln, held in Ann Arbor, Michigan; with the Address of Rev. E. O. Haven, D.D. ... *Ann Arbor.* 1865. 8vo, pp. 11. H. 41215

See also Pittsburgh, Pa.

Mr. Lincoln's Arbitrary Arrests. The Acts which the Baltimore Platform Approves. [n. p. n. d.] 8vo, pp. 24. B. 41216

Campaign Document, No. 13.

La Mort de Lincoln. Poème Dramatique. ... [Par L. Banet-Rivet.] *Paris.* 1867. 8vo, pp. 32. B. 41217

The Nation Weeping for the Dead. *See* Springfield, *Mass.*

Obsequies of Abraham Lincoln. *See* Newark and New York.

Old Abe's Jokes, fresh from Abraham's Bosom. Containing all his Issues, excepting the "Greenbacks," to call in some of which, this work is issued. *New York: T. R. Dawley.* [1864.] 12mo, pp. 19–140. Plate. BA. 41218

See "Old Abe, the Miller." Also: Only Authentic Life of Abraham Lincoln, *alias* "Old Abe" ... . [n. p. 1864.] 8vo, pp. 16.

Order of Services. *See* [Clarke (J. F.)], Vol IV., No. 13415.

Our Martyr President, Abraham Lincoln. Voices from the Pulpit of New York and Brooklyn. Oration by Hon. George Bancroft. Oration at the Burial, by Bishop Simpson. Eulogy by R. S. Storrs, Jun., D.D. *New York: Tibbals & Whiting.* [1865.] 12mo, pp. 420. BA. 41219

Twenty-one sermons by distinguished ministers of New York.

A Poetical Description of Lincoln's Assassination by James. ... *Valparaiso.* 1865. 8vo, pp. 58. 41220

Poetical Tributes to the Memory of Abraham Lincoln. *Philadelphia: J. B. Lippincott & Co.* 1865. 8vo, pp. 306. Portrait.

The President Lincoln Campaign Songster. *New York: T. R. Dawley.* 1864. 16mo, pp. 72. 2 Portraits. 41222

President Lincoln. From the Princeton Review. July, 1865. 8vo, pp. 23. 41223

The Private and Public Life of Abraham Lincoln. *New York: Beadle & Co.* [n. d.] 16mo, pp. 96. + [*Philadelphia.* n. d.] 8vo, pp. 12. 41224

Private Confession of the Murderer [J. W. Booth] of Lincoln. His connection with the Rebellion. ... [*London.* 1865.] 41225

"Advertisement of a catch-penny publication from a London paper."—BARTLETT.

Proceedings of a ... Meeting of Ministers of all Religious Denominations in the District of Columbia, ... April 17, In reference to the ... sudden Decease of our Beloved Chief Magistrate, Abraham Lincoln, with the Remarks of Rev. Dr. Gurley, addressed to the President ... Andrew Johnson, and the Reply ... *Washington: McGill & Witherow, Printers.* 1865. 8vo, pp. 14.

Proceedings of the City Council of Baltimore in Relation to the Death of Abraham Lincoln, late President of the United States. [n. p. n. d.] 8vo, pp. 24. 41227

Proceedings of the City Council of Boston, April 17, 1865, on occasion of the Death of Abraham Lincoln, President of the United States. *Boston: Published by Order of the City Council.* 1865. 8vo, 35 leaves. B. 41228

Two hundred copies printed on large paper in 4to. For other Proceedings *see our* Vol. III., No. 9174, *also* Pennsylvania, Philadelphia, Providence, Saco, St. Catherines, St. Johns, etc.

Les Procès des Conspirateurs de Washington ... . *New York: H. de Mareil.* 1865. 4to, pp. 87. 41229

Also: Republican Opinions about Lincoln. [n. p. n. d.] 8vo, pp. 16. B.

Sermons preached in Boston on the Death of Abraham Lincoln. Together with the Funeral Services in the East Room of the Executive Mansion at Washington. *Boston: J. E. Tilton and Company.* 1865. 12mo, pp. 379, (1). B. 41230

Services and Addresses at the Unveiling of the Statue of Abraham Lincoln, Brooklyn, N. Y., October 21st., 1869. ... *Brooklyn.* 1869. 8vo, pp. 32. B. 41231

A Sketch of the Life and Times of Abraham Lincoln ... [By Miss Bassett]. *Philadelphia: Bradly & Co.* [1865.] 8vo. Plate.

The Terrible Tragedy at Washington. Assassination of President Lincoln. ... *Philadelphia: Barclay & Co.* [1865.] 8vo, pp. 19–116. B. 41233

Trial of Abraham Lincoln by the Great Statesmen of the Republic. ... Abraham Lincoln, Prisoner at the Bar, his own Counsel. ... *New York: Metropolitan Record.* 1863. 8vo, pp. 29.

Trial of the Assassins and Conspirators for the Murder of Abraham Lincoln, and the Attempted Assassination of Vice-President Johnson and the whole Cabinet. Containing the Evidence in full, with Arguments of Counsel on both Sides, and the Verdict of the Military Commission. *Philadelphia.* [1865.] 8vo, pp. 102. 41235

See also Bingham (J. A.), Vol. II., No. 5451.

Tribute to the Memory of Abraham Lincoln by the American Citizens resident in Buenos Ayres. *Buenos Ayres.* [1865.] 8vo, pp. 25. 41236

Includes remarks by the Hon. R. C. Kirk, and the address by the Rev. William Goodfellow. *See also* [Hall (B. H.)], Vol. VII., No. 29736, *and* Savannah, Ga.

Vida de Abran Lincoln Decimo-sesto Presidente de los Estados Unidos. Precidida de una introduccion por D. F. Sarmiento. *New York: D. Appleton & Co.* 1866. 12mo, pp. xlviii, 306.

Von der Holzaxt zum Präsidentenstuhl oder Lebensgeschichte des Volksmannes Abraham Lincoln. ... *Berlin: C. F. Conrad.* 1865. 8vo, pp. 32. 2 Portraits. 41238

What will be the place assigned by History to Abraham Lincoln? [n. p. n. d.] 8vo, pp. 12. 41239

A Workingman's Reasons for the Re-Election of Abraham Lincoln. [n. p. n. d.] 8vo, pp. 8. 41240

See also "Good Words," June, 1865, *and our* Nos. 34180, 40350, 40454, etc.

LINCOLN (A. H.) Familiar Lectures on Botany ... With an Appendix containing descriptions of the Plants of the United States, and Exotics, &c. By Almira H. Lincoln. Twenty-first Edition. *New York.* 1844. 12mo. 41241

LINCOLN (B.) Narrative of the Capture, Sufferings and Escape of Capt. Barnabas Lincoln and his Crew, who were taken by a Piratical Schooner, December, 1821, off Key Largo; together with Facts Illustrating the Character of those Piratical Cruisers. *Boston: Printed by Ezra Lincoln.* 1822. 8vo, pp. 40.

Pages 41–46 were printed and subsequently added by Nathan Lincoln, of Cambridgeport.

LINCOLN (Benjamin). *See* [Kirkland (J. T.)], No. 38004.

LINCOLN (B.) Hints on ... Medical Schools in New England. With an Appendix ... . By Benjamin Lincoln. *Burlington: For the Author.* 1833. 8vo, pp. 76. B. 41243

Also: An Exposition of certain Abuses practised by some of the Medical Schools in New England. ... *Burlington.* 1833. 8vo.

LINCOLN (*Bishop of*), 1768. *See* [Green (John)], Vol. VII., No. 28540, *and* Reynolds (*Dr.*), 1727.

LINCOLN (C.) A Sermon ... in Hingham, January 8, 1865 .. after the Funeral of Mrs. Elizabeth Andrews Harding. By Rev. Calvin Lincoln. *Hingham: Blossom & Easterbrook.* 1865. 8vo, pp. 16. H. 41244

Lincoln (D. W.) An Oration, ... at Worcester, ... July 4th, 1805. By Daniel Waldo Lincoln, A.B. ... *Worcester: Printed by Sewall Goodridge.* 1805. 8vo, pp. 15. BA. 41245

Lincoln. An Oration, pronounced at Boston, on the Fourth Day of July, 1810, before the "Bunker-Hill Association" ... . By Daniel Waldo Lincoln ... . *Boston: Printed for Isaac Munroe.* 1810. 8vo, pp. 20. + Second Edition. *Boston.* 1810. 8vo.

Lincoln (*Dean of*), 1702. *See* Willis (*Dr.*)

[Lincoln (Enoch).] The Village; a Poem. With an Appendix. *Portland: Edward Little and Co.* 1816. 18mo, pp. 180.

Also: An Oration, pronounced at Worcester, ... July 4th, 1812. ... *Worcester: Printed by Henry Rogers.* 1812. 8vo, pp. 16. *See also* Maine Speeches.

Lincoln (F. W.) An Address ... before the Massachusetts Charitable Mechanic Association, on its First Semi-Centennial Anniversary ... October 2nd, 1845. By Frederick W. Lincoln, Jr. ... *Boston: Printed by Dutton and Wentworth.* 1845. 8vo, pp. 64. B. 41248

Also: An Address ... before the Mechanic Apprentices' Library Association, ... February 22d, 1844. ... *Boston.* 1844. 8vo, pp. 34.—The Inaugural Address ... to the City Council, January 4, 1858. ... *Boston: Geo. C. Rand & Avery ... Printers.* 1858. 8vo, pp. 15. Continued.

Lincoln (H.) ... A Sermon ... before the ... Congregations of Jamaica Plain, on Fast Day, April 5, 1855. By Rev. Heman Lincoln. *Boston: Gould and Lincoln.* 1855. 8vo, pp. 21. BA.

Lincoln (H.) A Sermon ... at the Ordination of the Rev. Nymphas Hatch ... in Tisbury, (Martha's Vineyard,) October 7, 1801. By Henry Lincoln ... . *Boston: Printed by Manning & Loring.* 1801. 8vo, pp. 31. BA. 41250

Lincoln (H. H.) School Discipline: ... An Address ... before the American Institute of Instruction ... Boston, August 31st, 1867. By Hosea H. Lincoln ... . *Boston.* 1867. 12mo, pp. 20. H. 41251

Lincoln (J.) Anti-Slavery Melodies; for the Friends of Freedom. ... By Jarius Lincoln. *Hingham: Elijah B. Gill.* [1843.] 12mo, pp. 96. B. 41252

Lincoln (J. L.) Fiftieth Anniversary Address before the First Baptist Sunday School, Providence, May 30, 1869. By John L. Lincoln. *Providence.* 1869. 12mo. 41253

Lincoln (L.) Address ... before the Worcester Agricultural Society, October 7, 1819 ... By Hon. Levi Lincoln, Jun. ... *Worcester: Printed by Manning & Trumbull.* 1819. 8vo, pp. 30.

[Lincoln.] A Farmer's Letters to the People. *Philadelphia: Robert Johnson.* 1802. 8vo, pp. 95. BA. 41255

[Lincoln.] Letters to the People. By a Farmer. ... *Salem: Printed by William Carlton.* 1802. 8vo, pp. 102. C. 41256

See previous title for another edition.

Lincoln. Speech ... on the Removal of the Treasury Building; ... April 17, 1838. *Washington.* 1838. 8vo, pp. 11.

Also: ... Address by ... Levi Lincoln ... January 8, 1833. *Boston: Dutton and Wentworth ... Printers.* 1833. 8vo, pp. 42.—Address ... at Worcester, (Mass.) March 4th, 1803. ... *Worcester: Printed by Sewall Goodridge.* 1803. 4to, pp. 14.—Address at Worcester, Oct. 21, 1807, before the 7th Division of the Massachusetts Militia. ... *Worcester.* 1807. 12mo.—An Address delivered on the Consecration of the Worcester Rural Cemetery, September 8, 1838. ... *Boston: Dutton and Wentworth, Printers.* 1838. 8vo, pp. 36.—Letter from the late Gov. Lincoln to Gov. Davis. [*Boston.* 1834.] 8vo, pp. 24.—Oration ... at Brookfield ... Fourth of July, 1807 ... . *Worcester: Printed by Henry Rogers.* [1807.] 8vo, pp. 16.—Speech ... Feb. 7, 1837, on the Resolution to Censure the Hon. John Q. Adams ... . *Washington: Printed by Gales and Seaton.* 1837. 8vo, pp. 9.

Lincoln. Reminiscences of the Original Associates and Past Members of the Worcester Fire Society, begun in an Address by Hon. Levi Lincoln, April, 1862, and continued in an Address by Hon. Isaac Davis, Jan. 1870. With Roll of Members. *Worcester.* 1870. 8vo, pp. 72. 41258

Lincoln. A Memorial of Levi Lincoln ... from 1825 to 1834. *Boston: Printed by J. E. Farwell & Company.* MDCCCLXVIII. 8vo, pp. 90. H. 41259

See also Massachusetts, and Worcester, Mass.

Lincoln (L. R.) *and* Eveleth (S.) Tariff: ... of March, 1833 ... . Compiled by Levi R. Lincoln and Samuel Eveleth ... . *Boston: Printed by Samuel Condon.* 1832. 12mo, pp. 163, 4. B.

Lincoln (L. B.) An Address delivered at South Deerfield, August 31, 1838, on the Completion of the Bloody Brook Monument, erected in memory of Capt. Lothrop and his Associates, who fell at that Spot, September 18, (O. S.), 1675. By Luther B. Lincoln. ... *Greenfield: Kneeland & Eastman.* 1838. 8vo, pp. 16, cover-title, pp. (4). B. 41261

The cover-title reads "Address delivered before the Society of Adelphi," etc.

Lincoln (R. W.) Lives of the Presidents of the United States; with Biographical Notices of the Signers of the Declaration of Independence; Sketches of the most remarkable Events in the History of the Country. By Robert W. Lincoln. *New York.* 1835. 8vo. + *Brattleboro', Vt.: Typographic Co.* 1839. 8vo, pp. vi, 522. Plate. + *New York.* 1842. 8vo. 41262

Lincoln (S.) An Address delivered before the Citizens of the Town of Hingham, on the Twenty-Eight of September, 1835, being the Two Hundredth Anniversary of the Settlement of the Town. By Solomon Lincoln. *Hingham: Jedidiah Farmer.* 1835. 8vo, pp. 63. BA. 41263

Lincoln. History of the Town of Hingham, Plymouth County, Massachusetts. By Solomon Lincoln, Jr. *Hingham: Caleb Gill, Jr.* ... 1827. 8vo, pp. 183. B., W. 41264

Lincoln. Notes on the Lincoln Families of Massachusetts, with some Account of the Family of Abraham Lincoln, late President of the United States. By Solomon Lincoln ... . *Boston: David Clapp & Son, Printers.* 1865. 8vo, pp. 10. 41265

[Lincoln.] Sketch of Nantasket: (now called Hull,) in the County of Plymouth. ... *Hingham.* 1830. 12mo, pp. 16. BA.

Also: An Oration delivered before the Citizens of Hingham, on the Fourth of July, 1826. ... *Hingham: Caleb Gill, Jr.* 1826. 8vo, pp. 23.—An Oration ... before the Citizens ... of Quincy, ... Fourth of July, 1835 ... . *Hingham: Jedidiah Farmer.* 1835. 8vo, pp. 31.—An Oration ... at Plymouth, at the Request of the Young Men of that Town, on the Centennial Anniversary of the Birth Day of George Washington. ... *Plymouth: Printed by Allen Danforth.* 1832. 8vo, pp. 23, (1). BA.

Lincoln (W.) History of Worcester, Massachusetts, from its Earliest Settlement to September, 1836: with Various Notices relating to the History of Worcester County. By William Lincoln. ... *Worcester: Moses D. Phillips and Company.* 1837. 8vo, pp. viii, 383, (1). Map. BA., C. + *Worcester: Charles Hersey.* 1862. 8vo, pp. 448. Plate. B. 41267

Also: An Address delivered before the American Antiquarian Society. ... October 23 1835, in ... Worcester, in relation to the Character and Services of their late Librarian, Christopher C. Baldwin, Esq. ... *Worcester: For the American Antiquarian Society.* 1835. 8vo, pp. 19.—An Address ... before the Massachusetts Horticultural Society ... September 20, 1837. ... *Boston: Dutton and Wentworth, Printers.* 1837. 8vo, pp. 56.—An Oration at Worcester, Mass. July 4th, 1816, in Commemoration of American Independence. *Worcester.* 1816. 8vo, pp. 10.—Report on Sundry Petitions respecting Distinctions of Color. February, 1839. ... [n. p. n. d.] 8vo, pp. 16.—Report on the Expediency of Publishing the Journal of the Provincial Congress. February, 1837. ... [n. p. n. d.] 8vo, pp. 8. *See also* Massachusetts and Worcester, Mass.

Lincoln (W. S.) Alton Trials: of Winthrop S. Gilman, who was Indicted with Enoch Long, ... for the Crime of Riot, ... on the ... 7th November, 1837, while engaged in defending a Printing Press, from an attack made on it at that time, by an Armed Mob. ... Also, the Trial of John Solomon, ... for a Riot Committed in Alton, ... November, 1837, in unlawfully and forcibly entering the Warehouse of Godfrey, Gilman & Co., and breaking up and destroying a Printing Press. ... By William S. Lincoln ... . *New-York: John F. Trow.* 1838. 12mo, pp. 158. Plate. BA. 41268

This trial bears on the slavery question.

Lincoln Academy, *Me.* Catalogue of Lincoln Academy: Newcastle, Maine, for ... 1847. *Bath.* [n. d.] 12mo, pp. 12.

Lincoln County, *Me.* Order ... of the Legislature ... to appoint Commissioners to Investigate the Causes of the Difficulties in the County of Lincoln; and the Report ... with the Documents ... . *Boston: Printed by Munroe & French.* 1811. 8vo, pp. 173, (1). BA., S. 41270

Also: Report of the Committee for promoting the due Observance of the Lord's Day. [n. p.] 1815. 8vo.

Lincoln Guard. Constitutional Articles ... of the Lincoln Guard ... . Adopted January 19, 1864. *Boston: Printed by Alfred Mudge & Son.* 1864. 24mo, pp. 18. B. 41271

Lincoln Institute, at Jefferson City, Mo. April, 1870. *Boston: Alfred Mudge & Son, Printers.* 1870. 8vo, pp. 19. H.

See also Roxbury, Washington, D. C., etc.

Lincoln Institution. *See* Philadelphia.

Lincoln, *Mass.* Dedication of Lincoln Grammar School House, Sept. 17, 1859. [n. p. n. d.] 8vo, pp. 24. 41273

Report of the Receipts and Expenditures of the Town of Lincoln, from March 1, 1869, to March 2, 1870. *Boston: Printed by Tolman & White.* 1870. 8vo, pp. 7. H. 41274

Report of the School Committee of ... Lincoln, April, 1854. *Concord: Press of S. B. Wilde.* 1854. 8vo, pp. 8. H. 41275

Lincoln University, *Pa.* Catalogue of ... Lincoln University ... 1865–66. *Oxford, Pa.: Press of H. L. Brinton.* 1866. 8vo, pp. 12. Plate. Continued. H. 41276

Lind (J.) An Essay on Diseases incidental to Europeans in Hot Climates ... . By James Lind, M.D. ... The Third Edition, ... *London: T. Becket.* MDCCLXXVII. 8vo, pp. xvi, 379, (8). H. + Sixth Edition. ... *London: J. and J. Richardson.* 1808. 8vo, pp. xiv, 402. B., BA. + First American from the Sixth London Edition. *Philadelphia: W. Duane.* 1811. 8vo, pp. viii, 268. C.

Lind. Jacob Lind's ... Versuch über die Krankheiten denen Europäer in heissen Climaten unterworfen sind. ... *Riga und Leipzig: Johann Friedrich Hartknoch.* 1773. 16mo, pp. (12), 328, (8). H. 41278

The Jenny Lind Mania in Boston; or a Sequel to Barnum's Parnassus. By Asmodeus. ... *Boston.* 1850. 12mo, pp. 40. B.

[Lind (Jonathan).] An Answer to the Declaration of the American Congress. *London: T. Cadell.* MDCCLXXVI. 8vo, pp. (4), xvi, 137. 41280

On the title of a copy belonging to the Brown Library is the following manuscript note: "By Jn Lind, of Lincoln's Inn, Esq. This is the work in its original state. A considerable part of this was left out at the desire of the Ministers in the published copy. Ex dono autoris J'y Bentham." Mr. Bartlett made a comparison of this with the following "published copy," and verified the above statement.

[Lind.] An Answer to the Declaration of the American Congress *London: T. Cadell.* M,DCC,LXXVI. 8vo, pp. 132. + The Second Edition. [*Ibid.*] + The Third Edition. [*Ibid.*] 8vo, pp. 117. + The Fourth Edition. [*Ibid.*] 8vo, pp. 132. + The Fifth Edition. [*Ibid.*] 8vo, pp. 132. B., H. 41281

In these later editions the outline of a counter declaration is omitted. With regard to the theory of government set forth in the preamble to the "Declaration," the writer adds, "a theory, as absurd and visionary, as the system of conduct in defence of which it is established, is nefarious;" indeed each article of the Declaration of Independence is carefully examined and every assertion disputed. *See* "M. Rev.," LV. 345. The following is a translation:

[Lind.] Réponse à la Déclaration du Congrès Américain. Traduite de l'Anglois par A. F. J. Fréville. *London: T. Cadell.* 1777. 8vo, pp. (2), v, 124, Index, 4. + *La Haye.* 1777. 8vo, pp. 205. 41282

[Lind.] A Letter to the Right Honourable Willoughby Bertie, by descent Earl of Abingdon ... . In which His Lordship's Candid and Liberal Treatment of the now Earl of Mansfield Is fully vindicated. *London: T. Payne and Son.* MDCCLXXVIII. 8vo, pp. xii, 86. 41283

Relates to his lordship's reply to Burke's letter to the sheriffs of Bristol.

[Lind.] Remarks on the Principal Acts of the Thirteenth Parliament of Great Britain. By the Author of Letters concerning the Present State of Poland. ... Vol. I. Containing Remarks on the Acts relating to the Colonies with a Plan of Reconciliation. *London: T. Payne.* MDCCLXXV. 8vo, pp. xvi, (4), 500. BA., C., H. 41284

"Constitutes part of a work which was never continued. Dr. Parr said it was the ablest book he ever read in defence of the American War; and that he knew and respected the author."—Rich, I. 210. The following is a translation.

[Lind.] Anmerkungen über die vornehmsten Acten des dreyzehnten Parlements von Groszbritannien. *Braunschweig: F. Waisenhaus.* 1778. 8vo, pp. 334. C. 41285

[Lind.] Three Letters to Dr. Price, containing Remarks on his Observations on the Nature of Civil Liberty, the Principles of Government, and the Justice and Policy of the War in America. By a Member of Lincoln's Inn, F. R. S. *London: T. Payne.* MDCCLXXVI. 8vo, pp. xxii, 163. 41286

"Probably the work of Mr. Lind. They discover great ability in the writer, though it does not seem to be always rightly or successfully employed."—*Monthly Review*, LV. 152. Dr. Lind has also been credited with the authorship of "The Rights of Great Britain asserted," *see* [Dalrymple (J.)], Vol. v., Nos. 18347–48, *and* "An Englishman's Answer," Vol. VI., No. 22624.

Lind University. First Annual Announcement of the Medical Department of the Lind University ... for 1859–'60. *Chicago: William H. Rand.* 1859. 8vo, pp. 12. Continued.

Linda (L. de). Lucæ de Linda | descriptio | Orbis | & omnium ejus Rerum Publi- | carum, | In qva Præcipua omnium Regnorum | & Rerum publicarum | Ordine & methodice pertractantur quorum seriem versa ostendit Pagina. | *Lugdvni Batavorvm,* | *Apud Petrvm Leffen.* 1655. 8vo, Engraved Title, Title, pp. (20), 1156, (12). + *Amsterdam.* 1665. 8vo, pp. 1150. + *Jenae: Matthias Birckner.* 1670. 18mo, pp. (6), 1448, (14). C. 41288

Lenglet-Dufresnoy asserts that this book is merely a translated extract from Davity's "Les Etats," etc. Liber XII. is by J. de Laet.

Lindemann (Johann Gottlieb). Geschichte der Meinungen älterer und neuerer Völker, im Stande der Roheit und Kultur, von Gott, Religion und Priesterthum. *Stendal, bey Franzen und Grosse.* 1786. 4 vols., 8vo. 41289

Contains a history of the religion of the natives of America.

Linden. Catalogue of ... Linden Hall, Litiz, Pa. From August 2, 1858, to June 16, 1859. *Lancaster: Printed by John Baer's Sons.* 1859. 8vo, pp. 10, (1). Plate. Continued. H.

Lindley (G.) A Guide to the Orchard and Fruit Garden; ... By George Lindley. With Additions of all the most Valuable Fruits cultivated in America ... . By Michael Floy ... . A New Edition, with an Appendix ... . *New York: C. M. Saxton.* 1852. 8vo, pp. xi, 420. Plates. H. 41291

Lindley (J.) Flora Medica; a Botanical Account of all the ... Important Plants used in Medicine in Different Parts of the World. By John Lindley ... . *London: Longman* ... 1838. 8vo, pp. xiii, (2), 655, (1). H. 41292

Lindley. Orchidaceæ Lindenianæ; Notes upon a Collection of Orchids formed in Colombia and Cuba, by J. Linden. By John Lindley. *London.* 1846. 8vo. C. 41293

Lindley (T.) Narrative of a Voyage to Brasil; terminating in the Seizure of a British Vessel, and the Imprisonment of the Author and the Ship's Crew, by the Portuguese. With General Sketches of the Country, its Natural Productions, Colonial Inhabitants, &c. And a Description of the City and Provinces of St. Salvadore and Porto Seguro. ... By Thomas Lindley. *London: J. Johnson.* 1805. 8vo, pp. xxxi, (2), 298. B. 41294

Mr. Lindley put into a port in the Brazils in distress, where his vessel was seized and himself and wife put under arrest. After a twelve month's detention they made their escape. The book was reissued, with a new title-page only, as:

Lindley. Authentic Narrative of a Voyage from the Cape of Good Hope to Brasil, ... in 1802, 1803; ... By Thomas Lindley. *London: W. Baynes.* 1808. 8vo, pp. xxxi, (2), 298.

Lindley. Voyage au Brésil; ... traduit de l'anglais par François Soulès. *Paris: Léopold-Collin.* 1806. 8vo, pp. xiv, 215.

Lindley. Lindley's Reise nach Brasilien und Aufenthalt daselbst in den Jahren 1802 und 1803. Nebst einer Beschreibung der Porto-Seguro und San Salvador. Aus dem Englischen von Ehrmann. *Weimar.* 1806. 8vo. 41297

Lindo (A.) Dr. Underhill's Testimony on the Wrongs of the Negro in Jamaica examined ... . By Abraham Lindo, Esq., ... *London: Effingham Wilson.* 1866. 8vo, pp. 32. B. 41298

Lindo (A. A.) Jamaica. Letter on promoting Immigration into that Colony. By A. A. Lindo. *London.* 1836. 8vo.

Also: Letter, connected with a pamphlet on "The Injurious Tendency of the Modifying of our Navigation Laws" ... . *London.* 1828. 8vo, pp. 38.—On the Injurious Tendency of the Modifying of our Navigation Laws, and the Necessity for revising Concessions made in favor of other Nations; with Letters and Documents. *London.* 1828. 8vo, pp. 38, 216.

Lindoe (R.) Observations on Slavery; setting forth that to hold the Principle of Slavery is to deny Christ. By Robert Lindoe, M.D. *London.* 1824. 8vo. P. 41300

Lindsay (*Col.*) History of the Seven Years War, with a Narrative of Events in St. Lucia and Gibraltar. By Col. Lindsay. *London.* 1793. 2 vols., 8vo. Plate. 41301

Lindsay (D.) The Claims of Pastors of Churches, and Preachers of the Gospel, for Maintenance; considered in the Light of Holy Scripture. By David Lindsay. *New York: C. McGowan.* 1843. 12mo, pp. iv, 165. C. 41302

Lindsay (E. G.) A History of the Events which transpired during the Navy Island Campaign; to which is added the Correspondence of Different Public Officers, with Affidavits. By E. G. Lindsay. *Lewiston.* 1838. 8vo, pp. 40. P. 41303

Lindsay (J.) A Voyage to the Coast of Africa, in 1758. ... By the Reverend Mr. John Lindsay ... . *London: S. Paterson.* MDCCLIX. 4to, pp. (8), 110. Plates. H. 41304

Relates to the slave-trade.

Lindsay (W.) View of America. To which is prefixed, A Narrative of a Voyage from Dumfries to Saint John, in New Brunswick, in the Year 1819. By William Lindsay. *Hawick: Printed by Robert Armstrong.* 1824. 12mo, pp. 104. 41305

This is the cover-title, the printed title differs.

Lindsay (W. S.) Report of ... Philadelphia Board of Trade, upon the Law of Collisions at Sea ... embraced in an Address ... November 10th, 1860. By W. S. Lindsay, Esq. ... . *Philadelphia: King & Baird, Printers.* 1861. 8vo, pp. 34. B. 41306

Lindsey (C.) The Life and Times of Wm. Lyon Mackenzie. With an Account of the Canadian Rebellion of 1837, and the Subsequent Frontier Disturbances, chiefly from Unpublished Documents. By Charles Lindsey. *Toronto, C. W.: Samuel Pike.* 1863. 2 vols., 8vo, pp. 401; 400. B. 41307

Lindsey. The Prairies of the Western States: their Advantages and their Drawbacks. By Charles Lindsey. *Toronto.* 1860. 12mo, pp. 100. 41308

Lindsey. Prohibitory Liquor Laws: their ... Operation in the United States. The subject discussed as a Question of State Policy and Legislation, with Suggestions for the Suppression of

Tipping Houses. By Charles Lindsey. *Montreal.* 1855. 8vo, pp. 35. 41309

Also: The Clergy Reserves: their History and Present Position ... With a full Account of the Rectories. Also an Appendix containing Dr. Rolph's Speech on the Clergy Reserves, delivered in 1836. ... *Toronto.* 1851. 8vo, pp. 74.

[Lindsey (H.)] New Bedford Harbor Signal Book. *New Bedford: Printed by Benj. Lindsey.* [1843?] 12mo. 41310

Various editions, revised and corrected. The last compiled by Geo. G. Coffin. 1860. 12mo, pp. 12.

Lindsley (A. L.) National Righteousness and National Sin: The Substance of A Discourse delivered in ... South Salem, ... November 20, 1856, By Aaron L. Lindsley ... . *New York: Printed by Edward O. Jenkins.* 1857. 8vo. S. 41311

Lindsley (J. B.) An Address on the Life ... of Robert M. Porter, M.D. ... By John Berrien Lindsley, M.D., ... Nov. 8, 1856. ... *Nashville, Tenn.: Printed by E. Vallette.* 1856. 8vo, pp. 47. H. 41312

[Lindsley.] Our Ruin: Its Causes and Cure. By a Poor-Rich Man. *Nashville.* 1868. 8vo. 41313

Also: Address ... before the Alumni Society of the University of Nashville. ... On the 3d of October, 1854. ... *Nashville: Cameron & Fall, ... Printers.* 1854. 8vo, pp. 25.—Appeal to the Citizens of Davidson County [Tenn.], in behalf of their University. ... June 12th, 1856. *Nashville: Cameron & Fall.* 1856. 8vo, pp. 8.—On Medical Colleges. ... Lecture ... Medical Department of the University of Nashville ... *Nashville: Printed by James T. Bell & Co.* 1858. 8vo, pp. 32. B.

Lindsley (P.) An Address ... in Nashville, January 12, 1825, at the Inauguration of the President of Cumberland College. By Philip Lindsley, D.D. ... *Nashville: Printed by Joseph Norvell.* 1825. 8vo, pp. 48. B. 41314

Lindsley. A Plea for the Theological Seminary at Princeton, N. J. By Philip Lindsly [*sic*]. *Trenton: Printed by George Sherman.* 1821. 8vo, pp. 34. + The Third Edition. [*Ibid.*] 1821. 8vo, pp. 31. BA., S. 41315

Also: An Address ... at Nashville, Ten. Feb. 22, 1832, ... on the ... Centennial Birth Day of George Washington. ... *Nashville: Hunt, Tardiff & Co., Printers.* 1832. 8vo, pp. 36.—Baccalaureate Address, ... on the Sixth Anniversary Commencement of the University of Nashville, October 5, 1831. ... *Nashville.* 1831. 8vo, pp. 36, (3).—Baccalaureate Address ... October 3, 1832. ... *Nashville: Printed by Hunt* ... 1832. 8vo, pp. 67.—The Cause of Education in Tennessee. An Address ... at ... Nashville, October 4, 1826. ... *Nashville: Hunt, Tardiff and Co., Printers.* 1833. 8vo, pp. 39, (1).—A Lecture on Popular Education. ... *Nashville: S. Nye & Co., Printers.* 1837. 8vo, pp. 38, (1). H.—Speech about Colleges, delivered in Nashville, on Commencement Day. October 4, 1848. ... *Nashville: John T. S. Fall ... Printer.* 1848. 8vo, pp. 32.—Speech in behalf of the University of Nashville ... October 4, 1837. *Nashville: S. Nye and Co., Printers.* 1837. 8vo, pp. 38. *See also* Nashville.

Lindsley. The Works of Philip Lindsley, D.D., formerly Vice-President and President Elect of the College of New Jersey, Princeton; and late President of the University of Nashville, Tennessee. Edited by Le Roy J. Halsey, D.D. ... *Philadelphia: J. B. Lippincott & Co.* 1866. 3 vols., 8vo, pp. 648; 720; 731. Facsimile and Portrait. B. 41316

Lindsly (H.) A Brief Sketch of Some of the Principal Universities of Europe and of the United States. By Harvey Lindsly, A.M. ... *Washington: Jacob Gideon, Jr., Printer.* 1836. 8vo, pp. 27, (1). B. 41317

Also: Address of Harvey Lindsly ... in ... Louisville, May, 3, 1859. *Philadelphia: Collins, Printer.* 1859. 8vo, pp. 12.—Medical Science and the Medical Profession in Europe and the United States. ... November, 1840. *Washington: Peter Force.* 1840. 8vo, pp. 35. B.

Line and Staff in our Navy Yards, from a Political Standpoint. [n. p. 1870?] 4to, pp. 3. H. 41318

"Line" and "Staff" [of the Navy. n. p. 1870.] 8vo, pp. 7.

Linen (J.) The Poetical and Prose Writings of James Linen. *New York: W. J. Widdleton.* 1864. 12mo, pp. 423. 41320

Linen (W.) Narrative of the Corruptions in the State Courts of South Carolina. By William Linen. *Charleston.* 1806. 12mo. C. 41321

Linen Trade. Evidence on the Linnen Trade with America ... *London.* 1774. 8vo. 41322

Lines made after the Great Earthquake in 1755, which shook North and South America. [n. p. n. d.] Folio, 1 l. 41323

Lines on Slaves killing their Masters, and the Song of Harmodius and Aristogeiton. *Portsmouth.* 1841. 8vo, pp. 12. H.

Linforth (J.) Route from Liverpool to Great Salt Lake Valley ... . Edited by James Linforth. *Liverpool: Franklin D. Richards.* MDCCCLV. 4to, pp. viii, 120. Map, Plates, Portraits.

Lingard (R.) A | Letter | of | Advice | To a Young | Gentleman | Leaving the | Vniversity, | Concerning his Behaviour and | Conversation in the World. | By R. Lingard. D.D.D.L. | *London | Printed for Benjamin Tooke, and | are to be sold at the Ship in | S. Pauls Church-Yard,* 1671. | 12mo, 35 leaves. BM. 41326

This title is introduced for the purpose of explaining the following:

L[ingard]. A | Letter of Advice | To A Young | Gentleman | Leaving the | University | Concerning his Behaviour | and Conversation in the | World. | By R. L. | *Printed and sold by W. Bradford, | Printer to his Majesty, King | William, at the Bible in | New York.* 1696. | 16mo, pp. (6), 45. 41327

The earliest book known to have been printed in the Colony of New York; the Laws of the Colony excepted. E. B. Corwin's copy sold for $12 in 1856; it was bought for Mr. Menzies, and sold in 1876 for $240. It is now in the possession of Mr. S. W. Phoenix of New York. Mr. Wallace, in his address on Bradford, and Thomas, in his "History of Printing," Second Edition, indulge in some curious speculations respecting the authorship, which are here dissipated. It is difficult to understand Bradford's motives in merely putting R. L. on the title-page when the book from which it was reprinted has the author's name in full on the title-page.

Lingard (W. H.) William H. Lingard's On the Beach at Long Branch Song Book. ... *New-York: Dick & Fitzgerald.* [1868.] 12mo. B. 41328

Lingham (E. J.) Vindiciæ Lusitanæ, or an Answer to a Pamphlet entitled "The Causes and Consequences of the late Emigration to the Brazils. By Edward James Lingham, Esq. *London: Budd.* 1808. 8vo, pp. 70. 41329

Relates to the transferment of the court of Portugal to the Brazils. *See* Rylance (J.)

Linieres (E. T. de). Establecimiento cientifico, agricola, fabril y comercial, que aprobó el supremo gobierno en 25 de Junio de 1844, y se propone fundar y dirigir Eduardo Turreau de Linieres. *Mexico.* 1844. 12mo, pp. 26. 41330

Liniers y Bremond, Santiago. ... Proclama. [Buenos-Ayres à 12 de Junio de 1809. *Buenos-Ayres.* n. d.] 4to, pp. 6. H.

Linguet [S. N. H.] Political and Philosophical Speculations on the Distinguishing Characteristics of the Present Century; and On the State of Legislation, Military Establishments, Finances, and Commerce, in Europe: with Occasional Reflections on the Probable Effects of American Independency. By M. Linguet, Late of the Parliament of Paris. *London: Fielding and Walker.* MDCCLXXVIII. 16mo, pp. 152. C., H. 41332

Translated from "Annales Politiques, Civiles et Littéraires du 18me siécle." For a reply *see* Burgoyne, Vol. III., No. 9267, and correct the date to read MDCCLXXVIII, 8vo, pp. 23.

Lining (J.) History of the Yellow Fever. By Dr. John Lining of Charleston *Charleston.* 1753. 8vo. 41333

The earliest account of this ease in America; *see* Thacher's "Medical Biography." Also: A Description of the American Yellow Fever ... at Charleston, ... 1748. ... *Philadelphia: Thomas Dobson.* 1799. 8vo, pp. 30. *See also* Philosophical Transactions, January, 1745.

Linn (A. L.) Oration at Schenectady on the Fourth of July, 1822. *Schenectady.* 1822. 8vo. S. 41334

Also: A Speech ... April 13, 1842, on the Annexation of Texas. *Washington.* 1842. 8vo.

Linn (E. A.) The Life and Public Services of Dr. Lewis F[ields] Linn, for Ten Years a Senator of the United States from the State of Missouri. By E. A. Linn and N. Sargent *New York: D. Appleton and Company.* M.DCCC.LVII. 8vo, pp. 441. Portrait. BA. 41335

Linn (J. B.) The Death of Washington. A Poem. In Imitation of the Manner of Ossian. By Rev. John Blair Linn, A.M. ... *Philadelphia: Printed by John Ormrod.* 1800. 8vo, pp. 26. BA. 41336

[Linn.] Miscellaneous Works, Prose and Poetical, by a Young Gentleman of New-York. *New-York.* 1795. 12mo.

Also: A Discourse occasioned by the Death of the Reverend John Ewing, D.D. ... *Philadelphia: John Conrad & Co.* 1802. 8vo, pp. 26.—The Powers of Genius, A Poem, in Three Parts. ... *Philadelphia: Asbury Dickins.* 1801. 8vo, pp. 127. B. + Second Edition, Corrected and Enlarged. ... *Philadelphia: John Conrad & Co.* 1802. 12mo, pp. 191. + *London.* 1804. 16mo, pp. 155.

Linn. Valerian, a Narrative Poem; intended ... to describe the Early Persecutions of Christians ... . By John Blair Linn, D.D. ... With a Sketch of the Life and Character of the Author. [By C. B. Brown]. *Philadelphia: Printed by Thomas and George Palmer.* 1805. 4to, pp. xxvi, (2), 97. Portrait. H. 41338

Linn [Lewis F.] ... Mr. Linn submitted the following Report: ... *Washington.* 1850. 8vo, pp. 22. 41339

Relative to Michael Armbrister's title to land purchased from Usse Yoholo, a Creek Indian.

Linn. ... Report ... on ... the Cultivation of Tropical Plants in the United States ... . [*Washington.* 1838.] 8vo, pp. 142. B.

Linn. Speech ... in Reply to McDuffie, on the Oregon Bill; delivered ... January 26, 1843. *Washington.* 1843. 8vo, pp. 15.

Also: Speech ... on ... the Sales of the Public Lands among the States. ... January 29, 1841. *Washington.* 1841. 8vo, pp. 7.—Speech ... Jan. 1841, on the prospective Pre-emption Bill. [n. p. n. d.] 8vo.—Speech ... Aug. 11, 1841, on National Defences. *Washington.* 1842. 8vo.—Speech ... on the Bill to Indemnify General Jackson, May 14, 1842. *Washington.* 1842. 8vo.

Linn (W.) The Blessings of America. A Sermon, preached ... On the Fourth July, 1791, being the Anniversary of the Independence of America: at the Request of the Tammany

Society, or Columbian Order. By William Linn, D.D. *New-York: Printed by Thomas Greenleaf.* M, DCC, XC, I. 8vo, pp. 39.

Linn. A Discourse delivered at Hackensack, June 28, 1796. On the Occasion of the Meeting of a Commission of Synod, to compose certain Differences in the Congregations of Hackensack and Schroenburgh. By William Linn, D.D. *New York.* 1796. 8vo, pp. 36. N. 41343

Linn. Discourses on the Signs of the Times. By William Linn, D.D. *New York: Printed by Thomas Greenleaf.* 1794. 8vo, pp. iv, 200. C., P. 41344

Linn. A Funeral Eulogy, occasioned by the Death of General Washington. Delivered February 22d, 1800, before the New-York State Society of the Cincinnati. By William Linn, D.D. ... *New-York: Printed by Isaac Collins.* 1800. 8vo, pp. 44.

Linn. A Military Discourse, delivered in Carlisle, March the 17th, 1776, to Colonel Irvine's Battalion of Regulars, and a very respectable number of the Inhabitants. Published at the request of the Officers. By William Linn, A.M. Chaplain. ... *Philadelphia: Printed in the Year* MDCCLXXVI. 12mo, pp. 16. 41346

[Linn.] Serious Considerations on the Election of a President: Addressed to the Citizens of the United States. *New-York: Printed by John Furman.* 1800. 8vo, pp. 36. BA. + *Trenton: Printed by Sherman, Mershon & Thomas.* M.DCCC. 8vo, pp. 31. C. 41347

Contains stories calculated to ruin Jefferson among all pious people. Dr. John M. Mason assisted in the performance.

Linn. Sermons, Historical and Characteristical. By William Linn, D.D. ... *New York: Printed by Childs and Swaine.* [1791.] 12mo, pp. xxiii, 360. BA., S. 41348

Also: A Discourse, Delivered on the 26th of November, 1795; ... a Day of Thanksgiving, ... on account of the removal of an Epidemic Fever ... . *New York: Printed by T. & J. Swords.* 1795. 8vo, pp. 38.—A Discourse on National Sins; Delivered May 9, 1798; ... a Day of General Fast. ... *New York: Printed by T. & J. Swords.* 1798. 8vo, pp. 37.—A Discourse before the New York Missionary Society, April 1st, 1800. ... *New York.* 1800. 8vo, pp. 40.—Remarks on Dr. Moore's Address to the Members of the Protestant Episcopal Church, in ... New-York. ... *New-York: Printed by Thomas Greenleaf.* M, DCC, XC, III. 8vo, pp. 46. B.

Linn, *and others.* A Collection of the Essays on the Subject of Episcopacy, which originally appeared in the Albany Centinel, and which are ascribed principally to Rev. Dr. Linn, Rev. Mr.

Beasley, and Th. Y. How. [Edited] With additional Notes and Remarks [by J. H. Hobart]. *New-York.* 1806. 8vo. 41349

Linn (W.) The Life of Thomas Jefferson, Author of the Declaration of Independence. And Third President of the United States. ... By William Linn. *Ithaca: Mack & Andrus.* 1834. 12mo, pp. 250. + *Mobile, Alabama.* 1835. 12mo. + Second Edition. *Ithaca: Mack & Andrus.* 1839. 12mo, pp. 267. Portrait. + Third Edition. *Ithaca: Andrus, Woodruff & Gauntlett.* 1843. 12mo, pp. 267. 41350

Linnæan Society. Report of a Committee of the Linnæan Society of New England, relative to a large Marine Animal, supposed to be a Serpent, seen near Cape Ann, Massachusetts, in August 1817. *Boston: Cummings and Hilliard.* 1817. 8vo, pp. 52. 2 Plates. BA. + *London: Souter.* [1818.] 8vo, pp. 59. Plate. 41351

See also our Vol. VI., No. 24920.

Linnæus (C.) Dissertatio sistens Specifica Canadensium. Respondente Johanne Coelln. *Scaræ.* 1756. 4to, pp. 28.

Johann von Coelln was the "Respondent." This is also contained in the "Amœnitates Academicæ" of Linnæus.

Linnæus. Plantarum Jamaicensium pugillus, quem consens. experient. fac. medicæ in Regia academia upsaliensi, præside viro nobilissimo et experientissimo Dn Doct. Carolo Linnæo ... . *Upsaliæ, Año* MDCCLIX. 4to, pp. 31. J.C.B. 41353

Linnæus. The Correspondence of Linnæus, with other Eminent Naturalists. Selected from the Original MSS. by Sir Jas. Edward Smith. *London.* 1821. 2 vols., 8vo. Facsimiles.

Full of matter relating to America, including memoir and correspondence of Dr. Alexander Gordon, of Charleston, S. C., letters from Catesby, Governor Cadwallader Colden, Dr. John Mitchell, Peter Collinson, Bartram, etc.

The Linnet; a Collection of Songs ... . *New York.* 1806. 18mo. 41355

Linonian Society. *See* Yale College.

Linschoten (J. H. van). Itinerario, | Voyage ofte Schipvaert, van Jan | Huygen van Linschoten naer Oost ofte Portugaels In- | dien, inhoudende een corte beschryvinghe der selver Landen ende Zee-custen, met aen- | wysinge van alle de voornaemde principale Havens, Revieren, hoecken ende plaetsen, tot noch | toe van de Portugesen ontdeckt ende bekent: Waer by ghevoecht zijn, niet

alleen die Conter- | feytsels vande habyten, drachten, ende wesen, so vande Portugesen aldaer residerende, als van- | de ingeboornen Indianen, ende huere Tempels, Afgoden, Huysinge, met die voornaemste | Boomen, Vruchten, Kruyden, Speceryen, ende diergelijcke materialen, als ooc die | manieren des selfden Volckes, so in hunnen Godts-diensten, als in Politie | eñ Huijs-houdinghe: maer ooc een corte verhalinge van de Coophan- | delingen, hoe eñ waer die ghedreven eñ ghevonden worden, | met die ghedenckweerdichste geschiedenissen, | voorghevallen den tijt zijnder | residentie aldaer. | Alles beschreven ende by een vergadert, door den selfden, seer nut, oorbaer, | ende oock vermakelijcken voor alle curieuse ende Lief- | hebbers van vreemdigheden. | *t'Amstelredam.* | *By Cornelis Claesz. op 't Water, in 't Schrijf-boeck, by de oude Brugghe.* | *Anno* CIↃ.IↃ.XCVI. | Folio. 41356

First edition. Collation: Part I. 4 prel. leaves; viz.: Title, on the reverse "Extract uyt't Register," etc.; "Aende Hooghende VVelghe borene," etc., pp. 2; "Prohemio ofte Voorreeden totten Leser," etc., 1 page; "Sonnet," 1 page; "Ode," 1 page, on the reverse Portrait of Linschoten; Text, pp. 160. Part II. "Reysgheschrift," etc., M.D.XCV, pp. 134; "Een seker Extract," etc., CIↃ.IↃ.XCVI, Title, reverse blank, "Aende VVelghebórene," etc., 1 page, on the reverse "Ad Io. Hvg. Linscotvm," etc. Text, pp. 135-147. Part III. "Beschryvinghe," etc., M.D.XCVI, pp. 82, followed by 5 leaves containing lists of Plates and Maps, Register, etc. 42 Maps and Plates.

For a full account and collation of this very rare first edition, *see* Tiele's "Mémoire Bibliographique sur les Journaux des Navigateurs," pp. 83-91, *also* J. R. Bartlett's Catalogue of J. C. Brown's Library. Part II. contains a description of the navigation of the Portuguese in India, comprising the coast of Brazil and the harbors. Part III. contains a description of the Cabo St. Augustin in Brazil, the peculiarities of the ocean, its islands, etc. With a description of West India at large. There are copies on large paper. "The thirty-six plates and six maps illustrating the book, are the same for the six editions in Dutch, the second and third French editions and (with exception of one map), for the Latin edition. The Latin and German translations, given by De Bry in the 'Petits Voyages,' II., III., IV., are crowded with faults, misunderstandings, quite fantastical translations, omissions, etc.; the plates are no less bad and often entirely drawn from imagination, etc., as is fully demonstrated by Camus' 'Mémoire,' p. 189, and Tiele's 'Mémoire,' p. 90."—Muller. Another edition of Part III. is described below:

Linschoten. Beschrijvinghe van de gantsche Custe | van Guinea ... met de ontdeckinghe ... gheleghentheyt van 't vaste | landt ... hebdy in t' boeck van Jan Huygen van Linschoten int langhe; | Met ooc alle de navigatien ... *t'Amstelredam.* | *By Cornelis Claesz. op 't Water, in 't Schrijf-boeck, by de oude* | *Brugghe, A* M.D.XCVI. Folio, 45 leaves. Map. 41357

An edition, *Fremeker,* 1601, is briefly described in Mr. H. C. Murphy's catalogue.

Linschoten. Itinerario, | Voyage ofte Schipvaert, van Ian | Huygen van Linschoten naer Oost ofte Portugaels In- | dien, [as in the edition dated 1596]. *t'Amstelredam,* | *By Cornelis Claesz. op't*

Water in't Schrijfboeck, by de oude Brugghe. | [1605.] Folio, Engraved Title, pp. (8), 160. Portrait of Linschoten, 10 Maps and Plans. 41358

Linschoten. Reys-Gheschrift | Van de Navigatien der Portugaloy- | sers in Orienten, ... Als oock van de gantsche | Custen van Brasilien, ende alle die Havens van dien: Item van't vaste landt ende die voor Eylanden (Las Antilas | genaemt) van Spaenschs Indien, met noch de Navigatie vande Cabo de Lopo Gonsalues, naer Angola toe, aen | de Custe van Æthiopien: Mitsgaders alle die Coursē, Havens, Eylanden, diepten ende ondiepten, sandē drooghten, Riffen ende Clippen, met die gelegentheyt ende streckinghe van dien. ... | Door Ian Huyghen van Linschoten. | *t'Amstelredam,* | *By Cornelis Claesz. op't water, in't Schrijfboeck, by de oude* | *Brugghe. Anno* 1604. | Folio, pp. 147. Map.

This is a reprint of Part II. of the "Itinerario," described No. 41356, *supra.*

Linschoten. Beschrijvinghe van de gantsche Custe | van Guinea, Manicongo, Angola, Monomotapa, | ende teghen over de Cabo de S. Augustijn in Brasilien, de eyghenschappen des ge- | heelen Occeanische zee: Midtsgaders haer Eylanden, als daer zijn S. Tho- | me, S. Helena, 't Eylant Ascencion, met alle hare Havenen, diepten, | droochten, zanden, gronden, wonderlijcke vertellingen van de | zee-vaerden van die van Hollandt, als oock de | Beschrijvinghe van de bin- | nen Landen. | ... tot de Roo-Zee toe, ende wat u dan | voort van de beschrijvinge ontbreeckt, hevdy int Boeck van Ian Huyghen van Linschoten int | langhe: Met oock alle de Navigatien van alle vaerden die de Portugische Pi- | loten ende Stier-lieden oyt beseylt hebben, uyt haer Zee-Caert- | Boecken ende gheexperimenteerde stucken ghe- | trocken, ende in ons tale int | licht ghebracht. | ... | Noch volght de beschrijvinghe van West-Indien int langhe, met haere Caerte. | *t'Amstelredam,* | *By Cornelis Claesz. opt Water int Schrijf-boeck,* | *by die oude Brugghe, Anno* xvj^{c}.v. | Folio, 45 leaves. Map. 41360

This is a second edition of Part III. of the "Itinerario," described No. 41356, *supra.* It is the rarest of the Dutch editions, and a reprint of the first, but without a separate title.

Linschoten. Itinerarium | Ofte | Schipvaert naer | Oost ofte Portugaels | Indien. | Inhoudende een beschrijvinge, dier Landen, | Zee-custen, havens, Rivieren, Hoecken ende plaet- | sen, met de ghedenckwaerdighste | Historien der selve. | Hier zijn by gevoeght de Conterfeytsels, van de | habijten, drachten, so van de Portugesen aldaer residerende, | als van de Ingeboorene Indianen: Ende van hare Tempe- | len, Afgoden, Huysingen, manieren, Godes-dienst, Politie, | Huys-houdingen ende Coophandel, hoe ende waer die | ghedreven wordt: Als oock van den Boomen | Vruchten, Cruyden, Speceryen, ende | dierghelijcke Materialen | van die Landen. | Alles beschreven door Ian Huygen | van Linschoten. | Op 't nieuwe gecorrigeert eñ verbetert. | *Tot Amsterdam,* | *By Jan Evertsz. Cloppenburch, in de vergulden Bybel, Anno* 1614, | *Met Previlegie voor* 12 *Iaren.* | Folio, pp. (8), 160. Portrait of Linschoten. 41361

Followed by: "Reys-gheschrift | Van de Navigatien der Por- | tugaloysers in Orienten" ... *Tot Amsterdam,* | *By Jan Evertsz. Cloppenburch* ... 1614. | ... Folio, pp. (8), 13–147; and "Beschrijvinge van de gantsche Custe | van Guinea" ... . *Tot Amsterdam,* | *By Jan Evertsz Cloppenburch, op't Water* | *by die oude Brugge in de Vergulden Bijbel. Anno* 1614. | Folio, 45 leaves. The text does not differ from the preceding editions, although on the title and in the license is "Op 't nieuwe gecorrigeert eñ verbetert."

This is, after the third, the rarest of the Dutch editions of Linschoten. "Reprint of the first edition; only some words changed, but the titles quite different; to Part III., that of the first part (first and second edition), is prefixed; Part III. has no paging; the title and dedication to Part IIb. are omitted."—MULLER.

LINSCHOTEN. Itinerarium, | Ofte | Schip-vaert [as the preceding title]. Van nieus ghecorrigeert ende verbetert. | *T' Amstelredam.* | *Ghedruckt by Jan Evertsz Cloppenburch, Boeck-verkooper, woonende op 't Water,* | *in den vergulden Bijbel. Anno* 1623. | *Met Previlegie voor* 12 *Jaren.* Folio, pp. (8), 160. 5 Maps, 36 Plates.

Followed by: "Reys-gheschrift | Van de Navigatien" ... *T'Amstelredam.* | *Ghedruckt by Jan Evertsz Cloppenburch* ... *Anno* 1623. ... Folio, pp. (8), 13–147; and "Beschrijvinge van de gantsche Cu- | ste van Guinea" ... . *Tot Amsterdam.* | *By Jan Evertsz Cloppenburch* ... *Anno* 1623. Folio, 45 leaves. An exact reprint of the edition of 1614.

LINSCHOTEN. Itinerarium, | Ofte | Schip-vaert [as in the edition of 1623]. Alles beschreven door Ian Huyghen | van Linschoten. | Van nieus ghecorrigeert ende verbetert. | *t'Amstelredam,* | *Ghedruckt voor Everhardt Cloppenburch, Boeck-verkooper woonende op't Water,* | *in den vergulden Bijbel Anno* 1644. | *Met Previlegie voor* 12. *Iaren.* | Folio, Engraved Title, pp. (8), 160. 10 Maps and Plans, Portrait of Linschoten. 41363

Followed by: "Reys-Gheschrift | Vande Navigatien" ... . *t'Amstelredam,* | *Ghedruckt voor Everhardt Cloppenburch, Boeck-verkooper woonende op't Water,* | *in den vergulden Bijbel Anno* 1644. | *Met Previlegie voor* 12. *Iaren.* | Folio, Engraved Title, pp. (8), 13–147. Map; and "Beschrijvinge vande gantsche Cu- | ste van Guinea" ... . *t'Amstelredam,* | *Ghedruckt voor Everhardt Cloppenburch, Boeck-verkooper woonende op't* | *Water, in den vergulden Bijbel Anno* 1644. | Folio, Engraved Title, 46 leaves. Map.

This last Dutch edition is scarcer than the first. The map of the two hemispheres, by Petrus Plancius, executed in 1594, and Langren's map of America, executed at the same time, are two remarkable efforts at cartography.

LINSCHOTEN. Journael | Van de derthien-jarighe Reyse, te Water en te Lande | Gedaen door | Jan Huygen van Linschooten, | na | Oost-Indien, | ... *'t Amsterdam, Gedruckt* | *By Gillis Joosten Saeghman, in de Nieuwe-straet,* | *Ordinaris Drucker van de Jour-*

nalen ter Zee, en de Landt-Reysen. | [*about* 1663.] 4to, pp. 208. Portrait of Linschoten and Plates. 41364

LINSCHOTEN. Beschryvinge van verscheyde Landen, gelegen onder | Africa en America, | Als t Coninckrijck Guinea, Congo, Angola, en voorts | tot voor by den Caep Bona Esperance, de eygenschappen des geheelen Oceani- | sche Zee en hare Eylanden, St. Thomae, St. Helena en Ascencion. Mitsgaders de | Beschryvingh van Brasilien, Nova Francia, Florida, de Eylanden Antillas, | Iucaya, Cuba, Iamaica ende van Peru, verhalende het Leven der Volckeren, Wetten, Zeden, | en Godts-dienst, als mede haer Ryckdom, de vreemdicheydt der Beesten, Voogelen, Visschen en | Aerdt-gewassen in de selve Landen. In dusdanigen ordre by een vergadert door | Jan Huygen van Linschooten. | *t' Amsterdam,* | *Gedruckt bij Gillis Ioosten Saeghman, Ordinaris Drucker van de Journalen.* [n. d.] 4to, pp. 36. Map. 41365

LINSCHOTEN. Navigatio | ac Itinerarivm | Iohannis Hvgonis Lin- | scotani in Orientalem sive Lvsitano- | rvm Indiam. Descriptiones eivsdem Terræ ac Tractvvm | Littoralivm. Præcipuorum Portuum, Fluminum, Capitum, Locorumque, Lusita- | norum hactenus navigationibus detectorum, signa & notæ. Imagines habi- | tus gestusque Indorum ac Lusitanorum per Indiam viventium, Tem- | plorum, Indolorum, Ædium, Arborum, Fructuum, Herbarum, | Aromatum, &c. Mores gentium circa sacrificia, Poli- | tiam ac rem familiarē. Enarratio Mercaturæ, quo- | modo & vbi ea exerceatur. Memorabilia | gesta suo tempore iis in partibus. | Collecta omnia ac descripta per eundem Belgicè; Nunc vero Latinè reddita, in vsum | commodum ac voluptatem studiosi Lectoris novarum memoriáque | dignarum rerum, diligenti studio ac operâ. | *Hagæ-Comitis,* | *Ex officinâ Alberti Henrici. Impensis Authoris & Cornelii Nicolai,* | *prostantque apud Ægidium Elsevirum. Anno* 1599. | Folio, Engraved Title. A., J.C.B. 41366

Collation: 4 prel. leaves; viz.: Title, on the reverse "Ad Illvstrissimvm," etc. Engraved Coat of Arms, 1 leaf; "Illvstrissimo atqve Serenissimo Principi ac Domino D. Mavritio Lantgravio Hessiæ," etc., pp. 2; "Praefatio ad Lectorem," 1 page, on the reverse Portrait of Linschoten; Text, pp. 124. Followed by "Descriptio Totivs Gvineae Trac- | tvs" ... . *Hagae-Comitis* | *Ex officinâ Alberti Henrici.* | *Anno* 1599. Folio, pp. 45, Index, pp. 3. 37 Maps and Plates.

This first Latin edition contains the "Itinerarium," slightly abridged in some portions, followed by a translation of pp. 1–16 of the third Dutch part, "Descriptio Guineae." The description of America, from the third Dutch part, pp. 17–25, is omitted. Pages 17–25 consist of a short narrative of three Dutch expeditions to the North, from the work of De Veer. Pages 26–36 contain a translation of pp. 124–134 of the Dutch bearings and distances; pp. 37–45 an abridgment of pp. 135–147 of the same work. The map illustrating the voyage of Barentsz is important, and exhibits the regions adjacent to the North Pole. "Très-rare et recherchée. On la réunit à la collection

des frères De Bry, attendu que leurs héritiers en ont fait faire une traduction moins exacte, qu'ils ont insérée dans la 2e partie des 'Petits Voyages.'"—LECLERC. *See also* Camus' "Mémoire," p. 189, Brunet, *and* Trömel.

LINSCHOTEN. Navigatio | ac Itinerarivm [same as the edition of 1599]. *Amstelodami apud Joannem Walschaert,* 1614. Folio.

We have not seen this edition, which is in the possession of Mr. James Lenox, but, with the exception of the title and preface, it does not differ from the first Latin version of 1599.

LINSCHOTEN. Histoire | de la Navi- | gation de Iean Hv- | gves de Linscot Hollandois et de | son voyage es Indes Orientales: contenante diuerses descriptions des | Pays, Costes, Haures Riuieres, Caps, & autres lieux iusques à présent | descouverts par les Portugais: Observations des coustumes des na- | tions de delà quant à la Réligion, Estat Politic & Domestic, de leurs | Commerces, des Arbres, Fruicts, Herbes, Espiceries, & autres | singularitez qui s'y trouuent: Et narrations des choses | memorables qui y sont aduenues de | son temps. | Avec Annotations de Bernard Palv- | danus Docteur en Medecine, specialement sur la matiere des plantes & | espiceries: & diuerses figures en taille douce, pour illu- | stration de l'œuure. | A qvoy sont adiovstées qvelqves av- | tres descriptions tant du pays de Guinee, & autres costes d'Ethiopie, | que des nauigations des Hollandois vers le Nord au Vay- | gat & en la nouuelle Zembla. | Le tovt recveilli & descript par le mesme | de Linscot en bas Alleman, & nouuellement traduict | en François. | *Amstelredam,* | *De l'Imprimerie de Henry Laurent.* | M DC.X. Folio, pp. (4), 275. 8 Maps and 58 Plates. C. 41368

"This edition is most probably printed at Frankfort by De Bry, as appears from the printing and bad paper; it contains fifty-eight plates (many with German inscriptions) printed in the text, as in the editions of De Bry. Of the six maps belonging to this edition, only one (facing page 14), is extant. The navigations of the Dutch to Waygat, though mentioned on the title, are omitted. Nearly all is an extract from the first Dutch edition. The notes of Paludanus, mentioned on the title, are also in all the Dutch editions but much fuller."—MULLER. Some copies of this edition have the following title:

LINSCHOTEN. Histoire | de la Naviga- | tion [as before]. *A Amstelredam,* | *De l'Imprimerie de Theodore Pierre.* | M DC.X. Folio, pp. (4), 275. 8 Maps, 58 Plates. C. 41369

LINSCHOTEN. Histoire | de la | Navigation | De | Iean Hvgves | de Linschot Hollandois, Aux | Indes Orientales. | Contenant diverses Descriptions des lieux | iusques à present descouverts par les Portu- | gais: Observations des Coustumes & singu- | laritez de delà, & autres declarations. | Avec annotations de B. Palvdanvs, Docteur | en Medecine sur la matiere des Plantes & | Espiceries:

Item quelques Cartes Geo- | graphiques, & autres Figures. | Deuxiesme edition | augmentee. | *A Amsterdam,* | *Chez Iean Evertsz Cloppenburch, Marchand libraire, demeu-* | *rant sur le Water à la Bible Doree. Avec Privilege pour* 12. *Ans.* 1619. | Folio, Engraved Title, pp. (8), 205. 5 Maps, Plates and Portrait. B., S.

Usually followed by the two works described below:

LINSCHOTEN. Le Grand | Rovtier | de Mer, | De | Iean Hvgves | de Linschot Hollandois. | Contenant une instruction des routes | & cours qu'il convient tenir en la Navigation | des Indes Orientales, & au voyage de la coste | du Bresil, des Antilles, & du Cap de Lopo Gonsalves. | Avec description des Costes, Havres, Isles, | Vents, & courants d'eaux, & autres particula- | ritez d'icelle Navigation. | Le tout fidelement recueilli des memoires & obser- | vations des Pilotes Espagnols & Portugais. | Et nouvellement traduit de Flameng en François. | *A Amsterdam,* | *Chez Iean Evertsz Cloppenburch, Marchand libraire, demeu-* | *rant sur le Water à la Bible Doree. Avec Privilege pour* 12. *Ans.* 1619. | Folio, Engraved Title, pp. (4), 181. B. 41371

LINSCHOTEN. Description | de l'Amerique | & des parties d'icelle, comme de la Nouvelle France, | Floride, des Antilles, Iucaya, Cuba | Iamaica, &c. | Item de l'estendue & distance des lieux, de la fertilité | & abondance du pays, religion & coustu- | mes des habitans, & autres | particularitez. | Avec vne Carte Geographique de l'Amerique | Australe, qui doit estre inseree en la | page suivante. | *A Amsterdam,* | *Chez Iean Evertsz Cloppenburch, Marchand libraire, demeu-* | *rant sur le Water à la Bible Doree. Avec Privilege pour* 12. *Ans.* 1619. | Folio, Engraved Title, pp. (2), 86. Map. B. 41372

LINSCHOTEN. Histoire | de la | Navigation | de | Iean Hvgves | de Linschot Hollandois: Aux | Indes Orientales | [as in the edition of 1619]. Troixiesme edition | augmentee. | *A Amsterdam,* | *Chez Evert Cloppenburgh, Marchand libraire, demeurant sur* | *le Water à la Bible Doree. Avec Privilege pour* 12 *Ans.* 1638. Folio, Engraved Title, pp. (8), 206. Maps, Plates, and Portrait.

Followed by: "Le grand | routier | de mer, | de | Iean Hvgves, | de Linschot Hollandois." | ... *A Amsterdam,* | *Chez Evert Cloppenburgh, Marchand libraire, demeurant sur* | *le Water à la Bible Doree. Avec Privilege pour* 12 *Ans.* 1638. | Folio, Engraved Title, pp. (4), 181; and "Description | de l'Amerique | & des parties d'icelle, comme de la Nouvelle France, | Floride, des Antilles, Iucaya, Cuba | Iamaica, &c." | ... *A Amsterdam,* | *Chez Evert Cloppenburch, Marchand libraire, demeurant* | *sur le Water à la Bible Doree. Avec Privilege pour* 12 *Ans.* 1638. | Folio, Engraved Title, pp. (2), 86. A reprint of the edition of 1619.

LINSCHOTEN. *See* Acosta (J. de), Vol. I., No. 126, correct the collation to read 389 leaves, *see also* No. 127.

LINSCHOTEN. ... Semper Eadem | Iohn | Hvighen Van | Linschoten. | his Discours of Voyages | into ye Easte & West | Indies. | Deuided into foure Bookes | *Printed at London by* | *Iohn Wolfe* | *Printer to ye Honorable Cittie of* | *London* | ... | *I. W.* | [1598.] Folio.

Collation: pp. (10); Text, pp. 197; "The Seconde Booke," etc., 1598, Title, and pp. 197–259 [*sic*] 295; "The Thirde Booke," etc., 1598, Title, and pp. 307–447; "The Fovrthe Booke," etc., 1598, Title, and pp. 451–462. 12 copperplate Maps.

As the maps are sometimes spurious, we append a list of those that are genuine: I. Typvs Orbis Terrarvm; II. Islandes and Castle of Mozambique, etc., p. 8; III. Caerd of the Coastes, etc., p. 12; IV. Coast of Abex, etc., p. 12; V. Coasts of China, etc., p. 32; VI. Sct Helena, etc., p. 172; VII. The true description of the Island St Helena, etc., p. 172; VIII. Island of Ascention, etc., p. 174; IX. Ægypt from Cair, etc., p. 197; X. Coast of Guinea, etc., p. 197; XI. South Seas of America, etc., p. 216; XII. Insvlae Molvccae, etc., p. 328. The maps are often supplied from the Dutch, Latin, or French edition; but, to be genuine, should be in English.

"This inestimable book, a treasure of all the learning respecting the East and West-Indies and the navigation thither, at the end of the sixteenth century, has been in the highest esteem for nearly a century, and was given to each ship sailing to India, as a log-book. Hence the many editions, which is also the cause why fine copies, especially with all the plates and maps, are so very rare. A large part of the book is occupied by translations of original Spanish and Portuguese documents on geography, ethnography, statistics, navigation, etc., and in these respects it is of the highest importance and authority. The description of America occupies pages 17 to 82 of the third part" —F. MULLER. *See also* Trömel.

LINSLEY (Daniel Chipman). Morgan Horses: A Premium Essay on the Origin, History, and Characteristics of this Remarkable American Breed of Horses ... . By D. C. Linsley ... . *New York: E. M. Sexton and Company.* 1857. 12mo, pp. viii, (2), 9–340. Plates. B. 41375

Also: Linsley's Report of his Survey of a Road from the Foot to the Summit of Mount Mansfield. Made October, 1865. *Montpelier.* 1866. 8vo, pp. 7. H.

LINSLEY (J. H.) ... A Catalogue of the Birds of Connecticut, arranged according to their Natural Families: ... By Rev. James H. Linsley, A.M. ... [n. p. n. d.] 8vo, pp. 26. H. 41376

From the "American Journal of Science and Arts," Vol. XLIV., No. 2.

LINSLEY. Memoir of the Rev. James H. Linsley, A.M. *Hartford: Robins and Smith.* 1845. 18mo, pp. 178. 41377

LINSLEY (J. H.) A Sermon ... at the Dedication of the Second ... Congregational Church, in Hartford ... April 11, 1827. By Joel H. Linsley ... . *Hartford: D. F. Robinson & Co.* 1827. 8vo, pp. 32. H. 41378

Also: The First Annual Address, ... before the Hartford Peace Society, March 18th, 1829. ... Second Edition. ... *Hartford: J. Hubbard Wells.* 1834. 8vo, pp. 24. H.

LINSTANT (S.) De l'émigration européenne dans ses rapports avec la prospérité future des colonies. *Paris: France.* 1850. 8vo. 41379

LINSTANT. Essai sur les Moyens d'extirper les Préjugés des Blancs contre la couleur des Africains et des Sang-Mêlés ... . Par S. Linstant ... . [*Paris:*] *Pagnerre, Éditeur.* 1841. 8vo, pp. (10), xiv, 170. B. 41380

LINSTANT-PRADINE (A.) Les Codes Haïtiens annotés ... Par Linstant-Pradine, avocat. Code de procédure civile et Code de commerce. *Lons-le-Saulnier: imp. Gauthier frères.* 1866. 8vo, pp. lxx, 593. 41381

LINSTANT-PRADINE. Recueil Général des Lois et des Actes du Gouvernement d'Haiti, depuis la Proclamation de son Indépendance jusqu'à nos jours, le tout mis en ordre et publié, avec des notes historiques de jurisprudence et de concordance. *Paris: A. Durand.* 1851–1865. 8vo. 41382

LINTNER (G. A.) The Early History of the Lutheran Church in the State of New York, a Discourse. By G. A. Lintner. *Albany.* 1867. 8vo, pp. 24. 41383

LINTNER. A Memoir of the Rev. Walter Gunn, late Missionary in India, from the Evangelical Lutheran Church of the United States. *Albany: E. H. Pease & Co.* 1852. 18mo, pp. 156. C. 41384

Also: A Historical Discourse ... before the Schoharie County Bible Society, at its Semi-Centennial Meeting. ... *Albany.* 1863. 8vo.

L[INTON] (A[nthonie]). Newes of the Complement of the Art of Navigation, and of the mightie Empire of Cataia, together with the Straits of Anian. By A. L. *London.* 1609. 4to, 23 l.

A very rare piece. I found it included in an English catalogue of Americana.

LINTON (J. J. C.) A Prohibitory Liquor Law for Upper Canada. Being A Bill for An Act to prohibit the Sale by Retail, &c. With Remarks ... . By J. J. C. Linton. *Toronto: Maclear & Co.* 1860. 12mo, pp. 48. Portrait. 41386

LINWOOD (W.) Great Men: their Characteristics, Influence, and Destiny. A Lecture, occasioned by the Death of the Rev. E. W. Channing, D.D. ... Nov. 20, 1842. By William Linwood ... *London: J. Green.* 1843. 12mo, pp. (2), 41. B. 41387

The Linwoods. *See* [Sedgwick (C. M.)]

LINZEE (J.) All Gentlemen Sailors ... . [*Philadelphia: J. Humphreys.* 1778.] Folio, 1 leaf. P. 41388

Advertisement for recruits to H. B. M. ship Pearl, Capt. J. Linzee: published Feb. 4, 1778.

LIOT (W. B.) Panama, Nicaragua, and Tehuantepec; or, Considerations upon the Question of Communication between the Atlantic and Pacific Oceans. By W. B. Liot ... . *London: Simpkin and Marshall.* 1849. 8vo, pp. (2), iv, 63. 2 folded Plates.

LIPENIUS (M.) Navigatio Salomonis ophiritica illustrata a Martino Lipenio ... . *Wittebergæ.* 1660. 12mo. 41390

Ophir is here located in South America; *see* pp. 499–538.

LIPPARD (G.) Blanche of Brandywine; or September the Eleventh, 1777. A Romance of the Revolution. By George Lippard. ... *Philadelphia: G. B. Zieber & Co.* 1846. 8vo, pp. 351. B. 41391

LIPPARD. The Empire City; or, New York by Night and Day. ... By George Lippard. ... *New York.* 1850. 8vo. + *Philadelphia: T. B. Peterson & Brothers.* [1864.] 8vo, pp. 205.

LIPPARD. Legends of the Revolution. By George Lippard. ... *New York.* 1850. 8vo. 41393

LIPPARD. The Life and Choice Writings of George Lippard. *New York.* 1855. 8vo, pp. 128. Portrait. C. 41394

LIPPARD. New York; its Upper Ten and Lower Million. By George Lippard. ... *Cincinnati.* 1853. 8vo, pp. 284. C.

LIPPARD. The Quaker City; ... By George Lippard, Esq. ... *Philadelphia: The Author.* [1845.] 8vo, pp. 4, (2), 494. Plate. H. 41396

LIPPARD. Die Quäkerstadt und ihre Geheimnisse. Amerikanische Nachtseiten. [*Philadelphia.* 184–.] 4 vols., 8vo. + Zweite Auflage. *Leipzig: O. Wigand.* 1846. 4 vols., 8vo. + [Aus dem Englischen] von Frdr. Gerstäcker. Dritte Auflage. *Leipzig: Vereins-Verlagsbuchhandlung.* 1847. 4 vols., 8vo, pp. 297; 262; 236; 250. + Vierte Auflage. *Leipzig Costenoble.* 1851. 4 vols., 8vo. 41397

[LIPPARD.] The Quaker Soldier; or, the British in Philadelphia. An Historical Novel. *Philadelphia.* [1858.] 12mo, pp. xxi, 569. 41398

LIPPARD. Washington and his Generals; or Legends of the Revolution. By George Lippard. With a Biographical Sketch of the Author, by Rev. C. Chauncey Burr. *Philadelphia: G. B. Zieber & Co.* 1847. 8vo, pp. iv, 538, xxvii. + [*Ibid.* n. d.]

Also: Belle of Prairie Eden. ... *Philadelphia.* 1845. 8vo.—Legends of Mexico. ... *Philadelphia.* 1847. 8vo.—Mysteries and Miseries of Philadelphia. ... *Philadelphia:* 184–. 8vo.—The Midnight Queen; or, Leaves from New York Life. ... *New York: Garrett & Co.* [*about* 1850.] 8vo, pp. 110.—The Nazarene; or, the Last of the Washingtons. ... *Philadelphia: G. B. Zieber & Co.* 1846. 8vo, pp. 240. + *Philadelphia: T. B. Peterson and Brothers.* [1854.] 8vo, pp. 239.—Paul Ardenheim, the Monk of Wissahikon ... *Philadelphia: T. B. Peterson & Brothers.* 1848. 8vo, pp. 536. + [*Ibid.*] 1867.

LIPPINCOTT (J. B.) Lippincott's Magazine of Literature, Science, and Education. Volume I. *Philadelphia: J. B. Lippincott & Co.* 1868. 8vo, pp. 680. Continued. B. 41400

LIPPINCOTT. Lippincott's Universal Pronouncing Gazetteer. *See* Baldwin (T.) *and* Thomas (J.), Vol. I., No. 2924.

[LIPPINCOTT (Sarah J. Clarke).] A Forest Tragedy and other Tales. By Grace Greenwood ... . *Boston: Ticknor and Fields.* M DCCC LVI. 16mo, pp. (8), 343. H. 41401

[LIPPINCOTT.] Poems. By Grace Greenwood. New and Enlarged Edition. *Boston: Ticknor & Fields.* 1850. 16mo, pp. viii, 196. Portrait. + *Boston: Ticknor, Reed and Fields.* M DCCC LI. 12mo, pp. viii, 190. Portrait. + [*Ibid.*] M DCCC LIV. 12mo, pp. viii, 196. Portrait. H. + *Boston.* 1860. 16mo. 41402

[LIPPINCOTT.] Recollections of my Childhood, and other Poems. By Grace Greenwood. *Boston.* 1852. 16mo. 41403

[LIPPINCOTT.] Records of Five Years. By Grace Greenwood ... . *Boston: Ticknor and Fields.* 1867. 16mo, pp. vi, 222.

Many articles relate to the Civil War. *See also* [Clarke (Sara J.)], Vol. IV., No. 13461, and *add*, Fourth Edition. [*Ibid.*] M DCCC LIII. 12mo, pp. (2), viii, 406. + Second Series. [*Ibid.*] M DCCC LIV. 12mo, pp. vii, 378. Portrait. H.

LIPS (Michael A.) Statistik von Amerika, oder Versuch einer historisch-pragmatischen und raisonirenden Darstellung des politischen und bürgerlichen Zustandes der neuen Staaten-Körper von Amerika, von D. Alexander Lips. *Frankfurt.* 1828. 8vo. Map. P. 41405

LIPSCOMB (A. A.) A Life of Rev. Charles W. Jacobs. By A. A. Lipscomb. *Baltimore: Matchett & Neilson.* 1839. 18mo, pp. 96. 41406

Lipscomb. Our Country: its Danger and Duty. By Rev. A. A. Lipscomb. *New York.* 1854. 18mo, pp. 144. 41407

The Liquor Law; its Uses and Abuses. By a Member of the New York Bar. *New York.* 1855. 8vo. P. 41408

La Lira Argentina; ó coleccion de las piezas poéticas, dadas a luz en Buenos-Ayres durante la guerra de su independencia. *Buenos-Ayres.* 1824. 8vo, pp. vii, 515. C. 41409

Lisardi (J. F.) *See* Lizardi (J. F.)

Lisboa (B. da S.) Annaes do Rio do Janeiro, contendo a descoberta e conquista deste paiz, a fundação da cidade com a historia civil e ecclesiastica, até a chegada d'el Rei Dom João vi; alèm de noticias topographicas, zoologicas, e botanicas. Por Balthazar da Silva Lisboa. *Rio de Janeiro: Seignot-Plancher et Cie.* 1834–35. 8 vols., 8vo. 41410

Lisboa (D.) Vida del P. Fr. Diego Romero, por Fr. Diego de Lisboa. *Mexico.* 1684. 4to. 41411

Lisboa (J. F.) Obras de João Francisco Lisboa, precedidas de uma noticia biographica por Antonio Henriques Leal. *San Luiz.* 1865–66. 3 vols., 4to, pp. cciv, 518; 520; 580. 41412

Lisboa (Jose Ant.) Reflexões sobre o Banco do Brasil. *Rio Janeiro.* 1821. 4to. 41413

Lisboa (J. da S.) Observações sobre o commercio franco no Brasil. Por José da Silva Lisboa. *Rio de Janeiro: Imp. Regia.* 1808. 2 vols., 4to. 41414

Lisboa y Lyon (D. de L.) Vida de D. Fernando Arias de Ugarte, arzobispo que murio de Lima, por D. Diego Lopez de Lisboa y Leon. *Lima.* 1638. 41415

Lisiansky (U.) A Voyage round the World, in the Years 1803, 4, 5, & 6; performed, by order of His Imperial Majesty Alexander the First, Emperor of Russia, in the Ship Neva. By Urey Lisiansky .... *London: John Booth.* 1814. 4to, pp. xxi, (2), 388. 14 Maps and Plates. BA., C., S. 41416

Lisiansky accompanied Krusenstern as far as the Sandwich Islands, when they parted company, from whence this work may be considered as new ground. There is of course a Russian edition.

L'Isle (J. N. de). Erklärung der Charte von den Neuen Entdeckungen welche gegen Norden des Süder-Meers durch den Herrn von L'Isle .... *Berlin: A. Haude.* 1753. 16mo, pp. 48.

A German version of *our* No. 35253, Vol. ix., which see, and for collation *read* pp. (2), 18. Map. *See also* No. 35254.

L'Isle. Schreiben eines Russischen Officiers von der Flotte an einen Herrn des Hofes, die Charte der neuen Entdeckungen gegen Norden des Süder-Meers .... *Berlin: A. Haude* ... [175–.] 16mo, pp. 54. H. 41418

[Lisle (H. M.)] Milton Hill; a Poem. ... *Boston: Printed by E. Lincoln.* 1803. 4to, pp. 15. BA., H. 41419

Lisle. An Oration, delivered at Hingham, ... on ... the 22d of February, 1800, the Anniversary of the Birth, and the Day appointed by the Government of the United States, for Public National Mourning, for the Death of ... General George Washington. By Henry Maurice Lisle .... *Boston: Printed by John Russell.* 1800. 8vo, pp. 22. B., BA., S. 41420

Also: An Address ... before the Grand Lodge of Massachusetts, ... December 27th, A.L. 5805 .... *Boston: Printed by Brothers Russell and Cutler.* 1805. 8vo, pp. 23. B. — An Address ... in Roxbury, by Request of the Charitable Society ... Sept. 19, 1808 .... *Boston: Munroe* ... 1808. 8vo, pp. 18, (2). — An Oration ... at Dorchester, on the 24th of June, A.L. 5807. ... *Boston: Printed by Belcher and Armstrong.* 1807. 8vo, pp. 15. BA., W.

Lisle (J. G. S.) The Life of Major J. G. Semple Lisle; containing a Faithful Narrative of his alternate vicissitudes of Splendour and Misfortune. *London.* 1799. 8vo. Portrait. + Second Edition. *London.* 1800. 8vo. 41421

Includes his adventures in South America, description of the Province of Rio Grande, etc.

Lisle (S.) Sermon before the Society for the Propagation of the Gospel in Foreign Parts, 1747. By the Rt. Rev. Samuel Bishop of St. Asaph. *London.* 1748. 8vo, pp. 84. M. 41422

Lislet (L. M.). *See* Louisiana—*Laws.*

Lisman (J. Æ.) Verslag van eene reis naar de rivier Marowijne en naar het etablissement Mana in fransch-Guyana. ... *Paramaribo.* 1849. 8vo. 41423

Lisman. Verslag van het onderzoek naar den toestand van het etablissement der Europesche kolonisatie te Groningen aan de Saramacca. ... *Paramaribo.* 1848. 8vo. 41424

Lisperguer (Mathias). Compendio Historial de la Vida de la Gloriosa S. Rita de Casia; Sermon Panegyrico en la Primera Solemne Festividad, que se hizo en el Convento Grand de Lima de el Orden de N. Padre San Augustin. *Lima, por Joseph Contreras.* 1699. 4to. 41425

Lissante (Pedro). Discurso del Tercer Aniversario de la Apertura del Instituto de Jalisco. ... *Guadalajara.* 1830. 8vo. 41426

List (F.) Outlines of American Political Economy, in a Series of Letters addressed by Frederick List, Esq. ... to Charles J. Ingersoll, Esq. ... To which is added The Celebrated Letters of Mr. Jefferson to Benjamin Austin, and of Mr. Madison .... *Philadelphia: Printed by Samuel Parker.* 1827. 8vo, pp. 40. BA. + Appendix ... *Philadelphia.* 1827. 8vo, pp. 13. P. 41427

Also: Professor List's Speech ... at the Philadelphia Manufacturers' Dinner, Nov. 3. [n. p. n. d.] 8vo, pp. 11. — Account of the Dinner given to Professor List, by the Pennsylvania Society for the Encouragement of Manufactures ... at Philadelphia, Nov. 3, 1827. [*Philadelphia.* 1827.] 8vo, pp. 15. BA.

List of Accounts required from the Collectors and Comptrollers in the Plantations. *London.* 1782. Folio, pp. xxxii. M.

A List of all the Officers of the Army; to which are likewise added the Officers of the Militia Forces, and of the Fensibles and Provincial Regiments in Great Britain, for the Year 1780. *London: J. Millan.* 1780. 8vo. Continued. 41429

This list gives the names of officers serving in the American colonies.

A List of Copies of Charters, from the Commissioners for Trade and Plantations, Presented to the Honourable the House of Commons, in Pursuance of their Address to His Majesty, of the 25th of April 1740. viz. Maryland Charter, granted by King Charles i. in the 8th Year of His Reign. Connecticut Charter, granted by King Charles ii. in the 14th Year of His Reign. Rhode-Island Charter, granted by King Charles ii. in the 15th Year of His Reign. Pensylvania Charter, granted by King Charles ii. in the 33d Year of His Reign. Massachusets Bay Charter, granted by King William and Queen Mary, in the 3d Year of Their Reign. Georgia Charter, granted by His present Majesty, in the 5th Year of His Reign. *London: Printed in the Year* M.DCC.XLI. Folio, pp. (2), 12, 10, 14, 12, 21, 18. H.

List of Diplomatic and Consular Officers of the United States ... *Washington.* 1862. 8vo. Continued annually. C. 41431

A List of Duties payable upon every Article imported into the United States of America .... *Birmingham: J. Belcher.* 1794. 12mo. 41432

A List of General and Staff Officers On the Establishment in North-America, within the Colonies laying on the Atlantic Ocean, from Nova-Scotia to West-Florida, inclusive. [n. p. n. d.] 8vo, pp. 54. P. 41433

An English official document; no title-page, but probably printed in 1778 at Philadelphia. It includes the Hessian troops.

A List of General Officers, nominated to the United States Senate during the Session of July, 1861, and January 1862. *Confidential, April* 7, 1862. 8vo, pp. 10. 41434

List of Inn-Keepers on the Road from Augusta (Ga.) to New York; and also from Boston to New York, with the distances from each. *New York.* 1814. 18mo. 41435

List of Light-Houses. *See* Light Houses, No. 41046.

List of Merchant Vessels of the United States, with the Official Numbers and Signal Letters awarded them, by the Chief of the Bureau of Statistics ... *Washington.* 1869. 8vo. Cont'd.

List of Ministers and Consuls and other Diplomatic and Commercial Agents of the United States in Foreign Countries, September 24, 1835. [n. p. n. d.] 8vo, pp. 17. 41437

A List of Numbers that Came up Prizes in the Second Class of the Newark Land and Cash Lottery, drawn at Christiana-Bridge, March 23. 1771. [n. p. n. d.] Folio, 1 leaf. P. 41438

List of Officers of the Navy and Marine Corps, who between December 1, 1860, and December 1, 1863, left the Service. *Washington.* 1863. 8vo, pp. 12. 41439

Senate Ex. Doc., No. 3, 38th Cong., 1st Session.

List of Officers who marched with the Army under the Command of Maj. Gen. Winfield Scott, from Puebla upon the City of Mexico, August, 1847. *Mexico.* 1848. 4to. C. 41440

A List of Officers. *See* Illinois, Vol. ix., No. 34301.

List of Patents. *See* Patents.

List of Post-Offices. *See* Post-Office.

List of Prices of the Journeymen House-Carpenters of the City of New York. *New York.* 1810. 8vo, pp. 44. 41441

List of Private Claims brought before the Senate, from the Commencement of the 14th to the Close of the 30th Congress. ... *Washington.* 1849. 8vo. C. 41442

... Alphabetical List of Private Claims ... presented to the House of Representatives, from the First to the Thirty-First Congress .... *Washington.* 1853. 3 vols., 4to, pp. (4), 782; (4), 620; (4), 721. B. 41443

List of Soldiers (Prisoners of War) belonging to Pennsylvania Regiments, who died at the Military Prison at Andersonville, Ga., ... 1864, to ... 1865. [*Philadelphia.* 1865.] 4to, pp. 24.

List of the Agricultural, Horticultural, and Pomological Societies, Farmers' Clubs, &c., on the Books of the Department of Agriculture, July 1, 1870. ... *Washington.* 1870. 8vo.

A List of the American Navy. ... *Boston: A. J. Allen.* [n. d.] 18mo. 41446

A List of the Delegates who attended the Congress held at Philadelphia, May 10, 1775, with Journal of their Proceedings from May 10 to July 31, 1775. *Philadelphia.* 1775. 8vo, pp. 138. 41447

A List of the Flag-Officers of his Majesty's Fleet. *London.* 1776. 16mo. 41448

Includes the names of officers who served in America.

List of the Fortunate Numbers drawn in the Washington Hotel Lottery. *Boston: Young and Nims.* MDCCXCIV. 8vo, pp. 523. 41449

A List of the General and Field Officers as they rank in the Army, of the Officers in the several Regiments of Horse, Dragoons and Foot, on the British and Irish Establishments; with the Dates of their Commissions, etc.; the Governors, Lieut.-Governors of His Majesty's Government at Home and Abroad. *London.* [1758.] 8vo. Continued annually. 41450

Includes the names and appointments of the officers who served in the French and Revolutionary War in America.

A List of the General and Staff Officers, and of the Officers in the several Regiments serving in North America, under the Command of His Excellency General Sir William Howe, K.B.

with the Dates of their Commissions as they rank in each Corps and in the Army. *New York: Printed by Macdonald and Cameron in Water Street.* 1777. 8vo, pp. 46. + *Philadelphia.* 1778. 8vo, pp. 56. C. 41451

See also Clinton (H.), No. 13755, Vol. iv.

A List of the Members of the Assembly, An Awe-ful Po'm by the Awe-thur the Capt'n. *Albany.* 1864. 8vo. 41452

List of the Minority in the House of Commons, who voted against the Bill to Repeal the American Stamp Act. *A Paris: Chez J. W., Imprimeur.* 1766. 8vo, pp. 8. 41453

A List of the Numbers that came out Prizes in the Second Class of the American Flint Glass Manufactory, Pettie's-Island Cash Lottery. [*Philadelphia, Sep.* 13, 1773.] Folio, 1 leaf. P.

List of the Numbers that Came up Prizes in the Third Class of the Newark Land and Cash Lottery, in the County of New-Castle upon Delaware, which was drawn the Fourth of June, 1773. [n. p. n. d.] Folio, 1 leaf. P. 41455

A List of the Officers of the Army serving in North America, under the Command of His Excellency General Sir Guy Carleton, K.B.; with the Dates of their Commissions, as they rank in each Corps and in the Army. For the year 1783. [Corrected to the 4th June, per Appendix.] *New York: James Rivington.* MDCCLXXXIII. 8vo, pp. 98, iv. 41456

Known as "Rivington's Army List." The New York Historical Society has a copy with manuscript additions.

A List of the Presbyteries, Ministers, Probationers, and Congregations, both Settled and Vacant, within the Bounds of the Synod of New York and Philadelphia, made in the year, 1788; ... The Presbyteries are placed in order in which they lye from New York to Georgia inclusive. *Philadelphia: Francis Bailey.* 1788. 8vo. 41457

A List of the Prize Numbers that came up Prizes in Bile's-Island Lottery, for the Benefit of a Place of Worship in Borden-Town. [*Philadelphia: Printed by Franklin & Hall.* 1755.] Folio, 1 leaf. P. 41458

A List of the Reported Dangers to Navigation in the Pacific Ocean, whose Positions are doubtful, or not found on the Charts in general Use. Compiled at the Bureau of Navigation, Navy Department, Washington City. *Washington.* 1866. 8vo, pp. 192. 41459

A List of those that have been Executed for the Late Rebellion in Virginia, by Sir William Berkeley, Governor of the Colony. Copied from the Original Manuscript, ... by Robert Greenhow. *Washington: Printed by Peter Force.* 1835. 8vo, pp. 4. 41460

Forms No. 10 of "Force's Tracts," Vol. i.

A List of those Tories. *See* Black List, Vol. ii., No. 5679.

A List of Two Hundred Indian Names. *See* [De Kay (J. E.)]

List of Vacancies in the Army, 1815–33. [n. p. n. d.] 12mo. B. 41461

List of Vessels. *See* [Dahlgren (J. A.)], Vol. v., No. 18277.

List of Volunteers from Passaic and Bergen Counties. *Paterson, N. J.: Van Derhoven & Holms.* 1862. 24mo, pp. 46. H.

Lista de los Sres. que han contribuido en las Islas de Cuba y de Puerto-Rico, en favor de los habitantes de la Guadalupe, víctimas del terremoto del 8 de febrero de 1843. *Habana: Imprenta del Gobierno por S. M.* 1844. 32mo, pp. (2), 77. B. 41463

Liste Chronologique. *See* Canada, Vol. iii., No. 10510.

Liston (J. K.) Niagara Falls: A Poem ... By James K. Liston. *Toronto.* 1852. 12mo. 41464

Lists of Distances; compiled for the Information and Guidance of Officers doing Duty in the Quartermaster's Department, in making Payments for Mileage. *Washington.* 1868. 12mo, pp. 132. C. 41465

Litchfield (H[arvey] T.) List of the Property of H. T. Litchfield destroyed by Fire ... East Boston, on the First Day of July, 1866. *Boston: Rockwell and Rollins, Printers.* 1866. 8vo, pp. 38. H. 41466

Litchfield (P.) A Sermon, ... before the Massachusetts Missionary Society ... in Boston, May 28, 1805. By Paul Litchfield, A.M. ... *Salem: Printed by Joshua Cushing.* 1805. 8vo, pp. 24. BA. 41467

Litchfield (*Bishop of*). *See* [Hurd (R.)], Vol. ix., 33991.

Litchfield, *Conn.* Articles of Association, By-Laws, etc., of the Agricultural Society, established at Litchfield, February 11, 1818. *Litchfield.* 1818. 8vo. N. 41468

Constitution of the Associated Churches of Litchfield, Conn. *Litchfield.* 1829. 12mo, pp. 24. 41469

Litchfield County Centennial Celebration, held at Litchfield, Conn., 13th and 14th of August, 1851. *Hartford: Edwin Hunt.* 1851. 8vo, pp. 212. Plate. BA., C. 41470

Manual of the ... Litchfield South Consociation. 1855. 12mo. 41471

Proceedings of the North and South Consociations of Litchfield County. Ct., In Convention at Litchfield, July 7 and 8, 1852, to commemorate the Centennial Anniversary of their Primitive Organization. *Hartford: Press of Case, Tiffany and Company.* 1852. 8vo, pp. 154. B. 41472

Report of the Registrar of Litchfield South Association ... for 1863. *Hartford: Press of Case* ... 1864. 8vo, pp. 7, (1). Cont'd.

The Sixth of August, or the Litchfield Festival. An Address to the People of Connecticut. *Hartford.* 1806. 8vo. 41474

A Literal Reprint of the Bay Psalm Book. *See* Psalms.

Literary and Critical Remarks, on sundry eminent Divines and Philosophers, of the Last and Present Age. Particularly Sir Walter Raleigh .... With an Appendix .... *London: B. Crosby.* [n. d.] 8vo, pp. (2), xvi, 489. B. 41475

Literary and Evangelical Magazine. *Richmond, Va.* 1819. 8vo. Continued. 41476

Literary and Historical Society of Quebec. *See* Quebec.

Literary and Philosophical Repertory ... *Middlebury, Vt.* 1812–1814. 2 vols., 8vo. S. 41477

Literary and Philosophical Society. *See* New York.

The Literary and Scientific Repository and Critical Review. No. 1. Published Quarterly. *New York: Wiley & Halsted, July,* 1820. 8vo, pp. iv, 280. Portrait. B. 41478

Edited by C. K. Gardner. Continued to four or more volumes.

The Literary and Theological Review. Conducted by Leonard Woods, Jun. Vol. 1. *New-York: D. Appleton & Co.* 1834. 8vo, pp. 702. Continued. BA. 41479

Literary Cabinet. ... Vol. I. No. I. Yale College, November 15, 1806, to October 31, 1807. [*New-Haven: For the Editors.* 1806.] 8vo, pp. 160. Continued. B. 41480

The Literary Companion. Edited by Howard, Jun. Vol. I. *New York: G. and J. Huntly.* 1821. 8vo, pp. 208. 41481

The Literary Focus. A Monthly Periodical. Edited and Published by the Erodeephian and Union Literary Societies of Miami University. Vol. I. *Oxford, Ohio.* 1827–28. 8vo.

The Literary Garland. *New York.* 1838–40. 2 vols., 8vo.

The Literary Garland, a Monthly Magazine, devoted to the Advancement of General Literature. 1838–1842. 4 vols., 8vo. + New Series, a Monthly Magazine of Tales, Sketches, Poetry, Music, Engravings. *Montreal: John Lovell and John Gibson.* 1843–1851. 9 vols., 8vo. 41484

This periodical was, for a time, the only literary magazine in the English language, published in British North America. Its contributions were chiefly original; and in numerous instances from the pens of esteemed Canadian writers. The editor, for the first thirteen years, was Mr. John Gibson, the associate publisher, after whose decease it was discontinued.

The Literary Gazette and American Athenæum. *New-York: Dixon & Sickles, Printers.* 1827. 2 vols., 4to. 41485

The Literary Gazette: or, Journal of Criticism, Science, and the Arts, being a Collection of Original and Selected Essays. January 6 to December 29, 1821. *Philadelphia.* 1822. 4to, pp. 830, (2). C., P. 41486

A third series of the Analectic Magazine; all that was published.

The Literary Journal. Vol. I. Latin School. *Boston.* 1829. 8vo. BA. 41487

The Literary Journal, or Universal Review of Literature, Domestic and Foreign, for the Year 1805. *Philadelphia.* 1805. 4to. 41488

For a curious account of George Washington, *see* page 1078.

The Literary Journal, and Weekly Register of Science and the Arts. Edited by Albert G. Greene. Vol. I. *Providence.* 1833–34. 4to. 41489

The Literary Magazine, and American Register. ... From October, 1803, to the Year 1808. Vol. I. *Philadelphia: John Conrad, & Co.* 1803. 8vo, pp. 480. BA. 41490

Edited by Charles B. Brown. Continued to eight or more volumes.

The Literary Magazine and British Review for 1788. Vol. I. *London: For the Proprietors.* 1788. 8vo, pp. (4), 480, (6). BA.

Includes several articles on American topics; continued to twelve or more volumes.

The Literary Miscellany ... Published Quarterly. *Cambridge: William Hilliard.* 1805–1806. 2 vols., 8vo, pp. (2), 402, (2); (2), 406, (2). Portrait. B., BA. 41492

By the Phi Beta Kappa Society of Harvard College.

The Literary Miscellany; or, Monthly Review ... *New York.* 1811. 12mo. N. 41493

Edited by Charles N. Baldwin.

The Literary Museum or Monthly Magazine. *Philadelphia.* 1797. 8vo. 41494

The Literary Panorama. A Review of Books, Register of Events, Magazine of Varieties. ... *London: C. Taylor.* 1807–8. 3 vols., 8vo. Maps. BA. 41495

Continued as "The Literary Panorama and National Register." *London.* 18—. 8vo. + *Boston, reprinted.* 1816. 8vo Embodies much interesting matter relative to America, particularly the War of 1812–14.

Literary Picture Gallery, and Admonitory Epistles to the Visitors of Ballston Spa. *Ballston Spa.* 1808. 12mo. 41496

Literary Record and Journal of the Linnæan Association of Pennsylvania College. *Gettysburg.* 1844–48. 4 vols., 8vo.

The Literary Union: a Journal of Progress in Literature and Education, Religion and Politics, Science and Agriculture ... . Vol. I. April 7–December 29, 1849. *Syracuse.* 1849. 4to. + New Series. Vol. I. January–July, 1850. *Syracuse.* 1850. 8vo. Continued. 41498

The Literary World. A Gazette for Authors, Readers, and Publishers. Edited by C. F. Hoffman. Vol. I. *New-York: Osgood & Co.* 1847. 4to, pp. v, 624. Continued. BA. 41499

The first volume, from Feb. 6, 1847, to July 31, was edited by C. T. Hoffmann, all the others by E. A. and G. L. Duyckinck.

The Literary World. ... No. I. Vol. I. *Boston.* 1870. 4to, pp. 16. Continued. B. 41500

LITKE (Tedor). *See* Lutke (Frederic).

LITTELL (E.) Littell's Living Age; conducted by E. Littell. Vol. I. ... *Boston: T. H. Carter & Company.* 1844. 8vo, pp. (2), iv, 766. Continued. B. 41501

LITTELL (J.) Family Records: or Genealogies of the First Settlers of Passaic Valley, (and vicinity,) above Chatham—with their Ancestors and Descendants, as far as can now be ascertained. By John Littell. ... *Feltville, N. J.: David Felt and Co.* 1851. 8vo, pp. (6), 504, (8). Plate. B. 41502

The woodcut title-page is dated 1852.

L[ITTELL] (J[ohn] S.) The Clay Minstrel; or, National Songster. To which is prefixed a Sketch of ... Henry Clay. *Philadelphia: Turner & Fisher.* 1842. 18mo, pp. 188. Plate.

See also Clay (H.), Vol. IV., No. 13555.

LITTELL [Squier]. Memoir of Francis West, M.D., read by Dr. Littell before the College of Physicians, December 2, 1868. [*Philadelphia.* n. d.] 8vo, pp. 13. B. 41504

LITTELL (W.) A Lecture ... at Frankfort, Ky. January 15th, 1818. By William Littell, Esq. L.L.D. on the Necessity of establishing Law Colleges in the United States. *Frankfort, Ky.: Printed by Bledsoe & Farnham.* 1818. 8vo, pp. 22. BA.

LITTELL. Political Transactions in and concerning Kentucky, from the First Settlement thereof, until it became an Independent State, in June, 1792. By William Littell, Esq. *Frankfort (K.): Press of William Hunter* ... 1806. 8vo, pp. 81, Appendix, 66. BA., S. 41506

A very rare pamphlet. *See also* Kentucky.

Litteræ Annuæ Societatis Jesu ad Patres et Fratres ejusdem Societatis. *Romæ.* 1581. 18mo. Continued. S. 41507

These letters of the Jesuits printed annually, and at various places, contain much valuable, important, and authentic information relative to the proceedings of the Society, and relate to Brazil, Mexico, Paraguay, Peru, Quito, etc. The volume 1613–14 was reprinted at *Albany*, 1871, 12mo. We enumerate below a few titles at greater length:

Annve Litteræ Societatis Iesv. *Dilingæ.* [n. d.] 16mo.

Relates to Brazil and South America.

Litterae Societatis Iesv Dvorvm Annorvm M.D.LXXXVI et M.D.LXXXVII Ad Patres et Fratres eiusdem Societatis. *Romæ In Collegio eiusdem Societatis.* M.D.LXXXIX. Sm. 8vo, pp. (4), 592.

Provincia Mexicana et Peru, pp. 471–528. *See also* our Vol. I., No. 1607.

La Littérature Canadienne de 1850 a 1860. Publiée par la Direction du "Foyer Canadien." Deuxième Édition. *Quebec: Desbarats et Derbishire.* 1863–64. 2 vols., 8vo, pp. 390; 389.

LITTLE (C.) ... A Discourse ... Thanksgiving, November 24th, 1864. By Rev. Charles Little ... . *New Haven: Printed by William H. Stanley.* 1864. 8vo, pp. 14. B. 41511

LITTLE (G.) American Cruiser. By George Little. *Boston: W. J. Reynolds & Co.* 1847. 12mo, pp. 390. Plates. C.

Also: The American Cruiser's Own Book. ... *New York.* 1851. 12mo.

LITTLE. Life on the Ocean; or, Twenty Years at Sea: ... By George Little ... . *Baltimore: Armstrong & Berry.* 1843. 12mo, pp. 395. Plate. C. + Second Edition. *Boston: Waite, Peirce, and Company.* 1844. 12mo, pp. 395. + *Boston.* 1846.

LITTLE (G. B.) Eulogy on Zachary Taylor, by Rev. George B. Little ... July 19, 1850. ... *Bangor: Smith & Sayward, Printers.* 1850. 8vo, pp. 16. H. 41514

LITTLE. A Memorial of Closing Scenes in the Life of Rev. George B. Little. ... *Riverside Press, Printed by H. O. Houghton, Cambridge.* 1861. 8vo, pp. 171. Portrait. B., BA. + *Boston: Massachusetts Sunday School Society.* 1865. 12mo, pp. 262. Port.

Also: The Kingdom of God. ... A Sermon at Bath, June 24, 1857, before the Maine Missionary Society, at its 50th Anniversary. ... *Augusta.* [n. d.] 8vo, pp. 64.

LITTLE (G. P.) The Fireman's Own Book: Containing Accounts of Fires throughout the United States, as well as other Countries; Remarkable Escapes, Heroic Conduct of Firemen in Cases of Danger, and Accounts of Firemen who have Lost their Lives while on Duty. By George P. Little. *New York.* 1860. 8vo. 41516

LITTLE (J.) Twenty-Seventh New Year's Sermon preached in the Congregational Church, Granville, Ohio, 1854. By Rev. Jacob Little. *Granville.* 1854. 8vo. 41517

LITTLE (J.) Obedience to Law. A Sermon ... By Rev. John Little. *New York.* 1851. 8vo. 41518

LITTLE (J. A.) The Autobiography of a New Churchman; or Incidents and Observations connected with the Life of John A. Little. *Philadelphia.* 1852. 12mo, pp. 258. S. 41519

LITTLE (J. P.) Richmond, the Capital of Virginia: its History. By Dr. J. P. Little. *Richmond.* 1851. 8vo, pp. 102.

Enlarged from the "Southern Literary Messenger."

[LITTLE (Josiah).] To the Members of the ... General Court of ... Massachusetts. [*Boston.* 1823.] 8vo, pp. 31. H.

A memorial respecting lands in Bakerstown.

LITTLE (L. J.) A Mother's Peace Offering to American Houses; or the Martyr of the Nineteenth Century. By Mrs. L. J. Little. *New York.* 1861. 12mo. 41522

[LITTLE (Otis).] State of Trade in the Northern Colonies considered; with An Account of their Produce, And a Particular Description of Nova Scotia. *London: G. Woodfall.* M.DCC.XLVIII. 8vo, pp. viii, 84. + *London, Printed,* 1748. *Boston Reprinted ... by Thomas Fleet* ... 1749. 8vo, pp. 43. BA.

LITTLE (R.) A Funeral Sermon on the Death of John Adams and Thomas Jefferson, ... July 16, 1826, in ... Washington City. By Robert Little. *Washington.* 1826. 8vo, pp. 22.

Also: The Duty of Public Usefulness. A Sermon ... in ... Washington ... February 16, 1823. ... *Washington: Pishey Thompson.* 1823. 8vo, pp. 20.—Ignorance, the Parent of Crime. A Sermon ... Death of William Seaver, Who was murdered ... July 6, 1821. ... *Washington: Printed by W. Cooper.* 1821. 8vo, pp. 20. BA.—The National Anniversary. In Two Sermons ... July 4th, 1824 ... in ... Washington ... *Washington: Way & Gideon, Printers.* 1824. 8vo, pp. 28. BA.

LITTLE (S. L.) The Branded Hand. A Dramatic Sketch, commemorative of the Tragedies at the South in the Winter of 1844–45. By Sophia L. Little. *Pawtucket.* 1845. 8vo, pp. 46.

LITTLE. Thrice through the Furnace. A Tale of the Times of the Iron Hoof. By Mrs. Sophia L. Little. *Pawtucket, R. I.: A. W. Pearce.* 1852. 12mo, pp. 190. 41526

LITTLE (W.) The Interesting Trials of the Pirates, for the Murder of William Little, Captain of the Ship American Eagle. *Newburyport.* [1796.] 12mo, pp. 59. BA. 41527

LITTLE (W.) ... The Trial of Doctor William Little ... for an Assault and Battery ... upon ... his ... Wife, Mrs. Jane Little, a Black Lady. ... The Second Edition. *New York: For the Purchasers.* 1808. 8vo, pp. 16. BA. 41528

LITTLE (W.) The History of Warren; a Mountain Hamlet, located among the White Hills of New Hampshire. By William Little. *Concord.* 1854. 12mo. + *Manchester (N. H.): William E. Moore, Printer.* 1870. 8vo, pp. 592. Plates and Portraits.

Also: Address ... at the Centennial Celebration of ... Warren, N. H. ... July 14, 1863. ... *Manchester: For the Town.* 1863. 8vo, pp. 18. H.

Little Bit of a Tid-Re-I; or, a Chorus for the Times. [By Roderick Roundelay. n. p. n. d.] 8vo. 41530

The Little Blue Book. *See* [Dimmick (R. A.)], Vol. V.

A Little Book for Little Children. *Boston.* 1702. 8vo, pp. 94.

This rare piece is one of the earliest of its kind printed in America.

LITTLE BRITAIN, *N. Y.* Centennial Memorials of the Associate Reformed Presbyterian Church. *New York.* 1859. 12mo.

LITTLE FALLS, *N. Y.* An Act Reincorporating the Village of Little Falls by the Name of Rockton. *Rockton.* 1850. 8vo, pp. 22. + The same as amended. *Little-Falls.* 1855. 8vo, pp. 24. S. 41533

Catalogue of the ... Academy at Little Falls, Herkimer County, N. Y. for ... 1846. *Little Falls, N. Y.: J. M. Lyon's Press* ... 1846. 8vo, pp. 20. B. 41534

Little Mac Campaign Songster. *New York: T. R. Dawley.* 1864. 16mo, pp. 72. 41535

LITTLE MIAMI, *O.* Annual Report of the Directors of the Little Miami Railroad Company for 1842. *Cincinnati.* 1842. 8vo. Continued. 41536

Annual Reports of the Directors of the Little Miami Railroad Company for the Years 1843 ... 1848. *Cincinnati: Re-printed by E. Shepard.* 1849. 8vo, pp. 87, (1). B. 41537

In the first five reports the paging is continuous.

The Little Osage Captive. An Authentic Narrative; to which are added some Interesting Letters, written by Indians. *York.* 1824. 18mo, pp. 182. 41538

A Little | Olive Leaf | Put in the Mouth of that | (So Called) | Noah's Dove, | And sent Home again to let her Master know | That the Waters are abated from off the face | of the Ground, | And that for the Sake of | Jesus Christ, | Whose Servant to the End of my Life I shall | Endeavour To Be. | *Printed and Sold by William Bradford at the Sign of the Bible* | *in New-York,* 1704. | 4to, pp. (4), 31. 41539

The first leaf consists of Texts of Scripture. It relates to Theophilus Brabourn and the Sabbath, and is of extreme rarity.

The Little Peace-maker, 1674. *See* [Morton (Charles)].

Little Pretty Pocket-Book ... First Worcester Edition. *Worcester: Isaiah Thomas.* 1787. 32mo. 41540

The Little Rebel. *Boston: J. E. Tilton & Co.* 1864. 18mo, pp. 295. 3 Plates. C. 41541

The Little Republic. Original Articles, by Various Hands. Edited by Mrs. T. P. Smith. *New York: Wiley & Putnam.* 1848. Sq. 18mo, pp. (2), vi, 228. Plate. C. 41542

LITTLE ROCK, *Ark.* Annual Report of the President of the Little Rock and Fort Smith Railroad Company, made to the Governor; including the Report of the Special Agent. *Little Rock, State of Arkansas.* 1866. 8vo, pp. 96. C. 41543

LITTLE SCHUYLKILL, *Pa.* Report of the President and Managers of the Little Schuylkill and Susquehanna Railroad Company. *Philadelphia.* 1838. 8vo. 41544

Report of the Little Schuylkill Navigation Railroad and Coal Company, January 8, 1855. *Philadelphia: John C. Clark & Son, Printers.* 1855. 8vo, pp. 8. Continued. H. 41545

LITTLEJOHN (A.) The Examination of Rev. Augustus Littlejohn ... at Almond, Allegany Co., N. Y., Feb. 2, 1841, for an alleged Assault and Battery ... and Trial before the Presbytery for Licentious Conduct. ... *Bath.* 1841. 8vo. 41546

LITTLEJOHN [F. J.] The Sovereign Right of Michigan to the Mines and Minerals within her borders. Report: By Mr. Littlejohn ... . [n. p. n. d.] 8vo, pp. 16. H. 41547

Legislature of 1846, Sen. Doc. No. 22.

LITTLEJOHN *vs.* GREELEY. The Case of De Witt C. Littlejohn against Horace Greeley, tried at the Oswego Term of the Supreme Court of the State of New York, at Pulaski; Sept. 10–13, 1861, before his Honor, William J. Bacon. ... Phonographically reported by James L. Crosby. *New York.* 1861. 8vo, pp. 56. H. 41548

LITTLEPAGE (L.) Answer to a Pamphlet, containing the Correspondence between The Honorable John Jay, ... and Lewis Littlepage, Esquire, Of Virginia ... . *New-York: Francis Childs.* [1786.] 4to, pp. 28. 41549

Very severe on Mr. Jay. *See our* Vol. IX., No. 35833.

LITTLETON (Mark), *pseudon.* *See* [Kennedy (J. P.)], Vol. IX.

LITTLETON, *N. H.* Assessors' Report of the Valuation and Taxes of ... Littleton for ... 1870. *Boston: Alfred Mudge & Son, Printers.* 1870. 8vo, pp. 46, (1), 80. B. 41550

Report of the School Committee ... 1849–50. *Groton: Geo. H. Brown, Printer.* 1850. 12mo, pp. (2), 11. Continued. H.

Report of the Selectmen ... of ... Littleton, for ... 1852. [n. p. n. d.] Folio, 1 leaf. + For ... 1868. *Boston: Alfred Mudge* ... 1868. 8vo, pp. 14. Continued. B. 41552

LITTON (A.) *See* Missouri—*Geology.*

A | Liturgy, | collected principally from the | Book of Common Prayer, | for the use of the | First Episcopal Church | in | Boston; | together with the | Psalter, or Psalms | of | David. | *Boston,* | *Printed by Peter Edes* ... MDCCLXXXV. | 8vo, 4 leaves, A to Bbb in fours.

Compiled by the Rev. James Freeman of Boston.

Liturgy for ... Warren Street Chapel in Boston ... . *Boston: Dutton and Wentworth, Printers.* 1840. 8vo, pp. vi, (1), 509.

Liturgy ... for ... King's Chapel, Boston. ... Second Edition. *Boston: Printed by Joshua Belcher.* 1811. 8vo, pp. (8), 360. B.

LIVERMORE (A. A.) ... A Discourse ... on the ... Death of Hon. John Quincy Adams ... March 5, 1848. By A. A. Livermore. ... *Keene: Printed by J. W. Prentiss & Co.* 1848. 8vo, pp. 19. BA. 41556

LIVERMORE. Discourses, by Abiel Abbot Livermore ... . *Boston: D. C. Colesworthy.* 1857. 12mo, pp. viii, 426. H.

LIVERMORE. The War with Mexico Reviewed. By Abiel Abbot Livermore. *Boston: American Peace Society.* 1850. 8vo, pp. xii, 310. BA. 41558

Also: ... A Discourse ... at the Dedication of the Unitarian Meeting-House in Windsor, Vt. ... December 9, 1846. ... *Boston: Wm. Crosby and H. P. Nichols.* 1847. 8vo, pp. 28.— ... A Discourse ... at the Installation of Rev. John Jay Putnam ... in Bolton, Mass. Sept. 26, 1849. ... *Keene, N. H.: Printed by J. W. Prentiss & Co.* 1849. 8vo, pp. 18. H.—A Discourse ... on Thanksgiving Day, Dec. 7, 1837, in ... Keene, N. H. ... *Keene: John Prentiss.* 1837. 8vo, pp. 19.— ... A Sermon ... at the Ordination of James Thurston ... . *Windsor: Printed by Tracy and Severance.* 1838. 8vo, pp. 16.— ... A Sermon preached ... in Keene ... Dec. 26, 1847. ... *Keene: Printed by J. W. Prentiss & Co.* 1848. 12mo, pp. 12. H. *See also* Livermore (J.), No. 41575, *infra.*

LIVERMORE (A.) The Trial of Alpheus Livermore and Samuel Angier, ... for the Murder of Nicholas John Crevay, an Indian, committed November 23, 1813. Containing the Evidence at large ... . *Boston: Watson & Bangs.* 1813. 8vo, pp. 50.

[LIVERMORE (C. W.)] ... Loss of the Sparrow-Hawk in 1626. ... Recent Discovery of the Wreck. *Boston: Printed by Alfred Mudge & Son.* 1865. 12mo, pp. 38. H. 41560

LIVERMORE (D.) The ... Almanack, for ... 1797. ... By Daniel Livermore. ... *Hallowell: The Author.* [n. d.] 12mo, pp. (24). H. 41561

LIVERMORE (E. St. L.) An Oration, in Commemoration of the Dissolution of the Political Union between the United States ... and France. Delivered on the Seventeenth of July, 1799 ... in Portsmouth, N. H. By Edward St. Loe Livermore ,... . *Portsmouth: Printed by Charles Peirce.* 1799. 4to, pp. 28. BA. 41562

Also: An Oration delivered July the Fourth, 1813. ... *Boston: Printed by Chester Stebbins.* 1813. 8vo, pp. 40. B.—An Oration ... before the ... Masons, of ... New-Hampshire ... the Twenty-Fifth ... of June ... 5792 ... . *Portsmouth: Printed by John Melcher.* M,DCC,XCII. 8vo, pp. 23.—Mr. Livermore's Speech, in the House of Representatives. ... Jan. 6. On ... the Embargo Law. [n. p. 1808.] 8vo, pp. 25.

[LIVERMORE (George).] A Brief Account of the Dana Hill Public Schools, Cambridge. 1849. [*Cambridge.* 1849.] 18mo, pp. 19, (1). Plate. B. 41563

LIVERMORE. An Historical Research respecting the Opinions of the Founders of the Republic on Negroes as Slaves, as Citizens, and as Soldiers. Read before the Massachusetts Historical Society, August 14, 1862. By George Livermore. *Boston: Printed by John Wilson and Son.* 1862. 8vo, pp. xiv, (2), 215. + Supplementary Note and Index printed in 1863. pp. 217–236.

Fifty copies printed on large paper in 4to.

LIVERMORE. An Historical Research [as before]. *Boston: A. Williams & Co.* 1862. 8vo, pp. xviii, (2), 184. + Third Edition. [*Ibid.*] 1863. 8vo. H. + Fourth Edition. [*Ibid.*] 1863. 8vo. BA. + Fifth Edition. [*Ibid.*] 1863. 8vo. 41565

Fifty copies printed on large paper. Included in the "Proceedings of the Massachusetts Historical Society," Vol. IV.

[LIVERMORE.] A Merchant of the Old School. A Tribute to the Memory of James Johnson. ... *Boston.* M.DCCC.LV. 8vo, pp. 19. BA. 41566

LIVERMORE. ... Opinions of the Early Presidents, and of the Fathers of the Republic, upon Slavery, ... By George Livermore. *New York: Wm. C. Bryant & Co., Printers.* 1863. 8vo, pp. 19. B. 41567

Loyal Publication Society, No. 18.

[LIVERMORE.] The Origin, History, and Character of the New-England Primer; being a Series of [eight] Articles contributed to the Cambridge Chronicle by "The Antiquary." *Cambridge.* 1849. 4to. 41568

Twelve copies only printed.

[LIVERMORE.] Remarks on Public Libraries. From "The North American Review" for July, 1850. For Private Distribution only. *Cambridge: Printed by Bolles and Houghton.* MDCCCL. 8vo, pp. 40. BA. 41569

Also: Remarks on the Publication and Circulation of the Scriptures. ... *Cambridge: University Press.* M.DCCC.XLIX. 8vo, pp. 31. BA.

LIVERMORE. Tribute of the Massachusetts Historical Society to the Memory of George Livermore. *Boston: Massachusetts Historical Society.* 1866. 8vo, pp. 19. BA. 41570

LIVERMORE (G. W[hitefield]). A Valedictory Address, ... before the Social Fraturnity, [*sic*] of Leicester Academy, (Mass.) ... Nov. 3d, 1818. By Geo. W. Livermore. ... *Leicester: Printed by Hori Brown.* 1818. 8vo. H., W. 41571

LIVERMORE (H.) The Harp of Israel, to Meet the Loud Echo in the Wilds of America. By Harriet Livermore ... . *Philadelphia: Printed for the Authoress, by J. Rakestraw.* 1835. 18mo, pp. 180. BA. 41572

[LIVERMORE (Isaac).] An Account of Some of the Bridges over Charles River. *Cambridge: Printed at the Chronicle Press.* 1858. 8vo, pp. 45. H. 41573

LIVERMORE (J.) An Address ... at Wilton ... July 4, 1828. By Jonathan Livermore. *Dunstable, N. H.: Printed by Thayer & Wiggin.* 1828. 8vo, pp. 16. BA. 41574

LIVERMORE. Two Dedication Sermons ... in Wilton, N. H., ... by Rev. Jonathan Livermore ... January 5, 1775; and by Rev. Abiel Abbot Livermore ... January 10, 1861. ... *New-York: John A. Gray, Printer.* 1861. 8vo, pp. 33. H. 41575

LIVERMORE (L. J.) Sermon ... at the Funeral of William Henry Harrington, in Clinton, Mass., May 20, 1855. By L. J. Livermore. [n. p. n. d.] 8vo, pp. 8. B. 41576

LIVERMORE. ... A Sermon ... on ... Thanksgiving ... at Lexington, Ms. August 6, 1863, by Rev. L. J. Livermore. *Boston: Press of T. R. Marvin & Co.* 1863. 8vo, pp. 16. H.

Also: The Increase of Immorality; a Sermon ... . *Clinton: Printed by E. Ballard, Jr.* 1852. 12mo, pp. 14.— ... A Sermon, preached in ... Lexington ... September 11, 1864. ... *Boston: Press of T. R. Marvin & Son.* 1864. 8vo, pp. 16. H.

LIVERMORE (S.) Dissertation on the Questions which arise from the Contrariety of the Positive Laws of Different States and Nations. By Samuel Livermore ... . No. 1, containing Two Dissertations. *New-Orleans: Printed by Benjamin Levy.* 1828. 8vo, pp. 172, (1). BA. 41578

LIVERMORE (S. K.) An Oration, ... at Temple, (N. H.) ... July 4, 1809. By Solomon Kidder Livermore. ... *Amherst, N. H.: Printed by Joseph Cushing.* 1809. 8vo, pp. 16. B. 41579

LIVERMORE (S. T.) A Condensed History of Cooperstown, with a Biographical Sketch of J. Fenimore Cooper. By Rev. S. T. Livermore, A.M. *Albany: J. Munsell.* 1862. 12mo, pp. 276.

LIVERMORE ASSOCIATION. Report. *Rutland, Vt.* 1865. 8vo.

LIVERPOOL (*Earl of*). *See* [Jenkinson (R. B.)], IX., 36025–6.

Declaration of the Objects of the Liverpool Society for promoting the Abolition of Slavery. ... *Liverpool.* 1823. 8vo. P.

LIVERYMAN, *pseudon.* *See* Vol. II., No. 7873.

Lives and Actions of British Admirals and Naval Heroes, with Accounts of their Victories over the Enemies of Old England, to the present time, including Memoirs of the Illustrious Lord Nelson. *Chester.* [n. d.] 8vo. 41583

Includes some American actions.

Lives and Confessions of John Williams, Francis Frederick, John P. Rog, and Peter Peterson, who were tried ... in Boston, for Murder ... Jan. 21, 1819; ... . *Boston: Printed by J. T. Buckingham.* [1819.] 8vo, pp. 36. + Second Edition. [*Ibid.*]

Lives and Exploits of the most Noted Highwaymen, Robbers and Murderers. *Hartford.* [n. d.] 12mo. 41585

The Lives and Portraits of Curious and Odd Characters. *Worcester.* 1852. 12mo, pp. 192. 41586

The Lives and Portraits of Remarkable Characters, drawn from the most Authentic Sources. A New Edition. *London: W. Lewis.* 1819. 2 vols., 8vo. 59 Portraits. 41587

Includes a "Memoir of John the Painter, who with a design to benefit the American insurgents, set fire to the English dock-yards in 1777."

Lives and Voyages. *See* Drake (F.), Vol. V., No. 20833.

Lives, Characters and Sufferings of the Fathers of New England. *Concord.* 1836. 8vo. 41588

Title from Colburne's "Bibliography of Massachusetts."

Lives, English and Forein: from the year 1550 to the year 1690. By several Hands. *London.* 1704. 2 vols., 8vo. N.

Includes the life of Sir Walter Raleigh.

Lives of American Merchants. *See* [Tuthill (*Mrs.*)]

Lives of Celebrated American Indians. *See* [Goodrich (S. G.)]

Lives of Distinguished Shoemakers. ... *Portland: Davis & Southworth.* 1849. 12mo, pp. 340. BA. 41590

Includes Roger Sherman, George Fox, and Noah Worcester.

Lives of Eminent Individuals, celebrated in American History. *Boston.* [1839.] 3 vols., 12mo. B. 41591

Selected from Sparks' "American Biography."

Lives of Eminent Men of Modern Times. *New York.* 1840. 2 vols., 16mo. 41592

... Lives of Eminent Persons ... . *London: Baldwin and Cradock.* MDCCCXXXIII. 8vo, pp. xv, 106, 54, 38, 32, 40, 32, 27, 32, 24, 32, 32, 32, 72. C. 41593

Lives of Grant and Colfax. *See* Vol. VII., No. 28319, *note.*

The Lives of Hernando Cortes, the Discoverer of Mexico, and Francisco Pizarro, the Conqueror of Peru. *Boston: B. H. Greene.* 1840. 16mo, pp. 194. 2 Plates. C. 41594

Lives of Illustrious Men. 16mo, pp. 227. 41595

Includes Columbus.

Lives of Missionaries. North America. New Edition. *London: Society for Promoting Christian Knowledge.* 1865. Fcap 8vo, pp. 252. 41596

Lives of Southern Heroes and Patriots, including General Marion, Governor Rutledge, etc. *Philadelphia: G. G. Evans.* 1859. 12mo. 41597

Lives of State Criminals who suffered for High Treason. *London.* 1759. 8vo. 41598

Includes Sir Walter Raleigh.

Lives of the Chief Fathers of New England ... . *Boston.* 1870. 6 vols., 16mo. 41599

A reproduction, in large paper, of a series of works which, in this dictionary, are described under the names of the respective authors; *see* Adams (N.), Albro (J. A.), Hooker (E. W.), McClure (A. W.), *and* Pond (E.)

Lives of the Discoverers and Pioneers of America. Containing Columbus, Vespucius, De Soto, Raleigh, Hudson, Smith, Standish, Arabella Stuart, Elliott, Penn. *New York.* 186–. 12mo.

Mostly taken from Bancroft's "History," Vol. I.

Lives of the Heroes of the American Revolution: comprising the Lives of Washington, and his Generals and Officers who were the most distinguished in the War of the Independence of the U. S. A.; ... and farewell addresses of Washington ... . *Boston: Phillips & Sampson.* 1848. 12mo, pp. 370. Portrait. + [*Ibid.*] 1849. 12mo. + [*Ibid.*] 1855. 12mo. H. 41601

Lives of the Illustrious. ... *London: Partridge, Oakey & Co.* 1852–54. 5 vols., 8vo, pp. (4), 280; (4), 326; (4), 277; (4), 282; (4), 282. C. + *London.* 1856. 5 vols., 8vo. BA. 41602

Includes George Washington.

Lives of the most Eminent and Evangelical Ministers from the beginning of the Reformation to the Present Time. Collected from Authentic Historians. *Newcastle: E. Walker for M. Heavisides.* 1813. 2 vols., 8vo, pp. (2), 437; (2), 473. 41603

The Lives of Vasco Nunez de Balboa, ... Hernando Cortez, ... and Francisco Pizarro ... . *Boston: Marsh, Capen, Lyon, and Webb.* 1840. 18mo, pp. (4), 276. + *New York.* 1847. 12mo, pp. (4), 276. 41604

Living Christianity delineated. *See* Bryan (H.), Vol. III., No. 8791, and *add, Boston: Hastings, Etheridge and Bliss.* 1809. 12mo, pp. 165. 41605

Living Martyr. *See* [West (Geo. M.)]

... The Living World ... . Vol. 1, No. 1 ... . July, 1854. ... *Cleveland: Steam Press of Harris, Fairbanks ...* [1854.] 4to, pp. 16. H. 41606

LIVINGSTON (A. W.) ... Wont we be a happy People, when this War is over. Words by A. W. Livingston ... . Music by Philip Phillips. *Cincinnati: John Church.* [1863.] 8vo, pp. 5.

[LIVINGSTON (Brockholst).] Democracy: An Epic Poem. By Aquiline Nimble-Chops, Democrat. Canto First. *New York: Printed for the Author* [*about* 1790]. 8vo, pp. 20. 41608

LIVINGSTON (E.) Address to the People of the United States, on the Measures pursued by the Executive with Respect to the Batture at New-Orleans; ... [with] Documents, etc. By Edward Livingston ... . *New-Orleans: Printed by Bradford & Anderson.* 1808. 8vo, pp. l, 50, 15, xxix, 68, lxxv. C., H. 41609

LIVINGSTON. An Answer to Mr. Jefferson's Justification of his Conduct in the Case of the New-Orleans Batture. By Edward Livingston ... . *Philadelphia: Printed by William Fry.* 1813. 8vo, pp. xi, 187. 2 Maps. BA., P. 41610

LIVINGSTON. Examen des Droits des États-Unis et des Pretension de Edward Livingston sur la batture en face du Faubourg St^e. Marie. *New Orleans.* 1808. 4to, pp. 48. N. 41611

LIVINGSTON. Project of a New Penal Code for the State of Louisiana. By Edward Livingston ... . *London.* 1824. 8vo.

LIVINGSTON. Rapport fait À l'Assemblée Générale sur le projet d'un Code Pénal de l'État de la Louisiane. Par Edward Livingston ... . *Nouvelle-Orleans: Benjamin Levy & Co.* 1822. 8vo, pp. 170, (1). + *Paris: A. Renouard.* 1825. 8vo, pp. xxii, 224. 41613

LIVINGSTON. Report made to the General Assembly of the State of Louisiana, on the Plan of a Penal Code for the said State. By Edward Livingston ... . *New Orleans: Printed by Benjamin Levy & Co.* 1822. 8vo, pp. 159. B., BA. + *London.* 1824. 8vo. 41614

See "N. A. Rev.," XVII. 242. Also: Code of Procedure, for giving Effect to the Penal Code of ... Louisiana. ... *New-Orleans: Printed by Benjamin Levy.* 1825. Folio, pp. 256.—Extracts from the ... Penal Code: ... *New-Orleans: Printed by Benj. Levy & Co.* 1823. Folio, pp. (2), 31, (2).

LIVINGSTON. A System of Penal Law, for ... Louisiana; ... A Code of Crimes and Punishments, A Code of Procedure, A Code of Evidence, A Code of Reform and Prison Discipline, A Book of Definitions. Prepared under the Authority of a Law of the said State. By Edward Livingston. To which are prefixed, a Preliminary Report on the Plan of a Penal Code, and Introductory Reports to the several Codes embraced in the System of Penal Law. *New-Orleans.* 1824. Folio. + *Philadelphia: James Kay, Jun. & Co.* [1833.] Rl. 8vo, pp. v, 745. B.

LIVINGSTON. Système de Loí Pénale pour État de la Louisiane ... . *Nouvelle-Orléans: Benjamin Levy.* 1825. Folio, pp. 157, 242, 25. BA. 41616

LIVINGSTON. A System of Penal Law for the United States of America: ... By Edward Livingston ... . *Washington: Printed by Gales & Seaton.* 1828. Folio, pp. x, (1), 187, 45, 21. A., C.

Also: [Code of Evidence. ... *New-Orleans.* 182–.] Folio, pp. 73.—Code of Reform and Prison Discipline ... for ... Louisiana. ... *New-Orleans: Printed by Benjamin Levy.* 1826. Folio, pp. (2), 65.—Commercial Code for ... Louisiana. *New-Orleans: Printed by Benjamin Levy.* 1825. 8vo, pp. (2), 260.—Definitions of all the Technical Words used in the System of Penal Law ... for ... Louisiana. [n. p. n. d.] Folio, pp. 27.—Introductory Report to the Code of Evidence of ... Louisiana. [*New-Orleans.* 182–.] Folio, pp. 68.—Introductory Report to the Code of Prison Discipline: Explanatory of the Principles on which the Code is founded. Being part of the System of Penal Law, prepared for ... Louisiana. ... *Philadelphia.* 1827. 8vo, pp. (2), 78. BA. —Introductory Report to the Code of Procedure. [*New Orleans.* 1827.] Folio, pp. 58.—Introductory Report to the Code of Reform and Prison Discipline. [*New-Orleans: Printed by Benjamin Levy.* n. d.] Folio, pp. 71.—Introductory Report to the System of Penal Law ... for the State of Louisiana. [*New-Orleans.* 182–.] Folio, pp. 185.—Letter ... to Roberts Vaux, on the Advantages of the Pennsylvania System of Prison Discipline ... . *Philadelphia: Jesper Harding, Printer.* 1828. 8vo, pp. 15. —Livingston's Motion respecting the Pirate Jonathan Robbins. *Philadelphia.* 1800. 8vo.—Remarks on the Expediency of Abolishing the Punishment of Death. ... *Philadelphia: Jesper Harding, Printer.* 1831. 8vo, pp. 42. BA.— ... Report [on French spoliations, January 14, 1831. n. p. n. d.] 8vo, pp. 16. B.—The Speech ... on the Third Reading of the Alien Bill. *Philadelphia: Printed by James Carey.* [n. d.] 8vo, pp. 16.—Speech ... on ... Internal Improvement. ... February 9, 1824. *Washington: Printed by Gales & Seaton.* 1824. 12mo, pp. 36.—Speech ... on Mr. Foot's Resolution, proposing an Inquiry into the Expediency of abolishing the Office of Surveyor General of Public Lands, ... February 29, 1830. *Washington: Printed by Duff Green.* 1830. 8vo, pp. 58. BA. + *Charleston: Printed by J. S. Burges.* 1830. 8vo, pp. 24. —Speech ... 1831 on The Turkish Mission in Answer to Mr. Tazewell ... *Washington.* 1831. 8vo, pp. 47.—*See also* Louisiana, Poydras (J.), *and* Thierry (M.)

LIVINGSTON. A Letter to Edward Livingston, Delegate from Louisiana to ... Congress ... on the ... Speech delivered by him, at Washington, at the late Celebration of the Anniversary of the 8th of January, 1815. *Natchez.* 1828. 8vo, pp. 24. 41618

LIVINGSTON. An Address delivered on the 1st of August, 1831, before the Philolexian and Peithologian Societies of Columbia College. By Edward P. Livingston ... . *New-York: G. & C. & H. Carvill.* M,DCCC,XXXI. 8vo, pp. 28. BA. 41619

Also: Letter from Edward P. Livingston to the Public, concerning Steamboats, etc. [n. p.] 1819. 8vo. N.

[LIVINGSTON (Henry).] "The Money-Maker;" or, how to get Rich. Being a Guide to Business Success, ... and designed as a Help to those out of Employment. *New-York: H. Livingston.* [1868.] 18mo, pp. 320. C. 41620

LIVINGSTON (J.) Refutation of the claim of John Livingston to Lands in the Western District of the State of New-York, under certain Indian Leases; Together with the Opinions of Counsel Thereon. [n. p.] 1811. 8vo. S. 41621

LIVINGSTON (J.) American Portrait Gallery. ... containing Portraits of Men now Living. By John Livingston. *New-York.* 1854. 8vo. 41622

LIVINGSTON. Biographical Sketches of Distinguished Americans, now living. ... By John Livingston. *New York.* 1853. 8vo, pp. viii, 504. BA. 41623

LIVINGSTON. Biographical Sketches of Eminent American Lawyers. By John Livingston. Part I. *New York.* 1852. 8vo. + Parts 2–4. [n. p. 1852.] 8vo. H. 41624

Also: ... Livingston's Biographical Magazine. No. 1., Vol. III. May 1st, 1853. *New-York: Publication Office.* [1853.] 8vo.

LIVINGSTON. Livingston's Law Register; containing the Name, Post Office, County and State of Every Lawyer in the United States: ... By John Livingston ... . *New York.* 1851. 8vo. 41625

Continued to 1868 or later.

LIVINGSTON. ... Livingston's Monthly Law Magazine. Vol. I. 1853. *New-York: Publication Office.* [1853.] 8vo.

Continued to four or more parts.

LIVINGSTON. The Official Directory and Law Register for the United States, for ... 1866: ... By John Livingston ... . *New York.* 1866. 8vo, pp. (2), xiv, 600. B. 41627

LIVINGSTON. Portraits of Eminent Americans now Living; with Biographical and Historical Memoirs of their Lives and Actions. By John Livingston ... . *New-York: Cornish, Lamport & Co.* 1853. 8vo, pp. xix, 391. Portraits. + *New York: Author.* 1853–54. 8vo, pp. xvi, 542. C. 41628

LIVINGSTON. ... The United States Lawyer's Directory and Official Bulletin for 1850 ... together with The Manual of the American Legal Association: compiled by John Livingston ... . *New-York: John Livingston.* 1850. 8vo, pp. vii, 144. 41629

Also: United States Law Register and Official Directory for 1860 ... *New York.* 1860. 8vo. C.

LIVINGSTON (J. H.) A Sermon, delivered before the New-York Missionary Society, ... April 3, 1804. By John H. Livingston, D.D. To which are added, an Appendix, ... and other papers relating to American Missions. *New-York: Printed by T. & J. Swords.* 1804. 8vo, pp. 97. + *Worcester: Printed by Thomas & Sturtevant.* 1807. 8vo, pp. 68. + *Greenfield.* 1809. 8vo, pp. 72. + Third Edition. *Providence.* 1832. 12mo.

The appendix contains the Speech of Red Jacket to Elkanah Holmes; Extract from an Indian Journal; Letter of W. H. Harrison, &c. Also: An Address delivered at the Commencement held in Queen's College, in New Jersey, September 25, 1810. ... *New Brunswick.* 1810. 8vo, pp. 32.—Two Sermons ... before the New-York Missionary Society ... April 23d ... by the Rev. Dr. Livingston. ... April 24th ... by the Rev. Dr. M'Knight. ... [with] a Charge ... by Rev. Dr. Rodgers ... . *New-York: Printed by Isaac Collins.* 1799. 8vo, pp. 104. H.

LIVINGSTON (J. R. *and* R. J.) Memorial of John R. and Robert J. Livingston to the Legislature of New York respecting Steamboats. [n. p. 1814?] 8vo, pp. 43. C. 41631

LIVINGSTON. Petition of John R. and Robert J. Livingston to the Legislature of New Jersey respecting Steamboats, with the Laws of New York and New Jersey [concerning them]. *New York: Pelsue & Gould.* 1814. 8vo, pp. 52. C., S. 41632

LIVINGSTON (M.) The Trial of the Hon. Maturin Livingston, against James Cheetham, for a Libel; ... Twenty-Eighth of Nov. 1807. ... Taken in Short Hand, by William Sampson, Esq. ... *New-York: S. Gould.* 1807. 8vo, pp. 63. BA. 41633

[LIVINGSTON (P.)] The Other Side of the Question; or, a Defence of the Liberties of North-America. In Answer to a late Friendly Address to All Reasonable Americans, on The Subject of our Political Confusions. By a Citizen. *New-York: Printed by James Rivington* ... M,DCC,LXXIV. 8vo, pp. 29, (1).

Written in a style of pleasantry, "but the arguments of the author, when he criticises, were too *reasonable* to be totally invalidated."—*Critical Review*, XXXIX. 156. Another edition has on the title "America, printed for the purchasers."

LIVINGSTON [Robert R.] The Address of Mr. Justice Livingston to the House of Assembly of New-York, in Support of his Right to a Seat. *New-York: Printed* M,DCC,LXIX. 8vo, pp. 15. BA. + *Boston.* M,DCC,LXIX. 4to, pp. 5. N. 41635

LIVINGSTON. Essay on Sheep; their Varieties—Account of the Merinoes of Spain, France, &c. Reflections on the Best Method of treating them, and raising a Flock in the United States; together with ... Remarks on Sheep and Woollen Manufactures. By Robert R. Livingston, LL.D. ... *New-York: Printed by T. and J. Swords.* 1809. 8vo, pp. 186. + Second Edition, much enlarged. *New York: ... Collins and Perkins.*

1810. 8vo. + *Concord, N. H.: Daniel Cooledge.* 1813. 12mo, pp. 143. BA. 41636

LIVINGSTON. The Opinions of the Judges of the Supreme Court, delivered in the Court of Errors, in the Cause of Robert R. Livingston and Robert Fulton, *vs.* James Van Ingen, and Twenty others. *Albany: Printed by S. Southwick.* 1812. 8vo, pp. 12, 12, 23, (1). B. 41637

LIVINGSTON. An Oration delivered before the Society of the Cincinnati of the State of New-York; in Commemoration of the Fourth Day of July. By the Honorable Robert R. Livingston, Esquire ... . *New York: Printed by Francis Childs.* M,DCC,-LXXXVII. 4to, pp. (4), 22. N. 41638

Also: Examination of the Chancellor's [John Lansing, Jr.] Opinion in the case of R. R. Livingston and R. Fulton *v.* Van Ingen, Lansing and Others. *Albany.* 1812. 8vo, pp. 54. C.

LIVINGSTON (T.) An Address ... at Jefferson College ... September 26, 1833. By Thomas Livingston, A.M. ... *Pittsburgh: Printed by Wilson and Marks.* 1834. 8vo, pp. 25. BA.

[LIVINGSTON (William).] An Address to his Excellency Sir Charles Hardy, Knt. ... By the Author of a Weekly Paper, entitled "The Watch-Tower." *New York.* 1755. Folio, pp. 13.

LIVINGSTON. A Funeral Eulogium on The Reverend Mr. Aaron Burr, Late President of the College of New-Jersey. By William Livingston ... . *New-York.* 1757. 4to, pp. 22. + *Boston: Re-printed for J. Winter.* MDCCLVIII. 8vo, pp. 23. BA.

LIVINGSTON. A Letter to the Right Reverend Father in God, John, Lord Bishop of Landaff [*sic*]; Occasioned by Some Passages in his Lordship's Sermon, on the 20th of February, 1767, in which the American Colonies are loaded with great and undeserved Reproach. By William Livingston. *New-York: Printed for the Author, and ... sold by Garrat Noel,* ... MDCCLXVIII. 8vo, pp. (4), 25. C. + *Boston: Re-printed by Kneeland and Adams.* MDCCLXVIII. 8vo, pp. 26. B. + *New-York Printed. London: Reprinted for J. Buckland.* MDCCLXVIII. 8vo, pp. 31. 41642

The sermon alluded to was delivered at the anniversary of the Society for the Propagation of the Gospel in Foreign Parts. The writer questions "whether there be a pamphlet in the nation, that, in proportion to the length of the sermon, contains so great a number of aberrations from the truth." Very severe, but courteous. *See* "M. Rev.," XXXIV. 87. The following is a Dutch translation:

LIVINGSTON. Brief aan den Lord Bisschop van Landaff. ... Uit het Engelsch vertaald. *Utrecht.* 1774. 8vo, pp. (4), 34.

It elicited the following reply:

A Vindication of The Bishop of Landaff's Sermon from the Gross Misrepresentations, and Abusive Reflections, contained In Mr. William Livingston's Letter to his Lordship: With Some Additional Observations On certain Passages in Dr. Chauncey's Remarks, &c. By a Lover of Truth and Decency. ... *New-York: Printed by J. Holt.* M,DCC,LXVIII. 8vo, pp. viii, 82. BA.

[LIVINGSTON.] Observations on Government; including some Animadversions on Mr. Adams's Defence of the Constitutions and Government of the United States of America, and on De Lolmes's Remarks on the Constitution of England. By a Farmer of New Jersey. *New York: Ross.* 1787. 8vo, pp. 56.

A very rare pamphlet, unknown to Rich, and apparently so to Sedgwick. The following is a translation:

[LIVINGSTON.] Examen du Gouvernement d'Angleterre, comparé aux Constitutions des États-Unis. Où l'on réfute quelques assertions contenues dans l'ouvrage de M. Adams, intitulé: Apologie de Constitutions des États-Unis d'Amérique, et dans celui de M. Delolme, intitulé: De la Constitution d'Angleterre. Par un Cultivateur de New Jersey. Traduit de l'Anglois, & accompagné de Notes. *Londres, et se trouve a Paris: Frouille.* 1789. 8vo, pp. viii, 91. 41646

Translated from the English by M. Fabre. The notes were written by Dupont de Nemours, Condorcet, and Gallois. *See* Rich, I. 359.

[LIVINGSTON.] Philosophic Solitude; or, The Choice of a Rural Life. A Poem. By a Gentleman educated at Yale College. *New-York: Printed by James Parker.* 1747. 8vo, pp. 42. + *Boston.* 1762. 8vo, pp. 46. + The Third Edition. *New-York: Printed by John Holt.* [1769?] 8vo, pp. 40. 41647

See Sedgwick's "Life of Livingston," p. 61. Reprinted with the following title:

LIVINGSTON. Philosophic Solitude, or the Choice of a Rural Life. Supposed to have been written by His Excellency William Livingston, Esq., Gov. of New Jersey. Progress of Science, spoken by Samuel Dexter, A.B. *New York: Greenleaf.* 1790. 8vo, pp. 48. N. 41648

[LIVINGSTON.] A | Review | of the | Military Operations | in | North-America; | from | The Commencement of the French Hostilities | on the Frontiers of Virginia in 1753, to the Surrender |

of Oswego, on the 14th of August, 1756. | Interspersed | With various Observations, Characters, and Anecdotes; necessary to | give Light into the Conduct of American Transactions in general; | and more especially into the political Management of Affairs in | New York. | In a Letter to a Nobleman. | *London: R. and J. Dodsley.* M.DCC.LVII. 4to, pp. (2), 144. BA. + *New England: Reprinted in the Year* MDCCLVIII. 4to, pp. 98. + *New York: Printed by Alexander & James Robertson.* M DCC LXX. 8vo, pp. 170. C., P. 41649

[LIVINGSTON. Same Title.] To which are added, Colonel Washington's Journal of his Expedition to the Ohio, in 1754, and several Letters and other Papers of Consequence, found in the Cabinet of Major General Braddock, after his Defeat near Fort Du-Quesne; and since published by the French Court. None of these Papers are contained in the English Edition. *Dublin: P. Wilson and J. Exshaw.* M.DCC.LVII. 8vo, pp. 276.

"The author's chief design is to vindicate Governor Shirley, and asperse the characters of those who opposed his measures."—*Monthly Review*, XVI. 524. The latter part of this work is a translation of the "Mémoire contenant le Précis des Faits," printed by the French Court, charging Washington with the assassination of Jumonville. The authorship has also been attributed to William Smith, of New York, who perhaps aided the author as did also J. M. Scott. The facts were supplied by W. Alexander, afterwards the *soi disant* Earl of Stirling, brother-in-law of Livingston, and secretary to Gen. Shirley. *See* Sedgwick's "Life of Livingston," p. 114. It was reprinted in the "Massachusetts Historical Collections," Vol. VII.

[LIVINGSTON.] A Soliloquy [of Lieut.-Governor Cadwallader Colden]. Second Edition. *New York.* 1770. 4to, pp. 15.

See Sedgwick's "Life of Livingston," p. 149. Sedgwick, p. 179, "cites an Address to the People of Ireland, July 28," perhaps the same as our No. 403. Mr. Livingston was also the projector and principal writer in the "Independent Reflector," *see our* No. 34452, and add to the note: A preface was put forth with the imprint *New-York: Printed until tyrannically suppressed.* M,DCC,LIII. Folio, pp. 31. This preface gives the proposed contents of many more numbers which were never published. *See* John Adams' Works, Vol. II. 349. "The Watch-Tower" was also edited by Mr. Livingston.

LIVINGSTON (W.) An Appeal to the Presbyterians of New Brunswick on the late Trial and Suspension of the Rev. David Syme, Provincial Missionary. By W. Livingston. *St. John, N. B.* 1836. 8vo, pp. 39. 41652

LIVINGSTON & WELLS. ... History of the Great Express Robbery of Livingston & Wells, in ... Rochester, ... 1845. *Rochester, N. Y.: Chas. H. M'Donell.* 1848. 8vo, pp. 23. B.

LIVINGSTON CO., *N. Y.* Proceedings of the Board of Supervisors of the County of Livingston, for 1863. 8vo. Continued.

View of the Livingston County High-School. To which are subjoined, Brief Remarks on ... Popular Education. *Geneseo: Printed by J. Percival.* 1828. 8vo, pp. 28. H. 41655

LIVIUS (P.) The Memorial of Peter Livius, Esq., one of His Majesty's Council for the Province of New Hampshire in New England, to the Lords Commissioners for Trade and Plantations; with the Governor's Answer and the Memorialist's Reply, printed Article by Article, also their Lordship's Report thereon to His Majesty, and the Opinion of the Attorney and Solicitor General in 1752, referred to by the Governor. [n. p.] 1773. 8vo, pp. 50. 41656

Relates to the controversy respecting the New Hampshire Grants. Excessively rare.

LIVIUS. Two Reports on the Matter of Complaint of Mr. Livius against Gov. Wentworth. *London.* 1773. 4to, pp. 15.

Livre de lecture, en dialecte créole-anglais. [*Amsterdam.* 1843.] 18mo, pp. 13, 8. 41658

Le Livre des Sauvages. *See* [Petzholdt (J.)]

Livres Curieux. *New York: Garrigue et Christern.* 1854. 8vo, pp. 37. 41659

Contains minute descriptions of parts of Thevenot, Hulsius, De Bry, "Relations," as well as the Letters of Columbus and Cortes [by James Lenox].

LIZANA Y BEAUMONT (F. X. de). Elogios latino y castellano del excellentisimo Señor D. Franc. Xav. de Lizana y Beaumont, Arzobispo y Virey de México. *Mexico: F. de Jauregui.* 1813. 4to, 41 leaves. Large Plate. 41660

LIZANA Y BEAUMONT. Exhortacion del Exmo. Illmo. Sr. Don Francisco Xavier de Lizana y Beaumont, Arzobispo de México, a sus fieles y demas habitantes de este Reyno. *Mexico.* 1810. 4to, pp. 10. 41661

A Pastoral of the Archbishop of Mexico against the revolutionary movements of that time.

LIZANA Y BEAUMONT. Instruccion Pastoral del Illmõ. Señor Don Francisco Xavier de Lizana y Beaumont, Arzobispo de México, del Consejo de S. M. ... Sobre la costumbre de llevar las Señoras el pecho y brazos desnudos. *Mexico: Doña Maria Fernandez de Jauregui.* 1808. 4to, pp. 42. 41662

Very severe on flesh-colored stockings and diabolical lace; as Stevens remarks it is "A funny book, very, and one well fortified with texts and authorities. This curious Pastoral Charge exhibits to us the queer spectacle of a presumably jolly old Mexican Archbishop running full tilt at the prevailing fashions of the fairer portions of his

flock. It seems that the Mexican ladies had adopted the new French fashion of allowing the wicked world to see too much of them by displaying their arms and charms without any covering save that of innocence, whereupon the wrath of the worthy Father is kindled."—*Bibl. Geographica*, No. 3090.

[LIZARDI (Joaquin Fernandez de).] Leben des Periquillo Sarmiento. Quarta edicion. *Mejico?* 1842. 4 vols., 8vo. 60 Illustrations. 41663

"A sort of imitation of Lazarillo de Tormes, Guzman de Alfarache, and Gil Blas, and considered a complete representation of the morals, customs, opinions, and tendencies of Mexican society."—*Jahrbuch für roman. Lit.*, III. 258.

[LIZARDI.] El Periquillo Sarmiento por el Pensador Mexicano. Primera edicion, corregida, ilustrada con notas y adornada con 56 laminas finas. *Mexico.* 1865. 4 vols., 8vo, pp. xxii, 218; 220; 208; 248. Portrait, 56 Illustrations. 41664

The author of these volumes has been styled the Cervantes of Mexico by some, while Dr. Beristain, in his "Biblioteca Hispano Americana Septentrional," calls him the American Quevedo. He has written much, and on the whole ranks perhaps as the best Mexican writer. The present work is one illustrative of Mexican character, satirizing the faults of the people, but always true to liberal and republican principles. Sixty lithographs illustrating the work are spirited and amusing. Lizardi was born in Mexico in 1771, and during the period of the Revoluion wrote very much, chiefly as the "Pensador Mexicano."

[LIZARDI.] Observaciones que el Pensador Mexicano hace à las Censuras que los Señores Doctores D. Ignacio Maria Lerdo, y D. Ignacio Grageda, hicieron de sus Conversaciones sexta, vigesima, y vigesima secunda, entre el payo y el sacristan. Con arreglo á los decretos del Señor Provisor, de 7 de junio de 1825. *Mexico.* 1825. 4to, pp. 87. 41665

L[IZARDI]. Pensador Mexicano, por D. J. F. de L. *Mexico.* 1813. 4to. 41666

A rare and curious political journal, composed of bizarre essays, which may not have lived beyond the year. It was published weekly, but the supplements, although as extensive as the chief work, were very irregular. The first number is called "Continuacion del Pensador," the others are simply "Pensador."

LIZARZABURU (J. A.) Observaciones meteorologicas correspondientes al año de 1862, hechas en el observatorio del Seminario de Guatemala. *Guatemala.* 1862. 12mo, pp. 17. 2 Tables.

LIZARZABURU. Los Temblores sentido en Guatemala, en Dec. de 1862–63. *Guatemala.* 1863. 41668

Llamamiento de la Isla de Cuba. *See* Cuba, Vol. V. 17787.

LLANDAFF (*Bishop of*). *See* [Cresset (E.)], [Ewer (J.)], [Gilbert (J.)], [Inglis (C.)], *and* [Newcomb (*Dr.*)]

LLANO Y ZAPATA (J. E. de). Carta o Diario que escribe D. Joseph Eusebio de Llano y Zapata a sus mas venerable amigo, el Doctor Don Ignacio Chirivoga. En que con la mayor verdad: y critica mas sagura de la cuenta de todo lo acaecido en esta Capital del Peru desde el Viernes 28 de Octubre de 1746, quando experimentó su mayor ruyna con el grande movimiento de Tierra que padeció á las diez, y media de la noche del mencionado dia, hasta 16 de Febrero de 1747 con una Tabla en que se dá el calculo exacto de todo el numero de Temblores que se han sentido en él tragico successo, que es lastimoso Assumpto de este Escrito. *Lima: Francisco Sobrino.* 1747. 4to, pp. 33. + *Madrid: Juan de Zuñiga.* 1748. 4to, pp. 33. 41669

A diary, giving a particular account of the great earthquakes which took place in Peru from October 28, 1746, to February 16, 1747.

LLANO Y ZAPATA. Preliminar y Cartas que preceden al Tomo 1° de las memorias historico-physicas critico-apologeticas de la America-Meridional. Su autor D. Joseph Eusebio Llano y Zapàta. *Cadiz.* 1759. Sm. 8vo. 41670

This author treats upon several heterogenous subjects, and incidentally endeavors to defend the humanity of the Spaniards against the good bishop Las Casas. At page 238 he says that rare and uncommon books are more abundant in America, particularly in Lima, than in Europe, and that Ciceros of 1465–6–7, etc., are so frequently met with that the finding of copies is not considered as anything so uncommon, which is an absurd statement.

LLANO Y ZAPATA. Memoria de los Acontecimientos Tristes y Lamentables en la Corte de Lima y su Puerto, con la Ruina total de esta, e Inundacion del Callo en el mes de Octubre, año de 1746. (Carta ó Diario que escribe D. José Eusebio de Llano y Zapata, [and] Carta del Padre Lozana, etc.) Segunda edicion. *Lima.* 1863. 4to, pp. 25, vi. 41671

LLANO Y VALDES (F. de). Oracion Panegyrica, que en la Solemnidad de N. Patrona Sañta Rosa de S. Maria de Lima, Dixolo en lo Iglesia Cathedral de la Ciudad de Quito. *Quito.* 1760. 4to, pp. 38. 41672

Perhaps the first book printed in Quito, the capital city of the kingdom of Quito.

LLERAS (*Dr.* Lorenzo M.) República de Columbia, ó Noticio de sus límites, extension, montañas, rios, producciones, comercio, poblacion, habitantes, educacion, leyes, religion é historia, publicada en la VII. edicion de la Enciclopedia británnica [*sic*] y traducida al castellano con varias notas. *Bogotá.* 1837. + *Reimpreso en Valencia.* 1841. 12mo, pp. viii, 184. 41673

[LLORENTE (——).] Proyecto de una constitucion religiosa considerada como parte de la civil de una nacion libre é independiente, escrito por un Américano; Apologia catolica del mismo proyecto. *Paris.* 1821. 2 vols., 8vo. 41674

[LLORENTE.] Saggio apologetico degli Storici e Conquistatori Spagnuoli dell' America. *Parma: Presso Luigi Mussi.* M.DCCC.IV. 12mo, pp. 91, (1). 41675

I have seen a notice of another edition, *Florence and Naples*, 1796.

LLOSA (M. E. de la). Proyecto de Constitucion Politica, con un Discurso Preliminar. *Lima.* 1827. 4to, pp. 20. 41676

[LLOYD (Caroline).] A Memorial of Lt. Daniel Perkins Dewey, of the Twenty-Fifth Regiment Connecticut Volunteers. *Hartford: Press of Case, Lockwood & Company.* 1864. 12mo, pp. 126. Portrait. B. 41677

[LLOYD (Charles).] *See* Conduct [etc.], Vol. IV. 15202–3.

See also "Two Papers."

[LLOYD.] Defence of the Majority in the House of Commons on the Question relating to general Warrants, in Answer to the Defence of the Minority. Second Edition. *London.* 1764. 8vo, pp. 66. C. + Sixth Edition. *Dublin.* 1765. 8vo, pp. 37. S. 41678

For a "Defence of the Minority," *see* [Townshend (Charles)].

Reply to the Defence of the Majority on the Question relating to general Warrants. *London.* 1765. 8vo. + Second Edition. [*Ibid.*] 1765. 8vo. 41679

[LLOYD.] An Examination of the Principles and boasted Disinterestedness of a late Right Honourable Gentleman [W. Pitt], in a Letter from an old Man of Business to a Noble Lord ***. *London.* 1766. 8vo, pp. 34. S. 41680

[LLOYD.] A True History of a late Short Administration. *London: J. Almon.* 1766. 8vo, pp. 22. BA., S. 41681

Also: An Honest Man's Reasons for declining to take part in the New Administration. ... *London.* 1765. 8vo.

LLOYD (C.) ... Lecture ... before the Soldiers' and Sailors' National Union League, Washington City ... November 14, 1865, by Clinton Lloyd ... . *Washington, D. C.: Chronicle Print.* [n. d.] 8vo, pp. 18. H. 41682

[Lloyd (David.)] The Legend of Captain Jones, relating his Adventure to Sea, his first Landing and Strange Combate, Furious Battles, his relieving of Kemper Castle, Admirable Sea Fight with the Gallies of Spain, his being taken Prisoner, and Hard Usage, Liberation and Return to England. *London.* 1648. 4to. 41683

First printed in 1636.

[Lloyd.] The Legend of Captaine Jones, the Two Parts, containing his incredible Adventures by Sea and Land, his strange Combat with a mighty Bear, his desperate Duels, his Loves ... . *London.* 1656. 12mo. 41684

[Lloyd.] The Wonderful, Surprising and Uncommon Voyages and Adventures of Captain Jones, to Patagonia. Relating his Adventure at Sea. ... His furious Battle with his Six-and-Thirty Men, against an Army of Eleven Kings, with their Overthrow and Deaths. His strange and admirable Sea-Fight with six huge Galleys of Spain, with 9000 Soldiers. ... His being set at liberty by the Kings' Command, in exchange for twenty-four Spanish Captains and return for England. ... Part the Second: His incredible Adventures and Atchievements by Sea and Land, particularly his Miraculous Deliverance from a Wreck at Sea, by the Support of a Dolphin. ... All which and more, is but the Tithe of his own relation, which he continued until he grew speechless and Died. With his Elegy and Epitaph. The Second Edition. *London: John Lever.* MDCCLXVI. 8vo, pp. (2), 74.

A very good burlesque, in imitation of a Welsh poem, entitled Owdl Rich, Greulon. Prefixed is a frontispiece representing the Captain, mounted on a war-horse, encountering an elephant with a castle on its back. "The said Captain Jones, on whom the legend was made, lived in the reign of Queen Elizabeth, when Sir John Norris, and his noble brethren, with Sir Walter Raleigh, were endeavouring, for the honour of their nation, to eternize their names by martial exploits."—Anthony à Wood. There are also other editions, *London*, 1656, 12mo; [*Ibid.*] 1659, 8vo; [*Ibid.*] 1671, 4to; [*Ibid.*] 1706, 4to.

Lloyd (H. H.) Lloyd's Battle History of the Great Rebellion, Complete, from the Capture of Fort Sumter, April 14, 1861, to the Capture of Jefferson Davis, May 10, 1865 ... . *New York: H. H. Lloyd & Co.* 1866. 8vo, pp. (2), viii, 566. Maps and Illustrations. B. 41686

Lloyd (J.) Address of General James Lloyd, To the Citizens of Kent and Queen-Anne's Counties, In Answer to a late Calumnious Charge ... by Robert Wright. ... *Annapolis: Printed by Frederick Green* ... [1794.] 8vo, pp. 38. BA. 41687

[Lloyd (James).] Remarks on the Report of the Committee of Commerce of ... Thirty-First of March, 1826, on the British Colonial Intercourse. [n. p. 1826.] 8vo, pp. (2), 51. BA.

Also: Hon. Mr. Lloyd's Letter, on Impressments [February 24, 1813. *Boston.* 1813.] 8vo, pp. 4.—Mr. Lloyd's Speech ... on the Bill "Concerning the Naval Establishment." February 28, 1812. [n. p. n. d.] 8vo, pp. 24. BA.—Mr. Lloyd's Speech ... Dec. 9 [1808], on the Bill making further Provisions for enforcing the Embargo. [n. p. n. d.] 8vo, pp. 7.—Mr. Lloyd's Speeches ... on Mr. Hillhouse's Resolution to repeal the Embargo Laws; November 21, 1808. [*Washington.* 1808.] 8vo, pp. 16.—Speeches of Mr. Lloyd, Mr. Hillhouse and Mr. Pickering in the Senate of the United States, in December, 1808. *Washington.* [n. d.] 8vo.

Lloyd (J. T.) American Guide. By James T. Lloyd. *Philadelphia.* 1857. Sq. 8vo. C. 41689

Lloyd. Lloyd's List of Post Offices in the United States and the Canadas. Alphabetically arranged. Also containing the Postal Laws and Regulations, classified by Subjects, omitting such as are not of Importance to the Public generally ... . *New York: J. T. Lloyd.* 1863. 12mo, pp. xxiv, 352. B. 41690

Lloyd. Lloyd's Steamboat Directory, and Disasters on the Western Waters, Containing the History of the First Application of Steam, as a Motive Power; the Lives of John Fitch and Robert Fulton, Likenesses & Engravings of their First Steamboats. Early Scenes on the Western Waters, from 1798 to 1812. ... Maps of the Ohio and Mississippi Rivers ... . By James T. Lloyd. *Cincinnati, Ohio: James T. Lloyd & Co.* 1856. 8vo, pp. 326. Maps and Plates. B., C. 41691

Lloyd (John Augustus). The Mines of Copiapo. Being a Report to the Foreign Office. By Col. J. A. Lloyd ... *London: Printed by Woodfall and Kinder.* 1857. 8vo, pp. 24. 41692

Lloyd. On the Facilities for a Ship Canal Communication, between the Atlantic and Pacific Oceans, through the Isthmus of Panama. With an Abstract of the Discussion upon the Paper. *London: W. Clowes & Sons.* 1850. 8vo, pp. (2), 34. 2 Plates.

An excerpt from the "Minutes of Proceedings of the Institution of Civil Engineers," Vol. IX. Also: On the Height of the Pacific Ocean at Panama, and of the Atlantic at Chagres, 1829. ... [n. p. n. d.] 8vo. *See also* "Philosophical Transactions," Vol. CXX., *and* "Journal of the Royal Geographical Society," Vol. I.

Lloyd (M. C.) Meditations on Divine Subjects. By Mrs. Mary Clarke Lloyd. With an account of her Life and Character, by E. Pemberton. *Boston.* 1745. 12mo. M. + *New York: J. Parker.* 1750. 12mo, pp. 116. C. 41694

Lloyd (O.) *See* Leoyd (O.), No. 40120.

Lloyd (Samuel). New-Jersey Annual Register and General Calendar ... 1846. *Trenton.* [1846.] 16mo. 41695

Lloyd (S. H.) Sketches of Bermuda. By Susette Harriet Lloyd. *London: James Cochrane and Co.* MDCCCXXXV. Post 8vo, pp. xv, 258. Map, 3 Plates. B. 41696

Lloyd (Thomas). *See* Budd (T.), Vol. III., No. 8957.

Lloyd (T.) Congressional Register. *See* Vol. IV. 15608.

Lloyd (T.) The Trial of the Boot & Shoemakers of Philadelphia, on an Indictment for a Combination and Conspiracy to raise their Wages. Taken in short-hand, by Thomas Lloyd. *Philadelphia: T. Lloyd, and B. Graves.* 1806. 8vo, pp. (4), 159.

See also Addison (A.), Vol. I., No. 381, Bright (M.), Vol. II., No. 7970, Pennsylvania, Selfridge (T. O.), Smith (W. S.), *and* Wentz (S.)

Lloyd (T.) Lloyd's Pocket Companion and Guide through New York City, for 1866–67. Published by Thomas Lloyd ... *New York: Torrey Brothers, Printers.* 1866. 12mo, pp. 150. Plates. B. 41698

Lloyd (W.) Letters from the West Indies, during a Visit in the Autumn of MDCCCXXXVI, and the Spring of MDCCCXXXVII; by William Lloyd, M.D. *London: Darton and Harvey.* [1837.] Post 8vo, pp. viii, 263. Map and 11 Plates. 41699

Lloyd (W. A.) Lloyd's Southern Railroad Guide, October 1863. *Mobile.* 1863. 12mo. Continued. 41700

Lloyd. Lloyd's Steamboat and Railroad Guide. *New York.* 1859. 8vo, pp. 196. 41701

Lloyd (W. F.) Sketch of the Life of Robert Raikes, Esq., and ... History of Sunday Schools. By W. F. Lloyd. ... *New-York: Sunday School Union* ... 1852. 16mo, pp. 125. B. 41702

Lloyd's Universal American Register of Shipping. ... Edited and issued under the direction of the Association. *New York.* 1866. Obl. folio, pp. xxxii, 689. 41703

Llufriu (J. J.) Manifestacion sobre la conducta que ha observado en la exaccion de la contribucion personal, y las imposturas con que ha informado sobre esto al Supremo Gobierno D. Paulino Garcia. Por José J. Llufriu, Prefecto del Distrito de Puebla. *Puebla.* 1844. 4to, pp. 26. 41704

Loaisaga (Manuel de.) Historia de la milagrosissima imagen de N. S. de Occotlan, que se venera extra muros de la ciudad de Tlaxcala. *Puebla.* 1745. 8vo, pp. (44), 182. 41705

"Livre de toute rareté."—Andrade.

The Loan, Revenue, and Currency Acts of 1863. ... *New York: Bankers' Magazine Office.* 186–. 8vo, pp. 12, 26, 38.

Acts of Congress relating to Loans and the Currency, from 1790 to 1867. *Washington: Government Printing Office.* 1867. 8vo, pp. 109. 41707

40th Cong., 2d Sess., Mis. Doc. No. 23.

The Acts of Congress relating to Loans and the Currency, from 1842 to 1863. *New York.* 1863. 8vo, pp. 74, 8. 41708

See also Congress, Vol. IV., No. 15507.

Foreign Loans and their Consequences considered ... . By a Member of the Stock Exchange, London ... . *London: Pelham Richardson.* 1854. 8vo, pp. 37. BA. 41709

Lobé (G.) Cuba et les Grandes Puissances Occidentales de l'Europe ... . Par M. Le Chevalier Guillaume Lobé ... . *Paris: E. Dentu.* 1856. 8vo, pp. (4), 220. BA. 41710

Lobé. Quelques mots aux habitants de Curaçao sur la culture du Nopal et sur la réproduction de la cochenille fine du Mexique. *Amsterdam.* 1839. 8vo. 41711

Also: Sur la culture du tabac dans l'Ile de Cuba. ... *Cayenne.* [1850.] 8vo.

Lobo Guerrero. *See* Guerrero (B. L.), Vol. VII. 29131.

Rich says it was "first printed at *Lima* in 1614." The edition of 1754 contains a reprint of the Synod of 1636, and various edicts issued in 1754.

Lobo (Manuel). Relacion de la Vida y Virtudes del V. Hermano Pedro de San Joseph Betancur primer fundador del Hospital de Convalecientes en la Ciudad de Guatemala. *Guatemala, por Joseph de Pineda Ybarra.* 1667. 12mo. + *Sevilla.* 1672. 12mo. + *Sevilla: T. Blasio.* 1673. 12mo. 41712

Excessively rare. The edition of 1667 is believed to be the earliest book printed at Guatemala.

Lobo (O. da G.) Indice alphabetico das Leis, Decretos, Avisos e Consultas do Conselho de estado sobre as Assembleas provinciaes, organisado por Ovidio da Gama Lobo. *San Luiz.* 1861. 8vo, pp. 82. 41713

See also Gama Lobo (O. da), Vol. VII., Nos. 26494–96.

Lobspruch. Ueber die Herrliche Victori. In Eroberung der Silberflotta, in dem Bay Matanca, unter dem Commando des E. unnd Manhafften Peters Heyn, wie auch die Eroberung der zwo Galleonen, so ausz Honduras kommen seyn. *Gedruckt im Jahr Christi Anno* 1629. 4to, 6 leaves. 41714

A very rare poem. A German translation of "Lof-Dicht," No. 41779, *infra.*

The Local Government. *See* Jamaica, Vol. IX., No. 35631.

Local Loiterings. *See* [Dix (J. R.)], Vol. V., No. 20344.

Lochinvar. Encouragements for such as shall have Intention to bee Vndertakers in the new Plantation of Cape Breton, near New Galloway, in America, by mee Lochinvar. *Edinburgh.* 1620. Sm. 4to. + [*Ibid.*] 1624. 4to. 41715

Sold at the Gordonstoun sale for £3; very rare, and now worth ten times as much.

Lock (D.) Essay on the Trade, Commerce, and Manufactures of Scotland. By David Lock ... . *Edinburgh: The Author.* M,DCC,LXXV. 8vo, pp. (1), vii, 92. 41716

Section V., "Disputes between Great Britain and her American Colonies."

Locke (C. S.) The Patriotic Volunteer: a Sermon ... October 19, 1862, at the Funeral of George F. Whiting ... . By Calvin S. Locke ... . *Boston: Press of John Wilson and Son.* 1862. 12mo, pp. 12. H. 41717

Also: ... A Sermon ... in ... West Dedham, Mass. ... May 30, 1858, at the Funeral of Mrs. Olive Morse Guild ... . *Providence.* 1858. 16mo, pp. 8. H.

[Locke (D. R.)] Divers Views, Opinions, and Prophecies of Yours Truly, Petroleum V. Nasby. ... *Cincinnati: R. W. Carroll & Co.* 1866. 8vo, pp. 424. + Sixth Edition. [*Ibid.*] 1867. 12mo, pp. xiv, (1), 25–424. B. 41718

[Locke.] Ekkoes from Kentucky. By Petroleum V. Nasby, P.M. at Confedrit × Roads (wich is in the State uv Kentucky), and professor uv biblikle polity in the Southern Military and classikle institoot, being a perfect record uv the ups and downs and experiences uv the dimocricy, doorin the eventful year 1867, ez seen by a naturalized Kentuckian. Illustrated by Thomas Nast. *Boston: Lee & Shepard.* 1868. 12mo, pp. 324. 41719

[Locke.] The Nasby Papers. ... *Indianapolis, Ind.: C. O. Perrine & Co.* 1864. 8vo, pp. 64. + With an Introduction by G. A. Sala. *London: Ward, Lock, & Tyler.* 1866. 12mo, pp. viii, 88. + *London: Routledge & Co.* 186–. Cr. 8vo, pp. viii, 88.

[Locke.] Swinging Round the Circle; or, Andy's Trip to the West, together with a Life of its Hero. By Petroleum V. Nasby. [*New York: American News Company.* 1866.] 12mo, pp. 38. 41721

[Locke.] "Swingin Round the Cirkle." By Petroleum V. Nasby, late Pastor of the Church of the New Dispensation ... . His Ideas of Men, Politics, and Things, as set forth in his Letters to the Public Press, during the year 1866. Illustrated by Thomas Nast. *Boston: Lee and Shepard.* 1867. 12mo, pp. 299.

Locke (E. W.) Three Years in Camp and Hospital. By E. W. Locke. ... *Boston: Geo. D. Russell & Co.* 1870. 8vo, pp. 408. B. 41723

[Locke (Jane E.)] Boston: a Poem. ... *Boston: Wm. Crosby and H. P. Nichols.* 1846. 16mo, pp. 46. H. + Second Edition. [*Ibid.*] 1846. 12mo, pp. 47. 41724

Dedicated to the names of Appleton and Lowell.

Locke. Daniel Webster, a Rhymed Eulogy. By Mrs. J. Ermina Locke. *Boston.* M.DCCC.LIV. 8vo, pp. 24. 41725

Also: Miscellaneous Poems. ... *Boston: Otis, Broaders & Co.* 1842. 12mo, pp. 300.—Rachel ... A Tale of Truth. ... *Lowell.* 1844. 16mo, pp. 16.—The Recalled; in Voices of the Past, and Poems of the Ideal. ... *Boston and Cambridge: James Munroe and Company.* MDCCCLIV. 12mo, pp. vii, 246. Portrait. + New Edition. [*Ibid.*] M DCCC LVI. 16mo, pp. vii, 246. H.

Locke (J.) A Collection of several Pieces of Mr. John Locke, Never before printed, or not extant in his Works. Publish'd by the Author of the Life of the ever-memorable Mr. John Hales, &c. *London: J. Bettenham for R. Francklin.* M.DCC.XX. 8vo, pp. (62), 362, Index and Errata, pp. 19. + *London.* 1739.

Contains the "Fundamental Constitutions of Carolina," the first instrument ever digested and written out, for the entire and perfect government of a political body. The plan was laid out by Lord Shaftesbury; but the labor of its composition was accomplished by Mr. Locke. Though impracticable in many particulars, it undoubtedly suggested to the colonists many hints which were beneficial in their civil and political organization.

Locke. An Essay concerning the True Original, Extent, and End of Civil Government. By the Late Learned John Locke, Esq. *Boston: Re-Printed ... by Edes and Gill.* 1773. 12mo, pp. 129. B. 41727

[Locke.] Histoire de la Navigation. *See* Churchill (J.), IV.

See also J. S. Clarke's "Progress of Maritime Discovery."

Locke. A Letter Concerning Toleration. By John Locke, Gent. The Third Edition. *Boston: Printed ... by Rogers and Fowle.* 1743. 8vo, pp. 77. B. + *Windsor, Vt.: Printed by Alden Spooner.* MDCCLXXXVIII. 12mo, pp. 71. 41728

Locke (J. G.) Book of the Lockes. A Genealogical and Historical Record of the Descendants of William Locke, of Woburn. With an Appendix, containing a History ... of the Family of John Locke, of Hampton, N. H., and kindred Families and Individuals. By John Goodwin Locke ... . *Boston and Cambridge: James Munroe and Company.* M DCCC LIII. 8vo, pp. 406. Plate and Portraits. B., C. 41729

"One of the best genealogies yet published."—Whitmore.

Locke. The Munroe Genealogy. By John G. Locke. *Boston and Cambridge: James Munroe and Company.* M DCCC LIII. 8vo, pp. 15. B. 41730

Locke (J. L.) Sketches of the History of the Town of Camden, Maine; Including Incidental References to the Neighboring Places and Adjacent Waters. By John L. Locke ... . *Hallowell: Masters, Smith & Company.* 1859. 12mo, pp. xii, 7–267, Errata, 1 leaf. BA. 41731

Also: History of Phœnix Lodge, ... of Belfast, Maine. ... *Belfast: T. J. & G. W. Burgess, Printers.* 1863. 8vo, pp. 25. B.

Locke (J.) An Oration ... at Billerica, July 5, 1802 ... . By Joseph Locke. *Young and Minus, Boston.* [1802.] 8vo, pp. 20.

Locke (N. C.) ... A Discourse, occasioned by the Death of Mrs. Margaretta Willoughby: delivered January 28, 1849. ... By Rev. N. C. Locke ... . *New-York: Leavitt, Trow & Co.* M.DCCC.XLIX. 8vo, pp. 48. H. 41733

Locke (S.) A Sermon preached before the Ministers of the Province of the Massachusetts-Bay, ... at their Annual Convention in Boston, May 28, 1772. By Samuel Locke, M.A. ... *Boston, New-England: Printed by Richard Draper.* M,DCC,LXXII. 8vo, pp. 51. BA. 41734

Locke (U.) Joy Days on Both Sides of the Water. By Una Locke and Zaida Yorke. *New York: Carlton & Lanahan.* 1870. 18mo, pp. 147. 3 Plates. 41735

Also: Highdays and Holydays in Old England and New England. ... *New York: Carlton & Porter.* 1870. 4 vols., 18mo, pp. 126; 159; 147; 142. 12 Plates.

Locke (W. E.) A Centennial Discourse, containing a History of the Scotch Plains Baptist Church, New Jersey, during the First Century of its Ecclesiastical Existence; preached August 8, 1847. By William E. Locke. *New York.* 1847. 8vo.

Locke (W. H.) The Story of the Regiment. By William Henry Locke, A.M. ... *Philadelphia: J. B. Lippincott & Co.* 1868. 12mo, pp. 401. 2 Plates. B. 41737

Relates to the Eleventh Regiment, Pennsylvania Volunteers.

L[ockerby] (E[lizabeth] N.) The Wild Brier: or, Lays by an Untaught Minstrel. *Charlottetown.* 1866. 8vo, pp. 196.

Lockhart (E.) Statement with reference to the Knights Baronets of Nova Scotia, their Creations, Privileges, and Territorial Rights of Property in that Colony. By Ephraim Lockhart. *Edinburgh.* 1831. 8vo. 41739

See also Stirling (*Earl of*), *and our* Nos. 741 and 9355.

Lockhart (J.) Speech of James Lockhart ... on the River and Harbor Bill. ... July 22, 1852. [n. p. n. d.] 8vo, pp. 8.

Lockman (J.) Vast Importance of the Herring Fishery, ... to those Kingdoms as respecting the National Wealth, our Naval Strength, and the Highlanders. Second Edition. *London.* 1750. 8vo. 41741

Refers to the settlements in North America. *See also* our Nos. 40708–709.

Lockport, *N. Y.* The Complete Directory ... 1859–60 ... By A. L. Jones. [n. p.] 1859. 12mo. S. 41742

Lockport and Middleport Directory for 1863 and 1864. Together with a History of Lockport. Compiled and published by A. De Lancey Brigham. *Lockport: Richardson & Barker, Printers.* 1864. 8vo. 41743

Also: Boyd's Lockport City Directory, with a Business Directory of Niagara County. 1866–7. Compiled by Andrew Boyd. *Lockport: The Author.* [n. d.] 12mo, pp. 160.

Lockport Union School: Catalogue ... 1858. [n. p. n. d.] 8vo. Continued. S. 41744

Summary of Faith and Rules of Discipline of the Evangelical Lutheran Church of Lockport, N. Y. *Albany: J. Munsell.* 1851. 18mo, pp. 8. 41745

Lockport and Niagara Falls Railroad Company: Report of Charles B. Stuart, Chief Engineer, January 1, 1846. *Rochester.* 1846. 8vo. S. 41746

LOCKWOOD (A.) A Brief Description of Nova-Scotia, with Plates of the Principal Harbors: including a particular Account of the Island of Grand Manan. By Anthony Lockwood ... . *London: The Author.* 1818. 4to, pp. (4), 134. 8 Plates. A., C.

[LOCKWOOD.] Report on the Projected Canal across the Istmus [*sic*] that divides Nova-Scotia and New-Brunswick, ... in ... 1819 ... . *Fredericton: Printed by George K. Lugrin.* 1820. 8vo, pp. 24. BA. 41748

LOCKWOOD. ... A Sermon, ... at the Ordination of the Reverend Mr. Eleazer May, at Haddam, June 30, 1756. By James Lockwood ... . *New-Haven: Printed by James Parker and Company.* [n. d.] 12mo, pp. (2), 34. B. 41749

Also: ... Discourse ... at Weathersfield July 27, 1755 ... after the Death of the Hon. Col. [Elisha] Williams ... With An Appendix ... . *New-Haven: Printed by James Parker, and Company.* 1756. 8vo, pp. 48, xv.—Sermon at Weathersfield, July 6, at a Public Thanksgiving. ... *New Haven.* 1763. 12mo, pp. 35.—Sermon before the General Assembly of Connecticut, Hartford, May 9, 1754. ... *New London.* 1754. 8vo, pp. 50.—Sermon on the Day of Election, May 10, 1759. ... *New London.* 1759. 12mo, pp. 36.— ... A Sermon, ... at Glassenbury, August 7, 1758. Being the Day of the Interment of the Reverend Mr. Ashbel Woodbride ... . *New-Haven: Printed by J. Parker and Company.* [1758?] 8vo, pp. 31. BA.

LOCKWOOD (L. C.) Mary S. Peake, the Colored Teacher at Fortress Monroe. By Rev. Lewis C. Lockwood ... . With an Appendix. *Boston: American Tract Society.* 1863. 18mo, pp. 64.

LOCKWOOD (P.) Memoir of John D. Lockwood. By Rev. Peter Lockwood ... . Second Edition ... . *New York: American Tract Society.* [n. d.] 16mo, pp. 231. Portrait. B. 41751

LOCKWOOD (R. A.) The Vigilance Committee of San Francisco. ... Speeches of R. A. Lockwood, Esq. *San Francisco, Cal.* M DCCC LII. 8vo, pp. 47, (1). H. 41752

LOCKWOOD (S.) ... A Sermon ... before the General Assembly of ... Connecticut, at Hartford; on ... their Anniversary Election, May 12th, 1774. By Samuel Lockwood, A.M. ... . *New-London: Printed by Timothy Green.* MDCCLXXIV. 8vo, pp. 39.

LOCKWOOD (S.) Defence of Commander S. Lockwood, before the Court of Inquiry ... at Washington City ... . Sept. 12th, 1857 ... . *Washington: F. H. Sage.* 1857. 8vo, pp. 8. H.

LOCKWOOD (S.) ... An Obituary Sermon, in relation to the late De La Fayette Schanck: preached in ... Keyport, N. J. Sept. 21st, 1862, By Samuel Lockwood ... . *New York: G. A. Whitehorne, Printer.* 1863. 8vo, pp. 24. 41755

LOCKWOOD (W.) A Sermon ... at the Funeral of Mrs. Jerusha Woodbridge ... Glasterbury, August 1st, 1799. By William Lockwood, A.M. ... *Middletown: Printed by Tertius Dunning.* 1799. 8vo, pp. 23, (1). BA. 41756

LOCKYER (E. H.) Memoirs of Celebrated Naval Commanders. By Edward Hawke Lockyer. Illustrated by Engravings from Original Pictures in the Naval Gallery of Greenwich Hospital. *London: Harding & Lepard.* MDCCCXXXII. Imp. 8vo.

Includes some who have figured in American history.

Loco-Focoism; as displayed in the Boston Magazine against Schools and Ministers ... . [*Albany.* 1840.] 8vo, pp. 32. B.

The Loco's Lament. *Boston.* 1841. 8vo. 41759

Locomotive Sketches, with Pen and Pencil, or Hints and Suggestions to the Tourist over the Great Central Route from Philadelphia to Pittsburg. *Philadelphia.* 1854. 12mo. 41760

LOCUST DALE, *Pa.* Report of the Directors of the Locust Dale Coal Company, February 6, 1867. *Boston: Wright & Potter, Printers.* 1867. 8vo, pp. 8. H. 41761

[LODDINGTON (William).] Plantation-Work the Work of this Generation, written in true love to all such as are weightily inclined to Transplant themselves and Families to any of the English Plantations in America. ... *London: Benjamin Clark.* 1682. 4to, pp. 20. 41762

LODDINGTON. Tythe no Gospel Maintenance, for Gospel Ministers. In an Epistle to all who conscientiously suffer for not paying them. By William Loddington ... . *London: ... T. Sowle* ... 1695. 8vo, pp. 28. 41763

LODE-STAR. Statement of the Lode Star Gold Mining Co. and Description of its Water-Powers and Lode-Claims ... . *New York.* 1865. 8vo, pp. 31. H. 41764

LODGE (T.) A Margarite of America. By Thomas Lodge. [*London:*] *Printed for John Busbie, and are to be sold in S. Dunston's church-yard in Fleet-Street, and at the little shop next Clifford's Inne.* 1596. 4to, pp. 139. 41765

A very rare tract. The author sailed with Captain Candish, or Cavendish, in his voyage around the world. He sailed on a second expedition from Plymouth, in 1591, the particulars of which are given by Southey, in his "History of Brazil." While at Santos he became acquainted with a friar in the Jesuit College where he lodged, with "many captains and young gentlemen." "Here it was," says Lodge, "my chance in

the library of the Jesuits in Santos to find this historie in the Spanish tong," of which he professes to give a translation. In his dedication to Lady Russell the author says: "Touching the place where I wrote this, it was in those straits christned by Magelan; in which place to the southward many wonderous isles, many strange fishes, many monstrous Patagones withdrew my senses; briefly, many bitter and extreme frosts at midsummer continually clothe and clad the discomfortable mountaines; so that as there was great wonder in the place wherein I writ this, so likewise might it be marvelled, that in such scantie fare, such causes of fear, so mightie discouragements, and so many crosses, I should deserve or eternize any thing." Twenty-six copies were reprinted with the following title:

LODGE. The Margarite of America. Edited by J. O. Halliwell. ... *London: T. Richards.* 1859. 8vo, pp. viii, 139. C.

LODI. An Act to incorporate the Lodi Manufacturing Company: ... passed 6th February, 1840. ... *New-York: Printed by H. Cassidy.* M,DCCC,XL. 8vo, pp. 35, (1). B. 41767

LODOWICK [Christianus]. A Letter from ... Mr. Lodowick [to Increase Mather, dated] Rhode-Island, Febr. 1. 1691, 2. [n. p. n. d.] 16mo, pp. 8. H., M. 41768

Also: An Almanac. By C. Lodowick. Physician. *Boston.* 1695. 8vo.

LOE (T.) A Divine Discourse, representing the Soul of a Believer Speaking by Faith, according to the Doctrine of the Scriptures. By Thomas Loe. *New London: Reprinted by T. Green.* 1717. Folio, 1 leaf. 41769

A very early specimen of Connecticut printing.

LOEBELL (——). Was die Militair-Journale über die Expedition nach Mexico erzählen. [n. p.] 1863. Map. 41770

LOEBER (E. C.) Auszug der Nachrichten von dem Englischen America, besonders von Carolina und Georgia. Von Emanuel Christian Loeber. *Jena.* 1750. 8vo. 41771

Title from Meusel, Vol. III., Part 1, p. 394.

LOEFLING (P.) Iter Hispanicum eller Resa til Spanska Länderna uti Europa och America, förrättad ifrån Ar 1751 til Ar 1756. Utgifven af Carl Linnæus. *Stockholm.* 1758. 8vo.

LOEFLING. Peter Loeflings Reise nach den Spanischen Ländern in Europa und America in den Jahren 1751 bis 1756. Nebst Beobachtungen und Anmerkungen über die merkwürdigen Gewächse; herausgegeben von Herrn Carl von Linné. Aus dem Schwedischen übersetzt von D. Alexander Bernhar Kölpin. *Berlin und Stralsund: Gottlieb August Lange.* 1766. 8vo, pp. (28), 406. 2 Plates. + Reisebeschreibung [as before]. Zweite

Auflage. *Berlin: Gottlieb August Lange.* 1776. 8vo, pp. 16, (16), 406, (2). 2 Plates. C. 41773

For a translation of a portion of this *see* Bossu (N.), Vol. II., No. 6466.

LOEHNIS (H.) Die Vereinigten Staaten von Amerika. Deren Vergangenheit und Gegenwart in socialer, politischer und finanzieller Beziehung. Von H. Loehnis. *Leipzig: Eduard Heinrich Meyer.* 1864. 8vo, pp. x, (2), xxxi, 352, v folded pages. BA.

LOEW (H.) ... Monographs of the Diptera of North America. Prepared for the Smithsonian Institution by H. Loew. Edited by R. Osten Sacken. *Washington: Smithsonian Institution.* 1862–1873. 3 parts, 8vo, pp. xxiv, 221; xi, 360; vii, 351, 13. 11 Plates. B., C. 41775

Included in the "Smithsonian Miscellaneous Collections," Vols. VI. and XI.

Loew's Bridge: A Broadway Idyl. *New York.* 1868. Square 18mo, pp. 78. 41776

LOEWENBERG (J.) Alexander von Humboldt's Reisen in Amerika und Asien. Eine ... Darstellung seiner wichtigsten Forschungen von J. Loewenberg. ... *Berlin.* 1835. 8vo. Map. + Zweite Auflage. *Berlin: Hasselberg'sche Verlagsbuchhandlung.* [1843.] 2 vols., 8vo, pp. x, 328; x, 412. Map. B. 41777

Lof der Oost-Indise | Compagnie, | Ende de E. Heeren | Bewinthebberen | Van dien. | Waer onder anderen aen-ghewesen wort, hoe nootsake- | lijck het is voor ons Vader-Land in dese Occurentie | van tijden haer versochte Octroy niet te weygheren. | *t'Amsterdam,* | *Gedruckt by Hendrick Jansz. Visscher, op de* | *Keysers gracht, by de Prince-straet, Anno* 1646. | 4to, pp. 18. 41778

This eulogium on the East India Company relates to the scheme for uniting the East and West India Company.

Lof-dicht. *See* Heyn (P. P.), Vol. VIII., No. 31659.

The following appears to be another edition:

Lof-Dicht, | Over de heerlijcke Vic- | torie, in het veroveren van de | Silver Vlote, in de Baey van Matanca, | onder het beleyt van den E. ende Manhaften Heer | Generael Pieter Pieterz Heyn, | Als oock het veroveren der twee Galioenen, | comende uyt de Honduras. | *Tot Middelburgh,* | *Voor Zacharias Roman, Kunst ende Boeckvercooper,* | *woonende in de Kerck-strate inden Vergulden Bybel,* | *Anno* 1629. | 4to, 6 leaves. C. 41779

Panegyric upon the glorious victory and the conquest of the silver-fleet by P. Heyn. Signed "Die wel doet, wel vint," the device of Willem Wynandts.

[LOFFT (Capel).] Observations on Mr. Wesley's Second Calm Address, and incidentally on other writings upon the American Question. Together with Thoughts on Toleration, and on the point how far the conscience of the subject is concerned in a War; ... and a recommendation of a plan of Peace. *London: E. and C. Dilly.* 1777. 12mo, pp. 124. 41780

"A plain, sensible, and dispassionate refutation of Mr. Wesley's pamphlet."—*Monthly Review*, LVI. 401.

[LOFFT.] A View of the Several Schemes with respect to America; and their comparative merit in promoting the dignity and interest of Great Britain. *London: W. Owen.* MDCCLXXV. 8vo, pp. 55. 41781

"After examining many of the plans suggested for terminating the American contest, the writer declares in favor of that which consists in restoring the colonies to the situation they were in before the Stamp Act, and waiving by an act of the Legislature the exercise of taxation, as inexpedient."—*Monthly Review*, LIII. 512.

LOFLAND (C.) A List of all the Entries in the Virginia Military District; and also, all the Entries in the United States Military District of 100 acre lots ... to the present year. By Charles Lofland ... . *Columbus: Printed by P. H. Olmsted.* 1821. 8vo, pp. 32. BA. 41782

LOFLAND (J.) The Poetical and Prose Writings of John Lofland, containing Moral, Sentimental, Humorous, and Patriotic Poems and Essays. *Baltimore: J. Murphy.* 1846. 12mo, pp. 332. Portrait. C. 41783

LOFLAND. The Poetical and Prose Writings of Dr. John Lofland, the Milford Bard, consisting of Sketches in Poetry and Prose. With a Sketch of his Life. Collected and Arranged by J. N. McJilton. *Baltimore.* 1853. 8vo, pp. 589. C. 41784

[LOFT] (Sa-sa-na). A Memorial of Sa-sa-na, the Mohawk Maiden. ... *Hamilton: Waldron & Baker, Printers.* 1852. 8vo, pp. 28. H. 41785

The Log Cabin. *See* [Lee (Hannah (F.)], No. 39736.

The Log Cabin & Hard Cider Melodies; A Collection of Popular and Patriotic Songs, ... dedicated to the Friends of Harrison and Tyler. ... *Boston: Charles Adams.* 1840. 16mo, pp. 72.

Published by the Whig Party during the electioneering campaign of 1840.

The Log Cabin Song-Book. A Collection of Popular and

Patriotic Songs. ... *New-York.* 1840. 12mo, pp. 72, cover, (4). Portrait of Harrison. 41787

Perhaps by Samuel D. Taylor. This is the title of the cover; the inner title differs slightly. Published during the candidacy of General Harrison.

Log of the Cruise of the Schooner Julius Webb, which sailed from Norwich, Conn., July 23, 1858, having on board "The Wachusett Club" of Worcester, Mass. *Worcester.* 1858. 8vo.

LOGAN (C. A.) ... Yankee Land. A Comedy ... . By C. A. Logan, Esq. ... . *Boston: William V. Spencer.* [n. d.] 8vo, pp. 31. B. 41789

LOGAN (G.) A Letter to the Citizens of Pennsylvania on the necessity of Promoting Agriculture, Manufactures, and the Useful Arts. By George Logan. *Lancaster: Dickson.* 1800. 8vo, pp. 28. + *Philadelphia.* 1800. 8vo, pp. 40. + Second Edition. [*Ibid.*] 8vo. 41790

Also: An Address on the Errors of Husbandry, in the United States. ... January 14, 1818. ... *Philadelphia: Printed by Lydia R. Bailey.* 1818. 8vo, pp. 11.—An Address ... before the Tammany Society, ... 12th of May, 1798. *Philadelphia: Printed by B. Franklin Bache.* [1798.] 8vo, pp. 12.—Fourteen Agricultural Experiments ... . *Philadelphia: Printed by Francis and Robert Bailey.* M,DCC,XCVII. 8vo, pp. (2), 41. For "Letters, addressed to the Yeomanry," also attributed to George Logan, *see* [Laughan (*Dr.*)], No. 39243.

LOGAN (H.) Hannah Logan. Memoirs of her Husband, and other Quakers; their Testimonies, &c. *Philadelphia.* 1839. 12mo. 41791

LOGAN (J.) The Antidote In Some Remarks on a Paper of David Lloyd's called A Vindication of the Legislative Power. Submitted to the Representatives of all the Freemen of Pennsylvania. By James Logan. Sep. 25, 1725. Folio, pp. 8.

[LOGAN.] The | Charge | Delivered from the Bench | to the | Grand-Jury, | At the Court of Quarter Sessions, | held for the County of Philadelphia, | the second day of September, 1723. | Published at the Desire of the Grand-Jury. | Together with Their Address. | *Philadelphia:* | *Printed and Sold by Andrew Bradford* ... MDCCXXIII. | Sm. 4to, pp. 16. J.C.B., C. 41793

[LOGAN.] The | Charge | Delivered from the Bench to the | Grand Inquest, | At a Court of Oyer and Terminer | and General Gaol Delivery | held for the City and County of Philadelphia, April 13, 1736. | *Philadelphia: Printed and Sold by B. Franklin.* M,DCC,XXXVI. 4to, pp. 24. 41794

A good specimen of Franklin's typography. The work was thought to be of sufficient importance to warrant a reprint, and was reproduced with the following title:

LOGAN. The Charge delivered from the Bench to the Grand Inquest, at a Court of Oyer and Terminer and General Goal Delivery, held for the City and County of Philadelphia, April 13th, 1736. By the Hon[ble] James Logan, Chief Justice of the Province of Pennsylvania. *Printed at Philadelphia. Reprinted at London, by J. Roberts.* 1737. 12mo, pp. 34. J.C.B. 41795

LOGAN. Experimenta et Meletemata de Plantarum Generatione. ... Experiments and Considerations on the Generation of Plants. By James Logan, President of the Council, and Chief Justice of the Province of Pensilvania. Translated from the Original Latin. *London: C. Davis.* 1747. 8vo, pp. viii, 39. P.

Also published in Latin at *Leyden*, 1739. Also: Part of a Charge delivered to the Grand Inquest at Philadelphia, 24th Sept. 1733. ... [n. p. n. d.] Folio, pp. 3.

LOGAN. Catalogus Bibliothecæ Loganianæ: Being a Choice Collection of Books, as well in the Oriental, Greek and Latin, as in the English, Italian, Spanish, French and other Languages. Given by the late James Logan Esq; of Philadelphia for the Use of the Publick. Numbered as they now stand in the Library; Built by him, in Sixth-street, over against the State-house Square. *Philadelphia: Printed by Peter Miller & Comp. in the Year* 1760. 8vo, pp. 116. P. 41797

The first catalogue of the Loganian library; *see* Cicero, *and* Philadelphia, *Pa.*

LOGAN (J.) Notes of a Journey through Canada, the United States of America, and the West Indies. By James Logan, Esq. ... *Edinburgh: Fraser and Co.* M.DCCC.XXXVIII. 12mo, pp. xii, 259. Map. B., C. 41798

"Mr. Logan swept rapidly through America, and the result is a conviction that our transatlantic friends are gross, rude, indecent, &c. The work in short, runs on the old rail-road of national prejudice, and contains no pictures vivid enough to make amends for its author's presumptuous uncharitableness."—*Athenæum*, 1838, p. 67.

LOGAN (J.) The Western Woodpecker, being the Journal of a Journey performed in ... 1818, from Georgetown, D. C. to the Miami in the State of Ohio, and back again. By John Logan. *Georgetown: The Author.* 1818. 12mo, pp. 38. 41799

A very rare pamphlet.

LOGAN (J. A.) Argument of John A. Logan ... on the Impeachment of Andrew Johnson ... . *Washington: Government Printing Office.* 1868. 8vo, pp. 55. H. 41800

LOGAN. Speech of Major General John A. Logan, at Duquoin, Illinois, July 31, 1863, on his return to Illinois after the

Capture of Vicksburg. *Cincinnati: Caleb Clark.* 1863. 8vo, pp. 32. 41801

Also in German. *Cincinnati.* 1863. 8vo, pp. 33. Also: Great Union Speech ... in Chicago, ... August 10th, 1863. *Chicago.* 1863. 8vo, pp. 16.— ... Oration ... upon the Occasion of the Decoration of the Soldiers' Graves, at ... Arlington, Va. ... May 30, 1870. *Washington.* 1870. 12mo, pp. 12.— ... Speech ... January 8, 1869. *Washington: F. & J. Rives & Geo. A. Bailey ... Printers.* 1869. 8vo, pp. 16.—Speech ... July 12, 1867, on Reconstruction. [n. p. n. d.] 8vo.—Speech ... July 16, 1868 [on the] Principles of the Democratic Party. *Washington, D. C.* [1868.] 8vo, pp. 8. H.— ... Speech ... January 22, 1870. *Washington: F. & J. Rives & Geo. A. Bailey ... Printers* ... 1870. 8vo, pp. 16.— ... Speech ... March 10, 1870. [n. p. n. d.] 8vo, pp. 15.— ... Speech ... June 15, 1870. *Washington: F. & J. Rives & Geo. A. Bailey ... Printers* ... 1870. 8vo, pp. 8. H.

LOGAN (J. H.) A History of the Upper Country of South Carolina, from the Earliest Periods to the close of the War of Independence. By John H. Logan, A.M. Vol. I. *Charleston: S. G. Courtenay & Co.* 1859. 12mo, pp. xi, 521. BA. 41802

No more printed.

LOGAN (*Mr.*) The Preamble and Resolution offered by Mr. Logan, ... on granting the Baltimore and Susquehanna Rail Road Company the privilege of extending their Rail Road into ... Pennsylvania. ... *Harrisburg.* 1829. 8vo, pp. 12. 41803

LOGAN (O.) Before the Footlights and Behind the Scenes: a Book about "The Show Business" in all its Branches ... . By Olive Logan. *Philadelphia: Parmelee & Co.* 1870. 8vo, pp. 612. 14 Plates, 10 Portraits. 41804

LOGAN (S.) Masonic Funeral Discourse, delivered at the Interment of Brother Samuel Works, Westmoreland, July 20, 1795. By Sheldon Logan. *Walpole, N. H.* 1795. 12mo.

LOGAN (T. M.) Memoir of C. A. Luzenberg, M.D. ... By Thomas M. Logan, M.D. ... *New-Orleans: Printed by J. B. Steel.* 1849. 8vo, pp. (2), 58. Portrait. B. 41806

LOGAN. [Extract from] Report on the Medical Topography and Epidemics of California. *Philadelphia.* 1865. 8vo, pp. 75.

LOGAN (W.) American Gold Mining Company, on the Portage River ... Canada East. Description of its Property by Sir William Logan ... with Surprising Statements of the Press respecting the Gold Fields ... &c. ... *Boston: Printed by Alfred Mudge & Son.* 1864. 8vo, pp. 16. Map. B. 41808

LOGAN. Geological Survey of Canada. Report of Progress, 1842–3 ... . *Montreal.* 1843. 8vo, pp. 159. + 1844. [*Ibid.*]

1846. 8vo, pp. 100. + 1845 ... [*Ibid.*] 1847. 8vo, pp. 125. + 1846. Geological Description of the North Shore of Lake Superior ... . [*Ibid.*] 1847. 8vo, pp. 66. + Report ... 1847. [*Ibid.*] 1849. 8vo, pp. 165. + 1848. [*Ibid.*] 1850. 8vo, pp. 65. + 1849 ... . *Toronto.* 1850. 8vo, pp. 115. + 1850 ... . *Quebec.* 1852. 8vo, pp. 54. + 1851. [*Ibid.*] 1852. 8vo, pp. 131. + 1852. [*Ibid.*] 1854. 8vo, pp. 179. + 1853 ... 56. *Toronto: Printed by John Lovell.* 1857. 8vo, pp. (4), 494. Maps. + 1857. [*Ibid.*] 1858. 8vo, pp. 240. + 1858. [*Ibid.*] 1859. 8vo, pp. 263. 41809

See also our Vol. III., No. 10459.

LOGAN. Commission Géologique du Canada. Rapport de Progrès depuis son Commencement jusqu'à 1863 ... . Membres de la Commission: Sir William E. Logan, LL.D. ... Traduit de l'anglais ... Par P. J. Darey, M.A. ... *Montréal: Dawson Frères.* 1864. 8vo, pp. (2), xxvi, 1043. B., C. 41810

For a translation *see* Taché (J. C.)

LOGAN. Atlas and Map to accompany the Geology of Canada. 1863. ... *Montreal.* 1865. 8vo, pp. 42. 41811

LOGAN. Canadian Organic Remains. Decade II ... . *Montreal.* 1865. 8vo, pp. 157. 41812

LOGAN. Descriptive Catalogue of a Collection of the Economic Minerals of Canada and of its Crystalline Rocks ... . *Montreal.* 1862. Rl. 8vo, pp. 88. 41813

LOGAN. Report of a Geological Exploration of Part of the North Shore of Lake Huron made by Mr. Logan in 1848; embracing a Special Examination of the Bruce Mines ... . *Montreal.* 1849. 8vo, pp. 51. 3 Folded Maps. 41814

LOGAN. Report of the Board of Engineers, as well as that of W. E. Logan, Esq. ... upon the Survey of Lake St. Peter, October, 1850. *Montreal.* 1850. 8vo. S. 41815

LOGAN. Rapport du bureau d'ingénieurs et de W. E. Logan, Ecr. sur le relevé du lac St. Pierre en Octobre 1850. *Montréal.* 1850. 8vo, pp. 24. 41816

LOGAN. Two Special Reports on the Mining Region of Lake Superior, addressed by Mr. Logan, the one to the Legislative Council and the other to the Commissioner of Crown Lands. *Montreal.* 1847. 8vo, pp. 31. 41817

LOGAN. Esquisse Géologique du Canada, pour servir à l'intelligence de la carte géologique et de la collection des minéraux économiques envoyées à l'Exposition Universelle de Paris, 1855. Par W. E. Logan et T. Sterry Hunt. *Paris: Hector Bossange et Fils.* 1855. Sm. 8vo, pp. 100. Map. + *Paris.* 1867. 8vo, pp. 72. 41818

See also Canada, Vol. III., No. 10457.

LOGAN, *pseudon.* *See* [Neal (John)].

LOGAN, *pseudon.* The Master's House; a Tale of Southern Life. By Logan. *New-York: T. L. McElrath & Co.* 1854. 12mo, pp. 391. 6 Plates. B., C. 41819

THE LOGAN COPPER MINING COMPANY. Reports of A. D. Hager, A.M. ... Charles Robb, Esq. ... *Boston: Press of Geo. C. Rand & Avery.* 1864. 8vo, pp. 16. B. 41820

LOGANIAN LIBRARY. *See* Philadelphia, *Pa.*

The Loggers; or, Six Months in the Forests of Maine. *Boston: H. B. Fuller.* [1870.] Sq. 16mo. C. 41821

LOGGIN (R.) The Case ... stated, representing great Frauds ... in relation to the Duty on Pepper and Tobacco ... offer'd to ... Parliament assembled. By Robert Loggin. *London.* [1718?] Folio, pp. 4. S. 41822

The Logic and Law of Col. Johnson's Report on Sabbath Mails, 1829. [n. p. n. d.] 8vo. 41823

LOGUEN (J. W.) The Rev. J. W. Loguen as a Slave and as a Freeman. A Narrative of Real Life. *Syracuse, N. Y.: J. G. K. Truair & Co. ... Printers.* 1859. 8vo, pp. 444. Portrait.

LOHENSCHIOLD (O. C.) Dissertatio de modo probabiliori quo primæ in Americam Septentrionalem immigrationes sunt factæ Ottonis Christi. de Lohenschiold. *Tubingæ.* 1754. 4to.

LÖHER (F.) Aussichten für gebildete Deutsche in Nordamerika. Von Franz Löher ... . *Berlin: Julius Springer.* 1853. 8vo, pp. vi, 91, (1). B. 41826

LÖHER. Geschichte und Zustände der Deutschen in Amerika. Von Franz Löher. *Cincinnati und Leipzig: Eggers & Wulkop.* ... 1847. 8vo, pp. (4), vii, 544. + Zweite Ausgabe. *Göttingen: Wigand.* 1855. 8vo, pp. iv, x, 544. B. 41827

LÖHER. Land und Leute in der Alten und Neuen Welt. Reiseskizzen. Von Franz Löher. *Göttingen: Wigand.* 1855. 3 vols., 8vo, pp. (4), 283; (4), 281; (4), 292. C. 41828

LOHMAN (A.) Trial of Madame Restell, alias Ann Lohman, for Abortion and Causing the Death of Mrs. Purdy; being a full account of all the Proceedings on the Trial, together with the Suppressed Evidence and Editorial Remarks. *New York.* 1841. 8vo. 41829

Also: Trial ... for Manslaughter, by producing Abortion on the Person of Maria Bodine, to which is added a full Account of her Life, and Horrible Practices, together with Prostitution in New York, its Extent, Causes and Effects upon Society. *New York.* 1847. 12mo, pp. 48. Portraits. — Wonderful Trial of Caroline Lohman, *alias* Madame Restell, with Speeches of Counsel, Charge of the Court, and Verdict of the Jury. *New York.* 1847. 8vo, pp. 38.

LOHMANN (Van C. W.) Reise nach Cayenne aus dem französischen. *Hamburg.* 1799. 8vo. 41830

Title from a French catalogue; not described by Boucher de la Richarderie.

The "Loil" Legislature of Alabama. *Montgomery.* 1868. 8vo.

[LOISEL (Francisco).] Demostracion de gozo que a obsequio del Señor D. Carlos Clemente de Borbon, principe sucesor de España. *Havana: en la Imprenta destinada para el computo eclesiastico.* 1772. 4to, pp. 52. 41832

Partly in verse.

LOMAS (J.) The Wealthy Men and Women of Brooklyn and Williamsburgh: ... with Brief Biographical Sketches ... . By John Lomas and Alfred S. Peace. *Brooklyn: Printed by A. S. Peace.* 1847. 16mo, pp. 48. 41833

LOMAX (J. T.) An Address to the Alumni ... of St. John's College, Annapolis. Delivered February 22, 1842. By John Taylor Lomax ... . *Baltimore: Woods and Crane, Printers.* 1842. 8vo, pp. 28. BA. 41834

LOMAX. Digest of the Laws respecting Real Property, generally adopted and in use in the United States; ... By John Taylor Lomax, LL.D. ... *Philadelphia.* 1839. 3 vols., 8vo. + Second Edition, ... greatly enlarged. ... *Richmond, Va.: Adolphus Morris.* 1855. 3 vols., 8vo, pp. viii, 821, iv; (4), 518, iv; (4), 452, cxxxvii. H. 41835

LOMAX (J.) The Notes of an American Lyre. By Judith Lomax, a Native of ... Virginia. ... *Richmond: Printed by Samuel Pleasants.* 1813. 16mo, pp. 70. B., C. 41836

LOMBARD (A.) Notice sur la position financière actuelle des États de l'Amérique du Nord accompagnée de quelques détails sur les dettes des principaux États européens. Par Alex. Lombard. ... *Geneva.* 1841. 8vo, pp. 64. 41837

[LOMBARD (Ammi Cutter).] Plan for forming a Warehouse Company ... . *Boston: Nathan Sawyer, Printer.* 1860. 8vo, pp. 12. Plan. H. 41838

[LOMBARD (Israel).] Remarks on the Tariff Bill ... . [n. p. n. d.] 8vo, pp. 8. 41839

LOMBARD UNIVERSITY. Catalogue of Lombard University, Galesburg, Ill., for ... 1859–60. *Galesburg.* 1860. 8vo. Cont'd.

LOMBARDO (N.) Arte de la Lengua Teguima vulgarmente llamada Opata. Compuesta por el P. Natal Lombardo de la Compañia de Jesus ... . *Con Licencia En Mexico, por Miguel de Ribera, Impressor y Mercader de libros, año de* 1702. 4to, 8 prel. leaves, 261 leaves. 41841

LOMBARDO. Vocabulario de la Lengua Teguima y Platicas doctrinales en ella. Por Natal Lombardo ... . *Mexico.* 1702. 4to.

This language is spoken in Sonora.

[LOMÉNIE (Ch. F. de).] Extrait des Registres du Conseil d'Estat | ... Le Roy s'estant fait representée en son Conseil, l'arrest rendu en iceluy le 7 mars 1657, portant réglement de la conduite qui doit être tenuë en la Traitte des Peleteries ... [Colophon:] *Paris le* 13 *May* 1659. 4to, 2 leaves. 41843

[LOMÉNIE.] Articles | accordez | entre | les Directevrs et Associez | en la Compagnie | de la Novvelle France; | et les Depvtez des habitans | dvdit pays: | Agreez et confirmez | par le Roy. | *A Paris,* | *chez Sebastien Cramoisy, Imprimeur* | *ordinaire du Roy, & de la Reyne Regente.* | M.DC.XLV. | *Auec Priuilege de sa Maiesté.* | Folio, pp. 14. 41844

LOMÉNIE (L. de). Beaumarchais et son Temps. Études sur la Société en France au XVIIIe Siècle d'après des Documents Inédits. Par Louis de Loménie. *Paris: Michel Lévy Frères.* 1856. 2 vols., 8vo, pp. (2), xi, 522; (2), 596, (1). + Deuxième Édition. [*Ibid.*] 1858. 2 vols., 8vo, pp. (4), xi, 522; (4), 596.

LOMÉNIE. Beaumarchais and his Times. Sketches of French Society in the Eighteenth Century from unpublished Documents. By Louis de Loménie. Translated by Henry S. Edwards. *Lon-*

don: Addey and Co. MDCCCLVI. 4 vols., post 8vo, pp. xxi, 17–313, (1); v, 9–290; 293; 375. BA. + *New York: Harper & Brothers.* 1857. 12mo, pp. 460. B. 41846

Vol. III., chapters 20–23 relate to Beaumarchais' transactions in America during the Revolution.

LOMOND (R.) A Narrative of the Rise and Progress of Emigration, from the Counties of Lanark and Renfrew to the New Settlements in Upper Canada. By Robert Lomond ... . *Edinburgh.* 1822. 8vo. 41847

LONCK (H. C.) Entwerffung von Eroberung der Stadt Olinda, so in der Hauptmannschafft Pharnambuco gelegen, vnd durch Heinrich Cornelis Lonck, General und Colonell Wartenburg, eingenommen: welche eygentlich abgebildet, vnd mit dem Jagd Schiff der Braeck genannt, überschicket worden. [*Amsterdam?* 1630.] Folio, 1 leaf. C. 41848

LONCK. Veroveringh | van | De Stadt Olinda | Gelegen in de | Capitania van Phernambuco, | Door den E.E. Manhaften | Gestrenghen | Heyndrick C. Lonck, Generael te | Water ende te Lande. Mitsgaders: | Diderick van VVaerdenburgh, Colonel over de Militie te | Lande, van wegen de Geoctroyeerde West-Indische Compagnie | onder de Hoog: Mo: Heeren Staten Generael, ende | den Prince van Orangen, Gouverneur General der | Vereenighde Neder-landen. | *T'Amsterdam, Voor Hessel Gerritsz. Pas-Caert-schryver* | *ende Boeck-* | *verkooper* ... [1630.] Sm. 4to, 6 leaves. C. 41849

Very rare. This conquest of the town of Olinda, in the Capitania of Pernambuco, by the courageous H. C. Lonck and Diderick van Waerdenburgh, in behalf of the West India Company, contains also the text of the treaty of surrender of the forts of S. Jorge and S. Francisco (in Spanish and Dutch). This text is of importance, as it rectifies, in some degree, the opinions of some historians on that subject. *See* Netscher's "Les Hollandais au Brésil," p. 48, *note.* Translated into German as:

LONCK. Beschreibung, welcher Gestalt die Hauptstatt desz Königreichs Brasilien, Phernambuco, in America gelegen, von Heinrich Cornelio Lonck, General, vnd Dieterich Wardenburg, verschienen Monat Febr. belägert, auch beneben den umbliegenden Castellen, im Monat Martio 1630, erobert worden. Auss dem Niederländischen in Hochteutsch vbergesetzt. *Erstlich getruckt zu Amsterdam, H. Gerritsz.* 1630. Sm. 4to, 4 leaves. C.

LONDON (D. H.) Speech of Daniel H. London on the Commercial, Agricultural & Intellectual Independence of Virginia and the South ... the 5th January 1860 ... . *Richmond, Va.* 1860. 8vo, pp. 52. H. 41851

LONDON (*Bishop of*). *See* [Gibson (Edmund)], Vol. VII., Nos. 27310–13, [King (J.)], Vol. IX., No. 37811, *also* Nos. 40461, 40537, *and* [Wilson] (T.)

LONDON. Address to the City of London with Continuation. 1762. 41852

Partly relates to the conquest of Canada. Title and note from an English catalogue.

Circular of the American Association in London, 1859–60. Folio. 41853

God's Terrible Voice in the City of London; wherein you have the Narration of the late dreadful Judgments of Plague and Fire; the former in the year 1665, and the latter in 1666. *Cambridge: Reprinted by M. Johnson.* 1668. 4to, pp. 32. 41854

A very rare Massachusetts reprint.

The London Calendar, or Court and City Register for England, Scotland, Ireland, and America, for the Year 1783. *London.* [1783.] 12mo. Continued. 41855

The London Chronicle. Vol. I. Jan.–June, 1757. *London.* 1757. 4to. Continued. 41856

Valuable for its accounts relative to the French and English war in Canada, on the Ohio, the Lakes, etc.

LONDON EMANCIPATION SOCIETY. Proceedings of the London Emancipation Society, an Anti-Slavery Meeting, at Spafield's Chapel, Oct. 14, 1859. *London.* 1859. 8vo. 41857

The London Gazette. A Reprint of a London Gazette, containing an account of an Engagement with the French. *New York: Printed by William Bradford.* 1696. Folio. 41858

"The first Newspaper printed in America."—*Historical Magazine*, III. 175.

The London Magazine: or, Gentleman's Monthly Intelligencer. *London: Printed for R. Baldwin.* 1732. 8vo. BA.

Continued to 1785. Contains many important historical, biographical, and political papers relative to the British North American Colonies. Some of the volumes have the title "The London Magazine and Monthly Chronologer."

LONDON MISSIONARY SOCIETY. *See* Smith (J.), *also* No. 15699.

London Review. *London.* 1777. 8vo. Continued. 41860

Relates many American historical incidents, etc.

London and Country Brewer; in Four Parts, including curious accounts of the Pensylvania manner of Brewing, the Carolina way of Brewing ... . *London: T. Astley.* 1759. 8vo. 41861

London *v.* New York. By an English Workman. ... *London: Bosworth & Harrison.* 1859. 8vo, pp. xi, 83. H. 41862

LONDON, *C. W.* Railton's Directory, for the City of London, C. W., for 1856–57. *London.* 1858. 8vo. Map. Continued.

LONDONDERRY, *N. H.* Celebration Exercises at the One Hundred and Fiftieth Anniversary of the Settled Part of Old Nutfield, comprising the Towns of Londonderry, Derry, Windham, Manchester, Hudson and Salem, N. H. *Manchester.* 1870. 8vo. 41864

LONDONIO (C. G.) Storia delle colonie Inglesi in America, dalla loro fondazion, fino allo stabilimento della loro independenza. Di C. G. Londonio. *Milano: Dalla Tipografia di Gio. Gius. Destefania.* MDCCCXII–XIII. 3 vols., 8vo, pp. (10), 299; 335; 381, (2). H. 41865

LONEY (F. B.) A Letter on the Financial Situation ... by Francis B. Loney ... . *Baltimore: Printed by Lucas Brothers.* 1869. 8vo, pp. 18. H. 41866

LONG (A.) The Present Condition and Future Prospects of the Country. Speech of Hon. Alexander Long, of Ohio, ... April 8, 1864. [n. p. n. d.] 8vo, pp. 20. BA. 41867

Also: ... Speech ... [on the State of the Union] April 7, 1864. [n. p. n. d.] 8vo, pp. 7.—Speech ... on the Policy of the Administration ... Feb. 7th, 1865. ... *Cincinnati: Johnson & Farrell, Printers.* 1865. 8vo, pp. 16. + [n. p. n. d.] pp. 16.

LONG (A. K.) Defence of Commander Andrew K. Long, U. S. N., before the Court of Inquiry No. 3 ... . *Carlisle.* 1857. 8vo, pp. 23. 41868

LONG (C.) ... A Sermon ... at the Funeral of the Rev. Jarvis Gregg, ... July 3, 1836. By Clement Long. *Hudson: Ansel R. Clark.* 1836. 8vo, pp. 21. B. 41869

Also: ... An Address at the Inauguration of the Author as Professor ... in the Theological Seminary at Auburn, June 15, 1853. ... *Auburn: J. C. Ivison.* 1853. 8vo, pp. 59.

LONG (D.) A Discourse, ... in Milford, (Mass.) ... Dec. 24, 1815, occasioned by the Death of Miss Betsy Tidd ... . By David Long, A.M. ... *Boston: Printed by Samuel T. Armstrong.* 1816. 8vo, pp. 16. BA. 41870

[LONG (Edward).] The History of Jamaica. Or, General Survey of the Antient and Modern State of that Island: With Reflections on its Situation, Settlements, Inhabitants, Climate,

Products, Commerce, Laws, and Government. ... *London: T. Lowndes.* MDCCLXXIV. 3 vols., 4to, pp. (2), 628; (2), 601; viii, 595–976. Plates. B., C. 41871

"The high station of the author at Jamaica, where he was Judge of the Admiralty Court, gave every opportunity of procuring authentic materials, which have been digested with ingenuity and candor. The work has now become exceedingly rare."—NICHOL'S *Literary Anecdotes*, III. 182. The book is not so rare as this remark seems to indicate. *See* "M. Rev.," LI. 129, 431.

LONG. Letters on the Colonies. By Edward Long, Esquire. *London.* 1775. 8vo. 41872

LONG (E. M.) The Union Tabernacle or Movable Tent-Church. By Edward Long. *Philadelphia: Parry & McMillan.* 1859. 8vo, pp. 234, 214. 41873

[LONG (George), *and others.*] The Geography of America and the West Indies. *London: Society for the Diffusion of Useful Knowledge.* 1841. 8vo, pp. xii, 648. BA. 41874

Reprinted with the following title:

LONG. ... America and the West Indies, Geographically Described. By Professor Long, ... George Richardson Porter, ... George Tucker ... . *London: Charles Knight and Co.* 1845. 8vo, pp. xii, 648. 3 Maps. B. 41875

LONG (H. C.) Report of Captain Henry C. Long, on the ... Prospects of ... Cairo. September 2, 1850. Submitted by Col. S. H. Long ... . *New York: Narine & Co., Printers.* 1850. 8vo, pp. 25, (1). BA. 41876

LONG (H. M.) The British Empire in America, containing the History of the Discovery, Settlement, Progress and Present State of all the British Colonies on the Continent and Islands of America. [n. p. n. d.] 2 vols., 12mo. 41877

Title from a Baltimore catalogue; it reads very much like John Oldmixon's work.

LONG (J.) Voyages and Travels of an Indian Interpreter and Trader, Describing The Manners and Customs of the North American Indians; with an Account of the Posts situated on the River Saint Laurence, Lake Ontario, &c. To which is added, a Vocabulary of The Chippeway Language. Names of Furs and Skins, in English and French. A List of Words in the Iroquois, Mohegan, Shawanee, and Esquimeaux Tongues, and a Table, shewing The Analogy between the Algonkin and Chippeway Languages. By J. Long. *London: Printed for the Author.* M,DCC,XCI. 4to, pp. (2), x, (2), 295. Map. BA. 41878

"A most faithful picture of the life and manners of the Indian and Canadian traders."—VOLNEY. It is also linguistically valuable. The author resided in the country for nineteen years, and has given a candid account of the injustice perpetrated on the Indians by the British. I have seen catalogues which describe large paper copies, but believe the statement to be erroneous; all the numerous copies I have seen have had a large margin.

LONG. Voyages chez différentes Nations Sauvages de l'Amérique Septentrionale; Renfermant des détails curieux sur les moeurs, usages, cérémonies réligieuses, le systême militaire, &c. ... Traduits de l'Anglois, avec des notes & additions intéressantes, par J. B. L. J. Billecocq, Citoyen Francais. *A Paris: Prault l'aîne, Imprimeur.* ... II. *Année de l'Ere Républicaine.* 8vo, pp. (4), xxxvi, 320. Map. BA. 41879

Some copies are dated *Paris*, 1810; they are the same work with a new title-page only.

LONG. Reisen eines Amerikanischen Dolmetschers und Pelzhändlers welche eine Beschreibung der Sitten und Gebräuche der Nordamerikanischen Eingebornen und einige Nachrichten von dem Posten an St. Lorenz-Flusse, dem See Ontario u. s. w. enthalten. *Berlin: In der Vossischen Buchhandlung.* 1792. 8vo, pp. vi, 176. Map. J.C.B. 41880

This German translation is by G. Forster.

LONG. See- und Land-Reisen; enthaltend eine Beschreibung der Sitten und Gewohnheiten der Nordamerikanischen Wilden; der Englischen Forts oder Schanzen längs dem St. Lorenz-Flusse, dem Ontario u. s. w.; ... Aus dem Englischen, von E. A. W. Zimmermann. *Hamburg: B. Gottlob Hoffmann.* 1791. 8vo, pp. xxiv, 334. Map. J.C.B. 41881

LONG (J. D.) Pictures of Slavery in Church and State; ... with an Appendix, containing the Views of John Wesley and Richard Watson on Slavery. By Rev. John Dixon Long ... . *Philadelphia.* 1857. 12mo, pp. 418. C. + Second Edition. ... [*Ibid.*] + Third Edition. ... [*Ibid.*] 12mo, pp. 4–418, 8. H.

LONG (M.) Historical Sketch of Warner, N. H. By Dr. Morris Long. *Concord: Jacob B. Moore.* 1832. 8vo. 41883

Republished in 1870. *See also* "N. H. Hist. Soc. Coll.," Vol. III.

LONG (R. C.) The Ancient Architecture of America, ... a Discourse ... April 3d, 1849. By R. Cary Long, A.M. ... *New York: Bartlett & Welford.* 1849. 8vo, pp. 37. 9 Plates. H.

The ninth plate is erroneously numbered XI.

LONG (R. H.) Hunt's Gazetteer of the Border and Southern States; containing a full Description of the Railroad Routes,

Turnpike Roads, Cities, Towns, etc. By R. H. Long ... . *Pittsburgh: John P. Hunt.* [1863.] 18mo, pp. 272. Map. C.

LONG (S. H.) Description of Col. Long's Bridges ... By S. H. Long ... . *Concord, N. H.: Printed by John F. Brown.* 1836. 8vo, pp. 72, (2). Plates. + *Philadelphia: Printed by Wm. F. Geddes.* 1841. 8vo, pp. 55. 10 Plates. A. 41886

LONG. Narrative of the Proceedings of the Board of Engineers, of the Baltimore and Ohio Railroad Company, from its Organization to its Dissolution ... . By Lt. Col. S. H. Long, and Capt. Wm. Gibbs McNeill ... . *Baltimore: Bailey & Francis.* 1830. 8vo, pp. 189, 95. H. 41887

LONG. Voyage in a Six-oared Skiff to the Falls of Saint Anthony in 1817. By Major Stephen H. Long. With Introductory Note by Edward D. Neill ... . *Philadelphia: Henry B. Ashmead, Printer.* 1860. 8vo, pp. 87, (1). Map. 41888

This voyage was made while the author was Superintendent of Indian Affairs for the Northwest Territories. Also: Report of the Canal Commissioners in Reply to the Strictures of Mr. Robinson. ... *Philadelphia.* 1831. 8vo. *See also* James (E.), Vol. IX., Nos. 35682–84, Keating (W. H.), No. 37137, Minnesota, *and* Tennessee.

LONG DOCK COMPANY. Charter and Laws relating to the Long Dock Company. ... [n. p. n. d.] 8vo, pp. 31. H. 41889

Also: First Report of the Directors of the Long Dock Company of New Jersey ... May, 1860. *New York: Wm. H. Trafton & Co. ... Printers.* 1860. 8vo, pp. 11, 25. Map. H.

LONG ISLAND, *N. Y.* Curtin's Directory of Astoria, East New York, Flatbush, Flushing, Glen Cove, Greenport, Hempstead, Huntington, Jamaica, Newtown, Patchogue, Port Jefferson, Riverhead, Sag Harbour, and Setauket. 1865–66. *New York.* 1866. 12mo. Continued. 41890

See also Curtin (C.), Vol. V., No. 18023.

Documents relating to the Conveyance of Land, ... on Long-Island. *New-York: Bell & Gould.* 1850. 8vo, pp. 24. 41891

Journal of the Third Convention of the Protestant Episcopal Church in the Diocese of Long Island, Brooklyn, May, 1870. *Brooklyn.* 1870. 8vo. Continued. B. 41892

Letter from a Long-Island Farmer. *See our* No. 40298.

LONG ISLAND BIBLE SOCIETY. The Second Annual Report of the Long-Island Bible Society, ... at Jamaica, ... 17th ... of September, 1817. *New-York: Printed by J. Seymour.* 1817. 8vo, pp. 20. BA. 41893

LONG ISLAND CANAL. Documents presented to the Legislature of the State of New York in relation to a Long Island Canal. ... *New York.* 1826. 8vo. Map. 41894

Reports of Committees in relation to the Long Island Canal Company. *Albany.* 1827. 16mo. 41895

LONG ISLAND COLLEGE HOSPITAL. Charter and By-Laws of the Long Island College Hospital ... . Incorporated March, 1858. *John F. Trow, Printer, N. Y.* 1858. 8vo, pp. 32.

Also: Circular and Catalogue of the Long Island College Hospital for 1861. ... *Brooklyn: Wilton, Printer.* [1861?] 8vo, pp. 8. Continued.

LONG ISLAND HISTORICAL SOCIETY. First Annual Report of the ... Long Island Historical Society, May, 1864. *Brooklyn.* 1864. 8vo, pp. 47, (1). Continued. B. 41897

Also: The By-Laws and Certificate of Incorporation, of the Long Island Historical Society. *Brooklyn: For the Society.* MDCCCLXIII. 8vo, pp. 22, (1). *See also* Dankers (J.), Vol. V., No. 18503, *and* Field (T. W.), Vol. VI., No. 24293.

The Long-Island Journal of Philosophy, and Cabinet of Variety. Conducted by Simon Fleet and others. *Huntington, L. I.* 1825. 8vo. S. 41898

LONG ISLAND RAILROAD COMPANY. ... Report of the ... Directors of the Long Island Railroad Company ... . [n. p.] 1843. 8vo, pp. 8. Continued. B. 41899

Also: An Act to incorporate the Long-Island Rail-Road Company. Passed April 24, 1834. [n. p. n. d.] 8vo, pp. 16. B.—Report of the Board of Directors of the Long Island Railroad Company to the Stockholders, in relation to the Condition of its Affairs and Prospects, when completed to Greenpoint. [n. p. n. d.] 8vo.—Strictures upon the Conduct of the President of the Long Island Rail-Road Company. [*New York.* 1845.] 8vo, pp. 18. H.

LONG ISLAND WATER WORKS COMPANY. *See* Vol. II. 8323.

Question of a South Ferry. *See* Vol. II., No. 8291, *note.*

Report on the Project of Uniting the Great Bays of Long-Island by Canals, from Coney-Island to Bridgehampton. *Brooklyn: E. B. Spooner, Printer.* 1848. 8vo, pp. 22, v. Map. H.

To the Clergy and Laity of Long Island. [n. p. 1872.] 8vo, pp. 12. 41901

An appeal for missions to the North American Indians.

LONG POND. *See* Boston, Vol. II., No. 6782.

Long-Rifle, Hunter; or, Adventures on the Frontier. ... *New York: G. Munro & Co.* 186–. 16mo, pp. 99. 41902

LONG-RUN. Minutes of the Annual Meeting of the Long-Run Association of Baptists [in Kentucky. n. p. 1840.] 8vo.

LONGACRE (J. B.) *See* Herring (J.), Vol. VIII., No. 31577.

LONGARO DEGLI ODDI. *See* Oddi (*P.* Longaro degli).

LONGCHAMP (*M.* de). Point de la question sur les colonies. *Paris.* 1720. 41904

LONGCHAMP (R. de). Essai historique. *See* Rengger (A.)

L[ONGCHAMPS (Pierre de).] Histoire Impartiale des Événemens Militaires et Politiques de la Dernière Guerre, dans les Quartre Parties du Monde. Par M. de L. *Paris: Chez la Veuve Duchesne.* 1785. 3 vols., 12mo, pp. 558; 523; (2), 620. + *Amsterdam.* 1785. 3 vols., 12mo. C. + Seconde Édition. *Paris: Chez la Veuve Duchesne.* 1787. 3 vols., 12mo. + Troisième Édition. [*Ibid.*] 1789. 3 vols., 12mo. 41905

The larger portion of this work relates to the military operations in North America. The author's name is mentioned in full on the title of the third edition.

LONGFELLOW (H. W.) Ballads and Other Poems. By Henry Wadsworth Longfellow ... . *Cambridge.* 1841. 16mo. + Second Edition. [*Ibid.*] 1842. 16mo. C. + Third Edition. *Cambridge: John Owen.* MDCCCXLII. 8vo, pp. 132. + Tenth Edition. *Boston: William D. Ticknor & Co.* 1848. 8vo, pp. 132.

A few copies of the third edition were printed on large paper.

LONGFELLOW. The Complete Works of Henry W. Longfellow. Revised Edition. *Boston.* 1866. 7 vols., cr. 8vo.

One hundred copies printed on large paper.

LONGFELLOW. The Courtship of Miles Standish, and Other Poems. By Henry Wadsworth Longfellow. *Boston: Ticknor and Fields.* MDCCCLVIII. 8vo, pp. 215. C. + Second Edition. *London: W. Kent & Co.* MDCCCLVIII. 12mo, pp. viii, 135. B. + *London: Bogue.* 1858. 8vo. + Illustrated by Absolon. *London: H. Bohn.* 1858. 8vo. + Illustrated by Gilbert. *London: Routledge.* 1858. 8vo. + *Boston: Ticknor and Fields.* MDCCCLIX. 8vo, pp. 215. BA. 41908

LONGFELLOW. Evangeline, a Tale of Acadie. By Henry Wadsworth Longfellow. *Boston: William D. Ticknor & Company.* 1847. 16mo, pp. 163. + Second Edition. [*Ibid.*] 1848. 16mo. + Third Edition. [*Ibid.*] 1848. + Sixth Edition. [*Ibid.*] + With an Introduction, Historical and Explanatory. *London.*

1848. 18mo, pp. 140. + *London: Clarke.* 18—. 18mo, pp. 156. + Eighth Edition. *Boston.* 1853. 12mo. + Illustrated by Foster. New Edition. *London: Bogue.* 1854. Post 8vo. + Illustrated by Gilbert. *London: Routledge.* 1856. 8vo. + Tenth Edition. *Boston.* 1856. 16mo. + New Edition, Illustrated by Gilbert and Dalziel. *Boston.* 1857. 8vo, pp. 159. + With Illustrations, by F. O. C. Darley. *Boston.* 1867. Sq. 16mo.

LONGFELLOW. Evangeline, a Tale of Acadie; The Belfrey of Bruges; Nuremberg, and additional Poems. By Henry W. Longfellow. *London.* 1848. 32mo, pp. 196. 41910

There are several other English editions.

A Review of Evangeline. From the American Review for February, 1848. [n. p. n. d.] 8vo, pp. 15. 41911

LONGFELLOW. Evangelina; poëme, traduit de l'anglais par M. le chevalier de Châtelain. *Londres: Rolandi.* 1853. 12mo.

LONGFELLOW. Évangéline; conte d'Acadie ... traduit par Ch. Brunel. *Paris: Meyrueis et Cie.* 1864. 12mo, pp. 125. 41913

LONGFELLOW. Évangéline traduction du poëme Acadien de Longfellow. Par L. Pamphile Lemay. Deuxième Édition. *Quebec: P.-G. Delisle.* 1870. 12mo, pp. 192. 41914

See also Lemay (L. P.), No. 39987.

LONGFELLOW. La Légende dorée et poëmes sur l'esclavage. ... Traduits par Paul Blier et Edward Mac-Donnel; suivis de quelques poésies par Paul Blier. *Paris: J. Gay.* 1864. 8vo, pp. x, 203. 41915

LONGFELLOW. Hypérion et Kavanagh. Traduction française; précédée d'une notice de l'auteur. *Paris: Dentu.* 1860. 2 vols., 12mo. 41916

LONGFELLOW. The New England Tragedies. By Henry Wadsworth Longfellow. ... *Boston: Ticknor and Fields.* 1868. 12mo, pp. 179. + *Leipzig: Bernhard Tauchnitz.* 1868. 12mo, pp. (4), 258, (2). B. 41917

LONGFELLOW. Poems. By Henry Wadsworth Longfellow. Tenth Edition. *Cambridge.* 1844. 12mo. + *Philadelphia.* 1845. 8vo. + *New York: Harper and Brothers.* 1846. 8vo, pp. 117. + Fifth Edition. [*Ibid.*] 1848. 8vo, pp. 117. + [*Ibid.*] 1849. 8vo, pp. 146. + A New Edition. *Boston: Ticknor and Fields.* MDCCCL. 2 vols., 16mo, pp. xv, 475; vi, 452. H. + [*Ibid.*]

MDCCCLII. 2 vols., 16mo. + [*Ibid.*] MDCCCLV. 2 vols., 16mo. + [*Ibid.*] MDCCCLVII. 2 vols., 16mo. + [*Ibid.*] MDCCCLVIII. 2 vols., 16mo. + [*Ibid.*] MDCCCL. 5 vols., 16mo, pp. xv, 144; vii, 151; 157; 183; iv, (2), 141. H. 41918

The last-mentioned edition is also printed on large paper.

LONGFELLOW. Poems, ... Illustrated with ... Engravings on wood from Designs by Birket Foster and others. *London.* 1854. 8vo. 41919

Some copies have the imprint *Boston*, 1854.

LONGFELLOW. Poems on Slavery. By Henry Wadsworth Longfellow. *Cambridge: J. Owen.* MDCCCXLII. 16mo, pp. 31. + Second Edition. [*Ibid.*] 16mo. + Third Edition. [*Ibid.*] MDCCCXLIII. 16mo, pp. 31. BA. 41920

LONGFELLOW. Poetical Works, ... Illustrated with upwards of one hundred Designs, drawn by J. Gilbert, engraved by Dalziel. *London: Geo. Routledge & Sons.* 1856. 4to. 41921

LONGFELLOW. Poetical Works, including his Translations and Notes. Illustrated with above two hundred Engravings on wood, from Designs by Birket Foster, John Gilbert, G. H. Thomas, John Absolon, etc. *London: Henry G. Bohn.* 1861. 8vo. 24 Engravings. + *Boston.* 1862. 8vo. 41922

This edition contains "Hiawatha" and the "Courtship of Miles Standish."

LONGFELLOW. The Poetical Works of Henry W. Longfellow. ... *Boston.* 1856. 12mo. + *Leipzig: Bernhard Tauchnitz.* 1856. 3 vols., 16mo, pp. viii, 399, Portrait; vi, 322; viii, 246. B. + *London.* 1864. 16mo. B. 41923

LONGFELLOW. The Poetical Works ... . Complete Edition. *London: Milner and Sowerby.* 1866. 24mo, pp. 402. Portrait. + *Boston.* 1867. Sq. 16mo, pp. viii, 363. + *London: Frederick Warne and Co.* 1868. 16mo, pp. xii, 628. B. 41924

There are other English editions which we have not seen.

LONGFELLOW. Prose Works of Henry Wadsworth Longfellow. ... *Boston.* 1857. 2 vols., 16mo. C. + *Boston: Ticknor and Fields.* MDCCCLXIII. 2 vols., 24mo, pp. 455; iv, 475. + *London: H. G. Bohn.* MD.CCC.LXIII. 16mo, pp. vii, (1), 580. Plates. B. 41925

LONGFELLOW. The Seaside and the Fireside. By Henry Wadsworth Longfellow. *Boston.* 1849. 12mo. + *Boston: Ticknor, Reed, and Fields.* MDCCCL. 12mo, pp. iv, (2), 141. BA.

LONGFELLOW. The Song of Hiawatha. By Henry Wadsworth Longfellow. *Boston: Ticknor and Fields.* MDCCCLV. 12mo, pp. iv, 316. + [*Ibid.*] MDCCCLVI. + [*Ibid.*] MDCCCLX. + *London: Low.* 1855. 12mo. + *London: Knight & Son.* 1856. 18mo. + [*Ibid.*] 1858. 18mo. + *London: Routledge.* 1859. 18mo. + Illustrated by Thomas. *London: Henry Bohn.* 1859. 8vo. 41927

Founded on an Indian tradition, respecting a person of miraculous origin, the benefactor and peace-maker. The scene is among the Ojibways, on Lake Superior. A Chippewa vocabulary is added. For parodies on this popular poem, *see* Henderson (M. A.), Vol. IX., No. 31325, Shortfellow (H. W.), *pseudon.*, *and* Ward (James W.)

LONGFELLOW. Hiawatha; poëme indo-américain. Traduction avec notes par H. Gomont. *Paris: Amyot.* 1861. 8vo.

LONGFELLOW. Hiawatha: Rendered into Latin. With Abridgment. By F. W. Newman. *London.* 1862. 12mo, pp. viii, 110. 41929

LONGFELLOW. Tales of a Wayside Inn. By Henry Wadsworth Longfellow. *Boston: Ticknor and Fields.* 1863. 16mo, pp. (2), v, (2), 225. B. + [*Ibid.*] 1864. 41930

LONGFELLOW. Un Village américain, par H. W. Longfellow; traduit de l'anglais par Mme Tourte-Cherbuliez. *Paris: Cherbuliez.* 1861. 12mo. 41931

LONGFELLOW. Works, Prose and Verse. 1854. 2 vols.

For a list of foreign editions of Longfellow, *see* "Allibone's Dictionary." Also: The Belfry of Bruges and other Poems. ... *Cambridge: Printed by John Owen.* 1846. 16mo, pp. vii, 151. BA. + Second Edition. [*Ibid.*] + Fourth Edition. [*Ibid.*]—The Building of the Ship. ... *Boston: Fields, Osgood & Co.* 1870 Sq. 16mo, pp. 79. Plates.—Christus. A Mystery ... *Boston.* 18—. 8vo.—Flower-de-Luce. ... *Boston: Ticknor and Fields.* 1867. 16mo, pp. 72. Plates. H.—Household Poems. ... *Boston: Ticknor and Fields.* 1865. 16mo, pp. 96. H.—Kavanagh, a Tale. ... *Boston: Ticknor Reed and Fields.* MDCCCXLIX. 12mo, pp. (2), 188. + Eighth Edition. *Boston: Ticknor and Fields.* MDCCCLVI. 12mo, pp. (2), 188.—Voices of the Night. ... *Cambridge: John Owen.* MDCCCXXXIX. 16mo, pp. xv, 144. + Second Edition. [*Ibid.*] MDCCCXL. 16mo. + Third Edition. [*Ibid.*] MDCCCXL. 16mo. BA. + Ninth Edition. [*Ibid.*] MDCCCXLIV. 16mo. B. + Twelfth Edition. *Boston: William D. Ticknor & Co.* 1848. 16mo. + *London.* 1848. 32mo, pp. 216.—The Waif. A Collection of Poems. ... *Cambridge: John Owen.* 1845. 16mo, pp. xi, 144. + Second Edition. [*Ibid.*] 1845. + Fifth Edition. *Boston.* 1846. 16mo.

LONGFELLOW (S.) ... A Sermon ... [in] Brooklyn ... April 23, 1853, at the Opening of their New Place of Worship. By Samuel Longfellow. ... *New-York: John C. Beale.* 1853. 8vo, pp. 16. H. 41933

Also: ... A Sermon ... at the Dedication of the Chapel of the Second Unitarian ... Society, in Brooklyn, N. Y., March 2, 1858. ... *New York: Mann, Stearns & Beale ... Printers.* 1858. 8vo, pp. 23. H.

LONGFELLOW (S. L.) An Oration ... July 4th, 1804 ... at ... Portland ... . By Stephen L. Longfellow. [n. p. n. d.] 16mo, pp. 18. H. 41934

LONGMAN (C.) *and others.* *See* Dean (J.), Vol. V., No. 19209.

LONGPÉRIER (A. de). Notice des Monuments exposés dans la Salle des Antiquités Américaines (Mexique et Pérou), au Musée du Louvre, par Adrien de Longpérier ... . *Paris: Vinchon.* 1850. Imp. 8vo, pp. 130. + Deuxième Édition. [*Ibid.*] 1852. 8vo, pp. 119, (1). B. 41935

[LONGSTREET (Augustus B.)] Georgia Scenes, Characters, Incidents, &c., in the First Half Century of the Republic. By a Native Georgian. *Augusta.* 1835. 12mo, pp. 235. + Second Edition. *New-York: Harper & Brothers.* 1840. 12mo, pp. 214. Plates. + [*Ibid.*] 1843. + [*Ibid.*] 1848. + [*Ibid.*] 1850. + [*Ibid.*] 1858. + [*Ibid.*] 1869. + *Macon, Ga.: Burke, Boykin & Co.* 1864. 8vo, pp. 239. 41936

LONGSTREET. Master William Mitten. By Judge Longstreet. *Macon, Ga.: Burke, Boykin & Co.* [18—.] 8vo.

LONGVIEW, *Ohio.* Annual Reports of the Board of Trustees and Officers of the Longview Asylum for the Insane, to the Governor of the State of Ohio. [n. p.] 1860. 8vo. Cont'd.

LONGWORTH (D.) Longworth's American Almanack, New York Register and City Directory for the Twenty-First Year of American Independence. *New York.* 1796. 12mo. 41939

Continued to 1820 or later. Afterwards by Thomas Longworth to 1843 or later; *see* New York City.

LONGWORTH. Longworth's Pocket Almanack and New York and United States Kalendar ... . *New York: D. Longworth, Jan.* 1, 1816. 18mo, pp. 167. Continued. S. 41940

LONGWORTH (N.) Memorial of the Golden Wedding of Nicholas and Susan Longworth, Christmas Eve, 1857 ... . *Cincinnati.* 1858. 4to. 41941

LONGYEAR (J. W.) ... Speech of Hon. J. W. Longyear ... on the Reconstruction of the Union. ... April 30, 1864. [n. p. 1864.] 8vo, pp. 8. H. 41942

Look before You Leap; or, a Few Hints to such Artizans, Mechanics, Labourers, Farmers and Husbandmen, as are desirous of Emigrating to America, being a genuine Collection of Letters from Persons who have Emigrated; Containing Remarks, Notes and Anecdotes, Political, Philosophical, Biographical and Literary, of the present State, ... Population, Prospects and Advantages, of America, together with the Reception, Success, Mode of Life, Opinions and Situation, of many ... who have Emigrated, particularly to the Federal City of Washington. ... *London: W. Row.* 1796. 8vo, pp. 144. + Second Edition. To which is Added an Appendix containing some Animadversions and Remarks on the Conduct of Popular Societies, and American Emissaries relative to this very interesting Performance. [*Ibid.*] 8vo, pp. 144, Appendix, 24. + Third Edition. [*Ibid.*]

"A series of letters, evidently forgeries, and purporting to be written by a carpenter, a mason, a plasterer, and a painter and glazier, decrying everything in America, with the view to discourage emigration."—*Monthly Review*, XXI. 343.

Look before you Leap. An Address to the People of Massachusetts. By a Washington Federalist. *Newburyport.* 1805. 8vo, pp. 12. 41944

A Looking Glass for a Right Honourable Mendicant; or, the Real Character of a certain great Orator: with political Observations. In particular the Marrow of the Slave Question. By an Old Member of Parliament. *London: W. Crosby.* 1794. 8vo, pp. 132. 41945

Mr. C. J. Fox is the Mendicant.

A Looking-Glass for Presbyterians. Or, A brief Examination of their Loyalty, Merit, and other Qualifications for Government. With some Animadversions on the Quaker unmask'd. Humbly Address'd to the Consideration of the Loyal Freemen of Pennsylvania. *Philadelphia: Printed in the Year* M,DCC,LXIV. 8vo, pp. 18. P. 41946

Relates to the Paxton Boys and The Presbyterians murdering the Indians at Lancaster, under the Protection of the Government.

The Looking-Glass. Nos. I and II. By a Pennsylvanian. With Appendix. [*Philadelphia.* 1764.] 8vo, pp. 17. 41947

Looking-Glass for the Modern Deists. Or Libertines, called Free Thinkers. *Philadelphia: Printed by Samuel Keimer.* 1728. 8vo. 41948

A very rare piece.

A Looking Glass for the Nullifiers. *See* [Carey (M.)], Vol. III.

Loomis (A. W.) Oration delivered at the Centennial Celebration of the Evacuation of Fort Duquesne. By Hon. A. W.

Loomis. Pittsburgh, November 25, 1858. *Pittsburgh: Printed by W. S. Haven.* 1859. 8vo, pp. 33. B., C., S. 41949

Loomis (C. A.) Free Thoughts on Politics and Politicians in Michigan. ... By C. A. Loomis. [n. p. n. d.] 8vo, pp. 16.

Loomis (D.) ... Speech of Hon. Dwight Loomis ... June 16, 1860. [*Washington.* 1860.] 8vo, pp. 8. H. 41951

Loomis (D. W.) A Memoir of Harriet Eliza Snow. By Mrs. D. W. Loomis. *Boston.* 1840. 18mo, pp. 288. + Second Edition. [*Ibid.*] 1845. 24mo, pp. 288. H. 41952

Loomis (E.) The Descendants of Joseph Loomis ... . By Elias Loomis, LL.D. ... *New Haven, Conn.: Tuttle, Morehouse* ... 1870. 8vo, pp. vii, 5–292. B. 41953

[Loomis.] Memoirs of American Missionaries, formerly connected with the Society of Enquiry respecting Missions, in the Andover Theological Seminary: embracing a History of the Society, etc. With an Introductory Essay by L. Woods. ... *Boston.* 1833. 12mo. Portraits. 41954

Loomis. The Recent Progress of Astronomy; especially in the United States. By Elias Loomis ... . *New York: Harper & Brothers.* 1850. 8vo, pp. 257. BA. + [*Ibid.*] 1851. + Third Edition. [*Ibid.*] 1856. 8vo, pp. 396. B. 41955

Also: ... Notice of the Hail Storm which passed over New York City, on the First of July, 1853. ... [n. p. n. d.] 8vo, pp. 21. Plates. *See also* "Contributions to Knowledge" of the Smithsonian Institution, Vol. II.

Loomis (G. J.) Albany Citizens Advertiser and General Directory; ... for 1834–5. Compiled by G. J. Loomis and T. G. Wait. *Albany: G. J. Loomis.* 1834. 12mo. 41956

Loomis (H.) A Sermon in Portland, June 25, 1823, before the Maine Missionary Society, at their 60th Anniversary. By Harvey Loomis. *Hallowell.* 1823. 8vo, pp. 40. 41957

Loomis (J. R.) An Inaugural Address ... July 27, 1859. By J. R. Loomis, LL.D. ... *Philadelphia: Wm. S. Young, Printer.* 1860. 8vo, pp. 40. H. 41958

Loomis. Loomis' Calendar, or New-York and Vermont Almanack. *Albany.* 1835. 12mo. S. 41959

Also: Loomis' Pittsburg Almanac, for the Year 1841. [n. p. n. d.] 12mo.

Loon (Geraard van). Klaer lichtende Noort Ster, ofte Zee-Atlas, waer in vertoont werde de Gelegentheyt van alle de

Zee-kusten des Aerdgebodens. *Amsterdam.* 1661. Rl. folio. Frontispiece, and 45 double Maps. 41960

The North American charts included in this atlas are much superior to, and different from those of Blaeu and Van Keulen.

Loose Leaves. *See* [Sutherland (Thomas Jefferson)].

Loosey (C. F.) Collection of the Laws of Patent Privileges of ... Europe, The United States ... and the Dutch West-Indies. Published by Charles F. Loosey ... . *London.* [1849.] 8vo, pp. (2), viii, 479. BA. 41961

Loosey. Recueil des Lois publiées dans tous les États de l'Europe, les États-Unis d'Amérique ... sur les Priviléges et les Brevets d'Invention. *Paris.* 1849. 8vo. 41962

Loosjes (A.) Gedenkzuil, ter gelegenheid der vry-verklaaring van Noord-Amerika. Door A. Loosjes P.Z. *Amsterdam: W. Holtrop.* 1782. 8vo, pp. (12), 64. BA. 41963

A Poem. Usually followed by: "Bylaagen ter opheldering van de gedenkzuil der vryverklaaring van de dertien vereenigde staaten van Noord-Amerika bestande in requesten, berichten, resolutien, enz." 8vo, pp. 176. Gives a full account of the negotiations between the United States and the States of Netherland concerning the acknowledgment of the independence of the former.

Loosjes. M. A. de Ruiter. In x boeken. *Amsterdam: W. Holtrop.* 1785. 4to. 41964

Loosjes. St. Eustatius genomen en hernomen. In v boeken. *Haarlem: C. Van der Aa.* 1782. 8vo. 41965

Lope (——). Copia di una lettera di Sybilia venuta al Signor Don Lope Imbasciadore Cesareo in Venetia. [n. p. n. d.] 8vo, 2 leaves. 41966

Loper (R. F.) R. F. Loper to Hon. E. M. Stanton, Secretary of War, in Self-Defence against the Aspersions of the Senate Committee. *Philadelphia.* 1863. 8vo, pp. 40. 41967

Lopez (——). Carta que Bernabeu escribe al Lopez. [n. p.] 1825. 8vo. 41968

Lopez (Abraham). Calendaria Manual. *Mexico.* 1827.

Lopez de Hinojoso (Alonso). Summa y Recopilacion de Cirugia, con un Arte para Sangrar, y Examen de Barberos. *Mexico: encasa de Pedro Balli, Año de* 1595. 4to. 41970

An extremely rare and curious work relating to the diseases and infirmities most common in Mexico, and incidentally to social customs.

[Lopez (A.)] Proposicion [de la Asamblea National por Andres Lopez y atros]. *Tegucigalpa.* 1852. 8vo, pp. 9.

Lopez (A. P.) Resena historica del derecho de ultramar por el Dr. D. Antonio Prudencio Lopez. *Habana.* 1864. 8vo, pp. 102. 41972

Lopez Cogolludo (D.) Los tres Siglos de la Domimnion Española en Yucatan, ò sea Historia de esta Provincia desde la Conquista hacta la Independencia. Escribiola el R. P. Fr. Diego Lopez Cogolludo. Vol. I. *Campeche: Imprenta de Jose Maria Peralta.* 1842. 4to, pp. ix, 481, (5). Vol. II. *Merida: Imprenta de Castilho y Cie.* 1845. 4to, pp. 717, (7). 41973

Corrected title of our No. 14211, Vol. IV., *see also* No. 14210.

Lopez de Escobar (D.) Relacion | de los Particvlares | seruicios que ha hecho a V. Magestad Don | Diego Lopez de Escobar Gouernador y Ca- | pitan general de la Isla de la Trinidad, y de las | Prouincias del Dorado, hijo del Capitan | Diego Lopez de la Fuente, en | el año de 1636. | *Con Licencia* | *En Madrid. Por la viuda de Iuan Gonçalez.* | *Año* M.DC.XXXVII. | Folio, pp. (2), 8.

Probably an official privately printed account.

Lopez del Castillo (D.) Oracion Funebre, que en las ecsequias celebrados en esta S. Iglesia Cathedral de Arequipa, por las Valientes de la Patria que Murieron en las gloriosas Journadas de Junin y Ayacucho, Dijo el F. Dom. Lopez del Castillo, 17 Dicemb. 1825. *Arequipa.* 1836. 4to, pp. 16. 41975

Lopez Pacheco y Bobalilla (D.) Viage por tierra y por mar del illº señor D. Diego Lopez Pacheco y Bobadilla, marques de Villena, duque de Escalona, ... aplausos y festejos a su venida por virrey de esta Nueva España. *Mexico.* 1641. 4to, 92 l.

Lopez (D. U.) El diabolo suelto y predicador. Periodico en miniatura, artistico y literario, en el que el diablo teniendo tiempo para todo, le adornara con muchas litografias que representaran los monumentos remarcablas, ... con los acontecimientos famosos de las historias, ... por D. U. Lopez. *Mexico.* 1854. 4to, pp. 72. Plates. 41977

A satirical journal, which contains a great number of lithographic caricatures of the actual condition of Mexico. Lopez is the author of other works, this was his last production.

Lopez de Castanheda. *See* Castanheda (F. Lopez de).

Lopez de Gomara (F.) *See* Gomara (F. Lopez de), Vol. VII.

Lopez (G.) Collectio Opusculorum de venerabili servo Dei Gregorio Lopesio, per Bernardinum Membrive dicata Ferdinando VI. *Romæ.* 1752. 4to. Plate. 41978

Lopez was an anchorite who wrought miracles in Mexico in the sixteenth century. For his biography *see* Loza (F.)

Lopez (G.) Oratoria Parentatio, qua Cæsareæ Angelorum vrbis Americanæ magnum, meritumq. dolorum testatus est in acerbo Philippi IV. Magni Hispaniarum et Indiarum Regis funere, D. Gregorius Lopez a Mendizabal. *Mexici, ex Typographia B. Calderon.* 1666. 4to. 41979

A very rare piece.

Lopez (G.) Tesora de Medicina y de las Plantas de la Nueva España. *Mexico.* 1673. 4to. 41980

Lopez (H. R.) Historical Eulogium on Don. Hipp. Ruiz Lopez, first Botanist and Chief of the Expedition to Peru and Chili, translated by Hatcher of Salisbury. *London.* 1831. 8vo.

Lopez (J. A.) Documentos oficiales relativos al estranamiento del R. Obispo de Durango D. José Antonio Lopez de Zubiria, a consecuencia de haberse resistido á cumplir la parte preceptiva de la ley general de 22 de abril del presente año sobre provision de curatos. *Victoria de Durango.* 1834. 4to, pp. 27. 41982

Lopez (J. F.) Defensa del Gobierno de Santa-Fé, y de los Derechos en esta Provincia, en la Cuestion del Matrimonio Civil, con el Obispo de Parana. Por el Dr. D. José Francisco Lopez. *Santa Fé.* 1867. Imp. 8vo. 41983

Lopez. Discurso pronunciado en la del 16 de Setiembre de 1861. *Aguascalientes.* 1861. 8vo. 41984

Lopez Aguado (Juan). Vozes, que hizieron eco en la Religiosa Pyra, que en las Honras del V. P. Fr. Antonio Margil de Jesus. *Mexico, por J. B. de Hogal.* 1726. 4to. 41985

Lopez Cancelada (Juan). Ruina de la Nueva España si se declara el comercio libre con los extrangeros. *Cadix.* 1811. 4to, pp. 84. 41986

Lopez Yepes (J.) *See* Yepes (J. Lopez).

Lopez (Juan Luis). Discurso juridico, historico-politico, en defensa de la Jurisdicion real sobre las Obenciones à los Indios, à fin solo de dar cuento con ellas no se contraviene à la Immunitad de la Iglesia. *Impresso con licencia del Govierno en Lima.* 1685. Folio. 41987

Lopez de Sousa (J. P.) *See* Sousa (J. P. Lopez de).

Lopez (L.) Documentos justificativos de los Servicios que el Ciudadano Lucio Lopez prestó a su patria en la Campaña de las Tamaulipas, contra la Invasion Española, desde Julio hasta 20 de Agosto de 1829. *Mexico.* 1832. 8vo, pp. 21. 41988

Lopez de Aragon (Manuel). El apostol de la paz, oracion panegyrica en la solemnidad fiesta de glorioso Señor Vicentio Ferrer. *Mexico: J. de Jauregui.* 1772. 4to, pp. (16), 20.

Lopez (M. A.) Compana del Perú, por el ejército Unido Libertador de Colombia, Perú, B. Aires y Chile à las órdenos del immortal Bolivar, en las anos de 1823, 24 y 25. Con mapas de los campos de batalla que dieron libertad à aquella república, y aseguraron la independencia del Nuevo Mundo. Por Manuel Antonio Lopez. *Caracas.* 1843. 8vo, pp. 86. 3 Maps.

Lopez. Manuel de la Istoria de Chile. *Valparaiso.* 1845. 16mo. 41991

Lopez (N.) El General Narcisco López y la isla de Cuba. Relacion historica de los últimos acontecimientos politicos de Cuba. *Caracas.* 1849. 8vo, pp. 32. 41992

Lopez. General Lopez, the Cuban Patriot. From the Democratic Review, for February, 1850. [n. p. n. d.] 8vo, pp. 16.

Lopez. Life of Gen. Narcisco Lopez, with History of the Attempted Revolution in Cuba. *New York.* [n. d.] 8vo.

[Lopez.] To the Public. [n. p.] 1849. 8vo, pp. 16.

Sketch of the Life of Lopez.

Lopez (P. A.) General aclamacion de la lealtad Mexicana; en las mas solemne jura del luminar mas flamante el Señor del Luis I. Por Don Patricio Antonio Lopez, Cazique de uno de los valles de Antequera. *Mexico.* 1724. Sm. 4to, pp. 8.

Lopez de Ayala (Pedro). Cronicas de los Reyes de Castilla D. Pedro, D. Enrique II., D. Juan I., D. Enrique III., con las Enmiendas del Secretario Geronimo Zurita, y las correctiones y notas, por de Eugenio de Llaguno Amirola. *Madrid.* 1780. 2 vols., 4to. 41997

Included in an English Catalogue of Americana.

Lopez Ruiz (Santiago José). La Insurreccion sin escuso ó sea discurso doctrinal sobre la obediencia debida al Soberano y á sus Magistrados. *Mexico.* 1814. 4to, pp. xxxv, 68. 41998

Lopez (T.) Atlas geographico de la America Septentrional y Meridional ... por ... Thomas Lopez ... . *Se hallarà en Madrid en Casa de Antonio Sanz, Plazuela de la Calle de la Paz.* [1757.] Sq. 12mo, Engraved Title, Portrait, pp. (8), 116. 37 Maps. + Another Edition. *Madrid.* [1758.] Sq. 12mo, pp. (14), 216. Portrait and Maps. H. 41999

Relates entirely to Spanish America.

Lopez (V. F.) La Novia del Hereje ó la Inquisicion de Lima. Por Vicente Fidel Lopez. *Buenos Aires: C. Casavalle.* 1870. 2 vols., 8vo, pp. (4), xvi, 352; (4), 420. C. 42000

Lopez. Les Races Aryennes du Pérou. Leur langue, leur religion, leur histoire. Par Vicente Fidel Lopez. *Paris: Franck.* 1871. 8vo, pp. 428. 42001

Lorain (J.) Hints to Emigrants, or a Comparative Estimate of the Advantages of Pennsylvania, and of the Western Territory, &c. By John Lorain ... . *Philadelphia: Littell & Henry.* 1819. 16mo, pp. (2), 144. B. 42002

Lorain (P.) Origine et Fondation des États-Unis d'Amérique par P. Lorain Ouvrage revu par M. Guizot (1497–1620) *Paris: ... L. Hachette et Cie.* 1853. 12mo, pp. (4), 267. B.

Loranger (T. J. J.) Mémoire composé de la Plaidoirie de T. J. J. Loranger, C.R., un des substituts du Procureur-Général devant la Cour Seigneuriale. *Montréal.* 1855. 8vo. 42004

Loranger. Suite du Mémoire de M. Loranger contenant sa réplique devant la Cour Seigneuriale. *Montréal.* 1856. 8vo.

Lorberry Coal Mine. ... Reports of Dr. Charles T. Jackson ... Prof. W. F. Roberts ... and Allen Fisher, Esq. ... June 1, 1863. *Boston: Wright & Potter, Printers.* 1863. 8vo, pp. 29. 2 Maps. H. 42006

Lord (B.) The Aged Minister's Solemn Appeal to God. Tenth and Eleventh Annual Discourses after the Half-century, Norwich, 1778. By Benjamin Lord, D.D. ... *Norwich.* 1783. 8vo, pp. 32. M. 42007

Lord. Believers in Christ, only, the true Children of God ... A Discourse Delivered at ... Boston, ... June 27. 1742. ... By Benjamin Lord, A.M. ... *Boston: J. Blanchard.* 1742. 8vo, pp. (4), iv, 42. B. 42008

Lord. God glorified in His Works, of Providence and Grace. A Remarkable Instance of it, in the various and signal Deliverances, that evidently appear to be wrought for Mrs. Mercy Wheeler, in Plainfield; lately restored from extreme Impotence and long Confinement. ... By Benjamin Lord, A.M. *Boston: Rogers & Fowle.* 1743. 12mo, pp. 44. + *Boston: J. Blanchard.* 1744. 12mo, pp. 44. + Second Edition. *New London, reprinted.* 1771. 8vo, pp. 30. + The Third Edition. [*Ibid.*] 1744. 12mo, pp. 40. BA. 42009

Also: Humble Importunity and Faith, Victorious ... . A Sermon, ... at Plainfield, June 14. 1743. Soon after the ... Deliverance of Mrs. Mercy Wheeler ... from long Confinement ... . *Boston: J. Blanchard.* 1743. 8vo, pp. 48. BA. Thomas says this passed through four or more editions.

Lord. Jubilee; An Half-Century Discourse ... . Delivered at Norwich ... Nov. 29th, 1767. ... By Benjamin Lord, A.M. ... *New-London: Printed ... by T. Green.* 1768. 16mo, pp. (2), 56.

Lord. The Parable of the Merchant-Man seeking goodly Pearls, &c. Explain'd & Improv'd: (In Substance) as delivered at Norwich, September 27th, 1772. ... Revised, and now published for Public Benefit. By Benjamin Lord, A.M. ... *Norwich: Printed by Green & Spooner.* 1773. 12mo, pp. 23. BA. 42011

Lord. ... A Sermon delivered ... on their Anniversary Election at Hartford, May 9th, 1751. ... *New-London: Printed ... by Timothy Green.* 1752. 8vo, pp. (4), 63. B. 42012

Lord. True Christianity Explained ... . A Discourse ... at Canterbury ... . By Benjamin Lord ... . *N. London: Printed by T. Green.* 1727. 8vo, pp. (2), vi, 88. B. 42013

An early Connecticut imprint. Also: ... A Funeral Sermon for the Honorable Hezekiah Huntington, Esq. ... Delivered at Norwich, Feb. 13th ... . *Norwich: Printed by Green & Spooner.* 1773. 16mo, pp. 31.—Funeral Sermon for Mrs. Anne Lord. ... *New London.* 1751. 12mo, pp. 32.— ... A Sermon, Preached ... in Norwich, December 13th, 1773. At the Funeral of Mrs. Martha Willes ... . [*Norwich:*] *Printed by Green & Spooner.* 1774. 8vo, pp. 24.— ... A Sermon ... at the Ordination of the Rev. Levi Hart, at Preston ... November 4, 1762. ... *Providence, in New-England: Printed ... by William Goddard.* M.DCC.LXIII. 8vo, pp. (2), 44. B.— ... A Sermon preached at the Ordination of Mr. Jabez Wight at East Norwich, October 27, 1726. ... *New London.* 1727. 12mo, pp. 55. + *New London.* 1752. 12mo.— ... A Sermon ... at the Instalment of the Reverend Nathanael Whitaker, At Chelsea, in Norwich, Feb. 25th, 1761. ... *New-London: Printed ... by Timothy Green.* 1761. 16mo, pp. 36.— ... Sermon delivered Jan. 3, 1759, after the Death of Rev. Henry Willes. ... *New London.* 1759. 8vo, pp. 32.— ... A Sermon ... June 25, 1761: at the Funeral of the Reverend Mr. Hezekiah Lord ... . *Providence, in New-England: Printed by William Goddard.* 1763. 8vo, pp. 26. B.— ... Sermon preached at the Ordination of Rev. J. Huntington at Salem, Sept. 28, 1763. ... *Boston.* 1763. 8vo, pp. 41. W.

Lord (C. E.) The Irrepressible Conflict: a Sermon for the Times ... Fast Day, April 7, 1864. By C. E. Lord. ... *Boston: Printed by John Wilson and Son.* 1864. 8vo, pp. 17. H. 42014

Lord. Sermons on the Country's Crisis, delivered in Mount Vernon, N. H., April 28, 1861, by C. E. Lord ... . *Milford: Printed at Boutwell's Newspaper ... Office.* 1861. 8vo, pp. 20.

Lord. Slavery, Secession and the Constitution. An Appeal to our Country's Loyalty. By Rev. Charles E. Lord ... . *Boston.* 1864. 8vo, pp. 58. H. 42016

Lord (C. E.), *Jun.* The Constitution and Slavery. By Rev. C. E. Lord, Jun. [n. p. n. d.] 8vo. 42017

[Lord (Daniel).] The Effect of Secession upon the Commercial Relations between the North and South, and upon each Section. ... *New York.* 1861. 12mo, pp. 72. Map. + Second Edition. [*Ibid.*] 1861. + *London.* 1861. 8vo. s. 42018

Lord. The Legal Effect of the Secession Troubles on the Commercial Relations of the Country. [*New York:*] *Privately Printed.* [1861.] 8vo, pp. 6. 42019

Also: Address ... New York Young Men's Christian Association. ... *New-York.* 1852. 8vo. s.

Lord (E.) A Compendious History of the Principal Protestant Missions to the Heathen. Compiled ... by E. Lord. *Boston: Samuel T. Armstrong.* 1813. 2 vols., 12mo, pp. x, 13–308; 336. B. 42020

Lord. Memoir of the Rev. Joseph Stibbs Christmas. By E. Lord. *New-York: John P. Haven, and Jonathan Leavitt.* 1831. 12mo, pp. vii, 13–213. B. 42021

Lord (E.) On Credit, Currency and Banking. By Eleazar Lord. *New York.* 1834. 12mo. + Second Edition. *New-York: G. & C. & H. Carvill.* 1834. 8vo, pp. 130. + Third Edition. *New-York.* 1834. 12mo, pp. 130, folded leaf. BA.

McCulloch remarks, in his "Literature of Political Economy," that "the general principles are unexceptionable; the practical measures suggested are different."

[Lord.] A Historical Review of the New-York and Erie Railroad. *New-York: Mason Brothers.* 1855. 8vo, pp. 223.

Lord. Six Letters on the Necessity and Practicability of a National Currency, and the Principles and Measures Essential to

it. By Eleazar Lord. *New York: Anson D. F. Randolph.* 1862. 12mo, pp. 53. 42024

Also: A Letter on National Currency, addressed to the Secretary of the Treasury ... . *New York: A. D. F. Randolph.* 1861. 12mo, pp. 24. H. — National Currency. A Review of the National Banking Law. ... *New York: A. D. F. Randolph.* 1863. 12mo, pp. 41. — Principles of Currency and Banking. ... *New York.* 1829. 16mo. — Theories of Currency. ... *New York.* 1864. — To the People and the Honorable the Legislature of the State of New York [on the N. Y. & Erie R. R. Co.] ... *New York, April* 12, 1851. 8vo, pp. 15. s.

Lord (G. A.) A Short Narrative of The Life and Conversion of Rev. G. A. Lord, formerly a French Canadian Roman Catholic. ... [n. p.] 1855. 12mo, pp. 103. 42025

Lord (H.) ... A Sermon ... at Williamsburgh, Nov. 30, 1828, ... after the Interment of Mrs. Fidelia Lord by ... Henry Lord. *Amherst: J. S. & C. Adams, Printers.* 1829. 8vo, pp. 21.

Lord (H. W.) The Highway of the Seas in time of War. By Henry W. Lord. *London: Macmillan & Co.* 1862. 8vo, pp. viii, 56. C. 42027

Lord (J.) A History of the United States of America ... . By John Lord, A.M. ... *Philadelphia: C. Desilver.* 1854. 12mo, pp. 479. + New Revised Edition. [*Ibid.* 1858.] 12mo, pp. 508. Map. H. 42028

Also: An Address, ... before the Peace Society of Amherst College, July 4, 1839 ... *Amherst: J. S. & C. Adams.* 1839. 8vo, pp. 31. H.

Lord (J. C.) Causes and Remedies of the Present Convulsions: A Discourse. By Rev. John C. Lord, D.D. *Buffalo: Joseph Warren & Co. ... Printers.* 1861. 8vo, pp. 25. B.

Lord. "The Higher Law" in its application to the Fugitive Slave Bill. A Sermon ... [at] Buffalo, on Thanksgiving day. By John C. Lord, D.D. ... *New-York: Union Safety Committee.* 1851. 8vo, pp. 16. BA. + *Buffalo: George H. Derby and Co.* 1851. 8vo, pp. 32. 42030

This elicited: "Slavery in its Relation to God. A Review of Rev. Dr. Lord's Thanksgiving Sermon in favor of Domestic Slavery, entitled 'The Higher Law.' ... By a Minister of the Gospel in Massachusetts." *Buffalo: A. M. Clapp & Co.* 1851. 8vo, pp. 56.

Lord. A Sermon on the Character and Influence of Washington, before the Union Continentals, of Buffalo, February 22, 1863. By J. C. Lord, D.D. *Buffalo: A. M. Clapp & Son.* 1863. 8vo, pp. 22. 42031

Lord. Signs of the Times. A Sermon ... November 26, 1837. By John C. Lord, A.M. *Buffalo: Press of Oliver G. Steele.* 1837. 8vo, pp. 18, (1). BA. 42032

Also: The Dead of the Present War. A Funeral Discourse, ... Buffalo, June 28, 1862. ... *Buffalo: Martin Taylor.* 1862. 8vo, pp. 28. — Discourse ... on Decease of Calhoun, Clay and Webster. ... *Buffalo.* 1852. 8vo. — Discourse ... on the Death of Rev. Norris Bull. ... *Buffalo.* 1852. 8vo. — A Discourse ... on the Death of the Hon. Samuel Wilkeson, of Buffalo. ... *Buffalo.* 1848. 8vo. — Discussion relative to Buffalo Hospital of the Sisters of Charity, between Rev. John C. Lord and Bernard O'Reilly. *Buffalo.* 1850. 8vo, pp. 38. — Human Government and Laws ... A Discourse ... Feb. 1, 1852. ... *Buffalo.* 1852. 8vo. — The Justice of our National Cause ... A Sermon ... in Buffalo ... September 26th, A National Fast Day. ... [n. p. 1861.] 8vo, pp. 8. — Lectures on the Progress of Civilization and Government, and other Subjects. ... *Buffalo.* 1851. 12mo. — Oration ... at Buffalo ... July 5, 1858. ... *Buffalo.* 1858. 8vo. — A Sermon ... at Buffalo, March 10, 1867. *New York.* 1867. 8vo. s.

Lord (J. K.) ... An Address ... before the Gamma Sigma Society of Dartmouth College, July 24, 1844. By the Rev. John K. Lord. *Boston: James Munroe and Company.* 1844. 8vo, pp. 32. BA. 42033

Also: The Influence exerted ... An Address before the Senior Class of Kimball Union Academy, Meriden, N. H. 5 May, 1845. ... *Windsor, Vt.* 1845. 8vo, pp. 24. — Sermons; With a Memoir by his Father. *Boston.* 1850. 12mo.

[Lord (J. K.)] At Home in the Wilderness ... . By 'The Wanderer.' *London: Robert Hardwicke.* 1867. 8vo, pp. xvi, 323. Portrait. B. 42034

Lord. The Naturalist in Vancouver Island and British Columbia. By John Keast Lord, ... Naturalist to the British North American Boundary Commission. ... *London: Richard Bentley.* 1866. 2 vols., cr. 8vo, pp. xiv, (2), 358; vii, (2), 375. 13 Plates. B. 42035

Lord (J. P.) Reference-Book of the State of Maine, for the Year 1845. By John P. Lord. *Portland.* 1845. 24mo.

Lord (J.) A Letter to the General Convention of the Ministers of ... Massachusetts-Bay ... in ... 1728. Together with the Sentence of Excommunication passed on Two ... Members of the Church in Chatham. And The Translation of a Latin Paragraph of Dr. Mather's Magnalia: Containing Mr. Nathanael Rodgers his Tho'ts of Impediments to Reformation. Written by Joseph Lord ... . *Boston.* 1734. 8vo, pp. (4), 12. B. 42037

The preface is signed "Nathanael Stone, Joseph Lord."

Lord. Reason Why, not Anabaptist Plunging but Infants-Believer's Baptism Ought to be approved, Is because the Lord

Jesus Christ, and His Apostles, Preached it and Practiced it. In Answer to the Anabaptist Reason Why. ... By Joseph Lord. *Boston: Samuel Gerrish.* 1719. 12mo, pp. (2), viii, 170. BA.

Also: ... Sermon preached in Eastham, 24th February, 1730–31. ... *Boston.* 1731. 12mo, pp. 29.

Lord (J. L.) Memorial addressed to the Trustees of the Massachusetts General Hospital, in behalf of Charles T. Jackson, M.D. By ... Joseph L. and Henry C. Lord. *Boston: Thurston.* 1849. 8vo, pp. 27. BA. 42039

Lord (N.) A Discourse Commemorative of Abiel Chandler ... delivered ... July 29, 1852. By Nathan Lord ... . *Boston: Printed by John Wilson & Son.* 1852. 8vo, pp. 32. B. 42040

Lord. A Eulogy on the Honorable John Quincy Adams, delivered March 24, 1848 ... . By Nathan Lord, D.D. ... . *Hanover: Printed at the Dartmouth Press.* 1848. 8vo, pp. 22. H.

[Lord.] A Letter of Inquiry to Ministers of the Gospel ... on Slavery. By a Northern Presbyter. *Boston: Little, Brown, and Company.* 1854. 8vo, pp. 32. + *Boston: Fetridge and Company.* 1854. 8vo, pp. 32. H. 42042

Lord. A Letter to the Alumni of Dartmouth College, on its Hundredth Anniversary. By Nathan Lord. *New York: Hurd and Houghton.* 1869. 8vo, pp. 89. B. 42043

Lord. A Northern Presbyter's Second Letter to Ministers of the Gospel of all Denominations on Slavery. By Nathan Lord ... . *Boston: Little, Brown and Company.* 1855. 8vo, pp. 99.

Lord. A Sermon ... at the Annual Election at Concord, 2 June, 1831 ... . By Nathan Lord, D.D. ... . *Concord: Printed by Hill and Barton.* 1831. 8vo, pp. (2), 34. BA. 42045

Also: An Address delivered at Hanover, October 29, 1828, at the Inauguration of the Author as President of Dartmouth College. ... *Windsor, Vt.: Simeon Ide, Printer.* 1828. 8vo, pp. 28. — ... A Baccalaureate Discourse to the Class of 1858, at Dartmouth College. ... *Hanover: Printed at the Dartmouth Press.* 1858. 8vo, pp. 39. — A Discourse on the Character of the late Stephen Chase ... . *Hanover.* 1851. 8vo, pp. 24. — Eulogium on Rev. J. Smith ... . *Hanover.* 1809. 8vo, pp. 15. — A Letter to the Rev. D. Dana, D.D., on Professor Park's Theology of New England ... . *Boston.* 1852. 8vo. — A Sermon, delivered at the Ordination of the Rev. Robert Page, Jr. ... in Bradford, N. H. May 22, 1822. ... *Amherst: Printed by Richard Boylston.* 1822. 8vo, pp. 23. — ... A Sermon ... April 3, 1859, on ... the Death of Rev. John Richards, D.D. ... *Concord: Printed by McFarland & Jenks.* 1859. 8vo, pp. 26. — Sermon ... at the Funeral of the Rev. David Peabody, A.M. ... October 20, 1839. ... *Hanover, N. H.: T. Mann, Printer.* [1839.] 8vo, pp. 15. — A True Picture of Abolition. ... *Boston: Press of the Daily Courier.* 1863. 8vo, pp. 16. *See also* our Vol. v., No. 18626.

Lord (N. J.) A Memorial of Nathaniel James Lord ... . *Salem: Essex Institute Press.* 1870. 8vo, pp. 45. Portrait. H.

Lord (O. P.) Fremont's Principles Exposed. Speech of Otis P. Lord ... at Faneuil Hall, Boston, Oct. 8, 1856. [n. p. n. d.] 8vo. 42047

Lord (W. B.), *Reporter.* Arguments ... upon the Power of Congress to make United States Treasury Notes a Legal Tender. Reported by William Blair Lord ... . *New York: Wm. C. Bryant & Co., Printers.* 1863. 8vo, pp. (2), 239. B. 42048

Lord (W. H.) ... A Sermon preached on the Fiftieth Anniversary of the Organization of the First Congregational Church in Montpelier, Vermont, July 25, 1858. By W. H. Lord ... . *Montpelier: E. P. Walton, Printer.* 1858. 8vo, pp. 32. H.

Lord. A Sermon on the Causes and Remedy of the National Troubles, preached at Montpelier, Vt., April 4th, 1861. By Rev. William H. Lord. ... *Montpelier: E. P. Walton, Printer.* 1861. 8vo, pp. 22. 42050

Also: ... A Sermon on ... the Death of Samuel Prentiss, LL.D. ... in ... Montpelier, January 18, 1857. ... *Montpelier: E. P. Walton, Printer.* 1857. 8vo, pp. 23.

Lord (W. W.) André: a Tragedy in Five Acts. By W. W. Lord. *New York: Charles Scribner.* 1856. 8vo, pp. 138.

Lord. Poems, by William W. Lord. *New-York: D. Appleton & Co.* MDCCCXLV. 12mo, pp. (2), vi, 158. H. 42052

Lord Ch——m's Prophecy. *See* [Pitt (W.)]

The Lords Protest against the Convention-Treaty. *London.* 1738. Folio. 42053

Title from John Russell Smith's Catalogue of Americana.

The Lords' Protest On the Treaty of Peace, Union and Friendship, between Great Britain, France and Spain; concluded at Seville on the 9th of November last. Die Martis Januarii 1729. *Boston.* 1730. Folio, pp. 4. 42054

Lorea (Antonio de). El bienaventvrado Toribio Alfonso Mogroveio Arzobispo de Lima, Istoria de su admirable vida, virtudes y milagros. *Madrid.* 1670. 4to. 42055

A very rare work; not quoted by Brunet, Rich, or Ternaux.

Lorea. Santa Rosa, religiosa de la tercera orden de S. Domingo, patrona vniversal del Nvevo Mvndo, milagro de la natv-

raleza y portentoso efecto de la gracia. Historia de sv admirable vida, y virtvdes, que empieza, desde la fvndacion de Lima, hasta sv canonizacion ... por Antonio de Lorea de la orden de Predicadores. *Madrid: Franc Nieto.* 1671. 4to, 14, 224 and 4 leaves.

This is a translation from the Latin of Hansen, *see our* No. 30249. "Pinelo, qui indique ces trois éditions donne la date de 1676 à la traduction du P. Lorea. Elle n'est pas citée dans Ternaux. Dédiée à D. Joseph Avellaneda Sandoval y Roja, elle contient dans la dédicace de nombreux renseignement généalogiques sur cette famille."—Leclerc, No. 1091.

Lorente (S.) Historia antigua del Peru. Por Sebastian Lorente. *Lima.* 1860. 8vo, pp. (4), 341. 42057

Lorente. Historia de la Conquista del Peru por Sebastian Lorente. *Lima.* 1861. 8vo, pp. 507. 42058

Really printed at *Poissy.*

Lorente. Historia del Peru bajo la dinastía austriaca 1542–1598. Por Sebastian Lorente. *Lima.* 1863. 8vo, pp. 386.

Lorente. Historia del Perú, compendiada para el uso de los colegios y de las personas ilustradas por Sebastian Lorente. *Lima.* 1867. 8vo, pp. 264. 42060

Lorente. Lecciones de geographia historica por Sebastian Lorente. *Lima.* 1866. 12mo, pp. 96. 42061

Also: Primeras Lecciones de Geografia para el Colegio de Guadalupe ... *Lima.* 1865. 18mo, pp. 126. — Primoras lecciones de geografia e historia del Peru. ... *Lima.* 1866 2 vols., 16mo, pp. 194; 90. — Primeras Lecciones de Geografia fisica ... *Lima.* 1865. 18mo, pp. 80. Also many other scholastic publications.

Lorenzana (F. A.) Cartas Pastorales, y edictos del Illmo. Señor D. Francisco Antonio Lorenzana y Buitron, Arzobispo de Mexico. *En Mexico, en la Imprenta del Superior Gobierno del Br. D. Joseph Antonio de Hogal, Año de* MDCCLXX. Folio, pp. (26), 229. 42062

"Among other things, this volume contains a most minute account of the portrait of the Virgin of Guadaloupe, which appeared miraculously on the *Filma* or blanket of Juan Diego, a converted Mexican, in the year 1531; and which was solemnly declared by a commission of painters and others, in 1751, not to have been painted by the hand of man. The good Archbishop comes to the conclusion that it must have been painted by millions of angels."—Stevens.

Lorenzana. Concilios Provinciales Primero, y Segundo, celebrados en la muy Noble, y muy leal Ciudad de México, Presidiendo en Illmo y Rmo Señor D. Fr. Alonso de Montufar, En los años de 1555, y 1566. Dalos a luz El Illmo Sr D. Francisco Antonio Lorenzana, Arzobispo de esta Santa Metropolitana Iglesia. Con las Licencias Necesarias *En México, en la Im-*

prenta de el Superior Gobierno, de el Br. D. Joseph Antonio de Hogal, en la Calle de Tiburcio, Año de 1769. Folio, pp. (10), 396, (12).

The first Council was originally printed in 1556, at Mexico, by Juan Pablos Lombardo. Besides the two Councils, the first volume contains an account of the Prelates of the Mexican Church. The second volume, containing the third Mexican Council, was printed in the following year, with the title:

Lorenzana. Concilium Mexicanum provinciale III. Celebratum Mexici, anno MDLXXXV. Præside D. D. Petro Moya, et Contreras Archiepiscopo ejusdem urbis. Confirmatum Romæ die XXVII. Octobris anno MDLXXXIX. Postea Jussu Regio editum Mexici anno MDCXXII. Sumptibus D. D. Joannis Perez de la Serna Archiepiscopi. Demum typis mandatum cura, & expensis D. D. Francisci Antonij a Lorenzana Archipræsulis. *Mexici Anno* MDCCLXX. *Superiorum Permissu. Ex Typographia Bac Josephi Antonij de Hogal.* Folio, pp. (12), 328, (4). 42064

This collection of Mexican Councils is of importance as containing those of 1555 and 1565, nowhere else to be found. That of 1585 is given in the great collections, but not from this edition. Fleury notices the last, and Rohrbacher only that of 1524. The Pastoral Letters, etc., of Lorenzana do not exist elsewhere. There are also appended to the Councils notices of the series of Mexican bishops.

Salva remarks "These two parts are rarely found together." "I have examined several copies of this work, but have found in one only an appendix of 53 pages, which contains copies of some original documents, giving an account of the first Apostolical Junta held in Mexico, in the year 1537, and of another in 1539, by the Bishops Zumarraga, Zarate, and Quiroga."—Rich, p. 183.

Lorenzana. Historia de Nueva-España, Escrita por su esclarecido Conquistador Hernan Cortes, Aumentada con otros Docvmentos, y notas, por el Ilustrissimo Señor Don Francisco Antonio Lorenzana, Arzobispo de Mexico. *En Mexico ... Joseph Antonio de Hogal ...* 1770. Folio, pp. xvi, 400, (18). Map, 36 Plates.

An important and highly esteemed work, containing the celebrated letters of Cortez to the Emperor Charles V. This edition is illustrated with copious notes and documents, together with facsimiles of the Mexican mode of representing the tributes paid by the different towns in Mexico. These pictures, more complete and colored like the originals, are included in Lord Kingsborough's "Antiquities of Mexico." *See* Cortes (H.), Vol. IV., where indeed this work should have appeared.

Lorenzana. Statuta Ordinata a Sancto Concilio Provinciali Mexicano III. Anno Domini MDLXXXV. Ex Præscripto Sacrosancti Concilij Tridentini Decreto Sess. 24. Cap. 12. de Reform. verbo Cetera. Revisa a Catholica Majestate, et a Sacrosancta sede Apostolica Confirmata, Anno Domini millessimo quingentissimo octuagessimo nono. Folio, pp. (2), 141, (4). 42066

Lorenzana died Cardinal-Archbishop of Toledo. Both as Archbishop of Mexico and of Toledo he displayed the same princely patronage of ecclesiastical literature as his predecessor in the latter see, Cardinal Ximenes. At his private expense, and for the purposes of distribution, not for sale, he edited and printed the above "Concilio," the

"Mozarabic Missal," the "Opera Patrum Toletanorum," the "Opera S. Martini Legionensis," etc., all of which are now of uncommon occurrence. Also: Aranzel para todos los curas de este Arzobispado, fuera de la Ciudad de Mexico. ... *Mexico.* 1767. Folio, 6 leaves. — Memorial que presentan á todas las Comunidades, y Gremios los Pobres Mendigos de Mexico por mano de su Arzobispo. [n. p. n. d.] 4to, pp. 29. — Memorial que presentan á todos Estados los Niños Expositos de la Imperial Ciudad de Mexico por mano de su Arzobispo. *Mexico.* 1770. 4to, pp. 21. — Reglas para que los Naturales de estos Reynos sean felices en lo espiritual, y temporal. ... *Mexico.* 1768. Folio, 2 leaves. — Tratado del Agua Mineral Caliente de San Bartholomé. ... [n. p.] 1772. 4to. *See also* "Missa Gothica seu Mozarabica."

Lorenzo de San Milian (F.) Por | D. Francisco Lorenzo | de San Milian, | Iuez oficiel de la Casa de | la Contratacion de la Ciudad de Seuilla, | y Contador de la Visita del Tribunal de | Quentas de la Ciudad de Mexico, y | de las caxas Reales della, y de las de- | mas del Reyno de Nueua | España. | En la Cavsa | qve en virtvd de cedvla de sv | Magestad se ha actuado, contra el dicho Don Fran- | cisco, sobre sus procedimientos en el juizio de vi- | sita de las caxas, y Minas de la Ciudad | da Zacatecas. | [*Mexico.* 1672.] Folio, 19 leaves. 42067

A privately printed official account.

Lorenzo (F.) El comun bienhechor predicado en la iglesia de los Carmelitas de Tehuacan. Por F. Lorenzo del S. Sacramento. *Mexico.* 1755. 4to, 68 leaves. 42068

Lorette. The History of Louise, daughter of a Canadian Nun, exhibiting the Interior of Female Convents. Second Edition. *New York: C. Small.* 1834. 16mo, pp. 208. Plate.

The Lorgnette. *See* [Mitchell (D. G.)]

Lorgues (Roselly de). *See* Roselly de Lorgues (A. F. F. V.)

[Lorimer (*Dr.* John).] An Account of the Surveys of Florida, &c. with Directions for sailing from Jamaica or the West Indies, by the West End of Cuba, and through the Gulph of Florida. ... *London: W. Faden.* M.DCC.XC. 4to, pp. (4), 27. Chart. BA. 42070

Lorimer (J. G.) Church Establishments Defended, or Church and State in America Exposed. *London.* 1835. 8vo.

This elicited: "Rev. J. Gordon Lorimer's 'Church and State in America' exposed and answered, or Church Establishments defended." 1835. Also: Democracy and Progress. ... *London.* 1857. 8vo.

Lorimer (M.) Among the Trees: a Journal of Walks in the Woods, and Flower-Hunting through Field and by Brook. By Mary Lorimer. *New York: Hurd and Houghton.* 1869. Sm. 4to, pp. (4), 153. BA. 42072

LORING (A.) A History of Shapleigh, By Rev. Amasa Loring. ... 1854. *Portland: Printed by B. Thurston.* 1854. 8vo, pp. 40.

LORING (B.) A Discourse ... on ... Thanksgiving ... November 27, 1828. By Bailey Loring ... . *Boston: Bowles and Dearborn.* 1829. 8vo, pp. 35. 42074

LORING (C. G.) England's Liability for Indemnity: Remarks on the Letter of "Historicus," dated November 4th, 1863 ... . By Charles G. Loring. *Boston: William V. Spencer.* 1864. 8vo, pp. vii, 46. BA. 42075

LORING. Memoir of the Hon. William Sturgis. ... By Charles G. Loring. *Boston: Press of John Wilson and Son.* 1864. 8vo, pp. (2), 64. B. 42076

[LORING.] Obituary Notices of the Late Chief Justice Shaw and Judge White. ... [n. p. 1861?] 8vo, pp. 11. H. 42077

[LORING.] A Reading upon the Personal Liberty Laws of Massachusetts. ... [n. p. 1861?] 8vo, pp. 15. H. 42078

Also: Argument ... on Behalf of the Eastern Rail-Road Company, ... before the ... Massachusetts Legislature, Boston, March 7, 1845. *Boston.* 1845. 8vo, pp. 88.—Argument ... at the Hearing of the Petition ... for a Rail-Road from Boston to Woonsocket ... . *Boston: Dutton and Wentworth, Printers.* 1847. 8vo, pp. 61. Map.—Neutral Relations of England and the United States. ... *Boston: William V. Spencer.* 1863. 8vo, pp. iv, 116. + *New York: D. Appleton and Company.* 1863. 8vo, pp. 116.—An Oration ... the Fourth of July, 1821, at ... Boston ... . *Boston: Charles Callender.* 1821. 8vo, pp. 19. + Second Edition. [*Ibid.*] H.—Reconstruction. ... *Boston: Little, Brown, and Company.* 1866. 8vo, pp. iv, 126. H.—Speech ... on the Troy and Greenfield Railroad Bill, in the Massachusetts Senate, ... April 16, 1862. [n. p. n. d.] 8vo, pp. 15. B. *See also* "Correspondence," Vol. IV., No. 16880, for collation *read* pp. (4), 153, *and* Wright (John S.)

LORING (E. G.) Report of the Joint Standing Committee on Federal Relations ... on the Case of Edward G. Loring. [n. p. 1855.] 8vo, pp. 38. S. 42079

House Document, on the Anthony Burns rendition affair.

LORING (F. W.) Cotton Culture and the South considered with reference to Emigration. By F. W. Loring and C. F. Atkinson. *Boston: A. Williams & Co.* 1869. 12mo, pp. (2), 183.

LORING (G. B.) Celebration at ... Salem, July 4, 1862. Oration by Dr. George B. Loring. *Boston: J. E. Farwell & Company.* 1862. 8vo, pp. 30. H. 42081

LORING. Celebration of the Birth-Day of Thomas Jefferson, at Salem, Mass., April 1st, 1859. Oration by Dr. Geo. B. Loring ... . *Salem.* 1859. 8vo, pp. 23. H. 42082

LORING. The Present Crisis. A Speech ... by Dr. Geo. B. Loring, at ... Salem ... April 26, 1865, on the Assassination of President Lincoln. ... *South Danvers: Printed ... by Charles D. Howard.* 1865. 8vo, pp. 12. H. 42083

Also: Address before the Essex Agricultural Society ... . *Newburyport: Herald Job Press.* 1858. 8vo, pp. 20.—Address ... before the Hampshire, Franklin and Hampden Agricultural Society, at Northampton, Oct. 14, 1858 ... . *Northampton: Printed by Metcalf & Company.* 1858. 8vo, pp. 22. H.—Address before the Merrimack County Agricultural Society ... at Concord, N. H., Sept. 28, 1864. ... *Concord: Fogg, Hadley & Co., Printers.* 1864. 8vo, pp. 20. H.—Constitutional Freedom the Genius of our Government. An Address ... before the Columbian Society of Marblehead, on the Eighth of January, 1856. ... *Boston: Printed at the Office of the Boston Post.* 1856. 8vo, pp. 32.—The New Administration. A Speech delivered at a Democratic Banquet at Chelsea, Mass., Jan. 8, 1857. ... *Boston.* 1857. 8vo, pp. 6.—An Oration ... at Bolton, Mass., December 20, 1866 ... . *Clinton.* 1867. 8vo, pp. 43.—An Oration ... at the Dedication of the Soldiers' Monument in North Weymouth, Mass. ... July 4, 1868 ... . *Weymouth: C. G. Easterbrook.* 1869. 8vo, pp. 44. Plate.— ... An Oration ... at Newburyport, July 4, 1866 ... . *South Danvers: Charles D. Howard, Printer.* 1866. 8vo, pp. 32.—A Speech ... at the Democratic ... Convention in Salem, ... October 10th, 1854, in Defence of the Administration of President Pierce. ... [n. p. n. d.] 8vo, pp. 8.—Speech ... upon the Resolutions on the State of the Union ... March 12, 1866. *South Danvers: Printed by Charles D. Howard.* 1866. 8vo, pp. 24.—A Speech ... in Support of James Buchanan ... . [*Boston.*] 1856. 8vo, pp. 22. B.

LORING (I.) The Duty of an Apostatizing People ... . A Sermon ... May 25th. 1737. Being the ... Election of his Majesty's Council ... . By Israel Loring, A.M. ... *Boston: Printed by S. Kneeland.* 1737. 8vo, pp. (2), 68. BA., M. 42084

LORING. Ministers insufficient of themselves ... . Shewed in a Sermon ... at the Convention of Ministers ... at Boston. ... May 27. 1742. By Israel Loring, A.M. ... *Boston: D. Henchman.* 1742. 8vo, pp. 39. B., W. 42085

LORING. Ministers must Certainly and Shortly Die. A Sermon ... at Marlborough, Feb. 7. 17 30/31. ... Occasioned by the Death Of the Reverend ... Mr. Robert Breck ... . By Israel Loring, M.A. ... *Boston, N. E.: Printed by S. Kneeland and T. Green.* M,DCC,XXXI. 8vo, pp. (4), 27. BA. 42086

LORING. ... A Sermon ... at the Ordination Of the Reverend Mr. Gideon Richardson, At Wells, Feb. 27. 1754. By Israel Loring, M.A. ... *Boston: Printed by S. Kneeland.* 1754. 8vo, pp. (2), 26. B. 42087

LORING. Two Sermons ... at Rutland, September 8th. 1723. After the Indians had ... Kill'd the Reverend Mr. Joseph Willard, With Two of Mr. Joseph Stevens's Children, and Captivated the other Two. By Israel Loring, M.A. ... *Boston: D. Henchman.* 1724. 8vo, pp. (4), 44. B. 42088

Also: False Hopes Discovered. A Sermon preached at Concord. ... *Boston.* 1738. 16mo, pp. 54.—Sermon at Lexington, to implore the Blessing of God on the Rising Generation, with a Preface by Dr. Increase Mather. ... *Boston.* 1718. 8vo.—The Service of the Lord must be chosen presently and without delay. Sermon at Concord Dec. 29, 1737. *Boston.* 1738. 16mo, pp. 53.—Sermon at Hopkinton, April 9, 1735. *Boston.* 1735. 8vo, pp. 26.—Three Discourses on Several Subjects. ... *Boston: D. Henchman.* 1731. 8vo. Also many other Sermons, Discourses, etc.

LORING (James). *See* Massachusetts Register.

LORING (J. S.) The Hundred Boston Orators appointed by the Municipal Authorities and other Public Bodies, from 1770 to 1852; comprising Historical Gleanings, illustrating the Principles and Progress of our Republican Institutions. By James Spear Loring. *Boston: John P. Jewett and Company.* 1852. 8vo, pp. viii, 694. + Second Edition Enlarged. [*Ibid.*] 1853. 8vo, pp. viii, 720. H. + Third Edition. [*Ibid.*] 1854. 8vo. + Fourth Edition, with an improved Index of Names. [*Ibid.*] 1855. 8vo, pp. viii, 730. B. 42089

LORING (J.) An Oration ... at Hingham, July 4, 1815. ... By Jerome Loring, A.B. *Boston: Printed by Rowe and Hooper.* 1815. 8vo, pp. 15. H. 42090

LORING (J.) A Discourse ... occasioned by the Death of Mr. John Loring ... . *Boston.* 1720. 8vo, pp. 43. 42091

LORING (J. G.) An Address ... before the First Christian Church in Boston, ... June 30th, 1844. ... the Fortieth Anniversary of the Organization of said Church. By John G. Loring. *Boston.* 1844. 8vo, pp. 26. B. 42092

[LORING (*Capt.* Joseph), *Jr.*] An Exhibition of Facts, supported by Documents, for the Information of the Militia Officers of ... Massachusetts. ... *Boston: Printed by David Carlisle.* 1806. 8vo, pp. (2), iv, 88. BA., S. 42093

Relates to the court-martial which condemned him.

LORING. Facts and Documents respecting Capt. Joseph Loring, jun. including ... the Last Trial, the Proceedings of the Legislature ... and the Governor's Objections. ... *Boston: Printed by Oliver and Munroe.* 1807. 8vo, pp. 59. H. 42094

LORING. Minutes and Proceedings of a Division Court Martial, ... at Boston, ... October 29, 1805, as they relate to the Trial of Capt. Joseph Loring, jun. ... *Boston: Printed by E. Lincoln.* 1806. 8vo, pp. (2), iii, 82. BA. 42095

LORING. Minutes and Proceedings of a General Court Martial, holden at Boston, ... before which, Major Joseph Loring, Jr. was ... Tried on a Complaint made by Brig. Gen. Arnold Welles, ... for not transmitting his Orders; ... By Joseph Loring, Jr. ... *Boston: Watson & Bangs,* ... 1813. 8vo, pp. 130, (2). B.

LORING (N. H.) An Address, ... Fourth July, A.D. 1822. Charlestown, Mass. By Nathaniel Hall Loring. ... *Boston: Printed ... by True and Greene.* 1822. 8vo, pp. 24. BA. 42097

LORING. Memorial of Nathaniel Hall Loring, and others, late Cadets at West Point; containing an Expose of Facts concerning recent Transactions relating to the Corps of Cadets ... . *Washington.* 1819. 8vo, pp. 72. 42098

LORING (T.) Speech of Thomas Loring, Esq. ... March 20, 1839, upon the Bill granting ... Aid in the Construction of the Western-Railroad. *Boston: Printed by Ezra Lincoln.* 1839. 8vo, pp. 28. M. 42099

LORING [W. W.] Report of Major General Loring, of Battle of Baker's Creek ... . *Richmond: R. M. Smith,* ... *Printer.* 1864. 8vo, pp. 29. BA. 42100

LORITZ. *See* Glareanus (H.), Vol. VII., Nos. 27536–46.

LORNER (M.) Wonderful Disclosure! ... Narrative of Dr. M. Lorner, one of the Passengers of the Steamship President! ... *New-York: W. L. Knapp* ... 1845. 8vo, pp. 26. B. 42101

LORRA BAQUIO (F. de). Manval Mexicano de la administracion de los santos Sacramentos, conforme al Manval Toledano. Compuesto en lengua Mexicana, por el Bachiller Francisco de Lorra Baquio Presbytero. Dirigido al Doctor Andres Fernandez de Hipença, Prothonotario Apostolico, Prouissor de los Naturales, ... en este Arçobispado de Mexico. Con privilegio. *En Mexico, por Diego Gutierrez, año* 1634. Sm. 8vo, 7 prel. and 136 leaves. Frontispiece. C. 42102

An extremely rare volume; not described by Brunet.

[LORRAINE (E.)] The Central Water-Line from the Ohio River to the Virginia Capes ... . *Richmond, Va.: Printed by Gary & Clemmitt.* 1868. 8vo, pp. 95. H. 42103

LORYEA (J.) Washoe Mines. A Directory of all Mines in Gold Hill, Virginia, Reese River, Humboldt River ... of Nevada Territory ... . By Joseph Loryea. [n. p.] 1864. 8vo. 42104

LORT (M.) Account of an antient Inscription in North America. By the Rev. Michael Lort, D.D. ... [With Col. Vallancey's Observations. n. p. n. d.] 4to, pp. 17. 2 Plates.

A Los Liberales de corazon.—La imprenta asaltada por Armona y su partida.—Conmovido el benéfico pueblo. *Puerto-Principe: Imprenta Patriótica de José Minuese. Reimpreso.* 1822. 8vo. 42106

LOS RIOS (E. J. de). *See* Rios (E. J. de los).

LOSA *or* LOSSA (F.) *See* Loza (F.)

LOSADA (J. M. de). La Batalla de Tampico, canto epico, original de Don Juan Miguel de Losada. *Mejico.* 1854. 4to, pp. 32. 42107

Also the following poems: El Libro de Oro. Leyenda Mistica tradicional ... . *Merida: Tipographia de R. Pedrera.* 1851. 16mo, pp. xiv, 46.—El Pajaro Negro. Leyenda ... . *Merida: Tipographia de R. Pedrera.* 1851. 16mo, pp. iv, 70.—Poesias ... *Mejico.* 1850. 16mo.

LOSANTIVILLE, *Ohio.* Record of the Distribution and Sale of Lots in the Town of Losantiville. Cincinnati, 1788–90. *Cincinnati.* 1870. 8vo. 42108

Losantiville is now named Cincinnati.

LOSKIEL (G. H.) Geschichte der Mission der Evangelischen Brüder unter den Indianern in Nordamerika durch Georg Heinrich Loskiel. *Barby, zu finden in den Brüdergemeinen.* 1789. 8vo, pp. (16), 783, (1). A., B. 42109

LOSKIEL. History of the Mission of the United Brethren among the Indians in North America. In Three Parts. By George Henry Loskiel. Translated from the German by Christian Ignatius La Trobe. *London: Printed for the Brethren's Society* ... 1794. 8vo, pp. xii, 159, 234, 233, (21). Map. BA.

The labors of this mission lay chiefly among the Delawares, the Nautikokes, the Shawanese, and other tribes in Pennsylvania and New York, upon which it is the best authority, both as to tradition and facts, having been drawn up from the accounts furnished by Gottlieb Spangenberg and David Zeisberger, missionaries among the Indian tribes during forty years. Among the subjects narrated is that of the massacre of Gnadenhutten and Salem. The translator has omitted some matter relative to former enemies of the mission.

LOSKIEL. Mission der Evangelischen Brüder in Grönland. ... *Gnadau.* 1831. 8vo. 42111

Loss of the "Sparrow-Hawk" in 1826. "Ye Ancient Wrecke." *Boston.* 1865. 8vo. + Second Edition. [*Ibid.*]

LOSSADA (D.) Compendio chronologico de los privilegios regulares de Indias, desde nuestro Santissimo Padre Leon X. creado el año de 1513, hasta nuestro Santissimo Padre Clemente XII. (que Dios prospère) creado en el año de 1730. Su autor el Rmo P. F. Domingo Lossada ... . *En Madrid, en la Imprenta de la Casa de la V. Madre de Agreda.* 1737. 4to, pp. (46), 467, (16).

LOSSING (B. J.) Biographical Sketches of the Signers of the Declaration of American Independence: the Declaration Historically Considered; and a Sketch of the Leading Events connected with the Adoption of the Articles of Confederation, and the Federal Constitution. By B. J. Lossing. ... *New York: George F. Cooledge & Brother.* [1845.] 12mo, pp. 384. + [*Ibid.* 1848, 1854, 1857.] + *Philadelphia: Davis, Porter & Co.* 1866. 12mo, pp. 384. BA. 42114

LOSSING. Eminent Americans: Comprising brief Biographies of Three Hundred and Thirty Distinguished Persons. By Benson J. Lossing. ... *New York: Mason Brothers.* 1857. 8vo, pp. 416. 42115

LOSSING. A History of the United States for Families and Libraries; Illustrated by nearly Three Hundred Engravings. By Benson J. Lossing. *New York: Mason Brothers.* 1857. 8vo, pp. 672. B., C. + [*Ibid.*] 1859 and 1860. 42116

LOSSING. The Home of Washington and its Associations, Historical, Biographical, and Pictorial. New Edition, Revised, with Additions. By Benson J. Lossing. Illustrated by Numerous Engravings. ... *New York: W. A. Townsend.* 1865. 8vo, pp. 376. + [*Ibid.*] 1866. 8vo. + *New York: Virtue & Yorston.* [1870?] 8vo, pp. 7–446. Plates and Portraits. H. + *Hartford, Conn.: A. S. Hale & Company.* 1870. 8vo, pp. 5–446. 2 Plates and Portrait. B. 42117

One hundred copies of the edition printed in 1865 are on large paper. It is a reproduction of No. 42125, *infra.*

LOSSING. The Hudson, from the Wilderness to the Sea. By Benson J. Lossing. Illustrated by Three Hundred and Six Engravings on Wood, from Drawings by the Author ... . *New York: Virtue & Yorston.* 1866. Sm. 4to, pp. vii, 464. B. 42118

A series of articles first published in the "Art Journal." This book was in fact printed in England.

LOSSING. The Illustrated New World; containing An Historical Sketch of Early Voyages and Discoveries; Settlements;

Colonial, Revolutionary, and Federal History of the United States; ... the South American States; the West India Islands; the British and Russian Possessions; and Greenland. ... By B. J. Lossing. *New York: H. Phelps & Company.* 1848. 8vo, pp. 64.

LOSSING. The Life and Times of Philip Schuyler. By Benson J. Lossing, LL.D. *New York: Mason Brothers.* 1860. 8vo, pp. 504. + *New York: Sheldon & Company.* [1860]–1873. 2 vols., 8vo, pp. 504; 548. Portraits. C. 42120

LOSSING. Life of Washington. *See* Vol. VII., No. 28901.

LOSSING. Lives of Celebrated Americans: Comprising Biographies of Three Hundred and Forty Eminent Persons. By Benson J. Lossing ... . Illustrated with over 100 Fine Portraits. ... *Hartford: Thomas Belknap.* 1869. 8vo, pp. 448. BA. 42121

This is "Eminent Americans," No. 42115, *supra*, with another title-page.

LOSSING. The Lives of the Presidents of the United States, embracing a Brief History of the Principal Events of their Respective Administrations. ... *New York: H. Phelps & Co.* 1847. 8vo, pp. 128. Portrait. + [*Ibid.*] 1848. + *New York: Phelps & Fanning.* 1853. 8vo, pp. iv, 7–128. Portrait. + [*Ibid.*] 1857.

LOSSING. Lives of the Signers of the Declaration of American Independence. ... By B. J. Lossing. *Philadelphia: Evans, Stoddart & Co.* 1870. 16mo, pp. 383. C. 42123

This is "Biographical Sketches," No. 42114, *supra*, with a new title.

LOSSING. Memoir of Lieut. Col. John T. Greble, of the United States Army. By Benson J. Lossing. *Philadelphia: Printed for Private Circulation.* 1870. Imp. 8vo, pp. 99.

LOSSING. Mount Vernon and its Associations, Historical, Biographical, and Pictorial. By Benson J. Lossing. Illustrated by Numerous Engravings ... . *New York: W. A. Townsend & Company.* 1859. 8vo, pp. 376. BA. 42125

LOSSING. The National History of the United States, from the Period of the Union of the Colonies against the French, to the Inauguration of Washington; together with Historical Sketches of the Continental Presidents ... . By Benson J. Lossing. Also the Lives of the Presidents, with the Acts of their Administrations; to which is added, valuable Historical and Statistical Documents. By Edwin Williams. *New York: Edward Walker.* 1855. 2 vols., imp. 8vo, pp. 1400. 42126

LOSSING. Our Countrymen; or Brief Memoirs of Eminent Americans. By Benson J. Lossing ... . Illustrated by One Hundred and Three Portraits ... . *Philadelphia: Lippincott, Grambo & Co.* 1855. 8vo, pp. 407. B., C. + [*Ibid.*] 1856. 42127

This is No. 42115, *supra*, with a third variation of the title-page.

LOSSING. A Pictorial Description of Ohio, comprising a Sketch of its Physical Geography, History, Political Divisions, Resources, Government and Constitution, Antiquities, Public Lands, &c. ... *New York: Ensign & Thayer.* 1848. 8vo, pp. 131. + [*Ibid.*] 1849 and 1850. 8vo. C. 42128

Allibone describes "The Ohio Book," pp. 100; probably the same as this.

LOSSING. The Pictorial Field-Book of the Revolution; or, Illustrations, by Pen and Pencil, of the History, Biography, Scenery, Relics, and Traditions of the War for Independence. By Benson J. Lossing. With ... Engravings on Wood ... chiefly from Original Sketches by the Author. *New York: Harper & Brothers.* 1851–52. 2 vols., rl. 8vo, pp. (2), 576, 16; (2), xvi, 9–880, 35. BA. 42129

First issued in thirty numbers. It contains many details and anecdotes which are not to be found in any other work; indeed, the great variety and numerous items of information contained in these volumes, make the work a cyclopædia of the American Revolution. The popularity of the work has made for it a great sale, consequently the earliest edition is much to be preferred on account of the clearness of the woodcuts. The second issue is *New York: Harper & Brothers.* 1855. 2 vols., imp. 8vo, pp. 783; 772. + [*Ibid.*] 1860. It is noticeable that the collation differs; the contents are the same. The change was made to insure a uniformity in the thickness of the volumes. It has been frequently reprinted with varying dates.

LOSSING. The Pictorial Field-Book of the War of 1812; or, Illustrations, by Pen and Pencil, of the History, Biography, Scenery, Relics, and Traditions of the Last War for American Independence. By Benson J. Lossing. With ... Engravings on Wood, ... Chiefly from Original Sketches by the Author. *New York: Harper & Brothers.* 1868. 8vo, pp. (4), 1084. C. + [*Ibid.*] 1869. H. 42130

First issued in twelve parts.

LOSSING. Pictorial History of the Civil War in the United States of America. By Benson J. Lossing. Illustrated by ... Engravings on Wood ... . *Philadelphia: George W. Childs.* 1866–1868. 3 vols., 8vo, pp. 608; 640; 640. BA. 42131

Vols. II. and III. were published at *Hartford: T. Belknap.* 1868–69.

LOSSING. Pictorial History of the United States. ... By Benson J. Lossing. *New York.* 1860. 8vo. + *Hartford.* 1867. 8vo. 42132

Lossing. A Pictorial History of the United States. For Schools and Families. By Benson J. Lossing. ... 200 Engravings. ... *New York.* [n. d.] 12mo, pp. 350. + [*Ibid.*] 1854. 12mo, pp. 344. + *New York: Mason Brothers.* 1857. 12mo, pp. 343. + Revised Edition. [*Ibid.*] 1858. 12mo, pp. 371. c. + [*Ibid.*] 1859, 1860, 1864. 42133

Lossing. Seventeen Hundred and Seventy-Six, or The War of Independence; a History of the Anglo-Americans, from the Period of the Union of the Colonies against the French, to the Inauguration of Washington .... By Benson J. Lossing. *New York.* 1840. 8vo. + *New York: Edward Walker.* 1847. 8vo, pp. (2), 510. B. + [*Ibid.*] 1848. + [*Ibid.*] 1849. + A New Edition. [*Ibid.*] 1850. 8vo, pp. 510. + [*Ibid.*] 1852. B.

Lossing. Vassar College and its Founder. By Benson J. Lossing. *New York: C. A. Alvord, Printer.* 1867. Rl. 8vo, pp. 175. Portrait. BA. 42135

Printed for private distribution only.

Lossing. Washington. *See* [Griswold], Vol. VII. 28901.

Also: The Cenotaph; or Brief Memoirs of Eminent Americans. ... New Edition. [n. p.] 1855. 8vo.—A Common School History of the United States; from the Earliest Period to the Present Time. ... *New York: Mason Brothers.* 1864. 12mo, pp. 372. + [*Ibid.*] 1865. 12mo, pp. 378.—The League of States. ... *New York: Charles B. Richardson.* 1863. 8vo, pp. 28.—The Marriage of Pocahontas. ... [n. p. n. d.] 8vo, pp. 8. Plate.—Martha Washington. ... *New York: J. C. Buttre.* 1861. 8vo, pp. 24. Portrait. + [*Ibid.*] 1864.—A Memorial of Alexander Anderson, M.D., the First Engraver on Wood in America. ... *New York.* 187–. 8vo.—Outline History of the Fine Arts ... in Five Parts. ... *New York: Harper and Brothers.* [1840.] 18mo, pp. 330. + [*Ibid.*] 1842. + [*Ibid.*] 1845. + [*Ibid.*] 1854.—A Primary History of the United States. ... *New York: Mason Brothers.* 1857. 16mo, pp. 222. + [*Ibid.*] 1858. + A New Edition, including a History of the Great Rebellion. ... [*Ibid.*] 1866. 16mo, pp. 238. *See also* Custis (G. W. P.), Vol. V., No. 18157, [Lyon (L.)], *and* [Strong (G. C.)]

Lost in the Forest or Wandering Will's Adventures in South America. ... *London: James Nisbet & Co.* 1869. 16mo, pp. (2), 126. B. 42136

The Lost Steamer; A History of the Amazon. *London: Partridge.* 1852. Post 8vo. C. 42137

Lotbinière, *Canada.* Minutes des Délibérations du comité sur l'élection de Lotbinière. *Québec.* 1854. 8vo, pp. 70.

Lothian (*Marquis of*). *See* [Kerr (W. S. R.)], IX. 37633.

Lothrop (Amy). *See* [Warner (Anna B.)]

Lothrop (S. K.) ... An Address ... before the Independent Company of Cadets, on their Centennial Anniversary, October 19, 1841 ... . By Rev. Samuel K. Lothrop ... . *Boston: John H. Eastburn, Printer.* 1841. 8vo, pp. 59. BA., M. 42139

Lothrop. The Causes, Principles and Results of the Present Conflict. A Discourse delivered before the Ancient and Honorable Artillery Company, on its CCXXIII. Anniversary, June 3, 1861. By S. K. Lothrop, D.D. ... *Boston: Press of Alfred Mudge & Son.* 1861. 8vo, pp. 70. B. 42140

Lothrop. ... A Sermon preached ... on the ... Death of Hon. Daniel Webster. By Rev. S. K. Lothrop ... . *Boston: Eastburn's Press.* 1852. 8vo, pp. 20. BA. 42141

Lothrop. A History of the Church in Brattle Street, Boston. By its Pastor, Samuel Kirkland Lothrop. *Boston: Wm. Crosby and H. P. Nichols.* 1851. 12mo, pp. vi, (1), 217, (1). 42142

Lothrop. Life of Samuel Kirkland, Missionary to the Indians. *Boston: C. C. Little and James Brown.* MDCCCXLVII. 12mo. 42143

Also included in Sparks' "American Biography," Vol. XXV.

Lothrop. Memoir of Nathaniel Ingersoll Bowditch. ... By Rev. S. K. Lothrop, D.D. *Boston: Printed by John Wilson and Son.* 1862. 8vo, pp. 15. Portrait. B. 42144

Lothrop. Memoir of William Lawrence. ... By Samuel Kirkland Lothrop, D.D. *Boston: Privately Printed.* M DCCC LVI. 8vo, pp. 33. Portrait. BA. 42145

[Lothrop.] Report on the Public Schools, and the Systems of Public Instruction in ... New York, Philadelphia, Baltimore and Washington. *Boston: Alfred Mudge & Son ... Printers.* 1867. 8vo, pp. 64. H. 42146

Lothrop. A Sermon preached before the Ancient and Honorable Artillery Company, at the Close of a Second Century from their Charter Incorporation, Boston, June 4, 1838, being the Occasion of their CCth Anniversary. By Samuel K. Lothrop ... *Boston: Weeks, Jordan and Company.* 1838. 8vo, pp. 36. B.

Lothrop. A Sermon, preached ... January 19, 1840, on the Destruction of the Lexington by Fire, January 13th. By S. K. Lothrop ... . *Boston: John H. Eastburn, Printer.* 1840. 8vo, pp. 24. BA. + Third Edition. *Boston.* 1840. 8vo. 42148

Lothrop. A Sermon ... at the Annual Election, ... January 3, 1855. By S. K. Lothrop, D.D. ... *Boston: William White, Printer.* 1855. 8vo, pp. 37. B., M. 42149

Also: An Address ... before the Massachusetts State Temperance Society, May 31, 1835. ... *Boston: Printed by John Ford.* 1835. 8vo, pp. 30, (2).—An Address ... at the Opening of the Rooms of the American Unitarian Association, ... March 9, 1854. ... *Boston.* 1854. 8vo, pp. 39.—An Address to the Benevolent Fraternity of Churches in Boston, Delivered April 27, 1856. ... *Boston.* 1856. 12mo, pp. (2), 30, (1).—Dangerous Tendencies of Civilization: a Sermon preached ... Fast Day, April 5th, 1855. ... *Boston: J. H. Eastburn's Press.* 1855. 8vo, pp. 16.— ... A Sermon, preached ... on the Sunday after the Interment of George Bond, Esq. May 29th, 1842. ... *Boston: Press of W. W. Clapp & Son.* 1842. 8vo, pp. 16. BA.— ... A Sermon preached ... January 9th, 1853, ... Funeral of Amos Lawrence. ... *Boston: Eastburn's Press.* 1853. 8vo, pp. 26. B.—Oration ... on the Fourth of July, 1866. ... *Boston: Alfred Mudge & Son, ... Printers.* 1866. 8vo, pp. 73.— ... A Sermon, ... March 5, 1843, ... after the Interment of Hon. Peter O. Thacher ... . *Boston: John H. Eastburn, Printer.* 1843. 8vo, pp. 20.— ... A Sermon ... at ... Dover, N. H. On the 28th of June, 1846, being the One Hundredth Birthday of Ezra Green, M.D. ... *Boston: Eastburn's Press.* 1846. 8vo, pp. 25.— ... A Sermon preached ... after the Interment of William Lawrence, Esq. October 22, 1848. ... *Boston: James Munroe and Company.* M DCCC XLVIII. 8vo, pp. 21.— ... A Sermon ... on the Sunday succeeding the Death of Moses Grant ... . *Boston: Printed by John Wilson and Son.* 1861. 8vo, pp. 38.— ... A Sermon ... Dec. 15, 1861, the Sunday succeeding the Death of Hon. Richard Sullivan. ... *Boston: Printed by John Wilson and Son.* 1862. 8vo, pp. 19. BA.— ... A Sermon preached ... on the death of the Hon. Harrison Gray Otis, November 5, 1848. ... *Boston: Eastburn's Press.* 1848. 8vo, pp. 25.— ... A Sermon, preached at ... Lynn, February 24, on the Occasion of the Death of Rev. William Gray Swett ... . *Boston: Printed by Samuel N. Dickinson.* 1843. 8vo, pp. 18. *See also* Boston, Vol. II., No. 6652.

Lott (J.) Oration, at Flatbush, on the Fourth of July, 1802. By Jeremiah Lott. *New York.* 1802. 8vo. 42150

Lotteries. A Brief Survey of the Great Extent and Evil Tendencies of the Lottery System, as existing in the United States. ... *Philadelphia: William Brown, Printer.* 1833. 8vo, pp. 48. BA. 42151

Lottery, For Effects to the full Value of 10,000 Dollars, or £3750, Without any Deduction. [*Philadelphia.* 1761.] Folio, 1 leaf. P. 42152

Over the final y in the first word is printed in small letters the words "Pettey's Island." *See also* Baltimore, Vol. II., No. 3064, List, Nos. 41438, 41449, 41454, 41455, 41458, *and* Pennsylvania.

The Lottery Magazine; Or, Compleat Fund of Literary, Political and Commercial Knowledge. For August and September, 1776. *London: Johnson and Co.* [1776.] 8vo. 42153

The number for August contains the Declaration of Independence, probably the earliest publication of it in England. The September number has a description of the City of New York, with a plan.

The Lottery; a Poem and an Ode to War. By St. Denis Le Cadet. *Baltimore.* 1815. 12mo. 42154

The Lottery Ticket: an American Tale. [*Cambridge:*] *Printed ... by Hilliard and Metcalf.* 1822. 12mo, pp. 51. BA.

Lotteries Exposed; or an Inquiry into the Consequences attending them ... . *Philadelphia.* 1827. 16mo, pp. 24. 42156

Lotz (G.) Wanderungen durch Portugal, Spanien und Nordamerika in die Jahren 1827–31. *Hamburg.* 1834. 4 vols., 8vo.

Louaillier (Lewis). ... The Appeal of L. Louaillier, Sen. against the Charge of High Treason, and explaining the Transactions at New Orleans. ... [*New Orleans.*] 1827. 8vo, pp. 28.

The offence of M. Louaillier, a distinguished citizen of Louisiana, consisted in his opposing in the Legislature the suspension of the Writ of Habeas Corpus, when General Jackson asked for it in 1815.

Louaillier. Speech delivered by Mr. Lewis Louaillier, at a Meeting of the Inhabitants of the County Opelousas, ... Louisiana ... held ... the Twentieth August, 1827. *New Orleans: Printed by John Gibson.* 1827. 8vo, pp. 30. H. 42159

Loubat (A.) The American Vine Dresser's Guide. By Alphonse Loubat. *New-York: G. & C. Carvill.* 1827. 12mo, pp. 137, iii. B. 42160

Loubat (J. F.) Official Papers relating to the Conduct of the Legation of the United States at Paris with regard to the Commissioners for the International Exposition of 1867. Second Edition. With the Complaint added. *Paris.* 1867. 8vo, pp. 23.

Loud (M. St. L.) Wayside Flowers: a Collection of Poems. By Mrs. M. St. Leon Loud. *Boston: Ticknor, Reed & Fields.* 1851. 12mo, pp. xii, 276. Portrait. C. 42162

A Loud Call to Mechanics; or the Wolves in Sheep-Skins Detected. By a Citizen. *New York.* 1801. 8vo, pp. 8.

[Louder (C. J.)] How this Administration Conducts this War. [n. p. n. d.] 8vo, pp. 5. H. 42164

Loudon (A.) A | Selection, | of Some | of the most interesting | Narratives, | of | Outrages, Committed | by the | Indians, | in | Their Wars, | with the White People. | Also, | An Account of their Manners, Customs, Traditions, | Religious Sentiments, Mode of Warfare, Military | Tactics, Discipline and Encampments, Treatment |

of Prisoners, &c., which are better Explained, and | more Minutely Related, than has been heretofore | done, by any other Author on that subject. Many | of the Articles have never before appeared in print. | The whole Compiled from the best Authorities, | By Archibald Loudon. | Vol. I. | *Carlisle:* | *From the Press of A. Loudon* | [*Whitehall, Pa.*] 1808. | Sm. 12mo, pp. *2, 5–355. + Vol. II. | *Carlisle,* | *From the Press of Archibald* | *Loudon,* | 1811. | Sm. 12mo, pp. iv, 13–369. C. 42165

In Vol. II. signature F is erroneously signed E, pp. 162–69 are incorrectly numbered 134, etc., but the mistake is corrected at page 169; page 217 is also wrongly numbered 215, and the error is continued up to the end of the volume, which should be, in fact, page 371. It is a work of extreme rarity, and rarely found complete, a circumstance partly owing to the time which elapsed between the publication of the first and second volumes. T. W. Field, in his "Essay," devotes a verbose and unnecessary note to an explanation of the collation, which is not at all an infrequent arrangement—the preliminary leaves not being printed until the text was completed. A perfect set is worth over $100, as not more than half a dozen are known to exist. It contains some narratives not elsewhere to be found, and is one of the most desirable works of its class.

Loudon. The Wonderful Magazine and Extraordinary Museum; being a Complete Repository of the Wonders, Curiosities and Rarities of Nature and Art. By Archibald Loudon. *Carlisle (Pa.): A. Loudon.* 1808. 8vo, pp. 504. C. 42166

[Loudon (*Earl of*).] The Conduct of a Noble Commander. *See* Vol. IV., No. 15197, and *add,* Second Edition. M,DCC,LVIII.

Loudon Park Cemetery. *See* Baltimore, Vol. I. 3084.

Loughborough (J.) The Pacific Telegraph and Railway, an Examination of all the Projects for the Construction of these Works, with a Proposition for Harmonizing all Sections and Parties of the Union and rendering these great Works truly National in their Character. By J. Loughborough. *St. Louis: Charles and Hammond.* 1849. 8vo. Map. 42167

"However visionary this scheme of a railway to the Pacific seemed to the blind eyes of some senators as late as 1849, their eyes have been moistened, they now see the great work accomplished."—Stevens.

Loughridge (R. M.) "Nakcokv Setempohetv." *See* Vol. IV., No. 17461.

Louie's Last Term at St. Mary's. *See* [Harris (*Mrs.* S. S.)]

Louis par la grace de Dieu Roy de France et de Navarre. | [n. p. 1654.] Folio, 1 leaf. 42168

Louis (D.), *pseudon.* Philosophische Gemälde von Westindien und dem Continent von Südamerika. In typographischen,

statistischen, historischen, anthropologischen und politischen Ansichten. ... *Hamburg: Herold.* [1810–11.] 2 vols., 8vo. + Zweite vermehrte Auflage. 1818. 42169

With a second title-page, "Westindien und der Kontinent von Südamerika."

Louis. Washington und der Französische Staat. *Giessen.* 1807. 8vo. 42170

Louis. Washington und die Nordamerikanische Revolution. *Giessen.* 1810. + 1818. 12mo. 42171

According to F. Rassmann's "Lexikon pseudonym Schriften," Louis is a pseudonym for Josias Ludwig Gosch, whose "Wash. u. d. Nordam. Rev." we gave in apparently a second edition under No. 28048. Gosch was imprisoned for his liberal opinions, and died in prison in 1811.

Louisa. Charter of the Louisa Rail Road Company. *Richmond: Printed by T. W. White.* 1836. 8vo, pp. 11–30. BA.

Although this has a separate title-page, it forms pages 11–30, of Moncure Robinson's report.

Louisbourg. An Accurate Journal and Account of the Proceedings of the New-England Land-Forces, during the Late Expedition ... to the Time of the Surrender of Louisbourg. ... *Exon: A. and S. Brice.* 1746. 8vo, pp. 40. H. 42173

An Authentic Account of the Reduction of Louisbourg, In June and July 1758. ... By a Spectator. *London: W. Owen.* 1758. 8vo, pp. 60. BA. 42174

See "M. Rev.," XIX. 499.

Journal of the Siege and Surrender of Louisbourg. Extracted from Major General Amherst's and Admiral Boscawen's Letters ... *Boston.* [1758.] 8vo. 42175

Title from an auctioneer's catalogue, probably incorrect.

Letter wherein the Demolition of Louisbourg is shewn to be absurd. [n. p.] 1761. 8vo. 42176

Louisiana. An Account of Louisiana, being an Abstract of Documents, in the Offices of the Department of State, and of the Treasury. *Philadelphia: John Conrad & Co.* 1803. 8vo, pp. 50. B. + *Philadelphia: Printed by William Duane.* 1803. 8vo, pp. 50. Folded Appendix. + *Philadelphia.* 1803. 8vo, pp. 48. + *Wilmington, Del.: James Wilson.* 1803. 12mo, pp. 76. + *Albany.* 1803. 8vo. + [n. p. n. d.] 8vo, pp. 48. BA. 42177

An Account of Louisiana; being an Abstract of Documents delivered in, or transmitted to, Mr. Jefferson, President of the

United States of America, and by him laid before Congress, and published by their order. *London: Hatchard.* 1804. 8vo, pp. 44.

An Account of Louisiana, laid before Congress by direction of the President of the United States. *Providence: Heaton and Williams.* [1804?] 18mo, pp. 72. C. 42179

An Account of Louisiana, Exhibiting a Compendious Sketch of its Political and Natural History and Topography, with a Copious Appendix, containing several Important Documents. *Newbern.* 1804. 12mo. 42180

For a French version *see* M***.

An Act to incorporate the New England Society of Louisiana. ... March 26, 1842. ... *New Orleans: Lumsden, Kendall & Co.* 1842. 12mo, pp. 12. H. 42181

Acts Passed at the First and Second Sessions of the Legislative Council of the Territory of Orleans, begun and held at the Principal, in the City of New Orleans, on Monday, the third day of December, 1804; and on Thursday, the 20th day of June, 1805. ... *New Orleans.* 1805. 8vo. C. 42182

Acts passed at the First Session of the First Legislature of the Territory of Orleans. *New Orleans.* 1806. 8vo, pp. 221. Continued. C. 42183

In French and English. Also: Acts of the Legislature of the Territory of Orleans. *New Orleans.* 1807. 8vo. C.

Acts of the General Assembly of the State of Louisiana. *New Orleans.* 1812. 8vo. Continued. C. 42184

Address of the Louisiana Native American Association, to the Citizens of Louisiana and the Inhabitants of the United States. ... *New-Orleans: Printed by D. Felt & Co.* 1839. 8vo, pp. 20.

Address of State Campaign Committee of the Republican Party of Louisiana. Official. New Orleans, La., Nov. 10, 1868. *New Orleans.* 1868. 8vo, pp. 10. 42186

Address to Chambers of Commerce, Board of Trade, and to Congress, as to Fort St. Philip Canal. [n. p. n. d.] 8vo, pp. 26. 42187

An Address to the Government of the United States, on the Cession of Louisiana to the French; ... including the Translation of a Memorial, on the War of St. Domingo, and Cession of the Mississippi to France, drawn up by a French Counsellor

of State. ... *Philadelphia: John Conrad, & Co.* 1803. 8vo, pp. (2), 92. + New Edition. [*Ibid.*] 1803. 8vo, pp. 56. 42188

The address is by Charles Brochedon Brown; *see also* Magruder (A. B.)

Addresse au Conseil Législatif du Territoire d'Orléans. *Nouvelle-Orléans.* 1808. 12mo. C. 42189

In French and English.

Analysis of the Third Article of the Treaty of Cession [of Louisiana. n. p. n. d.] 8vo. 42190

An Analytical Index. *See* [Forstall (E. J.)], Vol. VI. 25125.

Aperçu topographique de la Louisiane: Moyens d'y former des établissements utiles et agréables: Description de belles propriétés à vendre dans ce vaste état, par un Louisianais ... . *Paris.* 1816. 12mo, pp. 24. 42191

Appendix to an Account of Louisiana, being an Abstract of Documents in the ... Departments of State, and of the Treasury. *Philadelphia: Printed by T. & G. Palmer.* 1803. 8vo, pp. xc, folded sheet. + [Another Edition.] pp. 77. 42192

Report of the Attorney-General ... . *New Orleans: Printed by Emile La Sere.* 1854. 8vo, pp. 8. Continued. H. 42193

Report of the Auditor of Public Accounts to the General Assembly of Louisiana, for the years 1867 and 1868. Session of 1869. *New Orleans.* 1869. 8vo, pp. 383. 42194

Ausführliche historische ... Beschreibung. *See* Vol. VIII., No. 32104, and *add:* Dritte Auflage. *Leipzig: J. F. Gleditsch.* 1720. 16mo, pp. (6), 102. Map.

Bank Bill, as it passed The Louisiana Legislature, February 1, 1842. ... *New Orleans: Printed by Cook & Levy.* 1842. 8vo, pp. 22. H. 42195

Also: An Act to incorporate the Subscribers to the Bank of Louisiana. ... Second Edition. *New-Orleans: Printed by Benjamin Levy.* 1838. 16mo, pp. 52, (1). H.—The Banking Systems of Louisiana. The Free Banks and Chartered Banks compared. *New Orleans.* 1860. 8vo, pp. 26.—Documents relative to the Investigation of Banks, by the Joint Committee of the Houses of the Louisiana Legislature, 1840. [*New Orleans.* 1840.] 8vo.—Report of the Committee of Stockholders of the Louisiana Bank. *New Orleans.* 1820. 8vo, pp. 48.—Report of the ... Joint Committee on the Affairs of the Citizens' Bank of Louisiana ... for ... 1836. *New Orleans: T. Rea, Printer.* 1837. 8vo, pp. 8. H.

Report of the Board of Health, ... of Louisiana. January, 1859. *Baton Rouge: John M. Taylor ... Printer.* 1859. 8vo, pp. 62, (25). Continued. B. 42196

Annual Report of the Board of Public Works to the General Assembly of Louisiana, Dec. 31, 1869. *New Orleans.* 1870. 8vo, pp. 60. 42197

Report of the Board of Registration ... of Louisiana. ... 1869. *New Orleans: A. L. Lee ... Printer.* 1869. 8vo, pp. 40, lxii.

Annual Report of the Board of Swamp Land Commissioners ... of ... Louisiana. January, 1858. *New Orleans: John Claiborne ... Printer.* 1858. 8vo, pp. 38. H. 42199

Report of the Bureau of Immigration ... of Louisiana. February, 1869. *New Orleans: A. L. Lee ... Printer.* 1869. 8vo, pp. 30. H. 42200

Campaign Document No. 2. Issued by the Democratic State Central Committee of Louisiana. Letters from President Longstreet. [n. p. n. d.] 8vo, pp. 15. 42201

Catalogue of the Centenary College of Louisiana, for ... 1847. *Clinton.* 1848. 8vo. S. 42202

Report of the ... Charity Hospital ... of Louisiana. January, 1859. *Baton Rouge: John M. Taylor, ... Printer.* 1859. 8vo, pp. 26. Continued. H. 42203

Civil Code of the State of Louisiana. By Authority. *New Orleans: Printed by J. C. De St. Romes.* 1825. 8vo, pp. xxxi, 1348. 42204

Alternate pages are in French.

Civil Code of the State of Louisiana; with Annotations by Wheelock S. Upton, LL.B., and Needler R. Jennings. *New Orleans.* 1838. 8vo, pp. 676. C. 42205

In English and French. Also: Additions and Amendments to the Civil Code of ... Louisiana, ... 14th March, 1822 ... . *New-Orleans: Printed by Benj. Levy & Co.* 1823. Sm. folio, pp. (2), 219, 176, (3). B.

Civil Code of the State of Louisiana; with the Statutory Amendments, from 1825 to 1853, inclusive; and References to the Decisions of the Supreme Court ... . By Thomas Gibbes Morgan. *New-Orleans.* 1853. 8vo. C. 42206

The Civil Code of the State of Louisiana: with the Statutory Amendments from 1825 to 1866 inclusive ... . Compiled and Edited by James O. Fuqua. *New York: John F. Trow & Co.* 1867. 8vo, pp. xiv, 482, 72. 42207

Code de Commerce pour L'Etat de la Louisiane. *Nouvelle-Orleans: De l'Imprimerie de Benj. Levy.* 1825. Folio, pp. (2), 287, Table, ix. B. 42208

Code of Practice, in Civil Cases, for the State of Louisiana. *New Orleans.* 1830. 12mo. + [n. p. n. d.] Folio, pp. (6), 170.

Reproduced with "References to the Decisions of the Supreme Court of the State of Louisiana, and also the Statutory Law relating to Practice, by M. Greiner." *New Orleans.* 1844. 8vo. C.

Code of Practice in Civil Cases for ... Louisiana; with the ... Amendments ... to 1866, inclusive ... . Compiled ... by James O. Fuqua. *New York: John F. Trow & Co.* 1867. 8vo, pp. 440. C. 42210

Code of Procedure. *See* Livingston (E.), No. 41614, *note.*

Code of Reform and Prison Discipline. *See* No. 41617, *note.*

Code Pénal de la Louisiane. *See* Livingston (E.)

A Penal Code for the State of Louisiana. *See* Livingston (E.)

Commercial Code for ... Louisiana. *See* No. 41617, *note.*

A Compilation in which is comprised the Constitution of the United States, the Treaty by which Louisiana was ceded to the United States; the Laws and Ordinances of Congress for the government of the Territory of Orleans, together with two Ordinances of the Governor General Intendant of Louisiana. *New Orleans.* 1816. 8vo, pp. 159. 42211

In French and English.

Concession de la Louisiane à M. Crosat, pour 10 Années—Lettres Patentes du Roi 14 Septembre, 1712. *Paris.* 1719. 12mo. A. 42212

The Consolidation and Revision of the Statutes of the State ... prepared by Levi Peirce, Miles Taylor, Wm. W. King, Commissioners appointed by the State. February 5, 1852. *New Orleans.* 1852. 8vo, pp. 658. C. 42213

Constitution, or Form of Government of the State of Louisiana. *Washington City.* 1812. 12mo. C. 42214

Constitutions of Louisiana, 1812, 1845 and 1852. Also, the Constitution of the United States, with Amendments. Articles of Confederation and the Declaration of Independence. *New Orleans.* 1861. 8vo. 42215

A Confederate publication; now very rare.

Debates in the House of Representatives on the Bills for Carrying into Effect the Louisiana Treaty. *Philadelphia: J. Conrad & Co.* 1804. 8vo, pp. (2), 171. 42216

Debates in the Convention for the Revision and Amendment of the Constitution of ... Louisiana, ... at ... New Orleans, April 6, 1864. ... *New Orleans: W. R. Fish, Printer.* 1864. 8vo, pp. 643 [*sic*] 644. BA., C. 42217

Digest of the Civil Laws now in force in the Territory of Orleans; with Alterations and Amendments adapted to its present System of Government. By Authority. *New-Orleans.* 1808. 8vo. C. 42218

Documents of the ... Second Legislature of the State of Louisiana. *New Orleans: J. O. Nixon.* 1866–7. 2 vols., 8vo.

Documents of the General Assembly of Louisiana, 1866. *New Orleans.* 1866. 2 vols., 8vo. A. 42220

Documents relative to the Usury Bill. ... *New-Orleans: Printed by J. C. De St. Romes.* 1823. 8vo, pp. 34. H. 42221

Documents relatifs au bill sur l'usure. ... *Nouvelle-Orleans: Imprimé par J. C. De St. Romes.* 1823. 8vo, pp. 36. H. 42222

Education. Report of the Superintendent of Public Education for 1853. *New-Orleans.* 1854. 8vo. Continued. 42223

Also: Report on Public Instruction. [*New Orleans.*] 1853. 8vo.—Report of the Secretary of State, on Public Education. [n. p. n. d.] 8vo, pp. 8. B.

Report of the ... Superintendent of Public Education ... for 1852. ... *New Orleans: Printed by Emile La Sere.* 1853. 8vo, pp. 35. Continued. 42224

Also: Report of the Board of Education for Freedmen, for the year 1864. [n. p. n. d.] 8vo, pp. 27.

Laws for the Government of the College of Louisiana. *St. Francisville.* 1828. 8vo, pp. 26. + Adopted June, 1832. *New Orleans.* 1832. 8vo, pp. 23. + 1839. *Jackson.* 1839. 8vo, pp. 21. 42225

Les Emigrés Français. *See* Vol. VI., No. 22510.

A Few Remarks on the Cultivation of the Sugar Cane, in Louisiana and the diminution of the duties, on Foreign Sugar. [n. p. n. d.] 8vo, pp. 8. B. 42226

A General Digest of the Acts of the Legislature of the late Territory of Orleans and of the State of Louisiana, and the Ordinances of the Governor under the Territorial Government: preceded by the Treaty of Cession, the Constitution of ... the State, with the Acts of Congress relating to the Government of the Country and the Land Claims therein. By Francois Xavier Martin. *New Orleans.* 1816. 3 vols., 8vo. C. 42227

In French and English.

A General Digest of the Acts of the Legislature of Louisiana, passed from ... 1804 to 1827, inclusive. ... By L. Moreau Lislet. *New Orleans.* 1828. 2 vols., 8vo. C. 42228

Also in the French language.

A Geographical and Statistical Account of the Province of Louisiana. *Baltimore.* 1803. 12mo. 42229

Geology. Preliminary Report of a Geological Reconnoissance of Louisiana. By Eugene W. Hilgard. *New Orleans.* 1869. 8vo, pp. 15. C. 42230

Grand Celebration. *See* Vol. VII., No. 28256.

Guide and Directory for the State of Louisiana and the Cities of New Orleans and Lafayette, with Historical Notices of the State and the City. *New Orleans.* 1838. 12mo, pp. 384. 13 Plates and Map. 42231

Historical Collections. *See* French (B. F.), VII. 25852–54.

Historical Epitome of the State of Louisiana, with an Historical Notice of New Orleans, Views and Descriptions of Public Buildings ... . *New Orleans.* [n. d.] 12mo, pp. 372. 42232

Annual Report of ... the Insane Asylum at Jackson. ... 1859. *Baton Rouge.* 1859. 8vo. + For 1860. *Baton Rouge: J. M. Taylor, ... Printer.* 1860. 8vo, pp. 19. H. 42233

Inaugural Address of Governor Thomas O. Moore, ... January 23, 1860 ... of Louisiana. *Baton Rouge: J. M. Taylor ... Printer.* 1860. 8vo, pp. 7. BA. 42234

Inaugural Address of M[illegible]ael Hahn, Governor, at New Orleans, March 4, 1864. *New Orleans.* 1864. 8vo, pp. 4.

Interesting Account of ... Louisiana. *See* Vol. VIII. 34889.

Journal and Documents of the House of Representatives of Louisiana for 1850. [n. p. n. d.] 8vo. Continued. 42236

Journal and Documents of the Senate for 1850. [n. p. n. d.] 8vo. 42237

Journal de la Chambre des Représentans pendant la seconde session de la première de l'état de la Louisiane. ... 1812. *Nouvelle-Orléans.* 1813. 8vo. Continued. 42238

Journal d'un Voyage à Louisiane. *See* [Valette-Loudon].

Journal du Senat de l'état de la Louisiane, 1866. [n. p. n. d.] 8vo. A. 42239

Journal historique. *See* [La Harpe (Bénard de)], No. 38631.

Journal of the Convention called for the purpose of re-adopting, amending or changing the Constitution of the State of Louisiana, 1844–'45. *New Orleans.* 1845. 8vo. C. 42240

Journal of the House of Representatives of Louisiana, 1831. [n. p. n. d.] 8vo. Continued. A. 42241

Journal of the Proceedings of the Convention of the State of Louisiana, ... Held in ... New Orleans, ... January, 1845. ... *New Orleans: Besancon, Ferguson & Co.* 1845. Rl. 8vo, pp. (2), 960, Index, ii. 42242

Journal of the Senate for 1812. [n. p. n. d.] 8vo. Cont'd.

Laws. The Laws of Las Siete Partidas which are still in force in the State of Louisiana. Translated from the Spanish by L. Moreau Lislet and Henry Carleton. *New Orleans.* 1820. 2 vols., 8vo. C. 42244

"A curious and learned work."—TICKNOR's *Spanish Literature*, I. 51.

Laws of the State of Louisiana, from 1828. *New Orleans.* 1828. 8vo. Continued. 42245

The Laws of the Territory of Louisiana, comprising all those which are now actually in foree within the same. ... *St. Louis, (L.): Printed by Joseph Charless, Printer to the Territory.* 1808. 8vo, pp. 372. C. 42246

Believed to be the first book printed West of the Mississippi. *See also* No. 39411.

The Legal Bearings. *See our* No. 39849.

Letter of the Governor of ... Louisiana, communicating the Credentials of Charles Smith and R. King Cutler to the Congress of the United States ... . [*Washington.* 1864.] 8vo. 42247

Senate Document, No. 1, 38th Congress, 2d Session, 1864.

Lettres, etc. *and* Lettres Patentes. *See* Nos. 40634 and 40723.

Memorial from the ... Levee Commissioners of ... Louisiana ... *New Orleans.* 1866. 8vo, pp. 12. H. 42248

Louisiana and Mississippi Business Directory, 1870–71. With their State Governments, Post Offices, Telegraph Stations, Brief Sketches of the Principal States and Territories, and ... List of Farmers and Planters in Louisiana and Mississippi. *New Orleans: A. Boyd.* 1870. 8vo. C. 42249

Louisiana and the Tariff. By a Native of Louisiana. *New-Orleans: Printed by E. Johns & Co.* 1841. 8vo, pp. 24. BA.

Louisiana Digest, embracing the Laws of a General Nature, from 1804 to 1841; with an Abstract of the Decisions of the Supreme Court of Louisiana on the Statutory Law. By Meinrad Greiner. *New Orleans.* 1841. 8vo. C. 42251

Constitution and Statement of the Louisiana Homestead Aid Association. *Washington.* 1868. 16mo, pp. 15. H. 42252

The Louisiana Law Journal, ... Edited by Gustavus Schmidt, ... Vol. I. *New Orleans: E. Johns & Co.* 1841–42. 8vo. C.

No more published.

By-Laws, Rules and Regulations of the ... Louisiana Penitentiary ... February 5, 1868. *Baton Rouge.* 1868. 16mo, pp. 14, (4). H. 42254

Also: Report of the Penitentiary. [1839. n. p. n. d.] 12mo, pp. 4, (8). Folded leaf. Continued. H.

Louisiana State Colonization Society. Facts in regard to African Colonization; a Memorial ... to the Citizens of Louisiana. *New Orleans.* 1857. 8vo, pp. 23, (1). B. 42255

Louisiana State Gazetteer and Business Man's Guide, for 1866 and 1867. *New Orleans: Palmer, Buchanan & Smith.* [n. d.] 8vo, pp. 286, Index, xii. B. 42256

Catalogue of the Louisiana State Library, 1869. ... *New Orleans.* 1869. 8vo. C. 42257

Also: Report of the State Library ... of ... Louisiana. *Baton Rouge: J. M. Taylor ... Printer.* 1860. 8vo, pp. 36. H.

Report of the Board of Supervisors of the State Seminary of Learning ... . *Baton Rouge: J. M. Taylor ... Printer.* 1860. 8vo, pp. 15. B. 42258

Masonry. Grand Lodge of the State of Louisiana. Grand Annual Communication ... 1849. ... *New Orleans: Printed by B∴ J. L. Sollée.* 1849. 8vo, pp. 40. H. 42259

Also: Extract from the Proceedings of the Grand Lodge of Louisiana. *New Orleans.* 1820. 8vo.—Grand Lodge of Free and Accepted Masons of ... Louisiana ... . 1848. *New Orleans.* 1848. 8vo, pp. 32.—Report of Louisiana Relief Lodge, No. 1 ... at New Orleans. July 1, 1854 and 1857. [n. p. n. d.] 12mo, pp. 12.—Report of the Committee on Foreign Correspondence of Louisiana ... for ... 1849. [n. p. n. d.] 8vo, pp. 67.

Memorial and Remonstrance to Congress, on the Repeal of the Duties on Foreign Sugar, passed by both Houses of the Legislature of Louisiana, at its Session of 1831. *New-Orleans: Printed by A. T. Penniman & Co.* 1831. 8vo, pp. 15. B. 42260

Memorial presented by the Inhabitants of Louisiana to the Congress of the United States in Senate and House of Representatives Convened. Translated from the French. ... *Washington: Printed by Samuel H. Smith.* 1804. 8vo. 42261

Memorial of the People of Louisiana, to the Congress of the United States. [n. p. 1866?] 8vo, pp. 11. H. 42262

Memorials of the Citizens of Louisiana remonstrating against the Admission of Senators and Representatives from the State of Louisiana; and the Reception of an Electoral Vote from that State for President and Vice-President of the United States ... . [*Washington.*] 1864. 8vo, pp. 4. 42263

Message from the President ... relative to the Cession of Louisiana, Oct. 22, 1803. [*Washington.* 1803.] 8vo. 42264

Message from the President ... transmitting the Constitution of Louisiana, established by the Convention ... . *Washington.* 1812. 8vo. N. 42265

Message of the President ... communicating Documents respecting Louisiana. ... Dec. 10, 1805. *Washington.* 1805. 8vo, pp. 29. 42266

Message of the President and Documents on a Demand of the Spanish Government of Part of Louisiana, also the Message and Documents on the Negotiations for Peace with England. *Washington.* 1814–16. 2 vols., 8vo. 42267

Message of Governor Paul O. Hebert, to the General Assembly of ... Louisiana: January, 1854. [n. p. 1854.] 8vo, pp. 10. Continued. H. 42268

Annual Message of Robert C. Wickliffe, Governor ... of Louisiana, to the General Assembly. *Baton Rouge: J. M. Taylor, ... Printer.* 1860. 8vo, pp. 16. B. 42269

Message annuel ... à l'Assemblée Générale. *Baton Rouge: J. M. Taylor ... Printer.* 1860. 8vo, pp. 16. 42270

Message of the Governor ... October 7, 1864. [n. p. n. d.] 8vo, pp. 13. 42271

Relates to the Rebellion. Also: Annual Message of Governor Henry Watkins Allen, to the Legislature of ... Louisiana. January, 1865. [*Shreveport.* 1865.] 8vo, pp. 20. BA.

A New Digest. *See* Bullard (H. A.), Vol. III., No. 9119.

Observations on the Present Condition of Louisiana. *Washington.* 1865. 8vo, pp. 11. 42272

Official Journal of the House of Representatives of the State of Louisiana, Session of 1860. *Baton Rouge.* 1860. 8vo.

Official Register of the Officers and Cadets of the State Seminary, ... near Alexandria, Louisiana. ... 1866. *New Orleans.* 1866. 8vo, pp. 21. Continued. B. 42274

Afterwards known as the Louisiana State University.

Official Journal of the Proceedings of the Convention of the State of Louisiana. ... *New Orleans: J. O. Nixon, Printer.* 1861. 8vo, pp. 111, 330. BA., C. 42275

The Secession Convention. After page 111, follows this title (paging continuous to 330): "Journal Officiel de la Convention ... de la Louisiane." ... *Nouvelle Orléans: J. O. Nixon, Imprimeur.* 1861. 8vo. C.

Official Journal of the Proceedings of the Convention for the Revision and Amendment of the Constitution of ... Louisiana. ... *New Orleans: W. R. Fish, Printer.* 1864. 8vo, pp. 184, x.

This convention assembled by order of Gen. Nathaniel P. Banks. The French title is "Journal Officiel des Travaux de la Convention reunie pour reviser et amender la Constitution ... de la Louisiane." ... *Nouvelle Orleans: W. R. Fish, Imprimeur.* 1864. 8vo, pp. 187, x. Also: Auditor's Report to the State Constitutional Convention of 1864. *New Orleans: W. R. Fish, Printer.* [n. d.] 8vo, pp. 8.—Rules and Regulations of the Convention for the Amendment and Revision of the Constitution, 1864. [n. p. n. d.] 8vo, pp. 8.

Official Journal of the Proceedings of the Convention, for framing a Constitution for the State of Louisiana. ... *New Orleans: J. B. Roudanez & Co.* 1867–1868. 8vo, pp. 315, (1). B.

Official Report of Debates in the Louisiana Convention. August 5, 1844. [n. p. n. d.] 8vo, pp. 960. C. 42278

Official Reports of the Senate of ... Louisiana. ... 1855. *New Orleans: Printed by Emile La Sere.* 1855. 8vo, pp. 104.

On the Rock-Salt Deposit of Petit Anse: Louisiana Rock-Salt Company. Report ... . *New York: American Bureau of Mines.* 1867. 8vo. 42280

Petition of Sundry Inhabitants of Louisiana, asking redress of certain grievances. March 22, 1806. [*Washington.* 1806.] 8vo.

Platform of the Free State Party, January 30, 1865. [n. p. 1865.] 8vo, pp. 4. 42282

The Present State of the Country and Inhabitants, Europeans and Indians, of Louisiana, On the North Continent of America. By an Officer at New Orleans to his Friend at Paris. Containing The Garrisons, Forts and Forces, Price of all Manner of Provisions and Liquors, &c. also an Account of their drunken lewd Lives, which lead them to Excesses of Debauchery and Villany [*sic*]. To which are added, Letters from the Governor of that Province on the Trade of the French and English with the Natives. Also Proposals to them to put an end to their Traffick with the English. Annual Presents to the Savages; a List of the Country goods, and those proper to be sent there, &c. Translated from the French Originals, taken in the Golden Lyon Prize, Rasteaux, Master, by the Hon. Capt. Aylmer, Commander of his Majesty's Ship the Portmahon, and by him sent to the Admiralty Office. *London: J. Millan.* 1744. 8vo, pp. 55. + The Second Edition. [*Ibid.*] 42283

The Louisiana of this book included Alabama, the whole of the Mississippi Valley, the Great West, the Ohio Valley, and the country of the Illinois as far as Canada. The letters referred to are from M. de Vaudreil, Governor of New Orleans.

Proceedings of the Convention of the Republican Party of Louisiana, held at ... New Orleans, ... 1865, and of the ... Friends of Universal Suffrage of Louisiana ... . *New Orleans: Tribune Office.* 1865. 8vo, pp. 30. 42284

Protest of the State of Louisiana to the Senate of the United States. [n. p. n. d.] 8vo, pp. 8. W. 42285

Rapport Du Comité charge, en vertu de la résolution prise par les deux Chambres de la Législature de l'Etat de la Louisiane, le 5 Janvier 1815, de procéder à une enquête à l'effet de découvrir la cause des mesures militaires qui ont été exercées contre l'Assemblée Générale dudit Etat, pendant sa presente session. [n. p. n. d.] 8vo, pp. 80. 42286

Rapports Officiels Des Devats [*sic*] De la Convention De la Louisiane. James Foullouze, Rapporteur. *Imprimes par J. Bayon, ... Nlle.-Orleans.* 1845. Rl. 8vo, pp. 460, (2). C. 42287

Reflections on the Cause of the Louisianians; respectfully submitted by their Agents. [*Washington.* 1804.] 8vo, pp. 17.

Relations de la Louisiane. *See* [Tonti (*Chevalier* de)].

Remarks on a Dangerous Mistake made as to the Eastern Boundary of Louisiana. *Boston: Printed by J. T. Buckingham.* 1814. 8vo, pp. 28. B. 42289

Report of the Commissioner of the General Land-Office, on the Baron de Bastrop Crant in Louisiana. Dec. 1852. [*Washington.* 1852.] 8vo. S. 42290

Report of the Committee of the House of Representatives of Congress upon so much of the Presidents Message as relates to Louisiana. *Washington.* 1805. 8vo. 42291

Report of the Committee ... "To enquire into the Expediency of authorizing the President of the United States to employ Persons to explore such parts of the Province of Louisiana as he may deem proper." 8th March, 1804. ... [*Washington.* 1804.] 8vo. 42292

Report of the Finance Committee ... of Louisiana. *Baton Rouge: J. M. Taylor ... Printer.* 1861. 8vo, pp. 25. 42293

Report of ... the General Assembly of Louisiana on the Conduct of the Late Elections ... . *New Orleans: A. L. Lee ... Printer.* 1868. 8vo, pp. 68. Continued. H. 42294

Report of the Senate Standing Committee, March 21, 1850, on Levees, Drainage, etc. *New Orleans.* 1853. 8vo. 42295

Annual Report of the State Engineer ... of ... Louisiana. January, 1860. *Baton Rouge: J. M. Taylor ... Printer.* 1860. 8vo, pp. 15. H. 42296

Report of the State Treasurer ... . *Donaldson.* 1830. 8vo, pp. 15. Continued. 42297

Representation and Petition of the Representatives elected by the Freemen of the Territory of Louisiana. *Washington City.* 1805. 8vo, pp. 30. W. 42298

Revised Civil Code. *New Orleans.* 1870. 8vo, pp. xii, 503.

The Revised Statutes of ... Louisiana, compiled by U. B. Phillips ... . *New Orleans: John Claiborne, ... Printer.* 1856. 8vo, pp. xcv, 610. BA., C. 42300

The Revised Statute Laws of ... Louisiana, from the Organization of the Territory to the Year 1869 inclusive. *New Orleans.* 1870. 8vo, pp. xlii, 866. B. 42301

Rules and Regulations of the Quarantine, for the Protection of ... Louisiana. New Orleans, June 13, 1855. *New Orleans.* 1866. 8vo, pp. 18. B. 42302

Schilderung von Louisiana. *See* Berquin-Duvallon, II. 4964.

The Situation in Louisiana. The Legislature's Reply to Kellogg's Pronunciamento. ... [n. p. n. d.] 8vo, pp. 8. H. 42303

Sketches of Life and Character in Louisiana ... . By a Member of the New Orleans Bar. *New Orleans: Ferguson & Crosby.* 1847. 8vo, pp. 85, (1). B. 42304

Suggestions presented to the Judiciary Committee of the Senate of the United States, relating to the State of Louisiana. [*Washington.* 1865.] 8vo, pp. 8. 42305

38th Cong., Sen. Doc., No. 9.

Supplemental Report of the General Assembly of Louisiana on the Conduct of the Late Elections ... . *New Orleans: A. L. Lee ... Printer.* 1869. 8vo, pp. xl, 296. BA. 42306

A System of Penal Law. *See* Livingston (E.), No. 41615.

To the Citizens of ... Louisiana. [n. p. 1864.] 8vo, pp. 2.

By Gov. Henry W. Allen, July 5, 1864.

A Topographical and Statistical Account of the Province of Louisiana ... with ... particulars relative to the Indian Tribes ... and the recent Convention between the United States and the French Republic. *Printed for Jacob D. Dietrick. Hagerstown, Md.* 1803. 8vo, pp. 80. S. + *Baltimore: Martin & Pratt.* 16mo, pp. 80. Appendix, folded sheet. 42308

Very much like *our* No. 42180, with additions.

Travels in Louisiana. *See* [Berquin-Duvallon], Vol. II. 4965.

Treaty and Conventions entered into and ratified by the United States of America and the French Republic, relative to the cession of Louisiana. April 30, 1803. [n. p. 1803.] 8vo. A. 42309

Annual Report of the Administrators of the University of Louisiana. ... *New Orleans.* 1861. 8vo, pp. 28. B. 42310

Also: An Act to establish in ... New Orleans the University of Louisiana. [n. p. n. d.] 12mo, pp. 12.—Address of D. F. Boyd, Superintendent ... to the Graduating Class, 1869 ... . *New Orleans.* 1869. 8vo.—Annual Circular of the Medical Department of the University of Louisiana. ... 1853–54. *New Orleans.* 1853. 8vo, pp. 8. Plate. Continued. H.—Official Register of the Officers and Cadets, 1867 ... . *New Orleans.* 1867. 8vo. Continued.—Annual Report of the Board of Supervisors of the Louisiana State University for 1867 ... . *New Orleans.* 1868. 8vo, pp. 28. Continued.—Report of the Board of Supervisors of the Louisiana State Seminary of Learning and Military Academy. *New Orleans.* 1866. 8vo, pp. 30. Continued. S. Concerning Louisiana *see* "N. A. Rev.," XVII. 242, XXVIII. 389, XLIII. 297, LXV. 1, "Edinb. Rev.," XXXII. 231, *and* Hunt's "Magazine," IV., XI. 411.

LOUISVILLE, *Ky.* An Account of the Louisville City-School; with Ordinances of the City Council, and Regulations of the Board of Trustees. *Louisville.* 1830. 8vo, pp. 24. M. 42311

Address to the Non-Slaveholders of Kentucky. Read ... at ... Louisville, ... April 10, 1849. [*Louisville.* 1849.] 8vo, pp. 16.

Annual Communication of the Mayor, and Reports of Departments, of the City of Louisville. 1866. *Louisville: Bradley & Gilbert, Printers.* 1867. 8vo, pp. (4), 2, 10. Continued. B.

Annual Report of the Auditor of ... Louisville, for ... March 9, 1855. *Louisville, Ky.: C. Settle, Printer.* 1855. 8vo, pp. 20.

Constitution of the Catholic Benevolent Society of Louisville, Kentucky, 1840. *Louisville, Ky.* 1840. 12mo, pp. 12. M.

Charter of the City of Louisville of 1851, and Ordinances of the City in Force on the 24th of June, 1869 ... . Prepared by Robt. J. Elliott ... . *Louisville: Bradley & Gilbert.* 1869. 8vo, pp. (2), 9–1062. B. 42316

City of Louisville, *vs.* University of Louisville. ... July, 1852. ... [*Louisville:*] *Morton & Griswold, Prs.* [1852.] 8vo, pp. 46.

A Collection of the Acts of Virginia and Kentucky relative to the Town of Louisville. *Louisville, Ky.* 1823. 8vo, pp. 62.

A Collection of the Acts of Virginia and Kentucky relative to Louisville and Portland, with the Charter of the City of Louisville. *Louisville.* 1839. 8vo. M. 42319

A Collection of the State and Municipal Laws, ... of Louisville, Ky. Prepared ... by Oliver H. Strattan and John M. Vaughn ... . *Louisville: C. Settle, Printer.* 1857. 8vo, pp. 460.

Report on ... Education in ... Louisville. ... *Louisville, Ky.* 1833. 8vo, pp. 12. BA. 42321

Also: Annual Report of the ... Trustees of the ... Schools of Louisville ... for ... 1859–'60. *Louisville: Bradley & Gilbert.* 1860. 8vo, pp. 35, 29, 18, 5, 4, 35, (12), 36, 8, 13, 40, 4. Plates. Continued. H.

A Letter to the ... Louisville Journal. *See our* No. 40471.

Constitution and By-Laws of the Louisville and Jefferson Co. Horticultural Society. *Louisville: Printed by Henkle, Logan & Co.* 1841. 16mo, pp. 9. BA. 42322

Charter, By-Laws, &c., of the Louisville and Portland Canal Company. *Louisville, Ky.* 1825. 8vo, pp. 10. 42323

Constitution, By-Laws, and Regulations of the Louisville Chamber of Commerce; adopted November, 1839. *Louisville, Ky.* 1839. 8vo, pp. 16. M. 42324

Charter of the Louisville, Cincinnati, and Charleston Railroad Company; with Charter of the South-western Railroad Bank. *Charleston.* 1838. 8vo, pp. 32. M. 42325

Also: A Call to the Stockholders of the Louisville, Cincinnati and Charleston Rail Road ... By Robert Y. Heym, President. *Charleston: Printed by A. K. Miller.* 1838. 8vo, pp. 32.—Proceedings of the Stockholders ... at their Second Meeting ... With the First Annual Report ... . *Charleston.* 1837. 8vo.

The Louisville Directory for the Year 1832. By Richard W. Otis. *Louisville.* 1832. 16mo. Continued annually. 42326

The Directory for 1838–39 is by Gabriel Collins; for 1865 there are two, one by Edwards, the other by Williamson; for 1866 is by Edwards.

Act of Incorporation; with the By-Laws and Rules of the Louisville Gas and Water Company. [n. p. n. d.] 8vo, pp. 16.

Rules and Regulations of the Louisville Jockey Club. *Louisville, Ky.* 1838. 12mo, pp. 12. M. 42328

Catalogue ... of the Medical Institute of ... Louisville, January 1st, 1839. *Louisville, Ky.: Prentice and Weissinger.* 1839. 8vo, pp. 12, (2). Continued. B. 42329

Some Account of the Origin and Present Condition of the Medical Institute of Louisville, with Remarks on a Late Rejected Report. *Louisville, Ky.: Prentice and Weissinger.* 1842. 8vo, pp. 30. B. 42330

Catalogue of the Officers, Students and Graduates of the Louisville Medical Institute, 1839–40. *Louisville.* 1840. 8vo, pp. 16. Continued. 42331

Also: Annual Announcement of the Louisville Medical Institute, 1840–41. *Louisville.* 1841. 8vo, pp. 16.—Circular of the Louisville Medical Institute. *Louisville.* 1838. 8vo, pp. 8.

Louisville Municipal Reports for ... Dec. 31, 1867. ... *Louisville, Ky.: Bradley & Gilbert.* 1868. 8vo, pp. (6), 23. 2 Diagrams. Continued. B. 42332

Constitution, By-Laws, and Rules of Order of the Louisville Pilots' Benevolent Society. *Louisville.* 1841. 12mo, pp. 11.

Report of the Louisville Refugee Commission. *Louisville, Ky.: Civill & Calvert, Printers.* 1865. 8vo, pp. 16. H. 42334

Annual Report of the Louisville Temperance Society. *Louisville.* 1831. 8vo, pp. 20. 42335

Charter, Constitution, and By-Laws of the Mechanics' Institute, of Louisville. ... *Louisville: Printed by Morton & Griswold.* 1839. 12mo, pp. 10, (1). BA. 42336

Catalogue of the Louisville Mercantile Library; with an Appendix ... . *Louisville: Prentice and Weissinger.* 1843. 8vo, pp. 101, (2). BA. 42337

Also: Constitution, By-Laws, and Regulations of the Mercantile-Library Association of Louisville. *Louisville.* 1841. 8vo, pp. 22. M.

Constitution der National-Garde von Louisville. *Louisville.* [n. d.] 16mo, pp. 16. 42338

Proceedings of the Friends of Gen. Jackson at Louisville. *Louisville.* 1827. 12mo. W. 42339

Prospectus of the Collegiate Institute, Louisville, Ky. *Louisville.* [n. d.] 8vo, pp. 13. 42340

Constitution of the Protestant Episcopal Orphan Asylum of the City of Louisville, with Rules ... . *Louisville, Ky.: Prentice & Weissinger, Printers.* 1835. 8vo, pp. 12. H. 42341

Also: Annual Report of the Board of Managers, 1835. *Louisville.* 1835. 12mo.

University of Louisville: Medical Department. ... Annual Catalogue ... . *Louisville, Ky.: Prentice and Weissinger.* 1849. 8vo, pp. 14. Continued. B. 42342

History of the Medical Department. *See* Yandell (L. P.)

Constitution and By-Laws of the Washington Fire-Engine Company. *Louisville.* 1839. 8vo, pp. 8. M. 42343

LOUNSBERY (E.) ... A Sermon preached in ... Philadelphia, ... Sept. 7, 1862. By the Rev. Edward Lounsbery. ... *Philadelphia: Ringwalt & Brown.* 1862. 8vo, pp. 12. 42344

Relates to the Rebellion.

[LOUREIRO (João Bernardo da Rocha).] Exame critico do parecer que deu a Commissão especial das Côrtes, sobre os negocios do Brasil. [n. p. 1822.] Folio, pp. 8. 42345

LOUREIRO (Lorenço Trigo de). Instituições de Direito civil brasileiro, extrahidas das Instituições de Direito civil lusitano do eximio jurisconsulto portuguez Paschoal José de Mello Freire, na parte compativel com as instituições da nossa cidade, e augmentadas nos logares competentes com a substancia das leis brasileiras. Tomo I. *Pernambuco: Typ. da Viuva Roma & Filhos.* 1851. 8vo, pp. 190. + Tomo II. *Recife: Typ. Commercial de Meira Henriques.* 1851. 8vo, pp. 188. + Secunda edicão mais correcta e augmentada ... . *Recife: Typ. Universal.* 1857. 2 vols., 8vo, pp. 260; 300. 42346

LOUREIRO (P.) Tables showing the Approximate Cost of Tea ... laid down in New-York ... . *New-York.* 1828. 8vo.

LOUVERTURE (T.) Antwoord aan den Generaal Buonaparte. *'s Hage.* 1803. 8vo, pp. 8. 42348

In verse. Reply of Toussaint-L'Ouverture to General Buonaparte.

LOUVERTURE. Bonaparte in the West Indies; or, the History of Toussaint Louverture, the African Hero. In Three Parts. *London: Hatchard.* 1803. 8vo, pp. 48. + Third Edition. *London.* 1803. 8vo. + The Fourth Edition. *Dublin: Printed by Holmes & Charles.* 1804. 8vo, pp. 48. C. 42349

See "M. Rev.," New Series, XLII. 204.

LOUVERTURE. Extrait du Rapport addressé au Directoire Exécutif, par Toussaint l'Ouverture. *Cap Français.* [n. d.] 8vo.

LOUVERTURE. Histoire de Toussaint-Louverture, Chef des Noirs Insurgés de St. Domingue. Précédée d'un coup d'œil politique sur cette Colonie. *Paris.* 1802. 12mo, pp. 210. Port.

LOUVERTURE. The History of Toussaint Louverture. A New Edition ... . *London: J. Butterworth and Son.* 1814. 8vo, pp. viii, 93. B. 42352

LOUVERTURE. Life of Toussaint Louverture. *London.* 1802. 8vo. Portrait. 42353

LOUVERTURE. The Life and Military Achievements of Tousant Loverture, ... with an impartial Account of his political conduct ... to which is added a description of the ... conduct of General Le Clerc, until his death; also his successor General Rochambeau's Actions, until the Evacuation of that Colony ... . [n. p.:] *For the Author.* 1804. 8vo, pp. (2), 76. BA. + Second Edition. [n. p.] 1805. 8vo. 42354

See also "Pamphleteer," Vol. IV., p. 311, *and* Beard (J. R.)

LOUVERTURE. Memoires du Général Toussaint-Louverture, écrits par lui-même ... . Précédée d'une étude historique et critique, suivis de notes avec un appendice contenant les opinions de l'Empereur Napoléon Ier sur les événements de Saint-Domingue. Par Saint-Remy. *Paris: Pagnerre.* 1853. 8vo, pp. 160, or less. Portrait. 42355

LOUVERTURE. Toussaint L'Ouverture: a Biography [by J. R. Beard] and Autobiography [edited by J. Redpath]. *Boston: James Redpath.* 1863. 12mo, pp. 372. Map and Portrait. BA.

For an English edition *see our* Vol. I., No. 4125.

[LOUVET DE COUVRAY (Jean Baptiste).] Love and Patriotism! or, the Extraordinary Adventures of M. Duportail, Late Major-General in the Armies of the United States. Interspersed with many Surprising Incidents in the Life of the Late Count Pulaski [*sic*]. *Philadelphia: Printed by Carey & Markland.* 1797. 12mo, pp. 120. + *Boston: Printed by Samuel Etheridge.* 1799. 12mo, pp. 59. + [*Ibid.*] 1800. 12mo, pp. 59. + *From Sidney's Press. For I. Cooke & Co. New-Haven.* 1813. 18mo. + *Boston.* 1825. 12mo. B., C. 42357

Taken from the "Adventures of the Chevalier du Faublas."

[LOUVET DE COUVRAY.] Interesting History of the Baron de Lovzinski with a ... remarkable Occurrence in the Life of the ... Count Pulaski ... who ... fell ... before Savannah, 1779. *New York: Robert Moore.* 1807. 18mo, pp. 108. 42358

LOVE (A. H.) An Appeal in Vindication of Peace Principles, and against Resistance by Force of Arms, by Alfred H. Love ... . A Review in opposition to an Address ... by ... William J. Mullen ... June 17th, 1861. *Philadelphia: Maas & Vodges, Printers.* 1862. 8vo, pp. 17. + Second Edition. [*Ibid.*] 1862. 8vo, pp. 18. 42359

Also: Address before the Peace Convention, held in Boston, March 14 & 15, 1866; ... *Hopedale, Mass.: "Age" Office Print.* M DCCC LXVI. 8vo, pp. 24. H.

Love (C.) A Poem on the Death of General George Washington. Late President of the United States. In Two Books. By Charles Love. ... *Alexandria, Virginia*, A.D. M,DCCC. 12mo, pp. 60. BA., C. 42360

Very rare. The last four pages contain a list of subscribers.

Love (*Gen.*) Report of Major-General Love of the Indiana Legion. *Indianapolis: Joseph J. Bingham.* 1863. 8vo, pp. 72.

Love (H. T.) Circular of Horace T. Love, Agent of Brown University, in regard to the Disposal of the Lands in Kansas granted to that Institution. ... [n. p. 1863.] 4to, pp. 2.

Love (W. D.) Obedience to Rulers ... . A Discourse ... December 22d, 1850, on the Two Hundred and Thirtieth Anniversary of the Landing of the Pilgrims. By Wm. Deloss Love, ... *New Haven: Storer & Stone, Printers.* 1851. 8vo, pp. 16.

Love. Wisconsin in the War of the Rebellion: a History of all Regiments and Batteries the State has sent to the Field ... . By Wm. De Loss Love. *Chicago: Church and Goodman.* 1866. 8vo, pp. xxi, (1), 17–1144. 26 Plates. B., C. 42364

Love and Patriotism. *See* [Louvet de Couvray], No. 42357.

Love Triumphant. *See* [Mather (Cotton)].

The Loved and the Lost. Fourth Edition. *New York: W. G. Cordray.* 1860. 12mo, pp. 226. 42365

On cemeteries and burying grounds.

Lovejoy (J. C.) Memoir of the Rev. Elijah P. Lovejoy; who was murdered ... at Alton, Illinois, Nov. 7, 1837. By Joseph C. and Owen Lovejoy. ... *New York: John S. Taylor.* 1838. 12mo, pp. 382. B., C. 42366

Lovejoy. Memoir of the Rev. Charles T. Torrey, who died in the Penitentiary of Maryland, where he was confined for showing mercy to the Poor. By J. C. Lovejoy. *Boston.* 1847. 12mo, pp. 364. Portrait. 42367

Also: The Alliance of Jehoshaphat and Ahab. A Sermon, ... on the Annual Fast, ... April 4, 1844 ... . [*Boston.* 1844.] 8vo, pp. 7, (1).—The Baptism of Slavery. Speech ... April 5, 1860. *Washington.* 1860. 8vo, pp. 8.—The Fanaticism of the Democratic Party. Speech ... 21 February, 1859. *Washington.* 1859. 8vo, pp. 8: —The Law and the Offence: A Lecture on the Subject of Prohibitory Laws. ... *Boston: Printed by Charles C. P. Moody.* 1852. 8vo, pp. 16. This elicited: "Review of Rev. Mr. Lovejoy's 'Lecture on the Subject of Prohibitory Laws in regard to The Use of Intoxicating Drinks.' By a Citizen of Maine." *Boston.* 1852. 8vo, pp. 23. —The North and the South! Letter from J. C. Lovejoy, Esq., to ... Hon. Owen Lovejoy, ... March 16, 1859. [n. p. n. d.] 8vo, pp. 8.— ... A Sermon preached at the Interment of Rev. John Wilder, at Cambridgeport, March 8, 1844. ... *Boston: Wilder & Co.* 1844. 8vo, pp. 16.—Speech ... on ... the Repeal of the Liquor Law ... 1853. ... *Boston: R. C. Nichols.* [1853.] 12mo, pp. 22.—Speech ... at Watertown, August 1, 1855. [n. p. n. d.] 12mo, pp. 12.—The True Democracy. A Speech ... at East Cambridge, Sept. 29, 1856. ... [n. p. n. d.] 12mo, pp. 12. H.

Lovejoy (O.) The Barbarism of Slavery. Speech of Hon. Owen Lovejoy ... April 5, 1860. [*Washington.* 1860.] 8vo, pp. 8. BA. 42368

Lovejoy. Confiscation of Rebel Property. Remarks of Hon. Owen Lovejoy, in Reply to Messrs. Crittenden and Wickliffe of Ky. ... in the House of Representatives, April 24, 1862. [*Washington.* 1862.] 8vo, pp. 8. B. 42369

Also: Conduct of the War. Speech ... January 6, 1862. [*Washington, D. C.* 1862.] 8vo, pp. 7.—Human Beings not Property. Speech ... February 17, 1858. [*Washington, D. C.* 1858.] 8vo, pp. 8. H.—State of the Union. Speech ... in the House of Representatives, January 28, 1861. [n. p. n. d.] 8vo, pp. 8.

Lovejoy. Addresses on the Death of Hon. Owen Lovejoy, delivered in the Senate and House ... March 28, 1864. *Washington.* 1864. 8vo, pp. 60. 42370

Lovejoy *and* Dunn (W. M.) Remarks on the Bill to authorize the President to enlist Soldiers of African Descent. House of Representatives, January 29, 1863. [n. p. n. d.] 8vo, pp. 8. 42371

[Lovell (James).] Copy of a Letter of July 4, 1805, to the President of the United States, &c. *Boston: A. Newell, Printer.* [1805.] 8vo, pp. 8. H. 42372

Lovell. Oratio in Funere ... Henrici Flyntij, Arm. habita in Sacello Holdeniano. Coll. Harvard ... . A Jacobo Lovell, A.M. *Bostoni: Typis Z. Fowle et S. Draper.* 1760. 8vo, pp. 6. B., W.

Lovell. An Oration delivered April 2d, 1771. At the Request of the Inhabitants of the Town of Boston; to Commemorate the bloody Tragedy of the Fifth of March, 1770. By James Lovell, A.M. ... *Boston: Printed by Edes and Gill, by Order of the Town of Boston.* 1771. 4to, pp. 19. B., M. 42374

Also: Essay on the Eclipse. ... [*Boston.*] 1754. 4to, pp. 24.

Lovell. Propagation of Truth, or "Tyranny Anatomized" in Four Letters ... . With ... Notes ... . By James Lovell. ... *Boston: For the Author.* 1808. 8vo, pp. 29. BA. 42375

Also: Sketches of Man "As he is" connected with Past and Present Modes of Education. ... *Boston: For the Author.* 1808. 8vo, pp. 14. BA.

[Lovell (John).] Freedom the first of Blessings. [*Boston.* n. d.] 4to, pp. 7. BA. 42376

Lovell. A Funeral Oration deliver'd at the Opening of the Annual Meeting of the Town, March 14th. 1742. In Faneuil-Hall in Boston: Occasion'd by the Death of the Founder, Peter Faneuil, Esq; By John Lovell, A.M. ... *Boston: S. Kneeland and T. Green.* 1743. 4to, pp. 14. + The Second Edition. [*Ibid.*]

[Lovell.] The Seasons, An Interlocutory Exercise at the South Grammar School, June 26, 1765. *Boston.* 1765. 4to, pp. 8. 42378

Lovell (J. E.) Rhetorical Dialogues; or, Dramatic Selections, for ... Schools, Academies, and Families ... . By John E. Lovell ... . Second Edition. *New Haven: S. Babcock.* 1844. 12mo. H. 42379

Lovell. The United States Speaker ... : By John E. Lovell ... Stereotype Edition, revised and improved. *New Haven: S. Babcock.* 1845. 12mo, pp. 504. 5 Plates. 42380

Lovell. The Young Speaker: an Introduction to the United States Speaker ... . By John E. Lovell ... . Tenth Edition. *Cincinnati: Truman & Spofford.* 1852. 12mo, pp. 300. Plate. H.

Lovell (J.) Meteorological Register for the Years 1822, 1823, 1824 & 1825, from Observations made ... at the Military Posts of the United States. Prepared under the Direction of Joseph Lovell, M.D. Surgeon General ... . *Washington: Printed by Edward de Krafft.* 1826. 8vo, pp. 63. Map. B. 42382

Also: Meteorological Register; Fisheries, 1826–1830. ... *Philadelphia.* 1840. 8vo.

Lovell (L.) A Letter to a Friend, relative to the Present State of the Island of Dominica. By Langford Lovell, Esq. *Winchester: Printed by James Robbins.* 1818. 8vo, pp. 39. H.

Lover of Truth. An Address to the Rev. Dr. Alison, the Rev. Mr. Ewing, and others, Trustees of the Corporation for the Relief of Presbyterian Ministers, their Widows and Children: being a vindication of the Quakers from the Aspersions of the said Trustees in their Letter published in the London Chronicle, No. 1223. To which is prefixed, the said Letter. By a Lover of Truth. ... [n. p.:] *Printed in the Year* 1765. 8vo, pp. iii, 47.

Evidently printed in Pennsylvania. It relates to the dissensions caused by the Indian wars.

Loveridge (*Mrs.*) Report of the Sixth Annual Examination of Mrs. Loveridge's School ... June 20, 1861 ... . *Albany: Munsell & Rowland.* 1861. 8vo, pp. 36. H. 42385

Lovering (Joseph). ... On the American Prime Meridian. By Prof. J. Lovering. [n. p. n. d.] 8vo, pp. 15. H. 42386

[Lovett (John).] A Tribute to Washington, for February 22d, 1800. *Troy.* 1800. 4to, pp. 15. N. 42387

Dedicated to John Jay. Concerning the author of this rare poetical piece, *see* Woodworth's "Troy."

Lovett. Motion on the Subject of Retaliation. December 21, 1813. [n. p. n. d.] 8vo. 42388

Lovewell (J.) *See* Kidder (F.), *and* Symms (T.)

Lovis par la Grace de Dieu, roy de France et de Navarre: A nostre amé & feal Conseiller ... le Sieur de la Fosse. *Donné à Paris le vingt-quatriesme iour de iuin l'an de grace mil six cens cinquante-vn.* Folio, 1 leaf. 42389

Lövy (H.) Ueber Polarität. *Prag.* 1831. 8vo. 42390

Lovzinski. *See* [Louvet de Couvray], No. 42358.

Low (A. A.) Address by A. A. Low, Esq., ... [in] New-York, at the Annual Meeting of the Chamber of Commerce, May 3, 1866. *New-York: John W. Amerman, Printer.* 1866. 8vo, pp. 14. H. 42391

Löw (C.) Meer oder Seehanen Buch, | Darinn | Verzeichnet seind, die Wun- | derbare, Gedenckwürdige Reise vnd Schiffarhten, so | recht vnd billich geheissen Meer vnd Seehanen, der Königen von Hi- | spania, Portugal, Engellandt vnd Franckreich, inwendig den letst vergangnen hun- | dert Jahren, gethan. Auff vnd durch welche Schiffarten, ein Newe Welt gegen | Nidergang, vnd grosse Königreichen, Landtschafften vnd Insulen, | gegen Auffgang gelegen, erfunden vnd | entdeckt seind. | Hierzu seind noch gesetzt zwey seltzame vnd gedenckwürdige Stück. | Das eine ist, | Die Erzehlung der Schiffart, so im Jahr 1594. gethan siben Schiff, | welche die Vnierte Niderländische Ständ geschickt gegen Mitternacht, vmb von | dannen jren lauff nach China zu nemen. Dieselbige Schiff seind gefahren, durch die Enge oder | Strass zwischen den Landtschafften des Grossfürsten von der Moscow, vnd der Insel Waigatz, | bey Noua Zembla gelegen, biss ins grosse Tartarische Meer, Welches auff Latein Oceanus | Scythicus oder Mare Tabin genennet wirt, vnd haben entdeckt

den Fluss | Gilissy, nur 13. Meil vom grossen Fluss | Obij gelegen. | Das ander stück ist. | Ein Warhaffter, klarer, eigentlicher Bericht, von der weiten vñ wun- | derbaren Reise oder Schifffahrt, so drey Schiff vnd ein Pinass, auss Holland, biss in | Indien gegen Auffgang gethan. Dieselbe Schiff seind von Texel in Hollandt abgefaoren am an- | dern tag Aprilis, im Jar 1595. Haben vmbgesägelt das Vorhaupt Bonæ Spei, vnd seind ahn der | grossen Insel Madagascar, jetzt S. Laurentz Insel geheissen, angefahren. Von dannen seind sie | gesägelt gen Samatra, vorzeiten Taprobana, vnd fehrner gen Bantam, ein grosse Gewerbstatt | in der Insel Iaua Maior, weiter gen Sidaya, vnd der Insel Bally. Von dannen seind sie am 26. | Februarij 1597. wider nach Hollandt gefahren, vnd ohn jrgendts ahnzuländen, am 10. tag | Augstmonats desselben Jars mit freuden zu Hauss ankom̃en. Haben mit bracht | Pfeffer, Nägelein, Muscat Nüss vnd Blumen. Neben dem einen | wunderbarlichen Vogel, der Fewrkolen verschlucket. | Gantz lustig zulesen. | Dise Reisen vnd Schiffahrten seind zusamen, auss an- | dern Spraachen ins Teutsch gebracht, | Durch | Conrad Löw der Historien Liebhaber. | *Getruckt zu Cölnn, auff der Burgmauren, Bey | Bertram Buchholtz, Im Jahr* | 1598. | Folio, pp. (4), 110. 3 Maps. 42392

This book of the Ocean or Sea-Cocks relates the wonderful voyages and travels which the rightly and justly called Ocean or Sea-Cocks of the Kings of Spain, Portugal, England, and France have made within the hundred years preceding its date. It was compiled by Conrad Löw, and is so very rare that it seems to have been unknown until Brunet described it in his "Manuel." Although it contains nothing but extracts and translations, it will always occupy an elevated rank among the precious books which tell us of the great geographical discoveries of the fifteenth and sixteenth centuries. It includes the voyages of Columbus, Ponce de Leon, Hernando Cortez, Fernando de Magellan, Juan Sebastian del Cano, Garcia Jofre de Loaysa, Saavedra, Cedron, Vasco de Gama, Pedro Alvarez Cabral, Juan de Nova, Gaspar Cortereal, Sebastien Cabot, Martin Frobisher, Francis Drake, Richard Grenville, Thomas Cavendish, Walter Raleigh, John Hawkins, Verrazano, and Jacques Cartier. The maps are frequently wanting. Brunet, Grässe, and Trömel give the title at length, the first calling it, "Collection importante, et dont les exemplaires sont rares," and the last describing it fully. Trübner prices it at £10, 10s.

Low (D.) Appeal to the Common Sense of the Country regarding the present condition of the Industrious Classes ... . By David Low ... . *William Blackwood and Sons, Edinburgh.* MDCCCL. 8vo, pp. (2), 138. 42393

Contains many references to America.

Low (Edward Luther). Low's Pocket Almanack for the Year M.DCC.XCI. *St. Christopher.* [n. d.] 16mo. 42394

Low (F. F.) Inaugural Address of Fred'k F. Low, Governor of the State of California, at the Fifteenth Session of the Legislature. *Sacramento: O. M. Clayes, State Printer.* 1863. 8vo, pp. 12. H. 42395

Low (H. R.) The Governor's [H. Seymour] Message Reviewed. ... By Hon. Henry R. Low. In the Senate, Jan. 28, 1863. *Albany: Weed, Parsons and Company, Printers.* 1863. 8vo, pp. 24. BA. 42396

Low *vs.* Niven (A. C.) Testimony taken before the Committee of Privileges and Elections, of the Senate, in the matter of the Contested Election for the Office of Senator, from the 9th Senatorial District. ... [n. p. n. d.] 8vo. 42397

Also: In the Matter of the Petition of H. R. Low to the Senate of the State of New York, claiming his seat as Senator ... . *Albany.* 1864. 8vo.—Speech ... on ... the Present Condition of National Affairs. ... March 14, 1866. *Albany: Weed, Parsons and Company, Printers.* 1866. 8vo, pp. 19. BA.

Löw (Hermann). Diptera Americæ Septentrionalis indigena. (Centuria 1ma–5a.) *Berolini: Typis A. W. Schadii.* 1861. 8vo, pp. (2), 266. C. 42398

See also Loew (H.), *our* No. 41775.

Low (J. W.) Low's Railway Directory for 1858 ... . By James W. Low, Jr. *New York: Wynkoop, Hallenbeck & Thomas, Printers.* 1858. 12mo, pp. 151. Continued. H. 42399

Low (J.) An Alphabetical Table of the Situation and Extent of the different Streets, Roads, Lanes, Wharves, and Ships, Public Buildings, and Justices Courts of the City of New York. By John Low. *New York.* 1807. 12mo, pp. 52. + Second Edition, Improved. [*Ibid.*] 12mo, pp. 72. N. 42400

Low. An Impartial and Correct History of the Late War between the United States and Great Britain. By John Low. *New York.* 1815. 12mo. + Second Edition. [*Ibid.*] 42401

See also New York.

Low (Nathaniel). An Astronomical Diary; or, An Almanack. For the Year of Christian Æra, 1777. Being ... the first year of American Independence, which began July fourth, 1776 ... *America. Boston: Printed by J. Gill.* [1776.] 12mo, 12 leaves. 42402

Contains "A View of the Present Seat of War at and near New York," with "An Address to the Tories," by the author, October 8, 1776. Also patriotic mottoes at the head of each month's calendar. The first was printed in 1762, none were issued for 1766; it was continued to 1827 or later. Some have the imprint *Hartford & Boston.* In the Almanac for 1773, snow is predicted to fall on the fifth of June.

Low (S.) The American Catalogue of Books; or English Guide to American Literature, giving the full Title of Original Works published in the United States since the year 1800 ... . With especial reference to Works of Interest to Great Britain. *London: Sampson Low, Son, and Co.* 1856. 8vo, pp. 190. S.

Low (S.) Poems. By Samuel Low. ... *New York: Printed by T. & J. Swords.* 1800. 2 vols., 16mo, pp. 147; 168. B., C.

[Low.] The Politician Out-witted, a Comedy, in Five Acts. Written in the Year 1788. By an American. *New York: Printed ... by W. Ross.* M.DCC.LXXXIX. 8vo, pp. 71. N. 42405

[Low.] Winter Displayed, a Poem. By an American. *New York.* 1784. 8vo. S. 42406

Löwe (Andr. F.) Historisch-Geographische Beschreibung der zwölf vereinigten Kolonien von Nordamerika. Nebst eine Schilderung des gegenwärtigen Zustandes von Grossbritannien. *Bunzlau.* 1777. 8vo. 42407

Lowe (A. T.) The Columbian Class Book, consisting of Geographical, Historical and Biographical Extracts. By A. T. Lowe, M.D. ... *Worcester: Dorr & Howland.* 1824. 12mo, pp. 355. 4 Plates. + Second Edition. [*Ibid.*] 1825. B. 42408

Lowe (C.) The Condition and Prospects of the South. A Discourse ... in Somerville, Mass., June 4, 1865. By Rev. Charles Lowe. *Boston: Walker, Fuller, and Company.* 1865. 8vo, pp. 8. B. 42409

Lowe. Death of President Lincoln: a Sermon delivered in ... Charleston, S. C., ... April 23, 1865. By Rev. Charles Lowe, ... *Boston: American Unitarian Association.* 1865. 12mo, pp. 24.

Lowe (E. L.) ... Communication from E. Louis Lowe, Esq. Ex-Governor of Maryland. [n. p.] 1861. 8vo, pp. 8. B.

Relates to secession.

Lowe. Discourse delivered at the Commemoration of the Landing of the Pilgrims of Maryland, Celebrated May 12, 1845, at Mt. St. Mary's, near Emmittsburg, Md. By Enoch Louis Lowe, Esq. *Gettysburg.* MDCCCXLV. 8vo, pp. 37. 42412

Lowe. Ex-Gov. Lowe's Letter to the Virginia Legislature. Dated, Ashland, Virginia, December 16, 1861. [n. p. n. d.] 8vo, pp. 16. 42413

Also: Lecture on the Historical Destiny of Women ... . February, 1842. *Baltimore.* 1842. 8vo, pp. 15. *See also* Vol. I., No. 2995.

Lowe (J.) Liberty or Death. A Tract. By which is vindicated the obvious Practicability of trading to the Coasts of Guinea for its natural Products, in lieu of the Slave Trade ... . By John Lowe, Jun. *Manchester.* 1789. 4to, pp. 56. 42414

Lowe. A Letter to ... George Canning ... on ... Recognizing the Independence of the South American States. By John Lowe. *London.* 1822. 8vo. + [*Ibid.*] 1823. 8vo. BA.

Lowe. On the Recognition of Columbia by Great Britain. *London.* 1823. 8vo. C. 42416

See "Pamphleteer," Vols. XXI. and XXII.

Lowe (J.) An Enquiry into the State of the British West Indies. By Joseph Lowe, Esq. ... *London: C. and R. Baldwin.* 1807. 8vo, pp. xix, 160. H. + Second Edition. [*Ibid.*] BA. + Third Edition. [*Ibid.*] B. + Fourth Edition. [*Ibid.*] 1808. 12mo, pp. xix, 176. H. 42417

See "Edinb. Rev.," XI. 145, *and* "M. Rev.," February, 1808.

[Lowe (*Mrs.* M. A. P.)] The Olive and the Pine. ... *Boston: Crosby, Nichols, and Co.* 1859. 8vo, pp. viii, 156. H.

Lowe (P. P.) Oration delivered on the Fiftieth Anniversary of our National Independence, at Dayton, O., by P. P. Lowe, Esq. [n. p.] *Reprinted.* 1839. 8vo, pp. 8. 42419

[Lowell (Anna C.)] Poetry for Home and School. *Boston: S. G. Perkins.* 1843. 16mo, pp. 360. C. 42420

Lowell. Thoughts on the Education of Girls. By Mrs. Anna C. Lowell. *Boston: Ticknor, Reed, and Fields.* MDCCCLIII. 12mo, pp. 72. B. 42421

Lowell (C.) The Characteristicks of a Good Soldier: a Sermon, ... before the Ancient and Honourable Artillery Company, ... June 4, 1810. ... By Charles Lowell ... *Boston: Munroe & Francis.* 1810. 8vo, pp. 24. BA. 42422

Lowell. A Discourse delivered in ... Boston, December 31, 1820. By Charles Lowell ... . *Boston: Printed by Sewell Phelps.* 1820. 8vo, pp. 44. H. 42423

Lowell. A Discourse before the Society for propagating the Gospel among the Indians and others in North America: ...

Nov. 9, 1820. By Charles Lowell … . *Boston: Printed by Sewell Phelps.* 1820. 8vo, pp. 40. BA. 42424

LOWELL. A Discourse … in … West Church, in Boston, August 3, 1845. By Charles Lowell … . *Cambridge: Metcalf and Company.* 1845. 8vo, pp. 25. B. 42425

With an historical appendix.

LOWELL. … Down-East Commentator … a Dissertation upon … Liberty and Slavery … by Charles Lowell … . *Ellsworth, Me.* 1850. 8vo, pp. 24. H. 42426

LOWELL. … A Sermon, … at the Dedication of the Third Congregational Church in Cambridge, Dec. 25, 1827. By Charles Lowell … . *Cambridge: Hilliard, Metcalf, and Company, Printers.* 1828. 8vo, pp. 24. + Third Edition. *Boston: N. S. Simpkins & Co.* 1828. 12mo, pp. 18. BA. 42427

LOWELL. A Sermon, preached in … Boston, January 2, 1831, being a Quarter of a Century from the Settlement of the Present Minister. By Charles Lowell … . *Boston.* 1831. 8vo, pp. 20. B. 42428

LOWELL. Sermons: chiefly Occasional. By Charles Lowell, … *Boston: Ticknor and Fields.* M DCCC LV. 12mo, pp. vi, (1), 329. Portrait. H. 42429

LOWELL. The West Church. *See* Bartol (C. A.), I. 3794.

Also: A Discourse … March 16, 1817, … after the Execution of Henry Phillips Stonehewer Davis, for the Murder of Gaspard Denegri. … *Boston.* 1817. 8vo, pp. 16. + Second Edition. *Boston: Printed by John Eliot.* 1817. 8vo, pp. 16. BA. — … A Discourse … at the Ordination of Mr. Daniel M. Stearns … May 14, 1828. … *Boston: N. S. Simpkins & Co.* 1828. 12mo, pp. 35. — Extract from a Sermon preached … Aug. 7, 1842, … following the Death of Thomas Dennie, Esq. … *Boston: Dutton and Wentworth's Print.* 1842. 8vo, pp. 7. — An Important Letter to Henry C. Lowell … . *Ellsworth, Me.: Printed by Nathaniel K. Sawyer.* 1857. 8vo, pp. 14. — Man and his Destiny, Men, Politics, and Morals … Poem … . *Ellsworth, Maine.* 1855. 12mo, pp. 12. — … A Sermon … at the Ordination of Mr. Thomas B. Fox, … Newburyport, … August 3, 1831. … *Cambridge: Hilliard and Brown.* 1831. 8vo, pp. 44 — A Sermon … at the State Prison, in Massachusetts, November 29th, 1812. … *Boston: Printed by Joshua Belcher.* 1812. 12mo, pp. 14. + Another Edition. [n. p. 1812.] 8vo, pp. 19. — A Sermon preached at the Ordination of Mr. Samuel Barrett … in Boston, Feb. 9, 1825. … *Boston: Francis S. Carlile, Printer.* 1825. 8vo, pp. 24. — A Sermon … September 12, 1821, at the Ordination of … Rev. Richard Manning Hodges … in Bridgewater. … *Boston: Printed by Lincoln & Edmands.* [1821.] 8vo, pp. 24. — … A Sermon … at the Ordination of Mr. George Wadsworth Wells … . *Cambridge: Hilliard, Metcalf and Company.* 1827. 8vo, pp. 15, (1). BA. — A Sermon … at the Dedication of the Second Congregational Church in Milton, October 21, 1829. … *Boston: Dutton & Wentworth, Printers.* 1829. 8vo, pp. 24. — … A Sermon, preached in Berlin, at the Ordination of Mr. Robert Folger Wallcut, February 10, 1830. … *Boston: Leonard C. Bowles.* 1830. 8vo, pp. 32. — … A Sermon, … May 14, 1829,

at the Ordination of Mr. John L. Sibley … . *Boston: N. S. Simpkins & Co.* 1829. 8vo, pp. 24. — … A Sermon … at the Dedication of the South Congregational Church in Natick, November 20th, 1828. … *Boston: N. S. Simpkins & Co.* 1829. 8vo, pp. 24. — … A Sermon … at the Ordination of Mr. William Barry, Jr. … Nov. 17, 1830. … *Boston: N. S. Simpkins & Co.* 1831. 8vo, pp. 16. BA. *See also* "Mass. Hist. Soc. Colls.," Fourth Series, Vol. I.

LOWELL. Original Hymns for the Fiftieth Anniversary of the Ordination of the Rev. Charles Lowell, D.D. [n. p. n. d.] 12mo, pp. 3. 42430

LOWELL. Proceedings in the West Church on Occasion of the Decease of Charles Lowell, D.D. … *Boston: Walker, Wise, and Company.* 1861. 8vo, pp. 48. BA. 42431

[LOWELL (Francis C.)] To the President, … and Directors, of the Massachusetts Hospital Life Insurance Company. [*Boston.* 1859.] 8vo, pp. 16. BA. 42432

[LOWELL (J. R.)] … The Biglow Papers, edited … by Horace Wilbur, A.M. … . *Cambridge: George Nichols.* 1848. 16mo, pp. 12, xxxii, 163. + Third Edition. *Boston: Ticknor,* … M DCCC LIII. 16mo, pp. xxxii, 163. + *London.* 1859. 8vo. + *Boston.* 1860. B. + With additional Notes, Glossary and … Illustrations, by George Cruikshank. … *London.* 1861. 16mo. + With additional Notes and enlarged Glossary. *London: John Camden Hotten.* 1865. 16mo, pp. xvi, 200. + *Montreal: R. Worthington.* 1866. 8vo, pp. 8, xii, (2), 55. + Second Series. … *Boston: Ticknor and Fields.* 1867. 8vo, pp. (4), lxxx, 258.

LOWELL. … A Fable for Critics; or … a Glance at a Few of our Literary Progenies … from the Tub of Diogenes … . By a Wonderful Quiz … . [*New York:*] *G. P. Putnam.* 1848. 12mo, pp. 80. + *Boston: Ticknor and Fields.* MDCCCLVI. 8vo, pp. v, 80. H. 42434

[LOWELL.] … Mason and Slidell: a Yankee Idyll. … [n. p. 1862?] 8vo, pp. 12. H. 42435

LOWELL. Poems. By James Russell Lowell. *Cambridge: John Owen.* MDCCCXLIV. 12mo, pp. xii, 279. + Second Edition. [*Ibid.*] + Third Edition. [*Ibid.*] C. + *London: C. E. Mudie.* 1844. 12mo. + Second Series. *Cambridge: George Nichols.* 1848. 12mo, pp. viii, 184. + *Boston: Ticknor, Reed, and Fields.* M DCCC XLIX. 2 vols., 8vo, pp. xii, 251; vii, 354. H. + Sixth Edition. *Boston: Ticknor and Fields.* M DCCC LIV. 2 vols., 8vo.

LOWELL. The Poetical Works of James R. Lowell. … *Boston: Ticknor and Fields.* M DCCC LVIII. 2 vols., 16mo, pp. ix,

315; 322. Portrait. H. + *Boston.* 1863. 2 vols., 12mo. + *Boston: Fields, Osgood, & Co.* 1869. Sq. 18mo, pp. ix, 437. H.

LOWELL. Under the Willows and Other Poems. By James Russell Lowell. *Boston: Fields, Osgood, & Co.* 1869. 12mo, pp. 286. B. 42438

Also: Ode recited at the Commemoration of the Living and Dead Soldiers of Harvard University, July 21, 1865. … *Cambridge: Privately Printed.* 1865. 4to, pp. 25. — The President's Policy … . *Philadelphia.* 1864. 8vo, pp. 22. + [n. p. n. d.] 8vo, pp. 22. — A Year's Life. … *Boston: C. C. Little and J. Brown.* M DCCC XLI. 16mo, pp. viii, 182. BA.

LOWELL (J.) … A Sermon, … at Newbury, March 26, 1758. Occasioned by the Death of Mrs. Hannah Kent, … . By John Lowell, A.M. … *Boston; New-England: J. Edwards.* M.DCC.LVIII. 8vo, pp. 30. BA. 42439

LOWELL. … A Sermon, … at Newbury, May 22. 1755, … in the Audience of Col^o. Moses Titcomb, and Many Others, … going with him … against the French. By John Lowell, A.M. … *Boston: N. E. Printed by J. Draper.* 1755. 8vo, pp. (2), iv, 27. + *Newburyport: Press of E. W. Allen.* 1806. 8vo, pp. 30.

LOWELL. A Sermon, Occasioned by the … Death of Col. Moses Titcomb, who fell in Battle near Lake-George, September 8th, 1755. By John Lowell A.M. … *Boston: Printed … by Edes and Gill.* M,DCC,LX. 12mo, pp. 24. + *Newburyport: Press of E. W. Allen.* 1806. 8vo, pp. 23. BA. 42441

Also: A Sermon, … at the Ordination of Mr. Thomas Barnard … January 31, 1738 … . *Boston: Printed by J. Draper.* MDCCXXXIX. 8vo, pp. (2), 38. BA.

LOWELL (J.) An Eulogy, on the Honourable James Bowdoin, Esq. L.L.D. late President of the American Academy of Arts and Sciences. Who died at Boston, November 6, A.D. 1790. Delivered before the Society, January 26, 1791, by John Lowell, one of the Counsellors of the Academy. *Printed at Boston, by Isaiah Thomas and Ebenezer T. Andrews.* MDCCXCI. 4to, pp. 24. B., BA. 42442

Also included in "Memoirs of the American Academy," Vol. II., Part I.

[LOWELL (J.)] Analysis of the late Correspondence between our Administration and Great Britain & France. With an Attempt to shew what are the Real Causes of the Failure of the Negociation. … *Boston: Russell and Cutler, Printers.* [1809.] 8vo, pp. 52. BA. + *New York.* 1809. 8vo, pp. 56. 42443

[LOWELL.] Supplement to the late Analysis of the public correspondence between our Cabinet and those of France and G. Britain. [*Boston.* 1808.] 8vo, pp. 28. BA. 42444

[LOWELL.] The Antigallican. *See* Vol. I., No. 1691.

[LOWELL.] An Appeal to the People, on the Causes and Consequences of a War with Great Britain. *Boston: Printed by T. B. Wait and Company.* 1811. 8vo, pp. 36. H. 42445

[LOWELL.] The Diplomatic Policy of Mr. Madison Unveiled; in Strictures upon the late Correspondence between Mr. Smith and Mr. Jackson. … By a Bostonian. *London: J. J. Stockdale.* 1810. 8vo, pp. 78. BA. 42446

[LOWELL.] Essay on Hereditary Titles. *See* Vol. VI. 22941.

[LOWELL.] Further Remarks on the Memorial of the Officers of Harvard College. By an Alumnus of that College. *Boston: Printed by Wells and Lilly.* 1824. 8vo, pp. 36. B., H.

[LOWELL.] Gov. Strong's Calumniator Reproved: in a Review of a Democratic Pamphlet entitled, Remarks on the Governor's Speech. … By no Bel-Esprit. *Boston: W. W. Clapp, Printer.* 1814. 8vo, pp. 21. BA. 42448

[LOWELL.] Hints addressed to Wise Men; concerning the Dispute which ended, on Nov. 8, 1809, in the Dismission of Mr. Jackson, the British Minister to the United States. [*Boston.* 1809.] 8vo, pp. 115. S., W. 42449

[LOWELL.] The Impartial Inquirer; being a Candid Examination of the Conduct of the President [Madison] of the United States, in Execution of the Powers vested in him, by the Act of Congress of May 1, 1810: to which is added, some Reflections upon the Invasion of the Spanish Territory of West-Florida. … By a Citizen of Massachusetts. [*Boston:*] *Russell & Cutler, Printers.* 1811. 8vo, pp. 96. BA., W. 42450

[LOWELL.] An Inquiry into the Right. *See* Vol. IX. 34816.

[LOWELL.] Interesting Political Discussion. The Diplomatic Policy of Mr. Madison Unveiled. In a Series of Essays containing Strictures upon the Late Correspondence between Mr. Smith and Mr. Jackson. … By a Bostonian. [*Boston.* 1812.] 8vo, pp. 55. BA. 42451

[LOWELL.] Mr. Madison's War. A Dispassionate Inquiry into the Reasons alleged by Mr. Madison for declaring an Offensive and Ruinous War against Great-Britain. Together with some Suggestions as to a Peaceable and Constitutional Mode of averting that Dreadful Calamity. By a New-England Farmer. *Boston: Printed by Russell & Cutler.* 1812. 8vo, pp. 61, (2). + Second Edition. [*Ibid.*] 1812. 8vo, pp. x, 63. + Third Edition. [*Ibid.*] + Fourth Edition. [*Ibid.*] + *Hanover, N. H.: Charles Spear.* 1812. 8vo. + *London: Longman.* 1812. 8vo, pp. 87.

See "M. Rev.," LXIX. 269, *and* "Quart. Rev.," VIII. 193.

[LOWELL.] The New England Patriot: being a Candid Comparison, of the Principles and Conduct of the Washington and Jefferson Administrations. The whole founded upon indisputable Facts and Public Documents, to which Reference is made in the Text and Notes. *Boston: Printed by Russell and Cutler.* 1810. 8vo, pp. (2), 148, Notes, 12. C. 42453

LOWELL. An Oration, … July 4, 1799, at … Boston … . By John Lowell, jun. … *Boston: Printed by Manning & Loring.* 1799. 8vo, pp. 27. BA., W. 42454

More than an ordinary fourth of July oration.

[LOWELL.] Peace without Dishonour—War without Hope. Being A Calm and Dispassionate Enquiry into the Question of the Chesapeake, and the Necessity and Expediency of War. By a Yankee Farmer. *Boston: Printed by Greenough and Stebbins.* 1807. 8vo, pp. 43. BA., H., S. 42455

Reprinted in London as: "Peace without Dishonour. War without Hope. An Argument against War with Great Britain, recently published at Boston. By an American Farmer." *London: T. Butterworth.* 1807. 8vo, pp. 43.

[LOWELL.] Perpetual War, the Policy of Mr. Madison. Being a Candid Examination of his Late Message to Congress, so far as respects the following topicks: viz. the Pretended Negotiations for Peace, the Important and Interesting Subject of a Conscript Militia, and the Establishment of an Immense Standing Army of Guards and Spies, under the Name of a Local Volunteer Force. … By a New-England Farmer. … *Boston: Printed by Chester Stebbins.* 1812. 8vo, pp. 119. BA. + *Boston.* 1813. 8vo, pp. 78. B. 42456

[LOWELL.] The Recent Attempt to defeat the Constitutional Provisions in favour of Religious Freedom, considered in Reference to the Trust Conveyances of Hanover Street Church. By a Layman. *Boston: Wells and Lilly.* 1828. 8vo, pp. 24. +

Second Edition. *Boston: Sold by Hilliard, Gray, and Co.* 1828. 8vo, pp. 24. BA. 42457

[LOWELL.] Remarks on a Pamphlet printed by the Professors and Tutors of Harvard University … . By an Alumnus of that College. *Boston: Printed by Wells and Lilly.* 1824. 8vo, pp. 58.

[LOWELL.] Remarks on the Hon. John Q. Adams's Review of Mr. Ames's Works, with some Strictures on the Views of the Author. … *Boston: Printed by T. B. Wait and Co.* 1809. 8vo, pp. 50. BA. 42459

[LOWELL.] Review of a Treatise. *See* Hay (G.), Vol. VIII.

[LOWELL.] The Rights of the Congregational Parishes of Massachusetts. Review of a Pamphlet entitled "The Rights of the Congregational Churches of Massachusetts. The Result of an Ecclesiastical Council convened at Groton, Mass. July 17, 1826." From the Christian Examiner, Vol. IV. No. II. *Boston: Bowles and Dearborn.* 1827. 8vo, pp. 32. + Second Edition. [*Ibid.*] 1827. 8vo, pp. 36. B. 42460

See also [Beecher (L.)], Vol. II., No. 4338, *and* Groton, *Mass.*, Vol. VII., No. 28976.

[LOWELL.] Review of Dr. Morse's "Appeal to the Publick," … [n. p. 1814.] 8vo, pp. 42. BA. 42461

[LOWELL.] The Road to Peace, Commerce, Wealth and Happiness. By an Old Farmer. [*Boston.* 1813.] 8vo, pp. 16.

[LOWELL.] Thoughts upon the Conduct. *See* Vol. III. 12490

[LOWELL.] Vindication of the Rights of the Churches of Christ. … *Boston: Peirce and Williams.* 1828. 8vo, pp. 47. H.

Also: An Address … before the Massachusetts Agricultural Society … October 13, 1818. … *Boston: Printed by Wells and Lilly.* 1818. 8vo, pp. 22. H. — Biographical Notice of the late Hon. Dudley Atkins Tyng, Jr. By his Intimate Friend … . [n. p. n. d.] 8vo, pp. 17. *See also* [Everett (Edward)], *and* Vol. VIII., No. 30756.

LOWELL (J. A.) Memoir of Patrick Tracy Jackson. … By John A. Lowell, Esq. *New-York: Press of Hunt's Merchants' Magazine.* 1848. 8vo, pp. 14. Portrait. BA. 42464

LOWELL. Reply to a Pamphlet recently circulated by Mr. Edward Brooks. By John Amory Lowell. *Boston: Printed by Freeman and Bolles.* 1848. 8vo, pp. (4), 211. B. 42465

See our Vol. I. 1824 and Vol. II. 8344. Also: Review of Mr. Hooper's Pamphlet on Specie Reserves. … *Boston: Little, Brown, and Company.* 1860. 8vo, pp. 22. BA.

LOWELL (J. A.) Speech of Mr. Joshua A. Lowell, of Maine, on the Army Appropriation Bill: delivered … May 30, 1842. *Washington.* 1842. 8vo, pp. 12. 42466

Also: Speech … on the British Colonial Trade: … June 9, 1842. *Washington.* 1842. 8vo, pp. 13.

[LOWELL (R. Trail Spence).] The New Priest in Conception Bay. … *Boston: Phillips, Sampson and Company.* MDCCCLVIII. 2 vols., 12mo, pp. 309; 339. BA. + A New Edition. … *Boston: E. P. Dutton and Company.* 1864. 2 vols., 8vo, pp. 282; 284. 2 Plates. H. 42467

LOWELL. The Poems of Robert Lowell … . *Boston.* 1860. 16mo. + A New Edition (with Many New Poems). *Boston: E. P. Dutton and Company.* 1864. 16mo, pp. (2), 206. H.

LOWELL, *Mass.* Address of … Mayor of … Lowell, to the City Council, … April 3, 1837. [*Lowell:*] *Huntress—Printer.* [1837.] 8vo, pp. 8. Continued. B. 42469

The Auditor's Seventh Annual Report of the Receipts and Expenditures of … Lowell, … and the Treasurer's Annual Account. … *Lowell: Dearborn & Butterfield, Printers.* 1843. 8vo, pp. 53. Continued. B. 42470

Bill of Mortality of the City of Lowell, for the Year 1845. [*Lowell: Joel Taylor … Printer.* 1846.] 8vo, pp. 8. Continued.

The Charter of … Lowell, with the Rules and Orders … . [*Lowell:*] *Huntress & Knowlton, Printers.* 1836. 16mo, pp. 36. Continued. H. 42472

The Charter and Ordinances of … Lowell … . *Boston: J. E. Farwell and Company, Printers.* 1863. 16mo, pp. 240. H. 42473

City Documents. [n. p. 1836.] 8vo. Continued. 42474

Also: City Documents. *Lowell: Knapp & Morey.* 1866. 12 vols., 8vo.

Catalogue of the City School Library, Lowell, Mass. … *Lowell: Stearns & Taylor … Printers.* 1845. 16mo, pp. 66, 8. + *Lowell: S. N. Merrill.* 1868. 8vo, pp. (6), 214. 42475

Also: Supplement … *Lowell: Knapp & Morey, Printers.* 1869. 8vo, pp. 49. B. — Catalogue of the City Library [of Lowell]. *Lowell.* 1861. 8vo. — … Report of the Directors of the City Library for 1860. … *Lowell: Stone & Huse,* … *Printers.* 1860. 8vo, pp. 8. Continued. B.

The Lowell Directory … By B. Floyd. 1834. 12mo.

Continued by this editor to 1840 or later.

The Lowell Directory: containing The City Record … . By George Adams … . *Lowell: Oliver March.* 1851. 12mo, pp. 240. + For 1853. [*Ibid.*] 1853. 12mo, pp. 288. + For 1855. [*Ibid.*] 1855. 12mo. + [For 1861.] By Adams, Sampson & Co. *Lowell: J. Merrill and B. C. Sargeant.* 1861. 12mo. + For 1864–65. By Samuel A. McPhetres. *Lowell: Stone & Huse, Printers.* [n. d.] 12mo, pp. 248, 52. + For 1866. By Sampson, Davenport & Co. *Lowell: J. Merrill and B. C. Sargeant.* 1866. 8vo, pp. 384. Continued. 42477

A Farewell Address … before the … City Council … December 31, 1858, by E. Huntington, Mayor. *Lowell: Huse & Co. … Printers.* 1859. 8vo, pp. 16. H. 42478

Regulations for the Public Schools, of … Lowell … 1835. *Lowell: Huntress & Knowlton, Printers.* 1835. 24mo, pp. 17. Continued. H. 42479

Report of the School Committee, for … 1838. [*Lowell.* 1838.] 8vo, pp. 7. Continued. B. 42480

The annual report of the superintendent is included after 1864. Also: Rules and Regulations of the Public Schools, adopted May, 1839. *Lowell.* 1839. 12mo. B. — Rules of the School Committee, and Regulations of Public Schools, … of Lowell. … *Lowell: William Schouler, Printer.* 1842. 12mo, pp. 12. B.

Hand-Book for the Visiter [*sic*] to Lowell. … *Lowell: D. Bixby and Company.* 1848. 16mo, pp. (2), 46. H. 42481

Charter and By-Laws of the Howard Fire Insurance Company, Lowell, Mass., January, 1855. *Lowell.* 1855. 8vo. S.

The Inaugural Address of his Honor Hocum Hosford, Mayor of the City of Lowell … January 4, 1864. *Lowell: Knapp & Morey, Printers.* 1864. 8vo, pp. 22. Continued. 42483

The Lectures delivered before the American Institute of Instruction, at Lowell, Massachusetts, August, 1838: including the Journal of Proceedings, and a List of the Officers. Published under the direction of the Board of Censors. *Boston.* 1839. 8vo, pp. xxiv, 187. 42484

Lowell as It was and as It is. *See* [Miles (Henry A.)]

Annual Report to the Proprietors of the Lowell Cemetery … March 6, 1850. … *Lowell: B. H. Penhallow, Printer.* 1850. 8vo, pp. 18. H. 42485

Act of Incorporation, Constitution and By-Laws of the Lowell Dispensary .... *Lowell: Leonard Huntress, Printer.* 1840. 24mo, pp. 9, (1). H. 42486

Annual Report of the Chief Engineer of the Lowell Fire Department. March, 1858. ... *Lowell: Charles Hunt, Printer.* 1858. 8vo, pp. 20. Continued. B. 42487

Also: Rules and Regulations of the Fire Department of ... Lowell ... . *Lowell: Stone & Huse, Printers.* 1868. 8vo, pp. 18. B.

Lowell Five Cent Savings Bank. The Officers, Act of Incorporation, By-Laws, &c. ... 1854. *Lowell: S. J. Varney, ... Printer.* 1854. 12mo, pp. 23. H. 42488

Annual Report of the Lowell Hospital Association. May 1, 1841. *Lowell: Printed by L. Huntress.* 1841. 12mo, pp. 8. Continued. B. 42489

Also: Report ... from 1840 to 1849. ... By Gilman Kimball, M.D. ... *Lowell.* 1849. 8vo, pp. 16. H.

Lowell Hosiery Company. Act of Incorporation and By-Laws of the ... Company ... May, 1869. *Lowell: Stone & Huse ... Printers.* 1869. 16mo, pp. 7, (1). H. 42490

The Lowell Offering; A Repository of Original Articles, written exclusively by Females actively employed in the Mills. ... Vol. I. *Lowell, Mass.: Powers & Bagley.* 1841. 8vo, pp. iv, 380. Continued. B. 42491

Edited by A. C. Thomas and H. Farley. After 1845 it was called "New England Offering;" *see also* "Mind amongst the Spindles."

First Annual Report ... of the Lowell Sabbath School Union ... *Lowell: Leonard Huntress, Printer.* 1837. 8vo, pp. 7, (1).

Lowell Shakspeare Memorial. Exercises on the Ter-Centenary Celebration of the Birth of William Shakspeare, April 23, 1864 ... . *Lowell, Mass.: Stone & Huse, Printers.* 1864. 8vo, pp. 51. H. 42493

Memorial of Mary C. Rand and two thousand nine hundred and sixty-four others, female inhabitants in the town of Lowell, for the Repeal of the present Licence Law ... . [n. p. 1835.] 8vo, pp. 39. 42494

A Catalogue of the Library of the Middlesex Mechanic Association .... *Lowell.* 1840. 8vo. + *Lowell: S. J. Varney, Printer.* 1853. 8vo, pp. 165, (1). + *Lowell.* 1860. 8vo, pp. 299, (1).

Reports of the First Exhibition of the Middlesex Mechanic Association ... of Lowell, September, 1851. *Lowell: S. J. Varney, Printer.* 1852. 8vo, pp. xix, 102. Folded Plate. + Second Exhibition ... . *Lowell: S. N. Merrill, Printer.* 1859. 8vo, pp. xviii, (2), 101. B. 42496

Also: Constitution and By-Laws of the Middlesex Mechanic Association. Instituted October, 1825. *Lowell: Huntress and Knowlton, Printers.* 1835. 12mo, pp. 20. B.

The First Report of the Minister at Large in Lowell, to the Missionary Society connected with the South Parish. *Lowell: Joel Taylor, Printer.* 1845. 8vo, pp. 19. Continued. 42497

Municipal Register, containing Rules and Orders of the City Council, ... since 1851, and a List of the Government and Officers of ... Lowell, for 1853. *Lowell: S. J. Varney, ... Printer.* 1853. 12mo, pp. 36. Continued. B. 42498

Profits on Manufactures. *See* [Cary (T. G.)], III. 11219.

Report of the Joint Special Committee on a Supply of Water for ... Lowell, September, 1869. *Lowell: Marden & Rowell, Printers.* 1869. 8vo, pp. 81. Continued. B. 42499

Also: Report of the Joint Special Committee, on ... the Effects of Lead Pipes upon Well-Water in the City of Lowell. *Lowell: Printed by William Schouler.* 1842. 8vo, pp. 21. BA.

Salaries of the Officers of the City of Lowell for the Year 1870–71. *Lowell: Chase & Hildreth, Printers.* 1870. 8vo, pp. 8.

Statement in regard to the Moral Exposure and Spiritual Wants of Lowell. *Lowell.* 1850. 8vo. 42501

Statistics of Lowell Manufactures. January, 1855. Compiled from Authentic Sources. [n. p. n. d.] 8vo. Continued. S.

Statement of Deaths ... in ... Lowell during ... 1840. ... *Lowell.* 1840. 8vo. Continued. 42503

The Stranger in Lowell. *See* [Whittier (J. G.)]

LOWENÖRN (P.) Extrait de la Relation d'un Voyage fait par ordre de S. M. Danoise, pendant l'année 1786, pour la découverte de la côte orientale du Groenland ... . Par M. de Lowenörn, Capitaine ... . Traduit, en 1822, par l'auteur lui-même ... . Extrait des Annales Maritimes et Coloniales de 1823. *A Paris: De l'Imprimerie Royale.* 1823. 8vo, pp. 47. Map. 42504

The East coast of Greenland was not reached.

LÖWENSTERN (I.) Les États-Unis et la Havane. Souvenirs d'un Voyageur. Par M. Isidore Löwenstern. *Paris: A. Bertrand.* 1842. 8vo, pp. xii, 372. C. 42505

LÖWENSTERN. Le Mexique. Souvenirs d'un Voyageur. Par Isidore Löwenstern. *Paris: Arthus Bertrand.* 1843. 8vo, pp. viii, 466, (1). 42506

LOWER CANADA. ... Act for the Abolition of Feudal Rights and Duties in Lower Canada. [*Quebec.* 1854.] 8vo, pp. 22, (1).

An Act to provide for the Better Organization of Agricultural Societies in Lower Canada. ... *Quebec: Printed by Stewart Derbishire* ... 1852. 8vo, pp. 8. H. 42508

Also: An Act to amend ... the Laws relating to the Organization of Agricultural Societies in Lower Canada. ... *Toronto: Printed by Stewart Derbishire* ... 1857. 8vo, pp. 10. H.—Acts to amend the Municipal & Agricultural Acts of Lower Canada. ... *Toronto: Printed by Stewart Derbishire* ... 1858. 8vo, pp. v, 18, 26, 19, 15. H.

Report of the Special Committee ... of the Lower Canada Agricultural Society .... *Quebec: Printed by Rollo Campbell.* 1852. 8vo, pp. 117, (1). H. 42509

Civil Code of Lower Canada [adopted 1866]. *Ottawa: Printed by Malcolm Cameron.* 1866. 8vo, pp. xv, (4), 747. B.

See also Vol. III., No. 10477.

Code de Procédure Civile du Bas Canada .... *Ottawa: G. E. Desbarats.* 1866. 8vo, pp. xxxvii, 297. + *Ottawa: Printed by Malcolm Cameron.* 1867. 8vo, pp. xv, (4), 471. B. 42511

In French and English.

Code Rural à l'usage des habitants tant anciens que nouveaux du Bas-Canada, rédigé par J. F. Perrault Proton. *Québec.* 1832. 12mo. 42512

Complete Index to the Ordinances and Statutes of Lower Canada, to the 57th Year of King George the Third. *Quebec.* 1817. 8vo. 42513

A Correct Account. *See* Canada, Vol. III., No. 10407.

Acts for the Promotion of Education in Lower Canada. ... *Toronto: Printed by Stewart Derbishire.* 1857. 8vo, pp. 63. H.

The Journal of Education. *See* Vol. IX., No. 36708.

Report on Education in Lower Canada ... for ... 1849–50. ... *Toronto: Lovell and Gibson.* 1851. 8vo, pp. 92. H. 42515

Also in French. Also: Report of the Superintendent of Education for Lower Canada, for 1850–51. ... *Quebec: Printed by John Lovell.* 1852. 8vo, pp. 49, (1). Continued. H.

Rapport du Surintendant de l'Education pour le Bas-Canada ... 1855. ... *Toronto: Imprimé par John Lovell.* 1856. 8vo, pp. 221. Continued. H. 42516

Statutes relating to Elementary Education, and for the Establishment of Normal Schools ... [in] Lower Canada. *Quebec: Printed by Stewart Derbishire* ... 1852. 8vo, pp. 86, (1). H.

État des sommes dépensées. *See* Boutillier (T.), II. 6944.

Journal of the House of Assembly. *See* Vol. III., No. 10491.

Proceedings in the Assembly of Lower Canada on the Rules of Practice in the Courts of Justice and the Impeachment of Jonathan Sewell and James Monk, Esqrs. *Quebec.* 1814. 4to, pp. 64. 42518

Report of the Committee of ... Crown Lands. *See* No. 10410.

First & Second Reports of the Special Committee appointed to inquire into the Causes which retard the Settlement of the Eastern Townships of Lower Canada. ... *Quebec: Printed by Rollo Campbell.* 1851. 8vo, pp. 145, (1). 42519

Journal d'agriculture. *See* Vol. III., No. 10345.

Lower Canada Law Almanac. *Quebec.* 1859. 8vo. Cont'd.

The Lower Canada Watchman. [Edited by David Chisholme.] *Kingston (U. C.): James Macfarlane.* 1829. 18mo, pp. 491. 42521

Ordinances passed by the Governor and Special Council of Lower Canada in 1841. [n. p. n. d.] Folio. 42522

Parochial ... Subdivisions of Lower-Canada. *See* No. 10538.

Petition of ... Assembly of Lower Canada. *See* No. 10540.

Political ... Account. *See* [Laterriere (P. de S.)], No. 39157.

Public Documents. *See* Aylmer (M.), Vol. I., No. 2519, and *add* for collation, pp. 126.

Rapport du Comité special sur l'État de l'Agriculture du Bas-Canada. *Toronto.* 1850. 8vo. 42523

See also our Vol. III., No. 10347.

Report of Committee. *See* Vol. III., No. 10454.

Report of the Progress. *See* Boutillier (T.), Vol. II. 6945.

Report of ... Indians. *See* No. 10586.

Return with Despatches and Correspondence relative to the Seigniorial and Feudal Tenure in Lower Canada. [*Quebec.* 1852.] 8vo, pp. 40. 42524

The Revised Acts. *See* No. 10498.

Schedule. Resolutions Containing the Amendments to be made in the printed Roll of the Civil Code of Lower Canada ... [*Quebec: Printed by G. E. Desbarats.* 1865.] Folio, pp. 71, (1), 13, (1). B. 42525

In French and English.

Subdivisions du Bas-Canada. *See* No. 10612.

For other titles of books relating to Lower Canada, *see* Canada, Vol. III.

LOWER DUBLIN, *Pa.* Account of the Wheat Moth or Virginia Fly, as it appeared ... in the Township of Lower Dublin, in 1802–4. *Philadelphia.* 1805. 8vo. 42526

The Lower St. Lawrence or Quebec to Halifax, via Gaspé and Pictou. To which is appended Mr. Wood's Description of the River Saguenay, also Legends of the St. Lawrence ... . *Quebec: "Mercury" Office.* 1861. 18mo, pp. 122. 42527

LOWER WEST NOTTINGHAM. Historical Sketch of Lower West Nottingham Presbyterian Church. *Philadelphia.* 1865. 8vo. 42528

LÖWIG (Gustav). Die Freystaaten von Nordamerica. Beobachtungen und Bemerkungen für auswandernde Deutsche. *Heidelberg und Leipzig: Groos.* 1833 [1832]. 8vo. 42529

LOWNDES (J.) The Coffee-Planter; or, An Essay On the Cultivation and Manufacturing of that Article of West-India Produce. By John Lowndes ... . *London: C. Lowndes.* 1807. 8vo, pp. 76. 6 Plates. H. 42530

LOWNDES [W.] Speech of Mr. Lowndes ... Feb. 1819, on the Bank of the United States. [n. p. n. d.] 12mo, pp. 28. H.

Also: Speech ... on the Tariff Bill, ... April 24, 1820. [n. p. n. d.] 12mo, pp. 24.—Speech ... on the Admission of Missouri. ... Dec. 13, 1820. [n. p. n. d.] 12mo, pp. 23. H.

LOWNDES, *pseudon.* The Letters of Lowndes, addressed to the Hon. John C. Calhoun. *New-York: D. Appleton and Co.* MDCCCXLIII. 8vo, pp. 100. 42532

LOWNES (C.) An Account of the Alteration and Present State of the Penal Laws of Pennsylvania. ... By Caleb Lownes. ... *Boston: Printed by Young & Minns.* MDCCXCIX. 8vo, pp. 36.

See also Bradford (William), Vol. II., No. 7265.

LOWREY (G. P.) The Commander-in-Chief; a Defence upon Legal Grounds of the Proclamation of Emancipation; and an Answer to Ex-Judge Curtis' Pamphlet, entitled "Executive Power." By Grosvenor P. Lowrey .... *New York: G. P. Putnam.* 1862. 16mo, pp. 31. + Second Edition, with Additional Notes. [*Ibid.*] 1863. 12mo, pp. 34. B. 42534

Also: English Neutrality. Is the Alabama a British Pirate? ... *New York: A. D. F. Randolph.* 1863. 8vo, pp. 32. H.

LOWRIE (J. C.) A Manual of Missions; or Sketches of the Foreign Missions of the Presbyterian Church .... By John C. Lowrie .... *New-York.* 1854. Oblong 4to, pp. 74. 5 Maps.

Another edition is entitled: "A Manual of the Foreign Missions of the Presbyterian Church in the United States of America." ... *New York: William Rankin, Jr.* 1868. 8vo, pp. 359. Map. + Third Edition. [*Ibid.*] 1868. 12mo, pp. 359. 4 Maps, Plate. Includes missions among the Indian tribes.

LOWRIE (J. M.) ... A Discourse, ... Indianapolis, October 10, 1861. By John M. Lowrie, D.D. ... *Indianapolis.* 1861. 8vo, pp. 26. 42536

LOWRIE. The Lessons of our National Sorrow. A Discourse Delivered in ... Fort Wayne, Indiana, on the Sabbath Morning, April 16, 1865, Succeeding the Death of Abraham Lincoln. By John M. Lowrie .... *Fort Wayne: Jenkinson & Hartman, Printers.* 1865. 8vo, pp. 16. 42537

LOWRIE. The Prophet Elisha. To which is prefixed a Memoir of the Author. By the Rev. William D. Howard, D.D. *Philadelphia.* [1869.] 16mo, pp. 287. Plate. C. 42538

[LOWRIE (Walter).] Memoirs of the Rev. Walter M. Lowrie, Missionary to China. Edited by his Father. *New York.* 1849. 8vo, pp. 504. Portrait. + Fourth Edition. [*Ibid.*] 1851. 8vo, pp. vii, 456, (4). Portrait. + *Philadelphia.* 1854. 12mo. 42539

See "American State Papers," Vol. I., Nos. 1228–29.

LOWRY (M. B.) A Tribute of Gratitude to the Hon. M. B. Lowry ... Pennsylvania. *Philadelphia: Jas. B. Rodgers Co., Printers.* 1869. 8vo, pp. 36. H. 42540

LOWRY (R.) ... A Discourse delivered on the ... Fifth Anniversary of the Organization of the Church of the Messiah, Greenbush, N. Y. ... By ... Rev. Robert Lowry. *Albany: Joel Munsell.* 1858. 8vo, pp. 13. 42541

[LOWTH (Robert).] Sermon before the Society for the Propagation of the Gospel ... By the Lord Bishop of Oxford. *London.* 1771. 4to, pp. 29, 60. 42542

Contains memorials from America and the West Indies relative to converting the natives.

LOWVILLE, *N. Y.* Dedication Services of the Lowville Rural Cemetery, October 7, 1867 ... . Remarks by the President F. B. Hough. *Lowville, N. Y.* 1868. 8vo, pp. 24. S. 42543

LOWVILLE ACADEMY. Semi-Centennial Anniversary, Celebrated at Lowville, N. Y. July 21st and 22d, 1858. ... [Edited by F. B. Hough.] *Lowville.* 1859. Rl. 8vo, pp. 133. 4 Plates.

Twenty-three copies printed on large paper, and containing twelve engravings.

The Loyal Address of the Clergy of Virginia. *Williamsburg. Printed for Fr. Maggot, at the Sign of the Hickery Tree, in Queen Street.* 1702. Folio, 1 leaf. 42545

A poem. We do not recollect having seen any piece printed in Virginia with an earlier date than this.

To Loyal Democrats! Who are the Sympathizers with the Rebellion? What the Rebels say. [n. p. n. d.] 8vo, pp. 7.

In favor of the election of J. S. Wadsworth as governor of New York.

Loyal Heart: the Pale-face Hunter. *New York: American News Company.* [1868.] 12mo, pp. 100. C. 42547

Loyal International Bulletin. Good News! Good News from Home. [n. p. n. d.] 8vo. 42548

Address of the Loyal Leagues, Utica, October 20, 1863. [n. p. n. d.] 8vo. 42549

Proceedings of the Convention of Loyal Leagues ... at Mechanics Hall, Utica, ... 26 May, 1863. ... *New York: Wm. C. Bryant & Co., Printers.* 1863. 8vo, pp. 67, (1). BA. 42550

Loyal Meeting of the People of New-York, to Support the Government, Prosecute the War, and Maintain the Union.

Held at the Cooper Institute, ... March 6, 1863. ... *New-York: George F. Nesbitt & Co., Printers.* 1863. 8vo, pp. 80. + [*Ibid.*] 8vo, pp. 52, (1). BA. 42551

Address of the Loyal National League of the State of New York, ... to the American People. *New York.* [n. d.] 8vo, pp. 8. BA., C. 42552

The Loyal National League. Opinions of Prominent Men concerning the Great Questions of The Times ... On the Anniversary of Sumter. ... *New York: C. S. Wescott & Co., Printers.* 1863. 8vo, pp. 72. H. 42553

Also: Letter of the Loyal National League To Messrs. John Bright, John Stuart Mill, Richard Cobden, Newman Hall, E. B. Cairnes, Edward Dicey, and our other Friends in England. 8vo, pp. 8. For a letter to Friends of America in France, *see* Gasparin (A. de), Vol. VII., No. 26734, *note*.

Proceedings at the Organization of the Loyal National League ... March 20th, 1863. ... *New York: C. S. Wescott & Co., Printers.* 1863. 8vo, pp. 47, (1). BA. 42554

The Sumter Anniversary, 1863. Opinions of Loyalists concerning the Great Questions of the Times; expressed in ... Speeches and Letters ... on ... the Inauguration of the Loyal National League, in ... New York, on the 11th of April, 1863, ... *New York: C. S. Wescott & Co., Printers.* 1863. 8vo, pp. 144. H. 42555

Also: Dialogue Between an Old-fashioned Jackson Democrat and a Copperhead. [n. p. n. d.] 8vo, pp. 4.

The Loyal National Union Journal. April, 1864. *Brownsville, Texas.* 1864. Folio. 42556

Loyal Publication Society, ... Pamphlets ... *New York.* ... 1864. 2 vols., 8vo. B. 42557

Consists of eighty-four tracts, each with a distinct title-page; they are all described under their respective names in this Dictionary. Some of them were reissued as: "Loyal Reprints."

Proceedings at the First Anniversary Meeting of the Loyal Publication Society, February 13, 1864 ... . *New York.* 1864. 8vo, pp. 24. + Second Anniversary, Feb. 11, 1865. *New York.* 1865. 8vo, pp. 30. BA. 42558

Loyal Publications of the National Union Association of Ohio. *Cincinnati.* 1863. 42559

Eight or more numbers published.

Loyal National Repeal Association. *See* New England.

The Loyalist Poetry of the Revolution. *Philadelphia: Collins, Printer.* MDCCCLVII. 4to, pp. xi, 213, (4), and a leaf at page 126.

Nine-nine copies privately printed for the editor Winthrop Sargent. The leaf after page 125 contains a salacious verse. *See also* Stansbury and Odell.

LOYALISTS. Abstract of the Laws of the American States, now in Force, relative to debts due to Loyalists, subjects of Great Britain. *London: Printed in the Year* MDCCLXXXIX. 8vo, pp. xv, 45, 16. 42561

Case and Claim. *See our* Vol. III. 11306, and add for note: There are two different editions, neither of which have an imprint.

Case of the Uncompensated American Loyalists, as laid before Parliament ... . *London.* 1816. 4to. 42562

The Declaration and Address of his Majesty's Suffering Loyalists to the People of America. *London: T. Becket.* M,DCC,LXXXII. 4to, pp. (2), iv, 32. 42563

For another "Declaration and Address," *see our* No. 19156, and for the M. *read* His Majesty's. *See also* our Vol. I., No. 140, Vol. V., No. 20222, [Galloway (Joseph)], Vol. VII., Laws, No. 39417, Observations, *and* Reasons.

Laws ... against the Loyalists. *See our* No. 39417.

The Loyalist's Ammunition. *Philadelphia: Printed by Henry B. Ashmead.* 1863. 8vo, pp. 16. H. 42564

Contains seven pieces on the rebellion. Also in German as: "Die Munition des Loyalisten." *Philadelphia: H. B. Ashmead, Printer.* 1863. 8vo, pp. 16.

The Loyalty and Devotion of Colored Americans in the Revolution and War of 1812. *Boston: R. F. Wallcut.* 1861. 12mo, pp. 24. 42565

Loyalty and Disloyalty. [*Philadelphia: Ringwalt & Brown, Printers.* n. d.] 8vo, pp. 8. H. 42566

Loyalty for the Times. A Voice from Kentucky. April, 1864. [n. p. n. d.] 8vo, pp. 24. 42567

Loyalty. What is it? To whom or what due? [*Baltimore.* 1863.] 8vo, pp. 12. 42568

Loyalty Vindicated ... . *Boston.* 1698. 4to, pp. 28. N. 42569

All Boston imprints before 1700 have the merit of rarity.

LOYD (T. E.) Speech of Thomas E. Loyd ... on the Question of Negro Suffrage in the District of Columbia, December 14, 1865. [n. p. n. d.] 8vo, pp. 8. 42570

LOYER (R. F.) Letter of R. F. Loyer to E. M. Stanton, in Self-Defence against the Aspersions of the Senate Committee. *Philadelphia.* 1863. 8vo. 42571

LOYOLA COLLEGE, *Baltimore.* ... Catalogue ... 1857–8. *Baltimore: Printed by John Murphy & Co.* 1858. 8vo, pp. 27. Plate. Continued. H. 42572

LOYSEL (F.) Demostracion de gozo en las fiestas por el nacimiento del Príncipe D. Cárlos Clemente, por D. Francisco Loysel. *Imprenta destinada al cómputo eclesiástico.* 1772. 4to. 42573

LOYSEL. Simulacro y sitio de Atarés, plaza supuesta: verificado en la Habana en 12 de Abril de 1773. Dispuesto por el Sr. Marqués de la Torre su Gobernador y Capitan General, á quien lo dedica su mas reverente súbdito Francisco Loysel. ... *Habana: Imprenta de D. Blas de los Olivos.* 1773. 4to, pp. 16 [in verse].

[LOZA (F.)] La Vida que hizo el Siervo de Dios Gregorio Lopez, en algunos lugares de esta Nueva España. *Mexico, Emprenta de Juan Ruyz.* 1613. 12mo. 42575

Brunet, in mentioning an edition of *Seville*, 1618, which we have not seen, says, "Antonio, qui qualifie ce petit ouvrage *d'aureus libellus*, n'a pas connus cette edition de 1618, dont un bel exemplaire en *mar.* a été vendu £2. 12s, Heber, mais il cite une de *Mexico*, 1613, qui doit être encore plus rare que celle de *Séville*."

LOZA. Vida qve el siervo de Dios Gregorio Lopez hizo en algvnos lvgares de la Nueva España. Principalmente en el Pueblo de Santa Fè. Por el licenciado Francisco Lossa, Cura que fue de la Iglesia de Mexico. *Madrid, Imprenta Real.* 1642. 4to, 10 prel. leaves, 118 and 2 leaves. + *Madrid.* 1648. 4to, 117 leaves. + *Madrid.* 1649. 4to. + *Madrid.* 1674. 4to. + *Sevilla.* 1678. 4to. 42576

The edition of 1642 is dedicated to the celebrated Palafox. *See* Leclerc, No. 129.

LOZA. Vida | qve el siervo de Dios | Gregorio Lopez | hizo en algvnos lvgares de la | Nueua España. Principalmente en el Pueblo | de Santa Fè. | Por el licenciado Francisco Losa | Presbitero, Cura que fue en la Iglesia Catetralde Mexico. | ... | *Con licencia en Madrid, En la Impreta Real. Año* M. DC. LVIII. | ... | 4to, 8 prel. leaves, 114 and 2 leaves. 42577

This is the same as the first edition, with additions by Louis Munoz.

LOZA. Vida del Siervo de Dios Gregorio Lopez. Escrita por el Padre Francisco Losa ... . A qve se añaden los escritos del apocalypsi, y tesoro de medecina ... . Quarta Impression. *En Madrid. En la Imprenta de Juan de Ariztia. Año de* 1727. 4to, pp. (23), 441, (1). Portrait. C. 42578

LOZA. La Vida que hizo el siervo de Dios Gregorio Lopez en algunos lugares de la Nueva España, por el licenciado Francisco Lossa presbitero, cura que fue en la Iglesia Cathedral de Mexico. *En Lisboa, Por Pedro Crasbeeck, anno* 1618. 8vo, 9 p. l., Text, 107 leaves. 42579

This is the only Portuguese version we have seen.

LOZA. La Vie de Gregoire Lopez dans la Novvelle-Espagne, composee en Espagnol par François de Losa Prestre, Licencié, et mise en François, par vn Pere de la Compagnie de Jesvs. *Paris.* 1644. 12mo. 42580

LOZA. La vie | de | Gregoire | Lopez | dans la Novvelle | Espagne, | composee en espagnol | par François Losa Prestre, | Licentié, & iadis Curé de l'Eglise | Cathedrale de Mexico. | Et traduite nouuellement en François, | par vn Pere de la Compagnie de | Iesvs. | Seconde edition. | *A Paris*, | *Chez Iean Henavlt, Libraire Iuré*, | *ruë S. Iacques*, ... | M. DC. LVI. | *Auec Priuilege dv Roy.* | 12mo, pp. (24), 260, (4). S. 42581

Some copies have the date M.CD.LV. The first edition of this French translation was published in *Paris, Louis Conart*, 1644.

LOZA. La Vie dv bienhevrevx Gregoire Lopez, écrite Par François Losa Curé de l'Eglise Cathedrale de la ville de Mexico dans la nouvelle Espagne. De la Traduction de Mr. Arnavld d'Andilly. Sur l'Exemplaire imprimé à Madrid en 1658. *Paris, Pierre le Petit.* M.DC.LXXIV. 12mo, pp. (20), 420. Portrait. BA. + [*Ibid.*] 1684. 12mo. 42582

[LOZA.] Le Saint Solitaire des Indes, ou la Vie de Gregoire Lopez. *A Cologne.* 1717. 12mo. 42583

LOZA. The Holy Life of Gregory Lopez, a Spanish Hermite in the West Indies. Englished from the Spanish of Father Losa. [n. p.:] *Printed in the Year* 1675. 8vo. + Second Edition. [*Ibid.*] 1675. 8vo. 42584

Contains curious particulars of New Spain, the author's solitary life among the Indian Chichimecos, several testimonials of divers bishops in Mexico, etc.

[LOZA.] The Holy Life, Pilgrimage, and Blessed Death of Gregory Lopez; a Spanish Hermite in the West Indies. Second Edition. *London, W. C.* 1686. 18mo, pp. (56), 232. 42585

[LOZA.] The Life of Gregory Lopez. A Hermit in America. *New York: John Eyre.* 1841. 18mo, pp. 123. + *New York: Sold at Riker's Store.* 1852. 18mo, pp. 123. 42586

An abridgment; the preface is signed John Eyre.

LOZA. Vita Condatta dal servo di Dio Gregorio Lopez nello nuova Spagna composta dal Fran. Losa gia curato delle Chiesa Cattedrale del Messico, e poi suo Campagno. *Roma.* 1740. 4to. Folding Plate. 42587

The only Italian version which has come under my notice. Gregory Lopez, one of the most successful of the many early missionaries among the Indians of New Spain, was born at Madrid, July 4th, 1542, and is said to have been an illegitimate son of Charles V. or Philip II. At the age of twenty he landed at Vera Cruz, and soon after pitched his tent among the Chichimecos Indians. He died on the 20th of July, 1596, at Santa Fé, six miles from Mexico, where Father Losa wrote his life in 1613.

LOZA (L. R. de la). Descripcion del Aerolito de Yanhuitlan por L. Rio de la Loza. *México.* 1865. 8vo. 42588

LOZANO (A.) Coleccion de poesias originals por Abigail Lozano. [n. p.] 1864. 4to, pp. xvi, 472. 42589

Lozano is called "el bardo Venezolano."

[LOZANO (Pedro).] Individual y Verdadera Relacion de la extrema ruyna que padeciò la Ciudad de los Reyes Lima, Capitàl del Reyno del Perù, con el horrible Temblòr de tierra acaecido en ella la noche del dia 28. de Octubre de 1746, y de la totàl asolacion del presidio y puerto del Callao, por la violenta irrupcion del Mar, que ocasionò en aquella Bahia. *Lima, en la Imprenta que estaba en la Calle de los Mercadores. Año de* 1746. 4to, 13 l.

The original edition is a piece of extreme rarity. It relates one of the most dreadful convulsions of nature on record. The Port of Callao was inundated by the sea, and the entire population perished; Lima was almost destroyed. *See* Leclerc, No. 757.

[LOZANO.] Individual y Verdadera Relacion [etc., as in No. 42590]. *Mexico: Joseph Bernardo de Hogal.* 1747. 4to, 10 l.

Almost as rare as the Lima edition. The following is an English translation with additions:

[LOZANO.] A True and Particular History of Earthquakes. Containing a relation of that dreadful Earthquake which happen'd at Lima and Callao, in Peru, October 28, 1746; published at Lima by Command of the Vice-Roy, and now Translated from the Original Spanish; also of that which happen'd in Jamaica in

1692, and of others in different parts of the World. Accurately describing the dreadful Devastations that have been made by these dreadful convulsions of the Earth; whereby Mountains have been thrown down, or remov'd to great distances; Cities, with all their Inhabitants swallow'd up in a moment; whole flocks and herds, with their keepers, ingulp'd in the tremendous chasms and openings of valleys; and large forests sunk, and forever buried in an instant. Extracted from Authors of unexceptionable Reputation. By Philolethus. *London: Printed for the Author.* 1748. 8vo, pp. xvi, 176. 42592

[LOZANO.] A True and Particular Relation Of the Dreadful Earthquake Which happen'd At Lima, the Capital of Peru, and the neighbouring Port of Callao, On the 28th of October, 1746. With an Account likewise of every Thing material that passed there afterwards to the End of November following. Published at Lima by Command of the Viceroy, And translated from the Original Spanish, By a Gentleman who resided many Years in those Countries. To which is added, A Description of Callao and Lima before their Destruction; and of the Kingdom of Peru in General, with its Inhabitants; setting forth their Manners, Customs, Religion, Government, Commerce, &c. Interspersed with Passages of Natural History and physiological Disquisitions; particularly an Enquiry into the Cause of Earthquakes. The whole illustrated with A Map of the Country about Lima; Plans of the Road and Town of Callao, another of Lima; and several Cuts of the Natives drawn on the Spot by the Translator. The Second Edition. *London: T. Osborne.* M DCC XLVIII. 8vo, pp. xxiii, 341. 9 Plates and Maps. BA.

Concerning the author, *see* Funes' "Historia Civil del Paraguay," where he is commended as an exact and sincere writer. The translator was Henry Johnson, but the "Gentleman's Magazine", for 1748, says it is a pretended translation from the Spanish. The following are abridgments:

[LOZANO.] A True and Particular Relation of the Dreadful Earthquake, which happen'd at Lima, the Capital of Peru, and the neighboring Port of Callao, On the 28th of October, 1746. With an Account likewise of everything material that passed there afterwards to the end of November following. Published at Lima by command of the Viceroy, and translated from the Original Spanish. By a Gentleman who resided many Years in those Countries. *London Printed, and Philadelphia Reprinted and Sold by B. Franklin and D. Hall.* 1749. 8vo, pp. 52. 42594

[LOZANO.] A True and Particular Relation of the Dreadful Earthquake which happened at Lima, the Capital of Peru, and

the neighbouring Port of Callao, on the 28th of October, 1746. *Boston: Printed and Sold by D. and Z. Fowle.* [n. d.] 12mo, pp. 8.

[LOZANO.] Histoire des Tremblemens de Terre Arrive's a Lima, Capitale du Perou, et Autres Lieux; Avec la Description du Perou, Et des recherches sur les Causes Phisiques des Tremblemens de Terre, par M. Hales de la Société Royale de Londres, & autres Phisiciens. Avec Cartes & Figures. Traduite de L'Anglois, Premiere Partie. *A La Haye.* M. DCC. LII. 12mo, pp. xvi, 445, (9). Map and 6 Plates. S. 42596

A translation from the English by M. Hales. *See* "Quart. Rev.," XLIII. 155. In some copies the imprint reads: *Paris.* M.DCC.LII.

LOZANO. Carta del P. Pedro Lozano, de la Compañia de Jesus, de ... Paraguay, escrita al P. Bruno Morales, de la misma compañia, y provincia existente en esta corte de Madrid. [*Madrid.* 1747.] 4to, pp. 56. H. 42597

This letter is dated Nov. 1, 1746, at Cordova, in the province of Tucuman, and contains an account of the state of the missions of the Jesuits in Paraguay, at that time. It has no title-page, and was evidently printed for private distribution only.

LOZANO. Descripcion chorographica del terreno, rios, arboles, y animales de las dilatadissimas Provincias del Gran Chaco, Gualamba. Y de los ritos y costumbres de las innumerables Naciones barbaras è infieles, que la habitan: con una cabal relacion historica de lo que en ellas han obrado para conquistarlas algunos governadores, y ministros reales: y los missioneros Jesuitas para reducirlas à la fé del verdadero Dios. Escrita por el P. Pedro Lozano de la comp^a. de Jesus, chronista de su provincia del Tucuman. *En Cordoba: En el Colegio de la Assumpcion por Joseph Santos Balbas.* 1733. 4to, pp. (22), 485, (10). Map.

"An interesting account of a country very little known, even a century after it was printed."—RICH. "A very rare book," says Dr. Dibdin, "and in much request." "This description of the Province of Chaco and Countries of Paraguay, by one of the missionaries, is very much esteemed and sought after."—*Grenville Catalogue.* It has escaped Meusel, but is quoted as authority by Dr. Robertson. *See also* Leclerc, No. 917, *and* Pedro de Angeles' "Coleccion."

LOZANO. Historia de la Compañia de Jesus en la Provincia del Paraguay. Escrita por el Padre Pedro Lozano de la misma Compañia. *En Madrid: En la Imprenta de la Viuda de Manuel Fernandez.* M.DCC.LIV–V. 2 vols., folio, pp. (8), 760, (7); (4), 832. B. 42599

The author was a missionary in Paraguay. The present work, which is almost unknown, contains a history of the acts of the Jesuits in Paraguay, and appears to be but the beginning of a more extensive work contemplated by the author.

LOZERE (P. de la.) *See* Pélet de la Lozière.

LOZIER (J. Hogarth). The Nameless Graves where our Heroes lie. Words by John H. Lozier. Music by C. M. C. *Cincinnati: John Church, Jr.* [1864.] 4to, pp. 5. B. 42600

Also: The Old Union Wagon. ... *Cincinnati: J. Church, Jr.* [1863.] 4to, pp. 5.

LOZIÈRES (L. N.) *See* B[audry] d[es Lozières], Vol. I.

LUBBOCK (J.) The Origin of Civilisation [*sic*] and the Primitive Condition of Man. ... By Sir John Lubbock ... . *London: Longman, Green, and Co.* 1870. 8vo, pp. xvi, 380. 5 Plates. + Second Edition, with Additions. [*Ibid.*] 8vo, pp. xx, 426. 6 Plates. + *New York: D. Appleton and Company.* 1870. 8vo, pp. (2), xvi, 380. 5 Plates. H. 42601

The identity of the pagination of the editions of 1870, suggests the probability of both being the same, except in the imprint.

LUBBOCK. Pre-Historic Times, as Illustrated by Ancient Remains, and the Manners and Customs of Modern Savages. By Sir John Lubbock ... . *London: Williams and Norgate.* 1865. 8vo, pp. xxiii, (1), 512. 4 Plates. + Second Edition. [*Ibid.*] 1869. 8vo, pp. xxvii, (1), 619. 5 Plates. BA. 42602

See "Smithsonian Report," 1862 and 1869.

LUBELFING (J. von). *See* Leubelfing (J. von), IX. 40726.

LUBIN (Augustini). Orbis Augustinianus sive Conventuum Ordinis Eremitarum Sancti descriptio ... . *Paris.* 1659. 4to.

Includes seven maps of America.

LUCAS (A.) The Shaving Mill. [A Poem.] By Ansil Lucas. *Freetown.* [n. d.] 8vo. 42604

LUCAS (C.) A Letter to ... C. Lucas Esq. *See* No. 40348.

LUCAS (Charles). Du Système Pénitentiaire en Europe et aux États-Unis. ... *Paris: A. Bossange, et Charles-Béchet*; Vols. II. and III.: *Th. Dehay, et Veuve Charles-Béchet.* 1828–30. 3 vols., 8vo, pp. 460; 462; 164. 4 Plates and 2 Tables. C. 42605

Vol. III. is entitled "Conclusion générale de l'ouvrage sur le système," etc.

LUCAS. ... Exposé de l'état de la question pénitentiaire en Europe et aux États-Unis. Par M. Ch. Lucas ... *Paris: Imprimerie Panckoucke.* 1844. 8vo, pp. iv, 129. H. 42606

LUCAS. Historia do Systema Penitenciario na Europa, e nos Estados-Unidos da America, escripta em frances por Carlos Lucas, et traduzida em portuguez por José Cardoso Braga ... .

Lisboa: Na Typ. de Manuel de Jesus Coelho. 1836. 2 vols., 8vo, pp. 162; 162. 42607

LUCAS (D. R.) History of the 99th Indiana Infantry. By Rev. D. R. Lucas. *Lafayette, Ind.* 1865. 12mo. 42608

LUCAS (E.) Journal and Letters of Eliza Lucas. Now first printed. *Wormsloe.* MDCCCL. 4to, pp. 30, Colophon, 1 leaf. C.

Nineteen copies privately printed for Mr. George Wymberly-Jones, five of which were printed on T H paper. The inscription and the colophon are each printed on a leaf of vellum. The writer of this journal was the wife of Chief Justice Pinckney of South Carolina, and the mother of General Charles Cotesworth Pinckney, and General Thomas Pinckney. It was edited by Mrs. H. P. Holbrook.

LUCAS (F.) A New ... General Atlas, Containing Maps of each of the United States. *Baltimore: Fielding Lucas, Jun'.* [n. d.] 4to, pp. (6). 54 Maps. B. 42610

LUCAS. A New General Atlas of the West India Islands Comprehended in Twenty-one Maps from the best authorities. *Baltimore: ... Fielding Lucas, Jr.* [n. d.] 4to, pp. (4). 21 Maps.

Also: A General Atlas containing Distinct Maps of all the known Countries in the World. ... *Baltimore: Fielding Lucas, Jun'.* [1823.] Folio, pp. (6). 101 Maps.—A General Atlas, of all the Known Countries in the World. ... *Baltimore: Fielding Lucas, Jun'.* [n. d.] Folio, pp. (6). 67 Maps. BA.

LUCAS (G. W.) Remarks on Musical Conventions in Boston, ... By G. W. Lucas. *Northampton.* 1844. 8vo, pp. 27.

LUCAS (H.) Entomologie du Voyage dans l'Amérique du Sud de F. de Castelnau. *Paris.* 1857. 4to. 40 Plates. 42613

[LUCAS (J. B. C.)] Biography of Chas. Lucas, Esq. Late Attorney of the United States for Missouri Territory. [n. p. 1818?] 8vo, pp. 16. S. 42614

The subject of this biography was killed in a duel with T. H. Benton, in 1817.

LUCAS. Sketch of an Argument ... District Court of the U. States ... St. Louis, ... November, 1824. ... By John B. C. Lucas. *St. Louis: Printed by E. Charless.* 1825. 8vo, pp. 26.

LUCAS (R.) Remarkable Account of Mrs. Rachel Lucas ... of Durham (Conn.) As written by herself ... . *Boston: Printed by Samuel Avery.* 1811. 12mo. W. 42616

LUCAS (S.) Charters of the Old English Colonies in America. With an Introduction and Notes. By Samuel Lucas ... . *London.* 1850. 8vo, pp. xi, 123. A. 42617

See also our Vol. III., No. 12162–3.

Lucas. National Revolutions. A Prize Essay, read in the Sheldonian Theatre, Oxford, June 4th, 1845. *London.* 1845. 8vo, pp. 52. 42618

Lucas. Secularia; or, Surveys of the Mainstream of History. By Samuel Lucas ... . *London: John Murray.* 1862. 8vo, pp. vi, (2), 410. B. 42619

The English Alternative of 1640-41, Old or New England? pp. 182-210; The New England Theocracy, pp. 211-249; On some Preparations of the American Revolt, pp. 250-267.

Luccock (J.) Notes on Rio de Janeiro, and the Southern Parts of Brazil; taken ... from 1808 to 1818. By John Luccock. *London: Samuel Leigh.* MDCCCXX. 4to, pp. xv, (1), 639, (1). 3 Maps. C., H. 42620

See Stevenson's "Voyages," *also* "M. Rev.," XCVI. 80. Some copies are dated 1822.

Luccock. Bemerkungen über Rio de Janeiro und Brasilien, während eines zehnjährigen Aufenthaltes, vom Jahre 1808 bis 1818. Aus dem Englischen von C. Fl. Leidenfrost. *Weimar.* 1821. 2 parts, 4to. 2 Maps. 42621

"Neue Bibliothek der wichtigsten Reisebeschreibungen," Vol. XXVIII.

Luce (J.) Narrative of a Passage from the Island of Cape Breton across the Atlantic Ocean, with other interesting Occurrences in a Letter to a Friend. By John Luce. *London: James Forsyth.* 1812. 8vo, pp. viii, 86. 42622

Luce (S. B.) ... Address delivered at the United States Naval Academy, by Captain Stephen B. Luce ... . [n. p. n. d.] 8vo, pp. 15. H. 42623

Also: Seamanship. For the Use of the United States Naval Academy. Second Edition. *Newport, R. I.* 1863. 8vo.

El Lucero de Tacubaya. Periódico politico, cientifico y literario. *Tacubaya.* 1844. 42624

Luciennes (V.) Le Gibet de John Brown; épitre à Victor Hugo. Par Victor Luciennes. *Paris: Castel.* 1861. 8vo.

Lucifer's Decree, After a Fray. Or, a Friendly Warning To all Persons, of whatsoever Station, Nation, or Qualification, In the City of Deceit, and Province of Pennsylvania. [*Philadelphia:*] *Printed in the Year,* 1765. 8vo, pp. 8. 42626

Lucio (M. R.) Alegacion en Derecho por el Rmo. Padre Predicador Fr. Melchior Rodrigues Lucio, sobre la observancia del

orden hierarchico de la Iglesia. *Mexico, Año de* 1713. Folio, pp. 16. 42627

Luckenbach (A.) Memoirs of ... Abraham Luckenbach, who labored for about 43 Years ... among the American Indians, and departed at Bethlehem, Penna., March 8th, 1854 ... [n. p. n. d.] 8vo, pp. 15. H. 42628

Luckenbach. Newinachke & Guttasch Pipinasiki Gischekhaseiki Elekpanni Wedenastki Untschi Mechoweki Machgundowo agani Bambi ... . *New Fairfield, River Thames, U. C.* 1836. 8vo. 42629

In the language of the Delaware Indians, by Abraham Luckenbach, of said tribe. An uncertain title from an auctioneer's catalogue.

Luckenbach. ... A Thanksgiving Discourse ... Rhinebeck, ... November 28, 1861, By Rev. W. H. Luckenbach, ... *Albany: J. Munsell.* 1861. 8vo, pp. 24. 42630

Luckey (J.) Life in Sing Sing State Prison, as seen in a Twelve Years' Chaplaincy. By John Luckey. *New York: N. Tibbals.* 1860. 12mo, pp. 376. Plate. BA., C. 42631

[Luckey.] Prison Sketches. By a Chaplain. ... Edited by D. P. Kidder. *New York: S. S. Union Meth. Ep. Ch.* 1849. 18mo, pp. 105. S. 42632

Luckey (S.) A Sermon ... at the Annual Election in New-Haven, May 5th, 1824. By the Rev. Samuel Luckey ... . *New-Haven.* 1824. 8vo, pp. 34. H. 42633

Luckock (B.) The Terrors of the Storm at Barbadoes, practically remembered in a Thanksgiving Sermon, for Preservation from the Hurricane which desolated Barbadoes. Preached at St. John's, Antigua. By Benjamin Luckock. *Walsall.* 1831. 8vo.

In Luctuosum excessum ... Virginis ac Dominae Johannae van Aarssen, ... denatae ... epicedium. *Ultrajecti ad Rhenum, Just. à Stuyvesand.* 1707. 4to. 42635

In Latin and Dutch, by H. Brink. A very scarce piece.

Lucubrations during a Short Recess, by a Member of Parliament. With a Reply to the same. *London.* 1782. 8vo, pp. 65.

Luculentissima quædã. *See* [Schöner (John)].

Lucy (R. de). La Martinique en 1820, ou le Republicanisme oligarchique desapointé. Réponse à la Martinique en 1819,

mémoire rédigée par M. Richard de Lucy. *Paris.* 1820. 8vo, pp. 16. 42637

[Ludd (Walter).] Speculi Orbis succintiss. sed | neq3 poenitenda neq3 | inelegans Declara- | tio, et Canon | ... Renato Siciliae Regi. &c. dicatum. [Colophon:] *Decla- | rationis in spe- | culũ orbis p̃ Gualthe- | rũ Ludd Canonicũ diui | Deodati Illustrissimi Rena- | ti Solymorum ac Siciliae regis | &c. secretarium dignissimũ | diligenter paratum | et industria Joan- | nis Grũnigeri | Argẽtin, im- | pressum | ffinis.* | [1507.] Folio, 4 leaves. 42638

For further particulars, relative to this rare piece, *see* Harrisse's "Bib. Am. Vet.," No. 49.

Ludecus (E.) Reise durch die Mexikanischen Provinzen Tumalipas, Cohahuila und Texas im Jahre 1834. In Briefen an seine Freunde von Eduard Ludecus. *Leipzig.* 1837. 8vo, pp. xx, 356. S. 42639

Luden (H.) *See* Bernhard (K.), Vol. II., No. 4953.

Lũder (A. F.) Statistische Beschreibung der Besitzungen der Holländer in Amerika. *Braunschweig: In der Schulbuchhandlung.* 1792. 8vo, pp. 230. 42640

[Luders (Ludwig).] Das Continental-System Völker-Seerecht; Neutralität zur See; Contrebande; England und der Continent; Colonien und Colonial-System. *Leipzig: Brockhaus.* 1812. 8vo. 42641

Ludewig (B.) Ludewig's Wahrer Bericht de dato Germantown den 20sten Febr. 174½. An seine liebe Teutsche, Und Wem es sonst nützlich zu wissen ist, wegen sein und seiner Brüder Zusammenhanges mit Pennsylvania, Zu Prüfung der Zeit und Umstände ausgefertiget; Nebst einem P. S. de dato Philadelphia den 5ten Martii; Und einigen Unsere Lehre überhaupt und dieses Schriftgen insunderheit Erläuternden Beylagen. *Phila. Gedruckt bey Benjamin Franklin.* [1742.] 4to, pp. 26. 42642

Ludewig (H. E.) The Literature of American Aboriginal Languages. By Hermann E. Ludewig. With Additions and Corrections By Professor Wm. W. Turner. Edited by Nicolas Trübner. *London: Trübner and Co.* MDCCCLVIII. 8vo, pp. viii, (1), ix-xxiv, 258. BA., S. 42643

Forms No. 1 of Trübner's "Bibliotheca Glottica." It is based on the American portion of Vater's "Litt. der Gram., Lexica und Wörtersammlungen aller Sprachen der Erde," *Berlin,* 1847, 8vo. The amiable and learned author died while the work was passing through the press. It not only describes all known printed books which came

under the author's notice, but recounts the unpublished works or manuscripts which relate to the subject. It describes the literature of over five hundred languages and dialects spoken by about nine hundred tribes. As a monument of linguistic industry it is scarcely excelled. Much credit is due Dr. Nicolas Trübner of London, and Professor Turner of Washington, under whose auspices it was completed.

Ludewig. The Literature of American Local History; a Bibliographical Essay, By Hermann E. Ludewig ... . *New York: The Author.* MDCCCXLVI. 8vo, pp. xx, 180. BA. 42644

Privately printed and scarce. The entire edition was given away by the author who only received from thirty gentlemen an acknowledgment of the gift, which circumstance accounts for the small number of the following:

Ludewig. The Literature of American Local History. By Hermann E. Ludewig. First Supplement; New York. *New York: R. Craighead.* 1848. 8vo, pp. 20. 42645

Extracted from the "Literary World" of Feb. 19, 1848. Only thirty copies printed. The contents of this supplement relate exclusively to New York.

Ludington (C. V. R.) Remarks ... on Canals and State Finances, in Convention, Sept. 12, 1867. *Albany.* 1867. 8vo.

Ludlam (R.) On the Sources and Benefits of Professional Earnestness ... Address delivered in Jacksonville, Nov. 2d, 1859, ... By R. Ludlam, M.D. ... *Chicago: Halsey & King.* 1859. 8vo, pp. 15. H. 42647

Ludlow (E. G.) Observations on The Lake Fevers and Other Diseases of The Genesee Country, in the State of New-York. By Edward G. Ludlow. ... *New York: J. Seymour, Printer.* 1823. 8vo, pp. viii, 5-49. B. 42648

Ludlow (F.) The Heart of the Continent: a Record of Travel across the Plains and in Oregon, with an Examination of the Mormon Principle. By Fitz Hugh Ludlow. ... *New York: Hurd and Houghton.* 1870. 8vo, pp. vi, 568. 8 Plates. H.

Ludlow (H. G.) ... A Thanksgiving Sermon, ... in ... New Haven, Nov. 19, 1840. By ... H. G. Ludlow. *New Haven: Printed by B. L. Hamlen.* 1840. 8vo, pp. 23. B. 42650

Ludlow (J.) An Address ... December 22, 1834. By Rev. John Ludlow, D.D. on ... his Inauguration as Provost of the University of Pennsylvania. ... *Philadelphia: Printed by Joseph R. A. Skerrett.* 1835. 8vo, pp. 31. B., P. 42651

Also: An Address ... at the Opening of the New Female Academy in Albany, May 12, 1834. ... *Albany: Printed by Packard and Van Benthuysen.* 1834. 8vo, pp. 24. Plate. B.

Ludlow (J. L.) Address at the Opening of the New Clinical Lecture Room of the Philadelphia Hospital. By Dr. J. L. Ludlow. *Philadelphia.* 1861. 8vo. 42652

Ludlow (J. M.) Sermon commemorative of National Events, Delivered in ... Albany, N. Y. April 23, 1865, By ... Rev. James M. Ludlow. *Albany: Weed, Parsons and Company, Printers.* 1865. 8vo, pp. 27. B. 42653

Ludlow (J. M.) President Lincoln Self-Pourtrayed. By John Malcolm Ludlow ... . *London: Alfred W. Bennett.* 1866. 16mo, pp. (6), 239, (1). Portrait. BA. 42654

Ludlow. A Quarter of a Century of Jamaica Legislation. By J. M. Ludlow ... . *London.* 1866. 8vo. 42655

Ludlow. A Sketch of the History of the United States, from Independence to Secession. By J. M. Ludlow ... . To which is added, The Struggle for Kansas. By Thomas Hughes ... . *Cambridge: Macmillan and Co.* 1862. Post 8vo, pp. xxii, (2), 404.

Also: American Slavery. ... *London: Ladies' ... Emancipation Society.* 1864. 8vo, pp. 30.—The Southern Minister, and his Slave Convert. ... *Manchester: A. Ireland & Co.* [n. d.] 8vo, pp. 4.

Ludlow (P.) Eulogy on the late John P. Curran Sampson, Esq., Counsellor at Law ... Nov. 3d, 1820 ... . By Peter Ludlow. *New York.* 1820. 8vo, pp. 24. 42657

Ludlow, *N. Y.* Proceedings at the Laying of the Corner-Stone ... of St. Stephen's College, Annandale, N. Y., on June 13, 1866. *Cambridge.* 1866. 8vo, pp. 46. 42658

Ludolff (H.) Allgemeine Schaubühne der Welt oder Beschreibung der vornehmsten Weltgeschichte, so sich in 17. Jahrh. (bis 1688) in allen Theilen des Erdkreisses nach und nach begeben. Fortgesetzt von Chr. Juncker. *Frankfurt a. M.* 1701-31. 5 vols., folio. 42659

"L'ouvrage traite aussi des évènements hors de l'Europe, spécialement dans les deux Indes." Title and note from T. O. Weigel's Catalogue.

Ludovico (A.) A Review of the Scandalous and Impertinent Beale Pamphlet. By A. Ludovico. *Philadelphia.* 1855. 8vo.

Ludvigh (S.) Das Schwert der Revolution. ... Reise von New-York nach Paris, Hamburg, Leipzig ... 1847-48. Von Samuel Ludvigh. ... [n. p.] 1848. 12mo, pp. 120. B. 42661

Ludwig (J. F.) Herrn Johann Friedrich Ludwigs Neueste Nachrichten von Surinam. Als Handbuch für Reisende und Beytrag zur Länderkunde, herausgegeben und mit Anmerkungen erläutert, von M. Philipp Friedrich Binder ... . *Jena: In der akademischen Buchhandlung.* 1789. 16mo, pp. xxxii, 260. Map.

Ludwig (M. R.) Ludwig Genealogy: Sketch of Joseph Ludwig, who was born in Germany in 1699, and his Wife and Family, who settled at Broad Bay, Waldoboro, Maine, 1753. By M. R. Ludwig ... . *Augusta.* 1866. 8vo, pp. 223. 42663

Luff (L.), *pseudon.* The Texan Captain and the Female Smuggler. A Mexican Tale of Land and Water. By Lorry Luff. *New-York: W. F. Burgess.* 1850. 8vo, pp. 96. C.

Luffman (J.) A Brief Account of the Island of Antigua, together with the Customs and Manners of its Inhabitants as well White as Black; As also, an accurate Statement of the Food, Clothing, Labour, and Punishment of Slaves. In Letters to a Friend, written in ... 1786, 1787, 1788. By John Luffman. *London: T. Cadell.* 1789. 12mo, pp. (6), 180. Map. A. + The Second Edition, Revised. *London: J. Luffman.* [1790.] 12mo, pp. (4), 180. Map. B. 42665

"Contains nothing very interesting."—*Monthly Review,* Jan. 1790.

Luffman. Kurze Beschreibung der Insel Antigua, und Nachrichten von den Sitten und Gebräuchen der dortigen Einwohner. *Leipzig.* 1790. 8vo. Map. 42666

Also: Elements of History and Chronology shewing the Origin of States and Revolution of Empires, from the Creation to 1804. ... *London.* [n. d.] 2 vols., 8vo. Map.

Lugo (B. de). Gramatica | En la Lengua | General del Nvevo | Reyno, Llamada | Mosca. | Compuesto por el Padre Fray Bernardo | de Lugo, Predicador General del Orden | de Predicadores, y Catedratico de | la dicha lengua, en el Conuento | del Rosario de la ciudad | de Santa Fe | *Año* 1619. | *En Madrid por Bernardino de Guzman.* Sm. 8vo. 42667

Collation: Title, and 25 leaves, containing Privilegio, 4 leaves; a blank leaf; Licencia y Aprovacion, 10 leaves; Errata, 1 leaf; Soneti, 6 leaves; Prologo al Letor, 2 leaves; Text, irregularly numbered (159 leaves).

Excessively rare. Priced by Trübner at £40. The Mozka, also called the Muyska, or the Chibcha, is the language of a nearly extinct Indian race, inhabiting the neighborhood of Santa Fé de Bogota. *See* Ternaux, No. 411.

Luis I. Magestuosa, Real Pyra, que en las Funeral Exequias del N. S. D. Luis Primero. *Mexico.* 1727. 4to. 42668

Luis de Valdivia. Arte y Grammatica general de la lengua que corre en todo el reyno de Chile, por el Padre Luis de Valdivia. *Lima.* 1606. 12mo. 42669

Title from Ternaux, No. 296.

Luis de Valdivia. Arte Grammatica, Vocabulario, Catecismo y Confessionario en Lengua Chilena y en las dos Lenguas Allentiac y Milcocayac, que son las mas generales de la Provincia de Cuio en el reyno de Chili, y que hablan los Indios Guarpes y otros. *Lima.* 1607. 8vo. 42670

Brunet, Vol. IV., p. 547, gives a similar title as the above after Antonio, Vol. II., p. 67, but dated *Lima,* 1608, 8vo. Ternaux, No. 305, also adds, "1608 in 8vo."

Luis de Valdivia. Relacion de la entrada del Presidente D. Alonso de Ribera desde Arauco a concluir pazes con los Chilenos. *Lima.* 1607. Folio. 42671

Title from Ternaux, No. 304.

Luke Darrell, the Chicago Newsboy. *Chicago: Tomlinson Brothers.* 1866. 16mo, pp. 377. C. 42672

Lulli. Refutacion contra la Memoria presentada por Don Miguel Cabrera Nevares sobre las Americas. Escrita por Lulli. *Madrid: Don Lucis Olarieta.* 1821. Sm. 4to, pp. 24. 42673

Lumber. *See our* No. 40460, and *add*, pp. 10.

The Lumiere. Containing a variety of Topographical Views in Europe and America. *New York.* 1831. 12mo. 42674

Lumnius (J. F.) De Extremo Dei Judicio et Indorum vocatione. *Antverpiæ.* 1567. 12mo. 42675

The author of this treatise considers the Indians of America to be the lost tribes, and infers from the prophecies of Isaiah their conversion by the Jesuits. It seems to have escaped the notice of collectors, for I cannot find a copy in the United States.

Lumpkin (J. H.) Speech of Hon. John H. Lumpkin ... on the Army Appropriation Bill. ... May 18, 1846. *Washington.* 1846. 8vo, pp. 8. H. 42676

Lumpkin (J. H.) An Address ... before the South-Carolina Institute ... the 19th November, 1850. By Jos. H. Lumpkin, ... *Charleston, S. C.: Walker & James.* 1851. 8vo, pp. 52. H.

Lumpkin [Wilson]. Speech of Mr. Lumpkin, of Georgia, on the Indian Territory Bill. Delivered in the Senate of the United States, April 30, 1838. *Washington.* 1838. 8vo, pp. 7.

[Lumsden (James).] American Memoranda, by A Mercantile Man, during a Short Tour in the Summer of 1843. For Private Circulation. *Glasgow: Bell & Bain.* MDCCCXLIV. 8vo, pp. (4), 60. 42679

Luna (Lino de Monte Carmelo). Memoria historica e biographica do Clero Pernambucano. *Recife: Typ. de F. C. de Lemos e Silva.* 1857. 8vo, pp. 234, (4). 42680

Luna (J. G. de). Discurso Juridico que Propugna e Informa el derecho que â la propriedad del Mayorasgo, que fundaron J. G. de Luna y Doña Beatriz Gomes Davila ... . *Mexico.* 1710. Fol.

Lunan (J.) An Abstract of the Laws of Jamaica relating to Slaves. ... With the Slave Law ... . By John Lunan. *Jamaica.* 1819. 4to, pp. (4), xv, 192, (8). H. 42682

Lunan. Hortus Jamaicensis, or a Botanical Description, (according to the Linnæan System) and an Account of the Virtues, &c. of its Indigenous Plants hitherto known, as also of the most useful Exotics. Compiled from the best authorities, and alphabetically arranged, ... By John Lunan. *Jamaica.* 1814. 2 vols., 4to, pp. viii, 538; 402; Errata (2). A. 42683

The most complete system of Jamaican botany extant.

Lunar Hermit, *pseudon.* A Letter to the Rev. Samuel Hopkins ... and the Rev. Moses Hemminway ... . By a Lunar Hermit ... . [n. p.] 1774. 8vo, pp. 16. BA., W. 42684

Lund (J. J.) Förste Missionair paa Grönland, Biskop Hans Egedes levnet. *Kjöbenhavn.* 1778. 4to. Portrait. 42685

Lund (O.) The Order of the Sons of Temperance; its Origin—its History—its Secrets—its Objects—its Designs—its Influence; comprising a full, authentic history of this Deservedly Popular Institution, from its Origin to the Present Time. ... By Orlando Lund ... . Ninth Edition ... . *Syracuse.* 1850. 12mo, pp. 48. S. + Tenth Edition ... . *Syracuse: Agan & Summers, Printers.* 1850. 12mo, pp. 48. 42686

Lund (P. W.) Blik paa Brasiliens Dyreverden för sidste Jordomvaeltning. *Kjöbenhavn.* 1841-49. 4to. Plates. 42687

Lund. Brasiliens uddöde Dyrskabning. *Kjöbenhavn.* 1842. 4to. 42688

Lund. Om Huler i Kalksteen i d. Indre af Brasilien, d. tildeels indeholde fossile Knokler. [*Kjöbenhavn.*] 1837. 4to, pp. 65. 5 Plates. 42689

Titles from one of B. Quaritch's catalogues.

Lund (T.) The Children of the Frontier. By Theodore Lund. *New York.* 1867. 16mo. c. 42690

Edited by Mrs. L. B. Gow.

[Lundie (*Mrs.* J. C.) America as I found it. ... *London: James Nisbet & Co.* 1852. 16mo, pp. xii, 380. c. + *New York: Carter & Brothers.* 1852. 16mo, pp. 440. 42691

Lundt (J. H.) Oplysninger i Anledn. af Planen til Bjergværksdrift paa Grönland. *Kjöbenhavn.* 1853. 8vo. 42692

Lundy (B.) The Life, Travels, and Opinions of Benjamin Lundy, including his Journeys to Texas and Mexico; ... *Philadelphia: William D. Parrish.* 1847. 12mo, pp. 5–316. c.

Lundy was the pioneer of anti-slavery reform in North America. *See also* Vol. vii., No. 26951.

Lundy (J. P.) Loyalty to Government. Sermon by Rev. J. P. Lundy, preached at ... Holmesburg, ... April 21, 1861. *Philadelphia: Lindsay & Blakiston.* [1861.] 16mo, pp. 14.

[Lundy.] Review of Bishop Hopkins' Bible View of Slavery. By a Presbyter of the Church in Philadelphia. [n. p. 1863.] 8vo, pp. 15. 42695

Lundy's Lane. An Account of the Battle of Lundy's Lane, fought in 1814 ... . *Drummondville.* 1853. 12mo, pp. 13. s.

Lunenburg. ... Catalogue of Books in the Lunenburg Town Library ... . *Fitchburg.* [1868.] 8vo, pp. 30. B. 42697

A Copy of the Valuation and Taxes ... for ... 1855 ... . *Fitchburg: Printed by E. & J. F. D. Garfield.* 1856. 8vo, pp. 46. Continued. B. 42698

By-Laws of the Lunenburg Farmers' Club. *Fitchburg: Printed by W. J. Merriam.* 1849. 12mo, pp. 7, (1). H. + By-Laws, Premiums, Rules and Regulations ... [*Ibid.*] 1850. 12mo, pp. 7, (1). H. 42699

Report of the School Committee ... for ... 1839. *Worcester: Spooner & Howland, Printers.* 1839. 8vo, pp. 13. Continued.

Lunet (P.) Du Droit politique en Amérique et en Suisse, ou Essais sur les rapports de la constitution fédérale des États-Unis et de quelques constitutions suisses ... . Première Partie. Par Paul Lunet. *Genève: Gruaz.* 1848. 8vo. 42701

All that was published.

Lung (Peter). *See* Swift (Z.)

Lunt (G.) The Age of Gold, and other Poems. By George Lunt. *Boston: William D. Ticknor.* MDCCCXLIII. 12mo, pp. iv, 160. H. 42702

Lunt. The Origin of the late War; traced from the beginning of the Constitution to the Revolt of the Southern States. By George Lunt. *New York: D. Appleton and Company.* 1866. 12mo, pp. xiv, 491. BA. 42703

Lunt. Poems. By George Lunt. ... *New York: Gould and Newman.* 1839. 12mo, pp. xviii, (1), 25–160. H. 42704

Includes "Verses against the Removal of the Remains of Washington from Mount Vernon," "Lament of the Cherokee," and "Mount Hope."

[Lunt.] Radicalism in Religion, Philosophy, and Social Life; ... *Boston: Little, Brown, and Company.* 1858. 16mo, pp. 79.

[Lunt.] ... Report of the Proceedings of Professed Spiritual Agents and Mediums, in the Presence of Professors Peirce, Agassiz ... and Others ... the 25th, 26th and 27th of June, 1857. ... Second Edition. *Boston.* 1859. 12mo, pp. 24. 42706

Lunt. Three Eras of New England and other Addresses, with Papers Critical and Biographical, By George Lunt. *Boston: Ticknor and Fields.* 1857. 12mo, pp. 264. BA. 42707

[Lunt.] The Union. [A Poem.] *Boston: Crocker and Brewster.* 1860. 16mo, pp. 48. B. 42708

Also: An Address, delivered before the Massachusetts Charitable Mechanic Association, September 26, 1844. ... *Boston: Crocker and Brewster.* 1844. 8vo, pp. (2), 24. — An Address ... before the Massachusetts Horticultural Society, on the Dedication of Horticultural Hall, May 15, 1845. ... *Boston: Printed by Dutton and Wentworth.* 1845. 8vo, pp. 26. — A Lecture ... before the Newburyport Lyceum, ... October 15, 1830. ... *Newburyport: Printed by W. & J. Gilman.* 1830. 8vo, pp. 16. — Lyric Poems, Sonnets and Miscellanies. ... *Boston: Ticknor, Reed, and Fields.* MDCCCLIV. 12mo, pp. iv, 108. — An Oration ... in Newburyport, on the Fifty-Seventh Anniversary of American Independence. ... *Newburyport: J. G. Tilton, & B. E. Hale.* 1833. 8vo, pp. 16. — Oration delivered before the Newburyport Artillery Company, July 4, 1836. ... *Newburyport.* 1836. 8vo, pp. 24. — Patriotism a Moral Duty. A Lecture ... before the Democratic Union Association of East Boston ... March 21, 1858. ... *Boston: Press of T. R. Marvin & Son.* 1858. 8vo, pp. 16. — Speech ... on the Amendment offered ... to the Lowell Rail-Road Bill. February 18, 1836. *Boston: Printed by J.*

T. Buckingham. 1836. 8vo, pp. 16. — Washington and our own Times. A Lecture in aid of the Public Library, Newburyport. ... Feb. 22, 1861, ... *Boston: Press of Crocket and Brewster.* 1861. 12mo, pp. 29. BA.

Lunt (W. Parsons). ... A Discourse ... in ... Quincy, ... January 8, 1854, on the ... Death of Hon. Thomas Greenleaf. By William P. Lunt ... . *Boston: Little, Brown, and Company.* M DCCC LIV. 8vo, pp. 34. B. 42709

Lunt. A Discourse delivered ... in ... Boston, before the Ancient and Honourable Artillery Company, June 7, 1847, ... By William P. Lunt ... . *Boston: Eastburn's Press.* 1847. 8vo, pp. 35, (1). H. 42710

Lunt. A Discourse delivered in Quincy, March 11, 1848, at the interment of John Quincy Adams ... . By William P. Lunt ... . *Boston: Dutton and Wentworth, State Printers.* 1848. 8vo, pp. 61. + *Boston: Charles C. Little and James Brown.* MDCCCXLVIII. 8vo, pp. 60. H. 42711

Lunt. A Discourse ... in Quincy, ... Thanksgiving Day, Nov. 25, 1852, Commemorative of Daniel Webster. By William P. Lunt ... . *Boston: Little, Brown and Company.* 1852. 8vo, pp. 58. B. 42712

Lunt. Every Thing Beautiful in his Time: A Discourse delivered in ... Quincy, ... Sept. 15, 1850, By William P. Lunt, ... *Boston: Printed by John Wilson.* 1850. 8vo, pp. 29. B.

Pages 27–29 contain a biographical sketch of Eliza Susan Morton Quincy.

Lunt. Two Discourses ... September 29, 1839, on ... the Two Hundredth Anniversary of the ... First Congregational Church, Quincy ... . By William P. Lunt. *Boston: James Munroe and Company.* MDCCCXL. 8vo, pp. 147. BA. 42714

Also: Address before the Citizens and Schools of Quincy, Mass., July 4, 1838. ... *Quincy.* 1838. 8vo. — A Discourse delivered in ... Quincy, March 7, 1843, at the Funeral of Rev. Peter Whitney, ... *Quincy: John A. Green, Printer.* 1843. 8vo, pp. 29. — ... A Discourse ... at the Installation of Rev. George Whitney ... [at] Jamaica Plain, February 10, 1836. ... *Boston: Printed by D. Clapp, Jr.* 1836. 8vo, pp. 40. — ... A Discourse ... October 21st ... in Quincy ... . *Boston: Dutton and Wentworth, Printers.* 1849. 8vo, pp. 16. — ... A Discourse on the Twentieth Anniversary of his Installation, delivered ... in Quincy ... June 3, 1855. ... *Boston: Little, Brown and Company.* 1855. 8vo, pp. 32. — The Divine Right of Government: a Discourse ... in Quincy ... on the ... Annual State Fast, April 10, 1851 ... . *Boston: Wm. Crosby and H. P. Nichols.* 1851. 8vo, pp. 20. — Moral Education. An Address ... before the Teachers and Pupils of the Schools ... of ... Quincy, July 4, 1838. ... *Quincy: John A. Green.* 1838. 8vo, pp. 26. — ... A Sermon ... at the Ordination of Rev. Harrison G. O. Phipps, at Cohasset, Nov. 18, 1835. ... *Hingham: Press of J. Farmer.* 1836. 8vo, pp. 32. — The Union of the Human Race. A Lecture ... before the Quincy Lyceum ... February 7, 1850. ... *Boston: Ticknor, Reed, and Fields.* M DCCC L. 8vo, pp. 37. B.

Luque (Eduardo Malo de). *See* [Raynal (*l'Abbé*)].

Lurieu (G. de) *et* Romand (H.) Études sur les Colonies agricoles de mendiants, jeunes détenus, orphelins et enfants trouvés. ... *Paris: Dusacq.* 1851. 8vo. s. 42715

Lurting (T.) The Fighting Sailor Turned Peaceable Christian. Manifested in the Convincement and Conversion of Thomas Lurting, with a Short Relation of Many Great Dangers and Wonderful Deliverances he met withal. First written for private satisfaction, and now Published for General Service. *London: Printed, and Re-printed by Samuel Keimer* [*Philadelphia*]. 1725. 12mo, pp. 47. 42716

An extremely rare imprint.

Lury (J. E.) A Brief Sketch of the Life of William Penn. By John Elton Lury. *London.* 1853. 8vo, pp. 32. 42717

Lusher (R. L.) Recollections of the Outlines of a Sermon on the Death of Mrs. Waterman. By Rev. R. L. Lusher. *Halifax.* 1827. 8vo, pp. 8. 42718

Lushington (S. R.) The Life and Services of General Lord Harris ... during his Campaigns in America, the West Indies, and India. By the Right Hon. S. R. Lushington ... . *London: John W. Parker.* M. DCCC. XL. 8vo, pp. xv, (1), 551. + Second Edition, revised. [*Ibid.*] M DCCC XLV. Post 8vo, pp. xxiv, 387.

Capt. Harris was wounded at Bunker Hill, and served throughout the American war, respecting which his life includes many curious details, now first published.

Lushington (W.) The Interests of Agriculture and Commerce, inseparable. By William Lushington, Esq. Agent for the Island of Grenada. *London: Edmund Lloyd.* 1808. 8vo, pp. (4), 72. B. 42720

See "M. Rev.," New Series, LVIII. 87, *and* "Reply."

Lusignan (A.) L'Ecole Militaire de Québec. Par Alphonse Lusignan. *Montréal.* 1865. 8vo. 42721

Lusk (W.) A Discourse ... at Williamsburgh, January 24, 1836. By Rev. William Lusk. ... Prefixed is an Historical Sketch of that Church. ... *Northampton: John Metcalf, Printer.* 1836. 8vo, pp. 32. BA. 42722

Lusk (W.) Register and Western Calendar, for 1818, by William Lusk. No. 2. *Columbus.* [n. d.] 12mo. c. 42723

Lussága (J. Lucas de). Representacion que a nombre de la Minería de esta Nueva España. *Mexico.* 1774. Folio. 42724

Lussan (R. de). *See* Raveneau de Lussan.

Lustspiel. Die Ankunft der Deutschen aus Amerika, ein Lustspiel in einem Aufzuge ... . *Hof.* 1784. 12mo, pp. 55.

"This stupid play is built on the German mercenary soldiers in America (probably the Hessians), who were sold to the English by their Princes, and sent off like so many sheep to the slaughter, but who escaped that fate by surrendering with Burgoyne and his Army. Some lived to die in America, but some returned home to be laughed at." —Stevens.

Luther (M.) Lutheri Catechismus Öfwersatt på American-Virginiste Språket. *Stockholm, Tryckt vthi thet af Kongl. May*^{tt}. *privileg. Burchardi Tryckeri, af J. J. Genath f. Anno* MDCXCVI. 24mo, Engraved Title, pp. (14), 160. 42726

This translation of Luther's Catechism into the language of the Virginia (or more correctly the Delaware) Indians was made by Thomas Campanius. "Leclerc, No. 918, erroneously calls Thomas Campanius the author; he describes his copy as 'Exempl. au chiffre et aux armes de Charles xi,' but in Acrelius' work on New-Sweden, p. 423, we find it noticed, that all the copies were bound in this manner. Acrelius also remarks that the book was printed at the royal expense expressly for the conversion of the American heathen, and that five hundred copies were sent to New-Sweden."—Muller.

Luther. Catechismus-Mingnek D. M. Lutherim Aglega Innusuinnut Innungnullo Gum Okausianik illisimangangitout, suna operekullugo, Kannorlo innukullugit Tokorsub Kingornane Killangmut pekkullugit. *Kiöbenhavn ... G. Friderich Kisel.* 1756. 8vo, pp. 160. 42727

This is Luther's Catechism in Esquimaux by Paul Egede.

Luther. Der Psalter des Königs und Propheten Davids ... von D. Martin Luther ... . *Philadelphia.* 1762. 12mo, pp. 239, 9. + *Halle.* 1825. 8vo, pp. 140. H. 42728

Luther *vs.* Borden. Supreme Court of the United States, No. 124. Martin Luther, Plaintiff in error, *vs.* Luther M. Borden et al., in error to the Circuit Court of the United States for the District of Rhode Island. *Washington: J. & G. S. Gideon.* [1844.] 8vo, pp. 149. 42729

Concerning this *see* Bartlett's "Bibliography of Rhode Island."

Luther (S.) An Address on the Right of Free Suffrage, ... By Seth Luther. *Providence: Printed by S. R. Weeden.* 1833. 8vo, pp. 25, xvi. 42730

Partly in reply to Benjamin Hazard's report.

Luther. An Address to the Working-Men of New-England, on the State of Education ... in Europe and America. ... and on the Safety of Our Republic. By Seth Luther. ... *Boston: The Author.* 1832. 8vo, pp. 39. BA. 42731

For a Review *see* [Bigelow (Josiah)], Vol. II., No. 5318. Also: An Address ... before the Union Association of Working Men, in ... Charlestown, Mass., January 30, 1834. ... *Boston: The Author.* 1834. 8vo, pp. 43.

Luther, *Jr.* Right and Wrong of the Boston Reformers; showing them to be a bad Remedy. *New England: Published by the Author.* 1841. 18mo, pp. 42. 42732

The Lutheran Almanac for ... 1852–1855. ... *Baltimore.* 1855. 12mo. Continued. 42733

The Lutheran Home Journal June [1856]. *Philadelphia: Lindsay & Blakiston.* [1856.] 8vo. H. 42734

The Lutheran Pulpit, and Monthly Religious Magazine. *Albany: J. Munsell.* 1837. 8vo. Continued. s. 42735

Edited by Charles A. Smith.

Der Lutherische Calender. *Allentown, Pa.* 1857. 8vo. Cont'd.

Lutherland (T.) Blood Will Out; or an Example of Justice in the Tryal, Condemnation, Confession, and Execution of Thomas Lutherland, who barbarously murthered John Clark of Philadelphia, and was executed at Salem, in West Jarsey, 23rd Feb. 169½. *Philadelphia: W. Bradford.* 1692. 4to. 42737

Title from J. C. Hotten's Catalogue. One of the rarest pieces of its kind. Perhaps the name should be Sutherland.

Lutké (Frederic). Puteschestvie vokrug svjeta. *St. Petersburg.* 1834–1836. 3 vols., 8vo. 42738

I have not seen this Russian original; the following is a translation:

Lutké. Voyage autour du Monde, exécuté par ordre de Sa Majesté l'Empereur Nicolas Ier sur la corvette la Seniavine dans les Années 1826, 1827, 1828 et 1829, par Frederic Lutké. Partie historique; avec un Atlas lithographié d'après les dessins originaux d'Alexandre Postels ... et du Baron Kittlitz; traduit du Russe sur le MS. original, sous les yeux de l'auteur par le Conseiller de l'Etat F. Boyé. *Paris: Didot.* [1835–36.] 3 vols., 8vo, pp. 440; 394; 352, and Atlas in folio, pp. (2), 58. 3 Maps and 52 Plates. c.

"Contenant les travaux de MM. les Naturalistes."—*J. Lit.*, 1836, No. 5760. Printed in Belgium. Contains fifty-two beautiful plates, from drawings by Baron Kittlitz, including views of the Caroline Isles, discovered by the expedition, the natives, landscape plates of the tropical vegetation and forest scenery, portraits of savages, particularly on the Northwest coast of America, at Sitka, etc.

Lütken (Chr. F.) Oversigt ov. Grönlands Echinodermata. *Kjöbenhavn.* 1857. 8vo. Map. 42740

Lutyens (G. N.) Etwas über den gegenwärtigen Zustand der Auswanderungen und Ansiedlungen im Staate von Pennsylvanien ... . Von Gotthilff Nicolas Lutyens. *Hamburg: Bey Carl Ernst Bohn.* 1796. 12mo, pp. 23. H. 42741

Lützenkirchen (W.) West- vnnd Ost Indischer Lustgart: das ist Eygentliche Erzehlung, wann vnd von wem die Newe Welt erfunden ... . *Cöllen: Gedruckt ... bey Wilhelm Lützenkirchen.* MDCXVIII. 8vo, pp. (8), 436, 236. H. 42742

Luyts (J.) Joannis Luyts, Philosophiæ Professoris, Introductio ad Geographiam Novam & Veterem; in qua necessaria hujus Scientiæ Prolegomena; intermixto usu Globi Terrestris, necnon Oceani & Regionum constitutio perspicuo ordine pertractantur. Adjiciuntur suis locis Oceani, Terræ, & cujusq; Regionis Tabulæ, item Chartæ LXV Sansonis, inter quas quædam hac forma ante inedita. *Trajecti ad Rhenum ex officina Francisci Halma, Acad Typog.* M DC XCII. 4to, pp. 764. 65 Maps.

Part v. relates to America, and contains Sanson's maps of America, Canada, Florida, Guatemala, Guiana, Mexico, Paraguay, Peru, Carribbee Islands, Chili, Brasil, etc.

Luyts. General and Particular Description of America, from the Latin, improved with Particular Accounts of the English Plantations, and Maps by H. Moll. [*London.* n. d.] 4to.

Luz (José de la). Instituto Cubano. Informe presentado a la Real Junta de Fomento de Agricultura y Comercio de esta isla, en sesion de 11 de Diciembre de 1833. *Habana.* 1834. Folio. c. 42745

[Luzac (E.)] Het waare daglicht van het Politieek Systema der regeering van Amsterdam. *Middelburg.* [1781.] 8vo, pp. 92. 42746

This true light of the political system of the government of Amsterdam, relates in part to the American Colonies.

Luzac. Hollands rijkdom. *See* Vol. viii., No. 32521.

[Luzac.] Regtsgeleerde Memorie, waar in ... de gegrondheid der klagten van den Koning van Groot-Brittannien, over de geheime correspondentie tusschen Amsterdam en de amerikaansche colonien, en wederlegging van: Het politicq systema van de regeering van Amsterdam. [n. p.] 1781. 8vo. 42747

[Luzac.] Mémoire juridique ou l'on examine ... jusqu'à quel point sont fondé les plaintes du Roi de la Grande Bretagne, sur la secrète correspondance entre la ville d'Amsterdam et les colonies Anglaises dans l'Amérique, et ou l'on refute ... la brochure: Système politique de la régence d'Amsterdam. [n. p.] 1781. 8vo, pp. 48. 42748

A translation of the preceding. The following is a refutation:

[Luzac.] Breedvoerige Verhandeling waar in Het Politicq Systema onderzocht en de Rechtsgeleerde Memorie wederlegt worden door Alaethophilus. *Rotterdam.* 1781. 8vo, pp. 93.

Luzarche (Victor). Catalogue of the Valuable and Extensive Library, consisting in upwards of 6,000 lots of ... Books and Manuscripts, Travels, Works relating to America, ... sold by Auction in Paris, 1869, ... Parts II–III. *Paris.* 1869. 8vo, pp. (2), 304. c. 42750

Luzerne (César Henri, *Comte* de la). Mémoire (sur les affaires de St. Domingue) au Comité des Rapports de l'Assemblée Nationale. 18 Juin, 1790. [n. p. 1790.] 8vo. 42751

Relates to the revolution in Hayti.

Luzerne. Réponse Provisoire aux brillans extraits du Mémoire justificatif que M. de la Luzerne, Ministre de la Marine, a fait inserer dans plusieurs journaux. 7 Juillet, 1790. *Paris.* [1790.] 8vo, pp. 4. 42752

Luzerne. Supplément a la denonciation de M. de la Luzerne, Ministre de la Marine et des Colonies, ou Réponse par des pieces justificatives, sans réplique, au pretendu Mémoire justificatif qu'il a publié en Juin 1790. Par les Députés de Saint-Domingue à l'Assemblée Nationale. *Paris.* [1790.] 8vo, pp. 31. 42753

Lyceum of Natural History. *See* New York City.

Lycoming Coal Company. Brief Description of the Property belonging to the Lycoming Coal Co., with some general remarks on the subject of the Coal and Iron Business. *Poughkeepsie.* 1828. 8vo, pp. 8. 42754

Lycurgus, *pseudon.* War, or no War? Introduced with a View of the Causes of our National Decline and Present Embarrassments. ... By Lycurgus. *New-York: E. Sargeant.* 1807. 8vo, pp. 65. BA. 42755

LYDE (Augustus Foster). Buds of Spring. Poetical Remains, with Addenda. *Boston.* 1838. 12mo. 42756

[LYDIUS (Jac.)] Historie der beroerten van Engelandt, aengaende de veelderley secten, die aldaer in de kercke Jesu Christi zijn ontstaen. *Dordrecht: Hendr. van Esch.* 1647. Sm. 8vo.

A rare and interesting volume, containing many particulars on the Protestant Sects in America, including their dissensions at Boston, etc.

LYDIUS (J. H.) Some Reflections on the Disputes between New York, New Hampshire, and Col. John Henry Lydius of Albany, etc. *New Haven.* 1764. 8vo. N. 42758

LYELL (C.) The Geological Evidences of the Antiquity of Man ... . By Sir Charles Lyell, F.R.S. ... *London: John Murray.* 1863. 8vo, pp. xii, 420. Plate. + Second Edition. [*Ibid.*] 8vo, pp. xvi, 528. Plate. + *Philadelphia: George W. Childs.* 1863. 8vo, pp. x, 518. 2 Plates. H. 42759

LYELL. New York Industrial Exhibition. Special Report of Sir Charles Lyell. ... *London: Thomas Harrison.* 1854. 8vo, pp. (2), iii, 103. B. 42760

LYELL. Travels in North America in 1841–42; with Geological Observations on The United States, Canada, and Nova-Scotia. By Charles Lyell, Esq., F.R.S. ... *London: John Murray.* 1845. 2 vols., post 8vo, pp. xiii, (2), 316; viii, 272. Plates and Maps. + *New-York: Wiley and Putnam.* 1845. 2 vols., 12mo, pp. vi, vii, vi, 251; (2), 221. Plate. + *New York: John Wiley.* 1852. 2 vols., 12mo, pp. 251; vi, 197. + *New York: Wiley & Halsted.* 1856. 2 vols., 12mo, pp. vii, 251; vi, 197.

Interesting, valuable, and scientific.

LYELL. Reisen in Nord-Amerika, mit Beobachtungen über die geognostischen Verhältnisse der Vereinigten Staaten von Canada und Neu-Schottland. Deutsch von E. Th. Wolff. *Halle.* 1846. 12mo. 2 Maps, 9 Plates. 42762

LYELL. A Second Visit to the United States of North America. By Sir Charles Lyell, F.R.S. ... *London: John Murray.* 1849. 2 vols., post 8vo, pp. xii, 368; xii, 385, (1). H. + *New York: Harper & Brothers.* 1849. 2 vols., 8vo, pp. 273; 287. + Second Edition. *London: John Murray.* 1850. 2 vols., post 8vo, pp. xii, 368; xii, 385, (1). 42763

LYELL. Zweite Reise nach den Vereinigten Staaten von Nordamerika. Deutsch von E. Dieffenbach. *Braunschweig.* 1851. 2 vols., 8vo. 42764

Also: Lectures on Geology, ... Second Edition, ... With an Introduction. To which is added a Lecture on the different Races of Men, by J. Augustine Smith. Reported by H. J. Raymond. *New York.* 1843. 8vo, pp. 55. — ... Eight Lectures on Geology ... in ... New-York ... . *New-York: Greeley & McElrath.* 1842. 8vo, pp. 56. — Principles of Geology ... . The Seventh Edition. *Boston: Hilliard, Gray & Co.* 1842. 3 vols., 12mo, pp. xxi, (1), 442; xi, 479; xii, 476. Maps and Plates. + New and entirely Revised Edition. *New York: D. Appleton & Co.* 1862 8vo, pp. 834. Plates and Maps. *See* "Ed. Rev.," XCII. 339; "Fraser's Mag.," XLI. 563; "North Amer. Rev.," LXI. 498; LXIX. 325; "North British Rev.," XIV. 541; "Quart. Rev.," LXXXV. 183.

LYELL (T.) A Sermon ... for the Benefit of the New-York Bible and Common Prayer Book Society. By the Rev. Thomas Lyell, A.M. ... *New-York: Printed by T. and J. Swords.* 1818. 8vo, pp. 27. H. 42765

LYFORD (S. C.) An Address ... before the Strafford Agricultural Society, October 20, 1824, at Wolfborough. By Stephen C. Lyford. *Concord: Printed by Jacob B. Moore.* 1825. 8vo, pp. 16. H. 42766

LYFORD (W. G.) The Western Address Directory; ... Pittsburgh, (Pa.) Wheeling, (Va.) Zanesville, (O.) Portsmouth, Dayton, Cincinnati, (O.) Madison, (Ind.) Louisville, (K.) St. Louis, (Mo.), together with Historical, Topographical, and Statistical Sketches, for the year 1837, of the principal Cities and Towns in the Mississippi Valley. ... By William G. Lyford. *Baltimore: Printed by Jos. Robinson.* 1837. 12mo, pp. 468. C.

See also Baltimore, Vol. I., No. 2999, *and* "N. A. Rev.," January, 1838. Also: Mercantile Exchange Tables, and Pocket Book Companion ... . *New-York: Prior & Dunning.* 1816. 24mo, pp. 80. H.

LYGON (William), *1st Earl Beauchamp.* A Letter to Lord Beauchamp, on his Letter to the Belfast Volunteers. [n. p.] 1783. 8vo. S. 42768

Contains some allusions to the American Revolution.

LYKINS (J.) The Gospel according to Saint Matthew. Translated into the Shawannoe Language, by Johnston Lykins, aided ... by James Andrew Chute. *Shawannoe Baptist Mission Press.* 1842. 16mo, pp. 116. 42769

LYKINS. The Gospel According to St. Matthew, and The Acts of the Apostles translated into the Putawatomie Language. By Johnston Lykins. *Louisville, Ky.* 1844. 18mo. 42770

LYKINS. Siwinowe Eawekitake. Liekens Wastote. ... [Shawnee Speller and Reader, by Johnston Lykins.] *Shawannoe Mission: J. Meeker, Printer.* 1834. 18mo, pp. 54. BA. 42771

Also: Siwinowe Eawekitake. Liekens Wastote. ... By J. G. Pratt. *Shawannoe Mission: J. Meeker, Printer.* 1838. 18mo, pp. 24. BA.

LYLE (W. W.) Lights and Shadows of Army Life: or, Pen Pictures from the Battle Field, the Camp, and the Hospital. By Rev. W. W. Lyle, A.M. ... *Cincinnati: R. W. Carroll & Co.* 1865. 12mo, pp. 403. + Second Edition. [*Ibid.*] 12mo, pp. xii, 9–403. BA. 42772

LYLES (James H.) Official Railroad Manual of the Railroads of North America, for 1869–70. By J. H. Lyles. *New York: Thitchener & Gastaeter, Printers.* 1869. 8vo, pp. 471, clxxvi. Continued. 42773

LYMAN (A.) ... A Sermon, ... in Northyarmouth, (Maine,) at the Installation of the Reverend John Dutton, October 1, 1806, ... By Asa Lyman, A.M. ... *Portland.* 1807. 8vo, pp. 20.

LYMAN (A. S.) Historical Chart, Containing the Prominent Events of the Civil, Religious and Literary History of the World. By Azel S. Lyman. *Philadelphia: Doughty & Co.* 1845. Folio.

Another edition is [n. p. n. d.], folio, in which the title varies from this.

LYMAN (B. S.) Report on the Painter Tract, near Connellsville, Pa. ... By Benjamin Smith Lyman ... . *Philadelphia: Sherman & Co., Printers.* [n. d.] 8vo, pp. 13. Map. H. 42776

LYMAN (C. S.) ... An Address delivered at ... the Sheffield Scientific School of Yale College. July 15th, 1867. By Rev. C. S. Lyman, M.A. ... *New Haven: Printed by Tuttle, Morehouse & Taylor.* 1867. 8vo, pp. 30. H. 42777

[LYMAN (Caleb), *and others.*] A Vindication of the New-North-Church, From several Falshoods [*sic*] ... in ... Account of the Reasons [against] Mr. Peter Thacher's Ordination ... . By several of the Members of that Church. *Boston: D. Henchman.* 1720. 8vo, pp. (2), 14. BA. 42778

LYMAN (E.) A Sermon delivered on the Day of General Election ... Oct. 13, 1814, before the ... Legislature of Vermont. By Eliphalet Lyman. *Montpelier.* 1814. 8vo. 42779

LYMAN. Two Discourses ... at Woodstock, Nov. 10 and Dec. 1, 1793. With an Appendix. *Norwich.* 1794. 8vo. W.

LYMAN (G. C.) A Sermon preached ... before ... the ... Council and ... House of Representatives of ... Vermont, on the day of the Anniversary Election, Oct. 10, 1782. By Gershom C. Lyman. *Windsor.* 1784. 4to. 42781

[LYMAN (G. T.)] Copper Mines of the Pacific Coast of the United States. *New York: William H. Arthur ... Printer.* 1866. 8vo, pp. 11. H. 42782

LYMAN (H.) The Martyr of Sumatra: A Memoir of Henry Lyman. ... *New York: Robert Carter & Brothers.* 1856. 12mo, pp. 437. Plate. H. 42783

LYMAN (H.) An Address ... before the Temperance Society of Franklinville ... September, 1830. By Huntington Lyman. *New York: Henry C. Sleight.* 1830. 8vo, pp. 15. H. 42784

LYMAN (J. H.) An Address, ... before the New Hampshire, Franklin and Hampden Agricultural Society, at their Annual Meeting in Northampton, Oct. 25, 1820. By J. H. Lyman. *Northampton: Printed by Thomas W. Shepard & Co.* 1820. 8vo, pp. 31. BA., N. 42785

LYMAN (J.) Funeral Oration in Memory of Mr. Jonathan Lyman, at Hatfield, June 18, 1766. *New Haven.* 1767. 4to.

LYMAN (J.) A Sermon ... before ... The Honourable the Council ... Senate, and House ... Of ... Massachusetts, May 30, 1787, Being the Day of General Election. By Rev. Joseph Lyman, ... in Hatfield. *Boston: Printed by Adams and Nourse.* [1787.] 8vo, pp. 61. B., BA. 42787

LYMAN. ... A Sermon, ... Hatfield, November 7th, A.D. 1793. Being the Day of Public Thanksgiving. By Joseph Lyman, A.M. ... *Northampton: Printed by William Butler.* M,DCC,-XCIV. 8vo, pp. 22. BA. 42788

LYMAN. A Sermon, ... at Northampton, Nov. 11, 1819, at the Interment of the Hon. Caleb Strong, L.L.D. ... By Joseph Lyman, D.D. ... *Northampton: Printed by Thomas W. Shepard and Co.* 1819. 8vo, pp. 23. BA. 42789

LYMAN. A Sermon, ... at Hatfield, October, 20, 1807. At the Opening of Hatfield Bridge. By Joseph Lyman, D.D. ... *Northampton: Printed by William Butler.* 1807. 8vo, pp. 16. B.

LYMAN. The Two Olive-Trees: ... a Sermon ... at Hatfield, Nov. 4, 1804. Being the Day preceding the choice of

Electors in Massachusetts. Also ... a Thanksgiving Sermon ... Nov. 29, 1804. By Joseph Lyman, D.D. ... *Northampton: Printed by William Butler.* 1804. 8vo, pp. 29. BA., S. 42791

Also: Sermon at the Ordination of Eliphalet Lyman. Woodstock, Sept. 2, 1779. ... [n. p. n. d.] 8vo. — ... A Sermon, ... at the Introduction of the Reverend William Graves, To the ... Ministry, in ... North-Woodstock, August 31, 1791. ... *Northampton: Printed by William Butler.* 1791. 8vo, pp. 26. — ... A Sermon, ... at the Introduction of the Reverend Jonathan Grout ... at Hawley, October 23d. 1793. ... *Northampton: Printed by William Butler.* M, DCC, XCIII. 8vo, pp. 22. — ... Sermon ... Funeral of John Hubbard, Nov. 28, 1794. ... *Northampton.* 1795. 8vo. — ... A Sermon ... at Deerfield,—Jan. 1, A.D. 1799, at the Opening of the Academy ... . *Greenfield: Printed ... by Francis Barker.* M,DCC,XCIX. 8vo, pp. 19. — A Sermon ... at Northampton, before an Ecclesiastical Convention ... for ... forming a Missionary Society, for the Propagation of the Gospel ... September, A.D. 1801. ... *Northampton: Printed by William Butler.* 1801. 8vo, pp. 24. — A Sermon, at the Ordination of the Rev. Henry Lord ... in Williamsburgh; June 20, 1804. ... *Northampton: Printed by Thomas M. Pomroy.* 1804. 8vo, pp. 19. — A Sermon, preached before the Convention of the Clergy of Massachusetts, in Boston, May 29, 1806. ... *Boston: Printed by David Carlisle.* 1806. 8vo, pp. 24. — A Sermon ... in Halifax, (Vt.) Sept. 17, 1806. At the Installation of Reverend Thomas H. Wood ... . *Northampton: Printed by William Butler.* 1807. 8vo, pp. 23. BA. — A Sermon, at the Installation of Rev. Dan Huntington ... in Middletown. ... *Middletown: Printed by T. Dunning.* 1809. 8vo, pp. 24. — A Sermon, ... in Hadley, March 12, ... 1811. At the Interment of Rev. Samuel Hopkins, D.D. ... *Northampton: William Butler, Printer.* 1811. 8vo, pp. 16. — Sermon ... at Charlestown, Nov. 3, 1811 ... . *Boston.* 1811. 8vo. — A Sermon preached at Boston, before the American Board of Commissioners for Foreign Missions ... Sept. 16, 1819. ... *Boston: Samuel T. Armstrong.* 1819. 8vo, pp. 19. H. — ... A Sermon ... before the Ministers of the Central Association in the County of Hampshire ... May 1, 1821. ... *Northampton: Printed by Thomas W. Shepard and Co.* 1821. 8vo, pp. 19. — A Settled Ministry ... A Sermon ... at New-Braintree, October 26, A.D. 1796. At the Installation of the Rev. John Fiske ... . *Northampton: Printed by William Butler.* M,DCC,XCVII. 8vo, pp. 30. — Strictures upon the Comments of Rev. Samuel Willard, ... on a Pamphlet, entitled, A Counterpart, &c. ... *Greenfield: Printed by Denis and Phelps.* 1814. 12mo, pp. 35. — Thanksgiving Sermon at Hatfield, Dec. 15, 1774. ... *Boston.* 1775. 8vo, pp. 32.

LYMAN (J. B.) Cotton Culture. By Joseph B. Lyman. With an Additional Chapter on Cotton Seed and its Uses. By J. R. Sypher. *New York.* 1868. 12mo, pp. 190. Map.

LYMAN (P. Williston). History of Easthampton: its Settlement and Growth; ... with a Genealogical Record of its Original Families. By Payson W. Lyman. *Northampton: Trumbull & Gere.* 1866. 8vo, pp. (2), 192, 2. BA. 42793

LYMAN (R.) Genealogical Chart of the Richard Lyman Family, 1580–1869. [n. p. n. d.] Rl. 8vo. S. 42794

See also Dickinson (J. T.), Vol. V., No. 20035.

LYMAN (S. P.) Life and Times of Daniel Webster, including most of his great Speeches, Letters from Marshfield ... . By Gen. S. P. Lyman. *Philadelphia.* 1852. 2 vols., 12mo.

Reprinted as: "Life and Memorials of Daniel Webster." ... *New-York: D. Appleton & Company.* 1853. 2 vols., 16mo, pp. (2), 261; 300. B. + [*Ibid.*] 1855. It also appeared in the "New York Times." Also: Speech ... at Ithaca, July 11, 1839, on the N. Y. and Erie R. R. ... *New York.* 1839. 8vo.

[LYMAN (Theodore).] The Diplomacy of the United States. Being an Account of the Foreign Relations of the Country, from the First Treaty with France, in 1778, to the Treaty of Ghent, in 1814, with Great Britain. *Boston: Wells and Lilly.* 1826. 8vo, pp. xii, 379, (2). B. 42796

LYMAN. The Diplomacy of the United States. Being an Account of The Foreign Relations of the Country, From the First Treaty with France, in 1778, to the Present Time. Second Edition—With Additions. By Theodore Lyman, Jr. *Boston: Wells and Lilly.* 1828. 2 vols., 8vo, pp. xii, 470; xii, 517. BA.

See "N. A. Rev.," XXIV. 92.

[LYMAN.] Free Negroes and Mulattoes. ... [*Boston: True & Green, Printers.* n. d.] 8vo, pp. 16. H. 42798

LYMAN. Memoir of Theodore Lyman. [*Hartford.* 1861.] 8vo, pp. 14. Portrait. B. 42799

From Barnard's "American Journal of Education," for March, 1861.

LYMAN. An Oration delivered at ... Boston, on the Anniversary of American Independence, in ... 1820. By Theodore Lyman, Jun. *Boston: Printed by J. T. Buckingham.* [1820.] 8vo, pp. 20. H. 42800

LYMAN. Report of a Trial in the Supreme ... Court, ... at Boston, Dec. 16 and 17, 1828, of Theodore Lyman, Jr., for an Alleged Libel on the Hon. Daniel Webster. Taken in Short Hand by John W. Whitman. *Boston.* 1828. 12mo, pp. 76.

[LYMAN.] A Short Account of the Hartford Convention, ... [with a] Copy of the Secret Journal of that Body. *Boston: O. Everett.* 1823. 8vo, pp. 36. BA. 42802

LYMAN (T.) Illustrated Catalogue of the Museum of Comparative Zoology at Harvard College. ... No. I. Ophiuridæ and Astrophytidæ. By Theodore Lyman. *Cambridge.* 1864. Rl. 8vo, pp. viii, 200. 2 colored Plates. 42803

LYMAN (T.) Papers relating to the Garrison Mob. Edited by Theodore Lyman, 3d. *Cambridge: Welch, Bigelow, and Company.* 1870. 8vo, pp. 73. BA. 42804

LYMAN (T. P. H.) The Life of Thomas Jefferson, Esq., Late Ex-President of the United States; ... By T. P. H. Lyman. *Philadelphia: D. & S. Neall.* 1826. 8vo, pp. 111. 42805

LYMAN (W.) The Happy Nation. A Sermon, ... at the Anniversary Election, in Hartford, May 8th, 1806. By William Lyman, A.M. ... *Hartford: Printed by Hudson & Goodwin.* 1806. 8vo, pp. 42. BA., S. 42806

Also: The Design and Benefits of Instrumental Musick. ... a Sermon, ... at Lebanon Goshen, May 7, 1807. On the occasion of having an Organ introduced ... . *New-London: Printed by Ebenezer P. Cady.* 1807. 8vo, pp. 18. — A Missionary Sermon, delivered at Hartford, ... May 14, 1811. ... *Hartford: Peter B. Gleason and Co., Printers.* 1811. 8vo, pp. 19. — A Sermon ... at Hamden, Sept. 9th, 1802; at the Ordination of the Rev. Asa Lyman. ... *New Haven: Printed by William W. Morse.* 1802. 8vo, pp. 26. — ... Sermon ... at Lyme, Jan. 6, 1802; at the Funeral of Mrs. Sarah ... Griswold ... . *New-London: Printed by S. Green.* 1802. 8vo, pp. 23. — ... A Sermon ... at Lebanon ... at the Dedication of the New Brick Meeting House, January 21, 1807. ... *Hartford: Printed by Hudson and Goodwin.* 1807. 8vo, pp. 32. — A Sermon, ... in Goshen, October 24th, 1810, at the Ordination of the Rev. Joseph Harvey ... . *Hartford: Printed by Hudson and Goodwin.* [n. d.] 8vo, pp. 24.

LYMBURNER (Adam). The Paper read at the Bar of the House of Commons, By Mr. Lymburner, Agent for the Subscribers to the Petitions from the Province of Quebec. Bearing date the 24th of November, 1784. As read the 23d of March, 1791. Number I. *Quebec: Printed by William Moore.* 1791. Folio, pp. 32. 42807

LYNCH (A. Charlotte). Poems. By Anne C. Lynch. With Illustrations by Durand, Huntingdon ... . *New York.* 1849. 8vo. + Ninth Edition, Enlarged. *New York: George P. Putnam.* 1852. 8vo, pp. (2), 203, (1). B. 42808

See "Rhode Island Book."

LYNCH (E. H.) Address ... [at] Mount Saint Mary's College, near Emmittsburg, Maryland, at the Annual Commencement, June 24th, 1840. By Eugene H. Lynch, Esq. *Baltimore: Printed by John Murphy.* 1840. 8vo, pp. 27. H. 42809

LYNCH (F. T.) A Letter to John Sullivan, late Under-Secretary for the Colonial Department. By F. T. Lynch, M.D. *London.* 1808. 8vo, pp. 88. 42810

Relates to his official character.

LYNCH (H.) The Wonders of the West Indies. By Mrs. Henry Lynch. ... *London: Seeley, Jackson ...* MDCCCLVI. 12mo, pp. (2), iii, iv, 315. B., C. 42811

LYNCH (J.) Address, ... before the American Institute ... of New-York, ... October, 1829. By James Lynch, Esq. ... With a Report on the Fair ... . *New-York: Printed by John M. Danforth.* 1829. 8vo, pp. 31. B. 42812

LYNCH (J.) Correspondence between Jasper Lynch and Mr. Samuel B. Griswold: A Plain Statement to the Public. *Utica, Jan.* 31, 1824. 8vo. S. 42813

LYNCH (J.) Sermon ... before the Society for the Propagation of the Gospel in Foreign Parts, Feb. 20, 1735. By John Lynch, Dean of Canterbury. *London.* 1736. 8vo, pp. 74. S. 42814

LYNCH (J.) American Commerce. Speech of Hon. John Lynch ... May 11, 1870. *Washington: F. & J. Rives ...* 1870. 8vo, pp. 16. H. 42815

Also: Causes of the Reduction of American Tonnage and the Decline of Navigation Interests ... Report ... made ... the 17th of February, 1870. *Washington.* 1870. 8vo, pp. (1), xxi, 294. H. — Impeachment of the President. Speech ... February 24, 1868. [n. p. n. d.] 8vo, pp. 8. — Loan Bill and the Currency. Speech ... March 16, 1866. [n. p. n. d.] 8vo, pp. 7. — National Finances and a Resumption of Specie Payments. Speech ... March 7, 1868. *Washington: F. & J. Rives ... Printers.* 1868. 8vo, pp. 16. — Resumption of Specie Payments. Speech ... January 26, 1869. *Washington: F. & J. Rives ... Printers.* 1869. 8vo, pp. 14. H.

LYNCH (T. H.) An Address ... before the Masonic Fraternity, at Hamilton, Ohio, ... 24th of June, 1853. By Rev. Thomas H. Lynch, A.M. *Rossville: Barker & M'Cormick, Printers.* 1853. 8vo, pp. 24. H. 42816

LYNCH (W. F.) Narrative of the United States' Expedition to the River Jordan and the Dead Sea, By W. F. Lynch, U.S.N. ... A New and Corrected Edition. *Philadelphia: Lea and Blanchard.* 1849. 8vo, pp. xx, 13–508. 2 Maps and Plates. H. + Sixth Edition. [*Ibid.*] 1849. 8vo, pp. xx, 13–509. 2 Maps. + Seventh Edition, Revised. [*Ibid.*] 1850. Plates. + A New and Condensed Edition. [*Ibid.*] 1850. 12mo, pp. xvi, 25–332. Map. C. 42817

LYNCH. Naval Life; or, Observations Afloat and on Shore. The Midshipman. By W. F. Lynch, U.S.N. *New York: Charles Scribner.* 1851. 12mo, pp. 308. B. 42818

LYNCH. Official Report of the United States' Expedition to explore the Dead Sea and the River Jordan. By Lieut. W. F. Lynch, U.S.N. ... *Baltimore: Printed by John Murphy & Co.* 1852. 4to, pp. 235, (1). Map, 16 Plates, and Diagram. BA.

LYNCH (W. R.) The World Described, in Easy Verse. ... First American Edition with Additional Notes. *New-York: Samuel Wood and Sons.* 1822. 24mo, pp. viii, 215. Map. H.

LYNCHBURG, *Va.* Sketches and Recollections of Lynchburg. By the Oldest Inhabitant. *Richmond: C. H. Wynne* ... 1858. 12mo, pp. 363. 42821

Lynchburg and Tennessee Railroad Company. First Annual Report of the President to the Stockholders ... Nov. 27, 1848. *Richmond.* 1848. 8vo, pp. 40. S. 42822

Afterwards the Virginia and Tennessee Railroad. Also: Lynchburg and Tennessee Rail Road. Letters from T. S. Bocock, W. M. Cocke, J. A. Rogers, and V. K. Stevenson. *Richmond.* 1849. 8vo.

LYND (S. W.) Memoir of the Rev. William Staughton, D.D. By Rev. S. W. Lynd, A.M. *Boston: Lincoln, Edmands, & Co.* 1834. 12mo, pp. 311, (1). Portrait. S. 42823

[LYNDE (Samuel, *and others.*] A Vindication of the Bank of Credit Projected in Boston from the Aspersions of Paul Dudley, Esq. ... [*Boston.*] 1714. 8vo, pp. (2), 20. B., BA., M. 42824

LYNDON, *pseudon.* Margaret: a Story of Life in a Prairie Home. By Lyndon. *New York: Charles Scribner & Co.* 1868. 12mo, pp. 360. C., H. 42825

LYNDON ACADEMY. A Catalogue of the Officers & Students ... for ... November 23, 1832. [n. p. n. d.] 24mo, pp. 6, (2).

LYNE (C.) A Letter to the Right Honourable Lord Castlereagh, &c. &c. &c. on the North American Export Trade During the War, and during any time the Import and use of our Manufactures are interdicted in the United States. To which is added, the resolutions of the Manufacturers, Exporters of Goods, and Merchants, of the City of Glasgow. By Charles Lyne. *London: J. M. Richardson.* 1813. 8vo, pp. (2), 46. 42827

LYNE (T. A.) ... Assassination of Joseph & Hiram Smith, ... at Carthage, Illinois, June 27th, 1844. By ... T. A. Lyne, ... Annexed the Speech of H. L. Reid, also ... of James W. Woods. To which is added a Brief Outline of the Faith ... of the Latter Day Saints. *New-York: Printed by C. A. Calhoun.* 1844. 12mo, pp. 17. B. 42828

LYNN (D. The Trial of David Lynn and others ... for the Murder of Paul Chadwick. *Augusta.* 1809. 8vo, pp. 44. M.

LYNN, *Mass.* An Act to Establish the City of Lynn ... . *Lynn: H. J. Butterfield, Printer.* 1850. 12mo, pp. 12. H.

Annual Report of the Board of Health of Lynn ... . *Boston: Printed by Dutton & Wentworth.* 1850. 8vo, pp. 30. H. 42831

First Annual Report of Receipts and Expenditures for 1850–51. *Lynn.* 1851. 8vo. Continued. 42832

Annual Report of the School Committee of Lynn, March 4, 1846. *Lynn: J. B. Tolman, Printer.* 1846. 8vo, pp. 16. Continued. B. 42833

The Charter and Ordinances of the City of Lynn, and the Municipal Register for 1860. ... *Lynn: Printed by H. S. Cox.* 1860. 8vo, pp. xi, 169. B. 42834

City Documents. ... *Lynn: Thos. P. Nichols, Printer.* 1870. 8vo, pp. 107, (1), 48, 46. H. 42835

The City Hall of Lynn; being a History of Events leading to its Erection ... . *Lynn: Thos. P. Nichols, Printer.* 1869. 8vo, pp. xvii, (1), 132. H. 42836

The Directory of ... Lynn. ... By Alonzo Lewis. *Lynn: T. Herbert* ... 1851. 18mo, pp. 180, (4). BA. 42837

Also: The Lynn Directory and Town Register for 1832. ... By C. F. Lummus. *Lynn: Geo. Lummus.* 1832. 18mo, pp. 71, (1). Continued.—The Lynn Directory, ... with an Almanac for ... 1854. By George Adams ... . *Lynn: Thomas Herbert.* 1853. 18mo, pp. 194. Continued. BA. + For 1858. By Adams, Sampson & Co. *Boston: J. M. Munroe.* 1858. 18mo. + For 1865; also, Swampscott Directory. ... *Boston: J. M. Munroe.* 1864. 8vo, pp. 200, 58. Continued annually.

An Exposition of the Course. *See* King (S. W.), IX. 37836.

Extract from the Records of the Town of Lynn ... with the Division ... of Land at Nahant ... . *Lynn: W. W. Kellogg, Printer.* 1856. 8vo, pp. 24. H. 42838

... Inaugural Address of the ... Mayor, to the City Council of Lynn, delivered ... May 14, 1850. ... *Lynn: Press of L. Josselyn.* 1850. 8vo, pp. 12. Continued. H. 42839

LYNN HIGH SCHOOL. Catalogue of the Officers, Teachers, and Pupils ... February 18, 1853. *Lynn: W. W. Kellogg, Printer.* 1853. 12mo, pp. 12. Continued. H. 42840

LYNN LIBRARY ASSOCIATION. Catalogue of the Library ... *Lynn: W. W. Kellogg, Printer.* 1856. 16mo, pp. xi, (1), 84.

Also: Catalogue of the Free Public Library of Lynn, Mass. *Boston: A. Mudge & Son, Printers.* 1863. 8vo, pp. vii, (1), 181. + A Supplement ... . *Boston: Thos. P. Nichols, Printer.* 1868. 8vo, pp. 111. B.

The Municipal Register, containing the City Charter ... 1850–51. *Lynn: H. J. Butterfield, Printer.* 1850. 12mo, pp. 12.

A Review of Lynn; or Observations on the Manners and Customs of the Place. *Boston.* 1821. 12mo. 42843

Rules of the School Committee, and Regulations of the Public Schools of ... Lynn. *Lynn: P. L. & H. S. Cox.* 1855. 8vo, pp. 36. H. 42844

Third Annual Report of ... Commissioners of Pine Grove Cemetery, ... Feb. 16, 1857; ... *Lynn: W. W. Kellogg, Printer.* 1857. 8vo, pp. 28. B. 42845

LYNNFIELD, *Mass.* Expenses of ... Lynnfield, for ... 1857. With the Annual Report of the School Committee. *Boston: Kendall & Blaney, Printers.* 1857. 8vo, pp. 19. Continued. B.

LYON (C.) Narrative and Recollections of Van Dieman's Land, during a Three Years' Captivity of Stephen S. Wright. Together with an Account of the Battle of Prescott, from the Notes of Mr. Wright and other sources, by Caleb Lyon. *New York.* 1843. 8vo, pp. 80. + [*Ibid.*] 1844. 8vo. 42847

Also: An Address delivered September 28th, 1854 ... [before] the Queens County Agricultural Society, at Jamaica, Long Island ... . *Jamaica.* 1854. 8vo, pp. 11. H.—The Covenant of Freedom. Speech ... in the House of Representatives, May 8, 1854. [*Washington.* 1854.] 8vo, pp. 3.—No Government Bounty to Polygamy. Speech ... May 4, 1854. [*Washington.* 1854.] 8vo, pp. 2.—Speech ... March 30, 1854, on the Necessity for an Increase of the Navy. ... [n. p. n. d.] 8vo. S.

LYON (C. H.) Oration delivered ... near the ground on which Major Andre was taken, at Tarrytown, on the Fourth of July, 1839; by Charles H. Lyon, A.M. ... *New York: Bryant & Boggs.* 1839. 8vo, pp. 16. 42848

LYON (De C.) Almanach littéraire ou étrennes d'Apollon, par M. De Chateau Lyon. *Paris.* MDCCLXXXV. 16mo. P.

Contains, commencing page 24, an eulogium of General Washington.

LYON (D. S.) *See* Tariff.

LYON (E.) Trial of Edward Lyon, ... for Subornation of False Swearing; in which John Binns was endorsed as Prosecutor. ... *Philadelphia.* 1816. 8vo. + Second Edition. [*Ibid.*] 8vo, pp. 72. 42850

LYON (George Francis). A Brief Narrative of an Unsuccessful Attempt to reach Repulse Bay, through Sir Thomas Rowe's "Welcome," in His Majesty's Ship Griper, in the year MDCCCXXIV. By Captain G. F. Lyon, R.N. *London: John Murray.* MDCCCXXV. 8vo, pp. xvi, 198, (1). Map, 7 Plates. B.

Includes an account of the author's intercourse with the Esquimaux.

LYON. Journal of a Residence and Tour in the Republic of Mexico, in ... 1826. With some Account of the Mines in that Country. By Capt. G. F. Lyon ... . *London: John Murray.* 1828. 16mo, pp. viii, 323; iv, 304. A., BA., C. 42852

See "Quart. Rev.," XLII. 334.

LYON. The Private Journal of Captain G. F. Lyon, of H. M. S. Hecla, during the Recent Voyage of Discovery under Captain Parry. With a Map and Plates. *London: John Murray.* 1824. 8vo, pp. xiii, (1), 468. 7 Plates. BA. + *Boston: Wells and Lilly.* 1824. 12mo, pp. viii, 339. + A New Edition. *London: John Murray.* 1825. 8vo, pp. xiii, (1), 468. 7 Plates.

The work is principally devoted to the narration of the peculiarities of the aborigines of the Arctic regions. Captain Lyon's curiosity led him to observe with great attention the habits of life and traits of character of the different tribes of Esquimaux, who were attracted by his humane management to his winter quarters. Of Murray's first edition a few copies were printed on thick paper for presents only, containing three sets of the fine engravings by Finden, *i. e.* India proofs, etchings, and prints.

LYON. The Sketch Book of Capt. G. F. Lyon, R.N., during Eight Months' Residence in the Republic of Mexico. *London: J. Dickinson.* 1827. Folio, pp. (6). 10 Plates. [Unfinished.]

LYON (G. Parker). *See* New Hampshire.

LYON (I. S.) The Washington Monument. Shall it be Buit? An Address to the Citizens of New York. By I. S. Lyon. *New York: Printed by Wm. Oland Bourne.* 1846. 8vo, pp. 16.

LYON (J.) Urania; or, A Choice Collection of Psalm-Tunes, Anthems, and Hymns, from the most approv'd Authors, with some entirely new. By James Lyon, A.B. *Philadelphia.* 1761. Obl. 12mo, pp. (10), xii, 198. C. + [*Ibid.*] 1763. 42856

One of the earliest American books of its class.

LYON (J.) National Magazine; or, a Political, Historical, Biographical, and Literary Repository for 1799. By James Lyon. ... *Richmond (Va.): For the Editor.* 1799. 8vo. 42857

Continued to two or more volumes.

LYON (J.) A Republican Magazine; or, Repository of Political Truths. By James Lyon, of Fairhaven, Vermont. *Printed at Fairhaven, (Vt.)* M,DCC,XCVIII. 8vo, pp. (2), 192. 42858

LYON (J. A.) A Lecture on Christianity and the Civil Laws. By Rev. James A. Lyon, D.D. ... *Columbus.* 1859. 8vo, pp. 32.

[LYON (Lemuel) *and* HAWS (S.)] Military Journals of Two Private Soldiers, 1758–1775, with numerous Illustrative Notes; to which is added, a Supplement, containing Official Papers on the Skirmishes at Lexington and Concord. *Poughkeepsie.* 1855. 8vo, pp. 128. S. 42860

Lyon's journal contains some incidents of the expedition against Fort Ticonderoga in 1758. The work was edited by Abraham Tomlinson; the notes are by B. J. Lossing.

LYON (L.) Letter of Lucius Lyon to the Honorable Lewis Williams ... respecting the Boundary Line between Ohio and Michigan ... . *Washington: Printed by Gales & Seaton.* 1834. 8vo, pp. (1), 44. H. 42861

LYON (M.) Report of the Committee of Privileges, ... Relative to the ... Expulsion ... of Matthew Lyon, For a violent attack, ... upon ... Roger Griswold ... . [*Philadelphia.* 1798.] 8vo, pp. 4. B. 42862

Also: Circular-Letter to his Constituents, March 4, 1809. [*Washington.* 1809.] Folio, 1 leaf.—Mr. Lyon's Speech, in Favor of Peace. ... On the 7th of February [1813] ... . [n. p. n. d.] 8vo, pp. 10.

LYON (M.) Address, delivered before the Yorkville Lodge, ... December 27, 1853. By M. Lyon, Esq. *Carrollton.* [n. d.] 8vo, pp. 15. 42863

LYON (N.) The Last Political Writings of Gen. Nathaniel Lyon, U.S.A. With a Sketch of his Life and Military Services. ... *New York: Rudd and Carleton.* M DCCC LXI. 12mo, pp. 275. Portrait. H. 42864

LYON. Obituary Addresses of Messrs. Pomeroy, Dixon, and Foster, on the Death of Brig.-Gen. Lyon; delivered in the United States Senate, Dec. 20, 1861. *Washington: Globe Office.* 1861. 8vo. 42865

LYON (P.) The Narrative of Patrick Lyon, who suffered ... Imprisonment in Philadelphia Goal, on ... Suspicion of being concerned in the Robbery of the Bank of Pennsylvania. With his Remarks thereon. *Philadelphia: Francis and Robert Bailey.* 1799. 8vo, pp. 76. 42866

LYON. Robbery of the Bank of Pennsylvania in 1798. The Trial in the Supreme Court of the State of Pennsylvania. Reported from Notes by T. Lloyd. Upon which the President of that bank, ... were sentenced to pay Patrick Lyon twelve thousand dollars damages, for a false and malicious prosecution against him, without either reasonable or probable cause. *Philadelphia: For the Publishers.* 1808. 8vo, pp. (2), ii, 184. BA. 42867

[LYON (Sidney S.)] Hyko Silver Mining Company, located in the Pah-Ranagat Lake Silver Mining District ... Nevada, with Additional Facts ... . Also Statistics in reference to the Production of Silver in Various Countries. Compiled by Stuart Gwynn. *New York: Bogert, Kidder & Nexsen.* 1867. 8vo, pp. 36, (4). 2 Maps. C. 42868

LYON (T. C.) Do the Times demand a Southern Confederacy? By Theodore C. Lyon ... . [n. p. 1860.] 8vo, pp. 8.

LYON (T.) A Poem on the Lord's Day: Together with Acrostics on General Washington and President Adams. By Theophilus Lyon ... . [n. p. 1801.] 8vo. W. 42870

LYON (W. F.) Brigadier-General Thomas Francis Meagher: his Political and Military Career; with Selection from his Speeches and Writings. By Capt. W. F. Lyon. *Glasgow: Cameron & Ferguson.* [1870.] 12mo, pp. 186. + *New York: D. & J. Sadlier & Co.* 1870. 12mo, pp. 357. Portrait. B., S. 42871

LYON (W. N.) A Short and Comprehensive History of the United States ... By William N. Lyon, of Warsaw, Ky. [n. p.:] *Printed for the Author.* 1846. 12mo, pp. 124. 42872

LYONS (I.) An Hebrew Grammar, collected chiefly from those of Mr. Israel Lyons ... and the Rev. Richard Grey, D.D. ... *Boston: N. E. printed by R. and S. Draper, for the Honorable and Reverend the President and Fellows of Harvard-College.* 1763. 8vo. + Third Cambridge Edition. *Cambridge: Hilliard and Metcalf.* 1812. 8vo, pp. 47. 42873

Edited by Stephen Sewell.

LYONS (J.) Speech on the Basis Question. ... *Richmond.* 1851. 8vo. 42874

LYONS (J. A.) Silver Jubilee of the University of Notre Dame, June 23d, 1869. By Joseph A. Lyons. *Chicago: E. B. Myers & Co.* 1869. Sm. 4to, pp. 266. 4 Plates. + Second Edition. [*Ibid.*] 1869. Sm. 4to, pp. 344. 4 Plates. 42875

LYONS, *Lord.* Despatch from Lord Lyons respecting the Reciprocity Treaty. *London: Harrison and Sons.* [n. d.] Folio, pp. 25. 42876

Also other despatches relative to the Civil War.

Lyrics. By the Letter H. *New York.* 1854. 12mo.

Lyrics for Freedom; and Other Poems. Under the Auspices of the Continental Club. *New York: Carleton.* MDCCCLXII. 12mo, pp. xvi, 243. B. 42878

Lyrics of a Day, or Newspaper Poetry by a Volunteer in the United States Service. *New York: Carleton.* 1864. 12mo.

Lyrics of Loyalty. *See* [Moore (Frank)].

Lyrics of the War. *Philadelphia.* [n. d.] 4to, pp. 14.

LYSANDER, *pseudon.* Annals of the Corporation, relative to the late Contested Elections, with Strictures upon the Conduct of the Majority. In Seven Numbers. By Lysander. *New York.* 1802. 8vo, pp. 88. N. 42881

By James Cheetham. *See also* [Van Ness (W. C.)], *and* [Willis (Thomas)].

LYSCHANDER (Clauss Chrystopherson). Grönlandske Chronica. *Kiöpenhavn: B. Laurentz.* 1608. 12mo. 42882

Besides this work, which is in verse and very rare, although it has been reprinted in 1726, he has also published some other works, a list of which will be found in the "Dictionnaire de la littérature danoise, islandaise et norwegienne de Nyerup," *Copenhagen,* 1821, 2 vols., 4to, Vol. 1., p. 359.

LYSONS (D.) Parting Words on the Rejected Militia Bill. By Col. D. Lysons. *Quebec.* 1862. 8vo, pp. 14. 42883

Lyst van de Hollandse en Hamburger Groenlands- en Straat Davids-Vaarders, A°. 1764 uitgevaaren. *Amsterdam: J. M. Brouwer.* [1765.] 8vo. 42884

Lyst der Scheepen ... komende van Curaçao, St. Eustatius en de West-Indien, door de Engelschen genomen ... tegens het regt der volkeren. [n. p. 1758.] Folio. 42885

List of the Dutch ships captured by the English, against the law of nations, during their voyage from the West Indies. *See also* "Lijst," Nos. 41060–62.

Lysten van de Hollandse Scheepen zo veel deeze Stadt Amsteldam betreft. Welke op hunne Reisen, naar of van de West-Indiën, door de Engelschen in weerwil van de subsisterende Tractaten, genomen, opgebragt, en onregtmatig geconfisqueert zyn ... . *Amsteldam.* [1758.] Folio, pp. (4), 36. 42886

A different list from the preceding and more ample.

LYSTER. Report of the Lyster Copper Company, ... Canada East. ... *Boston: Press of Stacy & Richardson.* 1864. 8vo, pp. 15.

LYTTELTON (*Lord*). The Colonial Empire of Great Britain, especially in its Religious Aspect. A Lecture ... December 3, 1849. By Lord Lyttelton. *London: Simpkin, Marshall, & Co.* [1850.] 8vo, pp. 44. 42888

[LYTTELTON (George).] Considerations Upon the present State of our Affairs, at Home and Abroad, in a Letter to a Member of Parliament from a Friend in the Country. *London: T. Cooper.* MDCCXXXIX. 8vo, pp. (2), 39. + The Second Edition. [*Ibid.*] MDCCXXXIX. 8vo, pp. (2), 67, (2). BA. 42889

Denies the right of Spain to search American ships, and contains also the treaty with Spain regarding America. For "Farther Considerations," *see* Vol. VI., Nos. 23896–7. For a reply *see* "Popular Prejudices."

LYTTELTON. The Works of George Lord Lyttelton; ... Published by George Edward Ayscough, Esq. *London.* 1774. 8vo. + The Third Edition. *London: J. Dodsley.* MDCCLXXVI. 3 vols., 8vo, pp. xi, 413, Portrait; (4), 410, (1); ix, [*sic*] xi, 397.

LYTTELTON (T.) A Letter from Thomas Lord Lyttelton, to William Pitt, Earl of Chatham, on the Quebec Bill. *Boston: Printed by ... Cox and Berry.* M,DCC,LXXIV. 8vo, pp. 17. BA. + *New-York: Re-printed by James Rivington.* M,DCC,LXXIV. 8vo, pp. 20. 42891

See also No. 40468.

LYTTELTON. Letters of the Late Lord Lyttelton ... . *Troy, N. Y.: Printed by Wright, Goodenow & Stockwell.* 1807. 8vo, pp. 296. BA. 42892

Contains some selections from Lord Lyttelton's speeches on the American War.

LYTTELTON. The Speech of Lord Lyttelton, on a Motion made in the House of Lords for a Repeal of the Canada Bill, May 17, 1775. *London: J. Ridley.* MDCCLXXV. 4to, pp. 18.

See "M. Rev.," LII. 550.

[LYTTELTON (Thomas), *second Lord.*] Poems, | by | a Young Nobleman, | ... In a Letter from an American Traveller, | Dated from the Ruinous Portico of St. Paul's, | in the Year 2199, | to | A Friend settled in Boston, The Metropolis of the Western Empire. | Also, | Sundry Fugitive Pieces ... . The Second Edition. *London: G. Kearsly.* M.DCC.LXXX. 4to, pp. (6), iv, 60. 42894

Also included in Vol. LVI. of "The Works of the English Poets." This poetical prophet, appears to have anticipated Macaulay in his predictions concerning the downfall and desolation of London, the modern Babylon. Some of the poems are very free. *See* "M. Rev.," LXII. 128.

M ***. *See* B[uisson (*M.* du)], III. 9080.

M. ***. *See* [Dubuc (J. B.)], V. 21032.

M. ***. *See* [Fleurieu (C. P. C. de)].

M. ***. *See* [Vallette Laudun (*M.* de)].

M. ***. Mémoires sur la Louisiane et la Nouvelle-Orleans, accompagnés d'une Dissertation sur les avantages que le commerce de l'empire doit tirer de la stipulation fait par l'article VII. du traité de cession, du 30 Avril, 1803; par M. ***, suivis d'une traduction de diverses notes sur cette colonie, publié aux États-Unis peu de tems après la ratification du traité; terminé par un écrit traitent cette question; Est-il avantageux à la France de prendre possession de la Louisiane? *Paris.* 1804. 8vo, pp. 176. 42895

M***. Roman Politique sur l'état présent des affaires de l'Amérique, ou lettres de M***. à M***., sur les moyens d'établir une paix solide et durable dans les colonies. *Amsterdam.* 1757. 12mo. 42896

M*** (von). Der in dem wilden America von seiner Wildheit befreyte Europäer. *Franckfurt und Leipzig.* 1756. 8vo.

M****. Voyage au Kentoukey, et sur les bords du Genesée, précédé de conseils aux libéraux ... . Par M****. ... *Paris: M. Sollier.* 1821. 8vo, pp. (4), 243, (1). Map. B., C., S. 42898

M*******. Mémoires de Billaud-Varennes, ex-conventionnel, Écrits au Port-au-Prince en 1818, contenant la relation de ses voyages et aventures dans le Mexique, depuis 1806 jusqu'en 1817; avec des notes historiques et un précis de l'insurrection Américaine, depuis son origine jusqu'en 1820. Par M*******. *Paris: Plancher.* 1821. 2 vols., 8vo, pp. (4), iv, 211; (4), 228.

M. (A.) Reflections on the American Contest, in which the Consequences of a forced Submission, and the Means of a lasting Reconciliation are pointed out. ... By A. M. *London: J. Bew.* MDCCLXXVI. 8vo, pp. viii, 50. J.C.B. 42900

"Said to have been written in the year 1769, soon after the writer's return from America. It contains many candid, pertinent, and just reflections on the situation, circumstances, and dispositions of the colonists, and on the consequences of attempting to govern them by force."—*Monthly Review*, LV. 63.

M. (A.) Niagara: a Poem. By A. M. *New York.* 1822. 8vo, pp. 24. 42901

M. (A. B.) Guia de la ciudad de Nueva York. Por A. B. M. *Nueva York: N. Ponce de Leon.* 1872. 16mo, pp. (8), 236. Map and 48 Plates. C. 42902

M. (A. W.) The Smuggler's Son; and other Tales and Sketches. In Prose and Verse. By A. W. M. *Philadelphia.* 1824. 12mo. 42903

M. (C.) De la Tolerancia, o sea, del culto publico en sus relaciones con el Gobierno. Por El Lic. C. M. *Morelia.* 1847. 8vo, pp. 108. 42904

M*** (*le Comte* de). Mémoire sur les Colonies Occidentales de la France, ouvrage présenté au gouvernement en l'an X., contenant le projet d'un établissement national pour la restauration de la culture à Saint Domingue. Par le Comte de M***. *Paris.* 1814. 8vo, pp. 119. 42905

M. (E.) *See* M[elton] (E[dward]).

M. (E. C. M. J. D.) Proyecto de una Contribucion Nacional para engrosar y mantener la hacienda publica del Imperio Mexicano, por E. C. M. J. D. M. *Mexico.* 1822. Sm. 8vo, pp. 23.

M. (F.) Coup d'œil rapide sur la République de Costa Rica. Par F. M. *Paris.* 1849. 8vo, pp. 32. Map. 42907

M. A Brief Sketch of the Republic of Costa Rica. By F. M. *London: The Author.* 1849. 8vo, pp. 15. Map. C.

M. (J.) The Legislative Authority of the British Parliament, with respect to North America, and the privileges of the Assemblies there, briefly considered. By J. M. ... *London: W. Nicoll.* M.DCC.LXVI. 8vo, pp. 20. H., P. 42909

"A vindication of the legislative jurisdiction on the principles of law. The author, however, in common with almost every other writer, on whatever side the question, gives up the stamp act, as ineligible in some respect or degree."—*Monthly Review*, XXXIV. 156.

M. (J.) Grammatica over de Creoolske Sprog på de Danske Eilande i America. *Kjöbenhavn.* 1770. 8vo. 42910

The language of the inhabitants of the Danish West India Islands.

M. (J.) *See* M[orse] (J[ason]).

M. (J.) *See* Law (John), *and* Mortimer (J.)

M. (J. B.) Disertacion contra la Tolerancia religiosa. Por J. B. M. *Méjico.* 1831. 8vo, pp. 59. 42911

A curious pamphlet, chiefly directed against John Locke's views.

M. (J. L.) Native Bards; a Satirical Effusion: with other occasional pieces. By J. L. M. *Philadelphia: E. L. Carey, & A. Hart.* 1831. 12mo, pp. 114. C. 42912

The longest poem is a poor imitation of the Dunciad.

M**** (Julien). *See* M[ellet] (Julien).

M********* (Jh.) *See* [Mandrillon (Joseph)].

M (L. B. de). Coup d'œil sur l'état actuel des États-Unis d'Amérique, et sur les événemens qui s'y préparent. Par L. B. de M. *Paris.* 1834. 8vo, pp. 160. C. 42913

M. (M. L. L.) *See our* Vol. III., No. 9605.

By a mistake we have placed it under Butel-Dumont instead of Dumont.

M. (F. M.) Nouveau dictionnaire historique des sièges et batailles mémorables, et des combats maritimes les plus fameux De tous les Peuples du monde ... . Par F. M. M. *Paris.* 1808–1809. 6 vols., 8vo. BA. 42914

Includes some American battles and naval conflicts.

M. (M. V. D.) *See* Mezague (Vivant de).

M. (O.) Plain Reasons for Removing a Certain Great Man from His M——y's Presence and Councils forever. By O. M. Haberdasher. *London.* 1759. 8vo, pp. 36. W. 42915

Relates to William Pitt, Earl of Chatham.

M. (P.) Refutacion documentada del folleto titulado "Cuestion de limites entre el Ecuador y el Perú." Publicado en Santiago de Chile por P. M. Segunda edicion aumentada por Modesto Basadré. *Lima.* 1860. 4to, pp. iv, 227. 42916

M. (R.) A General Survey of that part of the Island of St. Christopher's which formerly belonged to France; and was yielded up to Great Britain forever by the late Treaty of Utrecht. Together with an estimate of the value of those Lands, and a Proposal and Scheme for raising a very considerable Sum of Money, for the use of the Publick, on the Produce thereof ... . By Mr. R. M., S.B. *London: J. Roberts.* MDCCXXII. 8vo, pp. 48.

M. (R.) A Relation of Mr. R. M's Voyage to Buenos Ayres: And from thence by Land to Potosi. ... *London: Printed by John Darby.* M. DCC. XVI. 16mo, pp. v, 117. Map. C., H. 42918

A reprint of the translation printed in 1698 of the voyage of Sieur Acarette to Buenos Ayres, from Thevenot's "Collection," without any acknowledgment of the source from whence it was taken.

M. (T. C.) The Priest's Turf-Cutting Day. A Historical Romance. By T. C. M. *New York: The Author.* 1841. 12mo, pp. 82. H. 42919

M. (W. T.) Reminiscences of a Trans-Atlantic Traveller. Being a sketch of Fourteen Months' Residence in North America, in the Years 1831–32. ... By W. T. M. ... *Dublin: William Frederick Wakeman.* MDCCCXXXV. 12mo, pp. (8), 188. 42920

M. y E. El Nuevo Viajero Universal, en América, ó sea Historia de viajes acerca el calendario de los Mejicanos. Por M. y E. *Barcelona: Imprenta de Bergnes y Compañia.* 1833. 12mo, pp. 151. Plate. 42921

Maandelijksche Nederlandsche Mercurius. *Amsterdam.* 1756–1790. 69 vols., 4to. 42922

This monthly Dutch Mercury contains many articles on American topics.

MABLY (Gabriel Bonnot de). Observations sur le Gouvernement et les Loix des États-Unis de l'Amérique. Par M. l'Abbé de Mably. *A Amsterdam: Chez J. F. Rosart & Comp.* MDCCLXXXIV. 12mo, pp. (2), 213. + Second Edition. [*Ibid.*] C. + Avec des Remarques d'un Republicain. *Dublin.* M.DCC.LXXXV. 12mo, pp. (8), 277. + Nouvelle Édition. *Amsterdam.* MDCCXC. 12mo, pp. (2), 213. BA. + *Paris.* 1791. 12mo, pp. (2), 213. BA. 42923

MABLY. Observations on the Government and Laws of the United States of America, translated from the French of the Abbé de Mably ... . *Amsterdam: J. F. Rosart and Comp.* MDCCLXXXIV. 24mo, pp. xxiv, 122. H. 42924

There is another translation with the following title:

MABLY. Remarks concerning the Government and the Laws of the United States of America: In Four Letters addressed to Mr. Adams; Minister Plenipotentiary from the United States of America to those of Holland; and one of the Negociators for the purpose of concluding a general Peace, from the French of the Abbé de Mably: With Notes, by the Translator. *London:*

J. Debrett. M,DCC,LXXXIV. 8vo, pp. (4), 280. BA. + *Dublin: Moncrieffe* ... MDCCLXXXV. 8vo, pp. (4), 280. C. 42925

"This work consists of four letters addressed to John Adams, with a preface by the translator, who does not seem to consider himself bound to adopt the opinions of his author. These, in fact, are not so liberal as was to be expected from a character so distinguished in the literary world. His work contains some observations which are the result of good sense and a great knowledge of mankind, yet amid these there are many things which betray the author's country and religious persuasion."—*Monthly Review*, LXXI. 371; LXXII. 146.

MABLY. Brieven over de regeeringsvorm en wetten der Vereenigde Staten van Nord America. *Amsterdam.* 1785. 8vo.

MCADAM (A.) Communications from Adam McAdam, originally published in the Montreal Herald, in Reply to Letters inserted therein under the Signature of Archibald Macdonald, respecting Lord Selkirk's Red River Colony. *Montreal.* 1816. 8vo, pp. 57. 42927

MCADAM (D.) The Marine Court of the City of New York: its Origin, Jurisdiction, and Practice. By D. McAdam. *New York: McAdam & Vannett.* 1868. 8vo, pp. xiv, 164.

[M'AFEE (Robert B.)] History of the Late War in the Western Country, comprising a Full Account of all the Transactions in that Quarter, from the Commencement of Hostilities at Tippecanoe, to the Termination of the Contest at New Orleans on the Return of Peace. *Lexington, K.: Worsley & Smith.* 1816. 8vo, pp. viii, 534, (2). BA. 42929

This valuable work is now scarce; it is one of the most authentic books on the subject, and is the source from which many subsequent writers have borrowed very freely.

MCALL (S.) Slavery a Curse and a Sin. A Speech ... at Bradford, Yorkshire ... October 20, 1852 ... . By Samuel McAll ... . *London: Charles A. Bartlett.* [n. d.] 12mo, pp. 12. H.

[MCALLISTER (F. M.)] A Memorial of Mrs. Louisa C. McAllister. ... *New York.* 1869. 8vo, pp. (1), 47. H. 42931

MCALPINE (J.) Genuine Narratives, and Concise Memoirs Of some of the most Interesting Exploits and Singular Adventures of J. McAlpine a Native Highlander, From the time of his Emigration from Scotland, to America 1773; during the long period of his faithful attachment to, and hazardous attendance on the British Army's under the Command of the Generals Carleton and Burgoyne, in their several operations that he was concerned in, till December 1779. ... *Greenock: W. McAlpine.* 1780. Sm. 8vo, pp. 65. P. + [n. p.] M,D,CCLXXXVIII. 16mo, pp. 72. C.

MCALPINE (W. J.) Report made to ... the City of Brooklyn, April 15th, 1852. On supplying the City with Water. By William J. McAlpine ... . *Brooklyn: Printed by I. Van Anden.* 1852. 8vo, pp. 139, (1). B. 42933

MCALPINE. Report on supplying Chicago with Water. ... [n. p.] 1851. 8vo. 42934

MCALPINE. Report on the Projects for supplying the City of Albany with Water ... . *Albany.* 1850. 8vo. S. 42935

MCALPINE. Reports and Estimates for a Ship Canal and Basin, from Albany to New-Baltimore. By William J. McAlpine ... . *Albany: Weed, Parsons & Company, Printers.* 1853. 8vo, pp. 64. Map. B., M. 42936

See also Vol. II., No. 8329, New Bedford, *and* Troy. Also: Address before the Chamber of Commerce, N. Y., on the Food-Producing Interior of the United States. ... *New York.* 1873. 8vo.—Transportation Routes from the West, Oswego Board of Trade. ... *Oswego.* 1873. 8vo.

M'ANALLY (D. R.) Life and Times of Rev. William Patton; and Annals of the Missouri Conference. By D. R. M'Anally. *St. Louis.* 1858. 12mo. C. 42937

MCANDREW (——). On the Geographical Distribution of Testaceous Mollusca, on the North Atlantic and Neighboring Seas. *Liverpool.* 1854. 8vo. 42938

MCARONE, *pseudon.* The Life and Adventures of Jeff. Davis. By McArone. *New York: J. C. Haney & Co.* 1865. 12mo, pp. 31. 42939

MACARTHUR (C. L.) An Address, St. John's Day, Dec. 27, 1853: Dedication of the New Masonic Hall. By Charles L. MacArthur. *Troy, N. Y.* 1854. 8vo. S. 42940

M'ARTHUR (J.) Financial and Political Facts of the Eighteenth Century; with Comparative Estimates of the Revenue, Expenditure, Debts, Manufactures, and Commerce of Great Britain. By John M'Arthur, Esq. Third Edition. With an Appendix of useful and interesting Documents. The whole Revised, Corrected, and Considerably Enlarged. *London: J. Wright.* 1801. 8vo, pp. xxiv, 337, (20). C., P. 42941

MACARTHY (H.) ... The Bonnie Blue Flag. ... By Harry Macarthy. ... *New Orleans: A. E. Blackmar & Brother.* [1861.] 4to, pp. 5. B. 42942

Also: Missouri or a Voice from the South. ... *Augusta, Ga.:* ... *Blackmar & Brother.* [1861.] 4to, pp. 5. B.

MACAULAY (A.) Rudiments of Political Science, Part the First; containing Elementary Principles: with an Appendix. By Angus Macaulay. *London: Tho. Egerton.* 1796. 8vo, pp. xxiv, 390, (2). 42943

Contains some account of the government of the American Indians.

MACAULAY (C.) An Address to the People of England, Scotland, and Ireland, on the Present Important Crisis of Affairs. By Catharine Macaulay. *Printed by R. Cruttwel, in Bath, for Edward and Charles Dilly.* MDCCLXXV. 8vo, pp. 29. + The Second Edition. [*Ibid.*] 8vo, pp. 31. B. + Third Edition. *New York, Reprinted.* 1775. 8vo. P. + *London: J. Williams.* [1775.] 8vo. 42944

Relates to the American Revolution, and is "a masterly specimen of accurate reasoning, and municipal information."—*Monthly Review*, LII. 87.

[MACAULAY.] Loose Remarks on Certain Positions to be found in Mr. Hobbes's Philosophical Rudiments of Government and Society. With a Short Sketch of a Democratical form of Government ... . *London: Printed for T. Davies.* M DCC LXVII. 8vo, pp. (1), 39, (1). H. + The Second Edition with Two Letters one from an American Gentleman to the Author which contains Some Comments on her Sketch of the Democratical Form of Government and the Author's Answer. *London: Printed for W. Johnston.* MDCCLXIX. 4to, pp. (2), 35. + Third Edition ... [n. p. 17—.] 8vo, pp. 120. BA. 42945

MACAULAY. Observations on a Pamphlet, entitled, Thoughts on the Cause of the Present Discontents. By Catharine Macaulay. *London: Edward and Charles Dilly.* MDCCLXX. 4to, pp. 20. + The Third Edition, Corrected. [*Ibid.*] 8vo, pp. 31. BA. + Fifth Edition. [*Ibid.*] + *Dublin.* 1770. 8vo, pp. 36. 42946

The various editions of this lady's "History of England" contain matter relative to America.

MACAULAY (G. H.) The Landed Credit System, or La Banque du Credit Foncier. By George Henry Macaulay. *Quebec.* 1863. 8vo, pp. 66. 42947

MACAULAY. The Political Past, Present and Future of Canada; an Essay. By George Henry Macaulay. *Montreal.* 1858. 8vo, pp. 40. 42948

French and English. Also: The Proposed British North American Confederation: a Reply to Mr. Penny's Reasons why it should not be imposed upon the Colonies by Imperial Legislation. ... *Montreal.* 1867. 8vo, pp. 13. *See also* Cauchon (J.), III.

MACAULAY (Thomas Babington). Macaulay on Democracy. Letter from Lord Macaulay on American Institutions and Prospects. *London, May* 23, 1857. 8vo, pp. 4. 42949

The various editions of Lord Macaulay's "History of England" contain references to America, particularly so in relation to William Penn, which have been answered by Dixon (W. H.), Forster (W. E.), [Gauntley (W.)], and others.

MACAULAY (W.) The Portraiture of a True and Loyal Orangeman; as Sketched in a Sermon, By Rev. W. Macaulay. *Toronto.* 1854. 8vo, pp. 26. 42950

[MACAULAY (Zachariah).] East and West India Sugar; or a Refutation of the Claims of West India Colonists to a Protecting Duty on East India Sugar. *London.* 1823. 8vo, pp. 128.

[MACAULAY.] Haiti, ou Renseignemens authentiques sur l'Abolition de l'Esclavage et ses Résultats à Saint-Domingue et à la Guadeloupe ... . Traduit de l'Anglais. *Paris: Chez L. Hachette.* 1835. 8vo, pp. (4), iv, 207. B. 42952

[MACAULAY.] A Letter to W. W. Whitmore, pointing out some of the Erroneous Statements contained in a Pamphlet by J. Marryatt. ... *London.* 1823. 8vo, pp. 38. S. 42953

MACAULAY. A Letter to ... President of the African Institution from Zachary Macaulay, Esq. Occasioned by a Pamphlet ... by Dr. Thorpe ... entitled "A Letter to William Wilberforce, Esq." ... Second Edition, Enlarged. *London: John Hatchard.* 1815. 8vo, pp. (4), 62, and Appendix. A., B. 42954

MCAULEY (C.) Life of Catherine McAuley, Foundress and First Superior of the Institute of Religious Sisters of Mercy. By a Member of the Order of Mercy. With an Introduction by Ven. R. B. O'Brien. *New York: D. & J. Sadlier & Co.* 1866. 12mo, pp. 500. 42955

MACAULEY (J.) The Natural, Statistical and Civil History of the State of New York. ... By James Macauley. *New-York: Gould & Banks.* 1829. 3 vols., 8vo, pp. xxiv, 539, (1); (2), xi, 459, (1); xvi, 451, (1). C. 42956

Of little value; it includes some Indian vocabularies.

MCBLAIR (C. H.) Proceedings of the Naval General Court Martial, in the case of Lieutenant C. H. McBlair: ... at ... Philadelphia, May 4th, 1840. *Baltimore.* 1840. 8vo, pp. 44.

M'BRIDE (——). Navy Appropriation Bill. Speech of Mr. M'Bride, of Oregon, ... Feb. 19, 1864. [n. p. n. d.] 8vo, pp. 16. 42958

McBRIDE (J.) Pioneer Biography. Sketches of the Lives of Some of the Early Settlers of Butler County, Ohio. By James McBride, of Hamilton. ... *Cincinnati: Robert Clarke & Co.* 1869. 8vo, pp. (2), xiv, 352. Portrait. BA. 42959

Also on large paper. The book is more than the title promises; it includes copious details of border life. Also: Speech ... Installing President Hall; with the Inaugural Address by Rev. J. W. Hall, D.D. [n. p. n. d.] 8vo, pp. 21.

McCABE (James D.) Substance of a Discourse ... September 12th, 1858, before the Old Defenders of Baltimore, By the Rev. J. D. McCabe, D.D. ... *Baltimore: Printed by Jos. Robinson.* 1858. 8vo, pp. 24. H. 42960

Also: Address ... Rogersville, Tenn. on the 4th ... of July, 1849, at the Laying of the Corner Stone of the Odd Fellows Female Institute. ... *Abingdon: Coale and Barr.* 1849. 8vo, pp. 24.

McCABE (J. D.), *Jr.* Life and Campaigns of General Robert E. Lee. By James D. McCabe, Jr. ... *Atlanta, Ga.* [1866.] 8vo, pp. 717. Maps and Portrait. B. + *New York: Blelock & Co.* 1867. 8vo, pp. 717. Portrait and 6 Maps. 42961

McCABE. The Life and Public Services of Horatio Seymour: ... with ... Life of Francis P. Blair, Jr. By James D. McCabe, Jr. *New York.* 1868. 8vo, pp. 503. 2 Portraits. B. 42962

Also: The Aid-de-Camp; a Romance of the War. ... *Richmond: W. A. J. Smith.* 1863. 8vo, pp. 113. — ... The Guerrillas: An Original Domestic Drama, in Three Acts. ... *Richmond: West & Johnston.* 1863. 12mo, pp. 44. B. — ... Planting the Wilderness; or, the Pioneer Boys. A Story of Frontier Life. ... *Boston.* 1869. 16mo, pp. 256. + *Boston: Lee and Shepard.* 1870. 16mo, pp. 256. 3 Plates. H.

M'CABE (J. C.) Scraps, By John Collins M'Cabe. ... *Richmond: Printed by J. C. Walker.* 1835. 12mo, pp. 192. H.

MACCABE (J. P. B.) *See our* No. 40882.

McCAFFERY (M. J. A.) The Siege of Spoleto; A Camp Tale of Arlington Heights. By Michael J. A. McCaffery, M.A. *New York: P. O'Shea.* 186–. 12mo, pp. 92. 42964

M'CAFFREY (J.) Oration ... at the Commemoration of the Landing of the Pilgrims of Maryland, Celebrated May 16, 1842, at Mt. St. Mary's, M.D. By Rev. John M'Caffrey ... . *Gettysburg.* MDCCCXLII. 8vo, pp. 32. 42965

Also: Church and State. A Lecture ... January 5, 1854. ... *Baltimore.* 1854.

8vo, pp. 27. — Discourse on the Rev. Simon Gabriel Brute, Bishop of Vincennes, with Sketch of his Life. ... *Emmittsburg.* 1839. 8vo.

M'CAINE (A.) The History and Mystery of Methodist Episcopacy ... . By Alexander M'Caine ... . *Baltimore: Printed by Richard J. Matchett.* 1827. 8vo, pp. 76. B. 42966

Also: A Defence of the Truth, as set forth in the "History and Mystery of Methodist Episcopacy" ... a Reply to John Emory's "Defence of our Fathers." ... *Baltimore: Printed by R. J. Matchett.* 1829. 8vo, pp. 144. H.

M'CAINE. Letters on the Organization and Early History of the Methodist Episcopal Church, By Rev. Alexander M'Caine, ... *Boston: Thomas F. Norris.* 1850. 8vo, pp. 206. H. 42967

McCAINE. Slavery Defended from Scripture, against The Attacks of the Abolitionists, in a Speech ... before the General Conference of the Methodist Protestant Church, in Baltimore, 1842. By Alexander McCaine. *Baltimore: Printed by Wm. Wooddy.* 1842. 8vo, pp. 28. BA. 42968

MACCALEB (Theodore H.) An Address ... Public Schools, ... New Orleans ... February 22, 1843. *New Orleans.* 1843. 8vo. 42969

McCALL (G. A.) Letters from the Frontiers. Written during a Period of Thirty Years' Service in the Army of the United States. By Major General George A. McCall, late Commander of the Pennsylvania Reserve Corps. *Philadelphia: J. B. Lippincott & Co.* 1868. 12mo, pp. 539. BA. 42970

Contains many particulars relative to the Seminole War. Also: Official Reports of the Battles of Mechanicsville, Gaines' Mills ... . [n. p. n. d.] 8vo. — The Seven Day's Contests. Pennsylvania Reserves. General McCall's Report, and Accompanying Documents. *New York: Office of the Rebellion Record.* 1864. 8vo, pp. (10), 4.

M'CALL (H.) An Oration, ... in ... Charleston, South-Carolina, on the Fourth of July, 1810. ... By Hext M'Call ... . *Charleston: Printed by W. P. Young.* 1810. 8vo, pp. 28. BA.

McCALL (H. S.) New Year's Address of the Carrier of the Albany Morning Express to its Patrons, Jan. 1, 1853. *Albany: J. Munsell, Printer.* 1853. 12mo, pp. 4. 42972

M'CALL (H.) The History of Georgia, containing Brief Sketches of the most Remarkable Events, up to the Present Day. By Capt. Hugh M'Call. ... *Savannah: Seymour & Williams.* 1811–16. 2 vols., 8vo, pp. viii, 376; vii, 424. Map.

One of the scarcest of state histories. Unfortunately unfinished; the history stops at 1783. Its details of border warfare with the Creeks and Cherokees are copious, authentic, and interesting. *See* "N. A. Rev.," LIII. 478.

McCALL (J.) Address, delivered before the New York State Medical Society in ... Albany, February 2, 1847. By John McCall, M.D. ... *Albany: Joel Munsell.* 1847. 8vo, pp. 17. B.

Also: Dissertation, ... before the New York State Medical Society, ... Albany, February 2, 1847. ... *Albany: Printed by Joel Munsell.* 1847. 8vo, pp. 20. B.

M'CALL (J. C.) The Troubadour and other Poems. By John C. M'Call. *Philadelphia: H. C. Carey & I. Lea.* 1822. 12mo, pp. 64. 42975

M'CALL (P.) Discourse ... before the Law Academy of Philadelphia, September 5, 1838. By P. M'Call. *Philadelphia.* 1838. 8vo, pp. 51. P. 42976

Relates to Andrew Bradford, the printer, judicial history of Pennsylvania, etc. Also: An Oration ... before the Zelosophic Society of the University of Pennsylvania. ... *Philadelphia: Joseph & William Kite, Printers.* 1836. 8vo, pp. 24. BA.

McCALL (S.) Who is responsible for Public Calamities? A Sermon preached in Old Saybrook, Conn., April 28, 1861. By Rev. S. McCall. *New York: Hall, Clayton & Co.* 1861. 8vo, pp. 20. 42977

McCALLA (D.) Sermon at the Ordination of Rev. James Adams to the Congregational Church of Dorchester and Beach Hill, May 8, 1799. By Daniel McCalla. *Charleston.* [n. d.] 8vo, pp. 42. N. 42978

McCALLA (W. L.) Adventures in Texas, chiefly in the Spring and Summer of 1840. *Philadelphia.* 1841. 18mo, pp. 199. S. 42979

Also: Review of Dr. Boardman's Address against Kossuth. ... *Philadelphia: William S. Young, Printer.* 1852. 8vo, pp. 31.

McCALLUM (D. C.) United States Military Railroads. Report of Bvt. Brig.-Gen. D. C. McCallum, Director and General Manager from 1861 to 1866. *Washington.* 1866. 8vo, pp. 37. Map. 42980

M'CALLUM (P. F.) Travels in Trinidad during ... 1803, ... By Pierre F. M'Callum. ... *Liverpool: W. Jones.* 1805. 8vo, pp. xvi, 354. Map. BA. 42981

See "M. Rev.," New Series, LXIX. 94.

McCALMONT (Robert). Letter to the Shareholders of the Grand Trunk Railway of Canada, with a Report to him by Mr. Liddell, on the best mode of bridging the St. Lawrence, at Montreal, together with Counter-Reports by MM. R. Stephenson, I. K. Brunel, Ed. Clark and A. M. Ross, and Replies to each, by Mr. Liddell. *London.* 1856. 8vo, pp. 77. 42982

McCANDLESS (Wilson). *See* Pittsburgh, *Pa.*

McCANN (W.) Two Thousand Miles' Ride through the Argentine Provinces; being an Account of the Natural Products of the Country, and Habits of the People; with a Historical Retrospect of the Rio de la Plata, Monte Video, and Corrientes. By William McCann ... . *London: Smith, Elder & Co.* 1853. 2 vols., post 8vo, pp. xiv, (2), 295; x, (2), 323, (1). 6 Plates and Map. BA. 42983

McCARDLE (W. H.) Case of William H. McCardle, for alleged Illegal Imprisonment ... . [n. p.] 1867. 8vo. 42984

MACCARGO (Thomas). T. Maccargo versus the Merchants Insurance Company. *New Orleans.* [1842.] 8vo. 42985

An argument in an action for the recovery of the value of certain slaves embarked on the Brig "Creole."

McCARRELL (J.) Answer to a Discourse ... by Dr. William E. Channing, at the Dedication of the Second Congregational Unitarian Church, New-York, Dec. 7th, 1826. By Joseph McCarrell. *New-York: Printed by J. Seymour.* 1827. 8vo, pp. 47. B. 42986

McCARRELL (J.) Speech ... General Assembly of the Presbyterian Church ... in Support of a Claim of the Associate Reformed Synod of New York. By Rev. Joseph McCarrell. *Newburgh.* 1831. 8vo, pp. 24. 42987

McCARTHER (J. M.) Border Methodism and Border Slavery. By Rev. J. M. McCarther. *Philadelphia.* 1858. 8vo. S.

MACCARTHY (Jacques *or* Jean). Choix de Voyages dans les Quartre Parties du Monde, ou précis des Voyages les plus intéressans, par terre et par mer, Entrepris Depuis l'Annés 1806 jusqu'à ce jour; Par J. MacCarthy ... . *Paris: Librairie nationale et étrangère.* 1821–22. 10 vols., 8vo. BA., P. 42989

Vols. v. and vi. are "Voyages en Amerique." 54 sheets, 4 Plates and Map.

M'CARTNEY (W.) The Origin and Progress of the United States. By Washington M'Cartney, Esq. *Philadelphia: E. H. Butler & Co.* 1847. 12mo, pp. 404. B., H. 42990

M'CARTY (J. H.) The American Union. A Discourse delivered in Concord, N. H., May 11, 1862. By Rev. J. H. M'Carty. *Concord [N. H.]: Fogg, Hadley & Co.* 1862. 8vo, pp. 29. 42991

M'CARTY (J. M.) A View of the Whole Ground: being the Whole Correspondence between Mr. John M. M'Carty and General A. T. Mason. *District of Columbia, September.* 1818. 8vo, pp. (2), 38. BA. 42992

McCARTY (J. W.) ... A Discourse ... in ... Cincinnati, O., on the Day of National Mourning, June 1st, 1865. By Rev. John W. McCarty, A.B. ... *Cincinnati: Printed by Jos. B. Boyd.* 1865. 8vo, pp. 18. H. 42993

MACCARTY (T.) ... Two Discourses ... at Worcester, April 5th, 1759. ... the Day preceding the General Muster ... throughout the Province, for ... Inlisting Soldiers ... [in an] Expedition against Canada. By Thaddeus Maccarty, A.M. ... *Boston: Printed by Thomas and John Fleet.* 1759. 16mo, pp. 39. H. 42994

MACCARTY. ... A Sermon ... at Worcester, ... November 23d, 1775. ... Thanksgiving ... . By Thaddeus Maccarty, A.M. ... *Massachusetts-Bay: Worcester: Printed ... by I. Thomas.* [n. d.] 8vo, pp. 28. H. 42995

Also: A Farewell Sermon ... at Kingston [Mass.], Nov. 3, 1745. ... *Boston: Printed by E. Lincoln.* 1804. 8vo, pp. 16. BA. — ... Sermon ... Worcester, June 10. 1747. ... *Boston: D. Henchman.* 1747. 8vo, pp. (4), 34. BA. — ... A Sermon ... at Worcester, October the Twentieth, 1768. Being the Day of the Execution of Arthur, a Negro of about 21 Years old ... . *Boston: Printed ... by Kneeland and Adams.* MDCCLXVIII. 16mo, pp. 28. — Sermon at Worcester, July 2, 1778, on ... the Execution of James Buchanan, William Brooks, Ezra Ross, and Bathsheba Spooner, for ... Murder ... with an Appendix. ... *Worcester.* 1778. 8vo, pp. 40. M. — ... A Sermon ... at Worcester, October 25th. 1770. On Occasion of the Execution of William Linsey ... . *Boston: Printed ... by Kneeland and Adams.* MDCCLXX. 16mo, pp. 28. — Two Sermons delivered at the Special Fast, Worcester, July 14, 1774. ... *Boston.* 1774. 8vo, pp. 38.

McCARTY (W.) National Songs, Ballads and other Patriotic Poetry, chiefly relating to the year 1846. Compiled by William McCarty. *Philadelphia.* 1846. 18mo, pp. 144. P. 42996

McCARTY. Songs, Odes, and Other Poems, on National Subjects; Compiled from Various Sources. By William McCarty. ... *Philadelphia: Wm. McCarty.* 1842. 3 vols., 12mo, pp. 468; 467; 468. C. 42997

Part First, Patriotic; Part Second, Naval; Part Third, Military.

McCAULEY (C.) ... Inaugural Sermon to the First Parish in Waltham, January 2, 1870. By Clay McCauley. *Waltham, Mass.* 1870. 8vo, pp. 16. B. 42998

McCAULEY (J. A.) Character and Services of Abraham Lincoln: A Sermon preached ... Eutaw ... on the day of National

Humiliation and Mourning ... June 1, 1865. By Rev. Jas. A. McCauley. *Baltimore: John D. Toy, Printer.* 1865. 8vo, pp 16.

McCAW (J. B.) Memoirs of Jas. McClurg, M.D., with Extracts from his Works. By J. B. McCaw. *Richmond.* 1854. 8vo. 43000

M'CAY (M.) Trial of Medad M'Cay, for the Murder of his Wife; Reported by M. T. C. Gould. *Albany.* 1821. 8vo.

M'CHESNEY (J.) An Antidote to Mormonism; ... and Truth Disentangled from error and delusion. By James M'Chesney. Revised by G. J. Bennet. *New-York.* 1838. 12mo, pp. 60, 4.

Also: A Brief Review of the Proceedings of the Annual Conference of the Methodist Episcopal Church, ... embracing a Historical Sketch of the Difficulties existing between Washington Street Church, Brooklyn, and some of the higher Powers ... . *New York: Burnett & Pollard.* 1839. 12mo, pp. 44.

McCHESNEY (J. H.) Description of New Species of Fossils from the Paleozic Rocks of the Western States. By J. H. McChesney. *Chicago.* 1859–65. 8vo, pp. 97. 43003

McCHESTNEY (J.) An Oration ... at the request of the City Guards of ... Albany, delivered July 4, 1818. By John McChestney. *Albany.* 1818. 8vo, pp. 16. 43004

M'CHORD (J.) National Safety: a Sermon ... before the Hon. the Legislature of Kentucky, ... 12th January, 1815. ... a Day of National Fasting. By James M'Chord. ... *Lexington, (Ky.): Thomas T. Skillman.* 1815. 8vo, pp. 32. BA. 43005

Also: A Last Appeal to the "Market Street Presbyterian Church and Congregation;" in Seven Sermons ... . *Lexington, Ky.* 1818. 8vo.

M'CLARY OWNERS. *See* [Hale (John)], Vol. VIII. 29638.

END OF VOLUME TEN.

A DICTIONARY OF BOOKS

RELATING TO AMERICA.

McCLEAN (C.) Dissertation on the Source of Epidemic and Pestilential Diseases. By Charles McClean. *Dover.* 1801. 8vo. 43006

One of the earliest medical works published in New Hampshire.

M'CLEAN (J. S.) A Report of the Trial, of James Sylvanus M'Clean, alias J. Melville, and William L. Graham, ... For a Conspiracy to extort Money from Stephen Girard, Esq. *Philadelphia: John Binns, Printer.* 1812. 8vo, pp. 47. BA. 43007

[McCLEARY (S. F.)] A Sketch of the Origin, Object and Character of the Franklin Fund, for the ... Young Married Mechanics of Boston. ... *Boston: Alfred Mudge & Son ... Printers.* 1866. 8vo, pp. 38. H. 43008

McCLELLAN (G.) A Statement of Facts. By George McClellan, M.D. *Philadelphia.* 1822. 8vo, pp. 24. 43009

Also: Valedictory Address ... to the Graduates of the Jefferson Medical College. ... March, 1836. *Philadelphia: Printed by William S. Martien.* 1836. 8vo, pp. 16. H.

McCLELLAN (G. B.) Army of the Potomac. Report of Maj. Gen. Geo. B. McClellan, August 4, 1863. With an Account of the Campaign in Western Virginia. *New York: Sheldon and Company.* 1864. 8vo, pp. 484. Plans. 43010

Two hundred and fifty copies printed on large paper, imp. 8vo.

McCLELLAN. The Army of the Potomac; Gen. McClellan's Report of its Operations while under his Command. *New York: G. P. Putnam.* 1864. 8vo, pp. 505–655. Maps and Plans.

From the "Rebellion Record." Also issued on thin paper as a campaign document.

McCLELLAN. ... Complete Report on the Organization and Campaigns of the Army of the Potomac, By Major-General George B. McClellan. [n. p. 1863.] 8vo pp. 142, (1). B.

This edition is a "Campaign Document," No. 3. There is another issue, with a title slightly different.

McCLELLAN. Document No. 15. ... The Harrison's Bar Letter of Gen. McClellan. ... [n. p. 1862.] 8vo, pp. 4. B.

McCLELLAN. Letter of the Secretary of War, transmitting report on the Organization of the Army of the Potomac, and of Its Campaigns in Virginia and Maryland, under the Command of Maj. Gen. George B. McClellan, from July 26, 1861, to November 7, 1862. *Washington.* 1864. 8vo, pp. (2), 242. + *Washington: Constitutional Union Office.* 1864. 8vo, pp. 175.

McCLELLAN. Oration by Gen. George B. McClellan [at West Point]. *New York: C. S. Westcott & Co.* 1864. 8vo, pp. 31. + [Another Edition.] *New York: Sheldon & Co.* 1864. 12mo, pp. 35, (2). 43015

McCLELLAN. Regulations and Instructions for the Field Service of the U. S. Cavalry in Time of War. By Geo. B. McClellan ... . *Philadelphia: J. B. Lippincott & Co.* 1862. 12mo, pp. 216. Plates. H. 43016

McCLELLAN. ... Report of the Secretary of War, communicating the Report of Capt. George B. McClellan ... sent to the Seat of War in Europe, in 1855 and 1856. *Washington: A. O. P. Nicholson, Printer.* 1857. 4to, pp. (2), 360. Map. H.

McCLELLAN. Report on the Organization and Campaigns of the Army of the Potomac: to which is added an Account of the Campaign in Western Virginia, with Plans of Battle-Fields. By George B. McClellan ... . *New York: Sheldon & Company.* 1864. 8vo, pp. 480. Maps. B. 43018

Another edition was issued on large paper, with the title as in our No. 43010. There is also a cheap edition, *New York: American News Company.* 1864. 8vo, pp. 480. The matter of the following is the same, with a variation in the title-page:

McCLELLAN. ... Report of Major-General George B. McClellan, upon the Organization of the Army of the Potomac, and of its Campaign in Virginia and Maryland, from July 26, 1861, to November 7, 1862 ... . *Boston.* 1864. 8vo, pp. 152.

Another edition is *Washington*, 1863, 8vo, pp. 242. *See also* Tribune War Tracts.

McClellan. West Point Oration, by Gen. George B. McClellan. [n. p. n. d.] 8vo, pp. 8. 43020

Also: The Armies of Europe: comprising Descriptions ... of the Military Systems of England, France, Russia, Prussia, Austria, and Sardinia, adapting their Advantages to all Arms of the United States Service ... . *Philadelphia: J. B. Lippincott & Co.* 1861. 8vo, pp. 499. Plates, Portrait. BA.—Letter ... to Chas. J. Biddle, Oct. 12, 1863. [n. p. n. d.] Folio, 1 leaf.

... General McClellan's Letter of Acceptance [together with his West Point Oration. *New York.* 1864.] 8vo, pp. 7, (1).

How McClellan took Manassas. [A Poem.] *New York: Privately Printed.* 1864. 4to, pp. (2), 4. 43022

Fifty copies printed, and ten on very large paper. *See also* [Boker (G. H.)], Vol. II. Also: "Leave Pope to get out of his Scrape." McClellan's Despatches. [*Washington, D. C.* n. d.] 8vo, pp. 8.—Letter from the Secretary of War, on the Subject of the Occupation of the "White House" in Va., July 8, '62. [*Washington.*] 1862. 8vo, pp. 7.

The Life and Public Services of Major-General McClellan. Which includes a Complete Summary of his Report. Written by a Gentleman who accompanied him through his Campaigns. *Philadelphia: Martin Tindale.* 1864. 12mo, pp. 84. 43023

The Life, Campaigns, and Public Services of General McClellan. The Hero of Western Virginia! South Mountain! and Antietam. With a full history of all his Campaigns and Battles ... . *Philadelphia: T. B. Peterson & Brothers.* [1864.] 8vo, pp. (2), 17–184. Portrait. 43024

"McClellan; Who he is." *See* [Wilkes (G.)]

Also: A Brief Sketch of the Life and History of General McClellan, with Incidents in his Illustrious Career. [*New York.* 1864.] 8vo, pp. 10.—Burlesque Campaign Life of Geo. B. McClellan. *New York.* [n. d.] 18mo.—The Life and Services of Gen. Geo. B. McClellan. [n. p.] 1864. 8vo, pp. 63, (1). B.—The Life of Maj.-Gen. Geo. B. McClellan. Including Campaign in Mexico, etc. *New York.* [1862.] 16mo, pp. 98.

McClellan and Fremont: a reply to "Fremont and McClellan, their Political and Military Careers Reviewed." By Antietam. .. *New York: Sinclair Tousey.* [n. d.] 8vo, pp. 16. 43025

McClellan's Campaign. ... *New York: Anson D. F. Randolph.* 1862. 12mo, pp. 12. 43026

McClellan's Military Career Reviewed and Exposed; The Military Policy of the Administration Set Forth and Vindicated. ... *Washington: Printed by Lemuel Towers.* 1864. 8vo, pp. 32.

Mai-Jour (translated May-Day,) General George Barnum McClellan, Militant-Homœopath to the Army of the Confederates. Attacked, after his own Mode, through Parallels. ... *London: John Lee.* 1864. 12mo, pp. 139. + *New York: American News Company.* 1864. 16mo, pp. 32. 43028

Major-General George B. McClellan, from August 1st, 1861, to August 1st, 1862. ... *New York: H. Dexter.* [1862.] 8vo, pp. 26. BA. 43029

Only Authentic Life of George Brinton McClellan, alias, Little Mac. With an account of his numerous Victories from Phillipi to Antietam. *New York: American News Company.* [n. d.] 12mo, pp. 16. 43030

This and the following are mostly campaign documents, which were published during General McClellan's candidacy for President of the United States: Did General McClellan ever Intend to hurt the Rebels? [n. p. n. d.] 8vo, pp. 4.—Facts for the People. Ben Wade on McClellan. And Gens. Hooker & Heintzelman's Testimony. A Crushing Review of Little Napoleon's Military Career. (From the Cincinnati Gazette, Oct. 24, 1864.) [*Cincinnati.* 1864.] 8vo, pp. 8. BA.—Gen'l McClellan's Record. His Sympathy with the South. Read for Yourselves. [*Cincinnati.* 1864.] 8vo, pp. 12.—Little Mac Campaign Songster. *New York: T. R. Dawley.* 1864. 16mo, pp. 72.—Little Mac, how he captured Manassas. [n. p. n. d.] 12mo.—The Little Mac Songster. ... *New York: Dick and Fitzgerald.* [n. d.] 18mo, pp. 72.—McClellan Campaign Songster for the Use of Clubs. ... *Philadelphia: Mason & Co.* 1864. 24mo, pp. 16.—McClellan Democratic Presidential Campaign Songster. No. 1, McClellan and Pendleton. *New York: J. F. Feeks.* 1864. 16mo, pp. 72.—McClellan, the Pride of the Nation! [Song. n. p. n. d.] 8vo, 1 leaf. *See also* No. 40612.

M'Clellan (R. G.) Republicanism in America: a History of the Colonial and Republican Governments of the United States of America, from ... 1607 to ... 1869. ... By R. Guy M'Clellan. ... *San Francisco: R. J. Trumbull & Company.* 1869. 8vo, pp. 665. 21 Portraits. + [*Ibid.*] 1870. H. 43031

McClellan [Robert]. Speech of Mr. McClellan ... on the United States Fiscal Bank Bill: ... August 2, 1841. *Washington: Printed by Blair and Rives.* 1841. 8vo, pp. 16. BA. 43032

M'Clelland (A.) A Sermon in vindication of the Religious Spirit of the Age: ... April 9, 1820, in ... New-York ... . By Alexander M'Clelland, A.M. ... *New-York: Printed by D. Fanshaw.* 1820. 8vo, pp. 47, (1). H. 43033

Also: ... A Sermon ... at the Anniversary of the Young Men's Missionary Society, of New-York ... 1817. ... *New-York.* 1818. 8vo, pp. 56. BA.

McClelland (R.) ... Speech of Hon. R. McClelland ... February 10, 1849 ... on the Bill to carry into effect the Treaty of Peace with Mexico. [n. p. n. d.] 8vo, pp. 8. H. 43034

Also: Letter on the Crisis. ... [*Detroit.* 1860.] 8vo, pp. 11. B.—Speech ... [on Appropriations for Harbors and Rivers] February 26, 1846. [n p. n. d.] 8vo, pp. 8.

McClenachan (C. T.) Detailed Report of the Proceedings ... in Commemoration of the ... Laying of the Atlantic Telegraph Cable ... . By C. T. McClenachan. New York, 1859. *New York: Edmund Jones & Co.* 1863. 8vo, pp. (2), ii, 282.

McClenachan (W.) The Christian Warriour. A Sermon ... In Boston, March 17th. 1744, 5. By Wm. McClenachan, A.M. ... *Boston: D. Gookin.* 1745. 8vo, pp. (6), 16. B. 43036

[McClenthen (C. S.)] Narrative of the Fall & Winter Campaign, by a Private Soldier ... containing a Description of the Battle of Fredericksburg ... . *Syracuse: Masters & Lee ... Printers.* 1863. 12mo, pp. 53. H. 43037

McClenthen. Sketch of the Campaign in Virginia. *Syracuse.* 1862. 18mo. C. 43038

M'Cleod [Malcolm, D.D., *pseudon?*] History of Witches. *New Haven: Sidney's Press.* 1811. 24mo, pp. 107. C. 43039

McClernand [John A.] Remarks of Mr. McClernand ... on the Bill to raise a Regiment of Mounted Riflemen, and to establish Military Posts on the Route to Oregon ... . April 10, & 23. *Washington.* 1846. 8vo, pp. 7. H. 43040

McClernand. Speech of Mr. McClernand ... . March 19, 1844—On the Resolution reported by the Select Committee on the Rhode Island Controversy ... . [n. p. n. d.] 8vo, pp. 8. H.

Also: Speech ... on the Oregon Question. ... January 8, 1846. *Washington.* 1846. 8vo, pp. 14.—Speech ... in review of the ... Policy of the Present Administration, ... January 10, 1848. *Washington.* 1848. 8vo, pp. 8. H.

McClintock (F. L.) ... Meteorological Observations in the Arctic Seas. By Sir Francis Leopold McClintock, R.N. Made on board the Arctic Searching Yacht "Fox," in Baffin Bay and Prince Regent's Inlet, in 1857, 1858, and 1859. Reduced and Discussed, ... by Charles A. Schott. [*Washington.* 1859.] 4to, pp. xii, 5, 146. Chart. B. 43042

Included in the "Smithsonian Contributions," Vol. XIII.

M'Clintock. ... A Narrative of the Discovery of the Fate of Sir John Franklin and His Companions. By Captain M'Clintock, R.N. ... *London: John Murray.* 1859. 8vo. + *Boston: Ticknor and Fields.* MDCCCLX. 12mo, pp. xxiii, (1), 375. 5 Maps, 15 Plates. + *Philadelphia: J. T. Lloyd.* 1860. 8vo, pp. 317.

+ *New York.* 1860. 12mo, pp. 314, (3). Followed by "Godfrey's Narrative," pp. 7, 173–213. 43043

M'Clintock. La Destinée de Sir J. Franklin dévoilée. *Paris.* 1860. 8vo. Map. 43044

M'Clintock (*Capt.*) John Beedle's Sleigh Ride, Courtship, and Marriage. *New York.* 1841. 12mo. 43045

McClintock (J.) Discourse Delivered on the Day of the Funeral of President Lincoln, ... April 19, 1865, In ... New York, By John M'Clintock, D.D., LL.D. Reported by J. T. Butts. *New York: Press of J. M. Bradstreet & Son.* 1865. 8vo, pp. 35. B. 43046

Twenty copies printed on large paper.

McClintock. Sketches of Eminent Methodist Ministers. By John McClintock. Portraits and Plates. *New York.* 1854. 8vo. 43047

Macclintock (S.) The Choice: A Discourse, occasioned by the ... Drought; the ... Fever, ... and the ... Prospect of ... War ... . Delivered at Greenland, Sept. 9, 1798. By Samuel Macclintock, D.D. *Boston: Thomas Adams.* 1798. 8vo, pp. 21.

McClintock. An Oration, Commemorative of the late Illustrious General Washington; Pronounced at Greenland, February 22d, 1800; ... By Samuel McClintock, D.D. *Portsmouth (New Hampshire): Printed by Charles Peirce.* 1800. 8vo, pp. 16. 43049

M'Clintock. A Sermon ... before the ... Council and ... the Senate, and House of Representatives of ... New-Hampshire, June 3, 1784. On occasion of the Commencement of the New Constitution and Form of Government. By Samuel M'Clintock, A.M. *New-Hampshire, Portsmouth, Printed by Robert Gerrish.* M,DCC,-LXXXIV. 8vo, pp. 47. N., W. 43050

Also: A Discourse ... at the Funeral of ... Alpheus Spring ... . *Dover, (New-Hampshire:) Printed by Eliphalet Ladd.* M,DCC,XCI. 12mo, pp. 24.—Agur's Choice. Sermon at Dover, N. H. Aug. 9, 1797, before the Piscataqua Association. ... *Dover.* 1797. 4to.— ... A Sermon preach'd at Greenland, ... New-Hampshire [to] Young People ... . *Portsmouth, New-Hampshire: Printed by Daniel and Robert Fowle.* 1770. 8vo, pp. 31.— ... A Sermon ... at the Ordination of the Rev. Jesse Appleton ... in Hampton, February 22d, 1797. ... *Portsmouth, N. H.: Charles Peirce.* 1797. 8vo, pp. 24.— ... Sermon preached Feb. 25, 1759. ... *Portsmouth, N. H.* 1759. 8vo, pp. 32. — ... A Sermon ... at Greenland, ... July 22, 1770. ... *Portsmouth, N. H.* 1770. 8vo, pp. 34.—Sermon at Portsmouth, N. H., June 14, 1772. ... *Portsmouth.* 1772. 8vo, pp. 24.—Sermon at the Ordination of Isaac Smith, at Gilmantown, N. H. Nov. 30, 1774. ... *Salem, Mass.* 1775. 8vo, pp. 45. W

McClune (J. H.) Camp Life. The Sayings and Doings of Volunteers. By J. H. McClune. *Baltimore: J. D. Toy.* 1862. 8vo, pp. 36. 43051

M'Clung (J. A.) Sketches of Western Adventure: containing an Account of the most Interesting Incidents connected with the Settlement of the West, from 1755 to 1794. Together with an Appendix. By John A. M'Clung. *Maysville, Ky.: L. Collins.* 1832. 12mo, pp. 360. 43052

Some copies have the imprint *Philadelphia: Grigg & Elliot.* 1832.

M'Clung. Sketches of Western Adventure [as before]. *Cincinnati: J. A. James & Co.* 1832. 12mo, pp. 321. + [*Ibid.*] 1836. + [*Ibid.*] 1839. + [*Ibid.*] 1851. 12mo, pp. 360. + *Dayton.* 1844. 12mo. + [*Ibid.*] 1847. + *Dayton, Ohio: F. F. Claflin & Co.* 1852. 12mo, pp. 315. + *Dayton: More, Clarke & Company.* 1854. 12mo. B. 43053

The last edition reads "Sketches of Western Adventure ... . Also, Additional Sketches of Adventure." ... *Covington, Ky.* 1872. 12mo.

McClung (J. W.) Report of the Special Committee to investigate the Charge made by the Hon. J. W. McClung, of Missouri, against F. P. Blair, Jr., of violating the Laws in the matter of an alleged Liquor Speculation. [n. p. n. d.] 8vo, pp. 75. 43054

House of Representatives Report No. 61, 38th Congress, 1st Session, 1864.

McClung (J. W.) Minnesota as it is in 1870. Its General Resources and Attractions for Immigrants, Invalids, Tourists, Capitalists, and Business Men, (Principally from Official Authorities.) With Special Descriptions of all its Counties and Towns, ... By J. W. McClung, St. Paul. ... [*St. Paul (Minn.):*] *By the Author.* 1870. 12mo, pp. 299. Map and 4 Plates. 43055

M'Clure (A.) Décision du Conseil Impérial des Prises, Dans l'affaire du navire naufragé l'Horison. [*Paris.* 1807.] 4to, pp. 9. 43056

M'Clure. Mémoire pour Alexander M'Clure, ... avec son frère John M'Clure, du navire américain the Horison, et propriétaire du chargement à bord dudit navire ... . [*Paris.* 1807.] 4to, pp. 27. BA. 43057

M'Clure. Nouvelles Observations pour Alexander M'Clure, ... avec son frère John M'Clure ... . [*Paris.* 1807.] 4to, pp. 17.

McClure (A. K.) Three Thousand Miles through the Rocky Mountains. By A. K. McClure. *Philadelphia: J. B. Lippincott & Co.* 1869. 12mo, pp. 456. 2 Plates and Portrait.

A clever book, including details of Indian warfare, etc. Also: Fusion in Pennsylvania ... [n. p. n. d.] 8vo, pp. 8.—The True Commercial and Revenue Policy of Pennsylvania. Speeches ... on the Act for the Commutation of Tonnage Duties upon all the Internal Improvements of the State. Delivered ... February 26th and 27th, 1861. [n. p. n. d.] 8vo, pp. 30. H.

[McClure (A. W.)] The Bi-Centennial Book of Malden. Containing the Oration [by James D. Green] and Poem ... May 23, 1849; ... *Boston: Printed by Geo. C. Rand & Co.* 1850. 12mo, pp. 251. BA. 43060

M'Clure. The Life of John Cotton. By A. W. M'Clure. ... *Boston.* 1846. 12mo, pp. 300. BA. 43061

M'Clure. The Lives of John Wilson, John Norton, and John Davenport. By A. W. M'Clure. ... *Boston.* 1846. 8vo, pp. 305. 43062

Also: The Christian Observatory, a Literary and Religious Magazine. ... *Boston.* 1847. 8vo.

M'Clure (D.) A Discourse; Commemorative of the Death of General George Washington, ... Delivered at East-Windsor, Connecticut, February 22, 1800. By David M'Clure, A.M. ... *East-Windsor: Printed ... by Luther Pratt, March 24th,* 1800. 8vo, pp. 23. 43063

M'Clure. An Oration on the Advantages of an Early Education, delivered at Exeter, ... New-Hampshire, May 1, 1783, at the Opening of the Phillips Exeter Academy ... . By David M'Clure, A.M. ... *New-Hampshire.* M,DCC,LXXXIII. 4to, pp. 28.

M'Clure. A Sermon, Delivered in East-Windsor, Connecticut, at the Interment of the Hon. Erastus Wolcott, Esq. Who Departed this Life September 14, 1793, in the 71st Year of his Age. By David M'Clure, A.M. *Hartford: Hudson and Goodwin.* MDCCXCIV. 12mo, pp. 28. 43065

M'Clure. Memoirs of the Rev. Eleazar Wheelock, D.D. Founder and President of Dartmouth College and Moor's Charity School; with a summary history of the College and School. To which are added, copious Extracts from Dr. Wheelock's Correspondence. By David M'Clure ... and Elijah Parish ... . *Newburyport: Edward Little & Co.* 1811. 8vo, pp. 336. Portrait.

Also: Sermon at the Ordination of Stanley Griswold. ... *Danbury.* 1790. 8vo.—A Sermon, delivered at Ellington in Connecticut at the Interment of the Reverend

John Elsworth, A.M. ... *Printed at Hartford, by Hudson & Goodwin.* MDCCXCII. 8vo, pp. 32.—A Sermon ... at Hebron, ... Connecticut, on the Death of ... Reverend Benjamin Pomeroy, D.D. ... *Hartford: Printed by Elisha Babcock.* MDCCXCII. 8vo, pp. 24.—Sermon at East Windsor, on the Death of Deacon Amasa Loomis, July 1, 1793. ... *Hartford: Elisha Babcock.* 1794. 8vo, pp. 18.—Sermon at the Installation of the Morning-Star-Lodge of Freemasons, in East-Windsor, Connecticut, Aug. 21, 1794. ... *Hartford.* 1794. 8vo.— ... A Sermon ... at the Funeral of Mr. Simeon Burge. .. *Hartford.* 1794. 8vo, pp. 20.— ... A Sermon ... at the Interment of the Rev. Eliphalet Williams, D.D. of East-Hartford, Connecticut, July 1, 1803. ... *Hartford: Printed by Hudson & Goodwin.* 1803. 8vo, pp. 15.— ... A Sermon, ... at the Interment of the Rev. Thomas Potwine, ... in East-Windsor. November 17, 1802. ... *Hartford: Printed by Hudson & Goodwin.* 1803. 8vo, pp. 18. B.

[M'Clure (David).] A Brief Exposition of the Philosophic Principles upon which the System of Education for the Girard College for Orphans is Founded. *Philadelphia: I. Ashmead & Co.* 1838. 8vo, pp. (2), 363. C. 43067

[M'Clure.] A System of Education for the Girard College for Orphans. ... By a Native of Philadelphia. *Philadelphia.* 1838. 8vo, pp. 16, 48. Table. C. 43068

M'Clure (D.) Report of the Survey of a Section of the River Delaware, from one mile below Chester to Richmond, above Philadelphia. By David M'Clure. *Philadelphia.* 1820. 8vo. P.

M'Clure. 1825. ... The United States National Almanac. ... By David M'Clure. *Philadelphia: R. Desilver.* 1825. 8vo, pp. 56. 2 folded Tables. BA. 43070

M'Clure (G.) Causes of the Destruction of the American Towns on the Niagara Frontier, and Failure of the Campaign of the Fall of 1813. By George M'Clure, Brigadier-General of New-York Militia. *Bath, N. Y. Printed in* 1817, *by Benjamin Smead.* Sm. 8vo, pp. 72. 43071

An extremely rare piece. The author's strictures on the powers that were are severe, and apparently well deserved.

M'Clure (*Sir* Robert John Le Mesurier.) The Arctic Dispatches containing An Account of the Discovery of the North-West Passage. By Captain Robert M'Clure, Commanding H. M. S. Investigator. With a Narrative of Proceedings of H. M. S. Resolute, Capt. Kellett, C.B. and the Dispatches of Capt. Sir Edward Belcher, C.B. Capt. Inglefield, and Commr. Pullen. ... *London: J. D. Potter.* [1853.] 8vo, pp. (4), 111. Map.

M'Clure. The Discovery of the North-West Passage by H.M.S. "Investigator," Capt. R. M'Clure, 1850, 1851, 1852, 1853, 1854. Edited by Commander Sherard Osborn, ... from

the Logs and Journals of Capt. Robert Le M. M'Clure. Illustrated by Commander S. Gurney Cresswell, R.N. *London: Longman* ... 1856. 8vo, pp. xix, 405, (1). Chart and 4 Plates. BA. + New Edition. [*Ibid.*] 1857. 8vo, pp. 450. + Third Edition. [*Ibid.*] 1859. 8vo, pp. 480. + Fourth Edition. *William Blackwood & Son, Edinburgh.* 1865. Cr. 8vo, pp. xxvi, 358. C.

The primary object of the voyage was to rescue Sir John Franklin and his companions (who sailed from England in 1845), but that object was not accomplished.

M'Clure. The North-West Passage. Capt. M'Clure's Despatches From Her Majesty's Discovery Ship, "Investigator," off Point Warren and Cape Bathurst. *London: John Betts.* 1853. 8vo, pp. 45. Map. C. 43074

Mac-Clure. Opdagelsen af Nordvestpassagen. Udg. af S. Osborn. Oversat af W. Bauditz. *Kjobenhavn: Reitzel.* 1858. 8vo. Portrait and Map. 43075

McClure (R.) Diseases in the American Stable, Field and Farm-Yard ... . By Robert McClure, M.D., VS. ... *Philadelphia: Porter & Coates.* [1866?] 8vo, pp. 414. H. 43076

McClure (W.) To the People of the United States, in relation to their Claims against France. By William McClure. *Philadelphia.* 1807. 8vo. C. 43077

McClure (W. J.) Poems. By William James McClure. *New York: P. O'Shea.* 1869. 12mo, pp. (2), 148, (2). 43078

McClurg (J. W.) Missouri Home Guards. Speech of Hon. Joseph W. McClurg, ... Dec. 22, 1863. [*Washington.* n. d.] 8vo, pp. 8. H. 43079

Also: Speech ... March 9th, 1864, in Reply to the Personalities of his Colleagues, Blair and King. ... [n. p. n. d.] 8vo, pp. 16.—Speech ... March 23, 1864, to refute the Charge ... of Forgery alleged by (Mr. Blair) against B. R. Bonner ... . *Washington, D. C.: Gibson Brothers, Printers.* 1864. 8vo, pp. 8.—Speech ... April 29, 1864, on motion to print the Evidence and Report of the Investigating Committee, in the Case of the Alleged Charge against Hon. F. P. Blair ... . *Washington, D. C.: Gibson Brothers, Printers.* 1864. 8vo, pp. 16. H.

McCollom (J. T.) ... A Sermon ... at the Funeral of Rev John E. Farwell, in Ashby, Mass., December 28, 1858, By James T. McCollom ... *Haverhill: E. G. Frothingham, Printer.* 1859. 8vo, pp. 11. H. 43080

M'Collum (W.) California As I Saw it. ... Pencillings by the Way of its Gold and Gold Diggers! And Incidents of Travel by Land and Water. By William M'Collum, M.D. a returned adventurer. *Buffalo: George H. Derby & Co.* 1850. 8vo, pp. 72. 43081

McComb (D. B.) Answers of David B. McComb, Esq. with an accompanying Letter of General Lafayette. *Tallahassee.* 1827. 8vo. 43082

These are answers to inquiries relative to Florida, and are rather climatically tinged. *See* "N. A. Rev.," xxvi. 494–496.

M'Combie (T.) Colonial Reform; being a comprehensive Plan for the Management of the British Colonies, in a Letter to Sir Robert Peel. By Thomas M'Combie. [*London.* n. d.] 8vo.

McConihe (Isaac). In Memoriam. *Troy, N. Y.* [1867.] 8vo, pp. 97. s. 43084

McConkey (H. E. B.) Dakota War Whoop; or, Indian Massacres and War in Minnesota, of 1862–'63. By Harriet E. Bishop McConkey ... . *St. Paul: D. D. Merrill.* 1863. 16mo, pp. vii, 13–304. 6 Portraits. c. + Revised Edition. *St. Paul: The Author.* 1864. 12mo, pp. 429. Portraits. 43085

McConnel (J. L.) The Glenns: A Family History. By J. L. McConnel. *New York.* 1851. 12mo. 43086

McConnel. Western Characters or Types of Border Life in the Western States By J. L. McConnel ... With Illustrations by Darley. *Redfield, New York.* 1853. 12mo, pp. (2), 378. 5 Plates. B. 43087

Of little value, and not in keeping with the promise in the title-page.

McConnel (W.) Life and Times of Old Billy McConnel, the Witch Doctor. *Cincinnati.* 1853. 8vo. 43088

M'Connell (M.) An Essay on the Domestic Debts of the United States of America. [With] a Statement of the Foreign Debt ... . By Matthew M'Donnell. *Philadelphia: Printed ... by Robert Aitken.* M.DCC.LXXXVII. 8vo, pp. (1), 90. H., P. 43089

McCook (D.) Trial of Daniel McCook on Articles of Impeachment for Breach of good Behavior in Office. *Cincinnati.* 1839. 8vo, pp. 72. 43090

[McCord (D.)] ... Political Economy — Manufactures: being a Review of 1. Message of President Polk ... . 2. Report of Mr. Walker ... . 3. Mr. Peel's Speech in the British Parliament ... . [n. p. 1856.] 8vo, pp. 43. H. 43091

[McCord (D. J.)] What is Fair and Equal Reciprocity? [n. p. n. d.] 8vo, pp. 15. B. 43092

McCord (J. S.) Report of Meteorological Observations made on the Island of St. Helen, River St. Lawrence. By John S. McCord. *Montreal.* 1842. 8vo. 43093

M'Cord (*Mr.*) Speech of Mr. M'Cord ... at ... Columbia, S. C. opposed to the proposed Woollens Bill, on the Second July, 1827. *Columbia, So. Ca.: Printed by Sweeny & Sims.* 1827. 8vo, pp. 50. BA., s. 43094

McCord (T.) Synopsis of the Changes in the Law effected by the Civil Code of Lower Canada. By T. McCord, Advocate, ... *Ottawa: G. E. Desbarats, Printer.* 1866. 8vo, pp. 39. H.

M'Corkle (S. Eusebius). A Sermon, on the Comparative Happiness and Duty of the United States ... Contrasted with other Nations ... . Delivered in Salisbury, ... February 18th; and at Thyatira, ... February 19th, 1795: ... By the Rev. Samuel E. M'Corkle, D.D. ... *Halifax: Printed by Abraham Hodge.* M,DCC,XCV. 12mo, pp. 43. BA. 43096

M'Corkle. True Greatness, a Sermon on the Death of Gen. George Washington; the Substance of which was delivered at Thyatira, Jan. 12th; and afterwards with some Additions in Salisbury, Feb. 11, 1800. By the Rev. Samuel E. M'Corkle, ... *Lincolntown (N. C.): J. M. Slump.* 1800. 8vo, pp. 27, 2.

McCorkle (W. A.) In Memoriam, George Duffield. By Rev. William A. McCorkle. *Detroit.* 1868. 8vo. 43098

M'Cormick (C.) Memoirs of the Right Honourable Edmund Burke; ... By Charles M'Cormick, LL.B. *London: The Author.* 1797. 4to, pp. 383. Portrait. A., B. 43099

A very bitter satirical work, containing some references to his views on American topics. Burke's family strove in vain to prevent its publication. Also: Reign of George III. to 1783. ... [n. p. n. d.] 8vo.

M'Cormick (R.) Narrative of a Boat Expedition up the Wellington Channel in the Year 1852, in Search of Sir John Franklin. By R. M'Cormick. *London.* 1854. 4to. Map. s.

McCormick (R. C.) Arizona: Its Resources and Prospects. ... By the Hon. Richard C. McCormick ... . *New York: D. Van Nostrand.* 1865. 8vo, pp. 22. Map. H. 43101

McCormick. Indians, Friendly and Unfriendly. Remarks of Hon. Richard C. McCormick ... delivered ... February 28, and March 2 and 3, 1870. *Washington.* 1870. 8vo, pp. 7.

A document of more interest and value than many more lengthy treatises. Also: The Duty of the Hour: An Oration delivered at Jamaica, Long Island, July 4th, 1863 ... . *New York: George A. Whitehorne, Printer.* 1863. 8vo, pp. 36.—Indian Affairs in Arizona. Speeches ... January 30, and April 13, 1872. *Washington.* 1872, 8vo, pp. 14.—The Patriotism of the Plough. An Address ... Flushing, Long Island. October 3, 1861. ... *Hempstead.* 1861. 8vo, pp. 31.—Surveys in Arizona. Remarks ... June 27, 1870. *Washington: F. & J. Rives ... Printers.* 1870. 8vo, pp. 7. H.

McCosh (J.) Inauguration of James McCosh, as President of the College of New Jersey. *New York.* 1868. 8vo, pp. 96.

Dr. McCosh is the well-known author of many theological works.

McCoskry (S. A.) The Blessings and the Sins of the Nation ... a Sermon, preached in ... Detroit, September 26, 1861, By the Rt. Rev. Saml. A. McCoskry, D.D. ... *Detroit: H. Barns & Co., Printers.* 1861. 8vo, pp. 15. H. 43104

McCoskry. ... The Sermon preached before ... the General Convention of the Protestant Episcopal Church, in ... New York, October 1, 1862. By Right Rev. Samuel Allen McCoskry, D.D. ... *New York: Baker & Godwin, Printers.* 1862. 8vo, pp. 19. H. 43105

Also: An Address ... at the Commencement, in the General Theological Seminary ... June 28, 1839. ... *New-York: Swords, Stanford & Co.* 1839. 8vo, pp. 14. H.—Sermon ... at the Jubilee ... 1853. ... [n. p. n. d.] 8vo.—Trust in God, the Strength of a Nation. A Sermon preached in Detroit, January 4, 1861. ... *Detroit.* 1861. 8vo, pp. 16.

McCoun (W. T.) Address ... before the Queen's County Agricultural Society, ... October 13th, 1842. By William T. McCoun. *New-York: Vinten, Printer.* 1843. 8vo, pp. 16. B.

McCoy (A. D.) Thoughts on Labor in the South, Past, Present, and Future, By A. D. McCoy ... . *New Orleans: Bleblock & Co.* 1865. 12mo, pp. 35. H. 43107

McCoy (A.) Funeral Oration on the Death of Hon. Daniel Webster, delivered ... in ... Ballston Spa, N. Y., ... November 8, 1852. By ... Amasa McCoy. *Boston: Charles C. P. Moody, Printer.* 1852. 8vo, pp. 16. + [*Ibid.*] 1853. 8vo, pp. 29. H. + Third Edition. [*Ibid.*] 1856. 8vo, pp. (4), 39. BA. 43108

[M'Coy (Isaac).] Address to Philanthropists in the United States generally, and to Christians in Particular, on the Condition and Prospects of the American Indians. [n. p. 1831.] 8vo, pp. 8. B., W. 43109

M'Coy. The Annual Register of Indian Affairs ... . Published by Isaac M'Coy. ... January 1, 1835. *Shawanoe Mission: J. Meeker, Printer.* 1835. 8vo, pp. 48. B. 43110

M'Coy. The Annual Register of Indian Affairs within the Indian (or Western) Territory. Published by Isaac M'Coy. ... May, 1837. *Shawanoe Baptist Mission, Ind. Ter.* 1835–38. 8vo, Nos. 1 and 2, pp. 85, 91; No. 3, pp. 81; No. 4, pp. 95, (1).

No. 4 is *Washington: Printed by Peter Force.* 1838.

McCoy. History of Baptist Indian Missions: embracing Remarks on the Former and Present Condition of the Aboriginal Tribes; their Settlement within the Indian Territory, and their Future Prospects. By Isaac McCoy. ... *Washington: William M. Morrison.* 1840. 8vo, pp. (8), 611. BA. 43112

A valuable record of the characteristic traits of the Indian tribes among whom the author labored.

M'Coy. Remarks on the Practicability of Indian Reform, embracing their Colonization. By Isaac M'Coy. *Boston: Printed by Lincoln & Edmands, December* 1827. 8vo, pp. 47. + With an Appendix. Second Edition. *New York: Printed by Gray and Bunce.* 1829. 8vo, pp. 72. C. 43113

Also: Periodical Account of Baptist Missions within the Indian Territory, for the year ending December 31, 1836. ... [n. p. n. d.] 8vo, pp. 52.

[McCrady (E.)] Minority Report of the Commission appointed ... to examine the Militia System of the State ... . *Columbia, S. C.: R. W. Gibbes ... Printer.* 1859. 8vo, pp. 25.

McCrady (J.) ... Address ... before the ... Alumni of the College of Charleston, at the Inauguration of the Charleston College Library. By Prof. John McCrady ... . *Charleston: Printed by A. J. Burke.* 1856. 8vo, pp. 23. H. 43115

McCrea (Robert Barlow). Lost amid the Fogs: Sketches of Life in Newfoundland, England's Ancient Colony. By Lieut.-Col. R. B. McCrea ... . *London: Sampson Low, Son, & Marston.* 1869. 12mo, pp. xv, 299. B., C. 43116

M'Cready (B. W.) Memoir of John A. Swett, M.D. ... By B. W. M'Cready, M.D. ... *New York: D. Appleton and Company.* 1855. 8vo, pp. 36. Portrait. BA. 43117

[McCreary (R. G.)] The Great Healing Springs on the Battle-Field of Gettysbourg ... . *N. Y.: J. Craft, Printer.* [1866?] 8vo, pp. 8. H. 43118

McCreery (T. C.) Arlington. Resolution and Speech of Hon. Thomas C. McCreery ... December 13, 1870. [n. p. n. d.] 8vo, pp. 4. H. 43119

Also: Finance. Speech ... January 27, 1869. *Washington.* 1869. 8vo, pp. 8.—Representation of Arkansas. Speech ... May 28, 1868. [n. p. n. d.] 8vo, pp. 10.

M'Cron (J.) A Sermon ... by Rev. John M'Cron, D.D. ... before the Association of Defenders of Baltimore in 1814. September 11th, 1859. *Baltimore: Printed by James Lucas & Son.* 1859. 8vo, pp. 13. H. 43120

M'Crum (James). *See* [Cramer (Zadock)], IV. 17384–6.

McCullagh (William T.) The Industrial History of Free Nations, considered in relation to their Domestic Institutions and External Policy. By W. Torrens McCullagh. *London: Chapman and Hall.* MDCCCXLVI. 2 vols., 8vo, pp. xviii, 336; xviii, 397. BA., C. 43121

Partly on American topics.

[McCulloch (——).] The Wisdom and Policy of the French in the Construction of their Great Offices, So as best to answer the Purposes of extending their Trade and Commerce, and enlarging their Foreign Settlements. With Some Observations in relation to the Disputes now subsisting between the English and French Colonies in America. *London: R. Baldwin.* MDCCLV. 8vo, pp. (2), 133. 43122

This performance seems more especially intended as an introduction to the following:

[McCulloch.] A Miscellaneous Essay, Concerning the Courses pursued by Great Britain, In the Affairs of her Colonies: With some Observations on the Great Importance of our Settlements in America and The Trade thereof. *London: R. Baldwin.* MDCCLV. 8vo, pp. (2), 134. 43123

"After having pointed out the inconveniences the inhabitants of our American colonies are exposed to, for want of sufficient checks on their government, our author hopes that it will be thought for the service of the crown and of the subject to regulate offices so as to bring every matter of importance to the view of the crown," etc.—*Monthly Review*, XII. 153. The writer recommends better treatment of the Indians and a closer alliance with them, after the manner of the French, particularly those of the Five Nations.

McCulloch (H.) Our National and Financial Future. Address of Hon. Hugh McCulloch, ... at Fort Wayne, Indiana, October 11, 1865. *Fort Wayne.* 1865. 8vo, pp. 16. 43124

Also: Mr. Hugh McCulloch and the Secretaryship of the Treasury. *Washington.* 1865. 8vo, pp. 8. H. *See also* Secretary of the Treasury.

[M'Culloch (John).] A Concise History of the United States, from the Discovery of America, till 1807. ... The Third Edition. *Philadelphia: John M'Culloch.* 1807. 16mo, pp. 300. Map. C. + Till 1813. ... The Fourth Edition. *Philadelphia: Printed by W. M'Culloch.* 1813. 12mo, pp. (4), 9–320. Map.

Also: M'Culloch's Pocket Almanack, For ... 1805. ... *Philadelphia: J. M'Culloch.* [n. d.] 12mo.

McCulloch (John Ramsay). A Descriptive and Statistical Account of the British Empire; ... By J. R. McCulloch, Esq. ... Third Edition, Corrected. ... *London.* 1847. 2 vols., 8vo. C. + Fourth Edition, Revised. With an Appendix of Tables. ... *London: Longman ...* 1854. 2 vols., 8vo, pp. xv, 766, (1); viii, 780, 36. B. 43126

Includes the American colonies.

McCulloch. A Dictionary, Geographical, Statistical, and Historical, of the Various Countries, Places, and Principal Natural Objects in the World. ... By J. R. McCulloch, Esq. ... *London: Longman, Orme, Brown ...* . MDCCCXLI–XLII. 2 vols., 8vo, pp. viii, 1020; (4), 948. Maps. BA. + Enlarged by Dr. Haskel. *New York.* 1845. 2 vols., 8vo. 7 Maps. + A New ... Edition, with a Supplement. *London: Longman ...* MDCCCLI. 2 vols., 8vo, pp. viii, 1020; (2), 970. Maps. + [*Ibid.*] 1854. + New Edition, carefully revised, with the Statistical Information brought up to the Latest Returns by Frederick Martin ... . *London: Longman ...* 1866. 4 vols., 8vo, pp. vii, (4), 670; (4), 603; (4), 600; (6), 502. B. 43127

The information on American subjects is copious and impartial.

McCulloch. A Dictionary, Practical, Theoretical, and Historical, of Commerce and Commercial Navigation ... . By J. R. McCulloch, Esq. ... *London.* 1832. 8vo, pp. xv, 1269, 16. Maps. + Second Edition. [*Ibid.*] 1835. 8vo, pp. 1296, 58. Maps. + A New Edition, corrected and improved: with an Enlarged Supplement ... . *London: Longman ...* . MDCCCXXXVII. 8vo, pp. xvi, 1269, 118. Maps. + [*Ibid.*] 1840. + *Philadelphia.* 1840. 2 vols., 8vo. C. + *Philadelphia: A. Hart.* 1851. 2 vols., 8vo, pp. xi, (1), 767; 803. B. 43128

Other editions are *London*, 1846, 1849, 1852, MDCCCLIV, 8vo, pp. xviii, 1484, Maps; *London: Longman, Brown ...* MDCCCLVI, 8vo, pp. xx, 1480, Maps; *Philadelphia: Parry & McMillan*, 1856, 2 vols., 8vo; and A New Edition, Edited by Hugh G. Reid, *London: Longman ...* 1869, 8vo, pp. xxiv, 1558, Maps. The American editions are edited by Henry Vethake, and contain much matter concerning America. There is a French translation, edited by Monbrion, 2 vols., 4to.

M'Culloch. A Statistical Account of the British Empire: ... By J. R. M'Culloch, Esq. ... *London: Charles Knight and Co.* MDCCCXXXVII. 2 vols., 8vo, pp. xi, (1), 630; viii, 692. BA. + Second Edition, Enlarged. [*Ibid.*] MDCCCXXXIX. 43129

See our No. 43126, *supra*, for later editions.

M'Culloch. Universal Gazetteer; a Dictionary, Geographical, Statistical, and Historical, of the Various Countries, Places, and Principal Natural Objects in the World. By J. R. M'Culloch, Esq. In which the Articles relating to the United States have been greatly Multiplied and Extended, ... by Daniel Haskel. *New York: Harper & Brothers.* 1843–44. 2 vols., 8vo, pp. 1148; 1109. Maps. + [*Ibid.*] 1845–49. + [*Ibid.*] 1851. B. 43130

Also: ... A Treatise on the Principles, Practice, & History of Commerce. ... *London: Baldwin and Cradock.* MDCCCXXXIII. 8vo, pp. (2), 128. H.

M'Culloch (T.) ... A Sermon, ... at Pictou, ... February 25, 1814, ... the Day appointed for a General Fast. By Thomas M'Culloch. ... *Halifax: Printed by John Howe and Son.* 1814. 8vo, pp. 24. BA. 43131

Also: ... Lecture ... at the Opening of the ... Pictou Academical Institute. ... *Halifax: A. H. Holland, Printer.* 1819. 8vo, pp. 24.

[M'Culloh (James H.)] Researches on America; being an Attempt to settle some Points relative to the Aborigines of America, &c. ... By an Officer of the United States' Army. *Baltimore: Coale and Maxwell.* 1816. 8vo, pp. (6), (1), 130, (1).

The original sketch of a work afterwards much amplified as below:

M'Culloh. Researches on America; being an Attempt to settle some Points relative to the Aborigines of America, &c. By James H. M'Culloh, Jun. M.D. *Baltimore: Joseph Robinson.* 1817. 8vo, pp. 220. 43133

McCulloh. Researches, Philosophical and Antiquarian, concerning the Aboriginal History of America. By J. H. McCulloh, Jr. M.D. *Baltimore: Fielding Lucas, Jr.* 1829. 8vo, pp. x, 13–535. Map. B. 43134

A meritorious work, containing some curious and learned speculations. *See* Prescott's "Mexico."

M'Culloh (R. S.) Letter to the Hon. Thomas Corwin, ... in Reply to a Report of the Director of the Mint upon Charges preferred against James C. Booth. ... By Professor R. S. M'Culloh. *Washington: Gideon and Co., Printers.* 1852. 8vo, pp. 24.

M'Culloh. Plan of Organization for the Naval Observatory ... . By Professor R. S. M'Culloh. *Washington: Printed by J. & G. S. Gideon.* 1844. 16mo, pp. 8. H. 43136

McCulloh. The Proceedings of the Late Director of the Mint, in relation to the Official Misconduct of Franklin Peale, Esq. ... and Other Abuses in the Mint. Reviewed by Prof. R. S. McCulloh ... . *Princeton, New Jersey.* 1853. 8vo, pp. 79.

M'Cullough (J. W.) Sacred Reminiscences. A Sermon ... August 21, 1842, in The Old Swedes' Church, Wilmington, Del.; with Historical Notes. By the Rev. John W. M'Cullough, A.M. ... *Wilmington, Del.: Printed by Porter & Naff.* 1842. 8vo, pp. 33. 43138

McDaniel (S. W.) An Address ... at the Funeral of Capt. William F. Brigham, in Feltonville, Mass., Feb. 18, 1865. By Samuel W. McDaniel. ... *Feltonville: Charles A. Wood, Printer.* 1865. 8vo, pp. 19. B. 43139

Macdill (D.) A Lecture delivered in the Mechanics Institute of Hamilton and Rossville. By D. Macdill ... . *Rossville, Ohio.* 184–. 8vo, pp. 20. 43140

Macdill. ... Three National Blessings. A Discourse ... in ... Hamilton, O.: December 2, 1841. ... Thanksgiving. By D. Macdill, D.D. ... *Rossville: J. M. Christy, Printer.* 1841. 12mo, pp. 22. H. 43141

Also: Sketch of the History of the Associated Reformed Church, delivered in Oxford, O., March 2, 1843. ... [n. p. n. d.] 8vo.—Three Questions: Why was the Continent of America not discovered till so late a period? Have we, the People of the United States, an Infidel or a Heathen System of Government? Does the Constitution of the United States sanction Slavery? ... *Oquaka (Illinois): Plaindealer Office.* 1863. 8vo, pp. 25.

McDonald (A.) A Narrative of some Passages in the History of Eenoolooapik, a young Esquimaux, who was brought to Britain in 1839, in the Ship "Neptune" of Aberdeen: an Account of the Discovery of Hogarths Sound: Remarks on the Northern Whale Fishery, and Suggestions for its Improvement, &c. &c. By Alexander McDonald. *Edinburgh: Fraser & Co.* MDCCCXLI. 12mo, pp. iii, 140. Map and Portrait. 43142

Macdonald (A.) America Central Reclamacion de la intervencion del Coronel Sr. Alejandro Macdonald, superintendente de Belize en el Coronel Sr. Man. Cuijano, administrador del Puerto de S. Juan del Norte. *Leon de Nicaragua.* 1842. 8 l.

McDonald (A.) American Steamship Lines. Speech of Hon. Alexander McDonald ... April 11, 1870. *Washington: F. & J. Rives, Printers.* 1870. 8vo, pp. 16. 43144

Macdonald (A.) Narrative respecting the Destruction of the Earl of Selkirk's Settlement upon Red River, in ... 1815. By Archibald Macdonald. *London: Printed by J. Brettell.* 1816. 8vo, pp. 14. H. 43145

Macdonald. Reply to the Letter, lately addressed to the ... Earl of Selkirk, by the Hon. and Rev. John Strachan, D.D. ... Being four Letters, ... containing a Statement of Facts, concerning the Settlement on Red River, in the District of Ossiniboia, ... properly called Rupert's Land. By Archibald Macdonald, ... *Montreal (Lower-Canada): Printed by W. Gray.* 1816. 8vo, pp. 50. 43146

See also McAdam (A.), Vol. x., No. 42927.

Macdonald (A. J.) Monuments, Grave Stones, Burying Grounds, Cemeteries, Temples, etc., By A. J. Macdonald ... . *Albany: Joel Munsell, Printer.* 1848. 12mo, pp. 22. 43147

[Macdonald (Angus W.)] The Two Rebellions; or, Treason Unmasked. By a Virginian. *Richmond: Smith, Bailey & Co.* 1865. 12mo, pp. 143, (1). B. 43148

Macdonald (D. G. F.) British Columbia and Vancouver's Island; comprising a Description of these Dependencies; their Physical Character, Climate, Capabilities, Population, Trade, Natural History, Geology, Ethnology, Gold Fields, and Future Prospects. Also, an Account of the Manners and Customs of the Native Indians. By Duncan George Forbes Macdonald, C.E. *London: Longman* ... 1862. 8vo, pp. 538. Map. C. + Second Edition. [*Ibid.*] 1863. 43149

Also: Lecture on British Columbia and Vancouver's Island. ... *London.* 1863. 8vo.

Macdonald (G.) Documents relating to Steam Navigation in the Pacific. *Lima.* 1836. 8vo. 43150

Macdonald (J. M.) President Lincoln; his Figure in History: A Discourse delivered in ... Princeton, New Jersey, June 1st, 1865. By James M. Macdonald, D.D. *New York: Charles Scribner & Co.* 1865. 8vo, pp. 23. 43151

Macdonald. A Sketch of the History of the Presbyterian Church in Jamaica, Long Island, which was established near the

middle of the Seventeenth Century. By James M. Macdonald. *New York.* 1847. 12mo, pp. 138. A., N. 43152

Macdonald. Two Centuries in the History of the Presbyterian Church, Jamaica, L. I., the Oldest Existing Church, of the Presbyterian Name, in America. By James M. Macdonald, D.D. ... *New York: Robert Carter & Brother.* 1862. 12mo, pp. 329. S. 43153

Also: ... A Discourse ... March 7, 1859, at the Funeral of the Rev. James Carnahan, D.D. ... *New York: Charles Scribner.* 1860. 8vo, pp. 39. B.

M'Donald (J.) Ebenezer: or Jehovah the Helper of America. A Sermon, ... July 4, 1814; ... By John M'Donald ... . *Albany: Printed by Ryer Schermerhorn.* 1814. 8vo, pp. 38. B.

M'Donald. Jehovah-Shalom: or The Peace sending Jehovah. A Thanksgiving Sermon, ... April 13th, 1815: ... for ... Peace. By John M'Donald, A.M. ... *Albany: E. & E. Hosford.* 1815. 8vo, pp. 32. B. 43155

M'Donald. Letters, by John M'Donald, addressed "To the Friends of Religion": Criminating the Presbytery of Albany, and the Synod of New-York and New-Jersey, with Answers, by Jonas Coe. *Albany: Printed by Charles R. and George Webster.* M.DCCCI. 8vo, pp. 51. BA. 43156

M'Donald. A Sermon on the Premature and Lamented Death of General Alexander Hamilton. By John M'Donald, A.M. ... *Albany: Printed by John Barber.* 1804. 8vo, pp. 32.

Also: Danger of America Delineated. Address at Cooperstown, April 25, 1799. ... *Cooperstown.* 1799. 8vo. — Duty of America Enforced. An Exhortation at Cooperstown, April 26, 1799. ... *Cooperstown.* 1799. 8vo. — Isaiah's Message to the American Nation. ... With Notes, Critical and Explanatory. ... *Philadelphia.* 1824. 12mo, pp. 107. — Sermon at the Ordination of Aaron Condict, Stillwater, January 15, 1793. ... *Albany.* 1793. 8vo. N.

M'Donald (J.) A Statement of the Opinions given in the Board of Commissioners, under the Sixth Article of the Treaty of Amity, Commerce, and Navigation, with Great Britain. By J. M'Donald, Esq. *Philadelphia.* 1800. 8vo. P. 43158

M'Donald (J.) Emigration to Canada. Narrative of a Voyage to Quebec, and Journey from thence to New Lanark, in Upper Canada. Detailing the hardships and difficulties which an Emigrant has to encounter, before and after his settlement; With an Account of the Country, as it regards its climate, soil, and the actual condition of its inhabitants. By John M'Donald. Eighth Edition. *London: H. Arliss.* 1826. 8vo, pp. 36. 43159

McDonald (J.) Biographical Sketches of General Nathaniel Massie, General Duncan McArthur, Captain William Wells, and General Simon Kenton: who were Early Settlers in the Western Country. By John McDonald, of Poplar Ridge, Ross County, Ohio. *Cincinnati: Morgan and Son.* 1838. 12mo, pp. 267. + *Dayton, O.: D. Osborn & Son.* 1852. 12mo, pp. 267. 43160

The author had personal communication with the families and neighbors of these Indian fighters, and has secured many details of their exploits among the savages.

Macdonald (J. A.) Address to the Electors of Kingston; with Extracts from Speeches made at Political Demonstrations during a Tour through the Province. By Sir John A. Macdonald. *Quebec.* 1860. 8vo, pp. 153. 43161

McDonald. The Crown and the Confederation. Three Letters to the Hon. John Alexander McDonald ... . By a Backwoodsman. ... *Montreal: John Lovell, Printer.* 1864. 8vo, pp. 36.

Macdonald (J. M.) Prayer for the Country. A Discourse preached November 29, 1860, in Princeton, N. J. By Rev. J. M. Macdonald. *New York: John F. Trow.* 1860. 8vo.

MacDonald. Charles Hodge Dod. A Memorial containing, in substance, the Address delivered in Princeton, New Jersey, August 31, 1864. *New York: Robert Carter & Brothers.* 1864. 12mo, pp. 36. 43164

The subject of this memorial was Assistant Adjutant-General in the Army of the Potomac, on the staff of Major-General Hancock.

McDonald (M. N.) Poems, by Mrs. Mary Noel McDonald. ... *New-York.* 1844. 8vo, pp. 208. BA. 43165

Macdonald (M.) Nebraska and Kansas. Speech of Hon. Moses Macdonald ... in the House ... April 10, 1854. [*Washington.* 1854.] 8vo, pp. 8. B. 43166

M'Donald (P.) A Surprising Account of the Captivity and Escape of Philip M'Donald & Alexander M'Lord. of Virginia, from the Chickkemogga Indians. and of their Great Discoveries in the Western World. From June 1779, to February 1786, when they returned ... to their friends after an absence of Six Years and a half. Written by Themselves. *Printed by Henry Blacke, &c. Co. Keene, Newhampshire.* M.DCC.XC.IV. 8vo, pp. 11.

M'Donald (W. K.) An Address ... before the Literary Societies of Washington College ... Sept. 23, 1851. By Wm. K. M'Donald, Esq. ... *Washington, Pa.* 1851. 8vo, pp. 18.

McDonald (—). The Manhattan Souvenir and New York Sketch Book for 1850. *New York.* 1850. 12mo, pp. 267.

M'Donell (A.) A Narrative of Transactions in the Red River Country; from the Commencement of the Operations of the Earl of Selkirk, till the Summer of the year 1816. By Alexander M'Donell, Esq. ... *London: Printed by B. M'Millan for Egerton.* 1819. 8vo, pp. xix, 85. Map. BA., H. 43170

Macdonell (A.) A Railroad from Lake Superior to the Pacific, the Shortest, Cheapest and Safest Communication for Europe with Asia. By Allan Macdonell. *Toronto.* 1851. 8vo.

M'Donnell (A.) Considerations on Negro Slavery. With Authentic Reports, illustrative of the Actual Condition of the Negroes in Demerara. ... By Alexander M'Donnell, Esq. ... *London: Longman, Hurst, Rees* ... 1824. 8vo, pp. xii, 338. H. + Second Edition. [*Ibid.*] 1825. 8vo, pp. xiv, 340. B. 43172

Also: An Address to The Members of Both Houses of Parliament on The West India Question. ... *London: James Ridgway.* 1830. 8vo, pp. (4), 108. + Second Edition. [*Ibid.*] — Letter to Thomas Fowell Buxton, in refutation of his allegations respecting the Decrease of the Slaves in the British West India Colonies ... . *London.* 1833. 8vo, pp. 80. C. — The West-India Legislatures Vindicated from the Charge of having resisted ... the Call for the Amelioration of Slavery. ... *London.* 1826. 8vo, pp. 104. S.

Macdonnell (A.) Colonial Commerce; comprising an Inquiry into the Principles upon which Discriminating Duties should be levied on Sugar, the Growth respectively of the West India British Possessions, of the East Indies, and of Foreign Countries. By Alexander Macdonnell, Esq. *London: John Murray.* MDCCCXXVIII. 8vo, pp. xix, 302. BA., C. 43173

M'Donnough (W.) Trial of William M'Donnough, ... for the Murder of his Wife, ... at Boston, ... 1817. ... *Boston: Printed by Thomas G. Bangs.* [1817.] 8vo, pp. 69. BA. 43174

McDonogh (J.) The Last Will and Testament of John McDonogh; Late of Macdonoghville ... Louisiana ... . *New Orleans.* 1851. 8vo, pp. 68. H. 43175

McDonogh. Report of Brantz Mayer [and others] Agents ... for the Sale ... of the McDonogh Estate, May 30th, 1859. *Baltimore: Printed by McCoull & Slater.* 1859. 8vo, pp. 63. + Second Report. [*Ibid.*] 1860. 8vo. 43176

McDonogh. Self-Emancipation. A Successful Experiment on a large Estate in Louisiana. Completed in 1840. [n. p. n. d.] 8vo, pp. 24. 43177

Also: Documents relative to the McDonogh Bequest. ... *Baltimore.* 1858. 8vo. — First Annual Report of Trustees of McDonogh Estate ... . *Baltimore.* 1859. 8vo. — Fundamental Rules for Administration of General Estate of John McDonogh ... . *New Orleans.* 1855. 8vo. — The Olographic Will of John McDonogh, of Louisiana ... *Baltimore: Printed by James Lucas.* 1850. 8vo, pp. 28. — Opinion on the Validity of the Devises and Bequests in the Will of John McDonogh ... . *Baltimore.* 1852. 8vo. Ordinance for the Appointment of Agents ... . *Baltimore.* 1854. 8vo. — Report ... on the M'Donogh Bequest ... . *Baltimore.* 1858. 8vo, pp. 16. — Reports of the Agents and Commissioners of the McDonogh Estate, ... and Opinion of Charles F. Mayer, Esq., on the Partition of the Estate. *Baltimore.* 1857. 8vo, pp. 61. H.

Macdonogh (T. M.) Memoirs of Nicholas Ferrar, collected from a Narrative by Dr. Turner, Bishop of Ely, by T. M. Macdonogh. *London.* 1837. Cr. 8vo. 43178

Ferrar was employed by the Virginia Company in the defense of their charter. *See also* Peckard (P.)

[Macdonough (A. R.)] A Statement of the Case of Brig.-Gen. Joseph W. Revere. *New York.* 1863. 8vo. 43179

Macdonough (*Capt.*) Letter from the Secretary of the Navy ... transmitting sundry Documents from Capt. Macdonough. Relating to the Captain of the British Fleet, on Lake Champlain. October 4, 1844. ... *Washington City: Printed by Roger C. Weightman.* 1814. 8vo, pp. 16. 43180

Macdouall (J.) Narrative of a Voyage to Patagonia and Terra del Fuégo, through the Straits of Magellan, ... in 1826 and 1827. By John Macdouall, R.N. ... *London: Renshaw and Rush.* MDCCCXXXIII. 16mo, pp. iv, 320. Plate. H. 43181

M'Dougall (G.) Petition of George M'Dougall, to Congress. *Detroit: Printed by Sheldon & Reed.* 1824. 8vo, pp. 17.

M'Dougall (G. F.) The Eventful Voyage of H.M. Discovery Ship "Resolute" to the Arctic Regions in Search of Sir John Franklin and the Missing Crews of H.M. Discovery Ships "Erebus" and "Terror," 1852, 1853, and 1854; ... By George F. M'Dougall ... . *London: Longman, Brown, Green* ... 1857. 8vo, pp. xl, 530. Map and 8 colored Plates. BA. 43183

McDougall (J.) God's Blessing of Peace. Discourse ... Thanksgiving Day ... 1866. By Rev. James McDougall. *Brooklyn.* 1866. 8vo. 43184

McDougall (J. A.) French Interference in Mexico. Speech of Hon. J. A. McDougall ... . February 3d, 1863. *Baltimore: Printed by John Murphy & Co.* 1863. 8vo, pp. 30. H. 43185

Mac-Dougall. Discurso pronunciado en el Senado de los Estados-Unidos por M. Mac-Dougall, apoyando las proposiciones que presentó para que la República del Norte auxilie á México en la actual guerra con Francio. *Mexico.* 1863. 8vo, pp. 84.

Also: Speech ... on the Arrest of Gen. Stone, and the Rights of the Soldier and Citizen. ... April 15, 16, & 22, 1862. *Washington: Printed by L. Towers & Co.* 1862. 8vo, pp. 32. — Speech ... advocating The Great Pacific Railroad. Delivered ... 29th ... of May, 1854. [n. p. n. d.] 8vo, pp. 16. — Speech ... on the Confiscation of Property. ... March 12, 1862. *City of Washington: L. Towers & Co., Printers.* 1862. 8vo, pp. 29. H. — Speech ... on the Expulsion of Mr. Bright ... January 31, 1862. [n. p. n. d.] 8vo, pp. 7.

MacDougall (P. L.) Emigration; its Advantages to Great Britain and her Colonies; together with a Detailed Plan for the Formation of the proposed Railway between Halifax and Quebec by Means of Colonization. By Col. P. L. MacDougall. *London.* 1848. 8vo, pp. 32. 43187

McDowall (J. R.) Charges preferred against the New-York Female Benevolent Society, ... In 1835 and 1836. By J. R. McDowall, ... Answered and Refuted by Himself!! In his own Journal!!! In the Year 1833. ... *New-York: Printed by Osborn & Buckingham.* 1836. 8vo, pp. 76. Plate. History, etc. pp. 7, (1). BA. 43188

McDowall's Defence, Nos. 1 and 2. *New York.* 1836. 8vo.

McDowall's Journal. [*New York.* 1833.] 4to, pp. 96. B.

M'Dowall. Memoir and Select Remains of the late Rev. John R. M'Dowall, the Martyr of the Seventh Commandment in the Nineteenth Century. *New-York: Leavitt, Lord & Co.* 1838. 12mo, pp. vi, 224. 43191

Also: History of Preliminary Proceedings of Third Presbytery in the Case of John R. M'Dowall, including the Charges, Specifications, Sentences ... . *New York.* 1836. 8vo. — Trial of the Rev. John Robert McDowall ... [in] New York, 1836 ... [n. p. n. d.] 8vo, pp. 16. H.

MacDowell (E. B.), *Compiler.* Republican Manual. *Philadelphia.* 1857. Sm. 8vo, pp. 137. B. 43192

McDowell (I.) Statement of Major-General Irwin McDowell, in Review of the Evidence before the Court of Inquiry ... *Washington: Printed by L. Towers, & Co.* 1863. 8vo, pp. 64, and cover. BA. 43193

McDowell (J.) Address ... before the Alumni Association of the College of New Jersey, September 26, 1838. By James McDowell. *Princeton: John Bogart.* [1838.] 8vo, pp. 51. + Second Edition. *Princeton: R. E. Hornor.* 1839. 8vo, pp. 37.

McDowell. A Lecture by the late Hon. James McDowell, of Lexington, Va., and an Address, by the Rev. A. Alexander, D.D. *Philadelphia: Joseph M. Wilson.* 1851. 8vo, pp. 48.

Also: Speech ... on the formation of governments for New Mexico and California. Delivered ... February 23, 1849. *Washington: Globe Office.* 1849. 8vo, pp. 16. — Speech ... on the Slave Question: ... January 21, 1832. Second Edition. ... *Richmond: Printed by Thomas W. White.* 1832. 8vo, pp. 33. B.

McDowell (J.) A Sermon occasioned by the Death of Alexander Henry. Preached in ... Philadelphia, ... August 17, 1847. By the Rev. John McDowell, D.D. *Philadelphia.* 1847. 8vo, pp. 16. B. 43196

McDowell (J. J.) Speech of ... Hon. Joseph J. McDowell, ... on the Oregon Territory ... January 5, 1846. *Washington: Blair & Rives, Printers.* 1846. 8vo, pp. 8. H. 43197

McDowell (J. N.) A Letter to the Rev. Henry Ward Beecher, and an Address to the Legislature of ... Missouri, By Joseph N. McDowell, M.D. *St. Louis, Mo.* 1860. 8vo, pp. 12.

Macdowell (T. C.) Speech of Col. T. C. Macdowell ... October 13th, 1863 ... at Harrisburg, Pa. [n. p. n. d.] 16mo, pp. 8. H. 43199

Macduff (J.) Soldiers Text Book, or Confidence in Time of War. By the Rev. J. Macduff, D.D. *New York: American Tract Society.* [n. d.] 16mo, pp. 64. 43200

McDuffie (G.) Conduct of George McDuffie, in relation to an Intended Meeting between himself and Col. Wm. Cushing, with some Allusions to a Former Affair between the Same Parties. *Augusta.* 1822. 8vo. 43201

M'Duffie. Defence of a Liberal Construction of the Powers of Congress, as regards Internal Improvement, etc. ... By George M'Duffie, Esq. in ... 1821. ... To which are prefixed an Encomiastic Advertisement of the work. By Major (now Governor) Hamilton, and a Preface by the Editor. *Philadelphia: Printed by Lydia R. Bailey.* 1831. 8vo, pp. (2), 22. + Second Philadelphia Edition. *Philadelphia: Printed by William F. Geddes.* 1832. 8vo, pp. 24. + Third Philadelphia Edition. *Philadelphia: Printed by Clark & Raser.* 1832. 8vo, pp. 24. BA. 43202

M'Duffie. A Eulogy upon the Life and Character of the late Robert Y. Hayne ... the 13th February, 1840 ... . By George M'Duffie. ... *Charleston: Printed by W. Riley.* 1840. 8vo, pp. 63. 43203

M'Duffie. National and State Rights Considered by the Hon. George M'Duffie, under the signature of One of the People in reply to the Trio ... . *Charleston.* 1821. 8vo. + *Charleston: W. S. Blain.* 1830. 8vo, pp. 40. BA. + *Columbia.* 1831. 8vo, pp. 40. 43204

McDuffie. The Reply of Mr. McDuffie on the Proposition to Amend the Constitution of the United States, Respecting the Election of President and Vice-President. Delivered in the House of Representatives, March 31, 1826. *Washington.* 1826. 8vo, pp. 56. 43205

Also: Bank of the United States. ... April 13, 1830. [Report of] Mr. M'Duffie, ... [n. p. n. d.] 8vo, pp. 31, (1), 2 folded leaves. — Mr. McDuffie's Speech, ... Feb. 14, 1826. On the Proposition to amend the Constitution of the United States, so that a Uniform System of voting by Districts shall be established ... . [n. p. n. d.] 8vo, pp. 36. — Mr. McDuffie's Speeches against the Prohibitory System; delivered ... April & May, 1830. [*Washington.* 1830.] 8vo, pp. 72. — Remarks ... delivered in the House of Representatives, April 3 & 4, 1834, on the Resolutions ... in Relation to the Public Deposites. *Washington.* 1834. 8vo, pp. 24. B. — Speech ... on Internal Improvements, with a few Introductory Remarks in answer to a Pamphlet, entitled "Consolidation." *Columbia.* 1824. 8vo. — Speech ... on the Proposition to clear the Galleries, during the Election of President ... . *Washington.* 1825. 8vo, pp. 24. H — Speech ... on the Amendment of the Constitution of the United States, ... February 15th, 16th, 1826. [n. p. n. d.] 12mo. — Speech ... on the Proposition to Amend the Constitution of the United States. Respecting the Election of President and Vice President. ... February 17, 1826. *Washington: Printed by Gales & Seaton.* 1826. 8vo, pp. 38. — Speech ... on the Woollens' Bill. February 7, 1827. *Washington.* 1827. 12mo, pp. 19. H. — Speech ... at a Public Dinner given to him by the Citizens of Charleston, (S. C.) May 19, 1831 ... . *Charleston: Printed by A. E. Miller.* 1831. 8vo, pp. 29. — Speech ... on the Bill proposing a Reduction of the Duties on Imports. ... May 28, 1832. *Charleston: Printed by A. E. Miller.* 1832. 8vo, pp. 39. + *Washington: Printed by Duff Green.* 1832. 8vo, pp. 48. BA. — Speech ... on the third reading of the Tariff Bill. ... 28th of June, 1832. [*Washington.* 1832.] 8vo, pp. 16. — Speech ... on the ... Removal of the Deposites. December 19, 1833. [*Washington.* 1833?] 8vo, pp. 16. B. — Speech ... on the Tariff, in reply to Messrs. Evans and Huntington: ... January 19, 1844. *Washington.* 1844. 8vo, pp. 15. — Speech ... on the Tariff. [January 29, 1844. *Washington.* 1844.] 8vo, pp. 8. — Speech ... On the Treaty for the Reannexation of Texas to the United States; ... in the Senate ... May 23, 1844. [*Washington.* 1844.] 8vo, pp. 8. BA.

Mace (F.) Familiar Dialogues on Shakerism; in which the Principles of the United Society are Illustrated and Defended. By Fayette Mace. ... *Portland: Charles Day and Co., Printers.* 1838. 8vo, pp. 120. BA. + *Concord: William White, Printer.* 1838. 8vo, pp. 120. 43206

Macedo (Antonio de). Vita patris Johannis de Almeida, societatis Jesus presbyteri provinciæ Brasiliensis. *Patavii.* 1669. 8vo. 43207

Macedo (F. a S. A.) Vita venerabilis Alfonsi Torrebio Mongrovegii archiepiscopi Limensis, autore Francisco a S. Augustino Macedo. *Patavii: Typis P. M. Framb.* 1670. 4to.

Macedo (I. J. de). Elogio ao Commercio [em verso]. Recitado no festim, que os negociantes da Bahia deram ao governador Conde dos Arcos em 6 de Septembro de 1817, por P. Ignacio José de Macedo. [n. p. n. d.] 4to. 43209

Macedo. Oração funebre nas exequias do muito alto e muito poderoso senhor D. João vi., imperador do Brasil, e rei de Portugal. Recitada na sancta Casa da Misericordia da cidade de Braga, por P. Ignacio José de Macedo. *Porto: Imp. de Gandra.* 1826. 4to, pp. 23. 43210

Macedo. Sermão em memoria do faustissimo dia em que Sua Alteza Real entrou a barra da Bahia. Recitado no antigo collegio dos Jesuitas da mesma cidade, em 22 de Janeiro de 1815, por P. Ignacio José de Macedo. *Bahia: na Typ. de Manuel Antonio da Silva Serva.* 1815. 4to, pp. 15. 43211

Macedo (J. M. de). Discurso proferido na Assembléa provincial do Rio de Janeiro, na sessão de 13 de Outubro de 1859. ... [*Rio de Janeiro:*] *Typ. Imperial de J. M. Nunes Garcia.* 1859. 8vo, pp. 58. 43212

Macedo. A Luneta magica por Joaquim Manoel de Macedo. *Rio de Janeiro.* 1870. 2 vols., 12mo, pp. 187; 208. 43213

Macedo. As Victimas-Algozes quadros da escravidão, romances por Joaquim Manoel de Macedo. *Rio de Janeiro.* 1869. 2 vols., 8vo, pp. xvi, 332; 389. 43214

Also: O primo da California: Opera em dous actos, imitação do francez. ... *Rio de Janeiro: Typ. de F. Brito.* 1858. 16mo, pp. 142.

Macedo (Joaquim Teixeira de). Legislação sobre a Alfandega dos Estados-Unidos da America Septentrional, com as formulas dos seus diversos expedientes. Traduzida do Digesto de Gordon. *Rio de Janeiro.* 1833. 4to. 43215

Macedo (J. A. de). Sermão das Dôres de N. Senhora, prégado de tarde, na real capella dos paços de Queluz, na festividade que mandou fazer a serenissima Princeza do Brasil viuva, no anno

de 1803, por P. José Agostinho de Macedo. *Lisboa, na Imp. Regia.* 1813. 8vo, pp. 49. + Segunda edição. [*Ibid.*] 1829. 8vo, pp. 46. 43216

Macedo (M.) Documentos que manifiestan la conducta que observó el C. Lic. M. Macedo como juez comisionado para ejecutar la sentencia de restitucion de tierras, dada á favor de la hacienda de Atenco contra los pueblos del partido de Tenango del Valle. *Mexico.* 1826. 4to, pp. 56. 43217

Macedo (*M.* de Souza de). *See* Souza de Macedo (*M.* de).

Macedo (M. A. de). Notice sur le Palmier Carnauba. Par M. A. de Macedo. *Paris.* 1867. 8vo, pp. 48. 43218

Macedon Academy, *N. Y.* Catalogue of the Macedon Academy, for ... 1851. *Rochester, N. Y.* 1851. 8vo. 43219

M'Elhiney (T.) Life of Martin Van Buren, by Thomas M'Elhiney. *Pittsburgh: Printed by J. T. Shryock.* 1853. 8vo, pp. 126. 43220

McElligott (J. N.) American Debater; being a Plain Exposition of the Principles and Practice of Public Debate. By James N. McElligott. *New-York.* 1855. 12mo. + Third Edition. *New York: Ivison and Phinney.* 1855. 12mo, pp. 323.

Mac El'Rey (J. A.) The Substance of Two Discourses, Occasioned by the National Bereavement, the Assassination of the President, the Position, the Lesson and the Duty of the Nation. Delivered in ... Wooster, Ohio, Easter Day, 1865, By the Rector, Rev. J. H. Mac El'Rey, M.D. ... *Republican Press, Wooster, Ohio.* 1865. 12mo, pp. 24. B. 43222

McElroy (A.) *See* Philadelphia, *and* Presbyterian Church.

McElroy (J.) The Judgment Seat; a Discourse on the Forty-seventh Anniversary of his Pastorate. By J. McElroy, D.D. *New York: R. Carter & Brothers.* 1869. 18mo, pp. 52.

M'Elroy (J.) Address, ... at the Funeral of John Johnston. By the Rev. Joseph M'Elroy, D.D. April 20, 1851. *New-York: Printed by Edward O. Jenkins.* M DCCC LI. 12mo, pp. 20.

M'Elroy. A Sermon, delivered Jan. 10, 1830, in ... New York, on the occasion of The Death of the Rev. John M. Mason, D.D. By Joseph M'Elroy, D.D. ... *New York: John P. Haven.* 1830. 8vo, pp. 36. B. 43225

Also: A Discourse occasioned by the Death of Mrs. Knox. ... July 29, 1855. ... [*New York.* 1855.] 8vo, pp. 41. B.

McElroy (S.) Report on the Silver Mines of Macate Valley, Peru. By Samuel McElroy, C.E. *New York.* 1865. 8vo, pp. 8.

Also: Report on the Improvement of the Valley of Chimbote. ... *New York.* 1865. 8vo, pp. 16.

McElroy (T.) Review of the Water Commissioners' Report for 1856. By Thomas McElroy. *Albany.* 1857. 8vo.

The McElroy Prize Compositions. Our Country; by Mary H. Cutter and Mary T. Reed. Woodbridge, July 4, 1863. *New York: W. C. Bryant & Co.* 1863. 8vo, pp. 16. 43228

Macer (J.) Les trois liures de | l'Histoire des | Indes, acomplie | de plusieurs choses memorables, | autant fidelement que sommaire- | ment composez en Latin, & depuis | nagueres faictz en Françoys. | Par Maistre Iehan Macer, | licencié en droict. | Avec Privilege. | *A Paris.* | *Chez Guillaume Guillard en rue* | *Sainct Iacques à l'enseigne* | *Saincte Barbe.* | 1555. | 16mo, 96 leaves. 43229

"Cette histoire des Indes occidentales a été écrite d'après le récit d'une personne qui avait séjourné fort longtemps en Amérique. L'original Latin (sous le titre 'Indicarum historiarum libri III.') a paru également à *Paris*, 1555, en 8vo."—Brunet. "In addition to what relates to the East and West Indies, this volume contains one of the earliest printed and most curious accounts of Japan."—Rich.

McEwen (A.) A Sermon Preached at the Anniversary Election, Hartford, May 8, 1817. By Abel McEwen ... . *Hartford: George Goodwin & Sons, Printers.* 1817. 8vo, pp. 22. H. 43230

McEwen. A Sermon, ... at the Funeral of Gen. Jedediah Huntington, of New-London, who died September 25, 1818; aged 75 Years. By Abel McEwen ... . *New York: Printed by Daniel Fanshaw.* 1818. 8vo, pp. 16. B. + [*Ibid.*] 1819. BA.

General Huntington commanded a regiment during the American Revolution.

M'Ewen. A Sermon, ... New London, Conn., on the Day of Thanksgiving, November 28, 1856. By Abel M'Ewen ... . *New London: Daniels & Bacon.* MDCCCLI. 8vo, pp. 16. 43232

Also: ... A Sermon ... in Stonington, at the Installation of the Rev. Ira Hart: December 6, 1809. ... *New-London: Printed by Samuel Green.* 1810. 8vo, pp. 20.

M'Ewen (J. A.) An Address ... at the laying of the Corner Stone of the University of Nashville, on the 7th of April, 1853. By John A. M'Ewen, A.M. *Nashville, Tenn.: John T. S. Fall.* 1853. 8vo, pp. 32. H. 43233

Also: Reform of Social Ranks: An Address ... before the Literary Societies of

Cumberland University ... June 21st, 1858. ... *Nashville: Smith, Camp & Co., Printers.* 1858. 8vo, pp. 23. H.

McEwen (M. H.) An Expose of the Case of the Commonwealth, or, John W. Simes & Co. *vs.* McEwen & Shee, By M. H. McEwen. *Philadelphia.* 1844. 8vo, pp. 34. 43234

M'Ewen (R. S.) The Mysteries, Miseries, and Rascalities of the Ohio Penitentiary, from the 18th of May, 1852, to the close of the Administration of J. B. Buttles. By R. S. M'Ewen. *Columbus: John Geary, Son & Co.* 1856. 8vo, pp. 75. 43235

MacFadyen (J.) Flora of Jamaica; or a Dissertation on the Plants of that Island, arranged according to the Natural Orders; with an Appendix containing an Enumeration of the Genera according to the Linnæan System, and an Essay on the Geographical Distribution of the Species. By James MacFadyen, M.D. Vol. I. *London: Longman* ... 1838. 8vo.

No more published.

McFalls (T. B.) We still Live as a Nation. A Thanksgiving Sermon, delivered November 28, 1862. By Rev. T. B. McFalls. *Washington.* [n. d.] 8vo, pp. 8. 43237

MacFarland (A.) The Escape or Loiterings amid the Scenes of Story and Song. By Andrew MacFarland. *Boston.* 1851. 12mo. 43238

M'Farland (A.) An Historical View of Heresies, and Vindication of the Primitive Faith. By Asa M'Farland, A.M. ... *Concord: Press of George Hough.* 1806. 12mo, pp. 274, (2).

M'Farland. A Sermon ... at Concord, before the Senate and House of Representatives of ... New Hampshire, June 2, 1808. By the Rev. Asa M'Farland, A.M. ... *Concord: Printed by George Hough.* 1808. 8vo, pp. 30. M. 43240

Also: An Oration ... before the Society of the Phi Beta Kappa ... at Hanover, August 25, 1802. ... *Hanover: Printed by Moses Davis.* 1802. 4to, pp. 24.— ... Sermon at Hanover, before the Franklin Lodge of Free and Accepted Masons . . . *Hanover.* 1797. 8vo.—A Sermon, ... at Concord, New-Hampshire, June 22, 1806, ... after the Total Eclipse of the Sun. ... *Concord: Printed by George Hough.* 1806. 8vo, pp. 18.—A Sermon at Concord, in New-Hampshire, Sabbath Day, April 25, 1813. ... *Concord, May,* 1813. 8vo, pp. 16.—A Sermon, ... at Epsom, New-Hampshire, at the Ordination of the Rev. Jonathan Curtis, ... February 22, 1815. ... *Concord: Printed by George Hough.* 1815. 8vo, pp. 32.—Sermon at Candia, N. H. Feb. 7, 1816, at the Ordination of Isaac Jones. ... *Concord.* [1816.] 8vo.— ... A Sermon Delivered at Concord, New-Hampshire ... . *Concord.* 1823. 8vo, pp. 14.

McFarland (D.) The Trial of Daniel McFarland for the Shooting of Albert D. Richardson ... . With a Preliminary Essay

on Medical Jurisprudence, by Dr. Wm. Hammond, and the *ex parte* Statement of Mrs. McFarland. Compiled by A. R. Cazauran. *New York.* [1870.] 8vo, pp. 209, and Appendix.

McFarland (J. B.) An Oration ... before the I. O. O. F., and Citizens, of Lafayette, Ind., September 10th, 1845. By ... Joel B. McFarland, M.D. *Lafayette, Ia.: Printed by Fry & Jackson.* 1845. 8vo, pp. 14. 43242

McFarland (W.) Browne's Western Calendar, or the Cincinnati Almanac, for the Year 1806. By William McFarland. *Cincinnati.* [n. d.] 8vo. C. 43243

MacFarland (W. H.) Address on the Life, Character and Public Services of B. W. Leigh, before the Virginia Historical Society, January, 1851. By W. H. MacFarland. *Richmond.* 1851. 12mo. 43244

MacFarland. Discourse on the Life of Honorable Henry Clay. By W. H. MacFarland, Esq. Delivered at ... Richmond. ... *Richmond: H. K. Ellyson, Printer.* 1852. 8vo, pp. 15.

MacFarlane (Charles). The Lives and Exploits of Banditti and Robbers in all Parts of the World. By C. MacFarlane, Esq. ... *New York: Harper & Brothers.* 1833. 2 vols., 12mo. + *London: Thomas Tegg and Son.* MDCCCXXXVII. Fcp. 8vo, pp. viii, 408. 4 Plates. + *London: John Murray.* 1839. Fcp. 8vo.

Also: Japan: ... and the Expedition fitted out in the United States ... . With Numerous Illustrations. *New York: George P. Putnam & Co.* MDCCCLII. 12mo, pp. xii, 9-365. BA.

MacFarlane (C.) The Comprehensive History of England, ... By Charles MacFarlane and the Rev. Thomas Thomson. *London.* 1860. 4 vols., rl. 8vo. 43247

Includes copious details of the old French War, 1759, the Revolution, and the War of 1812.

MacFarlane (J.) Britain's Victory, over the Combined Fleets of France and Spain Insured: as also, an Indissoluble Union with her Colonies. The Genuine Causes of all her Misfortunes, since the Commencement of her War in America. ... By James McFarlane. ... *Glasgow: Printed by Alex. Adam.* M DCC LXXIX. 8vo, pp. 38. BA. 43248

[MacFarlane (Robert).] The History of the First Ten Years of the Reign of George the Third, from ... 1760 to 1770; to which is prefixed a Review of the War which was terminated

by the Peace of Paris in 1763. Second Edition. *London.* 1783–1796. 4 vols., 8vo. 43249

See our Vol. VII., Nos. 26997–98, for the earlier editions of Vols. I. and II. The fourth volume has the author's name on the title-page. A considerable portion of the work relates to the war with America. *See the* "Diary of a Lover of Literature."

Mac Farlane (R.) Address delivered by Robert Mac Farlane, before the Mechanics of New-York, ... June 10th, 1847. *New-York: Huyler's Print.* 1847. 8vo, pp. 15, (1). 43250

Macfarlane. History of Propellers and Steam Navigation. With Biographical Sketches ... . By Robert Macfarlane, C.E. ... *New York: George P. Putnam.* 1851. 12mo, pp. 144. H. + [*Ibid.*] 1854. 43251

M'Farren (S.) Modern Slavery destitute of a Divine Warrant. A Sermon ... at Unity, April 14, 1863. By Rev. Samuel M'Farren, D.D. *Pittsburgh: W. S. Haven.* 1863. 8vo, pp. 16.

Macfie (M.) Vancouver Island and British Columbia. Their History, Resources, and Prospects. By Matthew Macfie, ... Five Years resident in Victoria, V. I. *London: Longman* ... 1865. 8vo, pp. xxi, (2), 574. 9 Maps and Plates. BA. 43253

Includes many interesting details of the life and customs of the Northwestern Indians.

McFingal. *See* [Trumbull (John)].

McGarrahan (William). The McGarrahan Memorial. ... *San Francisco: Smyth & Shoaff.* 1870. 8vo, pp. [270.] Map.

[McGarrahan.] The Quicksilver Mines of "Panoche Grandi," (... California,) and Attorney General Black. [n. p. n. d.] 8vo, pp. 8. H. 43255

Also: Brief Narrative of Facts in the McGarrahan Case ... . *Washington City: M'Gill & Witherow, Printers.* 1869. 8vo, pp. (2), 24. H.—Evidence to show that Beale's Survey is Correct. ... [*Washington: M'Gill & Witherow, Printers.* 1866.] 8vo, pp. 18.—A List of Papers before the Senate Committee. ... [n. p. n. d.] 8vo, pp. 16. —A Review of the Opinions of the Justices of the Supreme Court ... versus Vicente Gomez ... . *Washington: M'Gill & Witherow, Printers.* [n. d.] 8vo, pp. 28. H.

McGaughey (E. W.) Speech of Mr. E. W. McGaughey, ... on the Mexican War. ... Jan. 7, 1847. *Washington: Printed by J. & G. S. Gideon.* 1847. 8vo, pp. 14. H. 43256

MacGavock (R. W.) A Tennessean Abroad or Letters from Europe, Africa, and Asia. By Randal W. MacGavock, A.M. ... *Redfield, New-York.* 1854. 12mo, pp. 398. B. 43257

McGaw (J. F.) Philip Seymour or Pioneer Life in Richland County, Ohio. Founded on Facts. By Rev. James F. McGaw. *Mansfield: R. Brinkerhoff.* 1858. 8vo, pp. 296.

A skeleton of facts filled out from the author's imagination.

McGeachy (E.) Suggestions towards ... Shortening the Time of Transit between the Eastern and Western Hemispheres. By Edward McGeachy, Esq., ... Jamaica. ... *London: Smith, Elder & Co.* 1846. 8vo, pp. 17. 2 Maps. B. 43259

The author has anticipated many of the routes since adopted. Also a pamphlet "On Irrigation in the West Indies" ... . *Jamaica.* 1846. 8vo.

McGee (T. D'A.) Canadian Ballads, and Occasional Verses. By Thomas D'Arcy McGee ... . *Montreal: John Lovell.* 1858. 12mo, pp. 124. B. 43260

McGee. The Catholic History of North America. Five Discourses. ... By Thomas D'Arcy McGee ... . *Boston: Patrick Donahoe.* 1855. 12mo, pp. (2), 239. Plate. B. 43261

McGee. A History of the Irish Settlers in North America, from the Earliest Period to the Census of 1850. By Thomas D'Arcy McGee. *Boston: Patrick Donahoe.* 1851. 12mo, pp. 180. + Second Edition. [*Ibid.*] 1852. 12mo, pp. 240. A. + Fifth Edition. [*Ibid.*] 1852. + Sixth Edition. [*Ibid.*] 1855.

McGee. The Poems of Thomas D'Arcy McGee. With Copious Notes. Also an Introduction and Biographical Sketch. By Mrs. J. Sadlier. ... *New York: D. & J. Sadlier & Co.* 1869. 8vo, pp. 612. Portrait. 43263

McGee. Speeches and Addresses, chiefly on the Subject of British-American Union. By Hon. Thomas D'Arcy McGee. *London: Chapman & Hall.* 1865. Post 8vo. 43264

Also: The Irish Position in British and in Republican North America A Letter to the Editors of the Irish Press irrespective of Party. ... Second Edition. *Montreal: M. Longmoore & Co.* 1866. 8vo, pp. 45.—Notes on Federal Governments, Past and Present. ... *Montreal: Dawson Brothers.* 1865. 8vo, pp. 75.—The Political Cause and Consequences of the Protestant "Reformation" ... . *New York: D. & J. Sadlier & Co.* 1853. 8vo, pp. 27. BA.—The Present American Revolution. The Internal Condition of the American Democracy Considered ... . *London: Robert Hardwicke.* 1863. 8vo, pp. 19. B.—Two Speeches on the Union of the Provinces. ... *Quebec: Printed by Hunter, Rose & Co.* 1865. 8vo, pp. 34. *See also* Shea (J. G.)

McGeorge (R. J.) The Canadian Christian Offering. By Rev. Robert Jackson McGeorge. *Toronto.* 1848. 8vo, pp. 102.

Also: Tales, Sketches, and Lyrics. ... *Toronto.* 1858. 8vo, pp. 269.

McGhie (C.) Life and Surprising Adventures of Charles McGhie, or Mackey, a Negro Slave, afterwards Crossing Sweeper at Bridge Street, Blackfriars. [n. p. n. d.] 8vo. 43266

McGiffert (J. N.) A Discourse delivered at Clayville, June 4, 1863, at the Funeral of Corp. Robert Pettee ... . By Rev. Joseph N. McGiffert. *Utica, N. Y.: DeWitt C. Grove, Printer.* 1863. 8vo, pp. 8. 43267

McGiffert. Our Duty to our Country in the Present Crisis. A Discourse delivered in Sansquoit, May 5, 1861. By Rev. Joseph N. McGiffert. *Utica, N. Y.: DeWitt C. Grove.* 1862. 8vo, pp. 20. 43268

Also: A Sermon delivered in Manlius, N. Y., Sept. 29, 1861. ... *Syracuse: D. J. Halsted.* 1861. 8vo.

McGilchrist (J.) The Life of John Bright, M.P. By John McGilchrist. *London: J. Cassell.* 1865. Fcp. 8vo, pp. 124. + *New York: Felt and Dillingham.* [n. d.] 12mo, pp. 124. B.

Includes details of his services in favor of the North during the Rebellion. Also: Richard Cobden ... A Biography. ... *London: Lockwood and Co.* 1865. 16mo, pp. 294. Plates, Portrait. + *New York: Harper & Brothers.* 1865. 16mo, pp. 304 Plates, Portrait. BA.

McGill (A. T.) American Slavery as viewed and acted on by the Presbyterian Church in the United States ... . Compiled ... by the Rev. A. T. McGill, D.D. ... *Philadelphia: Presbyterian Board of Publication.* [1865.] 8vo, pp. 72. 43270

McGill. ... A Sermon ... April 11, 1841, ... at Carlisle, Pa. ... after the Decease of William Henry Harrison, late President ... . By Alexander T. McGill. *Philadelphia: William S. Martien.* 1841. 8vo, pp. 12. 43271

Also: The Hand of God With the Black Race. A Discourse ... before the Pennsylvania Colonization Society ... . *Philadelphia: William F. Geddes, Printer.* 1862. 8vo, pp. 19.— ... A Sermon, preached in ... New York, on the Day of National Fasting, January 4, 1861. ... *New York: John F. Trow, Printer.* 1861. 8vo, pp. 22.— Sermon before the Synod of New Jersey, Oct. 21, 1862. ... *New York.* 1862. 8vo.

McGill (P. M.) The Wrongs and Rights of Labor Shown, and a Remedy Proposed. By P. M. McGill, C.E. *Washington: Gibson Brothers.* 1857. 8vo, pp. 112. 43272

McGill College. Calendar of the University of McGill College ... . 1858–9. ... *Montreal: Printed by J. C. Becket.* 1858. 8vo, pp. 47. Plate. Continued. H. 43273

Also: Annual Announcement of the Medical Faculty, 1851–52. ... *Montreal.* 1852. 8vo.—Notice of the Natural History Collections of McGill University. ... [n. p. n. d.]

8vo. — Statement of the ... Governors of the University of McGill College; with other Publications ... . *Montreal: Printed by John C. Becket.* 1860. 8vo, pp. 12, 59, (1). — Statutes of the University of McGill College. [n. p. n. d.] 8vo, pp. 12. — Statutes, Rules, and Ordinances, made and established by the Principal and Governors. *Montreal.* 1832. 8vo.

[McGillivray (Simon)]. *See* [Douglas (T.)], No. 20699.

Macgillivray (W.) *See* Vol. viii., No. 33744.

McGinley (W. A.) ... A Discourse in ... Shrewsbury, Massachusetts, upon the Occasion of the Federal Triumphs over the Victories of February, 1862 ... . By Rev. William A. McGinley. *Worcester: Printed by Edward R. Fiske.* 1862. 8vo, pp. 25. 43274

McGinn (J.) Ten Days in the Tombs, or, A Key to the Modern Bastile! By John McGinn. *New-York: P. F. Harris.* 1855. 12mo, pp. 122. 43275

MacGinnis (J. Y.) Sketch of the Life, Character and Writings of Rev. James Y. MacGinnis. *Philadelphia.* 1854. 8vo. 43276

Macgowan (D. J.) Claims of the Missionary Enterprise on the Medical Profession: An Address ... before the ... College of Physicians ... of New-York, October 28, 1842. By Daniel J. Macgowan, m.d. *New-York: Printed by William Osborn.* 1842. 8vo, pp. 24. B. 43277

McGowan (E.) Narrative of Edward McGowan, including a full account of the Author's Adventures and Perils while persecuted by the San Francisco Vigilance Committee of 1856. *San Francisco: The Author.* 1857. 8vo, pp. 240. 43278

M'Gregor (J.) Letter from the Reverend Mr. James M'Gregor, Minister, at Pictou, Nova, Scotia, to the General Associate Synod, April 30th, 1793. ... *Paisley: Printed by John Neilson.* m.dcc.xciii. 8vo, pp. 16. 43279

McGregor (J.) British America, By John McGregor, Esq. *William Blackwood, Edinburgh.* mdcccxxxii. 2 vols., 8vo, pp. xxii, 484; xiv, 605. Maps. + Second Edition. [*Ibid.*] mdccc-xxxiii. 2 vols., 8vo, pp. xxiv, 561; xiv, (1), 606. 15 Maps.

Macgregor. The Commercial and Financial Legislation of Europe and America, with a Pro-Forma Revision of the Taxation ... . By John Macgregor ... . *London: Henry Hooper.* 1841. 8vo, pp. 320. BA. 43281

Macgregor. Commercial Statistics. A Digest of the Productive Resources, Commercial Legislation, Customs Tariffs, Navigation, Port, and Quarantine Laws, and Charges, Shipping, Imports and Exports, and the Monies, Weights, and Measures of All Nations. Including all British Commercial Treaties with Foreign States. ... By John Macgregor ... . *London: Whittaker and Co.* 1844–50. 5 vols., rl. 8vo, pp. xix, 1282, 7, (1); xii, 1195; ix, 1395; viii, 1036; vii, 399; Supplement, Vol. i. pp. 221. BA. + Second Edition. [*Ibid.*] 1850. 5 vols., imp. 8vo.

Vol. iii. relates to America, Spanish American Republics, Central and South America; Vol. iv. relates to Hayti and the foreign West Indies, the Brazils, British colonies in America and the West Indies.

Macgregor. Commercial Tariffs and Regulations of the several States of Europe and America. Together with the Commercial Treaties between England and Foreign Countries. By John Macgregor ... . *London: C. Whiting.* 1841–47. 21 parts in 12 vols., folio. A. 43283

Parts 15, 16, 20 and 21 are American.

Macgregor. Germany; ... With a Preliminary View of the Political Condition of Europe and America in 1848. By John Macgregor, m.p. ... *London: Whittaker and Co.* 1848. 8vo, pp. lxviii, 318, (1). H. 43284

Macgregor. Historical and Descriptive Sketches of the Maritime Colonies of British America. By J. McGregor. *London: Longman* ... 1828. 8vo, pp. (4), v, 266. BA. 43285

A second edition is entitled "British America."

Macgregor. The History of the British Empire, from the Accession of James i.; to which is prefixed, a Review of the Progress of England, from the Saxon Period to 1603. By John Macgregor ... . *London.* 1852. 2 vols., 8vo. 43286

Macgregor. Observations on Emigration to British America. By J. Macgregor. *London: Longman* ... 1829. 8vo, pp. (2), 68.

Macgregor. The Progress of America, from the Discovery by Columbus to ... 1846. By John McGregor ... . *London: Whittaker and Co.* 1847. 2 vols., 8vo, pp. (4), xii, 1520; viii, 1334, 84. H. 43288

Exhibiting a vast body of minute geographical, historical, and statistical information.

Macgregor. The States of Mexico, their Commerce, Trade, &c. By John Macgregor. *London: C. Whiting.* 1846. 4to, pp. 305. 43289

Also: Commercial Survey of Mexico, Oregon, and the Spanish American Republics. ... *London.* 1846. Folio. — Holland and the Dutch Colonies. ... *London.* 1848. 8vo. — Political Statistics of Nations. ... *Paris.* 1834. 8vo. — The Resources and Statistics of Nations. ... Vol. i. *London.* 1863. Rl. 8vo. — Sketches of the Progress of Civilization and Public Liberty; with a View of the Political Condition of Europe and America in 1848. ... *London.* 1848. Rl. 8vo, pp. 72. c.

Macgregor (J.) Our Brothers and Cousins: A Summer Tour in Canada and the States. By John Macgregor, m.a. ... *London: Seeley, Jackson* ... mdccclix. 12mo, pp. xix, 156. Plate.

McGregor (J. P.) Some Considerations upon the Financial Policy of the Government. By John P. McGregor. *Milwaukee: Starr & Son.* 1862. 8vo, pp. 16. 43291

McGregor Western Railway Directory for 1867. Comprising complete Business Directories of all Towns along the McGregor Western Railway. With Historical Sketches, etc. *Milwaukee: Bailey & Wolfe.* 1867. 8vo, pp. 205. 43292

MacGregore (D.) The Christian Soldier. A Sermon Preached at Newbury, at the Ordination of the Reverend Mr. Alexander Boyd; To the Pastoral Office at New-Castle, in the Province of the Massachusetts-Bay, September 24th, 1754. By the Reverend Mr. David MacGregore, Of Londonderry. ... *Boston: Edes and Gill.* 1754. 8vo, pp. 26. 43293

Also: Professors warn'd of their Danger. Sermon preach'd at Stratham [N. H.], Dec. 28, 1741. ... [n. p. 1741.] 8vo, pp. 26. — ... A Sermon preached ... in Boston, March the 11th and 12th ... . *Boston: Printed by S. Kneeland and T. Green.* 1747. 8vo, pp. 36. BA. — ... A Sermon Occasioned by the Death of The Rev. Mr. John Moorhead ... . *Boston: Printed by William M'Alpine.* m,dcc,lxxiv. 8vo, pp. 35. — The Spirits of the present Day Tried. A Sermon at the Tuesday-Evening Lecture in ... Boston, Nov. 3, 1741. ... *Boston: D. Henchman.* 1742. 12mo, pp. (6), 50. + Second Edition. With an ... Answer to the Preface of Mr. Caldwell's Sermon on the Trial of the Spirit. ... *Boston: D. Henchman.* 1742. 8vo, pp. (8), 30, xi.

McGuier (H.) A Concise History of High Rock Spring. By Henry McGuier. *Saratoga Springs: G. M. Davison.* 1867. 16mo, pp. 38. 3 Plates. H. + *Albany: C. Van Benthuysen & Sons.* 1868. 16mo, pp. 42. 3 Plates. 43294

McGuire (E. C.) Centennial Commemoration. A Sermon ... in ... Fredericksburgh, ... Oct. 4th, 1835 ... . By the Rev. Edward C. McGuire. *Fredericksburgh.* 1835. 8vo, pp. 43.

M'Guire. The Religious Opinions and Character of Washington. By E. C. M'Guire. ... *New York: Harper & Brothers.* m dccc xxxvi. 12mo, pp. 414. + Second Edition. [*Ibid.*] 1847.

[McGuire (*Mrs.* John P.)] Diary of a Southern Refugee during the War. By a Lady of Virginia. *New York: E. J. Hale & Son.* 1867. 12mo, pp. 360. + Second Edition. [*Ibid.*] 1868. 12mo, pp. 360. 43297

Machado (D. B.) Bibliotheca Lusitana, Historica, Critica, e Cronologica. Na qual se comprêhende a Noticia dos Authores Portuguezes, e das Obras, que compuzeraõ desde o tempo da promulgação da Ley da Graça até o tempo prezente. Offerecida à Augusta Magestade de D. João v. Nosso Senhor por Diogo Barbosa Machado. *Lisboa Occidental: A. Isidoro da Fonseca.* 1741–59. 4 vols., folio, Vol. i., pp. (80), 767, Portrait; Vol. ii. *Ignacio Rodrigues.* 1747. pp. (2), 927; Vol. iii. [*Ibid.*] 1752. pp. (2), 799; Vol. iv. *Fr. Luiz Ameno.* 1759. pp. (6), 725. 43298

The extreme rarity of this great work, the highest authority upon Portuguese bibliography, arises from the circumstance that a large proportion of the first three volumes was destroyed by fire at Lisbon in 1755. It describes many books relating to Brazil, etc. *See also* Leclerc, No. 110, and Petzholdt, p. 381.

Machado. Retratos de Varões Portuguezes, insignes em virtudes e dignidades, etc. Colligidos por Diogo Barbosa Machado, Abbade da parochial igreja de Sancto Adrião de Sever, e Academico Real. [n. p. n. d.] 4 vols., folio. 43299

Machado (I. B.) Theatro historico, universal e chronologico de todas as provincias ultramarinas do nosso reino, ou Annaes ecclesiasticos, politicos e militares da Africa, Asia, e America portugueza ... . Por Ignacio Barbosa Machado. [n. p. n. d.] Folio. 43300

Machado (Manuel Leite). Surpreza de Evora: drama historico em tres actos, approvado pelo Conservatorio Dramatico, e seguido das inspirações da juventude, e do poema heroi-comico "Os Sacripantes" ... . *Rio de Janeiro: Typ. de F. A. de Almeida.* 1855. 8vo, pp. viii–165. 43301

Also: Alvado de Abranches: drama original portuguez em quatro actos, approvado pelo Conservatorio Dramatico Brasileiro, precedido de um juizo critico pelo sr. Delfim Augusto Maciel do Amaral. ... *Rio de Janeiro: Typ. de F. A. de Almeida.* 1857. 8vo, pp. 74. — Os Pretendentes: comedia em um acto, approvada pelo Conservatorio Dramatico Brasileiro. ... *Rio de Janeiro: Typ. do Commercio de Brito & Braga.* 1860. 8vo, pp. 18.

Machault (J. de). Relation des missions du Paraguai, par le P. Jacques de Machault, de la compagnie de Jesus. *Paris.* 1636. 8vo. 43302

M'Henry (G.) ... The Cotton Supply of the United States of America. By George M'Henry. ... [Second Edition, with Additional Remarks.] *London: Spottiswoode & Co., Printers.* 1865. 8vo, pp. 66. H. 43303

McHenry. The Cotton Trade: its bearing upon the Prosperity of Great Britain and Commerce of the American Republics considered in connection with the System of Negro Slavery in the Confederate States. By George McHenry. ... *London: Saunders, Otley, & Co.* 1863. 8vo, pp. iii–lxix, (2), 292. + Second Edition. [*Ibid.*] 1863. 43304

The author was a vigorous partisan of the policy of recognizing the seceded States by England, for the sake of obtaining cotton.

[McHenry.] A Familiar Epistle to Robert J. Walker, ... From an old Acquaintance, to which is prefixed a Biographical Sketch. Tenth Thousand. *London: Saunders, Otley & Co.* 1863. 8vo, pp. xiii, 57. 43305

McHenry. ... A Paper Containing a Statement of Facts Relating to the Approaching Cotton Crisis, by George McHenry. *Richmond, Dec.* 31, 1864. 8vo, pp. 87. + Another Edition. [n. p. n. d.] 8vo, pp. 87. 43306

M'Henry. The Position and Duty of Pennsylvania: ... with Sketches of the Commercial, Financial, Geographical, and Political History of the Late American Union. By George M'Henry. ... *London: Henry F. Mackintosh.* mdccclxiii. 8vo, pp. (4), 91. H. 43307

[McHenry.] Why Pennsylvania should become one of the Confederate States of America. By a Native of Pennsylvania, 1861. *London: J. Wilson.* m.dccc.lxii. 8vo, pp. 15. 43308

Also: African Race in America, North and South. ... *London: Privately Printed.* 1861. 8vo. — The Cotton Question. ... *London.* 1864. 8vo.

M'Henry (J.) A Letter to the ... Speaker of the House of Representatives of the United States, with the Accompanying Documents; read in that ... House on the 28th December, 1802. By James M'Henry ... . *Baltimore: Printed by John W. Butler.* 1803. 8vo, pp. 91. BA. 43309

M'Henry. Waltham; An American Revolutionary Tale, in Three Cantos. By James M'Henry. *New York: E. Bliss & E. White.* 1823. 18mo, pp. 70. s. 43310

[M'Henry.] The Wilderness; or Braddock's Times: A Tale of the West. *New York.* 1823. 2 vols., 12mo. + *Pittsburgh.* 1848. 2 vols., 12mo, pp. 229; 230. 43311

Also: Baltimore Directory and Citizen's Register for 1807 ... . *Baltimore.* [1807.] 18mo. — The Pleasures of Friendship: a Poem in Two Parts, to which are added a few other Poems ... . *Philadelphia.* 1825. 12mo, pp. 96.

McHenry (J. H.) Speech of Mr. John H. McHenry ... on the ... Tariff. ... June 30, 1846. [*Washington:*] *J. & G. S. Gideon, Printers.* [1846.] 8vo, pp. 16. H. 43312

M'Henry (W.) State of the Accounts of William M'Henry, Esq. late Sub-Lieutenant of Bucks County; From ... 1781, until ... April, 1783 ... . *Philadelphia: Printed by Robert Aitken* ... m,dcc,lxxxv. 8vo, pp. 8. P. 43313

Machias, *Me.* Memorial of the Centennial Anniversary of the Settlement of Machias [May 20, 1863]. *Machias: Printed by C. O. Furbush.* 1863. 8vo, pp. 179, (1). BA. 43314

Machoni de Cerdeña (A.) Arte y vocabulario de la lengua Lule, y Tonocote ... . Por el Padre Antonio Machoni de Cerdeña, de la Compañia de Jesus. *Madrid: Por los herederos de Juan Garcia Infanzon.* 1732. 12mo, pp. 14, 97, 135, 17.

The last paging contains the "Catecismo, y doctrina Christiana en lengua Lulu, y Tonocoté."

Machpelah. A Book for the Cemetery. *New York.* 1865. 16mo, pp. 205. 43316

Machuca (Bernardo de Vargas). *See* Vargas Machuca (B. de).

McHugh (J.) ... Papers respecting the Arrest and Imprisonment of Mr. James McHugh in the United States. ... *London: Printed by Harrison and Sons.* [1864.] Folio, pp. (2), 17, (1). + Further Papers respecting the Arrest and Imprisonment ... . [*Ibid.*] Folio, pp. (2), 5, (1). + Further Papers ... . [*Ibid.*] Folio, pp. (2), 6. BA. 43317

Maciel da Costa (J. S.) *See* Costa (J. S. M. da), Vol. iv.

M'Ilvain (J.) ... Memorial of James M'Ilvain, praying that the Aid of Government may be extended to the Growers of Wool ... . February 20, 1828. ... *Washington: Printed by Gales & Seaton.* 1828. 8vo, pp. 10. H. 43318

McIlvaine (A. R.) Speech of Mr. A. R. McIlvaine ... on the Military Occupation of Texas. ... March 26, 1846. [*Washington:*] *J. & G. S. Gideon.* [1846?] 8vo. H. 43319

Also: Speech ... on the Mexican War. ... February 4, 1847. *Washington.* 1847. 8vo, pp. 8.

[M'Ilvaine (Charles Pettit).] Appeal on behalf of Kenyon College, Ohio ... . [*London.* n. d.] 8vo, pp. 5. H. 43320

McIlvaine. Bishop McIlvaine's Respectful Address to the Protestant Episcopalians of the City of Cincinnati. ... [n. p. n. d.] 8vo, pp. 7. 43321

Relates to the parish of St. Johns, Cincinnati.

McIlvaine. Correspondence between the Right Rev. C. P. McIlvaine, d.d., d.c.l. ... and the Rev. James A. Bolles, d.d., Rector of Trinity Church, Cleveland, with an explanatory Pastoral Letter to the Members of the Parish of Trinity Church, Cleveland, Ohio. *Cleveland: Harris, Fairbanks & Co., Printers.* 1857. 8vo, pp. 43. B. 43322

[McIlvaine.] Pastoral Letter of the Bishops of the Protestant Episcopal Church in the United States ... to the Clergy and Laity ... . Delivered before the General Convention ... New York, ... October 17, 1862. *New York: Baker & Godwin, Printers.* 1862. 8vo, pp. 14. B. 43323

M'Ilvaine. Rev. Mr. M'Ilvaine in Answer to the Rev. Henry U. Onderdonk, d.d. *Philadelphia: William Stavely.* 1827. 8vo, pp. 43. H. 43324

This elicited: "Some Remarks on a Pamphlet entitled, Rev. Mr. McIlvaine, in Answer to the Rev. Henry U. Onderdonk, d.d. By an Episcopalian of Maryland." *Baltimore: Printed by Lucas and Deaver.* 1829. 8vo, pp. 21. B.

Also: Baccalaureate Discourse, ... to the Senior Class of Kenyon College, ... Sept. 6th, 1837. ... *Gambier: George W. Myers, Printer.* 1837. 8vo, pp. 16. — Bishop McIlvaine's Address to the Convention of the Diocese of Ohio ... . In Newark, June 3d, 1858 ... . *Cincinnati: Printed by C. F. Bradley & Co.* 1858. 8vo, pp. 26, (1). H. — ... A Charge ... before the Clergy of ... the Diocese of Ohio ... September 13, 1839. ... *Columbus: Isaac N. Whiting.* m dccc xl. 16mo, pp. 156. — ... A Charge ... to the Clergy of the Diocese of Ohio ... October 11th, 1851. ... *New York: Harper & Brothers.* 1851. 8vo, pp. 53. — The Chief Danger of the Church in these Times: a Charge ... to the Clergy of the Diocese of Ohio ... September 8th, 1843. ... *New York: Harper and Brothers.* 1843. 8vo. — The Christians Duty in the Present Crisis. ... [*Cincinnati.* 1861.] 12mo, pp. 4. — An Earnest Word ... in behalf of the Church Institutions at Gambier, Ohio. *New-York: Printed by William Osborn.* 1843. 8vo, pp. 8. 2 Plates. — The Respectful Address of C. P. M'Ilvaine, d.d., ... to all who would Promote the Progress of Learning and Religion in the Western States. [n. p. n. d.] 8vo, pp. 8. — A Sermon, before the Domestic and Foreign Missionary Society ... August 24, 18-- ... *Philadelphia: Printed by Wm. Stavely.* 1835. 8vo, pp. 32.

— ... Sermon at the Consecration of the Right Reverend Leonidas Polk, d.d., ... in ... Cincinnati, December 9, 1838. ... *Gambier, O.: G. W. Myers.* m dccc xxxviii. 8vo, pp. 43. — The Sermon before the Bishops, Clergy, and Laity ... at the Consecration of the Rev. Alfred Lee, d.d. ... October 12, a.d. 1841. ... *New-York: Swords, Stanford, & Co.* mdccccxli. 8vo, pp. 24. — ... A Sermon ... at the consecration of the Rt. Rev. Alfred Lee, d.d. ... *Philadelphia: Edward Gaskill.* mdcccl. 8vo, pp. 31. — ... Sermon before the General Convention ... in ... New York ... October 5th, 1853. ... *New York: Printed ... by Billin and Brothers.* 1859. 8vo, pp. 25. — ... A Sermon ... on ... Thanksgiving ... November 29th, 1860, in ... Cincinnati ... . *Cincinnati: Bradley & Webb, Printers.* 1860. 8vo, pp. 24. — ... A Sermon ... at the Consecration of Calvary Church, Clifton, Ohio ... 5th of May, 1868 ... . *Cincinnati: Robert Clarke & Co., Printers.* 1868. 8vo, pp. 38. Plate. — The Work of preaching Christ. A Charge ... to the Clergy of the Diocese of Ohio ... in ... Akron ... 3d of June, 1863. ... *New York: Anson D. F. Randolph.* 1863. 16mo, pp. 72. H.

McIlvaine (J. H.) American Nationality. By J. H. McIlvaine. *Philadelphia.* 1861. 8vo. 43325

M'Ilvaine (J.) Report of The Engineers, employed to re-survey the location of the Contemplated Rail Road in the vicinity of Philadelphia. ... By Joseph M'Ilvaine, Esq. *Harrisburgh: E. F. Cryder & Co., Printers.* 1829. 8vo, pp. 26.

McIlvaine (W.) A New Plan of a Perpetual Civil Calendar. By William McIlvaine. *Burlington, N. J.* 1846. 4to.

Also: Memoir of the New Perpetual Calendar (not published). *Philadelphia.* 1849.

McIlvaine (W.) Sketches of Scenery and Notes of Personal Adventure in California and New Mexico. By William McIlvaine, Jr. *Philadelphia.* 1850. 8vo. 16 Plates. 43328

Mac-Intosh (A.) Address at the Interment of Sylv. Bourne, Consul-General of the United States in the Netherlands. By A. Mac-Intosh, d.d. *Harlem.* 1817. 8vo, pp. 16. 43329

McIntosh (D.) Some Account of an Entertainment given in honor of Duncan McIntosh, in Baltimore, January 9th, 1809. With a Collection of the Pieces delivered on that Occasion. [*Baltimore.*] 1809. 8vo. 43330

In French and English.

M'Intosh (G.) The Case of George M'Intosh, Esquire, A Member of the late Council and Convention of the State of Georgia; With The Proceedings thereon in the Hon. the Assembly and Council of that State. ... [n. p.] *Printed in the Year* mdcclxxvii. 4to, Half Title, pp. 29. 43331

McIntosh (J.) The Discovery of America by Christopher Columbus; and the Origin of the North American Indians. By John McIntosh. *Toronto: W. J. Coates.* 1836. 8vo, pp. 152.

McIntosh. The Origin of the North American Indians; with a faithful Description of their Manners and Customs, both Civil and Military; their Religion, Languages, Dress and Ornaments; including various specimens of Eloquence, as well as Historical and Biographical Sketches of almost all the distinguished Nations and celebrated Warriors, Statesmen and Orators among them. By John McIntosh. *New York: Nafis & Cornish.* 1843. 8vo, pp. 311. Plates. + [*Ibid.*] 1844. 8vo. + [*Ibid.*] 1849. 8vo, pp. 345. Plates. + [*Ibid.*] 1853. 8vo. + [*Ibid.*] 1858. 8vo. 43333

[M'Intosh (L.)] Class Despotism, as exemplified during the Four Years' Struggle for Freedom in the United States ... and the Evils of Individual Wealth Considered ... . *London: F. Farrah.* 1867. 16mo, pp. xxiii, (1), 337. 43334

M'Intosh (M. J.) Letter on The Address of the Women of England to their Sisters of America, in Relation to Slavery. By Miss M. J. M'Intosh ... . *New York: T. J. Crowen.* 1853. 24mo, pp. (1), 32. H. 43335

McIntosh. Woman in America. Her Work and her Reward. By Maria J. McIntosh ... . *New York: D. Appleton & Co.* 1850. 12mo, pp. 5–155. 43336

[M'Intyre (A.)] A Letter to ... Daniel D. Tompkins, Late Governor of ... New-York. *Albany: Printed by Jeremiah Tyron.* 1819. 8vo, pp. 112, xl. + *Albany: Printed by E. & E. Hosford.* 1820. 8vo, pp. 56, Appendix, xl. B., H. 43337

Also: Memorial relative to the Union Canal Company in Pennsylvania. [n. p.] 1832. 8vo. *See also* Union College.

M'Jilton (J. N.) God Speaketh. A Sermon, preached in ... Baltimore, ... June 22d, 1845, on the death of His Excellency, Andrew Jackson, late President ... . By Rev. John N. M'Jilton, A.M. ... *Baltimore: D. Brunner.* 1845. 8vo, pp. 16. 43338

M'Jilton. Poems. By Rev. John N. M'Jilton. *Boston: Otis, Broaders & Co.* 1840. 12mo, pp. 360. 43339

M'Jilton. Report of the Delegate to the Educational Conventions of Buffalo and Boston, to the Commissioners of Public Schools of Baltimore, and Address on the Teacher's Calling, Nationally Considered. By Rev. John N. M'Jilton. *Baltimore: Bull & Tuttle.* 1860. 8vo, pp. 126. B. 43340

Also: ... Address ... before ... Lafayette College ... at the Annual Commencement, September 22d, 1841. ... *Baltimore: Printed by John Murphy.* [n. d.] 8vo,

pp. 35. — Funeral Discourse in Memorial of Robert C. Morse ... Masonic Hall ... . *Baltimore.* 1849. 12mo. — ... A Funeral Sermon on the Death of the Rt. Rev. John Prentiss Kewley Henshaw, D.D., Bishop of Rhode Island. Delivered in ... Baltimore, July 25, 1852. ... *Baltimore: Jos. Robinson.* 1852. 8vo, pp. 20. — God's Controversy with the People of the United States. A Sermon ... September 26, 1861. ... *Baltimore: Joseph Robinson.* 1861. 8vo. — ... A Poem ... before the Philomathæan Society of Pennsylvania College, February 16, 1841. ... *Baltimore: Joseph N. Lewis.* 1841. 12mo, pp. 57. — The Prayer of the Republic in the Visitation of Calamity upon its Sins. A Sermon, April 30, 1863. ... *Baltimore: J. W. Bond & Co.* 1863. 12mo, pp. 21. — ... A Sermon ... Baltimore, on Thanksgiving Day, November 28, 1861. ... *Baltimore: J. W. Bond.* 1861. 16mo, pp. 27. — ... A Sermon, ... Thanksgiving Day, November 27, 1862. ... *Baltimore: J. W. Bond & Co.* 1862. 8vo, pp. 24.

Mack (A. W.) Speech of the Hon. A. W. Mack ... on the Slavery Question ... January 20, 1865. ... *Springfield: Baker & Phillips.* 1865. 8vo, pp. 20. 43341

Mack (Alexander). Kurze und einfältige Vorstellung der äussern, aber doch heiligen Rechten und Ordnungen des Hauses Gottes. Zweite Auflage. *Germantown* [*Pa.*]: *C. Saur.* 1774. 24mo, pp. (22), 133. 43342

Mack (D.) The Green Mountain Spring. ... Vol. I. ... *Brattleboro', Vt.* 1846. 8vo. Continued. 43343

Mack (E.) The Cat-Fight; a Mock Heroic Poem. Supported with Copious Extracts from Ancient and Modern Classic Authors ... . By Doctor Ebenezer Mack ... . *New York.* 1824. 8vo, pp. 276. Plate. C. 43344

Mack. The Life of Gilbert Motier de la Fayette, a Marquis of France; a General in the American and French Revolutions; the Compatriot and Friend of Washington, the Champion of American Independence, and of the Rights and Liberties of Mankind. From Numerous and Authentic Sources. By Ebenezer Mack. *Ithaca* (*N. Y.*): *Mack, Andrus & Woodruff.* 1841. 12mo, pp. (2), 371. Portrait. + Third Edition, Illustrated. *Utica, N. Y.: G. G. Brooks.* 1859. 12mo, pp. 376. 43345

Also: Character and Importance of Agriculture, and the Means directed to its Improvement: an Address. ... *Ithaca.* 1844. 8vo.

Mack (R.) Kyle Stuart; with other Poems. By Robert Mack, Esq. Vol. I. *Columbia, Tenn.: Printed ... by Felix K. Zollicoffer.* 1834. 16mo. 43346

Contains a poem on the Death of Washington, and on Col. Daviess, who fell at Tippecanoe. No more published.

Mack (R. C.) The Londonderry Celebration. Exercises on the 150th Anniversary of ... Old Nutfield ... June 10, 1869.

Compiled by Robert C. Mack. *Manchester: John B. Clarke.* 1870. 8vo, pp. 124. Portraits. B. 43347

Mack (W. G.) A Letter from the Eastern Townships of Lower Canada, containing Hints to intending Emigrants as to the Choice of Situation, &c. By W. G. Mack. *Glasgow.* 1837. 8vo, pp. 26. Map. 43348

Mackay (Alexander). Analysis of the Australian Colonies Government Bill. By A. Mackay, Esq. ... *London: James Ridgway.* 1850. 8vo, pp. (2), 68. 43349

Contains frequent references to America.

Mackay. Crisis in Canada; or, Vindication of Lord Elgin and his Cabinet as to the Correspondence by them in reference to the Rebellion Losses Bill. By Alexander Mackay, Esq. *London.* 1849. 8vo, pp. 68. 43350

Mackay. The Western World; or, Travels in the United States in 1846–47: exhibiting them in their Latest Development, Social, Political, and Industrial, and including a Chapter on California. By Alexander Mackay, Esq. ... *London.* 1849. 3 vols., post 8vo, pp. 340; 321; 374. Map. P. + Second Edition. [*Ibid.*] + From the Second London Edition. *Philadelphia: Lea & Blanchard.* 1849. 2 vols., 12mo, pp. 312; iv, 14–316. + Third Edition. *London.* 1850. 3 vols., post 8vo. + Fourth Edition. [*Ibid.*] 43351

"In extent and variety of subject it stands alone among American travels."—*Spectator.*

Mackay. Die Westliche Welt. Reise durch die Vereinsstaaten von Amerika. Aus dem Englischen von Marie Heine. Nebst einer Einleitung und 4 Illustrationen von Wilhelm Heine. *Leipzig: Kollmann.* 1861. 8vo, pp. 1006. 4 Plates. 43352

Mackay. Die Westliche Welt. Reisen in den Vereinigten Staaten. Deutsch bearbeitet und mit Zusätzen aus anderen Reisewerken, sowie nach den neuesten statistischen Quellen bis zum Jahre 1854 vervollständigt von O. L. H[eubner]. *Leipzig: G. Wigand.* 1855. 4 vols., 8vo, pp. viii, 328; (4), 330; (4), 316; viii, 343, 1 folding sheet. 43353

Mackay (C.) The History of the United States of America. With a Continuation, including the Presidencies of Pierce and Buchanan. By Charles Mackay, Esq. ... *London: Virtue & Co.* [n. d.] 2 vols., 8vo, pp. (4), iv, 816; (2), vi, 772. Maps, Portraits and Plates. 43354

Mackay. Life and Liberty in America: or, Sketches of a Tour in the United States and Canada in 1857–8. By Charles Mackay ... . *London: Smith, Elder and Co.* 1859. 2 vols., post 8vo, pp. vi, (2), 343; (2), 336. 10 Plates. + Second Edition. [*Ibid.*] + *New York: Harper & Brothers.* 1859. 12mo, pp. 413. 10 Plates. H. 43355

Mackay. Memoirs of Extraordinary Popular Delusions. By Charles Mackay ... . *London: Richard Bentley.* 1841. 3 vols., 8vo, pp. vi, (2), 400; (6), 406; (6), 404. 4 Portraits. 43356

Contains a graphic account of the Mississippi Scheme, South Sea Bubble, &c. This is the best edition in large type.

Mackay. Memoirs of Extraordinary Popular Delusions. By Charles Mackay ... . *Philadelphia: Lindsay and Blakiston.* 1850. 2 vols., 12mo, pp. viii, (2), 13–384; (4), 13–384. B. + [*Ibid.*] 1851. 2 vols., 12mo. 43357

Mackay. Memoirs of Extraordinary Popular Delusions and the Madness of Crowds. By Charles Mackay ... . Second Edition. *London.* 1852. 2 vols., post 8vo, pp. viii, 303; (2), viii, 324. + *London: G. Routledge & Co.* 1856. 2 vols., post 8vo, pp. (2), viii, 303, (1); (2), vi, 322. Plates. 43358

His "Memoirs of Commercial Delusions: embracing Historical Sketches of the Mississippi Scheme, and the South Sea Bubble" (*New York*, 1845), forms pp. 233–342, of "Hunt's Library of Commerce." Also: Street Tramways for London, ... with some Remarks, on the Working of Street Railways in the United States and Canada. ... 1868. 8vo. — Voices from the Mountains and from the Crowd. ... *London.* 1852. 8vo. + *Boston: Ticknor, Reed, and Fields.* MDCCCLIII. 16mo, pp. viii, 373. H. *See* [Mayhew (Henry).]

Mackay (C.) Death in the Pot: a Temperance Sermon ... December 12, 1847. By Rev. Charles Mackay. ... *Saint John, N. B.: Printed by J. & A. McMillan.* 1848. 12mo, pp. 22, (1).

McKay (D.) Description of the Largest Ship in the World, —the New Clipper Great Republic, of Boston. By Donald McKay. *Boston.* 1853. 8vo, pp. 24. M. 43360

McKay. La marine des États-Unis avant la guerre et la marine actuelle. Par Donald McKay. Traduit de l'anglais par M. Cavelier de Cuverville ... . *Paris: Corréard.* 1865. 8vo, pp. 14. 43361

Mackay (H.) A Letter from Lieut. Hugh Mackay, of General Oglethorpe's Regiment, to John Mackay, Esq. in the Shire of Sutherland in Scotland. *London.* 1742. 8vo, pp. 39.

Relates to the miscarriage of the siege of St. Augustine, and printed with a view to

correct some misstatements that had appeared in the London newspapers. Probably printed for private distribution.

Mackay (J.) Quebec Hill; or Canadian Scenery, a Poem, in Two Parts. By J. Mackay. *London.* 1797. 4to. 43363

Written in Canada.

McKay (N.) Centenary Sermon, By Rev. Neil McKay; and Discourse By James Banks, Esq. ... before the Presbytery of Fayetteville, ... October, 1858. ... *Fayetteville.* 1858. 8vo, pp. 19, 24. 43364

The discourse by Banks is replete with revolutionary incidents and the struggles with the Indians.

[Mackay (R.)?] Pocahontas: A Historical Drama in Five Acts; with an Introductory Essay and Notes. By a Citizen of the West. *New York.* 1837. 12mo, pp. 240. S. 43365

Mackay (R. W. S.) The Stranger's Guide to the Cities and Principal Towns of Canada ... . By Robert W. Stuart Mackay, ... *Montreal: C. Bryson.* 1854. 16mo, pp. 168. 2 Maps, Plates.

For Canada Directory, *see* Canada, Vol. III., No. 10416.

Mackay (S.) The Narrative of Captain Samuel Mackay, Commandant of a Provincial Regiment in North America; By the Appointment of Lieut. Gen. Burgoyne: ... *Kingston.* [1778.] 8vo, pp. 18. 43367

This very rare pamphlet relates to the Siege of Quebec.

Mackay (S.) Aperçu topographique de la Virginie, l'un des dix-sept États-Unis de l'Amérique septentrionale, situé au centre de cette belle république; par Samuel Mackay, A.M. *Paris: De l'Imprimerie de J.-Scherff.* 1816. 12mo, pp. 24. H. 43368

M'Kay (S. M.) An Address ... at Pittsfield ... July 4, 1822. By Samuel M. M'Kay. *Pittsfield: Printed by Phinehas Allen.* 1822. 8vo, pp. 20. H. 43369

Also: An Address, ... before the Berkshire Association ... of Agriculture ... at Pittsfield, October 3, 1822. ... *Pittsfield: Printed by Phinehas Allen.* 1822. 8vo, pp. 34. B.

[McKaye (J.)] ... The Birth and Death of Nations. ... *New York: G. P. Putnam.* 1862. 12mo, pp. 33. H. 43370

Reprinted from the "Rebellion Record," pp. 56–64.

McKaye (J.) ... The Mastership and its Fruits: the Emancipated Slave Face to Face with his Old Master. A Supplemental Report to Hon. Edwin M. Stanton, Secretary of War. By James McKaye ... . *New York.* 1864. 8vo, pp. 38. B. 43371

McKaye. Das Herrenthum und seine Früchte: der emancipirte Sklave und sein früherer Herr. Uebersetzt von F. Schultz. *New York: H. Ludwig.* 1864. 8vo, pp. 31. 43372

[McKean (Joseph).] Memoir towards a Character of Rev. John Eliot, S.T.D. ... *Boston.* 1793. 8vo, pp. 40. M. + [*Ibid.*] MDCCCXIII. 8vo, pp. 40. B. 43373

[McKean.] A Plea for Friendship and Patriotism; in Two Discourses, Preached ... in Boston, ... 27 March, and On the Annual Fast, 7 April, MDCCCXIV. ... *Munroe & Francis, Printers, Boston.* 1814. 12mo, pp. 59, (1). B., M. 43374

[McKean.] Remarks on the Hon. John Q. Adams's Review of Mr. Ames's Works ... . *Boston: Printed by T. B. Wait and Co.* 1809. 8vo, pp. 50. B. 43375

[McKean.] Sermon in which the Question of War with Great Britain is examined on Christian Principles. *Boston.* 1808. 8vo, pp. 14. 43376

[McKean.] A Sermon ... at ... Boston ... after the Decease of John Warren, M.D. ... who died IV. April, MDCCCXV. ... *Boston: Printed by John Eliot.* 1815. 8vo, pp. 23. H. 43377

[McKean.] A Sermon ... at the Ordination of Reverend John Burt Wight, A.M. ... in East Sudbury. XXV January, MDCCCXV. *Cambridge: Printed by Hilliard and Metcalf.* 1815. 8vo, pp. 36. H. 43378

[McKean.] A Valedictory Sermon, Preached at Milton, September 30th, 1804. *Boston: Printed by Manning and Loring.* 1804. 12mo, pp. 22. BA. 43379

Also: A Sermon ... at the Ordination of the Reverend Nathaniel Langdon Frothingham, A.M. ... Boston, XV. March, MDCCCXV. ... *Boston: Printed by Munroe, Francis & Parker.* 1815. 8vo, pp. 43. H. — A Sermon ... at Dorchester, June 25, 1817, on ... organizing the Third Church ... and the Installation of the Rev. Edward Richmond, D.D. ... *Dedham: Abel D. Alleyne, Printer.* 1817. 8vo, pp. 38. H.

[McKean (Thomas).] ... A Brief History of the Proposed Impeachment of the Governor of Pennsylvania; to which is added, His ... Message of January 28th, 1808. ... *Lancaster: Printed by William Hamilton.* 1808. 12mo, pp. (2), ii, 5–69.

See also Pennsylvania.

M'Kean. First Annual Report of the Directors of the McKean and Elk Land and Improvement Company. *Philadelphia: E. C. & J. Biddle.* 1857. 8vo, pp. 35. 8 Maps. Continued.

Also: Act of Incorporation ... *Philadelphia.* 1856. 8vo, pp. 39. Plan.

McKee (R.) Extract from Rev. Prof. McKee's Lecture, .. the Morning after the Funeral of the Misses Haven. *New York.* [1855.] 8vo, pp. 12. B. 43382

McKee. Lectures on Botany ... . By Rev. R. McKee, A.M. ... *Albany: Printed by J. Munsell.* 1839. 8vo, pp. 20. H.

McKee (S.) Speech of Hon. Samuel McKee ... on Reconstruction. ... March 3, 1866. [n. p. n. d.] 8vo, pp. 8. 43384

Also: Right of Suffrage. Speech ... January 28, 1869. [n. p. n. d.] 8vo, pp. 7. — Speech ... on Basis of Representation. ... January 26, 1866. [n. p. n. d.] 8vo, pp. 8. H.

McKee (S.) Reflections on the Law of 1813, for laying an Embargo on all Ships and Vessels in the Ports ... of the United States. By Samuel McKee, William P. Duvall, and Thomas Montgomery. [n. p.] 1814. 8vo, pp. 24. BA. 43385

McKee (W. H.) The Territory of New Mexico and its Resources. By Dr. W. H. McKee ... . *New York.* 1866. 8vo, pp. 12. Map. 43386

McKeehan (J. B.) The Crisis of the Country; the Duty of Republicans. By J. B. McKeehan. *Cincinnati.* 1860. 8vo.

McKeen (J.) A Discourse against speaking Evil of Rulers: ... Fast [Day] ... April 9th, 1801. By Joseph McKeen, A.M. ... *Salem: Printed by Joshua Cushing.* 1801. 8vo, pp. (2), 17.

McKeen. A Sermon ... on the Public Fast in ... Massachusetts, April 11, 1793. By Joseph McKeen, A.M. ... *Salem: Printed by Thomas C. Cushing.* M DCC XCIII. 8vo, pp. 22. H., S.

McKeen. A Sermon ... May 28, 1800, being the Day of General Election. By Joseph McKeen, A.M. ... *Boston: Printed by Young & Minns.* 1800. 8vo, pp. 30. B., W. 43390

M'Keen. Two Discourses ... at Beverly, on the Day of the National Fast, May 9, 1798. By Joseph M'Keen, A.M. ... *Salem: Printed by Thomas C. Cushing.* 1798. 8vo, pp. 31. H.

Also: Address at the Ordination of Mr. M'Keen, at Beverly in New England. [n. p.] 1785. 1 leaf. — The Inaugural Address, delivered in Brunswick, September 9th, 1802. ... at his Entrance on the Duties of President of Bowdoin College; with an Eulogy, ... at his Funeral, by the Reverend William Jenks. *Portland: Printed by Thomas B. Wait & Co.* 1807. 8vo, pp. 38. — A Sermon, preached at the Ordination of the Rev. Rufus Anderson, to the ... Second Church in North-Yarmouth, October 22, 1794. ... *Printed at Portland (Me.), by B. Titcomb, Jun.* MDCCXCV. 8vo, pp. 29. — A Sermon ... at the Ordination of ... Abraham Moore ... in Newbury, March 23, 1796. ... *Printed at Newburyport, by Blunt and March.* 1796. 8vo, pp. 32. B.

McKeen (S.) A Farewell Sermon, ... January 20, 1833, to the Congregational Church and Society in Bradford, Vt. By S. McKeen. *Haverhill, N. H.: Printed by J. R. Reding.* 1833. 8vo, pp. 16. BA. 43392

Also: A Sermon ... October 15, 1828, before the Vermont Colonization Society. ... *Montpelier: Printed by E. P. Walton.* 1828. 8vo, pp. 22. BA.

McKeen (S.) Heroic Patriotism. A Sermon, ... at Bradford, Vt., ... April 28, 1861, in the presence of The Bradford Guards, when under call to join the First Regiment Vermont Volunteers ... . By Rev. Silas McKeen. ... *Windsor.* 1860. 8vo, pp. 16. 43393

McKeen. ... A Sermon ... before the General Assembly of ... Vermont: October 9, 1857, By Rev. Silas McKeen ... . *Montpelier: E. P. Walton, Printer.* 1857. 8vo, pp. 34. H.

Also: A Scriptural Argument in favor of withdrawing Fellowship from Churches ... tolerating Slaveholding ... . *New York.* 1848. 12mo, pp. 37, (1). — ... A Sermon occasioned by the Death of Arthur H. Prichard, ... March 30, 1856. ... [n. p.:] *L. J. M'Indoe, Printer.* 1856. 8vo, pp. 17. — ... A Sermon ... March 23, 1858, at the Funeral of Oliver J. Hardy ... . *Bradford: L. J. McIndoe, Printer.* 1858. 8vo, pp. 15. — ... A Sermon ... before Orange County Conference, at West Fairlie, Vt., September 28, 1858. ... *Bradford, Vt.* [n. d.] 18mo, pp. 18. — ... A Sermon ... November 21, 1858, at the Funeral of Alfred Bliss King ... . *Bradford, Vt.: E. A. Fuller's ... Office.* [n. d.] 8vo, pp. 20. — ... A Sermon ... December 26, 1858; at the Funeral of Mrs. Martha T. Peckett ... . *Bradford, Vt.: E. A. Fuller's ... Office.* [1858?] 8vo, pp. 17. — ... A Sermon ... November 16th, 1859, at the Funeral of Mrs. Bertha B. Allbee ... . *Bradford.* 1860. 8vo, pp. 18. — ... A Sermon ... February 5, 1860 ... after the Funeral of Mrs. Nancy B. Farnum ... . *Windsor.* 1860. 8vo, pp. 17. H.

McKeever (H. B.) Twilight Musings, and Other Poems. By Harriet B. McKeever. ... *Philadelphia: Willis P. Hazard.* 1857. 12mo, pp. 263. H. 43395

M'Keevor (T.) A Voyage to Hudson's Bay, during the Summer of 1812. Containing a Particular Account of the Icebergs and other Phenomena which present themselves in those Regions; Also, a Description of the Esquimeaux, and North American Indians; their Manners, Customs, Dress, Language, &c. ... By Thomas M'Keevor, M.D. ... *London: Sir Richard Phillips and Co.* 1819. 8vo, pp. (4), 96. 8 Plates. B. 43396

Pages 76–96 consist of "La Poix de Fréminville's Voyage to the North Pole, in the Frigate the Syrene; including a Physical and Geographical Notice relative to ... Iceland."

McKell (Q.), *pseudon.* The Lament of Quinton McKell, of Irongray, Soothsayer. *New York: Privately Printed.* 1858. Sq. 18mo, pp. 48. 43397

Mackellar (P.) A Correct Journal of the Landing of His Majesty's Forces on the Island of Cuba, and of the Siege and Surrender of the Havannah, August 13, 1762. By Patrick McKellar. Together with a List of the Men of War taken and surrendered with the City, and the Return of Guns, Mortars, and Principal Stores. *London.* 1762. 8vo. + Second Edition. *Boston: Green & Russell.* 1762. 8vo, pp. 19. C., M. 43398

A very rare pamphlet. Included in his Majesty's forces were some New England troops under the command of Lyman and Putnam. Thomas says there were two *Boston* editions.

Mackellar (T.) Droppings from the Heart; or, Occasional Poems. By Thomas Mackellar. *Philadelphia: Sorin & Ball.* 1844. 12mo, pp. 144. H. 43399

Mackellar. Tam's Fortnight Ramble, and Other Poems. By Thomas Mackellar ... . *Philadelphia: Carey and Hart.* 1847. 12mo, pp. 216. B. 43400

McKendree College. Second Annual Catalogue of the Officers and Students. *Lebanon, Illinois.* 1838. 12mo, pp. 12. Continued. H. 43401

Also: ... The Seventh Triennial Catalogue ... . 1858–9. ... *St. Louis: R. P. Studley, Printer.* 1858. 8vo, pp. 40. Continued. H.

Mackenna (Benjamin Vicuña). *See* Vicuña Mackenna (B.)

[McKenney (T. L.)] Essays on the Spirit of Jacksonism, as exemplified in its Deadly Hostility to the Bank of the United States, and in the Odious Calumnies employed for its destruction. By Aristides. *Philadelphia: Jesper Harding, Printer.* 1835. 8vo.

M'Kenney. Memoirs, Official and Personal; with Sketches of Travels among the Northern and Southern Indians; embracing a War Excursion, and description of Scenes along the Western Borders. By Thomas L. M'Kenney ... . *New York: Paine & Burgess.* 1846. 8vo, pp. viii, 17–340; vi, 9–136. Plates. + Second Edition. [*Ibid.*] 8vo, pp. xi, (2), 17–340; v–ix, 9–136. 2 Portraits, 12 Plates. B. 43403

McKenney. Narrative of the Battle of Bladensburgh, in a Letter to Henry Banning, Esq. By Thomas L. McKenney. [n. p.] 1814. 8vo. W. 43404

McKenney. Reply to Kosciusko Armstrong's Assault upon Col. McKenney's Narrative of the Causes that led to General Armstrong's Resignation of the Office of Secretary of War in

1814. By Thomas L. McKenney. *New York: William H. Graham* ... 1847. 8vo, pp. 28. BA. 43405

McKenney. Reports and Proceedings of Col. McKenney, on the Subject of his Recent Tour among the Southern Indians, as submitted to Congress with the Message of the President U. S. *Washington: Printed by Gales & Seaton.* 1828. 8vo, pp. 37.

McKenney: Sketches of a Tour to the Lakes, of the character and customs of the Chippeway Indians, and of incidents connected with the Treaty of Fond du Lac. By Thomas L. McKenney ... . Also, A Vocabulary of the Algic, or Chippeway Language ... . *Baltimore: Fielding Lucas, Jun'r.* 1827. 8vo, pp. 493, (1). 8 Portraits, 19 Plates. A., H. 43407

See "N. A. Rev.," xxv. 334, xxxiii. 407.

M'Kenney. Sketches of Travels among the Northern and Southern Indians; ... Also the Questions Answered, "Who are the Indians," and whence the Origin of the Races, Ancient and Modern, that Peopled America prior to the Discovery of Columbus? By Thomas L. M'Kenney. ... Third Edition. *New York: Daniel Burgess & Co.* 1854. 8vo, pp. xi, (2), 17–340; vi, 9–136. Plates. 43408

This is *our* No. 43403 with a new title-page.

McKenney. To the Public. [n. p. 1828.] 8vo, pp. 16.

[M'Kenney *and* Hall (J.)] Catalogue of One Hundred and Seventeen Indian Portraits, ... accompanied by a Few Brief Remarks on the Character, &c. of Most of them. [n. p. n. d.] 8vo, pp 24. B. 43410

M'Kenney. History of the Indian Tribes of North America, with Biographical Sketches and Anecdotes of the Principal Chiefs. Embellished with One Hundred and Twenty Portraits from the Indian Gallery in the Department of War, at Washington. By Thomas L. M'Kenney, late of the Indian Department, Washington, and James Hall, Esq., of Cincinnati. *Philadelphia: Edward C. Biddle.* 1836–44. 3 vols., folio. 43410*a*

Collation: Vol. I. pp. (2), iv, 204, 48 Portraits; Vol. II. *Philadelphia: Frederick W. Greenough* ... 1838. pp. (2), 237, 48 Portraits; Vol. III. *Philadelphia: Daniel Rice and James G. Clark.* 1844. pp. (4), 196, (2), List of Subscribers, (22). 24 Portraits.

These are the imprints of the first issue, which was printed in 20 parts, and having been published by three several proprietors there is some confusion in the arrangement. In binding a set great care is necessary to secure accuracy, and the tables of plates should be consulted. The first 44 pages of the history (as distinguished from the biography) were issued in Parts I., II., and III.; then the biography commences. The

catch-words at the foot of the signatures of the third volume up to No. 39 read Vol. I. instead of Vol. III.; the error is corrected at the 40th sheet. The work was also issued with the imprint *Philadelphia: Frederick W. Greenough.* 1838–44. 3 vols., folio, pp. 4, 206, (1); 237, (1); (2), 196, (2), facsimiles, 18, (1). 120 Plates and Portraits. As early as 1824, the practice was begun of taking portraits of the principal Indians who came to Washington, and depositing them in the War Department. They were chiefly painted by Mr. King, an artist of high repute, who has been remarkably successful in transferring to his canvas the strong lineaments of the Indian countenance. Col. M'Kinney, who was for many years superintendent of Indian affairs at Washington, and was thus brought in constant association with the principal men of the nations and tribes which sent representatives to the seat of government, conceived the plan of making this rare and curious collection more valuable to the world by publishing a series of engraved portraits exactly copied and colored from these paintings. With each portrait is connected a biographical sketch of the individual whom it is intended to represent, interspersed with anecdotes and narrations. The work contains also a historical account of the various Indian tribes within the borders of the United States. *See also* "N. A. Rev.," XLVII. 134, LXIII. 481, *and* Rich, II. 307.

McKenney. History of the Indian Tribes of North America, with Biographical Sketches and Anecdotes of the Principal Chiefs. Embellished with One Hundred and Twenty Portraits from the Indian Gallery ... . By Thomas L. McKenney ... . *Philadelphia.* 1850. 3 vols., imp. 8vo, pp. iv, 333, 40 Portraits; pp. v, 319, 50 Portraits; pp. 339, 31 Portraits. + [*Ibid.*] 1854 and 1856.

In this edition the plates are on a reduced scale. The later issues have the imprint *Philadelphia: Rice & Hart.*

M'Kenney. A Letter addressed to Thomas L. M'Kenney, Esq. ... March, 1820, in reply to his Report of January, 1820. [n. p. n. d.] 8vo. 43412

Mackentosh (J.) Receipts for the cure of most diseases incident to the Human Family. By the celebrated Indian Doctor, John Mackentosh, of the Cherokee Nation; ... *New York.* 1827. 12mo, pp. 12. 43413

Mackenzie (A.) Voyages from Montreal, on the River St. Laurence, through the Continent of North America, to the Frozen and Pacific Oceans; In the Years 1789 and 1793. With a preliminary account of the Rise, Progress, and Present State of the Fur Trade of that Country. ... By Alexander Mackenzie, Esq. *London: T. Cadell, Jun.* M. DCCC. I. 4to, pp. viii, cxxxii, 412, Errata, (2). 3 Maps and Portrait. 43414

First and finest edition of the earliest expedition made by a white man in this direction. His investigations, although pursued at so early a period of Arctic exploration, were remarkable for their accuracy; Sir John Franklin more than once expressed his surprise at being able to corroborate their correctness in his own explorations. Some Indian vocabularies are included. "Of the vast region to which our Sovereign recently attached the name of British Columbia geographers have as yet but a scant and very imperfect account. Its first great explorer was my honoured countryman Mackenzie, who, traversing the Rocky Mountains and reaching the sea after incredible labour, left us an

excellent record of his exploits."—Sir R. I. Murchison's *Address to Rl. Geog. Soc., May* 23, 1859. *See also* "Edinb. Rev.," I. 141, "M. Rev.," XXXVIII. 225, 337, Rich, II. p. 1, *and* Twiss' "Oregon," p. 11.

Mackenzie. Voyages ... With original Notes by Bougainville, and Volney. *London: T. Cadell & W. Davies.* M. DCCC. II. 8vo, pp. xiv, 290; 332. 2 Maps and Portrait. + First American Edition. *New-York: Printed and Sold by G. F. Hopkins.* 1802. 8vo, pp. viii, [*sic*] ix, 94, 296. Map. + *Philadelphia: John Morgan.* 1802. 8vo, pp. (6), viii, cxxvi, 113; 115–392. Portrait and 3 Maps. + *New-York: Evert Duyckinck.* 1803. 12mo, pp. 437. + *New York: W. B. Gillen.* 1814. 8vo, pp. (6), viii, cxxii, 392. 43415

Also included in part in Mavor's "Voyages," Vol. XXIV.

Mackenzie. Voyages dans l'intérieur de l'Amérique septentrionale, faits en 1789, 1792 et 1793. Le 1er de Montréal au fort Chipiouyan et à la mer glaciale; le 2me du fort Chipiouyan jusqu'aux bords de l'Océan Pacifique. Précédés d'un tableau historique et politique sur le Commerce des Pelleteries, dans le Canada. Traduits de l'Anglais, par J. Castéra. Avec des notes, ... du vice-amiral Bougainville. *Paris: E. Dentu.* 1802. 3 vols., 8vo. Map and Portrait. 43416

The translator has added many notes which greatly enhances the value of the work.

Mackenzie. Tableau Historique et Politique du Commerce des Pelleteries dans le Canada, depuis 1608 jusqu'à nos Jours. Contenant beaucoup de détails sur les nations sauvages qui l'habitent, et sur les vastes contrées qui y sont contiguës; Avec un Vocabulaire de la langue de plusieurs peuples de ces vastes contrées. Par Alexandre Mackenzie. Traduit de l'Anglais, par J. Castéra. *Paris: E. Dentu.* M. D. CCC. VII. 8vo, pp. (4), 310, Table, 1 leaf. Portrait. 43417

A translation of part of the voyages. *See* Faribault, p. 420.

Mackenzie. Reisen von Montreal durch Nordwestamerika nach dem Eismeer und der Süd-See in den Jahren 1789 und 1793. Nebst einer Geschichte des Pelzhandels in Canada. Aus dem Englischen. *Hamburg.* 1802. 8vo. Map and Portrait. 43418

The English is omitted in the vocabularies, Knisteneaux, etc., pp. 118–131, and Chippeway, pp. 145–149, and German substituted.

McKenzie (A.) Address ... at the Funeral of Rev. Benjamin Tappan, D.D. ... with a Sermon ... December 27, 1863. By Alexander McKenzie ... . [Second Edition.] *Augusta.* 1864. 8vo, pp. 22. H. 43419

Also: An Introductory Sermon ... January 27, 1867 ... [in] Cambridge. ... *Cambridge: Welch, Bigelow, & Co.* 1867. 8vo, pp. 28.—Letter to the Rev. Samuel C. Aiken in Answer to his Sermon on Theatrical Exhibitions. ... *Cleveland, O.* 1836. 8vo, pp. 28.—Sermon and other Exercises at the Ordination of Alex. McKenzie, Aug. 28, 1861. ... *Augusta, Me.* 1861. 8vo.

[Mackenzie (A. S).] The American in England. ... *New-York: Harper & Brothers.* 1835. 2 vols., 12mo, pp. vii, 238; 239. + Fourth Edition. *New-York.* 1857. 2 vols., 12mo. B.

Mackenzie. Case of the Somer's Mutiny: Defence of Alexander Slidell Mackenzie, ... before the court-martial ... at ... Brooklyn. *New York.* 1843. 8vo, pp. 30, ii. H. 43421

Mackenzie. The Life of Commodore Oliver Hazard Perry. By Alex. Slidell Mackenzie ... . *New-York: Harper & Brothers.* 1840. 2 vols., 18mo, pp. viii, v, 322; 270. Portrait. + [*Ibid.*] 1841. 2 vols., 18mo. B. 43422

Mackenzie. The Life of Paul Jones. By Alexander Slidell Mackenzie, U.S.N. ... *Boston: Hilliard, Gray, and Company.* 1841. 2 vols., 16mo, pp. xiii, 260; ix, 308. + *New York: Harper & Brothers.* 1845. 2 vols., 16mo, pp. viii, vii–xiii, 260; ix, 308. + [*Ibid.*] 1848. 2 vols., 16mo, pp. xiii, 260; ix, 308. 43423

Mackenzie. Life of Stephen Decatur, A Commodore in the Navy of the United States. By Alexander Slidell Mackenzie, U.S.N. *Boston: Charles C. Little and James Brown.* 1846. 8vo, pp. (2), xi, 433. B. 43424

Some copies were printed on large paper, rl. 8vo. Another edition forms Vol. XXI. of Sparks' "Biography."

[Mackenzie.] Popular Essays on Naval Subjects. ... *New-York: George Dearborn.* 1833. 18mo, pp. 166. 43425

Mackenzie. Proceedings of the Naval Court Martial in the Case of Alexander Slidell Mackenzie, a Commander in the Navy of the United States, &c. ... To which is annexed, an Elaborate Review, By James Fennimore Cooper. *New York: Henry C. Langley.* 1844. 8vo, pp. (4), 344. H. 43426

Mackenzie (C.) Notes on Haiti, made during a Residence in that Republic. By Charles Mackenzie, Esq. ... *London: Henry Colburn and Richard Bentley.* 1830. 12mo, pp. xx, 335; vii, 306. Facsimile, Map, and 2 Plates. H. 43427

See "Blackwood's Magazine," XXVII. 240, 269; XXXIV. 615.

McKenzie. (C. D.) *See* [Bingham (L. D.)], Vol. II. 5455.

Mackenzie (E.) An Historical, Topographical, and Descriptive View of the United States of America, and of Upper and Lower Canada. With an Appendix containing a Brief and Comprehensive Sketch of the Present State of Mexico and South America, and also of the Native Tribes of the New World. ... By E. Mackenzie ... . *Newcastle-upon-Tyne: Mackenzie and Dent.* [1819.] 8vo, pp. xv, (1), 9–712. Map and 8 Plates. H. + Second Edition. [*Ibid.*] 8vo, pp. xv, 712. Map and 8 Plates.

Mackenzie (Henry). An Answer to Paine's Rights of Man. By H. Mackenzie, Esq. of Edinborough. To which is added A Letter from Peter Porcupine to Citizen John Swanwick, An Englishman, the Son of a British Waggon-Master, and Member of Congress for the City of Philadelphia. *Philadelphia: William Cobbett.* 1796. 8vo, pp. 96. P. 43429

See also [Dalrymple (Sir John)], No. 18,347, *and* [Germaine (George)], No. 27145.

McKenzie (J. A.) A Discourse against Life-taking. Delivered ... before the Rhode Island Quarterly Meeting, in Tiverton, August 24, 1842. By James A. McKenzie ... . *Providence: J. Whittemore & Batcheller.* 1842. 8vo, pp. 23. 43430

Mackenzie (R.) Strictures on Lt. Col. Tarleton's History of the Campaigns of 1780 and 1781, in the "Southern Provinces of North America." Wherein Military Characters and Corps are vindicated from Injurious Aspersions, and several Important Transactions placed in their proper point of view. In a series of Letters to a Friend, By Roderick Mackenzie late Lieutenant in the 71st Regiment. To which is added, a Detail of the Siege of Ninety Six, and the Re-capture of the Island of New-Providence. *London: Printed for the Author.* M.DCC.LXXXVII. 8vo, pp. (4), vi, 186. H. 43431

Scarce. The author defends Lord Cornwallis, and is very severe on Lieut. Col. Tarleton's "History," in which, he says, "Some facts have been withheld, and some mutilated, while others are raised to a pitch of importance, to which, if historical justice had been the author's object, they are by no means entitled." The account of the siege of Ninety Six and the capture of New Providence is by Lieut. Hatton. *See* Rich, I. 338, "European Magazine," for 1788, Hanger's "Reply," *and* Tarleton (B.)

Mackenzie (R.) America and her Army. By Robert Mackenzie. *London: T. Nelson and Sons.* 1865. 16mo, pp. 60. H.

Mackenzie. The United States of America: A History. By Robert Mackenzie. *London: T. Nelson and Sons.* 1870. 16mo, pp. (2), 278. H. 43433

A Dutch translation was published in 1872 as below:

Mackenzie. De Vereenigde Staten van Noord-Amerika, eene geschiedkundige schets. Naar het Engelsch door C. Koning Altman. *Sneek: H. Pyttersen.* 1872. 8vo, pp. viii, 260.

Mackenzie (W. L.) The Legislative Black-List of Upper Canada; or, Official Corruption and Hypocrisy Unmasked. By William Lyon Mackenzie. *York.* 1828. 8vo, pp. 40. 43435

Mackenzie. The Life and Times of Martin Van Buren: the Correspondence of his Friends, Family and Pupils; together with Brief Notices, Sketches, and Anecdotes, illustrative of the Public Career of James Knox Polk [and fifty-one other Americans]. By William L. Mackenzie. ... *Boston: Cooke & Co.* 1846. 8vo, pp. xii, 308. H. 43436

Mackenzie. The Lives and Opinions of Benj'n Franklin Butler, ... and Jesse Hoyt, ... [and others]. By William L. Mackenzie. ... *Boston: Cook & Co.* 1845. 8vo, pp. 152. H.

Mackenzie. Sketches of Canada and the United States. By William L. Mackenzie. ... *London: Effingham Wilson.* MDCCCXXXIII. 8vo, pp. xxiv, 504. BA. 43438

Mackenzie. Trial of W. L. Mackenzie, for an Alleged Violation of the Neutrality of the United States. *New York.* 1840. 24mo, pp. 104. 43439

See also Lindsey (C.), *and* Morgan's "Bib. Can.," pp. 243–45. Also: Petition of William L. Mackenzie, acting Executor to the Estate of the Late Robert Randall, Esq. ... [*Quebec: Printed by John Lovell.* 1852.] 8vo, pp. 70, (2).—The Seventh Annual Report of the Select Committee of the House of Assembly of Upper Canada, on Grievances. ... *Toronto.* 1835. 8vo, pp. 398.

McKeon (J.) The Administration Reviewed. Speech of the Hon. John McKeon before the Democratic Union Association, ... October 29, 1862. *New York: Van Evrie, Horton & Co.* 1862. 8vo, pp. 15. 43440

[McKeon.] To the Legislature of ... New York. [n. p. n. d.] 8vo, pp. 18. H. 43441

Also: Report ... in Relation to Protections to American Seamen. *Washington: Printed by Blair and Rives.* 1837. 8vo, pp. 16.—Speech ... on Nullification ... [n. p. n. d.] 8vo, pp. 7.—Speech ... on the Resolution ... proposing an Inquiry into the Condition of the Executive Departments. ... *Washington: Blair and Rives, Printers.* 1837. 8vo, pp. 8.—Speech ... on the Bill to distribute the Proceeds of the Public Lands among the States ... July 3, 1841. *Washington.* 1841. 8vo, pp. 6.—Speech ... May 30 and 31, 1842, on the Army Appropriation Bill. *Washington.* 1842. 8vo, pp. 11.—Speech ... Peace and Union; War and Disunion. *New York.* 1863. 8vo.

McKeon (J.) A Plea for Friendship and Patriotism in Two Discourses. By J. McKeon. *Boston.* 1814. 8vo. 43442

[MacKercher (Daniel).] A Memorial Relating to the Tobacco-Trade. Offer'd to The Consideration of the Planters of Virginia and Maryland. *Williamsburgh: Printed by William Parks.* M,DCC,XXXVII. 8vo, pp. 25. 43443

[McKerrell (R.)] Considerations on the Trade with America, extracted from the 'Times' of April 5th, 1813. *London.* 1813. 8vo. 43444

Mackey (A. G.) The Ahiman Rezon, or Book of Constitutions of the Grand Lodge of Ancient Freemasons of South Carolina; Edited by Albert G. Mackey, M.D. *Charleston: A. E. Miller.* 1852. 8vo, pp. 248. + Third Edition. *New York: Clark & Maynard.* 1871. 8vo, pp. 324, (20). 20 Plates.

Mackey. A Lexicon of Freemasonry; ... Notices of its History ... By Albert G. Mackey, M.D. *Charleston, S. C.* 1845. 12mo, pp. 360. + Third Edition ... . *Philadelphia: Moss & Brother.* 1855. 12mo, pp. 524. Portrait. 43446

Mackey. Washington as a Freemason. An Address ... at Charleston, S. C., ... November 4th, 1852, being the Centennial Celebration of the Initiation of George Washington. By Albert G. Mackey. *Charleston.* 1852. 8vo, pp. 23. 43447

Also: The Political Treason of ... F. A. Sawyer, and ... C. C. Bowen. Speech ... 28th July, 1869. *Charleston, S. C.* 1869. 8vo, pp. 6. H.

[Mackey (A. G.) *and* (T. J.)] The Political Record of ... F. A. Sawyer, and ... C. C. Bowen, of South Carolina. [n. p. n. d.] 8vo, pp. 83. H. 43448

[McKibbin (J. C.)] A Bill authorizing Mail Steamship Service in the Gulf of Mexico, between the Port of New Orleans, Louisiana, and certain Ports of ... Mexico. [n. p. n. d.] 8vo, pp. 25. H. 43449

Mackie (A.), *Jr.* An Address to the ... Sons of Temperance, By Andrew Mackie, Jr., M.A., on ... October 7th, 1862. *New Bedford: E. Anthony, Printer.* 1862. 8vo, pp. 20. 43450

Mackie (G.) Sermon preached at Quebec on National Schools in that City. By Rev. George Mackie. *Quebec.* 1840. 8vo, pp. 16. 43451

Mackie (J.) An Oration at Wareham, Mass. July 4, 1804 By John Mackie. *New Bedford.* 1804. 8vo. W. 43452

Mackie (J. M.) From Cape Cod to Dixie and the Tropics. By J. Milton Mackie ... . *New York: G. P. Putnam.* 1864. 12mo, pp. 422. B. 43453

[McKim (John). Appeal] To the Honorable Levi Woodbury, Secretary of the Navy. [n. p. n. d.] 8vo, pp. 56. B.

M'Kim (J. M.) The Freedmen of South Carolina. An Address ... by J. Miller M'Kim, ... July 9th, 1862. ... With a Letter ... to Stephen Colwell, Esq. ... *Philadelphia: Willis P. Hazard.* 1862. 8vo, pp. 32. H. 43455

M'Kinnen (D.) A Tour through the British West Indies, in the Years 1802 and 1803, giving a particular Account of the Bahama Islands. By Daniel M'Kinnen, Esq. *London: J. White.* 1804. Cr. 8vo, pp. (4), viii, 272. Map. C. 43456

Mac-Kinnen. Mac-Kinnen's Reise nach dem Brittischen Westindien, und besonders nach den Bahama-Inseln, in den Jahren 1802 und 1803. Aus dem Englischen mit einer Zugabe von Theoph. Fried. Ehrmann. *Weimar.* 1805. 8vo. 43457

See Edwards (B.) Dr. Allibone quotes some other works which I have not seen.

McKinney (M.) Our Governments: a View of the Government of the United States, and of those of the several States. By Mordecai McKinney. Second Edition. *Philadelphia.* 1856. 8vo. + Third Edition. [*Ibid.*] 1859. 8vo. 43458

M'Kinney. The United States Constitutional Manual; being a Comprehensive Compendium of the System of Government of the Country; ... By Mordecai M'Kinney. *Harrisburg: Hickok & Cantine.* 1845. 8vo, pp. xv, 304. 43459

M'Kinnon (J. D.) Descriptive Poems. By John D. M'Kinnon, containing Picturesque Views of the State of New-York. *New-York: Printed by T. & J. Swords.* 1802. 12mo, pp. (6), 79.

Mackinnon (L. B.) Atlantic and Transatlantic Sketches, Afloat and Ashore. By Commander Mackinnon, R.N. ... *London: Colburn and Co.* 1852. 2 vols., post 8vo, pp. xv, 288; ix, 292. + *New York: Harper & Brothers.* 1852. 12mo, pp. 324.

Mackinnon. Some Account of the Falkland Islands, from a Six Months' Residence in 1838 and 1839. By L. B. Mackinnon ... . *London: Baily and Co.* 1840. 8vo, pp. 79. Map.

Mackinnon. Steam Warfare in the Parana: a Narrative of Operations by the combined Squadrons of England and France, in forcing a Passage up that River. By Commander Mackinnon, R.N. ... *London: Charles Ollier.* 1848. 2 vols., post 8vo, pp. xii, 302; vii, 287. Map and Plates. BA., C. 43463

Contains an account of operations against Rosas, etc.

Mackinnon (W. A.) History of Civilization. By William Alexander Mackinnon. *London: Longman* ... 1846. 2 vols., 8vo, pp. (2), xiv, 388; xii, 402. BA. 43464

Mackinnon. On the Rise, Progress, and Present State of Public Opinion ... . By William Alexander Mackinnon. Second Edition. *London: Saunders and Otley.* MDCCCXXVIII. 8vo, pp. ix, 343. 43465

Public Opinion in America, pp. 300–311.

McKinnon (W. C.) St. George, or, the Canadian League; a Tale of the Outbreak in 1837, with an Introduction. By William Charles McKinnon. *Halifax.* 1852. 2 vols., 8vo.

McKinny (D.) The Union Preserved, or the Law-Abiding Christian. A Discourse, by David McKinny, D.D. *Philadelphia: William F. Geddes.* 1851. 8vo, pp. 27. 43467

McKinstry (E. W.) Oration at the Twenty-First Anniversary of the Society of California Pioneers. By E. W. McKinstry. *San Francisco.* 1870. 8vo. 43468

McKinstry (J.) Vindication of Brig. Gen. J. McKinstry, formerly Quartermaster of the Western Department. [*St. Louis.* 1862.] 8vo, pp. 102. B., H. 43469

Mackintosh (J.) Speech of Sir James Mackintosh ... on the Recognition of the Independence of the Spanish American Provinces. *London.* 1824. 8vo. 43470

Also: A Discourse on the Study of the Law of Nature and Nations. ... *London.* 1828. 16mo. c. + Second Edition. *London: Henry Goode and Co.* M. DCCC. XXVII. 16mo, pp. (2), 89. + *Boston: Pratt and Company.* 1843. 8vo, pp. (2), 103. H.

McKnight (G. H.) A Sermon on the Death of John M. Jackson, By Rev. Geo. H. McKnight ... October 25, 1863. ... *Springfield: Printed by Samuel Bowles & Company.* 1863. 16mo, pp. 20. H. 43471

McKnight (J.) A Discourse ... Aug. 26, 1826, Exposing Robert Owen's System, as practiced by the Franklin Community at Haverstraw, N. J. By James McKnight. *New York.* 1826. 8vo, pp. 20. 43472

M'Knight (J.) The Divine Goodness to the United States of America, particularly in the course of the last year. A Thanksgiving Sermon, ... in New-York, February 19, 1795. By John M'Knight, D.D. ... *New-York: Printed by Thomas Greenleaf.* 1795. 8vo, pp. 23, (4). B. 43473

"A dish of jumbled politics." Appended is a list of 250 subscribers, who had agreed to take 1400 copies of the discourse.

M'Knight. God the Author of Promotion, a Sermon ... at New York, July 4th, 1794, at the request of the Democratic Society and the Military Officers, By John McKnight, D.D. *New York.* 1794. 8vo, pp. 24. N. 43474

Also: Sermon before the New York Missionary Society, April 24, 1799. ... [n. p. n. d.] 8vo. — A View of the Present State of the Political and Religious World ... . In a Discourse, delivered January 1, 1802. ... *New-York: Printed by Isaac Collins and Son.* 1802. 8vo, pp. 39. B.

M'Knight (J.), *Jr.* An Address delivered before the Philolexian Society in New York, ... with a Notice of the Object of the Institution. By John M'Knight, Jr. *New York.* 1808. 8vo, pp. 16. 43475

McKnight (R.) Recognition of Liberia and Hayti ... . Speech of Hon. Robt. McKnight ... . June 3, 1862. [n. p. n. d.] 8vo, pp. 7. 43476

McKnight (T.) History of the Life and Times of Edmund Burke. By Thomas McKnight ... . *London: Chapman and Hall.* 1858–60. 3 vols., 8vo, pp. xxxi, 527, (1); (2), xvii, 556; xx, 764.

Contains references to his policy with regard to America. Also: Thirty Years of Foreign Policy: The Secretaryships of Aberdeen and Palmerston. ... *London.* 186–. 8vo.

M'Konochie (*Capt.*) Emigration: with Advice to Emigrants, especially those with small Capital. Addressed to the Society for promoting Colonization. By Capt. M'Konochie. *London.* 1848. 8vo, pp. 24. 43478

M'Konochie. A Summary View of the Statistics and Existing Commerce of the Principal Shores of the Pacific Ocean ... . By Captain M'Konochie ... . *London: J. M. Richardson.* 1818. 8vo, pp. xxi, 365, (1). Map. A., H., P. 43479

McKoy (Isaac). *See* McCoy (I.)

Mackrill (J.) History of the Yellow Fever. By Joseph Mackrill. *Baltimore.* 1796. 12mo. 43480

Mackworth (H.) A Proposal for Payment of the Publick Debts, For the Relief of the South-Sea Company ... . By Sir Humphrey Mackworth. The Fourth Edition. *London: W. Boreham.* [1720.] 8vo, pp. (7), xxiv, 38. J.C.B. 43481

Mackworth. Sir Humphrey Mackworth's Proposal in Miniature as it has been put in practice in New York, in America. *London: W. Boreham.* 1720. 8vo, pp. 18. S. 43482

M'Lachlan (A.) Poems. By Alexander M'Lachlan. *Toronto.* 1856. 12mo. 43483

M'Lain (W.) Discourse, Occasioned by the Death of John Coyle. ... Washington City ... . July 8, 1838. By W. M'Lain. *Washington City: Printed by Jacob Gideon, Jr.* 1838. 8vo, pp. 27.

M'Lane (D.) The Trial of David M'Lane for High Treason, ... at Quebec, on the 7th July 1797. *Quebec: J. Neilson.* 1797. 8vo, pp. 21. + *Quebec: W. Vondenvelden.* 1797. 8vo, pp. 127. 43485

M'Lane was an American citizen, employed by citizen Adet to bring about a revolution in Canada. He was found guilty, and executed July 21, 1797.

M'Lane (L.) Address of Mr. M'Lane, ... to the Stockholders of the Baltimore & Ohio R. Road Company ... the 5th of April, 1847 ... . *Baltimore: Printed by James Lucas.* 1847. 8vo, pp. 32. H., S. 43486

M'Lane. Oration delivered before the Artillery Company of Wilmington, Commanded by Captain Rodney, on the 5th of July, A.D. 1813. By Louis M'Lane, Esq'r. ... [n. p. n. d.] 12mo, pp. 23. 43487

Also: The Hon. Louis McLane and The British West-India Trade. [n. p. n. d.] 8vo, pp. 47. — Speech ... February 7th, 1820, on the Missouri Question. [n. p. n. d.] 12mo. — Speech ... on the Admission of Missouri. ... Dec. 12, 1820. [n. p. n. d.] 12mo, pp. 22. H.

McLane (R.) An Examination into the Cause of Explosions by Steam on the Western Waters. By R. McLane. *Louisville, Ky.* 1839. 8vo, pp. 15. M. 43488

McLane (R. M.) Sketch of the Remarks of Mr. McLane, ... on the Slave Trade in the District of Columbia. ... January 10, 1849. [n. p. n. d.] 8vo, pp. 8. H. 43489

Also: Speech ... on the War with Mexico. ... January 19, 1848. *Washington.* 1848. 8vo, pp. 8. — Speech ... February 27, 1850, on the Admission of California. [n. p.] 1850. 8vo.

McLaren (A.) The Negro Slaves; or, the Black Man and Black Bird. By Archibald McLaren. Second Edition. *London.* 1799. 24mo. 43490

McLaren (D.) The Pavilion Fountain at Saratoga. By D. McLaren. *New York: Thompson & Hart.* 1841. 12mo, pp. 100.

Maclaren (J.) Observations on the Effect of Californian and Australian Gold. By James Maclaren. *London.* 1852–3. 8vo. C. 43492

Maclaren. Impolicy of providing for a Family by Life Assurance since recent discoveries in California and Australia. By James Maclaren. *London.* 1853. 8vo. C. 43493

McLaren (W. E.) Detroit, June 3, 1869. Services at the Funeral of Martha, Wife of Hovey K. Clarke ... . Conducted by the Rev. W. E. McLaren ... . [*Cambridge: John Wilson and Son.* n. d.] 4to, pp. (2), 37. Portrait. B. 43494

McLaughlin (D.) Appointments of Auditors, ... by the Inferior Courts of Philadelphia, Briefly Reviewed. By Daniel McLaughlin. *Philadelphia.* 1851. 8vo. 43495

McLaughlin (D. D. T.) Re-Dedication. A Discourse ... in Sharon, Connecticut, March 2d, 1864, By ... D. D. Thompkins McLaughlin. ... *New York: Printed by F. Somers.* 1864. 8vo, pp. 29. H. 43496

McLaughlin (E. A.) ... Miscellaneous Poems. By E. A. McLaughlin. *Cincinnati.* 1841. 12mo. Portrait. 43497

M'Laughlin (J.) ... A Word with Bishop Hopkins. By John M'Laughlin. [n. p. 1864?] 8vo, pp. 17. H. 43498

[McLaughlin (J. Fairfax).] The American Cyclops, the Hero of New Orleans, and Spoiler of Silver Spoons. Dubbed L.L.D By Pasquino. *Baltimore: Kelly & Piet.* 1868. Sm. 4to, pp. 27. 12 Plates. 43499

Also: Address delivered before the Philodemic Society of Georgetown College, January 21st, 1854. ... *Baltimore.* 1854. 8vo, pp. 22.

McLaughlin (J. T.) Reply of John T. McLaughlin, ... to a Communication ... by William P. C. Barton, February 28, 1843. *Washington.* 1843. 8vo, pp. 16. BA. 43500

Maclaurie (——). A Narrative, or Journal of Voyages and Travels through the North-West Continent of America, in the years 1789 and 1793. *London.* 1802. 12mo, pp. 91. Plate.

Maclay (A.) ... A Sermon ... in ... New-York, on the ... Death of Mrs. Mary Delezenne ... . By Archibald Maclay. *New-York: Whiting & Watson.* 1812. 8vo, pp. 39. BA. 43502

Also: An Address ... before the Saratoga Baptist Association, at Middletown, ... N. Y. June 28, 1838. *New-York: Printed by John Gray.* 1838. 8vo, pp. 16. H.

Maclay (W. B.) An Address ... Fourth of July, 1835. By William B. Maclay. ... *New York: Printed by J. P. Wright.* MDCCCXXXV. 8vo, pp. 16. BA. 43503

Maclay. Address ... at the Democratic Republican Celebration ... July 4th, 1840, at ... Poughkeepsie. By William B. Maclay. *New-York.* 1840. 8vo, pp. 24. 43504

In defense of the Sub-Treasury.

Maclay. Oration ... at the Democratic Republican Celebration ... in ... New York, Fourth July, 1839. By William B. Maclay. *New York.* 1839. 8vo, pp. 24. S. 43505

Maclay. A Selection of Letters, written on Various Occasions. By Hon. William B. Maclay. *New York.* 1848. 8vo, pp. 47. 43506

On Oregon, the Annexation of Texas, and the War with Mexico. Also: Letters ... on the Admission of Kansas ... . [n. p. 1857?] 8vo, pp. 10. H. — Oration before the Literary Association, Fourth July, 1836. ... *New York.* 1836. 8vo.

M'Lean (A.) An Appeal to the Public, or an Exposition of the Conduct of Rev. Isaac Jennison and Others ... . By Alexander M'Lean ... . *Belchertown: Printed by C. A. Warren.* 1828. 8vo, pp. 56. H. 43507

Also: An Oration pronounced at Ludlow Factory Village, Mass., July 4, 1829. ... *Belchertown.* 1829. 8vo, pp. 16.

McLean (A.) The Clemency of the Divine Government a Cause for Thanksgiving. A Sermon ... Annual Thanksgiving, By Alexander McLean, Jr., ... Fairfield, Ct. *New York: George W. Wood, Printer.* 1861. 8vo, pp. 16. 43508

M'Lean (A.) A Discourse on the Fiftieth Anniversary of his Ordination ... in Simsbury, Conn. By Rev. Allen M'Lean. ... August 16, 1859. *Hartford: Press of Case, Lockwood and Company.* 1859. 8vo, pp. 35. H. 43509

M'Lean (C. B.) ... A Sermon ... at the Funeral of Rev. James Burt, of Canton, Conn., January 22, 1857. By Charles B. M'Lean. ... *Hartford: Press of Case, Tiffany and Company.* 1857. 8vo, pp. 31. H. 43510

M'Lean (C. G.) A Eulogium on General Lafayette. By the Rev. C. G. M'Lean. *Gettysburg: Printed by H. C. Neinstedt.* 1834. 8vo, pp. 16. BA. 43511

Maclean (*Gen.*) *See* Vol. IX., No. 36740.

M'Lean (H.) An Inquiry into the Nature and Causes of the Great Mortality among the Troops at St. Domingo; with Practical Remarks on the Fever of that Island; ... By Hector M'Lean, M.D. ... *London: T. Cadell.* M. DCC. XCVII. 8vo, pp. xxiii, (1), 358. H., P. 43512

M'Lean (J.) Seventeen Years History of the Life and Sufferings of James M'Lean, an impressed American Citizen and Seaman ... . Written by Himself. *Hartford.* 1814. 12mo, pp. 27.

M'Lean (J.) Notes of a Twenty-Five Years' Service in the Hudson's Bay Territory. By John M'Lean. ... *London: Richard Bentley.* 1849. 2 vols., 8vo, pp. 308; 328. H. 43514

Depicts with great fidelity and vivacity the manners and condition, the toils, privations, and perils of the Indian hunters. It includes also several interesting geographical and geological facts and Indian vocabularies.

Maclean (J.) Letters on the Elder Question. By John Maclean. [*Princeton:*] *Printed by John T. Robinson.* 1844. 8vo, pp. 55, (1). B. 43515

Also: The Inauguration of the Rev. John Maclean, D.D. ... President of the College of New Jersey, ... June 28, 1854. *Princeton, N. J.: Printed by John T. Robinson.* 1854. 8vo, pp. 52. — Lecture on a School System for New Jersey ... . [n. p. 1829.] 8vo.

M'Lean (J.) Sketch of Reverend Philip Gatch, an Early Western Methodist Preacher. Prepared by Hon. John M'Lean. *Cincinnati.* 1854. 16mo, pp. 190. + [*Ibid.*] 1856. 43516

Also: Address on the Consecration of the Spring Grove Cemetery, near Cincinnati, August 20, 1845. ... [n. p. 1845.] 8vo, pp. 29. — An Address, ... at the Request of the Union and Jefferson Societies of Augusta College. *Cincinnati: John Whetstone, Jr. & Co., Printers.* 1831. 8vo, pp. 28. BA. + Second Edition. *Philadelphia: Samuel C. Atkinson, Printer.* 1831. 8vo, pp. 16. BA. — A Sketch of the Life of John McLean, of Ohio. [n. p. n. d.] 8vo.

McLean (M.) Speech of Moses McLean ... on the Tariff. ... June 18, 1846. [n. p. n. d.] 8vo, pp. 7. H. 43517

Also in German, 8vo, pp. 8.

McLean (*Mr.*) Remove the Indians Westward. ... February 18, 1829. Mr. McLean ... made the following Report ... [*Washington.* 1829.] 8vo, pp. 48. 43518

M'Lean (O. O.) ... A Discourse ... before the Bible Society of Pennsylvania College ... Gettysburg, April, 16th, 1854. By Rev. O. O. M'Lean, A.M. ... *Gettysburg: Printed by H. C. Neinstedt.* 1854. 8vo, pp. 25. H. 43519

McLean Asylum, *Somerville, Mass.* Annual Report of the McLean Asylum for the Insane for ... 1854. *Boston.* 1854. 8vo.

Macleane (L.) An Essay on the Expediency of Inoculation and the Seasons most proper for it. ... By Laughlin Macleane, M.D. *Philadelphia: Printed by William Bradford.* 1756. 8vo, pp. 39, (1). 43521

One of the earliest American works on the subject.

McLelan (A. W.) Speech on the Union of the Colonies. ... By A. W. McLelan, Esq. ... 1865. [n. p. n. d.] 8vo, pp. 15. H. 43522

McLellan (I.) The Fall of the Indian, with other Poems. By Isaac McLellan, Jun. *Boston: Carter and Hendee.* M DCCCXXX. 18mo, pp. 99. H. 43523

M'Lellan. Mount Auburn, and other Poems. By Isaac M'Lellan, Jr. *Boston: W. D. Ticknor.* 1843. 16mo, pp. (4), 156. C. 43524

Also: The Year, with other Poems. ... *Boston.* 1832. 8vo, pp. 60. *See* Buckingham's "New England Magazine," Vol. v., 1833.

McLellan (R.) Speech of Robert McLellan ... on the United States Fiscal Bank Bill, 1811. [n. p. n. d.] 8vo. S.

McLelland (A.) ... "Plea for a Standing Ministry." A Sermon ... Dec. 28, 1817. By Alexander McLelland. *New York.* 1818. 8vo. 43526

McLelland (J.) True Sketches of Minnesota ... . By John McLelland. [n. p.:] *The Author.* 1858. 12mo, pp. 21. BA.

M'Leod (A.) Negro Slavery Unjustifiable. A Discourse by Alexander M'Leod, A.M. ... *New-York: Printed by T. & J. Swords.* 1802. 8vo, pp. 42. + *Glasgow: Stephen Young, Printer.* 1804. 8vo, pp. 35. + Eleventh Edition. *New York.* 1863. 12mo, pp. 48. 43528

McLeod. A Scriptural View of the Character, Causes, and Ends of the Present War. By Alexander McLeod, D.D. *New-York: Eastburn, Kirk and Co.* 1815. 8vo, pp. 224. B. + [Another Edition. *Ibid.*] 8vo, pp. 235. 43529

Also: An Oration delivered at Georgetown on the 4th day of July, 1816. ... *Georgetown: E. Waterman.* 1816. 8vo, pp. 17. — Review of the Opinion of Judge Cowen, of the Supreme Court of the State of New York. ... *Washington.* 1841. 8vo, pp. 28.

M'Leod (A.) Case of the Caroline and Arrest of M'Leod for the Murder of Durfee. *London.* 1837–41. 2 vols., folio.

M'Leod. Trial of Alexander M'Leod, for the Murder of Amos Durfee; and as an Accomplice in the Burning of the Steamer Caroline, in the Niagara River, during the Canadian Rebellion in 1837–8. *New York: Sun Office.* 1841. 8vo, pp. 32. + *Washington.* 1841. 8vo. B. 43531

For another and fuller account *see* "Stenographic Reporter," *also* [Pickering (J.)]

Mac-Leod. De la question de juridiction qui s'est présentée devant les cours des États-Unis dans l'affaire de Mac-Leod. *Paris.* [n. d.] 8vo, pp. 15. B. 43532

McLeod (C. D.) Phasmion, a Poem ... before the ... University of ... New-York. July 13, 1841. By C. Donald McLeod. *New-York: Press of Piercy & Reed.* 1841. 8vo, pp. (2), 22.

[McLeod (Daniel).] The Rebellion in Tennessee. Observations on Bishop Otey's Letter to the Hon. William H. Seward. By a Native of Virginia. ... *Washington: McGill, Witherow & Co., Printers.* 1862. 8vo, pp. 11. BA. 43534

McLeod (Donald). *See* [Thomson (William)].

McLeod (D.) A Brief Review of the Settlement of Upper Canada by the N. E. Loyalists and Scotch Highlanders in 1783; and of the Grievances which Compelled the Canadas to have recourse to Arms in Defence of their Rights and Liberties in the Years 1837 and 1838. Together with a Brief Sketch of the Campaigns of 1812–'13–'14: With an account of the Military Executions, Burnings, and Sackings of Towns and Villages, by the British, in the Upper and Lower Provinces, during the Commotion of 1837 and '38. By D. McLeod, Major General, Patriot Army, Upper Canada. *Cleveland: F. B. Penniman.* 1841. 16mo, pp. 292. 43535

McLeod. Biography of Hon. Fernando Wood, Mayor of the City of New York. By Donald McLeod. *New York.* 1856. 12mo, pp. 350. Portrait. 43536

McLeod. History of Wiskonsin, from its Discovery to the Present Period. Including a Geological and Topographical Description of the Territory, with a Correct Catalogue of all its

Plants. By Donald McLeod. *Buffalo: Steele's Press.* 1846. 16mo, pp. xii, 310. Map. 43537

[McLeod (*Miss* Isabella).] Westfield, a View of Home Life during the American War. *Edinburgh.* 1866. 8vo. 43538

McLeod (J. N.) ... A Discourse on the Death of the Rev. Samuel Brown Wylie, D.D. By John Niel McLeod ... . *New York: G. & H. Miller.* 1852. 8vo, pp. 31. 43539

McLeod. Presentation Address to, and Historical Discourse by, Rev. John N. McLeod, D.D., on the Completion of a Twenty-Five Years' Pastorate. *Philadelphia: C. Sherman & Son, Printers.* [1858.] 8vo, pp. 19. B. 43540

McLeod. ... A Sermon ... at the Opening of the First Reformed Presbyterian Church ... Philada. ... April 30, 1854. By John Niel McLord, D.D. ... *Philadelphia.* 1854. 8vo, pp. 17.

Also: ... A Discourse in Memory of the late Rev. Andrew W. Black, D.D. ... Nov. 21st, 1858. ... *New-York: W. H. Trafton & Co.* ... *Printers.* 1859. 8vo, pp. 30. — Protestantism, the Parent and Guardian of Civil and Religious Liberty. A Lecture ... March 26, 1843 ... . *New York: Robert Carter.* 1843. 8vo, pp. 38. — The Stone of Help; a Discourse, Historical and Commemorative, delivered Dec. 26, 1847. ... *New York.* 1848. 8vo, pp. 24.

[Macleod (Malcolm).] Practical Guide to Emigrants to the United States. By a Lancashire Artisan. *Manchester.* 1866. 12mo. 43542

Macleod (M.) History of Witches. ... By Malcolm Macleod. *Albany.* 1809. 18mo. + *Newark.* 1811. 8vo. 43543

McLeod (N.) Wee Davie, by Norman McLeod, D.D. ... From the Twenty-Seventh London Edition. *Richmond, Va.* 1864. 16mo, pp. 46. H. 43544

A Confederate publication.

Macleod (W.) Harper's New York and Erie Rail-Road Guide Book. ... By William Macleod. *New York: Harper & Brothers.* [1851.] 12mo, pp. 173, (1). B. 43545

Macleod (X. D.) Devotion to the Blessed Virgin Mary in North America. By the Rev. Xavier Donald Macleod. With a Memoir of the Author, by the Most Rev. John B. Purcell, D.D. *New York: Virtue & Yorston.* [1866.] 8vo, pp. xxiii, 467. Portrait. 43546

Maclise (D. M.) Historical Discourse at Montgomery, N. Y., Jan. 1, 1865, on the 125th Anniversary of the Pastorate of

the Goodwill Presbyterian Church. By Rev. D. M. Maclise. *New York.* 1865. 8vo, pp. 32. 43547

McLoud (A.) A Thanksgiving Discourse, ... in Topsfield, November 25th, 1852. By Anson McLoud ... . *Salem.* 1852. 8vo, pp. 29. B. 43548

McLowne (J.) Discourse on the Death of Abraham Lincoln. By J. McLowne. *Fort Wayne.* 1865. 8vo. 43549

Maclure (W.) Catalogue of Mineralogical and Geological Specimens at New-Harmony, Ind., collected in various Parts of Europe and America. By William Maclure. Arranged by D. D. Owen. *New-Harmony.* 1840. 8vo. 43550

Maclure. Essay on the Formation of Rocks ... . By William Maclure ... . *New-Harmony, Indiana: Printed for the Author.* 1832. 8vo, pp. 53. + *Philadelphia: J. Wilbank.* 1838. 8vo, pp. 32. H. 43551

Maclure. Observations on the Geology of the United States of America ... . By William Maclure. ... *Philadelphia: Printed ... by Abraham Small.* 1817. 8vo, pp. 127, (2). Map and Plate.

See "Edinb. Rev.," xxx. 374, *also* Rich, II. 92, No. 32.

Maclure. Observations on the Geology of the West India Islands, from Barbadoes to Santa Cruz, inclusive. By William Maclure. *New Harmony, Indiana: Printed for the Author.* 1832. 8vo, pp. 17. H. 43553

Maclure. Opinions on Various Subjects, dedicated to the Industrious Producers. By William Maclure. *New-Harmony, Indiana.* 1831–38. 3 vols., 8vo, pp. (4), 640; (8), 556; (2), iv, 320. BA. 43554

[Maclure.] Suite des Observations sur la Géologie des États-Unis ... . [n. p. 1811.] 4to, pp. 32. Map. BA. 43555

[Maclure.] To the People of the United States. *Philadelphia.* 1807. 8vo, pp. (2), 2, 4, (2), 2 folded pages, 9–145. BA.

Maclurian Lyceum. Contributions of the Maclurian Lyceum to the Arts and Sciences. Nos. 1 and 2. 8vo, pp. 60. Plates. A. 43557

McMcIntosh (J.) The Memorial of Commander James McMcIntosh, U.S.N., for Compensation; with Correspondence and Remarks. *New York.* 1843. 8vo, pp. 48. 43558

McMahon (B.) Jamaica Plantership. Compiled during Eighteen Years Residence. By Benjamin McMahon. *London: Effingham Wilson.* 1839. 12mo. P. 43559

A description of Jamaica planters, viz. attorneys, overseers, and book-keepers.

M'Mahon (B.) The American Gardener's Calendar; adapted to the Climates and Seasons of the United States. ... By Bernard M'Mahon ... . *Philadelphia: Printed by B. Graves.* 1806. 8vo, pp. v, 648, (18). + Third Edition. *Philadelphia.* 1819. 8vo. + Fourth Edition, Improved. *Philadelphia: T. P. M'Mahon.* 1820. 8vo, pp. 618. + Eleventh Edition. ... *Philadelphia: J. B. Lippincott and Co.* 1857. 8vo, pp. 637. Plate.

M'Mahon (J. V. L.) An Historical View of the Government of Maryland, from its Colonization to the present day. By John V. L. M'Mahon. Vol. I. *Baltimore: F. Lucas, Jr.* 1831. 8vo, pp. xvi, 539. A., B. 43561

No more published; perhaps suppressed. *See* Swearingen (G.)

MacMahon (T. O'B.) The Candor and Good Nature of Englishmen Exemplified. By Thomas O'Brien MacMahon. *London: J. Bew.* 1777. 8vo, pp. xii, 292. C. 43562

MacMahon (T. W.) Cause and Contrast: an Essay on the American Crisis. By T. W. MacMahon. *Richmond, Va.: West & Johnston.* 1862. 8vo, pp. xv, 192. BA. 43563

M'Manus (C.) A Correct Account of the Trials of Charles M'Manus ... and others; at Harrisburgh—June ... 1798. For the Murder of Francis Shitz ... 1797, at Heidelberg, ... Pennsylvania. Containing the Whole Evidence ... . *Printed at Harrisburg, by John Wyeth.* 1798. 8vo, Half Title, pp. 163. BA.

MacMaster (Erasmus D.) Integrity, Personal and Political: An Address ... in Hanover College, Indiana, ... July 27, 1842. By E. D. MacMaster ... . *Indianapolis: Printed by John Douglass.* 1842. 8vo, pp. 18. 43565

MacMaster. Speech of Mr. MacMaster in the Synod of Indiana, October 4, 1844, in relation to Madison University. *Madison: Jones and Lodge.* 1844. 8vo, pp. 39. 43566

This elicited a review which we have not seen.

MacMaster. A Sermon at Oxford, O., in 1849, on the Day of the National Fast. By Rev. E. D. MacMaster ... . [n. p.] 1849. 8vo. 43567

Also: Discourse before the Presbyterian Church at Ballston Spa, N. Y., on the Occasion of the Author's Resignation of his Pastoral Charge, April 29, 1838. ... *Albany.* 1838. 8vo. — A Discourse ... November 7th, 1838, on ... [his] Inauguration as President of Hanover College, Indiana. ... *Hanover, Ind.* 1838. 8vo, pp. 36. — The True Life of a Nation: An Address, ... July 2d, 1856. ... *New Albany.* 1856. 8vo, pp. 47. *See also* Miami University.

McMaster (G.) The Duty of Nations. A Sermon, ... Nov. 1, 1809, ... Thanksgiving ... . By Gilbert McMaster ... . *Ballston-Spa.* 1810. 8vo, pp. 52. S. 43568

McMaster. The Moral Character of Civil Government, considered with reference to the Political Institutions of the United States ... . By Gilbert McMaster, D.D. ... *Albany: W. C. Little.* 1832. 8vo, pp. 72. B. 43569

Also: Discourse on the Decease of S. B. Wylie, D.D. ... *Philadelphia.* 1852. 8vo, pp. 82. — "The Obligations of the American Scholar, to his Country, and the World." An Address ... Hanover College, Sept. 28, 1841. ... *Madison, Ind.* 1841. 8vo, pp. 24. — Remarks offered in illustration of a Report on the Doctrine of Civil Government. *Schenectady.* 1835. 8vo, pp. 24. — ... A Sermon, preached at the Ordination of the Rev. James Milligan, ... Coldenham. ... *New-York: Whiting and Watson.* 1812. 8vo, pp. 52.

M'Masters (G. H.) History of the Settlement of Steuben County, N. Y. Including Notices of the Old Pioneer Settlers and their Adventures. By Guy H. M'Masters. *Bath: R. L. Underhill & Co.* 1853. 12mo, pp. iv, 318. 43570

McMasters (S. Y.) A Methodist in search of the Church. By ... Rev. S. Y. McMasters, D.D. ... *Claremont, N. H.* 1862. 16mo, pp. 314. H. 43571

McMichael (J. B.) A Tribute to the Memory of the late Dr. Alexander Ingram, U.S.A. By Rev. J. B. McMichael. *Cincinnati: Moore, Wilstach & Baldwin, Printers.* 1867. 8vo, pp. 27. B. 43572

McMichael (W.) The Government of the Methodist Episcopal Church, Anti-Republican and Despotic. By Rev. William McMichael. Second Edition, Enlarged. *Pittsburgh.* 1855. 12mo, pp. 164. 43573

McMichael. Slavery, and its Remedy. By Rev. William McMichael. *Pittsburgh.* 1856. 12mo, pp. 221. 43574

McMicken (C.) The Will of Charles McMicken, of Cincinnati, Ohio. ... With ... an Index. *Cincinnati.* 1858. 4to, pp. 30. H. 43575

McMicken University. First Annual Report of the Directors of the McMicken University, for the year 1860. [n. p. n. d.] 8vo, pp. 18. Continued. 43576

McMillan (J.) Trial of the Rev. John McMillan for Defaming Thomas Leslie Birch. *Washington.* 1806. 8vo. 43577

McMullen (F.) Speech of F. McMullen, ... April 29, 1852, on the Homestead Bill. [n. p. n. d.] 8vo. 43578

MacMullen (J.) A Lecture on The Past, the Present, and the Future of the New York Society Library, ... February 15th, 1856, By John MacMullen ... . *New York: John F. Trow, Printer.* 1856. 8vo, pp. 42. BA. 43579

MacMullen. Nathan Hale, A Poem, ... before ... Columbia College, October 27, 1858. By John MacMullen, A.M. *New York: John F. Trow, Printer.* 1858. 8vo, pp. 31. H.

The cover-title has the date 1858. Also: To the Shareholders of the New-York Society Library. April 28, 1857. [*New York.* 1857.] 12mo, pp. 10.

McMullen (J.) The History of Canada, from its first discovery to the present time. By John MacMullen, Esq. ... *Brockville.* 1855. 8vo. + Second Edition, revised and improved. *Brockville: McMullen & Co.* 1868. 8vo, pp. xxxi, 613. H.

McMullen (R. B.) "Truth the Foundation of Genuine Liberty." An Address ... before the Alumni of the University of Alabama, July 13th, 1858. By R. B. McMullen, D.D. ... *Tuskaloosa.* 1858. 8vo, pp. 16. B. 43582

McMullin (F.) Letter of Hon. Fayette McMullin, to the People of ... Virginia. [n. p. 1856?] 8vo, pp. 7. H. 43583

Also: ... Speech ... April 29, 1852, on the Homestead Bill. [n. p. n. d.] 8vo, pp. 7. H.

[McMullin (M. A.)] Poems: by Una. *Cincinnati: L. G. Cobb.* 1863. 12mo, pp. 216. 43584

M'Murray (W.) A Sermon, ... in behalf of the American Colonization Society, ... New-York, July 10, 1825. By W. M'Murray. *New-York: Printed by J. Seymour.* 1825. 8vo, pp. 28. B. 43585

McMurray (W.) Democratic Policy in regard to the Canals and their Completion. Speech of William M'Murray ... March 26 & 28, 1853. [n. p. n. d.] 8vo, pp. 17. H. 43586

Also: Speech ... on the Governor's Message, January, 1843. [n. p. n. d.] 8vo. — Speech ... on the Proposition to Amend the Constitution of New York. *Albany.* 1853. 8vo. B.

M'Murtrie (H.) Sketches of Louisville And its Environs; including, ... a Florule Louisvillensis ... . By H. M'Murtrie, M.D. ... To which is added An Appendix ... . First Edition. *Louisville: Printed by S. Penn, Jun.* 1819. 8vo, pp. viii, 255. Map. H.

The first edition is the last.

McMyler (J. J.) History of the Eleventh Wisconsin Veteran Volunteer Infantry. By J. J. McMyler. *New Orleans.* 1865. 8vo. 43588

McN—— (T.) A Brief Review of the Past Sixty Years for the ... American People ... with the Letter of Andrew Jackson to Dr. Coleman, April 26, 1824 ... . [n. p. n. d.] 8vo, pp. 8.

McNair (J.) Eighty Original Poems; Secular and Sacred. By J. McNair. *Lancaster, Pa.* 1865. 12mo. 43590

Ten of these effusions were inspired (?) by the events of the rebellion.

M'Nair (T. J.) *See* St. Louis Magnet.

MacNair (R.) Case before the House of Lords between Robt. MacNair and others respecting trafficking to the Barbadoes and Virginia, ... with the Statements of John Hood of Virginia, who furnished the Cargoes ... . [n. p.:] *Privately Printed.* 1772. Folio. 43591

Title from J. C. Hotten's catalogue; sure to be incorrect.

McNally (W.) Evils and Abuses in the Naval and Merchant Service exposed, with Proposals for their Remedy and Redress. By William McNally ... . *Boston: Cassady and March.* 1839. 12mo, pp. viii, 201, (1). H. 43592

Macnamara (H. T. J.) Peace, Permanent and Universal ... A Prize Essay, By H. T. J. Macnamara. *London: Saunders and Otley.* 1841. 12mo, pp. vii, 354. H. 43593

Macnamara (M. H.) The Irish Ninth in Bivouac and Battle; or, Virginia and Maryland Campaigns. By M. H. Macnamara ... . *Boston: Lee and Shepard.* 1867. 12mo, pp. 306.

[McNaughton (J.)] An Enquiry into the Present System of Medical Education, in the State of New-York. ... By an Observer. *Albany: Printed by Websters and Skinners.* 1830. 8vo, pp. 16. B. 43595

Also: Address before the Kappa Alpha Phi Society of the College of Physicians of the Western District. ... *Albany.* 1830. 8vo. — Address ... before the Medical Society ... of New-York, February 8, 1837. ... *Albany: E. W. and C. Skinner.* 1837. 8vo, pp. 40. — Annual Address before the New-York State Medical Society. February 6, 1838. ... *Albany: Printed by J. Munsell.* 1838. 8vo, pp. 32. — Commentary on the Epistle of the Two Elders: To the Congregation of the First Presbyterian Church. [April 26, 1847. *Albany.* 1847.] 8vo, pp. 7. — A Discourse ... at the Anniversary Meeting of the Kappa Alpha Phi Society, of the College of Physicians and Surgeons of the Western District. ... *Albany: Printed by Websters and Skinners.* 1830. 8vo, pp. 23. — Vindication: To the Congregation of the First Presbyterian Church. [April 12, 1847.] *Albany.* 1847. 8vo, pp. 20.

McNeely (T. W.) Speech of Thompson W. McNeely ... Feb. 8, 1871, on National Education. [n. p. n. d.] 8vo.

M'Neely Normal School. The First Annual Catalogue of the Officers, Teachers and Students of the M'Neely Normal School of Ohio ... 1856. Circular of the Union Institute ... . *Columbus.* 1856. 8vo, pp. 14. H. 43597

Also: ... Catalogue of the Union Institute ... 1855. Circular of the McNeely Normal School. ... Hopedale ... Ohio ... . *Columbus.* 1855. 8vo, pp. 16. H.

McNeil (W. G.) Narrative of the Proceedings of the Engineers of the Baltimore and Ohio Rail Road. By William G. McNeil. Part II. *Baltimore.* 1830. 8vo. 43598

M'Neile (H.) ... A Lecture on the Life of Dr. Franklin, By The Rev. Hugh M'Neile, A.M. ... at ... Liverpool ... 17th Nov. 1841. With ... a Prefatory Note to the Reader, By John B. Murray, Esq. ... *Henderson Greene, New York.* 1841. 8vo, pp. 46, (2). Facsimile. H. 43599

M'Neile. Slave Labor versus Free Labor Sugar. Speech of The Rev[d]. Dr. M'Neile, ... at Liverpool, 13th June, 1848. *London: F. Syrett, Printer.* 1848. 8vo, pp. 18. 43600

McNeile (J.) Biography of Gen. John McNeile. [n. p. n. d.] 8vo. 43601

M'Neill (H.) Observations on the Treatment of the Negroes, in the Island of Jamaica, including some Account of their Temper and Character, with Remarks on the Importation of Slaves from the Coast of Africa. In a Letter to a Physician in England, from Hector M'Neill. *London: G. G. and J. Robinson.* [n. d.] 8vo, pp. vi, 46. 43602

Macneill (H.) The Poetical Works of Hector Macneill, Esq. A New Edition, corrected and enlarged. ... *Edinburgh: Printed by James Ballantyne & Co.* 1806. 2 vols., 12mo, pp. (2),

196; 172. 8 Plates and Portrait. + *Philadelphia: Benjamin Chapman.* 1815. 12mo, pp. 328, (1). H. 43603

McNeir (——). Maine Liquor Law Debate, at Clinton, New-Jersey ... October 9, 1852, between Rev. Mr. McNeir ... and G. J. Beebe ... . *Middletown, Orange County, N. Y.* 1853. 8vo, pp. 32. H. 43604

M'Nemar (R.) The Kentucky Revival; or, A Short History of the late extraordinary out-pouring of the Spirit of God, in the Western States of America, ... with a Brief Account of ... Shakerism ... in Ohio and Kentucky. ... By Richard M'Nemar. ... *Cincinnati.* 1807. 12mo, pp. 119. + *Albany: Re-Printed by E. and E. Hosford.* 1808. 12mo, pp. 119, 23. B. + *Pittsfield: Re-printed by Phinehas Allen.* 1808. 12mo, pp. 148. + *New York: Reprinted by Edward O. Jenkins.* 1846. 12mo, pp. 156.

M'Nemar. Observations on Church Government by the Presbytery of Springfield, to which is added the Last Will and Testament of that Reverend Body ... . *Albany.* 1808. 12mo, pp. 23. 43606

McNeven (W. J.) Chemical Examination of the Mineral Water of Schooley's Mountain. ... By William J. McNeven. *New York: Printed by Van Winkle and Wiley.* 1815. 4to, pp. 21.

McNiece (J.) Oration ... 4th July, 1802, at Stephentown, New York. By John McNiece. *Danbury.* 1802. 8vo. N.

McNutt (A. G.) An Account of the Origin of the Mississippi Doctrine of Repudiation; with a Review of the Arguments which his Exc. Alexander G. McNutt, late Governor of Mississippi, advanced in its Vindication. By a Member of the Boston Bar. *Boston.* 1842. 8vo, pp. 28. 43609

Macomb (A.) The Practice of Courts Martial. By Alexander Macomb ... . *New-York: Samuel Colman.* 1840. 8vo, pp. v–154. H. + *[Ibid.]* 1841. 43610

Macomb. A Treatise on Martial Law, and Courts-Martial; as practised in the United States of America. ... By Alexander Macomb, Esq. ... *Charleston (S. C.): The Author.* 1809. 8vo, pp. (2), 6, 5–6, 5–340. BA. 43611

Macomb (D. B.) Answer to Enquiries relative to Middle Florida, propounded by a Gentleman in Switzerland ... . By David B. Macomb, Esq. ... *Tallahassee.* 1827. 8vo, pp. 10.

[Macomb (*Gen.*)] Pontiac: or, the Siege of Detroit. A Drama, in Three Acts. *Boston: Samuel Colman.* M DCCC XXXV. 12mo, pp. 60. Portrait. B. 43613

[Macomb (Robert).] Address of "The United Whig Club" to their Fellow-Republicans of the State of New York. *New York.* 1809. 8vo. N. 43614

[Macomb.] A Reply to the Resolutions and Address of a Meeting convened at Martlings, in ... New-York, February 4, 1811. ... By a Whig of '76. *New-York: Printed by Henry C. Southwick.* 1811. 8vo, pp. 11. B. 43615

Macomb County, *Mich.* Meeting of Citizens of Macomb County, at Mt. Clemens, Dec. 1, 1849, for the Improvement of Clinton River. [n. p. n. d.] 8vo. 43616

[Macon (Nathaniel).] Letters to Chas. O'Conor. The Destruction of the Union is Emancipation. The Status of Slavery. The Rights of the States and Territories. *Philadelphia: John Campbell.* 1862. 8vo, pp. 38. 43617

There were copies [n. p. n. d.], also an edition with the author's name on the title-page.

Macon. The Rights of the States and Territories. By Nathaniel Macon. *Montgomery.* 1860. 8vo. 43618

Macon, *Ga.* Memorial of the Board of Trade of Macon, Georgia. December, 1867. [n. p. n. d.] 8vo, pp. 5. 43619

First Annual Report of the ... Macon & Brunswick Railroad Co. ... *Macon, Ga.: Burke, Boykin & Co., Printers.* 1864. 8vo, pp. 14, (1). 43620

Second Annual Report of the Macon and Western Railroad Company. *Macon.* 1848. 8vo. S. 43621

Maconochie (*Capt.*) *See* M'Konochie.

Macoy (R.) General History, Cyclopedia, and Dictionary of Freemasonry ... . By Robert Macoy. *New York.* 1869. 8vo, pp. 700. Portrait. 43622

Also: The Masonic Vocal Manual ... . *New York.* 1859. 18mo, pp. 72; and other masonic pieces.

McPhail (G. W.) Addresses at the Inauguration of the Rev. G. Wilson McPhail, D.D. as President of Lafayette College ... . *Philadelphia: William S. & Alfred Martien.* 1858. 8vo, pp. 30, (2). BA. 43623

McPhail (L.) On the Life and Services of William Henry Harrison, ... an Eulogium, pronounced before the Citizens of Eastport, Maine, By Dr. Leonard McPhail ... April 15, 1841. *Boston: B. B. Mussey.* 1841. 8vo, pp. 28. BA. 43624

McPheeters (S. B.) *See* St. Louis, Mo.

Macpherson (C.) Memoirs of the Life and Travels of the late Charles Macpherson, Esq., in Asia, Africa, and America. ... Investigation of the Nature, Treatment, and ... Improvement of the Negro, in the British and French West India Islands. Written by Himself ... . *Edinburgh.* 1800. 12mo, pp. 258. M.

See "M. Rev.," XXXIV. 106.

Macpherson (D.) Annals of Commerce, Manufactures, Fisheries, and Navigation, with Brief Notices of the Arts and Sciences connected with them. Containing the Commercial Transactions of the British Empire and other Countries, from the Earliest Accounts to the Meeting of the Union Parliament in January, 1801 ... . With a Large Appendix ... [and] a General Chronological Index. ... By David Macpherson. ... *London: Nichols and Son.* 1805. 4 vols., 4to, pp. (4), xvii, (1), 719; (4), 738; (4), 728; (4), 550, (198). Plate. A., B., H. 43626

McPherson (E.) Consolidated Index of the Reports of the Committees of the House of Representatives, from the Twenty-Sixth to the Fortieth Congress, inclusive. Prepared under the Direction of Edward McPherson ... . *Washington.* 1869. 8vo, pp. 158. + *[Ibid.]* 1870. 8vo, pp. 393. B. 43627

McPherson. A Handbook of Politics for 1868. By Edward McPherson, LL.D. ... *Washington City: Philp & Solomons.* 1868. 8vo, pp. 7, 387. Continued. H. 43628

McPherson. The Political History of the United States of America, during the Great Rebellion, from November 6, 1860, to July 4, 1864; Including ... the Important Executive, Judicial, and Politico-Military Facts of that Eventful Period; ... with the Organization, Legislation, and General Proceedings of the Rebel Administration; and an Appendix containing the Principal Political Facts of the Campaign of 1864; ... By Edward McPherson, ... *Washington, D. C.: Philp and Solomons.* 1864. 8vo, pp. vii, 440. + Second Edition. *[Ibid.]* 1865. 8vo, pp. viii, 653. H.

McPherson. The Political History of the United States during the Period of Reconstruction, April, 1865–July, 1870. *Washington.* 1871. 8vo. 43630

McPherson. A Political Manual for 1866 ... . By Edward McPherson ... . *Washington, D. C.: Philp & Solomons.* 1866. 8vo, pp. (4), 128. H. 43631

Continued to 1869 or later. Also: The Administration and its Assailants. Speech ... June 5, 1862. [n. p. n. d.] 8vo, pp. 8.—Disorganization and Disunion. Speech ... February 24, 1860. [n. p. n. d.] 8vo, pp. 8.—The Disunion Conspiracy. Speech ... January 23, 1861. *[Washington:] McGill & Witherow, Printers.* [1861.] 8vo, pp. 8.—The Growth of Individualism. ... *Gettysburg.* 1857. 8vo, pp. 39.— ... A Lecture before the Young Men's Christian Association of Gettysburg. February 13, 1858. ... *Gettysburg: Printed by Henry C. Neinstedt.* 1858. 8vo, pp. 23. H.—The Rebellion: Our Relations and Duties. Speech ... Delivered in the House of Representatives, February 14, 1862. *[Washington.* 1862.] 8vo, pp. 7.—The Rebellion. Two Speeches ... January 23, 1861, and February 14, 1862. ... *[Washington.]* 1862. 8vo, pp. 16.—Remarks ... on a Bill to Reorganize the Staff attached to Divisions of the Army ... March 6, 1862. [n. p. n. d.] 8vo, pp. 7.

Macpherson (J.) Original Papers; containing the Secret History of Great Britain, from the Restoration, to the Accession of the House of Hannover. ... Arranged and published by James Macpherson, Esq; ... . *London: W. Strahan.* MDCCLXXV. 2 vols., 4to, pp. viii, 711; x, 690. BA. + *Dublin.* 1775. 2 vols., 8vo. 43632

[Macpherson.] A Short History of the Opposition during the Last Session of Parliament. *London: T. Cadell.* MDCCLXXIX. 8vo, pp. vi, 58. BA. + The Second Edition. *[Ibid.]* + The Third Edition. *[Ibid.]* + The Fourth Edition. *[Ibid.]* + The Fifth Edition. *[Ibid.]* + Another Edition. [n. p. n. d.] 8vo, pp. vi, 58. + *Dublin.* 1779. 8vo. 43633

"Rather a picture than a history, and that picture a caricature; in which the anti-ministerial party makes but an awkward and scurvy appearance."—*Monthly Review,* LXI. 68. Also attributed to Edward Gibbon; *see also* "Observations," [Dalrymple (J.)], Vol. v., No. 18347, *and* [Germaine (G.)], Vol. VII., No. 27145.

McPherson (J.) Poems Descriptive and Moral, by John McPherson. Styled by Himself Harp of Acadia. With an Introductory Memoir of the Author by the Editor J. S. T. Thompson. *Halifax, N. S.: Printed by Theophilus Chamberlain.* 1862. 12mo, pp. (2), xlvi, 250, (2). 43634

Macpherson (J.) History of the Life, very strange Adventures, and Works of Captain John Macpherson. *Philadelphia.* 1789. 12mo. C. 43635

[Macpherson (John).] Letter to John Dickinson, Esq. [n. p. n. d.] 8vo, pp. 4. 43636

Dated "Phil. Nov. 13, 1770." The author was a poor half-crazed man who really was, or thought he was, harshly used by Mr. Dickinson and other public characters.

Macpherson. Macpherson's Letters, etc. *Philadelphia: Printed for the Author, in the Year* 1770. 8vo, pp. vii, 105, (1).

A curious correspondence between the author and John Dickinson, etc., May 9, 1770. The author complains of imprisonment as a madman, and published these letters in prose and verse to prove that he was not mad, and refers to Galloway and other prominent persons.

[Macpherson.] A Pennsylvania Sailor's Letters, alias the Farmer's Fall: With Extracts from a Tragic Comedy, called Hodge Podge improved: Or, The Race Fairly Run. The Author's Sympathy for an innocent Woman, prevents his publishing the Whole of that Dramatic Piece. ... Number 1. *Philadelphia: Printed for the Author.* 1771. 8vo, pp. 64. P. 43638

Against Dickinson. Thomas notices an "Address to the Public, May 5, 1766." *Philadelphia.* 1766, and "Reply to the above, May 19, 1766." *Philadelphia.* 1766.

McPhetres (S. A.) A Political Manual for the Campaign of 1868, for ... the New England States. ... By S. A. McPhetres. *Boston: A. Williams and Company.* 1868. 24mo, pp. 96.

McQueen (H.) An Address ... before the ... University of South Carolina ... June 26, 1839. By Hugh McQueen. *Raleigh.* 1839. 8vo, pp. 46. H. 43640

Macqueen (J.) The Colonial Controversy containing a Refutation of the Calumnies of the Anticolonists: the State of Hayti, ... the Production of Sugar, &c. and the state of the Free and Slave Labourers in those Countries; fully considered in a Series of Letters, addressed to The Earl of Liverpool; with a supplementary Letter to Mr. Macaulay. By James Macqueen. *Glasgow: Khull, Blackie, & Co.* 1825. 8vo, pp. 223. B. 43641

M'Queen. A General Plan for a Mail Communication by Steam between Great Britain and the Eastern and Western Parts of the World; ... To which are added Geographical Notices of Panama, Nicaragua, &c. By James M'Queen, Esq. *London: B. Fellowes.* 1838. 8vo. Charts. 43642

M'Queen. The West India Colonies; the Calumnies and Misrepresentations circulated against them by the Edinburgh Review, Mr. Clarkson, Mr. Cropper, &c., Examined and Refuted, By James M'Queen. ... *London: Baldwin, Cradock, and Joy.* 1824. 8vo, pp. xxvi, (10), 427, (1). + *[Ibid.]* 1825. H.

Also: A Geographical Survey of Africa ... . To which is prefixed, a Letter to Lord John Russell, regarding the Slave Trade ... . *London: B. Fellowes.* 1840. 8vo, pp. (4), xxiv, (2), 303, (1). Map. His "General Statistics of the British Empire" (*London: B. Fellowes.* 1836. 8vo, pp. 224.) contains 18 pages on the North British Colonies and Slave Colonies.

Macqueen (J. F.) Chief Points in the Laws of War and Neutrality, Search and Blockade; with the Changes of 1856, and those now proposed. By John Fraser Macqueen, Esq. ... *London and Edinburgh: William and Robert Chambers.* 1862. 12mo, pp. xii, 108. BA. + *Richmond: West & Johnston.* 1863. 12mo, pp. x, 102. 43644

MacRae (A.) A Manual of Plantership in British Guiana. By A. MacRae. *London.* 1856. 8vo. 43645

Macrae (D.) The Americans at Home: Pen-and-Ink Sketches of American Men Manners and Institutions. By David Macrae. *Edinburgh: Edmonston and Douglas.* 1870. 2 vols., 12mo, pp. xxiv, 332; vi, 408. B. 43646

McRae (D. K.) On Love of Country. An Address ... [at] Oxford Female College, June 2nd, 1862. By Col. D. K. McRae. *Raleigh: Strothne & Marcom.* 1864. 8vo, pp. 15. H.

Another edition is [n. p. n. d.] 8vo.

McRae (D. G.) Military Commission. Proceedings in the Case of the United States against Duncan G. McRae [and others], for the Murder of Archibald Beebee, at Fayetteville, N. C. 11th Feb. 1867 ... . Reported by C. Flowers and C. P. Young. *Raleigh: Robert Avery,* U.S.A. 1867. 8vo, pp. (2), 398. 43648

McRae (J. J.) Speech of Hon. J. J. McRae ... on the Compromise Question. ... January 29, and February 2, 1852. *Washington.* 1852. 8vo, pp. 24. H. 43649

Also: Speech ... on the Organization of the House ... December 13 and 14, 1859. *Washington.* 1859. 8vo, pp. 21. H.

Macreading (C. S.) Sermon on the Death of Otis Pettee, Esq., of Newton Upper Falls. ... By Rev. Charles S. Macreading, February 15, 1853. *Boston: Damrell & Moore.* 1853. 8vo, pp. 16. B. 43650

Macready (*Mrs.*) Memoir of Mrs. Macready ... . *New York.* 1855. 8vo, pp. 75. + *[Ibid.]* 1857. 8vo, pp. v, 108. Portrait. B. 43651

Also: Opinions of the American Press. ... *Albany.* 1855. 12mo, pp. 36.

Macready [William C.] The Replies from England, etc. to certain Statements circulated in this Country respecting Mr. Macready. *New York: Stringer & Townsend.* 1849. 8vo, pp. 21.

This elicited: "A Rejoinder to 'The Replies from England, etc. to certain Statements circulated in this Country respecting Mr. Macready;' together with an Impartial

History and Review of the Lamentable Occurrences at the Astor Place Opera House, on the 10th of May, 1849. By an American Citizen." *New York.* 1849. 8vo, pp. 119.

McRee (G. J.) Life and Correspondence of James Iredell, one of the Associate Justices of the Supreme Court of the United States. By Griffith J. McRee. ... *New York: D. Appleton and Company.* M.DCCC.LVII–LVIII. 2 vols., 8vo, pp. viii, 570; vii, 605. Portrait, Plate and Facsimile. A., BA. 43653

McRee. Memoirs of Maj.-Gen. J. McRee, and Col. W. McRee. [n. p. n. d.] 8vo. A. 43654

M'Robert (P.) A Tour through part of the North Provinces of America: ... a Series of Letters wrote ... in ... 1774, & 1775. ... By Patrick M'Robert. *Edinburgh: The Author.* 1776. 8vo, pp. 64. H. 43655

McRoberts (S.) Speech of Mr. Samuel McRoberts, ... on the Title of the United States to the Territory of Oregon, ... December 30, 1842, and January 9, 1843. *Washington.* 1843. 8vo, pp. 13. 43656

Also: Speech ... March 9, 1842, on the Pre-Emption Bill. *Washington.* 1842. 8vo.

Macrobius integer nitidus suoq̄ decori a Joanne Riuio restitutus. Cum indicio et amplo et veridico. *Parrhisiis, Venundatur ab Jodoco Badio & Ioanne Parvo.* 1515. [Colophon:] *Macrobii Aurelii viri consularis et illustris Saturnaliorum iLbri* [sic] *nouiter recogniti: infinitisq̄ erroribus expurgati. q̄ diligētissime nunc rursum impressi Parrhisiis accuratione Ascensiana. Ad Kalendas Februaris Calculo Romano* M.D.XV. Folio. 43657

On the reverse of D vii is a large map of the world surrounded by water, with a great boiling ocean between the Northern and Southern Continents. The artist has reversed it, putting India on the left. Another edition is *Parrhisiis, Badius Ascensius.* 1519.

McShea (J.), *Jr.* The War, its Causes and the Remedy. Speech of the Hon. John McShea, Jr. ... April 11, 1863. [n. p. n. d.] 8vo, pp. 16. 43658

McSherry (J.) History of Maryland; from its First Settlement in 1634, to the Year 1848. By James McSherry. *Baltimore: John Murphy.* MDCCCXLIX. 8vo, pp. 405. 4 Portraits and Plate. BA. + Second Edition, revised and corrected by the Author. *[Ibid.]* 8vo, pp. 418. C. 43659

Also in 12mo for the use of schools. It contains a very curious memorandum of the uniforms of the several corps of the Continental Army by the venerable Mr. Curtis. Also: Discourse ... at the Commemoration of the Landing of the Pilgrims of Maryland, ... May 11, 1846. ... *Emmittsburg.* 1846. 8vo, pp. 36.—Pere Jean; or, The Jesuit Missionary. [n. p.] 1849. 12mo.

McSherry (R.) El Puchero: or, A Mixed Dish from Mexico, embracing General Scott's Campaign, with Sketches of Military Life ... . By Richard McSherry, M.D., U.S.N. ... *Philadelphia: Lippincott, Grambo & Co.* 1850. 12mo, pp. (4), 247. Map, 6 Plates and 6 Portraits. C., H. 43660

McSherry. Essays and Lectures on 1. The Early History of Maryland. 2. Mexico and Mexican Affairs. 3. A Mexican Campaign. ... By Richard McSherry, M.D. ... *Baltimore: Kelly, Piet & Company.* 1869. 8vo, pp. (2), iv, 125. B. 43661

[Macsparran (James).] America Dissected, | being a | Full and True Account | of all the | American Colonies: | shewing, | The Intemperance of the Climates; excessive Heat and | Cold, and sudden violent Changes of Weather; ter- | rible and mischievous Thunder and Lightning; bad and | unwholesome Air, destructive to Human Bodies; Bad- | ness of Money; Danger from Enemies; but. above | all, the Danger to the Souls of the Poor People that | remove thither, from the multifarious wicked and pes- | tilent Heresies that prevail in those Parts. | In Several Letters, | From a Rev. Divine of the Church of England, | Missionary to America. and Doctor of Divinity. | Published as a Caution to Unsteady People who may | be tempted to leave their Native Country. | *Dublin:* | *Printed and sold by S. Powell, Dame Street,* | 1753. | 8vo, pp. (2), 48. BA., P. 43662

Very rare. These letters are signed James Macsparran, and addressed to the Hon. Col. Henry Cary, Esq. The author resided in the Narragansett country as a missionary for upwards of thirty years. Reprinted in Updike's "History of the Narragansett Church," with notes.

McSparran. An Answer to a Printed Letter said to be wrote from a Gentleman in Newport to his Friend in Boston Aug. 27; Pretending to find Fault with a Brief Representation of the Case between Dr. McSparran Plaintiff and Mr. Torrey Defendant, relating to the Ministry Land in South Kingstown, Narragansett, which was dated July 1739. [n. p. 1739.] Folio, pp. 10. B. 43663

An extremely rare piece.

Macsparran. The Sacred Dignity of the Christian Priesthood, Vindicated in a Discourse ... at St. Paul's in Narraganset, on ... the 4th Day of August, A.D. 1751. By the Rev. Dr. Macsparran. ... *Newport: Printed by J. Franklin.* M,DCC,LII. 12mo, pp. 46. BA. 43664

This elicited a reply for which *see* New England—"An Address." Also: Sermon at the Convention of the Episcopal Clergy at Newport, June 17, 1747. [n. p. n d.]

4to.—Sermon preached at Narraganset, March 15, 1741. ... *Newport.* 1741. 4to, pp. 24.

MACTAGGART (J.) Three Years in Canada: An Account of the Actual State of the Country in 1826–7–8. ... Including Sketches of the State of Society, Advice to Emigrants, &c. By John Mactaggart ... . *London: Henry Colburn.* 1829. 2 vols., post 8vo, pp. xi, 347; vii, (1), 340. BA., H. 43665

M'TAVISH [*and others*]. Northwest Company, carrying on Trade from Montreal to the Indian Territory ... . The Memorial of Messrs. M'Tavish, Fraser and Co. and Messrs. Inglis, Ellice and Co. on behalf of themselves and others. *London: B. M'Millan.* 1816. 4to, pp. 43. C. 43666

On the subject of the proceedings of the Earl of Selkirk in the Indian territories of North America.

MCTYEIRE (H. M.) Duties of Masters to Servants: Three Premium Essays. I. By the Rev. H. M. McTyeire. II. By the Rev. C. F. Sturgis. III. By the Rev. A. T. Holmes. *Charleston, S. C.* 1851. 12mo, pp. 151. B. 43667

MCVEAN (C.) Speech of Hon. Charles McVean ... on Bank Deposites. [n. p.] 1834. 8vo, pp. 7. S. 43668

MCVEY (W. G. D.) McVey's Literary and Professional Magazine. Vol. I. No. I. Oct. 1852. *Pittsfield, Ms.* [n. d.] 8vo, pp. 20. S. 43669

MCVICKAR (J.) A Biographical Memoir of the Rev. Edmund D. Griffin. By the Rev. John McVickar, D.D. ... *New-York.* 1832. 12mo, pp. 117. 43670

[MCVICKAR.] A Christian Memorial of Two Sisters [Maria Banyer and Ann Jay]. ... *New York: Stanford & Delisser.* 1858. 8vo, pp. 134. BA. 43671

[M'VICKAR (J.)] Considerations upon the expediency of abolishing Damages on Protested Bills of Exchange and the effect of establishing a Reciprocal Exchange with Europe: ... *New-York: Elliott and Palmer, Printers.* 1829. 8vo, pp. 67. S.

This elicited "Strictures on Professor M'Vickar's Pamphlet ... . By Publicola." *New-York.* 1829. 8vo, pp. 45. S.

MCVICKAR. A Domestic Narrative of the Life of Samuel Bard, M.D. LL.D. ... By the Rev. John McVickar, A.M. ... *New-York: A. Paul, Printer.* 1822. 8vo, pp. 244. B., S. 43673

MCVICKAR. The Early Years of the late Bishop Hobart. By John McVickar, D.D. ... *New-York.* M DCCC XXXVI. 12mo, pp. 228. BA. + [Another Edition.] pp. 245. H. 43674

MCVICKAR. The Early Life and Professional Years of Bishop Hobart, By John McVickar, D.D.; with a ... History of the Church in America, by Walter Farquhar Hook, D.D. *Oxford: D. A. Talboys.* MDCCCXXXVIII. 8vo. S. 43675

[MCVICKAR.] Hints on Banking, in a Letter to a Gentleman in Albany; By a New Yorker. *New York: Printed by Vanderpool & Cole.* 1827. 8vo, pp. 43. B. 43676

MCVICKAR. Outlines of Political Economy; ... With Notes Explanatory and Critical. *New York.* 1825. 8vo, pp. 188. B.

MCVICKAR. Political Economy. By John McVickar ... . *Boston.* 1835. 24mo. 43678

This piece has the honor of a translation into Chinese.

MCVICKAR. The Professional Years of John Henry Hobart, D.D.; being a Sequel to his Early Years. By John McVickar, D.D. ... *New York.* 1836. 18mo, pp. 500. S. 43679

Also: An Address ... before the ... Bible and Prayer Book Society ... the 29th ... of January ... 1818. ... *New-York: Printed by William A. Mercein.* 1818. 8vo, pp. 23.—Address on the Death of William Moore De Rham, at Columbia College, June 14, 1834. ... *New York.* 1834. 8vo.—Address ... 4th October, 1837. ... *New-York: G. H. Carvill & Co.* 1837. 8vo, pp. 40.—Dedication of the Chapel-School of St. Barnabas, (Dearman, ... N. Y.) ... with the Sermon ... by John McVickar, D.D., and ... Account of the Origin of the School and its Educational Arrangements. ... *New-York: Pudney & Russell, Printers.* 1853. 8vo, pp. 30.—"The Signs of the Times." Sermon for the General Theological Seminary. ... *New York.* 1833. 8vo, pp. 20. W.—Tribute to the Memory of Sir Walter Scott, [the proceedings of the Meeting of the Citizens of New York, to express their regret at his death, with an Eulogium]. ... *New York: Scott & Co.* 1833. 8vo.

MCVICKAR (W. A.) City Missions. By Rev. W. A. McVickar. Second Edition. *New York: Pott & Amery.* 1868. 12mo, pp. 96. C. 43680

MACWHORTER (A.) A Funeral Sermon, preached in Newark, December 27, 1799. A Day of Public Mourning, observed by the Town, for the universally Lamented, General Washington. ... To which is Subjoined, his Last Address, to his Beloved Countrymen. ... By Alexander Macwhorter, D.D. ... *Newark: Printed by Jacob Halsey.* MDCCC. 8vo, pp. (4), iv, Address, 22.

Also: Century Sermon, Newark, New Jersey, January 1, 1801; containing a brief History of the Presbyterian Church ... . *Newark.* 1807. 8vo, pp. 24. N.—A Festival Discourse occasioned by the Celebration of the Seventeenth Anniversary of American Independence. ... *Newark, N. J.* 1793. 8vo.— ... Sermon preached ... before the New-York Missionary Society at their first Institution, Nov. 1, 1796 ... . *New-York.* 1796. 8vo, pp. 28.—Sermon before the Female Charitable Society, Newark. ... *Newark.* 1805. 8vo. N.

MACWHORTER (A. C.) Oration, 4th July, 1794, Newark, New Jersey. By Alexander C. Macwhorter. [n. p.] 1794. 12mo. N. 43682

MCWILLIAM (J. O.) Report of the Fever at Buena Vista. By James Orniston McWilliam, M.D. *London.* 1847. Folio.

MCWILLIE (W.) Speech of Hon. W. McWillie, ... March 4, 1850, on the Admission of California. [n. p. n. d.] 8vo.

MCWRIGHT (A.) Sermons on the Sin of Slaveholding, preached in ... Madison, Wis. *Madison.* 1860. 8vo. 43685

MACY (B. F.) Lecture on Mysterious Knockings, Mesmerism, &c., with a Brief History of the Old Stone Mill, ... before the A N ti Quarian Society of Pappigassett. At Newport, R. I., February 14, 4199. By Benjamin Franklin Macy, ... *Newport, R. I.* 1851. 8vo, pp. 8. H. 43686

MACY (O.) The History of Nantucket; ... with the Rise and Progress of the Whale Fishery; and other Historical Facts relative to said Island and its Inhabitants. ... By Obed Macy. *Boston: Hilliard, Gray, and Co.* 1835. 8vo, pp. 300. Map and Plate. C. 43687

MACY (S. J.) Genealogy of the Macy Family from 1635–1868. Compiled by Silvanus J. Macy, New York. *Albany: Joel Munsell.* 1868. Sm. 4to, pp. (2), 457. B. 43688

[MACY.] Genealogy of the Early Generations of the Coffin Family in New England. ... *Boston: David Clapp & Son, Printers.* 1870. 8vo, pp. (2), 17. BA. 43689

MAD RIVER AND ERIE RAILROAD. Communication to the General Assembly of Ohio. March 1, 1843. By John H. James, late President. [n. p. 1843.] 8vo. S. 43690

Also: Report of the Committee ... made Feb. 8, 1858. [n. p. n. d.] 8vo, pp. 7. *See also* our Vol. X., No. 38657.

Mad River Valley Pioneer. Vol. I. No. I. *Mansfield.* 1870.

[MADAN (Cristobal).] Llamamiento de La Isla de Cuba a la Nacion Española ... . Por un Hacendado, en Diciembre de 1854. *Nueva-York: Imprenta de Estevan Hallett.* [n. d] 8vo, pp. (8), 233, (1); Appendice, pp. lv, (1). B. 43692

MADARIAGA (J. C.) Diario y observaciones del Presbitero José Cortes Madariaga, en su regreso de Santafe à Carácas, por la via de los rios Negro, Meta y Orinoco, despues de haber concluido la comision que obtuvo de su Gobierno, para acordar los tratados de alianza entre ambos Estados. *Carácas.* [n. d.] 4to, pp. 43. 43693

MADDEN (R. R.) The Island of Cuba: its Resources, Progress, and Prospects, considered in Relation especially to the Influence of its Prosperity on the Interests of the British West India Colonies. By R. R. Madden ... . *London: Partridge & Oakey.* 1853. 12mo, pp. xxiv, 252. B. 43694

MADDEN. A Letter to W. E. Channing, D.D. on the ... Abuse of the Flag of the United States in ... Cuba, and the Advantage taken of its Protection in promoting the Slave Trade. By R. R. Madden ... . *Boston: William D. Ticknor.* 1839. 8vo, pp. 32. BA. 43695

Also: A Letter to W. E. Channing, ... in Reply to one addressed to him by R. R. Madden, on the Abuse of the Flag of the United States in the Island of Cuba, for promoting the Slave Trade. By a Calm Observer. *Boston: William D. Ticknor.* 1840. 8vo, pp. 36. Very severe on Dr. Madden.

MADDEN. The Shrines and Sepulchres of the Old and New World ... Including the Funeral Customs of the Principal Nations ... By R. R. Madden ... . *London: T. C. Newby.* 1851. 2 vols., 8vo, pp. xii, 562, Plate; (4), 692. 43696

MADDEN. A Twelve months Residence in the West Indies, during the Transition from Slavery to Apprenticeship; with Incidental Notices of the State of Society, Prospects, and Natural Resources of Jamaica and other Islands. By R. R. Madden. ... *London: James Cochrane and Co.* 1835. 2 vols., 12mo, pp. xiv, 326; viii, 343, (1). Plate. + *Philadelphia: Carey, Lea and Blanchard.* 1835. 2 vols., 12mo, pp. 228; vii, 5–224. B.

Also: Address on Slavery in Cuba ... . [n. p. n. d.] 8vo, pp. 31. B.—The Life and Times of Robert Emmet ... With numerous Notes and Additions ... Also a Memoir of Thomas Addis Emmet ... . *New-York.* 1857. 12mo, pp. 328. + [*Ibid.*] 1858. 12mo. *See also* "Poems by a Slave."

MADDEN (S.) Memoirs of the Twentieth Century, being original Letters of State under George VI. By Samuel Madden, D.D. *London: W. Nicoll.* 1733. 16mo, pp. xxi, 192. 43698

[MADDOX] (I.) A Sermon ... before ... the ... Governors of the Hospital for the Small-Pox, and for Inoculation, ... March 5, 1752. By Isaac Lord Bishop of Worcester. ... *London: Printed. Boston; N. E. Reprinted by I. Draper.* 1752. 4to, pp. 15. BA.

The postscript gives an account of the small-pox and inoculation at Boston in New England.

[MADDOX.] A Vindication of the Government, Doctrine, and Worship, of the Church of England, Established in the Reign of Queen Elizabeth: Against the Injurious Reflections of Mr. Neal, in his late History of the Puritans. Together with a Detection of many false Quotations and Mistakes in that Performance. ... *London: ... A. Betteswortb.* M DCC XXXIII. 8vo, pp. 362. 43700

Relates to Vol. I. of Neal. *See* Grey (Z.), No. 28792. Also: A Sermon ... before the ... Society for the Propagation of the Gospel in Foreign Parts; ... 15th of February, 1733. ... *London: Printed by J. Downing.* M.DCC.XXXIV. 8vo, pp. 74, (1). BA.

MADIANA (J. B. R.) Recherches et Experiences sur les Poisons d'Amérique, des Trois Regnes de la Nature. *Bordeaux.* 1826. 4to. Plates. 43701

Title from an auctioneer's catalogue.

MADIEDO (M. M.) Hechos graves ejecutados en las Comarcas del Arauca por las autoridades de la República de Venezuela en el territorio de los Estados Unidos de Colombia, i contra la vida i propiedades de varios Colombianos, durante los anos de 1859 à 1863. Por Manuel Maria Madiedo. *Bogotá.* 1864. 4to, pp. 23. 43702

MADION (T. *fils*). Capitulation du Cap, 1803. Episode de l'Histoire d'Haïti. Par Thomas Madion fils ... . *Port-au-Prince.* 1845. 4to, pp. 29. M. 43703

MADION. Histoire d'Haiti. [1492–1803.] Par Thomas Madion fils ... . *Port-au-Prince: Imprimerie de Jh. Courtois.* 1847–1848. 2 vols., 8vo, pp. (2), viii, 369; (1), 447. BA. 43704

MADISON (J.) An Address, to the Members of the Protestant Episcopal Church, in Virginia. By Bishop Madison. *Richmond: Printed by T. Nicolson.* 1799. 12mo, pp. 24. H. 43705

MADISON. A Discourse, on the Death of General Washington, Late President of the United States; Delivered on the 22d of February, 1800, In the Church in Williamsburg. By James Madison, D.D. Bishop of the Protestant Episcopal Church in Virginia, and President of William and Mary College. *Richmond: Printed by T. Nicolson, just below the Capitol.* 1800. 8vo, pp. 25. BA. + The Second Edition Corrected. *New York: Printed by T. & J. Swords, for W. Prichard, Richmond.* 1800. 8vo, pp. 42. BA. + *New York: Printed. London: Reprinted for John Hatchard.* 1800. 8vo, pp. 48. + The Third Edition. [*Ibid.*] + Third Edition, with Additions. *Philadelphia: Printed by James Kay, Jun. and Co.* 1831. 8vo, pp. 40. + *Richmond.* 1844. 8vo. 43706

See "M. Rev.," XXXIV. 150.

[MADISON.] Letter to ... Jedediah Morse. *See* No. 40517.

Also: Manifestations of the Beneficence of Divine Providence towards America. A Discourse delivered on ... the 19th of February, 1795, being the day recommended ... for general Thanksgiving ... . *Richmond.* 1795. 8vo, pp. 23.—Oration in Commemoration of the Founders of William and Mary College, delivered on the Anniversary of its Foundation ... . *Williamsburgh.* 1772. 4to.—A Sermon ... before the Protestant Episcopal Church in ... Virginia. *Richmond.* 1786. 4to.

[MADISON (James).] An Examination of the British Doctrine which subjects to Capture a Neutral Trade not open in Time of Peace. Containing a Letter from the Minister Plenipotentiary of the United States, to Lord Mulgrave, late Secretary of State for Foreign Affairs. [n. p. 1806.] 8vo, pp. 204. B., C. + The Second Edition. *America, Printed. London, reprinted for J. Johnson.* 1806. 8vo, pp. (2), 200. 43707

See "M. Rev.," L. 199.

[MADISON.] An Examination of the Conduct of Great Britain, respecting Neutrals. ... *Philadelphia: Printed by B. Graves.* 1807. 8vo, pp. 72. N. + Second Edition. ... *Boston.* 1808. 8vo, pp. 72. H., W. 43708

MADISON. Jonathan Bull and Mary Bull. By James Madison. An Inedited Manuscript. Printed for Presentation by J. G. M'Guire. *Washington.* 1856. 8vo, pp. 14. B. 43709

MADISON. Letters and other Writings of James Madison Fourth President of the United States. ... Published by Order of Congress ... . *Philadelphia: J. B. Lippincott & Co.* 1865. 4 vols., 8vo, pp. li, 658; (2), xxxvii, 617; (2), lx, 670; (2), lvii, 694. Portrait. BA. 43710

MADISON. Letters on the Constitutionality of the Power in Congress to impose a Tariff for the Protection of Manufactures. By James Madison ... . *Washington City: Printed ... by S. C. Ustick.* 1828. 12mo, pp. 24. B., S. 43711

MADISON. Letters on the Constitutionality and Policy of Duties, for the Protection and Encouragement of Domestic Manufactures. By James Madison ... . *Richmond: Printed by Thomas W. White.* 1829. 8vo, pp. 27. B., M. 43712

MADISON. Letters ... to Mr. Monroe, on ... Impressments, &c. Also, Extracts from, and Enclosures in, the Letters of Mr. Monroe to the Secretary of State ... . *Washington City: A. & G. Way, Printers.* 1808. 8vo, pp. 130. B. 43713

MADISON. Letters from Mr. Madison, ... relative to the Treaty concluded ... on the 31 December, ... 1806. *Washington: Printed by R. C. Weightman.* 1808. 8vo, pp. 69. BA.

MADISON. Manifeste Du Gouvernement Américain, (10 Février 1815), ou Causes et Caractère de la dernière Guerre d'Amérique avec l'Angleterre; ... Par James Madisson, [*sic*] ... et traduit sur la 11e édition anglaise ... . *Paris, Chez Plancher.* 1816. 8vo, pp. 136. B. 43715

MADISON. The Papers of James Madison, purchased by Order of Congress; being his Correspondence and Reports of Debates during the Congress of the Confederation and his Reports of Debates in the Federal Convention; now published from the original manuscripts ... under the Superintendence of Henry D. Gilpin. *Washington: Langtree & O'Sullivan.* 1840. 3 vols., 8vo, pp. (2), lx, 580, xxii; (2), xxii, (2), 581–1242; (2), xiv, (2), 1243–1624, ccxlvi, Facsimiles, (22). C. 43716

Some copies have the imprint *New York: J. & H. G. Langley*, 1841, and others are dated *Mobile*, 1852.

MADISON. Report ... in relation to the Purchase and Publication of the Madison Papers. Dec. 23, 1847. [n. p. n. d.] 8vo. S. 43717

[MADISON.] Political Observations. *Philadelphia.* 1795. 8vo, pp. 24. C., N. 43718

MADISON. Religious Freedom. A Memorial and Remonstrance ... by his Excellency James Madison ... against the General Assessment, &c.; presented to the General Assembly of Virginia ... 1785. ... *Worcester.* 1786. 16mo, pp. 16. + *Boston: Printed ... by Lincoln & Edmands.* 1819. 12mo, pp. 12.

MADISON. The Resolutions of Virginia and Kentucky; Penned by Madison and Jefferson; in relation to the Alien and Sedition Laws. *Richmond.* 1826. 8vo, pp. 71. + [With] the Debates and Proceedings in the House of Delegates, of Virginia, on the same, in December, 1798. [*Ibid.*] 1835. 8vo, pp. 228.

MADISON. Selections from the Private Correspondence of James Madison, from 1813 to 1836. Published by J. C. McGuire ... . *Washington.* MDCCCLIX. 4to, pp. vi, 9–419. B., C.

Also: An Address delivered before the Agricultural Society of Albemarle, May 12th, 1818. ... *Richmond.* 1818. 8vo, pp. 31.—The Constitution A Pro-Slavery Compact, Or Selections from The Madison Papers, &c. Second Edition, Enlarged. *New York.* 1845. 8vo, pp. 131.—A Memorial and Remonstrance, on the Religious Rights of Man ... . *Washington City: Printed ... by S. C. Ustick.* 1828. 12mo, pp. 12. H.—Mr. Madison's Motion for Commercial Restrictions ... on the Commerce of the United States in Foreign Countries, Jan. 3, 1794. *Washington.* 1806. 8vo.—Report of Committee ... on Correspondence of Madison and Monroe. *Washington.* 1808. 8vo.—Speech ... January 14, 1794 ... in Support of his Propositions for the Promotion of the Commerce of the United States, and in Reply to William Smith, of South-Carolina. *New York.* 1794. 8vo, pp. 69. *See also* Elliot (J.), Vol. IV., No. 22233, Exposition, No. 23453, "The Federalist," Vol. IV., [Ingersoll (C. J.)], Vol. IX., No. 34734, [Lowell (John)], Vol. X., Messages, "Republican Crisis," *and* [Urquhart (D.)]

Madison Agonistes. *See* [Mauduit (I.)]

MADISON (J. M.) An Exposition of the Forms and Usages observed in the Various Lodges of the Independent Order of Odd Fellows ... . By James M. Madison ... . *New-York: The Author.* [1847.] 8vo, pp. 64. Plates. BA. + [*Ibid.*] 1848. S.

A satirical work.

MADISON COUNTY, *Ill.* Gazetteer of Madison County; with Directory of the Altons, and of the County. *Alton: J. T. Hair.* 1867. 8vo, pp. 292. 43723

MADISON, *Ind.* Catalogue of the Books of the Madison Library Association. *Madison (Ind.): Courier Office.* 1856. 8vo, pp. 106. C. 43724

Edwards' Annual Director to the Inhabitants, etc. of Madison, for 1867. *Madison, Ind.: Edwards, Greenough & Deved.* 1867. 8vo, pp. 255. 43725

First Annual Report of the President of the Madison, Indianapolis, and Peru Railroad Company. *New York.* 1855. 8vo.

MADISON COUNTY, *N. Y.* Proceedings of the Board of Supervisors of the County of Madison, for 1860. *Morrisville.* 1861. 8vo. Continued. S. 43727

To the Electors of the County of Madison. [Signed:] "A Number of Citizens," July 26, 1820. [n. p. n. d.] 8vo. S.

MADISON BAPTIST ASSOCIATION. Minutes of the Madison Baptist Association, ... in the Year ... [1820] ... . *Morrisville:*

Printed by John B. Johnson & Son. 1820. 8vo, pp. 11, (1). Continued. B. 43729

MADISON UNIVERSITY. Catalogue of Madison University, Hamilton, N. Y. *Hamilton.* 1852. 8vo. Continued. 43730

Charter of Madison University. 1865 [n. p. n. d.] 8vo, pp. 12. B. 43731

An Historical Sketch of Madison University, Hamilton, N. Y. *Utica: D. Bennett, Printer.* 1852. 8vo, pp. 16. B.

Madison Square. *See* New York City.

MADISON COLLEGE, *O.* Catalogue of the Officers, Course of Studies, etc., ... 1854. Antrim, Ohio. *Columbus.* 1854. 8vo, pp. 16. H. 43733

MADISON, *Wis.* An Act to consolidate and amend an Act, entitled, "An Act to Incorporate the City of Madison," approved March 4, 1856, etc. Approved March 23, 1865. [n. p. n. d.] 8vo. S. 43734

Annual Circular of the Madison Manufacturing Co. *Madison.* 1870. 8vo. 43735

Charter and Ordinances of the Village of Madison. *Madison.* 1851. 8vo. 43736

Charter of the City of Madison, Wisconsin. ... *Madison: Calkins & Proudfit, Printers.* 1856. 8vo, pp. 48. Map. H., S.

Charter and Constitution of the St. George's Society ... in ... Madison, Wisconsin ... . *Madison, Wis.: Atwood & Rublee ... Printers.* 1856. 16mo, pp. 8. H. 43738

Constitution and By-Laws of the Sacred Music Society, Madison. *Madison.* 1851. 12mo. 43739

... Directory for 1866, Compiled by B. W. Suckow, with a History of Madison by J. Y. Smith. *Madison: B. W. Suckow.* 1866. 12mo, pp. 175. 2 Maps. C. 43740

1855. Wm. N. Seymour's Madison Directory ... . First Annual Edition. *Madison: Atwood & Rublee, Printers.* 1855. 16mo, pp. 192. Map. Continued. C., H. 43741

First Annual Report of the Board of Education for ... 1855. *Madison, Wis.: Rublee & Gary, Printers.* 1856. 8vo, pp. 13, (1). Continued. H. 43742

Madison: the Capital of Wisconsin, its Progress, Capabilities and Destiny. *Madison, Wis.: Rublee & Gary, Printers.* 1855. 8vo, pp. 48. H. 43743

MADISON INSTITUTE. The Charter, Constitution and By-Laws of the Madison Institute ... . *Madison: J. T. Marston, & Co., Printers.* 1854. 8vo, pp. 13. H. 43744

Also: Catalogue of the Library. *Madison.* 1867. 8vo.

MADISON MUTUAL INSURANCE CO. Proceedings ... on the Death of Hon. Benjamin F. Hopkins, January 18, 1870. *Madison, Wis.: Atwood & Culver, Printers.* 1870. 8vo, pp. 14.

Manual of the First Congregational Church, Madison. *Madison.* 1869. 8vo. 43746

Ninth Annual Report of the Madison and Indianapolis Railroad Company, January, 1852. *Madison.* 1852. 8vo. S.

Report of the ... Committee, appointed to investigate into alleged Frauds ... in the Disposition of the Land Grant by the Legislature of 1856 ... . *Madison, Wis.: Calkins & Webb ... Printers.* 1858. 8vo, pp. 322, (1). H. 43748

MADISON AND DANE COUNTY. Statistics ... . *Madison: David Atwood, Printer.* 1853. 8vo, pp. 16. H. 43749

The Madmen's Chronicle; Exemplified in the Conduct of George the Third and his Ministers, towards the United States. ... To which are Annexed Biographic and Characteristic Sketches. ... *Philadelphia.* [n. d.] 8vo. 43750

MADOX (Isaac). *See* Maddox (I.)

MADOZ (P.) Diccionario Geografico, Estadistico, Historico de España y sus Possessiones de Ultramar. Por Paschal Madoz. *Madrid.* 1845–50. 16 vols., sm. 4to. 43751

A valuable gazetteer of Spain and its possessions in America, etc.

MADRAS. Annual Report of the ... Madras School in New-Brunswick, for ... 1820. *Saint John: Printed by William Durant.* [n. d.] 8vo, pp. 14. BA. 43752

MADRE DE DEOS (G. da). Memorias para a Historia da Capitania de S. Vicente, hoje chamada de S. Paulo, do estado do Brazil publicadas de Ordem da Academia R. das Sciencias por Fr. Gaspar da Madre de Deos, Monge Benedictino, e correspon-

dente da mesma Academia. *Lisboa: Na Typografia da Academia.* 1797. 4to, pp. (8), 242, 2. 43753

MADRE DE DEUS (M. da). Summa triumphal da nova e grande celebridade do glorioso e invicto martyr, o beato Garcia, pelos homens pardos de Pernambuco. Por Fr. Manual da Madre de Deus. *Lisboa: Na Officina de Pedro Ferreira.* 1753. 4to.

"Opusculo raro, que ainda não pude ver. Diz-se que sahira com o pseudonymo de Soterio de Silva Ribeiro."—SILVA.

MADRE DE DIOS (J. de la). Breve Summa de la Oracion Mental y de sú Exercicio conforme se Practica en los Noviciados de los Carmelitas desalcos por Fr. J. de la Madre de Dios. [n. p.] 1680. 4to. 43755

MADREGON (J. Adr.) De Imagine Guadalupensi Mexicana jambici Archilochii dimetri acatalectici. *Faventiæ: Archii.* 1774. 8vo, pp. viii. 43756

MADRID (J. F.) Breve Contestacion en que el Dr. J. F. Madrid, satisface con Documentos à los cargos que le ha hecho el Sr. Restrepo en su Historia de Colombia. *Londres.* 1827. 8vo, pp. 14. 43757

MADRID. Memorias sobre el comercio, cultivo y elaboracion del tabaco en esta Isla, por el Dr. D. José Fernandez Madrid. *Imprenta Fraternal.* 1821. 4to, pp. 19. 43758

MADRID. Poesias del ciudadano Dr. José Fernandez de Madrid. *Imprenta Fraternal.* 1821. 4to. 43759

MADRIGA (P. de). Beschryvinghe vande Regeringe van Peru, door Pedro de Madriga gebooren tot Lima. Als mede een verhael van Pedro Fernandez de Quir, van't Australia. *Amsterdam.* 1643. 4to. Maps. 43760

MADRIZ (F. T.) Cultivo del Café ó sea Manual teórico práctico sobre el beneficio de este fruto con las mejores ventajas para el Agricultor. *Paris.* 1869. Sm. 8vo, pp. viii, 170.

The author is a Venezuelan Coffee Planter; he had the book printed in Paris, but the whole edition came to Caràcas. The book contains from page 97–160 a reprint of "El Comercio de Café por H. Schoeffer, traducido del aleman por el jóven D. B. Urbaneja." *Caràcas.* 1869.

MAELEN (P. van der). Atlas universal de géographie physique, politique, statistique et minéralogique, sur l'echelle de 1/1641836, ou d'une ligne par 1900 toises; par Ph. van der Maelen et H. Ode. *Bruxelles.* 1827. 6 vols., atlas folio. 373 Maps.

Contains one hundred and twenty-two colored maps of America.

MAFFEI (Raffaello). Ad Iulium. II Orbis Romae episcopvm Sanctiss. Svm-|mvmque Pon. R. Volaterranvs Proemium.| [Recto of the first numbered leaf:] R. Volaterrani Commentariorvm Urbanorum | Liber. ii. Segmentorum coelestium breuis explicatio.| [Colophon:] *Impressum Romae per Ioannem Besicken Ale-|manum. Anno domini.* MDVI.| Folio, 18 prel. leaves, Text, DXLVII leaves. BM. 43763

Contains in Book XII. some reference to Columbus. *See* [Harrisse's] "Bib. Am. Vet.," I., No. 43; II., No. 22.

MAFFEI. Commentariorum Urbanorum Libri XXXVIII. *Paris.* 1510. Folio. 43764

See Meusel's "Bibliotheca Historica," Vol. I., Part I., page 281.

MAFFEI. Commentariorum Urbano-|rum Raphaelis Volaterra-|ni: octo & triginta libri cum | duplici eorūdem indice secundum | Tomos collecto. | Item Oeconomicus Xenophōtis | ab eodem latio donatus. | *Venundantur Parrhisiis in via Ia-|cobea ab Ioanne paruo & Iodoco | Badio Ascensio.* | [Verso of the title:] *Ex chalcographia nostra: in Parrhisiorum | lutetia: Ad Idus Augusti.* M.D.XI.| [Colophon:] *In aedibus Ascensianis ad Kalendas Iulias: Anno Salutis nostrę.* M.D.XI. | Folio, 26 prel. leaves, Text, CCCCXIIII leaves. 43765

The chapter relating to America begins on the verso of leaf CXXV.

MAFFEI. Commentarii rerum urbanorum libri XXXVIII. cum Oeconomico Xenophontis. *Paris, apud Jod. Badium.* 1526. Fol.

See Fabricius' "Bibl. Lat. Med.," Vol. VI., p. 142, where is also mentioned "a life of Alexander VI. by the same author ('Vitæ Sixti IV., Innocentii VIII., Alexander VI. & Pii III.,' *Venet.*, 1518, folio), which may contain additional details concerning Columbus."—HARRISSE.

MAFFEI. Commentariorvm | Vrbanorvm | Raphaelis Volaterrani, Octo | & triginta libri, accuratius quam antehac excusi, cum | duplici eorundem indice secundum | Tomos collecti. | Item Oeconomicus Xenophontis, ab eodem latio donatus. | *Basileae, in Officina Frobe-|niana, Anno* M.D.XXX. [Colophon:] *Basileae, in Officina Frobeniana, per Hieronymvm | Frobenivm, Ioannem Hervagivm, et Nicolavm | Episcopivm, Anno* M.D.XXX. *Mense Aug.* | Folio, 20 prel. leaves, Text, 468 leaves. 43767

MAFFEI. Commentariorvm | Vrbanorum Raphaelis Volater-| rani, octo & triginta libri, | accuratius quam antehac excusi, cum | dupli-| ci eorundem indice secundum | Tomos collecto. | Item Oeconomicus Xenophontis, ab eodem Latio donatus. | *Basileae* MDXLIIII. | [Colophon:] *Basileae, apvd Hieronymvm Frobenivm* |

et Nicolavm Episcopvm, Men-|se Avgvsto, Anno | MDXLIIII. | Folio, 22 prel. leaves, Text, 468 leaves. 43768

MAFFEI (J. P.) Ioan. Petri Maffeii, Bergomatis, è Societate Iesv, Historiarvm Indicarvm libri XVI. Selectarvm item ex India Epistolarum libri IV, eodem interprete. *Florentiæ, Ph. Juncta.* 1588. Folio, pp. (4), 570, (28). 43769

MAFFEI. Historiarum Indicarum libri XVI. Selectarum Epistolarum ex India, libri IV, Jo. Petri Maffeii interprete. Ejusdem de LII e Societate Jesu dum in Brasiliam navigant, pro catholica fide interfectis Epistolæ II. Item Vita Ignatii Loyolæ, lib. III. Eodem Maffeio auctore. *Venetiis.* 1588. 4to. 43770

Title from Carayon, No. 641. Leclerc quotes the same: "Accessit Ignatii Loiolæ vita postremo recognita et in opera singula copiosus Index." *Venetiis: D. Zenarium.* 1589. 4to, pp. (56), 283. Other editions are *Lugduni*, 1589, and *Coloniæ Agrippinæ*, 1589, folio. C.

MAFFEI. Ioan. Petri Maffeii, Bergomatis e Societate Iesu: Historiarvm Indicarvm Libri XVI. Selectarvm, item, ex India Epistolarvm Libri IV. Accessit Ignatii Loiolæ vita. Omnia ab auctore recognita, & emendata. In singula copiosus Index. *Coloniae Agrippinae. In Officina Birckmannica, sumptibus Arnoldi Mylij. Anno* M.D.XC. ... 8vo, pp. (88), 763, 461, Table (24). C.

There are copies of this edition which do not include the life of Loyola.

MAFFEI. Ioan. Petri | Maffeii, | Bergomatis, | e Societate Iesv, | Historiarvm | Indicarvm | Libri XVI. | Selectarvm, item, ex India | Epistolarum, eodem interprete, Libri IV. | Accessit Ignatii Loiolæ vita. | Omnia ab Auctore recognita, & nunc primùm in Germania excusa. | Item, in singula opera copiosus Index. | His nunc recèns adiecta est charta geographica, x renitidissimè expressa, qua Lectori vtriusq; | Indiæ situs, & longinqua ad eas nauigatio, accuratè ob oculos spectanda pro-|ponitur, non minus adspectu, quàm historia ipsa lectu incunda. | *Coloniæ Agrippinæ,* | *In Officina Birckmannica, sumptibus* | *Arnoldi Mylij.* | *Anno* M.D.XCIII. | ... | Folio, pp. (4), 541, (36). Map. C. 43772

MAFFEI. Ioan. Petri | Maffeii, | Bergomatis, | e Societate | Iesv, | Historiarvm | Indicarvm | Libri XVI. | Selectarvm, Item, ex In-| dia Epistolarvm Libri IV. | Accessit liber recentiorum Epistolarvm, a Ioanne Hayo Dalgattiensi | Scoto ex eadem Societate nunc primùm excusus, cum | Indice accurato. | Dvobvs Tomis Distribvti. | Omnia ab Auctore recognita & emendata. | In singula copiosus Index. | *Antverpiæ,* | *Ex Officina Martini Nutij, ad insigne dua-* | *rum*

Ciconiarum, Anno M.DC.V. | 2 vols., 8vo, pp. (72), 478; (2), 402, (6). BA. 43773

The best of the various editions in Latin. *See* Ternaux, p. 39.

MAFFEI. Joan. Petri Maffeii, ... Historiarvm Indicarvm libri XVI. Omnia ab auctore recognita & emendata. ... *Cadomi.* M.DC.XIIII. 12mo, pp. lxxx, 718. S. + *Lugduni. Apud Joannem Champion.* MDCXXXVII. 8vo, pp. 718. 43774

MAFFEI. Joannis Petri Maffeii ... Historiarum Indicarum libri XVI. acced. Selectarum epistolarum ex India libri quatuor; Joanne Petro Maffeio interprete. *Viennae Austriae.* 1751. Folio. + *Juarini.* [1752.] 8vo. BA. 43775

MAFFEI. Selectarum Epistolarum ex India libri quatuor; accessit vita Ignatii Loyolae. ... *Venetiæ.* 1588. 4to. 43776

Contains at the end "De 52 e societate Jesu, dum in Brasiliam navigant, pro catholica fide interfectis, epistolae duae." Another edition, *Olysipone.* 1571. 8vo.

MAFFEI. Le Istorie delle Indie Orientali scritte in latino dal P. Gio. Pietro Maffei, ... tradotte di Latino in lingua Toscana da M. da Francesca Serdonati. *Firenze.* 1589. 4to. A. 43777

MAFFEI. Le Historia delle India Orientali del P. Giovan. Pietro Maffei, ... Tradotte di latino in lingua Toscano da Francesco Serdonati. ... *Venetia: Dom Zenaro (Giunti).* 1589. 4to.

MAFFEI. Le Storie dell' Indie Orientali del P. Gio. Pietro Maffei, ... tradotte di latino in lingua Toscano da M. Francesco Serdonati. ... *Bergamo.* 1749. 2 vols., 4to. 43779

MAFFEI. Istorie dell' Indie Orientali ... tradotte de Latino in Lingua Italiana da M. Francesco Serdonati ... . *Milano.* 1806. 3 vols., 8vo. BA. + *Reggio.* 1826. 2 vols., 8vo. 43780

MAFFEI. Kurtze Beschreibung deren Dingen, so von der Societet Jesu in Orient von 1542–1568 gehandlet worden, jetzo neben etlichen Japonischen Sendtschreiben von 1548–1555 ins Teutsch gebracht durch J. G. Götzen. *Ingolstadt: G. Sartorius.* 1586. 8vo. 43781

MAFFEI. Histoire des Indes, de J. P. Maffei, Bergamesque, de la Société de Jesus, ou il est traicté de leur descouverte, navigation et conqueste faicte tant par les Portugais que Castillans. Ensemble de leurs mœurs, cérémonies, loix, gouvernements et reduction à la Foy Catholique. Traduict par F. Arnault de la Boirie, chanoine et archidiacre de Perigueux. *Lyon.* 1604. 8vo.

Title from Carayon, No. 752. Apparently the first edition in French.

MAFFEI. L'Histoire | des Indes | Orientales | et | Occidentales | Dv R. P. Iean Pierre Maffe'i, | de la Compagnie de Iesvs, | Traduite de Latin en Francois par M. M. D. P. Avec deux Tables, l'vne des Chapitres, & l'autre des matieres, tant geographiques | qu'Historiques. | *A Paris: Chez Robert de Ninville* ... M. DC. LXV. 4to, pp. (32), 353; Seconde Partie, (2), 292, (24), Privilege, (2).

The translator was Michel de Pure.

MAFFEI. Jo. Petri Maffeji ... Opera Omnia Latine Scripta, nunç primum in unum corpus collecta, variis illustrationibus exornata. Accedunt Maffeji vita P. A. Serassio auctore. ... *Bergomi.* CIↃIↃCCXLVII. 2 vols., 4to, pp. liv, 458, ii; viii, 516. S.

Includes "Vita Hist. Ind.," "Vita Gregorii," XVI. 64, and "De Rebus Indicis." Maffei also translated Acosta, and was specially distinguished for the purity of his style. His "Historiarum Indicarum" contains an account of Columbus' discovery of the New World; the voyage and discoveries of Americo Vespucci; Martin Behaim's voyage and astrolabe; Columbus' discovery of the Canaries, and other matters relating to America. *See* Backer, I. 472, *and* Carayon, No. 2121, etc.

Maffitt against Goldsborough. The Record compared by the Unconditional Union State Central Committee, Oct. 7, 1863. *Baltimore: Sherwood & Co.* 1863. 8vo, pp. 13. 43785

MAFFITT (J. P.) Poems by John Newland Maffitt. *Louisville: Prentice and Weissinger, Printers.* 1839. 12mo, pp. viii, 144. B. 43786

MAFFITT. Pulpit Sketches, Sermons, and Devotional Fragments. By Rev. John Newland Maffitt ... . *Boston: T. R. Marvin.* 1828. 12mo, pp. 300. Portrait. BA. 43787

MAFFITT. Pulpit Sketches. By Rev. John Newland Maffitt, ... First Series. *Louisville, Ky: W. Harrison Johnston.* 1839. 12mo, pp. 178. B. 43788

MAFFITT. Tears of Contrition; or Sketches of the Life of John N. Maffitt: with Religious and Moral Reflections. To which are appended Several Poetic Effusions. Written by Himself. ... *New-London: Printed by Samuel Green.* 1821. 12mo, pp. 260, Poems, pp. 40. Portrait. BA. 43789

"It is safe to say, that brother Maffitt's 'Poetic Effusions' may be read without profound emotion, though, perhaps, not without 'tears of contrition.'"

MAFFITT. Vindication of Public Justice and of Private Character, against the Attacks of a Council of Ministers of the Methodist Episcopal Church. By John N. Maffitt ... . *Providence, R. I.* 1823. 8vo. W. 43790

Also: An Address ... before the Literary Societies of the Wesleyan University, August 3rd, 1841. ... *Middletown, Conn.: George W. Conklin, Printer.* 1841. 8vo, pp. 23.—An Address ... before the Hibernian Relief Society ... April 7, 1828. ... *Boston: T. R. Marvin, Printer.* 1828. 8vo, pp. 16.—Brief Account of the Dreadful Occurrence at the laying of the Corner Stone of the Methodist Church in N. Bennet Street, April 30, 1828. ... *Boston.* 1828. 12mo, pp. 11.—Oration, May, 1832 ... over the grave of Philip Embury, the Earliest Minister in the American Methodist Church. ... *New-York.* 1832. 8vo. S.—A Plea for the Orphan; delivered ... 20 October, 1833. Before the Friends of the Female Orphan Asylum. ... *Baltimore.* 1833. 8vo, pp. 15.—A Plea for Africa. A Sermon ... in Behalf of the American Colonization Society. July 4, 1830. ... *Boston: E. W. Crittenden.* 1830. 8vo, pp. 14.—A Sermon, September 24, 1823, at the Dedication of the Second Methodist Chapel, Nantucket, R. I. ... *Nantucket.* 1823. 8vo, pp. 19.— ... Sermon delivered ... July 31, 1842, to the Memory of Rev. George G. Cookman. ... *Washington: Peter Force.* 1842. 8vo, pp. 31. *See also* Buckingham (J. T.), Vol. III., No. 8911, *and* Elsemore (Moses), Vol. VI., No. 22364.

This "gushing" clergyman was remarkable for the exuberance of his language, the warmth of his passions, and the power of his oratory. His popularity was scarcely inferior to that of Wesley or Whitefield. The following pieces also relate to him: Report of the Trial of Mr. John N. Maffitt, ... in Boston, December 26, 1822. ... *Boston: Printed by True and Greene.* 1823. 8vo, pp. 31.—Maffitt's Trial; or J. T. Buckingham acquitted. *New-York.* 1829. 8vo.—Startling Discoveries concerning the Death of John Maffitt. [n. p. n. d.] 8vo.—Theological Pretenders; or, an Analysis of the Character and Conduct of Rev. J. N. Maffitt. *New York.* 1830. 8vo.

Maga Excursion Papers. *New York: G. P. Putnam & Son.* 1867. 16mo, pp. 304. C. 43791

Reprinted from Putnam's monthly, also "Maga Social Papers," and "Maga Stories."

MAGALHANES (Domingos José Gonçalves de). Antonio José ou o poeta e a inquisição: Tragedia por D. J. G. de Magalhães. *Rio de Janeiro: P. Brito.* 1839. 8vo, pp. vi, 112, 12. 43792

MAGALHANES. A Confederação dos Tamoyos. Poema por D. J. G. De Magalhães. *Rio de Janeiro: Impresso pela Empreza Typografia.* 1857. 4to, pp. xii–324, 20. + Segunda Edição, revista, correcta e acrescentada pelo auctor. *Rio de Janeiro: Livraria de B. L. Garnier.* 1864. 4to, pp. xvi, 354. 43793

MAGALHANES DE GANDAVO (P. de). Historia da Prouincia de Sãcta-Cruz | a qui' vulgarmẽte chamamos Brasil: feita por Pero de | Magalhães de Gandauo, dirigida ao muito Illᵒ Sñoe Dom Li-|onis Pª gouernador que foy di Malaca & das mais partes | do Sul na India. ... [Colophon:] *Impresso em Lisboa, na officina de Antonio Gonsaluez. Anno de* 1576. Sm. 4to, 48 leaves, including the engraved title. J.C.B 43794

A volume of extraordinary rarity, curiosity, and interest, written in a pure, simple, and elegant style by an author who resided for many years in Brazil. He is the first if not the only Portuguese writer who has attempted to delineate the peculiar characteristics of the natives of Brazil. The work is so scarce that it is rarely cited by the Portuguese authors in Brazil; not even Vasconcelos, who teems with citations, mentions it, neither does Southey. In Pinelo's "Bibliotheca Oriental y Occidental," col. 673, a work very sparing of commendation, it is styled "Curiosa y Unica." Further interesting particulars occur in Machado's "Bibl. Lusitana," under Pedro de Magalhanes, and in the "Catalogue des Authores," prefixed to Vol. I. of the Dictionary of the Portuguese Academy, *Lisboa*, 1793. Davila, "Teatro das Grandezos de Madrid," entitles this work "Muy erudita y curiosa," p. 504; *see also* Ternaux, No. 121. Thorp priced a copy in 1835 at £15 15s; Quaritch gave £27 for a copy. There are not over two copies in the United States. There is no English version. Its value and importance suggested to Mr. Ternaux the propriety of including it in his "Relations et Memoires" under the following title:

Magalhanes de Gondavo. Histoire de la Province de Sancta-Cruz, que nous nommons ordinairement Le Brésil, par Pero de Magalhanes de Gondavo. *Paris.* 1837. 8vo, pp. 162.

[Magallanes (—).] Refutacion al papel titulado Bosquejo de la marcha de la Republica y de la influencia militar en sus destinos. *Santiago de Chile, abril* 17 *de* 1841. 4to, pp. (2), 9.

Magapica (M.), *pseudon.* The British and American Liturgy: ... adapted to the Three Kingdoms ... and the Thirteen United States of North America. Containing the Marrow of Modern Politics and Patriotism ... . By Magi Magapica. ... *London: For the Author.* M,DCC,LXXXIII. 8vo, pp. vi, 42. BA. 43797

Magariños Cervantes (A.) Estudios historicos, politicos y sociales sobre el Rio de La Plata, por D. Alejandro Magariños Cervantes ... . *Paris: Tipografia de Adolfo Blondeau.* 1854. 12mo.

Magasin du Bas-Canada, Journal Littéraire et Scientifique. Tome I. M. Bibaud, Éditeur. *Montreal.* 1832. 8vo. 43799

Magaw (S.) A Discourse ... July 17, 1794. In the African Church of ... Philadelphia, on ... opening the said Church, ... By Samuel Magaw, D.D. ... *Philadelphia: Printed by W. Woodward.* [n. d.] 8vo, pp. 24. H., P. 43800

Magaw. A Discourse occasioned by the Mournful Catastrophe, through Fire, which overwhelmed and destroyed Mr. Andrew Brown, his Wife, and three Children. Delivered in St. Paul's Church, ... February 5, 1797. By Samuel Magaw, D.D. *Philadelphia: Ormrod & Conrad.* [1797.] 8vo, pp. 22. 43801

Andrew Brown was the founder and editor of the "Federal Gazette."

[Magaw.] Notes on the ... Death, of a ... Friend [Mrs. Magaw]. *Philadelphia: Printed by William Young.* M,DCC,XC. 8vo, pp. 36. BA. 43802

Magaw. An Oration commemorative of the Virtues and Greatness of General Washington; Pronounced in ... Philadelphia ... before the Grand Lodge of Pennsylvania, on the Twenty-Second ... of February, Eighteen Hundred. By Samuel Magaw, D.D. ... *Philadelphia: Printed by J. Ormrod.* 1800. 8vo, pp. 45. + *Newfield: Printed by Lazarus Beach.* 1800. 8vo, pp. 23. H.

Magaw. A Sermon, delivered 28th of May, 1787, at the First Ordination held by the Bishop of the Protestant Episcopal Church, in the State of Pennsylvania. By Samuel Magaw, D.D. *Philadelphia: Printed by Prichard & Hall.* M.DCC.LXXXVII. 8vo, pp. 52. P. 43804

Also: Discourse Preached in Christ Church ... *Philadelphia.* 1775. 8vo, pp. 14.— A Sermon ... July 4, 1786, when the "Form of Prayer and Thanksgiving to Almighty God for the Inestimable Blessings of Religious and Civil Liberty" was first used. ... *Philadelphia.* 1786. 8vo. P.—A Sermon preached in ... Dover ... December 27th, 1779. ... Before the General Communication of Free and Accepted Masons of the Delaware State ... . *Philadelphia: Printed by John Dunlap.* [n. d.] 8vo, pp. 16.— Things Lovely and of good Report. A Sermon delivered in ... Philadelphia, ... 27th of December, 1793. In the presence of the Grand Lodge of Pennsylvania ... *Philadelphia: Printed by C. Orwald.* 1794. 8vo, pp. 24.

Magazin der neuesten und besten ausländischen Reisebeschreibungen. *Hamburg & Mainz: G. Vollmer.* 1804. 7 vols., 16mo.

Vols. V. and VI. contain C. F. Volney's "Reisen durch die Vereinigten Staaten von Nordamerika."

Magazin für die Literatur des Auslands. *Berlin.* 1856. 8vo.

Nos. 38 and 39 include "Die Sprache der Eskimos auf Grönland," by W. Schott.

Magazin für die neueste Geschichte der evangelischen Missions- und Bibelgesellschaften. *Basel.* 1822. 8vo. Continued.

Contains many articles relative to America, the Indians, life of Zeisberger, etc.

Magazin von merkwürdigen neuen Reisebeschreibungen, aus fremden Sprachen übersetzt und mit erläuternden Anmerkungen begleitet. *Berlin: In der Vossischen Buchhandlung.* 1797. 8vo, pp. 284, xxxvi, 232. 43808

Contains Hearne's "Travels to the Frozen Ocean," translated from the English by Forster, and Wansey's "Travels in the United States, in 1794," translated by Bottinger. *See also* Forster (J. R.), Vol. VI., No. 25139.

The Magazine of Horticulture, Botany, and all useful Discoveries and Improvements ... . Edited by C. M. Hovey. Vol. III. *Boston.* 1837. 8vo. Continued. 43809

For Vols. I. and II. *see* "American Gardener's Magazine," Vol. I., No. 1089. A new series commences with each tenth volume.

The Magazine of the Reformed Dutch Church. ... Edited by W. C. Brownlee [and others. April, 1826, to March, 1830.] *New Brunswick.* 1826–30. 4 vols., 8vo. S. 43810

... The Magazine for the Million ... . February 17, 1844. ... Vol. I. No. I. *New York: Burgess, Stringer, & Co.* [n. d.] 8vo, pp. 24. Continued. H. 43811

Magazine of Travel in various Countries both of the Old World and the New. *Detroit.* 1857. 8vo. 43812

Magazine of Wit, and American Harmonist. Songs ... composed in Honour of the Victories ... during the Late War. *Philadelphia: McCarty & Davis.* 1821. 24mo, pp. (4), 144.

Magdalena (Augustin de la). Arte de la Lengua Tagala ... *Mexico.* 1679. 8vo. 43814

Lord Kingsborough paid £10 10s for his copy, which was afterwards (1843) priced £6 6s by Thorp. It is introduced here as a very rare Mexican book.

Magdalena (J. B.) Privada y Oficial Correspondencia ... con el Marques de Casa Yrujo, para justa, debida, y natural vindicacion y defensa de su honor y conducta politica. *Philadelphia.* 1806. 8vo. C. 43815

Magdalena. Publica y Particular Correspondencia de Don Joseph Bruno Magdalena, Santin y Valcarce, ... y Posteriorment nombrado por J. M. Agregado al Ministerio di España en Saxonia, segun actualmento lo es ... . *Filadelfia.* 1813. 8vo, pp. 84, Appendice, pp. 35. 43816

Magee (J.) Memorial of John Magee. *New York.* 1870. 8vo. S. 43817

Magellan. *See* [Falkner (T.)], VI. 23737, *and* Relacion.

Conditions of the Magellanic Premium. *Philadelphia.* [n. d.] 8vo. 43818

Magie (D.) A Discourse delivered in ... Elizabeth, N. J. August 6th, 1863. On ... The Public Thanksgiving appointed ... to commemorate the signal Victories vouchsafed to the Federal Arms. By Rev. David Magie, D.D. *New-York: Printed by Francis Hart & Co.* 1863. 8vo, pp. 38. 43819

Magie. Public Thanksgiving. A Sermon, ... in ... Elizabeth, N. J. November 28th, 1861, By David Magie, D.D. ... *New-York: Printed by Francis Hart & Co.* 1861. 8vo, pp. 23.

Also: ... A Sermon ... at Buffalo, New York, September 8, 1847 ... before the American Board ... . *Boston: Press of T. R. Marvin.* 1847. 8vo, pp. 28.—Sermon on the Death of Gen. Zachary Taylor, President ... . *New York.* 1850. 8vo.

Magill (J.) A Historical Account of Kentucky. By John Magill. *Frankfort.* 1832. 8vo. 43821

A doubtful title from an auctioneer's catalogue.

Magin (A.) Histoire vniverselle. *See* [Wytfliet (Cornelius)].

Magini (J. A.) Geographiæ tum Veteris tum Novæ absolutissimum Opus, duobus voluminibus distinctum. I. Ptolomæi Geographicæ Enarrationis Libri viii.; et II. Ptolomæi Antiqui Orbis Tabulæ xxvii. et Tabulæ xxxvii. Recentiores, una cum ipsarum Tabularum Expositionibus, quibus singulæ Orbis Partes, provinciæ, regiones, imperia, regna, ducatus, et alia dominia, prout nostro tempore se habent, exacte describuntur a Jo. Antonio Magino. *Coloniæ: P. Keschedt.* 1597. 2 vols., 4to. Engraved Titles, 64 Maps engraved by Hieronymo Porro. 43822

The map of the World represents the whole of the South of the Globe, as occupied by "Terra Australis nondum cognita," excepting "Terra del Fuego," which forms part of it. This is repeated in the chart "ad Usum Navigantium," with the addition of mountain ranges. The description of America occupies twenty-five pages; but no mention is made of the then English possessions, though Canada ("Nova Francia") occupies eight lines. The Spanish and Portuguese territories, including the West Indies, occupy the rest of the space. "The various plates in which the New World is represented, do not show so much correction in the form of that continent as appears in the final edition of Ortelius, published in 1592, but adhere rather to the earlier types of the Antwerp geographer."—Quaritch. It was reprinted, *Arnhemi, Jo. Janssonius.* 1617. 2 vols., 4to.

Maginnis (J. S.) An Inaugural Address ... in ... Hamilton Literary and Theological Institution, August 21, 1839. By John S. Maginnis ... . *Utica: Bennett, Backus, & Hawley.* 1840. 8vo, pp. 26. H. 43823

[Maglathan (H. B.)] Company I, Fourth Massachusetts Regiment, Nine Months Volunteers, in Service, 1862–3. *Boston: Press of Geo. C. Rand & Avery.* 1863. 8vo, pp. 40, (1). H.

Magnenius (J. Chr.) De Tabaco Exercitationes XIV. *Amstelodami.* 1669. 12mo. 43825

De magnis thesauris spiritualibus ac temporalibus in Nova Hispania detectis, por Alphonsus de Benavides. *Salisburgo.* 1634. 8vo. 43826

Should have appeared under Benavides. *See* Ternaux, No. 558.

The Magnolia. Edited by H. W. Herbert. *New York.* 1835–37. 2 vols., 8vo. 43827

The Magnolia, An American Gift Book. Edited by H. H. Randall. *New York.* 1850. 8vo, pp. 380. Plates. 43828

Magnus (A.) Oratio in Fvnere | Regis Catholici. | [Recto of the second leaf:] M. Antonii Magni Oratio | Habita Neapoli in Fvnere | Ferdinandi Hispaniarvm | Regis Catholici | Calendis Martii MDXVI. | [Colophon:] *Neapoli: In ædibus Sigismundi Mayr | Germani An.* MDXVI. | 4to, 12 leaves. 43829

See [Harrisse's] "Bib. Am. Vet.," II., No. 47.

Magnus (Olaus). Historia de Gentibus Septentrionalibvs. *Romæ: Viotti.* 1555. Folio. 43830

First and best edition, with many wood-cuts in the text. This great work, by the Archbishop of Upsal, on the northern regions, includes Greenland with a map copied from the "Ptolemy" of 1482. The following is a reprint:

Magnus. Historia Olai Magni Gothi Archiepiscopi Vpsalensis, de gentivm Septentrionalium uariis conditionibus statibusue, & demorum, rituum, superstitionum, exercitiorum, regiminis, disciplinæ uictusque, mirabili diuersitate. Item de bellis, structuris, instrumentisq; mirabilibus. Item de mineris metallicis, & uarijs animalium generibus, in illis regionibus degentium. Opus omnibus cuiuscunq; conditionis hominibus magno usui futurum, rerum cognitione delectationeq; refertum, expressis figuris pictis illustratum. *Basileæ: ex officina Henric Petrina, anno salutis* MDLXVII. *mense martio.* Folio, pp. (44), 854, Colophon (2). 43831

There was an Italian version, *Venetia*, 1565, folio.

Magnus. A Compendious History of the Goths, Swedes and Vandals and other Northern Nations. Translated into English by J. S. *London: J. Streater.* 1658. Folio. C. 43832

Magnus. Gentium Septentrionalium Historiæ Breviarum. *Antverpiæ.* 1558. 8vo. + [*Ibid.*] 1562. + *Lugduni Batavorum.* 1652. 12mo. C. + *Amstelodami.* 1659. 8vo. 43833

This abridgment is by Corn. Scribon Graphæus. It was translated as below:

Magnus. Histoire des Pays Septentrionaux, en laquelle sont deduites les choses rares ou étranges qui se trouvent entre les Nations Septentrionales, traduit (en epitome) du Latin. *Anvers: Christ. Plantin.* 1561. 8vo. 43834

The dedication is signed by the printer. It is printed in the peculiar character known as "Lettres de Civilité." Some copies have the imprint *Paris: Martin le Jeune.* 1561.

Magnus. De vvonderlijcke Historie van de Noordersche Landen beschreuen door Heere Olaus de Grote Eerstbisschop

van Upsalen end Ouerste. Nu eerst ouerghestelt wten Latijn in ons Nederlantsche Duytsche Sprake. *Willem Siluius, Tantwerpen.* 1562. 8vo. 43835

The first edition in Dutch. The quaintness and beauty of the many wood-cuts in the text of this little book place it among the most interesting of all the works on the northern regions.

Magnus' Hand-Book of Travel, and Tourist's Guide through Canada and the United States. ... *Montreal: R. Worthington.* 1866. 16mo. 43836

Magoon (E. L.) The Eloquence of the Colonial and Revolutionary Times, with Sketches of Early American Statesmen and Patriots. Delivered before the New England Society of Cincinnati. By Rev. E. L. Magoon. *Cincinnati.* 1847. 12mo, pp. 91. 43837

Magoon. The Living Orators in America. By E. L. Magoon. *New York: Baker & Scribner.* 1849. 12mo, pp. ix, 462. 6 Portraits. + [*Ibid.*] 1850. B. 43838

Magoon. Orators of the American Revolution. By E. L. Magoon. *New York.* 1848. 12mo. + Second Edition. *New York: Baker and Scribner.* 1848. 12mo, pp. 456. 6 Portraits. + Third Edition. [*Ibid.*] 1849. + Fourth Edition. [*Ibid.*] 1850. B., BA. 43839

Magoon. Republican Christianity; or, True Liberty, as exhibited in the Life, Precepts, and Early Disciples of the Great Redeemer. By E. L. Magoon ... . *Boston: Gould, Kendall, and Lincoln.* 1849. 12mo, pp. 422. H. 43840

Magoon. Westward Empire; or, The Great Drama of Human Progress. By E. L. Magoon ... . *New York: Harper & Brothers.* 1856. 8vo, pp. 445. A., B., C. 43841

Also: Eloquence and Liberty. An Oration before the Literary Societies of Washington College, Lexington, Va. June 24, 1846. ... *Richmond.* 1846. 8vo, pp. 38.—Oration ... Delivered July 4th, 1848, at the Laying of the Corner Stone of the Ohio Mechanics' Institute, Cincinnati. *Cincinnati.* 1848. 8vo, pp. 23.—A Useful Life and a Peaceful Death; delivered before the Legislature of North Carolina, 18 December, 1842. ... *Richmond.* 1843. 8vo.

Magoon (J.) The Life of Major-Gen. John C. Fremont. With a Full Account of his Rocky Mountain Explorations and Adventures. By Lieut. Jas. Magoon. *New York: Beadle and Company.* [n. d.] 12mo, pp. 96. B. 43842

Magoun (G. F.) Historical Sketch of Iowa College. By President Magoun. [n. p. 1865?] 8vo, pp. 8. H. 43843

Magoun. The West; its Culture and its Colleges. An Oration ... at ... Iowa College ... July 18th, 1855. By George F. Magoun. ... *Davenport: Luse & Coles, Printers.* 1855. 12mo, pp. 34. 43844

Also: Addresses and Discourse at the Inauguration of ... Rev. George F. Magoun, A.M. ... July 19, 1865. ... *Chicago: Horton & Leonard, Printers.* 1865. 8vo, pp. 60, (1).—Architecture and Christian Principle. ... [n. p. 1859?] 8vo, pp. (2), 13.—A Ministry for the Northwest: An Address ... at the Triennial Convention ... of Chicago Theological Seminary, June 26, 1864. ... *Chicago.* 1864. 8vo, pp. 22.—President Magoun's College Statement. [n. p. n. d.] 8vo, pp. 7, (1).—The Relation of the Academy to our Educational System: an Address, Denmark, Iowa, July 3, 1867. ... *Denmark.* 1867. 8vo, pp. 28.

Magrath (A. G.) An Oration ... before the '76 Association ... 4th July, 1841. By A. G. Magrath ... . *Charleston: Printed by W. Riley.* 1841. 8vo, pp. (2), 32. H. 43845

Magrath (T. W.) Authentic Letters from Upper Canada; with an Account of Canadian Field Sports. By T. W. Magrath, Esq. The Etchings by Samuel Lover, Esq. Edited by the Rev. T. Radcliff. *Dublin: William Curry, Jun. and Company.* 1833. 8vo, pp. 334. 43846

See "Dublin University Magazine," I. 600.

Magre (P.) Le Pilote Américain, contenant la Description des Côtes orientales de l'Amérique du Nord, suivi d'une notice sur le "Gulph Stream," ... par P. Magre. *Paris.* 1826. 8vo.

Magruder (A. B.) Political, Commercial and Moral Reflections, on the Late Cession of Louisiana, to the United States. By Allan B. Magruder, Esquire ... . *Lexington: Printed by D. Bradford.* 1803. 8vo, pp. 150. BA. 43848

Magruder (H. R.) Sketches of the Last Year of the Mexican Empire. By Henry R. Magruder, M.D. ... [*Wiesbaden:*] *Printed for Private Circulation.* [1868.] 8vo, pp. viii, 135. Plates.

Magruder (J. B.) Major-General Magruder's Report of his Operations on the Peninsula, and of the Battles of "Savage Station" and "Malvern Hill," near Richmond. *Richmond: Chas. H. Wynne, Printer.* 1862. 8vo, pp. 46. H. 43850

Also: Presidential Contest of 1856, in Three Letters. ... [n. p.] 1857. 8vo.

Magruder (P.) *See* Vol. IV., No. 15563.

Magruder (W. B.) An Address to the Public, Accounting for the large Sum of Money which has been sunk in the hands of W. B. Magruder and W. B. Magruder and Company, and showing that their Failure and almost all their Losses were produced by the Misconduct of Messrs. Findlay, Bannatyne and Co. *Baltimore.* 1800. 8vo. 43851

Magruder (W. H. N.) The Young Minister; or, Memoirs and Remains of Stephen Beekman Bangs, of the New York East Conference. By W. H. N. Magruder. With a preface, by E. O. Haven. *New York.* 1853. 12mo, pp. 388. 43852

[Maguire (H. N.) *and* Horr (H.)] Historical Sketch and Essay on the Resources of Montana; including a ... Directory of the Metropolis. ... *Helena.* 1868. 8vo, pp. 168. H. 43853

Maguire (J. F.) America in its Relation to Irish Emigration. By John Francis Maguire ... . *Boston: Patrick Donahoe.* 1869. 12mo, pp. 24. B. 43854

Maguire. Father Mathew: A Biography. By John Francis Maguire ... . *London: Longman* ... 1863. 8vo, pp. (2), xv, 557. Portrait. BA. + *New York.* 1864. 12mo. 43855

Relates his travels and labors in America in the cause of temperance, etc.

Maguire. The Irish in America. By John Francis Maguire, M.P. ... *London: Longman, Green, and Co.* 1868. 8vo, pp. xvii, 653. BA. + *New York: D. & J. Sadlier & Co.* 1868. 12mo, pp. xiv, 653. 43856

[Maguire (Thomas).] Clergé Canadien vengé par ses ennemis; ou observations sur un ouvrage récent, intitulé: "Tableaux Statistique et Politique des Deux Canadas." Par Vindex. *Québec.* 1834. 8vo. 43857

[Maguire.] Observations d'un Catholique sur l'histoire du Canada de l'honorable William Smith. Par Vindex. *Québec.* 1827. 8vo. 43858

Magwire (J.) Letter to President Grant ... [on] the National Labor Union ... By John Magwire ... Feb. 17, 1869. *Washington: Joseph L. Pearson, Printer.* 1869. 8vo, pp. (2), 30. H.

Also: Address ... at ... St. Louis ... August 2, 1870 ... on ... Pauperism and Usury. *Saint Louis.* 1870. 8vo, pp. 8. H.

Mahaffy (J. P.) Twelve Lectures on Primitive Civilizations, and their Physical Conditions. ... By John P. Mahaffy, A.M. ... *London: Longmans* ... MDCCCLXIX. 16mo, pp. xix, 296, (1).

Mahan (A.) Modern Mysteries Explained and Exposed. ... By Rev. A. Mahan ... . *Boston: John P. Jewett and Company.* 1855. 12mo, pp. xv, 466. H. 43861

Mahan (D. H.) An Elementary Treatise on Advanced-Guard, Out-Post, and Detachment Service of Troops, ... By D. H. Mahan ... . *New Orleans: Bloomfield & Steel.* 1861. 16mo, pp. 143. 43862

Mahan. Summary of the Course of Permanent Fortification, and of the Attack and Defence of Permanent Works, for the use of the Cadets of the U. S. Military Academy. By D. H. Mahan, ... *Columbia, S. C.* 1863. 8vo, pp. 352. + *Richmond: West & Johnston.* 1863. 8vo, pp. 352. BA. 43863

This gentleman is also the author of many other works, the two we have introduced are only inserted here because they were published in the "Confederate States."

Mahan (J. B.) Trial of Rev. John B. Mahan, for Felony, in the Mason Circuit Court of Kentucky ... . *Cincinnati: Samuel A. Alley, Printer.* 1838. 8vo, pp. 88. B. 43864

Mahan (M.) ... An Address ... before the ... College of St. James, Maryland, June 10th ... 1851. By ... Rev. M. Mahan. ... *Philadelphia: King & Baird, Printers.* 1851. 8vo, pp. 15. H. 43865

Mahan. The Healing of the Nations: A Sermon ... in ... Albany, on Thanksgiving Day, Nov. 29, 1855. By M. Mahan, D.D. ... *Albany: J. Munsell.* 1855. 8vo, pp. 22. B. 43866

Mahan. Dr. Mahan's Speech. [n. p. n. d.] 8vo, pp. 16 + Second Speech. [n. p. n. d.] 8vo, pp. 16. 43867

Relates to the Civil War.

Mahan. ... Sermon in Memory of the Right Reverend George Washington Doane, Late Bishop of ... New-Jersey; ... in ... Burlington, ... May 25, A.D. 1859, By the Rev. M. Mahan, D.D. ... *New-York: Pudney & Russell, Printers.* 1859. 8vo, pp. 29. H. 43868

Malheiro e Mello (A. M. L. P.) Panegyrico gratulatorio ao Serenissimo Senhor D. José, Principe do Brasil, na occasião dos seus desposorios, por Antonio Manuel Leite Pacheo Malheiro e Mello. *Lisboa, na Regia Officina Typografia.* 1777. 4to, pp. 12.

Mahlmann (H.) Der Indianer-Sommer in Nord-Amerika verglichen mit gewöhnlichen Witterungserscheinungen Mittel-Europas. [n. p. n. d.] 8vo. 43870

Mahlmann. Karte von Amerika ... . *Berlin: Schropp und Compagnie.* 1838. Folio. + Berichtigungen. [*Ibid.*] 1844.

Mahlmann. Karte der Provinz Rio de Janeiro. *Berlin: D. Reimer.* 1848. 4to. 43872

The Mahogany Tree, its Botanical Characters, Qualities and Uses, with Suggestions for cutting it in the West Indies and Central America, with Notices of Panama, Nicaragua, Tehuantepec. *Liverpool.* 1850. 8vo. Map and Plates. 43873

See also Vol. III., No. 11775.

Mahon (Philip Henry), *Viscount.* *See* Stanhope (P. H.)

Mahoney (D.) Six Months in a House of Correction, or the Narrative of Dorah Mahoney, who was under the Influence of the Protestants about a Year. *Boston.* 1835. 18mo. 43874

Edited by William J. Snelling.

Mahoney (J. W.) The Cherokee Physician; or, Indian Guide to Health, as given by Richard Foreman, a Cherokee Doctor. By James W. Mahoney. Third Edition. *New York: J. M. Edney.* 1857. 12mo, pp. 304. C. 43875

Mahony (D. A.) The Four Acts of Despotism: comprising I. The Tax Bill, with all the Amendments. II. The Finance Bill. III. The Conscription Act. IV. The Indemnity Bill. With Introductions and Comments. By D. A. Mahony ... . *New York: Van Evrie, Horton & Co.* 1863. 8vo, pp. 160.

[Mahony.] Political Opinions in 1776 and 1863: a Letter to a Victim of Arbitrary Arrests and "American Bastiles." *New York: Anson D. F. Randolph.* 1863. 12mo, pp. 19. 43877

Mahony. The Prisoner of State. By D. A. Mahony. ... *New York: Carleton.* M DCCC LXIII. 12mo, pp. 414. H. 43878

Mahy (N.) Notas históricas de plan del Excmo. Sr. D. Nicolas Mahy. *Habana: Oficina de Bartolo.* 1818. 8vo.

Mahy. Pesame al Excmo. Sr. D. Nicolas Mahy. *Habana: Imprenta Fraternal.* 1818. 8vo. 43880

Mahy de Cormeré (J. F.) Observations sur les Colonies Françaises de l'Amérique. *Paris.* 1791. 8vo. C. 43881

Maia (J. J. da S.) O Brasileiro Imparcial, por Joaquim José da Silva Maia. *Rio de Janeiro: Typografia do Diario.* 1830 e 1831. 8vo. 43882

Maia (J. A. da S.) Memoria da origem, progressos e decadencia do quinto d'ouro na provincia de Minas-geraes, por José Antonio da Silva Maia. *Rio de Janeiro.* 1827. 4to. 43883

The Maid of Canal Street; and the Bloxhams. *Philadelphia.* 1851. 8vo. 43884

Mai-Jour. *See our* No. 43028.

Mailhe (J. B.) Discours ... sur la Grandeur et l'Importance de la Révolution qui vient de s'opérer dans l'Amérique septentrionale. Par M. Mailhe ... . *Toulouse: D. Desclassan.* M.DCC.LXXXIV. 8vo, pp. 40. BA. 43885

Maillard (N. D. The History of the Republic of Texas, from the Discovery of the Country to the Present Time; and the Cause of her Separation from the Republic of Mexico. By N. Doran Maillard, Esq. ... of Texas. *London: Smith, Elder, and Co.* ... 1842. 8vo, pp. xxiv, 512. Map. H. 43886

"My object is to present to the public an unvarnished account of what Texas and the Texans really are; of the true origin and history of their rebellion against Mexico, their lawful sovereign," etc.—Preface, p. iv.

Maillard (Pierre). Grammar of the Mikmaque Language of Nova Scotia, edited from the Manuscripts of the Abbe Maillard. By the Rev. Joseph M. Bellenger. *New York: Cramoisy Press.* 1864. 8vo, pp. 101. BA. 43887

Two titles, one of which is in French. The tribes of Mikmaks formerly occupied the peninsula of Nova Scotia and New Brunswick, and part of Maine. Forms No. XIII. of Shea's "Library of American Linguistics." One hundred copies only printed.

Maillard. Lettre sur les Missions de l'Acadie et particulièrement sur les Missions Micmaques. *Soir Canadian.* 1863. 8vo, pp. 136. 43888

Maillardière (Charles François), *Vicomte* de la. Abrégé des Principaux Traités conclus depuis le commencement du quatorzième siècle jusqu'à présent, entre les différentes puissances de l'Europe. *Paris.* 1778. 2 vols., 12mo. C. 43889

[Maillet Duclairon (Antoine).] Observations d'un Américain des Isles neutres au sujet de la négociation de la France et de l'Angleterre. *Geneve.* 1761. 12mo. 43890

See Barbier, II. 480.

Maillet (B. de). Telliamed ou Entretiens d'un Philosophe Indien avec un Missionnaire François Sur la Diminution de la Mer, la Formation de la Terre, l'Origine de l'Homme, &c. Mis en

ordre sur les Mémoires de feu M. de Maillet. ... *Amsterdam: Chez L'Honoré & Fils, Libraires.* M.DCC.XLVIII. 16mo, pp. (10), cxix, (8), 208; (2), 231, (2). H. 43891

[Maillet.] Telliamed; or, the World Explain'd: containing Discourses Between an Indian Philosopher and a Missionary, on the Diminution of the Sea—the Formation of the Earth—the Origin of Men & Animals: and other Singular Subjects, relating to Natural History & Philosophy. ... *London: T. Osborne.* MDCCL. 8vo, pp. liii, 284. H. + *Baltimore: D. Porter.* 1797. 8vo, pp. 268. BA. 43892

"This curious work was written by M. de Maillet, whose name is concealed in the word 'Telliamed.' It is supposed to have suggested to Mr. Darwin his celebrated theory."

Mailly (É.) Précis de l'histoire de l'astronomie aux États-Unis d'Amérique. Par Édouard Mailly. *Bruxelles: Hayez.* 1860. 12mo. 43893

Mails. *See* Mexico, Post-Office, etc.

Main (T.) Directions for the Transplantation and Management of Young Thorn or other Hedge Plants ... . With ... Operations on ... Hedging. By Thomas Main ... . *City of Washington: A. & G. Way, Printers.* 1807. 8vo, pp. 38. H. 43894

Maine District, and State of Maine,

Alphabetically arranged, except that the books relating to Banks, Education, Geology, Land, Masonry and Military matters are grouped.

An Abstract of Returns showing the amount of Money raised for ... Bridges. *Portland.* 1829. 8vo. W. 43895

An Abstract of the Returns of Corporations made to the Office of the Secretary of State in January, 1852, for the year 1851. *Augusta: State Printer.* 1852. 8vo. Continued. C.

An Act to apportion and assess a Tax on the Inhabitants ... for ... 1852. *Augusta: William T. Johnson, Printer.* 1852. 8vo, pp. 27. H. 43897

An Act to restrict the Sale of Intoxicating Drinks, 1846. [n. p. n. d.] 8vo, pp. 14. 43898

This is the celebrated "Maine Law." Also: An Act for the Suppression of Drinking Houses and Tippling Shops, passed ... 1851. [n. p. n. d.] 8vo, pp. 8.—An Appeal to the Public. From ... Results of the Maine Law. ... *New York.* 1853. 8vo. + Second Edition. [*Ibid.*] 1854. 8vo, pp. 32.— ... Report of the Committee on the Judiciary relative to the Sale of Intoxicating Liquors. ... February 29, 1856. [n. p.:] *Fuller & Fuller, Printers.* [1856?] 8vo, pp. 39, (1). H.

Acts and Resolves, passed by the Twentieth Legislature of the State of Maine, January Session, 1840. ... *Augusta: Wm. R. Smith & Co., Printers.* 1840. 8vo, pp. (10), 254, (12). Cont'd.

Additional Resolves respecting the North-Eastern Boundary. Passed January 23, 1832. *Augusta: I. Berry & Co., Printers.* 1832. 8vo, pp. 4. H. 43900

Address of a Convention of Delegates from Twenty Towns and five Plantations within the Counties of York, Cumberland and Lincoln, ... at Portland, ... the Twenty Eighth ... of January One Thousand Seven Hundred and Ninety Five ... on ... their Separation from Massachusetts. *Portland: Printed ... by Thomas B. Wait.* [1795.] 16mo, pp. 31. H. 43901

An Address of the Democratic Members of the Legislature, to the Democratic Party in ... Maine. [n. p. n. d.] 8vo, pp. 8.

An Address to the Inhabitants of the District of Maine, upon the Subject of their Separation from the Present Government of Massachusetts. By One of their Fellow Citizens. *Printed at Portland by Thomas B. Wait,* ... 1791. 8vo, pp. 54. BA., C.

An Address to the Inhabitants of Maine, shewing a Safe and Easy Method of extracting Good from Evil. By a Citizen. *Augusta: For the Proprietors.* 1805. 8vo, pp. 11. BA. 43904

An Address to the People of Maine, from the Convention of Delegates, assembled at Portland. [*Portland: F. Douglas, Printer.* 1819.] 8vo, pp. 7. H., W. 43905

An Address to the People. *See* [Lewis (A.), *and others*].

An Address to the People of Maine from M. Kinsley, Joshua Cushman, Ezekiel Whitman and Enoch Lincoln, relating to the Admission of that State into the Union. *Washington.* 1820. 8vo, pp. 14. H. 43906

Aggregate Amount of each description of Persons within the District of Maine. [*Washington.*] 1811. Folio. 43907

Agriculture. Digest of Returns from the Agricultural Societies in the State of Maine, for 1856. Prepared by S. L. Goodale ... *Augusta: Fuller & Fuller, Printers.* 1857. 8vo, pp. 288, (2). Plates. BA. 43908

Continued as: "Abstracts of Returns," etc. Also: Transactions of the Agricultural Societies ... for 1850, 1851, 1852. Arranged ... by E. Holmes ... . Part II. *Augusta: William T. Johnson, Printer.* 1853. 8vo, pp. vii, (2), 411-862. Continued.

An Appeal to the People of Maine on the Question of Separation ... from Massachusetts ... . [n. p.] 1816. 8vo, pp. 20. + Second Edition. [*Portland,*] *April,* 1816. 8vo, pp. 28. H.

Report of the Attorney General on ... the State Prison and Criminal Code, January, 1829. *Portland: J. and W. E. Edwards, Printers.* 1829. 8vo, pp. 22. H. 43910

Report of the Attorney General of ... Maine. 1859. *Augusta: Stevens & Sayward, Printers.* 1860. 8vo, pp. 11. H. 43911

Annual Report of the Bank Commissioners, 1848. ... *Augusta: William T. Johnson, Printer.* 1849. 8vo, pp. 37. Continued.

Also: Second Annual Report of the Bank and Insurance Examiner of ... Maine. December 31, 1869. ... *Augusta: Sprague, Owen & Nash, Printers.* [n. d.] 8vo, pp. 84. — ... Documents in relation to the Examination of Banks. *Portland: Printed ... by Thomas Todd.* 1828. 8vo, pp. 10.—List of Stockholders ... in the Banks of Maine. ... *Augusta: Wm. R. Smith & Co.* 1842. 8vo, pp. 87. Continued.—Report of the Bank Commissioners under a Resolve of March 6, 1826. *Portland: Printed ... by Thomas Todd, Printer.* 1827. 8vo, pp. 48.—Report of the Bank Examiner of ... Maine. 1870. *Augusta: Sprague, Owen & Nash, Printers.* 1870. 8vo, pp. 56. Continued. B.—Report of the Commissioners appointed ... to examine into the Doings and Transactions of the ... Banks in this State ... . *Portland: Printed by Thomas Todd.* 1827. 8vo, pp. 47, (1). Continued. H.

A Book for the Children of Maine ... . *Portland: S. Colman.* 1831. 12mo, pp. 119. 43913

A Brief Sketch of Parties. *See* Vol. II., No. 7897.

A Catalogue of Original Documents. *See* [Folsom (G.)]

Church Association of Maine. Report of the Convention held in Portland, September, 1852. *Bangor.* 1852. 8vo, pp. 20. 43914

Also: Report of the First Annual Meeting, Bangor, September, 1853. *Bangor.* 1853. 8vo, pp. 48. Continued.

Circular, dated Brunswick, Me., Aug. 16, 1832. [n. p. 1832.] 8vo, pp. 1. 43915

Signed by Marcellus Emery and seven others.

Address of the Board of Managers of the Colonization Society of the State of Maine. [*Portland.* 1855.] 8vo, pp. 8. H.

A Conspectus [etc.] *See* Vol. IV., No. 16040.

Constitution for the State of Maine; formed in Convention, at Portland, 29th of October, ... 1819 ... . *Portland: Printed by Francis Douglas.* 1819. 8vo, pp. 32. BA., C. 43917

The Constitution of the State. *Portland.* 1820. 8vo, pp. xxxvi, 48. 43918

The Constitution of the State of Maine, with Marginal References, the Census ... . *Portland.* 1831. 8vo. 43919

The Debates, Resolutions, and other Proceedings, of the Convention of Delegates, assembled at Portland on the 11th, and continued until the 29th day of October, 1819, for the Purpose of forming a Constitution for the State of Maine. To which is prefixed the Constitution ... . By Jeremiah Perley, Counsellor at Law. *Portland: A. Shirley, Printer.* 1820. 12mo, pp. 300, (1).

Decision of the King of the Netherlands considered in reference to the Rights of the United States and of the State of Maine. *Portland.* 1831. 8vo. C., W. 43921

Relates to the north-eastern boundary.

Defences of Maine. *See* [Poor (John A.)]

Defences of the North-Eastern Frontier. Report of the Select Committee to whom were referred the Resolutions of the Legislature of Maine. *Washington.* 1864. 8vo. S. 43922

A Description of the Situation, Climate, Soil and Productions of Certain Tracts of Land in the District of Maine, and Commonwealth of Massachusetts. [n. p. 1793.] 4to, pp. 44. BA.

Contains a letter from General Benjamin Lincoln to William Bingham, dated Feb. 26, 1793; also the certificate of Daniel Cony, John Gardiner, Francis Winter, and David Silvester, concerning the condition and resources of the District. Reprinted in the "Mass. Hist. Collections," Fourth Series.

Documentary History. *See* Maine Historical History.

... Documents, in relation to the Canada Road. ... *Portland: Printed ... by Thomas Todd.* 1828. 8vo, pp. 8. H. 43924

Documents printed by Order of the Legislature, ... 1841. *Augusta.* 1841. 8vo. Continued. 43925

Documents relating to the Boundary Line between Maine and New Brunswick. ... *Boston: True and Greene,* ... *Printers.* 1826. 8vo, pp. 18. BA. 43926

Documents, relating to the Maine Boundary; namely, President's Message, Letters that passed between the Secretary of State and the British Minister—Report made to Congress. *Washington.* 1838. 8vo, pp. 494. Map. 43927

Title from one of Mr. William Gowan's catalogues.

Documents relating to the North Eastern Boundary of ... Maine. *Boston: Dutton & Wentworth.* 1828. 8vo, pp. 275. H.

These documents cover the whole question respecting the disputed territories from the earliest period to this date. The matter was not finally settled till the Ashburton and Webster Treaty of 1840.

Documents relating to the Separation of Maine from Massachusetts. [n. p.] 1819. 8vo. W. 43929

... Documents relating to Trespassers on the Public Lands. [n. p.:] *Smith & Robinson, Printers.* [1839.] 12mo, pp. 47, (1).

Education. ... Abstract of the Returns of the Selectmen ... and Assessors ... of the Number of School Districts ... Scholars and Amount of Money raised for Schools. *Portland: Printed by Day & Fraser.* 1829. 8vo, pp. 20. H. 43931

Act to provide for the Education of Youth. *Augusta: W. T. Johnson.* 1851. 12mo, pp. 52. C. 43932

First Report of the Board of Education ... . 1847. *Augusta: W. T. Johnson.* 1847. 12mo, pp. 135. Plans. Continued.

Annual Report of the State Superintendent of Common Schools of ... Maine, ... 1855. *Augusta.* 1855. 8vo. Cont'd.

General Conference of the Congregational Churches in Maine. Churches and Ministers from 1672–1867. With the Minutes ... *Portland: Press of Brown Thurston & Co.* 1867. 8vo, pp. 157.

Geology. First Report on the Geology of the Public Lands in the State of Maine. By Charles T. Jackson, M.D. *Boston: Dutton and Wentworth, Printers.* 1837. 8vo, pp. 93, (1). BA.

First Report on the Geology of the State of Maine. By Charles T. Jackson, M.D. ... *Augusta: Smith & Robinson, Printers.* 1837. 8vo, pp. 127, (1). + Second Report. *Augusta: Luther Severance, Printer.* 1838. 8vo, pp. 168. BA. + Third Annual Report. *Augusta: Smith & Robinson.* 1839. 8vo, pp. xiv, 276.

See also Jackson (C. F.), Vol. IX., No. 35399-400.

Atlas of Plates, illustrating the Geology of the State of Maine, accompanying the First Report on the Geology of that State. By Charles T. Jackson, M.D. ... [*Augusta.* 1837.] 4to. 24 Plates.

Second Annual Report upon the Natural History and Geology of the State of Maine. 1862. [n. p. n. d.] 8vo, pp. 447. BA.

By Ezekiel Holmes and C. H. Hitchcock. Also included in the Seventh Report of the Maine Board of Agriculture. *Augusta.* 1862. 8vo.

[Report of] the Joint Select Committee to whom was referred "So much of the Governor's Message as relates to the Geological Survey" ... . [n. p. 1836.] 8vo, pp. 23, (1). H. 43940

Governor's Message and Documents ... with the Report ... in relation to the Northeastern Boundary. ... [n. p.:] *Todd and Holden, Printers.* 1831. 8vo, pp. 52. BA. 43941

Governor's Speech. [n. p. 1828.] 8vo, pp. 16. Continued.

Address of Governor Washburn to the Legislature of the State of Maine, January 3, 1861. *Augusta: Stevens & Sayward.* 1861. 8vo, pp. 25. + Address ... April 22, 1861. [*Ibid.*] 1861. 8vo, pp. 7. + Address ... January 2, 1862. [*Ibid.*] 1862. 8vo, pp. 30. 43943

These addresses relate chiefly to the Civil War in the South.

Address of Gov. Hamlin to the Legislature ... January 8, 1857. ... *Augusta: Stevens & Blaine, Printers.* 1857. 8vo, pp. 22. H.

Journal of the Constitutional Convention of the District of Maine: with the Articles of Separation and Governor Brooks' Proclamation, prefixed. 1819–20. *Augusta: Fuller & Fuller, Printers.* 1856. 12mo, pp. 112, (1). H. 43945

Journal of the Proceedings. *See* Smith (G. E.)

Lands. Documents showing the Division of the Public Lands, as far as made by the Commissioners under the Act of Separation. [*Portland.* 1822.] 8vo. W. 43946

Remarks on the two Last Reports of the Land Agent, together with some Particulars of his Conduct while in Office; addressed to the Governor, Council and Legislature of the State of Maine. [n. p. n. d.] 8vo, pp. 13, (1). W. 43947

See Honestus, *pseudon*, for a "Vindication," Vol. VIII., No. 32779.

A Reply to the "Vindication" of "the Land Agent," &c. By the Author of the Remarks. [n. p. n. d.] 8vo, pp. 23.

Report of the Commissioners on the Settlement of the Public Lands of Maine. *Augusta: Sprague, Owen & Nash, Printers.* 1870. 8vo, pp. 24. B. 43949

[Report of Committee appointed on a System for the Management of the Lands of this Commonwealth (Massachusetts) in the District of Maine. *Boston.* 1813.] 8vo, pp. 14, folded leaf. Continued. 43950

This is a made-up title.

... Report of the Committee on State Lands, made ... February 13th, 1829. *Portland: Printed by Day & Fraser.* 1829. 8vo, pp. 7. H. 43951

... Report of the Land Agent of Maine ... . [n. p. 1827?] 8vo, pp. 28, 3 folded leaves. Continued. H. 43952

Report on the State of the Land Office, for ... 1825. By James Irish ... . *Portland: A. W. Thayer, Printer.* [n. d.] 8vo, pp. 16. H. 43953

Laws of the State of Maine, passed by the Legislature at its Session ... May ... June, 1820; To which is prefixed, the Constitution of the State. ... *Portland: Printed by Francis Douglas.* 1820. 8vo, pp. xxxvi, 48, (8). BA. 43954

Laws of the State of Maine; To which are prefixed the Constitution of the U. States and of said State. ... Published according to resolves of the State, passed March 8, 1821, and March 30th, 1831. With an Appendix. ... *Brunswick: Printed by J. Griffin, for the State.* 1821–31. 3 vols., 8vo, pp. (2), lxx, 456, Index, xciii, (3); (2), xlii, 457–872, xciii, (3);

Laws ... with the Constitutions of the State and United States. *Portland.* 1822. 8vo. W. 43956

Laws of the State of Maine ... With an Appendix. *Hallowell.* 1830–38. 2 vols., 8vo. 43957

The title to Vol. II. reads: "Laws of the State of Maine from the Separation to 1833 inclusive."

Laws of the State of Maine; with the Constitution ... By Francis O. J. Smith. *Portland.* 1834. 2 vols., 8vo. C. 43958

Laws of Maine in Relation to the Education of Youth. ... *Augusta: William R. Smith & Co., Printers.* 1842. 12mo, pp. 27, (1). B. 43959

Also: Laws relating to the Public Schools in ... Maine. ... *Augusta: Wm. T. Johnson, Printer.* 1848. 8vo, pp. (6), 29. Continued.—Laws of the State of Maine relating to Manufacturing Corporations. *Kennebunk.* 1835. 24mo, pp. 12. M.

List of Government Officers for 1822 and 1826. [n. p. n. d.] 12mo. W. 43960

Minutes of the Forty-Fifth Session of the Maine Annual Conference of the Methodist Episcopal Church, ... May 5–10, 1869 ... . *Boston: James P. Magee.* 1869. 8vo, pp. 35, (1). Continued. B. 43961

First Annual Report of the Secretary of the Maine Board of Agriculture, 1856. Second Edition. ... *Augusta: Stevens & Blaine, Printers.* 1857. 8vo, pp. 135. Continued. BA. 43962

Minutes of the Maine Baptist Convention held ... October 12th and 13th, 1831. *Hallowell: Glazier, Masters & Co.* 1831. 16mo, pp. 21. Continued. H. 43963

The Maine Business Directory, for the Year commencing September 1, 1867. *Boston: Briggs & Co.* 1867. 8vo, pp. 280, 84.

Report of the Directors ... of the Maine Central Railroad Company. ... 1864. *Bangor: Printed by Samuel S. Smith.* 1864. 8vo, pp. 20, (1). Continued. B. 43965

MAINE CHARITABLE MECHANIC ASSOCIATION. First Exhibition and Fair ... held ... in ... Portland ... 1838. *Portland.* 1838. 8vo, pp. 82. Continued. B. 43966

MAINE CHARITY SCHOOL. Law ... . [*Bangor, Me.* n. d.] 12mo, pp. 12. H. 43967

Also: Account of the Maine Charity School. *Bangor.* [n. d.] 8vo. *See also* New Theological Seminary.

Maine Convention of Universalists. Proceedings ... June 25th, 26th and 27th, 1850 ... with the Transactions of the Missionary, Educational and Tract Societies, for ... 1850. ... *Augusta: Homan & Manley, Printers.* 1850. 8vo, pp. 71. H.

Maine Farmers' Almanac. By Daniel Robinson. *Augusta.* 1853. 12mo. 43969

MAINE HISTORICAL SOCIETY. Collections of the Maine Historical Society. Vol. I. *Portland: Printed by Day, Fraser & Co.* 1831. 8vo, pp. (8), viii, 416. Continued to 6 vols. B.

Vol. I. is scarce, as many of the copies were destroyed by fire. The series is important as it contains reprints of many rare books.

Collections of the Maine Historical Society. Second Series. Documentary History of the State of Maine. Edited by William Willis. Vol. I. Containing a History of the Discovery of Maine. By J. G. Kohl. With an Appendix on the Voyages of the Cabots, by M. d'Avezac, of Paris. ... *Portland: Bailey and Noyes.* 1869. 8vo, pp. (4), viii, (2), 9–535. 22 colored Maps.

Also: Report of the Joint Standing Committee on the Library, on the Memorial of the Maine Historical Society, March, 1856. [n. p.] 1856. 8vo, pp. 4.

First Annual Report of the Directors of the Maine Insane Hospital, ... 1840. *Augusta: Severance & Dorr, Printers.* 1841. 8vo, pp. 37, (1). Continued. B. 43972

... Report of the Trustees ... November 30, 1843. [n. p.:] *Wm. R. Smith & Co., Printers.* [n. d.] 8vo, pp. 38, (1). H.

Also: ... Reports of the Trustees, Steward and Treasurer, and Superintendent of the Insane Hospital, 1844. *Augusta: Wm. T. Johnson, Printer.* 1844. 8vo, pp. (2), 7, 47. Continued. H.

... The Maine Journal of Education. ... *Portland, Me.* 1867. 8vo. H. 43974

The Maine Law in New-York! Address of the Executive Committee of the New-York State Temperance Society. [n. p. n. d.] 8vo, pp. 15. B. 43975

The Maine Law in the Balance ... . By a Citizen of Maine. ... *Portland, Me.: Merrill and Whitman.* [1855.] 8vo, pp. 56.

... The Maine Law: its Constitutionality ... Operation and ... Acceptance. Also, Temperance Organization ... in Massachusetts ... . *Boston: George C. Rand.* 1851. 8vo, pp. 18, (1).

Also: ... Documentary History of the Maine Law ... . *New-York: Hall & Brother.* 1855. 8vo, pp. 128.

Maine Liquor Law. Documents relating to its Principles, Operation, etc. *Boston.* 1851. 8vo. 43978

Maine Legislative Manual, 1866. ... *Augusta: Stevens & Sayward, Printers.* 1866. 12mo, pp. iv, 4, 239. Continued.

The Maine Liquor Law. An Act for the Suppression of Drinking-Houses and Tippling-Shops. [*New York: Fowlers and Wells.* 1851.] 16mo, pp. 8. BA. 43980

Also: The Maine Liquor Law; with the Opinions of Prof. Stuart and L. M. Sargent. *New York.* 1851. 8vo. *See* Pitman (J. S.)

MAINE MEDICAL ASSOCIATION. Constitution, By-Laws, and Code of Medical Ethics of the Maine Medical Association. *Portland: Stephen Berry, Printer.* 1870. 8vo, pp. 29. B. 43981

Transactions of the Maine Medical Association, for ... 1866, 1867 and 1868. ... *Portland: Stephen Berry, Printer.* 1869. 8vo, pp. vi, 324. Continued. B. 43982

Also: Records of the Eleventh Annual Meeting of the Maine Medical Association, ... June 10, 1863. *Portland: Stephen Berry, Printer.* 1863. 8vo, pp. 33, (2). Cont'd.

Maine Medical School. *See* Bowdoin College.

MAINE MISSIONARY SOCIETY. Report of the Trustees ... at their Twentieth Annual Meeting ... 1827. *Portland.* 1827. 8vo, pp. 35, (1). Continued. H. 43983

... The Maine Normal ... . Volume I. Number I. ... December, 1866. *Farmington: J. Weston Swift & Co.* [n. d.] 8vo, pp. 46. Continued. H. 43984

The Maine Register, and United States' Calendar, for ... 1822: ... By William B. Sewall, Esq. *Portland: A. Shirley & T. Todd.* [n. d.] 12mo, pp. 142, (2). BA. 43985

Continued as: "The Maine Register and National Calendar, for ... 1841." ... *Augusta: Daniel C. Stanwood.* [n. d.] 24mo, pp. (2), 248, afterwards as: "The Maine Register, and State Reference Book. 1852." *Hallowell: Masters, Smith & Company.* 1852. 12mo, pp. 252, and finally continued as: "The Maine Register" ... . [*Boston:*] *G. Adams.* 1855. 8vo, pp. 432.

The Maine Teacher ... . 1859. *Portland.* [n. d.] 8vo. Continued. 43986

MAINE STATE LIBRARY. Catalogue of the Maine State Library, 1850. Arranged and prepared by Abner Oakes, Assistant Librarian ... . *Augusta.* 1850. 8vo, pp. 248. + With Appendix, 1854. *Augusta: W. T. Johnson.* 1854. 8vo, pp. 248, 47. C. + 1856. *Augusta.* 1856. 8vo, pp. 439. + 1862. By George G. Stacy, Librarian. *Augusta: Stevens & Layward, Printers.* 1862. 8vo, pp. 304. 43987

Also: ... Annual Report of the Librarian of the Maine State Library ... . *Augusta: Sprague, Owen & Nash, Printers.* 1870. 8vo, pp. 41. Continued. B.

Maine State Political Manual ... for ... 1870. Compiled by Edmund S. Hoyt. ... *Portland: Hoyt, Fogg & Breed.* [n. d.] 24mo, pp. 369. Map. H. 43988

MAINE STATE SEMINARY. Catalogue ... . 1857. *Lewiston.* 1857. 8vo, pp. 22. Continued. H. 43989

Maine Union in behalf of the Colored Race. Proceedings of Convention. *Portland.* 1835. 8vo. C. 43990

MAINE WESLEYAN SEMINARY. A Catalogue ... 1829. [*Hallowell.* n. d.] 8vo, pp. 11. Continued. H. 43991

Masonry. First Communication of the Grand Lodge of the State of Maine. 1820. [n. p. n. d.] Folio, pp. 7. Cont'd.

Also: Grand Lodge ... of ... Maine. ... *Portland: Printed by Arthur Shirley.* 1824. 4to, pp. 16. Continued.—Memorial of the Maine Grand Lodge. Signed W. Lord. [n. p.] 1820. Folio, pp. 7.—Proceedings of the Grand Lodge of the State of Maine, Portland, May 3, 1848. *Portland.* 1848. 8vo, pp. 38. M.—Quarterly and Annual

Communications of the Grand Lodge of the State of Maine, 1822–23. *Portland.* 1823. 4to, pp. 13.—Report of the Committee on Foreign Correspondence to the Grand Lodge of Maine, presented May 2, 1856. By Cyrus Pearl. [n. p. n. d.] 8vo, pp. 27.

Grand Royal Arch Chapter of Maine ... . *Portland: Printed by Arthur Shirley.* 1821. 12mo, pp. 10. Continued. H. 43993

... Memorial of the Trustees of the Mariners' Church for relief ... . *Portland: J. and W. E. Edwards, Printers.* 1829. 8vo, pp. 19. H. 43994

Message of the Governor of the State ... June 2, 1820. [n. p. n. d.] 8vo, pp. 7. Continued. H. 43995

Message of Gov. Kent, with Documents relating to the North Eastern Boundary of the State. [n. p. n. d.] 8vo. 43996

Military. Act to Organize, Govern, and Discipline the Militia ... . Passed ... 1821. ... *Portland: Printed by Thomas Todd & Co.* 1821. 12mo, pp. 82. H. 43997

Annual Report of the Adjutant General of the State of Maine, for ... 1834. [n. p.: *I. Berry & Co.* n. d.] 8vo, pp. 24, folded leaf, 8. + For ... 1861. ... *Augusta: Stevens & Sayward, Printers.* 1862. 8vo, pp. 633, (3), 191, (1), 64. + For ... 1862. [*Ibid.*] 1863. 8vo, pp. 164, and Appendix. + For ... 1863. [*Ibid.*] 1864. 8vo, pp. 947, and Appendix. Continued. 43998

Report of the Military Committee, Feb. 24, 1831. [n. p. n. d.] 12mo. 43999

Minutes of the General Conference at their Annual Meeting, ... 1828. *Portland: Shirley and Hyde.* 1828. 8vo, pp. 24. Continued. H. 44000

Minutes of the General Conference of the Congregational Churches in Maine, at their Thirty-Ninth Annual Meeting, ... 1865. *Portland: Printed by Brown Thurston.* 1865. 8vo, pp. 87. Continued. B. 44001

Private or Special Laws of the State of Maine, from 1820 to 1828 inclusive. Vol. I. *Portland.* 1828. 8vo. + From 1829 to 1835 ... . Vol. II. ... *Portland: Printed by Ira Berry and Company.* 1835. 8vo, pp. (22), 5–934, (55). BA. 44002

Private and Special Acts of ... Maine, passed by the Thirteenth Legislature ... . *Augusta: I. Berry & Co., Printers.* 1833. 8vo, pp. (5), 454–587, (13). Continued. B. 44003

Proceedings of the Convention. *See our* Vol. III., No. 8766.

Proceedings of the State Convention at Hallowell, Jan. 3, 4. *Hallowell.* 1834. 8vo. 44004

PROTESTANT EPISCOPAL CHURCH. Journal of the Thirty-First Annual Convention in the Diocese of Maine, Portland, July 10 and 11, 1850. *Augusta.* 1850. 8vo. 44005

Provisional Report upon the Water Power of Maine, By Walter Wells ... . *Augusta: Stevens & Sayward, Printers.* 1868. 8vo, pp. 327. Map. H. 44006

Register of the Executive and Legislative Departments of the Government of Maine. 1859. ... *Augusta.* 1859. 8vo, pp. 8.

Register of the House of Representatives of ... Maine, for ... 1865. *Augusta.* 1865. 8vo. 44008

Register of the Senate of Maine for ... 1867 ... . *Augusta: Stevens & Sayward, Printers.* 1867. 8vo, pp. 24. Plan. H.

Report and Resolves of the Legislature of ... Maine respecting International Literary Exchanges ... . *Augusta: Wm. T. Johnson, Printer.* 1847. 8vo, pp. 109. B., N. 44010

Report and Resolves relating to Divorces. 1844. [n. p. 1844.] 8vo, pp. 8. 44011

Report as to Mutual Fire and Marine Insurance Companies ... in ... Maine. ... *Augusta: William T. Johnson, Printer.* 1850. 8vo, pp. 33. H. 44012

Report of Charles S. Davies, Esq. Agent, ... to inquire into and report upon certain facts relating to aggressions upon the rights of the State, and of individual citizens thereof, by inhabitants of the Province of New-Brunswick. ... *Portland: Thomas Todd, Printer.* 1828. 8vo, pp. 35, (2). B. 44013

Report of the Commissioners appointed to settle the Line between New Hampshire and Maine, Nov. 1828. *Concord.* 1828. 8vo, pp. 18. 44014

Report of the Commissioners of the Hydrographic Survey of the State of Maine. 1867. *Augusta: Owen & Nash, Printers.* 1868. 8vo, pp. (4), 327. 2 Plans. BA. 44015

Report of the Commissioners ... May 26, 1842, "in relation to the North-Eastern Boundary of this State." *Augusta: W. R. Smith & Co., Printers.* 1843. 8vo, pp. 88. 44016

Report of the Commissioners on Equalization of the Municipal War Debts. *Augusta: Sprague, Owen & Nash, Printers.* 1870. 8vo, pp. 29. B. 44017

Report of the Committee appointed to Contract for State Printing. *Portland.* 1829. 8vo. W. 44018

... Report of the Committee on the North-Eastern Boundary. [n. p.:] *Severance & Dorr, Printers.* [1841.] 8vo, pp. 88. 2 Maps. H. 44019

... Report of the Committee of Elections, and Statement ... in the Case of Andrew Roberts ... . *Portland: Day & Fraser, Printers.* 1830. 8vo, pp. 10. H. 44020

Report of the Committee of the Legislature ... [on] the Kennebec and Portland Railroad. [n. p.:] *Wm. T. Johnson, Printer.* [1850?] 8vo, pp. 22. H. 44021

[Report of] the Committee ... [on] opening a Road from the ... Kennebec River to the British Provinces of Canada ... . 1827. [n. p. n. d.] 8vo, pp. 13. H. 44022

Report of the Joint Select Committee of the Senate and House of Representatives of ... Maine, in relation to the North-Eastern Boundary of the State. ... *Portland: Thomas Todd, Printer.* 1828. 8vo, pp. 62, Appendix, 56. B., BA. 44023

Jan. Sess., 1828. Doc. No. 13.

Report of the Joint Select Committee of the Legislature ... on ... the North-Eastern Boundary. *Augusta: I. Berry & Co., Printers.* 1832. 12mo, pp. 8. H. 44024

Report of the Joint Select Committee on the Infraction of the Treaty of Washington, March, 1845. [n. p.] 1845. 8vo, pp. 20

Report of the Joint Select Committee, on the Defalcation of Benj. D. Peck, Late Treasurer of ... Maine. *Augusta: Stevens & Sayward, Printers.* 1860. 8vo, pp. 66, (2). H. 44026

Also: Peck Defalcation—The Canada Company. Statement of the Canada Company. [*Augusta.* 1860.] 8vo, pp. 16.

[Report of] the Joint Standing Committee on Claims, to which was referred the Petition of Edward Russell ... . 1831. [n. p. n. d.] 8vo, pp. 15. H. 44027

Annual Report of the Warden of the State Prison; for ... 1826. [*Portland.* 1826?] 8vo, pp. 7, (1), folded leaf. Cont'd.

Also: ... [Report of] the Committee on the Judiciary to whom was referred the Message of the Governor ... with the Report of the Attorney General on the ... State Prison ... . February 24th, 1829. [n. p. n. d.] 8vo, pp. 15.—Reports of the Warden and Inspectors of the Maine State Prison, and of the Physician and Chaplain. *Augusta.* 1859. 8vo, pp. 35.

Report on ... the Governor's Speech relating to the Tariff, and on the Remonstrance and Resolutions of ... Georgia ... . *Portland: Printed by Day & Fraser.* 1829. 8vo, pp. 6. H. 44029

Reports and Negotiations on the North-Eastern Boundary of the State. *London.* 1831–40. 7 vols., folio. A. 44030

Made-up title to a collection of English Parliamentary reports in the Astor library.

Reports of Decisions in the Circuit Courts Martial ... . By Francis O. J. Smith ... . *Portland: Printed by Todd and Holden.* 1831. 8vo, pp. (2), 113. B. 44031

Reports of the Commissioners of Fisheries of ... Maine, for ... 1867 and 1868. *Augusta: Owen & Nash, Printers.* 1869. 8vo, pp 96, 43, (1). Continued. B. 44032

Resolutions of the Legislature of the State of Maine respecting the Advice of the King of the Netherlands on the North-Eastern Boundary. *Portland.* 1832. 8vo. C. 44033

Resolves of the Legislature of the State of Maine, passed ... May–June, 1820. *Portland.* 1820. 8vo, pp. 43. Continued.

Resolves of the Eighth Legislature of ... Maine ... . *Portland: Printed by Thomas Todd.* 1828. 8vo, pp. (5), 614–826. Cont'd.

Resolves of the State of Maine, from 1820 to 1828 inclusive. Volume I. ... *Portland: Printed by Thomas Todd.* 1828. 8vo.

... Returns made by the Trustees of ... Literary Institutions ... *Portland: J. and W. E. Edwards.* 1829. 8vo, pp. 16.

A Review of the Constitution of Maine. By an Elector. [n. p.] 1830. 8vo. S. 44038

The Revised Statutes of the State of Maine, passed October 22, 1840; to which are prefixed the Constitutions of the United States and of ... Maine, ... to which are subjoined the other Public Laws of 1840 and 1841, with an Appendix. ... *Augusta: William R. Smith & Co.* 1841. 8vo, pp. xv, (1), 896. B. + Second Edition. ... *Hallowell: Glazier, Masters & Smith.* 1847. 8vo, pp. xvi, 896. + Revised Statutes ... passed April 17, 1857. *Bangor.* 1857. 8vo. C. 44039

The Rights of Maine defended. Speech of Mr. Clay ... on the Boundary. [n. p. n. d.] 8vo, pp. 8. H. 44040

Omitted in our list of Henry Clay's works.

Rules and Orders to be observed in the House of Representatives ... . *Portland: Printed by Francis Douglas.* 1820. 12mo, pp. 24. Continued. H. 44041

Rules of the Supreme Judicial Court ... . *Portland: Printed ... by Thomas B. Wait, and Co.* 1806. 8vo, pp. 31. H. 44042

The Seventeenth Jewel. *See* Gorges (F.), Vol. VII. 28021.

Speech to the Legislature of Maine, Jan. 4, 1827. [By Enoch Lincoln. n. p. n. d.] 8vo. 44043

Proceedings and Speeches of the State Temperance Convention, held at Augusta, Me. January 21 and 22, 1852 ... . [n. p. n. d.] 8vo, pp. 16. H. 44044

To the People of Maine. [n. p. n. d.] 8vo, pp. 8. 44045

Proceedings of the Brunswick Convention on the Separation of this District from Massachusetts.

Statement on the Part of the United States of the case referred in pursuance of the Convention of the 29th Sept. 1827, between the said States and Great Britain to his Majesty the King of the Netherlands, for his Decision; with the First and Second Statements on the Part of Great Britain in relation to the same Subject. *Washington.* 1829. Folio. 44046

Relates to the settlement of the north-eastern boundary.

Tax for ... 1821. ... [n. p. n. d.] 8vo, pp. 12. Continued.

Letter from the Treasurer ... transmitting his Annual Report on the ... Finances ... December 31, 1822. *Portland: Printed by Todd & Smith.* 1823. 8vo, pp. 40. Continued. H. 44048

Annual Report of the State Treasurer for 1822. *Portland.* 1823. 8vo. Continued. 44049

Unitarian Church Association of Maine. Report of the First Annual Meeting, ... 1853. *Bangor: Samuel S. Smith, Printer.* 1853. 8vo, pp. 48. Continued. B. 44050

Also: Report of Convention, 1852 ... . *Bangor.* 1853. 8vo.

Valuation Lists of the State of Maine, including the Number of Polls, ... for the years 1850 and 1860. ... *Augusta.* 1860. 8vo, pp. 15. 44051

The Water-Power of Maine. Reports of the Commissioners and Secretary of the Hydrographic Survey of 1867. ... *Augusta: Owen & Nash, Printers.* 1868. 8vo, pp. (4), 30, (2), 327. Plan.

The Water Power of Maine, By Walter Wells ... . *Augusta: Sprague, Owen & Nash, Printers.* 1869. 8vo, pp. vii, (1), 526. Map and Plates. 44053

Western State Normal School, at Farmington, Me. Catalogue ... 1868–9. *Augusta: Sprague, Owen & Nash, Printers.* 1869. 8vo, pp. 16. H. 44054

MAINWARING [*and others*]. The Case of Mainwaring, Hawes, Payne, and others, concerning a Depredation made by the Spanish West India Fleete upon the Ship Elizabeth, going on a Trading Voyage to Virginia. [n. p.:] *Printed Anno* 1646. 4to.

MAIOLI (S.) Simonis Maioli Astensis Episcopi Vultvrarien Dies Canicvlares seu Colloquia Tria, & Viginti, Quibus pleraque naturæ admiranda, quæ aut in æthere fiunt, aut in Europa, Asia, atque Africa, quin etiam in ipso Orbe Nouo, & apud omnes Antipodas sunt, recensentur, ordine, quem sequens pagina indicabit. Svperiorvm permissv. *Romæ, Ex officina Ioan: Angeli Ruffinelli. Typis Zannetti.* M.D.XCVII. 4to, pp. (16), 1177, Errata and Colophon, pp. 3. + *Moguntiae.* 1614. Folio. + *Francoforti.* 1642. Folio. + *Moguntiae.* 1667. 4to. 44056

Contains many interesting notices relating to the New World.

MAIRE (J. le). *See* [Colijn (M.)], Vol. IV., Nos. 14348 and 14351, Herrera (A. de), Schouten (C.), Spilbergen (G.), *and* consult Tiele's "Mémoire Bibliographique," pp. 40–63.

MAIRE. Iournal & Miroir | de la | Navigation | Avstrale | Du vaillant & bien renommé Seigneur | Iaqves le Maire, | Chef & Conducteur de deux Navires | Concorde & Horne. [n. p. n. d.] Folio, pp. (4), 107–174. Plates and Maps. 44057

The maps and plates are from the Dutch edition. This is, in fact, part of our No. 31540, but having a separate title-page is sometimes found alone.

MAIRE. Relacion diaria del viage de Jacobo le Mayre y Guillelmo Cornelio Schouten, en que descubrieron nuevo estrecho y passage del mar del norte al mar del sur, a la parte austral del estrecho de Magellanes. *Madrid.* 1619. Sm. 4to. 44058

"The circumnavigation of Schouten and Le Maire was published in this year in English, French, Latin, etc.; but of all the versions, this in Spanish is, beyond a doubt, the rarest. I have never seen or heard of another copy. There is a reference to maps which were not in the book, but have been supplied from the French edition."—RICH, No. 149. *See also* Ternaux, No. 409.

MAIRE. Spieghel | der | Australische | Navigatie, | Door den | Wijt vermaerden ende cloeck- | moedighen Zee Heldt, | Iacob le Maire, | President ende Overste over de twee Schepen, d'Eendracht | ende Hoorn, uytghevaren den 14 Iunij 1615. | *t'Amsterdam,* | *By Michiel Colijn, Boeck-vercooper op 't Water* | *by de Oude Brugh, in 't Huys-Boeck.* | *Anno* 1622. | Folio, pp. (16), 98. Maps and Plates. 44059

Several errors in the pagination, *see* Tiele, p. 57. Portrait of Le Maire on the verso of the title-page.

[MAIROBERT (M. F. P. de).] *See* [Pidanzat de Mairobert].

MAIS (C.) The Surprising Case of Rachel Baker, who Prays and Preaches in her Sleep, Answers Questions during her Unconscious State. By Charles Mais. *New York.* 1814. 8vo, pp. 34. + Second Edition. [*Ibid.*] + *Baltimore.* 1815. 8vo.

MAISCH (J. M.) Report on Legislation regulating the Practice of Pharmacy in the United States. ... Sept. 10, 1868, By John M. Maisch ... . *Philadelphia: Merrihew & Son, Printers.* 1868. 8vo, pp. 48. H. 44061

MAISON (Hypolite). Précis historique sur la colonie française au Goazacoalcos (Mexique) ... . *Londres: Davidson & fils.* 1831. 12mo, pp. 260. 44062

MAISON (——). Speech of Mr. Maison, ... on the Power of Expulsion. [n. p. n. d.] 8vo. 44063

MAITIN (José A.) Obras poéticas. *Carâcas.* 1851. 8vo, pp. xviii, 163. Portrait. 44064

With a life of the poet, written by Simon Camacho.

MAIZ (C.) Juicio Imparcial que sirve de Respuesta al Papel de Da Carmen Maiz publicado hoy sobre el Asesinalo que proyecto su Marido D. Jose Moreno. *Lima.* 1835. 8vo. 44065

MAJOR (E.) A Serious Word to the Present and Succeeding Generation in New England. By Eleazer Major. *Cambridge, N. E.* 1671. 4to. 44066

[MAJOR (J. D.)] ... Vorstellung etlicher | Kunst- und Natura- | lien-kammern | in America und Asia. ... *Kiel: Gedruckt durch Joachim Reuman.* [1674.] Folio, pp. (24). H. 44067

MAJOR (J. R.) Bibliography of the First Letter of Columbus, describing his Discovery of the New World. By J. R. Major. *London.* 1872. 8vo. 44068

Seventy-five copies only privately printed. *See also* Colombo (C.)

MAJOR (R. H.) The Life of Prince Henry of Portugal, surnamed the Navigator; and its Results: Comprising the Discovery, within one Century, of Half the World. With New Facts in the Discovery of the Atlantic Islands; a Refutation of French Claims to Priority in Discovery; Portuguese Knowledge (subsequently lost) of the Nile Lakes; and the History of the Naming of America. From Authentic Cotemporary Documents. By Richard Henry Major ... . *London: A. Asher & Co.* 1868. 8vo, pp. (4), lii, 487. 11 Maps and Plates. C. 44069

Seventy copies printed on large paper, rl. 8vo. "'The Life of Prince Henry' is a piece of good work, full of new matter, and of high mark in European letters."—*Athenæum.* "Ein Klassisches Geschichtswerk."—DR. PESCHEL, in "Das Ausland."

MAJOR. Memoir on a Mappemonde by Leonardo da Vinci, being the earliest Map hitherto known containing the Name of America; now in the Royal Collection at Windsor. Communicated to the Society of Antiquaries by Richard Henry Major, Esq. ... *London: Printed by J. B. Nichols and Sons* ... 1865. 4to, pp. (1), 40. 2 Plates. 44070

From the "Archæologia," Vol. XL.

MAJOR. The True Date of the English Discovery of the American Continent under John and Sebastian Cabot. Communicated by Richard Henry Major. *London.* 1870. 4to, pp. 26.

Major and Brigadier Generals who are without Commands equal to a Brigade; also the number of Major and Brigadier Generals who are in Command of Departments and Posts in the Loyal States. Report of the Secretary of War. [*Washington.* 1863.] 8vo, pp. 6. 44072

38th Congress, 1st Session, 1863, Senate Exec. Doc., No. 5.

Majority and Minority Reports of the Board of Officers appointed under the Act approved July 15, 1862, entitled "An Act to authorize the Secretary of the Navy to accept League Island, in the Delaware River, for Naval Purposes." [*Washington.* 1862.] 8vo, pp. 29. 44073

38th Congress 3d Session, 1862, Senate Exec. Doc., No. 9. Also: Majority and Minority Reports of the Board of Officers appointed ... to Examine proposed Sites for a Navy Yard. *Washington.* 1862. 8vo.—Majority and Minority Reports of Naval Committee of ... House of Representatives, 1864. *Washington.* 1864. 8vo. *See also* Lincoln (A.) Vol. X., No. 41210.

The Majority and Minority Reports of the Committee of the Methodist Episcopal Church, on Slavery, May, 1860. *Buffalo.* 1860. 8vo, pp. 24. 44074

Majority Report of the Committee on Foreign Affairs on the True Policy of the War, and the Navigation of the Mississippi. [n. p. n. d.] 8vo, pp. 3. + [Another Edition. n. p. n. d.]

MAJOR (Johann Daniel). See-Farth nach der Neuen Welt, ohne Schiff- und Segel; Anno 1670, zuerst, und nu wiederumb der gelehrten Welt vorgestellet. *Hamburg: G. Wolf.* 1683. 18mo, pp. (22), 258, (6). Plate. C. 44076

MA-KA-TAI-ME-SHE-KIA-KIAK. *See* Black Hawk, Vol. II., No. 5675, [Leclair (A.)], Vol. X., No. 39646, *and* [Smith (E. H.)]

MAKEMIE (F.) An Answer to George Keith's Libel. Against a Catechism Published by Francis Makemie. To which is added, by way of a Postscript. A Brief Narrative of a Late Difference among the Quakers, begun at Philadelphia. *Boston: Printed by Benjamin Harris.* MDCXCIIII. 18mo, pp. (12), 103.

The Address to the "Christian Reader" is signed "Increase Mather, James Allen, Samuel Willard, John Baily, and Cotton Mather." Makemie's "Catechism has escaped the researches of American collectors." *See* Webster's "Presbyterian Church in America," p. 310.

MAKEMIE. A Good Conversation. A Sermon preached at the City of New York, January 19, 1706–7. *Boston: B. Green, for B. Eliot.* 1707. 16mo, pp. (4), 36. C. 44078

For preaching this sermon the author was imprisoned, and the following work appeared in reference to said imprisonment:

MAKEMIE. A | Narrative | Of a New and Unusual | American Imprisonment | Of Two | Presbyterian Ministers: | And Prosecution of | Mr. Francis Makemie | One of them, for Preaching one Ser- | mon at the City of New-York. | By a Learner of Law, and Lover of Liberty. | [*Boston:*] *Printed for the Publisher.* 1707. | 4to, pp. (4), 47. B. 44079

Reprinted with the following title:

MAKEMIE. A | Narrative | Of a New and Unusual | American Imprisonment, of | Two Presbyterian Ministers, and | Prosecution | of | Mr. Francis Makemie | One of Them, | For Preaching One Sermon in the City of | New-York. | By a Learner of Law, and Lover of Liberty. | *New-York: Re-printed and Sold by H. Gaine,* ... 1755. 4to, pp. (12), 52. P., W. 44080

Edited by the author of the "Watch Tower;" with an Epistle Dedicatory. The arrest took place 1706–7 for a violation of the laws, and was now reprinted to serve a political end and to influence the public mind. It is also reprinted in Force's "Tracts," Vol. IV., No. 4.

[MAKEMIE.] A Plain and Friendly Perswasive [*sic*] to the Inhabitants of Virginia and Maryland, for promoting Towns and Cohabitation. By a Well-wisher to both Governments. *London: Printed by John Humfreys.* 1705. 4to, pp. 16. H. 44081

See Webster's "Presbyterian Church in America," p. 301.

MAKEMIE. Truths in a True Light, or a Pastoral Letter to the Reformed Protestants in Barbados. By Francis Makemie. *Edinburgh.* 1699. 16mo. W. 44082

A very rare piece. Makemie also published about 1707, "Forget and Forgive," a Jersey paper, for which Lord Cornbury persecuted him, unjustly perhaps. "The Jersey Paper" of February, 1707, remarks "Colonel Morris and Jennings, with two or three others, had been very hard at work in hatching the most scandalous paper I ever saw in my life." It abused Lord Cornbury, and was widely dispersed.

MAKENZIE (H.) An Answer [etc.] *See* Mackenzie (H.)

MAKEPEACE (W.) The Genealogy of the Makepeace Families in the United States. From 1637 to 1857. By William Makepeace ... . *Boston: David Clapp.* 1858. 12mo, pp. 107.

Making Money by selling Rum. *Boston.* 1834. 12mo, pp. 8.

MAKO [von Keren-Gede (P.)] Descriptio Provinciæ Moxitarum in Regno Peruano, Quam e scriptis posthumis Franc. Xav. Eder ... digessit ... Mako. *Budæ: Typis Universitatis.* 1791. 8vo, pp. xviii, 383. Maps and Plates. BA. 44085

MALABAR. ... An Account of the Success of Two Danish Missionaries, ... with ... the Printer's Voyage to Brazil ... . *London.* 1718. 8vo. Map. 44086

MALACHI, 1717. *See* [Mather (Cotton).]

MALAGUETA. Carta ao redactor da Malagueta. [*Rio de Janeiro:*] *Imprensa Nacional.* [1822?] 8vo, pp. 24. 44087

[MALAN (*Rev.* Cæsar Henri Abraham).] The Swiss Peasant. [In Cherokee:] Asuwisi ageyo. [With] The One Thing Needful. Sudalegi udulvdiyu. *Park Hill: Mission Press.* 1848. 24mo, pp. 24. C. 44088

MALAPART (*Le Sieur*). La prise d'vn | Seigneur ecossois | et de ses gens qui pilloient | les Nauires pescheurs de France | ensemble du Razement de leur Fort, & l'establissement d'un autre pour le service du Roy, & l'assurance | des Pescheurs François en la Nouuelle France | Par Monsieur Daniel de Dieppe, Capitaine pour le Roy en la Marine, & General de | la Flotte en la Nouuelle

France. | Dedié à Monsieur le President de Lauzon, Intendant | de la Compagnie dudit Païs. | Par le Sieur Malapart Parisien, soldat dudit Sieur Daniel. | *A Rouen, chez Jean de Bovllenger, rue* | *des PP. Jesuites.* | M.D.C.XXX. | *Auec permission.* | 12mo, pp. (2), 22

MALASPINA (A.) Tablas de latitudes y longitudes de los principales puntos del Rio de la Plata, ... por D. Alejandro Malaspina ... . *Buenos Aires.* 1837. Folio, pp. vi, 10. 44090

[MALASPINA (M.)] Bacco in America. Componimento Ditirambico in Lode della Cioccolata. Colle Note fatte al Medesimo da G. Bianchini. [n. p. 1775?] 4to, pp. viii, 42, 2.

[MALCOLME (David).] A Collection of Letters, in which the Imperfection of Learning ... and a Remedy for it, are hinted ... The Affinity betwixt the Language of the Americans of the Terra Firma, and of the Ancient Britains, is proved. ... *Edinburgh: Printed in the Year* MDCCXXXIX. 8vo, pp. (2), 32, 8, 16, 8, 24, 32. H., P. 44092

Written partly in reply to a Mr. Innes.

[MALCOLME.] An Essay on the Antiquities of Great Britain and Ireland: Wherein they are Placed in a clearer Light than hitherto. Designed as an Introduction to a large Work, especially an Attempt to show an Affinity betwixt the Languages, &c. of the Ancient Britains, and the Americans of the Isthmus of Darien. In Answer to an Objection against Revealed Religion. ... *Edinburgh: Printed by T. and W. Ruddimans,* ... MDCCXXXVIII. 8vo, pp. 8, 16, 24, 32, 32, 48, 32, 8, 8, 8, 8, 8, 8, 8, 8. P.

"The first work which appeared in Scotland on the subject of the Celtic language."—PINKERTON.

MALCOLME. ... Letters, Essays, and other Tracts, illustrating the Antiquities of Great Britain and Ireland; together with many Curious Discoveries of the Affinity betwixt the Language of the Americans and the Ancient Britains to the Greek and Latin, &c. Also Specimens of the Celtic, Welsh, Irish, Saxon, and American Languages. By D. Malcolme. *London.* 1744. 8vo.

Probably the same work with a new title-page.

[MALCOM (Howard).] A Brief Memoir of ... Mrs. Lydia M. Malcom. Of Boston, Mass. *Boston.* 183–. 12mo. + Reprinted, with Additions ... . *Boston: John Putnam.* 1833. 12mo, pp. 52. B. + Fourth Edition. *Boston: W. D. Ticknor.* 1835. 16mo, pp. (2), 122. C. 44095

MALCOM. Signs of the Times favorable to Peace. An Address before the American Peace Society, ... May 26, 1862. By Howard Malcom, D.D. ... *Boston: American Peace Society.* 1862. 8vo, pp. 69–80. B. 44096

Also: ... A Discourse ... before the Boston Baptist Association, ... Sept. 19, 1832. .. *Boston: Allen and Ticknor.* 1833. 8vo, pp. 70. B.—Memoir of Mary Lothrop, who died in Boston, 18 March, 1831 ... . *Boston.* 1832. 18mo, pp. 103.

MALDEN, *Mass.* Annual Report of the Finances ... from March 1, 1860, to ... 1861 ... . *Boston: Printed by Charles C. P. Moody.* 1861. 8vo, pp. 48, 76, vi. H. 44097

Articles drawn up by the Members of the Church in Malden On a Day of Public Fasting and Prayer [December 21, 1727]. Occasioned by a Terrible Earthquake, on Lord's Day-Night, October 29th, 1727. [*Boston.* n. d.] 4to, pp. 4. 44098

Articles of Association of the Edgeworth Association ... . *Boston: George C. Rand & Co., Printers.* 1848. 12mo, pp. 14.

The Bi-Centennial Book. *See* [McClure (A. W.)], No. 43060, *see also* Green (J. D.), Vol. VII., No. 28528.

Malden Bridge to the People. *Boston.* 1829. 8vo, pp. 20.

Also: Rules and Regulations of the Corporation of Malden Bridge, ... July, 1808. *Charlestown: Printed by Samuel Etheridge.* 1808. 16mo, pp. 9.—Subscribers to Malden-Bridge. [*Boston: Printed by S. Hall.* 1787.] 32mo, pp. 13. BA.

Oration, Poem, Speeches, &c., at the Dedication of the Malden Town Hall, ... October 29th, 1857. *Malden: Charles C. P. Moody.* 1857. 8vo, pp. 52. H., S. 44101

Report of the School Committee ... for 1857–58. *Boston: Printed by T. W. Ripley & Co.* 1858. 8vo, pp. 23. H. 44102

See Woodlawn Cemetery.

MALDONADO (A.) Chronica Vniuersal de todas Las Naciones y Tiempos compuesta por Fray Alonso Maldonado ... . *En Madrid por Luys Sanchez ... Ano* M.DC.XXIIII. Folio, pp. (4), 218. B.

MALDONADO. Sueño intitulado Felipe el Grande en Jerusalen, en carta al Rey nuestro Señor. *Lima.* 1646. 4to. 44104

"This very rare book has escaped the notice of Nicholas Antonio."—SALVA. It is introduced here as an early Peruvian imprint.

MALDONADO (F. N.) Propuesto al Congreso para que todos los empleados publicos sirvan sus destinos sin disfrutar sueldo alguno. Por Fernando Nicolas Maldonado, Gobernador del Estado de Chiapas. *S. Cristobal Las Casas.* 1851. 4to, pp. 8.

MALDONADO (F. P.) Memoria justa del heroismo, que en el sitio de Gerona manifesto F. P. Maldonado, origin. de Mérida de Yucatan. *Mexico.* 1810. 4to, pp. (6), 66. 44106

MALDONADO (J. V. P.) No dia natalicio do muito alto e muito poderoso senhor D. Pedro IV, imperador do Brasil e rei de Portugal. Ode. Por João Vicente Pimentel Maldonado. *Lisboa: Na Imp. Regia.* 1826. Folio, pp. 4. 44107

MALDONADO (Lorenzo Ferrer). Imagen del Mundo sobre la Espera Geografia, Arte de Navigar, ... dirigido al Don Juan de la Serna, Arcobispo de Mexico. *Alcala.* 1626. Sm. 4to. Maps.

A very rare book by the famous Spanish navigator, whose pretended voyage in the Arctic regions in 1588, has excited so much controversy.

MALDONADO. Viaggio dal Mare Atlantico al Pacifico per la via del Nord-Ovest fatto dal Capitano Lorenzo Ferrer Maldonado l'Anno MDLXXXVIII. Tradotto da una Manoscritto Spagnuolo inedito da Carlo Amoretti ... . *Milano: Dalla Tipografia di Giovanni Silvestri.* MDCCCXI. 4to. Maps. B. 44109

There are those who still believe in the genuineness of this spurious voyage of Maldonado in 1588, from the Atlantic to the Pacific, and it is not impossible that Parliament may again be asked to subsidize with £20,000 or more a British ship, as it has done not very long ago, to re-find the passage.

MALDONADO. Viaggio dal Mare Atlantico al Pacifico ... tradotta da una Manoscritto Spagnuolo inedito della Bibliotheca Ambrosiana di Milano dal Sig. Cavaliere C. Amoretti ... *Bologna: Masi & Ca.* 1812. 4to, pp. (4), 96. 2 Maps. C. 44110

MALDONADO. Voyage de la Mer Atlantique à l'Océan Pacifique par le Nord-Ouest dans la Mer Glaciale par la Capitaine Maldonado l'An MDLXXXVIII traduit d'un Manuscrit Espagnol et suivi d'un discours qui en démontre l'authenticité et la veracité par Charles Amoretti, Membre de l'Institut Royal ... . *Plaïsance: de l'Imprimerie del Magno.* MDCCCXII. 4to, pp. (8), 84, (4), Appendix, 19. 5 Plates. N., S. 44111

Six hundred copies printed. This contains an appendix in answer to objections, *Milan*, 1813. "If we acquit Maldonado of imposture we must assign to him a considerable rank among the discoverers of the Northern Regions."—MURRAY.

MALDONADO (T. de S.) Elegia na morte do serenissimo senhor D. José, principe do Brasil, por Fr. Theodoro de Sousa Maldonado. *Porto: Na Officina de Antonio Alvares Ribeiro.* 1788. 4to, pp. 8. 44112

The Malefactors' Calendar, containing Genuine and Circumstantial Narratives of the Lives, Trials, and Dying Speeches of some of the Most Noted Criminals in Great Britain, ... and America. *New York.* 1813. 8vo. 44113

MALENFANT (*Col.*) Des Colonies, et particulièrement de celle de Saint-Domingue; Mémoire historique et politique ... . Par le Colonel Malenfant ... . *Paris: Chez Audibert.* 1814. 8vo, pp. (2), xii, 334, (3). B., H. 44114

MALESPINE (A.) Les États-Unis en 1865 D'après les Documents officiels communiqués au Congrès Par A. Malespine. *Paris: E. Dentu.* 1865. 8vo, pp. 48. C., H. 44115

MALESPINE. Solution de la Question Mexicaine par A. Malespine ... . *Paris: E. Dentu.* 1864. 8vo, pp. 31. Map. B.

See Sumner (Charles).

MALET (A.) The Canadas, the Nature of their Existing Connection with Great Britain Discussed, and a Remedy proposed ... . *London.* 1831. 8vo. 44117

MALET (W. W.) An Errand to the South in the Summer of 1862. By ... Rev. William Wyndham Malet. ... *London: Richard Bentley.* 1863. 8vo, pp. viii, 312. Plate. H. 44118

MALHAM (J.) The Naval Gazetteer; or, Seaman's Complete Guide. ... By the Rev. John Malham ... . First American Edition. ... *Boston: W. Spotswood and J. Nancrede.* 1797. 2 vols., 8vo, pp. xlvi, 7–436; 573, (1). 17 Maps. B. + Second Edition ... *London: Printed by M. Allen.* 1801. 2 vols., 8vo, pp. 560; (4), 644. Maps. BA. 44119

MALHAM. Dictionnaire Universel de Géographie Maritime; traduit de l'anglois de Malham. Par L. de Grandpré. *Paris.* 1802. 2 vols., 4to. S. 44120

MALHERBE (A.) Monographie des Picidés, ou Histoire naturelle ... des Picidés, Picuminés, Yuncinés ou Torcols, comprenant ... l'Origine mythologique, les Mœurs, les Migrations, ... la Physiologie, la Répartition géographique, les ... Systèmes de Classification ... la Synonymie, la Description ... l'Histoire de chaque Espèce ... . Par Alfred Malherbe. [*Metz: J. Verronnais.* 1861–3.] Text, 2 vols., 125 colored Plates, 2 vols., folio.

Only one hundred copies were printed, at the private expense of the author, who has spent 100,000 francs in raising this monument of science. What Gould has done for the humming-birds, M. Malherbe has done for the woodpeckers, some of which are American.

MALIN (W. G.) Some Account of the Pennsylvania Hospital, its Origin, Objects and Present State. By W. G. Malin ... *Philadelphia: Printed by Thomas Kite.* 1831. 8vo, pp. 46. Plate.

MALISEET. The Book of Matthew translated into the Maliseet Language. By Rev. S. T. Rand. *Charlottetown.* 1853. 8vo. 44123

Also: The Book of John ... . *Halifax.* 1855. 8vo.—The Books of Genesis, Psalms and Acts ... . *Bath, Eng.* [n. d.] 8vo.—The Ten Commandments, the Lord's Prayer, ... *Halifax.* 1863. 8vo.

MALL (T.) The History of the Martyrs Epitomized. A Cloud of Witnesses; or the Sufferers Mirrour ... . Collected out of the Ecclesiastical Histories of Eusebius, Fox, Fuller, Clark, Petrie, Scotland, And Mr. Samuel Ward's Life of Faith in Death ... . By Thomas Mall, M.A. ... *Boston, N. E. Printed ... by Rogers and Fowle.* MDCCXLVII. 2 vols., 8vo, pp. (16), 267, (2); (4), xi, (1), 292, (2). B., C., H. 44124

Prefixed are prefaces by J. Flavel and Rev. S. Lee, once minister of Bristol in New-England. A good specimen of American printing.

MALLALIEU (A.) Buenos Ayres, Monte Video, and Affairs of the River Plate, in a Letter to the Earl of Aberdeen. By Alfred Mallalieu, Esq. *London.* 1844. 8vo, pp. 72. 44125

MALLALIEU. Rosas and his Calumniators. Affairs of the River Plate considered ... . By Alfred Mallalieu. *London.* 1845. 8vo. 44126

MALLARD (J. B.) A Short Account of the Congregational Church, at Midway, Georgia. By John B. Mallard, A.M. ... *Savannah: Printed by Thomas Purse.* 1840. 8vo, pp. 28. H.

MALLARD. An Oration ... before the Midway and Newport Library Society ... March, 1839. By John B. Mallard, A.M. ... *Savannah: Printed by T. Purse & Co.* 1838. 8vo, pp. 21. H.

MALLARY (R. C.) An Oration ... at Rutland Fourth July, 1826; ... By R. C. Mallary. ... *Rutland: William Fay.* 1826. 8vo, pp. 24. B. 44128

Also: An Address ... before the ... Alumni of Middlebury College ... August 18, 1824. ... *Rutland: Printed by Wm. Fay.* 1824. 8vo, pp. 27. H.

MALLARY (——). Speech of Mr. Mallary, of Vt. on the Tariff Bill. ... March 3, 1828. *Washington: Printed by Gales & Seaton.* 1828. 12mo, pp. 34. H. 44129

Also: ... Tariff and Manufactures. January 13, 1831. ... Mr. Mallary, from the Committee ... made the following Report: ... [n. p. n. d.] 8vo, pp. 22.

MALLET (A. M.) Description de L'Univers, contenant Les Differents Systêmes du Monde ... . Par Allain Manesson Mallet, ... *A Paris, Chez Denys Thierry* ... M. DC. LXXXIII. 5 vols., 4to. Plates. C. + *Francfourt sur le Main, Chez Jean David Zunner.* M DC LXXXVI. 5 vols., 4to, pp. (18), 302, (10), 2 Portraits; (6), 299, (20); (6), 256; (8), 328, (44), 147 Plates; (10), 400, (44), 170 Plates. 44130

The only difference in these two editions consists in the inscriptions on the plates, which in the Frankfort edition are in German. Vol. v. relates to America.

MALLET (F.) Descriptive Account of the Island of Trinidad: made by order of Sir Ralph Abercrombie, K.B. ... By F. Mallet, Captain of the Surveying Engineers, 1797, &c. *London: J. Faden.* 1802. 4to, pp. 15. Map. 44131

Intended to accompany a four-sheet map.

MALLET (J. W.) Cotton; the Chemical, Geological, and Meteorological Conditions involved in its Successful Cultivation. With ... the Actual Conditions and Practice of Culture in the ... Cotton States of North America. By Dr. John William Mallet ... . *London: Chapman and Hall.* 1862. 8vo, pp. xvi, 183, (1). Map and Plate. BA. 44132

The first edition is *London.* 1827. 12mo. C.

MALLET (M.) Quinze Jours de Traversée; ou, Voyage en Amérique. Par Marie Mallet. *Paris: Alphonse Desesserts.* [n. d.] 8vo, pp. (6), 371. Plates. 44133

MALLET (P.) Remarks on a Speech made to the National Assembly of France by the Deputies from St. Domingo, with Observations. By Philip Mallet. *London.* 1791. 8vo. 44134

MALLETT *vs.* DEXTER. The Case in Equity, between Edward J. Mallett, et al., Complainants, and Samuel Dexter, Administrator, Respondent. *Providence: A. Crawford Greene.* 1852. 8vo, pp. 134. 44135

MALLEUS (Trepidantium), *pseudon.* *See* [Young (Samuel)].

MALLORCA. Exhortacion del Ilmo. Señor Obispo de Mallorca. *Mexico.* 1820. 8vo. 44136

MALLORY (Daniel). *See* Clay (H.), Vol. IV., No. 13543.

MALLORY (R. C.) Oration at Whitehall, N. Y., July 4, 1817. By R. C. Mallory. [n. p. n. d.] 8vo. 44137

MALLORY (S. R.) Effect of Naval Reform. Speech of Hon. S. R. Mallory ... . May 15 and 16, 1856. *Washington.* 1856. 8vo, pp. 30. H. 44138

Also: .. Report [of] the Committee on Naval Affairs ... [on] the Memorials of Captain Charles Stewart and other Officers ... . [n. p. 1856.] 8vo, pp. 50.— ... Speech ... Jan. 14 and 15, 1852. On the Restoration of Corporal Punishment in the Navy. [*Washington.* n. d.] 8vo, pp. 22.—Speech ... May 14th, 1858, on the Bill ... for the Relief of John Ericsson. [n. p. n. d.] 8vo, pp. 5, (1).—Speech ... on the Admission of Kansas; ... March 16, 1858. [n. p. n. d.] 8vo.

MALMGREN (Anders Johan). Spetsbergen, Grönlands, Islands och den Skandinaviska halföns hittills kända annulata polychæta. *Helsingfors: J. C. Frenckell & Son.* 1867. 8vo, pp. (2), 129. Table and 14 Plates. C. 44139

MALO (C.) Histoire de l'isle de Saint-Domingue, depuis sa découverte jusqu'à ce jour ... . Par M. Charles-Malo ... . *Paris: Louis Janet, Delaunay.* 1819. 8vo, pp. (4), ii, (2), 388. A. + Deuxième édition. [*Ibid.*] H. 44140

MALO. Histoire d'Haïti (Ile de Saint-Domingue), depuis sa Découverte jusqu'en 1824, Époque des Dernières Négociations entre la France et le Gouvernement haïtien. Par M. Charles-Malo ... . Nouvelle édition ... . *Paris: Chez Louis Janet, Ponthieu.* 1825. 8vo, pp. vii, 480. BA. 44141

MALO (J. R.) Funestos Recuerdos del Libertador de Mexico. *Mexico.* 1860. 8vo. 44142

MALO DE LUQUE (Eduardo). *See* Raynal (Guillaume-Thomas).

MALONE, *N. Y.* Kimball's Directory of Malone, with a Business Directory of Franklin County, for 1868. *Watertown: J. C. Kimball.* 1869. 16mo, pp. 119. 44143

Malone Sandstone Company. [n. p. n. d.] 8vo, pp. 16. H.

Description of the Malone Quarry, and By-Laws of the Company. Also: Report ... . 1854. [n. p. 1854?] 8vo, pp. 14.

MALOUET (V. P.) Collections de Mémoires et Correspondances Officielles sur l'Administration des Colonies, Et notamment sur la Guiane française et hollandaise, Par V. P. Malouet, ... *Paris: Baudouin, Imprimeur ... An* X [1802]. 5 vols., 8vo, pp. (2), 484; (2), 379; (2), 388; (2), 378; (2), 353. Plates.

"An unequal but valuable collection."—J. R. M'CULLOCH. The author was a member of the marine, and employed Guizan to write the following: "Traité sur les Terres noyées de la Guiane, appelées communément Terres Basses, par M. Guizan." This was reprinted by order of the Governor, at *Cayenne*, 1852. *See* "M. Rev.," XL. 482.

MALOUET. Examen de cette question: Quel sera pour les Colonies de l'Amérique le Résultat de la Révolution Françoise, de la Guerre qui en est la Suite, & de la Paix qui doit la terminer? Par M. Malouet ... . *A Londres: Baylis.* 1797. 8vo, pp. 29. + Cet ouvrage été fait sur un exemplaire imprimé à Londres. *Paris: Pougin.* [1797.] 8vo, pp. 40. 44146

See "M. Rev.," XXI. 579.

MALOUET. Lettre à M. S. D., Membre du Parlement, sur l'Intérêt de l'Europe, au Salut des Colonies de l'Amérique. Par M. Malouet ... . *Londres: Baylis.* 1797. 8vo, pp. (4), 36. BA.

MALOUET. Opinion, sur la Législation des Colonies, relativement à l'état des personnes et au régime interieur. [*Paris.* 1787.] 8vo, pp. 24. 44148

MALOUET. Seconde Lettre de M. Malouet, ... à ses Commettans. [n. p. 1798.] 8vo, pp. 8. P. 44149

Unnoticed by Quérard.

MALOUET. Beschreibung der West-Indischen Insel San Domingo. Aus dem Französischen. *Weimar.* 1808. 8vo. A.

MALOUET. Voyage dans les forêts de la Guyane française. *Paris.* 1802. 8vo. + Nouvelle édition, publiée par M. Ferdinand Denis. *Paris: G. Sandré.* 1853. 32mo. 44151

First appeared in Vol. III. of the "Collection." *See* Boucher, VI. 264; *see also* Vasty.

MALOUET. Reisen nach dem Französischen Guiana und nach Surinam. Aus dem Französischen. *Weimar.* 1805. 8vo. A.

MALTBY (E.) A Sermon ... on the Twenty-Fifth Anniversary of his Settlement ... in Taunton. By Erastus Maltby. *Boston: Phillips, Sampson & Company.* 1851. 8vo, pp. 32. H.

Also: Sermon ... at the Installation of the Rev. William M. Cornell, as Pastor ... in Woodstock, Conn., June 15, 1831. ... *Taunton.* 1831. 8vo, pp. 24.

MALTBY (I.) The Elements of War. By Isaac Maltby, ... *Boston: Printed by T. B. Wait and Co.* 1811. 12mo, pp. ix, (1), x–xxvi, 208. Plates. + Second Edition. [*Ibid.*] 1813. BA. + Third Edition. *Hartford: Printed by Peter B. Gleason and Co.* 1815. 12mo, pp. xxvii, 208. Plates. B. 44154

Also: Letter respecting some Military Orders of Gov. E. Gerry, addressed to Epaphras Hoyt of Deerfield, 29 Feb., 1812. [n. p. n. d.] Folio, 1 leaf.—A Treatise on Courts Martial and Military Law. ... *Boston: Printed by Thomas B. Wait and Company.* 1813. 8vo, pp. (8), 272. H., S.

MALTBY (J.) ... A Sermon, ... in Portland, at the Ordination of the Rev. Cyrus Hamlin, Missionary ... to Constantinople, October 3, 1838. By J. Maltby ... . *Bangor: E. F. Duren.* 1838. 8vo, pp. 40. B. 44155

Also: Sermon, ... Maine Missionary Society. ... *Augusta.* 1859. 8vo.

MALTE-BRUN (Conrad) [*properly* BRUUN (Malthe Conrad)]. Annales des Voyages, de la Géographie et de l'Histoire; ou Collection des Voyages nouveaux les plus estimés, traduits de toutes les langues Européennes; ... . Publiées par M. Malte-Brun. *Paris: Chez F. Buisson.* 1808–14. 24 vols., 8vo. Maps, Plates.

MALTE-BRUN. Table Générale et Raisonnée des Matières contenues dans les vingt premiers volumes des Annales des Voyages ... . Par M. Malte-Brun. *Paris: F. Buisson.* 1813. 8vo, pp. (4), iv, 448. BA. 44157

For a continuation *see* "Nouvelles Annales."

MALTE-BRUN. Diccionario geográfico universal, que contiene la descripcion de todos los paises de las cinco partes del mundo, ordenado con arreglo à la geografía de Malte-Brun. *Paris.* 1828. 2 vols., 8vo. 7 Maps. 44158

MALTE-BRUN. Précis de la Géographie universelle, ou Description de toutes les parties du monde ... . Par M. Malte-Brun. *Paris: Chez Fr. Buisson.* 1810–29. 8 vols., 8vo. Atlas in 4to. + Seconde édition, corrigée. ... [*Ibid.*] 1812–29. 8 vols., 8vo. + Nouvelle édition ... . *Paris.* 1831–37. 12 vols., 8vo. Atlas. + Cinquième édition revue, corrigée, et augmentée de toutes les nouvelles découvertes. Par M. J.-J.-N. Huot. ... *Paris: Furne et Cie.* 1841. 6 vols., 8vo, pp. (4), 611; (4), 649; (4), 691; (4), iii, 667; (4), ii, 773; (4), iii, 631. Atlas. + [Réimprimé] *Paris: Garnier Frères.* 1853. 6 vols., 8vo. Atlas of 72 Plates in folio. + Nouvelle édition, ... par V. A. Malte-Brun fils. *Paris: Penaud Frères.* 1852–56. 8 vols., 8vo. + Entièrement refondue et mise au courant de la science, por Th. Lavallée. *Paris: Furne et Cie.* 1855–57. 6 vols., 8vo. C. + [*Ibid.*] 1856–1862. 6 vols., 8vo. + Revue, rectifié et complétement mise au niveau de l'état actuelle des connaissances géographiques, par E. Cortambert. *Paris: Dufour, Mulat et Boulanger.* 1856–61. 8 vols., 8vo. Maps and Plates. 44159

MALTE-BRUN. Géographie universelle de Malte-Brun, illustrée par Gustave Doré. *Paris: G. Barba.* 1859. 2 vols., 4to. Atlas of 110 Maps. 44160

Of this edition the parts relative to each country may be purchased separately.

MALTE-BRUN. Le Mexique illustré Histoire et Géographie Par Malte-Brun ... Comprenant ... l'Histoire et la Géographie illustrées des États-Unis ... *Paris: Chez Azur-Dutil.* 1862. 4to, pp. 40, 81–96, 57–72 [*sic*]. Maps. H. 44161

MALTE-BRUN. Malte-Brun's neuestes Gemälde von Amerika und seinen Bewohnern. Aus dem Französischen übersetzt und mit Zusätzen vermehrt von E. W. von Greipel. *Leipzig.* 1819. 8vo. + [*Ibid.*] 1824. 2 vols., 8vo. 44162

MALTE-BRUN. New General Atlas, exhibiting the Five Great Divisions of the Globe, Europe, Asia, America, and Oceanica, with their several Empires, Kingdoms, &c. *Philadelphia.* 1828. 4to. 44163

MALTE-BRUN. Principles of Mathematical, Physical, and Political Geography. *Edinburgh.* 1834. 8vo. 44164

MALTE-BRUN. A System of Universal Geography, or a Description of ... the World ... . By M. Malte-Brun ... . With Additions and Corrections By James G. Percival. ... *Philadelphia: A. Finley.* 1827. 3 vols., 8vo. + *Boston.* 1828. 3 vols., 4to. + *Boston: Printed ... by Samuel Walker.* 1834. 3 vols., 4to, pp. (6), xx, viii, 3–6, 9–640; (6), xx, 3–680; (6), xv, 681–1394, (1). + [*Ibid.*] 1847, 1851, 1865. C. 44165

MALTE-BRUN. Universal Geography, or A Description of all the Parts of the World ... . By M. Malte-Brun. ... *Edinburgh: Adam Black.* 1822. 10 vols., 8vo. Plates. BA. + *Boston: Wells and Lilly.* 1824–31. 9 vols., 8vo. Plates. B. + *Philadelphia: Anthony Finley.* 1827–32. 6 vols., 8vo, pp. xxii, 503; xv, 529; xii, 439; x, 450; (2), 427; (2), 427–823, iii–xvii, xxvi. H. + *Philadelphia.* 1832–37. 5 vols., 8vo. Atlas, 4to. + New Edition ... . *Edinburgh: Adam and Charles Black.* MDCCCXLII. 8vo, pp. xxiii, 1063. BA. + *London: Henry G. Bohn.* 1851. 8vo, pp. xxiii, 1067. + [*Ibid.*] 1859. 44166

MALTE-BRUN (V. A.) Annales des voyages, de la géographie, de l'histoire et de l'archéologie, dirigées par M. V. A. Malte-Brun. Année 1866. *Paris: Challamel.* 1867. 8vo. 7 Maps. Continued. 44167

See "Nouvelles Annales."

MALTE-BRUN. Canal Interocéanique du Darien. Amérique. Notice Historique et Géographique sur l'État de la Question du Canal du Darien. Par M. V. A. Malte-Brun ... . *Paris: Arthus Bertrand.* [1865.] 8vo, pp. 32. Map. B. 44168

MALTE-BRUN. Un coup d'œil sur le Yucatan. Géographie, histoire et monuments. *Paris: Arthus Bertrand.* [n. d.] 8vo, pp. 34. Map. 44169

MALTE-BRUN. Coup d'œil d'ensemble sur les différentes expéditions arctiques entreprises à la recherche de Sir John Franklin, et sur les découvertes géographiques auxquelles elles ont donné lieu, par M. V. A. Malte-Brun ... . *Paris.* 1855. 8vo. Map. 44170

MALTE-BRUN. La destinée de Sir John Franklin dévoilée, rapport du capitaine MacClintock, suivi d'un résumé de l'expédition des navires "Erebus" et "Terror," et accompagné d'une carte des découvertes arctiques provoquées par la recherche de Franklin, de 1845 à 1849, par M. V. A. Malte-Brun. *Paris: Arthus Bertrand.* 1860. 8vo. Map. 44171

MALTE-BRUN. La France et ses colonies. Description géographique et pittoresque, esquisse de mœurs, merveilles de la nature et de l'art. *Paris: Morizot.* 1857. 8vo. 44172

MALTE-BRUN. La Sonora et Ses Mines. Esquisse Géographique. Par M. V. A. Malte-Brun ... . *Paris: Arthus Bertrand.* 1864. 8vo, pp. 31. Map. 44173

El Maltes al Historiador de Buenos Ayres. *Tucuman.* 1812. 4to. 44174

Curious as a specimen of printing at Tucuman. A criticism of Funes' "Ensayo."

MALVENDA (T.) Duodecim Fragmenta ad Sacram Scripturam pertinentia cum suis Indicibus a Nicolao Figures collecta et evulgata. *Valentiæ.* 1655. Folio. 44175

Relates incidentally to America.

MALVENDA. Thomae, Setabitani, Hispani Malvendae de Antichristo, Libri XI. *Romæ.* 1604. Folio. 44176

The question is here raised of America having been peopled by one of the lost tribes of Israel, and of the Gospel itself being preached there long anterior to its discovery by Columbus; which latter event is described in eight closely printed columns.

MALVINAS. Apendice a los documentos oficiales publicados sobre el asunto de Malvinas que contiene el esclarecimiento de los hechos perpetrados por el Comandante Silas Duncan, de la Corbeta de guerra de los E. U., contre aquel establecimiento y sus habitantes. *Buenos Ayres.* 1832. 4to, pp. 22. 44177

Mame Language. *See* [Raynosa (Diego de)].

MAMIANI (L. V.) Arte de Grammatica da lingua brasilica da nação Kiriri. Por Luis Vicencio Mamiani. *Lisboa, por Miguel Deslandes.* 1699. 8vo, pp. xvi, 124. 44178

Extremely rare; unknown to Brunet or Ternaux.

MAMIANI. Catecismo da doutrina Christão na Lingua Brasilica, da Nação Kiriri, composto pelo P. Luis v. Mamiani. *Lisboa: M. Deslandes.* 1698. 8vo. 44179

An exceedingly scarce volume.

MAMIANI. Grammatik der Kiriri-Sprache. Aus dem Portugiesischen des P. Mamiani übersetzt von H. C. von der Gabelentz. *Leipzig: F. A. Brockhaus.* 1852. 8vo, pp. 62. 44180

The Kiriri language is spoken by two Catholic tribes of Indians in the province of Bahia near Cochoeira.

Mammoth Cave. *See* [Croghan (Dr. John)], *and* No. 19723.

Mammoth Vein Consolidated Coal Company. ... Reports by P. W. Sheafer, Engineer ... . 1864. *Boston: Wright & Potter, Printers.* 1864. 8vo, pp. 67. Map. H. 44181

Also: ... Reports by Directors, Trustees ... etc. November 25, 1864. *Boston: Wright & Potter, Printers.* 1864. 8vo, pp. 61. H.

Mamvsse Wunneetupanatamwe. *See* Eliot (J.), 22154, *note*.

MAN (G. F.) An Oration, ... before the Citizens of ... Kent, at Apponaug, Warwick, July 4, 1838. By George F. Man. *Providence: Knowles, Vose, and Company.* 1838. 8vo, pp. 23. H.

MAN (Jan Willem Engelbert de). Suriname ontmaskerd of zaaklyke beschouwing waar aan het verval der Kolonie Suriname tans grootlyks toe te schryken is. *Amsterdam: J. A. Crayenschot.* 1778. Folio. 44183

MAN (T.) England's Treasure by Foreign Trade, or the Balance of our Foreign Trade is the Rule of our Treasure. By Thomas Man, Merchant of London. *Glasgow: R. and A. Foulis.* 1755. 8vo. 44184

MAN. Picture of a Factory Village; to which are annexed Remarks on Lotteries. By Sui Generis: alias, Thomas Man. *Providence: Printed for the Author.* 1833. 12mo, pp. 144. C.

MAN. A Picture of Woonsocket, or the Truth in its Nudity. ... By Thomas Man ... . *Providence: Printed for the Author.* 1835. 12mo, pp. 108. 44186

A scarce book, not mentioned in Bartlett's "Bibliography of Rhode Island."

A Man of Abilities for the Earl of B---------e or, Scotch Politics defeated in America. Accompanied with several interesting Anecdotes, and a Hint of the late intended ministerial changes. ... *London: ... J. Williams.* 1766. 8vo, pp. iv, 9–56.

"The 'Man of Abilities' here alluded to, is Lord George S——e; of whose conduct the author gives a most severe and libellous detail; he falls foul also on the Lords H——x and S—d—h."—*Monthly Review*, XXXIV. 239.

The Man of Two Lives. *See* [Sydenham (Edward)].

Man-of-War Life. *See* [Nordhoff (C.)]

MANAHAN (A.) Report of A. Manahan and G. A. Ridley ... on the removal of the Penitentiary from Kingston to Marmora. [n. p.: *J. H. Lawrence, Printer.* n. d.] Folio, pp. 15. H.

MANAMUSKIN, *N. J.* *See* [Cole (A.) & Co.], IV. 14283.

Mananas de la Alameda de Mexico. *Mexico.* 1835–36. 2 vols., 4to. 44189

MANASSEH BEN ISRAEL. An Account of the Ten Tribes of Israel being in America; originally published by Manasseh Ben Israel. With some Observations thereon, and Extracts from Sacred and Prophane, Ancient and Modern History, confirming the same; and the return from thence about the time of the return of the Jews. By Robert Ingram, A.M. ... *London: G. G. J. & J. Robinson.* 1792. 8vo, pp. 56. + *Colchester.* 1792. 8vo.

"Mr. Ingram believes that great numbers of the Israelites, after their dispersion, retired into a remote and uninhabited country, which he supposes to have been to the south of Hudson's Bay, and near California, between 53° and 60° N. lat., where their descendants, a numerous and distinct race, remain to this day, unconnected with the rest of mankind. All the difficulties in this long journey by sea and land are removed by the aid of miracles, of which the rev. author is not sparing. He has, however, used great diligence in examining and applying the Jewish prophecies, and other authorities, in support of his opinion, and of the evidence of Rabbi Manasseh."—*Monthly Review.*

MANASSEH BEN ISRAEL. Esto es Esperanca de Israel. Obra con suma Curiosidad Conquesta. *Amsterdam.* 1649. 12mo.

This book endeavors to prove that the lost tribes are to be found in America.

MANASSEH BEN ISRAEL. ... Hoc est, | Spes Israelis. | Authore | Menasseh Ben Israel. | Theologo & Philosopho Hebræo. | *Amstelodami.* | *Anno* 1650. | 12mo, pp. (12), 111. 44192

Concerning the identity of the Aborigines of America with the Hebrew race.

MANASSEH BEN ISRAEL. The Hope of Israel newly extant and printed in Amsterdam, Dedicated by the Author to the High Court, the Parliament of England, and the Council of State:

with the strange relation of Antony Montezinus, a Jew, of what befell him as he travelled over the "Mountaines Cordilliere," in America. *London.* 1650. 8vo. 44193

MANASSEH BEN ISRAEL. Jews in America. The Hope of Israel, written by Menasseh Ben-Israel, with Discoures by Moses Wall. *London.* 1651. 8vo. 44194

The address to the reader commences "There are as many minds as men about the original of the people of America, and of the first inhabitants of the New World, and of the West Indyes," and these words form a key to the entire tract.

MANATI. *See* Vol. IV., No. 14994; correct the date to 1862.

MANBY (G. W.) Journal of a Voyage to Greenland, in ... 1821. ... By George William Manby. *London: G. and W. B. Whittaker.* MDCCCXXII. 4to, pp. viii, 143. Map and Plates. H. + Second Edition. [*Ibid.*] 8vo. 44195

MANBY. Reise nach Grönland, ... 1821. Aus dem Englischen von C. F. Michaelis. *Leipzig.* 1823. Sm. 8vo. Map and Plates. 44196

MANBY. Reis naar Groenland, in het Jaar 1821. Gevolgd naar de hoogduitsche Vertaling van Dr. C. F. Michaëlis. *Amsterdam: Ten Brink & De Vries.* 1825. 8vo, pp. (4), 188. Map and 2 Plates. C. 44197

MANBY (T.) Collection of the Statutes of Charles I. and II. By Thomas Manby. *London.* 1667. Folio. 44198

Ship money, Newfoundland fisheries, etc., form part of the contents of this rare volume. The title-page is a fine specimen of a wood-cut title.

MANCE (*Mlle.*) *See* [Faillon], Vol. VI., No. 23653.

MANCHESTER (*Duke of*). The Speech of His Grace the Duke of Manchester, against the Bill, to prohibit all Intercourse with the Colonies. *London: G. Kearsly.* MDCCLXXV. Rl. 8vo, pp. 15. 44199

MANCHESTER (E.) The Principles upon which the Temperance Reform is Based, Examined and Defended, and Objections to Prohibitory Legislation, Discussed and Answered ... . By Elias Manchester. With an Appendix. *Auburn, N. Y.: William J. Moses.* 1854. 8vo, pp. 31. 44200

MANCHESTER, *Mass.* Brief History, Articles of Faith, Covenant, and Living Members, of the Orthodox ... Church ... . *Boston: Wright & Hasty, Printers.* 1851. 8vo, pp. 31. H.

Candid Enquiries, ... relative to the Difficulties ... in ... Manchester, Massachusetts, from ... 1816, to ... 1819. By a Friend to Truth. [n. p.] 1819. 8vo, pp. 8. BA. 44202

A Statement of Facts presented to an Ecclesiastical Council, October 5, 1858. ... Francis V. Tenney. ... *Manchester.* 1858. 16mo, pp. 44. H. 44203

In regard to F. V. Tenney's conduct.

MANCHESTER, *N. H.* ... An Act to establish the City of Manchester. [*Manchester?* 1846.] 16mo, pp. 16. H. 44204

... First Annual Report of the Committee on Finance ... for ... 1847. *Manchester, N. H.: James O. Adams, Printer.* 1847. 8vo, pp. 32. Continued. H. 44205

Annual Report of the ... School Committee ... for ... 1851. *Manchester.* 1851. 8vo, pp. 14, (2). Continued. 44206

A Business Directory of ... Manchester. ... 1848. *Manchester: J. O. Adams, Printer.* 1848. 16mo, pp. 206. H. 44207

The Charter ... as amended. ... *Manchester: Press of James O. Adams.* 1849. 12mo, pp. 27. H. 44208

The Charter with its Amendments, and the Revised Ordinances ... 1854. *Manchester: Abbott, Jenks & Co.* 1854. 8vo, pp. 91. Continued. H. 44209

Communication from his Honor the Mayor ... . before the City Council of Manchester, March 19th, 1856. ... *Manchester, N. H.: Abbott & Warren.* 1856. 8vo, pp. 14. Continued. B.

... Inaugural Address of ... Hon. Frederick Smyth ... 1852. *Manchester: H. A. Gage & Co., Printers.* 1852. 8vo, pp. 13. Continued. 44211

Catalogue of the ... Manchester Athenæum ... . *Manchester: Campbell & Gilmore.* 1853. 8vo, pp. xv, 112. B. 44212

Also: Constitution and By-Laws ... . *Manchester, N. H.: Wetmore & Wallace, Printers.* 1844. 12mo, pp. 11, (1).

Catalogue of the Manchester City Library ... . *Manchester: Printed by Abbott & Warren.* 1856. 8vo, pp. iv, 82. + *Manchester.* 1863. 8vo. Continued. 44213

Also: Twelfth Annual Report of the Trustees, Treasurer and Librarian of the Manchester City Library, for ... 1865. ... *Manchester, N. H.: Henry A. Gage.* 1866. 8vo, pp. 28. Continued.—Rules and Regulations ... of the City Library ... and a List of ... Officers ... 1854 ... . *Manchester.* 1854. 8vo, pp. 16. H.

Manchester Democrat—Extra. Containing ... the Political Phase of George Barstow, Esq. [n. p. n. d.] 8vo, pp. 8. H.

The Manchester Directory, containing The City Record, Names of the Citizens, and A Business Directory, ... for 1852. By George Adams ... . *Manchester.* [n. d.] 18mo. Continued. + For 1864. By Adams, Sampson & Co. *Manchester: Wm. H. Fisk.* [n. d.] 18mo, pp. 188. + For 1869. By Sampson, Davenport & Co. [*Ibid.*] 1869. 8vo, pp. 280. Continued.

MANCHESTER PUBLIC LIBRARY. Annual Report of the Officers and Trustees ... 1868. *Manchester, N. H.: ... Henry A. Gage, Printer.* 1869. 8vo, pp. 26. H. 44216

The Ordinances ... passed in 1846 & 1847. ... *Manchester: James O. Adams, Printer.* 1847. 8vo, pp. 52. Continued. H.

Proceedings of the Annual Meeting, of School District Number Two ... 1862 ... . *Manchester, N. H.: Gage, Moore & Co.* 1863. 12mo, pp. 11, (1). H. 44218

Also: Regulations and Course of Study, for ... District No. 2 ... 1846. *Manchester, N. H.: James O. Adams, Printer.* 1846. 16mo, pp. 8. H.

Reports of the Selectmen ... for ... 1841–42. *Manchester, N. H.* 1842. 12mo, pp. 15. Continued. H. 44219

Revised Ordinances of the City ... . *Manchester.* 1859. 12mo.

Rules and Orders of the City Council, and List of Officers ... *Manchester: James O. Adams, Printer.* 1846. 12mo, pp. 29. Continued. H. 44221

Valedictory Address of Mayor Weston, Jan., 1869. *Manchester.* 1869. 8vo. 44222

MANCHESTER, *Vt.* Catalogue of ... Burr Seminary, Manchester, Vt. June, 1844. *Troy, N. Y.: N. Tuttle.* 1844. 8vo, pp. 12. B. 44223

Manchester and its Vicinity; A Guide Book for the use of the Guests of the Equinox House. *Boston: Press of Geo. C. Rand & Avery.* 1862. 4to, pp. 11. 44224

Report of the Directors of the Manchester and Lawrence Railroad Corporation, ... to July 1, 1852. *Boston.* 1852. *Eastburn's Press.* 8vo, pp. 22. Continued. B. 44225

Also: Report of the Investigating Committee of the Stockholders ... Jan. 7, 1851. *Great Falls, N. H.* 1851. 8vo.

MANCILLA (A.) Imagen iris de N. Señ. de Valvanera. Sermon en la celebre dedicacion de vn Altar nuevo en Mexico. *Mexico.* 1725. 4to, 22 leaves. Plate. 44226

MANCIUS (G. W.) A Sermon, ... by Rev. Geo. Wilhelmus Mancius, ... Kingston, N. Y. ... 1754. ... Translated from the Dutch ... . *Kingston.* 1818. 8vo, pp. 12. BA. 44227

MANCUR (J. H.) Tales of the Revolution. By John H. Mancur. *New York.* 1844. 8vo, pp. 317. S. 44228

MANDAUILLA (Joanne de). Qual tratta delle piu marauegliosi cose e piu notabile che se trouino, e come presentitalmente ha cercato ... tutte le parte habitabile del mondo, et ha notato alcune degne cose ... che ha vedute in esse parte. *Venetia: A. Torti.* 1537. 12mo. 44229

"Very rare."—ASHER's Catalogue.

MANDEVILLE (G. H.) Flushing, Past and Present. A Historical Sketch, by Rev. G. Henry Mandeville ... . *Flushing, L. I.* 1860. 24mo, pp. 180. 3 Plates. BA., C. 44230

MANDEVILLE. My Country: A Discourse delivered in the Protestant Reformed Dutch Church at Newburgh, N. Y., Nov. 28th, 1861—Repeated Dec. 8th, 1861, By G. Henry Mandeville ... . *Newburgh: E. M. Ruttenber, Printer.* 1861. 8vo, pp. 22. 44231

Also: Discourse at the Funeral of Col. Benj. R. Hoagland. ... *Flushing, L. I.* 1858. 8vo.

MANDEVILLE (H.) Our Country. A Sermon, ... at Utica, ... December 10th, 1835. By H. Mandeville ... . *Utica.* 1835. 8vo, pp. 24. 44232

MANDEVILLE. Reflections on the Goodness of God to a Nation Three Score and Ten Years Old? A Sermon ... in ... Albany, on Thanksgiving Day, November 24, 1853. By Henry Mandeville, D.D. ... *Albany: Fisk & Little.* 1853. 8vo, pp. 25.

Also: ... A Sermon ... with reference to the Death of Prof. John Finley Smith ... Oct. 15, 1843 ... . *Utica: Press of Bennett, Backus, & Hawley.* 1843. 8vo, pp. 24.

MANDEVILLE (H. D.) Address on some of the Duties of the American Citizen ... April 5, 1842. By H. D. Mandeville, Jr., Esq. *Vidalia, La.* 1842. 12mo, pp. 39. H. 44234

MANDEVILLE (Marigni de). *See* Marigni de Mandeville.

MANDERVILLE (P.) Narrative of the Abduction, Captivity, Sufferings and Heart-rending Misfortunes of Payneta Manderville, Wife of Augustus H. Manderville, of Baltimore, who was abducted by the Spanish Bandits of New Grenada. *Richmond, Va.* [1854.] 8vo, pp. 36. Plates. 44235

MANDRILLON (Joseph H.) Fragmens de politique et de littérature, suivi d'un voyage à Berlin, en 1784. *Paris et Bruxelles.* 1788. 8vo, pp. 372. 44236

Contains "Remarques sur la Révolution Américaine; Crise de l'Amérique; Mémoires pour et Devise de la Société Américaine; Mémoire au Ministre Plénipotentiare des États-Unis; Société de Cincinnatus," etc.

M[ANDRILLON]. Précis sur l'Amérique Septentrionale et la République des Treize-États-Unis. Par M. J^h. M. *Amsterdam: J. Schuring.* 1782. 8vo, pp. 164. C. 44237

M[ANDRILLON]. Le Spectateur Américain. Ou Remarques Générales sur l'Amérique Septentrionale et sur la République des Treize-États-Unis. Suivi de Recherches Philosophiques sur la Découverte du Nouveau-Monde. Par M. J^h M********* ... *Amsterdam: E. van Harrevelt.* MDCCLXXXIV. 8vo, pp. xvi, 128, folded leaf, 307. Map. BA., J.C.B. 44238

In the same volume, with separate title and paging, is the following:

M[ANDRILLON]. Recherches Philosophiques sur la Découverte de l'Amérique, ou discours sur cette question, proposée par l'Academie des Sciences, ... de Lyon: "La découverte de l'Amérique a-t-elle été utile ou nuisible au genre-humain?" ... Par M. J^h. M*********. ... *Amsterdam: E. van Harrevelt.* MDCCLXXXIV. 8vo, pp. (2), 91, (4). H., P. 44239

M[ANDRILLON]. Le Spectateur Américain [as No. 44238]. Seconde Édition revue, corrigée, & augmentée ... . *Amsterdam: Emmanuel Flon.* 1785. 8vo, pp. xx, 519. Map and Table. C. + *Amsterdam: Chez De La Haye & Compagnie.* M. DCC. LXXXV. 8vo, pp. xx, 519. Map and Table. BA. 44240

Of the first edition there are copies on thick paper, there are also copies on thick paper in which the author's name is spelt out at length. The author was desirous of being a member of the Cincinnati, and thought that Congress could take away the difficulty which prevented his membership. *See also* [Cluny (A.)], Vol. IV. 13797.

MANEIRO (J. A.) Joannis Aloysii Maneiri Veracrucensis de Vitis aliquot Mexicanorum aliorumque, qui sive virtute, sive litteris, Mexici imprimis floruerunt. *Bononiæ: Ex Typographia Laelii a Vulpe.* 1791–2. 3 vols., 8vo, pp. 410; 412; 324.

This very rare book, by a native author "Veracrucensis," contains the lives of thirty-five distinguished literary men, missionaries, etc., of Mexico.

MANEIRO. De Vita Antonii Lopezii Portilli, Mexici primum, inde Valentiæ Canonici. *Bononiæ: Lælius a Vielpe.* 1791. 12mo, pp. 54, (2). C. 44242

MANEIRO. Joannes Aloysius Maneirus de Vita Michaelis Gutierri sacerdotis Mexicani. *Bononiæ.* 1795. 12mo. 44243

Also: Vita Petri Mali Sacerdotia Mexicani. *Bononiæ.* 1798. 8vo.

MANENT (G.), *pseudon.* *See* [Manley (J. R.)], No. 44301.

MANERO (José Mariano de) *and* HORTIGOSA (Tomas Lopez de). Solemnes Exequias del Illmo Señor Dr. José Gregorio Alonzo de Hortigosa, obispo que fue de la ciudad de Antequera, Valle de Oaxaca, celebradas en la santa iglesia catedral de la propia ciudad en los dias 1. y 2. del mes de Diciembre de 1796. *Nueva Guatemala: I. Beteta.* 1798. 4to, 14 leaves. 44244

MANETENSE (B.) Fr. Bernardo Manetense, Capuch., Catechismo para los Karitis, Indios de Brasil; en Portugues i Indio. 1709. 8vo. 44245

"Printed, according to Barcia-Pinelo." Title and note from Ludewig.

MANFORD (E.) Twenty-Five Years in the West. By Erasmus Manford. *Chicago: E. Manford.* 1867. 8vo, pp. (2), 359.

MANFREDO (——). Una Culpa. Drama en un acto. *Bogota.* 1866. 8vo, pp. 40. 44247

MANGANESE MINING COMPANY. Reports of the ... Company, New Brunswick. Organized ... 1869. [n. p. n. d.] 8vo, pp. 16. H. 44248

MANGIN (A.) Le Cacao et le chocolat considérés au point de vue botanique, chimique, physiologique, agricole, commercial, industriel et économique. Par Arthur Mangin. Suivi de la légende du Cacahuatl, par Ferdinand Denis. *Paris: Guillaumin et Cie.* 1860. 12mo. 12 Plates. + Seconde édition. [*Ibid.*] 1862. 8vo. 44249

MANGIN. Voyages et Découvertes outre-mer au XIXe siècle. Par Arthur Mangin. Illustrations de Durand-Brager. *Tours: Mame et Cie.* 1862. 8vo. 24 Plates. 44250

Also: Le Désert et le monde sauvage. ... Illustrations par MM. Yan' Dargent, Foulquier et W. Freeman. *Tours: Mame et fils.* 1865. 8vo.

MANGLES (J.) Papers and Despatches relating to the Arctic Searching Expeditions of 1850–1–2; together with a few brief

Remarks on the probable Course by Sir John Franklin. Collected and arranged by James Mangles. Second Edition. *London.* 1852. 8vo, pp. 94. Maps. C. 44251

MANGUM (Adolphus W.) Myrtle Leaves. A Book peculiarly adapted to the Times. By Rev. A. W. Mangum. *Raleigh, N. C.* 1864. 12mo, pp. 134. 44252

The second edition is entitled: "Myrtle Leaves; or Tokens at the Tomb. ... *Raleigh, N. C.: Branson & Farrar.* 1864. 16mo, pp. 132. B.

MANHATTAN, *pseudon.* *See* [Scoville (J. A.)]

MANHATTAN, *pseudon.* What Shall be Done with the Confiscated Negroes? ... A Letter to Hon. Abraham Lincoln, Gen. Winfield Scott ... and ... other Patriots. ... [n. p. n. d.] 8vo, pp. 15. H. 44253

MANHATTAN COLLEGE. Catalogue of Manhattan College. 1866–7. *New York: P. C. Devlin.* 1867. 8vo, pp. 50. Plate. Continued. B. 44254

Also: Documents on the Matter of Application to the Legislature of New York for a Charter for Manhattan College. *New York.* 1829. 8vo.

MANHATTAN COMPANY. Act of Incorporation of the Manhattan Company. *New York.* 1799. 8vo, pp. 12. N. 44255

MANHATTAN CO-OPERATIVE RELIEF ASSOCIATION. ... [Organization, Object, etc.] *New York City.* [n. d.] 24mo, pp. 12. H. 44256

MANHATTAN QUARTZ MINING COMPANY. Facts concerning Quartz and Quartz Mining; ... with the Charter of the ... Company ... . *New York: W. L. Burroughs' Steam ... Presses.* 1852. 8vo, pp. 30, (1). Plate. H. 44257

The Manhattan Souvenir. *See* Haven (C. W.), VIII. 30875.

MANHEIM (F.) Affecting History of the Dreadful Distresses of Frederic Manheim's Family. To which are added, The Sufferings of John Corbly's Family. An Encounter between a White Man and Two Savages. Extraordinary Bravery of a Woman. Adventures of Capt. Isaac Stewart. Deposition of Massey Herbeson. Adventures and Sufferings of Peter Wilkinson. Remarkable Adventures of Jackson Johonnot. Account of the Destruction of the Settlement at Wyoming. *Philadelphia: Printed (for Mathew Carey) by D. Humphreys.* 1794. 8vo, pp. 48. Plate. + [*Ibid.*] 1800. + *Bennington: Printed by Collins & Stockwell.* 1802. 8vo, pp. 33. 44258

The Maniacs; or, Fantasia of Bos Bibens, characteristic of some of the Fanatics who are Conspiring the Ruin of their Country at Home. By a West-Indian. [*Kingston, Jamaica?*] 1824. 12mo, pp. 128. C. 44259

MANIAU (J. N.) Oracion funebre de Señ. Don. Ignac. Paz. *Mexico.* 1829. 4to, 10 leaves. 44260

MANIERRE (G.) Testimonial of Respect of the Bar of Chicago to the Memory of Hon. George Manierre, ... also, the Funeral Discourse of Rev. R. W. Patterson. ... *Chicago: Dunlop, Sewell & Spalding, Printers.* 1863. 8vo, pp. 61. B. 44261

The Manifest Destiny of the American Union. Reprinted from the Westminster Review. *New York.* 1857. 12mo, pp. 72.

Manifest | Door d'Inwoonders van Pernambuco uytgegeven tot hun | verantwoordinge op 't aennemen der wapenen tegens | de West-Indische Compagnie; ghedirigeert aen alle | Christene Princen, ende besonderlijck aen de Hoogh- | Mo. H. H. Staten Generael van de Vereenighde Neder- | landen. | 't Heeft schijn van quaet | Maer niet de daet. | ... | Ghedruckt ende uyt het Portugies overgeset in onse Nederduytsche Tale. | *Tot Antwerpen,* | *Ghedruckt by Pieter van den Cruyssen, Boeckverkooper inde Lombertstraet. Anno* 1646. | 4to, pp. 12. 44263

This manifesto, by the inhabitants of Pernambuco, is a defense against the accusation of having taken part in the insurrection of the Portuguese. *See* Asher, Nos. 214–215.

Manifest | Ende redenen van Oorloge, tot | Lisbona | Vyt-ghegheven ende gepubliceert: Tusschen | Portugael ende de Geunieerde Nederlantsche Provintien | met de aenmerckinge ende den oorspronck waer uyt den self- | den gheprocedeert is. | Getrouwelijck uijt de Portugesche Tale over-geset: | *Gedruckt int Jaer onses Heeren* 1658. | 4to, pp. 16. C. 44264

Manifesto of war between Portugal and the United Provinces, with the origin of the war. *See also* Asher, No. 289.

Manifest, | ofte | Reden van den oorlogh tusschen Por- | tugael, ende de Vereenichde Provintien van de Nederlanden, | met de aenwijsinge vande oorsaeck waer uyt die ontstaen is. | Tot Lisbon in de Portugesche en Castiliaensche taelen | gedruckt ende uytgegeven, in 't Iaer 1657. Ende nu getrouwelijck | en verstandelijck inde Nederduytsche taele overgeset. | Mitsgaders | Manifestatie | Van de leugenen ende valsheden waer mede het is vervult, | Ende een | Kort ende waerachtich verhael | van des Conincks van Portugael, ende sijner onder- | saeten trouwloose ende meyneedyge

procedu- | ren, die de waere reden en oorsaeck, ende | selfs het begin, van desen oorlogh zin. | *In's Graven-Haghe,* | *By Henricus Hondius, inde* | *Hofstraet, inde nieuwe Konst-en-Boeck-Druckery.* 1659. | 4to, pp. 56. C. 44265

Manifesto or reasons of the war between Portugal and the United Netherlands, with numerous particulars of the mutual grievances in Brazil, etc. *See also* Asher, No. 290.

Het Manifest van George III., in een waar daglicht gesteld door Cato Batavius de Jonge. *Amsterdam.* 1781. 8vo. 44266

The war-manifest of George III., viewed in a true light by Cato Batavus Junior.

Manifest van pardon van de Koninck van Spaignen aende rebelle Portugesen. *Harderwyck.* 1662. 4to. 44267

Manifesto of pardon of the King of Spain to the rebellious Portuguese.

Manifest | van 't Koninghryck van | Portugael | In d'welcke verklaert wort de gerechte | oorsake en de reden waerom de Inwoonders sich | hebben getrocken uyt de gehoorsaemheit des Konings | van Castilien en nu aenghenomen den Serenissimo Heer | Don Joan IIII. van dien Name | wesende | den XVIII. gerechten Koningh van | dit Koninghryck. | Met Gratie ende Privilegie. | Gedruckt naer de Copye tot Lisbona, By Paulus van Craesbeecke. Ende nu getrou- | welyk overgheset in 't Nederlant's | Door C. F. Portugees. | En worden nu uytgegeven, | By Broer Jansz. Jan van Hilten, En C. de Pas. [*Amsterdam.*] *Anno* 1641. | 4to, pp. 23, (3). 44268

Manifesto of the kingdom of Portugal on its admitting D. Joan IV. as king. *See also* Asher, No. 173.

Manifestacion al Gobierno Supremo del Tribunal de Guerra y Marina, sobre la separacion de D. Augustin Buenrostos, y facultades para remover á los demas ministros letrados que lo componen. *Mexico.* 1835. 4to, pp. 28. 44269

Manifestacion de los Patriotas de Honduras contra los perturbadores de la paz Publica y los refractarios de la union. *Tegucigalpa.* 1853. Folio, 9 leaves. 44270

Manifestacion histórica y politica de la revolucion de la América y mas especialmente de la parte que corresponde al Perú, y Rio de la Plata. Obra escrita en Lima, centro de la opresion y del despótismo, en el año de 1816. *Impresa en Buenos-Ayres: Imprenta de los expositos.* 1818. 12mo. 44271

Manifestacion que hace al publico el de Santiago Bombalier relativa al Mandato que le confirio D. Manuel I Madrid para la

publicacion en Paris de los articulos cosas de Mexico y biografia de algunos individuos. *Mexico.* 1859. Sm. 8vo, pp. 23. 44272

Manifestacion que hace al publico el ex-general A. Alvarez. *Saltillo.* 1864. 8vo, pp. 10. 44273

Manifestacion que hace el Comandante en Gefe de la Seccion auxiliar de Chiapas sobre Pichucalco y S. J. Bautista de las comunicaciones habidas con los Gefes de ambos puntos desde el 13. de Setiembre en que arribó a Istacomitan hasta el 25 del propio mes en que entró en esta Capital con dicha seccion. *Tabasco.* 1845. 4to, pp. 19. 44274

Manifestacion que hace el gobierno eclesiastico de Guadalajara, contra las disposiciones dictadas en Veracruz. *Guadalajara.* 1859. 4to, pp. 34. 44275

Manifestacion que hace la Junta. *See* Jalisco, IX. 35553.

Manifestacion que hacen al Venerable Clero y Fieles de sus respectivas diocesis y á todo el mundo católico los Illmos. Señores Arzobispo de Mexico y Obispo de Michoacan, Linares, Guadalajara y el Potosi, ... en defensa del clero y de la Doctrina católica. *Mexico.* 1859. 8vo, pp. 38. 44276

A protest of the United Mexican clergy against the celebrated laws of Benito Juarez, on civil marriage and the disendowment of the church, which he published at Vera Cruz on the 7th, 12th, 13th, and 23d of July, 1859.

Manifestation or State and Case of the Quakers presented to all People, but especially to Merchants, Owners, and Masters of Ships, and Marriners, also to all Planters or occupiers of Lands in the English and Foreign Plantations, by T. D. *Printed at London in the year* 1664. 4to. 44277

Manifeste des motifs que légitiment la declaration de guerre contre le gouvernement du General Andres Santa Cruz, soi-disant Président de la Confédération Pérou-Bolivienne; traduit de l'espagnol. *Buenos Aires.* 1837. 4to, pp. 62. 44278

Manifeste du Rio. *See* Haiti, Vol. VII., No. 29580.

Manifeste sur l'infamie. *See* Leblanc (*M.*), *add* for note:

Also in Spanish, *Buenos Aires.* 1838. 8vo.

Manifesto á sus compatriotos hace J. de Ayala y Aguilar. *Mérida.* 1830. Sm. 4to. 44279

Manifesto de Ayala i Medrano sobre la cuestion bonos. *Bogotá.* 1865. 4to, pp. 22. 44280

Manifesto de las razones que legitiman de la Declaracion de Guerra contra el Gobierno del General Santa Cruz, titulo presidente de la Confederacion Peru-Boliviana. *Buenos Aires.* 1837. 4to. 44281

For a French version *see* No. 44278, *supra.*

Manifesto de los motivos en que se ha fundado la conducta del Rey Christianissimo respecto à la Inglaterra; con la exposicion de los que han guiado al Rey N. S. para su modo de proceder con la misma potencia. *Madrid.* 1779. 4to, pp. 43. 44282

Translated into French as: "Exposé des Motifs de la Conduite du Roi de France, relativement à l'Angleterre. Mémoire Justificatif pour servir à Réponse à l'Exposé, &c. de la Cour de France." *Londres: P. Elmsly.* M.DCC.LXXIX. 4to, pp. 16, 32. For another edition *see our* Vol. VI., No. 23428. For an English translation *see* "The Annual Register for 1779," pp. 337, 380, 386, 397. For a reply *see* [Gibbon (E.)], Vol. VII., Nos. 27282–83.

Manifesto documentado que el Supremo Gobierno Provisorio Del Estado de los Altos, dirige a Los Centro-Americanos. *Guatemala.* 1840. Folio, pp. (2), 28, (2). 44283

Manifesto of the Minister of Foreign Affairs of Chile on the Present War between the Republic and Spain. *London: Printed by Marchant Singer & Co.* 1866. Rl. 8vo, pp. 48. 44284

A Manifesto or Declaration. *See* Boston, Vol. II., No. 6635.

Manifesto sobre la Nulidad de las Elecciones. *Mexico.* 1820. 4to, pp. 26. 44285

Manifiesto del Congreso a los pueblos. *Buenos Aires.* 1816. 8vo, pp. 34. 44286

Manifiesto del Director provisorio de la Confederacion Argentina, con otros documentos correlativos. *Buenos Aires.* 1852. 4to, pp. 22. 44287

Manifiesto del Supremo Tribunal de Guerra y Marina. *Mexico.* 1848. 4to, pp. 38. 44288

Manifiesto de hecho con informe en derecho por la Justicia que assiste al Capitan D. Melchior Dias de Possada, Vezino y Minero, del Real de Santa Fee de Guanajuato, en el Pleyto que contra el suso dicho siguen D. Juan de Mendoza, Indio Cazique, y Nuñes de Villauscencio, sobre la Possession, y Propriedad de la Mina nombrada La Joya ... . *Mexico.* 1703. Folio. 44289

Manifiesto de la Nulidad con que se ha inciado y continuado en esta capital una causa que se versa con la Compañia del Rio

Janeiro que feneció por la variacion de Gobierno el año de 1821. *Lima.* 1835. 4to, pp. 20. 44290

Manifiesto de las Acusaciones. *See* Cochrane, IV. 14078.

Manifiesto de las sesiones tenidas en el pueblo de Miraflores para las transaciones intentadas con el General San Martin y Documentos presentados por parte de los comisionados en ellas. Se publican de órden de este Gobierno. *Lima.* 1820. Folio, 17 leaves. + *Mexico.* 1821. 8vo, pp. 51. 44291

Manifiesto de los antecedentes. *See* Cuba, Vol. V. 17788.

Manifiesto ó satisfaccion. *See* [Alvarez de Toledo], I. 978.

Manifiesto que hace á las Naciones el Congreso general constituyente de las Provincias-Unidas del Rio de la Plata, sobre el Tratamiento y Crueldades que han sufrido de los Españoles y Motivado la Declaracion de su Independencia. *Buenos Ayres.* 1817. 4to, pp. 12. + *Lima.* 1820. 4to, pp. 22. 44292

Manifiesto que hacen al público los diez oficiales del batallon de Tarragona, encausados por haber sido inminentemente adictos á la Constitucion. *Habana: Imprenta de Campe.* 1820. 4to.

Manifiesto y demas documentos relativos á la guerra que los Estados-Unidos han declarado á la Gran Bretaña, traducidos en esta ciudad. *Habana: Imprenta de Palmer.* 1812. 4to. 44294

MANIGNAULT (G.) The Signs of the Times. By G. Manignault, of South Carolina. *New York: Blelock & Co.* [n. d.] 8vo, pp. 60. 44295

MANITOWOC AND MISSISSIPPI R. R. Co. Report of the President to the Directors ... October, 1854. *Milwaukee.* 1854. 8vo. 44296

Manitowompae Pomantamoonk. *See* Bayly (L.), Vol. I. 4076.

MANJARRES (Fran. Cruz). Defensa de la Precedencia de los Hermanos ex Guardianes respecto de los solos Predicadores. *Mexico.* 1841. 8vo. 44297

[MANKIN (H.)] Thoughts on Labor, Capital, Currency, &c. With tables ... . By a Citizen of Maryland. *Baltimore: Printed ... by John Murphy & Co.* 1864. 8vo, pp. 16. B. 44298

MANLEY (J. R.) A Eulogium on De Witt Clinton, Late Governor of the State of New York. Delivered ... in ... Columbia

College ... 11th July, 1828. By James R. Manley, M.D. *New York: Printed by Gould & Jacobus.* 1828. 8vo, pp. (4), 22.

MANLEY. Exposition of the Conduct and Character of Dr. John Augustine Smith, President of the College of Physicians and Surgeons ... as exhibited in the Session of 1839–40. By James R. Manley, M.D. ... *New-York.* 1841. 8vo, pp. 48. + [*Ibid.*] 1842. 8vo, pp. 48. B. 44300

[MANLEY.] Letters on the College of Physicians and Surgeons By Graviora Manent. *New-York: Printed by Alex. S. Gould.* 1841. 8vo, pp. 16. B. 44301

Also: Anniversary Discourse before the New York Academy of Medicine, Nov. 8, 1848. ... *New York.* 1849. 8vo.—Address ... before the ... Alumni of Columbia College, ... May 4, 1831 ... . *New-York: G. & C. & H. Carvill.* M,DCCC,XXXI. 8vo, pp. 31.—An Address ... before the Medical Society of the County of New York, July 25, 1836 ... . *New York.* 1836. 8vo, pp. 24.—An Inaugural Address ... before the Medical Society of ... New-York ... 1826. ... *New-York: Printed by J. Seymour.* 1826. 8vo, pp. 28.—Introductory Address to the Students ... of the College of Physicians and Surgeons of the University of ... New York. ... Nov. 6, 1839. ... *New York: Printed by the Students.* 1839. 8vo, pp. 28.—Letters addressed to the Board of Health, and to Richard Riker, Recorder of the City of New York ... . *New-York: Printed by Peter Van Pelt.* 1832. 8vo, pp. 27. B.

MANLEY (J.) Cattaraugus County: embracing its Agricultural Society ... Biographies of the Old Pioneers ... and of Congressmen; ... Colonial and State Governors of New York ... with the Statistics of each Town. Compiled by John Manley ... *Little Valley, N. Y.: John Manley.* 1857. 8vo, pp. 136. 8 Portraits. H. + [*Ibid.*] 1858. 8vo, pp. 140. C. 44302

Manlius; with Notes. *See* [Gore (C.)], Vol. VII., No. 28016.

MANLY (B.) ... A Discourse, containing some Fragments of the History of the Baptist Church in Charleston, S. C. ... September 23d and 30th, A.D. 1832. By Basil Manly ... . [*Charleston.* 1837.] 8vo, pp. 80. BA. 44303

Also: Address ... University of North Carolina. ... *Raleigh.* 1838. 8vo.—Report on Collegiate Education, made to the ... University of Alabama, July, 1852. ... *Tuskaloosa: Printed by M. D. J. Slade.* 1852. 8vo, pp. 49.—A Sermon, preached by Appointment of the Senior Class of the University of North Carolina, June 2, 1856 ... [n. p.] 1856. 8vo, pp. 16. B.

MANLY (J. G.) Canada: its Geography, Scenery, Produce, Population, Institutions and Condition. By Rev. J. G. Manly. *Dublin.* 1860. 8vo, pp. 32. 44304

MANN (A). Original Letters ... of Abijah Mann ... and others, to J. W. Parkins, ex-sheriff of London, showing the

causes of his [Parkins'] unjust confinement for five years; and his unconditional discharge. *New York.* 1838. 8vo, pp. vi, 5–20.

Also: Correspondence ... in respect to the Payment of the Five-Twenty Bonds ... in Greenbacks ... . *Brooklyn.* 1868. 8vo.—Correspondence between A. Mann, jr., and Hon. A. C. Flagg, in relation to the General Bank Law of New York. *Brooklyn.* 1868. 8vo.

MANN [Ab.] Mr. Mann's Letter, &c. to the Merchants, Manufacturers, and others, interested in the Trade to the United States ... . [n. p.:] *Richard Taylor & Co.* [1808.] 8vo, pp. 20.

MANN (A.) An Address ... before the Medical Society of Maine ... Sept. 2, 1823. By Ariel Mann, M.D. ... *Bath: Printed* ... [*by*] *Joseph G. Torrey.* 1823. 8vo, pp. 12. H. 44307

MANN (A. D.) Letter to the Citizens of the Slave-Holding States, in relation to a weekly Atlantic Ferry Line between Chesepeake Bay and Milford Haven. By A. Dudley Mann. *London: J. Miller.* 1856. 16mo, pp. 30. C. 44308

MANN. Die Nordamericanischen Freistaaten. ... *Bremen: C. Schünemann.* 1845. 8vo, pp. viii, 326. C. 44309

MANN (C.) Poems by the Rev. Cameron Mann, ... February 19th, 1874. Illustrated with Alphabetical Designs By F. Burdge. [*New-York.* 1875.] 12mo, pp. 24. 44310

Historical; relates to the Civil War.

MANN (C.) ... A Sermon ... in Westminster, March 16, 1817. By Cyrus Mann, A.M. ... *Worcester: Printed by William Manning.* 1818. 8vo. 44311

Occasioned by the admission of a Universalist to preach in the Congregational Meeting-House in Westminster.

MANN. Memoir of Mrs. Myra W. Allen, who died ... the 5th of Feb. 1831 ... . *Boston.* 1832. 18mo, pp. 247. Portrait. + [n. p. n. d.] 24mo, pp. 256. Portrait. H. 44312

Also: The Clinton Family: or, the History of the Temperance Reformation. *Boston.* 1833. 18mo, pp. 263. Plate.— ... A Sermon, ... at Bristol, R. I. November 15, 1815. At the Ordination of the Rev. Joel Mann ... . *Warren, R. I.: Printed by Samuel Randall.* [1815.] 8vo, pp. (2), 32.—Sermon at the Ordination of Ebenezer Perkins at Royalston, Mass., Feb. 17, 1819. ... *Worcester.* [n. d.] 8vo.

MANN (E. J.) The Deaf and Dumb: ... their Education, and the Principal Asylums devoted to their Instruction. By Edwin John Mann ... . *Boston: D. K. Hitchcock.* 1836. 12mo, pp. 312. Plate. H. 44313

[MANN (H.)] The Female Review: | or, | Memoirs | of an | American Young Lady; | whose Life and Character are Peculiarly | Distinguished—being a Continental Soldier, | for nearly Three Years in the late Ameri- | can War. | During which Time, | she performed the Duties of every Depart- | ment, into which she was called with punc- | tual Exactness, Fidelity and Honor, and pre- | served her Chastity inviolate by the most | artful concealment of her sex. | With an | Appendix, | containing | characteristic Traits, by different Hands: | her taste for Economy, principles of Domes- | tic Education, &c. | By a Citizen of Massachusetts. | *Dedham: Printed by* | *Nathaniel and Benjamin Heaton,* | *For the Author.* | M,DCC,XCVII. | 12mo, pp. 258, (6). Portrait. 44314

This remarkable woman was twice severely wounded in action, was pensioned by Congress, and received a compensation from the State of Massachusetts, in consideration of her military services. Reprinted with the following title:

[MANN.] ... Life of Deborah Sampson the Female Soldier in the War of the Revolution With an Introduction and Notes by John Adams Vinton *Boston: J. K. Wiggin & Wm. Parsons Lunt.* M DCCC LXVI. 4to, pp. 267. Portrait. C., H. 44315

Two hundred and fifty copies printed. Also thirty-five copies on large paper and three on drawing paper.

MANN. Historical Annals of Dedham, from its settlement in 1635, to 1847. By Herman Mann. *Dedham, Mass: Herman Mann.* 1847. 8vo, pp. 136. B., H. 44316

Also: The Columbian Almanac and Agricultural Repository for the year 1804. *Dedham.* [n. d.] 18mo.—The Material Creation: being a Compendious System of Universal Geography and Popular Astronomy. ... *Dedham: H. & W. H. Mann.* 1818. 12mo, pp. 348.—Remarks, accompanying the reading of the Declaration of American Independence ... July 4, 1822. ... *Dedham: Printed by H. & H. W. Mann.* [n. d.] 8vo, pp. 20. H.

MANN (H.) Annual Reports on Education. By Horace Mann. *Boston: Horace B. Fuller.* 1868. 8vo, pp. xii, 758. H.

[MANN.] The Common School Controversy; consisting of Three Letters of the Secretary of the Board of Education, of the State of Massachusetts, in Reply to Charges preferred against the Board, by the Editor of the Christian Witness and by Edward A. Newton, Esq. ... to which are added Extracts from the Daily Press, in regard to the Controversy. *Boston.* 1844. 8vo, pp. 55.

MANN. Horace Mann's Letters on the Extension of Slavery into California and New Mexico; ... [*Washington.* 1850.] 8vo, pp. 32. BA. 44319

MANN. Lecture on Education. By Horace Mann ... . *Boston: Marsh, Capen, Lyon, and Webb.* 1840. 12mo, pp. 62. + *Boston: Wm. B. Fowle and N. Capen.* 1845. 12mo, pp. 338. + *Boston: Lemuel N. Ide.* 1850. 12mo, pp. 338. B. 44320

MANN. Lectures, and Annual Reports, on Education. By Horace Mann. *Cambridge: For the Editor.* 1867. 8vo, pp. (2), xii, 571. H. 44321

[MANN.] The Massachusetts System of Common Schools; being an enlarged and revised Edition of the Tenth Annual Report of the first Secretary of the Massachusetts Board of Education. *Boston.* 1849. 8vo. 44322

MANN. Slavery: Letters and Speeches, By Horace Mann, ... *Boston: B. B. Mussey & Co.* 1851. 12mo, pp. xii, 564. H. + [*Ibid.*] 1853. 12mo, pp. xii, 564. B. 44323

MANN. Thoughts selected from the Writings of Horace Mann ... . *Boston: H. B. Fuller and Company.* [1867.] 16mo, pp. (2), 240. B. 44324

Also: Abstract of the Massachusetts School Returns for 1837. ... *Boston.* 1838. 8vo. Continued.—Answer to the "Rejoinder" of Twenty-Nine Boston Schoolmasters ... *Boston: Wm. B. Fowle and Nahum Capen.* 1845. 8vo, pp. 124.—Baccalaureate delivered at Antioch College, 1857. ... [n. p. n. d.] 16mo, pp. 61.—Dedication of Antioch College, and Inaugural Address of its President ... with other Proceedings. *Yellow Springs, O.: A. S. Dean.* 1854. 16mo, pp. 144.—Demands of the Age on Colleges. Speech ... October 5, 1854. *New York: Fowler and Wells.* 1857. 16mo, pp. 86.—A Few Thoughts for a Young Man: a Lecture ... . *Boston: Ticknor, Reed, and Fields.* MDCCCL. 16mo, pp. 84. H.—A Few Thoughts on the Powers and Duties of Woman. Two Lectures. ... *Syracuse: Hall, Mills, and Company.* 1853. 24mo, pp. (2), 141.—Lectures on Various Subjects ... . *New York: Fowler and Wells.* 1859. 12mo. Portrait. B.—New Dangers To Freedom, and New Duties for its Defenders: ... *Boston: Redding and Company.* 1850. 8vo, pp. 32.—Observations on a Pamphlet, entitled "Remarks on the Seventh Annual Report of ... Horace Mann" ... . *Boston: Samuel N. Dickinson, Printer.* 1844. 8vo, pp. 16.—An Oration ... at Providence, September 6, 1825, before the United Brother's Society of Brown University. ... *Providence: Printed by Barnum Field & Co.* 1825. 8vo, pp. 30.—An Oration ... at Dedham, July 4th, 1823 ... . *Dedham: Printed by H. & W. H. Mann.* [n. d.] 8vo, pp. 25.—An Oration ... before the Authorities of ... Boston, July 4, 1842. ... *Boston: John H. Eastburn ... Printer.* 1842. 8vo, pp. 86. + Fourth Edition. [*Boston.* 1842.] 8vo, pp. 31. + *Boston: Wm. B. Fowle and Nahum Capen* ... 1842. 8vo, pp. 24. + Fifth Edition. [n. p. n. d.] 8vo, pp. 31.—Rejoinder to the "Reply" of ... Horace Mann, ... to the "Remarks" of the Association of Boston Masters, upon his Seventh Annual Report. *Boston: Charles C. Little and James Brown.* 1845. 8vo, pp. 55.—Rejoinder to the Second Section of the "Reply." [*Boston.* 1845.] 8vo, pp. 56.—Rejoinder to the Third Section of the "Reply." [*Boston.* 1845.] 8vo, pp. 40.—Rejoinder to the Fourth Section of the "Reply." [*Boston.* 1845.] 8vo, pp. 64. BA.—Reply to the "Remarks" of Thirty-One Boston Schoolmasters on the Seventh Annual Report of the Secretary of the Massachusetts Board of Education. ... *Boston: W. B. Fowle and Nahum Capen.* 1844. 8vo, pp. 176.—Rejoinder to the "Reply" of the Hon. Horace Mann ... to the "Remarks" of the ... Boston [School] Masters ... . *Boston: Charles C. Little*

... 1845. 8vo, pp. 55, 56, 40, 64.—Report of the Secretary of the Board of Education, on the Subject of School Houses, Supplementary to his First Annual Report. *Boston: Dutton and Wentworth,* ... *Printers.* 1838. 8vo, pp. 64.—Report and Resolution; on the "Code of Honor" ... [and] on Intemperance, Profanity, etc. *Columbus.* 1857. 8vo, pp. 16.—Report of an Educational Tour in Germany, and Parts of Great Britain and Ireland, being Part of the Seventh Annual Report of Horace Mann ... . With Preface and Notes, by W. B. Hodgson ... . *London: Simpkin, Marshall, and Company.* 1846. 16mo, pp. x, 272.—Seventh Annual Report of the ... Secretary of the Board [of Education of Massachusetts]. *Boston: Dutton and Wentworth ... Printers.* 1844. 8vo, pp. 199. Continued.—Remarks on the Seventh Annual Report of ... Hon. Horace Mann ... . *Boston: Charles C. Little* ... 1844. 8vo, pp. 144.—Sequel to the So Called Correspondence between Rev. M. H. Smith and Horace Mann, Surreptitiously published by Mr. Smith; Containing a Letter from Mr. Mann, suppressed by Mr. Smith, with the reply ... . *Boston: William B. Fowle.* 1847. 8vo, pp. 56. B.—Speech ... June 30, 1848, on the Right of Congress to Legislate for the Territories of the United States, and its Duty to exclude Slavery therefrom. *Washington: Printed by J. & G. S. Gideon.* 1848. 8vo, pp. 20. + Revised Edition. *Boston: William B. Fowle.* 1848. 8vo, pp. 31, (1). + [New and Revised Edition. n. p. n. d.] 8vo, pp. 31, (1). H. + To which is added, a Letter from ... Martin Van Buren, and ... Joshua Leavitt. *Boston: J. Howe, Printer.* 1848. 12mo, pp. 48.—Speech ... Feb. 23, 1849; on Slavery in the United States, and the Slave Trade in the District of Columbia. ... *Boston: Wm. B. Fowle.* [n. d.] 8vo, pp. 15. + *Philadelphia.* 1849. 12mo, pp. 48.—Speech ... on the subject of Slavery in the Territories, and the consequences of a Dissolution of the Union. ... February 15, 1850. ... *Washington: Gideon & Co., Printers.* 1850. 8vo, pp. 15. + *Boston: Redding and Company.* 1850. 8vo, pp. 35.—Speech ... on the Institution of Slavery ... August 17, 1852. *Boston: Charles List & Co.* 1852. 8vo, pp. 23. + *Washington: Buell & Blanchard, Printers.* [1852.] 8vo, pp. 24.— ... Speech ... Feb. 28, 1851, on the Fugitive Slave Law. [n. p. n. d.] 8vo. + *Boston: W. S. Damrell & Co.* 1851. 8vo, pp. 24.—Speech ... on the Fugitive Slave Law, ... at Lancaster, Mass., May 19th, 1851. *Boston.* 1851. 8vo, pp. 16.—Twelve Sermons: delivered at Antioch College ... . *Boston: Ticknor & Fields.* M DCCC LX. 12mo, pp. 314. + [*Ibid.*] M DCCC LXI.—Two Lectures on Intemperance. ... *Syracuse: Hall, Mills, and Company.* 1852. 16mo, pp. 127.—The Common School Journal, for the Year 1839. ... *Boston.* 1839. 8vo, pp. 396. H. Continued to 1847 or later. *See also* Massachusetts, *and* [Withington (L.)]

MANN. Inauguration of the Statue of Horace Mann, in the State-House Grounds, Boston, Massachusetts, July 4, 1865 ... . *Boston: Walker, Fuller, and Company.* 1865. 4to, pp. 29. H.

MANN. Life and Works of Horace Mann. Edited by Mrs. Mary Mann. ... *Boston and Cambridge: H. B. Fuller.* 1865–68. 3 vols., 8vo, pp. 602; (2), xii, 571; xii, 758. H. 44326

MANN. Review of the Life of Horace Mann. From the Biblical Repository ... for January, 1866. [n. p. n. d.] 8vo, pp. 24. B. 44327

MANN (J.) Medical Sketches of the Campaigns of 1812, 13, 14. To which are added, ... Observations on Military Hospitals; ... [With] An Appendix ... . By James Mann, M.D. ... *Dedham: Printed by H. Mann and Co.* 1816. 8vo, pp. 317, (1). 44328

Contains information relative to the war not found elsewhere. Also: An Eulogium Pronounced on Account of the Death of Brother Amos Haines, of Montgomery Lodge,

... *Providence.* 1804. 8vo.—An Oration, Addressed to the Fraternity of Freemasons, ... in Wrentham ... . *Printed at Wrentham, Massachusetts, by Nathaniel Heaton, Jun.* M,DCC,XCVIII 8vo, pp. 32. BA.—Oration at Wrentham, Mass. July 4, 1801. ... *Wrentham.* 1801. 8vo.

MANN (J.) The American Bird-Keeper's Manual; or Directions for the Proper Management of American ... Singing Birds By James Mann ... . *Boston.* 1848. 16mo, pp. 166. B. 44329

MANN (J.) ... A Discourse ... to the ... St. Alban's Lodge, ... in Bristol, R. I. Dec. 27, A.L. 5815 ... . By Joel Mann, A.M. ... *Warren, R. I.: Printed by S. Randall.* [n. d.] 8vo, pp. 24.

Also: Discourse at Bristol on the Landing of the Pilgrims at Plymouth, 22d Dec. 1820. ... *Warren, R. I.* 1821. 8vo.—Intemperance destructive of National Welfare. An Essay. ... [*Suffield?*] 1828. 12mo, pp. 12. M.

[MANN (J.)] ... To the Proprietors of Mount Auburn Cemetery. [n. p. n. d.] 16mo, pp. 10. H. 44331

MANN (Julius). Die Ansiedler in Amerika. Eine Erzählung für die christliche Jugend. *Stuttgart.* 1845. 8vo. 44332

MANN (J. A.) The Cotton Trade of Great Britain: its Rise, Progress, & Present Extent ... . By James A. Mann ... . *London: Simpkin, Marshall & Co.* 1860. 8vo, pp. (4), vii, 134, (1). Map and Tables. BA. 44333

[MANN (Mary).] Life of Horace Mann. By his Wife. *Boston: Walker, Fuller and Company.* MDCCCLXV. 8vo, pp. 602. + Second Edition. [*Ibid.*] M DCCC LXV. 8vo, pp. xi, 9–609.

MANN (S.) A Sermon preached in Wrentham, January 1, 1701. By ... Rev. Samuel Mann ... . And Now published at the Request of Several of his Descendants ... . *Dedham: Printed by Herman Mann.* 1801. 8vo, pp. 24. W. 44335

MANN (William). Mann's Emigrant's Complete Guide to Canada; containing the most recent Information ... . *Dublin: Grattan.* 1851. 12mo, pp. 40. Map. 44336

MANN. Mann's Emigrant's Complete Guide to the United States of America. *London: Strange.* 1850. 12mo, pp. 72.

MANN (W. J.) Lutheranism in America: an Essay on the present Condition of the Lutheran Church in the United States. By W. J. Mann, D.D. *Philadelphia: Lindsay & Blakiston.* 1857. 12mo, pp. (2), 7–152. C. 44338

MANN (W. W.) What are we coming to! or, The Veil removed. Peace–Reconciliation–Reconfederation. By W. W. Mann. [n. p. *Feb.*, 1863.] 8vo, pp. 8. B. 44339

MANNEQUIN (T.) A propos de la guerre contre le Paraguay par la Confédération Argentine, l'Uruguay et Brésil. Par M. Th. Mannequin. *Paris: Guillaumin et Cie.* 1866. 8vo, pp. 31.

MANNEQUIN. Aperçu moral et politique sur les sociétés hispano-américaines. Par M. Th. Mannequin. *Paris: Guillaumin.* 1855. 8vo. 44341

MANNEQUIN. La Nouvelle-Grenade et ses réformateurs. Étude économique, politique et financière. Par Th. Mannequin. *Paris: Guillaumin.* 1859. 8vo, pp. 21. 44342

MANNEQUIN. Les Provinces Argentines et Buenos-Ayres, depuis leur indépendance jusqu'à nos jours. Étude historique et économique au point de vue de l'état actuel des choses dans ces contrées; par M. Th. Mannequin. *Paris: Guillaumin.* 1856. 8vo. 44343

These four pieces, by Mannequin, are extracted from the "Journal des économistes."

MANNE-VILETTE (*M.* Daprès de). Mémoire sur la Navigation de France aux Indes. *Paris: De l'Imprimerie Royale.* 1765. 4to, pp. 131. J.C.B. + *Paris.* 1768. 4to, pp. 60. 44344

MANNERS (G.) The Conflagration, a Poem, written and published for the Benefit of the Sufferers by the Recent Disastrous Fires in the Province of New Brunswick. By George Manners. *Boston: Ingraham & Hewes.* 1825. 4to, pp. 18. W. 44345

MANNERS (Motley), *pseudon.* *See* [Duganne (A. J. H.)], *note.*

MANNERS (N.) A Concise Account of the Conduct ... of Nicholas Manners [a Methodist Minister] in ... America. ... *Leeds: T. Hannam.* [about 1770.] 18mo, pp. 208. 44346

Contains curious details of American religious life by a Yorkshireman. "This City (New York), though not so large as Philadelphia, seems to be more healthful."

MANNERS. A Word to the World in General, and to the North Americans in Particular ... . By Nicholas Manners. [n. p. n. d.] 8vo, pp. 12. N. 44347

The Manners ... of the Indians. *See* [Goodrich (S. G.)]

MANNI (M.) Dom. M. Manni de Florentinis Inventis Commentarium ... . *Ferrariæ.* 1731. 8vo. 44348

Who discovered America? is the subject of one of the chapters.

MANNING (J. M.) ... Oration ... before the City Authorities of Boston, on the Fourth of July, 1865. By J. M. Manning. ... *Boston: J. E. Farwell & Company.* 1865. 8vo, pp. 108.

MANNING. The Soldier of Freedom. A Sermon ... before the Officers of the Forty-Third Regiment, M. V., ... Boston, ... Oct. 5, 1862. By Jacob M. Manning. ... *Boston: J. E. Farwell and Company, Printers.* 1862. 8vo, pp. 20. B. 44350

Also: ... A Discourse, before the American Education Society, ... May 24, 1859. ... *Boston: T. R. Marvin & Son.* 1859. 8vo, pp. 22.—A New-Year's Address delivered before the Boston Young Men's Christian Association ... January 2, 1858. ... *Boston: Printed by Danviell and Moore.* 1859. 8vo, pp. 20.—Sermon and Addresses, at the Installation of ... Rev. Jacob M. Manning ... in Boston, Mar. 11, 1857. *Boston: T. R. Marvin & Son.* 1857. 8vo, pp. 91.— ... A Sermon in behalf of the American Home Missionary Society, ... May 10, 1870. ... *New York.* 1870. 8vo, pp. 24. B.

MANNING (J.) A Sketch of the Life and Writings of the Rev. Micaiah Towgood. By James Manning. *Exeter* [*Eng.*]: *The Author.* 1792. 8vo, pp. 191. C. 44351

Also: A Charge from the President to the Graduates at ... Providence, September 2, 1789. ... *Boston: Printed by Manning & Loring.* [1806.] 12mo, pp. 6. BA.

MANNING (J. W.) The Code of ... Atlanta ... . Compiled and arranged by Judge Jethro W. Manning ... . *Atlanta, Georgia.* 1863. 8vo, pp. 96, viii. H. 44352

MANNING (R.) Book of Fruits: ... a ... Catalogue of the most Valuable Varieties of the Pear, Apple, Peach, Plum & Cherry, for New-England Culture. By Robert Manning. ... *Salem: Ives & Jewett.* 1838. 12mo, pp. 120. Plates. BA.

MANNING. The New England Fruit Book. ... By Robert Manning. ... Second Edition enlarged. By John M. Ives. *W. & S. B. Ives, Salem.* 1844. 12mo, pp. (8), 133. Plates. B.

MANNING [R. J.] Speech of Mr. Manning ... on ... the Reception of Abolition Memorials. ... Feb. 23, 1836. *Washington: Printed by Blair & Rives.* 1836. 8vo, pp. 11. H.

MANOEL DA COSTA (C.) Villa Rica; Poema. Por Claudio Manoel da Costa. *Ouro-Petro: Typ. do Universal.* 1839. 4to, pp. (4), xix, 80. 44356

The date, at the end of the book, is 1841. "Ce poëme, composé en 1773, a pour sujet l'histoire de Villa Rica, maintenant Ouro Preto, chef-lieu de la province de Minas-Geraes."—LECLERC.

MANOEL DA CONCEICAO (J.) As Exequias de Abrahao Lincoln, com um Esboco Biographico do mesmo offerecido ao Povo Brasileiro, por seu Patricio José Manoel da Conceicao. *Rio Janeiro.* 1865. 8vo, pp. 40. 44357

Manomin. Rhythmical Romance of Minnesota. *Myron Colony, St. Louis.* 1866. 16mo, pp. 297. 44358

[Mañozca (Juan de).] Memorial; sobre las oposiciones del padre provincial del Piru. [n. p. 16—.] Folio, 26 leaves.

Mansfeldt (Julius). Meine Reise nach Brasilien im Jahre 1826. *Magdeburg.* 1828. 8vo. Maps and Plates. c. 44360

Mansfield (A.) ... A Sermon preached November 2, 1791, at the Ordination of the Reverend John Elliot ... in East Guilford. By Achilles Mansfield, A.M. *New Haven: Printed by Thomas and Samuel Green.* [1791.] 8vo, pp. 38. W. 44361

Also: Sermon ... at the Funeral of George Elliot, Esq. at Killingworth [Conn.], May 3, 1810. ... *Hartford.* 1810. 8vo. W.

Mansfield (C. B.) Paraguay, Brazil, and the Plate. Letters written in 1852–53. By C. B. Mansfield, Esq. ... With a Sketch of the Author's Life, By ... Rev. Charles Kingsley, Jun. ... *Cambridge: Macmillan & Co.* MDCCCLVI. 12mo, pp. (1), xxi, (1), 504. Map, Portrait and Illustrations. B., BA. 44362

See "New Quart. Rev.," Oct. 1856, p. 423.

Mansfield (D.) Two Sermons, ... on the Second Centennial Anniversary of the Organization of the First Church ... in Wenham. By Daniel Mansfield ... . *Andover: Printed by Allen, Morrill and Wardwell.* 1845. 8vo, pp. 72. H., S. 44363

Also: ... A Sermon ... at the Dedication of the New Meeting-House erected by the Congregational Society in Wenham, Dec. 20, 1843. ... *Andover: Allen, Morrill and Wardwell.* 1844. 8vo, pp. 24. BA.

Mansfield (E. D.) American Education, its Principles and Elements. ... By Edward D. Mansfield ... . *New York: A. S. Barnes & Co.* 1851. 12mo, pp. 330. + [*Ibid.*] 1853 and 1855.

[Mansfield.] Exposition of Mackinaw City and its Surroundings. [n. p. n. d.] 8vo, pp. 23. H. 44365

Mansfield. Exposition of the Natural Position of Mackinaw City, and the Climate, Soil, and Commercial Elements of the Surrounding Country. By E. D. Mansfield, Esq. *Cincinnati: Wrightson & Co., Printers.* 1857. 8vo, pp. 47, (1). 2 Maps.

Mansfield. The Life of General Winfield Scott. By Edward D. Mansfield, Esq. *New York: A. S. Barnes & Co.* 1846. 12mo, pp. 366. B., C. 44367

Mansfield. The Life of General Winfield Scott, embracing his Campaign in Mexico. By Edward D. Mansfield, Esq. *New*

York: A. S. Barnes & Co. 1848. 8vo, pp. 414. Maps, Portrait, and Plates. BA. 44368

Also: The only Authentic Edition. Life and Services of General Winfield Scott ... . *New York: A. S. Barnes & Co.* 1852. 8vo, pp. 538. Map, Plates and Portrait. H.

Mansfield. Memoirs of the Life and Services of Daniel Drake, M.D., Physician, Professor, and Author; With Notices of the Early Settlement of Cincinnati ... . By Edward D. Mansfield, LL.D. ... . *Cincinnati: Applegate & Co.* 1855. 12mo, pp. 408. Portrait. H. 44369

Mansfield. The Mexican War: A History of its Origin, and a detailed Account of the Victories ... With the Official Dispatches of the Generals. By Edward D. Mansfield ... . *New York: A. S. Barnes & Co.* 1848. 8vo, pp. 323. Maps and Plates. B. + [*Ibid.*] 1850. 12mo, pp. 365. Maps and Plates. + Tenth Edition. [*Ibid.*] 1858. + [*Ibid.*] 1860. B. 44370

Mansfield. The Political Grammar of the United States; or, a complete view of the Theory and Practice of the General and State Governments, with the relations between them. ... By Edward D. Mansfield ... . *New-York: Harper & Brothers.* 1834. 12mo, pp. viii, 13–275. C. + *Wiley and Long, New-York.* 1836. 16mo, pp. 292. + *Philadelphia.* 1836. 12mo. + New Edition ... *Cincinnati: Truman & Smith.* 1839. 12mo, pp. 336. + *Cincinnati.* 1843. 12mo, pp. 336. + *Cincinnati: W. T. Truman.* 1846. 12mo, pp. 336. + A New and Revised Edition ... . *Cincinnati: E. D. Truman.* 1849. 12mo, pp. 234. + [*Ibid.*] 1851. 44371

Mansfield. The Political Manual: ... a ... View of the Theory and Practice of the ... Governments of the United States. ... By Edward D. Mansfield ... . *New York: A. S. Barnes & Burr.* 1861. 12mo, pp. 347. B. 44372

The same as the foregoing with a new title-page.

Mansfield. A Popular and Authentic Life of Ulysses S. Grant. By Edward D. Mansfield. *Cincinnati: R. W. Carroll & Co.* 1868. 12mo, pp. 377. Map, Portrait, and Plate. B.

Mansfield. Popular and Authentic Lives of Ulysses S. Grant and Schuyler Colfax. By Edward D. Mansfield. *Cincinnati: R. W. Carroll & Co.* 1868. 12mo, pp. 425. 5 Maps, 2 Portraits, and Plate. 44374

Mansfield. Sketch of a Journey through the Western States of North America and the City of Cincinnati. *Cincinnati.* 1827. 12mo. Map. 44375

Mansfield. The Utility and Services of the United States Military Academy. A Discourse. By Edward D. Mansfield. *New York.* 1847. 8vo. S. 44376

Contains notices of some of its graduates who fell in Mexico. Also: The Annual Address delivered before the Cincinnati Astronomical Society, June, 1845 ... . *Cincinnati: Printed by R. P. Brooks.* 1845. 8vo, pp. 55, (1). B., M.—A Discourse on the Utility of History. ... *Cincinnati.* 1839. 4to. A.—Eulogy on ... William Henry Harrison ... 14th of May, 1841 ... . *Cincinnati: U. P. James.* 1841. 8vo, pp. 23.—The Issues and Duties of the Day. ... *Cincinnati: Caleb Clark.* 1864. 8vo, pp. 15. —Lecture on the Uses of History ... . *Cincinnati: Kendall and Henry, Printers.* 1838. 8vo, pp. 18.—The Legal Rights, Liabilities, and Duties of Women. ... *Salem.* 1845. 12mo. + [*Ibid.*] 1848.—A Letter in regard to the Tariff on Iron and Labor ... . *Cincinnati: Wrightson & Co., Printers.* 1869. 8vo, pp. 40.—On the Railway Connections of Philadelphia with the Central West. ... *Philadelphia: John C. Clark, Printer.* 1853. 8vo, pp. (2), 36.—[Articles on] The Tariff ... . [*Cincinnati?*] 1865. 8vo, pp. 16.—The United States Military Academy at West Point. ... *Boston: American Journal of Education, March,* 1863. 8vo, pp. 48. *See* Drake (B.), Vol. v., No. 20813.

Mansfield (I.) A Sermon, preached in the Camp at Roxbury, November 23, 1775; Being the Day ... for Thanksgiving ... By Isaac Mansfield, jun. ... *Boston: Printed by S. Hall.* 1776. 8vo, pp. 27, (1). BA. 44377

Published by request of the Officers of Gen. Thomas' regiment in the Continental Army.

Mansfield (J.) An Oration, ... at Western, ... July 4th, 1812. By Jacob Mansfield. ... *Printed at Worcester,* (*Mass.*) *By Henry Rogers.* 1812. 8vo, pp. 12. B. 44378

Mansfield (J. B.) Personal Sketches of the Members of the 40th Congress ... . Maine Delegation. By J. B. Mansfield and D. W. Kelsey. *Baltimore: The Author.* 1867. 12mo, pp. 12.

Mansfield (J. L.) Merits of the Dred Scott Decision. A Speech by ... Hon. John L. Mansfield ... Sept. 17, 1860. *Indianapolis.* 1860. 8vo, pp. 16. H. 44380

Mansfield (J.) Hope, A Poem, delivered in the Chapel of Harvard University, ... July 8th, 1800. By Joseph Mansfield, ... *Cambridge: Printed by William Hilliard.* 1800. 4to, pp. 15.

Contains some allusions to Washington.

Mansfield (Joseph K. F.) Memorial of Gen. J. K. F. Mansfield, who fell in the Battle at Sharpsburg, Sept. 17, 1862. *Boston: Press of T. R. Marvin & Co.* 1862. 8vo, pp. 67.

Mansfield (L. D.) Memorial of Charles Finney Mansfield; comprising Extracts from his Diary, Letters and other Papers. By Rev. L. D. Mansfield. *New York.* 1866. 8vo. 44383

[Mansfield (L. W.)] Up Country Letters. [By Z. P.] Edited by Prof. B——, National Observatory. *New York: D. Appleton & Co.* 1852. 12mo, pp. 331. Plate. 44384

Mansfield (*Lord*). *See* Murray (William), *Earl of Mansfield.*

Mansfield, *Mass.* Annual Report of the School Committee ... 1864–5. *Taunton.* 1865. 8vo, pp. 8. H. 44385

Mansfield, *O.* Business Guide and City Directory of Mansfield, Ohio, for 1867–8. *Mansfield, O.: L. D. Myers & Brother, Printers.* 1868. 8vo, pp. 92. 44386

Manship (A.) National Jewels: Washington, Lincoln, and the Fathers of the Revolution. By Rev. Andrew Manship. *Philadelphia: The Author.* 1865. 8vo, pp. 123. 44387

Manship. Thirteen Years' Experience in the Itinerancy. By Rev. Andrew Manship. Second Edition. *Philadelphia: Higgins and Perkinpine.* 1856. 12mo, pp. (4), 398. 2 Plates and Portrait. C. 44388

Mansie (A.) ... The Apprenticed Labourer's Manual: Or An Essay on the Apprenticeship System, and the Duties of the Apprenticed Labourers ... . By Alexander Mansie ... . *British Guiana.* 1837. 8vo, pp. xiv, 217, 13. 44389

Mansilla (Lucio V.) Una Escursion à los Indios Ranqueles. *Buenos Aires.* 1870. 8vo, pp. 347, vii, 428, x. Map. 44390

Mansion (H.) Précis Historique sur la Colonie Française au Goazacoalcos [Mexique]; avec la Réfutation des Prospectus publiés par MM. Laisne de Villevêque, Giordan et Baradère. ... Par M. Hypolite Mansion. *Londres: Davidson et Fils.* 1831. 8vo, pp. viii, 260. A. 44391

Evidently printed at Paris.

Manso de Contreras (C.) Relacion Cierta, y Verdadera de lo que sucediô, y a sucedido en esta Villa de Guadalcaçar, Provincia de Tehauntepeque, desde los 22 Março de 1660, hasta los 4 de Julio de 1661. Executado por el Snr. Don Juan Francisco de Montemayor a Cuenca del Cnsjo de su Magistad ... . Escribiala Don Christoval Manso de Contreras Regidor de la

Ciudad de Antequera ... . Cerca de que los Naturales Indios de estas Provincias, tumultuados y amotinados, mataron, á D. Juan de Avellan ... . *Mexico, por Juan Ruyz.* 1661. 4to, pp. 74.

An interesting account of the rising of the Tehuantepec Indians in 1660. Extremely rare.

Manso y Zuniga (Francisco). Regla y Ordenaciones de las Religiosas de la Limpia, e Immaculada Concepcion de la Virgin Sant. Nrã Señora. Que se an de Obseruar en los Conuentos de la dicha Orden de la Ciudad de Mexico ... . *Mexico, por Juan Ruysz.* 1635. 4to. 44393

Manso de Velasco (Joseph). El dia de Lima. Proclamacion real que de el nombre augusto de el supremo Señor D. Fernando VI. ... hizo la muy noble, y muy leal Ciudad de los reyes Lima ... . Con la relacion de la solemne pompa de tan fausto felice aplauso, y de las reales fiestas, con que se celebró. [*Lima?*] 1748. 8vo, pp. (4), 268, 21 leaves. Plate. C. 44394

Manso de Noronha (J.) Compendio de la historia de las provincias unidas del Rio de la Plata desde su descubrímiento hasta la declaracion de su independencia el 9 Julio de 1816. Por Juana Manso de Noronha. Segunda edicion. *Buenos-Aires.* 1865. 18mo, pp. 96. 44395

Also: Anales de la Educacion comun en la Republica Argentina, editados por Dr. Juana Manso de Noronha. *Buenos Aires.* 1862. 8vo. Continued.

Mante (T.) The | History | of the | Late War | in | North-America, | and the | Islands of the West-Indies, | including | the Campaigns of MDCCLXIII, and MDCCLXIV, | against his Majesty's Indian Enemies. | By Thomas Mante, | Assistant Engineer during the Siege of the Havanna, | and Major of a Brigade in the Campaign of 1764. | *London:* | *Printed for W. Strahan, and T. Cadell.* MDCCLXXII. 4to, pp. (4), viii, 542, (1). 18 Maps. H. 44396

Copies with all the maps are scarce. It is probable that but few were printed, though the large and beautiful plans and military maps (which gave it so great a value), must have made its production a work of much expense. The introduction contains an account of Washington's escape from assassination, in December, 1753. "An able and well-informed historian, distinguished for his accuracy and general impartiality."—Bancroft's *History,* Vol. v., Chap. x. "It is the best history of the war that has been written."—Sparks. *See also* "M. Rev.," XLVIII. 371.

Mantegazza (C.) Viaggio del cittadino Carlo Mantegazza ... a S. Domingo nell' anno 1802. ... *Milano.* 1803. 8vo, pp. (6), 136. H. 44397

Mantegazza (P.) Rio de la Plata e Tenerife, viaggi e studi. *Milano.* 1867. 8vo, pp. 736. 8 Plates. 44398

Mantegazza. Sulla América meridionale. Lettere mediche. *Milano.* 1860. 8vo. 44399

Mantovani (P. L.) Orazione Panegirica per la solennitá di S. Maria di Guadalupe recitada nella chiesa di S. Vito del abate Paolo Luigi Mantovani. *Ferrara, per gli Eredi Arnaldi.* [1784.] 8vo, pp. XXX. 44400

Mantovano *or* Guazzo (Marco). Historie di Tvtte le | Cose degne di Memoria qval del | Anño M.D.XXIIII. Sino questo presente sono occorse | nella Italia, ... nella Inghilterra, nella Spagna | ... | nella India, et altri lvoghi, | col nome di molti huomini scientiati, Noua- | mente con la giunta & la Tauola | ristampate & corrette. | *Con Gratia et Privilegio* | *in Venetia* M.D.XXXXV. | ... | [Colophon:] *In Vinegia per Cominvda* | *Trino de Monferrato* | *l'Anno* M.D.XXXXV. | 12mo, 8 prel. leaves, 408 leaves. 44401

Mantovano. Historie di | M. Marco Gvazzo | Di Tutti i Fatti Degni | Di Memoria nel Mon- | do Svccessi | Dell'Anno M.D.XXIIII. | Sino a Questo Presente | Con Molte Cose Nova- | mente giunte in piu luoghi de l'ope- | ra, & nel fine, che ne l'altre non | erano nouamente & con | diligenza ristampate. | *In Vinegia Appresso Gabriel* | *Giolito de Ferrari.* | MDXLVI. | 12mo, 8 prel. leaves, 375 leaves. 44402

See [Harrisse's] "Bib. Am. Vet.," Additions, Nos. 153 and 157.

Mantuanus (B.) Opera Noua Ba | ptistæ Mantuani Carmelitæ. | Georgius. | Cœcilia. | Brixia. | Siluarum Libri duo. | Exhortatio regũ christianorũ vt ducant in bar- | baros. | *Venundantur sub Pelicano & a Badio.* | [Colophon:] *Ex ędib9 Ascẽsianis Ad nonas Ianuarias* | *Anni.* M. D. IX. *ad calculũ Romanũ.* | 8vo, Title, 1 leaf, ii–xcv leaves, 1 leaf. 44403

See [Harrisse's] "Bib. Am. Vet.," Additions, No. 35.

Manual breve y forma de administrar los sacramentos a los Indios. *Mexico.* 1617. 8vo. 44404

Title from Ternaux, No. 391. I find no other account of it.

The Manual Exercise. *See* [Harvey (Edward)], VIII. 30771.

Manual Exercise and Evolutions of the Cavalry; as practised in the late American Army. *Concord: G. Hough.* 1806. 8vo.

Manual Guide des Voyageurs. *See* [Fernagus de Gelone].

Manual de Adultos [of which only the last leaves are known, bearing the following termination:] *Imprimiose este Manual de*

Adultos en la gran ciudad de Mexico por mandado do los Rev. Señores Obispos de la Nueva España y a sus expensas: en casa de Juan Cromberger. Año del nacimiento de nuestro Señor Jesu Christo de mil y quinientos y quarenta. A xiij dias del mes de Deziembre. 4to.

These fragments formed part of a volume in the Biblioteca Provincial of Toledo, from which they suddenly disappeared. They were accidentally discovered by Señor Don. Pascual de Gayangos at a book-stall in London in 1870, and purchased by him. Mr. Harrisse, in the additions to his "Bib. Americana Vetus.," No. 123, has given a facsimile of a portion of one of the leaves, being a series of verses; and of the colophon on the last leaf. There is a table of errata which refers to almost every page, and as the list ends with the thirty-sixth leaf, to which the two leaves in question should be added, Mr. Harrisse is of opinion that the book consisted of thirty-eight leaves.' It is certainly a work of the greatest rarity, and the discovery of a perfect copy will be an interesting addition to the history of printing in Mexico.

Manual of American Geography, designed to accompany the New Map of Our Country, Present and Prospective. *New York: J. G. Wells.* 1858. 12mo, pp. 132. 44407

Manual of Botany for the Northern States, to the north of Virginia, by the Members of the Botanical Class in Williams' College ... compiled by the Author of Richard's Botanical Dictionary. *Albany: Printed by Websters and Skinners.* 1817. 12mo, pp. vi, 164. H. 44408

Corrected title of our Vol. VI., No. 21706. For later editions *see* No. 21707–8.

A Manual of Horse-Breeding, for the Eastern Townships of Canada ... . *Melbourne: S. M. Taylor.* 1845. 12mo. 44409

A Manual of Military Surgery. Prepared for the use of the Confederate States Army. ... *Richmond: Ayres & Wade.* 1863. 12mo, pp. 297. 30 pages of Plates. 44410

Manual of Religious Liberty, By an Author, as yet, unknown. *New York: For Mr. Rivington.* 1767. 8vo. 44411

Manual of the Baptist Church in Columbus, Mississippi. [n. p. n. d.] 8vo, pp. 7. Plate. 44412

Manual of the House of Representatives of the United States; being a Digest of the Rules ... . *Washington.* 1859. 8vo, pp. (2), 166. C. 44413

Manual of the Lancasterian System of Teaching ... as practised in the ... Free School Society, of New York. *New York.* 1820. 8vo, pp. 63. 44414

Manual of the Lance and Lance Exercise for the Cavalry Service. By a Field Officer. *Savannah: John M. Cooper & Co.* 1862. 12mo, pp. 15. 44415

Manual on the Cultivation of the Sugar Cane, and the Fabrication and Refinement of Sugar. ... *City of Washington: Francis Preston Blair.* 1833. 8vo, pp. 122. 4 Plates. 44416

Manual para administrar los sacramentos. *Mexico.* [n. d.] 4to.

Manual | para administrar á los Indios | del Idioma Cahita | los santos | Sacramentos, | segun la reforma de NN. SS. P.P. | Paulo V. y Urbano VIII. | Compuesto | por un Sacerdote de la Compañia de Jesvs, | Missionero en las de la Provincia de Zynaloa. | Sacalo á luz | La piedad del Alferez D. Sebastian Lopez | de Guzman, y Ayala. | ... *Impresso en Mexico; con las licencias necessarias, en la Imprenta Real del Superior Gobierno de Doña Maria de Ribera, en el Empedradillo. Año de* 1740. 8vo. 44418

Collation: Title, 1 leaf; Dedicatoria, 6 leaves; Prólogo, Parecer, Aprobacion and Licencias, 6 leaves; Text, pp. 1–163 and 1 unnumbered page; Oràtio pro conversione infidelium, Albado and Errata, 2 unnumbered leaves.

Manual Serafico, o Libro de la Vida de los Frayles Menores, en que se contiene el Texto Latino de la Regla, y Testamento de S. Francisco, con la traduction Castellaña. Dispuesto para el uso de todos los Conventos de esta Santa Provincia de San Diego de Mexico, de Orden de Fr. Pedro de Oronsoro. *Reimpresso en México.* 1779. 4to. 44419

Manuale formarum Juramentorum ab his Præstandorum, qui in Rectores, Consiliarios, et Officiales in hac alma, Imperiali Mexicana eliguntur ... . Typis mandatum jussu D.D.D. Emmanuelis Ignatii Beye, Zisnoros, et Quixano. A.D. 1759, *Mexici, ex nova Typographiâ editioni Bibliothecæ Mexicanæ destinatâ.* 4to.

Manuale Secundum usum alme Ecclesie Mexicane: Summa diligentia novissime recognitum in multisq̃ locupletatum. *Mexicana, in edibus, Johãnis Pauli impressoris,* A.D. 1560. 4to.

A Mexican service-book of extreme rarity. The pagination is full of errors. Printed in red and black, with musical notes.

Manuductio ad Ministerium. *See* [Mather (Cotton)].

Manuel de Albuene (D.) Origen y estado de la causa formada sobre la Real orden de 17 de Mayo de 1810, que trata del comercio de América. *Cadiz: Vicente Lema.* 1811. 4to, pp. 122. 44422

Manuel de Herla. El Parnaso del real colegio de San Martin. *Lima.* 1694. 4to. 44423

Title from a New York catalogue.

Manuel de Mello (F.) Politica militar en avisos de Generales. Escrita al Conde de Liñares, Marquez de Viseo, capitan general del mar Oceano ... por D. Francisco Manuel de Mello. *Madrid, por Francisco Martinez.* 1638. 4to. 44424

Manuel de Mello. Relação dos successos da armada, que a Companhia geral de Commercio expediu ao estado do Brasil o anno passado de 1649, de que foi capitão geral o Conde de Castello-melhor, por D. Francisco Manuel de Mello. *Lisboa, na Officina Craesbeeckiana.* 1650. 4to, pp. 16. 44425

Manuel de la Sota (J.) Errores que contiene la memoria sobre la decadencia de las misiones jesuíticas, que ha publicado en la ciudad del Paraná el Dr. D. Martin de Moussy, en el presente ano de 1857; impugnados por Juan Manuel de la Sota. *Montevideo.* 1857. 8vo, pp. 26. 44426

Manuelde la Vega (F.) Historia del Descubrimiento de la América Septentrional por Cristobal Colón, escrita por Fr. Manuel de la Vega. Dala a luz con varias notas para mayor inteligencia de la historia de las Conquistas de Hernan Cortés que puso en mexicano Chimalpain, y para instruccion de la juventud mexicano Carlos Maria de Bustamante. *Mexico.* 1826. 8vo, pp. x, 238.

The Manufacture of Pot-Ash. *See* [Mascarene (John)].

Manufactures of the United States in 1860. Compiled from the Original Returns of the Eighth Census. *Washington.* 1865 [1866]. 4to, pp. ccxvii, 745. s. 44428

Manufactures and Statistics of the United States. Taken with the Census of 1810, 1820, 1830, 1840; as also from other sources. *Washington.* 1843. 4to. 44429

Manufactures, &c. No. 3. Central America (Financial Position) ... . *London.* 186–. 8vo. 44430

Manufacturing Interests of the United States: Essay, with Memorial of the Artists and Manufacturers of Philadelphia to Congress. *Philadelphia.* 1804. 8vo. c. 44431

The Manufacturing Interests of ... Buffalo: Including Sketches of ... [its] History ... . Second Edition. *Buffalo: C. F. S. Thomas.* 1866. 8vo, pp. iv, 99. h. 44432

The Manuscript. *See* [Griggs (*Rev. Mr.*)], vii. 28840.

The Manuscript. *See* Irving (W.), ix. 35192, *add* pp. 78.

Manuscript relating to Canada. *See* [Johnstone], ix. 36393.

Manuscrit Troano. Études sur le Système Graphique et la langue des Mayas, par M. Brasseur de Bourbourg. Vol. i. *Paris.* 1869. Imp. 4to, pp. viii, 224. 36 colored Plates.

Manutio (P.) Degli Elementi e di molti loro notabili effetti. *Venitia: P. Manutio.* 1557. 4to. 44434

In this scarce tract, Manuzio not only speaks of Columbus, but also of the stream in the ocean owing to the "moto diurno de cieli."

Manvill (*Mrs.* Elias F.) Lucinda, or the Mountain Mourner; being Recent Facts, in a Series of Letters from Mrs. Manvill, in the State of New York, to her Sister in Pennsylvania. *Johnstown.* 1807. 12mo. + Third Edition, with Additions. *Ballston Spa: Printed by J. Comstock.* 1817. 18mo, pp. 173. + *Albany: J. Munsell.* 1852. 12mo, pp. 168. s. 44435

Manwaring (C.) Essays, Historical, Moral, Political and Agricultural. By Christopher Manwaring. *New London: Samuel Green.* 1828. 12mo, pp. 204. c. + [*Ibid.*] 1829. 44436

Manwaring. Republicanism and Aristocracy contrasted; ... an Oration ... at New London, (Connecticut) July 4, 1804 ... . By Christopher Manwaring. *Norwich.* 1805. 8vo. + *Re-Printed at Boston* ... 1805. 8vo, pp. 12. ba. 44437

[Manypenny (George W.)] Les Hommes Rouges de l'Amérique du Nord. Rapport à M. le Ministre de l'Intérieur des États Unis, par M. le Chef du Bureau des Affaires Indiennes. *Paris: Imprimerie ... de Paul Dupont.* 1855. 8vo, pp. 27, (1). h.

[Manypenny.] Letter from the Commissioner of Indian Affairs to Colonel Benton. *Washington.* 1855. 8vo, pp. 15.

Manzaneda y Encinas (Diego Miguel Bringas de). Sermon que en las Solemnes Honras celebradas en obsequio de los V.V. P.P. Predicadores Apostólicos Fr. Francisco Tomas Hermenegildo Garcés: Fr. Juan Marcelo Diaz: Fr. José Matias Moreno: Fr. Juan Antonio Barreneche, Misioneros del Colegio de Propaganda Fide de la Santa Cruz de Queretaro, Fundadores de las Conversiones de la Purísima Concepcion, y de San Pedro y San Pablo del Rio Colorado entre los Gentiles Yumas, y muertos en ellas gloriosamente á manos de los mesmos Barbaros en los dias 17 y 19 de Julio de 1781. *Madrid: Villalpando.* 1819. 4to, pp. 94. 44440

Manzi (P.) Il Conquisto di Messico, ristretto de Pietro Manzi. *Roma.* 1797. 8vo. + [*Ibid.*] 1817. 44441

Very scarce. There are copies on thick paper.

Manzi. Storia della conquista del Messico fatta da Cortez. *Roma.* 1820. 8vo. 44442

Manzini (N. B. L.) Histoire de l'inoculation préservative de la fièvre jaune pratiquée par ordre du gouvernement espagnol à l'hopital militaire de la Havane rédigée par Nicolas B. L. Manzini ... . *Paris: J. B. Baillière et Fils.* 1858. 8vo, pp. xii, 243.

Map of the Battle Field of Fredericksburg ... also, Gen. Ro. E. Lee's Report of the Battle. *Lynchburg.* 1866. 8vo, pp. 33. Map. b. 44444

Map of the Military Bounty Lands. *See* Vol. ix. 34293.

Map of The Southern Part of Bergen Township, Hudson County, N. J. ... *Jersey City: Printed by J. Post.* 1860. 8vo.

A Map of the Whole World; or the Orb Terrestrial, in Four Parts, [viz.] Asia, Europe, Affrica [*sic*], America. ... *London:* ... *Thomas Jenner* ... 1668. 4to, pp. (8), 193. 44446

The description of America fills pages 171–191.

A Map: showing the location of the Sterling Iron Estate ... in Orange County, ... New York ... . *New York: Printed by Phair & Co.* 1856. 8vo, pp. 9. 44447

El Mapa de las Composiciones y nuevo descubrimiento, en que se assegura la caida del Reyno de Portugal por un Nautico ingenio, que ha venido de las Indias. *Madrid.* 1706. 8vo. 44448

A curious poem on a Voyage to South America and the West India Islands.

Mapes (J. J.) Inaugural Address, ... Jan. 7, 1845, before the Mechanics' Institute, ... of New-York. By James J. Mapes ... . *New York.* 1845. 8vo, pp. 23. ba. 44449

Mapimiha. Diligencia que el alcalde de Mapimiha practicado en el trance y remate de bienes de los Sres. Ortiz y Arriagas estrahidos del espediente original. *Durango.* 1831. 4to, pp. 24.

Maple Grove Cemetery Association. Rules and Regulations of the ... Association. *Albany.* 1865. 8vo. 44451

Maple Knot. *See* [Clemo], *pseudon*, Vol. iv., No. 13635.

"Maple Leaves from Canada: for the Grave of Abraham Lincoln": being a Discourse Delivered by Rev. Robert Norton, Pastor of the First Presbyterian Church, and Address by Rev. Robert F. Burns, Pastor of the Canada Presbyterian Church, at St. Catharines, Canada West, April 23rd, 1865. Together with Proceedings of Public Meetings, &c. *St. Catharines: Printed at E. L. Leavenworth's Book and Job Office.* 1865. 8vo, pp. 40.

Mapleson (T. W. Gwilt). A Hand-Book of Heraldry; with illuminated Illustrations, and illuminated pages of Arms of Distinguished American Families. By T. W. G. Mapleson. *New York.* [1851.] 4to. 13 Plates. c. 44453

Mapleson. Lays of the Western World. Illuminated by T. W. Gwilt Mapleson. *New York: Putnam.* [1847.] 4to.

Mapleson. Pearls of American Poetry. Illuminated by T. W. Gwilt Mapleson, Esq.; comprising the Choicest Selections from Longfellow, Halleck, Whittier, Percival, Sprague, Mrs. Sigourney, etc. *New York.* [n. d.] 4to. 44455

A fine specimen of book-making, every page being illuminated in gold and colors.

Mapleton; or, More Work for the Maine Law. *Boston.* 1853. 12mo. c. 44456

Mappas Geraes do Commercio de Portugal com suas Possessoes. 1848. *Lisboa.* 1851. Folio. + [*Ibid.*] 1855. Folio.

Maqueen (D.) A Sermon ... before the Society in Scotland for propagating Christian Knowledge, ... January 1. 1759. ... By Daniel Maqueen, d.d. ... *Edinburgh.* m,dcc,lix. 8vo, pp. 76.

Maraccio (P. H.) De Diva Copacavana in Peruano novi mundi regno celeberrima liber, unus. *Romæ.* 1654. Sm. 8vo. Plate. 44459

Marana, *pseudon.* The Future of America. Considered ... in View of ... re-opening the Slave Trade. By Marana. ... *Boston: Mansfield & Company.* [n. d.] 12mo, pp. 70. ba.

Maranhaõ. Regimento, & Leyes sobre as Missionens do Estado do Maranhaõ, & Parà, & sobre a liberdade dos Indios. Impresso por ordem de El-Rey nosso Senhor. *Lisboa Occidental: Antonio Manescal.* m.dccxxiv. Folio, pp. (4), 82. 44461

Marat (Jean Paul). ... Les Chaînes de l'Esclavage; par Marat ... . *Paris: Impr. de Mme. Dondey-Dupré.* 1850. 4to.

The first edition was published in 1792.

Maraviglia Americana osia complesso di rare maraviglie osservate colla direzione delle regole dell' arte della Pittura nella prodigiosa imagine della Madonna di Guadalupe del Signor Michele de Cabrera ... tradotta dello spagnuolo ... dall' abate D. G. M. de Gondra. *Ferrara: Stamperia Rinaldiana.* 1783. 8vo, pp. xlviii. 44463

See also Cabrera (M.), Vol. iii., No. 9814.

Maravilla (O.) Del Nuevo Mundo en la gran capilla del Rosario, dedicada y aplaudida en el convento de S. Domingo de la Ciudad de los Angeles, 16. Abril 1690. *Puebla.* 1690. 4to.

"Livre de toute rareté resté inconnu composé de 8 feuillets prélim. et 208 pages." Title and note from T. O. Weigel's catalogue.

Marban (P.) Arte | de la Lengua | Moxa, | con su Vocabulario, y Cathecismo. | Compuesto | por el M. R. P. Pedro Marban | de la Compañia de Jesvs ... . Con Licencia de los Svperiores. [*Lima:*] *En la Imprenta Real de Joseph de Contreras.* [1701.] Sm. 8vo, pp. (16), 664, 202, (1). a., c. 44465

The language of the nation of the province of "los Moxos," in Bolivia, South America. Their language is related to the Maipure. This is the only work on the subject.

Marble (M.) ... Freedom of the Press wantonly violated, Letter ... to President Lincoln ... . [n. p. n. d.] 8vo, pp. 8. b.

Marble. Letter to Abraham Lincoln, By Manton Marble, ... *New-York: Privately Printed.* 1867. 8vo, pp. 25. 44467

Ninety-nine copies only printed. Relates to the suppression of the "World"—an able argument. Mr. Marble was editor of "The World" newspaper from its commencement to 1876.

Marble (S. B.) Memoir of Susan B. Marble ... who Died February, 1821. *Philadelphia.* 1831. 8vo. 44468

The Marble Worker's Manual ... Translated ... by Mary L. Booth. With an Appendix concerning American Marbles. *New York.* 1856. 18mo. s. 44469

Marblehead, *Mass.* Annual Report of the Receipts and Expenditures ... . 1848. *Marblehead: J. K. Averill, Printer.* 1848. 8vo, pp. 32. h. 44470

Constitution and By-Laws of the Marblehead Union Moral Society. *Salem, Mass.* 1817. 12mo. 44471

Laws and Regulations of the Marine Society of Marblehead. ... Oct. 5, 1798. *Boston: Printed ... by Thomas Adams.* [n. d.] 16mo, pp. 14, and 4 ms. pages. h. 44472

Report of the School Committee ... . 1847–8. *Marblehead: Printed by R. Breare.* 1848. 8vo, pp. 12. Continued. h.

Also: ... Annual Report of Town Officers ... 1862–3. *Boston.* [n. d.] 8vo, pp. 14. Continued. h. *See* [Reed (William)].

[Marbois (Barbé de).] Voyage à la Guyane et à Cayenne fait en 1795 et année suivante; avec un Vocabulaire Français-Galibi, par L. M. B. *Paris, an* vi. 8vo. 44474

For other works by this author *see* Barbé-Marbois, Vol. i., p. 434.

Marbury *and* Crawford. Digest of the Laws of Georgia, from 1755 to 1800, inclusive. *Savannah.* 1802. 4to. c.

Marcandier (M.) An Abstract of the most Useful Parts of a later Treatise on Hemp. Translated from the French of M. Marcandier; ... To which is added some Account of the Use of the Horse-Chesnut, and a Plan of the Pennsylvania Hemp-Brake. *Boston: Edes and Gill.* 1766. 8vo, pp. 31. m.

The name of the inventor of the Pennsylvania Hemp Brake is not given, but the machine is described.

Marçay (de). Histoire de l'Amérique, par M. de Marçay. *Limoges: Barbou Frères.* 1860. 12mo, pp. 214. 44477

Marcellus; published in the Virginia Gazette, November and December, 1794. *Richmond.* 1794. 8vo, pp. 36. ba. 44478

Political disquisitions on the state of parties. Numbered i. to v.

Marcellus, *pseudon.* Essays on the Liberty of the Press. By Marcellus. Originally Published in the Virginia Argus ... . *Richmond: Printed by S. Pleasants, Jr.* 1804. 12mo, pp. 19.

Marcellus, *pseudon.* A Letter to the Hon. Daniel Webster on the Political Affairs of the United States. By Marcellus. *Philadelphia: Printed by J. Crissy.* 1837. 8vo, pp. 34 h.

March (A.) Address ... before the American Medical Association. By Alden March ... . *Philadelphia: Collins, Printer.* 1864. 8vo, pp. 14. h. 44481

March (A.) Semi-Centennial Address ... before the Medical Society of ... New-York, and ... the Legislature, in ... Albany, Feb. 4, 1857. By Alden March, m.d. ... *Albany: C. Van Benthuysen, Printer.* 1857. 8vo, pp. 20. h. 44482

Also: Lecture on the Expediency of establishing a Medical College and Hospital in the City of Albany. [n. p.] 1830. 8vo.—Sketch of the Life of Alden March. *New York.* [n. d.] 8vo.—Tribute to the Memory of Alden March, m.d., ll.d. *Albany: Charles Van Benthuysen & Sons.* 1870. 4to, pp. 112. Portrait. b.

March (Angier). Increase of Piety, or the Revival of Religion in the United States of America [1798–1802]; ... *Newburyport: A. March.* 1802. 12mo, pp. 128. c. 44483

March (C. W.) Daniel Webster and his Contemporaries. By Charles W. March. *New York.* 1852. 12mo, pp. 295. Portrait. + Sixth Edition. [*Ibid.*] 1859. 44484

March. Reminiscences of Congress. By Charles W. March. *New York: Baker and Scribner.* 1850. 12mo, pp. viii, 295. Portrait. + Second Edition. [*Ibid.*] + Third Edition. *New-York: Charles Scribner.* 1851. 12mo, pp. viii, 295. Portrait. 44485

This is the life of Daniel Webster with a new title-page.

March (D.) The Crisis of Freedom. Remarks on the Duty which all ... Good Citizens owe to their Country in the Present State of Public Affairs. By Rev. Daniel March. *Nashua, N. H.* 1854. 8vo, pp. 20. 44486

March. Yankee Land and the Yankee. By Daniel March. *Hartford: Printed by Case, Tiffany and Burnham.* 1840. 12mo, pp. 33. h. 44487

Also: The Presidential Election: Sermon ... Philadelphia, November, 1862. [n. p. n. d.] 8vo.—Steadfastness and Preparation in the Day of Adversity. A Sermon, ... in ... Philadelphia, September 14, 1862. ... *Philadelphia: C. Sherman & Son.* 1862. 8vo, pp. 20.

[March (Edmund).] Divine Providence (to appearance) visibly engaged in fulfilling Scripture Prophecies. *Boston.* 1762. 8vo, pp. 40. m. 44488

March (F. A.) The Scholar of To-day. An Address before the Phi Beta Kappa Society, at Amherst College ... July, 1868. By Francis A. March ... . *Springfield: Samuel Bowles & Company, Printers.* 1869. 8vo, pp. 24. h. 44489

March (*Major*). Faca; An Army Memoir. By Major March ... . *Boston: James French & Company.* 1857. 12mo, pp. vii, 11–338. h. 44490

March (Walter), *pseudon.* *See* [Wilcox (O. B.)]

March y Labores (J.) Historia de la marina real española, desde el descubrimiento de las Americas ... . *Madrid.* 1854. 4to.

Marchais. Voyage du Chevalier des Marchais en Guinée. *See* Labat (J. B.), Vol. ix., No. 38414.

Marchand (E.) Voyage autour du monde. *See* Fleurieu (C. P. C.), Vol. vi., No. 24748.

A sixth volume was published in 1800. There is another edition, *Paris: Imprimerie de la Republique. An* vi.–viii. [1798.] 3 vols., 4to, pp. cxliv, 628, (3); xvi, 676, (2); xi, 431, (3); (2), viii, 158, (1). 16 Maps. h.

Marchand. Die neueste Reise um die Welt in den Jahren 1790, 1791, und 1792. Aus dem Französischen. *Leipzig.* [n. d.] 2 vols., 8vo. Map and Plate. 44492

Marchant (J.) The Bloody Tribunal: or an Antidote against Popery. Being a Review of the Horrid Cruelties of the Inquisition, As practised in Spain, Portugal, Italy, and the East and West-Indies ... . By John Marchant, Gent. *Aberdeen: Gilbert Macpherson.* [1756.] 8vo, pp. 332. 44493

Marchant (W.) An Oration, pronounced at Newport, ... Rhode-Island, ... Fourth of July, 1797. By William Marchant. ... *Newport: Printed by Henry Barber.* 1797. Sm. 4to, pp. 18.

Marchese (M.) Vita della beata Rosa di Santa Maria Peruana. Por Dom. Maria Marchese, dell' ordine di San Domenico. *Napoli, ristampata appresso G. Fasulo.* 1668. 4to, pp. (10), 328, (4).

There is an edition printed at *Naples: G. Fasulo.* 1665. Neither of these editions is mentioned by Ternaux. According to Pinelo they were printed in Latin.

Marckmann (J. W.) Bogtrykkeren Benjamin Franklins Liv og Levnet. *Kjöbenhavn.* 1837. 8vo. 44496

Marco-Antonio, *pseudon.* Saldos contra o paiz. Reflexoes politicas de Marco-Antonio. *Recife.* 1866. 2 parts 18mo, pp. 38; 40. 44497

Marco Polo. Marco Polo Venetiano. In cvi si tratta le merav- | gliose cose del mondo per lui uedute, del costu- | me di uarij paesi, dello stranio uiuere di | quelli; della descrittione de diuerse | animale, e del trouar dell' oro | dell' argento, e delle pie- | tre preciose, cosa | non men utile, | che bel- | la. Senza di me l' hvom fassi a dio ribello. | [Colophon:] *In Venetia per Mathio Pagan, in Freza- | ria, al Segno della Fede.* | [n. d.] 12mo, Title, Text, 55 leaves. j.c.b. 44498

The travels of Marco Polo in the East claim a place in an American collection in consequence of the remarks of distinguished geographers that they were perused by Columbus, and that the revelations made by him of the wonders of Cathay and Zipanga stimulated the great navigator to accomplish through the sea, what the Venetian traveler had by land. We purposely omit the very numerous editions and translations of the work.

MARCONNAY (H. L. de). Valentine, ou la Nina Canadienne. Par H. Leblanc de Marconnay, Ecr. *Montréal.* 1836. 8vo, pp. 52. 44499

MARCOU (J.) American Geology. Letter on ... the Geology of Texas, New Mexico, Kansas, and Nebraska; ... By Jules Marcou. *Zurich: For the Author.* 1858. 8vo, pp. 16. 44500

MARCOU. Une Ascension dans les Montagnes Rocheuses. Par J. Marcou ... . *Paris: Imprimerie de E. Martinet.* 1867. 8vo, pp. 24. H. 44501

MARCOU. A Geological Map of the United States and the British Provinces of North America; ... By Jules Marcou ... . *Boston: Gould and Lincoln.* 1853. 8vo, pp. 5–92. 8 Plates.

MARCOU. Geology of North America, By Jules Marcou. ... with Two Geological Reports ... on the Prairies of Arkansas and Texas, the Rocky Mountains of New Mexico, and the Sierra Nevada of California ... . *Zurich: Zürcher & Furber.* 1858. 4to, pp. (6), 144. 3 Charts, 7 Plates. C. 44503

[MARCOU.] Le Terrain carbonifère dans l'Amérique du Nord. ... [*Genève?* 1855.] 8vo, pp. 23. Map. H. 44504

MARCOU. Über Die Geologie der Vereinigten Staaten und der Britischen Provinzen von Nord-Amerika. (Mit Karte.) Von Jules Marcou. Juli 1855. ... *Gotha: Justus Perthes.* 1855. 4to, pp. 11. H. 44505

Also: Dyas et Trias, ou le nouveau grès rouge en Europe, dans l'Amérique du Nord et dans l'Inde. [*Genève.* 1859.] 8vo, pp. 63. — Esquisse d'une classification des chaînes de montagnes d'une partie de l'Amérique du Nord ... . *Paris: Victor Dalmont.* 1855. 12mo, pp. 24. 2 Maps. — Le Niagara quinze ans après. Addition ... . *Paris: Société Géologique.* 1865. 8vo, pp. 15. Plate. — Notes on the Cretaceous and Carboniferous Rocks of Texas. ... *Boston: Geo. C. Rand & Avery.* 1861. 8vo, pp. (2), 86–97. — Notes pour Servir à une Description Géologique des Montagnes Rocheuses ... . *Genève: Imprimerie Ramboz et Schuchardt.* 1858. 8vo, pp. 22. — Notice sur les gisements des lentilles trilobitifères taconiques de la Pointe Lévis, au Canada. ... *Paris: Société Géologique.* 1864. 8vo, pp. 12. — Notice of a Geological Map of the United States and the British Provinces, with Explanatory Text ... . [n. p.] 1854. 8vo. — Une Reconnaissance géologique au Nebraska. ... *Paris: Société Géologique.* 1864. 8vo, pp. 16. — Reply to the Criticisms of James D. Dana. ... Including Dana's two Articles, with a Letter of Agassiz. *Zurich.* 1859. 8vo, pp. 40. — Résumé explicatif d'une carte géologique des États-Unis et des Provinces anglaises de l'Amérique du Nord ... . [*Paris: Imprimerie de L. Martinet.* 1855.] 8vo, pp. 124. — Sur le gisement de l'or en Californie. ... *Genève.* 1855. 8vo. — The Taconic and Lower Silurian Rocks of Vermont and Canada. ... *Boston.* 1862. 8vo.

MARCOY (P.) Scènes et Paysages dans les Andes. Par Paul Marcoy. ... *Paris: L. Hachette et Cie.* 1861. 12mo, pp. (4),

423, (1). B. + Deuxième Série. ... [*Ibid.*] 1861. 12mo, pp. (4), 331, (2). 44506

Paul Marcoy is a pseudonym for Lorenzo de Saint-Cricq.

MARCOY. Voyage a Travers L'Amérique du Sud de l'Océan Pacifique a l'Océan Atlantique Par Paul Marcoy Illustré de 626 Vues, Types et Paysages par E. Riou et accompagné de 20 Cartes gravées sur les dessins de l'auteur ... . *Paris: L. Hachette et Cie.* 1869. 2 vols., 4to, pp. (4), 704; (4), 519. Portrait. BA.

MARCOY. Travels in South America from the Pacific Ocean to the Atlantic Ocean. By Paul Marcoy. Illustrated by Five Hundred and Twenty-Five Engravings ... and Ten Maps ... . [Translated by Elihu Rich.] *London: Blackie & Son.* 1875. 2 vols., 4to, pp. 2, xii, 524, 2; viii, 496. 44508

In Field's "Essay" this work is eulogized in the glowing style peculiar to that gentleman. As a book of wood-cuts it is interesting, as a book of authorship it is a capital illustration of the use of a pair of scissors. The work of Mr. E. G. Squier furnished the author with a large proportion of the text, and Mr. Squier is a good authority. Some copies of the translation have a New York imprint.

MARCULLUS, *pseudon.* *See* [Kershaw (Philip G.)], IX. 37638.

MARCUS (M.) Address to the Members of the "United Church of England and Ireland," and of the Protestant Episcopal Church in the United States ... on ... Emigration ... . By ... Rev. Moses Marcus, B.D. ... *New-York: Printed by J. T. Crowell and Co.* 1846. 8vo, pp. 40. H., S. 44509

MARCUS, *pseudon.* A Reply to the Vindication of the Result of the late Council at Ipswich. By Marcus. *Newburyport: E. M. Blunt, Printer.* 1806. 12mo, pp. 52. BA., N. 44510

See also [Blunt (J.)], Vol. II., No. 6039, [Davis (Matthew L.)], Vol. V., Nos. 18863, 18866, *and* [Wolcott (Oliver)].

MARCY (R. B.) Border Reminiscences. By Randolph B. Marcy. *New York.* 1871. 12mo, pp. 396. Plates. 44511

MARCY. ... Exploration of the Red River of Louisiana, in the year 1852: By Randolph B. Marcy, ... assisted by George B. McClellan ... . With Reports on the Natural History of the Country, and numerous Illustrations. *Washington: Robert Armstrong, ... Printer.* 1853. 8vo, pp. xv, 320. 66 Plates and Maps. + *Washington: Beverly Tucker, Senate Printer.* 1854. 8vo, pp. xv, 310. 66 Plates. + *Washington: A. O. P. Nicholson, ... Printer.* 1854. 8vo, pp. xv, 286. Map and 66 Plates. H., C.

Contains authentic information regarding the peculiar customs of the Indians of the southern plains. Their mode of warfare, their invariable violation of the chastity of

female prisoners, and the construction of their dwellings and villages, are particularly described.

MARCY. Notes taken during the Expedition commanded by Capt. R. B. Marcy, U.S.A., through Unexplored Texas in the Summer and Fall of 1854. *Philadelphia.* 1856. 12mo. 44513

MARCY. The Prairie Traveller: a Handbook for Overland Expeditions; with Maps ... of the Principal Routes between the Mississippi and the Pacific. By Randolph B. Marcy ... . *New York: Harper & Brothers.* 1859. 16mo, pp. 340. Map and Plates. + New Edition. [*Ibid.*] 1861. 16mo, pp. 381. Map.

MARCY. ... The "Prairie Traveller," ... By Captain Randolph B. Marcy ... . Edited, with Notes, by Captain Richard F. Burton. *London.* 1863. Cr. 8vo, pp. 270. Map and Plates.

MARCY. Thirty Years of Army Life on the Border. Comprising descriptions of the Indian Nomads of the Plains; Explorations of New Territory; a Trip across the Rocky Mountains in the Winter; Descriptions of the Habits of different Animals found in the West, and the Methods of Hunting them; with Incidents in the life of different frontier men. ... By Colonel R. B. Marcy ... . *New York: Harper & Brothers.* 1866. 8vo, pp. 7–442. Plates. BA. 44516

MARCY (W. L.) An Oration on the Three Hundred and Eighteenth Anniversary of the Discovery of America, delivered before the Tammany Society ... . By William L. Marcy ... . With a Traditional Account of the Life of Tammany, an Indian Chief. *Troy, N. Y.* 1809. 8vo, pp. 71. 44517

MARCY. A Traditional Account of the Life of Tammany, an Indian Chief, famed for his Friendship toward the Whites, and for his virtues as a man. By William L. Marcy ... . *Providence: Phenix Press.* 1810. 8vo, pp. 20. 44518

An essay written in such grave historic strain as to be often taken for veritable biography. It is, however, nothing but fiction, and not even original at that, being extracted from Dr. S. L. Mitchell's account. Also: Correspondence between Wm. L. Marcy and Chev. Hulsemann, respecting Mark Koszta. [n. p. n. d.] 8vo.

Mardi Gras in New Orleans: Its Ancient and Modern Observance; History of The Mystick Krewe of Comus, the Twelfth-Night Revelers, and Knights of Momus, with Scenes, Sketches and Incidents of the Reign of His Majesty, the King of the Carnival. ... Atlanta, Georgia. *Barrow—The Printer—Atlanta.* [n. d.] 8vo, pp. 40 44519

MAREGNIER (——). Du Climat de Phernambuco. *Paris.* 1829. 4to. 44520

MARÈS (L.) Les Nouvelles Carabines Anglaises et Américaines, Par M. Léon Marès. ... *Paris: Imprimerie de L. Martinet.* 1858. 8vo, pp. 40. H. 44521

[MARESCHAL (Ambrose).] Pastoral Letter of the Archbishop of Baltimore ... on the Consecration of the Cathedral. *Baltimore: Printed by J. Robinson.* 1821. 8vo, pp. 16. BA. 44522

Finotti, p. 192, describes two editions, 1819 and 1820, which we have not seen.

MAREST (G.) *See* "Lettres Édifiantes," *and* "Die Neue Welt."

MARESTIER (M.) Mémoire sur les Bateaux à Vapeur des États-Unis d'Amérique; ... par M. Marestier ... . *Paris.* 1824. 4to, pp. 296. 44523

MARETZEK (M.) Crotchets and Quavers: or, Revelations of an Opera Manager in America. By Max Maretzek. *New York: S. French.* 1855. 12mo, pp. 346. C. 44524

MARGALLO [Pedro]. Phisices compendium | Clementissimo in Christo iesu patri ac illustrissimo do- | mino do. Iacobo So. Bracharensi archiepiscopo. ac Hispaniarum optimo iure patriarche Margallus | doctor theologus atque insignis collegij diui Bartholomei collega. S. P. D. | [Colophon:] ... 1520 ... *Uale Sal- | mantice.* 14. *Iunij.* | Folio, xxxvj leaves. 44525

Margaret. *See* [Judd (S.)], Vol. IX., No. 36840.

Margaret Percival in America. A Tale, edited by a New England Minister [E. E. Hale]. *Boston: Phillips, Sampson & Co.* 1850. 12mo. + Second Edition. [*Ibid.*] 44526

Margarita Philosophica. *See* [Reisch (G.)]

MARGIL (A.) El Peregrino | Septentrional Atlante | Delineado | en la exemplarissima Vida | Del Venerable Padre | Fr. Antonio Margil | de Jesus | Fruto de la gloridissima ciudad de Valencia | Hijo de su Serifica Observante Provincia Predicador Missionero. | ... *En Valencia, Ano de* 1742. 4to, pp. 420. 44527

The Texan missions of Father Margil are described on pages 248 to 265. Some curious matter relative to the Pagan rites, secretly preserved among the Indians, is found elsewhere. *See* "Hist. Mag.," VIII. 42.

MARGIL. Nuevas Empressas del peregrino Americano Septentrional Atlante, descubiertas en lo que hizo quando vivia, y aun despues de su muerte ha manifestado el V. P. F. Antonio Margil de Jesus. Casos Admirables de nuevo averiguados, que no están en la Vida de este Siervo de Dios estampada en el año de 1737, y pueden dessear los afectos de este Varon memorable, ... *Impressas en Mexico, en la Imprenta Real del Superior Gobierno.* 1747. 4to, pp. (24), 46. 44528

This account of the great earthquake in Lima was translated into English and published in London accompanied by other accounts. *See* [Lozano (Pedro de)], Vol. x.

MARGIL. Vozes que hizieron eco, en la religiosa pyra, que en las honras del V. P. Fr. Antonio Margil de Jesus, erigió N. R. P. Fr. Antonio de Harizon, el dia 21 de Agosto de 1726 en el Convento de N. S. P. S. Francisco de la Imperial Ciudad de Mexico. *Mexico, por J. B. de Hogal.* 1726. 4to, pp. (34), 56.

I have seen a similar title in which the authorship is credited to Juan Lopez Aguado.

MARGRAF (J.) Kirche und Sklaverei seit der Entdeckung Amerikas; oder, was hat die Katholische Kirche seit der Entdeckung Amerikas, theils zur Milderung theils zur Aufhebung der Sklaverei gethan? Von J. Margraf. *Tübingen: H. Laupp.* 1865. 8vo, pp. viii, 230. C., S. 44530

Margret Howth. A Story of To-day. ... [By Mrs. Rebecca Harding Davis.] *Boston: Ticknor and Fields.* 1862. 12mo, pp. (2), 266. C. + Second Edition. [*Ibid.*] 44531

MARGRY (P.) Les Navigations Françaises et la révolution maritime du XIVe au XVIe siècle, d'après les documents inédits tirés de France, d'Angleterre, d'Espagne et d'Italie. Par Pierre Margry. *Paris: Tross.* 1867. Sq. 8vo. 2 Plates. 44532

Some copies are printed on "papier de Hollande." Relates to Columbus. *See* Netscher's "Hollandais," XXIII.

[MARGRY.] Origines transatlantiques. Belain d'Esnambuc et les Normands aux Antilles d'après des documents nouvellement retrouvés. ... *Paris: Achille Faure.* 1863. 8vo, pp. (2), iv, 102, (1). 2 Plates. B. 44533

MARGRY. Relations et Mémoires inédits pour servir a l'histoire de la France dans les pays d'outre-mer ... Par Pierre Margry ... . *Paris: Challamel aîné.* 1867. 8vo, pp. (8), 376. B.

MARGUERITE DE VALOIS. L'Heptameron des nouvelles de tres illustre et tres excellente princesse Marguerite de Valois,

royne de Navarre, remis en son vray ordre, confus au parauant en sa premiere impression. *Paris: Vincent Sertenas, imprimé pour Benoist Prevost.* 1559. 4to, 6 prel., 206, and 2 leaves. 44535

See [Harrisse's] "Notes sur la Nouvelle-France," No. 382. It is scarcely necessary to say, there are very numerous editions and translations of this work.

MARGUERITE DE VALOIS. The | Memorialls | of | Margaret | de Valoys, | First Wife to Henry | the Fourth, King of | France and Navarre. | Compiled in French by her own | most Delicate and Royall hand: | And | Translated into English by Robert | Codington, Master | of Arts. | *London: Printed by R. H.* 1663. 18mo, pp. (8), 229. H.C.M. 44536

Partly relates to Canada.

MARIA (F.) Joseph Brown; or the Young Tennesseean, ... An Indian Tale. By Francis Maria. *Nashville, Tenn.: For the Author.* 1857. 24mo, pp. 126. Plate. H. 44537

MARIA (I. de). Apuntes biograficos de Don Francisco Antonio Maciel. Por Isidoro de Maria. *Montevideo.* 1860. 4to, pp. 20. Plate. 44538

MARIA DE ALCALA (Josef). Sermon ... celebrada en la santa iglesia Metropolitana de Mexico en honra y veneracion de la divina providencia, predicó el dia 29 de Julio de 1810. ... *Mexico: D. Mariano de Zuñiga y Ontiveros.* [1810.] 4to, pp. 24.

MARIA DE GUADELOUPE. Clamores de la America y recurso à la proteccion de Maria Santisima de Guadeloupe. *Mexico.* [About 1808.] Sm. 4to. 44540

MARIA DE HERAS (Bartolomé). Discurso que dirige á su grey D. Bart. Maria de Heras, arzobispo de esta metrópoli, con motivo de la abertura y bendicion solemne del cementerio general erigido en esta capital. [*Lima:*] *Impresso en la casa Real de Niños Expósitos. Y por su original en la Habana en la Imprenta de D. Estevan J. Boloña.* 1808. 4to, pp. (2), 16. 44541

Also: Reglamento provisional acordado por D. José Fern. de Abascal y Sousa, virey y capitan general del Perú ... . *Lima: Impreso en la casa de Niños Expósitos.* 1808. *Habana, reimpreso por D. Estevan José Boloña.* 1808. 4to, pp. 20.

MARIA AMALIA DE SAXONIA. Reales Exêquias del Da. Maria Amalia de Saxonia, Reyna de las Españas, ... celebradas en la Santa Iglesia Cathedral de la Imperial Corte Mexicana, los dias 17 y 18, de Julio de 1761, con Sermon Funebris, por J. M. Velez de Ulivarri, y Olasasso. *Imprenta Nueva Antuerpiana, de D. Christoval, y D. P. de Zuñiga.* 1761. 4to. 24 Engravings.

In prose and verse.

MARIANA (J. de). Historiæ de rebus Hispaniæ, Libri XX. *Toleti: Typis: P. Roderici.* 1592. Folio, pp. (8), 959, (12).

The first and extremely rare edition of this highly esteemed work, which includes some chapters on the West Indies. There are copies dated 1595, published by *Th. Guzman*, in which books XXI–XXV are added, continuing the volume to page 1168, and followed by 14 pages of index.

MARIANA. Historiæ de rebus Hispaniæ, Libri XXX, acc. J. E. Minianae continuationis novae libri X. *Hagae Comitatis.* 1733. 4 vols., folio. 44544

MARIANA. Historiæ Hispanicæ appendix, libri scilicet XXI–XXX, cvm indice. *Francofurti.* 1616. Folio. 44545

MARIANA. Historia general de España, por el padre Juan de Mariana. *Toledo.* 1601. 2 vols., folio. 44546

This first edition in Spanish is rare. The translation was made by the author. It was reprinted, *Madrid*, 1608, 1617, 1623, 1650, and 1678.

MARIANA. Historia general de España, compuesta, emendada y añadida por el padre Juan de Mariana ... . Decimaquarta impresion. ... *Madrid: D. Joachim de Ibarra, año* M.D.CC.LXXX. 2 vols., folio, pp. (24), 14, (14), 917; (10), 927, (32). B.

"This edition is very scarce, and does much honor to its celebrated printer.—SALVA.

MARIANA. Historia general de España ... ilustrada en esta nueva impresion de tablas cronologicas notas y observaciones criticas con la vida del autor. *Valencia: Benito Monfort.* M.DCCC.-LXXXIII–XCVI. 9 vols., 4to. BA. 44548

This edition is highly commended by Brunet, who also mentions the edition, *Valencia: Monfort.* 1794. 2 vols., folio. + [*Ibid.*] 1799.

MARIANA. Historia general de España, compuesta, emendada y añadida Por el P. Juan de Mariana ... y la continuacion que escribió en Latin el P. Fr. Joseph Manuel Miniana ... . Traducida nuevamente al Castellano. ... *Madrid: Don Benito Cano.* MDCCXCIV–V. 10 vols., 8vo. B. 44549

MARIANA. Historia general de España ... ilustrada con notas históricas y críticas ... por J. Sabau y Blanco ... . *Madrid.* MDCCC-XVII–XXII. 20 vols., 8vo. + *Valencia.* 1830–41. 18 vols., 4to.

MARIANA. Historia ... con una narracion ... hasta 1833 ... . *Barcelona.* 1823–40. 10 vols., sm. 8vo. 45 Plates. 44551

MARIANA. Historia ... Nueva edicion que contiene ... la narracion de los sucesos ... hasta ... 1808. *Madrid.* 1828–29. 9 vols., sm. 8vo. Portraits. 44552

"One of the good editions."—BRUNET. The "Historia" is also contained in the edition of Mariana's "Obras," *Madrid: Rivadaneyra.* 1854. 2 vols., 8vo.

MARIANA. The General History of Spain, from the first Peopling of it by Tubal, till the death of King Ferdinand; with a Continuation to the Death of King Philip III. To which are added, two Supplements; the first by Ferdinand Camargo y Salcedo, the other by Basil Varen de Soto, bringing it down to the present reign. The whole translated from the Spanish, by Capt. John Stevens. *London.* 1699. Folio, pp. (16), 563, Supplements, 95, and Index. C. 44553

Book XXVI. relates to the discoveries and conquests of the Spaniards in the West Indies, etc. The work is highly eulogized by Bouterweck.

MARIANA. Histoire Generale D'Espagne, du P. Jean de Mariana ... . Traduite en François; avec des Notes et des Cartes. Par le P. Joseph-Nicholas Charenton. ... *Paris: Chez Le Mercier, Pere,* ... M.DCC.XXV. 6 vols., 4to, pp. 8, xxxii, (8), 896; (2), 821, (15); (2), 900, Errata, 2; (2), 403, (24); (2), 544; (2), 545–899, Supplément, 105, (4). 3 Maps. B. 44554

MARIANA (J. de). Discurso de las Enfermedades de la Compagnie de Jesus, por P. Juan de Mariana. *Madrid.* 1768. 4to.

MARIANA (*P.*) Gloriosus Franciscus Redivivus, sive Chronica Observantiæ Strictioris, Reparatæ, Reductæ, ac Reformatæ; ejusdemque per Christianos Orbes non solum sed et Americam, Peru, ... diffusæ et Evangelio fructificantis. *Ingolstadt.* 1625. 4to. 29 Plates. 44556

An extract from Gonzaga's "Chronicle of the Franciscans," containing the parts relating to Asia and America. *See also* Vol. VII., No. 27790.

MARIANA (*Sor.*) Memorias de Sor. Mariana fundadora y abasida del Monasterio de Guadalupe, contiguo de Mexico. *Mexico.* 1808. 4to. 44557

MARIANO (J.) Carta de Consuelo que Ad. Antonio Zabala escribò el P. Jos. Mariano. *Mexico.* 1762. 8vo. 44557a

MARIANO DE ABARCA (J.) El Sol en Leon. Solemnes aplausos conque, el Rey Nuestro Señor D. Fernando VI., Sol de los Españas, fué celebrado el dia 11, de febrero del año de 1747. En que se proclamò su Magestad exaltada al Solio de dos Mundos por la ... Ciudad de Mexico ... . Escribe su relacion el P. Joseph Mariano de Abarca de la Compañia de Jesus ... . Con Licencia de los Superiores. *En Mexico, en la Imprenta del Nuevo Rezado de Doña Maria de Ribera, en el Empedradillo. Año de* 1748. 4to, pp. (36), 300. 44557b

MARIANO DE AGUIRA (J.) Necrologia de José Mariano de Aguira y Mayora, Dean de esta santiaglesia Metropolitana. *Lima.* 1835. 8vo. 44558

MARIÁTEGUI (F. J.) Reseña Historica de los Principales concordatos celebrados con Roma, y Breves réflexiones sobre el ultimo habido entre Pio IX. y el Gobierno de Bolivia, por F. J. Mariátegui. *Lima.* 1856. Sm. 4to, pp. (7), 286, (2). 44559

MARIE (J.) The Case of Jane Marie, exhibiting the Cruelty and Barbarous Conduct of James Ross, to a Defenceless Woman ... [*Philadelphia.*] 1808. 8vo, pp. 28. 44560

[MARIÉ (P.)] A Tribute to the Fair, Comprising a Collection of Vers de Société Published in Aid of the Sanitary Commission. *New York: D. Appleton & Co.* 1864. 12mo, pp. xiii, 7–253. B. 44561

MARIE DE L'INCARNATION. Lettres | de la venerable | Mere Marie | de l'Incarnation | première Superieure | des Ursulines | de la Nouvelle France. | Divisées en deux parties. | *A Paris,* | *chez Louis Billaine,* ... M.DC.LXXXI. | Avec ... Privilege de Sa Majesté. | 4to, pp. (10), 675, (1). 44562

Important for Canadian history. *See* Charlevoix (P. F. X.) *and* [Martin (D. C.)]

MARIE DE L'INCARNATION. Choix des lettres historiques de la vénérable mère Marie, de l'Incarnation, dédié aux élèves des Ursulines. *Paris: Clermont-Ferrand, Thibaut.* 1857. 12mo.

MARIETTA, *O.* The Act of Incorporation, and the Ordinances and Regulations ... . *Marietta, Ohio.* 1852. 8vo, pp. 29.

First Annual Report of the Marietta & Cincinnati Railroad Company. *Chillicothe: Ely, Allen and Looker.* 1851. 8vo, pp. 34. Map. Continued. B. 44565

Also: Semi-Annual Report ... 1st January, 1864. *New York: Latimer Bros. & Seymour.* 1864. 8vo, pp. 28.

Marietta and the Oil and Mineral Region of South-eastern Ohio and West Virginia. *Marietta, O.: Winchester & McGee.* 1864. 8vo, pp. 17. Map. 44566

Public Schools of Marietta. By-Laws and Report ... . *Marietta.* 1856. 8vo, pp. 42. Continued. 44567

MARIETTA COLLEGE. Addresses at the Inauguration of Israel W. Andrews, as President of Marietta College, July 26, 1855. *Marietta.* 1855. 8vo, pp. 30. H. 44568

Catalogue of the Officers and Students ... 1838–9. *Cincinnati: Isaac Hefley & Co., Printers.* 1838. 8vo, pp. 22. Cont'd.

Also: Catalogue of Marietta College Library. *Cincinnati: Moore, Wilstach ... & Co., Printers.* 1857. 8vo, pp. iv, 166. — Celebration of the Twenty-Fifth Anniversary of ... [the] College. ... June 27, 1860. *Marietta.* 1860. 8vo, pp. 60. — Second Annual Report of the Trustees ... . September, 1835. *Marietta: For the Trustees.* 1835. 8vo, pp. 23. H.

MARIETTA INSTITUTE. First Annual Report of the Trustees of the Marietta Collegiate Institute, and Western Teachers' Institute. 1834. *Cincinnati: Gregory & Smith, Printers.* 1834. 8vo, pp. 14. H. 44570

Catalogue of the English School ... 1839–40. *Marietta: G. W. Tyler & Co., Printers.* 1840. 8vo, pp. 8. H. 44571

MARIETTA FEMALE SEMINARY. Catalogue ... for ... 1839 ... *Marietta: ... I. Maxon, Printer.* 1839. 24mo, pp. (8). H.

MARIG (J.) Records of the Life of the Rev. John Marig, late Minister of the Reconciliation, ... Written by Himself. *Boston: Bowen and Cushing.* 1827. 12mo, pp. 348. Portrait.

MARIGNI DE MANDEVILLE (——). Mémoires ... de M. Marigni de Mandeville. *Paris: Guillaume Despies.* 1765.

MARIN (B. V.) Elogio del Senador Don Juan Egana pronunciado en la Capella del instituto nacional de Chile por Buena Ventura Marin. *Santiago.* 1836. Sm. 4to. 44575

MARIN BEN JESSE (D.) A Letter to the Independent Reflector. By David Marin Ben Jesse, Pastor at Aquenonka. *New York: Printed ... by Hugh Gaine.* 1753. 8vo, pp. 31. H.

MARIN BEN JESSE. A Remark on the Disputes and Contentions in this Province. ... By David Marin Ben Jesse ... . *New-York: Printed by H. Gaine* ... 1755. Folio, pp. 12. P. 44577

MARIN (Gom. M.) Oracion panegyrica en la funcion de S. Fel. Neri de Mexico. *Mexico.* 1836. 8vo, 13 leaves. 44578

MARIN (M. G.) Defensa Guadalupana, escrita por el P. Dr. y Mtrô. D. Manuel Gomez Marin, contra la Disertacion de D. Juan Bautista Muñoz. *Méjico.* 1819. Sm. 4to, pp. viii, 55.

MARIN (J.) Traité du Castor, dans lequel on Explique la Nature et l'Usage du Castoreum, ... par J. Marin, traduit par Eidous. *Paris.* 1746. 12mo. Plates. 44580

A curious book on the natural history of the beaver. Title from an auction catalogue.

MARIN (Miguel Angel). Vida de San Paphnucio. *Mexico.* 1810. 4to, pp. (4), 44. 44581

Marine Seizures, or a Vindication of the Rights of Jury Trial in the Federal Courts, in the Cases of Seizures made upon the Tide Waters under the Law of Imposts. *New York.* 1832. 8vo, pp. 28. 44582

MARINEO (L.) Obra Compuesta de las Cosas Memorables e Claros Varones de España. *Alcala.* 1530. Folio. 44583

Title from "Bibliotheca Heberiana," Part I., No. 4680.

MARINEO. Obra de las cosas memorables de España. *Alcala, Eguia.* 1533. Folio. 44584

MARINEO. L. Marinei Si- | cvli Regii Historiographi | opus de rebus Hispaniae Memorabili- | bus modo castigatum atq9 Cæsareae maie | statis iussu in lucem æditum. | ... [Colophon:] *Impres- | sum Compluti per Michaelum de Eguia, Absolutũq3 | est mense Maij. Anno ab orbe redempto.* | MD.XXXIII. | Folio, Title, 1 leaf, cxxviij leaves.

"Son ouvrage, qui a été imprimé assez souvent, est très-important pour l'histoire de l'Espagne, il renferme au verso du f. cvi une notice sur la découverte de l'Amérique; l'Amiral y est nommé Petrus Colonus."—LECLERC.

MARINEO. . Initvm . Sapiente . Timor . Domini | Obra Compuesta por Lucio Marineo Siculo Co- | ronista d' sus Majestades | de las cosas memora | bles de España. | *Año de* M.D.XXXIX. | [Colophon:] ... *Alcala de Henares. En | casa de Iuan de Brocar | a Catorze dias del | mes de Iulio. De Mil y Quinientos | y Treynta y Nueue Años.* | (.·.) Folio, 10 prel. leaves, 192 leaves. H. 44586

MARINEO. Sumario de la clarissima vida y heroicos hechos de los reyes don Fernando y doña Ysabel, sacado de la obra grande de las cosas memorables d'España compuesta por Lucio Marineo Siculo. *Toledo en casa de Juã de Ayala, mil y quiniẽto y qũarẽta y seyes años.* Sm. 4to, Title, 1 leaf, 77 leaves. 44587

The Mariner's Chronicle, containing Narratives of the most Remarkable Disasters at Sea. ... Also, Naval Engagements, Piratical Adventures, etc. [*New Haven.* 1834.] 8vo. 44588

MARINER'S CHURCH, *Boston.* History, Articles of Faith ... of the Mariner's Church. *Boston.* 1832.. 12mo, pp. 11.

Mariner's Dictionary, or American Seaman's Vocabulary. *Washington.* 1805. 18mo. 44590

Mariner's Library or Voyager's Companion, containing Narratives of the most popular Voyages, from the Time of Columbus to the Present Day; with Accounts of Remarkable Shipwrecks, Naval Adventures, the Whale Fishery, &c. ... *Boston: C. Gaylord.* 1834. 8vo, pp. 492. Plate. 44591

The Mariner's Marvellous Magazine, or Wonders of the Ocean, the most Remarkable Shipwrecks, Adventures, Disasters, Captivities, &c., of Mariners in Various Parts of the Globe. *London.* 1809. 3 vols., 12mo. Plates. 44592

Contains the struggles of Captain Thos. Keith in America and captivity among the Indians, sufferings of Capt. Fox among the Esquimaux, capture of the Gen. Washington by Barbary corsairs, and other American accounts.

MARINHO (J. A.) Historia de movimento politico, que no anno de 1842 teve logar na provincia de Minas-geraes. Por José Antonio Marinho. *Rio de Janeiro.* 8vo. 44593

MARION (M.) Nouveau Voyage a la Mer du Sud, commencé sous les ordres de M. Marion, Capitaine de brûlot; & achevé, apres la mort de cet Officier sous ceux de M. le Chev. Duclesmeur, on a joint a ce voyage un extrait de celui de M. de Sarville dans les même Parages. *Paris: Barois.* 1783. 8vo, pp. viii, 290. Map and 7 Plates. J.C.B. 44594

MARION (Francis). Life of General Marion, and Anecdotes Illustrative of his Character ... . *Philadelphia.* [1847.] 12mo.

See also Horry (P.), Vol. VIII., Nos. 33034–6.

MARION, *Mass.* Annual Report of the Selectmen ... 1862. *Boston: Wright & Potter, Printers.* 1862. 8vo, pp. 16. Cont'd.

MARION COLLEGE, *Mo.* First Annual Catalogue of the Officers and Students ... . *St. Louis.* 1835. 8vo, pp. 25. 44597

MARION UNION SCHOOL. Seventh Annual Report of the ... School ... for ... 1858 and '59. ... *Cleveland: Fairbanks, Benedict & Co., Printers.* 1859. 8vo, pp. 32. H. 44598

The Mariposa Company, ... New York ... . Organized 25th June, 1863. [Statement.] *New York: Wm. C. Bryant & Co., Printers.* 1863. 8vo, pp. 80. B. 44599

Also: Final Report of the Committee of the Bondholders of the Mariposa Company, June 4, 1868. *New York.* 1868. 8vo.

The Mariposa Estate: ... comprising the Official Report of J. Ross Browne ... upon its Mineral Resources ... . *New York.* 1868. 8vo, pp. 62. Map. B. 44600

MARIS (——). Souvenirs d'Amérique. Relations d'un voyage au Texas et en Haïti. *Bruxelles: Poot et Cie.* 1863. 8vo.

The Maritime Campaign of 1778. A Collection of all the Papers relative to the Operations of the English and French Fleets. To which are added, Strictures on the Publication made in France, by order of the Ministry, concerning the Engagement on the 27th of July; ... By J. M. a Lieutenant in the Fleet. *London: J. Faden.* 1779. Folio. Charts and Plans. 44602

"A very curious and instructive review."—*Monthly Review*, LX. 163.

Maritime Capture. Shall England uphold the Capture of Private Property at Sea? By a Lawyer. *London: Trübner & Co.* 1862. 8vo, pp. 40. C. 44603

The Maritime Flags of all Nations, together with a Geographical Sketch ... . *New York.* 1855. 24mo. 44604

Maritime Law. Correspondence relative to Neutral Rights between The Government of the United States and the Powers represented in the Congress at Paris. 1856. *Washington: A. O. P. Nicholson, Printer.* 1856. 8vo, pp. 18. B. 44605

Maritime Scraps, or Scenes in the Frigate United States during a Cruise in the Mediterranean. ... By a Man-of-War's-Man. *Boston: For the Author.* 1838. 12mo, pp. 108. B. 44606

MARIUS, *pseudon.* *See* [Day (T.)], Vol. V., No. 18985.

MARIZ CARNEIRO (Antonio de). Regimento de Pilotos, e roteiro de Navegaçam, e Conqvistas do Brasil, Angola, S. Thomé, Cabo Verde, Maranhão, Ilhas, et Indias Occidentaes. Agora novamente emendado et accressentado. *Lisboa: L. de Anueres.* 1642. Sm. 4to, 4 prel. leaves, 40 leaves, pp. 189, and 8 leaves. 6 Plates. C. + Quinta vez impresso com ... as emendas ... . Accrescentado com o roteiro do Maranhão e Itamaraca ... . [*Lisboa:*] *Por Manuel da Silva.* 1655. 4to, 111 leaves. 44607

MARIZ (Pedro de). Dialogos de varia historia. Em que summariamente se referem muytas cousas antiguas de Hespanha; e todas as mais notaueis q̃ em Portugal aconteceraõ em suas gloriosas Conquistas, antes & depois de ser leuantado a Dignidade Real. E outras muytas de outros reynos, dignas de memoria. Com os Retratos de todos os Reys de Portugal. *Em Coimbra: Na officina de Antonio de Mariz.* 1594. 8vo. 44608

The second edition, with the same title, is dated 1597, another 1598. It was also reprinted at *Lisboa, por Antonio Craesbeeck de Mello.* 1674. 4to. + *Lisboa, na Officina*

de Manuel da Silva. 1749. 2 vols., 4to. + *Lisboa, na Officina de José Filippe e Manuel Soares.* 1758. 2 vols., 4to. + *Lisboa, na Imp. Regia.* 1806. 2 vols., 4to.

MARJORIBANKS (A.) Travels in South and North America. By Alexander Marjoribanks. *Edinburgh.* 1852. Post 8vo, pp. 486. + *London.* 1853. P. + *Edinburgh.* 1854. Post 8vo, pp. 460. + Fifth Edition. *London: Simpkin, Marshall & Co.* 1854. 12mo, pp. xiv, 480. Plate. C. 44609

MARJORIBANKS (*Capt.*) Slavery: An Essay in Verse. By Captain Marjoribanks. *Edinburgh.* 1792. 8vo, pp. 31. S.

[MARKE (Desdemona).] An Appeal to the Women of America. [n. p. n. d.] 8vo, pp. 8. B. 44611

MARKHAM (C. Robert). Contributions towards a Grammar and Dictionary of Quichua. The Language of the Yncas of Peru. Collected by Clements R. Markham ... . *London: Trübner & Co.* 1864. Post 8vo, pp. (4), 223. B. 44612

The learned author was secretary to the French Royal Society of Geography, and composed his work during a long residence in Peru.

MARKHAM. Cuzco: A Journey to the Ancient Capital of Peru; with an Account of the History, Language, Literature, and Antiquities of the Incas. [And] Lima: a Visit to the Capital and Provinces of Modern Peru; with a Sketch of the Viceregal Government, History of the Republic, and a Review of the Literature and Society of Peru. ... By Clements R. Markham ... . *London: Chapman and Hall.* 1856. 8vo, pp. iv, 419. Map and Plates. BA. 44613

Principally devoted to a study of the works of the ancient rulers of Peru. Few persons have been better fitted for this task than Mr. Markham. *See* "Westminster Review," July, 1856.

MARKHAM. Expeditions into the Valley of the Amazons, 1539, 1540, 1639. Translated and Edited, with Notes, by Clements R. Markham ... . *London: Hakluyt Society.* M.DCCC.LIX. 8vo, pp. (8), lxiv, 190, Report, 4. Map. BA., C. 44614

Contents: Expedition of Gonzalo Pizarro to the Land of Cinnamon, 1539–42, by Garcilasso Inca de La Vega; Voyage of Francisco de Orellana, 1540–41, by A. de Herrera; New Discovery of the great River of the Amazons, by C. de Acuña, 1639; List of the principal Tribes of the Valley of the Amazons.

MARKHAM. Franklin's Footsteps; a Sketch of Greenland and of the Parry Isles. By Clements R. Markham ... . *London: Chapman and Hall.* 1853. 16mo, pp. vii, 143. Map. C.

MARKHAM. Travels in Peru and India ... . By Clements R. Markham ... . *London: John Murray.* 1862. 8vo, pp. xviii, 572. 2 Maps and 16 Wood-cuts. BA. 44616

The wonderful story of Tupac Amaru, the last of the Incas, his insurrection, defeat, and horrible execution, is here related at length. *See also* "Ollanta."

MARKHAM. Zwei Reisen in Peru. ... *Leipzig: G. Senf.* 1865. 8vo, pp. 316. C. 44617

MARKHAM (R.) Sympathy in Distress. ... A Sermon occasioned by the heavy Sufferings of our Fellow Subjects in the West-India Islands. ... By Robert Markham, D.D. *London: J. Rivington.* 1781. 4to. 44618

[MARKHAM] (W.) A Sermon Preached before the Incorporated Society for the Propagation of the Gospel in Foreign Parts; at their Anniversary Meeting in the Parish Church of St. Mary-le-Bow, On Friday February 21. 1777. By the Most Reverend Father in God, William Lord Archbishop of York. *London: T. Harrison and S. Brooke.* MDCCLXXVII. 8vo, pp. 104, (1).

"With the Charter of the Society and an account of its proceedings 1776–77. Above one hundred missionaries were scattered throughout the American Colonies at the breaking out of the Revolution. The report of their proceedings in 1776 reads strangely now: 'In July last, the Congress thought proper to make an explicit declaration of independence by which all connection with Great Britain was to be broken off, and the Americans released from any alliance to our gracious Sovereign.' ... To officiate publicly, and not pray for the king ... was against their duty and oath, ... therefore almost all of them shut up their churches."—STEVENS. *See also* [Maseres (Francis)].

MARKLEY (B. A.) An Oration ... on 4th July, 1809 ... . By B. A. Markley ... . *Charleston (S. C.): Printed by John Hoff.* 1809. 8vo, pp. 27, (1). BA. 44620

Also: An Oration ... on 4th July, 1811, ... before the '76 Association. ... Charleston, South-Carolina. ... *Charleston (S. C.): J. Hoff.* 1811. 8vo, pp. 24. BA.

MARKOE (P.) Miscellaneous Poems. By Peter Markoe. ... *Philadelphia: Printed by W. Prichard and P. Hall.* M.DCC.LXXXVII. 8vo, pp. (4), 30. P. 44621

[MARKOE.] The Patriot Chief. A Tragedy. *Philadelphia: William Prichard.* MDCCLXXXIV. 8vo, pp. 70. 44622

MARKOE. The Times, A Poem. By Peter Markoe. *Philadelphia: Printed for the Author.* M.DCC.LXXXVIII. 8vo, pp. 35. BA., P. + Second Edition. [*Ibid.*] 44623

The author writes

"Far from the tumult of the busy throng,
Where Schuylkill, gently winding, flows along."

Also: The Reconciliation; or, the Triumph of Nature; a Comic Opera. ... *Philadelphia: Prichard and Hall.* 1790. 12mo, pp. 48. C. *See our* Vol. I., No. 763, add, *Prichard and Hall*; *see also* Horatius (Quintus Flaccus), Vol. VIII., No. 33005.

MARKS (D.) The Life of David Marks ... . Written by Himself. ... *Limerick, Me.* 1831. 12mo, pp. 396. Portrait.

MARKS. Memoir of ... David Marks, Minister ... . Edited by Mrs. Marilla Marks. *Dover, N. H.* 1846. 12mo, pp. 516. Portrait. + Second Edition. [*Ibid.*] 1847. 44625

MARKS (E.) Hints on Female Education. By Elias Marks, M.D. *Columbia, S. C.: Printed by Isaac C. Morgan.* 1837. 8vo, pp. 41. H. 44626

MARKS. Hints on Female Education, with an Outline of ... the So. Ca. Female Institute; under the Direction of Dr. Elias Marks. ... *Columbia: Printed by David W. Sims.* 1828. 8vo, pp. 44, (1), 1 folded leaf. H. 44627

MARKS (I. D.) Memorial to Congress. [*Washington.* 1851.] 8vo, pp. 12. BA. 44628

For a reply *see* Mexican Indemnity Payments.

MARKS (J. J.) The Peninsula Campaign in Virginia; or Incidents and Scenes on the Battle-Fields and in Richmond. By Rev. J. J. Marks, D.D. *Philadelphia: J. B. Lippincott & Co.* 1864. 12mo, pp. 444. 8 Plates. + Fifth Edition. [*Ibid.*]

MARLBORO', *Mass.* The Case, William Hunter, in Equity, versus the Inhabitants of Marlboro', in the Circuit Court of the United States ... . *Worcester: H. J. Howland.* 1845. 8vo, pp. 5, 554. B. 44630

The Church Record. ... A ... Sketch of the Origin and History of the West Church in Marlborough; ... *Boston: Printed by John Wilson.* 1850. 12mo, pp. 22. B. 44631

Correspondence between the Comptroller of the Currency and First National Bank of Marlboro', Mass. ... *Boston: Geo. C. Rand & Avery, Printers.* 1867. 8vo, pp. 15. B. 44632

Annual Report of the Selectmen ... 1865. ... With the Report of the Treasurer ... &c. *Feltonville: Charles A. Wood,* ... *Printer.* 1865. 8vo, pp. 16. H. 44633

Report of the School Committee ... 1865. *Boston: Printed by John Wilson and Son.* 1855. 16mo, pp. 16. Continued. H.

MARLBOROUGH, *N. H.* Catalogue of the Frost Free Library ... 1867. *Boston: Alfred Mudge & Son, Printers.* 1867. 8vo, pp. 56. H. 44635

MARLBOROUGH, *Vt.* Second Annual Catalogue of the Marlborough High School ... 1862. *Brattleboro: Printed by D. W. Selleck.* 1862. 8vo, pp. 8. H. 44636

MARLE (Egb. van). De febre flava Indiæ Occidentalis. *Marburgi-Cattorum.* 1799. 8vo, pp. 78. 44637

MARLÈS (J. de). Histoire descriptive et pittoresque de Saint Domingo; par M. de Marlès. *Tours: Imp. de Mame.* 1846. 12mo. Plate. 44638

Title from an American catalogue, published by D. Appleton & Co.

MARLOE (——). Marloe's Tracts: the Molucco Nutts, Serpent Stones, Barbados Seeds, Mexico Seeds ... . *London.* 1672–1695. 8vo. 44639

The last tract contains "Observations on the Herb 'Cassing' imported from Carolina."

Marly; or, The Life of a Planter in Jamaica; with Sketches of Society and Manners in the West Indies. Second Edition. *Glasgow: Richard Griffin & Co.* 1828. 8vo, pp. (4), ii, 363, (1). Plate. B. 44640

[MARMAJON (A.)] Five Hundred Pounds Reward. ... *Philadelphia: Printed by John Dunlap.* [1778.] Folio, 1 leaf. P.

Advertisement by Antoine Marmajon, Philadelphia, July 16, 1778, for the recovery of his ship piratically captured by its crew.

MARMIER (X.) En Amérique et en Europe. Par Xavier Marmier. *Paris: L. Hachette et Cie.* 1860. 12mo, pp. (4), 447, (1). BA. 44642

MARMIER. Lettres sur l'Amérique, Canada, États-Unis, Havane, Rio de la Plata. Par Xavier Marmier. *Paris: Arthus-Bertrand.* [1851.] 2 vols., 12mo. C. 44643

See "Blackwood's Magazine," LXIX. 545.

MARMIER. Cartas sobre la America. ... *Mexico.* [n. d.] 2 vols., 8vo. 44644

MARMIER. Souvenirs d'un Voyageur. Par M. X. Marmier. En Amérique ... . En Allemagne ... . En Danemark. En Norvège ... . *Paris: ... Didier et Cie.* 1867. 8vo, pp. (4), 392. BA.

MARMIER. Les Voyageurs nouveaux, Études géographiques et historiques, d'après les voyages les plus récents, par M. X. Marmier. *Paris: Arthus-Bertrand.* [1851.] 3 vols., 12mo.

MARMOCCHI (F. C.) Raccolta di Viaggi dalla scoperta del Nuovo Continente fino a' dì nostri. Compilata da F. C. Marmocchi. ... *Prato: Fratelli Giachetti.* 1840–47. 8vo, pp. 551. Maps, Plates, and Portrait. Continued to 19 vols. 44647

MARMOL (Francisco). El Ilustrísimo Señor Obispo de Trícala. *Carácas.* 1865. 8vo, pp. 39. Portrait. 44648

MÁRMOL (J.) Poesias de José Mármol. *Buenos Aires.* 1854. 2 vols., 8vo, pp. vi, 194; 172. 44649

José Mármol is the founder of the historical novel in South America. His "Amalia" is a work of considerable merit.

MARMOLEJO (Alonso de Góngora). Historia de Chile, desde sú descubrimiento hasta el año de 1575. *Madrid.* 1852. 4to.

Documentos, Opúsculos y Antigüedades que publica la Real Academia de la Historia, Vol. IV.

MARMONT (*Le Maréchal* Auguste Frédéric Louis Viesse de). The Spirit of Military Institutions; or, Essential Principles of the Art of War. By Marshal Marmont. Translated ... by Frank Schaller, Col. 22d Reg. Miss. Inf. C. A. *Columbia, S. C.: Evans and Cogswell.* 1864. 12mo, pp. 278. 44651

MARMONTEL (Jean François). Les Incas, ou La Destruction De L'Empire Du Pérou; Par M. Marmontel ... . *A Paris, Chez Lacombe* ... M. DCC. LXXVII. 2 vols., 8vo. Plates. + [*Ibid.*] 2 vols., 12mo, pp. (2), viii, 252; (4), 280, (3). 2 Plates. H. + Another Issue has pp. xxvii, 207; (4), 257, (3). + *Liege, Chez Bassompierre, Fils.* M. DCC. LXXVII. 2 vols., 8vo, pp. (2), 271; (2), 278. Plates. B. + *Frankfurt.* 1777. 2 vols., 12mo. + *Neufchatel.* 1777. 2 vols., 12mo. + *Lausanne.* 1780. 8vo. + *Paris: Chez Lacombe.* MDCCLXXXIX. 2 vols., 12mo, pp. xxiv, 176; 205. + *Paris.* 1794. 3 vols., 12mo. + Revu et corrigé d'après les meilleures éditions de Paris, Par N. Wanostrocht ... . *À Londres: T. Boosey.* 1808. 12mo, pp. (2), ii, 416. Plate. + *Lyon.* 1810. 2 vols., 12mo. Plate. + *Paris.* 1810. 2 vols., 12mo. + *La Flèche: Voglet.* 1811. 3 vols., 18mo. + *Lyon: Ve Buynand.* 1812. 3 vols., 18mo. + [*Ibid.*] 1817. + *Paris: Guillaumin et Compagnie.* 1817. 2 vols., 16mo, pp. xxviii, 233, (3); 250, (4). Plate. + *Paris: Chassériau.* 1821. 3 vols., 18mo. + *London.* 1821. 2 vols., 12mo. + *Paris: Ledentu.*

1822. 2 vols., 18mo. Plates. + *Lyon: J. Janon.* 1822. 3 vols., 18mo. + *Paris: Touquet.* 1822. 2 vols., 12mo. + *Paris: Verdière.* 1824. 2 vols., 8vo. Plates. + *London: Printed by Whittingham.* 1826. 12mo. + *Paris: Hiard.* 1829. 2 vols., 18mo. + *Paris: Chassaignon.* 1832. 3 vols., 18mo. + *Paris: Ledentu, Libraire.* 1833. 2 vols., 12mo. + *Paris: Corbet.* 1834. 2 vols., 12mo. + *Tours: Mame.* 1843. 12mo. + *Limoges: Martial Ardant.* 1843. 12mo. + Édition ... corrigée par M. l'abbé Lejeune. *Paris: Lehuby.* 1844. 12mo. 20 Plates. + [*Ibid.*] 1845. + *Avignon: Offray aîné.* 1846. 3 vols., 18mo. + Nouvelle Édition, revue et corrigée avec soin, par M. l'abbé Lejeune; ... *Paris: Ducrocq.* 1864. 12mo, pp. xxiv–300.

MARMONTEL. The Incas; or, the Destruction of the Empire of Peru. By M. Marmontel. *London.* 1777. 2 vols., 12mo. + *Dublin.* M,DCC,LXXVII. 2 vols., 12mo, pp. xxxiii, (2), 263; (4), 296. + *Dublin: A. Stewart.* MDCCLXXVII. 2 vols., 12mo, pp. xxxii, (2), 263; x, 288. + *London.* MDCCLXXXVII. 2 vols., 12mo. + *Dublin.* 1792. 2 vols., 12mo. + [*London:*] *Lackington, Allen, and Co.* 1806. 2 vols., 12mo, pp. x, 260; 265. 44653

MARMONTEL. Gl' Incas o la distruzione del Peru ... . traduzida in Italiana. *London.* 1778. 2 vols., 12mo. A. 44654

MARMONTEL. Los Incas, ó La Destruccion Del Imperio del Perú Por Marmontel; traducida por la primera vez al Castellano Por Don F. de Cabello ... . *Paris: Masson y Hijo.* 1822. 2 vols., 12mo, pp. xl, 281; 285, (2). Plate. + [*Ibid.*] 1826. 2 vols., 12mo. + *Madrid.* 1830. 2 vols., 8vo. 44655

MARMONTEL. Le Huron, comédie en deux actes et en vers libres, mêlée d'ariettes. *Paris: Merlin.* 1768. 8vo. + *Parme: imprimerie royale.* 1787. 8vo. 44656

Words by Marmontel; Music by Grétry. It is founded on "L'Ingenu" of Voltaire. *See* Hogarth's "Musical Drama," chap. XXVIII.

Marmor Norfolciense: or, an Essay on an ancient prophetical Inscription in Monkish Latin, lately discovered near Lynn, in Norfolk, 1775. *London.* 17—. 8vo. 657

With a bantering dedication to Dr. S. Johnson, on whom the tract is very severe and satirical, on account of his "False Alarm" and "Taxation no Tyranny."

MARPLE (P. B.) Funeral Address on the Occasion of the Execution of Peter, Slave of J. Douglass, for Murder. Delivered at Dade Court House, Mo., May 26, 1848. By Rev. P. B. Marple. *Springfield.* [1848.] 8vo. S. 44658

MARQUAND (H. E.) John Brown; sa vie, l'affaire de Harper's-Ferry, capture, captivité et martyre du héros et de ses compagnons, ... par Henri E. Marquand. *Paris: E. Dentu.* 1860. 12mo. 44659

MARQUAND. Souvenirs des Indes Occidentales, et Impressions Intimes suivis de Eliza et Maria. Par Henri E. Marquand. *Paris.* 185–. 8vo, pp. 264. 44660

MARQUARD (J.) Iohannis Mar-|quardi I. Cti.|de|Iure Merca-|torum et|Commerciorum.|Singulari|Libri IV|*Francofurti.*|*Impensis*|*Thomæ Matthiæ*|*Götzij.*|*Cum Privi: S. C. Maij:*|[1662.] 2 vols., folio, pp. xiv, 572; iv, 744. 44661

A politico-juridical treatise on commercial law. It is one of those books whose importance is by no means indicated by the title, and is of interest for the history of the Swedish South Company and its settlement in Pennsylvania. It contains an exact reprint of the extremely scarce first edition of the "Argonautica Gustaviana," published by W. Usselincx in 1633. The original editions of some documents reprinted in this collection are lost. For an analysis and for a table of contents, *see* Asher's "Bibliographical Essay," pp. 83–84 and 93–96.

MARQUARDSEN (H.) Der Trent-Fall. Zur Lehre von der Kriegscontrebande und dem Transportdienst der Neutralen. Von Dr. Heinrich Marquardsen ... . *Erlangen: Ferdinand Enke.* 1862. 8vo, pp. xii, 194, (1). H. 44662

MARQUES (C. A.) Apontamentos para o diccionario historico, geographico e estatistico da provincio do Maranhao por Cezar Augusto Marques. *San Luiz.* 1864. 4to, pp. xiv, 376.

MARQUES (S.) Brasilia Pontificæ, sive speciales facultates pontificiæ, quæ Brasiliæ Episcopis conceduntur et singulis decenniis renovantur, cum notationibus evulgatæ, et in quatuor libros distributæ per R. P. Simonem Marques Conimbricensem Societatis Jesu in Provincia Brasilica. Accessit Appendix pro casibus in Brasilia reservatis cum desiderata eorum expositione. Opus omnibus confessariis, parochis, causidicis, et judicibus ultramarinis, præsertim Ecclesiasticis, in ultraque India tam Orientali, quam Occidentali perquam utile, ac necessarium. *Ulyssipone: Ex typis Michaelis Rodrigues Eminentissimi Domini Cardinalis Patriarchae Typogr.* 1749. Folio. J.C.B. 44664

Collation: Half Title and Title, pp. (4); Dedication, (12); Ad Lectorem, (4); Facultates, etc., (4); Series Librorum, (12); Text, 486; Index, (69); Errata, p. 70. A volume of great rarity. *See* Carayon, No. 2800.

MARQUETTE (J.) Recit des Voyages et des Decouvertes du R. Père Jacques Marquette de la Compagnie de Jesus, eñ l'année

1673 et aux suivantes; la Continuation de ses Voyages par le R. P. Claude Alloüez, et le Journal-Autographe du P. Marquette en 1674 & 1675. [*Albanie, N. Y.: Imprimerie de Weed, Parsons & Cie.* 1855.] 12mo, pp. (10), 169, (2). Facsimile and Map. H.

A few copies only privately printed from the original MSS. for James Lenox, exclusively for presentation. *See* B. F. French's "Historical Collections," *and* Shea (J. G.)

MARQUETTE. Voyage et Découverte de Quelques Pays et Nations de l'Amérique Septentrionale. Par le P. Marquette et Sr. Joliet. *A Paris: Chez Estienne Michallet* ... M.DC.LXXXI. 8vo, pp. (4), 43. Map. BA. 44666

A volume of extreme rarity and value. One hundred and twenty-five copies were reprinted for Mr. Obadiah Rich, *Paris: Maulde et Renou.* 1845. 16mo. Also reprinted in Thévenot's "Recueil de Voyages." *See* Faribault, No. 435. A Dutch version is included in Van der Aa's Collection, *Leyden*, 1707.

MARQUETTE, *Wis.* Baptist Association ... Minutes of Session of 1855. *Berlin.* 1855. 8vo. Continued. 44667

DES MARQUETZ. Mémoires chronologiques pour servir à l'histoire de Dieppe. *Paris.* 1785. 2 vols., 12mo. 44668

Contains some particulars concerning the early voyages of the French to Brazil.

MARQUEZ (J. A.) El Perú y la España moderna por J. Arnaldo Marquez. *Lima.* 1866. 2 vols., imp. 8vo, pp. 160; 282. 44669

The most complete collection relating to the history of the last Peruvian war against the Spaniards.

MARQUEZ. Recuerdos de Viaje a los Estados-Unidos de la America Norte (1857–1861). Por José Arnaldo Marquez. *Lima.* 1862. 8vo, pp. (vi), 135, (1). 44670

MARQUEZ (L.) Ejercito imperial Mexicano. Division Marquez. Cuartel General en Morelia. Diciembre 20 de 1863. *Morelia.* 1863. 4to, pp. 27. Plan and 20 Tables. 44671

MARQUEZ. Manifiesto á la Nacion. *Guadalajara.* 1859. 4to, pp. 42. 44672

MARQUEZ (P.) Due Antichi Monumenti di Architetura Messicana Illustrati da D. Pietro Marquez ... . *Roma: Presso li Salomoni.* 1804. 8vo, pp. (2), iv, 47. 4 Plates. H. 44673

Also on large paper in folio.

MARR (W.) Reise nach Central-America, von Wilhelm Marr. *Hamburg.* 1863. 2 vols., 8vo, pp. xii, 322; viii, 276.

MARRACCI (Ippolyte). De diva virgine, Copacavana, in peruano novi mvndi Regno celeberrima. Liber vnvs. Quo eius Origo, et Miracula compendio descripta. *Romæ, Apud Hæred. Colinij.* 1656. 8vo, pp. 125, (26). 44675

"Non mentionné par Ternaux, et cité par Pinelo sous la date de 1658."—LECLERC, No. 1639.

MARRANT (J.) Journal of Rev. John Marrant, from August 18, 1785, to March 16, 1790; and two Sermons preached at Ragged Island and Boston. *London.* 1790. 8vo. S. 44676

MARRANT (J.) An Interesting Narrative, of the Life of John Marrant (A man of Color). Containing an Account of his Birth, Extraordinary Conversion, and Remarkable Success among the Cherokee Indians, his Arrival in England, and Departure as a Missionary to America. Compiled originally By the Rev. J. Aldridge ... . A New Edition. *Brighton: T. Sharp.* 1813. 12mo, pp. 27. 44677

MARRANT. A Narrative of the Life of John Marrant, of New York, in North America; ... his ... religious motives, wandering several Days in the Desert without Food, and being at last taken by an Indian Hunter among the Cherokees ... . With an account of his Conversion of the King of the Cherokees, and his Daughter, &c. The whole authenticated by the Rev. W. Aldridge. *Leeds.* 1810. 8vo, pp. 24. 44678

MARRANT. A Narrative of the Lord's wonderful Dealings with John Marrant, a Black, (Now going to Preach the Gospel in Nova-Scotia) Born in New-York, in North-America. Taken down from his own Relation, Arranged, Corrected, and Published By the Rev. Mr. Aldridge. The Second Edition. *London: Gilbert and Plummer.* 1785. 8vo, pp. 38. + *London.* 1787. 8vo. + Sixth Edition. *London.* 1788. 8vo. 44679

MARRANT. A Sermon Preached on the 24th ... of June 1789, ... at the Request of ... the African Lodge ... in Boston. By The Reverend Brother Marrant ... . *Boston.* [n. d.] 8vo, pp. 24. BA. 44680

MARRERO (Abraham). Causa célebre del hospital militar de S. Ambrosio de la ciudad de la Habana. [*Madrid.* n. d.] 8vo, pp. 37. 44681

MARRIAGE (F.) The Career of Modern Liberty: being an Extract from a Treatise on Chili; shewing the Important Position

which the Pennsylvanians have maintained in the Cause of Freedom as regards the Old World as well as America, and the service rendered by William Penn to Civil and Religious Liberty. By Francis Marriage. *London.* 1849. 8vo, pp. 24. 44682

Marriage Ceremonies as now used in all Parts of the World, .. *London.* 1744. 12mo. 44683

Marriage Rites, Customs, and Ceremonies, of the Nations of the Universe. *London: J. Robins & Co.* 1824. 8vo, pp. viii, 400. Plate. 44684

MARRIOTT (C.) An Address to the Members of the Religious Society of Friends, on the Duty of declining the Use of the Products of Slave Labour. By Charles Marriott. ... *New-York: Isaac T. Hopper.* 1835. 8vo, pp. 18. BA. 44685

Also: Testimony of the New-York Association of Friends for the Relief of those held in Slavery, &c. concerning Charles Marriott ... . *New-York: Piercy & Reed, Printers.* 1844. 24mo, pp. 15. H.

MARRIOTT (G.) A Sermon preached December 13, 1776, being the Fast Day on account of the Troubles in America; ... By G. Marriott ... . *London: J. Flexney.* 1777. 4to. 44686

Differs from most fast-day sermons in this respect, that popery is the chief object of the author's fears. *See* "M. Rev.," LVI. 237.

[MARRIOTT (James).] The Case of the Dutch Ships considered. *London.* 1758. 8vo. + The Fourth Edition. *London: T. Harrison.* 1778. 8vo. 44687

Relates to neutral rights, during the Seven Years War between England and France, 1754–1760, carried on chiefly in America.

MARRIOTT. Examinations of Doctor Marriot, and Messrs. Maseres and Hey at the Bar of Parliament, concerning the Religion and Laws of Quebec. *Philadelphia.* 1774. 8vo. 44688

[MARRIOTT.] Mémoire Justificatif de la Conduite de la Grande Bretagne, En arrêtant les Navires Étrangers et les Munitions de Guerre destinées aux Insurgens de l'Amérique. *Londres: Imprimé par T. Harrison et S. Brooke.* MDCCLXXIX. 4to, pp. vii, 60. + *Londres: G. Cooke.* 1804. 8vo, pp. x, 106.

There are copies on thick paper, signed at the end by J. Marriott.

[MARRIOTT.] Plan of a Code of Laws for the Province of Quebec; Reported by the Advocate General. *London.* MDCCLXXIV. 8vo, pp. (4), 292. C., H. 44690

MARRIOTT. The Singular and Diverting Behaviour of Doctor Marriot, His Majesty's Advocate General: Who was examined concerning the Religion and Laws of Quebec: and found means from his incomparable Wit and Subtilty, to defeat the Purposes for which he was brought to the Bar of Parliament, on the 3d of June, 1774. *Philadelphia: James Humphreys, junr.* 1774. 12mo, pp. 16. P. 44691

MARRIOTT (J.) Poems, by John Marriott. To which is prefixed a Short Account of the Author ... . *New-Bedford: Reprinted by A. Shearman, Jr.* 1805. 16mo, pp. xlii, (2), 141. C.

MARRON (P. H.) Regi Pacifico, Ludovico XVI. *Paris.* 1783. 8vo, pp. 3. 44693

An ode on the success of the American war.

MARROQUIN (F.) Doctrina Christiana en Lengua Utlatleca, por Fr. Francisco Marroquin, Obispo de Guatemala. *Mexico, apud Joannem Paulum.* 1556 or 1566. 4to. 44694

This very rare book is in the language spoken by the Indians on the Pacific side of Guatemala, north of Nicaragua. Its author was the first Bishop of Guatemala, 1533–1563. It is an early specimen of Mexican typography. *See* Ternaux, No. 98.

MARRYAT (F.) Mountains and Molehills; or, Recollections of a Burnt Journal in California ... . By Frank Marryat. *London: Longman.* 1855. 8vo, pp. 442. + *New York: Harper & Brothers.* 1855. 12mo, pp. 319. P. 44695

MARRYAT [Frederick]. A Diary in America, with Remarks on its Institutions. By Capt. Marryat, C.B. *London: Longman, Orme* ... 1839. 3 vols., post 8vo, pp. (4), 321; (4), 319; (4), 311, (1). + *Paris: Baudry.* 1839. 8vo. + *New York: Wm. H. Colyer.* 1839. 8vo, pp. 263. + *New York: Harper & Brothers.* 1839. 12mo, pp. 247. + *Philadelphia.* 1839. 2 vols., 12mo, pp. 242; 228. + *Philadelphia: Carey & Hart.* 1839. 12mo, pp. 263. + *New York: D. Appleton & Co.* 1839. 12mo, pp. 263.

See also "Waldie's Circulating Library," XIV. The work elicited some controversy and two replies, viz: Lie-ary on America, with Yarns on its Institutions. By Captain Marry-it, C. B., (Common Bloat). *Boston.* 1840. 18mo, pp. 36. Reply to the Illiteral and Incorrect Statements in Marryat's Diary in America, relative to the coloured West Indians. *London.* 1840. 8vo. *See also* our No. 40392.

MARRYAT. A Diary in America. By Capt. Marryat, C.B. The Second Part: with Canada and the Present Condition of the Indians. With a Map of Aboriginal America, and of the Seat of War in Florida. *London: Longman.* 1839. 3 vols., post 8vo, pp. (4), 304; (4), 293; (4), 362. + [*Ibid.*] 1840. + *Philadelphia: T. K. & P. G. Collins.* 1840. 12mo, pp. (2), 300. B.

See "Edinburgh Review," LXX. 123, and "Blackwood's Magazine," XV. 424.

MARRYAT. Narrative of the Travels and Adventures of Monsieur Violet, in California, Sonora, & Western Texas. Written by Capt. Marryat ... . *London.* 1843. 3 vols., post 8vo. + *Leipzig: Bernhard Tauchnitz.* 1843. 12mo, pp. vi, 384. Map. + *New York.* 1843. 8vo. 44698

Reprinted, *London: Geo. Routledge.* 1849. 12mo, pp. 354. It is mainly appropriated from Gregg (J.), and Kendall (G. W.)

MARRYAT. Monsieur Violette, ou Aventures d'un jeune émigré français en 1830; traduites par J. Robaglia. *Paris: Gosselin.* 1845. 2 vols., 8vo. 44699

MARRYAT. The Settlers in Canada: written for Young People. By Captain Marryat. *London.* 1844. 2 vols., fcap 8vo, pp. 730. + *New York.* 1844. 18mo. + *Leipzig: Bernhard Tauchnitz.* 1844. 16mo, pp. (2), 324. 2 Plates. + *New York: D. Appleton & Co.* MDCCXLVI. 2 vols., 18mo. + [*Ibid.*] 1856. + New Edition. *London.* 1849. 12mo, pp. 398. + *London: H. G. Bohn.* 1854. 12mo, pp. 396. 44700

MARRYAT. Les Colons du Canada. Ouvrage pour la jeunesse. Traduit de l'anglais par E. P. *Paris: Ducloux.* 1852. 2 vols., 18mo. + Seconde Édition. *Paris: Meyrueis et Cie.* 1855. 2 vols., 12mo. 44701

MARRYAT. Sigismund Ruestig, ou le Naufrage du Pacifique. Nouveau Robinson; traduit de l'anglais par Charles Brandon. *Leipzig: Teubner.* 1844. 16mo. 44702

Also published with the title: "Le Naufrage du Pacifique, ou les Nouveaux Robinsons. ... *Paris: Lécrivain et Toubou.* 1861. 2 vols., 4to.

[MARRYAT (Joseph).] Concessions to America the Bane of Britain; or the Cause of the Present Distressed Situation of the British Colonial and Shipping Interests explained, and the Proper Remedy suggested. *London: W. J. and J. Richardson.* 1807. 8vo, pp. 63. BA. 44703

MARRYAT. An Examination of the Report of the Berbice Commissioners, and an Answer to the Letters of James Stephen, Esq. respecting the Crown Estates in the West-Indies, published in the Courier, under the Signature of "Truth." By Joseph Marryat, Esq. M.P. ... *London: Printed by Hughes & Baynes.* 1817. 8vo, pp. (2), 122. B. 44704

MARRYAT. More Thoughts, occasioned by Two Publications which the Authors call "An Exposure of some of the numerous Misstatements and Misrepresentations contained in a Pamphlet ... entitled Thoughts, &c." and "A Defence of the Bill for the Abolition of Slaves." By Joseph Marryat, Esq. M.P. ... *London: J. M. Richardson.* 1816. 8vo, pp. vii, 143. B. 44705

MARRYAT. More Thoughts still on the state of the West-India Colonies, and the Proceedings of the African Institution. with Observations on the Speech of James Stephen, Esq. ... By Joseph Marryat, Esq. M.P. ... *London.* 1817. 8vo, pp. (4), 147. + Second Edition. *London: J. M. Richardson.* 1818. 8vo, pp. (4), 147. B. 44706

MARRYAT. Observations on the West India Dock Charter. By Joseph Marryat. *London.* 1837. 8vo. 44707

This elicited "Reply to the Observations of Jos. Marryat, on the West India Dock Charter." *London.* 1832. 8vo, pp. 107.

MARRYAT. A Reply to the Arguments contained in various publications recommending an Equalization of the Duties on East and West-India Sugar. *London.* 1823. 8vo, pp. 111. 44708

For a reply see [Larpent (G.)], "On Protection to West India Sugar," No. 39068.

MARRYAT. Thoughts on the Abolition of the Slave Trade, and Civilization of Africa; with Remarks on the African Institution, and an Examination of the Report of their Committee, Recommending a General Registry of Slaves in the British West India Islands. ... By Joseph Marryat, Esq. M.P. *London: J. M. Richardson.* 1816. 8vo, pp. vii, 235. + Fourth Edition, revised and corrected. [*Ibid.*] 1816. 8vo, pp. vii, 243. B. 44709

This brought out "An Exposure of ... Misstatements and Misrepresentations contained in ... Mr. Marryat's Pamphlet, entitled 'Thoughts on the Abolition of the Slave Trade and the Civilization of Africa'" ... . *London: Printed by Ellerton and Henderson.* 1816. 8vo, pp. (2), 65. B., C. Also: Speech, ... June 5, 1820, upon ... alteration in the Duties of Timber. *London.* [1820.] 8vo. S.—Speech, ... July 25, 1822. ... on the state of the Island of Trinidad. *London.* 1823. 8vo, pp. 115. S.—Substance of a Speech in the House of Commons upon the second reading of the Martinique Trade Bill. *London.* 1809. 8vo. *See also* [Macaulay (Z.)], No. 42953.

MARS (J.) Life of James Mars, a Slave born and sold in Connecticut. Sixth Edition. Written by himself. *Hartford: Case, Lockwood & Company.* 1868. 12mo, pp. 38. B. 44710

MARSDEN (J. B.) The History of the Early Puritans: from the Reformation to ... 1642. By J. B. Marsden, M.A. *London.* 1850. 8vo. S. + Second Edition. *London: Hamilton, Adams,*

& Co. M.DCCC.LIII. 8vo, pp. xvi, 460. H. + [*Ibid.*] MDCCCLIV. 8vo, pp. viii, 473. + Third Edition. [*Ibid.*] 1860. 8vo, pp. xv, 462. BA. 44711

MARSDEN. The History of the Later Puritans, from the opening of the Civil War in 1642, to the Ejection of the Non-conforming Clergy in 1662. By J. B. Marsden, M.A. *London.* 1852. 8vo. C. + Second Edition. *London: Hamilton, Adams, & Co.* MDCCCLIV. 8vo, pp. viii, 473. BA. 44712

MARSDEN (J.) An Extract from the Rev. J. Marsden's Journal, during his Passage from New-York to England. To which are added, Lines on the ... Death of the Rev. Thomas Coke, L.L.D. ... By Joshua Marsden. *New-York: David Seabury.* 1815. 8vo, pp. 24. BA. 44713

MARSDEN. Grace Displayed: an Interesting Narrative of the Life, and Missionary Labours of Joshua Marsden. *New-York.* 1813. 12mo, pp (4), 240. Portrait. + Second Edition. [*Ibid.*] 1814. 12mo. S. 44714

MARSDEN. Leisure Hours; or Poems, Moral, Religious, & Descriptive. By Joshua Marsden, Missionary. ... *New-York: Griffin & Rudd.* 1812. 8vo, pp. 12, (8), 13–160. C. 44715

MARSDEN. The Narrative of a Mission to Nova Scotia, New Brunswick, and the Somers Islands; with a Tour to Lake Ontario. To which is added, The Mission, An Original Poem, with copious Notes. Also a brief account of Missionary Societies. And much interesting Information on Missions in general. By Joshua Marsden, late Missionary to Nova Scotia, &c. *Plymouth-Dock: J. Johns.* 1816. 8vo, pp. xiv, 289. Portrait. + Second Edition. *London.* 1827. 12mo. C. 44716

[MARSDEN (Peter).] An Account of the Island of Jamaica; with Reflections on the Treatment, Occupation and Provisions of the Slaves. To which is added a Description of the Animal and Vegetable Productions of the Island. By a Gentleman lately resident on a Plantation. *Newcastle: Printed for the Author.* 1788. 8vo, pp. 87. N. 44717

MARSDEN (William). A Catalogue of Dictionaries, Grammars, and Alphabets, in two parts. I. Alphabetical Catalogue of Authors. II. Chronological Catalogue of Works in each Class of Language. *London.* 1796. 4to, pp. vi, 156. 44718

Privately printed, and scarce; contains but little about American languages. *See also* the "Bibliotheca Marsdeniana." *London: Printed by J. L. Cox.* 1827. 4to.

MARSDEN. Miscellaneous Works. *London: Cox and Son.* 1834. 4to, pp. 104. 44719

Includes some Araucanian words at page 104. *See* Ludewig, p. xix.

MARSELLUS (N. J.) ... A Sermon ... in the Reformed Dutch Church, at Greenwich in the City of New York, on ... the Death of the Rev. John H. Livingston ... . By Nicholas Marsellus. *New-York: Printed by E. Conrad.* 1825. 8vo, pp. 19.

MARSH (A.) The Liquor Traffic, and Prohibitory Law. By Rev. Abram Marsh ... . [n. p. n. d.] 8vo, pp. 16. H. 44721

Also: Discourse ... Reasons for Law with special reference to the Traffic in Intoxicating Drinks. ... *Hartford.* 1846. 8vo.

[MARSH (Anne).] The Protestant Reformation in France, or History of the Huguenots. ... *London.* 1847. 2 vols., 8vo. + *Philadelphia.* 1851. 2 vols., 12mo. 44722

Contains some particulars relative to the emigration of the Huguenots to America.

MARSH (*Mrs.* Caroline Crane). Wolfe of the Knoll, and Other Poems. By Mrs. George P. Marsh. *New York: Charles Scribner.* 1860. 12mo, pp. 327. H. 44723

[MARSH (*Miss* C.)] The Aspects of Religion in the United States of America. ... *London: Sampson Low* ... . 1859. 16mo, pp. (6), 189. B. 44724

[MARSH.] The Life of the Rev. William Marsh, D.D. By his Daughter ... . *New York: Robert Carter and Brothers.* 1867. 8vo, pp. (4), 580. 4 Plates. B. 44725

Also: The Brave and Happy Soldier. ... *New York: Military Post Library Association.* [n. d.] 24mo, pp. 16. B.

MARSH (C.) The Speech of Charles Marsh, Esq., in a Committee of the House of Commons, July 1st, 1813. *London.* 1813. 8vo. 44726

MARSH (C.) An Essay on the Amendments proposed to the Constitution of the State of Vermont by the Council of Censors, delivered at the Celebration of Washington's Birth-day at Norwich, on the 22d of February, 1814. By Charles Marsh, Esquire. *Hanover, N. H.: Printed by Charles Spear.* 1814. 8vo, pp. 24. H. 44727

MARSH (D.) A Sermon preached on the Day of General Election ... before the ... Legislature of Vermont. By Rev. Daniel Marsh, A.M. *Montpelier.* 1813. 8vo, pp. 30. 44728

MARSH (D.) Report, on the Diversion of the Water of the enesee River, for the supply of the Erie and Genesee Valley anals. By Daniel Marsh ... . *Rochester: Printed by A. Strong Co.* 1847. 8vo, pp. 16. H. 44729

[MARSH.] Report on the Importance and Best Mode of curing an Ample Supply of Water from Lake Erie for the ... Erie Canal. *Rochester: A. Strong & Co., Printers.* 1854. 8vo, pp. 16. H. 44730

Also: Report of a Survey of the Genesee Valley Canal, made Sept. 1854, by D. Marsh and S. Cornell. Rochester, Jan. 1, 1855. [n. p. n. d.] 8vo. S.

MARSH (E. G.) An Oration ... before the Φ B K Society, ... in New Haven, at the Fifth of December, A.D. 1797. By Ebenezer Grant Marsh. *Hartford: Hudson & Goodwin.* 1798. 8vo, pp. 32. H. 44731

MARSH. An Oration, delivered at Wethersfield, February 22, 1800; on the Death of General George Washington. ... By Ebenezer Grant Marsh. ... *Hartford: Printed by Hudson and Goodwin.* 1800. 8vo, pp. 16. BA. 44732

MARSH (E.) Letter. Sept. 10, 1856. By Ephraim Marsh, President of the Convention which nominated Fillmore. [n. p. 1856.] 8vo. 44733

MARSH (G. P.) ... Address, ... before the New England Society of ... New-York, December 24, 1844. By George P. Marsh. ... *New York: M. W. Dodd.* 1845. 8vo, pp. 54. H.

This elicited "Remarks on an Address ... before the New England Society ... December 23, 1844, By George P. Marsh." *Boston: C. Stimpson.* 1845. 12mo, pp. 23. H.

MARSH. The Camel his Organization Habits and Uses considered with reference to his Introduction into the United States By George P. Marsh *Boston: Gould and Lincoln.* 1856. 12mo, pp. 224. H. 44735

MARSH. The Goths in New-England. A Discourse . Middlebury College, August 15, 1843. By George P. Marsh. ... *Middlebury: Printed by J. Cobb, Jr.* 1843. 8vo, pp. 39.

MARSH. Remarks of George P. Marsh, ... on Slavery in the Territories of New Mexico, California and Oregon; ... August 3d, 1848. [*Burlington.* 1848.] 8vo, pp. 12. B. 44737

Also: Address before the Agricultural Society of Rutland County, September 30, 1847. ... *Rutland.* 1847. 8vo. + [*Ibid.*] 1848. 8vo, pp. 24.—Address ... American Institute, Oct. 25, 1855. ... [n. p. n. d.] 8vo.—The American Historical School:

a Discourse ... before The Literary Societies of Union College. ... *Troy, N. Y.: Kneeland and Co.* 1847. 8vo, pp. 29.—Discourse before the Philomathesian Society of Middlebury College, Aug. 15, 1843. ... [n. p. n. d.] 8vo.—Human Knowledge: a Discourse ... before the ... Phi Beta Kappa Society at Cambridge, August 26, 1847. ... *Boston: Charles C. Little and James Brown.* 1847. 8vo, pp. 42.—Report made under Authority of the Legislature of Vermont, on the Artificial Propagation of Fish ... . *Burlington: Free Press Print.* 1857. 8vo, pp. 52, Appendix, 62, Index, (2).—Speech ... on the Tariff Bill ... . April 30, 1844. ... *Washington.* [1844.] 8vo, pp. 16. + *St. Albans, Vt.: Printed by E. B. Whiting.* 1844. 8vo, pp. 15.—Speech ... on the Bill for establishing the Smithsonian Institution ... April 22, 1846. *Washington: Printed by J. & G. S. Gideon.* 1846. 8vo, pp. 15.—Speech ... on the Mexican War; ... February 10, 1848. *Washington: Printed by J. & G. S. Gideon.* 1848. 8vo, pp. 16.—Speech ... on The Tariff Question. ... June 30th, 1846. [n. p.:] *J. & G. S. Gideon, Printers.* [n. d.] 8vo, pp. 16. H.

MARSH (H.) A History of the Translations ... of the Scriptures, from the Earliest to the Present Age, throughout Europe, Asia, and America. ... By Herbert Marsh, D.D. F.R.S. ... *London: Printed by Law and Gilbert.* 1812. 8vo, pp. vii, (1), 120. H.

MARSH (J.) The Remains of the Rev. James Marsh, D.D. Late President ... in the University of Vermont; with a Memoir of his Life. [By J. Torrey.] ... *Boston: Crocker and Brewster.* 1843. 8vo, pp. 642. + Second Edition. *Burlington: Chauncey Goodrich.* 1845. 8vo, pp. 642. 44739

Also: An Address ... in Burlington ... [at his] Inauguration ... [as] President of the University of Vermont, Nov. 28, 1826. *Burlington: Printed by E. & T. Mills.* 1826. 8vo, pp. 31. B.

MARSH (J. W.) The Turning Point, or shall America be ruled by a Monarch or by the People? *New York.* [n. d.] 12mo, pp. 32. 44740

Also: Washington's Prophecy; or Facts concerning the Rebellion. ... *Louisville.* 1866. 8vo.

MARSH (J.) A Discourse, ... in Wethersfield, at the Funeral of the Honourable John Chester, Esq. ... By John Marsh, D.D. ... *Hartford: Printed by Hudson and Goodwin.* 1809. 8vo, pp. 24.

MARSH. A Discourse ... at Wethersfield, December 11th, 1783. Being a Day of Public Thanksgiving. By John Marsh, A.M. ... *Hartford: Printed by Hudson and Goodwin.* [1784.] 8vo, pp. 22. BA. 44742

MARSH. ... A Sermon ... at Wethersfield, December 13th, 1782. At the Funeral of Mrs. Lydia Beadle, Wife of the Late William Beadle, and their Four Children, who were all murdered by his Own Hands ... . By John Marsh, A.M. ... *Hartford: Printed by Hudson and Goodwin.* [1782.] 8vo, pp. 39. H., M. + *Middleborough.* 1788. 8vo, pp. 38. 44743

MARSH. A Sermon, Preached ... at Hartford, on the Day of the Anniversary Election, May 12th, 1796. By John Marsh, A.M. ... *Hartford: Printed by Hudson and Goodwin.* M.DCC.XCVI. 8vo, pp. 34. BA., M. 44744

MARSH (J.) The Cause of Temperance as connected with Home Evangelization; An Address ... at the Conference of Churches ... June 10 & 11, 1863. By Rev. John Marsh, D.D. ... *New-York.* 1863. 12mo, pp. 23. H. 44745

MARSH. A Discourse on the Extent and Evils of the Sunday Liquor Traffic in Cities ... By Rev. John Marsh ... . *New York: American Temperance Union.* 1848. 8vo, pp. 24. B. 44746

MARSH. A Half Century Tribute to the Cause of Temperance. An Address ... at New Paltz ... January 8, 1851, By Rev. John Marsh ... . *New-York.* 1851. 8vo, pp. 32. 44747

MARSH. The Napoleon of Temperance. Sketches of the Life and Character of the Hon. Neal Dow ... . By Rev. John Marsh ... . *New-York.* 1852. 8vo, pp. 24. Portrait. H. 44748

MARSH. Temperance Recollections. Labors, Defeats, Triumphs. An Autobiography. By John Marsh, D.D. ... *New York: Charles Scribner.* 1866. 12mo, pp. (6), vii, 7–373. Port.

Also: The Actings of Faith in Moral Reforms. A Word to the Friends of Temperance. ... *New York.* 1856. 12mo, pp. 24.—An Address ... before the Marine Temperance Society ... July 4th, 1840. *New York.* 1840. 8vo, pp. 20. H.— ... An Address ... at Pomfret, Con., October 28, 1829, before the Windham Co. Temperance Society. ... *Hartford: D. F. Robinson & Co.* 1830. 12mo, pp. 24.—The Drunkard's Heart and the Devil's Palace: captured and reclaimed by the Son of God. ... *New York: American Temperance Union.* 1865. 16mo, pp. 16.—The Hand of God in the Reformation of Drunkards. A Sermon. ... [n. p.] 1842. 8vo.—Letter to Rev. Howard Crosby, D.D., on his Denial of Teetotalism as a Bible Rule. ... *New York: Charles Scribner & Co.* 1867. 8vo, pp. 20.—Letter on the Promotion of Moral Reforms by Secret Societies. ... *New York.* 1868. 8vo.—Letter to the Rev. Leonard Bacon, D.D. ... *New York.* 1865. 8vo.—The Temperance Battle not Man's but God's. ... *New-York.* 1858. 8vo, pp. 23, (1).—The Triumphs of Temperance. A Discourse ... *New-York: John P. Prall, Printer.* 1855. 8vo, pp. 16.—Two Hundred Temperance Anecdotes. ... *New York.* 1848. 18mo.

MARSH (J.) ... A Sermon ... before the General Court of Election at Hartford ... May 11th, 1721. By Jonathan Marsh, A.M. ... *N. London: Printed ... by T. Green.* [1721.] 24mo, pp. (2), 53. H. 44750

MARSH. ... A Sermon ... before the General Assembly of ... Connecticut, On the Day of their Election, ... May 13. 1736. By Jonathan Marsh, A.M. ... *N. London: Printed ... by T. Green.* 1737. 24mo, pp. (4), 27. H. 44751

MARSH. A Sermon ... in Barkhemstead, ... Christmas, ... 1787 ... . By Jonathan Marsh, A.M. ... *Hartford: Printed by Nathaniel Patten.* M,DCC,LXXX,VIII. 16mo, pp. 24. H. 44752

Also: The Great Care and Concern of Men under Gospel-Light. Sermon at Windsor [Conn.], Dec. 14, 1720. *New London.* 1721. 12mo, pp. 27. W.

MARSH (J.) An Address on Temperance ... at West Sandwich, Mass. March 24, 1833. By Joseph Marsh. *Boston: Printed by Perkins & Marvin.* 1833. 16mo, pp. 16. H. 44753

MARSH (J.) A Popular Life of George Fox, the first of the Quakers. Compiled from his Journal and other Authentic Sources; ... By Josiah Marsh. *London: Charles Gilpin.* 1847. 8vo, pp. 426. + *Philadelphia.* [1848.] 12mo, pp. 446. P.

This produced: Review of a work entitled, "A Popular Life of George Fox, the first of the Quakers, by Josiah Marsh," (in the "Westminster and Foreign Quarterly Review," No. 93, for July, 1847). Reprinted, *London.* 1847. 12mo.

[MARSH (Lennard).] The Apocatastasis; or Progress Backwards. ... *Burlington: Chauncey Goodrich.* 1854. 8vo, pp. 202, (1).

Also: On the Relations of Slavery to the War; and on the Treatment of it necessary to permanent Peace. A few Suggestions for Thoughtful and Patriotic Men. ... [n. p. n. d.] 8vo, pp. 8.—Review of a Letter from Bishop Hopkins, Vermont, on the Bible View of Slavery. ... *Burlington: Free Press.* 1861. 8vo, pp. 28.—The Third Party in the War. ... [n. p. n. d.] 8vo.—To the Hon. F. P. Blair of Missouri. ... [n. p. n. d.] 8vo. *See also* "A Bake-Pan," *our* Vol. I., No. 2816.

MARSH (L. R.) ... An Oration on the Life, Character, and Public Services, of General Nathaniel Woodhull. With an Account of the Origin of the Woodhull Monument Association. By Luther R. Marsh, Esq. ... *New-York: Leavitt, Trow & Co., Printers.* 1848. 8vo, pp. 30. 2 Plates. H. 44756

MARSH (O. C.) ... Description of an Ancient Sepulchral Mound near Newark, Ohio. By O. C. Marsh, F.G.S. [n. p. n. d.] 8vo, pp. 11. B. 44757

MARSH (R.) A Comparison of the Present with the Former Doctrines of the General Government, on ... Slavery, the Territories, &c. By Roswell Marsh. ... *Steubenville, O.* 1856. 8vo, pp. 23. H. 44758

MARSH. Important Correspondence. Friendly Discussion of Party Politics in 1860–1. Letters of Hon. Roswell Marsh, ... and Hon. Charles Reemelin ... . [n. p. n. d.] 8vo, pp. 51.

MARSH (S. H.) An Inaugural Discourse, By Sidney H. Marsh ... . *Burlington.* 1856. 8vo, pp. 20. H. 44760

MARSH (W.) Wegweiser für Auswanderer nach den Vereinigten Staaten von Nord-Amerika. Nach officiellen Documenten von W. Marsh ... . *Altona.* 1866. 8vo, pp. 24. + Zweite vergrösserte Ausgabe. [*Ibid.*] 12mo, pp. 28. + Dritte Ausgabe. *Altona: L. Hestermann.* 1866. 16mo, pp. 64. + Vierte Ausgabe. [*Ibid.*] 16mo, pp. 60. H. 44761

MARSH (W. H.) ... A Sermon ... in Relation to the Fugitive Slave Law ... at Woodstock, Conn. ... Thanksgiving, Nov. 28, 1850; ... By Rev. William H. Marsh. ... *Worcester: Printed by Henry J. Howland.* [n. d.] 8vo, pp. 30. B., H. 44762

MARSH (——). Marsh's Masonic Register. *New York.* 1846. 18mo. 44763

MARSHAL (R.) *and* THOMPSON (J.) A Brief Historical Account of sundry things in the Doctrines ... of the Newlight Church. By R. Marshal & J. Thompson ... . *Cincinnati: J. Carpenter & Co.* 1811. 12mo, pp. 24. B. 44764

MARSHALL (A. E.) Debates. *See* Georgia, VII. 27036.

MARSHALL (A. K.) Speech of Hon. Alexander K. Marshall ... on the Slavery Question, &c. ... Feb. 4, 1857. *Washington.* 1857. 8vo, pp. 8. H. 44765

MARSHALL (B.) Memorial of B. Marshall, Tuckahatchee Mico, G. W. Stedham and Geo. Scott, Delegates to the Creek Nation, June 19, 1848. [n. p. n. d.] 8vo, pp. 5. 44766

MARSHALL (C. H.) *See* [Butler (W. A.)], III. 9663.

MARSHALL (C.) Passages from the Diary of Christopher Marshall, kept in Philadelphia and Lancaster during the American Revolution. Edited by William Duane ... . Volume I. 1774–1777. *Philadelphia: Hazard & Mitchell.* 1839–1849. 12mo, pp. 174, xix, Errata. 44767

MARSHALL. Passages from the Remembrancer of Christopher Marshall, Member of the Committee of Observation and Inspection, of the Provincial Conference, and of the Council of Safety. Edited by William Duane, Jr. ... *Philadelphia: Printed by James Crissy.* 1839. 12mo, pp. 124, xvi, Errata. M., P. 44768

MARSHALL (E. C.) The Ancestry of General Grant, and their Contemporaries. By Edward Chauncey Marshall, A.M. ... *New York: Sheldon & Company.* 1869. 12mo, pp. xiii, 186.

MARSHALL. History of the United States Naval-Academy, with Biographical Sketches, and the Names of all the Superintendents, Professors, and Graduates ... . By Edward Chauncey Marshall, A.M. ... *New York: D. Van Nostrand.* 1862. 8vo, pp. 156. 2 Plates. H. 44770

Also: Are the West Point Graduates Loyal? ... [*New York.*] 1862. 16mo, pp. 8. —American Progress—Judge Davis and the Presidency. Speech ... March 11, 1852, ... [*Washington.* 1852.] 8vo, pp. 8.—The Book of Oratory: ... Selections from American and English Orators, Divines and Poets. ... *New York.* 1851. 12mo.

MARSHALL (E.) Johnny Weston; or, Christmas Eve at the White House. By Mrs. Emma Marshall. *Philadelphia: J. P. Skelly & Co.* 1868. 18mo, pp. 216. 44771

MARSHALL (G.) ... Practical Marine Gunnery; containing ... the ... Description & Use, of Every Article used in the ... Navy of the United States. By George Marshall. *Norfolk: Printed by Thomas G. Broughton.* 1822. 8vo, pp. 136. 44772

MARSHALL (H.) Memoir of Herbert Marshall, a Presbyter of the Protestant Episcopal Church. ... *Boston: R. P. & C. Williams.* 1828. 18mo, pp. 126. B. 44773

MARSHALL (Humphry). An Address to the People of Kentucky. By H. Marshall. *Philadelphia: Printed by Ormrod & Conrad.* 1796. 8vo, pp. 48. 44774

MARSHALL. The Aliens, a Patriotic Poem. By H. Marshall ... occasioned by the Alien Bill now before the Senate. *Philadelphia: The Author.* 1798. 8vo, pp. 24. 44775

MARSHALL. Arbustrum Americanum: the American Grove, or, an Alphabetical Catalogue of Forest Trees and Shrubs, natives of the American United States ... . Compiled ... By Humphry Marshall. *Philadelphia: Printed by Joseph Crukshank.* M DCC LXXXV. 8vo, pp. xx, 174. BA. 44776

See "M. Rev.," LXXIX. 74.

MARSHALL. Catalogue alphabetique des arbres et arbrisseaux, qui croissent naturellement dans les États-Unis de l'Amérique Septentrionale ... . Traduit de l'Anglois, de M. Humphry Marshall, avec des Notes & Observations sur la culture; par M. Lézermes ... . *Paris: Chez Cuchet.* M DCC LXXXVIII. 8vo, pp. vii, (1), xxii, 278, (2). A., H. 44777

This translation contains additional notes and remarks.

[MARSHALL.] A Reply to the Address, of the Hon. George Muter and Benjamin Sebastian. [n. p.] M,DCC,XCV. 8vo, pp. 31.

MARSHALL (H.) The History of Kentucky; including an account of the Discovery, Settlement, Progressive Improvement, Political and Military Events, and the Present State of the Country. By Humphrey Marshall. *Frankfort, Ky.* 1812. 8vo, pp. 407. 44779

Of this first edition Vol. I. only was printed. It is very scarce.

MARSHALL. The History of Kentucky. Exhibiting an account of the Modern Discovery; Settlement; Progressive Improvement; Civil and Military Transactions; and the Present State of the Country. By Humphrey Marshall. *Frankfort: Geo. S. Robinson, Printer.* 1824. 2 vols., 8vo, pp. v, iii–465, 8; v, 524. H. 44780

Includes the "Ancient Annals of Kentucky," by C. S. Rafinesque. Largely composed of minute relations of the border wars and the massacres by the Indians. *See* "N. A. Rev.," XXXV. 1–18.

MARSHALL (H.) Speech of Hon. Humphrey Marshall ... January 19, 1859. [n. p. n. d.] 8vo, pp. 16. H. 44781

Also: Remarks ... on the Report of the Conference Committee on the Kansas Question ... April 29, 1858. [*Washington, D. C.: C. W. Fenton, Printer.* 1858.] 8vo, pp. 8.—Speech ... on the Bill to appropriate the proceeds of the Sales of the Public Lands ... . July 6, 1841. *Washington.* 1841. 8vo, pp. 16.—Speech ... April 3, 1850, on the Admission of California and New Mexico. [n. p. n. d.] 8vo.—Speech ... March 11, 1852, on the Homestead Bill. [n. p. n. d.] 8vo.—Speech ... March 18, 1852. [*Washington.* n. d.] 8vo, pp. 7.—Speech ... on the Deficiency Bill. *Washington.* 1853. 8vo.

MARSHALL *and* HALLETT (B. F.) ... Speeches of Hon. Humphrey Marshall & Hon. B. F. Hallett ... on the Nomination of Breckinridge and Lane. [n. p. n. d.] 8vo, pp. 5, 2–4.

MARSHALL (J.) Statistical Illustrations of the Territorial Extent and Population, Commerce, Taxation, &c., of the British Empire. With an Appendix. By James Marshall. *London.* 1825–26. 2 vols., 8vo. C. 44783

MARSHALL. Statistics of the British Empire, of the various Countries of Europe, and of the United States. By James Marshall. *London.* 1833. 4to. C. 44784

MARSHALL (J.) The Nation's Grief. Death of Abraham Lincoln. A Discourse delivered in the ... United States General Hospital, near Fort Monroe, Va., ... April 29th, 1865, and Repeated ... in St. Paul's Church, Norfolk, Va., By James Marshall ... . Published by Battery 'F.' 3d Pa. H. Artillery. *Syracuse, N. Y.* 1865. 8vo, pp. 40. 44785

Also: The Nation's Changes. A Discourse ... in the Chesapeake General Hospital, ... Thanksgiving, Nov. 26th, 1863. ... *Baltimore: John F. Wiley, Printer.* 1863. 8vo, pp. 30, (2). H.—The Nation's Gratitude. A Discourse ... at the United States General Hospital, November 24, 1864. ... *Philadelphia: King & Baird.* 1865. 8vo, pp. 32.—The Nation's Inquiry. A Discourse ... in the Chesapeake General Hospital, ... National Fast, April 30th, 1863. ... *Philadelphia: King & Baird, Printers.* 1863. 8vo, pp. 34. BA.—The Nation's Prospects of Peace. A Discourse at the Officers' General Hospital ... Thanksgiving ... September 11, 1864. ... *Philadelphia: King & Baird, Printers.* 1864. 8vo, pp. 32. H.

MARSHALL (J. V.) The United States Manual of Biography and History: comprising Lives of Presidents and Vice-Presidents of the United States, and the Cabinet Officers, from the Adoption of the Constitution ... . By James V. Marshall. *Philadelphia.* 1855. 8vo, pp. 720. + [*Ibid.*] 1857. 8vo. 44786

MARSHALL (J.) A History of the Colonies Planted by the English on the Continent of North America, from their Settlement, to the Commencement of the War, which terminated in their Independence. By John Marshall. *Philadelphia: Abraham Small.* 1824. 8vo, pp. xv, 9–486. H. 44787

"Originally published as an Introduction to the 'Life of Washington,' by the same author, that work having been published with great precipitation, numerous errors and mistakes were unavoidable, which have been corrected in the present work, several alterations made, the whole revised."—RICH.

MARSHALL. The Life of George Washington, Commander in Chief of the American Forces, during the War which established the Independence of his Country, and First President of the United States, Compiled under the Inspection of the Honourable Bushrod Washington, from Original Papers ... . To which is prefixed a compendious view of the Colonies planted by the English on the Continent of North America ... . By John Marshall ... . *Philadelphia: C. P. Wayne.* 1804–7. 5 vols., 8vo, pp. (2), xxii, 488, 45, Portrait; viii, 560, 72; viii, 580, 28; iii–viii, 626, (1), 16; vii, 779, 36. 4to Atlas of 10 Maps, and Subscribers' Names, pp. 22. + [*Ibid.*] 1805–7. 5 vols., 8vo, pp. xxii, 459, 43, Portrait; vii, 516, 67; vii, 527, 28; iii–viii, 567, (1), 16; vii, 779, 36. H. + *London: Richard Phillips.* 1804–7. 5 vols., 4to, pp. xxxii, 458 (pp. 257–308 are repeated); vii, 541; viii, 470; vii, 589; vii, 669, (1). 16 Plates. + [*Ibid.*] 5 vols., 8vo, pp. xxxvi, 576; viii, 633, (1); viii, 570 [for 572]; viii, 684; viii, 843, (1). 10 Maps, Plates, and Portrait. H. 44788

The only complete editions of this indispensable work, the Colonial History being omitted in the later American editions. "After the able, accurate, and comprehensive work of Chief Justice Marshall, it would be presumptuous to attempt a historical biography of Washington."—SPARKS' *Washington*, I. 12. *See also* "N. A. Rev.," XXVI. 1., and XLII. 217; "M. Rev.," XLIV. 337; XLVII. 128; XLIX. 237.

MARSHALL. The Life of George Washington ... . By John Marshall ... . Second Edition, revised and corrected by the Author. *Philadelphia: James Crissy.* 1832. 2 vols., 8vo, pp. iv, 460, 42, viii; 448, 32, v. Maps and Portrait. + [*Ibid.*] 1836. + *Philadelphia: Carey & Lea.* 1840. 2 vols., 8vo. BA. 44789

The maps are sometimes bound up separately, making three volumes. These editions omit the early Continental History. It has been frequently reprinted.

MARSHALL. The Life of George Washington. Written for the use of Schools. By John Marshall ... . *Philadelphia.* 1838. 12mo, pp. 379. C. 44790

MARSHALL. Georg Washington's ... Lebensbeschreibung ... Nach den Original-Papieren unter der Aufsicht des Herrn Bushrod Washington zusammengetragen und mit einer historischen Darstellung der englischen Bilderfassungen in Nordamerika begleitet. Von John Marshall ... . Aus dem Englischen übersetzt ... . *Hamburg: August Campe.* 1805–6. 4 vols., 8vo, pp. xvi, 280; viii, 296; vi, 289; viii, 358. B. 44791

MARSHALL. Het Leven van George Washington, uit deszelfs oorspronklijke papieren, onder toezigt van Bushrod Washington zamengesteld. Door John Marshall ... . Uit het Engelsch door I. Werninck. *Haarlem: Bij A. Loosjes.* MDCCCV–IX. 10 vols., 8vo, and Atlas in 4to. Portrait. B. 44792

MARSHALL. Vie de George Washington, général en chef des armées américaines ... . Précédée d'un précis de l'histoire des Colonies fondées par les Anglais, sur le continent de l'Amérique septentrionale. Par J. Marshall ... . Traduite de l'anglais, par T. F. Henry. *Paris.* 1807. 5 vols., 8vo, and Atlas in 4to. S.

MARSHALL. Opinion of the Supreme Court of the United States, January, 1832, ... by Mr. Chief Justice Marshall, in the Case of Samuel A. Worcester, ... versus The State of Georgia. *Washington.* 1832. 8vo, pp. 20. 44794

MARSHALL. Opinion of the Supreme Court of the United States ... by Mr. Chief Justice Marshall, ... with the Opinion of Mr. Justice McLean, in the Case of Samuel A. Worcester, ... versus The State of Georgia. ... *Washington: Printed by Gales and Seaton.* 1832. 8vo, pp. 39. BA., N. 44795

In this case of the Cherokee Indians against Georgia, the whole history of Indian treaties with the United States is reviewed.

MARSHALL. The Writings of John Marshall, Late Chief Justice of the United States, upon the Federal Constitution. ... *Boston: James Munroe and Company.* M DCCC XXXIX. 8vo, pp. xvii, (2), 728. H. 44796

Also: Opinions of ... Chief Justice ... John Marshall, concerning Freemasonry. [n. p. n. d.] 8vo, pp. 4. H.—Speech ... on the Resolutions of the Hon. Edward Livingston, relative to Thomas Nash, alias Jonathan Robbins. *Philadelphia.* 1800. 12mo, pp. 45.

MARSHALL (J.) Royal Naval Biography; or, Memoirs of the Services of ... Flag-Officers, Superannuated Rear-Admirals, Retired-Captains, Post-Captains, and Commanders. ... Illustrated by ... Historical and Explanatory Notes ... . By John Marshall. ... *London: Longman* ... 1823–30. 12 vols., 8vo. BA. 44797

Contains numerous details relative to the Revolutionary War, etc., not to be found in any other work.

MARSHALL (J. A.) American Bastile. A History of the Illegal Arrests and Imprisonment of American Citizens during the Late Civil War. By John A. Marshall. ... *Philadelphia: T. W. Hartley.* 1869. 8vo, pp. 728. 5 Plates. C. + Fourth Edition. *Philadelphia: Evans, Stoddart & Co.* 1870. 8vo. 8 Plates. H. 44798

MARSHALL (J. G.) An Examination of the Proposed Union of the North American Provinces. By John G. Marshall ... . *Halifax.* 1865. 8vo, pp. 71. 44799

MARSHALL. The Justice of the Peace, and County and Township Officer in Nova Scotia; being a Guide to them in the Discharge of their Official Duties. By John G. Marshall ... . *Halifax.* 1837. 8vo, pp. 669. + Second Edition. [*Ibid.*] 1845. 8vo, pp. 800. 44800

MARSHALL. A Patriotic Call to Prepare in a Season of Peace for one of Political Danger; suggested by Reflections on the Policy and Designs of the United States towards Great Britain and her American Colonies; with a view of the Principal Advantages of Nova Scotia. By John G. Marshall ... . *Halifax.* 1819. 8vo, pp. 151. 44801

MARSHALL (J. G.) The Outlaw Brothers; or, The Captive of the Harpes. A Tale of the Early Kentucky Settlements. By John G. Marshall. *New York: Beadle & Co.* 1865. 8vo, pp. 40. 44802

Also: The Deer Hunters; or, Life and Love in the Ottawa Country. ... *New York: Beadle & Co.* [1865.] 8vo, pp. 40.

[MARSHALL (Joshua).] Ode on the Bones of the Im-mortal Thomas Paine, Newly Transported from America to England by the No Less Im-mortal William Cobbett, Esq. *London: Tho. Rodd.* 1819. 4to, pp. 8. 44803

MARSHALL (J. T.) The Dignity of the Agricultural Occupation. An Address ... at Plessis, Jefferson County, N. Y. ... 26th September, 1838. By Josiah T. Marshall. *Watertown: Printed by Knowlton & Rice.* 1838. 12mo, pp. 15. B. 44804

MARSHALL. The Farmer's and Emigrant's Handbook; being a full and complete Guide for the Farmer and the Emigrant ... . By Josiah T. Marshall. *New York: D. Appleton & Co.* 1845. 12mo. + Second Edition, revised. *New York.* 1847. 12mo, pp. 498. + *Cincinnati.* 1857. 12mo, pp. 492. 44805

MARSHALL (Mary). *See* Dyer (Mary M.), Vol. VI. 21597.

MARSHALL (*Mrs.*) A Sketch of My Friend's Family. By Mrs. Marshall. *Northampton.* 1821. 24mo. 44806

MARSHALL (O. H.) The Niagara Frontier: embracing Sketches of its Early History, and Indian, French and English Local Names. ... By Orsamus H. Marshall. *Printed for Private Circulation.* [*Buffalo.* 1865.] 8vo, pp. 46. H. 44807

An excellent monograph; reprinted in 1866. Also: The First Visit of La Salle to the Senacas, in 1669. ... [n. p. n. d.] 8vo.

MARSHALL (S. V.) An Address to the Young Ladies of the Natchez Female Academy, May 17, 1838. By Rev. S. V. Marshall. With Catalogue. *Natchez.* 1838. 8vo, pp. 38, 7.

MARSHALL (T.) Speech of Thomas Marshall ... on the Abolition of Slavery, Jan. 20, 1832. *Richmond.* 1832. 8vo, pp. 12. S. 44809

MARSHALL (T. F.) Letters to the Editors of the Commonwealth: ... . By Thomas F. Marshall. [*Louisville:*] *A. G. Hodges, Printer.* [1840.] 8vo, pp. 37. BA. 44810

MARSHALL. Life and Character of Richard H. Menifee. By Thomas F. Marshall. *Lexington, Ky.* 1841. 8vo. 44811

MARSHALL. Speeches and Writings of Hon. Thomas F. Marshall. Edited by W. L. Barre. *Cincinnati: Applegate & Company.* 1858. 8vo, pp. iv, 3–462. B., C. 44812

Also: Speeches ... on Alcohol and Intemperance, and Fashionable Wine Drinking, ... New-York ... May 4 and 7 [1842]. ... [n. p.: *Greeley & McElrath.* 1842. 8vo, pp. 10.—Speeches ... Jan. 25, 26 and 28, 1842, on the Resolutions to Censure J. Q. Adams. *Washington.* 1842. 8vo.—Substance of an Address on Temperance, ... May 16, 1842. ... *New-York: J. B. Swain, Printer.* 1842. 8vo, pp. 23.—Two Speeches ... at the Temperance Meeting. *Louisville.* 1842. 8vo. P.

MARSHALL (T. W. M.) Christian Mission: their Agents, and their Results, including Comparisons between Protestant and Catholic Missions throughout the World, brought down to 1863. By T. W. M. Marshall. *London: James Burns.* 1862. 3 vols., 8vo. + *New York: D. & J. Sadler & Co.* 1865. 2 vols., 8vo, pp. (2), vi, 644; 479, xxxv. B. 44813

MARSHALL (W.) Memoirs of ... Rev. William Marshall, ... *Philadelphia: John M'Culloch.* 1806. 12mo, pp. 50. B. 44814

MARSHALL ACADEMY. Catalogue of the Officers and Students ... . 1842–3. *Marshall: Lewis & Simonds, Printers.* 1843. 18mo, pp. 6, (1). H. 44815

MARSHALL COLLEGE. Catalogue of the Members and Library of the Goethean Literary Society of ... [the] College ... to March, 1844. *Chambersburg, Pa.* [1844.] 8vo, pp. 32. H.

Also: Catalogue of the Officers and Students ... 1846–7. *Mercersburg, Pa.: Printed by D. J. Schnelby.* 1847. 8vo, pp. 28. Plate. H.

MARSHFIELD. Report of the School-Committee ... April 5, 1847. ... *Boston: Benjamin H. Greene.* 1847. 16mo, pp. 16. Continued. H. 44817

Transactions of the Marshfield Agricultural and Horticultural Society during the Year 1869. ... *Plymouth.* 1869. 8vo, pp. 56.

Also: First Annual Report ... for 1868 ... . *Hingham: Blossom and Easterbrook, Printers.* 1868. 8vo, pp. 16. Continued.

MARSHPEE INDIANS. Memorial of the Marshpee Indians. [n. p.] 1834. 8vo, pp. 14. Continued. BA. 44819

Also: Documents relative to the Marshpee Indians. [*Boston.* 1833.] 8vo, pp. 43.

MARSILLAC (J.) La Vie de Guillaume Penn, Fondateur de la Pensylvanie; Premier Législateur connu des États-Unis de l'Amérique. Ouvrage contenant l'Historique des premiers fondemens de Philadelphie, des Loix et de la Constitution des États-Unis de l'Amérique, des Principes et des Actions de la Société des Amis (vulgairement connus sous le nom de Quakers, etc.) Par J. Marsillac, Docteur en Médecine ... . *A Paris: De l'Imprimerie du Cercle Social.* 1791. 2 vols., 8vo, pp. 264; 294. P.

MARSILLAC. Leben Wilhelm Penns, des Stifters von Pensylvanien. ... *Strassburg.* 1793. 8vo. 44821

[MARSTON (Edward).] To The Most Noble Prince Henry Duke of Beaufort, Marquiss and Earl of Worcester, Baron Herbert, Lord of Ragland, Chepstow and Gower, Palatine of the Province of South Carolina in America. [*London.* 1712.] 4to, pp. 12. 44822

Probably privately printed. The author solicits redress on account of his ejection from his rectory in South Carolina. *See also* Vol. III., No. 10966.

MARSTON (G.) Argument of Hon. George Marston ... in behalf of the ... Incorporation of the Boston and Cape Cod Marine Telegraph Co. March 12, 1856. *Boston: Printed by Dutton and Wentworth.* 1856. 8vo, pp. 44. H. 44823

MARSTON (M.) The Trial of Brevet Major Morrill Marston, ... in Sept. 1818 ... . *Philadelphia.* 1818. 8vo, pp. 32. 44824

MARSY (*l'Abbé* François Marie de) *and* RICHER (Adrien). Histoire Moderne des Chinois, ... et des Américains, pour servir de suite à l'Histoire Ancienne de M. Rollin, par l'Abbé de Marsy et M. Richer. *Paris: Saillant.* 1775–1778. 30 vols., 12mo.

The first eleven or twelve volumes are by Marsy, the later by Richer. The last seven volumes contain "l'Histoire des Américains, et des Terres Polaires."

MARTEL (M.) Rapport et projet de décret, sur les Lettres-du-change tirées par l'Ordonnateur des Finances à Saint Domingue, fait au nom du Comité de Marine et des Colonies dans le séance du 28 pluviôse, l'an 2e de la République. ... [*Paris:*] *l'Imprimerie Nationale.* [1794.] 8vo, pp. 24. J.C.B. 44826

MARTELO Y OTERO (J. R.) El Regidor D. José Ramon Martelo y Otero, presenta al Excmo. Ayuntamiento Constitucional de la ciudad de la Habana las noticias de los ramos que le están consignados. [*Habana:*] *Imprenta de D. Pedro Nolazco Palmer.* 1821. Folio, pp. 124. 44827

MARTELS (H. von). Briefe über die Westlichen Theile der Vereinigten Staaten von Nord Amerika. Von Heinrich v. Martels Premier Lieutenant im 8ten. Konigl. Hannoverschen Linien-Bataillon. *Osnabrück: Rackhorst.* 1834. 8vo, pp. 195. Map of Missouri. 44828

MARTEN (Anthony). The Seconde Sounde or Warning of the Trumpet vnto Iudgement: wherein is proved that all the tokens of the Latter Day are not onelie come, but wel neere finished. *London: Imprinted by Thomas Orwin, for Andrew Maunsell.* 1589. 4to. 44820

On folio 17 is noticed the neglect of teaching "the Gospel to the people of America and the Lower India, by the Spanyards and Portingals, when they first found out those nations."

MARTENET [Simon J.] Appeal to the Legislature in behalf of Martenet's Map of Maryland. [*Baltimore.* 1865.] 8vo, pp. (1), 8. Map. 44830

MARTENS (C. de). Causes Célèbres du Droit des Gens, Rédigées par le Bn. Charles de Martens ... . *Leipzig: F. A. Brockhaus.* 1827. 2 vols., 8vo, pp. xx, 424, (1); vi, 496, (1). B. + Nouvelle Édition, revue, rectifiées et emélioréе dans tous ses parties ... . Par M. de Hoffmanns. ... *Paris: J. P. Aillaud.* 1837. 3 vols., 8vo, pp. (4), xxi, (2), 344; (4), 345–760; (4), xxx, 507. + Deuxième Édition, revue, corrigée et augmentée par l'auteur. ... *Leipzig: F. A. Brockhaus.* 1858–61. 5 vols., 8vo, pp. xix, 499, (1); viii, 461, (2); vi, 529, (1); vi, 400; viii, 630, (2). B. + Quatrième Édition, entièrement refondue par l'auteur, avec la collaboration de Ferdinand de Wegmann ... . *Paris: Gravelot Jeune.* 1851. 2 vols., 8vo, pp. xxvi, (2), 512; xi, (2), 607. + Cinquième Édition, entièrement refondue par M. F. H. Geffeken, ... *Leipzig: F. A. Brockhaus.* 1866. 3 vols., 8vo, pp. xix, 300, (1); x, 305, (2); vi, 388. H. 44831

MARTENS. Nouvelles Causes Célèbres du Droit des Gens, Rédigées par le Baron Charles de Martens ... . *Leipzig: F. A. Brockhaus.* 1843. 2 vols., 8vo, pp. xxii, 595, (2); viii, 592, (2).

MARTENS *et* DE CUSSY (Ferd. de). Recueil manuel et pratique des Traités, Conventions et autres Actes diplomatiques, sur lesquels sont établis les relations et les rapports existant aujourd'hui entre les divers États souverains du globe, depuis l'année 1760 jusqu'à l'époque actuelle. ... *Leipzig: F. A. Brockhaus.* 1846–56. 7 vols., 8vo. 44833

See also Martens (G. F. de), Nos. 44841, etc.

MARTENS (F.) Friderich Martens | von Hamburg | Spitzbergische oder Groenlandische | Reise Beschreibung | gethan im Jahr 1671. | Aus | eigner Erfahrunge beschrieben, die dazu erforderte | Figuren nach dem Leben selbst abgerissen, (so hierbey in | Kupffer zu sehen) und jetzo durch den | Druck mitgetheilet. | *Hamburg,* | *Auff Gottfried, Schultzens Kosten, gedruckt, Im Jahr* 1675. | 4to, pp. (8), 132, (3). 16 Plates. B., C. 44834

MARTENS. Fredrik Martens Nauwkeurige Beschryvinge van Groenland of Spitsbergen, waer in de Walvisch-Vangst, gelegentheyt vant 't Ys, en haer wonderlijke kragt en Figuren, duydelijk word aengewesen: Nevens den Aard van't Land, Gewassen, Ys-Bergen, Gevogelte, Viervoetige Dieren, en Visschen deser Contryen. Oock hoe de Walvisschen gevangen, gekapt, en gesneden worden: Benevens verscheyde Avontuurlijke voorvallen in Groenland. Met een Verhael van de gevange Walvisch by St. Anne Land. Als mede De Walvisch-Vangst op Rym. *Tot Amsterdam: By de Wed: van Gysbert de Groot.* 1710. 4to, Engraved and Printed Titles, pp. (6), 88. 3 Plates. 44835

This accurate description of Greenland, in which the whale-fishery is clearly described, contains a poetical description of Greenlandish ships.

MARTENS. [Engraved Title:] Vojagie naar | Groenland of Spitsbergen | mits gaders een net verhaal der | Walvis vanghst | en der zelve behandeling. | Met veel Avontuurlyke voorvallen door F. Martens. | *Te Dordrecht,* | *Gedrukt by Hendrik Walpot, boekverkooper overt Stadhuys.* | [Printed Title:] Fredrik Martens | Nauwkeurige Beschryvinge | van | Groenland | of | Spitsbergen, | Waer in de Walvisch-Vangst, gelegentheyd van | 't Ys, en haer wonderlyke kragt en Figuren duydelyk worden | aengewesen: | Nevens | Den Aard van't Land, Gewassen, Ys-Bergen, Gevogelte, | Viervoetige Dieren, en Visschen deser Contryen. | Ook hoe de Walvisschen gevangen, gekapt en gesneden worden: | Benevens verscheyde Avontuurlyke voorvallen in Groenland. | Met een Verhael van de gevange Walvisch by St. Anne-Land. | Als mede een Gevegt en springen van twee Schepen, een Frans en een En- | gels: Nevens alle de Gevaaren haar overgekomen. | Met Kopere Platen Verçiert. | *Te Dordrecht,* | *Gedrukt by Hendrik Walpot, Boekdrukker en Boekverkooper* | *over 't Stadthuys.* | [1710?] 4to, pp. (10), 88. 3 Plates. + [Another Edition. *Ibid.* 1760?] 4to. + *Amsterdam: A. Cornelis.* 1770. 4to, pp. (10), 88. 3 Plates. C. 44836

"The last two editions differ from the preceding. They contain, instead of a description of the Greenlandish ships (pp. 75–88), an account of a voyage of Montaubain, Captain of the Freebooters, on the coast of Guinea, in 1695."—MULLER.

MARTENS. Viaggio di Spizberga o' Grolanda, fatto da Frederico Martens amburghese l'anno 1671. Con una copiosa relazione di' quell' aggiacciato Clima, e degli uccelli, quadrupedi, pesci, e piante rare, che vi nascono, colla descrizione delle Balene e lor Pesca, ... portato dalla lingua Alemana nell' Italiana dal signor Jacobo Rautenfens, gentilhuomo curlandese. *Venetia: J. Prodocimo.* 1680. 12mo, pp. 264. A. 44837

A very rare edition.

MARTENS. Viaggio di Spizberga o' Grolanda fatto ... l'anno 1671. ... *Bologna.* 1680. 12mo. 44838

See also La Martinière (P. M. de), Vol. x., No. 38712, *and* Narborough (*Sir* John).

MARTENS (Georg Friedrich von). Cours diplomatique, ou tableau des relations extérieures des Puissances de l'Europe, tant entre elles, qu'avec d'autres États dans les diverses parties du globe, Par G. F. de Martens. *Berlin: A. Mylius.* 1801. 3 vols., 8vo, pp. 691; 627; 501. C. 44839

MARTENS. Précis du droit des gens modernes de l'Europe, fondé sur les traités et l'usage; pour servir d'introduction à un cours politique et diplomatique, Par G. F. de Martens. *Paris.* 1789. 2 vols., 8vo. + Troisième Édition ... . *Gottingue: Dieterich.* 1821. 8vo, pp. xl, 608. + Nouvelle Édition, avec des Notes de M. S. Pinheiro-Ferreira ... . *Paris: J. P. Aillaud.* 1831. 2 vols., 8vo, pp. (4), 460; (4), 447. + *Paris: Guillaumin et Cie.* 1858. 2 vols., 8vo. + Deuxième Édition ... . [*Ibid.*] 1864. 2 vols., 12mo, pp. (4), lv, 432; (4), 463. + [*Ibid.*] 2 vols., 8vo.

MARTENS. Recueil des Principaux Traités d'Alliance, de Paix, de Trêve, de Neutralité, de commerce, de limites, d'échange &c. conclus par les Puissances de l'Europe tant entre elles qu'avec les Puissances et États dans d'autre parties du monde depuis 1761 jusqu'à présent. Tiré des copies publiées par autorité, ... Par Mr. de Martens ... . *Gottingue: Chéz Jean Chretien Dieterich.* 1791–1801. 7 vols., 8vo. BA. 44841

There is perhaps no more important source for the history of America than the great collection of Martens. The colonies in the New World were, up to a very recent date, considered by the European powers as a kind of property that might be obtained, transferred and exchanged almost with equal facility as any description of movable goods. Every great war between European states led therefore to some changes in the colonies. Even in time of peace many sales and exchanges were concluded, besides the still more numerous commercial treaties in which the colonies were concerned. The deeds of all these transactions are laid down in the collection of Martens.

MARTENS. Supplément ... Précédé de Traités du XVIIIme Siècle antérieurs à cette époque, et qui ne se trouvent dans ... autres recueils ... Par George Frédéric de Martens ... . *Gottingue: Dieterich.* 1802–20. 8 vols., 8vo. 44842

MARTENS. Recueil de Traités d'Alliance, ... et plusieurs autres actes, servant à la connaissance des relations étrangères des Puissances et États de l'Europe, tant des leur rapport mutuel que dans celui envers les Puissances et États dans d'autres parties du globe, depuis 1761 jusqu'à présent. Seconde Édition, revue et augmentée. *Gottingue: Dieterich.* 1817–35. 8 vols., 8vo.

MARTENS. Nouveau Recueil de Traités ... depuis 1808 jusqu'à présent. ... Par Geo. Fréd. de Martens. *Gottingue: Dieterich.* 1817–41. 16 vols., 8vo. BA. 44844

MARTENS. Nouveaux Supplémens au Recueil de Traités ... depuis 1761 jusqu'à présent. ... Continué Par Frédéric Murhard. *Gottingue: Dieterich.* 1839–42. 3 vols., 8vo, pp. xviii, 810; (2), 662; (2), 904. BA. 44845

MARTENS. Table générale, chronologique, et alphabétique du Recueil de Traités ... . Commencé par Geo. Fréd. de Martens et continué jusqu'à nos jours. *Leipzig.* 1837–45. 2 vols., 8vo. + *Gottingue: Dieterich.* 1837–43. 2 vols., 8vo, pp. iv, 383; iv, 428. BA. + [*Ibid.*] 1838–45. H. 44846

MARTENS. Nouveau Recueil Général de Traités, Conventions et autres Transactions remarquables ... . Continuation ... . *Gottingue: Dieterich.* 1843–75. 20 vols., 8vo. BA. 44847

MARTENS. Summary of the Law of Nations ... with a List of the Principal Treaties, concluded since the Year 1748 down to the Present Time, [1788] ... . By Mr. Martens ... . Translated from the French by William Cobbett. *Philadelphia: Thomas Bradford.* 1795. 8vo, pp. xix, (1), 379. C., H. + *Philadelphia.* 1805. 8vo. 44848

MARTENS. A Compendium of the Law of Nations, ... a ... List of ... Treaties ... &c. from ... 1731 to 1788 ... . By G. F. Von Martens ... . Translated, and the List of Treaties, &c. ... to June, 1802, By William Cobbett. *London: Cobbett and Morgan.* 1802. 8vo, pp. xxxii, 454. H. + Fourth Edition. *London.* 1829. 8vo. C. 44849

MARTENS (M.) *and* GALEOTTI (H.) Mémoire sur les Fougéres du Mexique, et considérations sur la Géographie Botanique de cette contrée. [n. p. n. d.] 4to. Plates. 44850

Also: Enumeratio synoptica plantarum phanerogamicarum ... in regionibus Mexicanis collectarum. ... [n. p. n. d.] 3 parts, 8vo.—Notice sur les plantes des familles de vacciniées et d'éricacées recueillies au Mexique ... . [n. p. n. d.] 8vo.

MARTENZE (C.) Cannon-Flashes and Pen-Dashes. By Claes Martenze. *New York: W. H. Kelley & Co.* 1861. Sm. 4to, pp. 110. 44851

MARTHA'S VINEYARD AGRICULTURAL SOCIETY. Transactions ... 1865. *Martha's Vineyard.* 1865. 8vo, pp. 34. Continued. H. 44852

Martial Achievements of Great Britain and her Allies, from 1799 to 1815. *London.* 1815. 4to. Plates. 44853

Martial Law in the Colonies; with Special Regard to its Regulation and Restraint. ... *London: Stevens & Sons.* 1867. 8vo. 44854

MARTIN (A.) Essays on Woman's True Destiny, Responsibilities and Rights ... By Angelique Le Petit Martin. ... *Warren, O.: J. Dumars, Printer.* 1851. 8vo, pp. 43. H. 44855

MARTIN (B.) Speech of Barkley Martin ... on our Right to Oregon ... . February, 1846. [n. p. n. d.] 8vo, pp. 8. H.

MARTIN (B.) Miscellaneous Correspondence, ... Relative to Natural and Civil History ... . By Benjamin Martin. *London: W. Owen.* MDCCLIX. 4 vols., 8vo. 44857

Includes several articles on American subjects.

MARTIN (B. E.) In Memoriam Joseph Gilbert Totten. By Benjamin Ellis Martin. ... *New York: C. B. Richardson.* 1866. 8vo, pp. 8. H. 44858

MARTIN (C.) Précis des événements de la Campagne du Mexique en 1862 Par Ch. Martin ... . Précédé d'une Notice Géographique et Statistique sur le Mexique Par Léon Deluzy. ... *Paris: Ch. Tanera.* 1863. 8vo, pp. (4), 372. Map, Plan.

MARTIN (C. B.) Mount Desert, on the Coast of Maine. By Mrs. Clara Barnes Martin. *Portland: B. Thurston and Company, Printers.* 1867. 12mo, pp. 36. + *Portland: Loring, Short & Harmon.* 1870. 12mo, pp. 36. H. 44860

[MARTIN (Claude).] La Vie de la Venerable Mere Marie de l'Incarnation Premiere Superieure des Ursulines de la Nouvelle France. Tirée de ses Lettres & de ses ecrits. *Paris: Chez Loüis Billaine.* M.DC.LXXVII. 4to, pp. (36), 757, (6). Portrait. 44861

For another life *see* [Charlevoix (P. F. X.)] The present work consists of two "Relations," written by the mother herself in 1633 and 1654, with "Additions" by Martin.

MARTIN (D.) Trial of the Rev. Jacob Gruber, Minister in the M. E. Church, in ... 1819, for a Misdemeanor. Reported by David Martin. *Fredericktown, Md.* 1819. 12mo. 44862

Rare. The misdemeanor was preaching against slavery, and inciting the negroes to escape or rebel.

MARTIN (Edward Winslow). The Life and Public Services of Schuyler Colfax, together with his most Important Speeches. By E. W. Martin. *New York: United States Publishing Co.* 1868. 8vo, pp. 512. Plate. 44863

MARTIN. The New Administration: containing Complete and Authentic Biographies of Grant and his Cabinet. *New York: G. S. Wilcox.* 1869. 12mo, pp. 155. 44864

MARTIN. The Secrets of the Great City: ... descriptive of the Virtues, ... Vices, ... Mysteries, Miseries and Crimes of New York City. By Edward Winslow Martin. ... *Philadelphia, Pa.* [1869?] 8vo, pp. 11–552. 33 Plates. B. 44865

MARTIN (E.) An Essay on the Epidemics of the Winters of 1813 and 1814, in Talbot and Queen Anne's Counties in the State of Maryland. By Ennalls Martin, M.B. *Baltimore: Joseph Robinson.* 1815. 8vo, pp. 78. 44866

MARTIN (Felix). Manuel du Pélerin de Notre Dame de Bonsecours à Montréal ... Par le R. P. Martin. *Montréal.* 1848. 8vo, pp. 178. C., P. 44867

Extracted in part from a very curious notice of the ancient monuments of Montreal, published in the "Mélanges Religieux" by Jacques Viger, first mayor of Montreal, to whom the country is indebted for the most ancient and most interesting archæological researches.

[MARTIN.] De Montcalm en Canada ou les dernières années de la Colonie Française (1756–1760). Par un Ancien Missionaire. *Paris: P. M. Laroche.* 1867. 8vo, pp. x, 354. Portrait.

See also Bressany (J.), II. 7735, Carayon (A.), III. 10792, *and* O'Callaghan (E. B.)

[MARTIN *and* MONTÉZON (F. de).] Mission du Canada. Relations inédites de la Nouvelle-France (1672–1679) pour faire suite aux anciennes relations (1615–1672) Avec deux Cartes Géographiques. *Paris: Charles Douniel.* 1861. 2 vols., 12mo, pp. (2), xxviii, 356; (2), 384. 2 Maps. BA. 44869

MARTIN (F. X.) A Collection of the Statutes of the Parliament of England in Force in ... North-Carolina. Published ... By Francois-Xavier Martin, Esq. ... *Newbern.* 1792. 4to, pp. xxvi, 424, (3). H. 44870

MARTIN. General Digest. *See* Louisiana, Vol. x. 42227.

MARTIN. The History of Louisiana, From the Earliest Period. By François-Xavier Martin. ... *New Orleans: Printed by Lyman and Beardslee.* 1827–9. 2 vols., 8vo, pp. lxxxiii, 364; iii–xv, 429. BA. 44871

MARTIN. The History of North Carolina, From the Earliest Period. By Francois-Xavier Martin. ... *New Orleans: A. T. Penniman & Co.* 1829. 2 vols., 8vo, pp. xii, 325, (1), civ; (4), 411, (1). C., H. 44872

MARTIN. Notes of ... Decisions in the Superior Courts of ... North-Carolina, and in the Circuit Court of the U. States, for North-Carolina ... . *Newbern: Francois-Xavier Martin.* 1797. 8vo, pp. (8), 78, 83, (12), 275, (20). H. 44873

MARTIN. The Office and Authority of a Justice of the Peace ... &c. according to the Laws of ... North-Carolina. ... *Newbern: François-Xavier Martin.* 1791. 8vo, pp. (4), 6, 307, (5). H.

MARTIN (F.) The Statesman's Year-Book, a Statistical, Genealogical, and Historical Account of the States and Sovereigns of the Civilized World for the Year 1864. By Frederick Martin. *London and Cambridge: Macmillan and Co.* 1864. 8vo, pp. xiii, (2), 684, (2). Continued. BA. 44875

Also: Handbook of Contemporary Biography ... . *London: Macmillan and Co.* 1870. 16mo, pp. 287, (1). H.

MARTIN (F. S.) Speech of Frederick S. Martin, of New York, on the Public Lands. *Washington.* 1852. 8vo. 44876

MARTIN (*Gen.*) El General Martin. *Buenos Aires.* 1863. Folio. 44877

In verse and prose. Contains also a very ample account of the books and tracts relating to the revolution, and the times of General Martin.

[MARTIN (Gershom).] The Military Route to Richmond. [n. p. 1862.] 8vo, pp. 4. BA. 44878

MARTIN (H.) Letter of Henry Martin, Esq. ... to the Senate ... in Opposition to the Bill increasing the Duty on Imported Copper Ores. *Baltimore.* 1869. 8vo, pp. 12. H. 44879

MARTIN (*Sir* H. W.) A Counter Appeal to an Appeal from William Wilberforce. By Sir Henry William Martin, Bart. *London.* 1823. 8vo. 44880

MARTIN (H.) Pictorial Guide to the Mammoth Cave, Kentucky. By ... Rev. Horace Martin. ... *New York: Stringer & Townsend.* [1851.] 12mo, pp. (2), 116. 8 Plates. + [*Ibid.*] 1852. C. 44881

MARTIN (I.) A Journal of the Life, Travels, Labors, and Religious Experience of Isaac Martin, late of Rahway, in East Jersey. *Philadelphia.* 1804. 12mo, pp. 160. 44882

MARTIN (J.) Oration at Jamaica, Long Island, on the 4th of July, 1796. By James Martin. [n. p.] 1796. 8vo. C.

MARTIN (J. H.) Smith and Pocahontas. A Poem. By J. H. Martin. *Richmond: West & Johnston.* 1862. 12mo, pp. 135.

M[ARTIN] (J. L.) Native Bards; A Satirical Effusion; with Other Occasional Pieces. By J. L. M. *Philadelphia: E. L. Carey & A. Hart.* 1831. 12mo, pp. 114. 44885

MARTIN (J. R.) The Influence of Tropical Climates on European Constitutions; including practical observations on the nature and treatment of the diseases of Europeans on their return from tropical climates. By James Ranald Martin. A New Edition. *London: J. & A. Churchill.* 1856. 8vo. + [*Ibid.*] 1861.

MARTIN (J. S.) The Hero and the Slave. Founded on Fact. By Rev. J. Sella Martin. *Boston: Printed by W. F. Brown & Co.* [n. d.] 12mo, pp. 12. H. 44887

MARTIN (J.) Familiar Dialogues between Americus and Britannicus; in which The Right of Private Judgment; the Exploded Doctrines of Infallibility, Passive Obedience, Non-Resistance; With The leading Sentiments of Dr. Price, on the Nature of Civil Liberty, &c. are Particularly Considered. By John Martin. ... *London: J. Wilkie.* MDCCLXXVI. 8vo, pp. iv, 74.

"These dialogues afford scarcely anything worthy of attention. Mr. Martin must have known little respecting America, or he would not have censured the colonists for considering the wild Indians as their own slaves!"—*Monthly Review*, LV. 64.

MARTIN (J.) Succinct account of the Case Sarah Walker *vs.* John Martin, in which a System of Spunging and Fraud is Exposed. With an Appendix by John Martin, Broker. [n. p.:] *The Author.* 1827. 8vo, pp. 36. 44889

MARTIN (J. P.) The Triumph of Truth. History and Vision of Clio. ... By John Paul Martin, A.M. ... *Printed ... Boston: by Isaiah Thomas and Ebenezer T. Andrews.* MDCCXCI. 8vo, pp. 62. H. 44890

MARTIN (J.) Speech of Hon. Jonas Martin upon the Subject of Federal Relations, ... February 12, 1863. *Frankfort: Major & Co., Printers.* 1863. 8vo, pp. 8. 44891

MARTIN Y GUZMAN (José). Oracion Funebre que en las magnificas, y sumptuosas Exequias, que hicieron los Reales Batallones de Marina á los Individios de sú Illustro Cuerpo. *Mexico.* 1758. 8vo. 44892

MARTIN DE CHAVES (J.) Breve Descripcion de las Solemne. Exequias en los dias 25 y 26 de Junio de este Año de 1779, en se Celebraron en la Santa Iglesia Catedral de Mexico al Exc. Señor Baylio Fr. Don Antonio Maria de Bucareli y Ursua. Dispuestos por los Nobles Caballeros D. Jos. Martin de Chaves, y D. Joachin Ant. Dongo, sus Albaceas testamentarios. *Mexico.* 1779. 8vo. Portrait. 44893

MARTIN (J.) A Comprehensive Description of Virginia, and the District of Columbia: containing a Copious Collection of Geographical, Statistical, Political, Commercial, Religious, Moral, and Miscellaneous Information, chiefly from original sources, by Joseph Martin. To which is added a History of Virginia, from its first settlement to the year 1754, with an abstract of the principal events from that period to the Independence of Virginia, by W. H. Brockenbrough ... . *Richmond: J. W. Randolph.* [n. d.] 8vo, pp. 636. Map. B., C. 44894

Reprinted as: "A New and Comprehensive Gazetteer of Virginia and the District of Columbia: ... To which is added a History of Virginia from its First Settlement to the year 1754; ... Written ... by a Citizen of Virginia. *Charlottesville: Joseph Martin.* 1835. 8vo, pp. 636. Map. + [*Ibid.*] 1836.

MARTIN (J. G.) Twenty-One Years in the Boston Stock Market, or Fluctuations therein from January 1, 1835 to January 1, 1856 ... . By Joseph G. Martin ... . *Boston: Redding and Company.* 1856. 8vo, pp. 80. H. 44895

MARTIN (L. C.) The Current Gold and Silver Coins of All Countries, Their Weight and Fineness, and their Intrinsic Value in English Money. With Facsimiles of the Coins. By Leopold C. Martin, ... and Charles Trübner. *London: Trübner & Co.* 1863. 8vo, pp. xx, 140, (1). Plates. BA. 44896

MARTIN (Louis Aimé). *See* Lettres édifiantes, Vol. X.

MARTIN (L.) The Genuine Information, delivered to the Legislature of the State of Maryland, Relative to the Proceedings of the General Convention, Lately held at Philadelphia; by Luther Martin, Esquire, Attorney-General of Maryland, and One of the Delegates in the said Convention. Together with A Letter to the Hon. Thomas C. Deye, Speaker of the House of Delegates, An Address to the Citizens of the United States, And some Remarks relative to a Standing Army and a Bill of Rights ... . *Philadelphia: Printed by Eleazer Oswald.* M,DCC,-LXXXVIII. 8vo, pp. viii, 93. BA. 44897

MARTIN. Modern Gratitude, in Five Numbers: addressed to Richard Raynall Keene, Esq. ... By Luther Martin, Esq. of Maryland. [*Baltimore.* 1801.] 8vo, pp. (2), 163, (1). 44898

Martin was a leading Federalist, and Attorney-General of Maryland; his daughter married R. R. Keene, a democrat, much against his wishes; this volume relates to that affair, and was privately printed by Martin, for distribution among his friends. Also: The Charge delivered to the Grand Jury, on the Fourth ... of October, 1813. ... [*Baltimore.* 1813.] 8vo, pp. 11. BA.—An Inroad upon the sacred Trial by Jury; or the Case of John Bentley and Isaiah Green, against whom Summary Proceedings for Contempt of Court were begun ... . *Baltimore.* 1811. 8vo. *See also* Keene (R. R.), Vol. IX., No. 37155, National Portrait Gallery, Vol. IV., *and* Yates (R.)

[MARTIN (Manuel M.)] A Venezuela. Rápida ojeada sobre nuestros disturbios, sus causas y remedios. *Carácas.* [n. d.] 8vo, pp. 19. 44899

MARTIN (M.) History of the Captivity and Sufferings of Mrs. Maria Martin, who was Six Years a Slave in Algiers ... . Written by Herself. *Boston.* 1807. 8vo, pp. 72. Plate.

MARTIN (M.) Confession of Michael Martin, or Captain Lightfoot, who was hung at Cambridge, Massachusetts, in ... 1821 ... . Also, An Account of Dr. John Wilson ... believed by many to be ... Captain Thunderbolt. *Brattleboro', Vt.: J. B. Miner.* 1847. 8vo, pp. 30, 12. Portrait and Vignette.

MARTIN. Life of Michael Martin, who was Executed for Highway Robbery, December 20, 1821. As given by himself. *Boston: Russell & Gardner.* 1821. 8vo, pp. 102. B. 44902

MARTIN. Trial of Michael Martin, for Highway Robbery ... Reported by F. W. Waldo, Esq. *Boston: Russell and Gardner.* 1821. 8vo, pp. 36. BA. 44903

Also: Review of the "Life of Michael Martin, who was executed for Highway Robbery" ... . *Boston: Wells and Lilly.* 1822. 8vo, pp. 12. BA.

MARTIN (Morgan L.) Address ... before the State Historical Society of Wisconsin, Madison, January 21, 1851. By M. L. Martin. *Green-Bay: Robinson & Brother, Printers.* 1851. 12mo, pp. 44. N. 44904

MARTIN (M.) A Treatise on the Fullness of the Everlasting Gospel, setting forth its first Principles, Promises, and Blessings. By Elder Moses Martin, [Mormon] Minister of the Gospel. *New York.* 1842. 16mo, pp. 64. 44905

MARTIN DE NANTES (*Le Père*). Relation succinte et sincère de la mission du Père Martin de Nantes, Missionaire Apostolique

dans le Brézil, parmis les Indiens appelés Cariris. *À Quimper: Jean Perier* [about 1706]. 24mo, pp. (16), 233, (2). C. 44906

MARTIN (R. M.) The British Colonial Library, comprising a Popular and Authentic Description of all the Colonies of the British Empire. By Robert Montgomery Martin. *London: G. B. Whittaker.* 1836–7. 10 vols., fcap 8vo. + *London: H. G. Bohn.* 1844. 10 vols., fcap 8vo. 44907

Vols. I., IV., V., and VI. relate to America.

MARTIN. The British Colonies, their History, Extent, Condition, and Resources. By R. Montgomery Martin ... . *London: London Printing ... Company.* [1849.] 4to, pp. (4), ii, xxiv, 360. Continued to 6 vols. B. 44908

Vol. I. treats of British North America, and Vol. IV. of Africa and the West Indies. First published in 1843.

[MARTIN.] Colonial Policy of the British Empire. ... Part I. Government. *London.* 1837. 8vo, pp. 87. 44909

MARTIN. History of the British Colonies. By R. Montgomery Martin ... *London: Cochrane and M'Crone.* MDCCCXXXIV. 5 vols., 8vo. Maps. + Second Edition. [*Ibid.*] MDCCCXXXV. 5 vols., 8vo, pp. (2), xvi, (2), 630, (2); (6), xxiv, 522, (5); (4), xx, 604, (6); (4), xii, 624, (60); xv, (1), 596. Maps. BA., H.

MARTIN. History of the Colonies of the British Empire in the West Indies, South America, North America, Asia, Austral-Asia, Africa, and Europe; comprising the Area, Agriculture, Commerce, ... &c., of Each Colony; with the Charters and the Engraved Seals. ... By Robert Montgomery Martin, Esq. *London: Wm. H. Allen and Co.* 1843. Rl. 8vo, pp. v, (3), 602, Appendix, 304. Maps, Plates and Tables. BA. 44911

The same as *our* No. 44917, described *infra*, except that the first word is History instead of Statistics.

MARTIN. History of Nova Scotia, Cape Breton, the Sable Islands, New Brunswick ... . By R. Montgomery Martin ... . *London: Whittaker & Co.* MDCCCXXXVII. Fcap 8vo, pp. viii, 363, (1). Plate and 2 Maps. H. 44912

MARTIN. History of the West Indies. Comprising Jamaica, Honduras, Trinidad, Tobago, Grenada, the Bahamas, and the Virgin Isles. By R. Montgomery Martin, F.S.S. ... *London: Whittaker & Co.* MDCCCXXXVI–VII. 2 vols., fcap 8vo, pp. xxxvi, 308, (2); viii, 344, Appendix, (7). 2 Plates and 4 Maps. B.

MARTIN. History, Statistics, and Geography of Upper and Lower Canada. By R. Montgomery Martin. *London: Whittaker & Co.* 1836. Fcap 8vo. + [*Ibid.*] 1838. 44914

MARTIN. The Hudson's Bay Territories and Vancouver's Island: with an Exposition of the Chartered Rights, Conduct, and Policy of the Honble Hudson's Bay Corporation. By R. M. Martin, Esq. ... *London: T. and W. Boone.* MDCCCXLIX. 8vo, pp. vii, (1), 175, (1). Map. H. 44915

MARTIN. The Past and Present State of the Tea Trade of England, and of the Continents of Europe and America; and a Comparison between the Consumption, Price of, and Revenue derived from, Tea, Coffee, Sugar, Wine, Tobacco, Spirits, &c. By R. Montgomery Martin ... . *London: Parbury, Allen, & Co.* 1832. 8vo, pp. xi, 222. Table. BA., C. 44916

MARTIN. Statistics of the Colonies of the British Empire in the West Indies, South America, North America ... with the Charters and ... Seals; ... By R. Montgomery Martin, Esq. *London: Wm. H. Allen and Co.* MDCCCXXXIX. 8vo, pp. v, (3), 602, Appendix, 304. Map and Plates. B., C. + [*Ibid.*] 1840.

MARTIN. Taxation of the British Empire. By R. Montgomery Martin ... . *London: Effingham Wilson.* MDCCCXXXIII. 16mo, pp. xxvi, (2), 264. BA. 44918

Also: The Sugar Question in relation to Free Trade and Protection. ... *London.* 1848. 8vo, pp. 21. *See also* "The Colonial Magazine," Vol. IV., No. 14492.

MARTIN-MAILLEFER (P. D.) Les Fiancés de Caracas: Poëme eclectique, en deux chants. Par P. D. Martin-Maillefer. *Paris.* 1829. 8vo, 10 leaves. S. 44919

MARTIN DE LA BASTIDE. *See* La Bastide (M. de), 38408.

MARTIN (S.) An Essay upon Plantership ... inscribed to ... George Thomas, Esq., Chief Governor of All the Leeward Islands. By Samuel Martin. *Antigua.* 1756. 8vo. + The Fourth Edition. *London: Reprinted for A. Millar.* MDCCLXV. 8vo, pp. xvi, 62. + *Antigua.* 1767. 8vo. + With a Preface upon the Slavery of Negroes in the British Colonies. *London.* 1773. 8vo. + Seventh Edition, with all the Additions, from the Author's Experiments to the Time of his Death. *Antigua: Printed by R. Mearns.* 1785. 4to. 44920

MARTIN (T.) Speech of Hon. Thomas Martin, delivered ... February 17th, 1870, on a bill ... for the appropriation of ...

money to bury ... the Remains of the Confederate Dead, at Point Lookout, in St. Mary's County, Md. *Annapolis.* 1870. 8vo, pp. 12. 44921

MARTIN (T. M.) The National Crisis. A Sermon ... in Philadelphia, By Rev. Thomas M. Martin, M.A. ... January 4, 1861 ... a Day of Fasting ... . [n. p. n. d.] 8vo, pp. 16. H.

MARTIN DE MOUSSY (V.) Description Géographique et Statistique de la Confédération Argentine Par V. Martin de Moussy, ... *Paris: Firmin Didot Frères, Fils et Cie., Imprimeurs.* 1860–64. 3 vols., 8vo, pp. (4), 582; (4), 671; (8), 752. Atlas, 1869. Folio, pp. (4), 20. 30 Plates. B. 44923

MARTIN DE MOUSSY. Mémoire historique sur la décadence et la ruine des missions des Jésuites dans le bassin de la Plata, leur état actuel, Par V. Martin de Moussy. *Paris: Douniel.* 1865. 8vo, pp. 92. 2 Maps. 44924

MARTIN (W.) The Self Vindication, of Col. William Martin, against certain Charges ... made against him by Gen. Andrew Jackson and others, in relation to ... Transactions in the Campaign against the Creek Indians in ... 1813. *Nashville: Printed by John S. Simpson.* 1829. 8vo, pp. 48. B. 44925

MARTIN (William Charles Linnæus). A General History of Humming-Birds, or the Trochilidæ: with special reference to the Collection of J. Gould ... . By W. C. L. Martin ... . *London. H. G. Bohn.* 1852. 16mo, pp. vii, (1), 232. Plates. A., B.

Many of these are American birds.

MARTIN (W. F.) The Geographical Magazine; ... of Asia, Africa, Europe, and America; ... By William Frederick Martin. *London: Harrison and Co.* MDCCLXXXII. 2 vols., 4to.

America occupies over one hundred pages in Vol. II.

MARTIN (W. T.) Franklin County Register; with a Brief History of the Settlement of the County. By William T. Martin. *Columbus.* 1834. 32mo. Map. 44928

MARTIN. History of Franklin County; a Collection of Reminiscences of the Early Settlement of the County; with Biographical Sketches, and a Complete History of the County to the Present Time. By William T. Martin. *Columbus: Follett, Foster & Company.* 1858. 8vo, pp. v, 449, (1). 8 Plates. H.

[MARTIN DE VALENCIA.] El Lutero de las almas de Kuketan [*sic*] y Nueva España 1532. Folio. 44930

[MARTIN DE VALENCIA.] Passio gloriosi marty | ris beati patris fratris Andree de | Spoleto ordinis minorū regula- | ris obseruãtie p̄ catholice fideive | ritate passi in Affrica civitate Fez. | *Anno dñi* M.D.xxxij | [Colophon:] *Impressum Tholose expensis honesti viri Johannis | barril mercatoris Tholose.* | *Laus deo.* | 4to, 4 leaves.

See also Vol. X., No. 40960, Menesses (F. de) *and* Olave (A. S. de).

[MARTIN DE VALENCIA.] Lettres envoyees au chapitre general des freres mineurs de la reguliere obseruance, celebre ... en la cite de Tholose ... lan mil. D. xxxij ... touchant les affaires des Indes et parties orientalles. nouuellement translatees de latin en francoys ... joincte a icelles vne salutaire exhortation a tous bons et loyaulx chrestiens vtile et profitable. [*Tholose, par Jean Barril, vers* 1532.] 4to, 10 leaves. 44932

"Apparently a translation into French of the previous title."—[HARRISSE'S] *Bib. Am. Vet.*, Additions, No. 98; *see also* Nos. 97 and 99.

MARTINDALE (H. C.) Oration ... at West Granville, ... N. Y., July 5, 1830 ... . By Henry C. Martindale. *Union-Village, N. Y.: P. S. Mills and W. Lansing.* 1830. 8vo, pp. 28. B.

MARTINDALE (J. C.) A History of the Townships of Byberry and Moreland, in Philadelphia, Pa. By Joseph C. Martindale, M.D. ... *Philadelphia: T. Ellwood Zell.* 1867. 8vo, pp. 379.

MARTINDALE. A History of the United States from 1492 to 1866, for the Use of Schools. By Joseph C. Martindale, M.D. ... *Philadelphia: J. K. Simon.* 1866. 12mo, pp. 171. 44935

MARTINEAU (Eyquem du). *See* Eyquem du Martineau, VI.

MARTINEAU (H.) A History of the American Compromises: ... By Harriet Martineau. *London: J. Chapman.* 1856. 8vo, pp. 36. 44936

MARTINEAU. The Hour and the Man. A Romance of Hayti. By Harriet Martineau. *London.* 1841. 3 vols., post 8vo. Map. + *New-York: Harper & Brothers.* 1841. 2 vols., 12mo, pp. 224; 209. + *London: Routledge & Co.* 1843. 12mo. + [*Ibid.*] 1855. 44937

A historical romance descriptive of the career of Toussaint Louverture.

MARTINEAU. Illustrations of Political Economy. By Harriet Martineau. ... *London: Fox.* 1832. 19 vols., 24mo. + *Boston:*

Leonard C. Bowles. 1832–35. 19 vols., 18mo. B. + *London: Routledge* ... 1859. 9 vols., 24mo. H. 44938

Contents: No. I. Life in the Wilds; IV. Demerara; X. Homes Abroad.

MARTINEAU. The Martyr Age in the United States of America. By Harriet Martineau. *New York.* 1839. 8vo, pp. 36. + *Boston: Weeks, Jordan & Co.* 1839. 12mo, pp. 84. + *Newcastle upon Tyne: Finlay and Charlton.* 1840. 8vo, pp. xix, 44.

First appeared in the "London and Westminster Review," for December, 1838, being a review of a work entitled "Right and Wrong in Boston," and of various matters connected with the slavery societies of that period.

MARTINEAU. Retrospect of Western Travel By Harriet Martineau ... . *London: Saunders & Otley.* 1838. 3 vols., post 8vo, pp. vi, (2), 318, (1); (6), 292; (6), 293, (1). + *New York: Harper & Brothers.* 1838. 2 vols., 12mo, pp. (6), 13–276; 239.

"No one who wishes to form a correct and enlarged view of the character, institutions, resources, and prospects of America, should fail to peruse Miss Martineau's volumes."—*Eclectic Review.* *See also* "N. A. Rev.," XIV, 15, XLV, 418; "Frazer's Magazine," XIX. 557.

MARTINEAU. Society in America By Harriet Martineau ... . *London: Saunders & Otley.* 1837. 3 vols., post 8vo, pp. xix, 364; vi, 369; vi, 365. H. + *New York: Saunders and Otley.* 1837. 2 vols., 12mo, pp. (2), xv, iv, 395; ii, 420. + Fourth Edition. [*Ibid.*] B., H. 44941

It elicited: "Miss Martineau on America, Reviewed. From the American Quarterly Review, for September, 1837." [n. p. n. d.] 8vo, pp. 43. *See also* [Otis (J. F.)], "Slavery in America," *and* [Wilks].

MARTINEAU. De la Société Américaine, par Miss Martineau; traduit de l'anglais Par M. Benjamin Laroche ... . *Bruxelles.* 1836. 3 vols., 18mo. + [*Ibid.*] 1838. 44942

MARTINEAU. Voyage aux États-Unis; ou tableau de la Société Américaine, par Harriet Martineau. Traduit de l'anglais, par B. Laroche. *Paris.* 1839. 2 vols., 8vo. 44943

MARTINEAU. Views of Slavery and Emancipation; from "Society in America." By Harriet Martineau ... . *New York: Piercy Reed, Printers* [*sic*]. 1837. 8vo, pp. (4), 79. BA. 44944

Also: Biographical Sketches ... . *London: Macmillan & Co.* 1869. 12mo, pp. ix, (2), 445. + *New York: Leypoldt & Holt.* 1869. 12mo, pp. 458.—Miscellanies. ... *Boston: Hilliard, Gray and Company.* M DCCC XXXVI. 2 vols., 8vo, pp. xii, 352; (4), 402.

MARTINEAU (J.) Miscellanies. By the Rev. James Martineau. *Boston: Wm. Crosby and H. P. Nichols.* 1852. 12mo, pp. vi, (2), 472. H. 44945

Contents the life, character, and works of Dr. Priestley, etc.

MARTINELLI (V.) Istoria del Governo d'Inghilterra e delle sue Colonie in India, e nell' America settentrionale Scritta da Vincenzio Martinelli Seconda Edizione ... . *Pescia.* MDCCLXXVII. 8vo, pp. viii, 190. H. 44946

[MARTIÑENA (Juan Martin de Juan).] Verdadero Origen, Carácter, Causas, Resortes, Fines y Progresos de la Revolucion de Nueva España, y Defensa de los europeos en general residentes en ella, y especialmente de los autores de la aprehension y destitucion del virey D. José Iturrigaray en la noche del 15 de setiembre de 1808, contra los falsos calumniadores que los infaman, y atribuyen al indicado suceso, á opresion, agresiones y ofensas de su parte contra los americanos, la desastrosa revolucion que ha asolado este reino. Folio, pp. 17. [Followed by:] Manifiesto e todas las Naciones por el superior gobierno de Nueva España. *Mexico.* 1820. Folio, pp. 114, 66. 44947

"An angry condemnation of the insurrection of Ydalgo, but contains the most interesting documents for any one who intends to write the history of that revolution."

MARTINEZ (A. J. P.) Oracion Funebre que en las Solemnes Exequias en la Iglesia del Espiritu Santo de la Puebla, á devocion y expensas de los hijos y Oriundos de Vizcaya de Navarra, por todos los que murieron en la Gloriosa Defensa de Buenos-Ayres, dixo 24 de Feb. de 1808. El D. A. J. Perez Martinez. *Mexico.* 1808. 8vo. Plate. 44948

MARTINEZ. Sermon predicado en la Santa Iglesia Metropolitana de Megico el dia 21 de Julio de 1822 por el Exmo. e Illmo. Sr. Dr. D. Antonio Joaquin Perez Martinez, ... con motivo de la solemne coronacion del Señor D. Augustin de Iturbide, primer Emperador constitucional de Megico. *Puebla.* 1839. 4to, pp. 28.

Also: Panegirico de S. Augustin. ... *Puebla.* 1817. 4to, pp. (6), 19.—Panegirico de Santa Clara, predicado en la iglesia de su convento de la Puebla de los Angeles. ... *Puebla.* 1819. 4to, pp. (4), 28.

MARTINEZ (Caro). Ramon, Verdadera idea de la primera Campaña de Tejas, y sucesos ocurridos despues de la accion de San Jacinto. *Mexico.* 1837. 4to, pp. 162. 44950

[MARTINEZ DE PINILLOS (Claudio).] Alcabalatorio de la Isla de Cuba, ó Recopilacion Sumaria de las Leyes y Reales Ordenes, que rigen en dicha Isla ... . *Habana.* 1830. 8vo, pp. (2), 42. B.

MARTINEZ (Henrico). Repertorio de los Tiempos, y Historia Natvral desta Nveva España. *Mexico.* 1606. Sm. 4to, pp. (22), 342, (numbered 278). Plate. C. 44952

"Livre d'une rareté excessive dont on ne connait que quelques exemplaires."—ANDRADE. "Libro muy curioso i de grandes noticias por tenerlas su Autor, que oy vive en Mexico, i tiene otros escritos, que nunca llegaran a España, pues el impresso no se halla."—LEON PINELO, p. 102; ANTONIO, Vol. I., p. 564.

MARTINEZ DE LA PUENTE (J.) Compendio | de las Historias | de los Descubrimien- | tos, Conquistas, y Guerras de la | India Oriental, y sus Islas ... . Por D. Joseph Martinez de la Puente. ... *Madrid: Por la Viuda de Joseph Fernandez de Buendia.* 1681. 8vo, pp. (14), 380, 30. H. 44953

Includes an account of the discovery of Brazil. Lord Stuart de Rothesay's copy, with the date *Madrid*, 1680, sold in 1844 for £3 3s.

MARTINEZ (J.) Sermon de San Felipe de Jesus. *Mexico.* 1781. 4to, 22 leaves. 44954

The subject of this sermon suffered martyrdom in Mexico.

MARTINEZ (J.) El P. Maestro Fray Juan Martinez, Vocabulario en la Lengua general del Peru, llamada Quichua y en la Lengua Española. [*Lima:*] *En los Reyes.* 1604. Sm. 8vo.

Title from "Bibliotheca Heberiana, VI. 35, No. 512, as quoted by Ludewig.

MARTINEZ DE ARAUJO (J.) Manual de los Santos Sacramentos en el Idioma de Michuacan. Dedicalo al Ilstmo y Revmo Señor Doctor D. Juan Ortega Montañes mi Señor del Consejo de su Magestad, Obispo que fue de Durango, Guatemala ... . El Bachiller Iuan Martinez de Aravjo, primer Colegial de el Colegio de S. Ramon Nonnato ... . Con licencia de los Superiores. *En Mexico: por Doña Maria de Benavides, Viuda de Juan de Ribera en el Empedradillo. Año de* 1690. 4to, 7 prel. leaves, Text, 93 leaves, Table, 1 leaf. 44956

Not mentioned by Brunet, Rich, Brockhaus, or Stevens.

MARTINEZ (Juan Chrys.) El Phenix de la Africa Augustino, breve relacion de su sagrado cuerpo. *Mexico: B. de Hogal.* 1729. 4to, pp. (2), 56. 44957

MARTINEZ (J. G. de C.) Amorosa contienda de Francia, Italia, y España sobre la augusta persona de el Señor Don Carlos III. exaltado al trono Español ... Propone al a El Dr. T. Mro. Don Juan Gregoria de Campos Martinez ... Protho-Medico por sa Majestad de esta Nueva España. ... *Impressa en el Rl y mas Antiguo Colegio de Ildefonsa de Mexico, año de* 1761. 4to, pp. (26), 208. 44958

See also Campos Martinez (J. G.), Vol. III., No. 10323.

[MARTINEZ DE] L[EJARZA] (J. J.) *See* L[ejarza] (J. J.)

MARTINEZ (M.) Sermon de Gracias con que el ill. Cabildo de la ciudad de Santa Fe real y minas Guanaxoato. *Mexico.* 1784. 4to, 20 leaves. 44959

Also: Sermon panegirico en la dedicacion de la nueva iglesia del convento de S. Petro de Alcantura de la ciudad de Santa Fe y minas de Guanaxoato. ... *Mexico.* 1785. 4to, 16 leaves.

MARTINEZ (M. L.) Memoirs of Dona Maria Loretto Martinez, the Black Malibran, Native of Cuba. *London.* [1850.] 8vo. 44960

MARTINEZ (M. G.) Oracion funebre pronunciada por el Sr. Prebendado Lic D. Miguel G. Martinez, en las honras que en sufragio por el alma del Señor Dr. D. Francisco Javier Miranda, se celebraron por acuerdo del Exmo. Ayuntamiento de Pueblo cuto Iglesia de N. S. P. S. francisco de la misma ciudad el dia 13 de Julio de 1864. *Puebla.* 1864. 4to, pp. 22. Portrait.

MARTINEZ (P.) Bref discours d'aucunes Missions, tant d'Orient que d'Occident, tiré d'aucunes lettres des PP. Pierre Martinez ... . *Douai.* 1593. 12mo. 44962

MARTINEZ. Brevis et compendiosa narratio Missionum quarundam Orientis et Occidentis. Excerpta ex quibusdam letteris a PP. Petro Martinez ... P. Joanne de Atienza, Provinciale Peruanæ, et P. Pietro Diaz, Provinciale Mexicanæ. Provinciarum datis anno 1590 et 1591 ad reveren. P. Generalem Societatis Jesu. Et collecta per P. Gasparum Spitelli ... . *Antverpiæ.* 1593. 8vo. 44963

MARTINEZ. Ragguaglio d'alcune missioni dell' Indie Orientali et Occidentali cavato da alcuni avisi scritti gli anni 1690 et 91. da i PP. P. Martinez, G. d'Atienza, P. Diaz. *Roma.* 1593. 8vo. 44964

MARTINEZ. Recueil de quelques missions des Indes-Orientales et Occidentales, par les pères Pierre Martinez, proviseur des Indes-Orientales, Jean d'Atienza, provincial du Pérou, et Pierre Diez, provincial du Mexique. *Lyon.* 1594. 12mo. 44965

MARTINEZ DE LA TORRE (Rafael). Alegato de bien probado en el juicio promovido por algunos aviados de la mina de Jacal contra la compañia aviadora. *Mexico.* 1861. 8vo, pp. 138.

Also: Alegato de puena prueba por parte de la compañia aviadora del mineral del Monte y Pachuca, en el negocio promovido por varios accionistas de la mina del Jacal. *Mexico.* 1862. 8vo, pp. 49.—Copia de las sentencias pronunciadas por D. Manuel

Siliceo, D. Miguel Atristain y D. Hilario Elguero, en el juicio arbitral que los aviados de la mina del Jagal han seguido contra la compañia aviadora del Monte y Pachuca, etc. *Mexico.* 1862. 8vo, pp. 70. C.

MARTINGALE (Hawser), *pseudon.* *See* [Sleeper (Jacob S.)]

MARTINHO DE MESQUITA. Estreum fulmen in Batavorum classem a Jove Gallico Ludovico XIV Galliarum rege invictissimo jaculatum, tanti fulminis a ministro illustrissimo et excellentissimo comite Joanne de Estrees, ejusdem regis in toto Occidentali Oceano pro architalasso, ad insulam Tabacum in America Meridionali, heroico reditum carmine. *Roma: M. Barnabo.* 1677. Fol.

MARTINI (F.) Argo-Navta | Batavvs, | Sive expeditionis Navalis, quam alter noster | Jason, & Heros fortissimus, Petrvs | Heinivs, sub auspicijs Illustrissimorum & | potentissimorum DD. Ordd: & | Illustrissimi Principis Auraici, In- | clytæq; Societatis Indiæ Occi- | dentalis ductu nuper | suscepit: | Et Victoriæ in sinu Matanzæ divinitus | reportatæ | Historia | Carmine heroico descripta, & publicè recitata, | à | Francisco Martini | Scholæ Campensis Discipulo. | *Campis.* | *Ex officina Petri Henrici Wyringani,* | *sub signo Typographiæ.* | CIↃ IↃ CXXIX | 4to, pp. (2), 28. 44968

This account of the Dutch expedition to Brazil, under Peter Heyn, is a poetical volume of great rarity.

[MARTINIANO DE ALENCAR (J.)] Cartas sobre a Confederação dos Tamoyos, por I. G. *Rio de Janeiro: Empreza Typographia Nacional do Diario.* 1856. 8vo, pp. 96, 16. 44969

MARTINICO. Genuine Account. *See* No. 26960, *add* Map.

MARTINIÈRE (Bruzen de la). *See* Bruzen de la Martinière, Vol. III., No. 8783, and La Martinière, Vol. X., Nos. 38711-16.

MARTINIQUE. Affaire des Déportés de la Martinique, Mémoires, consultation, pièces justificatives, &c. *Paris.* 1827. 8vo.

Annales de la Société d'Agriculture et d'Économie politique à la Martinique. [v. d.] 8vo. Continued. 44971

Articles de la capitulation de l'isle Martinique, entre son Excellence M. Le Vassor de la Touche, et leurs Excellences Messieurs G. B. Rodney & Robert Monckton, Généraux des Armées de Mer & de la Terre de S. M. Britannique. *Martinique: Pierre Richard.* 1762. 4to, pp. 7. J.C.B. 44972

Bulletin des actes administratifs de la Martinique, 1re série, contenant les arrêtés et actes du gouvernement pendant les années

1828-31. *Saint-Pierre, Martinique: J. A. Fleurot.* 1829-32. 4 vols., 8vo, pp. xvj, 274; xvj, 944; xvj, 286; xix, 308. 44973

Rare, as two hundred copies only were printed.

Code de la Martinique. Nouvelle édition par M. Durand Molard, sous-commissaire des Colonies. *Saint-Pierre (Martinique).* 1807-14. 5 vols., 8vo. 44974

Another collection of laws was published in 1757, with a supplement in 1772, folio.

Compte général de l'Administration de la Justice dans les Colonies de la Martinique, la Guadeloupe, la Guyane, et Bourbon, 1834-39. *Paris.* 1842-45. 2 vols., 4to. A. 44975

Essai sur l'état actuel de l'administration de la Colonie de la Martinique. *Bordeaux.* 1817. 8vo. C. 44976

Lettre d'un Dominicain de la Martinique à un de ses supérieurs en France; contenant le récit de la persecution que le P. de Lavalette, Jésuite, a suscitée aux Missionaires de cet ordre. [n. p. 1763.] 12mo, pp. viii, 32. J.C.B. 44977

Lettres sur la prise de la Martinique par les Anglois, en 1762. [*Paris.* 1763.] 8vo, pp. vii, 55. J.C.B. 44978

Written by an inhabitant of the Island of Guadalupe to an inhabitant of Martinique.

Mémoire des officiers, bas-officiers, &c du régiment de la Martinique; et détail exact de la conduite que ce corps a tenue à l'occasion des excès commis envers deux officiers du régiment par une partie de la ville de St. Pierre. *Paris.* 1790. 8vo. 44979

Pièces du procès instruit contradictoirement au conseil supérieur de la Martinique, entre le procureur général, en la société des Jésuites. [n. p. about 1763.] 12mo, pp. 191. C. 44980

Précis historique des Événemens arrivés à la Martinique, depuis 1789 jusqu'à la prise de la Colonie par les Anglois, en 1794. [*Paris.* 1794.] 4to, pp. 20. J.C.B. 44981

"Seul et unique exemplaire pour la premier Consul."—J. C. BROWN'S Catalogue. *See also* [Chanvalon (J. B. T. de)], [Deshalles], *and* D[ouble] (M.)

MARTINSBURG, *Va.* Discourse delivered in the Protestant Episcopal Church ... November 23, 1806, Martinsburg, Virginia. *Martinsburg.* [1806.] 18mo, pp. 14. N. 44982

MARTIR (P.) Informe de Una Comision Del M. I. A. de la Habana, Sobre Poblacion Blanca. Publicado y Anotado por Pedro Martir. *Nueva Orleans.* 1847. 8vo, pp. 19. BA. 44983

MARTIRE D'ANGHIERA (Pietro). *See* Anghiera (P.), Vol. I.

MARTIUS (Carl Friedrich Philipp von). Beiträge zur Ethnographie und Sprachenkunde Brasiliens. Wörtersammlung brasilianischer Sprachen. *Erlangen: Junge.* 1863. 8vo, pp. xxi, 548. + *Leipzig: F. Fleischer.* 1867. 2 vols., 8vo, pp. ix, 202; xxi, 548. C. 44984

MARTIUS. Beiträge zur Naturgeschichte von Brasilien. ... *Weimar.* 1825-33. 4 vols., 8vo. 44985

MARTIUS. Catalogue de la Bibliothéque américaine de Mr. de Martius. *Munich.* 1848. 4to, 34 leaves. C. 44986

Lithographed; describes four hundred and seventy-eight works.

MARTIUS. Flora Brasiliensis seu Enumeratio Plantarum in Brasilia tam sua sponte quam accedente cultura provenientium, quas in itinere ... annis 1817-1820 peracto collegit, partim descripsit ... C. F. Ph. de Martius. ... *Stuttgartiae: Sumptibus J. G. Cottae.* 1833, 1829. 8vo, pp. iv, 390; (6), ii, 608. H.

These are Part I. of Vol. I. and Part I. of Vol. II.

MARTIUS. Flora Brasiliensis sive Enumeratio Plantarum in Brasilia ... Edidit Car. Frid. Phil. de Martius. Accedunt ... Musei C. R. Pal. Vindob. Eduardi Fenzl. *Lipsiae: F. Fleischer.* 1857. 8vo, pp. 170. Plate. C. 44988

For parts I.-X. *see* Endlicher (S.), Vol. VI., 22562. The seventieth fasciculus was published in 1876.

MARTIUS. Genera et Species Palmarum quas in itinere per Brasiliam annis 1817-1820 ... collegit, descripsit, et iconibus illustravit C. F. P. de Martius. *Monachii.* 1823-37. 3 vols., folio. 245 Plates. + *Lipsiæ: T. O. Weigel.* 1856-57. 3 vols., folio. Plates. 44989

"One of the grandest botanical works ever published. The plates are of very large size, and some copies were published with them exquisitely colored. The expense of producing it was so enormous that a great portion of the funds for the purpose was contributed by the Bavarian Government." The second issue sold for 196 thaler, plain, 328 thaler, colored.

MARTIUS. Herbarium Floræ Brasiliensis. Plantæ Brasilienses exsiccatæ ... . *Monachii.* 1837-[40]. 8vo, pp. 352. 44990

Pages 1-72 relate to the literary history of the "Flora Brasiliensis."

MARTIUS. Historia naturalis Palmarum, opus tripartitum, cujus volumen primum Palmas generatim tractat; Volumen secundum Brasiliæ Palmas singulatim descriptiones et icones illus-

trat; Volumen tertium Characteres ordinis Palmarum generum recensuit, Species selectas describit, et figuris adumbrat adjecta omnium Synopsi. Acc. Tabulæ CCXLV. *Lipsiæ: T. O. Weigel.* 1823-50. 3 vols., folio. A. 44991

MARTIUS. Icones Selectæ Plantarum Crytogamicarum quas in itinere per Brasiliam annus MDCCCXVII-MDCCCXX ... collegit et descripsit Dr. C. F. P. de Martius ... . *Monachii: Impensis Autoris.* 1828-34. 4to, pp. (6), 138. 76 colored Plates. 44992

MARTIUS. Nova Genera et Species Plantarum quas in itinere per Brasiliam, annis MDCCCXVII-MDCCCXX ... suscepto collegit et descripsit C. F. P. de Martius ... . *Monachii: Typis Lindaueri.* 1824-29. 3 vols., 4to, pp. (8), 158; (6), 148; (8), 198. 300 colored Plates. A., H. 44993

MARTIUS. Das Naturell, die Krankheiten, das Arzthum und die Heilmittel der Urbewohner Brasiliens. *München: Wolf.* [1844.] 8vo, pp. 192. 44994

MARTIUS. Die Physionomie des Pflanzenreichs in Brasilien, eine Rede ... am 14 Februar 1824 ... von Dr. C. F. Ph. von Martius. *München.* 1824. 4to, pp. 36. 44995

MARTIUS. Reise in Brasilien auf Befehl Sr. Maj. Maximilian Joseph I., Königs von Baiern, in den Jahren 1817-20. *München.* 1823-31. 3 vols., 4to. Atlas in folio. 44996

There are copies on large paper, and one or more with the atlas colored by hand.

MARTIUS. Specimen Materiæ Medicæ Brasiliensis, exhibens Plantas Medicinales, quas in itinere per Brasiliam annis 1817-20 ... observavit Dr. C. F. P. de Martius ... [*Monachii:*] *Typis J. E. de Seidel.* 1824. 4to, pp. 20. 9 Plates. H. 44997

MARTIUS. Systema Materiæ Medicae Vegetabilis Brasiliensis. Composuit Car. Frid. Phil. de Martius. *Lipsiae: Frid. Fleischer.* 1843. 8vo, pp. (2), xxvi, 155, (1). B., C., H. 44998

MARTIUS. Von dem Rechtszustande unter den Ureinwohnern Brasiliens. Eine Abhandlung von Dr. C. F. Ph. von Martius. Mit Anhang. *München.* 1832. 4to, pp. iv, 86, 20. 44999

Also: Beitrag zur Flora Brasiliens. Mit Beschreibung von Nees von Esenbeck und von Martius. [n. p. n. d.] 4to. 6 Plates.—Brasilianische Volkslieder und Indianische Melodien. ... [n. p. n. d.] 4to.—Glossaria Linguarum Brasiliensium. ... *Erlangen: Junge & Sohn.* 1863. 8vo, pp. xxi, 544, 547-8.—Syllabus praelectionum de botanica pharmaceutico-medica. ... *München: Verfasser.* 1852. 8vo, pp. 34.—Die Thiere und Pflanzen des tropischen America. ... *München: Verfasser.* 1831. 4to. 4 Plates, folio. This was reprinted from the "Reise," No. 44996.—Die Vergangenheit und Zukunft

der Amerikanischen Menschheit. ... [n. p.] 1838. 8vo, pp. 34. + [n. p.] 1839. 8vo, pp. (2), 36.—Versuch eines Commentars über die Pflanzen in den Werken von Marcgrav und Piso über Brasilien nebst weiteren Erörterungen über die Flora ... . I. Kryptogamen. *München.* 1853. 4to, pp. 60. *See also* Spix (J. B.)

The Martling-Man. *See* [Clinton (De Witt)], IV. 13717.

[MARTYN (Benjamin).] An | Account | Shewing | the Progress of the | Colony of Georgia | in America | from its first establishment. | *London: Printed in the Year* M.DCC.XLI. Folio, pp. (2), 71. + *Maryland: Reprinted and Sold by Jonas Green, at his Printing Office. in Annapolis.* 1742. 4to. + *Washington: Peter Force.* 1836. 8vo, pp. v, 56. 45000

First published by order of the trustees of the colony, and forms Vol. I. of "Force's Tracts." It is also reprinted in the "Georgia Historical Society Collections," Vol. II.

[MARTYN.] An | Impartial Enquiry | into the | State and Utility | of the | Province of Georgia. | *London: W. Meadows.* MDCCXLI. 8vo, pp. (2), 104. BA., H. 45001

"A well-written tract, defending the colony from the malignant reports that had been circulated."—RICH. It includes an account of South Carolina. Reprinted in the "Georgia Historical Society Collections," Vol. I. Its authorship has also been attributed to Lord John Percival.

[MARTYN.] Reasons For Establishing the Colony of Georgia, With Regard to the Trade of Great Britain, The Increase of our People, and the Employment and Support it will afford to great Numbers of our own Poor, as well as foreign persecuted Protestants. With some Account of the Country, and the Design of the Trustees. *London: W. Meadows.* MDCCXXXIII. 4to, pp. 39. Map and Plate. 45002

MARTYN. Reasons For Establishing the Colony of Georgia, ... By Benjamin Martyn, Esq. The Second Edition. *London: W. Meadows.* MDCCXXXIII. 4to, pp. 48. Map and Plate.

This second edition contains letters of Gen. Oglethorpe, with resolutions of the Assembly relative to his arrival. A well-written tract; plausible in its arguments, glowing in its descriptions, valuable for its information, and pertinent in its appeals to the philanthropic and benevolent. Reprinted in "Georgia Historical Society Collections," Vol. II., pp. 203-238.

MARTYN (J.) Joannis Martyn Historia Plantarum Rariorum. ... *Londini: Ex Typographia Richardi Reilly.* MDCCXXVIII. Folio, pp. (4), 52. 50 colored Plates. H. 45004

The plants described are chiefly American. Two other parts were printed.

MARTYN (J. H.) A Narrative of the Origin and Progress of the First Free Congregational Church, in Buffalo, New-York:

... By J. H. Martyn. ... *Buffalo: Printed by H. A. Salisbury.* 1834. 8vo, pp. 16. BA. 45005

MARTYN (S. T.) The English Exile; or, William Tyndale at Home and Abroad. By Mrs. S. T. Martyn. *New York.* 1867. 16mo, pp. 237. C. 45006

[MARTYN.] Our Village in War Time. ... *New York.* 1867. 18mo, pp. 125. 45007

MARTYN (W. Carlos). The Pilgrim Fathers of New England. A History. By W. C. Martyn. *New York.* [1867.] 12mo, pp. 432. C. 45008

Also: A History of the English Puritans. ... *New York.* [1867.] 12mo, pp. 496. —History of the Huguenots. ... *New York.* [1866.] 12mo, pp. 528. C.

MARTYR (Peter). *See* Anghiera (Pietro Martire d'), Vol. I.

MARTYR. Die schiffung mitt|dem Lanndt der|Gulden Insel gefundē durch|Hern Johan vō Angliara|Hawptman des Cristen-|lichen Künigs vō His-|pania, gar hübsch|ding zū hörē mit|allen yren leben|vnd sit-|ten.| [n. p. about 1520.] Sm. 4to, 3 leaves.

This is a corrected title of *our* No. 1560, Vol. I. *See also* Græsse's "Trésor," I. 130, *and* Harrisse's "Bib. Am. Vet.," No. 102.

MARTYR. De Orbe No-|uo Petri Martyris ab | Angleria Mediolanen-|sis Protonotarij | Cesaris sena-|toris de-|cades | ... . *Compluti apud Micha-|elē d' Eguia Anno* MD.XXX | [Colophon:] ... *Anno Virginei | partus* M.D.XXX. | *Mense Decēbri.* | Folio, Text, cxij leaves, Vocabula Barbara, 3 leaves. Map. H. 45010

First complete edition of the eight decades. It is in some respects more correct than Hakluyt's, which is usually considered the best. This is the correct title of *our* No. 1551. *See* Harrisse's "Bib. Am. Vet.," No. 154.

MARTYR. De|orbe novo| ... M.D.LXXXVII.

See our No. 1552, and add to the note: There are copies on thick paper.

MARTYR. Relationi [*our* No. 1559].

E. Tross of Paris quotes a copy of this work dated 1561, which may be an error.

MARTYR. The Decades|of the newe worlde or|west India.

Title as in *our* No. 1561, but with the imprint *W. Powell*, 1557.

[MARTYR.] The|Historie Of|The West-Indies,|Containing the Actes and Aduentures|of the Spaniards, which haue conquered | and peopled those Countries, inriched with vari-|etie of pleasant relation of the Manners,|Ceremonies, Lawes, Gouernments, | and Warres of the | Indians. | Published in Latin by Mr. Hakluyt, | and translated into English by M. Lok. Gent. | ... |

London, | *printed for Andrew Hebb, and are to be sold at the Signe* | *of the Bell in Paul's Church-yard.* [1597?] 4to, 3 prel. leaves, Text, 318 leaves. 45011

The "Epistola Dedicatoria," 2 leaves, is sometimes inserted from the edition dated 1612. Its date is uncertain; White Kennett, a good authority, places it at 1597, Rich gives the date as 1612. It is, in fact, the same edition as *our* Nos. 1563–64, with another title, and from the fact that the "Epistola Dedicatoria" is not usually found with it, we incline to the belief that it is even later than 1628. The change of title was merely a publisher's trick. In noticing this edition T. W. Field remarks "The name of the author of this work was Pietro Martir, of Anghiera, in Milan, a name which he latinized into Angleria. There is no more warrant for styling him Anglerius than Milanoise. He is recognized by all Spanish writers by his patronymic, anglicized to Peter Martyr." Our answer to which is that Brunet and other authorities of far more repute than Mr. Field, index him under the name "Anghiera."

MARTYR. Histori von der Newen Welt, und Indianischen Nidergängischen Königreichs; aus dem Latein in das Teutsch gebracht durch Nicolaum Höniger von Königshofen. *Basil: Sebastian Henicpetri.* 1582. 2 vols., folio. 45012

[MARTYR.] L'Histoire. *See* Vol. VIII., No. 32018.

MARTYR. P. Martyris ab | angleria | Mediolanensi. | Opera. | Legatio babilonica|Occeanea decas.|Poemata.|Cum priuilegio.| [Colophon:] *Impressum Hispali cū diligencia per Jacobū corumberger alemanū. Anno. Millessimo quingentessimo. xj. mēse vero* | *Aprili.* | Folio, 74 leaves. Map. 45013

Another version of *our* No. 1565, Vol. I. Harrisse thinks that this was the first issue; *see* "Bib. Am. Vet.," Additions, No. 41.

The Martyr Age of the United States of America, with an Appeal on behalf of the Oberlin Institute in aid of the Abolition of Slavery. Re-published from the London and Westminster Review ... . *Newcastle upon Tyne: Finlay and Charlton.* 1840. 8vo, pp. xix, 44. 45014

The Martyr President. *See* No. 41211, *also* [Newell (R. H.)]

Martyrologium magnum oder il cudesch grands dels Martyrs. Jl qual contegna: La historia dellas persecutions dalla Baselgia et dels martyrs con lur excellentes confessions contra ils jnimis della evangelica veritat in Germania, ... et America. ... Parte prime chi contegna la historia fin ano 1560. Huossa in noss Romansch verti et contract da Conradino Riolano. *Stampa in Strada in Engadina bassa: L. C. et J. Janet.* 1718. 4to, pp. (20), 55, Index, 8. 45015

The only volume of this very rare Romanish translation of Crespin's "Histoire des Martyrs" published. The index, which was published separately at Scuol, is usually wanting. "Volume d'une grande rareté."—BRUNET.

The Martyr's Monument. *See* [Lieber (F.)], Vol. X. 40981.

Martyrs to the Revolution. *See* [Taylor (George)].

The Martyrs, Who for our Country gave up their Lives in the Prison Pens, in Andersonville. *Washington.* 1866. 8vo.

MARURE (A.) Bosquejo historico de las revoluciones de Centro-America, desde 1811 hasta 1834. Escrito por Alejandro Marure. Tomo primero. *Guatemala: Imprenta de la Nueva Academia de Estudios. Año de* 1837. 4to, pp. (6), 295, lxvi, (15). Plate. 45017

MARURE. Efemerides de los hechos notables acaecidos en la República de Centro-America, desde el año de 1821 hasta el de 1842. Seguidas de varios catálogos de los Presidentes de la República, Gefes de los Estados, cet, por Alejandro Marure. *Guatemala, año de* 1844. 8vo, pp. (1), 8, (2), 79. 45018

MARURE. Memoria Historica sobre el Canal de Nicaragua. Seguida de algunas observaciones de Mr. I. Bailey sobre el mismo asunto. Escrita por Alexandro Marure ... . *Guatemala.* 1845. 4to, pp. (2), 44, (1). Map. 45019

[MARURE.] Memorias para la Historia de la Revolucion de Centro-America. Por un Guatemalteco. *Jalapa: Aburto y Blanco.* 1832. 12mo, pp. xxxii, 257. 45020

MARVEL (Ik.), *pseudon.* *See* [Mitchell (D. G.)]

MARVELL (A.) No. 1. Philadelphia, June 10th, 1773. To my Fellow-Citizens, Friends to Liberty, and Enemies to Despotism. ... Andrew Marvell. Folio, 1 leaf. P. 45021

Violently opposing the proposed shambles in Market Street, as also does the following:

MARVELL. Andrew Marvell's Second Address to the Inhabitants of Philadelphia. ... *Philadelphia: Printed Anno* 1773. 8vo, pp. 16. P. 45022

MARVIN (A. P.) Essay by Rev. Abijah P. Marvin ... . The Christian Element Essential to the Truest Patriotism; ... . [*Worcester?* 1863.] 8vo, pp. 15. H. 45023

MARVIN. Fugitive Slaves: A Sermon ... in ... Winchendon ... Fast [Day], April 11, 1850. By A. P. Marvin ... . *Boston: John P. Jewett & Co.* 1850. 8vo, pp. 24. H. 45024

MARVIN. History of ... Winchendon (Worcester Co. Mass.), from the grant of Ipswich Canada, in 1735, to the Present Time,

By Rev. A. P. Marvin. ... *Winchendon: The Author.* 1868. 8vo, pp. 528. Map, 14 Plates, 9 Portraits and 3 Plans. H.

MARVIN. History of Worcester in the War of the Rebellion. By Abijah P. Marvin ... . *Worcester: The Author.* 1870. 8vo, pp. 582. 9 Plates. C., H. 45026

MARVIN (D.) ... An Address to the ... Law School of the University of Albany ... February 25, 1857. By Dan. Marvin. ... *Albany: W. C. Little & Co.* 1857. 8vo, pp. 38. H. 45027

MARVIN (D.) Letter of the Hon. Dudley Marvin ... . [n. p.:] *J. & G. S. Gideon, Printers.* [1848.] 8vo, pp. 8. H. 45028

This letter was addressed to James Parker, Esq., against supporting the nominees of the Buffalo convention.

MARVIN (E. P.) Home. A Sermon ... Thanksgiving Day. By Rev. Elihu P. Marvin ... . *Boston: Press of T. R. Marvin & Son.* 1859. 8vo, pp. 23. H. 45029

MARVIN. ... A Sermon ... in the First Trinitarian Church, Medford, Mass. January 29, 1860. By Rev. Elihu P. Marvin, ... *Boston: T. R. Marvin & Son.* 1860. 8vo, pp. 31. 45030

MARVIN (H.) A Complete History of Lake George ... intended as a descriptive Guide ... . By Henry Marvin. *New York: Sibells & Maigne, Printers.* 1853. 24mo, pp. 102. Map.

MARVIN (J. G.) Legal Bibliography, or a Thesaurus of American, English, Irish, and Scotch Law Books. Together with some Continental Treatises. Interspersed with Critical Observations upon their various Editions and Authority. To which is prefixed a Copious List of Abbreviations. By John G. Marvin, Counsellor at Law. ... *Philadelphia: T. & T. W. Johnson.* 1847. 8vo, pp. vii, 800. C. 45032

MARVIN (T. R.) Genealogical Sketch of the Descendants of Reinold and Matthew Marvin, who came to New England in 1635. Compiled ... by T. R. Marvin. *Boston.* 1848. 12mo, pp. 56. B. 45033

MARVIN (W.) Report to the Chamber of Commerce ... of New-York, on the Proceedings of the International Congress held at York, in England ... September, 1864 ... . With an Appendix ... . By William Marvin, Delegate. *New-York: John W. Amerman, Printer.* 1866. 8vo, pp. 136. H. 45034

MARVIN (W.) Address of the Hon. William Marvin, ... Governor of Florida, ... Dec. 22, 1865, on ... the Inauguration of ... Hon. D. S. Walker, Governor elect. [n. p. 1865.] 8vo, pp. 12. BA. 45035

MARVIN (W. F.) The Battle of Monterey, and other Poems. By William F. Marvin. *Danville, Ky.: A. S. McGroberty.* 1851. 12mo, pp. 219. Portrait. C. 45036

MARWADE (C. G.) ... Observations on the State of the Cotton Market, ... from ... 1801, to the Present Time; ... . By Chr. G. Marwade. *Liverpool: Printed by J. Lang.* [n. d.] 8vo, pp. 30. Map. BA. 45037

MARY EDMOND SAINT GEORGE. An Answer to Six Months in a Convent, Exposing its Falsehoods and Manifold Absurdities. By the Lady Superior. With some Preliminary Remarks. Second Edition. *Boston: Printed ... by J. H. Eastburn.* 1835. 8vo, pp. xxxvii, (1), 67. BA. 45038

MARY (J.) New French and English Grammar. ... By John Mary ... . *Printed for ... the Author, Boston.* M,DCC,LXXXIV. 8vo, pp. 141, (22), 88. H. 45039

One of the earliest books of its class printed in America.

MARY. Our Nation; By Mary. ... *Bangor: Printed by Samuel S. Smith.* 1860. 16mo, pp. 16. H. 45040

Mary Clifton, a Tale of the Late War. By the Author of Ethel Somers. *Augusta* [*Ga.*]. 1865. 12mo, pp. 73. C.

Mary Hollis. An Original Tale. ... *New-York.* 1822. 12mo, pp. 22. H. 45042

Mary Lyndon. *See* [Nichols (Mary Gove)].

Mary Staunton. *See* [White (*Mrs.* J. W.)]

MARYLAND.

In the following list the titles, with a few exceptions, viz.: Banks, Boundary, Canals, Education, Geology, Militia, etc., are alphabetical. In the preparation of the list I am under special obligations to Mr. Lee, Librarian of the Baltimore Mercantile Library Association, for his valuable assistance.

Abridgment and Collection. *See* Bisset (J.), Vol. II. 5643.

An|Abridgment|of the|Laws|of|Maryland,|Now in force.| Under Proper Heads. [*London: John Nicholson.* 1704.] Small 8vo, pp. 71 [for 87]. 45043

From page 81–87 the pagination is 65–71.

An Act for Granting a Supply of Twenty Thousand Pounds for His Majesty's Service, and the more immediate Defence and Security of the Frontier Inhabitants of this Province. [Colophon:] *Annapolis: Printed by Jonas Green, Printer to the Province.* 1758. Small folio, pp. 58. 45044

Acts of Assembly, passed in the Province of Maryland, from 1692 to 1715. *London: Printed by John Baskett,* ... MDCCXXIII. Folio, pp. xi, (viii), 183. H. 45045

Acts of Assembly,|Of the Province of|Maryland,|Enacted| At a Session of Assembly, begun and held|at the City of Annapolis, in the said Province,|on Tuesday the 12th Day of July, in the Eleventh|Year of the Dominion of the Right Honourable | Charles Lord Baron of Baltemore, abso-|lute Lord and Proprietary of the Provinces of | Maryland and Avalon, &c. Annoq; Dom' 1726. | By Authority. | *Annapolis: Printed by W. Parks.* [n. d.] Small folio, pp. 8. 45046

Continued annually and semi-annually, under the title of "Acts, and Laws," in small folio, until 1762; after this in folio, until 1798; from 1799 to 1811 in quarto form, though folio in fold; after 1812 all were in octavo form.

Acts, Of the Province of Maryland, Made and Passed At a Session of Assembly, begun and held at the City of Annapolis, on Tuesday the Second Day of October, in the Third Year of the Dominion of the Right Honourable Frederick, Lord Baron of Baltimore, Absolute Lord and Proprietary of the Province of Maryland, and Avalon, &c. Annoque Domini, 1753. Published by Authority. *Annapolis: Printed by Jonas Green, Printer to the Province; and are to be Sold at his Printing-Office in Charles-Street.* 1754. Folio, pp. 84. 45047

Acts passed at Different Sessions ... concerning the Navigation of the River Susquehanna ... . *Baltimore: Printed by W. Pechin.* 1797. 8vo, pp. 37. H. 45048

Address and Resolutions adopted at the Meeting of the Southern Rights Convention of Maryland, held in ... Baltimore, February ... 1861: ... *Baltimore: Printed by J. B. Rose & Co.* 1861. 8vo, pp. 14. H. 45049

Address of the Convention of National Republicans, at Baltimore, to the Voters of Maryland. [*Baltimore.* 1830.] 8vo, pp. 8.

Signed by S. C. Leakin, and others.

Address of the Democratic Members of the Legislature to the People of Maryland. *Annapolis: Geo. Johnston, Printer.* 1843. 8vo, pp. 16. 45051

Address of the Jackson Central Committee to the People of Maryland, on Subjects connected with the approaching Elections in the State. *Baltimore.* 1830. 8vo, pp. 16. 45052

Address of the Jackson State Convention ... on the late and approaching Election for President. *Baltimore: Printed at the Jackson Press.* 1827. 8vo, pp. 19, (1). 45053

Relative to Andrew Jackson.

Address of the Unconditional Union. *See* [Hill (W. B.]

Address of the Union State ... Committee. *See* [Mayer (B.)]

Address of the Union State Central Committee, with the Proceedings of the Meeting, at Temperance Temple, August 26, 1863, with the Resolutions of the State Convention. *Baltimore: Printed by Bull & Tuttle.* 1863. 8vo, pp. 16. 45054

Address of the Vestry of Christ Church, Hagerstown, to the Protestant Episcopalians of the Diocese of Maryland. *Hagerstown: Printed by Fleaner & Boyd.* 1844. 16mo, pp. 24. 45055

Address of the Young Men of the National Republican Party, or the Fifth Congressional District, to the Young Men of ... Maryland. [n. p. about 1832.] 8vo, pp. 10. 45056

Address to the Free and Independent Citizens of Maryland; and particularly ... of Baltimore, being a Statement of Facts, and a Brief Exposition of Chartered Monopoly, Usurpation and Outrage, under the Sanction of Law. *Baltimore.* 1820. 8vo, pp. 43. 45057

Relates to charges on turnpike roads. Another address, on the same subject, was published in 1860.

An Address to the Members of the Protestant Episcopal Church in Maryland on the Condition of the Diocese. By a Layman [John I. Donaldson]. *Baltimore: Lucas and Deaver.* 1829. 8vo, pp. 67. 45058

An Address to the People of Charles, Calvert, and St. Mary's Counties, Maryland. [n. p. n. d.] 8vo, pp. 35. 45059

Signed by P. Emerson, and others. A Jackson document.

Address to the People of Maryland, by a Farmer and Landholder of Jessup's Cut, Maryland. [On Emancipation. *Baltimore:*] *Bull & Tuttle.* 1863. 8vo, pp. 8. 45060

Address to the People of Maryland by the General Assembly, in Extra Session. *Frederick: Beale H. Richardson, Printer.* 1861. 8vo, pp. 4. 45061

Address to the People of Maryland, by the Whig Central Committee of the State. [*Baltimore.* 1840.] 8vo, pp. 8.

An Address to the People of Maryland, from Their Delegates in the late National Republican Convention: ... . *Baltimore: Printed by Sands & Neilson.* 1832. 8vo, pp. 62. 45063

An Address to the People of Maryland, on the Origin, Progress and Present State of French Aggression, with a Sketch of the Infamous Attempts to degrade the Government of the United States, and some Reflections on the late Proceedings in Congress; By [L. P. Dennis] a Member of the House of Representatives. *Philadelphia: Printed by John Fenno.* 1798. 8vo, pp. 76, (1), Appendix, iv. 45064

An Address to the People of Maryland, on the subject of the Presidential Election. [In favor of Calhoun. *Baltimore.* 1827.] 8vo, pp. 17. 45065

An Address to the People of Maryland, Respecting Some Abuses that Exist, and Improvements that may be made in the Laws of the State. By a Citizen. [n. p.:] *Printed for the Author.* [1804.] 18mo, pp. 27. 45066

Address to the Voters ... Residing within the first Five Wards of ... Baltimore, also a Reply to the Hon. Isaac McKim ... . *Baltimore: Printed by Sands & Neilson.* 1834. 8vo, pp. 30, (1).

An Address to the Voters. *See* [Spence (Carroll)].

Annual Message of the Executive, to the Legislature of Maryland. December Session, 1836. *Annapolis: Jeremiah Hughes, Printer.* 1836. 8vo, pp. 15. Continued. 45068

An Answer to the Queries on the Proprietary Government of Maryland, inserted in the Public Ledger. Also, An Answer to Remarks upon a Message sent by the Upper to the Lower House of Assembly of Maryland, 1762. Published in 1763. Containing a Defence of the Lord-Proprietor from the Calumnies and

Misrepresentations of the Remarker, and also a Vindication of the Upper House, in their Conduct relative to a Supply Bill for his Majesty's Service. By a Friend to Maryland. [n. p.:] *Printed in the year* 1764. 8vo, pp. (2), 160. c. 45069

The copy of this tract, in the Library of Congress, is credited to Mr. Calvert. *See also* "A Bill for raising a Supply," No. 45085, *and* "Remarks upon a Message."

An Appeal to the Bar and the Freemen of Maryland from the refusal of Baltimore City Court to grant a Rule requiring Richard N. Allen to shew cause why an information of Quo Warranto should not be exhibited against him for usurping the office of Commissioner of Insolvent Debtors for the City and County of Baltimore. *Baltimore.* 1823. 12mo, pp. 16. 45070

Appeal to the Citizens of the Commonwealth of Maryland on the License Question. [*Baltimore.* 1846.] 8vo, pp. 8. 45071

Appeal to the People of Maryland on the subject of the Proceedings of the House of Delegates on the Contested Election of Calvert County. [*Annapolis:*] *Printed by J. Green.* 1820. 8vo, pp. (2), 30, Appendix, (2). 45072

Articles | of | Agreement | made and concluded upon between | The Right Honourable The | Lord Proprietary of Maryland, | and The Honourable The Proprietarys of Pensilvania, &c. | touching the Limits and Boundaries of the Two Provinces. | With | The Commission, | Constituting Certain Persons to Execute the same. | *Philadelphia:* | *Printed by B. Franklin, at the New Printing Office* | *near the Market.* M,DCC,XXXIII. | Folio, pp. 19. Map. c.

At a Meeting of the Committee appointed by the several Counties of the Province of Maryland, at ... Annapolis, the 22d Day of June, 1774, and continued ... . [*Annapolis.* 1774.] Folio, pp. (2). 45074

Resolutions, and a list of delegates to the general Congress.

At a Meeting of the Delegates ... of the Province of Maryland, at the City of Annapolis, ... 26th of July, 1775, and continued till the 14th day of August, in the same year ... . [n. p. n. d.] Folio, pp. (4). 45075

This is a resolution relative to the enrollment of minute-men, etc., consequent upon the acts of Great Britain in Massachusetts.

At a Meeting of the Deputies appointed by the several Counties of the Province of Maryland, at the City of Annapolis, by Adjournment, on the 8th day of December, 1774, and continued

till the 12th day of the same month. [*Annapolis.* 1774.] Folio, 1 leaf. 45076

Probably a supplement to the "Maryland Gazette." The three above titles are a part of the Proceedings of the Conventions of 1774–5, and are reprinted in Annapolis and Baltimore.

Report of the Auditor General to the Legislature of the State of Maryland, December Session, 1826. Published by Authority. *Annapolis: Printed by J. Hughes.* 1826. 8vo, pp. 6. 2 folded Accounts. 45077

Bank of Maryland. Extracts from the Correspondence and Minutes of the Trustees of the Bank of Maryland, published by J. B. Morris & R. W. Gill, two of the Trustees, having relation principally to their intercourse with Poultney, Ellicott & Co. and Evan Poultney. *Baltimore: Jas. Lucas & E. K. Deaver.* 1835. 8vo, pp. 6, 65. 45078

Report of the Case of the Bank of Maryland *vs.* Samuel Poultney and William M. Ellicott, trading under the firm of Poultney, Ellicott & Co., tried before Harford County Court, March Term, 1836. *Baltimore.* 1836. 8vo, pp. 166. 45079

Also: The Report and Testimony taken before the Joint Committee ... of Maryland, to which was referred the Memorials of John B. Morris, ... and others, praying indemnity for losses sustained by reason of the Riots in Baltimore in ... [1835] ... . *Annapolis: William M'Neir, Printer.* [1836.] 8vo, pp. 77. + Testimony only. [*Ibid.*] 8vo, pp. 93. — Statement of the Condition of the Bank of Maryland. [*Baltimore.*] 1835. Folio, pp. (4). — Statement of the Judgments confessed by Evan Poultney, at the suit of the Trustees of the Bank of Maryland. And Report of the Trial of Evan Poultney, William M. Ellicott, and Samuel Poultney, for a Conspiracy. Harford County Court, March Term, 1836. *Baltimore.* 1836. 8vo, pp. iii, 15. — Testimony of William G. Read, taken before the Joint Committee ... of Maryland in behalf of the Civil Authorities of Baltimore, to which was referred the Memorial of John B. Morris, ... and others, praying indemnity for losses sustained by reason of the Riots in Baltimore in ... [1835]. *Annapolis: William M'Neir, Printer.* [1836.] 8vo, pp. 28. — Testimony of Francis M. Fowler and Evan Poultney, in the Case of the Bank of Maryland *vs.* Samuel Poultney & William M. Ellicott: Tried before Harford County Court. ... 1836. *Baltimore.* 1840. 8vo, pp. 63, 97. — To the Creditors of the Bank of Maryland. [*Baltimore.* 1834.] 8vo, pp. 7. *See also* Ellicott (Thomas), Vol. VI., No. 22220, Johnson (R.), Vol. IX., No. 36271–2, *and* [Poultney (Evan)].

Bank Statement. Western Shore Treasury. *Annapolis.* 1835. 8vo. 45080

Charter of the Union Bank of Maryland, and its Supplements, together with the Acts of Assembly applicable thereto, and the By-Laws. *Baltimore: Jas. Lucas & E. K. Deaver.* 1835. 8vo, pp. v, 154. 45081

Also: Proceedings of the Stockholders of the Union Bank of Maryland, in General Meeting, in June and July, 1830. *Baltimore: John D. Toy.* 1830. 8vo, pp. (3), 68.

... Report of the Select Committee ... [on] ... the Memorials and Petitions of ... Citizens ... Praying the establishment of a Financial Institution under the style of the Bank of the State of Maryland. *Annapolis: Printed by J. Green.* 1830. 8vo, pp. 48.

Report of the Select Committee relative to the Establishment of a [Maryland] State Bank and a National Currency. January 26, 1835. *Annapolis.* 1835. 8vo, pp. 52. 45083

Testimony taken by the Committee of the House of Delegates, appointed to investigate the condition of the several Banks in the State of Maryland. [*Annapolis.* 1838.] 8vo, pp. 247, lxii. 3 folded Tables. 45084

A | Bill | for raising a | Supply | for | his Majesty's Service: | which was | Framed by the Lower House of Assembly of the Pro- | vince of Maryland, at a Session held at the City of Anna- | polis, in March 1762, and Rejected by the Up- | per House. | To which is prefixed, | All the Messages which passed between the Two Houses, | relating thereto. | *Annapolis:* | *Printed by Jonas Green, Printer to the Province,* | MDCCLXII. | Sm. 4to, pp. 10, (4), [11]–59.

See also "An Answer to the Queries," No. 45069, *and* "Remarks upon a Message."

Boundary. Communication of E. F. Chambers, Esq. One of the Commissioners on the Western Boundary to the Legislature. *Annapolis: J. Hughes, Printer.* [1825.] 8vo, pp. 7. 45086

Copy of a Correspondence between Governor Thomas of Maryland, and Governor Tazewell of Virginia, in relation to the Unsettled Divisional Boundary Lines between the two States. ... *Annapolis: Jeremiah Hughes, Printer.* 1835. 8vo, pp. 24.

Indenture of Agreement. *See* Vol. IX., No. 34439.

Message from the Governor [P. F. Thomas] of Maryland, transmitting the Reports of the Joint Commissioners, and of Lt. Col. Graham, U. S. Engineers, in relation to the Intersection of the Boundary Lines of the States of Maryland, Pennsylvania & Delaware. *Washington: Printed by Gideon and Co.* 1850. 8vo, pp. 87. Map. B. 45088

The cover-title to this differs slightly. *See also* Pennsylvania.

Messages from the Governors of Maryland and Pennsylvania, transmitting the Reports of the Joint Commissioners, and of Lieut. Col. Graham, ... in relation to the Intersection of the Boundary Lines of the States of Maryland, Pennsylvania and

Delaware, being a portion of Mason and Dixon's Line. ... Second Edition. *Chicago: F. Fulton & Co.* 1862. 8vo, pp. 95. Map.

Report of the Commissioners appointed by the Legislature of Maryland and Virginia to Run and Mark the Division Line between Maryland and Virginia, on the Eastern Shore of Chesapeake Bay. ... *Annapolis: Wm. Thompson, Printer.* 1868. 8vo, pp. 36. 45090

Also: Communication from the Attorney General [Josiah Bayly] relative to the Suit of Maryland against Virginia. *Annapolis: Wm. M'Neir—Print.* 1836. 8vo, pp. 38. — The Depositions of Witnesses taken in the Arbitration respecting the Boundary Line between the States of Maryland and Virginia. *Baltimore: Charles Harvey & Co.* 1875. 8vo, pp. 159, (1). — Documents relative to the Southern and Western Boundaries of this State. [*Annapolis.* 1834.] 8vo, pp. 8. — Executive Message on the Western Boundary of the State. *Annapolis: J. Hughes, Printer.* [1825.] 8vo, pp. 4. — Mr. Maulsby. ... Report ... on the Bill to Settle and Adjust the Western Boundary Line of the State ... . *Annapolis: Jeremiah Hughes, Printer.* 1837. 8vo, pp. 5. — Mr. Pigman. Report and Resolutions relative to the Southern and Western Limits of this State. *Annapolis: Wm. M'Neir—Print.* 1832. 8vo, pp. 52. — Mr. Pigman's Second Report ... with the Accompanying Documents. [*Annapolis.* 1834.] 8vo, pp. 11. — Report and Journal of Proceedings of the Joint Commissioners to adjust the Boundary Line of ... Maryland and Virginia. ... *Annapolis: Wm. T. Iglehart & Co., Printers.* 1874. 8vo, pp. 344. — Report of Progress of the Survey of the Sounds lying on the Eastern Shore of Virginia, Maryland and Delaware: ... [*Annapolis: William M'Neir, Printer.* 1835.] 8vo, cover-title, pp. 23. — Report of Wm. J. Aydelott, a Member of the Joint Committee appointed by the General Assembly of Maryland to adjust and mark the Eastern Shore Boundary between Maryland and Virginia. *Annapolis: S. S. Mills, L. F. Colton & Co., Printers.* 1872. 8vo, pp. 11. — Report of the Commissioners concerning the Western Limits of the State. *Annapolis: J. Hughes, Printer.* [1825.] 8vo, pp. 19. — Report of the Special Committee, on ... Retracing and Marking the Western and Southern Boundary. [*Annapolis.* 1858.] 8vo, pp. 4. — Report on the Survey of the Boundary between Maryland and Virginia. By Thomas J. Lee, Commissioner. *Annapolis: Thomas J. Wilson.* 1860. 8vo, pp. 8. — The Southern Boundary of Maryland. [A Report by T. J. Lee. *Baltimore.* 1860.] 8vo, pp. 24. Map. *See also* Pennsylvania and Virginia.

A Brief Exposition of the Leading Principles of a Bank. Humbly submitted to the Consideration of the Honourable the Legislature of Maryland. *Baltimore: Printed by Edwards & Allen.* 1795. 8vo, pp. 45. 45091

A Brief Sketch, of Maryland, its Geography, Boundaries, History, Government, Legislation, Internal Improvements, &c. [By Jeremiah Hughes. *Annapolis:*] *Printed for the Publisher.* 1845. 18mo, pp. vi, 256. 45092

Usually found with "The Maryland Pocket Annual," for 1846.

Brief Statements of Facts shewing the Origin, Progress and Necessity of African Colonization. Addressed to the People of ... Maryland. *Annapolis.* 1836. 12mo, pp. 36. 45093

By his Excellency The Governor and Council, 10th July, 1761. [Colophon:] *Annapolis: Printed by Jonas Green, Printer to the Province.* 1761. Sm. folio, pp. 8. 45094

A message to the Lower House, in reference to the accounts of a Mr. Darnall, late Naval Officer of Patuxent.

By his Excellency Horatio Sharpe, Esq; Governor and Commander in Chief in and over the Province of Maryland. A Brief. [n. p. n. d.] Folio, 1 leaf. 45095

Dated "6th May, 1760;" in reference to the fire in Boston, 20th March, 1760.

Bystander: or a Series of Letters on the subject of the "Legislative Choice" of Electors in Maryland: ... Addressed to the People of Maryland. *Baltimore: Printed by Yundt and Brown.* M,DCCC. 16mo, pp. 30. 45096

By Robert Goodloe Harper. *See* Tyler's "Life of R. B. Taney."

Canals. Minority Report [by J. C. Le Grand] of the Committee on Internal Improvements, on the subject of the Chesapeake and Ohio Canal. [*Annapolis.* 1841.] 8vo, pp. 38.

See also Baltimore, Vol. I., *and* our Vol. III., p. 573.

Report by the Maryland Commissioners on a proposed Canal from Baltimore to Conewago. ... *Baltimore: Fielding Lucas, Jr.* 1823. 8vo, pp. 84, (1). 2 Maps. 45098

Also: Approximate Estimate of that Portion of the "Brookville Route," of the Maryland Canal, surveyed during the Summer of 1838, under the direction of Col. J. J. Abert. [*Annapolis.* 1839.] 8vo, pp. 52. — Report of the Commissioners appointed to examine into the practicability of a Canal from Baltimore to the Potomac, together with the Engineer's Report. *Baltimore: Fielding Lucas, Jun.* 1823. 8vo, pp. 69. Map. — Report of the Engineer [I. Trimble] appointed by the Commissioner of the Mayor ... of Baltimore, on the subject of the Maryland Canal. *Baltimore: Printed by Lucas & Deaver.* 1837. 8vo, pp. 27. — Statement in reply to an order of the House ... 9th February, 1839. ... Relative to Surveys made in ... 1838, for the Route of the Maryland Canal. [*Annapolis.* 1839.] 8vo, pp. 39. Map.

Case of Charles Lord Baltemore. *See* [Calvert (G.)], 10083.

The Case of the Province of Maryland, touching the outrageous Riots which have been Committed in the Borders of that Province, by the Inhabitants of Pensilvania. [*London.* 1737.] Folio, pp. 3. 45099

Signed by J. Strange. *See also* Pennsylvania.

Catalogus Provinciæ Marylandiæ Societatis Jesu ineunte anno MDCCCLVII. *Baltimori.* 1857. 8vo, pp. 36. Continued. H.

Catechism, confuting Popery, &c., for Christians in Maryland. *Boston.* 1707. 12mo. 45101

Imperfect title from Thomas' "History of Printing," Vol. II.

The Central Committee of National Republicans of ... Baltimore, to the People of Maryland. [Colophon:] *Baltimore: Printed by Sands & Neilson.* [n. d.] 8vo, pp. 18. 45102

Signed by Luke Tiernan, and others.

The Chancellor's Memorial to the General Assembly of Maryland. *Baltimore: Printed by John D. Toy.* 1825. 8vo, pp. 73.

By Theodorick Bland. In reference to a reduction of the salary of the Chancellor. Corrected title of our No. 5862, Vol. II.

The Charter | of | Maryland. | [*London.* 1632.] 8vo, pp. 23.

This is probably the first publication of the Charter of Maryland. It has no date of publication; but the charter itself is dated June 20, 1632.

The Charter of Maryland; with an Abridgment of the Acts of their Assembly. [n. p. n. d.] 8vo. P. 45105

Charter of the Colony of Maryland; together with the Debates and Proceedings of the Upper and Lower Houses of Assembly, in the Years 1722, 1723, 1724, and 1725. *Philadelphia: Printed by Andrew Bradford.* 1725. Folio. 45106

A Collection of the British Statutes in Force in Maryland, according to the Report thereof made to the General Assembly by the late Chancellor Kilty; with Notes and References to the Acts of Assembly and the Code, and to the principal English and Maryland Cases. By Julian J. Alexander ... . *Baltimore: Cushings & Bailey.* 1870. 8vo, pp. xlvi, (1), 847. 45107

A Collection of the Governor's Several Speeches and the Addresses of each House, at a Convention of the Assembly, begun the first of May, 1739. [*Annapolis: Printed by Jonas Green.* 1739.] Folio, pp. (2), 80. C. 45108

Communication from the Executive of Delaware, to the Governor of Maryland ... Relative to a Union with the Eastern Shore of Maryland. *Annapolis: J. Hughes, Printer.* 1833. 8vo, pp. 4.

Communication from the Messrs. Howard and M'Neill in reply to a request from the Committee on Internal Improvements ... of the House of Delegates, to ascertain the ... Advantages of a Rail Road from Baltimore to Washington ... . *Annapolis: Jonas Green, Jan.* 1831. 8vo, pp. 12. 45110

A Compleat Collection of the Laws of Maryland. With an Index and Marginal Notes ... . *Annapolis: Printed by William Parks.* MDCCXXVII. Folio, pp. (4), 300, (6). H. 45111

The first complete collection of laws.

A Compilation of the Insolvent Laws of Maryland ... with the Decision of the Court of Appeals ... on ... Insolvency .. By a Member of the Baltimore Bar. ... *Baltimore: John J. Harrod.* 1831. 8vo, pp. iv, 3–235. 45112

Considerations on the ... Removal. *See* [Hanson (A. C.)]

The Constitution of the State of Maryland. *Abingdon (Md.): Printed by Daniel P. Ruff.* 1806. 16mo, pp. 93. + *Annapolis: Printed by J. Green.* 1821. 16mo, pp. 34. 45113

Also: Mr. Carroll. ... Chairman. Report of the Select Committee of the House ... on the Constitution of Maryland. *Annapolis: Jeremiah Hughes, Printer.* 1836. 8vo, pp. 8.

The Constitution of ... Maryland, ... adopted by the Convention ... at ... Annapolis, November 4th, 1850 ... . *Baltimore: Printed by John Murphy & Co.* 1851. 8vo, pp. 70. + With Marginal Notes ... and an Appendix ... By Edward Otis Hinkley, Esq. ... *Baltimore: John Murphy & Co.* 1855. 8vo, pp. 108. + [*Ibid.*] 1862. 8vo, pp. 71, (1). 45114

The Constitution of the State of Maryland, ... Adopted ... April 27, 1864, and ... Ratified ... October, 1864. With ... Notes ... By Edward Otis Hinkley. *Baltimore: John Murphy & Co.* 1864. 8vo, pp. 107, (1). 45115

The Constitution of the State of Maryland, ... Adopted ... May 8th, 1867 ... . Submitted ... September 18th, 1867. ... *Annapolis: George Colton.* 1867. 8vo, pp. (2), 32. + [The same, in German.] *Baltimore.* 1867. 8vo, pp. (2), 32. 45116

The Constitution of the State of Maryland, ... Ratified by the People, September 18, 1867. With ... Notes ... . By Edward Otis Hinkley ... . *Baltimore: John Murphy & Co.* 1867. 8vo, pp. 156. 45117

Copies of Some Records & Depositions Relating to the Great Bohemia Mannor [*sic*] lying on Bohemia River in Maryland. Memorandum, with two Patents granted to Augustine Herman, the one for 6000 Acres, called Bohemia Mannor [*sic*] and the other for 1000 Acres, called Little Bohemia. ... [*London,* after 1722.] Folio, pp. over 8. 45118

Copy of Proposed Amendment to the Constitution of the United States [April 30, 1861]. *Frederick: Beale H. Richardson.* 1861. 8vo, pp. 4. 45119

Correspondence between the Governor of Maryland and the Sheriff of Frederick County. *Frederick: Beale H. Richardson.* 1861. 8vo, pp. 4. 45120

Correspondence between the Treasurer of the W. Shore of Maryland, and the ... United States Treasury, on the ... Claim of the State oe [*sic*] Maryland upon the United States, for Interest due upon Sums advanced by the State during the late War. *Annapolis: Printed by Jeremiah Hughes.* 1827. 8vo, pp. 35. 3 folded Accounts. BA., C. 45121

Correspondence relative to the Insurrection at Harper's Ferry, 17th October, 1859. *Annapolis: B. H. Richardson.* 1860. 8vo, pp. 79. 45122

Debates and Proceedings of the Maryland Reform Convention to Revise the State Constitution; to which are prefixed the Bill of Rights and Constitution, as adopted. Published by order of the Convention. *Annapolis: William M'Neir, Official Printer.* 1851. 2 vols., 8vo, pp. 20, 52, [25]–550; 890, Index, 52. C.

The Debates of the Constitutional Convention of ... Maryland, Assembled at ... Annapolis, ... April 27, 1864: Being a ... report of the debates and proceedings of the Convention, together with the old Constitution ... . Official: Wm. Blair Lord, Reporter. ... *Annapolis: Printed by Richard P. Bayly.* MDCCCLXIV. 3 vols., 8vo, pp. 744; (2), [745]–1384; (2), 1385–1988. 45124

A | Declaration | of | Rights, | and the | Constitution | and | Form of Government, | Agreed to by the Delegates of Maryland, in | free and full Convention assembled. | [August 14, 1776.] *Annapolis: Printed by Frederick Green.* [1776.] 16mo, pp. 43. C.

The Declaration of Rights and the Constitution of Maryland ... with the several Amendments by Acts of the Assembly. Prepared and Revised by George Hebb. *Baltimore: Willam Wooddy.* 1824. 18mo, pp. 56. 45126

The Declaration of the Reasons. *See* our Vol. V., No. 19180.

A Digest of the Laws. *See* Herty (T.), Vol. VI., No. 31596.

Diocese of Maryland. Amendments proposed for the Constitution. ... [*Baltimore.* 185–.] 8vo, pp. 4. 45127

By John H. Alexander. *See* Protestant Episcopal Church.

Documents accompanying the Governors [*sic*, A. W. Bradford] Message to the Legislature of Maryland. *Annapolis: Bull & Tuttle.* 1864. 8vo, pp. 195, (1). 45128

Relates entirely to the Civil War. 1861–5. Also: Documents of the House of Delegates of Maryland, in Extra Session, April, 1861. [*Frederick: E. S. Riley.* 1861.] 8vo, pp. 24, 4, 4, 8, 48, 16. Consists of important matters relating to the Civil War.

Documents of the House of Delegates for 1840. *Annapolis.* 1840. 8vo. Continued. 45129

Documents of the Senate of Maryland, in Extra Session, April, 1861. [*Frederick: B. H. Richardson.* 1861.] 8vo, pp. 24, 4, 4, 4, 5. 45130

An Earnest Appeal to the People of Maryland upon the Important Issues of the Times. ... Issued by the State Democratic Executive Committee, Baltimore City, October 8, 1860. *Baltimore: Printed by J. B. Rose & Co.* 1860. 8vo, pp. 16. 45131

Education. An Act providing a Uniform System of Free Public Schools for ... Maryland. Passed ... 1865. *Annapolis: Richard P. Bayly, Printer.* 1865. 8vo, pp. 35. 45132

Documents accompanying the Governor's Message ... 1822, respecting the Proceedings of several States, upon the subject of appropriating the Public Lands for the support of Schools. *Annapolis.* 1823. 8vo. 45133

Report of the Committee on Public Instruction. ... 1824. *Annapolis: J. Hughes, Printer.* [n. d.] Folio, pp. 16. 45134

Report of the Principal of the State Normal School showing the Condition of the Public Schools of Maryland, with the Reports of the County School Commissioners, for ... 1869. *Annapolis: Wm. Thompson, Printer.* 1870. 8vo, pp. 237. Continued. 45135

Report ... [by V. Maxcy] relative to Appropriations of Public Lands for ... Education. ... January 30, 1821. ... [*Annapolis:*] *J. Green—Print.* 1821. 8vo, pp. 23. + *Concord: Printed by Hill and Moore.* 1821. 8vo, pp. 29. H. 45136

Also: Report and Resolutions on the subject of the Maryland Report, ... relative to School Lands. Published by Authority. *Columbus.* 1822. 8vo, pp. 21. *See* [Sparks (Jared)].

The School System of Maryland. *See* [Van Bokkelen (L.)]

State Education not radically wrong; Being a Reply to an Article in the Presbyterial Critic, 1855. By a Friend of Education. *Baltimore.* 1856. 8vo, pp. 31. 45137

Also: First Annual Report of the Superintendent of Public Instruction, ... of Maryland, ... 31st December, 1827. *Annapolis: J. Hughes—Printer.* 1828. 8vo, pp. (2), 37. BA.—First Report of the State Superintendent of Public Instruction, ... with an Appendix containing Reports of the ... School Commissioners ... . *Baltimore: Printed by William K. Boyle.* 1866. 8vo, pp. 86, (1). Continued. H.—First Annual Report of the State Superintendent of Public Instruction, with the Reports of the ... School Commissioners, and ... other Documents, ... June 30, 1866. *Annapolis: Henry A. Lucas, Printer.* 1867. 8vo, pp. 264, lxv, (4). + Second Report ... 1867. *Annapolis: Wm. Thompson.* 1868. 8vo, pp. 224. Continued.—Erster Jahres Bericht des Stadts Superintendenten des öffentlichen Schulwesens ... von Maryland, 1866. *Annapolis.* 1867. 8vo.—Report of the Committee on Education establishing a Uniform System of Instruction in the Public Schools of this State. Reported ... By M. Kerney, Chairman. *Annapolis: Thomas E. Martin, Printer.* 1852. 8vo, pp. 12.— ... Report of the State Superintendent of Public Instruction ... with a Bill entitled "A Uniform System of Public Instruction," etc. *Annapolis: Richard P. Bayly, Printer.* 1865. 8vo, pp. 128.—Report upon ... a Code for the support of Common Schools, prepared by J. C. Le Grand, J. S. Owens & J. H. T. Magruder ... . *Annapolis: Printed by George Johnston.* 1843. 8vo, pp. 47. H.

Election Laws of the State of Maryland. Published by order of the Governor and Council, in pursuance of a resolve of the General Assembly, ... 1819. *Annapolis.* 1820. 8vo. C.

Election Laws of the State of Maryland, ... With such Portions of the Constitution as relate to the Elective Franchise. *Baltimore: George W. Bowen & Co.* 1856. 8vo, pp. 45. 45139

Emancipation in Maryland. [*Philadelphia.* 1864.] Folio, Illustrated Title, pp. (2). 45140

The title is a view in commemoration of emancipation in Maryland, November 1, 1864. *See also* our Vol. IV., No. 22401.

... Executive Communication ... Inclosing the Correspondence with the Executive of Pennsylvania, and other Papers in Relation to the Demand made by the latter for the delivery of Nathan & Bemis, and others, as offenders against the laws of that State. [On Kidnapping. *Annapolis.* 1838.] 8vo, pp. 42.

Executive Communication to the General Assembly, ... December Session, 1818, on ... Turnpike Roads. ... *Annapolis: John Chandler, Printer.* 1819. 8vo, pp. 45. 45142

Executive Communication to the House of Delegates relative to the State's Claim against the General Government for Monies Expended during the late War. February 1, 1819. [n. p.] 1819. 8vo, pp. 55. 45143

These executive communications, on various subjects, are published at each session.

Extracts from the Proceedings of the Committee of Observation for the Elizabethtown (now Hagerstown) District during 1775–76–77. *Baltimore.* 1862. 8vo, pp. 12. 45144

"The Federal Union, it Must be Preserved!" The Crisis ... The Remedy! Address of the State Central Committee of the National Union Democracy to the People of Maryland. [*Baltimore.* 1860.] 8vo, pp. 8. 45145

Forms of Government, containing an abstract of the original Charter of Maryland, the Bill of Rights and Constitution of the State. *Annapolis.* 1827. 16mo. 45146

Four Letters to the People, on the undue Influence of Bank Directors, in the Political Affairs of the State of Maryland. *Baltimore.* 1804. 8vo. C. 45147

Fraternal Appeal and other Documents, from the Maryland Tract Society. [On Slavery. *Baltimore.* 1858.] 8vo, pp. 7.

The Free Negro Question. *See* [Jacobs (C. W.)], VI. 35498.

Freedmen's Convention at Annapolis, July, 1864. [n. p. n. d.] 8vo. 45149

General Public Statutory Law and Public Local Law ... from the year 1692 to 1839, inclusive, with Annotations thereto, and a Copious Index. By Clement Dorsey. ... *Baltimore: Printed by John D. Toy.* 1840. 3 vols., 8vo, pp. (2), li, 922; (2), 923–1944; (2), [1945]–2848. C. 45150

General Report of the Committee on Internal Improvement. *Annapolis: Printed by Jonas Green.* 1831. 8vo, pp. (2), 3, 3, 5, 12. 45151

A series of documents, numbered from 1 to 5, each with title and paged separately.

Geology. Wm. D. Merrick, Chairman, Report of the Committee on Internal Improvemet [*sic*], relative to a Map and Survey of the State of Maryland. *Annapolis: Printed by Jeremiah Hughes.* 1834. 8vo, pp. 6. 45152

Annual Report of the Geologist [J. T. Ducatel] of Maryland. 1837. [*Annapolis.* 1838.] 8vo, pp. 39, (1). 2 Maps. + For 1838. 8vo, pp. 33, (1). 4 Plates. + For 1839. 8vo, pp. 45, (1). 2 Maps. + For 1840. 8vo, pp. 59, (1). 3 Maps. C. + [*Ibid.*] 8vo, pp. 46, (1). 3 Maps. 45153

Report of the Select Committee relative to the Expediency of Procuring a Map of the State. ... *Annapolis: Printed by J. Hughes.* 1833. 8vo, pp. 10. 45154

Report on the Projected Survey of the State of Maryland ... . [By Julius T. Ducatel and J. H. Alexander.] *Annapolis: Printed by Jeremiah Hughes.* 1834. 8vo, pp. 34. Table. + [Another] Report. *Annapolis: Printed by Wm. M'Neir.* 1834. 8vo, pp. 58. 2 Maps, Table, (1). 45155

Report [by J. H. Alexander and J. T. Ducatel] on the New Map of Maryland, 1834. [n. p. n. d.] 8vo, pp. 15. Map.

Also: Report on the New Map of Maryland, 1835. [n. p. n. d.] 8vo, pp. 84, (1). 6 Maps and Errata. + [*Ibid.*] 8vo, pp. 42. 2 Maps.—Report of the Engineer [J. H. Alexander] and Geologist [J. T. Ducatel] in relation to the New Map, to the Executive of Maryland. *Annapolis: William M'Neir.* 1835. 8vo, pp. 96, Index, 1. 6 Maps and Plate.—Report of the Engineer and Geologist in relation to the New Map ... . *Annapolis: William M'Neir, Printer.* 1836. 8vo, pp. 89, (1). 6 Maps and Plan. + [*Ibid.*] 8vo, pp. 104. 5 Maps. + [*Ibid.*] 8vo, pp. 117. 6 Maps.—Report of Select Committee ... [on] Expediency of repealing the Act to provide for completing a New Map and Geological Survey of this State. [*Annapolis.* 1838.] 8vo, pp. 4. + [*Ibid.*] 8vo, pp. 8.—Trigonometrical Survey for the New Map of Maryland [By J. H. Alexander], 1841. *Baltimore, February* 2, 1841. 8vo, pp. 8. + Another Report. *Baltimore, February* 19, 1841. 8vo, pp. 4.

... Report of James Higgins, M.D., State Agricultural Chemist, to the House of Delegates ... [*Annapolis:*] *Wm. M'Neir, Printer.* [1851.] 8vo, pp. 92. M. + The Second Report ... . *Annapolis: Printed by Thomas E. Martin.* MDCCCLII. 8vo, pp. 126. + The Third Report ... . *Baltimore: Sands & Mills.* 1853. 8vo, pp. 160. + The Fourth Report ... . *Baltimore: Sherwood & Co.* 1854. 8vo, pp. 92. + The Fifth Report ... . *Annapolis: Requa and Wilson.* 1856. 8vo, pp. 90. + The Sixth Report ... . *Annapolis: Bull & Tuttle.* 1858. 8vo, pp. 96, xxii. H. 45157

First Report of Philip T. Tyson, State Agricultural Chemist ... of Maryland, ... 1860. [*Annapolis: Printed by Elihu S. Riley.*] 1860. 8vo, pp. xi, 5–145, Appendix, 20. Map. + Second Report ... January, 1862. *Annapolis: Thomas J. Wilson, Printer.* 1862. 8vo, pp. 92. C. 45158

Also: Communication from John H. Alexander, Esq. Topographical Engineer ... . *Annapolis: William M'Neir, Printer.* 1838. 8vo, pp. 5. + [Another. *Annapolis.* 1838.] 8vo, pp. 4. + Report. [*Annapolis.* 1842.] 8vo, pp. 5.— ... Report of the Committee on Agriculture, in Relation to the Appointment of an Agricultural Chemist. [*Annapolis.* 1847.] 8vo, pp. 8.—Report of the Treasurer ... Expenses ... in making the Geographical and Geological Surveys of the State. [*Annapolis.* 1838.] 8vo, pp. 3. + [Another. *Annapolis.* 1839.] 8vo, pp. 2.— ... Mr. Wharton. Report of Select Committee appointed ... to Report a Bill to Abolish the Office of State Geologist. [*Annapolis.* 1839.] 8vo, pp. 3.

Proceedings of the Grand Lodge of Free and Accepted Masons of Maryland ... 1853. ... *Baltimore.* 1853. 8vo, pp. 90. Continued. 45159

Also: General Laws. *Baltimore.* 1853. 18mo.

A Historical and Physical Sketch of a Malignant Epidemick, prevalent in Maryland, and some other States, within the last few years. With a brief notice of some opinions which have been published on its nature and treatment. ... *Baltimore: Printed by R. W. Pomeroy & Co.* 1815. 8vo, pp. 168. 45160

History of a Session of the General Assembly of ... Maryland, held at ... Annapolis ... in November, 1785. *Printed in the Year* M,DCC,LXXXVI. 8vo, pp. 44. H. 45161

The History of Maryland. *See* Vol. VIII., No. 32142.

The Hoop-Pole Law: entitled "An Act to declare certain Trespasses Felony, and for other purposes," passed December Session, 1826. [*Baltimore.* 1827.] 8vo, pp. 8. 45162

House of Delegates ... Baltimore ... . Contested Election. Papers on the Contested Election Case from Baltimore. ... Adam Denmead [and others] *vs.* Charles L. Krafft [and others. *Annapolis.* 1860.] 8vo, pp. 334. 45163

See also "Report of the Committee," No. 45328.

Immediate Emancipation in Maryland. *See* Vol. IX. 34362.

The Inaugural Address of Governor P. F. Thomas. Delivered January 3rd, 1848. *Annapolis: Riley & Davis, Printers.* 1848. 8vo, pp. 14. 45164

Also: Inaugural Address ... January 8, 1862. *Annapolis: Thomas J. Wilson.* 1862. 8vo, pp. 15. + Another Edition. *Annapolis: Schley & Cole, Printers.* 1862. 8vo, pp. 15.—Inaugural Address ... January 11th, 1865. [*Annapolis.* 1865.] 8vo, pp. 15.

Index to the Journals of the Senate and House of Delegates ... of Maryland. ... *Annapolis: Requa & Wilson.* 1856–7. 3 vols., 8vo, pp. 1030; 990; 1707. 45165

Index to the Laws of Maryland, from 1818 to 1825. By William Kilty. *Annapolis: Jeremiah Hughes, Printer.* 1827. 8vo, pp. (4), 232. C. 45166

Index to the Laws and Resolutions of Maryland, from 1800 to 1813 inclusive. Published by Authority. *Annapolis: Printed by J. Green.* 1815. 8vo, pp. (2), (227). + From 1826 to 1831.

Annapolis: William M'Neir, Printer. 1832. 8vo, pp. (2), (344). + From 1832 to 1837. [*Ibid.*] 1838. 8vo, pp. (2), (534). + From 1838 to 1845. *Annapolis: Riley & Davis, Printers.* 1846. 8vo, pp. 754. C. 45167

Also: Index to the Printed Bills of the House of Delegates of Maryland, from ... 1824 to ... 1849 inclusive. *Annapolis: Riley and Davis, Printers.* 1850. 8vo, pp. 215.—Index to the Public Documents of the House of Delegates, from ... 1834, to ... 1844, ... *Annapolis: Riley and Davis, Printers.* 1845. 8vo, pp. 144.

The [Maryland] Inebriate Asylum, Report of the Committee on the Temporary Organization of the Asylum, submitted to the ... Trustees ... 1870. *Baltimore: John W. Woods.* 1870. 8vo, pp. (2), 8. 45168

An Inquiry into the Principles of the late Act of the Legislature, for Incorporating the Precincts with the City of Baltimore. *Baltimore.* 1817. 16mo, pp. 35. 45169

Internal Improvements. The Relation of the State to the Baltimore and Ohio Rail Road Company. In the New Constitution. [*Baltimore.* 1867.] 8vo, pp. (4). 45170

Journal of the House of Delegates of Maryland. December Session, 1825. ... *Annapolis: Printed by J. Green.* 1826. 8vo, pp. 420. Continued. 45171

Journal of the Proceedings of the Convention on Internal Improvements of Maryland, held in Baltimore, May 2, 1836. *Baltimore: John D. Toy.* 1836. 8vo, pp. 15. 45172

See also our Vol. I., No. 3039, *and* "Proceedings," No. 45287.

Journal of the Proceedings of the House of Delegates. In Extra Session. *Frederick: E. S. Riley.* 1861. 8vo. + Special Session, December, 1861. *Annapolis: Thomas J. Wilson.* 1861. 8vo, pp. 117. 45173

Journal of the Proceedings of the House of Delegates ... January Session, 1862. *Annapolis: Thomas J. Wilson.* 1862. 8vo, pp. 992. + January Session, 1864. *Annapolis: Bull & Tuttle.* 1864. 8vo, pp. 1144. 45174

This and the following contain much matter relative to the Civil War.

Journal of the Proceedings of the Senate of Maryland, January, 1860. *Annapolis.* 1860. 8vo, pp. 2122. + Special Session, December, 1861. *Annapolis: Schley & Cole.* 1861. 8vo, pp. 569. + January Session, 1864. *Annapolis: Mittag & Sneary.* 1865. 8vo, pp. 564. C. 45175

Journal of Proceedings of the Senate of Maryland, in Extra Session, April, 1861. *Frederick: Beale H. Richardson, Printer.* 1861. 8vo, pp. 365, Secret Proceedings, 6, Rules, 8. 45176

Journal of the Senate of Maryland. December Session, 1825. ... *Annapolis: Printed by J. Green.* 1826. 8vo, pp. 259. Cont'd.

A Journal of the Votes and Proceedings of the Lower House of Assembly of the Province of Maryland, at their Session begun May 1, 1739. *Annapolis: Printed and Sold by Jonas Green.* 1739. Sm. 4to, pp. 197. Continued. 45178

Report of the Ladies' Southern Relief Association ... September 1st, 1866. *Baltimore: Printed by Kelly & Piet.* 1866. 8vo, pp. 46. H. 45179

The Late Maryland [P. E.] Convention. [By Hugh Davey Evans. *Baltimore.* 1850.] 8vo, pp. 19. 45180

A Law of Maryland concerning Religion. [n. p. n. d.] Folio, 1 leaf. 45181

Written in Lord Baltimore's time.

The Laws of the Province of Maryland, Collected into one Volumn [*sic*], By Order of the Governour and Assembly of the said Province, At a General Assembly begun at St. Mary's the 10th Day of May, 1692, and continued by Several Assemblies to the Year 1718. *Philadelphia: Printed by Andrew Bradford, and are to be Sold by Evan Jones at the City of Annapolis in Maryland.* 1718. Folio, pp. (4), Index (7), 248. P. 45182

Laws of Maryland, Enacted At a Session of Assembly, begun and held at the City of Annapolis, March the 15th, 1725. [*Annapolis: Printed by William Parks.* 1725.] Sm. folio, pp. 20.

The earliest law-book I have seen, printed in the State with a title-page, is the "Acts of 1726," *our* No. 45046.

Laws of Maryland, Enacted at a Session of Assembly, ... held at ... Annapolis ... the Tenth Day of October, ... 1727. ... *Annapolis: Printed ... by W. Parks.* MDCCXXVII. Folio, pp. (2), 32. Continued. H. 45184

Laws of Maryland, Enacted ... at the City of Annapolis, ... in the Twenty Second Year of the Dominion of the Right Honourable Charles Lord Baron of Baltimore, Absolute Lord and Proprietary of the Province of Maryland and Avalon, &c. Annoq; Domini 1737. ... *Printed by William Parks, ... Annapolis.* M,DCC,XXXVII. Folio, pp. (2), 15, (1). 45185

Laws of Maryland at large, ... Collected into One Compleat Body ... . Together with Notes and other Matters, relative to the Constitution thereof, extracted from the Provincial Records. To which is prefixed, The Charter, with an English Translation. By Thomas Bacon ... . *Annapolis: Printed by Jonas Green, Printer to the Province.* MDCCLXV. Folio, pp. (6), Charter, (17), Laws, (624), Index, (91). 45186

Also on large paper; handsomely printed.

Laws of Maryland, Made and Passed at a Session of Assembly, held at Annapolis, 17th October, 1780. *Annapolis: Printed by Frederick Green, Printer to the State.* [1780.] Folio, pp. (2), (103). Continued. 45187

Laws of Maryland, Made and Passed at a Session of Assembly, Convened by the Council of Safety, and begun and held at the City of Annapolis, on Wednesday the fifth of February, in the year ... [1777]. *Annapolis: Printed by Frederick Green.* [n. d.] Small folio, pp. (2), (55). 45188

Laws of Maryland, Made Since M,DCC,LXIII, consisting of Acts of Assembly under the Proprietary Government, Resolves of Convention, the Declaration of Rights, the Constitution and Form of Government, the Articles of Confederation, and, Acts of Assembly since the Revolution. ... *Annapolis: Printed by Frederick Green* ... MDCCLXXXVII. Folio, pp. (4), (438), (12), (1).

One hundred copies printed. Edited by A. C. Hanson.

The Laws of Maryland, ... 1692 ... to ... 1799. To which are prefixed the Original Charter ... . Revised and Collected by William Kilty. *Annapolis: Printed by Frederick Green.* 1799–1800. 2 vols., 4to. A., C. + Vols. III–VII. *Annapolis.* [n. d.] 5 vols., 8vo. C. 45190

[Laws made] At a Session of the General Assembly of Maryland, ... November ... 1799, [to] ... January, 1800. [*Annapolis: F. Green.* 1800.] 4to, 40 leaves. 45191

The Laws of Maryland ... . Revised by Virgil Maxcy. *Baltimore.* 1811. 3 vols., 8vo. C. 45192

Letter from the Governor and Council of Maryland, transmitting A Report of the Commissioners appointed to Survey the River Potomac. January 28, 1823. ... *Washington: Gales & Seaton.* 1823. 8vo, pp. 46. 45193

A Letter to a Gentleman, concerning the Boundaries of the Province of Maryland, wherein is shewn, that no part of the 40th degree of latitude is, or can be, any part thereof. *London: For the Author* [about 1735]. 12mo, pp. 15. C. 45194

Letter to the Hon. Reverdy Johnson, on the Proceeding at the Meeting at Maryland Institute, Jan. 10, 1861. *Baltimore.* 1861. 8vo. 45195

List of Members of the Constitutional Convention of Maryland, of 1867 ... . *Annapolis: George Colton, Printer.* 1867. 8vo, pp. (2), 8. 45196

... Maffit against Goldsborough. The Records compared. By the Unconditional Union State Central Committee. October 7th, 1863. *Baltimore: Printed by Sherwood & Co.* [1863.] 8vo, pp. 13. H. 45197

A corrected title of *our* No. 43785.

Transactions of the Maryland Academy of Science and Literature. Vol. I. Published by the Academy. *Baltimore: John D. Toy.* 1837. 8vo, pp. xii, 17–190. Map. 45198

No more published. Also: Constitution and By-Laws of the Maryland Academy of Science and Literature. *Baltimore: John D. Toy.* 1825. 18mo, pp. 10, (1).

Report of the Register of the Maryland Agricultural College, ... *Baltimore: Samuel S. Mills.* 1858. 8vo, pp. 29. Plate.

Also: Catalogue of the Maryland Agricultural College ... . *Baltimore: John Murphy & Co.* 1870. 8vo, pp. 12. Folded Table. Continued.

The Maryland Ahiman Rezon, of Free and Accepted Masons, containing the History of Masonry, from the Establishment of the Grand Lodge to the Present Time. *Baltimore.* 1799. 8vo, pp. 266. 45200

The Maryland Almanack for ... 1759. *Annapolis: Jonas Green.* [1759.] 12mo, pp. 32. Continued. 45201

Maryland and Massachusetts. *See* Massachusetts.

First Annual Report of the President and Directors ... of the Maryland and Delaware Rail Road Company. ... *Baltimore: Sherwood & Co.* 1856. 8vo, pp. 32. Continued. 45202

The Charter and By-Laws of the Maryland Anthracite Coal Company of the Wyoming Coal Region, with Reports on the Geology and Mining Resources of their Coal Lands. ... *Baltimore: John W. Woods.* 1856. 8vo, pp. 46, (1). 2 Maps.

Minutes of the ... Maryland Baptist Union Association, ... in Newton, Md. November 10th, ... 1859. *Baltimore: William M. Innes, Printer.* 1859. 8vo, pp. 32. Continued. H. 45204

Maryland Central Railroad. To the Citizens of Baltimore and others interested. *Baltimore: J. B. Rose & Co.* [1869.] 8vo, pp. 8. 45205

Constitution and By-Laws of the Maryland Club, 1857. *Baltimore: Lucas Brothers.* 1865. 18mo, pp. 21. 45206

The Maryland Code: Public General Laws. Compiled by Otho Scott and Hiram McCullough, Commissioners. ... With an Index ... . By Henry C. Mackall ... . *Baltimore.* 1860. 2 vols., 8vo, pp. 822; 965. + Supplement. ... 1861 ... 1862. ... By H. C. Mackall. ... *Baltimore: Printed by John Murphy & Co.* 1862. 8vo, pp. 102, 128, 71, (1), 31. + Supplement. [*Ibid.*] 1863. 8vo, pp. 486. + Supplement. ... 1864 ... By Lewis Mayer ... . [*Ibid.*] 1865. 8vo, pp. 79, 111, (1), 102, (1). + Supplement. ... 1865 ... By Lewis Mayer ... . [*Ibid.*] 1865. 8vo, pp. 127, 63. + Supplement. ... 1861, 1861–2, 1864, 1865, 1866 and 1867. ... By Lewis Mayer ... . [*Ibid.*] 1868. 8vo, pp. 670. + Supplement. ... 1868 ... By Lewis Mayer ... . [*Ibid.*] 1868. 8vo, pp. 426. + Supplement. ... 1870 ... By J. J. Cohen and Thomas Rowland ... . [*Ibid.*] 1870. 8vo, pp. 466. 45207

Maryland Colonization Journal. Vol. I. *Baltimore.* 1841. 8vo. Continued. 45208

The Maryland Educational Journal ... . E. S. Zevely, Editor. Vol. I. *Baltimore: E. S. Zevely.* 1867–68. 8vo, pp. 376. Map.

No more published.

First Annual Report of the Maryland Eye [and Ear] Infirmary, Baltimore, Maryland. ... *Baltimore: John Murphy & Co.* 1870. 8vo, pp. 16. Continued. 45210

... The Maryland Farmer and Mechanic ... . Vol. II. No. I. January, 1864. *Baltimore, Md.: S. S. Mills & Co.* [n. d.] 8vo.

MARYLAND HISTORICAL SOCIETY. Publications. *Baltimore.* 1844–67.

The various publications of this society are described in this Dictionary under the names of their respective authors. Complete sets are scarce. In order to assist the collector we append a brief list of the works in the order of their publication: I. Constitution, etc.; II. Mayer (C. F.), Discourse; III. Latrobe (J. H. B.), Banneker; IV. Carroll (C.), Journal; V. Kennedy (J. P.), Calvert; VI. Harris (J. M.), Raleigh; VII. Wynne (Dr. J.), Ringgold; VIII. Mayer (B.), Commerce; IX. Donaldson (T.), Ameri-

can Colonial History; X. Harris (J. M.), California; XI. Report; XII. Brown (G. W.), Origin of Civil Liberty; XIII. Tiffany (O.), Williams; XIV. Dodge (R.), Columbus; XV. Mayer (B.), Tah-gah-jute; XVI. Streeter (S. F.), Maryland Two Hundred Years Ago; XVII. Burnap (G. W.), Democracy; XVIII. B[uchanan] (W. B.), Baltimore; XIX. Report; XX. Mayer (L.), Catalogue; [Tyson (*Mrs.* M. E.)], Banneker; XXII. [Sheppard (Moses)], Slave Trade; XXIII. Morris (J. G.), Behaim; XXIV. Smith (J. S.), DeKalb; XXV. Report; XXVI. Davis (G. L. L.), Japan; XXVII. Norris (J. S.), Early Friends; XXVIII. Allen (E.), Early Settlers; XXIX. [Mayer (B.)], Maryland Historical Society, etc.; XXX. Giles (W. F.), Discourse, two editions; XXXI. Mayer (B.), Sparks; XXXII. Mayer (B.), History, etc., Maryland Historical Society, 1867; XXXIII.–XXXVIII. Exhibitions of Paintings, etc., during 1848–58; XXXIX. Pinkney (Rev. W.), Alexander; XL. Constitution [1867], 8vo, pp. 24. After XL. the issues are Fund Publications.

Annual Report of the President ... . 1850. *Baltimore: John D. Toy.* [1850.] 8vo, pp. 21. Continued. H. 45212

Catalogue of the Manuscripts, [etc.] and an Account of the Library of the Maryland Historical Society, ... in 1854 ... . By Lewis Mayer ... . *Baltimore: Printed ... by John D. Toy.* 1854. 8vo, pp. 49, (2). H. 45213

Catalogue of Paintings, Engravings, &c. at the Picture Gallery of the Maryland Historical Society. First Annual Exhibition. 1848. *Baltimore: Printed by John D. Toy.* [1848.] 8vo, pp. 12. Continued. 45214

Constitution, By-Laws, ... and Members of the Maryland Historical Society. *Baltimore: Printed by John Murphy.* 1844. 8vo, pp. 19, (1). H. 45215

Fund Publication, No. 3. The Maryland Historical Society. In Memory of George Peabody. January, 1870. [*Baltimore.* 1870.] 8vo, pp. 33. 45216

The Maryland Historical Society and the Peabody Institute Trustees. A Report ... March 5th, 1866. *Baltimore: Printed by John Murphy & Co.* 1866. 8vo, pp. 15. H. 45217

Report of the President and Board of Visiters [*sic*] of the Maryland Hospital, ... for 1843. *Baltimore: John D. Toy.* 1844. 8vo, pp. 24. Continued. 45218

Second Annual Report of the Maryland Industrial School for Girls. January, 1869. *Baltimore: Rhodes Bros.* [1869.] 8vo, pp. 13. Continued. 45219

Charter, Constitution ... of the Maryland Institute of Education. *Baltimore: Woods & Crane, Printers.* 1841. 12mo, pp. 27.

Also: A Plan for a System of Public Education; Submitted by the Maryland Institute of Education to the General Assembly of ... Maryland. *Baltimore: Printed by John Murphy.* 1843. 8vo, pp. 15, 15.

Annual Opening and Concluding Addresses delivered before the Maryland Institute for the Promotion of the Mechanic Arts, during the Annual Exhibitions ... in 1848–1849 and 1850. *Baltimore: James Young.* [1850.] 8vo, pp. 77. 45221

Annual Report of the Board of Managers and Treasurer of the Maryland Institute ... for ... October, 1848. *Baltimore.* 1848. 8vo. Continued to 1860. 45222

The Book of Exhibition. Fourth Annual Exhibition of the Maryland Institute. Baltimore, 1851. ... *Baltimore: Printed by John Murphy & Co.* 1852. 8vo, pp. 24, 80, 36, 14, 93. H.

Continued to the Thirteenth Exhibition, 1860.

Catalogue of the First Annual Exhibition of the Maryland Institute ... 1848. ... *Baltimore.* 1848. 8vo, pp. (2), 21.

Continued to the Thirteenth Exhibition, 1860.

Catalogue of Books in the Library of the Maryland Institute ... In Two Parts. Part First—Alphabetical. *Baltimore.* 1857. 8vo, pp. (4), 132. 45225

The second part was never published. Also: Annual Report ... on the Library Department of the Maryland Institute, ... for 1857. *Baltimore: Samuel Sands Mills.* 1857. 8vo, pp. 18.—Catalogue of Books ... Classified and Alphabetically Arranged by Titles. *Baltimore: James Young.* 1865. 8vo, pp. 176.—Constitution of the Maryland Institute ... . [*Baltimore.* 1825.] 8vo, pp. 7.—Constitution and By-Laws ... . *Baltimore: Samuel Sands Mills.* 1848. 8vo, pp. 12. Continued.—Judges' Catalogue of the Articles Deposited at the Fourth Annual Exhibition of the Maryland Institute, ... October 20th, 1851. *Baltimore: Murphy & Co., Printers.* [1851.] 8vo, pp. 96.—Proposals of the Maryland Institute ... for the Exhibition of ... 1827 ... . *Baltimore: John D. Toy.* 1827. 8vo, pp. 11.

Second Annual Report of the Maryland Institution for the Education of the Deaf and Dumb, ... 1869–70. *Frederick: Keefer, Smith & Co.* 1871. 8vo, pp. 28, (2). Continued.

First Report of the Directors of the Maryland Institution for the Instruction of the Blind. ... *Baltimore: Printed by Samuel S. Mills.* 1858. 8vo, pp. 20. 45227

Maryland Jockey Club [Rules. *Baltimore.* 1830.] 8vo, pp. 6.

Description of the Property of the Maryland Marble Company, of Baltimore. *Baltimore: Cushings & Medairy.* 1866. 16mo, pp. 15. 45229

Catalogue of the Officers and Cadets of the Maryland Military Academy, for ... 1854–55. *Baltimore: Printed by John Murphy & Co.* 1855. 8vo, pp. 12. H. 45230

Maryland Muster Roll. War of 1812. *Baltimore.* [n. d.] 12mo. 45231

A doubtful title from an auction catalogue.

Maryland not a ... Catholic Colony. *See* N[eill] (E. D.)

Report of the Committee appointed by the Board of Directors of the Maryland Penitentiary to visit the Penitentiaries and Prisons in the City of Philadelphia and State of New York. *Baltimore: Printed by Lucas & Deaver.* 1828. 8vo, pp. 26.

Report of the Joint Committee appointed by the General Assembly ... to investigate the Affairs of the Maryland Penitentiary. [*Annapolis.* 1838.] 8vo, pp. 118, (1). + [*Ibid.*] 8vo, pp. 120. 45233

Also: First Annual Report of the Committee of the Relief Association of the Maryland Penitentiary ... . *Baltimore: Printed by James Lucas & Son.* 1860. 8vo, pp. 32. Continued.—Reply of the Directors to the Charges against the Penitentiary. *Baltimore: Printed by J. W. Woods.* 1837. 8vo, pp. 18.—Report of the Committee ... appointed to prepare Plans for the ... Maryland Penitentiary. *Baltimore.* 1835. 8vo.—Report of the Committee on Prison Manufactures. September, 1842. *Baltimore: Printed by Lucas & Deaver.* 1842. 8vo, pp. 22.—Report of the Directors of the Penitentiary, to the Legislature of Maryland, December, 1825. *Annapolis: J. Hughes, Print.* 1826. 8vo, pp. (2), (9). Folded Account. Continued.—Testimony taken before the Joint Committee of the Legislature of Maryland, on the Penitentiary. [*Annapolis.* 1838.] 8vo, pp. 430.

Maryland Pension Roll. Doc. 514. [*Washington.* n. d.] 8vo, pp. 52. 45234

The Maryland Pocket Annual, for ... 1834. *Annapolis: J. Hughes.* [1833.] 18mo, pp. 127, (2). Continued to 1846.

The Maryland Pocket Magazine; ... 1796. ... *Baltimore: George Keatinge.* [1796.] 12mo. H. 45236

... Report of the ... Maryland Reform Convention, on the Late Acts of Congress forming the Compromise, etc. [*Annapolis.* 1850.] 8vo, pp. 4. H. 45237

The Maryland Register, for 1856 and 1857; A Legal, Political and Business Manual, By James Wingate ... . *Baltimore.* 1856. 8vo, pp. 37, (1), x, 301, 30, 13. + 1860–61. [*Ibid.*] 1860. 8vo, pp. xxvi, 37, 215, 26, 17*. 45238

The Maryland Resolutions. *See* [Maxcy (Virgil)].

The Maryland Scheme of Expatriation Examined. By a Friend of Liberty. *Boston: Garrison & Knapp.* 1834. 8vo, pp. 20. BA. 45239

The Maryland School Journal ... . Edited ... by Levi & Galligher ... . Vol. II. *Hagerstown: Levi & Galligher.* [n. d.] 8vo.

Constitution | of the | Maryland Society, | for Promoting the | Abolition of Slavery, | and the relief of | Free Negroes, and Others, | unlawfully held in | Bondage. | *Baltimore:* | *Printed by William Goddard and James Angell* | ... | M.DCC.LXXXIX. | 8vo, pp. 8. 45241

Reprinted in W. F. Poole's "Anti-Slavery Opinions before 1800." Also: [Resolutions passed] At a Meeting of "The Maryland Society for promoting the Abolition of Slavery, and the Relief of Free Negroes, and others, unlawfully held in Bondage," held at Baltimore, the 4th of February, 1792. *Baltimore: Printed by William Goddard and James Augell.* [n. d.] 4to, pp. 8.

Fourth Annual Report of the Board of Managers of the Maryland State Bible Society, for 1837. *Baltimore: J. W. Woods.* 1837. 8vo, pp. 56. Continued. 45242

Act of Incorporation and By-Laws of the Maryland State Colonization Society: ... *Baltimore: Printed by J. D. Toy.* 1834. 12mo, pp. (2), 32. BA. 45243

Addresses delivered at the Sixth Anniversary Meeting of the Maryland State Colonization Society, held at Annapolis, February 2d, 1838. *Baltimore.* 1838. 12mo, pp. 45. 45244

African Colonization. Proceedings of a Meeting of the Friends of African Colonization, held in the City of Baltimore, on the Seventeenth of October, 1827. [*Baltimore.* 1827.] 8vo, pp. 19. + *Baltimore: B. Edes.* 1828. 8vo, pp. 24. 45245

This meeting resulted in the formation of the Maryland State Colonization Society. Also: Colonization of the Free Colored Population of Maryland, and of such Slaves as may hereafter become free. Statement of Facts ... on this ... subject. *Baltimore.* 1832. 8vo, pp. 16.

The Third Annual Report of the Board of Managers of the Maryland State Colonization Society, to the Members and the Public. *Baltimore: Printed by John D. Toy.* 1835. 8vo, pp. 36. Continued. 45246

This was the first published.

Maryland State Gazetteer and Business Directory, 1867–8. Compiled by Geo. W. Hawes. *Baltimore.* 1867. 8vo, pp. 557.

Maryland State Business Directory; with ... Sketch of Annapolis ... . *New York: Webb & Fitzgerald.* 1866. 8vo, pp. viii, 17, 161, 81. 45248

Sixth Annual Report of the Maryland State Temperance Society. [n. p. 1837.] 16mo, pp. 22. 45249

Report of the Maryland Union Commission, May 1, 1866. *Baltimore: Sherwood & Co.* 1866. 8vo, pp. 20. 45250

Also: Services held by the Maryland Union Commission, ... June 1st, 1865, ... the Day of Humiliation ... appointed by the President ... . *Sherwood & Co., Printers, Baltimore.* [1865.] 16mo, pp. 22.

The Maryland, Virginia, Pennsylvania, ... Almanack for 1780, by M. K. Goddard. *Baltimore.* 1780. Continued. 45251

Maryland's Crisis: A Political Outline. By W. Jefferson Buchanan. ... *J. W. Randolph, Richmond, Va.* 1863. 8vo, pp. 16.

This and the following were omitted under Buchanan.

Maryland's Hope: Her Trials and Interests in Connexion with the War. By W. Jefferson Buchanan. ... *West & Johnston, Richmond.* 1864. 8vo, pp. 62. 45253

A Summary of Proceedings from the Organization of the Medical and Chirurgical Faculty of Maryland, in 1799, to the Convention of 1807. ... *Baltimore: Printed by Fryer and Rider.* 1807. 8vo, pp. 23, (1). 45254

Continued as "Transactions." Also: Catalogue of Books belonging to the Library of the Medical and Chirurgical Faculty, of Maryland. *Baltimore: John W. Woods.* 1852. 8vo, pp. 66.

Meeting of Young Men in Maryland, Dec. 20th, 1831. [*Baltimore:*] *Printed by Sands & Neilson.* [n. d.] 8vo, pp. 16.

Memorial of John Chandler, Late Printer to the State, to the General Assembly ... his Claims for Services ... 1812 ... '16. ... [*Annapolis.*] 1819. 8vo, pp. 26. 45256

Memorial to the General Assembly of Maryland, by James M'Evoy, Vindicatory of his Testimony, ... to the Joint Committee on the Affairs of the Penitentiary ... . [n. p. 1837.] 8vo, pp. 23. 45257

Memorial to the General Assembly of Maryland on behalf of the Baltimore and Susquehanna Rail Road. [n. p.] 1834. 8vo.

Message from the Executive to the General Assembly of Maryland. December Session, 1830. *Annapolis: Printed by Jeremiah Hughes.* 1830. 8vo, pp. 15. 45259

Continued at each session. Those delivered in 1861, etc, contain important matter relative to the Civil War.

Message of the Governor [Wm. Grason] in Relation to the Report ... of the Committee on the Public Lands. [n. p.] 1841. 8vo, pp. 7. BA. 45260

Message of the Governor of Maryland, communicating the Report of the Commissioners ... to Survey the River Potomac. ... *Annapolis: Printed by J. Hughes.* 1822. 8vo, pp. 92. Tables.

See also under Boundary, No. 45077–8, *supra*.

Militia. An Act to provide for the Organization and Discipline of the Militia of Maryland; ... 1864. *Baltimore: Printed by John D. Toy.* [n. d.] 16mo, pp. 77. 45262

Also: An Act to Regulate and Discipline the Militia of this State ... . *Baltimore: Printed by Samuel Magill.* 1807. 18mo, pp. 45. + *Annapolis: Printed by John Chandler.* 1812. 8vo, pp. 30.

Message of the Governor in relation to Disarming the State Militia, in Extra Session, 1862. [n. p. n. d.] 8vo, pp. 4.

Proceedings of the Officers of the Thirty-Ninth Regiment of Maryland Militia, on an Inquiry into the Conduct of the Adjutant [Jonathan Meredith]: Including the Statement made by him in explanation: Together with his Letter of Resignation, and the Answer of Colonel Mosher. *Baltimore: Printed by G. Dobbin & Murphy.* 1808. 8vo, pp. 24. 45264

Report of the Adjutant General, May 8, 1861. [n. p. n. d.] 8vo, pp. 16. 45265

Report of the Committee on the Message of the Governor, giving his reasons for disarming the State Militia. [n. p. n. d.] 8vo, pp. 7. 45266

Report of the Quartermaster General, February 1, 1862. [n. p. n. d.] 8vo, pp. 10. 45267

A New Arrangement of the Courts of Justice, of the State of Maryland Proposed. [By John Leeds Bozman.] *Maryland: Printed for the Author.* 1802. 8vo, pp. 66. S. 45268

The New Constitution and its Relation to Railroads. [*Baltimore.* 1867.] 8vo, pp. 7. 45269

Notes for an Essay on some of the Effects and Abuses of the Constitution of Maryland, and on its proposed Reform. *Baltimore: J. W. Woods.* 1836. 8vo, pp. 16. 45270

Notes of Reference to certain Maryland Statutes passed since the Compilation of Dorsey's Laws of Maryland. [By C. J. M.

Gwinn.] *Baltimore: Printed by John D. Toy.* 1857. 16mo, pp. 28. 45271

Objections to yielding to Northerners. *See our* No. 2992, *note.*

Observations | on the | Present | State of Religion | in | Maryland. | By a Clergyman. | [Rev. William Duke.] ... *Baltimore: | Printed by Samuel & John Adams.* | M, DCC, XCV. | 16mo, pp. 53. 45272

Official Census of Maryland, ... 1830; Also the Aggregate Census for ... 1790, 1800, and 1810; Accompanied by an Abstract of the Census of the United States, for ... 1830. ... *Annapolis: J. Hughes, Print.* 1838. 8vo, pp. 63. 9 folded Tables.

Oyster Law of the State of Maryland, passed ... 1868 ... . *Annapolis: Printed by Wm. Thompson.* 1868. 8vo, pp. 18.

Papers relating chiefly to the Maryland Line. *See* Balch (T.)

Paragraphs on Judicial Reform in Maryland. *See* [Price (W.)]

Petition of Richard B. Carmichael and others, against the Adjournment of the Legislature, sine die. [Jan. 18, 1861. n. p. n. d.] 8vo, pp. 5. 45275

Petition to th[e] General Assembly of Maryland, by Citizens of the State, praying to be relieved from Illegal Exactions of Toll on the ... Roads; leading to Baltimore. *Baltimore.* 1819. 8vo, pp. 20. 45276

Plan of a Code of Laws for the Province of Maryland, reported by the Advocate General. *London.* 1774. 8vo. 45277

Preamble and Resolutions in regard to the Objects of the Present War, passed by the General Assembly, December 23, 1861. [n. p. n. d.] 8vo, pp. 4. 45278

The Present State of Maryland. By the Delegates of the People. *Baltimore Printed: London Reprinted. For John Stockdale.* M DCC LXXXVII. 8vo, pp. 28. H. 45279

Address to the people of Maryland, signed by order of the House of Delegates, by Thomas Cockey Deye, Speaker. *See* "M. Rev.," LXXVIII. 66.

Proceedings of the Convention of the Province of Maryland, Held at ... Annapolis, ... December, 1775. *Annapolis: Printed by Frederick Green.* [1776.] 4to, pp. 62. C. 45280

This convention sat until January 18, 1776, when it adjourned to meet on the second Tuesday in April following.

Proceedings of the Convention of the Province of Maryland, Held at ... Annapolis, ... May, 1776. *Annapolis: Printed by Frederick Green.* [1776.] Sm. 4to, pp. (2), 29. C. 45281

Proceedings of the Convention ... Held at ... Annapolis, ... June, 1776. *Annapolis: Printed by Frederick Green.* [1776.] Sm. 4to, pp. (2), 33. 45282

Proceedings of the Convention ... Held at ... Annapolis, ... August, 1776. *Annapolis: Printed by Frederick Green.* [1776.] 4to, pp. (2), 91. C. 45283

Proceedings of the Conventions of the Province of Maryland, Held at ... Annapolis, ... June, 1774; ... November, 1774; ... December, 1774; ... April, 1775; and ... July, 1775. *Annapolis: Printed by Frederick Green.* [1775.] Sm. 4to, pp. 26. C.

Proceedings of the Conventions of the Province of Maryland, Held at ... Annapolis in 1774, 1775, & 1776. *Baltimore: James Lucas & E. K. Deaver.* 1836. 8vo, pp. (2), 378. C., H. 45285

"There is no indication in this work of whether it was printed from a manuscript or from an older edition, it having neither introduction or preface."—RICH.

J. Green, Proposes to Publish The Journals of the Conventions of the Province of Maryland. Held ... Annapolis, in the years 1774, 1775 and 1776. *[Annapolis.* 1825.] Folio, 1 leaf.

Mr. Green proposed to print from the original manuscripts, but failed to get a bill through the legislature.

Proceedings of the Convention on Internal Improvements, held Dec. 1825. By T. Phenix. *Baltimore.* 1826. 8vo, pp. 44, 19. 45287

Proceedings of the Electors of President, 1840. *Annapolis.* [n. d.] 8vo. S. 45288

Proceedings of the Great Meeting of the Friends of Civil and Religious Liberty, held in Baltimore, 1837. *Baltimore.* 1837. 8vo. 45289

Proceedings of the House of Assembly of Maryland, with Governor Eden's Proclamations, Addresses, &c. ... *Annapolis.* 1771. Folio. 45290

Title from an English catalogue.

Proceedings of the Maryland Administration Convention, ... held in Baltimore, ... July ... 1827. *Printed at the Office of the Baltimore Patriot.* 1827. 8vo, pp. 24. 45291

Proceedings of the two Houses of Assembly of Maryland, on the Subject of Confiscation of British Property, &c. *Annapolis: Printed by Frederick Green, Printer to the State.* [1780.] 8vo, pp. 69. 45292

Proceedings of the State Convention of Maryland to frame a New Constitution. ... April 27, 1864. *Annapolis: Richard P. Bayly, Printer.* 1864. 8vo, pp. 856. 45293

Proceedings of the State Convention, of Maryland, to frame a New Constitution, Commenced at Annapolis, May 8, 1867. *Annapolis: George Colton, Printer.* 1867. 8vo, pp. 850, 16, 66, 14.

Proposals for a Tobacco-Law, In the Province of Maryland. Humbly offered to the Consideration of the Legislature, and all Lovers of their Country. In a Letter from a Gentleman to William Parks, Printer in Annapolis. *Annapolis: Printed in the Year* 1726. 4to, pp. 21. 45295

Also: Proposals for Tobacco Warehouses, and Accompanying Documents. *Annapolis: Printed by Jeremiah Hughes.* 1827. 8vo, pp. 16. Folded Plan.

Protest and Argument against a Subscription on the Part of the State to the Baltimore and Ohio Railroad Company. By a Citizen of Baltimore. [n. p.] 1827. 8vo. 45296

Protest of the General Assembly against the Illegal Arrest and Imprisonment, by the Federal Government, of Citizens of Maryland. [n. p. n. d.] 8vo, pp. 4. 45297

Protestant Episcopal Church. An Abstract of the Proceedings of the Corporation for the relief of the Widows and Children of the Clergy of the Protestant Episcopal Church in Maryland. *Baltimore: Printed by Philip Edwards.* 1797. 16mo, pp. 12.

Address of the Board of Trustees. *See* [Johns (John)].

Articles of Religions of the Protestant Episcopal Church ... together with the Canons ... in ... Maryland, which respect discipline: ... prefixed a Pastoral Letter from the Bishop [T. J. Claggett] of the said Church. ... *Baltimore: Cole & Hewes.* 1805. 8vo, pp. 8. 45299

The Charter, Laws and Regulations of the Corporation for the relief of the Widows and Children of the Clergy of the Protestant Episcopal Church in Maryland. *Baltimore: J. Robinson.* 1827. 8vo, pp. 12. 45300

A Compilation containing the Constitution and Canons of the Protestant Episcopal Church, ... the Constitution and Canons of the ... Church in Maryland; together with other documents interesting to churchmen, and the Laws of Maryland relating to the duties of clergymen and vestries, &c. ... *Baltimore: Printed by Jos. Robinson.* 1849. 18mo, pp. 340. + *Baltimore: H. A. Robinson.* 1863. 8vo, pp. vii, 121. 45301

Constitution and Canons of the Protestant Episcopal Church, in Maryland. ... *Baltimore: Joseph Robinson.* 1809. 8vo, pp. 16.

Constitution of the Free Church Association of the Diocese of Maryland. *Baltimore: John D. Toy.* 1863. 18mo, pp. 4.

The Convention of the Protestant Episcopal Church, in the State of Maryland, to the Vestries and other Members of the said Church. [*Baltimore.* 1794.] 8vo, pp. 8. 45304

Written by the Rt. Rev. Thomas J. Claggett.

First Annual Report of the Prayer Book and Homily Society of Maryland, M. DCCC. XIX. with the Constitution and ... Subscribers and Benefactors. ... *Baltimore: Printed by William Warner.* [n. d.] 18mo, pp. 16. 45305

Journal of the Convention of the Protestant-Episcopal Church of Maryland; May, 1808. *New York.* 1808. 8vo. Continued.

Notices and Journals, and remains of Journals, of the Two preliminary Conventions of the Clergy, and of the first Five Annual Conventions and two adjourned Conventions of ... Maryland, in the years 1783, ... 1788. ... From the Papers of the Rev. Dr. West, Secretary ... . [*Baltimore.* 1855.] 8vo, pp. 43.

Reprinted and appended to the journal of 1855.

The Report of the Committee on the Proposed Division of the Diocese of Maryland. ... 1859. [*Baltimore:*] *J. D. Toy, Print.* [1859.] 8vo, pp. 20. Map. 45308

Also appended to the journal of this year.

Report of the Committee on the Question of the Episcopate of Maryland, touching the Interests of the District of Columbia. [*Baltimore.* 1867.] 8vo, pp. (2), 8. 45309

A Statement of Facts. *See* [Parkman (C. M.)]

To the Clerical and Lay Members of the Convention of the Diocess of Maryland. [*Baltimore.* 1824.] 8vo, pp. 4. 45310

Signed by "A Churchman" on a theological seminary.

Queries about the Practicability of Codifying the Laws of Maryland. *Baltimore: Printed by James Lucas.* 1854. 8vo, pp. 46. 45311

Page 35 was reprinted and pasted over the original.

Reasons for an Extra Session of the Legislature. [*Frederick.* 1854.] 8vo, pp. 13. 45312

Signed by Wm. Price, Samuel Tyler and Frederick Stone.

Record of Proceedings of the Investigation ... in the case of Samuel Hindes and Nicholas L. Wood, Commissioners of the Board of Police of ... Baltimore, upon the Charges preferred against them for Official Misconduct. *Baltimore: Willam K. Boyle, Printer.* 1866. 8vo, pp. lxx, 201. 45313

A | Relation | of | Maryland; | Together, | With A Map of the Countrey, | The Conditions of Plantation, | His Majesties Charter to the | Lord Baltemore, translated | into English. | *These Bookes are to bee had, at Master William | Peasley Esq; his house, on the backside of Dru- | ry-Lane, neere the Cock-pit Playhouse; or in | his absence, at Master Iohn Morgans house in | High Holbourn, over against the Dolphin, London.* | *September the* 8. *Anno Dom.* 1635. | Sq. 16mo, pp. (2), 56, the Charter, pp. 25. Map. C., H. 45314

The map is usually wanting. It is the second printed account of the Lord Baltimore's plantation, and is a volume of unusual rarity and value.

A Relation of Maryland, Reprinted from the London Edition of 1635, With a Prefatory Note and Appendix, By Francis L. Hawks, D.D. ... *New York: Joseph Sabin.* 1865. 4to, pp. vii, 103. Map. BA. 45315

Two hundred and fifty copies printed, of which fifty are on large paper. Forms No. II. of Sabin's Reprints, 4to Series. Some copies were issued without the "Charter," pp. vii, 73. Dr. Hawks' notes contain some errors. The Privy Council did not decide that Kent Island belonged to Lord Baltimore till 1638. There are also errors in his statement relative to Claiborne. *See* White (Andrew).

A Relation of The successfull beginnings of the Lord Baltemore's Plantation in Mary-Land; Being an extract of certaine Letters written from thence, by some of the Aduenturers to their friends in England. [*London.*] *Anno Domini* 1634. 4to. BM.

A volume of extreme rarity; no copy is known in the United States. It contains a description of the natives. It was reprinted with the same title, with a prefatory note by Brantz Mayer, as "Shea's Early Southern Tracts, No. 1," pp. (2), 23, (1). One hundred and fifty copies printed, of which thirty were on large paper.

Remarks on the Majority and Minority Reports of the Select Committee on Secret Societies, of the House of Delegates of

Maryland. *New York: M. B. Wynkoop, Printer.* 1856. 8vo, pp. 37. 45317

Remarks on the Proposed Plan. *See* [Hanson (A. C.)]

Remarks | upon a | Message, | sent by the | Upper to the Lower | House of Assembly | of Maryland, 1762. | Containing a Vindication of the latter, | in their Conduct relative to a Supply | Bill for His Majesty's Service; and | occasionally interspersed with some curious and in- | teresting Particulars, respecting the Constitu- | tion of the said Province. | By a Friend to Maryland. | ... | *Printed in the Year* MDCCLXIII. | Sm. 8vo, pp. 71. 45318

See also "Answer to the Queries," No. 45069, *and* "A Bill," No. 45085.

Report and Resolutions. *See* Baltimore, Vol. I., No. 3078.

... Report from the Select Committee, to whom was referred the Subject of the Removal of the Free Colored Population from Charles County. [*Annapolis.* 1844.] 8vo, pp. 51. 45319

Report of all such English Statutes as existed at the time of the first Emigration of the People of Maryland, and which by experience have been found applicable to their ... circumstances; ... Made ... By William Kilty, Chancellor of Maryland. To which are prefixed an Introduction ... . *Annapolis: John Chandler.* 1811. Sm. 4to, pp. 289, (1). 45320

Report of Attorney General Brent, to ... Gov. Lowe, in relation to the Christiana Treason Trials, ... at Philadelphia. *Annapolis: Thomas E. Martin, Printer.* 1852. 8vo, pp. 19.

Report of the Commissioners appointed to wait on the President of the United States, to the ... Assembly of Maryland. ... 1861. *Frederick.* 1861. 8vo, pp. 4. 45322

Report of the Commissioners authorized to Build an Hospital for Insane Persons. *Baltimore: Printed by John D. Toy.* 1853. 8vo, pp. 27. 45323

Report of the Committee of Claims to the Legislature of Maryland. *Annapolis.* 1835. 8vo. 45324

Report of the Committee of Grievances. *See* Vol. I. 3072.

Report of the Committee of Ways and Means on the Finances and Resources of the State of Maryland. [*Annapolis.*] 1819. 8vo, pp. 18. 45325

Report of the Committee of Ways and Means on the State of the Finances. January 24, 1825. *Annapolis: J. Hughes, Printer.* [n. d.] 8vo, pp. 31. Continued. 45326

Report of the Committee on Agriculture, relative to the Application of Lime to the Different Qualities of Soil, and Use of Calcareous Matter for Agricultural Purposes. ... *Annapolis: Riley & Davis, Printers.* 1844. 8vo, pp. 15. 45327

Report of the Committee on Elections, in relation to Contested Elections. [*Annapolis.* 1860.] 8vo, pp. 27. 45328

Case of Denmead [and others] *vs.* Krafft [and others]. New election ordered. *See also* No. 45163.

Report of the Committee on Federal Relations upon the Messages of the Governor, in regard to the Arbitrary Proceedings of the United States Authorities, and the Governor's Correspondence with the United States Government. *Frederick: Elihu S. Riley.* 1861. 8vo, pp. 5 or 8. 45329

Report of the Committee on Federal Relations in regard to the Calling of a Sovereign Convention. *Frederick, Md.: E. S. Riley, Printer.* 1861. 8vo, pp. 22. 45330

Report of the Committee on the Coloured Population, of Answers of the President of the Colonization Society ... on the 4th January, 1841. [*Annapolis.* 1841.] 8vo, pp. 26. 45331

Report of the Committee on the Fugitive Slave Case. By the Convention. April 23, 1851 ... . [*Annapolis.* 1851.] 8vo, pp. 20.

Case of James Mitchell, indicted by the State of Pennsylvania for capturing slaves in this State. A requisition was made on the Governor of Maryland for the arrest and return of Mitchell, which requisition was refused.

Report [by J. V. L. McMahon] of the Committee on Internal Improvement. ... 1827. [*Annapolis.* 1828.] 8vo, pp. 22.

Relates entirely to the Baltimore and Ohio Rail-Road.

Report of the Committee on Lotteries; to the House of Delegates. February 9, 1835. [n. p. n. d.] 8vo. 45334

Report of the Committee on Ways and Means, in relation to sundry Sugar Refiners in Maryland. [n. p.] 1803. 8vo.

... Report of the Joint Committee on Federal Relations, ... proposing an Amendment to the Constitution of the United States. ... *Annapolis: Henry A. Lucas, Printer.* 1867. 8vo, pp. 26.

Report of the Majority of the Committee on Secret Societies, made to the House of Delegates ... . March 3, 1856. *Annapolis: Requa & Wilson, Printers.* 1856. 8vo, pp. 16. 45337

Report of the Peace Commissioners appointed to wait on Presidents Lincoln and Davis, by the General Assembly, 1861. *Annapolis.* 1861. 8vo. 45338

Report of the Rev. Dr. Ethan Allen in relation to Records of the Executive Department; and Letter from John H. Alexander, Esq. in reference to Calendar of Domestic State Papers. [*Annapolis.* 1861.] 8vo, pp. 8. 45339

Report of the Select Committee appointed to consider so much of the Governor's Message as relates to the Murder of Edward Gorsuch, and the Trial of the Treason Cases in Philadelphia. [*Annapolis.* 1852.] 8vo, pp. 16. 45340

... Report of the Select Committee ... in Relation to the Resources of Maryland. *Annapolis: Richard P. Bayly, Printers.* 1865. 8vo, pp. 51. H. 45341

Report of the Select Committee on Benevolent and Reformatory Institutions which are beneficiaries of the State. *Annapolis.* 1870. 8vo, pp. 22. 45342

Report of the Select Committee on the Claims of the Nanticoke Indians. Made to the House of Delegates. Wm. A. Stewart, Chairman. *Annapolis: Thomas E. Martin.* 1853. 8vo, pp. 8. 45343

Report of the Senate Committee on Internal Improvement. *Annapolis: Wm. Thompson, Printer.* 1868. 8vo, pp. 4. 45344

Report of the Special Committee appointed for the purpose of Examining the Condition of the Public Records of this State. [*Annapolis.* 1853.] 8vo, pp. 5. 45345

Report [by J. H. Alexander] on Certain Documents touching the Provincial History of Maryland: ... *Baltimore: John D. Toy.* 1860. 8vo, pp. 11. 45346

Also: Report on the Board of Police of Baltimore, in Extra Session, 1861. [n. p. n. d.] 8vo, pp. 8, 48.

Report on the Condition of the Public Records. By Ethan Allen. *Annapolis: Thomas J. Wilson.* 1860. 8vo, pp. 5.

Report on the Manufacture of Iron; Addressed to the Governor of Maryland. By John H. Alexander. *Annapolis: Wm. M'Neir, Printer.* 1840. 8vo, pp. xxiv, [17]–269, (6). 3 Plates. + Second Report. [*Ibid.*] 1844. 8vo, pp. xvii, [9]–189.

Report on the Standards of Weight and Measure for the State of Maryland; ... By J. H. Alexander. [*Baltimore: John D. Toy.* 1846.] 8vo, pp. iv, 213. 45349

Report on the Subject of the Chancery Records. ... March, 1829. *Annapolis: Jeremiah Hughes, Printer.* 1829. 8vo, pp. 67.

Resolutions from the Committee on Federal Relations, January 19, 1850. [n. p. n. d.] 8vo, pp. 4. 45351

Resolutions of the Committee on Federal Relations of the House of Delegates ... . 1861. *Frederick.* 1861. 8vo, pp. 4.

Resolutions of the Legislature of Maryland, approving the Views of the President in his ... Message ... . January 2, 1861. ... [*Washington.* 1861.] 8vo, pp. 2. 45353

Resolutions [relating to the Public Lands] and the object of them considered. By a Citizen of Maryland. *Baltimore.* 1822. 8vo. 45354

The Revenue Laws of Maryland ... . *Baltimore: John Murphy & Co.* 18—. 8vo. 45355

Rules and Orders for the Regulation and Government of the Constitutional Convention, Assembled at Annapolis, April 27, 1864. *Annapolis: Richard P. Bayly, Printer.* 1864. 8vo, pp. 14. + Constitutional Convention of 1867. *Annapolis: George Colton.* 1867. 8vo, pp. 12. 45356

Brief History of St. George's Parish, Harford County. ... [By Rev. S. W. Crampton.] *Baltimore: Printed by John D. Toy.* [1851.] 16mo, pp. 42. Plate. 45357

Secret Correspondence illustrating the Condition of Affairs in Maryland. *Baltimore.* 1863. 8vo, pp. 42. 45358

Very rare; consisting of letters from prominent Union men in Maryland, giving information regarding Southern sympathizers; which letters were captured by Stonewall Jackson from General Banks.

Services held by the Maryland Union Commission, ... June 1st, 1865, being the Day of ... Prayer appointed by the President ... . *Baltimore: Sherwood & Co., Printers.* [1865.] 12mo, pp. 22, (1). H. 45359

A Short Address to the Aged Union Citizens of Maryland, Read at a Meeting of the "Aged Guard of '62." By the Captain [Samuel Child], ... January 4th, 1865. [*Baltimore.* 1865.] 8vo, pp. 3. 45360

A Short History of the Public Debt of Maryland, and of the Causes which Produced it. By a Citizen of Maryland. *Baltimore: Printed by Bull & Tuttle.* 1845. 8vo, pp. 95. 45361

Sketch of Proceedings in the Legislature of Maryland, December Session, 1818, on what is commonly called The Jew Bill; ... and the Speeches of Thomas Kennedy, Esq., ... and H. B. Brackenridge, Esq. ... *Baltimore: Printed by Joseph Robinson.* 1819. 8vo, pp. 86. 45362

Slavery in Maryland. An Anti-Slavery Review. By a Virginian. *Baltimore.* 1846. 8vo, pp. 24. 45363

Society of Friends. Extracts from the Minutes of our Yearly Meeting, ... in Baltimore ... 1829. [n. p. n. d.] 12mo, pp. 16.

Also: Revised Discipline approved by the Yearly Meeting of Friends, held in Baltimore for Western Shore of Maryland and adjacents parts of Pennsylvania and Virginia. *Baltimore.* 1794. Sm. 4to.

Soldier's Home. Annual Report of the Maryland Soldiers' Relief Association. February 5, 1868. ... [*Baltimore.* 1868.] 8vo, pp. 8. 45365

"Southern Rights." *See* [Johnson (S. M.)], Vol. IX. 36319.

The | Speech | of His Excellency | Samuel Ogle, | Governor and Commander in Chief, in and | over the Province of Maryland, to | both Houses of Assembly: At a Session, | begun and held at the City of Annapolis, | on Tuesday, the Eleventh Day of July, in | the Eighteenth Year of the Dominion of | the Right Honourable Charles, Lord | Baron of Baltemore, Absolute Lord and | Proprietary of the Province of Maryland | and Avalon, &c. Annoq; Dom' 1732. | By Authority. | *Annapolis: Printed by William Parks and Edmund Hall.* M,DCC,XXXII. | Sm. folio, pp. (2), (6). 45366

State Armory & Town Hall. An Act in aid of the Construction of a State Armory and Town Hall, in ... Baltimore, and the re-building ... of the Hanover Market House ... . [*Baltimore.* 1840.] 8vo, pp. 11. 45367

The State Convention on Internal Improvements containing the Resolutions, &c. offered by the different Gentlemen composing the Convention. Together with an Appendix containing the

Views of T. Ellicott ... . By T. Phenix, Assistant Secretary to the Convention. *Baltimore.* 1825. 8vo, pp. 44, 20. S. 45368

STATE LIBRARY. Catalogue of the Library of the State of Maryland. ... 1833. *Annapolis: Printed by Jeremiah Hughes.* 1833. 8vo, pp. 111. + [*Ibid.*] 1837. 8vo, pp. 132. 45369

Report from the Committee on the Library on the Manuscript in the Library relating to the Early History of the State. [*Annapolis.* 1840.] 8vo, pp. 16. 45370

Three letters of Gov. Sharpe, 1754–5. Also: Catalogue of the Maryland State Library. By Richard Swan. *Annapolis.* 1851 8vo.—Mr. Pigman's Report upon the Autographical Manuscript of the History of Maryland. By John Leeds Bozman. [*Annapolis.* 1836.] 8vo, pp. 7.—Report of the Joint Committee on the State Library to the Legislatu ... . *Annapolis: J. Hughes, Printer.* 1833. 8vo, pp. 15.— ... Report of the Joint Committee on the State Library, enclosing a Letter from John Leeds Kerr, Esq., relative to the History of Maryland [by Bozman]. *Annapolis: Jeremiah Hughes, Printer.* 1834. 8vo, pp. 7.— ... Report of D. Ridgely, State Librarian, ... in relation to the ... Documents, Papers, &c. ... January 13th, 1836. ... *Annapolis: Jeremiah Hughes, Printer.* 1836. 8vo, pp. 13. + Second Report. [*Ibid.*] 8vo, pp. 17. + Third Report. [*Ibid.*] 8vo, pp. 8.—Report relative to the State Library made by the Committee, ... L. D. Teackle, Chairman. *Annapolis: Printed by Jeremiah Hughes.* 1832. 8vo, pp. 8.—Rules and Regulations, to be observed in the Library of the Legislature of Maryland. *Annapolis.* 1827. 8vo, pp. 6.

STATE NORMAL SCHOOL. First Annual Catalogue ... July, 1866. *Baltimore: William K. Boyle, Printer.* 1866. 8vo, pp. 16.

The State of Maryland, against the Vestry of St. Peter's Church; in which a portion of the Members of the Church prayed for a Mandamus, ... enjoining and prohibiting them from further permitting George Dashiell to occupy the parsonage house, ... *Baltimore: Joseph Robinson.* 1817. 8vo, pp. 80. 45372

A Summary View of the Courses of Crops, in the Husbandry of England & Maryland; ... and a System ... proposed for Farms in America. *Printed by Charles Cist, at Philadelphia.* M,DCC,-LXXXIV. Sm. 4to, pp. 22. H. 45373

By John Beale Bordley. This is a corrected title of *our* No. 6416, Vol. II.

A Succinct Exposition of the Industrial Resources and Agricultural Advantages of the State of Maryland. By James Higgins, A.M., M.D. ... *Annapolis.* 1867. 8vo, pp. 109, iii. 45374

Testimony taken before a Committee of the House of Delegates of Maryland, on Contested Elections. [*Annapolis.* 1860.] 8vo, pp. 31, 126. 45375

Jarrett *vs.* Purnell, and Kerr *vs.* Gaither. Contains full accounts of the Know Nothing, Plug Ugly, and Blood Tub Riots.

Testimony taken before a Special Committee of the House of Delegates of Maryland, ... to inquire into the Allegations of Discriminations against the Citizens of Maryland, by the B. and O. R. R. ... *Baltimore.* 1863. 8vo, pp. 32. 45376

The Three Patriots; or, the Cause and Cure of Present Evils. Addressed to the Voters of Maryland. *Baltimore: For the Author, B. Edes, Printer.* 1811. 8vo, pp. 55. BA. 45377

Jefferson, Madison and Monroe are the patriots.

To the Landholders of the State of Maryland. *Baltimore: Printed for the Consideration of Landholders.* 1825. 8vo, pp. 23.

Five hundred copies printed. Signed for a meeting of citizens by Col. John Eager Howard and James Carroll, Jr. On the claim for quit rents said to be due Louisa Browning, as one of the heirs of Lord Baltimore. For others on this subject, *see* Browning (Charles).

To the Voters of Maryland. [*Baltimore.* 1840.] 8vo, pp. 16.

A Harrison election document. Signed by O. C. Tiffany and others.

Treasurer. Annual Report of the Treasurer of ... Maryland, for ... 1847, to the General Assembly ... . *Annapolis: Riley & Davis, Printers.* 1847. 8vo, pp. 37. 5 folded Accounts. Continued. 45380

Also: ... Report of Mr. Carey, ... on ... the Finances of the State. *Annapolis: Riley & Davis, Printers.* 1844. 8vo, pp. 15. H.—Report of the Comptroller of the Treasury Department for ... 1853. To the General Assembly of Maryland. *Annapolis: Thomas E. Martin, Printer.* 1854. 8vo, pp. 78. 3 folded Accounts. Continued.—Annual Report of the Comptroller of the Treasury Department, for ... 1863, to the General Assembly of Maryland. *Baltimore: John D. Toy, Printer.* [n. d.] 8vo, pp. 48. 4 folded Tables. Continued.

Report of the State's Agent [S. DuVal] of the Western Shore of Maryland. [*Annapolis.* 1827.] 8vo, pp. (2), 4. 4 folded Accounts. 45381

Also: The Annual Report of the Treasurer of the W[estern] Shore for December Session, 1830. To the General Assembly ... . *Annapolis: Printed by Jeremiah Hughes.* 1830. 8vo, pp. 38. Continued to 1846.

The Union State Executive Committee versus the Union City Convention. [*Baltimore, May,* 1864.] 8vo, pp. 4. 45382

Also: Union State Central Committee. Proceedings Dec. 16, 1863, in reference to Emancipation. [n. p. n. d.] 8vo.

Union Prayer Meeting, held by the Christian Commission on the ... National Fast, April 30, 1863, in ... Baltimore. [*Baltimore:*] *James Young.* [1863.] 16mo, pp. 24. 45383

[First] Report of the Committee of the Christian Commission in charge of the District of Maryland. *Baltimore: Printed by Jos. Robinson.* 1862. 16mo, pp. 16. 45384

United States Christian Commission. Second Report of the Committee of Maryland. *Baltimore: Printed by Sherwood & Co.* 1863. 8vo, pp. 146. 45385

Rev. A. B. Cross' account of the Battle of Gettysburg forms pp. 113–144, but is paged separately, pp. 32, and Map. Also: Third Report [to September 1, 1864]. *Baltimore: James Young.* 1864. 8vo, pp. 286. + Fourth Report. *Baltimore: Innes & Maguire.* 1866. 8vo, pp. 279.

UNIVERSITY OF MARYLAND. Address of the University of Maryland, to the Public. [*Baltimore.* n. d.] 8vo, pp. 22. W.

... Annual Circular of the Faculty of Physic of the University ... 1846–47. *Baltimore: Printed by John Murphy.* 1846. 8vo, pp. 14, (1). Continued. H. 45387

... Annual Circular and Catalogue of the Medical Department of the University of Maryland, 1849–50. *Baltimore.* 1849. 8vo, pp. 20. 45388

Memorial of the Trustees of the University of Maryland, and the Trustees of Baltimore College, to the Legislature of Maryland. *Baltimore: John D. Toy, Printer.* 1830. 8vo, pp. 31.

Also: Catalogue ... of the University of Maryland ... . 1862–3. [n. p. n. d.] 8vo, pp. 14.—Memorial of the Medical Faculty ... to the Legislature ... . *Annapolis: William M'Neir, Printer.* 1837. 8vo, pp. 7.—Memorial of the Professors of the Medical School, to the Legislature ... . [*Annapolis.* 1826.] 8vo, pp. 4.—One of the Reports of the Joint Committee on the Memorial of the Regents ... . *Annapolis: Jeremiah Hughes, Printer.* 1839. 8vo, pp. 16. + [*Ibid.*] *William M'Neir, Printer.* 1839. 8vo, pp. 15, (1).—Register of the Faculty, Officers and Students of the Academic Department ... 1857–58. *Baltimore: Printed by John D. Toy.* 1858. 8vo, pp. 20. H.—Report of Mr. Stewart, one of the Joint Committee on the Memorial of the Regents ... . [*Annapolis.* 1839.] 8vo, pp. 2.—Report of the Joint Committee of the Legislature, Respecting the University ... February 24th, 1826. *Annapolis: Printed by Jeremiah Hughes.* 1826. 8vo, pp. 10.—Report of the Joint Committee on the Memorial of the Regents ... . *Annapolis: William M'Neir, Printer.* 1839. 8vo, pp. 10.—Report of the Majority of the Committee ... [on] ... the Bill for the Relief of the University ... . *Annapolis: William M'Neir, Printer.* 1839. 8vo, pp. 5. + Report of the Minority ... . [*Ibid.*] 1836. 8vo, pp. 7.—Report of the Trustees ... to the General Assembly. Dec. Sess. 1830–31. *Annapolis: Printed by J. Green.* 1831. 8vo, pp. 7. 1 folded Table. Continued.— ... Mr. Ridgely ... Report of the Joint Committee on the Memorial of the Regents ... . [*Annapolis.* 1839.] 8vo, pp. 10.—Statement shewing that the University Lottery has not been Exhausted. *Annapolis: Printed by Jeremiah Hughes.* 1826. 8vo, pp. 7.

A View of the Finances of the State of Maryland, and of Several Other States: in Letter Addressed to Governor Stevens,

By Thomas Kennedy ... . *Baltimore: Printed by Joseph Robinson.* 1824. 8vo, pp. 28. 45390

Votes and Proceedings of the Lower House of Assembly of the Province of Maryland. At ... Annapolis, on Tuesday ... 1750. ... [Colophon:] *Annapolis: Jonas Green.* MDCCL. Sm. folio, pp. 56. Continued. 45391

Votes and Proceedings of the Senate of the State of Maryland. February Session. 1777 ... . [*Annapolis.* 1777.] Folio, pp. 63. Continued. 45392

Votes and Resolves of the Lower House of Assembly of the Province of Maryland. July–August, 1729. [*Annapolis.*] 1729. Folio. 45393

See also "Journal."

The Constitution of the Washington Society of Maryland. *Baltimore: Printed by John L. Cook.* 1810. 8vo, pp. 15. 45394

The Western Maryland Rail Road, its Agricultural and Mineral Resources—its future Importance to ... Baltimore— ... *Baltimore: Printed by John D. Toy.* 1859. 16mo, pp. (2), xii, 39.

The Western Maryland Railroad and His Honor the Mayor of Baltimore, versus The Balt. & Ohio Railroad. *Baltimore.* 1863. 8vo, pp. 14. 45396

Signed "Expositor." A comparison of the roads. Also: Laws and Ordinances relating to the Western Maryland Rail Road Co. Compiled by Wm. A. Fisher, Attorney for the [Road]. *Baltimore: Wm. M. Innes.* 1861. 8vo, pp. 34. + *Baltimore: William K. Boyle.* 1868. 8vo, pp. 52.—Report and Ordinance submitted by the Committee on Ways and Means and passed by the City Council of Baltimore ... . *Baltimore: E. G. Armiger.* 1869. 8vo, pp. 20.—Fifth Annual Report of the President and Directors to the Stockholders for ... 1867. *Baltimore: William K. Boyle.* 1867. 8vo, pp. 20. Continued.—Report of the Surveys and Location for the Extension of the Western Maryland Rail Road. By Joseph S. Gitt, Civil Engineer. *Baltimore: Printed by John D. Toy.* 1865. 8vo, pp. 57. 2 Maps.

Constitution of the Women's Maryland Branch of the U. S. Sanitary Commission, with a List of the Officers ... . *Baltimore: John W. Woods.* 1865. 8vo, pp. 12. 45397

MARYLANDER, *pseudon.* Letters to Gov. Bradford, by a Marylander. *Baltimore.* 1863. 8vo, pp. 21. H. 45398

MAS (J. F.) The End of the Miserable World ... . *New York: J. F. Mas, Printer* ... 1864. 24mo, pp. 40. H. 45399

MAS. La fin du monde misérable. ... *New York: J. F. Mas ... Imprimeur.* 1864. 24mo, pp. 60. H. 45400

MAS Y RUBI (J. F.) Elogio fúnebre pronunciado el 26 de Abril de 1849 en las Exequias consagradas por la I. Universidad di Mérida al Ilustrísimo y Reverendísimo Señor Dr. Ignacio Fernandez Pena, dignísimo Arzobispo de Carácas y Venezuela. *Carácas.* 1850. 8vo, pp. 16. 45401

[MASCARENE (John).] The Manufacture of Pot-Ash in the British North-American Plantations Recommended. *Boston: Printed by Z. Fowle for T. Leverett,* ... 1757. 4to, pp. (4), 11.

[MASCARENHAS (Antonio).] Relação dos procedimentos que teve sendo Commissario Geral da Bulla da Sancta Cruzada, na declaração e decisão de algumas duvidas que moveu o collector João Baptista Palloto ... Dirigida ao Sanctissimo P. Urbano VIII nosso senhor. [*Lisboa.* 1625.] 4to, 60 leaves. 45403

[MASCARENHAS (Fernando).] Cort verhael vande ordre die sijne conincklicke Majesteyt van Spagnien aen sijn Generalissimo den Graef de la Torre inde Bay de todos los Sanctos gegeven heeft, om int werck te stellen al t'ghene hy tot recuperatie van Brasil noodigh achten soude. Mitsgaders 't remarcabelste dat op de custe van deselve capitania, soo int ghevecht vande Spaensche Vlote stercke 87 zeylen ... . *Amsterdam: I. van Hilten.* [1640.] Sm. 4to, 6 leaves. C. 45404

MASCARENHAS. Relacion nueva y verdadera de los felizes sucessos que ha tenido el Señor D. Fernando Mascareñas, General de la Armada de Portugal. Dase cuenta de la Batalla que tuvieron contra 36 vavios de Olanda, que iban á socorrer la plaza de Pernambouc, adonde murio en ella el General de Olanda. [n. p. 1640.] 4to, pp. 4, in verse. 45405

MASCARENHAS (I. M. da C.) Oração funebre, panegyrica e historica, nas exequias que celebraram os Irmãos da veneravel Irmandade de S. Pedro da cidade do Rio de Janeiro, á saudosa memoria do fidelissimo rei de Portugal D. João V, no dia 26 de Fevereiro de 1751. Por Ignacio Manuel da Costa Mascarenhas. *Lisboa, na Officina dos Herdeiros de Antonio Pedroso Galrão.* 1752. 4to, pp. xvi, 22. 45406

[MASCARENHAS (José Freire de Monteroyo).] Os Orizes conquistados, ou noticia da conversão dos indomitos Orizes Procazes, povos barbaros do certão do Brasil ... . *Lisboa, por Antonio Pedroso Galrão.* 1716. 4to, pp. 14. 45407

[MASCARENHAS.] Relação da embaixada que o poderoso Rei de Angomé ... mandou ao ... Sr. D. Luis Peregrino de Ataide, Conde de Atouguia, vice-rei do Estado do Brasil. Por J. F. M. M. *Lisboa, por Francisco da Silva.* 1751. 4to, pp. 11. 45408

Also: Guimarães festiva, ou relação do festejo publico, com que na villa de Guimarães se applaudiram os reaes desposorios do serenissimo Principe do Brasil, e da serenissima senhora Infanta D. Maria Barbara, Princeza das Asturias, no mez de Fevereiro de 1728. *Lisboa, por Pedro Ferreira.* 1728. 4to, pp. 16.—Relação de um prodigio succedido em uma das cidades da provincia do Paraguay n'este anno passado de 1735. *Lisboa, por Antonio Corrêa Lemos.* 1735. 4to, pp. 6.

MASCARENHAS (J.) Carta que o Vice-Rei do Brasil D. Jorge Mascarenhas, Marquez de Montalvão, escreven do Excellentissimo Conde de Nassau, General das Hollandezas em Pernambuco. *Lisboa, por Jorge Rodrigues.* 1641. 4to, pp. 3. 45409

Maschill, or The Faithful Instructor, offering Memorials of Christianity, in Twenty-Six Exercises upon the New English Catechism, &c., with an Addition [to render the work yet more universally acceptable and serviceable,] of the like operation upon the Assemblies Catechism. *Boston: Printed by B. Green and J. Allen, for Samuel Phillips, at the Brick Shop.* 1702. 12mo, pp. 192.

[MASCRIER (J. B.)] *See* Dumont (M.), Vol. III., No. 9605.

[MASERES (F.)] An | Account | of the | Proceedings | of the | British, | And other Protestant Inhabitants, | of the | Province of Quebeck, | In North-America, | In order to obtain | An House of Assembly | In that Province. | *London:* | *B. White.* | MDCCLXXV. 8vo, pp. 294. BA., C. + Additional Papers ... Being an Appendix ... . *London: W. White.* M.DCC.LXXVI. 8vo, pp. 510.

"This volume is the work of Francis Maseres, Esq. lately Attorney-General of Quebec, and now Cursitor Baron of the Court of Exchequer."—*Monthly Review,* LIII. 46. *See also* "M. Rev.," LV. 397, *and* our Vol. II., No. 4947.

[MASERES.] The Canadian Freeholder: A Dialogue shewing the Sentiments of the Bulk of the Freeholders of Canada concerning the late Quebeck-Act, with some Remarks on the Boston-Charter Act, and an Attempt to shew the great Expediency of immediately repealing both those Acts of Parliament, as a ground for a Reconciliation with the United Colonies in America. *London: B. White.* M.DCC.LXXVI. 8vo, pp. 483. 45412

This was reissued the following year with an additional volume (pp. xxii, 404), and the title changed to read "in Two Dialogues," and on the publication of Vol. III. (pp. xlii, 399–810) in 1779, the title was made to read "in Three Dialogues;" there are also other verbal changes. The dialogues are between a sensible and substantial Canadian freeholder of the Roman Catholic religion and an English Protestant gentleman, and are intended to convey a true representation of the sentiments of the French, or Canadian, inhabitants of that province, etc. *See also* "M. Rev.," XLIII. 161, LVII. 467, LVIII. 149, LXI. 171, LXII. 239, LXIII. 355, 439, "London Review," *and* Bishop Watson's "Anecdotes," p. 55.

MASERES. A | Collection | of | several Commissions, | and | other Public Instruments, | Proceeding from His Majesty's Royal Authority, | and | other Papers, | Relating to the State of the Province in Quebec in North | America, since the Conquest of it by the British Arms | in 1760. | Collected by | Francis Maseres, Esquire, | His Majesty's Attorney General in the said Province. | *London:* | *Printed by W. and J. Richardson*, ... MDCCLXXII. 4to, pp. xv, 311.

[MASERES.] Considerations on the Expediency of Admitting Representatives from the American Colonies into The British House of Commons. *London: B. White.* M.DCC.LXX. 8vo, pp. (2), 41. BA. 45414

[MASERES.] An Enquiry into the Extent of the Power of Juries on Trials of Indictments or Informations for publishing Seditious or other Criminal Writings or Libels, extracted from ... "Additional Papers concerning the Province of Quebec," etc. *London.* 1785. 8vo. S. 45415

MASERES. Mémoire | à la | Défense d'un Plan d'Acte de Parlement | Pour l'Établissement des Loix de la Province | de Québec, | Dressé | Par Mr François Masères, | ... | Contre | Les Objections de Mr François Joseph Cugnet ... . *A Londres: Imprimé chez Edmond Allen.* M.DCC.LXXIII. Folio, pp. (2), 159, (1). H.

[MASERES.] Occasional Essays on Various Subjects, chiefly Political and Historical: ... *London: R. Wilks.* 1809. 8vo, pp. xvi, 607. 45417

Contains several pieces relating to America, as: Proposal for a Reconciliation with the Revolted Colonies; Inexpediency of establishing Bishops in America; State of North America after the Capture of Lord Cornwallis' Army; Charters of Massachusetts; Proceedings of the Town of Boston, 1772; Account of the Noblesse or Gentry in Canada, Slavery, etc.

[MASERES.] A | Paraphrase | on | A Passage | in | A Sermon | preached by the | Most Reverend Dr. Markham, | ... the 21st of February, 1777; | When it was expected by the Persons who had | advised the American War, that the re- | volted Colonies in America would soon | be intirely subdued, and reduced | to the obedience of the | British Parliament. | [n. p. 1777.] 8vo, pp. (2), 38. H. 45418

MASIAS (F.) Curso elemental de economia-politica por Felipe Masias ... . *Lima.* 1860. 4to, pp. 152. 45419

The Masked Lady of the White House. *See* Ku-Klux-Klan.

MASKELYNE (N.) Astronomical Observations made at the Island of Barbados, at Willoughby Fort, and at the Observatory on Constitution Hill. By Nevil Maskelyne. 1765. Sm. 4to.

MASON (——). Mason's Handbook to California; its Gold, and how to get it; a Description of the Country, &c. *London.* 1850? 8vo, pp. 16. 45421

MASON (——). Brother Mason, the Circuit Rider; or, Ten Years a Methodist Preacher. *Cincinnati: H. M. Rulison.* 1855. 12mo, pp. 310. Plate. C. 45422

MASON (A. T.) Controversy between Armistead Thompson Mason and Charles Fenton Mercer. *Washington.* 1813. 8vo, pp. 36. S. 45423

MASON (A.) The Quackery of the Age: A Satire on the Times. By Augustus Mason, M.D. ... *Boston: White, Lewis & Potter, Printers.* 1845. 8vo, pp. 44. H. 45424

MASON (B.) Light rising out of Obscurity, or, a Reply to Francis Herr's Pamphlet, intitled A Short Explication of the written Word of God: likewise of the ... Peaceable Kingdom of Christ against the People called Quakers. By Benjamin Mason. *Philadelphia: Printed by Joseph Crukshank* ... . 1790. 8vo, pp. 48. P. 45425

[MASON] (C. A. B.) Utterance; or, Private Voices to the Public Heart. ... Poems. By Caroline A Briggs [Mason]. *Boston: Phillips, Sampson, and Company.* 1852. 8vo, pp. 255. H.

MASON (C.) A Discourse ... in ... Salem ... February 19, 1843, on the Death of the Rt. Rev. Alexander V. Griswold, D.D. ... By Charles Mason. *Salem: W. and S. B. Ives.* M.D.CCC.XLIII. 8vo, pp. 23. BA. 45427

Also: A Discourse ... on the National Fast Day, January 4th, 1861, in ... Boston. ... *Boston: Printed by David Clapp.* 1861. 8vo, pp. 18.—A Discourse on the Death of Daniel Webster, ... Oct. 31, 1852. ... *Boston: Printed by John Wilson & Son.* 1852. 8vo, pp. 25. BA.

MASON (C.) An Elementary Treatise on the Structure and Operations of the National and State Governments of the United States. ... By Charles Mason, A.M. ... *Boston: David H. Williams.* 1842. 12mo, pp. 233. B. + Second Edition. *Boston: James Munroe and Company.* 1843. 12mo, pp. 233. H. 45428

MASON (C.) A Brief History of the Duane Street late Cedar Street Presbyterian Church; ... Cyrus Mason, Pastor. ... *New-York: James Van Norden, Printer.* 1835. 18mo, pp. 27.

Also: Eulogy on Mr. John Leckie, A.M., ... delivered ... October 20th, 1841 ... . *New-York: Hopkins and Jennings, Printers.* 1841. 8vo, pp. 15.—The Growth and Prospects of the University of the City of New York: a Discourse ... before the Alumni ... . *New York: Bartlett & Welford.* 1847. 8vo, pp. 32.—The Oration on the Thirteenth Anniversary of the American Institute, ... October 15th, 1840. ... *New-York: Printed by Hopkins & Jennings.* 1840. 8vo, pp. 53. + Second Edition. [*Ibid.*] 8vo.

MASON (D.) Observations on the Present State and Future Prospects of the Island of Jamaica. By D. Mason. *London.* 1837. 8vo. P. 45430

MASON (D. H.) Address at the Centennial Celebration of the Settlement of ... Lancaster, N. H. July 14, 1864. By David H. Mason. ... *Concord, N. H.: Printed by McFarland & Jenks.* 1864. 8vo, pp. 16. 45431

MASON (E.) Impartial Account of the Trial of Ebenezer Mason ... for the Murder of William Pitt Allen. ... *Dedham: Printed by H. Mann.* 1802. 12mo, pp. 28. H. 45432

Also: The Last Words ... , *Dedham.* 1802. 12mo, pp. 18. + Third Edition. [*Ibid.*]

MASON (E. P.) Life and Writings of Ebenezer Porter Mason; ... By Denison Olmsted ... . *New York: Dayton & Newman.* 1842. 12mo, pp. 252. BA. 45433

MASON (E. R.) Argument of Edwin R. Mason, in Support of the Act of the Surveyor General of Illinois and Missouri ... . *Washington.* 1857. 8vo, pp. 17. B. 45434

MASON (E.) Discourse ... April 2, 1868; on the Life and Character of Hon. John Albion Andrew, LL.D. ... By Rev. Elias Mason, M.A. *Boston.* 1868. 8vo. S. 45435

MASON (E. V.) The Southern Poems of the War. Collected and arranged by Miss Emily V. Mason. *Baltimore: John Murphy & Co.* 1867. 12mo, pp. 456. + Second ... Edition. [*Ibid.*] 1868. 8vo, pp. 524. Plate. + Third Revised and Enlarged Edition. [*Ibid.*] 1869. 12mo, pp. 524. Plate. 45436

MASON (E.) God's Hand in Human Events. A Sermon, ... on the 14th July, 1850. In reference to the death of President Taylor. By Erskine Mason, D.D. *New York: R. Craighead, Printer.* 1850. 8vo, pp. 19. BA., C. 45437

MASON. A Pastor's Legacy; being Sermons on Practical Subjects. By the late Rev. Erskine Mason, D.D. ... With a Brief Memoir of the Author, by Rev. Wm. Adams, D.D. *New York: Charles Scribner.* 1853. 8vo, pp. liv, 471. Portrait. B.

Also: An Evangelical Ministry, the Security of a Nation: A Sermon ... in behalf of the American Home Missionary Society ... January 2, 1848. ... *New York: Printed by William Osborn.* 1848. 8vo, pp. 24.—The Inconsistencies of Christian Professors. A Sermon ... Nov. 12th, 1837. ... *New York: E. French.* 1837. 8vo, pp. 32.—A Rebuke to the Worldly Ambition of the Present Age. ... *New York.* 1836. 8vo, pp. 30.—A Sermon ... Oct. 19th, 1834. ... *New York.* 1835. 8vo, pp. 24.—"Signs of the Times." A Sermon, ... before the Foreign Missionary Society of New York and Brooklyn. ... April 7, 1850 ... . *New-York: Printed by John A. Gray.* 1850. 8vo, pp. 31.—The Subject and Spirit of the Ministry. A Sermon ... before the Synod of New-York, at ... Newburgh, Oct. 16th, 1838. ... *New-York: E. French.* MDCCCXXXVIII. 8vo, pp. 34.— ... A Sermon ... February 2d, 1845; occasioned by the Death of John E. Hyde ... . *New York: Wm. A. Wheeler.* 1845. 8vo, pp. 24. H.

MASON (F.) The Story of a Working Man's Life: With Sketches of Travel in Europe, Asia, Africa, and America. ... By Francis Mason, D.D. With an Introduction by William R. Williams, D.D. ... *New York: Oakley, Mason & Co.* 1870. 12mo, pp. xxvii, (1), 462. 4 Plates. BA. 45439

MASON (G.) The Life of Richard, Earl Howe. By George Mason ... . *London: White.* 1803. 8vo, pp. 111. S. 45440

See "M. Rev.," XLVI. 101.

MASON (G.) The Tariff Controversy, or the Promotion of American Industry in the Farming, Manufacturing, and Mechanical Walks of Life. By George Mason. *Wells River, Vt.* 1842. 12mo. 45441

[MASON (George Champlin).] Newport and its Environs, Illustrated by a Series of Views. ... Vol. I. *Newport.* 1848. Oblong folio. 45442

[MASON.] Newport Illustrated in a Series of Pen and Pencil Sketches. By the Editor of the Newport Mercury. ... *D. Appleton & Co., New York.* [1854.] 12mo, pp. 110. Plates. C.

Some copies have the imprint *Newport, R. I.: C. E. Hammett, Jr.* [1854.]

MASON. Re-Union of the Sons and Daughters of Newport, R. I., August 23, 1859. By George C. Mason. Compiled and printed by Order of the General Committee of Arrangements. *Newport, R. I.: Fred. A. Pratt & Co., Printers.* 1859. 12mo, pp. 297, (1). BA. 45444

Contains a history of the "Redwood Library and Athenæum," from its establishment in 1730, to its enlargement in 1859.

MASON (G. E.) Catalogue of ... Books and Tracts, wholly relating to America and the West Indies, ... formed by Mr. G. E. Mason, ... sold by Auction, by Messrs. Puttick and Simpson, ... November 27th, and Four following Days. [1860.] 8vo.

There are in all three parts. This G. E. Mason was an English barrister and an amateur bookseller.

MASON (H.) A Poem, ... at the Fifth Anniversary of the Franklin Debating Society, on the Birth-Day of Benjamin Franklin, January 17, 1827. By Henry Mason. *Boston: [Isaac R. Butts & Co. Printers.* 1827.] 8vo, pp. 8. 45446

Also: Poetry. A Poem before the Franklin Debating Society, ... January 17, 1830, being ... their Seventh Anniversary. ... *Boston: For the Society.* M DCCC XXX. 8vo, pp. 9.

MASON (H. M.) The City of God. A Sermon, ... in ... Newark, before an Annual Convention of the Church, ... May 28, 1834. By Henry M. Mason ... . *Camden: Josiah Harrison.* MDCCCXXXIV. 8vo, pp. 17. B. 45447

MASON. The City of God in the Anglo-Saxon Church. A Sermon before the Clergy and Laity of the Eastern Shore of Maryland, Oct 10, 1866. By Rev. H. M. Mason, D.D. *New York: Pott & Amery.* 1867. 16mo, pp. 42. 45448

Also: An Address ... May 21, 1840. *Easton, Md.: Printed by E. G. Dorsey.* 1840. 8vo, pp. 16. P.

MASON (James M.) Mr. Mason made the following Report of Committee on Foreign Relations, in the Senate, Feb. 11, 1853. [*Washington.* 1853.] 8vo, pp. 17. 45449

Relates to Central America.

MASON. Speech of Hon. J. M. Mason ... on the Admission of Kansas. ... March 15, 1858. [*Washington.* 1858.] 8vo, pp. 16. B. 454[illegible]

MASON. Correspondence relative to the Case of Messrs. Mason and Slidell. [*Washington.* 1862.] 8vo, pp. 15. 45451

Between Mr. Seward, Mr. Adams, Lord Lyons, and Mr. Thouvenel. Also: Correspondence with Mr. Mason respecting the Blockade and Recognition of the Confederate States. [*London.*] 1863. Folio, pp. 17.—Correspondence respecting the Seizure of Messrs. Mason, Slidell, McFarland and Eustis, from on board the Royal Mail Packet, "Trent," by the Commander of the United States Ship of War, "San Jacinto." [n. p. n. d.] Folio, pp. 37.—A Legal View of the Seizure of Messrs. Mason and Slidell. *New York.* 1861. 8vo, pp. 27. *See also* our Vol. IV., No. 16887, *note*, and [Lowell (John)], Vol. X., No. 42435.

MASON (J.) Proceedings in Massachusetts and New Hampshire on the Death of the Hon. Jeremiah Mason. *Boston: Printed by John Wilson.* 1849. 8vo, pp. 41. BA., S. 45452

MASON (J.) A briefe Discourse of the New-found-land, with the Situation, Temperature, and Commodities thereof. By John Mason. *Edinburgh: Andro Hart.* 1620. 8vo, 7 leaves.

Title from Lowndes, so rare that we have been unable to find a copy.

MASON (J.) A | Brief History | of the | Pequot War: | Especially of the memorable Taking of their Fort at Mistick in Connecticut | In | 1637. | Written by | Major John Mason, | A principal Actor therein, as then Chief Captain and Com- | mander of Connecticut Forces. | With an Introduction and some Explanatory Notes, | By the Reverend | Mr. Thomas Prince. | ... *Boston: Printed & Sold by S. Kneeland & T. Green, | in Queen-Street*, 1736. 12mo, pp. (2), vi, x, 22. BA. 45454

Very rare. Major Mason was one of the first settlers of Dorchester, in 1630. From that place he removed about the year 1635, and assisted in laying the foundation of a new colony. After the Pequot War, in which he took a prominent part, he was appointed by the Governor of Connecticut, Major-General of all their forces, which office he continued to hold till his death.

MASON. A Brief History of the Pequot War ... . *New York: Reprinted by J. Sabin and Sons.* 1869. 8vo. 45455

Also reprinted in the "Mass. Hist. Soc. Coll.," Second Series, Vol. VIII., and appended to the "Case of the Governor and Company of Connecticut and Mohegan Indians." *London.* 1769. 4to, pp. 254–283.

[MASON (John).] Recollections of the Early Days of the National Guard comprising the Prominent Events in the History of the Famous Seventh Regiment New York Militia By an Ex-Orderly Sergeant A Veteran of the National Guard *New York J. M. Bradstreet & Son* 1868 Large 8vo, pp. (4), iv, 201. Plate. 45456

MASON (J.) ... To the Hon. Abraham Lincoln, President Elect of the United States. By J. Mason ... . [n. p. 1861?] 8vo, pp. 12. H. 45457

MASON (J. L.) Remarks of John L. Mason and Joseph S. Bosworth, on the Rights and Powers of the Public School Society. March, 1847. [n. p. n. d.] 8vo. 45458

MASON (J. Mitchell). A Funeral Oration, Delivered in the Brick Presbyterian Church in the City of New-York, on the 22d Day of February, 1800, being the Day recommended by Congress to the Citizens of the United States, Publicly to testify their Grief for the Death of Gen. Washington: By Appointment of a Number of the Clergy of New-York ... . By John M. Mason, A.M. ... *New-York: Printed by G. F. Hopkins.* 1800. 8vo, pp.

23. BA. + The Second Edition. *New-York: George Folliolt Hopkins.* 1800. 8vo, pp. 32. 45459

The half title to the second edition reads "Mr. Mason's and Mr. Ames' Orations on George Washington."

MASON. An Oration Commemorative of the Late Major-General Alexander Hamilton; pronounced before the New-York State Society of the Cincinnati, ... the 31st July, 1804. By J. M. Mason, D.D. ... *New-York: Printed by Hopkins and Seymour.* 1804. 8vo, pp. 40. BA. + *London: R. Edwards.* 1804. 8vo, pp. 38. 45460

This elicited "A Review of Dr. John M. Mason's Oration on the Death of Gen. Hamilton." ... *New-York: Printed by James Oram.* 1807. 8vo, pp. 10. First printed in the "Christian Observer," 1805, and reprinted in this form. A very unjust and unfair criticism. *See* "M. Rev.," XLVII. 446.

MASON. A Sermon, Preached September 20th, 1793; A Day set apart, in the City of New-York, for Public Fasting, ... on account of a Malignant and Mortal Fever prevailing in ... Philadelphia. By John Mitchel Mason ... . *New York: Printed by Samuel Loudon & Son.* MDCCXCIII. 8vo, pp. 64. BA. 45461

MASON. ... A Sermon ... December 2, 1821, on the Occasion of Resigning his Charge ... By John M. Mason, D.D. With an Appendix. ... *New-York: ... Abraham Paul, Printer.* 1822. 8vo, pp. 39. H. 45462

[MASON.] The Voice of Warning, to Christians, on the Ensuing Election of a President of the United States. ... *New-York: Printed by G. F. Hopkins.* 1800. 8vo, pp. 40. B. 45463

An Anti-Jefferson tract. *See also* [Linn (W.)], X. 41347. Also: Christian Mourning: A Sermon occasioned by the Death of Mrs. Isabella Graham: ... preached on ... the 14th Aug. 1814. ... *New-York: Whiting and Watson.* 1814. 8vo, pp. 50. BA.—Dr. Mason's Speech, Relative to the Resignation of his Pastoral Charge, in the City of New-York. ... *Philadelphia: Printed by Jane Aitken.* 1810. 8vo, pp. iv, 64. B.—First Ripe Fruits; being a Collection of Tracts, To which are added Two Sermons. With a ... Short Memoir of the Author. *London.* 1803. 8vo.—Hope for the Heathen: A Sermon, ... before the New-York Missionary Society, ... November 7, 1797. ... *New-York: Printed by T. & J. Swords.* 1797. 8vo, pp. 49. BA.—Living Faith: A Sermon preached before the Society for the Destitute Sick ... . *New York.* 1802. 8vo, pp. 35.—Mercy Remembered in Wrath. A Sermon ... on the 19th of February, 1795, ... a Day of Thanksgiving ... . *New York: Printed by J. Buel.* M,DCC,XCV. 8vo, pp. 33. BA.

MASON. The Writings of the Late John M. Mason, D.D. consisting of Sermons, Essays, and Miscellanies ... . Selected and arranged by Rev. Ebenezer Mason. ... *New York: The Editor.* 1832. 4 vols., 8vo, pp. xiv, 405; vii, 414; iv, 438; iv, 447.

MASON. The Complete Works of John M. Mason, D.D. ... Edited by his Son, Ebenezer Mason. Second Enlarged Edition. *New York: Baker and Scribner.* 1850–1849. 4 vols., 8vo, pp. xvii, (1), 557, Portrait; (4), 593; (2), 604; (4), 579. 45465

See E. B. Williston's "Eloquence of the United States," Vol. V., *also* Van Vechten (J.) The following relate to J. M. Mason: An Appeal from the Denunciation of the Rev. Dr. Mason against Rational Christians. By a Unitarian of New York. *New York.* 1822. 8vo, pp. 24. W.—Letter to John M. Mason in answer to his Speech, at the Thirteenth Anniversary Meeting of the British and Foreign Bible Society. By a Soldier of the American Revolution. *Elizabethtown, N. J.* 1818. 8vo. W.

MASON (J. T.) Speech of Mr. John Thomson Mason, ... on the United States Fiscal Bank Bill: ... August 3, 1841. [*Washington.* 1841.] 8vo, pp. 16. BA. 45466

Also: ... An Address upon ... the late Dr. Frederick Dorsey, of ... Maryland ... . Second Edition. *Baltimore: William K. Boyle.* 1867. 12mo, pp. 50. Portrait. B.—Speech ... July 7, 1842, on the Tariff. *Washington.* 1842. 8vo.

MASON (J. Y.) Address before the Alumni Association of the University of North Carolina, ... June 2, 1847, ... By Hon. John Y. Mason, L.L.D. *Washington: Printed by J. & G. S. Gideon.* 1847. 8vo, pp. 24. B. 45467

MASON (J.) An Oration, delivered March 6, 1780. At the Request of the Inhabitants of the Town of Boston, to commemorate the Bloody Tragedy of the Fifth of March, 1770. By Mr. Jonathan Mason, Jun. ... *Boston: Printed by John Gill.* M DCC LXXX. 4to, pp. 23. BA. 45468

[MASON.] Report of the Select Committee ... [on] a Resolution relating to the Claim of Massachusetts, for Expenditures of their Militia ... . March 10, 1818. ... [n. p. n. d.] 8vo, pp. 38. H. 45469

MASON (J.) Argument of Joseph Mason, Esq. against the Petition of Nathaniel Wood and others, for the Establishment of Courts ... at Fitchburg; ... 1852. ... *Worcester: Printed by Henry J. Howland.* [n. d.] 8vo, pp. 36. H. 45470

MASON (J.) Trial of Joseph Mason for the Murder of William Farrel; Reported by M. T. Gould. *Onondaga.* 1820. 8vo. 45471

MASON (L.) Address on Church Music; ... October 7, 1826, in ... Boston. By Lowell Mason. *Boston: Hilliard, Gray, and Company.* 1826. 8vo, pp. 42. BA. 45472

Also various music-books, some of which include national airs, patriotic songs, etc.

[MASON (Lyman).] Report on the Red Slate Quarry ... at Hampton, N. Y. *Boston: Press of Geo. C. Rand & Avery.* 1864. 8vo, pp. 15. H. 45473

MASON (M.) An Oration pronounced ... at Bethel [Maine], ... July 4th, 1809. By Moses Mason, Junior. *Sutton, Massachusetts: Printed by Sewall Goodridge, for Edmund Chapman, Bethel.* 1810. 12mo, pp. 12. W. 45474

MASON (R. B.) The Georgian Bay Canal. Reports of Col. R. B. Mason, ... and Kivas Tully ... with an Appendix, Profile, and Map. *Chicago.* 1858. 8vo, pp. 63. BA. 45475

MASON. Report of the Survey and Examination of a Route for a Railroad from Bridgeport, in the direction of New York City to Sawpitt's Village. By R. B. Mason. *New York.* 1838. 8vo. N. 45476

MASON (R. H.) Pictures of Life in Mexico. By R. H. Mason. *London.* 1851. 2 vols., post 8vo. + [*Ibid.*] 1852.

With anecdotes of General Santa Anna, and etchings by the author.

MASON. Mexikanische Bilder. Aus dem Englischen von M. B. Lindau. *Dresden: R. Kuntze.* 1853. 2 vols., 12mo, pp. viii, 239; (2), iv, 205. C. 45478

MASON (R. M.) A Sketch of ... the late Ebenezer Francis, of Boston. By R. M. Mason. ... *New York: Printed by George W. Wood.* 1859. 8vo, pp. 15. BA. 45479

MASON (R. R.) Slavery in America. An Essay for the Times. By Richard R. Mason. *Boston: Press of Crocker and Brewster.* 1853. 8vo, pp. 34. B. 45480

[MASON (R. S.)] A Letter to the Bishop of North Carolina on ... his late Pastoral on the Salisbury Convention; By the Chairman of the Committee on the State of the Church. *New York.* 1850. 12mo, pp. 71. B. 45481

Also: Inaugural Address before ... Newark College ... April 26th, 1836 ... . *Philadelphia: Jesper Harding, Printer.* 1836. 8vo, pp. 27, (1). H.

MASON (Samson). Speech of Mr. S. Mason, ... on the Objections of the President to the Bill to establish a Fiscal Corporation. ... House of Representatives, September 10, 1841. *Washington.* 1841. 8vo, pp. 16. B. 45482

MASON (T.) A Sermon, ... at Northfield, on the Day of ... Thanksgiving: November 29, 1804. By Thomas Mason, A.M.

... *Greenfield, Mass.: Printed by John Denio.* MDCCCIV. 8vo, pp. 16. BA. 45483

Also: A Discourse ... at Northfield, Mass. ... Feb. 28, 1830. ... on ... the Close of his Ministerial Labors ... . *Greenfield, Mass.: Phelps & Ingersoll, Printers.* 1830. 8vo, pp. 11, (1).—Thanksgiving Sermon at Middlebury, 1798 ... . *Rutland, Vermont.* 1799. 8vo.

MASON (W.) A Sermon ... at Castine, January 13th, 1799. Being ... the Interment of a ... Lady ... . By William Mason, A.M. ... *Printed at Castine, (Maine,) by David J. Waters.* MDCCXCIX. 8vo, pp. 17. BA. 45484

MASON (W.) An Occasional Discourse, ... in ... York, Jan. 27, on the Subject of the African Slave Trade. By William Mason, M.A. ... *York.* 1788. 4to. 45485

See "M. Rev.," LXXVIII. 270.

MASON (W.) A Collection of Psalms and Hymns. Translated into the Language of the York Indians of the Diocese of Rupert's Land, North-West America. *London: Society for Promoting Christian Knowledge.* 1860. 18mo, pp. 163. 45486

[MASON (W.)] The Improvement of Taunton River. [*Taunton, Mass.* n. d.] 8vo, pp. 8. H. 45487

MASON (W. P.) The Case of the Jeune Eugenie, determined by the Circuit Court of the United States, ... at Boston, December, 1821. With an Appendix. By William P. Mason ... . *Boston: Wells and Lilly.* 1822. 8vo, pp. (4), 108. B. 45488

MASON. An Oration ... July 4, 1827, ... before the ... City of Boston. By William Powell Mason. ... *Boston: Nathan Hale, Printer.* 1827. 8vo, pp. 31. BA. 45489

Mason and Dixon's Line. *See* Maryland, No. 45088.

MASON, *N. H.* Report of the School Committee ... for ... 1857. *Groton Junction: Printed by Brown & Son.* 1857. 8vo, pp. 15. Continued. H. 45490

Report of the Selectmen ... for ... 1854. *Groton Junction: Geo. H. Brown's Press.* 1854. 8vo, pp. 9. Continued. 45491

MASONRY. *See also* under the names of the various States.

An Address. *See* [Lathrop (John H.)], Vol. x., No. 39191.

The Address of the National Anti-Masonic Convention, held in Philadelphia, September 11, 1830, to the People of the United States. *Philadelphia.* 1830. 8vo, pp. 24. M., W. 45492

The American Masonic Register ... being a Periodical devoted to Masonry ... . *Albany, N. Y.* 1838–40. 8vo. 45493

Anti-Masonic Almanac. *See* Giddins (E.), VII. 27332, *note.*

Anti-Masonic Almanac, for New England. *Boston.* 1829–35. 12mo. + Gest's Anti-Masonic Almanac for ... 1837: ... . *Philadelphia: Printed by William K. Boden.* 1837. 12mo, pp. 48. B.

The Anti-Masonic Review and Monthly Magazine. ... H. Dana Ward, Editor. Vol. I. *New York.* 1828. 8vo. S.

Anti-Masonic Tracts. *Boston.* 1829. 8vo. 45496

Five or more printed.

Catalogue of Books. *See* [Gassett (Henry)], VII. 26745.

Constitution and Abstract of Proceedings of the Grand Lodge of Georgia, A.L. 5820. *Savannah.* 1820. 2 vols., 8vo. 45497

The Constitution of the Free Masons. Containing the History, Charges, Regulations, &c., of that ... Fraternity. ... *Boston: Reprinted.* 1750. 4to, pp. 94. + *New York.* 1855. 4to.

See also Freemasons. Our No. 25798, Vol. VII., has pp. 288.

Constitution of the General Grand Royal Arch Chapter, of the Northern States of America. *Albany: Thomas S. Webb.* 1799. 12mo, pp. 19. + [n. p.] 1844. 12mo, pp. 14. + [n. p.] 1853. 12mo, pp. 10. H. 45499

A Discourse on Masonry ... . *Philadelphia: Printed by D. Humphreys.* M. DCC. XCVII. 8vo, pp. 10. H. 45500

Free Masonry. ... Exposed in ... Extracts of its Standard Authors; with a Review of Town's speculative Masonry: ... . By a Master Mason. ... *New-York.* 1828. 8vo, pp. xvi, 399. Plate. B. 45501

Funeral Service of the Free ... Masons of ... California ... at the Burial of ... Brother Thomas Starr King, ... March 6, A.L. 5864, A.D. 1864. [n. p. n. d.] 24mo, pp. 15. H. 45502

Grand Lodge of the State of Louisiana. Report of the Committee appointed to inquire into the use and progress of Free-Masonry in Louisiana ... . [n. p. 1849.] 8vo, pp. 27, folded leaf. H. 45503

See also Louisiana, Vol. x., No. 42259.

Grand Lodge of the United States. Adjourned Session, Sept. 1850. *Cincinnati.* 1850. 8vo. S. 45504

Also: Annual Communication, Baltimore, Sept. 1854. *Baltimore.* 1854. 8vo.

Illustrations of Masonry. *See* [Morgan (W.)]

An Investigation into Free-Masonry by a Joint Committee of the Legislature of Massachusetts. ... March, 1834. *Boston: Dutton and Wentworth, Printers.* 1834. 8vo, pp. 76, 54. H.

Legislative Investigation into Masonry; ... Examination ... of more than Fifty Adhering and Seceding Masons, before ... the General Assembly of Rhode Island ... . *Boston.* 1832. 8vo, pp. 85, (2). H. 45506

Letters addressed to W. L. Stone. *See* Vol. x., No. 40568.

List of the Grand Officers and Members of the Supreme Council of the Grand Inspectors General of the 33d Degree. *New York.* 5813. 16mo. + [*Ibid.*] 1816. 45507

The Lodge of Saint Andrew, and the Massachusetts Grand Lodge. ... 5756–5769. *Boston.* 1870. 8vo, pp. 292. Plates.

Masonic Almanac for 1828. *Boston.* [1828.] 8vo. 45509

The Masonic Chronicle; Devoted to Freemasonry, its History, Jurisprudence, and Philosophy. *New York.* 1859. 8vo, pp. 174. Continued to 1860. 45510

The Masonic Eclectic; or Gleanings from the Harvest Field of Masonic Literature ... . Edited by John W. Simons and Rob. Macoy. ... *New York: Masonic Publishing and Manufacturing Company.* 1865–67. Vols. I. and II., 12mo, pp. 571, 488; Vol. III., 8vo, pp. 380. 45511

The Masonic Gavel. By John W. Reams. *Annapolis, Md.* 1865. 4to, 3 Nos. 45512

The Masonic Jewel; ... A. J. Wheeler, Editor and Proprietor. *Memphis, Tenn.* [n. d.] Vol. I., rl. 8vo; Vol. II., 4to, pp. 192.

The Masonic Journal; Devoted to Masonry, Science, and Literature ... . *Marietta, Georgia.* 1849–52. 5 vols., 8vo.

The Masonic Messenger; Devoted to Masonic Intelligence, Business, Jurisprudence ... . *New York: M. J. Drummond.* 1855–60. 6 vols., 4to. 45515

The Masonic Mirror; ... Levi & Nevin, Editors. ... Vol. V. [n. p.] 1868. 8vo. Discontinued. 45516

The Masonic Mirror; ... Amasa W. Bishop, P.M., Editor. Vol. I. *San Francisco: Fred. B. Cornish.* 1870. 8vo, pp. 440. Continued. 45517

The Masonic Mirror and American Keystone; ... *Philadelphia: Leon Hyneman.* 1852. 8vo. Continued. 45518

Masonic Mirror and Mechanic's Intelligencer. ... *Boston, Mass.: Moore & Powers.* [n. d.] 3 vols., 4to. S. 45519

The Masonic Mirror and Organ of the Grand Lodge of Kentucky. [n. p. n. d] 3 or more vols., 8vo. 45520

The Masonic Miscellany and Ladies' Literary Magazine ... . [By W. G. Hunt.] *Lexington, Ky.: William Gibbes Hunt.* 1822–1823. 2 vols., 8vo, pp. vi, 480; vi, 480. B. 45521

Masonic Monitor. Edited by J. A. Bonitz. *Goldsboro, N. C.* [n. d.] Folio. 45522

The Masonic Monthly. [S. Evans, Editor.] Vol. I. *Boston: Edward L. Mitchell.* [1864.] 8vo, pp. 572. Continued. B.

The Masonic Record; A Monthly Magazine ... . John Frizzell & Co., Editors ... . *Nashville, Tenn.* 1868–70. 4 vols., 8vo. 45524

Masonic Register and Union. ... Devoted to Freemasonry; Its History, Jurisprudence, and Philosophy. ... *New York: J. F. Adams & Co.* 1854–55. 8vo. Discontinued. 45525

The Masonic Review. Vol. I. *Cincinnati: C. Moore.* 1846. 8vo. Continued. 45526

The Masonic Review and Keystone. ... [n. p.] 1867–8. 2 vols., 4to. 45527

Masonic Signet and Journal; ... *Marietta, Ga.* 1855–9. 4 vols., 8vo. Discontinued. 45528

Masonic Song Book, containing a large collection of the most approved Masonic Songs, Odes, Anthems, etc. *Philadelphia: M. Carey.* 1814. 12mo, pp. 164, (4). 3 Plates. 45529

The Masonic Sun; ... Thomas B. Carr, M.D. ... Editor. ... *Wilmington, N. C.* 1867. 4to. 45530

Masonic Tidings ... . *Warsaw.* 1865. 4to. 45531

Continued at Lockport, N. Y., January 1, 1867.

Masonic Token; ... *Portland, Maine: Stephen Berry.* 1867. 4to. Continued. 45532

The Masonic Trowel; H. G. Reynolds, Editor. *Springfield, Ill.* 1862. 4to, pp. 192. Continued. 45533

The Masonic Union, ... Finlay M. King, Editor. *Auburn, N. Y.* 1850–51. 8vo, pp. 368. 45534

Continued at Port Byron till 1854.

"Masonry the same all over the World." Another Masonic Murder. [*Boston?* 1830?] 8vo, pp. 8. H. 45535

Case of William Miller. For other anonymous works on masonry *see* under the first word of the title, *also* Freemasonry.

Maspeth Poems. *See* [Furman (Garrit)], Vol. VII. 26221.

MASSA (J. A.) A Mascara descoberta, ou antidoto contra as maximas do Governador e Capitão-General de Moçambique, Sebastião Xavier Botelho e seus satelites. Offerecido e dedicado a SS. MM. [*sic*] o Imperador do Brasil e Rei de Portugal, por seu auctor João Alves Massa. *Rio de Janeiro: Typographia da Astrea.* 1829. 4to, pp. 100. 45536

Massachusee Psalter: asuh Uk-kuttoohomaongash David weche wunnaunchemookaonk ne ansukhogup John ut Indiane kah Englishe nepatuhquonkash ne woh sogkompagunukhettet kakoketahteaekuppannegh, aketamannat kah wohwohtamunat Wunnetuppantamwe Wussukwhongash. *Boston, N. E. Uppointhomunneau B. Green, kah J. Printer wutche quhtiantamwe Chapanukkeg wutche onchekehtouunnat wunnaunchummookaonk ut New England, &c.* 1709. 12mo, pp. (101). J.C.B. 45537

The English title reads "The Massachuset Psalter: Or Psalms of David, with the Gospel according to John, in Columns of Indian and English. Being an Introduction for Training up the Aboriginal Natives in Reading and Understanding the Holy Scriptures." *Boston, N. E. Printed by B. Green and J. Printer for the Honourable Company for the Propagation of the Gospel in New England, &c.* 1709. "Next to Eliot's Bible, this is the most important monument of the Massachuset language. The translation was made by the Rev. Experience Mayhew."—J. H. TRUMBULL, *in A. A. S. Proceedings*, No. 61.

Massachusettensis. *See* [Leonard (D.)], x. 40097 and 40100.

MASSACHUSETTS, *pseudon.* The New States, or a Comparison of the Wealth, Strength, and Population of the Northern and Southern States; ... with a View to Expose the Injustice of

Erecting New States at the South. By Massachusetts. *Boston: J. Belcher, Printer.* 1813. 8vo, pp. 36. BA. 45538

MASSACHUSETTS JUNIOR, *pseudon.* A Plea for the South. By Massachusetts Junior. *Boston.* 1847. 12mo. C. 45539

MASSACHUSETTS.

With a few exceptions the following list of anonymous books are alphabetical under the first word of the book or the name of the institution or society which puts forth the book. The geology is grouped under that head.

Abstract Exhibiting the Condition of the Banks in Massachusetts, ... 1838: ... *Boston: Dutton and Wentworth, Printers.* 1838. 8vo, pp. 60, (2). Continued. H. 45540

Also: Abstract Exhibiting the Condition of the Institutions for Savings of Massachusetts, ... October, 1846. *Boston.* 1846. 8vo. Continued.

Abstract from the Returns of Agricultural Societies in Massachusetts for ... 1845 and 1846. By J. G. Palfrey. *Boston.* 1846. 8vo. Continued. 45541

Abstract of Criminal Laws of Massachusetts. ... *Boston: Wright & Potter, Printers.* 1866. 12mo, pp. 120. + Supplement. [*Ibid.*] 1868. 8vo, pp. 16. + Revised Edition. 1869. [*Ibid.*] 1869. 8vo, pp. 173. BA. 45542

... Abstract of Returns of Inspectors and Keepers of Jails and Houses of Correction. [n. p.] 1839. 8vo, pp. 12, 1 folded leaf. Continued. H. 45543

Abstract of School Returns, 1829. [n. p. n. d.] Folio, pp. 16, (1). Continued. B. 45544

Abstract of the Census of ... Massachusetts, taken ... 1855. With Remarks ... [by N. B. Shurtleff, M.D.] ... . *Boston: William White, Printer.* 1857. 8vo, pp. xiii, 252, (1). Continued.

Abstract of the Laws of the Colony of Massachusetts. *Boston: Printed by T. Green.* 1704. Sm. 8vo, pp. 56. 45546

Abstract of the Norfolk Exercise. A Plan of Exercise for the Militia of Massachusetts Bay. Third Edition. *Boston.* 1771. 8vo, pp. 92. + *Boston: R. Draper.* 1772. M. 45547

An Abstract of the Proceedings of the Anti-Masonic State Convention of Massachusetts. ... 1829 and ... 1830. *Boston: John Marsh.* 1830. 8vo, pp. 32. + 1831. *Boston.* 1831. 8vo, pp. 78. M. 45548

... Abstract of the Return of Paupers. 1833. [n. p. 1834.] 8vo, pp. 23. Continued. H. 45549

Also: Abstract of Returns of Joint-Stock Companies for the Years 1851–54 ... . [*Boston.* n. d.] 8vo, pp. 11. A., M.

Abstract of the Returns and Statements of Foreign Insurance Companies for the Year 1854. ... *Boston.* 1855. 8vo, pp. 51, xv.

... Abstract of the Returns of Insurance Companies, ... 1837: ... *Boston: Dutton and Wentworth, Printers.* 1838. 8vo, pp. 8. Continued. H. 45551

Abstract of the Returns of the Overseers of the Poor ... for 1837 ... . [*Boston.* 1837.] 8vo. Continued. 45552

Abstract of the Statements of the Several Banks in the Commonwealth of Massachusetts. 1811–1837. [n. p. n. d.] Folio, 1 leaf. 45553

Abstracts of Returns of Assessors ... on the Shares of Corporations, and Deposits in Savings Institutions; ... 1860. Prepared ... By Oliver Warner ... . *Boston: William White, Printer.* 1861. 8vo, pp. 261. BA., H. 45554

... Abstracts of the Returns from the Banks, and ... Institutions for Savings ... . 1862. ... *Boston: Wright & Potter, Printers.* 1863. 8vo, pp. 128. H. 45555

An Account of the Rise, Progress, and Consequences of the Land Bank and Silver Schemes in the Province of Massachusetts Bay. [*Boston.*] 1744. 8vo, pp. 91. M. 45556

... An Account of the State of the Treasury of ... Massachusetts. *Boston: Dutton and Wentworth, Printers.* 1843. 8vo, pp. 47. BA. 45557

An Act codifying the Laws of Massachusetts relating to aid to Families of Soldiers and Seamen in the Service of the United States. *Boston: Wright and Potter, Printers.* 1865. 12mo, pp. 7.

An Act concerning the Manufacture and Sale of Spirituous ... Liquors, May 22, 1852. [n. p. n. d.] 18mo. + 1855. 8vo.

This is the Massachusetts Liquor Law.

An Act for Regulating and Governing the Militia, 1778. [n. p. 1778.] 4to. + *Boston: J. Gill.* 1781. 4to. + *Boston.* 1785. 4to, pp. 19. + *Boston.* 1786. 4to, pp. 49. M. + *Boston.* 1793. 8vo, pp. 84. + An Act for Regulating, Governing and Training the Militia ... March 6, 1810. *Boston.* 1810. 12mo, pp. 50. + [n. p. 1814.] 8vo, pp. 56. BA. 45560

Also: An Act in addition to an Act for forming and regulating the Militia within the Commonwealth of Massachusetts, 1783. *Boston.* 1783. 8vo, pp. 8. M.

An Act for repealing Certain Parts of an Act postponing the Payment of Government Securities. *Boston.* 1781. 8vo, pp. 7.

Act providing for the more easy Payment of the Specie Taxes, etc. [n. p.] 1786. 8vo, pp. 23. 45562

An Act providing Remedy for Bankrupts and their Creditors, printed and referred to the People of the Province of Massachusetts Bay, April, 1757. [n. p.] 1757. 4to. 45563

An Act to prevent Monopoly and Oppression. [n. p.] 1774. 8vo. 45564

Also: Act in addition to an Act intitled "An Act to prevent Monopoly and Oppression." [n. p.] 1777. 8vo, pp. 8. — Act to Restrain the Trade and Commerce of Massachusetts and other Provinces in America. [n. p.] 1774. Folio. — An Act to supply the Treasury with the Sum of Four Hundred Thousand Pounds Money. *Boston.* 1781. 8vo, pp. 8. — Act to suppress the Riots in Massachusetts, Jan., 1774. [n. p. n. d.] Folio. — Act for better Regulating the Province of Massachusetts Bay, Jan., 1774. [n. p. n. d.] Folio.

Acts | and | Laws, | Passed by the Great and General Court | ... of the Massachusetts-Bay, in | New-England. | Begun ... the Eighth ... of June, 1692. And Con- | tinued ... unto ... the Twelfth | ... of October ... . *Boston:* | *Printed by Benjamin Harris.* | 1692. | Folio, pp. (2), 90. Continued. BA. 45565

This earliest edition of the Laws of the Province contains also the Charter, as also do many other editions. *See* Charter, *infra*, No. 45673.

Acts and Laws of His Majesty's Province of the Massachusetts-Bay in New-England. *Boston: Printed by Barthol. Green and John Allen.* 1699. Folio, pp. 192. C. + *Boston ... Printed by B. Green, ... for Benjamin Eliot* ... 1714. Folio, pp. 370.

Acts and Laws, Passed by the Great and General Court ... Of the Province Of the Massachusetts-Bay in New-England, From 1692 to 1719. To which is Prefix'd, The Charter, Granted by their late Majesties King William and Queen Mary, ... A.D. 1691. ... *London: Printed by John Baskett.* MDCCXXIV. Folio, pp. xvi, xvi, 359. C. 45567

Acts and Laws of His Majesty's Province of the Massachusetts Bay in New England. *Boston in New England: Printed by*

B. Green, ... for Benjamin Eliot ... 1726. Folio, Charter, pp. 14, Table, 7, 483. Continued. C. 45568

The collations of copies of this edition differ, owing to the fact that at each session the additional laws were continuously paged; other editions, *Boston*, 1742, 1759, etc., are subject to the same variation.

Acts and Laws passed by the Great and General Court or Assembly of the Colony of the Massachusetts Bay in New-England, from the 19th of July 1775, to the 25th of March 1783. *Boston: Benjamin Edes & Sons.* 1776–83. Folio. S.

Of these laws, passed during the revolutionary period, some were printed at Watertown.

Acts and Laws of the Commonwealth of Massachusetts, 1786–1789. *Boston.* 1786–89. Folio. Continued. 45570

The Acts and Resolves ... of the Province of Massachusetts Bay: to which are prefixed the Charters of the Province. ... *Boston: Wright & Potter, Printers.* 1869. 2 vols., 8vo, pp. xxix, (2), 904; 1187. BA. 45571

Acts and Resolves passed by the Legislature of Massachusetts; together with the Rolls and Messages, 1839 to 1842. ... Vol. I. *Boston.* 1839–42. 8vo. Continued. 45572

Also: The Acts ... ordered to be left out of the last Impression of Temporary Laws ... . *Boston.* 1763. 4to, pp. 52.

Acts regulating Banks and Banking. Passed in 1829 and 1831. *Boston: Printed by Beals and Homer.* 1831. 16mo, pp. 32. H.

An Addition | To the Present Melancholy Cir- | cumstances of the Province | Considered, &c. March 6th. | 1718, 9. Exhibiting Considerations about Labour, Commerce, Money, Notes, or Bills of Credit. [*Boston: B. Green.*] 1719. 16mo, pp. 28. C.

... Address and Resolutions, adopted at the Whig State Convention, Worcester, October 3, 1849, ... with ... Speeches ... . *Boston: Eastburn's Press.* 1849. 8vo, pp. 32. H. 45575

Address and Resolves of the Democratic Members of the Massachusetts Legislature of 1838, with A Sketch of Some Debates. [n. p. n. d.] 8vo, pp. 48. H. 45576

Address adopted by the Whig State Convention at Worcester, September 13, 1848. ... [n. p. n. d.] 8vo, pp. 16. H. 45577

Address before the Legislature to the People of ... Massachusetts. [n. p.] 1809. 8vo. N. 45578

An Address from the Convention of Congregational Ministers in the Commonwealth of Massachusetts, to their Christian Brethren of the several Associations, and others not associated throughout this State ... . [n. p.] 1799. Folio, pp. 3. 45579

An Address from the General Court, to the People of the Commonwealth of Massachusetts. *Boston: Printed by Adams and Nourse.* M,DCC,LXXXVI. 8vo, pp. 40, (1). H. 45580

Address of a Convention of Delegates. *See* Vol. x. 43901.

Address of a Convention at Worcester, March, 1812. [n. p. n. d.] 8vo. 45581

... Address of His Excellency Edward Everett, to the ... Legislature, on the Organization of the Government, ... 1837. *Boston: Dutton and Wentworth, Printers.* 1837. 8vo, pp. 20. Continued. H. 45582

The annual addresses of the respective governors include topics of political and historical interest.

Address of the Central Committee, Appointed by ... the Legislature friendly to the election of John Q. Adams, as president ... June 10, 1828 ... . [*Boston.* 1828.] 8vo, pp. 24. BA.

An Address of the Convention, For Framing a new Constitution of Government, for the State of Massachusetts-Bay, to their Constituents. *Boston: Printed by White and Adams.* M,DCC,LXXX. 8vo, pp. 18, Constitution, pp. 53. BA. 45584

Address of the Democratic Members of the Massachusetts Legislature, to the People, at the Close of the Session for 1841. [n. p. n. d.] 8vo, pp. 24. BA. 45585

Also: Address ... to their Constituents ... with a History of the Proceedings of the ... Session 1843. [*Boston: Printed by Beals & Greene.* 1843.] 8vo, pp. 22, (1). + Address ... to the People, ... at the Close of the Session of 1844. ... *Boston: Wright & Ballou.* 1844. 8vo, pp. 12.

Address of the House of Representatives to the Inhabitants ... on the Act for calling in the Bills of Credit. *Boston.* 1777. Folio, pp. 4. M. 45586

Address of the House of Representatives to the People of Massachusetts. [*Boston.* 1812.] 8vo, pp. 14. B., H. 45587

On the War with England.

An Address of the Legislature to the Inhabitants of the Commonwealth of Massachusetts. *Boston: Printed by Beniamin Edes*

and Sons. M,DCC,LXXXI. 8vo, pp. 22. BA. + Another Edition. *Boston.* 1781. 8vo, pp. 37. M. 45588

An Address of the Legislature to the People of ... Massachusetts: ... Reports ... on the late Treasury's Accounts, and General Wilkinson's Table. *Worcester.* 1809. 12mo, pp. 31. BA.

Address of the Whig, etc. *See* [Quincy (J.)], [Winthrop (R.)]

Address of the Worcester Convention to the Electors of Massachusetts. *Worcester.* 1837. 8vo. 45590

Address to the Antimasonic Republicans of ... Massachusetts. [n. p. 1836.] 8vo, pp. 24. BA. 45591

An Address to the Citizens of Massachusetts, on The Approaching State Elections. [n. p. 1807?] 8vo, pp. 8. BA.

An Address to the Citizens of Massachusetts on the Causes and Remedy of our National Distresses. By a Fellow Sufferer. *Boston.* 1808. 8vo, pp. 28. 45593

An Address to the Electors of Massachusetts. ... [*Boston.* 1804?] 8vo, pp. 8. H. 45594

Also: Address to the Electors of Massachusetts. *Boston.* 1814. 8vo.

An Address To the Electors of the Ninth Congressional District of Massachusetts. [By Rev. George Allen. *Worcester.* 1860.] 8vo, pp. 14. B. 45595

Address to the Free and Independent People of Massachusetts. [n. p. 1812.] 8vo, pp. 8. BA. 45596

In favor of the election of Caleb Strong. Also: Address to the Free and Independent People of Massachusetts. With a Protest against the Bill for Districting the Commonwealth. [*Boston.* 1812.] 8vo, pp. 15. M.

An Address to the Freeholders and Inhabitants of the Province of the Massachusetts-Bay, in New-England. [*Boston:*] *Printed in the Year* 1751. 8vo, pp. 8. W. 45597

Signed "Phileleutheros," and very rare.

Address to the Freemen of Massachusetts. By a Freeman. [Antimasonic.] *Worcester: M. Spooner and Co., Printers.* 1832. 8vo, pp. 16. B. 45598

Address to the Independent Electors of Massachusetts by a Meeting of Citizens, Boston, 27th February, 1815. *Boston.* 1815. 8vo, pp. 16. M. 45599

An Address to the Independent Citizens of Massachusetts, on the ... approaching Election. Exhibiting a View of the leading Measures of the Jefferson & Madison Administrations. *Worcester.* 1810. 8vo, pp. 23. B., BA. 45600

Address to the Inhabitants of Massachusetts Bay, occasioned by a late Attack on their Liberties. *Boston.* 1729. 4to. 45601

From Thomas' "History of Printing;" the following is perhaps the correct title:

An | Address | to the | Inhabitants of the Province | Of the Massachusetts-Bay in New-England; | More Especially, | To the Inhabitants of Boston; Occasioned by the late | Illegal and Unwarrantable Attack | Upon their Liberties, | and the unhappy | Confusion and Disorders consequent thereon. | By a Lover of his Country. ... *Boston: Rogers and Fowle.* [1747.] 4to, pp. 8. M.

Signed "Amicus Patriæ." Relates to the proceedings of an English press-gang in the town of Boston.

Address ... to the ... Legislature of Massachusetts ... [on] "the Annexation of a part of Deerfield to Greenfield." *Greenfield: Charles A. Mirick, Printer.* 1850. 8vo, pp. 27. B. 45603

By P. Temple, and others.

An Address to the People of Massachusetts. February, 1805. [n. p. 1805.] 8vo, pp. 24. H. 45604

By the Federalists. The following is by the Republicans:

An Address to the People of Massachusetts. February, 1805. [n. p. 1805.] 8vo, pp. 24. S. 45605

Address to the People ... with the Report of the Committee of the Senate on the Votes for Governor for 1806, and the Protest of the 19 Members who were opposed to the Same. *Boston.* 1806. 8vo. W. 45606

Address to the People of Massachusetts. [n. p. *March,* 1809.] 8vo, pp. 24. H., S. 45607

An Address to the People of Massachusetts. [n. p. n. d.] 8vo, pp. 22. + [n. p. n. d.] 8vo, pp. 8. BA., H. 45608

Recommends Sullivan and Heath for Governor and Lieutenant-Governor.

Address [of the Legislature] to the People of Massachusetts. [*Boston.* 1809.] 8vo, pp. 15, 24. 45609

On the Embargo; with a Memorial to Congress.

Address to the People of Massachusetts, February 15, 1812. *Boston.* [1812.] 8vo. W. 45610

Address to the People of Massachusetts. [n. p. 1851.] 8vo, pp. 16. BA. 45611

By Whig members of the Legislature.

Address to the People of Massachusetts on the Choice of Electors of President and Vice-President. [n. p. n. d.] 8vo, pp. 12. 45612

Address to the People of Massachusetts. By Members of the Legislature. [n. p. n. d.] 8vo, pp. 16. M. 45613

On the coalition of 1851–52.

An Address to the People. By the General Court, January 26, 1777. [*Boston.*] 1777. Folio, 1 leaf. 45614

An Address to the People of Massachusetts, by the Friends of Temperance and of the Statute of 1838. *Boston.* 1838. 8vo, pp. 24. M. 45615

Address to the People of Massachusetts by the House of Representatives upon the News of the Declaration of War by the United States against Great Britain. *Boston.* 1812. 8vo. W.

Address to the People of Massachusetts on the Justice and Importance of a Law for the Relief of Insolvent Debtors. ... *Boston.* 1813. 8vo, pp. 23. M., W. 45617

Address to the People of this Commonwealth. [*Boston.* 1807.] 8vo, pp. 20. BA. 45618

By the Federal members of the Legislature, 1807. Also: Address to the People of the Commonwealth. *Boston.* 1809. 8vo.

Address to the Republicans. *See* [Davis (G. T.)], v. 18823.

Address to the Voters of the Fourth Congressional District. A Business View of the Question before us. *Boston.* 1860. 8vo, pp. 11. B. 45619

Report of the Adjutant General of the Massachusetts Militia, ... *Boston: Printed by True and Greene.* 1824. 8vo, pp. (2), 24. Continued. BA. 45620

... Annual Report of the Adjutant-General, of ... Massachusetts, with Reports from the Quartermaster-General, Surgeon-General, and Master of Ordnance, for ... 1862. *Boston: Wright & Potter, Printers.* 1863. 8vo, pp. 470, 10, 9, 29, 6 folded leaves. + For 1863. [*Ibid.*] 1864. 8vo, pp. 1022. + For 1864. [*Ibid.*] 1865. 8vo, pp. 1099, 80. BA. 45621

The volumes for the years 1862–5 contain copious details of the Civil War.

Affidavits and Depositions relative to the Commencement of Hostilities in the Province of Massachusetts Bay. [n. p.] 1775. 8vo. M. 45622

Agricultural Statistics of Massachusetts, arranged by Towns and Counties. ... [n. p. 1862.] 8vo, pp. 71. 45623

Also: First Annual Report of the Secretary of the Board of Agriculture, together with Reports of Committees, appointed to visit the County Societies. With an Appendix, containing an Abstract of the Finances of the County Societies. *Boston: William White, Printer.* 1854. 8vo, pp. (4), 186. Plate. Continued. *See* our No. 14585, *note, also* Flint (C. L.), Vol. vi., No. 24765.

Aliens. [Whether aliens are rateable polls. *Boston.*] 1811. 8vo, pp. 8. S. 45624

Almanac for 1669. By J. B[rown]. *Cambridge: Printed by S. G. and M. J.* [1669.] 45625

Amendments of the Constitution of Massachusetts, proposed by the Convention of Delegates, assembled at Boston, ... November, ... Eighteen Hundred and Twenty; With their Address to the People of this Commonwealth. *Boston: Russell and Gardner, Printers.* 1821. 8vo, pp. 32. M. 45626

Amendments to the Report of the Commissioners appointed to revise the General Statutes of the Commonwealth: ... *Boston: Dutton and Wentworth, Printers.* 1835. 8vo, pp. (8), 170.

Annual Register of the Executive and Legislative Departments of the Government of Massachusetts, 1859. *Boston.* 1859. 8vo, pp. 19, (1). Continued. H. 45628

Previously "Poole's Annual Register," etc., and still earlier, "Poole's Statistical View," etc.

Annual Report of the Bank Commissioners, 1838. *Boston.* 1838. 8vo. Continued. 45629

Also: ... Schedule exhibiting the condition of the Banks in Massachusetts ... From 1803 to 1837, inclusive. [n. p. n. d.] 8vo, pp. 30. H.

... Annual Report of the Superintendent of Alien Passengers for the Port of Boston, 1859. [n. p. n. d.] 8vo, pp. 8. Cont'd.

Another Letter, From One in the Country, to his Friend in Boston. [On the Governor's Salary. *Boston.* 1714?] 4to, pp. 11.

Answer of the Elders and other Messengers of the Churches assembled at Boston in the year 1662 to the Question propounded to them by Order of the Honoured General Court. *Cambridge: Printed by S. Green.* 1662. 4to, pp. 60. M. 45632

Answer of the House of Representatives to the Speech of Governor Dudley, June, 16th, 1702. With the Address of Divers Ministers of the Province to Governor Dudley. *Boston.* 1703. 4to, pp. 3. 45633

See also New England.

Answer of the Whig Members. *See* [King (D. P.), *and others*].

An Answer to a Letter addressed to a Republican Member of the House of Representatives of ... Massachusetts, on ... a Petition for a New Corporation, to be entitled the College of Physicians. [*Boston:*] *True & Rowe, Printers.* 1812. 8vo, pp. 16.

Answer to an Advertisement in the Boston Gazette, Feb. 20, 1721, dated, N. E. Castle-William, February, 1720, 21. *Boston.* 1721. M. 45635

Relates to paper-money.

Appeal to Democrats and Union Men. From the Democracy of Boston and Suffolk. *Boston.* 1855. 8vo. 45636

An Appeal to the Good Sense of the People of Massachusetts. [n. p. n. d.] 8vo, pp. 8. H. 45637

An Appeal to the Old Whigs of Massachusetts. 1806. [*Boston.* 1806.] 8vo, pp. 20. BA. 45638

An Appeal to the People of Massachusetts, on the Texas Question. *Boston: Charles C. Little and James Brown.* 1844. 8vo, pp. 20. BA. + [Second Edition. *Ibid.*] 1844. 8vo. B.

An Appeal to the Republicans of Massachusetts, against Gag Resolutions and forced Pledges. By a Republican. *Boston.* 1862. 8vo, pp. 12. B. 45640

The Appendix. *See our* Vol. I., No. 1792, *add* pp. 15.

Appendix to Massachusetts in Agony. By Cornelius Agrippa, L.L. [*Boston.*] 1751. 4to, pp. 20. M. 45641

Sixth Annual Report of the Associated Banks of Massachusetts, for the Suppression of Counterfeiting. *Boston.* 1859. 8vo, pp. 40. S. 45642

Constitution of the Associated Mechanics and Manufacturers of Massachusetts. *Boston.* 1800. 12mo. 45543

Report of the Attorney General ... January 2, 1833. *Boston: Dutton and Wentworth, Printers.* 1833. 8vo, pp. 40. Cont'd.

Report of the Attorney General of Massachusetts respecting claims for Confiscated Debts. *Boston.* 1808. 8vo, pp. 22.

Also: Report on the Libels contained in the Boston Newspapers. [n. p.] 1812. 8vo. W.

... Report of the Auditor of Accounts of ... Massachusetts, for ... 1849. *Boston: Dutton and Wentworth, Printers.* 1850. 8vo, pp. 70, (1). Continued. B. 45646

A Circular Address from the Bible Society of Massachusetts. With the Constitution, etc. *Boston: Printed by J. Belcher.* 1809. 8vo, pp. 24. BA. 45647

Also: Report of the Executive Committee ... prepared for the Anniversary ... 1812. *Boston: Printed by John Eliot, Jun.* 1812. 8vo, pp. 19, (1). Continued. BA.

... Report on providing for the Appointment of a Board of Agriculture, and a State Chemist ... . [n. p. n. d.] 8vo, pp. 23.

First Annual Report of the Board of Education, ... with the First Annual Report of the Secretary of the Board. *Boston: Dutton and Wentworth, Printers.* 1838. 8vo, pp. 75. Cont'd.

See also Mann (Horace), No. 44324, *note*, page 167.

First Annual Report of the Board of Health ... January, 1870. *Boston: Wright & Potter, Printers.* 1870. 8vo, pp. viii, 58. Continued. H. 45650

... First Annual Report of the Board of State Charities: January, 1865. *Boston: Wright & Potter, Printers.* 1865. 8vo, pp. xlviii, 456. Continued. BA. 45651

The Body of Liberties. *Cambridge: Printed by John Daye.* 1641. Folio. 45652

It contained one hundred laws drawn up by Rev. Natthl Ward of Ipswich, pursuant to an order of the General Court. *See* Thomas' "History of Printing," I. 47, *note*. Mr. Thomas is probably mistaken in supposing that "The Body of Liberties," established in 1641, was printed at that time. A pamphlet, entitled "An Abstract of the Laws of New England," was printed in London in 1641, and has by many writers been supposed to be substantially the same as "The Body of Liberties." There is good reason to believe that the last named compilation was published by distribution to the towns in manuscript. One of these copies, discovered by Mr. Francis C. Gray, and accompanied by his learned essay on the early Laws of Massachusetts Bay, was printed in the "Massachusetts Historical Collections," Third Series, Vol. VIII.

The | Book of the General | Lawes and Libertyes | concerning the Inhabitants of the | Massachusetts, | collected Out of the Records of | the General Court, | for the several Years | wherein they were made and | Established. | And Now Revised by the same Court, and disposed into an | Alphabetical order, and pub-

lished by the same | Authority in the General Court holden | at Boston, in May, | 1649. | ... | *Cambridge: | Printed according to Order of the General Court.* | 1660. | Folio, pp. (4), 88, Table, (8).

Of extreme rarity. The preface is signed, "By Order of the Generall Court, Edward Rawson, Secret:" It was printed by Samuel Green. The earliest volume of Massachusetts Laws extant. An edition is supposed to have been printed in 1648 or 1649, but there is no known copy in existence. It is referred to in the "Massachusetts Records" of May, 1648, as "now at the presse." *See* "Massachusetts Records," II. pp. 239, 246, 262. Johnson, in "Wonder Working Providence," p. 205, says it was printed in 1648. Its discovery would be a bibliographical wonder.

A Book for Massachusetts Children, in Familiar Letters, For the use of Families and Schools. *Boston.* 1831. 12mo. Maps.

The Boston Opposition to the New Law for the Suppression of Rum Shops ... being an Appeal to the Country People of Massachusetts to protect themselves. ... *Boston: Printed by Perkins & Marvin.* 1838. 12mo, pp. 28. H. 45655

Our No. 6501, Vol. II., seems to be another edition.

Brief of the Governor and Council of Massachusetts, for Collections for Propagating the Gospel. [n. p.] 1718. 4to, pp. 1.

A Brief Account of the State of the Province of Massachusetts Bay. By a Lover of his Country. *Boston.* 1717. 12mo, pp. 8. 45657

A Brief History of the Evangelical Missionary Society of Massachusetts. With the Last Report of the Trustees. [n. p. 1820.] 8vo, pp. 7. H. 45658

Brief Remarks on the Rail Roads. *See* [Sedgwick (T.)]

Brief Report of the Debates in the Anti-Masonic Convention of the Commonwealth of Massachusetts. Held in Faneuil Hall, Boston, December 30, 31, 1829, and January 1, 1830. *Boston: John Marsh.* MDCCCXXX. 8vo, pp. 48. B. 45659

A Brief Review of the Rise, etc. *See* Vol. II., No. 7896.

A Brief State of the Services and Expences of the Province of the Massachusett's Bay, In the Common Cause. *London: J. Wilkie.* M DCC LXV. 8vo, pp. 24. 45660

The claims here set forth are, first, the part taken by the Colony in the Indian wars, and next for the large sums contributed, and men furnished for the several expeditions against Canada, Cape Breton, and other French Colonies on the northern frontier.

Briefs in the Controversy between Massachusetts Bay and New Hampshire. *Boston.* 1739. Folio. 45661

Imperfect title from Thomas' "History of Printing."

Business Register of Manufacturers in the States of Massachusetts, Connecticut, Rhode Island, and New Hampshire, and the Principal Manufacturers in New York, New Jersey, Ohio, Pennsylvania, Maine, and Vermont. 1868–9. *New York.* 1869. 4to, pp. 410. 45662

By-Laws for the Government of the State Alms-Houses, together with the Statute Laws establishing the same. *Lowell.* 1854. 8vo. 45663

The Capital Laws of the Massachusetts Bay, with the Freeman's Oath. 1642. 45664

"Ordered to be printed, 18th 3d month, 1642. Col. Rec. mentioned as printed in the Preface to 'New England's Jonas Cast up at London.'" Title and note from Thomas' "History of Printing."

The Case of His Majesty's Province of the Massachusetts-Bay, upon two Appeals relating to the Boundaries between that Province and the Colony of Rhode Island and Providence Plantations. To be heard before the Right Honorable the Lords of the Committee of His Majesty's most Honorable the Privy Council, at the Council Chamber at the Cockpit. *Whitehall, [London.]* 1743. Folio, pp. 9. J.C.B. 45665

The Case of His Majesty's Province of the Massachusetts Bay in New England, with respect to the Expences they were at in taking and securing Cape Breton. *London.* 1744. Folio, pp. 4.

The Case of the Provinces. *See* [Hutchinson (T.)], IX. 34068.

The Case of the Provinces of Massachusetts Bay ... respecting a Bill for Preservation of His Majesty's Woods in America. [n. p. n. d.] Folio, 1 leaf. 45667

Catalogue of the Fraternity of Φ B K, Alpha of Massachusetts, Harvard University, Cambridge, 1846. *Cambridge.* 1846. 8vo, pp. 48. Continued. 45668

Catalogue of the Library of the General Court. *Boston: Dutton and Wentworth, Printers.* 1831. 8vo, pp. 43. + *Boston.* 1839. Rl. 8vo, 52 leaves. + *[Ibid.]* 1846. 8vo. 45669

A Catechism agreed upon by the Elders at the Desire of the General Court. *Cambridge: Printed by John Daye.* 1641.

Concerning this rare catechism *see* "Winthrop's Journal," II. 37.

The Central Committee of the State, to the Federal Electors. [n. p. n. d.] 8vo, pp. 8. BA. 45671

Chapters and Dates of the Laws of Massachusetts. ... [*Boston: Munroe, Francis, & Parker.* 1809.] 8vo, pp. (44). BA.

The Charter | Granted by their Majesties | King William | And | Queen Mary, | to the | Inhabitants | of the | Province | of the | Massachusetts-Bay, | in New-England. | *Printed at London, and Re-Printed at Boston in New-England, By | Benjamin Harris.* 1692. Folio, pp. (2), 13. BA. + *Printed at Boston ... by Bartholomew Green and John Allen.* 1699. Folio. + *Boston ... Printed by B. Green ...* 1714. Folio, pp. 13. H. + [*Ibid.*] 1726. Folio, pp. (2), 14. + *Boston ... Printed ... by Samuel Kneeland and Timothy Green, ...* MDCCXLII. Folio, pp. (2), 14. + *Boston.* M,D,CC,LIX. Folio, pp. 14. + *Printed in the Year* MDCCLXXV. 8vo, pp. 45.

This is usually found with the "Acts and Laws," for 1692 and following years. Also: The Charter of the Massachusetts Colony. [n. p. n. d.] 4to, pp. 26. BA.—The Charter of the Province of the Massachusetts Bay. [n. p. n. d.] 18mo.

The Charters and General Laws of The Colony and Province of Massachusetts Bay. Carefully collected from the Publick Records and Ancient Printed Books. To which is added An Appendix, tending to explain the Spirit, Progress and History of the Jurisprudence of the State; ... . *Boston: T. B. Wait and Co.* 1814. 8vo, pp. vii, 830, (30). A., B., C., H. 45674

Chronological Table of the Most Remarkable Events in the Province of the Massachusetts Bay, from 1602 to 1770. *Boston.* 1771. 8vo, pp. 8. 45675

Circular. *See* [Blanchard (J. P.)], Vol. II., No. 5827.

Circular Letter, relating to Lyceums in Massachusetts. [n. p. 1830.] 8vo, pp. 7. W. 45676

Circular of the Board of Missions of the Diocese of Massachusetts, March, 1856. *Boston.* 1856. 8vo, pp. 4. 45677

Claim for Military Service, with Documents relating to the late War. *Boston.* [n. d.] 8vo. W. 45678

A Collection of Acts or Laws passed in the State of Massachusetts Bay, relative to American Loyalists and their Property. *London: John Stockdale.* M.DCC.LXXXV. 8vo, pp. 35. C., H.

A | Collection | Of the Proceedings of the | Great and General Court or Assembly | Of His Majesty's Province of the | Massachusetts-Bay, | in | New-England; | Containing several Instructions from the Crown, to the | Council and Assembly of that Province

for fixing a | Salary on the Governour, and their Determinations | thereon. | As also, | The Methods taken by the Court for Supporting the several | Governours, since the Arrival of the present Charter. | Printed by Order of the House of Representatives. | *Boston: Printed by T. Fleet, ...* | 1729. | 4to, pp. 112. BA., W.

Commissioners for the ... Survey of the State. *See* [Dewey (C.)], [Gould (A. A.)], [Harris (T. W.)], Storer (D. H.)

Commissioner's Report on ... Matrons and Labor in the Common Jails. By C. W. Bellows ... . *Boston: William White, Printer.* 1854. 8vo, pp. 12. B. 45681

The Common School Controversy. *See* [Mann (H.)], 44318.

Commonwealth of Massachusetts against the State of Rhode Island and Providence Plantations. ... *Taunton: C. A. Hack.* 1861. 8vo, pp. 14. Map. BA., H. 45682

... Commonwealth of Massachusetts. Aggregates of Polls, Property, Taxes, &c., ... 1862. Compiled by Oliver Warner, ... *Boston: Wright & Potter, Printers.* 1863. 8vo, pp. 25. B.

Commonwealth of Massachusetts. [*Boston.* 1818.] 45684

This is a letter from A. Stearns, inquiring if his acceptance of a professorship of law is incompatible with a seat in the House of Representatives. *See also* [Bidwell (Barnabas)], Vol. II., No. 5253. Many historical pamphlets published during the sessions of the State Legislature have this general title.

Communication of ... the Governour [Sullivan] to the ... Council, Relative to the Removal of Sheriff Lithgow; and the Report and Advice of Council Thereon. [*Boston.*] 1808. 8vo, pp. 18. BA. 45685

Communication of Gov. Briggs to the House of Representatives of Massachusetts, ... 1846; and a Letter from Daniel Webster, accompanying the Opinion of Judge McLean delivered in the Supreme Court of the United States, ... 1845, in the Case of the State of Rhode Island *vs.* Massachusetts. Also, Resolves concerning the Boundary Line between Massachusetts and Rhode Island. [n. p. 1846.] 8vo, pp. 22. 45686

A Compendium and Digest of the Laws of Massachusetts. By William Charles White ... . *Boston: Munroe, Francis and Parker.* 1809–11. 4 vols. in 7 parts, 8vo, pp. 4, 198, viii; (2), 199–1361. BA., W. 45687

The parts are paged continuously.

... Compilation of the Laws regulating Taxation in Massachusetts ... . *Boston: Wright & Potter, Printers.* 1870. 8vo, pp. 39.

A | Conference | Between the | Commissaries | of | Massachusets-Bay, | And the | Commissaries | of | New-York; | at | New-Haven in the Colony of Connecticut. | 1767. | *Boston; New-England: | Printed by Richard Draper ...* | MDCCLXVIII. | 4to, pp. (2), 26, (1). + [*Ibid.*] 4to, pp. (2), 26, (1), 9. H. 45689

Thomas describes this with the date 1767, 4to, pp. 35, and I have a memorandum of another edition, pp. (2), 57. *See also* Vol. IV., No. 15441.

Considerations and Documents. *See* 15941, 15950, 15954.

A Constitution and Form of Government for the State of Massachusetts-Bay, Agreed upon by the Convention of said State, February 28, 1778, to be laid before the several Towns and Plantations in said State, for their Approbation, or Disapprobation. *Boston: J. Gill.* MDCCLXXVIII. 8vo, pp. 23. M.

A | Constitution | Or | Frame of Government, | Agreed upon by the Delegates of the People of the State of Massachusetts-Bay, | In | Convention, | Begun and held at Cambridge on the First of September, 1779, | and | Continued by Adjournments to the Second of March, 1780. ... | *Boston: | State of Massachusetts-Bay: Printed by Benjamin Edes & Sons.* | M,DCC,LXXX. | 8vo, pp. 43. H. + [*Ibid.*] M,DCC,LXXXI. Folio, pp. 24. M. + The Third Edition. [*Ibid.*] M,DCC,LXXXIV. 8vo, pp. 43. H. + *Worcester: Printed by Isaiah Thomas.* 1787. 18mo, pp. 107. B. 45691

The Constitution of the State of Massachusetts ... . *Boston: Manning and Loring.* 1805. 12mo, pp. 119. + *Northampton.* 1806. 12mo. + *Pittfield.* 1806. 12mo. + *Brookfield.* 1807. 12mo. + *Boston: Printed by Adams and Rhoades.* 1807. 12mo, pp. 94. H. + *Salem: Printed by Thomas C. Cushing.* 1811. 12mo, pp. 112. + With the Amendments annexed. ... *Boston: Benjamin Russell.* 1822. 8vo, pp. 86. BA. + *Boston: Dutton and Wentworth, Printers.* 1833. 8vo, pp. 5–90. H. 45692

Constitution of the Commonwealth of Massachusetts ... April 26, 1853. ... *Boston: White and Potter, Printers.* 1853. 8vo, pp. 46. BA. + [n. p. n. d.] 12mo. 45693

The Constitutional Propositions, adopted by the Convention of Delegates, assembled at Boston, ... May, ... 1853. ... With an Address ... . *Boston: White & Potter, Printers.* 1853. 8vo, pp. 50. H. 45694

The Constitutions ... of Free ... Masons. *See* Vol. VII., No. 25798, for collation *read* pp. 288.

A Continuation of the Proceedings of the House of Representatives Of the Province of the Massachusetts-Bay, relative to the Convening, Holding, and Keeping The General Assembly at Harvard-College, in Cambridge. ... *Boston: Printed by Edes and Gill.* 1770. 8vo, pp. 66. H., W. 45695

Convention of Congregational Ministers in Massachusetts. Report of the Committee on Slavery, presented May 30, 1849. *Boston.* 1849. 8vo, pp. 92. 45696

Copy of the Complaint. *See* Bernard (F.), Vol. II. 4922.

A Copy of the King's Majesties Charter for Incorporating the Company of the Massachusetts Bay in New England in America. Granted ... 1628. *Boston in New England. Reprinted by S. Green, for Benjamin Harris.* 1689. 4to, pp. 26. M. 45697

Correspondence between the Agent of the Commonwealth [George Sullivan] and ... the Governor, [Levi Lincoln] on the ... Massachusetts Claim on the General Government. *Boston: True and Greene, Printers.* 1826. 8vo, pp. 14. B. 45698

Correspondence between the ... Bishop, etc. *See* Boston, II.

Counter Report of the ... Committee, on so much of the Governor's Message, as relates to Capital Punishment. [n. p. n. d.] 8vo, pp. 11. B. 45699

The County and Town Officer: or an Abridgement of the Laws of the Province of the Massachusetts-Bay, relative to County and Town Officers. By a Gentleman. *Boston: Printed by T. and J. Fleet.* 1768. 8vo, pp. (2), ii, 149. H. 45700

The Cow Pox Act with the Order of the Legislature; and a Communication ... from the Selectmen of ... Milton. ... *Boston: Printed by Joshua Belcher.* 1810. 8vo, pp. 16. B., W. 45701

Debates, Resolutions and other Proceedings, of the Convention of the Commonwealth of Massachusetts, convened at Boston, on the 9th of January, 1788, and continued until the 7th of February following, for the purpose of assenting to and ratifying the Constitution recommended by the Grand Federal Convention. Together with the Yeas and Nays on the decision of the Grand Question. To which the Federal Constitution is prefixed. *Bos-*

ton: Adams and Nourse. M,DCC,LXXXVIII. 8vo, pp. 219. + To which are added the Amendments which have been made therein. *Boston: Printed ... by Oliver & Munroe.* 1808. 12mo, pp. 236.

Debates and Proceedings in the Convention of the Commonwealth of Massachusetts, held in the Year 1788 ... . *Boston: William White, Printer.* 1856. 8vo, pp. vii, (8), 442. A., H.

Edited by Bradford K. Peirce and Charles Hale.

Debates and Proceedings in the Massachusetts Legislature ... 1856. Reported for the Boston Daily Advertiser. *Boston: C. Hale.* 1856. 8vo, pp. viii, 424. Continued. C. 45704

A Declaration Against Prophaneness and Immoralities. *Boston: Printed by Barth. Green.* 1704. Folio, 1 leaf. 45705

By Gov. Joseph Dudley. *See also* our Nos. 18470 and 19157. Also: A Declaration against the Penicooke and Eastern Indians. *Boston: Printed by B. Green and John Allen.* [n. d.] Folio, 1 leaf.

A Declaration of Former Passages and Proceedings Betwixt the English and the Narrowgansets, with their Confederates, wherein the grounds and justice of the Ensuing Warre are opened and cleared. Published by order of the Commissioners for the united Colonies: At Boston the 11th of the sixth month, 1645. [*Cambridge, N. E.* 1645.] 4to, pp. 7. 45706

Printed without a separate title-page. Signed "Jo: Winthrop, *President, in the name of all the Commissioners.*" In Hutchinson's "Collection of Papers" this "Declaration" is printed from manuscript. Hutchinson says in a foot-note, page 138, "I never met with it in print." The only copy known was in the possession of the late George Brinley.

Declaration of Independence, by the Colony of Massachusetts Bay, May 1, 1776. *New York.* 1862. 8vo, pp. 12. 45707

A Declaration of Rights of the Inhabitants of the Commonwealth of Massachusetts. [*Boston.* 1786.] 18mo, pp. 5. M.

A Defence of the Legislature. *See* Vol. V., No. 19248.

Defence of the Third Article of the Massachusetts Declaration of Rights; ... in the Case of Barnes vs. Falmouth. ... *Worcester: Printed by Manning & Trumbull.* 1820. 8vo, pp. 7. H. 45709

A Description of the Situation. *See* Maine, No. 43923.

A Detailed Account of the Receipts into, and Expenditures from the Treasury of the Commonwealth of Massachusetts, 1818–1824. [n. p. n. d.] Folio. M. 45710

Discussions on The Constitution proposed to the People of Massachusetts by The Convention of 1853. *Boston: Little, Brown, and Company.* 1854. 8vo, pp. (4), 306. BA. 45711

Contents: The Letters of Phocion, by G. T. Curtis; Letters of Silas Standfast, by G. S. Hillard; Address of Samuel Hoar at Fitchburg; Address of Marcus Morton at Taunton; Address of C. F. Adams at Quincy; Remarks of J. G. Palfrey.

Documents prepared and submitted to the General Court ... . By the Secretary of the Commonwealth. *Boston: Dutton and Wentworth, ... Printers.* 1846. 8vo. B. 45712

Each document is paged separately.

Documents printed by Order of the Constitutional Convention of the Commonwealth of Massachusetts ... A.D. 1853. *Boston: White & Potter, Printers.* 1853. 8vo. BA. 45713

Documents printed by Order of the House of Representatives, ... Session ... 1808. *Boston.* 1808. 8vo. Continued. 45714

Documents printed by Order of the Senate of the Commonwealth of Massachusetts ... 1834. *Boston.* 1834. 8vo. Continued. 45715

These documents, printed annually, are usually known as House and Senate Documents. They contain matter indispensable to the student of Massachusetts history.

Documents printed by Order of the Valuation Committee, during their Session in 1850. *Boston.* 1850. 8vo. Continued.

Documents relating to the Boundary Line and Disputed Territory between Massachusetts and Rhode Island. *Fall River.* 1847. 8vo, pp. 64. 45717

... Documents relating to the State Survey. [n. p. 1835.] 8vo, pp. 23. B. 45718

... Documents relating to the State Prison. [n. p. 1831.] 8vo, pp. 30. Continued. H. 45719

... Documents relative to the Marshpee Indians. [n. p. 1833.] 8vo, pp. 43. BA. 45720

Documents respecting the Resolutions. *See* [Bigelow (T.)]

Enlargement of the State House, in Boston. General and Mechanical Description, by the Architect, G. J. F. Bryant. *Boston.* 1853. 8vo, pp. 14. S. 45721

An Epistle to a Member of the General Court of Massachusetts, For 1809. [n. p. n. d.] 8vo, pp. 32. BA. 45722

An Essay on the Establishment of a Chancery Jurisdiction in Massachusetts. *Boston: Farrand, Mallory & Co.* [n. d.] 8vo, pp. 90. BA. 45723

The Address and Constitution of the Evangelical Missionary Society. *Cambridge: William Hilliard.* 1807. 8vo, pp. 9. BA.

Also: An Address, from the Trustees ... to the People of the New Settlements, in the United States. May, 1809. *Worcester: I. Thomas, Jun.* [1809.] 8vo, pp. 14. — Address of the Trustees of the Evangelical Missionary Society in Massachusetts. 1823. *Boston: R. M. Peck.* 1823. 12mo, pp. 12. — The Constitution of the Evangelical Missionary Society ... . *Worcester: Printed by William Manning.* 1818. 8vo, pp. 8, 16. — Report of the Proceedings of the Trustees of the Evangelical Missionary Society ... 1812. ... *Worcester: Isaac Sturtevant.* 1812. 8vo, pp. 23. Continued. BA.

Evidence before the Street Railway Commissioners appointed by the Massachusetts Legislature ... . *Boston: Wright & Potter, Printers.* 1864. 8vo, pp. 173. B. 45725

Exact Table to bring Old Tenor into Lawful Money, from 15d to a Thousand Pounds, &c. *Boston.* 1750. 8vo. + [Another Edition. *Ibid.*] 1750. 8vo. 45726

Also: Exact Table. Shewing how Provisions ought to be sold when the Dollars pass for Six Shillings a piece, which they must do according to the Act of the General Court. *Boston.* 1750. 8vo.

Examination of the Banking System. *See* [Appleton (N.)]

The Exercise of the Militia of the Province of Massachusetts Bay. *Boston.* 1750. 8vo. 45727

Also: The Exercise of the Musket, and Forming of Battalions. *Boston.* 1702. 8vo, pp. 22.

Exhibition of Facts Supported by Documents for Information of the Militia Officers of Massachusetts. *Boston.* 1806. 8vo.

The Explanatory Charter Granted by King George I. To the Province of the Massachusetts-Bay, in New-England. Accepted by the General Court, Jan. 15, 1725. [*Boston.* 1725.] 8vo, pp. 8. 45729

Extract from the Journal of the Honble House of Representatives, May [30th] 1755. Relating to the Imprisonment of Daniel Fowle and Royall Tyler [1754. *Boston: D. Fowle.* 1755.] 16mo, pp. 14. C. 45730

Contains a list of the names of all who voted *pro* and *con*, on the question of the rightful imprisonment of Fowle. *See* [Church (B.)], 12982, *and* Fowle (D.), 25296.

Extract of a Letter. *See* Vol VI., No. 23507.

Extracts and Collections of Acts. *See* Vol. VI., No. 23517.

Extracts from the Records of the Provincial Congress, Held at Cambridge in ... October, November and December, ... 1774. Also Extracts from the Minutes of the Proceedings of the Congress, Held at Cambridge, February, ... 1775. ... *Boston: Printed by Edes and Gill.* M,DCC,LXXV. 8vo, pp. 14. BA., C. 45731

Facts for the People. The Massachusetts Anti-Liquor Law no failure. [By W. B. Spooner. n. p. n. d.] 12mo, pp. 12.

A Faithful Monitor. Offering an Abstract of the Laws in the Province of Massachusetts, against those Disorders, the Suppression whereof is desired and pursued by them that wish well to the Worthy Designs of Reformation. ... *Boston.* 1704. 12mo, pp. 56. W. 45733

Constitution and By-Laws of the First Massachusetts Infantr Veteran Association. *Boston: Alfred Mudge & Son.* 1869. 18mo, pp. 18. H. 45734

Form of Constitution and By-Laws for Auxiliary Societies. [n. p. n. d.] 8vo, pp. 4. H. 45735

The Emigrant Aid Company of Massachusetts. Relates to Kansas.

Free Negroes and Mulattoes. ... Report ... concerning ... [their] admission into this State ... . [n. p. 1822.] 8vo, pp. 16.

The Freeholder's Address. *See* [Wise (John)].

A Full Statement of the Reasons ... why there should be no penal laws enacted, and no condemnatory resolutions passed ... respecting Abolitionits [*sic*] and Anti-Slavery Societies. *Boston: Massachusetts Anti-Slavery Society.* 1836. 8vo, pp. 48. H.

Minutes of the General Association of Massachusetts Proper, ... 1809. *Boston.* 1809. 8vo. Continued. S. 45738

Also: Extracts from the Minutes of the General Association of Massachusetts Proper ... June ... 1815 ... . [*Boston.*] 1815. 8vo, pp. 23. BA.

Extracts from the Minutes of the General Association of Congregational Ministers in Massachusetts ... 1814. ... *Boston: Printed by Samuel T. Armstrong.* 1814. 8vo, pp. (2), 22. Continued. H. 45739

Minutes of the General Conference of the Congregational Churches in Massachusetts, at its first annual session ... Sept.

11-13, 1860. ... *Boston: Crocker and Brewster.* 1860. 8vo, pp. 57. Continued. H. 45740

Also: First Report ... on Home Evangelization. Presented to the General Conference, September 13, 1866. [n. p. n. d.] 8vo, pp. 36. Continued. H.

General Lavves of the Massachusetts Colony. Revised and Published by Order of the General Court, October, 1658. [n. p. n. d.] Folio. 45741

The General | Laws | And | Liberties | Of the | Massachusets | Colony: | Revised & Re-printed, | By Order of the General Court Holden at Boston | May 15th. 1672. | Edward Rawson, Secr. | ... | *Cambridge | Printed by Samuel Green, for John Vsher of Boston.* | 1672. | Folio, pp. (2), 170, Summary, 14 leaves, Several Laws, pp. 15, 19-21, 41-43, 49-59. Woodcut Coat of Arms, 1 leaf.

The collation of the several laws varies in the few copies known to exist. Thomas devotes a couple of pages to this important book, and relates that it "produced the first nstance in America of the security of copyright by law." Usher having obtained permission to print the edition, and "suspecting that Green might print additional copies for himself, or that Johnson, at Cambridge, would reprint from his copy," at his request "two laws were passed to secure to him this particular work." Thomas adds copies of those laws, the second of which extended the right for seven years. *See* "History of Printing," I. 248-9, and new edition, I. 71.

General Laws and Liberties of the Massachusetts Colony, Revised and Corrected and Alphabetically arranged, to which are added Precedents and Forms of Things frequently used, with a complete Index to the whole. *Cambridge: Printed by S. Green.* 1672. Folio, pp. 200. 45743

Title from Thomas' "History of Printing," probably the same as the foregoing. The catalogue of the Worcester Antiquarian Society describes an edition dated 1675, which is probably an error as to date.

The General Laws of Massachusetts, from the Adoption of the Constitution, to February, 1822; with the Constitution of the United States and of this Commonwealth, together with their respective Amendments prefixed; Revised and published by Authority of the Legislature, by Asahel Stearns & Lemuel Shaw, Esquires, Commissioners. Theron Metcalf, Esq. Editor. *Boston: Wells & Lilly.* 1823. 2 vols., 8vo, pp. iv, 580; (2), 599, Index, 68. H. + Vol. III. Continued to 1831. *Boston.* 1832. 8vo. 45744

The General Laws of the Commonwealth of Massachusetts, ... Session, 1832. *Boston.* 1832. 8vo, pp. 56. Continued.

General Laws of the Commonwealth of Massachusetts, passed subsequently to the Revised Statutes, containing the Statutes from

1836 to 1859. Edited by Theron Metcalf, Luther S. Cushing, and Horace Gray, Jr. *Boston.* 1854-59. 2 vols., 8vo. C.

General Laws and Resolves of the Legislature of the Commonwealth of Massachusetts, ... Session of 1854. *Boston.* [1854.] 8vo, pp. 76. Continued. 45747

The General Statutes of the Commonwealth of Massachusetts, revised by Commissioners ... . *Boston.* 1860. 8vo, pp. xiv, 1126.

Edited by Joel Parker, W. A. and A. A. Richardson.

The General Statutes of the Commonwealth ... relating to the Public Schools, with the Alterations and Amendments to 1868. *Boston.* 1868. 8vo. C. 45749

Geology. Report of a Geological Survey of Massachusetts. By Edward Hitchcock ... . Part I. Economical Geology. *Amherst.* 1832. 8vo, pp. 70. 45750

Republished with three other parts as follows:

Report on the Geology, Mineralogy, Botany, and Zoology of Massachusetts, made and published by order of the Government of the State: in four parts: Part I. Economical Geology. Part II. Topographical Geology. Part III. Scientific Geology. Part IV. Catalogue of Animals and Plants. With a descriptive List of the Specimens of Rocks and Minerals, collected for the Government. Illustrated by numerous Woodcuts, and an Atlas of Plates. By Edward Hitchcock ... . *Amherst.* 1833. Rl. 8vo, pp. 700. Atlas of 18 Plates in folio. C. + Second Edition, Corrected and Enlarged. *Amherst: J. Adams.* 1835. Rl. 8vo, pp. (4), 702. Atlas of 19 Plates in folio. BA. 45751

... Report, &c. relating to the Geology of the State. [n. p. 1837.] 8vo, pp. 16. H. 45752

Report on a Re-Examination of the Economical Geology of Massachusetts. By Edward Hitchcock ... . *Boston: Dutton and Wentworth, State Printers.* 1838. 8vo, pp. 139. H. 45753

Reports of the Commissioners on the Geological Survey of the State. *Boston.* 1838. 8vo. 45754

Final Report on the Geology of Massachusetts: ... Containing—I. Economical Geology. II. Scenographical Geology. III. Scientific Geology. IV. Elementary Geology. With an appended Catalogue of ... Specimens ... in the State Collection. By Edward Hitchcock, LL.D. ... *Northampton: J. H. Butler.* 1841.

4to, pp. xii, 831. 55 Plates and Map. + *Amherst: J. S. & C. Adams.* 1841. 4to, pp. xii, 299, 14 Plates; 299-831, 37 Plates and Map. H. 45755

Report on certain Points in the Geology of Massachusetts. By Edward Hitchcock ... . *Boston.* 1853. 8vo, pp. 44. 45756

See also Jackson (C. T.), Vol. IX., Nos. 35399 and 35400.

George Town. *See* Vol. IX., No. 34654.

Graduated Tables, showing the Comparative Amount of Money appropriated by the Different Towns for Education. [n. p. n. d.] 8vo, pp. 16. 45757

Department of Massachusetts, Proceedings of the ... Grand Army of the Republic, ... at New Bedford, ... 1870. ... *Boston: B. F. Bennett & Co.* 1870. 8vo, pp. 16. H. 45758

Constitution, etc., of the Grand Consistory of the State of Massachusetts, Valley of Boston. *Charlestown.* 1863. 12mo.

The Act of Incorporation, By-Laws, Rules and Regulations ... of the Grand Lodge of Massachusetts. ... *Boston: Printed by E. G. House.* 1819. 8vo, pp. 32. Continued. H. 45760

Also: Annual Communication of the Grand Lodge of Massachusetts. *Boston.* 1826. Folio. — Circular Letter of the Grand Lodge of Massachusetts, relative to forming an Asylum for Female Orphans. *Boston.* 1822. Folio. W. — Constitution, adopted 1811. [*Boston.* 1811.] 4to, pp. 8. — The Constitutions of the ... Grand Lodge of Massachusetts, and General Regulations ... . *Boston.* [n. d.] 8vo, pp. 78. Continued. H. — Grand Lodge ... of Free and Accepted Masons, of ... Massachusetts ... from March 9 to Dec. 27, 1864 ... . *Boston: Hugh H. Tuttle.* 1865. 8vo, pp. 119, (1). Continued. BA. — Journal of Proceedings of the Grand Lodge of the State of Massachusetts, 1823 to 1847. *Boston.* 1847. 8vo. — Proceedings of the Grand Lodge ... February 5, 1846. *Boston.* 1846. 8vo, pp. 42. Continued. — Report on the Condition of the Charity Fund of the Grand Lodge of Massachusetts; March 11, 1857 ... . *Boston: William White.* 1857. 8vo, pp. 64. H. — Report on the State of the Grand Lodge and Lodges under its Jurisdiction, made Dec. 27, 1823, by John Dixwell. *Boston.* 1824. 8vo. *See also* [Dexter (S.)], Vol. V., No. 19901.

Grand Royal Arch Chapter of Massachusetts ... 1819. *Boston.* 1819. 8vo. Continued. H. 45761

... Third Annual Report of the ... Harbor Commissioners. January, 1869. *Boston: Wright & Potter, Printers.* 1869. 8vo, pp. 39. Continued. H. 45762

An Historical Sketch. *See* Vol. VIII., No. 32084.

History of the Gaols in this State; with Tables. [*Boston.* 1827.] 8vo. 45763

House No. 19. Papers relating to the Coal Mines of this State. [*Boston.* 1842.] 8vo. 45764

It is scarcely necessary to say that a series of the "House" documents include many papers of historical interest. *See also* [Kinnicutt (T.)], Vol. IX., No. 37934.

The Humane Society of ... Massachusetts. [History, List of Officers, etc.] *Boston: Barker, Cotter & Co., Printers.* 1869. 8vo, pp. 18. Plate. B. 45765

Also: ... An Act to incorporate ... a Society by the name of The Humane Society of ... Massachusetts. [n. p. 1810?] 8vo, pp. 44. — A Continuation of the Proceedings of the Humane Society ... June, 1788-June, 1789. [n. p. n. d.] 12mo, pp. 7. — History of The Humane Society of Massachusetts: with a ... List of Premiums ... from its commencement to the Present Time: ... and a List of the Officers and Members. ... *Boston: Samuel N. Dickinson, Printer.* 1845. 8vo, pp. 95, (1). B. — The Institution of the Humane Society of ... Massachusetts: with the Rules ... . *Boston: Printed in the Year* 1788. 16mo, pp. 27. — A Statement of Premiums awarded by the Humane Society ... from July 1817, to April 1829 ... . With an Appendix. *Boston: Freeman & Bolles, Print.* 1829. 8vo, pp. 60. H.

The Improvements of the State House. The Investigations thereof investigated ... . *Boston.* 1868. 8vo, pp. 93. 45766

In Provincial Congress, Watertown, May 5, 1775. 4to, 1 leaf.

Resolutions disqualifying General Gage as Governor, etc.

In the House of Representatives, February 8, 1784. [*Boston.* 1815.] 8vo. 45768

Relates to a grant of land to Captain John Flint, in Baldwin, Maine.

Incomes of the Citizens of Boston and other Cities and Towns in Massachusetts. *Boston.* 1866. 8vo. 45769

The Constitution of the Independent Company of Cadets, attached to the First Division Mass. Volunteer Militia. [n. p.] 1857. 12mo, pp. 27, (2). H. 45770

See also Vol. IX., No. 34449.

Constitution, By-Laws, and Rules of Groton Lodge, No. 71, I[ndependent] O[rder of] O[dd] F[ellows]. *Boston.* 1845. 12mo, pp. 38. 45771

An Index to the Laws of Massachusetts: from the Adoption of the Constitution to the Year 1796. By Benjamin Whitman. *Worcester.* 1797. 8vo, pp. 152. W. 45772

Report of the Industrial School for Girls, at Winchester, January, 1856. *Boston.* 1856. 12mo, pp. 12. Continued. M.

Inquiries by the Agricultural Society. [*Boston.* MDCCC.] 8vo, pp. 29. Continued. H. 45774

An Inquiry into the right. *See* Vol. IX., No. 34816.

Inquiry into the State of the Bills of Credit of the Province of Massachusetts-Bay in New-England. [*Boston.*] 1743. 8vo, pp. 52. 45775

... First Annual Report of the Insurance Commissioners, December, 1855. *Boston: William White, Printer.* 1856. 8vo, pp. 235. Continued. BA. 45776

Also: ... First Annual Report upon Loan and Fund Associations, by the Insurance Commissioners. 1857. *Boston: William White, Printer.* 1857. 8vo, pp. 33, folded leaf. Continued. H. — ... Report relative to Insurance Companies. [n. p. 1836.] 8vo, pp. 27. H.

[Report of] The Joint Special Committee, to whom was recommitted the Report and Bill relating to the Suppression of the Evils of Intemperance ... . [n. p. *February* 15, 1855.] 8vo.

Journal and Documents of the Valuation Committee of the Year 1860: ... with Acts of 1861, to secure a uniform Description & Appraisal of Estates in the Commonwealth. ... *Boston: William White, Printer.* 1861. 8vo, pp. 523. B., H. 45778

Journal of the Constitutional Convention of ... Massachusetts, ... held in Boston, ... the Fourth ... of May, 1853. ... *Boston: White & Potter, Printers.* 1853. 8vo, pp. (2), 560, (1). H.

Journal of the Convention for framing a Constitution of Government for the State of Massachusetts Bay, from ... September 1, 1779, to ... June 16, 1780. Including a List of the Members. With an Appendix ... . *Boston: Dutton and Wentworth, Printers.* 1832. 8vo, pp. 264. C., H. 45780

Journal of the Debates and Proceedings in the Convention of Delegates, chosen to revise the Constitution of Massachusetts, ... November 15, 1820, ... to January 9, 1821. ... *Boston.* 1821. 8vo, pp. 292. BA., C. + New Edition, Revised and Corrected. [*Ibid.*] 1853. 8vo, pp. vii, (1), 677. H. 45781

By Nathan Hale and Charles Hall. Corrected title of *our* No. 29654, Vol. VIII.

Journal Of the Honourable House of Representatives, Of His Majesty's Province of the Massachusetts-Bay in New-England, begun and held at Boston, 1715 ... . *Boston.* 1715. Folio. Continued. 45782

Journal of the Honourable House of Representatives, ... Begun and held at Harvard-College in Cambridge, ... the Thirtieth of

May ... 1770 [and continued by adjournment to April 26, 1771]. *Boston: Printed by Edes and Gill.* M,DCC,LXX–[71]. Folio, pp. 253. H. 45783

Journal of the Proceedings. *See* [Hutchinson (T.)] *and* Indians

Journal of the Proceedings of the Honourable House of Representatives of His Majesty's Province of the Massachusetts Bay in New England, begun at Boston, 31st of May, 1769, to the 25th of April, 1772. *Printed at Boston, in New England.* 1772.

The Journals of each Provincial Congress of Massachusetts in 1774 and 1775, and of the Committee of Safety, with an Appendix, containing the proceedings of the County Conventions —Narratives of the Events of the nineteenth of April, 1775— Papers relating to Ticonderoga and Crown Point, and other Documents, illustrative of the early History of the American Revolution. ... *Boston: Dutton and Wentworth, Printers.* 1838. 8vo, pp. lix, 778. A., C., H. 45785

Journals of the Committees on the Revised Statutes. *Boston: Dutton and Wentworth, State Printers.* 1835. 8vo, pp. (2), xi, 43, 467, Appendix. B. 45786

Journals of the House of Representatives of the Colony of the Massachusetts-Bay, July, 1775–Feb. 1776. *Watertown, (New England): B. Edes.* 1775–76. 2 vols., folio, pp. 271; 332.

The Laws "agreed upon to be printed" by Order of the General Court, Oct. 15, 1650. 45788

"Not extant. Probably particular Laws only." Title and note from Thomas' "History of Printing."

The Laws, such as were ordered to be printed by Order of the General Court, May 3d, 1654. *Cambridge.* 1654. 45789

"No copies of this edition of the Laws are to be found. They were probably only particular Laws."—THOMAS.

Laws and Orders made at Several General Courts in the years 1661, 1662, & 1663. Printed and published by Order of the General Court. *Cambridge: Printed by S. Green.* 1664. Folio, pp. 8. 45790

Continued to 1668, or later.

Laws for Regulating and Governing the Militia ... . *Boston: Printed by Young & Minns.* 1800. 12mo, pp. 73, iv. Cont'd.

The Laws for the Government of the Massachusetts Militia, ... amended ... 1868. Published by the Adjutant-General ... . *Boston: Wright & Potter, Printers.* 1868. 12mo, pp. 92, (2), 2.

Laws of the Commonwealth of Massachusetts, passed by the General Court, holden at Boston, Suffolk Co., 1789, 1791, 1792. *Boston: T. Adams.* 1791–1792. Folio. + Vol. II. 1789–1796. + [Vol. III.] 1796–1802. + [Vol. IV.] 1802–1805. Folio.

Continued after this date in octavo.

The Laws of the Commonwealth of Massachusetts, Passed from the Year 1780, to ... 1800, with the Constitutions of the United States ... and of the Commonwealth ... . To which is added, an Appendix ... . *Printed by Thomas & Andrews, Boston.* 1801. 3 vols., 8vo. + *Boston: Printed by Manning & Loring.* 1801. 2 vols., 8vo, pp. (4), 520, Index, (56); 521–1073, (56).

The Laws of the Commonwealth of Massachusetts from November 28th, 1780, to February 16th, 1816. *Boston.* 1807–16. 4 vols., 8vo. C. 45795

Laws of the Commonwealth ... establishing the Boston Board of Health; with Rules and Regulations. *Boston.* [n. d.] 8vo, pp. 33. 45796

Laws relating to the Boston Board of Health. [n. p. 1811.] 8vo, pp. 38. 45797

Letter addressed to Caleb Strong. *See* Strong (C.)

A Letter addressed to the Congregational Clergy of Massachusetts, on Episcopacy. *Boston.* 1829. 12mo, pp. 24. 45798

A Letter from the Elders. *See* [Breck (R.)], Vol. II. 7655.

Letter of the Justices of the Supreme Judicial Court to ... the Governor, with two Judiciary Bills drawn by them; ... *Boston: ... Printed by Young and Minns.* 1804. 8vo, pp. 28. BA.

Letter to a Gentleman chosen to be a Member of the Hon. House of Representatives, to be assembled at Boston, Feb. 10, 1731. [n. p. n. d.] 12mo. W. 45800

See also under Letter, in our Vol. X.

A Letter to a Gentleman in the Massachusetts General Assembly, Concerning Taxes to support Religious Worship. ... [By Isaac Backus. *Boston:*] *Printed in the Year* 1771. 8vo, pp. 22.

A Letter ... to the Chairman of the Committee of the Legislature on the License Law. By Homo. *Boston: Printed for the Author.* [1839.] 8vo, pp. 8. BA. 45802

Letter to the Governor. *See* [Cabot (J. E.)], Vol. III. 9801.

Liability of Stockholders in Manufacturing Corporations. Reasons for repealing the Laws of Massachusetts which render the Members of Manufacturing Companies personally Liable for their Debts. *Boston.* 1830. 8vo, pp. 12. M. 45803

The License Law. [*Boston.* 1838.] 8vo, pp. 8. B. 45804

List of Members of the House of Representatives, 1809. *Boston.* 1809. Folio. Continued. 45805

List of Officers in Commission in Massachusetts since 1833. [n. p.] 1843. 8vo, pp. 48. 45806

A List of Shareholders ... with the ... Values of Shares, in the National Banks in the Commonwealth. ... *Boston: Wright & Potter, ... Printers.* 1867. 4to, pp. xi, 573. + [*Ibid.*] 1869. 4to, pp. xiii, 582. B. 45807

... Manual for the Use of the General Court: ... with the Constitution of the Commonwealth ... . Prepared ... By William Stowe ... . *Boston: William White, Printer* ... 1858. 16mo, pp. 232. Continued. B. 45808

Maryland and Massachusetts. Proceedings in the Legislature of Massachusetts, upon the Act of the State of Maryland appropriating seven thousand dollars for the families of those belonging to the Sixth Regiment of Massachusetts Volunteers, who were killed or disabled by wounds received in the riot at Baltimore, April 19th, 1861. *Boston: Wright & Potter, Printers.* 1862. 8vo, pp. 15. B. 45809

Massachusetts, or the First Planters. *See* [Dudley (T.)], V.

The Second Annual Report of the Massachusetts Abolition Society ... 1841. *Boston: David H. Ela, Printer.* 1841. 12mo, pp. 12. Continued. H. 45810

Also: The True History of the late Division in the Antislavery Societies, being Part of the Second Annual Report of the Executive Committee ... . *Boston: David H. Ela, Printer.* 1841. 12mo, pp. 45. H.

... Annual Report of the Massachusetts Agricultural College. [*Boston.* 1865.] 8vo, pp. 10. Continued. B. 45811

Massachusetts Agricultural Journal. 1810. [n. p. n. d.] 8vo.

Continued as the "Massachusetts Agricultural Repository and Journal, Published by the Trustees of the Massachusetts Society for Promoting Agriculture." Vol. III *Boston.* 1815. 8vo.

Massachusetts Almanack for 1790. By Poor Richard. *Boston: Joseph Hovey.* [n. d.] 45813

Printed with red ink, and on one side of the leaf only.

Massachusetts Almanac, or the Merchant's and Farmer's Calendar, for 1832. *Boston.* [n. d.] 12mo. H. 45814

Massachusetts Anti-Liquor Law; ... also the Proceedings of the ... Convention held at Worcester, June 23d and 24th ... . *Boston.* 1852. 8vo, pp. 36. B. 45815

Massachusetts Anti-Slavery Society. Proceedings ... at the Annual Meetings held ... 1854, 1855, & 1856; ... *Boston.* 1856. 8vo, pp. 67. H. 45816

Fourth Annual Report of the ... Massachusetts Anti-Slavery Society, ... 1836. *Boston: Isaac Knapp.* 1836. 8vo, pp. 72. Continued. B. 45817

For preceding Reports *see* "New England Anti-Slavery Society." Also: An Account of the Interviews which took place ... between a Committee of the Massachusetts Anti-Slavery Society, and the Committee of the Legislature. *Boston: Massachusetts Anti-Slavery Society.* 1836. 4to, pp. 26. BA.—Address of the Committee appointed for the purpose of considering the recent case of Kidnapping from our Soil ... . *Boston.* 1846. 8vo.—An Address to the Abolitionists of Massachusetts, on ... Political Action. By the ... Managers of the Mass. A. S. Society. [n. p. n. d.] 16mo, pp. 20. BA.—Report of the Committee on Slavery to the Convention of Congregational Ministers. *Boston.* 1849. 8vo.—Report of the Twenty-Fourth National Anti-Slavery Festival. *Boston: Printed for the Managers.* 1858. 16mo, pp. 32. H.

Constitution and By-Laws of the Massachusetts Army Association. *Boston: Geo. C. Rand & Avery, Printers.* 1865. 12mo, pp. 11. H. 45818

Constitution of the Massachusetts Army and Navy Union. Adopted January 17, 1866. ... *Boston: Printed by Calkins & Goodwin.* [n. d.] 12mo, pp. 12. H. 45819

Constitution and Minutes of the Massachusetts Baptist Convention, held in Boston, Nov. 11 and 12, 1824. *Worcester.* [n. d.] 12mo, pp. 28. 45820

Minutes of the Massachusetts Baptist Convention, held in Worcester, October 26th and 27th, 1825. *Boston.* 1825. 8vo. Continued. W. 45821

Also: Annual Report of the Massachusetts Baptist Convention. *Boston.* 1802. 8vo. Continued.—Constitution and By-Laws of the Massachusetts Baptist Charitable Society, with an Appendix, containing ... the Transactions of the Society ... . *Boston: J. M. Hewes & Co., Printers.* 1853. 12mo, pp. 12. H.

The Massachusetts Baptist Missionary Magazine. Vol. I. ... 1803. ... *Boston: Printed by Manning & Loring.* 1803. 8vo. Continued. BA. 45822

Reports of the ... Massachusetts Baptist Missionary Society, presented ... May 28, 1834. ... *Boston: Press of Jonathan Howe.* 1834. 8vo, pp. 16. 45823

First State Exhibition by the Mass. Board of Agriculture ... Boston, October, 1857. ... *Boston: William White, Printer.* 1857. 8vo, pp. 31. H. 45824

Also: The Proceedings and Reports of the Massachusetts Board of Agriculture, ... 1851–2. ... *Boston: Dutton and Wentworth, Printers.* 1852. 8vo, pp. 141. H.

The Massachusetts Business Directory, for ... 1856: ... By George Adams. ... *Boston.* 1856. 8vo, pp. 288. H. 45825

The Massachusetts Calendar & Thomas' New England Almanac, 1772. *Boston.* [n. d.] Continued. 45826

Act of Incorporation and By-Laws of the Massachusetts Charitable Eye and Ear Infirmary. With an Historical Sketch ... *Boston: T. R. Marvin.* 1840. 12mo, pp. 20. B. 45827

Also: Acts and Resolves ... with the By-Laws ... . *Boston: Dutton & Wentworth, Printers.* 1850. 8vo, pp. 16.—By-Laws ... . [n. p. n. d.] 8vo, pp. 8.—Annual Report of the Surgeons ... 1825. *Boston.* 1825. 8vo. Continued.—Statement of a Committee ... . *Boston: T. R. Marvin, Printer.* 1828. 8vo, pp. 8. BA.

Act of Incorporation, Laws and Regulations, Catalogue, &c., of the Massachusetts Charitable Fire Society. *Boston: Manning & Loring.* 1800. 8vo, pp. 19. + *Boston.* 1805. 8vo, pp. 22. + [*Ibid.*] 1824. 12mo. W. 45828

Also: Act of Incorporation, additional Acts and By-Laws ... . *Boston: Damrell & Moore, Printers.* 1852. 16mo, pp. 23. B.—Bye-Laws ... . *Boston: Printed by J. B. Chisholm.* 1861. 16mo, pp. 36.— ... Constitution ... . [n. p. n. d.] 8vo, pp. 15.—Constitution, State of the Funds, and Charitable Disbursements. ... *Boston.* 1813. 16mo, pp. 16. C.

Constitution of the Massachusetts Charitable Mechanic Association ... . *Boston: Printed by Samuel N. Dickinson.* 1838. 18mo, pp. 47. Continued. H. 45829

Also: First Exhibition and Fair of the Massachusetts Charitable Mechanic Association, ... in ... Boston, September 18, 1837. *Boston: Dutton and Wentworth.* 1837. 8vo, pp. 104, (2). Continued.—Official Catalogue and Journal of the Eleventh Exhibition of American Manufactures, ... under the direction of the ... Association, ... Boston, ... 1869 ... . *Boston: G. Coolidge.* 1869. 4to, pp. 64.—Proceedings on ...

laying the Corner Stone of a Building for the Use of the ... Association, September 30, 1857. *Boston: Geo. C. Rand & Avery, ... Printers.* 1857. 8vo, pp. 16.—Report of the ... Committee ... on ... An Annual Fair. ... *Boston: Printed by Homer & Palmer.* 1837. 8vo, pp. 7, (1).—Report of the Committee ... on ... the relation of Apprentices to their Employers. Read ... Jan., 1869. *Boston: For the Association.* 1869. 8vo, pp. 20.—Rules and Articles of the ... Society, ... with the Charter ... . *Boston: Printed by Adams and Rhoades.* 1803. 8vo, pp. 16. BA.—Sixteenth Triennial Festival ... Oct. 11, 1854. *Boston: For the Association.* 1854. 8vo, pp. 56. BA.

First Anniversary of the Massachusetts Church Missionary Society, ... 1863. *Boston: E. P. Dutton and Company.* 1864. 8vo, pp. 16. Continued. B. 45830

Constitution and By-Laws of the Massachusetts College of Pharmacy; with a List of the Members, etc. *Boston: Printed ... by Bannister & Marvin.* 1824. 12mo, pp. 12. H. + *Boston.* 1831. 12mo, pp. 18. + [*Ibid.*] 1851. 18mo. 45831

Also: Act of Incorporation and By-Laws ... . *Boston: Printed by David Clapp.* 1853. 24mo, pp. 24.—Proceedings ... at the Annual Meeting ... March 6, 1854. With the ... List of Members ... . *Boston: Printed by David Clapp.* 1854. 8vo, pp. 15, (1).—Prospectus of the Course of Instruction ... . 1869–70. *Boston: Alfred Mudge & Son, Printers.* 1869. 12mo, pp. 12. Continued. B.

Massachusetts Colonization Society. ... American Colonization Society, and the Colony at Liberia. ... *Boston: Printed by Perkins & Marvin.* 1832. 8vo, pp. 16. H. 45832

Also: Proceedings of the Annual Meeting of the Massachusetts Colonization Society, ... 1833. ... With the Speeches ... . Also the Letters of ... Governor Lincoln and ... Samuel Lathrop ... . *Boston: Peirce and Parker.* 1833. 8vo, pp. 28.—Third Annual Report of the Board of Managers of the ... Society. Presented May ... 1844. *Boston.* 1844. 8vo. Continued.—Statement of Facts relating to Slavery, by the ... Society. *Boston.* 1831. 8vo. + [*Ibid.*] 1832. 8vo.

Annual Register of the Military Order of the Loyal Legion of the Massachusetts Commandery. *Boston.* 1870. 12mo.

Massachusetts Compiler of Sacred Vocal Music. *Boston: Isaiah Thomas.* 1795. Oblong 4to. 45834

Act of Incorporation and By-Laws of the Massachusetts Congregational Charitable Society. *Boston: Printed by I. R. Butts.* 1853. 8vo, pp. 8. B. 45835

Also: Act of Incorporation, Regulations, and Members of the ... Society. With a Brief Sketch of its Origin ... . *Boston: John Eliot.* MDCCCXV. 8vo, pp. 20. H., M.

Articles of the Massachusetts Constitutional Society. [n. p. 1794.] 12mo. W. 45836

Rules of the Massachusetts Convention of Congregational Ministers. Adopted May, 1830. *Boston: T. R. Marvin, Printer.* 1831. 16mo, pp. 8. H. 45837

Constitution and By-Laws of the Massachusetts Dental Society. ... *Boston: T. R. Marvin and Son.* 1865. 24mo, pp. 11, (1). B. 45838

Constitution and By-Laws of Massachusetts Division, No. 71, Sons of Temperance ... . *Boston: Stacy and Richardson, Printers.* 1853. 24mo, pp. 24. BA. 45839

Fourth Annual Report of the Massachusetts Domestic Missionary Society ... . *Boston: Crocker & Brewster, Printers.* 1822. 8vo, pp. 19. Continued. H. 45840

Massachusetts Election! ... American Nomination. Major-General Henry Dearborn, for Governor ... . [n. p. about 1815.] 8vo, pp. 24. BA. 45841

Massachusetts Emigrant Aid Company. *See* Nebraska *and* "Organization."

The Annual Report of the Massachusetts Episcopal Missionary Society ... 1823. With an Appendix ... . *Boston: Printed by Joseph W. Ingraham.* 1823. 12mo, pp. 56. Continued. H.

Also: Address to the Members of the Episcopal Church, Oct. 11, 1828. *Boston.* 1828. 8vo, pp. 4.—First Semi-Annual Report of the Rev. Asa Eaton, D.D. ... Boston, ... 1829. *Boston: Press of Putnam & Hunt.* 1830. 12mo, pp. 20.—Proceedings of the ... Society, June 20, 1827. *Boston.* 1827. 8vo, pp. 24. M.—Report of the Board of Directors, April 1, 1823. *Boston.* 1823. 8vo, pp. 56. Continued.

First Annual Meeting of the Massachusetts Episcopal Society for the Religious Instruction of Freedmen, held ... March 1, 1865. *Boston: Geo. C. Rand & Avery.* 1865. 12mo, pp. 17.

The Massachusetts Family Almanac, or the Merchants & Farmers Calendar ... 1833; ... *Boston: Allen & Company.* [1832.] 16mo, pp. (36). Continued. H. 45844

Acts of Incorporation of the Massachusetts Fire and Marine Insurance-Company. 1795 and 1799. [n. p. n. d.] 8vo, pp. 13.

Massachusetts General Hospital. Acts, Resolves, By-Laws, and Rules and Regulations. *Boston: James Loring.* 1837. 8vo, pp. 44. H. + *Boston.* 1846. 8vo, pp. 58. 45846

Also: ... An Act to incorporate certain Persons by the Name of the Massachusetts General Hospital. [n. p. 1816?] 8vo, pp. (2), 8. B.—Account of the Medical School in Boston, and of the Hospital. *Boston.* 1824. 8vo.—Address of the Board of Trustees of the ... Hospital to the Public. ... *Boston: Printed by J. Belcher.* 1814. 8vo, pp. 14. Continued.—Address of the Trustees ... to the Subscribers and to the Public. [*Boston.* 1822.] 8vo, pp. 34.—Address to the Citizens of Boston [December, 1816. *Boston.* 1816.] 8vo, pp. 8.—Annual Report of the Board of Trustees ...

for 1828. [*Boston.*] 1828. 8vo, pp. 8. Continued.—By-Laws ... with ... Rules and Regulations ... for the Government of the Asylum for the Insane in Charlestown, and the Hospital in Boston. *Boston: Charles Crocker, Printer.* 1821. 8vo, pp. 24. + *Boston.* 1830. 8vo, pp. 28.—Civil, Religious, and Masonic Services, at the Laying of the Corner-Stone of the ... Hospital, ... July 4, 1818. [*Boston.*] 1818. 8vo, pp. 8.—History of the Massachusetts General Hospital. *Boston.* 1857. 8vo.—Report of the Committee of By-Laws. ... [n. p. 1811?] 8vo, pp. 36.—The Report ... upon the Financial Condition of the ... Hospital. [*Boston.* 1865.] 4to, pp. 6.—Report of the ... Hospital, ... 1823. [n. p. n. d.] 8vo, pp. 14. Continued. H.—The Trustees of the ... Hospital, to the Public. *Boston: Eastburn's Press.* 1844. 8vo, pp. 14. B. *See also* "Some Account."

Massachusetts Health Insurance Co. [Act of Incorporation, etc. n. p. 1847.] 16mo, pp. 16. B. 45847

Also: Exposition of the Objects of the ... Company, Boston. *Boston: Printed by Alfred Mudge.* 1847. 16mo, pp. 12. B.

Proceedings of the First Semiannual Session of the Massachusetts Grand Lodge, of the Order of Knights of St. Crispin ... Boston ... May 12 and 13, 1869. *Boston.* 1869. 8vo, pp. 24.

Centennial Festival of Massachusetts Lodge ... including the Historical Address by ... Charles W. Slack ... . May 12, 1870. *Boston.* 1870. 8vo, pp. 73. H. 45849

Also: The History, Charter and By-Laws of Massachusetts Lodge ... . *Boston.* 1863. 12mo, pp. 36. H.

MASSACHUSETTS HISTORICAL SOCIETY. The Act of Incorporation, the Laws, and the Circular Letter of the Massachusetts Historical Society. With an Appendix. ... *Boston: Printed ... by Joseph Belknap.* MDCCXCIV. 8vo, pp. 14. Continued. H.

Also: Act of Incorporation, ... Catalogue of Members, and Circular Letter of the Massachusetts Historical Society. *Boston.* 1853. 8vo, pp. 26.—Act of Incorporation and By-Laws of the ... Society. [*Boston.*] 1853. 8vo, pp. 12.—The Act of Incorporation, with the additional Acts, and By-Laws ... *Boston.* 1857. 8vo, pp. 19. B.

Catalogue of the Library of the Massachusetts Historical Society. *Boston: Printed for the Society.* M.DCCC.LIX. 2 vols., 8vo, pp. vii, 732; vii, 651. 45851

A valuable work of reference for books and pamphlets printed in and relating to America. A few copies were printed on large paper in quarto. Also: Catalogue of Books in the Massachusetts Historical Library. *Boston: Printed by S. Hall.* 1796. 8vo, pp. 40. Continued.—Catalogue of the Books, Pamphlets, Newspapers, Charts, Manuscripts, &c. in the Library ... . *Boston: John Eliot, Jun.* 1811. 8vo, pp. vi, (2), 96.—Catalogue of the ... Library of Thomas Dowse, ... Presented to the ... Society, July 30, 1856. *Boston: Printed by John Wilson & Son.* 1870. 8vo, pp. (2), 214.—Circular Letter, addressed in 1794, ... to Gentlemen of Science in America, requesting Historical Information, and Contributions to the Library and Cabinet. [n. p. n. d.] 4to, pp. 3.—Circular Letter soliciting the Co-operation of the Members and others in collecting a Series of the Laws of Massachusetts. *Boston.* 1854. 8vo, pp. 3.—Circular Letter to the Resident and Corresponding Members, soliciting Contributions to the Library and Cabinet. [n. p. n. d.] 4to, pp. 3.

Collections of the Massachusetts Historical Society, for ... 1792. Volume I. *Boston: Printed ... by Belknap and Hall.* MDCCXCII. 8vo, pp. (4), 288. H. + *Boston: ... Re-printed by Munroe & Francis*, ... 1806. 8vo, pp. (2), 288. Continued. BA.

This valuable collection of important documents, relating to the history of America, is issued in series of ten volumes each. Some of the earlier volumes [I., II., III., IV., V., XVII., XVIII., XIX., XX.] have become scarce, and some others have been reprinted. Of course it is desirable to secure a set of the original edition. Mr. Bartlett's catalogue of J. C. Brown's library contains a detailed list of the contents. The last volume of each series contains a general table of contents of the series and an index of authors, a chronological table of the most remarkable events recorded in the text and a general analytical index. The fifth series is now (1879) in course of publication. *See* "N. A. Rev.," II. 109, XLIV. 260, LVII. 352, etc.

The Dowse Library. *See* Vol. V., No. 20793.

An Historical Journal of the American War. Extracted from the Publications of the Massachusetts Historical Society. *Boston.* 1795. 8vo, pp. 246. + [*Ibid.*] 1810. + [*Ibid.*] 1813. 45853

Lectures delivered in a Course before the Lowell Institute in Boston, by Members of the Massachusetts Historical Society, on Subjects relating to the Early History of Massachusetts. *Boston: The Society.* 1869. 8vo, pp. viii, 498. C. 45854

Memoir of the Hon. Abbott Lawrence. Prepared for the Massachusetts Historical Society. *Boston.* 1856. 8vo, pp. 21.

Memorial of the ... Society to the Legislature ... February, 1858. *Boston.* 1858. 4to, pp. 3. 45856

Also: Laws and Regulations of the ... Society; ... April 25, 1833. *Cambridge.* 1833. 8vo, pp. 8.—List of Portraits in the Hall of the ... Society. [*Boston.* 1838.] 8vo, pp. 8.—Order of Services, 22d of December, MDCCCXIII, in Commemoration of the Landing of the Forefathers. *Boston.* 1813. 8vo, pp. 4.

Proceedings of the Massachusetts Historical Society. 1855–1858. ... *Boston: For the Society.* M. DCCC. LIX. 8vo, pp. xi, (1), 412. 5 Portraits, Facsimile and Plate. Continued. BA. 45857

For a list of the contents of this series, *see* Bartlett's catalogue of J. C. Brown's library.

Proceedings of the Massachusetts Historical Society in Respect to The Memory of William Hickling Prescott, February 1, 1858. *Boston: Massachusetts Historical Society.* 1859. 8vo, pp. 53. H.

Also: Prospectus of the Collections of the Massachusetts Historical Society. *Boston.* 1814. Folio, 1 leaf.—Regulations for the Library ... April, 1841. [n. p. n. d.] 8vo, pp. 2.—Report of a Committee appointed by the ... Society on Exchanges of Prisoners during the American Revolutionary War. ... December 19, 1861. *Boston: For the Society.* 1861. 8vo, pp. 26.—Report of the Proceedings at the Annual Meeting of the Massachusetts Historical Society. Address of Hon. Robert C. Winthrop,

and the Remarks of Hon. Edward Everett, with a Description of the Dowse Library. *Boston.* 1857. 8vo, pp. 8.

Tribute of the Massachusetts Historical Society To the Memory of Josiah Quincy, July 14, 1864. *Boston: Massachusetts Historical Society.* 1864. 8vo, pp. 32. H. 45859

See Everett (E.), Vol. IV., No. 23278, *also* Livermore (E.), Vol. X., No. 41570.

Forty-Fifth Annual Report of the Massachusetts Home Missionary Society ... . *Boston: T. R. Marvin.* 1844. 8vo, pp. 48. Continued. B. 45860

Also: Semi-Centennial Report ... Presented at the Annual Meeting. *Boston.* 1849. 8vo, pp. 60.

Massachusetts Homœopathic Medical Society. Publications ... For 1861–62. [n. p. 1862.] 8vo, pp. 105. H. 45861

Somewhat historical: containing List of Officers, Proceedings of Annual Meetings, Reports, etc. Also: Report of a Committee of the Massachusetts Homœopathic Medical Society, occasioned by a Report of a Committee of the ... Mass. Medical Society. *Boston: David Clapp, Printer.* 1851. 8vo, pp. 8. H.

Massachusetts Horticultural Society. ... *Boston: Isaac R. Butts.* MDCCCXXIX. 8vo, pp. 51, (1). B. 45862

Also: Addresses of the retiring President and President Elect of the ... Society, ... with the Schedule of Prizes for 1852. ... [*Boston:*] *Dutton & Wentworth, Printers.* [n. d.] 8vo, pp. 19, (1). B.—By-Laws of the ... Society. [n. p. n. d.] 8vo, pp. 16. Continued.—A Catalogue of ... the Library ... January, 1854. *Boston: Cross & Freeman, Printers.* 1854. 24mo, pp. 33. H.—Constitution and By-Laws of the ... Society. *Boston.* 1829. 8vo. + *Boston.* 1836. 8vo, pp. 24. + With the Act of Incorporation, &c., &c. *Boston: Dutton and Wentworth's Print.* 1842. 8vo, pp. 88, x.—Premiums and Gratuities awarded by the ... Society, ... 1850. [n. p. n. d.] 8vo, pp. 20. Continued.—Proceedings ... . Vol. I. [No. I.] *Boston: ... William D. Ticknor & Company.* MDCCCXLVII. 4to.—Properties of Plants and Flowers compiled by the Flower Committee of the ... Society ... . *Boston: The Society.* 1862. 12mo, pp. 33, (1). B.—Report of the Transactions of the ... Society, for ... 1837–8, with Preliminary Observations. By John Lewis Russell ... . *Boston: Tuttle, Dennett ... Printers.* 1839. 8vo, pp. 116. H.—Report of the Twentieth Annual Exhibition of the ... Society, and Third Triennial Festival, ... 1848. *Boston: Printed by Tuttle & Dennett.* 1848. 8vo, pp. 61. H.—Reports of the Committees for 1852, of the ... Society, with the Schedule of Prizes for 1853. *Boston: Printed by Dutton and Wentworth.* 1853. 8vo, pp. 35, (1). Continued.—Schedule of Prizes offered by the ... Society, ... 1851. [n. p. n. d.] 12mo, pp. 14. Continued.—Transactions of the ... Society ... 1842–1843. To which is added the Address ... by J. E. Teschemacher, Esq. ... *Boston: Dutton and Wentworth's Print.* 1843. 8vo, pp. 78, Address, 22.—Transactions of the ... Society. ... Volume I. No. I. *Boston: ... William D. Ticknor & Company.* MDCCCXLVII. 4to. 5 colored Plates. H.

Proposals of the Massachusetts Hospital Life Insurance Company, to make Insurance on Lives ... August 18, 1823. ... [*Boston:*] *Printed by James Loring.* 1823. 8vo, pp. 51, (1). Cont'd.

See also [Lowell (Francis (C.)], Vol. X., No. 42432.

Massachusetts in Agony: or, Important Hints To the Inhabitants of the Province: Calling aloud for Justice to be done to the Oppressed; and avert the Impending Wrath over the Oppressors. By Vincent Centinel. ... *Boston: Printed by D. Fowle.* 1750. 4to, pp. 19, (1). BA. 45864

Corrected title of our Vol. III., No. 11679. *See also* "Appendix," No. 45641.

First Annual Report of the Massachusetts Infant Asylum. ... 1868. *Boston: Alfred Mudge & Son, Printers.* 1868. 8vo, pp. 45, (1). Continued. H. 45865

Second Annual Report ... of the Massachusetts Infirmary for Diseases of the Lungs. *Boston: Isaac R. Butts, Printer.* 1839. 12mo, pp. 10. BA. 45866

Massachusetts Institute of Technology. Officers. Extracts from Act of Incorporation. Objects and Plan. By-Laws. *Boston: Printed by John Wilson and Son.* 1862. 8vo, pp. 12. B.

Also: An Account of the Proceedings preliminary to the organization of the ... Institute ... with ... an Appendix ... . *Boston: Printed by John Wilson and Son.* 1861. 8vo, pp. 23.—First Annual Catalogue of the Officers and Students, and Programme of the Course of Instruction, ... of the Massachusetts Institute of Technology, 1865–6. *Boston: John Wilson and Sons.* 1865. 8vo, pp. 39. Continued.—By-Laws. [n. p. n. d.] 8vo, pp. 7. B.—Objects and Plan of an Institute of Technology; including a Society of Arts, a Museum of Arts, and a School of Industrial Science. ... *Boston: Printed by John Wilson and Son.* 1860. 8vo, pp. 29. H. + Second Edition. [*Ibid.*] 1861. 8vo, pp. 29.—Outline of Studies in the ... School of Industrial Science of the ... Institute ... . *Boston: Printed by John Wilson and Son.* 1864. 8vo, pp. 10. B.—School of the ... Institute ... . Semi-Annual Examination Papers for ... 1865–66. *Boston: Thomas Kirwan, Printer.* 1866. 8vo, pp. 25. B.

Constitution and By-Laws of the Massachusetts Journeymen Shipwright's Union ... . *Boston: Printed by R. H. Blodgett.* 1864. 18mo, pp. 12. B. 45868

The Massachusetts Justice: Being A Collection of the Laws of the Commonwealth ... . With an Appendix ... . By Samuel Freeman ... . *Printed at Boston, by Isaiah Thomas* ... 1795. 8vo, pp. iv, 396. B. + The Second Edition, ... enlarged. [*Ibid.*] 1802. 8vo, pp. 334. BA. 45869

Massachusetts Lawyer, *pseudon.* *See* [Lowell (J.)], Vol. X., *and* [Hay (G.)], Vol. VIII., No. 30998, *note.*

The Massachusetts Magazine: or, Monthly Museum of Knowledge and Rational Entertainment. ... Vol. I. ... 1789. *Printed at Boston, by Isaiah Thomas* ... . MDCCLXXXIX. 8vo, pp. (4), 802. Plates. Continued. A. 45870

The Massachusetts Manual. *See* Burdick (W.), III. 9215.

... An Act, to Incorporate ... the Massachusetts Manufacturing Company. [*Boston.* 1813.] 8vo, pp. 8. B. 45871

Constitution of the Massachusetts Mechanical Association. Instituted March 15, 1795. *Boston.* 1795. 12mo. + *Boston: Printed by Gilbert & Dean.* 1804. 16mo, pp. 64. BA. 45872

Act of Incorporation and By-Laws of the Massachusetts Medical Society; with the Rules and Regulations, and ... Members. *Boston: John Wilson and Son.* 1867. 8vo, pp. 20. B. 45873

The Acts of Incorporation ... with the By-Laws and Orders, of the Massachusetts Medical Society. *Salem: Printed by Joshua Cushing.* 1806. 8vo, pp. (2), 27, (2). + *Boston.* 1816. 8vo, pp. 54. + [*Ibid.*] 1822. 8vo, pp. 92. + [*Ibid.*] 1826. 8vo, pp. 100. + [*Ibid.*] 1840. 8vo, pp. 96. + [*Ibid.*] 1850. 8vo, pp. 47. M. 45874

Also: Acts of the Legislature ... for regulating the Practice of Physick ... . With the Regulations adopted by the Massachusetts Medical Society, for carrying these Acts into Operation. ... *Boston: Printed by Wells and Lilly.* 1819. 8vo, pp. 21. Continued.—Address of the Counsellors to the Fellows of the ... Society. *Boston: Printed by John Eliot, Jun.* 1812. 8vo, pp. 11.—Address to the Community, on the Necessity of Legalizing the Study of Anatomy. By Order of the ... Society. *Boston: Perkins & Marvin.* 1829. 8vo, pp. 27.—Address to the Members of the ... Society. [*Boston.* 1844.] 8vo, pp. 16.—Amendments of the By-Laws of the ... Society ... 1837. *Boston: John Putnam.* 1837. 8vo, pp. 32.—Annual Circular of the ... College, ... History ... Catalogue of Graduates, &c. *Boston: Printed by David Clapp.* 1846. 8vo, pp. 32. 2 Plates.—By-Laws of the ... Society. [n. p. 1849.] 8vo, pp. 8. Cont'd.—A Catalogue of Books, belonging to the ... Society. 17th June, 1822. [n. p. n. d.] 12mo, pp. 12.— ... Circular of the Medical Faculty of Harvard University ... . *Boston: Printed by David Clapp.* 1849. 8vo, pp. 12. BA.—Constitution, Bye-Laws, and Regulations, of the ... Society ... . With a List of the Officers and Fellows, ... 1804. *Charlestown: Printed by Samuel Etheridge.* 1804. 8vo, pp. 32. + *Boston.* 1816. 8vo.—A Digest of the Acts of the Commonwealth ... relating to the ... Society ... . *Boston: Printed by David Clapp.* 1861. 8vo, pp. 27, (1).—Fellows of the ... Society. [n. p. 1812.] 8vo, pp. 12. Continued.—Fellows of the ... Society, 1787 to 1854. Alphabetically arranged. *Boston: Printed by John Wilson and Son.* 1855. 8vo, pp. 50.—Proceedings of the Counsellors of the ... Society. [n. p. 1826.] 12mo, pp. 10.—Remonstrance of the ... Society, on the Petition for the Establishment of a College of Physicians: ... . *Boston: Printed by Thomas B. Wait and Co.* 1811. 8vo, pp. 12.—Remonstrance of the Board of Censors of Suffolk District against the Privilege acceded to Harvard and Berkshire Medical Schools in the Admission to Fellowship of the Massachusetts Medical Society. [*Boston.* 1827.] 8vo, pp. 4. H.—Report of a Committee on the Charter and By-Laws of the ... Society. [*Boston.* 1848.] 8vo, pp. 8.—Speeches of Drs. Thompson, James Jackson, John Homans, O. W. Holmes, S. Durkee, and H. W. Williams, at the Annual Dinner of the Massachusetts Medical Society, May, 1856. *Boston.* 1856. 8vo, pp. 12.

Articles of Association and By-Laws of the Massachusetts Medical Benevolent Society. Instituted 1857. *Boston: Printed by David Clapp.* 1857. 8vo, pp. 8. H. 45875

Correspondence relating to the Operations of the Massachusetts Mining Company. [n. p.] 1837. 8vo, pp. 6. 45876

The Massachusetts Missionary Magazine for ... 1803. ... Volume I. *Salem: Printed by Joshua Cushing, for the Editors.* [1804.] 8vo, pp. 482, (1). Continued. H. 45877

The Massachusetts Missionary Register ... . Vol. I. *Salem.* 1803. 8vo. Continued. 45878

The Constitution of the Massachusetts Missionary Society: with ... the Officers and Members, etc. *Salem: Printed by Thomas C. Cushing.* 1818. 8vo, pp. 20. BA. 45879

Also: The Twenty-Fifth Annual Report of the ... Massachusetts Missionary Society. ... *Salem: Printed by Warwick Palfray, Jun.* 1824. 8vo, pp. 15. BA.

Massachusetts National Democratic Convention, and Speeches of Gen. Cushing, ... and others. September 12th, 1860. *Boston: Beals, Greene and Company, Printers.* 1860. 8vo, pp. 71, (1).

Title from the cover; the inside title differs slightly.

Second Annual Report of the Massachusetts Peace Society. *Cambridge: Printed by Hilliard and Metcalf.* 1819. 8vo, pp. 14. Continued. H. 45881

Reports and Resolves of the Massachusetts Peace Society in relation to a Congress of Nations, April 4, 1837. [*Boston.* 1837.] 8vo, pp. 18. 45882

Also: A Catalogue of the Officers and Members ... including Nine Branches ... . March 1, 1819. *Cambridge: Printed by Hilliard & Metcalf.* 1819. 8vo, pp. 12, Constitution, 3. Continued.—A Circular Letter from the ... Society ... addressed to the various Associations ... of the Ministers of Religion in the United States. *Cambridge: Printed by Hilliard and Metcalf.* 1816. 8vo, pp. 16.—Circular Letter in behalf of the ... Society, to the Friends of Peace of all Denominations. *Boston: Printed by John Eliot.* 1817. 8vo, pp. 8.—Constitution of the ... Society. [n. p. n. d.] 8vo, pp. 8.

Massachusetts Personal Liberty Bill. [Report of] Joint Standing Committee on Federal Relations [on] ... Trial by Jury and the Writ of Habeas Corpus ... . [n. p. *April* 25, 1855.] 8vo, pp. 21. S. 45883

Constitution and Addresses of the Massachusetts Philo-Italian Society. *Boston: Printed by Samuel N. Dickinson.* 1843. 8vo, pp. 20. H. 45884

Massachusetts Psalter. *See* Massachusee Psalter, 45537, *note.*

The Massachusetts Quarterly Review. ... *Boston: Coolidge & Wiley.* 1848–50. 3 vols., 8vo, pp. (4), 528; (4), 528; (4), 526.

Massachusetts Register: a State Record for 1852. By G. Adams. *Boston.* 1852. 8vo, pp. 336. Continued. B. 45886

The Massachusetts Register and United States Calendar; For 1801 ... . *Boston: Printed by Manning & Loring.* [1801.] 12mo, pp. 180. Continued. B. 45887

For preceding years *see* Fleet (T. *and* J.), "A Pocket Almanac," etc., Vol. VI., No. 24688, of which this is a continuation.

Massachusetts Reports on Life Insurance: 1859–1865. By the Insurance Commissioners. With an Appendix, by Elizur Wright. *Boston: Wright & Potter.* 1865. 8vo, pp. iv, 382, folded leaf. B. 45888

First Annual Report of the Massachusetts Rifle Club. [For 1861.] *Boston: Mudge & Son, Printers.* [1862.] 8vo, pp. 12. Continued. H. 45889

Also: By-Laws of the ... Club. Adopted ... 1861. *Boston: Printed by John Wilson and Son.* 1861. 32mo, pp. 11, (1).—Rules and Regulations of the ... Club. ... 1863. *Boston: Printed by Alfred Mudge & Son.* 1863. 32mo, pp. 9. H.

First Annual Report of the Massachusetts Sabbath-School Society, May 30, 1833. *Boston.* 1833. 8vo, pp. 20. 45890

Also: Brief History of the Massachusetts Sabbath School Society. *Boston.* 1850. 8vo.—Plans and Objects of the ... Society. Addresses by Rev. J. P. Langworthy and C. T. Russell, Esq. ... 1848. [n. p. 1848.] 12mo, pp. 18. S.

First Annual Report of the Massachusetts Sabbath School Union, ... June 1, 1826. *Boston.* 1826. 8vo, pp. 40. Cont'd.

Massachusetts School of Agriculture. ... [Circular and By-Laws.] *Boston: J. H. Eastburn's Press.* 1858. 8vo, pp. 8. B.

First Annual Report of the Massachusetts School for Idiotic and Feeble-minded Youth. *Boston.* 1848. 8vo. 45893

Also: Constitution of the ... School ... . *Boston.* 1851. 8vo.—Third and Final Report on the Experimental School for teaching and Training Idiotic Children; also, the First Report of the Trustees of the Massachusetts School ... . *Cambridge.* 1852. 8vo. S.

Massachusetts School Fund. Extract from the Twenty-Second Annual Report of the Secretary of the Board of Education. [n. p. n. d.] 8vo, pp. 20. B. 45894

Massachusetts Senate Report on the Petition of the Trustees of Amherst College, 1837. *Boston.* 1837. 8vo, pp. 16. M.

Laws and Regulations of the Massachusetts Society for promoting Agriculture. Names of its Present Officers and Mem-

bers, List of Premiums, &c. With ... Extracts from Foreign and Domestick Publications. By the Trustees. *Boston: Printed by Isaiah Thomas* ... MDCCXCIII. 8vo, pp. 56. Continued. H.

Also: Georgick Papers for 1809: consisting of Letters and Extracts communicated to the ... Society ... . *Boston: Russell & Cutler.* 1809. 8vo, pp. 91. Continued. M.—Inquiries by the ... [Society. *Boston.* 1805?] 8vo, pp. 29.—Papers on Agriculture, consisting of Communications, made to the ... Society ... . *Boston: Printed by Young and Minns.* 1799. 8vo, pp. 103. Plate. Continued.—Report of the Trustees of the ... Society ... on ... Reports made to them ... 1860, 1861, and 1862 ... . *Boston: J. H. Eastburn's Press.* 1863. 8vo, pp. 4, (3).—Rules and Regulations of the ... Society ... containing, the Names of its Present Members and Officers, ... Communications, ... Extracts, from Foreign and Domestick Publications, &c. *Boston.* 1793. 8vo, pp. 76. + *Boston: Printed by Thomas Fleet, Jun.* MDCCXCVI. 8vo, pp. 78. B.—Transactions of the ... Society ... for 1856 ... . *Boston: William White, Printer.* 1857. 8vo, pp. 106. BA. + New Series. Vol. I. *Boston: J. H. Eastburn's Press.* 1858. 8vo, pp. (4), 160, 20, 27, 16, 21, 26. B. Continued.

An Account of the Massachusetts Society for promoting Christian Knowledge. ... *Cambridge: Printed by William Hilliard.* 1806. 12mo, pp. 34. BA. + *Andover: Printed by Flagg and Gould.* 1815. 12mo, pp. 83, 1 sheet. BA. 45897

Exhibits the deplorable condition of Rhode Island, with regard to learning, religion, and morals. Also: Annual Report of the Directors ... May 24, 1831. *Boston.* [n. d.] 8vo, pp. 15.—Constitution of the ... Society ... . *Charlestown.* 1803. 8vo, pp. 16. S. + Amended May, 1844. *Boston: T. R. Marvin.* 1844. 12mo, pp. 20. B.

The Second Annual Report Of the Massachusetts Society for suppressing of Intemperance. [n. p. 1814.] 8vo, pp. 11. H.

Also: Circular addressed to the Members of the ... Society ... . *Boston: Printed by Samuel T. Armstrong.* 1814. 8vo, pp. 15.—Constitution of the ... Society ... . And Report ... May 28, 1813. 8vo. Continued.—A Letter to the Mechanics of Boston, respecting the formation of a City Temperance Society. *Boston.* 1831. 12mo, pp. 26.—Report of a Committee of the ... Society ... . 1831. *Boston.* 1831. 8vo, pp. 12.—Report of the Board of Counsel to the ... Society ... June 2, 1820. *Boston: Printed by Sewell Phelps.* 1820. 12mo, pp. 21, (1). H.—When will the day come? *Boston: Massachusetts Temperance Society.* [n. d.] 12mo, pp. (4), 181. 3 Portraits. H.

Report of a Meeting of the Massachusetts Soldier's Relief Association, held ... December 8th, 1862. ... *Washington: M'Gill & Witherow, Printers.* 1863. 8vo, pp. 16. H. 45899

Catalogue of the Massachusetts State Cabinet, under the Charge of the Sec'y of the Board of Agriculture. 1859. *Boston: William White, Printer.* 1859. 8vo, pp. cii, xii. H. 45900

Massachusetts State Charities. Report of the ... Committee appointed to investigate the ... system of the Public Charitable Institutions of ... Massachusetts ... . *Boston: William White, Printer.* 1859. 8vo, pp. 153, folded leaf. B. 45901

An Account of the Massachusetts State Prison. Containing a Description and Plan of the Edifice; the Law, Regulations, Rules, and Orders: ... . By the Board of Visitors. *Charlestown: Printed by Samuel Etheridge.* 1806. 8vo, pp. 47, (1). 2 folded Plates. + *Charlestown: Printed by S. Etheridge, Jr.* 1816. 8vo, pp. 83. 2 folded leaves. H. 45902

Also: Abstract of the Number of Convicts ... during the Year ending Sept. 30, 1817. [*Boston.* 1817.] Folio, 1 leaf. Continued.—Annual Report of the ... Inspectors ... September 30th, 1851, ... with the Annual Reports of the Officers of the Institution. *Boston: Dutton and Wentworth, State Printers.* 1852. 8vo, pp. 55. Continued.—Annual Report of the Convicts ... 1827 and 1828. [n. p. n. d.] Folio, 1 leaf.—An Extract from the Report of the Directors ... October 18, 1827. Reviewing ... the Second Annual Report of the Prison-Discipline Society. ... *Boston: Dutton and Wentworth, Printers.* 1827. 8vo, pp. 28.—Laws of the Commonwealth for the Government of the Massachusetts State Prison; with the Rules and Regulations ... . *Charlestown.* 1830. 8vo, pp. 112. Continued. H.—Regulations of the Governor and Council ... . [*Boston.* 1806.] 8vo.—Rules and Regulations for the Government of the Massachusetts State Prison. *Boston.* 1811. 8vo, pp. 32. + [*Ibid.*] 1823. 8vo, pp. 62. + *Charlestown.* 1830. 8vo, pp. 12. Plate. + *Boston.* 1832. 8vo.

The Massachusetts State Record. *See* Vol. III., No. 10747.

Documents of the Massachusetts Reform School for ... 1849. *Boston.* 1849. 8vo. Continued. 45903

Annual Report of the Secretary of the Massachusetts State Temperance Alliance ... . 1864. *Boston: Wright & Potter, Printers.* 1865. 8vo, pp. 16. Continued. H. 45904

Proceedings of the Massachusetts State Temperance Convention, Boston, Feb. 12, 1840. *Boston.* 1840. 8vo, pp. 31. M.

The Massachusetts System of ... Schools. *See* [Mann (H.)]

The Massachusetts Teacher. Vol. I. [*Boston.* 1848.] 8vo, pp. 384. Continued. H. 45906

Constitution and By-Laws of the Massachusetts Teachers' Association. *Boston.* 1858. 8vo, pp. 15. 45907

Also: Transactions ... . Edited by the Secretary [Charles J. Capen] ... . Vol. I.—1845–1847. *Boston: Samuel Coolidge.* 1852. 12mo, pp. 304. H.

Journal of the Proceedings of the Massachusetts Temperance Convention, ... at Worcester, ... September 18, 1833. *Boston: Ford and Damrell.* 1833. 8vo, pp. 36. Continued. H. 45908

Address of the Council of the Massachusetts Temperance Society, to the Friends of Temperance. *Boston: Printed by John Ford.* 1836. 8vo, pp. 19. B. 45909

Also: ... Addresses. *Boston: Massachusetts Temperance Society.* 1861. 12mo, pp. 98. Portrait. — ... Doings of the Council of the Massachusetts Temperance Society. ... *Boston: Ford and Damrell.* 1834. 12mo, pp. 24. — The Twenty-Fourth Annual Report of the Massachusetts Temperance Society, ... May 27th, 1836. ... *Boston: Printed by John Ford.* 1836. 8vo, pp. 16. Continued. BA.

Address to the People of Massachusetts, on the ... Temperance Reformation. By Mark Hopkins, D.D., Samuel B. Woodward, M.D., Hon. Samuel Hoar. Published by the Massachusetts Temperance Union. *Boston: Daniel Kimball, Printer.* 1846. 8vo, pp. 20. H. 45910

Constitution, By-Laws, and Rules ... of the Massachusetts Tin-Plate, Copper, and Sheet-Iron Workers' Association, Boston. ... *Boston: Printed by Alfred Mudge & Son.* 1864. 18mo, pp. 18. B. 45911

Massachusetts Universalist Convention. Minutes of the First Session of the Council ... 1859, with Act of Incorporation, and By-Laws, ... and a Historical Sketch ... . *Boston: J. S. Spooner, Printer.* [n. d.] 8vo, pp. 24. B. 45912

Address of the Government of the Massachusetts Washington Total Abstinence Society to the Society, and to the Public. *Boston:* ... *R. Newcomb.* 1842. 8vo, pp. 8. H. 45913

... The Memorial and Remonstrance of the Legislature of Massachusetts [against the Embargo. n. p. 1809.] 8vo, pp. 15.

Memorial for an Act to render Masonic and Extrajudicial Oaths penal. ... *Boston.* 1834. 8vo, pp. 9. M. 45915

Memorial of sundry Inhabitants of the State of Massachusetts, on the Subject of Privateering. January 26, 1821. ... *Washington: Printed by Gales & Seaton.* 1821. 8vo, pp. 32. 45916

Memorial of the House of Representatives of the Commonwealth of Massachusetts. *Washington.* 1812. 8vo. 45917

... Memorial [of the President and Fellows of Harvard College]. To the ... House of Representatives of ... Massachusetts. [n. p. 1851.] 8vo, pp. 54. BA. 45918

Message of Gov. Levi Lincoln, communicated to the Legislature, Jan. 4, 1826. Together with Communications from the Secretary and Treasurer and the Adjutant-General. *Boston.* 1826. 8vo, pp. 43. M. 45919

Also: Message ... for regulating ... the Militia of this Commonwealth ... March 28, 1833. *Boston: Dutton and Wentworth, State Printers.* 1833. 8vo, pp. 31. B.

Message ... relative to Arms loaned to Rhode Island, Sept 1842. [n. p. 1842.] 8vo, pp. 13. 45920

Message [transmitting the Report on the Boundary Line between Massachusetts and Rhode Island. n. p. 1848.] 8vo, pp. 95. BA. 45921

Message ... transmitting the Report of B. P. Poore, employed in France as Historical Agent of ... Massachusetts, with Letters ... in relation to the subject. [*Boston.* 1848.] 8vo. 45922

Message ... accompanying the Report of the Massachusetts Commissioners on the Boundary Line between the States of Rhode Island and Massachusetts, March 15, 1851. [n. p. 1851.] 8vo, pp. 14. 45923

The annual messages of the respective governors are included in the documents of the State, and often include matters of much historical interest.

The Militia Act; together with the Rules and Regulations for the Militia. ... *Boston: Printed by J. Gill.* 1776. 4to. 45924

This famous Militia Act of Massachusetts was passed at Watertown in 1775, after the Battles of Lexington and Bunker's Hill, when the General Court had been expelled from Boston by the British Army, and were just in the grieved spirit to cause them to do the work thoroughly. Appended are the 69 Articles of War, passed the 16th of April, 1776, signed by Warren, as Speaker, concurred in by the Council two days later, the very reading of which, it is said, made patriots into soldiers.

Militia Act passed by the Great and General Court or Assembly of the Colony of the Massachusetts-Bay, in New-England, ... *Boston.* 1776. 8vo, pp. 40. 45925

Also: Militia Acts for 1781–6. *Boston.* 1781–6. 4to. — Militia Law of Massachusetts, 1866: with the Articles of War. ... *Boston: Wright & Potter, State Printers.* 1866. 12mo, pp. xii, 83. — Militia Report of William H. Sumner, Adjutant General & Acting Quarter Master General to ... Levi Lincoln, Governor ... . *Boston: Dutton & Wentworth, Printers.* 1828. 8vo, pp. 31, folded leaf. BA. *See* Militia Laws, *infra.*

Annual Report of the Mount Pleasant State Prison. [n. p. 1832.] 8vo. Continued. 45926

A Narrative of the Planting. *See* [Scottow (Joshua)].

Observations on the Finances of Massachusetts. *Boston.* 1786. 8vo. W. 45927

Official Report of the Debates and Proceedings in The State Convention, assembled May 4th, 1853, to Revise and Amend the Constitution of ... Massachusetts. *Boston: White & Potter, Printers.* 1853. 3 vols., 8vo, pp. (4), 3–994, (1); (2), 840; (2), 797. 45928

See "N. A. Rev.," LXXXV. 255.

An Order of Council for issuing a Quo Warranto against the Charter of the Colony of the Massachusets Bay in New-England, with his Majesty's Declaration that in case the said Corporation of the Massachusets Bay, shall before Prosecution had upon the said Quo Warranto make a full Submission and entire Resignation to his Royal Pleasure, He will then regulate their Charter in such manner as shall be for his Service, and the good of that Colony: Given at Whitehall the 26th day of July, 1683. *London, Printed by the Assignes of John Bill deceas'd, &c.* 1683. Folio, 1 sheet. 45929

Order of ... the Legislature. *See* Vol. x., No. 41270.

Papers relating to the Public Events in Massachusetts preceding the American Revolution. *Philadelphia: Seventy-Six Society.* 1856. 8vo, pp. (4), 199. B. 45930

The Patriotick Proceedings of the Legislature of Massachusetts, ... from Jan. 26, to March 4, 1809. ... *Boston: Printed by Joshua Cushing.* 1809. 8vo, pp. 130, (1). BA. 45931

The Perpetual Laws of the Commonwealth of Massachusetts, from the establishment of its Constitution to the first Session of the General Court, A. D. 1788. Compiled, Arranged and Printed To the Wishes of many respectable Law Characters, and the Approbation of the Honourable Judges of the Supreme Judicial Court. *Printed at Worcester, by Isaiah Thomas.* MDCCLXXXVIII. 12mo, pp. (4), 389. B. + *Boston.* 1789. Folio, pp. 48, 493, vi. + [*Ibid.*] 1800. 8vo. + *Boston: I. Thomas & E. T. Andrews.* 1801. 3 vols., 8vo. + *Boston.* 1801–1817. 5 vols. 8vo.

Petition and Representation of the House of Representatives of Massachusetts Bay to the King and His Majesty's Ministers, 20th, Jan. 1768 ... With Letters to Lords Shelburne, Rockingham, Camden, Chatham, and to D. De Berdt, Agent for the Province. Also a Letter from Lord Shelburne to Gov. Bernard, Sept. 17, 1767. *Boston.* 1768. Folio. 45933

This protest against British taxation is one of the most important of revolutionary papers.

A Plan of Exercise for the Militia of Massachusetts Bay; Extracted from the Plan of Discipline of the Norfolk Militia. *Boston: R. Draper.* 1768. 8vo. 45934

For two other editions *see* No. 45547.

... Preliminary Report of the Commissioners on Criminal Law. [n. p. 1839.] 8vo, pp. 59. BA. 45935

The Present Political State. *See* [Leonard (D.)], x. 40098.

First Annual Report of the Board of Managers of the Prison Discipline Society, Boston, ... 1826. *Boston.* 1826. 8vo, pp. 88. Continued. H. 45936

Circular of the Prisoner's-Friend Association. *Boston.* [n. d.] 12mo, pp. 11. 45937

Private and Special Statutes of the Commonwealth of Massachusetts, from ... 1780 to ... 1805. With an Appendix ... . *Boston: Printed ... by Manning & Loring.* 1805. 3 vols., 8vo, pp. xiv (2), 540, Index, (20); 537, Index, (20); 622, Appendix, 42, Index, (20). Continued. B. 45938

Proceedings of a Convention ... on ... the Proposed Annexation of Texas. *Boston.* 1845. 8vo, pp. 18. 45939

Proceedings of His Majesty's Council of the Province of Massachusetts-Bay, relative to The Deposition of Andrew Oliver, Esq; Secretary of the said Province, Concerning what passed in Council in Consequence of the unhappy Affair of the 5th of March 1770. *Boston, New England: Printed by Edes and Gill.* MDCCLXX. Folio, pp. (2), 33. BA. 45940

This deposition of Secretary Oliver was inserted in a pamphlet entitled "A Fair Account of the late unhappy Disturbances at Boston," which was made up from depositions of a large number of persons, with a view to prove that the firing of the soldiers upon their assailants, if not wholly unavoidable, was at least excusable. Mr. Oliver's deposition relative to what passed in Council, gave great offense in Boston, and the proceedings contained in this volume were instituted in consequence.

Proceedings of the Anti-Masonic State Convention, in Faneuil Hall, Boston, Dec. 30 and 31, 1829, and Jan. 1, 1830. *Boston.* 1830. 8vo, pp. 32. Continued. S. 45941

Proceedings of the Convention of the People of Massachusetts, holden at Faneuil Hall, Boston, Oct. 7, 1862. *Boston: Printed by C. J. Peters.* 1862. 8vo, pp. 31. B. 45942

Proceedings of the Convention of Congregational Ministers in ... Massachusetts; together with a Statement of the Names of the Associations, ... &c. MDCCXCV. *Boston: Printed by Samuel Hall.* [1795.] 4to, pp. 18. H. 45943

Proceedings of the Convention of the Congregational Churches of Massachusetts, in regard to Sabbath Schools, ... 1860. *Boston: Wright & Potter, Printers.* 1860. 8vo, pp. 61. H. 45944

Proceedings of the Council. *See* [Hutchinson (T.)], IX. 34084

The Proceedings of the General Assembly, and of the Council of ... Massachusetts-Bay, relating to the Penobscot Expedition: and the Orders of the Continental Navy-Board to the Commander of the Naval Forces. ... With the Report of a Committee Appointed to enquire into the Cause of the Failure of the .. Expedition. ... *Boston: Printed by J. Gill.* 1780. 4to, pp. 29.

Proceedings of the Legislature of the Commonwealth of Massachusetts, in Session at Boston, in the year 1810. [n. p. n. d.] 8vo. Continued. 45946

Proceedings of the Massachusetts National Democratic Convention, and of the Mass Meeting for the Ratification of the Nominations of Breckinridge & Lane, held at ... Boston, Sept. 12, 1860. ... *Office of the Boston Post.* 1860. 8vo, pp. 72.

Proceedings of the Senate and House of Representatives, upon the Petition of George M. Withington and Others, ... that James G. Carter be removed from his Office of Justice of the Peace, ... *Boston: George C. Rand & Co., Printers.* 1849. 8vo, pp. 74.

Proceedings of the State Board of Agriculture, ... 1852. *Boston: White & Potter, Printers.* 1853. 8vo, pp. (2), 123, (1).

Proceedings of the State Disunion Convention, ... at Worcester, Massachusetts, January 15, 1857. Phonographically reported by J. M. W. Yerrington. *Boston.* 1857. 8vo, pp. 60, 19. H.

Proceedings of the State Military Convention, held at Worcester, Jan. 28, 1835. ... *Worcester: Printed by S. H. Colton & Co.* 1835. 8vo, pp. 20. W. 45951

Proceedings of the Whig State Convention held at Springfield, Mass., Sept. 10, 1851. [n. p. n. d.] 8vo, pp. 24. M. 45952

Also: Proceedings of the Whig State Convention held at Worcester, Oct. 2, 1855. *Boston.* 1855. 8vo, pp. 16.

Proclamation by the Council for a Fast on the Death of Lieut.-Gov. William Stoughton, 1701. [*Boston.* 1701.] Folio, 1 leaf.

Also: A Proclamation for a General Fast ... given at the Council Chamber in Boston, the twenty-third day of August, 1701. [n. p. n. d.] 8vo, 1 leaf. — Proclamation of Gov. Andros, January 10, 1688–9. *Boston.* 1868. 8vo. — Proclamation by the Council of His Majesties Province of the Massachusetts Bay in New England. *Boston: Printed by B. Green, and J. Allen.* 1702. Folio, pp. 4. — Proclamation for a General Fast. Given at the Council Chamber, April 5th, 1766. *Boston.* 1766. Folio, 1 leaf. — Proclamation by the Great and General Court, Jan. 23, 1776. [n. p. n. d.] Folio, 1 leaf. — Proclamation for a Day of Public Humiliation and Prayer, 15th October, 1779. [n. p. n. d.] Folio, 1 leaf. — Proclamation by John Hancock, Governor, for a Day of Thanksgiving, 22d November, 1781. [*Boston.* 1781.] Folio, 1 leaf. —

Proclamation by James Bowdoin, Governor, for a General Thanksgiving, 3d November, 1786. [*Boston.* 1786.] Folio, 1 leaf.

Protest of the Minority of the House of Representatives against the Bill dividing the State into Districts for Councillors and Senators, Feb. 20, 1812. *Boston.* [1812.] 8vo. W. 45954

Protest of the Minority of the Senate of Massachusetts against the Resolutions appointing Delegates to the Hartford Convention. *Boston.* 1814. 8vo. W. 45955

Constitution of the Protestant Episcopal Church in the Commonwealth of Massachusetts. Adopted 1709. Revised 1817. [n. p. n. d.] 4to, pp. 11, (1). H. 45956

... Constitution of the Protestant Episcopal Church in the Diocese of Massachusetts. [n. p. 1844.] 8vo, pp. 16. H.

Also: Journal of the Proceedings of the Annual Convention ... Boston, June, 1829. *Cambridge.* 1829. 8vo, pp. 15. Continued.

The Public and General Laws of the Commonwealth of Massachusetts, from ... 1807, to ... 1816. ... Vol. IV. *Boston: Printed by Wells and Lilly.* 1816. 8vo, pp. (4), 529, Index, xxii. Continued. B. 45958

Public Documents, containing Proceedings of the Hartford Convention ... ; Report of the Commissioners ... at Washington; Letters from Massachusetts Members in Congress. ... [*Boston.*] 1815. 8vo, pp. 54. B. 45959

Public Documents of the Legislature of Massachusetts; containing the Speech of ... Governor Strong; with the Answer of the Senate and House of Representatives; Reports ... and a Remonstrance ... to Congress on the Present Unhappy War. ... *Boston: Printed by Russell and Cutler.* 1813. 8vo, pp. 86. N.

Question of Order. Interested Members. [Decision of the Speaker of the] Massachusetts House of Representatives, Feb. 19, 1840. [n. p. n. d.] 8vo, pp. 4. B. 45961

The Question, Will the Christian Religion be Recognized as the Basis of the System of Public Instruction in Massachusetts? Discussed in Four Letters to the Rev. Dr. [Heman] Humphrey ... . *Boston: Whipple and Damrell.* 1839. 8vo, pp. 25.

... Annual Reports of the Rail-Road Corporations of Massachusetts. [For 1837.] *Boston: Dutton and Wentworth, Printers.* 1838. 8vo, pp. 53. Continued. H. 45963

Also: Annual Report of the Board of Railroad Commissioners. ... 1870. *Boston: Wright & Potter, State Printers.* 1870. 8vo, pp. 124, (1). Continued. — ... Returns of the Railroad Corporations in Massachusetts, 1859. ... With an Abstract ... prepared by Oliver Warner ... . *Boston: William White, Printer.* 1860. 8vo.

Record of the Massachusetts Volunteers. 1861–65. Published by the Adjutant-General ... . *Boston: Wright & Potter, Printers.* 1868. 2 vols., 4to, pp. (6), 793; (4), 1085, (1). BA. 45964

Records of the Company of the Massachusetts Bay, to the Embarkation of Winthrop and his Associates for New England, as contained in the First Volume of the Archives of ... Massachusetts. *Cambridge: Printed by Bolles and Houghton.* 1850. 8vo, pp. viii–cxxxviii, 107. B. 45965

Records of the Governor and Company of the Massachusetts Bay in New England. [1628–1686.] Printed by Order of the Legislature. Edited by Nathaniel B. Shurtleff, M.D. ... *Boston: From the Press of William White.* 1853–4. 6 vols., 4to, pp. xii, (4), 479; (12), 344; (2), ix, (6), 510; (12), 578; (10), 647; (12), 615. A., H. 45966

Highly important for the history of Massachusetts. A few copies only printed at the public expense, and now scarce. *See* "N. A. Rev.," LXXIX. 53.

Reflections On the Present State of the Province of the Massachuset-Bay in General, And Town of Boston in Particular; Relating to Bills of Credit And the Support of Trade by Them: As the same has been lately represented in several Pamphlets. *Boston: Benjamin Eliot & Daniel Henchman.* 1720. Sm. 8vo, pp. 22. B. 45967

Remarks on the ... State of the Laws in Massachusetts, respecting Violations of the Sabbath. *Boston: Printed by Nathaniel Willis.* 1816. 8vo, pp. 15. BA., S. 45968

Remarks on the Governor's Speech. *See* [Everett (A. H.)]

Remarks on the Judiciary System of Massachusetts, and the necessity of a Change, with a Review of certain recent Decisions. By a Member of the Bar. [*Boston.* 1844?] 8vo, pp. 48. H.

Reply to a Pamphlet, purporting to be an Answer to a Letter addressed to a Republican Member of the House of Representatives, on the subject of a Petition for a New Incorporation ... . *Boston.* 1812. 8vo. 45970

For the "Letter" *see* Vol. x., No. 40255, for the "Answer" *see* No. 45634.

Report. [*Boston.* 1821.] 8vo, pp. 36. BA. 45971

Relative to the Pauper Laws.

Report and Resolves adopted by the Democratic State Central Committee of Massachusetts, 1851. [n. p. 1851.] 8vo, pp. 6.

... Report and Resolves providing for a Board of Agriculture. [n. p. 1838.] 8vo, pp. 12. B. 45973

... Report and Resolves relating to the Massachusetts Claim. *Boston: Dutton and Wentworth, Printers.* 1830. 8vo, pp. 16.

Report and Resolves relative to qualifying Teachers for Common Schools. [*Boston.* 1838.] 8vo, pp. 8. 45975

Report, April 18, 1848, ... from the Committee on Public Lands, to whom was referred the bill to promote the Education of the Deaf and Dumb. *Boston.* 1848. 8vo, pp. 16. 45976

Report, by a Joint Committee of the Legislature of Massachusetts. *Boston.* 1834. 8vo, pp. 76, 54. M. 45977

On Freemasonry.

Report by the State Commission on cheap Railway Transportation between Boston and Lake Ontario ... . *Boston: Wright & Potter, Printers.* 1870. 8vo, pp. 129. H. 45978

Report, House of Representatives, Relating to the ... use of Spirituous Liquors in the State House, March 2, 1853. [n. p. n. d.] 8vo. 45979

Also: Report ... Amendments to Act of 1852, concerning the Manufacture and Sale of Spirituous Liquors. April 14, 1853. [n. p. n. d.] 8vo.

Report in the Legislature on Imprisonment for Debt. *Boston.* 1840. 8vo. 45980

Also: Report ... on Capital Punishments. *Boston.* 1843. 8vo. — Report ... on the State Finances. *Boston.* 1843. 8vo.

Report made to the House of Representatives of ... Massachusetts, by a Committee appointed to consider the Expediency of Abolishing Capital Punishments, January 12, 1836. *Boston.* 1836. 8vo. C. 45981

Report of a Committee ... Respecting certain Military Orders issued by ... Levi Lincoln, ... [to enforce the embargo]; with ... Documents ... . [n. p. 1809.] 8vo, pp. 11, (1). BA. 45982

Report of a Committee of the Massachusetts Legislature, concerning the Loan of Arms by the Adjutant-General [to Rhode Island], Feb. 8, 1843. [*Boston.*] 1843. 8vo, pp. 37. 45983

Report of a Committee of the Peace Convention on the Injustice and Inequality of the Militia Law of Massachusetts. *Boston.* 1838. 12mo, pp. 16. M. 45984

The Report of a Constitution or Form of Government for the Commonwealth of Massachusetts: Agreed upon by the Committee—to be laid before the Convention of Delegates, assembled at Cambridge, on the First Day of September, A. D. 1779; and continued by Adjournment to the Twenty-Eighth Day of October following. *Boston: Printed by Benjamin Edes & Sons.* 1779. 4to, pp. 50. BA., N., W. 45985

Report of a General Plan for the Promotion of Public and Personal Health, ... by the Commissioners appointed ... to a Sanitary Survey of the State. Presented April 25, 1850. *Boston: Dutton & Wentworth, Printers.* 1850. 8vo, pp. 544. Plans and Maps. B. 45986

By Lemuel Shattuck, and others.

... Report of a Joint Special Committee on Capital Punishment. [n. p. 1851.] 8vo, pp. 33. B. 45987

Report of Commissioners appointed under a Resolve of the Legislature of Massachusetts, to superintend the Erection of a Lunatic Hospital at Worcester, ... Made January 4th, 1832. *Boston: Dutton and Wentworth, Printers* ... 1832. 8vo, pp. 32. Continued. BA. 45988

Also: Annual Report of the Trustees ... *Boston.* 1833. 8vo. Continued. *See also* [Hovey (William)], Vol. VIII., No. 33215.

... Report of Commissioners concerning an Agricultural School. January, 1851. [n. p. n. d.] 8vo, pp. 105. B. 45989

Report of Committee on Petitions of Tufts College, Wesleyan Academy and ... Harvard University ... and on the Museum of Natural History. March 7, 1859. [n. p. n. d.] 8vo. S. 45990

... Report of Committee on the Petition of the President and Fellows of Harvard College. [n. p. 1836.] 8vo, pp. 15, (1).

Report of Contested Elections, in the House of Representatives of Massachusetts. [D. Everett.] *Boston: True & Rowe, Printers.* 1812. 8vo, pp. 52, (1). Continued. H. 45992

Report of ... John Davis, Agent for the Prosecution of the Claim of Massachusetts upon the United States, for Militia services during the last war ... May 30, 1831. *Boston: Dutton and Wentworth, Printers.* 1831. 8vo, pp. (2), 76. BA. 45993

Report of One of the Commissioners [J. G. Rogers] appointed to reduce the ... Law of Crimes and Punishments to a Systematic Code. [n. p. 1844.] 8vo, pp. (4), 48. BA. 45994

Report of Special Committee on the State Liquor Agency, ... 1859. *Boston: William White, Printer* ... 1859. 8vo, pp. xxx, 3–395. B. 45995

... Report of the Board of Commissioners, of Internal Improvement, in relation to ... a Railway from Boston to Providence. With a Memoir of the Survey. *Boston: Dutton & Wentworth, Printers.* 1828. 8vo, pp. 72. Map. H. 45996

Report of the Board of Commissioners of Internal Improvements, in relation to ... a Route for a Canal, from Boston to the Blackstone Canal, and thence to the Line of Connecticut, &c. *Boston: Dutton & Wentworth, Printers.* 1828. 8vo, pp. 51. Map. + *Boston: True & Greene, Printers.* 1829. 8vo, pp. 51. Map.

Report of the Board of Directors of Internal Improvements of ... Massachusetts, on the Practicability and Expediency of a Rail-Road from Boston to the Hudson River, and from Boston to Providence. January 16, 1829. To which are annexed the Reports of the Engineers, Maps, Plans and Profiles of the Routes. *Boston: ... W. L. Lewis, Printer.* 1829. 8vo, pp. 76, 11. H. 45998

The modest advantages of these great enterprises, as set forth in this volume, read strangely in these days of private extravagance and public stealings. This was afterwards known as the Western Railroad.

Report of the Boundary Commissioners, transmitting Simeon Borden's Survey of the Line from Burnt Swamp corner, in Wrentham, to a monument in Thompson, Connecticut, January, 1847. [n. p. n. d.] 8vo. 45999

Report of the Bureau of Statistics of Labor, ... from August 2, 1869, to March 1, 1870 ... *Boston: Wright & Potter, Printers.* 1870. 8vo, pp. 423. BA. 46000

Report of the Commissioners of the State of Massachusetts and Rhode Island, appointed to ascertain, ... the true Boundary

Line between said States, from the Atlantic Ocean to the northwest corner of Rhode Island. *Boston.* 1847. 8vo, pp. 4.

Also: Report of the ... true Boundary Line between Massachusetts and Rhode Island, from Pawtucket Falls to Bullock's Neck; and a Minority Report. With an Appendix of twenty-four Documents .... *Boston.* 1848. 8vo, pp. 132. Map.

... Report of the Commissioners on the Boundary Line between ... Massachusetts and Rhode Island, made ... 1867. *Providence.* 1867. 8vo, pp. 23. B. 46002

See also Rhode Island.

Report of the Commissioners ... upon the Practicability and Expediency of reducing to a ... Systematic Code the Common Law of Massachusetts ... . Made ... January, 1837. *Boston: Dutton and Wentworth, Printers.* 1837. 8vo, pp. 48. BA. 46003

Report of the Commissioners appointed ... Feb. 29, 1832, on the ... Pauper System of ... Massachusetts. *Boston: Dutton and Wentworth, Printers.* 1832. 8vo, pp. 97, 3 folded leaves. + [*Ibid.*] 1833. H., S. 46004

... Report of the Commissioners, appointed ... [to prepare a System for the Establishment of a Seminary of Practical Arts and Sciences. n. p. 1826.] 8vo, pp. 55. BA. 46005

Report of the Commissioners appointed to revise the General Statutes of the Commonwealth. Part 1. *Boston: Dutton and Wentworth, Printers.* 1835. 8vo, pp. xx, 343, (1). Continued.

Also: Report of the Commissioners on the Revision of the Statutes, ... 1858. *Boston.* 1858. 8vo.— ... Report of the Commissioners appointed to revise and reform the Proceedings in the Courts of Justice ... . [n. p. 1851.] 8vo, pp. 74.—Report of the Commissioners appointed to Revise the Militia Laws. *Boston.* 1839. 8vo.

... Report of the Commissioners for the Establishment of a State Reform School for Girls ... . *Boston: William White, Printer.* 1855. 8vo, pp. 66. B. 46007

Also: Report of the Commissioners appointed to consider the subject of Reform Schools for Girls. March 5th, 1851. *Boston.* 1851. 8vo. S.

Report of the Commissioners for the Enlargement of the State House for the Library. *Boston.* 1854. 8vo, pp. 23. Plans. S.

... Report of the ... Commissioners, for the Survey of ... a Railway from Boston to Albany. *Boston: Dutton & Wentworth, Printers.* 1828. 8vo, pp. 56. H. 46009

... Report of the Commissioners in relation to the Flats in Boston Harbor. January, 1850. [n. p. n. d.] 8vo, pp. 72. 2 Plans. BA. 46010

Report of the Commissioners of Alien Passengers and Foreign Paupers, Jan. 1852 ... . [n. p. n. d.] 8vo, pp. 20. Continued.

... Report of the Commissioners of Fisheries. [*Boston.* 1867.] 8vo, pp. 7. Plate. Continued. B. 46012

Report of the Commissioners of ... Massachusetts, on the Routes of Canals from Boston Harbour, to Connecticut and Hudson Rivers. *Boston: True and Greene, Printers.* 1826. 8vo, pp. 185, (1), Appendix, 62. Map. BA., H. 46013

Report of the Commissioners on "Matrons and Labor in Common Jails," ... May 11, 1853. *Boston.* 1853. 8vo.

... Report of the Commissioners on Mystic River, Boston Harbor and Dorchester Bay. 1854. *Boston: William White, Printer.* 1855. 8vo, pp. 80. B. 46015

Report of the Commissioners upon the Troy and Greenfield Railroad and Hoosac Tunnel, to ... the Governor, and ... Council of ... Massachusetts. *Boston: Wright & Potter, ... Printers.* 1863. 8vo, pp. viii, 229. Plates. BA. 46016

... Report of the Commissioners relating to the Condition of the Indians in Massachusetts. [*Boston.* 1849.] 8vo, pp. 88. H.

Report of the Commissioners to Determine the Title of Certain Lands claimed by Indians at Deep Bottom, in the Town of Tisburg, ... [at] Martha's Vineyard. ... *Boston: William White, Printer.* 1856. 8vo, pp. 52. B. 46018

Report of the Committee appointed ... to take into Consideration the Judiciary System. [n. p.] 1808. 8vo, pp. 18. S.

Report of the Committee appointed to Examine and report whether monies drawn from the Treasury, have been faithfully applied, &c. April 29, 1802. *Salem, Mass.* [1802.] 8vo. W.

... Report of the Committee appointed ... 1864, to improve the Ventilation of the Representatives' Hall. [n. p. n. d.] 8vo, pp. 106. B. 46021

Report of the Committee appointed to make a Valuation of the Polls and Property of the Commonwealth. *Boston: Dutton and Wentworth, Printers.* 1841. 8vo, pp. 30. Continued. BA.

Also: Report of the Valuation Committee as corrected in the Legislature. [*Boston.*] 1841. Folio.

... Report of the Committee ... in relation to the Commonwealth Flats near South Boston. *Boston: Wright & Potter, ... Printers.* 1868. 8vo, pp. 105. Plan. B. 46023

Report of the Committee ... of Interdicting Slavery in the New States ... beyond the River Mississippi. Feb. 1, 1820. [n. p. n. d.] 8vo, pp. 7. S. 46024

Report of the Committee ... on the present Alarming State of our Foreign Relations. [n. p. 1811.] 8vo, pp. 14. S.

Respecting the alleged offense of the British minister Francis James Jackson, etc.

Report of the Committee ... to meet the Exigency resulting from the Secession of Maine ... Jan. 18, 1820. [n. p. n. d.] 8vo, pp. 8. S. 46026

Report of the Committee of Conference in the House of Representatives of Massachusetts, on the Choice of Electors of President and Vice-President. *Boston.* 1812. 8vo. 46027

Also: Report of the Committee of Elections on the Boston Elections. Feb. 26, 1811. [n. p. n. d.] 8vo, pp. 5. S.

Report of the Committee of Valuation. [*Boston.* 1793.] 8vo, pp. 15. Continued. B. 46028

Report of the Committee of the House of Representatives of Massachusetts, on ... Impressed Seamen: with the Evidence and Documents ... . *Boston: Russell and Cutler, Printers.* 1813. 8vo, pp. 84. BA., M. 46029

Also: Report ... on the Deficiency in the Treasurer's Accounts. [*Boston.*] 1812. 8vo. W.

Report of the Committee of the Legislature on the subject of the War with England, and for Selecting Delegates to meet in Convention. [n. p.] 1814. 8vo. W. 46030

Report of the Committee of the Senate of Massachusetts; comprising the President's Message of the 1st of June;—the Report of the Committee of Foreign Relations;—the Act declaring War;—the Proclamation of the President announcing that event;—and the Address of the Senate to the People of this Commonwealth. June 26th, 1812. ... *Boston: Adams, Rhoades & Co., Printers.* 1812. 8vo, pp. 28. H. 46031

... Report of the Committee on Agriculture, on ... allowing a Bounty for the Production of Wheat. [n. p. 1838.] 8vo, pp. 12.

... [Report of] The ... Committee ... on as much of the Governor's Address as relates to "the Emigration of Young Women to the West" ... . [n. p. 1865.] 8vo, pp. 52. B.

... Report of the Committee on Cape Cod Harbor, ... 1857. *Boston: William White, Printer.* 1857. 8vo, pp. 26. Plan. BA.

... Report of the Committee on Claims, on the Alterations and Repairs upon the State House: ... with a Phonographic Report of the Testimony ... . 1869. *Boston: Wright & Potter, Printers.* 1869. 8vo, pp. 34, Appendix, 598. B. 46035

... Report of the Committee on Education, relative to the Education of Children employed in Manufacturing Establishments. [n. p. 1836.] 8vo, pp. 16. H. 46036

Also: Report ... on so much of the Governor's Message as relates to the School Fund. *Boston.* 1835. 8vo.

Report of the Committee on Mr. Browninshield's two Resolutions [on the Embargo. n. p. 1808.] 8vo, pp. 9. S. 46037

Report of the Committee on Railways and Canals, ... relative to the Public Use of Railroads. ... 1837. *Boston: Dutton and Wentworth, Printers.* 1838. 8vo, pp. 20. BA. 46038

Report of the Committee on the Judicial Reform, made to the Legislature ... June 21, 1798. [*Boston.* 1798.] 8vo, pp. 36.

Also: Report ... on the subject of Jurors. [n. p. 1808.] 8vo, pp. 20. S.

Report of the Committee on the subject of the Embargo. [n. p. 1809.] 8vo, pp. 16. BA., S. 46040

Report of the Committee to prevent the Admission of Texas as a Slave State. [*Boston.* 1845.] 8vo. 46041

Report of the Committee ... relating to the Southern Boundary of Massachusetts. *Boston: Dutton and Wentworth, Printers.* 1832. 8vo, pp. 15, (1). BA. 46042

... Report of the Committee to whom was referred the Memorial of the Boston Sanitary Association ... . [n. p. 1861.] 8vo, pp. 80. B. 46043

... Report of the Joint Committee of the Legislature ... on the State Prison. ... *Boston: Dutton & Wentworth, ... Printers.* 1828. 8vo, pp. 35. H. 46044

... Report of the Joint Committee ... appointed April 20, 1848, on the Subject of Insanity in the State ... . *Boston: Dutton and Wentworth, Printers.* 1849. 8vo, pp. 28. B. 46045

Also: ... Report ... relative to ... Banks ... and ... the Law against Usury. [n. p. 1834.] 8vo, pp. 31. BA.

... Report of the Joint Committee, relative to calling a Convention to amend the Constitution. [n. p. 1834.] 8vo, pp. 15.

... Report of the Joint Committee of 1860 upon the proposed Canal to unite Barnstable and Buzzard's Bays ... . *Boston: Wright & Potter, ... Printers.* 1864. 8vo, pp. 165. 2 Maps, 6 Plates, and 6 Plans. BA. 46047

... Report of the Joint Special Committee of the Legislature of 1867, on the Education of Deaf-Mutes: ... [*Boston:*] *Wright & Potter, Printers.* 1867. 8vo, pp. iv, 236. BA. 46048

Also: Report of the Joint Special Committee on State Lunatic Paupers, February, 1848. [n. p. 1848.] 8vo, pp. 37.—Report ... on the State Pauper Laws, February, 1848. [n. p. 1848.] 8vo, pp. 25. M.

Report of the Joint Special Committee on ... modifying the Laws relating to the Registration of Births, Marriages, and Deaths. *Boston.* 1849. 8vo. 46049

Report of the Joint Special Committee, ... [on the Eastern Boundary,] made in April, 1848. [*Boston.* 1848.] 8vo, pp. 140.

Report of the Joint Special Committee, ... on the Boundary Question (upon the Petitions from Pawtucket, Seekonk, Rehobeth and Fall River), with accompanying Resolves. April, 1852. [*Boston.* 1852.] 8vo, pp. 15. 46051

Report of the Legislature on the Observance of the Sabbath. [n. p. 1814.] 8vo, pp. 8. BA. 46052

Report of the Massachusetts Commissioners ... upon the Boundary Line between Rhode Island and Massachusetts, from Pawtucket Falls to Bullock's Neck, Jan. 23, 1846, together with the Report of Simeon Borden. [*Boston.* 1846.] 8vo, pp. 21.

Report of the Penal Code of Massachusetts ... . *Boston: Dutton and Wentworth, Printers.* 1844. 8vo. 46054

By Willard Phillips and Samuel Baker Walcott.

Report of the Select Committee ... on ... legalizing the Study of Anatomy: ... *Boston: Dutton and Wentworth, Printers.* 1831.

8vo, pp. 118. C. + *New Haven: Whitmore and Minor.* 1833. 8vo, pp. 46. BA. 46055

Report of the Select Committee ... upon the Late Resolutions of the General Assembly of ... Georgia. *Boston: Dutton and Wentworth.* 1831. 8vo, pp. 24. BA. 46056

See also [Mason (Jonathan)], No. 45469.

... Report of the Special Commission on the Hours of Labor, and the Condition ... of the Industrial Classes. ... *Boston: Wright & Potter, Printers.* 1866. 8vo, pp. 70. B. 46057

... Report of the Special Joint Committee on the Message of the Governor ... transmitting Resolutions of South Carolina proposing a Convention ... to revise the Constitution ... . *Boston: Dutton and Wentworth, Printers.* 1833. 8vo, pp. 19, Resolves, 11–13. BA. 46058

Report of the Treasurer. To the Honorable House of Representatives of Massachusetts. *Boston.* 1816. 8vo. Continued.

... Report on Capital Punishment. [n. p. 1846.] 8vo, pp. 28.

Report on Gaols and Houses of Correction in ... Massachusetts ... . [By John W. Lincoln and Louis Dwight.] *Boston: Dutton and Wentworth, Printers.* 1834. 8vo, pp. 120. H.

... Report on Insanity and Idiocy in Massachusetts ... . *Boston: William White, Printer.* 1855. 8vo, pp. x, 7–213, 15. H.

... Report on the Annexation of Texas to the United States. [n. p. 1838.] 8vo, pp. 39. B. 46063

Report on the Burial of Massachusetts Dead at Gettysburg; with the Oration of Edward Everett. *Boston.* 1863. 8vo, pp. 93. + [Another Edition.] 8vo, pp. 30. 46064

Report on the Classification of the Schools. *Boston.* 1852. 8vo, pp. 10. 46065

... Report on the Hoosac Tunnel and Troy and Greenfield Railroad, by the ... Committee of 1866. *Boston: Wright & Potter, Printers.* 1867. 8vo, pp. 97. B. 46066

Report on the Insects. *See* [Harris (T. W.)], VIII. 30523.

Report on the Invertebrata. *See* [Gould (A. A.)], 28086–7.

Report on the Memorials of the Seneca Indians and others, accepted November 21, 1840, in the Council of Massachusetts. *Boston: Dutton & Wentworth, Printers.* 1840. 8vo, pp. 28. B.

Report on the Merits of the Claim of ... Massachusetts, on the National Government, for Expenses of the Militia, during the late War, ... January, 1821. *Boston: Printed by Russell and Gardner.* 1822. 8vo, pp. 30. BA. 46068

Also: Documents upon the "Merits," etc., accompanying the President's Message to Congress, Feb. 23, 1824. *Washington.* [1824.] 8vo, pp. 177. W.

Report on the Ornithology. *See* Peabody (W. B. O.)

Report on the Quadrupeds of Massachusetts. Published agreeably to an Order of the Legislature, By [E. Emmons, one of] the Commissioners on the Zoological and Botanical Survey of the State. *Cambridge: Folsom, Wells, and Thurston.* 1840. 8vo, pp. (2), 86. BA., H. 46069

Report on the Stockbridge Indians, by Charles Adams, Attorney General of Massachusetts, to the Legislature. *Boston: Wright & Potter, ... Printers.* 1870. 8vo, pp. 23. 46070

A statement of the various sales of land made by the Stockbridge tribe of Indians.

... Report on the Suspension of Specie Payments. [n. p. 1838.] 8vo, pp. 24. BA. 46071

A Report on the Trees. *See* [Emerson (G. B.)], VI. 22429.

... Report relating to Capital Punishment. [n. p. 1836.] 8vo, pp. 112. BA. 46072

... Report relating to Incompetency of Witnesses on account of Religious Belief. [n. p. 1838.] 8vo, pp. 58. BA. 46073

... Report relating to State Paupers. [n. p. 1836.] 8vo, pp. 28. H. 46074

Report relative to establishing the State Bank of Massachusetts with a Capital of Ten Millions. [*Boston.* n. d.] 8vo, pp. 10. M. 46075

First Annual Report of the Secretary ... under the Act of March, 1842, relating to the Registry and Returns of Births, Marriages and Deaths in Massachusetts. February, 1843. *Boston: Dutton and Wentworth, Printers.* 1843. 8vo, pp. (8), 119. Continued. BA. 46076

Report to the Massachusetts Legislature, by the Committee on Education, in favor of an Appropriation to the Female Medical Education Society ... . *Boston.* 1851. 8vo, pp. 15, (1). B.

Also: Mr. Child's Report ... relative to Gayhead ... Indians. *Boston.* 1827. 8vo.

Reports and Bills relating to Spirituous Liquors, March 6, 1839. [n. p. n. d.] 8vo, pp. 46. S. 46078

Reports concerning Property in Trust, in ... Massachusetts, as held by Certain Corporations, and by Trustees under Acts of Incorporation. ... *Boston: Wright & Potter, Printers ...* 1866. 8vo, pp. 239. B. 46079

Reports in the Legislature on the Reduction of Salaries, and the Abolishing of Commissions. *Boston.* 1840. 8vo. 46080

Reports of Controverted Elections in the House of Representatives of ... Massachusetts, from 1780 to 1852: the Cases from 1780 to 1834, inclusive, compiled ... by Luther S. Cushing: and the Cases from 1835 to 1852, inclusive, ... by Luther S. Cushing, Charles W. Storey, and Lewis Josselyn. *Boston: White & Potter, Printers.* 1853. 8vo, pp. xx, 757. B. 46081

See also Cushing (L. S.), Vol. v., No. 18119.

Reports of the Commissioners on the Zoological Survey of the State ... . *Boston: Dutton and Wentworth, ... Printers.* 1838. 8vo, pp. 107. BA., H. 46082

By Dr. Ebenezer Emmons, Dr. T. W. Harris, and A. B. Gould.

Reports on Contested Elections by the House of Representatives of ... Massachusetts. Printed under the Direction of Theron Metcalf. *Dedham.* 1814. 8vo, pp. 71. W. 46083

... Reports on the Abolition of Capital Punishment. ... *Boston: Dutton and Wentworth, Printers.* 1837. 8vo, pp. 136. BA.

By Robert Rantoul, Jr. and others.

Reports on the Fishes, Reptiles [by D. H. Storer] and Birds [by W. B. O. Peabody] of Massachusetts. ... *Boston: Dutton & Wentworth, Printers.* 1839. 8vo, pp. xii, (4), 426. 4 Plates.

Reports on the Herbaceous Plants and on the Quadrupeds of Massachusetts. ... By the Commissioners on the Zoological and Botanical Survey ... . *Cambridge: Folsom, Wells, and Thurston.* 1840. 8vo, pp. viii, 277, (2), 86. B. 46086

... Reports on the subject of a License Law, by a Joint ... Committee of the Legislature of Massachusetts; with ... the

Testimony ... 1867. *Boston: Wright & Potter, Printers.* 1867. 8vo, pp. 69, Appendix, 898. BA., C. 46087

Republican Address to the Electors of Massachusetts. [*Boston.* 1812.] 8vo, pp. 8. BA. 46088

Republican Documents. Massachusetts Republican Resolutions, 1855. [n. p. n. d.] 8vo, pp. 16. B. 46089

Republican Ticket. ... E. Gerry for Governor, W. King for Lieut.-Governor. [*Boston.* 1812.] 8vo, pp. 8. 46090

Resolutions Adopted by the Anti-Masonic Members of the Legislature of Massachusetts, and other Citizens of Boston and the vicinity, opposed to the nomination of Martin Van Buren and Richard M. Johnson for President and Vice President ... at a Meeting held in the Chamber of the House of Representatives, March 9, 1836. With an Address to their Anti-Masonic Fellow-Citizens throughout the State. *Boston: D. Hooton, Printer.* 1836. 8vo, pp. 24. + *New Bedford: J. C. Parmenter, Printer.* 1836. 8vo, pp. 25. 46091

The New Bedford edition contains Mr. Van Buren's letter to the Pennsylvania Committee.

Resolve concerning the Boundary Line between the States of Massachusetts and Rhode Island, 1843. With the Petition of Church Gray and [79] others. [*Boston.*] 1844. 8vo, pp. 8. + [Another] Resolve ... . [*Boston.*] 1847. 8vo. 46092

Resolve for Districting the Commonwealth for the Purpose of choosing Electors of President, 1792. *Boston.* 1792. 4to, pp. 4.

Also: Resolve for Districting the Commonwealth for the Purpose of choosing Federal Representatives, 1792. [*Boston.* 1792.] 4to, pp. 7.

Resolve of his Majesty's Council relating to the Disorders on the Days of Ordination of Ministers; with Proceedings of the Convention of Ministers thereupon. *Boston.* 1759. 4to, pp. 4.

Resolves and Orders of the Congress and General Court, ... collected for the use of the several Towns in the said State. *Boston.* 1776. 8vo. 46095

Resolves and Orders of the Congress, Council and General Court of Massachusetts, for the Use of Committees of Correspondence. *Boston.* [1777.] 8vo, pp. 16. M. 46096

Resolves concerning the Boundary Line between Massachusetts and Rhode Island. [*Boston.*] 1846. 8vo. 46097

Resolves of Congress concerning Trade; with the Act for establishing a Naval Office in the State of Massachusetts Bay. *Boston.* 1777. 8vo, pp. 27. Continued. M. 46098

Resolves of the General Assembly of the Colony of Massachusetts-Bay, Begun and held at Watertown, ... 29th ... of May, ... 1776. *Boston, New-England: Printed by B. Edes.* M,DCC,-LXXVI. Folio, pp. 59, 21, 25, 40, 37, 51, Appendix, 15. Continued. BA., C. 46099

Resolves of the General Court of ... Massachusetts, ... 1781. *Boston: Printed by Nathaniel Willis.* M,DCC LXXXI. Folio, pp. 245. B. 46100

Continued; after 1806 in octavo.

Resolves of the General Court of ... Massachusetts, respecting the sale of Eastern Lands: with the Reports of the Committees appointed to sell said Lands; ... *Boston: Printed by Young and Minns.* 1803. 8vo, pp. 287. B. + *Boston.* 1810. 8vo, pp. 410, (4). + [*Ibid.*] 1811. 8vo. 46101

Resolves of the Massachusetts House of Representatives relating to the Letter of Thomas Hutchinson and others, June 15, 1773. [n. p. 1773.] 12mo, pp. 8. W. 46102

The Result of the Convention. *See* [Parsons (Theophilus)].

The Results of Three Synods Held by the Elders and Messengers of the Churches of Massachusetts Province, New England. Containing I. The Platform of Church Discipline, in the Year 1648. II. Propositions concerning the Subject of Baptism, in 1662. III. The Necessity of Reformation, ... in Answer to two Questions, in 1679. ... *Boston: Re-printed for B. Eliot and D. Henchman ...* . 1725. Sm. 8vo, pp. (2), vi, 118. B. 46103

Return from the Quarter Master General's Department. 1833. [n. p. n. d.] 8vo, pp. 11. BA. 46104

Returns relating to the Poor ... Nov. 1, 1852. [n. p. n. d.] 8vo, pp. 20. 46105

Review of the Proceedings in the Massachusetts Legislature for 1843; with an Appeal to the People against the violent course of the Majority. By The Whig Minority. *Boston: John H. Eastburn, Printer.* 1843. 8vo, pp. 48. BA. 46106

The Revised Statutes of ... Massachusetts, passed November 4, 1835. ... Printed and published ... under the Supervision and

Direction of Theron Metcalf and Horace Mann. *Boston.* 1836. 8vo. 46107

Revised Abstract, exhibiting the Condition of the Banks, 1853. ... *Boston.* 1854. 8vo. 46108

The Rich Men of Massachusetts; containing a Statement of the reputed wealth of about two thousand persons, with brief Sketches of nearly fifteen hundred Characters. Second Edition Enlarged. *Boston: Redding & Co.* 1852. 8vo, pp. 224. 46109

Rights of the Congregational Churches. *See* [Beecher (L.)], II., 4338, Groton *Mass.*, VII. 28976, *and* [Lowell (J.)], 42460.

Rules and Forms in Bankruptcy in ... Massachusetts. ... Second Edition. *Boston: Charles C. Little and James Brown.* 1842. 8vo, pp. 58. BA. 46110

Rules and Orders of the Constitutional Convention of Massachusetts, met May 4, 1853. *Boston.* 1853. 12mo. S. 46111

... Rules and Orders of the General Court of ... Massachusetts [1856], ... with the Constitution of the Commonwealth, and that of the United States, etc. *Boston: William White, Printer.* 1856. 16mo, pp. (2), 180. BA. 46112

Rules and Orders of the House of Representatives, 1804. *Boston.* [1804.] 8vo, pp. 24. Continued. 46113

Rules and Orders to be observed in the Convention of Delegates, for ... Massachusetts ... 1820. ... *Boston: B. Russell.* 1820. 12mo, pp. 36. H. + *Boston.* 1853. 16mo. 46114

Rules and Orders to be observed in the House of Representatives of ... Massachusetts, For ... 1831. ... *Boston.* 1831. 12mo.

Rules and Orders to be observed in the Senate of ... Massachusetts, for ... 1809. *Boston.* 1809. 12mo, pp. 36. Cont'd.

Rules and Regulations for the Massachusetts Army. ... *Salem: Printed by Samuel and Ebenezer Hall.* 1775. 8vo, pp. 15. + *Cambridge.* [*Ibid.*] B. + *Watertown.* 1775. 8vo, pp. 16.

Rules of the General Association in Massachusetts. [n. p.] 1825. 8vo. W. 46118

Proceedings of the Fourth Annual Convention of the Sabbath School Teachers of Massachusetts, held in ... 1858. *Boston: State Central Committee.* 1859. 16mo, pp. 79. Continued. B.

Several | Acts | and | Laws | Passed by the Great and General Court ... | of the Massachusetts-Bay, in | New England. | ... Held ... the Eighth ... of June. 1692. | ... *Boston:* | *Printed by Benjamin Harris.* | 1692. Folio, pp. (2), 16. BA. 46120

Several Laws and Orders made at the General Courts in May 3. August 1 & October 11, 1665. *Printed and Published by order of the General Court held at Boston the 11th of October*, 1665. Folio, pp. 3. W. 46121

These "Several Laws" were printed annually; a complete series is not known to exist. They are supposed to have been printed at Cambridge, by Samuel Green, his name as the printer first appears on the issue for 1672.

A Short View of the History. *See* [Mauduit (Israel)].

Rules of the Society for Encouraging Industry and Employing the Poor. [*Boston.* 1754.] 4to. W. 46122

Something in answer to a Law lately made at the First Sessions of the General Court held at Boston in New England, May 28, 1679. [n. p. n. d.] 8vo. 46123

Some Observations Relating to the Present Circumstances of the Province of the Massachusetts-Bay: Humbly offered to the Consideration of the General Assembly. ... *Boston: Printed and Sold by D. Fowle.* 1750. 8vo, pp. 20. M., P., S., W. 46124

A sound practical work. It relates to the great expenses incurred by Massachusetts for the military expeditions to Canada and Cape Breton, and to her issues of paper money, with suggestions as to the duties and taxes for revenue. It is also proposed to offer bounties for the raising of wheat, barley, hemp, flax, etc.

Special Message of Gov. Andrew, Jan. 3, 1866. [*Boston.* 1866.] 8vo. 46125

For other messages relative to the rebellion *see* Andrew (J. A.), Vol. I.

... Special Report on Prisons and Prison Discipline, made under authority of the Board of State Charities. By the Secretary ... [F. B. Sanborn]. *Boston: Wright & Potter, ... Printers.* 1865. 8vo, pp. 141. B., BA. 46126

Speech intended to have been delivered. *See* [Shipley (J.)]

Speech of Governor Dudley to the Council and House of Representatives, Convened at Boston June 16th, 1702. *Boston.* 1703. 4to, pp. 3. 46127

See also New England.

Speech of ... [Elbridge Gerry] the Governor ... to ... the Legislature ... January, 1812. ... *Boston: State Press.* 1811–[12]. 8vo, pp. 20. B., BA. 46128

Also: His Excellency Governor Gerry's Speech to the Legislature of Massachusetts, ... June 7, 1810. [*Boston,* 1810.] 8vo.

The Speech of his Excellency Governor Strong, ... Oct. 16, 1812; with the Documents which accompanied the same. To which is added, the Answer of the House of Representatives. *Boston.* 1812 8vo. 46129

These speeches relate specially to the War of 1812.

Speeches in the Legislature of Massachusetts on Incorporating the Town of Belmont. *Boston.* 1857. 8vo. 46130

Speeches of the Governors of Massachusetts, from 1765 to 1775; and the Answer of the House of Representatives, to the same; with their Resolutions and Addresses for that period. And other Public Papers, relating to the Dispute between this Country and Great Britain, which led to the Independence of the United States. *Boston: Russell and Gardner.* 1818. 8vo, pp. 424. B.

Very scarce. Known as the "Massachusetts State Papers." Collected and edited by Alden Bradford.

Speeches, &c. ... [of] the Governor ... [and] Council ... . [n. p. 1773?] 8vo, pp. 126. BA. 46132

State of the Treasury of Massachusetts, Jan. 1, 1810. [n. p. n. d.] Folio, 1 leaf. Continued. M. 46133

... First Report of the Inspectors of the State Alms House at Bridgewater. ... 1854. *Boston: William White, Printer.* 1855. 8vo, pp. 34. Continued. H. 46134

Also: ... [First] Report of the Inspectors of the State Almshouse, at Monson, for ... 1854. *Boston: William White, Printer.* 1855. 8vo, pp. 14. Continued. B.— ... Sixth Annual Report of the Inspectors of the State Almshouse, at Tewksbury. October, 1859. *Boston: William White, Printer.* 1859. 8vo, pp. 26. Continued. H.— By-Laws for the Government of the State Alms-Houses ... . *Lowell: S. J. Varney, Printer.* 1854. 16mo, pp. 16. H.

... First Annual Report of the Trustees of the State Industrial School for Girls, at Lancaster ... . *Boston: William White, Printer.* 1857. 8vo, pp. 92. Plate. Continued. H. 46135

Also: By-Laws ... Prepared ... October, 1855. ... Amended Nov. 14, 1859. *Boston: Printed by John Wilson & Son.* 1860. 16mo, pp. 32. H.

Catalogue of Books in the State Library [of Massachusetts], October, 1825. [n. p. n. d.] 8vo, pp. 8. 46136

Catalogue of the State Library of Massachusetts. *Boston: William White, Printer.* 1858. 8vo, pp. xxiv, 338. B., H., M.

Also: ... Annual Report of the Librarian of the State Library. ... [n. p. 1850.] 8vo, pp. 12. Continued. H.

Reports and other Documents relating to the State Lunatic Hospital at Worcester, Mass. ... *Boston: Dutton and Wentworth, Printers.* 1837. 8vo, pp. (2), 200. H. 46138

Also: By-Laws, established by the Trustees of the State Lunatic Hospital, in Worcester, 1848. *Boston.* 1848. 8vo.— ... Third Annual Report of the State Lunatic Hospital, at Northampton. ... 1858. *Boston: William White, Printer.* 1858. 8vo, pp. 38. Continued. H.— By-Laws of the State Lunatic Hospital, at Taunton, Mass. *Taunton: Printed by C. A. Hack.* 1854. 16mo, pp. 21.— ... [First] Report of the Trustees of the State Lunatic Hospital, at Taunton, ... 1854. *Boston: William White, Printer.* 1855. 8vo, pp. 47. Continued. H.

Catalogue and Circular of the State Normal School. Bridgewater. ... 1859. *North Bridgewater: George Phinney.* 1859. 8vo, pp. 11, (1). Continued. H. 46139

Also: General Catalogue of the Bridgewater State Normal School, from ... 1840, to ... 1855. *Boston: S. K. Whipple & Company.* 1855. 12mo, pp. 45, (2). H.— Catalogue and Circular of the State Normal School at Framingham, Mass. 1859–1860. *Boston: Press of Geo. C. Rand and Avery.* 1860. 8vo, pp. 15. Plate. Continued.— Course of Training, ... at the State Normal School, West-Newton; being the substance of the last two Reports of the Principal, July, 1851. [n. p. n. d.] 8vo. S.— General Catalogue of the State Normal School, at West Newton, Mass. July, 1850. *Boston: Printed by Charles C. P. Moody.* 1850. 8vo, pp. 28. Continued.— Catalogue and Circular of the State Normal School, at Westfield, Mass. ... 1848. *Springfield: Printed by Horace S. Taylor.* 1848. 12mo, pp. 12. Continued. H.

State Papers on Nullification. ... Collected ... by order of the General Court of Massachusetts ... . *Boston: Dutton and Wentworth, Printers.* 1834. 8vo, pp. vii, 381. B. 46140

State Reform School at Westborough. Fifth Annual Report of the Trustees, ... with ... Reports of the Officers of the Institution. *Boston: Dutton and Wentworth, Printers.* 1852. 8vo, pp. 48. Continued. H. 46141

Also: ... Documents relating to the State Reform School. [*Boston.* 1849.] 8vo, pp. 113. Plan and Plate. Continued.— Fifth Annual Report of the Trustees of the Nautical Branch of the State Reform School; ... . 1864. *Boston: Wright & Potter, State Printers.* 1865. 8vo, pp. 30. Continued. H.— Report ... on the State Reform School ... May 1, 1856. [n. p. n. d.] 8vo, pp. 4.

Address of the State Temperance Alliance, to the People of Massachusetts, on a State Police for the City of Boston. *Boston: Wright & Potter, Printers.* 1864. 8vo, pp. 19. 46142

Also: Reports of the Work of the State Temperance Alliance For 1862–3. [n. p. n. d.] 8vo, pp. 20. B.

Address of the State Temperance Committee to the Citizens of Massachusetts on the ... Anti-Liquor Law. [n. p. 1853.] 8vo, pp. 8. B. 46143

Also: Report of the State Temperance Committee, for ... 1854; ... Address; and Resolutions ... List of Members ... . *Boston.* 1854. 8vo, pp. (2), 13, (1). Cont'd.

Statistical Information relating to Certain Branches of Industry in Massachusetts, for ... 1865. Prepared by Oliver Warner, Secretary of the Commonwealth. *Boston.* 1866. 8vo, pp. xxv, 805. 46144

This is the fourth of a series of statistical publications relating to the manufactures and producing interests of Massachusetts.

A Statistical View of the Population of Massachusetts, from 1765, to 1840. *Boston.* 1846. 8vo. N. 46145

Statistics of the Condition and Products of Certain Branches of Industry in Massachusetts, for ... 1845. Prepared ... by John G. Palfrey, Secretary of the Commonwealth. *Boston: Dutton and Wentworth, Printers.* 1846. 8vo, pp. vi, (2), 391. H.

See also Vol. II., No. 5315.

... Report of the Street Railway Commissioners, to the General Court. ... 1865. *Boston: Wright & Potter, Printers.* 1865. 8vo, pp. 66. 2 Maps. B. 46147

A Supplement to the Digest of the Militia Laws of Massachusetts, and Resolves ... passed 1852: ... Compiled ... By Ebenezer W. Stone, Adjutant-General ... . *Boston: White and Potter, Printers.* 1852. 12mo, pp. 52. Continued. H. 46148

Supplementary Bill in Equity, the Commonwealth of Massachusetts *vs.* The State of Rhode Island, December Term, 1860. *Boston.* 1861. 8vo, pp. 11. 46149

Relates to the boundary line between Massachusetts and Rhode Island.

Supplementary Report ... [to] the Penal Code of Massachusetts, Reported to the Legislature, January 27, 1844. [n. p. n. d.] 8vo, pp. 51. BA. 46150

By Willard Phillips and S. B. Walcott.

Supreme Court of the United States, September Term, 1852. [Bill of Complaint.] The Commonwealth of Massachusetts *vs.* The State of Rhode Island and Providence Plantations. *Boston: Wright & Potter, Printers.* 1852. 4to, pp. 200. Maps and Plans.

Supreme Court of the United States: December Term, 1852. Bill: The Commonwealth of Massachusetts *vs.* The State of

Rhode Island and Providence Plantations. *Boston: Wright & Potter, Printers.* 1852. 4to, pp. 105, (2). H. 46152

Supreme Court of the United States, at its December Term, at Washington, A. D. 1855. (In Equity.) The Commonwealth of Massachusetts *vs.* The State of Rhode Island and Providence Plantations. *Providence.* 1855. Folio, pp. 37, 40. 46153

Answer to the State of Rhode Island.

Supreme Court of the United States, No. 3. The Commonwealth of Massachusetts, Complainant, *vs.* The State of Rhode Island. Bill in Chancery. [*Washington:*] *Government Printing Office.* 1862. 8vo, pp. 261. 46154

Also: Supreme Court of the United States. Rhode Island *vs.* Massachusetts. Papers put into the Case by Massachusetts. [*Washington:*] *J. & G. S. Gideon.* [n. d.] 8vo, pp. 54.

Report of the Surgeon-General ... . 1863. [*Boston.* 1863.] 8vo, pp. 22. Continued. H. 46155

Synopsis of Debates in the Massachusetts Legislature [in Oct. 1814. n. p. n. d.] 8vo, pp. 23. BA. 46156

Relates to the Hartford convention.

Tables of Bearings, Distances, Latitudes, Longitudes, &c. ascertained by the Astronomical and Trigonometrical Survey of Massachusetts. Published ... By John G. Palfrey, Secretary of the Commonwealth. *Boston: Dutton and Wentworth, ... Printers.* 1846. 8vo, pp. (4), xxxviii, (2), 73. Map. H. 46157

See also Vol. II., No. 6407–8.

A Tabular View of Representation in the Commonwealth of Massachusetts, from 1780 to 1853. Prepared by Ephraim M. Wright ... . *Boston: William White.* 1854. 8vo, pp. (2), 162.

Temporary Acts and Laws Of His Majesty's Province of the Massachusetts-Bay in New-England. [1736–1753.] *Boston: Printed ... by Samuel Kneeland ... .* MDCCXLII–[1753]. Folio, pp. (2), 4, 400. Continued. B. 46159

The Testimony of the Pastors of the Churches in ... Massachusetts-Bay, ... May 25, 1743. Against several Errors in Doctrine, and Disorders in Practice ... . *Boston: Printed by Rogers and Fowle, for S. Eliot.* 1743. 8vo, pp. 13. H. 46160

Third Article in the Declaration of Rights. [n. p. n. d.] 8vo, pp. 20. M. 46161

To the Electors of Massachusetts. [*Worcester.* 1837.] 4to, pp. 40. W. 46162

To the Honorable General Court of the State of Massachusetts Bay to be convened at Boston, 31 May, 1778. *Boston: Draper and Folsom.* 1778. 4to, pp. 3. 46163

To the Hon. the Senate ... of ... Massachusetts, ... the Memorial of the undersigned [E. Bacon and others], sureties of T. J. Skinner, late Treasurer ... of said Commonwealth, etc. *Boston.* 1811. 8vo. 46164

To the Hon. the Senate and ... Representatives ... in Congress assembled, the Representatives of ... Massachusetts. [n. p. 1812.] 8vo. 46165

Relates to the war with Great Britain.

To the Members of the General Court of Massachusetts, friendly to Temperance. [n. p. n. d.] 8vo, pp. 22. B. 46166

Draft of a bill for the present session of the legislature, 1855. *See also* [Little (J.)]

To the ... Senate. *See* [Kirkland (J. T.)], Vol. IX. 38005.

To the Whig Voters of the Fourth Congressional District, of ... Massachusetts. [n. p. 1848?] 8vo, pp. 16. 46167

Transactions of the Agricultural Societies of Massachusetts, for 1847. ... *Boston.* 1847. 8vo. Continued. 46168

Treasurer's Statement, Jan. 1, 1825. [n. p. n. d.] Folio, 1 leaf. Continued. 46169

Also: Treasurer's Statement of the Annual Expense of Printing for the Legislature, 1819–1829. *Boston.* 1829. Folio.

The True Whig Sentiment of Massachusetts. ... [n. p. 1846.] 8vo, pp. 24. H. 46170

Votes of the Honourable House of Representatives of the Province of the Massachusetts Bay, 1721–1722. *Boston.* 1721–1722. Folio. 46171

Who shall be Governor? The Contrast, containing Sketches of the Characters and Public Services of the Two Candidates [Christopher Gore and Levi Lincoln] for the Office of Chief Magistrate of ... Massachusetts. *Worcester: Spy Office.* 1809. 8vo, pp. 11. BA. 46172

A Word of Comfort. *See* [Wise (John)].

MASSE (E. M.) L'Isle de Cuba et la Havane, ou Histoire, Topographie, ... de cette Colonie, d'après un Journal écrit sur les lieux. Par E.-M. Masse. *Paris: Lebègue, Imprimeur.* 1825. 8vo, pp. (2), 410. H. 46173

MASSERAS (E.) El Programa del Imperio. *Mexico.* 1864. 8vo, pp. 34. 46174

MASSETT (S. C.) "Drifting About;" or, What "Jeems Pipes of Pipesville" Saw—and—Did. An Autobiography. By Stephen C. Massett. With Comic Illustrations by Mullen. *New York: Carleton.* 1863. 12mo, pp. 371. 46175

Also: Biographical Sketch, Words of the Songs, Ballads, &c., of ... Mr. Stephen Massett, "Jeems Pipes of Pipesville." ... *New-York.* 1858. 12mo, pp. 52. H.

MASSEY (E.) Sermon against the Dangerous and Sinful Practice of Inoculation. By Edmund Massey. Third Edition. *Boston, reprinted.* 1730. 8vo, pp. 32. 46176

MASSEY (T. E.) Mexico As it Is. By Thomas E. Massey, ... Lecture: ... February 20th, 1866; ... . *Washington, D. C.* 1866. 8vo, pp. 28. H. 46177

MASSEY (W.) A History of England during the Reign of George the Third. By William Massey, M.P. ... *London: John W. Parker and Son.* 1855–63. 4 vols., post 8vo, pp. (2), xxviii, 552; xix, 472; (2), xvi, 511; xii, 647. H. + Second Edition, Revised and Corrected. *London: Longmans.* 1865–66. 4 vols., post 8vo. 46178

MASSIAS (G.) Vita del Beato Giovanni Massias converso della Provincia di S. Giovanni Battista del Perú nell Ordine de' Predicatori. *Roma.* 1837. 4to. 46179

MASSIE (J.) Brief Observations on the Management of the War, and the means to Prevent the Ruin of Great Britain, with notices of the Gold Mines of Peru and Mexico, the Possessions of the French in America, 1761. *London.* 1761. Folio.

Title from one of Thomas Thorpe's catalogues.

MASSIE. Calculations and Observations relating to an Additional Duty upon Sugar. Dated Westminster, 20th January, 1759. [n. p. n. d.] Folio, 1 leaf. 46181

MASSIE. An Historical Account of the Naval Power of France, ... With a State of the English Fisheries at Newfoundland, for a hundred and fifty years past. ... To which is added,

A Narrative of the Proceedings of the French at Newfoundland, from the Reign of King Charles the First, to the Reign of Queen Anne, shewing what Measures were taken on the Part of England, during that Interval, in relation to the said French Proceedings, &c. First Printed in the year 1712, and now Reprinted for general Information. By J. Massie. *London: T. Payne.* [1763.] 4to. 46182

I have never seen the first edition. *See* "M. Rev.," XXVII. 461.

MASSIE. A State of the British Sugar-Colony Trade; shewing, That an Additional Duty of Twelve Shillings per 112 Pounds Weight may be laid upon Brown or Muscovado Sugar (and proportionably higher Duties upon Sugar refined before imported) without making Sugar dearer in this Kingdom than it hath been of late Years, and without Distressing the British Sugar-Planters; for their Profits will then be Twice as much Money per acre of Land, as the Landholders of England receive for their Estates. All which Matters are plainly made appear, and the vast losses which this Kingdom hath suffered by the Sugar-Colony Trade, written Thirty Years last past, are particularly pointed out. Most humbly submitted to the consideration of the Honourable House of Commons. By J. Massie. *London: T. Payne.* MDCCLIX. 4to, pp. (2), 40. 46183

MASSIE (J. W.) An Address ... before the ... Virginia Military Institute, July 3rd, 1857. By James W. Massie, Esq. ... *Richmond: Macfarlane & Fergusson, Printers.* 1857. 8vo, pp. 53, (2). 46184

Severely criticises the military spirit of Massachusetts in the revolutionary war.

MASSIE (J. W.) America: The Origin of her Present Conflict; her Prospect for the Slave, and her Claim for Anti-Slavery Sympathy; Illustrated by Incidents of Travel during a Tour in the Summer of 1863, throughout the United States, from the Eastern Boundaries of Maine to the Mississippi. By James W. Massie, D.D. ... *London: John Snow.* MDCCCLXIV. 8vo, pp. viii, 472. Map. H. 46185

MASSIE. The American Crisis, in relation to the Anti-Slavery Cause. Facts and Suggestions addressed to the Friends of Freedom in Britain. By William Massie, D.D. ... *London: John Snow.* MDCCCLXII. 16mo, pp. 11. B. 46186

Also: The Case Stated. The Friends and Enemies of the American Slave. ... *Manchester.* 1863. 8vo, pp. 8.—International Sympathies. Report of the Farewell Meeting for Dr. Massie, of London. New York, September 27, 1863. *New York: Anson D. F. Randolph.* 1863. 8vo, pp. 31.—The Slave: Hunted, Transported, and

Doomed to Toil; a Tale of Africa. ... *Manchester: J. Lowndes.* 1846. 16mo, pp. iv, 176.—Slavery the Crime and Curse of America: an Expostulation with the Christians of that Land. ... *London.* 18—. 8vo.

MASSON (E.) Olla Podrida, condimentada en México, ó coleccion de todos los remitidos que, desde 1844, y en varios periódicos de México, publicó bajo diferentes seudónimos como los de Gilles Gogo, Anti-Pierna-Seca y otros muchos. *Paris.* 1864. 8vo, pp. 684. 46187

MASSOW (F. van). De servitute conventionali secundum juris hodierni rationem. *Lugduni Batavorum.* 1821. 4to. 46188

MASTERMAN (G. F.) Seven Eventful Years in Paraguay. A Narrative of Personal Experience amongst the Paraguayans. By George Frederick Masterman ... . *London: Sampson Low, Son, and Marston.* MDCCCLXIX. 8vo, pp. xv, (1), 356. Map. BA.

MASTERS (T.) Sketches of the Life and Death of Isabella Sarah Wilbur; eldest daughter of Jeremiah and Sarah R. Wilbur, and granddaughter of Thomas Masters. ... *New York.* 1858. 12mo, pp. 148. 46190

MASTERS (W.) Advertisement. For the Satisfaction of the Adventurers in Pettie's Island Land and Cash Lottery, &c. ... Their obligated Friend, William Masters. [*Philadelphia, August,* 1771.] Folio, 1 leaf. P. 46191

MASTERS. Advertisement. ... William Masters. [*Philadelphia, August* 29, 1771.] Folio, 1 leaf. P. 46192

This is more of Pettie's Island Lottery. Also: Pettie's Island Land and Cash Lottery, &c. ... W. M. [*Philadelphia, April* 4, 1771.] Folio, 1 leaf.—Pettie's Island Land and Cash Lottery. ... William Masters. [*Philadelphia, Oct.* 1, 1771.] Folio, 1 l.

Het Matappika landbouwkundig Genootschap: De Eensgezindheid in de Devisie, te Suriname. Verzameling van uitgezochte Verhandelingen, betreffende de Landbouw in de Kolonie Suriname. *Amsteldam: Gartman & Uylenbroek.* 1804. 8vo, pp. (8), 128. C. 46193

MATAMORA. Histories of the Indian King Matamora, the last of the Wampanoags ... . *Baltimore.* [n. d.] 16mo. Plates.

MATAMORAS. Correspondence respecting Trade with Matamoras. [*London.* n. d.] Folio, pp. 5. 46195

MATANZAS. La milicia nacional local de Matanzas á D. Gabriel Sequeira. [n. p. n. d.] Folio, 1 leaf. 46196

Manual de Forasteros en la la Ciudad de Matanzas. *Matanzas.* 1836. 12mo. 46197

A Match for a Widow. *See* [Atkinson (Joseph)], I. 2184.

The Match Girl; or, Life Scenes as they are. *Philadelphia: W. W. Smith.* 1858. 12mo, pp. 418. Plates. 46198

Includes some particulars relative to Edwin Forest.

MATCHETT (Richard J.) The Baltimore Director, for the year 1829 ... . *Baltimore.* 1829. 46199

Continued to 1856 or later.

MATEO (J.) Poema joco-serioso en el que bajo el titulo del Chiton se impugna el antiguo abuso de inponer silencio á las verdaderas noticias que se communicaron como favorables a la justisima causa de la Patria, en los calamitosos tiempos de la barbara Dominacion Española, etc. Por D. José Mateo de Otero. *Lima.* [n. d.] 4to, pp. 8. 46200

MATEOS (J. A.) El cerro de las Campanas (Memorias de un Guerillero), Novela histórica por Juan A. Mateos. *Mexico.* 1868. Sm. 4to, pp. 758, vii. Plate and Portrait. 46201

MATEOS. El sol de Mayo. (Memorias de la intervencion.) Novela histórica por Juan A. Mateos. Segunda Edicion. *Mexico.* 1868. Rl. 8vo, pp. vi, 756. 46202

MATEOS (N. M.) La tolerancia, opusculo politico. Por Nicomedes Martin Mateos. *Mexico.* 1847. 4to, pp. 48.

The Material Bearing of the Tennessee Campaign in 1862 upon the Destinies of our Civil War. *Washington, D. C: W. H. Moore, Printer.* [n. d.] 8vo, pp. 19. H. 46204

Materiales para la Historia de Sonora (1658–1778). Copia de las tomos XVI y XVII de la coleccion de MSS. del Archivo general de Mexico. *Mexico.* 1851. Folio, pp. 940, (14). 2 Maps.

Materials for a Catalogue of the Masters and Scholars who have belonged to the Public Latin School, Boston, Massachusetts, From 1635 to 1846. ... *Boston: Wm. Crosby and H. P. Nichols.* 1847. 8vo, pp. vii, 72. H. 46206

This school publishes annual catalogues.

In the preparation of the following list of works by the Mather family, I am under special obligations to Mr. J. A. Lewis, of Boston, who has made their collection a specialty; also to Dr. J. H. Trumbull, of Hartford, Conn. The titles which are obviously imperfect are mostly taken from Thomas' "History of Printing," second edition; a few are from Samuel Mather's List of his father's books, which is a very untrustworthy source, and probably includes some works never printed.

MATHER (A.) Good Rulers a choice Blessing. A Sermon ... before the ... General Assembly of ... Connecticut, at Hartford, ... May 12th, 1725. The Day for the Election of the ... Governour ... . By Azariah Mather, A.M. ... *New London: T. Green.* 1725. 8vo, pp. (2), 50. H. 46207

MATHER. None but Christ. A Discourse on John VI. 67, 68. Preach'd Privately, to a Religious Society in Say-brook. By Azariah Mather, A.M. ... *New London: T. Green.* 1722. 8vo, pp. (2), 22. 46208

MATHER. The | Sabbath-Day's | Rest | Asserted, Explained, Proved, and | Applied. | By Azariah Mather, A.M. ... | *Boston, N. E.* | *Printed by B. Green, Jun. for* | *S. Gerrish* ... . 1725. 8vo, pp. (2), 4, 38 (1). B. 46209

"An Attestation," pp. 4, is signed "Co. Mather." Very rare.

MATHER. Wo to | Sleepy | Sinners. | Or, A | Discourse ... in | Saybrook, | January 6. 1719, 20. | By Azariah Mather, A.M. ... | *New-London: Printed ... by T. Green.* 1720. 8vo, pp. (2), 29.

Also: A Discourse Concerning the Death of the Righteous; at Lyme, Occasion'd by the Decease of the Rev. Mr. Moses Noyes, who dyed November 10th, 1729. ... *New London: T. Green.* 1731. 16mo, pp. (4), 24.—The Gospel-Minister Described. Sermon at Newent in Norwich Dec. 10th. 1723, at the Ordination of the Rev. Daniel Kirtland There. ... *New London: T. Green.* 1725. 16mo, pp. 32, (1).—Sermon at the Ordination of Mr. George Beckwith, in Lyme, Jan. 22, 1729, 30. ... *New London: T. Green.* 1730. 12mo, pp. 18.

[MATHER (Cotton).] The A, B, C, of Religion. Lessons relating to the Fear of God, Fitted unto the Youngest & Lowest Capacities, and Children suitably instructed in the Maxims of Religion. *Boston: Timothy Green.* 1713. 12mo, pp. (2), 42.

At the end, pp. 37–42, "Instructions for Children," in verse, including "The Body of Divinity Versifyed." Very rare. Mr. Brinley had the only copy.

[MATHER.] The Accomplished Singer. | Instructions | How the Piety | of Singing | with a | True Devotion may be | obtained and expressed; the Glor | ious God after an uncommon | manner glorified in it, and His | people Godified. | Intended for the Assistance of all that would | sing Psalms with Grace in their Hearts; | But more particularly to accompany the | Laudable Endeavours of those who are | Learning to sing by Rule … . *Boston: Printed by B. Green, for S. Gerrish,* | … 1721. 16mo, pp. (4), 24. H. 46212

One of the rarest of Cotton Mather's tracts; no copy, as far as the writer knows, having occurred for sale in this country. Mather remarks: "It has been found in some of our congregations, that in length of time, their singing has degenerated into an odd noise, that has had more of what we want a name for than any regular singing in it; whereby the Celestial Exercise is dishonoured; and indeed the Third Commandment is trespassed upon."

[Mather.] An Account of the Method and further Success of Inoculating for the Small Pox in London. *Boston.* 1714. 8vo.

Thomas says there were two editions, but I have been unable to find either.

Mather. Addresses | To Old Men, and Young Men, and | Little Children. | In Three Discourses | … . To which may be added, A short Scriptural Cate- | chism … . By Cotton Mather. | *Boston: Printed by R. Pierce, for Nicholas Buttolph.* 1690. 8vo, pp. (4), 122. BA. 46214

Mather. Adversus Libertinos. | Or, | Evangelical Obedience | Described and Demanded; | In an Essay | To Establish, the Holy Law | of | The Glorious God, | … | By Cotton Mather, D.D. | … | *Boston: Printed by B. Green, for Samuel Gerrish,* | … 1713. 8vo, pp. (4), 49, (1). BA. 46215

Mather. Advice from Taberah. | A Sermon | Preached | After the Terrible | Fire, | Which, (attended with Some very | Lamentable and Memorable Cir- | cumstances, On Oct. 2, 3. 1711.) | Laid a Considerable Part of Boston, | in Ashes. | Directing a Pious Improvement of Every | Calamity, but more Especially of so | Calamitous a Desolation. | By Cotton Mather, D.D. | … | *Boston in N. E.: Printed by B. Green:* | … 1711. 16mo, pp. iv, 33, (1).

[Mather.] Advice from the Watch Tower. | In a Testimony against | Evil Customes. | A brief Essay | To declare the Danger & Mischief of all | Evil Customes, | … With certain Methods for the Prevention and Suppression of them. | … | *Boston: Printed by J. Allen, for N. Boone.* 1713. 8vo, pp. 40. BA.

"Liberavi Animam Meam," says Mather, by way of Finis. Doubtless it was a great comfort to him, to "free his mind," about the "Infamous Rum" which was "the usual Entertainment of a Friend at our Houses," the "Flood of Strong Drink," the too great frequency of "Games of Hazard, such as Cards and Dice, among our Children" [in Boston!]; "Christmas-Revels, beginning to be taken up;" the "diversions at many Weddings—improved into such Revels, as are not well consistent with the Sobriety of Christianity;" the "very common usage" of Drinking Healths, "even among professors of our Holy Religion," and the whole "Black List of some Evil Customes which begin to appear among us."—*Brinley Catalogue.*

[Mather.] An Advice, | to the Churches of the Faithful: | … Reporting, | the Present State of the | Church, | Throughout the World; … *Boston: Printed by B. Green, & J. Allen.* | 1702. | 16mo, pp. 16. H. 46218

Mather. Agreeable Admonitions for Old and Young. *Boston.* 1703. 8vo, pp. 48. 46219

Title from Thomas' "History of Printing."

[Mather.] Agricola. | Or, the | Religious Husbandman: | The Main Intentions of | Religion, | Served in the | Business and Language | of | Husbandry. | A Work Adapted unto the Grand | Purposes of Piety; | And Commended therefore by a Number | of Ministers, to be Entertained in | the Families of the Countrey. | … *Boston:* | *Printed by T. Fleet, for D. Henchman,* … 1727. 16mo, pp. (6), 221, (1). H. 46220

[Mather.] The Ambassadors Tears. | A | Minister of the Gospel, | Making his Just and Sad | Complaint | of an | Unsuccessful Ministry. | … | *Boston:* | … *T. Fleet.* 1721. 12mo, pp. 27.

[Mather.] American Tears upon the Ruins of | the Greek Churches. | A Compendious, but Entertaining | History | of the | Darkness come upon the | Greek Churches, | in | Europe and Asia. | Composed by an American. | … | With An Appendix containing a Relation | of the Conversion of a Jew, | Named Shalome Ben Shalomoh. | *Boston in N. E.: Printed by B. Green & J. Allen,* | *for … Samuel Sewall Junior.* 1701. 16mo, pp. 80. H. 46222

The appendix has (p. 56) a separate title and imprint, with a preface (3 pp.) signed, "Cotton Mather."

[Mather.] The Angel of Bethesda, | Visiting | the | Invalids | of a Miserable | World. | … | By a Fellow of the Royal Society. | *New-London:* | … *Timothy Green.* | 1722. 8vo, pp. (2), 17, (1).

[Mather.] Another Tongue brought in, to confess the great Saviour of the World; or, Some Communications of Christianity, put into a Tongue used among the Iroquois Indians in America. And put into the hands of the English and Dutch Traders. To accommodate the Great Intention of communicating the Christian Religion unto the Salvages among whom they may find anything of this language to be intelligible. *Boston: Printed by T. Green.* 1707. 8vo, pp. 16. J.C.B., N. 46224

Sentences in relation to God, Jesus Christ, and the Trinity, in the Iroquois, Latin, English, and Dutch languages.

[Mather.] The Armour of Christianity. | A | Treatise, | Detecting first, the Plots of the | Devil against our Happiness. | Declaring then, the Wiles by | which those Plots are managed. | And Propounding, lastly, the | Thoughts by which those | Wiles may be Defeated. | … | *Boston, in N. E. Printed by Timothy* | *Green, for Benjamin Eliot* … . 1704. 12mo, pp. (2), 234. B. 46225

Mather. Awakening Thoughts on the Sleep of Death, with a debt paid to the Memory of that Sleep in Jesus. Preached at a Thursday Lecture Decr. 1711. *Boston.* 1712. Sm. 8vo, pp. viii, 34. 46226

The preface is a tribute to the Memory of Mrs. Mary Higginson. Title and note from Thomas' "History of Printing." I am unable to locate a copy.

[Mather.] The Balance of the Sanctuary. | … A Lecture; In the Audience of the | General Assembly at Boston, | Oct. 5. 1727. … *Boston: Printed … by T. Fleet.* 1727. 12mo, pp. (2), 24.

[Mather.] Baptismal Piety. Two brief Essays. I. The Angel of the Waters. … II. The Angel of the Little Ones … . *Boston: Printed in the Year* 1727. 12mo, pp. 48. H. 46228

M[ather]. Baptistes: | A Conference | About the | Subject and Manner | of | Baptism. | Between C. M. and D. R. | [*Boston.* 1704.] 8vo, pp. (3), 32. H. + The Second Edition. … *Boston: Printed by T. Fleet, for J. Phillips* … . 1724. 12mo, pp. (3), 32.

The title to the second edition is lengthened and varies.

Mather. Batteries upon the Kingdom | of the Devil. | Seasonable | Discourses | upon Some Common, but Woful | Instances, | wherein | Men Gratifie the Grand Enemy of | their Salvation. | By Mr. Cotton Mather … . | *London,* | *Printed for Nath. Hiller* … . 1695. Sm. 8vo, pp. (16), 192. 46230

The first sermon in the volume, "Sacred Exorcisms: Or, The Case and Cure of Persons Possessed by the Devil," alludes (p. 21) to cases "we have seen," of "bodily molestations by Evil Spirits."

Mather. Benedictus. | Good Men | Described, | And the Glories of their | Goodness, declared. | With | Some Character & History of | One who belonged unto the Tribe; | Namely, | Mr. Thomas Bridge, | A Late Pastor of the First-Church in | Boston; who Expired, | 26 d. VII m. 1715. | Whereto there is added, An Instru- | ment, which he wrote, when he | drew near his End, and Left as a | Legacy to Survivers, relating some of his Experiences; And offering some | Testimonies to the cause of Religion. | By Cotton Mather, D.D. & F.R.S. | *Boston: Printed by B. Green, for Samuel Gerrish* … . 1715. 12mo, pp. (2), 58. H. 46231

[Mather.] The Best Ornaments of Youth. A Short Essay on the Good Things, which are found in Some, and should be found in All, Young People. … which Wherever they are found, Heaven will take a Favourable Notice of them. A Sermon … . *Boston, in N. E. … Timothy Green* … . 1707. 12mo, pp. 36. W.

Mather. The Best Way of Living; | Which is to | Die Daily: | … a … Discourse, | … at a Time, when the Au- | thor had newly seen Repeat- | ed Strokes of Death, on his | own Family. | … By Cotton Mather, D.D. … *Boston: Printed by J. Allen.* 1713. 12mo, pp. (2), 26. B. 46233

[Mather.] Bethiah. The Glory Which Adorns the Daughters of God. And the Piety, Wherewith Zion wishes to see her Daughters Glorious. *Boston: Printed by J. Franklin, for S. Gerrish* … . 1722. 12mo, pp. 60. 46234

Mather. Blessed Unions. | An Union | With the Son of God by | Faith, | And, an Union | In the Church of God by | Love, | Importunately Pressed; in a | Discourse | Which makes Divers Offers, for those Unions; | Together with | A Copy of those Articles, where-upon a most | Happy Union, has been lately made | between those two Eminent Parties in | England, which have now Changed | the Names of Presbyterians, and | Congregationals for that of | United Brethren. | By Cotton Mather. | … | *Boston: Printed by B. Green, & J. Allen,* | *for Samuel Phillips.* 1692. 24mo, pp. (10), 86, 12. B., H. 46235

The "Articles" were also printed in the "Magnalia," v. 58–61.

[Mather.] Boanerges. | A Short Essay | to preserve and strengthen the | Good Impressions | Produced by | Earthquakes | On the Minds of People that have been | Awakened with them. | … | Address'd unto the Whole People of New- | England, who have been Terrified | with the Late Earthquakes; | And more especially the Towns that have had a more singular Share in the Terrors of them. | … | *Boston:* | … *S. Kneeland* … . 1727. 8vo, pp. (2), 53. B. 46236

Mather. The Bonds of the Covenant. *Boston.* 1709. 8vo, pp. 33. 46237

This imperfect title is from Thomas' "History of Printing," Vol. II.

[Mather.] Bonifacius. | An Essay | Upon the Good, | that is to be Devised and Designed, | by those | Who Desire to Answer the Great End | of Life, and to Do Good | While they Live. | A Book Offered, | First, in General, unto all Christians, | … . Then

… | Unto Magistrates, … Ministers, … Physicians, … Lawyers, | … Schoolmasters, … | *Boston in N. England: Printed by B. Green, for Samuel Gerrish.* 1710. 16mo, pp. (2), 206. B., BA. 46238

This is the original edition of "Essays to Do Good," *infra.* A perfect copy is rare. It contains Mather's proposal for the "Biblia Sacra," which was written but not published. At the end is "An Appendix Concerning the Essays that are made for the Propagation of Religion among the Indians."

[Mather.] M.DC.LXXXIII. The Boston Ephemeris. | An | Almanack | for | the | Dyonisian | Year of the Christian | Æra. M.DC.LXXXIII. | And of the World's Creation 5632. | *Anno oppidi inchoati* 53. | Of which the vulgar Notes are, | Cycle of the Sun 12. | Dominic Let. G. F. | Golden Numb. 12. | Epac 12. | Num. of Direct. 18. | Serving the Meridian of Boston in New Engl. | Latitude 42 qr. 30 min. | Longitude 315 qr. | … | (*Boston in New-England.*) *Printed by S*[*amuel*] *G*[*reen*] *for S*[*amuel*] *S*[*ewall*]. 1683. 16mo, pp. (24). 46239

"There is much internal evidence that this is by Cotton Mather. The style, the learning, and the spirit of the book are his; and no writer displays more marked individuality than he."—W. F. Poole. It is Mather's second publication. *See* "Mather Papers," 479.

[Mather.] The Bostonian Ebenezer. | Some | Historical Remarks, | On the State of | Boston. | The Chief Town of New-England, | and of the English America. | With Some, | Agreeable Methods, | for | Preserving and Promoting, the Good | State of That, as well as any | other Town, in the like Circumstances. | Humbly Offer'd, By a Native of Boston. | … | *Boston, Printed by B. Green & J. Allen, for* | *Samuel Phillips,* … 1698. 12mo, pp. 82.

Concerning this rare work, *see* Samuel Mather's Life of his father, p. 164.

Mather. Brethren dwelling together in | Unity. | The True Basis for an | Union | Among the | People of God, | Offered and Asserted; | In | A Sermon | Preached at the Ordination of a | Pastor, in the Church of the | Baptists. | At Boston in New-England. | On 21 d. III m. 1718. | By Cotton Mather, D.D. | With a Preface of the Reverend | Dr. Increase Mather. | … | *Boston: Printed for S. Gerrish* … 1718. 8vo, pp. (2), iv, 42. BA. 46241

Elisha Callendar was the pastor who was ordained.

[Mather.] A Brief Memorial, | of Matters, and Methods for | Pastoral Visits. | *Boston: Printed in the Year,* MDCCXXIII. 4to, pp. 3. B. 46242

[Mather.] Brontologia Sacra: | the | Voice | of the | Glorious God | in the | Thunder: | Explained and Applyed | In a Sermon

uttered by a Minister of the Go- | spel in a Lecture unto an Assembly of Chri- | stians abroad, at the very same time when | the Thunder was by the Permission and | Providence of God falling upon his own | House at home. | Whereto are added | some Reflections formed on the Lords-Day following | by the Voices of Thunders, upon the great things | which the great God is now a doing in the World. | A Discourse useful for all Men at all times, but especi- | ally intended for an Entertainment in the Hours of | Thunder. | *London,* | *Printed by John Astwood.* 1695. 16mo, pp. (4), 38. 46243

Mather. The | Call of the Gospel | Applyed | unto All Men in general, | and | unto a Condemned Malefactor in particular. | In | A Sermon | Preached on the 7th d. of the 1st. m. 1686. | At the Request, and in the Hearing of [James Morgan] a man, | under a just Sentence of Death for the hor- | rid Sin of Murder. | By Cotton Mather, | … | *Printed at Boston, by R. P. Anno Supradict.* [1686.] Sm. 8vo, pp. (2), 94. B. 46244

Joshua Moody's "Exhortation to a Condemned Malefactor, Delivered March 6th, 1685–6." *Printed at Boston in N. England. Anno praedict,* forms pp. 55–94. This work stands first in Samuel Mather's catalogue of the books published by his father. In his "Letters from New-England," John Dunton quotes extensively from these sermons. He also had a hand in bringing them out. *See* page 80, Prince Society edition of Dunton's Letters: "He [Brunning] was my Partner in Printing Mr. Mather's and Mr. Moody's Sermon on condemned Morgan." For a second edition, *see* Mather (Increase). It is, in fact, Mather's fourth publication; *see* "A Poem" and "Elegy," *infra,* and No. 46239, *supra.*

[Mather.] Cares about the Nurseries. | Two brief | Discourses. | The One, offering | Methods and Motives for | Parents | To Catechise their Children | While yet under the Tuition of | their Parents. | The other, offering | Some Instructions for | Children, | How they may do well, when | they come to Years of Doing for themselves. | … | *Boston, N. E. Printed by T. Green,* | *for Benjamin Eliot.* 1702. 12mo, pp. (2), 88. B., M. 46245

Mather. The Case of a troubled Mind. | A brief Essay, | … Which apprehends the Face of … God | Hidden from it. | By Cotton Mather, D.D. | … *Boston: Printed by B. Green, for S. Gerrish.* 1717. 18mo, pp. (2), 27. + The Second Edition. … *Boston: Printed by G. Rogers for N. Proctor.* 1741. 8vo, pp. 23.

[Mather.] The Choice Wisdom. | A | Brief … Essay | on the | best of Blessings, | To be Obtained | By the Chusing [*sic*] of them | and Asking for them. | … | *Boston: Thomas Hancock.* 1726. 12mo, pp. 23. B. 46247

[Mather.] A Christian at his Calling. Two brief Discourses. One Directing a Christian in his General Calling; Another Directing him in his Personal Calling. *Boston: Printed by B. Green & J. Allen, for S. Sewall, Jun.* 1701. 12mo, pp. 72.

[Mather.] A Christian Conversing with the Great Mystery of Christianity. The Mystery of the Trinity In the One Infinite and Eternal God, Practically Improved and Applied, and Plainly brought into the Life of Christianity. [*Boston:*] *Printed & Sold by T. Green.* 1709. 16mo, pp. 56. 46249

[Mather.] The Christian Cynick. | A brief Essay | On a | Merciful Saviour, | … With | Directions … | For the | Addresses, | Which will obtain His Favours. | … | *Boston.* 1716. 12mo, pp. (2), 42. B. 46250

[Mather.] A Christian Funeral. A brief Essay, On that Case, What should be the Behaviour of a Christian at a Funeral? *Boston: Timothy Green.* 1713. 12mo, pp. (2), 36, (1). 46251

Mather. Christian Loyalty. | Or, | Some Suitable Sentiments | On the Withdraw of | King George the First, | Of Glorious Memory, | And the Access of | King George the Second, | Unto the Throne of the | British Empire. | By Cotton Mather. … *Boston:* | *Printed … by T. Fleet* … . 1727. 16mo, pp. (2), ii, 25.

Mather. The | Christian Philosopher: | A | Collection | of the | Best Discoveries in Nature, | with | Religious Improvements. | By Cotton Mather, D.D. | And Fellow of the Royal Society. | *London:* | … *Eman. Matthews* … . M.DCC.XXI. 8vo, pp. vii, (1), 304. H. + *Charlestown: … J. M'Kown, Printer.* 1815. 12mo, pp. 324.

"Hereby hangs a funny tale. About the year 1714, Cotton Mather in Boston was dubbed with F.R.S., a trinity of capitals which flattering his vanity he adopted and wore, though somewhat against his previous teachings in regard to worldly distinctions. The first of his 383 books that came out after the receipt of this polished handle bore F.R.S. after his name, much to the astonishment of his rivals, and amusement of his fellow citizens. He immediately wrote to the Secretary of the Royal Society thanking him, and continued through life to be an active correspondent, all but the first letter being still preserved by the Society. The letter of thanks, however, for some reason never got among the records, but eventually fell among autograph-mongers, and found its way to New York. Some, in the Doctor's lifetime, said he had been hoaxed, and never was really elected, while others, and among them his son, manfully contended that he was really one of the Philosophers. This book was written during the controversy to show that he was both competent and willing to be an F.R.S. To this day the question is not settled—Was Cotton Mather an F.R.S.? There is nothing in the Society's records to show it, though the names of a dozen other Americans are recorded."—Stevens.

[Mather.] The Christian Temple, | or, | An Essay | upon a | Christian | Considered as a | Temple. | A Consideration of great

Consequence | to the Interests of | Christianity. | … | *Boston: Printed and Sold by* | *Bartholomew Green.* 1706. 8vo, pp. (2), 38. 46254

Mather. The Christian Thank-Offering. A Brief Discourse … Made on a Solemn Thanksgiving, kept in a Private Meeting of Christians, on the Occasion of some Deliverance. *Boston: Printed by B. Green & J. Allen, for Michael Perry.* 1696. 8vo, pp. 32. 46255

Rare. A versified paraphrase of the 103d Psalm, by Mather, is prefixed.

[Mather.] Christianity Demonstrated | An Essay | to Consider the Sanctifying | Work of Grace | On the Minds of the Faithful, | as a Noble Demonstration to the | Truth of our Holy Religion | With | an Exhortation unto All | but especially unto Young | Persons to seek after that | Work of God. | *Printed at Boston in N. E. Sold by* | *Timothy Green* … . | 1710. 16mo, pp. 60.

Mather. Christianity to the Life; Our Imitation of our Saviour. *Boston.* 1702. 8vo, pp. 60. 46257

Title from Thomas' "History of Printing."

[Mather.] Christianus per Ignem: | Or, A Disciple | Warming of himself | and | owning of His Lord, | With Devout and Useful Meditations, | Fetch'd out of the | Fire, | By a Christian in a Cold Season, | Sitting before it. | … | *Boston: Printed by B. Green, and J. Allen, for Benjamin Eliot.* 1702. 16mo, pp. 198, (2). B.

"This is in S. Mather's list of his father's works under the date of 1700. Yet it has been attributed to Nicholas Noyes, because he signs the "Præfatory Poem," although that is evidently not by the author of the book."—*Catalogue of the Prince Library.* It is "one of the most curious volumes in the Mather library;" some of the "Meditations" are on the most puerile subjects.

Mather. Christodulus. | A Good Reward | of | A Good Servant. | Or, The Service of a | Glorious Christ, | Justly Demanded and Commended, from a | View of the Glory with which it shall | be Recempensed [*sic*]. | With some Commemoration of | Mr. Thomas Walter, | Lately a Pastor to a Church in Roxbury: | Who had an Early Dismission from what of | that Service was to be done in This | World. Jan 10. 1724–5. | By Cotton Mather, D.D. and F.R.S. | … | *Boston: Printed by T. Fleet, for S. Gerrish* … . 1725. 8vo, pp. (3), iii, 33. B., BA., C., M., W. 46259

The Rev. Thomas Walter was a grandson of Increase and a nephew of Cotton Mather.

[Mather.] The City of Refuge. | The | Gospel of the City | Explained; | And the Flight of a | Distressed Sinner | Thereunto, | Directed and Quickened; | With a special Aspect on … | Early

Piety. | ... | *Boston: Printed by T. Fleet and T. Crump, for Daniel Henchman.* 1716. 12mo, pp. 33. B. 46260

[MATHER.] Cœlestinus. | A | Conversation in Heaven, | Quickened and Assisted, | with | Discoveries | Of Things in the | Heavenly World. | And some Relations of the | Views and Joys | That have been granted unto Several | Persons in the Confines of it. | Introduced by Agathangelus, Or, An | Essay on the Ministry of the Holy | Angels. | And Recommended unto the People of God, by the | very Reverend | Dr. Increase Mather; | Waiting in the Daily Expectation of his Departure | to that Glorious World. | *Boston: Printed by S. Kneeland, for Nath. | Belknap* ... . 1723. 12mo, pp. (2), viii, 27, ii, 162. B., H. 46261

Published by Dr. Cotton Mather, with a dedication to Mr. Thomas Hollis.

[MATHER.] Coheleth. | A Soul | upon | Recollection; | Coming into | Incontestible Sentiments | of | Religion: | Such as all the Sons of Wisdom | will and must forever Justify. | Written by a Fellow of the | Royal Society. | Offering the Advice of a Father | going out of the World, unto a | Son coming into it. | *Boston: Printed by S. Kneeland, | for S. Gerrish* ... . 1720. 12mo, pp. (2), 46. H.

[MATHER?] A | Collection, | Of Some | Of the Many | Offensive | Matters, | Contained in a | Pamphlet, | Entituled, | The Order of the Gospel Revived. | *Printed at Boston, Sold by T. Green.* 1701. 12mo, pp. 24. H., W. 46263

"I have thought it not worth while for me to take notice of the impotent Allatrations of so little a thing as that which is famed to be the Author of their Pamphlet. But a *Friend* of mine having, as he perused it, set a *Remark* on *some* of the Scandalous violations of the third, fifth, and ninth Commandments which he observed therein, I supposed it might be a service to the Churches to have them set before them," etc.—I. MATHER. Dr. Sibley attributes the work to Increase Mather, who wrote the prefatory matter only. Very rare.

[MATHER.] Columbanus. Or, The Doves Flying to the Windows of their Saviour. A Sermon, to a Religious Society of Young People. June 4th. 1722. *Boston: Printed by S. Kneeland, for J. Edwards* ... . 1722. 12mo, pp. (2), 22. N. 46264

[MATHER.] The Comfortable Chambers, | Opened and Visited, | upon | the Departure of that | Aged and Faithful | Servant of God, | Mr. Peter Thatcher, | The Never-to-be-forgotten Pastor | of Milton. | Who made his flight thither, | On December 17. 1727. | ... | *Boston: Printed for J. Edwards,* | ... 1728. Sm. 8vo, pp. (2), 31, (6). + *Boston: Re-printed by Thomas Fleet, jun.* MDCCXCVI. 8vo, pp. 28. H. 46265

"This was the last Sermon my Father deliver'd from the Pulpit: and truly such a Sermon as a good Minister wou'd desire shou'd be his last."—S. MATHER. An obituary

of Mr. Thacher is given in "Addenda from the 'Weekly Journal,' No. XL. Milton, December 23, 1727," pp. 4. "A short account of the Town of Milton" (2 pp.) is appended to the second edition.

[MATHER.] A Comforter of the Mourners. | An Essay | For the Undoing of | Heavy Burdens, | In an Offer of such Good Words | As have a Tendency to cause | Glad Hearts, | ... | *Boston, in N. E.: Printed ... by Timothy | Green.* 1704. | 8vo, pp. (6), 34.

MATHER. A | Companion for Communicants. | Discourses | Upon | The Nature, the Design, and the | Subject of the | Lords Supper; | With | Devout Methods of Preparing for, | and Approaching to that | Blessed Ordinance. | By Cotton Mather, | ... | *Printed at Boston by Samuel Green for Ben- | jamin Harris* ... . 1690. Sm. 8vo, pp. (8), 167, (1). B., W. 46267

[MATHER.] A Companion for the Afflicted. | The | Duties | and the | Comforts | of Good Men, under their Afflictions. | In | Two Brief and Plain | Discourses. | ... | *Boston, in N. E.: Printed by T. Green, | for,* ... *Samuel Sewall Junior.* | 1701. 16mo, pp. 56.

[MATHER.] Compassions Called For. | An Essay | of | Profitable Reflections | On Miserable | Spectacles. | To which is added, | A Faithful Relation of Some | Late, but Strange Occurrences | that call for an awful and | useful Consideration. | Especially, | The Surprising Distresses and | Deliverances, of a company | lately Shipwreck'd on a Desolate | Rock, on the coast of New-England. | ... | *Boston: Printed by B. Green, for Eleazer Phillips.* 1711. 8vo, pp. 60. BA. 46269

Some copies have the imprint, *Boston, in N. E. Printed: Sold by Timothy Green, at the Lower End of Middle Street.* Either editions are very rare. It contains the first account of Capt. John Dean's Narrative of the shipwreck of the Nottingham Galley, on Boone Island; appended to Mather's Boston Lecture, Dec. 28, 1710. The narrative has a half title (p. 49): "The Mariner Call'd upon." *See also* Vol. V. 19025-9.

MATHER. Concio ad Populum. | A | Distressed People | Entertained with | Proposals | For the Relief of their | Distresses | In a Sermon at Boston; made | in the Audience of His Excellency | the Governour, and the General | Assembly of the Massachusetts-Bay, | New-England. | 12d. 1m. 1719. | By Cotton Mather ... | *Boston, New-England: | Printed by B. Green, for Benj. Eliot,* | ... 1719. 8vo, pp. (2), 29. B., BA. 46270

[MATHER.] The Converted Sinner. The Nature of a Conversion to Real and Vital Piety ... A Sermon preached in Boston, May 31. 1724. In the Hearing of certain Pirates, a little before their Execution. Added, A more Private Confer-

ence of a Minister with them. *Boston: Printed for Nath'l. Belknap.* 1724. 8vo, pp. (4), 49. 46271

"These pirates, John Rose Archer and William White, executed June 2, 1724, belonged to the crew of the dreaded Capt. John Phillips. *See* Drake's 'History of Boston,' p. 570. Phillips was killed and his vessel captured by a few young men whom he had compelled to sail with him. One of these (whom Mather names) 'John Philmore of Ipswich,' was the great-grandfather of President Millard Fillmore."—J. H. TRUMBULL.

[MATHER.] Corderius Americanus. | An Essay | upon | The Good Education of Children. | And what may Hopefully be Attempted, for | the Hope of the Flock, | in a | Funeral Sermon | upon | Mr. Ezekiel Cheever. | The Ancient and Honourable Master of the | Free-School in Boston | ... | With an Elegy and an Epitaph upon him. | By one that was once a Scholar to him. | ... | *Boston, Printed by John Allen, for Nicholas Boone,* | ... 1708. 8vo, pp. (6), 34. H. + *Boston: Printed by Ezekiel Russell.* M,DCC,LXXIV. Sm. 8vo, pp. 30. BA., M. 46272

MATHER. Corderius Americanus. A Discourse on the Good Education of Children ... at the Funeral of Ezekiel Cheever ... who died August, 1708 ... . By the Rev. Cotton Mather, D.D. ... To which is ... added, A Selection from the Poems of Cheever's Manuscript ... . *Boston: Printed by Dutton & Wentworth.* 1828. 8vo, pp. 32. Facsimile. H., S. 46273

[MATHER, *and others.*] A Course of Sermons on Early Piety. By the Eight Ministers who carry on the Thursday Lecture in Boston. With a Preface by the Reverend Dr. Increase Mather. And also clos'd with a Discourse lately had by him to Young People. ... *Boston in N. E.: Printed by S. Kneeland, for N. Buttolph, B. Eliot and D. Henchman.* 1721. 12mo, pp. (2), vi, 44, 30, 36, 26, 52, 36, 32, 66, 16. 46274

The eight ministers were Cotton Mather, B. Wadsworth, B. Colman, J. Sewall, T. Prince, J. Webb, W. Cooper, and T. Foxcroft.

MATHER. The Curbed Sinner. | A Discourse | Upon the Gracious and Wondrous Restraints | Laid by the | Providence | Of the Glorious God | On the Sinful Children of Men, to | Withold them from Sinning against | Him. | Occasioned by a Sentence of Death, | passed on a poor Young Man, | for the Murder of his Companion. | With some Historical Passages refer- | ring to that Unhappy Spectacle. | By Cotton Mather, D.D. | ... | *Boston, N. E. Printed by John Allen, for Nicholas Boone* ... . 1713. 12mo, pp. (2), xiv, 64.

A sermon preached after the condemnation of David Wallis.

[MATHER.] The Cure of Sorrow. An Essay directing Persons under Sadness, what Course to take, that they may be no more Sad. *Boston: Printed by B. Green.* 1709. 12mo, pp. 46.

MATHER. The Day, & the Work of the Day. | A Brief Discourse, | on | What Fears, we may have at | This Time to quicken us; | What Hopes there are for us at | This Time to comfort us: | and | ... Collections of certain Prophecies | relating to the present Circum- | stances of New-England. | Uttered on a Fast, kept in | Boston, July 6th. 1693. | By Cotton Mather. | *Boston: Printed ... by B. | Harris.* 1693. 12mo, pp. 71. B. 46277

[MATHER.] The Day which the Lord hath made. | A | Discourse | Concerning | the Institution | and | Observation | of the | Lords-Day. | Delivered ... | 4d. 1m. 1703. | *Boston, N. E.: Printed by B. Green, and | J. Allen.* 1703. Sm. 8vo, pp. (2), 46. B., H. + *Boston, N. E.: Reprinted by B. Green.* 1707. Sm. 8vo.

It was translated into Indian by Rev. Sam'l Danforth as "Ne Kesukod Uttiyen Jehovah Kessehtunkup," etc.

MATHER. Death made Easie & Happy. | Two ... | Discourses on the | Prudent Apprehensions | of | Death; | ... With | Serious Thoughts in Dying Times: | or, A | Discourse upon Death; | ... By Cotton Mather. ... *London: Printed by Tho. Parkhurst.* 1701. 24mo, pp. (2), 106. B., W. 46279

[MATHER.] Decennium Luctuosum. | An | History | of | Remarkable Occurrences, | In the Long | War, | which | New-England hath had with the | Indian Salvages, | From the year 1688. | to the Year 1698. | Faithfully Composed and Improved. | *Boston: Printed by B. Green & J. Allen, for Samuel Phillips.* 1699. 8vo, pp. 254, (1). 46280

After p. 198, a second title-page: "Observable Things. | The | History | of | Ten Years | Rolled away under the great | Calamities of | A War, | with | Indian Salvages: | Repeated and Improved, in a Sermon, | at Boston-Lecture. 27d. 7m. 1698. | ... *Boston, Printed for Samuel Phillips* ... . 1699. Very rare. Reprinted in the "Magnalia," 1702, and with Increase Mather's "History," as edited by S. G. Drake, 1862.

MATHER. Decus ac Tutamen. | A Brief Essay | on the | Blessings | Enjoy'd by a People | that have | Men of a Right Character | Shining among them. | Offered in Commemoration of that | Good and Great Man | the Honourable | Gurdon Saltonstall Esq; | Late Governour of Connecticut-Colony | New-England. | Who Expired, at New-London; | Sept. 20th. 1724. | In the Fifty-ninth Year of his Age. | By Cotton Mather ... . *New-London: Printed by T. Green.* 1724. 8vo, pp. (4), iv, 34. 46281

MATHER. Desiderius. | Or, | A Desireable Man | Describ'd; | In the Characters of One Worthy to be, | A | Man Greatly Beloved. | ... | Given in ... Commemoration of ... | Mr. James Keith, | Late Minister of the Gospel | in Bridgwater; | Who Expired, on 23. d. v. m. 1719. ... | By Cotton Mather ... . | *Boston: Printed by S. Kneeland.* 1719. 12mo, pp. (2), 34. B., H. 46282

MATHER. Detur Digniori. | The Righteous Man | described & asserted | as the | Excellent Man; | and | The Excellencies of Each | an One demonstrated. | In a Sermon, upon the Death | of the Reverend | Mr. Joseph Gerrish, | Late Pastor to the Church in | Wenham: | Who was Received, where the weary | are at Rest, On the 6 d. XI m. 1719. | In the Seventieth Year of his Age. | By Cotton Mather ... . | *Boston: Printed by B. Green.* 1720. 8vo, pp. (2), 29. 46283

[MATHER.] Deus Nobiscum. | A | Very brief Essay, | on the | Enjoyment of God. | ... | *Boston: S. Gerrish.* 1725. 12mo, pp. 24.

[MATHER.] Diluvium Ignis. | De | Secundo ac Optando | Jehovæ-Jesu | Adventu; | Deque | Secundo ac Tremendo | Illum Comitante | Deluvio; | Atque de Fine omnium instante; | Monita quaedam Scripturaria, | et Salutaria, atque summe | Necessaria: | Mundo alte consopito, et haec | porro omnia susque deque ha- | bituro, oblata. | ... | [n. p.] Editur, A. D. Vulgariter, 1726, Realiter, 1729. Sm. 8vo, pp. (2), xiv. B., H. + *Reprinted at Boston, for Benjamin Indicott* 1730. 46285

MATHER. Discipline Practised in the Churches of New England, containing the Principles owned and the Endeavours used by them. By Cotton Mather. *Whitchurch, Salop.* 1823. 8vo. 46286

[MATHER.] Divine Afflations. | An Essay, | To Describe and Bespeak | Those | Gracious Influences | of the | Holy Spirit | Which | Will Produce & Confirm the Eter- | nal Happiness of those who | find that Blessed Spirit of Life | so Entring into them, and making | them to Live unto God. | ... | *New-London: | Printed and Sold by Timothy Green.* | 1717. 8vo, pp. (2), 38. + [*Ibid.*] 1722. M.

[MATHER.] Duodecennium Luctuosum. | The History of a Long | War | With Indian Salvages, | And their Directors and Abettors; | From the Year, 1702. To the Year, 1714. | Comprised in A | Short Essay, to declare the Voice of the | Glorious God, in the Various Occurrences | of that War, which have been thought

Mat- | ters of more Special Observation. | A Recapitulation made in the Audience, | of His Excellency the Governour, | and the General Assembly of the | Massachusett Province; At Boston, | 30. d. VII. m. 1714. | ... | *Boston: Printed by B. Green, for Samuel Gerrish,* | ... 1714. 8vo, pp. (2), 30. BA., J.C.B., M., W. 46289

MATHER. Durable Riches. | Two Brief | Discourses, | Occasioned | By the Impoverishing Blast of Hea- | ven, which the Undertakings of | Men, both by Sea and Land, | have met withal. | The One, handling, | The true Cause of Loosing; | The other, giving, | The True Way of Thriving. | By Cotton Mather. | ... | *Boston: Printed by John Allen, for | Vavasour Harris* ... . 1695. 12mo, pp. (2), 33, (1), 34, (2). H. + *Boston.* 1715. 12mo.

[MATHER.] Dust and Ashes. An Essay upon Repentance to the Last. *Boston: Printed by B. Green.* 1710. 12mo, pp. (2), 34. 46291

MATHER. The Duty of Children Whose Parents have Pray'd for them. Or, Early and Real Godliness Urged; Especially upon such as are descended from Godly Ancestors. A Sermon, preached May 19. 1703. [on a Day of] Prayer with Fasting for the Rising Generation. By Cotton Mather ... . *Boston: Printed for the Booksellers.* 1703. 12mo. 46292

For a second impression *see* Increase Mather's "The Duty of Parents," *infra.*

[MATHER.] Early Piety, | Exemplified | in the | Life and Death | of | Mr. Nathanael Mather, | who | Having become at the Age of | Nineteen, an Instance of more | than common | Learning and Virtue, | Changed Earth for Heaven, Oct. 17. 1688. | Whereto are added | Some Discourses on the true Nature, | the great Reward, and the best | Season of such | a walk with God | as he left a Pattern of. | ... | *London, | Printed by J. Astwood for J. Dunton.* 1689. 8vo, pp. (10), 60. + The Second Edition. With a Prefatory Epistle by Mr. Matthew Mead. [*Ibid.*] 1689. 8vo, pp. (14), 60. C. + *Boston: Reprinted from the London Edition of 1689.* 1690. 12mo. + *Boston: Congregational Board of Publication.* [1857?] 16mo, pp. 74. H. 46293

The "Discourses" announced were not printed.

MATHER. Early Piety exemplified in Elizabeth Butcher of Boston, who was born July 14th, 1709, and died June 13th, 1718, being just 8 years and 11 months old. Fourth Edition. *Boston.* 1718. 16mo. 46294

Title from Thomas' "History of Printing."

MATHER. Early Religion, | Urged in a | Sermon, | Upon | The Duties Wherein, | And the Reasons Wherefore, | Young People, | Should Become | Religious, | Whereto are Added, | The Extracts of several Papers, Written | by several Persons, who here Dying in their | Youth, left behind them those Admonitions for | the Young Survivers, with Brief Memoirs rela- | ting to the Exemplary Lives of some such, | that have gone from hence to their | Everlasting Rest. | By Cotton Mather. | ... | *Boston, Printed by B. H. for Michael Perry,* | ... 1694. 8vo, pp. (2), 117, (1). 46295

[MATHER.] Ecclesiæ Monilia. | The | Peculiar Treasure | of the | Almighty King | opened: | ... | At Boston Lecture, July 14. 1726. | ... | Exhibited, in the Character of | Mrs. Elizabeth Cotton, | Who was Laid up a few Days before. | And Certain Instruments and | Memorials of | Piety, | Written by that Valuable and Honourable | Gentlewoman. | *Boston: ... Daniel Henchman* ... 1726. 8vo, pp. (2), 42. H. 46296

Mrs. Cotton was the widow of Rev. Roland Cotton, of Sandwich, Mass., and a sister of Gurdon Saltonstall, Governor of Connecticut.

MATHER. Ecclesiastes. | The Life | of the | Reverend & Excellent, | Jonathan Mitchel; | A Pastor of the Church, | and | A Glory of the Colledge, | in | Cambridge, New-England. | Written by Cotton Mather. | ... | *Massachuset: | Printed by B. Green, and J. Allen.* 1697. Sm. 8vo, pp. 111. C., H. 46297

Very rare. At the end of the sermon are two elegies, in verse, one by Cotton Mather, the other, with an "Epitaphium," signed "F. D." [Francis Drake]. There were two issues, one of which has five lines of errata on the last page, not in the other. Thomas says it was reprinted, *Boston,* 1724. 8vo.

MATHER. The Echoes of Devotion. A very brief and plain Essay on those Acts of Compliance, which all calls to Piety are to be entertained withal. *Boston.* 1716. 12mo, pp. 36. 46298

A sermon, so rare that I am unable to quote a perfect copy.

[MATHER.] Edulcorator. Or the Waters of Marah Sweetened. An Essay on the Death of Capt. Josiah Winslow. *Boston.* 1725. 12mo, pp. 38. 46299

Title from Thomas' "History of Printing."

[MATHER.] An | Elegy | on The Much-to-be-deplored Death | of that Never-to-be-forgotten Person, | The Reverend | Mr. Nathanael Collins; | Who After he had been many years a faithful | Pastor to the Church at Middletown of Connecticut in New-England, | about the Forty-third year of his Age Expired; On

28th. 10. moneth 1684. | ... | *Boston, N. E.: Printed by Richard Pierce for Obadiah Gill.* 1685. 8vo, pp. (4), 20. 46300

This extremely rare and curious poem abounds in extravagant hyperbole, though by no means remarkable for poetic talent. The following lines are a fair specimen:

"There,
Grov'ling in ashes, with dishev'led hair,
Smiting her breast, *black'd* with a *mourning* dress,
Resembling mother *Sion in distress;*
Pitty, the Church of Middletown *bespeaks*
Set in the midst *of swoons and sobs and shrieks.*
With Bowells full of *it* I hastned to
The *Wet place,* asking *why she grieved so?*
And had this Answer:
Sir, *ask* you this? Are you a Sojourner
Within *New-England's* bounds and know *not why?*
I've lost great COLLINS, man! O that, O there,
From this *Tears-Fountain* is my misery."

[MATHER.] Eleutheria: | or, | An Idea of the Reformation | In | England: | and | A History of Non-Conformity in | and since that Reformation. | With Predictions of a more glorious | Reformation and Revolution at | hand. Written in the year 1696. | Mostly compiled and maintain'd from unexceptionable Writings of Conformable Di- | vines in the Church of England. | To which is added, | The Conformists Reasons for joining with the | Nonconformists in Divine Worship. | By another Hand. | *London.* | *Printed for J. R. and sold by Sam. Phillips Bookseller | at Boston in New-England.* 1698. 8vo, pp. iv, 135. B., BA., M., W. 46301

[MATHER.] Elijah's Mantle. *See* [Mitchel (J.)], *and others.*

MATHER. Elizabeth in her Holy Retirement; an Essay to prepare a Pious Woman for her Lying-in. *Boston: N. Boone.* 1710. 12mo. 46302

Title from an English auctioneer's catalogue. I find no other trace of the work.

[MATHER.] El-Shaddai. | A brief Essay, | on | All Supplied in an Alsufficient | Saviour. | Produced by the Death | Of ... Mrs. Katharin Willard, | ... . | *Boston, in N. E.: Printed by B. Green.* 1725. 8vo, pp. (2), ii, 25. BA. 46303

[MATHER.] An Epistle | To the Christian | Indians, | Giving them | A Short Account, of what the | English | Desire them to Know and to Do, | In order to their Happiness. | Written by an English Minister, at the | Desire of an English Magistrate, | who sends unto them this | Token of Love. | *Boston, | Printed by Bartholomew Green, and | John Allen.* 1700. Sm. 8vo, pp. (4), (28).

+ The Second Edition. | *Boston,* | *Printed by Bartholomew Green.* | 1706. 8vo, pp. (4), (28). H., M. 46304

Recto of each leaf in English, verso in Indian.

MATHER. An Essay on Remarkables in the Way of wicked Men. *Boston.* 1723. 46305

Title from Samuel Mather's list. I find no other account of it.

MATHER. An Essay upon the Good that is to be Devised ... by those who desire to Answer the Great End of Life ... . By Cotton Mather. ... *Boston: Massachusetts Sabbath School Society.* 1845. 18mo, pp. 314. H., S. 46306

For the original edition, *see* "Bonifacius," No. 46238, *supra.*

MATHER. Essays to do Good .... By the late Cotton Mather, ... Revised and Improved by George Burder. *London.* 1807. 12mo, pp. 172. + Second Edition. *London.* 1808. 12mo, pp. xii, 167. C. + A New Edition, Improved by George Burder. From the Latest London Edition. *Boston: Printed ... by Lincoln & Edmands.* 1808. 12mo, pp. 148. BA. + *New-York: Whiting and Watson.* 1815. 18mo, pp. 132. S. + *Johnstown: Printed ... by Asa Child.* 1815. 12mo, pp. 195, (1). H. + *London: Williams and Son.* 1816. 12mo. + *New-York: American Tract Society* [*about* 1820]. 24mo, pp. 108. H. + *Lexington, Ky.* 1823. 12mo. + *London: Francis Westley.* 1824. 12mo, pp. xvi, 215. + *Portsmouth.* [*N. H.*] 1824. 12mo, pp. 148. + *Glasgow: Chalmers and Collins.* 1825. 12mo, pp. xc, 31–214. BA. + *Dover: Samuel C. Stevens.* 1826. 12mo, pp. 148. + *Lexington, Ky.: T. T. Spillman.* 1829. 12mo, pp. 238. 46307

See Sparks' "Franklin," x. 83. For the first edition, *see* "Bonifacius," No. 46238.

MATHER. Ευρηκα. Or a Virtuous Woman found. An Essay on the Death of Mrs. Mary Brown. *Boston.* 1703. 8vo.

[MATHER.] Euthanasia. | A | Sudden Death | Made | Happy and Easy | to the | Dying Believer. | Exemplified in | John Frizell, Esq; | Who so Expired, April 10. 1723. | ... | *Boston: Printed by S. Kneeland.* MDCCXXIII. 8vo, pp. (4), 27. B., H. 46309

MATHER. The Everlasting Gospel. | The Gospel of | Justification | By the | Righteousness of God; | As 'tis | Held and Preach'd in the Churches | of New-England: Expressed in | a Brief Discourse on that | Important Article; made at Boston | in the Year, 1699, | by Cotton Mather. | ... | *Boston: Printed by B. Green, and*

J. Allen, for Nicholas Buttolph .... 1700. 12mo, pp. (32), 76. B. + Second Edition. *Philadelphia.* 1767. 18mo. 46310

Dedicated "To the Reverend Ministers ... in London, sometimes honoured with the Name of United Brethren." For a later edition, *see* "Gospel of Justification."

MATHER. The Evident Tokens of Salvation. *Boston.* 1727. 8vo. 46311

Perhaps the same as "Signatus," *infra.*

MATHER. Fair Dealing | between Debtor and Creditor. | A very brief Essay | upon | The Caution to be used, | about coming in to | Debt, | And getting out of it. | Offered at Boston-Lecture; | 5. d. XI. m. 17 15/16. | By Cotton Mather ... . *Boston:* | *Printed by B. Green, for Samuel Gerrish* ... . 1716. 8vo, pp. (2), 30. 46312

MATHER. Fair Weather. Or Considerations to Dispel the Clouds, & Allay the Storms of Discontent. ... Whereto there is prefixed a Catalogue of Sins against all the Commandments ... By Cotton Mather ... . *Boston: Printed by B. Green and John Allen, for Nicholas Buttolph.* 1691. 12mo, pp. (2), 93. + Second Edition. [*Ibid.*] 1694. 46313

Appended (pp. 83–92) is "A Narrative of a Very Tragical Accident, which happened while the foregoing Treatise was in the Press,"—the assault on York, by the Eastern Indians; with an Epitaph on Rev. Shubael Dummer who was killed.

[MATHER.] Faith at Work. | A | Brief and Plain | Essay, | Upon ... | Good Works, | by which | the Faith of a Christian is | to be evidenced. | ... | *Boston in New-England:* | *Printed by B. Green and J. Allen.* | 1697. | Sm. 8vo, pp. 23. H. 46314

[MATHER.] Faith Encouraged. | A | Brief Relation | of a | Strange Impression from | Heaven, on the Minds of some | Jewish Children, | at the City of Berlin, | (in the Upper Saxony.) | And some Remarks, for the | Improvement of so Marvellous an | Occurrence. | *Boston:* | *Printed by J. Allen, for T. Fleet* ... . 1718. | Sm. 8vo, pp. 32. 46315

MATHER. The Faith of the Fathers. | Or, | The Articles of the | True Religion, | All of them Exhibited | In the Express Words of the | Old Testament. | Partly, | To Confirm those who do not profess that Reli- | gion, and His Messiah. | But Chiefly, | To Engage the Jewish Nation, unto | the Religion of their Patriarchs; | And, Bring down the Hearts of the Fathers into | the Children, and the Disobedient unto the | Wisdom of the Just, and so, To make Ready | a People prepared for the Lord. | By Cotton Mather. | ... | *Boston in New-England. Printed by B. Green, and J. Allen.* 1699. | 8vo, pp. 24. B., H. 46316

MATHER. A Faithful Man, | Described and Rewarded. | Some | Observable & Serviceable | Passages in the | Life and Death | of | Mr. Michael Wigglesworth. | Late Pastor of Maldon; | Who Rested from his Labours, on the | Lords-Day, June 10th. 1705. In the | Seventy Fourth year of his Age. | And | Memorials of Piety, | Left behind him among his Written | Experiences. | With a Funeral Sermon Preached | (for him) at Maldon; June 24. 1705. | By Cotton Mather. | ... | *Boston: Printed by B. Green, for Benj. Eliot.* 1705. 12mo, pp. (6), 48. B., H., M. 46317

"The Dedication," pp. 4, is signed "Increase Mather." The "Written Experiences" fill pp. 27–48. On page 48 is a punning epitaph on Wigglesworth, in verse.

[MATHER.] A Faithful Man described and rewarded. A Sermon preached at Malden, June 24, 1705, occasioned by the Death of that faithful and aged Servant of God, Mr. Michael Wigglesworth. [Second Edition.] *Boston.* 1849. 8vo, pp. 52. + *Boston.* 1850. 8vo, pp. 52. 46318

The title-page erroneously credits this sermon to Increase Mather.

[MATHER.] A Faithful Monitor. | Offering, An | Abstract | of the | Lawes | in the Province of the Massachusett-Bay, | New-England, | Against those Disorders, the Suppression | whereof is desired and persued by them | that wish well to the worthy Designs of | Reformation. | With some Directions and Encouragements, | to dispense due Rebukes, & Censures | unto all Censurable Actions. | ... | *Boston: Printed ... by Timothy Green.* | 1704. Sm. 8vo, pp. 56. H., M. 46319

MATHER. Faithful Warnings to prevent Fearful Judgments. *Boston.* 1704. 8vo, pp. 48. 46320

[MATHER.] The Fall of Babylon. *See* Frontiers, etc. 46332

[MATHER.] Family-Religion, Excited and Assisted. The Second Impression. [*Boston: Reprinted by B. Green.* 1707.] 12mo, pp. 23. + The Third Impression. *Newport: Widow Franklin.* [1740.] Sm. 8vo, pp. 16. + [The Fourth Impression. Colophon: *Boston: Reprinted by S. Kneeland, for S. Gerrish.* 1720.] 8vo, pp. (2), 20. + [Another Impression.] *Boston.* 1727. 8vo. 46321

Also translated into the Massachusetts Indian language. *Boston.* 1714. 16mo, pp. 20. For the first edition, *see* "A Family Sacrifice," No. 46323, the third edition is entitled:

MATHER. Family Religion Urged. ... To which is added, A select number of choice Hymns ... . By Cotton Mather, D.D. ... *Boston.* 1709. 12mo, pp. 24. + The Third Edition. *Boston: Re-printed for D. Henchman.* 1747. 8vo, pp. 23. H. 46322

[MATHER.] A Family Sacrifice. | A | Brief Essay | To | Direct and Excite | Family Religion; | and | Produce the Sacrifices of | Righteousness in our | Families. | *Boston: Printed by B. Green, and* | *J. Allen. Sold by B. Eliot.* 1703. Sm. 8vo, pp. (2), 40.

MATHER. A Family Well-Ordered. | Or | An Essay | To Render | Parents and Children | Happy in one another. | Handling Two very Important | Cases. | I. What are the Duties to be done by Pi- | ous Parents, for the promoting of Pie- | ty in their Children. | II. What are the Duties that must be | paid by Children to their Parents, | that they may obtain the Blessings of | the Dutiful. | By Cotton Mather. | ... | *Boston, Printed by B. Green, & J. Allen, for* | *Michael Perry* ... . 1699. 12mo, pp. 79, 5. B. 46324

At the end is "An Address *Ad Fratres in Eremo,*" of five pages, separately paged.

[MATHER.] Fasciculus Viventium. | Or, | All Good Wishes | in One. | A brief Essay | on, | A Soul Bound up in the Bundle | of Life; ... | *Boston: Printed by T. Fleet, for* | *Alford Butler.* 1726. 8vo, pp. 24. B. 46325

[MATHER.] A Father Departing. | A Sermon | On the Departure of the | Venerable and Memorable | Dr. Increase Mather, | Who Expired Aug. 23. 1723. | In the Eighty Fifth Year of his Age. | By One who, as a Son with a Fa- | ther, served with him in the Gospel. | ... | *Boston:* | *Printed by T. Fleet, for N. Belknap,* ... 1723. 8vo, pp. 31. B., BA. 46326

MATHER. La Fe | del Christiano: | En Veyntequatro Articulos | de la Institucion de Christo. | Embiada | A Los Espanoles, | ... Por C. Mathero, | ... . *Boston.* 1699. Sm. 8vo, pp. 16. H.

See "La Religion Pura," *infra.*

MATHER. Fibufugium. An Essay for the Cure of Ungodly Anger. *Boston.* 1717. 8vo. 46328

From S. Mather's list. Perhaps the same as "The Case of a Troubled Mind," *supra.*

MATHER. The Fisher-man's Calling. A Brief Essay to Serve the Great Interests of Religion among our Fisher-men. By Cotton Mather ... . *Boston: T. Green* 1712. 8vo, pp. (2), iv, 49, (1). 46329

MATHER. A Flying Roll, | Brought forth, to Enter into the House | and Hand of the Thief. | The | Crime & the Doom | Of the Thief declared; | The various Wayes of his | Theft | Detected and Exposed; | And a Repentance demanded | from the Malefactor.

| In a Sermon ... at Boston, | P. M. Lords-Day, 11 d. 11 m. 1712. | By Cotton Mather, D. D. | ... | *Boston in New-England: Printed by B. Green* ... . | 1713. 12mo, pp. (2), 34. B., H., W. 46330

[MATHER.] Free-Grace, Maintained & Improved. | Or, | The General Offer | of the | Gospel, | Managed with Considerations of the | Great Things done by | Special Grace, | in the | Election and Redemption | and Vocation | Of those who Embrace that Offer, | and | The Illustrious Doctrines of Divine | Predestination and Humane | Impotency, Rescued from the Abuses, | which they too frequently meet withal; | And rendered (as they are) highly Useful | to the Designs of Practical Piety. | In Two brief Discourses; | Published at the Desire | of Some, who have been greatly Apprehensive | of Growing Occasions for such Treatises. | *Boston: Printed by B. Green.* 1706. Sm. 8vo, pp. (2), 70. H. 46331

[MATHER.] Frontiers Well-Defended. | An | Essay | to Direct the | Frontiers | of a | Countrey Exposed unto the Incur- | sions of a Barbarous Enemy. | How to behave themselves in their | Uneasy Station? | Containing Admonitions of Piety, | Propos'd by the Compassion of | some Friends unto their Welfare, | to be Lodg'd in the Families of | our Frontier Plantations. | *Boston, in N. E. Printed by T. Green.* | 1707. Sm. 8vo, pp. 52. W. 46332

Usually followed by "The Fall of Babylon," pp. (2), 20.

[MATHER.] Genethlia Pia; Or, Thoughts for a Birth-Day. *Boston.* 1719. 12mo, pp. (2), 37. 46333

MATHER. Genuine Christianity. | Or, | A True Christian | Both in Life and in Death, | Glorifying the ... Lord. | A Sermon, | On the Departure of | Mrs. Frances Webb, ... September 14. 1721. ... | By C. Mather ... . | *Boston: Printed by S. Kneeland, for S. Gerrish.* 1721. 8vo, pp. (4), 20. B. 46334

[MATHER.] A Glorious Espousal. A Brief Essay to Illustrate the Marriage, wherein Our Great Saviour offers to Espouse unto Himself the Children of Men; And there upon to Recommend ... a Good Carriage in the Married Life. An Essay ... Seasonably to be presented, where a Marriage is upon a Celebration. *Boston: Printed by S. Kneeland, for B. Gray.* 1719. 12mo, pp. (2), 46. 46335

MATHER. The Glorious Throne. | A Short View of Our Great | Lord-Redeemer, | ... Ordering ... all the | Changes in the World: | ... Particularly, ... in the Death of Our ... | Sovereign, | and the ... | Succession of the British Crown, | to the Illustrious

House of | Hanover. | ... A Sermon ... | at Boston in New-England, | on 23 d. VII m. 1714. | By Cotton Mather ... . *Boston: Printed by B. Green.* 1714. Sm. 8vo, pp. (2), 37. B. 46336

MATHER. The Glory of Goodness, in the Redemption of the English in Barbary. *Boston.* 1703. 8vo, pp. 51. 46337

Title from Thomas' "History of Printing," Vol. II.

MATHER. A Golden Curb, | For the Mouth, which ... | Rushes into the Sins of Profane | Swearing and Cursing. | ... [*Boston: John Allen.* 1709.] 12mo, pp. 12. H. 46338

"You Disguise, you Curtail, you Abbreviate your Swearing: As *Dod;* and many other such Strokes in the Jargon of Oath-mongers ... This is a poor Evasion. What is it, that these Fictitious words Originally Signify? In these *Mongrel Oathes,* your *God us,* is as much as to say, *By God's Soul.* Your *Ods me,* is as much as to say, *As God sees me.* *'Slife,* is as much as to say, *By God's Life.* *'Zounds,* is as much as to say, *By God's Wounds.* Yea, when you say, *Marry,* 'tis, *By Saint Mary.* And thus for the rest." (p. 10.) "The Golden Curb: or, Sober Checks given to Rash Passions," was the title of another work of Mather's (published in "Batteries upon the Kingdom of the Devil," 1695), No. 46230, *supra.*

MATHER. Golgotha. | A Lively | Description of Death. | With | Such Thoughts, as are to | be Entertained by Men, that | they may not Perish, in that | very Day, when the Thoughts of | Men do Perish. | Occasioned | By some fresh Instances of | Early Mortality. | With | A more particular Memorial | of One of them; Namely, | Mr. Recompence Wadsworth, a | late School-Master in Boston. | By Cotton Mather, D.D. | ... | *Boston in N. E. Printed by B. Green, for* | *Daniel Henchman* ... . 1713. 12mo, pp. (2), 46.

[MATHER.] A Good Character. | Or, A Walk with God | Characterized. | With some Dues paid unto the | Memory of | Mr. Joseph Belcher, | The late Reverend & Excellent Pastor | of Dedham, who Expired April 27, 1723. | By One of the Ministers in Boston. | ... | With an Elegy by the Reverend Mr. John Danforth. | *Boston, N. E.* | *Printed by B. Green.* 1723. 8vo, pp. (2), 24. B.

[MATHER.] A Good Evening for the Best | of Dayes. | An Essay, | To Manage an | Action of Trespass, | against | Those who Mispend the | Lords-Day | Evening, | In such Things as have a Tendency to | Defeat the Good of the Day. | A Sermon ... in the Audience | of the General Assembly, | at Boston, 4 d. 9 m. 1708. | ... | *Boston: Printed by B. Green.* 1708. 8vo, pp. (6), 26. C., H.

[MATHER.] Good fetch'd out of Evil. A Collection of Memorables relating to our Captives. *Boston.* 46342

Title from an imperfect copy in the Boston Public Library

[MATHER.] Good Lessons for Children; in Verse. *Boston.* 1706. Sm. 8vo. 46343

MATHER. A Good Man making a Good End. | The | Life and Death, | of the Reverend | Mr. John Baily, | ... in a | Sermon, | On the Day of his Funeral, | ... 16 d. 10 m. 1697. | By Cotton Mather. | ... *Boston in N. E.:* | *Printed by B. Green* ... . 1698. Sm. 8vo, pp. 88. BA. 46344

MATHER. A Good Master Well Served. | A Brief | Discourse | on the Necessary | Properties & Practices | Of a Good | Servant | In every Kind of Servitude; And of the | Methods that should be taken by the | Heads of a Family, to Obtain such | a Servant. | By Cotton Mather. | ... | *Boston in New England.* | *Printed by B. Green, and J. Allen.* 1696. Sm. 8vo, pp. 55, (1). M., W.

[MATHER.] A Good Old Age. | A Brief Essay | on | The Glory | of | Aged Piety. | ... | *Boston: Printed by S. Kneeland and T. Green, for S. Gerrish.* 1726. Sm. 8vo, pp. (2), 42. B., H.

[MATHER.] The Good Old Way. | Or, | Christianity | Described, | From the Glorious Lustre of it, | Appearing | In the Lives of the | Primitive Christians. | An Essay | Tending, from Illustrious Examples | of a Sober, & a Righteous, | and a Godly Life, Occurring | In the Ancient Church- | History, to Revive the | Languishing Interests of Genuine | and Practical Christianity. | ... | *Boston: Printed by B. Green,* | *for Benj. Eliot* ... . 1706. 12mo, pp. (2), 94.

MATHER. Gospel for the Poor. *Boston.* 1697. Sm. 8vo.

MATHER. The Gospel of Justification by the Righteousness of God. By Cotton Mather. *Wilmington: Printed by Bonsal & Niles.* [n. d.] 12mo, pp. 60. B. 46349

First published under the title of "The Everlasting Gospel," No. 46310, *supra.*

MATHER. Grace Defended. | A Censure | on ... Ungodliness, ... A Sermon Preached on the | Twenty fifth Day of December, 1712. | Containing Some Seasonable | Admonitions of Piety. | And Concluded, with a brief Dissertation | on ... the Penitent Thief on the Cross ... . | By Cotton Mather, D.D. ... | *Boston: Printed by B. Green, for Samuel Gerrish.* 1712. 8vo, pp. (2), 35, (2). B.

"We lay the charges of God upon you, that if any People take *this Time,* for any thing of a *riotous tendency,* you do not associate with them in such *Ungodliness.* ... The Grace of God in sending us a Great Saviour calls for more Pious Acknowledgments" (p. 20). "One of the earliest—perhaps the first—*Christmas Sermon* preached from a puritan pulpit in New England."—J. H. TRUMBULL.

[MATHER.] The Grand Point of Solicitude. A very brief Essay upon Divine Desertions; the Symptoms of them, and The Methods of Preventing them. A Sermon Published for the Service of Others, by One of the Hearers, more particularly affected in the Hearing of it. *Boston: Printed by B. Green.* 1715. 12mo, pp. (2), 31. 46351

MATHER. Grata Brevitas. | An Essay | Made in a Few Words, | To demonstrate that a | Few Words | May Have | Much comprised in them. | With | The most Weighty Matters of | Religion, offered in general | Abridgments, as particular | Demonstrations of it. | A Winter-Sermon Preached at | Boston-Lecture 27. d. 9. m. 1712. | By Cotton Mather, D.D. | ... | *Boston: Printed by B. Green, for Samuel* | *Gerrish* ... . 1712. 12mo, pp. (2), 20. H. 46352

MATHER. Great Consolations; Or a Tempted Christian Triumphing over his Temptations. *Boston.* 1703. 8vo. 46353

[MATHER.] The Greatest Concern in the World. A Short and Plain Essay to answer [the] Enquiry, What must I do to be Saved? The Second Edition. *New London: Printed by T. Green.* 1718. 8vo, pp. (2), 22. 46354

The first edition was printed in 1707. *See* S. Mather's list.

MATHER. Hades Look'd into. | The Power of Our Great | Saviour | Over the | Invisible World, | and the | Gates of Death | which lead into that World. | Considered, In | A Sermon | Preached at the Funeral | of the Honourable, | Wait Winthrop Esq; | Who Expired, 7 d. IX m. 1717. | In the LXXVI Year of his Age. | By C. Mather ... . *Boston: Printed by T. Crump,* 1717. 8vo, pp. (2), vi, 46. W. 46355

The preface is by Increase Mather.

[MATHER.] Hatzar-Maveth. | Comfortable Words; | In a Short Essay | on | The Comforts | Of One ... | Walking through the Valley | of the | Shadow of Death; | ... | *Boston.* 1726. 12mo, pp. (4), 28. B., W. 46356

[MATHER.] The Heavenly Conversation, | An Essay | upon the Methods of Conversing | With a Glorious | Christ, | In Every Step of our Life. | ... *Boston.* 1710? 18mo, pp. (2), 14. 46357

Title taken from a copy with the imprint torn off.

MATHER. Help for Distressed Parents. Sermon at Lecture, Boston, Dec. 14, 1694. *Boston.* 1695. Sm. 8vo, pp. 62, (2).

MATHER. Hezekiah. A Christian armed with Strength. Sermon at the Boston Lecture, Nov. 26, 1713. *Boston.* 1713. 12mo, pp. 37. 46359

MATHER. The High Attainment. A Discourse on Resignation. *Boston.* 1703. 8vo. 46360

[MATHER.] Honesta Parsimonia; Or, Time Spent as it should be. Proposals, To prevent that Great Folly and Mischief, The Loss of Time; And Employ the Talent of Time So Watchfully and Fruitfully that a Good Account may at Last be given of it. *Boston: Printed by S. Kneeland, for J. Edwards* ... . 172[2?] 12mo, pp. (4), 23. W. 46361

MATHER. Hor-Hagidgad. | An Essay | upon, | An Happy Departure. | Occasioned | By the Decease of the Valuable | Mr. William Waldron, | Late Pastor to one of the Churches in | Boston; | Who Departed, Sept. 11. 1727. | By Cotton Mather, D.D. | and F.R.S. | ... | *Boston: ... S. Gerrish* ... . 1727. 8vo, pp. (4), 8, 28.

[MATHER.] Humiliations followed with Deliverances. ... With an Appendix containing a Narrative of Wonderful Passages relating to the Captivity and Deliverance of Hannah Swarton. *Boston: Printed by Joseph Wheeler.* 1697. 12mo, pp. 72.

MATHER. Icono-clastes. | An Essay | upon the | Idolatry, | too often committed under the | Profession of the | most Reformed | Christianity; | And a Discovery of the | Idols which all | Christians are | Every where in danger of. | By Cotton Mather ... . *Boston: Printed by John Allen.* | 1717. | 24mo, pp. (8), 37. H. 46364

[MATHER.] Ignorantia Scientifica. | A brief Essay | On | Mans not knowing his | Time: | The | Just Inferences from it, | And the | Great Advantages of it. | Upon a Special and Mournful | Occasion. | ... | *Boston in N. E.* | *Printed by B. Green, for Samuel Gerrish,* | ... 1727. Sm. 8vo, pp. (4), 24. B., H. 46365

MATHER. The Impenitent Sinner disarmed of his Plea. *Boston.* 1706. 8vo. 46366

MATHER. India Christiana. | A Discourse, | Delivered unto the | Commissioners, | for the | Propagation of the Gospel among | the American Indians. | Which is | Accompanied with several Instru- | ments relating to the Glorious | Design of Propagating our Holy | Religion, in the Eastern | as well as the Western, Indies. | An Entertainment which they that are | Waiting for the Kingdom of God | will receive as Good News | from a far Country. | By

Cotton Mather, D.D. | and F.R.S. | *Boston in New-England:* | *Printed by B. Green.* 1721. Sm. 8vo, pp. (2), ii, 94, (1). B., H., P.

The "Corrigenda," at the end, is usually wanting. "That the more Curious may have a Taste of the Language wherein" the Indians are instructed in Religion, Mather prints (pp. 52–55, *doubled,*) "The Religion which all good men are united in," in *Indian*, with English translation opposite.

[MATHER.] Insanabilia; | or an | Essay | Upon | Incurables; | Handling that Case, | What shall People do under | their Griefs, when there is | no Curing of them? | And Aimed at the | Comfort and Counsil | Of the many, who Encounter those | Grievous Things, | For which there is no Remedy | but | Patience. | ... | *Boston: Printed by T. Fleet, for Samuel Gerrish* ... . 1714. 12mo, pp. 48. 46368

[MATHER.] Instructions to the Living, | from the Condition of the | Dead. | A Brief Relation of Remarka- | bles in the Shipwreck of a- | bove One Hundred Pirates, | Who were cast away in the Ship | Whido, on the Coast of New- | England, April 26. 1717. | And in the Death of Six, who af- | ter a Fair Trial at Boston, were | Convicted & Condemned, Octob. | 22. And executed, Novemb. 15. | 1717. With some Account of | the Discourse had with them on | the way to their Execution. | And a Sermon Preached on | their Occasion. | *Boston: Printed by John Allen, for Nicholas Boone* ... . 1717. Sm. 8vo, pp. 64. M. 46369

MATHER. Jedidiah: Or a Favorite of Heaven Described. *Boston.* 1703. Sm. 8vo. 46370

MATHER. Johannes in Eremo. | Memoirs, Relating to the | Lives, | of the | Ever-Memorable, | Mr. John Cotton, | Who Dyed, 23. d. 10. m. 1652. | Mr. John Norton, | Who Dyed, 5. d. 2. m. 1663. | Mr. John Wilson, | Who Dyed, 7. d. 6. m. 1667. | Mr. John Davenport, | Who Dyed, 15. d. 1. m. 1670. | Reverend and Renowned Ministers of the | Gospel, All, in the more Immediate Service | of One Church, in Boston; | and | Mr. Thomas Hooker, | Who Dyed, 7. d. 5. m. 1647, | Pastor of the Church at Hartford, New-England. | Written by Cotton Mather. | ... | [*Boston:*] ... *Michael Perry* ... . 1695. Sm. 8vo, pp. 32, 80, 39, 46, 30, 45, (2)

"To the Reader," 10 pp., by Increase Mather. After the Introduction, is the Advertisement of the author's projected "Church History of New England" (the "Magnalia"), with "A Schæme of the Whole Work" (pp. 28–32).

MATHER. Juga Jucunda. | A Brief Essay | to Obtain from | Young People, | An Early ... Submission | to the | Yoke of their Saviour ... . | With a Relation of the ... Dying Hours of Mrs.

Abiel Goodwin; ... . The Second Edition. *Boston: D. Henchman.* 1728. 8vo, pp. (4), 36. 46372

For the first edition, *see* Mather's "Some Remarkables," *infra.*

[MATHER.] Just Commemorations. | The Death | of | Good Men, Considered; | and | The Characters | of Some who | have lately Died in the Service of | the Churches, Exhibited. | Unto which is added, | A Brief Account of the Evangelical | Work among the Christianized | Indians of New England; | Whereof One of the Persons here | Commemorated, was a Valuable | and Memorable Instrument. | ... | *Boston in N. E. Printed by B. Green:* ... [1715.] Sm. 8vo, pp. (2), iv, 58. C., H., M. 46373

Another issue has the date on page 58. This is a funeral sermon on John Cotton and Grindal Rawson. "The Appendix contains an account of the Progress of the Gospel among the Indians, from Eliot's death to 1715."—G. BRINLEY.

[MATHER.] Lampadarius. | A very Brief Essay, | To Show the | Light, | Which Good Men have in | Dark Hours | Arising to them. | ... | *Boston: Printed in the Year* 1726. 12mo, pp. 24. B.

[MATHER.] Lapis e Monte. *See* "The Stone cut," *infra.*

MATHER. Late | Memorable Providences | Relating to | Witchcrafts and Possessions, | Clearly Manifesting, | Not only that there are Witches, but | that Good Men (as well as others) | may possibly have their Lives shortned | by such evil Instruments of Satan. | Written by Cotton Mather Minister of the | Gospel at Boston in New-England. | The Second Impression. | Recommended by the Reverend Mr. Richard | Baxter in London, and by the Ministers of | Boston and Charlestown in New-England. | *London,* | *Printed for Tho. Parkhurst* ... . 1691. Sm. 8vo, pp. (22), 144. B. 46375

One of the earliest American works referring to the subject. "The latest witchcraft frenzy was in New England in 1692, when the execution of witches became a calamity more dreadful than the sword or the pestilence."—ROBINSON'S *Theol. Dict.* For the First Impression, *see* Mather's "Memorable Providences," No. 46407, *infra.*

[MATHER.] A Letter | About a Good Management under the Distemper of the Measles, at | this time Spreading in the Country. Here Published for the Benefit of | the Poor, and such as may want the Help of Able Physicians. | [*Boston.* 1713.] Folio, pp. 4.

[MATHER.] A | Letter of Advice | to the | Churches | of the | Non-Conformists | in the | English Nation: | Endeavouring their Satisfaction in that Point, | Who are the True Church of England? | ... | *London,* | *Printed, and sold by A. Baldwin* ... . 1700. 4to, pp. (4), 30. 46377

Signed "Philalethes," one of Mather's pseudonyms.

MATHER. Letter on the Character of the Inhabitants of New England, and of Col. Shute, their Governor, Nov. 4, 1718. [*Boston.* 1718.] Folio, 1 leaf. H. 46378

[MATHER.] A | Letter | to a | Friend in the Country, | Attempting a Solution of the | Scruples & Objections ... | against the New Way of | receiving the Small-Pox. | By a Minister in Boston. | ... | *Boston: Printed by S. Kneeland, for* | *S. Gerrish.* | MDCCXXI. | 12mo, pp. (2), 13. H. 46379

[MATHER.] A Letter to the Ungospellized Plantations. Briefly Representing the Excellency and Necessity of a People's Enjoying the Gospel of the Lord Jesus Christ among them. *Boston: Printed by B. Green & J. Allen.* 1702. 8vo, pp. 16.

[MATHER.] Lex Mercatoria. | Or, The Just Rules | of | Commerce | Declared. | And Offences against the Rules of | Justice ... Detected. | ... Given ... [before] the General Assembly of the | Province of the Massachusetts-Bay, ... Nov. 9. 1704. | ... | *Boston: Printed ... by Timothy Green.* 1704. Sm. 8vo, pp. 40. BA.

MATHER. The | Life and Death | Of The Renown'd | Mr. John Eliot, | Who was the | First Preacher | of the | Gospel | to the | Indians in America. | With an Account of the Wonderful Success which the Gospel has had amongst the Hea- | then in that part of the World: And of the | many strange Customes of the Pagan Indians, | In New-England. | Written by Cotton Mather. | .. | The Second Edition carefully Corrected. | *London:* | *Printed for John Dunton* ... . M DC XCI. | Sm. 8vo, pp. (6), 138. 46382

For the first edition, *see* "The Triumphs of the Reformed Religion," *infra.*

MATHER. The | Life and Death | of the Reverend | Mr. John Eliot, | Who was the | First Preacher | of the | Gospel | to the | Indians in America. | With an Account of the Wonderful Success | which the Gospel has had amongst the Heathen | in that Part of the World: And of the many | strange Customs of the Pagan Indians, | In New-England. | Written by Cotton Mather. | The Third Edition carefully Corrected. | *London:* | *Printed for John Dunton* ... . MDCXCIV. Sm. 8vo, pp. (8), 168, (4). 46383

MATHER. The Life of the Rev. John Eliot, the First Missionary to the Indians in North-America. By Cotton Mather. A New Edition. *London: D. Jaques* ... . 1820. 18mo, pp. (4), 112. 46384

MATHER. The Life of Mr. Thomas Dudley, several times Governor of ... Massachusetts. Written, as is supposed, By Cotton Mather. Edited by Charles Deane. *Cambridge: John Wilson and Son.* 1870. 8vo, pp. 20. BA. 46385

MATHER. A Life of Piety Resolv'd upon. | A brief and plain | Essay, | Upon, A Life of Religion, | in, | A Walk before the Glorious God. | And the | Resolutions | Wherewith such a Walk | is to be come into. | Made, upon the Death of that | Honourable and Religious | Gentlewoman, | Mrs. Sarah Thig; | Who after many Steps in that | Walk, arrived unto the | Blessed End of it; | 28. d. 12. m. 1713, 14. | By Cotton Mather, D.D. | ... | *Boston: Printed by John Allen,* | *for Michael Boone* ... . 1714. 12mo, pp. (2), 34.

MATHER. Life swiftly Passing and quickly Ending. | A ... | Sermon, | ... after the Death of Mrs. Mehitable Gerrish, | ... Who died 111 d. XI m. 1715–16. ... | By C. Mather ... . | *Boston: Printed by T. Fleet and T. Crump.* | 1715–16. | Sm. 8vo, pp. 20. H.

[MATHER.] Light in Darkness. | An Essay | On the | Piety | Which by Remembring the | Many Days of Darkness, | Will Change them into a | Marvellous Light. | With a Notable Example of it, in a | Young Person | Mrs. Rebeckah Burnel, | ... . | *Boston: Printed by S. Kneeland, for Nath.* | *Belknap.* 1724. 8vo, pp. (4), 20

MATHER. Little Flocks Guarded against | Grievous Wolves. | An Address | Unto those Parts of New-England which are | most Exposed unto Assaults, from the Mo- | dern Teachers of the misled Quakers. | In a Letter, | Which impartially Discovers the manifold Hai- | resies and Blasphemies, and the Strong De- | lusions of even the most Refined | Quakerism; | And thereupon Demonstrates the Truth of those | Principles and Assertions, which are most | opposite thereunto. | With just Reflections upon the extream Igno- | rance and Wickedness, of George | Keith, Who is the Seducer that | now most Ravines upon the | Churches in this Wilderness. | Written by Cotton Mather. | ... | *Boston: Printed by Benjamin Harris, & John* | *Allen* ... . 1691. 8vo, pp. (2), 110.

[MATHER.] The Lord-High-Admiral | of all the Seas, Adored. | A Brief Essay | upon the | Miracle of our Saviour | Walking upon the Water. | ... | *Boston: Printed by S. Kneeland.* MDCCXXIII. | 12mo, pp. (2), 22. BA. 46390

[MATHER.] Love Triumphant. | A | Sermon | at the Gathering | of a | New Church, | And the | Ordaining | Of their | Pastor; | In the North Part of Boston; | May 23. 1722. | With Copies of other

Things Offered in the | Publick Actions of that Solemn Occasion. | ... | *Boston: Printed by S. Kneeland, for Nath. Belknap* ... . 1722. Sm. 8vo, pp. (4), 39. H. 46391

MATHER. Magnalia Christi Americana: | or, the | Ecclesiastical History | of | New-England, | from | Its First Planting in the Year 1620. unto the Year | of our Lord, 1698. | In Seven Books. | I. Antiquities: In Seven Chapters. With an Appendix. | II. Containing the Lives of the Governours, and Names of the Magistrates | of New-England: In Thirteen Chapters. With an Appendix. | III. The Lives of Sixty Famous Divines, by whose Ministry the Churches of | New-England have been Planted and Continued. | IV. An Account of the University of Cambridge in New-England; in Two | Parts. The First contains the Laws, the Benefactors, and Vicissitudes of | Harvard College; with Remarks upon it. The Second Part contains the Lives | of some Eminent Persons Educated in it. | V. Acts and Monuments of the Faith and Order in the Churches of New-Eng- | land, passed in their Synods; with Historical Remarks upon those Venerable | Assemblies; and a great Variety of Church-Cases occurring, and resolved by | the Synods of those Churches: In Four Parts. | VI. A Faithful Record of many Illustrious, Wonderful Providences, both | of Mercies and Judgments, on divers Persons in New-England: In Eight | Chapters. | VII. The Wars of the Lord. Being an History of the Manifold Afflictions and | Disturbances of the Churches in New-England, from their Various Adversa- | ries, and the Wonderful Methods and Mercies of God in their Deliverance: | In Six Chapters: To which is subjoined, An Appendix of Remarkable | Occurrences which New-England had in the Wars with the Indian Salvages, | from the Year 1688, to the Year 1698. | By the Reverend and Learned Cotton Mather, M.A. | ... | *London:* | *Printed for Thomas Parkhurst,* ... MDCCII. Folio, pp. (30), 38; (2), 75; (2), 238; (2), 125–222; 100; (2), 88; 118, Errata, (2). Map. B., H., P. 46392

A leaf of "Books printed for Thomas Parkhurst" sometimes precedes the title-page, and another leaf of advertisements follows the text. The map is often wanting, or supplied by a facsimile lithographed by Messrs. Day & Sons. There are copies on large paper. "To those who are interested in the early history of our country, it may be well to remark, that for accuracy in historical occurrences they will do well to rely upon other authorities; but if they wish to obtain a general view of the state of society and manners, they will probably nowhere find so many materials for this purpose, as in the work of this pedantic and garrulous writer." "One of the most singular books in this or any other language. Its puns and its poems, its sermons and its anagrams, render it unique in its kind."—SOUTHEY in the *Quarterly Review.* "Liber quidem superstitionis plenus, utilis tamen illis, qui nasum habent."—MEUSEL. *See also* "N. A. Rev.," VI. 255.

MATHER. Magnalia Christi Americana: or, the Ecclesiastical History of New England, from its First Planting in the year 1620, ... to 1698. ... First American Edition, from the London Edition of 1702. *Hartford: Roberts & Burr, Printers.* 1820. 2 vols., 8vo, pp. 573; 595. H. + *Hartford: Silas Andrus and Son.* 1855. 2 vols., 8vo, pp. xli, (2), 13–626; 682. Portraits. BA. + With a Memoir and Index. *Hartford.* 1870. 2 vols., 8vo. Portrait. 46393

Some copies of the edition of 1820 have the imprint, *Hartford: Silas Andrus.*

[MATHER.] Malachi. Or, The Everlasting Gospel Preached unto the Nations. And those Maxims of Piety, which are to be the Glorious Rules of Behaviour, The Only Terms of Communion, and The Happy Stops to Controversy, among all that Moved. Meet and Serve those Advances which the Kingdom of God is Now Making in the World ... . *Boston: Printed by T. C[rump] for Robert Starke* ... 1717. Sm. 8vo, pp. (2), 93. W.

MATHER. Man Eating the Food of | Angels. | The | Gospel | of the | Manna, | To be Gathered in the | Morning. | With diverse famous & wondrous | Examples of Early Piety, | Especially, the Surprising History, | of Christlieb Leberecht Von Extor, | Late Son to the Physician of the | King of Prussia. | Delivered, part of it, in Boston-Lecture; | part of it on another Occasion. | By C. Mather, D.D. | ... | *Boston: ... Benj. Eliot.* 1710. 12mo, pp. (2), 85, (1). B. 46395

[MATHER.] The Man of God Furnished. | The | Way of Truth, | Laid out, with a Threefold | Catechism, | ... | To which are added; Several other In- | struments of Piety; To Serve the | great Interests of Religion; which ly near | to the Hearts of all Faithful Ministers | and all Godly Householders. | Offered unto the Publick Service, by several | Ministers of the Gospel in the | Churches of New-England. | ... [With "Supplies," etc.] *Boston: Printed by B. Green, for Samuel* | *Phillips* ... . 1708. 24mo, pp. (2), 140, (2). 46396

Of extreme rarity. The "Supplies," etc., commences at page 47, with a title-page of its own. For a second edition, *see* "The Way of Truth," *infra.*

[MATHER.] A Man of his Word. A very brief Essay, on Fidelity In Keeping of Promises and Engagements ... Boston-Lecture; in the Audience of his Excellency the Governour, and of the General Assembly 11 d. 4 m. 1713. *Boston: Printed by John Allen, for N. Boone.* 1713. 8vo, pp. (2), 22. W. 46397

[MATHER.] A Man of Reason. | A Brief Essay | to demonstrate, | That all Men should hearken to | Reason; | And | What a World of Evil would | be prevented in the World, if | Men would once become so Reasonable. | ... | *Boston: in N. E.* | *Printed for John Edwards* ... . 1718. 12mo, pp. (2), 34. M. 46398

[MATHER.] Manly Christianity. | A brief | Essay | on the | Signs of Good Growth | and Strength | In ... | Christianity. | ... | *London: For Ralph Smith.* | 1711. | Sm. 8vo, pp. 34. H., W. 46399

[MATHER.] Manuductio ad Ministerium. | Directions | for a | Candidate | of the | Ministry. | Wherein, First, a Right Founda- | tion is laid for his Future Improvement; | And, Then, | Rules are Offered for such a Ma- | nagement of his Academical & Preparatory | Studies; | And thereupon, | For such a Conduct after his | Appearance in the World; as may | Render him a Skilful and Useful | Minister of the Gospel. | ... | *Boston, Printed for Thomas Hancock* ... . 1726. 8vo, pp. (2), xviii, (2), 151. H. 46400

On pp. 148–149 is a short English poem, entitled, "Filii, quum legisset, Gratulatio," signed "S. Mather." For a later edition, *see* "Student and Preacher," *infra.*

[MATHER.] Marah Spoken to. A Brief Essay to do Good unto the Widow. By one of the Ministers of Boston. *Boston.* 1716. 8vo. + Second Edition. With a Preface by Increase Mather. [*Ibid.*] 1721. 8vo. 46401

[MATHER.] The Marrow of the | Gospel. | A very brief | Essay, | on the | Union | Between the | Redeemer | And the | Beleever. | ... | *Boston: ... N. Belknap* ... . 1727. 8vo, pp. 24. B. 46402

[MATHER.] Maschil, | Or, | The Faithful Instructor. | Offering, | Memorials of Christianity | In Twenty-Six | Exercises | Upon the New-English Catechism. | ... | *Boston: Printed by B. Green and J. Allen, for Samuel Phillips.* 1702. 8vo, pp. 192. B. 46403

MATHER. Maternal Consolations. | An Essay | on | The Consolations | of God | whereof, | A Man whom his Mother | comforteth ... on the Death of | Mrs. Maria Mather | the Consort of the Eminent | Dr. Increase Mather ... . | By Cotton Mather ... | *Boston: Printed by T. Fleet, for Samuel* | *Gerrish* ... . 1714. 12mo, pp. 44, (4). 46404

MATHER. Meat out of the Eater. | Or, Funeral-Discourses, | Occasioned By the Death of several | Relatives. | ... | By Cotton Mather. ... *Boston: Benjamin Eliot.* | 1703. | 24mo, pp. (6), 222.

[MATHER.] Memoirs | of the | Life | of the late Reverend | Increase Mather, D.D. | Who died August 23, 1723. | With a Preface by the Reverend Edmund | Calamy, D.D. | *London: | Printed for John Clark and Richard | Hett* ... . MDCCXXV. 8vo, pp. (8), 88. Portrait by R. White. C. 46406

Contains a list of Increase Mather's writings. *See* "Parentator," No. 46447, *infra.*

MATHER. Memorable Providences, | Relating to | Witchcrafts | And Possessions. | A Faithful Account of many Wonderful and Sur- | prising Things, that have befallen several Be- | witched and Possessed Persons in New-England. | Particularly, A Narrative of the marvellous | Trouble and Releef [*sic*], Experienced by a pious Fa- | mily in Boston, very lately and sadly molested | with Evil Spirits. | Whereunto is added, | A Discourse delivered unto a Congregation in | Boston, on the Occasion of that Illustrious Pro- | vidence. As also | A Discourse delivered unto the same Congrega- | tion; on the occasion of an horrible Self-Mur- | der Committed in the Town. | With an Appendix, in vindication of a Chapter | in a late Book of Remarkable Providences, from | the Calumnies of a Quaker at Pen-silvania. | Written By Cotton Mather, Minister of the Gospel. | And Recommended by the Ministers | of Boston and Charleston. | *Printed at Boston in N. England by R. P.* 1689. | *Sold by Joseph Brunning, at his Shop at the Cor- | ner of the Prison-Lane next to the Exchange.* Sm. 8vo, pp. (10), 75, 21, 40, (2), 14. B. 46407

Of extreme rarity. For the Second Impression, *see* "Late Memorable Providences," No. 46375, *supra.* The first of the two appended discourses is "On the Power and Malice of the Devils;" the second is "A Discourse on Witchcraft." The Appendix (pp. 14) contains a reply to George Keith's "Churches in New-England brought to the Test," etc. *See also* "Speedy Repentance urged," No. 46528, *infra.*

MATHER. Memorable Providences, | Relating to | VVitchcrafts and Possessions: | A Faithful Account of many Wonderful and Surprising | Things, that have befallen several Bewitched and Pos- | sessed-Persons in New-England. | Particularly, A Narrative of the marvellous Trouble | and Relief, Experienced by a pious Family in Boston, | very lately and sadly molested with Evil Spirits, | Whereunto is added, | A Discourse delivered unto a Congregation in Boston, on | the Occasion of that Illustrious Providence. | As also, A Discourse delivered unto the same Congre- | gation; on the occasion of an horrible Self-Murder | Committed in the Town. | With an Appendix, in Vindication of a Chapter in a | late Book of Remarkable Providences, from the Ca- | lumnies of a Quaker at Pen-silvania. | Written by Cotton Mather, Minister of

the Gospel. | And Recommended by the Ministers of Boston and Charleston. | *Printed at Boston in New-England, and Re-printed at | Edinburgh by the Heirs and Successors of Andrew An- | derson, Printer to His most Excellent Majesty, Anno Dom.* 1697. Sm. 8vo, pp. (6), 102. J.C.B. 46408

MATHER. Memoria Wilsoniana. | Or, | Some Dues | Unto | The Memory of the | Truly | Reverend & Renowned | Mr. John Wilson, | The First | Pastor of Boston: Who Expired | August 7. 1667. Aged 79. | Paid by Cotton Mather. | ... | *Printed for and Sold by Michael Perry,* | ... *in Boston, in N. E.* 1695. Sm. 8vo, pp. (2), 46. M. 46409

Reprinted in "Johannes in Eremo," No. 46371, *supra.*

[MATHER.] Memorials of Early Piety. | Occurring in the | Holy Life & Joyful Death | of | Mrs. Jerusha Oliver | ... With Some Account of her | Christian Experiences, | Extracted from her ... Papers: | ... | *Boston in N. E.: Printed ... by T. Green.* 1711. 12mo, pp. (4), 54, (1). B. 46410

Mrs. Oliver was one of Cotton Mather's sisters.

MATHER. Menachem. | A very brief Essay, | on | Tokens for Good; | wherein, | Together with the Good Signs | which all Good Men have to | Comfort them, there are Exhibited, | also some | Good Things of a late Occurrence, | ... which have a Comfortable | Aspect on the Protestant Religion ... . A Sermon, | Delivered in an Honourable Audience, | At Boston. | II D. VIII M. 1716. | By Cotton Mather, D.D. ... | *Boston: Benjamin Gray.* 1716. 12mo, pp. 45. B. 46411

MATHER. Mens sana in Corpore sano. A Discourse on Recovery from Sickness. *Boston: Printed by B. Green and J. Allen.* 1698. 12mo, pp. 68. 46412

MATHER. Methods and Motives for a Society to Suppress Disorders. *Boston.* 1703. 8vo, pp. 12. 46413

MATHER. A Midnight Cry. An Essay for our Awakening out of a Sinful Sleep ... A Discourse given on a Day of Prayer, kept by the North-Church in Boston. By Cotton Mather ... . *Boston: Printed by John Allen, for Sam. Phillips.* 1692. 12mo, pp. 72. 46414

"I have ordered a *Small Impression* ... So that perhaps I may say of this Book, as the Philosopher did of his, '*Tis Published, but Scarce made Publick.*'—*Preface.* Excessively rare. It is quoted in the Am. Antiq. Soc. catalogue with the date 1691, which is probably an error.

MATHER. Military Duties, | Recommended | to an | Artillery Company; | at their Election of Officers, | in Charles-town, | 13. d. 7. m. 1686. | By Cotton Mather, Pastor of | a Church in Boston. | ... | *Boston in New England.* | *Printed by Richard Pierce: And are to be sold* | *by Joseph Brunning, at his Shop at the Corner* | *of Prison Lane near the Exchange.* 1687. Sm. 8vo, pp. (8), 78, (2). H.

[MATHER.] The Minister. | A Sermon, | Offer'd unto the | Anniversary Convention | of | Ministers, | From several Parts of | New-England, | Met at Boston, 31 d. III m. | 1722. | By One of their Number. | And published at the Request of them that heard it. | ... | *Boston: Printed in the Year* 1722. 8vo, pp. (2), 45. B., C.

MATHER. Mirabilia Dei. | An Essay | On the very | Seasonable & Remarkable | Interpositions | of the | Divine Providence, | To | Rescue & Relieve | Distressed People, | Brought unto the very Point | of Perishing; Especially relating | to that Twice-Memorable | Fifth of November. | Offered in the Audience of His Ex- | cellency the Governour | and the General Assembly of | the Massachusetts-Province, New-England, On the Fifth of | November. 1719. | By Cotton Mather, DD. & F.R.S. | *Boston: Printed by B. Green,* | *Printer to His Excellency the Go- | vernour & Council.* 1719. 8vo, pp. (2), 34. BA., W. 46417

[MATHER.] Monica Americana. | A | Funeral Sermon, | Occasioned | by the Death of | Mrs. Sarah Leveret, | Once the Honourable Consort of | John Leveret Esq. | Governour of the Massachu- | set-Colony, New-England. | Who changed Earth for Heaven. | 2d. 11m. 1704. | With an Elegy upon her Memory. | ... *Boston:* | *Printed for Samuel Phillips* ... . 1705. 8vo, pp. 32. M.

[MATHER.] A Monitor for Communicants. | An Essay | To Excite and Assist | Religious Approaches | to the | Table of the Lord. | Offered by an Assembly of the New | English Pastors, unto their | own Flocks, and unto all the | Churches in these American Colonies: | ... | *Boston.* 1714. 12mo, pp. 21. W. + *Printed, by T. Fleet and T. Crump, for Samuel Gerrish and Daniel Henchman, and sold at their shops, Boston.* 1715. 12mo, pp. 24. + The Third Edition. [*Ibid.*] 1715. 12mo, pp. 24. H. + The Fourth Edition. *New London: T. Green.* 1732. 12mo, pp. (4), 18. + *Boston.* 1750. 12mo, pp. 21. 46419

[MATHER.] A Monitory, and Hortatory | Letter, | To those English, who debauch the | Indians, | By Selling | Strong Drink

unto them. | ... | *Boston, N. E.: Printed in the Year* 1700. | Sm. 8vo, pp. (2), 16. B., H., W. 46420

[MATHER.] A | Monitory Letter | To them who Needlessly and Frequently | Absent themselves from the | Publick Worship of God. | *Boston.* 1712. 8vo. + The Second Edition. *Boston: Printed by S. Kneeland and T. Green, for D. Henchman.* 1738. 12mo, pp. (4), 17, (2). B., W. 46421

MATHER. Much in Little; or three Brief Essays to sum up the whole Christian Religion. *Boston.* 1702. 12mo. W. 46422

MATHER. The Mystical Marriage. | A Brief Essay, | on, | The Grace of the Redeemer | espousing | The Soul of the Believer. | By the Late Reverend | Dr. Cotton Mather. | Approved by Several Pastors of our Churches ... . *Boston, N. E.:* | *N. Belknap.* | MDCCXXVIII. 12mo, pp. (4), 16. BA. 46423

[MATHER.] Nails Fastened. | Or, | Proposals of Piety | Reasonably and Seasonably | Complyed withal. | A Brief Essay | on | The Conduct | Exposed of such as have | had their Duty Proposed | unto them. | Designed more Particularly to be | Lodg'd and Left, where Pasto- | ral Visits, have Watched for | the Souls of a Gospellized People. | ... | *Boston: ... Joseph Edwards* ... MDCCXXVI. 12mo, pp. (2), 22. B., BA. 46424

[MATHER.] Necessary Admonitions. | Containing | Just Thoughts upon some Sins, | Too Little Thought of, | or, | A Brief Discourse | Concerning | Sins of Omissions. | Made 11 d. 4 m. 1702. | ... | *Boston in N. E.* | *Printed by B. Green, and J. Allen, for | Samuel Phillips* ... . 1702. 12mo, pp. (2), 34. W. 46425

[MATHER.] The | Negro Christianized; | An Essay | to | excite and assist ... | The Instruction | of | Negro-Servants | in Christianity. | ... | *Boston: Printed by B. Green.* 1706. 12mo, pp. (2), 46. B. 46426

MATHER. Nehemiah. | A Brief Essay on | Divine Consolations, | How Great they are; | And | How Great the Regards to be Paid unto them. | With An | Application thereof to Some | frequent Cases; | Especially | The Death of Relatives. | Offered, at the Lecture in Boston. 30 d. 9 m. 1710. | By Cotton Mather, D.D. | ... | *Boston in New-England.* | *Printed by Bartholomew Green.* 1710. 4to, pp. (4), 24. B., H., M. 46427

[MATHER.] Nepenthes Evangelicum. A brief Essay, upon A Soul at Ease ... A Sermon occasion'd by the Death of a Re-

ligious Matron, Mrs. Mary Rock. *Boston: Printed by Thomas Fleet, for D. Henchman.* 1713. 12mo, pp. 48. 46428

Mrs. Rock was the daughter of Rev. John Wilson of Boston, and "one of the First-born, if not the *very First* of her Sex that was born in this famous Metropolis of the English-America: and who deserves to be honourably mentioned as long as *Boston* shall endure, which, I hope, will be unto the Second Coming of our Saviour" (p. 4). The Rev. Samuel Danforth, of Roxbury, was her first husband.

[MATHER.] The Nets of Salvation. A Brief Essay upon the Glorious Designs & Methods of Winning the Minds of Men unto Serious Religion. *New London: Timothy Green.* 1704. 8vo, pp. 56. 46429

At the end, a poem: "The Language of a Soul taken in the Nets of Salvation," pp. 2.

[MATHER.] A New Offer to the Lovers of Religion and Learning. *Boston.* 1713. Sm. 8vo, pp. 16. 46430

The Prospectus of Cotton Mather's "Biblia Americana."

[MATHER.] A New-Year Well-begun. | An | Essay | Offered on | A New-Years-Day; | To Provide a | Good Work for such a Day, | And Advise, | How a Good Year may certainly | follow the Day. | Boston, January 1. 1718–19. | ... | *New-London: | Printed ... by T. Green.* | 1719. 8vo, pp. (4), 29, 1. M. 46431

Dedicated to John Winthrop.

[MATHER.] The Nightingale. | An Essay | on | Songs among Thorns. | Or the | Supports & Comforts | of the | Afflicted Believer. | Thankfully Published by One that | has had Experience of them. | ... | *Boston in New-England:* | *Printed by B. Green.* 1724. 8vo, pp. (4), 19. B. 46432

[MATHER.] Nunc Dimittis, | briefly descanted on. | The Happy Dismission, | of the | Holy Believer, | from | The Work of Earth, to the Joy | of Heaven; | Considered in a | Funeral Sermon, | For that Venerable and Memorable | Servant of Christ, | Mr. John Higginson, | The Aged Pastor of the Church in | Salem; | [with Memoirs of his Life,] | Who, on 9 d. 10 m. 1708. in the Ninety | Third Year of his Age, went from the | Earthly Salem, to the Heavenly. | ... | *Boston in N. E. Printed by B. Green, for | Eleazar Phillips* ... . 1709. | Sm. 8vo, pp. (6), 42. N. 46433

MATHER. Nuncia Bona | e Terra Longinqua. | A Brief Account of some | Good & Great Things | a doing | For the Kingdom of God, | In the Midst of | Europe. | Communicated in a Letter to —— | From Cotton Mather, D.D. & F.R.S. | *Boston in New-England:* | *Printed by B. Green, for Samuel Gerrish* ... . 1715. 8vo, pp. (2), 14. B., BA., N., W. 46434

MATHER. The Obedient Sufferer. *Boston.* 1718. 12mo, pp. 42. 46435

[MATHER.] Observanda. | The | Life and Death | Of the Late | Q. Mary. | Prefaced, with some Observations | upon the Turns of the Divine | Providence, now bringing of | mighty Changes, upon the | World. | Whereto is added, | The Address of Condolence, | made unto His Majesty, | on the Decease of that Illustrious Queen. | *Boston in N. E. Printed by B. Green,* | *for Samuel Phillips* ... . 1695. Sm. 8vo, pp. 56. 46436

MATHER. The Old Man's Honour; or, The Hoary Head found in the Way of Righteousness. ... *Boston.* 1691. 12mo, pp. 122. 46437

[MATHER.] The Old Paths Restored. | In a brief Demonstration | that | the Doctrines of Grace hitherto Pre- | served in the Churches of the Non-Conformists | are not only Assert- | ed in the Sacred Scriptures, but | also in the Articles and Homilies | of the Church of England; | ... | *Boston, Printed and Sold by T. Green,* | ... 1711. 12mo, pp. (2), 25. + ... *Reprinted at London;* | 1712. With a Preface by Will. Whiston, A.M. | *To be sold by A. Baldwin* ... . Sm. 8vo, pp. 12, 24. W. 46438

[MATHER.] The Old Principles of New-England. Or, Thirty-Three Articles Extracted from, and Contracting of, The [Cambridge] Platform of Church-Discipline ... . [*Boston.* 1700?] 8vo, pp. 16. 46439

MATHER. Optanda. | Good Men Described, | and | Good Things propounded. | A | serious Consideration | of | Two very Important Cases: | I. What should be our Spirits, | and | II. | What should be our Studies, | That so | All Things may Go well among us. | By Cotton Mather. | In Two Sermons; | Whereof One was | Preached unto the Governour, | and General Court, of the Pro- | vince of the Massachusetts-Bay, in New- | England; at their First Session: June 9. | 1692. | Published by Authority. | *Boston, Printed and Sold by Benjamim* | *Harris, at the London-Coffee-House.* 1692. Sm. 8vo, pp. (6), 99. H. 46440

[MATHER.] The Order of the Churches in New-England. Vindicated. [*Boston.* 1700?] 12mo, pp. 144. 46441

MATHER. Ornaments for the Daughters of Zion. | Or | The Character and Happiness | of a | Vertuous [*sic*] Woman: | ... A | Discourse | ... . Written By Cotton Mather | ... . *Cambridge:*

Printed by S. G. & B. G., for Samuel Phillips ... . 1691. 12mo, pp. 104, (1). + [*Ibid.*] 1692. 12mo, pp. 104, (1). BA. + *London,* | *Printed for Tho. Parkhurst* ... . 1694. 12mo, pp. (12), 144. + The Third Edition. *Boston: Re-printed ... by S. Kneeland* ... . 1741. 12mo, pp. (4), 116. B. + The Fifth Edition. [*Ibid.*] 1741. 46442

Thomas in his "History of Printing" mentions an edition, 1682.

MATHER. Orphanotrophium. | Or, | Orphans Well-provided for. | An Essay, | On the Care taken in the | Divine Providence | For Children when their | Parents forsake them. | With Proper Advice to both | Parents and Children, that | the Care of Heaven may be the | more Conspicuously & Comforta- | bly Obtained for them. | Offered in a Sermon, on a Day | of Prayer, kept with a Religious | Family, [28 d. 1 m. 1711,] whose | Honourable Parents [John and Abigail Foster] were late- | ly by Mortality taken from them. | By Cotton Mather, D.D. | ... | *Boston: Printed by B. Green.* 1711. 8vo, pp. (4), 68. B., C. 46443

[MATHER.] The Palm-Bearers. | A brief | Relation | of | Patient and Joyful | Sufferings; | and of | Death | ... Triumphed over; | In the History of the Persecution | which the Church of Scotland | suffered, from the Year 1660, to ... 1668. | *Boston: Printed by T. Fleet, for S. Gerrish.* 1725. Sm. 8vo, pp. (2), viii, 58. B., C.

[MATHER.] Parental Wishes and Charges. Or, The Enjoyment of a Glorious Christ, Proposed, as the great Blessedness which Christian Parents desire for themselves, and for their Children ... . *Boston: Printed ... by T. Green.* 1705. 12mo, pp. 60. 46445

With a poem entitled "The Consent."

MATHER. Parentalia. | An Essay | upon the | Blessings and Comforts | Reserved for | Pious Children | after the Death | of their | Pious Parents. | And a Commemoration of Two | such Parents; in a Sermon | Preached on a Time of Prayer, attend- | ed by some Christians in the Neighbour- | hood, with the Children of an Honou- | rable and Religious Family; whose Fa- | ther first, and then at some distance of | Time, their Mother, having been taken | from them. | By Cotton Mather, D.D. F.R.S. | ... | *Boston, Printed by J. Allen, for N. Boone* ... . 1715. 12mo, pp. (2), 34. 46446

[MATHER.] Parentator. | Memoirs | of | Remarkables | in the | Life | and the | Death | of the | Ever-Memorable | Dr. Increase Mather. | Who Expired, August 23. 1723. | ... | *Boston: Printed by*

B. Green, for | *Nathaniel Belknap* ... . 1724. Sm. 8vo, pp. (2), x, xiv, 239, (6). Portrait by Sturt. + *Boston.* 1741. 8vo, pp. 256.

Rewritten and issued as "Memoirs of the Life of the late Reverend Increase Mather," No. 46406, *supra.*

MATHER. Pascentius: | A very brief Essay | upon | The Methods | of | Piety. | Wherein | People in whom the Difficulties of the | Times have caused Anxieties, | may have a Comfortable Assu- | rance of being at all Times | Comfortably Provided for. | Offered | unto the Inhabitants of Boston, at | their Lecture 23. d. x m. 1714. | By C. Mather, D.D. & F.R.S. | *Boston in N. E. Printed by B. Green, for* | *Benj. Eliot and Joanna Perry* ... . 1714. 18mo, pp. (2), 33. J.C.B. 46448

It may be, that the rarity of this tract has prevented such a "comfortable assurance" as it offers, from being universally entertained. The running title is: "How to live in Hard Times." A reprint would not be unseasonable at any time.

[MATHER.] Pastoral Desires. | A Short Catalogue | of | Excellent Things, | which | A True Pastor, will Desire to | see Approved and Practised, and | Abounding, among his People. | A Book, design'd to be Lodg'd | and Left in their Hands, by One | Desirous to be Such an One, in | his Pastoral Visits, | to the Houses of all his People. | ... | *Boston: Printed by B. Green, for* | *Nicholas Boone* ... . 1712. 12mo, pp. (2), 116. 46449

One of the rarest of Cotton Mather's works.

[MATHER.] A Pastoral | Letter | to the | English | Captives, | in Africa. | From New-England. | *Boston: Printed by B. Green,* | *and J. Allen.* 1698. Sm. 8vo, pp. 16. H. 46450

[MATHER.] A Pastoral Letter, to Families Visited with Sickness. From several Ministers of Boston, At a time of Epidemical Sickness Distressing of the Town. The Third Impression. [Colophon:] *Boston: Printed by B. Green, for S. Gerrish* ... . 1721. 12mo, pp. (2), 24. 46451

[MATHER.] A Perfect Recovery ... A Brief Discourse to the Inhabitants of a Place that had passed thro' a very Sickly Winter, and a Time of much Adversity ... . [*Boston.* 1714.] 12mo, pp. 60. 46452

Mr. Brinley's (the only known copy) lacked the imprint.

MATHER. Perswasions [*sic*] from the Terror of the Lord. | A Sermon | concerning, | The Day of Judgement; | Preached on a Solemn Occasion, 15.d. 2.m. 1711. | By Cotton Mather, D.D. ... *Boston in New-England: Printed ... by Timothy Green.* 1711. 8vo, pp. (2), 38. BA. 46453

[Mather.] Pia Disideria. Or, The Smoaking Flax, raised into a Sacred Flame; In a Short and Plain Essay upon those Pious Desires, Which are the Introduction and Inchoation of all Vital Piety, Delivered unto a Religious Society of Young People; On the Lord's-Day-Evening, Aug. 5. 1722. *Boston: Printed by S. Kneeland for S. Gerrish* ... . 1722. 12mo, pp. (2), 22. 46454

[Mather.] Pietas in Patriam: | The | Life | of His | Excellency | Sir William Phips, Knt. | Late Captain General, and Governour | in Chief of the Province of the Massachu- | set Bay, | New-England. | Containing the Memorable Changes Under- | gone, and Actions Performed by Him. | Written by one intimately acquainted with Him. | ... | *London:* | *Printed by Sam Bridge in Austin Friers,* | *for Nath.* | *Hiller at the Princes-Arms in Leaden-Hall street,* | ... 1697. Sm. 8vo, pp. (10), 110, (8). 46455

Calef is so unkind as to remark that Mather wrote this book anonymously, in order to praise himself. A second edition was printed in 1699. It is reprinted entire in the "Magnalia." *See* "N. A. Rev.," III. 308. Thomas quotes a Boston edition, 1696, which I have not seen.

[Mather.] Pietas Matutina. | One Essay more, | to bespeak and engage | Early Piety, | made | on an Occasion taken from the | Early Departure | of | Mrs. Elizabeth Cooper, | at the age of Twenty-Two, | August 7, 1726. | By her Father. | ... | *Boston: Printed for J. Phillips.* | MDCCXXVI. Sm. 8vo, pp. (2), 46.

With a Poem by Samuel Mather.

Mather. Piety and Equity United. In Two Essays ... . By Cotton Mather ... . *Boston: Printed by J. Allen, for Robert Starke.* 1717. 12mo, pp. (2), 44, 42. 46457

The running titles are: "The Desires of Piety" and "The Measures of Equity."

Mather. A Pillar of Gratitude. | Or, | A brief Recapitulation, of the Match- | less Favours, with which the | God of Heaven hath obliged the | Hearty Praises of His | New-English Israel. | A Sermon delivered in the Audi- | ence of His Excellency, the | Earl of Bellomont, Captain | General, and Governour in | Chief, and of the Council & | Representatives, of the Gene- | ral Assembly of the Pro- | vince of the Massachusetts-Bay, Con- | vened at Boston, in New-England. | On May 29 1700 the Day, for Election | of Counsellors, in that Province. | By Cotton Mather. | Whereto there is Appendiced, an Extract of | Some Accounts, concerning the Won- | derful Success of the Glorious Gos- | pel, in the East Indies. | ... | *Boston: Printed by B. Green, & J. Allen.* 1700. 12mo, pp. 48. H., M. 46458

[Mather.] Pillars of Salt. | An History | of some | Criminals executed in this Land. | For | Capital Crimes. | With some of their Dying | Speeches; Collected and Published, | For the Warning of such as Live in | Destructive Courses of Ungodliness. | Whereto is added, | for the better improvement of this History, | a Brief Discourse about the Dreadful | Justice of God, in Punishing of | Sin, with Sin. | *Boston in New England.* | *Printed by B. Green and J. Allen, for Samuel Phillips.* 1699. Sm. 8vo, pp. 111. W.

Mather. Piscator Evangelicus. Or, The Life of Mr. Thomas Hooker, The Renowned, Pastor of Hartford-Church, and Pillar of Connecticut-Colony ... . By Cotton Mather. [*Boston:*] *Printed in the year* 1695 [*for Michael Perry*]. 8vo, pp. 45, (2). 46460

Rare. The last two pages have "A Catalogue of some other Books, all by this Author," comprising thirty-four titles.

Mather. The Pleasures of True Piety. ... *Boston.* 1716. 12mo, pp. 90. 46461

[Mather.] A Poem | Dedicated to the Memory | of The Reverend and Excellent | Mr. Urian Oakes, | the late Pastor to Christ's Flock, | and Præsident of Harvard-Colledge, | in Cambridge, | Who was gathered to his People on 25d 5mo 1681. | In the fifty'th Year of his Age. | ... | *Boston in New-England,* | *Printed for John Ratcliff.* 1682. Sm. 4to, pp. (4), 16. 46462

A sub-title reads: "Memoirs | of the Life and Worth: | Lamentations | for the Death, and Loss | of | the every way admirable | Mr. Vrian Oakes." The initials *N. R.*, subscribed to the Poem (p. 16), are the last letters of the name Cotto*n* Mathe*r*. This poem was, probably, Cotton Mather's first published work. It was printed three years before the "Elegy" on Collins (No. 46300), and *four years* before "The Call of the Gospel" (No. 46244), the first work named in Samuel Mather's list. Mr. Brinley's is the only known copy, and is believed to be unique. In May, 1683, Nathanael Mather, of Dublin, wrote to his brother Increase: "The last I had from you was dated 9ber 15. 82. & with it Mr. Oaks his Sermon on Eccles. and two of *your son's Poems on him*, for which I thank you."—*The Mather Papers* (4 *Mass. Hist. Coll.*, VIII.), p. 55.

[Mather.] The Pourtraiture of | a Good Man, | Drawn | With the Pencils of the Sanctuary, | in such Colours as | the Oracles of the | Sacred Scriptures | have given him. | At a Lecture, in the Audience of | the General Assembly, | at Boston, | June 25, | 1702. | *Boston: Printed for, and sold by* | *Benjamin Eliot.* 1702. Sm. 8vo, pp. 34. W. 46463

Mather. A Present of Summer-Fruit. | A very brief Essay | To Offer | Some Instructions of | Piety, | Which the Summer-Season | more Particularly and Empha- | tically Leads us to; But

such | also as are never out of Season. | Being | The short Entertainment of an | Auditory in Boston, on a Day | distinguished with the Heat of | the Summer; 5d. 5m. 1713. | By Cotton Mather, D.D. | ... | *Boston: Printed and Sold by* | *B. Green* ... . 1713. 12mo, pp. (2), 29. 46464

Mather. The Present State of New-England. | Considered in a | Discourse | On the Necessities and Advantages of a | Public Spirit | In every Man; | Especially at such a time as this. | Made at the Lecture in Boston | 20.d. 1.m. 1690. | Upon the News of an Invasion by bloody | Indians and French-men, begun, | upon Us. | By Cotton Mather. | ... | *Boston:* | *Printed by Samuel Green.* 1690. Sm. 8vo, pp. (2), 52. C., H., M. 46465

Of much rarity and equal interest.

[Mather, *and others.*] The Principles | of the | Protestant | Religion | Maintained, | And Churches of New-England, in the | Profession and Exercise thereof | Defended, | Against all the Calumnies of one George Keith, | a Quaker, in a Book lately Published at | Pensilvania, to undermine them both. | By the Ministers of the Gospel in Boston. | ... | *Boston, in New-England,* | *Printed by Richard Pierce* ... . MDCXC. Sm. 8vo, pp. (10), 156. BA., C.

The preface is signed "James Allen, Joshuah Moodey, Samuel Willard, Cotton Mather." This is the correct title of our Vol. I., No. 828.

[Mather.] Private Meetings Animated and Regulated. A Short Essay, To Preserve and Revive the Ancient Practice of Lesser Societies, Formed among Religious People to Promote the Great Interests of Religion. ... *Boston: Printed ... by T. Green.* 1706. 12mo, pp. 23. 46467

[Mather.] A | Proposal | for an | Evangelical Treasury; | Humbly tendered unto the Churches. | [*Boston.* 1725.] 4to, pp. 4. B. 46468

The author's name and the imprint are given from Mr. Prince's MS. catalogue.

[Mather.] Proposals to Lawyers. From Essays to do Good. *Barnard, Vt.* [n. d.] 12mo, pp. 8. 46469

Mather. Providence Asserted and Adored. A Sermon occasioned by the Death of Several who were Drowned. *Boston.* 1716. 12mo. 46470

[Mather.] Psalterium Americanum. | The Book of | Psalms, | In a Translation Exactly conformed | unto the Original; | but all in | Blank Verse, | Fitted unto the Tunes commonly used | in our Churches. Which Pure | Offering is accompanied with | Illustra-

tions, digging for Hidden | Treasures in it; And Rules to | Employ it upon the Glorious and | Various Intentions of it, | Whereto are added, | Some other Portions of the Sacred | Scripture, to Enrich the | Cantional. | *Boston: in N. E.* | *Printed by S. Kneeland, for B. Eliot,* | *S. Gerrish, D. Henchman, and* | *J. Edwards, and Sold at their Shops.* 1718. Sm. 8vo, pp. (2), xxxv, (1), 426. H. 46471

Some copies have the prospectus "Proposals | For Printing by | Subscription | Psalterium Americanum," etc., pp. 7. "In this singular publication, which is a close translation of the Hebrew, Dr. Mather has not only disregarded the modern practice of breaking the lines, whether rhymed or not, but he has run out (to use a printer's phrase) the whole matter; so that while each psalm looks exactly like prose, and may be read as such, it is, in fact, modulated so that it may be sung as lyric verse. The learned Doctor says that in the 'twice seven versions' which he has seen, the authors 'put in as large an Heap of poor Things, which, are intirely their own,—meerly for the sake of preserving the *Clink* of the *Rhyme;* Which after all is of small consequence unto a Generous Poem; and of none at all unto the Melody of Singing.'"

[Mather.] The pure Nazarite. | Advice | to a | Young Man, | concerning | An Impiety and Impurity ... . *Boston: Printed by T. Fleet, for John Phillips.* 1723. 8vo, pp. (4), 19. B., BA. 46472

[Mather.] The Quickened Soul. A Short and Plain Essay on, The Withered Hand Revived & Restored. ... *Boston: Printed by B. Green.* 1720. 12mo, pp. (2), 30. 46473

"Aimed, more Particularly at the Direction of them whose Conversion to Piety may be in Danger, thro' wretched and foolish *Pamphlets,* which the Enemies of Grace & of Souls, industriously scatter about the Country." This perhaps refers to John Checkley's "Choice Dialogues." *See* our Vol. III., No. 12361.

[Mather.] Ratio Disciplinæ Fratrum | Nov-Anglorum. | A | Faithful Account | of the | Discipline | Professed and Practised; | in the | Churches | of | New-England. | With Interspersed and Instructive Reflec- | tions on the Discipline of the | Primitive Churches. | ... | *Boston: ... S. Gerrish* ... . 1726. Sm. 8vo, pp. (2), iv, 207, (3). 46474

In a postscript, on page 208, Cotton Mather owns himself the author of this book, a sort of historical relation of the church discipline of New England. Preceding is an attestation of four pages, dated the 10th Oct. 1719, and signed by Increase Mather.

[Mather.] Ratio Disciplinæ, or the Constitution of the Congregational Churches. [Edited by T. C. Upham.] *Portland.* 1829. 12mo. 46475

[Mather.] Reason Satisfied: and Faith Established. The Resurrection of a Glorious Jesus Demonstrated by many infallible Proofs ... . *Boston: Printed by J. Allen, for N. Boone.* 1712. 24mo, pp. 47. B., H. 46476

Mather. Reasonable Religion. | Or, | The Truth of the | Christian | Religion, | Demonstrated. | The Wisdom of its Precepts | Justified: | And the Folly of Sinning against those | Precepts, Reprehended. | With | Incontestable Proofs, | That Men, who would Act | Reasonably, must Live Religiously. | By Cotton Mather. | *Boston, in N. E. Printed by T. Green,* | *for Benjamin Eliot* ... . 1700. 12mo, pp. 72. B. + To which is prefix'd A Preface, by the Reverend Dr. Williams. *London: ... N. Cliff and D. Jackson.* 1713. 12mo, pp. (20), 135. B. 46477

[Mather.] The Religion of an Oath. | Plain Directions | How the Duty of | Swearing, | May be Safely Managed, | When it is Justly Demanded. | And | Strong Persuasives | To avoid the Perils of | Perjury. | Concluding with a most Solemn Expla- | nation of an Oath, which the Laws | of Denmark have provided for the con- | sideration of them, whom an Oath | is propos'd unto. | Published at the Desire of Some, who | apprehended Oaths to be too frequently | and faultily trifled with. | *Boston, N. E.: Printed by B. Green, for* | *D. Henchman* ... . 1719. Sm. 8vo, pp. (2), 30.

[Mather.] The Religion of the Closet. | An Essay, | on the Holy Employments | Which are proper for a Christian in his | Daily Retirements. | ... The Second Edition. | *Boston: Printed ... by T. Green.* 1706. 12mo, pp. 42, (2). + The Fourth Edition. | ... | *Boston: Printed by T. Fleet,* ... | *for Samuel Gerrish.* 1715. 12mo, pp. 44. H. 46479

[Mather.] The Religion of the Cross. | A Brief Essay | Upon the | ... Death of ... [his Wife] Mrs. Elizabeth Mather. | ... | *Boston: Printed by John Allen.* | 1714. 12mo, pp. (4), 47, (1).

Mather. La Religion pura. To which is added La Fe del Christiano: En Veynte quatro articulos de la Institucion de Christo. An Essay to convey Religion into the Spanish Indies. *Boston.* 1699. 8vo, pp. 18. 46481

Title from Thomas' "History of Printing." *See also* "La Fe," No. 46327, *supra.*

[Mather.] Religious Societies. | Proposals | For the Revival of | Dying Religion, | by Well-Ordered Societies | ... . | With a brief Discourse, Offered | unto a Religious Society ... . | *Boston: Printed by S. Kneeland, for John* | *Phillips* ... . 1724. 12mo, pp. (4), 8, 19. B. 46482

[Mather.] Renatus. | A brief Essay | on, | a Soul passing | From Death to Life: | ... And the Mystery of the | Two Adams, | Explained ... . | *Boston: S. Gerrish.* 1725. 12mo, pp. 34. B.

[Mather.] Repeated Admonitions. | In a | Monitory Letter, | About the | Maintainance | Of an Able and Faithful | Ministry; | Directed unto those People, who Sin against | and Sin away the Glorious Gospel, | by not supporting the worthy Dispenses | of it: | First Published some Years ago; and now Re- | printed; | In concomitancy with the pious Concern about | this Matter, expressed by the General Assembly | of the Province. | ... | *Boston: Printed by J. Franklin, for S. Gerrish* ... . 1722. 8vo. + *Boston: Printed by T. Fleet* ... . 1725. 8vo, pp. (2), iii, 19.

Mather. Repeated Warnings. Another Essay, to Warn Young People against Rebellions that must be Repented of. ... With a Pathetical Relation, of what occurr'd in the Remarkable Experiences of a Young Man, who made an Hopeful End lately at Lyme in Connecticut. By Cotton Mather, D.D. *Boston: Printed by B. Green, for S. Gerrish.* 1712. 12mo, pp. (2), 34.

Mather. The Resolved Christian; Pursuing the Designs of Holiness and Happiness ... . By Cotton Mather. *Boston: Sold by Nicholas Boone.* 1700. 8vo, pp. (2), 128. 46486

Rare. This is identical—the title-page and the omission of the errata and dedication excepted—with "Small Offers," etc., No. 46513, *infra.*

[Mather.] The Resort of Piety. | Our Saviour | Considered and Exhibited, as a | Tree of Life, | Which All may and must Resort | unto. | And an Early Flight unto | Him, very particularly called for. | An Essay | offered unto a Society of Young | Men, United in the Intentions of | Early Piety. | On the Lord's-Day Evening, | 18d. 1m. 1716. | *Boston: Printed in the Year* 1716. 12mo, pp. 47. J.C.B. 46487

[Mather.] Restitutus. | The | End of Life Persued, | And then, The | Hope in Death Enjoyed, | by the | Faithful. | Both of them Described | in A | Discourse | Made upon a | Recovery from Sickness. | Or, The | Declaration | Of One Returning from the Gates of the Grave. | ... | *Boston: ... S. Gerrish,* | ... 1727. 12mo, pp. (2), 54. H. 46488

Mather. The Retired Christian. *Boston.* 1707. 12mo, pp. 46. W. 46489

Title from the catalogue of the American Antiquarian Society. The book has been lost.

[Mather.] Right Thoughts in Sad Hours, | Representing the | Comforts and the Duties | of | Good Men under all their | Afflictions: | And Particularly, | That one, the Untimely Death of |

Children: | in a Sermon ... at Charls-Town, New-England ... . *London: Printed by James Astwood.* 1689. Sm. 8vo, pp. (6), 54, (2). + *Dunstable.* 1811. 24mo. BA. 46490

[Mather.] The Right Way to Shake off a Viper. | An | Essay, | upon a | Case | Too commonly calling for | Consideration; | What shall Good Men do, when they are | Evil Spoken of? | With a Preface of | Dr. Increase Mather, | The Second Impression. | ... | *Boston: Printed by S. Kneeland, for S.* | *Gerrish* ... . 1720. | 12mo, pp. (2), xiv, 64. BA. 46491

First printed at London about 1711. The catalogue of the American Antiquarian Society quotes an edition, *Boston,* 1711.

[Mather.] The Rules of a Visit. | An Essay | Upon that | Case, | how the | Visits | Of Christians to one another, may | be so Managed, as to Answer the | Noble Designs of Christia- | nity. | ... *Boston, in N. E. Printed ... by Timothy Green* ... . 1705. 12mo, pp. 40. B. 46492

[Mather.] The Sad Effects of Sin. | A True Relation of the | Murder | Committed by | David Wallis, | On his Companion | Benjamin Stolwood: | On Saturday Night, the first of Au- | gust, 1713. With his Carriage af- | ter Condemnation; His Confessi- | on and Dying Speech at the Place | of Execution, &c. | To which are added, The Sermons | Preached at the Lecture in Boston, | in his Hearing, after his Condem- | nation; And on the Day of his | Execution, being Sept. 24. 1713. | *Boston, N. E. Printed by John Allen,* | *for Nicholas Boone* ... . 1713. 12mo, pp. 14. 46493

[Mather.] The Sailours Companion | and Counsellour. | An Offer of | Considerations | for the | Tribe of Zebulun; | Awakening the | Mariner, | to Think and to Do, | Those things that may render his | Voyage Prosperous. | ... | *Boston in N. E.* | *Printed by B. Green, for Samuel Gerrish.* | 1709. Sm. 8vo, pp. (2), 62. H.

[Mather.] The Salvation of the Soul considered ... With Directions ... and Incentives ... . *Boston: Printed by B. Green.* 1720. 12mo, pp. (2), 22. 46495

Mather. The Saviour with his Rainbow. A Discourse concerning the Covenant which God will remember in the Times of Danger passing over his Church. By Cotton Mather ... . *London.* 1714. 8vo, pp. 23. 46496

The Dedication is by Samuel Mather. This London edition is very rare. It was reprinted from the Boston edition. *See* "Thoughts," etc., No. 46551, *infra.*

Mather. A Scriptural Catechism. | The Heads of the Christian | Religion | Plainly, briefly, and fully delivered in a | Catechism, | Which endeavours a sufficient Answer to every | Question, barely with a pertinent Sentence of | Sacred Scripture, and Enables the Learner at | once with ease to confirm as well as assert the | great Articles of the Faith once delivered unto | the Saints. | By Cotton Mather. | ... | *Boston, Printed by R. Pierce, for Nicholas Buttolph* ... 1691. Sm. 8vo, pp. (2), 21. BA. 46497

[Mather.] A Seasonable Testimony | to the Glorious Doctrines of Grace, | At this Day many ways undermined | in the World. | Considered, by a General Convention of | Ministers, Meeting at Boston, May 28th | 1702. And Voted by them, to be Pub- | lished, for the Establishment of the | Churches in the present Truth. | *Boston.* 1702. Sm. 8vo, pp. 15. W. 46498

Mather. Seasonable Thoughts upon | Mortality. | A Sermon | Occasioned by the raging of a | Mortal Sickness | in the Colony of | Connecticut, | and the many Deaths of | our Brethren there. | Delivered at Boston-Lecture, | 24.d. 11.m. 1711, 12. | By Cotton Mather, D.D. | ... | *Boston Printed: Sold by T. Green.* 1712. 12mo, pp. (2), 56, (2). 46499

[Mather.] A | Serious Address | To those | Who unnecessarily frequent | The | Tavern, and | Often spend the Evening | in | Publick Houses. | By several Ministers. | To which is added, | A private Letter on the Subject, by the | late Rev. Dr. Increase Mather. | ... | *Boston, N. E. Printed for S. Gerrish,* | ... 1726. 8vo, pp. (2), iv, 30. 46500

Edited by Cotton Mather. Increase Mather's Letter (pp. 27–36) is in answer to the Question, "Whether it be Lawful for a Church-Member among us, to be frequently in Taverns?"

[Mather.] The Serious Christian: | or, | Three Great Points of | Practical Christianity | ... . In Three Brief Discourses. | By an American. ... *London: Printed by Benj. Harris.* 1699. 12mo, pp. (4), 116. B. 46501

"The Epistle to the Reader" is signed "Daniel Burgess."

Mather. The Servant of Abraham: With Motives for the Instruction of Servants. *Boston.* 1716. 12mo. 46502

Mather. A Servant of the Lord not ashamed of his Lord. *Boston.* 1704. Sm. 8vo. 46503

Mather. The Serviceable Man. | A | Discourse | Made unto the | General Court | of the | Massachusets Colony, New-England,

[At the Anniversary | Election | 28 d. 3 m. 1690. | By Cotton Mather ... . *Boston, Printed by Samuel Green, for Joseph | Browning* ... . 1690. Sm. 8vo, pp. (4), 64. B., H., W. 46504

MATHER. Seven Select Lectures, | of Mr. Cotton Mather, | of New-England. | Or, | Seasonable Discourses | upon | Some Common but Woful Distem- | pers ... And, upon, | the Remedies of those Distempers. | ... | *London: For Nath. Hiller.* | 1695. Sm. 8vo, pp. (16), 192. H., W. 46505

MATHER. Several | Sermons | Concerning | Walking | with | God, | and that | In the Dayes of Youth : | Preached | At Boston in New-England. | By Cotton Mather ... . *London,* | *Printed by J. Astwood for J. Dunton* ... . 1689. Sm. 8vo, pp. (2), 86. B.

The last sermon is on the death of the author's brother Nathanael. Usually bound up with Mather's "Early Piety," No. 46293, *supra.*

MATHER. Shaking Dispensations. | An Essay | Upon the Mighty Shakes, | which | The Hand of Heaven, hath given, | and is giving, to the World. | With some | Useful Remarks | On the Death of the | French King. | Who left off to make the World a | Wilderness, and to destroy the Cities | thereof ; on the Twenty-first of | August. 1715. | In a Sermon on that Great Occasion, | At Boston, New-England. | 13 d. VII. m. | By Cotton Mather ... . *Boston: Printed by B. Green. Sold by S. Gerrish,* | ... 1715. 8vo, pp. (2), 50. 46507

[MATHER.] A Short | Discourse | Shewing | That our | Salvation | is of | Meer [*sic*] Grace. | ... | *Printed in the Year* 1716. 8vo, pp. (4), 32. B. 46508

Prince in his MS. list says "By Mr. Warham Mather."

MATHER. The Short History of New England. | A | Recapitulation | of | Wonderfull Passages | Which have Occurr'd, | First in the Protections, and | then in the Afflictions of | New England. | With a | Representation | of Certain Matters calling for the | Singular Attention of that Country. | Made at Boston-Lecture, in the Audience | of the Great and General Assembly | of the Province of the Massachu- | setts-Bay. June 7. 1694. | By Cotton Mather. | *Boston: Printed by B. Green for S. Phillips.* 1694. 12mo, pp. 67.

MATHER. A Short View of our glorious Redeemer on his Throne. ... *Boston.* 1714. 12mo. 46510

[MATHER.] Signatus. | The | Sealed Servants | Of our God, | Appearing with | two Witnesses, | To produce a Well-Established |

Assurance | Of their being the | Children of the Lord Almighty | ... At Boston Lecture, 1726–7. *Boston: Daniel Henchman.* 1727. 8vo, pp. 40. + With a Preface and Appendix by the Rev. Mr. Croswell. The Second Edition. *Boston: Printed ... by Rogers and Fowle.* 1748. 8vo, pp. viii, 31. B., W. 46511

[MATHER.] Silentiarius. A brief Essay on the Holy Silence and Godly Patience, that Sad Things are to be Entertained withal. A Sermon at Boston-Lecture, On the Death of Mrs. Abigail Willard, And the Day before her Interment ; who Expired Septemb. 26. 1721. By her Father. Whereto there is added, A Sermon on, The Refuge of the Distressed, which was Preached on the Lord's-Day preceding. *Boston: Printed by S. Kneeland.* 1721. 12mo, pp. 34, 28. 46512

MATHER. Small Offers | Towards the Service of the Tabernacle | in the Wilderness. | Four Discourses, accommodated unto the Designs of | Practical | Godliness. ... | Preached partly at Boston, partly at Charleston. | By Cotton Mather ... . Published by a Gentleman lately Restored from threat- | ning Sickness, ... in Gratitude unto God for his Recovery. | *Boston, Printed by R. Pierce.* MDCLXXXIX. Sm. 8vo, pp. (8), 128. BA. 46513

[MATHER.] Sober Considerations, on a growing Flood of Iniquity. Or, An Essay, To Dry up a Fountain of, Confusion and every Evil Work ; and to Warn People, particularly of the Woful Consequences [of] the Prevailing Abuse of Rum. *Boston: Printed by John Allen.* [1708.] 8vo, pp. (2), 20. 46514

[MATHER.] Sober Sentiments. | In an Essay | ... . Produced by the | Premature and much lamented Death of | Mr. Joshua Lamb, | ... [who fell from Stoughton Hall, Harv. Coll.] July 15. 1722. By One of the Ministers in Boston. | ... With an Appendix by another hand [Thomas Walter]. ... *Boston: Printed by T. Fleet.* 1722. 12mo, pp. 37. BA. 46515

See "New England Genealogical and Historical Register," VIII. 260–61.

MATHER. Solution of the Scruples of a Religious or Conscientious Nature against Inoculation. *Boston.* 1722. 12mo.

[MATHER.] Some Few | Remarks, | upon | A Scandalous Book, against the | Government and Ministry of | New-England. | Written, | By one Robert Calef. | Detecting the Unparrellel'd Malice & Falsehood | of the said Book. | Defending the Names of several particular | Gentlemen, by him therein aspersed & abused. | Composed and Published by several Persons | belonging to the Flock

of some of the | Injured Pastors and concerned for | their Just Vindication. | Truth will come off Conquerer. | *Boston, N. E. Printed by T. Green, Sold by* | *Nicholas Boone.* 1701. 8vo, pp. 71, (1). 46517

The postscript, pp. 67–71, is signed "Increase Mather, Cotton Mather," and dated "Jan. 9th. 1700, 1." A letter, pp. 34–59, signed "Cotton Mather," contains information about the witchcraft delusions.

MATHER. Some Remarkables on the Peaceful and Joyful Death of Mrs. Abiel Goodwin. Together with a Sermon preached to Young People at the Request of the Deceased. *Boston: ... D. Henchman.* 1727. 8vo. 46518

For the second edition, *see* "Juga Jucunda," No. 46372, *supra.*

[MATHER.] Some Seasonable Advice unto the | Poor ; | To be annexed unto the | Kindnesses of God, that are dispensed | unto them. [*Boston: T. Fleet.* 1726?] 12mo, pp. 12. B. 46519

[MATHER.] Some Seasonable | Enquiries | Offered, | For the Consideration and Satisfaction of | them that are willing to Weigh things | in Even Balances. | And for the Establishment of the Re- | formed Churches ; ... [Colophon:] *Printed in the Year* 1723. 12mo, pp. 12. B., S. 46520

MATHER. The Songs of the Redeemed. *Boston.* 1697. Sm. 8vo. 46521

MATHER. A Sorrowful Spectacle. | In Two Sermons. | Occasioned by a Just Sentence of | Death, on a ... Woman, | for the Murder of a Spu- | rious Offspring. | ... With some Remarkable Things, relating to | the Criminal ; proper for All to be In- | formed of. | By Cotton Mather ... . *Boston: Printed by T. Fleet & T. Crump, for Samuel Gerrish.* 1715. 12mo, pp. (2), vii, 3–92.

For the second sermon, which has a separate title-page, paging, and register, *see* Colman (B.), "The Divine Compassions," our Vol. IV., No. 14525, *note.*

[MATHER.] The Soul upon the Wing. | An Essay | on | The State of the | Dead. | Answering | That Solemn Enquiry, | How the Children of Men are at | their Death disposed of ? | In | a Sermon | Occasion'd by the Decease of some | Desirable Friends lately Departed. | By One of the Ministers in | the North-part of Boston. | ... | *Boston, N. E.* | *Printed by B. Green.* 1722. 8vo, pp. (4), 24.

[MATHER.] A Soul Well-Anchored. A Little Manual for Self-Examination ; To assist a Christian In Examining his Hopes of a Future Blessedness ... . *Boston: Printed by B. Green.* 1712. 12mo, pp. 24. 46524

MATHER. The Souldier told what he Should do. ... *Boston.* 1707. 12mo. 46525

Title from Samuel Mather's list.

MATHER. Souldiers Counselled and Comforted. | A Discourse | Delivered unto some part of | the Forces | Engaged in the Just War of | New-England | Against the Northern and Eastern | Indians. | Sept. 1. 1689. | By Cotton Mather, Minister of the | Gospel in Boston. | ... | *Boston, N. E.* | *Printed by Samuel Green.* [1689.] Sm. 8vo, pp. (10), 38. M., W. 46526

[MATHER.] Sound Words, | to be held fast, in Faith and Love. | Or, | The Christian Religion, | Epitomized and Inculcated, | in | Three Essayes. [n. p. n. d.] 12mo, pp. 28. B. 46527

MATHER. Speedy Repentance Urged. | A | Sermon | Preached at Boston, Decemb. 29. 1689. | In the Hearing, and at the Request of | One Hugh Stone ; | A Miserable Man | Under a just Sentence of Death, for a | Tragical and Horrible Murder. | Together with some Account concern- | ing the Character, Carriage, and | Execution of that Unhappy Ma- | lefactor. | To which are Added certain Memorable | Providences Relating to some other Mur- | ders ; & some great Instances of Repen- | tance which have been seen among us. | By Cotton Mather, Pastor of a | Church in Boston. | *Boston: Printed by Samuel Green, and* | *Sold by Joseph Browning ... and Benj. Harris* ... . 1690. 12mo, pp. (6), 87, (8), 15, 75, 21, 40, (2), 14. J.C.B., H. 46528

This exceedingly rare and interesting volume also contains "A little history of several very astonishing Witchcrafts, and Possessions, which partly from my occular observation, and partly my undoubted information, hath enabled me to offer unto the publick notice of my neighbours," pp 75, which is, perhaps, the first appearance of his treatise on witchcraft. Then follows "A Discourse on the Power and Malice of Devils," and "A Discourse on Witchcraft," the volume concluding with an appendix in defense of Increase Mather's "Remarkable Providences." *See also* "Memorable Providences," No. 46407, *supra.*

[MATHER.] The Spirit of Life entering into the Spiritually Dead. | An Essay, | to bring a | Dead Soul | into the Way, wherein the Quicken- | ing Spirit of God & of Grace, | is to Hoped and Waited for ; | And | to Prophesy over the | Dry Bones | in the | Valley of Death, | such Words of the Lord, as use | to be the Vehicles of Life unto them. | *Boston in N. E. Printed and Sold by* | *Timothy Green* ... . 1707. Sm. 8vo, pp. 40. W. 46529

MATHER. Stimulator ; Or the Case of a Soul walking in Darkness. *Boston.* 1724. Sm. 8vo. 46530

[MATHER.] The Stone Cut out of the | Mountain. | And | The Kingdom of God, | in | Those Maxims of it, that | cannot be shaken. | ... | Exhibited in the Year, | Seventeen Hundred & Sixteen. | [Latin Title :] Lapis e Monte Excisus. | Atque | Regnum Dei, | Ejusdemque Principia in æternum | Stabilienda. | ... | Editur Anno Domini, M DCC XVI. Sm. 8vo, 14 leaves. H., M., W.

This treatise is in English and Latin.

MATHER. Strange Phenomena. *See* Jones (H.), IX. 36506.

MATHER. Dr. Cotton Mather's | Student and Preacher. | Intituled, | Manuductio ad Ministerium ; | or, Directions for a Candidate of the Ministry. | ... | Republished by John Ryland, A.M. | of Northampton. | *London: Charles Dilly.* MDCCLXXXI. 8vo, pp. xx, 216. H. + [To which is] Added, a Literal Translation of Dr. Cotton Mather's famous Latin Preface : with an Abridgement of Mr. Ryland's Preface to his edition. *London: T. Scollick & J. Matthews.* 1789. 12mo, pp. xvi, 260. J.C.B., C. 46532

For the first edition, *see* "Manuductio ad Ministerium, No. 46400, *supra.*

MATHER. Successive Generations. | Remarks | Upon the Changes of a | Dying World, | ... [To] the | General Assembly | of the Massachusetts-Province, | New-England. 8 d. x m. 1715. | By C. Mather, D.D. & F.R.S. | ... | *Boston: Printed by B. Green.* | 1715. 24mo, pp. (2), 42. H. 46533

MATHER. The Sum of the Matter. An Abridgment of the Assembly's Catechism. *Boston.* 1709. Sm. 8vo. 46534

[MATHER.] Suspiria Vinctorum. Some Account of the Condition to which the Protestant Interest in the World is at this Day reduced. ... *Boston: Printed by ... T. Fleet.* 1726. 12mo, pp. (2), 22. B., H. 46535

MATHER. Tabitha Rediviva. | An | Essay | To Describe and Commend the | Good Works | of a | Vertuous Woman ; | Who therein approves her self a | Real Disciple | of an | Holy Saviour. | With some Justice done to the Memo- | ry of that Religious and Honoura- | ble Gentlewoman, | Mrs. Elizabeth Hutchinson. | Who Expired, 3. d. 12. m. 1712, 13. | In the LXXI Year of her Age. | By Cotton Mather, D.D. | ... | *Boston: Printed by J. Allen.* 1713. 8vo, pp. (2), 56, (2). M. 46536

MATHER. Tela Prævisa. | A Short Essay, | on | Troubles to be Look'd for. | A Wise | Expectation of, | and | Preparation for, | Troublesome Changes, | Recommended unto the Strangers and |

Pilgrims in this Present Evil World. | By Cotton Mather, D.D. | ... *Boston in New-England: | Printed by B. Green, for Thomas Hancock,* | ... 1724. Sm. 8vo, pp. (2), 22. H. 46537

[MATHER.] The Temple Opening. | A | Particular Church | Considered as a | Temple | of the | Lord. | In a Sermon Preached on a | Day, when such a Church | was Gathered, and a Pastor | to it Ordained. | ... | *Boston: Printed by B. Green, for S. Phillips.* 1709. 24mo, pp. (2), 34. H., W. 46538

[MATHER.] Terra Beata. | A Brief Essay, | on the | Blessing of Abraham ; | Even the | Grand Blessing | Of a Glorious | Redeemer, | ... | *Boston: J. Phillips.* MDCCXVI. 12mo, pp. (2), 54.

MATHER. Terribilia Dei. Remarkable Judgments of God, on several sorts of Offenders, in several Scores of Instances ; among the People of New-England. Observed, Collected, Related, and Improved ; In Two Sermons, at Boston-Lecture in the Month of July 1697. By Cotton Mather. ... *Boston: Printed by B. Green.* 1697. 8vo. 46540

This was reprinted in the "Magnalia," Book VI. 23.

[MATHER.] The Terror of the Lord. | Some Account of the | Earthquake | That shook New-England, | In the Night, | Between the 29 and the 30 of October. 1727. | With a Speech, | Made unto the Inhabitants of Boston, | Who Assembled the Next Morning, for | the proper | Exercises of Religion, | On so Uncommon, and so Tremendous | an Occasion. | ... | *Boston: Printed by T. Fleet, for S. Kneeland* ... . 1727. 8vo, pp. (4), 37, 6. B. + The Second Edition. | With a Second Appendix. [*Ibid.*] 1727. 12mo, pp. (4), 42. + The Third Edition. With an Appendix and a Further Appendix. [*Ibid.*] 1727. 12mo, pp. (4), 42.

[MATHER.] A | Testimony | against Evil Customs. | Given by Several Ministers ... . [*Boston.* 1713.] 4to, pp. 4. B. 46542

[MATHER.] The Thankful Christian. | A brief Essay, | Upon those returns of | Thankfulness and Obedience | to the Glorious God, ... | ... for His benefits. | Addressed ... | ... more especially un- | to them, | who after the good | Success of a Whaling- | Season, would Express their | Gratitude unto God ... . *Boston: Printed by B. Green, for Samuel Gerrish.* 1717. 12mo, pp. (2), 43, (1). B.

[MATHER.] Thaumatographia Christiana. | The Wonders | of Christianity ; | Discoursed, | In a brief Recapitulation of Many | Wonderful Mysteries, | in our Lord Jesus Christ ; | ... | *Boston:*

Printed by B. Green ... | *for Samuel Sewall, junior.* | 1701. Small 8vo, pp. 55. H. 46544

[MATHER.] Theopolis Americana. An Essay on the Golden Street of the Holy City ; publishing a Testimony against the Corruptions of the Market-Place ... In a Sermon to the General Assembly of the Massachusett-Province ... 3 d. 9 m. 1709. *Boston: Printed by B. Green: ...* 1710. 12mo, pp. (4), 51, (2).

MATHER. Things for a Distress'd People to think upon. Offered in the Sermon to the General Assembly of the Province of the Massachusetts-Bay, at the Anniversary Election, May 27, 1696. By Cotton Mather. *Boston: Printed by B. Green and J. Allen, for Duncan Campbel.* 1696. Sm. 8vo, pp. (2), 84. 46546

[MATHER.] Things that Young People should | Think upon. | Or, | The Death of | Young People | Improved, | In some Lively | Admonitions | to the Living. | With | Consolations, to the Bereaved | Parents of such Young People, | as are by an Early, (and perhaps a | Sudden) Death, taken from them. | *Boston in N. E. Printed by B. Green* | *& J. Allen*: ... 1700. Sm. 8vo, pp. 16 and over. W.

MATHER. Things to be Look'd for. | Discourses | on the Glorious Characters, | With Conjectures on the Speedy | Approaches of that State | Which is | Reserved for the Church of God in the | Latter Dayes. | Together with an Inculcation of Several | Duties, which the Undoubted Cha- | racters and Approaches of that State | Invite us unto : | Delivered unto the Artillery | Company of the Massachusets | Colony : New England ; at their | Election | of Officers, for the Year 1691. | By Cotton Mather. | ... | *Cambridge:* | *Printed by Samuel Green, and Barth. Green, for* | *Nicholas Buttolph,* ... *in Boston.* 1691. 12mo, pp. 83, (1). 46548

[MATHER.] Things to be more thought upon. | A Brief | Treatise | on the | Injuries Offered unto | the ... Saviour | ... With a more Particular Conviction of the | Jewish and Arian Infidelity. | ... *Boston: Printed by Thomas Fleet, for Daniel* | *Henchman.* 1713. 12mo, pp. 108. B. 46549

[MATHER.] Thirty | Important Cases, | Resolved, | With Evidence of | Scripture | and | Reason. | [Mostly] | By several Pastors of Adjacent Churches, | meeting in Cambridge, | New-England. | ... *Boston in New-England.* | *Printed by Bartholomew Green, & John Allen,* | ... 1699. Sm. 8vo, pp. 78, (2), 4. B., C., H. 46550

An "Advertisement," pp. 4, is signed by "Cotton Mather," who edits the book. At the end is a Declaration "of Ministers from Divers parts of Massachusetts, Assembled at Boston, May 27. 1697."

MATHER. Thoughts for the Day of Rain. | In Two Essay's : | I. The Gospel of the Rainbow. | In the Meditations of Piety, | on the Appearance of the Bright | Clouds, with the Bow of God | upon them. | II. The Saviour with His | Rainbow. | And the Covenant which God | will Remember to His People in the | Cloudy Times that are passing | over them. | By Cotton Mather, D.D. | ... | *Boston in N. E. Printed by B. Green: Sold* | *by Samuel Gerrish* ... 1712. 8vo, pp. (2), vi, 64. H., M., W. 46551

The second Essay was reprinted in *London,* 1714. *See* No. 46496, *supra.*

[MATHER.] The Thoughts of a Dying Man. A Faithful Report of Matters uttered by many, in the Last Minutes of their Lives ... . *Boston: Printed by B. Green & J. Allen, for J. Wheeler.* 1697. 12mo, pp. 47, (1). 46552

[MATHER.] Three | Letters | from | New-England, | Relating to the | Controversy | of the | Present Time. | *London: | Printed for Eman. Matthews* ... . 1721. | ... 8vo, pp. (2), 30, (2). H. 46553

Two letters, pp. 3–27, are by Cotton Mather ; pp. 28–30, a letter by Increase Mather. "I do not find the above title in any list of Cotton or Increase Mather's writings."—J. A. LEWIS.

[MATHER.] To the truly Honourable, & Venerable, | ... Rector. ... And the rest of the Learned & Worthy | Professors, of the ... | University of Glasgow. | [*Boston.* 1710.] 12mo, pp. 12. B. 46554

A letter acknowledging the degree of Doctor of Divinity conferred upon him by the University.

[MATHER.] A Token for the Children of New-England. Or, Some Examples of Children in whom the Fear of God was Remarkably Budding, before they Dyed, In Several Parts of New-England ... . Added as Supplement, unto the Excellent Janewayes Token for Children : Upon the Re-printing of it, in this Countrey. *Boston in N. E. Printed by Timothy Green, for B. Eliot.* 1700. 12mo, pp. 36. 46555

For other editions, *see* Janeway (J.), Vol. IX., No. 35754.

[MATHER.] A Town in its truest Glory. A Discourse wherein the State of all our Towns is Considered. ... *Boston: Printed by B. Green, for D. Henchman.* 1712. 12mo, pp. 58.

[MATHER.] A Treacle fetch'd out of a Viper. | A Brief Essay | Upon | Falls into Sins ; | Directing, | How a Recovery out of such | Falls, | May be attended with a Revenue | of Special | Service and Glory to God, | From the | Fallen Sinner. | ... | *Boston in N. E. Printed by B. Green, for* | *Benj. Eliot* ... . 1707. 12mo, pp. (2), 32.

[MATHER.] A Tree planted by the Rivers of Water. Or, An Essay, upon the Godly and Glorious Improvements, which Baptised Christians are to make of their Sacred Baptism. *Boston: Printed by Bartholomew Green ....* 1704. 12mo, pp. (2), 69.

[MATHER.] Tremenda. | The | Dreadful Sound | with which | The Wicked are to be | Thunderstruck. | In a Sermon | Delivered unto a great Assembly, | in which was present, a Miserable | African, Joseph Hanno, just going to be Exe- | cuted, for a most Inhumane and | Uncommon Murder, | at Boston, May 25th, 1721. | To which is added A Conference between a Minister | and the Prisoner, on the Day | before his Execution. | *Boston: Printed by B. Green ....* 1721. 8vo, pp. (2), 41. W. 46559

[MATHER.] The Tribe of Asher. | A brief Essay | on the | Conspicuous Blessings | with which | the People of God | and their Off-Spring | are known to be the | Blessed of the Lord. | A Sermon preached on the | Baptism of a Grand-Child. | ... | *Boston: | Printed in the year* 1717. 12mo, pp. 34. 46560

MATHER. The Triumphs of the Reformed Religion, | in America. | The Life of the Renowned | John Eliot; | A Person justly Famous in the | Church of God, | Not only as an Eminent Christian, | and an Excellent Minister, among the | English, | But also, | As a Memorable Evangelist among the | Indians, of New-England; | With some Account concerning the late and | Strange Success of the Gospel, in those parts | of the World, which for many Ages have | lain Buried in Pagan Ignorance. | Written by | Cotton Mather. | ... | *Boston: Printed by Benjamin Harris, and John | Allen, for Joseph Brunning ...* 1691. 8vo, pp. (8), 152. H.

Very rare. For later editions, *see* "The Life and Death," Nos. 46382–84, *supra*.

MATHER. Triumphs over Troubles. Sermon ... January 9. 1700–1. *Boston.* 1701. 8vo, pp. 41. 46562

[MATHER.] A | True Account | of the Tryals, Examinations, | Confessions, Condemnations, | and Executions of divers | Witches, | At Salem, in New-England, | for | Their Bewitching of sundry People and Cattel | to Death, and doing other great Mischiefs, | to the Ruine of many People about them. | With | The Strange Circumstances that attended | their Enchantments: | And | Their Conversation with Devils, and other | Internal Spirits. | In a Letter to a Friend in London. | ... | *London, Printed for J. Conyers, in Holborn.* | [1693.] 4to, pp. 8. 46563

Signed "C. M.," and dated "Salem, 8th. Month, 1692." Very rare.

[MATHER.] The True Riches. | A Present | of | Glorious and Immense | Riches, | Plainly and Freely Tendered unto | those that are willing to Accept | of them. | In a brief Essay | on the | Unsearchable Riches | of Christ. | ... | *Boston: Printed by B. Green, for Nathaniel Belknap.* 1724. 8vo, pp. (2), vi, 31. B. 46564

[MATHER.] A true Survey & Report | of the Road. | A brief Essay | to Rectify the Mistakes of Men, | about the Way taken by them. | The Whole | Way of Transgression, | and Particularly, | the Wrong Way, wherein Men | Transgress the Rules of Honesty, | Proven an | Hard Way. | And | the Good Way of Religion | therefore Preferred & Commended. | In a Lecture at Boston, on a | Special & Mournful Occasion. | *Boston.* 1712. Sm. 8vo, pp. 46.

[MATHER.] The Tryed Professor. | A very Brief Essay, | to Detect and Prevent | Hypocrisy, | and make sure of | Sincerity, | in the Profession of | Religion. | A Plain, Short, and Useful Manual | for the | Self-Examination | which every Christian has Frequent | and Solemn Occasion for. | *Boston: in N. E. Printed by S. Kneeland.* 1719. Sm. 8vo, pp. 16. W. 46566

MATHER. Undoubted Certainties | ... A Sermon ... on the | Death of | Mrs. Abigail Sewall, | ... By Cotton Mather ... . *Boston: Printed by B. Green.* 1720. | Sm. 8vo, pp. (2), 28. H.

MATHER. Unum Necessarium. | Awakenings | for the | Unregenerate; | or | the Nature and Necessity | of | Regeneration. | Handled in a | Discourse designed for the Service of | any that may be thereby assisted in the | Grand Concern of Conversion | unto God; but especially the | Rising Generation. | With an Addition of some other Sermons relating | to that Important Subject. | By Cotton Mather. | *Boston Printed, by B. H. for Duncan Campbel,* | ... 1693. 8vo, pp. vi, 154. G.B., W. 46568

[MATHER.] Utilia. | Real and Vital | Religion | Served, | In the Various & Glorious Intentions of it. | With Eight Essays | Upon important Subjects, which | have a Serviceable Aspect upon it. | ... | *Boston: | Printed by T. Fleet & T. Crump, for Daniel | Henchman ....* 1716. 24mo, pp. (8), 288. W. 46569

[MATHER.] Valerius; or Soul Prosperity. The Prosperity of the Soul proposed and promoted ... . *Boston: Printed by T. Fleet, for S. Gerrish.* 1723. 8vo, pp. 24. 46570

MATHER. The Valley of Baca. | The | Divine Sov'reignty, | Displayed and Adored; | More Particularly, in | Bereaving Dispen-

sations, | of the | Divine Providence. | A Sermon | ... on the Death of | Mrs. Hannah Sewall, | The Religious & Honourable Consort | of | Samuel Sewall Esq; | Which befell us, on the 19 d. VIII m. 1717. | ... | By Cotton Mather ... . *Boston: Printed by B. Green.* 1717. Sm. 8vo, pp. (4), 28. H. 46571

[MATHER.] The Valley of Hinnom. | The Terrours of | Hell | demonstrated; | And the Methods of Escaping the | Terrible Miseries of the | Punishments on the Wicked | there, declared. | In a | Sermon | Preached in the Hearing, and at the | Request, of a Man under a Sen- | tence of Death for a Murder; | Just before the Execution of the | Sentence; and upon a Text by | himself assigned for the Sermon | to insist upon. | At Boston, 13. d. IV. m. 1717. | ... | *Boston, Printed by J. Allen, for Robert | Starke ....* 1717. 12mo, pp. (2), 49, 6. M. 46572

MATHER. Vanishing Things. An Essay on Dying Man, ... In A Sermon Preached on the Departure of ... Mr. Thomas Bernard, the late Pastor of a Church in Andover ... . *Boston: Printed by S. Kneeland, for D. Henchman.* 1718. Sm. 8vo, pp. (2), 35, (1). 46573

MATHER. Verba Opportuna. The Circumstances of Boston considered, with fresh Inculcations of Early Piety. *Boston.* 1714. Sm. 8vo. 46574

[MATHER.] Verba Vivifica. Some Words of Life, produced by the death of Some Young Persons. *Boston.* 1714. Sm. 8vo. 46575

[MATHER.] A Very Needful Caution. | A Brief | Essay, | To Discover the Sin that | Slayes its Ten Thousands; | And Represent the Character | and Condition of the | Coveteous. | With some Antidotes against | the Infection of Coveteousness | and Earthly-Mindedness. | ... | *Boston, in N. E. Printed and Sold | by Timothy Green ....* 1707. 12mo, pp. 60. M. 46576

[MATHER.] The Vial poured out upon the Sea. | A | Remarkable Relation | Of certain | Pirates | Brought unto a Tragical and Untimely | End. | Some Conferences with them ... . | Their Behaviour at their Ex- | ecution. | And a | Sermon | Preached on that Occasion. | ... | *Boston: Printed by T. Fleet, for N. Belknap.* 1726. 8vo, pp. (2), 51. BA. 46577

[MATHER.] Victorina. | A Sermon | Preach'd, | On the Decease | and | At the Desire, | of | Mrs. Katharin Mather, | By her Father. |

Whereunto there is added, | A further Account of that | Young Gentlewoman, | By another Hand. | *Boston: Printed by B. Green, | for Daniel Henchman ....* 1717. 24mo, pp. (2), viii, 86. B., H.

[MATHER.] Vigilantius. | Or, | A Servant of the Lord | Found Ready for the | Coming of the Lord. | A Discourse | Occasioned by the Early Death | of Seven Young | Ministers, | With a Little while One of another; | With some Essay, upon their | very Commendable and Imitable | Character. | And an Elegy upon them. | ... | *Boston: Printed & Sold by B. Green,* | ... . 1706. Sm. 8vo, pp. (2), 38. 46579

[MATHER.] Vigilius. | Or, The Awakener, | Making a Brief Essay, | To Rebuke first the Natural Sleep | Which too often proves a Dead Fly, | in the Devotions of | them that indulge it. | And then the | Moral Sleep, | Wherein the Souls of Men frequently | Omit the Duties, and Forfeit the Com- | forts, of Religion In Earnest. | ... *Boston: Printed by J. Franklin.* 1719. 12mo, pp. (2), 14. B., H. 46580

This exceedingly scarce piece was printed by Benjamin Franklin while a boy, managing the business of his brother, James Franklin, while he was in difficulties. He was then in his fourteenth year. It is an unusually neat specimen of Boston printing.

[MATHER.] Virtue in it's Verdure. | A | Christian | Exhibited as a | Green Olivetree, | in the | House of God; | with a | Character | of the Virtuous | Mrs. Abigail Brown: | ... Who Expired Feb. 18. 1724, 5. | ... | *Boston, N. E.* | *Printed by B. Green.* 1725. 8vo, pp. (4), iv, 28. B., BA., H. 46581

An appendix, partly by "another hand," forms the last four pages of the tract.

MATHER. A Vision in the Temple. | ... On a Day of Prayer kept May | 10. 1721 at the Opening of the New | Brick Meeting House in the North | part of Boston ... . | By Cotton Mather ... . *Boston: Robert Starkey.* 1721. 12mo, pp. (2), 45. B. 46582

MATHER. Vita Brevis. An Essay upon Withering Flowers. *Boston.* 1714. Sm. 8vo. 46583

Evidently on the same subject as "Verba Vivifica." I have not been able to find either of the books.

[MATHER.] Vital Christianity: | A brief | Essay | On the Life of God, | in the | Soul of Man; | Produced and Maintained by a | Christ living in us: | and | The Mystery of a Christ | within, Explained. | ... | *Printed by Samuel Keimer, for Eleazer | Phillips, in Charles-Town in New-England.* 1725. 8vo, pp. (4), 30. B.

[MATHER.] The Voice of God | in a Tempest. | A | Sermon | Preached in the Time of the | Storm; | Wherein many and heavy and | unknown Losses were Suffered | at Boston, (and Parts | Adjacent,) Febr. 24. 1722–3. | By One of the Ministers in Boston. | ... | *Boston: N. E.* | *Printed by S. Kneeland.* MDCCXXIII. 12mo, pp. (4), 19. B., BA., N., W. 46585

[MATHER.] Le Vrai Patron des Saines Paroles. [*Boston.* 1704.] 8vo, pp. 15. B. 46586

"Designed for the Instruction of our French Captives."—MATHER'S *Catalogue of his own writings.*

MATHER. A Warning to the Flocks against Wolves in Sheeps-Cloathing. Or, A Faithful Advice from several Ministers of the Gospel, in and near Boston, unto the Churches of New-England, relating to the Dangers that may arise from Impostors, pretending to be Ministers. With a Brief History of some Impostors ... . By Cotton Mather. *Boston: Printed for the Booksellers.* 1700. 16mo, pp. 79. W. 46587

"A Letter Containing a Remarkable History of an Impostor" [Samuel May], dated 25 d. 10 m. 1699, signed by C. Mather, pp. 29–52; A Postscript, "Something to be Known by all the Churches," etc. "A Faithful Advice from Several Ministers," dated Boston, Dec. 28, 1699, is signed by Increase Mather and twelve others (pp. 3–10).

MATHER. Warnings from the Dead. | Or | Solemn Admonitions | unto | All People; | but Especially unto | Young Persons | to Beware | of such Evils as would bring | them to the Dead. | By Cotton Mather. | In Two Discourses, | Occasioned by a Sentence of Death, | Executed on some Unhappy Ma- | lefactors. Together with the | Last Confession made by a | Young Woman, who Dyed on June | 8. 1693. One of these Malefactors. | *Boston in New-England; Printed by Bartholomew Green, for | Samuel Phillips ....* 1693. 12mo, pp. (2), 67. 46588

MATHER. The Way of Truth laid out. A Catechism which, as with Supplies from the Tower of David, Arms Christians of all Ages, to Refute the Errors which most commonly assault the Cause of Christianity: and To Preserve the Faith once delivered unto the Saints. In Seven Essays ... . By Cotton Mather ... . The Second Edition. *Boston: Printed by S. Kneeland.* 1721. 12mo, pp. (2), 8, 95, (2). 46589

"One of the very rarest of Mather's works. The title is not in S. Mather's list, nor in any library catalogue which has been consulted. It seems to be the second edition, with additions and change of title, of 'The Man of God furnished with Supplies from the Tower of David,' named by S. Mather, under the year 1706 (No. 46396). Of the Seven Essays, the first, entitled 'The Fall of Babylon,' was appended to

'Frontiers well Defended,' printed in 1707 (No. 46332), with a prefatory note headed 'The Protestant Armed from the Tower of David.' At the end of the volume is 'The Body of Divinity Versified' (2 pp.), which was (first?) printed in 'Maschil,' 1702 (No. 46403). 'An Addition,' pp. 91–95, contains 'A Short Catechism for the Conscience, on the Condition of Ungospellized Plantations.'"—J. H. TRUMBULL.

MATHER. The Way to Excel. | Meditations, | Awakened by the Death of | the Reverend | Mr. Joshua Moodey; | With some Short Character | of that | Eminent Person: | Who slept in Jesus, 4. d. 5. m. 1697. | In the Sixty-fifth year of his Age. | By Cotton Mather. | ... | *Boston, in N. E.* | *Printed by B. Green, and J. Allen.* 1697. 8vo, pp. 32. 46590

MATHER. The Way to Prosperity. | A | Sermon | Preached to the Honourable | Convention | Of the | Governour, Council, and Representatives | of the Massachuset-Colony in New-England; | on May 23. 1689. | By Cotton Mather. | ... | *Boston.* | *Printed by Richard Pierce, for Benjamin | Harris. Anno Domini* MDCXC. Sm. 8vo, pp. (7), 26 [*i. e.* 36], 5, (7). B., H., W. 46591

Usually bound up with "The Wonderful Works," No. 46602, which *see* for a note.

MATHER. The Wayes and Joyes of | Early Piety. | One Essay More, | To Describe and Commend, | A Walk in the Truth | Of our Great | Saviour, | Unto | The Children of His People. | ... In the Audience of the | General Assembly of the | Massachusett-Province. | By Cotton Mather, D.D. | ... | *Boston in N. E. Printed by B. Green, Sold by Samuel Gerrish ....* 1712. 12mo, pp. (2), 54, (2), (4). H., W. 46592

[MATHER.] A Weaned Christian. | ... A brief Essay ... . *Boston, in N. E. Printed ...* | *by Timothy Green.* 1704. 12mo, pp. 42. H., W. 46593

[MATHER.] What should be most of all Tho't upon. | A | Brief Essay, | To Awaken in a Dying Man, | ... a Proper and a Lively Concern for, | A Good State | after | Death. | ... | *Boston.* | *Printed by T. Green, for D. Henchman.* | 1713. | 12mo, pp. (2), ii, 42. H. 46594

MATHER. What the Pious Parent | wishes for. | By Dr. Cotton Mather. | Boston Lecture 23 d. 1 m. 1721. | *Boston.* 1721. 8vo, pp. 34. 46595

This is the first sermon in "A Course of Sermons," No. 46274, *supra*.

[MATHER.] Wholesome Words. A Visit of Advice, Given unto Families That are Visited with Sickness; By a Pastoral Letter, briefly declaring the Duties incumbent on all Persons in

the Families that have any Sick Persons in them. *Boston: ... D. Henchman.* 1713. 12mo, pp. (2), 24. 46596

Very rare. In S. Mather's list the date is 1702; Dr. Trumbull says that "may be the date of the first edition."

MATHER. The | Widow of Naim. | Remarks | On the Illustrious | Miracle | Wrought by Our Almighty | Redeemer, | On the behalf of a Desolate | Widow. | By the Late Reverend Cotton Mather, | ... | *Boston: Printed in the Year* | MDCCXXVIII. 8vo, pp. (4), 30. B., M. 46597

This was written in 1724, and dedicated to Mrs. Dorothy Frizzel.

[MATHER.] The Will of a Father submitted to. | The Duty of | Patient Submission | to every Condition, | which the Providence of God, | Orders for the Children of Men. | Enforced from the | Glorious Pattern of the | Blessed Jesus, | Readily and Cheerfully Submitting to | take the Cup, which His Father | had given Him. | In a very Brief Discourse, | made with a special Regard unto a | Religious Family, Burying an Only | Son. | And at a Time of much Affliction in | the Neighborhood. | *Boston: Printed by T. Fleet, for D. Henchman.* 1713. Sm. 8vo, pp. 40. W. 46598

MATHER. Winter-Meditations. | Directions | How to employ the Liesure [*sic*] of the | Winter | For the Glory of God. | Accompanied with Reflections, as well Historical, | as Theological, not only upon the | Circumstances of the | Winter, | But also, upon the Notable Works of God, | Both in, | Creation, and Providence: | Especially those, which more immediately Con- | cern every Particular Man, in the whole course | of his Life: | And upon the Religious Works, wherewith e- | very Man should acknowledge God, in and | from the Accidents of the Winter. | By Cotton Mather. | With a Preface of the Reverend, | Mr. John Higginson. | *Boston, Printed ... by Benj. Harris ....* 1693. 8vo, pp. (16), 82.

MATHER. Winter Piety. | A Very Brief Essay, | in the | Methods of Piety, | wherein | A Serious Christian may Propose to meet with his Blessed | Saviour, at the Temple | in the Winter. | Made in a Sermon, at Boston-Lecture, 27. d. 10. m. 1711. ... By Cotton Mather, D.D. | *Boston in N. E. Printed by B. Green: Sold by* | *T. Green ....* 1712. 12mo, pp. (2), 33. 46600

MATHER. Winthropi Justa. | A | Sermon | At the Funeral of the Honble | John Winthrop, Esq. | Late Governour of the Colony of Connecticut in New- | England. Who Died at Boston, | Nov. 27, 1707. in his 69th Year. | ... | By Cotton Mather. | ... | *Boston.* 1708. 8vo, pp. 40. + *Printed at Boston in New-England,*

and Reprinted | *at London, by B. Harris ...* 1709. 8vo, pp. 16, (1). + A Second Impression. [*Ibid.*] 1710. 8vo, pp. (18), (1). BA.

MATHER. The Witchcraft Delusion. *See* Drake (S. G.)

MATHER. The Wonderful Works of God | Commemorated. | Praises | Bespoke for the God of Heaven, | In a Thanksgiving | Sermon; | Delivered on Decemb. 19. 1689. | Containing | Just Reflections upon the Excel- | lent Things done by the Great God, | more Generally in Creation and Re- | demption, and in the Govern- | ment of the World; But more Par- | ticularly in the Remarkable Revolu- | tions of Providence which are every | where the Matter of present Observation. | With a Postscript giving an Account of some very | stupendous Accidents, which have lately happened | in France. | By Cotton Mather. | To which is Added a Sermon Preached unto the | Convention of the Massachusetts Colony in | New-England. | With a short Narrative of several Prodigies, which New- | England hath of late had the Alarms of Heaven in. | *Printed at Boston by S. Green. & Sold by Joseph | Browning at the corner of the Prison Lane and | Benj. Harris at the London Coffee-House.* 1690. Sm. 8vo, pp. (8), 62, 7, 26 [36], 5, 7. B. + Second Edition. *Boston.* 1703. 46602

The Convention Sermon has a separate title-page and paging; *see* "The Way to Prosperity," No. 46591, *supra*. The appendix (and its introductory "Mantissa") "touching Prodigies in New-England," are also separately paged. Some of the prodigies narrated are very striking: "In the summer of the year 1688, just before the first eruption of our unhappy *War*, we had growing in Boston a *Cabbage-Root*, out of which there sprouted three very wonderful Branches, one of them exactly resembling a *Curtlace* [Cutlass], another of them as exactly resembling a *Rapier*, and a third, extreamly like to the *Club* used by the Indians in their barbarous Executions. I was myself one among the many who visited this Curiosity." This work of Mather's is of peculiar interest, as containing (in the dedicatory epistle to Sir Henry Ashurst) a copy, cut in wood or type metal, of a portion of the famous Dighton Rock Inscription.

MATHER. The Wonders of the Invisible World. | Observations | As well Historical as Theological, upon the Nature, the | Number, and the Operations of the | Devils. | Accompany'd with, I. Some Accounts of the Grievous Molestations, by Dæ- | mons and Witchcrafts, which have lately | annoy'd the Countrey; and the Trials of some eminent | Malefactors Executed upon occasion thereof: with several | Remarkable Curiosities therein occurring. | II. Some Counsils, Directing a due Improvement of the ter- | rible things, lately done, by the Unusual & Amazing | Range of Evil Spirits, in Our Neighbourhood: & | the methods to prevent the Wrongs which those Evil | Angels may intend against all sorts of people among us: | especially in Accusations of the Innocent. | III. Some Conjectures upon the great Events, likely | to befall, the

World in General, and New-En-|gland in Particular; as also upon the Advances of | the Time, when we shall see Better Dayes. | IV. A short Narrative of a late Outrage committed by a | knot of Witches in Swedeland, very much Resem-|bling, and so far Explaining, That under which our parts | of America have laboured! | V. The Devil Discovered: In a Brief Discourse upon | those Temptations, which are the more Ordinary Devices | of the Wicked One. | By Cotton Mather. | *Boston Printed by Benj. Harris for Sam. Phillips.* 1693. | Sm. 8vo, pp. (32), 151, (1), 32 [24]. B. 46603

Of all works by the Mathers, this is probably the rarest; it is, perhaps, also one of the most important, as exhibiting the prevalence of the delusion which at that time infected New England.

MATHER. The Wonders of the Invisible World: | Being an Account of the | Tryals | of Several Witches, | Lately Executed in | New-England: | And of several remarkable Curiosities therein Occurring. | Together with, | I. Observations upon the Nature, the Number, and the Operations of the Devils. | II. A short Narrative of a late outrage committed by a knot of Witches in | Swede-Land, very much resembling, and so far explaining, that under which | New-England has laboured. | III. Some Councels directing a due Improvement of the Terrible things lately | done by the unusual and amazing Range of Evil-Spirits in New-England. | IV. A brief Discourse upon those Temptations which are the more ordinary Devi-|ces of Satan. | By Cotton Mather. | Published by the Special command of his Excellency the Governour of | the Province of the Massachusetts-Bay in New-England. | *Printed first, at Bostun in New-England; and Reprinted at Lon-|don, for John Dunton, at the Raven in the Poultry.* 1693. | 4to, pp. (4), 98.

Very rare. This is the first and only complete London edition. The last page is numbered 98, but the pagination is irregular, the number of pages being, in fact, 106, exclusive of the four preliminary pages not numbered. A leaf preceding the title, has the half-title: "The | Tryals | of | Several Witches, | Lately Executed | in | New-England: | Published by the | Special Command of the Governour;" | and, on the verso, is the "Imprimatur. Dec. 23. 1693. Edmund Bohun."

MATHER. The Wonders of the Invisible World: | Being an Account of the | Tryals | of | Several Witches | Lately Executed in | New-England: | And of Several Remarkable Curiosities | therein Occurring. | By Cotton Mather. | Published by the Special Command of his Excellency the | Governour of the Province of the Massachusetts-Bay in New-| England. | The Second Edition. | *Printed first, at Boston in New-England, and reprinted at London, for | John Dunton, at the Raven in the Poultry.* 1693. 4to, pp. 62.

The pagination of this edition is very irregular.

MATHER. The Wonders of the Invisible World: | Being an Account of the | Tryals | of | Several Witches | Lately Executed in New-England: | And of several Remarkable Curiosities | therein Occurring. | By Cotton Mather. | Published by the Special Command of his Excellency | the Governour of the Province of the Massachusetts-Bay in | New-England. | The Third Edition. | *Printed first at Boston in New-England, and reprinted at London, | for John Dunton, at the Raven in the Poultry.* 1693. 4to, pp. 64.

MATHER. The Wonders of the Invisible World, Being an account of the Tryals of Several Witches lately executed in New-England. By Cotton Mather, D.D. To which is added a Further Account of the Tryals of the New-England Witches. By Increase Mather, D.D. ... *London: John Russell Smith.* 1862. F'cap 8vo, pp. xvi, 291. BA. 46607

[MATHER.] The Words of Understanding. | Three Essays: | I. The Philomela. | With, The Notes of | Morning-Piety. | II. The Ephemeron. | Or, Tears drop'd on | Dust and Ashes. | III. Jonah: Or, The | Dove in Safety. | Occasioned by some Early | Deaths which require such | Notice to be taken of them. | ... | *Boston: Printed by S. Kneeland, | for J. Edwards* ... . 1724. 12mo, pp. (2), 105, (1). B. 46608

"These sermons wre published & some of ym at least Preach'd on occasion of ye Loss of *Increase* ye eldest son of Dr *Cotton Mather* of Boston; we havg set sail from Barbadoes sm time last Fall for Newfoundland, was never after heard of, & so concluded to be founder'd in ye sea."—*MS. note of* Mr. Prince.

MATHER. Work upon the Ark. Meditations upon the Ark as a Type of the Church; Delivered in a Sermon at Boston, [Nov. 17, 1689,] ... . By Cotton Mather. *Boston: Printed by Samuel Green.* 1689. 8vo, pp. (10), 54. 46609

[MATHER.] Work Within Doors. An Essay To Assist the Serious in the Grand Exercise of Conversing with Themselves, and Communing with their own Hearts ... . *Boston: Printed by T. Green.* 1709. 12mo, pp. 40. 46610

[MATHER.] The World Alarm'd. | A | Surprizing Relation, | Of a New | Burning-Island | Lately raised out of the Sea, | near Tercera; | with | A Geographical and Theological | Improvement of So astonishing | an Occurrence. | And | A brief History of the other Ignivomous Mountains at | this day flaming in the World. | In a Letter to an Honourable | Fellow of the Royal | Society at London. | From a Member of the same | Society, at Boston. | *Boston: Printed by B. Green, | for S. Gerrish* ... 1721. 12mo, pp. (2), 10, (2). BM.

[MATHER.] Wussukwhonk. *See* "An Epistle," No. 46304.

[MATHER.] A Year and a Life Well Concluded. A brief Essay, On the Good Things Wherein The Last Works Of a Christian, may be, and should be, His Best Works. A Sermon Preached on the Last Day of the Year, 1719. *Boston: Printed by S. Kneeland, for B. Gray* ... . 1719–20. 12mo, pp. 24.

[MATHER.] A Young Follower of a Great Saviour. *Boston.* 1706. 8vo, pp. 36. 46613

Perhaps the same as "Vigilantius," No. 46579, *supra.*

MATHER. The Young Man Spoken to. Another Essay, to Recommend & Inculcate the Maxims of Early Religion, unto Young Persons ... In a Sermon preached unto them on a Special Occasion ... . By Cotton Mather. *Boston: Printed by T. Green, for Samuel Gerrish.* 1712. 12mo, pp. (4), 43. 46614

Occasioned by the death of Mr. Peter Oliver, "an Hopeful, and a Pious Young Man, One well beloved in the Vicinity" (p. 38). Very rare.

[MATHER.] The Young Man's Monitor. *Boston.* 1700. 8vo, pp. 43. 46615

Perhaps the same as "Things that Young People," etc., No. 46547, *supra.*

[MATHER.] Youth in its Brightest Glory. An Essay, Directing them that are Young ... to become strong in Grace, by the Word of God abiding in them. ... *Boston: Printed ... by T. Green.* 1709. 12mo, pp. 36. H. 46616

[MATHER.] Zalmonah. | The Gospel of the | Brazen Serpent, | In the Mosaic History. | Offered | With some Uncommon Sentiments | upon it; | ... *Boston: J. Phillips.* 1725. 8vo, pp. (2), 106.

MATHER. Zelotes. | A Zeal | For the | House of God; | ... a Sermon ... in | ... | Boston. | On 8 d. XI m. 1716, 17. ... By Cotton Mather ... . *Boston: Printed by J. Allen, for Nicholas Boone.* 1717. 12mo, pp. 44. BA. 46618

The sermon relates to "their First Entrance into a New Edifice for Publick Worship."

Since going to press with the earlier pages of Cotton Mather's works, I have received from the Rev. Dr. Cox, of the Bodleian Library at Oxford, correct titles of the following:

MATHER. Awakening Thought on the | Sleep of Death. | A short Essay, | on the | Sleep, | which | By Death all men must fall into; ... | With a Debt paid unto the Memory of | some that sleep in Jesus. | By Cotton Mather, D.D. | ... | *Boston in N. E. Printed ... by Timothy | Green* ... . 1712. Sm. 8vo, pp. viii, 34. BD. 46619

[MATHER.] The Echo's of Devotion. | A very brief and plain | Essay | on those Acts of Compliance | which all | Calls to Piety | are to be entertained withal. | ... | Now published ... . | *Boston: Printed by T. Fleet and T. Crump, for | Samuel Gerrish.* 1716. | 12mo, pp. 36. BD. 46620

[MATHER.] Elizabeth in her Holy Retirement; | An Essay | To Prepare a Pious | Woman | for her | Lying In | or Maxims and Methods | of Piety | To direct and Support an | Handmaid of the Lord | who expects a | Time of Travail. | ... | *Boston in N. E. Printed by B. Green, for | Nicholas Boone* ... . 1716. 12mo, pp. 36.

[MATHER.] Hezekiah. | A Christian | Armed with | Strength | from above; | to keep him from Fainting | in a day of | Adversity. | In a brief Essay ... . | *Boston: Printed by B. G. for Benj. Eliot.* 1713. 12mo, pp. 37. BD. 46622

The following relate to Cotton Mather:

MATHER. Cotton Mather & Witchcraft Two Notices of Mr. Upham his Reply *Boston: T. R. Marvin & Son.* 1870. 24mo, pp. 30. H. 46623

MATHER. The Life of Cotton Mather. Containing an account of the uncommonly Early Piety of Dr. Mather, his Method of Teaching his Children, and of his Peculiar Habits, Religious Exercises, &c. With an Original Preface by Dr. Watts. *Leeds.* 1802. 18mo, pp. 108. 46624

MATHER. The Life of the late Rev. and Learned Dr. Cotton Mather, of Boston. *Philadelphia.* 1829. 24mo. 46625

MATHER. Life of Cotton Mather, Abridged. *Boston.* 1744. 12mo. 46626

MATHER (E.) A Serious | Exhortation | to the | Present and Succeeding | Generation | in | New-England, | Earnestly calling upon all to Endeavour that the Lords | Gracious Presence may be continued with Posterity. | Being the Substance of the | Last Sermons | Preached | By Eleazer Mather, late Pastor of the Church in | Northampton in New-England. | ... | *Cambridge: Printed by S. G. and M. J.* 1671. 4to, pp. (8), 31. + The Second Edition. *Boston: Printed by John Foster.* 1678. 4to, pp. (4), 31. B., C.

The address "To the Church and Inhabitants of Northampton" (pp. 5), in the first edition, and the letter "To the Reader" (pp. 2), in the second, are by Increase Mather. Both editions of the work are very rare.

MATHER (E.) Antimasonic Tracts, No. 5. Masonic Obligations unlawful: as proved and substantiated in a Court of Justice on empannelling the Jury at the Trial of Elihu Mather for a Conspiracy to kidnap Wm. Morgan, at the Orleans County Court, Nov. 11th, 1829. ... *Boston.* 1829. 12mo, pp. 16.

MATHER (I.) Advice to the Children of Godly Ancestors. Given July 9. 1721. By Increase Mather ... . And taken in Short-Hand, by one of the Hearers. *Boston: Printed by S. Kneeland* ... . 1721. 12mo, pp. 16. 46629

This "Advice," given in his eighty-third year, "without using any notes," is in "A Course of Sermons," No. 46274, *supra.*

MATHER. Angelographia, | or | A Discourse | Concerning the Nature and Power of the | Holy Angels, and the Great Benefit | which the True Fearers of God Receive | by their Ministry: | Delivered in several | Sermons: | To which is added, A Sermon concerning the Sin and | Misery of the Fallen Angels: | Also a Disquisition concerning | Angelical-Apparitions. | By Increase Mather, President of Harvard | Colledge, in Cambridge, and Preacher of the | Gospel at Boston in New-England. | *Boston in N. E. Printed by B. Green & J. Allen, | for Samuel Phillips* ... . 1696. Sm. 8vo, pp. (16), 132, 44. Portrait. B. 46630

The portrait in this volume is said to have been the first ever engraved in this country. The "Disquisition" has a separate title-page and paging.

[MATHER.] The | Answer | Of Several | Ministers | in and near | Boston, | To that Case of Conscience, | Whether it is Lawful for a Man | to Marry his Wives own Sister? | *Boston in N. E.* | *Printed and Sold by Bartholomew Green.* 1695. Sm. 8vo, pp. 8, (1). C.

The "Answer" is signed by Increase Mather, Charles Morton, James Allen, Samuel Willard, James Sherman, John Danforth, Cotton Mather, Nehemiah Walter; and is against such marriages. It is followed by an obituary notice of Mrs. Judith Hull, which may be a separate publication, and is probably by Cotton Mather.

[MATHER.] An Arrow | against | Profane and Promiscuous | Dancing. | Drawn out of the Quiver of the | Scriptures. | By the Ministers of Christ at Boston | in New-England. | *Boston: Printed by Samuel Green* ... . 1684. Sm. 8vo, pp. 30. M. 46632

In November, 1684, the Ministers of Boston "come to the Court and complain against a Dancing Master [Mr. Francis Stepney] who seeks to set up here, and hath mixt Dances, and his time of meeting is *Lecture-Day*, and 'tis reported he should say that by one Play *he could teach more Divinity than Mr. Willard* or the Old Testament. Mr. Moody said 'twas not a time for N. E. to dance. Mr. *Mather* struck at the Root, speaking against mixt Dances."—SEWALL'S *Diary.* "Mr. Stepney was ordered not to keep a dancing school. Disregarding the prohibition, in February, 1685–6, he was

prosecuted and fined £100, for 'speaking blasphemous words,' but the payment of all but £10, was remitted on condition that he should leave Boston before the last of March. Just then, a second impression of the 'Arrow against Dancing' was published." —BRINLEY *Catalogue.* I am unable to find any other account of the second edition.

MATHER. Awakening Soul-Saving Truths Plainly Delivered In Several Sermons in which is shewed, I. That Many are Called, who are not effectually Called. II. That Men may be of the Visible Church, and yet not be of the Lords Church. III. That the Chosen of God are comparatively but Few. By Increase Mather, D.D. *Boston: Printed by S. Kneeland for B. Gray, and J. Edwards* ... . 1720. 12mo, pp. (2), ii, 100, (1). C.

MATHER. Awakening Truths | Tending to | Conversion. | Delivered | In several Sermons | Wherein is Shewed, | I. That the greatest Sinners may | be Converted and Saved. | II. That Sinners who cannot | Convert themselves, ought to | Pray for Converting Grace. | III. That Sinners who neglect Spiritual Blessings until the | Day of Grace is past will wish | for them but in vain, when it | is too late. | In Which Sermons notice is taken of | some late Remarkable Conversions. | By Increase Mather, D.D. | *Boston in N. E. Sold by Timothy Green.* 1710. 12mo, pp. (10), 120.

MATHER. The | Believers | Gain by | Death: | Opened and Applyed | In a Sermon. | ... | Upon | The Death of a Valuable Relative. | By I. Mather, D.D. | ... | *Boston: Printed by B. G. for S. Gerrish.* 1713. Sm. 12mo, pp. (2), 34. H., M. 46635

This sermon was preached on the death of his daughter-in-law, Nov. 22, 1713.

MATHER. The Blessed | Hope, | And the Glorious Appearing of the | Great God our Saviour, | Jesus Christ. | Opened & Applied, | In several | Sermons. | By Increase Mather, | ... . | *Boston: Printed by Timothy Green, for N.* | *Boone.* 1701. Sm. 8vo, pp. 142. H.

[MATHER.] A Brief | Account | concerning | Several of the Agents | of | New-England, | their | Negotiation at the Court | of | England: | With | Some Remarks on the New Charter | Granted to the Colony of Massachusets. | Shewing | That all things duely Considered, Greater Priviledges | than what are therein contained, could not at this | Time rationally be expected by the People there. | ... | *London, Printed in the Year* 1691. 4to, pp. 24. BA., H., M.

A piece of uncommon rarity. Reprinted in the "Andros Tracts," II. 271–296.

MATHER. Brief Animadversions on the Narrative of the New England Anabaptists. *Boston* ⌜*Printed by John Foster*⌟. 1681. 4to. 46638

[MATHER.] A | Brief Discourse Concerning the | unlawfulness of the | Common Prayer | Worship. | and Of Laying the Hand on, and | Kissing the Booke in | Swearing. | By a Reverend and Learned Divine. | [*Boston:*] *Printed in the Year, &c.* [1689]. 12mo, pp. (4), 21. + The Second Impression. *Reprinted at London in the Year* 1689. Sm. 8vo, pp. (2), 43. W. 46639

One of the most rare of Increase Mather's pieces. The preface to the first edition is signed "T. P." It has been erroneously attributed to John Cotton. *See* "Some Remarks on a Pretended Answer," *infra*, in which Mather acknowledges the authorship, and points out an error in the spelling of a Hebrew word. For a reply, *see* [Williams (J.)]

MATHER. A | Brief History | of the | Warr | With the Indians in | Nevv-England. | (From June 24, 1675. when the first English-man was mur-|dered by the Indians, to August 12, 1676. when *Philip*, aliàs | *Metacomet*, the principal Author and Beginner | of the Warr, was slain.) | Wherein the Grounds, Beginning, and Progress of the Warr, | is summarily expressed. | Together with a serious | Exhortation | to the Inhabitants of that Land, | By Increase Mather, Teacher of a Church of | Christ, in Boston in New-England. | ... | *Boston. Printed and Sold by John Foster over* | *against the Sign of the Dove.* 1676. 4to, pp. (6), 51, (8); (4), 26. 46640

"An Earnest Exhortation" has a separate title-page and paging. Mather was stimulated to this literary labor by the knowledge that his reverend brother, Wm. Hubbard, was engaged upon a similar work. Indeed, the two treatises were probably almost simultaneously passing through the press of John Foster. Mr. Drake observes: "When it is considered that the war was not ended until the autumn of 1676, the year in which it was printed, it must be apparent to every reader that the work was a hurried performance." In his preface, Mather exhibits a little trace of acerbity, when he asserts, "This following relation was written neer upon a year ago; since which a reverend author hath emitted a narrative of the troubles which happened by the Indians: ... nevertheless ... most of the things here insisted on, are not so much as once taken notice of in that narrative." Of this exceedingly rare book two copies only are known: Mr. Brinley's and one in England. The following is a reprint:

MATHER. A Brief | History | of the | War | with the | Indians | in | New-England. | From June 24. 1675. (when the first English-man was Murder-|ed by the Indians) to August 12. 1676. when Philip, | alias Metacomet, the principal Author and | Beginner of the War, was slain. | Wherein the Grounds, Beginning, and Progress of the War, is summarily | expressed. Together with a serious Exhortation to the | Inhabitants of that Land. | By Increase Mather, Teacher of a Church of | Christ, in Boston in New-England. | ... | *London, Printed for Richard Chiswell, at the Rose and Crown in St. Pauls* | *Church-Yard, according to the Original Copy Printed* | *in New-England.* 1676. 4to, pp. (8), 51, (1), 8. C.

The half-title reads: "The Wars of New-England." The "Serious Exhortation,"

though named in the title, is not given is this edition. The preface refers to John Eliot as "this now aged servant of the Lord." Extremely rare. For a modern reprint, *see* "History," *infra.*

[MATHER.] A Brief | Relation | of the | State | of | New-England, | From the Beginning of that | Plantation | To this Present Year, 1689. | In a Letter to a Person of Quality. ... | *London: Printed for Richard Baldwine, near the Black Bull* | *in the Old Baily.* 1689. 4to, pp. 18. 46642

Reprinted in the "Mass. Hist. Soc. Collections," XXI. 93; Force's "Tracts," IV., No. 11; and "Andros Tracts," II. 149.

MATHER. Ein Brieff | von dem | Glücklichen Fortgang | des Evangelii | Bey den | West-Indianern in Neu-Engeland | An den berühmten | Herrn Johann Leusden | Der H. Sprache Professor auff der hohen Schule | zu Utrecht geschrieben | von | Crescentius Matherus, | Diener des Worts Gottes bey den Bostoniensern | und Rectore des Harvardinischen Collegii zu Cantabrig | in Neu-Engeland | London druckts J. G. 1688. | Zum andernmahl gedruckt und mit dem glücklichen | Fortgang des Evangelii bey den Ost-Indianern | vermehret | Utrecht gedurckt [*sic*] bey W. B. 1693. | ... Aus dem Lateinischen ins Hochteutsche übersetzet | Von einem Bekenner der Wahrheit die nach der | Gottseligkeit ist. | *Halle, Gedruckt bey Christoph Salfelden.* 1696. | Sm. 8vo, 24 leaves. H.

This is a German translation of "De Successu Evangelii," *infra.*

MATHER. Burnings | Bewailed: | In a | Sermon, | Occasioned by the | Lamentable Fire | Which was in Boston, Octob. 2. | 1711. | In which the Sins which Provoke | the Lord to Kindle Fires, | are Enquired into. | By Increase Mather, D.D. ... | *Boston Printed: Sold by Timothy Green.* 1711. Sm. 8vo, pp. (4), 36. B., BA. + The Second Edition. *Boston in N. E. Printed and Sold by Timothy Green* ... . 1712. Sm. 8vo, pp. (4), 36. 46644

MATHER. A Call from Heaven | To the Present and Succeeding | Generations | Or A | Discourse | Wherin [*sic*] is shewed, | I. That the Children of Godly Parents are under | special Advantages and Encouragements to | seek the Lord. | II. The exceeding danger of Apostasie ... . [Delivered in a Sermon, preached in the Audi-|ence of the general Assembly of the Massachu-|sets Colony, at Boston in New-England, | May 23. 1677. being the day of Election | there. | ...] III. That Young Men ought to Remember God | their Creator. | By Increase Mather ... . *Boston: Printed by John Foster.* 1679. Sm. 8vo, pp. (6), 114. + The Second Impression. *Boston: Printed by R*[*ichard*] *P*[*ierce*] *for I. Brunning.* 1685. Sm. 8vo, pp. (8), 198. B., W. 46645

MATHER. A Call to the Tempted. | A Sermon | On the horrid Crime | of | Self-Murder, | Preached on a Remarkable Occasion, | by the Memorable | Dr. Increase Mather. | And now Published from his Notes, | for a Charitable Stop to Suicides. | ... | *Boston: Printed by B. Green, March 12th*, 1723, 4. Sm. 8vo, pp. (4), ii, 17. BA. 46646

At the end is "Boston, 23d. V.m. 1682." "The Occasion of the Publication" prefixed, was evidently written by Cotton Mather.

[MATHER.] A Case of Conscience | Concerning Eating of Blood, | Considered and Answered. | [Colophon:] *Boston in New-England, Printed by B. Green, and J. Allen.* 1697. 8vo, pp. 8.

MATHER. Cases of Conscience | Concerning evil | Spirits | Personating Men, | Witchcrafts, infallible Proofs of | Guilt in such as are accused | with that Crime. | All Considered according to the Scriptures, | History, Experience, and the Judgment | of many Learned men. | By Increase Mather, President of Harvard | College, at Cambridge, and Teacher of | a Church at Boston, in New-England. | *Boston Printed, and sold by Benjamin | Harris, at the London Coffee-House.* 1693. Sm. 8vo, pp. (8), 67, (7). Portrait.

Reprinted with "A Further Account," *infra*, and with Cotton Mather's "Wonders of the Invisible World," *London*, 1862, No. 46607, *supra*. Very rare.

[MATHER.] A Collection. *See* Mather (C.), No. 46263.

MATHER. David | Serving His | Generation. | Or, A Sermon | Shewing | What is to be done in order to our so | Serving our Generation, as that when we | Dy, we shall Enter into a Blessed Rest. | ... | Occasioned by the Death, of the Reverend | Mr. John Baily, | ... | December 12th. 1697. | By Increase Mather ... | *Boston, Printed by B. Green, & J. Allen.* 1698. Sm. 8vo, pp. 39. BA.

MATHER. The Day of Trouble is near. | Two | Sermons | Wherein is shewed, | What are the Signs of a Day of Trouble being near. | And particularly, | What reason there is for New-England to expect | A Day of Trouble. | ... | Preached (the 11th day of the 12th Moneth, 1673. being a day of | Humiliation | in one of the Churches in Boston. | By Increase Mather, Teacher of that Church. | ... | *Cambridge: Printed by Marmaduke Johnson.* 1674. 4to, pp. (4), 31. B., S. 46650

See Cotton Mather's "Magnalia," II. 46.

[MATHER.] The Declaration of the Gentlemen, Merchants, and Inhabitants of Boston, and the Country Adjacent. *Boston: Printed by Samuel Green.* 1689. Folio, pp. 4. 46651

Ascribed by Hutchinson ("Hist. of Mass.," I. 381, *note*,) to Increase Mather.

MATHER. Diatriba | de signo | Filii Hominis, | et de | Secundo Messiæ Adventu; | Ubi de modo futuræ Judæorum Conversionis; | Nec non de signis Novissimi diei, disseritur. | Authore | Crescentio Mathero | V.D.M. apud Bostoniensis in Novâ Angliâ. | *Amstelodami, | Apud Mercy Browning Juxta Bursam.* 1682. | Sm. 8vo, pp. (8), 98, (6). B., J.C.B., N. 46652

MATHER. A | Discourse | Concerning | Earthquakes. | Occasioned by the Earthquakes which | were in New-England, in the Province | of Massachusets-Bay, June 16. and in | Conecticot-Colony, June 22. 1705. | Also, Two | Sermons, | shewing, | That Sin is the Greatest Evil; | And, | That to Redeem Time is the Greatest | Wisdom. | By Increase Mather. | *Boston: Printed by Timothy Green, for | Benjamin Eliot* ... . 1706. 12mo, pp. 131. B.

MATHER. A Discourse | Concerning | Faith and Fervency | in | Prayer, | And the Glorious Kingdom of the | Lord Jesus Christ, on | Earth, Now Approaching. | Delivered in several Sermons, | in which the Signs of the present | Times are Considered, | with a true | Account of the late wonderful and | Astonishing Success of the Gospel | in Ceilon, Amboina, and Malabar. | By I. Mather, D.D. ... | *Boston in N. E. Printed by B. Green, for Benj. Eliot* ... . 1710. 12mo, pp. (2), xix, (1), 112, (6). B., J.C.B., S. 46654

Mr. Brinley's copy has the imprint: *Boston in N. E. Printed by B. Green, for Samuel Gerrish.* Reprinted in London with the following title:

MATHER. A | Discourse | Concerning | Faith and Fervency | in | Prayer; | Especially | Respecting the Glorious Visible Kingdom | of our | Lord Jesus Christ | Over All the Earth. | Together with a Vindication of the Only true | Scriptural Mode of Standing in Singing | the Praises of God. To which is added, | An Ample Confirmation of the foregoing Discourse | by sundry suitable Quotations. | ... | [*London.* n. d.] Sm. 8vo, pp. xvi, viii, 80. W.

The "Epistle Dedicatory," by Joseph Jacob, is dated "30th 11th Mo. 1713."

MATHER. A Discourse | Concerning the Death of the | Righteous. | Occasioned by the Death of the | Honourable, | John Foster Esqr. | ... And of ... Mrs. Abigail Foster. | ... By I. Mather, D.D. ... *Boston: Printed by B. Green.* 1711. 8vo, pp. (2), 29. B., M.

MATHER. A | Discourse | Concerning the | Existence and the Omniscience | of | God. | ... | Being the Substance of several | Sermons. | By Increase Mather ... . | [*Boston.* 1716.] 12mo, pp. (6), 86, (1). 46657

MATHER. A Discourse | Concerning the Grace of | Courage, | Wherein | the Nature, Beneficialness, and | Necessity of that Vertue for | all Christians, is described. | Delivered in a | Sermon | Preached at Boston in New-England [at the Artillery Election]. | June 5th. 1710. | By Increase Mather, D.D. ... *Boston: Printed by B. Green, for Samuel Phillips* ... . 1710. 12mo, pp. (4), 44. BA.

MATHER. A Discourse | Concerning the | Maintenance | Due to those | That Preach the Gospel: | In Which, | That Question Whether | Tithes | Are by the | Divine Law the Ministers Due, | Is Considered, | And the Negative Proved. | By I. Mather, D.D. ... | *Boston: N. E. Printed by B. Green.* 1706. Sm. 8vo, pp. (2), 60.

Contains curious anecdotes of Thomas Shepard and John Davenport; notes on the salaries paid to Richard Mather, John Cotton, etc. "My Father, John Cotton, would sometimes say pleasantly that there was nothing cheap in New England besides Milk and Ministers" (p. 32). Reprinted in London with some variations in the title as:

MATHER. A Discourse Concerning the Maintenance, Due to those that Preach the Gospel: In which The Question, Whether Tithes Are by the Divine Law, the Ministers Due? is considered: and the Negative Prov'd. By J. Mather, D.D. *Boston, N. E. Printed* 1706, *and Reprinted at London*, 1709. Sm. 8vo, pp. (4), 32. C., W. 46660

MATHER. A | Discourse | Concerning | the Subject of Baptisme | Wherein the present Controversies, that are agitated in | the New English Churches are from | Scripture and Reason modestly enquired into | By Increase Mather, Teacher of a Church | in Boston in New-England. | ... *Cambridge | Printed by Samuel Green.* 1675. | 4to, pp. (4), 76. B., BA., S., W. 46661

Concerning this, *see* J. S. Clark's "Historical Sketch," Chap. V. and VI., and Mather's "Magnalia," Bk. V., p. 82.

MATHER. A Discourse | Concerning the Uncertainty of the | Times of Men, | ... | In a Sermon Preached | at Cambridge in New-England. | Decemb. 6. 1696. On Occasion of | the Sudden Death of Two Scholars [Eyre and Maxwell] | belonging to Harvard Colledge. | By Increase Mather ... . | *Boston in New England, Printed by B. Green and J. Allen* ... . 1697. Sm. 8vo, pp. (4), 40.

MATHER. A Discourse on Sacramental Occasions. *Boston.* 1711. 12mo, pp. 200. 46663

Title from Thomas' "History of Printing," Vol. II.

MATHER. A Discourse | Proving that the | Christian Religion, | Is the only | True Religion: | Wherein, | The necessity of Divine

Revelation | is Evinced, in several Sermons. | By Increase Mather. ... *Boston: Printed for & sold by the Booksellers.* 1702. 12mo, pp. 96, (4). B., W. 46664

[MATHER (I. *and* N.)] A Disputation. *See* Vol. V. 20274.

This very rare tract was published by the agency of Nathaniel and Increase Mather.

MATHER. Disquisition. *See* Angelographia, No. 46630, *supra*.

MATHER. A | Disquisition | Concerning | Ecclesiastical Councils. | Proving, that not only Pastors, But | Brethren delegated by the Curch- | es [*sic*], have equally a Right to a deci- | sive Vote in such Assemblies. To | which is added, Proposals concern- | ing Consociation of Churches, A- | greed upon by a Synod, which Con- | vened at Boston, in New-England. | With a Preface, containing a further | Vindication of the | Congregational Discipline. | By Increase Mather, D.D. | ... | *Boston, Printed for N. Boone* ... . 1716. 12mo, pp. (2), xx, 47. B. 46665

An important and very rare work, which Dr. Mather says (p. 38) he leaves as his dying farewell to the churches in this land, after having served them "in a poor weak manner for more than five above a *Jubilee of Years*." Reprinted with some variations in the title as below:

MATHER. A | Disquisition | Concerning | Ecclesiastical Councils. | ... To which | is added, Proposals concerning Consociation of Churches, Agreed | upon by a Synod, which Convened at Boston, in New-England. | With a Preface, containining [*sic*] a further Vindication of the | Congregational Discipline. | By Increase Mather, D.D. | ... | *Boston, Printed for N. Boone* ... . 1716. 8vo, pp. 36. B. 46666

This was also reprinted in the "Congregational Quarterly," Vol. XII., and again put forth as a so-called "Privately printed" book, *Boston*, 1870 (8vo, pp. 36), of which edition one hundred and twenty-five copies were printed.

MATHER. A Disquisition concerning the State of the Souls of Men, (especially of Good Men) when separated from their Bodies, in which some late very Remarkable Providences relating to Apparitions, are considered. By Increase Mather ... . *Boston: Printed by B. Green, for Benj. Eliot and Nich. Boone.* 1707. Sm. 8vo, pp. (2), 45. C. + With a Postscript ... . *London, Printed for T. Parkhurst.* 1707. 8vo, pp. 36. 46667

The only account I can find of the English edition is in White Kennett's "Bibliothecæ Americanæ Primordia"—a very good authority however.

MATHER. A | Dissertation | Concerning the | Future Conversion | of the | Jewish Nation. | Answering the Objections of ... Mr. Baxter, Dr. Lightfoot, and others. | With an Enquiry into

the first Resurrection. | By Increase Mather ... . *London: Printed by R. Tookey for Nath. Hillier.* M DCC IX. 4to, pp. (4), 35, (1).

In Chap. VIII. are some curious "Conjectures about the *Americans*," the probability that "the Apocalyptical *Gog* and *Magog*" will come from America, etc. (pp. 32, 33). Compare Sewall's "Phænomena Apocalyptica." Thomas says, *Boston. Reprinted from the London edition.* 1709. 4to.

MATHER. A Dissertation, | wherein | The Strange Doctrine | Lately Published in a Sermon, | The Tendency of which, is, to Encourage | Unsanctified Persons (while such) | to Approach the Holy | Table of the Lord, | is Examined and Confuted. | With an | Appendix, | ... | By I. Mather, D.D. | ... | *Boston: Printed by B. Green, for Benj. Eliot* ... . 1708. Sm. 8vo, pp. (12), 135. B., W.

The preface is historical. It is in answer to Solomon Stoddard, who replied in "An Appeal to the Learned." The sermon and appendix were reprinted, *Edinburgh, Printed by the Heirs ... of Andrew Anderson.* 1710. 4to, pp. 32; also, *Edinburgh. Reprinted by John Reid* ... . 1713. 4to, pp. 28.

MATHER. The | Divine Right | of | Infant-Baptisme | Asserted and Proved from | Scripture | And | Antiquity. | By Increase Mather, | Teacher of a Church of Christ in Boston in New-England. | ... | *Boston, | Printed by John Foster, in the Year* 1680. 4to, pp. (8), 27.

The address "To the Christian Reader," is signed "Urian Oakes."

MATHER. The | Doctrine | of Divine | Providence | opened and applyed: | Also Sundry Sermons on ... other Subjects. | By Increase Mather. | ... *Boston in New-England [sic] | Printed by Richard Pierce for Joseph Brunning*, | ... 1684. Sm. 8vo, pp. (8), 148. B.

MATHER. The | Doctrine | of | Singular Obedience, | As the Duty and Property | of the True | Christian: | Opened & Applied. | In a Sermon, | Preached by I. Mather, D.D. | *Boston in New-England, Printed ... by Timothy Green* ... 1707. 12mo, pp. 39, (1).

Extremely rare. Mr Sibley gives the title from Mr. Brinley's copy, and had seen no other.

MATHER. The Duty of | Parents | To | Pray | For their | Children, | Opened & Applyed in a Sermon, | Preached May 19 1703. | Which Day was set apart by One | of the Churches in Boston, New- | England, humbly to Seek unto God by Prayer with Fast- | ing for the Rising Generation. | By Increase Mather. | *Boston: Printed by B. Green and J. Allen.* ... 1703. 12mo, pp. (4), 66. + [*Ibid.*] 1703. 12mo, pp. 54. + The Second Impression. *Boston: Printed by John Allen, for John Edwards* ... . 1719. 12mo, pp. vi, 40. B 46673

Paged continuously (pp. 41–99) with the second impression, but with a separate title, *see* C. Mather's "Duty of Children," No. 46292, *supra*.

MATHER. A Dying | Legacy | of a Minister | To his ... | People, | ... Being the Three Last Sermons Preached | By Increase Mather, D.D. ... *Boston: Printed by S. Kneeland, | for J. Edwards.* 1722. Sm. 12mo, pp. (2), 4, 90. B. 46674

MATHER. Early History of New England; being a Relation of Hostile Passages between the Indians and European Voyagers and First Settlers: and a full Narrative of Hostilities, to the Close of the War with the Pequots, in the year 1637; Also a Detailed Account of the Origin of the War with King Philip. By Increase Mather. With an Introduction and Notes, By Samuel G. Drake. *Boston: Printed for the Editor.* 1864. 4to, pp. 319. Portrait. BA. 46675

For the first edition, *see* "A Relation of the Troubles," No. 46726, *infra*.

MATHER. An | Earnest Exhortation | to the | Children | of | New-England, | To Exalt the | God of their Fathers. | Delivered in a Sermon. | By Increase Mather ... . *Boston, in N. E.* ... *Benjamin | Eliot.* | 1711. 12mo, pp. (4), 39. B., W. 46676

MATHER. An Earnest | Exhortation | To the Inhabitants of | New-England, | To hearken to the voice of God | in his late and present | Dispensations | As ever they desire to escape another Judgement, seven times | greater then any thing which as yet hath been. | By Increase Mather; Teacher of a Church | in Boston in New-England. | ... | *Boston | Printed by John Foster:* ... 1676. 4to, pp. (4), 26. 46677

This is the "Serious Exhortation" mentioned in the "Brief History," No. 46640.

[MATHER.] Elijah's Mantle. *See* [Mitchel (J.)], *and others.*

MATHER. An | Essay | For the Recording of | Illustrious | Providences, | Wherein an Account is given of | many Remarkable and very Me- | morable Events, which have hap- | pened in this last Age; | Especially in | New-England. | By Increase Mather, | Teacher of a Church at Boston in | New-England. | ... | *Boston in New-England | Printed by Samuel Green for Joseph Browning, | And are to be sold at his Shop at the corner of | the Prison Lane.* 1684. Sm. 8vo, pp. (22), 372, (8). B., BA., M. 46678

A very singular collection of remarkable Sea Deliverances, Accidents, Remarkable Phenomena, Witchcrafts, and Apparitions, connected with the Inhabitants of New England. *See* a long notice of the volume in the "New Retrospective Review," No. I, Nov., 1852, p. 30. Another edition has the following title:

MATHER. An Essay | for the | Recording | of Illustrious | Providences: | Wherein an Account is given of many Re- | markable

and very Memorable Events, | which have hapned this last Age; | Especially in | New-England. | By Increase Mather ... . *Boston* ... *Printed by Samuel Green for Joseph Browning* ... 1684. Sm. 8vo, pp. (22), 372, (8). 46679

MATHER. An | Essay | for the | Recording | of | Illustrious Providences: | wherein | An Account is given of many Re- | markable and very Memorable Events, | which have happened in this last Age; | Especially in | New-England. | By Increase Mather, | Teacher of a Church at Boston in New- | England. | *Printed at Boston in New-England, and are to | be sold by George Calvert at the Sign of the | Half-Moon in Pauls Church-Yard, London*, 1684. Sm. 8vo, pp. (22), 372, (8). M. 46680

The same as the preceding with another title-page. Reprinted in 1856, *see* "Remarkable Providences," No. 46728, *infra*.

MATHER. The | Excellency | of a | Publick Spirit | Discoursed: | In a Sermon, Preached in the | Audience of the General Assembly | of the Province of the Massachu- | setts Bay in New-England May 27. | 1702. Being the day for Election | of Counsellors in that Province. | By Increase Mather. | [Followed by:] The | Righteous Man | A | Blessing: | Or, | Seasonable Truths | ... In Two Sermons. | [And] The Morning Star. | *Boston in New-England: Printed by B. Green, & J. Allen, for Nicholas Boone* ... . 1702. 12mo, pp. (12), 84 B., BA., C. 46681

[MATHER, *and others.*] A faithful Advice from several Ministers of the Gospel, relating to Dangers that may arise from Impostors. *Boston.* [1699.] Sm. 8vo, pp. 79. M. 46682

MATHER. The | First Principles | of | New-England, | Concerning | The Subject of Baptisme | & | Communion of Churches. | Collected partly out of the Printed Books, but chiefly | out of the Original Manuscripts of the First and chiefe | Fathers in the New-English Churches; With the Judg- | ment of Sundry Learned Divines of the Congregational | Way in England, Concerning the said Questions. | Published for the Benefit of those who are of the Rising Gene- | ration in New-England. | By Increase Mather, Teacher of a Church | in Boston in New-England. | *Cambridge | Printed by Samuel Green.* 1675. | 4to, pp. (8), 40, 7. B., P.

The last paging contains a letter of the Rev. J. Mitchel.

MATHER. Five Sermons | on | Several Subjects, I. A Birth Day Sermon, Preached | on the Day when the Author | attained to the Eightieth Year of his Age. | II. A dying Testimony to the

So- | vereign Grace of God in the | Salvation of His Elect, Con- | taining Three Sermons. III. Believers encouraged to Pray | ... | *Boston: Printed by B. Green, for Daniel Henchman* ... . 1719. 12mo, pp. v, 148. W. 46684

MATHER. The Folly | of Sinning, | Opened & Applyed, | In Two Sermons, | Occasioned by the Condemnation | of one that was executed at | Boston ... on | November 17th. 1698. | By Increase Mather ... . *Boston: Printed by B. Green, & J. Allen, | for Michael Perry ... and Nicholas Buttolph* ... . 1699. 12mo, pp. 95.

MATHER. Four Sermons, viz., I. The Glorious Throne. II. The Excellency of a Public Spirit. III. The Righteous Man a Blessing. IV. The Morning Star. ... *Boston: Printed for N. Boone.* 1708. 12mo, pp. (2), 97–122, 84. 46686

"The Glorious Throne," which has a separate title-page, was printed in 1702, appended to "Ichabod," No. 46694. The other three sermons were published together, in 1702, *see* No. 46681. This volume, made up by the publisher, under a new general title, is not in Sibley's list or in Thomas' "History of Printing," second edition.

MATHER. A Further | Account | of the | Tryals | of the | New-England Witches. | With the Observations | Of a Person who was upon the Place several | Days when the suspected Witches were | first taken into Examination. | To which is added, | Cases of Conscience | Concerning Witchcrafts and Evil Spirits Per- | sonating men. | Written at the Request of the Ministers of New-England. | By Increase Mather, President of Harvard Colledge. | Licensed and Entred according to Order. | *London: Printed for J. Dunton, at the Raven in the Poultrey* | 1693. ... | 4to, pp. 10, (4), 40, (4). 46687

The first part of the work (pp. 1–10) is Deodat Lawson's "Brief and True Narrative" (No. 39442, Vol. X.), taken from Cotton Mather's "Wonders of the Invisible World." Thomas quotes an edition, *Boston*, 4to, pp. 50, which I have not seen. It is reprinted in Cotton Mather's "Wonders," *London*, 1862.

[MATHER.] A Further | Testimony | Against the Scandalous Proceed- | ings of the New-North Church | in Boston. [Colophon:] *Boston: Printed for B. Gray, and J. | Edwards, at their Shops on the North | and South side of the Town-House.* 1720. pp. 3

Signed "Increase Mather." Not in Mr. Sibley's list of Mather's books.

MATHER. The Glorious Throne. *See* Ichabod, *infra*.

MATHER. The Great | Blessing, | of | Primitive | Counsellours. | Discoursed in a | Sermon, | Preached in the Audience of the Governour, Council, | and Representatives, of the Province of the

Massachusets-|Bay, in New-England. May 31st. 1693. Being the Day for the|Election of Counsellours, in that Province.| By Increase Mather ... . | *Boston: Printed ... by Benjamin Harris*, ... 1693. 4to, pp. 23. B. 46689

Pages 3–8 are reprinted in the "Andros Tracts," II. 301.

MATHER. The Greatest|Sinners|Exhorted and Encouraged| To Come to Christ and that|Now|Without Delaying.|Also, The Exceeding Danger of Men's De-|ferring their Repentance. |Together with a Discourse about The Day | of Judgement. And on Several|other Subjects.|By Increase Mather ... . |*Boston: Joseph Browning*. 1686. Sm. 8vo, pp. (4), 146. W. 46690

MATHER. Heavens Alarm to the World. | Or | A Sermon| Wherein is shewed,|That fearful Sights and Signs in Heaven| are the Presages of great Ca-|lamities at hand. | By Increase Mather; Teacher of a Church|in Boston in New-England.|...| *Boston: Printed by John Foster*. 1681. 4to, pp. (6), 17. B. + The Second Impression. ... *Boston in New-England, Printed for Samuel Sewall*. ... 1682. Sm. 8vo, pp. (8), 38. BA. 46691

The first edition is probably the last work printed by John Foster. The second impression forms part of the Κομητογραφια, No. 46696, *infra*. It was also reprinted, *London*, 1812. 8vo.

MATHER. An|Historical Discourse|Concerning the|Prevalency | of | Prayer | Wherein is shewed that New-Englands late Deliverance from the | Rage of the Heathen, is an Eminent Answer of Prayer. | By Increase Mather | Teacher of a Church in Boston in New-England.|...|*Boston: Printed and sold by John Foster*. 1677. 4to, pp. (6), 19. M. 46692

This has a separate title and collation, but is part of Mather's "Relation of the Troubles," No. 46726, *infra*. There is another edition in which the title reads the same, but the length of the lines differ.

MATHER. The History of King Philip's War. By the Rev. Increase Mather, D.D. Also, a History of the Same War, by the Rev. Cotton Mather, D.D. To which is added An Introduction and Notes, By Samuel G. Drake. *Boston: Printed for the Editor, ... by J. Munsell*. 1862. 4to, pp. 281. 2 Portraits, Pedigree of the Mather family, folded sheet. BA. 46693

This is a new edition of "A Brief History," No. 46640, *supra*. Two hundred and sixty-one copies printed, of which eleven are on large paper. The editor has marred the completeness of this edition by reproducing the abridged text of Cotton Mather's "Troubles ... had with the Indian Salvages," from Book VII. of his "Magnalia," blended with the material of the other work. Pages 227–264 consist of narratives, etc., now first printed.

MATHER. Ichabod.|Or,|A Discourse,|Shewing what Cause there is to Fear|that the|Glory|Of the Lord, is Departing from| New-England.|Delivered in Two Sermons,|By Increase Mather, ...|*Boston: Printed by Timothy Green*. ... 1702. 12mo, pp. 122. Portrait. B. + *Boston: Printed, for N. Boone* ... . 1729. 12mo, pp. 88. 46694

The second sermon has a separate title-page: "The Glorious Throne: | Or, | A Sermon | Concerning | The Glory of the Throne of the | Lord Jesus Christ, | Which is now in Heaven, and | shall quickly be seen on The Earth," pp. 92–122. Mr. Sibley does not notice the edition of 1729.

[MATHER.] The|Judgment|Of Several Eminent|Divines| Of The|Congregational VVay.|Concerning A|Pastors Power.| Occasionally to Exert Ministerial Acts|in another Church, besides|that which is his Own Particular|Flock.|*Boston: Printed by Benjamin Harris* ... . 1693. Sm. 8vo, pp. (2), 13. M. 46695

MATHER. Κομητογραφια. | Or a | Discourse Concerning | Comets;|Wherein the Nature of Blazing Stars|is Enquired into: |With an Historical Account of all the Comets | which have appeared from the Beginning of the | World unto this present Year, M.DC.LXXXIII. | Expressing | The Place in the Heavens, where they were seen, | Their Motion, Forms, Duration; and the Re-|markable Events which have followed|in the World, so far as they have been|by Learned Men Observed.|As also two Sermons, | Occasioned by the late Blazing Stars. | By Increase Mather, Teacher of a Church | at Boston in New-England.| *Boston In New-England.|Printed by S[amuel] G[reen] for S[amuel] S[ewall]. And sold by J. Browning|At the corner of the Prison Lane next the Town-|House*. 1683. Sm. 8vo, pp. (12), 143, (1); (8), 38; (2), 32. BA., H., M., W. + *London*. 1811. 8vo. 46696

An address "To the Reader," p. 4, is signed "John Sherman." The "two Sermons" are "Heaven's Alarm," Second Impression, 1682, which has a separate title-page, and "The Latter Sign," which has continuous signatures with "Heaven's Alarm." The original edition is very scarce, but I have never met with the reprint.

MATHER. The Latter|Sign|Discoursed of,|in a|Sermon|... at ... Boston in New-England;|August, 31. 1682.| ... By Increase Mather ... . [n. p. n. d.] Sm. 8vo, pp. (2), 32. B.

This is usually found with the preceding work, without which that is not complete, but, having a separate title, it is sometimes bound up separately.

[MATHER.] A|Letter,|About the Present State of Christianity, among the Christianized | Indians | of | New-England.| Written,|To the Honourable,|Sir William Ashurst,|Governour of the Corporation, for|Propagating the Gospel among the|Indians, in New-England, and|Parts Adjacent, in|America.|*Boston, in N. E.: Printed by Timothy Green*. 1705. Sm. 8vo, pp. 15.

Signed "Increase Mather, Cotton Mather, Nehemiah Walter."

MATHER. A Letter concerning the Success of the Gospel, amongst the Indians in New-England. Written by Mr. Increase Mather, Minister of the Word of God at Boston, and Rector of the College at Cambridge in New-England, to Dr. John Leusden, Hebrew Professor in the University of Vtrecht. Translated out of Latin into English. *London*. 1689. 4to, pp. 4. 46699

An English version of "De Successu Evangelii," No. 46749, *infra*. *See* "Magnalia," Book III. 194.

[MATHER.] The|Life and Death|Of|That Reverend Man of God,|Mr. Richard Mather,|Teacher of the Church|in|Dorchester | in | New-England. | *Cambridge: Printed by S[amuel] G[reen] and M[armaduke] J[ohnson]*. 1670. 4to, pp. (4), 38.

Excessively rare. The *second* of Increase Mather's acknowledged publications. Reprinted, *Dorchester: D. Clapp*. 1850. 12mo.

MATHER. Masukkenukeeg|Matcheseaenvog|Wequetoog kah Wuttooanatoog|Uppevaonont Christoh kah ne|Yeuyeu|Teanuk |Wonk, ahche nunnukquodt missinninnuk|uk-|quohquenaount wutaiuskoianatamoooonganoo.|Kah Keketookaonk papaume Wussittum-|wae kesukodtum. Kah papaume nawhutch|onkatogeh Wunnomwayeuongash|...|Nashpe Increase Mather.|Kukkootomwehteaenuh ut oomoeuwehkomong-|anit ut Bostonut, ut New England. | Yeush kukkookootomwehteaongash qushkinnumunash en Indiane unnontoowaonganit nashpe S. D[anforth]. *Bostonut, Printeuoop Bartholomew Green kah John Allen*. 1698. Sm. 8vo, pp. 164. W. 46701

Five sermons by Increase Mather, translated into the Indian language by Rev. Samuel Danforth. "The first Indian book known to have been printed after the removal of the press to Boston."—J. H. TRUMBULL in *A. A. S. Proceedings*, No. 61.

MATHER. Meditations | on | Death. | Delivered in Several | Sermons.|Wherein is shewed: | I. That some True Believers on| Christ are afraid of Death,|but that they have no Just|Cause to be so.|II. That Good Men as well as ot-|hers may be taken out of the|World by a Sudden Death.|III. That not Earth but Heaven is|the Christians Home.|By Increase Mather ... .|*Boston, in N. E. Printed ... by Timothy Green*. 1707. 8vo, pp. v, 171, (5).

MATHER. Meditations | on the | Glory | of the | Heavenly World. | I. On the Happiness of the Souls of | Believers, at the Instant of their|Separation from their Bodies. II. On the Glory

of the Bodies of|God's Children, in the Resurrecti-|on World, when they shall be as|the Angels of Heaven. III. On the Glory of both Soul and|Body in the Heaven of Heavens,|after the Day of Judgment, to all|Eternity.|By Increase Mather, D.D. ...|*Boston in N. E. Printed: Sold by Benjamin Eliot* ... . 1711. Sm. 8vo, pp. (2), v, (1), 276, (4). B., BA., J.C.B. 46703

"These Sermons were Pluckt out of the Burning; when Seven Book-sellers Shops in Boston were Consumed in those Flames, which on the Second of this Instant October, made a dismal Desolation in the midst of this Great Town."—*Preface*, pp. ii, iii.

MATHER. Meditations | on the | Glory | of the | Lord Jesus Christ: | Delivered in several | Sermons. | By Increase Mather.| *Boston in New-England: Printed by Bartholomew Green, for Benj. Eliot* ... . 1705. 16mo, pp. (2), viii, 165, (1). B., W. 46704

In the Epistle Dedicatory, to his Congregation, April 2, 1705, the author says: "You are to look upon these as *the Last Words*, which I shall ever, *by the Press*, Speak and Dedicatate [*sic*] unto you." Nevertheless, he lived to publish more than thirty works after this (besides prefaces, dedications, etc.) Some copies have the imprint, *Boston in New-England: Printed by Bartholomew Green, for Nicholas Buttolph, at the Corner of Gutteridges Coffee-House.*

MATHER. Meditations|On the Sanctification|of the|Lord's Day:|And|On the Judgements which|attend the Profanation of it.|To which is Added,|Seasonable Meditations both for|Winter and Summer.|By I. Mather, D.D|...|*Boston: Printed by T. G. for S. Gerrish*,| ... 1712. 12mo, pp. (2), x, 71, (3), iv, 51. B., W.

The "Seasonable Meditations" have a separate title-page, and were printed by *John Allen*.

MATHER. The|Mystery|of|Christ|opened and applyed.|In several Sermons, Concerning the|Person, Office, and Glory of Jesus Christ.|By Increase Mather,|Teacher of a Church at Boston in N. England.| [*Boston:*] *Printed in the year* MDCLXXXVI. Sm. 8vo, pp. (2), 6, 212, (1). B. 46706

MATHER. The | Mystery | of | Israel's Salvation, | Explained and Applyed: | Or, | A Discourse | Concerning the General Conversion of the | Israelitish Nation. | Wherein is Shewed, | I. That the twelve Tribes shall be saved. | 2. When this is to be expected. | 3. Why this must be. | 4. What kind of Salvation the Tribes of Israel | shall partake of. (viz.) A Glorious, Wonder-|ful, Spiritual, Temporal Salvation. | Being the Substance of several Ser-|mons Preached. | By Increase Mather, M.A. | Teacher of a Church in Boston in New-England. | [*London:*] *Printed in the year* 1669. Sm. 8vo, pp. (46), 181, (10). B., C. 46707

A second title-page precedes the text with the imprint: *London, Printed for John Allen in Wentworth-street, near Bell-Lane*, 1669. This is the first work by its cele-

brated author, and is very rare. Rice's copy sold, in 1870, for $22. "Isaiah Thomas ('Hist. of Printing,' I. 286) says: 'There is in an ancient library in Boston, a copy of Increase Mather's *Mystery of Israel's Libation* [*sic*] printed in London, by John Allen. It is supposed he came to Boston by encouragement from the Mathers.' But Allen's name does not appear on the first title-page, and on the second the imprint is '*for*'—not as Thomas has it—*by* Allen. The work *may* have been printed by Green at Cambridge, and some copies may have been provided with a special title-page for the London market. It is certain that both title-pages were printed from the *same types*."—J. H. TRUMBULL.

[MATHER.] A Narrative of the Miseries of New-England, By Reason of an Arbitrary Government Erected there Under Sir Edmund Andros. *London, Printed for Richard Janeway* ... . *And Reprinted at Boston in New-England by Richard Pierce*. 1688.

This very rare piece was again reprinted as:

[MATHER.] A Narrative of the Miseries of New-England, By Reason of An Arbitrary Government Erected there. Printed in the Tyranic [*sic*] Reign of Sir Edmund Andross. *Boston: Re-Printed* ... . 1775. 4to, pp. 8. BA. 46709

It is also included in Part VI. of *our* No. 9371. *See also* "Andros Tracts," II. I. I have never seen the original English edition. The "Narrative" relates an interview with the Prince of Orange, 21 September [December] 1688.

[MATHER?] The Necessity|of|Reformation|With the Expedients subservient | thereunto, asserted; | in Answer to two| Qvestions | I. What are the Evils that have provoked the Lord to bring his Judg-|ments on New-England?|II. What is to be done that so those Evils may be Reformed?|Agreed upon by the | Elders and Messengers | Of the Churches assembled in the| Synod|At Boston in New-England,|Sept. 10. 1679.|...|*Boston; Printed by John Foster. In The Year* 1679. 4to, pp. (8), 15. B.

"$4 to be drawn up by Mr. Increase Mather."—PRINCE'S *MS. catalogue*. The preface is certainly by him. Reprinted with "The Result of Three Synods," 1728.

[MATHER?] Needful Caution against a Sin that easily besets us. Sermon at Boston Lecture June 15th, 1706. *Boston*. 1706. Sm. 8vo, pp. 56. 46711

Title from Thomas' "History of Printing."

[MATHER.] New-England Vindicated From the Unjust Aspersions cast on the former Government there, by some late Considerations Pretending to shew that the Charters in those Colonies were Taken from them on Account of their Destroying the Manufactures and Navigation of England. *London*. [1688.] 8vo, pp. 8. 46712

See "Andros Tracts," II. 111–121, 150, *and* Palfrey's "New England," III. 515.

MATHER. Now or Never|Is the|Time for Men to make Sure of their|Eternal Salvation.|Several|Sermons,|In which is Declared;|I. That now is the Day of Sal-|vation.|II. That it is Wisdom, for Men to|Consider their Latter End.|III. That Impenitent Sinners, will|be found Guilty of their Own|Destruction.|By Increase Mather ... .|*Boston: Printed ... by T. Green*. 1713. 12mo, pp. (2), ii, 113. C. 46713

MATHER. The Order of the | Gospel, | Professed and Practised by the | Churches of Christ in | New-England, Justified, by the|Scripture, and by the Writings|of many Learned men, both| Ancient and Modern Divines;|In Answer to several Questions,| relating to Church Discipline.|By Increase Mather, President of| Harvard Colledge, in Cambridge, and | Teacher of a Church at Boston | in New-England.|...|*Boston, Printed by B. Green, & J. Allen,|for Nicholas Buttolph* ... . 1700. 12mo, pp. 143, (1). H. + ... *Reprinted at London, and sold by A. Baldwin*. 1700. 8vo, pp. (2), viii, 86. 46714

More commonly cited by its running title, "The Order of the Churches in N. England Vindicated." For a reply, *see* our Vol. VII., No. 28052. In some copies the imprint reads: *Boston. Printed by B. Green and J. Allen, for B. Eliot.* The London reprint is very rare. It is not in Mr. Sibley's list.

M[ATHER?] The|Original|Rights|Of|Mankind|Freely to Subdue and Improve the|Earth.|Asserted and Maintained|By I. M.|*Boston: For the Author*. 1722. 12mo, pp. 22. 46715

"Attributed to Mather, in the Am. Antiq. Society (Haven's) catalogue, and by Mr. Sibley (No. 157), on the authority of a copy on which I. M. is extended to 'I. *Mather, D.D.*' in a nearly contemporary hand-writing. Mr. Brinley's copy is so inscribed, and is probably the one to which Mr. Sibley refers. The main argument of the tract is, that 'Monopolizing dormant lands subjects the Colony to Slavery,' and that all 'dormant (unimproved) Lands ought to be Taxed for the support of government,' and it appeals to the General Assembly to 'undo heavy Burdens, break every Yoke, make us a free People, to *Enjoy without Price or Purchase what God hath freely given us*,' &c. It is extremely rare. *If* by Mather (which seems *very* doubtful) it is the last work (independently) published by him."—J. H. TRUMBULL.

MATHER. A Plain Discourse, | shewing | who shall, & who shall not,|Enter into the|Kingdom of Heaven,|and|How far Men may go and yet|fall short of|Heaven,|After their seeming to be|Converted and Religious.|By Increase Mather ... . [Followed by:] A Sermon|Wherein is Declared|That the|Blessed God is Willing to be|Reconciled|to the|Sinful Children of Men. |Preached at Dorchester ... .|*Boston: Printed by B. Green, for B. Eliot* ... . 1713. 12mo, pp. v, 112. W. 46716

Thomas quotes another edition, *Boston*, 1721.

[MATHER.] A Plea | for the | Ministers | Of the | Gospel,| Offered to the Consideration of the|People of New-England.| ... |By a Friend to the Churches.|*Boston: Printed by B. Green*. 1706. Sm. 8vo, pp. 29. H. 46717

MATHER. Practical Truths,|Plainly Delivered:|Wherein is Shewed,|I. That true Believers on Jesus|Christ, shall as certainly enjoy|Everlasting Life in Heaven, as|if they were there already. |II. That there is a blessed Mar-|riage between Jesus Christ the| Son of God, & the true Believer.|III. That Men are Infinitely| concerned, not only to hear|the Voice of Christ, but that|they do it, To Day.|IV. The Work of the Ministry,|described, in an Ordination | Sermon. | By Increase Mather, D.D. | *Boston, N. E. Printed by B. Green, for Daniel Henchman* ... . 1718. 12mo, pp. (4), 138. B. 46718

"The Work of the Ministry" has an independent title-page.

MATHER. Practical|Truth's,|Tending to Promote|Holiness| in the|Hearts & Lives|of|Christians.|Delivered in several|Sermons. | By Increase Mather. | ... | *Boston, in N. E. Printed by Barth. Green*, | *for Benj. Eliot* ... . 1704. Sm. 8vo, pp. (2), 102, (4). BA. 46719

MATHER. Practical Truths|Tending to Promote the|Power of Godliness:|Wherein|Several Important Duties, are|Urged, and the Evil of divers com-|mon Sins, is Evinced:|Delivered in Sundry|Sermons.|By Increase Mather ... . |*Boston In New-England*|*Printed by Samuel Green upon Assignment of* | *Samuel Sewell* [sic]. 1682. Sm. 8vo, pp. (14), 220. BA., H., W. 46720

Thomas quotes a second edition with the same imprint.

MATHER. Pray for the Rising Generation,|Or A|Sermon| Wherein Godly Parents are Encou-|raged to Pray and Believe| for their Children,|Preached the third Day of the fifth Moneth, 1678.|which Day was set apart by the second Church in Boston in New-England,| humbly to seek unto God by Fasting and Prayer,|for a Spirit of Converting Grace, to be poured|out upon the Children and Rising Generation in | New-England. | By Increase Mather, Teacher | of that Church. | ... | *Cambridge: Printed by Samuel Green* ... . 1678. 4to, pp. 23. + The Second Impression. *Boston: Printed by John Foster*. 1679. Sm. 8vo, pp. 29. M. 46721

The second and third impressions are appended to Mather's "Call from Heaven," No. 46645, *supra*.

[MATHER.] The Present State of New England impartially considered in a Letter to the Clergy. [*London*. 1689.] 4to, pp. 44. M. 46722

[MATHER.] The Present State of | New-English Affairs.| This is Published to prevent False Reports.|*Boston: Printed ... by Samuel Green*. 1689. Folio, 1 leaf. 46723

Reprinted in "Andros Tracts," II. 15.

[MATHER.] Reasons for the Confirmation of|the Charters belonging to the several|Corporations in New-England.| [n. p. n. d.] 4to, pp. 4. 46724

Reprinted in the "Andros Tracts," II. 223.

[MATHER.] Reasons|for the|Confirmation|of the|Charter| Belonging to the|Massachusets Colony|in|New-England.| [n. p. n. d.] 4to, pp. 4. 46725

This also is reprinted in the "Andros Tracts," II. 223.

MATHER. A Relation|Of the Troubles which have hapned in | New-England, | By reason of the Indians there. | From the Year 1614. to the Year 1675. | Wherein the frequent Conspiracyes of the Indians to cutt off the | English, and the wonderfull providence of God, in disappointing | their devices, is declared.| Together with an Historical Discourse concerning the | Prevalency of Prayer; shewing that New-Englands | late deliverance from the Rage of the Heathen is an eminent | Answer of Prayer. | By Increase Mather | Teacher of a Church in Boston in New-England.|...| *Boston, Printed and sold by John Foster*. 1677. 4to, pp. (6), 76; An Historical Discourse, (6), 19. C., M. 46726

A very rare work. The "Historical Discourse" (No. 46692, *supra*,) appears to have been printed before the "Troubles," the putting of both under one title being an afterthought. There is another issue of this edition in which the title reads as below:

MATHER. A Relation | Of the Troubles which have hapned in | New-England, | By reason of the Indians there. | From the Year 1614. to the Year 1675. | Wherein the frequent Conspiracyes of the Indians to cutt off the | English, and the wonderfull providence of God, in | disappointing their devices, is declared.| Together with an Historical Discourse concerning the Prevalency of | Prayer; | shewing that New-Englands late deliverance from the Rage of the | Heathen is an eminent Answer of Prayer. | By Increase Mather, | Teacher of a Church in Boston in New-England.|...| *Boston*, | *Printed and sold by John Foster*. 1677. 4to, pp. (6), 76; An Historical Discourse, (4), 19. G.B. 46727

MATHER. Remarkable Providences Illustrative of the Earlier Days of American Colonisation. By Increase Mather. With Introductory Preface, By George Offor. *London: John Russell Smith.* 1856. Fcap 8vo, pp. xix, (18), 262. Portrait. BA.

For the original edition, *see* "An Essay," etc., No. 46678, *supra*.

MATHER. Renewal of Covenant the great Duty | incumbent on decaying or distressed | Churches. | A Sermon | ... | Preached at Dorchester in New-England, the 21. Day | of the 1. Moneth 1677. being a Day of | Humiliation | There, on that Occasion. | By Increase Mather, Teacher of | a Church in Boston. | ... | *Boston; Printed by J. F. for Henry Phillips* .... 1677. 4to, pp. (8), 21.

An extremely rare piece.

MATHER. Returning unto God the great concernment | of a Covenant People. | Or | A Sermon | Preached to the second Church in Boston in | New-England, March 17. 16 79/80. when | that Church did solemnly and explicitly | Renew their Covenant with | God, and one with another. | By Increase Mather Teacher of that Church. | ... | *Boston, Printed by John Foster.* 1680. 4to, pp. (6), 21

[MATHER.] The | Revolution | in | New England | Justified, | and the People there Vindicated | from the Aspersions cast upon them | by Mr. John Palmer, | in his Pretended Answer to the | Declaration, | Published by the Inhabitants of Boston, and the | Country adjacent, on the day when they se- | cured their late Oppressors, who acted by an | Illegal and Arbitrary Commission from the | Late King James. | *Printed for Joseph Brunning at Boston | in New England.* 1691. 4to, pp. (6), 48. M. 46731

"To the Reader," is signed by "E. R." and "S. S.," which, Palfrey, "Hist. of New England," III. 514, says undoubtedly represent Edward Rawson, and Samuel Sewall.

[MATHER.] The Revolution in New-England Justified [as before]. To which is added, A Narrative of the Proceedings of Sir Edmond Androsse and his Accomplices. Who also acted by an Illegal and Arbitrary Commission from the late King James, during his Government in New-England. By several Gentlemen who were of his Council. Printed in the Year 1691. *Boston: Re-printed and sold by Isaiah Thomas* .... M,DCC,LXXXIII. 8vo, pp. 59. 46732

Another edition forms No. 9, of Force's "Tracts," Vol. IV. *Washington: Reprinted* 1846.

MATHER. The Righteous Man. *See* "Excellency," etc. *supra*

MATHER. Seasonable Meditations. *See* "Meditations on the Sanctification," etc., No. 46705, *supra*.

MATHER. A Seasonable | Testimony | To Good Order | in the | Churches | Of the Faithful. | Particularly | Declaring the Usefulness & Necessity | of Councils in Order to | Preserving Peace and Truth in | the Churches. | By Increase Mather, D.D. | With the Concurrence of Other | Ministers of the Gospel in Boston. | ... | *Boston, N. E. Printed by B. Green, for D. Henchman* .... 1720. Sm. 8vo, pp. (4), 20. B., BA. 46733

MATHER. A | Sermon | Concerning | Obedience & Resignation | to the Will of God | in Every Thing. | Occasion'd by the Death | of that Pious Gentlewoman | Mrs. Mariah Mather | Late Consort of | Increase Mather, D.D., | ... | on the Lord's Day, April 4, 1714. *Boston: Printed ... by T. Green* .... 1714. 12mo, pp. (2), vi, 40.

The running title is: "Let the Will of the Lord be Done." Extremely rare. Mr. Sibley had seen no other copy than Mr. Brinley's. Thomas gives the title differently, probably a half-title.

MATHER. A Sermon Occasioned by the Execution of [James Morgan] a Man found Guilty of Murder: Preached at Boston, in New England, March 11th, 168 6/8 [*sic*]. (Together with the Confession, Last Expressions, and Solemn Warning of that Murderer ... .) By Increase Mather .... *Boston, Printed for Joseph Brunning, corner of Prison Lane near the Town Hall. Anno* 1686. 8vo, pp. (4), 44. + The Second Edition. ... *Boston, Printed by R[ichard] P[ierce]. Sold by J. Brunning. Anno* 1687. 8vo, pp. (4), 124. B. 46735

Pages 37–82 of the second edition, whose title varies somewhat from the first, contain "The Call of the Gospel," with a title-page, for which *see* Mather (C.), No. 46244; pp. 83–124, "An Exhortation," with a title-page, for which *see* Moodey (J.) The first edition contains, besides the above-mentioned, "The Penitent Murderer," by Randolph Yearwood. Reprinted in *London, ... for John Dunton*, 1691, pp. 32, in "Wonders of Free Grace."

MATHER. A | Sermon | (Preached at the Lecture in Boston in New- | England the 18th of the 1. Moneth 1674. | When two men were Executed, who | had Murthered their Master). | Wherein is shewed | That Excess in Wickedness doth bring | Untimely Death. | The Second Impression. | By Increase Mather, | Teacher of a Church of Christ | .... *Printed by R. P[ierce], for J. Brunning in Boston.* 1685. Sm. 8vo, pp. (2), 38. B., BA. 46736

For the first edition, *see* "The Wicked mans Portion," No. 46758, *infra*.

MATHER. A Sermon | Shewing | That the present Dispensations of | Providence declare that wonderful | Revolutions in the World are near at | Hand; | With | An Appendix, shewing some Scripture Ground | to hope, that within a few Years, glorious

Prophecies | and Promises will be fulfilled. By | The very Reverend Mr. Increase Mather, D.D. Minister | of the Gospel at Boston in New-England. | *Edinburgh, Printed by the Heirs ... of Andrew Anderson* .... 1710. 4to, pp. 32. + *Edinburgh, Reprinted by John Reid* .... 1713. Sq. 8vo, pp. 28. 46737

Reprinted from "A Dissertation," etc., No. 46669, *supra*.

MATHER. A | Sermon | Wherein is Shewed, | I. That the Ministers of the Gospel | need, and ought to desire the | Prayers of the Lord's People | for them. | II. That the People of God ought | to Pray for his Ministers. | Preached at Roxbury, October 29. 1718. | When | Mr. Thomas Walter | Was Ordained a Pastor in that Church, by | his Grand-Father, Increase Mather, D.D. ... *Boston: Printed by S. Kneeland, for J. Edwards* .... 1718. 8vo, pp. (2), ii, 35. BA., M. 46738

MATHER. A Sermon | Wherein is shewed that the Church of God | is sometimes a Subject of | Great Persecution; | Preached on a Publick | Fast | At Boston in New-England: | Occasioned by the Tidings of a great Persecution Raised against | the Protestants in France. | By Increase Mather .... | *Boston, in New-England: ... Samuel Sewall, in the Year*, 1682. 4to, pp. (6), 24. B., C., W.

MATHER. Sermons | wherein | Those Eight Characters of the Blessed | Commonly called the | Beatitudes, | Are Opened & Applyed | in | Fifteen Discourses. | To which is added, | A Sermon concerning Assurance of the | Love of Christ. | By Increase Mather .... | *Boston, N. E. Printed by B. Green, for Daniel Henchman* .... 1718. 8vo, pp. (2), iv, 298. W. + The Second Edition. ... *Dublin, reprinted.* 1721. 8vo, pp. (6), 211. 46740

This has a copper-plate engraving of the author, which is perhaps the first thing of the kind attempted in New England. The second edition is not known to Mr. Sibley. Very rare.

[MATHER?] Several Reasons proving that Inoculating or Transplanting the Small Pox is a lawful Practice, and that it has been blessed by God for the Saving of many a Life. *Boston.* 1721. Folio, 1 leaf. + *Boston, Reprinted.* 1726. 8vo. 46741

MATHER. Several | Sermons | Wherein is shewed, | I. That Jesus Christ is | a Mighty Saviour. | II. That God Converts His | Elect some at one Age, and | some at Another, | Commonly before Old Age. | III. That when Godly Men dye, | Angels carry their Souls to | another and a better World. | With | A Preface in which there is a brief | and true Character of the Reverend | Mr. Thomas

Bridge a Lately deceased | Pastor in one of the Churches in Boston. | By Increase Mather, D.D. | ... | *Boston: Printed by B. Green, for | Benjamin Eliot.* 1715. 12mo, pp. (2), ix, (1), 126. B.

MATHER. Solemn Advice to Young Men, Not to Walk in the Wayes of their Heart .... *Boston.* 1695. Sm. 8vo. W.

MATHER. Some further Account | from London, of the Small- | Pox Inoculated. | The Second Edition. | With some Remarks on a late Scan- | dalous Pamphlet Entituled, In- | oculation of the Small Pox as | practis'd in Boston, &c. | By Increase Mather .... [Colophon:] *Boston: ... J. Edwards* .... 1721. Sm. 8vo, pp. 8. H., M. 46744

MATHER. Some Important | Truths | About | Conversion, | Delivered in Sundry | Sermons, | By Increase Mather .... | *London: Richard Chiswell.* 1674. Sm. 8vo, pp. (28), 248. B. + With a Preface by Dr. Owen. | The Second Edition. | ... | *London Printed.* 1674. *Boston, in N. E. Re-Printed by John Allen, for John Edwards* .... 1721: 12mo, pp. (2), xxii, 260, (1). B., W. 46745

Sibley quotes a second edition, *Boston*, 1684, pp. 151, which I have not seen.

MATHER. Some Remarks | On a late Sermon, | Preached at Boston | in New-England, | by | George Keith, M.A. | Shewing | That his pretended Good Rules in | Divinity, are not built on the foun- | dation of the Apostles & Prophets. | By Increase Mather. ... | *Boston, ... Nicholas Boone* .... 1702. Sm. 8vo, pp. (2), 36. B.

MATHER. Some Remarks, | On a Pretended | Answer, | To a Discourse concerning the | Common-Prayer Worship. | With | An Exhortation to the Churches | in New-England, to hold fast the Pro- | fession of their Faith without Wavering. | By Increase Mather, D.D. ... [Followed by:] An Appendix, containing Some Remarks on a Book written by the Bishop of Derry. *Printed for Nath. Hillier ... in London, and for the Book-sellers in Boston, in New-England.* [1712.] 8vo, pp. (2), 36, 10. BA. 46747

This defense is scarcely less rare than the original tract. In the preface Mather gives his reasons for not before admitting his authorship; and mentions an error of the New England printer (corrected, as he says, in the London edition of 1689) who put "Jephilleth" for "Tephilloth." The appendix is dated, Dec. 2, 1712. Its title-page has the imprint: *Sold by Several of the Book-sellers in Boston*, MDCCXIII. *See* "A Brief Discourse," No. 46639, *supra*.

MATHER. Soul-Saving | Gospel Truths. | Deliver'd in several Sermons: | Wherein is shew'd, | I. The Unreasonableness of those | Excuses which Men make for | their Delaying to come to the |

Lord Jesus Christ for Salvation. | II. That for Men to Despair of | the Forgiveness of their Sins | because they have been Great, | is a great Evil. | III. That every Man in the World | is going into Eternity. | By Increase Mather .... | Second Edition. | *Boston.* 1712. 24mo, pp. iv, 135. W. + *Philadelphia: Printed by B. Franklin.* 1743. 18mo, pp. 167. J.C.B. 46748

The first edition was probably printed in 1703.

MATHER. De | Successu Evangelij | Apud Indos | in | Novâ-Angliâ | Epistola. | Ad Cl. Virum | D. Johannem Leusdenum, | Linguæ Sanctæ in Ultra- | jectinâ Academiâ Pro- | fessorem, Scripta. | A Crescentio Mathero | Apud Bostoniensis V.D.M. nec non | Collegij Harvardini quod est Canta- | brigiæ Nov-Anglorum, Rectore. | *Londini, Typis J. G.* 1688. 12mo, pp. (2), 13.

In the "Brief Relation of the State of New-England" it is stated that this piece of Mather's had been translated into several of the native American dialects. For an English version, *see* No. 46699, *supra*, also included in the "Magnalia," III. 194, and in part in the "Andros Tracts," II. 166. For a German translation, *see* "Ein Brieff," etc., No. 46643, *supra*. The following contains additional matter:

MATHER. De | Successu Evangelii | Apud | Indos | Occidentales, | In Novâ-Angliâ; | Epistola. | Ad Cl. Virum | D. Johannem Leusdenum | Linguæ Sanctæ in Ultrajectinâ Acade- | miâ Professorem, Scripta, | A Crescentio Mathero. | Apud Bostoniensis V.D.M. nec non Collegii | Harvardini quod est Cantabrigia Nov-An- | glorum, Rectore. | Londini Typis J. G. 1688, | Jam recusua, & successu Evangelii apud In- | dos Orientales aucta. | *Ultrajecti, | Apud Wilhelmum Broedeleth, | Anno* 1699. Sm. 8vo, pp. 16. 46750

Field says "This is the third edition, having been printed in London in 1688, and at the same place as this in 1697. Copies of either edition are not easy to procure, but that of 1698 is rarer than the others." A blundering note, which, if it proves anything, proves there are *four* editions; moreover, he translates *Crescentius* as Cotton.

MATHER. The | Surest way to the Greatest | Honour: | Discoursed in a Sermon, | Delivered | In the Audience of His Excellency the | Earl of Bellomont, Captain | General and Governour in Chief, | and of the Council, and Repre- | sentatives of the General Assembly | of the Province of Massachusetts- | Bay, Convened at Boston in New- | England, May 31st. 1699. Being | the day for the Election of | Counsellors in that Province. | By Increase Mather. | *Boston. Printed by Bartholomew Green, & John Allen, | for Samuel Phillips* .... 1699. Sm. 8vo, pp. (8), 42. B.

MATHER. A | Testimony | Against several Prophane and Superstitious | Customs, | Now Practised by some in | New-England, | The Evil whereof is evinced from the | Holy Scriptures,

and from the | Writings both of Ancient | and Modern Divines. | By Increase Mather .... | *London: Printed in the Year* 1687. Sm. 8vo, pp. (8), 41 [*i. e.* 31]. B., M. 46752

Very rare. Thomas quotes an edition, "With a Preface. *Boston: Reprinted from the London Edition.* 1688."

MATHER. The Times of men are in the hand | of God. | Or | A Sermon | Occasioned by that awfull Providence which hapned in | Boston in New England, the 4th day of the 3d | Moneth 1675. (when part of a Vessel was blown up in | the Harbour. and nine men hurt, and three mortally | wounded) wherein is shewed how we should | sanctifie the dreadfull Name of God | under such awfull | Dispensations. | By Increase Mather .... | *Boston, Printed by John Foster.* 1675. 4to, pp. (6), 21. BA., M. 46753

The second work printed in Boston. Extremely rare.

MATHER. Two Discourses | Shewing, | I. That the Lord's Ears are | open to the Prayers of the | Righteous. | II. The Dignity & Duty of | Aged Servants of the Lord. | Also, | A Preface in which the | Congregational Discipline of | the Churches in New-England | is Vindicated, with the Authors | Dying Testimony there-unto. | By I. Mather, D.D. ... | *Boston in N. E. Printed by B. Green, | for Daniel Henchman.* 1716. 12mo, pp. (2), ix, 141, (1).

The Preface (pp. ix) is dated July 26, 1716. "Nine and Fifty Years are Lapsed, since I began to Preach the Gospel, in my Youth, in lands afar off ... Since God brought me to Boston, Five and Fifty Years are within a few Weeks expired. What Changes have I lived to see!"

MATHER. Two Plain and Practical | Discourses | Concerning | I. Hardness of Heart. | Shewing, | That some, who live under the Gospel, | are by a Judicial Dispensation, given | up to that Judgment; and the Signs | thereof. | II. | The Sin and Danger | of | Disobedience to the Gospel. | By Increase Mather, President of Harvard- | College in Cambridge, and Preacher of | the Gospel at Boston in New-England. | *London. Printed for J. Robinson, and are to | be Sold by Samuel Phillips, Bookseller in Boston, | in New-England.* 1699. 12mo, pp. 187. M. 46755

[MATHER.] A | Vindication of Nevv-England, | from the | Vile Aspersions Cast upon that | Country | By a Late Address of a Faction there, | Who Denominate themselves | of the | Church of England | in | Boston. | Printed with Allowance. | [n. p. 1688?] 4to, pp. 27. H., W. 46756

Excessively rare. Probably Increase Mather furnished much of the material for this work, though indirectly. *See* "Andros Tracts," II. 19–82, *and* Sibley, No. 44.

MATHER. The Voice of | God, | in | Stormy Winds. | Considered, in Two | Sermons, | Occasioned by the Dreadful and Un- | parallel'd Storm, in the European | Nations. Novemb. 27th. 1703. | By Increase Mather. ... | [Followed by:] A | Brief Discourse | Concerning the | Prayse | Due to God, for His Mercy, in giving | Snow like Wool. | *Boston in N. E. Printed by T. Green, | for Nicholas Buttolph.* 1704. 12mo, pp. 95. B. 46757

In the first tract, the address "To the Reader" contains a brief notice of the attack on Deerfield and the capture of Mr. Williams and his family. The discourse makes frequent allusions to recent events: the great snow of Dec. 1703, and the loss of a Boston ship, in the harbor (p. 8), the storm of April 7th and 8th, 1704, which wrecked the French privateer "designing to do us hurt" (p. 28), the terrible "windy tempest" at Cambridge, in 1682 (pp. 63–4), etc.

MATHER. The Wicked mans Portion. | Or | A Sermon | (Preached at the Lecture in Boston in New England the | 18th day of the 1 Moneth 1674, when two men | were executed, who had murthered | their Master.) | Wherein is shewed | That excesse in wickedness doth bring | untimely Death. | By Increase Mather, Teacher | of a Church of Christ. | ... | *Boston, Printed by John Foster.* 1675. 4to, pp. (4), 25. W. 46758

Excessively rare. This appears to have been the first work printed in Boston. The preface is dated "15. of 2. Moneth [April 15]. 1675." "The Times of Men," No. 46753, *supra*, have the same date of imprint, but the preface is dated "9th of 4th Moneth [June 9th] 1675," and the accident which occasioned it occurred *May 4th*, 1675. There is another issue in which two lines are added to the errata, on the last page (25), and an error in a marginal note on the same page is corrected. For the second impression, *see* "A Sermon (Preached at the Lecture ...)," No. 46736, *supra*.

MATHER. Wo to Drunkards. | Two | Sermons | Testifying against the Sin of | Drunkenness: | Wherein the Wofulness of that Evil, and the Misery of all | that are addicted to it, is Discovered from the | Word of God. | By Increase Mather, D.D. | *Cambridge, Printed by Marmaduke Johnson*, 1673. *And sold by Edmund Ranger Bookbinder in Boston.* 4to, pp. (4), 35. + The Second Edition. ... *Boston, Printed ... by Timothy Green*, ... 1712. Sm. 8vo, pp. (4), 58, (1). BA. 46759

The *third* of Mather's published works. Hebrew type is used in a marginal note, p. 9, and Greek type on p. 3, in the first edition. "*Cyder*, and a Spirit Extracted out of it, has been much abused to Intemperance. Some observe, that since it has been so, a strange Blast has been upon the fruit Trees, in many Places; so as that some whose Orchards have yielded 500 Barrels of Cyder in a Year, now produce very little. But there is another sort of Strong Drink imported from the Sugar Islands, which has been of all others the most fatal. It is now called *Rum*, but it once had another name, and a ridiculous one, viz. *Kill Devil.* Renowned Mr. Wilson said, it should rather have been called, *Kill Men for the Devil.*"

MATHER. Word to the Present and Succeeding Generations of New England. *Printed at Cambridge by Sam'l Green, and are to be sold by John Tappan of Boston.* 1672. 4to, pp. 32. 46760

Title from Thomas' "History of Printing."

MATHER. The Work of the Ministry. *See* "Practical Truths," No. 46718, *supra*.

MATHER (J.) A Sermon Occasioned by the Great Fire, Boston, N. England, 1760, by J. Mather. *Boston.* 1760. 8vo.

MATHER (J.) The Constitutions of Great Britain, France, and the United States of America, from the most Authentic Sources. ... By James Mather, Esq. *London: Effingham Wilson.* 1834. 8vo, pp. viii, 76. 46762

MATHER (J. M.) The Christian Record, edited and published by James M. Mather. Vol. I. *Bloomington, Indiana.* 1843. 8vo, pp. 286. 46763

[MATHER (John).] Genealogy of the Mather Family, from about 1500 to 1847, with sundry Biographical Notices. *Hartford: Press of Elihu Geer.* 1848. 12mo, pp. 76. 46764

This little book, by John Mather of Manchester, Conn., is but an outline of such a genealogy of the family as we trust will yet be written.

MATHER (J. C.) Trial of John C. Mather ... in the Court for the Trial of Impeachments, held at the Capitol in the City of Albany, commencing July 27, 1853. By R. Sutton. *Albany.* 1853. 8vo. 46765

Also: Speech ... on Repeal of the Metropolitan Police Law. *Albany.* 1858. 8vo, pp. 14. — Speech ... on the Bill authorizing the New York Protestant Episcopal Public School to sell a part of their Lands. *Albany.* 1859. 8vo, pp. 9. S.

MATHER (J. H.) Geography of the State of New York. Embracing its Physical Features, Climate .... With Statistical Tables, and a Separate Description and Map of Each County. Accompanied by a Large Outline Map and Geological Chart ... By J. H. Mather .... And L. P. Brockett, M.D. ... *Hartford: J. H. Mather & Co.* 1847. 12mo, pp. 432. + *Utica: H. H. Hawley & Co.* 1848. 12mo, pp. 432. + *Utica.* 1851. 12mo. + *Utica.* 1853. 12mo. 46766

MATHER (M.) A Brief View of the ... Controversy about Terms of Communion in the Visible Church .... By Moses Mather, A.M. ... *New Haven: Printed by Samuel Green.* 1772. 8vo, pp. 20. 46767

The Rev. Moses Mather, D.D., minister of Middlesex (a parish in Stamford, now the town of Darien,), was the great-great-grandson of Richard of Dorchester.

MATHER. Connecticut Election Sermon, May 10, 1781. By Moses Mather .... *New-London.* 1781. 4to. 46768

MATHER. The Visible Church, in Covenant with God: or, an Inquiry into the Constitution of the Visible Church of Christ. ... By Moses Mather, A.M. ... *New-York: Printed by H. Gaine.* M,DCC,LIX. 8vo, pp. 60. BA., N. 46769

A defense of the "Half-way Covenant," against the Rev. Dr. Bellamy.

MATHER. The Visible Church, in Covenant with God; Further Illustrated. Containing Also, a brief Representation of some other Gospel-Doctrines, which affect the Controversy. Interspersed with Remarks upon some Things advanced by Dr. Bellamy, and Mr. Hopkins ... By Moses Mather, A.M. ... *New-Haven: Printed by Thomas and Samuel Green.* M,DCC,LXX. 8vo, pp. 84. BA. 46770

"America's Appeal," Vol. I., No. 1276, is probably by Moses Mather.

MATHER (N.), *of Dublin and London.* A | Discussion | Of the Lawfulness of a | Pastor's Acting as an | Officer | In Other | Churches | Besides that which He | is specially Called to | take the Oversight of. By the late Reverend | Mr. Nathanael Mather. | *London: Nath. Hiller.* M DC XC VIII. 12mo, pp. (20), 155. + The Second Edition. *Boston: Re-printed ... by Thomas Fleet.* 1730. 12mo, pp. (2), x, 83. B. 46771

MATHER. A | Sermon | Wherein is shewed | That it is the Duty and should be the Care | of Believers on Christ, to Live | in the Constant Exercise of | Grace. | By Mr. Nathanael Mather | ... . *Printed at Boston in New-England* | *By R. P[ierce], for Joseph Browning.* 1684. Sm. 8vo, pp. (2), 28, (1). B., M. 46772

The first work independently published by him. This Nathanael is the author of other sermons which have no special relation to America.

MATHER. Twenty-Three | Select Sermons, | Preached ... at | Pinners-Hall, and in Lime-Street. | Wherein Several | Cases of Conscience, | and | Other Weighty Matters, are | propounded, and handled. | By ... | Mr. Nathanael Mather. | *London: N. Hiller.* 1701. 8vo, pp. (8), 480. 46773

[MATHER (Nathanael), *of Salem.*] The Boston Ephemeris. An Almanack ... for the Year of the Christian Æra 1685. *Boston: Samuel Green.* 1685. 12mo, pp. 16. M. 46774

The author was a brother of Cotton Mather. He prepared this almanac when he was but fifteen years of age. It is devoted strictly to the legitimate purposes of an almanac, and no attempt is made at religious instruction. "His Piety and Learning was beyond his Years. He dyed here at *Salem*, and over his Grave there is written,

'The Ashes of an Hard Student, a Good Scholar, and a Great Christian.'"—REV. JOHN HIGGINSON, *in his Attestation to Cotton Mather's Magnalia.*

MATHER (R.) A | Catechism | or, | The Grounds and Princi- | ples of Christian Religion, set forth by way of Question | and Answer, Wherein the summe of the Doctrine of | Religion is comprised, familiarly opened, | and clearly confirmed from the | Holy Scriptures. | By Richard Mather; Teacher to the | Church at Dorchester in | New-England. ... | *London: | Printed for John Rothwell* ... 1650. 12mo, pp. 124. 46775

Concerning this rare volume, *see* C. Mather's "Magnalia," *also* "Hist. Mag.," III. 26.

[MATHER.] Church-Government | and | Church-Covenant | Discvssed, | In an Answer of the Elders of the seve- | rall Churches in | New-England | To two and thirty Questions, sent over | to them by divers Ministers in England, to de- | clare their judgements therein. | Together with an Apologie of the said Elders in | New-England for Church-Covenant, sent over | in Answer to Master Bernard in the | yeare 1639. | As also in an Answer to nine Positions about Church- | Government. | And now published for the satisfaction of all who desire | resolution in those points. | *London, | Printed by R. O. and G. D. for Benjamin Allen.* | *Anno Dom.* 1643. 4to, pp. (4), 84, (2), 78. B., C., W. 46776

The "Apologie" has a separate title-page and paging; the "Answer unto nine Positions" is by John Davenport and has a separate title-page, but is paged continuously with the "Apologie," omitting pp. 47, 48. As the address "To the Reader" is signed "H. Peter," the work has sometimes wrongly been ascribed to him. *See* Ball (J.)

MATHER Collections of the Dorchester Antiquarian and Historical Society. Number Three. Journal of Richard Mather. 1635. His Life and Death. 1670. *Boston: David Clapp.* 1850. 12mo, pp. 108. BA. 46777

Also included in Young (A.), "Chronicles of Massachusetts."

[MATHER.] A Defence of the Answer and Arguments of the Synod met at Boston in the Year 1662. Concerning The Subject of Baptism and Consociation of Churches. Against the Reply made thereto, by the Reverend John Davenport, ... in his Treatise Entituled, Another Essay for Investigation of the Truth, &c. Together with An Answer to the Apologetical Preface set before that Essay [by Jonathan Mitchel]. By some of the Elders who were Members of the Synod ... . *Cambridge: ... S. Green and M. Johnson for Hezekiah Usher.* 1664. 4to, pp. (2), 46, 102.

MATHER. A | Farewel-Exhortation | to the Church and People | of Dorchester in | New England. | ... By Richard Mather Teacher

to the | Church above mentioned. | ... | *Printed by Samuel Green at Cambridg in | New-England* 1657. 4to, pp. (4), 27. B. 46779

The preface "To the Reader," p. 2, is signed "Charles Chauncy." *See* Mather's "Magnalia," Bk. III., p. 128. Excessively rare. Mr. Brinley's copy is the only one which has been sold in New York.

MATHER. An | Heart-Melting | Exhortation, | Together | with a Cordiall | Consolation, | Presented in a Letter from New- | England, to their dear Coun- | treymen of Lancashire; | Which may as well concern all others | in these suffering times. | By Richard Mather Teacher of | the Church at Dorchester, | and William | Tompson Pastor of the Church | at Braintry in New England. | ... | *London, | Printed by A. M. for J. Rothwell, at the Sun and | Fountain in Pauls-Church yard, near the little | North-door.* 1650. Sm. 8vo, pp. (2), 84, (6). 46780

MATHER. A | Modest & Brotherly | Ansvver | To Mr. Charles Herle his Book, | against the Independency of Churches. | Wherein his foure Arguments for the Govern- | ment of Synods over particular Congregati- | ons, are friendly Examined, and | clearly Answered. | Together, with Christian and Loving Ani- | madversions upon sundry other observable passa- | ges in said Booke. | All tending to declare the true use of Synods, and the | power of Congregational Churches in the points of | electing and ordaining their owne Officers, | and censuring their Offendors. | By Richard Mather Teacher of the | Church at Dorchester; and William | Tompson Pastor of the | Church at | Braintree in New-England. | ... | *London, Printed for Henry Overton in Popes-head alley.* 1644. 4to, pp. (4), 58. M. 46781

MATHER. A | Reply | to | Mr. Rutherfurd, | or, | A defence of the Answer to Re- | verend Mr. Herles Booke against the | Independency of Churches. | Wherein such Objections and | Answers, as are returned to sundry passages | in the said Answer by Mr. Samuel Rutherfurd, | a godly and learned Brother of the Church of Scotland, in his Booke Entituled The Due | Right of Presbyters, are examined and removed, and the Answer justified | and cleared. | By Richard Mather Teacher to | the Church at Dorchester in New | England. 1646. | *London, | Printed for J. Rothwell, and H. Allen* ... . 1647. 4to, pp. (8), 109. 46782

MATHER. The Summe of Certain Sermons upon Genes: 15. 6. Wherein Not only the Doctrine of Justification by Faith is Asserted and Cleared, And sundry Arguments for Justification before Faith, discussed and Answered, But Also The nature and the meanes of Faith, with the Imputation of our Sins to Christ,

and of Christs Righteousness to us are briefly Explained and Confirmed. By Richard Mather ... . *Cambridg, Printed by Samuel Green.* 1652. 4to, pp. (12), 47. 46783

"To the Christian Reader," by John Cotton and John Wilson, 1 p. This exceedingly rare book is the first work of Richard Mather's printed in New England, except a catechism of which no copy is known to be extant.

MATHER. Will of Rev. Richard Mather. Transcribed from the Record, in Suffolk Probate Office, ... by William B. Trask, ... [*Boston.* 1866.] 8vo, pp. 8. Genealogical Chart. 46784

Also: Massachusetts Election Sermon. [*Boston.* 1660.] 8vo. *See also* No. 46700.

MATHER (S.), *of Dublin.* The | Figures | or | Types | of the | Old Testament, | By which | Christ and the Heavenly Things of the | Gospel were preached and shadowed to | the People of God of old; | Explained and Improved in sundry | Sermons, | By | Mr. Samuel Mather, sometime Pastor of a Church | in Dublin. | [*Dublin?*] *Printed in the Year* M.DC.LXXXIII. 4to, pp. (6), 678.

MATHER. The | Figures | [as before]. Explain'd and Improv'd in sundry | Sermons. | By Samuel Mather, sometime Pastor | of a Church in Dublin. | The Second Edition, To which is annex'd, (more than | was in the former Edition) a Scheme and Table of the whole, | whereby the Reader may readily turn to any Subject treated | of in this Book. | *London, | Printed for Nath. Hillier* ... . 1705. 4to, pp. vii, (1), 4, 540, 11, (1). BA., H.

This book was edited by the author's brother, and successor, Nathaniel Mather, of Dublin. *See* Sibley's "Biographical Sketches," I. 86.

MATHER. A | Testimony | from the | Scripture | against | Idolatry & Superstition, | In Two Sermons; | Upon the Example of that Great Reformer Hezekiah, | ... | The first, Witnessing in generall against all the Idols and | Inventions of Men in the Worship of God. | The second, more particularly against the Ceremonies, and | some other Corruptions of the Church of England. | Preached, the one September 27. the other September. 30. 1660 | ... . By Mr. Samuel Mather, Teacher to a | Church ... in Dublin ... . [*Cambridge: Printed by Samuel Green.* 1670.] 4to, pp. (6), 75. BA. + [*Boston.* 1725.] 4to, pp. (6), 88. BA., M. 46787

The address "To the Reader" is by Increase Mather. Samuel Mather was silenced for his ardent preaching against the established church. *See* C. Mather's "Magnalia," IV. 146-....

MATHER (S.), *of Windsor, Conn.* A Dead Faith Anatomized. A Discourse on The Nature, and the Danger, with the Deadly Symptoms of a Dead Faith in those who profess the Faith of Christ. By Samuel Mather ... . *Boston: Printed by Bartholomew Green, and John Allen.* 1697. 8vo, pp. 108. B. + The Second

Edition. *Boston: Re-Printed for D. Henchman.* MDCCXL. 8vo, pp. (2), 108. BA. 46788

The preface (pp. 3-24) is by Cotton Mather.

MATHER. The Self-Justiciary Convicted and | Condemned. | Or, A | Discourse | Concerning the | Difficulty & Necessity | of | Renouncing our own | Righteousness; | and the ... Method of Repairing | to the | Righteousness | of ... Christ, | ... . By Samuel Mather, | ... . | *Boston in N. E. Printed by B. Green* | *for N. Porter.* 1707. 8vo, pp. (2), 27, (1), 94. B. + *Boston: Printed by J. Draper, for D. Henchman.* 1740. 12mo, pp. (2), 14, 82. C.

"The Epistle Dedicatory," in the edition of 1707, contains (pp. 19-27) "A Testimony to the Order of the Gospel, in the Churches of New-England," signed "John Higginson. William Hubbard."

[MATHER (Samuel), *of Witney*).] A Compendious History of the Rise and Progress of the Reformation of the Church here in England, from Popish Darkness and Superstition. Together with an Account of Nonconformity ... Also, King Charles II's Declaration about Religion, October, 1660 ... . By a Gentleman. *London.* 1715. 8vo, pp. (16), 148. 46790

A great part of this book is (almost verbatim) a transcript of Dr. Cotton Mather's "Eleutheria: or, An Idea of the Reformation" (No. 46301, *supra*), London, 1698. This third Samuel Mather was the son of Increase Mather. He is the author of several other works, which do not relate to American topics.

MATHER (S.), *of Boston.* An | Apology | For the Liberties of the Churches in | New England: | To which is prefix'd, | A Discourse concerning | Congregational Churches. | By Samuel Mather, M.A. | Pastor of a Church in Boston, New England. | ... | *Boston: | Printed by T. Fleet, for Daniel Henchman,* | ... 1738. 8vo, pp. (8), ix, (1), 116 [*i. e.* 216]. BA., H. 46791

[MATHER.] An | Attempt to Shew, | That America must be Known to the | Ancients; | Made at the Request, and to gratify the Curiosity, of | an Inquisitive Gentleman: | To which is added | an Appendix, | Concerning the American Colonies, | and some | Modern Managements against | them. | By an American Englishman. | Pastor of a Church in Boston, New-England. | ... | *Boston New-England: | Printed by J. Kneeland, ... for T. Leverett, and H. Knox* ... . MDCCLXXIII. 8vo, pp. 35. A., BA., P., W. 46792

The preface, which precedes the title-page, is signed by the author, Samuel Mather. "A work of equal Learning and Patriotism." "It maintains that the posterity of Japhet, by Magog, were the primary inhabitants of America; a warlike people, well qualified to make those Ancient Encampments which have been discovered at the West."—THOMAS. For a reply, *see* [Prout (Timothy)].

MATHER. The | Departure and Character | of Elijah | Considered and Improved. | A Sermon | After the Decease of the | very

Reverend and Learned | Cotton Mather, D.D. | F.R.S. | And Minister of the North Church, | Who expired Feb. 13. 1727, 8. | In the Sixty Sixth Year of his Age. | By Samuel Mather, M.A. | And Chaplain at Castle William. | ... | *Boston, Printed by G. Rogers, for* | *S. Gerrish* ... . 1728. 8vo, pp. (4), 26. BA., C., H. 46793

[MATHER.] The Dying Legacy of an Aged Minister of the Everlasting Gospel, to the United States of North-America. ... *Boston: Printed by Benjamin Edes and Sons.* M,DCC,LXXXIII. Sm. 8vo, pp. (2), ii, 7-29. BA., W. 46794

MATHER. The Faithful Man abounding with Blessings. | A | Funeral Discourse | Upon the Death of the | Honourable | Thomas Hutchinson, Esq; | ... December ... 1739. ... By Samuel Mather, A.M. | ... | *Boston:* | *Printed by J. Draper, for N. Procter.* | MDCCXL. 8vo, pp. (2), 32. B., H., M., W. 46795

MATHER. The Fall of the Mighty lamented. A Funeral Discourse upon the Death of Her ... Majesty Wilhelmina Dorothea Carolina, Queen-Consort to His Majesty of Great-Britain, ... Preach'd on March 23d 1737,8, In the Audience of ... the Governour, the ... Lieutenant-Governour, and the honourable His Majesty's Council, ... in Boston, New-England. By Samuel Mather, M.A. ... *Boston, in New-England: Printed by J. Draper.* 1738. 8vo, pp. (2), 33. B., BA., M., W. 46796

MATHER. A Funeral Discourse Preached on the Occasion of the Death of ... Prince Frederick Lewis, ... In the Audience of ... the ... Council, of the Province of the Massachusetts-Bay: On May 22d. 1751. At Boston, New-England. By Samuel Mather, A.M. ... *Boston: Printed by John Draper.* 1751. 8vo, pp. 31. BA., C., H., N. 46797

[MATHER.] The Holy Walk and Glorious Translation of Blessed Enoch. A Sermon preached at the Lecture in Boston, two days after the Death of the Reverend and Learned Cotton Mather. *Boston.* 1728. 8vo. 46798

MATHER. The | Life | of the | Very Reverend and Learned | Cotton Mather, | D.D. & F.R.S. | Late Pastor of the North Church in Boston. | Who Died, Feb. 13. 1727, 8. | By Samuel Mather, M.A. | ... | *Boston, New-England: Printed for Samuel Gerrish* ... . MDCCXXIX. 8vo, pp. (4), iv, 6, 10, 186. BA., H. 46799

At the end of the volume is a badly compiled list of the several works published by Dr. Mather, chronologically arranged from 1686 to 1727, which, with two sermons published after his death, prepared by him for the press, make three hundred and eighty-three. This Dictionary describes four hundred and eleven works.

MATHER. Of the Pastoral Care: | A | Sermon | Preached to the | ... Ministers of the Province | of the | Massachusetts-Bay in New-England, | at their | Annual Convention in Boston, on May 27. 1762. | ... By Samuel Mather, M.A. | ... *Boston, New-England:* | *Printed by Thomas and John Fleet.* 1762. 8vo, pp. 31. BA.

[MATHER.] The Sacred Minister: A New Poem, in Five Parts; representing his Qualifications for the Ministry, and his Life and Death in it. By Aurelius Prudentius, Americanus. ... *Boston: Printed by John Boyles.* MDCCLXXIII. 8vo, pp. 22, (1).

MATHER. ... A Sermon, ... in Boston, On October, 21st. 1773. When Levi Ames, a Young Man, under a Sentence of Death for Burglary, ... was present to hear the Discourse: By Samuel Mather, D.D. ... *Boston: Printed ... by E. Russell.* M,DCC,-LXXIII. 8vo, pp. 36. BA. 46802

MATHER. The State of Religion in New England. Letters from S. Mather and other Eminent Divines, in 1742. *Glasgow.* 1743. 12mo. 46803

MATHER. Two Discourses delivered October 25th, 1759, the day of Thanksgiving for the Reduction of Quebec, with an Appendix containing a Brief Account of two former Expeditions. By Samuel Mather ... . *Boston: ... R. Draper.* 1759. 8vo, pp. 67, (12). C. 46804

MATHER. Vita B. Augusti Hermanni Franckii ... . Cui adjecta est, Narratio Rerum Memorabilium in Ecclesiis Evangelicis per Germaniam, &c. Revisa, et, Cura Samuelis Mather, A.M. ... *Bostoni, Nov-Anglorum, Thoma Hancock.* MDCCXXXIII. 8vo, pp. (2), iv, 31, 11, (1). BA., C. 46805

MATHER. The Walk of the Upright, with its Comfort. | A | Funeral Discourse | After the Decease of the Reverend | Mr. William Welsted, | ... | and | Mr. Ellis Gray; | ... | Colleague Pastors of a Church in Boston. | Preached | ... May 6. 1753. By Samuel Mather, A.M. | ... *Boston: ... Michael Dennis.* | 1753. 8vo, pp. 34.

MATHER. War is lawful, and Arms are to be proved. | A | Sermon | Preached to the Ancient and Honourable | Artillery Company, | on June 4. 1739. | The ... Day for Electing their Officers, | at Boston, New England. | By Samuel Mather, M.A. | ... *Boston: Printed by T. Fleet, for Daniel Henchman.* 1739. 8vo, pp. 33. BA., H. 46807

Also: A Dissertation Concerning the most venerable Name of Jehovah. ... *Boston: Printed ... by Edes and Gill.* M,DCC,LX. 8vo, pp. (6), 101. + — An Essay concerning

Gratitude. ... *Boston, N. E.: T. Hancock.* M,DCC,XXXII. 8vo, pp. (8), 53. — The Lord's Prayer: or, A New Attempt to recover the Right Version and genuine Meaning of that Prayer. ... *Boston: Printed by Kneeland & Adams.* MDCCLXVI. 8vo, pp. (4), iv, 67.

MATHER (T. G.) Address ... before the Middlesex County Agricultural Society, ... October 13th, 1843. By Thomas G. Mather, Esq. *Middletown, Conn.: Wm. D. Starr, Printer.* 1843. 8vo, pp. 19, (1). H. 46808

[MATHER (Warham).] A Short Discourse. *See* [Mather (C.)]

M[ATHER] (W.) A Brief Character of the Antient Christian Quakers. Written by W. M. a Witness for the Truth, as it was in the beginning. *London: ... S. Clarke* ... 1695. Sm. 8vo, pp. 24. 46809

MATHER (W. W.) Elements of Geology, for the Use of Schools. By Wm. W. Mather. *Norwich.* 1833. 16mo, pp. 139. 46810

MATHER. Geology of New-York. *See* New York.

MATHER. On Diluvial Deposits by W. W. Mather. Lithographed. [n. p. 1835.] 4to, pp. 47. B. 46811

MATHER. ... On the Physical Geography of the United States East of the Rocky Mountains ... . By William W. Mather ... . [n. p. n. d.] 8vo, pp. 39. H. 46812

MATHER. Report on the Geological Reconnoissance of Kentucky, made in 1838. By W. W. Mather. [n. p. 1839.] 8vo, pp. 40. 46813

MATHER. Report on the ... Survey of ... Ohio. *See* Ohio.

MATHER. Report on the State House Artesian Well, at Columbus, Ohio. By W. W. Mather ... . *Columbus.* 1859. 8vo.

MATHER. Sketch of the Geology and Mineralogy of New-London and Windham Counties, Connecticut. By Wm. W. Mather. ... *Norwich: Printed by J. Dunham.* 1834. 8vo, pp. 36.

[MATHER *and* CONRAD (T. A.)] Geological Survey of the State [of New York. Questions proposed to observers. n. p. n. d.] 8vo, pp. 8. B. 46816

Mather Papers. [Being the Correspondence, mainly, of Increase, Samuel, and Cotton Mather.] *Boston: Massachusetts Historical Society.* 1865. 8vo, pp. xvi, 736. C. 46817

"Massachusetts Historical Society's Collections," Fourth Series, Vol. VIII.

MATHERS (W.) The Rise, Progress and Downfall of Aristocracy. By William Mathers. *Wheeling.* 1831. 12mo, pp. 200

MATHETEES ARCHAIOS, *pseudon.* A Serious Letter to the Young People of Boston, which may be serviceable to others, to guard them against Error, to establish them in the present Truth, and excite them to the prosecution of their Duty and best Interest. By Mathetees Archaios. *Boston: Benjamin Edes & Sons.* MDCCLXXXIII. 8vo, pp. 27. 46819

MATHEVET (Jean Claude). Aimie Tipadjimo8in Masinaigan ka ojitogobanen kaiat ka niina8isi mekate8ikonaie8igobanen kanactageng, 8ak8iena8indibanen. *Montreal.* 1859. 12mo, pp. 337. 46820

History of the Old Testament, in the Algonquin language.

MATHEVET. Ka Titc Tebeniminang Jezos ondaje aking. *Montreal.* 1861. 12mo, pp. 396. 46821

Life of Jesus Christ, in the Algonquin language.

MATHEWS (A. E.) Canyon City, Colorado, and its Surroundings. By Alfred E. Mathews. *New York: Privately Printed.* 1870. 4to. 46822

MATHEWS. Gems of Rocky Mountain Scenery, containing Views along and near the Union Pacific Railroad. By Alfred E. Mathews. *New York: The Author.* 1869. 4to, 23 leaves. 20 Plates. C. 46823

MATHEWS (Anne Jackson). The Life and Correspondence of Charles Mathews, the Elder, Comedian. By Mrs. Mathews. A New Edition, Abridged ... by Edmund Yates. *London: Routledge ...* . 1860. Post 8vo, pp. xvi, 480. B. 46824

MATHEWS. The London Mathews; Containing an Account of this Celebrated Comedian's Trip to America ... . By Mrs. Mathews. *Philadelphia.* 1824. 12mo, pp. 36. Plate. + *New York.* 1824. 12mo, pp. 34. Plate. + *Baltimore.* 1824. 12mo.

MATHEWS. Memoirs of Charles Mathews, Comedian. By Mrs. Mathews. *London.* 1838–39. 4 vols., 8vo. C. 46826

Includes his Journal, American Tours, etc.

MATHEWS. A Continuation of the Memoirs of Charles Mathews, Comedian. By Mrs. Mathews. Including his Correspondence and an Account of his Residence in the United States.

Philadelphia: Lea & Blanchard. 1839. 2 vols., 12mo, pp. 8, 13–395; 319. B., P. 46827

Also: Memories of Youthful Days of Mr. Mathews, the celebrated Actor. ... *Philadelphia.* 1822. 12mo.—Sketches of Mr. Mathews's Celebrated Trip to America; comprising a full Account of his admirable Lectures on Peculiarities, Characters, and Manners ... . *London: J. Limbird.* [n. d.] 12mo, pp. 24. 4 Plates.

[MATHEWS (Cornelius).] Behemoth: a Legend of the Mound-Builders. *New York: J. & H. G. Langley.* 1839. 12mo, pp. vi, (2), 192. B. + [*Ibid.*] 1843. 46828

MATHEWS. ... Big Abel and The Little Manhattan. By Cornelius Mathews. *New York: Wiley and Putnam.* MDCCCXLV. 12mo, pp. (6), 93. H. + [*Ibid.*] 1847. 12mo. 46829

[MATHEWS.] Chanticleer: a Thanksgiving Story of the Peabody Family. Second Edition. *Boston: B. B. Mussey & Co.* 1850. 12mo, pp. 155. C. 46830

MATHEWS. Chanticleer: a Thanksgiving Story of the Peabody Family. By Cornelius Mathews. ... *New-York.* [n. d.] 16mo, pp. 132. Plates. + *New York: Brown, Loomis & Co.* 1856. 16mo, pp. 130. 2 Plates. + *New York: American News Company.* [1868.] 12mo, pp. 130. 2 Plates. C. 46831

[MATHEWS.] The Indian Fairy Book. From the Original Legends. With Illustrations by J. McLenan, Engraved by V. S. Anthony. *New York: Mason Brothers.* 1854. 12mo, pp. 338.

Includes some of the legends introduced into Longfellow's "Hiawatha." Reprinted in 1856, and again as below:

MATHEWS. The Indian Fairy-Book. From the Original Legends. ... By Cornelius Mathews. *New York: Allen Brothers.* 1869. 12mo, pp. 338. 4 Plates. 46833

MATHEWS. Légendes indiennes recueillies chez les peuplades sauvages de l'Amérique. ... Traduit de l'anglais, ... par Mlle Frappaz. *Paris: Hachette et Cie.* 1861. 12mo. 46834

[MATHEWS.] The Motley Book: a Series of Tales and Sketches. By the Late Ben. Smith. With Illustrations by Dick and Others. New Edition. *New-York: J. & H. G. Langley.* MDCCCXXXVIII. 8vo, pp. (2), 190. 10 Plates. B., C.

[MATHEWS.] The Motley Book: a Series of Tales and Sketches of American Life. By the Author of "Behemoth," ... With Illustrations by Dick, Gimber, and Others. Third Edition ... . *New York: Benj. G. Trevett.* 1840. 8vo, pp. (4), 190. 9 Plates. C. 46836

MATHEWS. A Pen-and-Ink Panorama of New-York City. By Cornelius Mathews. *New-York: John S. Taylor.* 1853. 18mo, pp. 209. C. 46837

MATHEWS. Poems on Man, in his Various Aspects under the American Republic. By Cornelius Mathews ... . *New York: Wiley and Putnam.* MDCCCXLIII. 16mo, pp. 112. B. + A New Edition. *New York.* 1846. 12mo. 46838

[MATHEWS.] The Politicians, a Comedy. *New York.* 1840. 12mo. 46839

MATHEWS. The Various Writings of Cornelius Mathews; Embracing The Motley Book, Behemoth, The Politicians, Poems ... Wakondah, Puffer Hopkins, Miscellanies, Selections from Arcturus, International Copyright. ... *New York: Harper & Brothers.* MDCCCLXIII. 8vo, pp. viii, 11–370. BA. 46840

Also: Americanism. Address ... . *New York.* 1845. 8vo.—An Appeal to American Authors and the American Press, in Behalf of International Copyright. ... *New-York: Wiley & Putnam.* MDCCCXLII. 12mo, pp. 16. B.—The Better Interests of the Country, in connexion with International Copy-right: ... *New-York: Wiley & Putnam.* MDCCCXLIII. 12mo, pp. 30. B.—Moneypenny, or, the Heart of the World: A Romance of the Present Day. ... *New York: Dewitt & Davenport.* 1850. 8vo, pp. 270, (1).—A Speech on International Copyright, delivered ... at the City Hotel, New York, February 19, 1842. ... *New York: George L. Curry and Company.* MDCCCXLII. 8vo, pp. 16.—Wakondah; the Master of Life. A Poem. ... *New York.* 1841. 8vo. Witchcraft; a Tragedy in Five Acts. ... *New York.* 1852. 12mo. *See* "Arcturus."

MATHEWS (E.) American Slavery and the War. A Lecture ... the 15th August, 1864, By ... Rev. Edward Mathews ... . *Wirksworth: J. Buckley, Printer.* [n. d.] 8vo, pp. 8. 46841

MATHEWS. The Autobiography of ... Rev. Edward Mathews, the "Father Dickson," of Mrs. Stowe's "Dred." Also a Description of the Influence of the Slave Party on the American Presidents ... . *London: Houlston and Wright.* [n. d.] Post 8vo, pp. xii, 444. 46842

MATHEWS (J. M.) The Bible and Civil Government. By J. M. Mathews, D.D. *New-York.* 1850. 12mo. + [*Ibid.*] 1851.

MATHEWS. Fifty Years in New-York; A Semi-Centennial Discourse preached in the South Dutch Church, By J. M. Mathews, D.D. *New-York: Printed by D. Fanshaw.* 1858. 8vo, pp. 48. B., S. 46844

MATHEWS. Recollections of Persons and Events, chiefly in ... New York: ... By J. M. Mathews, D.D. ... *New York: Sheldon and Company.* M DCCC LXV. 8vo, pp. 368. B. 46845

Also: ... A Sermon, ... on the Loss of the Lexington. ... *New-York: Printed by George F. Hopkins.* 1840. 8vo, pp. 20. BA.

MATHEWS (J. H.) Guy Hamilton: a Story of our Civil War. By Joanna H. Mathews. *New York.* 1866. 8vo, pp. 99.

Also: The Bessie Books. ... *New York: R. Carter & Brothers.* 1869. 16mo, etc.

MATHEWS (S. A.) The Lying Hero,—or an Answer to J. B. Moreton's Manners and Customs in the West Indies. By Samuel Augustus Mathews. *St. Eustatius: E. L. Low & Co.* 1793. 4to, pp. 160. W. 46847

MATHEWS (W.) A Pamphlet on the Washington Miracle. [n. p.] 1824. 46848

See "The Washington Miracle refuted," *and* Mattingly (A.), No. 46900.

MATHIES (J.) Rochester, a Satire; and other Miscellaneous Poems. By James Mathies. *Rochester.* 1830. 18mo. 46849

MATHIESEN (J.) Den grönlandske Handel og Grönlands Colonisation. *Kjöbenhavn.* 1846. 8vo. Map. 46850

MATHIESEN. Om Grönland, dets Indbyggere, Producter og Handel. *Kjöbenhavn.* 1852. 8vo. 46851

[MATHIESON (A.)] An Appeal to the Democracy of Wisconsin. [*Milwaukee.* 1849.] 8vo, pp. 12. BA. 46852

MATHIESON (A.) Discourse delivered on board the Transport Ship Java, off Quebec, ... to the 1st Battalion of the 71st Highland Light Infantry ... . By Alexander Mathieson, D.D. *Montreal.* 1843. 8vo, pp. 41. S. 46853

Also: Anniversary Sermon before the St. Andrew's Society. ... *Montreal.* 1863. 8vo, pp. 19.—The Moral and Religious Influences of Autumn. A Sermon ... Saint Andrew's Church, Montreal, 1849. ... *Montreal.* 1850. 8vo, pp. 72.—Sermon on the Death of Mr. Robert Watson. ... *Montreal.* 1827. 8vo.—Sermon on St. Andrew's Day. ... *Montreal.* 1837. 8vo.—Sermon ... at the opening of the Synod at Quebec. ... *Montreal.* 1861. 8vo, pp. 29.—A Tribute of Respect to the Memory of a Good Man. A Sermon on the Death of Hugh Brodie, Esq. ... *Montreal.* 1852. 8vo, pp. 44. S.

MATHIOT (G.) On the Electrotyping Operations of the U. S. Coast Survey. By George Mathiot ... . Nov. 29, 1851 ... . *New Haven: Printed by B. L. Hamlen.* 1852. 8vo, pp. 15. Chart. B. 46854

MATHISON (G.) Critical View of a Pamphlet [by Mr. J. T. Barham], entitled, "The West India Question practically considered," with Remarks on the Trinidad Order in Council. By Gilbert Mathison ... . *London.* 1827. 8vo, pp. 78. 46855

MATHISON. Notices Respecting Jamaica, in 1808–1809–1810. By Gilbert Mathison, Esq. *London: John Stockdale.* 1811. 8vo, pp. vii, 117. C., H. 46856

See "Q. Rev.," VI. 147, *also* "M. Rev.," LXVIII. 426.

MATHISON. A Short Review of The Reports of the African Institution, and of the Controversy with Dr. Thorpe. With some Reasons against the Registry of Slaves in the British Colonies. By Gilbert Mathison, Esq. *London: Wm. Stockdale.* 1816. 8vo, pp. x, 78. A. + Second Edition. *London: W. Stockdale & J. Asperne.* 1816. 8vo, pp. 123. C. 46857

MATHISON (G. F.) Narrative of a Visit to Brazil, Chile, Peru, and the Sandwich Islands, during the Years 1821 and 1822. With Miscellaneous Remarks on the Past and Present State and Political Prospects of those Countries. By Gilbert Farquhar Mathison, Esq. *London: Charles Knight.* M DCCC XXV. 8vo, pp. xii, 478. Map and 4 Plates. C., H. 46858

MATIAS (P.) Exequias de la reyna doña Margarita de Austria, por Pedro Matias. *Lima.* 1612. 4to. 46859

Matias Campanillas y Roque Pechuga; o los camaleones politicos. Descriptos por un curioso parlante. *Buenos Aires.* 1857. 8vo, pp. 16. 46860

MATIGNON (F. A.) Obituary Notice of Rev. Francis Anthony Matignon, D.D. ... *Boston.* 1818. 16mo, pp. 16. M.

Matilda Berkely; or, Family Anecdotes. *Raleigh, N. C.* 1804. 12mo, pp. 224. 46862

MATILDA, *pseudon.* *See* [Smiley (*Miss*)].

MATILE (C. A.) Les Écoles de Droit aux États-Unis. ... Par M. G.-A. Matile. *Paris: Auguste Durand.* 1864. 8vo, pp. 19. B. 46863

Also: ... American Ethnology. A Paper on a General Society for the Study of American Antiquities. ... 1865 ... [n. p. n. d.] 8vo, pp. 425–432. H.

MATIN Y MATORRAS (J. de San). Elogio del Excel. Señor D. Jose de San Matin y Matorras, Protector del Peru. *Lima.* 1822. 4to, pp. 42. 46864

MATLACK (L. C.) The History of American Slavery and Methodism, from 1780 to 1849: and History of the Wesleyan Methodist Connection of America; in Two Parts, with an Ap-

pendix. By Lucius C. Matlack. ... *New York.* 1849. 12mo, pp. 368, 16. B. 46865

MATLACK. Life of the Rev. Orange Scott. Compiled from his Personal Narrative, Correspondence, and other Authentic Sources of Information. By Lucius C. Matlack. *New York: C. Prindle & L. C. Matlack.* 1847. 12mo, pp. 307. Portrait.

Also: Narrative of the Life and Adventures of Henry Bibb, an American Slave. Written by Himself. With an Introduction by Lucius C. Matlack. *New York: The Author.* 1849. 12mo, pp. 204, and Index.—A Personal Narrative of Proscription for being an Abolitionist. ... *Syracuse.* 1856. 24mo. S.—Sermon ... at the Funeral of Rev. Orange Scott, August 4, 1847. ... *Lowell: Pillsbury & Knapp, Printers.* [1847.] 12mo, pp. 24. BA.

MATLACK (R. C.) The Loyalty of the Episcopal Church Vindicated: An Address ... November 5th, 1865, by the Rev. Robert C. Matlack ... . *Philadelphia.* 1865. 8vo, pp. 36.

MATLACK (T.) An Oration ... March 16, 1780, before the ... American Philosophical Society ... . By Timothy Matlack, Esquire ... . *Philadelphia: Printed by Styner and Cist.* M.DCC.LXXX. 4to, pp. 27. C., P. 46868

MATORRAS (G.) Diario de la Expedicion hecha en 1774 a los paises del grand Chaco, desde el fuerte del valle, por D. Geronimo Matorras, Gobernador del Tucuman. *Buenos Aires.* 1837. Folio, pp. xiv, 34. 46869

See Angelis (Pedro de), "Coleccion de Obras y Documentos," Vol. VI.

MATRAT (J. B.) Practical Emigration to the United States ... systematized: ... By J. B. Matrat. Edited by Thomas Egerton Browne. *Louisville, Kentucky, U. S.* 1835. 16mo, pp. 52. BA., M. 46870

MATRAYA Y RICCI (J. J.) El Moralista Filalethico Americano, o el Confesor Imparcial instriudo las Obligaciones de su Ministerio segun los preceptos de la Mas Solida Theologio Moral, conforme a las limitaciones Indispensables en la America España. Por Juan Jos. Matraya y Ricci de la Provincia de S. Antonio de los Charcas en el Peru. Tomo I. *Lima.* 1819. Folio.

The second part of this volume contains a compendium of the Indian Laws. No more published.

Matrimonial Brokerage in the Metropolis; being True Narratives of Strange Adventures in New York ... . By a Reporter of the New York Press. *New York: Thatcher & Hutchinson.* 1859. 12mo, pp. 355. 6 Plates. H. 46872

Matrimony; or, Love Affairs in our Village Twenty Years Ago. By Mrs. Caustic. Second Edition. *New York: M. W. Dodd.* 1853. 12mo, pp. 316. 46873

MATSON (H. T.) Remarks on the Slave Trade and African Squadron. By Commander H. J. Matson, R.N. Third Edition. *London.* 1854. 8vo, pp. 94. 46874

MATSON (N.) Superior Court for the Counties of Plymouth, Barnstable, &c. The Case of Nathaniel Matson against Nathaniel Thomas. Arguments for the Defendant, on a Special Verdict. (John Valentine, Attorney for Defendant.) [n. p. 1720.] Sm. 4to, pp. 20. 46875

See "Washburn's Judicial History," 186.

MATSON (N.) Map of Bureau County, Illinois, with Sketches of its Early Settlement. By N. Matson. *Chicago: G. H. Fergus.* 1867. Sm. 4to, pp. 88. 8 Plates and 26 Maps. C. 46876

MATSON (W. A.) ... An Address before the House of Convocation of Hobart Free College, Geneva, July 19, 1854. By ... Rev. William A. Matson, M.A. ... *Utica: D. C. Grove, Printer.* 1854. 8vo, pp. 21. H. 46877

MATTAPAN. Constitution and By-Laws of the Mattapan Literary Association; ... and a Catalogue of the Library. ... *Boston: Printed by David Clapp.* 1857. 12mo, pp. 60. B.

MATTAPOISETT. Register of Mattapoisett Academy, for the Quarter commencing April 2d, 1860 ... . *New-Bedford.* 1860. 16mo, pp. 8. H. 46879

Matters of Fact relative to late Occurrences among Professional Quakers. *Philadelphia.* 1827. 12mo, pp. 24. 46880

Relates to the Hicksite controversy.

MATTESON (F. F.) The Fragment; or, Letters and Poems. By Mrs. Frances F. Matteson. *Rome [N. Y.]: A. Sandford.* 1855. 16mo, pp. 144. Portrait. C. 46881

MATTESON (O. B.) Speech of Hon. O. B. Matteson, of New York, on the Presidential Question and Kansas Affairs. [n. p. n. d.] 8vo, pp. 16. 46882

Also: Speech ... on the Cheap Postage Bill. *Washington.* 1851. 8vo, pp. 15.—Speech ... against The Repeal of the Missouri Prohibition, North of 36° 30′. ... April 4th, 1854. [n. p. n. d.] 8vo, pp. 16.

MATTHAEI (C. Chr.) Untersuchung über das gelbe Fieber. ... *Hannover.* 1827. 2 vols., 8vo. Map. 46883

MATTHEW (P.) Emigration Fields: North America, the Cape, Australia, and New Zealand, describing these Countries, and giving a comparative view of the Advantages they present to British Settlers. By Patrick Matthew. *Edinburgh.* 1839. Post 8vo. 2 Maps. 46884

MATTHEWS (C. J.) How do you Like our Country? or an Autumn in America. By Charles J. Matthews, Esq. *London: R. Bentley.* 1839. 8vo. 46885

MATTHEWS (Eliza Jane), *and* JENKINS (Mary H.) A Statement of Facts, together with some Observations relating to the Merits and Demerits of the Englishbe Case [of lands]. *New York.* 1849. 8vo, pp. 12. S. 46886

MATTHEWS (J. M.) *See* Vol. IV., Nos. 15342–6, 15417, *also* Virginia.

[MATTHEWS (J.)] Twenty-one Plans, with Explanations, of Different Actions in the West Indies, during the late War: By an Officer of the Royal Navy ... . *Chester: Printed by J. Fletcher.* MDCCLXXXIV. 4to, pp. 24. 21 Plans. A., H. 46887

The dedication to Lord Hood is signed by John Matthews.

MATTHEWS. A Voyage to the River Sierra-Leone ... . By John Matthews ... . with ... Letter on the ... African Slave Trade. *London: B. White and Son.* 1788. 8vo, pp. iv, 183. 2 Plates. A. 46888

MATTHEWS (J. T.) Sermon at Plymouth Church, Milwaukee, Wis., September 11, 1864, on the Rebellion. By Rev. J. T. Matthews. *Milwaukee.* 1864. 8vo, pp. 16. 46889

MATTHEWS (L.) History of the Town of Cornwall, Vermont. By Rev. Lyman Matthews. ... *Middlebury: Mead and Fuller.* 1862. 8vo, pp. 356. Portraits. B., C., S. 46890

MATTHEWS. Memoir of the Life and Character of Ebenezer Porter, D.D. late President of the Theological Seminary, Andover. By Lyman Matthews ... . *Boston: Perkins & Marvin.* 1837. 12mo, pp. 396. Portrait. B., C. 46891

Also: ... A Sermon ... before the ... Education Society of Norfolk County, at their Annual Meeting ... June 13, 1838. ... *Boston: Printed by Perkins & Marvin.* 1838. 8vo, pp. 33, (2). H.

MATTHEWS (M.) The Christian's Daily Exercise [in verse]. By Mordecai Matthews. *Newport: Widow Franklin.* 1738. 12mo, pp. 12. 46892

[MATTHEWS (Nathan).] An Address to the Stockholders of the Winnisimmet Company, by one of the Directors. *Boston: Printed ... by Beals & Greene.* 1852. 8vo, pp. 16. H. 46893

Also: A Letter to the Stockholders of the Winnisimmet Company ... . *Boston: Printed ... by Beals, Greene & Co.* 1852. 8vo, pp. 11. H.

[MATTHEWS (William).] An Address to the Public. [n. p. 179–.] 16mo, pp. 94. BA. 46894

[MATTHEWS.] A General Epistle ... to the People called Quakers, in Great Britain, ... and America, issued ... Anno 1803 ... . By Theophilus Freeman. *London: ... J. Johnson ...* 1803. 8vo, pp. 24. M. 46895

MATTHIAS. The False Prophet! The very interesting and Remarkable Trial of Matthias, the False Prophet, at White Plains, Westchester County, New-York, for the alleged Murder of Mr. Elijah Pierson, Reported ... By W. E. Drake ... . *New-York: W. Mitchell ...* . 1835. 8vo, pp. 16. + Third Edition. *New York.* 1835. 8vo. 46896

MATTHIAS. Memoirs of Matthias the Prophet, with a Full Exposure of his Atrocious Impositions, and of the Degrading Delusions of his Followers. *New York.* 1835. 8vo. Portrait.

MATTHIAS. The Prophet! A Full and Accurate Report of the Judicial Proceedings in the ... Case of Matthews, alias Matthias, charged with having Swindled Mr. B. H. Folger, ... Also A Sketch of the Impostor's Character. ... *New-York: W. E. Mitchell.* 1834. 8vo, pp. 16. 46898

MATTHIAS (B.) The Politician's Register; containing a brief sketch of the Executive, Legislative and Judicial Departments of the Federal and State Governments; ... By Benjamin Matthias. *Philadelphia: Key and Biddle.* 1835. 12mo, pp. 104. 46899

Also: The Traveler's Guide from New York to Philadelphia ... . *Philadelphia.* 1843. 12mo, pp. 96. BA.

MATTINGLY (A.) A Collection of Affidavits and Certificates, relative to the Wonderful Cure of Mrs. Ann Mattingly, Which took place in the City of Washington, D. C. on the tenth of March, 1824. *Washington: James Wilson.* 1824. 8vo, pp. 41.

MATTISON (H.) The Impending Crisis of 1860; or the Present Connection of the Methodist Episcopal Church with Slavery, And our Duty in Regard to it. By H. Mattison ... . *New York: Mason Brothers.* 1859. 12mo, pp. 136. B. 46901

Also: The Abduction of Mary Ann Smith by the Roman Catholics, and her Imprisonment in a Nunnery, for Becoming a Protestant. ... *Jersey City: The Author.* 1858. 16mo, pp. 150.— ... The Church, the Ministry and the Gospel, the best means for promoting Moral Reformation. ... *Troy, N. Y.: Press of N. Tuttle.* 1844. 8vo, pp. 40. B. — A Defence of American Methodism against the Criticisms, Inculpations, and Complaints of a Series of Sermons by Rev. E. D. Bryan. ... *New York: John A. Gray & Green, Printers.* 18—. 8vo, pp. 64.—Spirit-Rapping Unveiled! An Exposé of the Origin, History, Theology and Philosophy of certain alleged Communications from the Spirit World, by means of "Spirit-Rapping," "Medium Writing," "Physical Demonstrations," etc. ... *New York: Mason Brothers.* 1853. 12mo, pp. 192. B. + A New Edition, with an Appendix ... . *New York: J. C. Derby.* 1855. 12mo, pp. 240.

MATTISON (I.) Finney's Lectures on Human Governments Reviewed, By Israel Mattison; ... Sandwich, Illinois, 1864. [n. p. n. d.] 12mo, pp. 20. H. 46902

MATTISON (S.) ... Discourse occasioned by the Death of the Rev. Joseph Tomkinson; ... Lockport, October 20, 1835. By Seth Mattison. ... *Geneva, N. Y.: Printed by Ira Merrell.* 1837. 8vo, pp. 36. BA. 46903

MATTOON (C. S.) Pacific Ocean Commerce. Letter from C. S. Mattoon, U. S. Consul at the Sandwich Islands ... . [n. p. n. d.] 8vo, pp. 8. H. 46904

MATTOS (J. F. de) Diario historico das celebridades que na cidade de Bahia se fizeram em acção de graças pelos felicissimos casamentos dos serenissimos Principes de Portugal e Castella. Por José Ferreira de Mattos. *Lisboa, por Manuel Fernandes da Costa.* 1729. 4to, pp. xviii, 124. 46905

MATTOSO CAMARA (E. de Q. C.) Relatorío apresentado á Assembléa geral legislativa, ... pelo Ministro e Secretario d'Estado dos negocios da Justiça, Eusebio de Queiroz Coitinho Mattoso Camara. *Rio de Janeiro.* 1852. 8vo, pp. 36, 8, 16. 46906

MATUGÈNE DE KERALIO. Voyage dans l'Afrique et les deux Indes, pendant les années 1809, 10, 11 & 12. *Paris.* 1814. 2 vols., 12mo. 46907

MATURIN (E.) Montezuma; the Last of the Aztecs. ... By Edward Maturin. ... *New-York: Paine & Burgess.* 1845. 2 vols., 12mo, pp. 270; 287. B. 46908

MATURINO GILBERTI. Grammatica latina. *Mexico: Antonio de Spinoza.* [1575.] 8vo. 46909

For other works by this author, *see* Vol. VII., Nos. 27357–61.

[MAUBERT DE GOUVEST (J. H.)] Lettres Chérakéesiennes. Mises en François de la Traduction Italienne. Par J. J. Rufus, ... *Rome.* MDCCLXIX. 8vo, pp. viii, 164. H. 46910

[MAUBERT DE GOUVEST.] Lettres Iroquoises. *À Irocopolis, Chez Les Vénérables.* MDCCLII. 2 vols., 12mo, pp. (2), 166; (2), 164. + Nouvelle édition revue et corrigée. [*Ibid.*] 46911

Of these forty-three letters thirty-six were reprinted in 1769 under the title "Lettres chérakéesiennes."

[MAUBERT DE GOUVEST.] Lettres Iroquoises, ou Correspondance politique, historique et critique entre un Iroquois voyageant en Europe, et ses Correspondans dans l'Amérique Septentrionale. *Londres: Au Berceau de la Vérité.* [1781.] 8vo, pp. 70. 46912

The "Lettres Iroquoises" were the medium which their author assumed for his political criticisms.

[MAUDE (John).] A Visit to the Falls of Niagara, in 1800. *London: Longman ...* . MDCCCXXVI. 8vo, pp. (2), viii, (2), v, 313, xxvi, (1). 8 Plates. BA. 46913

Includes travels in New York. Three hundred copies only printed, of which fifty were on large paper with proof-plates, rl. 8vo, four copies on India paper, and four on Whatman's thick ribbed paper. Some copies contain additional notes (pp. 16), which were printed after the book had been published.

MAUDE, *pseudon.* *See* [Jennings (Clotilda)], Vol. VIII. 36037.

MAUDUIT (I.) An Apology for the Life and Actions of General Wolfe, against Misrepresentations. By Israel Mauduit, Esq. *London.* 1765. 8vo. 46914

Of this interesting memoir only twenty-five copies were printed for presents. The only copy which I have seen is now in the British Museum. *See* "Bibliotheca Grenvilliana," *and* "Heb. Cat.," III. 287.

MAUDUIT. The Case of the Dissenting Ministers. Addressed to the Lords Spiritual and Temporal. By Israel Mauduit. ... The Third Edition. *London: J. Wilkie.* MDCCLXXII. 8vo, pp. (2), 65. + The Fourth Edition. [*Ibid.*] + The Fourth Edition. *Boston: N. E. Printed by E. Russell.* M, DCC, LXXIII. 8vo, pp. 55. BA. 46915

[MAUDUIT.] Considerations on the Present German War. *London.* 1760. 8vo, pp. 136. + The Third Edition. *London: John Wilkie.* 1760. 8vo, pp. 144. H., N. 46916

This elicited "A Full and Candid Answer to 'Considerations'" ... . *London.* 1760. 8vo, pp. 86. *See* Walpole's "George III.," I. 33.

[MAUDUIT.] Madison Agonistes; or, the Agonies of Mother Goose. Fragment of a Political Burletta as acting or to be acted, on the American Stage. To which are added, Sundry other Monologues, Dialogues, Songs, &c., as Spoken or Sung on the Boards of the Great Political Theatre of Europe. *London: Printed by D. Deans, for John Cawthorpe.* 1814. 8vo, pp. 103. 46917

Among the *dramatis personæ* are Randolpho and Adamo, Members of Congress, Mother Jeff, Miss Paterson, King of Westphalia, etc.

[MAUDUIT.] Observations upon the Conduct of S— W——m H——e at the White Plains; as related in the Gazette of December 30, 1776. *London: J. Bew.* MDCCLXXIX. 8vo, pp. 44.

[MAUDUIT.] Remarks upon Gen. Howe's Account of his Proceedings on Long Island, in the Extraordinary Gazette of October 10, 1776. *London: Fielding and Walker.* 1778. 8vo, pp. (4), 54. + The Second Edition. [*Ibid.*] BA. 46919

[MAUDUIT.] A Short View of the History of the Colony of Massachusett's Bay, With Respect to their Original Charter and Constitution. *London: J. Wilkie.* 1769. 8vo, pp. (2), 71.

MAUDUIT. A Short View of the History of the Colony of Massachusetts Bay, With Respect to their Charters and Constitution. By Israel Maudit. The Second Edition, To which is now added the Original Charter granted to that Province in the 4th of Charles I. and never before printed in England. *London: J. Wilkie.* MDCCLXXIV. 8vo, pp. (4), 93. + The Third Edition. [*Ibid.*] 46921

MAUDUIT. A Short View of the History of the New England Colonies, With Respect to their Charters and Constitution. By Israel Mauduit. The Fourth Edition, To which is now added, An Account of a Conference between the late Mr. Grenville and the several Colony Agents, in the Year 1764, previous to the passing the Stamp Act. Also the Original Charter granted in the 4th of Charles I. and never before printed in England. *London: J. Wilkie.* MDCCLXXVI. 8vo, pp. (2), 100. 46922

The "Conference" forms duplicate pages 95 to 100. "The object of its author was to show that the colonists have no charter exemption from the authority of Parliament. Mauduit was the agent for Massachusetts in England, and a warm partisan in the disputes with the mother country."—*Monthly Review*, XL. 94.

[MAUDUIT.] Some Thoughts on the Method Of Improving and Securing the Advantages which accrue to Great-Britain from

the Northern Colonies. *London: J. Wilkie.* MDCCLXV. 8vo, pp. (4), 23. M. 46923

Purports to have been reprinted from the "New York Mercury."

[MAUDUIT.] Some trifling Thoughts on Serious Subjects. Addressed to the Earl of S(andwic)h, to which is added Liberty's Dream, with a Description of Modern Patriotism, &c. *London: Newell.* 1765. 8vo, pp. 78. 46924

[MAUDUIT.] Strictures on the Philadelphia Mischianza or Triumph upon leaving America Unconquered. With Extracts containing the Principal Part of a Letter, published in the "American Crisis." In order to shew how far the King's Enemies think his General deserving of Public Honours. N.B. A flattering Account of this Mischianza was published in the "Philadelphia Gazette," and copied into the "Morning Post," the 13th of July last; and a Larger one by a still more flattering Panegyrist, may be found in the "Gentleman's Magazine" for August last. *London: J. Bew.* M.DCC.LXXIX. 8vo, pp. (2), 42.

For an extended note respecting this scarce tract, from the "Monthly Review," XL. 393, *see* Rich I. 277. These "Strictures" are rather upon the conduct of General Howe, than upon the entertainment given him by his officers before leaving Philadelphia. *See* the "Ladies' Magazine," August, 1792, Smith's "American Curiosities," 1850, "Gentleman's Magazine," August, 1779.

MAUDUIT. Substance of a Speech at a General Court of the Company for Propagation of the Gospel in New England and Parts adjacent in America. By Israel Mauduit. [*Privately*] *printed in the Year* 1785. 8vo. 46926

[MAUDUIT.] Three Letters to Lieutenant-General Sir William Howe. With an Appendix. *London: G. Wilkie.* MDCCLXXXI. 8vo, pp. (4), 48. Map. H. 46927

A different pamphlet to the following:

[MAUDUIT.] Three Letters to Lord Viscount Howe. To which are added, Remarks on the Attack at Bunker's Hill. *London: G. Wilkie.* MDCCLXXX. 8vo, pp. (4), 47. + The Second Edition. To which is added a Comparative View of the Conduct of Lord Cornwallis and General Howe. *London: G. Wilkie.* MDCCLXXXI. 8vo, pp. 48. Map. 46928

"These letters contain many strong articles of impeachment of the conduct of Lord and Sir William Howe, during their command in America. The particulars are too well known, and the silence of the noble brothers is, by many, considered as a strong presumption that the charge implied in them *is not to be answered.*"—*Monthly Review*, LXIII. 65. *See* our No. 34072. Mauduit is supposed to have had a hand in the author-

ship of "The Present State of the Nation." *See* [Grenville (*Lord*)]. His reply to Burke's Speech on American Taxation, is characterized as "a most artful attempt to mislead."—BANCROFT, V. 190.

MAUDUIT-DUPLESSIS. Description nautique de la côte du Labrador, depuis le Cap Saint-Louis jusqu'à la Grande-Pointe, comprenant le détroit de Belle Ile. Traduit de l'Anglais par M. de Mauduit-Duplessis. *Paris.* 1852. 8vo. + [*Ibid.*] 1853. 8vo.

MAUGÉ (A. P.) Directoire Français et Guide des Affaires en Amérique ... . Par Augustin P. Maugé. *New York: A. P. Maugé.* 1864. 12mo, pp. 164. 46930

MAULE (J. E.) Some Extracts and Remarks on Acknowledging Meetings of Separatists, as though they were ... Friends. By Joseph E. Maule. *Philadelphia: William S. Young, Printer.* 1859. 8vo, pp. 15. H. 46931

Also: A Serious Review, affectionately recommended to the careful examination of Friends. ... *Philadelphia: William S. Young, Printer.* 1860. 8vo, pp. 16.

M[AULE] (T[homas]). An Abstract of a Letter to Cotton Mather, of Boston, in New England, By T. M. [n. p.] *Printed in the Year* 1701. 4to, pp. 20. 46932

[MAULE.] For the Service of Truth, against George Keith. [n. p.] 1703. 4to, pp. 8. 46933

[MAULE.] New England Persecutors Mauld With their own Weapons; Giving Some Account of the bloody Laws made at Boston against the Kings Subjects that dissented from their way of Worship. Together with a brief Account of the Imprisonment and Tryal of Thomas Maule of Salem, for publishing a Book entitled, Truth held forth and maintained, &c. By Theo. Philathes. ... [n. p. 1697.] 4to, pp. (6), 62. 46934

Probably printed by William Bradford, in New York, *see* p. 61.

MAULE. Truth held forth and maintained According to the Testimony of the Holy Prophets, Christ and his Apostles, recorded in the Holy Scriptures. With Some Account of the Judgments of the Lord lately inflicted upon New England by Witchcraft. To which is added, Something concerning the Fall of Adam, his State in the Fall, and way of Restoration to God again, with many other weighty things necessary for People to weigh and consider. Thomas Maule. [*New York:*] *Printed* [*by William Bradford*] *in the Year* 1695. Sm. 4to, pp. xvi, 260.

The foot of the last page is dated 4th 1st mo. 1694, and signed "Tho. Maule."

MAULEY (J.) Cattaraugus County, N. Y., embracing its Agriculture, Society, Newspapers and Biography of Pioneers. By John Mauley. *Little Valley, N. Y.* 1857. 8vo. 46936

MAULL (D. W.) The Life and Military Services of the late Brigadier General Thomas A. Smyth. By D. W. Maull, M.D. ... *Wilmington, Del.: H. & E. F. James, Printers.* 1870. 8vo, pp. 50. Portrait. B. 46937

MAUMEE, *O.* Minutes of the Maumee Baptist Association, June, 1856. [n. p. n. d.] 8vo. 46938

MAUND (G. C.) Responsibilities of the American Citizen. An Address ... before the Alumni of Pennsylvania College, ... August 10, 1864. By G. C. Maund, A.M., of Baltimore, Md. *Gettysburg: H. C. Neinstedt, Printer.* 1864. 8vo, pp. 23. B.

MAUNDER (S.) The Treasury of History. ... By Samuel Maunder ... . To which is added a History of the United States, by John Inman, Esq. *New York.* 1847. 2 vols., 8vo. 46940

Reproduced as:

MAUNDER. The History of the World: ... . By Samuel Maunder ... . Including a Complete History of the United States to the Present Time ... . Edited by John Inman, Esq. ... *New York: Henry Bill.* 1852. 2 vols., 8vo, pp. x, 19–771, 20 Plates; 741, 20 Plates. B. 46941

MAUNDER. The Treasury of Geography, Physical, Historical, Descriptive, and Political; containing a Succinct Account of Every Country in the World: ... Designed and commenced by the late Samuel Maunder; continued and completed by William Hughes ... . *London: Longman ...* . MDCCCLVI. 12mo, pp. x, (2), 924. Maps and Plates. BA. 46942

The author's "Biographical Treasury" includes many Americans.

MAUN-GWU-DAUS. An Account of the North American Indians, written for Maun-gwu-daus, A Chief of the Ojibway Indians, Who has been traveling in England, France, Belgium, Ireland, and Scotland. ... *Leicester: Printed by T. Cook.* 1848. 8vo, pp. 24. 46943

MAUNY (*Comte* de). Essai sur l'Administration des Colonies. Par M. le Comte de Mauny. *Paris.* 1840. 8vo, pp. 204.

[MAUPERTUIS (Pierre Louis Moreau de).] Dissertation Physique à l'occasion du Negre Blanc. *Leyde.* 1744. 8vo, pp. (6), 132. 46945

We think, after examination, that the work is by Maupertuis, and that Guil. Rey (to whom it has been attributed) is the collaborator spoken of in the "Advertissement." The work is not included in the "Œuvres de Maupertuis," *Lyon, Barbier.* 1754. 4 vols., 8vo.

MAUPERTUIS, *and others.* The Figure of the Earth, Determined from Observations Made by Order of the French King, at the Polar Circle: by ... Maupertuis, Camus, Clairaut, Le Monnier, ... Outhier ... and ... Celsius ... . Translated from the French ... . *London.* 1738. 8vo, pp. 7, (1), 232. 9 Plates and Map. B. 46946

See also his "Œuvres," Nouvelle Édition, *Lyon*, 1756, Vol. III., *and* Pinkerton's "Voyages," Vols. I. and IV.

MAURAN (E. C.) *See* Rhode Island.

MAURAN (J.) An Address ... before the Alumni Association of the College of Physicians ... of ... Columbia College, New-York, ... March 10, 1864. ... By J. Mauran, A.M. ... *Providence: A. Crawford Greene, Printer.* [1864.] 8vo, pp. 24.

Also: Anniversary Address ... before the Alumni Association of ... Columbia College ... March 2d, 1869. ... *Providence: Hammond, Angell & Co., Printers.* 1869. 8vo, pp. 24.—Remarks on the Cholera, embracing Facts ... collected at New-York, ... Second Edition. *Providence: W. Marshall and Co., Printers.* 1832. 8vo, pp. 34. + Third Edition. [*Ibid.*] B.

MAURAULT (J. A.) Histoire des Abenakis, depuis 1605 jusqu'à nos jours. Par L'Abbé J. A. Maurault. ... *Imprimé à l'atelier typographique de La "Gazette de Sorel."* 1866. 8vo, pp. (2), iii, x, (1), 631, (8). BA., C. 46948

MAURE (A.) Les Indiens de la Province de Mato-Grosso [Brésil]. Par M. le docteur Am. Maure ... . [n. p. n. d.] 8vo.

MAUREL (——). Maurel et consorts à MM. les commissaires nationaux civils envoyés á Saint-Domingue, en vertu du décret du 24 mars, sanctionné le 4 avril 1792. *Port-au-Prince: Imprimerie nationale.* [n. d.] 4to, pp. 48, or less. 46950

MAURELLE (F. A.) Journal of a Voyage in 1775. To explore the Coast of America, Northward of California. By the Second Pilot of the Fleet, Don Francisco Antonio Maurelle, in the Kings Schooner, called the Sonora, and commanded by Don Juan Francisco de la Bodega. [*London.* 1780?] 4to, pp. ix, 67. Map. C. 46951

Also included in Barrington's "Miscellanies," 1781, our Vol. I., No. 3628.

Maurer (U.) Betrachtungen über die amerikanische Frage und ihre wahrscheinliche Lösung. ... *Darmstadt: Gustav G. Lange.* 1862. 8vo, pp. 16. 46952

Maurice (F. D.) The Religions of the World and their Relations to Christianity. By the Rev. F. D. Maurice. Third Edition Revised. *Cambridge.* 1852. 12mo. A. 46953

[Maurice (Henry).] The Antithelemite, or an Answer to certain Queries by the D[uke] of B[uckingham] and to the Considerations of an unknown author concerning Toleration. *London: Printed for Sam. Smith.* 1685. 4to, pp. 76. 46954

Contains references to Roger Williams and the persecutions in New England.

Maurice (J.) *vs.* Judd (S.) Is a Whale a Fish? An Accurate Report of the Case of James Maurice against Samuel Judd, tried in ... 1818, wherein the above Problem is discussed theologically, scholastically, and historically. By William Sampson ... . *New-York: C. S. Van Winkle.* 1819. 8vo, pp. 83. BA.

Mauritiados Libri VI in quibus Belgica describitur civilis belli causæ illust. ac fortis herois Mauritii Nassovi, &c. opera et studio Gasparus Ens. *Coloniæ.* 1612. 12mo. 46956

"Book v. relates to the Dutch discoveries in America." Title and note from J. R. Smith's catalogue. Compare with our No. 22656, Vol. VI.

Maurolycus (F.) Cosmographia | Francisci Mavrolyci Mes- | sanensis Sicvli, | In tres dialogos distincta: in qvibus de forma, | situ, numeroq; tam cœlorum q̈ elemento- | rum, alijsq; rebus ad astronomica | rudimenta spectantibus sa- | tis disseritur. | Ad Reverendiss. Cardinalem | Bembvm | *Venetiis* M.D.XXXXIII. [Colophon:] ... *Venetijs apud hæredes Lucæ' antonij Iuntæ Florentini* | *mense Ianuario.* | *anno*. M. D. XLIII. | 4to, 4 leaves, Text, 103 leaves, 1 blank leaf, 4 leaves. J.C.B. 46957

A very rare volume, containing several passages concerning America. Mr. Harrisse's description ("Bib. Amer. Vet., Additions," pp. 144–145,) is incorrect. After the printer's mark is a blank leaf, followed by four others printed in gothic characters, containing astronomical tables, signed at the end: "Franciscus Maurolycus hec scribebat Messane in freto siculo Nonis De[ce]mbris MDXXXXII."

Maurolycus. Cosmogra- | phia Francisci | Mavrolyci Messa- | nensis Sicvli, | In tres dialogos distincta: in quibus de for- | ma, situ, numeroq; tam cœlorum quàm | elementorum, aliisque rebus ad astro- | nomica rudimenta spectantibus satis | disseritur. Ad reuerendiss. Cardinalem Bembum. | *Parisiis,* | *Apud Gulielmum Cauellat, in pingui* | *Gallina ex aduerso Collegij* | *Camerensis.* | 1558. | 12mo, 8 leaves, Text, 168 leaves. J.C.B. 46958

Maury (A. P.) Address of the Honorable Abram P. Maury, on the Life ... of Hugh Lawson White, ... at Franklin, May 9, 1840. ... *Franklin.* 1840. 8vo, pp. 15. B. 46959

Maury (D. H.) Skirmish Drill for Mounted Troops. By Capt. D. H. Maury, C.S.A. *J. W. Randolph, ... Richmond, Va.* 1861. 8vo, pp. 24. 46960

Maury (Mathew Fontaine). The Amazon, and the Atlantic Slopes of South America. ... By M. F. Maury ... . Revised and Corrected. *Washington: Franck Taylor.* 1853. 8vo, pp. 63. Map. BA. 46961

Maury. Captain Maury's Letter on American Affairs. Hon. J. C. Breckinbridge's Address to the People of Kentucky. Ex-Gov. Lowe's Letter to the Virginia Legislature. Address of Geo. N. Sanders to the Democracy of the North West. Gov. Letcher's Message to the Virginia Legislature. Message of Jefferson Davis to the Confederate Congress. [*Baltimore.* 1862.] 8vo, pp. 16. 46962

Maury. Explanations and Sailing Directions to accompany the Wind and Current Charts ... . By Lieut. M. F. Maury, U.S.N. ... *Washington: C. Alexander, Printer.* 1851. 4to, pp. 318. 12 Plates. + Fourth Edition. [*Ibid.*] 1852. 4to, pp. 413. 19 Plates. + Fifth Edition, Enlarged and Improved. [*Ibid.*] 1853. 4to, pp. 492, xxx. 8 Charts, 16 Plates. + Sixth Edition ... . *Philadelphia: E. C. and J. Biddle.* 1854. 4to, pp. 772. 17 Plates. B. + Seventh Edition ... . [*Ibid.*] 1855. 4to, pp. xxvi, 869, (68). 23 Plates. C. + Eighth Edition. *Washington: C. Wendell.* 1858–59. 2 vols., 4to, pp. xxxvi, 383, 39 Plates, 12 Charts; vii, 874, 7 Plates. C. 46963

Maury. Instructions nautiques destinées à accompagner les cartes de vents et de courants. ... Traduites par E. Vaneechout, ... *Paris: Imp. Dépôt des Cartes de la Marine.* 1859. 4to, pp. xxxvi, 496. 23 Plates. 46964

Maury. Maury's Wind and Current Charts. Gales in the Atlantic. *Washington.* 1857. 4to, pp. (4). 24 Maps. H., S.

[Maury.] ... The National Observatory. [n. p. 1849.] 12mo, pp. 12. B. 46966

[Maury.] ... National Observatory. The Isthmus Line to the Pacific. [n. p. 1849.] 8vo, pp. 7. H. 46967

[Maury.] On the establishment of an Universal System of Meteorological Observations, by Sea and Land. *Washington: C. Alexander, Printer.* 1851. 12mo, pp. 30. H. 46968

Maury. The Physical Geography of the Sea. By M. F. Maury ... . *New York: Harper & Brothers.* 1855. 8vo, pp. 274. + Third Edition ... . [*Ibid.*] 1855. 8vo, pp. 287. 12 Plates. + Fifth Edition ... . [*Ibid.*] + An entirely New Edition. [*Ibid.*] 1856. 8vo, pp. 348. 13 Plates. + An entirely New Edition, with Addenda. [*Ibid.*] 1857. 8vo, pp. 360. 13 Plates. B. + [*Ibid.*] 1858. 8vo. + Eighth Edition, Revised and greatly Enlarged. [*Ibid.*] 1861. 8vo, pp. (2), xxxii, 474. 15 Plates. C. + Twelfth Edition. Being the Third Edition of the Author's Reconstruction of the Work. *London.* 1858. Cr. 8vo, pp. xx, 474. Plates. + [*Ibid.*] 1867–9. 46969

Maury. Géographie physique de la Mer. ... Traduit par P. A. Terquem. *Paris: J. Corréard.* 1858. 8vo. 13 Plates. + Seconde Édition, revue et complétée ... . [*Ibid.*] 1861. 8vo, pp. 586. 13 Plates. 46970

Maury. Géographie physique ... traduit par MM. Zurcher et Margollé. *Paris: Hetzel.* 1865. 18mo, pp. x, 282. + Seconde Édition. [*Ibid.*] 1868. 18mo, pp. x, 279. 46971

Also: Extrait de la Géographie physique ... . Par M. E. Tricault ... . *Paris: Imp. Paul Dupont.* 1858. 8vo, pp. 39. 2 Maps.

Maury. Observations sur les navigations des paquebots qui traversent l'Atlantique. Routes à suivre pour éviter les abordages en mer. *Paris: Ledoyen.* 1856. 8vo, pp. 24, or less. 2 Maps. 46972

Reproduced for the "Annales hydrographiques" by A. Le Gras, and separately published as above.

Maury. Physical Survey of Virginia. Geographical Position; its Commercial Advantages and National Importance. Preliminary Report by M. F. Maury, LL.D. ... *Richmond: W. A. R. Nye, ... Printer.* 1868. 8vo, pp. 90, (1). 3 Maps. C. + Second Edition. *New York: D. Van Nostrand.* 1869. 8vo, pp. 100. 3 Maps. BA. 46973

[Maury.] ... Sailing Directions from Sea to Sandy Hook. ... May, 1855. *Philadelphia: E. C. & J. Biddle.* 1855. 4to, pp. 8. Map. H. 46974

Also: Abstract Log; prepared for the use of American Navigators ... . *Washington.* 1848. 4to. — Address ... before the Literary Societies of the University of Virginia,

on the 28th June, 1855, ... *Richmond.* 1855. 8vo, pp. 24. — Astronomical Observations, made during the years 1845–50, at the ... Observatory, Washington ... . *Washington.* 1846–59. 5 vols., 4to. — Conséquences ... . De la mer. ... *Paris: imp. Paul Dupont.* 1857. 8vo, pp. 89. Map. — Instructions générales pour naviguer dans les différents océans. Extrait de ... "Sailing Directions" ... par M. Le Gras ... . *Paris: Ledoyen.* 1857. 8vo, pp. 132. — Letter concerning Lanes for the Steamers crossing the Atlantic. ... *New York.* 1855. 4to, pp. 12. Map and Chart. — Letter on American Affairs, addressed to Rear-Admiral Fitz Roy, of England. ... *Richmond, August,* 1861. 8vo, pp. 10. — Lieut. Maury's Investigations of the Winds and Currents of the Sea. ... *Washington: C. Alexander, Printer.* 1851. 4to, pp. 126. — Notice to Mariners: ... *Washington: C. Alexander, Printer.* 1850. 4to, pp. 19. + Second Edition. [*Ibid.*] 1850. 4to, pp. 51. H. — Paper on the Gulf Stream and Currents of the Sea. Read before the National Institute, at its Annual Meeting, April 2d, 1844. ... *Richmond.* 1844. 8vo, pp. 16. — The Petition ... to the Senate and House of Representatives [concerning certain aspersions upon his reputation by a Board of Naval Officers. With appendix of Correspondence. *Washington.* 1856.] 8vo, pp. 17, 18. — Résumé de la partie physique et descriptive des "Sailing Directions" ... par M. Tricault ... *Paris: Ledoyen.* 1857. 8vo, pp. 208. 5 Plates and Maps. — ... The World We Live In. (Intermediate.) *New York: Richardson & Co.* 1868. 4to, pp. 104.

Maury (L. F. A.) La terre et l'homme ou aperçu historique de géologie, de géographie et d'ethnologie générales. Par L. F. Alfred Maury. *Paris: L. Hachette.* 1857. 12mo, pp. viii, 601.

Maury (S. M.) An Englishwoman in America. By Sarah Mytton Maury. ... An Appendix contains the History of the Emigrant Surgeons' Bill. *London: Thomas Richardson and Son.* 1848. 8vo, pp. (4), cxviii, 251; (2), 204, (2), 16. BA. + *London: John Murray.* 1856. Post 8vo, pp. 576. 46976

Maury. The Statesmen of America in 1846. By Sarah Mytton Maury. ... *London: Longman ...* . 1847. 12mo, pp. (2), vi, (2), 548. C. + *Philadelphia: Carey.* 1847. 12mo, pp. 261.

Dr. Allibone quotes "Progress of the Catholic Church in America," 1847, 8vo, which I have not seen.

Maussion Candé (*M.* de). Notice sur le Golfe de Honduras et la République du Centre-Amérique, par M. de Maussion Candé. *Paris.* 1860. 8vo, pp. 28. 46978

Maverick (A.) Henry J. Raymond and the New York Press, for Thirty Years. Progress of American Journalism from 1840 to 1870. With ... Appendix. By Augustus Maverick. *Hartford (Conn.): A. S. Hale and Company.* 1870. 8vo, pp. 501. Portrait and Plates. B., C. 46979

[Mavor (William).] A General Collection of Voyages and Travels, from the Discovery of America to the Commencement of the Nineteenth Century. *London.* 1810. 28 vols., 12mo. S.

[Mavor.] A General Collection of Voyages and Travels, ... from the Discovery of America, ... to the Travels of Lord Valentia. *London: Sherwood, Neely, and Jones.* 1813. 28 vols., 12mo. B. 46981

Mavor. Historical Account of the most Celebrated Voyages, Travels, and Discoveries, from the Time of Columbus to the Present Period. ... By William Mavor, LL.D. *London: E. Newbery.* 1796–7. 20 vols., 12mo. C. + [*Ibid.*] 1797–1800. 25 vols., 12mo. + *Philadelphia.* 1802–3. 20 vols., 12mo.

See "M. Rev.," XXVI. 348.

Mavor. The History of the Discovery and Settlement to the Present Time of North and South America, and of the West Indies. By William Mavor ... . *London.* 1806. 12mo, pp. xii, 459. Map. 46983

Mavor. Mavor's Travels in North America, and the Duc de la Rochefaucault Travels through the United States, the Country of the Iroquois, and Upper Canada. *London.* 1807. 18mo. 46984

Mavor. Universal History, Ancient and Modern; from the Earliest Records of Time, to the General Peace of 1801 ... . By William Mavor, LL.D. ... *London.* 1802–4. 25 vols., 12mo. + *New York: Samuel S. Bradford.* 1803–5. 25 vols., 12mo.

Mavor (W. F.) Elegy to the Memory of Captain James King. By the Rev. William Fordyce Mavor. *London: J. Nichol.* 1785. 4to. 46986

See "M. Rev.," LXXIII. 233.

Mavrile de S. Michel. Voyage des isles Camercanes, en l'Amériqve. Qvi font partie des Indes Occidentales. Et vne relation diversifiee de plusieurs Pensées pieuses, et d'agreables Remarques tant de toute l'Amerique que des autres Païs. Avec l'établissement des RR. PP. Carmes Reformez de la Province de Touraine et dites Isles: Et un discours de leur Ordre. Composé par F. Mavrile de S. Michel Religieux Carme de la mesme Prouince: Partie pendant son voyage: Partie depuis son retour. *Av Mans, chez Hierôme Olivier, Imprimeur et libraire demeurant près l'Eglise S. Jvlian.* 1652. 8vo, pp. (34), 378, Table geographiqve, 379–434. 46987

A very rare and little-known work. "Brunet indique une édition de 1653, imprimée à Paris, petit in-4°: La 'Biblioth. des Voyages' en annonce une de Paris, 1654, in-8°, sous un titre défectueux; ainsi qu'une traduction anglaise imprimée à Londres, en 1740." Title and note from Leclerc, No. 951.

Maw (H. L.) Journal of a Passage from the Pacific to the Atlantic, crossing the Andes in the Northern Provinces of Peru, and descending the River Marañon, or Amazon. By Henry Lister Maw, Lieut. R.N. *London: John Murray.* MDCCCXXXIX. 8vo, pp. xv, 486. Map. A., BA., P. 46988

Rich in facts relating to the condition, history, and character of the Indians of Peru and Brazil, particularly of the unexplored districts, in the valley of the Marañon.

Maw. Narrativa da passagem do Pacifico ao Atlantio a travez dos Andes, nas provincias do norte do Peru, e descendo pelo rio Amazonas até ao Pará. Por Henrique Lister Maw. Traducido inglez por Antonio Julião da Costa. *Liverpool.* 1831. 8vo. Map. 46989

Also: Letter in Answer to a Criticism of the Edinburgh Review. ... [n. p.] 1830. 8vo.

Mawe (J.) Descriptive Catalogue of Minerals. By John Mawe. *London.* 1816. 8vo. N. 46990

Mawe. Travels in the Interior of Brazil, particularly in the Gold and Diamond Districts of that Country, ... Including a Voyage to the Rio de la Plata, and Historical Sketch of the Revolution of Buenos Ayres. ... By John Mawe ... . *London: Longman ...* . 1812. 4to, pp. vii, 366, (2). Map and 9 Plates. + *Philadelphia: M. Carey.* 1816. 8vo, pp. 373, (3). 5 Plates.

Mawe. Travels in the Interior of Brazil; with Notices of its Climate, Agriculture, Commerce, Population, Mines, Manners, and Customs, and a Particular Account of the Gold and Diamond Districts, including a Voyage to the Rio de la Plata. By John Mawe ... . *London: Longman ...* . 1821. 8vo, pp. x, (1), 493, (1). 6 Plates. + [*Ibid.*] 1822. + [*Ibid.*] 1823. + A New Edition. *London.* 1825. 8vo. C. 46992

The work of Mr. Mawe contains the first authentic information which the jealousy of the Portuguese Government ever allowed a foreigner to acquire respecting the mineral treasures of the Brazils. *See* "M. Rev.," LXXII. 337, "London Rev.," VII. 343, *and* "British Critic," June, 1813.

Mawe. Voyages dans l'intérieur du Brésil, particulièrement dans les districts de l'Or et du diamant, faits avec l'autorisation du Prince Régent en 1809 et 1810, contenant aussi un voyage au Rio-de-la-Plata, et un essai historique sur la révolution de Buenos Ayres por Jean Mawe. Traduits de l'Anglais, por J. B. Eyriés. *Paris: Gide Fils.* 1816. 2 vols., 8vo, pp. xlii, 358; 381, (2). Map and 4 Plates. 46993

Mawe. Viaggio nell' interno del Brasile, e particolarmente nei distretti dell' oro e dei diamanti, fatto nel 1809–10. Coll' aggiunta di un appendice. Tradotto dall' Inglese dall'ab. Lorenzo Nesi. *Milano: Sonzogno e Comp.* 1817. 2 vols., 16mo, pp. xix, 335, (2); (2), 292. 10 Plates. C. 46994

Included in "Raccolta de' Viaggi," v. 39–40.

Mawe. Reisen in das Innere von Brasilien, vorzüglich nach den Gold- und Diamant-Districten. Nebst einer Reise nach dem La Plata Fluss, und einer Auseinandersetzung der Revolution in Buenos Ayres. Nach dem Englischen, mit Anmerkungen begleitet, deutsch herausgegeben von E. A. W. von Zimmermann. *Bamberg und Leipzig.* 1816–17. 8vo. 46995

Mawe. Reizen in de Binnendeelen van Braziliё, vooral in deszelfs goud- en diamantrijke Streeken ... Reis naar Rio de la Plata en ... Omwenteling van Buenos-Ayres. Uit het Engelsch. *Haarlem.* 1817–18. 2 vols., 8vo. Map and Plates. 46996

[Mawson] (Matthias). A Sermon ... before the ... Society for the Propagation of the Gospel in Foreign Parts; ... February 18, 1742–43. By Matthias Lord Bishop of Chichester. *London: Somerset Draper.* 1743. 4to, pp. 72. J.C.B. + [*Ibid.*] 1743. 8vo, pp. 48. BA., W. 46997

Maxan. ***. Military Reflections, on Four Modes of Defence, for the United States ... . By Maxan. *** ... Translated by Eliza Anderson. *Baltimore: Printed by Joseph Robinson.* 1807. 8vo, pp. 42. BA. 46998

Maxcy (J.) American Eloquence, consisting of Orations, Addresses and Sermons, being the Literary Remains of the Rev. J. Maxcy; with A Memoir of his Life by R. Elton, D.D. *New York.* 1845. 8vo, pp. 452. 46999

The appendix contains addresses, etc., by A. Messer.

Maxcy. The Last Enemy Destroyed. A Funeral Sermon, ... in the Baptist Meeting-House in Providence, July 31, A. D. 1791, Occasioned by the Death of The Rev. James Manning, D.D. President of Rhode-Island College. By Jonathan Maxcy, A.M. *Providence: Printed by John Carter.* [1791.] 8vo, pp. 43. + Second Edition. *Providence: Bennett Wheeler.* MDCCXCVI. 8vo, pp. 30. 47000

Maxcy. The Literary Remains of the Rev. Jonathan Maxcy, D.D. ... With a Memoir of his Life, By Romeo Elton, D.D. ... *New York: A. V. Blake.* 1844. 8vo, pp. 452. H. 47001

Maxcy. An Oration delivered in ... Providence, July 4. A. D. 1795 ... . By Jonathan Maxcy, A.M. ... *Providence: Printed by Carter & Wilkinson.* 1795. 8vo, pp. 20. 47002

Maxcy. A Poem on the Prospects of America. ... By Jonathan Maxcy, A.B. *Printed at Providence by Bennett Wheeler.* [1787.] 8vo, pp. 40. 47003

Maxcy. Proposals for printing by subscription a Poem, on the "Prospects of America," with the Valedictory Addresses subjoined. Spoken at the public Commencement, in Providence, September 5, 1787. By the author, Jonathan Maxcy. ... To which is added, Notes and Observations, with an appendix by another hand, containing a short topographical and historical account of the State of Rhode Island, but more particularly of the Town of Providence—of the College, its Regulations and the Studies pursued there ... . [n. p. n. d.] 8vo. 47004

"So rare that no complete copy has ever come to our knowledge. It is not certain that the entire work was ever printed."—J. R. Bartlett.

Maxcy. A Sermon delivered in the Chapel of Rhode-Island College, to the Senior Class, Commencement, September 3, 1800. By Jonathan Maxcy ... . *Providence: Bennett Wheeler.* 1801. 8vo, pp. 15. 47005

The last page contains a catalogue of the Baccalaureate of Rhode Island College, 1800. Also: An Address to the Graduates at the Commencement of Rhode-Island College, September 3, 1794. ... *Providence: Bennett Wheeler.* 1794. 8vo, pp. 8. — An Address, ... to the Graduates of Rhode-Island College, at the ... Commencement, ... September 5, A. D. 1798. ... *Providence: Printed by Carter and Wilkinson.* [1798.] 8vo, pp. 12. — An Address ... to the Candidates for the Baccalaureate in Rhode-Island College, at the ... Commencement, September 2. 1801. ... *Wrentham (Mass.): Printed by Nathaniel Heaton, Jun.* 1801. 8vo, pp. 20. — An Address ... to the Graduates of Rhode-Island College, at the Public Commencement, September 1, 1802. ... *Wrentham (Mass.): Printed by Nathaniel Heaton, Jun.* 1802. 8vo, pp. 14. — Anniversary Sermon, December 1, 1816. ... *Columbia, S. C.* [1816.] 8vo. — Collegiate Addresses ... with a Biographical Introduction, by R. Elton, D.D. *London.* 18—. 18mo. — A Discourse, ... South-Carolina College, July 4th, A. D. 1819. ... Second Edition. *Columbia, S. C.* 1819. 8vo. — Funeral Sermon, ... December 17, 1817, ... before ... the Legislature of ... South Carolina. ... *Columbia, S. C.* 1818. 8vo, pp. 50. — Funeral Sermon, occasioned by the Death of Mr. John Sampson Bobo, of the South Carolina College. ... *Columbia, S. C.* 1819. 8vo, pp. 16. — Oration delivered before the Providence Association of Mechanics and Manufacturers, April 13, 1795. ... *Providence: Bennett Wheeler.* 1795. 8vo, pp. 17. — An Oration, ... in Providence, on the Fourth of July, 1799. ... *Providence: Printed by John Carter, Jun.* 1799. 4to, pp. 16. — A Sermon, ... September 14, 1796, at the Dedication of the Meeting-House, belonging to the Catholic Baptist Society in Cumberland. ... *Providence: Printed by Carter & Wilkinson.* M.DCC.XCVI. 8vo, pp. 22. — A Sermon, ... in Boston, at the Annual Convention of the Warren Association, ... September 12, A. D. 1797. ... *Boston: Printed by Manning & Loring.* 1797. 8vo, pp. 22. — A Sermon, ... Providence, ... October 14, A. D. 1798. Occasioned by the Death of Welcome Arnold, Esq; One of the Trustees of

Rhode-Island College ... . *Providence: Printed by Carter and Wilkinson.* 1798. 8vo, pp. 15. — ... A Sermon, ... in Providence, ... December 14, 1800. Occasioned by the Decease of Mrs. Mary Gano ... . *Providence: Printed by J. Carter.* [1800.] 8vo, pp. 19. — A Sermon preached in the Baptist Meeting House in Providence, before the Female Charitable Society, September 21, 1802. ... *Providence: Bennett Wheeler.* 1802. 12mo, pp. 13.

MAXCY (M.) An Oration, ... in Schenectady, ... on the 4th of July, 1803. By Milton Maxcy, A.B. *Albany: D. & S. Whiting.* 1803. 8vo, pp. 23. B., S. 47006

[MAXCY (Virgil).] Democratic National Convention. [n. p. n. d.] 8vo, pp. 12. H. 47007

MAXCY. A Discourse before the Phi Beta Kappa Society of Brown University. Delivered September Fourth, 1833. By Virgil Maxcy. *Boston: Lilly, Wait, Colman, and Holden.* 1833. 8vo, pp. 31. B. 47008

[MAXCY.] The Maryland Resolutions, and the Objections to them Considered. By a Citizen of Maryland. *Baltimore: E. J. Coale & Co.* 1822. 8vo, pp. 39. BA. 47009

[MAXCY.] Report with sundry Resolutions relative to Appropriations of Public Land for the Purposes of Education, To the Senate of Maryland, January 30, 1821. ... [*Annapolis:*] *Green—Print.* 1821. 8vo, pp. 23. H. 47010

Also: Address to the Agricultural Society of Maryland. ... at Annapolis, ... 15th December, 1819. ... *Printed by J. Green, Annapolis.* 1820. 8vo, pp. 19. *See also* Maryland, No. 45192.

MAXIMILIAN (Alexander Philipp). Abbildungen zur Naturgeschichte Brasiliens, von Maximilian, Prinz zu Wied. ... *Weimar.* 1822–30. Folio. 90 Plates. 47011

MAXIMILIAN. Beiträge zur Naturgeschichte von Brasilien, von Maximilian, Prinzen zu Wied. ... *Weimar.* 1825–33. 4 vols., 8vo, pp. xxii, 612; (4), 620; (2), xii, 1277, (3); (2), viii, 964. 11 Plates. B., C., H. 47012

MAXIMILIAN. Brasilien. Nachträge, Berichtigungen und Zusätze zu der Beschreibung meiner Reise im östlichen Brasilien, von Maximilian ... . *Frankfurt am Main: H. L. Brönner.* 1850. 8vo, pp. (4), 144. C. 47013

MAXIMILIAN. Reise in das Innere Nord-America in den Jahren 1832 bis 1834, von Maximilian, Prinz zu Wied. Mit 48 Kupfern, 33 Vignetten, vielen Holzschnitten und einer Charte. *Coblentz,* 1839, *bei J. Hölscher.* 2 vols., 4to, pp. xvi, 653, (1);

[Vol. II. 1841,] pp. xxii, (2), 687, (1). 33 small and 48 large Plates. Key-plate, Plan, Table and Map. C. 47014

Of this beautiful work there are copies on large paper. The plates of scenery, costume, portraits, etc., are after drawings by Ch. Bodmer. Pages 455–645 relate to North American Indian languages. *See* No. 47017, *infra.*

MAXIMILIAN. Voyage dans l'intérieur de l'Amérique du Nord, exécuté pendant les années 1832, 1833 et 1834, par le prince Maximilien de Wied-Neuwied. Ouvrage accompagnée d'un Atlas de 80 planches (format demi-colombier) dessinées sur les lieux par M. Charles Bodmer. *Paris: Arthus Bertrand.* 1840–43. 3 vols., 8vo. C. 47015

There are copies with the plates tinted. The errors of the translator were sufficiently numerous to warrant the following:

MAXIMILIAN. Liste des Fautes d'Impression et de Traduction de l'Édition française de la Description du Voyage ... par le prince Maximilien ... . [n. p. n. d.] 8vo, pp. 43. S. 47016

MAXIMILIAN. Travels in the Interior of North America. By Maximilian, Prince of Wied. With Numerous Engravings on Wood, and a large Map. Translated from the German, by H. Evans Lloyd. To accompany the Original Series of Eighty-One Elaborately Coloured Plates, Size, Imperial Folio. *London: Ackermann and Co.* MDCCCXLIII. 4to, pp. x, (2), 520. 81 Plates in folio, and Map. BA. 47017

Caveat emptor is good advice always, especially so in purchasing this work. The *original* edition of the atlas of plates is one of the most interesting publications ever issued from the press; the details of the costume of the various tribes of Indians, their warlike and musical instruments, smoking apparatus, etc., are given with the utmost minuteness; the bison, dog, scalp, and other dances, with their huntings, are represented in the most spirited manner, and the extraordinary natural features of the country are delineated with the greatest truth, by an artist who accompanied the prince in his travels, and they are exactly reproduced in the brilliantly colored plates of the work, conveying the most vivid and faithful impression of the scenery of the West, between the Mississippi and the Rocky Mountains. The demand for the work overran the supply, and Edward Lumley, a London bookseller, reproduced the plates, without altering the title-page; but the buyer who mistakes this last and inferior issue for the original edition, must not congratulate himself on his own intelligence. It is a matter of regret that the translator omitted the extensive vocabularies contained in the German edition.

MAXIMILIAN. Reise nach Brasilien in den Jahren 1815 bis 1817, von Maximilian, Prinz zu Wied-Neuwied. *Frankfurt am M.: H. L. Brönner.* 1820–21. 2 vols., 4to, pp. xxxvi, 385; xviii, 346. 19 Vignettes. Atlas of 22 Plates and 3 Maps. B., C.

The atlas is in folio. There are copies on large vellum paper, with the nineteen vignettes printed on separate leaves; in the ordinary copies they are printed in the text. Vol. II., pp. 302–32, contains an essay on the Brazilian languages, with vocabularies.

MAXIMILIAN. Reise nach Brasilien [as before]. *Frankfurt am M.* 1820–21. 2 vols., 8vo, pp. iv, (2), 376, (4); vi, 345, (1). 2 Maps. 47019

This edition lacks the illustrations of the quarto edition, the text is the same.

MAXIMILIAN. Reize naar Braziliē, in de jaren 1815 tot 1817, door Maximiliaan, Prinz van Wied-Neuwied. Uit het Hogduitsch. ... *Groningen: W. Van Boekeren.* MDCCCXXII–XXIII. 2 vols., 8vo, pp. (2), xvi, 448; (2), 416. Plate, Map and Portrait.

MAXIMILIAN. Travels in Brazil, in the Years 1815, 1816, 1817. By Prince Maximilian, of Wied-Neuwied. ... *London: Henry Colburn & Co.* 1820. 4to, pp. x, 335. Map, 6 Plates. A.

See "M. Rev.," XCIV. I.

MAXIMILIAN. Travels in Brazil, in 1815, 1816, and 1817. By Prince Maximilian, Neuwied. Translated from the German, ... *London: Sir Richard Phillips, and Co.* 1820. 8vo, pp. iv, 112. 9 Plates. 47022

MAXIMILIAN. Voyage au Brésil, dans les années 1815, 1816 et 1817, Par S. A. S. Maximilien, Prince de Wied-Neuwied; traduit de l'Allemand Par J. B. B. Eyriès. ... *Paris: Arthus Bertrand.* 1821–22. 3 vols., 8vo, pp. xvi, (2), 399; (4), iii, 400; (4), iii, 384. Atlas of 41 Plates and 3 Maps in folio. B., C., H.

MAXIMILIAN. Brésil. Quelques corrections indispensables à la Traduction française de la description d'un Voyage au Brésil par le prince Maximilien de Wied. *Francfort sur le Mein: H. L. Brönner.* 1853. 8vo, pp. 109. C. 47024

MAXIMILIAN. Recueil de planches coloriées d'animaux du Brésil. ... *Weimar.* 1822–31. Folio. A. 47025

Ninety-six beautiful colored plates, with descriptions in French in German. A work of great scientific value.

MAXIMILIAN. Verzeichniss der auf seiner Reise in Nord-Amerika beobachteten Säugethiere. ... *Berlin.* 1822. 8vo, pp. 240. 4 Plates. B., C. 47026

Also: Verzeichniss der Reptilien welche auf einer Reise im nördlichen Amerika beobachtet wurden. ... *Dresden.* 1865. 4to. 7 Plates. S. — Ueber die Selbstständigkeit der Species der Ursus ferox. ... *Dresden.* 1857. 4to. 3 Plates.

MAXIMILIAN (Ferdinand Joseph). Aus meinem Leben. Reiseskizzen, Aphorismen, Gedichte. ... Zweite Auflage. *Leipzig: Verlag von Duncker und Humblot.* 1867. 7 vols., 12mo.

Vol. VI. relates to Bahia. The following is a translation:

MAXIMILIAN. Recollections of My Life. By Maximilian I. Emperor of Mexico. *London: Richard Bentley.* 1868. 3 vols., post 8vo, pp. (4), 291; (4), 354; (4), 408. BA., C. 47028

MAXIMILIAN. Maximilian and the Mexican Empire. By an American. *New York.* 1866. 8vo. 47029

MAXIMILIAN. Maximilien, Empereur du Mexique. Sa vie, sa mort, son procès: détails intimes et inédits. *Paris: Lebigre-Duquesne.* [1867.] 18mo, pp. (2), 157. Portrait. C. 47030

MAXIMILIAN. Maximilien et la Monarchie au Mexique. ... *Paris: Amyot.* 1867. 8vo, pp. 91. 47031

The following works relate to Maximilian:

Advenimiento de SS. MM. I. I. Maximiliano y Carlota al Trono de México. Documentos relativos y Narracion del Viaje de Nuestros Soberanos de Miramar á Veracruz y del Recibimiento que se les hizo en este ultimo puerto y en las Ciudades de Cordoba, Orizara, Puebla, y Mexico. Edicion de "la Sociedad." *Mexico.* 1864. Rl. 8vo, pp. 368. 7 Plates. 47032

Alocuciones Cartas oficiales é instrucciones del Emperador Maximiliano durante los años de 1864, 1865, y 1866. *México: Imprenta Imperial.* 1867. 8vo. 47033

Carta pastoral que los Ilmos Sres. Arzobispos de Mejico y Michoacan, y Obispos de Puebla, Queretaro, etc., dirigen a sus diocesanos con motivo de la entrada de sus Majestades Maximiliano I y la emperatriz Carlota a la capital. *Merida.* 1864. 8vo, pp. 8. 47034

Causa de Fernanda Maximiliano de Hapsburgo y sus Generales Miguel Miramon y Tomas Mejia. *Mexico.* 186–. 8vo. Maps and Portraits. 47035

Memorandum sobre el proceso del Archiduque Fernando Maximiliano de Austria—Defensa del Archiduque de Austria por los C. C. Lics, J. M. Vazquez y E. M. Ortega, en el proceso que se le formo en la ciudad de Queretaro. *Mexico.* 1867. Folio, pp. 696. 47036

Also: Anuario de las Ordenes Imperiales, 1865. *Mexico.* 1865. Folio. — Breve Noticia del recibimiento y permanencia de S. M. el Emperador y la Emperatriz de Mexico en la Ciudad de Puebla. *Puebla.* 1864. 4to, pp. 36. 7 Plates. — Ceremonial para la Fiesta Nacional del 16 de Sept. de 1866. *Mexico.* 1866. 8vo. — Discursos pronunciados en las festividades celebradas en la ciudad del Carmen por el feliz arribo al puerto de Veracruz y advenimiento al trono de Mejico de SS. MM. Maximiliano I. y su

augusta esposa. *Carmen.* 1864. 4to, pp. 13. — Documentos relativos á la mision politica encomendada á la Asamblea general de Notables, que dio por resultado la adopcion del sistema monarquico en Mexico, y la eleccion para Emperador del Archiduque Fernando Maximiliano de Austria. *Mexico.* 1864. 4to, pp. 74. — Documents offic. rec. dans la secrét. privée de Maximilien. Histoire de l'intervention française au Mexique. *Paris.* 1868. 2 vols., 8vo. — Inscripciones, poesias y otras piezas literarias, colocadas en el instituto literario de Toluca al 28 de Octubre de 1864 en que se digno visitarlo S. M. J. Maximiliano I. *Toluca.* 1864. 12mo, 7 leaves. — Memoria presentada á S. M. el Emperador por el Ministro de formento Luis Robles Pezuela de los Trabajos ejecutados en sú Ramo el año de 1865. *Mexico.* 1866. Folio. — Reflexiones sobre la Carta escrita por F. de Arrangoiz y Berzabal á S. M. el Emperador de Mejico. *Madrid.* 1866. 8vo. — Reglamento para los Servicios de Honor y Ceremonial de la Corte. *Mexico: Imprenta de J. M. Lara.* 1866. Folio. — Reglamentos de los Cabinets Civil y Militar del Emperador. *Puebla.* 1865. 8vo. — Viaje de Emperador Maximiliano y de la Emperadriz Carlota, desde su Palacio de Miramar cerca de Trieste, hasta la capital del Imperio Mexicana, con una relacion de los festejos publicos con que fueron obsequiados en Vera Cruz, Cordoba, Orizaba, Puebla, Mexico, y en las demas poblaciones del Transito. *Orizaba.* 1864. Sm. 4to, pp. 412. 6 Portraits, 2 Views.

Catalogue de la ... Bibliothèque de D. Jose Maria Andrade, 1869. *Leipzig.* 1869. 8vo, pp. ix, (1), 368. 47037

Forms the so-called Maximilian Library; it is rich in books relating to Mexico, etc.

MAXIMILIAN OF TRANSYLVANIA. De Molvccis in-|sulis, intemq; alijs pluribus mirãdis, quæ | nouissima Castellanorum nauigatio Se-|reniss. Imperatoris Caroli . V . auspicis|suscepta, nuper inuenit: Maximiliani | Transyluani ad Reuerendiss. Cardina-|lem Saltzburgensem epistola lectu per-|quam iucunda. | [Colophon:] *Datum Vallisoleti die* XXIIII *Octobris* M.D.XXII. *Coloniæ in ædibus Eucharij Ceruicorni. Anno uir-|ginei partus* . M . D .-XXIII . *mense* | *Ianuario.* Sm. 8vo. 16 leaves. J.C.B. 47038

This is the original edition of the celebrated voyage of Ferdinand Magellan, a Portuguese navigator, who, being dissatisfied because the King refused to add half-a-crown a month to his pay, entered into the service of the Emperor Charles V. The author was a relation of Christopher Haro, the friend and companion of Magellan, in this voyage "Frater mei Soceri." He sailed from Seville with five ships, August, 1519; discovered and passed the straits to which he gave his name; went by the South Sea to the Islands; and was murdered, for his severity, by his own men, 1520, in the island of Duran, after having conquered that of Cebu. The voyage ended September 6, 1522. Of this original edition I have only been able to trace the existence of two other copies, one of which was purchased in the Lucca sale for £16 16s. For an interesting notice of this rare work, *see* [Harrisse] "Bib. Am. Vet.," No. 122.

MAXIMILIAN. Maximiliani Transyluani Cæsaris | a secretis Epistola, de admirabili | & nouissima Hispanorũ in Orien|tem nauigatione, qua uariæ, & nul|li prius accessæ Regiones inuẽtæ | sunt, cum ipsis etiã Moluccis insu|lis beatissimis, optimo Aromatũ |genere refertis. Inauditi quoq. in|colaȓ mores exponuntur, ac mul|ta quæ Herodotus, Plinius, Soli|nus atque alii tradiderunt, fabulo|sa esse arguunȶ. Contra nonnulla|ibidẽ|uera, uix tamen

credibilia ex|plicanȶ. quibuscum historiis Insu|laribus ambitus describiȶ alterius|Hemisphaerii, qua ad nos tandem|hispani redierunt incolumes. | *Roma* [Colophon:] *Romae* | *in aedibvs . F .* | *Minitii Calvi* | *Anno* . M.D.XXIII | *Mense Novembri.* | Sm. 4to, 19 leaves. J.C.B. 47039

In this edition, the date, "Vallisoleti die XXIIII Octobris M.D.XXII," is omitted.

MAXIMILIAN. Maximiliani Transyluani Cæsaris | a secretis Epistola, de admirabili | & nouissima Hispanorũ in Orien|tem nauigatione, qua uariæ, & nul|li prius accessæ Regiones inuẽtæ | sunt, cum ipsis etiã Moluccis insu|lis beatissimis, optimo Aromatũ |genere refertis. Inauditi quoq. in|colaȓ mores exponuntur, ac mul|ta quæ Herodotus, Plinius, Soli|nus atque alii tradiderunt, fabulo|sa esse arguunȶ. Contra nonnulla|ibidẽ|uera, uix tamen credibilia ex|plicanȶ. quibuscum historiis Insu|laribus ambiusdescribiȶ alterius|Hemisphaerii, qua ad nos tandem|hispani redtie runt incolumes.|*Roma* [Colophon:] *Romae in ædibvs*|*F. Minitii Calvi*|*Anno* M.DXXIIII.|*Mense*|*Feb.*| Sm. 4to, 18 leaves. 47040

A literal copy of the preceding, as far as signature B ii, which, in this copy, ends with "inuenerint," instead of "qua." The signature D ii is correctly given.

MAXIMILIAN. Il Viaggio fatto dagli Spagnuoli atorno al mondo. *Venise.* 1534. 4to. 47041

Title from [Harrisse] "Bib. Am. Vet.," No. 192. The following is probably the correct title:

MAXIMILIAN. Il Viaggio|fatto da gli Spa|gnivoli a|torno a'l| Mondo.|Con Gratia per Anni. XIIII.| [*Venetia?*] MDXXXVI. 4to, 52 leaves. J.C.B. 47042

This first Italian edition contains two accounts of the Spanish expedition round the world, 1519 to 1522, under Magellan; the first by Maximilian, the other, a diary, by Pigafetta. The recto of the last leaf contains a short vocabulary of the language of Brazil. *See* [Harrisse] "Bib. Am. Vet.," No. 215, *and* Brunet's "Manuel," v. 1167.

Maxims for the Promotion of the Wealth of Nations: being a Manual of Political Economy ... . [By Mathew Carey.] *Philadelphia: Clark & Raser, Printers.* 1830. 12mo, pp. 32. BA.

MAXSON (D. E.) Speech of Hon. D. E. Maxson ... on the Personal Liberty Bill, ... March 14, 1860. *Albany: Weed, Parsons & Company, Printers.* 1860. 8vo, pp. 11. H. 47044

MAXSON (E. R.) Hospitals, British, French, and American. [With] a Glance at the British Islands, France, and America. Ethnological, Climatic, and General. By Edwin R. Maxson. *Philadelphia: The Author.* 1868. 18mo, pp. 122. C. 47045

MAXSON (W. B.) A Discourse delivered at the Constitution of the Seventh-Day Baptist Church, in Plainfield, N. J., February 9th, 1838, By William B. Maxson ... . *New York: J. P. Callender.* 1838. 8vo. 47046

MAXWELL (A. M.) A Run through the United States, during the Autumn of 1840. By Lieut.-Col. A. M. Maxwell ... . *London: Henry Colburn.* 1841. 2 vols., post 8vo, pp. xx, (1), 310; xii, 261. 2 Portraits. C., S. 47047

Also: My Adventures in Italy, ... the West Indies, North America ... . *London.* 1845. 2 vols., post 8vo. Portraits.

MAXWELL (H.) The Christian Patriot. Some Recollections of the late Col. Hugh Maxwell; Collected by a Daughter. *New York.* 1833. 16mo. S. 47048

MAXWELL (H.) An Oration, ... February 22d, 1811, before the Washington Benevolent Society, of ... New-York. By Hugh Maxwell, Esq. ... *New-York: J. Hardcastle.* 1811. 8vo, pp. 16. BA. 47049

See Verplank (G. C.), *and* Barker (J.), Vol. I., No. 3392, *note.*

MAXWELL (J.) The American Patriot and Hero. Or, a brief Memoir of ... His Excellency General Washington; ... By John Maxwell ... . [n. p.:] *Printed for the Author.* 1785 [*i. e.* 1795]. 12mo, pp. 94 [*i. e.* 64], Errata, 1. 47050

One of the earliest biographies of Washington.

MAXWELL (J.) Remarks on the Present State of Jamaica: with a Proposal of Measures for the Resuscitation of our West Indian Colonies. By James Maxwell, M.D. *London.* 1848. 8vo, pp. 52. 47051

MAXWELL (M.) Ernest Grey; or, the Sins of Society. A Story of New York Life. By Maria Maxwell. ... *New York: T. W. Strong.* 1855. 12mo, pp. 335. 47052

MAXWELL (S.) Case and Complaint of Samuel Maxwell, Pastor of a Church in Rehoboth [Mass.] *Newport, R. I.* 1750. 16mo. N., W. 47053

Also: An Almanac for the Year 1731. ... *Newport, R. I.* 1731. 12mo.

MAXWELL (S. D.) Cincinnati Suburbs in 1870. Sketches, Historical and Descriptive. By Sidney D. Maxwell. *Cincinnati.* 1870. 4to. 47054

MAXWELL. History of the Exposition of Textile Fabrics, held in Cincinnati, August, ... 1869. By Sidney D. Maxwell. ... *Cincinnati: Gazette Co. Print.* [n. d.] 8vo, pp. 97, (3). BA.

MAXWELL (S. H.) Voices of the Spirit, the Inner and Outer Life of Miranda Elliot. By S. H. Maxwell. *Philadelphia.* [n. d.] 12mo. 47056

MAXWELL (W.) A Memoir of the Rev. John H. Rice, D.D. ... By William Maxwell. *Philadelphia: J. Whetham.* 1835. 12mo, pp. vii, 412. Portrait. 47057

MAXWELL. Poems by William Maxwell, Esq. *Philadelphia: M. Thomas.* 1816. 18mo, pp. 168. 47058

Also: An Oration Commemorative of the Rev. John Holt Rice, D.D. ... *Richmond: R. J. Smith.* 1832. 8vo, pp. 33. *See also* Letters, Vol. X., No. 40595, *and* Virginia.

MAXWELL, WRIGHT & CO. Commercial Formalities of Rio de Janeiro. By Maxwell, Wright & Co. *Baltimore.* 1830. 8vo, pp. 79. 47059

MAY (*Capt.*) Le Capitaine May et Le Général de la Vega sur le Bords du Rio Grande, Opera Comique ... . Représenté à la Nouvelle-Orléans ... le 27 Mai 1847. *Nouvelle-Orléans: J. L. Sollée.* 1847. 8vo, pp. 16. 47060

In French and English.

MAY (C.) The American Female Poets: with Biographical and Critical Notices. By Caroline May. *Philadelphia: Lindsay & Blakiston.* [1848?] 8vo, pp. 559. 11 Plates and Vignette.

Contains biographies of, and selections from, no less than eighty female poets. Reprinted in 1856, 1859, 1865, etc.

[MAY (Charles).] Remarks on Bishop Hopkins' Letter on the Bible View of Slavery. [n. p. n. d.] 8vo, pp. 20. 47062

MAY (C. S.) Sustain the Government. Speech of Hon. Charles S. May, ... February 9, 1863. *Lansing: John A. Kerr & Co.* 1863. 8vo, pp. 22. 47063

Also: Union, Victory and Freedom: Speech ... Lansing, ... January 25, 1864. *Lansing: John A. Kerr & Co., Printers.* 1864. 8vo, pp. 22.

MAY (E.) ... Sermon at the Opening of the New Meeting House at Haddam, Ct., Oct. 24, 1771. By Eleazer May. *Hartford.* 1772. 8vo, pp. 35. W. 47064

MAY (G. R.) Trial of George Ryan May, for Highway Robbery ... . *Keene, N. H.* 1811. 8vo, pp. 24. 47065

MAY (G. T.) A Suggestion towards a Navy. By Geo. T. May. *New York: Beadle and Company.* 1862. 8vo, pp. 16.

MAY (H.) ... Speeches of the Hon. Henry May ... . *Baltimore: Printed by Kelly, Hedian* ... . 1863. 8vo, pp. 45. H.

Also: Speech, ... against the War and Arming Negroes, and for Peace and Recognition; ... Feb. 2, 1863. [n. p. n. d.] 8vo, pp. 7. + [The same, February 20th, 1863.] *Baltimore: Kelly.* 1863. 8vo, pp. 18.

MAY (H.) A Thanksgiving Sermon, ... at Bath, ... Maine, November 25, 1802. By Hezekiah May, A.B. ... *Portland: Printed by E. A. Jenks.* 1802. 8vo, pp. 28. H. 47068

Also: An Oration, ... before ... the ... Masons, at Bangor, ... June 24, 5808. ... *Augusta: Printed by Peter Edes.* 1808. 8vo, pp. 16. — ... A Sermon, in Braintree, at the Installation of the Rev. Sylvester Sage, Nov. 4, 1807. ... *Boston: Printed by Lincoln & Edmands.* 1808. 8vo, pp. 28. B., BA., N.

MAY (J.) Sermon delivered at the Diocesan Convention, May 19, 1847, By James May. *Winchester, Va.* 1847. 8vo.

MAY (J.) Journal and Letters of Colonel John May, of Boston, relative to Two Journeys to the Ohio Country in 1788 and '89 with a Biographical Sketch By Rev. Richard S. Edes of Bolton, Mass. and Illustrative Notes By Wm. M. Darlington of Pittsburgh, Penn *Cincinnati: Robert Clarke & Co.* 1873. 8vo, pp. 160. H. 47070

MAY (J.) Explanation of a Project for Navigating the River Magdalena by Steam. By John May. [n. p.] 1855. 8vo, pp. 16

MAY (J. F.) The Sectional Difficulties. Opinions ... by John F. May ... . [n. p. 1861.] 8vo, pp. 8. H. 47072

MAY (L. du) Le prudent voyageur, contenant la description politique de tous les etats du Monde, l'Asie, de l'Afrique, et de l'Amérique ... . Par Louis du May. *Geneve, H. Widerhold.* 1681. 2 vols., 12mo, pp. (44), 830; (8), 758. W. 47073

MAY (R.) A Voice from Richmond ... . By the late Rev. Robert May. With a brief account of the Author. ... *Philadelphia: American Sunday-School Union.* [1842.] 24mo, pp. 300. 3 Plates. H. 47074

MAY (S. J.) A Discourse on Slavery in the United States, ... Brooklyn [Conn.], July 3, 1831. By Samuel J. May ... . *Boston: Garrison and Knapp.* 1832. 8vo, pp. 29. BA. 47075

MAY. The Flood. A Sermon. By Rev. Samuel J. May. *Boston: Leonard C. Bowles.* 1849. 8vo, pp. 13. B. 47076

MAY. Letters to Rev. Joel Hawes, D.D. in Review of his Tribute to the Memory of the Pilgrims. By Samuel J. May ... . *Hartford: Printed by Philemon Canfield.* 1831. 8vo, pp. 72. BA.

MAY. Some Recollections of our Anti Slavery Conflict. By Samuel J. May. *Boston: Fields, Osgood, & Co.* 1869. 12mo, pp. viii, 408. BA. 47078

Also: An Address ... before the American Peace Society, in ... Boston. May 28, 1860. ... *Boston.* 1860. 8vo, pp. 24. — A Brief Account of his Ministry, ... in a Discourse ... in Syracuse, N. Y., September 15th, 1867 ... . *Syracuse, N. Y.: Masters & Lee ... Printers.* 1867. 8vo, pp. 52. — A Discourse on the Life and Character of the Rev. Charles Follen, ... April 17, 1840. ... *Boston: Henry L. Devereux, Printer.* 1840. 8vo, pp. 30. — Emancipation in the British W. Indies, August 1, 1834. An Address, delivered in ... Syracuse, on the First of August, 1845. ... *Syracuse: Printed by J. Barber.* 1845. 8vo, pp. 24. — Letter addressed to the Editor of the Christian Examiner. ... *Boston: Printed by Garrison & Knapp.* 1835. 8vo, pp. 8. — Liberty or Slavery, the only Question. Oration ... Fourth of July, 1856, at Jamestown ... New York ... . *Syracuse: J. G. K. Truair, Printer.* 1856. 18mo, pp. 30. — Memoir of Cyrus Peirce, First Principal of First State Normal School in the United States. ... *Hartford: F. C. Brownell.* 1857. 8vo, pp. 38. Portrait. — The Revival of Education. ... Address to the Normal Association, Bridgewater, Mass. August 8, 1855. ... *Syracuse, N. Y.: J. G. K. Truair, Printer.* 1855. 8vo, pp. 40. — The Right of Colored People to Education, Vindicated. Letter to Andrew T. Judson and others in Canterbury [Conn.], Remonstrating with them on their Unjust and Unjustifiable Procedure relative to Miss Crandall and her School for Colored Females. ... *Brooklyn.* 1833. 8vo, pp. 24. — The Rights and Condition of Women; A Sermon, ... in Syracuse, Nov., 1845. ... Third Edition. [*Syracuse.* n. d.] 8vo, pp. 16. — The Rights and Condition of Women; ... November, 8, 1846. ... *Syracuse: Stoddard & Babcock.* [n. d.] 8vo, pp. 16. + Fourth Edition. *London.* 1859. 8vo. — The Second Revolution. An Oration ... in Dryden, Tompkins County, N. Y. July 4, 1855 ... . *Syracuse.* 1855. 8vo, pp. 20. — A Sketch of the Character ... of the late Mrs. Adelia E. Smith, of Borodino ... . *Boston: Leonard C. Bowles.* 1850. 16mo, pp. 16. — A Sermon, ... at Hingham, March 19, 1837; ... after the Death of Mrs. Cecilia Brooks. ... *Hingham: Press of J. Farmer.* 1837. 8vo, pp. 31. — Speech ... to the Convention of Citizens of Onondaga County, in Syracuse, on the 14th of October, 1851, Called To consider the Principles of the American Government ... . *Syracuse: Agan & Summers, Printers.* 1851. 12mo, pp. 23. — These Bad Times the Product of Bad Morals. Sermon preached May 21, 1837. *Boston.* 1837. 12mo, pp. 20. *See also* Thayer (Nathaniel), *and* Walker (James).

[MAY (Sam'l), *Jr.*] ... Fugitive Slave Law. *See* No. 26128.

MAY (S.) Dotty Dimple Out West. By Sophie May. *Boston: Lee & Shepard.* 1868. 18mo, pp. 171. Plates. 47079

MAY (Thomas). To the Memory of John Woolman, late of Mount-Holly, in the Province of New-Jersey. [In verse. n. p.:] *Printed for the Author.* 1772. Folio, 1 leaf. 47080

MAY (T. E.) The Constitutional History of England since the Accession of George the Third. 1760–1860. By Thomas Erskine May ... . *London: Longman* ... . 1861–63. 2 vols., 8vo, pp. xvi, 512; xvii, 640. BA. + *Boston.* 1863. 2 vols., 12mo.

Includes a discussion on American topics.

MAY. Histoire constitutionelle de l'Angleterre depuis l'avénement de George III, 1760–1860; ... traduite et précédée d'une introduction par Cornelis de Witt. *Paris: Lévy frères.* 1865–1866. 2 vols., 8vo, pp. 599; 739. 47082

MAY (W. W.) A Series of Fourteen Sketches made during the Voyage up Wellington Channel in search of Sir John Franklin, with a short Account of each Drawing. By Commander Walter W. May. *London: Day & Son.* 1865. Folio, pp. 7. 14 Plates. C. 47083

MAY (W.) Record of Proceedings of a Naval Court Martial, Convened ... 25th July, 1842, on board the U. S. Ship North Carolina, at New York, in the trial of Passed Midshipman William May ... . [n. p. 1842.] 8vo, pp. 34. H. 47084

Also: Trial of Passed Midshipman May, ... before a Naval Court Martial, at New York, 1842. To which is added his affidavit of the falsity of the first charge preferred against him by Lieut. Charles Wilkes, U.S.N. *Washington.* 1842. 8vo.

MAY (W. H.) The Old Flag. Fac-simile of a paper in imitation of print published during an Imprisonment of Thirteen Months at Camp Ford, Tyler, ... Texas. With List of Officers, Privates, at Camp Ford. By William H. May. Vol. I. *New York.* 1864. 4to. 47085

The May Be. *See* Vol. v., No. 20050.

May Martin [etc.] 1852. *See* [Thompson (Daniel P.)]

MAYA. El Ejercécio del Santo Via crucis Puerto en Lengua Maya. ... *Merida.* 1869. 16mo, pp. 31. 47086

MAYALL (S.) Speech of Hon. S. Mayall ... on the Financial and Territorial Policy of the Administration. ... January 2, 1855. *Washington.* 1855. 8vo, pp. 8. H. 47087

MAYBERRY (D. F.) Trial of David F. Mayberry for the Murder of Andrew Alger; ... July 10th & 11th, 1855. ... *Janesville, Wis.: Baker, Burnett & Hall, Printers.* 1855. 8vo, pp. 48. H. 47088

MAYCOCK (J. D.) Flora Barbadensis; a Catalogue of Plants, Indigenous, Naturalized, and Cultivated, in Barbados. To which is prefixed a Geological Description of the Island. By James Dottin Maycock. *London.* 1830. 8vo, pp. 450. 2 Maps. A.

MAYER (A. A.) Mémoires sur la Guyane Française. *Cayenne.* 1820. 4to. 47090

[MAYER (Brantz).] Address of the Union State Central Committee of Maryland. [*Baltimore.* 1861.] 8vo, pp. 8.

MAYER. Calvert and Penn; or the Growth of Civil and Religious Liberty in America, as disclosed in the Planting of Maryland and Pennsylvania. A Discourse ... by Brantz Mayer ... 8 April, 1852. [*Baltimore.* 1852.] 8vo, pp. 49, (1). BA.

MAYER. Captain Canot; or, Twenty Years of an African Slaver; being an account of his Career and Adventures on the Coast, in the Interior, on Shipboard, and in the West Indies. ... Edited from the Captain's Journals, ... By Brantz Mayer. *New York: D. Appleton and Company.* M. DCCC. LIV. 12mo, pp. (2), xvii, 448. Plates. BA., C. + [*Ibid.*] 1864. 47093

Reprinted in London as "Adventures of an African Slave Trader" ... . *London: Geo. Routledge and Sons.* [n. d.] 12mo.

MAYER. Le Capitaine Canot; ... Illustré par Pauquet. Traduction Raoul Bourdier. *Paris: Barba.* 1855. 4to.

MAYER. Commerce, Literature and Art: A Discourse by Brantz Mayer, at the Dedication of the Baltimore Athenæum, October 23, 1848. *Baltimore: Printed by John Murphy.* MDCCC-XLVIII. 8vo, pp. 52. BA. 47095

The cover of some copies reads: *Printed by John D. Toy.*

MAYER. ... The History, Possessions and Prospects of the Maryland Historical Society. Inaugural Discourse of Brantz Mayer ... March 7th, 1867. [*Baltimore.* 1867.] 8vo, pp. 36.

Contains a list of the society's publications.

MAYER. History of the War between Mexico and the United States, with a view of its origin. By Brantz Mayer ... . *New York.* 1848. 8vo. Portrait. C. 47097

MAYER. Memoir of Jared Sparks, LL.D. ... By Brantz Mayer ... . [*Baltimore.* 1867.] 8vo, pp. 36. Portrait. 47098

Fifty copies were printed on large paper, in 4to, with the imprint, *Baltimore: Printed for the Author.* 1867.

MAYER. Mexico as it Was and as it Is: By Brantz Mayer, Secretary of the U. S. Legation to that Country in 1841 and 1842. ... *New-York: J. Winchester.* MDCCCXLIV. 8vo, pp. (2), xii, 390. 28 Plates. BA. + Third Edition, revised and corrected, with the historical portion brought down to the present time. *Philadelphia: G. B. Zieber & Company.* 1847. 8vo, pp. vii–xv, ix–xii, 390. Plates. H. 47099

Highly commended in Rich's "Bibliotheca Americana," Vol. II.

MAYER. Mexico; Aztec, Spanish and Republican; a Historical, Geographical, Political, Statistical and Social Account of that Country, from the Period of the Invasion by the Spaniards to the Present Time; with a View of the Ancient Aztec Empire and Civilization; a Historical Sketch of the Late War; and Notices of New Mexico and California. By Brantz Mayer ... . *Hartford: S. Drake and Company.* MDCCCLI. 2 vols., 8vo, pp. (4), 433; 398. Portrait, Plates and Map. H. + [*Ibid.*] MDCCCLII. C. + [*Ibid.*] MDCCCLIII. BA. 47100

MAYER. ... Observations on Mexican History and Archæology, with a special notice of Zapotec Remains, as delineated in Mr. J. G. Sawkins's Drawings of Mitla, etc. By Brantz Mayer. [*Washington City: Smithsonian Institution.* 1856.] 4to, pp. (2), 33. 4 Plates. BA. 47101

Some copies have the imprint, *New York: G. P. Putnam.*

MAYER. Revelations of A Slave Trader; or, Twenty Years' Adventures of Captain Canot. *London: Richard Bentley.* 1854. 18mo, pp. xvii, 352. 47102

[MAYER.] Romanism in Mexico, being a Reply to an Article by the Rev. Mr. Verot, against Mayer's Mexico, in U. S. Catholic Magazine, March, 1844, by John Smith, Jr. *Baltimore.* 1844. 8vo, pp. 31. 47103

MAYER. Tag-Gah-Jute or Logan and Captain Michael Cresap; A Discourse by Brantz Mayer; delivered in Baltimore, before the Maryland Historical Society ... 9 May, 1851. *Baltimore: John Murphy & Co.* 1851. 8vo, pp. 86. 47104

Some copies have the imprint of the society.

MAYER. Tah-Gah-Jute; or, Logan and Cresap, an Historical Essay. By Brantz Mayer. *Albany: Joel Munsell.* 1867. 8vo, pp. (4), x, 204. C., H. 47105

An amplification of the former work, and a vindication of Capt. Cresap against the charge of murdering the family of Logan, which leaves some odium on the name of Thomas Jefferson. This edition forms No. VII. of "Munsell's Series of Local American History." Also: Address ... [before] the Central High School of Baltimore, August 1st, 1853. ... *Baltimore: Printed by James Lucas.* 1853. 8vo, pp. 18. — The Emancipation Problem in Maryland. ... [*Baltimore.* 1862.] 8vo, pp. 4. H. — The Maryland Historical Society and the Peabody Institute. ... [*Baltimore.* 1866.] 8vo. *See also* McDonogh (J.), No. 43176.

MAYER (C. F.) First Discourse ... before the Maryland Historical Society, ... 20 June, 1844, By Charles F. Mayer, A.M. ... *Baltimore: Printed by John D. Toy.* 1844. 8vo, pp. 32.

Also: An Address ... [before] the Maryland State Temperance Society ... 15th January, 1833. ... *Annapolis: W. M'Neir—Print.* 1833. 8vo, pp. 21. — Address at Loudon Park Cemetery. ... *Baltimore.* 1853. 8vo.

MAYER (Charles Joseph). Les Ligues Achéenne, Suisse et Hollandoise; et Révolution des États-Unis de l'Amérique. Comparées ensemble. Par M. de Mayer. ... *À Genêve, et se trouve à Paris, chez Cuchet.* M.D.CC.LXXXVII. 2 vols., 12mo, pp. xxiv, 259; (4), 328. BA., C. 47107

The title of the second volume is "États Unis de l'Amérique Septentrionale, comparées avec les Ligues Achéenne, Suisse et Hollandoise." Also: Asgill, ou Désordres des Guerres Civiles. ... *Paris.* 1784. 12mo, pp. 130. S.

MAYER (D.) Neu aufgerichteter Americanischer Mayerhof, das ist: Schwere Arbeiten und reiffe Seelen-Früchten ... gesammelt in neu aufgerichteten Missionen in America. *Augspurg.* 1747. 8vo. 47108

These are missionary accounts from Peru.

MAYER *or* MAYR (Johann). Compendium cronologicum seculi à Christo nato decimi sexti ... . *München.* 1598. 4to.

In German. Includes numerous references to America.

MAYER. Epitome Cronicorum seculi moderni, das ist: Kurtzer Begriff und Inhalt aller gedenckwürdigen Sachen, so von 1500 bisz zu dem 1604 Jar Christi, auff dem gantzen Erdenkreiss, zu Wasser und Landt sich verlauffen, an jetzt durch den Authorn selbst corrigiert, mit vilen Historien, sonderlich der Newen Welt Americae, und Ost-Indien vermehret. *München: N. Henricus.* 1604. 4to, 10 leaves, Text, 339. Map on Title.

MAYER (J.) Address to the Members of the Historical Society of Lancashire and Cheshire. By Joseph Mayer ... . *Liverpool: Printed by Thomas Brakell.* 1868. 8vo, pp. 20. H.

Includes American topics.

MAYER (L.) History of the German Reformed Church. By Lewis Mayer. To which is prefixed a Memoir of the Author; by Elias Heiner. Vol. I. *Philadelphia.* 1851. 8vo. C. + Second Edition. Vol. I. [*Ibid.*] 1851. 8vo. 47112

Also: Inaugural Address ... at his Inauguration as Principal in the Theological Seminary ... in Carlisle, Pa. ... April 6, 1825. [n. p. 1825.] 8vo, pp. 16. BA.

MAYER (L.) Digest of the Decisions, construing the Statutes of Maryland, of which the Code of Public General Laws is composed. By Lewis Mayer. *Baltimore.* 1866. 8vo. C. 47113

MAYER (P. F.) Sermon of the Rev. Philip F. Mayer, D.D., first Pastor of the Evangelical Lutheran Church of St. John ... October 5, 1856, the Fiftieth Anniversary of his Pastoral Charge ... . *Philadelphia: Joseph Rakestraw, Printer.* 1856. 8vo, pp. 15, (1). H., S. 47114

MAYER VON ESSLINGEN (——). Album von Combe-Varin. Zur Erinnerung an Theodor Parker und Hans Lorenz Küchler. ... *Zürich.* 1861. 8vo, pp. (4), xvi, 331, (1). 2 Portraits, 2 Plates, and Map. B. 47115

Also with a title-page in French.

MAYERHOFFER (V. P.) Twelve Years a Roman Catholic Priest; or, the Autobiography of the Rev. V. P. Mayerhoffer, M.A. ... Late ... Grand Chaplain of the ... Orangemen in Canada ... . *Toronto.* 1861. 12mo, pp. 340. 47116

[MAYERNE-TURQUET (Louis de).] Histoire Générale d'Espagne, Comprinse en XXVII liures ... M.D.LXXXVII. *Povr Iean de Tovrnes Imprimevr dv Roy A Lyon.* Folio, 32 leaves, one of which is blank, pp. 1526. 47117

[MAYERNE-TURQUET.] The Generall Historie of Spaine, ... unto the year 1583. Translated into English, and continued unto these times by Edward Grimestone, Esq. *London.* 1612. Folio. S. 47118

MAYES (D.) An Address delivered on the First Anniversary of Van Doren's Collegiate Institute, Lexington, Ky., 1832. By Hon. Daniel Mayes. *Lexington.* 1832. 8vo, pp. 14. M.

Also: Address to the Students of Law in Transylvania University, delivered 1835. ... *Lexington, Ky.* 1835. 8vo, pp. 30. M.

MAYFIELD (M.), *pseudon.* Progression; or, The South Defended. By Millie Mayfield ... . *Cincinnati, O.: Applegate & Co.* 1860. 12mo, pp. 226. H. 47120

A Poem. Also: Carrie Harrington; or, Scenes in New Orleans. A Novel. ... *New York: A. Atchison.* 1857. 12mo, pp. 354. C.

THE MAYFLOWER. Correspondence relating to the Wreck of the Mayflower, Dec. 13, 1851. *Buffalo.* 1852. 8vo.

MAYHAM (S. L.) The Condition of the Country. Speech of Hon. S. L. Mayham ... New York Assembly, March 2, 1863. [n. p. n. d.] 8vo, pp. 12. 47122

MAYHEW (E.) A Discourse shewing that God dealeth with Men As with Reasonable Creatures in a Sermon ... at Boston, N. E. Nov. 23. 1718. With a brief Account of the State of the Indians on Martha's Vineyard, & the Small Islands adjacent ... from ... 1694. to 1720. By the Reverend Experience Mayhew ... . *Boston: Printed by B. Green, for Samuel Gerrish.* 1720. 8vo, pp. (2), 34, 12. B. 47123

MAYHEW. Indian Converts: or, some Account of the Lives and Dying Speeches of a considerable Number of the Christianized Indians of Martha's Vineyard, in New England. ... By Experience Mayhew, M.A. Preacher of the Gospel to the Indians of that Island. To which is added, Some Account of those English Ministers who have successively presided over the Indian work in that and the adjacent Islands. By Mr. Prince. ... *London: Printed for Samuel Gerrish, in Boston in New England:* ... M.DCC.-XXVII. 8vo, pp. xxiv, 310, Books, 1 leaf. B., H. 47124

Prince's Account has a separate title at page 277. A specimen sheet and proposals were issued in Boston, May 25, 1726. *See* "Historical Magazine," II. 232.

MAYHEW. Narratives of the Lives of Pious Indian Children, who lived on Martha's Vineyard ... . By Experience Mayhew, A.M. ... *Boston: James Loring.* [1829.] 24mo, pp. 108.

A reprint of part of the fourth division of the "Indian Converts." Also: ... A Sermon Preach'd at the Public Lecture in Boston. On Thursday, Dec. 3. 1724. ... *Boston: Samuel Gerrish.* 1725. 8vo, pp. (2), ii, 28. — Grace Defended ... . In Which The Doctrine of Original Sin and Humane Impotence, ... and other Important Points, are considered and cleared. ... *Boston: Printed by B. Green, and Company, for D. Henchman.* 1744. 8vo, pp. (2), vi, 7, (1), 208. *See also* Nos. 22166, *and* 45537, *note.*

[MAYHEW (Henry).] The Mormons: or Latter-Day Saints. With Memoirs of the Life and Death of Joseph Smith, the "American Mahomet." *London.* [1851.] Post 8vo, pp. 326. + [*Ibid.*] 1852. Post 8vo, pp. 320. + Third Edition. [*Ibid.*] + [*Ibid.*] 1855. + Fourth Edition. *London: Ward & Lock.* 1856. Post 8vo. 47126

Edited by Charles Mackay. Some copies have the title: "The Mormons or Latter-Day Saints: A Contemporary History." *London.* [n. d.]

MAYHEW. Young Benjamin Franklin. *London: R. Griffin & Co.* 1858. Post 8vo. + *New York.* 1862. 12mo. 47127

MAYHEW (I.) The Means and Ends of Universal Education. By Ira Mayhew, A.M. ... *New York: A. S. Barnes & Burr.* 1860. 12mo, pp. 5–474. H. 47128

MAYHEW. Popular Education: ... By Ira Mayhew, A.M. ... *New York: Harper & Brothers.* 1850. 12mo, pp. 467. Plate.

Mayhew (J.) A Defence Of the Observations on the Charter and Conduct of the Society for the Propagation of the Gospel in Foreign Parts, against An anonymous Pamphlet falsly intitled, A Candid Examination Of Dr. Mayhew's Observations, &c. And also against The Letter to a Friend annexed thereto, ... By Jonathan Mayhew, D.D. ... *Boston: ... R. and S. Draper*, ... 1763. 8vo, pp. 144. BA., C. + ... *London: Reprinted for W. Nicoll.* M.DCC.LXIV. 8vo, pp. 120. 47130

See [Caner (H.)], No. 10681, for the title of the work to which this is a reply.

Mayhew. A Discourse concerning Unlimited Submission and Non-Resistance to the Higher Powers: with ... Reflections on the Resistance made to King Charles I. and on the Anniversary of his Death; In which the Mysterious Doctrine of that Prince's Saintship and Martyrdom is unriddled: ... delivered ... on the Lord's Day after the 30th of January, 1749–50. ... By Jonathan Mayhew, A.M. ... *Boston: Printed by D. Fowle* ... . 1750. 8vo, pp. 55. C. + *Boston: ... Re-printed by Hall & Goss.* 1818. 8vo, pp. 48. B., BA. 47131

A few copies of the 1750 edition were printed in 4to. Also reprinted in Thornton's "Pulpit of the American Revolution," and in Baron's "Pillars of Priestcraft shaken," Vol. II., pp. 259–335. The writer boldly asserts that resistance to tyranny is obedience to God, as well in Church as in State. "He speaks strongly and historically against the Saintship and Martyrdom of Charles, with an irreverent glibness of tongue, akin to the feeling which until recently caused the bells of New Haven in Connecticut to ring a merry peel every year on the 30th of Jan., in honour of the regicides buried there."—Stevens. *See* Tudor's "Otis," Chp. x., *and* Bancroft's "History," IV. 60.

Mayhew. A Discourse ... Occasioned by the Earthquakes In November 1755. Delivered in the West-Meeting-House, Boston, ... December 18, following. ... By Jonathan Mayhew, D.D. ... *Boston: N. E. Printed by Edes & Gill.* M,DCC,LV. 8vo, pp. 72, (2). BA., C. 47132

Mayhew. A Discourse Occasioned by the Death of The Honourable Stephen Sewall, Esq; Chief-Justice of the Superiour Court of Judicature, ... as also A Member of His Majesty's Council for the Province of the Massachusetts-Bay in New-England: Who departed this Life On ... September 10. 1760. Ætatis 58. Delivered the Lord's-Day after his Decease. By Jonathan Mayhew, D.D. ... *Boston: Printed by Richard Draper*, ... MDCCLX. 8vo, pp. 66. B., C., W. 47133

Mayhew. A Discourse Occasioned by the Death of ... George II. and the ... Accession of ... George III. ... Delivered Jan. 4th. 1761. ... By Jonathan Mayhew, D.D. ... *Boston: New-England, Printed by Edes & Gill.* M,DCC,LXI. 8vo, pp. 43.

Mayhew. Eclogue ... to ... Mayhew. *See* [Green (Jos.)]

Mayhew. Elegy on the Death of the Reverend Jonathan Mayhew, D.D., who departed this life July 9th, ... 1766. ... *Boston: Printed ... by Edes and Gill.* [1766.] 4to, pp. 15. H.

By Benjamin Church. Corrected title of *our* No. 12979.

Mayhew. The expected Dissolution of all Things, a Motive to universal Holiness. Two Sermons Preached in Boston, N. E. on the Lord's Day, Nov. 23, 1755; Occasioned by the Earthquakes, which appeared on the Tuesday morning and Saturday evening preceding. By Jonathan Mayhew, D.D. ... *Boston: N. E. Printed by Edes & Gill* ... . M,DCC,LV. 8vo, pp. 76, 5.

Mayhew. God's Hand ... . A Sermon Occasioned by The Great Fire in Boston, New-England, ... March 20. 1760. ... By Jonathan Mayhew, D.D. ... *Boston: Printed by Richard Draper.* 1760. 8vo, pp. 38. BA., H., W. 47137

Mayhew. The Late Smiles of Providence represented ... . Two Discourses Delivered November 23d. 1758. Being the Day ... of public Thanksgiving: Relating, more Especially, to the Success of His Majesty's Arms, ... the last Year. By Jonathan Mayhew, D.D. ... *Boston: N. E. Printed by R. Draper.* [1759.] 8vo, pp. 57. BA. 47138

Mayhew. A Letter of Reproof to Mr. John Cleaveland of Ipswich, occasioned by A defamatory Libel Published under his Name ... . By Jonathan Mayhew, D.D. ... *Boston: Printed by R. and S. Draper.* 1764. 8vo, pp. 49. BA., W. 47139

Mayhew. Observations on the Charter and Conduct of the Society for the Propagation of the Gospel in Foreign Parts; designed to shew their Non-Conformity to each other. With Remarks on the Mistakes of East Apthorp, M.A. Missionary at Cambridge, in Quoting, and Representing the Sense of said Charter, &c. As also, Various incidental Reflections relative to the Church of England, and the State of Religion in North-America, particularly in New-England. By Jonathan Mayhew, D.D. ... *Boston, New-England: Printed by Richard and Samuel Draper.* M,DCC,LXIII. 8vo, pp. 176. B., BA. + ... *London, reprinted for W. Nicoll.* MDCCLXIII. 8vo, pp. 164. C. 47140

"The designs of a certain Society to introduce [the Canon] have been well exposed by a writer of great abilities—Dr. Mayhew."—John Adams. For "An Answer," *see* [Secker (Thomas)], *see also* [Browne (Arthur)], No. 8641, *and* [Caner (H.)], No. 10681. It also elicited:

The Claims of the Church of England seriously examined: In a letter to the Author of an Answer to Dr. Mayhew's Observations on the Charter and Conduct of the Society for Propagating the Gospel in Foreign Parts. By a Protestant Dissenter of Old England. *London: W. Nicoll.* MDCCLXIV. 8vo, pp. 28.

Verses on Dr. Mayhew's Book of Observations on the Charter and Conduct of the Society for the Propagation of the Gospel in Foreign Parts. With Notes Critical and Explanatory. By a Gentleman of Rhode Island Colony [William Goddard]. *Providence: William Goddard.* 1763. 8vo, pp. 19. M. 47142

Mayhew. Practical Discourses delivered on Occasion of the Earthquakes in November, 1755. By Jonathan Mayhew, D.D. ... *Boston: R. Draper.* 1760. 12mo, pp. (6), 378. C., S. 47143

Mayhew. Remarks on an Anonymous Tract, entitled An Answer to Dr. Mayhew's Observations On the Charter and Conduct of the Society for the Propagation of the Gospel in Foreign Parts. Being a Second Defence of the said Observations. By Jonathan Mayhew, D.D. ... *Boston: ... R. and S. Draper* ... . 1764. 8vo, pp. 86, (1). C. 47144

With an advertisement on a fly-leaf, dated Boston, June 20. 1764, respecting the burning of the library of Harvard College.

Mayhew. Remarks [as before]. In which the Scheme of sending Bishops to America, is particularly considered; and the Inconveniences that might result from it to that Country, if put into Execution, both in Civil and Religious Respects, are represented. By Jonathan Mayhew, D.D. ... *Boston: Printed* 1764. *London: Reprinted for W. Nicoll.* MDCCLXV. 8vo, pp. 87.

For "A Review," *see* Apthorp (E.), Vol. I., No. 1856. *See* "M. Rev.," XXXI. 396.

Mayhew. A Sermon Preached at Boston in New-England, May 26, 1751. Occasioned by The much-lamented Death of His Royal Highness, Frederick, Prince of Wales ... . By Jonathan Mayhew, D.D. ... *Boston; New-England: Printed by Richard Draper.* 1751. 8vo, pp. 39. 47146

Mayhew. A Sermon Preach'd in the Audience of His Excellency William Shirley, Esq; Governour, ... the Council, And the ... Representatives Of the Province of the Massachusetts-Bay, in New-England. May 29th, 1754. Being the Anniversary for the Election of His Majesty's Council for the Province. ... By Jonathan Mayhew, D.D. ... *Boston: N. E. Printed by Samuel Kneeland* ... . 1754. 8vo, pp. (2), 52. BA., C. 47147

Said to have been reprinted in London, 1755.

Mayhew. The Snare broken. A Thanksgiving-Discourse, Preached at the Desire of the West Church in Boston, N. E. Friday May 23, 1766. Occasioned by the Repeal of the Stamp-Act. By Jonathan Mayhew, D.D. ... *Boston: Printed by R. & S. Draper.* 1766. 8vo, pp. viii, 44. BA. + The Second Edition. [*Ibid.*] 8vo, pp. viii, 52. P. + *London: G. Kearsley.* [1766.] 8vo, pp. vi, 41. H. 47148

Mayhew. Two Discourses delivered October 25th. 1759. Being the Day appointed by Authority to be observed as a Day of public Thanksgiving for the Success of His Majesty's Arms, more particularly in the Reduction of Quebec, the Capital of Canada. With an Appendix, Containing a brief Account of two former Expeditions against that City and Country, which proved unsuccessful. By Jonathan Mayhew, D.D. ... *Boston; New-England: ... Richard Draper* ... . 1759. 8vo, pp. 67, (12).

Mayhew. Two Sermons ... Delivered December 9. 1762. Being the Annual Thanksgiving of the Province ... . By Jonathan Mayhew, D.D. ... *Boston: N. E. Printed by D. and J. Kneeland.* 1763. 8vo, pp. 91. BA. 47150

Also: Christian Sobriety: being Eight Sermons ... Preached ... to the ... Young Men, ... attending the ... West Church, in Boston. ... *Boston: New-England: Printed by Richard and Samuel Draper.* 1763. 8vo, pp. xvi, 343, (1). H.—Five Sermons on Several Subjects. ... *Boston.* 1755. 12mo.—Popish Idolatry: A Discourse ... in the Chapel of Harvard-College ... May 8. 1765. ... *Boston: Printed by R. & S. Draper.* MDCCLXV. 8vo, pp. 52.—Sermons ... . *Boston: Printed by Richard Draper.* MDCCLV. 8vo, pp. (2), iv, (2), 510, (1). H. + *London: A. Millar.* 1756. 8vo.—Sermons to Young Men. ... *London: ... T. Becket and P. A. De Hondt* ... . MDCCLXVII. 2 vols., 12mo, pp. xx, 275; (2), iv, 304.—Seven Sermons ... Preached at a Lecture in the West Meeting-House in Boston ... . *Boston, N. E.: ... Rogers & Fowle.* MDCCXLIX. 8vo, pp. (4), 157. B. + ... *London Reprinted, John Noon.* MDCCL. 8vo, pp. (6), 132.

Mayhew (M.) A Brief | Narrative | Of | The Success which the Gospel | hath had, among the | Indians, | of | Martha's Vineyard (and the Places adjacent) | in New-England. | With | Some Remarkable Curiosities, concerning the | Numbers, the Customes, and the present Cir- | cumstances of the Indians on that Island. | Further Explaining [*sic*] and Confirming the Ac- | count given of those matters, by Mr. Cotton | Mather in the Life of the Renowned | Mr. John Eliot. | By Matthew Mayhew. | Whereto is added, | An Account concerning the Present State of | Christianity among the Indians, in | other Parts of New-England: Expressed | in the Letters of several Worthy Persons, | best Acquainted therewithall. | *Boston in N. E. Printed by Bartholomew Green, | Sold by Michael Perry* ... . 1694. Sm. 8vo, pp. 55. M. 47151

A volume of extreme rarity. Reprinted with the following title:

Mayhew. The | Conquests and Triumphs | of | Grace: | Being | A Brief Narrative of the Success which the | Gospel hath had among the Indians of | Martha's Vineyard (and the Places adjacent) | in New-England. | With | Some Remarkable Curiosities, concerning the | Numbers, the Customs, and the present Cir- | cumstances of the Indians on that Island. | Further Explaining and Confirming the Account | given of those Matters, by Mr. Cotton Mather, | in the Life of the Renowned Mr. John Eliot. | By Matthew Mayhew. | Attested by the Reverend Mr. Nath. Mather, and others. | Whereunto is Added | An Account concerning the Present State of Christianity | among the Indians, in other Parts of New-England: | Expressed in the Letters of several Worthy Persons. | best acquainted therewithal. | *London, Printed for Nath. Hiller, at the Princes Arms | in Leadenhall-street, over against St. Mary Axe*, 1695. Sm. 8vo, pp. 68, (1). 47152

Menzies' copy sold for $105. We cannot record the public sale of any other copy in the United States.

Mayhew (T.) Upon the Joyfull and vvelcome Return of his Sacred Majestie, Charles the Second, of England, Scotland, France and Ireland King, Defender of the Faith, &c. To his due and indubitate Right of Government, over these His Majestie's Kingdoms and Dominions. A Panegyrick. By Tho. Mayhew Gent. *London: Printed for Abel Roper.* 1660. 4to.

Very rare. *See also* Eliot (J.), *and* Mayhew (T.), No. 22166, *and* Winslow (E.)

Maylem (J.) The Conquest of Louisbourg. A Poem. By John Maylem, Philo-Bellum. [*Boston.* 1758.] 4to, pp. 10. M.

Maylem. Gallic Perfidy: A Poem. By John Maylem, Philo-Bellum. *Boston: New-England: ... Benjamin Mecom*, ... *July* 13. 1758. ... 8vo, pp. 15. P. 47155

Dated "March 10. '58." The author was captured by Montcalm's Indians.

Maylins (Robert). A Letter which was delivered to the King (Charles) on the second day of the second Moneth 1660, sent (From the Barbadoes, on the Behalf of many Thousands in the West-Indies.) *London, Printed for Giles Calvert at the West-end of Pauls.* 1661. Folio, 1 leaf. 47156

Maynadier (W.) Oration prepared for delivery at West Point, N. Y. July 4, 1826. By William Maynadier. *Newburgh.* 1826. 8vo. W. 47157

[Maynadier (W.)] Remarks on the Circular Letters to the Secretary of War, to be signed by Artillery Officers. *Washington.* 1852. 8vo, pp. 32. S. 47158

Maynadier Reply of Lt. Col. Maynadier, to the Charges in the Report of the Potter Committee. *Washington: Printed by H. S. Bowen.* 1862. 8vo, pp. 8. 47159

Maynard (A.) The New Farmer's Almanac for 1849. By Aaron Maynard. *Boston.* [1848.] 8vo. 47160

Maynard ... The Select Manual Almanac: ... for ... 1846. ... By Aaron Maynard. ... [n. p. 1845.] 12mo, pp. 48.

Also: The Farmer's Almanac, for ... 1851; ... *Boston: Phillips, Sampson & Co.* [1850.] 8vo, pp. 48.

Maynard (C. J.) The Naturalist's Guide in collecting and preserving Objects of Natural History, with a Complete Catalogue of the Birds of Eastern Massachusetts. By C. J. Maynard. ... *Boston: Fields, Osgood & Co.* 1870. 12mo, pp. ix, 170. 10 Plates. 47162

The author also announced "The Birds of Florida."

Maynard (F.) Voyages et Aventures au Chili; par le docteur Félix Maynard. *Paris: Jaccottet, Bourdilliat et Cie.* 1858. 18mo, pp. 312. 47163

Maynard (H.) An Address: ... before the Literary Societies of Mossy Creek Baptist College, June 19th, 1857. By Horace Maynard. ... *Knoxville, Tenn.: Hiram Barry.* 1857. 8vo, pp. 23. B. 47164

Maynard. A Discourse, Commemorating ... Daniel Webster: ... in ... Knoxville, January 1st, 1853. ... By Horace Maynard. *Knoxville, Tenn.: A. Blackburn & Co.* 1853. 8vo, pp. 47, (1). BA. 47165

Maynard. An Oration ... before the Order of United Americans, at ... New York, Feb. 22, 1861, on the Celebration of the ... Birthday of Washington By Hon. Horace Maynard, ... *New York: Chas. E. Gildersleve.* 1861. 8vo, pp. 32.

Also: An Address to the Slaveholders of Tennessee, delivered in Nashville, on the 4th of July, 1863. ... [n. p. n. d.] 8vo, pp. 23.—How, by Whom, and for What was the War begun? Speech ... in ... Nashville, ... March 20, 1862. [n. p. n. d.] 8vo, pp. 24.—Let us Remain one People! An Appeal to the North. Speech ... February 6, 1861. [n. p. n. d.] 8vo, pp. 11.—Political Education. An Address, ... August 8, 1860. ... *Boston: Press of Geo. C. Rand and Avery.* 1661. 8vo, pp. 42.—The Punishment of Treason. Speech ... delivered in the House of Representatives, March 23, 1862. [n. p. n. d.] 8vo, pp. 12.—Speech ... on the Negro Enlistment Bill, in the House of Representatives, January 31, 1862. [n. p. n. d.] 8vo, pp. 12.—Speech ... on the Admission of Kansas under the Lecompton Constitution. ... March 20, 1858. *Washington: G. S. Gideon, Printer.* 1858. 8vo, pp. 16.—Speech ... on the Claim of Joseph Segar to a Seat in the House; ... February 11, 1862. *Washington.* 1862. 8vo,

pp. 8.—Speech ... Dec. 12, 1867, on Reconstruction ... Tennessee. ... [n. p. n. d.] 8vo. *See also* [Mayo (R.)], No. 47190, *infra.*

Maynard (*Judge*). Extract from the Charge of Judge Maynard to the Grand Jury of Northampton County, ... 1863. [n. p. n. d.] 8vo, pp. 7. 47167

Relates to the Rebellion in the South.

Maynard (S.) The Experience of Sampson Maynard, Local Preacher of the Methodist E. Church. (Written by himself.) ... *New-York: Printed for the Author, by Wm. C. Taylor.* 1828. 16mo, pp. 252. 47168

Maynard (T.) Histoire des États-Unis d'Amérique. Par Théophile Maynard. *Tours: Mame et Cie.* 1857. 8vo, pp. 240. Vignette. 47169

Maynard (W. H.) The Speech of William H. Maynard, on the Bill for the Construction of the Chenango Canal, ... in the Senate of New-York, 23d and 24th February, 1831. *Albany: Printed by B. D. Packard & Co.* 1837. 8vo, pp. 56. B., S.

Also: A Speech in the Senate of New-York, Third and Fourth of February, 1832. ... on Renewing the Charter of the Bank of the United States. *Albany: Printed by Packard* ... . 1832. 8vo, pp. 38. B., S.

Maynarde (T.) Sir Francis Drake his Voyage, 1595. By Thomas Maynarde, together with the Spanish Account of Drake's Attack on Puerto Rico. Edited, from the Original Manuscripts, By W. D. Cooley. *London: Printed for the Hakluyt Society.* M.DCCC.XLIX. 8vo, pp. (2), viii, 65, 12. BA. 47171

Forms Vol. IV. of the Publications of the Hakluyt Society.

Maynas. Copia de dos Cartas Escritas de vn | Missionero, y del Superior de las Missiones de los Maynas, | en el Rio Marañon, jurisdiccion de la Real Audiencia de Qui- | to, aviendo al Padre Vice-Provincial de la Compañia de | Iesvs, del Nuevo Revno de Granada; el vno, el estado del | Pueblo en que assiste; y el otro, el que tiene parte de aquella | gloriosa Mission, que avia visitado el año passado de 1681. | Primera Carta. | [n. p. n. d.] Folio, 2 leaves. 47172

Mayne (F.) Voyages and Discoveries in the Arctic Regions. Edited by F. Mayne. *London: Longman* ... . 1855. 12mo, pp. 140. C., P. 47173

Mayne (R. C.) Four Years in British Columbia and Vancouver Island. An Account of their Forests, Rivers, Coasts,

Gold Fields, and Resources for Colonisation. By Commander R. C. Mayne. ... With Map and Illustrations. *London: John Murray.* 1862. 8vo, pp. xi, 468. BA. 47174

The facts narrated are chiefly derived from William Duncan's letters. *See* Vol. VI., No. 21264.

Mayo (A. D.) The American Cemetery. An Address, ... at the Dedication of Green Hill Cemetery, ... Amsterdam, ... N. Y., ... Sept. 1, 1868. By Rev. A. D. Mayo ... . *Amsterdam, N. Y.* 1858. 8vo, pp. 17. H. 47175

Mayo. Herod, John and Jesus; or American Slavery, and its Christian Cure. A Sermon ... in ... Albany, N. Y. By Rev. A. D. Mayo. *Albany: Weed, Parsons & Company, Printers.* 1860. 12mo, pp. 29. 47176

Mayo. The Nation's Sacrifice. Abraham Lincoln. Two Discourses, ... April 16, and ... April 19, 1865, in the Church of the Redeemer, Cincinnati, Ohio. By A. D. Mayo, Pastor. *Cincinnati: Robert Clarke & Co.* 1865. 8vo, pp. 28. H. 47177

Mayo. Religion in the Common Schools. Three Lectures delivered in ... Cincinnati, ... October, 1869. By Rev. A. D. Mayo. *Cincinnati: Robert Clarke & Co., Printers.* 1869. 8vo, pp. 51. C., S. 47178

Mayo. The Scholar's Vocation in the New Republic. An Address ... before ... Antioch College, June 30, 1863. By A. D. Mayo ... . *Cincinnati: Robert Clarke & Co.* 1863. 8vo, pp. 28

Relates to the Rebellion.

Mayo. A Sermon on Daniel Webster, preached at Gloucester, Mass., By A. D. Mayo ... . *Gloucester: John S. E. Rogers, Printer.* 1852. 8vo, pp. 19. B., BA. 47180

Mayo. Symbols of the Capital; or, Civilization in New York. By A. D. Mayo. *New-York: Thatcher & Hutchinson.* 1859. 12mo, pp. 368. C., H. 47181

Also: The Aged Christian. A Discourse, ... after the Decease of Mr. Richard Friend ... . *Gloucester.* 1849. 8vo, pp. 13.— ... American Dangers and Duties. ... *Albany: Weed, Parsons & Company, Printers.* 1861. 12mo, pp. 19.—The Capitol; or, the Higher Law: A Lecture ... in ... Albany, ... February 21st, 1858. ... [n. p. n. d.] 8vo, pp. 6.—The Death Penalty. A Sermon, ... June 3, 1855 ... . *Cleveland: Harris, Fairbanks & Co., Printers.* 1855. 8vo, pp. 16.—A Discourse ... at the Funeral of Rev. Thomas Jones, ... Gloucester, Ms., Aug. 22, 1846. ... *Boston: A. Tompkins.* 1846. 8vo, pp. 8.— ... A Discourse ... after the Decease of Mrs. S. C. E. Mayo. ... *Boston: Eastburn's Press.* 1848. 8vo, pp. 23.—East and West. ... [n. p. n. d.] 8vo, pp. 33.—The Gold Dollar: a Discourse, ... Nov. 29, 1857. ... [n. p. n. d.] 12mo.— ... Liberal Christianity ... . *Albany: Weed, Parsons & Company, Printers.* 1859.

12mo, pp. 11. — Man and his Modern Inventions: A Discourse ... Albany, ... 1858. ... *Albany*. 1858. 8vo. — Pedantry and Power. An Address ... before ... State Normal School, ... July 7, 1856. ... *Albany: Weed, Parsons and Co., Printers*. 1856. 8vo, pp. 14. — The Personal Liberty Bill. An Address to the Legislature and People of New York. ... *Albany: Weed, Parsons & Company, Printers*. 1859. 12mo, pp. 17. — The Relations of Liberal Christianity to ... the West. ... *Cambridge: Press of John Wilson and Son*. 1866. 8vo, pp. (2), 27. — A Review of the Year: A Sermon, ... Dec. 31, 1854 ... . *Cleveland: Printed by Harris, Fairbanks & Co.* 1855. 8vo, pp. 24. — ... A Sermon, ... on assuming the Duties of Pastor of the Church of the Redeemer, Cincinnati, Ohio, ... February 1, 1863. ... *Cincinnati*. 1863. 8vo, pp. 16. — ... Sermon at the Installation of Rev. C. Cravens, June 29, 1853. ... *Boston*. 1853. 8vo. — ... Theodore Parker. ... *Albany: Weed, Parsons & Company, Printers*. 1860. 12mo, pp. 18. — Theology in America. A Sermon ... March 15, 1857, in ... Albany. ... *Albany: Weed, Parsons & Company, Printers*. 1857. 8vo, pp. 24. — Thomas Starr King. A Sermon at Cincinnati, March 13, 1864. ... *Cincinnati*. 1864. 8vo.

MAYO, *and* VICKERS (T.) ... The Bible in the Public Schools. Addresses of Rev. A. D. Mayo and Rev. Thos. Vickers ... . *New York: J. W. Schermerhorn & Co.* 1870. 24mo, pp. 223. B.

MAYO, *and* WHITMAN (E. B.) Liberal Christianity The Religion for the South-West, By Rev. A. D. Mayo. Christian Work at the South, By Maj. E. B. Whitman. *Louisville: Hill & Brother, Printers*. 1867. 8vo, pp. 26, (1). H. 47183

MAYO (C.) A Compendious View of Universal History. From the Year 1753 to ... 1802. By C. Mayo. *Bath*. 1804. 4 vols., rl. 4to. 47184

"Very important for the History of America." So says an English catalogue. We cannot endorse the statement.

MAYO (H. B.) Address delivered before the Citizens of Oxford, 4th July, 1839. By H. B. Mayo. *Oxford, Ohio*. 1839. 8vo, pp. 16. 47185

MAYO (R.) The Affidavit of Andrew Jackson, taken by the Defendants in the Suit of Robert Mayo *vs*. Blair & Rives for a Libel, Analysed and Refuted. By Robert Mayo, M.D. ... *Washington*. 1840. 8vo, pp. 23. + Third Edition, with Supplementary Notes. ... *Washington City, D. C.: For the Plaintiff*. 1840. 8vo, pp. 80. BA., S. 47186

MAYO. Pension Laws of the United States, including Sundry Resolutions of Congress, from 1776 to 1833. By Robert Mayo, M.D. *City of Washington*. 1833. 8vo. C. 47187

MAYO. Political Sketches of Eight Years in Washington; In Four Parts, with Annotations to each. Also a General Appendix; An Alphabetical Index; and a Series of Charts, giving a Comparative Synopsis of the Constitutions of the Several

States, and the United States. By Robert Mayo, M.D. *Baltimore: Fielding Lucas, Jr.* 1839. 8vo, pp. viii, v, 216. A., BA.

See "N. A. Rev.," April, 1839. This elicited: "A Reply to the Sketches of an Eight Years' Resident in the City of Washington, By Dr. R. Mayo ... . By a Member of the Hickory Club." *Washington*. 1837. 8vo, pp. 14, 4, (1). To which Mr. Mayo responded in the following:

MAYO. The Misrepresentations of "A Member of the Hickory Club," in reply to Dr. Mayo's "Sketches," &c., refuted. Second Edition. *Washington: Printed for the Author, By Garret Anderson*. 1837. 8vo, pp. 36. 47189

[MAYO.] ... A Review of the Report of Hon. Horace Maynard, Chairman of the Committee of Investigation, into the conduct and accounts of William Cullom, late Clerk of the House of Representatives; ... [n. p. n. d.] 8vo, pp. 16, 31. H.

MAYO. A Synopsis of the Commercial and Revenue System of The United States, as developed by Instructions and Decisions of the Treasury Department for the administration of The Revenue Laws; accompanied with A Supplement of Historical and Tabular Instructions of the Origin, Organization, and Practical Operations of the Treasury Department, Audits, various Bureaus, in fulfilment [*sic*] of that System. ... with An Appendix. By Robert Mayo, M.D. Extra Edition. *Washington: Printed by J. & G. S. Gideon*. 1847. 4to, pp. xxiv, 440, 42. A., C., H.

MAYO. The Treasury Department and its Various Fiscal Bureaus, their Origin, Organization, and Practical Operations, illustrated; being A Supplement to the Synopsis of Treasury Instructions ... . By Robert Mayo, M.D. Extra Edition. *Washington: Printed by Wm. Q. Force*. 1847. 4to, pp. xvi, 262, viii, 8, 2 folded leaves. B., C., H. 47192

MAYO, *and* MOULTON (F). Army and Navy Pension Laws, and Bounty Land Laws of the United States, including sundry Resolutions of Congress, from 1776 to 1852: ... With an Appendix, containing the Opinions of Attorneys General of the United States ... . Compiled by Robert Mayo, M.D., and Ferdinand Moulton ... . *Washington: Printed by Jno. T. Towers*. 1852. 8vo, pp. (4), lii, 754. + Second Edition. *Baltimore: Lucas Brothers*. 1854. 8vo, pp. (10), lxxxvi, 836. C., H. 47193

MAYO (S. M.) The Trials of Samuel M. Mayo and William Love, for the Murder of David Whittemore. ... *Augusta*. 1807. 8vo, pp. 36. BA. 47194

MAYO (S. C. E.) Selections from the Writings of Mrs. Sarah C. Edgarton Mayo; With a Memoir, by her Husband [A. D. Mayo]. ... *Boston: A. Tompkins*. 1849. 12mo, pp. 432. Port.

MAYO (W.) A Discourse ... in ... Ludlow, Mass., on ... the Burial of Capt. Henry A. Hubbard, of Company I., 27th Reg. Mass. Vol. ... By ... Rev. Warren Mayo. *Springfield: Samuel Bowles & Company, Printers*. 1862. 8vo, pp. 12. H.

MAYO (W. S.) Romance Dust from the Historic Placer. By William Starbuck Mayo, M.D. *New-York: G. P. Putnam*. 1851. 12mo, pp. 284. C. 47197

Also: Kaloolah, or Journeyings to the Djébel Kumri. An Autobiography of Jonathan Romer. Edited by W. S. Mayo, M.D. Third Edition. *New York: George P. Putnam*. 1850. 12mo, pp. xii, 514. + Fifth Edition—Ninth Thousand. [*Ibid.*] 1850. 8vo, pp. 185. H. + *New York*. 1861. 12mo.

MAYORA (J.) Relacion de la Vida, y Virtudes del P. Antonio Herdoñana de la Compañia de Jesus, Zeloso Missionero por espocio de veinte y quatra años en el Apostolico Colegio de S. Gregorio de Mexico. Sacala à la Publica Luz el Padre Juan Mayora ... . *Mexico*. 1758. Sm. 4to, pp. 78. 47198

MAYORGA (M. de). Ordenanza de la Division de la Nobilisima Ciudad de Mexico en Quarteles, Creacion de los alcaldes de ellos, y reglas de su govierno, dada y mandada observar por el Exmo. Señor Don Martin de Mayorga, Virrey Governador, y Capitan General de esta Nueva-España ... . *Mexico*. 1782. Folio, pp. 41. Map. 47199

The map represents the city of Mexico in 1782, with the thirty-two divisions decreed by the Governor, M. de Mayorga. An explanatory leaf is prefixed.

... Maysville Road. Message from the President ... returning To the House ... the ... bill, entitled "An Act authorizing a subscription of stock in the Maysville, Washington, Paris, and Lexington Turnpike Road Company" ... . May 27, 1830. [n. p. n. d.] 8vo, pp. 22. B. 47200

MAZE (H.) La République des États-Unis d'Amérique. Par M. H. Maze. Sa fondation. *Paris: Degorce-Cadot*. 1869. 18mo, pp. 59. 47201

MAZATLAN. Informe á la Nacion. *See* Vol. IX. 34709.

MAZÈRES (——). Le nouveau Paysan du Danube, ou Doléances d'un citoyen à l'assemblée coloniale. Par M. Mazères, ainé ... . *Le Cap*. 1792. 8vo, pp. 40, or less. 47202

MAZÈRES. De l'utilité des colonies, des causes intérieures de la perte de Saint-Domingue, et des moyens d'en recouvrir la possession. ... *Paris*. 1814. 8vo. 47203

MAZERO (F.) El General Felipe Mazero al público. *Carácas*. 1850. 8vo, pp. 11. 47204

MAZOIS (E.) De Saint Domingue. Reflexions extraites d'un Mémoire sur le Commerce maritime et les Colonies. Par E. Mazois. *Paris*. 1824. 8vo. 47205

[MAZZEI (Filippo).] Recherches | Historiques et Politiques | Sur les États-Unis | de | L'Amérique Septentrionale, | Où l'on traite des établissemens des treize Colonies, | de leurs rapports & de leurs dissentions avec la | Grande-Bretagne, de leurs gouvernemens avant & | après la révolution, &c. | Par un Citoyen de Virginie. | Avec quatre Lettres d'un Bourgeois de New- | Heaven [*sic*] sur l'unité de la législation. | ... | *A Colle*, | *Et se trouve a Paris*, | *Chez Froullé* ... . 1788. 4 vols., 8vo, pp. (4), xvi, 383, (1); (4), 259; (4), 292; (4), 366. A., C. 47206

"M. Mazzei was assisted in this work by the celebrated Condorcet. The second and third volumes are occupied by criticisms on the works of Mably and Raynal. Mazzei was an Italian by birth, who migrated to America before the Revolution and established himself in Virginia, near Monticello, where he planted a vineyard. He was intimate with Mr. Jefferson, through whose influence he was sent on a mission to the Grand Duke of Tuscany."—RICH, I. 350.

MAZZEI. Memorie della Vita e delle Peregrinazioni del fiorentino Filippo Mazzei ... . *Lugano*. 1845. 2 vols., 8vo, pp. (4), 547; 352. 47207

With historical documents connected with his political missions, as agent of the United States of America and of Stanislaus King of Poland.

MAZZUCHELLI (Samuele). Memorie Istoriche ed Edificanti d' uno Missionario Apostolico dell' ordine dei Predicatori fra varie tribù di Selvaggi e fra i Cattolici e i Protestanti negli Stati Uniti d' America. *Milano: Boniardi-Pogliani*. 1844. 8vo, pp. 364. 47208

MDCXLVI. An Almanack for the Year of our Lord 1646. *Cambridge: Stephen Day*. 1646. 16mo, pp. 16. 47209

A conjectural title. The only known copy formed lot 699 in Mr. Brinley's catalogue. For the almanac for 1647, *see* Danforth, No. 18473. Danforth is also the author of the almanac for 1648 and 1649. A very early colonial imprint.

MDCL. | An | Almanack | for the Year of | our Lord | 1650 | Being the third after Leap year | and from the Creation 5582. | — | Calculated ... . *Printed at Cambridge.* | 1650. 16mo, pp. 16. 47210

MEACHAM (A. C.) A Compendious History of the Rise and Progress of the Methodist Church, both in Europe and America. By A. C. Meacham. *New York*. 1835. 12mo, pp. 503.

Also: Rise and Progress of Methodism in Canada. ... *Picton, C. W.* [18—.] 8vo, pp. 900.

MEACHAM (A. G.) Summer: A Poem. By A. G. Meacham. *Rushville Illinois*. 1856. 16mo, pp. 16. BA. 47212

MEACHAM (H. H.) The Empty Sleeve: or the Life and Hardships of Henry H. Meacham, in the Union Army. By Himself. *Springfield, Mass.* [n. d.] 12mo, pp. 24. + [*Ibid.*] 12mo, pp. 32. B., H. 47213

MEACHAM (J.) Speech of Hon. James Meacham ... June 9 and 10, 1851, on the ... Tariff. [*Washington*. 1852.] 8vo, pp. 7. BA. 47214

Also: Defense of the Clergy. Speech ... in the House of Representatives, May 17, 1854. [*Washington*. n. d.] 8vo, pp. 8. — Speech ... on Kansas Affairs ... . April 30, 1856. *Washington*. 1856. 8vo, pp. 8. — ... Speech, ... Feb. 15, 1854, Against the Nebraska and Kansas Territorial Bill ... . [*Washington*. 1854.] 8vo, pp. 7. BA.

[MEAD (Asa).] Memoirs of John Mooney Mead, who died at East Hartford, Conn. April 8, 1831 ... . *New-York: American Tract Society*. [1831.] 12mo, pp. 118. Portrait. H. 47215

MEAD. A Sermon, ... July 5, 1829. On Taking Leave of the First Church ... in Brunswick. By Asa Mead ... . *Brunswick, Me.: John W. Moore, Printer*. 1829. 12mo, pp. 12.

Also: ... A Sermon ... before the Hartford County Peace Society, ... in East Windsor, Sept. 30, 1830. ... *Hartford: Printed by Philemon Canfield*. 1830. 8vo, pp. 18. — A Sermon, Addressed to the Temperate. ... *Portland*. 1827. 8vo, pp. 20.

MEAD (C.) American Minstrel. Consisting of Poetical Essays on Various Subjects. By Charles Mead. *Philadelphia: J. Mortimer*. 1828. 12mo, Engraved Title, pp. 175. C. 47217

MEAD. Mississippian Scenery; A Poem, descriptive of the Interior of North-America. By Charles Mead. *Philadelphia: S. Potter and Co.* 1819. 12mo, pp. 113. 47218

MEAD (D. M.) A History of the Town of Greenwich, Fairfield County, Conn., with Many Important Statistics. By Daniel M. Mead ... . *New York: Baker & Godwin, Printers*. 1857. 12mo, pp. 7, 13–318. BA. 47219

MEAD (E. C.) Genealogical History of the Lee Family of Virginia and Maryland from ... 1300 to ... 1866 With Notes

and Illustrations Edited by Edward C. Mead *New York: Richardson and Company*. 1868. 4to, pp. 114. B. 47220

[MEAD (H.)] ... A Sermon, ... in ... South Hadley, on Thanksgiving ... Nov. 21, 1861. *Northampton: Printed by Trumbull & Gere*. 1861. 8vo, pp. 21. H. 47221

MEAD (H. E.) Kentucky and Tennessee. A Complete Guide to their Railroads, ... Rivers, Landings ... . By H. E. Mead. *Louisville: H. E. Mead*. 1867. 24mo, pp. 147. Maps.

[MEAD (H. H.)] The Soldier's Sacrifice. [n. p. n. d.] 8vo, pp. 4. 47223

A biographical sketch of Henry H. Mead, 10th Connecticut Volunteers.

MEAD (Joel K.) *See* National Register, Vol. XII.

MEAD (J.) An Essay on Currents at Sea; By which it appears, There is Reason to apprehend, that the Sea is not a Fluid in a State of Rest, except those Motions which are caused by the Impulse of Winds, and that known by the Name of Tides: And consequently, That this Earth is not of a uniform Density, according to the Supposition of Sir Isaac Newton; but that the Currents of the Gulph of Florida, also on the Coast of Brasil, and the Northern In-draught on this Western Coast, are Currents of Circulation, kept up by different Densities in this Earth, and its Motion round its Axis. By Joseph Mead. *London: J. Marshall*. M,DCC,LVII. 8vo, pp. (2), 48. 47224

MEAD (*Mrs.*) Mrs. Mead's School. Catalogue ... for ... 1845–6. *Richmond: Printed by H. K. Ellyson*. 1846. 12mo, pp. 22, (1). H. 47225

MEAD (P. B.) ... Treatise on American Grape Culture and Wine Making. By Peter B. Mead. ... *New-York: Harper & Brothers*. 1867. 8vo, pp. (2), 483. 47226

MEAD (S.) A Sermon, Delivered December 29, 1799; Occasioned by the Death of General George Washington, who Died December 14, 1799 ... . By Samuel Mead, A.M., Pastor of a Church in Danvers. *Printed by Joshua Cushing, Salem*. 1800. 8vo, pp. 24. 47227

MEAD. A Sermon on the War, delivered in Amesbury, August 20, 1812, ... Fast [Day]. By Samuel Mead. ... *Newburyport: E. W. Allen*. 1812. 8vo, pp. 18. B. 47228

MEAD (W.) Travels in North America. By Whitman Mead, A.M. *New-York: C. S. Van Winkle*. 1820. 8vo, pp. 160

[MEAD (William).] Letter to the American Colonization Society. *Washington*. 1819. 8vo, pp. 4. 47230

MEADE (George Gordon). Life and Public Services of Major-General Meade, the Hero of Gettysburg; and Commander of the Army of the Potomac. ... *Philadelphia: T. B. Peterson & Brothers*. [1864.] 12mo, pp. 17–80. BA. 47231

MEADE. Report of Major General Meade's Military Operations ... in the Third Military District and Dep't of the South, for ... 1868 ... . *Atlanta, Ga.* 1868. 8vo, pp. 105. 47232

MEADE. Report of the Survey of the North and Northwest Lakes. By Capt. George G. Meade ... . 1860. *Detroit*. 1861. 8vo, pp. 190. 6 Plates. B., C. 47233

Also: Major General Meade's Report on the Ashburn Murder. [n. p. 1868.] 12mo, pp. 130. H.

MEADE (Richard K.) Speech of Mr. Meade ... on the Bill to pay to the ... Representatives of Pacheco the Value of a Slave hired by the Government during the Seminole War ... . January 13th, 1849. [*Washington:*] *J. & G. S. Gideon, Printers*. [n. d.] 8vo, pp. 8. H. 47234

Also: Speech ... on ... Restricting Slavery in the Territories ... August, 1849. [n. p. n. d.] 8vo, pp. 13.

MEADE (R. W.) The Case of R. W. Meade, Esq. A Citizen of Pennsylvania, U. S. A. Seized and Imprisoned, 2d of May, 1816, by the Government of Spain, and still detained. *Cadiz, November 27th*, 1817. 8vo, pp. 25. 47235

Meade was United States Consul at Cadiz for many years.

MEADE. The Claim of Richard W. Meade upon the United States ... Concisely Stated; with ... the Documents ... . *Philadelphia: Printed by John Norvell*. 1825. 8vo, pp. 194. 47236

Also: An Address to the Roman Catholics of ... Philadelphia, in reply to Mr. Harold's Address. ... *Philadelphia*. 1823. 8vo, pp. 33. — Argument ... in the Case of R. W. Meade, Washington, D. C. February 28, 1867. By Caleb Cushing. ... *Washington, D. C.: McGill & Witherow, Printers*. 1867. 8vo, pp. 32. — Argument of Counsel in the Case of R. W. Meade, &c. ... [*Washington*. 1823.] 8vo, pp. 17. — Defence of Richard W. Meade, before the Court of Inquiry, convened at Washington City ... . Read March 30, 1857. *Washington*. 1857. 8vo, pp. 16. — Defense of Capt. Richard W. Meade, tried for the Loss of the ... Steamer San Jacinto ... January 1, 1865. Read by his Counsel John W. Ashmead, ... before a Naval Court-Martial ... Philadelphia. *New York: Press of Wynkoop & Hallenbeck*. 1866. 8vo, pp. 65. — Remarks on the Report of the ... Committee of the Senate to whom was referred the Memorial of

Richard W. Mead. [n. p. n. d] 8vo, pp. 26. — Statement of Facts. [Relating to] Richard W. Meade ... . [n. p. n. d.] 8vo, pp. 12. H.

MEADE (W.) An Experimental Enquiry into the Chemical Properties and Medicinal Qualities of the Principal Mineral Waters of Ballston and Saratoga, in the State of New-York. ... To which is added an Appendix, containing a Chemical Analysis of the Lebanon Spring in the State of New-York. By William Meade, M.D. ... *Philadelphia: Harrison Hall*. 1817. 8vo, pp. xv, 195. 2 Plates. BA., P. 47237

Also: Chemical Analysis of the Waters of New Lebanon, N. Y. ... *Burlington, N. J.* 1818. 12mo.

MEADE (W.) A Counter Statement of the Case of Bishop H. U. Onderdonk. In reply to one signed "A Member of the Church." By William Meade, D.D. *Philadelphia: Printed by T. K. and P. G. Collins*. 1854. 8vo, pp. 31. B. 47238

This elicited: "A Review of Bishop Meade's Counter Statement of the case of Bishop H. U. Onderdonk. By a Member of the Church." *Philadelphia*. 1854. 8vo.

MEADE. Statement of Bishop Meade, in reply to ... Bishop Onderdonk's Statement of Facts connected with his Trial. *New-York: Stanford and Swords*. 1845. 8vo, pp. 21. B. 47239

Also: Bishop Meade's Second Pamphlet in the case of Bishop H. U. Onderdonk. *Winchester: Printed by Senseney & Coffroth*. 1854. 8vo, pp. 24. B.

MEADE. Old Churches, Ministers and Families of Virginia. By Bishop Meade. *Philadelphia: J. B. Lippincott & Co.* 1857. 2 vols., 8vo, pp. 490; 495. Plates. B. + [*Ibid.*] 1861.

"Contains a fund of information extremely valuable and interesting to the genealogist."—WHITMORE.

MEADE. ... Scriptural Duties of Masters. ...' A Pastoral Address of the Rt. Rev. William Meade, D.D. ... A Sermon of the Rev. John C. Young, D.D. ... [n. p. n. d.] 12mo, pp. 76.

Also with another title-page, preceding it, which reads thus: "To all Evangelical Christians. The Suppressed Tract! and The Rejected Tract!" etc., with the imprint *New-York: John A. Gray, Printer*. 1858.

MEADE. Sermon, ... University of Virginia, ... May 24, 1829, on the ... Deaths of Nine Young Men, who fell Victims to the Diseases which visited that Place during ... 1828. By Rev. William Meade. *Charlottesville: F. Carr, and Co.* 1829 8vo, pp. 48. 47242

Also: A Brief Review of the Episcopal Church in Virginia, from its first establishment to the present time; Being part of an Address of the Right Rev. William Meade, D.D. ... May 22nd, 1845. *Richmond: Printed by Wm. Macfarlane*. 1845.

8vo, pp. 15.— ... A Charge to the Clergy of the Protestant Episcopal Church of Virginia. ... *Richmond: H. K. Ellyson, Printer.* 1850. 8vo, pp. 96.—Pastoral Letter to the ... Friends of the Protestant Episcopal Church in the Diocese of Virginia, on the Duty of affording Religious Instruction to those in Bondage. ... *Alexandria, D. C.* 1834. 8vo. + *Richmond.* 1854. 18mo.—A Sermon ... Convention of the Protestant Episcopal Church of Virginia, ... May the 15th, 1828. ... *Richmond: Printed by John Warrock.* 1828. 8vo, pp. 24.—A Sermon ... in ... Alexandria, ... 18th of Sept. 1825, ... on the ... Death of the Rev. Oliver Norris ... . *Alexandria: Printed by S. Snowden* ... 1825. 8vo, pp. 23, 6.—Sermon ... at the consecration of The Right Reverend Stephen Elliott, D.D. for the Diocese of Georgia, In ... Savannah, February 28th, 1841. ... *Washington: Printed by J. and G. S. Gideon.* 1841. 8vo, pp. 143.—The True Churchman. An Address ... to the Convention of the Protestant Episcopal Church of Va. ... May 21st. 1851. *Charlottesville: James Alexander, Printer.* 1851. 8vo, pp. 23.—Two Letters ... to the Board of Managers and Executive Committee of the Episcopal Sunday School Union. Second Edition. *Baltimore: Printed by John D. Toy.* 1847. 8vo, pp. 62. B.

MEADE, *and others.* Reply of Bishops Meade, M'Ilvaine, and Burgess to the Argument presented by the Committee of the Convention of the Diocese of New Jersey, to The Court of Bishops, in session at Burlington for the Trial of Bishop Doane. *Philadelphia: Printed by T. K. and P. G. Collins.* 1852. 8vo, pp. 136. P. 47243

MEADER (J. W.) The Merrimack River; its Source and its Tributaries. Embracing a History of Manufactures, and of the Towns along its Course; their Geography, Topography, and Products, with a Description of the Magnificent Natural Scenery about its Upper Waters. By J. W. Meader. *Boston: B. B. Russell.* 1869. 8vo, pp. 307. Map. C. 47244

[MEADS (Orlando).] What ought the Diocese to do? Considerations addressed to Churchmen of the Diocese of New-York. By a Layman. [n. p.] 1845. 8vo, pp. 15. B., S.

Also: An Address to ... Graduates of the Albany Medical College, ... December 26, 1854 ... . *Albany: J. Munsell.* 1855. 8vo, pp. 19. B.

MEADVILLE. A Catalogue of the Officers and Students of Meadville Academy ... 1855–6. *Meadville, Pa.* 1855. 12mo, pp. 24. 47246

Catalogue of the Meadville Theological School, for ... 1845–6. *Meadville: Printed by Lewis L. Lord.* 1845. 16mo, pp. 8. Continued. H. 47247

Also: Catalogue of the Library of the Meadville Theological School. *Meadville, Penn.* 1870. 8vo, pp. 134.—Report of the Treasurer of the Meadville Theological School. *Meadville: Clark, Printer.* 1864. 8vo, pp. 8. H.—A Report, by the Rev. Rufus P. Stebbins, to the Executive Committee of the American Unitarian Association. *Boston.* 1845. 12mo, pp. 16. S.

MEAGHER (T. F.) The Last Days of the 69th in Virginia. A Narrative ... . By Thomas Francis Meagher, Captain ... . *New York.* 1861. 8vo, pp. 15. Portrait. 47248

MEAGHER. Letters on our National Struggle. By Brig.-Gen. Thos. Francis Meagher. ... [*New York: Loyal Publication Society.* 1863.] 8vo, pp. 15. 47249

Meaning of the Terms in the Constitution "No State shall pass any Ex post Facto Laws," &c. [n. p. n. d.] 8vo. W.

MEANS (J. H.) Dorchester, Past and Present. A Sermon ... in the Second Church, Dorchester, December 26, 1869. By Rev. James H. Means. *Boston: Moses H. Sargent.* 1870. 8vo, pp. 24. H. 47251

MEANS. An Historical Discourse on occasion of the Fiftieth Anniversary of the ... Second Church, Dorchester, ... January 3, 1858. By Rev. James Howard Means ... . *Boston: Press of T. R. Marvin & Son.* 1858. 8vo, pp. 32. 47252

MEANS. The Power of the Past. A Sermon, ... before the ... Artillery Company, on their CCXIX. Anniversary, ... 1857. By Rev. James H. Means ... . *Boston: Press of T. R. Marvin & Son.* 1857. 8vo, pp. 63. H. 47253

MEANS. Sermons preached in ... Dorchester, By James H. Means. *Boston: Printed by Alfred Mudge and Son.* 1865. 8vo, pp. 122, (1). B. 47254

Also: Address at the Funeral of Mrs. Elizabeth Thompson ... November 26, 1867. ... *Boston: Gould and Lincoln.* 1867. 8vo, pp. 15.—Duties of Parents in aid of the Teacher: A Lecture ... . *Boston.* 1852. 12mo. S.— ... A Sermon ... Death of Mrs. Mary Codman ... April 12, 1857. ... *Boston: Press of T. R. Marvin.* 1857. 8vo, pp. 36.—Sermon ... in ... Dorchester, after the Death of Lieutenant William R. Porter ... . September 7, 1862. ... *Boston: T. R. Marvin & Son.* 1862. 8vo, pp. 21.

MEANS (John O.) ... A Discourse at the Funeral of Lieut. Edgar M. Newcomb, of the Mass. 19th Regm't, ... December 27, By Rev. J. O. Means ... . *Boston: Printed by Alfred Mudge & Son.* 1863. 12mo, pp. 15. H. 47255

Also: Soldiers and their Mothers. ... *American Tract Society.* [n. d.] 18mo, pp. 32.

MEANWELL (——) Meanwell's Town and Country Almanack for 1774. *New York.* 1774. 12mo. 47256

MEARES (J.) An Answer to Mr. George Dixon, late Commander of the Queen Charlotte, in the service of Messrs. Etches and Company; By John Meares, Esq. In which the Remarks

of Mr. Dixon on the Voyages to the North West Coast of America, &c., lately published, are fully Considered and Refuted. *London: Printed ... by J. Walter.* M.DCC.XCI. 4to, pp. 32. H.

See Dixon (G.), Vol. v., No. 20363, for a reply.

MEARES. Authentic Copy of the Memorial to ... William Wyndham Grenville, one of his Majesty's Principal Secretaries of State. By Lieutenant John Meares, ... dated 30th April 1790, and presented to the House of Commons, May 13, 1790, containing every particular respecting the Capture of the Vessels in Nootka Sound. *London: J. Debrett.* 1760 [*i. e.* 1790]. 8vo, pp. 65. J.C.B. + *London.* 1810. 8vo. C. 47258

See "M. Rev.," XI. 458.

MEARES. Mr. Meares' Memorial, dated 30th April 1790. [14 inclosures.] To the Right Honourable William Wyndham Grenville ... . [*London.* 1790.] Folio, pp. 28. J.C.B. 47259

MEARES. Voyages made in the Years 1788 and 1789, from China to the North West Coast of America. To which are prefixed, an Introductory Narrative of A Voyage performed in 1786, from Bengal, in the Ship Nootka; Observations on the Probable Existence of a North West Passage; and some account of the Trade between the North West Coast of America and China; and the Latter Country and Great Britain. By John Meares, Esq. *London: Printed by J. Walter.* M.DCC.XC. 4to, pp. viii, (12), xcv, (1), 372, Appendix, (108). 3 Maps, and 23 Plates by Stothard. A., J.C.B., P., W. 47260

There are copies on large paper. The voyages of Meares are an important link in the chain of American discovery, of which he was one of the pioneers. The English claim to Oregon depended mainly on his discoveries, and the seizure of his ships by the Spaniards, led to the convention by which the Spanish claims to any Northern territory were finally disallowed. *See* Dixon (G.), Vol. v., Nos. 20361 and 20363; *also* "M. Rev.," IV. 182, 249.

MEARES. Voyages made in ... 1788 and 1789 ... . With an Introductory Narrative of A Voyage performed in 1786 ... . To which are annexed, Observations on the Probable Existence of a North West Passage ... . By John Meares, Esq. *London: Printed by J. Walter.* 1791. 2 vols., 8vo, pp. xii, lxxii, 363; (4), 332, (63). Portrait, 9 Maps, and 4 Plates. BA., C. 47261

In this edition some of the plates from the quarto edition are omitted.

MEARES. Voyages de la Chine à la Côte du Nord-Ouest D'Amérique, faits dans les années 1788 et 1789; Précédés de la relation d'un autre voyage exécuté en 1786 sur le vaisseau le

Nootka, parti du Bengale; D'un Recueil d'Observations sur la Probabilité d'un Passage Nord-Ouest; Et d'un Traité abrégé du Commerce entre la Côte Nord-Ouest et la Chine ... . Par le Capitaine J. Meares ... . Traduits de l'Anglois Par J. B. L. J. Billecoq ... . *Paris, Chez F. Buisson, An 3e de la République.* [1794.] 3 vols., 8vo, pp. xxiv, 391; (4), 386; (4), 371. Atlas in 4to. A., H., S. 47262

MEARES. Viaggi dalla China alla Costa Nord Ouest d'America fatti negli Anni 1788 e 1789 ... . *Napoli.* 1796. 4 vols., 8vo. Maps and Plates. 47263

MEARES. Reisen nach der Nordwestküste von Amerika, in den Jahren 1786 bis 1789. Aus dem Englischen übersetzt und mit Anmerkungen erläutert von Georg Forster. Nebst einer Abhandlung von eben demselben über die Nordwestküste von Amerika, und den dortigen Pelzhandel. *Berlin: Voss.* 1796. 4to, pp. (2), 130, 302. 2 Maps and 7 Plates. C. 47264

See also our Nos. 20367 and 25126. The following is a Swedish version:

MEARES. Tvänne Resor fran Ostindien till Americas nordvästra kust ären 1786, 1788 och 1789. Sammandrag uter Engelska Originalet Tryckt i. *Stockholm: J. S. Ekmanson.* 1797. 12mo, pp. (10), 404. J.C.B. 47265

MEASE (J.) Description of ... Medals struck in relation to Important Events in North America, before and since the Declaration of Independence by the United States. By James Mease, M.D. ... *New-York: Printed by James Seymour.* 1821. 8vo, pp. 20. B., C., N. + *Boston.* 1834. 8vo. 47266

See New York Historical Society's "Collections," Vol. III., 1st Series.

MEASE. A Geological Account of the United States; comprehending a Short Description of their Animal, Vegetable, and Mineral Productions, Antiquities and Curiosities. By James Mease, M.D. ... *Philadelphia: Birch & Small.* 1807. 16mo, pp. (8), 496, xiv. 5 Plates. BA., C., P. 47267

MEASE. The Picture of Philadelphia, giving an account of its Origin, Increase and Improvements ... . With a compendious View of its Societies, Literary, Benevolent, Patriotic, & Religious. Its Police—the Public Buildings—the Prison and Penitentiary System—Institutions, Monied and Civil—Museum. By James Mease, M.D. *Philadelphia: B. & T. Kite.* 1811. 12mo, pp. xii, 376. Plate. BA. 47268

MEASE. Picture of Philadelphia for 1824, containing the "Picture of Philadelphia for 1811, By James Mease, M.D." With all its Improvements since ... . By Thomas Wilson. *Philadelphia: T. Town.* 1823. 12mo, pp. 96, xii, 358. 2 Plates. + Continued by Thomas Porter. *Philadelphia.* 1831. 2 vols., 12mo, pp. xii, 358; viii, 128. S. 47269

MEASE. A Reply to the Criticisms by J. N. Barker, on the Historical Facts in the Picture of Philadelphia. By James Mease, M.D. ... *Philadelphia: Clark & Raser, Printers.* 1828. 8vo, pp. 18. BA., P., W. 47270

Also: 'An Address on the Progress of Agriculture, ... January 14th, 1817. [n. p.] 1817. 8vo, pp. 45.—Address on ... Establishing a Pattern Farm in the Vicinity of Philadelphia: ... *Philadelphia.* 1818. 8vo, pp. 14.—Letter ... transmitting a Treatise on the Rearing of Silkworms; by Mr. De Hazzi ... . *Washington.* 1828. 8vo, pp. 108. Plates.—Life of Robert Morris. ... [n. p. n. d.] 8vo.—Observations on the Penitentiary System, and Penal Code of Pennsylvania: ... . *Philadelphia: Clark & Raser, Printers.* 1828. 8vo, pp. vi, 95.—On the Utility of Public Loan Offices and Savings Funds, established by City Authorities. ... [n. p. 1836.] 8vo, pp. 6.—On William Penn's Treaty with the Indians. ... [*Philadelphia.* 1836.] 8vo, pp. 4. P.

MEASON (C. F. H.) Narrative of the Massacre of Counterfeiters, Gamblers, etc., in Coahoma Co., Mississippi. By C. F. H. Meason. [n. p.] 1841. 12mo. 47271

Measures adopted in Boston, Massachusetts, for the Relief of the Suffering Scotch and Irish. *Boston, N. E.* 1847. 8vo, pp. 23

Measures, Not Men. By a Citizen of New York. Illustrated by some Remarks on the Public Conduct and Character of John C. Calhoun. *New York.* 1833. 8vo, pp. 49. 47273

A Mechanic. America's Offering. A Recitative Ode on Events of Revolutionary Times. Dedicated to the American People. By a Mechanic. In Five Cantos, with Historical Notes. *Philadelphia.* 1849. 8vo. 47274

A Mechanic. "Common Sense" especially addressed to the most suffering portion of our Fellow-Citizens, The "Bone and Sinew" of our Country, the Mechanics. By a Mechanic. *Philadelphia: Charles Bell.* 1837. 8vo, pp. 31. 47275

The Mechanick's Address to the Farmer: being a short Reply to some of the Layman's Remarks on the Eighteen Presbyterian Ministers Letter to the Archbishop. *Philadelphia: Printed by Andrew Steuart.* 1761. 12mo, pp. 14. P. 47276

This elicited the following: A Bridle for the Ass; being a second Letter to the Congregations of the Eighteen Presbyterians (or New Light Ministers) who wrote the late

contradictory Letter to the Archbishop of Canterbury. By an old Covenanting and true Presbyterian Layman. *Philadelphia.* 1767. 12mo, pp. 28.—Conduct of Presbyterian Ministers; in Reference to a Letter addressed to the Archbishop of Canterbury. *Philadelphia.* 1767. 12mo, pp. 19.—Letter of a Farmer on the Above. *Philadelphia.* 1767. 12mo.

Mechanics & Agricultural Fair Association of Louisiana. Report of their Fourth Grand State Fair, held ... April 23, 1870. *New Orleans: Steel & Company ... Printers.* 1870. 8vo, pp. 64, ii. H. 47277

Mechanics' and Farmers' Magazine of Useful Knowledge. Conducted by Sargeant and Halsey. *New York.* 1830. 2 vols., 8vo. 47278

Mechanics' and Gardeners' Mutual Education, and Manual Labour Association, at Woodville, Long Island. *New-York: Printed by P. Miller.* 1841. 8vo, pp. 7. Plates. 47279

The Mechanics' and Inventors' Pocket Almanac for 1861. *New York: Fowler and Wells.* [n. d.] 18mo, pp. 30. H. 47280

Mechanics' Magazine. *New York.* 1825–6. 2 vols., 8vo.

The Mechanics' Magazine, and Journal of Public ... Improvement; ... Vol. I. *Boston: Samuel N. Dickinson.* 1830. 8vo, pp. 384. Diagrams. B. 47282

Mechanic's Magazine and Register of Inventions and Improvements. *New York.* 1833. 8vo. 47283

Edited by J. Knight, D. K. Minor, and G. C. Schaeffer. Eight or more volumes published.

Mechanics' Mirror. *Albany: J. Munsell.* 1846. 8vo.

MECHLIN (A. H.), *and* WINDER (C. M.) A General Register of the Navy and Marine Corps of the United States, alphabetically arranged ... . With an Index. Compiled from the Official Records of the Navy Department, ... By Mechlin & Winder, Attorneys and Agents ... . *Washington: C. Alexander, Printer.* 1848. 8vo, pp. (4), x, 539. B., C., H., M. 47285

MECKLENBURG CO., *N. C.* The Declaration of Independence by the Citizens of Mecklenburg County on the twentieth day of May, 1775, with accompanying Documents, and the Proceedings of the Cumberland Association. ... *Raleigh.* 1831. 8vo, pp. 32.

Corrected title of our No. 19178.

Documents shewing that Mecklenburg County, North-Carolina, declared her Independence of Great-Britain, May 20, 1775. ... *Raleigh: Printed by J. Gales & Son.* 1822. 8vo, pp. 15.

MECKLENBURG CO., *Va.* ... Memorial of Inhabitants of Mecklenburg County, ... Virginia, against an Increase of Duty on Imported Goods. January 2, 1828. ... *Washington: Printed by Gales & Seaton.* 1828. 8vo, pp. 10. H. 47288

Act of Incorporation and Report of the Mecklenburgh Gold Mining Company. [n. p.] 1833. 8vo. S. 47289

[MECORNEY (W.)] ... Address before the Grand Division of Sons of Temperance of Massachusetts, January 21, 1863. [n. p. n. d.] 8vo, pp. 7, (1). H. 47290

MED. Report of the Boston Anti-Slavery Society; being a Concise History of the Cases of the Slave Child, Med, and of the Women demanded as Slaves of the Supreme Court of Massachusetts. *Boston: Isaac Knapp.* 1836. 12mo, pp. 90. 47291

See also Vol. I., No. 2490.

La Médaille de la Liberté, avec les Lettres de Folcon, Edgar Quinet, Victor Hugo, Schœler, Louis Blanc, et la Vie d'Abraham Lincoln. *Paris: A. Lacroix.* 1866. 8vo. 47292

MEDARY (S.) The New Constitution [of Ohio]. By Samuel Medary. *Columbus.* 1849. Sm. folio, pp. 408. C. 47293

MEDBERY (J. K.) Men and Mysteries of Wall Street. By James K. Medbery. ... *Boston: Fields, Osgood & Co.* 1870. 12mo, pp. iv, (2), 344. 6 Plates. C. 47294

MEDBERY (Rebecca B.) Memoir of Mrs. Sarah Emily York, formerly Miss S. E. Waldo; ... By Mrs. R. B. Medbery ... . *Boston: Phillips, Sampson and Company.* 1853. 12mo, pp. xii, 420. Portrait. H. 47295

Also: Memoir of William G. Crocker, late Missionary in West Africa among the Bassas ... . *Boston.* 1848. 18mo, pp. 300. Portrait.

Mededeelingen betreffende den Galveston Houston en Henderson spoorweg. *Amsterdam: M. Schooneveld en Zoon.* 1867. 8vo, pp. 13. 47296

MEDEIROS (F. L. d'A.) Curiosidades Brasileiras por F. L. d'Abreu Medeiros. *Rio de Janeiro.* 1864. 2 vols., 8vo, pp. 226; 230. 47297

MEDFIELD, MASS. Annual Report of the School Committee ... 1860. *Dedham: Printed by John Cox, Jr.* 1860. 8vo, pp. 16. Continued. H. 47298

Also: Report of the Receipts and Expenditures ... for ... 1867. [n. p. n. d.] 8vo, pp. 8.

MEDFIELD LIBRARY. Constitution and Catalogue of Books of the Medfield Library. *Dedham.* 1816. 8vo, pp. 24. 47299

MEDFORD (M.) Details of the Commercial Transactions of Michael Medford in London, with John Lisle, Jun., of Philadelphia. *London.* 1807. 8vo, pp. 77. 47300

MEDFORD (M.) Oil without Vinegar, and Dignity without Pride: or, British, American, and West-India Interests considered. By Macall Medford, Esq. *London.* 1807. 8vo, pp. 87. + The Second Edition. With a Preface, and Additions. ... *London: W. J. and J. Richardson.* 1807. 8vo, pp. (2), xv, (1), 110, (14). BA. 47301

For an "Answer," *see* "A True Picture." Also: Observations on European Courts, and Outlines of their Politics. ... *London and Philadelphia.* 1807. 8vo, pp. 52. S.

MEDFORD, *Mass.* Catalogue of the Public Library of ... Medford. 1867. *Boston: W. F. Brown & Co., Printers.* [n. d.] 12mo, pp. 89. Continued. B. 47302

Also: Catalogue of ... the Medford Tufts Library. 1856. *Boston: Printed by James M. Usher.* 1856. 12mo, pp. 36.—List of Town, County, and State Taxes ... for ... 1862. ... With a Statement of the Town ... Expenses, from ... 1862, to ... 1863 ... . *Boston: Printed by Bazin & Chandler.* 1863. 8vo, pp. 119, (1). Contin'd.—Report of the Auditing Committee, to the Committee of Thirteen. [n. p. n. d.] 8vo, pp. 8. H.—Report of the School Committee ... . *Boston: Printed by Bazin & Chandler.* 1863. 8vo, pp. 24. Continued. H.—Statement of ... Expenses, from ... 1852, to ... 1853, ... &c. *Boston: C. C. P. Moody, Printer.* 1853. 8vo, pp. 46, 18. *See* Tufts College.

Mediation Position of France. *See* [Jewett (W. C.)], 36119.

The Mediator between North and South; or, The Seven Pointers of the North Star. Thoughts of an American in the Wilderness. Sixth Edition, revised. *Baltimore.* 1862. 8vo, pp. 4. + *Baltimore: Chas. H. Anderson.* 1863. 8vo, pp. 11.

The Medical Adviser. Vol. I. [n. p. 1828.] 8vo. H.

... The Medical and Agricultural Register, for the Years 1806 and 1807. ... Edited by Daniel Adams ... . *Boston: Printed by Manning & Loring.* [n. d.] 8vo, pp. (2), 378, (6). BA. 47305

Medical and Philosophical Journal and Review. *New York.* 1809–11. 3 vols., 8vo. W. 47306

The Medical and Surgical History of the War of the Rebellion. [1861–65.] Prepared under the Direction of Surgeon General Joseph K. Barnes ... . *Washington: Government Printing Office.* 1870. 4to, pp. clv, 650, xiv. 13 Plates. C. 47307

Medical and Surgical Journal; Edited by James Ryan. ... 1858. *Philadelphia.* 1858. 8vo. 47308

The Medical and Surgical Register ... . *New York.* 1818–20. 8vo, pp. 406. 47309

... The Medical and Surgical Reporter. Edited by S. W. Butler, M.D. ... January, 1856. Vol. IX. No. I. *Burlington, N. J.: S. W. Butler.* 1856. 8vo. Continued. + *Philadelphia: Crissy & Markley, Printers.* 1859. Vol. I. 8vo, pp. 463. Continued. B., H. 47310

A Medical Apocalypse, being Revelations and Expositions of the New York Academy of Medicine. *New York.* 1850. 8vo.

Transactions of the Medical Association of Southern Central New York, ... Ithaca, ... 1847. *Ithaca.* 1847. 8vo. Cont'd.

... The Medical Chronicle, or, Montreal Monthly Journal of Medicine & Surgery. Edited by Wm. Wright, M.D., & D. C. MacCallum, M.D. Vol. I. ... 1853. *Montreal: Printed ... by Moore, Owler & Stevenson.* 1853. 8vo. Continued. H. 47313

The Medical Companion and Temperance Advocate, Edited ... by B. F. C. Brooks and George Wyche. ... *Yazoo City, Miss.* [1853.] 8vo. Continued. H. 47314

The Medical Counselor: ... R. Hills, M.D., Editor ... . *Columbus, Ohio.* [1856.] 8vo. Continued. H. 47315

The Medical Examiner. ... Edited by J. B. Biddle, M.D. [and others]. *Philadelphia: For the Editors.* MDCCCXXXVIII. 8vo, pp. iv, 424. Plate. Continued. B. 47316

The Medical Examiner. ... *Philadelphia.* 1845–56. 8vo. S.

The Medical Gazette. ... Vol. I. ... *New York: A. Simpson & Co.* 1867. 4to. Continued. H. 47318

Medical Intelligencer, from April 29, 1823, to May 9, 1826. Edited by J. V. C. Smith. *Boston.* 1823–6. 3 vols., 4to. W.

... The Medical Investigator ... . *Chicago.* [1863.] 8vo. Continued. 47320

The Medical Magazine. Conducted by A. L. Peirson, J. B. Flint ... . Vol. I. *Boston: Allen & Ticknor.* 1833. 8vo, pp. iv, 760. 2 Plates. Continued. B. 47321

The Medical News. ... *Philadelphia.* 1843–58. 16 vols., 8vo.

The Medical Record. A Semi-Monthly Journal ... . Edited by George F. Shrady, M.D. ... *New York: William Wood & Company.* [1867.] 8vo, pp. (2), 591. Continued. BA. 47323

The Medical Register of the City of New York and Vicinity, for the Year commencing June 1, 1867. ... By John Shrady, M.D., Editor. *New York: New York Printing Company.* 1867. 16mo. Continued. 47324

The Medical Reporter. A Quarterly Journal, ... of the Chester and Delaware County Medical Societies. *Westchester, Pa.: H. S. Evans.* [1853–56.] 3 vols., 8vo. C. 47325

... The Medical Reporter, a semi-monthly record ... . Edited by J. S. B. Alleyne, M.D., and O. F. Potter, M.D. July 1, 1866. *Saint Louis: P. M. Pinckard.* 1866. 8vo. Continued. H.

The Medical Repository. ... *New-York: Printed by T. & J. Swords.* 1797. 8vo, pp. 584. BA. 47327

Continued to 1824. Of the first hexade (6 vols.) there were three editions of Vols. I. and II., dated 1797, 1800 and 1804. After Vol. III. the name of E. H. Smith is omitted; after Vol. IV. the title reads "Medical Repository and Review." The second hexade consists of six and the third of nine volumes. A new series was commenced in 1813, which was conducted at various times by S. L. Mitchill, F. Pascalis, J. P. Manley, and C. Drake. Besides taking into review all the publications of the day on physic, surgery, chemistry and natural history, it embraces civil history, politics, topography, voyages and travels, more particularly those that relate to America.

The Medical Review, and Analectic Journal. ... Conducted by John Eberle, M.D. ... and George M'Clellan, M.D. ... *Philadelphia: A. Sherman.* 1824–26. 3 vols., 8vo, pp. 631, (1); 412; (2), 436, (2). Plates. 47328

Continued in Vol. II. as "American Medical Review."

The Medical World: ... By J. V. C. Smith, M.D. and Edward Sutton Smith, M.D. *Boston: Damrell & Moore* ... . 1857. 2 vols., 4to, pp. (2), iv 684; (6), 288. 47329

The Medicinal Waters of Saratoga. *New-York: A. B. & D. Sands.* 1841. 18mo, pp. 8. 47330

MEDICUS (F. C.) Ueber nordamerikanische Bäume und Sträucher, als Gegenstände der deutschen Forstwirthschaft und der schönen Gartenkunst. Von Fried. Cas. Medicus. *Manheim.* 1792. 8vo, pp. 96. 47331

MEDILL (W.) Letter from William Medill to the Senecas. [n. p. 1848.] 8vo, pp. 8. 47332

MEDILL. Speech ... April 5, 1842, on the Appropriation Bill. *Washington.* 1842. 8vo. 47333

In relation to the salary of Gov. Doty, of Wisconsin.

MEDINA (A. de) Sermon | predicado en | el Castillo de San Felipe | del Puerto del Callao, a su Dedicacion y benedi- | cion; estando descubierto el Santissimo Sacra- | mento, y en presencia de todo el | Presidio. | Por el P. F. Antonio de Medina del Orden | de Predicadores, ... Mayo de 1625. años. | A Don Fernando de Castro Cavallero | del Abito de Santiago, y Teniente de Capitan General, por el | Excellentissimo Señor Marques de Guadalcaçar. | Virrey destos Reynos del Pirù. | Con licencia. | *Impresso en Lima; por Geronymo de Contreras.* | *Ano de* 1625. | 4to, 18 leaves. 47334

MEDINA (A. de) Exposicion al Soberano Congreso Mexicano sobre el Estadado de la Hacienda Pública y Conducta del Ciudano Ant. de Medina ... . *Mexico.* 1823. 4to. 47335

MEDINA (B. de). Chrónica de la Santa Provincia de San Diego de Mexico, de Religiosos Descalços de N. S. P. S. Francisco en la Nueva España. Vidas de Illustres y Venerables Varones, que la han edificando con excelentes virtudes. Escrivelas y consagralas al glorioso San Diego de Alcala, Patron y tutelar de la misma provincia, Fr. Balthasar de Medina, Natural de la Ciudad de Mexico ... . *En Mexico, por Iuan de Ribero, Año de* 1682. Folio, Engraved Title, 21 leaves, Text, 259 leaves, Table, 9 leaves. Map. C. 47336

A volume of extreme rarity. The map at fol. 230 is the earliest specimen of copperplate engraving done in Mexico. *See* Brasseur de Bourbourg "Bibliothèque," p. 98.

MEDINA. Vida, Martyrio, y Beatificacion del Invicto Proto-Martyr de el Japon San Felipe de Jesus, Patron de Mexico, su Patria. Segunda Impression. *Madrid: Herederos de la Viuda de J. G. Infanzon.* 1751. 4to, pp. (28), 176. Portrait. C. 47337

MEDINA (Bernardo de). Vida de F. Martin de Porras. *Lima.* 1663. 4to. 47338

Title from Ternaux, No. 810.

MEDINA (F.) Vida y Milagros del glorioso S. Nicolas Tolentino, en lengua mexicana, por el P. Fr. Francisco de Medina, Predicador, y Guardian del Convento de N. P. S. Francisco de la Villa de Carrion. [*Mexico.* 1604?] 8vo, 1 leaf, 80 leaves.

MEDINA (F. G. de). La Miscelanea, ó coleccion de macsimas y pensamientos critico-politico-morales, por el Ciudadano Francisco G. de Medina. *Jalapa.* 1836. Sm. 8vo, pp. (4), 36.

MEDINA RINCON (J. de). Doctrinalis fidei in Mechvacanensivm indorvm lingva: aeditus ab admodvm Reverendo Patre fratre Ioanne Metinensi, Bethico, Augustiniani ordinis & Priore conuentus Cuisensis. Tomus Primus. Ad Illustrissimum ... D. Dominum Fratrem Ioannem à Medina Rinconeum Michuacanensem Episcopum, eiusdē instituti. Accessere sermones qvattuor. ... *Mexici. Cum licencia. In ædibus Antonij Ricardi Typographi. ... Anno* 1577. Folio. 47341

MEDINA RINCON. Thesoro Spiritual de Pobres, in Lengua Michuacan ... . *Mexico: Antonio Spinosa.* 1575. 4to. 47342

An extremely rare and early specimen of Mexican typography.

MEDINA (J. M.) Juycio de Cometas, determinado por los dos, que prometen Ubisiton para el año de 58 y Christiani Uvolfi para el presente de 54 por Octubre, escrito à un Amigo por el Br. Joseph Mariano Medina. [Colophon:] *Con licencia en Puebla, en la Imprenta de la Viuda de Miguel Ortega, y Bonilla. Año de* 1754. 4to, 4 leaves. 47343

MEDINA (P. de). Arte de nauegar | en que se contienen todas las Reglas, Declara- | ciones, Secretos, y Auisos, q̄ a la buena nauegaciō son necessarios, y se deuē saber, hecha por | el maestro Pedro de Medina. Dirigida al sere- | nissimo y muy esclarescido señor, don Phelipe | principe de España, y delas dos Sicilias. &c. | Con preuilegio imperial. | [Colophon:] ... *Valladolid ... Im- | primio se enla dicha villa, en casa de Francisco fernan- | dez de Cordoua impressor, junto a las escuelas mayo- | res: Acabo se primero dia del mes de Octubre. Año del | nascimiento de nuestro señor Jesu christo, de mil y qui- | nientos y quarenta y cinco años.* Folio, 5 leaves, Text, C leaves, Colophon, 1 leaf. Map. J.C.B., H. 47344

MEDINA. L'Art de Navigeur de Maistre Pierre de Medine Espaignol, contenant toutes les Reigles Secrets, & enseignements necessaires à la bonne Navigation. Traduict de Castillan en Françoys, auec augmentation & illustration de plusieurs figures &

annotations, par Nicolas de Nicolai du Dauphinè Geographe du tres Chrestien Roy Henri II. *A Lyon, chez Guillaume Roville.* 1554. Folio, Engraved Title, 5 leaves, Text, 115 leaves. C.

Brunet quotes an edition 1553. Other editions: *Rouen, J. Crevel,* 1573, 4to; *Lyon, G. Roville,* 1569; + [*Ibid.*] 1576, and *A Rouen, chez David Ferrand,* MDCXXXIII.

MEDINA. L'Arte del | Navegar, | In laqval si contengono lere | gole, dechiaration, secreti, & auisi, alla bona nauegation ne- | cessarij. Composta per l'Eccel. Dottor M. Pietro da Me- | dina, & tradotta de lingua Spagnola in volgar Italia- | no, a beneficio, & vtilita de ciascadum Nauigante. | *In Vinetia, ad instantia di Gionbattista Pedrezano, libraro | al segno della Torre, à pie del ponte di Rialto.* | *Con Priuilegio del Illustriss. Senato Veneto. Per anni* XV. | M D LV. | [Colophon:] *In Vinetia. Nella Stamparia de Aurelio Pincio, de* MDLIIII. 4to, 12 leaves, Text, cxxxvii leaves. Map.

MEDINA. The Arte of Navigation, translated out of Spanish into English by John Frampton. *London.* 1581. Folio. + *London: Thomas Dawson.* 1595. 4to. 47347

"The author was the official examiner of pilots for the Indies, in the service of Spain, and acquired high repute as a cosmographer and historian."—HARRISSE. There is also a German version by M. Coignet, 1576.

MEDINA. Libro de grandezas y cosas memora | bles de España, Agora de nuevo fecho y copilado por el Maestro Pedro | de Medina vezino de Seuilla. Dirigido al Serenissimo y muy esclarecido | Señor. Don Filipe Principe de España &c. Nuestro Señor. | M. D. xlviij. Folio, 8 leaves, Text, clxxxij leaves. Map.

Pinelo says, "Pedro de Medina, en las Grandeças de España, trae algunas cosas de el Decubrimiento de Colon;" this circumstance will partly account for the extreme scarcity of this work, even in Spain. It is a curious work and contains many interesting particulars relating to the discoveries by Columbus. *See* [Harrisse] "Bib. Am. Vet.," No. 281, and his "Additions," No. 165.

MEDINA (S. de) The Decree in the Case of Solomon De Medina, et al, in London, and Roderigo Pacheco, Jacob de Lara, and Manual de Costa, bearers of their orders, Complainants; against Rene Het, and the Executors of Andrew Fresneau, deceased, Defendants, in Cancellaria Nova Eborac. *New York.* 1728. Folio, pp. 44. N., W. 47349

MEDINA ACADEMY. Constitution of the Burroughsian Lyceum ... . *Buffalo.* 1853. 8vo. S. 47350

MEDINILLA (M. E. de) Relacion de la feliz entrada en Mexico del marques de Villena, ce 28 de agosto de 1640, y las fiestas

de toro, cañas y alcancias, por D. Maria Estrada de Medinilla. *Mexico.* 1641. 4to. 47351

Mediterranean and Oriental Steam Navigation Company. ... Testimony ... on the Causes of the Decadence of American Tonnage, House of Representatives. [n. p. 1870.] 8vo, pp. 22.

Also: ... American Commerce—Southern Emigration. ... [n. p. n. d.] 8vo, pp. 8.

Medizinische und chirurgische Bemerkungen über das Klima, die Lebensweise und Krankheiten der Einwohner der holländischen Kolonie Rio-Essequebo. *Frankfurt.* 1796. 8vo. 47353

MEDLEY (J.) The Sermon at the Consecration of Thomas Frederick Davis, D.D., and Thomas Atkinson, D.D., ... in St. John's Chapel, New York, ... October 17, 1853, By John Medley, Lord Bishop of Fredericton. ... *New-York: Daniel Dana, Jr.* MDCCCLIII. 8vo, pp. 25. H. 47354

Also: A Charge delivered in ... Fredericton, ... at the Second Triennial Visitation, ... *Saint John, N. B.: Printed by W. L. Avery.* 1850. 8vo, pp. 63.—Two Ordination Sermons ... By the Lord Bishop of Fredericton. *Fredericton: John Simpson, Printer.* 1846. 8vo, pp. 23. *See also* No. 25697.

The Medley: a Monthly Periodical conducted by an Association of the Students of Yale College. ... Vol. I., No. I. *New Haven.* 1833. 8vo. H. 47355

The Medley, or Monthly Miscellany. *Printed by Daniel Bradford, Lexington, Ky.* [1801.] 12mo. Continued. 47356

Contains an ode by Thomas Paine.

MEDRANO (P. de). Gazophylacium Divinæ Dilectionis. Petra Pretiosior Coeli, Soli, et Sali, ... Por Petro de Medrano, Soc. Jesu. Peruano, Limensi. *Matriti.* 1720. 4to. 47357

MEDRANO (S. F. de). Breve Descripcion del Mundo, y sus partes, ò Guia Geographica, y Hydrographica ... Por el Capitan D. Sebastian Fernandez de Medrano ... . *En Brusselas.* 1686. 18mo, pp. xxx, 412. 5 Plates. S. 47358

MEDRANO. Breve | descripcion del | Mundo | o Guia Geographica | de Medrano. | Lo mas principal de ella en Verso. | Dirigida | A la Catholica Magestad del Rey Nuestro Señor | Don Carlos Segundo, | Monarcha de las Españas. | Debajo | De la protecion del Excelentissimo Señor | Marques de Jodar. | *En Brusselas,* | *En casa de Lamberto Marchant,* | *Mercader de Libros* | M.DC.LXXXVIII. | 12mo, pp. 108. 47359

MEDRANO. Breve Tratado de Geographia, en tres partes que la una contiene la Descripcion del Rio y Imperio de las Amazonas Americanas con su Carta Geographica; la otra lo que poseen Franceses y Ingleses, etc. en el nuevo Mundo, y la tercera del Estado presente del Imperio del Gran Mogor y Reyne de Siam. *Brusselas, Lamberto Marchant.* 1700. 12mo. 47360

Reprinted in 1701.

MEDWAY, MASS. Annual Report of the Receipts and Expenditures ... for ... 1858. *Holliston: E. G. Plimpton, Printer.* 1858. 8vo, pp. 20. Continued. H. 47361

Constitution of Medway Social Library. [n. p. n. d.] 8vo, pp. 14. H. 47362

MEECH (A.) An Oration, ... July 4th, 1805, at ... Bridgewater ... . By Asa Meech. ... *Boston: Printed by Manning & Loring.* 1805. 8vo, pp. 16. H. 47363

Also: A Farewell Sermon at Bridgewater, 1811, and another at Canterbury, 1822.

MEEHAN (C. H. W.) Catalogue of the Law Department of the Library of Congress. By Charles H. W. Meehan. *Washington.* 1860. 8vo, pp. viii, 225. B. 47364

MEEHAN (T.) The American Handbook of Ornamental Trees. By Thomas Meehan. *Philadelphia.* 1853. 12mo. C.

MEEK (A. B.) The Red Eagle. A Poem of the South. By A. B. Meek. *New York: D. Appleton & Company.* M.DCCC.-LV. 12mo, pp. 108. B. 47366

Accompanied with notes on Indian life. Some copies have a *Mobile* imprint.

MEEK. Romantic Passages in Southwestern History; including Orations, Sketches, and Essays. By A. B. Meek ... . *New York: S. H. Goetzel & Co.* 1857. 12mo, pp. 330. + Second Edition. *Mobile: S. H. Goetzel & Co.* 1857. 12mo, pp. 330. + Third Edition. [*Ibid.*] + Fourth Edition. *New York: S. H. Goetzel & Co.* 1857. 12mo, pp. 330. B., BA. 47367

"Pages 210 to 330 are occupied with a biography of Weatherford, the Creek chief, massacre of Fort Mimms, and other sketches of Indian history, bearing marks of personal research, as they convey information that is novel and evidently authentic."—FIELD.

MEEK. Songs and Poems of the South. By A. B. Meek ... . *New York.* 1857. 12mo. + *Mobile: S. H. Goetzel & Co.* 1857. 8vo, pp. x, 282. + Fourth Edition. [*Ibid.*] B., C., H. 47368

Also: Address ... before the Alabama University, on the Early History of the State, ... *Tuscaloosa.* 1840. 8vo.—A Poem ... before the Ciceronian Club, ... Tuscaloosa,

Alabama, July 4, 1838. ... *Tuscaloosa.* 1838. 12mo, pp. 35.—A Supplement to Aikin's Digest of the Laws of Alabama, to 1841. ... *Tuscaloosa: White & Snow.* 1841. 8vo, pp. 409. C.

MEEK (Fielding Bradford). Check List of the Invertebrate Fossils of North America. Cretaceous and Jurassic. By F. B. Meek ... . *Washington.* 1864. 8vo, pp. ii, 240. 47369

Also: Check List of the Invertebrate Fossils of North America. Miocene. ... *Washington.* 1864. 8vo, pp. ii, 32.

MEEK. Descriptions of New Organic Remains. Collected in Nebraska Territory in ... 1857. ... By F. B. Meek and F. V. Hayden. *Philadelphia: Merrihew and Thompson.* 1858. 8vo, pp. 18. 47370

MEEK. Palæontology of the Upper Missouri. A Report upon Collections made principally by the Expeditions under the command of Lieut. G. K. Warren, U. S. Topographical Engineers in 1855 and 1856. Invertebrates by F. B. Meek and F. V. Hayden, M.D. Part I. *Washington.* 1865. 4to, pp. ix, 135. 5 Plates.

Also: Descriptions of New Organic Remains from North-Eastern Kansas, indicating the Existence of Permian Rocks ... . [n. p. n. d.] 8vo, pp. 16.— ... Descriptions of New Species and Genera of Fossils, collected ... in Nebraska Territory ... . *Philadelphia: Merrihew & Thompson, Printers.* 1857. 8vo, pp. 34.—A Reply to some Remarks ... by Prof. Swallow on Certain Disputed Points in the Geology of Kansas and other North Western Localities. ... [n. p. n. d.] 8vo, pp. 9. H. *See also* California, Vol. III., No. 10008, *and* Geological Survey of Illinois, Vol. IX., No. 34253, *note.*

MEEKER (B. B.) A Plan for the Speedy Construction of a Pacific Railroad, with the Draft of a Bill. By Hon. B. B. Meeker ... . *St. Louis: George Knapp & Co., Printers.* 1860. 8vo, pp. 15. H. 47372

MEEKER (E.) Washington Territory West of the Cascade Mountains, containing a Description of Puget Sound, &c. By E. Meeker. *Olympia, W. T.* 1870. 8vo, pp. 52. B. 47373

MEEKER (J.) An Inaugural Dissertation on the Principal Mineral Waters of the States of New York and New Jersey ... . By John Meeker ... . *New York.* 1815. 8vo, pp. 37. 47374

MEEKER (J.) Original and Select Hymns, in the Ottawa Language. By Jotham Meeker ... . *Shawanoe, Ind. Ter.* 1845. 24mo, pp. 96. BA. + Third Edition. *Ottawa Baptist Mission Station.* 1850. 24mo, pp. 127. 47375

MEEKER. Ottawa First Book. Prepared by Jotham Meeker, ... *Shawanoe Mission: J. G. Pratt, Printer.* 1838. 18mo, pp. 229

MEEKER. Ottawa First Book. Containing Lessons for the Learner; Portions of the Gospels by Luke, omitted by Matthew and John; and the Ottawa Laws. By Jotham Meeker, Missionary ... . Second Edition. *Ottawa Baptist Mission Station: J. Meeker, Printer.* 1850. 24mo, pp. 128. BA. 47377

Also: The Gospel according to John. Translated into the Ottawa Language, by Jotham Meeker, ... Revised ... by Rev. Francis Barker ... . *Shawanoe: Press of American Baptist Board of Foreign Missions.* 1844. 16mo, pp. 98. C.—Lenapee Spelling-Book, Shawanoe Mission. ... *For the Baptist Society.* 1834. 12mo, pp. 24.—Lenapi Wawipoetakse ave Apwatuk. First Lessons in Delaware. ... *Baptist Shawanoe Mission.* 183 . 18mo, pp. 48.

MEEKER (N. C.) Life in the West; or, Stories of the Mississippi Valley. By N. C. Meeker ... . *New York: S. R. Wells.* 1868. 12mo, pp. 360. C. 47378

Meeting of Delegates at Carlisle [Pa. 1816]. 8vo, pp. 7.

Meeting of Irishmen in New York. To the People of Ireland. *New York.* [1825.] 8vo. 47380

MEGIA (F.) La Fayette in Mount Vernon. A Drama in Two Acts. By Felix Megia ... . *Philadelphia: Printed by Stavely,* .. 1825. 24mo, pp. 23. BA. 47381

MEGINNESS (J. F.) Otzinachson; or, a History of the West Branch Valley of the Susquehanna: embracing a full Account of its Settlement—Trials and Privations endured by the first Pioneers—Full Accounts of the Indian Wars, Predatory Incursions, Abductions, Massacres, &c. Together with an Account of the Fair Play System; and the Trying Scenes of the Big Runaway; interspersed with Biographical Sketches of some of the leading Settlers, Families, etc., together with Pertinent Anecdotes, Statistics, and much valuable matter entirely new. By J. F. Meginness. *Philadelphia: Henry B. Ashmead.* 1857. 8vo, pp. 518. C., H. 47382

A better book than the long title would lead one to expect.

MEGISER (Hieron.) Septentrio Novantiquus, oder die newe Nort-Welt, das ist: Gründliche vnd warhaffte Beschreibung aller Mitternächtigen vnd Nortwerts gelegenen Landen und Insulen, so vnsern Vorfahren ... vnbekandt gewesen. ... Sampt Relation welcher gestalt in 1612 ... eine newe Schiffarth nach der China gegen Nortwerts, vnd eine vnsegliche grosse Landschaft in ... der Magellanica erfunden worden. *Leipzig: H. Gross.* 1613. 8vo, pp. 471. 12 Maps and Plates. 47383

A rare and very interesting collection of voyages to the North, including also some information relative to America, especially Virginia. Reprinted in 1638.

MEGISER. Specimen Quadraginta diversarum Linguarum et Dialectorum ... . *Francofurti.* 1593. 8vo. 47384

The Lord's Prayer in forty different languages, including some North American Indian languages.

[MEIER (Adolphus).] U. S. Treasury Notes to be the Circulation of the Country, in lieu of Bank Notes. ... *St. Louis: R. P. Studley & Co., Printers.* 1861. 8vo, pp. 8. H. 47385

MEIGHAN (T. W.) California as it Is; Comic Song, written by Thaddeus W. Meighan ... . *New York: William Hall & Son.* 1849. 4to, pp. 5. 47386

MEIGS (C. D.) A Biographical Notice of Daniel Drake, M.D., of Cincinnati. ... By Charles D. Meigs, M.D. Read ... July, 1853. *Philadelphia: Lippincott, Grambo, and Co.* 1853. 8vo, pp. 38. B. 47387

MEIGS. A Memoir of Samuel George Morton, M.D. ... By Charles D. Meigs, M.D. ... *Philadelphia: T. K. and P. G. Collins, Printers.* 1851. 8vo, pp. 48. Portrait. C. 47388

Also: Address delivered before the Union League of Philadelphia, October 31, 1864. ... *Philadelphia: Collins.* 1864. 8vo, pp. 19.

MEIGS (H.) Address ... at the ... Annual Fair of the American Institute. By Hon. H. Meigs. ... October, 1849. *New York: William E. Dean, Printer.* 1849. 8vo, pp. 10. B. 47389

Also: Address ... before the American Institute, October 9, 1845, on Agriculture and Horticulture. ... *New York.* 1845. 8vo.

MEIGS (J. A.) Catalogue of Human Crania, in the Collection of the Academy of Natural Sciences, Philadelphia. By J. Aitken Meigs, M.D. *Philadelphia: J. B. Lippincott & Co.* 1857. 8vo, pp. 112. A. 47390

MEIGS. Observations upon the Cranial Forms of the American Aborigines, based upon Specimens contained in the Collection of the Academy of Natural Sciences of Philadelphia. By J. Aitken Meigs, M.D. *Philadelphia.* 1866. 8vo, pp. 39.

Also: Address before the Alumni Association of Pennsylvania Cent. High School, 1854. ... *Philadelphia.* 1854. 8vo.—Hints to Craniographers ... . *Philadelphia: Merrihew & Thompson, Printers.* 1858. 8vo, pp. 8. H.

MEIGS (J.) An | Oration | pronounced | Before a public Assembly in New-Haven, | On the 5th Day of November 1781, | At the Celebration of the glorious Victory | over Lieutenant-General Earl Cornwal-| lis, at York-Town in Virginia, on the

19th | Day of October, 1781. | By Josiah Meigs, A.M. | *New-Haven: Printed by Thomas and Samuel Green.* MDCCLXXXII. | Sm. 4to, pp. 14. BA., J.C.B. 47392

MEIGS (M. C.) The Three Days' Battle of Chattanooga, 23d, 24th, 25th November, 1863. An Unofficial Dispatch from General Meigs ... . *New York: Presented to the U. S. Sanitary Commission by Julius Bien and Wm. M. Franklin.* 1864. 8vo, pp. 10. + Now first correctly printed. *Washington, D. C.: McGill & Witherow, Printers.* 1864. 8vo. 47393

The date of the *event* on the "correctly printed" edition reads November, 1864. Also: Report of Quartermaster Gen. Meigs, relative to the Purchase of Horses for Pennsylvania Cavalry. [37th Cong., Doc. No. 60.] 8vo, pp. 38.

[MEIGS (R. J.)] A Brief Sketch of the State of Ohio, ... Giving the Opinion of Thomas Hutchison, Esq. By a Resident of Twelve Years at Marietta, in that State. *Glasgow: A. Penman & Co.* 1822. 8vo, pp. 16. Map. 47394

MEIGS. A Journal of Occurrences which happened within the Circle of Observation in the Detachment commanded by Colonel Benedictine Arnold, consisting of two Battalions, which were detached from the Army at Cambridge, in the Year 1775. By Major Ret. J. Meigs. [n. p. n. d.] Sm. 4to, pp. 11.

"This interesting tract contains an account of the attack on Quebec, in which General Montgomery was killed. It has no place, date, or printer's name, but has the appearance of having been printed in America. A part of this journal is printed in the 'Remembrancer', III.; said to be taken from the American copy, 'supposed to be written by Major Meigs.'"—RICH, I. 211. Reprinted in "Mass. Hist. Soc. Colls.," II., 2d Series, and announced in Hildreth (S. P.), "Biographical Sketches."

MEIGS. Journal of the Expedition against Quebec, under Command of Col. Benedict Arnold, in the Year 1775, by Maj. Return J. Meigs, with An Introduction and Notes, by Charles I. Bushnell. *New York: Privately Printed.* 1864. 8vo, pp. 57. Portrait. C. 47396

Forms No. 6 of Bushnell's "Crumbs for Antiquarians," Vol. I.

[MEIGS.] Letter from the Postmaster General, transmitting a List of Contracts, made by the Post Office Department ... 1817. ... *Washington: Printed by E. De Krafft.* 1818. 8vo, pp. 24. BA. 47397

MEIGS. A Poem spoken in the Chapel of Yale-College, at the Quarterly Exhibitions, March 9th, 1784. By R. J. Meigs. *New-Haven: Printed by Meigs, Bowen and Dana.* 1784. 4to, pp. 16. BA. 47398

MEIGS. Report of the Committee ... to whom were referred ... the Memorial of Return Jonathan Meigs, Junior ... . December 20, 1805. ... *City of Washington: A. & G. Way, Printers.* 1805. 8vo, pp. 7, (1). B. 47399

MEIJER (H. A.) De Boekanier. ... *Amsterdam: J. D. Sybrandi.* 1840. 8vo. + Tweede Druk. 1847. 8vo. 47400

MEIKLE (J.) The Miscellaneous Works of James Meikle, ... *Pittsburgh: R. Patterson & Lambdin.* 1818. 12mo, pp. 297, (2)

MEIKLE. The Select Remains of James Meikle; or, Extracts from Manuscripts found among his Papers ... . *Pittsburgh: R. Patterson & Lambdin.* 1819. 12mo, pp. 299. C. 47402

Also: The Traveller; or, Meditations on various Subjects; written on board a man of war. ... To which is prefixed, a Life of the Author. *New York.* 1811. 16mo. P. + *New York.* 1813. 16mo.

MEIKLE (W.) The Canadian Newspaper Directory; or, Advertiser's Guide: containing a complete List of all the Newspapers in Canada, the circulation of each, and all information in reference thereto. By W. Meikle. *Toronto.* 1858. 8vo, pp. 60

MEILLEUR (J. B.) Mémorial de l'Education du Bas-Canada, ... Par J. B. Meilleur, A.M. ... *Montreal: J. B. Rolland & Fils.* 1860. 16mo, pp. xiv, 389. H. 47404

[MEIN (John).] Sagittarius's Letters | and | Political Speculations. | Extracted | From the Public Ledger. | Humbly Inscribed | To the Very Loyal and Truly Pious Dr. Samuel | Cooper, Pastor of the Congregational Church in Brattle | Street. | *Boston: | Printed by Order of the Select Men and Sold at Dona-| tion Hall, for the Benefit of the distressed Patriots.* | MDCCLXXV. 8vo, pp. 127.

"A strong Tory, anti-Puritanical publication, full of hits against the Pilgrim Fathers and their descendants, with a great deal of personal gossip, and, on the whole, a book of considerable historic interest. To the New York, Philadelphia, and Southern antiquarian explorers after scraps against the early New Englanders, this little volume will prove a mine, and afford salt and spice enough for many Fourth of July orations."—STEVENS.

[MEIN.] A State of the Importations from Great-Britain into the Port of Boston, From the beginning of Jan. 1769, to Aug. 17th 1769. With the Advertisements of ... "all the Well Disposed Merchants," ... . *Boston: Printed by Mein and Fleeming.* 1769. 4to, pp. (4), 130. BA., W. 47406

This rare tract contains much curious matter relative to the non-importation agreement of the Boston merchants. Also: A Catalogue of Mein's Circulating Library, Boston. *Boston.* 1765. 8vo, pp. 56. M.

Mein and Fleeming's Massachusetts Register, with an Almanack for ... MDCCLXVII. ... *Boston: Printed by Mein and Fleeming.* [1767.] Sm. 16mo, pp. 54. Continued. BA. 47407

The first Register printed in Massachusetts.

Mein and Fleeming's Register for New England and Nova Scotia; and an Almanack for 1768. *Boston.* [n. d.] Sm. 16mo. Continued. B. 47408

MEINECKE (C.) Frühlings-Kuren. Eine mineral-wäss'rige Centralpark- und Charakter-Studie, in schlechten herametern abgefasst von C. Meinecke. Zweite Auflage. *New-York: Verlag von C. Steiger.* 1869. 8vo, pp. 16. H. 47409

MEINERS (Christoph). Geschichte des weiblichen Geschlechts von C. Meiners. ... *Hannover: Helwing.* 1788–1800. 4 vols., 16mo, pp. viii, 398, (2); xviii, 470; viii, 576; xvi, 376. H.

The Carib language as spoken by females.—Vol. I., p. 47.

MEINERS. History of the Female Sex, comprising a View of the Habits, Manners, and Influence of Women among all Nations. Translated from the German, by F. Shoberl. *London.* 1808. 4 vols., 12mo. C. 47411

MEINERS. Göttingisches Historisches Magazin ... . Herausgegeben von C. Meiners und L. T. Spittler. *Hannover.* 1787–1793. 11 vols., 8vo. 47412

This valuable Historical Magazine contains some articles on America.

MEINICKE (C. E.) Versuch einer Geschichte der europäischen Colonien in Westindien, nach den Quellen bearbeitet. ... *Weimar.* 1831. 8vo, pp. 785. 47413

MEISNER (L. F. F.) De Caffe, Chocolatæ, Herbæ Thee ac Nicotianæ Natura, Usu et Abusu Anacrisis Medico-Historico-Diæletica ... . *Norimbergæ.* 1721. 8vo. Plates. 47414

MEISSNER (J. P.) Wahre Erklärung des "Buches der Wilden. Ein Schreiben an den Abbé Domenech" von Vitzputzli. Aus dem Aztekischen von J. P. Meissner. *Leipzig: Friedrich Ludwig Herbig.* 1862. 8vo, pp. 31. B. 47415

See also Domenech (E.), Vol. v., No. 20550, *note*, and No. 20551.

MEISSNER (R.) *and* SMITH (Wed.) Verhaal van den zendingpost der Evang. Broedergen, in het Boschnegerland van Suriname. Uit het Hoogduitsch vertaald. *Amsterdam: H. Hövker.* 1848. 8vo. 47416

MEJIA (Pero). *See* Mexia (Pero).

MEJORDA (*Marques* de). Ideas Importantes acerca del Patronato. *Lima.* 1831. 4to. 47417

MELBOURN (J.) Life and Opinions of Julius Melbourn; with Sketches of the Lives and Characters of Thomas Jefferson, John Quincy Adams, John Randolph, and several other eminent American Statesmen. Edited by a late Member of Congress. *Syracuse: Hall & Dickson.* 1847. 12mo, pp. 239. Plate. A., C.

MELBOURNE. Celebration ... of the Independence of the United States, by the American Citizens ... in Melbourne, Australia. *Melbourne: Goodhugh & Hough, Printers.* 1857. 8vo, pp. 34. BA. 47419

MELCHOR DE CASTRO MACEDO (El Contador) Contra los Frutos Caydos que dexo el Obispo de los Charcas, tio de sus hijos. [*Madrid.* 1610?] 8vo, pp. 10. 47420

Relative to ecclesiastical disputes in Peru.

MELCHORA. Carta Encyclica de edificacion, en que se anuncia la exemplar Vida y Santa muerte de la V. M. Sr. Melchora de Jesus Religiosa del Monasterio de N. S. de la Merced de esta ciudad de Lima. *Lima.* [1781.] 4to, pp. 57. J.C.B. 47421

MELENDEZ. Pompa que huvo por la beatificacion de Santa Rosa de Lima en el convento del Rosario. *Lima.* 1622.

Title from Ternaux, No. 446.

MELENDEZ (J.) Tesoros Verdaderos de las Yndias En la Historia de la gran Prouincia de San Ivan Bavtista del Perv De el Orden de Predicadores ... . Por el maestro F. Ivan Melendez Natural de Lima ... . *Roma: Nicolas Angel Tinassio.* M.DC.LXXXI–M.DC.LXXXII. 3 vols., folio, pp. (48), 643, (24); (24), 669, (15); (34), 857, (19). 3 Engravings and 2 Plans. C., H. 47423

The work of Melendez contains much important information that is not to be met with in any other chronicle, and it must always occupy a prominent position in every American library. It is a work of much rarity.

MELGAR (E. S. de). Arte de la Lengua general del Ynga, llamada Qquechhua. Por el Bachiller Don Esteban Sancho de Melgar. *Lima: Diego de Lyra.* 1691. 16mo. A. 47424

MELGUIZO (A.) El Sacerdocio y la civilizacion ó sea vindicacion del clero catôlico. *Mexico: Andrade.* 1858–59. 4 vols., 8vo. 47425

[MELILLANCA Y GUANALCOA.] Cartas pehuenches; ó, correspondencia de dos Indios naturales del Pire-Mapu, ó sea la quarta thetrarquia en los Andes, el uno residente en Santiago, y el otro en las cordilleras pehuenches. [*Santiago: Imprenta del Gobierno,* about 1820.] 12 Núm., sm. 4to. C. 47426

MELINE (J. F.) Two Thousand Miles on Horseback. Santa Fé and Back. A Summer Tour through Kansas, Nebraska, Colorado, and New Mexico, in ... 1866. By James F. Meline. *New York: Hurd and Houghton.* 1868. 12mo, pp. x, 317. Map

The author examined with great care a vast mass of documents relating to the early occupation of New Mexico by the Spaniards.

MELISH (J.) A Description of East and West Florida and the Bahama Islands; with an Account of the most Important Places in the United States, bordering upon Florida and the Gulf of Mexico. ... By John Melish. *Philadelphia: Printed by T. and G. Palmer.* 1813. 8vo, pp. 18. Map. B., W. 47428

MELISH. A Description of the British Possessions in North America, and of the most important places along the lines in the United States: ... By John Melish. *Philadelphia: Printed by T. and G. Palmer.* 1812. 8vo, pp. 132. Map. W. + Third Edition, enlarged and improved; ... . [*Ibid.*] 1813. 8vo, pp. 26. Map. BA. 47429

MELISH. A Geographical Description of the United States; with Topographical Tables of the Counties, Towns, Population, &c. ... By John Melish. *Philadelphia: John Melish.* 1815. 12mo, pp. 32. 3 Maps. BA. 47430

MELISH. A Geographical Description of the United States, with the contiguous British and Spanish Possessions ... . By John Melish. *Philadelphia: The Author.* 1816. 8vo, pp. 182. Errata, 8 lines. 5 Maps. H. + Second Edition. [*Ibid.*] 1816. 8vo, pp. 180. 4 Maps. + Third Edition. [*Ibid.*] 1818. 8vo, pp. 186. 4 Maps. + A New Edition, greatly improved. [*Ibid.*] 1822. 8vo, pp. (2), 491, 15. Map. BA. + *New York: A. T. Goodrich.* 1826. 8vo, pp. 497, (15). Maps. H. + *Philadelphia.* 1850. 8vo. 47431

MELISH. A Military and Topographical Atlas of the United States; ... British Possessions & Florida: ... By John Melish. *Philadelphia: Printed by G. Palmer.* 1813. 8vo, pp. 6, 34, 3–20,

3–29. 12 Maps. + *Philadelphia: John Melish.* 1815. 8vo, pp. 6, 34, 3–20, 3–29. BA. 47432

Curious and scarce, showing the operations of the late war in Canada, the Creek Country, New Orleans, etc.

[MELISH.] Military Documents; ... the South Section of the United States; Operations of the British Army, 1759–60; Military Districts of the United States ... . *Philadelphia.* 1817. 8vo. 3 Maps. 47433

Title from J. R. Smith's catalogue. Probably made up by J. R. S.

MELISH. The Sine Qua Non: A Map of the United States, shewing the Boundary Line proposed by the British Commissioners at Ghent, with ... Documents ... and Remarks on the extent and effect of the British pretensions ... . By John Melish. *Philadelphia.* 1815. 12mo. Map. + Second Edition ... . *Philadelphia: John Melish.* 1815. 12mo, pp. iv, 3–120. B. 47434

MELISH. The Traveller's Directory through the United States: Consisting of a Geographical Description of the United States ... and a Description of the roads ... . By John Melish. *Philadelphia: For the Author.* 1815. 2 Parts. 1815–14. 12mo, pp. (4), 32, 82. Maps. + Fifth Edition. [*Ibid.*] 1819. 12mo, pp. 134, and Calendar, (14). Maps. + To which is added an Appendix ... . [*Ibid.*] 1822. 18mo, pp. xix, 183. 2 Maps. + A New Edition, Revised and Enlarged. *New York.* 1825. 12mo. 47435

"A Statistical View of the United States" (pp. 39) is usually appended to the last-mentioned edition.

MELISH. Travels in the United States of America, in the years 1806 & 1807, and 1809, 1810, & 1811; including an account of passages betwixt America and Britain; and Travels through ... Upper Canada. ... By John Melish. *Philadelphia: Printed for the Author.* 1812. 2 vols., 8vo, pp. xxii, (2), 444; ix, 492. 8 Maps. + [*Ibid.*] 1815. + With Corrections and Improvements till 1815. By John Melish. With an Appendix, containing a Letter from Clements Burleigh, Esq., to Irish Emigrants removing to America, and Hints by the Shamrock Society, New York, to Emigrants from Europe. *Philadelphia.* 1818. 8vo, pp. 648. Maps and Plans. + *London.* 1818. 8vo. Map and Plates. + *Dublin.* 1818. 8vo. 47436

See "M. Rev.," XCIII. 113.

MELISH. John Melish's Reisen durch die Vereinigten-Staaten von America, in den Jahren 1806, 1807, 1809, 1810 und 1811.

Aus dem Englischen, und mit Anmerkungen begleitet von J. Ernst Ludw. Brauns ... . *Weimar.* 1819. 16mo, pp. xviii, 378. Maps. H. 47437

Also: A Description of the Roads in the United States. ... *Philadelphia: Printed by G. Palmer.* 1814. 12mo, pp. 82. + [*Ibid.*] 1815. 12mo, pp. iv, 97.—A Description of the Seat of War in the Southern Section of the United States, &c. ... [n. p. n. d.] 8vo, pp. 20.—A Geographical Description of the World ... . *Philadelphia: John Melish.* 1818. 8vo, pp. xiii, (2), 9–280. 3 Maps.—Information and Advice to Emigrants to the United States, &c. ... *Philadelphia.* 1819. 16mo.—Letter to James Monroe, Esq. President ... on the State of the Country; with a Plan for Improving the Condition of Society. ... *Philadelphia: John Melish.* 1820. 8vo, pp. 32.—The Necessity of Protecting and Encouraging the Manufactures of the United States. ... *Philadelphia: John Melish.* 1818. 8vo, pp. 30.—A Statistical View of the United States; containing a Geographical Description of the United States, and of each State and Territory. ... *Philadelphia: The Author.* 1822. 18mo, pp. 45. + *New York.* 1825. 18mo, pp. 39.—Views on Political Economy, from the Description of the United States. ... [n. p.] 1822. 8vo, pp. 27.

MELLEN (G. W. F.) An Argument on the Unconstitutionality of Slavery, Embracing an Abstract of the Proceedings of the National and State Conventions on this Subject. By George W. F. Mellen. ... *Boston: Saxton & Peirce.* 1841. 12mo, pp. 440. A., B., C. 47438

Dr. Mellen is known as a candidate for the presidency, in opposition to Daniel Pratt the great American Traveler.

MELLEN (G.) A Book of the United States: exhibiting its Geography, Divisions, Constitution, ... Government, etc., with a Condensed History of the Land; ... the Biography of about Two Hundred of the Leading Men; a Description of the Principal Cities and Towns; with Statistical Tables ... . Edited by Grenville Mellen. With Engravings ... . *New York: George Clinton Smith and Co.* 1839. 8vo, pp. vi, 13–824. + *New York.* 1841. + *Hartford.* 1835. 8vo. + [*Ibid.*] 1837. 8vo, pp. 804. + *Hartford: H. F. Sumner & Co.* 1838. 8vo, pp. vi, 13–804. Plate and 7 Portraits. + [*Ibid.*] 1842. B. 47439

MELLEN. Ode for the Celebration of the Battle of Bunker-Hill, at the Laying of the Monumental Stone, June 17, 1825. By Grenville Mellen. *Boston: Cummings, Hilliard, & Company.* 1825. 8vo, pp. 16. B. 47440

[MELLEN.] Our Chronicle of '26. A Satirical Poem. ... *Boston: Wells and Lilly.* 1827. 8vo, pp. 40. H. 47441

[MELLEN.] Sad Tales and Glad Tales; by Reginald Reverie. ... *Boston: S. G. Goodrich.* MDCCCXXVIII. 12mo, pp. vi, 185.

Also: Address ... before the Citizens of North-Yarmouth, ... July 4, 1825. ... *Portland: Printed by D. & S. Paine.* 1825. 8vo, pp. 20.—An Address ... before the

Maine Charitable Mechanic Association, ... 8th Nov. 1821. ... *Portland: Printed by T. Todd & Co.* 1821. 8vo, pp. 18.—The Age of Print: A Poem ... before the Phi Beta Kappa Society, at Cambridge, 26 August, 1830. ... *Boston: Carter and Hendee.* 1830. 8vo, pp. 40, (1).—The Light of Letters. A ... Poem. ... [n. p.] 1828. 8vo.—The Martyr's Triumph; Buried Valley; and Other Poems. ... *Boston: Lilly, Wait* ... . 1833. 12mo, pp. 300.—Poem ... before the Literary Societies in Amherst College, August 27, 1839. ... *Amherst: J. S. & C. Adams.* 1839. 8vo, pp. 35.—The Rest of the Nations: a Poem. ... *Portland: Hill, Edwards & Co., Printers.* 1826. 8vo, pp. 28. H.

MELLEN (J.) A Discourse ... October 31, 1756 ... in Lancaster: On Occasion of the late Mortality in that and the neighboring Places. ... By John Mellen, A.M. ... *Boston: Printed ... by Edes and Gill.* M,DCC,LVII. 8vo, pp. (2), 49. 47443

MELLEN. ... A Discourse ... at Wellfleet, ... 13th of April, 1785. At the Ordination of Mr. Levi Whitman ... . By John Mellen, A.M. ... *Plymouth, Massachusetts: Printed by Nathaniel Coverly.* M,DCC,LXXXV. 8vo, pp. 45. B., M., W. 47444

MELLEN. The Duty of all ... . A Sermon ... June 16, 1756. At ... Lancaster, occasioned by the General Muster and Inspection of Arms on that Day. By John Mellen, A.M. ... *Boston: S. Kneeland.* 1756. 8vo, pp. 23. M. 47445

MELLEN. Religion productive of Music. A Discourse, ... at Marlborough, March 24th, 1773. At a Singing Lecture. ... By John Mellen, A.M. ... *Boston: Printed ... by Isaiah Thomas.* MDCCLXXIII. 8vo, pp. 34. W. 47446

MELLEN. A Sermon ... in Lancaster, October 9. 1760. On The General Thanksgiving for The Reduction of Montreal and ... Conquest of Canada. Containing a brief Account of the War, ... By John Mellen ... . *Boston: Printed by B. Mecom.* [1760.] 8vo, pp. 46, (1). M., N., W. 47447

Also: A Discourse ... at Hingham ... at an association of ... Ministers ... April 8, 1789. ... *Boston: Printed by Joseph Bumstead.* MDCCXC. 8vo, pp. 32.—The Duty of Ministers ... . A Sermon Preach'd at Norton, January 3d, 1753. At the Ordination of the Reverend Mr. Joseph Palmer. ... *Boston: N. E. Printed by S. Kneeland.* 1753. 8vo, pp. (2), 30.—Fifteen Discourses for the Liberties of the Churches of New England. ... *Boston.* [n. d.] 8vo, pp. 220.—The Merit of doing Good. A Funeral-Sermon, ... in Lancaster, ... March 31, 1765. On the Death of Mr. Sebastian Smith ... . *Boston: Printed by Edes and Gill.* 1765. 8vo, pp. 24. M., W.

MELLEN (J.), *Jun.* The Great and Happy Doctrine of Liberty. A Discourse ... at Hanover, ... February 19, 1795, on the Day of ... Thanksgiving ... . By John Mellen, A.M. ... *Boston: Printed by Samuel Hall.* 1795. 8vo, pp. 34. BA.

MELLEN. A Sermon, ... at Harwich, January 21, 1791, at the Funeral of the Reverend Isaiah Dunster ... . By John Mellen, Jun. A.M. ... *Boston: Printed by Samuel Hall.* MDCCXCI. 8vo, pp. 22. BA. 47449

Also: Affection for the House of God recommended. Sermon ... at Yarmouth, Jan. 1, 1795, at the Opening of a new Meeting-house. ... *Boston.* 1795. 12mo, pp. 18.—Non-conformity to the World, in Moral Character. A Discourse, ... at Hanover, ... June 24th, 1793. To ... the Old Colony Lodge ... . *Boston: Printed by Brother Benjamin Russell.* 5793. 8vo, pp. 40.—A Sermon, ... at Barnstable, ... on ... Thanksgiving, November 20, 1794. ... *Boston: Printed by Samuel Hall.* MDCCXCIV. 8vo, pp. 21.—A Sermon, ... at Yarmouth [Mass.], November 13, 1796, occasioned by the ... Death of Mrs. Sarah Alden ... . *Boston: Printed by S. Hall.* 1797. 12mo, pp. 28.—A Sermon ... at Barnstable, April 28th, 1799; Occasioned by the Death of Hon. Daniel Davis, Esq. ... *Boston: Printed by Manning & Loring.* 1799. 8vo, pp. 23.—A Sermon, ... on the Annual Election, May 31, 1797. ... *Boston: Printed by Young & Minns.* 1797. 8vo, pp. 36. B., M.

MELLEN (W. P.) Report relative to Leasing Abandoned Plantations and Affairs of the Freed People ... . By William P. Mellen. ... *Washington, D. C.: McGill & Witherow, Printers.* 1864. 8vo, pp. 19. H. 47450

MELLER (Henry James). Nicotiana; or the Smoker's and Snuff-Taker's Companion; containing the History of Tobacco; Culture—Medical Qualities ... . Third Edition. *London: E. Wilson.* 1833. 18mo, pp. xvi, 128. Plate. C. 47451

M[ELLET] (J.) Voyage dans l'Amerique Méridionale, a l'intérieur de la Cote-ferme, et aux iles de Cuba et de la Jamaique, depuis 1808 jusqu'en 1819; ... Par M. Jullien M.****. *Agen: De l'imprimerie de Prosper Noubel.* 1823. 8vo, pp. 291, (4). 2 Plates. + Seconde Édition. Par Jullien Mellet. *Paris: Masson.* 1824. 8vo, pp. 295, (4). H. 47452

MELLICHAMPE, 1836. *See* [Simms (William G.)]

MELLINI (Domenico). Descrizione dell' entrata della Sereniss. Reina Giouanna d'Austria Et dell' Apparato, fatto in Firenze nella venuta et per le felicissime nozze di S. Altezza Et dell' Illustr. et Eccellent. S. Don Francesco de Medici. *Fiorenza, appresso i Giunti.* 1566. 8vo, pp. (16), 128, (10), Printer's Mark, &c., 2 l.

Contains a notice of Vespuccius. "Volume fort rare, dont il a été fait trois éditions la même année. La première est in-4°; la seconde in-8° 'Ristampata et riveduta;' la troisième 'Riveduta corretta stampata la terza volta.'"—LECLERC, No. 959.

MELLISH (J. H.) Exhortation to Youth. A Sermon ... in Kingston, N. H. Feb. 24, 1867. By John H. Mellish ... . *Newton, N. H.: E. A. Carter, Printer.* [n. d.] 8vo, pp. 9. H.

MELLO (A. d'A.) A libertade no Brasil, seu nascimento, vida, morte e sepultura. *Recife.* 1864. 8vo. 47455

MELLO MORAES [Alexandre J.] Apontamentos Biographicos do Barão de Cayru ... . Pelo Dr. Mello Moraes ... . *Rio de Janeiro: J. J. Do Patrocinio.* 1863. 8vo, pp. 112. H. 47456

MELLO MORAES. O Brazil historico escripto pelo Dr. A. J. de Mello Moraes. Primeiro Anno. *Rio de Janeiro.* 1864. Folio. + 2ª Serie. *Rio de Janeiro.* 1867. 2 vols., folio, pp. 295; 262.

The first twenty numbers of the first series bear the title "O Medico do Povo." Original documents and much information on the discovery and settlement of Brazil are contained in the work.

MELLO MORAES. Corographia historica, chronographica, genealogica, nobiliaria e politica do Imperio do Brasil, contendo noções historicas e politicas, a começar do descobrimento da America e particularmente do Brasil ... . *Rio de Janeiro.* 1858–63. 5 vols., 8vo. Portrait. 47458

A valuable encyclopædia of information on the social and commercial history of Brazil, its mines, and the development and extent of its resources and their first discovery. The rise of the most important towns, the chief families, and the Political History of the country from the conquest downward, are also copiously treated.

MELLO MORAES. Ensaio corografico do Imperio do Brasil ... Por Alexandre José de Mello Moraes, ... e Ignacio Accioli de Cerqueira e Silva ... . *Rio de Janeiro: P. Brito Impressor.* 1854. 16mo, pp. 353, 2 folded leaves. H. 47459

Also: Biographia do Exm. Conselheiro Joaquim Marcellino de Brito ... . *Rio de Janeiro: J. J. Do Patrocinio.* 1861. 8vo, pp. 23.—Biographia do Senador Diogo Antonio Feijo ... . *Rio de Janeiro: J. J. Do Patrocinio.* 1861. 8vo, pp. 8.—Biographia do tenente-coronel e cirurgião mor reformado do exercito Dr. Manoel Joaquim de Menezes, ... *Rio de Janeiro: J. J. Patrocinio.* 1861. 8vo, pp. 35.—Discurso Historico ... 29 de Setembro 1858 por occasião de solemnisarse a posse dos GGR ∴ officiaes e dignatarios que compoem o Grande Oriente do Brasil. ... *Rio de Janeiro: J. J. Patrocinio.* 1860. Sm. 4to, pp. 38, (2). H.

MELLO (F. F. de). Exercitação na qual plenamente se prova que D. Pedro I, imperador do Brasil, é estrangeiro para Portugal: que nenhum direito tem á corôa portugueza; e que esta pertence ao sr. rei D. Miguel I pelas leis fundamentaes do Estado. Por Francisco Freire de Mello. *Lisboa: Na Imp. Reg.* 1828. 4to, pp. 19. 47460

MELLO (Francisco Manuel de). *See* Manuel de Mello (F.)

MELLO (J. R. de). Josephi Rodrigues de Mello ... De Rusticis Brasiliae Rebus Carminum libri IV. Accedit Prudentii

Amaralii Brasiliensis de Sacchari Opificio Carmen *Romae: Ex Typographia Fratrum Puccinelliorum.* MDCCLXXXI. 8vo, pp. vii, (1), 206. 4 Plates. H. 47461

MELLO. De Rebus Rusticis Brasilicis Carminum libri quatuor quibus accedit Prudentii Amaralii de Sacchari Opificio singulare carmen. *Olysipone.* 1798. 4to. Plates. + *Romæ.* 1798. 4to. 47462

MELLO (Urbano Sabino Pessoa de). Apreciação da revolta praieira em Pernambuco. *Rio de Janeiro.* 1849. 8vo. 47463

MELLON (M.) The Mail Robbers. Report of the Trials of Michael Mellon, ... and George Wilson and James Porter *alias* May ... . Taken in Short Hand, by John Mortimer. *Philadelphia: J. Mortimer.* 1830. 8vo, pp. (4), 160. BA., P. 47464

MELMOTH (S.) Bunker Hill. A Poem ... . By Sydney Melmoth. *Boston.* 1827. 16mo. 47465

Melodies for the Craft, or Songs for Freemasons, suitable for every occasion. Compiled by a Past Master. *Cincinnati.* 1852. 18mo. 47466

MELODY (G. H. C.) Notice sur les Indiens Ioways, et sur le Nuage Blanc, 1er Chef de la Tribu, Venus des plaines du Haut-Missouri, près des Montagnes Rocheuses ... sous la conduite de G. H. C. Melody, Esqre, et accompagnés Par Jeffrey Doraway, Leur Interprète Favori. ... *Paris: Imprimerie de Wittersheim.* 1845. 12mo, pp. 24. 8 Plates. H. 47467

MELROSE, *Mass.* Constitution and By-Laws of Endeavor Engine Company, ... Melrose, Mass. *Boston: Alfred Mudge & Son, Printers.* 1854. 18mo, pp. 11. B. 47468

Also: Report of the School Committee ... 1863–4. *Boston: Prentiss & Deland, Printers.* 1864. 8vo, pp. 22.—Report of the Selectmen ... for ... 1868 ... . *Boston: Joseph McIntire, Printer.* 1868. 8vo, pp. 8. H.

MELSHEIMER (F. E.) Catalogue of the described Coleoptera of the United States. By Frederick Ernst Melsheimer, M.D. Revised by S. S. Haldeman and J. L. Le Conte. *Washington: Smithsonian Institution.* 1853. 8vo, pp. xvi, 174. H. 47469

MELSHEIMER (F. V.) A Catalogue of Insects of Pennsylvania. By Fred. Val. Melsheimer. Part I. *Hanover, York Co., Pa.* 1806. 8vo. P. 47470

MELSHEIMER (F. V.) Tagebuch von der Reise der Braunschweigischen Auxiliär Truppen von Wolfenbüttel nach Quebec entworfen von F. V. Melsheimer ... . *Minden: Justus Henrich Körber.* 1776. 16mo, pp. 40, 32. H. 47471

MELTON (E.) [Engraved Title:] Edward Meltons | Zee en Land | Reizen | Door | verscheide Gewesten des Werelds. [Printed Title:] Edward Meltons, | Engelsch Edelmans, | Zeldzaame en Gedenkwaardige | Zee- en Land- | Reizen; | Door | Egypten, West-Indien ... . Aangevangen in den jaare 1660. en geëindigd in den jaare 1677. | Vertaald uit d'eigene Aanteekeningen en Brieven van den gedagten Heer Melton; | en met verscheidene schoone Kopere Figuuren versierd. | *T'Amsterdam,* | *By Jan ten Hoorn, Boekverkooper over 't Oude Heeren-* | *Logement, Anno* 1681. 4to, pp. (6), 495, (8). 20 Plates. C. 47472

Who this Melton was, is an unsettled problem. His travels in the West Indies relate partly to the buccaneers. The chapter on New Netherland is made up from Van der Donck and A. Montanus. All the natural productions of the country are described, and the names given in the Indian dialects of Guyana, with occasional observations on the pronunciation of the words. The map is reversed, the south being at the head of the page, and the north at the foot, with west on the right, and east on the left. The text is in Friesic Dutch, to which the author calls particular attention in the preface. Several of the plates are by the celebrated Jan Luiken, and are among his best productions; one of them is a view of the Cohoes Falls in the Mohawk river. *See* Asher's "Essay," Nos. 16 and 17, *also* F. Muller's catalogue.

MELTON. Edward Meltons Engelsch Edelmans Zeldzaame en Gedenkwaardige Zee- en Land-Reizen; door Egypten, West-Indien ... . *T'Amsterdam. By Jan Verjager, Boekverkooper in de Harte-straat, by Heeregraft.* 1702. 4to, pp. (4), 495, (8). 19 Plates. J.C.B. 47473

This second edition is a reproduction of the first, with the addition of a new preface. Some copies have the imprint: *By Jan ten Hoorn, Boekverkooper over 't Oude Heeren-Logement.* 1702.

M[ELTON]. Aenmerkenswaardige en Zeldzame | West-Indische | Zee- en Land-Reizen, | Door de Caribische Eylanden, Nieuw-Nederland, | Virginien, en de Spaansche West-Indien: | Behelsende: | Een seer naukeurige Beschryving der genoemde Landen, be- | neffens derzelver Inwoonderen, Godsdienst, Regeering, Zeden en Gewoonten, | vreemde Geschiedenissen en Voorvallen, Mitsgaders de Grouwelyke Wreed- | heden der Spajaarden aan de Indianen gepleegt in 't ontdekken van Nieuw Span- | jen, enz. en Wreedheyd der Amerikaanse Zee-Rovers tegens de Spanjaarden. | Met Koopere Platen Verciert. | Door een Voornaam Engels Heer E. M. en andere, Opmerkelijk Beschreven. | *t'Amsterdam, by de Weduwe van Gysbert de Groet, Boekverkoopster op de* |

Nieuwe-Dyk op de hoek van d'Engelsche Steeg, in de groote Bybel. 1705. 4to, pp. 96. C. 47474

This is a reprint of the second part of No. 47472 (pp. 121–225), with several cleverly drawn plates; those on New Netherland are copied from D. P. de Vries. T. W. Field expresses himself in an *ex cathedra* and somewhat clumsy style as to the rarity of the work; he would have done well to quote from Frederic Muller, who is an authority, and from whose catalogue he obtained his information. *See also* our Vol. II., No. 5046.

MELVIL (C.) L'Emigration, colonisation dans l'Amérique ... *Paris: Schiller.* 1852. 8vo, pp. 32. 47475

MELVIL (P.) Le Moniteur des Indes-Orientales et Occidentales, recueil de Mémoires et de Notices Scientifiques et Industriels, concernant les possessions Néerlandaises d'Asie et d'Amérique. *La Haye.* 1848. Rl. 4to. Map and Plates. 47476

MELVILL (T.) Address of Thomas Melvill, jun. ... before the Berkshire Society ... of Agriculture ... Pittsfield, October 3, 1815 ... . *Pittsfield: Printed by Phinehas Allen.* 1815. 8vo, pp. 31.

MELVILLE (D.) An Expose of Facts, ... Relating to the Conduct of Winslow Lewis, of Boston, "Superintendent for lighting the United States' Light-House" ... . By David Melville, ... *Providence, R. I.: Miller & Hutchins, Printers.* 1819. 8vo, pp. 48. BA. 47478

See [Lewis (W.)], Vol. X., No. 40865.

MELVILLE (H.) The Rise and Progress of Trinity College, Toronto; with a Sketch of the Life of the Lord Bishop of Toronto, as connected with Church Education in Canada. By Henry Melville. *Toronto.* 1852. 8vo, pp. 265. 47479

MELVILLE (H.) Battle-Pieces and Aspects of the War. By Herman Melville. *New York: Harper & Brothers.* 1866. 12mo, pp. 272. H. 47480

MELVILLE. Israel Potter: his Fifty Years of Exile. By Herman Melville. *New York: G. P. Putnam & Co.* 1855. 12mo, pp. 276. + Third Edition. [*Ibid.*] 47481

MELVILLE. White-Jacket; or the World in a Man-of-War. By Herman Melville ... . *New York: Harper & Brothers.* [1850.] 12mo, pp. 465. B., BA. + [*Ibid.*] 1855. 47482

Consists of Experiences in a U. S. Frigate, in 1843. Also: The Confidence-Man; his Masquerade. ... *New York: Dix, Edwards & Co.* 1857. 12mo, pp. vi, 394.—Redburn; his First Voyage; being the Sailor-Boy Confessions and Reminiscences of the Son-of-a-Gentleman, in the Merchant Service. ... *New York: Harper & Brothers.* 1849. 12mo, pp. 390. + [*Ibid.*] 1855.

MELVILLE (L.) Edith Allen, or Sketches of Life in Virginia, By Lawrence Melville. *Richmond: J. W. Randolph.* 1855. 12mo. 47483

MELVILLE, *pseudon.* Ethan Allen; or the King's Men, an Historical Novel. By Melville. *New York.* 1836. 8vo.

MELVIN (J.) A Journal | of the | Expedition to Quebec, | in the Year 1775, | under the Command of Colonel Benedict Arnold. | By | James Melvin, | a Private in Captain Dearborn's Company. | *New York.* 1857. Rl. 8vo, pp. 30. BA. 47485

This volume, of which only one hundred copies were printed, is now rare. It was privately printed by "The Club," the organization from which sprung "The Bradford Club." The following is a reprint:

MELVIN. A Journal of the Expedition to Quebec, in the Year 1775, under the Command of Colonel Benedict Arnold. By James Melvin, A Private in Captain Dearborn's Company. *Philadelphia: The Franklin Club.* MDCCCLXIV. 8vo, pp. (4), iv, 34

The edition consisted of one hundred copies in octavo, and twenty in quarto.

Members of The City Council of Baltimore, Their Clerks, and Officers of the Corporation. For The Year 1860. [*Baltimore.* 1860.] 8vo, pp. 16. Continued. 47487

MEMMI (Juan Bapt.) Vida del Padre Francisco Maria Galluzzi de la Compania de Jesus, traducida en Lengua Castellana por el P. Bernardo Pazuengos, Procurador General de la Provincia de Philipinas. *Mexico: Imprenta Colegio de S. Ildefonso.* 1761. 4to. 47488

MEMMINGER (C. G.) ... Address of the Hon. C. G. Memminger, ... before the assembled Authorities of ... Virginia, January 19, 1860. [n. p. 1860.] 8vo, pp. 43. H. 47489

[MEMMINGER.] The Mission of South Carolina to Virginia. [n. p. 1860.] 8vo, pp. 34. BA. 47490

Also: Lecture ... April 10th, 1851. Showing African Slavery to be Consistent with the Moral and Physical Progress of a Nation. ... *Augusta, Ga.: W. S. Jones, ... Printer.* 1851. 8vo, pp. 25.—Speech ... upon the Proposition relative to a Railroad from Charleston to the Ohio River. *Frankfort, Ky.* 1839. 8vo, pp. 28.—Speech ... upon the Bill and Resolutions relating to Bank Issues and Suspensions, December, 1857. *Charleston, S. C.: ... Press of Walker, Evans & Co.* 1858. 8vo, pp. 57, Appendix 9.—Speech ... on the Bill to Afford Aid to the Blue Ridge Rail Road. ... 1858. *Charleston: ... Press of Walker, Evans & Co.* 1859. 8vo, pp. 26. H.

Memoir and Character of Sarah, a Pious Woman of Connecticut, who died in the year 1818. *Bridgenorth.* [n. d.] 24mo.

Memoir concerning the Commercial Relations of the United States with England; also, an Essay on the Advantages to be Derived from new Colonies. *Boston.* 1809. 8vo. 47492

Memoir of, etc., if not found *infra*, *see* under the *subject*.

Memoir of Colonel John Allan, an Officer of the Revolution, born in Edinburgh ... Jan. 3, 1746. Died in Lubec, Maine, Feb. 7, 1805. With a Genealogy by George H. Allan ... . *Albany: Joel Munsell.* 1867. 8vo, pp. 32. M. 47493

Memoir of Mrs. Jane Greenleaf, of Newburyport, Mass. Third Edition. *Boston: Massachusetts Sabbath School Society.* [1855.] 18mo, pp. 247. 47494

Memoir of Ginevra Guerrabella. *New York.* 1863. 8vo.

A few copies only printed for distribution among personal friends. She is the daughter of Samuel Ward the banker. Her romantic marriage, and subsequent career on the stage, form the principal items of interest in this work.

A Memoir of Rev. Joseph Badger; containing an Autobiography, and Selections from his Private Journal and Correspondence. *Hudson, Ohio.* 1851. 12mo, pp. 185. S. 47496

Rev. H. N. Day wrote the preface. Badger was a missionary in Ohio, among the Indians from 1800 to 1844.

Memoir of T. Brand Hollis. *See* [Disney (J.)], v. 20268.

Memoir of the British Doctrine of Neutral Trade. *Washington.* 1806. 8vo. C. 47497

Memoir of the Committee of the Free Trade Convention, Held at Philadelphia in September and October, 1831, remonstrating against the ... Tariff ... . *Philadelphia.* 1831. 8vo.

Memoir of the Naval Life and Services of Admiral Durham. *London.* [n. d.] 8vo. 47499

The subject of this memoir served under Lords Howe and Rodney in the American Revolution.

Memoir of the Pilgrimage to Virginia of the Knights-Templar of Massachusetts and Rhode Island, May, 1859. ... *Boston: A. Williams and Company.* 1859. 12mo, pp. xi, 211. BA. 47500

Memoir of the Public and Private Life of Fanny Elssler. *New York.* 1840. 12mo. 47501

Relates some of her American experiences.

A Memoir on the Antiquities of the Western Part of the State of New York ... . *Albany.* 1817. 8vo, pp. 16. 47502

Memoir on the Navigation of South-America, to accompany a Chart of that Station. Parts 1, 2. *London: Hydrographical Office of the Admiralty.* 1825. 8vo, pp. 50, 117. S. 47503

Memoir on the Organization of the Army of the United States, with a view to its giving effect to the Militia, when called into actual Service. *Georgetown, D. C.* 1826. 8vo. 47504

Memoir on the Subject of a General Bible Society for the United States. By a Citizen of New York. *New Jersey.* 1816. 8vo, pp. 16. 47505

A Memoir on the Subject of the Wheat and Flour in the State of New York. ... *New York: Kirk and Mercien.* 1820. 8vo, pp. 46. 47506

Memoir ... of Rev. John Eliot. *See* [McKean (J.)], 43373.

Memoir upon the Negociations between Spain and the United States, which led to the Treaty of 1819, with a Statistical Notice of that Country [Florida]. *Washington.* 1821. 8vo. 47507

Mémoire à consulter, et consultation, &c. contre la Nouvelle Compagnie des Indes. *Paris.* 1786. 4to. C. 47508

Mémoire à consulter. *See* Guiana, Vol. VII., 29177.

Mémoire accompagnant. *See* Canada, Vol. III., No. 10512.

Mémoire adressé a l'Assemblée. *See* Bosque (*S.*), II. 6455.

Mémoire concernant le feu Sr. de Rochemore, Commissaire Générale de la Marine, Ordonnateur à la Louisiane, contre la Sieur de Kerlerec, Gouverneur de la même Colonie. *Paris.* 1765. 4to. 47509

Mémoire concernant les prises faites par les vaisseaux de guerre et les armateurs anglois, des vaisseaux hollandois allant à l'Amérique, ou en revenant. *Amsterdam.* 1758. Folio, pp. (2), 13.

Mémoire | contenant le | Précis des Faits, | avec leurs | Pièces Justificatives, | Pour servir de Réponse aux Observations | envoyées par les Ministers d'Angleterre, | dans les Cours de l'Europe. | *A Paris,* | *De l'Imprimerie Royale.* | M.DCCLVI. 4to, pp. vi, 198. H. + *[Ibid.]* 12mo, pp. viii, 275. Map. + *[Ibid.]* 12mo, pp. 292.

The very curious history of this "mémoire" deserves special attention. At the surrender of Fort Necessity by Washington, his Journal of the Expedition, together with the letters of Braddock to the British Ministry, and his instructions to Washington, were seized by the French victors. They were immediately transmitted to France, and

by order of the French king, printed and sent to every court of Europe, as indicating the aggressive character of the British. From evidence drawn from these documents, they charge Washington with the murder of Jumonville. This "mémoire" proves that Jumonville was approaching Washington on an embassy of peace, but that Washington, unwilling to trust him, had ordered his advance to be fired upon. It includes a translation of the "Journal of Major George Washington" (pp. 73–100), printed in 1754. It was of so much consequence that no less than five editions of a translation were published; for one of them, *see* "The Conduct of the late Ministry," our Vol. IV., No. 15205, which was reproduced as "The Mystery Revealed." The American editions are entitled:

A Memorial containing A Summary View of Facts, with their Authorities. In Answer to The Observations Sent by the English Ministry to The Courts of Europe. Translated from the French. *Philadelphia: Printed by James Chatten.* 1757. 8vo, pp. iv, 338. + *New York: J. Parker* ... 1757. 8vo, pp. iv, 190. B. + *New York: Printed ... by Hugh Gaine.* 1757. 8vo, pp. iv, 190. C., H. 47512

The Philadelphia edition is in larger type than the New York editions, and has a half-title which reads: "Memorial and Papers concerning the Expedition to the Ohio, containing General Braddock's Register, Journals of Major Washington, M. de Villiers," etc. The work was reprinted in the second volume of Craig's "Olden Time," and is appended to the Dublin edition of [Livingston's] "Review," *see* our Vol. X., No. 41650. Some of the papers are re-translations from the French.

Mémoire contenant un aperçu. *See* [Obert (*M.*)]

Mémoire de la Chambre de Commerce d'Aunis, que la Rochelle soit un des ports francs promis par le roi aux États-Unis de l'Amérique. [n. p. n. d.] 4to. 47513

Mémoire des Habitans des Colonies Françaises, &c., sur la question de reduire les droits sur les sucres étrangers. *[Paris.] Avril* 19, 1829. 8vo, pp. 34. 47514

Mémoire Des Habitans & Négocians de la Louysiane, sur l'événement du 29 Octobre 1768. [n. p. n. d.] 8vo, pp. 90.

Mémoire des officiers. *See* Martinique, No. 44979.

Mémoire historique. *See* Basse-Terre, Vol. I., No. 3890.

Mémoire Historique sur la Négociation de la France & de l'Angleterre, depuis de 26 Mars 1761 jusqu'au 20 Septembre de la même année; avec les pièces justificatives. *Paris: Imprimerie Royale.* 1761. 8vo, pp. iv, 196. + *Imprimée selon l'édition publiée à Paris, par l'autorité. A Londres de D. Wilson.* MDCCLXI. 4to, pp. 60. J.C.B. 47516

A collection of state papers relative to the cession of Canada, the limits of Louisiana, the fisheries off Newfoundland, Cape Breton, Guadeloupe, and other islands of the

West Indies, etc., preliminary to the treaty of 1762, which ended the old French war. Translated as:

An Historical Memorial of the Negotiation of France and England, From the 26th of March, 1761, to the 20th of September of the same Year, With the Vouchers. Translated from the French Original, published at Paris by Authority. *London: Printed for D. Wilson, and T. Becket, and P. A. Dehondt.* MDCCLXI. 4to, pp. 63, (1). J.C.B., P. 47517

Mémoire historique sur les Indes Braves et les Forbans François du Golfe de Darien. *Amsterdam.* 1743. 12mo, pp. xx, 252.

Mémoire instructif, adresse aux Notables, sur le Régime et l'importance de la Colonie de Saint-Domingue. *Paris.* [1788.] 8vo, pp. 47. P. 47519

Signed by le Duc de Choiseul-Praslin, le Comte de Vaudreuil, etc., Commissaires de la Colonie de Saint-Domingue, et le Marquis de Gouy D'Arsy, Commissaire-Rapporteur.

Mémoire instructif des droits et des justes motifs que le Gouvernement des États-Unis Mexicains a pour refuser de reconnaitre la validité du privilège accordé à D. José Garay, d'ouvrir une voie de communication entre les océans Atlantique et Pacifique par l'isthme de Tehuantepec ... . Publié par le Ministre des Affaires Étrangères. *Washington: Imprimé chez R. A. Waters.* 1852. 8vo. 47520

For other editions, *see* Vol. VII., Nos. 26547–48.

Mémoire juridique. *See* [Luzac (E.)], Vol. X., No. 42748.

Mémoire justificatif. *See* [Marriott (James)], No. 44689.

Mémoire justificatif. *See* [Gibbon (E.)], Vol. VII. 27283.

END OF VOLUME ELEVEN.

A Dictionary of Books

RELATING TO AMERICA.

MÉMOIRE justificatif des hommes de couleur de la Martinique, condamnés par arrêt de la cour royale de cette colonie, contenant: l'Histoire des hommes de couleur dans les colonies françaises. Rapport fait à la chambre des pairs par M. le comte de Cornet, sur la pétition des trois hommes de couleur de la Martinique. *Paris.* 1826. 8vo, pp. 600.

Mémoire pour Daniel de Joncaire-Chabert, ci-devant Commandant au petit Fort de Niagara. Contre M. le Procureur-Général de la Commission établié pour l'affaire du Canada. [*Paris? De l'Imprimerie de Grange.* n. d.] 4to, pp. 23, 47, 23.

Mémoire | pour Mr Charles de Saint Estienne Chevalier Seigneur de la | Tour & ses freres et sœurs, enfans & heritiers de Messire Charles de Saint Estienne | Seigneur de la Tour, Gouverneur et Lieutenant General pour le Roy en l'Acadie & | légataires universels de Dame Marie de Menou d'Aunay de Charnizay, Chanoinesse | de Poussay, leur soeur utérine, fille et seule héritiere bénéficiaire du sieur d'Aunay, de Charnizay | & de Dame Jeanne Motive, Demandeurs & Deffendeurs. | [*Paris.* 1690.] Folio.

Mémoire pour des Négocians de l'Orient, intéressés au Commerce des États-Unis; contre la Ferme Générale. [*Paris: L. F. Prault.* 1788.] 4to, pp. (2), 155. 12 Tables. C. 47524

Mémoire pour le Sieur de Boishebert, Capitaine, Chevalier de St. Louis, ci-devant Commandant à l'Acadie. *Paris: De l'Imprimerie de Moreau.* [1763.] 4to, pp. 59. H. 47525

Signed "Clos." Corrected title of our No. 6156, Vol. II.

Mémoire pour les Colonies Françaises. *St. Pierre, Martinique.* 1821. 8vo. 47526

Mémoire pour les citoyens Verneuil. *See* [Baillio], I. 2765.

Mémoire pour les États-Unis d'Amérique demandeurs; contre MM. Arman Erlanger, Voruz, Dubigeon, Jollet et Babin, Mazeline, et la société des chantiers et ateliers de l'Océan, defendeurs. *Paris.* 1868. 4to, pp. 220. 47527

Relates to the vessels built in the French ship-yards on account of the Confederates, during the rebellion.

Mémoire pour Messire François Bigot, ci-devant Intendant de Justice, Police, Finance, & Marine en Canada, Accusé: Contre Monsieur le Procureur-Général du Roi ... Accusateur. ... *Paris: De l'Imprimerie de P. Al. Le Prieur.* M DCC.LXIII. 2 vols., 4to, pp. xvi, 303; lii, 780. H. 47528

Signed by M. Dupont and two others. Very rare, and of the highest historical interest. Corrected title of our No. 38696, Vol. X.

Mémoire pour servir à l'histoire de l'Église de l'Amérique du Nord. *Paris.* 1853. + *Villemarie.* 1852–54. 5 vols., 8vo.

These five volumes are out of print, and difficult to find, they consist of "Vie de la sœur Bourgeoys," 2 vols., "Vie de Madame Mance," 2 vols., and "Vie de Madame d'Youville," 1 vol.

Mémoire presenté a son Altesse Royale M. le Duc D'Orleans, concernant la precieuse Plante du Gin seng de Tartarie, découverte en Canada par le P. Joseph François Lafitau, ... Missionnaire des Iroquois du Sault Saint Louis. *A Paris, chez Joseph Monge.* M DCC XVIII. 18mo, pp. 88, (4). Map. 47530

Corrected title of our No. 38595.

Mémoire présenté au protecteur d'Angleterre, par le marquis de Leyde et D. Alonse de Cardenas, ambassadeurs du Roy catholique en Angleterre, le 21 may 1665. ... [n. p. n. d.] 4to, pp. 16

Mémoire sur Cette Question: Est-il avantageux à la France de prendre possession de la Louisiane? [n. p. 1802?] 4to, pp. 16. BA. 47532

Mémoire sur la Colonie. *See* Guiana, Vol. VII., No. 29178.

Mémoire sur la Conduite de la France et de l'Angleterre à l'égard des neutres. *Paris.* 1810. 8vo, pp. 243. S. 47533

Mémoire sur le Canada. *See* No. 10515.

Mémoire sur le Commerce, 1789. *See* [Tolosan (M. de)].

Mémoire sur le commerce étranger avec les colonies françaises de l'Amérique; Présenté à la Chambre d'Agriculture du Cap, le 17 Février 1784. *Paris: Cuchet.* M.DCC.LXXXV. 8vo, pp. (2), 51

Mémoire sur le Commerce Maritime et Colonial. Extrait des Annales Maritimes et Coloniales. Juillet 1832. *Paris: Imprimerie Royale.* M DCCC XXXII. 8vo, pp. 56. H. 47535

Mémoire sur l'exploitation. *See* Guiana, Vol. VII. 29181.

Mémoire sur le Guatemala et la colonisation du département de Vera Paz, Amérique du centre. *Bruxelles.* 1840. 8vo.

Mémoire sur les Nègres pour servir de materiaux aux cahiers des Colonies. *Paris: Clousier.* 1790. 8vo, pp. 41. J.C.B.

Mémoire sur les Principes et les Lois de la Neutralité Maritime, accompagné de Pièces Officielles Justificatives. *Paris.* 1812. 8vo. 47538

Mémoire sur un nouvel equipage de Chaudières à sucre pour les Colonies, avec le plan dudit equipage. *Paris: Hardouin et Gattey.* [1786.] 4to, pp. 14. 2 Plates. J.C.B. 47539

Mémoire touchant l'établissement des Peres Jésuites dans les Indes d'Espagne. [*Amsterdam.*] 1712. 12mo, pp. 47. 47540

Relative to the missions of Paraguay, and against the Jesuits. Very rare. *See* Frézier (A. F.), Vol. VII., No. 25924, *note.*

Mémoires chronologiques, pour servir a l'histoire de Dieppe et à celle de la navigation françoise, avec un recueil abrégé des privilèges de cette ville. *Paris.* 1785. 2 vols., 12mo. 47541

Very interesting on account of the history of the expeditions from Dieppe to America. The author was a M. Desmarquet.

Mémoires de l'Institut National.

Vol. VI. contains Buache de Neuville's "Recherches sur l'Ile Antilla," etc.

Mémoires de la Société d'Agriculture du département de la Seine. Tome I. *Paris.* 1800. 8vo. 47543

Contains many articles relating to the French colonies.

Mémoires de la Société Ethnologique. *Paris: Veuve Dondey-Dupré.* 1845. 8vo. 47544

Contains many articles on the American Indians.

Mémoires de la Société Royale des Antiquaires du Nord. 1840–1844. *Copenhague: Au Secrétariat de la Société.* [1844.] 8vo, pp. 176, 16. 10 Plates. Continued. H. 47545

Many of the memoirs are on America topics.

Mémoires d'un Américain. *See* [La Croix (J. V.)], X. 38502.

Mémoires des Commissaires de sa Majesté très-chrétienne et de ceux de sa Majesté Britannique, Sur les possessions & les droits respectifs de deux couronnes en Amérique; Avec les Actes publics & Pièces justificatives. ... *A Copenhague, Chez Joh. Benj. Ackermann.* MDCCLV. 3 vols., 12mo, pp. xii, 502; (4), iv, 400; (4), xvi, 568. Map. J.C.B. + *A Amsterdam et a Leipzig, Chez J. Schreuder & Pierre Mortier le jeune.* MDCCLV. 3 vols., 12mo, pp. xii, 502; xv, 154, 400; xvi, 568. Map.

The collation or arrangement varies in some copies; I have seen one with pp. xii, 502; xvi, 568; (2), iv, 400, 154. Probably extracted from the following:

Mémoires des Commissaires du Roi et de ceux de sa Majesté Britannique, Sur les possessions & les droits respectifs de deux Couronnes en Amérique; Avec les Actes publics & Piéces justificatives. Contenant les Mémoires sur l'Acadie & sur l'isle de Sainte-Lucie. *A Paris, de l'Imprimerie Royale.* M.DCCLV–LVII. 4 vols., 4to, pp. viij, lxxv, 181, 61, cvij, 120; xiij, 646; xvj, 319; (6), xxv, 654. 3 Maps. + *Paris.* M.DCCLVI. 6 vols., 12mo, pp. viii, 321; vi, 363; vi, 278; vii, 331; x, 335; xxi, 438. Map.

The fourth volume (1757, of the first-mentioned edition) of this valuable work is very scarce, and seldom found with the others. "An invaluable collection of official papers and documents."—HOLMES' *Annals.* "The authors of these memoirs were MM. de Silhouette, de la Galissonière, and particularly the Abbé de la Ville, an ex-Jesuit."—BARBIER. The English commissioners were Messrs. W. Shirley and Wm. Mildmay. It is an interesting collection, the English documents, with translations, being given as well as the French ones. There is a continual examination and discussion of the early maps and geographers, and of books of travel in North America. For a translation, in part, *see* "Memorials of the English and French," 47741, *infra.*

Mémoires du cercle des Philadelphes. Tome Premier. *Port-au-Prince: De l'Imprimerie de Mozard.* M. DCC. LXXXVIII. 8vo, pp. 264, Table, &c., (8). H. 47548

"The only one published. Extremely rare."—MULLER.

Mémoires et Documents relatifs a l'Histoire du Canada; Publiés par La Societe Historique de Montreal. *Montreal.* 1859. 8vo. 47549

Mémoires et essais pour servir à l'histoire des nations espagnole et portugaise. I. échantillon. [n. p. n. d.] 8vo. 47550

Mémoires et Observations Géographiques. *See* [Engel (S.)]

Mémoires Géographiques, 1767. *See* [Rousselet de Surgy].

Mémoires historiques sur la Louisiane. *See* Vol. III., No. 9605

Mémoires militaires. *See* [Vimeur (J. B. de)].

Mémoires particuliers pour servir à l'histoire de l'Église de l'Amérique du Nord. *Paris: Veuve Poussielgue-Rusand.* [1853.] 2 vols., 8vo, pp. (4), cxviii, 406; (2), xii, 519. Fac-simile and 10 Plates. C. 47551

Contains "la Vie de la sœur Bourgeoys et l'Histoire de la congrégation de Villemarie."

Mémoires pour la carte intitulée Canada, Louisiane, et les terres Anglaises. Par J. B. Bourguignon d'Anville. *Paris.* 1755. 4to, pp. 26. Map. 47552

Omitted in its proper place.

Mémoires pour les hommes de couleur. *Paris.* 1826. 8vo.

Five or more parts published.

Mémoires sur la vie de Mgr de Laval. *See* La Tour (B. de), Vol. x., Nos. 39216, *and* 39279.

Mémoires sur l'Administration de la Marine et des Colonies; par un Officier General de la Marine. *Paris: Ph. D. Pierres.* 1790. 8vo, pp. 248. + Suites des Mémoires .... [*Ibid.*] 1790. 8vo, pp. 70, 12. J.C.B. 47554

By Gabriel de Bory. *See also* our Vol. II., No. 6437.

Mémoires sur l'Amérique et sur l'Afrique. Donnés au mois d'Avril, 1752. *Paris.* 1752. 4to, pp. 58. 47555

Mémoires sur le Canada, depuis 1749 jusqu'a 1760, avec cartes et plans. ... *Québec: Imprimerie de T. Cary & Cie.* 1838. 8vo, pp. 207, (4). C. 47556

Mémoires sur le Commerce des Hollandois, dans tous les États et Empires du Monde. ... *Amsterdam: Chez Emanuel du Villard.* MDCCXVII. 12mo, pp. xx, (4), 283, (12). 47557

Mémoires sur les colonies occidentales de la France. *Paris.* 1814. 8vo. 47558

Mémoires sur les Finances. Pièces Justificatives. [*Paris.* 1791.] 4to, pp. 91. 47559

Mémoires sur les parties du monde avec des réflexions sur la régie des esclaves et autres objets. *Cayenne.* 1788. 4to.

Mémoires tovchant l'Establissement. *See* [Paulmyer (J. J.)]

Memoirs and Autobiography of some of the Wealthy Citizens of Philadelphia, with a fair estimate of their Estates and particu-

lar accounts of Stephen Girard, Jacob Ridgway, and Obed Coleman. By A Merchant of Philadelphia. *Philadelphia.* 1846. 8vo, pp. 80. P. 47561

Memoirs of a Grandmother. By a Lady of Massachusetts .... *Boston.* 1854. 12mo, pp. 141. 47562

Memoirs of a late ... Bookseller. *See* [Almon (J.)], No. 954.

Memoirs of a late Officer in the Army of the United States. By an officer in the same service. ... *Philadelphia: American Sunday-School Union.* [n. d.] 24mo, pp. 69. Plate. H. 47563

Memoirs of a Life. *See* [Graydon (A.)], Nos. 28418–19.

Memoirs of a New England Village Choir. With Occasional Reflections. By a Member [Samuel Gilman]. ... *Boston: S. Goodrich, & Co.* 1829. 12mo, pp. (4), 149. + *Boston.* 1834. 12mo, pp. 152. + Second Edition. [*Ibid.*] + Third Edition. *Boston.* 1846. 16mo. C. 47564

For another edition, *see* Gilman (S.), Vol. VII., No. 27436, *note*.

Memoirs of a Nullifier; Written by Himself. By a Native of the South. *Columbia, S. C.* 1832. 8vo, pp. (2), 110. + To which is added, An Historical Sketch of Nullification in 1832–3. *New York: James O. Noyes.* 1860. 12mo. 47565

This has been attributed to Dr. Thomas Cooper, also to A. S. Johnson.

Memoirs of American Missionaries. *See* [Loomis (E.)], 41954

The Memoirs of an American, with a Description of the ... Island of St. Domingo, translated from the French. *London: F. and J. Noble.* MDCCLXXII. 2 vols., 12mo, pp. xx, 216; (4), 225.

See "Monthly Review," XLVII. 411.

Memoirs of an American Lady *See* [Grant (A.)], No. 28296.

Memoirs of an American Loyalist. *London: Privately Printed.* 1826. Post 8vo. 47567

Memoirs of an Unfortunate Young Nobleman. *See* [Annesley (James)], Vol. I., Nos. 1599–1603.

Memoirs of Darien, 1715. *See* [Borland (F.)], Vol. II. 6428.

Memoirs of Distinguished Americans. ... *New York: G. W. Casilear.* 1853. 8vo, pp. 48. S. 47568

Memoirs of Eminent Female Writers. *See* [French (B. F.)]

Memoirs of Eminent Persons. *See* [Hall (J. E.)], No. 29813.

Memoirs of Four Brothers engaged in the Service of their Country in the New World and Africa. Second Edition. *London: William Sams.* M.DCCC.XXX. 8vo, pp. xi, 275. 7 Plates.

Relates to the capture of Buenos-Ayres.

The Memoirs of Lafitte, or the Barritarian Pirate. A Narrative founded on Fact. *Providence.* 1826. 16mo, pp. 125. Portrait. 47570

Memoirs of North Britain. *London.* 1715. 8vo. 47571

Contains an account of the Colony of Darien, with a Vindication of King William's Honor and Justice therein. *See also* [Borland (F.)], Vol. II., No. 6428.

Memoirs of the Administration. *See* Vol. III., No. 10516.

Memoirs of the American Academy of Arts and Sciences: ... *Boston: Printed by Adams and Nourse.* M, DCC, LXXXV. 4to, pp. xxxii, 568, (2). 6 Plates. Continued. 47572

Memoirs of the Connecticut Academy. *See* Vol. IV. 15703.

For other memoirs of societies, *see* under the respective names of the societies.

Memoirs of the Dead, and Tomb's Remembrancer. *Baltimore: The Editors.* 1806. 12mo, pp. 300. 47573

Epitaphs from Maryland cemeteries.

Memoirs of the Dutch Trade in all the States, Kingdoms, and Empires of the World. *London.* [n. d.] 8vo. 47574

Includes the trade of the Dutch Company in the West Indies, etc.

Memoirs of ... Barbados. *See* Vol. I., No. 3278.

Memoirs of the Life of a Modern Saint. Containing his Adventures in ... America. *London: Ranger.* 1760. 8vo.

See "Monthly Review," XXIII. 524.

Memoirs of the Long Island Historical Society. *See* Vol. V., No. 18503, *and* Vol. VI., No. 24293.

Memoirs of the Pillory, being a Letter of Consolation to Dr. Shebbeare. *London: Cabe.* 1759. 8vo. 47576

Partly on American topics. *See also* "Monthly Review," XIX. 583.

Memoirs of the Principal Transactions. *See* [Shirley (W.)]

Memoirs of the Young Prince of Annamaboe, his Slavery in Barbadoes .... [*London.* n. d.] 8vo. 47577

Title from an English auctioneer's catalogue.

Memoirs read before the Anthropological Society of London. 1863–4. ... *London: Trübner and Co.* 1865. 8vo, pp. viii, 533. 4 Plates, 4 folded sheets. Continued. 47578

Contains "Bollaert's Ancient Population of the New World," "Ancient Picture Writing of America," and "Astronomy of the Red Men of the New World."

Memoirs read before the Boston Society of Natural History; being a New Series of the Boston Journal of Natural History. *Boston.* 1868. 8vo. Map and Plates. Continued. 47579

Memorable Accidents, and Unheard of Transactions, Containing an Account of Several Strange Events, Shipwrecks, Dismal Misfortunes, Stratagems, Deliverances, &c. Translated from the French; printed at Brussels 1691. Published in England by R. B[urton]. *London: A. Bettsworth.* 1833. 16mo. Portrait.

Made up from the early voyages of the Dutch, English and French to the North, and to the East and West Indies. Another edition is abridged and entitled:

Memorable Accidents and Remarkable Transactions: containing an Account of several strange Events; as deposing of Tyrants, Shipwrecks, Misfortunes, Stratagems of War, Perilous Adventures, Happy Deliverances ... . Translated from the French, and published in English, by R. B. *Worcester.* 1795. 18mo, pp. 142. C. 47581

Memoranda concerning Baltimore. *See* No. 3041, *add* pp. 93.

Memoranda, Historical. *See* [Dexter (H. M.)], No. 19895.

Memoranda of a Settler. *See* [Abbott (J.)], I. 29.

Memoranda of some of the Proceedings of the Friends of Baltimore Yearly Meeting ... and of the Yearly Meetings of Philadelphia, New York, Ohio, Indiana, and Genesee ... in Relation to the Western Indians. [*Philadelphia:*] *Printed for Private Circulation among Friends only.* 1869. 12mo, pp. 27. H.

Memoranda of the Experience. *See* [Rogers (——)].

Memoranda respecting the French Slave Trade in 1820. *London.* 1820. 8vo. 47583

Memoranda respecting the Families of Quincy and Adams. [n. p. n. d.] 8vo, pp. 9. 47584

Memorandum de Négociations pendantes entre le Méxique et l'Espagne. *Poissy.* 1857. 8vo. 47585

Memorandum des los negocios pendientes entre México y España presentado al E. S. ministro de estado por el representante de la república el dia 28 de 1857. *Poissy.* 1857. 8vo. 47586

Memorandum del gobierno. *See* Buenos Ayres, III. 9021.

Memorandum on the Relative Importance of the West and East Indies to Great Britain. *London.* 1823. 8vo, pp. 32.

Memoria acerca de los medios que se estiman justos para el fomento y pronto restablecimiento de la Mineria. *México.* 1824. 4to. 47588

Memoria acerca de los terrenos de Metlabtoyuca, por D. Ramon Almaraz. *Mexico: Imprenta Real.* 1866. 8vo, pp. 33. Map and 10 Plates. 47589

Memoria apologetica do Arcebispo da Bahia ... em resposta a um opusculo do D. Man. do Monte Rodrigues di Araujo, Bispo do Rio de Janeiro, sobre a questão; A qual dos dois Prelados competia fazer a ceremonia de sagração do mesmo Augusto Senhor. *Bahia.* 1842. 8vo, pp. 145. 47590

Memoria de la Municipalidad de la Ciudad de Buenos Aires ... 1860. ... *Buenos Aires.* 1861. 8vo, pp. 200, iv. 8 Plates. B.

See also Vol. III., No. 9021, *note*.

Memoria de la Secretario de Estado. *See* Columbia, IV. 14602

Memoria de las operaciones que han tenido lugar en la oficina especial de desamortizacion del distrito, desde el 7. de Enero, hasta el 5. de Diciembre de 1861. *Mexico.* 1862. Folio, pp. 162

Memoria de los abonos. *See* Caracas, III. 10778.

Memoria de los Trabajos. *See* Almaraz, No. 945, *and* 29088

Memoria de Relaciones Exteriores. 1860. Documentos. *Carácas.* 1860. 8vo, pp. 80. 47593

Memoria del Despacho de Guerra. *See* Peru.

Memoria del Ministro de Relaciones y Gobernacion de Costa-Rica. [n. p.] 1852. Folio, pp. (2), 15. 47594

Memoria del Ministro de Interior y Relaciones Esteriores presentada á las Cámaras de 1833. *Chuquisaca.* 1833. Folio, pp. 15

See also Republica Arjentina.

Memoria del secretario del tesoro y crédito nacional al congreso de 1866. *Bogotá.* 1866. 4to, pp. 68. 47596

Memoria documentada. *See* Brazil, II. 7601.

Memoria en que el Ministro. *See* Argentina, I. 1956.

Memoria general. *See* Peru.

Memoria instructiva. *See* [Garay (J.)], VII. 26547.

Memoria Leida á lás Córtes por el encargado del despacho de Gobernacion de Ultramar en 1813–14. *Madrid.* 1814. 4to, pp. 32. 47597

Memoria ofrecida á la consideracion de los Honorables Senadores y Dispudados al próximo Congreso, y á toda la República, sobre el tratado de límites y navegacion fluvial ajustado y firmado por Plenipotenciarios del Brasil y de Venezuela en 5 de Mayo de 1859. *Carácas.* 1860. 8vo, pp. 210. 47598

Memoria Politica sobre si conviene en Chile la Libertad de Cultos reimpresa en Lima, con du Breve Apologia del Art. 8 y 9 de la Constitucion Politica del Perù de 1823, y con Notas y adiciones. *Lima.* 1827. 4to, pp. 150. 47599

On the liberty of conscience and worship.

Memoria politico-instructiva. *See* [Rocha Fuerte].

Memoria presentado por el Ministro de Relaciones y de lo Interior de la Republica de Costa Rica ... 1854. *San José.* [1854.] Folio, pp. (2), 15. 47600

See also Buenos Ayres, Chili, Mexico, Peru, etc.

Memoria que dirije á la Asamblea legislativa de Guayana el Presidente del Estado, 1865. *Ciudad-Bolivar.* [1865.] 8vo, pp. 56. 47601

Memoria que dirige a la legislatura nacional de 1865, el ministro de hacienda. *Carácas.* 1865. 4to, pp. 180. 47602

Also: Memoria que dirije á la legislatura nacional de 1865 el ministro de crédito público. *Carácas.* 1865. 8vo, pp. 24, lxiii. *See also* our No. 10779.

Memoria que el Ministro de Estado en el departamento de marina presenta al Congreso Nacional de 1868. *Santiago de Chile: Imprenta Nacional.* 1868. 8vo. + [*Ibid.*] 1869. 8vo, pp. 230. Plates. 47603

See also Chili, Peru, Venezuela, etc.

Memoria que presenta á la H. Diputacion provincial de Carácas en 1851 la Junta de Caminos de la Provincia. *Carácas.* 1851. 8vo, pp. 64. 3 Tables. 47604

Memoria que presenta el Secretario del Interior de los negocios de su departamento al Congreso de 1832. [*Carácas.* 1832.] 8vo, pp. 30. 47605

Also: Memoria que presenta el Secretario del Interior al Congreso de 1835. *Carácas.* [1835.] 4to, pp. 16. *See also* Bolivia, Peru, etc.

Memoria que presentó al Congreso Federal de Centro-America el secretario de estado y del despacho de hacienda del Supremo Gobierno de la Republica el 26. de marzo de 1831. en la legislatura ordinaria del mismo año. *Guatemala: Imprenta Nueva.* 1831. Folio, pp. 28. 12 Tables. 47606

Signed P. José de Valencia.

Memoria sobre a conspiração de 1817, vulgarmente chamada a conspiração de Gomes Freire, escripta e publicada por um Portuguez [Joaquim Ferreira de Freitas], amigo da justiça e da verdade. *Londres.* 1822. 8vo. + *Lisboa: Na Imprensa Liberal.* 1822. 4to, pp. x, 281. 47607

Relates to Portuguese America.

Memoria sobre a nobreza no Brasil, por um Brasileiro. *Rio de Janeiro.* 1841. 4to. 47608

Memoria sobre la conservation del Puerto de la Habana. *Cuba.* 1852. 8vo. A. 47609

Memoria sobre la utilidad é influjo de la mineria en el reino: Necessidad de su fomento, y arbitrios de verificarlo. *Mexico.* 1819. 4to, pp. 98. 47610

Memoria sobre las immensas ventajas que resultarian de introducir y generalizar en esta Isla el uso de los Camellos. *Habana: Imprenta de Roquero.* 1831. 8vo, pp. 8. 47611

Memoria sobre. *See* Chili, [Gama e Castro (J. de)], Guatemala, Peru, etc.

Memoria sobre os trabalhos da commissão mixta brasileira e portugueza na execução dos artigos 6.º e 7.º do tractado de 29 de Agosto de 1825, celebrado entre o Brasil e Portugal para o reconhecimento da independencia do Brasil. *Rio de Janeiro: Typographia Imparcial de F. de P. Brito.* 1847. 8vo, pp. 28. Maps. 47612

Memorial. [n. p. n. d.] 8vo, pp. 19. 47613

Relates to Georgia. *See also* [Sackett (N.)]

Memorial adjustado contra los Officiales de Casa de Monedo a Mexico de el año 1729. [n. p.] 1729. Folio. 47614

See also Vol. IV., No. 14658.

Memorial ajustado de los diversos espedientes seguidos sobre la provision de obispos en esta iglesia de Buenos Aires, hecha por el solo sumo potifice sin presentacion del gobierno, y sobre un breve presentado en materia de jurisdiccion, y reservas retenido, y suplicado. ... Dispuesto por el fiscal general del estado [Pedro Jose Agrelo]. *Buenos-Aires: Imprenta Argentina.* 1834. 8vo, pp. 246

Memorial a-justado que de Orden del Consejo Supremo de Indias ... sobre visitar, y exercer los Actos de la Jurisdiccion Diocesana en la Custodia del Nuevo España, poner Vicario Foraneo, y otras cosas. [n. p.] 1738. Folio. 47616

Memorial and Affidavits showing Outrages perpetrated by the Apache Indians, in the Territory of Arizona, during the years 1869 and 1870 ... *San Francisco: Francis & Valentine, Printers.* 1871. 8vo, pp. 32. H. 47617

The Memorial & Petition of the People of Rupert's Land and North-West Territory, British America, to ... U. S. Grant, President ... . [n. p. 1870.] 8vo, pp. 11. H. 47618

The Memorial and Petition of the Society of Friends, ... to the Legislature of Virginia, on the subject of Militia Fines, Together with the Letter of Benjamin Bates ... . *New York.* 1812. 8vo, pp. 16. + [n. p. 1817.] 12mo, pp. 16. + *New York: Samuel Wood & Sons.* 1818. 8vo, pp. 20. 47619

See Bates (B.), I. 3922, *note*, and "Memorial of the Religious Society of Friends."

Memorial and Remonstrance of the Committees appointed by the Yearly Meetings of Friends, of Genesee, New York, Philadelphia, and Baltimore, to the President of the United States; in Relation to the Indians of the State of New York. *New York: Mercein & Posts' Press.* 1840. 8vo, pp. 19. H. 47620

The Memorial ... of the Public Creditors who are Citizens of the Commonwealth of Pennsylvania ... to the ... Congress ... *Philadelphia: Zachariah Poulson.* MDCCXC. 8vo, pp. 28. J.C.B.

Memorial and Remonstrance to the General Assembly of Virginia, against supporting Religious Teachers by Law: With the

Act establishing Religious Freedom: and Mr. Madison's Letter. [n. p.] 1826. 8vo. C., M., W. 47622

Memorial and Remonstrance. *See* Louisiana *and* Virginia.

A Memorial and Remonstrance, Presented to the General Assembly Of ... Virginia, ... in 1785, in Consequence of a Bill ... for the Establishment of Religion by Law. *Reprinted at Worcester by Isaiah Thomas.* MDCCLXXXVI. 16mo, pp. 16. C. 47623

A Memorial and Representation, of ... Merchants, ... of the City of New-York, to the Hon. the Legislature of the State of New-York [on the Merchants' Bank], 1804. *Albany: C. R. & G. Webster.* [1804.] 8vo, pp. 8. S. 47624

The Memorial and Resolutions adopted at the Anti-Tariff Meeting, held at Sumter District, South-Carolina, ... September 3, 1827. ... [*Charleston:*] *Printed by A. E. Miller.* 1827. 8vo, pp. 16. + *Washington: Printed by Duff Green.* 1828. 8vo, pp. 9

Memorial aos Habitantes da Europa sobre a iniquidade do commercio da Escravatura. Publicado pela Religiosa Sociedade de Amigos, vulgarmente chamados Quakers, na Gram Bretanha e Irlanda. *Londres: Impresso na officina de Jorge Smallfield.* 1822. 8vo, pp. 16. + *Londres: Harvey e Darton.* 1824. 8vo, pp. 16.

Also in Swedish, Portuguese, Italian, and Danish.

Memorial concerning Several Ministers, Deceased, of the ... Society of Friends, within the limits of Baltimore Yearly Meeting. *Baltimore.* 1833. 12mo, pp. 176. 47627

See also [Clinton (De W.)], No. 13719, Society of Friends, *and* [Sparks (J.)]

A Memorial containing a Summary View. *See* No. 47512, *supra*

Memorial|de lo Svcedido en|la ciudad de Mexico, desde el dia pri-|mero de Nouiembre, de 1623. has-|ta quienze de Enero de |1624.| [*Mexico.* 1624.] Folio, 28 leaves. C. 47628

D. Diego Carillo de Mendoza y Pimentel, twenty-fourth viceroy of Peru, assumed his title September, 1621. He was cruel and passionate. The disputes which he had with the archbishop Juan Perez de la Serna, of a no less violent temper than that of the viceroy, caused a rebellion to break out January, 1624, which obliged the viceroy to retire to the convent of S. Francisco, from where he embarked for Spain at the end of 1624.

Memorial del que succedio entre el opispo de Cartagena y la audiencia real, año de 1681. [n. p.] 1695. Folio. 47629

Memorial for an Act. *See* Massachusetts, No. 45915.

A Memorial for the Establishment of a Homœopathic Military Hospital. [n. p. n. d.] 8vo, pp. 4. 47630

Memorial from California on the Ship-Building Interests of the United States ... to the Senate and House ... from the Association for the Restoration of American Shipping Interests. *San Francisco: ... Printing Office of Trumbull & Smith.* 1870. 8vo, pp. 31. H. 47631

Memorial from the United Society of Believers, or Shakers, asking for Exemption from Service of such Members as may be Drafted. [n. p. n. d.] 8vo, pp. 8. 47632

Memorial Histórico Espanol. Coleccion de documentos, opúsculos y antigüedades, que publica la Real Academia de la Historica. *Madrid.* 1851. Sm. 4to. Continued. 47633

This valuable collection of unedited documents, published by the Royal Academy of Madrid, contains some interesting contributions to the early history of the Spanish colonies in South America.

Memorial humbly shewing the Past and Present State of the Land lying waste and uninhabited between Nova Scotia and the Province of Main in New England in America. *London.* 1721. Folio. 47634

Title from one of Thomas Thorpe's catalogues.

Memorial i Informacion por las Iglesias Metropolitanas i Catedrales de las Indias, sobre que sean proveidas sus Prelacias en los Naturales, i Capitulares dellas. *Madrid: Por Francisco Martinez.* 1634. Folio, 24 leaves. 47635

In Andrade's catalogue this is attributed to Luis de Betancurt y Figueroa.

Memorial most humbly Addressed. *See* [Pownall (T.)]

The Memorial of a Convention of Delegates Representing the Merchants and others interested in Commerce, assembled at Philadelphia, to the Congress ... [Nov. 4, 1820. *Philadelphia.* 1820.] 8vo, pp. 11. 47636

Memorial of a Delegation to the Cherokee Tribe of Indians. [*Washington.*] 1832. 8vo, pp. 5. 47637

... Memorial of certain ... Tailors of Boston, praying that additional duty be imposed on Ready Made Clothing ... . May 5, 1828. ... *Washington: Printed by Duff Green.* 1828. 8vo, pp. 5.

... Memorial of Citizens of Chesterfield, ... against a Further Increase of Duties on Imported Articles. ... 1828. ... *Washington.* 1828. 8vo, pp. 8. H. 47639

The Memorial of Common-Sense, upon the present Crisis between Great-Britain and America. ... *London: J. Almon.* M.DCC.LXXVIII. 8vo, pp. 29. H. 47640

The writer gives up all hope of subduing the colonies. He fears the intrigues of France, which can only be counteracted by Great Britain "by a wise acknowledgment of that, which she cannot deny to be a fact, and which she hath no power to prevent." *See* "Monthly Review," LVIII. 239.

Memorial of French Citizens of Wayne County, Territory of Indiana. *Washington.* 1805. 8vo. 47641

An imperfect title from a Baltimore catalogue.

... Memorial of Inhabitants of ... Albany and County of Sullivan; on ... affording protecting duties, to Domestic Manufactures. ... 1828. ... *Washington.* 1828. 8vo, pp. 5. H. 47642

Also: ... Memorial of Inhabitants of Newberry District, ... South Carolina, against further protecting Duties ... 1828. ... *Washington.* 1828. 8vo, pp. 6.— ... Memorial of Inhabitants of Otsego County, upon ... Duties on ... Imported Manufactures, ... 1828. ... *Washington.* 1828. 8vo, pp. 5. H.— ... Memorial of Inhabitants of Dutchess County ... New York, upon ... the Bill ... imposing duties on Imports. ... 1828. ... *Washington.* 1828. 8vo, pp. 7.— ... Memorial of Inhabitants of ... Albany ... praying further protection to Agricultural and Manufacturing Interests. ... *Washington.* 1828. 8vo, pp. 6. H.

Memorial of Inhabitants of ... Philadelphia to Congress, on the Missouri Slave Question, November, 1819. *Philadelphia.* 1819. 4to, pp. 10. M. 47643

Memorial of Manufacturers of Naval Machinery for the United States ... . *Washington: Gibson Brothers, Printers.* 1868. 8vo, pp. 13, (1). H. 47644

Memorial of Mr. David L. Dodge, consisting of an Autobiography, ... with a few Selections from his Writings. *Boston: Published only for the Family.* 1854. 8vo, pp. 325. C. 47645

Memorial of Officers of the Army of the United States, praying that the Bill to abolish Brevet Rank may not become a Law. *Washington.* 1832. 8vo. S. 47646

Memorial of Officers. *See* [Walker (W. W.)]

Memorial of Officers of the United States Navy, for an Increase of Pay. *New York.* 1866. 8vo. 47647

A Memorial of Some of the Part-Owners and Proprietors of the Patents of Minisink and Wawayanda, bordering on the Crown-Lands in the Colony of New-York, that lie between these Patents and the true Boundaries of New-Jersey. In Be-

half of themselves, and the other Owners and Proprietors of the Patents ranging with the said Patents of Minisink and Wawayanda, between Hudson's and Delaware Rivers. Respecting the Controversy between the Colonies of New-York and New-Jersey. ... *New-York: Printed and Sold by J. Parker and W. Weyman, at the New-Printing-Office in Beaver-Street.* MDCCLVII. Folio, pp. 20. N., P. 47648

A very rare and important tract.

Memorial of Sugar Refiners, asking for a New Classification of Sugars for Tariff Purposes. [n. p.] 1869. 8vo. 47649

... Memorial of Sundry Citizens of Alleghany County ... Pennsylvania, in favor of an increase of the Tariff for ... Domestic Manufactures. ... 1828. ... *Washington.* 1828. 8vo, pp. 11. H. 47650

Memorial of Sundry Inhabitants of the Counties of Randolph and St. Clair, in the Indiana Territory. January 17, 1806. ... *City of Washington: A. & G. Way, Printers.* 1806. 8vo, pp. 12. H.

Memorial of sundry Inhabitants. *See* Massachusetts, 45916.

Memorial of sundry Proprietors ... of American Steam Vessels, on the Policy ... of Certain Enactments contained in the Law relative to Steamboats. *New York.* 1840. 8vo, pp. 12.

Memorial of the Agents. *See* N. England Mississippi Land Co.

Memorial of the American Philosophical Society, and of the Historical Society of Philadelphia, recommending the publication of certain Ancient Records, and the Report of a Committee of the House of Representatives upon the subject. *Harrisburg.* 1836. 8vo. P. 47653

Also: Memorial ... praying a repeal of the existing Duty on Books imported. *Washington.* 1822. 8vo, pp. 7.

Memorial of the American Society for the Diffusion of Useful Knowledge, praying the attention of Congress to the important objects of that Institution. February 19, 1839. *Washington.* 1839. 8vo, pp. 83. 47654

Memorial of the American Society for the Encouragement of Domestic Manufactures. January 19, 1822. ... *Washington: Printed by Gales & Seaton.* 1822. 8vo, pp. 5. 47655

... Memorial of the Boston Sanitary Association to the Legislature of Massachusetts, asking for ... a Board of Health and ... Vital Statistics. *Boston.* 1861. 8vo, pp. 31. B. 47656

A Memorial of the Case. *See* [Franklin (B.)], VII. 25554.

Memorial of the Cherokee Indians, with a Letter of John Ross, Chief of the Nation, to a Gentleman in Philadelphia. *Washington, D. C.* 1838. 8vo. 47657

... Memorial of the Citizens of Abbeville District, S. C. against an increase of Duties on Imported Goods. ... 1827. *Washington.* 1827. 8vo, pp. 16. H. 47658

Memorial of the Citizens of Boston, ... in Favor of Further Protection to Manufactures. *Washington.* 1828. 8vo, pp. 9.

Also: Memorial ... in Favor of the Increase of Duty on Woollen Goods ... . *Washington.* 1828. 8vo, pp. 59.

Memorial of the Citizens of Cairo and Vicinity, relating to the permanent location of a Western Navy and Dock Yard, and Naval Depot. *Cairo, Illinois.* 1864. 8vo, pp. 5. H. 47660

... Memorial of the Citizens of Chester District, South Carolina, adverse to an increase of Duty on Woollen Goods ... . 1828. ... *Washington.* 1828. 8vo, pp. 5. H. 47661

Memorial of the Citizens of Cincinnati to ... Congress ... relative to the Navigation of the Ohio and Mississippi Rivers. *Cincinnati: L'Hommedieu & Co.* 1843. 8vo, pp. 36. + *Cincinnati.* 1844. 8vo, pp. 53. H. 47662

... Memorial of the Citizens of Edgefield, against the Woollen Bill. ... 1827. ... *Washington.* 1827. 8vo, pp. 7. H. 47663

Also: ... Memorial of the Citizens of Georgetown, South Carolina, adverse to the increase of Duties on Coarse Woollens ... . 1828. ... *Washington.* 1828. 8vo, pp. 7.

Memorial of the Citizens of Laurens District, South Carolina, adverse to the Present Tariff, and to the Passage of the Woollens Bill. January 10, 1828. ... *Washington: Printed by Duff Green.* 1828. 8vo, pp. 8. H. 47664

... Memorial of the Citizens of Laurens District, South Carolina, against any Increase of the Tariff, &c. January 22, 1828. ... *Washington: Printed by Gales & Seaton.* 1828. 8vo, pp. 6.

Memorial of the Citizens of New-York. *See* Vol. VI. 22747.

Memorial of the Citizens of the Counties of St. Lawrence, Franklin and Clinton, ... praying for an Act, authorizing a Survey of the Route of a Canal to connect Lakes Ontario, Champlain, etc., presented the 28th of January. [n. p. 1837.] 8vo.

The catalogue of the Albany Institute describes a work with a similar title, dated 1824.

... Memorial of the Citizens of Union District, South Carolina, against the System of Protecting Duties adopted by Congress. ... 1828. ... *Washington: Printed by Duff Green.* 1828. 8vo, pp. 4. H. 47667

Memorial of the Clerks in the Executive Departments, at Washington City. [*Washington:*] *Polkinhorn's ... Press.* [1857.] 8vo, pp. 16. 47668

Memorial of the Committee Appointed by the "Free Trade Convention" ... . *Washington.* 1832. 8vo, pp. 55. P. 47669

See Gallatin (A.), Vol. VII., No. 26399, *note*, for another edition.

Memorial of the Creek Nation of Indians. *Washington.* 1832. 8vo, pp. 8. 47670

Memorial of the Dedication of Monuments erected by the Moravian Historical Society, to mark the sites of Ancient Missionary Stations in New York and Connecticut. *New York: C. B. Richardson.* 1860. 8vo, pp. viii, 184. Plates. 47671

... Memorial of the Delegation of the Cherokee Nation, March 9, 1840. [*Washington.* 1840.] 8vo, pp. 117. 47672

See also Vol. III., No. 12467.

Memorial of the First Great South-Western Turnpike Road Company. *Albany.* 1823. 8vo. 47673

A Memorial of the Goodness of God, in Two Discourses, delivered at the Opening of the First Presbyterian Church in ... New York, Jan. 11, 1846, By the Pastor. ... *New York: Robert Carter.* 1846. 12mo, pp. 120. 47674

... Memorial of the Head Men and Warriors Of the Creek Nation of Indians, February 6, 1832. ... [*Washington.* 1832.] 8vo, pp. 5. 47675

... Memorial of the Inhabitants of Dutchess County, ... New York, against an increase of Duty on Imported Merchandise, &c. ... 1828. ... *Washington: Printed by Gales & Seaton.* 1828. 8vo, pp. 7. H. 47676

Memorial of the Inhabitants ... on the Niagara Frontier, ... to the Senate and House of Representatives ... . *City of Washington: Printed by Jonathan Elliot.* 1817. 8vo, pp. vii, 5–56. BA.

Memorial of the Masonic Festival ... held at Dubuque, Iowa. *Dubuque.* 1867. 8vo, pp. 46. 47678

Memorial of the Memphis, El Paso and Pacific Railroad Comp'y, of Texas, Praying for a Grant of Public Lands, and a Loan ... to aid in constructing a ... Railroad ... from Jefferson, in Texas, to San Diego, in California, ... under the title of The Southern Trans-Continental Railroad. *Philadelphia: King & Baird, Printers.* 1868. 8vo, pp. 72. Map. H. 47679

The Memorial of the Merchants, ... in Salem ... to ... Congress ... on the Discontinuance of Credits on Revenue Bonds, the Abolition of Drawbacks, and other Restrictions on Commerce. *Salem.* 1820. 8vo, pp. 19. W. 47680

Memorial of the Merchants of Boston Praying the Repeal or Modification of the Non-importation Act. April 30, 1812. *Washington City.* [1812.] 8vo, pp. 15. 47681

See also our Vol. II., No. 6524.

Memorial of the Merchants of ... Boston, in ... Massachusetts. February 3, 1806. Referred to the Committee of the Whole House, on the State of the Union. *City of Washington: A. & G. Way, Printers.* 1806. 8vo, pp. 17. H. 47682

Memorial of the Owners and Underwriters of the American Ship, New Jersey, respectfully accompanied by certain Documents to establish the Facts therein represented. *Philadelphia.* 1806. 8vo, pp. 66. 47683

For an "Examination of the Memorial," *see* Vol. VI., No. 23361.

Memorial of the Owners of Real Estate in the vicinity of the Washington Military Parade Ground, for relief from the assessments ... . *New-York: Printed by Clayton & Van Norden.* 1828. 8vo, pp. 8. H. 47684

Memorial of the Paper Manufacturers. [n. p. 1862.] 8vo, pp. 8. 47685

Memorial of the present deplorable State. *See* New England.

Memorial of the Quarter-Centennial Celebration of the establishment of Normal Schools in America, ... at Framingham, July 1, 1864. *Boston: Printed by C. C. P. Moody.* 1866. 18mo, pp. 59

Memorial of the Religious Society of Friends to the Legislature of Virginia, on the Militia Laws. With a Letter from Benjamin Bates, ... to a Member of the Legislature. ... *New Bedford: Printed for A. Shearman, Jun.* 1813. 12mo, pp. 18. H. + [n. p. n. d.] 12mo, pp. 18. + *New York: Samuel Wood & Sons.* 1818. 8vo, pp. 20. 47687

See also Bates (Benjamin), Vol. I., No. 3922.

Memorial of the Semi-Centennial Anniversary of the American Colonization Society, celebrated at Washington, January 15, 1867. ... *Washington.* 1867. 8vo, pp. 190, (2). H. 47688

Memorial of the Society of Friends in regard to the Indians. [*Baltimore.* 1867.] 8vo, pp. 7. + [*Ibid.* 1870.] 8vo, pp. 8, and cover. H. 47689

Memorial of the Thirteenth General Assembly of Iowa ... relative to Water Communication between the Atlantic and Mississippi. *Des Moines.* 1870. 8vo. 47690

Memorial of the Town of Deerfield, &c. and the Report of the two Houses thereon against the Existing War and Embargo. [n. p.] 1814. 8vo, pp. 12. W. 47691

A State Document. Reported February 4, 1814, in Senate and House.

Memorial of the United Illinois, etc. *See* Vol. IX. 34296.

Memorial of the United States Naval Engineers, to ... Congress ... . *New York: C. A. Alvord, Printer.* 1864. 8vo, pp. 14.

Memorial of the William Penn Parlor, in the Great Central Fair, ... June, 1864, for the benefit of the U. S. Sanitary Commission ... . *Philadelphia.* [1864.] 8vo, pp. 14. 47693

... Memorial of the Wool Growers and Manufacturers of Berkshire ... Massachusetts. December 31, 1827. *Washington: Printed by Gales & Seaton.* 1828. 8vo, pp. 5. H. 47694

... Memorial of the Workers in Iron of Philadelphia, Praying that the ... Duty on Imported Iron may be repealed, &c. ... 1831. ... [n. p. n. d.] 8vo, pp. 16. B. 47695

Memorial on behalf of the Surviving Officers of the Revolutionary Army of the United States to the Congress of the United States. N. 47696

Memorial on Personal Representation. Addressed to the ... Convention of the State of New York, by the Personal Representative Society. *New York: A. Simpson & Co.* 1867. 8vo, pp. 9. 47697

Memorial on Slavery in America, from Ministers and Office Bearers in the County of Lancaster, etc. to Churches in America. *Manchester: Printed by Prentice and Cathrall.* [1844.] 12mo, pp. 12. BA. 47698

Memorial on the Sixteenth Census. *Washington.* 1845. 8vo.

Memorial Papers. The Memorial; with Circular and Questions of the Episcopal Commission; Report of the Commission; Contributions of the Commissioners; and Communications from Episcopal and Non-Episcopal Divines. With an Introduction by Rt. Rev. A. Potter, D.D., one of the Commissioners. *Philadelphia.* 1857. 12mo, pp. 444. S. 47700

Mémorial présenté. *See* Cardenas (B. de), III. 10806.

Memorial Presented to the Legislature of ... New-York, on behalf of the Scientific Commission convened ... in Albany ... in relation to a National University to be Established in the State of New-York. [*Albany.* 1852.] 8vo, pp. 11. H. 47701

Memorial que presentan a todas las Comunidades, y Gremios los Pobres Mendigos de Mexico por Mano de su Arzobispo. *Mexico* [about 1770]. 4to, pp. xxix. 47702

A Memorial Relating. *See* [MacKercher (D.)], XI. 43443.

Memorial reported to have been laid before the "General Council" of the Bishops, Clergy and Laity of the Protestant Episcopal Church in the Confederate States of America, held in St. Paul's Church, Augusta, Georgia, November 22, 1862. [n. p. n. d.] 8vo, pp. 8. 47703

"An amusing squib."—J. R. BARTLETT.

Memorial Service for Three Hundred Thousand Union Soldiers, with the Commemorative Discourse, by Rev. J. P. Thompson. *New York.* 1866. 8vo, pp. 28. 47704

A Memorial setting forth. *See* [Garay (J.)], VII. 26548.

Of this work there is another edition, pp. (1), 44.

Memorial; sobre las oposiciones. *See* [Mañozca (Juan de)].

A Memorial to Congress against An Increase of Duties on Importations, By Citizens of Boston ... . *Boston: Dutton.* 1827. 8vo, pp. 15. S. 47705

A Memorial ... against the Tariff Law of 1828, by Citizens of Boston. *Boston: Beals, Homer and Co., Printers.* 1829. 8vo, pp. 16. H. 47706

Memorial ... by Citizens of Boston and Vicinity, on the Extension of Slavery. *Boston.* 1819. 8vo. 47707

Memorial ... by Natives of Ireland. ... *New York.* 1801. 8vo.

Memorial ... from the Canal Convention at Chicago, to facilitate Commerce between the East and West. [n. p. n. d.] 8vo, pp. 16. 47709

Memorial ... from the Chamber of Commerce of New York, in favor of enlarging the Canals for the Defence of the Lakes. *New York: W. C. Bryant & Co.* 1863. 8vo, pp. 14. 47710

Memorial ... from the Union League of Philadelphia, on the System of Recruiting by means of Local Bounties. December, 1864. [n. p. n. d.] 8vo, pp. 6. 47711

Memorial ... of the Clerks ... of the Executive Departments at Washington, for an Increase of Compensation. ... 1866. [*Washington:*] *McGill & Witherow, Printers.* [1866.] 8vo, pp. 15. H. 47712

Memorial ... of the Society of Paper Makers of Pennsylvania and Delaware, Jan. 15, 1820. [*Philadelphia.* 1820.] 8vo, pp. 15

Memorial ... on Steamboat Navigation in the West. *Cincinnati.* [1848.] 8vo, pp. 10. H. 47714

Memorial ... submitted by various Canal Conventions. *Madison.* 1870. 8vo. 47715

On Wisconsin and Fox Rivers improvement.

A Memorial to Sir Robert Peel and the Earl of Aberdeen on the Oregon Dispute with the United States of America. [n. p.] 1846. 4to, pp. 4. 47716

Title from Joseph Smith's catalogue. A Quaker document.

Memorial to the Commissioners of the Albany Basin, by Owners of Ground lying on the inland side of the Upper Part of the Basin. [n. p. n. d.] 8vo. 47717

Memorial to ... Congress on the Contract made with Messrs. Ramsey and Carmick for the Transportation of the Mails between New Orleans and San Francisco. *New-York: Printed by Baker & Godwin.* 1855. 8vo, pp. 28. 47718

A Memorial to the Congress of the United States for a General Bankrupt Law. New York, Oct. 1, 1861. *New York: Baker & Godwin.* 1861. 8vo, pp. 14. 47719

Memorial to ... Congress ... regarding the Abolition of the Presidency. [*New York.* n. d.] 8vo, pp. 8. H. 47720

Memorial to ... Congress. *See* Vol. II. 6527, Vol. VII. 28799

Memorial to the Government of the United States, from the Citizens of Chicago, Ill. Setting forth the Advantages of that City as a site for a National Armory and Foundry. ... 1861. *Beach & Barnard, Printers, Chicago.* [n. d.] 8vo, pp. 22.

Memorial to the ... Legislature of New-York by the Claimants of the Lands purchased of Connecticut, commonly called the Gore [dated Connecticut, March 9, 1801]. 8vo. 47722

Memorial ... to the Honourable, etc. *See* Vol. III. 12487.

A Memorial to the ... Senate and House of Representatives of the United States ... . By a Company of Swiss Settlers. *Philadelphia: J. F. Hurtell.* 1820. 8vo, pp. 27. 47723

A Memorial to the Legislature. *See* Vol. V., No. 18516.

A Memorial to the Legislature of the State of New York upon The Effects of the Passage of the Trade of the Western States, through the Welland and Oswego Canals, upon the Income of the State and the Interests of its Citizens. *Rochester: Press of E. Shepard.* 1845. 8vo, pp. 24. S. 47724

A Memorial to the Legislature of the State of New York upon the Present State of the Canals; the Necessity of their Enlargement ... . January 24, 1857. [n. p. n. d.] 8vo, pp. 15.

Memorial to the Legislature of Rhode-Island, in favor of the prohibition of all Lotteries. February, 1844. [n. p. 1844.] 8vo, pp. 12. H. 47726

Memorial to the Massachusetts. *See* [Le Barnes (John W.)]

A Memorial to the Queen, on the subject of ... Slavery, presented by the Meeting for Sufferings on behalf of the Society of Friends, ... 1849. *London.* 1849. 4to, pp. 2. 47727

Memorial to the Senate ... from the Tobacco Cutters' Association, of Michigan, relative to the Tax on Tobacco. ... *Detroit.* 1866. 8vo, pp. 6, (1). H. 47728

Memorial to the United States Senate. and House of Representatives. [n. p. 1866?] 8vo, pp. 8. H. 47729

Memorial ultramarino e maritimo: Publicação mensal, redigida pela Secretaria d'Estado dos Negocios de Marinha e Ultramar. N.º 1.º Março de 1836. *Lisboa: Na Imprensa Nacional.* 1836. 8vo, pp. 52. 47730

Memorial Upon the Free Admission of Foreign Copper Ores. [*Baltimore?* 1868.] 8vo, pp. 8. H. 47731

Memorial Volume of the first Fifty Years of the A. B. C. F. M. ... Fourth Edition. *Boston.* 1861. 8vo. 47732

Prepared by R. Anderson.

... Memorial with the Resolutions adopted at the Anti-Tariff Meeting, ... at Abbeville Court-House, South-Carolina, ... 1827. ... *Washington: Printed by Duff Green.* 1828. 8vo, pp. 17.

See Ballard (E.), No. 2953, New York, and other names of States, etc.

The Memorialists Reply. *London.* 1773. 8vo. 47734

Memorials and Resolutions of Sundry Merchants relative to the Infringements of our Neutral Trade. With Resolutions. Nov. 18, 1808. *Washington.* 1808. 8vo, pp. 138. 47735

Memorials concerning Deceased Friends: being a Selection from the Records of the Yearly Meeting for Pennsylvania, &c., from ... 1788 to 1819 inclusive. *Philadelphia.* 1821. 12mo, pp. 186. + Second Edition. [*Ibid.*] + ... *London, Reprinted ... by William Phillips.* 1821. 12mo, pp. 188. + *Philadelphia.* 1843. 12mo. + From 1788 to 1850. *Philadelphia: Printed by Joseph Rakestraw.* 1850. 12mo, pp. 168. 47736

Memorials concerning Deceased Friends, Members of the Yearly Meeting of Philadelphia. ... *Philadelphia: Printed by Joseph and William Kite.* 1842. 12mo, pp. 96. + ... *London, Reprinted: Charles Gilpin.* 1842. 12mo, pp. 96. + *Philadelphia: Printed by Joseph Rakestraw.* 1850. 12mo, pp. 56.

Memorials concerning several Ministers, and Others, Deceased; of the Religious Society of Friends ... . [Of the New York Yearly Meeting.] *New York.* 1814. 12mo, pp. 127. + *London: Reprinted ... by W. Phillips.* 1816. 12mo, pp. 127. + *New York: Mahlon Day.* 1825. 12mo, pp. 127. + *York: Alexander & Son.* 1827. 12mo. + *New York: Mahlon Day.* 1829. 12mo, pp. 78. + *York: Alexander & Son.* 1829. 12mo, pp. 84.

+ *New York: Isaac T. Hopper.* 1832. 12mo, pp. 45. + [For 1846.] *New York: Baker, Crane & Dey.* 1846. 12mo, pp. 60. + [For 1848.] *New York: William J. Baner.* 1848. 12mo, pp. 36. 47738

Memorials of Deceased Friends, of New-England Yearly Meeting. ... *Providence: Knowles & Vose.* 1841. 8vo, pp. 96. Continued. B. 47739

Memorials of Early Piety. *See* [Mather (C.)], No. 46410.

Memorials of Margaret Elizabeth, ... Daughter of Rev. Albert Des Brisay, of the Province of New Brunswick. By a Friend. *New York: Carlton & Phillips.* 1856. 18mo, pp. 236. 6 Plates.

All the Memorials. *See* Vol. I., No. 774, and *add*, *Hague: Printed in the Year* M DCC LVI. 4to, pp. (2), 349, Memorials concerning St. Lucia, pp. (2), 188. H., P.

The | Memorials | of the | English and French | Commissaries | concerning St. Lucia. | *London: Printed in the Year* MDCCLV. 4to, pp. (4), 520. A., C. 47741

"Some of the memorials which have been respectively delivered by the English and French Commissaries, concerning the limits of Acadia or Nova Scotia, and the right to St. Lucia, having been printed at Paris, it has been thought necessary to print at London this edition of all the memorials upon these points, in the same form in which they were delivered." *See* "M. Rev.," XIV. 264.

The | Memorials | of the | English and French | Commissaries | Concerning the | Limits of Nova Scotia or Acadia. | *London: Printed in the Year* MDCCLV. 4to, pp. (4), 771. Map. 47742

"This work, containing the various papers drawn up by the English and French Commissioners, respecting the history and geography of Eastern Canada, Maine, New Brunswick, Nova Scotia, the Gulf of St. Lawrence, etc., is of the utmost importance to the historian of these districts. It was drawn up by Charles Townsend, and published by order of the Lords of Trade, as a full exhibit to the English title of that part of America." *See* Livingston's "Review of Military Operations," *see also* Shirley (W.), "Political Register," January, 1753, *and* Bancroft's "History," IV. 100.

Memorials of the Proprietors. *See* Vol. IV., No. 15869.

Memorials [Poetical] on Several Occasions. *New York.* 1843. 8vo. 47743

Memorials presented by the Deputies of the Council of Trade, in France to the Royal Council, in 1701, concerning the Commerce of that Nation to their American Islands ... . *London.* 1737. 8vo. 47744

In French and English. Title from a London bookseller's catalogue.

Memorials presented to the Congress of the United States of America, by the different Societies instituted for promoting the Abolition of Slavery, ... in the States of Rhode Island, Connecticut, New York, Pennsylvania, Maryland, and Virginia. ... *Philadelphia: Printed by Francis Bailey.* M DCC XCII. 8vo, pp. (4), 31. BA., P. 47745

Memorials presented to the Legislature for the Repeal of a Section of a Law granting peculiar Privileges to the Bethel Baptist Church in the Apportionment of the Common School Fund. *New York.* 1823. 8vo. 47746

Memorials written on Several Occasions, during the Illness and after the Decease of Three Little Boys. By Those who Loved Them. ... *New York: Privately Printed.* 1843. 8vo, pp. 52. 47747

Memorias. *See* [Montufau (M.)]

Memorias da Academia Real das Sciencias de Lisboa. ... *Lisboa.* 1797–1837. 12 vols., 4to. 47748

Includes some particulars relative to the Portuguese settlements in America.

Memorias de la junta inspectora de instruccion primaria del estado de San Luis Potosi, acerca de sus trabajos desde 4 de Julio de 1859 en que fue nombrada, hasta Diciembre de 1861 en que termina su periodo. *San Luis Potosi.* 1861. 12mo, pp. 47. + 1862. [*Ibid.*] 1863. 12mo, pp. 24. 47749

Memorias de la Real Academia de la Historia. Tomo I. *Madrid.* 1796. 8vo, pp. (4), 6, clxi, (1), 408, Errata, (1). Plates. Continued. BA. 47750

Includes many papers on Spanish-American topics.

Memorias de Litteratura Portugueza, publicadas pela Academia Real das Sciencias de Lisboa. *Lisboa.* 1792–1814. 8 vols., 4to.

Contains matters relative to Portuguese America.

Memorias de lo acontecido en Córdova. *See* [Isassi (J. D.)]

Memorias de los diversos Departamentos de la Administracion de la Provincia de Buenos Ayres, y de las Municipalidades de Campaña. 1867. *Buenos Aires.* 1868. 8vo. Continued. C.

Memorias de los Vireyes. *See* [Fuentes (M. A.)], VII. 26119

Memorias de um Sargento de milicias. Por um Brasileiro. [Manuel Antonio de Almeida.] *Rio de Janeiro: Typographia Brasiliense de Maximiano Gomez Ribeiro.* 1854–55. 2 vols., 8vo, pp. 142; 159. 47753

Memorias do Instituto da Ordem dos Advogados Brasileiros. *Rio de Janeiro.* 1843. 8vo. Continued. 47754

Memorias do Instituto Historico e Geographico Brasileiro. Tomo I. *Rio de Janeiro: Typographia de Laemmert.* 1839. 4to. Continued. 47755

Memorias Historicas. *See* [Cobarrubias (Josef de)].

Memorias Históricas sobre la Legislacion Gobierno del Comercio delos Españoles sus Colonias en las Indias Occidentales. *Madrid.* [n. d.] 4to. 47756

Memorias para a Historia da Capitania de S. Vicente hoje chamadu de S. Paulo do estado do Brazil. *Lisboa.* 1797. 4to.

Memorias para la Historia. *See* [Marure (A.)], *and* Mexico.

Memorias sobre los sucesos que tuvieron lugar en el Paraguay, a consecuencia del tratado entre España y Portugal de 1750 ... . *Mexico.* 1850. 4to. 47758

Memorias y Noticias. *See* Vol. I., No. 1957.

Memorie. Aanmerkingen over de Zogenaamde Antidotael Memorie tot nadere Verdediging van de Goode Zaak der Hollandsche Kooplieden. *Amsterdam: Isaac Tirion.* 1758. Folio.

A memorial demolishing the arguments of the Antidotal Memorie, which had defended the English for their capture of Dutch ships trading to and from the West Indies.

Memorie aan H. Hoog Mog. de Staaten Generaal der Vereenigde Nederlanden. [n. p. 1781.] 8vo, pp. 16. 47760

This is the first edition of the memorial of John Adams as Ambassador of the United States, proposing an alliance of the two republics. *See also* our Nos 247–8.

Memorie betreffende. *See* [Wagenaar (J.)]

Memorie d'un Giovane Nobile Sventurato che ritorna finalmente da una lunga Schiavitù sofferta nell' America, per l'Arti pessime d'un crudele Zio. *Venezia.* 1745. 12mo. 47761

A romance founded on the well-known hardships undergone by Annesley, who was shipped as a slave to America by his uncle the Earl of Anglesey. *See* Vol. I. 1603.

Memorie, gedaan maaken, en overgegeeven aan de Staaten Generaal der Vereenigde Nederlanden, door ofte van wege Hope en Compagnie, Kooplieden, woonende te Amsterdam, om de dienen tot eene compleete Verificatie van de voordragt, door dezelve, by twee Requesten, aan Hunne Hoog Mogende, gedaan,

nopens het arivement van het Americaansch Fregat-Schip, genaamt The Illustrious President, gevoert by Capt. Dennis Buttler, binnen Texel; en nopens de redenen, welken het gemelde Schip van Duins naar Texel hebben doen steevenen. [n. p. n. d.] Folio, pp. (6), 20. 47762

Memorie istoriche per servire alla vita de piu uomini illustri della Toscana raccolta da una societa' di letterati. *Livorno.* 1757–58. 2 vols., 4to. 47763

Contains a portrait and memoir of Amerigo Vespucci.

Memorie over de achterstallighe subsidien by den Staat geconsenteert aan de West-Indische Compagnie ... . [n. p. 1674.] 4to, pp. 14. 47764

This memorial regarding the subsidies in arrears, granted by the State, contains all the publications from the year 1631 to 1654, which treat of the subsidies granted by the States General to the West India Company.

Memorie van consideratien van Bewindhebberen der West Indische Compagnie indien deeze zoude moeten worden gedissolveerd. [n. p.] 1791. Folio, pp. 46. 47765

Considerations of the directors on the dissolution of the West India Company.

Memorie van de Bewint-hebberen der West-Indische Compagnie ter Kamer van Amsterdam ... 21 julii 1664 aen de ... Staten-Generaal der Vereenigde Nederlanden. Neffens een beëedigde verklaring van Andries Cornelissen Vertholen. *Amsterdam.* 1664. 4to. 47766

This rare piece is not described by Asher.

Memorie van de Consideratien der Gecommitteerdens uyt de Hollandsche Raden en Ministers in de Collegien ter Admiraliteyt in Holland residerende op de Motiven, Bedenkingen en Advisen van de Leden van het groot Besogne, over het different nopens het Regt van de Westindische Compagnie tot de recognitie van de Carolina Ryst. Exhibitum 7 November 1765. [n. p. 1765.] Folio, pp. 28. 47767

Memorie van de ghevvichtighe redenen. *See* [Usselincx (W.)]

Memorie van elucidatien, concerneerende de discrepeerende sentimenten van haar Edele Groot Mog. Gecommitteerden zo als dezeloe voorkomen in het nader Rapport op den 27 January laatsleeden ter Vergadering van Hoogst dezelve uitgebragt ... . [n. p. 1776.] 47768

Concerning the Greenland and Davis's Straits fishery.

Memorie van Remarques. *See* Vol. VI., No. 22993.

Memorie vervattende een Vertoog der Grondregelen strekkende tot Duidelyke Opheldering en Verklaring der Traktaten Wegepast op het Traktaat van 1674; Overgegeven aan de Wel Edele Geskenge Heeren Boseel, van de Poll, en Meerman, buitengewone Afgezanten van dezen Staat aan het Hof van Engeland. *Amsterdam.* 1759. Folio. 47769

A memorial touching the infringement of various treaties by the English in capturing Dutch ships trading to and from the West Indies.

Memorie wegens het belang dezer Republicq in het sluiten van een tractaat van Commercie met de Vereenigde Staaten van America. *Rotterdam.* 1781. 8vo, pp. 20. 47770

Memorial on the interest of Holland in a treaty with the United States.

MEMPHIS, *Tenn.* Annual Report of the Memphis Chamber of Commerce and Merchants' Exchange, ... 1869. Compiled by W. L. Trask. *Memphis: Cowperthwait, Chapman & Co., Printers.* 1869. 8vo, pp. 64. Continued. 47771

Fifth Annual Report ... of the Memphis City Schools, for ... 1856–7. *Memphis.* 1857. 8vo, pp. 24. Continued. H.

First Annual Statement of the Trade and Commerce of Memphis, for ... 1861. Reported ... by Jno. S. Toof, Secretary. *Memphis: O'Neill & Parrish, Printers.* 1861. 8vo, pp. 37. B.

Denson's Memphis Directory, for 1865. *Memphis: [P. M. Pinckard.]* 1865. 8vo. C. 47774

Halpin's City Directory Memphis, 1867–8. Containing also: a ... Business Register, etc. T. M. Halpin, Compiler. *Memphis.* 1867. 8vo, pp. 21–339. Continued. B. 47775

The Memphis Almanac for 1856. *New York: Printed by Baker & Godwin.* [1856.] 12mo. 47776

Sixth Annual Report of the Directors of the Memphis and Charleston Railroad Company, to the Stockholders; March 1, 1856. *Memphis.* 1856. 8vo. Continued. 47777

The Charter of the Memphis and Ohio Railroad Company, with the ... laws ... by which said R. R. Co. is Governed. *Memphis: Mosely & Finnie, Printers.* 1854. 8vo, pp. 47. H.

Memorial of the Memphis, El Paso ... R. R. *See* No. 47679

Statement of the Memphis, Helena and St. Louis Levee Railroad. 1869. [n. p. n. d.] 8vo. 47779

Annual Announcement and Circular of the Memphis Medical College ... 1852–53. ... and Catalogue ... 1851–52. *Memphis.* 1852. 8vo, pp. xv. H. 47780

Also: Catalogue of the Second Session of the Memphis Medical College, 1847–48. *Memphis.* 1848. 8vo, pp. 12.

... Memphis Medical Recorder, Published ... by the Memphis Medical College. ... 1852. *Memphis.* [1852.] 8vo. Cont'd.

Memphis Riots. Report of the Select Committee of the House of Representatives. *Washington.* 1866. 8vo. 47782

Minutes and Proceedings of the Memphis Convention, assembled Oct. 23, 1849. *Memphis.* 1850. 8vo, pp. 68. BA.

Proceedings of the Chamber of Commerce of ... Memphis, in favor of the Repeal of the Cotton Tax. ... 1867. *Memphis.* [1867.] 8vo, pp. 8. H. 47784

Proceedings of the Commercial Convention at Memphis, May, 1869. [n. p. n. d.] 8vo. 47785

Report on the Health and Mortality of Memphis for 1852. *Memphis.* 1853. 8vo. Continued. 47786

... Report ... on the Debts and Revenues of the City of Memphis. ... 1850. *Memphis: Van Pelt & McClanahan, Printers.* 1850. 8vo, pp. 8. H. 47787

Men and Manners in America. *See* [Hamilton (T.)], 30034.

Men of Color to Arms! Now or Never! [n. p. 1863?] 4to, pp. 1. 47788

Men of History. By Eminent Writers. *Edinburgh: William P. Nimmo.* 1866. Post 8vo, pp. 319. 47789

Includes Washington and Franklin.

The Men of Old. *Philadelphia.* 1836. 8vo, pp. 60. 47790

The Men of the Time in 1852; or, Sketches of Living Notables. *London.* 1852. Post 8vo. + *Redfield, New York.* 1852. 12mo, pp. 564. C. + Fourth Edition. [*Ibid.*] 1856. H.

Reproduced as: "Men of the Time. Biographical Sketches of Eminent Living Characters:" ... *London: David Bogue.* 1856. Post 8vo, pp. xv, 926, (2); and again as: "Men of the Time. A Biographical Dictionary of Eminent Living Characters of both Sexes. A New Edition, ... revised" ... . *London: George Routledge and Sons.* 1865. 8vo, pp. xxxix, (1), 860. B. + A New Edition, ... By Edward Walford, M.A. ... *London: Routledge, Warne, & Routledge.* 1862. 8vo, pp. vi, (2), 842.—Men of

the Time: A Dictionary of Contemporaries ... . [Revised by G. H. Townsend.] Seventh Edition ... . *London: George Routledge and Sons.* 1868. 8vo, pp. vii, 859, (1). Includes many Americans.

Men of the Time: Being Biographies of Generals Halleck, [and others]. *New York: Beadle and Company.* [1862.] 12mo, pp. 100. + [No. II.] Biographies of Generals Butler [and others. *Ibid.* 1862.] 12mo, pp. 6–100. + [No. III.] Biographies of Generals Hooker [and others. *Ibid.* 1863.] 12mo, pp. 99.

The Men who Advertise; An Account of Successful Advertisers ... . *New York: Nelson Chesman.* 1870. 8vo, pp. (2), 872.

Men who have Risen. ... Illustrated by C. A. Doyle. *New York: W. A. Townsend & Company.* 1860. 8vo, pp. (2), 315. 8 Plates. H. 47794

MENARD (J. W.) Black and White. No Party—No Creed. A Lecture. By J. Willis Menard. [n. p. n. d.] 8vo, pp. 6.

MÉNARD (T.) Histoire des États-Unis d'Amérique; par Théophile Ménard. Troisième Édition. *Tours.* [n. d.] 12mo, pp. 240. 47796

MENASSEH BEN ISRAEL. *See* Manasseh Ben Israel, 44190–4

MENCKE (J. B.) Catalogue des principaux historiens avec des remarques critiques sur la bonté de leurs ouvrages et sur le choix des meilleures éditions. Par J. B. Mencke. *Lipsic* [sic]. M DCC-XIV. 12mo, pp. 426. 47797

Includes works relating to America.

MENDELL (*Miss* ——), *and* HOSMER (Harriet). Notes of Travel and Life [in the United States]. By ... Misses Mendell and Hosmer. ... *New York: The Authors.* M.DCCC.LIV. 12mo, pp. 288. B., C. 47798

MENDENHALL (T.) An Entire New Plan for a National Currency; ... To which is added a Plan for a Real National Bank. By Thomas Mendenhall. *Philadelphia: Printed by Joseph Rakestraw.* 1834. 8vo, pp. 32. 47799

MENDENHALL (W.) History, Correspondence, and Pedigrees of the Mendenhalls of England and the United States ... . by William Mendenhall, of Bath, England. Extended by ... Tables of Pedigrees of the American Family, by his Son, Edward Mendenhall, of Cincinnati ... . *Cincinnati: Moore, Wilstach & Baldwin.* 1866. 8vo, pp. 65. 47800

MENDES DE ALMEIDA (C.) Altas do Imperio do Brazil, comprehendendo as respectivas divisões administrativas, ecclesiasticas eleitoraes e judiciarias. ... por Candido Mendes de Almeida, ... *Rio de Janeiro: Just, philomathico.* 1868. Sq. folio, pp. 37. 28 Maps. C. 47801

MENDES (Luis Antonio de Oliveira). Discurso preliminar historico á descripção economica da comarca da cidade da Bahia, em que se entra no paralello do commercio e da navegação antiga e moderna ... . [n. p. n. d.] 8vo. 47802

MENDES (R. I.) Documentos oficiales que dan el justo concepto acerca de la expulsion del Illmo. Sr. Dr. Ramon Ignacio Mendes, dignisimo Arzobispo de Carácas, y sobre otras circunstancias interesantes que occurrieron en ella. *Carácas.* 1830. 4to, pp. 77. 47803

MENDES. Repuesta á la Contestacion sobre la estincion de Conventos y Establecimiento de Colegios que corre inserta en la Gaceta de Venezuela del Sábado 8 de Febrero de 1834. Por Ramon I. Mendes Arzobispo de Carácas. *Carácas.* 1834. 8vo, pp. 15. 47804

Also: Reflexiones que el Arzobispo de Carácas y Venezuela, Dr. Ramon Ignacio Mendez, dirige á sus Diocesanos sobre varios errores que se propagan en las diocesis. *Carácas: C. F. Devisme.* 1832. 8vo, pp. 128.—Representacion que el Clero de Carácas hace al Sob. Congreso de Venezuela sobre la expulsion de su digno Prelado, el Illmo. Sr. Dr. Ramon I. Méndez. *Carácas.* 1831. 8vo, pp. 13.—Representacion que el Clero de Carácas preparó para darla al Soberano Congreso de Venezuela con motivo de la expulsion de su digno Prelado el Illmo. Sr. Dr. Ramon Ignacio Méndez, ocurrida el 30 de Noviembre de 1836. *Carácas.* 1837. 8vo, pp. 19.

MENDEZ (Andres). Discurso sobre la centinela del reyno de Chile. *Lima.* 1641. 4to. 47805

MENDEZ (Juan Francisco). Panegyrico funeral a D. Tomas Tamaio de Vargas, chronista mayor de las Indias. [n. p.] 1641. 4to. 47806

MÉNDEZ (Juan de Dios). Contestacion á la Protetas que contra el acuerdo del Ve. Cabildo metropolitano de la Catedral de Carácas de 21 de Junio ultimo han públicado los Srs. Canónigos Sucre, Alpizar y Castillo. *Carácas.* 1864. 8vo, pp. 16.

MENDEZ (L.) Gaceta de las Tribunales de la Republica Mexicana. Tomo I. *Mexico.* 1860. 4to, pp. 864. 47808

MENDEZ Y LACHICA (Tomas de). Panegirico del San Philipe Neri, Pronunciado en Lima. *Lima.* 1818. 8vo, pp. 68.

MENDIBIL (P. de). Resúmen Histórico de la Revolucion de los Estados Unidos Mejicanos, por D. Pablo de Mendibil. *Londres.* 1828. 8vo. 47810

MENDICTA (M.) Manifesto Legal por D. Maximo Mendicta en el sigue contra D. Carlos Bispham Socio director de la casa consignataria de Alsop y Compania pidiendole cuenta con pago del cargamento del Bergantin Occeana pata que la Ilma Corte, en Sala de comercio confirme en segunda instancia la sentencia que el Juez de Comercio y colegas de Valparaiso pronuncia von con dictamen del Asesor titular del Consulado. *Santiago di Chili.* 1834. Sm. 4to. 47811

MENDIETA (G. de). Historia Eclesiástica Indiana. Obra escrita á fines del siglo XVI Por Fr. Gerónimo de Mendieta de la Orden de San Francisco. La publica por primera vez Joaquin García Icazbalceta. *México.* M.DCC.LXX [*i. e.* 1870]. 4to, pp. xlv, 790. C. 47812

Of this important work only four hundred and twenty copies were printed, of which twenty-six are on fine paper. It had slumbered in MS. for two hundred and fifty years, when the eminent Mexican scholar and archæologist Señor Icazbalceta brought it to light. Its importance can scarcely be overestimated. Mendicta was sent to Mexico in 1554, and remained there till 1571, having spent much of his time in the study of the Mexican languages. Torquenada evidently had access to the MS., for he has reproduced a large portion of it without giving credit to Mendieta.

MENDIVE Y GARCIA. Revista de la Habana, Periodico-quincenal, por Mendive y I. Q. Garcia. ... *Habana.* 1854. 4to. Plates. 47813

Vol. III. contains extracts from Squier and Davis' "Ancient Monuments," in Spanish.

MENDIZABAL (H.) Primeros versos de Horacio Mendizabal. *Buenos Aires.* 1865. 8vo, pp. ii, 190. 47814

[MENDIZABAL (L. de), *y* VASQUEZ (P.)] Solemnes exequias de D. Manuel Ignacio Gonzalez del Campillo, obispo de la Puebla de los Angeles. *Mexico.* 1814. 4to, 12 leaves. 47815

MENDIZABAL (P. J. de). Sermon que en el tercer dia del solemne novenario de Nuestra Señora del Pueblito conducida en secreto a la iglesia del serafico Patriarca San Francisco de Queretaro para implorar su favor en las actuales necessidades predicó en dicha Iglesia el dia 30 de Septiembre, de 1810. El Dr. D. Pedro Josef de Mendizabal. *Mexico.* 1810. 4to, pp. (4), 11.

MENDO (Andres). Crisis de los Compañia de Jesus, de su piedad, doctrina, y multiplicado fruto, que hà cogido en el universo

mundo. Escrita en lengua latina; y traducida en castellano por un discipulo afecto de esta sagrada religion. [*Mexico:*] *En la Imprenta del Colegio de S. Ildefonso.* 1765. Sm. 8vo, pp. (16), 284, (4). C. 47817

"This very earnest book is substantially a defense of the Jesuits, and their conduct and usefulness in all parts of the world. The author gives a list of above one hundred and seventy authors whom he quotes, many of them bearing testimony to the valuable services of the Order as missionaries among the heathen of both hemispheres, strongly fortified by many historical allusions to services in the new world from the time of the entrance of the Dominicans into Mexico in the time of Cortes."—STEVENS.

MENDO (H.) The Injustice and Cruelty of the Slave Trade considered; A Sermon preached at Plymouth, Feb. 22, 1789. By Herbert Mendo. *London: Law* ... . 1789. 4to, pp. 37.

See "Monthly Review," LXXX. 469.

MENDON, *Mass.* An Address, by Rev. Carlton A. Staples, of Milwaukee, Wis.; A Poem, by Hon. Henry Chapin, of Worcester, Mass., and Other Proceedings, in commemoration of The Two Hundredth Anniversary of the Incorporation of Mendon, Massachusetts. *Worcester: Printed by Chas. Hamilton.* 1868. 8vo, pp. 89, (1). 47819

The Christian Magazine conducted by Members of the Mendon Association. For ... 1824. Volume I. *Providence: Printed by Barnum Field.* 1824. 8vo, pp. (2), 383, (1). Continued. B.

A Short Account Of the State of Mendon Third Parish, Relative to Mr. Balch's settling there in the Work of the Ministry, September 14, 1768; Of His Conduct while with said People; and The Manner of his leaving them, March 27, 1773. By an Inhabitant Of said Parish. *Boston: Printed in the Year* 1773. 8vo, pp. 16. 47821

Also: Constitution of the Fraternal Communion, with an Exposition of the same; ... [n. p. n. d.] 8vo, pp. 16. *See also* "Whig Songs."

MENDONÇA (Antonio Pedro Lopes de). A Questão Financeira em 1856. *Lisboa: Na Imprensa Nacional.* 1856. 8vo, pp. 55. 47822

MENDONZA (A. de). Instruction à F. de Al. Mendonza au sujet des désordres que les Jesuites ont commis dans le Bresil et dans le Nord et dans le Sud de l'Amérique Portugaise, 8 Oct. 1757. [n. p. n. d.] 8vo. 47823

Also: Memoire de Sa Majesté au Pape Clement XIII. sur le même sujet, Ap. 1759. [n. p. n. d.] 8vo.

MENDOÇA CORTE-REAL (D. de). Examen et réponse à un écrit publié par la Compagnie des Indes Occidentales sous le titre de Réfutation des Argumens et Raisons alléguées par M. Diogo de Mendoça Corte-Real, Envoié Extraordinaire de Portugal à la Haye, dans son mémoire et l'écrit annexe presenté à leurs hautes puissances le 15 septemb. 1727 ... . [*Paris.*] 1727. 4to, pp. 64. Map. C. 47824

MENDOÇA CORTE-REAL. Traduction de la Demonstration de la Compagnie des Indes Occidentales, contenant les raisons pourquoi les Portugais ne sont point en droit de naviguer vers les côtes de la Haute et Basse Guinée, ... et examen et réfutation de toutes ces raisons. *Paris.* 1727. 4to, pp. 34. C. 47825

MENDOÇA (J. G. de). *See* Gonçalez de Mendoça (J.)

MENDOÇA. Historia | de las Cosas | mas Notables, | Ritos y Costvmbres, | Del gran Reyno dela China, sabidas assi por los libros | delos mesmos Chinas, como por relacion de Religio- | sos y otras personas que an estado en el dicho Reyno. | Hecha y ordenada por el mvy R. P. Maestro Fr. Ioan Gonçalez de Mendoça dela Orden de S. Augustin, y peniten- | ciatio Appostolico a quien la Magestad Catholica embio con su real | carta y otras cosas para el Rey de aquel Reyno el año. 1580. | Al Illvstrissimo S. Fernando | de Vega y Fonseca del consejo de su Magestad y su | presidente en el Real delas Indias. | Con vn Itinerario del nueuo Mundo. | Con Priuilegio y Licencia de su Sanctidad. | *En Roma, a costa de Bartholome Grassi.* 1585 | *en la Stampa de Vincentio Accolti.* | 8vo, 15 leaves, 1 blank leaf, Text, pp. 440. 47826

This is the correct title of our No. 27775, which *see* for a note.

MENDOÇA. Historia de las Cosas mas notables [as in our No. 27776]. *En Medina del Campo, por Sātiago del Canto.* M.D.XCV. *Por los herederos de Benito Boyer.* 12mo, 12 leaves, Text, 348 leaves, Table, 9 leaves. 47827

MENDOÇA. Dell' Historia | della China, | Descritta nella lingua Spagnuola, dal P. Maestro | Giouanni Gonzalez di Mendozza, | dell' Ord. di S. Agostino. | Et tradotta nell' Italiana, dal Magn. M. Francesco | Auanzo, cittadino originario di Venetia. | Parti dve, | Diuise in tre libri, & in tre viaggi, fatti in quei paesi, | da i Padri Agostiniani & Franciscani. | Doue si descriue il sito, & lo stato di quel gran Regno, | & si tratta della religione, de i costumi, & della | disposition de suoi popoli, & d'altri luochi | più conosciuti del mondo nuouo. | Con due Tauole, l'vna de' Capitoli, & l'altra

delle cose notabili. | *In Venetia*, MDLXXXVI. | *Appresso Andrea Muschio.* | 8vo, 15 leaves, 1 blank leaf, Text, pp. 462, 1 blank leaf, Table, etc., pp. 40. 47828

Correct title of our No. 27779. Another edition: *In Vinegia.* 1587. *Per Andrea Muschio.* 12mo, pp. 508, (1), Table, 77, (1). Stevens' "Nuggets," No. 1896, describes a variation in the imprint of our No. 27780.

MENDOÇA. Histoire dv Grand Royavme de la Chine [as in our No. 27780]. *A Paris, Chez Ieremie Perier, ruë S. Iean de Beuuais, au franc Meurier.* 1589. *Avec privilege dv Roy.* 8vo, 12 leaves, Text, 323 leaves, Index, pp. 48, (1). 47829

MENDOÇA (Lorenço de). Supplication a su Magestad Catolica del nuestro señor ante sus Reales Consejos de Portugal y de las Indias, en defensa de los Portugueses. *Madrid.* 1630. 4to.

MENDOÇA CATAÑO Y ARAGON (L. de). Excelent.^mo^ señor. El doctor don Luis de Mendoça Cataño y Aragon, suplica a V. Excelencia se le sirua de hazerle merced en la Consulta de la Mastrescolia de la santa Iglesia de Lima, ya que no huuo lugar de hazersela en el Arcedianato. [*Lima.* 1633.] 8vo, 4 leaves.

See Pinelo, Vol. II., col. 772.

MENDOSSE (T. de). Le bon advis, | Mesprisé ou la lettre | De Monsr. | Tristan de Mendosse Jadis, | Ambassadeur pour le nouveau Eletto | Don Joan El Quarto: | par grace de trahison Roy de | Portvgal. | Escrite à son successeur l'Ambassadeur de | Portugal, | Francisco de Sousa Cotinho: presente a la Haye. | [n. p.] 1649. | 4to, pp. 8. 47832

MENDOZA (A. de). Con preuilegio Ordenācas y copilacion de leyes: hechas por el muy Illustre señor don Anto- | nio d' mēdoça Uisorey y Gouernador desta nueua Espa | ña: y Presidēte dela Audiēcia Real q̄ en ella reside: y por los | señores Oydores d' la dicha audiēcia: p̄a la buēa gouerna- | ciō y estilo d' los oficiales della. *Año d'* M. d. xlviij. | [Colophon:] ... *Y* | *fuerō por su mādo impres- | sas ē la muy leal y grā ciu- | dad d' Mexico ē casa | d' Iuā pablos: aca | baronse d' imp̄mir | a xxij. dias d'l | mes d' mar | ço d'.* M. | d. xlviij. | *años.* | Folio, 48 leaves. 47833

The forty-sixth leaf is erroneously numbered xlv. It is a very early specimen of printing in Mexico. The only known copy belongs to Señor Icazbalceta of Mexico. *See* Ramusio, Vol. III., *and* Hakluyt, Vol. III.

MENDOZA (D. P.) Tratado del sistema de marcacion para los ganados del estado de Buenos-Aires, con la cartilla esplicativa y reglas para aprender á decifrar el valor de las marcas y su composicion acompanado de un numero de laminas con muchos ejemplos. Inventado por Daniel Perez Mendoza. *Buenos-Aires.* 1854. 4to, pp. vi, 19. Plates. 47834

MENDOZA (D. de). Chronica | de la Provincia de S. Antonio | de los Charcas | del orden de Nrõ. Seraphico P. | S. Francisco | En la Indias Occidentales Reyno del Peru | Escrita | por el R. P. Predicador F. Diego de Mendoza | Chronista y Padre de la mesma Prouincia. | Dedicala | Al Illmo. Yr^{mo}. S. D. F. Gabriel | de Guillestegui del Consejo de su Mag^{d}. | y Obispo del Paraguay. | *P'a Villafranca sculptor Regius, sculpsit Matriti,* 1664. | Folio, Engraved Title, 14 leaves, Text, pp. 601, (1), (6). 47835

A work of importance for the history of the provinces of Cuzco and Bolivia. There are copies dated *Matriti*, 1665.

MENDOZA (E.) Nociones de cronologia universal, formadas para los alumnos del "Liceo del Estado," por el C. Lic. Eufemio Mendoza. *Guadalajara.* 1869. 8vo, pp. 268. 47836

MENDOZA (G. H. de). Ordenanzas que mando hacer D. Garcia Hurtado de Mendoza, marques de Cañete, para el remedio de los excesos que los corregidores de los naturales hacen en tratar y contractar con los Indios, i otras cosas dirigidas al bien de ellos. *Lima.* 1594. Folio. 47837

Title from Ternaux, No. 192.

MENDOZA (Javier de). La Cuestion de Mejico y el Conde de Reus. *Madrid.* 1859. 4to, pp. 108. 47838

MENDOZA (J. de). Historia de Nuestra Señora de los Angeles de Tesaxique, por Fr. Juan de Mendoza. *Mexico.* 1672. 4to.

MENDOZA. Relacion de el Santuario de Tecique, en que está colocada la milagrosa Imagen de Nuestra Señora de los Angeles. *Mexico, por J. de Ribera.* 1684. 4to. 47840

MENDOZA (J. de). Letras de los Villancios, que se han de Cantar en la Santa Iglesia Cathedral de la Ciudad de Valladolid, en los Maytines de la Solemne Festividad del San Pedro, Año 1776–7, por Juan de Mendoza. *Mexico.* 1776–7. 4to. 47841

MENDOZA AYALA (Juan de). Conjuncion magna. Stigmaticacion mister. de San Francisco. *Mexico.* 1667. 4to, 22 leaves

MENDOZA AYALA. Virtud juiziosa, santidad prudente de San Gregorio Thaumaturgo, Obispo de Neocesaria, patron de esta

ciudad de Mexico. *Mexico: Viuda de Juan de Ribera.* 1686. 4to, 7 prel. and 13 leaves. 47843

MENDOZA (L. H. de). Memorial al rey pidiendo remedio a los excesos que se cometen en el Brasil; por D. Lorenço Hurtado de Mendoza, obispo de Rio de Janeyro. [n. p.] 1638. Folio.

MENDOZA (*Obispo del Cuzco*). Pastoral sobre el Jubileo de 1847. *Cuzco.* 1847. 4to, pp. 12. 47845

MENENDEZ (B.) Manual de geografia y estadistica del alto Perú ó Bolivia, por D. Baldomero Menendez. *Paris.* 1860. 12mo, pp. 323. + [*Ibid.*] 1861. 12mo, pp. 383. 47846

MENENDEZ. Manual de historia y cronologia de Chile. Por D. Baldomero Menendez. *Paris.* 1860. 12mo, pp. 380.

MENENDEZ DE SAN PEDRO (D. A.) Aneages mas comunes en America. Varas extrangeras, reducidas a catellanas ... . Por Don Diego Antonio Menendez de San Pedro. *Mexico.* 1810. Sm. 8vo, pp. 40. 47848

MENENDEZ DE SAN PEDRO. Meses y dias liquidos dirigidos a ajustar las cuentes a los operarios de Haciendas de campo y minas, asi como a los dependientes de comercio criados domesticos, etc. Con arreglo al sueldo que cada individuo goce por Don Diego Antonio Menendez de San Pedro. *Mexico.* 1810. Sm. 8vo, 35 leaves. 47849

MENESES BRACAMONTE (B. de). Relacion de la Vitoria de las Armas de su Magestad en la Ciudad de S. Domingo, Isla Española, contra la Armada Inglesa de Guillermo Pen, por D. B. de Meneses Bracamonte. *Sevilla.* 1655. Folio. 47850

Ternaux, No. 746, gives the title differently.

MENESES (F. de), *and* OLAVE (A. S. de). A Gloria y loor de dios, 1544.

This reference in our Vol. VII., p. 287, is an error. The work is only a portion of our Vol. X., No. 40960; for further particulars *see* [Harrisse] "Bib. Am. Vet.," No. 244.

MENEZES (F. de P.) Discurso biographico-necrologico, recitado na Academia Imperial de Medicina do Rio de Janeiro. Por Francisco de Paula Menezes. *Rio de Janeiro: Na Typographia Imparcial de Francisco de Paulo Brito.* 1841. 4to. 47851

MENEZES. Proposições sobre a degeneração cancerosa dos ossos em geral, ou osteo-sarcoma e suas diversas fórmas. These

apresentada á Faculdade de Medicina do Rio de Janeiro, por occasião do concurso ao logar de Substituto da secção cirurgica. Por Francisco de Paula Menezes. *Rio de Janeiro: Na Typographia Imparcial de Francisco de Paulo Brito.* 1839. 4to, pp. 23.

MENEZES (F. de Sá de). Malaca conquistada por o grande Affonso de Albuquerque. Poema heroico. Offerecido á catholica magestade d' elrei Filippe III de Portugal. Por Francisco de Sá de Menezes. *Lisboa, por Mathias Rodrigues.* 1634. 8vo.

The second edition is entitled: "Malaca conquistada: poema heroico. Antigamente impresso, agora reformado. Offerecido á real magestade d' el-rei D. Affonso VI nosso senhor." *Lisboa, por Paulo Craesbeeck.* 1658. 4to. + Terceira edição, mais correcta que as antecedentes. *Lisboa, na Officina de José de Aquino Bulhões.* 1779. 4to, pp. viii, 461.

MENEZES (F. X. de). Relação da victoria que os portuguezes alcançaram no Rio de Janeiro contra os francezes em 19 de Septembro de 1710. Por D. Francisco Xavier de Menezes. *Lisboa, por Antonio Pedroso Galrão.* 1711. 4to, pp. 12. 47854

MENEZES (J. de A. de). Poema heroico á felicissima jornada d' el-rei D. Joã V nosso senhor, nas plausiveis entregas das serenissimas princezas do Brasil e Asturias. Por D. Jorge de Almeida de Menezes. *Lisboa: Na Officina de Musica.* 1734. 4to, pp. xxx, 48. 47855

MENEZES (Luis de, *Conde de Ericeyra*). Historia de Portugal restaurado. *Lisboa, na Officina de João Galrão.* 1679. Folio.

This volume is of interest for the history of the Portuguese colonies in America, and the wars in Brazil with the Dutch. The second volume appeared in 1698, at which time the first volume had become so scarce that it was thought necessary to reprint it, which was done in 1710; for this reason most sets have not the original edition of the first volume.

MENEZES. Historia de Portugal restaurada. *Lisboa, na Officina de Domingos Rodrigues.* 1751. 4 vols., 4to, pp. xx, 494; 568; xxiv, 520; viii, 608. 47857

The imprint in Vols. III. and IV. is *Lisboa, na Officina dos Herdeiros de Antonio Pedroso Galrão,* 1751. Silva, v. 307, quotes "Sahiu terceira vez: Tomo I. *Lisboa, na Offic. de Domingos Rodrigues* 1751 (aliás 1759, como consta das licenças). 4to.—Tomo II, *ibi, na Offic. de Antonio Vicente da Silva* 1759. 4to.—Tomo III, *ibi, na Offic. de José Filippe* 1759. 4to.—Tomo IV, *ibi, na Offic. de de Ignacio Nogueira Xisto* 1759. 4to."

MENEZES (Manuel de). Relação do successo e batalhas que teve com a nau S. Julião, com a qual, sendo capitão-mór d'aquella viagem, se perdeu na ilha do Comero, além de Madagascar ou S. Lourenço, no anno 1616. [n. p. n. d.] 4to. 47858

MENEZES (M. J. de). Exposição historica da Maçonaria no Brasil, particularmente na provincia do Rio de Janeiro, em relação com a independencia e integridade do imperio. Por Manuel Joaquim de Menezes. *Rio de Janeiro: Empreza Nacional do Diario.* 1857. 8vo, pp. 67. 47859

MENEZES (Manuel Jacome Bezerra de). A Gratidão Parnambucana [*sic*] ao seu bemfeitor, o ex.^{mo} e rev.^{mo} sr. D. José Joaquim da Cunha de Azeredo Coutinho, bispo de Elvas ... . *Lisboa: Na nova Officina de João Rodrigues Neves.* 1808. 4to, pp. viii, 207, (1). 47860

MENGARINI (G.) A Selish or Flat-Head Grammar, [*or*] Grammatica Linguæ Selicæ. By the Rev. Gregory Mengarini, of the Society of Jesus. *New York: Cramoisy Press.* 1861. Imp. 8vo, pp. viii, 122. C. 47861

Forms No. II. of Shea's "Library of American Linguistics." The title-page is in English and Latin.

Mengwe, a Tale of the Frontier. A Poem. [By D. A. Borrenstein.] *Philadelphia: H. C. Carey & I. Lea.* 1825. 12mo, pp. 76. 47862

Contains notes of incidents and historical data relating to the American Indians.

MENIN (*Abbate* Lodovico). Sulla guerra testi scoppiata fra gli Stati Uniti d' America. Memoria. *Venezia: G. Ebhardt.* 1862. 4to, pp. 17. 47863

See also "Memorie dell' Istituto Veneto," Vol. X., part 3.

MENKEN (A. I.) Infelicia. By Adah Isaacs Menken. *New York: H. L. Williams.* 1868. 24mo, pp. v, 141. 2 Plates. + *London.* 1868. 18mo. 47864

Many copies contain fifty-four characteristic photographs.

MENKEN. Notice Biographique sur Miss Adah Isaacs Menken, Artiste Américaine. ... *Paris: Imp. Morris et Cie.* [n. d.] 8vo, pp. 14. 47865

Also: Life and Remarkable Career of Adah Isaacs Menken. Edited by G. L. Barclay. *Philadelphia.* 1868. 8vo, pp. 64.

Menologium Societatum Jesu oder lobs. Gedächtnuss der Patrum so die Societät mit h. Leben oder glorwürdigem Tod erleuchtet haben. *München.* 1669. 4to. 47866

Contains principally the martyrs in America, Asia, England, etc. *See also* Florencia (F. de), Vol. VI., No. 24811.

MENONVILLE (T. de). *See* Thiery de Menonville (N. J.)

MENORES. Advertencias y Preceptos utiles para la Classe de Menores ... . *Mexico.* 1721. 4to. 47867

Mensage del encargado. *See* Buenos Aires, II. 9022.

The Mental Elevator. [In the Seneca Language.] *Cattaraugus Reservation Mission Press.* 1846. 47868

Fourteen or more numbers of eight pages each published. The only miscellaneous work of its kind ever attempted.

The Mental Novelist, and Amusing Companion, a Collection of Histories, Essays, and Novels. *London.* 1783. 12mo.

Contains an historical description of the Indians of North America, the unheard of sufferings of David Menzies among the Cherokee Indians, etc.

MENTELLE (*M.*), *et* MALTE BRUN (*M.*) Géographie Universelle, Ancienne et Moderne, ... des cinq Parties du Monde. Par Une Societe de Savans. *Paris.* 1816. 16 vols., 8vo. Atlas in folio. 47870

Mons. Mentelle has contributed several articles to the "Feuille de la Guyane Française."

The Mentor and Fireside Review. Vol. I. ... Under the supervision of Rev. E. G. Smith ... . *New-York: John S. Taylor.* 1839. 12mo, pp. iv, 216. Continued. BA. 47871

Mentor's Reply to Phocion's Letter; with Some Observations on Trade. Addressed to the Citizens of New-York. *New-York: Printed by Shepard Kollock.* 1782. 12mo, pp. 20. 47872

Corrected title of our Vol. VIII., No. 29963.

Mentoriana, or A Series of Communications published in the Kingston Herald ... on the subject of the Statute Law of the Province, ... establishing the True Boundaries and Lines of Survey ... securing the Rights of Land ... to the Loyalists and their heirs. *Kingston: Printed at the Herald Office.* 1843. 8vo, pp. 62, xiii, Communications, 16. Map. 47873

MENU DE SAINT-MESMIN (E.) Le percement de l'isthme américain. Par E. Menu de Saint-Mesmin ... . *Paris: Bourdier et Cie.* 1865. 8vo, pp. 35. 47874

Reprinted from the "Revue nationale."

MENZEL (G.) Die Vereinigten Staaten von Nordamerika mit besonderer Rücksicht auf deutsche Auswanderung dahin nach eigener Anschauung beschrieben. *Berlin: G. Reimer.* 1853. 8vo, pp. viii, 364. 47875

MENZIES (G.) The Posthumous Works of the late George Menzies, being a Collection of Poems, Sonnets, &c., written at various times when the Author was connected with the Provincial Press. *Woodstock, U. C.* 1850. 8vo. 47876

MENZIES (J. W.) Speech of Hon. John W. Menzies, of Kentucky, on the Military Academy Bill. Delivered in the House of Representatives, January 27, 1862. [n. p. n. d.] 8vo, pp. 8. 47877

MEPHISTOPHILES, *pseudon.* A Review of Mr. Cambreling's Report from the Committee of Commerce in the House of Representatives. By Mephistophiles. *Baltimore.* 1830. 8vo, pp. 72. P. 47878

The Mercantile Agency and United States Business Directory for 1867 ... . *New York: John F. Trow.* [1867.] 4to, pp. 15–788. Continued. B. 47879

Mercantile Honor. *See* [Dexter (John H).], v. 19897.

The Mercantile Library Reporter. Edited ... by the Members of the Mercantile Library Association. [Vol. I.] *Boston: Mercantile Library Association.* 1855. 8vo, pp. (2), 96. Continued.

MERCATOR, *or* KAUFMANN (G.) Gerardi Mercatoris Atlas sive Cosmographicæ Meditationes de fabrica Mundi et fabricati Figvra. ... *Duisburgi Clivorum.* [1595.] Folio. Colored Maps.

This volume contains several plates concerning America; the large map (the fifth) of this part of the world is remarkable for its exactness.

MERCATOR. Gerardi Mercatoris | Atlas | sive | Cosmographicæ | Meditationes | de | fabrici Mundi et | fabricati Figvra. | Iam tandem ad finem perductus, quamplurimus æneis ta- | bulis Hispaniæ, Africæ, Asiæ & Americæ auctus ac | illustratus à Iudoco Hondio. Quibus etiam additæ (præter Mercatoris) dilucidæ & accuratæ omnium tabu- | larum descriptiones novæ, studio et opera Pet. Montani. | *Excusum in ædibus Iudoci Hondij Amsterodami.* 1606. Folio, pp. (20), 354, (36). Maps. + Editio qvarta. *Amsterodami: Iudoci Hondij.* 1613. Folio, pp. (18), 365, (35). Maps. + [*Ibid.*] 1619. Folio. + Editio qvinta. *Amsterodami: Henrici Hondij.* 1623. Folio, pp. (20), 374, (35). Maps. BA. + [*Ibid.*] 1628. Folio. 47882

Other editions: *Amsterodami.* 1609. Folio. + *Amsterodami: J. Cloppenburg.* 1632. 4to.

MERCATOR. Atlas Novus sive Descriptio Geographica Totius Orbis Terrarum, Tabulis aeneis luculentissimis et accuratissimis exornata. ... *Amstelodami.* 1638. 3 vols., imp. folio. 318 Colored Maps. 47883

"A splendid work bearing the highest testimony to the learning and labour of the editors. The latest geographical discoveries are incorporated in this work, and contributions by the best authorities in each country are used. It is the first Atlas containing anything like a fair description of the now United States; the settlements of the Pilgrim Fathers at Plymouth, the establishment of James' City, and the position of Fort Orange and New Amsterdam (the future city of New York), being all clearly laid down, although then but a few years in existence. It is interesting to observe the records on the map of New England, of the recent English investigations. Besides the general map of the world, there are seventeen special maps for America and its parts. A voyage from Bermuda to Ireland in an open boat, by five Englishmen, is noticed as an unprecedented fact."—QUARITCH.

MERCATOR. Atlas ou Représentation du Monde universel et des parties d'icelui; faictes en tables et descriptions très amples et exactes. *Amsterdam.* 1633–39. 3 vols., folio. 47884

"In many respects a better edition than the Latin. The text is only in part a translation, and contains a great number of details omitted in the Latin issue. It is evidently the work of a superior hand, and in many places disagrees in judgment from the statements of the other edition; as, for instance, may be observed in the remarks on Seneca's prophecy about America. The text to the general map of America is also quite different. There is in this edition a notice of the Pilgrim Fathers' voyage, and the founding of the town of Plymouth, which does not appear in the Latin one. Again, Smith's adventures in Virginia are not alluded to in the latter, while they are in the French copy."—QUARITCH.

MERCATOR. [Engraved Title:] Historia lvx ævi | Geographia Mvndi. | Historia Mvndi | or Mercators Atlas. Containing his Cosmographicall Descriptions | of the Fabricke and Figure of the world. | Latelij rectified in diuers places, as also beutified | and enlarged with new Mapps and Tables | by the Studious industrie of Iodocvs Hondy | Englished by W[ye] S[altonstall] Generosus & Regin: Oxoniæ. | *London* | *Printed for* | *Michaell* | *Sparke, and are to be sowld in* | *greene Arbowre* | 1637 | Second Edytion. | [Printed Title:] Historia Mvndi: | Or | Mercator's | Altas. | Containing his Cosmographicall | Description of the Fabricke and | Figure of the World. | Lately rectified in divers places, as also beautified | and enlarged with new Mappes and Tables; | By the Studious industry, | Of | Ivdocvs Hondy. | Englished | By | W[ye] S[altonstall]. | Generosus, & Coll. Regin. Oxoniæ. | *London* | *Printed by T. Cotes, for Michael Sparke and* | *Samuel Cartwright.* 1635. Folio, pp. (24), 56, (2), 930, (32). 191 Maps. C. 47885

The buyer should be careful to secure a copy of the second issue with the rare map of Virginia and New England, engraved by Ralph Hall in 1636, which is seldom found in the book, and a portrait of Captain John Smith, by Pass. All the copies were issued

with simply a duplicate of the map of New Spain impressed opposite the text to Virginia, this being mentioned in the errata with a statement that a correct map of New England was then being prepared in America, which would be published on its arrival in England. Sometimes the map of New England from Smith's "Virginia" is subsituted. A change of owners took place two years after the first publication, and the frontispiece was re-engraved, having Sparke's name alone, with "Second Edytion" added, and the date changed.

MERCATOR. Atlas; or, A Geographicke Description of the Regions, Countries, and Kingdomes of the World. Translated by Henry Hexham. *Amsterdam.* 1636. 2 vols., folio. S.

A work of uncommon occurrence with the descriptions in English.

MERCATOR. Atlas | Minor | Gerardi Mercatoris | à I. Hondio plurimis æneis tabulis | auctus atque illustratus. | *Amsterodami* | *Excusum in ædibus Iudoci Hondij.* | *veneunt etiam apud Corneliũ Nicolai.* | *item apud Ioannem Iansoniũ Arnhemi.* | [Colophon:] *Dordrechti* | *Excudebat Adrianus Bottius* | *Anno* CIƆ IƆ CX. | Oblong 4to, pp. (8), 684. B., S. + *Arnhemii.* 1621. 4to. + *Amsterdam.* 1628. 4to.

MERCATOR. Atlas minor, | Ou | Briefve, & vive description de tout le | Monde & ses parties: | Composee premierement en Latin par Gerard Mercator, | & depuis revue, corrigè, & augmentè de plusieurs Tables nouvelles, | par Ivdocvs Hondivs: & traduict en Francois | par le sieur de la Popeliniere Gentilhome Francois. | *A Amsterdam* | *Chez Iean Iansson.* | *L'An* M. DC. XXX. | Oblong 4to, pp. (8), 644, (4). 47888

This is an abridgment of the Grand Atlas. It was reprinted, *Amsterdam,* 1636 and 1644, 4to.

MERCATOR. Atlas Minor, das ist: Ein kurtze, jedoch gründliche Beschreibung der gantzen Welt. Aus dem Latein durch Jodocum Hondium mit vielen Kupffern gebessert und vermehrt; und in unsere hochteutsche Sprache versetzt. *Amsterodami, J. Janssonii.* 1631. Oblong 4to. Maps. 47889

MERCATOR, *pseudon.* Les Communications de Mercator, sur la conteste entre le Comte de Selkirk et la Compagnie de la Baye d'Hudson et la Compagnie du Nord-Ouest d'autre part. *Montreal.* 1817. 8vo. 47890

For an English version, *see* [Douglas (T.)], No. 20697.

MERCATOR, *pseudon.* The Financial Problem: Being Suggestions on the Money, Paper Currency, Public Revenue, and Debt of the United States. By Mercator. *New York.* 1868. 8vo, pp. 43. H. 47891

Mercator, *pseudon.* Letters on the Abolition of Slavery. By Mercator. *London.* 1807. 8vo. 47892

For a reply, *see* our Vol. ix., No. 40257.

Mercator, *pseudon.* Several New, Pressing and Weighty Considerations for an Immediate War with Spain. With a reasonable Plan of making the Operations effectual, to the Reparation of our Merchants, the securing the whole Effects of the South Sea Company in America ... and the promoting of the Happiness of Great Britain, and all her Dominions at Home and Abroad. ... By Mercator. *London: Champion St. George.* 1739. Folio, pp. 8. J.C.B. 47893

Merced. Fundacion e Indulgencias de la orden de la Merced. *Mexico.* 1595. 8vo. 47894

Mercedes: or, The Outlaw's Child ... . *New York: T. R. Dawley.* [n. d.] 12mo. 47895

A strange story of California life.

Mercein (T. F. R.) The Masses: Saved, with the Sabbath-School—without it, Lost. A Discourse, By T. F. Randolph Mercein, ... Dec. 17, 1854 ... . [n. p. 1854.] 8vo, pp. 12. H.

Mercein (T. R.) An Address, ... on the opening of The Apprentices' Library of the City of New-York, ... 1820. By Tho. R. Mercein ... . *New-York: Printed by W. A. Mercein.* 1820. 8vo, pp. 22. 47897

Also: Remarks on laying the Corner-stone of the Mechanic Institution, in New-York, in 1821. [n. p. n. d.] 8vo.

Mercer (A. G.) American Citizenship, ... A Sermon ... National Fast, January 4, 1861, By Alexander G. Mercer ... . *Boston: Little, Brown and Company.* 1861. 8vo, pp. 41.

Mercer (A. S.) Washington Territory. The Great North-West, her Material Resources, and Claims to Emigration. ... By A. S. Mercer ... . *Utica, N. Y.: L. C. Childs, ... Printer.* 1865. 8vo, pp. 38. 47899

[Mercer (Charles Fenton).] An Exposition of the Weakness and Inefficiency of the Government of the United States, ... [n. p.:] *The Author.* 1845. 12mo, pp. 380. B., BA. 47900

Reprinted as:

[Mercer.] The Weakness and Inefficiency of the Government of the United States ... By a Late American Statesman.

Edited by a Member of the Middle Temple, London. *London: Houlston & Wright.* 1863. 16mo, pp. xiv, 17–382. B. 47901

Mercer. Mémoire relatif a l'Abolition de la Traite Africaine addressé aux Puissances Maritimes de l'Europe et de l'Amérique, au nom de la Société Américaine de Colonisation, Par C.-F. Mercer, L.L.D. ... Traduit de l'Anglais, par Hippolyte Vattemare. *Paris: Imprimerie de Paul Dupont.* 1855. 4to, pp. 20

Also: A Discourse on Popular Education; ... at Princeton ... College of New Jersey September 26, 1826. ... *Princeton: Printed by D. A. Borrenstein.* 1826. 8vo, pp. 86, Appendix, xli, (2). — An Oration ... on the Twenty-Second of February, 1806. ... *Alexandria: Printed by Cottom and Stewart.* 1806. 12mo, pp. 28. — Speech ... on Internal Improvement, ... March 12, 1818. *Philadelphia.* 1818. 8vo, pp. 49. — Speech ... on the Seminole War. [*Washington.* 1818.] 8vo. — Speech ... on the subject of the Chesapeake and Ohio Canal, ... in the Convention of Delegates, ... November 7, 1823. *Washington: Printed by Gales & Seaton.* 1823. 12mo, pp. 47.

Mercer (J.) An Oration ... 4th of July, 1792. Before The President, Professors and Masters of William & Mary College, by John Mercer, Student. *Richmond: Printed by T. Nicolson.* [n. d.] 8vo. M. 47903

John Mercer was a son of General Hugh Mercer. *See also* Virginia.

Mercer (J. F.) An Introductory Discourse to an Argument in Support of the Payments made of British Debts into the Treasury of Maryland During the Late War, By John Francis Mercer ... . *Annapolis: Printed by Frederick Green, Printer* ... . [1789.] 8vo, pp. 44. 47904

This elicited: Strictures on Mercer's Introductory Discourse relative to the payments made of the British Debts into the Treasury of Maryland during the Late War. *London: A. Grant.* 1790. 8vo, pp. 44.

Mercer (——). Substitute ... proposed by Mr. Mercer, of Loudoun, to that proposed by Leigh of Dinwiddie, relative to the Right of the State Legislature to instruct Senators in Congress. ... [n. p. 1812.] 8vo. N. 47905

Mercer (N.) The Chemistry of Gold; with a Sketch of its Natural History and Geological Distribution ... . By Nathan Mercer. *Liverpool.* 1853. 12mo, pp. 58. 47906

Mercer (S.) Tyranny Exposed, True Liberty Discovered. Wherein is contained the Scripture Doctrine concerning Kings; Their Rise, Reign and Downfall. Together with the total Overthrow of Anti-Christ. By Silas Mercer ... . *Halifax.* 1783. 12mo. 47907

Mercer, *pseudon.* *See* [Cheetham (James)], iii. 12376.

Mercer University. Catalogue ... . 1857–58. *Penfield, Georgia: The University.* 1858. 8vo, pp. 35, (4). H. 47908

The Mercersburgh Review; ... *Mercersburgh, Pa.* 1849. 8vo. Continued. 47909

A Merchant, *pseudon.* *See* [Bird (H. M.)], ii. 5542.

A Merchant of the Old School. *See* [Livermore (G.)]

The Merchant's and Banker's Almanac for 1852. *Boston: Phillips, Sampson & Co.* [n. d.] 8vo. B. 47910

Continued at New York by J. Smith Homans.

... The Merchant's and Banker's Register for 1859. ... *New York: J. Smith Homans, Jr.* 1859. 8vo, pp. (4), 96, 156. Continued. BA. 47911

The Merchants' & Farmers' Almanack, for ... 1859 ... . *Saint John, N. B.: Printed ... by William L. Avery.* [1858.] 16mo, pp. 61. H. 47912

Merchants' and Manufacturers' Business Register for the Principal States of the Great West. Including a Commercial Register of the Principal Merchants and Manufacturers in the East and West. *New York.* 1869. Rl. 8vo, pp. 388. 47913

Merchants' and Manufacturers' Magazine. Vol. i., No. i. *Boston.* 1856. 8vo. S. 47914

Acts of Incorporation and By-Laws of the Merchants' and Miners' Transportation Company, of Baltimore, Norfolk, and Boston. *Baltimore.* 1869. 8vo, pp. 34. 47915

Merchants' and Travellers' Directory, or a Table of the principal Roads and Distances throughout the United States ... . [n. p. n. d.] 8vo. 47916

The Merchant's Complaint against Spain: containing i. Their Behaviour towards England, in the peaceable reign of King James i. ... ii. A Letter from a Gentleman in the West Indies to a Merchant in London, concerning Trade, the pretensions of Spain to Georgia, the Depredations and Cruelties committed by their Guarda Costa on the English Merchants and Sailors. ... To which is added, A Letter from Queen Mary in Elysium, to the famous Count Gondamar, ... who was the principal cause of the Death of the Great Sir Walter Raleigh. *London: W. Lloyd.* 1738. 8vo, pp. (2), 63. J.C.B. 47917

The Merchants, Factors and Agents, residing at Kingston, in ... [Jamaica], Complainants, against The Inhabitants of Spanish-Town, ... adjacent Parishes, and against the Members of the ... Assembly, ... and against the Planters, Freeholders, Settlers, and Chief Body of the People of the Island of Jamaica, Respondents. The Respondents' Case. ... *London: Printed in the Year* M.DCC.LV. 4to, pp. viii, (2), 72. B., N. 47918

The Merchants' Magazine, and Commercial Review. Freeman Hunt, Editor. *New York: Freeman Hunt.* MDCCCXXXIX. 8vo. 47919

Continued as:

The Merchant's Magazine and Commercial Review. Edited by William B. Dana. *New York: William B. Dana.* 1870. 63 vols., 8vo, in all. 47920

Discontinued after December, 1870, and consolidated with the "Commercial and Financial Chronicle." Also: A Comprehensive Index to the Merchants' Magazine ... embracing the First Ten Volumes, from ... July, 1839, to June 1844 ... . *New York.* 1846. 8vo, pp. 37. H.

Merchant's Memorandum Book, and Pocket Almanac, for 1810. *New York.* [n. d.] 18mo. 47921

The Merchants of this City are ... requested to meet ... to consider of a matter of great Importance, that will then be laid before them. [*Philadelphia,*] *February* 4, 1769. Folio, 1 leaf.

... November, 1866. First Monthly Report of the Merchants' Union Law Company, giving its Organization, Officers, and Members: ... *New York.* 1866. 8vo, pp. 80. H. 47923

Mercier (Alfred). Histoire du Pierre Soulé, sénator à Washington. *Paris: Dentu.* 1848. 18mo, pp. 108. 47924

Mercier. La fièvre jaune, sa manière d'être à l'égard des étrangers à la Nouvelle-Orléans et dans les campagnes, ... par le docteur Alfred Mercier ... . *Paris: A. Delahaye.* 1860. 8vo, pp. 48 or less. 47925

Also: La Rose de Smyrne et l'Ermite de Niagara, poèmes. ... *Paris: Labitte.* 1842 18mo, pp. 286.

Mercier de Lacombe (H). Le Mexique et les États-Unis Par H. Mercier de Lacombe. Deuxième Édition, revue et augmentée. *Paris: E. Dentu.* 1863. 8vo, pp. 162, (1). H.

For the first edition, *see* our Vol. ix., No. 38472.

Mercur (U.) True Basis of a Restored Representation. ... Speech of Hon. Ulysses Mercur, ... February 16, 1867. *Washington.* 1867. 8vo, pp. 8. H. 47927

Le Mercure Amériquain, ou Nouvelles de l'Amérique ... . *Rouen.* 1676. 16mo. 47928

Doubtful title from an American auctioneer's catalogue, prepared by C. Welford.

Mercure de la Nouvelle France, ou Abregé de tout ce qui s'y est passé depuis que les François l'ont découverte par Gourdin. *Paris.* [n. d.] 8vo. 47929

Mercure des Isles du Vent ou Essaix philosophiques ... . No. 1er. Janvier 1783. *Guadeloupe.* 1783. 8vo. 47930

Le Mercvre François, ov, la Svite de l'Histoire de la paix. Commençant l'an M.DC.V. pour suitte de Septenaire du D. Cayer, & finissant au Sacre du ... Loys XIII. *Paris: Jean Richer.* M.DC.XII–XLVIII. 25 vols., 16mo. Plates and Maps. 47931

This work is an annual register of occurrences, and gives the first published account of the voyages of Champlain, and of the establishment of the Jesuits in Canada, Louisiana, etc. It is a continuation of the "Chronologie novenaire," etc. *Paris.* 1608.

Le Mercure hollandois, contenant les choses les plus remarquables qui se sont passees pendant l'année 1677 ... . *Amsterdam.* 1679. 12mo. 47932

Contains many articles relative to America. *See also* Vol. x., No. 40661.

Mercurio Britannico. *See* [Hall (Joseph)], viii. 29819.

El Mercurio Chileno. *Santiago de Chili.* 1820. 2 vols., sm. 4to. 47933

A journal of arts, sciences, belles lettres, etc., but not political.

Il Mercurio Italico ... . The Italian Mercury: or, A General Account concerning the Literature, Fine Arts, Useful Discoveries, &c. of all Italy. *London: Couchman & Fry.* M DCC LXXXIX. 2 vols., 8vo, pp. (2), 504; (16), 488. Plates. BA. 47934

In English and Italian. Contains a history of discovery in America, with a facsimile of the map of Andrea Bianco, a Venetian, of 1436, in which the Antilles are delineated, before the discovery of Columbus, etc.

Mercurio Peruano de Historia, Literatura, y Noticias públicas que da á luz la Sociedad Academica de Amantes de Lima. Y en su nombre D. Jacinto Calero y Moreira. *Lima: En la Imprenta Real de los Niños Huerfanos.* 1791–94. 12 vols., 4to. C.

An important work, by a learned society at Lima, the object of which was to illustrate the topography and local history of Peru, as well as its arts, agriculture, mines,

natural history, manners, etc. It is seldom found complete. "Some numbers have been omitted, while the pagination remains correct; and sometimes there are two with the same number, although the text runs on correctly. The last part of vol. xi. is number 582, yet the first of vol. xii. receives the number 583, from which the numeration proceeds to the end (No. 611), although nothing is deficient. The periodical seems to have been produced under great difficulties and discouragements; it was suppressed by the Spanish government, as the enlightened opinions which the French Revolution had first set afloat were winning popularity amongst the educated youths of Spanish Peru. There is a sort of indignant bitterness in the title of the last volume which is stated to be 'dado a luz por uno de los individuos de la Sociedad.'"—Quaritch. *See* "N. A. Rev.," *also* "Ed. Rev.," ix. 433. Skinner's "Present State of Peru" is extracted from this work. It was reprinted with the following title:

Mercurio Peruano. Biblioteca Peruana de Historia Ciencias y Literatura. Coleccion de Escritos del anterior y presente siglo de los mas acreditados autores Peruanos, por Manuel A. Fuentes. ... Antiguo Mercurio Peruano. *Lima: Felipe Bailly.* 1861–1864. 9 vols., 8vo, pp. (8), 315, 3 Tables; (8), 359; (6), 332; (6), 321; (6), 318; (6), 328; (6), 359, Table; (6), 385; (6), 325. Map. 47936

For a German version of part of the work, *see* "Peru nach seinem," etc.

Mercurio Peruano del Dia 17 de Marzo de 1793, continuacion del tratado sobre las Aguas de los valles de Lima. *Lima.* 1793. 4to. 47937

A facsimile reprint of the scarce suppressed number.

De Americaansche Mercurius. *Amsterdam.* 1678. 47938

Mercurius Anti-Mechanicus. *See* [Ward (N.)]

Mercurius Politicus; comprising the Summe of all Intelligence, with the Affairs now on Foot in ... England, Ireland and Scotland ... . *London.* 1660. 4to. Continued. 47939

No. 63 contains a letter by John Eliot, and some of the other numbers relate to American topics.

Mercurius Ponticus ... 1716–17. [n. p. 1717.] 8vo.

Contains "Tidings of Barbarous Murders in New England," "Pyrates in the West Indies," etc.

Merda (R. D.) Representacion del Rafael D. Merda al Congresso de Venezuela, Instalado en la Ciudad de Santo Tomas de Angostura en 1819. *Burdeos.* [n. d.] 8vo. 47941

Meredith (E. A.) Essay on the Oregon Question, ... By Edmund A. Meredith ... . *Montreal.* 1846. 8vo, pp. 43. S.

[Meredith (Jonathan).] *See* Maryland, xi. 45264.

Meredith (T.) Christianity and Slavery. Strictures on the Rev. William Hague's Review of Doctors Fuller and Wayland on Domestic Slavery. By Thomas Meredith ... . *Boston: Gould, Kendall and Lincoln.* 1847. 18mo, pp. 72. B. 47943

Also: Sermon at the Consecration of T. F. Davis, and T. Atkinson, to the Episcopate, October 17, 1853. ... *New York.* 1853. 8vo, pp. 25. — Two Discourses, October 19, 1851. ... *Boston.* 1851. 8vo, pp. 31.

[Meredith (William).] Historical Remarks on the Taxation of Free States, in a Series of Letters to a Friend. *London: Printed the sixteenth of November* MDCCLXXVIII. 4to, pp. 82.

"An answer to a tract [by W. Barron] entitled: 'An History of the Colonization of the Free States of Antiquity.' [*See* our No. 3644*a*.] The point labored at in the latter was to show that Great Britain was fully justified by the precedents. Sir William refutes the work, and shows the author to be totally mistaken in all his premises. Candour must allow that the 'Historical Remarks,' is not only a very learned but very able performance. It was never published. Only about thirty copies were printed, which the author gave away."—Almon's *Anecdotes*, i. 81. *See also* Walpole's "Correspondence," *and* Symond's "Remarks," 1778, p. 473.

[Meredith.] A Letter to the Earl of Chatham, on the Quebec Bill. *London: T. Cadell.* MDCCLXXIV. 8vo, pp. (2), 36.

See our Vol. x., No. 40468. This elicited:

Meredith. A Letter to Sir William Meredith, ... in Answer to his late Letter to the Earl of Chatham. *London: J. Kearsly.* 1774. 8vo, pp. 52. 47946

See "Monthly Review," li. 149 and 393. Also: Speech of Sir William Meredith, May 13, 1777. *London.* 1777. 8vo.

[Meredith (William).] Fugitive Slaves. [n. p. n. d.] 16mo, pp. 7. H. 47947

Meredith (W. M.) Eulogium on ... the late John Sargent, ... at ... Philadelphia, ... April 22, 1853. By Hon. William M. Meredith. *Philadelphia: Crissy & Markley, Printers.* 1853. 8vo, pp. 34. H., P. 47948

Meredith. An Oration ... before the Whigs of Philadelphia, on the Fourth of July, 1834. By William Morris Meredith. *Philadelphia.* 1834. 8vo, pp. 22. B. 47949

Meredith; or, the Mystery of the Mischianza. A Tale of the American Revolution. By the Author of "The Bethroted of Wyoming." *Philadelphia.* 1831. 8vo. 47950

Meredith Association. Minutes of the Meredith Association held at Sandbornton, Sept. 1792. *Concord.* 1792. Cont'd.

Mereno (J. J.) Fragmentos de la Vida, y virtudes del V. Illmo. y Rmo. Sr. Dr. D. Vasco de Quiroga primer obispo de la Santa Iglesia de Michoacan; con notas criticas, en que se aclaran muchos puntos historicos, y antiguedades Americanas especialmente Michoacanenses. Por Juan Joseph Mereno, Rector del Colegio de San Nicolàs. *Mexico, Imprenta del Real Colegio de S. Ildefonso.* 1766. 4to. 47952

Merewether (Henry Alworth). Speech ... April 23, 1839, against the Bill making temporary provisions for the Government of Jamaica. *London.* 1839. 8vo. S. 47953

Meriam (J.) A Sermon ... at Falmouth, at the Ordination of the Reverend Mr. Samuel Dean, ... with The Rev[d]. Mr. Thomas Smith, By Jonas Meriam, A.M. ... October 17, 1764. *Boston: Printed ... by Edes and Gill.* M,DCC,LXV. 8vo, pp. 38.

Meriam (M.) Sermon preached to Joshua Abbot at York, 3 September, 1792, preparatory to the 6th, the day appointed for his Execution, with an Address to John Hancock by Matthew Meriam ... and Joseph Buckminster, ... of Portsmouth. [n. p.] 1792. 8vo. N. 47955

Merian (*le Baron* de). Principes de l'Étude comparative des Langues, par le Baron de Merian. Suivis d'Observations sur les racines des langues sémitiques, par M. Klaproth. *Paris.* 1828. 8vo, pp. viii, 240. S. 47956

American languages are compared with those of the old word.

Merian (M. S.) Metamorphosis Insectorum Surinamensium. In qua erucæ ac Vermes Surinamenses, cum omnibus suis transformationibus, ad vivùm delineantur & describuntur singulis eorum in Plantas, Flores & Fructus Collocatis, in quibus reperta sunt; Tum etiam Generatio Ranarum, Bufornum rariorum, Lacertarum, Serpentum, Araneorum & Formicarum exhibentur; Omnia in America ad vivùm naturali magnitudine picta atque descripta. ... Mariam Sibyllam Merian. *Amsterdami: Gerardum Valk.* MDCCV. Imp. folio, pp. 66. Frontispiece and 70 Plates. J.C.B.

Reprinted in 1719 with the following title:

Merian. Dissertatio de Generatione et Metamorphosibus Insectorum Surinamensium: in quâ præter vermes & erucas surinamenses, earum que admirandam metamorphosin, plantæ, flores & fructus, quibus vescantur, & in quibus fuerunt inventæ, exhibentur. ... Mariæ Sibillæ Merian. Accedit appendix transformationum Piscium in Ranas & Ranarum in Pisces. *Amsterdam: Joannem Oosterwyk.* 1719. Imp. folio, pp. 66. 72 Plates. J.C.B.

Engraved and printed titles in Latin and Dutch. "Mad. Merian made the voyage to Surinam on purpose to study its Natural History. Her entomological and botanical drawings are considered to be among the finest ever made." The work was reproduced *Amsterdam*, 1730, folio, of which edition there are copies on large and thick paper, with the following title:

MERIAN. Over de Voortteeling en Wonderbaerlyke Veranderingen der Surinaemsche Insecten. Benevens een Aenhangsel van de Veranderingen van Visschen in Kikvorschen en van de Kikvorschen in Visschen. *Amsterdam.* 1730. Folio. 72 Plates.

MERIAN. Dissertation sur la Generation et les Transformations des Insectes de Surinam, les Plantes, Fleurs, et Fruits dont ils Vivent; aussi des Crapauds, Lezards, Serpents .... Par Marie Sibille Merian. *La Haye.* 1726. Folio. 72 Plates. B. 47960

MERIAN. Histoire générale des Insectes de Surinam, contenant leurs descriptions, leurs figures, leurs différentes métamorphoses, de même que les descriptions des plantes, fleurs et fruits dont ils se nourrissent. *Amsterdam.* 1726. Folio. + Troisième Édition, revue ... par Buchoz. *Paris: L. C. Desnos.* 1771. 3 vols., folio. C. 47961

MÉRIDA (R. D.) Representacion del Señor Rafael D. Mérida, al Congreso de Venezuela, instalado en la Ciudad de Santo Tomas de Angostura, el año de 1819, la que fué mandada archivar por resolucion de dicho congreso. *Burdeos.* 1819. 4to, pp. 38. + 1820. C., S. 47962

MERIDA DE YUCATAN, *Mexico.* Informe presentado en 13 de Setiembre de 1833, al R. Ayuntamiento de esta ciudad sobre la viciosa administracion de los fondos de su comun y urgente necesidad de su reforma. *Merida de Yucatan.* 1837. 8vo, pp. 22

MERIDA, *Venezuela.* Constituciones sinodales de Mérida. Impresas de órden del Ilustrísimo Señor Obispo. *Carácas.* 1839. Sm. 8vo, pp. 73. 47964

MERIDEN, *Conn.* Apology for Abolitionists, addressed by the Anti-Slavery Society of Meriden, Conn., to their Fellow-Citizens. Second Edition. *Middletown.* 1837. 8vo. 47965

Annual Reports of the several Departments for the year ending June 1, 1871. *Hartford.* 1871. 8vo, pp. 55. 47966

Catalogue of the Meriden Institute ... April 13, 1860. *Hartford: Press of C. Montague.* 1860. 24mo, pp. 12. H. 47967

MÉRILHOU (François Xavier). Rapport à la Chambre des Pairs, par M. Mérilhou, sur le régime législatif des colonies. *Paris.* 1844. 8vo. P. 47968

MERINO (Antonio). Manifestacion que hace al publico para vindicar su conducta en todo el tiempo que sirvió la segunda comandancia del resguardo de la aduana maritima de Veracruz. *Mexico.* 1842. 4to, pp. 45. 47969

MERIÑO (Fernando A. de). Elementos de Geografia fisica, politica e historica de la republica dominicana, precedidos de las nociones generales de geografia. *Santo Domingo: Garcia Hermanos.* 1867. 18mo, pp. 124. C. 47970

MERITON (G.) A Geographical Description of the World, with a brief Account of the several Empires, Dominions and parts thereof, with Directions for Travellers. By George Meriton, Gent. *London.* 1674. 12mo. Plate. + Third Edition. *London.* 1679. 16mo. 47971

Part of the work is devoted to America.

The Merits of the New Administration duly stated. *London.* 1765. 8vo, pp. 48. M. 47972

MERIVALE (H.) Lectures on Colonization and Colonies. ... Before the University of Oxford in 1839, 1840, and 1841. By Herman Merivale, A.M. ... *London: Longman* ... 1841–42. 2 vols., 8vo, pp. xv, (2), 329, (1); iv, 329, (1). B., C. + Second Edition, with Notes and Additions. [*Ibid.*] 1861. 47973

MERIWETHER (David). Speech ... in the House of Representatives of Kentucky, on the Bill to grant Banking Privileges to the Cincinnati and Charleston Railroad Company. [n. p. n. d.] 8vo, pp. 7. M. 47974

MERIWETHER (J. A.) Extract from the Speech of Hon. J. A. Meriwether, ... 1841, in reply to the Charge of Extravagant Expenditures ... by the Whig Party. [n. p. n. d.] 8vo, pp. 20.

Also: Speech ... 1842, on Discriminating Duties. *Washington.* 1842. 8vo.

MERLE (J.-A.) De l'Émigration aux États-Unis d'Amérique, Par J.-A. Merle ... *Genève: Imprimerie Ch. Gruaz.* 1849. 8vo, pp. 46. Map. B. 47976

MERLET (L.) Histoire des relations des Hurons et des Abnaquis du Canada, avec Notre-Dame de Chartres, suivie de documents inédits sur la Sainte-Chemise, par Lucien Merlet. *Chartres: Petrot-Garnier.* 1858. 8vo. 2 Plates. 47977

MERLIN, [Mercedes de Santa Cruz]. La Havanne. Par Madame la Comtesse Merlin. *Paris: Amyot.* 1844. 3 vols., 8vo. B., C. + *Bruxelles.* 1844. 5 vols., 8vo. 47978

A reunion of articles which have appeared in the journal "la Presse."

MERLIN. Viaje a la Habana por la Condesa de Merlin, precidio de una biografia de cota ilustre cubana por la Señorita Da Gertrudio Gomez de Avellaneda. *Madrid: Imprenta de la Sociedad Literaria y Tipografica.* 1844. 8vo, pp. xvi, 106, (2). H.

The Mermaid's Release: or Inchanted Lady's Prophecy; being the Speech of an Inchanted Lady, who appear'd in the form of a Mermaid, ... in ... Liverpool, who gives an account of the Northern Brazille, to be called New Ireland, and that the people who of late have flocked to America will hasten back there. [n. p. n. d.] Folio, 1 leaf. 47980

MERRELL (W. H.) Five Months in Rebeldom; or Notes from the Diary of a Bull Run Prisoner, at Richmond. ... By Corporal W. H. Merrell ... . *Rochester, N. Y.: Adams & Dabney.* 1862. 8vo, pp. 64. Plate. BA., S. 47981

MERREM (K. Th.) Ueber den Cortex adstringens Brasil. *Köln.* 1828. 8vo. Plate. 47982

MERRIAM (G. *and* C.) Have we a National Standard of English Lexicography? or, some comparison of the claims of Webster's ... and Worcester's Dictionaries. *Springfield: Geo. & Chas. Merriam.* 1854. 8vo, pp. 15. B., H. 47983

Messrs. Merriam have published several tracts relative to Noah Webster's Dictionary.

MERRICK (J. L.) An Appeal to the American Board of Commissioners for Foreign Missions. By Rev. J. L. Merrick, ... *Springfield: Printed by John M. Wood.* 1847. 8vo, pp. 125.

MERRICK (J.) Trial of David Lynn ... and [others], for the Murder of Paul Chadwick, at Malta, in Maine, on September 8th, 1809; ... held at Augusta ... Nov. 16, 1809. Taken in short hand, by John Merrick, Esq. *Hallowell: Ezekiel Goodale.* 1810. 8vo, pp. 188. H. 47985

See Lynn (D.), Vol. x., No. 42829, for another account of the trial.

MERRICK (J. M.) A Discourse ... at the Dedication of the Congregational Church, in Sandwich, Mass. October 30th, 1833. By John M. Merrick ... . *Boston: Printed by Samuel N. Dickinson.* MDCCCXXXIII. 8vo, pp. 30. H. 47986

Also: Address delivered before Mount Zion Lodge, Hardwick [Mass.], Jan. 14, 1829. ... *Athol.* 1829. 8vo, pp. 16. W.

MERRICK (P.) An Eulogy on the Character of the late Gen. George Washington: The Pride of America, the Glory of the World. Pronounced ... [at] Brookfield ... the 22d of February, 1800. By Pliny Merrick, Esq. ... *Brookfield, Mass.: E. Merriam & Co.* 1800. 8vo, pp. 14. BA., M., W. 47987

Also: Address delivered at the Installation of Social Harmony Lodge of ... Masons, at Middleborough, Aug. 19, 1823. ... *New Bedford.* 1823. 8vo, pp. 20. W.—Anti-Masons of Massachusetts, Listen to the voice of those who have always been foremost in your cause. Letter of Pliny Merrick to the Editor of the Worcester Palladium. [n. p. n. d.] 12mo, pp. 8.—Eulogy on General Jackson, ... July 9, 1845 ... . *Boston: J. H. Eastburn, ... Printer.* 1845. 8vo, pp. 32.—A Letter on Speculative Free Masonry, by Pliny Merrick, Esq. Being his Answer to Gen. Nathan Heard and Col. Gardner Burbank upon their application for his views on that subject. *Worcester: Dorr and Howland.* 1829. 8vo, pp. 20. H. + Second Edition. [*Ibid.*] 1830.—An Oration, ... at Worcester, July 4, 1817. ... *Worcester: Printed by Henry Rogers.* 1817. 8vo, pp. 16. BA., W.

MERRICK (R. T.) Oration delivered by Richard T. Merrick, Esq. ... July 5th, 1852. *Baltimore: Printed by Sands & Mills.* 1852. 8vo, pp. 22. C. 47988

MERRICK (W. D.) Speech of Mr. Merrick ... on the Sub-Treasury Bill. ... January 23, 1840. *Washington: Printed by Gales and Seaton.* 1840. 8vo, pp. 16. H. 47989

Also: Speech ... on the Bill to reduce the Rates of Postage ... . January 27, 1845. *Washington: Printed by Gales and Seaton.* 1845. 8vo, pp. 16. H.

Merrick Genealogy. A Genealogical Circular, Very Respectfully Addressed to all the Merricks in America. [n. p. n. d.] 4to, pp. 9. 47990

MERRILL (A. P.) [Plan for establishing] the City School [at Memphis, Tenn.]. By Dr. Merrill. [n. p. 1851.] 8vo, pp. 24.

[MERRILL (Catherine).] The Soldier of Indiana in the War for the Union. *Indianapolis: Merrill & Company.* 1866. 8vo, pp. vi, 690. 9 Plates, 4 Maps. C. 47992

MERRILL (D.) Autobiography of Daniel Merrill. *Philadelphia: Baptist General Tract Society.* [1832.] 12mo, pp. 12. H.

MERRILL (D.) ... A Discourse ... before ... the Governor ... Council, etc. of ... New-Hampshire, June 5, 1817. Being the Anniversary Election. By Daniel Merrill, A.M. ... *Concord: Printed by Isaac Hill.* 1817. 8vo, pp. 44. H. + Third Edition. *Arlington: The Author.* 1818. 8vo, pp. 22. H. 47994

Also: The Gospel Rangers. A Sermon ... at the Ordination of Elder Henry Hale. ... *Buckstown: Printed ... by William W. Clapp.* 1807. 12mo, pp. 36. B. + Second Edition. *Springfield.* 1807. 8vo, pp. 20.—... A Thanksgiving Sermon, ... at Nottingham-West, April 13, 1815. ... *Concord: Printed by Isaac & W. R. Hill.* 1815. 12mo, pp. 30. H. + Second Edition. *Concord, N. H.* 1816. 12mo, pp. 35. W.

MERRILL (D.) Sermons, By the late Rev. David Merrill, Peacham, Vt. With a Sketch of his Life. *Windsor Vt.* 1855. 12mo, pp. 288. Portrait. H. 47995

MERRILL (E. *and* P.) A Gazetteer of the State of New Hampshire, In three parts: ... Compiled from the best Authorities, by Eliphalet Merrill and the late Phinehas Merrill, Esq. *Exeter: Printed by C. Norris & Co.* 1817. 8vo, pp. 218, (13).

The first gazetteer of the State.

MERRILL (I.) Faith in Divine Providence the Great Support of God's People. Sermon ... Lexington, April 19, 1780. By Rev. Isaac Merrill, A.M. *Boston.* 1780. 8vo, pp. 30. 47997

MERRILL (J. L.) History of Acworth, N. H.; with The Proceedings of the Centennial Anniversary, Genealogical Records, and Register of Farms. Edited by the Rev. J. L. Merrill, ... *Acworth: Published by the Town.* 1869. 8vo, pp. 306. 56 Plates. B. 47998

MERRILL (J. W.) The People's Cabinet: containing a ... History of the United States; Government and Law; ... and Biographical Sketches of Distinguished Characters in all Ages of the World. Edited by Joseph W. Merrill. *Boston: The Editor.* 1844. 12mo, pp. 344. C. 47999

MERRILL. Records of the 24th Independent Battery, N. Y. Light Artillery, U. S. V. Compiled by J. W. Merrill. [*New York:*] *For the Ladies' Cemetery Association of Perry, N. Y.* 1870. 12mo. 48000

MERRILL (J.) A Sermon ... in Wiscasset, Me., on ... the Death of Mrs. Hannah Cushman, ... Jan. 23, 1859. By Rev. Josiah Merrill. ... *Boston: Printed by Damrell & Moore.* 1859. 8vo, pp. 16. H. 48001

MERRILL (O. C.) An Oration delivered at the Meeting-House in Bennington, on the 4th of July, 1806. By Orsamus C. Merrill. *Bennington [Vt.]: Benjamin Smead.* [1806?] 16mo, pp. 56. C. 48002

MERRILL (O. N.) True History of the Kansas Wars, and their Origin, Progress and Incidents. By O. N. Merrill. *Cincinnati: J. R. Telfer.* 1856. 8vo, pp. 54. Portrait, 3 Plates.

[MERRILL (Rufus).] 150 Stories about Indians. *Concord, N. H.: Rufus Merrill.* 1853. 32mo, pp. 192. 48004

MERRILL (S. H.) The Campaigns of the First Maine and First District of Columbia Cavalry. By Samuel H. Merrill ... . *Portland: Bailey & Noyes.* 1866. 12mo, pp. 436. 3 Portraits.

MERRILL (T. A.) Semi-Centennial Sermon, containing a History of Middlebury, Vt. ... Dec. 3, 1840; being the first Thanksgiving Day after the Expiration of Half a Century from the Organization of the Congregational Church, Sept. 5, 1790. By Thomas A. Merrill, D.D. ... *Middlebury: Printed by E. Maxham.* 1841. 8vo, pp. 92. B., C. 48006

MERRILL. A Sermon preached at the Audience of ... Governor ... Council, etc. of ... Vermont, ... on the Day of the Anniversary Election, Oct. 9, 1806. By Thomas A. Merrill, ... *Middlebury.* 1806. 8vo. S. 48007

MERRILL. A Sermon ... before the Vermont Domestic Missionary Society, at their Annual Meeting, held at Royalton, Sept. 12, 1833. By Thomas A. Merrill ... . *Windsor.* 1834. 8vo, pp. 28. W. 48008

MERRIMACK. [Merrimack and Boston Canal.] To Members of the General Court. [*Boston.* 1814.] 8vo. 48009

Charter of the Merrimack & Connecticut River Railroad, with the By-Laws of the Corporation ... . *Concord.* [1853?] 12mo, pp. 39, (1). H. 48010

Account of the Receipts and Expenditures of the Merrimack County Agricultural Society, from ... 1859, to ... 1867 ... . *Concord: Printed by A. G. Jones.* 1867. 8vo, pp. 22. H.

The Institution of the Merrimack Humane Society; with the Rules, &c. *Newburyport: Printed by E. M. Blunt.* 1803. 16mo, pp. 24. H. + *Newburyport.* 1809. 12mo, pp. 30. 48012

Also: Laws of the Merrimack Humane Society. *Newburyport.* 179–. 8vo.—By-Laws of the Merrimack Humane Society. *Newburyport.* 1792. 8vo.

The Attorney General ex relatione Rector, Wardens and Vestry of St. Anne's Church, in Lowell, vs. the Merrimack Manufacturing Company. ... *Lowell.* 1856. 4to, pp. 91 [*i. e.* 93].

Also: Report of the Proprietors of the Merrimack Manufacturing Company, ... and ... of the Directors' Committee in relation to that Report. *Boston: J. H. Eastburn's Press.* 1861. 8vo, pp. 33. Continued.—By-Laws of the Merrimack Mutual Fire-Insurance Company. *Andover.* 18–. 16mo, pp. 8.

Catalogue of the Merrimack Normal Institute, for ... 1849–50. *Manchester, N. H.: Gage and Forsaith, Printers.* [1850.] 8vo, pp. 15, (1). H. 48014

Act Incorporating the Proprietors of the Locks and Canals on the Merrimac River. *Boston.* 1792. 8vo, pp. 12. 48015

Also: By-Laws, passed August 8, 1792. *Newburyport.* 1792. 8vo, pp. 14.

Report of the Committee on the Subject of a New Canal, to the Proprietors of the Locks and Canals on Merrimac River. *Boston.* 1848. 8vo, pp. 20. H. 48016

MERRIMAN (T. M.) ... A Sermon on the Moral Aspect of the Kingston Tragedy, ... by Rev. T. M. Merriman, A.M., ... July 12, 1868. ... *Plymouth: W. W. Avery, ... Printer.* 1868. 8vo, pp. 31. H. 48017

Also: The Trail of History: or, History of Religion and Empire in Parallel from the Creation to the Present Time. With a Historical Diagram. ... *Johnson [Vt.]: The Author.* 1860. 8vo, pp. (2), 11–520. C.

MERRITT (E. A.) Government Aid to American Shipping Interests. The Bounty Plan ... [of] Gen. E. A. Merritt ... . [*New York.* 1870.] 8vo, pp. 14. H. 48018

Also: Maps of the Racket River and its Head Waters, with descriptions of the Several Routes to the principal bodies of Water. ... *Albany.* 1860. 18mo, pp. 12. 2 Maps. S.

MERRITT (H. W.) Trial of Henry W. Merritt, a Special Justice ... of New-York, containing the Opinions of the Judges, ... and an Opinion ... by Judge Irving in the Case of Abraham M. Valentine. *New-York.* 1840. 8vo, pp. 211. C. 48019

MERRITT (J. King). Report on the Region of Mineral de Veraguas and its Gold Mines. *New York.* 1854. 8vo, pp. 33.

Also: Report on the Huacals [*sic*], or Ancient Graveyards of Chiriqui ... . [n. p. n. d.] 8vo, pp. 8.

MERRITT (J. P.) The Historic Tree of British North America, an emblematic tree, shewing the various periods of British American Colonial History, from 1492 to the present time. By J. P. Merritt. *St. Catharines.* 1866. 8vo. 48021

MERRITT (T.) A Discourse on the Horrid Murder of Capt. James Purrington's Family, of Augusta (Maine), delivered in Bowdoinham, July 20, 1806. By Timothy Merritt. *Augusta: Printed by Peter Edes.* 1806. 8vo, pp. 23. H. 48022

Also: Camp Meeting Discourse at East Hartford. ... *Palmer: E. Terry's Press.* 1816. 8vo. *See also* Avery, I. 2486.

MERRITT (W. H.) A Brief Review of the Revenue, Resources and Expenditures of Canada, compared with those of ... New York, with a Remedy to relieve the Province from Extravagant Expenditure ... . By W. H. Merritt ... . *St. Catharines, C. W.* 1845. 8vo, pp. 22. 48023

MERRITT. Journal of Events principally on the Detroit and Niagara Frontiers, during the War of 1812. By Capt. W. H. Merritt ... . *St. Catharines, C. W.* 1863. 8vo, pp. 82. 48024

Also: A Concise View of the Inland Navigation of the Canadian Provinces. ... *St. Catharines.* 1832. 8vo, pp. 20.—Letter addressed to the Inhabitants of the Niagara District on Free Trade, &c. ... *Niagara.* 1847. 8vo, pp. 32.—Review of the Origin, Progress, Present State and Future Prospects of the Welland Canal. ... [n. p. n. d.] 8vo, pp. 48.

MERRY (R.) The Pains of Memory. A Poem, By Robert Merry, A.M. ... *Boston: Printed by Manning & Loring.* 1797. 4to, pp. 39. H. + *Cambridge: Printed ... by W. Hilliard.* 1807. Sm. 8vo, pp. 27. + [n. p. n. d.] Sm. 8vo, pp. 27. B. 48025

Merry Andrew's New Almanac. *New York.* 1774. 12mo. Continued. 48026

Also: Merry Andrew's Gentleman and Lady's Pocket Almanac. *New York.* 1775. 12mo.

The Merry Fellows Companion, being the Second Part of the American Jest Book. *Philadelphia: M. Carey* ... . M,DCC,LXXXIX. 12mo, pp. 96. Plate. + *Printed at Harrisburgh for C. Carey of Philadelphia.* 1797. 12mo. Plate. 48027

Merry's Museum. Edited by S. G. Goodrich. *Boston.* 1841. 8vo. 48028

Continued as: "Merry's Museum and Parley's Magazine."

MERRYMAN (John). Decision of Chief Justice Taney, in the Merryman Case, upon the Writ of Habeas Corpus. ... *Philadelphia: John Campbell.* 1862. 8vo, pp. 16. 48029

See also Vol. VII., No. 29463.

Merry-Mount. *See* [Motley (John L.)]

MERRYWEATHER (George, *pseudon.?*) Kings the Devil's Viceroys and Representatives on Earth. [*New York:*] *The Author.* 1838. 8vo, pp. 456. C. 48030

MERSHON (S. L.) The Christian Sanctuary; or the Church of the Colony and Town of East Hampton, L. I., A. D. 1642–1861. By Rev. Stephen L. Mershon. *New York: Geo. F. Nesbitt & Co., Printers.* 1861. 8vo, pp. 44. 48031

Also: Causes for Thanksgiving in the midst of Civil War. A Discourse delivered at East Hampton, Long Island, November 28, 1861. ... *New York: Geo. F. Nesbitt & Co., Printers.* 1861. 8vo, pp. 24. — Funeral Sermon preached at the burial of the Crew of the John Milton, ... Feb. 28. 1858, at East Hampton, L. I. Third Edition. ... [*New York:*] *G. F. Nesbitt & Co., Printers.* 1858. 8vo, pp. 24.

MERSON (E.) La Guerre d'Amérique et la Médiation Par M. Ernest Merson. *Paris: Dentu.* 1862. 8vo, pp. 111. B., BA.

MERULA (Gaud.) Memorabilium opus cum emendatione et scholiis P. Castalii. *Lugduni.* 1556. 8vo. 48033

Pages 417 and 418 contain a short notice of the "insulae Americae."

Merveilles de la nature et de l'art dans les cinq parties du monde. *Paris.* 1836. — vols., 12mo. 48034

Vol. II. relates to America.

MERWIN (H.) Merwin's Connecticut River Business Directory, for 1867–8. Containing a ... List ... of Business Firms, Manufacturing Establishments, etc. of the Cities, Towns, etc. on the River, from Saybrook, Conn., to Newport, Vt. *Hartford: H. Merwin.* 1867. 8vo, pp. 457. 48035

MERWIN (S.) A Discourse on the Completion of Fifty Years Service in the Ministry of the Gospel; ... in ... New Haven, February 25th, 1855, By Samuel Merwin. *New Haven: T. H. Pease.* 1855. 8vo, pp. 72. Portrait. B., M. 48036

Also: Funeral Sermon ... on the Death of Rev. John Summerfield. ... *Baltimore.* 1825. 8vo. — A Missionary Sermon, ... in Hartford, ... May 17, 1814 ... . *Hartford: Peter B. Gleason and Co., Printers.* 1814. 8vo, pp. 15. — Sermon on Opening the Methodist Church in John St., New York, January 4, 1818. [n. p. n. d.] 8vo.

MÉRY (Joseph), CHAUBET (C.), *and* SAINT-ÉTIENNE (S.) Christophe Colomb, ou la découverte du Nouveau-Monde, ode-symphonie en quatre parties, paroles de MM. Méry, Charles Chaubet et Sylvain Saint-Étienne, musique de M. Félicien David, ... *Paris: Imprimerie de Guyot.* 1847. 8vo, pp. 24. + Deuxième Édition. [*Ibid.*] + Troisième Édition. [*Ibid.*] + Quatrième Édition. [*Ibid.*] 48037

MERY (M. de St.) *See* Moreau de Saint-Mery.

Mes de Maria en la parroquia de Sasaima. Ano de 1866. *Bogotá.* 1866. 18mo, pp. 16. 48038

MESA (Franc. de Paula). Breve manifestacion que hace al publico, de su conducta como gobernador que fué del Estado de Queretaro. *Mexico.* 1849. 8vo, pp. 47. 48039

MESA Y LEOMPART (J.) Compendio de la historia de América desde su descubrimiento hasta nuestros dias. *Paris: Rosa & Bouret.* 1871. 2 vols., 18mo, pp. vii, 1252. 48040

MESANGE (Pierre de). *See* [Tyssot de Patot (S.)]

MESEGUER (Fran.) El Diablo Predicador. Discurso que en la Catedral de Longroño Pronunció el mas erudito y sabio Capellan de Baco D. Josef Botella. *Reimpresso en Mexico.* 1809. 8vo.

MESERVE (A. L.) The Indian Spirit; ... A Story of Indian Warfare. By Arthur L. Meserve ... . *New York: George Munro.* [1868?] 16mo, pp. 7–100. H. 48042

MESNIL (E. M. du). Memoria que dirije Don Emilio Mangel Du Mesnil al ministro de relaciones esteriores de la República Oriental del Uruguay, etc., sobre la espulsion á mano armada de la colonia Du Mesnil. *Montevideo.* [n. d.] 4to, pp. 40.

MESQUITA (J. J. de). Ontwerp ter verbetering van den financielen toestand der kolonie Suriname, uitgegeven door J. W. Tydeman. *Amsterdam.* 1842. 8vo. 48044

MESQUITA (Martinho de). *See* Martinho de Mesquita, 44967.

A | Message | of the | President | of the | United States | to | Congress | relative | to | France and Great-Britain. | Delivered December 5, 1793. | With the papers therein referred to. | To which are added | the | French Originals. | ... | *Philadelphia: Printed by Childs and Swaine.* M,DCC,XCIII. 8vo, pp. 102, (2), 116, 32, (4), 11, 26, 4. + *London: J. Butterworth.* 1794. 8vo, pp. 103. 48045

This is the official account of the celebrated Genet affair. Rich I. 386, quotes a long commendatory note from the "Monthly Review," XIX. 103. The English reprint omits the documents which accompanied the message.

This is the first of a series of messages from the Presidents of the United States, which are, of course, important as State Papers illustrative of the history of the United States, and especially so of the individual views of each President. In the following list we purposely omit a majority of them, and enumerate only those which we consider worthy of special mention. Our list is chronological. Some are to be found under their respective subjects. The messages are usually followed by "Documents" illustrative of the subject of the message.

A Message ... transmitting certain Documents relative to Hostile Threats against the Territories of Spain, in the Neighbourhood of the United States. ... *Philadelphia: Printed by Francis Childs* ... . M, DCC, XCIV. 8vo, pp. 24. BA. 48046

Relates to Louisiana.

Messages ... relative to France and Great Britain, ... January, 1794; ... *Philadelphia.* 1794. 8vo. P. 48047

Message ... transmitting a Report of the Secretary of State. *Philadelphia.* 1794. 8vo, pp. 8. Continued. 48048

See also Secretary of State, etc.

... Message ... accompanying an Official Statement of the Expenditure to ... 1795 ... . [n. p. n. d.] 8vo, pp. 11. + [Another.] *Philadelphia.* [n. d.] 8vo, pp. 7. 48049

Message ... relative to the French Republic; ... Jan. 19, 1797, with the papers therein referred to. *Philadelphia: Printea by W. Ross.* [n. d.] 8vo. 48050

Also: Message ... containing Observations on some of the Documents, communicated on the 18th January. [n. p. 1797.] 8vo. N.

Message ... Relative to the Affairs of the United States on the Mississippi; the Intercourse with the Indian Nations, ... the Treaty between the United States and Spain, 23d January, 1798, ... *Philadelphia: Printed by W. Ross.* [1798.] 8vo, pp. 91.

Message ... inclosing a letter ... from the Governor of South Carolina, accompanying a number of Depositions of Witnesses to several Captures and Outrages, committed within and near the Limits of the United States by a French Privateer, called the Vertitude, or Fortitude. February 5, 1798. *Philadelphia: Joseph Gales.* [n. d.] 8vo, pp. 22. 48052

Message ... relative to the Military Establishment. ... 31st December, 1798. ... [n. p. n. d.] 8vo, pp. 27. P. 48053

Message ... April 3, 1798; with Despatches from the Envoys to the French Republic. *Philadelphia.* [1798.] 8vo, pp. 60. + [n. p. n. d.] 8vo, pp. 71. B. 48054

Also: Message ... accompanying a Communication, No. 8, from the Envoys ... to the French Republic ... . *Philadelphia: Joseph Gales.* [1798.] 8vo, pp. 72. — Message ... accompanying sundry Papers relative to the Affairs ... with the French Republic, 18th January, 1799. *Philadelphia.* 1799. 8vo. + 22d January, 1799. [n. p. n. d.] 12mo.

Message ... inclosing A Report ... from the Director of the Mint, on the State of the Business committed to his Superintendence and A Statement of the Coinage at the Mint, during ... 1798. 31st January, 1799. ... *Printed ... by Way & Groff, Philadelphia.* [n. d.] 8vo, pp. 7. 48055

Message ... Transmitting ... Documents on the ... Insurrection in Pennsylvania; The Renewal of Commerce with St. Domingo, and the Mission to France. 5th December, 1799. ... [n. p. 1799.] 8vo, pp. 42. P. 48056

Message ... Transmitting a Roll of the Persons having Office or Employment under the United States. *Washington City: W. Duane.* 1802. 8vo, pp. 52, 21, 32, 22, 8, 15, 13. C., P., S.

Message ... Transmitting Plans and Estimate of a Dry Dock. *Washington.* 1802. 8vo. 48058

Message ... accompanying a Statement of Expenditures from January 1, 1797, by the Quarter Master General, and the Navy Agents. ... *Washington.* 1803. Folio. 48059

Message ... inclosing a Treaty and Conventions, ... by the United States of America and the French Republic relative to the cession of Louisiana, 22 Oct. 1803. [n. p. n. d.] 8vo.

Message ... transmitting sundry Documents, relative to the Affairs of the City of Washington. *Washington.* 1803. 8vo.

Message ... accompanying Copies of Treaties concluded with the Delaware and Piankeshaw Indians. *Washington.* 1804. 8vo.

Message ... transmitting a List of the Names of Patentees, &c. *Washington.* 1805. Folio. 48063

Message ... [on] the Act of Congress ... 1806, appropriating Two Millions of Dollars, for defraying any extraordinary expenses attending the intercourse between the United States and Foreign Nations. ... *Washington City: Printed by R. C. Weightman.* 1809. 8vo, pp. 14. B. 48064

Message ... on a Military Expedition, January 26, 1807. *Washington.* 1807. 8vo, pp. 8. 48065

Relates to Aaron Burr. *See also* Vol. III., No. 9428–9. Also: Message ... November 8th, 1808. *City of Washington.* 1808. 8vo, pp. 111. — Message transmitting Copies of all Acts, Decrees, ... affecting the Commercial Rights of Neutral Nations, issued since 1791. ... *Washington.* 1808. 8vo, pp. 123. — Message ... Extracts from the Correspondence of Mr. Pinkney: December 18, 1809. *City of Washington: A. & G. Way, Printers.* 1809. 8vo, pp. 14.

Message ... November 5th, 1811. *Washington.* 1811. 8vo. + *London.* 1812. 8vo. 48066

Contains interesting particulars of the action between Little Belt and the President.

Message ... relative to the Orders in Council. *Washington.* 1811. 8vo. 48067

Message ... transmitting ... Documents ... from a secret Agent of the British Government, employed ... to destroy the Union of the United States. March 9, 1812. *Washington: R. C. Weightman.* 1812. 8vo, pp. 50. 48068

Message ... communicating ... Letters ... between the Secretary of State and the Envoy ... of Great Britain, on the ... Orders in Council and Impressed Seamen. June 8, 1812. *Washington City: R. C. Weightman.* 1812. 8vo, pp. 17.

Also: Message ... transmitting Documents on British Impressments ... 6 July, 1812. *Washington City.* 1812. 8vo, pp. 54.

Message ... transmitting ... Correspondence ... relating to the alleged Encouragement by the British Government of the Indians to commit Depredations on the Inhabitants of the United States ... . *Washington.* 1812. 8vo, pp. 24. 48070

Message ... to Explain the Causes of the Failure of the Arms of the United States on the Northern Frontier, February 2d, 1814. ... *Washington.* 1814. 8vo, pp. 115, 114. + [Another Edition.] *New York: At the Office of "The Examiner"* ... 1814. 8vo, pp. (2), 65. + *Albany.* 1814. 16mo, pp. 175. 48071

Message ... showing the Progress of the Negotiations for Peace with Great Britain. *Washington.* 1814. 8vo. 48072

Message ... transmitting the Treaty of Peace and Amity between the United States and his Britannic Majesty. *Washington.* 1815. 8vo. 48073

Message ... transmitting an extract from the Occurrences at Fort Jackson, in August, 1814, during the negotiation of a

Treaty with the Indians; and recommending the ratification of certain Donations of Land, made By the said Indians ... . *Washington: Printed by William A. Davis.* 1816. 8vo, pp. 11.

Message ... transmitting the Correspondence between the Department of State, and the Spanish Minister, ... Showing the Present State of the Relations between the two Governments. March 14, 1818. ... *Washington: Printed by E. De Krafft.* 1818. 8vo, pp. 91. 48075

Message ... transmitting Information in relation to the War with the Seminoles. ... March 25, 1818. *Washington: Printed by E. De Krafft.* 1818. 8vo, pp. 29. 48076

Also: Message ... December 3, 1818, with Documents in relation to the Seminole War. *Washington.* 1818. 8vo.

Message ... in relation to our Affairs with Spain ... December 28, 1818. *Washington: Printed by E. De Krafft.* 1818. 8vo, pp. 215. 48077

Contains copious details illustrating the origin of a war of the United States with a tribe of Indians, which lasted over a quarter of a century, and includes minutes of the trial of Arbuthnot and Ambrister. Lord Castlereagh told the American minister (Mr. Rush) that the excitement was so great in England, at the treatment of Arbuthnot and Ambrister, by General Jackson, that the holding up of his finger would have caused a declaration of war against America. *See also* our Vol. I., Nos. 1894–6.

Message ... transmitting ... Communications from the Agents of the United States with the Governments south of the United States which have Declared their Independence; ... and the State of the War between them and Spain, March 8, 1822. ... *Washington.* 1822. 8vo, pp. 74. 48078

Message ... transmitting ... Information of the Annual Disposition ... Of the Sum of Fifteen Thousand Dollars, ... To promote Civilization among friendly Indian Tribes; ... *Washington: Printed by Gales & Seaton.* 1822. 8vo, pp. 7. 48079

Message ... transmitting ... a Report from the Attorney General [Wirt] relative to the Introduction of Slaves into the United States ... . May 6, 1822. ... *Washington.* 1822. 8vo, pp. 53.

Message ... with ... Objections to the Bill for the Preservation and Repair of the Cumberland Road; also a Paper containing ... Views on Internal Improvements. 4 May, 1822. *Washington.* [1822.] 8vo, pp. 60. 48081

Message ... transmitting Information in relation to certain Christian Indians, ... on the Muskingum, in ... Ohio, granted ...

June 1st, 1796, to the Society of the United Brethren, for propagating the Gospel among the Heathen. December 10, 1822. *Washington: Printed by Gales & Seaton.* 1823. 8vo, pp. 58.

Message ... Communicating the Report of the Commissioners appointed to survey the River Potomac. *Annapolis: Printed by J. Hughes.* 1823. 8vo, pp. 92. 48083

Message ... transmitting a Digest of the Commercial Regulations of the different foreign Nations, with which the United States have Intercourse. ... *Washington.* 1824. 8vo. 48084

Message ... transmitting sundry documents, in relation to the various Tribes of Indians ... and recommending a plan for their future location and Government. January 27, 1825. ... *Washington: Printed by Gales & Seaton.* 1825. 8vo, pp. 13. 4 Tables.

Message ... transmitting Copies of Treaties between the United States and the Quapaw and Choctaw Nations of Indians. February 26, 1825. ... *Washington: Printed by Gales & Seaton.* 1825. 8vo, pp. 11. 48086

Message ... transmitting a Report of the Board of Engineers on Internal Improvements. *Washington.* 1825. 8vo. 48087

Message ... transmitting ... Instructions to the Ministers of the United States to the Government of France, ... having reference to the Spoliations committed by that Power on the Commerce of the United States, anterior to September 30, 1800, &c. ... *Washington: Printed by Gales & Seaton.* 1826. 8vo, pp. 804.

Message ... transmitting Information in relation to the proposed Congress to be held at Panama. *Washington.* 1826. 8vo.

Message ... in relation to ... a road from Little Rock to Cantonment Gibson. *Washington.* 1826. 8vo. 48090

Message ... providing for the Settlement and Confirmation of private Land Claims in Florida. *Washington.* 1828. 8vo.

See also Florida for other messages.

Message ... relative to the Free Navigation of the River St. Lawrence. Jan. 7, 1828. ... *Washington.* 1828. 8vo, pp. 54.

Message ... in relation to the formation of a new Government by the Cherokee Tribe of Indians, within the States of North Carolina, Georgia, Tennessee, and Alabama, &c. March 22, 1828. *Washington.* 1828. 8vo, pp. 19. 48093

Message ... upon the ... Award ... under the Treaty of Ghent. *Washington.* 1828. 8vo. 48094

Message ... transmitting the Correspondence between this Government and that of Great Britain on the ... Claims of the two Governments to the Territory west of the Rocky Mountains. *Washington.* 1828. 8vo. 48095

Message ... returning the bank bill, with ... objections, &c. July 10th, 1832. ... Likewise, a Biographical Sketch of Martin Van Buren. *New-York.* 1832. 12mo, pp. 48. 48096

Message ... transmitting Copies of the Proclamation and Proceedings in relation to South Carolina, January 16, 1833. *Washington.* 1833. 8vo, pp. 112. 48097

Message ... in relation to the Consular Establishment of the United States; ... March 2d, 1833. *Washington.* 1833. 8vo.

Message ... December 2, 1834. *Washington.* 1834. 8vo, pp. 370. 48099

Contains Wheelock's Journal of the Campaign of United States Dragoons for the summer of 1834, among the Indians. Also, Lewis Cass' Reports on Indian Affairs.

Message ... in relation to the Boundary Line between Ohio and Michigan Territory. ... *Washington.* 1835. 8vo. 48100

Message ... Frauds, &c. in the Sale of Indian Reservation of Land. [*Washington.* 1836.] 8vo, pp. 388. 48101

Message ... on our Relations with France, including the Debates in the French Chambers. January, 1836. *Washington.* [1836.] 8vo. 48102

Message ... Indian Hostilities in Florida. [*Washington.* 1836.] 8vo, pp. 52. 48103

Message ... in relation to the ... Exploring Expedition. *Washington.* 1837. 8vo. 48104

Message ... in reference to the Imprisonment of Mr. Greely in New-Brunswick, and the Maine Boundary. *Washington.* 1838. 8vo. 48105

Message ... on the State of Affairs between Maine and New Brunswick, 1839. *Washington.* [n. d.] 8vo. 48106

Message ... Dec. 7, 1842. With ... Documents; containing Negociation and Treaty of Washington, Texan and North-Eastern Boundary Reports. *Washington.* 1842. 8vo. Maps.

Message ... suppression of hostilities in Florida. [*Washington.* 1842.] 8vo, pp. 2. 48108

Message ... Communicating Copies of Correspondence with ... Mexico. [*Washington.* 1842.] 8vo. 48109

Message ... relative to the employment of the United States Troops in Rhode Island, and ... Documents ... April 10, 1844. [n. p. n. d.] 8vo, pp. 179. 48110

Message ... with ... Documents. *Washington.* 1845. 8vo, pp. 893. 48111

Includes correspondence and papers relating to the annexation of Texas, the Oregon controversy, etc.

Message ... in relation to the Construction of Floating Dry Docks at Pensacola, Philadelphia and Kittery. ... [n. p.] 1847. 8vo, pp. 152. s. 48112

Message ... December 7, 1847. *Washington.* 1847. 8vo, pp. 1369, Appendix, 249. 48113

Partly relates to Mexican affairs.

Messages ... on the Subject of the Mexican War. *Washington: Wendell and Van Benthuysen, Printers.* 1848. 8vo, pp. 1277. B. 48114

Perhaps the most important collection of material we have for the history of the Mexican War.

Message ... to the Two Houses of Congress ... of the First [and Second] Session ... . *Washington.* 1848. 8vo, pp. 1237; 1275. 48115

Contains full details of the Mexican War. Also: Message ... communicating a copy of the Treaty with the Mexican Republic of February 2, 1848, and of the Correspondence. *Washington.* 1848. 8vo, pp. 74. — Message ... and Documents from which the injunction of secrecy has been removed, relating to the Treaty between the United States and Mexico. *Washington.* 1848. 8vo.

Message ... in relation to a Postal Arrangement. ... 1848. [n. p. 1848.] 8vo, pp. 45. s. 48116

Message ... transmitting Information relative to California and New Mexico. *Washington.* 1850. 8vo, pp. 976. 48117

Message ... relative to Rank, &c., in the Army and Navy. Jan. 21, 1851. ... [n. p. n. d.] 8vo, pp. 12. s. 48118

Message ... in relation to the Difficulties between the British Authorities and San Salvador. *Washington.* 1851. 8vo, pp. 99.

Contains the dispatches of E. G. Squier, as U. S. Minister to Central America.

Message ... on the Seizure and Confiscation of the Barque Georgianna and Brig Susan Loud. Jan. 28, 1852. [n. p. n. d.] 8vo. 48120

Message ... in relation to the Inter-Oceanic Canal—Nicaragua Route. 1853. *Washington.* 1853. 8vo. 48121

Message ... [relative to Central America] January 21, 1853. *Washington.* 1853. 8vo, pp. 108. + December 31, 1853. [*Ibid.*] 8vo, pp. 19. 48122

Message ... July 31, 1854. [*Washington.* 1854.] 8vo, pp. 30

Relates to the bombardment of Greytown.

Message ... communicating Documents in Case of the Black Warrior, and Spanish Violations of the Rights of American Citizens. *Washington.* 1854. 8vo. 48124

Message ... transmitting ... Correspondence, etc. growing out of the Seizure and Rescue of Martin Koszta. [*Washington.* 1854.] 8vo, pp. 92. c. 48125

... Message ... calling for correspondence between the ... United States and Great Britain, relative to the enlistment of Soldiers ... . *Washington.* 1856. 8vo, pp. 251. 48126

Message ... communicating the Proceedings of the Commissioners for the Adjustment of Claims under the Convention ... between Great Britain and the United States ... . *Washington.* 1856. 8vo. N. 48127

Message ... communicating cessation of Intercourse with the ... Minister Plenipotentiary of Great Britain. May 29, 1856. [n. p. n. d.] 8vo, pp. 80. 48128

Message ... relative to Neutral Rights ... August 12, 1856. [n. p. n. d.] 8vo, pp. 18. s. 48129

Message ... relative to the seizure ... in Peru, ... of the ... cargo of the brig Macedonian ... . [*Washington.* 1858.] 8vo, pp. 466. BA. 48130

Message ... communicating ... information in regard to the occupation by American citizens of the Island of Navasca, in the West Indies. April 13, 1860. ... *Washington.* 1860. 8vo, pp. 25. 48131

... Message ... communicating, ... the correspondence of Lieutenant General Scott, in reference to the island of San Juan, and of Brigadier General Harney, in command of the department of Oregon. [*Washington.* 1860.] 8vo, pp. 75. 48132

Messages ... relative to the Compulsory Enlistment of American Citizens in the Army of Prussia, &c. *Washington: G. W. Bowman.* 1860. 8vo, pp. 237. c. 48133

Message ... communicating the Instructions to, and Dispatches from, the ... Ministers in China, ... to the ... Treaty of Tientsin. *Washington.* 1860. 8vo, pp. 624. 48134

Message ... communicating, ... information in relation to the massacre at Mountain Meadows, and other massacres in Utah Territory. ... [*Washington.* 1860.] 8vo, pp. 139. 48135

Message ... [to] Senate and House of Representatives. [July 4, 1861. n. p. n. d.] 8vo, pp. 15. B. 48136

The messages for 1861–5 are chiefly on the subject of the rebellion in the South, and on that subject they are voluminous and important state papers.

Message ... transmitting Correspondence relative to the attempted seizure of M. Fauchet, Envoy ... of France, by the Commander of the British Sloop-of-War Africa, within the waters of the United States. *Washington.* 1862. 8vo, pp. 53.

This correspondence was called for, from its bearing on the case of the seizure of Mason and Slidell.

Message ... in relation to a Military Appointment of the Hon. Francis P. Blair, Jr., representing ... Missouri. [n. p. n. p.] 8vo, pp. 2. 48138

Message ... in relation to the Indian Barbarities in Minnesota. [*Washington.*] 1862. 8vo, pp. 9. 48139

Message ... with Information relative to a Conference held at Hampton Roads, with Messrs. A. H. Stephens, R. M. T. Hunter and J. A. Campbell. [n. p. n. d.] 8vo, pp. 10.

Message ... communicating, ... information in relation to the States of the Union lately in rebellion ... . also a report of Lieutenant General Grant. [*Washington.* 1864.] 8vo, pp. 108.

Message ... March 20, 1866, relating to the Condition of Affairs in Mexico ... . Part I. *Washington.* 1866. 8vo, pp. 706.

Message ... December 3, 1866; together with Papers relating to Mexico. [*Washington.* 1866.] 8vo, pp. 30. 48143

Message ... transmitting a Report ... concerning the International ... Monetary Conference at ... Paris ... 1867. *Washington.* 1868. 8vo, pp. 110. 48144

Message ... transmitting a Treaty between the United States and the Great and Little Osage Tribe of Indians, ... 1868. [*Washington.* 1868.] 8vo, pp. 14. 48145

Message of the President [of the Confederate States], February 12, 1864, ... relative "to the Trial and Conviction of W. E. Coffman by a military court," and the Interposition of the Circuit Court of Rockingham County, Virginia, by Habeas Corpus, to prevent the execution of Coffman. [n. p. n. d.] 8vo, pp. 10. 48146

Message ... February 15, 1864. [n. p. n. d.] 8vo, pp. 41.

Transmitting copies of charges and specifications in Case of Major H. C. Guerin, C. S. A. *See also* under Confederate States and President's Message.

Messages of the Presidents of the United States from the formation of the ... Government ... to the close of the Administration of President Van Buren. ... *Columbus, Ohio: Jonathan Philips.* 1841. 8vo, pp. 704. 48148

See also our Nos. 3299, 4946, 5864, 6001, 12488, 17791, 24888, 25840, 27072–3, 35378, 37023, 37456.

Messages from the Governors of Maryland and Pennsylvania, *See* Vol. XI., No. 45089.

See also under the names of the various States.

MESSE (——). The History of Dungeon Rock, completed September 17th, 1856. By Messe. *Boston.* 1856. 12mo.

MESSENIUS (Johannes). ... Scondia illustrata, Seu Chronologia de rebus Scondiæ, Hoc est, Sueciæ, ... Atque una Islandiæ, Gronlandiæque, tam Ecclesiasticis quam Politicis; â mundi Cataclysmo, usque annum Christi MDCXII. gestis. Primum edita ... â J. Peringskiöld. *Stockholmiæ: Typis Olai Enei.* 1700–5. 15 vols., folio. BA. 48150

The fourteenth part has never been printed. It was lost in MS. as we see from a notice in the "Emendanda": "Tom. XIV. de Gothis extra patriam, perditus est."

MESSER (A.) An Address, ... to the Graduates of Brown University, ... September 5, 1810. By Asa Messer, D.D. ... *Providence: ... Dunham & Hawkins, Printers.* [1810.] 8vo, pp. 11, (1). B. 48151

Also: An Address ... to the Graduates of Rhode Island College, ... Sept. 7, 1803. ... *Providence: Nathaniel Heaton, Jun.* 1803. 8vo, pp. 12. — A Discourse ... in the

Chapel of Rhode Island College, to the Senior Class, ... 1799. ... *Providence: John Carter, Jun.* 1799. 8vo, pp. 16. — A Discourse ... before the Warren [R. I.] Association, ... September 8, 1812. ... *Providence: D. Hawkins.* 1813. 8vo, pp. 18. — An Oration ... before the Providence Association of Mechanics and Manufacturers, at their Annual Election, April 11th, 1803. ... *Providence: John Carter.* 1803. 8vo, pp. 15. — An Oration ... at Providence, ... Fourth of July, 1803. ... *Providence: John Carter.* 1803. 8vo, pp. 14. *See also* our Vol. II., No. 8600.

MESSIA *or* MESSIE (P. de). *See* Mexia (P. de).

MESSIAE (P.) *and* VERDIER (A. du). Verscheyden Lessen, waarin beschreven worden de weerdichste Gheschiedenissen aller Keyzeren, Koningen ende loflycker mannen ... . *Amsterdam.* 1629. 2 vols., 8vo. 48152

Various lessons, wherein are described the histories of all emperors, etc. Vol. II., pp. 210–215, treats of Columbus and the discovery of America.

MESSINGER (G. W.) Genealogy of the Messinger Family, compiled by Hon. George W. Messinger. *Albany: J. Munsell.* 1863. 8vo, pp. 14. B. 48153

[MESSINGER.] The Hinckley Family. [*Washington.* 1859.] 8vo, pp. 7. 48154

MESSINGER (R.) An Oration, ... at Old York, on the Death of George Washington ... . By the Rev. Rosewell Messinger, Pastor ... in Old York, Maine. *Charlestown: Printed by Samuel Etheridge.* 1800. 8vo, pp. 16. H. 48155

Also: Sentiments on Resignation. ... *Portsmouth, N. H.: The Author.* 1807. 12mo, pp. 225, (9). — A Sermon ... at York, Me., Oct. 21, 1798; being the first after his Inauguration into the Gospel Ministry. ... *Boston.* 1799. 8vo, pp. 23. — Sermon at the Ordination of the Rev. James Boyd, Bangor, September 10, 1800. ... *Newburyport.* [n. d.] 8vo. N.

MESSIRE-JEAN. Plus d'Esclavage! Par Messire-Jean. *Paris: Amable Rigaud.* 1863. 8vo, pp. 12. H. 48156

Messis Paraquariensis á Patribus Societatis Jesu per Sexennium in Paraquaria collecta, annis videlicet 1638, 39, 40, 41, 42 ét 43, conscripta à P. Adamo Schirmbeck, Societatis ejusdem Sacerdote. *Monachii: S. Straubii.* 1649. 12mo, pp. (8), 366, (2). 48157

MESSLER (A.) A Brief History of the Reformed Dutch Church of Raritan, from its Organization to ... 1834. ... By Abraham Messler, Pastor. *Somerville, N. J.* 1834. 12mo, pp. 22

MESSLER. ... A Sermon ... at the Dedication of The Reformed Dutch Church of Raritan, February 25, 1835. By Rev. Abraham Messler ... . *Somerville.* MDCCCXXXV. 8vo, pp. 28.

Also: Discourse ... Death of J. H. Castner. ... *Somerville, N. J.* 1841. 8vo. — ... A Sermon ... before the Classis of New Brunswick ... April 2d, 1845 ... . *New-York: Printed by Daniel Fanshaw.* 1845. 8vo, pp. 40. N. — Sermon ... at the Installation of John Steele. ... *New Brunswick.* 1853. 8vo.

MESTRE (M.) Vida, y Milagros del Glorioso S. Antonio de Padua. Sol Brillante de la Iglesia, Lustre de la Religion Serafica, Gloria de Portugal, Honor de España, Tesoro de Italia, terror del Inferno, martillo perpetuo de la heregia, entre los Santos por excelencia et Milagrero. Por El R. P. Miguel Mestre. *Madrid.* 1724. 4to, pp. (16), 308, (8). Portrait. 48160

Some of these miracles of San Antonio of Padua are located in the West Indies.

MESSONIER (H.) Report of the Committee of Commerce and Manufactures, ... on ... the Memorial of Henry Messonier. 6th January, 1803. ... [n. p. n. d.] 8vo, pp. 10. B. 48161

MESTRE (J. M.) De la filosofia en la Habana: Discurso ... por José Manuel Mestre. Seguido de una carta inedita del Félix Varela, y uno articulo del José Z. Gonzalez del Valle. *Habana: Imprenta "la Antillo."* 1862. 12mo, pp. 149. c. 48162

MESZLENYI (S. K.) Memorial of Mad. Susanne Kossuth Meszlenyi. ... *Boston: N. C. Peabody.* 1856. 16mo, pp. 64. B.

The last half of the book relates her life in America.

METCALF (E. W.) Genealogy of a branch of the Metcalf Family, who originated in West Wrentham, Mass. ... . Prepared by E. W. Metcalf ... 1867. [n. p. 1867.] 8vo, pp. (2), 12.

METCALF (J. G.) An Oration ... at Indian Rock, in Franklin, July 4th, 1823 ... . By John George Metcalf. *Dedham: Printed by H. & W. H. Mann.* [1823.] 8vo, pp. 23. H.

METCALF (S. L.) A Collection of some of the most interesting Narratives of Indian Warfare in the West, Containing an Account of the Adventures of Colonel Daniel Boone, one of the first Settlers of Kentucky, Comprehending the most important occurrences relative to its early history—Also, an account of the Manners, and Customs of the Indians, their Traditions and Religious Sentiments, their Police or Civil Government, their Discipline and method of War: to which is added, an Account of the Expeditions of Genl's Harmer, Scott, Wilkinson, St. Clair, & Wayne: The whole compiled from the best authorities, By Samuel L. Metcalf. *Lexington, Ky.: Printed by William G. Hunt.* 1821. 8vo, pp. 270. 48166

This rare work is a compilation, principally from available sources, of the narratives which in their original form had even at the date of its publication, become scarce. It

includes Boone's, Knight and Slover's, and James Smith's narratives. Also: A New Theory of Terrestial Magnetism. ... *New-York: G. & C. & H. Carvil.* MDCCCXXXIII. 8vo, pp. (2), 158. H.

METCALF (T.) An Address to the Phi Beta Kappa Society of Brown University ... 5th September, 1832. By Theron Metcalf. *Boston: Lilly, Wait, Colman* ... . 1833. 8vo, pp. 28. B.

Also: An Oration, ... at Dedham, July 4th, 1810 ... . *Boston: Printed by Joshua Belcher.* 1810. 8vo, pp. 18. H., M. *See also* Massachusetts, Vol. XI., No. 46083.

METCALFE (Charles). Selections from the Papers of Lord Metcalfe, late ... Governor of Jamaica, and Governor-General of Canada. Edited by John William Kaye. *London.* 1855. 8vo. c. 48168

Also: Addresses to Sir Charles Metcalfe on the occasion of the Resignation of his late Advisers. *Toronto.* 1844. 8vo. — Report of the Proceedings of a Meeting of the Friends and Admirers of Lord Metcalfe in Montreal, 1st February, 1847. *Montreal.* 1847. 8vo, pp. 15. *See also* Vol. V., No. 17586, Vol. IX., Nos. 37123 and 35579, [Wakefield (E. G.)], Zeno, *pseudon.*, Parliamentary Papers for 1847–8, *and* "Blackwood's Magazine," LX.

METCALFE (J.) Memoir of the Rev. William Metcalfe, M.D. ... By his Son, Rev. Joseph Metcalfe. *Philadelphia.* 1866. 12mo, pp. 38. 48169

METELLUS (J. M.) America, | sive | Novvs Orbis, | Tabvlis Æneis Secvndvm | Rationes Geographicas | delineatvs. | ... Ioannes Matalivs Metellvs ... . *Coloniæ Agrippinæ*: | *Stephanus Hemmerden.* | M.DC. | Folio, 52 leaves, containing 20 Maps. H. 48170

Also: Insvlarivm orbis aliqvot, tabulis aeneis delineationem continens. In quo describvntur multa per Oceanum sparsae insulae ... Continet hoc opus tabulas geographicas aeri incis. 264, earumque dorsis res Historicae impressae sunt. ... *Coloniae Agrippinae.* 1601. Folio.

The Meteor of Light, containing the Minutes of the ... Infidel Convention, held in the City of New York, May ... 1845. Vol. I. June 1, 1845. No. I. *Boston: Printed by J. P. Mendum.* 1845. 8vo, pp. 41, (1). BA. 48171

Meteorological Register for the Years 1822–25, from Observations made by the Surgeons of the Army, at the Military Posts of the United States. *Washington: E. De Krafft.* 1826. 8vo, pp. 63. c. 48172

Meteorological Register, for Twelve Years, from 1831 to 1842, compiled from Observations made by the Officers of the Medical Department of the Army, at the Military Posts of the United States. *Washington.* 1851. 8vo. A. 48173

... Meteorological Sketches. By an Observer. ... [n. p. n. d.] 8vo, pp. 20. H. 48174

METEREN (E. van). Belgische ofte Nederlantsche Oorlogen ende Geschiedenissen beginnende van't jaer 1595 tot 1611, mede vervatende enighe gebueren handelinghe. Beschreven door Emanuel Van Meteren. Bij hem voor de leste reyse oversie verbetert ende vermeerdert na die copie gedruckt op Schotlant buyten Danswyck by Hermes van Loven. [*Dordrecht?*] *Voor den Autheur Anno* 1611. 4to, 360 leaves. H.C.M. 48175

"Contains the first account that appeared in print of Hudson's voyage for the East-India Company."—[HARRISSE] *Bib. Am. Vet.* p. XXXVII.

METEREN. Historie der Nederlandschen en haar nabueren oorlogen. *Amsterdam.* 1652. Folio. 48176

"This work contains very valuable materials for the life of Henry Hudson, and for the history of W. Usselincx and his first attempts to establish the West-India Company."—MULLER.

METEREN. Meteranus novus, dass ist: Warhafftige Beschreibung dess Niederländischen Krieges: so wol was sich Denckwürtiges in dem gantzen Römischen Reich auch in Franckreich, Hispanien, Engelland und anderen Königreichen, dessgleichen in Ost- und Westindien zugetragen. Biss 1638 continuirt. *Amsterdam: J. Jansson.* 1640. 4 vols., folio. Plates. 48177

This work also treats of the events in the East and West Indies. The fourth volume contains, for example, a description of the capture of Pernambuco.

Methodism Anatomiz'd; or an Alarm to Pennsylvania. By a lover of true Piety, in opposition to Enthusiasm. With some remarks on a Discourse deliver'd September 24th, 1763. ... [*Philadelphia*:] *Printed for the Author, and sold by John Morris, at the Green-Man in Fishamble-street.* MDCCLXIII. 12mo, pp. 16. P.

Written on occasion of Mr. Whitefield's late visit to Pennsylvania.

Methodism Inspected. *Philadelphia.* [n. d.] 12mo. 48179

A series of tracts in refutation of Methodism.

Methodism in the State of New York, as represented in State Convention, held in Syracuse, N. Y., February 22–24, 1870. *New York: Carlton & Lanahan.* 1870. 8vo, pp. 150. 48180

Methodist Church. The Doctrines and Discipline of the African Methodist Episcopal Church. Fifth Edition. *Brooklyn, N. Y.: ... George Hogarth.* 1840. 32mo, pp. 223, (4). H. 48181

Also: Articles of Agreement between the General Conference of the Methodist Episcopal Church, and the Trustees of the African Methodist Episcopal Church in ...

New York. *Brooklyn.* 1801. 8vo, pp. 8. — Minutes of the General and Annual Conferences of the African Methodist Episcopal Church, from 1836–1839 inclusive. *Brooklyn, N. Y.* 1839. 12mo. Continued.

The Doctrines and Discipline of the Methodist Episcopal Church in America; Revised and approved at the General Conference held at Baltimore, in the State of Maryland, in November, 1792, in which Thos. Coke and Francis Asbury presided. Eighth Edition. *Philadelphia.* 1792. 12mo, pp. 263. + With Explanatory Notes by Thomas Coke and Francis Asbury. *Philadelphia.* 1798. 12mo, pp. (192). + *New York.* 1821. 12mo. + *New York: B. Waugh & T. Mason.* 1832. 24mo, pp. 196. + *New York.* 1836. 32mo, pp. (2), 60, (2). + *New York: T. Mason & G. Lane.* 1840. 24mo, pp. 206. 48182

The Doctrines and Discipline of the Methodist Episcopal Church South. *Nashville, Tenn.: E. Stevenson & F. A. Owen.* 1856. 16mo, pp. vi, 267. + *New York: Carlton & Porter.* 1856. 32mo, pp. 240. + *New York: Carlton & Lanahan.* 1868. 32mo, pp. 374. + *Nashville, Tenn.: Publishing House of Methodist Episcopal Church South.* 1870. 12mo, pp. 291. 48183

Doctrines and Discipline of the Methodist Episcopal Church. [In Cherokee.] *Park Hill: ... John Candy, Printer.* 1842. 24mo, pp. 45. BA. 48184

An Exposition. *See* Vol. VI., No. 23454, [Jennings (S. K.)], IX. 36049, *and* [Kingman (J.)], IX. 37869.

A Form of Discipline ... of the Methodist Episcopal Church in America .... *London.* 1779. 8vo. + *New-York.* 1789. 12mo. + *Philadelphia.* 1791. 12mo. 48185

General Rules of the United Societies of the Methodist Episcopal Church. Translated into the Chahta Language. Mehlotist Iska i Nana Ulhpisa Puta. ... *Park Hill: ... John Candy, Printer.* 1841. 24mo, pp. 24. BA. 48186

History of the Organization of the Methodist Episcopal Church South, comprising all the Official Proceedings of the General Conference, the Southern Annual Conference, and the Convention; ... *Nashville.* 1845. 8vo, pp. 267. 48187

Journals of the General Conference .... 1796–1836. ... Volume I. *New-York: Carlton & Phillips.* 1855. 8vo, pp. 504. Continued. H. 48188

The Methodist Almanac, ... 1835: ... By David Young .... *New-York: B. Waugh and T. Mason.* 1834. 12mo, pp. 36. Continued. B. 48189

Methodist Chapel Property Case. Report of the Trial of an Action brought by persons calling themselves "The Methodist Episcopal Church in Canada," to obtain possession of the Wesleyan Methodist Chapel in Belleville. Tried before the Hon. Mr. Justice Jones at Kingston, October 11th, 1837. With brief Notes and Remarks, by Rev. E. Ryerson. *Toronto.* 1837. 8vo, pp. 103. 48190

Methodist Church Property Case. Report of the Suit of Henry B. Bascom and others *vs.* George Lane and others, ... May 17–29, 1851. By R. Sutton, ... Reporter. *New-York.* 1851. 8vo, pp. 372. S. 48191

On the affairs of the "Book Concern." Also: Brief Appeal to Public Opinion in a Series of Exceptions to the course and action of the Methodist Episcopal Church from 1844 to 1846, affecting the Rights and Interest of the Methodist Episcopal Church South; By H. B. Bascom and A. L. P. Greene and C. B. Parsons. *Louisville, Ky.* 1848. 8vo, pp. 202.

Methodist Episcopacy. A Religious Colloquy; being an Examination of an Important Subject of Religion, etc. By a Friend to Truth. *Annapolis.* 1800. 12mo, pp. 26. 48192

The Methodist Episcopal Church in the United States; or an account of its Present Organization and Influence. ... [n. p.:] *The Author.* 1833. 8vo, pp. 32. H. 48193

Methodist Episcopal Church ... *vs.* New organization, called "Methodist Episcopal Church South," formed 1845. [n. p. n. d.] 8vo, pp. 30. 48194

Catalogue of the Officers and Students of the Methodist General Biblical Institute ... 1850. *Boston: George C. Rand and Company.* [1850.] 16mo, pp. 16. Continued. H. 48195

The Methodist Magazine ... . 1798. *London.* 1798. 8vo. Continued. 48196

Contains many biographies and notices of the church in America.

The Methodist Magazine, for ... 1818. Volume I. *New York: J. Soule and T. Mason.* 1818. 8vo, pp. 478, (2). B.

Continued as "The Methodist Magazine and Quarterly Review." ... New Series. Vol. I. *New York.* 1830. 8vo. After 1840, continued as "The Methodist Quarterly Review."

Annual Report of the Methodist Missionary Society, ... 1820. *New-York.* 1820. 8vo. Continued. S. 48198

Annual Report of the Methodist Tract Society ... 1854. *New-York: Carlton & Phillips.* [1854.] 8vo, pp. 56. Cont'd.

Minutes of Several Conversations between the Rev. Thomas Coke, LL.D., the Rev. Francis Asbury, and others; at a Conference begun in Baltimore, on Monday, the 27th day of December, in the year 1784. Composing a form of Discipline for the Ministers, Preachers, and other Members of the Methodist Episcopal Church in America. *Philadelphia: [Printed by Charles Cist].* 1785. 12mo. 48200

Minutes of the Methodist Conferences, annually held in America, From 1773 to 1794 .... *Philadelphia: Printed by Henry Tuckniss.* M DCC XCV. 12mo, pp. 214. B. 48201

Minutes of the Annual Conferences of the Methodist Episcopal Church for the years 1773–1828. Volume I. *New-York: T. Mason and G. Lane* 1840. 8vo, pp. 574. Continued. H.

Minutes taken at the several Conferences of the Methodist Episcopal Church in America for the year 1794. *Philadelphia.* 1794. 16mo, pp. 22. Continued. S. 48203

The minutes of the Wesleyan conferences contain information relative to Methodism in the American colonies.

Minutes taken at the several Annual Conferences ... for ... 1804. *New York: Printed by T. Kirk.* 1804. 12mo, pp. 24. Continued. BA. 48204

Annual Report of the Sunday-School Union of the Methodist Episcopal Church. *New-York: Lane & Scott.* 1851. 8vo, pp. 158. Continued. H. 48205

Also: A Brief Exposition of the Character, Operations, and Claims, of the Sunday-School Union of the Methodist Episcopal Church. *New-York: Lane & Scott.* 1852. 12mo, pp. 47. — Constitution, By-Laws, etc., of the Sunday-School Union of the Methodist Episcopal Church. *Albany.* 1860. 12mo. — Manual of the Sunday-School Union, for Ministers of the Methodist Episcopal Church. *New-York.* 1855. 16mo, pp. 8, 8. — Annual Report of the Sunday-School Union of the Methodist Episcopal Church. *New York.* 1850. 8vo.

Constitution of the Methodist Protestant Church, adopted by a General Convention ... held in Baltimore, November, 1830. ... *Baltimore: John J. Harrod.* 1830. 8vo, pp. 30. H. 48206

Also: Constitution and Discipline of the Methodist Protestant Church. *Baltimore: John J. Harrod.* 1830. 18mo, pp. 159. Continued.

Constitution and Discipline of the Methodist Protestant Church of British North America. *Stanbridge, Canada.* 1835. 16mo, pp. 47. S. 48207

Also: Account of the Exercises at a Methodist Camp-Meeting. [n. p.] 1813. 8vo. — Annual Report of the Missionary Society of the Methodist Episcopal Church. *New York.* 1819. 8vo. Continued. — Connectional Centenary Documents. No. 1. Resolutions of the General Conference on the Centenary of American Methodism. ... *New York: The Committee.* 1865. 8vo, pp. 8. Continued. — Loan Fund of the Church Extension Society. *New York.* 1869. 8vo. — Ritual of the Methodist Episcopal Church. *New York: Carlton & Porter.* 1864. 8vo, pp. 152.

Methods for Improving. *See* Vol. III., No. 10937.

METHUEN, *Mass.* Annual Report of the School Committee ... 1850. *Lawrence.* 1850 8vo, pp. 16. Continued. B. 48208

Also: Annual Report of the Receipts and Expenses ... from ... 1848 to ... 1849. *Lawrence: Hayes, Printer.* 1849. 8vo, pp. 13. Continued B.

Metlahkatlah. *See* [Duncan (William)], VI. 21264.

[METLAR (George W.)] Northern California. Scott and Klamarth Rivers, &c. *Yreka, Cal.* 1856. Sm. 8vo, pp. 24.

Metodo curativo de las Viruelas formado a consecuencia de ecsitacion del Gobierno del estado de Puebla por la academia medico quirurgica establecida en la capital del Mismo, para uso de los Pueblos en que no hay facultativos. *Puebla.* 1830. Sm. 8vo, pp. 15. 48210

MÉTRAL (A.) Histoire de l'Expédition des Français, a Saint-Domingue, sous le consulat de Napoléon Bonaparte, Par Antoine Metrat; suivie des mémoires et notes d'Isaac Louverture, sur la même expédition, et sur la vie de son père ... . *Paris: Fanjat Aîné.* 1825. 8vo, pp. xii, 348. Map and Portrait. H. 48211

MÉTRAL. Histoire de l'Insurrection des Ésclaves dans le Nord de Saint-Domingue. Par Antoine Metral. *Paris: Scherff.* 1818. 8vo, pp. 100. C. 48212

Metrica Panegyrica descripcion de las fiestas que se celebraron el la ciudad de Mexico al felix casamiento del Rey N. S. D. Carlos II. ... *Mexico: Maria Benavides.* 1691. 4to, 20 leaves.

A Metrical Description of a Fancy Ball given at Washington, 9th April, 1858. Dedicated to Mrs. Senator Gwin. *Washington: F. Philp.* 1858. 4to, pp. 40. C. 48214

Metrology Universalized; or, a Proposal to Equalize ... the Weights, ... of Great Britain and America; ... *London: J. A. Hessey.* 1828. 8vo, pp. 23. P. 48215

... The Metropolitan: edited by a Committee of Literary Gentlemen. May, 1856. *Baltimore: John Murphy & Co.* [1856.] 8vo. Continued. H. 48216

Metropolitan Catholic Almanac, and Laity's Directory, for ... 1839. *Baltimore: Fielding Lucas, Jr.* [1838.] 12mo, pp. 195, (1). Continued. H. 48217

Constitution, By-Laws and List of Members of the Metropolitan Club ... . Organized ... 1863. [n. p. 1863?] 12mo, pp. 20. H. 48218

Also: Annual Report. [n. p. 1866.] 8vo, pp. 7. H.

Metropolitan Fair. *See* New York City Guide.

A Record of the First Exhibition of the Metropolitan Mechanics' Institute, ... 1853. *Washington: H. Polkinhorn, Printer.* 1853. 8vo, pp. 52, 14, 68, 11, 6, (2), 3, (2). Continued. B.

The Metropolitan Merchants' and Manufacturers' Business Directory, for 1866 and '67 ... . *New York: Fitzpatrick & Co.* 1866. 4to, pp. 299. 48220

First ... Report of the ... Directors of the Metropolitan Railroad Company to the Stockholders. July 3, 1854. *Georgetown: A. L. Settle.* 1854. 8vo, pp. 43. Map. Continued. 48221

Articles from the Metropolitan Record. *New York.* 1863. 8vo, pp. 130. 48222

Relates to the Rebellion.

MEULEN (M. E. v. d.) Vlugtige blik op Noord-Amerika en een boek daar verschenen. *Utrecht.* 1853. 8vo. 48223

A cursory view of North America and "Uncle Tom's Cabin."

MEUNIER (V.) Les grandes chasses; par Victor Meunier. ... *Paris: L. Hachette et Cie.* 1866. 18mo, pp. 301. 21 Vignettes. + [*Ibid.*] 1868. 18mo, pp. 311. 38 Vignettes. 48224

MEUNIER Adventures on the Great Hunting Grounds of the World. By Victor Meunier. ... *New York: Charles Scribner & Co.* 1869. 16mo, pp. vii, (2), 297. 22 Plates. H. 48225

MEUNRIOS (F. X. de). Description historique d'un monstre symbolique, pris vivant sur les bords du lac Fagua, près de Santa-Fé, par les soins de Francisco Xaveiro de Meunrios, comte de Barcelona. *Santa-Fé.* 1784. 8vo, pp. 29. 2 Plates. 48226

This allegorical pamphlet is directed against magnetism. The author is Monsieur, comte de Provence (Louis XVIII). Meunrios is the anagram for Monsieur.

MEURSINGE (A.) Proeve eener Hollandsche Spraakkunst ten gebruike der algemeene armenschool in de gemeente van de H. Rosa op Curaçao. *Gedrukt te Santa Rosa.* 1849–51. 2 parts, 8vo. 48227

Also: Gemeenzame Zamenspraken behoorende bij behovest. Proeve. Door J. J. Putnam. *Santarosa.* 1853. 8vo. Grammar and dialogues in the Dutch language, written in the dialect of Curaçao and the neighboring islands in use by the inhabitants.

MEUSEL (J. G.) Bibliotheca Historica *See* Struve (B. G.)

MÉVIL (C.) L'Émigration Colonisation dans l'Amérique Centrale. Par Charles Mévil. ... Deuxième Édition. *Paris: Imprimerie de Schiller Aîné.* 1852. 8vo, pp. 32. BA. 48228

MEW (W. M.) ... Report of Captain W. M. Mew ... relative to ... Life-Saving Apparatus, ... with Remarks ... [on] the preservation of Life at Sea. *Washington.* 1868. 8vo, pp. 48. 4 Plates. H. 48229

Me-won-i-toc: A Tale of Frontier Life and Indian Character. *New York.* 1867. 18mo. 48230

MEXIA (Diego). Primera parte del Parnaso Antartico de obras amatorias. *Sevilla: Alonso Rodr. Gamarra.* 1608. 4to.

No more published than this part, which is written, according to Ticknor, "in pure and elegant Castilian verse." The Discurso "en loor de la Poesia" was composed by a lady of high rank in Mexico.

MEXIA Y OCON (J. R.) Arte de la Lengua general de los Indios de Peru. Por D. Juan Roxo Mexia y Ocon, Natural de la Ciudad del Cuzco. *Impresso en Lima, por Jorge Lopez de Herrera.* 1648. Sm. 8vo, pp. (18), 88. 48232

MEXIA (P. de). Libro llamado sil|ua d' varia leciõ dirigido|a la S. C. C. M. d'l Empe|rador y rey nr̃ señor dõ|Carlos quinto deste nom|bre. Cõpuesto por un ca|uallero de Sevilla llama|do Pero Mexia. En el q̃l|a manera de siluas sin guardar hordẽ en los|propositos, se tratan por capitulos muchas y|muy diuersas materias, historicas, exemplos|y questiones de varia lecion, y erudicion. |Con preuilegio Imperial. |M.D.XL.| [Colophon:] *Deo gratias.|fue imprimido el presente libro en la muy noble y muy leal ciudad de|Seuilla por Dominico de Robertis impressor, ... aca|bosse en el mes d' Iulio|de mil y quinientos|y q̃renta años.|* Folio, 8 leaves, Text, cxxxvj leaves. 48233

MEXIA. Silua de varia le-|cion cõpuesta por|Un Cauallero de|Seuilla llamado|Pero Mexia segũ-|da vez Impressa y|añadida por el|mismo auctor.|MDXL.| [Colophon:] *Fue impresso el presente libro en la muy|noble y muy leal ciudad de Seuilla en las casas de luã Cröber-|ger: con licencia ... Año de mill y|quinientos y quarenta|A. xxij. dias d'|deziẽbre.|* Folio, 8 leaves, Text, cxlj leaves.

"Both of these editions are extremely rare, and unknown to bibliographers, but we are unable to state whether they contain in the chapter 'Coloquio del sol,' the passage which, in the edition of 1547, refers to Magellan."—[HARRISSE] *Bib. Am. Vet., Additions*, p. 139. The catalogue of the Ticknor Collection describes one dated 1543, and states that the first edition is *Seville*, 1537.

MEXIA. Con priuilegio|Coloquios o|Dialogos nueuamente cõ|puestos por el Magnifico|Cauallero Pero Mexia|Uezino de Seuilla en los|quales se disputan y tratã|varias y diuersas cosas d'|mucha erudicion y doctri|na. Son dedicados al|Illustrissimo Señor don|Perafan de Ribera Mar|ques de Tarifa, Adelanta|do Mayor del Andaluzia.|&c. M.Dxlvij.| [Colophon:] *Fueron impre-|ssos los presentes Dialogos en la|muy noble y muy leal Ciudad|de Seuilla por Dominico d' Robertis, A siete dias del mes de abril de mil|& quinientos y qua|rẽta y siete años,|* ... 12mo, 1 leaf, Text, ij–clxxiij leaves. 48235

The passage referring to Magellan's voyage is on the verso of leaf cii.

MEXIA. Los dialogos o colloquios nueuamẽte corregidas por el y añadido vn excelẽte tratado de Isocrate philosopho llamado parenesis o exortacion a virtud. Traducido de Latin en Castellano por el mismo autor. *Seuilla.* 1548. 48236

Title from Salva's Catalogue, No. 3471.

[MEXIA.] Silva de|varia lecion|agora nueuamente enmendada, y|añadida por el autor de la quarta|parte, con diligencia corregida, y|adornada de algunos cosas utiles, que en las otras impressiones le|faltaua.|*Imprimose|en Leon de Francia,|por los herederos de|Diego de Iunta,*|M. D. LVI. 8vo, pp. (32), 666, (5).

MEXIA. Silua de varia lection:|Compuesta por el Magnifico cauallero Pe|dro Mexia. Nueuamente agora añadida ene|lla la quarta parte, por el mismo Autor: en|la qual se tratan muchas cosas, y muy|agradables y curiosas.|*En Seuilla en casa de Hernãdo Diaz. Año.* 1570.| [Colophon:] *Fue impresso en Seuilla en casa de Hernando Diaz|en la calle de la Sierpe, y a su costa con poder irre-|uocable que tiene del Señor de Francisco Mexia,|para podello imprimir, durante el tiempo de la merced de los diez años. Acabose a quinze|dias del mes de Febrero. Año de|*M.D.LXX.| Folio, 8 leaves, Text, clxxxvij leaves, Authors quoted, 2 leaves. J.C.B. 48238

MEXIA. Della selva di varia lettione parti V. Ampliate per Fr. Sansouino. *Venetiæ: Rampazetto.* 1571. 8vo. 48239

MEXIA. Nvova Seconda Selva de Varia Lettione, che segve Pietro Messia: Nella quale sono gloriosi fatti, & detti degni di cognitione; tratti con breuità dalli più nobili, & eccellenti Autori, Antichi, & Moderni. Nvovamente posta in luce, & con somma diligenza coretta. Con tavola delle cose notabili. *In Venetia, Apresso Christoforo Zanetti.* M.D.LXXIII. 12mo, pp. (24), 207.

[MEXIA.] Silva de varia Lecion vltimamente agora enmendada, y añadida la quarta parte della por el autor. *Anvers. M. Nutio* [*sic*]. 1593. 8vo, pp. (31), 929 [907]. B. 48241

There are also editions: *Anvers, M. Nucio,* 1555, 1564, 1603, and one without date, all in 8vo; also *Lyons,* 1556, 8vo; *Saragossa,* 1554, 8vo; *Madrid: Garcia de Olmeda,* 1643 and 1673, 4to. Some of these contain four and others six parts. Brunet, referring to a folio edition in Spanish, printed by *Cromberger* at *Seville*, in 1542, says that is the first edition—which is an error.

[MEXIA.] Silva de varia Leccion. Van añadidas en esta vltima impression quinta, y sexta parte, y vn parenesis de Isocrates, traducido de latin en lengua castellana por el mismo autor. *Madrid: Imprenta Real.* 1669. 4to, pp. (7), 555, (13), 159, (5).

"The fifth and sixth books were first added, I think, in the edition of 1554, two years after his death, and do not seem to be his."—TICKNOR.

MEXIA. Les|Diverses|Lecons de|Pierre Messie.|Gentilhomme de|Seuile|Mises de Castillan en|François, par Claude Gruget Parisien.|Avec Sept Dialogves de|l'Autheur, dont les quatre derniers ont|esté de nouueau traduits en ceste|quatriesme Edition.|Ensemble quatre Tables, deux de Chapitres, & les autres des principales matières y traictées.|Reueu de nouueau en ceste derniere Edition.|*A Lion,*|*Par Clavde Michel.*|M.D.XXVI.| 4to, pp. (16), 1032, (14). + *A Roven,*|*De l'Imprimerie,*|*de Iean Roger, ruë Mars-Parlus.*|M.D.XXVI.| 4to, pp. (16), 1032, (14).

"These two books are unquestionably dated 'M.D.XXVI,' but it must be a mistake of the printer."—[HARRISSE] *Bib. Am. Vet., Additions*, p. 92. The passage referring to Magellan is found on page 854 in the "Dialogue du Soleil."

MEXIA. Les Diverses Leçons de Pierre Messie Gentilhomme de Seuille. Contenans variables & memorables histoires, mises en François par Claude Gruget Parisien. De nouueau reueuës, corrigees & augmentees de la V. partie & de trois Dialogues, touchant la nature du Soleil, de la Terre, & des Meteores. *Se vendent A Paris. Chez Claude Micard* .... 1580. [Colophon:] *A Roven De l'Imprimerie de George l'Oyselet.* 12mo, 620 leaves, Register, 10 leaves, Colophon, 1 leaf. J.C.B. + *Lyon: T. Soubron.* M. D. XCII. 2 vols., sm. 8vo, pp. (13), 7–738 [764], (1); (19), 602, (39). Portrait. B. 48244

The reference to Magellan and his voyage round the world is in the "Dialogues."

[Mexia.] Les diverses Leçons d'Antoine du Verdier suivant celles de Pierre Messie. Contenant plusieurs histoires, discours et faicts mémorables. Augmentées de trois discours. *Tournon, Claude Michel.* 1610. 8vo. 48245

Pages 324–336 contain a notice of the new world and the voyages of Columbus. Brunet also mentions French translations: *Paris: Sertenas,* 1554; *Morel,* 1571 and 1577; *Lyons,* 1584 and 1593; *Tournon: Michet et Soubron,* 1604 and 1616, all in 8vo.

[Mexia.] The Foreste or Collection of Histories, no lesse profitable, then pleasant and neassarie, dooen out of French into Englishe. [By Thomas Fortescue.] *Imprinted at London by Jhon Kyngston, for William Iones.* 1571. Sm. 4to, 5 leaves, Text, 187 leaves, Table, 4 leaves. J.C.B. 48246

Mexia. The | Treasvrie | of Avncient | and Moderne | Times. | Containing the Learned Collections, Iudicious Rea- | dings, and Memorable Obseruations: Not only Diuine, | Morrall and Phylosophicall. But also Martiall, | Politicall, Historicall, Astrologicall, &c. | Translated [by Thomas Mills] out of that Worthy Spanish Gentleman, Pedro Mexio [*sic*] | And M. Francisco Sansouino, that Famous Italian. ... *London:* | *Printed by W. Laggard.* | 1613. Folio, pp. (10), 965, (5). H. 48247

[Mexia.] Times Store-Hovse | containing | The learned Collections, Iuditious | Readings, and memorable Obserua | tions of sundry worthy Personages | English, French, Italian, Spanish, | &c. vpon diuers Subiects, as will ap | peare by the seuerall heades in the | page following; all of them no lesse vsefull then | delight- | full. | VVhervnto | is annexed: | A speciall Treatise of that kind of | Nobility which Soverayne Grace, | and fauor, and Contryes Customes, | haue made meerly Politicall | and peculiarly Civill, | (neuer so | distinctly handled before) | *London:* | *Printed by W. Laggard.* | 1619. Folio, pp. (12), 977, (8). Portrait and Plates. H.

At page 916 will be found a curious "Discourse how those Parts and Countries, commonly called The New World, were first found. Also by whom, and what things were there found, and seene, and brought away thence." The address of "The Printer to the Reader" in this volume, makes it clear that it is Vol. II. of No. 48247, *supra.* For a Dutch version, *see* Messiae (P.) *and* Verdier (A. du), No. 48152, *supra.*

Mexia. The Rarities of the World, with Discourses of Creatures bred in the Sea, Translated by J. Baildon. *London.* 1651. 4to. 48249

The author's "Historia Imperial y Cesarea;"— ... *Sevilla, por Dominico de Robertis* 1547, folio, and another edition, *Anvers, M. Nucio,* M.D.LXI, folio, pp. (4), 366, (10), of which there is an English translation, *London, M. Lovvnes,* 1604, folio, pp. (9), 890—contains a reference to America. The author repeatedly calls himself Pero instead of Pedro.

Mexico.

The following list of anonymous books relating to Mexico is, with a few exceptions, alphabetically arranged; for others, *see* under the first word of the title.

Accion de Gracias que la Academia de Derocho Español, Publico y Privado de la Capital de Mexico, celebrada el Dia 15 de Marzo de 1813. [*Madrid.*] 1814. 4to. 48250

Accion solemne de gracias que tributaron al todo-poderoso en la Metropolitana de Mexico los caballeros del orden de Carlos III. *Mexico.* 1809. 4to, 53 leaves. 48251

Acta Constitucional presentado al Soberano Congreso Constitùvente por su Comision, el 20 Nov., 1823. *Mexico.* 1823. 4to, pp. 8. 48252

Acta Constitutiva de la Federacion Mexicana. *Mexico.* 1824. 24mo, pp. 25. + [n. p. 1824?] 24mo, pp. (2), 12. B. 48253

Actas de las sesiones de las camaras despacho diario de los ministerios, sucesos notables, documentos oficiales importantes y rectificacion de hechos oficiales. *Mexico.* 1852. 2 vols., 4to.

Actas del congreso constituyente mexicano. *México: Alejandro Valdes.* 1822. Sm. 4to. Continued. 48255

Also: Actas del congreso constituyente del estado libre de México, revisadas por el mismo congreso ... . [*México.*] 1824–1825. 4 vols., 4to.

Actas formadas en el capitulo general de N. Sagrado Orden Bethlemitico, celebrado en este su Convento Hospital de Convalecientes de la Ciudad de Mexico el dia 30. de Abril de 1768. *Mexico: Ph. de Zuniga y Ontiveros.* 1768. 4to, pp. (2), 59.

Aduanas Maritimas. A los Ives. Diputados y Senadores al Congreso General y de las Legislaturas de los Estados. [n. p. n. d.] 8vo, pp. 28. 48257

Also: Reformas al Arancel de aduanas maritimas de 30de Abril del presente anno, decretadas in 2de Diciembre.—Aclaracion al Arancel General de aduanas maritimas y fronterizas.—Aclaracion al Articulo 38 del arancel de aduanas maritimas de 30de Abril del presento anno. *Mexico.* 1842. 8vo, pp. 14.

Advenimiento de SS. MM. II. Maximiliano. *See* No. 47032.

Affaires étrangères. Documents diplomatiques. 1866. *Paris: Imprimerie Impériale.* 1856. Sm. folio, pp. (4), 38. H. 48258

Contains "États-Unis. Suite de la correspondance relative aux affaires de Mexique," and "Mexique."

La Aguila Mejicana. Periódico cuotidiano politico y literario. *Mexico.* 1823. Folio. Continued. 48259

Also: Coleccion de Articulos selectos sobre Politica, sacados del Aguila Mexicana del Año de 1822. *Mexico.* 1828. 4to.

Album Méjicano Tributo de gratitud al Civismo nacional Retratos de los Personages ilustres de la primera y segunda época de la Independencia Mejicana y notabilidades de la présente. *Méjico: C. L. Prudhomme Editor.* 1843. 4to, pp. 2. 21 Plates. 48260

El Album Mexicano, periodico de literatura, artes y bellâs letras, publicado por Ignacio Cumplido. *Mexico.* 1849. 2 vols., 4to, pp. iv, 620; iv, 620. B. 48261

Alegato por el Colegio Mayor de Santa Maria de todos Santos de la ciudad de Mexico contra la Real Universidad de dicha ciudad, sobre la observancia, y subsistencia de diferentes privilegios concedidos por su Magestad á el referido Colegio Mayor. [*Mexico,* about 1750.] Folio, 26 leaves. 48262

Algunas Indicaciones acerca de la intervencion europea en Mejico. *Paris.* 1859. 8vo, pp. 27. 48263

Algunas Observaciones sobre el opusculo intitulado "El Imperio y Clero." *Mexico.* 1865. 8vo. 48264

Also: Segundas Observaciones. ... *Mexico.* 1865. 8vo. + Terceras Observaciones. [*Ibid.*] 1865. 8vo.

Almacen Universal. Articulos de historia, geografia, viajes, literatura y variedades. *Mejico.* 1840. 2 vols., 8vo. 48265

Almanaque Imperial para el año de 1866. *Mexico.* 1866. 8vo.

Also: Almanaque de la Corte. *Mexico.* 1866. 8vo.

Alocuciones. *See* Maximilian, Vol. XI., No. 47033.

Alverna Seraphico, Tropheo de la Victoria mas celebre, por Juan de Abrev, Predicador en el Convento de S. Francisco de Mexico. *Mexico.* 1725. 4to. 48267

The American Star. From the 20 of September 1847 to the 30 of May 1848. *Mexico.* 1847–48. Folio, 207 Numbers.

This interesting journal appeared during the occupation of Mexico by the United States Army.

El Amigo de la patria. *Mexico.* 1812–13. 4to, 26 Numbers.

An important journal for the history of America. No more published.

El Amigo de los hombres. A todos los que habitan las islas y el vasto continente de las Americas. *Reimpreso en Mexico.* 1823. 12mo, pp. 14. 48270

El Amigo del pueblo. Periódico seminario literario, cientifico, de politica y comercio. *Mexico.* 1827–28. 5 vols., 8vo.

El Amigo del pueblo. Periódico de religion, variedades y anuncios. *Mexico.* 1861. Folio. 48272

Amorosa contienda de Francia. *See* Martinez (J. G. de C.)

Anales de la minería mexicana, ó sea: revista de minas, metalurgica mecánica, y de las ciencias de aplicacion a la mineria. Publicada por los antiguos profesores de la escuela practica de miñas y a espensas del gobierno del· Guanajuato. Tomo I. *Mexico: I. Cumplido.* 1861. 8vo, pp. 324. Map, 8 Plates, and 12 Tables. Continued. C. 48273

Also: Anuario del colegio nacional de mineria. Año 1845. *Mexico.* 1846. 4to. Continued.

Anales del Ministerio de Fomento. Industria agrícola, Minera, Fabril, Manufacturera y Comercial, y Estadística general de la República Mexicana. *México.* 1854. 8vo, pp. iv, 726; 32.

Anales Mexicanos de ciencias, literatura, mineria, agricultura, artes, industria y comercio en la República Mexicana. *Mexico: Andrade.* 1860. 8vo, pp. 346. Plates. 48275

Analysis of the Memorial presented by the Secretary of the Treasury, to the first Constitutional Congress of the United Mexican States: ... Translated from the official copy published in Mexico. *London: T. Cowie and Co.* 1825. 8vo, pp. vi, 96.

Report of the Directors of the Anglo-Mexican Mining Association. *London.* 1826. 8vo, pp. 51. 48277

Annales du Commerce Extérieur, publiées Par la Département de l'Agriculture, du Commerce et des Travaux publics ... . Mexique. (Législation commerciale.—Nos 1 à 16.) 1843 à 1856. *Paris: Imprimerie ... de Paul Dupont.* 1856. 8vo. B.

Each number is paged independently.

Antiquités Mexicaines. *See* Lenoir (A.), X. 40038.

El Apuntador semanario de teatros, costumbres, literatura y variedades. *Mexico.* 1841. 4to. Portraits. 48279

Apuntamientos sobre derecho público ecclesíastico. *Mexico.* 1857. 4to. 48280

Apuntes para la Historia de la Guerra entre México y los Estados-Unidos. *Mexico: [Tipografia de Manuel Payno].* 1848. Rl. 8vo, pp. v, 401. 23 Lithographs. 48281

Extremely rare. General Santa Anna, when last in power, ordered the edition to be destroyed, and imprisoned the authors. Corrected title of our No. 1858, Vol. I.

Arancel de los honorarios y derechos judiciales que se han de cobrar en el Departamento de Chiapas, de Durango, de Guanajuato, de Jalisco, de Mexico ... . Mandado observer por la suprema Corte de Justicia de la Republica Mexicana. Conforme a lo prevenido en el articulo, 55 de la ley de 23 de Mayo de 1837. *Mexico.* 1840. 4to, pp. 44, 44, 44, 44, 46, 44, 47, 44, 44, 44, 44, 44. 48282

Arancel general de aduanas maritimas y fronterizas y panta de comisos para el gobierno interior de la Republica Mexicana. *Mexico.* 1837. 8vo, pp. 80. Continued. + Nueva edicion arreglada para el Corredor del Comercio, por J. M. Y. Y. *Mexico.* 1851. 12mo, pp. 471. Tables. 48283

Arancel general interino e instruccion para gobierno de las aduanas maritimas en el comercio libre del Imperio Mexicano. *Mexico.* 1821. 8vo, pp. 44. Continued. 48284

Aranzel para todos los curas de este arzobispado, fuera de la ciudad de Mexico. *Mexico.* 1676. 4to, pp. 9. 48285

Archives de la Commission scientifique du Mexique, publiées sous les auspices du ministère de l'instruction publique. *Paris: Auguste Durand et Pedone Lauriel.* 1865–9. 3 vols., 8vo. Maps, Plans, and Plates. 48286

Archivio Mexicano. Documentos para la Historia de Mexico. ... *Mexico: Tipografia de Vicente Garcia Torres.* 1852–3. 2 vols., 8vo, pp. (4), v, 456, (1); 509, Indice, vi. B. 48287

"In these volumes, the Process against Cortes, with the important testimony of all the witnesses—illustrating not merely the conqueror's life and character, but also many obscure questions in the history of the conquest, etc.—is published for the first time." —Quaritch.

El Archivo Mexicano. Coleccion de Leyes y Decretos Circulares y otros Documentos. *Mexico.* 1856–62. 6 vols., 4to.

Important to the historian and student.

El Arco-Iris mexicano. Tomo I. *Mexico.* 1844. 8vo.

Arreglo del Cuerpo Permanente de Ingenieros. *México.* 1838. 8vo. 48290

Also: Arreglo del Cuerpo Permanente de Artilleria. *México.* 1838. 8vo. C.

Articulo sobre los fundamentos en que debe apoyarse el Arreglo definitivo y general de los Pesos y Medidas mas convenientes en la República Mexicana. *Mexico.* 1852. Sm. 8vo, pp. 55.

El Ateneo Mexicano. *Mexico.* 1844. 2 vols., folio. 48292

Contributions by the most celebrated Mexican writers, Alaman, Bustamente, etc.

El Atleta. Periodico Mexicano. *Mexico.* 1830. 8vo.

Die Auswanderung nach Mexico mit Unterstützung durch die mexicanische Regierung zur Niederlassung Deutscher in der Republik Mexico, nach Verfügung vom 16. Febr. 1854. Beschreibung des Landes, seines Klimas und Bodens, seiner Eintheilung, Producte und Industrie, so wie Vorschläge in Beziehung auf Reise, Bedarf, Einrichtung und gesicherte Niederlassung. *Leipzig: Hunger.* [1854.] 16mo, pp. 68. Map in 4to. 48294

Avto General de la Fee, ... Celebrado en la Plaça mayor de la muy noble, y muy leal ciudad de Mexico, á los 19. de Noviembre de 1659. años. *Con licencia, En Mexico, En la Imprenta del Secreto del Santo Officio. Por la Viuda de Bernardo Calderon, en la calle de San Agustin.* [1659.] 4to, 76 leaves. 48295

Also: Sermon en el solemnissimo Avto de la Fee qvel el Tribunal del Santo Officio de la Inquisicion de los Reynos, y Provincias de la Nueva España celebró à 19 de Noviembre de 1659. Predicole por Fr. Diego de Arellano. [*Mexico.* 1659.] 4to, 8 l.

Balanza general del comercio maritimo por los puertos de la República Mexicana, en el año 1810. *Mexico.* 1811. 4to, pp. 24. Continued. 48296

Very important for the commercial statistics of Mexico.

Balanza mercantil de la Plaza de Mexico, correspondiente al año de 1843, formada y publicada por la Junta de Fomento. *Mexico.* 1844. 4to. Continued. 48297

Balanza mercantil de las plazas de la Paz y S. José del cabo de San Lucas, correspondiente al ano de 1849, que forma la Aduana Maritima de la Paz, de orden del gobierno politico de esta territorio, de fecha 5 de febrero, de 1850. *Mexico.* 1850. 8vo, pp. 14. 48298

Banquete dato. *See* [Romero (Matias)].

Bases de la contrata de limpia de calles y barrios, celebrada entre el Es. Ayuntamiento de esta Capital, y los Contratistas Don Luis Bracho y Don José Maria Barrera en 21 de Octubre de 1843, y aprobada por la Superioridad con la puja del medio diezmo admitida en el presente año. *Mexico.* 1844. 12mo, pp. 16. 48299

Bases de Organization Politica de la Republica. *Mexico.* 1842. 8vo. 48300

Bases orgánicas de la república mexicana, acordadas por la junta legislativa, etc. *Mexico.* 1843. 12mo. 48301

Bases sobre las que se ha formado un plan de Colonizacion en el ysmo de Hoazacoalco o Tehuantepec ... . *Mexico.* ... 1823. 8vo, pp. (8), 21. 48302

Bases y leyes constitucionales de la Republica Mexicana, decretadas por el Congreso General de la Nacion en el año de 1836. *Mexico.* 1837. Sm. 8vo, pp. 127. 48303

Bibliotheca Mexicana Catalogue d'une Collection de Livres Rares (principalement sur l'histoire et la linguistique) Réunie au Mexique Par M. *** [Fischer] ... *Paris Librairie Tross* 1868 8vo, pp. (8), 47. B. 48304

See also [Fischer (Augustin)], VI. 24417, for another catalogue.

A Bill authorizing. *See* [McKibbin (J. C.)], XI. 43449.

La Bocina Periódico. *Mexico.* 1850. 4to, 4 Numbers.

Boletin de las Leyes del Imperio Mexicano. *Mexico.* 1865. 8vo. Continued. 48306

Also: Boletin de las Leyes, ordenes y disposiciones particulares. *Mexico.* 1865. 8vo, pp. 64.

Boletin del Instituto Nacional de Geografia y Estadistica de la República Mexicana. *Mexico.* 1850. 2 vols., 4to, pp. 352; 280.

Of Vol. I. there were three editions. Continued as the

Boletin de la Sociedad Mexicana de Geografia y Estadistica. *Mexico.* 1851–1866. 9 vols., 4to, pp. 472; 376; 462; 426; vi, 598; 728; 510; 716; 658; 131. Maps. B. 48308

Continued to Vol. XII., No. 2. A very important collection, containing a vast amount of geographical, statistical, and philological information regarding Mexico; it is now out of print. For the description and contents, *see* Trübner's "Record," Nos. 11, 17, 19, 40.

Bosquejo. *See* Vol. II., No. 6459, *and* [Rocafuerte (V.)]

Breve Defensa de las Exenciones y Privilegios Regulares. *Mejico.* 1841. 8vo. 48309

Breve Diseño Critico. *See* [Iturbide (A. de)], IX. 35287.

Breve Manifestacion del que suscribe [Sebastian Camacho]. *Impreso en Jalapa por Aburto y Blanco.* 1832. 4to, pp. 92.

Sebastian Camacho was for some time at the head of the State of Veracruz, and in connection with all the political men of Mexico. The present volume, written shortly after the fiery struggle between Bustamente and Santa Anna, which it describes, is a most valuable contribution to the history of the time. Pages 50 to 92 contain historical documents, such as letters by Santa Anna, Bustamante, etc. Corrected title of our No. 10099, Vol. III.

La Bruja, Periodico y trata de todo. *Mexico.* 1841–2. 4to, 50 Numbers. 48311

A scarce satirical publication.

Bulla Erectionis Sanctæ Metropolitanæ Ecclesiæ Mexiceæ. Executoria en el Pleyto de los dotales con la Sagrada Compañia de Jesus. *Mexico.* 1635. Folio, pp. 4, 7. 48312

Calendario de las Señoritas Megicanos. *Megico.* [n. d.] 18mo.

Calendario Manual y Guia de Forasteros en México, para el año de 1811. Por Don Mariano de Zúñiga y Ontiveros. ... [n. p.:] *En la Oficina del Autor.* [n. d.] 12mo. 48314

Continued to 1817 or later.

Campana sin gloria tenida en el recinto de Mexico, causada por haber persistido Don Valentin Gomez Farias, Vice-Presidente, por Bustamente. *Mexico.* 1847. 8vo, pp. 44. 48315

Cancion Patriotica ... . *Mexico.* 1812. 8vo. 48316

Cancionero Spiritual en que de contierien obras muy provechosas y edificantes, etc. *Mexico: Juan Pablos.* 1546. 8vo.

Title from Sr. Pascqual de Gayangos, the Spanish translator of Ticknor's "History of Spanish Literature."

Carta de un Ciudadano Mexicano a un oficial del ejercito Norte-Americano, en respuesta á las observaciones à los habitantes de la república, que escribió hace pocos dias en Puebla, y corren impresas. *Atlixco.* 1847. 12mo, pp. 28. 48318

Carta gratulatoria del Ecxmo. é Illmo. Sr. Arzobispo de Méxco al Clero Secular y Regular de la Capital. [Colophon:] *Mexico y Octubre 9 de* 1810. Franzisco Arzobispo de Mexico. 4to, pp. 2. 48319

Carta pastoral. *See* Maximilian, Vol. xi., No. 47034.

Carta pastoral del Illmo. y Excmo. Sr. Arzobispo de Mexico. *Mexico.* 1855. 12mo, pp. 36. 48320

Cartilla de Comisarios del Santo Oficio de la Inquisicion de Mexcio. Instruccion que deben observar los Comisarios en el despacho de los negocios de fe, y demas tocantes á su conocimiento. [n. p. n. d.] 4to, pp. 36. 48321

Cartilla de policia para el mas puntual servicio publico de los coches de Providencia. *Mexico.* 1840. Sm. 8vo, pp. 20.

Cartilla mayor en Lengua Castellana, Latina, y Mexicana. Nuevamente Corregida, y Enmendada, y Reformada en esta vltima Impression. [Colophon:] ... *Con Licencia. En Mexico: por la Viuda de Bernardo Calderon en la calle de S. Augustin.* [1683.] 4to, 12 leaves. 48323

Catálogo de los objetos de bellas artes, de que consta la esposicion annual de la academia nacional de S. Carlos de Mexico. *Mexico.* 1850. 8vo. Continued. 48324

Catalogue des produits naturels, industriels et artistiques, exposés dans la section mexicaine, à l'exposition universelle de 1855. *Paris.* 1855. 8vo. 48325

Catalogue of a valuable Portion of the very interesting Collection of Mexican Antiquities lately exhibited in Pall Mall. Sold ... April, 1856. [*London.* n. d.] 8vo, pp. 14. 48326

Catecismo breve en el idioma Mejicano. *Orizaba.* 1842. c.

Also: Devocionario en Mejicano. *Orizaba.* 1842. 16mo. c.

Catecismo Breve, en Lengua Mexicana, con el Acto de Contricion, en Idioma Mexicana. [n. p. n. d.] Folio, 1 leaf.

Catecismo para usu de los Párrocos hecho por el iv. Concilio Provincial Mexicano, celebrado Año de 1771. *Mexico: J. de Jauregui.* 1772. 4to. 48329

Catecismo político arreglado a la constitucion de la monarquia española para ilustracion del pueblo, ... por D. J. C. *Méjico.* 1820. 16mo, pp. 94. 48330

Catecismo politico de la federacion Mexicana. *Mexico.* 1831. Sm. 8vo, pp. 104. 48331

Causas para Declarar la Guerra a los Estados-Unidos del Norte, y Delitos del Ministro Poinsett, por un Amante de su Pátria. *Mexico.* 1829. 4to, pp. 22. 48332

Causas y Efectos de la última revolucion de Mégico. *Mégico: [Imprenta de la Lima].* 1841. 2 parts, sm. 8vo, pp. 32, 23.

Cedula concerniente al Teatro de Mexico y á la representacion de comedias etc. *Mexico.* 1786. Folio, pp. 28. 48334

Ceremonial y rubricas general con la orden de celebrar las misas. *Mexico.* 1579. 8vo. 48335

An early Mexican imprint. Title from [Harrisse] "Bibliotheca Amer. Vetus."

Certamen cientifico que el nacional y mas antiguo Colegio de S. Ildefonso de Mexico, dedica a su antiguo alumno El ciudano Guadalupe Victoria, primer Presidente. *Mexico.* 1825. 8vo, pp. vi, 3, 29, 36, 72. s. 48336

Contains a poem by Barquera, and essays by Bocanegra, Barquera and de la Torre.

Christian Martyr and Child, Victims of the Spanish Inquisition of 1595, or, 274 years ago; as found in the Convent of Santo Domingo, City of Mexico .... [*New York.* 1866.] 8vo, pp. (2) 5

Circular que el Senor Gobernador de la Sagrada Mitra (D. Isidro Sainz de Alfaro y Beaumont) dirige a los Parrocos y Eclesiasticos del Arzobispado de Mexico. *Mexico.* 1810. 4to.

Ciudadanos. *Mexico.* 1820. Sm. 4to, pp. 4. 48339

Issued by the Junta Provisional the year prior to Iturbide's Declaration of Independence. *See also* our Vol. iv., No. 13161.

Claim of Bertram H. Howell of ... New Jersey, U. S. A., against the Republic of Mexico for breach of Contract, With copies of Official Agreements, and Correspondence ... . *Paris.* 1868. 8vo, pp. viii, 203. 48340

Claimants on Mexico ... . [n. p. 1845.] 12mo, pp. 4, 8, 12, 12. BA., s. 48341

A Series of Papers reviewing the ... Conduct of the Executive ... towards American Citizens having Claims upon the Mexican Government.

Claims of Mexican Citizens against the United States for Indian Depredations, being the opinion of the Mexican Commissioner in the joint claims commission, Under the Convention of July 4, 1868, between Mexico and the United States. *Washington, D. C.* 1871. 8vo, pp. 162. 48342

Clara y sucinta. *See* Vol. iv., No. 13233.

Código Civil [1866]. Libro Segundo. *México: M. Villanueva.* 1866. 18mo, pp. 46. c. 48343

Codigo de comercio de México. *Mexico: Mariano Lara.* 1854. 8vo, pp. 282, (4). 48344

Codigo de la Restauracion—Boletin de las Leges del Imperio Mexicano, desde Mayo 1863 hasta Dec. 1864, publicado por J. S. Segura. *Mexico.* 1863–64. 3 vols., 8vo. 48345

Código fundamental de los Estados Unidos Mexicanos. *Mexico: V. G. Torres.* 1847. 18mo, pp. 92, (4). c. 48346

Codigo penal decretado por las Cortes, sancionado y promulgado en 19. de Marza de 1848. *Mexico.* 1848. 8vo. 48347

Coleccion de articulos selectos sobre politica, sacados del Aguila Mexicana del año de 1828. [n. p. n. d.] 4to, pp. 78. 48348

Coleccion de Constituciones de los Estados-Unidos Mexicanos. *México.* 1828. 3 vols., 16mo. c. 48349

Coleccion de cuadros para estadistica general de la Republica Mexicana, formada por la Secretaria de Estado y del Despacho de Fomento, Colonizacion, Industria y Comercio. *Mexico.* 1853. Folio, 50 leaves. 48350

Coleccion de decretos del Congreso constituyente de México espedidos en su primera reunion los años de 1824–1827, y en su reinstalacion en 1830. *Toluca.* 1850. 2 vols., 4to. 48351

Coleccion de decretos, ordenes y circulares espedidas por los Gobiernos Nacionales de la federacion Mexicana desde el ano de 1821 hasta el de 1826 para el arreglo del ejercito de los Estados-Unidos Mexicanos, y ordenas por el Teniente coronel de Caballeria J. R. Y. S. *Mexico.* 1827. 4to, pp. 350. Tables.

Coleccion de Documentos oficiales relativos a la construccion y demolicion del Parian, y a la propriedad reconocida é incontestable que turo el escmo. ayuntamiento de Mexico en aquel edificio. *Mexico.* 1843. 8vo, pp. xxvii, 97. Plate. 48353

Coleccion de documentos para la historia de México. Tomo i. *México.* 1858. 8vo. 48354

No more published.

Coleccion de leyes, decretos, circulares ... que se han publicado desde 30. de mayo de 1848. Tomo i. *Mexico.* 1849. 8vo, pp. 817, 7. 48355

No more published.

Coleccion de las Leyes fundamentales que han regido en la Republica Mexicana, y de los Planes que han tenido el mismo caracter desde el año de 1821, hasta el de 1857. *Mexico.* [n. d.] 8vo, pp. 379. 48356

Coleccion de las Leyes y Decretos expedidos por el Congreso General de los Estados-Unidos Mejicanos, en los Años de 1829 y 1830. Comprende tambien los reglamentos del gobierno para la ejecucion de varias leyes y decretos; ... los decretos expididos por el poder ejecutivo en virtud de las facultades extraordinarias que se le concedieron en 25 de agosto de 1829 ... . *Méjico: Mariano Arevalo.* 1831. 4to, pp. (4), xx, 212. Continued. c.

Coleccion de las leyes, 1861. *See* [Payno (M.)]

Coleccion de los Decretos y Ordenes de las Cortes de España, que se Reputan Vigentes en la Republica de los Estados-Unidos Mexicanos, 1811 à 1821. *Mexico:* 1829. *Mariano Arévalo.* 4to, pp. (2), xvi, 216. c. 48358

Coleccion de los Ultimos Decretos sobre Contribuciones Directas, Potestad Coactiva y Papel Sellado. *México.* 1842. 16mo

Also: Coleccion de los decretos espedidos por el Supremo Gobierno, relativos a los tribunales mercantiles y reglamento para el regimen interior del de esta capital, publicada por acuerdo del mismo. *Mexico.* 1844. 12mo, pp. 56.

Coleccion de los documentos mas interesantes relativos al prestamo de Medio Millon de Pesos, ofrecido por el venerable clero secular y regular de este Arzobispado. *Mexico.* 1839. 4to, pp. 16. + Continuacion ... . [*Ibid.*] 4to, pp. 7. 48360

Coleccion de memorias instructivas sobre los ramos de agricultura, artes y manufacturas, cuyo fomento es importante para la prosperidad de los Estados-Unidos Mexicanos. *Mexico.* 1830. 4to. 48361

Coleccion de Ordenes y Decretos de la Soberana Junta Provisional Gubernativa, y Soberanos Congresos Generales de la Nacion Mexicana. ... Segunda Edicion, Corregida y aumentada ... *Mexico:* 1829. *Mariano Arévalo.* 4 vols., 4to, pp. (4), xvi, 150; (6), xiv, 220; (6), x, 172; (6), viii, 198. Continued. c. 48362

Coleccion de Poesías Mejicanas. *Paris: Rosa.* 1836. 12mo, pp. (2), iv, 457. 5 Plates. B. 48363

Coleccion de Sentencias pronunziadas por los tribunales y juzgados de la Republica Mexicana. *Mexico.* 1850. 4to. 48364

Coleccion de tratados con las naciones estranjeras, leyes decretos y ordenes, que forman el derecho internacional Mexicano. *Mexico.* 1854. 4to. 48365

Coleccion Eclesiastica Mejicana. *Mexico.* 1834. 4 vols., 16mo, pp. xiv, 242; 328; 401; 308. 48366

Coleccion Polidiómica Mexicana que contiene la Oracion Dominical vertida en cincuenta y dos idiomas indígenos de aquella República. Dedicada á N. S. P. el Señor Pio ix., Pont. Max. Por la Sociedad Mexicana de Geografía y Estadística. *México: Libreria de Eugenio Maillefert y Comp.* [1859.] Sm. folio, pp. vii, 52. 48367

The Lord's Prayer in fifty-two of the languages of Mexico and California, collected from mss. in the convents and libraries in those countries. With description, introduction, and locality where each is, or was spoken.

La Columna de la constitucion federal de la republica mexicana. *Mexico.* 1832–1833. 2 vols., folio. 48368

No more published; the journal was suspended by the government.

Commission on Claims against Mexico, under Act of Congress of March 3, 1849. Treaty ... of February 2, 1848 ... Convention ... of April 11, 1839: Act of Congress of March 3, 1849 ... Rules and orders established ... . *Washington: J. and G. S. Gideon, Printers.* 1849. 8vo, pp. 40. BA., s. 48369

Compañia Zacateno-Mexicana. *Mexico.* 1837. Continued.

Compendio de las Constituciones, y Reglas de la M. Iltre. V. Apostolico Congregacion de N. G. P. Sr. S. Pedro, canonicamente fundada por el Exemplar Clero Secular de esta Ciudad de Mexico ... et año de 1577. *Mexico.* 1747. 4to, pp. (10), 17. 48371

The Complaint of Mexico. *See* Vol. iv., No. 15048.

El Conciliator. *Mexico.* 1850–51. 8 Numbers. 48372

Concilium Sanctum Provinciale Mexici celebratum Anno 1585. Præsidente Petro Moya de Contreras, Archiepiscopo Mexicana. [Followed by:] Statuta Ordinata, a Sancto Concilio Provinciali Mexicana iii. Anno 1585. *Mexici, apud Jo. Ruiz.* 1622.

Folio, Engraved Title by Stradan, pp. (6), 102 leaves, (2), Statuta, pp. (2), 39 leaves. 48373

The first edition of the third Mexican Council. Extremely rare. It was reprinted, *Paris,* 1725, 8vo, and again in 1770. *See* Lorenzano (A.), x. 42063–66.

Concilio iii. provincial Mexicano, celebrado en Mexico el año de 1585 confirmado en Roma por el Papa Sixto v., y mandado observar por el Gobierno Español en diversas reales ordenes. Ilustrado con muchas notas R. P. Basilio Arrillaga, de la Compañia de Jesus, y un appendice con los decretos de la Silla Apostolica relativos a esta Santa Iglesia, que constan en el Fasti novi orbis y otros posteriores y algunos mas documentos intresantes; con cuyas adiciones formara un codigo de derecho Canonico de la Iglesia Mexicana. Publicado con las licencias necessarias por Mariano Galvan Rivera. Primera edicion en Latin y Castellano. *Mexico.* 1859. 8vo, pp. 6, 608; Estatutos ordenados ... clii, 22.

This important collection of documents is now out of print. Also: Opusculo sobre los Catorce Casos reservados, y otras tantas Excomuniones Sinodales del Concilio Mexicano Provincial tercero, celebrado en el año 1585, y aprobado en Roma por el Papa Sixto v. en 1589. *Mexico.* 1816. 4to.

Confessionario Mayor, y Menor en lengua Mexicana. Y platicas contra las Supresticiones [*sic*] de idolatari, que el dia de oy han quedado a los Naturales desta Nueua España, è instruccion de los Santos Sacramentos &c. Al Illustrissimo Señor D. Erancisco [*sic*] Manso y Zuñiga, Arzobispo de Mexico, del Consejo de su Magestad, y del Real de las Indias &c. Mi Señor. Nuevamente compuesto por el Bachiller don Bartholome de Alua, Beneficiado del Partido de Chiapa de Mota. Año de 1634. *Con licencia. Impresso en Mexico, por Francisco Salbago, impressor del Secreto del Sancto Officio. Por Pedro de Quiñones.* [Colophon:] *En Mexico En la Imprenta de Francisco Salbago librero, Impressor del Secreto del Sancto Officio. En la Calle de San Francisco. Año* m.dc.-xxxiii. 4to, 4 leaves, Text, 52 leaves. 48375

Extremely rare. *See* [Fischer's] Catalogue, No. 57.

The Conquest of Mexico! An Appeal to the Citizens of the United States, on the Justice and Expediency of The Conquest of Mexico; with historical and descriptive information respecting that country. ... *Boston: Jordan & Willey.* 1846. 8vo, pp. 32. Map. BA. 48376

Consolidacion de la Republica Mexicana. Recopilacion de algunos impresos publicados y bien recibidos en esta Capital el año proximo pasado. *Mexico.* 1850. 4to, pp. 12, 12, 24, (4).

Constitucion de los Esclavos Cocheros del Santiss. Sacramento, establecidos en la parroquia del Salto del Agua. *Mexico.* 1845. 4to, pp. 13. 48378

Also: Constitucion de la Congregacion de Esclavos del Divinisimo Señor Sacramentado, fundada en la primitiva parroquia de San José de esta Capital. *Mexico.* 1842. 8vo, pp. 16.

Constitucion Federal de los Estados-Unidos Mexicanos, Sancionado por el Congreso General Constituyente, el 4. de Octubre de 1824. *Imprenta del Supremo Gobierno de los Estados-Unidos Mexicanos.* [1824.] 4to, pp. (4), 28, (2). BA. + [*Mexico.* n. d.] Sm. 8vo, pp. (4), xviii, 62, (4), iii. B., H. 48379

Constitucion política del estado de Mexico, sancionada por su congreso constituyente en 14 de febrero de 1827, publicada en ... Tezcoco. *Mexico: M. Rivera.* 1827. 8vo, pp. (2), x, 41.

Also: Decreto constitucional para la libertad de la America Mexicana, sancionado en Apatzingan a 22 de Ocubre 1814. *Mexico.* 1821. 12mo, pp. 68.

El Constitucional. *Mexico.* 1844. Folio, 37 Numbers.

El Constitucional. Periódico oficial del gobierno de los Estados-Unidos Mexicanos. *Mexico.* 1851–2. 2 vols., folio.

Constituciones de la Cofradia del Apostol Santiago en la Ciudad de Mexico. *Mexico.* 1768. Folio, pp. 27 [*i. e.* 28]. 48383

Also: Constituciones de la Archicofradia del Arcangel San Miguel, fundada en la Parroquia del mismo glorioso Arcangel de Mexico. *Mexico.* 1794. 4to, pp. 48.—

Constituciones de la Congregacion de Nuestra Señora con el titulo De Covadonga, ... fundada ... por los naturales y originarios del Principado de Asturias, y Obispado de Oviedo. Con una breve noticia de la Antiguedad, y Situacion del Santuario de Santa Maria de Covadonga ... . *Mexico.* 1785. 4to, pp. 83. Plate.

Constituciones de la imperial orden de Guadalupe, instituida por la Junta Provisional Gubernativa del Imperio, á propuesta de D. Agustin de Iturbide, en 18. de Febrero de 1822. *Mexico.* 1822. 8vo, pp. 25. 4 Plates. 48385

Constituciones de las Señoras de la ilustre Archicofradia de San Miguel, fundada en la Parroquia del mismo Santo Arcangel de esta Capital de Mexico. *Mexico.* 1838. 8vo, pp. (2), 5. Plate.

Constituciones del arçobispado y pronuncia de la muy ynsigne y muy leal ciudad de Temixtitla Mexico de la Nueva España. [Colophon:] ... *Mexico ... Jua Pablos ...* M. d. lvi. Folio, 49 l.

A piece of extreme rarity.

Constituciones del Colegio de S. Ignacio de Loyla de Mexico, fundado y dotado por la Congregacion de N. Señora de Aranzazu de la misma ciudad, para la manutencion, y enseñanza de niñas huerfanas, y Viudas pobres. *Madrid.* 1766. Folio, pp. 55. Portrait. 48388

Constitution fédérative des États-Unis Mexicains, sanctionnée par le Congrès Général constituant, du 4 Oct. 1824. ... *Paris.* 1825. 18mo, pp. 162. s. 48389

The Constitution of the Aztec Club. To which is appended a List of the Members of that Club. ... *Mexico: Printed at the Office of the American Star.* 1848. 18mo, pp. 16. s. 48390

The club consisted of military officers of the United States.

Constitution of the Republic. *See* Vol. iv., No. 16084.

Constitutiones Ecclesiasticæ, disputandæ propugnandaeque in Aula Reg. et Antiq. SS. AA. Petri et Pauli S. Q. Ildefonsi Colegii pro hujus Statuto adimplendo a Bac. Faustino de S. Juan Hermoso et Rio de Loza ibi convictore. *Méxici: P. de Zuniga et Ontiveros.* 1792. 4to. 48391

Constitutiones ordin. fratr. eremit. S. Aug. *Mexico.* 1587. 8vo. 48392

Title from [Harrisse] "Bibliotheca Americana Vetustissima."

Contestacion al Folieto la Oposicion y el gobierno. *Aguascalientes.* 1853. 8vo, pp. 34. 48393

Contestacion de la segunda comision de Hacienda de la Camara de Diputados. *Mexico.* 1850. 8vo. 48394

Contestacion del Illmo Sr. Arzobispo. *Morelia.* 1856. 8vo.

On the nationalization of church property.

Contestaciones habidas entre el Arzobispo de Mexico, D. Lazaro de la Garza y Ballesteros, y el Ministro de Justicia, D. Ezequiel Montes, con motivo de la ley espedida en 25 de Junio de 1856, sobre la desamortizacion de los bienes de las Corporaciones civiles y eclesiasticas de la Republica. *Mexico.* 1856. 4to, pp. 54. 48396

See also Vol. vii., Nos. 26719–21.

Contestaciones habidas entre el supremo gobierno mexicano, el General en Gefe del ejercito americano, y el Comisionado de los Estados-Unidos. *Mexico.* 1847. 4to, pp. 36. 48397

Contract of the Mexican Government. *See* [Cushing (C.)]

Convention between the United States ... and the Mexican Republic, concluded April 10th, 1829. [*Washington.* 1829.] Folio. 48398

Le Corpes belge du Mexique. *See* [Brialmont (A. H.)]

Correo, semanario politico y mercantil de Mexico. *Mexico.* 1809–11. 3 vols., 4to. 48399

A very curious and important journal.

Correo Semanario de Mexico, por el Pensador Mexicano. *Mexico.* 1826. 8vo. 48400

Correspondance entre la Légation. *See* Vol. IV., No. 16848.

Correspondence respecting the Affairs of Mexico. *London.* 1862. Folio. 48401

Correspondence with Mexico. May 19, 1836. [*Washington.* 1836.] 8vo, pp. 61. 48402

Correspondencia que ha mediado. *See* Vol. IV., No. 16908.

Cosas de Mexico. *Veracruz.* 1858. 12mo, pp. 91. C. 48403

Cronica Mexicana, o teoamoxtli. *Mexico.* 1822. 4to, pp. 136

El Cronista de Mexico. Periódico de noticias religiosas, nacionales y extrangeras ... . *Mexico.* 1862–66. 9 vols., folio.

Cuentas Generales de la Republica durante el año economico de 1 de Julio de 1847, à 3 de Junio de 1848; certificadas y finiqui tadas por el Consejo Administrativo ... . *Mexico.* 1848. 8vo. 48406

See also Payno (M.)

Cuestion de Francia. El Presidente de la Republica Mexicana a sus Habitantes. *Mexico.* 1838. 8vo. C. 48407

Decreto constitutional [del Supremo Gobierno Mexicano] para la libertad de la América Mexicana dato 22 de octubre [1814]. [n. p. n. d.] 8vo. 48408

Decreto de 4 de diciembre de 1860 y oficio de remision de la misma fecha sobre Libertad de Cultos en la Republica Mejicana. *Merida.* 1861. 8vo, pp. 32. 48409

Decreto del Supremo Gobierno concediendo el Pase el Breve en que nuestro Santisimo Padre el Señor Pio IX. nombra su delegado apostolico en la Republica Mexicana a Monseñor Luis Clementi, Arzobispo de Damasco, y dictamen de una comision especial ... . *Mexico.* 1853. 4to, pp. 36. 48410

Decreto sobre extincion de Alcabalas en el Estado de Mexico. *Toluca.* 1847. 8vo, pp. 46. 48411

Decretos del Congreso Constituyente del Estado de México, revisados por el mismo congreso e impresos de su orden, 1824 à 1830. *Tlalpam.* 1830. 8vo. C. 48412

Decretos del Rey Don Ferdinando VII.; expedidos desde su restitucion al trono Español hasta el restablecimiento de la constitucion de 1812. Se refieren todas las resoluciones generales que se suponen vigentes en la República Megicana, con expresion de los diferentes ministerios y Consejos por cuyo conducto se expidieron, y del dia en que fueron recibidos de oficio en Mégico para su publicacion y observancia, 1814 à 1820. *Mexico.* 1836. 4to. C. 48413

Defensa de la Manifestacion de los Sres. Arzobispos y Obispos de la Republica Mexicana. *Mexico.* 1860. 4to, pp. 95.

See also our Vol. V., Nos. 19258–61.

Defensa de la Peticion hecha al Soberano Congreso por varios individuos solicitando la restitucion de la Compañia de Jesus en la Republica Mexicana. *Mexico.* 1841. 8vo. 48415

Defensa de las exenciones y privilegios regulares, hecha por los Prelados del Convento de S. Diego de esta capital. *Mexico.* 1841. 4to, pp. vii, 88. 48416

Defensa del Ex-Ministro de Relaciones D. Lucas Alaman, en ha causa formado contra él y contra los Ex-ministros de Guerra y Justicia del Vice-presidente D. Anastasio Bustamente, con unas noticias preliminares que dan idea del origin de esta. Escrita por el mismo Ex-Ministro, quien la dirige a la nacion. *Mejico.* 1834. Sm. 4to, pp. xxii, 126. 48417

The introductory letter is addressed, "Al Exmo. Sr. Presidente de la Republica, General D. Antonio Lopez de Santa Anna."

Defensa, Juridica Alegacion, y Manifestacion con que en Derecho, Justicia, y razon satisface D. A. A. Montero Prieto de Bonilla, à la demanda, y Pleito, que se le ha puesto por D. Alonso Cavallero de los Olivos, sobre la succession del Mayorazgo ... . *Mexico: J. B. de Hogal.* 1736. 8vo. 48418

De la revolution au Mexique. *See* [Cañedo (E.)], III. 10677.

Derrotero de las Islas Antillas, de las Costas de Tierra-Firme, y de las del Seno Mejicano. ... Tercera Edicion. ... *Madrid.* 1837. 8vo, pp. (4), 421, (4). B. 48419

For other editions, see our Vol. V., No. 19678–9.

Description of the Panorama of the Superb City of Mexico, and the Surrounding Scenery, Painted ... by Robert Burford, Esq. from Drawings made ... by Mr. W. Bullock, Junior. ... *London.* 1826. 8vo, pp. 12. + *Boston.* 1828. 8vo, pp. 16. + *New York.* 1828. 8vo. + *Washington.* 1832. 8vo, pp. 16. Map. B. + *Philadelphia.* 1833. 8vo, pp. 16. 48420

Also: Descriptive Catalogue of Mexican Antiquities. *Leamington.* 1854. 8vo, pp. 38.

Diario de avisos de religion, politica, literatura, artes, ciencias, industria, comercio, medicina, tribunales, agricultura y teatros. *Mexico.* 1856–1860. 8 vols., folio, or more. 48421

A journal which appeared in the place of the journal "l'Omnibus," suppressed by the government, November 5, 1856.

Diario de la junta nacional instituyente del imperio mexicano. Vol. I. *Mèxico: Alejandro Valdes.* 1822. Sm. 4to, pp. 442.

Diario de las sesiones de la soberana junta provisional gubernativa del imperio mexicano, instalada segun previenen el plan de Iguala y tratados de la villa de Cordova. *México: Alexandro Valdes.* 1821. Sm. 4to, pp. 354. C. 48423

Diario de Mexico, desde su principio en el año de 1805 hasta el de 1810 ... . *Con Licencia de Superior Govierno.* 1805–17. 13 vols., sm. 4to. 48424

Rare, even in Mexico, as in the troubles and revolutions that supervened, many of the copies were destroyed.

Diario del Imperio. *Mexico.* 1865. 2 vols., folio. 48425

Diario Literario de Mexico. Dispuesto para la Utilidad publica, á quien se dedica. Por D. J. A. de Alzate y Ramirez. *Mexico: Imprenta de la Bibliotheca Mexicana.* 1768. 4to. 48426

The earliest work edited by this celebrated savant, and of much rarity.

Diario Notable de la Marquesa de las Amarillas, Virreyna de Mexico. *Mexico.* 1757. 12mo. 48427

Diccionario Español y Mexicano. [n. p.] 1742. 8vo, pp. 248.

Title from Ludewig's "Literature of American Aboriginal Languages."

Diccionario Universal de Historia y de Geografia. ... Por una sociedad de literatos distinguidos, y refundida y aumentada ... con noticias historicas, geografias, estadisticas, biographicas sobre las Americas en General, y especialmente sobre da Republica Mexicana ... . *Mexico: Tipografia de Rafael.* 1853–55. 7 vols., 8vo. + *Mexico: Imprenta de J. M. Andrade y F. Escalante.* 1855–56. 3 vols., 8vo. B. 48429

Un Dictador en México confundiendo á los partidos politicos, y formando el suyo con las personas mas notables por su sabiduria y por su honradez. *Mexico.* 1853. 8vo, pp. 24. 48430

Dictamen de la Comision de Credito publico sobre el Arreglo de la Deuda Inglesa. *Mexico.* 1850. 8vo. 48431

In Spanish and English, with appendixes. Also: Deuda y Credita Publico: Junta Direccion de Credito Publico. Aduana maritima del Manzanillo. *Mexico.* 1851. Cr. 8vo.

Dictamen de la Comision de Crédito Público de la Cámara de Diputados, sobre arreglo de la Deuda interior de la Nacion. *Mexico.* 1859. 4to. 48432

Dictamen de la comision primera de la camara de representantes del Congreso General de la Federacion Mexicana, sobre arreglo de aranceles para las aduanas maritimas. *Mexico.* 1827. 8vo, pp. 54. 48433

See also our Vol. V., pp. 417–418.

Dictamen de la comision y acuerdo del Cabildo Metropolitano de Mexico, sobre hipotecar los bienes eclesiasticos para el emprestito que solicita el Supremo Gobierno. *Mexico.* 1837. 4to, pp. 28. 48434

Dictamen noticia historica de Soconusco y su incorporacion a la Republica Mexicana. *Mexico.* 1843. Sm. 8vo, pp. 194.

Dictamen presentado á la Sociedad de Geografia y Estadistica de Mexico sobre la obra de Brasseur de Bourbourg, cuyo titulo es: "Si ecsiste el origen de la historia primitiva de Mexico en los monumentos egipcios" etc. *Mexico.* 1865. 8vo. 48436

Dimision del ministerio. *Mexico: V. G. Torres.* 1852. 8vo, pp. 12. 48437

Documentos importantes tomados del espediente instruido sobre la ocupacion por el gobierno general a las Temporalidades del Estado libre de Mexico: impresos de orden de su legislatura. *Tlalpam.* 1829. 4to, pp. 53. 48438

Documentos oficiales que se publican par órden del Supremo Gobierno ... . *Mexico.* 1840. 8vo. 48439

Documentos para la Historia de Mejico. *Mexico.* 1853–57.

First series, 6 vols. Vol. I. of this series contains the Diary of D. Gregorio Martin de Guijo, a Spanish lawyer residing in Mexico, comprising from the year 1648 to 1664. Vols. II. and III., the Diary of D. Ant. de Robles, 1665 to 1703. Vols. IV., V., and VI., the Diary of D. Jose Manuel de Castro Santa Anna, from 1752 to 1758; and Vol. VII., an Anonymous Diary from 1675 to 1696, and the Diary of Jose Gomez, from 1776 to 1798. The second series, 7 vols. (1854–55), contains a selection of various historical documents, one volume being entirely occupied by papers on the tumult of 1624, proceeding from a dispute between the Viceroy of Mexico and the Archbishop of that See. The third series, 1 vol., folio (1856), contains a selection of papers on the History, Chronology, and Mexican System of Astronomy; also on the Discovery and History of Texas and New Mexico. The fourth series, 7 vols. (1856–57), comprises materials for the history of Sonora and Sinaloa: History of "la Nueva Vizcaya" (Durango), and the History of the Missions in California, by Palou, etc. It is a most important series for the student of Mexican history. The publication of these documents reflects the highest credit upon the Mexican administration, as it places within the grasp of the scholar a body of information which no amount of individual enterprise and industry could possibly obtain. They were first published in the "Diario official," and form 17 vols., 8vo, 4to, and folio. *See* Berendt, in "Peterman's Mittheilungen," for August, 1856.

Documentos relativos á la Instalacion del Presidente de la Suprema Corte de Justicia. *Mexico.* 1847. 8vo. 48441

Documentos relativos a la primera exposicion de flores, arbustos, frutas ... . *Mexico.* 1849. 8vo. 48442

Documentos relativos a la reunion en esta capital de los gobernadores de los estados, convocados—para proveer á las exigencias del erario federal. *Mexico: J. M. Lara.* 1851. 8vo. C.

Documentos relativos á la sublevacion del General D. Juan Alvarez en el Sur del Estado de Mexico, y á los ultimos sucesos del Estádo de Zacatecas. *Mexico.* 1835. 4to, pp. 44. 48444

Documentos relativos al ingreso y a la separacion de la Primera Secretaria de Estado de la República Mexicana ... . *Mexico.* 1835–40. 8vo. 48445

Documents relatifs à la protection des sujets étrangers résidant au Mexique après le départ de Mr. de Wagner Ministre Résident de S. M. le Roi de Prusse. *Mexico.* 1864. 8vo, pp. 41.

Dos años en Mejico. *See* Vol. V., No. 20662.

Dudas Acerca de las Ceremonias Sanctas de la Missa. Resueltas por los Clerigos de la Congregacion de Nuestra Señora, fundada con Authoridad Apostolica en el Collegio de la Compañia de Jesus de Mexico. *Mexico: Por H. Martinez.* 1606. 4to.

Edicto del Arzobispo de Mexico, para la Publicacion del Jubileo Universal, que N. S. P. Clemente XIII. *Mexico.* 1760. 8vo.

Ensayo para la materia medica Mexicana, arreglado por una comision nombrada por la Academia Medico-quirurgica de esta capital ... . *Puebla.* 1832. 4to, pp. xi, 101. 48449

Espediente de la Cuenta Enviada por el Ejecutiro al Quinto Congreso de la Union el 14 de Diciembre de 1869, y Discusion que Respecto de Dicha Cuenta ... . *Mexico: Imprenta de Ignacio Cumplido.* 1870. Folio, pp. 223. H. 48450

Esposicion que el Cabildo Metropolitano de Mexico ha elevado al Soberano Congreso contra la Tolerancia de Cultos. *Mexico.* 1856. 4to, pp. 14. 48451

Esposicion que los conservadores de las provincias dirigen al General Almonte, á sus correligionarios y proprietarios de la Capital, sobre las bases de la futura organizacion politica del pais. *Mexico.* 1863. 4to, pp. 20. 48452

Esposiciones verificadas en 1850. *Mexico.* 1850. 8vo.

Also: Acta y documentos relativos a la exposicion general de industria, verificada en 1853. *Mexico.* 1853. 8vo.

Estadas que acompañan la Memoria del Ministro de Hacienda D. Bonifacio Gutierrez. *Mexico.* 1849. 8vo. 48454

Estadistica del colegio de Abogados. *Mexico.* 1808. 4to.

Also: Constituciones de l'academia de jurisprudencia. *Mexico.* 1811. 4to.—Estadistica del colegio Abogados. *Mexico.* 1830. 4to.—Proyecto de estatutos del colegio de Abogados. *Mexico.* 1827. 4to.

Estadistica del imperio Mexicano. *Mexico.* 1822. 12mo.

Estado demostrativo ó Indice Alfabético con los Nombres de las Calles, &c. que comprehenden los ocho Quarteles mayores, ... in que su halla repartida la Ciudad de Mexico, &c. [n. p.:] *Impreso por D. Felipe de Zúñiga y Ontiveros.* 1793. 24mo, pp. (37).

Estado Mayor General del Ejercito. Escalafon General que comprende a los Sres. Capitan General, Generales de Division, á los de Brigada, Coroneles, Oficiales y Subalternos etc. *Mexico.* 1854. Folio, pp. 323. 48458

Estado Provisional del Imperio Mexicano. *Mexico.* 1865. 8vo. 48459

Estatutos de la Compañia del Ferro-Carril de México á Puebla, autorizada por decreto de 5 de Abril de 1861. *Mexico.* 1861. 4to, pp. 51. 48460

Estatutos de la Santa Iglesia de México, 1585, Revisados. [Latin and Spanish.] *México.* 1859. 8vo. 48461

Estatutos de la sociedad economica de Mexico. *Mexico.* 1831. 12mo, pp. 14. 48462

Estatutos del Real Colegio de Escribanos de Mexico ... . *Mexico: Felige de Zúñiga.* 1793. 4to. 48463

Estatutos gencral de Barcelona. *Mexico.* 1585. 4to. 48464

An early Mexican publication. Title from [Harrisse] "Bibliotheca Amer. Vetus."

Estatutos y constituciones del colegio de Abogados establecido en la Corte de Mexico. *Madrid.* 1760. Folio, 12 leaves.

Études historiques sur le Mexique au point de vue politique et social. *Paris.* 1859. Rl. 8vo. 48466

La Europea Intervencion en Mexico. *Filadelfia.* 1859. 4to, pp. 8. 48467

Exequias militar. celebradas por la plaza de Mexico. *Mexico.* 1787. 8vo. 48468

Also: Exequias reales celebradas en la santa iglesia catedral de México del Señor D. Carlos III. *Mexico.* 1789. 4to, 8 leaves.—Exêquias reales en Mexico, de D. Isabel de Braganza, D. Maria Luisa de Borbon, Carlos IV. ... *Mexico.* 1820. Folio. Plate.

Explicacion de el arco erigido en la puerta de el palacio arzobispal de Mexico a la gloria de Carlos III. ... 25 de Junio de 1760. *Mexico.* 1760. 4to, pp. 19. 48469

Exposicion de una persona. *See* Vol. VI., No. 23434.

Exposicion del Ex-Ministro que la suscribe, sobre las differcias con Francia. *Mexico.* 1839. 8vo. 48470

Exposicion del pequeño Catecismo, impreso en el Idioma Mexicano, para la mejor instruccion de los Indios. [Mexican and Spanish.] *Puebla.* 1819. 12mo. 48471

Exposicion hecha por la comision especial de mineria a la soberana junta gubernativa, sobre la necesidad de fomentar este ramo principal de Industria con la baja de derechos que propuso en su dictamen de 24 de octubre proximo pasado. *Mexico.* 1822. 4to, pp. 36. 48472

Exposicion de varias personas de Mexico dirigido al Soberano Congreso de esta Capital solicitando la reposicion de la Compañia de Jesus en la Republica. *Mexico.* 1841. 8vo, pp. 24. 48473

Exposicion que el ejecutivo dirige al Congreso de la Union, dando cuenta del uso que hizo de las facultades que le concedío el Articulo 11 de la Ley de 17 de Enero de 1870 ... . *Mexico: Imprenta ... de José M. Sandoval.* 1870. 8vo, pp. 27, (2). H.

Exposicion que hace al Publico. *See* Vol. VI., No. 23442.

Exposicion que los Conservadores. *See* Vol. VI., No. 23444.

Exposiciones de la Suprema Corte. *See* Vol. VI., No. 23446.

Extracto ... de la causa criminal formada por la sala del crimen de Mejico a. — D. Antonio Ygnacio Lopez Matoso ... la cual comenzò en 28. de Febrero de 1815. [n. p. n. d.] 4to, 148 l.

Extracto del hecho, y breves Apuntes de Derecho en el Pleyto qui sigue D. E. M. Faxardo, como marido de D. Doña Ysabel de Andrade, contra D. Pedro Valbuena, sobre aver Fallecido Intestada. *Mexico: J. B. de Hogal.* 1732. Folio. 48476

The Fall of Mexico. [n. p. n. d.] 4to. 48477

Title from Raetzel [*i. e.* Ternaux-Compans] Catalogue, No. 1670.

Folletin del Diario Official del Gobierno de la República Mejicana. *Mejico.* 1853. Rl. 8vo, pp. 184. 48478

A diary kept in Mexico in the seventeenth century.

Forma brev. administr. ap. Indios S. Baptismi Sacramentum. *Mexico.* 1583. 8vo. 48479

Title from [Harrisse] "Bibliotheca Americana Vetustissima."

Funcion dramatica en el Palacio Imperial de México el de 4 de Noviembre de 1865. *Mexico.* 1865. 8vo. 48480

Gaceta del Gobierno de Mexico. *Mexico: J. M. de Benavente.* 1816. Sm. 4to. Continued. C. 48481

Galeria de Antiguos principes Mejicanos ... . *Puebla.* 1821. 4to, pp. 30. + Segunda Parte. pp. 21, (1). 48482

Gazeta de Mexico, Compendio de Noticias Mexicanas, con Indice General de todas, en la Impression de las Gazetas de Mexico ... sú Autor J. F. Sahagum de Arevalo, Ladron de Guevara. *Mexico.* 1728–39. 3 vols., sm. 4to. 48483

Extremely rare and curious, being a collection of the first regular newspaper established in Spanish America.

Gazetas de Mexico, Compendio de Noticias de Nueva-España, desde principios del año de 1784, por D. Manuel Antonio Valdes.

Mexico: [Felipe de Zúñiga y Ontiveros]. 1784–85. Sm. 4to, pp. 474. + Supplement and Engravings. [*Ibid.*] 1784–5. Cont'd.

Geschichte der Entdeckung. *See* [Haeberlin (C. L.)], 29496

El Gobierno Supremo de la Republica á los Mexicanos. *Mexico.* 1858. 8vo. 48485

Gran Almanaque y directorio del comercio de la Republica Mexicana, publicado por E. Maillefert, ano 1869. *Mexico.* 1869. 4to, pp. 320. 48486

Guia de la Hacienda de la Republica Mexicana; año de 1826. *Mexico.* 1826. 16mo. Map and Tables. Continued. C.

Guia de los forasteros de México de 1788. *Mexico.* 1788? 8vo. Continued. 48488

Histoire ancienne. *See* [Solis (A. de)].

Historia de la Revolucion de Mexico contra la dictadura del General Santa-Anna, 1853–1855. *México: V. Garcia Torres.* 1855. 4to, pp. (8), 335, 12 Portraits, 1 Plan, Apéndice, clviii, 2 Tables between pages 104 and 105, Indice, 6 leaves. Plan of Puebla. 48489

There are copies on vellum paper. Corrected title of our No. 38612.

History of the Conquest of Mexico, by Hernan Cortes, to which is added the Voyage of Vasco de Gama. *London.* 1759. 12mo. 48490

Probably from Antonio de Solis, or perhaps a translation from Prévost's "Histoire général des Voyages," XII. 1754.

The History of the raising of the First American Flag on the Capitol of Mexico. ... *Washington: Printed by C. Wendell.* 1856. 8vo, pp. 34. B. 48491

Honras de Felipe IV en el convento de Santo Domingo de Mexico. *Mexico.* 1666. 4to. 48492

... Hostilities by Mexico. Message from the President of the United States ... . May 11, 1846. ... [n. p. n. d.] 8vo, pp. 130

Ilustracion de el derecho. *See* Vol. IX., No. 34347.

Ilustracion de las pinturas del Arco. *See* Vol. IX., No. 34348

Imperialis Mexicana Universitas illustrata ipsius per Constitutionum Scholia, Academico Generali Commentario, Theorico Practico, Fundationis, Patronatus, Instituti, Privilegiorum, Ex-

emptionum, Consuetudinum Pontificij, ac Cæsarej Universi Juris studia concernentis, et Rerum ejus insignium. Par Josepho Adame et Arriaga. *Hispali, ex Typographia Hæredum Thomæ Lopez de Haro.* 1698. Folio. 48494

Very scarce; not mentioned by Brunet, Rich, Stevens, Salva, or Ternaux, but alluded to by Eguiara in his article on the Mexican Academy as an important work, ("Bibl. Mex.," p. 3).

El Imperio y la Intervencion. *Mexico.* 1867. 8vo. 48495

Independencia de Mexico. *Mexico.* 1842. 12mo, pp. 31.

El Indicador de la Federacion Mexicana. *México.* 1833. 3 vols., 8vo. 48497

Informe de la Administracion General de Correos, al ... Ministro de Hacienda. *Mexico: Imprenta de Ignacio Cumplido.* 1857. 16mo, pp. 81, folded leaf. B. 48498

Also: Informe de la Comision Nombrada por el Gobernador de Mexico ... . *México.* 1843. 8vo. — Informe de la Junta de Fomento y Administrativa de Mineria, dado al Ministro de Relaciones, sobre el estado en que se encuentren los fondos de azogues y dotal de los mineros. *Mexico.* 1850. 8vo, pp. 32. — Informe de la Junta de Fomento y Administrativa de Mineria, al Ministro de Relaciones sobre el estado que han guardado los fondos, de azogue y dotal en el año de 1850, con apuntes para formar la estadistica minera de los Estados-Unidos Mexicanos. *Mexico.* 1851. 8vo, pp. 64. — Informe ... de relaciones sobre la comision de que esta encargado por el Supremo Gobierno de la Republica Mejicana. *Campeche.* 1828. 8vo. S.

Informe General que ... de real órden instruyó entregó el ... Marques de Sonora, siendo Visitador general de este Reyno, al ... Virrey D. Antonio Bucarely y Ursua, ... 31 Diciembre de 1771; lo publica el Secretario del Emperador Maximiliano, D. Eduardo Pierron. *Mexico.* 1866. Sm. folio. Tables. + Publicado por la Seccion de Fomento del Ministerio de Gobernacion. *México: [Imprenta de S. White].* 1867. 4to, pp. 411. Tables.

"Of this valuable work only twenty copies were printed, which had remained in MS. until the liberality of the unfortunate Maximilian allowed it to see the light in this limited form. It was prepared for the secret instruction of the Viceroy and his successors in the due administration of the government, to enable them to secure just imposition of taxes, the verification of revenue-receipts, and to control the entire financial system of the Mexican dominion. The Marquis de Sonora, better known as Don José de Galvez, is said by Aleman to have as it were created the 'Board of Trade' ministry in Mexico, and the historian goes even so far as to attribute all the material and commercial prosperity of the country to that statesman."—STEVENS. The second edition was also printed at the expense of the Imperial Government, but only for private circulation.

Informe presentado al Excmo. Sr. presídente de la Republica, por el ministro de hacienda, sobre los puntos de que en el se tratá. *Mexico.* 1853. 8vo, pp. 90. Tables. 48500

Also: Informe presentado á la Junta general de la Industria mexicana en la sesion de 13 de Diciembre de 1844, por el Director general del ramo. *Mexico.* 1844. 8vo, pp. 56. 7 Tables. — Informe que dan al Sr. Gobernador D. Miguel M. Azcarate, los Comisionados del desagué de la Capital y su distrito. *Mexico.* 1853. 4to, pp. 22.

Informe, qve la Real Vniversidad, y Clavstro Pleno de Ella de la Ciudad de Mexico de esta Nueva-Espana haze Á el Excellentissimo Señor Virrey de ella en conformidad de orden de su Excelencia de 3. de Iulio de este año 1692. Sobre los inconvenientes de la bebida de el Pulque. *Mexico.* 1692. Folio, 18 leaves.

Informe que por orden de Su Alteza Serenisima presenta al Supremo Gobierno sobre el estado de la Hacienda publica y sus reformas, M. Olasagarre. *Mexico.* 1855. 8vo, pp. 67. Tables.

Iniciativas presentadas a la camara de diputados por el ministerio de Hacienda para la formacion de una acta de navegacion de la republica, y su comercio exterior por las fronteras. *Méjico.* 1849. 8vo, pp. 40. 48503

Instruccion formada en virtud de Real Orden de S. M., que se dirige al Comandante General de Provincias internas D. Jacobo Ugarte y Loyola para gobierno y puntual observancia de este Superior Gefe y de sus immediatos Subalternos. *Mexico.* 1786. Folio, pp. 60. 48504

Instruccion para. *See* Vol. IX., Nos. 34831–35.

Instruccion que debe observarse para el arreglo, regimen y servicio del Resguardo unido de rentas reales de Mexico. *Mexico.* 1794. Folio, pp. 39. 48505

Instrucciones para el jusgado de bienes de difuntos de la Real Audiencia de Mexico. *Mexico.* 1805. Folio, pp. 20. 48506

The Insurrection of 1810. *Mexico.* 1810. 8vo. 48507

L'Intervention française. *See* our Vol. IX., No. 34945, and add, *Paris: Amyot.* 1868. 8vo, pp. (4), xvi, 414, (1).

Los Jesuitas. *See* Vol. VIII., Nos. 36083, '84, and '86.

La Junta Suprema del Reyno á la Nacion Española. *Mexico.* 1810. 8vo. 48508

Kalendario manuel Americano ecclesiastico y literario para el anno de 1827. Dispuesto con arreglo al meridiano de la Ciudad de Meyico por Dn. M. R. F. de la B. *Hamburg: Hoffmann und Campe.* [n. d.] 48509

Lamenta la Ciudad de Mexico. [Poetical.] *Mexico.* 1771. 8vo. 48510

A Letter to a Member. *See* Vol. X., No. 40407.

Ley, justicia y verdad. *See* [Guridi y Alcozer (J. M.)]

Ley sobre derechos y obvenciones parroquiales. *Mexico.* 1857. 4to, pp. 11. + Coleccion de los aranceles ... [*Ibid.*] pp. xii, 124.

Leyes relativas a papel sellado y ultimas sobre administracion de Justicia y modo de enjuiciar a los ragos y la organica de guardia Nacional. *Mexico.* 1848. Sm. 8vo, pp. 72. 48512

Leyes y reglamento, para al arreglo de la instruccion publica, en el distrito federal. *Mexico.* 1834. 12mo, pp. 132. C.

Ligero Bosquejo de la actual Situacion en Mejico articulo publicado por "El Veracruzano." *Madrid.* 1862. 8vo. 48514

Liquidacion General de la Deuda Esterior de la República Mexicana hasta fin de Deciembre de 1841. *Mexico.* 1845–52.

Lista alfabetica de los professores de medicina y cirugia, ... autorizados legalenente por medio de examen paro ejercer su profesion que existen en esta capital. *Mexico.* 1859. 12mo, pp. 12

Lista alfabetica y cronologica de los individuos que forman el illustre y nacional colegio de Abogados de Mexico, en el año de 1838. *Mexico.* 1838. Sm. 8vo, pp. 58. Continued. 48517

Also: Lista alfabética de los Señores empleados é individuos, matriculados en el ... Colegio de Abogados. *Mexico.* 1840. 32mo, pp. 42. — Lista de los generos frutos y efectos de procedencia extrangera, cuya importacion se prohive en el territorio de la federacion mexicana, por decreto del soberano congreso de 20 de Mayo de 1824. *Mexico.* 1824. 8vo, pp. 6, 4. — Lista de los individuos matriculados en el ilustre y nacional colegio de Abogados de Mexico. *Mexico.* 1837. Sm. 8vo, pp. 36.

Manifestacion. *See* Vol. XI., Nos. 44269 and 44272.

Manifestacion que hacen al Clero y Fieles de sus Diocesis los Señores Arzobispo de Mexico y Obispos de Michoacan, Linares, Guadalajara y el Potosi, y D. Francisco Serrano como Representante de la Mitra de Puebla, en defensa del Clero ... con ocasion del manifiesto y Decretos expedidos por ... Benito Juarez en Veracruz en los dias 7, 12, 13 y 23 de Julio de 1859. *Mexico.* 1859. 4to, pp. 38. 48518

Manifesto de la riqueza de la Negociacion de Minas conocida por la veta vizcaina, Ubicada en el Real del Monte jurisdiccion

de Pachuca, de las grandes obras ... y del estado actual ... para la Compañia de Accionistas ... su actual poseedor El Senor D. Pedro Josef Rodriguez Saenz de Pedroso, ... Lo escribió de su Orden D. Josef Rodrigo de Castelazo ... *Méjico: Casa de Ontiveros, año de* 1820. 4to, pp. 63. 48519

Manifesto del gobierno a la Nacion. *Mexico.* 1857. Sm. 8vo, pp. 208. 48520

By Ignacio Comonfort, president of the republic.

Manifesto del presidente de la Republica [A. L. de Santa Anna] a la Nacion. *Mexico.* 1855. 4to, pp. 16. + *Puebla.* 1855. 4to, pp. 14. 48521

Manifesto in Defence of the Policy of General Comonfort during his Administration in Mexico. *New York.* 1858. 8vo.

Manifiesto al publico que hace el Ayuntamiento de 1840. *Mexico.* [n. d.] 8vo. 48523

Manifiesto de la Cámara de Diputados en la legíslatura de 1831 y 1832. *Mejico.* 1832. 4to, pp. 30. Continued. 48524

Manifiesto del Congreso General á los Mejicanos. *Mexico, 4. de Octubre de* 1824. Folio, pp. 6. Continued. 48525

Manifiesto del Gobernador Constitucionel del Estado [Antonio Juille], al separase del egercicio del poder. *Veracruz.* 1833. 4to, pp. 6, (4). 48526

Manifiesto que dirige a la Nacion el General Juan Alvarez, con motivo de la representacion calumniosa que unos emigrados de la villa de Chilapa hicieron a la augusta cámara de diputados en Febrero último. *Mexico.* 1845. 4to, pp. 180. 48527

Also: Manifiesto que el soberano Congreso constituyente hizo á los pueblos, en los momentos de publicarse el Acta Constitutiva de la Federacion. *Mexico, 31. de Enero de* 1824. Folio, pp. 16. *See also* Vol. XI., Nos. 44285 and 44288.

Manualito para Administrar el Viatico y Extremauncion, en Idioma Mexicano ... . *Mexico: A. Valdés.* 1817. 8vo. 48528

Mappe de Tepechpam, Mappe Tlotzin and Mappe Quinatzin. *Paris: Privately lithographed for Mr. Aubin.* [n. d.] Imp. folio, 18 folded leaves. 48529

Martirologio de los primeros Insurgentes por la libertad Mexicana. *Mexico.* 1841. 8vo. 48530

Lo Maximo. *See* Carillo y Perez (I.), III. 10897.

La Mejico intervencion y la monarquia. *Washington.* 1862. 4to, pp. 18. 48531

Mémoire instructiv des Droits et des Justes Motifs du Gouvernement des ... Mexicains Por ne point reconnaître l'existence légale ni la continuation du privilége accord à D. José Garay, pour ouvir une ... communication entre les océans Atlantique et Pacifique, par l'isthme de Tehuantepec, etc. *Paris: Imprimerie Serriere et Cᵉ.* 1852. 8vo, pp. 48. H. 48532

See also Vol. VII., p. 154, for other works relative to this subject.

Memoranda of Four Claims against Mexico ... submitted to the Late Board and rejected. *Washington, D. C.: Buell & Blanchard, Printers.* 1853. 8vo, pp. 87. H. 48533

There is another edition entitled: "Four Claims against Mexico, rejected by the Board of Commissioners." *Washington.* 1853. 8vo.

Memorandum de négociations pendantes entre le Mexique et l'Espagne. *Poissy.* 1857. 8vo, pp. 365. 48534

Not published. For a Spanish version, *see* [Lafragua (J. M.)], Vol. X., No 38614.

Memoria de Hacienda y Credito Publico, que el Secretario del Rama presenta al Congreso de la Union, el 28 de Setiembre de 1868. *Mexico: Imprenta ... de José María Sandoval.* 1868. Folio. Continued. H. 48535

Memoria de Marina: presentada a las Camaras par el Secretario de Estado. ... *Mexico.* 1826. Folio, pp. (6), 82. Tables. Continued. C., M., 48536

Memoria de Nacionalizacion ... . *Mexico.* 1829–40. Folio.

Memoria de Relaciones Interiores y Esteriores della Republica, 1826. *Mexico.* 1826. Folio. Continued. 48538

Memoria de la corporacion municipal que funcionó el año de 1851. *Mexico.* 1852. 4to. Continued. 48539

Memoria de la Direccion de colonizacion é industria. Año de 1849. *Mexico.* 1850. 8vo, pp. 46. 48540

Also: Memoria de la direccion general de la Industria Nacional. *Mexico.* 1845. 8vo. Continued.

Memoria de la Hacienda Nacional de la Republica Mexicana. *Mexico.* 1838. Folio. Continued. 48541

Memoria de la Secretario de Estado y del Despacho de Relaciones Interiores y Esteriores de la Republica Mexicana. ... *Mexico.* 1829. 8vo. Continued. 48542

Memoria de la Secretario de Estado y del Despacho de Fomento, Colonisacion, Industria, y Comercio de la Republica Mexicana, escrita por el Ministro del Ramo. C. Manuel Siliceo, para dar Cuenta con ella al Soberano Congreso Constitucional. *Mexico.* 1857. Folio, pp. 129, 170, 6, 66, 159, 7, 105, with 21 Maps, 7 Plans, 1 View, and 17 Statistical Tables. 48543

Copies with the maps are scarce.

Memoria de los Ramos del Ministerio de Relaciones Interiores y Esteriores de la Republica, Enero, 1826. *Mexico.* 1826. Folio, pp. (2), 33. Continued. M. 48544

Memoria de los Ramos municipales formada por el Exnio Ayuntamiento en 1846. *Mexico.* 1846. 8vo. Continued.

Memoria del Ministerio de Justicia y Negocios ecclesiasticos de la Republica Mexicana, presentada á las Cámaras del Congreso de la Union ... . Año de 1835. *Mexico.* 1835. Folio, pp. 71. Continued. 48546

Also: Memoria del Ministro de Justicia è Instruccion publica presentada por el Secretario, Año de 1845. *Mexico.* 1845. 8vo. Continued. — Memoria del Ministro de Relaciones Exteriores y gobernacion, el 12 de Marzo de 1845. *Mexico.* 1845. 8vo. Continued.

Memoria del Ramo de Hacienda Federal de los Estados-Unidos Mexicanos, leida en la Cámara de Diputados el 13 de Enero, y en la de Senadores el 16 del mismo, por el Ministro respectivo, año de 1826. *Mexico.* 1826. Folio, pp. 82. 96 Tables. Cont'd

Also: Memoria de Ramo de la Hacienda Federal da los Estados Unidos Mexicanos. *Mexico.* 1828. 8vo.

Memoria del Secretario de Estado y del Despacho de Justicia é Instruccion Pública, Leida á las Cámaras del Congreso Nacional de la República Mexicana en Enero de 1844. *Mexico: Impresa por Ignacio Cumplido.* 1844. Folio, pp. 88, Appendix. 85. Statistical Tables. Continued. BA. 48548

Memoria del Secretario de Estado y del Despacho de la Guerra, pres. a las Camaras, Enero, 1826. *Mexico.* [1826.] Folio, pp. 15. Tables. Continued. 48549

Also: Memoria del Secretario de Estado de la nacion mexicana. *Mexico.* 1851. Folio. — Memoria del Secretario de Estado al Congreso de la Union. *México.* 1868. 8vo.

Memoria del Secretario del Despacho de Hacienda. Leida en la cámara de senadores el dia 15, y en la de diputados el 17 de Febrero de 1832. *Mexico.* 1832. Folio. 59 Tables. Cont'd.

Memoria Instructiva. *See* Garay (J. de), VII., 26547.

Memoria leida en las camaras en 1851. *Mexico: V. G. Torres.* 1851. Folio, pp. 43. C. 48551

Memoria presentada á S. M. el Emperador por el Ministro de fomento Luis Robles Pezuela de los trabajos ejecutados en su ramo el año de 1865. *México: Andrade y Escalante.* 1866. 4to, pp. (4), 657. 9 Plates and 2 Maps. 48552

Also: Memoria presentada a las dos Cameros del Congreso general de la Federacion Por el Secretario de Estado al abrirse las Sessiones del ano de 1825. *Mexico.* 1825. 8vo. — Memoria presentada al Soberano Congreso Mexicano, por el Secretario de Estado y del Despacho de Relaciones Interiores y Exteriores. *Mexico.* 1822. Folio. — Memorial Provisional presentada al Soberano Congreso, por el Ministerio de Hacienda en 2 de Junio de 1823. [*Mexico:*] *Imprenta Nacional del Supremo Gobierno, en Palacio.* 1823. Folio.

Memoria que el Secretario de Estado y del Despacho de Hacienda ... . *Mexico.* 1844. Folio, pp. 52. Continued. 48553

Also: Memoria que el Secretario de Estado y del Despacho de Justicia e Instruccion pública presenta al Congreso de la Union en Marzo de 1868. *Mexico.* 1868. 8vo, pp. 107. Continued. — Memoria que el Secretario de Estado y del Despacho de Relaciones esteriores é interiores ... . *Mexico: Imprenta del Supremo Gobierno, en Palacio.* [n. d.] 4to. Continued.

Memoria que en Cumplimiento del Articulo 120, de la Constitucion Federal de los Estados Unidos Mexicanos. *Mexico: Imprenta del Supremo Gobierno.* 1825. 8vo, pp. 28. 8 Tables. C. + [n. p. 1826.] Folio, pp. (2), 13. Tables. 48554

Also: Memoria que la Direccion de Colonizacion é Industria presentó al Ministerio. *Mexico.* 1851. 8vo.

Memoria que presenta el Gobernador de Guanajuato al Congreso Constituyente, del Estado de los Negocios Publicos, 1824–1825. *Mexico.* 1826. Folio. M. 48555

Memoria que sobre el Estado de la Hacienda Nacional de la Republica Mexicana ... . *Mexico.* 1846. Folio, pp. 160. Tables. Continued. 48556

Also: Memoria sobre el estado de la agricultura é industria de la Republica, que la direccion general de estos ramos presenta al Gobierno supremo. *Mexico.* 1843. 8vo, pp. 74. 8 Tables. Continued. — Memoria sobre la propriedad eclesiastica, riqueza publica destruida, y victimas hechas por los demagoges de 1858 hasta junio 1863. *Mexico.* 1864. 8vo.

Memoria sobre las Casas de Moneda de la Republica. *Mexico.* 1849. 8vo. Plates. 48557

Memoria sobre reformas del arancel mercantil ... . *Mexico.* 1824. 8vo, pp. 26, 23, 8. 48558

Memorial que presentan a todos estados los niños expósitos de la Imperial Ciudad de Mexico por mano de su Arzobispo. *Mexico.* 1770. 4to, pp. xxi. 48559

A Memorial setting forth. *See* Garay (J. de), VII. 26548, and add, *Nueva-York: Imprenta de W. G. Stewart.* 1852. 8vo, pp. (2), 44.

Memorial. *See* Vol. XI., Nos. 47628 and 47702.

Memorias de la primera Secretaria de Estado y del Despacho de Relaciones Interiores y Esteriores de Mexico, leida al Congreso por el Ministro Lafragua .... *Mexico.* 1847. 4to. 48561

Memorias de las operaciones que han tenido la oficina de desamortizacion del distrito de México. *Mexico.* 1862. 8vo.

Memorias Historicas de la Congregacion de el Oratorio fundada en Mexico. [*Mexico.* 1740?] Folio. 48563

The lives of Juan de la Pedrosa, M. de la Llana Partida, C. A. Diaz de Castro, Salvador Rodriguez de la Fuente Salzedo, Pedro de Arellano y Sossa, and Joseph Montano, are contained in this rare volume of biographies and form the second and third parts of the Memorias.

Memorias para la historia Megicana, ó los ultimos dias del Castillo de San Juan de Ulua. *Jalapa.* 1826. 4to, pp. (4), 18.

Mensage del C. Guadalupe Victoria, Presidente de los Estados-Unidos Mexicanas, a las Camaras del Congreso General, 1826. *Mexico.* [1826.] Folio, pp. 4. Continued. 48565

El Mensagero Comercial de Mexico. Periodico de comercio, politica y literatura. Domingo 10 de Octubre de 1826. ... [n. p. n. d.] 4to. Continued. 48566

El Mensajero de los Estados-Unidos Mexicanos. ... Tomo I. *Mexico.* 1850. Folio. 48567

Forty-four numbers only published.

Message of the President [etc.] *See* Nos. 48109, 48113–15, 48142–43.

Metrica Panegyrica. *See* No. 48213.

The Mexican Empire, 1865. *See* [Parker (F. J.)]

Mexican Extraordinary, a tri-weekly Newspaper, edited by William Moran .... *Mexico.* 1861. 48568

Contains details of the American rebellion, and of the imbroglio which led to the

establishment and downfall of Maximilian's empire. The editor is like many other writers who suppose that tri-weekly means three times a week.

Mexican Indemnity Payments. Remarks on Mr. Marks' "Memorial." [*Washington: Gideon, Print.* 1851.] 8vo, pp. 5.

Mexican Letters, Containing Humorous and Satirical Observations on the Manners, Customs, Religion, and Policy of the English, French, Spaniards, and Americans. Interspersed with a Great Variety of Interesting and Entertaining Anecdotes, Illustrated by Moral and other suitable Reflections. Compiled from Original Letters. *London: W. Goldsmith.* MDCCLXXIII. 2 vols., 12mo, pp. ix, 264; xii, 280. C., N. 48570

Mexican Ocean Mail and Inland Company. ... Report .... The Shortest Route to California, via Vera Cruz and Acapulco. *Philadelphia.* 1854. 8vo, pp. 22. Map. H. 48571

Also: First Annual Report of the Mexican Ocean Mail and Inland Company. *New York: Hall, Clayton and Co., Printers.* 1853. 8vo, pp. 43. 2 Maps. H.

Reports of the Mexican Pacific Coal and Iron Mining and Land Company's Exploring Expedition to the States of Guerrero and Michoacan, Republic of Mexico, 1856–'57. [By ——. Plumb.] *New York.* 1858. 8vo, pp. iv, 171. 12 Maps.

Also: Prospecto de la compañia denominada "Mexican Pacific Coal and Iron and Land Company." *Nueva-York.* 1856. 8vo, pp. 14, 40.

... Mexican Treacheries and Cruelties. Incidents and Sufferings in the Mexican War; ... Also, ... the particulars of the Death ... of Capt. George Lincoln, of Worcester. By a Volunteer returned from the War. *Boston.* 1847. 8vo, pp. 32. H.

The Mexican War. Review of the Annual Message of the President of the United States to Congress, December 7, 1847. *Washington.* 1848. 8vo, pp. 32. B., H. 48574

The Mexican War and its Heroes ... with a Biography of the Officers. Also, an Account of the Conquest of California and New Mexico .... *Philadelphia: Lippincott, Grambo & Co.* 1850. 12mo, pp. vi, 9–224. H. 48575

Mexicanische Zustände in den Jahren 1830 bis 1832 vom Verfasser der Briefe in die Heimath. *Stuttgart.* 1837. 2 vols., 8vo. 48576

Los Mexicanos pintados por si mismos, por varios Autores. [*Mexico.* 1855.] 4to. 35 Plates. 48577

Los Mexicanos y su pas. Articulo tomado del "Atlantico." Trasladado al Español. *Nueva Orleans.* 1860. 4to, pp. 39.

Mexico. Statistical and Financial Items: [n. p. n. d.] 8vo, pp. 8. 48579

Mexico and Mr. Poinsett. Reply to a British Pamphlet, entitled "Observations on the Instructions given by the President of the United States of America to the Representatives of that Republic, at the Congress of Panama" .... *Philadelphia.* 1829. 4to, pp. 13. 48580

Mexico and the Munroe Doctrine. [n. p. 1862?] 8vo, pp. 24

Mexico como nacion independente. Descripcion de su presente estado, y esperanzas de su condicon futura. Articulo traducido del periodico; Revista trimestre de Filadelfia. *Mexico.* 1828. 4to, pp. 32. 48582

This elicited: Contestacion á este articulo infamatorio contra la Republica Mexicana. *Mexico.* 1828. 4to, pp. 16.

Mexico dividida en quarteles. *Mexico.* 1811. 12mo. Plate.

México el Imperio y la Intervencion. ... *Mexico.* 1867. 8vo.

Mexico en 1847. Contiene una relacion de las revoluciones y de algunos sucésos ocurridos entre nosotros, desde que comenzó la guerra contra los Estados-Unidos .... *Mexico.* 1847. 4to, pp. 40. 48585

Report of the Chief Engineer to the Directors of the Mexico Gulf Railway Company. *London.* 1846. 8vo. Plans. 48586

Mexico in 1842. *See* [Folsom G. F.)], Vol. VI., No. 24968.

Mexico plausibile con la triumphal demostracion por la victoria de muy alto Philipo V. en los Campos de Brihuega y Villaviciosa. *Mexico.* [1711.] 4to, 9 leaves. 48587

Mexico: the Country, History, and People. *London: Religious Tract Society.* 1863. 16mo, pp. viii, 340. B. 48588

Mexico y la Intervencion. Opusculo publicado en Paris a principios de Noviembre, y traducido del Frances por Francisco Elorriaga. *Mexico.* 1861. Sm. 8vo, pp. 123. 48589

México y sus Alrededores. Coleccion de monumentos, trajes y paisajes dibujados al natural y litografiados por los artistas mex-

icanos C. Castro, J. Campillo, L. Nuda y E. Rodriguez, bajo la direccion de decaen. *México.* 1856. Folio, pp. 32. 18 Plates.

Le Mexique conquis. *See* [Boesnier], II. 6124.

Le Mexique et l'Intervention *Paris: Imprimerie de L. Tinterlin et Cᵉ.* 1861. 8vo, pp. 72. B. 48591

Le Mexique L'Empire et l'Intervention. *Leipzig: F. A. Brockhaus.* 1869. 8vo, pp. vi, 55, (1). H. 48592

Mexique et Texas. Documens Officiels publiés par le Noticioso de ambos Mundos de New York du 2 Avril. *Paris.* 1842. 4to, pp. 16. 48593

Le Mexique, ses ressources et son avenir. *Paris.* 1864. 8vo, pp. 32. 48594

Le Mexique. Un mot sur l'exposé des principes de "l'Ère nouvelle," journal des intérêts franco-mexicains, publié à Mexico, par un Mexicain. *Paris: Lainé et Harvard.* 1865. 8vo.

Corrected title of our No. 29261, Vol. VII.

Notes on Mexico. *See* [Poinsett (Joel R.)]

Noticia breve de la Solemne, deseada, ultima dedicacion del Templo Metro. de Mexico, Corte Imperial de la Nueva-España, edificado por la magnificencia de los Reyes de España Celebrada, en 22, de Diziembre de 1667; y Sermon que predicò el Doctor Ysidro Sariñana. *Mexico.* 1668. 4to. 48596

Noticia de las fincas pertenecientes á Corporaciones civiles y eclesiasticas del distrito de Mexico. *Mexico.* 1856. Folio, pp. 43

Noticia sobre su Hacienda Publica bajo el Gobierno Español y despues de la Independencia 1845 el Ayuntamiento de Mexico de 1840. [n. p. n. d.] 8vo. 48598

Noticias de la Ciudad de México y de sus alrededores. Articulos tomados del "Diccionario Universal de Historia y de Geografia," que actualmente se publica en esta capital. *Mexico: Tipografia de F. Escalante y Cª.* 1855. Folio, pp. 423, (1). 2 Maps and Plate. BA. 48599

Nueva forma de Gobierno en Mexico o sea su Verdadera e indispensabile reforma. *Amules.* 1862. 12mo, pp. 40. 48600

Nueva y curiosa guia para dentro y fuera de este corte de Mexico. *Mexico.* 1823. 12mo. 48601

Nuevos Documentos relativos á la cuestion de Mexico. *Mexico.* 1863. 8vo. 48602

Obediencia que Mexico dio al rey D. Felipe IV con un discurso en verso del estado de la misma ciudad desde el mas antiguo de su fundacion, imperio y conquista hasta hoy. *Mexico.* 1623. 4to. 48603

Observaciones del Cabildo Metropolitano de Mexico sobre el Dictamen que las Comisiones reunidas presentaron á la Camara de Senadores en 28 de Febrero de 1826, para las instrucciones del Enviado por la republica romana al Pontifice Romano. *Mexico.* 1827. 4to, pp. 51. 48604

Observaciones que el Pensador. *See* [Lizardi (J. F. de)].

Observaciones que hace el ejecutivo al Proyecto de Arancel de Aduanas Maritimas y Fronterizas declarado ... por el Quinto Congreso de la Union .... *Mexico: Imprenta ... de Jose M. Sandoval.* 1870. 8vo, pp. 139. H. 48605

Observador Judicial y de Legislacion; periodico que contiene todas las leyes y decretos dados por el Exmo. Señor Presidente Provisional D. Antonio Lopez de Santa-Anna, desde la epocha de nuestra regeneracion politica, 1842 à 1844. *Mexico.* 1842–3. 4 vols., 4to. C. 48606

Operaciones ocurridas en la Defensa de la Capital de la Republica. *Mexico.* 1847. 8vo. 48607

Ordenancas de la Ciudad de Mexico, hechas en virtud de real Cedula por Gatica Cerda, Maldonado, y Valdes. *Mexico.* 1683. 4to. 48608

Ordenanza de la division de la ... ciudad de Mexico en quarteles, creacion de los Alcaldes de ellos y reglas de su gobierno. *Mexico.* 1782. Folio, pp. (2), 41. Plan of Mexico. + *Mexico: F. de Zuñiga y Ontiveros.* 1793. Folio, pp. (2), 41. Plan.

Ordenanza general de aduanas maritimas y fronterizas de la Republica Mexicana. *Mexico.* 1856. 8vo, pp. 89. 48610

Ordenanza Militar para el Regimen, Disciplina, Subordinacion y Servicio del Ejercito. ... *Mexico.* 1842. 2 vols., sm. 4to. C.

Ordenanzas de la fiel executoria, formadas por la nobilissima ciudad de Mexico en el año de 1718, para el mejor regimen, y gobierno de aquella republica, aprobadas, y confirmadas por la

Magestad del Señor Rey D. Luis Primero por su real despacho de 6. de Mayo de 1724. [*Madrid.* 1726.] Folio, 31 leaves.

Ordenanzas del Consulado de Mexico Universidad de Mercaderes de esta N. E., confirmadas por el Rey en el año de 1607, impresas la primera vez, en el de 1636, la segunda, en el de 1772, la tercera en el de 1816. *Mexico.* 1816. Folio, pp. 61.

Ordenanzas municipales para los ayuntamientos constitucionales de los pueblos, adaptables à sus differentes situaciones politicas y morales. *Mexico.* 1822. 12mo, pp. 32. 48614

Ordenanzas para el gobierno de la labor de monedas, que se fabricaren en la Real Casa de Moneda de Mexico, y demas de las Indias. *Mexico.* 1771. Folio, pp. (6), 59. 48615

Ordenanzas para el gobierno del hospicio de pobres de la ciudad de México en sus quatro departamentos. *Mexico: D. Mariano de Zuñiga y Ontiveros.* 1806. Folio, pp. 52. Continued. 48616

Ordenanzas para el regimen y gobierno de los tenderos y tiendas de pulperia, dadas por la ... ciudad de Mexico. *Mexico.* 1758. Folio, pp. 12. 48617

Ordenanzas, que se han de observar, y guardar en la muy nobilissima, y leal ciudad de Mexico, ... aprobadas, y confirmadas por el Señor Rey D. Phelipe Quinto ... por su real Cedula de 4. de Noviembre de 1728. [*Madrid.* 1729–31.] Folio, pp. (2), 43 leaves, pp. 10. C. 48618

Ordenes y circulares espedidas por el Supremo Gobierno desde el año de 1829 hasta la fecha, para el arreglo y legitimudad del comercio maritimo nacional. *Mexico.* 1830. 8vo, pp. 18.

Papers relative to Mexican Affairs. Communicated to the Senate, June 16, 1864. *Washington.* 1865. 8vo, pp. vii, 496. Map. 48620

Patronata en la Nacion. *Méjico.* 1835. 8vo, pp. 28.

Pauta de comisos para el comercio interior de la república. *Mexico.* 1843. 8vo, pp. 40. 48622

El Pensador Mexicano. *See* L[izardi] (J. F. de), X. 41666.

Periódico oficial del supremo gobierno de los Estados-Unidos Mexicanos. *Mexico.* 1849–1864. 4 vols., folio. 48623

In the years 1863 and 1864 this journal was published in Spanish and French.

El Periquillo Sarniento. *See* [Lizardi (J. F. de)], X. 41664.

Piezas Justificativas de Mexico. *Mexico.* 1849. 8vo.

Plan de Hacienda para la Republica Mexicana. *Mexico.* 1847. 8vo. 48625

Plan de la constitucion politica de la nacion mexicana. [*Mexico:*] *Imprenta Nacional.* 1823. 18mo, pp. (2), 84, (2). C.

Plana mayor general del Ejército Escalanon General. *Mexico.* 1845. 8vo. C. 48627

El Presidente de la Republica Mexicana a sus Habitantes. *Mexico.* 1838. 8vo. C. 48628

Proclama del arzobispo virey de México, contra los engaños pérfidos de los Bonapartes. *Mexico.* 1810. 4to, pp. 22. C.

Prontuario por materias y orden alfabetico, para la mas facil inteligencia de los cuatro tomos de la parte legislativa de Hacienda. *Mexico.* 1828. 12mo. 48630

Proyecto de arancel de aduanas maritimas, que a la Camara de Diputados presenta la comision encargada de su formacion. *Mexico.* 1826. 8vo, pp. 55. 48631

Also: Proyecto de bases de organizacion para la república mexicana, presentado á la junta nacional legislativa, por la comision nombrada al efecto. *Mexico.* 1843. 8vo. — Proyecto de constitucion presentado al Congreso por la comision especial nombrada con este objeto. *Mexico.* 1842. 8vo. — Proyecto de constitucion que presenta al soberano Congreso constituyente la mayoria de su comision especial, y voto particular de la minoria. *Mexico.* 1842. 8vo. — Proyecto de decreto y ordenanza que consulto al supremo Gobierno desde el año de 1842, la junta nombrada por el mismo para arreglar el cuerpo medico militar. *Mexico.* 1846. Sm. 8vo, pp. 60, (16). Plate. — Proyecto de reglamento para el Gobierno interior del Congreso General. *Mexico.* 1824. 12mo, pp. 42. Continued.

Proyectos de colonization presentados por la junta directiva del ramo, al ministerio de relaciones de la Republica Mexicana en 9 de Julio de 1848. *Mexico.* 1848. Sm. 8vo, pp. 40. Table.

Al Pueblo Mexicano. Relacion de las causas que influyeron en los desgraciados sucesos del dia 20 de Agosto de 1847. *Mexico.* 1847. 4to, pp. 36. 48633

Real Cedula concerniente á las Carcelas y Reos en la ciudad de Mexico. *Mexico.* 1768. Folio, 7 leaves. 48634

Real Cedula para la fundacion de la Cofradia de Santiago en la ciudad de Mexico. *Mexico.* 1768. Folio, pp. 27. 48635

Recopilacion de Leyes, Decretos, Bandos, Reglamentos, Circulares y Providencias de los Supremos Poderos y otras autoridades, de la República Mexicana; formada de orden del supremo gobierno, de Enero de 1828 a Diciembre de 1838. Por B. J. Arillaga. *Mexico.* 1838–42. 13 vols., 8vo. C. 48636

Recopilacion de las Leyes del Gobierno Español, que rigen en la República, respectivas à los años de 1788 y siguientes, à 1813. (Cuarta parte del Semanario Judicial.) *México.* 1851. 8vo. C.

Récueil de Pièces. *See* Ternaux-Compans.

Registro oficial del gobierno de los Estados Unidos Mexicanos. *Mexico.* 1830. Folio. Continued. 48638

Reglamento de aduanas maritimas frontarizas y de cabotage, con arreglo á lo dispuerto en la ley de 24 de Noviembre de 1849. *Mexico.* 1849. 8vo, pp. 82. 48639

Reglamento de auxiliares para la seguridad de las personas y bienes de los vecinos de esto capital, y observancia de las leyes de policia. *Mexico.* 1824. 12mo, pp. 13. Continued. 48640

Reglamento de la Compañia General Mexicana para la Exploitacion de la Seda en la Republica Mexicana. *Mexico.* 1841. 12mo, pp. 36. 48641

Reglamento de la Milicia Nacional Mexicana. Segunda edicion. *Mexico.* 1823. Sm. 8vo, pp. 28. 48642

Reglamento de libertad de imprenta mandado observar en la República Mexicana. *Mexico.* 1828. 12mo, pp. 48. 48643

Also: Reglamento de libertad de imprenta de la República Mejicana, ó collecion de las leyes vigentes en el la hasta el presente anno sobre esta materia. *Mexico.* 1833. 12mo, pp. 50.

Reglamento del Tribunal de Revision de Cuentas y su Contaduria Mayor. *México.* 1840. 8vo. C. 48644

Also: Reglamento de la Milicia Activa, y General de la Civica de la Republica Mejicana, con el particular de la Segunda en el Distrito Federal. *Méjico.* 1833. 16mo. — Reglamento del colegio militar. *Mexico.* 1854. 8vo. — Reglamento del gremio de panaderos de Mexico para su abasto y ereccion de un pósito de trigos y harinas à beneficio de su conum. *Mexico.* 1770. Folio, pp. 17. — Reglamento interior del Soberano Congreso Mexicano. *Mexico.* 1823. 16mo, pp. 52. — Reglamento interior para el Gobierno de la Sociedad Mexicana, promovedora de mejoras materiales en la republica. *Mexico.* 1851. 12mo, pp. 12. — Reglamento Interior para el Servicio de la Administracion General de Correos ... 1865. *Mexico.* 1865. 8vo, pp. 24. — Reglamento para el Desempeño del Servicio de la Mayoria de la Plaza de México. *Mexico.* 1839. 8vo. — Reglamento para el Ejercicio y Maniobras de la Infanteria. *Mexico.* 1840. 12mo. — Reglamento para el Gobierno interior de la Sociedad Mexicana. *Mexico.* 1862.

8vo. — Reglamento para el Gobierno Interior del Congreso General. *Mexico.* 1824. 12mo, pp. 47. Continued. — Reglamento para el Gobierno interior del consejo. *Mexico.* 1859. Sm. 8vo, pp. 23. — Reglamento para la Tesoreria General de los Estados-Unidos-Mejicanos, sus Comisarias Generales, de Division, y Subcomisarias. *Mejico.* 1831. Folio, pp. 38, 33 leaves. — Reglamento para los mercados de Mexico. *Mexico: F. de Zuñiga y Ontiveros.* 1791. Folio, pp. 10. — Reglamento para precaver y estinguir en Mexico los incendios de casas y edificios publicos. *Madrid.* 1782. 4to, pp. 90, 14. — Reglamento provisional para el Gobierno Interior del Congreso General. *Mexico.* 1837. Sm. 8vo, pp. 48.

Reglamentos de los Cabinetes Civil y Militar del Emperador. *Puebla.* 1865. Folio, pp. 26. 48645

Very rare. Only printed for private distribution. Also: Reglas de Gobierno de la Sociedad de Subscritores del Teatro de la Ciudad de Mexico. [n. p.] 1786. Folio, pp. 28.

Reglement général des douanes maritimes et frontieres de la République Mexicaine. Traduction officielle. *Mexico.* 1856. 8vo, pp. 88. Tables. 48646

Relacion descriptiva de la fundacion, dedicacion ... de las iglesias y conventos de Mexico. *Mexico.* 1863. 4to. 48647

The author was L. Alfaro y Piña.

Relacion sumaria del Auto Particular de Fee, celebro en la Ciudad de Mexico en 1646 [etc.] *Mexico.* 1646, etc. 4to.

Report on Mexico and her Financial Questions with England, Spain, and France. ... *Mexico.* 1862. Folio. 48649

Report of the Mexican Chamber on the Adjustment of the Mexican Debt. Translated ... *London.* 1850. 8vo. 48650

Representacion del Ilmo. Sr. Arzobispo de Mejico concerniente a algunos sucesos Anteriores a la Independencia proclamada en Aquella Capital. *Habana: 1822. Impreso por Campe en la Oficina Liberal.* 4to, pp. 43. 48651

Representacion dirigida al Virey de Nueva España por la Junta de Policia de México en Diciembre 31 de 1811. *Mexico.* 1812. 8vo. 48652

Reseña de las festividades nacionales de los dias 15. y 16. de Setiembre solemnizadas, en la Capital del Imperio por orden del Emperador Maximiliano. *Mexico.* 1864. 8vo. 48653

Second Report of the Committee of Mexican Bondholders. *London.* 1850. 8vo. + [Another] Report. [*Ibid.*] 1854. 8vo.

Segunda Exposicion de objetos naturales e industriales, en la capital del Estado de Mexico. *Toluca.* 1851. 8vo. 48655

Sesiones extraordinarias del Congreso Constituyente, con Motivo del arresto de Algunos Señores Diputados. *Mexico: D. Mariano de Zúñiga y Ontiveros.* 1822. 8vo, pp. (2), cxcviii. B.

Solemne Accion de Gracias que Tributaron al todopoderoso en la Metropolitana de Mexico los Caballeros de la real y distinguida Orden Española de Carlos III. ... *Mexico.* 1809. 4to, 52 leaves.

Semblanzas de los individuos de la camara disputados de los años de 1825 y 26. *Mexico.* 1827. Sm. 8vo, pp. 20. 48658

Also: Semblanzas de los miembros que componen el honorable congreso del estado de Megico en el Bienio de 1829 y 1830. *Nueva Orleans.* 1829. Sm. 8vo, pp. 10. Continued.

Solemne accion de Gracias que la Academia de Derocho Español, ... de la Capital de Mexico, da al supremo Congreso de las Cortes ... celebrada el dia 15 de Marzo de 1813. *Mexico.* 1814. 8vo. 48659

Tarifa o Arancel que para la esaccion del derecho de Alcabala debe observarse por ... los articulos del ramo del riento en la administracion principal de Rentas del departamento de Mexico ... comenzo á regir en 1° de enero de 1840. [n. p. n. d.] Folio, 8 leaves. 48660

Testamento de la Federacion Mexicana. Año de 1853. *Mexico.* 1853. 12mo, pp. 36. 48661

Constituciones de la real y pontificia Universidad de Mexico. Segunda edicion. ... *Mexico.* 1775. Folio, pp. xxxii, 238, xxi. + Suplemento ... . *Mexico.* 1839. Folio, pp. 14. 48662

Also: Estatos y Constituciones Reales de la Imperial y Regia Universidad de Mexico. *Mexico, por la Viuda de B. Bernardo Calderon.* [n. d.] Folio.

Vando sobre limpieza de las calles de Mexico, ... fecha en Mexico á 26 de Octre. de 1769. *Mexico.* 1769. 4to, pp. 18.

Varias observaciones contra un opúsculo titulado: Apuntamientos sobre derecco público ecclesiástico. *Mexico.* 1857. 4to.

See also No. 48280, *supra.*

Vindicacion de la Primera Sala de la Suprema Corte de Justicia de los Estados Unidos Mexicanos, sobre la acusacion hecho contra ella ante la Camara de Diputados del Congreso general, por la legislatura del Estado de Mexico. *Mexico.* 1834. 4to, pp. 38.

See "North American Review," XIV. 420; XXII. 461; XXXII. 317; XLIII. 226; *also* 'Quarterly Review," XXX. 152.

MEYEN (F. J. F.) Outlines of the Geography of Plants: with particular inquiries concerning the Native Country, the Culture, and the uses of the Principal Cultivated Plants on which the Prosperity of Nations is based. By Franz Julius Ferdinand Meyen, PH.D.M.D. ... Translated by Margaret Johnston. *London: For the Ray Society.* MDCCCXLVI. 8vo, pp. (2), x, 422, (16). A., C., H., S. 48666

Also with a title-page in German, with the imprint *Berlin*, 1836.

MEYEN. Reise um die Erde ausgeführt auf dem Königlich Preussischen Seehandlungs-Schiffe Prinzess Louise, commandirt von Capitain W. Wendt, in den Jahren 1830, 1831, und 1832. Von F. J. F. Meyen. *Berlin.* 1834–35. 2 vols., 4to, pp. vi, v–viii, 493; vi, 414, (2). Map and 3 Plates. A. 48667

MEYEN (J. J.) Franklin der Philosoph und Staatsmann. In fünf Gesängen, von Johann Jacob Meyen ... . *Alt-Stettin, bey Strucks Wittwe.* 1787. 8vo. 48668

A biography of Dr. Franklin in bad hexameters.

MEYER (A.) The Introduction of Paper Money involves the Abolishment of Taxation. By Albertus Meyer. [n. p. n. d.] 8vo, pp. 12. 48669

Dated, Oakland, California, March, 1865.

[MEYER.] ... The National Problem solved! ... *San Francisco.* 1867. 8vo, pp. 12. H. 48670

Also: An Address to the People. [n. p. 1869.] 8vo, pp. 18. H.

MEYER (E.) De plantis Labradoricis Libri Tres. ... *Lipsiæ.* 1830. 12mo. A. 48671

MEYER (Edward). Ministerial Perplexities and Solaces: ... Sermon ... Delaware and Chester Convocation, in the Diocese of Pennsylvania ... . *Philadelphia.* 1853. 8vo. S. 48672

MEYER (Georg Friedrich Wilhelm). Primitiæ Floræ Essequeboensis, adjectis descriptionibus centum circiter Stirpium novarum. Cum tabulis æreis duabus. *Goettingæ.* 1818. 4to, pp. 318. 2 Plates. 48673

MEYER (H. J.) Meyer's Universum, or Views of the remarkable Places and Objects of all Countries. Edited by C. A. Dana. Vol. I. *New York.* 1852. Obl. 4to. 48674

Includes some American views.

[MEYER (Isaac).] Presidential Power over Personal Liberty. A Review of Horace Binney's Essay on the Writ of Habeas Corpus. [*Philadelphia:*] *Imprinted for the Author.* 1862. 8vo, pp. 94, (2). 48675

MEYER (M.) Der Handel New York's im Jahre 1855. ... *New York.* 1856. 8vo. 48676

MEYERS (L.) Speech of Leon Meyers, on Compensation to American Ship Builders. February 28, 1865. [n. p. n. d.] 8vo.

MEYNARD DE QUEILHE (L. le). Outre Mer. *Paris.* 1835. 2 vols., 8vo. 48678

Relates to the war in Martinique. Printed on colored paper.

MEYNARDIE (E. J.) The Siege of Charleston; Its History and Progress. A Discourse, ... in ... Charleston, S. C., November 19, 1863, (Thanksgiving Day.) By Rev. E. J. Meynardie. *Columbia: Evans & Cogswell.* 1864. 8vo, pp. 15. BA. 48679

MIALL (C.) The Proposed Slave Empire: its Antecedents, Constitution, and Policy. By Charles Miall. *London.* 1863. 8vo. C. 48680

MIALL (J. G.) Footsteps of our Forefathers: What they Suffered and what they Sought. ... By James G. Miall. ... *Boston: Gould and Lincoln.* 1852. 12mo, pp. 352. H. 48681

MIAMI, *Ohio.* Laws relating to The Miami University, together with the Ordinances ... to which is added a Table of the Lots and Lands belonging to the University. ... *Cincinnati: Printed by F. S. Benton.* 1833. 8vo, pp. 148. C. 48682

Also: Addresses at the Inauguration of Rev. E. D. MacMaster, as President of Miami University, Ohio, August 13th, 1845. *Cincinnati: Printed ... by E. Shepard.* 1845. 8vo, pp. 64. — A Catalogue of the Honorary and Ordinary Members of the Erodelphian Society of Miami University ... . *Cincinnati: Corey & Webster.* 1835. 8vo, pp. 17. — Two Addresses ... at Oxford, Ohio, on Occasion of the Inauguration of Rev. Geo. Junkin, D.D. as President ... . *Cincinnati.* 1841. 8vo, pp. 48. — Third Triennial Catalogue of the Officers and Graduates ... . *Oxford, Ohio.* 1840. 12mo, pp. 42. Continued.

Manifesto and Declaration of the Free Associate Presbytery of Miami. *Xenia.* 1843. 8vo, pp. 21. 48683

Minutes of Anniversaries of the Miami Association of Regular Baptists held in ... 1850. *Cincinnati.* 1850. 8vo. Continued. 48684

MIAMI COUNTY. Report by G. C. Swallow, State Geologist, on the Survey of Miami County. *Kansas City, Mo.* 1865. 8vo.

Michael Bonham. *See* [Simms (W. G.)]

MICHAELER (K.) Ueber die ältesten Völkerstämme und ihre Wanderungen nebst Verpflanzung nach Amerika. *Wien.* 1802. 8vo. 48686

MICHAELIS (G.) De Antipodibus. *Wittebergae.* 1677. 4to.

I find this title in a European catalogue of Americana.

MICHAELIUS (J.) The First Minister of the Dutch Reformed Church in the United States. Letter from Jonas Michaelius from Manhatas in New Netherland, 11th August, 1628. Translated and printed for private distribution by Henry C. Murphy, Esq. *The Hague.* [1858.] 8vo, pp. 25. 48688

Very scarce, as but few copies were printed, all for presentation.

[MICHAUS (J. M.)] Certamen cientifico. *See* No. 48336.

MICHAUX (A.) Mémoire sur les causes de la fièvre jaune. Le concours simultané de trois causes est nécessaire au développement de la fièvre jaune, ou Résultat d'observations faites dans les ports de mer des États-Unis de l'Amérique du Nord. Par André-Michaux ... . *Paris: J. B. Baillière.* 1852. 12mo, pp. 48 or less.

MICHAUX (A.) Flora Boreali-Americana, sistens caracteres Plantarum quas in America Septentrionali collegit et detexit Andreas Michaux, ... Tabulis æneis 51 ornata. *Typis Caroli Crapelet Parisiis & Argentorati, Apud fratres Levrault. Anno* XI–1803. 2 vols., 4to, pp. x, (1), 330; (4), 340. 51 Plates. A., C.

Also on large vellum paper. The collation varies slightly in some copies. The work was republished with new titles only, *Paris*, 1820, and copies are sometimes made up of both issues. *See also* Brunet (O.), III. 8754–55.

MICHAUX. Histoire des Chênes de l'Amérique, ou Descriptions et Figures de toutes les espèces et variétés de Chênes de l'Amérique Septentrionale, Considérées sous les rapports de la Botanique, de leur culture et de leur usage. Par André Michaux, ... *A Paris, de l'Imprimerie de Crapelet. An* IX–1801. Folio, pp. (4), 7, (44). 36 Plates of Oaks by Redouté. A., B., C. 48691

Some copies are printed on fine paper.

MICHAUX. Andreas Michaux Geschichte der Amerikanischen Eichen ... Uebersetzt und mit illuminirten Abbildungen begleitet von Hofr. und Prof. J. S. Kerner ... . *Stuttgart.* 1802–4. 2 parts, 4to. 14 Plates, mostly colored. 48692

MICHAUX (F. A.) Histoire des Arbres Forestiers de l'Amérique Septentrionale, Considérées principalement sous les rapports de leur usage dans les Arts et de leur introduction dans le Commerce ... . Par F^s^. André-Michaux ... . *Paris, de l'Imprimerie de L. Haussmann et d'Hautel.* M.D.CCC.X–XIII. 3 vols., rl. 8vo, pp. (8), 222, (1); (4), 280; (4), 408, (2). 145 Plates. C., P. 48693

Rich and two other catalogues say 156 plates. Some copies of this edition were printed in 4to, with the plates plain and colored, making four volumes. Indeed, the work has assumed so many variations both as to its titles and dates, as well in English as in French, that I can do no more than caution the buyer to carefully collate before buying, and remark that for beauty in the coloring of the plates the Paris editions are preferable, having been executed under the author's supervision. Some copies are complete in two volumes.

MICHAUX. The North American Sylva, or, A Description of the Forest Trees of the United States, Canada and Nova Scotia; ... . To which is added a Description of the most useful of the European Forest Trees. Illustrated by 156 Coloured Engravings. Translated from the French of F. Andrew Michaux ... [by Augustus L. Hillhouse]. *Paris: Printed by C. D'Hautel.* 1819–18–19. 3 vols., 8vo, pp. (6), v, 268; (4), 247; (4), 285, (1). 156 Plates. C., H., P. 48694

Of the various editions with the text in English this, notwithstanding some typographical errors, is the best. Some copies of this edition were issued complete in *two* volumes, pp. (6), v, 383; (4), 417, (1). 156 Plates.

MICHAUX. The North American Sylva [as before]. *Philadelphia: Thomas Dobson.* 1817–19. 3 vols., imp. 8vo, pp. (4), xii, 268, (1); (4), 250; (4), 285, (1). 150 Plates. A., BA. + With Notes, by J. Jay Smith. *Philadelphia: Robert P. Smith.* 1850–51. 3 vols., imp. 8vo, pp. viii, 123; 128; (2), 143. 156 Plates. B. 48695

Reprinted in 1852, 1853, 1859, 1865, and other later dates, with collations which vary somewhat. The early editions are preferable. Rich, II. 364, remarks: "In 1840, a new edition of the English translation was printed at New Harmony, on very bad paper, and with a worn out type, and, contrary to the intentions of Mr. Maclure, put at so high a price, that few copies were sold. Latterly, all the remaining copies were destroyed by a fire on the premises where they were stored." I have never seen a copy of this Indiana edition. For a continuation, *see* Nuttall (T.), which continuation is now always added by the publisher. Of the two works united, it is no exaggeration to remark that it is the most complete work of its kind, and is a production of unrivalled interest and beauty, giving descriptions and illustrations of all the forest trees of North America, from the arctic limits of arborescent vegetation to the confines of the tropical circle.

MICHAUX. Histoire des Chênes de l'Amérique Septentrionale, considérés principalement sous les Rapports de leur usage dans les Arts et de lear Introduction dans le Commerce, Par F^s^. André-

Michaux ... . *Paris: L. Haussmann et D'Hautel.* M.D.CCC.XI. Imp. 8vo, pp. (4), 128, (1). B. 48696

MICHAUX. Histoire des Pins et des Sapins de l'Amérique Septentrionale ... Par F^s^. André-Michaux ... . *Paris.* 1810. Folio. 48697

MICHAUX. Mémoire sur la naturalisation des Arbres Forestiers de l'Amérique Septentrionale ... . Par F. A. Michaux. *Paris: De l'Imprimerie de Madame Huzard. An* XIII–1805. 12mo, pp. 36, folded leaf. C., H. 48698

Extracted from the "Mémoires de la Société du département de la Seine," tome VII.

MICHAUX. Notice sur les Isles Bermudas, et particulièrement sur l'Isle St. George. [n. p. n. d.] 4to. 48699

MICHAUX. Oaks of the United States and of Canada. *Sold at Philadelphia, London, Paris.* 18—. Text, pp. 2. 26 Plates, folded as 8vo. P., S. 48700

MICHAUX. Quercus; or, Oaks. From the French of Michaux, Histoire des Chênes de l'Amérique Septentrionale. With Notes and an Appendix by Walter Wade, Esq., M.L.S. ... *Dublin.* 1809. Rl. 8vo, pp. 73. C., N. 48701

MICHAUX. Rapport sur les voyages de M. Michaux pour la naturalization des Arbres Forestiers des États-Unis, fait à la Société d'Agriculture du departement de la Seine par MM. Allaire, Bosc, etc. *Paris.* 1809. 8vo, pp. 11. P. 48702

A corrected title of our No. 776, Vol. I.

MICHAUX. Voyage à l'ouest des Monts Alléghanys, dans les États de l'Ohio, du Kentucky, et du Tennessée, et retour à Charleston par les Hautes-Carolines ... . Entrepris pendant l'an X–1802, sous les auspices de ... M. Chaptal ... . Par F. A. Michaux, M.D. ... *Paris: Levrault, Schoell et Compagnie.* 1804. 8vo, pp. (4), vi, 312. Map. BA., C. + *Paris: Dentu.* 1808. 8vo, pp. (4), vi, 312. Map. H. 48703

MICHAUX. Travels to the Westward of the Allegany Mountains, in the States of the Ohio, Kentucky, and Tennessee, and return to Charlestown, through the Upper Carolinas; containing details on the present State of Agriculture and the Natural Productions of these Countries; as well as information relative to the commercial connections of these States with those situated to the Eastward of the Mountains and with Lower Louisiana. Undertaken in the year X, 1802 ... . By F. A. Michaux, M.D. ...

Faithfully Translated from the Original French, by B. Lambert. *London: J. Mawman.* 1805. 8vo, pp. xv, 350. Map. C., P.

MICHAUX. Travels to the West of the Alleghany Mountains, in the States of Ohio, Kentucky, and Tennessea, and back to Charleston, by the Upper Carolines; comprising The most interesting Details on the present State of Agriculture, and the Natural produce of those Countries: Together with Particulars relative to the Commerce that exists between the above-mentioned States, and those situated East of the Mountains and Low Louisiana, Undertaken, in the Year 1802, ... By F. A. Michaux ... . Second Edition. *London: B. Crosby & Co.* 1805. 8vo, pp. xii, 294.

See "Monthly Review," LI. 272. The following is a different translation:

MICHAUX. Travels to the Westward of the Allegany Mountains, in the States of the Ohio, Kentucky, and Tennessee, in the Year 1802. ... By F. A. Michaux. Translated from the French. *London: Richard Phillips.* 1805. 8vo, pp. 96. 48706

Included in Vol. I. of Phillips' "Collection of Voyages."

MICHAUX. Michaux Reise in das Innere der Nordamerikanischen Freistaaten, westlich der Alleghany-Gebirge. Aus dem Französischen, mit Zusätzen von T. F. Ehrman. *Weimar.* 1805. 8vo. Map. 48707

MICHAUX (——). Mémoires et pièces justificatives adressées à la convention. *Paris.* [1793.] 8vo. 48708

MICHELBACHER (M. J.) A Sermon delivered On the Day of Prayer, Recommended by the President of the C. S. of A., the 27th of March, 1863, ... by the Rev. M. J. Michelbacher. *Richmond: Macfarlane & Fergusson.* 1863. 8vo, pp. 16.

MICHELENA Y RÓJAS (F.) Exploracion oficial ... desde el Norte de la America del Sur ... bajada del Amazonas hasta el Atlántico ... . Comprendiendo ... Viaje a Rio de Janeiro ... En los años, de 1855 hasta 1859 Por F. Michelena y Rójas ... . *Bruselas: A. Lacroix, ... y C^o^.* 1867. Rl. 8vo, pp. 684. B., S.

Account of an expedition undertaken by order of the Venezuelan Government. The expedition started from the mouth of the Orinoco and went up that river, crossed Ecuador and Peru on the Maranon and the Ucayali; thence down the river Amazon to Para, then to Rio de Janeiro by the Atlantic.

MICHENER (E.) A Retrospect of Early Quakerism; being Extracts from the Records of Philadelphia Yearly Meeting and the Meetings composing it. ... By Ezra Michener. *Philadelphia: T. Ellwood Zell.* 1860. 8vo, pp. 432. C. 48711

MICHIGAN.

Acte pour l'organization de la Milice de Michigan, approved April 21, 1825. *Detroit.* 1825. 8vo. 48712

Actes relatifs aux Townships, aux Grands Chemins, aux Elections, publié conformement a certaines Resolutions passées dans la Seconde Session du Second Conseil Législatif du Michigan. *Detroit.* 1827. 8vo. 48713

Acts passed at the Second Session of the First Legislative Council of the Territory of Michigan, 1825. *Detroit.* 1825. 8vo. Continued. 48714

Acts of the Legislature of the State of Michigan, passed at the Annual Session, 1831. *Detroit.* 1831. 8vo. Continued.

The Agricultural College of the State of Michigan. *Lansing, Michigan: Hosmer & Fitch, ... Printers.* 1857. 8vo, pp. 58.

Also: Catalogue of Officers and Students ... . *Lansing.* 1857. 8vo. — State Agricultural College, Michigan. 1866. Report of the President. [n. p. n. d.] 8vo, pp. 30.

Annual Report of the Secretary of the State Board of Agriculture ... for ... 1862. ... *Lansing: John A. Kerr & Co., Printers ...* 1862. 8vo, pp. 50. Continued. B. 48717

Also: Report of the Committee on Agriculture. February 22, 1839. [n. p. n. d.] 8vo, pp. 3. — Transactions of the State Agricultural Society ... . *Lansing: R. W. Ingals, ... Printer.* 1850. 8vo, pp. 234. Continued.

Annual Report of the Acting Superintendent of Indian Affairs for Michigan, made to the Bureau of Indian Affairs at Washington, ... 30th September, 1840. ... *Detroit.* 1840. 8vo, pp. 28.

Annual Report of the Adjutant and Quarter-Master General, for ... 1848. [*Lansing.* 1848.] 8vo, pp. 35, 12 folded leaves. Continued. B. 48719

The Reports for 1861–4 contain copious details relative to the Civil War.

Annual Report of the Attorney-General, January 1, 1850. [n. p. 1850.] 8vo, pp. 52. Continued. 48720

Also: Annual Report ... of the Auditor General for ... 1844. [*Detroit?* 1844.] 8vo, pp. 25. Continued. — ... Annual Report of the Board of Internal Improvement. ... 1844. [n. p. 1845] 8vo, pp. 40. H.

Annual Report of the Commissioner of the Land Office ... for ... 1857. ... *Lansing: Hosmer & Kerr, Printers.* 1857. 8vo, pp. 21. H. 48721

... Annual Report of the Superintendent of Public Instruction. ... 1837. [By John D. Pierce. *Detroit.* 1837.] 8vo, pp. 78. Continued. B. 48722

Also: Annual Report of the Baptist Convention of the State ... . *Detroit.* 1835. 8vo. Continued. — Proceedings of the Baptist Convention of ... Michigan. *Detroit.* 1843. 8vo.

Appeal by the Convention of Michigan to the People of the United States, with other Documents, in relation to the Boundary Question between Michigan and Ohio. ... *Detroit: Sheldon McKnight, Printer.* 1835. 8vo, pp. 176. 48723

Des Auswanderers Wegweiser. *See* [Thomson (E. H.)]

Census and Statistics, condensed for publication by Secretary of State, May, 1854. *Lansing: G. W. Peck.* 1854. 8vo, pp. 413. Continued. C. 48724

A Compilation from the Annual Reports of the Superintendent of Public Instruction of ... Michigan, for ... 1845 and '46, with ... Additions ... . Prepared ... By Ira Mayhew ... . *Detroit: Bagg & Harmon, Printers ...* . 1848. 8vo, pp. 176. B. 48725

The Compiled Laws of the State of Michigan. ... Compiled and Arranged, ... By Thomas M. Cooley. ... *Lansing: Hosmer & Kerr, Printers.* 1857. 2 vols., 8vo, pp. viii, 807; vii, 811–1785. H. 48726

Constitution of the State of Michigan, as adopted in Convention, Detroit, ... 1835. *Detroit.* 1835. 8vo, pp. 20. P.

Also: Constitution of Michigan, adopted in 1850. In Dutch and English [n. p.] 1851. 8vo. + Constitution ... 1867. *Detroit.* 1867. 8vo.

The Debates and Proceedings of the Constitutional Convention of ... Michigan ... 1867. Official Report by W. B. Lord, and D. W. Brown. *Lansing: John A. Kerr & Co., Printers.* 1867. 2 vols., 4to, pp. lxiv, 664; 1072. C., S. 48728

Documents accompanying the Journal of the Senate of ... Michigan at the Annual Session of 1836. *Detroit.* 1836. 8vo. Continued. C. 48729

Documents communicated to the Senate and House of Representatives, Session 1842–[43]. *Detroit.* 1842–3. 8vo. Cont'd.

Also: Documents accompanying the Journal of the House of Representatives of the State of Michigan, for 1838. *Detroit.* 1838. 8vo. Continued.

The Emigrant's Guide. *See* [Thomson (E. H.)]

Executive Journal of the Senate of ... Michigan at the Annual Session of 1835. *Detroit.* 1835. 8vo. Continued.

A Gazetteer of Michigan, including a History of that State. *Detroit.* 1840. 12mo. 48732

Geology. ... Report of the State Geologist [Douglass Houghton. n. p. 1838.] 8vo, pp. 37, (1). + Second ... Report. *Detroit.* 1839. 8vo, pp. 39, 123. B. 48733

Third Annual Report of the Geological Survey of the State of Michigan. [*Detroit.* 1840.] 8vo, pp. 124. + Fourth ... Report. *Detroit.* 1841. 8vo, pp. 184. Continued. H. 48734

First Biennial Report of the Progress of the Geological Survey of Michigan, embracing Observations on the Geology, Zoölogy and Botany of the Lower Peninsula. Made [by A. Winchell] to the Governor, December 31, 1860. ... *Lansing: Hosmer & Kerr, Printers ...* . 1861. 8vo, pp. 339. C., S. 48735

... Geological Report of Bela Hubbard on Survey of Township Lines in 1845–46. *Washington.* 1849. 8vo, pp. 132. 7 Plates, 5 Maps. 48736

... Report on the Geological and Mineralogical Survey of the Mineral Lands of the United States in ... Michigan. By Charles T. Jackson ... . *Washington.* 1849. 8vo, pp. 234. 6 Maps.

... Synopsis of the Exploration of the Geological Corps in the Lake Superior Land District in ... Michigan under the Direction of J. W. Foster and J. D. Whitney ... . *Washington.* 1849. 8vo, pp. 196. 48738

Also: Communication from the State Geologist, March 11, 1839. [n. p. n. d.] 8vo. — ... Report of the Joint Committee relative to the Geological Survey. [n. p. 1846.] 8vo, pp. 7, (1). — ... Report of the State Geologist in relation to the improvement of State Salt Springs. ... 1839. [n. p. 1840.] 8vo, pp. 8. *See also* Foster (J. W.), Vol. VI., No. 25249.

Historical and Scientific Sketches. *See* Vol. VIII., No. 32062.

Inaugural Address of the Governor. [n. p. 1846.] 8vo, pp. 30. Continued. H. 48739

In English and French.

The Inaugural Message of the Governor of Michigan. ... January 4, 1855. *Lansing: Geo. W. Peck, Printer.* 1855. 8vo, pp. 26. Continued. H. 48740

Also: Gov. Blair's Inaugural Message to the Legislature, for ... 1861. *Lansing: Hosmer & Kerr.* 1861. 8vo, pp. 24. + Message ... Extra Session, January 2, 1862. [n. p. n. d.] 8vo, pp. 11. Continued.

The Iron Resources of Michigan. *See* Vol. IX., No. 35098.

Joint Documents of the Senate and House of Representatives. Session 1841. *Detroit.* 1841. 8vo. Continued. 48741

Journal of the House of Representatives ... 1837. *Detroit: John S. Bagg, ... Printer.* 1837. 8vo, pp. 629. Continued. H.

Journal of the Proceedings of the Convention, held at Ann Arbor, 14th December, 1836, in regard to the Admission of Michigan into the Union. *Ann Arbor, Michigan.* 1836. 8vo.

Journal of the Legislative Council of the Territory of Michigan, ... 1825. *Detroit.* 1825. 8vo. Continued to 1834.

Journals of the Senate of the State of Michigan, ... 1835 and 1836. ... *Detroit: John S. Bagg, Printer.* 1836. 8vo, pp. 396, (6), 45, xxxiii. Continued. H. 48745

Laws of Michigan. Vol. I. *City of Washington.* 1806. 8vo.

Laws of the Territory of Michigan; with Marginal Notes and an Index; To which are prefixed, the Ordinance and several Acts of Congress relating to this Territory. ... *Detroit: Printed by Sheldon & Reed.* 1820. 8vo, pp. 517. BA., C., S.

Also: Laws of the Territory of Michigan ... revised by Commissioners appointed by the First Legislative Council and passed by the Second Council. ... *Detroit.* 1827. 8vo, pp. 709. — Laws of the Territory of Michigan, condensed, arranged and passed by the Fifth Legislative Council. *Detroit.* 1833. 8vo.

Laws of the State of Michigan, passed at the adjourned session of 1837, and the regular session of 1838. *Detroit.* 1838. 8vo. Continued. 48748

Also: Laws concerning the Record, ... of Marriage. *Lansing.* 1867. 8vo. — Laws ... relative to Highways and Bridges, and the Duties of Highway Commissioners ... . *Lansing: Hosmer & Fitch, Printers.* 1857. 8vo, pp. 29. H.

Legislative Excursion, February, 1869. *Lansing.* 1869. 8vo.

Manual, containing the Rules of the Senate and House of Representatives ... . And other matter. *Detroit: Bagg and Harmon, Printers.* 1846. 16mo, pp. 55, (1). Continued. H. 48750

Manual of the Grand Army of the Republic, together with Memorial Day in the Department of Michigan. May, 1869. *Lansing.* 1869. 8vo. 48751

Memorial of the Legislative Council of the Territory of Michigan, to the Congress of the United States, Adopted Aug. 4, 1824. *Detroit: Printed by Sheldon & Reed.* 1824. 8vo, pp. 15.

Also: Memorial for erecting Wisconsin Territory, 1832. [n. p. n. d.] 8vo. — — Memorial to Congress [by the Legislative Council], in favor of Erection of the Territory of Wisconsin. [*Washington.* 1834.] 8vo. — [Another Memorial by the same,] for the Establishment of a separate Territorial Government for Wisconsin. [*Washington.* 1834.] 8vo. *See also* Vol. XI., No. 47728.

... Message of Governor Stevens T. Mason, to the Senate ... of Michigan, February 1, 1836. *Detroit: L. Le Grand Morse,* ... 1836. 8vo, pp. 27. Continued. B. 48753

Message of the Acting Governor Stevens T. Mason to the Legislative Council of the Territory of Michigan, August, 1835. *Detroit.* 1835. 8vo. 48754

Message from the President ... transmitting a Report from the Governor, and Presiding Judge of ... Michigan, relative to the State of that Territory. ... *City of Washington: A. & G. Way, Printers.* 1805. 8vo, pp. 16. BA. 48755

... Michigan, seine Vorzüge und Hülfsquellen. ... Herausgegeben von M. L. Allardt ... . *Frankfurt am Main: Im Selbstverlage des Herausgebers.* 1869. 8vo, pp. 80. Map. H. 48756

The Michigan Almanac ... 1870. Charles K. Backus, Compiler. *Detroit.* 1869. 12mo. C. 48757

Minutes of the Nineteenth Session of the Michigan Annual Conference of the Methodist-Episcopal Church, Ann Arbor, 1854. *Ann Arbor.* 1854. 8vo, pp. 48. Continued. 48758

Biennial Report of the Trustees of the Michigan Asylum for the Insane, for ... 1859 and 1860. *Lansing.* 1861. 8vo. Continued. 48759

Catalogue of the Officers and Students of the Michigan Central College ... 1850. *Jackson: Printed by R. S. Cheney.* 1850. 8vo, pp. 16. H. 48760

First Annual Report of the Directors of the Michigan Central Railroad Company, June, 1847. *Detroit.* 1847. 8vo, pp. 13. Continued. 48761

Also: Circular of the Treasurer of the ... Company, ... December 26, 1855. *Boston: J. H. Eastburn's Press.* 1855. 8vo, pp. 20. — Contract between the Mich. Central R. R. Co. and the Galena and Chicago Union Rail Road. *Detroit.* 1851. 8vo, pp. 14. — Laws and Charters in Michigan, Indiana, and Illinois, under which the Michigan Central Road, and its Connections with Chicago, have been constructed.

Detroit: W. F. Storey. 1856. 8vo, pp. (2), 107. — Report upon the Merits of the Michigan Central Railroad. By J. W. Brooks. With the Charter. *New York.* 1846. 8vo, pp. 24, 31. + *Detroit: Charles Willcox, Printer.* 1846. 8vo, pp. 5–64. — Verslag van de directie der Michigan Central spoorweg-maatschappij, aan de aandeelhouders ... Junij 1869. ... *Amsterdam: Loman en Verster.* 1869. 8vo, pp. 15.

The Michigan Farmer. ... November, 1852. ... Warren Isham, Editor. *Detroit.* 1852. Folio. Continued. H. 48762

Annual Catalogue of the Officers and Pupils of the Michigan Female Seminary ... 1862–63; ... *Detroit, Mich.* 1863. 8vo, pp. 21. Continued. H. 48763

Michigan First Regiment. Incidents, Marches, Battles and Camp Life; and the Adventures of the Author, known as the Indiana Banker ... . *Detroit: The Author.* 1861. 8vo, pp. 9.

The Michigan Freemason; A Monthly Magazine ... . *Kalamazoo, Michigan: Chaplin, Ibling & Rix.* 1869. 8vo. Cont'd.

Also: Proceedings of the Grand Council of Royal and Select Masters of the State of Michigan ... June 5, 1861. *Detroit: H. Barns & Co.* 1861. 12mo, pp. 20, (3).

... The Michigan Journal of Education and Teachers' Magazine ... . Edited ... by John M. Gregory, A.M. ... *Detroit.* 1853. 8vo. Continued. H. 48766

Circular Statement of the Condition and Prospects of the Michigan Southern Railroad, ... 1849. *New York.* 1849. 8vo.

The Michigan Southern and Northern Indiana Railroad Business Gazetteer. Compiled ... by C. E. Brown. Vol. I. *Chicago.* 1868. 8vo. C. 48768

Also: Charter and Laws of the States of Ohio, Indiana, Michigan and Illinois, relating to the Michigan Southern and Northern Indiana Railroad Company. *New York.* 1855. 8vo. — Report of the Directors ... March 28, 1859. *New York.* 1859. 8vo. Continued.

Michigan State Gazetteer and Business Directory for 1863–4, embracing Historical and Descriptive Sketches of all the Cities, Towns, and Villages throughout the State ... . *Detroit: Charles F. Clarke.* 1863. 8vo, pp. 611. Plates. + Second Edition. [*Ibid.*] Continued. B. 48769

Michigan State Gazetteer, Shippers' Guide, and Business Directory for 1865. *Indianapolis: George W. Hawes.* [n. d.] 8vo, pp. 393. 48770

Catalogue of the Michigan State Library ... 1855. *Lansing.* 1855. 8vo, pp. 42. + For ... 1859. *Lansing.* 1859. 8vo, pp. 63. 48771

Catalogue of the Michigan State Normal School, Teachers' Institute, Teachers' Association ... . *Detroit.* 1853. 8vo. S.

Also: Fourth Annual Report of the ... State Reform School ... . 1860. ... *Lansing: Hosmer & Kerr, Printers.* 1861. 8vo, pp. 51. Plate. Continued. — Catalogue of State Teachers' Institute. ... 1859. *Lansing.* 1859. 8vo.

... The Michigan Teacher ... . William H. Payne, ... C. L. Whitney, ... [Editors]. Vol. I. ... *Niles, Michigan: Payne & Whitney.* 1866. 8vo. Portrait. Continued. H. 48773

The Militia Laws of the Territory of Michigan. *Detroit.* 1833. 8vo. 48774

Minutes of the General Association of Michigan, ... 1847. *Detroit.* 1847. 8vo. Continued. 48775

Opinion of the Attorney General [J. M. Howard] of ... Michigan, construing the General Banking Law of the State. ... *Lansing: John A. Kerr & Co., Printers ...* . 1863. 12mo, pp. 12.

Pastoral Letter of the Synod of Michigan. *Detroit.* 1862. 8vo, pp. 11. B. 48777

Signed by George Duffield, Chairman; Alanson Scofield, and Elder Wood, Committee.

Primary School Law with Notes and Forms. *Detroit.* 1847. 8vo. 48778

Journal of the Annual Convention of the Protestant Episcopal Church of the Diocese of Michigan. [n. p.] 1834. 8vo. Continued. 48779

Report of a Committee of the House of Representatives, transmitting a Report from the Governor and Presiding Judge of the Territory of Michigan, relative to the State of the Territory. *City of Washington.* 1806. 8vo. C. 48780

Report of Committee of Ways and Means. [n. p. 1846.] 8vo, pp. 13, Errata, 6 lines. H. 48781

Report of the Committee on Internal Improvements; made to the House of Representatives of ... Michigan, January 24, 1837. *Detroit: John S. Bagg, Printer ...* . 1837. 8vo, pp. 17.

Report of the Finance Committee. [n. p. 1846.] 8vo, pp. 21

On the canals and railroads of Michigan.

Report of the Great Conspiracy Case. The People of the State ... *versus* Abel F. Fitch and Others, commonly called The

Rail Road Conspirators: ... *Detroit.* 1851. 8vo, pp. 175, 283, 399, (1), Index and Appendix, (8). B. 48784

Report of the Quartermaster General, November 30, 1861. [n. p. n. d.] 8vo. + For 1862. 8vo, pp. 24. + For 1863. 8vo, pp. 19. Continued. 48785

... Report of the Special Committee appointed to inquire into the Military Expenditures of the State during ... [1861.] [n. p. 1862.] 8vo, pp. 104. H. 48786

Report of the Special Committee appointed ... to investigate the Proceedings, &c., of the ... Boards of Internal Improvement. *Detroit: Dawson & Bates, Printers.* 1840. 8vo, pp. x, (2), 618 [*i. e.* 518]. 48787

Report of the State Librarian of Michigan, ... 1867 and 1868. ... *Lansing: John A. Kerr & Co., Printers ...* . 1868. 8vo, pp. 30. Continued. B. 48788

... Report of the Superintendent of Public Instruction. ... 1839. [n. p. n. d.] 8vo, pp. 40. Continued. B. 48789

Report relative to the Contested Election for Delegate to Congress ... . *Detroit.* 1825. 4to. 48790

Report to the Governor of the State of Michigan, on the Soldiers' National Monument at Gettysburg, 1864. [n. p. n. d.] 8vo, pp. 6. 48791

Reports of Clinton and Kalamazoo Canal, April 11, 1839. [n. p. n. d.] 8vo. 48792

Revised Constitution of Michigan, 1850. [n. p. n. d.] 8vo.

The Revised Statutes of ... Michigan. Passed at the ... Sessions of 1837, and ... 1838. Printed and published ... under the Supervision and Direction of E. B. Harrington and E. J. Roberts. *Detroit: John S. Bagg, Printer.* 1838. 8vo, pp. 817. H. + Under the Superintendence of Sanford M. Green. *Detroit.* 1846. 8vo, pp. 829. C., S. 48794

School Funds and School Laws of Michigan: with Notes and Forms. ... *Lansing: Hosmer & Kerr, Printers.* 1859. 8vo, pp. viii, (1), 448. Plate. + *Lansing.* 1864. 8vo. + *Lansing: W. S. George & Co.* 1869. 8vo, pp. 186. 12 Plates. C. 48795

First Annual Report of the Secretary of State ... relating to ... Births, Marriages and Deaths, for ... 1868. *Lansing: John A. Kerr & Co., Printers* ... . 1868. 8vo, pp. vii, 96. Continued.

Also: Annual Report of the Secretary of State relating to Insurance. *Lansing*. 1870. 8vo. Continued.— ... Annual Report of the State Treasurer. ... 1844. [*Detroit?* 1845.] 8vo, pp. 10. Continued. H.

Some of the Acts of the Territory of Michigan, and now in force, March 20, 1816. *Detroit*. 1816. 8vo. 48797

State of Michigan. Message ... [on] admitting Michigan into the Union as an independent State. December 27, 1836. [n. p. 1836.] 8vo, pp. 60. 48798

State of Michigan. Legislature, 1847. Governor's Message. [n. p. n. d.] 8vo, pp. 18. H. 48799

Statistics of the State of Michigan, compiled from the Census of 1860 ... . *Lansing: John A. Kerr & Co., Printers*. 1861. 8vo, pp. 334 [*i. e.* 344]. Continued. H. 48800

Statutes of the State ... relating to Primary Schools, ... with explanatory Notes, &c. prepared ... By Ira Mayhew ... . *Detroit: Bagg & Harmon, Printers* ... . 1847. 8vo, pp. 102. B. 48801

System of Public Instruction and Primary School Law of Michigan ... . Prepared by Francis W. Shearman ... . *Lansing, Michigan: Ingals, Hedges & Co., Printers*. 1852. 8vo, pp. xv, 640. Plate. H. 48802

To Emigrants; John Almy, State Agent, 1845. *New-York*. 1845. 12mo, pp. 7. S. 48803

UNIVERSITY OF MICHIGAN. A General Catalogue of the Officers and Graduates from ... 1837 to 1864. *Ann Arbor: The University*. 1864. 8vo, pp. 40. H. 48804

Also: Annual Report of the President for 1866 ... . *Ann Arbor: Dr. Chase's ... Printing House*. [1866.] 8vo, pp. 18.—Catalogue of the Library of the University of Michigan. 1846. *Ann Arbor*. 1846. 8vo, pp. 48.—Catalogue of the Officers & Students, of the University of Michigan, 1850–51. *Detroit: Duncle, Wales & Co., Printers*. 1851. 8vo, pp. xxxii. Continued.—Catalogue of the Officers and Students in the Department of Arts and Sciences, 1843–4. *Ann Arbor*. 1843. 8vo. Continued.—Constitutional Provisions, Laws and By-Laws of the University of Michigan. Revised edition; adopted February 16, 1864. *Ann Arbor: The University*. 1864. 8vo, pp. 31.— ... Petition of the Board of Regents ... . [n. p. 1867.] 8vo, pp. 12.—Report of the Board of Regents on Public Instruction. *Detroit*. 1841. 8vo.—Report to the Board of Regents of the University of Michigan, made November 15th, 1853, by Henry P. Tappan, D.D., Chancellor ... . *Ann Arbor: Cole & Gardiner, Printers*. 1853. 8vo, pp. 32. Continued.— ... President Haven's Annual Message to the Fourth Moot Congress of the Law Department. ... Dec. 3, 1864. ... [n. p.] 1865. 8vo, pp.

20. *See also* "North American Review," XLIV. 55; "Journal of Sciences," x. 304; "Hunt's Magazine," VI. 333 and XIX. 9.

MICHILIMACKINAC. Ancient and Modern Michilimackinac, including an Account of the Controversy between Mackinac and the Mormons. [n. p.] 1854. 8vo, pp. 48. C. 48805

See also "Letters to an Officer," Vol. IX., No. 40638.

MICHLER (N.) Report ... Lieutenant Michler's Report of his Survey for an Interoceanic Ship Canal near the Isthmus of Darien ... 1861. *Washington*. 1861. 8vo, pp. 457. Maps.

MICHOACAN. El Cabildo de Michoacan, para manifestar que no fue arbitraria la declaracion que hizo contra D. Martin Gil y Garces, privandole de la Dignidad de Dean de aquella santa iglesia, presenta al publico los hechos é irrefragables constancias que justifican sus procedimientos. *Mexico*. 1831. 8vo. 48807

See also Gil y Garces (M.), Vol. VII., No. 27344, *and* [Queipo (Manuel Abad)].

Constitucion politica del estado de Michoacan, sancionada por el Congreso Constituyente en 19 de Julio de 1825. *Mexico: J. Ximeno*. 1825. 18mo, pp. 78, (4). 48808

Decretos del Congreso Constituyente del Estado de Michoacan, desde 6 de Abril de 1824, hasta 21 de Julio de 1825, en que cesó, los decretos del segundo congreso constitucional, 1827–29. *Mexico*. 1828. 8vo. Continued. C. 48809

Dictamen sobre diezmos y vacantes, presentado por la comision de justicia del honorable congreso del estado de Michoacan, y aprobado por este en el mes de septiembre de 1852. [Escrito por Francisco Garcia Anaya.] *Mexico: I. Cumplido*. 1856. 18mo, pp. 93. C. 48810

Esposicion hecha al Exmo. St. General D. Epitacio Huerta, por el C. Juan Aldaiturreaga al separarse de la Secretaria del Supremo Gobierno de Michoacan. *Morelia*. 1860. 4to, pp. 50

Expression de Michoacan que haze D. Rodrigo Alvarez de Sobrino, para la revocacion que pretende de la Sentencia pronunciada por esta Real Audiencia en 3 Sept. de 1720 ... en el Pleyto con la Provincia de San Nicolas de Michocan. *Mexico*. 1721. Folio. 48812

Historia de la Provincia de Michoacan del Ordre de S. Augustin, de San Nicolas de Tolentino, en el tiempo que fue una con la del S. Nombre de Jesus de Mexico. *Mexico*. [1533.] Sm. 4to.

An imperfect title from "Trübner's Record."

Informes dados al Supremo Gobierno de la Republica por las autoridades superiores del departamento de Michoacan, acerca de la solicitud del S. Ayuntamiento de Colima, y sub-prefectura de Almoloyan, dirigida a que aquel distrito sea declarado nuevamente territorio. *Morelia*. 1845. 4to, pp. 28. 48814

Relacion sencilla del funeral y exequias de Antonio de San Miguel Iglesias, obispo ... de Michoacan. *Mexico*. 1805. 8vo.

Renuncia justificada del Gobernador interino del estado de Michoacan, Senador al Congreso de la Union, Joaquin Caballero. *Morelia*. 1833. 4to, pp. 38. 48816

Also: La Banderar roja. Periódico semioficial del Estado de Michoacan. *Morelia*. 1859–62. 2 vols., folio. *See also* our Vol. IV., No. 13789.

MICHOACANOS. De el Sr. Cevallos, de la situacion actual, del Plan de Jalisco, y de General Uraga. Por unos Michoacanos. *Mexico*. 1853. 4to, pp. 11. 48817

MICKLE (I.) Reminiscences of Old Gloucester: or Incidents in the History of the Counties of Gloucester, Atlantic and Camden, New Jersey. ... By Isaac Mickle ... . *Philadelphia: Townsend Ward*. 1845. 8vo, pp. (4), 98, Errata, 21 lines. Plate.

MICKLEY (J. J.) Dates of United States Coins, and their Degrees of Rarity. ... [By] Jos. J. Mickley. ... [*Philadelphia?*] *Auner, Printer*. [1858.] 8vo, pp. (4). H. 48819

Also: Catalogue of the Numismatic Collection formed by Joseph J. Mickley, Esq. [By W. E. Woodward.] *Roxbury*. 1867. 8vo, pp. 196, (1), Errata.

[MICKLEY (J. M.)] *See* Vol. VI., No. 25181, for pp. 8 *read* 88

MICMAC. The Report ... on the Micmac Mission. From Nov. 1849, to Oct. 1850. ... *Halifax, N. S.* 1850. 8vo, pp. 11

Also: The Fifth Annual Report of the Micmac Missionary Society. From ... 1850, to ... 1851. *Halifax, N. S.* 1851. 8vo, pp. 15. Continued. H. *See also* our Vol. I., No. 94, *and* Maillard (P.), Vol. XI, No. 43887.

[MICOUD D'UMONS (Ch. E.)] Sur les finances, le commerce, la marine et les colonies. *Paris: H. Agasse*. *An* X.–1802. 2 vols., 8vo, pp. (2), 223; (2), 267. H. 48821

Middelen en motiven. *See* [Muys van Holy (D.)]

The Middle District Association met at Cedar-Creek Meeting-House, May, 1791. *Richmond: Printed by Augustine Davis, Printer for the Public*. [1791.] 8vo. 48822

The Middle Line: or, an Attempt to Furnish Some Hints for ending the Differences subsisting between Great-Britain and the Colonies. *Philadelphia: Printed and sold by Joseph Crukshank* ... M.DCC.LXXV. 12mo, pp. 48. M., P. 48823

MIDDLEBOROUGH, *Mass.* Book of the First Church of Christ, in Middleborough, Plymouth County, Mass. With notices of other churches in that town. *Boston: C. C. P. Moody, Printer*. 1852. 8vo, pp. 72. S. 48824

Contains a historical notice of the First Church and two discourses by Israel W. Putnam, also chronological notice and catalogue from 1695 to 1853. *See also* [Eddy (Z.)], VI. 21819. Also: Catalogue of the Members of the First Church. *Boston*. 1854. 8vo.

Celebration of the Two-Hundredth Anniversary of the incorporation of Middleborough, Massachusetts, October 13, 1869. ... With an Appendix. ... *Middleborough*. 1870. 8vo, pp. 51, (1). Plate. H. 48825

The Confession of Faith and Church Covenant ... made ... by the Church of Middleborough, December 26, 1694. ... [*Boston: Re-printed in the Year* 1771.] 8vo, pp. 10. H., N., W. 48826

First Church in Middleborough, Mass: Mr. Putnam's Century and half Discourses: An Historical Account; and a Catalogue of Members. ... *Boston: C. C. P. Moody, Printer*. 1854. 8vo, pp. (4), 124. B., S. 48827

History of Middleborough, Mass. *Boston*. 1849. 8vo.

Report of the School Committee of the Town ... 1848. *Boston: Press of T. R. Marvin*. 1849. 8vo, pp. 8. Continued. H.

Also: Manual of the First Congregational Church. *Middleborough*. 1825. 8vo. *See also* Vol. I., No. 3240, *and* Peirce Academy.

MIDDLEBROOK (E.) Middlebrook's Astronomical Diary, Calendar, or Almanac, for ... 1811 ... . By Elijah Middlebrook. *New-Haven: Increase Cooke & Co.* [1810.] 12mo, pp. (36). H.

Continued to 1845 or later.

MIDDLEBROOK (G.) One Year of my Life. Eleanor Winthrop's Diary for 1869. By Grace Middlebrook. *Boston: D. Lothrop & Co.* 1870. 16mo, pp. 321. 3 Plates. C. 48831

MIDDLEBURY, *Vt.* Addresses and Proceedings at the Semi-Centennial Celebration of Middlebury College, held at Middlebury, Vermont, August 20, 21, and 22, 1850. *Middlebury: Printed by Justus Cobb*. 1850. 8vo, pp. viii, 179. H. 48832

Also: Addresses ... at the Inauguration of the Professors ... March 18, 1839. ... *Middlebury*. 1839. 8vo, pp. 56.—Addresses at the Inauguration of Rev. H. D. Kitchel, DD., President ... . *Middlebury*. 1866. 8vo, pp. 32. B.

Catalogue of ... the Library of Middlebury College. 1833. [n. p. 1833.] 8vo, pp. 29. H. 48833

Also: Catalogue of ... the Library of the Philological Society ... . *Middlebury: Printed by J. W. Copeland*. 1824. 8vo, pp. 60. H.

Catalogue of the Graduates ... embracing a Biographical Register and Directory. ... By Thomas Scott Pearson, A.B. *Windsor*. 1853. 8vo, pp. 144. B. 48834

Also: Catalogue of the Officers and Students of Middlebury College. October, 1818. *Middlebury, Vt.: Printed by Francis Burnap*. 1818. 8vo, pp. 8. Continued.

Catalogus Senatus Academice, et eorum, qui munera et officia academica gesserunt, quique alicujus gradus laurea exornati fuerunt, in Collegio Medioburiensi ... ab ... 1802 ad ... 1814. *Mediouriæ: Typis Timothei C. Strong*. 1814. 8vo, pp. 8. Continued. H. 48835

Concise Account of the Institution, Transactions and present Condition of the Middlebury College Charitable Society. *Middlebury, Vt.* 1817. 8vo. 48836

... Laws ... . *Middlebury: Printed by J. W. Copeland*. 1823. 8vo, pp. 24. Continued. H. 48837

Middlebury College and Vermont Academy of Medicine. Catalogue of the Faculty and Students ... 1821. ... [*Rutland: Wm. Fay's Print*. 1821.] 8vo, pp. 8. Continued. H. 48838

Necrological Report of Middlebury College for 1867. [n. p. n. d.] 8vo, pp. 8. 48839

Also: ... Inaugural Address of the Rev. Benjamin Labaree, President of Middlebury College ... May 18, 1841. ... *Middlebury: Printed by Ephraim Maxham*. 1841. 8vo, pp. 32. B. *See* "The Philomathesian."

MIDDLESEX, *Mass.* Transactions of the Middlesex Agricultural Society for ... 1856. *Concord*. 1856. 8vo, pp. 83. M.

Report of the Agent of the Middlesex Canal to the Proprietors, January, 1809. [*Boston*. 1809.] 8vo, pp. 8. Continued.

Also: Report of a Committee of the Directors ... 1811. [n. p.] 1811. 8vo, pp. 15. M.—Report of the Board of Directors ... by a Committee, April, 1817. *Boston*. [1817.] 8vo, pp. 20.—Report respecting the Business done on the Middlesex Canal, Mass. in 1805. [By James Sullivan. *Boston*. 1806.] 8vo. W. *See also* Vol. VI., No. 21804.

The Middlesex Collection of Church Music: or, Ancient Psalmody revived. ... Second Edition, revised ... . *Boston: Printed ... by Manning & Loring*. 1808. Oblong 8vo, pp. 167, (1). H.

Also: The Middlesex Harmony. A Collection of Sacred Music. *Boston*. 1795. Oblong 4to.

Address to the Churches of the Middlesex Consociation; with ... the Pilgrim's Legacy: ... Second Edition. *Hartford: Printed by D. B. Moseley*. 1844. 18mo, pp. 36. B. 48843

Address to the Clergy and the People of ... Middlesex, from the Middlesex Massachusetts Auxiliary Society, ... in aid of the American Society for educating Pious Youth for the Gospel Ministry. *Cambridge: Printed by Hilliard and Metcalf*. 1819. 8vo, pp. 16. H. 48844

Also: Annual Report of the Directors of the Middlesex Auxiliary Society for the Education of Pious Youth ... . 1830. *Boston: Printed by Jonathan Howe*. 1830. 12mo, pp. 12. Continued. B.

Proceedings of the Middlesex Convention for Suppressing Violations of the Lord's Day: ... *Andover: Printed by Flagg and Gould*. 1814. 12mo, pp. 24. B. 48845

MIDDLESEX CO., *Mass.* First Annual Report of the Bible Society of Middlesex County, Mass., June, 1846. *Lowell*. 1846. 8vo, pp. 16. Continued. 48846

Also: Constitution ... . *Concord: Allen and Atwill, Printers*. 1826. 8vo, pp. 8. B.

Statement of Receipts and Expenditures of the County of Middlesex, for ... 1864. ... *Charlestown: W. & E. Howe, Printers*. 1865. 8vo, pp. 18. Continued. B. 48847

The Middlesex County Directory, for ... 1867. *Boston: Briggs & Co.* 1867. 8vo, pp. 224, 60. 48848

Catalogue of the Middlesex Mechanic Association, at Lowell, Mass., with the Act of Incorporation ... . *Lowell: Leonard Huntress, Printer*. 1840. 8vo, pp. 168. Continued. H. 48849

See also Lowell, Vol. X., Nos. 42495–6.

First Report of the Middlesex Sunday School Society; made ... September 27, 1843. *Concord: Hazewell & Simonds, Printers*. 1843. 16mo, pp. 16. Continued. B. 48850

Society of Husbandmen and Manufacturers. Transactions for 1851. Including the Speeches of E. Everett and R. C. Winthrop. [n. p.] 1852. 8vo, pp. 57. B. 48851

To the Electors of the County of Middlesex. [n. p. n. d.] 8vo, pp. 8. BA. 48852

An Address of the Whig Convention at Concord, Mass., dated October 25, 1838.

MIDDLETON (A.) An Oration ... Fifth of July, 1824, before the '76 Association. By A. Middleton. *Charleston: Printed by A. E. Miller*. 1824. 8vo, pp. 23. 48853

Favors nullification.

MIDDLETON (C. T.) A New ... | System | of | Geography. | Containing | A full ... Description | of | Europe, Asia, Africa, and America; | ... | By Charles Theodore Middleton, Esq. | ... | *London:* | ... *J. Cooke* ... . MDCCLXXVIII. 2 vols., folio, pp. v–xxviii, 5–546; 548, (4). 120 Engravings, Maps, etc. H. 48854

MIDDLETON (C.) Forgery Detected. By which is evinced how groundless are All the Calumnies cast upon the Editor, in a Pamphlet published under the Name of Arthur Dobbs, Esq; By Capt. Christopher Middleton, late Commander of his Majesty's Ship, Furnace, when sent upon the Search of a North-West Passage to the Western American Ocean. *London:* M.DCC.XLV. 8vo, pp. (2), v, 35. J.C.B. 48855

MIDDLETON. A Rejoinder to Mr. Dobb's Reply to Capt. Middleton; In which is expos'd, both his Wilful and Real Ignorance of Tides; &c. his Jesuitical Prevarications, Evasions, Falsities and false Reasoning; ... By Christopher Middleton, Esq. *London: M. Cooper*. 1745. 8vo, pp. 156. J.C.B. 48856

MIDDLETON. A Reply to the Remarks of Arthur Dobbs, Esq; on Capt. Middleton's Vindication of his Conduct on board his Majesty's Ship the Furnace, when Sent in Search of a North-west Passage, by Hudson's-Bay, to the Western American Ocean. ... By Christopher Middleton, Esq; *London: George Brett*. MDCCXLIV. 8vo, pp. x, 192, Appendix 94, Errata and Index, (8).

Rich, Vol. I., describes "A Reply to Mr. Dobbs's Answer, by Capt. Middleton"—*London*, 1745, 8vo—which is probably our No. 48856, *supra*. *See also* North-West Passage.

MIDDLETON. A Vindication of the Conduct of Captain Christopher Middleton, in a Late Voyage on Board His Majesty's Ship the Furnace, for Discovering a North-west Passage to the Western American Ocean. In Answer To certain Objections and Aspersions of Arthur Dobbs, Esq; with an Appendix: Containing ... Letters between Mr. Dobbs, Capt. Middleton, &c. Affidavits and other Vouchers refer'd to in the Captain's Answers,

&c. With as much of the Log-Journal as relates to the Discovery. The Whole as lately deliver'd to the Lords Commissioners of the Admiralty. To which is annex'd, An Account of the Extraordinary Degrees and Surprizing Effects of Cold in Hudson's-Bay, North America, read before the Royal Society. By Christopher Middleton, Late Commander of the Furnace, and F.R.S. *London: Jacob Robinson*. 1743. 8vo, pp. (4), 206, (1), Log, 48. + *Dublin: Isaac Jackson*. M,DCC,XLV. 8vo, pp. 168, 48. J.C.B. 48858

Also on large paper. The objections and aspersions of Mr. Dobbs, which gave rise to this controversy, were made in writing to the Lords of the Admiralty. Also: Table of Meteorological Observations from 1721 to 1729 in nine voyages to Hudson's Bay. *London*. 1730. 4to, pp. 8.

MIDDLETON (E.) Biographia Evangelica ... . By the Rev. Erasmus Middleton ... . *London: Printed by J. W. Pasham*. 1779–86. 4 vols., 8vo, pp. (2), iv, (6), 520; (4), 512; (4), 512; (4), 512, (2), vi. 52 Portraits. + A New Edition ... with Fifty-One Portraits. ... *London: For W. Baynes*. 1816. 4 vols., 8vo, pp. (4), iv, (2), 520; (6), 512; (4), 512; (4), 512. H. 48859

Includes a Life of Cotton Mather.

MIDDLETON (H.) A Clear Idea of the Genuine and Uncorrupted British Constitution, in an Address to the Inhabitants of the Province of Quebec, from the 49 Delegates in the Continental Congress at Philadelphia. By H. Middleton. *London*. 1774. 8vo. 48860

[MIDDLETON (H.)] Economical Causes of Slavery in the United States, and Obstacles to Abolition. By a South Carolinian. *London: Robert Hardwicke*. 1857. 8vo, pp. (4), 56. H.

[MIDDLETON (Henry), *Jr.*] Four Essays: The Science of Political Economy; Political Economy and Industry, and their Relations; Impolicy of Protective Duties. A Portion of the Friends of the High Tariff Examined. *Philadelphia, Reprinted*. 1847. 8vo. N. 48862

MIDDLETON (H.) The Government and the Currency. New Edition, with Alterations. By Henry Middleton. *New York: Charles B. Norton*. 1850. 12mo, pp. 190. A., B., C., H.

MIDDLETON (J.) Motives to Gratitude. A Discourse delivered before the Baptist Church and Society of Wheatland, New York, on Thanksgiving Day, December, 1841. By Rev. John Middleton. *Rochester*. 1842. 16mo, pp. 28. 48864

[MIDDLETON (J. C.)] Poem read before the Delta Kappa Sigma, of Williston Seminary, June 28th, 1865. ... *New Haven: Tuttle, Morehouse ... Printers.* 1865. 8vo, pp. 24. H.

MIDDLETON (P.) A Medical Discourse, or an Historical Inquiry Into the ancient and present State of Medicine ... . By Peter Middleton, M.D. *New-York: Printed by Hugh Gaine.* M,DCC,LXIX. 8vo, pp. (2), ii, 72. H. 48866

MIDDLETON (R. T.) ... Records of the Life, Character and Achievements of Adoniram Judson. By Robert T. Middleton. *New York: Edward H. Fletcher.* 1854. 12mo, pp. 456. Portrait and Map. 48867

MIDDLETON (William Henry). The History of My Friend; shewing how he was deprived of his Military Commission ... because a great man thought my friend called him a Nincompoop. ... *New-York.* 1816. 8vo, pp. 27. S. 48868

MIDDLETON, *Mass.* Annual Report of the School Committee, for 1862–3. *South Danvers.* 1863. 8vo. Continued.

See also Vol. XI., No. 46090.

MIDDLETOWN, *Conn.* The Addresses delivered at the Dedication of the Indian Hill Cemetery, with the Articles of Association, By-Laws ... . *Middletown: Pelton.* 1850. 8vo. 48870

Prospectus of the American Literary, Scientific and Military Academy, to be opened at Middletown, Ct. [n. p.] 1825. 8vo.

Also: Catalogue of Officers and Cadets of the American Literary, Scientific and Military Academy. *Middletown, Ct.* 1826. 8vo. — Report on the Suspension Bridge at Middletown. *Middletown.* 1848. 8vo. *See also* "Journal," IX. 36694, *and* Wesleyan University.

MIDDLETOWN, *N. Y.* A Brief Historical Sketch of the Middletown Lyceum ... . *Middletown, N. Y.: John W. Hasbrouck, Printer.* 1853. 8vo, pp. 15, (1). B. 48872

Directory for 1857–8, with various Historical Sketches of Middletown. By John W. Hasbrouck. *Middletown, N. Y.* 1857. 12mo, pp. 110, (161). S. 48873

MIDGLEY (R. L.) Boston Sights; or Hand-Book for Visitors. By R. L. Midgley. *Boston: James Munroe and Company.* 1857. 12mo, pp. (2), 2, 5, 224, (1). H. + *Boston: A. Williams and Company.* 1865. 12mo, pp. (2), 2, 5, 214. 2 Maps. B.

Midnight, and Other Poems. *New-York.* 1858. 12mo, pp. 90

The Midnight Cry. ... *New York.* 1842. 4to, 26 or more Numbers. N. 48876

This organ of the Millerites was a daily paper, comprising the lectures of William Miller, relative to Christ's coming in 1843.

A Midsummer's Fete at Woodland Hall. *New-York.* 1850. 12mo, pp. 30. 48877

Midwinter's Day Dream. By Aliquis. *Troy.* 1845. 12mo.

MIELZINER (M.) Slavery among the Ancient Hebrews. By M. Mielziner. *New York.* 1861. 8vo. C. 48879

Mientras no hay Inquisicion, se acaba la Religion. *Mexico.* 1833. 8vo. 48880

A vigorous plea for the restoration of the Inquisition in Mexico in 1833.

MIER CAZO Y ESTRADA (Francisco de). Voces el Silencio, mudo Llanto, con que la Cesarea de los Angeles como en sombras, diò á luz sú inexplicable pena en fallecimiento de el Catholico Monarcha de las Españas Don Phelipe V. ... y Poëmas ... . *En la Puebla.* 1747. 8vo. 48881

MIER Y GUERRA SERVANDO (J. de). Historia de la Revolucion de Nueva España. Por Don José de Mier y Guerra Servando. *Londres.* 1813. 2 vols., 8vo. C. 48882

MIER QUATEMOCZIN (J. R. de). Manifiesto sobre la inutilidad de los Provinciales de las Religiones en esta America. Por Fr. Juan Rosillo de Mier Quatemoczin. *Puebla.* 1821. 4to, pp. 16. 48883

MIER (M. de). Cartas de un Americano al "Español," sobre su Numero XIX. Por Dr. Manual de Mier. *Londres.* 1811–12. 2 vols., 8vo. C. 48884

MIER Y TERAN (M. de). Diario de Viage de la Comision de Limites que puso el Gobierno de la Republica, baja la direccion del D. Manuel de Mier y Teran. *Mexico.* 1850. 8vo. Portrait.

MIER Y TERAN. Manifestacion del Ciudadano Manuel de Mier y Teran al Publico. *Mexico.* 1825. 4to, pp. 31. + *Jalapa.* 1825. 4to, pp. 31. + Segunda Manifestacion. *Mexico.* 1825. 4to, pp. 127. 48886

MIER Y TRESPALACIOS. Exequias celebradas por el S. C. de Mier y Trespalacios. *Mexico.* 1806. 8vo. Portrait and Plate.

MIER (Servado Teresa de). Vida, Adventuras, y Viages, precedidos de un Ensayo Historico, por M. Payno. *Mexico.* 1865. 4to, pp. over 112. 48888

MIERS (J.) Travels in Chile and La Plata, including Accounts respecting the Geography, Geology, Statistics, Government, Finances, Agriculture, Manners and Customs, and the Mining Operations in Chile. Collected during a residence of several years in these Countries. By John Miers. Illustrated by Original Maps, Views, &c. *London: Baldwin, Cradock, and Joy.* 1826. 2 vols., 8vo, pp. xv, 494; vii, 536. 3 Maps, 19 Plates. H. 48889

See "Quarterly Review," XXXV. 114.

MIERS (J.) Contributions to Botany [of South America], Iconographic and descriptive. ... Vol. I. *London.* 1851–61. Rl. 4to, pp. 312. 48890

No more published.

MIERS. Illustrations of South American Plants. ... *London.* 1847–57. 2 vols., 4to. 87 Plates. 48891

First published in parts. Also: On new Genera of Plants from Brazil and Chile. [*London.* 1842.] 4to. 2 Plates.

MIERTSCHING (J. A.) Reise-Tagebuch des Missionars Johann August Miertsching, welcher als Dolmetscher die Nordpol-Expedition zur Aufsuchung Sir John Franklins auf dem Schiffe Investigator begleitete. In den Jahren 1850 bis 1854. *Gnadau.* 1855. 8vo. Map. + Zweite Auflage. *Gnadau: H. L. Menz.* 1856. 8vo, pp. xvi, 206. Map. C. 48892

MIERTSCHING. Journal de Voyage au Pole Nord. ... Deuxième Édition. *Genève: J. Cherbuliez.* 1857. 12mo, pp. 143. Map. C. 48893

MIETTE DE VILLARS *and* CLÉRAMBAUT. Manuel des Émigrants en Californie, par Miette de Villars et Clérambaut. *Paris: Veuve Louis Janet.* 1849. 8vo. 48894

[MIFFLIN (Thomas).] Sir, In the present state ... . *Philadelphia.* 1794. Folio, 1 leaf. P. 48895

Circular from Gov. Mifflin on the Excise. Thomas quotes a similar title dated 1772, which is, I think, an error as to the date.

MIFFLIN (W.) Account of Warner Mifflin, who liberated his Slaves, and of an African Prince, who sold a Negro Boy for a metal Watch. *Wisbech.* . 12mo. 48896

[MIFFLIN.] A Serious Expostulation with the Members of the House of Representatives of the United States. *Philadelphia: Printed ... by Daniel Lawrence.* 1793. Sm. 8vo, pp. 24. + *Reprinted by J. Spooner, in New Bedford.* 1793. 12mo, pp. 16. + *Poughkeepsie, ... Reprinted by Nicholas Power ...* . 1794. Sm. 8vo, pp. 24. 48897

A remonstrance respecting the abolition of slavery.

Might and Right. By a Rhode Islander. *Providence: A. H. Stillwell.* 1844. 12mo, pp. 324. Portrait of Dorr. 48898

Relates to the Dorr Rebellion. It has been ascribed to F. H. Green, also to Catherine R. Williams.

Might, not Right; or, Stories of the Discovery and Conquest of America. ... *London: Griffith & Farran.* 1857. Sq. 16mo, pp. 240. 48899

Issued with the plates plain or colored.

The Mighty Destroyer. *See* [Benezet (A.)], II. 4674.

MIGNARD (J.) Apperçu [*sic*] des Crimes commis par les Anglo-Américains envers les Français. Par Jacques Mignard, ... *Paris: Chez l'Auteur.* [1800.] 8vo, pp. 52. H. 48900

A most violent diatribe against the Americans, called by Mr. Jacques Mignard "peuple de Barrington (fameux voleur Anglois)." England is called a nation composed of pirates and brigands, and is condemned to live upon potatoes; the Americans upon Indian corn; whilst the luxuries of the world are to be for the exclusive use of France.

MIGNARD. La Politique Anglaise devoilée, ou les moyens de rendre les Colonies à la France. Presenté à la Convention Nationale, le 24 Vendemaire l'an 3e. *Paris: Chez les Marchands de Nouveautés, l'an 3 de la Republique* [1795]. 8vo, pp. 55. J.C.B.

Also: Remarques, sur les maladies vénériennes, le virus vénérien et la maniere d'agir du mercure. ... *A la Martinique.* 1790. 8vo. P.

MIGNET (F. A. M.) Portraits et Notices historiques et littéraires Par M. Mignet ... . Deuxième Édition ... . *Paris: Didier.* 1852. 2 vols., 8vo, pp. (4), iv, 399, (1); iv, 456. B. 48902

Includes Livingston and Franklin.

MIGNET. ... Vie de Franklin ... . Par M. Mignet ... . *Paris: Pagnerre.* 1848. 12mo, pp. 230. + Nouvelle Édition. *Paris: Didier.* 1868. 12mo, pp. 200. 48903

Forms parts VII. and VIII. of the "Petits Traités publiés par L'Académie des Sciences Morales et Politiques."

MIGNET. Benjamin Franklin. Eine Biographie von F. A. Mignet. Aus dem Französischen von Dr. Ed. Burckhardt. *Leipzig: Verlag von Carl B. Lorck.* 1855. 16mo, pp. (4), 143.

Also: Antonio Perez and Philip II. ... *London.* 1846. 12mo. P.

[MIGT *or* MICH.] La Richesse de la Hollande, ouvrage dans lequel on expose, l'origine du commerce & de la puissance des Hollandois; l'accroissement successif de leur commerce & de leur navigation; les causes qui ont contribué à leur progrès, celles qui tendent à les détruire; & les moyens qui peuvent servir à les relever. *Londres, aux dépens de la Compagnie.* 1778. 2 vols., 4to, pp. xvi, 384; (4), 372, (8). C. 48905

MIGUEL (J. R. de). La Republica Mexicana en 1846, ó sea Directorio General de los supremos Poderes y de las principales Autoridades, Corporaciones y Oficinas de la Nacion. Por Juan Rodriguez de S. Miguel. *Mexico.* 1845. 8vo. 48906

Also: Tercera Guia Judicial, ó sea Colleccion de las Leyes de mas frecuente uso en la Administracion de Justicia. ... *Mexico.* 1850. 8vo.

MIGUEL (P. A. G.) Stirpes Surinamenses selectae. *Lugduni Batavorum.* 1850. 4to. 65 Plates. 48907

MIJANGOS (I. de). Espeio Divino en Lengva Mexicana, en qve pveden verse los Padres, y tomar documento para acertar á doctrinar bien á sus hijos, y Aficionallos a las Virtudes. Compuesto por el Padre F. Ioan de Mijangos, Religioso Indigno, y ... Obispo de Yponia, &c. ... *En Mexico, con licencia. En la Emprenta de Diego Lopez Daualos.* 1607. 4to, pp. (16), 562, (6). C.

Extremely rare, not mentioned by Brunet, Rich, Brochaus, or Stevens. Quaritch marks a copy £16 16s.

MIJANGOS. Primera Parte del Sermonario, Dominical, y Sanctoral en Lengua Mexicana. ... Compuesto por el P. Maestro. Fr. Ivan de Miiangos ... . *En Mexico en la Imprenta del Licenciado Iuan de Alcaçar, Año 1624. Vendese en la Libreria de Diego de Ribera.* 4to, pp. (18), 564, Index, (92). 48909

The author, a native of Oaxaca, dedicated himself chiefly to the wants and necessities of the native Indians, whose language he mastered to an admirable degree. His works are looked upon as specimens of the most elegant Mexican language. Priced by Quaritch at £10.

[MIJST (Gerardus de la).] Verloren Arbeyt | ofte | Klaar en kortbondigh vertoogh | van de | Colonie | In de Lantstreke Guiana, aan de vaste kuste | Van | America, | Op de Revier | Wiapoca. | Desselfs | Verkiesinge, bebouwinge, versterckinge, mitsga- | ders, oneenigheden, Disordres, en verlies. | Verciert | Met Kopere Platen. | Synde de ware Afbeeldinge, soo van de Rivier, en Streec- | kinge, desselfs. | Als de Lantstreke, neffens de Stadt, en Fortificatie, | alles naar 't leven afgeteeckent. | Gedruckt voor den Autheur. | *t' Amsterdam, by Pieter Timmers, Boeckdrucker en Verkoper,*

op de | Haerlem'er-straet, omtrent de Brouwer-straet. | [1678.] 4to, two Titles, one of which is engraved, pp. (6), 60. Map.

Gerardus de la Mijst, the author of this work, furnishes us with exact details of this unfortunate attempt at colonization; and his account is the most important for the history of the colonization of America by the Dutch.

MIKAN (J. C.) Delectus Floræ et Faunæ Brasiliensis ... . Auctore J. C. Mikan ... . *Vindobonæ: Typis Antonii Strauss.* 1820. Folio, pp. (54). 24 Plates. B. 48911

MIKAN. Kinder meiner Laune, ältere und jüngere, ernste und scherzhafte, von Joh. Chr. Mikan. *Prag.* 1833. 8vo.

This work also contains the voyages of the author in Brazil.

MILAM, *pseudon.* Texas: Sketches of Character; Moral and Political Condition of the Republic; the Judiciary ... . By Milam. *Philadelphia: Brown, Bicking & Guilbert, Printers.* 1839. 18mo, pp. 95. S. 48913

MILANÉS (J. J.) .Obras de Don José J. Milanés, coleccion de sus Poesias, Dramas, Leyendas, y articulos literarios. *Habana.* 1846. 4 vols., 8vo. 48914

Milanés was a native of Cuba, and his works are among its finest literary productions.

MILBERG (J. H.) Ueber die Werthlosigkeit eiserner Panzerschiffe. ... *München.* 1862. 8vo, pp. 38. 48915

MILBERT (J[acques Gérard].) Itinéraire pittoresque du Fleuve Hudson et des parties latérales de l'Amérique du Nord, d'après les dessins originaux pris sur les lieux, Par J. Milbert, ... et lithographiés par Adam, Bichebois, Deroy, Dupressoir, Jacottet, Joly, Sabatier, Tirpenne et Villeneuve. ... *Paris: Henri Gaugain et Cie.* 1828–29. 2 vols., 4to, pp. (4), xxxvi, 146 [*i. e.* 246], (2); (4), 257, (2). Atlas in folio, Title and 54 Plates. BA., C. 48916

Twenty-five copies of the atlas were issued as proof impressions on India paper before the letters. The work includes views on the Hudson, in New Jersey, New York, Pennsylvania, Falls of Niagara, etc.

MILBURN (W. H.) The Pioneers, Preachers and People of the Mississippi Valley. By William Henry Milburn ... . *New York: Derby & Jackson.* 1860. 12mo, pp. 465. H. 48917

MILBURN. The Rifle, Axe, and Saddle-Bags, and Other Lectures. By William Henry Milburn. With Introduction by Rev. J. McClintock, D.D. ... *New York: Derby & Jackson.* 1857. 12mo, pp. 309. Portrait. + With a Preface and Life of the Author by the Rev. T. Binney. *London: Sampson Low, Son & Co.* 1857. Post 8vo, pp. 264. 48918

MILBURN. Ten Years of Preacher Life: Chapters from an Autobiography. By William Henry Milburn ... . *New York: Derby & Jackson.* 1859. 12mo, pp. 363. Portrait. + [*Ibid.*] 1860. + With an Introduction by the Rev. William Arthur ... *London: Sampson Low, Son & Co.* 1859. Post 8vo, pp. xviii, (2), 286. 48919

MILBURN (*Mrs.* W. H.) Poems of Faith and Affection. By Mrs. Wm. H. Milburn. ... *New York: Hurd and Houghton.* 1866. 16mo, pp. (2), vi, 103. B. 48920

The author sympathizes warmly with the South in its struggle.

[MILCENT (C. L. M.)] Sur les Troubles de Saint-Domingue. [n. p. 1791.] 18mo, pp. 19. H. 48921

Signed at the end, "Milscent, créole."

MILES (D. H.) Message of the President of the United States, with copies of the Charges, Testimony and Finding of the recent Court of Inquiry, in the Case of Col. Dixon H. Miles, U.S.A. *Washington.* 1861. 8vo, pp. 56. 48922

MILES (G. D.) Memoir of Ellen May Woodward. By the Rev. Geo. D. Miles, A.M. ... *Philadelphia: Lindsay and Blakiston.* 1850. 12mo, pp. 174. Portrait. + Second Edition. With a Preface by Rt. Rev. A. Potter, D.D. *Philadelphia.* 1852. 12mo.

MILES (G. H.) A Discourse in Commemoration of the Landing of the Pilgrims of Maryland, Pronounced at Mt. St. Mary's College, May 10, 1847. By George H. Miles, Esq. *Emmittsburg.* 1847. 8vo, pp. 39. 48924

Also: Oration at St. Mary's College. ... *Baltimore.* 1850. 8vo.

MILES (G. I.) A Glance at the Baptists. By Rev. G. I. Miles. *West Chester (Penn.): H. S. Evans.* 1836. 18mo, pp. 264. C. 48925

MILES (H. A.) A Discourse ... at the Dedication of the Union Meeting-House, in Dresden, Me. June 27, 1833. By Rev. Henry A. Miles ... . *Hallowell: Glazier, Masters & Co.* 1833. 8vo, pp. 16. BA. 48926

[MILES.] Genealogy of the Miles Family. [*Lowell: Norton, Printer.* 1840.] Sm. 4to, pp. 12. B. 48927

MILES. Lowell, as it was, and as it is. By Rev. Henry A. Miles. ... *Lowell: Powers and Bagley.* 1845. 18mo, pp. 234.

Map and Plate. + Second Edition. *Lowell: Nathaniel L. Dayton.* 1846. 18mo, pp. 234. Map. B. + [*Ibid.*] 1847. 48928

Also: ... An Address ... to the Worcester County Agricultural Society, ... September 20, 1866 ... . *Worcester.* 1866. 8vo, pp. 17. — A Discourse on the Life and Character of Rev. Joseph C. Smith, delivered in ... Newton, ... March 28, 1858. *Boston: Crosby, Nichols ...* . 1858. 8vo, pp. 27. — Fidelity to our Political Idea ... A Discourse before the Ancient ... Artillery Company, June 5th, 1843. ... *Boston.* 1843. 8vo, pp. 24. — On Natural Theology as a Study in Schools. A Lecture ... . *Boston: Marsh, Capen ...* . 1840. 8vo, pp. 14. — Sermon ... in Lowell, on the Sabbath following the Funeral of the Hon. Luther Lawrence ... . *Lowell: Leonard Huntress, Printer.* 1839. 8vo, pp. 14. — A Sermon ... in ... Concord, December 10, 1858, at the burial of Rev. Barzillai Frost. ... *Cambridge: Metcalf and Company.* 1859. 8vo, pp. 23. — ... Thanksgiving Discourse ... Lowell, November 30, 1843. ... *Lowell: Printed by Stearns & Taylor.* 1844. 8vo, pp. 16. H.

MILES (H. H.) Canada East at the International Exhibition. ... To which is added A Succinct Account of the Eastern Townships of Lower Canada, by Henry H. Miles, M.A. *London.* 1862. 8vo, pp. 88. Map and Plates. 48929

MILES (J. B.) Address at the Funeral ... of Sergeant Henry Todd, By Rev. James B. Miles. *Charlestown.* 1866. 12mo, pp. 12. B. 48930

MILES. Discourse Commemorative of James Hunnewell, ... By Rev. James B. Miles, ... in Charlestown, May 9, 1869. *Charlestown, Mass.: James F. Hunnewell.* 1869. 8vo, pp. 32.

Privately printed. Also: ... A Discourse addressed to the Members of Concordia Lodge, No. 8, I. O. of G. T. ... Nov. 23, 1862. ... *Boston: Geo. C. Rand & Avery.* 1862. 8vo, pp. 22. — A Sermon, ... in Charlestown, October 21st, 1866, ... after the Funeral of Mrs. Roxanna Glidden ... . [n. p. n. d.] 8vo, pp. 20. — ... A Sermon ... in ... Charlestown, On Fast Day, April 16, 1857. ... *Charlestown: Abram E. Cutter.* 1857. 8vo, pp. 24. H.

MILES (J. W.) The Discourse ... [at] the ... Funeral of the Hon. John C. Calhoun ... Charleston, ... April 26th, 1850. By the Rev. James W. Miles. ... *Charleston: John Russell.* 1850. 8vo, pp. 39. H. 48932

[MILES.] Relation between the Races at the South. *Charleston: Evans & Cogswell.* 1861. 8vo, pp. 20. B. 48933

Also: ... Annual Oration ... before ... South-Carolina College, ... December 7th, 1852. ... *Charleston: John Russell.* 1853. 8vo, pp. 51, (1). — Farewell Sermon ... August 20, 1843. ... *Charleston.* 1843. 8vo.

MILES (J.) Review of Bishop Hughes's Sermon on the Decline of Protestantism: A Lecture. By John Miles. *Albany.* 1851. 8vo. S. 48934

Miles (P.) Advantages of Direct Steam Communication between Europe and America, via Galway, Ireland. By Pliny Miles .... *London.* 1859. 8vo. Map. 48935

Miles. The Advantages of Ocean Steam Navigation, Foreign and Coastwise, to the Commerce of Boston, and the Manufactures of New England. By Pliny Miles .... *Boston: Printed by Emery N. Moore & Co.* 1857. 8vo, pp. xii, 96. H. 48936

Miles. Postal Reform: its Urgent Necessity and Practicability. By Pliny Miles. ... *New York: Stringer & Townsend.* 1855. 8vo, pp. xii, 112. C., H. 48937

Also: The New York Chamber of Commerce, and Suggestions for an Enlarged Sphere of Action. ... *New York.* 1857. 8vo, pp. 8. — The Statistical Register and Book of General Reference .... *New York.* 1846. 12mo. + Second Edition. *New York: Mark H. Newman & Co.* 1849. 12mo, pp. 200. C.

Miles (T. J.) ... The Conspiracy of Leading Men of the Republican Party to destroy The American Union proved by their words and acts ... . By Thomas Jefferson Miles ... . *New York: J. Walter & Co.* 1864. 8vo, pp. 35. 48938

Miles [W. A.] The Author of a Letter to the Duke of Grafton Vindicated from the charge of Democracy. With Notes. By Mr. Miles. *London: J. Owen.* MDCCXCIV. 8vo, pp. 68. H. 48939

Miles. A Letter to the Duke of Grafton, with Notes. Including a complete Exculpation of M. de La Fayette from the Charges indecently urged against him by Mr. Burke, In the House of Commons, on the 17th March, 1794. By Mr. Miles. To which is annexed a Vindication of the Author from the Charge of Democracy. *London: J. Owen.* MDCCXCIV. 8vo, pp. 95.

Miles. Remarks on An Act of Parliament, ... intituled [*sic*], "An Act for the Encouragement of the Fisheries "carried on from Great Britain, Ireland," &c. to Newfoundland, &c. For the Repeal or Amendment of which, A Petition ... has ... been presented ... . [With the] State of the Fishery in 1771. ... By William Augustus Miles. *London: H. Payne.* 1779. 4to, pp. xiii, 15. H. 48941

Miles (W. P.) Admission of Kansas. Speech of Hon. W. Porcher Miles, ... March 31, 1858. [n. p. n. d.] 8vo, pp. 8.

Also: Oration, ... Charleston, July 4th, 1849. ... *Charleston.* 1849. 8vo.

Miles Standish, *Jr.*, *pseudon.* The Times: A Poem, addressed to the Inhabitants of New England and New York. By Miles Standish, Jr. *Plymouth.* 1809. 8vo. N. 48943

On the anti-commercial system of the present administration.

Milet (P.) Relation de sa Captivité parmi les Onneiouts en 1690–1. Par le R. P. Pierre Milet de la Compagnie de Jésus. *Nouvelle York: De la Presse Cramoisy de Jean-Marie Shea.* M.DCCC.-LXIV. 8vo, pp. v, 9–56. BA. 48944

Forms No. XVIII. of Shea's Cramoisy Series. This and Father Jogues' narrative gives us nearly all we know from personal observation, of the Five Nations at this period.

Milford, *Mass.* Annual Report of the Receipts and Expenditures ... [and other] Reports ... . *Milford.* 1863. 8vo, pp. 28, (1). Continued. B. 48945

Brief Sketch of the First Congregational Church in Milford. *Milford.* 1852. 8vo, pp. 22. 48946

Minutes of the First Anniversary of the Milford Baptist Association, ... Oct. 15 & 16, 1828. *Concord: Printed by Isaac Hill.* 1828. 8vo, pp. 16. Continued. B. 48947

The Milford Directory; to which is added a History of Milford, by Rev. Adin Ballou. *Milford: C. C. Drew.* 1869. 8vo.

Also: Report of the School Committee ... For 1856. *Milford.* 1856. 12mo, pp. 23. Continued. B.

Milfort (*Gen.*) Mémoire ou Coup-d'œil Rapide Sur mes différens voyages et mon séjour dans la nation Crëck. Par le G^al. Milfort, Tastenegy ou grand Chef de guerre de la nation Crëck, et Général de brigade au service de la République française. *A Paris: De l'Imprimerie de Giguet et Michaud An* XI. [1802.] 8vo, pp. (4), 331, (1). H. 48949

A very curious book. Gen. Milfort resided many years among the Creeks, was adopted into their nation, and made "Tastenegy," or Great War Chief. *See* Field's "Essay," No. 1065.

Militão (G.) Elogio Historico do Finado Marquez de Abrantes Presidente da Sociedade Auxiliadora da Industria Nacional. Recitado pelo Dr. Gabriel Militão de Villa Nova Machado em sessão d'Assembléa Geral de 6 de Novembro de 1865. *Rio de Janeiro.* 1865. 8vo, pp. (2), 57. 48950

The Military Academy at West Point. *Washington.* 1860. 8vo. 48951

The Military Academy at West Point, Unmasked; or Corruption and Military Despotism Exposed. By Americanus. *Washington.* 1830. 8vo, pp. 28. C. 48952

See also United States *and* West Point.

The Military and Naval Magazine of the United States. ... *Washington, D. C.: Benjamin Homans.* 1833–36. 6 vols., 8vo, pp. 384; (4), 392; 480; (4), 480; (4), 480; 444. BA. 48953

The Military and Naval Situation, and the Glorious Achievements of our Soldiers and Sailors. *Washington: Union Congressional Committee.* 1864. 8vo, pp. 15, (1). H. 48954

The Military Bill. Provisions for Despotism in the South! ... [n. p. n. d.] 8vo, pp. 8. H. 48955

Military College. Catalogue of the Officers and Students for the year 1853. *Wilmington, Del.* 1853. 8vo. Continued.

Military Control. *See* [Gardner (John L.)], VII. 26650.

The Military Defences of Canada, considered in respect to our Colonial Relations with Great Britain. ... By an Upper Canadian. *Quebec.* 1862. 8vo, pp. 43. S. 48957

Military Despotism! Arbitrary Arrest of a Judge!! [n. p. n. d.] Folio, 1 leaf. 48958

A folio broadside referring to General Jackson at New Orleans.

Military Despotism! or Observations on the Law for enforcing the Embargo. [n. p. n. d.] 8vo, pp. 8. BA. 48959

Military Despotism! Suspension of the Habeas Corpus! Curses coming Home to roost! ... *New York: Wm. C. Bryant & Co., Printers.* 1863. 8vo, pp. 16. BA. 48960

Military Discipline, 1701. *See* [Boone (N.)], II. 6375.

Military Districts. Letter from the Secretary of War [on Freedmen. *Washington.* 1862.] 8vo. 48961

The Military Execution of American Citizens, by Order of the President. An Appeal to the People of the United States, by Citizens of the District of Columbia. *Washington, D. C.* 1857. 8vo, pp. 44. 48962

In reference to the riot at the election in 1857.

The Military Gazette. *New York.* 1858. 8vo. Continued.

The Military Glory of Great Britain, an Entertainment given by the late candidates for Bachelor's Degree at the close of the Anniversary Commencement held in Nassau Hall, College of New Jersey, Sept. 27th, 1762. *Philadelphia: William Bradford.* 1762. 4to, pp. 15. 48964

The Military History of Great Britain, for 1756, 1757. Containing A Letter from an English Officer at Canada, Taken Prisoner at Oswego. Exhibiting the Cruelty and Infidelity of the French, and their Savage Indians, in Times of Peace, and War. Shewing their superior advantages, and the only means of redress: and impartially delineating the present state of our Colonies in America, with some hints for their future regulation. Also A Journal of the Siege of Oswego, and the Articles of Capitulation; with a particular table of their Inhabitants ... . *London: J. Millan.* 1757. 8vo, pp. 125. Plan. 48965

"A collection of different papers, from various quarters, and very improperly entitled a History. However, as the materials have the appearance of authenticity, they may possibly be of use in future compilations; but certainly the public ought to be told what authority they come from."—*Monthly Review*, XVII. 375.

Military Journals. *See* [Lyon (Lemuel) *and* Haws (S.)], Vol. X

Military Laws, and Rules and Regulations for the Armies of the United States. *Washington.* 1813. 12mo, pp. 247. C. + [*Ibid.*] 1814. 12mo. 48966

Military Laws of the Confederate States. *See* Vol. IV. 15318.

Military Laws of the United States; ... Compiled ... by Truman Cross. *Washington.* 1825. 8vo. 48967

For two later editions, *see* Cross (T.), Vol. V., Nos. 17664–5.

Military Memoirs of Four Brothers, (Natives of Staffordshire,) Engaged in the Service of their Country, ... in the New World and Africa ... . By the Survivor. *London.* MDCCCXXIX. 8vo.

Military Monitor and American Register. Containing a correct Record of the Events of the War between the United States and Great Britain from 1812, to Aug. 23, 1813. *New York: J. Desnoues.* 1813. 4to. C., S. 48969

Fifty-three or more numbers published.

The Military Monitor; or, Advice to the Officers and Soldiers of the American Army ... . *Baltimore.* 1813. 12mo, pp. 184. 48970

Military Operations on the Delaware during the Late War. ... *Philadelphia.* 1820. 12mo. 48971

Constitution and By-Laws of the Military Orders of the Loyal Legion of the United States. *Philadelphia.* 1866. 12mo, pp. 62, (1). 48972

Military Post Library Association. The Muster-Roll, and Other Sketches. ... *New York: Military Post Library Association.* [n. d.] 32mo, pp. 20. H. 48973

Also: Out on Picket! ... *New York.* [n. d.] 32mo, pp. 12. — The Roll Call; or, How will You Answer it? Dedicated to the Soldiers of the United States Army. ... *New York.* [n. d.] 32mo, pp. 16. — The Soldier's Knapsack: ... *New York.* [n. d.] 32mo, pp. 44. H.

Military Preparations. *Boston: American Peace Society.* [n. d.] 12mo, pp. 4. 48974

Military Pyrotechny, for the Use of the Cadets of the United States Military Academy, West-Point. Lithographed by G. Aspinwall. [n. p.] 1839. 4to. S. 48975

Military Reflections. *See* Max^an. ***, XI. 46998.

The Military Reporter; containing the Trials of Capt. Jos. Loring, Jun. ... Capt. Amos Binney, ... Capt. Thomas Howe, ... From authentic documents. For the information of the Officers of the Militia. *Boston: Printed by T. Kennard.* 1810. 8vo, pp. 299. C., H. 48976

Military Repository. *See* Smith (Charles).

Military Route to Richmond. *See* [Martin (G.)], XI. 44878.

Military System of the Republic of Switzerland; or, how to raise an Efficient Army, without Offering Bounty or Resorting to Draft. *Washington: Franck Taylor.* 1864. 8vo, pp. 15. H.

Militia. Bill to provide for Organizing, Arming and Disciplining the Militia of the United States. Feb. 18th, 1795. [n. p. 1795.] 8vo. + *Philadelphia.* 1798. 8vo, pp. 18. 48978

Exercise for the Militia. *See* Vol. XI., No. 45727, and add, *Boston.* 1758. Folio.

The Militia Act. *See* Vol. XI., Nos. 45924–5.

Militia of the United States. *See* [Lee (H.), *Jr.*], X. 39757.

Militia Laws of the United States, and ... Massachusetts. ... *Dedham.* 1815. 12mo, pp. 254, (2). B. 48979

Militia Laws of the United States and ... Massachusetts ... . Compiled ... by William H. Sumner ... . *Boston: Printed by Simon Gardner.* 1824. 12mo, pp. iv, 99, Index, xv. + Second Edition, revised ... . *Boston: True and Greene, ... Printers.* 1829. 12mo, pp. vi, 91. xi. + Edited by H. A. S. Dearborn. *Boston: Dutton and Wentworth ... Printers.* 1836. 12mo, pp. x, 108. + [*Ibid.*] 1840. 12mo, pp. 119. B. 48980

The Militia Soldier's Pocket Companion; ... for the ... Troops of the United States. ... Also, Extracts from the Militia Laws of Massachusetts. *Worcester: Printed by Thomas & Sturtevant.* 1807. 24mo, pp. 24. BA. 48981

Milius (A.) De Origine | Animalium, | et Migratione | Populorum | Scriptum Abrahami Milii. | Ubi inquiritur, quomodo quaque via Homines cætera-|que Animalia Terrestria provenerint; & post De-|luvium in omnes Orbis terrarum partes & regiones: | Asiam, Europam, Africam, utramque Americam, | & Terram Australem, sive Magellanicam, pervene-|rint. | *Genevæ: | Apud Petrum Columesium.* | M. DC. LXVII. | 12mo, pp. (2), 68. 48982

Includes a curious dissertation on the origin of the American races. The following is a German translation:

Milius Merckwürdiger Discurss von dem Ursprung der Thier, und Ausszug der Völcker ... . *Saltzburg.* 1670. 16mo.

Mill (J.) Commerce Defended. ... By James Mill, Esq. *London: C. and R. Baldwin.* 1808. 8vo. + Second Edition. [*Ibid.*] 8vo, pp. 154. 48984

Mill (J. S.) The Contest in America. By John Stuart Mill. Reprinted from Fraser's Magazine. *Boston: Little, Brown and Company.* MDCCCLXII. 16mo, pp. 32. + Second Edition. [*Ibid.*]

Also in "Harper's Magazine," April, 1862, and reprinted in the following work.

Mill. Dissertations and Discussions Political, Philosophical, and Historical ... . By John Stuart Mill. ... *London: John W. Parker and Son.* M.DCCC.LIX. 3 vols., 8vo. + *Boston: William V. Spencer.* 1865. 3 vols., 8vo. + Second Edition. *London: Longmans, Green ...* . M.DCCC.LXVII. 3 vols., 8vo. 48986

Mill. On Liberty. By John Stuart Mill. *London.* 1859. 8vo. C + The Second Edition. *London: John W. Parker and*

Son. M. DCCC. LIX. 8vo, pp. 207, (1). + *Boston: Ticknor and Fields.* 1863. 8vo, pp. 223. H. 48987

This elicited: "Individual Liberty, Legal, Moral and Licentious; in which The Political Fallacies of J. S. Mill's Essay 'On Liberty' are Pointed out." By Index. ... *London: George Vasey.* 1867. 12mo, pp. xii, 172.

Also: Considerations on Representative Government. ... *London: Parker, Son, and Bourn.* MDCCCLXI. 8vo, pp. viii, 340. BA. + *New York: Harper & Brothers.* 1862. 12mo, pp. 365. B. — Personal Representation. Speech ... May 29, 1867. ... Second Edition. *London: Printed by Henderson ...* . 1867. 8vo, pp. 71. — The Slave Power; its Character, Career, and probable Designs. ... *New York: T. J. Crowen.* 1862. 8vo, pp. 16.

Mill, *and* Hare (Thomas). True and False Democracy. Representation of all, and Representation of the majority only. A brief Synopsis of Recent Publications on the subject. *Boston: Prentiss & Deland.* 1862. 8vo, pp. 16. 48988

Mill (N.) The History of Mexico, from the Spanish Conquest to the Present Æra; containing a condensed ... View of the Manners, Customs, ... and a ... Review of the Changes affected in that Country, with its present Form of Government, ... By Nicholas Mill, Esq. ... *London: Sherwood, Jones, and Co.* 1824. 8vo, pp. xii, 300. Map. B., C. 48989

Curious, as exhibiting the strange and absurd ideas entertained by the English generally in reference to the importance of Mexico.

Mill Creek Cannel Coal and Oil Company. Statement to the Stockholders. *Boston: Rockwell & Rollins.* 1867. 8vo, pp. 23.

The Mill-Girls. *Philadelphia.* [1862.] 18mo, pp. 162. C.

Mill Pond Wharf Corporation. Catalogue of 278 Lots of Land to be Sold at Auction. *Boston.* 1840. 8vo, pp. 20. B.

Milla (J.) Don Bonifacio. Leyenda antigua por Don José Milla. *Guatemala: Imprenta de la Concordia.* 1862. 4to, pp. 94.

A satirical poem on the manners of the Guatemalans.

Millan de Poblete (Juan). Sermon Funebre que en las Exequias del P. San Phelipe Neri, en su Oratorio de Mexico. ... *Mexico, por Miguel de Ribera.* 1701. 8vo. 48994

Millar (R.) The History Of the Propagation of Christianity, And the Overthrow of Paganism. By Robert Millar ... *Edinburgh.* 1723. 2 vols., 8vo. + The Third Edition Corrected, with Additions. *London: A. Millar.* M DCC.XXXI. 2 vols., 8vo, pp. xii, 447, (12); (2), 404, (12). 48995

Contains interesting particulars relating to the introduction of Christianity in New England.

Millard (N.) A Discourse ... Thanksgiving Day. By Rev. Nelson Millard ... . *New York.* 1863. 8vo. 48996

Millbury, *Mass.* Annual Reports of the ... Town Officers of ... Millbury, for ... 1856. *Boston: Printed by Damrell and Moore.* [n. d.] 8vo, pp. 28. Continued. H. 48997

Also: Report of the School Committee ... for ... 1855. ... *Worcester: Printed by Henry J. Howland.* [n. d.] 8vo, pp. 16. H.

Milledoler (P.) A Sermon, ... in ... New-York, ... August 8, 1810; at the Ordination ... of the Rev. Gardiner Spring, ... By Philip Milledoler, D.D. ... *New-York: Williams & Whiting.* 1810. 8vo, pp. 60. B. 48998

Also: Address ... before the Alumni of Columbia College, on the Seventh of May, 1828. ... *New-Brunswick: Terhune & Letson.* 1828. 8vo, pp. 23. — Address ... to the Graduates of Rutgers College, ... July 20, 1831 ... . *New York: William A. Mercein, Printer.* 1831. 8vo, pp. 20. — A Discourse ... at Hackensack, N. J. before the Rev. Classis of Paramus, ... July 6, 1824. ... *New-York: Printed by G. F. Hopkins.* 1824. 8vo, pp. 32. — Discourse ... in New York, March 23, 1806, for a Society of Ladies instituted for the Relief of Poor Widows with Small Children. ... *New York.* 1806. 8vo, pp. 24. — A Sermon, ... at the Installation of the Rev. John B. Romeyn ... . *New-York: Printed by J. Seymour.* 1808. 8vo, pp. 29. B. — ... Sermon ... Albany ... General Synod of the Reformed Dutch Church. *New York.* 1823. 8vo. S.

The Millennial Harbinger. ... *Bethany, Va.: A. Campbell.* 1855. Continued. P. 48999

Millennial Institutions; ... . *New-York.* MDCCCXXXIII. 8vo, pp. lix, 160, (1). Plan. B. 49000

The Millennium: or, The Age to come. By a Presbyter of Massachusetts. *Philadelphia.* 1864. 16mo, pp. 23, (1). B.

The Millennium; or, The American Consummation of Equality. In which the Big Pot is put in the Little one ... . By Tempora Mutantur, Esq. ... [*Savannah?*] 1870. 16mo, pp. 20. 49002

The Millennium: the Good Time Coming. With a History of Experiments on the Odic Force. By the Author of Millennial Institutions, etc. *Springfield, Mass.: Samuel Bowles & Company.* 1862. 8vo, pp. 196. H. 49003

Miller (——). Military Sketch of the Present War in America. ... *London.* 1862. 8vo. Map. C. 49004

Miller (A.) Origin and Progress of the German Missions of the Methodist Episcopal Church. ... By Adam Miller. *Cincinnati.* 1843. 12mo. C. 49005

Miller (A.) A Sermon Occasioned by the Death of General Washington. Delivered at Greenbush, On the 22d Day of February, 1800. By Alexander Miller, A.M. *Albany: Printed by Charles R. and George Webster.* 1800. 8vo, pp. 15. J.C.B.

Very rare. Also: An Essay on Church Government. ... *Albany.* 1801. 8vo, pp. 30.

Miller (A.) Memoir of Rev. Alexander Gordon, ... Johnstown, ... N. Y. Compiled by Amanda Miller. *Philadelphia: William S. Young.* 1846. 18mo, pp. 170. S. 49007

Miller (A.) New States and Territories; or the Ohio, Indiana, Illinois, Michigan, North-Western, Missouri, Louisiana, Mississippi and Alabama, in their Real Characters in 1818; ... and the Advantages and Disadvantages of each, and of their particular parts; and of the new parts of York State, Pennsylvania, Virginia and Kentucky; ... By Andrew Miller. [n. p.:] *Printed for the benefit of Emigrants, and others, intending to visit the Western Country.* 1819. 24mo, pp. 96. Folded Table. + *Keene, N. H.* 1819. 8vo, pp. 32. S. 49008

A small volume of much rarity but of little use.

Miller (A. E.) Miller's Planter's and Merchant's Almanac for ... 1824; ... *Charleston, S. C.: A. E. Miller.* [1823.] 12mo, pp. (46). Continued. H. 49009

[Miller.] Notices of the Early History of South Carolina. [*Charleston: A. E. Miller.*] 1832. 8vo, pp. 14 49010

From the appendix to the reprint of Archdale's "Carolina."

Miller (A. G.) A Paper on the Judicial and Legal Condition of the Territory of Wisconsin, at and after its Organization, By Andrew G. Miller, D. A. J. Upham and W. A. Prentiss, ... Read ... July 4, 1870. ... *Milwaukee: Starr & Son, ... Printers.* 1870. 8vo, pp. 17. H. 49011

Miller (A. H.) Address before the Western Institute. By A. H. Miller. *Pittsburgh.* 1840. 8vo. 49012

Miller (A. S.) ... An Oration before the ... Alumni of Hamilton College, ... July 21, 1858, By Anson S. Miller. ... *Utica: Roberts, Printer.* 1858. 8vo, pp. 24. BA. 49013

Miller (C. W.) Address on re-opening the Slave Trade, By C. W. Miller, Esq., ... to the Citizens of Barnwell at Wylde-Moore [S. C.], August 29, 1857. *Columbia, S. C.* 1857. 8vo, pp. 10. B. 49014

Miller (E.) Report on The Malignant Disease, which prevailed in the City of New York, in ... 1805 ... . By Edward Miller, M.D. ... [*New York.* 1806.] 8vo, pp. 48. H. 49015

Miller (E. H.) The Royal Road to Fortune. By Emily Huntington Miller. *Chicago: A. L. Sewell & Co.* 1869. 16mo, pp. 333. 5 Plates. C. 49016

Miller (G. B.) Harmonious Action ... A Sermon, preached before the New York Ministerium of the Evangelical Lutheran Church, at its Semi-Centennial Anniversary in Albany, September 7, 1845. By George B. Miller. *Albany: Joel Munsell.* 1845. 8vo, pp. 25. N. 49017

Miller (G. F.) Reconstruction. Speech of Hon. George F. Miller, ... January 19, 1867. [n. p. n. d.] 8vo, pp. 7. H.

Also: True Mode of Reconstruction. Speech ... April 21, 1866. [n. p. n. d.] 8vo, pp. 8. H.

Miller (G. W.) The Political Record of the Hon. John Bell. Speech of G. W. Miller, M.D. ... at Indianapolis, Ind., September 17th, 1860. [n. p. n. d.] 8vo, pp. 8. H. 49019

Miller [Guillermo]. Resumen de los Servicios del General Miller en Sud America ... . *Lima: Imprenta de J. M. Masias.* 1861. Folio, pp. (4), 49, 5. B. 49020

See Miller (John), Nos. 49028–29, *infra.*

Miller (H.) An Address ... before the American Medical Association, ... in ... New Haven, Conn., ... 5th of June, 1860, By Henry Miller, M.D. ... *Philadelphia: Collins, Printer.* 1860. 8vo, pp. 28. B. 49021

Miller (J. W.) ... Address, ... before the New Jersey Historical Society, ... Jan'y 19th, 1854. By Hon. Jacob W. Miller. *Newark: The Society.* 1854. 8vo, pp. 16. H. 49022

Also: An Address delivered before the New-Jersey-State Agricultural Society, Sept. 21, 1855. ... *Somerville, N. J.* 1855. 8vo, pp. 53.—Oration ... on the Fourth of July, 1851, at Morristown, New Jersey. ... *Newark, N. J.* 1851. 8vo, pp. 20.—Speech ... March 15, 1842, on the Clay Resolutions. *Washington.* 1842. 8vo.—Speech ... on the Oregon Question; ... March 23, 1846. *Washington.* 1846. 8vo, pp. 16.—Speech ... on the Mexican War ... . February 2, 1847. [n. p. n. d.] 8vo, pp. 16.—Speech ... . On the Ten Regiment Bill. ... February 8, 1848. [n. p. n. d.] 8vo, pp. 16.—Speech ... relative to the Compromise Measures. ... February 12, 1852. *Washington.* 1852. 8vo, pp. 7.—Speech ... in Favor of sustaining the Collins Line of ... Steamers. ... April 22, 1852. *Washington.* 1852. 8vo, pp. 24.—Speech ... in favor of recognizing the Independence of Liberia. ... March 3, 1853. [n. p. n. d.] 8vo, pp. 7. B.

Miller (Jas.), *publisher.* *See* New York *and* Richards (T. A.)

[Miller (James M.)] Remarks on Marine Life-Saving Inventions, in connection with the Report made to Congress, March 2, 1868. *New York: William J. Read.* 1868. 8vo, pp. 11. H. 49023

Miller (J. P.) Biographical Sketches and Sermons, by some of the first Ministers of the Associate Church in America. To which is prefixed a Historical Introduction ... . By James P. Miller. *Albany: Printed by Hoffman & White.* MDCCCXXXIX. 8vo, pp. 512. 49024

Miller (J. W.) Poems and Sketches. By the late James William Miller. *Boston: Carter & Hendee.* 1830. 12mo, pp. (2), 165. H. 49025

Miller (J.) A Description of the Province and City of New York; with Plans of the City and Several Forts as they existed in the Year 1695. By the Rev. John Miller. Now first printed from the Original Manuscript. (To which is added, a Catalogue of an extensive Collection of Books relating to America ... .) *London: Thomas Rodd.* MDCCCXLIII. 8vo, pp. iv, 43. 6 folded Plans. Rodd's Catalogue, pp. (4), 21–116. + A New Edition With an Introduction and Copious Historical Notes. By John Gilmary Shea, LL.D. ... *New York: William Gowans.* 1862. 8vo, pp. 127. 6 Plans. B. 49026

Contains some curious particulars respecting the state of society in the province at that time. Fifty copies of Gowans' edition were printed in quarto size.

Miller (J.) The Case of John Miller, Esq; One of His Majesty's Council for the Bahama Islands, respecting the Surrender of the said Islands to the Arms of His Catholic Majesty, and the subsequent violation of the Article of the Capitulation by the Spanish Officers ... . *London: Printed in the Year* M.DCC.LXXXVI. 8vo, pp. viii, 54. 49027

Miller (J.) Memoirs of General [William] Miller, in the Service of the Republic of Peru. By John Miller. ... *London: Longman ...* . 1828. 2 vols., 8vo, pp. xxiii, (1), 389, (1); vii, (1), 460. 8 Maps and Portrait. + Second Edition. ... [*Ibid.*] 1829. 2 vols., 8vo, pp. ii, (1), 452; vii, (1), 557, (1). 7 Maps and 3 Portraits. B., H. 49028

A most interesting description of the war of independence of the Spanish colonies. *See* "Quarterly Review," XXXVII. 448.

Miller. Memorias del General Miller, al Servicio de la República del Perú. Traducidas al Castillano por el General Torrijos. *Londres.* 1829. 2 vols., 8vo. Maps and Plans. 49029

Miller (J. B.) Oration delivered at Utica, N. Y., July 5, 1847. By John B. Miller, Esq. ... *Utica, N. Y.: Welch & Grove, Printers.* 1847. 8vo, pp. 19. 49030

Miller (J. G.) Speech of Hon. J. G. Miller, February 19, 1852, on the Public Lands. [n. p. n. d.] 8vo. 49031

Miller (J.) Concio ad Clerum: a Sermon ... [at] Yale-College, ... September 9th, 1812. By Jonathan Miller, A.M. ... *New-Haven: Howe & Deforest.* 1812. 8vo, pp. 23. BA.

Also: ... A Sermon delivered in the Chapel of Yale College, ... Commencement Evening, Sept. 9, 1812. ... *New Haven.* 1812. 8vo.

Miller (J.) Singers and Songs of The Church: being Biographical Sketches of the Hymn-Writers in all the Principal Collections. ... By Josiah Miller, M.A. ... Second Edition. ... *London: Longmans, Green and Co.* 1869. 8vo, pp. xviii, 617. H.

Contains sketches of numerous American hymn-writers.

Miller (J. R.) History of Great Britain from the Death of George II. to the Coronation of George IV. ... By J. R. Miller. *London.* 1825. 8vo. C. + *Philadelphia.* 1836. 8vo. 49034

Includes some particulars relating to America.

Miller (L.) The Great Conflict; or Cause and Cure of Secession, by Leo Miller, Esq. Delivered at ... Providence, R. I. ... Dec. 8, 1861 ... . *Boston: Bela Marsh.* 1862. 8vo, pp. 24.

Miller (L. M.) Perfect through Suffering. A Thanksgiving Sermon delivered November 28, 1861. By Rev. L. Merrill Miller. [n. p. n. d.] 8vo, pp. 8. 49036

Also: The Spirit of our Fathers, The Nation's Hope. An Oration delivered at Ogdensburgh, July 4, 1861. ... [n. p. n. d.] 8vo, pp. 12.—The Union a Blessing ... A Sermon ... April 28, 1861. ... *Ogdensburgh.* 1861. 8vo, pp. 8.

Miller (L. W.) Notes of an Exile to Van Dieman's Land, comprising incidents of the Canadian Rebellion in 1838, Trial of the Author in Canada ... . By Linus W. Miller. *Fredonia, N. Y.* 1846. 12mo, pp. 378. C. 49037

Miller (M.) The Wild Flowers of Nova Scotia. By Mrs. Maria Miller. *London.* 1840. 4to. + Second Series. [*Ibid.*] 1853. 49038

Miller (M.) Slavery and the American War. A Lecture ... by the Rev. Marmaduke Miller ... . *Manchester: William Bremner & Co.* [1863.] 16mo, pp. 46. H. 49039

Miller (M. S.) Speech of the Hon. Morris S. Miller, ... on the Army Bill, ... January, 1814. *Georgetown: Printed by Robert Alleson.* 1814. 8vo, pp. 20. H. 49040

Also: Speech ... on the Army Bills, 8th December, 1814 ... . *Georgetown, D. C.: Richards and Mallory.* 1814. 8vo, pp. 31 H.

Miller (M.) A Sermon ... before the Hampshire Missionary Society, at ... Northampton, August 19, 1824. By Rev. Moses Miller ... . *Northampton: Printed by H. Ferry.* 1824. 8vo, pp. 40. H. 49041

Also: An Historical Discourse. ... *Shelburne Falls.* 1853. 8vo.

Miller (O.) Address of Hon. Oliver Miller, Speaker of the House of Delegates of Maryland. ... January 3, 1867. *Annapolis: Henry A. Lucas, Printer.* 1867. 8vo, pp. 6. H.

Miller (O. D.) ... An Occasional Discourse ... before the New Hampshire Convention of Universalists ... June 15, 1859. By Rev. O. D. Miller. ... *Boston: Printed by Bazin and Chandler.* 1859. 16mo, pp. 15. 49043

Miller (R.) Chronicon Ephratense, enhaltend den Lebenslauf des Ehrwürdigen Vater in Cristo Friedsham Gottrecht weyland ... Vosteher des geistlichen Ordens der Eersamen in Ephrata, der Graftschaft Lancaster in Pennsylvania. *Ephrata.* 1786. 8vo. 49044

Miller (R. A.) ... Sermon ... in ... Worcester, Mass. on ... Thanksgiving ... November 29, 1832. By Rodney A. Miller, ... *Worcester: Dorr and Howland.* 1833. 8vo, pp. 27. 49045

Also: Speech ... on the Plummer Professorship ... April 12, 1855, before the ... Overseers of Harvard University. *Boston: John P. Jewett and Company.* 1855. 8vo, pp. 38. H.

[Miller (Rutgers B.)] In Ejectment: The People of the State of New York *vs.* The Rector, &c. of Trinity Church. January, 1858. [n. p. n. d.] 8vo, pp. 9. 49046

See also "Nebular Hypothesis," Vol. v., No. 21100, *note.*

Miller. Letter and Authentic Documentary Evidence in relation to Trinity Church Property ... submitted to the Commissioners of the Land Office, June 21, 1855. By Rutgers B. Miller. *Albany.* 1855. 8vo, pp. 86. Map. C., S. 49047

Miller (S.) A Brief Retrospect of the Eighteenth Century. ... Containing a Sketch of the Revolutions and Improvements in Science, Arts, and Literature, during that Period. By Samuel

Miller, A.M. ... *New-York: Printed by T. and J. Swords.* 1803. 2 vols., 8vo, pp. xvi, 544; vi, (2), 510, (1). H., P. + *London.* 1805. 3 vols. 8vo. 49048

Contains a large amount of historical matter relative the United States.

Miller. A Discourse designed to commemorate the Discovery of New-York by Henry Hudson; ... before the New-York Historical Society, September 4, 1809; ... By Samuel Miller, D.D. ... *New-York: I. Riley.* 1810. 8vo, pp. 28. B. 49049

Also included in the New York Historical Society "Collections," Vol. I. pp. 17–45.

Miller. An Essay, on the Warrant, Nature and Duties of the Office of the Ruling Elder in the Presbyterian Church. By Samuel Miller, D.D. ... *New-York: Jonathan Leavitt.* 1831. 12mo, pp. 322. + *Philadelphia: Presbyterian Board of Publication.* [1832?] 24mo, pp. 339. H. 49050

Miller. A Letter to A Gentleman of Baltimore, in reference to the case of The Rev. Mr. Duncan. [Relative to Creeds.] By Samuel Miller, D.D. ... *Princeton Press: Printed by D. A. Borrenstein.* 1826. 8vo, pp. 89. 49051

This elicited "A Reply to Dr. Miller's Letter to a Gentleman of Baltimore, in reference to the Case of Rev. Mr. [John M.] Duncan." *Baltimore.* 1826. 12mo.

Miller. Letters concerning the Constitution and Order of the Christian Ministry ... addressed to the Members of the United Presbyterian Churches in ... New-York. By Samuel Miller, D.D. ... *New-York: Printed by Hopkins and Seymour.* 1807. 12mo, pp. 355. + Second Edition. *Philadelphia.* 1830. 8vo, pp. 485. 49052

Also: A Continuation of Letters ... . *New York.* 1809. 12mo.

Miller. Letters to Presbyterians, in the Present Crisis in the Presbyterian Church in the United States. By Samuel Miller. *Philadelphia: Anthony Finly.* 1833. 12mo, pp. vi, 314. 49053

Miller. Life of Jonathan Edwards, President of the College of New Jersey. By Samuel Miller ... . *Boston.* 1837. 12mo.

Also included in Sparks' "American Biography," VIII.

Miller. Memoir of ... Rev. Charles Nisbet, D.D. Late President of Dickinson College, Carlisle. By Samuel Miller, D.D. ... *New York: Robert Carter.* 1840. 12mo, pp. 357. Portrait. + [*Ibid.*] 1849. B. 49055

Miller. Memoirs of the Rev. John Rodgers, D.D., Late Pastor of the Wall-Street and Brick Churches in the City of

New-York. By Samuel Miller, D.D. ... *New-York: Whiting and Watson.* 1813. 8vo, pp. 432. Portrait. B. + Abridged from the Original Edition of 1813. *Philadelphia: Presbyterian Board of Publication.* [1840?] 18mo, pp. 240. Portrait. H.

Miller. A Sermon, ... in New-York, July 4th, 1793. ... At the request of the Tammany Society, or Columbian Order. By Samuel Miller. *New-York: Printed by Thomas Greenleaf.* [1793.] 8vo, pp. 38. BA. 49057

Miller. A Sermon Delivered December 29, 1799; occasioned by the Death of General George Washington, late President of the United States. ... By Samuel Miller, A.M. ... *New-York: Printed by T. and J. Swords.* 1800. 8vo, pp. 39.

Miller. A Sermon, ... before the New York Missionary Society, ... April 6th, 1802. By Samuel Miller, A.M. ... To which are added, the Annual Report of the Directors, and other papers relating to American Missions. *New York: Printed by T. & J. Swords.* 1802. 8vo, pp. 81. H. 49059

Pages 63–81, are occupied with reports of Indian councils.

Miller. A Sermon, ... January 19, 1812, at the request of a Number of Young Gentlemen of the City of New York, who had assembled to express their condolence with the Inhabitants of Richmond, on the late ... dispensation of Providence in that City. By Samuel Miller, D.D. ... *New-York: Whiting and Watson.* 1812. 8vo, pp. 42. B. + *New York: Printed by T. and J. Swords.* 1812. 8vo, pp. 50. BA. 49060

Miller. A Sermon ... on the Burning of the Theatre at Richmond. By Samuel Miller, D.D. ... *New York: Whiting and Watson.* 1812. 16mo, pp. 45. 49061

See also Witherspoon (J.), "Serious Inquiry."

Miller. ... A Sermon, ... in ... Baltimore, October 19, 1820; at the Ordination and Installation of the Reverend William Nevins ... . By Samuel Miller ... . *Baltimore: Printed by J. Robinson.* 1820. 8vo, pp. 60. BA. 49062

This sermon elicited the following:

A Letter to the Rev. Samuel Miller, D.D. ... on the charges against Unitarians, contained in his late Ordination Sermon in Baltimore. ... *Baltimore.* 1821. 12mo, pp. 24. + Second Edition. *Baltimore: John D. Toy, Printer.* 1821. 12mo, pp. 24.

This was followed by a "Second and [to the] Tenth Letters" ... . *Baltimore,* 1821–22, 12mo; to the first of which Dr. Muller replied in the following:

Miller. A Letter to the Editor of the Unitarian Miscellany, in reply to an Attack, by an Anonymous Writer in that Work, on a late Ordination Sermon ... in Baltimore. By Samuel Miller, D.D. ... *Baltimore: E. J. Coale.* 1821. 12mo, pp. 34. + Second Edition. *Boston: Samuel T. Armstrong.* 1821. 12mo, pp. 24.

Also: An Address, ... Elizabethtown, Nov. 24, 1845 ... Dedication of a Monument to Rev. James Caldwell. ... *Elizabethtown.* 1846. 8vo.—Christian Weapons ... A Sermon, ... Baltimore, October 13, 1826; at the Installation of the Reverend John Breckinridge ... . *Princeton Press: Printed by D. A. Borrenstein.* 1826. 8vo, pp. 55.—A Discourse ... before the Literary and Philosophical Society of New Jersey, ... September 27, 1825. ... *Princeton: D. A. Borrenstein.* 1825. 8vo, pp. 39, (1). B.—Discourse ... in ... New York, before the Grand Lodge of Free and Accepted Masons of the State of New York, June 24, 1795. ... *New York.* 1795. 8vo, pp. 32. + *Birmingham.* 1802. 8vo.—A Discourse ... April 12, 1797, before the New York Society for promoting the Manumission of Slaves, and protecting such of them as have been or may be liberated. ... *New York: Printed by T. and J. Swords.* 1797. 8vo, pp. 36.—The Divine Appointment, ... Duties, and ... Qualifications of Ruling Elders: a Sermon ... in ... New-York, May 28, 1809. ... *New-York: Samuel Whiting & Co.* 1811. 8vo, pp. 47.—The Guilt, Folly, and Sources of Suicide. Two Discourses ... in ... New-York, February, 1805. ... *New-York: Printed by T. and J. Swords.* 1805. 8vo, pp. 72.— ... Sermon ... in ... Albany, August 26, 1829; at the Installation of ... Reverend William B. Sprague, D.D. ... *Albany: Printed by Packard and Van Benthuysen.* 1829. 8vo, pp. 49.— ... An Introductory Lecture, ... at the opening of the Summer Session of the Theological Seminary ... Princeton, July 2, 1824. ... *Princeton, N. J.: D. A. Borrenstein.* 1824. 8vo, pp. 84. + July 3, 1829. ... *Andover: Mark Newman.* 1830. 8vo, pp. 30.—A Letter ... to the Members of the Presbyterian Churches in the United States, on the Present Crisis in their Religious ... Concerns. *Hartford: Printed by P. B. Gleason & Co.* 1833. 18mo, pp. 20.—Letters from a Father to his Sons in College. ... *Philadelphia: Presbyterian Board of Publication.* [1852?] 8vo, pp. 240. Portrait. H.—Letters on Clerical Manners and Habits; addressed to a Student in the Theological Seminary at Princeton, N. J. ... *New York: G. & C. Carvill.* 1827. 12mo, pp. xiv, 13–476. C., H. + Second Edition. [*Ibid.*] 12mo. + Third Edition, revised. *Princeton.* 1835. 12mo. + A New Edition, revised. *Philadelphia: Presbyterian Board of Publication.* [1852?] 12mo, pp. 384. Portrait.—The Literary Fountains healed: a Sermon, ... [at] the College of New-Jersey, March 9th, 1823. ... *Trenton: Printed by George Sherman.* 1823. 8vo, pp. 42.—A Sermon ... in ... New-York, July Fourth, 1795, ... before, the Mechanic, Tammany, and Democratic Societies, and the Militia Officers. ... *New-York: Printed by Thomas Greenleaf.* 1795. 8vo, pp. 33.—A Sermon, ... May 9, 1798, ... a Day of General Humiliation, Fasting and Prayer. ... *New-York: Printed by T. & J. Swords.* 1798. 8vo, pp. 46.—A Sermon, ... February 5th, 1799, ... a day of Thanksgiving, ... on account of the Removal of a Malignant and Mortal Disease ... . *New York: ... George Forman.* 1799. 8vo, pp. 36.—A Sermon, ... New-York, July 4th, 1799. ... at the Request of the Tammany Society ... . *New-York: Printed by Thomas Greenleaf.* [n. d.] 8vo, pp. 38.—A Sermon Preached March 13th, 1808, for the benefit of the Society, instituted in the City of New York, for the Relief of Poor Widows with Small Children. *New York.* 1808. 8vo, pp. 31.— ... Sermon, ... at the Inauguration of the Rev. Archibald Alexander, D.D. as Professor ... in the Theological Seminary of the Presbyterian Church [at Princeton,] &c. [With] the Professor's Inaugural Address, and the charge ... . *New-York: Whiting and Watson.* 1812. 8vo, pp. 122.—A Sermon ... in the Middle Church, New Haven, Con. Sept. 12, 1822, at the Ordination of the Rev. Messrs. William Goodall, William Richards, and Artemas Bishop, as Evangelists and Missionaries to the Heathen. ... *Boston: Crocker and Brewster.* 1822. 8vo, pp. 48.—Sermon ... before the Synod of New Jersey, for the Benefit of the African

School. ... *Trenton.* 1823. 8vo.— ... Sermon ... in ... Baltimore, September 15, 1836; at the Installation of ... Rev. John C. Backus ... . *Baltimore: Armstrong & Berry.* 1836. 8vo, pp. 46.

MILLER (S.) The Life of Samuel Miller, D.D. LL.D., Second Professor in the Theological Seminary of the Presbyterian Church, at Princeton, New Jersey. By Samuel Miller. *Philadelphia: Claxton, Remsen and Haffelfinger.* 1869. 2 vols., 8vo, pp. 381; 562. 2 Portraits. B. 49065

MILLER (S.) Prayer for our Country. Three Sermons. By Samuel Miller. *Philadelphia: Henry B. Ashmead, Printer.* 1862. 8vo, pp. 46. 49066

[MILLER (Samuel), *Jr.*] Report of the D'Hauteville Case: the Commonwealth of Pennsylvania, at the Suggestion of Paul Daniel Gonsalve Grand D'Hauteville, *versus* David Sears, Miriam C. Sears, and Ellen Sears Grand D'Hauteville. ... *Philadelphia: Printed by William S. Martien.* 1840. 8vo, pp. 295. BA. 49067

MILLER (Samuel F.). Life and Character of Abraham Lincoln. A Memorial Oration by S. F. Miller, ... at Franklin, N. Y., June 1st, 1865. *Delhi: Sturtevant & McIntosh, Printers.* 1865. 8vo, pp. 16. B. 49068

MILLER. Speech of Hon. S. F. Miller, ... on the Bill to secure to Persons in the Military or Naval Service of the United States, Homesteads or confiscated or forfeited Estates in Insurrectionary Districts. ... May 4, 1864. [n. p. n. d.] 8vo, pp. 8.

MILLER (S. B.) Historical Sketches of Hudson, embracing the Settlement of the City, City Government, Business Enterprises, Churches, Press, Schools, Libraries, etc. By Stephen B. Miller. *Hudson: Bryan & Webb, Printers.* 1862. 8vo, pp. 120.

MILLER (S. D.) Speech of the Hon. Stephen D. Miller (of South Carolina), on the Tariff. Delivered ... on the 21st & 23d of February, 1832. On Mr. Clay's Resolution in Relation to the Tariff. [n. p. n. d.] 8vo, pp. 37. 49071

MILLER (S. F.) The Bench and Bar of Georgia; Memoirs and Sketches. With an Appendix, containing a Court Roll from 1790 to 1857 ... . By Stephen F. Miller. ... *Philadelphia: J. B. Lippincott & Co.* 1858. 2 vols., 8vo, pp. 483; 454. H. 49072

MILLER. Memoir of Gen. David Blackshear, including Letters from Governors Irwin, Jackson, Mitchell, Early, and Rabun, and from Maj.-Gen. McIntosh, Brig.-Gen. Floyd, and other

Officers of the Army in the War of 1813–14 on the Frontier and Sea-Coast of Georgia; ... By Stephen F. Miller. *Philadelphia.* 1858. 8vo. C. 49073

Also: Remarks ... at ... Macon County, Ga., ... August 8th, 1850, on the Southern Question. [n. p. n. d.] 8vo, pp. 7.—Wilkins Wylder; or, The Successful Man. ... *Philadelphia: J. B. Lippincott & Co.* 1860. 12mo, pp. 420. H.

MILLER (S.) A Letter from Silvanus Miller to De Witt Clinton, L.L.D. on the Fossil Bones of the Mammoth, discovered in the State of New-York ... . *New-York: Nicholas Van Riper, Printer.* 1815. 8vo, pp. 15. B. 49074

Also: An Address ... in behalf of the New-York Institution for the Instruction of the Deaf and Dumb, ... December 24, 1818 ... . [*New York:*] *Printed by E. Conrad.* 1819. 8vo, pp. 15. Plate.—Report of the Trial of an Action on the Case, brought by Silvanus Miller, Esq. ... against Mordecai M. Noah, Esq. ... for an alleged Libel. ... By L. H. Clarke. *New-York: Printed by J. W. Palmer and Co.* 1823. 8vo, pp. 72.

MILLER (W.) Evidence from Scripture and History of the Second Coming of Christ, about the Year 1843; exhibited in a Course of Lectures. By William Miller. *Syracuse.* 1835. 12mo. + *Troy, N. Y.* 1838. 12mo, pp. 280. + *Boston.* 1840. 12mo, pp. 300. + *Boston: Moses H. Dow.* 1841. 12mo, pp. 300

Introduced here on account of its connection with "Millerism" in the United States.

MILLER. Miller's Works. ... With a Memoir of his Life. Edited by Joshua V. Himes. ... *Boston: Joshua V. Himes.* 1841. 2 vols., 18mo, pp. 252; 300, Supplement, 4. BA. 49076

[MILLER (William).] A Thrilling Narrative of the Life, Adventures, and Terrible Crimes of James Bagwell; who was tried at Somerset (Pa.) for the Murder of Solomon Jones. *Cincinnati: William Miller.* [1851.] 8vo, pp. 42. 3 Plates. C.

MILLER (W. A.) The Lessons of the Atlantic Telegraph. A Sermon ... . By Rev. William A. Miller. *Albany.* 1858. 8vo, pp. 28. 49078

MILLER (W. S.) Remarks of Hon. W. S. Miller, ... on the Bill "authorizing the Issue of Treasury Notes," &c.; passed ... January 21, 1847. *Washington: Printed by J. & G. S. Gideon.* 1847. 8vo, pp. 15. H. 49079

Also: Speech ... on the Bill to reduce the Duties on Imports. ... July 1, 1846. [n. p. n. d.] 8vo, pp. 8.—Speech ... on the War and Mail Steamer Bill. ... *Washington.* 1847. 8vo, pp. 8. H.

MILLER (W. W.) An Address, ... before the Newark Bible Society, ... 13th June, 1824 ... . By Wm. W. Miller, Esq. ... *Newark, N. J.: Printed by W. Tuttle & Co.* 1824. 8vo, pp. 26.

With the Annual Report. Also: Address ... Oct. 24, 1820 ... . *Morristown.* 1820.

MILLERN (A. von). All about Petroleum, and the Great Oil Districts of Pennsylvania, West Virginia, Ohio, &c. ... By Alexander von Millern, LL.D. ... *New York.* 1864. 12mo, pp. 87.

[MILLET (C. F. A.)] Liberté, égalité [etc.] *See* No. 40930.

MILLET (J.) A History of the Baptists in Maine ... . By Rev. Joshua Millet. *Portland: Printed by Charles Day & Co.* 1845. 12mo, pp. 472. C. 49082

[MILLET (Th.)] Nouvel Examen du Rapport de M. Barnave sur l'Affaire de Saint-Domingue ... . *Paris.* [1791?] 16mo, pp. (2), 109. H. 49083

MILLETT (D. C.) History of the Parish of St. Thomas' Church, Whitemarsh, Montgomery County, Penn'a, By the Rev. D. C. Millett, A.M. ... June 30, A. D. 1864. *Doylestown, Pa.: J. D. Mendenhall.* 1864. 8vo, pp. 12. 49084

Contains some curious epitaphs.

MILLIET DE SAINT-ADOLPHE (J. C. R.) Diccionario Geographico, Historico e Descriptivo do Imperio do Brasil, contendo a origem e historia de cada provincia, cidade, villa e aldêa; sua população, commercio, industria, e productos mineralogicos; ... Obra colligida e composta por Milliet de Saint-Adolphe, e trasladada em Portuguez do mesmo manuscripto inedito Francez, pelo Dr. Caetano Lopes de Moura, com numerosas observações e addições; ... publicada pelas diligencias e debaixo da direcção litteraria, de J. P. Aillaud. *Pariz.* 1845. 2 vols., 8vo, pp. 1375. Map. C. 49085

[MILLIGAN (*Dr.*)] A Short Description of the Province of South-Carolina, with an Account of The Air, Weather, and Diseases at Charlestown. Written in the Year 1763. *London: John Hinton.* MDCCLXX. 8vo, pp. 96. 49086

Reprinted in Carroll's "Historical Collections," II. 463–535. *See* "Monthly Review," XLIII. 484, *also* our Vol. III., No. 12039.

MILLIGAN (L. P.) Decision of the United States Supreme Court on Military Commissions. Case, Ex parte Lambdin P. Milligan et al. December Term, 1866. *Washington: W. H. & O. H. Morrison.* 1867. 8vo, pp. 23. 49087

This elicited "Review of the Decision of the United States Supreme Court, in the Case of Lambdin P. Milligan and others. [n. p. 1867.] 8vo. Also: Arguments and Decisions in the Indiana Conspiracy Case. United States Supreme Court, 1866 [*Washington: R. Sutton.* 1866.] 8vo. C.

MILLIGAN (R.) Examination of the alleged Expediency of the American Intercourse Bill. By R. Milligan. *London.* 1806. 8vo. 49088

[MILLIKEN (James).] Rejoinder. To the Stockholders of The Little Schuylkill Navigation Railroad and Coal Company. [*Philadelphia?* 1862.] 8vo, pp. 8. H. 49089

MILLIKIN (T.) Address delivered before the Graduates of the Erodelphian Society of Miami University, August 10th, 1841. By Thomas Millikin. *Rossville.* 1841. 8vo, pp. 21. 49090

Millions of Dollars Tendered Gratis, and not accepted on those terms. *Washington.* 1813. 8vo, pp. 19. 49091

Relative to the loan to promote the war of 1812.

MILLIROUX (F.) Demerary, transition de l'Esclavage à la Liberté. Colonies françaises, future abolition. Par Felix Milliroux. *Paris.* 1843. 8vo. 49092

MILLIROUX. Emigration à la Guyane Anglaise. Par Felix Milliroux. *Paris.* 1842. 8vo, pp. 92. Map. 49093

MILLIROUX (J. F.) Aperçus sur les Institutions et les Mœurs des Américains Par J.-F. Milliroux. *Paris: E. Dentu.* 1862. 8vo, pp. vii, 172, (1). BA. 49094

Written to bring into disrepute republican institutions, in the course of which De Tocqueville is assailed and the Monroe doctrine expounded.

MILLIROUX. Confédération Américaine Revue de son passé Conjectures Suggestions Par J.-F. Milliroux. *Paris: E. Dentu.* 1861. 8vo, pp. 48. B., H. 49095

Attributes the success of the American Revolution to France.

Millon de Carácas. *See* Vol. III., No. 10780.

Mills and Hicks' British and American Register, with an Almanack For ... 1774; Calculated for ... New York. *New York: Mills and Hicks.* [n. d.] 24mo, pp. 95, (1). 49096

Continued to 1780 or later.

[MILLS (Alfred), *and* HALSEY (S. S.)] In Memory of Edward W. Whelpley, Late Chief-Justice of New-Jersey. ... [n. p. 1864.] 8vo, pp. 55. Portrait. H. 49097

MILLS (A.) Colonial Constitutions; an Outline of the Constitutional History and Existing Government of the British Dependencies ... . By Arthur Mills, Esq. ... *London: John Murray.* 1856. 8vo, pp. lxxi, 399. C., H. 49098

MILLS (C.) A Sermon, ... at Crawfordsville, ... before the Commencement in Wabash College, July 18th, 1841. By Rev. Caleb Mills, M.A. ... *Indianapolis: G. A. & J. P. Chapman, Printers.* 1841. 8vo, pp. 20, (3). B. 49099

MILLS (E.) An Oration, ... in Sutton, ... July 4th, 1809. By Edmund Mills. *Sutton (Mass.): Printed by Sewall Goodrich.* 1809. 8vo, pp. 16. B., W. 49100

Also: A Sermon, ... at the Ordination of the Rev. Nathan Holman, ... in Attleborough. October 15, 1800. ... *Wrentham (Mass.): Printed by Nathaniel Heaton, Jun.* 1801. 8vo, pp. 31. H.

MILLS (E.) Statement of Edward Mills in relation to his Mail Contract with the United States Government ... . [n. p. 1848.] 8vo, pp. 15. H. 49101

MILLS (E. H.) An Oration ... at Northampton, at the request of the Washington Benevolent Society ... [July 4,] 1813. By Elijah H. Mills. *Northampton: Simeon Butler.* 1813. 8vo, pp. 24. H., W. 49102

MILLS (F. D.) Fate of Major Frederick D. Mills, ... who is supposed to have been assassinated by the Mexicans, ... immediately after the Battle of Churubusco, ... 20th of August, 1847. [n. p. n. d.] 8vo, pp. 16. B. 49103

MILLS (F. J.) Life of John Carter. By F. J. Mills. *New York.* 1868. 12mo. 49104

An interesting biography. Carter attained notoriety from the fact that he painted holding his brush in his mouth, having lost the use of his limbs. The illustrations are specimens of his work and implements.

MILLS (H.) Narrative of the Pious Death of the Penitent Henry Mills, executed for Murder, with a Solemn Address to Youth. *Boston.* 1827. 18mo. 49105

MILLS (H. F.) Natural Resources and their Development. Memorial of Hiram F. Mills, Civil Engineer, to the Governor and Council of Maine. ... *Augusta: Stevens & Sayward, Printers.* 1867. 8vo, pp. 23. Map. H. 49106

MILLS (J. B.) Report of J. B. Mills and J. H. Hopkins, upon the Surveys for the Louisa Rail Road. *Richmond.* 1836. 8vo, pp. 12. BA. 49107

MILLS (J. H.) Chronicles of the Twenty-First Regiment N. Y. S. V. ... By J. H. Mills ... . *Buffalo: J. M. Johnson.* [1863.] 4to. Portraits. BA. 49108

MILLS (J. H.) Poetic Trifles. By John Henry Mills. *Baltimore: G. Dobbin & Murphy.* 1808. 16mo, pp. 116, (14). C.

MILLS (J. L.) Two Funeral Sermons. ... In Otis, at the Interment of Mrs. Naomi D'Wolf: ... in Becket, at the Funeral of Mrs. Irene Nichols. By Joseph L. Mills ... . *Stockbridge: Printed by H. Willard.* 1811. 8vo, pp. 37. BA. 49110

MILLS (L. E.) General Pope's Virginia Campaign of 1862. ... By Lewis Este Mills. *Cincinnati: Robert Clarke & Co.* 1870. 8vo, pp. 32. BA. + *Detroit.* 1870. 8vo, pp. 32. H. 49111

MILLS (R.) The American Pharos, or Light-House Guide: founded on official reports received at the Treasury Department Also, a General View of the Coast, from the St. Lawrence to the Sabine. ... By Robert Mills, P.A. ... *Washington: Thompson & Homans.* 1832. 8vo, pp. 184. C. 49112

MILLS. Atlas of the State of South Carolina, made under the Authority of the Legislature; prefaced with a Geographical, Statistical and Historical Map of the State. By Robert Mills, ... *Philadelphia.* 1826. Folio. Map. A. + *Philadelphia: J. & W. Kite, Printers.* [1838?] Folio. 29 Maps. H. 49113

MILLS. Guide to The Capitol of The United States, embracing every Information useful to the Visiter ... . By Robert Mills, ... *Washington.* 1834. 16mo, pp. 62. S. 49114

MILLS. Guide to the Capitol and to the National Executive Offices of the United States. Illustrated by Diagram Plans ... . By Robert Mills ... . *Washington: P. Force.* 1842. 12mo. Plans. + *Washington: Wm. Greer, Printer.* 1847–8. 12mo, pp. (2), 94, (2). B. + *Washington: J. C. Greer, Printer.* 1854. 8vo, pp. 82, Index, (4). 6 Plates. C., H. 49115

MILLS. Internal Improvement of South Carolina, Particularly Adapted to the Low Country. ... By Robert Mills ... . *Columbia: Gazette Office.* 1822. 8vo, pp. 28. 49116

MILLS. Plan for a Great Canal between Charleston and Columbia, and for Connecting our Waters with those of the Western Country. By Robert Mills ... . *Columbia, S. C.* 1821. 8vo, pp. 95. 49117

MILLS. Statistics of South Carolina, including A View of its Natural, Civil, and Military History ... . By Robert Mills ... .

Charleston, S. C.: Hurlburt and Lloyd. 1826. 8vo, pp. vii, 17–782, Appendix, 47, (1). H. 49118

This book is, in fact, a history of every thing connected with the State of South Carolina, of general or local interest. Also: Memorial, submitting a new Plan of Roadway [to the Pacific. n. p. 1846.] 8vo, pp. 27. Map.—Memorial ... respecting a new Route to the Pacific Ocean. [n. p. n. d.] 8vo, pp. 7. Map. S.—A Treatise on Land Navigation. ... *Baltimore.* 1820. 8vo. Map.—Water-Works for the Metropolitan City of Washington. ... *Washington: Printed by Lemuel Towers.* 1853. 8vo, pp. 36. H.

MILLS (R. C.) A Historical Discourse delivered on the Fiftieth Anniversary of the Formation of the First Baptist Church, Salem, Mass., December 24, 1854. By Robert C. Mills. *Boston: Gould and Lincoln.* 1855. 8vo, pp. 78. A., M. 49119

Also: The Southern States Hardened until Ruined. A Sermon preached in Salem, April 13, 1865. ... *Boston: J. M. Hewes.* 1865. 8vo, pp. 21.

MILLS (S. J.) Sermon at Litchfield, at a Public Meeting of Singers, March 22, 1775. By Samuel John Mills. *Hartford.* 1775. 8vo, pp. 19. 49120

[MILLS (Samuel J.), *and* SCHERMERHORN (J.)] Communications relative to the Progress of Bible Societies in the United States. With other Articles of Information ... . *Philadelphia Bible Society.* 1813. 8vo, pp. 24. BA. 49121

MILLS. Report of a Missionary Tour through that part of the United States which lies West of the Allegany Mountains; performed under the direction of the Massachusetts Missionary Society. By Samuel J. Mills and Daniel Smith. *Andover: Flagg and Gould.* 1815. 8vo, pp. 64. 49122

See Schermerhorn (J. F.), *and* Spring (Gardiner).

MILLS (W. H.) ... A Sermon ... at the re-opening of St. Andrew's Church, Providence, R. I., July 6, 1854. By Rev. William H. Mills. *Providence: Knowles, Anthony & Co.* 1854. 8vo, pp. 18. 49123

MILLSON (J. S.) Speech of Hon. J. S. Millson ... April 28, 1852, on the Homestead Bill. [n. p. n. d.] 8vo, pp. 7. H.

Also: Nebraska and Kansas. Speech ... March 23, 1854 ... . [n. p. n. d.] 8vo, pp. 8.—Speech ... on the Late Navy Board. ... March 24, 1856. *Washington.* 1856. 8vo, pp. 12.— ... Speech ... December 14, 1852, on the Tariff Question. ... [n. p. n. d.] 8vo, pp. 7. H.

MILLSON. Remarks of Messrs. Millson, ... and [others] ... against the Abolition of the Franking Privilege. ... February 11th & 14th, 1860. [n. p. n. d.] 8vo, pp. 8. H. 49125

MILNE (A. D.) Uncle Sam's Farm Fence. By A. D. Milne. *New-York.* 1854. 12mo. C. 49126

Also: The Woman That Lives Without Eating. ... An Authentic Narrative of Mrs. Simeon Hays, of Chester, Warren Co., N. Y. ... *Glen's Falls.* 1858. 16mo, pp. 47. BA.

MILNER (T.) The Gallery of Geography: a Pictorial and Descriptive Tour of the World. By Rev. T. Milner. *London.* 1850. 2 vols., rl. 8vo, pp. xvii, 956. 49127

Also: The Gallery of Nature: a Pictorial and Descriptive Tour through Creation, illustrative of the Wonders of Astronomy, Physical Geography, and Geology. ... *London.* 1846. Rl. 8vo, pp. 804. Maps and Plates. + A New Edition, ... revised. *London: Wm. S. Orr & Co.* MDCCCXLIX. Rl. 8vo, pp. xii, 803. Maps and Plates. B.—A Universal Geography ... . *London.* 1850. 12mo, pp. 552.

MILNER (T. H.) The Present and Future State of Jamaica Considered. By T. H. Milner, Esq. *London: Hooper.* 1839. 8vo, pp. 96. 49128

MILNER (V. L.) Religious Denominations of the World; with Sketches of the Founders of various Religious Sects. By Vincent L. Milner. *Philadelphia: J. W. Bradley.* 1860. 8vo, pp. 512. 6 Portraits. + A New Edition brought up to the Present Time, by J. Newton Brown, D.D. *Philadelphia: Bradley & Co.* 1871. 12mo, pp. 609. 7 Portraits. + *Philadelphia: Bradley, Garretson & Co.* 1874. 12mo, pp. 629. 7 Portraits.

MILNOR (J.) Charitable Judgment of the Opinions and Conduct of Others, recommended; being the Last Sermon preached ... April 6, 1845; By ... Rev. James Milnor, D.D. ... *New-York: Stanford and Swords.* MDCCCLV. 8vo, pp. 24. B. 49130

MILNOR. A Sermon ... in ... New-York, ... November, 1817, being A Public Day of Thanksgiving ... . By the Rev. James Milnor ... . *New-York: Robert and Wm. A. Bartow.* 1817. 8vo, pp. 28. 49131

Also: Address ... before the ... Sunday Schools ... [of] St. George's Church, ... New York, on ... their entering into the ... Apartments prepared for their Accommodation ... November 9, 1817. ... *New-York: Printed by John C. Totten.* 1817. 8vo, pp. 30.—Plea for the American Colonization Society: A Sermon ... July 9, 1826. ... *New York.* 1826. 8vo. C.—Sermon, occasioned by the Death of His Excellency DeWitt Clinton, late Governor ... February 24, 1828. ... *New York: Printed by Gray and Bunce.* 1828. 8vo, pp. (2), 26.—The Widow and her Mites: A Sermon, ... 7th of November, 1819 ... . *New-York: Printed by T. and J. Swords.* 1819. 8vo, pp. 23.—The Address of the Rev. Dr. Tyng, at the Funeral of the Rev. Dr. Milnor; and the Funeral Sermon of the Rev. Dr. Stone; together with the Proceedings of various Religious Bodies, occasioned by the death of the Rev. James Milnor, D.D. ... *New-York: Stanford and Swords.* 1845. 12mo, pp. 66.

Milnor (J.) Oration on Masonry, ... at ... Philadelphia ... [before] the ... Grand Lodge of Pennsylvania, ... June 24, 1811, By James Milnor, Esquire ... . *Philadelphia: J. Maxwell, Printer.* 1811. 8vo, pp. 41. B. 49132

Also: Circular Charge ... by James Milnor, R.W.G.M. of the Grand Lodge of Pennsylvania, to the Subordinate Lodges in ... Philadelphia. ... *Philadelphia: James Maxwell, Printer.* 1812. 8vo, pp. 28. BA.

[Milnor (William).] An Authentic Historical Memoir of the Schuylkill Fishing Company of the State, in Schuylkill. From its Establishment on that romantic stream near Philadelphia, in the year 1732, to the present time. By a Member. *Philadelphia.* 1830. 8vo, pp. viii, 127. 2 Portraits. [Followed by:] Memoir of the Gloucester Fox Hunting Club, near Philadelphia. *Philadelphia.* 1830. pp. 56, (1). 49133

Milo, *pseudon.* Letters ... to a Friend at Pittsburgh, on the Character and Conduct of De Witt Clinton, Esq. By Milo. *New York.* 1812. 8vo, pp. 15. BA. 49134

Miltenberg (R. J.) Die Deutsche Kolonie Dona Francisca in der südbrasilischen Provinz Santa Catharina. Dargestellt nach authentischen Quellen und den neuesten Berichten von R. J. Miltenberg. ... *Berlin: Fr. Schneider & Comp.* 1852. 8vo.

Miltimore (J.) A Discourse ... in New market [N. H.], at the particular request of a Respectable Musical Choir, to a numerous Assembly, convened for Celebrating the Birth-day of the Illustrious Washington. By James Miltimore, A.M. ... *Printed at Exeter, by Henry Ranlet.* MDCCXCIV. 8vo, pp. 24.

Miltimore. A Sermon ... in Newbury-port, April 7, 1793, occasioned by the ... Death of the Rev. John Murray, A.M. ... *Exeter: Printed ... by Henry Ranlet.* 1793. 8vo, pp. 62. Port.

Also: An Anniversary Lecture; .. Nov. 27, 1810, in ... Belleville, Newbury. ... *Newburyport: E. Little & Co.* 1811. 8vo, pp. 21.—A Discourse ... before the ... Female Charitable Society of Newburyport, ... May 20, 1807. ... *Newburyport: Printed by E. W. Allen.* 1807. 8vo, pp. 19.—Oration ... in Stratham, N. H., July 4, 1806. ... *Exeter.* 1806. 8vo, pp. 16. M.—Sermon ... at the Ordination of Rev. James Thurston, New Market, October 15, 1800. ... *Exeter.* 1800. 8vo, pp. 28.—Sermon ... at the Ordination of the Rev. William Gregg, Cape-Elizabeth, July 15th, 1801. ... *Portland.* 1801. 8vo.—Sermon at the Ordination of the Rev. Jeremiah Noyes, ... Gorham, November 16, 1803. ... *Portland.* 1804. 8vo. N.—A Sermon preached ... before ... the Governor, ... Council, &c. of ... New Hampshire. ... *Concord.* 1806. 8vo.—A Sermon, ... at Belle-Ville in ... Newbury, November 24. 1807, at the Dedication of the New Meeting House ... . *Newburyport: William Sawyer & Co.* 1807. 8vo, pp. 23.—Two Discourses ... at Belle-Ville, April 9, 1812, on ... the Annual Fast ... . *Haverbill, Mass.: Printed by W..B. and H. G. Allen.* 1812. 8vo, pp. 22. B.

Miltimore (W.) A Sermon ... March 18, 1812. At the Installation of ... Rev. Elijah Kellogg. ... In Portland. By William Miltimore. ... With the Result of the Council, and other Proceedings ... . *Portland: Printed by J. M'Kown.* 1812. 8vo, pp. 30. + Second Edition. [*Ibid.*] BA. 49138

Also: A Sermon, occasioned by the Death of Mrs. Clarissa Webber ... . *Portland: Printed by A. & J. Shirley.* 1815. 8vo, pp. 16. H.

Miltitz (Alex. de). Manuel des Consuls. ... *Londres and Berlin.* 1837–42. 5 vols., 8vo. 49139

Contains items of interest useful to commerce, and treats of the commercial and maritime legislation, and the consulates established abroad, by the principal States of Europe and the United States of North America.

Milton (Charles William). Narrative of the Gracious dealings of God in the Conversion of W. Mooney Fitzgerald and John Clark, two malefactors, Who were Executed on Friday, Dec. 18, 1789, At St. John's New Brunswick, Nova Scotia, for Burglary; in a Letter from The Reverend Mr. Milton to the ... Countess Dowager of Huntingdon. *London: Printed in the year* 1790. 12mo, pp. 22. + *Exeter, N. H.* 1793. 12mo. W.

[Milton (John).] A Declaration of His Highness, setting forth the Justice of the Commonwealth's Cause against Spain. *London.* 1655. Folio, pp. (30). 46141

This very interesting tract details a great number of instances of cruelty and oppression towards English mariners and others, at Hispaniola, Providence, Tortugas, etc. Reprinted in 1738 as below:

Milton. A Manifesto of the Lord Protector of the Commonwealth ... wherein is shewn the Reasonableness of the Cause of this Republic against the Depredations of the Spaniards. Written in Latin by John Milton, and first printed in 1655. Now translated into English. The Second Edition. ... *London: A. Mellar.* 1738. 8vo, pp. 40. J.C.B. 49142

This differs sufficiently in style to render the inference almost conclusive that the English folio is the original, and was translated by Milton into Latin when first published by order of Council, October 26, 1655.

Milton. An Old Looking-Glass for the Laity and Clergy of all Denominations, Who either give or receive Money under Pretence of the Gospel: ... By John Milton, Author of Paradise Lost. *Philadelphia: Robert Bell.* M,DCC,LXX. 12mo, pp. x, 74. + *New Haven: Printed by Thomas and Samuel Green.* M,DCC,LXXIV. 8vo, pp. 100. H. 49143

Milton (*le Vte.*) Voyage de l'Atlantique au Pacifique à travers le Canada, les Montagnes rocheuses et la Colombie anglaise.

Traduit de l'anglais par M. J. Belin-Delaunay. *Paris: Hachette.* 1866. 8vo. 2 Maps. 49144

For the English edition, *see* [Fitzwilliam (W. W.)], Vol. VI., No. 24631.

Milton (W.) Report on the Claims of William Milton, and others. *Philadelphia.* 1800. 8vo. P. 49145

Milton Hill. *See* [Lisle (H. M.)], X. 41419.

Milton, *Mass.* A Collection of Papers relative to the Transactions of the Town of Milton, in ... Massachusetts, to Promote a General Inoculation of the Cow Pox, or Kine Pock, as a never-failing preventive against Small-Pox Infection. *Boston: Printed ... By J. Belcher.* 1809. 8vo, pp. 48. B., M., W. 49146

Also: The Cow Pox Act ... and a Communication, relative to the subject, from the Selectmen of ... Milton. ... *Boston: Printed by Joshua Belcher.* 1810. 8vo, pp. 16.—Auditor's Report of Receipts and Expenditures ... . *Milton, Mass.* 1855. 8vo. Continued.—A Report of the Expenses of the Town ... for ... 1838. ... *Dedham: H. Mann ... Printer.* 1838.. 8vo, pp. 8. Continued.—School Report of the Town ... for ... 1841. [n. p. n. d.] 12mo, pp. 12. Continued. *See also* Vol. I, No. 1568, *and* Vol. XI., No. 43379.

Milton College, *Wis.* Catalogue of Milton College, Wis., for ... 1865. *Janesville.* 1865. 8vo. Continued. 49147

Milwaukee, *Wis.* Annual Report of the Commerce, Manufactures, Public Improvements, and Rail Road System of Milwaukee, for ... 1855. Prepared by a Committee of the Board of Trade. *Milwaukee.* 1855. 8vo, pp. 8. Continued. H.

Annual Report of the School Commissioners ... for ... 1848. *Milwaukee.* 1848. 8vo. Continued. 49149

Annual Statement of the Trade and Commerce, ... with the General Business, of ... Milwaukee. For ... 1858. ... *Milwaukee: S. M. Booth, ... Printer.* 1859. 8vo, pp. 30. Cont'd.

Charter of the City of Milwaukee ... . *Milwaukee.* 1849. 12mo, pp. 84. H. 49151

Reprinted in 1853 and 1856.

Commissioners of the Public Debt. Circular to Holders of Municipal Bonds ... . *Milwaukee.* 1861. 8vo. 49152

Act of Incorporation, Constitution and By-Laws of the Chamber of Commerce, Milwaukee, Wis. ... *Milwaukee.* 1858. 8vo, pp. 15. H. 49153

Directory of the City of Milwaukee for ... 1847–48. By Julius P. Bolivar Maccabe. *Milwaukee.* 1847. 12mo. Cont'd.

Also: 1854–55. Col. Van Slyck's Milwaukee City Directory, and Business Advertiser. ... First Annual Edition. *Milwaukee.* 1854. 12mo. Continued.—Erving, Burdick & Co.'s Milwaukee City Directory for 1857 and 1858. *Milwaukee: King, Jermain & Co.* 1857. 8vo, pp. xxiv, 336. Continued.—Milwaukee City Directory for 1863. ... Compiled by A. Bailey. *Milwaukee: Starr & Son.* 1863. 8vo, pp. 320.—Edwards' Annual Director to ... Milwaukee, for 1865. Richard Edwards, Editor, ... *Milwaukee: Starr & Son.* 1865. 8vo.—Milwaukee Business Directory, City Guide, and Almanac, for 1867. *Milwaukee: A. Bailey.* 1867. 8vo, pp. 252.—Edwards' Annual Director ... 1868–9. *Milwaukee: Edwards & Co.* 1868. 8vo, pp. 400.—Directory, 1868–9. By J. Thickens. *Milwaukee: Hawks & Burdick.* 1868. 8vo, pp. 300. C.

Inaugural Address of ... Mayor of ... Milwaukee. ... 1848. *Milwaukee.* 1848. 12mo, pp. 18. Continued. H. 49155

Jahres-Bericht von Handel, Manufakturwesen, ... der Stadt Milwaukee für ... 1856. Zusammengestellt ... von Andrew J. Aikens, Sekretär. *Milwaukee.* 1857. 8vo, pp. 46, (1). H.

First Annual Report of the Ladies' Association, for the Aid of Military Hospitals. *Milwaukee.* 1862. 8vo. Continued.

First Annual Report of the Ladies' Bible and Benevolent Association. *Milwaukee.* 1868. 8vo. Continued. 49158

Manual of the First Presbyterian Church. With a Concise History of its Formation. *Milwaukee.* 1846. 12mo. 49159

Also: Manual of the Spring Street Congregational Church ... of Milwaukee. With Historical Sketch and Catalogue. ... *Milwaukee.* 1859. 8vo, pp. 64.

Mayor's Messages to the Common Council ... and Annual Report of the Comptroller, for ... 1863. *Milwaukee.* 1863. 8vo, pp. iv, 204. Continued. B. 49160

A Memorial from the City of Milwaukee, on the subject of a Naval Depot, an Armory and an Arsenal. *Milwaukee: Starr & Son.* 1861. 8vo, pp. 15. 49161

Memorial of ... Citizens of Milwaukee, Praying Congress not to confirm an act of the Legislative Council of Wisconsin, "to incorporate the stockholders of the Bank of Milwaukee." January 31, 1837. [*Washington.* 1837.] 8vo, pp. 22. 49162

Also: Memorials to Congress ... 1861–2. *Milwaukee.* 1862. 8vo.

Milwaukie: Report on its Commerce, and the navigation of Lake Michigan. [n. p.] 1842. 8vo. S. 49163

First Annual Catalogue of the Milwaukee Academy, for ... 1852–3. *Milwaukee.* 1852. 8vo. Continued. 49164

By-Laws of the Milwaukee and Beloit Rail Road Company, ... 1856; also Charter ... . *Milwaukee.* 1856. 8vo, pp. 30. H.

Also: Statement of the President on the Affairs of the ... Company. *Milwaukee.* 1857. 8vo, pp. 65. Map. S.

Exhibit of the Milwaukee & Horicon Railroad Company, with ... the Charter ... . *New-York: John W. Oliver.* 1856. 8vo, pp. 32. H., S. 49166

Also: First Annual Report of the Milwaukee and Horicon Railroad Company. *Milwaukee.* 1855. 8vo. Continued.

Annual Report of the Directors of the Milwaukee and Mississippi Rail Road Company, with Reports of the Treasurer, Secretary and Superintendent. January, 1849. *Milwaukee.* 1849. 8vo. Continued. 49167

Also: Engineer's Report ... . For ... 1850. [n. p. 1851.] 8vo, pp. 15. H.—Exhibit of the ... Company. June, 1852. *New York.* 1852. 8vo, pp. 36. S.

First Annual Report of the Milwaukee and Prairie du Chien R. R. Co. ... 1861. *Milwaukee.* 1862. 8vo. Continued.

Memorial of the Milwaukee and Rock River Canal Company, to Congress. December, 1857. *Milwaukee.* 1857. 8vo, pp. 24.

Also: Acts relating to the ... Company, from 1841 to 1861, inclusive. *Milwaukee.* 1861. 8vo.—Report of Commissioners appointed to ascertain and settle the Liabilities of the State ... to the ... Company. *Madison.* 1863. 8vo.—Report of the Chief Engineer of the Territory, on the ... Canal. [n. p. 1839.] 8vo, pp. 8.—Statement of the Claim of the ... Company. *Madison.* 1861. 8vo. + *Milwaukee.* 1863. 8vo.

First Annual Report of the Milwaukee and St. Paul Railway Co., ... From June ... 1863, to December ... 1864 ... . *New York: Wm. C. Bryant & Co., Printers.* 1865. 8vo, pp. 28, 2 folded leaves. Continued. B. 49170

Prospectus, Charter, etc., of the Milwaukie [*sic*] & Superior R. R. Co. May, 1856. *New York: R. C. Root* ... . [1856.] 8vo, pp. 17. H. 49171

Also: Report of the Select Committee of the Wisconsin Legislature to Investigate the Affairs of the ... Co. *Madison.* 1858. 8vo.

Charter and By-Laws of the Milwaukee Female College ... 1856. *Milwaukee.* 1856. 8vo. Continued. 49172

Also: Catalogue of the ... College, for ... 1855–6. *Milwaukee.* 1855. 8vo. Continued.—First Annual Report of the ... College, for ... 1852–3. *Milwaukee.* 1853. 8vo. Continued.

Acts incorporating the Milwaukee, Fond du Lac & Green Bay R. R. Co. *Milwaukee.* 1853. 8vo. 49173

First Annual Report of the Milwaukee Musical Society. *Milwaukee.* 1851. 8vo. Continued. 49174

First Annual Report of the Milwaukee Orphan Association. *Milwaukee.* 1851. 8vo. Continued. 49175

Milwaukee River. Resolutions of the Legislative Council for the construction of a Harbor at the Mouth of the Milwaukee River. [*Washington.*] 1834. 8vo. 49176

Acts incorporating the Milwaukee, Waukesha, and Miss. R. R. Co., with Preliminary Report, May 19, 1849. *Milwaukee.* 1849. 8vo. 49177

Also: Exhibit of the present Condition of the ... Co. ... 1851. *Milwaukee.* 1851. 8vo. Continued.—Annual Report of the Directors ... for 1849. *Milwaukee.* 1850. 8vo. Continued.—Report by Byron Kilbourn on the Flanders Fraud. *Milwaukee.* 1849. 8vo.

Proceedings and Addresses at the Twenty-fifth Anniversary of the Founding of the Plymouth Church of Milwaukee, May 27, 1866. *Milwaukee: J. H. Yewdale, Printer.* 1866. 12mo, pp. 65

Report of the Joint Committee of Citizens and Common Council on the Corporate Debt of the City. *Milwaukee.* 1861. 8vo. 49179

To Capitalists, relative to Milwaukee City Loan. *Milwaukee.* 1859. 8vo, pp. 26. Map. 49180

Valedictory and Inaugural Addresses of the Mayor before the Common Council of Milwaukee, April 21st, 1868. *Milwaukee.* 1868. 8vo. 49181

Catalogue of the Library of the Young Men's Association of ... Milwaukee ... . *Milwaukee.* 1861. 8vo, pp. 179, (1). H. + First Supplement ... . *Milwaukee.* 1863. 8vo, pp. 80. + Second Supplement ... . *Milwaukee.* 1865. 8vo, pp. 91. + *Milwaukee.* 1868. 8vo, pp. 391, (1). 49182

Charter ... of the Young Men's Association of the City of Milwaukee; with a Catalogue of the Library, and List of Members. *Milwaukee.* 1855. 8vo. 49183

Mina (C. E. de). The Life and Confession of Carolino Estrados de Mina, executed at Doylestown, June 21, 1832, for poisoning William Chapman. Written by himself in the Spanish language. Translated from the Original MS. in Spanish by C. G. *Philadelphia.* 1832. 8vo. C., P. 49184

Mina (*Gen.*) Short Extract from the Life of General Mina, published by himself. *London.* 1825. 8vo. 49185

With the Spanish text on the opposite pages.

Mina de S. Nicolas, alias el Jacal, en el mineral de Pachuca, 1841. *Pachuca.* 1841. 8vo. 49186

Mina (F. X. de). Resumen historico de la insurreccion de Nueva España, desde su origen hasta el desembarco de D. Francisco Xavier de Mina. Traducida del frances. *Mexico.* 1821. 4to, pp. 32. 49187

Miñana (J. M.) Continuacion de la Historia General de España del P. Juan de Mariana, escrita en Latin por José Manuel Miñana, y traducida al Castellano por Don Vicente Romero. *Madrid.* 1804. Folio. + *Valencia.* 1836–41. 4 vols., 4to. C.

Minas del Rincon del mineral de Temascaltepec. *Mexico.* 1851. 8vo. Map. 49189

Minas-Geraes, *Brazil.* Almanak Administrativo, Civil Industrial da Provincia de Minas-Geraes do Anno de 1869 ... 3.° Anno. *Rio de Janeiro.* 1870. Rl. 8vo, pp. 569, 12, 38, 14, 5.

Minaya (F. V.) Esfera, forma del Mundo con una breve descripcion del Mapa. Por D. Francisco Velasquez Minaya. Dividido en dos libros: en el primero la Esfera en dos tratados. *Madrid.* 1628. 8vo. 49191

This work contains a nomenclator of places in the New World, occupying 200 pages.

Mind amongst the Spindles. A Miscellany wholly composed by the Factory Girls. Selected from the Lowell Offering. With ... a Letter from Harriet Martineau. *Boston: Jordan, Swift & Wiley.* 1845. 16mo, pp. 214. B., C., S. 49192

Mind amongst the Spindles: A Selection from The Lowell Offering, a Miscellany wholly composed by the Factory Girls of an American city. With an Introduction, by the English Editor. *London: Charles Knight & Co.* 1845. 16mo, pp. 240. B. 49193

Report of the ... Managers to the Stockholders of the Mine Hill and Schuylkill Haven Rail Road Company ... 1848. *Philadelphia: Kite & Walton, Printers.* 1848. 12mo, pp. 11, (1).

Miner (Alonzo A.) Right and Duty of Prohibition. Argument before a ... Committee of the Massachusetts Legislature ... By A. A. Miner, April 2, 1867. ... *Boston: Wright & Potter, Printers.* 1867. 8vo, pp. 122. H. 49195

[Miner.] A Sermon ... at South Carver, Mass., at the Funeral of Thomas Barrows, Esq., ... May ... 1860. ... *Boston: Printed by Bazin & Chandler.* [n. d.] 8vo, pp. 15. B. 49196

Also: Annual Address ... before the American Peace Society ... May 20, 1869. ... *Boston: American Peace Society.* 1869. 16mo, pp. 32.—A Discourse, ... in ... Boston, June 9, 1852, at the Funeral of the Rev. Hosea Ballou ... . *Boston: The Society.* 1852. 8vo, pp. 56.— ... A Discourse, ... March 6, 1853, ... after the Funeral of Mrs. Ruth Ballou ... . *Boston: J. M. Usher.* 1853. 8vo, pp. 21.—An Oration ... Boston, July 4, 1855. *Boston.* 1855. 8vo, pp. 38. B., M., P.

Miner. Addresses at the Inauguration of Rev. Alonzo A. Miner, A.M. as President of Tufts College, ... July 9, 1862. *Boston: Printed by John S. Spooner.* 1862. 8vo, pp. 39. BA.

Miner. ... Shall Criminals Sit on the Jury? A Review of Governor Andrew's Veto, by Rev. A. A. Miner, D.D., and by Hon. R. C. Pitman ... With other Documents ... . *Boston: Massachusetts Temperance Alliance.* 1865. 8vo, pp. 70. H.

Miner (A.) Life and Confession of Amos Miner, who was tried and convicted ... for the Murder of John Smith, Esq., Town Sergeant of Foster ... . *Providence.* 1833. 8vo, pp. 24.

Miner (C.) History of Wyoming, in a Series of Letters, from Charles Miner, to his Son William Penn Miner, Esq. ... *Philadelphia: J. Crissy.* 1845. 8vo, pp. 488, (2), 104. 2 Maps, 2 Plates. C., H. 49200

The most complete of all the histories of this valley, which has been the scene of many tragic events. It includes a "Copy of Lt. Col. Adam Hubley's Journal on the Western Expedition, against the Indians under the Command of Major General Sullivan, 1779.

[Miner.] Letter, to the Citizens of Lancaster County, on the Woolens Bill. [n. p. 1827?] 12mo, pp. 15. B. 49201

Also: An Address, ... at ... Wilkes-Barre, Penn., December 4, 1840. In honor of the election of Gen. Wm. Henry Harrison. ... *Wilkes-Barre: Amos Sisty, Printer.* 1841. 8vo, pp. 8.—The Olive Branch; or, The Evil and the Remedy. ... *Philadelphia.* 1856. 8vo, pp. 35.—Speech ... in Defence of the Constitution, ... March 28, 1826. *Washington.* 1826. 8vo, pp. 29.—Speech ... on ... Constitutional Power to make Internal Improvements. *Washington.* 1828. 8vo.—Speech ... 6th and 7th January, 1829, on the Subject of the Slave-Trade in the District of Columbia. With Notes. *Washington.* 1829. 8vo, pp. 24.

Miner (T.) Typhus Syncopalis, ... or the Spotted-Fever of New-England, as it appeared in the Epidemic of 1823, in Middletown, Connecticut. By Thomas Miner, M.D. ... *Middletown, (Conn.): The Author.* 1825. 8vo, pp. 48. B. 49202

Also: Address to the Annual Convention of the Medical Society of Connecticut, ... at Hartford, May 10, 1837. ... *New Haven: Printed by B. L. Hamlin.* 1837. 8vo, pp. 12.—The Annual Address to the Candidates for Degrees and Licenses, in the Medical Institution of Yale College, February 26, 1839. ... *New Haven: Printed by B. L. Hamlin.* 1839. 8vo, pp. 20. H.

MINER, *and* TULLY (W.) Essays on Fevers, and other Medical Subjects. By Thomas Miner, M.D. and William Tully, M.D. *Middletown (Conn.): Printed by E. & H. Clark.* 1823. 8vo, pp. 484. B. 49203

MINER. An Examination of the Strictures in the New-England Journal ... and in the North American Review, ... 1823, on Essays on Fevers, &c. By Thomas Miner, M.D. and William Tully, M.D. ... *Middletown (Conn.): Printed by E. & H. Clark.* 1823. 8vo, pp. 22. H. 49204

MINER (T. B.) The American Bee Keeper's Manual; being a practical Treatise on the History and Domestic Economy of the Honey-Bee ... . By T. B. Miner. ... *New York.* 1849. 12mo. + Fourth Edition. *New York: C. M. Saxton.* 1852. 12mo, pp. 349. + Fourth Edition. *New York: C. M. Saxton & Company.* 1855. 12mo, pp. 349. + *New York.* 1857. 12mo.

Also: An Essay on Winter Management of Bees, with ... Rules for Feeding ... . *Clinton, Oneida County, N. Y.: The Author.* 1851. Sm. 8vo, pp. 24. B.

Mineral Lands of the Ohio Great Vein Mining Company in the Sunday Creek Valley of Perry County, Ohio. *Zanesville.* 1870. 8vo, pp. 12. 49206

Mineral Lands of the United States. Message of the President of the United States, June 6, 1846. [*Washington.* 1846.] 8vo, pp. 161. 3 Charts. P. 49207

MINERAL POINT, *Wis.* Charter and Ordinances of the City of Mineral Point; ... with the ... Rules and Regulations of the Common Council. ... 1858. *Mineral Point: Printed by Bliss & Son.* 1858. 8vo, pp. 96. H. 49208

Also: Act of Incorporation of the Village of Mineral Point. ... *Mineral Point, Wis.: George W. Bliss, Printer.* 1855. 8vo, pp. 19. H.

Directory of ... Mineral Point, for ... 1859. ... Compiled by T. S. Allen. *Mineral Point: Bliss & Son, Printers.* 1859. 12mo, pp. 64. Map and Plate. H. 49209

Also: Constitution of the Mineral Point Guards. *Madison.* 1846. 12mo.—Third Annual Fair of the Mineral Point Industrial Art Union ... September 11th, 12th, and 13th, 1860. *Mineral Point: Bliss & Son, Printers.* 1860. 12mo, pp. 17, (1). Continued.

Mineral Point Mining Company. Reports by Professor George I. Chace and Dr. Charles T. Jackson. November, 1863. *Boston: Press of Geo. C. Rand & Avery.* 1863. 8vo, pp. 8. H.

Also: Charter and Scheme of Mineral Point Mining Company. *Milwaukee.* 1865. 8vo.

Mineral Spring of Bellevue de la Cataracte [Niagara]. *Buffalo.* 1842. 18mo. S. 49211

The Miner's Hand-Book and Guide to Pike's Peak. *St. Louis.* 1859. 16mo. Map. 49212

The Miners' Journal Coal Statistical Register, for 1869: ... . *Pottsville, Pa.* 1869. 8vo, pp. 24, folded leaf, 17–20. Cont'd.

The Miner's Progress. A Series of Humorous Illustrations of the "Ups and Downs" of a Gold Digger, in pursuit of his "Pile." *Sacramento.* 1853. 8vo. 49214

The Minerva; or, Weekly Literary, Entertaining, and Scientific Journal, Devoted to the Drama, Arts, Literature, etc. By George Houston. *New York.* 1822–23. 2 vols., 4to. 49215

Continued as: "The Minerva, or Literary and Scientific Journal of Original and Select Articles. Edited by James G. Brooks." *New York.* 1824. 2 vols., rl. 8vo. Afterwards entitled: "The Minerva; or Literary, Entertaining and Scientific Journal, ... by George Houston and James G. Brooks. New Series." *New York.* 1824–25. 2 vols., 8vo. S.

Minerva Brasiliense. *See* Vol. II., Nos. 7603–4.

MINES (F. S.) A Presbyterian Clergyman looking for the Church. By the Rev. Flavel S. Mines ... . *New York: Daniel Dana, Jr.* 1858. 12mo, pp. (4), xvii, 5–580. Portrait. H.

[MINES (J. F.)] The Heroes of the Last Lustre. A Poem. *New York.* 1858. 12mo. S. 49217

Mines and Mining. *Philadelphia: American Sunday-School Union.* [n. d.] 24mo, pp. 192. H. 49218

Mines d'Or et d'Argent du Mexique. Compagnie Franco-Mexicaine pour la reprise de leur exploitation. [*Paris.* 1822.] 8vo, pp. 31. S. 49219

A prospectus in Spanish and French.

Report of the ... Directors of the Minesota [*sic*] Mining Company, presented ... 1853. *New-York: Francis Hart, Printer.* 1853. 8vo, pp. 15. Continued. H. 49220

MING (Alexander). Ming's United States Register, and New York Pocket Almanac for 1805. *New York.* 1805. 18mo. Continued. 49221

Also: Ming's Hutchin's Improved Almanac. *New-York.* 1822. 12mo. Cont'd. *See also* Gaine (H.), Vol. VII., No. 26331.

Miniature Almanack, for ... 1820. ... *Boston: Charles Ewer.* [1819.] 32mo, pp. (24). Continued. H. 49222

MINIÈRES (E. Bellot des). *See* Bellot des Minières (Ernest).

The Mining Magazine: devoted to Mines, Mining Operations, Metallurgy, &c., &c. Edited ... by William J. Tenney. Volume I. ... 1853. *New York: John F. Trow, Printer.* 1853. 8vo, pp. (2), iv, 3–672. Continued. BA. 49223

MINISCALCHI-ERIZZO (F.) Le Scoperte artiche narrate ... . *Venezia: Gio Cecchini.* 1855. 8vo, pp. xvi, 643. 4 Maps. B.

Contains a succinct history of Arctic discoveries.

MINISINK. Message of Gov. Bernard to the Minisink Indians; and a Conference in consequence thereof, held at Burlington, August, 1758. *Philadelphia.* 1758. Folio, pp. 6.

For "A Memorial of some of the Part-Owners," *see* our No. 47648.

The Minister *and* Minister in Boston. *See* [Mather (C.)]

Ministère de la marine et des colonies. *See* Vol. IV. 14717.

A Ministerial Catechise, Suitable to be Learned by all Modern Provincial Governors, Pensioners, Placemen, &c. Dedicated to T----- H---------, Esq. *Boston: Printed ... by Isaiah Thomas,* ... MDCCLXXI. 8vo, pp. 8. M., W. 49226

Governor Hutchinson is the individual at whom this is aimed, in the form of a parody or imitation of the Assembly's Catechism. One of the first books printed by Thomas.

The Ministerial Crisis and Mr. Viger [of Canada]. *Kingston.* 1844. 8vo. 49227

Ministerial Prejudices in favour of the Convention, Examin'd and Answer'd. *London: T. Cooper.* MDCCXXXIX. 8vo, pp. (2), 30. J.C.B. 49228

O Ministerio de 31 de Agosto. Uma Pagina da Historia. *Rio de Janeiro.* 1867. 8vo, pp. 31. 49229

The Ministry and the Sugar Duties. *London.* 1844. 8vo, pp. 50. 49230

Ministry at large for the Poor in Cities. *New York.* 1832. 8vo. 49231

MINNEAPOLIS, *Minn.* Merwin's Directory of ... Minneapolis, for ... 1867. *Minneapolis: H. Merwin.* 1867. 8vo, pp. 264.

Also: Charter and By-Laws of the Minneapolis Mill Company ... . *Saint Paul: Goodrich & Somers, Printers.* 1856. 16mo, pp. 14. H. *See also* No. 32081, Vol. VIII.

The Tribune's Annual Exhibit of the Manufacturing and Commercial Industry of Minneapolis and St. Anthony. *Minneapolis.* 1871. 8vo. 49233

MINNESOTA.

Act to provide Township Organization in the State of Minnesota. *St. Paul.* 1858. 8vo. 49234

Acts, Joint Resolutions and Memorials passed by the First Legislative Assembly. ... September 3d, 1849. *Saint Paul.* 1850. 8vo. Continued. 49235

... Address of the Republican Committee. The Second Congressional District of Minn. [n. p. 1868?] 8vo, pp. 20. H.

Address to Holders of Minnesota State Bonds. *New York.* 1870. 8vo. 49237

Annual Report of the Adjutant General ... for ... 1862. *St. Paul: W. R. Marshall.* 1862. 8vo, pp. 300. + Appendix to ... Report. *St. Paul: W. R. Marshall.* 1863. 8vo, pp. 392. Continued. 49238

The report for 1866 contains names of all Minnesota troops, 1861–65.

Annual Report of the Auditor ... made in ... 1864. *St. Paul.* 1864. 8vo. Continued. 49239

Annual Report of the Superintendent of Public Instruction, for ... 1865. *Saint Paul.* 1865. 8vo. 49240

Bulletin of the Minnesota Academy of Natural Sciences ... for ... 1874. ... *Minneapolis: Johnson & Smith, Printers.* 1874. 8vo, pp. 152. Continued. 49241

Catalogue of the Territorial Library ... . *St. Paul.* 1850. 8vo.

Constitution of Minnesota in the Dakota Language. Translated by S. R. Riggs. *Boston.* 1858. 12mo. 49243

Debates and Proceedings of the Minnesota Constitutional Convention, including the Organic Act of the Territory; with the Enabling Act of Congress, the Act of the Territorial Legislature relative to the convention, and the Vote of the People on the Constitution; Reported by Francis H. Smith. *Saint Paul.* 1857. 8vo. C. 49244

Debates and Proceedings of the Constitutional Convention for the Territory of Minnesota, to form a State Constitution preparatory to its Admission into the Union as a State. Reported by T. F. Andrews. *Saint Paul.* 1858. Rl. 8vo. C. 49245

No. 49244 was the "Democratic Wing," No. 49245 the "Republican Wing."

Executive Documents ... for ... 1860. ... *Saint Paul: William R. Marshall, ... Printer.* 1860. 8vo. Continued. H. 49246

The Geological and Natural History Survey of Minnesota. The First Annual Report for ... 1872. By N. H. Winchell, State Geologist. *St. Paul.* 1873. 8vo, pp. 112. Map. Continued. 49247

Also: Report of Anderson and Clark on the Geology of the State ... January, 1861. [n. p. n. d.] 8vo, pp. 26.—Report of Hanchett and Clark, November, 1864. [n. p. n. d.] 8vo, pp. 82.—Report of H. H. Eames on some of the Northern and Middle Counties of ... Minnesota, 1866. [n. p. n. d.] 8vo, pp. 58.

General and Special Laws of the State of Minnesota, passed and approved during the First Session of the State Legislature, 1857–58. *Saint Paul.* 1858. 8vo. Continued. C. 49248

The General Statutes of the State of Minnesota: revised under ... Acts ... passed at the Session of 1866. *St. Paul: Davidson & Hall, State Printers.* 1867. Rl. 8vo, pp. xi, 874.

E. C. Palmer was commissioner to revise.

Guide for Emigrants to Minnesota, by a Tourist. *Saint Paul: Goodrich, Somers & Co.* 1857. 8vo, pp. 23, (1). Map. H.

The Guide to Minnesota. ... *Saint Paul: E. H. Burritt & Co.* 1868. 12mo, pp. 81. H. 49251

Hand Book of Minnesota. *Chicago.* 1867. 12mo. 49252

The Immigrant's Guide to Minnesota in 1856. By an Old Resident. *St. Anthony: W. W. Wales* ... . 1856. 12mo, pp. 116, viii. Map. H. 49253

Inaugural Message of Governor Ramsey to the Senate and House of Representatives ... . *St. Paul: Minnesotian ... Printing Company.* 1860. 8vo, pp. 23. Continued. 49254

Independent Order of Odd Fellows. Journal of the Grand Lodge of Minnesota, held at ... St. Paul, Minnesota Territory. *St. Paul: Minnesotian Office.* 1855. 8vo, pp. 62. Continued.

Journal of the Constitutional Convention, of the Territory of Minnesota, ... held in ... Saint Paul, ... 1857. *Saint Paul.* 1857. 8vo. C. 49256

Journal of the Council during the first session of the Legislative Assembly ... September Third, One Thousand Eight Hundred and Forty-Nine. ... *Saint Paul: M'Lean & Owens, ... Printers.* 1850. 8vo, pp. 255, (1). Continued. H. 49257

Journal of the House of Representatives. First Session of the Legislative Assembly ... held at St. Paul, ... the Third ... of September, One Thousand Eight Hundred and Forty-Nine. *St. Paul: Printed by James M. Goodhue.* 1850. 8vo, pp. 250. Continued. H. 49258

Journal of the Proceedings of the First Annual Convention of the Protestant Episcopal Church in the Diocese of Minnesota, held in ... St. Paul, ... May 19th & 20th, 1858. *St. Anthony: Express Office.* 1859. 8vo, pp. 31. Continued. 49259

Journal of the Senate [and] House of Representatives, during the First Session of the Legislature of the State of Minnesota, held at Saint Paul, 3d of December, 1857. *Saint Paul.* 1858. 2 vols., 8vo. Continued. C. 49260

Journal of the Senate of Minnesota, sitting as a High Court of Impeachment, for the Trial of Hon. Sherman Page, Judge of the Tenth Judicial District. *Ramaley & Cunningham, St. Paul.* [n. d.] 3 vols., 8vo, pp. 754; 549; 389. 49261

The Legislative Manual of the State of Minnesota. Compiled for the ... Twelfth Legislature. *St. Paul: Press Printing Co.* 1870. 12mo, pp. 133. Continued. 49262

Manual of the House of Hope Presbyterian Church, Saint Paul, Minnesota, 1869. *St. Paul.* 1869. 12mo, pp. 35.

Materials for the future History of Minnesota: being a Report of the Minnesota Historical Society ... . *Saint Paul: Joseph R. Brown, Printer.* 1856. 8vo, pp. 141, 17. 5 Plates. BA., C.

The cover has the title "Annals of the Minnesota Historical Society, MDCCCLVI."

Memoirs of the State Officers, Judiciary and Members of the Twentieth Legislature of Minnesota. By C. L. Hall. *St. Paul: Pioneer Press Co.* 1878. 8vo, pp. 64. 49265

Merrill's Minnesota Guide. Prepared Expressly for Tourists and the Season of 1870. *St. Paul: D. D. Merrill, Randall & Co.* 1870. 16mo, pp. 66, (1). 49266

Message of the Governor of Minnesota, delivered to the Legislative Assembly, with accompanying Documents. January, 1852. [n. p. n. d.] 8vo. Continued. 49267

The messages delivered during 1861–65, contain much information relative to the Rebellion of 1860–65, and to the Indian massacre.

Message ... in relation to the Indian Barbarities. *See* No. 48139

Minnesota, as a Home for Immigrants. Being the first and second Prize Essays awarded by the Board of Examiners appointed ... [by] the Legislature of ... Minnesota, ... March 4, 1864. *Saint Paul.* 1865. 8vo, pp. 84. + [*Ibid.*] 1866.

First Report of the Minnesota & Pacific R. R. Co. ... January 12, 1858. *Saint Paul: Goodrich, Somers & Co., Printers.* 1858. 8vo, pp. 20. H. 49269

Minutes of the Minnesota Baptist Association, September, 1853. *St. Anthony.* 1853. 12mo. 49270

First Annual Report of the Minnesota Central Railway Co. ... January 1, 1866. *Minneapolis, Minn.* 1866. 8vo, pp. 87, (1).

Proceedings of Second Annual Meeting of the Minnesota Editorial Convention ... Saint Paul, ... January 21, 1868. *Saint Paul: Pioneer Printing Company.* 1868. 8vo, pp. 22. Continued.

Minnesota Gazetteer and Business Directory, for 1865. Containing a List of Cities, Villages, and Post Offices in the State; ... *Saint Paul: Groff & Bailey.* 1865. 8vo, pp. 399. 49273

Annals of the Minnesota Historical Society. ... *St. Paul: Printed by James M. Goodhue.* 1850. 8vo, pp. 28. + Second Edition. [*Ibid.*] 1850. 8vo, pp. 32. + 1850–1. 8vo, pp. 184. + 1852. 8vo, pp. 64. + 1853. 8vo, pp. 72. Continued.

Annual Report of the Minnesota Historical Society, ... for ... 1867. ... *St. Paul.* 1868. 8vo, pp. 32. Continued. B. 49275

Also: Charter, Constitution and By-Laws ... . *Saint Paul: Ramaley & Hall, Printers.* 1868. 8vo, pp. 11. H. *See also* Long (S. H.), Vol. X., No. 41888.

Proceedings of the First Annual Meeting of the Minnesota Horticultural Society, ... St. Paul, Jan. 27th & 28th, 1869. *St. Paul: Dispatch Printing Company.* 1869. 8vo, pp. 11. 49276

By-Laws, Rules and Regulations, of the Minnesota Hospital for the Insane. *Saint Paul.* 1867. 8vo, pp. 22. B. 49277

Also: First Annual Report ... for ... 1867. *Saint Paul.* 1868. 8vo.

First Annual Report of the Minnesota Institution for the Deaf and Dumb, for ... 1863. ... *Saint Paul: Frederick Driscoll.* 1864. 8vo, pp. 21. Continued. B. 49278

Minnesota: its Advantages. *See* [Hewitt (G.)], VIII. 31639.

Minnesota; its Place among the States. Being the First Annual Report of the Commissioner of Statistics, for ... 1860. ... *Hartford: Case, Lockwood and Company.* 1860. 8vo, pp. 174.

Minnesota: Its Progress and Capabilities. Being the Second Annual Report of the Commissioner of Statistics, for ... 1860 and 1861. *Saint Paul: Wm. R. Marshall, ... Printer.* 1862. 8vo, pp. 126, (1). H. 49280

Minnesota: its Resources and Progress; its Beauty, Healthfulness and Fertility; and its Attractions and Advantages as a Home for Immigrants. Compiled by the Commissioner of Statistics, ... *St. Paul: Press Printing Company.* 1870. 8vo, pp. 72. C.

Report of the President of the Minnesota Magdalen Society to the Legislature of 1875. *St. Paul: Pioneer Company Print.* 1875. 8vo, pp. 8. 49282

The Minnesota Messenger, containing Sketches of the Rise and Progress of Minnesota ... . *Saint Paul: A. D. Munson.* 1855. 8vo, pp. 78. 49283

Premium List and Rules and Regulations of the Ninth Annual Fair of the Minnesota State Agricultural Society, October, 1867. *Winona.* 1867. 8vo, pp. 36. H. 49284

Fourteenth Annual Report of the Minnesota State Bible Society ... . *St. Paul: David Ramaley, Printer.* 1864. 8vo, pp. 32.

Minnesota State Business Directory, containing a brief description of many of the Towns, &c. ... *H. E. Newton & Co., Minneapolis.* [1873.] 8vo, pp. 367. 49286

Minnesota State Gazetteer and Business Directory, 1878–9. *Detroit: R. L. Polk & Co.* [1878.] 8vo, pp. 810. 49287

Minnesota State Library. Annual Report. *St. Paul.* 1863. 8vo. C. 49288

Transactions of the Minnesota State Medical Society. *St. Paul: Pioneer Printing Co.* 1870. 8vo, pp. 46. Continued.

Annual Report of the Minnesota State Normal School Board, for ... 1864. *St. Paul.* 1864. 8vo. 49290

Report and Accompanying Documents of the Minnesota State Railroad Bond Commission. January 14, 1867. [*St. Paul.* 1867.] 8vo, pp. 24. H. 49291

Proceedings of the Tenth Annual Convention of the Minnesota State Sabbath School Association, ... at Faribault, June 16, 17, & 18th, 1868. *St. Paul: Press Print.* 1868. 8vo, pp. 73.

... The Minnesota Teacher and Journal of Education. ... Vol. I. January, 1868. *Saint Paul.* 1868. 8vo. Continued.

Minnesota Tourist's and Traveller's Guide, with Maps. *St. Paul: James Davenport.* 1872. 16mo, pp. 77. 2 Maps.

The Minnesota Year Book. *See* Le Duc (W. G.), X. 39689.

Minutes of the Minnesota Annual Conference of the Methodist Episcopal Church, held ... Sept. 19–24, 1866. ... *Saint Paul.* 1866. 8vo, pp. 74. H. 49295

Minutes of the Fifth Annual Session of the General Conference of Congregational Churches. ... 1860, with a Sermon. *Winona, Minn: ... D. Sinclair & Co., Printers.* 1860. 8vo, pp. 31, folded leaf. Continued. H. 49296

Proceedings of a Public Meeting of Citizens of Minnesota, in favor of a Semi-Weekly Overland Mail from Saint Paul to Puget Sound. Held January 3, 1850. *Saint Paul.* 1859. 8vo, pp. 16.

Proceedings of Encampments of the Grand Army of the Republic, Department of Minnesota, for ... 1869, '70 and '71. *St. Paul.* 1871. 8vo. 49298

Proceedings of the Grand Lodge of Ancient Free and Accepted Masons of Minnesota ... . *Saint Paul.* 1869. 8vo, pp. (2), 695. Table. C. 49299

Public Statutes of the State of Minnesota. 1849 to 1858. Compiled by Moses Sherburne and William Hollinshead, Commissioners. *Saint Paul.* 1859. 8vo. C. 49300

... Report from a Select Committee of the House of Representatives, on the Overland Emigration Route from Minnesota to British Oregon. With an Appendix. ... *Saint Paul: Earle S. Goodrich, ... Printer.* 1858. 8vo, pp. 100. H. 49301

Report of the Select Committee, to which was referred that part of the Message of the Governor ... relating to Duluth, as a Harbor, etc. *Saint Paul.* 1870. 8vo, pp. 21. Map. H. 49302

Report of the Special Emigration Agent, to ... Governor of Minnesota. ... *Saint Paul: Pioneer Printing Company.* 1867. 8vo, pp. 14. H. 49303

Report of the Committee on Schools of the Council, accompanied by the Report of the Superintendent of Common Schools. *Saint Paul.* 1852. 8vo. S. 49304

Revised Statutes of the Territory of Minnesota, passed at the Second Session of the Legislative Assembly, ... 1851. ... under the Supervision of M. S. Wilkinson. *Saint Paul.* 1851. 8vo.

Rise and Progress of Minnesota Territory. Including a Statement of the Business Prosperity of Saint Paul; and Information in regard to the different Counties, Cities, Towns and Villages in the Territory, etc. *Saint Paul: C. L. Emerson.* 1855. Rl. 8vo, pp. 64. S. 49306

Session Laws of the Territory ... passed ... 1851. ... *Saint Paul: Printed by James M. Goodhue.* 1851. 8vo, pp. 53. Continued. H. 49307

A Sketch of the Organization, Objects and Membership of the Old Settlers Association of Minnesota ... . *St. Paul: Ramaley, Chaney & Co., Printers.* 1872. 8vo, pp. 29. 49308

Special Laws of the State of Minnesota, passed and approved during the First Session of the State Legislature, 1857–58. *Saint Paul.* 1858. 8vo. 49309

Statistics of Minnesota ... for 1869. Being the First Annual Report of the Assistant Secretary of State ... . *Saint Paul.* 1870. 8vo, pp. 152. Continued. BA. 49310

The Statutes at Large, of ... Minnesota, comprising ... all Laws of a General Nature in force, March 7, A. D. 1873. ... Compiled and arranged by A. H. Bissell. *Chicago: Callaghan and Company.* 1873. 2 vols., rl. 8vo, pp. xiii, 718; 657.

The Annual Report of The Board of Regents of the University of Minnesota, to the Governor ... for ... 1872. ... *Saint Paul: Press Printing Company.* 1873. 8vo. 49312

Also: The Addresses at the Inauguration of William W. Folwell as President of the University ... December 22, 1869 ... . *Minneapolis.* 1870. 8vo, pp. 40.—Report of the Committee on Organization ... to the ... Regents of the University ... May 7, 1869. ... *Minneapolis.* 1869. 8vo, pp. 38. H. *See also* Vol. III., No. 11192.

Minnie Myrtle, *pseudon.* *See* [Johnson (Anna C.)], IX., 36183

MINNIGERODE (C.) Power: A Sermon preached at St. Paul's Church, Richmond, on the 13th November, 1864. By Rev. Charles Minnigerode, D.D. ... *Richmond, Va.: W. H. Clemmitt, ... Printer.* 1864. 8vo, pp. 20. 49313

MINOR (J. D.) Arguments in the Case of John D. Minor et al. *versus* The Board of Education of the City of Cincinnati et al. Superior Court of Cincinnati. With the Opinions and Decisions of the Court. *Cincinnati: Robert Clarke & Co.* 1870. 8vo, pp. 420. B. 49314

MINOR (L.) Discourse on the Life and Character of the late John A. G. Davis ... June 29th, 1847. By Lucian Minor, Esq. ... *Richmond: Printed by Shepherd and Colin.* 1847. 8vo, pp. 32. H. 49315

Also: An Address on Education, as connected with the Permanence of our Republican Institutions: delivered before ... Hampden Sidney College, ... September 24, 1835 ... . *Richmond: Printed by T. W. White.* 1835. 8vo, pp. 10. H.—Reasons for Abolishing the Liquor Traffic. Addressed to the People of Virginia ... . *Richmond: H. K. Ellyson.* 1853. 16mo, pp. 23. H.

MINOR (P.) Notes on the Cultivation and Management of Tobacco. By Peter Minor. *Baltimore.* 1822. 8vo. 49316

The Minor Prophets. *See* Vol. VI., No. 22871.

Minority Report, of a Committee of the General Association of Connecticut, on the Sin of Slavery. [n. p. n. d.] 8vo, pp. 20

Also: Minority Report on the Currency. December 30, 1863. [n. p. n. d.] 8vo, pp. 4.—Minority Report of the Committee on the Judiciary on the Suspension of the Habeas Corpus, May 28, 1864. [n. p. n. d.] 8vo, pp. 17.—Minority Report touching the propriety of "Recalling our Commissioners to Foreign Powers" ... . [n. p. n. d.] 8vo, pp. 8. B. [Confederate publications.] *See also* Vol. IV., No. 15320.

MINOT (G.) Public Laws of the United States of America, passed at the First Session of the Twenty-Ninth Congress, 1845–1846. *Boston.* 1846. Rl. 8vo. Continued. 49318

Also: Private Laws of the United States of America ... 1845–6. *Boston.* 1846. Rl. 8vo. Continued.

MINOT. A Memorial of George Minot, Esq. *Boston: Geo. C. Rand & Avery.* 1858. 8vo, pp. 8. H. 49319

MINOT (——). Mr. Minot's Address, ... at the Dedication of the Smith School House ... March 3, 1835. ... *Boston: Webster and Southard, Printers.* 1835. 12mo, pp. 12. H. 49320

MINOT (G. R.) Continuation of the History of the Province of Massachusetts Bay, from the Year 1748. With an Introductory Sketch of Events from its Original Settlement. By George Richards Minot ... . *Boston: Printed by Manning & Loring.* 1798. 8vo, pp. 304. Vol. II. *Boston: James White & Co. June,* 1803. pp. 222. 49321

"The second volume was published after the death of the author. It brings the history down to the year 1765, and was apparently intended as a continuation of Hutchinson."—RICH. *See also* Mass. Hist. Soc. "Collections," VIII. 86–109.

MINOT. An Eulogy on George Washington, ... who died December 14, 1799. Delivered before the Inhabitants of ... Boston, ... By George Richards Minot, A.M. *Boston: Manning & Loring.* [1800.] 8vo, pp. 24. + Second Edition. [*Ibid.*] H.

Reprinted in London, 1800, with Lee's "Oration." *See* "Columbian Phœnix."

MINOT. Mindetale over Washington. Oversat af Engelsk ved Christian Sörenssen. *Christiansand.* 1805. 8vo. 49323

MINOT. The History of the Insurrections in Massachusetts, In the Year MDCCLXXXVI, and the Rebellion consequent thereon. By George Richards Minot, A.M. *Printed at Worcester, Massachusetts, by Isaiah Thomas.* MDCCLXXXVIII. 8vo, pp. 192. H. + Second Edition. *Boston: James W. Burdett & Co.* 1810. 8vo, pp. 192. H. + Third Edition. *Boston.* 1840. 8vo. 49324

Rich says, "This insurrection is more generally known as 'Shay's Rebellion,' from the name of the person who took the lead in it, and relating to whom there is a ballad extant in Massachusetts commencing:

'My name is Shays; in former days
In Pelham I did dwell, sirs,'" etc.

MINOT. An Oration, ... March 5th, 1782. At the Request of the Inhabitants of ... Boston; to Commemorate the Bloody Tragedy of the Fifth of March, 1770. By George Richards Minot. ... *Boston: Printed by B. Edes and Sons.* 1782. 4to, pp. 15

Also: An Address to the Members of the Massachusetts Charitable Fire Society, ... May 29, 1795. ... *Boston: Printed by Alexander Martin.* 1795. 8vo, pp. 23. H. *See* [Jackson (J.)], Vol. IX., No. 35441, which is sometimes accredited to Minot.

MINOT, *Me.* Report of the ... School Committee of ... Minot, March, 1853. *Lewiston Falls: Chase & Merrill—Printers.* 1853. 16mo, pp. 11, (1). H. 49326

MINSHALL (T.) *and* (M.) Thomas and Margaret Minshall who came from England to Pennsylvania in 1682, and their early Descendants: ... [with] Accounts of Griffith Owen and Descendants ... . By One of the Sixth Generation. [n. p.] 1867. 12mo, pp. (4), 8. B., S. 49327

MINSHULL (J.) The Sprightly Widow, with the Frolics of Youth ... . A Comedy. By John Minshull. *New York.* 1803. 8vo, pp. 64. 49328

The author, an Englishman by birth, resided in New York, and wrote a number of plays, nearly all of which were performed at the old Park Theatre. The scene of the "Sprightly Widow" was laid in New York City.

Mint. Annual Report of the Director of the Mint for the Fiscal Year ending 30th June, 1859. [n. p. n. d.] 8vo. Continued. 49329

Communication relative to a proposed Branch Mint at New York. *Philadelphia.* 1808. 8vo. 49330

Also: Communication from the Director of the Mint to the Secretary of the Treasury. Relative to a Proposed Branch Mint at New York. *Philadelphia Board of Trade.* 1860. 8vo, pp. 12. C.

Letter from the Director of the Mint accompanying A Report, and sundry statements, ... December, 19, 1797. ... *Philadelphia: Joseph Gales.* [n. d.] 8vo, pp. 8. P. 49331

Message ... transmitting Report ... of the Mint ... for 1855. [n. p. n. d.] 8vo, pp. 47. S. 49332

Contains a descriptive list of the dies of medals.

The Mint at Philadelphia. ... December, 1861. *Philadelphia: Collins, Printer.* [n. d.] 8vo, pp. 14. 49333

Report of the Treasury Board on a Mint; ... *Annapolis.* 1786. 8vo. 49334

See also Secretary of State, etc.

MINTHORNE (M.) Reply to the Resolutions and Address of a Meeting at Martlings, ... New York, February 4th, 1811. Containing the Proceedings of the Committee of Safety of 1776 against Mangle Minthorne. By a Whig of '76. *New York.* 1811. 8vo. C., N. 49335

MINTO (W.) An Inaugural Oration, on the Progress and Importance of the Mathematical Sciences. Delivered at Princeton, ... 1788, By Walter Minto, LL.D. ... *Trenton: Printed by Isaac Collins.* M.DCC.LXXXVIII. 8vo, pp. 51. BA., N. 49336

MINTURN (R. B.), *Jr.* From New York to Delhi, By way of Rio de Janeiro, Australia and China. By Robert B. Minturn, Jr. *New York: D. Appleton & Co.* 1858. 12mo, pp. 488. Map. + Second Edition. [*Ibid.*] + *London: Longman ...* . 1858. 8vo. + *New York.* 1859. 8vo. BA., C. 49337

A Minute Description of the Philadelphia, Wilmington and Baltimore Rail Road ... . Also, a detailed account of the various modes of Duck Shooting, &c. as now practised on the waters of the Chesapeake Bay. ... *Baltimore: Printed by John Murphy & Co.* 1850. 16mo. 49338

Minute expressing Sympathy and Brotherly Love for our Brethren on the American Continent. Signed Josiah Forster, Clerk. [*London:*] *Printed by Harvey and Darton.* 1829. 4to, pp. 2. + *Manchester: Printed by John Harrison.* 1829. 4to, pp. 4. 49339

The Minute Gun. *Worcester.* 1845. 8vo. 49340

Edited and printed by Samuel Foster Haven, Jr., aged 14, afterwards killed in the Civil War of 1861–5.

Minute on the Slave Trade and Slavery, 1st of 12th month, 1848. [n. p.] 1848. 4to, pp. 4. 49341

Also: Minute on the presentation of the Address on Slavery. [n. p.] 1849. 4to, pp. 4. + Report on the same. [n. p.] 1850. Folio, pp. 4.—Minute on a subscription for the Negro Fund. [n. p.] 1851. 4to, 1 leaf. + 1856. 4to, 1 leaf.—Minute on Immigration Slave Trade. ... [n. p.] 1858. 4to, pp. 2.—Minute on African Slave Trade and Slavery. ... [n. p.] 1854. 8vo, pp. 2.—Minute, On the distribution of "The Address to Sovereigns, &c., on the Slave Trade and Slavery," issued by the Yearly Meetg. of 1849. 6th of 9th mo., 1850. [n. p.] 1850. 8vo, pp. 2.—Minute recommending Subscription for the Abolition of Slave Trade and Slavery. [n. p.] 1825. 4to.—Minute recommending Subscription for the Education of the Negroes and for the Aborigines. ... [n. p.] 1845. 4to, pp. 2.

Minutes and Proceedings of the First Annual Convention of the People of Colour, held ... in ... Philadelphia, ... 1831. *Philadelphia.* 1831. 8vo, pp. 16. Continued. H. 49342

See also Vol. I., No. 1334.

Minutes of a Conference. *See* Vol. IV., No. 15321.

Minutes of a Conspiracy. *See* "Minutes of the Trial," *infra.*

Minutes of a Court Martial held on board His Majesty's Ship Dodo, in Halifax Harbour, Nova Scotia, ... May 1788: ... to try Isaac Coffin, Esq., Captain of H. M. Ship Thisbe, on the charge exhibited against him ... for false Musters on the said Ship's Books. With the Minutes of the Board of Admiralty,

and Captain Coffin's Memorial; ... *London: Printed in the year* MDCCLXXXIX. 8vo, pp. 42. J.C.B. 49343

Minutes of a Court of Inquiry. *See* Vol. I., No. 1457.

Minutes of a General Convention of the Christian Church, held at Marion, New York, October, 1850. ... *Philadelphia.* 1851. 8vo, pp. 24. H. 49344

Minutes of Conferences, held with the Indians, at Easton, in the Months of July and November, 1756; Together with the Messages sent by the Government to the Indians residing on Susquehannah; and the Report of the Committee appointed by the Assembly to attend the Governor at the last of the said Conferences. *Philadelphia: Printed and Sold by B. Franklin, and D. Hall, at the New-Printing-Office, near the Market.* MDCCLVII. Folio, pp. 32. 49345

Minutes of Conferences, held with the Indians At Harris's Ferry, and at Lancaster, in March, April, and May, 1757. *Philadelphia: Printed and Sold by B. Franklin, and D. Hall, at the New-Printing-Office, near the Market.* MDCCLVII. Folio, pp. 22.

With the proprietary arms on the title-page, and one of the scarcest of a scarce series.

Minutes|of|Conferences,|held with the|Indians,|at|Easton,| In the Months of July, and August, 1757.|*Philadelphia:|Printed and Sold by B. Franklin, and D. Hall, at the|New-Printing-Office, near the Market.* MDCCLVII.| Folio, pp. 24. 49347

Minutes|of|Conferences,|held at|Easton,|In October, 1758, |With the Chief Sachems and Warriors of the Mohawks,|Oneidoes, Onondagoes Cayugas, Senecas, Tuscaroras, Tuteloes, Skaniada-|radigronos, consisting of the Nanticokes and Conoys, who now make one|Nation; Chugnuts, Delawares, Unamies, Mahickanders, or Mohickons;|Minisinks, and Wapingers, or Pumptons.| *Philadelphia:|Printed and Sold by B. Franklin, and D. Hall, at the |New-Printing-Office, near the Market.*|MDCCLVIII.| Folio, pp. 31. P. + Second Edition. [*Ibid.*] 1759. Folio. + *Woodbridge, N. J.* 1759. Folio. P. 49348

Minutes of Conferences, held at Easton, in August, 1761. With the Chief Sachems and Warriors of the Onondagoes, Oneidas, Mohickons, Tuteloes, Cayugas, Nanticokes, Delawares, Conoys. *Philadelphia: Printed and Sold by B. Franklin, and D. Hall, at the New-Printing-Office, near the Market.* MDCCLXI. Folio, pp. 18. P. 49349

Minutes of Conferences, held at Fort-Pitt. *See* Vol. V. 17589.

Minutes|of|Conferences,|held at|Lancaster,|In August, 1762.|With the Sachems and Warriors of several Tribes of| Northern and Western Indians.|*Philadelphia:|Printed and Sold by B. Franklin, and D. Hall, at the|New-Printing-Office, near the Market.* MDCCLXIII. Folio, pp. 36. P. 49350

Minutes of Debates in Council on the Banks of the Ottowa River, November —, 1791. ... *Baltimore.* 1800. 8vo, pp. 23.

Said to have been held there by the Chiefs of the several Indian Nations who defeated the Army of the United States on the 14th of the month.

Minutes of Evidence on Ceylon and British Guiana. [*London.*] 1849. Folio, pp. 704. 49352

Minutes of Evidence taken at the Bar of the House of Lords, before a Committee of the whole House, to whom it was referred to consider the Orders in Council recommended by His Majesty, ... *London.* 1808. 8vo. N. 49353

Also: Minutes of Evidence taken before the House of Commons, to whom were referred the Petitions against the Orders in Council. *London.* 1812. Folio.

Minutes of Evidence taken before the Committee on Manufactures, 1st Session 20th Congress. [*Washington.*] 1828. 8vo.

Minutes of Proceedings of the Requited Labor Convention ... Philadelphia, ... 1838. *Philadelphia.* 1838. 8vo, pp. 36. H.

Minutes of Proceedings of the Supreme Grand Council ... for the Northern Masonic Jurisdiction of the United States ... . *Boston: Printed by Tuttle & Dennett.* 1851. 8vo, pp. 30. Cont'd.

Minutes of Several Conversations. *See* Methodist, No. 48200

Minutes of the Alabama Conference ... held ... December 5th, 1855, ... with the Annual Sermon ... by Phil. P. Neely, D.D. *Montgomery.* 1856. 8vo, pp. 48. H. 49357

Minutes of the Eighteenth Session of the American Convention for promoting the Abolition of Slavery, and improving the Condition of the African Race. Convened at Philadelphia, ... 1823. *Philadelphia: Printed ... By Daniel Neall* ... 1823. 8vo, pp. 65. 49358

Also: Minutes of the Proceedings of a Special Meeting ... Philadelphia, December 10, 1818. *Philadelphia.* 1818. 8vo, pp. 68, iv.—Minutes of an Adjourned Session ... at Baltimore, 1826. *Baltimore.* 1826. 12mo.—Minutes of the Adjourned Session of the Twentieth Biennial Convention ... . *Philadelphia.* 1828. 8vo. N.

Minutes of the Annual Conferences. *See* No. 48202, *supra.*

Minutes of the Baptist General Committee, holden at Muddy-Creek Meeting-House, Powhatan County, Virginia, May, 1793. *Richmond, Virginia: T. Nicholson.* 1793. 8vo. 49359

Minutes of the Baptist Yearly Meeting of the Ancient Order of Six Principles of the Doctrine of Christ, held at Coventry, R. I., 11th, 12th, and 13th Days of September, 1812. *Providence.* 1812. 8vo, pp. 8. 49360

Also: Minutes of the Baptist Committee held at Nuckols's Meeting-House, in the County of Goochland, May, 1791. *Richmond: Printed by John Dixon.* 1791. 8vo. *See also* Vol. I., No. 3239.

Minutes of the Charleston [S. C.] Association, ... 1788. *Charleston.* 1788. 4to. Continued. 49361

Also: Minutes of the Charleston Baptist Association, ... 1802. *Charleston.* 1802. 8vo. Continued.

The Minutes of the Christian Anti-Slavery Convention. ... 1850. Cincinnati, Ohio. [*Cincinnati.* 1850.] 8vo, pp. 84. H. + 1851. ... *Chicago, Ill.* 1851. 8vo, pp. 31. 49362

Minutes of the Christian Convention, held at Aurora, Illinois, Oct. 31 and Nov. 1, 1867; with Proceedings, Resolutions, Addresses ... . *Chicago: Dean and Ottaway, Printers.* 1867. 12mo, pp. 56. + Second Edition. *Chicago: E. A. Cook.* 1868. 16mo, pp. 108. C. 49363

Minutes of the Convention of Delegates from the Synod of New-York and Philadelphia, and from the Associations of Connecticut, held annually from 1766 to 1775 inclusive. *Hartford.* 1843. 8vo, pp. 68. 49364

Minutes of the Convention of Delegates met to Consult on Missions in ... Cincinnati, A. D. 1831. ... *Lexington, Ky.* 1831. 8vo, pp. 22. 49365

Minutes of the Discussion at a Meeting at the Board of Council for Trade and Foreign Plantations, 5th March, 1813, on the Propriety of admitting Cotton Wool, the growth of the United States, during the War. *London.* 1813. 8vo. 49366

Minutes of the Dover Baptist Association met at the Diamond Meeting-House, in Essex County, Virginia, October, 1790. *Richmond: Printed by Thomas Nicholson.* 1790. 8vo. Cont'd.

Minutes of the East Maine Conference of the Methodist Episcopal Church, held ... June 23, 1852. ... *Bangor: Smith & Sayward, Printers.* 1852. 8vo, pp. 41, (1). Continued. H.

Minutes of the Evidence and Proceedings of the Select Committees on the Saguenay, Argenteuil, Kamouraska and Laval Contested Elections. *Quebec.* 1854. 8vo, pp. 54. 49369

Minutes of the Evidence taken in Committee of the House of Commons, ... [on] the Slave Trade ... . *Printed in the Year* M.D.CCLXXXIX. Folio, pp. 286. + For 1790. Folio, pp. 640.

There are four or more volumes with this general title. Also: Minutes of the Evidence taken at the Bar of the House of Lords, upon the Order for taking into consideration the ... Trade to Africa, and particularly the Trade in Slaves ... . [*London.*] 1792. Folio. *See also* Slavery.

Minutes of the General Association. *See* Vol. IV., No. 15820, *also* Vol. XI., No. 45738.

Minutes of the General Conference. *See* Vol. XI., No. 45740.

Minutes of the General Convention of Universalists in the United States, at New York, 1861. *Boston.* [n. d.] 8vo.

Minutes of the Illinois Conference of the Methodist Episcopal Church, for ... 1862. *Quincy, Illinois.* 1862. 8vo, pp. 48. H.

Minutes of the Third Session of the Kansas and Nebraska Annual Conference, ... held ... April 15–19, ... 1858. ... *St. Joseph, Mo.: Printed by Prouts and Cundiff.* 1858. 8vo, pp. 12, folded leaf. Continued. H. 49373

Minutes of the Maine Conference of the Methodist Episcopal Church, held ... June 30, 1847. *Boston: G. C. Rand & Co., Printers.* 1847. 12mo, pp. 24. Continued. H. 49374

See Vol. XI., Nos. 43961 and 43963, *also* No. 48201.

Minutes of the Particular Synod of Albany; convened at Schenectady, May, 1837. *Albany.* 1837. 8vo, pp. 29. Cont'd.

Minutes of the Proceedings of a Convention of Baptist Churches at New York, October 19–21, 1791, in forming the New York Association. *New York: Printed by Wm. Durrell.* 1791. 4to. Continued. 49376

Minutes of the Proceedings of the Bank Convention, held in ... New York, ... November, 1837. *New York.* [n. d.] 8vo, pp. 24. S. 49377

Minutes of the Proceedings of the Committee appointed on the 14th September, 1793, by the Citizens of Philadelphia, ... to attend to and to alleviate the Sufferings of the Afflicted with the Malignant Fever, prevalent in the City and its vicinity, with an Appendix, containing a list of the deceased. *Philadelphia.* 1794. 12mo, pp. 223. + *Philadelphia.* 1848. 8vo, pp. 243. Table.

Minutes of the Proceedings of the Convention of Delegates from the Abolition Societies established in different parts of the United States, assembled at Philadelphia ... . *Philadelphia.* 1794. 8vo, pp. 30. + Second Convention. *Philadelphia.* MDCCXCV. 8vo, pp. 32. + *Wilmington, Reprinted.* 1862. 8vo, pp. 19.

Continued to 1821 or later.

Minutes of the Proceedings of the Court Martial held at Portsmouth, August 12, 1792, on the ten persons charged with Mutiny on board the ship Bounty; with an Appendix, containing an account of the Real Causes of that Transaction. *London.* 1794. 4to, pp. 79. P. 49380

For an answer, *see* Bligh (W.), Vol. II., No. 5913.

Minutes of the Proceedings of the Quarantine Convention, held at Philadelphia, by invitation of the Philadelphia Board of Health, May 13–15, 1857. *Philadelphia: Crissy & Markley.* 1857. 8vo, pp. 60. Continued. 49381

Minutes of the Session of the Evangelical-Lutheran Synod of Maryland and Virginia, held in Shepherdstown, November, 1823. *Philadelphia.* 1824. 8vo. 49382

Minutes of the Shaftsbury Association at their Annual Convention, held at the Meeting House in Shaftsbury, 1788. *Bennington, Vermont: Haswell and Russell.* 1788. 8vo. 49383

Continued to 1809 or later.

Minutes of the Synod of South Carolina and Georgia; Columbia, S. C., December, 1833. *Charleston.* 1834. 12mo, pp. 84.

Minutes of the ... Synod of the Evangelical Lutheran Ministerium of the State of New York, and Adjacent Parts; Sept. 9, 1837. *Albany.* 1837. 8vo, pp. 16. Continued. 49385

Minutes | of the | Trial and Examination | of | Certain Persons, | in the | Province of New York, | Charged with being Engaged in a | Conspiracy against the Authority | of the Congress, | and | The

Liberties of America. | *London: Printed for J. Bew.* MDCCLXXXVI. 8vo, pp. iv, 45. 49386

In the preface to those "Minutes," it is stated that they were "discovered (on the late capture of New York by the British troops) among the papers of a person who appears to have been Secretary to the Committee." They relate to a conspiracy, known as "the Hickey Plot," against Congress, and particularly against Washington, whom the conspirators proposed to carry off. "A Mr. Matthews," late Mayor of New York, says the *Monthly Review,* LVI. 232, "who was prominent in the conspiracy, was condemned to suffer death, but Congress resolved to postpone the execution of the sentence, and ordered him to be carried into Connecticut, there to be imprisoned till further orders." Hickey, the ringleader, and one of Washington's life-guards, was publicly executed in New York City. The work contains some curious scandal about Washington, and Mary Gibbons, "a girl from New Jersey, of whom General Washington was very fond, and whom he maintained genteelly at a house near Mr. Skinner's." It was reprinted as:

Minutes of a Conspiracy against the Liberties of America. *Philadelphia: John Campbell.* MDCCCLXV. 8vo, pp. xiv, iv, iii, Names, 1 leaf. 49387

Twenty-five copies printed in folio, seventy-five in quarto, and one hundred and fifty in octavo.

Minutes of the Warren Association, held at Sutton, in the Province of Massachusetts-Bay, September, 1771. *Boston: Printed by John Bogles.* 1771. 4to, pp. 7. Continued. 49388

See also our Nos. 7040, 18463, 25745, 48203–4, 48758, and under the names of the organizations referred to in the various titles.

MINUTOLI *or* MINUTHOLY (J. H. van). *See* Rio (A. del).

MIQUEL (F. A. G.) Stirpes Surinamenses selectae. ... *Lugduni Batavorum.* 1850. 4to. 65 Plates. 49389

MIQUEL. Over de geografische Verspreiding der Fichtenader onderzoek omtrent de soorten, welke in Amerika, und in de landengte van Panama, voorkomen. ... *Amsterdam.* 1862. 8vo.

MIQUEORENA (A. de). Vida de la venerable madre Michaela Josepha de la Purification, religiosa de Velo, y choro de el osservantissimo convento de Señor S. Joseph de Carmelitas descalzas de la ciudad de la Puebla. *Puebla.* 1755. 4to. 49391

[MIRABEAU (Honoré Gabriel Riquetti), *Compte de).*] Avis aux Hessois et autres Peuples de l'Allemagne vendus par leur Princes a l'Angleterre. *A Cleves, Chez Bertot.* 1777. 8vo, pp. 16

Relates to the employment of the Hessians by the British during the Revolutionary War.

MIRABEAU. Considérations | sur l'ordre de | Cincinnatus, | ou, | Imitation | D'un Pamphlet Anglo-Américain. | Par le Comte de

Mirabeau. | Suivies | De plusieurs Pièces relatives à cette Institution; | D'une Lettre signée du Général Washington, | accompagnée de Remarques par l'Auteur François; | D'une Lettre de feu Monsieur Turgot, Ministre d'État en | France, au Docteur Price, sur les Législations Améri- | caines; & de la Traduction d'un Pamphlet du Docteur | Price, intitulé: Observations on the Importance of the | American Revolution, and the means of making it a benefit | to the world; accompagnée de Reflexions & de Notes | du Traducteur. | ... | *A Londres: J. Johnson.* M,DCC,LXXXIV. 8vo, pp. xii, 385, Errata, (3). + [*Ibid.*] M,DCC,LXXXV. H. 49393

Not allowed to be printed at Paris. Contains matter not in the English version.

MIRABEAU. Considerations on the Order of Cincinnatus; To which are added, As well several Original Papers relative to that Institution, As also A Letter from the late M. Turgot, Comptroller of the Finances in France, To Dr. Price, On the Constitutions of America; and an abstract of Dr. Price's Observations on the Importance of the American Revolution; With Notes and Reflections upon that Work. Translated from the French of the Count de Mirabeau [by Samuel Romilly]. *London: J. Johnson.* M,DCC,LXXXV. 8vo, pp. xii, 284. 49394

The order of "the Cincinnati" was considered inimical to American principles—and this rare piece gives the Count Mirabeau's views on the subject. "The language of the Count relating to the new order is animated and indignant, though clear and precise; the translator frequently soars above him, and sometimes seems to be lost in the clouds into which he is raised."—*Critical Review. See also* "M. Rev.," July, 1758.

MIRABEAU. Considerations on the Order of Cincinnatus. To which are added several Original Papers relative to that Institution. Translated from the French of the Count de Mirabeau. ... A New Edition with considerable Corrections. *Philadelphia: Printed by T. Seddon.* M.DCC.LXXXVI. 8vo, pp. iv, 68. BA. + [n. p. n. d.] 8vo, pp. iv, 76. 49395

MIRABEAU. Des Grafen von Mirabeau Sammlung einiger philosophischen und politischen Schriften die Vereinigten Staaten von Nord-America betreffend. Nebst einem Schreiben von demselben an den Uebersetzer. Aus dem Französischen. *Berlin und Lebau: Lagarde und Friedrich.* 1787. 8vo, pp. vi, 324. Plate. J.C.B. 49396

[MIRABEAU.] An Essay on the Nature of Colonies, and the Conduct of the Mother Country towards them. *London: Printed for J. Johnson.* MDCCLXXV. 8vo, pp. 57. J.C.B. 49397

"This performance consists of extracts from the writings of the Marquis of Mirabeau, tending to discourage the present pursuit of coercive measures towards the colonies."—*Monthly Review,* LII. 454.

[MIRABEAU.] The Glory of Soldiers cannot be completed without acting well the part of Citizens. La Gloire des Guerriers ne sauroit être complète, que lorsqu'ils savent remplir les devoirs des citoyens. Lettre circulaire aux Sociétés d'État de l'Ordre des Cincinnati, signée du Général Washington. *A Londres, Chez J. Johnson, St. Paul's Church-Yard, & Chez C. R. Hake, à Rotterdam.* M.DCC.LXXXV. 8vo, pp. xii. + Deuxième Édition. *Paris: Chaigneau Jeune.* 1815. 8vo. P. 49398

This was the first publication of le Comte de Mirabeau. He is highly unfavorable to the Society. Querard says, S. R. N. Chamfort aided in this book, which statement is confirmed in Sparks' "Life of Franklin," I. 584.

MIRABEAU. Mémoires biographiques littéraires et politiques de Mirabeau, écrits par lui-même, par son frère, son oncle et son fils adoptif; et précédés d'une Étude sur Mirabeau, Par Victor Hugo. ... *Bruxelles: Louis Hauman et Compe.* 1834–6. 12 vols., 24mo. A. + *Paris.* 1834–5. 8 vols., 8vo. C., P. 49399

MIRABEAU. Memoirs of Mirabeau: Biographical, Literary, and Political. By Himself, his Father, his Uncle, and his adopted Child. ... *London: Edward Churton.* MDCCCXXXV–XXXVI. 4 vols., 8vo, pp. xiii, 417, (1); ix, 377, (1); viii, 436; xi, 413, (1). H.

No more published.

MIRABEAU. Opinion de M. le Vicomte de Mirabeau, député du Limousin, sur la petition des villes du commerce des colonies, l'esclavage et la traite des noirs. *Paris: Vezard & le Normant.* 1790. 8vo, pp. 30. J.C.B. 49401

MIRABEAU. Reflections on the Observations on the Importance of the American Revolution, and the means of making it a Benefit to the World. By Richard Price, D.D. LL.D. Translated from the French of the Count de Mirabeau. A New Edition with considerable Corrections. *Philadelphia: Printed by T. Seddon.* M.DCC.LXXXVI. 8vo, pp. 19. BA. 49402

MIRÆUS *or* LE MIRE (A.) De Statv | Religionis | Christianæ, | per Evropam, | Asiam, Africam, et | Orbem Nouum, | Libri IV. | Avbertvs Miraevs Brv- | xellensis Ser.mis Archiducibus Alberto, | & Isabellæ Claræ Evgeniæ, | Belgarum Principibus à sacris | Oratorij, & Bibliotheca, | publicabat. | *Coloniæ Agrippinæ,* | *Sumptibus Bernardi Gualtheri.* | M. DC. XIX. | 8vo, pp. (16), 222, (6). 49403

The fourth book (pp. 200–222) is dedicated to America. For another edition, *see* Le Mire (A.), Vol. X., No. 40002.

MIRÆUS. Notitia episcopatuum orbis Christiani. *Antverpiæ: J. Plantin.* 1613. 8vo. 49404

Chapter XXVI. is "India occidentalis seu Orbis Novus," etc.

MIRÆUS. Politiae ecclesiasticae seu Status religionis Christianae, per Europam, Asiam, Africam et Orbem Novum. *Lugduni: Ant. Pillehotte.* 1620. 12mo, pp. (26), 348, (44). 49405

The fourth book "Orbis Novus" (pp. 313–348) contains a list of the Collegia Societate Jesu in the West Indies and Brazil.

MIRALLA (J. A.) Analisis del papel titulado "Lo mas y lo ménos" ... su autor D. José Antonio Miralla. *Habana: Imprenta de Palmer é hijo.* 1820. 4to, pp. 20. 49406

MIRALLA. Observaciones políticas por D. José Antonio Miralla. *Habana: Imprenta de D. Pedro Nolasco Palmer.* 1821. 4to. 49407

MIRAMON (Miguel). Á là Nacion. *Mexico.* 1859. 8vo.

MIRANDA (A. de la Torre). *See* Torre Miranda (A. de la).

MIRANDA (——). Reflexiones sobre la cuestion de la paz. *Mexico.* 1860. 8vo, pp. 22. 49409

MIRANDA (——). Schriftelycke | Notificatie | en | Protest | Van den | Graef de Miranda | Portugees Ambassadeur, | Voor sijn vertreck, aende Heeren Staten | gegeven, &c. | Naer de copye tot Delft | voor Michel Michielsen, | achter 't Stadthuys 1663. [n. p. n. d.] 4to, pp. 16. 49410

MIRANDA (F. de). Catecismo breve en lengua Otomi, dispuesto por el P. Francisco de Miranda de la Compañia de Jesus. *Impresso en Mexico, en la Imprenta de la Bibliotheca Mexicana. Año de* 1759. 8vo, pp. 16. 49411

MIRANDA (F. de). *See* [Biggs (Jas.)], *also* [Sherman (J. N.)]

It has also, with less probability, been attributed to H. A. Bullard.

MIRANDA (Fr. J.) Panegirico de San Ignacio de Loyola. ... *Mexico.* 1850. 8vo, 8 leaves. 49412

Also: Panegirico de la doctora mistica S. Teresa de Jesus. ... *Puebla.* 1859. 8vo, 8 leaves.

[MIRANDA (F. X.)] Réponse à Jean Skei Eustace, se disant Citoyen des États-Unis d'Amérique, par Junius. *Paris.* [n. d.] 8vo, pp. 20. 49413

Also: Esposicion publica (concerniente à su destierro de la ciudad de Puebla. [*Nueva-Orleans.* 1856.] 4to, pp. 68.

MIRANDA (J. A. de). Discurso recitado pelo Exm. Snr Doutor Joaõ Antonio de Miranda. Prezidente da Provincia do Pará. Na abertura da Assemblea legislativa provincial. No dia 15 de Agosto de 1840. *Pará.* 1840. 8vo, pp. 114, (30). 49414

MIRANDA (José Antonio de). Memoria constitucional e politica sobre o estado presente de Portugal e do Brasil. Dirigida a El-rei nosso senhor. *Rio de Janeiro: Typographia Regia.* 1821. 4to, pp. 91. 49415

[MIRANDA (Rafael).] Alocucion del Supremo Delegado a los Centro-Americanos. *Guatemala.* 1845. 8vo, pp. 27. 49416

[MIRANDA.] Sr. Ministro, Señores Hermanos. [n. p. n. d.] 8vo, pp. 12. 49417

MIRANDA (R.) Causa de Roque Miranda. *Mexico.* 1848. 2 parts, sm. 4to, pp. 12, 8. 49418

MIRBECK (Frederic Ignace de). Compte Sommaire de l'état actuel de la Colonie de Saint-Domingue, rendu a l'Assemblée Nationale le 26 Mai 1792, par M. de Mirbeck, Commissaire national civil, délégué par le roi aux isles françaises de l'Amérique sous-le-vent; ... . *A Paris: De l'Imprimerie Nationale.* 1792. 8vo, pp. 44. P. 49419

MIRBECK. Lettre a l'Assemblée Coloniale de la partie française de Saint-Domingue, par M. de Mirbeck. *Cap François.* 1792. 8vo. 49420

Miriam Coffin, or the Whale-Fisherman. A Tale. [By Joseph C. Hart.] *New York.* 1834. 2 vols., 12mo. + *London: G. B. Whitaker.* 1834. 3 vols., post 8vo. 49421

MIRICK (B. L.) The History of Haverhill, Massachusetts. By B. L. Mirick. ... *Haverhill: A. W. Thayer.* 1832. 12mo, pp. 277. Plate. C., H. 49422

MIRMONT (A. J. J. D. de). *See* Delaville de Mirmont (A. J. J.)

Le Miroir de la Cruelle. *See* Casas, Vol. III., No. 11270.

Miron and Florilla: a Poetic Tale. The Scenery American. *New York: Thomas J. Crowen.* 1835. 12mo, pp. 148. + *New York.* 1838. 12mo. 49423

The Mirror. ... *Newburyport: Angier March.* 1803. 2 vols., 12mo, pp. (2), 286, Index, (3); 332. 4 Plates. H. 49424

The Mirror and Casket of the Davghters [*sic*] of Indvstry [*sic*]. ... [May, 1848. *Newburyport:*] *Abel Whitton, Print.* [1848.] 8vo. H. 49425

"A Mirror for the Pretended Democracy." With a Report on Executive Patronage; ... May 4, 1826. [*Washington.* 1840.] 8vo, pp. 16, 15. M. 49426

Mirror of Merit and Beauty. *See* [Smith (James)].

The Mirror of Misery; or, Tyranny Exposed. Extracted from Authentic Documents; exemplified by Engravings. *New York.* 1807. 12mo. 49427

On slavery and the slave-trade.

Mirror of Parliament, from ... 1828 to ... 1837 ... . Edited by John Henry Barrow. *London.* 1828–37. 36 vols., folio. S.

Contains reports in full of all the speeches, many of which relate to America.

The Mirror of Taste, and Dramatic Censor. ... *Philadelphia: Bradford and Inskeep.* 1810. 8vo, pp. (2), 510, Music, (1). Portraits. Continued. BA. 49429

The Mirror of the Philomathean Society. ... Phillips Academy, Andover, ... Fall Term of 1855. [n. p. 1855.] 8vo, pp. 34.

Mirval (C.-H. de). L'Ermite du Chimboraço, ou les Jeunes Voyageurs Colombiens. ... *Paris.* [n. d.] 12mo, pp. 292.

The Misanthrope of the Mountain. A Poem. *New Haven.* 1833. 12mo. 49432

Miscegenation: The Theory of the Blending of the Races, applied to the American White Man and Negro. ... [By D. G. Croly, George Wakeman and E. C. Howell.] *New York: H. Dexter, Hamilton & Co.* 1864. 12mo, pp. ii, 72. BA. 49433

Miscelánea Hispano-Américana de ciencias, literatura i artes. Obra especialmente dirijida, a dar a conozer el estado i a promover los progresos de la instruccion en Hispano-América. *Londres.* 1827–9. 4 vols., 8vo, pp. 320; 320; 314; 314. Plates.

Contains: Noticia de la Victoria de Junin, canto a Bolivar; El Orinoco entre la cascada de Guaharivos i la embocadura del Guaviare; Cascadas del Parana; Descripcion de la Cordilleras de la America Meridional; Vida i escritos de Las-Casas, noticia importante—Sobre la Lengua de los Salvajes de la America del Norte por Morénas; Historia de la Conquista de Mejico escrita por un Indio, etc.

Miscelánea Militar Mejicana. Année 1820. *Mexico.* 1820. 8vo. 49435

Miscelánea política y literaria. *Carácas.* 1839. 8vo, pp. 190.

Miscellanea Curiosa. | Being a | Collection | Of some of the Principal | Phænomena | in | Nature, | Accounted for by the Greatest | Philosophers of this Age. | ... | *London:* | *Printed by J. B. for Jeffery Wale* ... . 1705–7. 3 vols., 8vo, pp. (8), 361; (8), 320, 41; (8), 430. Plates. BA. 49437

Vol. III. is entitled: "Miscellanea Curiosa. | Containing a | Collection | of | Curious Travels, | Voyages, | and | Natural Histories | of | Countries," | ... *London:* | *Printed by J. B. for Jeffery Wale* ... . 1707. pp. (8), 430. + [*Ibid.*] 1708. 8vo.

Miscellanea Curiosa. | Containing a | Collection | [as before]. The Second Edition, | Revised and Corrected by W. Derham, F.R.S. | *London:* | *Printed for James and John Knapton* ... . MDCCXXIII–XXVII. 3 vols., 8vo, pp. 401; 372; (8), 430. Plates. + Third Edition. *London.* 1726–27. 3 vols., 8vo. 49438

The third volume contains, among other things, five letters from Mr. John Clayton, "Observations in Virginia, and in his Voyage thither," and "Part of a Journal kept from Scotland to New Caledonia in Darien; with a Short Account of the Country. By Dr. Wallace, F.R.S.

Miscellanea Economica, Politica, etc. 1749. 49439

Title from the "Bibliotheca Americana," p. 130.

Miscellanea Poetica, ou Collecção de Poesias diversas de Auctores escolhidos. *Rio de Janeiro.* 1853. 8vo, pp. 198. 49440

Miscellaneous ... Pieces. *See* [Johnson (Sam'l)], IX. 36299.

A Miscellaneous Collection, consisting of an Original Letter from the Pen of Columbus, never before published, some Original Poetry, and detached pieces of Prose; ... *London: For the Editor.* 1803. 4to, pp. (10), 132, (4). 49441

The dedication is signed "M. H." This is a corrected title of our No. 29396.

A Miscellaneous Collection. *See* [Russell (John)].

Miscellaneous Correspondence ... . *London.* 1742. 8vo.

Contains a letter from Boston, in 1741, concerning the new preachers in New England. Title and note from one of Thomas Thorpe's catalogues.

The Miscellaneous Documents of The Senate of the United States, for ... 1854–'55. ... *Washington: Beverley Tucker, Senate Printer.* 1855. 3 vols., 8vo. Continued. 49443

A Miscellaneous Essay. *See* [McCulloch], XI. 43123.

... Miscellaneous Observations. *See* [Hildreth (S. P.)], 31796

Miscellaneous Poems. ... [n. p.] 1828. 12mo, pp. 108. H.

These poems are mostly political. A slip pasted on the title-page says, "By John Agawam." I find nothing to prove that he is the author.

Miscellaneous Poems selected from the United States Literary Gazette. *Boston: Cummings, Hilliard and Company.* 1826. 24mo, pp. (4), iv, 172. B., H. 49445

See also [Murden (Eliza)], *and* Osander, *pseudon.*

Miscellaneous Remarks. *See* Vol. II., No. 6529.

Miscellaneous Thoughts: or some Occasional Observations. Pen'd at the Desire of a Minister. *Boston.* 1740. 8vo. 49446

Miscellaneous Thoughts. *See* [Hervey (John), *Lord*)], Vol. VIII., No. 31607, *also* [Hoffman (David)], No. 32395.

Miscellaneous Works, Prose and Poetical. By a Young Gentleman of New-York [J. B. Linn]. ... *New-York: Printed by Thomas Greenleaf.* 1795. 12mo, pp. (12), 7–353, Errata, (1). B.

Miscellanies. *See* [De Peyster (A. S.)], *and* Tudor [W.]

Miscellanies, Moral and Instructive ... . *Philadelphia: Printed by Joseph James.* M.DCC.LXXX.VII. 12mo, pp. 202. H. + *New Bedford: Printed by John Spooner.* 1794. 12mo, pp. 200.

Miscellanies, viz. I. The Time-Piece; or, An honest Servant's Advice to his Master. II. Verses on the Month of May. III. An affectionate Father's dying Advice. ... *Philadelphia: Printed for the Author, by John M'Culloch.* M.DCC.XC. 12mo, pp. 24. P.

The Miscellany containing choice Specimens in Poetry and Prose; an Account of several modern Shipwrecks, and two extensive Chronological Tables. By a Gentleman of Baltimore. *Cincinnati.* 1826. 18mo, pp. 98. 49450

Miscellany, entertaining and useful. ... [*Charlestown* (*Mass.*): *Printed by Samuel T. Armstrong.* 1802.] 12mo, pp. 24. BA.

Miscellany of Knowledge; ... by several Gentlemen, ... Poetry, ... by an Irish Gentleman, now in America. A Twelve Month's Tour of Observations, through America ... . *London.* 1792. Post 8vo, pp. (12), 302, (2). + Second Edition. [*Ibid.*]

Miscowaulik Mining Co. Report of the Directors ... and others; also Articles of Association ... . *Boston: Geo. C. Rand and Avery, Printers.* 1865. 8vo, pp. 40. H. 49453

Mis Deberes para con la sociedad, o bien sea necesidad de la religion para la organizacion, estabilidad, civilizacion de las naciones. Por un abogado de los tribunales nacionales. *Mexico: Andrade.* 1860. 8vo. 49454

The Miserable Case of the British Sugar Planters; Wherein is contained, Some Remarks on the Poverty, Distress, and other Difficulties, which they labour under; &c. And Some Comparisons are made between the French and the English in regard to the Sugar Trade. With a Proposal for Relief. By a Well-wisher to the Trade and Navigation of Great-Britain. *London: R. Willock.* M DCC XXXVIII. 4to, pp. vii, 26, (2). H. 49455

Mishaps of an Indian Agent. *See* [De Puy (H. W.)], 19652.

Las Misiones del Paraguay. Su establecimiento. Sus progresos. Su destruccion. *Mexico.* 1853. 8vo. 49456

Misiones de la antigua y nueva California, para la conversion de las tribus barbaras. *Mexico.* 1833–45. 2 vols., 8vo. 49457

Misisquoi. Reports of Thomas Petherick, Esq. ... [and 3 others] on the Misisquoi Copper Mine, Canada East. ... *Boston: Printed by Cutter, Tower, and Company.* 1864. 8vo, pp. (2), 15. Map and Plate. H. 49458

Misrepresentations corrected. *See* [Porter (N.), *Jr.*]

Missa Gothica seù Mozarabica, et Officium itidèm Gothicum diligentèr ac dilucidè explanata ad Usum Percelebris Mozárabum Sacelli Toleti á Munificentissimo Cardinali Ximenio erecti; et in Obsequium Ill[mi]. Perindè ac Venerab. D. Decani et Capituli Sanctae Ecclesiae Toletanae, Hispaniarum et Indiarum Primátis. *Angelopoli: Typis Seminarii Palafoxiana Anno Domini* MDCCLXX. Folio, pp. (8), 137, 198. 3 Copperplates by J. Nava. 49459

Contains some musical notation printed from copperplates, and is particularly interesting for its rubrics and very numerous hymns. As a specimen of Mexican typography alone the volume is one of considerable interest. Angelopolis is the same as La Puebla de los Angeles, or more briefly, La Puebla.

Missale Romanum. *Mexico.* 1561. Folio. 49460

Title from [Harrisse] "Bibliotheca Americana Vetustissima."

Missão especial do Visconde de Abrantes de Outubro de 1844 á Outubro de 1846. *Rio de Janeiro.* 1853. 2 vols., 8vo, pp. x, 324; x, 440. 49461

Relates to his mission to the Courts of Berlin and London.

Mission de Cayenne. *See* Vol. III., No. 11620.

Mission du Canada. *See* [Martin *and* Montézon (F. de)].

The Mission of South Carolina to Virginia. *From the Press of James Lucas & Son, Baltimore.* [1861.] 8vo, pp. 34. 49462

From "De Bow's Review." For another edition, *see* [Memminger (C. G.)], 47490.

Mission Schools. Shall they be abolished or sustained? [*Philadelphia.* 1856.] 8vo, pp. 43. S. 49463

Mission scientifique au Mexique et dans l'Amérique Centrale, Linguistique. Manuscrit Troano. Études sur le Système graphique et la Langue des Mayas, por M. Brasseur de Bourbourg. Tome premier. *Paris: Imprimerie Impériale.* 1869. Imp. 4to. pp. viii, 224. Colored Plates in facsimile. 49464

Contains a monograph of the Palanque MSS., an elucidation of the character in Diego de Landa's Maya Alphabet and Calendar, a collection of variants, and an interlineal explanation of seven or eight leaves of the Troan MS. one of the finest specimens of the "Codex Americanus," which is faithfully reproduced. For part I., *see* Vol. V., No. 20542.

Missionary Anecdotes. Series First. ... North America and the West Indies. *Philadelphia.* 18—. 16mo, pp. 233. 49465

The Missionary Chronicle; containing the Proceedings of the Boards of Foreign and Domestic Missions. *Pittsburgh.* 1833–1849. 17 vols., 8vo. 49466

Vols. I.–V. published at Pittsburgh, Pa., by "Western Foreign Missionary Society," afterwards at New York.

Missionary Chronicle of the Presbyterian Church. *New York.* 1833. 8vo. Continued. 49467

Missionary Geography; or, the Progress of Religion traced round the World. By an Irish Clergyman. Second Edition. *Nisbet, London.* 1827. 18mo, pp. 108. Map. 49468

The Missionary Herald for the Year 1821. Vol. XVII. ... *Boston: Samuel T. Armstrong.* [n. d.] 8vo, pp. 400, viii.

A continuation of the "Panoplist." Contains a large amount of information relative to the Indians.

The Missionary Jubilee. An Account of the Fiftieth Anniversary of the American Baptist Missionary Union, at Philadelphia, May 24–26, 1864. With Commemorative Papers and Discourses. *New York: Sheldon & Co.* 1864. 8vo, pp. 500.

The Missionary Link. Eighth Number, for the Woman's Union Missionary Society of America ... . July, 1864. *New*

York: Edward O. Jenkins, Printer. [1864.] 12mo, pp. 44. Continued. H. 49471

Missionary Magazine. Published by the American Baptist Missionary Union. Vol. I. *Boston.* 1817. 8vo. Continued.

The Missionary Memorial: a Literary and Religious Souvenir. ... *New York: E. Walker.* M DCCC XLVI. 12mo, pp. xii, 372. Plate. H. 49473

Missionary Paper. Number Six. By the Associate Mission for Minnesota. Bishop Whipple. *Faribault, Minn.: Holley & Brown, Printers.* 1860. 8vo, pp. 7, (1). + No. 16. The Future Destinies of America as affected by the Present Generation. ... [n. p. 1831?] 12mo, pp. 16. H. 49474

Missionary Record, detailing the Proceedings of the Church Missionary Society. *London.* 1832. 8vo. Continued. 49475

Includes the North American colonies.

Missionary Record of the Domestic and Foreign Missionary Society ... . Vol. I. ... 1833. *Philadelphia: Printed by William Stavely.* 1833. 8vo. Continued. H. 49476

Missionary Records. North America. *London: Religious Tract Society.* [n. d.] 18mo, pp. viii, 423. + Northern Countries. *London.* 1839. 18mo, pp. viii, 195. Map. C. 49477

Missionary Remains; or, Sketches of the Lives of [Jeremiah] Evarts, [Elias] Cornelins, and [Benjamin B.] Wisner. With an Introduction by Samuel H. Cox. *New York: Taylor & Gould.* 1835. 18mo, pp. 143. C., S. 49478

Missionary Scapegoat, employed by Convert hunting Nimrods riding on the backs of beastly crowing roosters. *Baltimore, Md.* [n. d.] 8vo. 49579

Title from a Baltimore catalogue of Americana.

Missionary Society of Connecticut. *See* Vol. IV., Nos. 15633, 15639, 15805–6, 15812.

A | Missionary Voyage | to the | Southern Pacific Ocean, | performed in the years 1796, 1797, 1798, | in the | ship Duff, | commanded by | Captain James Wilson. | Compiled from Journals of the Officers and the Missionaries, | and illustrated with | Maps, Charts, and Views, | Drawn by Mr. William Wilson, and engraved by the most eminent Artists. | ... | By a Committee appointed ...

by the Directors of the Missionary Society. ... *London: T. Chapman.* 1799. 4to, pp. (12), c, 395, (5). 13 Plates. A., S., P.

Also on large paper. *See* "Monthly Review," XXXI. 331, XXXII. 1. Also included in Cavendish Pelham's "The World; or, the Present State of the Universe," Vol. I. The following are translations:

Reise in das südliche Stille Meer. *Weimar.* 1800. 8vo. + *Berlin.* 1800. 8vo. 49481

Zendelingsreis naar den Stillen Oceaan. Uit het Engelsch door J. Heringa. *Dordrecht.* 1801–2. 3 vols., 8vo. Maps and Platès. 49482

Un Missionnaire russe. *See* Galitzin, Vol. VII., No. 26375.

Missions of the Moravians among the North American Indians inhabiting the Middle States of the Union. *Philadelphia: American Sunday School Union.* 1831. 18mo, pp. 162. C. 49483

Missions to the North American Indians. New Edition, abridged. *London.* 1848. 18mo, pp. 244. Map. 49484

Missionsbilder. 4. Heft. Nordamericanische Indianer. *Stuttgart: J. F. Steinkopf.* 1865. 8vo, pp. 132. + 5. Heft. Die Mission in den Polarländern. *Calw: Vereinsbuchhandlung.* 1866. 8vo, pp. 119. + 7. Heft. Jamaika und die Bahamas. 1868.

The Missisquoi Spring Water and its Wonderful Cures. *New York: Anson Herrick & Sons.* [1867.] 16mo, pp. 16. H. 49486

Also: The Missisquoi Springs [Sheldon, Vermont,] and their Wonderful Cures. *New York: Anson Herrick & Sons, Printers.* [1868.] 12mo, pp. 48. H.

Mississippi.

An Account of the Origin. *See* McNutt (A. G.), XI. 43609.

An Act to Establish a Bank in the Mississippi Territory, passed the 23rd Dec. 1809. *Natchez: J. W. Winn & Co.* 1811. 8vo.

Acts and Resolutions, from October, 1817, to February, 1819. *Natchez.* 1818–19. 8vo. W. 49488

Address of the Commissioners of the Gulf and Ship Island Railroad ... June 7th, 1858. ... *Jackson.* 1858. 8vo, pp. 35.

Le bassin du Mississipi. *See* [Chaix (Paul)], III. 11740.

Case of the Mississippi Territory. *See* Vol. IX., No. 37434.

Catalogue of the ... State Library. *Jackson.* 1858. 8vo.

The library was burnt in 1863.

Charter of the Grand Gulf Rail Road and Banking Company, ... Mississippi. ... *Port Gibson.* 1834. 12mo, pp. 8. 49491

Code of Mississippi; being an Analytical Compilation of the Public and General Statutes of the Territory and of the State; with ... Cession of the Country by the Choctaw and Chickasaw Indians, and Acts of Congress for the survey and sale of the Lands, and granting donations thereof to the State; By A. Hutchinson. *Jackson.* 1848. 8vo, pp. 1111. C. 49492

Constitution and Ordinances of ... Mississippi, adopted in Convention assembled ... in 1868. *Jackson.* 1868. 8vo, pp. 48.

The Constitution of the State of Mississippi, as revised in Convention on the 26th of October, 1832. *Jackson, Miss.: Printed by Peter Isler.* 1832. 8vo, pp. 27. 49494

The Constitution of the State of Mississippi. *Natchez.* [n. d.] 12mo. W. 49495

Constitution of the State of Mississippi, as amended with the Orvinances [*sic*] and Resolutions adopted ... August, 1865. ... *Jackson, Miss.: E. M. Yerger, State Printer.* 1865. 8vo, pp. 56.

Description de l'Amérique et des parties d'icelle, comme de la Nouvelle-France, Floride, des Antilles, Lucaya, Cuba, Jamaica, ... *Amsterdam: Cloppenburg.* 1619. Folio. 49497

A Digest of the Laws of Mississippi, comprising all the Laws of a General Nature, including the Act of the Session of 1839. By T. J. Fox Alden and J. A. Van Hoesen. ... *New York.* 1839. 8vo. A., C., S. 49498

Digest of the Statutes of the Mississippi Territory, containing the Ordinance for the Government of the Territory of the United States Northwest of the River Ohio, and such Acts of Congress as relate to the Mississippi Territory. ... By Harry Toulmin. *Natchez.* 1807. 8vo. C. 49499

Extracts from the Records of the Synod of Mississippi, from 1835 to 1837. *Natchez.* 1838. 8vo, pp. 54. 49500

Geology. Report on the Geological Age of the Mississippi Delta; by E. W. Hilgard. ... *Washington.* 1870. 8vo, pp. 10.

Preliminary Report of the Geology and Agriculture of ... Mississippi, By L. Harper, LL.D. ... *Jackson: E. Barksdale, ... Printer.* 1857. 8vo, pp. 4–8, 350, (1). Maps and Plates. B. 49502

Annual Report on the Geology and Agriculture of ... Mississippi. By E. W. Hilgard. *Jackson.* 1858. 12mo, pp. 22.

Report on the Geology and Agriculture of ... Mississippi. By E. W. Hilgard, State Geologist. *Jackson.* 1860. 8vo, pp. xxiv, 391. Map and 2 Plates. 49504

Constitution of the M. W. Grand Lodge of the State of Mississippi of Free and Accepted Masons. ... [n. p. n. d.] 8vo, pp. 16. 49505

The Inaugural Address of William M'Willie, November 16, 1857. *Jackson: E. Barksdale, ... Printer.* 1857. 8vo, pp. 8. Continued. H. 49506

Indians—Choctaw Citizens. *See* Vol. IX., No. 34658.

Journal of the House of Representatives of the State of Mississippi ... 1840. *Jackson: Printed by C. M. Price.* 1840. 8vo, pp. 967. Continued. B. 49507

Journal of the Proceedings and Debates in the Constitutional Convention of ... Mississippi, August, 1865: ... *Jackson, Miss.: E. M. Yerger, State Printer.* 1865. 8vo, pp. 296, (2). C., S.

Journal of the Senate of ... Mississippi. *Jackson.* 1838. 8vo. Continued. C. 49509

Journal of the Senate and House of ... Mississippi. *Jackson.* 1858. 2 vols., 8vo. C. 49510

Journal of the State Convention and Ordinances and Resolutions adopted in January, 1861, with an Appendix. ... *Jackson, Miss.: E. Barksdale, State Printer.* 1861. 8vo, pp. 256.

The Confederate convention.

Laws of the Mississippi Territory. ... 1799–1800. ... *Natchez* 1799–1800. Folio. 49512

Laws of the State of Mississippi, 1817–18 ... . *Natchez.* 1818. 8vo. Continued. C. 49513

Laws of ... Mississippi, embracing all Acts of a Public Nature, from ... 1824, to ... 1838: ... *Jackson.* 1838. 8vo, pp. 932.

Laws of ... Mississippi. Passed at a called session of the Mississippi Legislature, held in Macon, August, 1864. *Meridian, Miss.: J. J. Shannon & Co., ... Printers.* 1864. 8vo. pp. 64.

These are the Confederate Laws.

Majority and Minority Reports of the Committee on State and Federal Relations, to the Legislature of the State. ... *Jackson.* 1867. 12mo, pp. 8. C. 49516

... Memorial ... upon the Subject of the Lands acquired by Treaty from the Choctaw Nation of Indians. [*Washington.*] 1832. 8vo, pp. 7. 49517

Message of the Governor to the Legislature of ... Mississippi, delivered January 8, 1839. ... *Jackson: Printed by B. D. Howard.* 1839. 8vo. Continued. 49518

Message from the President ... transmitting copies of the Laws of the Mississippi Territory. [*Washington.* 1801.] 8vo, pp. 16.

Mississippi. Nederlands tegenwoordige financiële nood. *Arnhem: C. A. Thieme.* 1839. 8vo. 49520

Report of an Experimental Survey of the Mississippi and Atlantic Railroad. February, 1851. *Indianapolis: Elder & Harkness, Printers.* 1851. 8vo, pp. 15. H. 49521

Report of the Preliminary Survey of the Mississippi and Missouri River Air-Line R. R. Co. *Canton.* 1868. 12mo.

An Act to provide for the Construction of the Mississippi and Pacific Rail Road, passed by the Legislature of Texas. Approved Dec. 21, 1853. [n. p. n. d.] 8vo. 49523

Also: ... Circular Address to the People of the United States. *Memphis, Tenn.: Twyman & Tannehill, Printers.* 1849. 8vo, pp. 24. H.

Minutes of the Mississippi Annual Conference, Natchez, December, 1839. *Natchez.* 1840. 8vo, pp. 28. M. 49524

Annual Report of the Mississippi Railroad Comp'y ... for ... 1866. *Jackson, Tenn.: W. W. Gates & Co., Printers.* 1866. 8vo, pp. 16, 2 folded leaves, (4). H. 49525

Catalogue of the Officers and Students of the Mississippi College. 1857–58. *Jackson, Miss.* 1858. 8vo, pp. 36. Cont'd.

Report of the Board of Trustees of the Mississippi Institute for the Deaf and Dumb. *Jackson.* 1857. 8vo. 49527

The Mississippi Navigator; Revised and Corrected. *Philadelphia: Printed by B. T. G. Bradford.* 1815. 12mo. Plates.

Report of the Officers of the Mississippi Penitentiary. *Jackson.* 1854. 8vo, pp. 24. Continued. H. 49529

Mississippi Question. *See* Vol. III. 10172, *and* Vol. V. 20990.

Official Proceedings of the Mississippi State Colored Convention held at Vicksburg, Miss., ... Nov. ... 1865. *Vicksburg, Miss.* 1865. 12mo, pp. 8. H. 49530

Petition of a Portion of the Inhabitants of the Mississippi Territory. ... 1802. [n. p. n. d.] 8vo, pp. 8. 49531

The Charter, and Amendments Thereto; of the Planters' Bank, of ... Mississippi. ... *New York: J. M. Elliot, Printer.* 1833. 16mo, pp. 35. 49532

Proceedings of a Meeting of Citizens of Central Mississippi, ... [on] the Slavery Question: also, the Proceedings of the State Convention ... . *Jackson, Miss.: Fall & Marshall, Printers.* 1850. 8vo, pp. 20. H. 49533

Proceedings of the Second Annual Meeting of the Convention of the Baptist Denomination, of ... Mississippi. ... May, 1838. *Natchez.* 1838. 8vo, pp. 24. Continued. H. 49534

Report of Auditor of Public Accounts. [n. p. 1855.] 8vo, pp. 8. H. 49535

Report of the Bank Commissioners of ... Mississippi, on the condition of the Brandon Bank. Columbus, Aug. 22, 1838. *Natchez: Printed by Besançon & Haliday.* 1838. 8vo, pp. 12.

Also: Report of the Bank Commissioners ... for 1839. *Jackson.* 1840. 8vo. Continued.

Report of the Committee, ... [on] the Propriety of admitting the Mississippi Territory into the Union ... . January 9th, 1811. ... *Washington City: Printed by R. C. Weightman.* 1811. 8vo, pp. 6. BA. 49537

Report of the Committee on the Collection of the Revenue, &c., Jan. 16, 1841. *Jackson.* 1841. 8vo, pp. 15. 49538

Also: Report of the Select Committee of the Legislature appointed to Examine the Mississippi Bank, 1840. [n. p. n. d.] 8vo. — Report of the Select Committee of the Constitutional Convention, on the Proclamation of Gov. Humphreys. *Jackson.* 1868. 8vo. — Report of the Select Committee on Banks and Currency to the Legislature of Mississippi, January, 1841. *Jackson.* 1841. 8vo, pp. 7. — Report of the Select Com-

mittee on State Bonds to the Legislature of Mississippi, 1841. *Jackson.* 1841. 8vo, pp. 28. — Report of the Select Committee of the Legislature on the Tariff; presented Jan. 18, 1841. *Jackson.* 1841. 8vo, pp. 8.

Report of the Treasurer ... January 13th, 1855. *Jackson.* 1855. 8vo, pp. 11. H. 49539

Report on the Agriculture and Geology of Mississippi. ... By B. L. C. Wailes ... . [n. p.:] *Lippincott, Grambo and Co.* 1854. 8vo, pp. xx, 17–371. 17 Plates. H. 49540

Resolutions of the General Assembly of the Mississippi Territory ... and A Memorial, ... to the President, Senate, and House of Representatives ... . 10th February, 1803. ... *Washington City: Printed by William Duane & Son.* 1803. 12mo, pp. 6. BA.

Revised Code of the Laws of Mississippi, comprising all such Acts of a public nature as were in force at the end of the year 1823. ... *Natchez.* 1824. 8vo, pp. 743. C., S. 49542

Revised Code of the Statute Laws of ... Mississippi. Published by Authority of the Legislature. *Jackson.* 1857. 8vo.

Constitution and other Documents in relation to the State Historical Society of Mississippi. *Jackson.* 1859. 8vo, pp. 15.

... The State of Mississippi, *vs.* Hezron A. Johnson. Involving the Liability of the State ... for the Payment of the Bonds ... of the Mississippi Union Bank. ... *Jackson: Thomas Palmer, Printer.* 1853. 8vo, pp. 55. H. 49545

Report of the Commissioners on the State University; presented Jan. 21, 1841. *Jackson.* 1841. 8vo, pp. 8. 49546

Statutes of the Mississippi Territory; the Constitution of the United States, with the several Amendments thereto; the Ordinance for the Government of the Territory of the United States north-west of the River Ohio; the Articles of Agreement and Cession, between the United States and the State of Georgia and such Acts of Congress as relate to the Mississippi Territory. Digested by ... Edward Turner. ... *Natchez.* 1816. 8vo. C.

Statutes of ... Mississippi, of a Public and General Nature Compiled by V. E. Howard and A. Hutchinson, 1840. ... *New-Orleans.* 1840. Rl. 8vo, pp. 885. C., S. 49548

Catalogue of the Officers and Students of the University of Mississippi; ... 1856–57. [n. p. 1867.] 8vo, pp. 49, (1). Continued. H. 49549

Also: Laws of the University of Mississippi ... . Fourth Edition. *Holly Springs.* 1857. 8vo, pp. 22. — Minutes of a Meeting of the ... Trustees of the University of Mississippi ... 1870. *Louisville, Ky.: Printed by John P. Morton and Company.* 1870. 8vo, pp. 23, (6). H.

Mississippi River. Documents relating to the Improvement of the Navigation of the Mississippi River; printed by order of the New Orleans Chamber of Commerce. *New Orleans.* 1837. 8vo, pp. 82, xii. Map. 49550

A Journey on the Mississippi River, being a Lecture delivered before the Lyceum of the Lane Street Public School, Philadelphia. By a Director. April 10, 1847. *Philadelphia: Crissy & Markley.* 1847. 8vo, pp. 24. 49551

Proceedings of the Mississippi River Improvement Convention, held ... February ... 1866. *Dubuque.* 1866. 8vo, pp. 52. 2 Maps. H. 49552

Also: ... Memorial of the Mississippi River Improvement and Manufacturing Company. ... [n. p. 1865.] 8vo, pp. 7, (1). H.

Mississippi Valley Business Directory, containing a Short History of all the Towns on the Ohio and Mississippi Rivers. *Cincinnati.* 1844. 8vo. A. 49553

Official Proceedings of the Mississippi Valley Railroad Convention ... at ... St. Louis, ... November, 1852 ... . Also, the ... Proceedings of the North Missouri Railroad Convention ... at ... St. Charles ... . *St. Louis: Printed by M. Niedner.* [1852.] 8vo, pp. 63. H. 49554

Catalogue of Autograph Letters, Documents, and Signatures, Relics and Curiosities, etc., donated to The Mississippi Valley Sanitary Fair, and to be sold ... October 7th and 8th, 1864. ... *St. Louis: R. P. Studley & Co., Printers ...* . 1864. 8vo, pp. 37.

Missive aan ... *See* Irhoven van Dam (W.), IX. 35064.

This writer published at least seven letters on this subject.

Missive aen den Koninck van Groot-Brittangien van den Staten-Generael der Vereenighde Nederlanden, 24 junii 1664. Uyt het fransch. *Amsterdam.* 1664. 4to. 49556

In this letter the States General demands a prompt reparation for the capture of Cap-vert and for capturing some vessels belonging to the West India Company.

Missive. | Daer in | Kortelijck ende grondigh | werdt vertoont, hoeveel de Vereenighde | Nederlanden gheleghen is aen de Oost | ende West Indische Navigatie. | Mitsgaders | 't Profijt, dat men

van de Oost Indische Com- | pagnie, gheduerende den tijt van vierentwintich | jaren herwaerdts, daer wt heeft | ghetrocken. | Ende | Met fondamentale redenen werdt bewesen, dat door de | geoctroyeerde West Indische Navigatie, meer voordeel | voor de Participanten met meerder dienste voor | de Nederlantsche Provintien, grooter schade | ende afbreuck voor de Koninck | van Spaengien zij te | verwachten. | Gheschreven aen een seker Vriendt ende Lief-hebber | van de Wel-standt des Vader-landts, ēn tot ghemeenen | dienst der Inghesetene van dien. | *Tot Arnhem,* | *By Ian Iansz. Boeck-Verkooper.* | *Anno* 1621. | 4to, 18 leaves. C. 49557

A letter in which is succinctly and thoroughly proved, of how much importance it is to the United Nederlands to preserve the East and West India navigation.

Missive | daer in | Kortelijck ende grondigh wert | verthoont hoe veel de Vereenighde Nederlanden | gelegen is aen de Oost- ende West-Indische Navigatie. | Mitsgaders | 't Profijt, datmen van de Oost-Indische Compagnie, geduyrende | den tijdt van 24 Jaren herwaerts, daer uijt heeft ghetrocken. | Ende | Met sondamentale redenen werd bewesen, dat door de gheoc- | troyeerde West-Indische Navigatie, meer voordeel voor de Participanten | met meerder dienste voor de Nederlantsche Provintien, grooter schade | ende afbreuck voor den Coninck van Spaengien zij te verwachten. | Gheschreven aen een seeke Vrient ende Lief-hebber van de Welstant | des Vader-lants, ende tot ghemeenen dienst der Inghesetene van dien. | *Eerst tot Aernhem by Jan Jansz.* | *Ende nu tot Amsterdam bij Broer Jansz.,* *woonende op de* | *Nieu zijds Achter Burchwal in de silvere Kan.* *Anno* 1621. | 4to, pp. 28. 49558

An exact reprint of the preceding pamphlet. For another reprint, *see* Vol. V. 20233.

Missive | Van de | Bewint-hebberen der West- | Indische Compagnie ter Camere | van Amsterdam, | geschreven den 10 July 1664, | Aen de | Ho. Mo. Heeren Staten Gene- | rael der Vereenighde Nederlanden. Neffens een Extract | Uyt de Heer Matthias | Becks, Vice Directeur op 't Eylandt Curacao | in 't Fort Amsterdam, dato den 12 Martij | Anno 1664. | Raeckende de Engelsche Capers, ende haer Commissie | in de West-Indien. | *Tot Gouda* | *By Pieter Klaerbeeck.* 1664. | 4to, pp. 4. 49559

Letter of the directors of the West India Company. With an extract from the letter of Matthias Becks, on the English cruisers and their commission in the West Indies.

Missive van Bewindhebberen der West-Indische Compagnie, met een deductie door J. de Graaf, Commandeur van St. Eustatius, ten opzigte van de klagten door het Hof van Engeland tegens

hem, als hetgeen geduurende zijn Commando is verrigt. [n. p.] 1779. Folio, pp. 344. 49560

This letter contains also a justification by J. de Graaf, Governor of St. Eustatius, against the complaints of England concerning the favors shown to the Americans.

Missive van Bewinthebberen der West Indische Compagnie ter Kamer Amsterdam, betreffend het voorval met den Ambassadeur Yorke. [n. p.] 1777. Folio, pp. 54. 49561

Missive van de Hoofd. *See* Vol. VI., No. 22994.

Missive van de Staten van Hollandt aen de Bewinthebberen van de West Indische Compagnie [20 Oct. 1673]. 4to, pp. 21.

Letter to the directors of the West India Company.

Missive van de Staten Generael aen den Koninck van Groot-Brittannien, den 19 Dec. 1673. [*Hague.* 1673.] 4to, pp. 8.

This letter is important from its reference to New Netherland, as it contains the offer of restitution of all the places of New Netherland conquered during the last war.

Missive van den Commandeur J. Binckes, ... aan den Prince van Orange, in 's Landts schip de Bescherminge, ... aen 't Eylandt Tabago, 22 Martii 1677. [n. p. n. d.] Folio, 1 leaf.

Contains a journal of the battles and the conquest of Tabago, February 18 till March 12, 1677. Very rare. For another edition, *see* our Vol. II., No. 5426.

Missive van den Secretaris F. Valckenier aen HH. MM. tot Madrid, 2 Sept. 1671. *'sHage.* 1671. 4to. 49565

This letter imparts the news of the arrival of a fleet freighted with silver from New Spain, etc.

Missive van een Amsterdamsch Burger ... rakende de Memorie ... van den Ridder Yorke. [n. p.] 1780. Folio, pp. 8.

An ardent defense of the Amsterdam Burgomaster P. J. van Berckel, one of the most zealous friends of America, at whose instigation the "Preparatoirlyk Plan" was made.

Missive van een burger te Amsterdam aan den schrijver van den Post van den Neder-Rhijn: behelzende verscheide gewigtige aanmerkingen ... ter Vergad. van HH. MM. gedaan 31 Julij 1782. *'sHage.* [1782.] 8vo. 49567

Missive van G. Fagel 1684, ... zeer toepasselijk op het gehouden gedrag der Regeering van Amsterdam, ... zoo ten aanzien van haare geheime correspondentie met den Ambassadeur van zeker uitheemsch vorst, als van haare onbetamelyke onderhandelingen met den Amerikanschen commissaris W. Lee ... . [n. p.] 1782. 8vo. 49568

Relates to unbecoming negotiations with the American commissioner W. Lee, etc.

Missive van twee Indiaensche Coninghen, aen den Vorst Mauritius van Oranje, by dewelcke sy versoecken dat haere soonen, welcke sy mede overghesonden hebben, in de Christel. religie mochten opgetrocken worden, 1 Aug. 1620. *'s Hage: A. Meuris.* 1621. 4to, pp. 4. 49569

Message of two Indian kings to Prince Maurice of Orange, requesting that their sons, whom they have sent over with this letter, might be educated in the Christian religion. A very rare piece.

Missive van Z. Hoogheid. *See* Vol. IX., No. 36562.

MISSOURI.

Account of the Wapeti, or Gigantic Elks of the Missouri, lately discovered in the Interior of North America, and now Exhibiting ... . *Dublin.* 1822. 12mo, pp. 15. Plate. 49570

An Act for the consolidation of the Railroad State Debt, ... with the Report of the Joint Committee on State Credit ... . *Jefferson City: Emory S. Foster, ... Printer.* 1866. 8vo, pp. 16.

An Act to Dispose of the Southwest Pacific Railroad, ... securing the Early Completion of said Road. Passed ... March 17, 1868. *St. Louis.* 1868. 18mo, pp. 18. H. 49572

Act of the General Assembly of the State of Missouri, Incorporating the American Iron Mountain Company. ... *New York.* 1843. 8vo. S. 49573

An Act to regulate Banks and Banking Institutions ... . [n. p. n. d.] 8vo, pp. 28. H. 49574

Also: An Act to charter the Bank of ... Missouri. [n. p. 1837.] 8vo, pp. 27. — Bank Law. An Act for the relief of the Banks of ... Missouri ... . Passed ... 1861. *St. Louis: George Knapp & Co., Printers ...* . 1861. 8vo, pp. 11. H. — Report of the Committee of the Bank of Missouri. *Jefferson.* 1851. 8vo.

Acts of the General Assembly of the State of Missouri, ... 1820. *St. Charles.* 1820. 8vo. Continued. 49575

Address of the Committee from ... Missouri to President Lincoln. [n. p. Dated] September 30, 1863. 12mo, pp. 12.

An Address to the People of Missouri in Vindication of the Independence of the Judiciary, and the ... Principles of Free Government ... . [n. p. n. d.] 8vo, pp. 24. H. 49577

Annual Report of the Adjutant General ... December 15, 1862. *St. Louis.* [1862.] 12mo, pp. 12. H. 49578

Also: Adjutant General's Report of Missouri State Militia, ... for ... 1861. *St. Louis: George Knapp & Co., Printers.* 1862. 12mo, pp. 9. Tables. Continued. B.

First Annual Report of the Commissioner of Statistics, ... for ... 1866. ... *Jefferson City: Emory S. Foster, ... Printer.* 1867. 8vo, pp. 296. Table. Continued. B. 49579

First Annual Report of the Superintendent of the Insurance Department. 1870. *Jefferson City: H. Wilcox.* 1870. 8vo. Continued. C. 49580

Appeal to the Patriotism of the Citizens of Missouri. [n. p. n. d.] 8vo. 49581

First Report of the Board of Immigration of ... Missouri ... for ... 1865 and 1866. ... *Jefferson City: Emory S. Foster, ... Printer.* 1867. 8vo, pp. 296. Folded leaf. H. 49582

Report of the Board of Public Works and State Engineer, upon the condition of the various Railroad Companies ... *Jefferson City.* 1857. 8vo. Continued. 49583

Botschaft des Gouverneur's Thomas C. Fletcher an die Mitglieder der Drei und zwanzigsten General-Assembly ... *Jefferson City, Mo.: Emory S. Foster, ... Drucker.* 1865. 8vo, pp. 24.

Brief Narrative. *See* Vol. II., No. 7881.

Constitution of the State of Missouri. ... *St. Louis.* 1820. 8vo. + *Washington: Printed by Gales & Seaton.* 1820. 8vo, pp. 25.

Correspondence and Documents relative to the Financial Condition of ... Missouri, and the County and City of St. Louis, with ... reference to the North Missouri Railroad Company. *St. Louis.* 1855. 8vo, pp. 28. H. 49586

Desultory remarks on the Question of extending Slavery into Missouri: ... *West Chester, Pa.: Lewis Marshall, Printer.* 1856. 8vo, pp. 37. B. 49587

Extracted from the American republican newspaper of 1819–20.

Digest of the Laws of the State of Missouri, ... 1812–1817. By H. S. Geyer. *St. Louis: J. Charless.* 1818. 8vo. C.

Discovery and Settlement of Missouri Territory. *Paris, Ky.* 1817. 8vo. 49589

A doubtful title from an auctioneer's catalogue.

Documents relating to the Indians, from the State of Missouri. *Washington.* 1826. 8vo. 49590

Another doubtful title.

Geology. Report of a Geological Reconnoissance of part of the Missouri River, adjacent to the Osage River, made ... by H. King. [n. p. 1841.] 8vo, pp. 19. 49591

Memorial to the Fifteenth General Assembly of Missouri, concerning a Geological Survey of the State. *Jefferson City.* 1849. 8vo. 49592

The First and Second Annual Reports of the Geological Survey of Missouri. By G. C. Swallow ... *Jefferson City: James Lusk ... Printer.* 1855. Rl. 8vo, pp. 207, 239, (1). 5 Maps, 34 Plans, etc. + Third Report. 1857. 8vo. + Fourth Report of Progress of the Geological Survey of Missouri. 1859. 8vo. + Fifth Report. 1861. 8vo. 49593

Geological Report of the Country along the Line of the South-western Branch of the Pacific Railroad, State of Missouri. By G. C. Swallow. *St. Louis.* 1859. 8vo. 49594

Constitution and By-Laws of the General Emancipation Society of ... Missouri. ... 1862. *St. Louis.* 1862. 16mo, pp. 16.

Proceedings of the Grand Royal Arch Chapter of Missouri, at the Annual Commandery at St. Louis, May 23, 1855. *St. Louis.* 1855. 8vo, pp. 53. 49596

Also: Proceedings of the Grand Lodge of Missouri, at ... St. Louis ... A. D. 1845. *St. Louis, Mo.: Printed by Chambers & Knapp.* 1845. 8vo, pp. 43. Continued. H.—The Book of Constitutions of Missouri. *St. Louis, Mo.* 1853. 12mo, pp. 57.—Constitution and By-Laws of the Grand Lodge of Missouri ... *St. Louis.* 1840. 12mo, pp. 16. + 1842. 12mo, pp. 36. + 1851. 12mo, pp. 53.

Inaugural Message of Governor Fletcher. *See* Vol. VI. 24741.

The Internal Improvement System of the State of Missouri, showing the Enormous Frauds practised. *St. Louis.* 1859. 8vo.

Journal of the Convention assembled November 17, 1845, to Revise the Constitution. *Jefferson City.* 1845. 8vo. 49598

Journal and Proceedings of the Missouri State Convention, held ... March, 1861. *St. Louis: George Knapp & Co., Printers,* ... 1861. 8vo, pp. 136. C., H. 49599

Continued in July, 1861, October, 1861, June, 1862, and June, 1863.

Journal of the House of Representatives of the State of Missouri, for ... 1838–9. *Jefferson City.* 1839. 8vo. Continued.

Journal of the Senate of the State of Missouri, for ... 1838–1839. *Jefferson City.* 1839. 8vo. Continued. 49601

Journal of the Senate Extra Session [of the Rebel Legislature, Oct. 21, 1861. n. p. n. d.] 8vo. 49602

Journal of the State Convention, held at St. Louis, January–April, 1865. *St. Louis: Democrat Office.* 1865. 8vo, pp. 287.

Laws of the State of Missouri; revised ... by authority of the General Assembly. *St. Louis.* 1825. 2 vols., 8vo. C. 49604

Laws of the State of Missouri, ... 1836–37 and 1838–39. Second Edition. *Saint-Louis and City of Jefferson.* 1841. 8vo.

Local Laws and Private Acts of the State of Missouri, 1844–1845. *City of Jefferson.* 1845. 8vo. Continued. C. 49606

Letter from the Presidents of the Atchison & St. Joseph and Weston & Atchison R. R. Co.'s to the Governor of Missouri. *St. Louis.* 1865. 8vo. 49607

Memorial of Inhabitants. *See* No. 47643.

Memorial of the State of Missouri, and Documents in relation to Indian Depredations upon Citizens of that State. *Washington.* 1826. 8vo. 49608

Memorial to Congress, on the ... Northern Boundary of Missouri. ... [n. p. n. d.] 8vo, pp. 11. BA. 49609

Message of Governor Gamble, December 30, 1862. *Jefferson City.* 1862. 8vo, pp. 20. Continued. 49610

Report of the Second Fair held by the Missouri Agricultural and Mechanical Association. *St. Louis.* 1857. 8vo. Contin'd.

Minutes of the Eighth Session of the Missouri Annual Conference of the Methodist Episcopal Church. *St. Louis.* 1862. 8vo. 49612

Minutes of the Nineteenth Annual Meeting of the General Association of the Baptists of Missouri, ... 1858. *St. Louis.* 1858. 8vo. 49613

Minutes of the Thirty-Third Annual Meeting of the South District Baptist Association ... *St. Louis.* 1853. 8vo. 49614

... The Missouri and Illinois Farmer's Almanac, ... for ... 1844 ... By Cheney Howe, A.M., M.D. *St. Louis: Turnbull & Pray.* [1843.] 12mo, pp. (24). Continued. H. 49615

Annals of the Missouri Historical and Philosophical Society. No. I. [1845–48.] *Jefferson City: Metropolitan Print.* 1848. 8vo. C. 49616

See also St. Louis, Mo.

Fifth Biennial Report of the Missouri Institution for the Deaf and Dumb, ... 1863–4. *Jefferson City.* 1865. 8vo. 49617

Prospectus of the Missouri Iron Company and Missouri and Iron Mountain Cities ... *Hartford: Printed by P. Canfield.* 1837. 8vo, pp. 40. Map. B. + *Boston: Marden & Kimball, Printers.* 1837. 8vo, pp. 40. H. 49618

Also: Prospectus of the Missouri Iron Company. *Philadelphia.* 1837. 8vo, pp. 32. + [The same.] With the Acts of Incorporation. [n. p. 1837.] 8vo, pp. 36. Map and Plate. B.

The Charter of the Missouri Juvenile Reform School, with a Statement of the Design and Advantages of the Institution. ... *St. Louis.* 1851. 8vo, pp. 23. H. 49619

Missouri Medical and Surgical Journal. Edited by T. Barbour, M.D. ... *St. Louis.* 1845. 8vo. Continued. 49620

Charter and Laws of the Missouri Petroleum and Mining Company. *St. Louis: R. P. Studley and Co., Printers.* 1865. 12mo, pp. 11. B. 49621

The Missouri State Gazetteer and Business Directory. [J.] Sutherland & [H. N.] McEvoy, Publishers and Compilers. *St. Louis.* 1860. 8vo. 49622

Missouri State Gazetteer, Shipper's Guide, and Business Directory for 1866. *Indianapolis: Geo. W. Hanes & Co.* [n. d.] 8vo, pp. xxxvi, 414, 112. 49623

Report of the ... Missouri State Lunatic Asylum, for ... 1855–1856. *Jefferson City.* 1856. 8vo. Continued. 49624

Missouri und Illinois. Taschenbuch für Einwanderer. *Dresden.* 1835. 8vo. Map. 49625

The New Constitution ... as revised, amended, and adopted ... June, 1865. *St. Louis: McKee, Fishback & Co., Printers* ... 1865. 8vo, pp. 20. H. 49626

Official Register of Missouri Troops for 1862. ... *St. Louis.* 1863. 8vo, pp. xx, 120. H. 49627

Also: Official Report of Missouri Troops, for 1862. *St. Louis.* 1863. 8vo, pp. 204

Proceedings and Address of the Anti-Jackson Convention of Missouri, to their Fellow-Citizens. *Fayette: Printed by Nathaniel Patten.* [1828.] 8vo, pp. 47. B., B.M. 49628

Proceedings of the Colored People's Educational Convention, held ... January, 1870. *St. Louis.* 1870. 8vo, pp. 35. H.

Proceedings of the Emancipation Convention held at Jefferson City, June, 1862. *Jefferson City.* 1862. 8vo, pp. 8. 49630

Proceedings of the First Annual State Sunday-School Convention ... held ... October ... 1866. ... *St. Louis, Mo.: Clayton & Babington, Printers.* 1866. 8vo, pp. 68. H. 49631

Report of the Auditor of Public Accounts, ... to the Nineteenth General Assembly. *Jefferson City: James Lusk, State Printer.* 1856. 8vo, pp. 47. H. 49632

Report of the Colonel of Ordnance in relation to the Mineral Lands of Missouri. [*Washington.* 1836.] 8vo. 49633

Report of the Committee on the Financial Affairs of the State ... February 4, 1865, By George K. Budd ... *St. Louis: M'Kee, Fishback and Co., Printers* ... 1865. 8vo, pp. 15. H.

... Report of the Committee ... appointed to Investigate the Conduct and Management of the Militia. Majority and Minority Reports, with the Evidence. *Jefferson City, Mo.: W. A. Curry, ... Printer.* 1864. 8vo, pp. 159, (1). H. 49635

Report of the Paymaster General of Missouri, relative to Disbursements ... *Jefferson City: Emory S. Foster, ... Printer.* 1865–6. 8vo, pp. 11. Continued. B. 49636

Annual Report of the Quartermaster General ... for ... 1863, ... to the Governor ... *St. Louis, Mo.: R. P. Studley and Co., Printers* ... 1864. 8vo, pp. 44, (4), Tables, clxxviii. Cont'd.

Report of the Superintendent of Common Schools to the Sixteenth General Assembly of ... Missouri. *Jefferson City.* 1851. 8vo. Continued. 49638

Report of the Superintendent of Public Instruction ... *Jefferson City: Emory S. Foster, ... Printer.* 1865. 8vo, pp. 12. Continued. H. 49639

Report on ... Prisons ... 1853. *Jefferson City: James Lusk, ... Printer.* 1853. 8vo, pp. 24. H. 49640

The Revised Statutes of the State of Missouri, revised ... by the Eighth General Assembly during the Years One Thousand Eight Hundred and Thirty-Four, and ... Thirty-Five. ... With the Constitutions of Missouri and of the United States. Printed and published under the Direction of [A. A. King] the Superintendent appointed by the General Assembly for that Purpose. *St. Louis.* 1835. 8vo, pp. (4), 699, (1). A., B., C., 49641

The Revised Statutes of the State of Missouri. ... Printed under the Superintendence of William Claude Jones, Commissioner. ... *St. Louis.* 1845. 8vo, pp. 1215. C. 49642

Revised Statutes of ... Missouri. ... Charles H. Hardin, Commissioner. *City of Jefferson.* 1856. 2 vols., 8vo. C.

Shall the New Constitution be adopted? Explanation of Votes ... on the Final Passage in the State Convention, April 8th, 1865. [n. p. n. d.] 8vo, pp. 8. H. 49644

First Annual Report of the State Board of Agriculture ... for ... 1865. ... *Jefferson City: Emory S. Foster, ... Printer.* 1866. 8vo, pp. 480. 2 Plates. Continued. H. 49645

Also: First Annual Report on the Noxious, Beneficial and other Insects, of ... Missouri ... By Charles V. Riley, State Entomologist. *Jefferson City: Ellwood Kirby, ... Printer.* 1869. 8vo, pp. 181, (1), Index, 7. Continued. H.

Report of the State Treasurer ... January 8, 1867. ... *Jefferson City: Emory S. Foster, ... Printer.* 1867. 8vo, pp. 33. H.

Also: Special Report of the State Treasurer ... *Jefferson City: Ellwood Kirby, ... Printer.* 1868. 8vo, pp. 36. H.

Report of the ... Curators of the State University ... 1867. ... *Jefferson City: Emory S. Foster, ... Printer.* 1867. 8vo, pp. 24. Continued. B. 49647

To the Citizens of Missouri. *Boston.* 1855. Folio, pp. 2.

Address by the New England Emigrant Aid Society, relative to Kansas.

To the Voters. *See* [Bishop (W.)], II. 5623.

Catalogue of the Officers and Students of the University of ... Missouri, for ... 1843. *Columbia: Printed by Switzler & Williams.* 1843. 8vo, pp. 8. Continued. B. 49649

Annual Catalogue of the Medical Department of the University ... and Circular for the Ensuing Session; With an Address

by Dr. Samuel Cartwright ... *St. Louis: T. W. Ustick, Printer.* 1848. 8vo, pp. 19, (1), 12. B. 49650

University of Missouri. Installation Exercises. Address by J. W. Tucker, Esq., of St. Louis. ... and Response by Benj. B. Minor, A.M., President ... 1860. *Columbia, Mo.: Wm. P. Switzler.* 1860. 8vo, pp. 32. 49651

MISTICA. Vocabulario en Lengua Misteca, hecho por los Padres de la Orden de Predicadores, que residen en ella, y vltimamente recopilado, y acabado por el Padre Fray Francisco de Alvarado, Vicario de Tamaçulapa, de la misma Orden. *En Mexico. Con licencia, En casa de Pedro Balli.* 1593. [Colophon:] *Acabose este presente Vocabulario, En Tamaçulapa, a 6. de Septiẽbre de* 1592 *años. El qual con su auctor, se somete y subiecta a la correction de la Sancta madre Yglesia Romana. En Mexico. En casa de Pedro Balli. Año de* 1593. 4to, 6 leaves, Text, 203 leaves, Colophon, 1 leaf. 49652

Corrected title of No. 971, Vol. I.

Misteca Theologia ... por ... J. E. de Buenaventura. *Mexico.* 1575. 8vo. + *Mexico.* 1594. 8vo. 49653

Mistick Krewe of Comus; or, Missing Links to Darwin's Origin of Speeches. *New Orleans.* 1868. 12mo. 49654

The portrait of a gentleman not wholly unconnected with spoons [B. F. Butler] is visible at page 18.

[MITCHEL (Jonathan).] A Defence [etc]. *See* Vol V. 18704.

Pages 1 to 46 are by Mitchel.

MITCHEL. A | Discourse | of the | Glory | To which God hath called | Believers | By Jesus Christ. | Delivered in some Sermons out | of the 1 Pet. 5 Chap. 10 Ver. | Together with an annexed Letter. | Both, by that Eminent and Worthy Mi- | nister of the Gospel, Mr. Jonathan | Mitchil, late Pastor to the Church | at Cambridge in New-England. | *London: Printed for Nathaniel Ponder at the | Peacock in the Poultry, Anno Dom.* 1677. | Sm. 8vo, pp. (16), 263, 21. H., W. 49655

MITCHEL. A | Discourse | of the | Glory | To which God hath called | Believers | By Jesus Christ. | Delivered in some Sermons | out of the 1 Pet. v. Chap. 10 v. | Together | with an annexed Letter | Both, by that Eminent & Worthy | Minister of the Gospel, Mr. Jonathan Mitchel, | late Pastor of the Church at | Cambridge in New-England. | The Second Edition with a Preface | by

Increase Mather, D.D. | *Boston: Reprinted by B. Green* ... 1721. Sm. 8vo, pp. (2), viii, 10, 291, (1). B., BA. + Third Edition. *Boston.* 1721. 12mo, pp. 300. 49656

[MITCHEL.] Elijah's Mantle. | A Faithful | Testimony, | to the | Cause and Work of God, | in the Churches of | New-England. | And | The Great End and Interest | of these Plantations, | Dropt and Left by Four Servants of God, | Famous in the Service of the Churches. | Highly Seasonable to be Offered unto the People, | now succeeding in the New-English Colonies, | for their Serious Consideration. | *Boston: Printed by S. Kneeland for S. Gerrish.* 1722. Sm. 8vo, pp. (2), ii, 17, (2). B., BA., C., W. 49657

The "Four Servants of God," are Jonathan Mitchel, John Higginson, William Stoughton, and Increase Mather. It was edited by Cotton Mather.

[MITCHEL.] Elijah's Mantle. | A Faithful | Testimony, | to | New-England, | containing | I. The Great End and Interest of | New-England, Stated by the memo- | rable Mr. Jonathan Mitchel, extrac- | ted from an Instrument of His, which | bears date, December 31. 1662. | II. The Cause of God and His | People in New England; Stated in | a Sermon of the Memorable | Mr. John Higginson, unto the General | Court of the Massachuetts-Colony, May | 27. 1663. ... | III. New England's True Interest, | further Declared, | in the Words of | the Hon. William Stoughton, Esq; | in a Sermon preach'd by Him, | [in the Audience of the General | Court April, 1668.] when He was a | Preacher of the Gospel at Dorchester: | From which he was called Successively | to many Stations of the highest | Figure in the Civil Government, | and when he died was Commander | in Chief of the Province. | IV. The Testimony Finished by Dr. | Increase Mather: Who says (I do | now, with my Dying Hand, sign my | Concurrence to the above Testimonies; | and am now in the Eighty-Fourth | Year of my Age, and under a feeble- | ness in the Valley of the shadow of | Death, &c.) | Highly seasonable to be offered unto the People, now | succeeding in the New-English Colonies, for their serious Consideration, at this gloomy Day of darkness | and Trial: When by Artful Schemes and Inventions of a Corrupt Set of Tyrannical Arbitrary Men, our most | Sacred and Religious Privileges are in eminent | Danger. | *Boston: Printed and Sold by Nathaniel Coverly* ... M,DCCLXXIV. 8vo, pp. 31. B.

MITCHEL. Letter to a Friend in New England in 1649. *Boston.* 1732. 12mo. 49659

This is doubtless a different edition of the following.

Mitchel. Mr. | Mitchel's | Letter | To | his Brother. [Dated May 19, 1649. *Boston.* n. d.] 12mo, pp. 22, (1). BA., W. + [*Boston: Printed by Z. Fowle*, about 1764.] 12mo, pp. 22, (1)

The edition of 1764 includes a letter by John Eliot.

Mitchel. Nehemiah | on the | Wall | in | Troublesom Times; | or, | A Serious and Seasonable Improvement of that great | Example of Magistratical Piety and Prudence, Self-denial | and Tenderness, Fearlesness and Fidelity, unto In- | struction and Encouragement of present and | succeeding Rulers in our Israel. | As it was delivered in a Sermon Preached at | Boston in N. E. May 15. 1667. being the | Day of Election | there. | By that faithful Servant of Christ, | Mr. Jonathan Mitchel, late Pastor of | the Church of Christ at Cambridge. | ... | *Cambridge:* | *Printed by S[amuel] G[reen] and M[armaduke] J[ohnson].* 1671. Sm. 4to, pp. (4), 34. B.

Exceedingly rare, and one of the earliest Massachusetts election sermons.

[Mitchel.] Propositions | concerning the | Subject of Baptism | and | Consociation of Churches, | Collected and Confirmed out of the Word of God, | By a | Synod of Elders | and | Messengers of the Churches | in Massachusets-Colony in New-England. | Assembled at Boston, according to Appointment of the | Honoured General Court, | In the Year 1662. | ... | *Cambridge. Printed by S[amuel] G[reen] for Hezekiah Usher at Boston in* | *New-England.* 1662. 4to, pp. 16, 32. B. 49662

Mitchel (M.) History of the County of Fond du Lac, Wis. ... from its earliest settlement, to the present time, By Martin Mitchel. *Fond du Lac: Printed by J. A. Smith.* 1854. 12mo, pp. 96. H., S. 49663

Mitchel. Geographical and Statistical History of the County of Winnebago ... with ... a General View of the State of Wisconsin ... . Published by Martin Mitchel and Joseph H. Osborn. *Oshkosh: Printed by Mitchel & Smith.* 1856. 16mo, pp. 120. S.

Mitchel (O. M.) Address at the Dedication of the Astronomical Observatory of Hamilton College, July 16, 1856. By Ormsby McKnight Mitchel, LL.D. *Utica, N. Y.* 1856. 8vo.

Mitchell (A. M.) The Freed Boy in Alabama. By Anne M. Mitchell. *Philadelphia: Presbyterian Publication Committee.* [1869.] 18mo, pp. 152. 3 Plates. 49666

[Mitchell] (A. W.) *See* Vol. x., No. 42903.

Mitchell (B. G.) Consanguinity of the Families of Gibbs and Mitchell ... . Some Remarks on the Settling of the Island of Bermuda and Virginia. By B. Gibbs Mitchell. *Baltimore.* 1864. 8vo. 49667

Mitchell (B. R.) Vocabulary of the Jargon or Trade Language of Oregon. By Dr. B. Rush Mitchell, U. S. Navy; with Additions by Professor W. W. Turner. *Washington.* 1853. 8vo, pp. 22. 49668

Mitchell (C.) Exposition, Historical and Legal, of the Title of Colin Mitchell, and others, to Lands in Florida, now depending in the Supreme Court of the United States. *Washington.* 1834. 8vo. N. 49669

Mitchell (D. M.) A Sermon ... June 22, 1825, before the Maine Missionary Society ... . By David M. Mitchell ... . *Portland.* 1825. 8vo, pp. 40. H. 49670

Mitchell (D. W.) Ten Years in the United States: Being an Englishman's Views of Men and Things in the North and South. By D. W. Mitchell ... . *London: Smith, Elder and Co.* M.DCCC.LXII. Post 8vo, pp. xii, 332. BA. 49671

[Mitchell (Donald Grant).] A Bachelor's Reverie: in Three Parts. ... By Ik: Marvel. *Wormsloe.* MDCCCL. 8vo, pp. 40, (1). H. 49672

Of this edition twelve copies only were printed. It has been frequently reprinted as "Reveries of a Bachelor," No. 49677, *infra.*

[Mitchell.] Dr. Johns: being A Narrative of certain Events in the Life of an Orthodox Minister of Connecticut. ... *New York: Charles Scribner and Company.* 1866. 2 vols., 8vo, pp. (2), 300; (2), 295. B., S. 49673

[Mitchell.] The Lorgnette; or, Studies of the Town. By an Opera Goer. ... *New York: Henry Kernot.* 1850. 2 vols., 12mo. + Second Edition. *New York: Stringer & Townsend.* [1850.] 2 vols., 12mo, pp. 294; 298. 12 Plates. + Eleventh Edition. ... *New York: Charles Scribner.* 1854. 2 vols., 12mo, pp. xviii, 294; 298, 6. B. 49674

[Mitchell.] My Farm of Edgewood: a Country Book. ... Eighth Edition. *New York.* 1863. 12mo. + *New York: Charles Scribner.* 1864. 8vo, pp. x, (2), 319. BA. + *New York.* 1867. 12mo, pp. x, (2), 319. 49675

[Mitchell.] Pictures of Edgewood. In a Series of Photographs, with Illustrative Text. ... *New York.* 1869. Folio, pp. 69. 49676

Three hundred copies only printed.

[Mitchell.] Reveries of a Bachelor: or a Book of the Heart. By Ik Marvel. *New York.* 1850. 12mo. C. + Third Edition. *New York: Baker & Scribner.* 1851. 12mo, pp. iv, 298. + *New York.* 1852. 12mo. + A New Edition. *New York: C. Scribner.* 1863. 16mo, pp. 271. + [*Ibid.*] 1864. + [*Ibid.*] 1869. 49677

[Mitchell.] Rêveries d'un Célibataire; ... traduit de l'anglais et précédé d'une lettre à un homme marié, par Paul Ithier. Notice biographique sur l'auteur. *Bruxelles: Van Meenen et Cie.* 1860. 12mo. 49678

[Mitchell.] Rural Studies with Hints for Country Places. ... *New York: Charles Scribner & Co.* 1867. 12mo, pp. (2), viii, (2), 295. C., H. 49679

[Mitchell.] Wet Days at Edgewood: with Old Farmers, Old Gardeners, and Old Pastorals. ... *New York: Charles Scribner.* 1865. 8vo, pp. (2), vii, 324. Diagram. BA. 49680

Also: Seven Stories, with Basement and Attic. ... *New York: Charles Scribner.* 1864. 12mo, pp. viii, 314. H.

Mitchell (E.) A Sermon before the Fifth Regiment of New York State Infantry and Artillery, commanded by C. D. Colden, Esq. 9th October, 1814. By Edward Mitchell. *New York.* 1814. 8vo, pp. 12. N. 49681

Also: The Installation of Reverend Edward Mitchell, as Colleague with Rev. John Murray, ... in Boston, September 12, 1810. ... *Boston: Printed by Munroe and Francis.* 1810. 8vo, pp. 19. — ... A Sermon, ... before the Society of United Christian Friends, ... New York, November 19, 1820. ... *New-York: Printed by J. Seymour.* 1820. 8vo, pp. 19. — Two Sermons. On the National Fast, Twelfth of Jan. 1815; and ... Thanksgiving, Thirteenth of April, 1815. ... *New-York: The Society.* 1815. 8vo, pp. 44. B.

Mitchell (E. L.) Memoir of Lieut. E. L. Mitchell, who Fell at the Battle of Shiloh aged 22 years. [By Mrs. Fitch.] *New York.* 1864. 8vo. 49682

Mitchell (E.) Elements of Geology, with an Outline of the Geology of North Carolina ... . By Elisha Mitchell ... . [n. p.] 1842. 12mo, pp. 141. Map. H. 49683

Mitchell [E.] Remarks on Bishop Ravenscroft's Answer to the Statements contained in Professor Mitchell's printed Letter, Of the 12th of February ... . *Raleigh: Printed by J. Gales & Son.* 1825. 8vo, pp. 48. BA. 49684

Mitchell. A Memoir of Rev. Elisha Mitchell, D.D., ... [by Charles Phillips,] with the Tributes of Respect to his Memory, ... and the Addresses ... at the Re-Interment of his Remains, by Rt. Rev. James H. Otey, D.D., ... and Hon. David L. Swain, LL.D. ... *Chapel Hill: J. M. Henderson.* 1858. 8vo, pp. 88. Portrait. H. 49685

Mitchell (H.) Two Letters to the Colonial Secretary, from Hector Mitchell, in Answer to the Yellow Book. *Jamaica.* 1828. 8vo. 49686

Mitchell (H.) ... On the Reclamation of Tide-Lands, and its Relation to Navigation. By Henry Mitchell ... . [n. p. 1869.] 4to, pp. 32. 2 Maps. B. 49687

From the Coast Survey Report for 1869. Also: ... Tides and Tidal Phenomena: for the use ... of U. S. Naval Officers. ... *Washington.* 1868. 8vo, pp. 56. H.

Mitchell (I.) The Asylum; or, Alonso and Melissa. An American Tale, founded on Fact. By I. Mitchell. *Poughkeepsie: J. Nelson.* 1811. 2 vols., 12mo. C. 49688

[Mitchell (James).] Letter on the relation of The White and African Races in the United States, showing the necessity of the Colonization of the latter. ... *Washington.* 1862. 8vo, pp. 28. H. 49689

First issued as: "Letters," etc., *Springfield: ... Press of Bailhache & Baker.* 1860. 8vo, pp. 32. — Also: Report on Colonization and Emigration. ... *Washington.* 1862. 8vo. C. *See also* Vol. xi., No. 45332.

Mitchell (J.) ... An Answer to the Southern Pastoral of April 18, 1867; ... A Sermon on The Great Schism of 1844, ... in Richmond, Va., July 28, 1867. By Rev. James Mitchell. [n. p. 1867.] 16mo, pp. 16. H. 49690

Mitchell [James C.] Speech of Mr. Mitchell, of Ten. on the proposition to amend the Constitution, ... respecting the Election of President and Vice-President. ... March 22, 1826. [n. p. n. d.] 12mo, pp. 43. H. 49691

Mitchell (J. C.) A Bible Defence of Slavery, and The Unity of Mankind, By Rev. J. C. Mitchell, ... of ... Mobile. *Mobile: J. Y. Thompson.* 1861. 8vo, pp. 31. H. 49692

[Mitchell (John).] The | Contest | in | America | between | Great Britain and France, | with | Its Consequences and Importance; | Giving an Account of the | Views and Designs of the French, | with the Interests of Great Britain, and | the Situation of the British and French | Colonies, in all parts of America: | in which | A proper Barrier between the two | Nations in North America is pointed out, | with a Method to Prosecute the War, | so as to obtain that necessary security for our | Colonies. | By an Impartial Hand. | ... | *London: A. Millar.* M,DCC,LVII. 8vo, pp. (2), xlix, (1), 17–244. A., C., H. 49693

The "Monthly Review," XVII. 172, says, "that this work abounds with truths, hitherto perhaps not generally attended to, and with observations and proposals that indicate the author's knowledge of the subject." This book has also been ascribed to Dr. Oliver Goldsmith. It shows an unusual knowledge and familiarity with the internal geography of America and the affairs of the French on the lakes, the Ohio, and in Western Virginia.

Mitchell. D. Johannis Mitchell Dissertatio brevis de Principiis Botanicorvm et Zoologorvm deque novo stabiliendo natvræ rervm congrvo cvm Appendice aliqvot genervm plantarvm recens conditorvm et in Virginia observatorvm. *Norimbergæ: Wolfgangi Schwarzkopfii.* MDCCLXIX. 4to, pp. (2), 46. H. 49694

The first of these two tracts is dedicated to Sir Hans Sloane, and dated "Virginia, 1738:" the second, "Nova Plantarum genera," is dedicated to Peter Collinson, and dated "Virginia, $17\frac{40}{41}$."

Mitchell. A Map of the British and French Dominions in North America, with the Roads, Distances, Limits and Extent of the Settlements. By John Mitchell. *London: For Jefferys and Faden, Feb.* 13, 1755. Atlas folio, 8 sheets. J.C.B. 49695

[Mitchell.] The Present State of Great Britain and North America, with regard to Agriculture, Population, Trade, and Manufactures, impartially considered: ... the want of staple commodities in the Colonies; the decline of their trade; increase of people; and necessity of manufactures, as well as of a trade in them hereafter. ... The proper Regulations for the Colonies, and the taxes imposed upon them, are considered, and compared with their condition and circumstances. *London: T. Becket and P. A. de Hondt.* MDCCLXVII. 8vo, pp. (8), xvi, 363, (1). C., H.

"The author of this treatise appears to be well acquainted with the true interest, nature, and state of our different colonies, in some of which he is supposed to have resided many years, though at present in England."—*Monthly Review*, XXXVI. 429. *See also* Sparks' "Franklin," IV. 355.

Mitchell (J.) The Practical Church Member. A Guide to the Principles and Practice of the Congregational Churches of

New England. By John Mitchell. *New Haven.* 1835. 12mo, pp. 252. 49697

Reprinted as:

Mitchell. A Guide to the Principles and Practice of the Congregational Churches of New England: With a Brief History of the Denomination. By John Mitchell ... . *Northampton: J. H. Butler.* 1838. 12mo, pp. 300. B., BA. 49698

[Mitchell.] Reminiscences of Scenes and Characters in College. By a Graduate of Yale College, of the Class of 1821. *New Haven: A. H. Maltby.* 1847. 12mo, pp. 229. Plate.

Also: My Mother; or, Recollections of Maternal Influence. ... *New York.* 1849. 12mo. + *Boston: Gould and Lincoln.* 1855. 12mo, pp. 254. Plate. — Rachel Kell. or The Disowned; A Tale of Country Life. ... *New York.* [n. d.] 12mo. — Sermon, ... at Northampton, ... Fast Day, September 1, 1837. ... *Northampton.* 1837. 8vo.

Mitchell (J.) The Sower Blessed. A Discourse delivered on Thanksgiving Day, at West Galway, Nov. 29, 1860. By Rev. John Mitchell. *Amsterdam, N. Y.* 1861. 8vo, pp. 14.

Mitchell (J.) Report on Colonization and Emigration, made to the Secretary of the Interior. By J. Mitchell. *Washington: Government Printing Office.* 1862. 8vo, pp. 29. 49701

Mitchell (J. K.) Indecision, a Tale of the Far West; and other Poems. By J. K. Mitchell, M.D. ... *Philadelphia: E. S. Carey & A. Hart.* MDCCCXXXIX. 12mo, pp. 212. C., H. 49702

Mitchell. On the Cryptogamous Origin of Malarious and Epidemic Fevers. By J. K. Mitchell, A.M., M.D. ... *Philadelphia: Lea and Blanchard.* 1849. 12mo, pp. 137. H. 49703

Also: A Lecture on some of the Means of elevating the Character of the Working Classes, in the Winter of 1833–4. ... *Philadelphia.* 1834. 8vo, pp. 17. — An Oration ... before the Philadelphia Medical Society ... . February 23, 1825. ... *Philadelphia: Printed by I. Ashmead & Co.* 1825. 8vo, pp. 28. B. — Proceedings of R. W. Grand Lodge of Pennsylvania, ... April 13, 1858, on the Occasion of the Death of the R. W. Grand Master, John K. Mitchell, M.D. *Philadelphia.* 1858. 8vo, pp. 8.

Mitchell (J.) The Missionary Pioneer, or a brief Memoir of the Life, Labours, and Death of John Stewart, (Man of Colour,) Founder, under God of the Mission among the Wyandotts at Upper Sandusky, Ohio. Published by Joseph Mitchell. *New York: Printed by J. C. Totten.* 1827. 24mo, pp. 96. C.

Field says "There are few in any generation of men, who may not envy the labors of this negro missionary and his reward. Some details of his labors will be found in Finley's autobiography."

Mitchell (J. W. S.) The History of Freemasonry and Masonic Digests: ... By J. W. S. Mitchell, M.D. ... *Marietta, Ga.* 1859. 2 vols., 8vo. + Eleventh Edition, thoroughly revised and reduced to one volume. *Griffin (Ga.): The Author.* 1871. 8vo, pp. 740, vi. Portrait. 49705

Mitchell (M.) A Short Account of the Early Part of the Life of Mary Mitchell, late of Nantucket, deceased, written by Herself. ... *New Bedford: Abraham Shearman, Jr.* 1812. 12mo, pp. 74. J.C.B. 49706

Mitchell (N.) History of the Early Settlement of Bridgewater, in Plymouth County, Massachusetts, including an extensive Family Register. By Nahum Mitchell. ... *Boston: Kidder & Wright.* 1840. 8vo, pp. 400. H. 49707

Mitchell (N.) Oration delivered before the Fourth of July Association, By Nelson Mitchell, Esq. on the Fourth of July, 1848. *Charleston, S. C.* 1849. 8vo, pp. 30. S. 49708

Mitchell (O. M.) Views for Freedom. By General O. M. Mitchell. *Cincinnati: American Reform Tract and Book Society.* 1862. 8vo, pp. 4. 49709

Also: Survey of the Little Miami Rail Road. Reports and Estimates made ... August 24th, 1837. ... *Cincinnati: Pugh and Dodd, Printers.* 1837. 8vo, pp. 16. H.

Mitchell (O. P.) The Olive Branch. ... By O. P. Mitchell. *Marysville: California Express Office.* 1862. 8vo, pp. 97.

Mitchell (R. C.) Extracts from the Army Regulations, etc. ... Compiled by R. Charlton Mitchell ... . *Annapolis, Md.: Elihu S. Riley, Printer.* 1861. 8vo, pp. 24. H. 49711

Mitchell (S.) Curious Particulars concerning the Osages. By S. Mitchell. [n. p. n. d.] 8vo. 49712

Mitchell (S. A.) An Accompaniment to Mitchell's Map of the World, ... containing an Index to the various Countries, Cities, Towns, Islands, ... Also, A General Description of the Five great Divisions of the Globe ... . *Philadelphia.* 1838. 8vo, pp. 572. + *Philadelphia: R. L. Barnes.* 1839. 8vo, pp. 572. + *Philadelphia: S. Augustus Mitchell.* 1846. 8vo, pp. 572, (4).

Mitchell. Accompaniment to Mitchell's New Map of Texas, Oregon, and California ... . *Philadelphia: S. Augustus Mitchell.* 1846. 18mo, pp. 46. Map. B. 49714

Mitchell. An Accompaniment to Mitchell's Reference and Distance Map of the United States; containing an Index of all the Counties, Districts, Townships, Towns, ... with an Index of the Rivers; ... [and] a General View of the United States, and the several States and Territories; ... *Philadelphia: Mitchell and Hinman.* 1834. 12mo, pp. 324. + [*Ibid.*] 1835. 12mo, pp. 324. + [*Ibid.*] 1836. 8vo, pp. 344. + [*Ibid.*] 1838. 8vo, pp. 344. + *Philadelphia: S. A. Mitchell.* 1845. 8vo. A.

[Mitchell.] Description of Oregon. *See* Vol. v. 19712.

Mitchell. A General View of the United States. Comprising, also, a description of each State and Territory in the Union ... . By S. A. Mitchell. *Philadelphia.* 1846. 8vo.

[Mitchell.] Illinois in 1837. *See* Vol. ix., No. 34260.

Mitchell. Mitchell's Traveller's Guide through the United States ... . *Philadelphia: Thomas, Cowperthwait, & Co.* [1836.] 16mo, pp. 74, (4). Map. Continued. B., H. 49717

Mitchell. Mitchell's New Traveller's Guide through the United States and the Canadas ... . *Philadelphia: Thomas, Cowperthwait, & Co.* 1850. 24mo, pp. 118. Map. Continued.

Mitchell. New General Atlas, containing Maps of the Various Countries of the World, Plans of Cities, etc. ... In Forty-Seven ... Maps, forming a Series of Seventy-Six Maps and Plans, ... with valuable Statistical Tables. *Philadelphia: S. A. Mitchell.* 1860. 4to, pp. (4), 22, (4). B. + [*Ibid.*] 1867. 4to, pp. 27. 91 Maps. C. 49719

Mitchell. New Universal Atlas, ... with a special Map of each of the United States, Plans of Cities, &c. ... *Philadelphia.* 1849. Folio. + [*Ibid.*] 1851. Folio. + [*Ibid.*] 1852. Folio. + *Philadelphia: Charles Desilver.* 1857. Folio. 49720

Mitchell. The Stage, Steamboat and Canal Routes in the United States, with the Population of each State. ... *Philadelphia.* 1834. 24mo, pp. 96. 49721

Mitchell. Die Vereinigten Staaten und die andern Länder Amerikas. *Philadelphia.* 1849. Rl. 8vo. 49722

Also: An Accurate Synopsis of the Sixth Census of the United States ... . *Philadelphia.* 1833. 8vo. + *Philadelphia: S. A. Mitchell.* 1845. 8vo, pp. 91–208, iv. C. — General View of the World; comprising a Physical, Political and Statistical Account of its Grand Divisions. ... *Philadelphia.* 1846. 8vo. — Key for Exercise on Mitchell's

Series of Outline Maps ... . *Hartford: Mather, Case* ... . 1842. 18mo, pp. 106. B.—Manual of Geography. *Hartford.* 1834. 18mo.—Mitchell's Geographical Question Book; ... containing Questions on ... Mitchell's School Atlas. ... [With] an Appendix, ... *Philadelphia: Thomas, Cowperthwait & Co.* 1852. 12mo, pp. 140. + *Philadelphia: E. H. Butler & Co.* 1866. 12mo, pp. 140.—Mitchell's Geographical Reader: a System of Modern Geography ... . *Philadelphia: Thomas, Cowperthwait & Co.* 1840. 12mo, pp. 600.—Mitchell's Intermediate or Secondary Geography. ... *Philadelphia: Thomas, Cowperthwait & Co.* 1850. 4to, pp. 80.— ... Mitchell's Primary Geography. ... *Philadelphia: Thomas, Cowperthwait & Co.* 1851. Sq. 16mo, pp. 176. + Third ... Edition. [*Ibid.*] 1853.—Mitchell's School Atlas: ... to Illustrate Mitchell's School and Family Geography. ... *Philadelphia: Thomas, Cowperthwait & Company.* MDCCCXXXIX. 4to, pp. (6). Maps. + *Philadelphia: E. H. Butler & Co.* 1866. 4to, pp. (8). Maps. B.—Mitchell's School Geography, A System of Modern Geography ... . *Philadelphia: Thomas, Cowperthwait & Co.* 1841. 8vo, pp. 336. + [*Ibid.*] 1855. 8vo, pp. 336.—Mitchell's Series of Geographies. ... [n. p. 1860?] 8vo, pp. 15. H.

MITCHELL (S. S.) Presbyterian Church of Harrisburg, April 19, 1865. In Memoriam. An Address by the Pastor, Rev. S. S. Mitchell. *Harrisburg: Singerly & Myers, Printers.* 1865. 8vo, pp. 15. B. 49723

On the assassination of Abraham Lincoln.

MITCHELL (S. T.) The Spirit of the Old Dominion. By S. T. Mitchell. No. 1. *Richmond.* 1827. 8vo. C. 49724

MITCHELL (T. D.) The Past, ... Present, and ... Future of the Medical Profession in the United States ... By Thomas D. Mitchell, M.D., ... November 2, 1852. ... *Louisville: Haldeman & Co.* 1852. 8vo, pp. 23. BA. 49725

Also: The Annual Oration of the Ohio Medical Lyceum: ... in the Medical College ... January 1, 1834. ... *Cincinnati: Truman, Smith & Co.* 1834. 8vo, pp. 32.—Professor Mitchell's Farewell to The Graduating Class of Jefferson Medical College, of Philadelphia, ... 9th ... of March, 1861. ... *Philadelphia: Collins, Printer.* 1861. 8vo, pp. 12, (4).—The Reciprocal Obligations of Professors and Pupils: an Introductory Lecture ... . *Lexington: N. L. Finnell, Printer.* 1845. 8vo, pp. 16. BA.

MITCHELL [T. R.] Speech of Mr. Mitchell, of South Carolina, on a motion to postpone, indefinitely, The Tariff Bill, Delivered ... April 15, 1828. *Washington.* 1828. 8vo, pp. 16.

Also: Speech ... on the Resolution of Mr. Mercer, to appoint a ... Committee on Roads and Canals. ... Dec. 15, 1831. *City of Washington.* 1831. 8vo, pp. 12. BA.

MITCHELL (W.) Our Reasons for Thankfulness: A Sermon delivered in ... Stamford, ... November 28, 1861, By the ... Rev. Walter Mitchell. ... *New York.* 1862. 8vo, pp. 15.

Also: Poems. ... *New York: John F. Trow, Printer.* 1860. 12mo, pp. 35. H.

MITCHELL (W.) The Astronomical Observatory of Harvard University. By William Mitchell. ... *Boston: Wm. Crosby and H. P. Nichols.* 1851. 8vo, pp. 16. H. 49728

MITCHELL (W.) The Claims of Africa. A Discourse ... at Montpelier, ... [before] the Vermont Colonization Society, October 19, 1843. By William Mitchell ... . *Burlington: Printed by Stilman Fletcher.* 1843. 8vo, pp. 24. H. 49729

MITCHELL. The Progress of the African Race; A Lecture by Rev. W. Mitchell ... . *Toronto, Canada West.* [1857.] 8vo, pp. 14. 49730

MITCHELL (W. H.) Geographical and Statistical History of the County of Olmstead, ... with a ... View of ... Minnesota, from its Earliest Settlement to the Present Time, By W. H. Mitchell. *Rochester, Minn.: Shaver & Eaton, Printers.* [1866.] 16mo, pp. 121. B., S. 49731

MITCHELL. Geographical and Statistical Sketch of ... Wabasha County, ... with a ... View of ... Minnesota. By W. H. Mitchell, and U. Curtis. *Rochester.* 1870. 16mo, pp. 164.

MITCHELL. Historical Sketches of Dodge County, Minn. By W. H. Mitchell, and U. Curtis. *Rochester.* 1870. 12mo.

MITCHELL. Sketch of Dacotah County, Minn. By W. H. Mitchell. *Minneapolis.* 1869. 12mo. 49734

MITCHELL (W. M.) The Under-ground Railroad, from Slavery to Freedom. By W. M. Mitchell. Second Edition. *London.* 1860. 18mo. C. 49735

Sketch of an Anniversary Festival of the Mitchell Family, held at South Britain, New Haven Co., Ct., October 5th, 1858, with an Historical Notice of the Life and Character of Dea. Eleazar Mitchell. ... *New York: Henderson & Stoothoff, Printers.* 1859. 18mo, pp. 28. 49736

[MITCHILL (S. L.)] The Case of the Manufacturers of Soap and Candles, in the City of New York, Stated and Examined. To which are prefixed, the Laws of the State of New York, concerning Infectious Diseases. With ... an Appendix, containing several Documents and Papers relative to these subjects. ... *New York.* 1797. 8vo, pp. 62. 49737

MITCHILL. Catalogue of the Organic Remains, which, ... were presented to the New-York Lyceum of Natural History, in August 1826, by ... Samuel L. Mitchill ... . *New-York: Printed ... by J. Seymour.* 1826. 8vo, pp. 40. B., W. 49738

MITCHILL. A Chemical Examination of the Mineral Water of Schooley's Mountain Springs ... with a Physical Geography, of the ... Mountains extending across New Jersey, from the Hudson to the Delaware. By Drs. Samuel L. Mitchell [*sic*], and James McNeven ... . *Morristown: S. P. Hull, Pr.* 1841. 12mo, pp. 24. + [*Ibid.*] 1845. 8vo, pp. 20. H. 49739

MITCHILL. A Concise Description of Schooley's Mountain, in New Jersey, with some Experiments on the Water of the Chalybeate Spring. By Samuel L. Mitchill ... . *New York: Printed by J. Seymour.* 1810. 8vo, pp. 14. H., N. 49740

MITCHILL. A Discourse on the Character and Services of Thomas Jefferson, more especially as a promoter of Natural and Physical Science. ... Before the New-York Lyceum of Natural History, on the 11th October, 1826. By Samuel L. Mitchill, ... *New York: G. & C. Carvill.* 1826. 8vo, pp. 67. B. 49741

MITCHILL. A Discourse on the Character and Scientific Attainments of De Witt Clinton, late Governor of the State of New-York; ... at the Lyceum of Natural History, ... 14th July, 1828 ... . By Samuel L. Mitchill. *New-York: Printed by E. Conrad.* [1828.] 8vo, pp. 28. BA., N. 49742

[MITCHILL.] An Historical Summary of the several Attacks that have been made upon the City of New York, since its first Settlement, and of the Measures that have been adopted, from time to time, for its defence. *New York.* 1812. 8vo. N.

MITCHILL. A Lecture on some parts of the Natural History of New Jersey, delivered ... June 3, 1828. By Samuel L. Mitchill, M.D. ... *New York: Printed by Elliot and Farmer.* 1828. 8vo, pp. 34. N. 49744

MITCHILL. The Life, Exploits, and Precepts of Tammany; the Famous Indian Chief. ... Anniversary Oration ... before the Tammany Society, or Columbian Order, ... the 12th May, 1795. By Samuel Latham Mitchill, M.D. ... *New York: Printed by J. Buel.* M,DCC,XCV. 8vo, pp. 36. Portrait. BA. 49745

[MITCHILL.] The Picture of New York; or, the Traveller's Guide through the Commercial Metropolis of the United States. By a Gentleman residing in this City. *New York: J. Riley & Co.* 1807. 16mo, pp. viii, 223. Map. C. 49746

With a plan of New York City, engraved by Peter Maverick, dated 1807.

[MITCHILL.] The Present State of Learning in the College of New York. *New York: T. & J. Swords.* 1794. 8vo, pp. 16.

MITCHILL. Report, in Part, of Samuel L. Mitchill, M.D. ... on the Fishes of New-York. ... *New-York: Printed by D. Carlisle.* 1814. 12mo, pp. 28. BA., P. 49748

MITCHILL. Some of the Memorable Events and Occurrences in the Life of Samuel L. Mitchill, of New York, from 1786 to 1821. [n. p. n. d.] 8vo, pp. 8. 49749

Also: Address [Fourth of July, 1800,] at New York. ... *New York.* 1800. 8vo, pp. 27.—Address to the Officers composing the Medical Staff [of the Militia in New York]. ... *New York: Printed by E. Conrad.* 1820. 8vo, pp. 38.—Address delivered before the New York Horticultural Society, ... August 29th, 1826. ... *New York.* 1826. 8vo.—Address to the Fredes, or People of the United States, on the 28th Anniversary of their Independence. ... *New York.* 1804. 8vo.—Concise Memorandum of certain Articles in the Museum ... . *New York.* [n. d.] 12mo.—A Discourse ... [before] the Society for Instructing the Deaf and Dumb, ... in the City of New-York, ... 24th day of March, 1818. ... *New York: Printed by E. Conrad.* [1818.] 8vo, pp. 32, (3).—A Discourse on the Life and Character of Samuel Bard, M.D. ... 5th ... of Nov. 1821. ... *New-York: Printed by Daniel Fanshaw.* 1821. 8vo, pp. 40.—A Discourse on the State and Prospects of American Literature; ... at Schenectady, July 24th, 1821, before the New-York Alpha of the Phi-Beta-Kappa Society. ... *Albany: Printed by Websters and Skinners.* 1821. 8vo, pp. 36.—Discourse on ... Thomas Addis Emmet, ... in ... New-York ... First ... of March, 1828. ... *New-York: Printed by E. Conrad.* 1828. 8vo, pp. 26.—Observations Anatomical ... . To which are added Geological Remarks on the Maritime Parts of the State of New York. ... *New York.* 1787. 12mo.—Observations on the Canada Thistle ... . [n. p. 1810.] 8vo, pp. 16. Plate.—Oration before the Society of Black Friars, New York, at their Anniversary Festival, 11th November, 1793. ... *New York.* 1793. 8vo, pp. 34.—Outline of the Doctrines in Natural History, Chemistry, and Economics, now delivering in the College of New York. ... *New York.* 1792. 12mo.—Present State of Medical Learning in the City of New York. ... *New York.* 1797. 8vo.

A | Mite Cast into the Treasury: | or, | Observations on Slave-Keeping. | ... | *Philadelphia, printed* 1772. 12mo, pp. iv, 24. P. + *Philadelphia: Joseph Crukshank.* [1785.] 12mo. 49750

Probably by Anthony Benezet, *see* our Vol. II.

MITFORD (M. R.) Lights and Shadows of American Life. Edited by Mary Russell Mitford. ... *London: Henry Colburn* ... . 1832. 3 vols., post 8vo, pp. vi, 340; (4), 339, (1); (4), 344.

MITFORD. Recollections of a Literary Life; or, Books, Places, and People. By Mary Russell Mitford ... . *London.* 1832. Post 8vo. C. + *New York: Harper & Brothers.* 1852. 12mo, pp. xii, 558. Portrait. B. 49752

This work includes extracts from American poets and authors.

MITFORD. Stories of American Life; by American Writers, Edited by Mary Russell Mitford. *London.* 1830. 3 vols., post 8vo. 49753

Probably "Lights and Shadows" is a new edition of this, or the same work with a differing title-page. Also: The Life of Mary Russell Mitford, ... in a Selection from her Letters ... . Edited by the Rev. A. G. L'Estrange. ... *London: Richard Bentley.* 1870. 3 vols., 8vo, pp. viii, 344; vii, 339; vii, 307. + *New York: Harper & Brothers.* 1870. 2 vols., 12mo, pp. 378; 365. B., H.

MITHRIDATE (H.), *pseudon.* Some Serious Thoughts on the Design of erecting a College in the Province of New York. Shewing the eminent Advantages of a liberal Education, etc. By Hippocrate Mithridate, Apoth. *New York.* 1749. 8vo.

Title from Thomas' "History of Printing," Vol. II.

Mitigation of Slavery, in two parts: Part 1, Letters and Papers of the late Hon. Joshua Steele; Part 2, Dickson's Letters to Clarkson. *London.* 1814. 8vo. S. 49755

MITRE (B.) Estudios históricos sobre la Revolucion Argentina. Belgrano y Güemes. Por Bartolomé Mitre. *Buenos Ayres.* 1864. 4to, pp. 264. 49756

MITRE. Galeria de Celebridades Argentinas. Biografias de los personages mas notables del Rio de la Plata. Por los Senores B. Mitre, D. F. Sarmiento, F. M. Gutierrez, M. Lozano, M. R. Garcia, T. J. Guido, M. Moreno, L. Dominguez, P. Lacasa. Con retratos litografiados por Narciso Desmadryl. *Buenos Aires.* 1857. Folio, pp. iv, 276. 9 Plates. 49757

Contains the biographies and lithographic portaits of the following celebrities: José de San Martin, D. Bernardino Rivadavia, General Manuel Belgrano, Gregorio Funes, Guillermo Brown, D. Manuel José Garcia, D. Mariano Moreno, D. Florencio Varela, General D. Juan Lavalle.

MITRE. Historia de Belgrano y de la Independencia Argentina. Por Bartolomé Mitre, Président de la République Argentine. *Buenos Aires.* 1859. 2 vols., 8vo, pp. 644, (2); 553. + Tercera y unica edicion completa. *Buenos Aires.* 1876–77. 3 vols., 8vo. 49758

A masterly work of which the two earlier (and incomplete) editions were speedily sold.

MITRE. Rimas de Bartolomé Mitre, con un prefacion del autor. *Buenos Aires.* 1854. 4to, pp. 320. 49759

The Mitre and Crown. *London.* 1750. 2 vols., 8vo.

Contains "A Description of Nova Scotia," account of "Cape Breton," etc.

MITTELBERGER (G.) Gottlieb Mittelberger's | Reise | nach | Pennsylvanien | im Jahr 1750. | Und | Rükreise nach Teutschland | im Jahr 1754. | Enthaltend | nicht nur eine Beschreibung des Landes | nach seinem gegenwärtigen Zustande, son- | dern auch eine ausführliche Nachricht von den | unglükseligen und betrübten Umständen der meisten | Teutschen, die in dieses Land gezogen sind, | und dahin ziehen. | *Stuttgard: | gedrukt bey Gottlieb Frederich Zenisch.* 1756. | 16mo, pp. (8), 120. C., H. 49761

This interesting narrative treats of the German colonists in Pennsylvania.

MITTEN (Wilhelm). Musci austro-americani. Enumeratio muscarum omnium austro-americanorum auctori hucusque cognitorum. ... *London.* 1869. 8vo, pp. (4), 659. C. 49762

MITTERMAIER (C. J. A.) Das englische, schottische und nord-amerikanische Strafverfahren im Zusammenhange mit den politischen, sittlichen und socialen Zuständen und in den Einzelnheiten der Rechtsübung dargestellt von Dr. C. J. A. Mittermaier, ... *Erlangen: Ferdinand Enke.* 1851. 8vo, pp. xii, (2), 560. H.

MITTERMAIER. Traité de la Procédure Criminelle en Angleterre, ... et dans l'Amérique du Nord, envisagée dans l'ensemble de ses Rapports avec les Institutions Civiles et Politiques de ces Pays, et dans les Détails Pratiques de son organisation, Par Le Dr C.-J.-A. Mittermaier ... augmentée des Additions de l'Auteur; traduit Par A. Chauffard ... . *Paris: E. Thorin.* 1868. 8vo, pp. xci, 644. B., C. 49764

Mittheilungen aus Justus Perthes' Geographischer Anstalt über wichtige Neue Erforschungen auf dem Gesammtgebiete der Geographie von Dr. A. Petermann. *Gotha: Justus Perthes.* [1855.] 4to, pp. vi, 378. 23 Maps. Continued. B., C. 49765

Many of the articles are on American topics.

MIX (J. B.) The Biter Bit; or the Robert Macaire of Journalism. ... By James B. Mix. ... *Washington, D. C.* 1870. 8vo, pp. 69. H. 49766

A narrative of the blackmailing operations of C. A. Dana's "Sun."

MIX (L. C.) Alida: Sketches of the late American War. By L. C. Mix. *New York.* 1841. 12mo. 49767

MIX (S.) An Oration, ... at the National Celebration, at New-Haven, Con., July 3, 1830. By Silas Mix. ... *New-Haven: Printed by Charles Adams.* [1830.] 8vo, pp. 20. H.

MIX (S.) Extraordinary Displays of the Divine | Majesty & Power, are to Try | Men, and Impress the Fear of God on | their Hearts, that they sin not. | Being the Substance of | Two Sermons | Occasioned by a Terrible | Earthquake | in New-England, | and other parts of Northern America; | In the Night immediately following the | Sabbath-Day, October 29. 1727. | Publickly Delivered in Wethersfield, on No- | vember the 5th. and 12th. ... | By Stephen Mix, M.A. | ... | *N. London: Printed by T. Green.* 1728. 8vo, pp. (2), 2, 36. B. 49769

Mixteca Language. Catecismo en Idioma Mixteco, segun se habla en los Curatos de la Mixteca baja que pertenecen al Obispado de Puebla, formado nuevamente de oren [*sic* for órden] del Exmo. é Illmo. Sr. Obispo Dr. D. Francisco Pablo Vasquez. E impreso á sus espensas. Por una Comision de Curas. *Puebla. Imprenta del Hospital de San Pedro.* 1837. 4to, pp. (14), 21.

Catecismo en el Idioma Mixteco Montañez, para el uso de los Curatos que van señalados en la lista que se inserta. Formado de oren [*sic*] del Exmo. é Illmo. Sr. Obispo de la Puebla Dr. D. Francisco Pablo Vasquez. Traducido al Castellano, por una Comision unida de Curas de la Misteca baja y Montañez. *Puebla. Imprenta del Hospital de San Pedro.* 1837. 4to, pp. (4), 20

Manual en Lengua Mixteca de ambos dialectos Bajo y Montañez, para los Curatos de la Sagrada Mitra de Puebla en los que se habla este Idioma. Formado por una Comision de Curas, de órden de Su Excelencia Illma. el Sr. D. D. Francisco Pablo Vasquez, Dignísimo Obispo de esta Diócesis. *Puebla. Imprenta del Hospital de San Pedro.* 1837. 4to, pp. 75, (2). 49772

Mizaldi de Mundi Sphærâ seu Cosmographiâ libri tres. [*Paris:*] *Lutetiæ.* 1552. 12mo. Diagrams. 49773

This poem, in which America is mentioned, is dedicated to the learned lady Margaret of Valois, Duchess of Berry, who afterwards married Emanuel Philibert of Savoy. She is not to be confounded with the other two Margarets of Valois, who were equally accomplished and are better known.

MIZNER (L. B.) Oration before the Society of California Pioneers ... By L. B. Mizner. *San Francisco.* 1870. 8vo.

Mnemonika; or, Chronological Tablets, exhibiting the most remarkable Occurrences from the Creation to the Present Period. *Baltimore.* 1812. 18mo. Plate. S. 49775

MOBERLY (W.) British Columbia. Columbia River Exploration, 1865. Instructions, Reports, and Journals, relating to

the Government Exploration of Country lying between the Shuswap and Okanagan Lakes and the Rocky Mountains. By W. Moberly. *New-Westminster: Government Printing Office.* 1866. Folio, pp. (4), 36. C. 49776

MOBILE, *Ala.* Charter of the Planters and Merchants Bank of Mobile. *Mobile.* [1836.] 12mo, pp. 12. 49777

The Code of Ordinances of the City of Mobile, with the Charter, and an Appendix. ... *Mobile: S. H. Goetzel & Co.* 1859. 8vo, pp. (4), 442, (2). C. + Compiled by Reuben A. Lewis. *Mobile: Advertiser and Register Office.* 1866. 8vo, pp. 274. C.

Digest of Acts of the Legislature, incorporating the City of Mobile. *Mobile.* 1849. 8vo. 49779

Mobile Directory, or Strangers' Guide for 1839. By T. C. Fay. *Mobile: R. R. Dade.* [1839.] 12mo, pp. 104, 96. C.

Directory and Register for 1844. ... With a variety of ... Statistical Matter, etc. By E. F. Wood. *Mobile.* 1844. 12mo.

Prefixed is a short historical sketch of Mobile and Louisiana.

Directory of the City of Mobile for the year 1866. By Henry Farrow and W. B. Dennett. [*Mobile.* 1866.] 8vo, pp. 116. Continued. 49782

Proceedings of the First Annual Meeting of the Stockholders of the Mobile and Ohio Railroad Company. *Mobile.* 1849. 8vo. 49783

Also: List of Lands donated to the Mobile and Ohio Rail Road, by Congress, 1850. *Mobile.* 1853. 8vo, pp. 132.

Organization of the Board of Mobile School Commissioners, and Regulations of the Public Schools. *Mobile.* 1860. 8vo.

Report of the Commissioners appointed to Examine the Bank of Mobile, Nov. 3, 1841. *Tuscaloosa.* 1841. 8vo. Cont'd

Also: Report of the Commissioners appointed to Examine the Planters and Merchants Bank of Mobile. *Tuscaloosa.* 1841. 8vo. + [Another Report.] *Tuscaloosa.* 1842. 8vo.—Report of the Commissioners appointed to Examine the Mobile Branch Bank. *Tuscaloosa.* 1846. 8vo.—President's Reply of the Branch Bank at Mobile, to the Resolution of the House of Representatives, of the 7th inst. [*Tuscaloosa.* 1843.] 8vo.

Report of the Committee appointed to investigate the ... Late ... Mortality in ... Mobile. [*Mobile.*] 1819. 12mo, pp. 12.

The Mock Auction. Ossawatomie Sold, a Mock Heroic Poem. *Richmond.* 1860. 12mo. Portraits. 49787

Relates to John Brown's Invasion of Virginia.

The Mocking Bird; a Collection of the Most Admired Songs. *Alexandria.* 1814. 24mo. 49788

Mocorosi Language. Arte y Vocabulario de la Lengua Mocorosi. *Mexico.* 1599. 4to. 49789

Title as given by Barcia. "The language of the Indians of Mexico now perhaps extinct."—LUDEWIG.

MOCQUET DE MEAUX (J.) Voyages en Afrique, Asie, Indes Orientales et Occidentales, Faits par Jean Mocqvet, ... divisez en six livres, et enrichiz de Figures. *Paris.* 1616. 8vo, pp. (8), 442. 9 Plates. + *Paris.* 1617. 8vo, pp. (8), 442, (14). 9 Plates. + *Rouen: Jacques Caillové.* 1645. 8vo, pp. (8), 442, (12). 5 Plates. C. + *Rouen: Antoine Ferrand.* 1665. 8vo, pp. (8), 442, (12). 9 Plates. S. + *Paris: Imprimé aux frais du Gouvernement.* 1830. 8vo, pp. (6), 381. 49790

The original edition is rare. Some copies of the edition of 1665 have the imprint: *Rouen, Jacques Besogne.* They all include the voyage of the author in Guiana and the province of Cumana. The following are translations:

MOCQUET DE MEAUX. Reysen | in | Afrique, Asien, Oost-en West-Indien, gedaen door | Jan Mocquet, | Bewaerder van 't Cabinet der ongemeene Aerdigheden | van den Koninck van Vranckrijck in de Tuillerie binnen Paris. | Gedeylt in ses Boecken, ende verciert met Koopere Platen, | overgeset uyt de Fransche Tale. | *Tot Dordrecht,* | *Voor Abraham Andriessz. Boeck-verkooper.* 1656. | 4to, pp. (14), 153. 10 Plates. C. 49791

MOCQUET DE MEAUX. De Grote Nieuw Bereisde Wereld: Begrypende zes Reyzen zo na Lybien, d'Eilanden van Kanarien en Barbaryen; Stroom der Amazonen, Karipouzen en Karibanen; ... Den Tweeden Druk. *Te Leeuwarden: By Jan Klassen.* 1717. 4to, pp. (20), 195. 3 Plates. + Den Derden Druk. [*Ibid.*] 1718. 4to, pp. (20), 195. 3 Plates. J.C.B. 49792

MOCQUET DE MEAUX. Wunderbare | Jedoch | Gründlich- und warhaffte Geschichte | und | Reise Begebnisse | In Africa, Asia, Ost- und | West-Indien | von | Jan Mocquet aus Frankreich, | Ihrer Königlichen Majestät Heinrichs des Grossen oder IV. | und Ludwigs des XIII. daselbst gewesnen geheimen Hof- und Cammer- | Apotheckers, ... in dero Königlichen Residenz-Stadt zu Paris, | in der Tuillerie. | Nebst eigentlicher Beschreibung derer Städte,

Königreiche, Inseln und | Provinzen, wie selbige itziger Zeit annoch zu befinden, und Er zu verschiednen | malen mit langwirigen Sorgen, Mühe und Beschwernissen zu Wasser und Lande, ... ganzer zwanzig Jahr, durch Gottes Gnade, durchzureisen | über sich genommen, ausgestanden und geendiget. | Allen Liebhabern verwundersamer Begebnissen und Reise-Geschichten | zu angenehmer Ergötzlichkeit in unterschiednen Büchern aus dem Französischen | in Hochteutsche Sprache übersetzet und entdecket | durch | Johann Georg Schoeben. | *Lüneburg,* | *In Verlegung Johann Georg Lippers.* | [1688.] 4to, pp. (60), 632. Plates. A. 49793

MOCQUET DE MEAUX. Travels and Voyages into Africa, Asia, and America, the East and West-Indies; ... Performed by Mr. John Mocquet ... . Enriched with Sculptures. Translated from the French, by Nathaniel Pullen, Gent. *London: William Newton.* 1696. Sm. 8vo, pp. (32), 352. Cuts. A., H. 49794

A | Model | For Erecting a | Bank of Credit; | with a | Discourse | In Explanation thereof. | Adapted to the Use of any Trading | Countrey, where there is a Scarcity | of Moneys: | More Especially for His Majesties Plantations | in America. | ... | *London. Printed in the Year* 1688. Sm. 8vo, pp. (2), 38. B. + ... *Reprinted at Boston, in New England, in the Year* 1714. Sm. 8vo, pp. (2), 30.

The preface to the Boston edition, dated Feb. 26, 1713–14, announces that, "a scheme of a Bank of Credit, founded upon a Land Security, has been projected; and will be humbly offered to the Consideration of the General Assembly, at their next Session." The tract sets forth in a plain and familiar way, not only the nature, but the feazibleness and utility of such a fund of credit. This seems to have been the first gun fired in the land bank war of 1714–21. For other works on this subject, *see* Vol. II., Nos. 6708–11.

Model of Government, 1685. *See* [Scot (George)].

El Modelo de los Cristianos presentado á los Insurgentes de America. *Mexico.* 1814. 8vo. 49796

Modelo para llevar las Cuentas de la Tesoreria General y Administraciones de Reutas maritimas y terrestres de la Republica, por un sistema de cargo y data seneillo, general y exacto. *San Salvador.* 1860. 8vo. 49797

MODENA. Discourse of the Dukedom of Modena, containing the Origin, Antiquity, Government, Manners, and Qualities of the People ... . *London.* 1674. 4to. 49798

With notices of Columbus, Vespuccius, and other discoveries in America.

MODENA (Angelo Vincenzo). Vita del B. Martino de Porres, Terziario Professo dell ordine de' Predicatori nella Provincia di S.

Giovanni Battista del Perú. *Roma: Salviucci.* 1837. 4to, pp. 210. 49799

MODERA (J.) Zeevaartkundige Beschrijving van de Nederlandsche West-Indische Bezittingen. [*Amsterdam.*] 1843. 8vo. Map. 49800

Los Moderados y el Estado de Mexico. *Toluca.* 1861. 8vo.

A Moderate and Safe Expedient to remove Jealousies and Feares, of any Danger, or Prejudice to this State by the Roman Catholicks of this Kingdome. *London.* 1646. Sm. 4to.

"Objections answered touching Mariland," is one of the topics.

... The Modern Age. July, 1865. ... Published by B. J. Butts ... . *Boston.* M DCCC LXV. 4to. Continued. H. 49803

Modern Battle of the Keys. By the Poet Laureate of the Know Nothings. *Philadelphia.* 1854. 16mo. 49804

Modern Geography, and a Compendious General Gazetteer. ... *Berwick.* 1811. 8vo. 49805

Includes portraits of Washington and Franklin.

Modern Geography, ... with Brief Notices of European Discovery and Colonization. By a Member of the Society of Friends. *London.* 1846. 16mo, pp. 230. 49806

The Modern Gilpin. A Ballad of Bull Run. *New York.* 1866. 12mo, pp. 19. 49807

Modern Government, and its True Mission. A Few Words for the American Crisis. [n. p.] 1862. 8vo, pp. 16. 49808

Modern History, or the Present State of all Nations, embracing a Description of Cuba, Hispaniola, Porto Rico, Spanish America, Brazil, and the British Plantations, particularly Virginia, Maryland, New-England, Nova Scotia and New Britain. *Dublin: Printed for George Grierson.* 1737. 2 vols., 12mo, pp. 351, (14); 334, (6). + *Dublin.* 1739. 4to. + [*Ibid.*] 1755.

Forms vols. XXV. and XXVI. of "Modern History." *See also* Moll (Herman).

Modern Patriotism Exemplified, in a late Convention, after the Capture of our outward-bound East and West India Fleets. *London: R. Faulder.* 1780. 8vo. 49810

See "Monthly Review," LXIII. 228.

Modern Protestant Church Courts Unmasked. *Providence.* 1838. 12mo, pp. 154. 49811

The Modern Quaker. *Philadelphia* [*about* 1790]. 12mo.

Modern Songster; consisting of a Collection of American and English Songs ... . The Second Baltimore Edition. *Baltimore.* 1816. 12mo. 49813

The Modern Thinker: ... . D. Goodman, Editor and Publisher. *New-York.* 1870. 8vo, pp. (2), 247, (1). Continued.

Modern Toleration. Tyranny in Disguise. [n. p.] 1816. 8vo. 49815

Relates to politics in Connecticut.

The Modern Traveller. A Popular Description, Geographical, Historical, and Topographical, of the Various Countries of the Globe. Mexico and Guatemala. *London: James Duncan.* 1825. 2 vols., 18mo, pp. vi, iii–iv, 371; 320. Map and 6 Plates. BA. + *Boston: Wells & Lilly.* 1830. 2 vols., 12mo, pp. 350; 301. + Columbia. *London.* 1825. 12mo. + Brazil and Buenos Ayres. *London.* 1825. 2 vols., 12mo. 49816

See also Conder (Josiah), IV. 15169.

The Modern Taveller: being a Collection of useful and entertaining Travels, lately made into various Countries, abridged. *London.* 1777. 6 vols., 12mo. 49817

Modern Women and what is said of them ... . With an Introduction by Mrs. Lucia Gilbert Calhoun. *New York: J. S. Redfield.* 1868. 12mo, pp. 371. + Second Series. [*Ibid.*] 1870. 12mo, pp. 404. B. 49818

A Modern View of the Thirteen United States of America; ... containing A concise account of their First Settlement, Principal Cities and Towns, Air, Soil, Produce, Manufactures, and Commerce, ... with A short account of the Independent State of Vermont, and of East and West Florida. ... To which is added, an account of the ... Original Inhabitants of America. *London: David Walker.* [1784.] 8vo, pp. (2), 101. 49819

A Modest Address ... occasioned By the ill success of our present Naval War with France ... . *London: J. Scitt.* MDCCLVI. 8vo, pp. 34. 49820

Contains some reference to American topics.

A Modest Apology for My Own Conduct ... . *London.* 1748. 8vo. 49821

Included in an English catalogue of Americana.

A | Modest Enquiry | into the | Grounds and Occasions of a Late | Pamphlet, | intituled, a | Memorial | of the | Present Deplorable State | of | New-England. | By a Disinterested Hand. | *London:* | *Printed in the year,* 1707. 4to, pp. (2), 30. 49822

"A violent pamphlet in defence of Gov. Dudley."—RICH. It also contains the "Memorial" itself, which was written by Gov. Dudley. See a curious letter from Cotton Mather (Oct. 2, 1706), with the answer (13–16) accusing Mather of improper intimacy with "a Gentlewoman of Gayety near Boston," his resolutions "to avoid her conversation, being frustrated by Vicious Inclinations."! Curious and very rare.

A Modest Enquiry. *See* [Franklin (B.)], VII. 25556.

A Modest Enquiry into the Present State of Foreign Affairs. ... By a Lover of his Country. *London.* [1742.] 8vo, pp. 71.

A Modest Proof. *See* [Checkley (J.)], III. 12364.

A | Modest Vindication | of the late | New-Jersey Assembly, | in | Answer | To a printed Paper against them, | call'd a | Representation. | *Printed in the year* MDCCXLV. 4to, pp. 32. P. 49824

Probably printed by B. Franklin.

MODTIBOLT, *pseudon.* The Republic of North America. By Modtibolt. ... *Detroit.* 1863. 8vo, pp. 70. S. 49825

A scheme for its government.

MOENS (J. B.) Manuel du collectionneur de Timbres-Poste ou Nomenclature générale de tous les timbres adoptés dans les divers pays de l'univers, Par J.-B. Moens. *Bruxelles: Moens.* 1862. 24mo, pp. 72. H. 49826

MOENS (Petronella). Aardenburg, of de onbekende volkplanting in Zuid-Amerika. ... *Haarlem: F. Bohn.* 1817. 8vo, pp. (2), viii, 320. C. 49827

MOERBEECK (J. A.) Redenen | Wâeromme de West- | Indische Compagnie dient te trachten het Landt van Brasilia den Co- | ninck van Spangien te ontmach- | tigen, en dat ten eersten. | Wesende een ghedeelte der Propositie | ghedaen door Jan Andries Moerbeeck, aen zijn Vor- | stelijcke Ghenade Mauritio Prince van Orange, etc. | ende eenighe andere Heeren Ghecommitteerden van | de Hooghe ende Groot Moghende Heeren de Staten | Generael der Vereenichde Nederlanden, ins Graven | Haghe de 4, 5, ende 6 April Anno 1623. | *t' Amsterdam* | *By Cornelis Lodewijcksz van der Plasse, Boeck-verkooper, op de* | *hoeck van de Beurs, in den Italiaenschen Bijbel. Anno* 1624. | 4to, pp. 16. 49828

Reasons why the West India Company ought to try to conquer Brazil. Concerning this rare piece, *see* Asher's "Bibliographical Essay," No. 105.

MOERENHOUT (J. A.) Voyages aux Iles du Grand Océan, contenant des Documens nouveaux sur la Géographie physique et politique, la Langue et la Littérature, la Religion, les Mœurs, les Usages et Coutumes, l'Histoire ancienne et moderne, et le Gouvernement de leurs Habitants, par M. J. A. Moerenhout, Consul des États-Unis á Otaïti ... . *Paris.* 1837. 2 vols., 8vo. 4 Plates and Map. A. 49829

MOESTA (C.) Informe Sobre las Observaciones hechas durante el Eclipse Solar de 30 Noviembre de 1853. ... Por Cárlos Moesta. *Santiago de Chile: Imprenta de Julio Belin i Ca.* 1854. 8vo, pp. 22. Plate. H. 49830

MOESTA (C. G.) Observaciones astronómicas hechas en el Observatorio nacional de Santiago de Chile en los años de 1853, 1854, 1855. Por el Dr. Cárlos Guillermo Moesta. Tomo I. ... *Santiago de Chile.* 1859. 4to, pp. xlii, 301, (1). Plate.

Moeurs et Coutumes des Peuples ou collection de tableaux, représentant les usages remarquables, les mariages, funérailles, supplices et fêtes des diverses nations du monde. *Paris.* 1811–14. 2 vols., 4to. 144 colored Plates 49832

MOFFAT (J. C.) Liberal Education: an Address ... [at] Hanover College, ... August 6th, 1856, By James C. Moffat, ... *Philadelphia: Parry and McMillan.* 1857. 8vo, pp. 24. H.

[MOFFATT (Mary Anne Ursula).] *See* [Mary Edmond St. George], XI. 45038.

See also Reed (M. T.), for a "Review."

MOFFETTE (J. F.) Territories of Kansas and Nebraska. By Joseph F. Moffette. *New-York.* 1855. 16mo. Maps. C.

MOFRAS (Duflot de). *See* Duflot de Mofras, V. 21144.

[MOGRIDGE (George).] Indians of North America. By Old Humphrey. *London.* [n. d.] 16mo. 49835

Reprinted as: North American Indians. By Old Humphrey. *Boston.* [n. d.] 18mo.

MOGROVEIUS (T. A.) Toribio Alfonso Mogrovesio Il Santo Arcivescovo di Lima compendio di vita e di Massime adattate a tutti i Principi e Prelati ecclesiastici con un ritiro di otto giorni de esercizi Spirituali ... . *Roma.* 1728. 4to. Engraved Title and Portrait. 49836

For an earlier edition, *see* Haroldus (F.), Vol. VIII., No. 30416, *see also* No. 30415, *and* Vol. XI., No. 43208.

Mohawk Language. The Acts of the Apostles, in the Mohawk Language, Translated by H. A. Hill, with Corrections by William Hess and John A. Wilkes, Jr. *New York: Young Men's Bible Society.* 1835. 12mo, pp. 121. 49837

The Book of Common Prayer, ... of the Protestant Episcopal Church in the United States of America. Translated into the Mohawk or Iroquois Language, ... By the Rev. Eleazer Williams, V.D.M. Revised Edition of his Former Translation. *New York.* 1853. 12mo, pp. 108, Hymns, pp. 67. + *New York: H. B. Durand.* 1867. 12mo, pp. 101, 38. 49838

For other editions, *see* Vol. II., No. 6351–2.

A Collection of Hymns for the use of Native Christians of the Mohawk Language. Ne karoronh ne teyrighwaghkwatha ne ne enyontste ne yagorihwiyoghstonh kanyengehaga niyeweantenh. Translated by A. H. Hill. *New York.* 1829. 32mo, pp. 39, 68. + To which are added, a number of Hymns for Sabbath Schools. *New-York: Printed by D. Fanshaw.* 1835. 24mo, pp. 147.

Some copies are without date.

A Collection of Psalms and Hymns, in the Mohawk Language, for the use of the Six Nation Indians. By the New England Corporation. Mohawk and English. *Hamilton: Printed ... [by] Ruthven.* 1839. 18mo, pp. 80 *bis.* BA. 49840

The Epistle of Paul ... to the Romans, in the Mohawk Language, translated by H. A. Hill, with corrections by William Hess and John A. Wilkes, Jr. *New York: Young Men's Bible Society.* 1835. 12mo, pp. 56. 49841

Usually follows the "Acts," our No. 49837, *supra.*

The Epistle of Paul to the Galatians, in the Mohawk Language. Translated by William Hess, and Corrections by J. A. Wilkes, Jr. *New York: Howe and Bates.* 1835. 8vo, pp. 18. + To the Ephesians. [*Ibid.*] 8vo, pp. 18. 49842

The Epistles of Paul. Translated by William Hess, and Corrections by J. A. Wilkes, Jr. *New York: Howe & Bates.* 1836. 12mo, pp. 104. 49843

The Gospel, ... according to St. Matthew, Translated into the Mohawk Language, by A. Hill, and Corrected by J. A. Wilkes, Jr. Grand River, U. C. *New York.* 1831. 12mo. + *New York.* 1836. 12mo, pp. 197. 49844

The Gospel according to St. Mark, into the Mohawk Tongue, by Capt. Brant; also several Portions of the Sacred Scriptures. *New York: Printed by McElrath and Bangs ... .* 1829. 12mo, pp. 239, (1). 49845

This is a reprint of Brant's translation, published in 1787.

Morning and Evening Prayer. *See* Vol. IV., Nos. 13180–81.

Nene karighwiyoston tsinihorighhoten ne Saint John. The Gospel according to St. John. *London: ... Phillips & Fardon* [*about* 1805]. Sm. 8vo, pp. 125, (1), 125, (1). H. + *New-York: D. Fanshaw.* 1818. 18mo, pp. 116, 116. C. 49846

In English and Mohawk, printed on opposite pages. The translator was a young educated Mohawk, named Teyoninhokarawen, commonly called John Norton. *See* Janson's "Stranger in America," p. 278; *also* the address of Teyoninhokarawen, prefixed to some copies of the work, and Drake's "Book of the Indians."

Ne Kagh-ya-dough-se-ra, ne Royadadokenghdy, ne Isaiah. *New York: American Bible Society.* 1839. 18mo, pp. 243.

The book of Isaiah, translated into the Mohawk dialect.

Ne Raorihwadogenghti ne Shongwayaner Yesus Keristus jiniihorihoten ne Royatadogenhti Luke. *New York: Printed by McElrath, Bangs and Herbert.* 1833. 12mo. 49848

The Gospel of St. Luke in Mohawk, by A. H. Hill, corrected by J. A. Wilkes, Jr., of Grand River, C. W.

Ne Raowenna Teyoninhokarawen Shakonadonire ne rondaddegenshon ne rondadhawakshon Rodinonghtsyoni Tsiniyoderighwagennoni ne Raorighwadogenghte ne ne Sanctus John. Address to the Six Nations; recommending the Gospel of Saint-John. By Teyoninhokarawen, The Translator.——London. *London: Printed by Phillips & Fardon.* 1805. 12mo, 8 prel. leaves, Text, 125 leaves; Errata, 1 leaf. 49849

Ne tsinihhoweyea-nenh-onh orighwa do geaty, roghyadon royadado geaghty, Saint Luke. *New-York: A. Hoyt.* 1827. 12mo, pp. 314. 49850

"The Gospel according to Saint Luke translated into the Mohawk tongue, By H. A. Hill."

Ne totyerenhton kahyatonhsera ne royatadogenhti Paul shagohyatonni ne Corinthians. First Epistle of Paul the Apostle to the Corinthians. Translated by H. A. Hill. *New York: Young Men's Bible Society.* 1834. 12mo, pp. 50, 50. C. 49851

Mohawk and Hudson Rail Road. [n. p.] 1840. 4to, pp. (2).

Act to Incorporate the Mohawk and Hudson Railroad Company ... 1826–28. *New-York.* 1830. 8vo, pp. 20. S. 49853

Also: Charter of the Mohawk and Hudson Rail-Road Company ... . *Albany: Alfred Southwick, Printer.* 1838. 8vo, pp. 33.—Report to the President and Directors ... by Peter Fleming ... . *New York: G. & C. Carvill.* 1829. 8vo, pp. 15.—Report to the Stockholders of the ... Company: ... 1838. *Albany: Printed by Alfred Southwick.* 1838. 8vo, pp. 18.—Report on the Affairs of the Mohawk and Hudson Railroad Company; ... January, 1840. *Schenectady: Riggs & Morris, Printers.* 1840. 8vo, pp. 24.

Papers and Documents relating to the Mohawk and St. Lawrence Rail Road and Navigation Company. *Albany.* 1838. 8vo, pp. 25. Map. 49854

Articles of Association of the Mohawk Valley Railroad Company. ... *New York.* 1850. 8vo. S. 49855

Also: By-Laws. ... *New-York.* 1851. 8vo.—Report of the Survey, ... May 1, 1851. [n. p. n. d.] 8vo. S.

The Mohawk Chief. By the author of "The Fall of the Nau Soung." *London: T. Cautley Newby.* 1857. 3 vols., post 8vo, pp. vi, 265; 290; 247. 49856

The Mohawks; a Satirical Poem with Notes. *London.* 1822. 8vo, pp. 164. 49857

MOHEGAN INDIANS. Memoir written in the year 1804. [n. p. n. d.] 8vo. C. 49858

See also under Connecticut, Vol. IV., Nos. 15748–52.

Moheakunnuk Language. Assembly's Shorter Catechism. *Stockbridge, Mass.* 1795. 8vo, pp. 31. 49859

In the Moheakunnuk, or Stockbridge Indian language.

MOHL (R. von). Das Bundes-Staatsrecht der Vereinigten Staaten von Nord-Amerika. *Stuttgart und Tübingen.* 1824. 8vo.

MOHL. Die Geschichte und Literatur der Staatswissenschaften. In Monographieen dargestellt von Robert von Mohl. ... *Erlangen: Verlag von Ferdinand Enke.* 1855–58. 3 vols., 8vo, pp. xvi, 599; xii, 602, (1); xv, 851. BA. 49861

Part of Vol. I. relates to the United States.

The Mohocks. *See* [Gay (J).], VII. 26788.

MOKE (H. J.) Histoire des peuples américains, par H. J. Moke. *Bruxelles: F. Deoroede.* 1847. Sm. 8vo, pp. iv, 262. 2 Maps. 49862

MOLAS (Mariano Antonio). Descripcion Historica de la antigua Provincia del Paraguay, correjida, aumentada y anotada por A. T. Carranza. *Buenos-Aires: Imprenta de Mayo de C. Casavalle.* 1868. 8vo, pp. 388. C. 49863

MOLESWORTH (W.). Speech of Sir William Molesworth, Bart. M.P. in the House of Commons, on ... July 25, 1848, on Colonial Expenditure and Government. *London.* 1848. 8vo, pp. 40. 49864

MOLESWORTH. Speeches of Sir William Molesworth, ... on the ... Government of the Australian Colonies. *London: James Ridgway.* [1850.] 8vo, pp. 75. 49865

With frequent references to America. Also: Speech ... in the House of Commons on the State of the Colonies. *London.* 1838. 8vo.—Speech ... on the Second Reading of the Canada Bill, 23d January, 1838. *London.* 1838. 8vo, pp. 48.—Speech ... June 25th, for a Royal Commission on the Colonies. [n. p.] 1849. 8vo, pp. 32.

MOLGUIN (D. de Goncalez). *See* Goncalez Molguin (D. de).

MOLINA (A. de). Aqui comiença vn vocabula-|rio enla lengua Castellana y Mexicana, Compuesto|por el muy reuerendo padre fray Alonso de|Molina: Guardiā d'l cōueto d' sant Antonio d'| Tetzcuco d'la ordē delos frayles Menores.|...|[Colophon:] *A honrra y gloria de nues-|tro señor Iesu xpo y de su bēdita madre aq se aca-|ba la presente obra: la q̄ fue compuesta por el|muy reuerēdo padre fray Alōso d' molina.|Imprimio se ē la muy grāde & insigne y|muy leal ciudad de Mexico, en casa de|Iuā pablos, cō licencia del Illustrissi-|mo señor Dō Luys de Velasco|Visorrey y Gouernador d'sta|Nueua España, y de la Au-|diēcia Real q̄ ē ella resi-|de. Y assimismo cō|licencia del Reue-|rendissimo Se-|ñor dō fray|Alōso de|Montufar por la gracia de Dios Arçobispo meri-|tissimo d'la dicha ciudad de Mexico. Fue|vista y examinada esta presente obra|por el reuerēdo padre fray Francis-|co de Lintorne, Guardian del|monesterio de sant Francisco|de Mexico, y por el Reue-|rēdo padre fray bernar-|dino d' Sahagū, dela|dicha ordē, a quiē|el examē della|fue cometido. Acabo se d'|imprimir a q̄tro di-|as del mes de|Mayo. de|*1555.| 4to.

Collation: Title, in alternate lines of red and black letters, with woodcut in the centre; reverse, a large woodcut filling the page, with the letters *ihs* in the centre; 6 prel. leaves; Text, 259 leaves; Colophon, 1 leaf.

The author, a native of Spain, was taken in early life to Mexico (1523), where he soon learnt the Mexican language, and even as a child he acted as interpreter between the first missionaries and the native Indians. He afterwards devoted his life to the propagation of useful knowledge in the Mexican language, and this first edition of his dictionary is one of the earliest books published in the new world, and is a work of such extreme rarity that it escaped the researches of Ludewig, who supposed Antonio's reference to it to be a mistake. The only perfect copy in the United States is in the Lenox Library; most of the other known copies lack the title and colophon. In cataloguing one Quaritch remarks "Only five other copies are believed to be extant; all of them imperfect," which remark must be taken *cum grano salis.*

MOLINA. Vocabvlario|en lengva Castellana y Mexicana, com-|puesto por el muy Reuerendo Padre Frav Alonso de Molina, dela|Orden del bienauenturado nuestro Padre sant Francisco.|Dirigido al mvy Excelente Senor|Don Martin Enriquez, Visorrey destanueua España.|*En Mexico,*|*En Casa de Antonio de Spinosa.*|1571.| [Colophon:] *Soli Deo honor et Gloria.*|*Aqui hazen fin los dos vocabvlarios, en lengva Caste|llana y nahual o Mexicana que hizo y recopilo el muy Reuerendo padre, fray Alonso de Mo-|lina: de la orden de señor san Francisco. Imprimieronse enla muy insigne y gran ciudad|de Mexico: en casa de Antonio de Spinosa. enel Año de nuestra redēpcion. de.* 1571.| Folio. J.C.B., C. 49867

Collation: 4 prel. leaves, Text, 121 leaves, and 1 leaf with printer's mark on the verso, being the first device used by a Mexican printer; followed by another title-page: "Vocabvlario en lengva Mexicana y Castellana" (as above), 2 leaves, Text, 162 leaves.

This second and enlarged edition is so scarce that forty years ago Lord Kingsborough paid 50 guineas for it. The buyer should be careful to secure a copy with title-pages to both parts, for sometimes the first title-page being deficient the enterprise of a dealer induces him to put the second in its place, as it reads nearly the same; the woodcut, however, represents San Francisco, and differs from the escutcheon on the first title. Rich and other bibliographers erroneously supposed that this was the first book printed in America. M. L. Leon de Rosny, of Paris, announced a new edition, but it has not yet appeared.

MOLINA. Arte de la lengua Mexi-|cana y Castellana, compuesta por el muy Re-|uerendo padre fray Alonso de Mo-|lina de la orden de Señor|sant Francisco.|*En Mexico en casa de Pedro Ocharte.* 1571. Sm. 8vo. J.C.B., C. 49868

Collation: Title and "Epistola nuncupatoria," 3 leaves, Text, 82 leaves; Segunda parte, 35 leaves.

"This copy was purchased by the late Lord Kingsborough for 25*l.*, and it is the only one I can trace."—*Note in one of Thomas Thorpe's catalogues.* It is certainly a work of very great rarity.

MOLINA. Arte de la lengva Mexicana y Castellana, compuesta por el muy R. P. Fray Alonso de Molina, de la orden de Señor sant Francisco, de nueuo en esta segunda impression corregida, emendada y añadida, mas copiosa y clara que la primera. Dirigida al muy Excelente Señor Visorrey. &c. *Mexico, en casa de Pedro Balli.* 1576. Sm. 8vo. J.C.B. 49869

Collation: Title, License, and "Epistola," 7 leaves, Text, 112 leaves.

This second edition of Molina's Grammar is also very rare, being unknown to Antonio, Pinelo, Brunet, and Ludewig.

MOLINA. Confessionario breue, en lengua|Mexicana y Castellana: compuesto por el muy reuerēdo|padr efray [*sic*] Alonso de Molina, de la ordē del sera-|phico padre Sant Francisco.|*En Mexico en casa de Antonio de Espinosa, Impssor.* 1565. [Colophon:] *Acabose de imprimir este confessionario en xxvj de Henero. Año de* 1565. 4to, 20 leaves. J.C.B. 49870

This extremely rare book is usually found bound up with the following:

MOLINA. Confessionario mayor, en lengua Mexicana y Castellaña.|*En Mexico, por Antonio de Espinosa.* 1565. [Colophon:] *Acabose de impri-|mir este Confessionario, en la muy in-|signe y gran ciudad de Mexico: en casa de An-|tonio de Espinosa impressor de libros, jun-|ta a la yglesia de Señor Sant Augu-|stin: a quinze de Mayo. Año de* 1565. *Laus Deo.* 4to, Title and "Epistola nuncupatoria," dated 1564, 2 leaves, Text, 121 leaves, Table, 3 l.

Both works were reprinted as below:

MOLINA. Confessionario Breue, en lengua Mexicana y Castellana. Compuesto por el muy Reuerendo padre Fray Alonso de Molina, de la orden del Seraphico sant Francisco. *En Mexico. En casa de Pedro Balli.* 1577. 4to, 20 leaves. 49872

MOLINA. Confessionario Mayor, en la lengna [*sic*] Mexicana y Castellana. Compuesto por el muy Reuerendo padre Fray Alonso de Molina, de la orden del Seraphico sant Francisco. *En Mexico. En casa de Pedro Balli. Año de* 1578. 4to, 132 leaves, Table and "privilegio," 4 leaves. 49873

MOLINA. Doctrina Christiana en lengua Mexicana muy necessaria: en la qual se contienen todos los principales misterios de nuestra Sancta Fee catholica. Compuesta por el muy Reuerendo Padre Fray Alonso de Molina, de la orden del glorioso Padre Sant Francisco. Con Priuilegio. *En Mexico, En casa de Pedro Ocharte.* MDLXXVIII. 8vo, xci leaves, Table, 4 leaves. 49874

Extremely rare, unmentioned by Brunet, Rich, Stevens, and other bibliographers. Eguiara says it was reprinted, *Seville,* 1584, 4to; it was again reprinted in part as:

MOLINA. Doctrina Christiana y Cathecismo en Lengua Mexicana. Nueuamente Emendada, Dispuesta, y Añadida; para el vso, y enseñança de los Naturales. Compuesta Por el P. Fr. Alonso De Molina, de la Orden Del Glorioso Padre San Francisco. Año de 1675. Con licencia. *En Mexico, Por la Viuda de Bernardo Calderon.* 8vo, 16 leaves. 49875

MOLINA. Doctrina Christiana, y Cathecismo, en Lengua Mexicana. Compuesta por el P. Fr. Alonso de Molina, de la Orden del Glorioso Padre S. Francisco. Corregida ahora nuevamente por el R. Padre Lector Fr. Manuel Perez, Cathedratico de Lengua Mexicana en esta Real Vniversidad, del Orden de San Augustin. Para la buena enseñança de los Naturales. Año de 1718. Con licencia: *En Mexico, por Francisco de Ribera Calderon.* 8vo, 16 leaves. 49876

MOLINA. Doctrina Christiana, y Cathecismo En Lengua Mexicana. Compuesta por el P. Fr. Alonso de Molina, de la Orden del Glorioso, y Seraphico Padre San Francisco. Corregida fielmente, por su original. Año de 1732. *Reimpressa en Mexico: Por la Viuda de Francisco de Ribera Calderon* ... . 8vo, 16 leaves. 49877

MOLINA. Doctrina Christiana y Cathecismo En Lengua Mexicana. Compuesta por el P. Fr. Alonso de Molina, de la Orden del Glorioso Seraphico Padre San Francisco. Corregida fielmēte, por su original. Año de 1735. *Reimpressa en Mexico: Por la Viuda de Francisco de Rivera Calderon* ... . 8vo, 16 leaves.

MOLINA (F.) Bosquejo de la Republica de Costa Rica, seguido de Apuntamientos para su Historia. Con varios Mapas, Vistas y Retratos. Por Felipe Molina. *Madrid: Imprenta de la Viuda de Catero.* 1850. 8vo, pp. 44. Map. + *Nueva York: Imprenta de S. W. Benedict.* 1851. 8vo, pp. (2), 128. 9 Maps, 2 Plates, and 3 Portraits. C., H. P. 49879

MOLINA. Costa-Rica y Nueva Granada Examen de la Cuestion de Limites, que hay pendiente entre las dos republicas mencionadas Con un Mapa, ... y Testimonios de los Titulos Antiguos de Costa-Rica. Por Felipe Molina ... . *Washington: Imprenta de R. A. Waters.* 1852. 8vo, pp. 50. Map. B., P.

MOLINA. Costa Rica and New Grenada. An Inquiry into the Question of Boundaries, ... with ... an Appendix ... containing a Brief Account of the Question between Costa Rica and Nicaragua, By Felipe Molina ... . *Washington: R. A. Waters, Printer.* 1853. 8vo, pp. 54. Map. B., C. 49881

M[OLINA]. Coup d'œil rapide sur la République de Costa-Rica. Par F. M. *Paris: D. Dupré.* 1849. 8vo, pp. 32. Map. + *Paris: Aubusson.* 1850. 8vo, pp. 32. Map. 49882

M[OLINA]. A Brief Sketch of the Republic of Costa Rica. By F. M. *London: The Author.* 1849. 8vo, pp. 15. Map.

MOLINA. Memoria sobre les Cuestiones de Limites que se versan entre la República de Costa Rica y el Estado de Nicaragua. Por Felipe Molina ... . *Madrid: Imprenta de la Viuda de Catero.* 1850. 8vo, pp. 46. Map. 49884

MOLINA. Memoir on the Boundary Question pending between The Republic of Costa Rica and the State of Nicaragua; By F. Molina ... . *Washington: Gideon and Co., Printers.* 1851. 8vo, pp. 40. Map. B., C., P. 49885

MOLINA (Francisco Xavier). El Llanto de los Ojos de los Jesuitas de Guathemala en la muerte de sú luz, el Dr. Francisco Joseph de Figueredo y Victoria, Obispo, Primero de Popayan, y despues Arzobispo dignissimo de Guathemala. [*Mexico:*] *En el Colegio Real de San Ignacio de la Puebla de los Angeles.* 1766. 4to.

Also: El Rey de las Luces, Luz de los Reyes, Encendida sobre el Candelero de la Funebre Pyra, para aclarar desengaños à los Soberanos, y ensenarles las mas Heroycas Virtudes Philipo V. *Mexico.* 1747. 4to.

MOLINA (G. I.) Saggio sulla Storia Civile del Chili del Signor Abate Giovanni Ignazio Molina. *Bologna.* 1787. 8vo. Map.

MOLINA. Saggio sulla Storia Naturale del Chili del Signor Abate Giovanni Ignazio Molina. *Bologna: Stamperia di S. Tommaso d'Aquino.* MDCCLXXXII. 8vo, pp. 367, (1). H. + [*Ibid.*] MDCCLXXXVII. 8vo, pp. 333, (1). Map. B. + Seconda Edizione accresciuta e arricchita di una nuova Carta Geografica e del ritratto dell' Autore. ... *Bologna: Fratelli Masi e Comp.* 1810. 4to, pp. (6), v, 306, (2). Map and Portrait. A., B., C. 49888

MOLINA. Compendio de la Historia Geografica, natural y civil del Reyno de Chile, escrito en Italiano por el Abate Don Juan Ignacio Molina. Primera Parte, que abraza la Historia Geografica y Natural, traducida en español por Don Domingo Joseph de Arquellada Mendoza ... . Parte Segunda, traducida al español, y aumentada con varias notas por Don Nicolas de la Cruz y Bahamonde. *En Madrid, por Don Antonio de Sancha.* M.DCC.-LXXXVIII–MDCCXCV. 2 vols., 4to, pp. xx, 418; xvi, 382, (1). 4 Maps, 3 Tables. A., C., H. 49889

This Spanish translation is more complete than the Italian original, many notes being added by the translator to the second part. It contains a philological sketch of the Chilian language, comparative vocabularies, and a list of writers upon Chili.

MOLINA. Essai sur l'Histoire Naturelle du Chili, Par M. l'Abbé Molina; Traduit de l'Italien, & enrichi de notes, Par M. Gruvel, D.M. *A Paris, Née de la Rochelle.* M.DCC.LXXXIX. 8vo, pp. xvi, 352. C., S. 49890

Includes a Chilian and French vocabulary

MOLINA. Geschichte der Eroberung von Chili durch die Spanier. Nach dem Italienischen des Herrn Abbe J. I. Molina. *Leipzig: Bey Friedrich Gotthold Jacobäer.* 1791. 8vo, pp. (12), 308

MOLINA. Versuch einer Naturgeschichte von Chili. Von Abbé J. Ignaz Molina. Aus dem Italiänischen übersetzt von J. D. Brandis. *Leipzig: Bey Friedrich Gotthold Jacobäer.* 1786. 8vo, pp. (18), 328. Map. H. 49892

MOLINA. The Geographical, Natural and Civil History of Chili. By Abbe Don J. Ignatius Molina. ... With Notes from the Spanish and French Versions, and an Appendix, containing copious extracts from the Araucana of Don Alonzo de Ercilla. Translated from the original Italian, by an American Gentleman. ... *Middletown (Conn.): For I. Riley.* 1808. 2 vols., 8vo, pp. (8), xii, 271, (1); (4), viii, 305, (1), 68. H. 49893

MOLINA. The Geographical, Natural and Civil History of Chili. Translated from the original Italian of the Abbe Don J. Ignatius Molina. To which are added, Notes from the Spanish and French Versions, and two Appendixes, by the English Editor; the first, an Account of the Archipelago of Chiloe, from the Descripcion Historial of P. F. Pedro Gonzalez de Agueros; the second, an Account of the Native Tribes who inhabit the Southern extremity of South' America, extracted chiefly from Falkner's Description of Patagonia. ... *London: Longman.* 1809. 2 vols., 8vo, pp. xx, 321; xii, 385. Map. A., P. 49894

This translation is apparently a copy of the American edition of the preceding year, with a few alterations and some additions, but without any acknowledgment of the American original. The "Edinburgh Review" says the translator has leaned to the French version. The translators were Richard Alsop and William Shaler, Esq. "Excellent and full of information."—PINKERTON.

MOLINA (J. I.) Peru. El cumplimiento de la Ley por el Organo Republicano. Proyecto formado por el Ciudadano Jose Ignacio de Molina ... . *Lima: Imprenta ... por J. M. Concha.* 1827. Folio, pp. (4), iv, 76. BA. 49895

Also: Report of the Soil and Mineral Productions of Chili, extracted from the Italian of the Abbe Molina. *London.* 1825. 8vo.

MOLINA (Luis de). Reglas de Ortographia Dicionario y Arte del Ydioma Othomi ... . *Mexico.* 1767. 12mo. 49896

The Othomi language differs entirely in structure from those spoken in Mexico, North America, etc., having more resemblance to the languages of Eastern Asia than any other.

MOLINA (M.) Segunda publicacion. (Carta de varios vecinos de San Francisco de Yare al Presidente de la República, al Arzobispo y al Ministro de lo Interior y Justicia, acusacion de un indigno Presbítero Marcos Molina.) *Carácas.* 1866. 8vo, pp. 18

MOLINA (Tirso de). Gloria de loz Pizarros. 1622.

Title from Ternaux's "Bibliothèque Américaine," No. 443.

MOLINE, *Ill.* Directory ... for 1858 and '59. *Moline.* 1858. 12mo. 49899

Moll Pitcher, A Poem. ... *Boston: Carter and Hendee.* 1832. 8vo, pp. 27, (1). BA. 49900

MOLL (G.) Verhandeling over eenige vroegere zeetogten der Nederlanders. ... *Amsterdam: J. vander Hey et Zoon.* 1825. 8vo, pp. 220. 49901

This treatise of some early voyages of the Dutch "is of importance, as it contains valuable notices of the voyages and books of Linschoten, Cornelis and Frederick Houtman, Peter Plancius, Voyages to the Northern Regions, Voyages to the Pacific, Jacob Mahu, Simon de Cordes, and Sebald de Weerdt, Oliver van Noort, Joris van Spilbergen, Le Maire, William Schouten, L'Heremite, Roggewien, Tasman and De Vries."

MOLL (H.) Atlas Geographus; or a Complete System of Geography, ... with Discoveries and Improvements to this time, ... Done by Herman Moll. *London.* 1711–17. 5 vols., 4to.

Volume V. relates to America.

MOLL. Atlas Manuale: or, a New Sett of Maps of all the Parts of the Earth, as well Asia, Africa and America, as Europe. Wherein Geography is Rectified. ... *London: A. & J. Churchill.* 1709. 8vo, pp. v, (2). 43 Maps. C. + [*Ibid.*] 1713. 4to.

MOLL. Atlas Minor: or ... Sixty two Maps, in which are shewn all the Empires, Kingdoms, Countries, States, in all the known Parts of the Earth; ... Composed and laid down by Herman Moll Geographer. ... *London: Thoˢ. Bowles.* [1732.] 4to.

MOLL. Compleat Geographer or the Chorography and Topography of all the known Parts of the Earth. To which is premis'd an Introduction to Geography and a Natural History of the Earth and the Elements. ... *London.* 1709. Folio. 9 Maps. + Third Edition. *London.* 1719. Folio. + Fourth Edition. *London.* 1723. Part I. Folio, pp. 402. Part II. 1722, pp. 288, Index, xx. 49905

MOLL. Modern History: or the Present State of All Nations, including a Dissertation on the first Peopling of America; the Discovery ... by Columbus; the Conquest by Cortez; an Account of Florida, and of the British Plantations ... . *Dublin.* 1727–1739. 6 vols., 4to. Maps and Plates. 49906

Volumes V. and VI. relate to America.

Moll. A System of Geography: or, a New and Accurate Description of the Earth .... *London.* 1701. Folio. 9 Maps.

Includes a general and particular description of America, by Joan Luyts. The "British Empire in America," is sometimes attributed to Moll—it is by [Oldmixon (John)], which see. *See also* "A View," etc.

Molleda y Clerque (G. de). Representacion, | que pone reverente | a los reales pies | de la Catholica magestad | de el Señor | Don Fernando vi. | El D. D. Gregorio de Molleda | y Clerque, Arzobispo de la Metropolitana | Iglesia de la Ciudad de la Plata, en los Rey- | nos del Perù, Prelado domestico de su | Santidad, y asistente à su Sacro | Pontificio Salio: | En Solicitud | de las Providencias mas Propor- | cionades, y convenientes à la salud espiritual de los In- | dios .... [*Madrid.* 1755.] Folio, 1 leaf, 70 leaves. + Segunda Representacion .... [*Ibid.*] Folio, 1 leaf, 51 leaves. H.

Möllhausen (B.) Die in Texas und Virginien gelegenen, der Londoner allgemeinen Auswanderungs- und Colonisations-Gesellschaft gehörigen Ländereien ... von Balduin Möllhausen. ... *Berlin: Schneider & Co.* 1850. 8vo, pp. 55. 2 Maps.

Möllhausen. Der Flüchtling. Erzählung aus Neu-Mexico und dem angrenzenden Indianergebiete; ... von Baldwin Möllhausen. ... *Leipzig: Hermann Costenoble.* 1862. 4 vols., 8vo, pp. 273; 264; 271; 307. B. 49910

Möllhausen. Der Halbindianer. Erzählung aus dem westlichen Nordamerika von Balduin Möllhausen. ... *Leipzig: Hermann Costenoble.* 1861. 4 vols., 16mo, pp. 280; 265; 291; 282. + [*Ibid.*] 1864. 8vo. 49911

Möllhausen. Das Mormonenmädchen. Erzählung aus den Zeiten des Kriegszuges der Vereinigten Staaten von Nord-Amerika gegen die "Heiligen der letzten Tage" in den Jahren 1857–58; von Balduin Möllhausen. *Jena und Leipzig: Hermann Costenoble.* 1864. 6 vols., 8vo. + Zweite Auflage. [*Ibid.*] 1868. 6 vols., 8vo, pp. 893. 49912

Möllhausen. Reisen in die Felsengebirge Nord-Amerikas bis zum Hoch-Plateau von Neu-Mexico ... von Balduin Möllhausen ... . Eingeführt durch zwei Briefe Alexander von Humboldt's in facsimile. *Jena: Costenoble.* 1861. 2 vols., 8vo, pp. xxvi, 861. 12 Plates and Map. 49913

Möllhausen. Tagebuch einer Reise vom Mississippi nach den Küsten der Südsee .... Von Baldwin Möllhausen ... . Ein-

geführt von Alexander von Humboldt. *Leipzig: Mendelssohn.* 1858. 4to, pp. (10), xv, 496. Map and 13 Plates. C. 49914

Möllhausen. Diary of a Journey from the Mississippi to the Coasts of the Pacific with a United States Government Expedition. By Baldwin Mollhausen ... . With an Introduction by Alexander Von Humboldt and Illustrations in Chromo-Lithography. Translated by Mrs. Percy Sinnett. ... *London: Longman,* ... 1858. 2 vols., 8vo, pp. xxx, (2), 352; x, (2), 397, (1). 18 Plates and Map. C., H. 49915

The narration of the author's personal examination of Indian life, and aboriginal antiquities, occupy almost the whole of these volumes.

Möllhausen. Wanderungen durch die Prairien und Wüsten des westlichen Nordamerika vom Mississippi nach den Küsten der Südsee ... . Von Baldwin Möllhausen ... . Zweite Auflage. *Leipzig: Mendelssohn.* 1860. 8vo, pp. xvi, 492. Map. 49916

Also: Der Mayordomo. Erzählung aus dem südlichen Californien und Neu-Mexico. ... *Leipzig.* 1863. 4 vols., 8vo, pp. 1004. — Nord und Süd. Erzählungen und Schilderungen aus dem westlichen Nordamerika. *Jena: Costenoble.* 1867. 2 vols., 8vo, pp. 419. — Palmblätter und Schneeflocken. Erzählungen aus dem fernen Westen. ... *Leipzig.* 1863. 2 vols., 8vo, pp. x, 461. — Reliquien. Erzählungen und Schilderungen aus dem westlichen Nordamerika. *Berlin: Janke.* 1865. 3 vols., 8vo, pp. 688.

Mollien (G.) Voyage dans la République de Colombia, en 1823; Par G. Mollien. Ouvrage accompagné de la carte de Colombia et Orné de Vues et de divers Costumes. ... *Paris: Arthus Bertrand.* 1824. 2 vols., 8vo, pp. (4), iv, 307, (1); (4), 316, (1). 8 Plates and Map. B. + Deuxième Édition. [*Ibid.*] 1825. 2 vols., 8vo, pp. (2), vii, 315, (1); (2), 341, (3). Map and 8 Plates. H. 49917

Mollien. Travels in the Republic of Columbia, in the Years 1822 and 1823. By G. Mollien. Translated from the French. *London: C. Knight.* 1824. 8vo, pp. iv, 460. Map and Plate.

This map, extending down to the Amazon and East to the Essequibo River, is a curiosity in 1872. The political changes in that vast territory since 1824 remind one of the innumerable boundary lines of the ducal farms of Germany, now brushed into Prussia.

Mollien. Reise nach Columbia, in den Jahren 1822 und 1823 ... . Aus dem Französischen übersetzt von Fr. Schoell. *Berlin: Duncker und Humblot.* 1825. 8vo, pp. (2), xviii, 390.

Mollien. Reis door de Republik van Columbia, in het jaar 1823. ... Uit het Fransch vertaald door A. Bruggemans. *Dordrecht.* 1825. 8vo. Plates. 49920

Mollien. Viaggio alla Repubblica di Colombia eseguito nell' anno 1823 Dal Sig. Mollien Opera Cui va unita la Carta Geografica della Colombia ... . Tradotta dal Francese dal Prof. Gaetano Barbieri ... *Milano: dalla Tipografia de' Fratelli Sonzogno* 1825. 2 vols., 12mo. 49921

Mollineux (M.) Fruits of Retirement, or Miscellaneous Poems, Moral and Divine. Being Some Contemplations, Letters, etc., written on variety of Subjects and Occasions. By Mary Mollineux. To which is prefixed; Some Account of the Author. *Philadelphia: Printed and sold by Samuel Keimer, in the Second Street.* 1729. 12mo, pp. (40), 182. 49922

Very rare, in which respect it is like all Keimer's imprints.

Mölling (P. A.) Reise-Skizzen in Poesie und Prosa. Gesammelt auf einer siebenmonatlichen Tour durch die Vereinigten Staaten von Nord-Amerika. Von Peter August Mölling. *Galveston (Texas): Offices des "Apologeten."* [1857?] 8vo, pp. 384. 8 Portraits and Plate. C. 49923

Molloy (C.) De Jure | Maritimo | et | Navali: | or, | A Treatise | of | Affairs Maritime, | And of Commerce. | ... | By Charles Molloy. | *London.* 1676. 8vo. + The Third Edition much inlarged ... *London: Thomas Passenger.* 1682. 4to, pp. (18), 302, Table, (22). H. + Fourth Edition. *London: John Bellinger* ... 1688. 8vo, pp. 433. + Sixth Edition. *London.* 1707. 8vo. H. + Seventh Edition. *London.* 1722. 8vo. C. + Eighth Edition. *London.* 1744. 8vo, pp. 501. + Ninth Edition, with ... Additions. *London.* 1769. 2 vols., 8vo. + Tenth Edition, with Additions. *London.* 1778. 2 vols., 8vo. 49924

Refers to Columbus, etc.

Molyneux (T. M.) Conjunct Expeditions: or Expeditions that have been carried on jointly by the Fleet and Army, with a Commentary on a Littoral War. By Thomas More Molyneux. *London: R. & J. Dodsley.* M.DCC.LIX. 2 parts, 8vo, pp. 253; viii, 202, (2). 3 Maps. J.C.B. 49925

The various expeditions to Canada and the West Indies are mentioned and commented upon. *See* "Monthly Review," XXI. 185.

Mombert (J. I.) An Authentic History of Lancaster County, ... Pennsylvania. By J. I. Mombert, D.D. ... *Lancaster, Pa.: J. E. Barr & Co.* 1869. 8vo, pp. vii, 617, Appendix, 175. 8 Maps. B. 49926

Mombert. ... Sermon on the Death of the Rt. Rev. Samuel Bowman, D.D. ... at Lancaster, Pa. ... August 11th, 1861, with Biographical Notice, By Rev. J. Isidor Mombert ... . *Lancaster: Pearsol & Geist, Printers.* 1861. 8vo, pp. 16. H. 49927

Momus, Formerly of Mount Olympus. *New York.* 1860. Folio, 23 or more numbers. 49928

Mon Droit, *pseudon.* Criticisms on the Declaration of Independence as a Literary Document. By Mon Droit. *New York.* 1846. 8vo. 49929

Monacho (R.) *See* Robertus Monachus.

Monágas (José R.) Encargado de la Presidencia de la República, A la Nacion. *Carácas.* 1869. 8vo, pp. 15. 49930

Monágas (J. T.) El General José Tadeo Monágas. Apuntes biográficos. Documentos políticos. Funerales. Honores oficiales. Edicion oficial. *Carácas.* 1868. 4to, pp. xl, 46. Portrait and 2 Plates. 49931

The author is the editor of "El Federalista," Ricardo Becerra.

Monágas. Ofrenda al Excelentísimo Señor José T. Monágas. *Carácas.* 1858. 8vo, pp. 26. 49932

Monagas and Paez. *See* [Williams (Thomas)].

Monarch. ... Correspondence respecting the Visit of Her Majesty's Ship "Monarch" to the United States. ... *London: Printed by Harrison and Sons.* [1870.] Folio, pp. (2), 5. BA.

Monarchial Projects. *See* Buenos Ayres, III. 9024.

Monarcho-Republicanism. Why does the History of the World oscillate between Monarchial and Republican Forms of Government. *London.* 1848. 8vo. 49934

Monarchs of Ocean: Columbus and Cook. Two Narratives of Maritime Discovery. *Edinburgh: Nimmo.* 1868. F'cap 8vo, pp. 227. 49935

Monarchy v. Republic. *See* Vol. II., No. 7606.

Monardes (N.) Dos Libros, el vno qve trata de todas las cosas | que traen de nuestras Indias Occidentales, que siruen | de vso en la Medicina, y el otro que trata de la | Piedra Bezaar, y de la yerua Escuerçonera. | Cõpuestos por el doctor Nicoloso de

Monardes Medico de Seuilla. | *Impressos en Sevilla en casa de | Hernandez Diaz, en la calle de la Sierpe. Con Licencia y Priuilegio de su Magestad.* | *Año de* 1569. 2 vols., 12mo, 4 leaves, Text, 137 leaves; Vol. II. 131 leaves. J.C.B. 49936

The first and perhaps the rarest of all the editions of Monardes.

Monardes. Segvnda | parte del libro | de las cosas qve se | traen de nuestras Indias Occidentales, | que siruen al vso de medicina. Do se tra- | ta del Tabaco, y de la Sassafras: y del Carlo Sancto, y de otras muchas yeruas y Plantas, Simientes, y Licores; q̄ ago- | ra nueuamente han venido de a quellas | partes, de grandes virtudes, y marauillosos effectos. | Hecho por el Doctor Monardes Medico de Seuilla. | Va añedido vn libro de la Nieue. Do veran los q̄ beuen frio conella, cosas dignas de saber, y de grande admiracion, cerca | del vso del enfriar con ella. Fecho por el mismo Doctor Monardes. | *En Seuilla. En casa Alonso Escriuano. Impressor. Año de* 1571. *Con Preuilegio de su Real Magestad.* 12mo, 131 leaves. Followed by: "Libro qve trata de la nieue," 47 leaves. J.C.B.

Monardes. Primera y | Segvnda y Tercera | Partes de la Historia | Medicinal de las cosas | que se traen de nuestras Indias Occi- | dentales que siruen en | Medicina. | Tratado de la Piedra | Bezaar, y dela yerua Escuerçonera. | Dialogo de las Gran- | dezas del Hierro, y de sus virtudes | Medicinales | Tratado de la Nieve y del beuer frio. | Hechos por el Do- | ctor Monardes Medico | de Seuilla. | Van en esta impression | la Tercera parte y el Dialogo del Hierro nueua- | mente hechos, que no han sido impressos | hasta agora. Do ay cosas grandes | y dignas de saber. | Con licencia y Preuilegio de su Magestad. | *En Sevilla | En casa de Alonso Escriuano.* | 1574. | 4to, 6 leaves, Text, 206 leaves, 1 leaf. + *En Seuilla, en casa de Fernando Diaz.* 1580. 4to, 7 leaves, on the second a Portrait of Monardes, Text, 162 leaves. J.C.B. 49938

The edition of 1574 is most rare, and that of 1580 is not common; both of them include the contents of the former editions, with a third part added.

Monardes. Delle Cose che vengono portate dall' Indie Occidentali pertinenti all' vso della Medicina. Raccolte, & trattate dal Dottor Nicolò Monardes ... . Nouamente recata della Spagniola nella nostra lingua Italiana. Doue ancho si tratta de' Veneni, & della lor cura. ... *Venetia, Giordano Ziletti.* 1575. 2 parts, 8vo, pp. 159, (16); (16), 140. 49939

"The original Italian translation, by Annibale Briganti, is very rare. Not cited by Ternaux, nor by Haym."—Leclerc.

Monardes. Delle cose, | che vengono | portate dall' Indie | Occidentali pertinenti all' vso | della Medicina. | Raccolte, & trattate dal Dottor Nicòlo | Monardes, Medico in Siuiglia, | Parte Prima. | Nouamente recata dalla Spagnola nella nostra | lingua Italiana. | Doue ancho tratta de Veneni, & della lor cura. | Aggiuntiui doi Indici; vno de' Capi principali; l'altro delle cose piu ri- | leuanti, che si ritrouano in tutta l'opera. | Con privilegio. | *In Venetia, Appresso Giordan Ziletti.* 1582. | Sm. 8vo, pp. (16), 249, Table, (13). C. 49940

The second part has a special title-page. This edition of Monardes is generally appended to the Italian translation of Garcia d'Orto.

Monardes. De Simplicibvs | Medicamentis | ex Occidentali India | delatis, qvorvm in Medicina vsvs est. | Auctore D. Nicolao Monardis | Hispalensi Medico; | Interprete Carolo Clvsio Atrebate. | *Antverpiæ,* | *Ex officina Christophori Plantini,* | *Architypographi Regij.* | M. D. LXXIIII. | Sm. 8vo, pp. 88, (8). 49941

The Latin translation of the first two books of Monardes by Charles de l'Écluse. The third book was published in 1582.

Monardes. Simplicivm Medicamentorvm ex Novo Orbe delatorvm, qvorvm in Medicina vsvs est, Historia, Hispanico Sermone descripta à D. Nicolao Monardis; latio deinde donata à Carolo Clvsio. Editio secunda. *Antverpiæ: Ex officina Christophori Plantini.* 1579. 8vo, pp. 84, (4). + Editio tertia. *Antverpiæ.* 1593. 49942

Monardes. Simplicivm | Medicamentorvm | ex Novo Orbe delato- | rvm, qvorvm in Medicina | vsvs est, Historia | Liber tertivs: | Hispanico sermone nuper descriptus à D. Nico- | lao Monardes, Hispalensi Medico: | Nũnc verò primùm Latio donatus, & notis illustratus | à Carolo Clvsio A. | *Antverpiæ,* | *Ex officina Christophori Plantini,* | M. D. LXXXII. | 8vo, pp. 47. 49943

Latin translation of the third book of the work.

[Monardes.] Ioyfvll | Nevves ovt of | the newe founde worlde, wherein is | declared the rare and singular vertues of diuerse | and sundrie Hearbes, Trees, Oyles, Plantes, and Stones, with their aplications, as well for Phisicke as Chirurgerie, the saied be- | yng well applied bryngeth suche present remedie for | all deseases, as maie seme altogether incredible: | notwithstandyng by practize founde out, | to bee true: Also the portrature of the saied Hearbes, very apt- | ly discribed: Engli- | shed by Jhon |

Framp- | ton | Marchaunt. | *Imprinted at London in | Poules Churcheyarde, by | Willyam Norton.* | *Anno Domini.* | 1577. | 4to, 3 leaves, Text, 109 leaves, Table, 1 leaf. A. 49944

Black letter. The first edition in English, and is more rare than the following. Among other curious matter this volume states the medical properties of the "Gumme called Tacamachaca, the Oyle of the Figge-tree of Hell, Tobaco, Sassafras, Amber Gryse," etc.

[Monardes.] Joyfull Newes | out of the new found world, wherein are declared the rare and | Singular vertues of diuers and sundrie | Herbs, Trees, Oyles, Plants, & Stones, | with their applications, aswell to the vse | of Phisicke, as Chirurgery; which being wel | applied, bring such present remedy for | all diseases, as may seeme altoge- | ther incredible: notwith- | standing by practize found | out, to be true. | Also the portrature of the sayde | Herbes, very aptly described: En- | glished By John Frampton | Merchant, | Newly corrected as by conference with | the olde copies may appeare. Whereunto are | added three other bookes treating of the Bezaar stone, | the herbes Escuerçonera, the properties of | yron and steele, in medicine and the benefite of | snowe. | *Imprinted at London, in Paules | Churchyard at the Signe of the Quenes | Armes, by William Norton.* | 1580. 4to, 3 leaves, 181 leaves, 2 leaves.

Contains three additional books, not in the former edition. It commences with a notice of Columbus' discovery, and among other curious matters contains a long article on tobacco. After folio 181, there is a second title which is sometimes substituted for the proper one when that has been lost. I have seen more than one English catalogue in which this fraud has been euphonized to read thus: "This is one of the copies with the variation in the title from that quoted by Lowndes;" a judicious buyer will reject such a copy as *imperfect.*

[Monardes.] Ioyfvll Newes | Out of the New-found | VVorlde. | Wherein are declared, the rare and | singuler vertues of diuers Herbs, Trees, | Plantes, Oyles & Stones, with their ap- | plications, as well to the vse of Phisicke, as of | Chirurgery: which being well applyed, bring | such present remedie for all diseases, as may | seeme altogether incredible: notwith- | standing by practice found out | to be true. | Also the portrature of the said Hearbs, | verie aptly described: | Englished by John Frampton Marchant. | Newly corrected as by conference with | the olde copies may appeare. Wher- | vnto are added three other bookes | treating of the Bezaar stone, the herb | Escuerconera, the properties of Iron | and Steele in Medicine, and the be- | nefit of Snow. | *London,* | *Printed by E. Allde. by the assigne of* | *Bonham Norton.* | 1596. | 4to, 3 leaves, Text, 187 leaves. 49946

There are errors in the numbering of the leaves.

Monardes. Histoire des Simples Médicamens apportés des terres neuves, desquels on se sert en la Médicine. ... *Lyon.* 1602. 8vo. 49947

Monardes. Histoire des | Simples Medica- | mens Apportés de l'A-meriqve, desqvels | on se sert en la Medicine. | Escrite premierement en Espangnol, par M. Nicolas | Monard, Medecin de Siuille. | Du despuis mise en Latin, & illustrée de plusieurs Annota- | tions, par Charles l'Ecluse d'Arras. | Et nouuellement traduicte en François par Anthoine Colin | Maistre Apoticaire Iuré de la ville de Lyon. | Edition seconde augmentée de plusieurs fi- | gures & Annotations. | *A Lyon,* | *Aux despens de Iean Pillehotte,* | *à l'enseigne du nom de Iesvs.* | M.DC.XIX. | *Auec Priuilege du Roy.* | 8vo, pp. 262, (6). 49948

Monatsbericht der Kön. Preussischen Akademie der Wissenschaften. *Berlin.* 1856–76. 8vo. 49949

Contains many articles on American linguistics, etc. There are two indexes: to 1836–58 published in 1860, and to 1859–73, published in 1875.

Moncada (A.) Sermon que en la toma de hábito de Doña Mariana Samaniago y Canal, dijo en la Santa Iglesia de la muy RR. MM. Capuchinas de la ciudad de Santiago de Querétaro, el R. P. ex-Difinidor y Guardian Er. Antonio Moncada. *Mexico.* 1846. 8vo, pp. (4), 14. 49950

Moncada (Balthasar de). Descripcion de la Casa Fabricada en Lima, Corte de el Perù, para que las Señoras Ilustres de ella, y las demàs Mugeres Devotas, y las que desean servir à Dios, puedan tener en total retiro ... los exercicios de San Ignacio de Loyola. ... *Sevilla: Padrina.* 1757. 4to, pp. (56), 85, (2).

Moncade. Histoire de Moncade. *See* Vol. VIII. 32019.

Monchy (S. de). An Essay on the Causes and Cure of the usual Diseases in Voyages to the West-Indies: Together with the Preservatives against them. In answer to the Questions proposed by the Society of Sciences in Holland; What are the Causes of the usual Diseases among Seamen in Voyages to the West-Indies? and, What are the Means of preventing, and of curing them? To which Essay the Prize was adjudged. Written by Solomon De Monchy, City Physician at Rotterdam. And Translated from the Dutch Philosophical Transactions. *London: Printed for T. Becket and P. A. De Hondt.* MDCCLXII. 8vo, pp. x, 175. P. 49952

Monckton (R.) By Order of the Honourable Brigadier General Robert Monckton .... [n. p. n. d.] Folio, 1 leaf. P.

A proclamation for hire of wagons to transport stores.

Monckton. Proceedings of a General Court Martial, held at the Judge Advocate's Office, in the Horse-Guards, ... April 1764, for the Trial of a Charge preferred by Colin Campbell, Esq. against the Honourable Major General Monckton. *London: James Robson.* MDCCLXIV. 8vo, pp. 98. J.C.B. 49954

Relative to transactions in the Island of Martinique. The Court decided the charges to be entirely unsupported by evidence, and further, that the complaint was groundless, malicious, and scandalous in the highest degree. General Mockton was Governor of New York, 1762–63. He also served as Brigadier-General in the Expedition of General Wolfe against Quebec. *See* "Monthly Review," XXXI. 158.

[Moncrief (*Major*).] A Short Account of the Expedition against Quebec, commanded by Major-General Wolfe in the year 1759. By an Engineer upon that Expedition. With a Plan of the Town and Basin of Quebec, and part of the adjacent Country, showing the principal Encampments and Works of the British Army, and those of the French Army, during the Attack in 1759. [*London.* n. d.] 8vo. 49955

Moncure (R. C. L.) Argument of R. C. L. Moncure in Bank of Virginia *vs.* Adams. *Fredericksburg.* 1849. 8vo. P.

Monday Morning, December 27. 1773. The Tea-Ship having arrived, every Inhabitant, who wishes to preserve the Liberty of America, is desired to meet at the State-House, This Morning, precisely at Ten o'Clock, to advise what is best to be done on this alarming Crisis. [*Philadelphia.* 1773.] 12mo, 1 leaf. P.

Probably unique. This apparently trifling affair of one leaf is, in fact, the opening paragraph of the history of the American Revolution.

Mondelet (C.) Letters on ... Education. By Charles Mondelet, Esq. ... [With] a French Translation. *Montreal: John James Williams.* 1811. 8vo, pp. (1), 59, (1); 60, (4). BA.

Also: Address, ... before the American Association for the Advancement of Learning, ... 19th August, 1857, at ... Montreal ... . *Montreal: Printed by John Lovell.* 1857. 8vo, pp. (2), 9. *See also* "Report of the Commissioners."

[Mondelet (Dominique).] Traité sur la Politique Coloniale du Bas-Canada. Réflexions sur l'état actuel du Pays. Par un Avocat. *Montréal.* 1835. 8vo, pp. 67. 49959

Monderie (Thiébault de). Voyages faits dans l'intérieur de l'Oyapock en 1819, 1822, 1836, 1842–47. ... *Nantes.* 1856. 8vo, pp. 96. Map. 49960

Mondidier (*Count*). Catalogue of the ... Library of the Count Mondidier ... [with] Works relating to America. Sold by Auction ... December ... 1851. *London: Puttick and Simpson.* [1851.] 8vo, pp. 167. S. 49961

There never was such a person as the Count Mondidier; he is an imaginary individual, so called by Mr. Henry Stevens, who probably edited the catalogue which describes some of the rarest of books relating to America, many of which were purchased by Mr. Stevens and are included in his "Nuggets."

Mondot (A.) Histoire des Indiens des États-Unis faite d'après les statistiques et les rapports officiels que le Congrès a publiés en 18:1. Par Armand Mondot ... . *Montpellier: Boehm, Imprimeur.* 1858. 8vo, pp. (4), 352. 4 Plates. H. 49962

A digest of Vols. I.–III. of Schoolcraft. Some copies have a Paris imprint.

Mone (F.) Treatise on American Engineering. By F. Mone, C.E. ... *New York.* 1856. 4to, and Plates in folio.

Monell (J. J.) The School Question in the United States. An Address ... By the Hon. John J. Monell. ... In ... Newburgh, ... February 26, 1867 ... . *Newburgh: Ruttenber & Co., Printers.* 1867. 12mo, pp. 28. B. 49964

The Monetary Policy of England and America. *London.* 1842. 8vo. 49965

Monette (J. W.) History of the Discovery and Settlement of the Valley of the Mississippi, by the Three Great European Powers, Spain, France, and Great Britain, and the Subsequent Occupation, Settlement, and Extension of Civil Government by the United States, until the Year 1846. By John W. Monette, M.D. ... *New York: Harper & Brothers.* 1846. 2 vols., 8vo, pp. xxiii, 567; xv, 595. 3 Maps, 4 Plans and 2 Plates. A., BA. + [*Ibid.*] 1848. H. 49966

Includes a relation of the French and Spanish discovery of the territory, and the association of the colonial governments of these nations with the Indians, and their wars with the various tribes inhabiting it, and a narration of the Indian wars of the States bordering the Ohio. Probably the best of the numerous books on western history. It is now out of print and scarce.

Monette. Observations on the Epidemic Yellow Fever of Natchez and the Southwest. By John W. Monette, M.D. ... *Louisville (Ky.): Prentice & Weissinger.* 1842. 8vo. pp. 155. C.

Money (C. F. S.) Mormonism Unmasked. By the Rev. C. F. S. Money. *London: Wertheim.* 1857. Post 8vo, pp. 16.

Money and Banking, or their Nature and Effects Considered. Together with a plan for the universal diffusion of their Legitimate Benefits without their Evils. *Cincinnati.* 1839. 12mo.

Money by Steam. John Law—his body moulders in the ground, but his soul is marching on. MDCCCLXIV. [n. p. n. d.] 8vo, pp. (2), 40. H. 49970

Money; its Nature, History, Uses, and Responsibilities. *Philadelphia: American Sunday-School Union.* [n. d.] 24mo, pp. 192.

"The Money-Maker." *See* [Livingston (H.)], x. 41620.

The Money Question in 1813 and 1863. What some did then, others are seeking to do now. By A Loyal Citizen. *New York: Anson D. F. Randolph.* 1863. 8vo, pp. 11. 49972

Money the Sinews of Trade. The State of the Province of the Massachusetts-Bay Considered, with respect to its Trade for want of a Medium of Exchange wherewith to manage it. Recommended to the serious Consideration of the Trading part in general, more especially to the Merchants and Traders of the Town of Boston. By a Lover of his Country. *Boston, N. E.: Printed by S. Kneeland & T. Green.* 1731. 16mo, pp. 16. BA.

The author proposes that merchants and traders shall enter into copartnership for issuing bills or notes for circulation, to be loaned on land security, etc. He dwells on the bad effects that have resulted from giving currency in Massachusetts to Rhode Island bills: "We have given the bread out of our own mouths, and enrich'd them, who now despise us for so doing."

Moneypenny (George W.) Rapport à M. le Ministre de l'Intérieur des États-Unis sur les hommes rouges de l'Amérique du Nord. Traduite par Maunsel B. Field de New York. *Paris.* 1855. 8vo. 49974

Monge (M.) Lettre du Ministre de la Marine a la Convention Nationale, du 11 Mars 1793, l'an III. de la République française. Suivie d'autres pièces relatives à la reunion des Isles-du-Vent à la mère patrie. *Paris: l'Imprimerie Nationale.* 1793. 8vo, pp. 33. J.C.B. 49975

Monglave (E. de). Résumé de l'histoire du Mexique, Par Eugène de Monglave. ... *Paris: Lecointe et Durey.* 1826. 18mo, pp. (4), iii, 307. C., H. 49976

The Mongrelites: or the Radicals—So-called. A Satiric Poem. ... *New York: Van Evrie, Horton & Co.* 1866. 12mo, pp. 59. 49977

Mongrolle (*Citoyen*). La France Équinoxiale, ou Exposé sommaire des possessions de la République sous l'Équateur ... . Par le Citoyen Mongrolle ... . *Paris: Fuchs. An* XI.–(1802.) 8vo, pp. 122, (1). Plan. H. 49978

A defense of the French colony of Guiana.

Monica Americana. *See* [Mather (C.)], XI. 46418.

Monis (J.) ... A Grammar of the Hebrew Tongue, being An Essay To bring the Hebrew Grammar into English ... . Published more especially for the Use of the Students of Harvard-College at Cambridge, in New-England. ... Composed and ... Corrected, By Judah Monis, M.A. *Boston, N. E.: Printed by Jonas Green.* MDCCXXXV. 4to, pp. (4), 94, (2). B., W. 49979

The first Hebrew Grammar published in America. The author was an Italian Jew, who emigrated to America about 1720. In 1722, he was appointed Hebrew Instructor in Harvard University, and occupied this position for forty years. He made a profession of Christianity, and put forth three discourses as described *infra* by way of proof: The Truth, Being a Discourse Which the Author delivered at his Baptism ... . Prefaced by Increase Mather, D.D. *Boston: Printed by S. Kneeland, for D. Henchman.* 1722. 8vo, pp. (2), iv, vi, 36.—The Whole Truth: ... *Boston: Daniel Henchman.* 1722. 8vo, pp. (2), 40.—Nothing but The Truth: ... *Boston: Daniel Henchman.* 1722. 8vo, pp. (2), 27. B.

Monita Secreta. Instucções Secretas que devem, guardar todos os religiosos da Companhia. Auctor o rev.mo P. Claudio Aquaviva, da mesma Companhia. Fielmente traduzida da lingua hespanhola na portugueza por J. S. de A. *Lisboa: Na Officina de Simão Thaddeo Ferreira.* 1820. 8vo, pp. 75. 49980

Monita Secreta Societatis Jesu. Instrucciones secretas de los Jesuitas. Su Codigo El Juramento de los Padres de la Fé, sus palabras de Pruncimiento. *Paris* [*Lima*]. 1869. 8vo, pp. 158.

Le Moniteur des Indes-Orientales et Occidentales, Recueil de Mémoires et de Notices Scientifiques et Industriels, de nouvelles et de faits importants concernant les Possessions Neerlandaises d'Asie et d'Amérique, publié par Ph. Fr. de Siebold et P. Melville. Pour les années 1846–49. *La Haye.* 1846–49. 2 vols., 4to. Maps and Plates. A. 49982

Complete copies are rare. This is a corrected title of our No. 47476.

Moniteur. Analyse des Discussions qui se sont élevées dans les Assemblées Legislatives depuis le 24 Avril, 1790, jusqu'au 20 Mai, 1802, concernant l'impôt du Tabac. Extrait du Moniteur. *Paris: Agasse.* 1819. 8vo, pp. 110. 49983

The Monikins [etc]. *See* [Cooper (J. F.)], IV. 16481.

Monitor (E.), *pseudon.?* The Stranger's Apology for the General Associations. Supposed to have been written by Elias Monitor ... for several Years a Resident ... of New England. ... *Boston: William Wells.* 1812. 12mo, pp. 23. BA. 49984

The Monitor ... . *Boston: R. Bannister.* 1823–24. 2 vols., 12mo, pp. viii, 424; iv, 428. BA. 49985

Edited by Hervey Wilbur. The preface in vol. II. states, that in future the "Monitor" and "Guardian" were to be united.

A Monitor for Communicants. *See* [Mather (C.)], XI. 46419.

The "Monitor" Iron Clads. ... *Boston: S. H. Eastburn.* 1864. 8vo, pp. 17. 49986

The Monitor: or British Freeholder ... . *London.* 1756–8. 3 vols., 8vo. 49987

Chronicles the whole period of the Canadian disturbances, and sides throughout with the Colonists. Gives an account of the troubles at "Kebec," Cape Breton, New Scotland, etc.

Monitor's Letter. *See* [Lee (Arthur)], x. 39701.

A Monitory, and Hortatory Letter. *See* [Mather Cotton).]

Monitory Hints to the Ministers, on the present State of the Nation, the Dismemberment of the Empire, ... with occasional Observations, elucidating many Passages in a Pamphlet ... entituled, A Defence of the Earl of Shelburne, &c. *London: J. Bew.* 1782. 8vo. 49988

See "Monthly Review," LXVIII. 363.

A Monitory Letter. *See* [Mather (C.)], XI. 46421.

Moniz Barretto (F.) Classicos e Romanticos. Exercicios Poeticos. Por Francisco Moniz Barretto, Natural de Bahia. *Bahai: C. de Lellis Masson et C.* 1855. 2 vols., 8vo, pp. xviii, 297; 281. 49989

Moniz (Nuno Alvares Pereira Pato). Versos gratulatorios, que aos srs. subscriptores para a beneficencia a favor dos officiaes e companhia do navio Balsemão, incendiado em Pernambuco, em 23 de Janeiro de 1816 ... . *Lisboa, na Imprensa Regia.* 1816. 8vo, pp. 13. 49990

Moniz (Patricio). Sermão sobre a Piedade de Nossa Senhora, prégado na egreja de Sancta Cruz dos Militares do Rio de Janeiro, em presença de SS. MM. II. ... *Rio de Janeiro: Typographia de F. de Paulo Brito.* 1860. 8vo, pp. 23. 49991

Monk (M.) Awful Disclosures of Maria Monk, as Exhibited in a Narrative of her Sufferings during a Residence of Five Years as a Novice, and Two Years as a Black Nun, in the Hotel Dieu Nunnery at Montreal. [*New York.* 1836.] 18mo, pp. 231. + Revised, with an Appendix ... . Also, a Supplement ... . *New York: For Maria Monk.* 1836. 12mo, pp. 376. Plan. + *New York: Dewitt & Davenport.* 1855. 12mo, pp. xxiv, 13–262.

The authorship is attributed to the Rev. J. J. Slocum. Reprinted in London as:

Monk. The Character of a Convent, displayed in the Awful Disclosures of Maria Monk ... to which is added Confirmatory Notes and Affidavits. ... *London: Houlston & Stoneman.* 1851. 8vo, pp. (2), iv, 174. 49993

The work elicited the following replies:

Awful Exposure of the Atrocious Plot formed by certain Individuals against the Clergy and Nuns of Lower Canada, through the intervention of Maria Monk. With an authentic Narrative of her Life, from her Birth to the present moment and an account of her Impositions, etc. ... *New-York: Jones & Co.* 1836. 12mo, pp. 11, 131. B. 49994

An Exposure of Maria Monk's pretended Abduction and Conveyance to the Catholic Asylum, Philadelphia, by six Priests, on the night of August 13, 1837. [n. p. n. d.] 12mo. 49995

Maria Monk's Show-up, or the "Awful Disclosures," a Humbug. *New York: Go-a-head Press.* [n. d.] 12mo, pp. 24.

Also: Maria Monk and her Impositions. [By——Perkins. n. p. n. d.] 12mo.

Monk. Further Disclosures by Maria Monk, concerning the Hotel Dieu Nunnery of Montreal; also, her Visit to Nun's Island, and Disclosures concerning that Secret Retreat. Preceded by a reply to the Priests' Book, By Rev. J. J. Slocum. *New York: For Maria Monk.* 1837. 12mo, pp. 194. Portrait.

Scarce, scurrilous and rather bordering on the salacious.

Monmonier (J. F.) Public Education in Baltimore. Address ... *Baltimore: J. Lucas.* 1847. 8vo, pp. 16. 49998

Also: Address before the Young Ladies of Western Female High School of Baltimore. ... *Baltimore: J. Lucas.* 1848. 8vo, pp. 15.

Monmouth (*Duke of*). An | Abridgment | of the | English | Military | Discipline, | Compiled by the Late Duke of Monmouth. | Printed by Especial Command, for the Use of | Their Majesties Forces. | *Printed at London by their Majesties Printers; | Reprinted at*

Boston by Samuel Green, And sold by | Benjamin Harris at the London Coffee House, 1690. | 16mo, pp. 167. 49999

The first book of its kind printed in the British American Colonies.

Monmouth College. Ninth Annual Circular and Catalogue .... For ... 1865. *Monmouth, Ill.: John S. Clark, Printer.* 1865. 8vo, pp. 31. Continued. H. 50000

Monnick (Joan). *See* Munk (Jens).

Monnier (P.) Description Nautique des Côtes de la Martinique précédée d'un Mémoire sur les opérations hydrographiques et géodesiques exécutées dans cette île en 1824 et 1825. *Paris: de l'Imprimerie Royale.* M.DCCC.XXVIII. 8vo. 50001

Monnier *and* Duperré (B.) Atlas de plusieurs Cartes de cette Ile [Martinique], faites par ordre du Roi, par MM. Monnier et B. Duperré. *Paris.* 1827. Folio. 50002

A Monody in honor of the Chiefs who have fallen in the cause of American Liberty, and a Rondelay celebrating American Independency. *Philadelphia.* [1783.] 4to. 50003

Monograph of the Fluviatile Bivalve Shells of the River Ohio. *Philadelphia.* 1832. 12mo. 50004

Monongahela. Directory of the Monongahela and Youghiogheny Valleys. *Pittsburg.* 1860. 8vo. 50005

Monro (A.) History, Geography, and Statistics of British North America. ... By Alex. Monro, Esq. ... *Montreal: Printed by John Lovell.* 1864. 8vo, pp. iv, (6), 324. B. 50006

Monro. New-Brunswick; with a Brief Outline of Nova-Scotia, and Prince Edward Island. Their History, Civil Divisions, Geography, and Productions; with Statistics of the several Counties ... . By Alexander Monro, Esq. ... *Halifax, N. S.: Printed by Richard Nugent.* 1855. 8vo, pp. vi, (1), 384, Errata, (1). 2 Maps. C., H., S. 50007

Monro. Statistics of British North America. By Alexander Monro, Esq. ... *Halifax.* 1862. 8vo, pp. 228. 50008

Monro (R.) A Description of the Genesee Country, in the State of New York: in which the Situation, Dimensions, Civil Divisions, Soil, Minerals, Produce, Lakes and Rivers, Curiosities, Climate, Navigation, Trade and Manufactures, Population, and other interesting matters relative to that country, are impartially

described. ... By Robert Monro. *New York: The Author.* 1804. 8vo, pp. 16. Map. 50009

Monroe (A. F.) The Life and Writings of A. F. Monroe, who was hung by a Blood-Thirsty Mob in Charleston, Ill. on the 15th. Feb., 1856, for Killing his Father-in-Law, Nathan Ellington, Esq., in Self-Defence. *Cincinnati.* 1857. 8vo, pp. 118.

Monroe (James). Correspondence in relation to the British Treaty of 1806. ... *Washington.* 1808. 8vo. C. 50011

Monroe. Defense of the Mission to England ... . *Washington.* 1808. 8vo. 50012

Monroe. Letter from Mr. Monroe to the Secretary of State ... February 28, 1808. Part IV. Accompanying the message of the president ... . March 23, 1808. ... *Washington City: A. & G. Way, Printers.* 1808. 8vo, pp. 47. 50013

I have not met with the other parts. *See* Secretary of State.

Monroe. A Letter from James Monroe, in answer to ... Questions [on War and Slavery, etc.]; ... [n. p. 1863?] 8vo, pp. 32. H. 50014

Monroe. Letters between James Monroe, Esq., Secretary of State of the United States, and Augustus J. Foster, Esq., ... Minister Plenipotentiary, of His Britannic Majesty; in relation to the Orders in Council, and the affair of the Little Belt. To which is added, the Declaration of War. *New-York: J. Peters, jun.* 1812. 12mo, pp. 59. B. 50015

Monroe. Letters from Messrs. Monroe and Pinkney to Mr. Madison. With the Treaty [with Great Britain, 1806. n. p. n. d.] 8vo. 50016

Monroe. The Memoir of James Monroe, Esq. relating to his Unsettled Claims upon the People and Government of the United States. *Charlottesville, Va.: Gilmer, Davis and Co.* 1828. 8vo, pp. 60. BA. 50017

Monroe. ... Mr. Monroe's Letter on the Rejected Treaty, between the United States and Great Britain ... . Also, the Treaty itself; ... *Portland.* 1813. 8vo, pp. 52. H. 50018

Monroe. The People, the Sovereigns Being a Comparison of the Government of the United States with those of the Republics which have existed before, with the Causes of their

Decadence and Fall. By James Monroe .... Edited by Samuel L. Gouverneur .... *Philadelphia: J. B. Lippincott & Co.* 1867. 12mo, pp. 274. BA. 50019

Monroe. A View of the Conduct of the Executive, in the Foreign Affairs of the United States, connected with the Missions to the French Republic, during the years 1794, '5 & '6. By James Monroe ... Illustrated by his Instructions and Correspondence and other Authentic Documents. ... *Philadelphia: Benj. Franklin Bache.* M,DCCXCVII. 8vo, pp. (4), lxvi, 407. B., H. + The Second Edition. ... *London: Reprinted for James Ridgway.* 1798. 8vo, pp. viii, 117. + The Third Edition, with Additions. [*Ibid.*] 1798. 8vo, pp. xvi, 117. 50020

The London edition was reprinted, with some omissions, from the Philadelphia edition, and republished for the purpose of counteracting the pernicious representations of Mr. Harper, in his "Observations on the Dispute," etc. *See* "Monthly Review," xxv. 232. For a review, *see* [Hamilton (A.)], Nos. 29982–83, *and* [Tracy (Uriah)]. The following relate to James Monroe:

Exposition of Motives for opposing the Nomination of Mr. Monroe for the office of President of the United States. *Printed in the City of Washington, by Jonathan Elliot.* 1816. 8vo, pp. 14.

Monroe's Embassy, or, The Conduct of the Government, in relation to our Claims to the Navigation of the Mississippi, considered, By the Author of an Address to the Government of the United States, on the Cession of Louisiana, &c. &c. ... [Signed "Poplicola."] *John Conrad, & Co., ... Philadelphia*; ... 1803. 8vo, pp. 57. BA. 50022

A Narrative of A Tour of Observation, made during the Summer of 1817, By James Monroe, ... through the North-Eastern and North-Western Departments of the Union: with a view to the Examination of their several Military Defences. With An Appendix. *Philadelphia: S. A. Mitchell & H. Ames.* 1818. 12mo, pp. 228, Appendix, xxxvi. B., C. 50023

Narrative of the Grand Civic and Military Demonstration in honor of the Removal of the Remains of James Monroe, ... from New York to Virginia, in 1858. *New York: Udolpho Wolfe.* 1858. 12mo, pp. 324. 50024

Order of Exercises at the Old South Church, commemorative of ... James Monroe, ... August 25, 1831. *Boston: J. H. Eastburn, ... Printer.* 1831. 8vo, pp. 8. B. 50025

See also Nos. 280, 12489, 35883, 38082, [(Pinkney (C.)], Virginia, *and* Waldo (S. P.)

Monroe (J.) The American Botanist, and Family Physician: ... By John Monroe. Compiled by S. Gaskill. *Wheelock (Vt.): Jonathan Morrison.* 1824. 12mo, pp. 203. B. 50026

Monroe (J. A.) Description of the Piers of the New Railroad Bridges of the Boston and Providence Railroad over the Seekonk River ... . By J. A. Monroe. *Providence: Hammond, Angell & Co., Printers.* 1868. 8vo, pp. 22. 50027

Monroe (M.) Only Copy of the Life, and the Testimony that convicted Michael Monroe alias James Wellington, at a Court ... held at Chester, Pennsylvania, on the 20th of October, 1824, for the Murder of Wm. Bonsall. *Philadelphia.* 1824. 8vo. C. 50028

Monroe, *N. Y.* Minutes of the Thirty-Third Anniversary of the Monroe Baptist Association, October, 1860. *Rochester.* 1860. 8vo. 50029

Annual Report of the ... Monroe County Agricultural Society ... [with] the Address ... October 26, 1842, By Henry Colman, ... and ... Officers and Members, ... for 1842. ... *Rochester: Strong & Dawson, Printers.* 1842. 8vo, pp. 68. H. 50030

Also: History of the Exhibition ... of 1857. *Rochester.* 1857. 8vo.—Annual Session of the Teachers' Institute of the Third Assembly District of Monroe County, held ... October 29, 1866 ... . *Rochester: E. Darrow & Kempshall.* 1867. 8vo, pp. 24, (3).—First Report of the Monroe County Workhouse, October, 1855. *Rochester.* 1856. 8vo, pp. 60.—Rules and Regulations for the Government ... of the Monroe County Insane Asylum adopted ... 1863. *Rochester: ... Press of Curtis, Butts & Co.* 1863. 8vo, pp. 8. H.

Proceedings of the Board of Supervisors of the County of Monroe. For 1860. ... *Rochester, N. Y.: Press of C. D. Tracy & Co.* 1861. 8vo, pp. 199, (1), folded leaf. Continued. H.

Monroe, *Mich.* Proceedings of the Horticultural Association of Monroe, Michigan. ... 1863. *Monroe: M. D. Hamilton, Printer.* 1863. 8vo, pp. 48. H. 50032

Monroe, *Pa.* Report of the Monroe Coal and Iron Company's Estate in M'Kean County, Pa. *Pottsville.* 1856. 8vo.

Monroux (P.) Mémoire pour Pierre Monroux, Capitaine de Frégate dans la Marine française, et ci-devant Chef des mouvemens du port, a la Pointe-à-Pitre, île de la Guadaloupe. [*Paris, about* 1800.] 8vo, pp. 78. 50034

Monroy (A. de). Oraciones Panegyricas Funebres, en las Exequias del Fr. Antonio de Monroy, Metropolitana Yglesia, de Santiago de Galicia, 27 y 28 de Julio Año de 1716. *Mexico, por F. R. Lupercio.* 1716. 4to. 50035

Monroy (Jos.) Estado del Convento de Goatemala, del Orden de nuestra Señora de la Merced, Redempcion verdadera de los aumentos, que en lo temporal, y espiritual ha tanido, desde el año de sesenta y cinco, hasta el de sesenta y siete. ... *Guatemala, por Joseph de Pinede Ybarra, Impresor de Libros, Año de* 1667. Folio, 6 leaves. 50036

A rare specimen of early printing in Guatemala.

Monsalve (M. de). Reduccion Universal de todo el Piru y demas Indias, con otros muchos avisos, para el bien de los naturales dellas, y en aumento de las Reales Rentas. Compuesto por el P. F. Miguel de Monsalve, de la orden de Predicadores, morador del Reyno del Piru. Dirigido à la Catolica Magestad del Rey don Felipe Tercero deste nombre N. S. [*Lima?* 1604.] Sm. 4to, 46 leaves. 50037

Commences as above, without any other title or preliminaries. Nicolas Antonio cites it from Pinelo, who gives it the above date of 1604. Neither mentions where printed, but it has the appearance of being printed at Lima.

Monsigny (M.) Mythology: or, A History of the Fabulous Deities of the Ancients: ... By Madame Monsigny. First American Edition. *Randolph [Vt.]: Printed by Sereno Wright, for Thomas and Merrifield.* 1809. 12mo, pp. 298. B. 50038

An interesting specimen of early Vermont typography.

Monson (A. S.) An Address ... before The New Haven Horticultural Society, May 25, 1843. By Alfred S. Monson, M.D. ... *New Haven: Printed ... by William Storer.* 1843. 8vo, pp. 72. H. 50039

Monson, *Mass.* Annual Report of the Selectmen ... 1867. [n. p. n. d.] 8vo, pp. 6, (4). H. 50040

Monson Academy. Discourses, and Speeches, ... at the Celebration of the Semi-Centennial Anniversary of Monson Academy, ... July 18th and 19th, 1854. ... *New York: Printed by John A. Gray.* 1855. 8vo, pp. 90. H. 50041

Contains History of Monson, by Charles Hammond; Discourse, by Richard Storrs, on "Relation of Commerce to Literature;" and an Account of the Jubilee of Monson Academy. Also: Catalogue of Trustees, Instructors, and Students ... for ... 1839. *Springfield: Merriam, Wood & Co., Printers.* 1839. 12mo, pp. 12. Continued. H.—Catalogue of the Trustees, Instructors, and ... Students ... from its foundation in 1804. ... *Springfield: H. S. Taylor's ... Press.* 1851. 8vo, pp. 24. H.

Montagne (C.) Botanique, Plantes Cellulaires de l'Ile de Cuba, par C. Montagne. [n. p. n. d.] 8vo. Atlas of 20 Plates in folio. 50042

Montagne. Fungorum species novae Surinamenses. ... [n. p. n. d.] 8vo. 50043

See also Orbigny (A. de), *and* Valliant (*M.*)

Montagu (M.) England Victorious.—A Poem upon the Capture of the American Frigate Chesapeake by the British Frigate Shannon, June 1st 1813. By Lieutenant M. Montagu, ... To which is prefixed A Copy of Captain Broke's Official Letter relating the Action. From the London Gazette. And, a Correct Copy of his written Challenge to the American Captain Laurence. ... Also Verses to the Memory of Captain Samuel Blyth ... . *London: J. Hatchard.* 1814. 8vo, pp. 47. B.

M[ontagu] (M. R.) Peace the best Policy or Reflections upon the Appearance of a Foreign War, the present state of Affairs at Home and the Commission for Granting Pardons in America. In a Letter to a Friend by Matt. Robinson M. *London: J. Almon.* MDCCLXXVII. 8vo, pp. (2), 112. N. + Second Edition. [*Ibid.*] C. 50045

"This patriotic writer does not trouble himself much about systematic arrangement, or classic purity of style; he abounds with peculiarities and redundances of expression; but his compositions are the productions of a vigorous comprehensive mind, deeply impressed by the subject, and filled with just, bold, liberal, and reflected ideas."—*Monthly Review*, LVI. 308. *See also* Robinson (Matthew).

Montagu (R.) A Mirror in America. By Lord Robert Montagu, M.P. *London: Saunders, Otley & Co.* 1861. 8vo, pp. 108. C. 50046

Montague (Emily). Voyage dans le Canada, ou Histoire de Miss Montague ;. traduit de l'Anglais par Madame J. G. M. *Paris.* 1809. 4 vols., 12mo. 50047

A romance. It is a translation of our Vol. II., No. 8240.

Montague (E. J.) A Directory ... and Sketches of Randolph County: ... with brief notes of the pioneer settlers. By E. J. Montague. *Alton, Ill.* 1859. 12mo, pp. 246. H.

Montague (W. L.) Montague's Illinois and Missouri State Directory for 1854–5, ... A Register ... . To which is appended A New and Complete Business Directory of the City of St. Louis. The whole carefully compiled from authentic sources. *St. Louis: Wm. L. Montague.* 1854. 8vo, pp. xxi, (2), 17–504.

[Montalboddo (Fracanzano) *or* Fracanzano da Montalboddo (Antonio).] Cum Priuilegio | Paesi Nouamente retrouati. Et Nouo Mondo da Alberico vesputio Florentino intitulato. [Colophon:] *Stampato in Vicentia cū la impensa de Mgrō | Henrico Vicentino: & diligente cura & indu- | stria de Zāmaria suo fiol nel* M.CCCCCVII. *a | di iii. de Nouembre. | Cum gratia & | priuilegio p̄ ani.* X. *como nella | sua Bolla appare: che p̄ | sōa del Dominio Ve- | neto nō ardisca i | primerlo.* | 4to. J.C.B., L. 50050

In some copies the colophon ends with the word "priuilegio." Collation: Title, 1 leaf, "Tabula Cõmunis," (9) pages, "Montalbobdo Fracan. al suo amicissimo Ioānimaria Anzolello Vicentino. S.," 1 page, Text, (120) leaves, Primo Libro to Libro Sexto, being signatures a to D in fours, the last leaf blank.

In crediting this very early collection of voyages to Montalboddo, I have followed the illustrious footsteps of Brunet, Græsse, Harrisse, Tiraboschi, and other bibliographers. I am aware that Count Baldelli and others have ascribed it to Alessandro Zorzi, who probably did add some notes to a later edition. The subject of the authorship is discussed at length, and with much ability, in [Harrisse] "Bib. Am. Vet.," No. 109. *See also* "Bulletin de la Société de Géographie," Paris, for October, 1857, Note x., page 312. Unlike most modern works, its contents exceed the promise of its title. It commences with the celebrated voyage of Alovise da Ca da Mosto in Ethiopia, etc., which appeared for the first time in this volume, followed by the voyage of de Cintra in 1462, of Vasco da Gama, 1497–1500, of Cabral in 1500–1501, of Columbus, 1492–1498, of Alonso Negro and the Penzons, of Vespucci, third voyage, 1501–1502, of Cortereal, 1500–1501, etc. Its great value to us, however, consists in its containing the voyages of Columbus and Vesputius. It has been frequently reprinted and translated, and serves to this day, in the Latin repertory of Huttich, as a trustworthy and interesting source of information. This first edition is particularly valuable, from the changes which were made in those which followed, and which are referred to by Mr. Biddle, in his "Life of Cabot." Ternaux, No. 11, refers to an edition, *Vicenza*, 1508, so also Brunet—probably an error as to date.

[Montalboddo.] Paesi nuouamente retrouati. & Nouo Mōdo da Alberico Vesputio Flo- | rētino intitulato. | [Colophon:] *Stampato in Milano con la impensa de Io. Iacobo & fratelli da | Lignano: & diligente cura & industria di Ioanne Angelo scinzen- | zeler. nel.* M.CCCCCVIII. *a di xvii. de Nouembre.* | 4to, (83) leaves. H.

[Montalboddo.] Paesi nouamēte retrouati. & No- | uo Mondo da Alberico Vespu- | tio Florentino intitulato. | [Colophon:] *Stampato in Milano con la impēsa de Io. Iacobo & fratelli da Ligna- | no: & diligente cura & industria de Ioanne Angelo scinzē- zeler: nel.* M. | CCCCCXII. *adi. xxyii. de Mazo* | 4to, (75) leaves.

An extremely rare edition; only one copy known to be in the United States.

[Montalboddo.] Paesi nouamente ritrouati per | la Nauigatione di Spagna in Calicut. Et da Alber- | tutio Vesputio Fiorentino intitulato Mon- | do Nouo: Nouamente Impressa. | [Colophon:] *Stampata in Venetia per Zorzi de Rusconi milla- | nese: Nel.*

M.CCCCC.XVII. *adi. xviii. Agosto.* | 8vo, (124) leaves, woodcut of Venice on the title. 50053

The Lenox Library possesses the only copy in the United States.

[Montalboddo.] Paesi nouamente retrouati. & Nouo Mōdo da Alberico Vesputio Flo- | rē.ino intitulato. | [Colophon:] *Stampato in Milano con la impensa de Io. Iacobo & fratelli di | Lignano: & diligente cura & industria de Ioanne Angelo scinzen- | zeler: nel.* M.CCCCCXIX. *a di. v. de Mazo.* | 4to, 4 leaves, Text, (79) leaves.

"This edition is said to be the best known, and hence more frequently referred to by early writers than any other."—J. R. Bartlett. By a curious mistake, Faribault, No. 18, credits this to Jean Marie Angiadelo, which is apparently a misprint for Angiolelo. The words written hastily are very much alike. Montalboddo dedicated his work in 1507 to Giammaria Angiolelo, and, perhaps, the edition of 1519 has been attributed to Angiolelo by the blunder of some cataloguer ignorant of Italian. *See* Tiraboschi, 2ª ediz. moden., VII. 269.

[Montalboddo.] Paesi nouamente ritrouati per | la Nauigatione di Spagna in Calicut. Et da Alber- | tutio Vesputio Fiorentino intitulato Mon- | do Nouo. Nouamente Impresso. | [Colophon:] *Stampata in Venetia per Zorzo de Rusconi Milla- | nese. Nel.* M.D.XXI. *adi. xy. de Febraro.* | 4to, (124) leaves. C., L. 50055

Mr. Hanrott states that this edition, "though not so rare as the preceding (Nos. 50050 and 50051), contains more at the end." *Per contra*, Nodier (Catalogue of 1844, Part I., No. 1042,) says that all the editions, except these two, "ont éprouvé, dans plusieurs endroits du texte, des altérations sensibles, et pour des causes particulières," while Brunet (Vol. v., col. 1159) calls this number a "simple réimpression de l'édit. de 1517" (No. 50053).

[Montalboddo.] Newe | vnbekanthe | landte | Und | ein | newe | weldte | in | kurtz | verganger | zeythe | erfunden | [Colophon:] *Also hat ein endte dieses Büchlein, wel- | ches ausz wellischer sprach in die dewtschen | gebrachte vnd gemachte ist worden, durch | den wirdigē vnd hochgelarthen herrē Job- | sten Ruchamer der freyen künste, vnd artz- | enneien Doctorē &c. Vnd durch mich Geor- | gen Stüchszen zu Nüreinbergk, Gedrückte | vnd volendte nach Christi vnsers lieben her- | ren geburdte.* M.CCCCC.viij. *Jare, am Mit- | woch sancti Mathei, des heiligen apostols | abenthe, der do was der zweyntzigste tage | des Monadts Septembris.* | Folio, (68) leaves. J.C.B., C., L. 50056

This German translation is by Ruchamer, and is the first collection of voyages printed in that language. "We have seen a copy of the same date, which contains on the verso of the title, and immediately after the preface, a woodcut, representing a man, probably Ca da Mosta, kneeling before a king who is surrounded by a retinue of armed men, some of whom are mounted on an elephant. The table of contents is not reliable. The third book is therein called the second, the fourth is taken from the third. Chapters 80–90, 91–101, and 105–108, contain the first three voyages of Columbus; the fourth voyage is not inserted at all. This work is not as rare as the Italian and Latin versions."—[Harrisse] *Bib. Am. Vet.*, No. 57.

[Montalboddo.] Nye unbekande Lande unde ein nye Werldt in korter fortgangener tyd gefunden. [Colophon:] *Also hefft dyt Boeck einen ende welker | vth Walsher Sprake in de hoechdüdeschen | gebrächt vnde gemaket is durch den werdi- | gen vnde hochgeleerden heren Josten Rü- | chamer vryen Künste unde arstenyen Doc- | torem &c. Dar na dörch Henningū Ghetelen | vth der keyserliken Stadt Lübeck geboren in | desse sine Moderliken Sprake verwandelt. | Vnde dörch my Jürgen Stüchszen to Nü- | reinberch Gedrücket vñ Vulendet na Christi unses leuen Heren gebort* M.CCCCC viij *jare | am Auende Elizabeth des hilligen Wedewed | dede dar was am achteynden dage Novē- | bris des Wintermaens.* | ... | Folio, (68) leaves. 50057

"Translation of Ruchamer's German version of the 'Paesi' into the Low Saxon Dialect (*Platt-Deutsch*) by Henning Ghetel of Lübeck, and printed by the same printer, with the same types and justification" as No. 50056, *supra.* *See* [Harrisse] "Bib. Am. Vet."—*Additions*, No. 29.

[Montalboddo.] Itinerariū Portugallēsiū e Lusitania in Indiā & in- | de in occidentem & demum ad aquilonem. | [Colophon:] *Operi suprema manus imposita est kalendis quintilibus. Ludouico gal- | liar. rege huius urbis Iclite iceptra regēte. Iulio secūdo pōtifice maxi- | ma orthoˀoxā fidē feliciter moderāte: anno nīæ salutis* .M.D.VIII. | Folio. J.C.B., C., H., L. 50058

Collation: (10) leaves, Text, 88 leaves, the last erroneously marked LXXVIII. The last signature is N iii, followed by three unnumbered leaves.

Camus and Ebert say that there should be eleven preliminary leaves, but we have not found one with over *ten.* *See* [Harrisse] "Bib. Am. Vet.," No. 58. This book is of excessive rarity. Bolton Corney's copy sold for £137. It is a Latin translation of the "Paesi nouamente," by Archangelo Madrignano, a Milanese monk. The map of Africa is the earliest known in which that continent is represented as surrounded by the ocean. After Columbus' letters, this is the most important contribution to the early history of American discovery. The two leaves of Index give an analysis of the contents together with the names of the discoverers, while the text of the book runs on from chapter to chapter without distinction. The narratives of Columbus, Pinzon, and Vespucci, concerning America, begin on leaf 52 and end on 75. Quaritch's cataloguer remarks: "The eighth preliminary leaf ends with a metrical eulogium upon Madrignano by Quintianus Stoa. These verses close with a semicolon at the bottom of the reverse page, so that many persons have been led to think there ought to be some further preliminary matter in continuation of the iambics. But the semicolon is simply intended for a mark of interrogation, set at the end of a question in which the verses are brought to a conclusion and a climax thus:

'An credis ergo dignior mortalibus
Sit qui labores superet et vivens deum?'"

[Montalboddo.] Sensuytle Nou- | ueau mōde & na- | uigations: fai- | ctes par Emeric de vespuce Florentin, Des | pays & isles nouuellemēt trouuez, au pauāt | a no⁹ incōgneuz Tant en lethiope q̄ arrabie | Calichut et aultres plusieurs regions estrā- | ges Trāslate de Italien en Lāgue frācoise | par mathurin du redouer licencie es loix. | XIX. | [Verso of the fourth leaf:] *On les vent*

a paris en la rue neufue no- | stre dame a lenseigne de lescu de France. [1515.] 4to. L. 50059

Collation: Title, 1 leaf, (3) leaves, Text, LXXXVIII leaves, the last of which is marked by mistake LXXXX.

A literal translation, in primitive French, of No. 50050, *supra.* Concerning this, *see* [Harrisse] "Bib. Am. Vet.," No. 83.

[Montalboddo.] Sensuyt le Nou- | ueau mōde [as before] Trālate de Italien en Lāgue frācoise | par marthurin du redouer licencie es loix. | *On les vent a Paris enla rue neufue nostre | dame a lenseigne de Lescu de France.* | [1515.] 4to, 4 leaves, Text, LXXXVIII leaves. 50060

Harrisse ("Bib. Am. Vet."—*Additions*, No. 46,) says "there is still another issue with greater differences."

[Montalboddo.] Sensuyt le Nou- | ueau monde & na- | uigations: Fai- | ctes par Emeric de vespuce Florentin, Des | pays & isles, nouuellemēt trouuēz au pauāt a | no⁹ īcongneuz Tāt en lethiope q̄ arabie cali- | chut, & aultres plusieurs regiōs estrāges. xix | *On les vend a Paris a lenseigne Sainct iehn bap- | tiste en la Rue nuefue Nostre dame pres Saincte gene- | uiefue des ardans. Jehan iannot.* | [1515.] 4to, 4 leaves, Text, LXXXVII leaves. L. 50061

From its resemblance to our No. 50059, *supra*, and the fact that Jehan Janot became the partner of Trepperel's widow, we place it here. The Lenox copy, the only one in the United States, is slightly imperfect. "Cette édition ne porte, ni privilège, ni date, en sorte qui'l est difficile de savoir si elle a précédé on suivi celle de Galliot du Pré; cependant Jean Janot ne vivait plus en 1522."—Brunet, v. 1160.

[Montalboddo.] Le nouueau monde et nauigacions fai- | tes p̄ Emeric de Vespuce florētin, Des | pays et isles nouuellemēt trouuez, au | parauāt a nous incongneuz, Tāt en le- | thiope q̄ arabie Calichut & aultres plu- | sieurs regions etranges, Translate de italien en Lāgue | francoyse par Mathurin du redouer licencie es loix. ... | Cum priuilegio regis | *Imprime a Paris pour Galliot du pre, marchant li- | braire demourant sus le pont nostre dame, a lenseigne de | la gallee, ayant sa Boutique en la grand salle du Pallays | au second Pillier.* | [Privilege dated Jan. 10th, 1516.] 8vo, 6 leaves, Text, CXXXII leaves. J.C.B., L. 50062

[Montalboddo.] Sensuyt le Nou- | ueau mōde et na- | uigations: Fai- | ctes par Emeric de vespuce Florentin, Des pays et isles nouuellemēt trouuez, au pauāt | ano⁹ icōgneuz Tant en lethiope q̄ arrabie, ca- | lichut, & aultres plusieurs regions estranges | Translate de ytaliē en langue francoyse par | mathurin du redouer licēcie es loys XX. | [Colophon:] *Cy finist le liure intitule le nouueau mōde & nauigation | de Emeric de vespuce des nauigatiōs faictes p̄ le roy de por-|tugal es pays des mores et aultres regions et diuers pays |Imprime a Paris par Phelippe le Noir.*| [1521.] 4to, 4 leaves, Text, 88 leaves. H. 50063

[MONTALBODDO.] Sensuyt le nouue-|au Monde & Na-|uigations. Faictes par Emeric|de vespuce Florentin, Des pays & iles, nou-|uellement trouuez, au parauant a nos incon-|gneuz.| Tant en lethiope q̄ arrabie, Calichut|Et aultres plusieurs regiõs estrãges. Trãs-|late de ytaliē en langue francoyse, par Ma-|thurin du redouer licencie es loix. xxj.|*On les vend a Paris en la rue neufue nostre Dame a lensei-|gne sainct Jēhan baptiste par Denis ianot.*| [Colophon:] *Cy finist le liure intitule le nouueau Monde & uauigaci-|tions* [sic] *de Almeric de vespuce: des nauigations faictes par|le roy de Portugal es pays des mores et aultres &|diuers pays. Imprime nouuellement a Paris.*| [1528.] 4to, 4 leaves, Text, LXXXVIII leaves. 50064

MONTALEMBERT (Charles Forbes, *Comte de*). Discours prononcé sur l'abolition de l'esclavage dans la discussion générale du projet de roi relatif aux colonies; séance [de la Chambre des Pairs] du 7 Avril, 1845; extrait du Moniteur Universel du Avril, 1845. *Paris.* [1845.] 8vo. A. 50065

MONTALEMBERT. La Victoire du Nord aux États-Unis Par le Comte de Montalembert ... . *Paris: E. Dentu.* 1865. 8vo, pp. 160. H. + *New York: H. de Mareil.* 1865. 8vo, pp. 51.

MONTALEMBERT. The Victory of the North in the United States. By Count de Montalembert ... . Translated from the French ... . *Boston: Little & Gay.* [1865?] 8vo, pp. 32. H.

MONTALEMBERT. La Victoria del Norte, en los Estados Unidos. [n. p.] 1865. 8vo. C. 50068

MONTALVO (F. A. de). Breve Teatro|De las acciones mas notables|de la vida|del Bienaventvrado|Toribio|Arçobispo de Lima.|Por el Doctor|D. Francisco Antonio de Montalvo ... . *En Roma, Por el Tinasi Ympr. Cam.* 1683. 4to, pp. 224. 40 Plates by Thiboust. C. 50069

Two titles, one of which is engraved. The work is dedicated to the Queen of Spain.

MONTALVO. Concilia Limana, Constitvtiones synodales, et alia vtilia monumenta: qvibvs Beatvs Toribivs archiepisc. Limanvs ecclesias Peruani imperij mirificè illustrauit. ... *Romæ, Ex*

Typographia Josephi Vannaccij. 1684. Folio, pp. (32), 255. 2 Portraits. 50070

This volume is as rare as the following. Pinelo and Ternaux do not mention it, and Antonio does not even cite the author's name. For another Latin version, *see* Vol. VIII., No. 30415.

MONTALVO. El Sol del Nvevo Mvndo ideado y compvesto en las esclarecidas operaciones del bienaventvrado Toribio Arçobispo de Lima. Ofrecido a D. Melchor de Navarra y Rocafvll, por el Doctor D. Jvan Francisco de Valladolid. ... *En Roma, En la Imprenta de Angel Bernavò.* 1683. Folio, Engraved and Printed Titles, pp. (16), 540, (28). Portrait of Torribio. 50071

So rare that it has escaped the researches of Ternaux and Brunet.

MONTALVO. Vida admirable y muerte preciosa dei ven. herm. Pedro de S. Joseph Betancur, fundador de la Compañia Bethlemitica en las Indias Occidentales. ... *Roma.* 1683. 4to. 50072

For an Italian version, *see* Vol. II., No. 5062.

MONTALVAN (Perez de). Monja Alferez. 1622.

See Ternaux, No. 443.

MONTALVO (——). Clamor de amante de los milicianos, al Sr. General Montalvo. [*Habana:*] *Imprenta del Gobierno.* 1812. 4to. 50074

MONTALVO (J. O.) Arte o Nuevo Modo de beneficiar los Metales de Oro y Plata, y de Plata con ley de Oro, por Azogue, ... Lo inventò el Br. D. Juan Ordonez Montalvo ... . Lo saca a luz D. Juan Moreno y Castro Marquès de Valle-Ameno. [n. p.:] *Imprenta de la Biblioteca Mexicana.* 1758. 8vo, pp. (6), 65.

MONTALVO (Luis Berrio de). Informe del nuevo beneficio que se ha dado a los Metales ordinarios de Plata por Azogue ... . *Mexico.* 1643. Folio. 50076

An important scientific work on the proper method of working silver mines. *See also* Berrio de Montalvo (Luis), II. 4987.

MONTALVO (P.) Sermon de la dedicacion del hospital de los terceros hijos de S. Francisco de Mexico. *Mexico.* 1760. 4to, 20 leaves. 50077

MONTAÑA (Jos. Isidro). El Corazo de las Rosas Sepultado entre Fragrancias, Relacion Poetica de las Solemnes Funerales Exequias de el Domingo Pantaleon Alvarez de Abreu, 23 y 24 de Enero. *Mexico.* 1765. 4to. 50078

MONTANA TERRITORY. Acts of the First Assembly of Montana Territory, ... 1864. *Virginia City.* 1866. 8vo. Cont'd.

Contributions to the Historical Society of Montana; with its Transactions, Act of Incorporation, Constitution, Ordinances, Officers and Members. Vol. I. *Helena, Montana: Rocky Mountain Publishing Company.* 1876. 8vo, pp. 357. Portrait.

Historical Sketch. *See* [Maguire (H. N.) *and* Horr (H.)]

Laws, Memorials, and Resolutions ... passed at the Sixth Session of the Legislative Assembly, ... 1869, and ... 1870. ... *Helena, M. T.: Robert E. Fisk, ... Printer.* 1870. 8vo, pp. 163, Errata, 15 lines. Continued. H. 50081

Message of the Governor of Montana ... December 7, 1868. *Montana Democrat Print.* [1868.] 8vo, pp. 14. Continued. H.

Report of the Auditor, Treasurer, and Superintendent of Public Instruction ... . 1868. *Virginia City, M. T.: Printed ... [by] John P. Bruce ... .* [1868.] 8vo, pp. 22. H. 50083

MONTANO (B. A.) Relacion Cierta y Verdadera,|del famoso sucesso y vitoria que tuvo el Capitan|Benito Arias Montano, sobrino del doctissimo Arias Montano, natural de Estremadura, Gover-|nador y Capitan general de la Provincia de la nue-|va Andaluzia, y ciudad de Cumana, y Alcayde de|la fuerea de Araya, por el Rey nuestro señor, con-|tra los enemigos Olãdeses, q̃ estavan fortificados|en una salina que está riberas del rio Vnare, que es|en esta governacion, veynte y quatro leguas de la|ciudad de Cumana, este año de 1633.| [Colophon:] *Con licencia, impresso en Sevilla por Francisco de Lyra,*|*Año de* 1634.| Folio, pp. 4.

MONTANO (J.) Sermon de la Santidad el Señ. San Pedro ... . *Mexico.* 1723. 4to, 18 leaves. 50085

MONTANUS (A.) [Engraved Title:] America|*T'Amsterdam*|*By Jacob van Meurs, Plaetsnyder en Boeckverkooper op de Keysers graft in de Stadt Meurs.* 1671.| [Printed Title:] De Nieuwe en Onbekende|Weereld:|of|Beschryving|van|America|en|'t Zuid-Land,|Vervaetende|d'Oorsprong der Americaenen en Zuid-|landers, gedenkwaerdige togten derwaerds,|Gelegendheid|Der vaste Kusten, Eilanden, Steden, Sterkten, Dorpen, Tempels, |Bergen, Fonteinen, Stroomen, Huisen, de natuur van Beesten, Boomen,|Planten en vreemde Gewasschen, Gods-dienst en Zeden, Wonderlijke|Voorvallen, Vereeuwde en Nieuwe Oorloo-

gen:|Verciert met Af-beeldsels na 't leven in America gemaekt, en beschreeven|Door|Arnoldus Montanus.|*t' Amsterdam,*|*By Jacob Meurs Boek-verkooper en Plaet-snyder, op de Kaisars-graft,*|*schuin over de Wester-markt, in de stad Meurs. Anno* 1671. *Met Privilegie.*| Folio, pp. (8), 585, 27. 70 Plates, 32 folded Views, 16 Maps and 7 Portraits in the Text. BA., C., H. 50086

Also on large paper. Sought for chiefly for its plates, especially for the engraved view of New Amsterdam which "is, without any doubt, the handsomest, and at the same time the most agreeable view of Dutch New York.—ASHER's *Bibliographical Essay*, p. 23. The plates in the text are the same as those in the following translations, but are earlier and therefore better impressions, and represent the games, festivals, occupations, battles, religious rites, cannibalism, habitations, manners and customs of the Indians.

[MONTANUS.] Die Unbekante|Neue Welt,|oder|Beschreibung|des Welt-teils|Amerika,|und des|Sud-Landes:|Darinnen vom Vhrsprunge der Ameriker und Sudlän-|der, und von den gedenckwürdigen Reysen der Europer darnach zu.|Wie auch|Von derselben Festen Ländern, Inseln, Städten, Festungen, Dörfern,|vornähmsten Gebeuen, Bergen, Brunnen, Flüssen, und Ahrten der Tiere,|Beume, Stauden, und anderer fremden Gewächse; Als auch von den|Gottes- und Götzen-diensten, Sitten, Sprachen, Kleider-trachten,|wunderlichen Begräbnissen, und so wohl alten als neuen|Kriegen, ausführlich gehandelt wird;|Durch und durch mit vielen nach dem-Leben in Ameriken selbst|entworfenen Abbildungen gezieret.|Durch D^{r}. O. D[apper].|*Zu Amsterdam,*|*Bey Jacob von Meurs, auf der Keysersgraft, in der Stadt Meurs,*|1673.| Folio, Engraved and Printed Titles, pp. (4), 658, (22). 6 Portraits, 32 Folded Views, 16 Maps, and 70 large Plates in the Text. BA. 50087

This German translation is much scarcer than the Dutch original. Asher says that he had met with only one copy in the Netherlands, viz. that in the Royal Library of the Hague. This publication is, besides, a specimen of the most impudent plagiarism, the translator O. Dapper calling himself the author and concealing the real author's name. It forms part of Dr. O. D[apper]'s collection of voyages, or descriptions of foreign countries.

[MONTANUS.] America:|being an|Accurate Description|of the|New World;|containing|The Original of the Inhabitants; the Remarkable|Voyages thither:|The Conquest of the vast Empires|of|Mexico and Peru,|Their ancient and later Wars.| With their several|Plantations,|Many, and Rich Islands;|Their Cities, Fortresses, Towns, Temples,|Mountains, and Rivers:| Their Habits, Customs, Manners, and Religions,|their Peculiar Plants, Beasts, Birds, and Serpents.|Collected and Translated from most Authentick Authors,|And Augmented with later Observations;|Illustrated with Notes, and Adorn'd with peculiar

Maps, and Proper Sculptures,|By John Ogilby, Esq;|...|*London:|Printed by Tho. Johnson for the Author ... .* M.DC.LXX. Folio, pp. (6), 629. Plates, Maps and Plans. H. 50088

Another issue has the following title:

[MONTANUS.] America:|being the Latest, and most|Accurate Description|of the|New World;|containing|The Original of the Inhabitants, and the Re-|markable Voyages thither.|The Conquest of the Vast|Empires|of|Mexico and Peru,|and other Large|Provinces and Territories,|with the several European| Plantations|in those Parts.|Also|Their Cities, Fortresses, Towns, Temples,|Mountains, and Rivers.|Their Habits, Customs, Manners, and Religions.|Their Plants, Beasts, Birds, and Serpents.| With|An Appendix, containing, besides several other considerable|Additions, a brief Survey of what hath been discover'd of the|Unknown South-Land and the Arctick Region.|Collected from most Authentick Authors, Augmented with later Observations, and|Adorn'd with Maps and Sculptures,|By John Ogilby, Esq; ... . *London:|Printed by the Author, and are to be had at his House in|White Fryers.* M.DC.LXXI. Folio, pp. (10), 674, (1). 65 Plates, 6 Portraits, 30 folded Views and 19 Maps. B., BA.

Also on large paper. This English translation is, like Dapper's, "an impudent plagiarism" from Montanus, plates included. The plates include portraits of Columbus, Vespucius, Magellan, etc. Ogilby may be considered the English De Bry. His works are similar in their objects, compilation, and mode of illustration.

MONTCALM [SAINT-VÉRAN (L. J. de)] *Marquis de.* Éloge Historique de Monsieur le Marquis de Montcalm. (Extrait du "Mercure de France," de 1760.) *Québec.* 1855. 8vo, pp. 16. Portrait. S. 50090

MONTCALM. Lettres de Monsieur Le Marquis de Montcalm, Gouverneur-General en Canada; a Messieurs de Berryer & de la Molé. Ecrites dans les Années 1757, 1758, & 1759. Avec une Version Angloise. *A Londres: J. Almon.* M.DCC.LXXVII. 8vo, pp. (2), 28 *bis.* H. 50091

The English title reads: "Letters from the Marquis de Montcalm, Governor-General of Canada; to Messrs. De Berryer & De la Molé, In the Years 1757, 1758, and 1759. With an English Translation." ... *London: J. Almon.* M.DCC.LXXVII.

French and English on opposite pages. These letters, purporting to have been written by so distinguished a man as the Governor General of Canada, the last of them but a few days before the fall of Quebec and the death of both Generals Montcalm and Wolfe, have attracted great interest, while their genuineness has been suspected. But "it has been reserved," says Mr. Henry Stevens in an extended note on the subject, "for Mr. Francis Parkman, the historian, in 1869, to settle almost to a demonstration that the Montcalm letters are forgeries." *See* Mr. Stevens's long and exceedingly interesting note on this scarce work, in his "Bibliotheca Historica," *also* "Monthly Review," LVI. 306. *See also* [Martin (Felix)], XI. 44868.

MONTCLAIR (J. W.) Real and Ideal: a Collection of Metrical Compositions, By J. W. Montclair. [*New York.* 1864?] 12mo, pp. (2), 95. B. 50092

MONTE Y TEJADA (Antonio del). Historia de Santo Domingo, desde su descubrimiento hasta nuestros dias. ... Tomo I. *Habana: Soler.* 1853. 8vo, pp. (6), xxi, 600. Portrait, 6 Maps, and 5 Plates. C. 50093

MONTEAGUDO (Bernardo). Ensayo sobre la Necesidad de una Federacion Jeneral entre los Estados Hispano-Americanos. ... *Lima.* 1825. 4to, pp. 22. M. 50094

MONTEAGUDO. Peruvian Pamphlet; being an Exposition of the Administrative Labours of the Peruvian Government, from the time of its formation, till the 15th of July, 1822; presented to the Council by the Minister of State and Foreign Relations, Don Bernardo Monteagudo. Translated from an Official Copy printed at Lima. *London: Ridgway.* 1823. 8vo, pp. 99. M.

[MONTEAGUDO (Matias), *and others.*] Dictamen de la Comision y Acuerdo del Illmo. Cabildo Metropolitano de México, ... *Mexico: Imprenta de Luis Abadiano y Valdés.* 1837. 8vo, pp. (2), 28. BA. 50096

MONTEATH (W.) Brotherly-Love. A Sermon At a meeting of the Grand Lodge of Free-Masons, of the State of New-Jersey, ... 24th Day of June, 1788. By Rev. Walter Monteath. *New-Brunswick: Printed by Shelly Arnelt.* M.DCC.LXXXIX. 8vo, pp. 20. N. 50097

Monte-Christo. Periódico politico, literario, económico y mercantil. *Mexico.* 1850. Folio. 50098

MONTEFIORE (J.) The American Trader's Compendium; containing the Laws, Customs, and Regulations of the United States, relative to Commerce. ... By J. Montefiore ... . *Philadelphia: Samuel R. Fisher, Jun.* 1811. 8vo, pp. xii, 304. BA.

MONTEFIORE. A Commercial Dictionary: containing the Present State of Mercantile Law, Practice and Custom. By Joshua Montefiore ... . First American Edition; with ... Additions relative to the Laws, Usages, and Practice of the United States. ... *Philadelphia: Printed ... by James Humphreys.* 1804. 3 vols., 8vo, pp. ix–562; (2), 481; 479. B. 50100

MONTEIRO BAENA (Antonio Ladislau). Compendio das Eras da provincia do Pará. ... *Pará: Na Typographia de Sanctos & menor.* 1838. 4to, pp. vi, 650. 50101

MONTEIRO BAENA. Proposições resumidas dos principios em que se estriba o direito das Sociedades Civis. ... *Maranhão.* 1848. 8vo. 50102

MONTEIRO (J. M. de Sousa). *See* Sousa Monteiro (J. M. de).

MONTEIRO (Manuel). Brevissimo compendio da vida e excellencias de S. Francisco Xavier, apostolo da India; com a devoção da sua novena, e das dez sextas feiras. ... *Evora: Na Officina da Universidade.* 1675. 16mo, pp. 58. 50103

MONTEIRO DA VIDE (Sebastião). Historia da vida e morte da madre Soror Victoria da Encarnação, religiosa no convento de Sancta Clara da cidade da Bahia ... *Roma, por João Domingos Chracas.* 1720. 8vo. 50104

MONTEITH (J.) Youth's History of the United States ... . By James Monteith. *New York: A. S. Barnes & Co.* 1860. 4to, pp. (4), 88. C. 50105

MONTEMAIOR DE CUENCA (J. F. de). Discvrso Politico: Historico|Juridico Del derecho, y Repartimiento|de presas, y despojos apprehendidos en Justa|guerra. Premios, y castigos de los soldados.|Lo dedica, y offrece a la Grandeza, y proteccion| del|Exmo. S^{or}. D. Fran^{co}. Fernandez de la Cueva ... .|D. Juan Fran^{co}. de Montemaior de Cuenca,|Oydor mas antiguo, q̄ fue de la Real Audiencia|de Santo Domingo y como tal, Presidente| della, Gouernador, y Capitan General de la|Isla Español, y de la Tortuga, y oi Oydor|de la Real Chancilleria de Mexico|*Con Licencia, En Mexico: Por Jvan Rrviz, Impressor. Año de* 1658.| 4to, Engraved Title, pp. (52), 192, (40). Map. H. 50106

A very rare and precious volume. It contains an account of the expulsion of the buccaneers from the Island of Tortuga, with a separate title-page. The map represents the attack on the Island of Tortuga, also St. Domingo, Cuba, and Jamaica. The title of this work is not given by Pinelo, who mentions a narrative of the Island of Tortuga, by this author, printed in 1654, folio, and reprinted in his "Tratado de las presas maritimas," 1658, 4to, which is probably the work enumerated above. Brunet cites the book after Salva and Antonio. The last-mentioned gives the title as follows: "Investigacion del origin, y privilegios de los ricos hombres, o nobles Cavalleros Infanzones, o hijosdalgo y señores de vasallos de Aragon, y del absoluto poder que en ellos tienen. Parte primera, Discurso politico ... . *Mexici* 1658, *typis Joannis Ruiz.*" 4to, which is perhaps the same as our No. 50111. Salva quotes the title as Antonio, but under the date of 1664.

MONTEMAIOR. Excvbationes|Semicentvm|ex Decicisionibvs Regiæ|Cancellariæ|Sancti Dominici, Insulæ vulgo dictæ|Español |totius Noui Orbis Primatis|D. D. D. Ioannes Franciscvs|a Montemaior de Cuenca.|...|*Mexici: Franciscum Rodriguez Lupercio.* 1667. 8vo, (16) leaves, Text, 165 leaves. H. 50107

MONTEMAIOR. Pastor Bonus: Dominus Jesvs: sacerdos in æternvm, christus, secundum ordinem Melchisedech; exemplum dedit crucem suam baiulantibus, illius vestigia sequentibus. Præsvli sanctissimo divo Nicolao, Myræ archiepiscopo ipsi ex corde addictvs servvs D. D. Joannes Franciscus a Montemaior, ... *Mexici, ex Typographia Francisci Rodriguez Lupercio.* 1676. 8vo, (18) leaves, Text, 67, 81, 75 leaves, "Repertorium," 10 leaves. 50108

This volume is still rarer than the "Discvrso Politico." It has escaped the researches of Antonio and Brunet.

MONTEMAIOR. Relacion de lo svcedido en las provincias de Nexapa, Yztepex, y la villa Alta. Inquietudes de los Indios sus Naturales. *Mexico.* 1662. 4to. 50109

MONTEMAIOR. Recopilacion Sumaria de algunos autos acordados de la Real Audiencia y Chancilleria de la Nueva España, que rende en la ciudad de Mexico para la mejor expediciõ de los negocios de su cargo, desde el año de mil quiniẽtos y veinte y ocho en que se fundo hasta este presente año de mil seiscientos y setenta y siete, con las ordenanças para su Govierno. Recogidos por el Dr. Don J. F. de Monte-Mayor de Cuenca. [*Mexico.* 1787.] Folio. C. 50110

Perhaps a part of our No. 4419. There is a continuation to 1786. [Harrisse] "Bib. Am. Vet.," p. 395, credits this to J. F. de Montemavor y Cordova. *See also* "Sumario."

MONTEMAIOR. Summaria|Investigacion|de el origen, y privi, legios, de los Ricos Hombres,|o Nobles, Caballeros, Infanzones-o Hijos dalgo, y Seño-|res de Vassalos Aragon, y del absoluto poder queen|ellos tienen.| ... Don Iuan Francisco de Montemaior de Cuenca ... . [*Mexico.* 1664.] 2 vols., 4to, pp. (22), 135 *bis*; (12), 321 *bis*, (28). Plate. H. 50111

A most rare and important work. *See* Mayans, Brunet, III. 1852, and Salva.

MONTE MAYOR (G. de). Dones del Espiritu Santo, Oraciones Evancelicas. Por Geronimo de Monte Mayor, Natural de Ciudad de Cuenca. *Madrid.* 1667. 4to. 50112

MONTEMAYOR Y CORDOVA (J. F.) *See* Sumarios de las Cedulas

MONTÉMONT (A.) Bibliothèque Universelle des Voyages effectués par Mer ou par Terre dans les diverses Parties du Monde, depuis les Premières Découvertes jusqu'a nos jours; contenant la Description des Mœurs, Coutumes, Gouvernemens, Cultes, Sciences et Arts, Industrie et Commerce, Productions Naturelles et autres. Revues ou Traduits Par M. Albert-Montémont ... . *Paris: Armand-Aubrée.* MDCCCXXXIII–XXXVI. 46 vols., 8vo. A., BA. 50113

Vol. XLVI. has an Index. An atlas of 22 maps is in folio. It was also issued with the title:

MONTÉMONT. Histoire Universelle des Voÿages effectués par Mer et par Terre dans les cinq Parties du Monde, sur les divers points du Globe, contenant la Description des Mœurs ... . Traduits par M. Albert-Montémont ... . *Paris: Armand-Aubrée.* [1833–37.] 46 vols., 8vo. 46 colored Plates, and Atlas of 22 Maps in folio. H. 50114

Five volumes relate to America, and twenty-one are voyages around the world.

MONTÉMONT. Voyages en Amérique; par Christophe Colomb, Fernand Cortez, Pizarre, Cabral, Humboldt, Basil Hall, Mistress Trollope, Ross, Parry, Franklin, Bulloch, Watterton, Head, Walsh. Traduit par Albert Montémont. *Paris: J. Bry ainé.* 1854. Folio, pp. 320. Map and 8 Plates. C. 50115

MONTÉMONT. Voyages Nouveaux par Mer et par Terre, effectués ou publiés de 1837 à 1847, dans les diverses Parties du Monde, analysés ou traduits par Albert Montémont. *Paris.* 1847. 5 vols., 8vo. C. 50116

MONTENEGRO (A. de la Peña). *See* Peña Montenegro (A. de la)

MONTENEGRO (Antonio Casimiro). Judith Religiossa, reproducida en los virtuossos hechos de la M. R. M. Josepha Maria de Christo. ... *Mexico.* 1733. 4to. 50117

[MONTENEGRO COLON (Feliciano).] *See* [Colon (F. M.)]

MONTENEGRO (J. G.) Á sus Conciudadanos. Por J. G. Montenegro, Comandante General del Estado de Jalisco. *Guadalajara.* 1856. 4to, pp. 23. 50118

MONTENGON (P.) La Conquista del Megico por Hernan Cortès. Poema épico. ... *Napoli.* 1820. Sm. 8vo. 50119

MONTEREY, *Cal.* Constitution and Rules of the Monterey Library Association, together with Catalogue of Books. *San Francisco.* 1854. 8vo. C. 50120

MONTEROS (I. E. de los). *See* Espinosa de los Monteros (I.)

[MONTEROYO (J. F. de).] *See* [Mascarenhas (J. F. de M.)]

MONTES DE OCA (J.) Fiesco. Poema Historica. ... *Mexico.* 1850. 8vo. 50121

MONTESANO (R. R.) Redstick; or, Scenes in the South. By R. R. Montesano. *Cincinnati.* 1856. 8vo. C. 50122

MONTESCLAROS. Relacion de la inundacion de la laguna de Mexico y del desaguadero hecho por el verrey Marques de Montesclaros. *Mexico.* 1611. 4to. 50123

Title from Ternaux, No. 339.

MONTESINOS (F. de). Avto|de la Fe|celebrado en|Lima a 23. de Enero|de 1639.|Al Tribvnal del Santo Ofi-|cio de la Inquisicion, de los Reynos del Perù,|Chili, Paraguay, y Tucuman.|Por el licenciado D. Fer-|nando de Montesinos Presbitero, natural de Ossuna.|Con Licencia|de sv Excelencia, del Ordi-|nario, y del santo Oficio.|*Impresso en Lima,|por Pedro de Cabrera; Año de* 1639.|*Vendense en la tienda de Simon Chirinos, Mercader de Libros.*| 4to, 4 leaves, and Text, signatures A to G in fours.

[MONTESINOS.] Libro segundo de las Memorias Antiguas Historiales del Peru. [n. p. about 1652.] Folio, 66 leaves.

MONTESINOS. Mémoires Historiques sur l'Ancien Pérou (traduits sur le manuscrit espagnol), publiés par H. Ternaux-Compans. *Paris: Arthus Bertrand.* 1840. 8vo, pp. 234. C. 50126

Forms Vol. XVII. of Ternaux's "Relations."

MONTEVIDEO. Esposicion sobre el estado de los Bancos existentes en la Capital. ... *Montevideo.* 1865. 8vo, pp. 24. 50127

Gazeta Extraordinaria de Montevideo. *Montevideo.* 1810. 4to

See also Nos. 9000, 20441, "Narrative," *and* [Wright (A.)]

MONTEZ (L.) Lectures of Lola Montez ... . Including her Autobiography. *New York: Rudd & Carleton.* 18—, 12mo, pp. 282. 50129

Also: The Story of a Penitent, Lola Montez. *New York.* 1867. 24mo, pp. 46. *See* Papon (*Marquis*).

MONTEZUMA (F. G. B.) *See* Brandao Montezuma (F. G.)

MONTGAILLARD (Jean Gabriel Maurice Roques de). Situation of England in 1811. By M. Mie. de Montgaillard. Translated from the French, by A Citizen of the United States. *New York: C. Van Winkle.* 1812. 8vo, pp. 279, (2). 50130

Relates partly to the questions which were determined by the War of 1812.

[MONTGOLFIER (*M.*)] Vie de la Vénérable Sœur Marguerite Bourgeoys, institutrice, fondateur et premiere Supérieure de la Congrégation de Notre Dame de Villemarie en Canada. *Villemarie* [i. e. *Montreal*]. 1818. 12mo. C., P. 50131

See also Faillon (*l'abbé*), VI. 23655.

MONTGOMERY (C.) Eagle Pass; or, Life on the Border. By Cora Montgomery. ... *New York: George P. Putnam & Co.* MDCCCLII. 12mo, pp. 188. H. 50132

MONTGOMERY. The King of Rivers, with a Chart of our Slave and Free Soil Territory. By Cora Montgomery. ... *New-York: Charles Wood.* 1850. 8vo, pp. 19. C. 50133

MONTGOMERY. The Queen of Islands, and the King of Rivers. By Cora Montgomery. ... *New-York: Charles Wood.* 1850. 12mo, pp. 50. BA. 50134

MONTGOMERY (C.) Texas and Her Presidents. With a glance at her Climate and Agricultural Capabilities. By Corinne Montgomery. *New-York: E. Winchester.* 1845. 18mo, pp. 122.

MONTGOMERY (C.) The Missionary Memorial: a Gift Book for all Seasons. Edited by Cuthbert Montgomery. *Philadelphia: G. Collins.* 1855. 12mo, pp. (10), 372. 4 Plates. C. 50136

[MONTGOMERY (*Dr.*)] Decius' Letters on the Opposition to the New Constitution of Virginia. *Richmond.* 1789. 8vo.

MONTGOMERY (E.) Reminiscences of Wilmington, in familiar Village Tales, Ancient and New. By Elizabeth Montgomery. ... *Philadelphia: T. K. Collins, Jr.* 1851. 8vo, pp. xii, 7–367. Portrait and 3 Plates. BA. 50138

Very scarce. Nearly the entire edition destroyed by fire.

MONTGOMERY (G. W.) Narrative of a Journey to Guatemala, in Central America, in 1838. By G. W. Montgomery. *New York: Wiley & Putnam.* 1839. 8vo, pp. 195. A., H. 50139

Concerning this writer, *see* a long note in Rich, II. 329.

MONTGOMERY (H.) The Life of Major General William Henry Harrison, ninth President of the United States of America. By H. Montgomery. *Auburn, N. Y.* 1848. 12mo. BM. + *Cleveland.* 1852. 12mo. + Second Edition. *Cleveland, O.: Tooker & Gatchell.* 1853. 12mo, pp. 465. + *New York.* 1857. 12mo. + *Cleveland, Ohio.* 1858. 12mo. + *New York.* 1859. 12mo. + [*Ibid.*] 1860. 12mo. C. 50140

MONTGOMERY. The Life of Major General Zachary Taylor, By H. Montgomery. ... *Buffalo.* 1847. 12mo. + *Auburn, N. Y.: J. C. Derby & Co.* 1847. 12mo, pp. 350. + [*Ibid.*] 1849. 8vo, pp. 425. + Twentieth Edition, revised and enlarged. *Auburn: Derby, Miller & Company.* 1851. 12mo, pp. (2), xiv, 13–463. 8 Portraits and 6 Plates. B. 50141

MONTGOMERY. Montgomery's Tippecanoe Almanac, for the year 1841. Fourth edition, enlarged and improved. Containing a short history of the Life and Services of General William Henry Harrison; ... . *Philadelphia: M'Carty & Davis.* [n. d.] 8vo, pp. 79. 50142

MONTGOMERY (J.) The Abolition of the Slave Trade, A Poem in Four Parts. By James Montgomery. Embellished with Engravings by the First Artists, from Pictures Painted by R. Smirke, Esq., R.A. *London: Printed by T. Bensley.* 1814. 4to, pp. 53. 12 Plates. 50143

Also on large paper.

MONTGOMERY. Greenland, and other Poems. By James Montgomery. *London.* 1819. 16mo. + *New-York: Kirk & Mercein.* 1819. 24mo, pp. (2), 207. + Third Edition. *London: Longmans.* 1825. 12mo, pp. viii, 252. C. 50144

MONTGOMERY. Poems on the Abolition of the Slave Trade; written by James Montgomery, James Grahame, and E. Benger. ... Engravings from Pictures ... by R. Smirke ... . *London: R. Bowyer.* 1809. 4to, pp. (16), 141. 12 Plates. H. + [n. p. n. d.] 4to, pp. (2), 53. 12 Plates. B., C. 50145

MONTGOMERY. The West Indies, and other Poems. By James Montgomery. *London.* 1810. 12mo. + The Second Edition. *London: Longman, Hurst* ... . 1810. 12mo, pp. (2), ii, (2), 175. + *Boston: Printed by Munroe & Francis.* 1810. 12mo, pp. 156. + The Third Edition. *Philadelphia: James P. Parke.*

1811. 18mo, pp. 126. + Fourth Edition. *London.* 1810. + *London.* 1814. 12mo. 50146

Written in honor of the abolition of the African slave-trade by the British Legislature, in 1807.

MONTGOMERY. The West Indies and Other Poems, on the Abolition of the Slave-Trade, by James Montgomery; James Grahame, and E. Benger. *New York: Prior & Dunning.* 1810. 8vo, pp. (4), 127. BA. 50147

These various poems are, of course, included in all the collected editions of the author's works, which editions are numerous. Longman's edition, *London*, 1841, and Little, Brown & Co.'s edition, 1858, are among the best.

MONTGOMERY (J.) ... A Sermon, preached in ... Philadelphia, May 8th, 1822, before the Annual Convention of the Protestant Episcopal Church in ... Pennsylvania ... . By the Rev. James Montgomery, A.M. ... *Philadelphia: S. Potter & Co.* 1822. 8vo, pp. 22. 50148

MONTGOMERY (J.) A Practical Detail of the Cotton Manufacture of the United States of America; and the state of the Cotton Manufacture of that country contrasted and compared with that of Great Britain; with comparative estimates of the cost of manufacturing in both countries. Illustrated by ... Engravings. Also, a brief Historical Sketch of the Rise and Progress of the Cotton Manufacture in America, and Statistical Notices of various Manufacturing Districts in the United States. By James Montgomery ... . *Glasgow: John Niven, Jun.* MDCCCXL. 8vo, pp. 219. Plates. A., B., C., H. 50149

The author was superintendent of the York factories, Saco. The work elicited the following:

Strictures on Montgomery on the Cotton Manufactures of Great Britain and America. Also, A Practical Comparison of the Cost of Steam and Water Power in America. By the Author. *Newburyport: Printed by Morss and Brewster.* 1841. 8vo, pp. 75, Errata, 6 lines. B., H. 50150

MONTGOMERY (J. E.) Our Admiral's Flag Abroad. The Cruise of Admiral D. G. Farragut ... in 1867–8, in the Flag-Ship Franklin. By James Eglinton Montgomery, A.M. ... *New York: G. P. Putnam & Son.* 1869. 8vo, pp. (2), xvi, 464. 20 Plates. H. 50151

[MONTGOMERY (John T.)] The Writ of Habeas Corpus, and Mr. Binney. *Philadelphia: John Campbell.* 1862. 8vo, pp. 29.

+ Second Edition. [*Ibid.*] 1862. 8vo, pp. 29. BA. + [*Philadelphia.* 1862.] 8vo, pp. 35. H. 50152

Forty-nine copies printed on large paper, 4to. Also: In the matter of the Claim of the Girard Bank, against the Estate of Charles S. Boker, Dec'd. Argument of John T. Montgomery, Esq., on behalf of Mr. Boker's Estate. Before Furman Sheppard, Esq., Auditor. *Philadelphia: Sherman & Co., Printers.* 1866. 8vo, pp. xii, 806.

MONTGOMERY (J.) A Sermon, preached at Christiana Bridge and New Castle, the 20th of July, 1775. Being the Day appointed by the Continental Congress, as a Day of Fasting, Humiliation and Prayer. ... By Joseph Montgomery, A.M. ... *Philadelphia: Printed by James Humphreys, junr.* M. DCC. LXXV. 8vo, pp. 30. P. 50153

MONTGOMERY (M. W.) History of Jay County, Indiana. By M. W. Montgomery. *Chicago: The Author.* [1862.] 12mo, pp. 288. Map. B. 50154

MONTGOMERY (R.) Articles of Capitulation, Made and entered into between Richard Montgomery, Esquire, Brigadier General of the Continental Army, and the Citizens and Inhabitants of Montreal, &c. ... [*Philadelphia:*] *Printed by John Dunlap.* [1775 or 1776.] Folio, 1 leaf. P. 50155

Probably unique. *See* [Brackenridge (H. H.)], II. 7185, and add, *Norwich: Printed by J. Trumbull, for and Sold by J. Douglass M'Dougall, on the West Side of the Great-Bridge, Providence,* 1777. 8vo, pp. 68.

MONTGOMERY. Entretiens de Guillaume de Nassau, Prince d'Orange, et du Général Montgomery, sur ... les Affaires de l'Amérique. *Londres.* 1776. 12mo. S. 50156

See also Vol. VI., No. 22673.

MONTGOMERY (Robert). *See* Mountgomery (*Sir* R.)

MONTGOMERY (T.) Literary Societies: their Uses and Abuses. An Address ... before The Wesleyan Literary Association, of ... Charlotteville, ... N. Y., September 28th, 1852. By Thomas Montgomery. *Albany: Gray, Sprague & Co.* 1853. 8vo, pp. 32.

MONTGOMERY (T. H.) A Genealogical History of the Family of Montgomery, including the Montgomery Pedigree. Compiled by Thomas Harrison Montgomery. ... *Philadelphia: Printed for Private Circulation.* 1863. Rl. 8vo, pp. xii, 5–158. Chart.

MONTGOMERY (W.) The Extraordinary Adventures of William Montgomery in the Unexplored Regions of Amazonia; An account of his Captivity among the Oromana Indians, a Description of their Manners, Customs, and Wars; and the Escape of

the Captive with the daughter of their Chief. *London: Printed by W. Nicholson.* [n. d.] 16mo, pp. 30. 50159

Probably a fiction. *See* Field's "Essay," No. 1083.

MONTGOMERY [William]. Speech of Mr. Montgomery ... on the ... Issue of Treasury Notes; ... April 25, 1840. *Washington.* 1840. 8vo, pp. 16. BA. 50160

Also: Speech ... on the Admission of Kansas ... . March 19, 1858. [n. p. n. d.] 8vo, pp. 16. H.

Montgomery, or the West Indian Adventurer. By a Gentleman resident in the West Indies. *Jamaica.* 1812. 3 vols., post 8vo. 50161

Exhibits a curious picture of life in the West Indies. *See* "Monthly Review," LXXVI. 101.

MONTGOMERY, *N. Y.* Catalogue of the Teachers, Pupils and Patrons of Montgomery Academy ... 1848–9 ... . *Montgomery.* 1849. 8vo, pp. 12. H. 50162

Proceedings of the Board of Supervisors of Montgomery County ... 1867. *Fonda.* 1868. 8vo. Continued. 50163

Also: Thirty-Third Annual Report of the Auxiliary Bible Society of the Counties of Montgomery, Fulton and Hamilton. *Amsterdam.* 1840. 8vo. S.

MONTGOMERY Co., *Pa.* State of the Accounts of Jacob Auld, Esquire, Collector of Excise, for the County of Montgomery; From ... 1784, until ... 1786. *Philadelphia: Printed by Robert Aitken.* M. DCC. LXXXVI. 8vo, pp. 5. P. 50164

A Month of Freedom. An American Poem. *New York.* 1837. 12mo, pp. 90. 50165

Partly descriptive of American scenery.

Monthly American Journal of Geology and Natural Science. July, 1831, to January, 1832. Conducted by G. W. Featherstonhaugh. *Philadelphia.* 1831–2. 8vo. BM. 50166

The Monthly Anthology, and Boston Review, Containing Sketches and Reports of Philosophy, Religion, History, Arts and Manners ... . Vol. I. 1804. *Boston: For the Proprietors by Munroe & Francis.* 1804. 8vo. A., B., H., P. 50167

Continued to ten volumes. The forerunner of the "North American Review," into which it was merged at the completion of the tenth volume, and is now scarce. "Whoever indulges in the history of American literature must not fail to consult these ten muses of the Hub. It is delightful even now to dip for an hour into them and see the mental activity of Boston half a century ago, before a single one of its numerous brain clubs had been organized."—STEVENS.

The Monthly Assembly. A Farce. *Boston.* 1770. 8vo.

Monthly Bulletin. *See* Vol. IV., No. 13097.

Monthly Chronicle for the British Colonies. Vol. I. ... *Philadelphia: William Bradford.* 1758. 8vo. 50169

The Monthly Chronicle, for the Years 1728–31. *London: Aaron Ward.* 1728–31. 4 vols., 4to. 50170

Continued to 1731 or longer. Contains an Appendix of curious Trials, Papers relating to the American Colonies, Treaties with the Indians, Original Letters from America, Speeches of the Governors, etc.

The Monthly Chronicle, of Events, Discoveries, Improvements and Opinions ... . Illustrated with Maps and Drawings. Vol. I. *Boston: For the Proprietors by Samuel N. Dickinson.* 1840. 8vo, pp. iv, 588. BA. 50171

Edited by Nathan Hale. Continued to three volumes.

The Monthly Chronicle of Original Literature. Vol. I. No. I. July, 1839. *New-York.* 1839. 8vo, pp. 66. BA. 50172

... Monthly Chronicle of the Merchants' Protective Union, Organized ... for the Promotion and Protection of Trade, throughout the United States and British Provinces. ... No. I.—July, 1868. *New-York.* 1868. 8vo, pp. 60. H. 50173

Monthly Commercial Record and Business Directory of San Francisco, Sacramento, San Jose and Oakland. [*San Francisco:*] *F. R. Voigt.* 1868. 2 or more vols., 8vo. 50174

The Monthly Indiana Freemason; ... Edited by Sol. D. Bayless, P.G.M. Vol. I. *Fort Wayne, Indiana: R. C. F. Rayhouser.* 1859. 8vo, pp. 580. 50175

"Indiana" dropped from the title in Vol. II.

Monthly Journal. *See* American Unitarian Association, Vol. I.

Monthly Journal of Agriculture, ... John S. Skinner, Editor. Volume I. ... *New-York: Greeley & McElrath.* 1846. 8vo, pp. (2), iv, 612. 3 Portraits and 9 Plates. H. 50176

Continued to three or more volumes.

Monthly Journal of Education. Edited by E. C. Wines. Vol. I.—No. I. January. ... *Princeton, N. J.: Moore Baker.* 1835. 8vo. H. 50177

The Monthly Journal of Medical Literature. Vol. I. January 1, 1832. No. I. [n. p. 1832.] 8vo. H. 50178

Also: The Monthly Journal of Medicine .... Conducted by an Association of Physicians. ... Vol. I. No. I. *Hartford: Philemon Canfield.* 1823. 8vo. Continued. B.

... The Monthly Jubilee. ... 1852. *Philadelphia.* [1852.] Folio. Continued. H. 50179

Monthly Law Magazine: Edited by John Livingston ... . *New-York.* 1850. 8vo. Continued. 50180

Also: Monthly Law Reporter. ... *Boston,* 184–. 8vo. Continued.—The Monthly Legal Examiner. [Conducted by] John Livingston: ... Vol. I. May, 1850. No. I. *New-York: John Livingston.* 1850. 8vo, pp. 31. H. (No more published.)

Monthly Magazine; ... . Vol. I. January, 1806. No. I. ... *Danbury (Conn.): John C. Gray & Co.* [1806.] 8vo. Cont'd.

Monthly Magazine and American Review, for ... 1799: ... . *New-York: Printed ... by T. & J. Swords.* 1800. 3 vols., 8vo, pp. iv, 480; iv, 480; viii, 480, 7. B., H., S., W. 50182

Edited by C. Brockden Brown. For a continuation, *see* "American Review," our Vol. I., No. 1213.

Monthly Magazine. Edited by W. M. Reynolds. Vol. I. *Gettysburg.* 1840. 8vo. 50183

The Monthly Mercury. ... or, the Historical and Political Monthly Mercury ... . *London.* 1702–1728. 20 vols., 4to. C.

This first English magazine includes communications from the British Colonies in America.

The Monthly Military Repository. Respectfully inscribed to the Military of the United States of America. By Charles Smith. *New York: William A. Davis.* 1796–7. 2 vols., 8vo, pp. 336; 314. Portraits of Washington and Greene. 6 Maps and Plans. 50185

The revolutionary descriptions in this scarce work "were said to have been supplied by Baron Steuben and General Gates."—Dr. J. W. Francis.

The Monthly Miscellany of Religion and Letters. Volume I. *Boston: William Crosby & Co.* 1839. 8vo, pp. vii, (1), 288. Continued. H. 50186

The Monthly Miscellany, or Memoirs for the Curious. *London.* 1707. 4to. 50187

Contains articles on Virginia, Jamaica, American Botany, etc.

Monthly Miscellany or Vermont Magazine. Vol. I. *Bennington: Anthony Haswell.* 1794. 8vo. 50188

The Monthly Nautical Magazine ... . Vol. I. October, 1854. No. I. *New-York: Griffiths & Bates.* [1854.] 8vo. Cont'd.

In 1855 the title was changed to "U. S. Nautical Magazine," etc.

The Monthly Offering. February, 1841. [Edited by John A. Collins. n. p. n. d.] 12mo. H. 50190

... The Monthly Phonographic Magazine. ... Vol. I. ... March, 1868. ... *New York: James E. Munson.* [1868.] 12mo. Continued. H. 50191

Monthly Record of Church Missions in connection with the Society for Propagation of the Gospel in Foreign Parts. *London.* 1852. 12mo. Plates. 50192

The Monthly Recorder, for April, 1813. [*New York.* 1813.] 8vo. Portrait. H., S. 50193

The Monthly Register and Review of the United States. ... Vol. I. ... *Charleston (S. C.): For the Proprietor, By G. M. Bounetheau.* [1805.] 8vo. H. 50194

Edited by John Bristed. *See* "History of the American Revolution," VIII. 32156.

The Monthly Religious Magazine. Volume I. *Boston: Leonard C. Bowles.* 1844. 12mo, pp. vii, 432, iv. Continued.

Monthly Report of the Department of Agriculture. ... J. R. Dodge, Editor. *Washington: Government Printing Office.* 1866. 8vo. Continued. C. 50196

Monthly Report of the Deputy Special Commissioner of the Revenue, in Charge of the Bureau of Statistics, Treasury Department. Commerce and Navigation ... . *Washington.* 1869. Folio, pp. 27. Continued. 50197

The Monthly Review: or, Literary Journal: ... . Volume I. *London.* M,DCC,XLIX. 8vo. B., BA., C. 50198

Continued to 1845, 249 volumes. The most valuable existing record of contemporary literature for nearly a century, replete with the most important events; embracing the whole period of the American Revolution, it chronicles every production of the press connected with the subject, many of which, indeed, are only known to have existed from its pages. It is constantly referred to by Mr. Rich in his "Bibliotheca Americana," and by myself in this Dictionary, for particulars of works relating to this country. The Indexes by S. Ayscough, etc., *London,* 1786–96 and 1818, form 5 vols., 8vo, and should always accompany a set of the work. During the American Revolution, it was edited by a Dr. Bancroft, who is said to have resided in America several years. The bias of most of its criticism is American, without being disloyal to Great Britain.

Monthly Review and Literary Miscellany of the United States. Vol. I. *Charleston, S. C.* 1806. 8vo. 50199

The Monthly Review: devoted to the Civil Government of Canada. Vol. I. February, 1841. ... *Toronto: H. Scobie.* [1841.] 8vo. H. 50200

Monthly Rose; A Periodical conducted by the present and former Members of the Albany Female Academy. *Albany.* 1841. 8vo. 50201

The Monthly Scientific Journal ... . Conducted by W. Marrat, A.M. ... *New-York: W. Marrat.* 1818. 8vo. H. 50202

The Monthly Traveller ... . *Boston.* [1830.] 8vo. Cont'd.

MONTICELLO. Thirteenth Annual Catalogue of Monticello Female Seminary ... 1851. *Alton, Ill.* 1851. 12mo, pp. 22.

Catalogue of Monticello Academy, Sullivan County, N. Y. ... 1859. [n. p. n. d.] 8vo. S. 50205

MONTIGNY (*M. de*). *See* [Buisson (J. F.)], III. 9079.

MONTILLA (M.) Biografia del General de Division Mariano Montilla, del órden de libertadores. [Por Col. Juan Austria.] *Carácas.* 1851. 8vo, pp. 23. 50206

MONTIZAMBERT (E. L.) A Lecture on the Mercantile Law of Lower Canada, ... Montreal, January 27, 1848. By Edward L. Montizambert. *Montreal.* 1848. 8vo, pp. 28. 50207

Also: Rapport sur l'Administration de la Justice. ... *Montréal.* 1842. 8vo.

M[ONTLEZUN (*Baron de*)]. Souvenirs des Antilles: Voyage en 1815 et 1816, aux États-Unis, et dans l'Archipel Caraïbe; apperçu de Philadelphie et New-Yorck; Descriptions de la Trinidad, la Grenade, Saint-Vincent, Sainte-Lucie, Martinique, Guadeloupe, Marie-Galante, Saint-Christophe, Sainte-Croix et Saint-Thomas. Par M. ... *Paris: Gide Fils.* 1818. 2 vols., 8vo, pp. viii, 406; (4), 590. A., H. 50208

See "Monthly Review," LXXXVII. 483.

[MONTLEZUN.] Voyage Fait dans les Années 1816 et 1817, De New-Yorck a la Nouvelle-Orléans, et de l'Orénoque au Mississipi; par les Petites et les Grandes-Antilles ... . Par l'Auteur des Souvenirs des Antilles. ... *Paris: Gide Fils.* 1818. 2 vols., 8vo, pp. (4), 372; (4), 406, (2). C., H., S. 50209

See "Monthly Review," LXXXVIII. 504. It elicited the following:

Examen Impartial d'un ouvrage intitulé: Voyage fait dans les Années 1816 et 1817, de New Yorck a la Nouvelle-Orléans, ... où l'on réfute les calomnies du voyageur sur les Américains des États-Unis et les réfugiés Français, etc. *Paris: Renaudière.* 1818. 8vo, pp. (4), 23. BA. 50210

MONTLINOT (C.) Essai sur la transportation comme récompense, et de la déportation ... . *Paris: An* V. 8vo, pp. 100.

MONTLONG (W. von). Authentische Enthüllungen über die letzten Ereignisse in Mexico. ... Von Wilhelm v. Montlong ... . *Stuttgart: Hoffmann.* 1868. 8vo, pp. vi, 233, (1). 2 Plates. B.

[MONTMIGNON (*l'Abbé* Jean Baptiste).] Choix des Lettres Édifiantes, Écrites des Missions Étrangères; avec des Additions, des Notes Critiques, et des Observations pour la plus grande intelligence de ces Lettres. Par M. *** ... *A Paris: Chez Maradan.* M. DCCC. VIII–1809. 8 vols., 8vo, pp. (4), cviii, 400; (4), lxiv, 451; (4), 458; (4), lxxxiv, 568; (4), lxxii, 427; (4), 507; (4), lxxxviii, 490; (4), iv, 514. B., BA. + Seconde Édition, augmentée. *Paris: Grimbert.* 1824–26. 8 vols., 8vo. + Troisième Édition, augmentée ... . *Paris.* 18—. 8 vols., 8vo. 50213

Vols. VII. and VIII. include the "Missions de l'Amérique. Précédées d'un Tableau historique de la découverte du nouveau Monde, et des premiers établissemens des Espagnols, des Anglais et des Français," etc.

MONTÓRO (Reinaldo Carlos). Relatorio do Gremio Litterario Portuguez no Rio de Janeiro. ... *Rio de Janeiro.* 1858. 4to, pp. 15. 50214

MONTOTO (G.) Vindicacion de D. Genaro Montoto injustamente difamado por los Sres. Oidores de Puerto-Principe. *Habana: Imprenta de D. Pedro Palmer.* 1812. 4to, pp. 8. 50215

MONTOYA (Antonio Ruiz de). *See* Ruiz de Montoya (A.)

MONTOYA (I. J.) Teatro Histórico, Juridico, y Politico-Militar, de la Isla Fernandina de Cuba, principalmente de su Capital La Havana. ... Por el Dr. D. Ignacio Jph. de Urruha Montayo, ... Tomo I. ... *En la Havana.* M.DCC.LXXXIX. 8vo, pp. (14), xxxviii, 64. 50216

MONTPALAU (A.) Diccionario Geografico Universal, que comprehende la descripcion de las quatro partes del Mundo; ... Quinta edicion, corregida y enmendada por D. Antonio Montpalau. *Madrid,* 1793. 3 vols., sm. 4to, pp. viii, 474; iii, 424; iii, 400. S. 50217

MONTPELIER, *Vt.* Proceedings of the Montpelier Congregational Association, in reply to ... Statements of Henry Jones, ... in relation to Freemasonry in the Churches. *Danville, Vt.: E. Eaton, Printer.* 1830. 12mo, pp. 22. B. 50218

Services at the Dedication of Green Mount Cemetery, Montpelier, Vt., Sept. 15, 1855, with the Rules and Regulations. ... *Montpelier: E. P. Walton, Jr.* 1855. 8vo, pp. 40. H. 50219

Also: Lectures delivered before the American Institute of Instruction. *Boston.* 1850. 8vo, pp. xi, 232.—Report of the Farmer's Mutual Fire Insurance Company. *Montpelier, Vt.* 1851. 8vo. Continued.

[MONTPLEINCHAMP (*l'Abbé* J. Chr. B. de).] Vie de Phil. Emm. de Lorraine, duc de Mercœur; par G. G. D. M. *Cologne: Marteau.* 1689. 12mo. + [*Ibid.*] 1692. 8vo. + Deuxième Édition. *Londres.* 1737. 2 vols., 12mo. 50220

Contains information relative to the Canadian Indians. The second edition was retouched, but abridged. The first edition is the same as the anonymous "L'histoire de Philippe Emmanuel de Lorraine, duc de Mercœur." *Cologne: Marteau.* 1689. 12mo.

MONTRESOR (*Col.* J.) Journal of a Tour from the St. Lawrence to the Kennebec, about 1760. *Portland: Day, Frazer & Co.* 1831. 8vo. C. 50221

This Journal fell into the hands of Col. Benedict Arnold, and suggested the Expedition through Maine by the Kennebec and Chaudiere rivers, in 1775. *See* "Collections of Maine Historical Society," Vol. I.

MONTROND (M. de). Histoire de Christophe Colomb, d'après D. Fernand Colomb, Robertson et Washington Irving; par Maxime de Montrond. Troisième Édition. *Lille: Lefort.* 1853. 12mo, pp. 200. Plate. 50222

Also: Missions d'Amérique, d'Océanie et d'Afrique .... *Lille: Lefort.* 1846. 12mo, pp. 288. Plate. + Seconde Édition. *Lille.* 1853. 8vo.

MONTS (*Sieur de*). Commissions dv | Roy & de Monseigneur l'admiral | au Sieur de Monts, pour l'habi- | tation ès terres de Lacadie, | Canada, & autres en-droits en la nouuelle | France. | Ensemble les defenses premieres et secon- | des à tous autres de trafiquer auec | les sauuages desdites terres | auec la verification en la Cour de Parlement à Paris. | *A Paris.* | *Par Philippes Patisson.* | 1605. | *Auec Permission.* | 8vo, pp. 39. 50223

Concerning this rare piece, *see* [Harrisse] "Notes sur la Nouvelle-France," No. 14. An English version will be found in Churchill's "Voyages," Vol. II., Supplement.

MONTSERRAT. An Abridgement of the Acts of Assembly, passed in the Island of Montserrat; From 1688, to 1740, inclusive. *London: Printed in the Year* 1790. Folio, pp. (4), 81–102.

Acts of Assembly, passed in the Island of Montserrat; From 1668, to 1740, inclusive. *London: Printed ... by John Baskett.* M.DCC.XL. Folio, pp. x, 146. C., H. 50225

Also on large paper.

Montserrat Code of Laws: From 1688, to 1788. *London: Printed ... by Robert Hindmarsh.* MDCCXC. Folio, pp. x, 76. H.

Rich says pp. 243, and another authority pp. 251—probably these collations represent sequent laws added to the first issue.

MONTT. Cuadro histórico de la Administracion Montt, escrito segun sus propios Documentos. *Valparaiso.* 1861. 12mo.

MONTUFAR (Manuel). Réfutation d'assertions erronées publiées par le Moniteur Universel du 16 mai dernier, contre San Salvador. ... *Paris.* 1863. 8vo, pp. 32. 50228

"Memorias para la Historia de la Revolucion de Centro-America," our No. 45020, Vol. XI., is sometimes attributed to this author.

MONTULÉ (Edouard de). Voyage en Amérique, en Italie, en Sicile et en Egypte, pendant les années 1816, 1817, 1818 et 1819; Par Ed. de Montulé ... . *Paris: Delaunay.* 1821. 2 vols., 8vo, pp. 466, (1); viii, 448, (1). Atlas of 51 Plates in obl. folio. H.

MONTULE. A Voyage to North America, and the West Indies, in 1817; by E. Montule ... . *London: Sir R. Phillips & Co.* 1821. 8vo, pp. 102. 2 Plates. C. 50230

Forms Part VI. of Vol. V. of Phillips' "Collection of Voyages."

MONTUVAL (*Marquis de*). Copyen van drie Missiven, | Een door den Marquis de Montuval, Vice-Roy vande | Bay, gheschreven ende ghesonden aen sijn Excell: Grave | Mauritius van Nassau, tot Fernambock. | Mitsgaders: | Noch een vanden Colonel Hinderson ende Capi- | teyn Day, aen sijn Excell: voorsz. Inhoudende in wat ma- | niere den voorsz. Vice-Roy sich verclaert den Koninck | van Portegael aen te nemen; Ende hoe hy de | Spanjaerden ende Italianen daer op gedisarmeert heeft. | Noch een Missive gheschreven van Fernanbock, | dat van daer gheordineert ende vertrocken waren Gecom- | mitteerden aen den voorsz. Marquis, om met den | selven te handeln. | *T' Amsterdam,* | *Gedruckt voor Ian van Hilten woonende inde Beurs-* | *straet. Anno* 1641. 4to, pp. 8. + Tweede Druck. *Amsterdam.* 1642. 4to. 50231

Copy of three letters: one by the Marquis of Montuval, Vice-Roy of the Bay, one by Col. Hinderson and Capt. Day, to Count Maurice of Nassau at Fernambuco, containing in what manner the Vice-Roy has declared for the King of Portugal.

The Monument. Vol. I. September 8th, 1840. No. I. Edited by Mrs. S. J. Hale. *Boston: Printed by S. N. Dickinson.* 1840. Folio. Continued. H. 50232

Monument of a Beneficent Mission from Boston to St. Johns. ... [*Boston.* 1818?] 12mo, pp. 24. BA. 50233

Appendix to Vol. I. of the "Friend of Peace."

Act of Incorporation, By-Laws, Rules and Regulations of the Monument Cemetery of Philadelphia. ... And the Second Annual Report. *Philadelphia: J. Van Court, Printer.* 1839. 8vo, pp. 24. Plan. Continued. H. 50234

Monument to the Victims. *See* [Murphy (H. C.)]

A Monumental Gratitude attempted, In a Poetical Relation of the Danger and Deliverance of Several of the Members of Yale-College, in Passing the Sound, from South-hold to New-Haven, Aug. 20th. 1726. *New-London: Printed ... by T. Green.* 1727. 12mo, pp. (4), 10. BA., N. 50235

Monumental Inscriptions to the Seven Mutineers. July 4, 1828. [n. p. n. d.] 8vo, 7 leaves. S. 50236

A Jacksonian presidential campaign document.

Monumental Memorials of the Appleton Family. *Boston: Privately Printed.* 1867. 4to, pp. 29. 50237

By John Appleton. One hundred and fifty copies printed for private distribution.

Monuments of Washington's Patriotism. *See* Washington (G.)

MONTREAL, *Canada.* The Act of Incorporation and the Bye Laws of the Boston and Montreal Turnpike Company. *Peacham, Vt.: Samuel Goss.* 1806. 8vo. 50238

Annales de la Temperance. Tous le Patronage du Conseil Central de l'Association Diocésaine de Ville-Marie. *Montreal.* 1854. 8vo, pp. 80. 50239

Annual Report of the Canada Education and Home Missionary Society. *Montreal.* 1836. 8vo. Continued. S. 50240

Also: Annual Report of the Chief of Police for ... 1868. ... *Montreal.* 1869. 8vo, pp. 17. Continued.— ... Annual Report of the Inspector of Buildings ... for ... 1868. ... *Montreal: Printed by J. Starke & Co.* 1869. 8vo, pp. 30. Continued. —Annual Report of the Ladies' Benevolent Society. *Montreal.* 1833. 8vo. Continued.—Fourth Annual Report of the Mercantile Library Association of Montreal. *Montreal: Printed by Lovell & Gibson.* 1844. 12mo, pp. 46. Continued.—Annual Report of the Montreal Auxiliary Bible Society. *Montreal.* 1820. 8vo. Continued.

—Annual Report of the Montreal Protestant Orphan Asylum ... 1821. *Montreal.* 1822. 12mo. Continued.—Second Annual Report of the Montreal Sanitary Association, ... 1868 .... *Montreal.* 1868. 8vo, pp. 16, 8. Continued. H.

Annual Report of the Superintendent of the ... Water Works For ... 1869; also ... estimates for the Enlargement of the Aqueduct, with a Report ... by Thos. C. Keeeer [*sic* Keefer], Esq., C.E. ... *Montreal: Printed by J. Starke & Co.* 1869. 8vo, pp. 44, Appendix, (2), 21, 7 folded leaves. Continued. B.

Annual Report of the Treasurer of the City of Montreal, for 1848. [n. p. n. d.] 8vo. Continued. 50242

Business Sketches with a Description of the City of Montreal; the Grand Trunk, Victoria Bridge ... . *Montreal.* 1864. 12mo, pp. 225. 50243

By-Laws fixing the Rates of Assessment for 1847. *Montreal.* 1847. 8vo, pp. 22. Continued. 50244

Also: By-Laws, Rules and Regulations ... of the University Lying-in Hospital, Montreal, ... 1859; ... *Montreal: Printed by Salter & Ross.* 1859. 12mo, pp. 20.

The Case of the Canadians at Montreal distressed by Fire. *London.* [1765.] 8vo, pp. 47. + Second Edition. [n. p. 1765.] 8vo. 50245

Privately printed. This pamphlet has a second title as follows: "Motives for a Subscription towards the Relief of the Sufferers at Montreal in Canada, by a Dreadful Fire," etc.

The Charter and Bye-Laws of the City of Montreal: ... Compiled ... by Chas. Glackmeyer, City Clerk. *Montreal.* 1865. 8vo, pp. viii, 518. 50246

Circulaire, École de Médecine de Montreal. *Montreal.* 1858. 8vo. 50247

Compilation of the By-Laws and Police Regulations in Force in the City of Montreal ... . Part I. *Montreal.* 1842. 8vo.

La Convention anti-seigneuriale de Montreal au Peuple. ... *Montreal.* 1854. 8vo, pp. 24. 50249

Evidence Demonstrating the Falsehoods of William L. Stone concerning the Hotel Dieu Nunnery of Montreal. *New York.* 1837. 12mo, pp. 31. S. 50250

Financial Report of the Mayor, ... for the Year ... 1849. [*Montreal.* 1849.] 8vo, pp. 8. 50251

Guide to Montreal and its Environs. ... *Montreal.* 1854. 12mo, pp. 56. Map. 50252
See also Vol. vii., No. 29205.

Hochelaga Depicta. *See* Vol. ii., No. 6793.

... Journal of a Visitation. *See* Vol. iv., No. 13005.

The Journal of the Bishop. *See* Mountain (J. G.), *and* West (J.)

Laws for the Government of the Advocate's Library, Montreal. *Montreal.* 1828. 8vo, pp. 12. 50253

Catalogue of ... the Library of the Mechanics' Institute ... with the Rules .... *Montreal: Printed by A. A. Stevenson.* 1869. 12mo, pp. 142. 50254

Also: Report of the General Committee of the Mechanics' Institute of Montreal, to the Members at the 16th Annual General Meeting, 5 Nov. 1855. [n. p. n. d.] 18mo, pp. 34. s.

Mémoires et Documents relatifs a l'Histoire du Canada; Publiés par La Société Historique de Montreal. [Première Livraison.] *Montreal: Imprimé par Duvernay, Frères.* 1859. 8vo, pp. 63. Continued. H. 50255
See also Vol. ii., Nos. 5159–60.

Meteorological Observations made at Montreal, L. C., 21st December, 1835. [n. p. n. d.] 8vo. Continued. 50256

Montreal and Kingston Railway. Report on the Construction of a Railway Bridge at Montreal over the St. Lawrence ... . *Montreal.* 1853. 8vo. Map. s. 50257

The Montreal Almanack, or Lower Canada Register, for 1829 ... . *Montreal: Printed by Robert Armour.* MDCCCXXIX. 12mo. Continued. 50258

Montreal City Advertiser and Monthly Visitor. Gratis. Dec. 1852. Vol. i. No. i. *Montreal.* [1852.] 8vo, pp. 32. s.

Montreal Directory (Doige's). *Montreal.* 1820. 12mo.

Montreal City Directory, ... 1842. By Robert W. S. Mackay [to 1853 or later]. *Montreal.* 1842. 12mo. 50261

Montreal et ses Principaux Monuments Edition illustrée *Montreal: Eusèbe Senécal, Imprimeur.* 1860. 8vo, pp. 46. 13 Plates. B. 50262

Montreal Horticultural Society. Circular relative to the Provincial Exhibition, September, 1857. *Montreal.* 1857. 4to, pp. 2. 50263

Montreal in 1856. A Sketch prepared for the Celebration of the opening of the Grand Trunk Railway of Canada. By a Sub-Committee of the Celebration Committee. *Montreal: Printed by John Lovell.* 1856. 8vo, pp. 51, (1). H., s. 50264

Catalogue of the Montreal Library. *Montreal.* 1821. 8vo.

Report of the Trustees of the Montreal Mining Company ... 1846. *Montreal.* 1846. 8vo, pp. 50. Continued. H. 50266

Montreal Museum. Vol. i. ... *Montreal.* 1832. 8vo. Continued. 50267

The Montreal Pilot. (Extra) Speeches and Papers relating to Losses by the Rebellion, Montreal, Feb. 26, 1849. [n. p. n. d.] 8vo. 50268

The Montreal Pocket Almanack, and General Register, for 1842 ... . *Montreal: Printed by Jas. Starke & Co.* [1842.] 64mo, pp. 84. Continued. B. 50269

Articles of Association of the Montreal River Mining Company of Lake Superior. *New-York.* 1846. 8vo. s. 50270

Catalogue of the Library and Museum of the Natural History Society of Montreal. *Montreal.* 1846. 8vo, pp. 37. 50271

Also: Constitution and Bye-Laws of the Natural History Society of Montreal. With Directions for preserving and forwarding Objects of Natural History. *Montreal.* 1828. 8vo, pp. (2), 25.—First Annual Report of the ... Society ... 1828. *Montreal.* 1828. 16mo, pp. 7. Continued.—Report of Meteorological Observations made on the Island of St. Helen ... under ... the direction of John S. McCord. *Montreal.* 1842. 8vo.—Transactions of the ... Society. *Montreal.* 1820. 16mo.

The New Guide to Montreal and its Environs. ... *Montreal: Armour & Ramsay.* 1851. 24mo, pp. 57, (2). Map. H. 50272

Prospectus du Chemin de fer de Montréal et Bytown. *Montréal.* 1853. 8vo. s. 50273

Rapport de l'Inspecteur des Chemins sur les ouvrages faits en 1854. *Montréal.* 1855. 8vo, pp. 40. s. 50274

Rapport sur une Exploration préliminaire faite dans la vue de fournir de l'eau à la ville de Montréal. Par T. C. Keefer. [n. p.] 1852. 8vo, pp. 29. s. 50275

Rapports de l'Association de la Propagation de la Foi, établie à Montréal, en vertu d'un indult du Saint Siége, et annoncée au diocèse par le mandement du 18 avril 1838. *Montréal.* 1839. 8vo. Continued. 50276

Report of the Board of Works, ... 1844. ... *Montreal: Printed by Desbarats and Derbishire.* 1845. Folio, pp. (2), 82, (1), 4 folded leaves. Map and 3 Plans. B. 50277

Report of the City Surveyor; ... 1842. *Montreal: Printed by James Starke & Co.* 1843. 8vo, pp. 43, (4). Continued. B.

Report of the Special Sanitary Committee upon Cholera and Emigration, 1834. [n. p. n. d.] 8vo. s. 50279

Report of the Water Committee, submitting the Reports of the Engineers on the New Water-Works. *Montreal.* 1854. 8vo, pp. 92. s. 50280

Reports on the Accounts of the Corporation ... and Reports of City Officials for the Year ending ... January, 1869. *Montreal.* [n. d.] 8vo, pp. (4), 4. Continued. B. 50281

Report on the Trade and Commerce of Montreal for 1864; including ... Reports on the Progress and Local Advantages of the City, &c., &c. By Wm. J. Patterson ... . *Montreal: Printed by J. Starke & Co.* 1865. 8vo, pp. 136. Continued. B. 50282

The scope of the later reports is much wider, and includes the "Trade Relations of British North America, Trade with the West Indies, Brazil, etc., Immigration to British North America," etc. *See also* "Statements," No. 50287, *infra.*

Representation against the Title of the Seminary to the Seignory of Montreal; and Objections to the ... Extinction of Seignorial Dues ... . *Montreal.* 1839. 8vo, pp. 14. H. 50283

Résumé du Recensement de la Cité de Montréal. [*Montreal.* n. d.] Folio, 1 leaf. 50284

The Riot and Outrage of the 9th June, in Montreal. ... By an Eye Witness. *Montreal: Printed ... by Francis Wayland Campbell.* 1853. 8vo, pp. 24. Plate. H. 50285
Relative to the disturbances growing out of Father Gavazzi's visit.

An Act to Incorporate Saint-Andrew's Church, Montreal ... . *Montreal.* 1849. 8vo. s. 50286

Also: Narrative of the Proceedings ... from ... March 1835 ... . *Montreal.* 1844. 8vo. s.

Statements relating to Trade, Navigation, Mining, etc., ... of the Dominion of Canada; and Annual Report on the Commerce of Montreal, for 1867. ... By Wm. J. Patterson ... . *Montreal: Starke & Co., Printers.* 1868. 8vo, pp. 140. Cont'd.

The Stranger's Guide through the City of Montreal, with Engravings ... . *Montreal: Salter & Ross.* 1857. 12mo, pp. 40. c.

Thoughts on the Last Election, and Matters connected therewith. By an old Citizen. *Montreal.* [n. d.] 8vo, pp. 16.

The Traveller's Guide for Montreal and Quebec. *Montreal: Daniel Rose.* 1866. 18mo, pp. 40. 50290

1856. Traveller's Guide to Montreal and its Vicinity. *Montreal: Printed by J. C. Becket.* 1856. 24mo, pp. 32. Cont'd.

Les | Veritables Motifs | de | Messievrs et Dames | de la Societé | de Nostre Dame | de Monreal. | Pour la Conuersion des Sauuages de la | nouuelle France. | [*Paris.*] M.DC.XXXXIII. 4to, pp. 127.

[Mooar (George).] Historical Manual of the South Church in Andover, Mass. August, 1859. *Andover: Printed by Warren F. Draper.* 1859. 12mo, pp. 200. Portrait and Plate. H.

Also: The Prominent Characteristics of the Congregational Churches. A Lecture. ... *San Francisco.* 1866. 16mo, pp. 60.

Mood (F. A.) Methodism in Charleston, S. C., a Narrative of the Rise and Progress of the Methodist Episcopal Church in Charleston. By F. A. Mood. *Nashville.* 1856. 12mo. c.

Moodey (J.) The Believers happy Change by Dying, A Sermon preached on the occasion of the Death of Capt. Thomas Daniel Esq., who was interred the day before, November 17th, 1683. By Joshua Moodey ... . *Boston: Printed by B. Green and J. Allen.* 1697. Sm. sq. 8vo, pp. 32. 50295
A posthumous publication, and very rare.

Moodey. An | Exhortation | to a Condemned | Malefactor | Delivered March the 7th, 1686. | By Joshua Moody ... . *Printed at Boston, by R[ichard] P[ierce]. Anno* 1687. Sm. 8vo. 50296

Forms pp. 55–94 of "The Call of the Gospel," by Cotton Mather, Vol. xi., No. 46244, and pp. 83–124 of "A Sermon Occasioned," by Increase Mather, No. 46735.

Moodey. The Great Sin of Formality in God's Worship: being The Subject of a Sermon preacht on the Weekly Lecture in Boston. By Joshua Moodey ... . *Boston: Benj. Harris and J. Allen.* 1691. 12mo. N. 50297

Moodey. A | Practical | Discourse | Concerning the Choice Benefit | of Communion with God in his | House, | Witnessed unto by the Experience of Saints as | The best Improvement of Time. Being the | Summe of Several Sermons on Psal. 84. 10. Preach'd in Boston on Lecture-Dayes. | By Joshua Moody ... . *Boston: Printed by Richard Pierce, for Joseph Brunning.* 1685. 16mo, pp. (8), 109. B. + *Boston: D. Henchman.* 1746. Sm. 8vo, pp. (2), 6, 88. H., M. 50298

Moodey. Souldiery Spiritualized, | Or | the Christian Souldier | Orderly, and Strenuously Engaged in the | Spiritual Warre, | and So fighting the good Fight: | Represented in a Sermon Preached at Boston in | New England on the Day of the Artil- | lery Election there, June 1. 1674. | By Joshua Moodey ... . *Cambridge: Printed by Samuel Green.* 1674. 4to, pp. (4), 47. H., W. 50299

Also: The People of New England Reasoned with ... . An Election Sermon ... May 4. 1692. ... *Boston.* 1692. 8vo.—Catalogue of Rare and Valuable Books. Being the Greatest Part of the Library of the late Reverend and Learned Joshua Moodey and Daniel Gookin. *Boston.* 1718. 12mo. *See also* Vol. i., No. 828.

Moodey (S.) ... A Funeral Discourse, Occasioned by the Death of Thomas Sewall; ... 1716. By Samuel Moodey, M.A. ... *Boston: Printed by John Allen.* 1716. 24mo, pp. xii, 52. H.

Moodey. Judas the Traitor | Hung up in Chains, | To Give | Warning | To Professors, That they | beware of | Worldlymindedness, | And Hypocrisy: | A Discourse concluding with a | Dialogue; | Preach'd at York in New-England. | By Samuel Moodey, M.A. | ... | *Boston: Printed & Sold by B. Green.* 1714. 12mo, pp. (2), x, 84. B., C., W. 50301

Moodey. A Sermon ... May 31. 1721. Being the Day for the Election ... . By Samuel Moodey, A.M. ... *Boston in N. E.: Printed by Nicholas Boone.* 1721. 8vo, pp. (4), 64. H. 50302

Moodey. Summary Account of the Life and Death of Joseph Quasson, Indian, who, on the 28th day of August, 1725, at Arundel, in the County of York, and Province of Maine, in New England, Shot his Fellow Soldier and Kinsman, John Peter, for which being Apprehended, Tried and Condemned at York, he was there executed on the 29th of June, 1726. By Samuel Moodey ... . *Boston: Printed for S. Gerrish.* 1726. 12mo, pp. (4), 41. C. 50303

Also: The Vain Youth Summoned to Appear at Christ's Bar. | Or, | An Essay | To Block up the Sinful Wayes | of | Young People, | By most Solemn Considerations, Relating to that Judgment unto | which they are Hastening. | ... Lecture-Sermon (June 25.

1701.) | Preached at York, in the Province | of Main. | ... | *Boston in N. E. Printed and Sold | by Timothy Green,* ... 1707. 12mo, pp. 64. B. + Second Edition. [*Ibid.*] + Third Edition. *New London.* 1760. 12mo. W.—Extract from a late Sermon on the Death of Rev. Samuel Moodey. *Boston.* 1748. 8vo.

Moodie (Susanna Strickland). Flora Lyndsay: or, Passages in an Eventful Life. By Mrs. Moodie ... . *London: Richard Bentley.* 1853. 2 vols., post 8vo. + *New York: DeWitt & Davenport.* [1854.] 12mo, pp. 343. H. 50304

Moodie. Life in the Clearings versus the Bush. By Mrs. Moodie ... . *London: Richard Bentley.* 1853. Post 8vo, pp. 390. + *New York.* [1854.] 12mo, pp. 300. H. 50305

Moodie. Roughing it in the Bush; or, Life in Canada. By Susanna Moodie. ... *London: Richard Bentley.* 1852. 2 vols., post 8vo, pp. 608. + Second Edition. [*Ibid.*] + Part i. *New York: George P. Putnam.* M.DCCC.LII. 12mo, pp. vi, (2), 211. + New Edition. *London.* 1853. 2 vols., post 8vo. + *London.* 1854. 2 vols., post 8vo. + *New York.* 1854. 12mo. + New Edition. *London: Richard Bentley.* 1857. Post 8vo, pp. 260. Plate. 50306

Moody (C. C. P.) Biographical Sketches of the Moody Family: embracing notices of ten Ministers and several Laymen, from 1633 to 1842. ... By Charles C. P. Moody. *Boston: Samuel G. Drake.* 1847. 16mo, pp. 168. B., C., H. 50307

Moody (G.) Letters of Col. G. Moody, Feb. 5, 1863, [and] Maj. Gen. W. S. Rosecrans, Feb. 2, 1863. [n. p. n. d.] Folio.

Moody (J.) Lieutenant James Moody's Narrative of his Exertions and Sufferings in the Cause of Government, since the year 1776. *London, Printed in the year* 1782. 8vo, pp. 59. W.

Extremely rare. "Moody, a New Jersey farmer, was so much harassed by mobs, associations and committees, that, driven into the British lines, he became an active, and in some instances successful partizan against his countrymen." *See* "Monthly Review," lxix. 78. From 1776 to 1782, he was a spy, a ranger and scout in the service of the British. A portion of the time he was attached to General Skinner's New Jersey Tory Brigade.

Moody. Lieut. James Moody's Narrative of his Exertions and Sufferings in the Cause of the Government, since the year 1776; Authenticated by Proper Certificates. The Second Edition. *London: Richardson & Urquhart.* MDCCLXXXIII. 8vo, pp. (2), 57, (7). 50310

This second and best edition is very scarce, and contains matter not embraced in the first. It was reprinted [*Morisania: H. B. Dawson*], 4to, pp. (4), 57, (8); also with the following title:

Moody. Narrative of the Exertions and Sufferings of Lieut. James Moody, in the Cause of Government since the Year 1776. Written by Himself, with the Author's Last Corrections, etc. With an Introduction and Notes, by Charles I. Bushnell. *New York.* 1865. 8vo, pp. 98. 4 Portraits. BA. 50311

One hundred copies were privately printed. It forms No. i of Bushnell's "Crumbs for Antiquarians," Vol. ii. It is also reprinted in "the Excitement," *Boston, Lilly, Wait & Co.* 1833. 32mo, pp. 30.

Moody (S.) The Doleful State of the Damned; Especially such as go to Hell from under the Gospel; Aggravated from their Apprehensions of the Saints in Heaven. Being the Substance of Several Sermons preached at York, in the Province of Main. By Samuel Moody, M.A. Pastor of the Church of Christ there. *Boston: Printed ... by Timothy Green.* 1710. 16mo, pp. vi, 184. BA. + Second Edition. [*Ibid.*] 16mo, pp. iv, 172.

Also: A [Massachusetts] Election Sermon, ... 1748. ... *Boston.* 1748. 8vo.

Moody (J.) Joseph Embalmed. An Attempt to preserve the Memory of ... Rev. Joseph Moody of York, who deceased March 20th, 1753. ... [n. p. n. d.] Sm. 8vo, pp. 7, (1). H.

Moody (L.) The Destruction of Republicanism the Object of the Rebellion. The Testimony of Southern Witnesses. By Loring Moody ... . [*Boston:*] *Emancipation League.* [1863.] 8vo, pp. 16. + Second Edition. [*Ibid.*] + Third Edition. *Boston: Wright & Potter, Printers.* 1863. 8vo, pp. 20. H. 50314

Of the third edition there is a variation in the title, "Destruction of Democratic Republicanism."

Moody. The Destruction of the Republic, and of all Constitutional Liberty, the Object of the Rebellion. The Testimony of Southern Witnesses. Compiled by Loring Moody ... . *London: Reprinted ... for the Ladies' London Emancipation Society.* 1866. 16mo, pp. 35. BA. 50315

Moody. Facts for the People; showing the Relations of the United States Government to Slavery, embracing a History of the Mexican War ... . Compiled ... . By Loring Moody. *Boston.* 1847. 18mo, pp. 142. B., H. 50316

Moody. A History of the Mexican War, or Facts for the People, showing the relation of the United States Government to Slavery. Compiled from Official and Authentic Documents. By Loring Moody. Second Edition, with Additions and Corrections. *Boston: Bela Marsh.* 1848. 12mo, pp. 120. C., H.

Moody. A Plain Statement addressed to all Honest Democrats. By Loring Moody. *Boston: Geo. C. Rand & Avery, Printers.* 1868. 16mo, pp. 48. H. 50318

Moody (R. B.) The Evil and the Remedy. A Discourse ... on the ... National Fast, April 30, 1863. By Rev. Ruel B. Moody ... . *Boston: J. M. Hewes, Printer.* 1863. 8vo, pp. 15.

Moody (S.) A Sermon, preached at Arundel, January 12, 1800, On the Death of George Washington, By Silas Moody, A.M., Pastor of the Church in said town. ... *Portsmouth.* 1800. 8vo, pp. 16. N. 50320
One of the rarest of the Washington eulogies.

Moody (T.) Compendium of the Art of Surveying; or the Surveyor's Pocket Companion. By Thomas Moody. *Burlington, N. J.* 1771. 8vo. 50321
The first work of its kind printed in New Jersey.

Moon (C. W.) Address, Delivered on the Centennial Anniversary of St. John's Lodge, No. 1, at Portsmouth, N. H., June 24, 1836. By Chas. W. Moon. [n. p. n. d.] 8vo, pp. 80.

Mooney (T.) Nine Years in America: By Thomas Mooney ... *Dublin: James McGlashan.* 1850. 12mo, pp. 154. + Second Edition. [*Ibid.*] C. 50323

Moor (C. R.) ... A Discourse ... in Watertown, Mass. ... Oct. 14, 1853, at the Funeral of Deacon Stephen W. Trowbridge. By C. R. Moor. *Boston: Abel Tompkins.* 1854. 8vo, pp. 24. H. 50324

Moore (A.) An Oration, ... at Westmoreland, ... July 4th, 1798. By Alpheus Moore. *Walpole, Newhampshire: Printed by David Carlisle.* 1798. Sm. 4to, pp. 13. BA. 50325

Moore (A. Y.) The Life of Schuyler Colfax. By Rev. A. Y. Moore ... . *Philadelphia: T. B. Peterson & Brothers.* 1868. 8vo, pp. 21–394. Portrait. B. 50326

Moore (A.) A Memoir of the Late Rev. Savillion W. Fuller, By Rev. Asher Moore. ... *Philadelphia: J. H. Gihon & Co.* 1840. 12mo, pp. 214. Plate. C., H. 50327

Moore (A.) Notes from Plymouth Pulpit: a Collection of Memorable Passages from the Discourses of Henry Ward Beecher. By Augusta Moore. *New York.* 1859. 12mo. +

New Edition, revised and greatly enlarged. *New York: Harper & Brothers.* 1866. 12mo, pp. xxiv, 374. 50328

MOORE (B.) The Charge of the Right Reverend Benjamin Moore delivered to the Convention of ... [the Protestant Episcopal Church in New-York], ... Fifth ... of October, ... 1802. *New-York: Printed by T. and J. Swords.* 1803. 8vo, pp. 22.

Also: A Charge, delivered to the Convention of the Protestant Episcopal Church in ... New-York, ... October 5, 1808. ... *New-York: Printed by T. & J. Swords.* 1809. 8vo, pp. 22.—Pastoral Letter. ... *New York.* 1801. 8vo, pp. 16. N.—Sermon occasioned by the Death of Rev. Dr. Auchmuty, March 9, 1777. ... *New York.* 1777. 12mo.—Sermon in St. George's Chapel, New York, July 15, 1787, at the First Ordination by Bishop Provost. ... *New-York.* 1787. 4to. N.—A Sermon, ... before the General Convention of the Protestant Episcopal Church in ... New-York, ... September 12, 1804. ... *New-York: Printed by T. & J. Swords.* 1804. 8vo, pp. 15.—A Sermon, ... before the Convention of the Protestant Episcopal Church ... New-York, October 3, 1809. ... *New-York: Printed by T. and J. Swords.* 1809. 8vo, pp. 23.—A Sermon, ... before the Bible and Common Prayer Book Society of New-York, ... Feb. 27, 1810; ... . *New-York: Printed by T. and J. Swords.* 1810. 8vo, pp. 22.—... A Sermon ... preached at the Consecrating of Trinity Church, Newark, New Jersey, May, 1810. *New York?* 1810. 8vo, pp. 41.

MOORE (B. F.) An Address on the Life, Character and Public Services of Henry Clay, delivered ... August ... 1852, at Weldon, North Carolina. By B. F. Moore. *Raleigh.* 1853. 8vo, pp. 37. 50330

MOORE (C. B.) Town of Southold, Long Island. Personal Index, prior to 1698, and Index of 1698, compiled ... for the purpose of having corrections. By Charles B. Moore. *New York: John Medole, Printer.* 1868. Obl. 4to, pp. 145. 50331

Privately printed and very rare.

MOORE (C. W.) Address ... on the Centennial Anniversary of St. John's Lodge, No. 1. at Portsmouth, N. H. June 24, 1836. By Charles W. Moore ... . *Boston: Tuttle, Weeks* ... . 1836. 8vo, pp. 80. + Second Edition. *Boston.* 1846. 8vo. Plates. 50332

MOORE. To the Ingenious and Candid. The Masonic Character and Correspondence of General George Washington. By Charles W. Moore ... . *Boston.* 1830. 12mo, pp. 18. W.

Also: Address ... before the Boston Encampment of Knights Templars, April 17, 1833. ... *Boston: Printed by Moore and Sevey.* 1833. 8vo, pp. 74.—Amaranth, or Masonic Garland. Vol. I. ... *Boston.* 1828–9. 8vo.—Constitutions of the Grand Lodge of Massachusetts, and General Regulations for the Government of the Craft under its jurisdiction. With an Appendix. ... *Boston.* 1857. 8vo. C.—The Masonic Trestle-Board ... . *Boston.* 1843. 8vo, pp. 87. Plates.—The New Masonic Trestle-Board ... . *Boston: Charles W. Moore.* 1856. 12mo, pp. 98; 104. Plates. H.—The Pocket Trestle-Board ... . *Boston: Chas. W. Moore.* 1861. 32mo, pp. 80. Plate. B.

MOORE *and* SEVEY (Edwin). Trial of Moore & Sevey for a Libel on Samuel D. Greene, in the Municipal Court, Boston, July Term, 1833. Reported by Charles H. Locke. *Boston: Moore & Sevey.* 1833. 8vo, pp. 78, (1). B., S. 50334

[MOORE (Clement C.)] An Inquiry into the effects of our Foreign Carrying Trade upon the Agriculture, Population, and Morals of the Country, By Columella. ... *New-York: Printed by D. and G. Bruce.* 1806. 8vo, pp. 61. BA., S. 50335

[MOORE.] Observations upon certain passages in Mr. Jefferson's Notes on Virginia, which appear to have a tendency to Subvert Religion, and establish A False Philosophy. *New-York.* 1804. 8vo, pp. 32. B. 50336

[MOORE.] A Plain Statement, addressed to the Proprietors of Real Estate in the City and County of New York. By a Landholder. *New York.* 1818. 8vo. N. 50337

MOORE. Poems By Clement C. Moore, LL.D. ... *New York: Bartlett & Welford.* 1844. 12mo, pp. 216. BA. 50338

Printed for private distribution. Includes a "Trip to Saratoga" and "'Twas the Night before Christmas."

[MOORE.] A Sketch of our Political Condition. Addressed to the Citizens of the United States, without Distinction of Party. By a Citizen of New-York. *New-York: The Author.* 1813. 8vo, pp. 47. B., N. 50339

Also: Address ... before the Alumni of Columbia College, ... 4th of May, 1825, ... *New-York: E. Bliss & E. White.* 1825. 8vo, pp. 37. B., H.

[MOORE (Cornelius).] Masonic Biography; or Sketches of Eminent Freemasons. By one of the Craft. *Cincinnati: Masonic Review Office.* 1862. 12mo, pp. 126. 50340

MOORE. Leaflets of Masonic Biography; or Sketches of Eminent Freemasons. Edited by Cornelius Moore, A.M. *Cincinnati: Masonic Review Office.* 1863. 12mo, pp. 420. + Third Edition. *Cincinnati: Macoy & Sickels.* 1864. 12mo, pp. 420.

MOORE (D.) A Representation of Facts, Relative to the Conduct of Daniel Moore, Esquire, Collector of His Majestys Customs at Charles-Town, In South Carolina. From the Time of his Arrival in March, 1767, to the Time of Departure in September following. Transmitted By the Merchants of Charles-Town, to Charles Garth, Esquire, in London, Agent for the Province of South-Carolina; and, Recommended in a Letter

from the Honourable The Committee of Correspondence. *Charlestown, South Carolina: Printed by Charles Crouch* ... . 1767. Folio, pp. viii, 3–43. 50342

MOORE (D.), *Jr.* A Thanksgiving Sermon preached in Buffalo, New York, November 28, 1861. By Rev. D. Moore, Jr. *Buffalo: Breed, Butler & Co.* 1861. 12mo, pp. 25. 50343

MOORE (D. D. T.) A Manual of Flax Culture and Manufacture: ... also an Essay by a Western Man [C. D. Bragdon], on Hemp and Flax in the West: ... . With Botanical Descriptions and Illustrations. *Rochester, N. Y.: D. D. T. Moore.* 1863. 8vo, pp. 48. BA. 50344

Also: Moore's Rural New-Yorker. A National Illustrated Rural ... Newspaper ... Conducted by D. D. T. Moore. ... *New York.* 1849. Folio. Continued.

MOORE (D.) The African, a Tale; and other Poems. By Dugald Moore. *Glasgow: Robertson & Atkinson.* 1829. 12mo. + Second Edition. [*Ibid.*] 12mo, pp. ix, 216. C. 50345

Partly on slavery.

MOORE (E.) Oriental Fragments ... . By Edward Moore ... . *London.* 1784. 8vo. 50346

Pages 238 to 438 contain a dissertation on Sanskrit Etymologies which he traces in North and South America.

MOORE (E.) Address ... before the General Trades Union of ... New York, ... Dec. 2nd, 1833. By Ely Moore. *New York.* 1833. 8vo, pp. 32. 50347

MOORE. Speech of the Honorable Ely Moore, in reply to the Honorable Waddy Thompson and others. ... May 5, 1836. *Washington: Blair and Rives, Printers.* 1836. Rl. 8vo, pp. 15.

Another issue is entitled "Speech of Mr. Moore of New York" [as before. n. p. n. d.] 8vo, pp. 8. Also: Remarks ... on Slavery in the District of Columbia ... *Washington.* 1839. 8vo.

MOORE (E. D.) ... A Farewell Sermon ... in Barre, Mass., October 2, 1842. By Rev. E. D. Moore ... . *Boston: Printed by David H. Ela.* 1842. 8vo, pp. 32. H. 50349

Also: Life Scenes from Mission Fields: a Book of Facts, Incidents, and Results, the most material and remarkable in Missionary Experience. Condensed and arranged for popular use. ... *New York: Charles Scribner.* 1857. 12mo, pp. 358. BA.

MOORE (E. W.) Action of the Legislature of ... Texas, in reference to ... Commodore E. W. Moore, and the construction put upon the "Annexation Resolutions," by the Government of

the United States. *Washington: T. Barnard, Printer.* 1849. 8vo, pp. 14. BA. 50350

MOORE. A Brief Synopsis of the Doings of the Texas Navy under the command of Com. E. W. Moore ... . *Washington: Printed by T. Barnard.* 1847. 8vo, pp. 32. 50351

MOORE (F.) A | Voyage | to | Georgia. | Begun in the Year 1735. | Containing, An Account of the Settling the Town of | Frederica, in the Southern Part of the | Province; and a Description of the Soil, | Air, Birds, Beasts, Trees, Rivers, | Islands, &c. | With | The Rules and Orders made by the Honour- | able the Trustees for that Settle- | ment; including the Allowances of Provisions, | Cloathing, and other Necessaries to the Families | and Servants which went thither. | Also | A Description of the Town and County of Savannah, | in the Northern Part of the Province; the manner of | dividing and granting the Lands, and the Improve- | ments there: With an Account of the Air, Soil, | Rivers, and Islands in that Part. | By Francis Moore ... . | *London:* | ... *Jacob Robinson.* 1744. 8vo, pp. (2), 108, (2). 50352

"The number of the Indian tribes, the location of their territories, and the dealings of the wise and pacific Oglethorpe with them, form the subject of much of the volume. Many incidents in the life of Tomo-chi-chi are given."—FIELD. Reprinted in the "Collections of the Georgia Historical Society," Vol. I.

MOORE (F.), *Jr.* Map and Description of Texas, containing Sketches of its History, Geology, Geography and Statistics: ... And some brief remarks upon the character and customs of its inhabitants. By Francis Moore, Jr. ... *Philadelphia: H. Tanner, Junr.* 1840. 18mo, pp. 143, (1). + Second Edition. *New York: Tanner & Disturnell.* 1844. 18mo, pp. 143, (1). C.

MOORE (F.) American Eloquence: A Collection of Speeches and Addresses, by the Most Eminent Orators of America; with Biographical Sketches and Illustrative Notes, by Frank Moore. ... *New York: D. Appleton and Company.* 1857. 2 vols., 8vo, pp. vi, 576; 614. 16 Portraits. + [*Ibid.*] 1862. C. + [*Ibid.*] 1864. 2 vols., 8vo, pp. vi, 576; 614. 14 Portraits. BA. 50354

MOORE. Anecdotes, Poetry and Incidents of the War: North and South. 1860–1865. Collected ... by Frank Moore ... . *New York.* 1866. 8vo, pp. 560. 10 Portraits. + [*Ibid.*] 1867.

MOORE. ... Companion to the Rebellion Record; Being a Supplementary Volume. Edited by Frank Moore. ... *New York: G. P. Putnam.* 1862. 8vo. Portraits. BA. 50356

MOORE. Diary of the American Revolution. From Newspapers and Original Documents. By Frank Moore. ... *New York: Charles Scribner.* MDCCCLX, MDCCCLIX. 2 vols., 8vo, pp. 528; 559. 8 Portraits, 6 Maps, and 4 Plates. H. + [*Ibid.*] MDCCCLX. H. + New Edition. *New York: Charles T. Evans.* 1863. 2 vols., 8vo, pp. 528; 559. 8 Portraits, 6 Maps, and 4 Plates. B. 50357

In 1865, a so-called "Privately Printed" edition of one hundred copies was put forth, which is the same work on larger paper, impl. 8vo, with the portraits and views on India paper, and more recently a cheap edition, without the plates, has been issued in one volume, 8vo.

MOORE. Heroes and Martyrs; Notable Men of the Time. Biographical Sketches of the Military and Naval Heroes, Statesmen and Orators, distinguished in the American Crisis of 1861–62. Edited by Frank Moore. With Portraits ... . *New York: G. P. Putnam.* [1861.] 4to, pp. iv, 3–253. 40 Plates. BA., C.

First published in 20 parts; no more issued.

MOORE. Lyrics of Loyalty. Arranged and Edited by Frank Moore. *New York: George P. Putnam.* 1864. 16mo, pp. xvi, 336. H. 50359

MOORE. Materials for History Printed from Original Manuscripts. With Notes and Illustrations. By Frank Moore. First Series. *New York: Printed for the Zenger Club.* 1861. 4to, pp. (4), 9–240. Portrait of Henry Laurens. 50360

Two hundred and fifty copies printed, and not often found complete. Contains the Laurens Correspondence. The Zenger Club consisted of one person, and for some unexplained reason many copies terminate abruptly. The Club collapsed with this publication.

MOORE. Memorial Ceremonies at the Graves of our Soldiers. ... May 30, 1868. Collected ... By Frank Moore. *Washington City.* 1869. 8vo, pp. (2), 736. H. 50361

MOORE. Notable Men; a Series of Comprehensive Biographies. Edited by Frank Moore. *New York.* [n. d.] 4to.

This is "Heroes and Martyrs," No. 50358, *supra*, with a new title-page only.

MOORE. Patriot Preachers of the American Revolution, with Biographical Sketches. Edited by F[ran]k Moore. *New York.* 1862. 12mo. 50363

MOORE. Personal and Political Ballads ... Edited by Frank Moore *New York: George P. Putnam.* 1864. 16mo, pp. xv, 368. H. 50364

MOORE. The Portrait Gallery of the War, Civil, Military, and Naval: A Biographical Record. Edited by Frank Moore. *New York: Derby & Miller.* 1864. Rl. 8vo, pp. iv, 353. 60 Portraits. + [*Ibid.*] 1865. Rl. 8vo, pp. iv, 353. 60 Portraits.

MOORE. The Pulpit Record; a Collection of Sermons, by Eminent Divines, North and South with reference to the American Crisis of 1861–'62. *New York.* [n. d.] 8vo. 50366

MOORE. Rebel Rhymes and Rhapsodies. ... Edited by Frank Moore. *New York: George P. Putnam.* 1864. 16mo, pp. xiv, 299. H. 50367

MOORE. The Rebellion Record: A Diary of American Events, with Documents, Narratives, Illustrative Incidents, Poetry, etc. Edited by Frank Moore ... . With an Introductory. Address, on the Causes of the Struggle, and the Great Issues before the Country By Edward Everett. ... *New York: G. P. Putnam.* 1861–1868. 11 vols., impl. 8vo. Portraits, Maps and Diagrams. + Supplement—First Volume. ... *New York: D. Van Nostrand.* 1869. 8vo, pp. (2), vi, 759, Index, iv. Portraits, Maps and Diagrams. H. 50368

First published in parts. No. 1. appeared with a red, white, and blue cover, which style was discontinued after the first number. The work is an impartial embodiment of all that is valuable on the subject, and is for the Rebellion what Almon's "Remembrancer" is for the Revolution.

MOORE. Songs and Ballads of the American Revolution. With Notes and Illustrations by Frank Moore. ... *New York: D. Appleton & Company.* MDCCCLVI. 12mo, pp. (2), xii, 394. Plate. H. 50369

MOORE. Songs of the Soldiers ... Edited by Frank Moore *New York: George P. Putnam.* 1864. 16mo, pp. xv, 318. H.

MOORE. Women of the War; their Heroism and Self-Sacrifice. By Frank Moore ... . Illustrated ... . *Hartford, Conn.: S. S. Scranton & Co.* 1866. 8vo, pp. 596. BA. 50371

See also Barnum (H. L.), Vol. I., No. 3562.

MOORE (F.) A Treatise on American Engineering. By F. Moore ... . Illustrated by Large and Detailed Engravings. *New York.* 1855. 4to, pp. 44. Atlas in folio. 50372

MOORE (F.) Thanksgiving Sermon, ... in ... Harrisburg, Pa. By Rev. Franklin Moore, D.D. November 27th, 1862. *Philadelphia: James H. Bryson, printer.* 1862. 8vo, pp. 35. H.

MOORE (F. A.) Gems for you; from New Hampshire Authors. By F. A. Moore. *Manchester, N. H.: William H. Fisk.* 1850. 12mo, pp. (2), 312. Plate. B. 50374

MOORE (G.) Address of Gabriel Moore, to the Freemen of Alabama, in Reply to the Resolutions of the General Assembly, ... *Washington: Printed by Duff Green.* 1835. 8vo, pp. 18.

MOORE. Letter from Gabriel Moore, ... of Alabama, in Reply to the Resolutions adopted by ... his Constituents ... at Courtland. [Dated] *Washington, March* 8, 1832. 8vo, pp. 24.

MOORE (G.) Journal of a Voyage across the Atlantic, with Notes on Canada and the United States, and return to Great Britain. By George Moore. *London: Privately Printed.* 1845. Post 8vo. 50377

MOORE (G. C.) The Life of Alexander Carson, LL.D. By George C. Moore. *New York.* 1851. 12mo, pp. 156. 50378

MOORE (G. H.) Historical Notes on the Employment of Negroes in the American Army of the Revolution. By George H. Moore ... . *New York: Charles T. Evans.* 1862. 8vo, pp. 24.

MOORE. "Mr. Lee's Plan—March 29, 1777." The Treason of Charles Lee Major General Second in Command in the American Army of the Revolution. By George H. Moore ... . *New-York: Charles Scribner.* M.DCCC.LX. 8vo, pp. xii, 115, (1). 2 Portraits and 2 Facsimiles. H. 50380

A manuscript, accidentally discovered, has at length settled this vexed question, to the shame of the treacherous officer. Mr. Moore has presented the subject, with notes and facsimiles, in the most careful manner.

MOORE. Notes on the History of Slavery in Massachusetts By George H. Moore ... . *New York: D. Appleton & Co.* MDCCCLXVI. 8vo, pp. iv, 256. H. 50381

Also: ... Additional Notes on the History of Slavery in Massachusetts. [n. p. 1866.] 8vo, pp. 15. (From the "Historical Magazine," December, 1866.) H.—Slavery in Massachusetts. Two Letters from the Historical Magazine, September and October, 1866. I. From George Davis, Esq. II. From George H. Moore, Esq. *New York.* 1866. 8vo, pp. 12. The catalogue of the New York Historical Society was prepared by Dr. Moore, who is now the Superintendent of the Lenox Library in New York.

MOORE (H.) The Life of the Rev. John Wesley; ... comprehending an Account of the Great Revival of Religion, in which they were the first and chief Instruments. By the Rev. Henry Moore. *London.* 1824. 2 vols., 8vo. A. + *New York.* 1826. 8vo. 50382

MOORE (H.) Presidential Campaign of 1860. Argument on the Popular Sovereignty of Mr. Douglas. By Henry Moore, M.A. ... *Lynn: H. S. Cox, Printer.* 1860. 8vo, pp. 8. H. 50383

MOORE (H. D.) Our Country ... . A Discourse; on ... the National Fast, September 26th, 1861. By Rev. Henry D. Moore ... . *Portland: Hezekiah Packard.* 1861. 8vo, pp. 21.

MOORE. ... A Sermon ... on ... Thanksgiving, December 7, 1865, in ... Pittsburgh, Penn'a. By Rev. Henry D. Moore, ... *Pittsburgh: Printed by W. S. Haven.* 1866. 8vo, pp. 20.

Also: ... A Sermon ... at ... Portsmouth, N. H. on the Anniversary of the City Missionary Society, ... Dec. 3, 1854. ... *Portsmouth: Wm. B. Lowd.* 1854. 8vo, pp. 31

MOORE (H. J.) Scott's Campaign in Mexico, from the Rendezvous on the Island of Lobos to the taking of the City, including an account of the Siege of Puebla, with Sketches of the Country, and Manners and Customs of the Inhabitants. By H. Judge Moore. *Charleston: J. B. Nixon.* 1849. 12mo, pp. xii, 234. C. 50386

MOORE (H. J.) Wild Nell, the White Mountain Girl. By Mrs. H. J. Moore ... . *New York: Sheldon & Company.* 1860. 12mo, pp. 293. 5 Plates and Portrait. BA., C. 50387

MOORE (H. N.) Life and Services of Gen. Anthony Wayne. Founded on documentary and other evidence, furnished by his son, Col. Isaac Wayne. By H. N. Moore. ... *Philadelphia: John B. Perry.* [1845.] 18mo, pp. 210. 8 Plates. B., BA.

MOORE. The Life and Times of Gen. Francis Marion, with an Appendix; containing Biographical Notices of ... other Distinguished Officers of the Southern Campaign during the American Revolution. By H. N. Moore. *Philadelphia.* 1845. 12mo.

MOORE (H.) Memoir of Col. Ethan Allen; containing the most Interesting Incidents connected with his Private and Public Career. By Hugh Moore. *Plattsburgh, N. Y.: O. R. Cook.* 1834. 12mo, pp. 252. H. 50390

MOORE (H.) Address ... before Hollis Branch of Massachusetts Peace Society. July 4th, 1821. By Humphrey Moore ... . *Amherst: Printed by Richard Boylston.* 1821. 8vo, pp. 23. H.

Also: An Address ... before the Hillsborough Society for the promotion of Agriculture ... October 17, 1821. ... *Amherst, N. H.: Printed by Elijah Mansur.* 1822. 8vo, pp. 14.—An Address ... before the Temperance Society in Pembroke, July 4, 1836. ... *Concord: Printed by Asa McFarland.* MDCCCXXXVI. 8vo, pp. 16.—A Discourse, ... at Milford, August 20th, 1812, the Day ... for National Humiliation. ... *Amherst, N. H.: Printed by Richard Boylston.* 1812. 8vo, pp. 16.—A Discourse ... at Milford, N. H. January 12, 1815; the Day ... for National Fasting ... . *Amherst: R. Boylston, Printer.* 1815. 8vo, pp. 16.—Farewell Sermons, ... at Milford, N. H. January 10, 1836. ... *Nashua, N. H.: Printed by Alfred Beard.* 1836. 8vo, pp. 24. —An Oration, prepared to be delivered at Nottinghamwest, N. H. April 11, 1815, in celebration of the Late Peace ... between Great-Britain and the United States ... . *Amherst: R. Boylston, Printer.* 1815. 8vo, pp. 16 —An Oration, ... at Milford, N. H. March 9, 1815, occasioned by the Treaty of Peace, ... between Great-Britain and the United States. ... *Amherst: R. Boylston, Printer.* 1815. 8vo, pp. 16.—A Sermon, ... at the Funeral of the Rev. Timothy Fuller, of Merrimack ... . July 4th, 1805. ... *Amherst, N. H.: Printed by Joseph Cushing.* 1805. 8vo, pp. 15.—A Sermon, ... November 4, 1812, at the Dedication of the Meeting-House, in Dunstable, N. H. ... *Amherst, N. H.: Printed by Richard Boylston.* 1812. 8vo, pp. 16. H.—Thanksgiving Sermon ... in Milford, N. H. December 25, 1817. ... *Amherst.* 1818. 8vo, pp. 15. — ... A Sermon ... June 4, 1829, before the ... Authorities of ... New-Hampshire, on the Anniversary Election. ... *Concord: R. H. Sherburne and Co., Printers.* 1829. 8vo, pp. 32. BA.

MOORE (J. B.) Annals of the Town of Concord, in the County of Merrimack, and State of New-Hampshire, from its first Settlement, in the Year 1726, to the Year 1823. With several Biographical Sketches. To which is Added, a Memoir of the Penacook Indians. By Jacob B. Moore. ... *Concord: Jacob B. Moore.* 1824. 8vo, pp. 112. H. 50392

First published in the "Collections of the New Hampshire Historical Society," Vol. I., pp. 153–218.

[MOORE.] "The Contrast." *See* our Vol. VIII., No. 30577.

MOORE. Lives of the Governors of New Plymouth and Massachusetts Bay, from the Landing of the Pilgrims ... in 1620 to ... 1692. By Jacob Bailey Moore. *New-York.* 1848. 8vo. A. + *Boston: C. D. Strong.* 1851. 8vo, pp. ix, 439, (1). Portrait.

First published with the following title:

MOORE. Memoirs of American Governors. By Jacob Bailey Moore. Vol. I. *New-York: Gates & Stedman.* 1846. 8vo, pp. 439, (1). 4 Portraits. B., C., H. 50394

No more published.

[MOORE.] "A Peep behind the Curtain" ... . Proceedings of the State Treasurer of New Hampshire (1827). *Concord.* 1827. 8vo. N. 50395

[MOORE.] The Principles and Acts of Mr. Adams' Administration Vindicated, against the Aspersions contained in the Address of the Jackson Convention, assembled at Concord, 11th and 12th June, 1820. By a Freeman. *Concord.* 1828. 8vo.

MOORE. A Topographical and Historical Sketch of the Town of Andover, in the County of Hillsborough, N. H. By Jacob B. Moore. *Concord: Printed by Hill & Moore.* 1822. 8vo, pp. 24. W. 50397

Also included in Farmer and Moore's "Collections," Vol. I., pp. 9–24.

[MOORE.] A Vindication of Mr. Adams's Oration [Washington, July 4th, 1821]. *Concord, N. H.* 1821. 8vo, pp. 26.

Also: The Laws of Trade in the United States; being an Abstract of the Statutes of the several States and Territories concerning Debtors and Creditors. ... *New York.* 1840. 12mo. A., C., N. *See also* Vol. VI., Nos. 23837–39, *and* New Hampshire.

MOORE (James). Letter to Mr. John Stancliff, containing some Remarks on his Vindication of his Account of the Murrinitish Plague, ... in a Letter to the Author. *Philadelphia.* 1788. 8vo. W. 50399

MOORE (J.) Masonic Constitutions, or Illustrations of Free Masonry; Compiled by the direction of the Grand Lodge of Kentucky ... . By James Moore and Carey L. Clarke ... . *Lexington: Printed by Daniel Bradford.* 1808. 12mo, pp. 190. + [*Ibid.*] 1818. 50400

MOORE (J.) Complete History of the Great Rebellion; or, the Civil War in the United States, 1861–1865. By James Moore, M.D. ... With Introduction by R. Shelton Mackenzie. *Philadelphia.* 1867. 12mo. C. 50401

MOORE. History of the Cooper Shop Volunteer Refreshment Saloon. By James Moore, M.D. ... *Philadelphia: Jas. B. Rodgers.* 1866. 12mo, pp. 212. Plate. H. 50402

MOORE. Kilpatrick and our Cavalry: comprising a Sketch of the Life of General Kilpatrick, with an Account of the Cavalry Raids, Engagements, and Operations under his command, from the beginning of the Rebellion to the surrender of Johnston. By James Moore, M.D. ... *New York: W. J. Widdleton.* 1865. 12mo, pp. 3–14, 26–245. Portrait and 12 Plates. BA. 50403

Also: The World's Battle. ... *Philadelphia: Brown's ... Printing Office.* 1857. 16mo, pp. 47. H.

MOORE (J. B.) & Co. Memorial of James B. Moore and Company, asking the aid of the Government in the establishment of a regular Line of Mail Steamers from California to China and the East Indies. [*Washington:*] *Towers, printer.* [1849.] 8vo, pp. 8. H. 50404

MOORE (J. Lovell). The Columbiad: An Epic Poem on the Discovery of America and the West Indies by Columbus. In Twelve Books. By the Rev. James L. Moore ... . *London: F. and C. Rivington.* 1798. 8vo, pp. (2), 455. C. 50405

[MOORE] (J.) Of the Truth & Excellency of the Gospel.| A|Sermon|Preach'd before the|Society|for|Propagation of the Gospel|in|Foreign Parts,|at their|Anniversary Meeting,|... 20th of February, $17\frac{12}{13}$. By the Right Reverend Father in God,| John Lord Bishop of Ely. *London: Printed by Joseph Downing.* 1713. 8vo, pp. 56. B. 50406

[MOORE] (J.) A Sermon preached before the Incorporated Society for the Propagation of the Gospel in Foreign Parts, ... Feb. 15, 1782. By the Right Reverend John Lord Bishop of Bangor. *London: Printed by T. Harrison and S. Brooks.* 1782. 4to, pp. 84. M., S., W. 50407

MOORE (J.) On the Causes, Nature, and Cure of Consumptions, to which is prefixed the Character of the Massachusetts Medical Society. By John Moore, M.D. *Boston: R. Hodge.* [n. d.] 8vo. 50408

MOORE (J. G.) The Patent Office and Patent Laws; or, a Guide to Inventors ... . By J. G. Moore. *Philadelphia: Parry & M'Millan.* 1855. 12mo, pp. 342. C. 50409

[MOORE (J. H.)] The Mariner's Dictionary, or American Seaman's Vocabulary ... . Illustrated ... . *Washington City: William Duane.* 1805. 16mo, pp. iv, (2), 257. B. 50410

MOORE. A New and Complete Collection of Voyages and Travels ... and ... Geography, Describing ... Europe, Asia, Africa, and America: ... . By John Hamilton Moore ... . With ... Plates, Maps, Charts, Plans, &c. ... *London: Allard Hogg.* [1778?] 2 vols., folio, pp. (2), viii, 592; (2), 593–1172, Index, etc., (16). BA. 50411

MOORE. The Practical Navigator, and Seaman's New Daily Assistant. ... Exemplified in a Journal kept from London to the Island of St. Maries, and back again to Falmouth: ... By John Hamilton Moore ... . *London.* 1772. 8vo. + The Ninth Edition, with ... Additions. *London: B. Law.* M,DCC,XCI. 8vo, pp. (8), 296, (195). + The Eleventh Edition. [*Ibid.*] 1795. 8vo, pp. viii, 309, (203). H. + The New Practical Navigator; ... First American, from the Thirteenth English Edition ... .

Newburyport: Printed by Edmund M. Blunt. [1799?] 8vo, pp. 574. Plates and Diagrams. + Second Edition. [*Ibid.*] 1800. 8vo, pp. 570. Plates and Diagrams. B. 50412

MOORE. Sailing Directions for the West Indies and Coast of America ... . By John Hamilton Moore. ... *London.* M,DCCXCIII. 8vo, pp. 72. 50413

MOORE (J. W.) Complete Encyclopædia of Music, Elementary, Technical, Historical, Biographical, Vocal, and Instrumental. By John W. Moore. *Boston: Oliver Ditson & Co.* [1854.] Rl. 8vo, pp. 1004. Plate. B., H. 50414

The only American work of its class. The author was a bookseller and druggist, at or near Bellows Falls, Vt.

MOORE (J.) A New Systeme of the Mathematicks. By Sir Jonas Moore. *London.* 1681. 2 vols., sm. 4to. C. 50415

Contains geography, and includes maps of North and South America.

MOORE (J.) An Address ... at Pembroke, Mass. February 23, 1836, on ... the simultaneous meeting of Temperance Societies, in the United States. By Josiah Moore ... . *Plymouth: J. Thurber, printer.* 1836. 8vo, pp. 32. H. 50416

Also: A Discourse, ... in Duxbury, August 31st, 1838, on ... the burial of Samuel Alden Frazer, Esq. ... *Boston: Joseph A. Stearns.* MDCCCXXXVIII. 8vo, pp. 16. H.—Funeral Discourse commemorative of Dr. John Porter ... . April 2, 1865. *Plymouth.* 1865. 8vo, pp. 12. B.

MOORE (L. M.) An Address on the Encroachments of the Slave Power, ... in Rochester, By Lindley Murray Moore. ... *Rochester: Printed by Canfield & Warren.* 1845. 12mo, pp. 12.

MOORE (M.) A Wonderful, Startling and Thrilling Narrative of the Adventures of Miss Madeline Moore, who, in order to be near her Lover, joined the Army, was elected Lieutenant and fought in West Virginia. *Philadelphia: Barclay & Co.* [1862.] 8vo, pp. 40. 50418

The cover title reads "The Lady Lieutenant, or the Strange and Thrilling Adventures of Miss Madeline Moore."

MOORE (M.) The Memoirs and Adventures of Mark Moore, late an Officer in the British Navy. Interspersed with a Variety of original Anecdotes, selected from his Journals, when in the Tuscan, Portuguese, Swedish, Imperial, American, and British Service, in each of which he bore a Commission. Written by Himself. ... *London: The Author.* 1795. 8vo, pp. xi, 267. P.

Moore was by birth an American, and an officer in the British navy, afterwards an "itinerant play-house adventurer," etc. *See* "M. Rev.," Second Series, XVIII. 115.

MOORE (M.) Boston Revival, 1842. ... History of the Evangelical Churches of Boston, ... with ... the Revival of 1842. By Martin Moore. ... *Boston: John Putnam.* 1842. 24mo, pp. iii–148. Plate. B. 50420

MOORE. Memoirs of the Life and Character of Rev. John Eliot, Apostle of the N. A. Indians. By Martin Moore ... . *Boston: T. Bedlington.* 1822. 24mo, pp. 174 + Second Edition, revised and corrected. *Boston: Seth Goldsmith.* 1842. 24mo, pp. 144. Plate. H. 50421

MOORE. Pastoral Reminiscences. By the late Rev. Martin Moore. *New York: American Tract Society.* 1866. 18mo, pp. 84

MOORE. A Sermon, ... at Natick, January V., MDCCCXVII, containing a History of said Town, from MDCLI, to the day of delivery. By Martin Moore, A.M. ... *Cambridge: Printed by Hilliard and Metcalf.* 1817. 8vo, pp. 27. H. 50423

A rare piece of local history. It describes the labors of Eliot, and gives an exceedingly interesting account of the progress of the Gospel among the Indians there, explaining the "Natootomutcackesuk," or day of asking questions, etc.

MOORE. ... A Sermon ... at the Dedication of the Vestry of the Second Congregational Parish in Cohasset, Dec. 4, 1833. And at the Organization of the First Trinitarian Congregational Church in North Marshfield, July 4, 1835. By Martin Moore, A.M. ... *Hingham: J. Farmer, Printer.* [1835.] 8vo, pp. 24.

Also: ... A Sermon, ... in Natick, June 13, 1819. Occasioned by the death of Mrs. Hannah Coolidge ... . *Dedham: Printed by H. & W. H. Mann.* [1819.] 8vo, pp. 15. H.

MOORE (M. A.) Life of Gen. Edward Lacey, with a List of Battles and Skirmishes in South Carolina, during the Revolutionary War. By M. A. Moore, M.D. *Spartanburg, S. C.* 1859. 8vo. 50425

MOORE (M. B.) The Dixie Primer ... . By Mrs. M. B. Moore. Third Edition. *Raleigh, N. C.: Branson, Farrar & Co.* 1863. 24mo, pp. 32. + [*Ibid.*] 1864. + Fourth Edition. [*Ibid.*] 1866. 8vo, pp. 24. B. 50426

Also: The Dixie Speller. To follow the First Dixie Reader. ... *Raleigh: Branson & Farrar.* 1864. 16mo, pp. 120.—The Dixie Elementary Spelling Book ... . *Raleigh, N. C.: Branson & Farrar.* 1864. 16mo, pp. 120.—The First Dixie Reader; ... *Raleigh: Branson, Farrar & Co.* 1863. 16mo, pp. 62, (1).—The Geographical Reader, for the Dixie Children. ... *Raleigh: Branson, Farrar & Co.* 1863. Sm. 4to, pp. 48. Maps. BA.

MOORE. Primary Geography ... . By M. B. Moore. (Second Edition.) *Raleigh, N. C.: Branson, Farrar & Co.* 1864. 4to, pp. 47, (1). 6 Maps. H. 50427

I introduce these Confederate school books because they illustrate a phase of educational history, very much warped by the circumstances of the civil war. The last question and answer is a sample: "Q. What is the present drawback to our trade? A. An unlawful blockade by the miserable and hellish Yankee nation."

MOORE (M. E.) Minding the Gap and other Poems. By Mollie E. Moore. *Houston, Texas: Cushing & Cave.* 1867. 12mo, pp. 240. Portrait. B. 50428

MOORE (N. F.) An Historical Sketch of Columbia College, in the City of New-York. By N. F. Moore. *New-York: Printed for Columbia College.* 1846. 12mo, pp. 126. B. 50429

Also: Address to the Alumni of Columbia College. ... March 16, 1844. *New York.* 1848. 12mo. C.

MOORE (R. W.) Journal kept during a Tour to the West Indies and South America in 1863–64. By Rachel Wilson Moore. With Notes from the Diary of Her Husband; [and] his Memoir, by G. Truman. *Philadelphia: T. E. Zell.* 1867. 12mo, pp. 274. C. 50430

MOORE (R.) The Redemption of the Seed of God at Hand: declaring the Return of the True Church out of the Wildernesse into her former State of Glory. By Richard Moore. [n. p.:] *Printed in the Year* 1677. 8vo, pp. 168. 50431

Richard Moore was born at Worle in Somersetshire. He visited America, and wrote this piece while staying at Barbadoes.

MOORE (R.) New York Pocket Almanack. By Richard Moore. *New York.* 1762. 12mo. Continued. 50432

MOORE (R.) Addresses ... . By R. Mocre. *Trenton.* 1867. 8vo. 50433

MOORE (R.) Poor Roger's Almanack. By Roger Moore. *New York.* 1762. 12mo. Continued. 50434

MOORE (Samuel). *See* Barbadoes, I. 3280.

MOORE (S. M.) Remarks of ... Hon. Samuel M. Moore, of Virginia, ... March 10, 1834. On ... the Removal of the Public Deposites [*sic.* n. p. n. d.] 8vo, pp. 8. B. 50435

MOORE (S. S.), *and* JONES (T. W.) The Traveller's Directory; or, A Pocket Companion, shewing the Course of the Main

Road from Philadelphia to New York, and from Philadelphia to Washington. ... By S. S. Moore and T. W. Jones. *Philadelphia.* 1802. 8vo Maps. + Second Edition. *Philadelphia: Mathew Carey.* 1804. 8vo. pp. (4), 37, 19. Maps. BA. 50436

MOORE (S. W.) A Memoir of ... John Watts, M.D. ... With an Address, ... April 5th, 1831. By Samuel W. Moore, M.D. ... *New-York: G. & C. & H. Carvill.* M,DCCC,XXXI. 8vo, pp. 26. 50437

MOORE (S.) Speech of ... Hon. Sydenham Moore, ... 25th March, 1858, on Kansas, And the Evil Effects of the Slavery Agitation. *Baltimore: Printed by John Murphy & Co.* 1858. 8vo, pp. 16. BA. 50438

MOORE (T.) Marriage Customs and Modes of Courtship of the Various Nations of the Universe ... . By Theophilus Moore. With Penn's Maxims ... . Second Edition. *London: J. Bumpus.* 1820. 18mo, pp. 364. Plate. C. 50439

MOORE (T.) Mangora, King of the Timbusians. Or the Faithful Couple. A Tragedy. By Sir Thomas Moore. *London: W. Harvey.* 1718. 4to, pp. (8), 54. 50440

The scene of this curious play is laid in Spanish America. The characters are Spaniards and Indians.

MOORE (*Sir* Thomas). *See* More (T.)

MOORE (T.) The New-York Pocket Almanack for ... 1761. Calculated for the use of the Province of New York, and the neighboring Provinces. By Thomas Moore, Philo. *New York: H. Gaine.* [n. d.] 18mo, pp. 46. S. 50441

Continued to 1801. Corrected title of our No. 26331.

MOORE. Gaine's New York Pocket Almanack for ... 1802: ... By T. Moore. *New York: Printed by Ming and Young, successors to H. Gaine.* [n. d.] 18mo, pp. (90). S. 50442

Continued to 1804? *See also* Ming (A.), No. 49221.

MOORE (Thomas). Moore's American Country Almanack. *Philadelphia.* 1746. 18mo. 50443

Continued to 1768 or later. Some years have a New York imprint.

MOORE (T.) The Great Error of American Agriculture Exposed, and Hints for Improvement Suggested. By Thomas Moore. *Baltimore: The Author.* 1801. 8vo pp. 72. C. 50444

MOORE (T.) Epistles, Odes, and Other Poems. By Thomas Moore, Esq. ... *Philadelphia: John Watts.* 1806. 8vo, pp. xii, 306. + Second Edition. To which is prefixed, by the American Editor, A Notice, Critical and Biographical of the Author. [*Ibid.*] 1806. 8vo, pp. (2), xii, lxxiv, 306. BA., H. 50445

The principal poems in this collection were written during his stay in America—suggested by the character and manners of the people. Henry Stevens remarks "His own youthful importance seems to have been dwarfed for the first time in his life by Niagara, and hence his dislike to the whole country. He was nowhere properly appreciated, not even in Washington, with its Tiber, and streets of magnificent distances, but in Canada he stood on his own soil [dirt] and threw it, and felt happier. Some of his finer poems, as, for instance, the "Canadian Boat Song," are in this volume, but they are so mixed up with Tom Moore unrefined, that the volume as a whole is an unfortunate monument to the great Irish poet." The publication of this volume elicited:

An Attempt to vindicate the American Character, being ... a Reply to the ... Animadversions of Thomas Moore, Esq. *Philadelphia: Benjamin Johnson.* 1806. 8vo, pp. 43. BA. 50446

MOORE. The Life and Death of Lord Edward Fitzgerald. By Thomas Moore. ... *London: Longman, Rees* ... . 1831. 2 vols., post 8vo, pp. xi, 307, (1); 305, (1). Portrait and Map. H. + *New York: J. & J. Harper* ... . 1831. 2 vols., 12mo, pp. 220; 223. + *Paris.* 1831. 12mo. + *London.* 1832. 2 vols., post 8vo. + *New York.* 1855. 12mo, pp. 312. 50447

Fitzgerald served in the English army in the South during the American Revolution. The "Memoirs, Journal, and Correspondence of Thomas Moore. Edited by ... Lord John Russell, M.P." ... (*London: Longman, Brown* ... . 1853–56. 8 vols., 8vo. Plates. + *New York: D. Appleton and Company.* M.DCCC.LVII. 2 vols., 8vo, pp. (2), 512; (2), 513–1079. Portrait.) contain some matter relative to America.

MOORE (T. L.) Sermon before the Convention of the Protestant Episcopal Church, in the State of New York, November 3, 1789. By Rev. Thomas L. Moore. *New York.* 1789. 8vo, pp. 20. N. 50448

MOORE (T. V.) The Conservative Elements of American Civilization. An Address ... Jefferson College, Canonsburg, Pa. ... By the Rev. T. V. Moore, D.D. *Pittsburgh: J. T. Shryock.* 1853. 8vo, pp. 28. 50449

MOORE. ... A Discourse, ... at the Funeral of Samuel Taylor, Esq. in ... Richmond, Va., Feb. 24th, 1853. By Rev. T. V. Moore. *Richmond: Chas. H. Wynne, Printer.* 1853. 8vo, pp. 16

Also: ... A Discourse ... at the Funeral of Richard W. Flournoy, Esq., in ... Richmond, Va., December 1st, 1857. ... *Richmond: MacFarlane & Fergusson.* 1858. 8vo, pp. 24. BA.—Warning Words to Young Men: A Discourse, ... Richmond, Virginia, February 29th, 1852. ... *Richmond.* 1852. 8vo. S.

Moore (T.) A Universal Biographical Dictionary. By Thompson Moore. *Columbus, O.* 18—. 8vo. 50451

Moore (W.) The Addresses for Blood and Devastation, and the Addressers Exposed, in Answer to "Taxation no Tyranny," "Wesley's Calm Address" .... By W. Moore. *London.* [1776.] 8vo. 50452

Moore (W. T.) The Living Pulpit of the Christian Church: a Series of Discourses, ... from Representative Men .... With a Biographical Sketch and ... Portrait of each Contributor. ... Edited by W. T. Moore. *Cincinnati: R. W. Carroll & Co.* 1869. 8vo, pp. 589. 28 Portraits. B., C. 50453

Moore. Radicalism and Conservatism: their Influence on the Development of a True Civilization. A Discourse ... Thanksgiving Day, November 29, 1866. By Rev. W. T. Moore .... *Cincinnati.* 1866. 12mo. 50454

Also: Views of Life. Addresses on the Social and Religious Questions of the Age. ... *Cincinnati: R. W. Carroll & Co.* 1869. 16mo, pp. 351. C.

Moore (W. V.) Indian Wars of the United States, from the discovery to the present time. With accounts of the Origin, Manners, Superstitions, &c., of the Aborigines. By William V. Moore. *Philadelphia.* 1855. 8vo. 50455

John Frost is the real name of the author. It is a variation of our No. 26035.

Moore (W. W.) Address to the Public and especially the Printers of the United States. By W. W. Moore. *Washington.* 1835. 8vo. 50456

Moore (W. W.) The Non-Essentialism and the War. The Non-Essentialism of the American Church, the Cause of our Present National Calamity. By Rev. W. W. Moore. *Chicago: J. W. Dean.* 1863. 8vo, pp. 20. 50457

Moore (Z. S.) An Oration ... at Worcester, ... July 5, 1802, By Zephaniah Swift Moore, A.M. *Worcester, Massachusetts: Isaiah Thomas, Jun.* 1802. 8vo, pp. 24. H. 50458

Moore. The Sabbath .... A Sermon, ... at the Annual Election, May 27, 1818 .... By Zephaniah Swift Moore, D.D. ... *Boston: Printed by Russell, Cutler and Co.* 1818. 8vo, pp. 27.

Also: Address to the Public on Amherst Collegiate Institution, March 1, 1823. ... [n. p. n. d.] 8vo, pp. 6. — ... A Sermon, ... at the Ordination of ... Rev. Simeon Colton ... in Palmer, Massachusetts, June 19, 1811. ... *Brookfield: Printed by E. Merriam & Co.* 1811. 8vo, pp. 24. — A Sermon at the Ordination of Lemuel P.

Bates, in Whately, February 14, 1822: ... *Boston: Printed by Crocker and Brewster.* 1823. 8vo, pp. 32.

Moore's Hand-Book of Montreal, Quebec, and Ottawa; ... *Montreal.* 1860. 16mo, pp. 192. Map and 3 Plates. H. 50460

Third Annual Catalogue of Moore's Hill Male and Female Collegiate Institute. 1858–9. ... *Cincinnati: Bradley & Webb, ... Printers.* 1859. 8vo, pp. (16). Plate. H. 50461

Moorhead (J.) A Fair Narrative of the Proceedings Of the Presbytery of Boston Against ... Reverend Mr. Robert Abercrombie, ... With ... Remarks on a Pamphlet of his, in ... a Letter to a Friend. By John Moorhead, A.M. Jonathan Parsons, A.M. David MacGregore. ... *Boston: Printed by D. & Z. Fowle.* 1756. 8vo, pp. 43. BA. 50462

See Vol. I., No. 54 and 55, for other pieces on this subject. *See also* Whitefield (G.)

Moorhead (J. K.) The Nation and its Labor. Speech of Hon. J. K. Moorhead, ... April 28, 1866. *Washington.* 1866. 8vo, pp. 15. H. 50463

Also: The Perpetuity of the Union. Speech ... March 26, 1864. *Washington: McGill & Witherow, Printers.* 1864. 8vo, pp. 15. — The Rights of Labor. Speech ... March 7, 1860. [n. p. n. d.] 8vo, pp. 8. *See also* Broomall (J. M.), II. 8382.

[Moorhead (*Mrs.*)] Lines addressed to the Rev. James Davenport, on his Departure from Boston, By a Female Friend. *Boston.* 1741. 16mo. 50464

Moorhead (T.) A Second Letter to George W. Jones, Esq., in Disproof of his Falsehoods and Slanders. By Thomas Moore. *Cincinnati.* 1838. 8vo, pp. 46, 10. M. 50465

It is fair to infer there is a first letter, but I have not seen it.

Moorman (J. J.) A Directory for the ... White Sulphur Waters; with ... Remarks on their Medical Properties .... By J. J. Moorman, M.D. ... *Philadelphia: Printed by T. K. & P. G. Collins.* 1839. 12mo, pp. 35. B. 50466

Moorman. The Mineral Waters of the United States and Canada, with a Map and Plates, and General Directions for reaching Mineral Springs. By J. J. Moorman, M.D. ... *Baltimore: Kelly & Piet.* 1867. 12mo, pp. 507. Map and 5 Plates.

Moorman. The Ohio White Sulphur Springs, by J. J. Moorman, M.D., ... with observations at the Ohio White Sulphur, in 1858, by W. W. Dawson, M.D. ... *Cincinnati: Moore,*

Wilstach, Keys & Co., Printers. 1859. 8vo, pp. 72. Map and Plate. 50468

Moorman. The Virginia Springs, with their Analysis; and ... a Directory for the Use of the White Sulphur Water, ... [with] a Review of a Portion of Wm. Burke's Book on the Mineral Springs of Western Virginia, etc. and an Account of the Different Routes to the Springs. By John J. Moormann [*sic*], M.D. ... *Philadelphia: Lindsay & Blakiston.* 1847. 12mo, pp. xii, 17–219, (1). 2 Maps. B. + Second Edition. *Richmond.* 1854. 12mo. + Second Edition, ... enlarged. With ... an Account of the Natural Curiosities of Virginia. *Richmond.* 1857. 12mo. Map and Plates. A. 50469

Moorman. The Virginia Springs, and Springs of the South and West. By J. J. Moorman, M.D. ... *Philadelphia: J. B. Lippincott & Co.* 1859. 12mo, pp. xxvii, 25–403. 5 Plates and 2 Maps. B., C. 50470

Also: A Brief Notice of a Portion of a Work by William Burke, entitled "The Mineral Springs of Western Virginia." ... With ... remarks on the ... White Sulphur Water. ... *Philadelphia: Printed by Merrihew and Thompson.* 1843. 12mo, pp. 52. — Guide to the Virginia Springs and Natural Curiosities .... *Richmond.* 1854. 18mo. Map and Plates. + *Philadelphia.* 1864. 18mo. — Virginia White Sulphur Springs, with the Analysis of its Waters, etc. ... *Baltimore: Kelly, Piet & Company.* 1869. 12mo, pp. 27. — Water from the White Sulphur Springs, Greenbrier County, Va. ... [n. p. n. d.] 8vo, pp. 8. B.

Moors (J. F.) A Discourse ... at the funeral of Mr. Luther B. Lincoln, in ... Deerfield, May 13, 1855. By John F. Moors, ... *Boston: William White, Printer* .... 1855. 8vo, pp. 21. H.

Also: ... A Sermon ... at the dedication of a House of Worship, in Bernardston, October 31, 1850. ... *Greenfield: Printed by Charles A. Mirick.* 1850. 8vo, pp. 15.

Moorsom (W.) Letters from Nova Scotia; Comprising Sketches of a Young Country. By Captain W. Moorsom .... *London: Henry Colburn and Richard Bentley.* 1830. Post 8vo, pp. viii, 371. Map and 3 Plates. H. 50472

M[oosmüller] (O[swald].) St. Vincenz in Pennsylvanien. Von O. M. *New York: F. Pustet & Co.* [1873.] 8vo, pp. (4), 385. 19 Plates. C. 50473

Mooy (M.) Omstandig Journaal van de reize naar Groenland, gedaan door Commandeur Maarten Mooy, met het schip Frankendaal. *Amsterdam.* 1787. 4to, pp. 71. 50474

Circumstantial journal of a voyage to Greenland.

Mora (A.) Copia fiel de la representacion dirigida al Rey Constitucional el Sr. D. Fernando VII., por D. Antonia Mora. *Habana: Imprenta de Palmer é hijo.* 1824. Folio. 50475

Relates to the slave-trade.

Mora (——). Reimpresion del Articulo en la Miscelanea denunciando el Curso de Derocho que enseña el Señor Mora. *Lima.* 1833. 4to, pp. 42. 50476

Mora (Gerónimo). Reglas ciertas para Jueces de las Indias y sus confesores. ... *Mexico.* 1732. 8vo. 50477

Mora (J. A. de). Anagrammas en Aplauso y Gloria de la Concepcion Purissima de Maria Señora Nuestra, concebida sin la culpa original. ... *Mexico.* 1731. 8vo. 50478

Mora. Espejo Crystalino de Paciencia: la Vida, y Virtudes de la Ven. Madre sor Maria Ynes de los Dolores, Religiosa Professa en el Religioso Convento de San Lorenzo de la Ciudad de Mexico. ... *Mexico.* 1729. 4to. 50479

Mora. Vida y Virtudes Heroycas de el Exemplar y Fervoroso Hermano Juan Nicolas, coadjutor temporal de la Compañia de Jesus, y Procurador, por espacio de trienta y ochos años, en el Colegio de S. Pedro, y S. Pablo de Mexico. ... *Mexico: J. B. de Hogal.* 1726. 4to. Portrait. 50480

Mora (J. J. de). De la Libertad del comercio. ... *Mexico.* 1853. 8vo. 50481

Mora (J. M.) Memoria que para informar sobre el Origen y Estado Actuel de las Obras emprendidas para el Desagüe de las Lagunas del Valle de Méjico, presentó a la Excma. Diputacion Provincial el vocal Dr. D. José Maria Mora. *Méjico.* 1823. 8vo, pp. 62. Maps. C. 50482

Also: Defensa de J. M. Mora contra las accusaciones mentirosas y contra las intrigas de D. J. Reinosa. *Mexico.* 1838. 8vo, pp. 58.

Mora (J. M. L.) Mejico y sus Revoluciones, obra escrita por Jose Maria Luis Mora, ciudadano de los Estados-Unidos Mexicanos. *Paris: Rosa.* 1836. 8vo, Vol. I., pp. xvi, 538; Vol. III., pp. xv, 450; Vol. IV., pp. viii, 449, xliii. 50483

Vol. II. was never published. "To be completed in eight volumes."—Rich.

Mora. Obras sueltas de Jose Maria Luis Mora, ciudadano Mejicano. (Revista Politica. Credito publico.) *Paris: Librairie de Rosa.* 1837. 2 vols., 8vo, pp. (4), ccxcix, 468; (2), 513.

Mora (J. G. de). *See* Gomez de Mora (J.), VII. 27765.

Moraes y Vasconcelos. *See* Botello de Moraes, II. 6797.

Moraes (A. J. M.) *See* Mello Moraes [A. J.], XI. 47456–59

Moraes (E. J. de). Navegação interior do Brasil, Noticia dos projectos apresentados para a juncção de diversas bacias hydrographicas do Brasil, ou rapido esboço da futura rêde geral de suas vias navegareis, por Eduardo José de Moraes. *Rio de Janeiro.* 1869. 8vo, pp. 248. Map. 50485

Moraes Navarra (José Gregorio de). Discurso sobre o melhoramento da economia rustica do Brazil, pela introducção do arado, refórma das fornalhas conservação de suas mattas .... *Lisboa.* 1799. 12mo, pp. 20. 50486

[Moragne (*Miss*).] The British Partizan: a Tale of the Olden Time. By a Lady of South Carolina. *Macon, Ga.: Burke, Boykin & Company.* 1864. 8vo, pp. 157. C. 50487

Moragne (W. C.) An Address, ... at New Bordeaux, ... S. C., November 15, 1854, on the 90th Anniversary of the Arrival of the French Protestants .... By W. C. Moragne, Esqr. ... *Charleston, S. C.: Printed by James Phynney.* 1857. 8vo, pp. 48.

Morais (S.) A Discourse ... before the Congregation Mikvé Israel of Philadelphia, at their Synagogue ... June 1, 1865, the day ... for Fasting, Humiliation, and Prayer, for the Untimely Death of the late lamented President of the United States, Abraham Lincoln. By Rev. S. Morais .... *Philadelphia: Collins, Printer.* 5625=1865. 8vo, pp. 8. 50489

Morais. A Thanksgiving Sermon, ... By the Rev. S. Morais, ... November 26, 5624=1864. The National Thanksgiving Day .... *Philadelphia: Collins, Printer.* 5624. 8vo, pp. 11.

Moral y Castillo (Jose Antonio de). Sermon Panegyrico Funebre, que en las Reales Exequias de la Sra. D. Isabel Farnesio, en ... Puebla de los Angelos, il dia 29 Jan. 1767. ... *Mexico, et en Puebla de los Angeles. Año* 1767. 4to, 22 leaves. 50491

The Moral Almanac, for ... 1852. ... *Philadelphia: Tract Association of Friends.* [1851.] 18mo, pp. (36). Continued. B.

The Moral Character of the American Government. *New York.* 1838. 8vo. 50493

Moral Education. By a Disciple of the Old School Philosophy. *New-Haven: Simeon Jocelin.* 1804. 8vo, pp. 45, (1).

The Moral State of Nature, or Travels over the Most Interesting Parts of the Globe. *Middletown, N. J.* 1790. 12mo.

Morales (Ambrosio de). Continuacion de la Coronica General de España de Ocampo. Prossiguiendo adelante de los Cinco Libros de la Coronica de Ocampo, hasta el Rey don Bermudo el tercero deste nombre. ... *Alcala.* 1573.–*Cordova.* 1586. Folio.

These Chronicles are of considerable rarity. "Florian de Ocampo ought to be read, as the information he gives is an indispensable requisite to the understanding the old historians. The continuation of Morales should follow; he has excelled all others in the indefatigable diligence with which he has collected all the documents that were worthy of any consideration, from the most remote period up to his own time."—Mondexar, *in Noticia.*

Morales (J. A. D.) Practica de la Doctrina Christiana. Obra vtilissima para los curas, y Confessores de Yndios, y de rusticos. Por J. Antonio Davila Morales, Rector del Colegio Seminario de la Ciudad de la Plata. *Lima: F. Sobrino.* 1730. 4to. 50497

On page 85 commences a Catechism in the Quichua language.

Morales (J. B.) Esposicion que hace con el objeto de escitar el patriotismo de los habitantes del Departamento de Guanajuato, á que contribuyan para los gastos que deben erogarse en la guerra contra Tejes y los Estados-Unidos de America. Por J. B. Morales, Gobernador de Guanajuato. *Guanajuato.* 1845. 4to, pp. 7. 50498

Morales (J. B.) El Gallo Pitagórico. ... [*Mexico.*] 1845. 8vo. Plates. + Nueva edicion .... *Mexico.* 1857. 8vo. 100 Plates. 50499

A series of curious and amusing caricatures of Mexican society. Also: Disertacion contra la Tolerancia Religiosa .... *Mejico.* 1831. 8vo.

Morales (Jose de). Exposicion del Secretario de Estado, del Despacho de Negocios Eclesiasticos al Congreso General Constituyente del Peru .... *Lima.* 1827. 4to, pp. 18. 50500

Morales. Manifestacion del estado de la hacienda de la Republica del Peru enfin de Abril de 1827. Presentada al soberano congreso constituyente por el ciudadano encargado de la direccion del ministerio Jose de Morales y Ugalde. *Lima.* 1827. 4to, pp. 53. 50501

Morales (L.) Oracion gratulatoria que en la solemne funcion dispuesta por el beneficio incomparable de la libertad y gloriosa independencia Mejicana. ... *Puebla.* 1821. 4to, 21 leaves.

Morales y Duarez (V.) Honores Patrios consagrados a la tierna memoria del Señor Don Vicente Morales y Duarez, Presidente del augusto congreso de Córtez, por el excmo. cabildo de esta Capital de Lima, en VII. de Noviembre de 1812. *Lima: Imprenta ... por Don Bernardino Ruiz.* 1812. 8vo, pp. lii. Port.

Morales (V.) Compendio de la Vida del V. P. Juan de Santiago .... *Córdoba.* [n. d.] 8vo. 50504

The Morality of a Citizen, a Visitation Sermon; with a View to the present alarming Situation of Public Affairs. *London: J. Kearsly.* 177–. 8vo. 50505

"The American dispute is the author's great object."—*Monthly Review*, LIV. 167.

... The Morality of the Nebraska Bill. [n. p. n. d.] 8vo, pp. 32. B. 50506

From the "New Englander" for May.

The Morality of Public Men. *See* [Vernon-Harcourt (W. G.)]

Moran (C.) Money. By Charles Moran. ... *New York: D. Appleton and Company.* 1863. 12mo, pp. 228. BA. 50507

Morán de Butròn (J.) La Azvcena de Qvito, que brotò en el florido Campo de la Iglesia en las Indias Occidentales, la Venerable Virgin Mariana de Jesus, Flores, y Paredes, Beata Jesuita, esclarecida en Virtudes, Profecias y Milagros. Consagrada à las Aras de Maria Santissima, en su prodigiosa Imagen de Loreto. Breve Epitome sacado de la vida, que latamente escriviò el Padre Jacintho Morán de Butròn, de la Compañia de Jesus. *Con licencia en Lima, por Joseph de Contreras, Impressor Real.* 1702. 12mo, pp. (26), 192. Portrait. + [*Ibid.*] 1732. J.C.B. + *Reimpresa en Mexico.* 1732. 50508

A corrected title of our No. 9665, Vol. II.

Morán de Butròn. Vida de la Beata Mariana de Jesus de Paredes y Flores, conocida vulgarmente bajo el nombre de la Azucena de Quito. ... *Madrid.* 1854. 8vo. 50509

Moran y Crivelli (Tomas). Juicio Critico sobre el Sistema de Hacienda en Mexico, segun la Teoria Francesa .... *Mexico.* 1865. 4to. 50510

Morancy (A.) Monsieur de la Crocheterie, ou la nouvelle du sept Decembre mil sept cent quatre vingt-dix, comédie en un acte et en prose, avec un divertissement, par M. Alexandre Morancy. *Cape Français.* 1791. 8vo. P. 50511

Morange (W. D.) A Poem delivered ... on the Opening of Tweddle Hall, June 28th, 1860. By William D. Morange. *Albany: J. Munsell.* 1860. 8vo, pp. 15. C. 50512

[Morato (Francisco Manuel Trigoso de Aragão).] Elogio historico da Princeza do Brazil D. Maria Francisca Benedicta, escripto em Fevereiro de 1834. *Paris: Paul Renouard.* 1836. 4to, pp. 14. 50513

Moravians. An Account of the United Brethrens' Missions among the Heathen [in South Carolina, St. Thomas, etc.]. *London.* 1788. 8vo. 50514

Anecdotes of Missionary Worthies, in the Moravian Church. ... *Philadelphia: American Sunday School Union.* 1832. 16mo, pp. 116. C. 50515

Briève et Fidèle. *See* Vol. II., No. 7935.

Catalogue of the Officers and Students of the Moravian College. *Bethlehem.* 1868. 8vo, pp. 16. H. 50516

Catalogue of the Officers, Teachers, and Pupils of the Moravian Young Ladies' Seminary, Bethlehem, Pa. From July 1st, 1860, to March 1st, 1861. *Bethlehem.* 1861. 8vo, pp. 24. Continued. H. 50517

A Collection of Hymns, for the use of the Christian Indians of the United Brethren in North America. Translated from the German by David Zusberger. *Philadelphia.* 1803. 12mo, pp. 358. + *Reprinted, Bethlehem.* 1847. 12mo. 50518

Concise Historical Account of the Present Constitution of the Protestant Church of the United Brethren adhering to the Confession of Augsburg. *London.* 1775. Post 8vo. + *Philadelphia.* 1836. 12mo, pp. 71. 50519

The Fourth Centennial Anniversary of the Moravian Church. Three Sermons ... March 1, 1857, ... Philadelphia, by the Rev. Edmund De Schweinitz, Pastor; Rev. J. F. Berg, D.D. ... Rev. R. Newton .... *Philadelphia.* 1857. 18mo, pp. 67. S. 50520

The History of the Moravians, From their first Settlement ... to the present Time; ... . Translated from the German. *London: J. Robinson.* 1754. 8vo, pp. (8), 208. H. 50521

See also Vol. VIII., Nos. 32082 and 32185.

Instructions for the Members of the Unitas Fratrum, who minister in the Gospel among the Heathen. *Printed for the Brethren's Society.* 1784. 8vo. 50522

A Letter to a Friend. *See* Vol. x, No. 40386.

Memorial of the Dedication. *See* No. 47671.

Memorials of the Moravian Church. Edited by William C. Reichel. Vol. I. ... *Philadelphia: J. B. Lippincott & Co.* 1870. 8vo, pp. 366. 50523

Missions of the Moravians. *See* No. 49483.

The Moravian Church Miscellany. A Monthly Journal of the United Brethren in America. ... 1850. ... *Bethlehem, Pa.* [n. d.] 8vo. 50524

Contains reports on the Indians.

The Moravian Indian Boy. A Tale of the Pilgrimage of the Moravian Indians from the Susquehanna to the Muskingum. ... *Philadelphia: Presbyterian Board of Publication.* [1870.] 18mo, pp. 206. 3 Plates. C. 50525

The Moravian Missions. *See* [Hagen (F. F.)], VII. 29509.

Transactions of the Moravian Historical Society. 1857–58. *Nazareth.* 1859. 8vo, pp. 31. Continued. 50526

[MORAZAN (F.)] Al Pueblo Centro-Américano. *David, Julio* 16, 1841. 8vo, pp. 16. 50527

Also: A la Memoria de Morazan. [Par Quinonez. *San Salvador.*] 1852. Folio, 1 leaf. — Testamento del jeneral Francisco Morazan; San Jose, Sept. 15 de 1842. [*San Salvador.* n. d.] Folio, 1 leaf. — Articulos publicados en el Diario de la Marina de la Habana ... . *Leon: Imprenta de Minerva, Año de* 1848. 25 leaves.

MORCILLO RUBIO DE AUÑON (Pedro). Magnifica Parentacion, y Funebre Pompa, en la occasion de transladarse de el Sepvltvra de los Sres. Arzobispos y Venerables Prebendados, al Sepulchro, y Monumento, que se erigió en la Capilla de la Purissima Concepcion de esta Sta. Iglesia Metropolitana de Lima, el cuerpo de el Exmo é Ilmo Sr. Dr. Diego Morcillo Rubio de Avñon, Obispo de Nicaragua y Arzobispo de las Metropolitanas de la Plata y de Lima, etc. Por D. Alfonso Carrio y Morcillo Rubio de Auñon. *Lima: Por Antonio Gutierres de Zeballos.* 1744. 4to, 60 leaves. Plate. J.C.B. 50528

MORCILLO RUBIO. Oracio qve se dixo en la solemne y magnifica translacion, ... de el Cadaver de el Exmo. y Illmo. Diego Morcillo Rubio de Auñon, su Tio, Obispo, que fué de las Santas Iglesias Cathedrales de Nicaragua; Arzobispo de S. Iglesias de la Plata y Lima: dos veces Virrey Governador y Capitan General de estos Reynos de el Peru. *Lima.* 1744. 4to, 24 leaves. J.C.B.

MORDACQUE (L. H.) History of the Names of Men, Nations and Places in their connection with the Progress of Civilization. By L. H. Mordacque. *London.* 1864. 2 vols., 8vo.

MORDECAI (A.) Artillery for the United States Land Service, as devised and arranged by the Ordnance Board. Prepared by Major Alfred Mordecai. *Washington.* 1848–49. 8vo. 141 colored Plates. C., S. 50531

MORDECAI. ... Military Commission to Europe, in 1855 and 1856. Report of Major Alfred Mordecai ... . *Washington.* 1860. 4to, pp. vii, 232. 21 Plates. C. + *Washington: George W. Bowman, Printer.* 1861. 4to, pp. vii, 232. Plates. B. 50532

[MORDECAI (Samuel).] Richmond in By-Gone Days; being Reminiscences of An Old Citizen. ... *Richmond, Va.* 1856. 12mo, pp. 321. S. 50533

MORDECAI. Virginia, especially Richmond, in By-Gone Days; with a Glance at the Present: being Reminiscences and Last Words of An Old Citizen. By Samuel Mordecai. ... Second Edition, with many Corrections and Additions. *Richmond: West & Johnston.* 1860. 12mo, pp. 359. H., S. 50534

MORDEN (R.) Geography Rectified: or, a Description of the World, in all its Kingdoms, Provinces, Countries ... . By Robert Morden. *London: Robert Morden.* 1680. 4to. 60 Maps. + Second Edition. [*Ibid.*] 1688. 4to. + The Third Edition Enlarged ... . *London: Robert Morden and Thomas Cockirell.* MDCXCIII. 4to, pp. (8), 626, Index, (72), Advt. (2). + Fourth Edition, Enlarged. ... *London: R. Morden and T. Cockirell.* MDCC. 4to, pp. (10), 626, (72). B. 50535

America occupies about sixty pages. So much as relates to West New Jersey was reprinted in the "Historical Magazine," VI. 191.

MORE (C.) The War in New-England, visibly ended. King Philip, that barbarous Indian, now Beheaded, and most of his Bloudy Adherents submitted to Mercy, the rest fled far up in the Countrey, which hath given the Inhabitants Encouragement to prepare for their settlement. Being a True and Perfect Account brought in by Caleb More, Master of a Vessel newly arrived from Rhode Island, and published for general satisfaction. *London: Printed by J. B., for Francis Smith.* 1677. Folio, pp. 4. J.C.B.

A piece of uncommon rarity.

MORE (F. J.) Nachrichten über die Früheren Einwohner von Nord Amerika und ihre Denkmäler. Von Franz Joseph More. *Heidelberg.* 1827. 12mo. 50537

Contains a plan of the western mounds, antiquities, etc.

MORE (H.) Slavery. A Poem. By Hannah More. *London: T. Cadell.* M.DCC.LXXXVIII. 4to, pp. (2), 20. + *Philadelphia.* 1788. 12mo, pp. 12. + *New York: J. & A. McLean.* 1788. 12mo, pp. 19. 50538

See "Monthly Review," LXXVIII. 246.

MORE (J.) Relation de deux caravelles envoyées en 1618 par le roi d'Espagne sous la conduite de D. Juan de More pour découvrir le détroit de Lemaire. *Amsterdam.* 1622. 50539

Title from Ternaux, No. 448.

[MORE (John J.)] Five Years in a Lottery Office; or, an Exposition of the Lottery System in the United States. By Thomas Doyle [pseudonym]. *Boston: S. N. Dickinson.* 1841. 12mo, pp. 62. N., P. 50540

MORÉ (J. L.) Le Brésil en 1852 et sa colonisation future. Notice écrite sur des documents communiqués par le consulat suisse a Rio de Janeiro. *Genève et Paris.* 1852. 8vo, pp. (6), 318, (2). C. 50541

MORE (T.) Libellus vere aureus nec|minus salvtaris qvam festi-|uus de optimo reip. statu, deq3 noua Insula Vtopia|authore clarissimo viro Thoma Moro inclytæ|ciuitatis Londinensis ciue & viscomite cu-|ra M. Petri Aegidii Antuerpiesis, & arte|Theodorici Martini Alustensis, Ty-|pographi almæ Louaniensium| Academiæ nunc primum|accuratissime edi-|tus ... . [*Lovanii:*] *Theodorico Martini.* [1516.] 4to, 53 leaves. 50542

First edition; of the greatest rarity. The only copy I have seen is in the British Museum.

MORE. De opti-|mo reipv. statv, deqve|noua insula Vtopia, libellus ue|rè aureus, nec minus salutaris|quam festiuus, clarissimi disertis-|simique uiri Thomae Mori in-|clytæ ciuitatis Londinensis ciuis|& Vicecomitis.|... [Colophon:] *Basileæ apvd Io.| Frobenivm men-|se Decembri|an.* M.D.XVIII. Sm. 4to, pp. 355, (1). H. + *Lovanii,|Excudebat Servatius Sassenus impensis viduæ Arnoldi Birkmanni. Anno Salutis* 1548. *Mense Iunio.* 12mo, pp. 182. J.C.B. 50543

MORE. A fruteful and pleasaunt worke of the beste state of a publyque weale, and of the newe yle called Utopia: written in Latine by Syr Thomas More Knight, and translated into Englyshe by Raphe Robynson Citizein and Goldsmythe of London, at the procurement, and earnest request of George Tadlowe Citizein and Haberdassher of the same Citie. *Imprinted at London by Abraham Vele, dwelling in Pauls churchyarde at the sygne of the Lambe. Anno,* 1551. 12mo. J.C.B. 50544

Of the very numerous editions of this philosophical romance, we take notice only of a few, and content ourselves with a brief extract as below:

"One Raphael Hythlodaye, a native of Portugal, for the desire that he had to see, and know farre countreys of the worlde, joyned himself in company with Amerike Vespuce, and in the iii last voyages of those iiii that be nowe in printe, and abrode in every mannes handes, he continued styll in his company, saving that in the last voyage he came not home agayne with him. For he made such meanes and shift as to be one of the xxiiii whiche in the ende of the last voyage were left in the countrey of Gulike."

MORE. A frutefull|pleasaunt, & wittie worke,|of the best state of a publique|weale, and of the newe yle, called Uto-|pia: written in Latine, by the right wor-|thie and famous Syr Thomas More|Knyght, and translated into Englishe by|Raphe Robynson, sometime fellowe|of Corpus Christi College in Ox-|ford, and nowe by him at this se-|conde edition newlie peru-|sed and corrected, and|also with diuers no-|tes in the margent|augmented.| *Imprinted at London, by|Abraham Uele, dwellinge in|Paules churchyarde, at the signe|of the Lambe.*| [Colophon:] *Imprinted at London in Paules Church yarde, at the sygne of the Lambe, by Abraham Veale.* M.D.LVI. 4to, pp. 2no, (9), 131, and (5) leaves. H. 50545

MORE. Utopia:|Written in Latin by|Sir Thomas More,|...| Translated into English.|*London;|Printed for Richard Chiswell* ... MDCLXXXIV. Sm. 8vo, pp. (22), 206. 50546

This edition was translated by G. Burnet.

MORE. The Common-Wealth of Utopia. Containing a learned and pleasant Discourse of the best State of a Publick Weal, as it is found in the new Island called Utopia. Written by the Right Honourable Sir Thomas Moore ... . *London; Printed. Philadelphia: James Chattin.* 1753. 8vo, pp. (2), 126. P.

More Light on Masonry, or Morgan Revived, with an Appendix, by one of the Fraternity ... . *Rochester.* 1827. 8vo, pp. 88. 50548

"More than Conqueror," or Memorials of Col. J. Howard Kitching, Sixth New York Artillery, Army of the Potomac. ... *New York.* 1873. 12mo. 50549

... More than One Hundred Reasons why William Henry Harrison should and will have the Support of the Democracy, for President ... in preference to Martin Van Buren. By a Workingman. *Boston: Printed by Tuttle* ... . 1840. 8vo, pp. 16.

MOREAU DE JONNÈS (Alexandre). Aventures de Guerre au temps de la République et du Consulat. ... *Paris.* 1858. 2 vols., 8vo. 50551

Relates to the war in the Antilles, and contains interesting information and historical facts.

MOREAU. Le Commerce au Dix-Neuvième Siècle: État actuel et ses Transactions dans les Principales Contrées des deux Hemisphères: Causes et Effets de son Agrandissement et sa Décadence, moyens d'accroître et de consolider la prospérité agricole, industrielle, coloniale, et commerciale de la France. Par Alexandre Moreau de Jonnès. *Paris: l'Auteur.* 1825. 2 vols., 8vo, pp. xii, 395; (4), 362, (2). C. 50552

MOREAU. Essai de l'hygiène militaire des Antilles. ... *Paris.* 1816. 8vo, pp. 84. 50553

MOREAU. Estadistica de España ... . Escrita en francés por Mr. Moreau de Jonnés. Traducida y adicionada. Por el Lic. D. Pascual Madoz é Ifañez ... . *Barcelona: Imprenta de M. Rivadeneyra y Compañia.* 1835. 8vo, pp. 416, folded leaf. H.

MOREAU. Histoire Physique Des Antilles Françaises; savoir: la Martinique et les Iles de la Guadeloupe; ... Par Alexandre Moreau de Jonnes ... . Tome Premier. *Paris: Imprimerie de Migneret.* 1822. 8vo, pp. (2), 560. Table. 50555

No more published.

MOREAU. Monographie Historique et Médicale de la Fièvre Jaune des Antilles; et Recherches physiologiques sur les lois du développement et de la propagation de cette Maladie Pestilentielle. Lues à l'Académie ... . *Paris.* 1820. 8vo, pp. 10, 384. A., S. + [*Ibid.*] 1821. 8vo, pp. 24. 50556

MOREAU. Monographie du Trigonocephale des Antilles, ou grande Vipère fer-de-lance de la Martinique. ... *Paris.* 1816. 8vo, pp. 42. 50557

MOREAU. Recherches Statistiques sur l'Esclavage Colonial et sur les moyens de le supprimer, Par Alex. Moreau de Jonnès, ... *Paris: Imprimerie de Bourgogne et Martinet.* 1842. 8vo, pp. (4), 275. A., C. 50558

MOREAU. Statistique de l'Espagne. ... Par Alex. Moreau de Jonnès. *Paris: Imprimerie de Cosson.* 1834. 8vo, pp. viii, 318. Map. A., H. 50559

Includes the Spanish colonies.

MOREAU. Tableau du Climat des Antilles. Par A. Moreau de Jonnès. *Paris.* 1817. 8vo, pp. 83. N. 50560

Also: Observations sur les Géophages des Antilles. ... *Paris.* 1816. 8vo, pp. 12. — Précis Historique ... de La Fièvre Jaune a la Martinique, en 1802 (1); ... [n. p. n. d.] 8vo, pp. 16. H.

MOREAU (C.) Les Prêtres Français Émigrés aux États-Unis, Par M. C. Moreau. *Paris: Charles Douniol.* 1856. 12mo, pp. (4), 520. B. 50561

MOREAU (César). Chronological Records of the British Royal and Commercial Navy, 827–1827, founded on Official Documents ... . *London: Treuttle & Wurtz.* 1827. Oblong folio, pp. (2), 85. C. 50562

Also: State of the Trade of Great Britain with all parts of the World, from the year 1697 to 1822 ... . *London.* 1824. 8vo. Chart. C.

[MOREAU (*M.*)] Lettres d'un François à un Hollandois Au sujet des Differends Survenus entre la France & la Grande-Bretagne, Touchant leurs Possessions respectives dans l'Amérique Septentrionale. [n. p.] MDCCLV. Sm. 8vo, pp. 174. A., B., H. + *Paris: P. la Rive.* 1755. 4to, pp. 90. 50563

See Vol. IV., No. 16023, for another work on this subject.

[MOREAU.] Mémoir contenant le précis [etc.] *See* No. 47511

MOREAU (H.) Plaidoirie de Me Henry Moreau pour les États-Unis d'Amérique contre MM. Arman et Consorts ... 1868. *Paris: Imprimerie Simon Raçon et Compagnie.* 1868. 4to, pp. (4), 84. H. 50564

MOREAU. La Politique Française en Amérique 1861–1864 Par M. Henry Moreau *Paris: E. Dentu.* 1864. 8vo, pp. 176.

MOREAU DE DAMMARTIN. Explication de la Pierre de Taunston [*sic*]. Par Moreau de Dammartin. *Paris.* [n. d.] 8vo, pp. (2), 28 (autographié). 2 Plates. 50566

MOREAU (J. N.) Testimonials to the merits of Thomas Paine, ... compiled by Joseph N. Moreau. ... *Burlington, N. J.: F. L. Taylor.* 1861. 12mo, pp. 60. Portrait. H. 50567

MOREAU DE SAINT-MÉRY (Médéric Louis Élie). Considerations présentées aux vrais amis du repos et du bonheur de la France à l'occasion des nouveaux mouvemens de quelques soi-disant Amis des noirs. Par M. L. E. Moreau de Saint Mery, deputé de la Martinique ... . *Paris.* 1791. 8vo, pp. 74. C.

MOREAU. De la Danse. ... *A Parme: Imprimé par Bodoni.* 1801. 16mo. + [*Ibid.*] 1803. 12mo. Portrait. 50569

Both editions are the same, in fact. Treats almost exclusively on the dancing of the Creoles. The author was a native of Port Royal.

MOREAU. Description topographique et politique de la partie Espagnole de l'Isle Saint-Domingue; Avec des Observations générales sur le Climat, la Population, les Productions, le Caractère et les Mœurs des habitans ... . Par M. L. E. Moreau de Saint-Méry ... *Philadelphie: l'Auteur.* 1796. 2 vols., 8vo, pp. 8, xlix, (3), 307, (1); 311 [*i. e.* 311], (1). Map. C., H. 50570

MOREAU. Description topographique, physique, civile, politique et historique de la partie Française de Saint-Domingue. Avec des Observations générales sur sa Population, sur le Caractère & les Mœurs de ses divers habitans; sur son Climat, sa Culture, ses Productions, son Administration ... . Accompagnées des détails les plus propres à faire connaître l'état de cette colonie à l'époque du 18 Octobre 1789 ... . Par M. L. E. Moreau de Saint-Méry. ... *A Philadelphie: l'Auteur.* 1797–98. 2 vols., 4to, pp. xix, (1), 788; viii, 856. Map and Table. A., H. 50571

This narrative, more than any other, gives us a correct idea of the last state of the colony of Saint Domingo before the insurrection. Also: Extrait de la Description Topographique, Physique, et Historique de Partie Française de l'île St. Domingue. ... *Paris: Imprimerie de Goetschy.* 1828. 8vo, pp. 40.

MOREAU. A Topographical and Political Description of the Spanish Part of Saint-Domingo, containing General Observations on the Climate, Population, and Productions; ... By M. L. E. Moreau de Saint-Mery. ... Translated from the French by William Cobbett. ... *Philadelphia: The Author.* 1796. 2 vols., 8vo, pp. 8, 8, liv, 314; 318, (1). Map. BA., H. + [*Ibid.*] 1798. 2 vols., 8vo, pp. 8, liv, 314; 318, (1). B., C. 50572

The edition dated 1798 is really the same as the earlier, but with new title-pages.

MOREAU. Loix et Constitutions des Colonies Françoises de l'Amérique sous le vent; suivies, 1°. d'un Tableau raisonné des différentes parties de l'Administration actuelle de ces Colonies: 2°. d'Observations générales sur le Climat, la Population, la Culture, le Caractère et les Mœurs des Habitans de la partie Françoise de Saint-Domingue: 3°. d'une Description Physique, Politique et Topographique des différens Quartiers de cette même partie; le tout terminé par l'Histoire de cette Isle et de ses dépendances, depuis leur découverte jusqu'à nos jours. Par M. Moreau de Saint-Méry ... *Paris: Chez l'Auteur* ... . [1784–'90.] 6 vols., 4to, pp. lij, 770, (2); xvj, 851; viii, 936; x, 914; xiv, 976; xvi, 962, xv. A., C., H. 50573

The title calls for a History of the Island of St. Domingo, but this history is not contained in these six volumes.

MOREAU. Mémoire sur une espèce du Coton nommé à Saint-Domingue, Coton de soie, ou Coton de Sainte-Marthe. Par M. Moreau de Saint-Mery; ... *A Paris: De l'imprimerie de la Veuve D'Houry & Debure* ... . 1790. 8vo, pp. 20. P. 50574

MOREAU. Opinion de M. Moreau de St-Méry, député de la Martinique sur la motion de M. de Curt, député de la Guadeloupe. *Paris: Imprimerie Nationale.* 1789. 8vo, pp. 20. 50575

Relative to the establishment of a committee to be particularly intrusted with the examination of all colonial matters. Not mentioned by Quérard.

[MOREAU.] Des Prisons de Philadelphie. Par un Européen. *Philadelphie: Imprimé & se trouve chez Moreau De St-Méry, Janvier,* 1796. 8vo, pp. 44. P. 50576

[MOREAU.] On the Prisons of Philadelphia. By an European. *Philadelphia: Printed & Sold by Moreau de Saint-Méry, January,* 1796. 8vo, pp. 46. P. 50577

MOREAU. Recueil de Vues des Lieux Principaux de la Colonie Françoise de Saint-Domingue, gravées par les soins de M. Ponce, ... accompagnées de Cartes et Plans de la même Colonie, gravés par les soins de M. Phelipeau, Ingénieur Géographe; Le tout principalement destiné à l'Ouvrage intitulé: Loix et Constitutions des Colonies Françoises de l'Amérique sous le Vent, avec leur Description, leur Histoire, &c. Par M. Moreau de Saint-Méry, ... *Paris.* 1791. Folio, pp. (2). 31 Plates. B. 50578

MOREAU (P.) Histoire | des | Derniers Trovbles | dv Bresil. | Entre les Hollandois | et les Portvgais. | Par Pierre Moreau ... . *Paris: Avgvstin Covrbé.* M.DC.LI. Sm. 4to, pp. (6), 158. H., S.

This rare work forms Part III. of [Morisot's] "Relations veritables et cvrieuses," but, having a title and separate pagination, it is sometimes found alone.

MOREAU. Klare en Waarachtige | Beschryving | Van de leste Beroerten en Afval der Portugezen in | Brasil; | Daar in d'oorsprong dezer zwarigheden en oor- | logen klarelijk vertoont worden. | In de Fransche taal beschreven door Pierre Moreau van Parrey | in Charollois, die zelf in dat Lant geweest, en d'oorzaken dezer beroerten | naaukeuriglijk onderzocht, en getrouwelijk beschreven heeft. | Met de Reisbeschrijving van de zelve Schrijver naar Brasil, en | de vreemdigheden, die hem daar in ontmoet zijn. | Door J. H. Glazemaker vertaalt. | *t'Amsterdam,* | *Voor Jan Hendriksz. en Jan Rieuwertsz. Boekverkopers.* 1652. | 4to, pp. (8), 94. Plate.

Concerning this clear and true description of the troubles of the Portuguese in Brazil, *see* Asher, No. 277.

MOREHEAD (C. S.) Remarks ... on the Necessity of organizing Governments for our recently acquired Territories: ... February 24, 1849. *Washington: J. & G. S. Gideon, Printers.* 1849. 8vo, pp. 16. H. 50581

Also: Address delivered on the Second Anniversary of Van Doren's Collegiate Institute, Lexington, Ky., 1833. ... *Lexington.* 1833. 8vo, pp. 16.—Speech ... on the Bill to incorporate the Subscribers to the Fiscal Bank of the United States. ... July 27, 1841. *Washington.* 1841. 8vo, pp. 28.—Speech ... on the Loan Bill, ... February 16th, 1848. *Washington: Printed by J. & G. S. Gideon.* 1848. 8vo, pp. 15. H.—Speech ... on the Admission of California, and the Question of Slavery. ... April 23, 1850. *Washington: Printed by Gideon & Co.* 1850. 8vo, pp. 15. B. *See also* Vol. IX., No. 37535.

MOREHEAD (D. C.) Morehead's Family Almanac for ... 1859. *New York: D. C. Morehead.* [1858.] 8vo, pp. 36. H.

MOREHEAD (J. T.) An Address in Commemoration of the First Settlement of Kentucky: ... at Boonesborough the 25th May, 1840, By James T. Morehead. *Frankfort, Ky.: A. G. Hodges, ... Printer.* 1840. 8vo, pp. 181. H., N. 50583

Also: ... Report [of the Committee on Retrenchment. *Washington.* 1844.] 8vo, pp. 448.— ... Report ... [on] French Spoliations ... . February 10, 1847. ... [n. p. n. d.] 8vo, pp. 8.—Speech ... on French Spoliations. ... August 10, 1846. *Washington: Printed ... [by] Blair and Rives.* 1847. 8vo, pp. 23. H.

MOREHOUSE (H. L.) Evil, its own Destroyer. A Discourse Delivered ... in ... East Saginaw, April 19th, 1865, on the ... Death of President Abraham Lincoln, by H. L. Morehouse ... . *East Saginaw, Mich.: Enterprise Print.* 1865. Sm. 8vo, pp. 16.

MOREIRA (C.) Relatorio sobre a Exposição Internacional de 1862, apresentado a S. M. O. Imperador pelo Conselheiro Carvalho Moreira, Presidente de Commissão Brasileira. *Londres: Impresso por Thomas Brettel.* MDCCCLXII. 4to, pp. (2), lxxxii, 516. 3 Plates. 50585

Includes copious details of Brazilian products, etc.

MOREIRA (J. de C.) Fourteen Views of Rio de Janeiro and Neighbourhood, By J. de C. Moreira. *Rio de Janeiro.* 1814. 4to. 50586

MOREIRA (N. J.) Diccionario de Plantas medicinaes Brasileiras contendo o nome da planta, seu genero, especie, familia e o botanico que a classificon. Por Nicolão Joaquim Moreira. *Rio de Janeiro.* 1862. 4to, pp. 146. 50587

MOREIRA. Vocabulario das Arvores Brasileiras que podem fornecer Madeira para construcções civis, navaes e marcenaria seguido de um indiculo botanico de algumas plantas do Paraguay, pelo Dr. Nicolau Joaquim Moreira. *Rio de Janeiro.* 1870. 8vo, pp. 63. 50588

MOREJON (J. A.) Memoria sobre los medios que podrán adoptarse para fomentar las Haciendas en órden al ganado vacuno y mular, escrita por D. Juan Antonio Morejon ... . *Havana, por D. Estéban Boloña.* 1800. 4to, pp. 27, and Appendix. 50589

[MOREL DE STA. CRUZ (Pedro Agustin).] Carta Pastoral del Illmo. Sr. Obispo de Cuba á su diócesis, con motivo del terremoto acaecido en la ciudad de Santiago y lugares adyacentes. *Habana: Imprenta del Cómputo Eclesiástico.* 1766. 4to, pp. 11.

MORELET (A.) Voyage dans l'Amérique Centrale, l'Ile de Cuba et le Yucatan. Par Arthur Morelet. *Paris: Gide et J. Baudry.* 1857. 2 vols., 8vo, pp. (4), 337, (2); (4), 323, (6). Map and Plates. C. 50591

MORELET. Travels in Central America including Accounts of some Regions Unexplored since the Conquest from the French of the Chevalier Arthur Morelet By Mrs. M. F. Squier Introduction and Notes by E. Geo. Squier. *London: Trübner & Co.* 1871. 8vo, pp. 430. Map and 8 Plates. C. 50592

"The *Tierra de Guerra* of the time of Las Casas remained for three centuries not only the Land of War, but the land of mystery. A vast tract of territory in Guatemala, inhabited by the fierce Itzas and Locandons, whose wars are recorded by Villaguatierre, was for the first time visited by a peaceful traveler in 1846. The adventurous Frenchman, whose literary thirst impelled him to explore this mysterious country, recorded his observations in a manner which entitles them to more credence than could be fairly claimed by many of his countrymen."—FIELD. Some copies have the imprint *New York: Leypoldt, Holt & Williams.* 1871.

MORELET. Reisen in Central-Amerika, von Arthur Morelet. In deutscher Bearbeitung von Dr. H. Hertz. *Jena.* 1872. 8vo, pp. viii, 362. Map and Plates. 50593

MORELET. Testacea novissima insulæ Cubanæ et Americæ centralis. ... *Paris.* 1849–51. 2 vols., 8vo. 50594

[MORELLET (André).] Examen de la Réponse de M. N..... [Necker] au Mémoire de M. l'Abbé Morellet sur la Compagnie des Indes; par l'Auteur du Mémoire. Sept. 1769. *Paris: Desaint.* 1769. 4to, pp. 151. S. 50595

MORELLET. Mémoire sur la Situation actuelle de la Compagnie des Indes: Seconde Édition, augmentée d'une Histoire de la Compagnie, depuis 1723, jusqu'à présent; par M. l'Abbé Morellet. *Paris.* MDCCLXIX. 4to, pp. 260, xxvii. S. 50596

MORELLET. Memoires relatifs a la Discussion du Privilege de la Nouvelle Compagnie des Indes. ... *Amsterdam.* 1787. 4to, pp. (2), 140. C. 50597

MORELLI (C.) *See* [Muriel Domingo)].

MORELLI (J.) Operette di Jacopo Morelli ora insieme raccolte con oposcoli di antichi scrittori (per cura di B. Gamba). Col ritratto dell' autore. *Venezia.* 1820. 3 vols., 8vo. Portrait.

Contains "Lettera rarissima di Christoforo Colombo riprodotta e illustrata." *See also* our Vol. IV., No. 14643.

MORELOS (J. M.) Elegia a la muerte del Excmo. Sr. D. Jose Maria Morelos. Dedicada al Sr. D. Vicente Guerrero. *Puebla.* 1821. Sm. 8vo, pp. 7. 50599

Also: La Abispa de Chilpancingo. Dedicada para perpetuar la Buena Memoria del muy Hon. y Excel. Señor D. José Maria Morelos. *Mexico.* 1821–22. 4to, 30 Numbers and Supplement.

MORÉNAS (J.) Précis historique de la Traité des Noirs et de l'Esclavage colonial, contenant l'origine de la Traité, ses progrès, son état actuel, et un exposé des horreurs produites par le despotisme des colons; ouvrage dans lequel on prouve qu'on a exporté

d'Afrique, depuis 1814 jusqu'à present, plus de 700,000 esclaves, ... *Paris.* 1828. 8vo, pp. 424. 3 Portraits. A. 50600

Proving that in 1814–28 more than 700,000 slaves were imported from Africa, and a large proportion under the French flag.

MORENO (A. F.) El Rey Pacifico gloriosamente coronado de Marciales tropheos. Sermon Panegyrico, en la accion de gracias, que la Santa Iglesia Metropolitana de Mexico solemnizò el dia 12. de Febrero de 1747. Por la feliz Coronacion de N. Rey, y Señor D. Fernando VII. ... predicò el Dr. D. Alonso Francisco Moreno, y Castro ... . [n. p. n. d.] 4to, pp. (2), 20. 50601

MORENO (A. M.) Documentos Justificativos de la Conducta del A. M. Moreno. *Mexico.* 1845. 4to. 50602

MORENO (C. C.) American Interests in Asia. By Celso Cesare Moreno. *New York: Westcott & Co.* 1869. 8vo, pp. 40

MORENO (D.) Manifiesto sobre la Conducta observada por Diego Moreno, al dejar el Gobierno del estado soberano de Michoacan. *Mexico.* 1833. 4to, pp. 23. 50604

MORENO (G.) Reglas Ciertas, | y Precisamen- | te Necessarias para | Ivezes, y Ministros de Ivs- | ticia de las Indias, y para sus Confessores. | Compuestas por el muy Docto P. M. Fr. Geronymo | Moreno ... . [*Mexico: Emprenta de Francisco Salbago.*] 1637. 4to, (8) and 59 leaves. H. + *Mexico.* 1732. 4to, pp. (16), 136.

A rare production of the Mexican press; not mentioned by Salva, Rich or Stevens.

MORENO (J. Demetrio). Oracion Fúnebre que en las Solemnes Exequias celebradas en esta Santa Iglesia Catedral de Puebla de los Angeles el dia 12 de Oct. 1819, en Sufragio del Alma de la Reyna Madre de les Españos, Doña Maria Luisa de Borbon. ... *Habana: Arazora y Soler.* 1819. 4to, pp. 26. 50606

Also: Panegirico de San Felipe Neri. ... *Puebla.* 1819. 4to, 11 leaves.—El Triunfo de la Iglesia, Oracion panegirica del gran principe de los apostoles San Pedro. ... *Mexico: Zuñiga.* 1801. 4to, pp. (8), 21.

MORENO (Jose Ignacio). Discurso que el Dia 1. de Enero de 1813, en que se Celebró la Misa Solemne de Accion de Gracias, y se juró la Constitucion Política de la Monarquía Española. ... *Lima.* 1813. 4to. 50607

MORENO. Exhortacion a la submission y concordia, que hizo a sus feligreses en el dia 10 de Mayo del presente año El Dr. D. Jose Ignacio Moreno, ... a consequencia de la Proclama del

Excmo. Señor vrey del Peru, que se remitio por el Gobierno de la intendencia de Tarma ... . *Lima: Imprenta de los Huerfanos.* 1812. 4to, pp. 24. 50608

MORENO (J. M.) Estudios sobre las Quiebras. Disertacion por José Maria Moreno. *Buenos Aires: Imprenta del Comercio del Plata.* 1864. 8vo, pp. 268. C. 50609

MORENO (J. B.) Relacion del Funeral Entierro, y Exequias de el Illmo. Sr. Dr. D. Manuel Rubio y Salinas Arzobispo que fué de esta Santa Iglesia Metropolitano de Mexico. Dispuesta por el Br. D. Juan Becerra Moreno. *Mexico: Imprenta del Colegio de S. Ildefonso.* 1766. 4to, pp. (8), 155. Plate. 50610

MORENO (J. J.) Fragmentos de la Vida, y Virtudes del V. Illmo. y Rmo. Sr. Dr. D. Vasco de Quiroga primer Obispo de la Santa Iglesia Cathedral de Michoacan, escritos, por el lic. D. Juan Joseph Moreno colegial Real de Oposicion del mas Antiguo de S. Ildefonso de Mexico. ... Con notas criticas en que se aclaran muchos puntos historicos, y antiguedades Americanas especialmente Michoacanenses. Sacaloz a Luz el Mencionado Colegio, y los dedica al mui ilustre, venerable Sr. Dean, y Cavildo de la misma Santa Iglesia Cathedral, por ... D. Ricardo Joseph Gutierrez Coronel ... . *Impressos en Mexico en la Imprenta del Real, y mas Antiguo Colegio de S. Ildefonso, Año de* 1766. 4to, pp. (24), 202. J.C.B. 50611

Usually followed by: "Reglas y Ordenanzas para el gobierno de los Hospitales de Santa Fé de Mexico, y Michoacan, dispuestas por su fundador el Rmo. y Venerable Sr. Don Vasco de Quiroga primer Obispo de Michoacan." pp. (2), 29. Portrait of Quiroga. Also: Sermon en la solemne accion de gracias, que de la eucaristia celebró, ... *Mexico.* 1789. 4to, 31 leaves.

MORENO DE TEXADA (J. P.) Tablas acomodadas à la moneda de Indias ... . Sacadas á luz para utilitad de ambas Americas. Por D. J. Prudencio Moreno de Texada. *Madrid.* 1864. 12mo, pp. 63. 50612

MORENO (M.) Late Military Revolution in Buenos Ayres, and Assassination of Governor Dorrego; being the Translation of an Exposition, addressed to the United Provinces of the River Plate, By Citizen Dr. Manuel Moreno, Envoy Extraordinary ... . In answer to Attacks published in the Buenos Ayres Journals, called the "Tiempo" & "Pampero," accompanied by Illustrative Documents. *London: John Richardson.* 1829. 8vo, pp. 95, (1). BA., C. 50613

MORENO. Vida y Memorias del Dr. Don Mariano Moreno secretario de la Junta de Buenos Ayres, con una idea de su revolucion, y de la de Mexico, Caracas, &c. Por Don Manuel Moreno. *Londres: En la Imprenta de J. McCreery.* 1812. 8vo, pp. 333. Portrait. P. 50614

See also Vol. X., No. 38996.

MORENO (M.) Sermon panegyrico del ange. Joven Sán Luis Gonzaga. ... *Mexico.* 1839. 8vo, 16 leaves. 50615

MORENO Y JOVE (Manuel). Oracion Funebre del Sr. D. Augustin de Iturbide. ... *Mexico.* 1850. 8vo. 50616

MORÉNO (M. A.) Carta Apologética de las Reflexîones sobre el uso de las Lagartijas que escribieron el Lic. D. M. Antonio Moréno, y el Br. D. Alejo Ramon Sanchez. *Mexico.* 1782. 4to. 50617

MORETO *et* LANINI. Santa Rosa del Peru, par Moreto et Lanini. 1622. 50618

Title from Ternaux, No. 443. I find no other account of this.

MORETON (J. B.) Manners and Customs in the West India Islands. Containing various Particulars respecting the Soil, Cultivation, Produce, Trade, Officers, Inhabitants, &c. With the method of establishing and conducting a Sugar Plantation; ... Also the Treatment of Slaves; and the Slave-Trade. By J. B. Moreton. *London: W. Richardson.* 1790. 8vo, pp. 192. H.

"The author was a negro driver. He has given a strange jumble of good advice, gross descriptions, licentious remarks, and bad poetry, mixed occasionally with texts of Scripture."—*Monthly Review*, IV. 337. The title of the "new edition" is as follows:

MORETON. West India Customs and Manners, containing Strictures on the Soil, Cultivation, Produce, Trade, Officers, and Inhabitants; with the method of establishing and conducting a Sugar Plantation. To which is added, the Practice of training new Slaves. By J. B. Moreton, Esq. A New Edition. *London: J. Parsons.* 1793. 8vo, pp. 192. 50620

MORETON. Schilderung des häuslichen Lebens, der Sitten und Gebräuche der Einwohner auf der Insel Jamaika. Aus dem Englischen. *Prag: Johann Herrl.* 1793. 12mo, pp. 126.

MORETON (J.) Life and Work in Newfoundland; Reminiscences of Thirteen Years spent there. By the Rev. Julian Moreton ... . *London: Rivingtons.* 1863. Post 8vo, pp. xv, 106. Map and Plates. B. 50622

With Glossary of Words and Phrases peculiar to Newfoundland.

MOREWOOD (S.) An Essay on the Inventions of both Ancients & Moderns in the use of Inebriating Liquors ... . By Samuel Morewood ... . *London.* 1824. 8vo, pp. xi, 375. 50623

Includes an account of the liquors used in America. The following is an amplification:

MOREWOOD. A Philosophical and Statistical History of the Inventions and Customs of Ancient and Modern Nations in the Manufacture and use of inebriating Liquors; ... By Samuel Morewood, Esq. ... *Dublin: William Curry, Jun. and Company.* 1838. 8vo, pp. xii, 745. Plate. A., BA. 50624

MOREYRA (M.) Cuestion entre el Perú y la España. Exposicion dirigida al Cuerpo Legislativo de la Nacion Peruana, por Don Mariano Moreyra ... . *Madrid: Imp. de el Clamor.* 1864. Folio, pp. 30. H. 50625

[MOREY (George), *and others.*] Annexation of Roxbury and Boston. Remonstrance of Bostonians against the Measure. ... *Boston: Press of Geo. C. Rand & Avery.* 1865. 8vo, pp. 8. H.

MORFI (J. A.) La Nobleza y Piedad de los Montañeses, demonstrada por el S. Cristo de Burgos. Sermon que sú Primera fiesta, celebrada en el Convento Grande de N. S. Francisco de México el dia 3 de Mayo 1775 años. ... *Mexico.* 1775. Folio.

MORFORD (H.) The Coward. A Novel of Society and the Field in 1863. By Henry Morford ... . *Philadelphia: T. B. Peterson & Brothers.* [1864.] 12mo, pp. (4), 21–520. C., H.

MORFORD. Democracy and the Nation. A Poem delivered on the 4th of July, 1863, before the Tammany Society, New York. By Henry Morford. With Oration of the Hon. H. C. Murphy, and Proceedings on the occasion. *New York: Baptist & Taylor.* 1863. 8vo, pp. 67. 50629

[MORFORD.] Red-Tape and Pigeon-Hole Generals, as seen from the Ranks during a Campaign in the Army of the Potomac. *New York: Carleton.* 1864. 12mo, pp. 318. 50630

Also: The Days of Shoddy. A Novel of the Great Rebellion in 1861. ... *Philadelphia: T. B. Peterson & Brothers.* 1863. 8vo, pp. 17–478. Portrait.—The Great Rebellion ... . *Chicago.* 1863. 8vo, pp. 32.—Music of the Spheres. ... *Middletown.* 1840. 8vo.—Rhymes of Twenty Years. ... *New York: H. Dexter & Co.* 1859. 12mo, pp. 240. Portrait.—Shoulder Straps. A Novel of New York and the Army, in 1862. ... *Philadelphia: T. B. Peterson & Brothers.* [1862.] 12mo, pp. (4), 15–482. 2 Plates. + [*Ibid.* 1868.]—Sprees and Splashes; or, Droll Descriptions of Town and Country. ... *New York: Carleton.* 1862. 12mo, pp. 240. Plate.—Turned from the Door. A Christmas Story for 1869–70. ... *New York: American News Com-*

pany. 1869. 8vo, pp. 80.—Utterly Wrecked; a Novel of American Coast Life. ... *New York.* 1866. 8vo.

MORGA (A. de). Sucesos de las Islas Filipinas dirigido a Don Cristoval Gomez de Sandoval y Rojas, Duque de Cea, por el Doctor Antonio de Morga, Alcalde del Crimen, de la real Audiencia de la Nueva Espana ... . *En Mexico, en casa de Geronymo Babi, Ano* 1609. *Por Cornelio Adriano Cesar.* 4to, (10), and 172 leaves. 50631

Includes notices of different parts of America, etc. This original edition is of excessive rarity, neither Brunet nor Ebert had ever seen it, as they both state it to be in folio.

MORGA. The Philippine Islands, ... Translated from the Spanish, with Notes and a Preface; ... *London: Hakluyt Society.* 1868. 8vo, pp. xxx, 413. 2 Plates. C. 50632

MORGAN (A.) Anti-Paedo-Rantism; | or | Mr. Samuel Finley's | Charitable Plea for the Speechless | Examined and Refuted: | The Baptism of Believers | Maintain'd; | And the Mode of it, by Immersion, | Vindicated. | By Abel Morgan, at Middletown, | in East-Jersey. | *Philadelphia:* | *Printed by B. Franklin, in Market Street,* M,DCC,XLVII. 12mo, pp. 174, (2). 50633

The first book written in America relative to the baptismal controversy.

MORGAN. Cyd-Gordiad | Egwyddorawl o'r | Scrythurau: | neu | Daflen Lythyrennol o'r Prif Eiriau | yn y Bibl Sanctaidd. | Yn Arwain, dan y Cyfryw eiriau, i fuan | ganfod pob rhyw ddymunol ran o'r | Scrythurau. | A Gyfan-soddwyd Drwy Lafurus Boen | Abel Morgan, | Gwenidog yr Elengyl er lle's y Cymru. | *Argraphwyd in Philadelphia, gan Samuel Keimer,* | *a Dafydd Harry.* | MDCCXXX. Folio, Title, Dedication, etc., 4 leaves, Text, A to LLL, in fours, unpaged. P. 50634

The earliest Welsh Concordance to the Bible. It was composed by the author while he was a minister in Monmouthshire. He took the manuscript with him to America about 1711. It served as the basis to Peter Williams' concordance, printed at Carmarthen, by J. Ross, in 1773. One of the preliminary pieces is signed John Cadwalader, Philadelphia, 1730. David Harry was Keimer's apprentice. He bought Keimer out in July, 1729, and during the year 1730, followed him to Barbados. This is one of the few works he printed, and is very rare.

MORGAN (E. B.) Mr. Fillmore's Political History and Position. Speech of Hon. E. B. Morgan, of New York. ... August 4, 1856. [n. p. n. d.] 8vo, pp. 7. 50635

MORGAN [E. D.] International Coinage. Report of Senator Morgan. [n. p. 1868.] 8vo, pp. 11. H. 50636

Also: Remarks ... at ... Cooper Institute, New York, ... Oct. 16, 1867, on Republican State Nominations. [n. p. n. d.] 8vo. — ... Remarks ... at ... Cooper Institute, ... New York, ... Oct. 8, 1868. [n. p. n. d.] 8vo, pp. 12. H.

MORGAN (F.) A Temperance Address, ... in West Chester, Conn. July 4, 1834. By Frederick Morgan, M.D. ... *Hartford: Printed by Peter B. Gleason and Co.* 1834. 8vo, pp. 14.

MORGAN (G. D.) Report of the Committee on Naval Affairs, relative to the Employment of George D. Morgan, to purchase vessels for the Government. [*Washington.*] 1862. 8vo.

MORGAN (G. G. W.) The Boston Token: a Memento of Friendship. By George G. W. Morgan. *Boston: The Author.* 1855. 12mo, pp. 34, (1). B. 50639

MORGAN. Poems, or Metrical Gossamer Thoughts. By George G. W. Morgan. Second Edition. *Boston.* 1855. 18mo, pp. 144, (1), 34, (1). B. 50640

Contents: The Rochester Token, the Boston Token, etc.

MORGAN (G. C.) Landscape Views of New England. Edited by George C. Morgan. No. 1. *New York: Morgan & Waterhouse.* 1847. Impl. 8vo, pp. 24. 2 Plates. 50641

Apparently the only number published. Contains two views of Danbury, Conn., and accompanying descriptive poems.

MORGAN (G. H.) Annals: Comprising Memoirs, Incidents, and Statistics of Harrisburg, from the Period of its First Settlement. Compiled by George H. Morgan. *Harrisburg.* 1858. 12mo. 50642

See also St. Louis, Mo.

MORGAN (G. W.) Report of the Occupation of Cumberland Gap. By General George W. Morgan. [*Washington.*] 1864. 8vo, pp. 19. 50643

Also: Speech ... June 7, 1870, on Banking and Currency. [n. p. n. d.] 8vo.

MORGAN (G.) Report on Public Instruction in Pennsylvania. By the Rev. Gilbert Morgan, A.M. ... *Philadelphia: E. G. Dorsey, Printer.* 1836. 12mo, pp. 24. B. 50644

See also Western University of Pennsylvania.

MORGAN (*Sir* H.) Sir Henry Morgan; or, the Knight of the Black Flag. [A Tale.] *London.* 1865. 8vo. 50645

See [Exquemelin (A. O.)], Vol. VI., Nos. 23467–23494, *also* [Howard (E. G. G.)], Vol. VIII., No. 33245.

MORGAN (H.) Music Hall Discourses, Miscellaneous Sketches, Ministerial Notes, and Prison Incidents. Also, Song

of Creation, A Poem. By Henry Morgan ... . To which is added a Sketch of his Life. *Boston: H. W. Swett & Co.* 1859. 12mo, pp. xvi, 344. Portrait, 2 Plates. C. + Second enlarged Edition. *Boston: H. V. Degen and Son.* 1860. 12mo, pp. xvi, 356. Portrait, 2 Plates. B. 50646

Also: Ned Nevins, the Newsboy; or, Street Life in Boston. ... Third Edition. *Boston: Lee & Shepard.* 1867. 16mo, pp. 428. — Preaching for the Times. ... [*Boston:*] *H. W. Swett & Co.* [n. d.] 12mo, pp. 32. B.

MORGAN (H. J.) Bibliotheca Canadensis: or A Manual of Canadian Literature. By Henry J. Morgan ... . *Ottawa: Printed by G. E. Desbarats.* 1867. Impl. 8vo, pp. xiv, 3–411. C. 50647

Rather a crude performance, but very rare; most of the copies having been destroyed by fire. A new edition is said to be in the press [December, 1879].

MORGAN. Sketches of Celebrated Canadians, and Persons connected with Canada, from the Earliest Period in the History of the Province down to the Present Time. By Henry J. Morgan ... . *Quebec: Hunter, Rose & Co.* MDCCCLXII. 8vo, pp. xiii, 779. + *Montreal: R. Worthington.* 1865. 8vo, pp. xiii, 779

Mr. Morgan's notions of *celebrity* are certainly very provincial. Also: The Canadian Parliamentary Companion. ... Third Edition. *Montreal: John Lovell, Printer.* 1864. 32mo, pp. 95. — The Place British Americans have won in History. A Lecture, ... at Aylmer, L. C., ... 22nd February, 1866. ... *Ottawa: Printed by Hunter, Rose & Co.* 1866. 12mo, pp. 22. H.

MORGAN (J.) State of the Accounts of Jacob Morgan, Senior, late Lieutenant of Berks County, from ... 1777 to ... 1780. In which is exhibited the amount of the monies received by him within that time for militia fines ... . *Philadelphia: Printed by Robert Aitken.* M.DCC.LXXXIII. 8vo, pp. 54. P. 50649

MORGAN (J.) A Discourse Upon the Institution of Medical Schools In America; Delivered at a Public Anniversary Commencement, held in the College of Philadelphia May 30 and 31, 1765. With a Preface Containing, amongst other things, the Author's Apology, For attempting to introduce the regular mode of practising Physic in Philadelphia: By John Morgan, M.D. ... *Philadelphia: Printed ... by William Bradford,* MDCC,LXV. 8vo, pp. vii, xxvi, (2), 63. B., C., N., P. 50650

One of the earliest American works on the subject. *See* "M. Rev.," XXXIV. 222.

MORGAN. A Recommendation of Inoculation according to Baron Dimsdale's Method. By John Morgan, M.D., Director General of the Hospitals and Physician in Chief of the American Army. *Boston: Printed by J. Gill.* M. DCC. LXXVI. 8vo, pp. 18.

MORGAN. To His Excellency General Washington, Commander in Chief of the American Army. The Memorial and Representation of Doctor John Morgan, respecting his Care of the Sick, and Manner of conducting the Department of the General Hospital committed to his care. *Fishkill, Feb. 1st.,* 1777. 8vo, pp. 24. P. 50652

MORGAN. A Vindication of his Public Character in the station of Director-General of the Military Hospitals, and Physician in Chief of the American Army; Anno 1776. By John Morgan, M.D. ... *Boston: Printed by Powers and Willis.* M, DCC, LXXVII. 8vo, pp. xliii, 158. BA. 50653

Also: Oration which might have been delivered on rupture of Medical Schools. *Philadelphia.* 1789. 4to, pp. 19. P. *See also* Vol. VI., Nos. 25279–80.

MORGAN (J.) The Manufacturer's Book of Wages, and Work-People's Companion ... . *Baltimore.* 1825. 8vo, pp. 46.

[MORGAN (J.)] Trinity Church Case: Dr. Tyng and others against Trinity Church. By Presbyter. *New-York.* 1856. 8vo, pp. 30. S. 50655

MORGAN (J.) O Tram Road a vapordo Paraguassi na Provincia de Bahia ... por John Morgan ... . *Bahia.* 1867. 8vo, pp. 48. Map. 50656

MORGAN (J. B.) Fluctuations in the Price of Middling and Fair New Orleans Cotton during 1857 ... 1860. [*London.* 1861.] Folio, 1 leaf. 50657

[MORGAN (Joseph).] A Brief History of the Country of Humanity. ... *Boston.* 1728. 8vo, pp. 58. M. 50658

MORGAN. The General Cause of all Hurtful Mistakes. Sermon ... . By Rev. Joseph Morgan, A.M. *Philadelphia: Printed by B. Franklin.* 1741. 16mo, pp. 24. + *Reprinted, New London.* 1741. 16mo. 50659

MORGAN. Gospel Ordinances. Sermon at the Ordination of Jonathan Dickinson ... 29th Sept. 1709. By Rev. Joseph Morgan, A.M. *Philadelphia: Printed by William and Andrew Bradford.* 1712. 12mo, pp. 44. 50660

MORGAN. The | Portsmouth Disputation | Examined, | being | A brief Answer to the Arguments | used by the Anti-Pædo-Baptists in Dr. | Russel's Narrative of the Disputation held | at Portsmouth, between some Baptists | and Presbyterian Ministers. | By

Joseph Morgan. | ... | *Printed, ... by William Bradford in | New-York.* 1713. 12mo, pp. (10), 98. H. 50661

Also: The Duty, and a Mark of Zion's Children. A Discourse at Freehold, N. J. Dec. 1. 1723, upon the sorrowful occasion of the Death of his son Joseph Morgan, of Yale College. ... *New London, Con.: T. Green.* 1723. 12mo, pp. (2), 32. — Love to our Neighbour recommended ... . A Sermon preached at Freehold in the Jersies. ... *N. London.* 1749. 12mo, pp. 15. + Third Edition. *Boston.* 1749. 16mo, pp. 15. — The Only Effectual Remedy Against Mortal Errors Held forth in a Discourse, ... Shewing the Cause of all the Heresies, Apostasies, Soul-murdering Errors, & contrary Articles of Faith. ... *New-London: Printed ... by T. Green.* 1725. 8vo, pp. (2), 49, (1). — Sermon Preached at Norwich ... . *New London.* 1727. 8vo. — Sin its own Punishment. ... *Boston, N. E.: Printed by Gamaliel Rogers, for Samuel Gerrish.* 1728. 8vo, pp. (6), 24. BA.

MORGAN (J. C.) The Emigrant's Note Book and Guide; with Recollections of Upper and Lower Canada, during the late War. ... By Lieutenant J. C. Morgan, H.P. ... *London: The Author.* 1824. 12mo, pp. xxiii, 348, (1). 2 Plates. H. 50662

MORGAN (L. H.) The American Beaver and his Works. By Lewis H. Morgan ... . *Philadelphia: J. B. Lippincott & Co.* 1868. 8vo, pp. 330. Map and 23 Plates. H. 50663

Incidentally treats of some of the phases of American Indian life.

MORGAN. Circular in reference to the Degrees of Relationship among different Nations. By L. H. Morgan. *Washington.* 1860. 8vo, pp. 34. 50664

Forms part of Vol. II. of the "Miscellaneous Collections" of the Smithsonian Institute.

MORGAN. Laws of Descent of the Iroquois. By Lewis H. Morgan ... [n. p. n. d.] 8vo, pp. 16. + *Rochester, N. Y.* 1859. 12mo, pp. 12. 50665

MORGAN. League of the Ho-dé-no-sau-nee or Iroquois. By Lewis H. Morgan ... . *Rochester: Sage & Brother.* 1851. 8vo, pp. xviii, 477. 23 Maps, Plates and Plans. B. 50666

The work of a writer more than ordinarily fitted for the task.

MORGAN. [Begins] Rochester, Monroe County, N. Y., January —, 1859. [n. p. n. d.] 12mo, pp. 12. 50667

On the consanguinity of the Iroquois.

MORGAN. [Begins] Rochester, Monroe Co., N. Y., October 1, 1859. [n. p. n. d.] 8vo, pp. 8. 50668

A sheet designed to be sent to persons having some knowledge of Indian history, and domestic or social customs, in order to elicit information regarding them. It contains an analysis of their tribal divisions, marital relations, and a series of questions regarding the same. *See also* annual reports of the Regents of the University of New York.

MORGAN (M.) Plan for the Abolition of Slavery in the West Indies. By Morris Morgan. *London.* 1772. 4to. 50669

MORGAN (N. H.) Morgan Genealogy. A History of James Morgan, of New London, Conn. and his Descendants; From 1607 to 1869. With an Appendix, containing the History of his Brother, Miles Morgan, of Springfield, Mass.; and some of his Descendants. ... By Nathaniel H. Morgan. *Hartford: Case, Lockwood & Brainard.* 1869. 8vo, pp. 280, (1). 13 Portraits.

MORGAN. Our Family Genealogy. Printed for the Family, but not published. Morgan. Avery. ... *Hartford: Case, Tiffany and Company.* 1851. Rl. 8vo, pp. 16. H. 50671

MORGAN (P. B.) The Coming Conflict: With the inquiry, —Ought Christians to bear arms? A Discourse ... May 12, 1861, By P. B. Morgan. ... *Boston: Redding & Co.* 1861. 12mo, pp. 24. H. 50672

MORGAN (R. P.) Report of the Survey of the Route of the Galena and Chicago Union Rail Road, By Richard P. Morgan, Engineer. *Chicago.* 1847. 8vo, pp. 17. Map. H. 50673

Also: Report to the Hudson River Railroad Committee, August, 1842. ... *Poughkeepsie.* 1842. 12mo. S.

MORGAN (Thomas Gibbes). *See* Louisiana, X. 42206.

MORGAN (W.) Memoirs of the Life of the Rev. Richard Price, D.D. ... By William Morgan, F.R.S. *London: R. Hunter.* 1815. 8vo, pp. viii, 189. H., P. 50674

See "Monthly Review," LXXXIII. 77. Dr. Price participated quite actively in American questions. *See* Price (R.)

MORGAN. A Review of Dr. Price's Writings, on the Subject of the Finances of this Kingdom; to which are added the Three Plans communicated by him to Mr. Pitt, in the year 1786, for redeeming the National Debt ... . *London: G. Stafford.* MDCCXCII. 8vo, pp. viii, 72. J.C.B. + Second Edition. 1795. 8vo. P.

[MORGAN (W.)] Illustrations of Masonry, By one of the Fraternity ... . *New York.* 1826. 12mo. + Second Edition. With an Account of the Kidnapping of the Author. *New-York: The Author.* 1826. 12mo, pp. 84. B., S. + *Cincinnati: Matthew Gardiner.* [1826?] 8vo, pp. 5–80. + [n. p.:] *The Author.* 1827. 8vo, pp. 92. + Third Edition. *Rochester: The*

Author. 1827. 12mo, pp. 95, (1). Plate. + *New York.* 1828. 12mo. + *Boston: Frederick A. Sumner.* 1829. 12mo, pp. 84.

The first edition of this work is extremely rare. There are other editions. The following is a German version:

MORGAN. Eine Geschichte der Thatsachen und Umstände die Entführung und vermuthete Ermordung des William Morgan betreffend. Und auch von dem Versuch der gemacht wurde, David C. Müller zu entführen, und seine Druckerey zu verbrennen oder zu zerstören. Vorbereitet unter der Direction der verschiedenen Committeen, welche von Versammlungen der Bürger der Caunties Genesee, Livingston, Ontario, Monroe, und Niagara, in dem Staate Neu-York gehalten wurden. [n. p.] 1828. 16mo, pp. 80. C. 50677

MORGAN. Free Masonry Revealed and Exposed, by Eleven Seceeding Members; with a Sketch of the Life, Abduction and Murder of William Morgan. *Cincinnati.* [n. d.] 8vo, pp. 131.

A reprint of "Illustrations of Masonry," No. 50676, *supra.*

MORGAN. The Mysteries of Free Masonry: ... By Captain William Morgan: ... Revised and Corrected ... . By George R. Crafts ... . *New York: Wilson and Company.* [n. d.] 8vo, pp. 112

MORGAN. Erläuterung der Frey-Maurerey. Aus dem Englischen übersetzt, nebst einem Meisterschlüssel zu den Geheimnissen des höhern Ordens, von einem Frey-Mauren ... . *Waterloo: W. Child.* 1828. 8vo, pp. 96. C. 50680

The excitement relating to the alleged murder of Morgan, led to the publication of many pamphlets. We enumerate the following:

Confession of the Murder of William Morgan, as taken down by Dr. John L. Emery, of Racine County, Wisconsin, in the Summer of 1848, now first given to the Public, by Henry L. Valance. *New York.* 1849. 12mo, pp. 23, (1). 50681

... Extracts from the Proceedings of the First U. States Anti-masonic Convention: embracing an Account of the Abduction and Murder of William Morgan; ... *Boston.* 1833. 8vo, pp. (1), 18, 5. H. 50682

Light on Masonry: A Collection of all the most Important Documents on the Subject of Speculative Freemasonry: Embracing the Reports of the Western Committees in relation to the Abduction of William Morgan. ... By Elder David Bernard ... .

Utica. 1829. 12mo, pp. 506, Appendix, 55. Portrait and Plate. 50683

Corrected title of our No. 4919, Vol. II.

A Narrative of the Facts ... relating to the Kidnapping and Presumed Murder of William Morgan. ... With an Appendix. ... [*Batavia, N. Y.* 1827.] 8vo, pp. 36. + To which is added, the late Trials at Canandaigua. *Brookfield: E. and G. Merriam, Printers.* 1827. 12mo, pp. 84. + Third Edition. *Rochester.* 1828. 12mo, pp. 72. 50684

Report of the Select Committee on that part of the Governor's Message relating to the Abduction of William Morgan. ... *Albany: Printed by Croswell and Van Benthuysen.* 1829. 8vo, pp. 68.

Also: Report ... Feb. 14, 1829. *Albany: Printed by Croswell and Van Benthuysen.* 1829. 8vo, pp. 27. — Supplemental Report of the Committee appointed to Ascertain the Fate of Capt. William Morgan. *Rochester.* 1827. 8vo, pp. 10. *See also* Vol. IX., No. 38467.

MORGAN (W. F.) Discourses upon Christian Duties in connection with National Dangers. By William F. Morgan ... . *New York: Wm. M. Taylor.* 1861. 12mo, pp. 27. 50686

MORGAN. Francis Lister Hawks, D.D. ... A Commemorative Discourse ... on the Anniversary of his Burial, Sept. 29th, 1867. By William F. Morgan, D.D. [*New York: Wynkoop & Hallenbeck.* n. d.] 8vo, pp. 21. B. 50687

[MORGAN.] In Memoriam. [n. p. 1865.] 8vo, pp. 47, (1).

Sermons occasioned by the death of Abraham Lincoln.

[MORGAN.] A Letter addressed to the Members of the Parish of Christ Church, Norwich. [n. p. 1845.] 8vo, pp. 8. H.

[MORGAN.] Obituary Notice of ... George L. Duyckinck, Esq. *New York: Gen. Prot. Episc. Sunday School Union.* 1863. 24mo, pp. 26. H. 50690

Also: ... An Address, ... before the House of Convocation of Trinity College, in ... Hartford, July 28th, 1852. ... *Hartford: S. Hanmer & Co.* 1852. 8vo, pp. 35. — Centenary Discourse, at Christ's Church, Norwich, April 22, 1849. ... *New-York.* 1849. 8vo, pp. 20. — ... Sermon ... in ... Norwich, on ... the death of Edward B. Chappell ... . *Norwich: Press of James N. Perry.* 1856. 8vo, pp. 20. H. — Sermon preached before the St. George's Society of New York, April 23, 1858. ... *New York.* 1858. 8vo, pp. 28.

MORGAN COUNTY, *Ill.* Minutes of the Morgan County Sabbath School Convention, held in ... Jacksonville, Ill., ... August ... 1866. *Jacksonville.* 1866. 8vo, pp. 10, (2). H. 50691

Morganiana, or the Wonderful Life and Terrible Death of Morgan. Written by Himself. Illustrated with Gritholaphic Plates, by Hassan Straight-Shanks. By Baron Munchausen, Jr. *Boston.* 1828. 8vo. 50692

MORGRIDGE (C.) A Discourse ... at the Opening of the Christian Chapel in Salem, May 1st, 1828. By Charles Morgridge. *Boston.* 1828. 12mo, pp. 24. 50693

[MORHARD (——).] Plan d'une agence, pour la réception, la direction et le placement des prolétaires européens dans l'Amérique du Nord. *Genève: J. Fick.* 1846. 8vo, pp. 16. 50694

MORHARD. Travail, liberté, propriété pour tous. Appel d'un Américain aux riches et aux prolétaires de l'Europe. ... [*Genève*] *Chez les principaux libraires.* 1846. 8vo, pp. 35. 50695

MORHOUSE (Abraham). The Writings of a Pretended Prophet, ... *Rutland, Vt.* 1796. 12mo. 50696

MORI (A.) Life and Resources in America. Prepared under the direction of Arinori Mori. For Circulation in Japan. *Washington, D. C.* 1871. 12mo, pp. 404, (1). Portrait of U. S. Grant

MORIANA Y ZAFRILLA (M.) Solemnes Exequias que celebró la Santa Yglesia Catedral de ... Michoacan. La Mañana del 9, y 10, de Mayo de 1810. Por la alma del Illmo. Señor Doctor Don Marcos Moriana y Zafrilla, su ... Obispo. *Mexico.* 1810. Sm. 4to, pp. (10), 113. 50698

MORIARTY (*Dr.*) ... A Sermon ... in ... Kensington, by Very Rev. Dr. Moriarty at the funeral ... of Rev. Daniel Sheridan, ... July 19, 1856. *Philadelphia: Thomas McLoughlin.* 1856. 8vo, pp. 14. H. 50699

MORILLA (J. M.) Breve Tratado de derecho administrativo Espanol general del reino, y especial de la Isla de Cuba. Por el Dr. Jose Maria Morilla. *Habana.* 1852. 4to, pp. viii, 390.

MORILLAS (P.) Aguinaldo Habanero, por Pedro J. Morillas y Manuel Costales. *Habana.* 1857. 8vo, pp. 234. 50701

MORILLO (A.) Causa criminal seguida contra el coronel graduado Apolinar Morillo, y demas autores y cómplices del asesinato perpetrado en la persona del Sr. Jeneral Antonio José de Sucre, ... *Bogotá: Imprenta del Estado.* 1843. Folio, pp. (4), 147. C.

Morillo [Pablo]. Mémoires du Général Morillo, Comte de Carthagène, ... relatifs aux principaux événemens de ses Campagnes en Amérique de 1815 à 1821; Suivis de deux précis de Don José Domingo Diaz, ... et du Don Miguel de la Torre. Traduit de l'Espagnol [par E. de Blosseville]. *Paris: P. Dufart.* 1826. 8vo, pp. (4), xvi, 452. c., p. 50703

Morin (A. N.) Lecture sur l'Education, devant l'Institut Canadien, le 18 Décembre 1845. ... *Montréal.* 1845. 8vo, pp. 30. 50704

Morin (M.) A Funeral Sermon, on Michael Morin, Master and Verger of the Church of Beausojour, in Champagne, Deceas'd the first of May, 1718. Preached by the Parson of the aforesaid Parish, before the body of the deceased in presence of the Parishioners. ... *New-York: Printed by James Parker, in Beaver Street.* 1748. 12mo, pp. 7. p. 50705

A burlesque performance, supposed to refer to the Morin family, then residents in the colony.

Morineau (A. de). Essai statistique et politique sur les États-Unis d'Amérique, d'après les documens recueillis sur les lieux. ... *Paris.* 1848. Folio. 50706

Moring (H. E.) Suggestions to Congress on the Finances of the United States, ... By H. E. Moring. ... [*N. Y.: John W. Amerman, Printer.*] 1869. 8vo, pp. 71. h. 50707

Mori-Ortiz (M. E.) Resultado de las Exploraciones Practicadas para establecer una Via de Comunicacion, entre el Pueblo de Tayabamba, Provincia de Pataz, y el Puerto de Pizana, á las márjenes del Hallago. Por el Teniente Coronel D. Manuel E. Mori-Ortiz. *Lima.* 1870. 8vo, pp. 68. 50708

Moris (G.) Copye. | Van 't Journael gehou-|den by Gedeon Moris, Koopman op het | Schip vande West-Indische Compagnie, | genaemt de Princesse, uytgevaren naer Bre-|silien van Zeelandt den 27 Februarij 1640. | daer Capiteyn op is Pieter Constant van | Middleburg. Gesonden uyt Poortland in En-|gelant aende Kamer van Zeelandt per Mis-|sive in dato 2 Martij 1640. | Daer in verhaelt staet, hoe couragieus ende | Mannelijck sy hun gedragen hebben tegen elf Duyn-|kercksche Fregatten, die sy naer eenighe uren ge-|vechts so gematteert ende ghetracteert heb-| ben, datse 't selve Schip hebben | moeten verlaten. | *t'Amsterdam,* |

Voor Francois Liesbout, Boeckverkooper op | den Dam in 't Groot-Boeck. | *Anno* 1640. | 4to, 4 leaves. 50709

This journal of G. Moris, merchant on the West India ship the Princess, which sailed for Brazil, etc., is very rare.

Morison (J. H.) An Address, ... at the Centennial Celebration, in Peterborough, N. H., Oct. 24, 1839. By John Hopkins Morison. *Boston: Printed by Isaac R. Butts.* 1839. 8vo, pp. 99. b. 50710

This address and the accompanying documents and notes contain a history of the township of Peterborough.

Morison. Life of the Hon. Jeremiah Smith, ll.d. ... By John H. Morison. *Boston: Charles C. Little and James Brown.* 1845. 12mo, pp. (2), viii, 516. Portrait. c., m. 50711

[Morison.] Memoir of Robert Swain. [*Boston.*] mdcccxlvi. 12mo, pp. (4), 259. + *Boston: James Munroe and Company.* mdccxlvii. 16mo, pp. (8), 259. ba. 50712

The edition of 1847 was published for general circulation. Of the first edition a small number of copies was printed for friends only.

Morison. A Memorial of Rev. Ephraim Peabody, d.d. By J. H. Morison. ... *Boston: Crosby, Nichols, and Company.* 1857. 8vo, pp. 42. b. 50713

Morison. A Sermon ... before the First Congregational Society, in New-Bedford, ... November 27, 1842. By John H. Morison. ... *New Bedford: Benjamin Lindsey.* 1842. 8vo, pp. 16. h. 50714

Occasioned by the death of Mary, and of Edward Everett, children of John H. and Sarah P. Clifford.

Morison. A Sermon, ... at The Installation of Rev. George W. Briggs, as pastor ... in Salem, January 6, 1853. By John Hopkins Morison, ... Milton. ... [With Notices of the First Church and its Ministers, By a Member.] *Salem.* 1853. 8vo, pp. 62, (1). h. 50715

Morison. Two Sermons ... in ... Milton, ... suggested by the Centennial Celebration, on the 11th of June, 1862. By John H. Morison, d.d. *Boston: Joseph G. Torrey, Printer.* 1862. 8vo, pp. 55. h. 50716

Also: An Address ... before the Golden Branch Society of Phillips Exeter Academy, August 22, 1839. ... *Boston: Printed by I. R. Butts.* 1839. 8vo, pp. 23.—A Sermon ... in ... Milton, June 4, 1854. [After the rendition of Anthony Burns.] ... *Boston: Benjamin H. Greene.* 1854. 8vo, pp. 18.— ... A Sermon on the Death of Capt. J. Sewall Reed and Rev. Thomas Starr King; ... March 13, 1864. ... *Boston:*

Printed by John Wilson and Son. 1864. 8vo, pp. 28.—Sermon ... in ... Boston, on the death of Mary E. Robbins ... June 26, 1870. ... *Boston: John Wilson and Son.* 1870. 8vo, pp. 20. h.

Morison (*Mr.*) Account of the Slavery Times in Virginia.

I have never seen this book. It is referred to in Nichols' edition of Dean Swift's Works, xv. 97.

Morison (W.) A Sermon, delivered at Dover, State of New Hampshire; before the Honorable General Court, at the Annual Election, June 7th, 1792. By William Morison, Minister of ... Londonderry. *New-Hampshire: Exeter, Printed by Henry Ranlet, for the General Court of said State ...* 1792. 8vo, pp. 43. n.

Morison. A Sermon, ... January 20, 1796, at the Ordination of ... Rev. William Pidgin, ... in Hampton, New-Hampshire: By William Morison ... . *Newburyport: Printed by Blunt and March.* [n. d.] 8vo, pp. 40. ba. 50719

Morison. A Sermon, Delivered at the request of the Elders ... of the Presbyterian Society in the West Parish of Londonderry, January 1st, 1800. On the Death of General George Washington. By William Morison. ... *From the Press of Angier March, Newburyport.* [1800.] 8vo. 50720

This is followed by:

An Oration, Delivered at the request of the Officers of the Assembled Cavalry and Infantry, and Other Militia Officers, On the 22d of February, 1800; In the West Parish of Londonderry, In Commemoration of the Death of General George Washington. By William Morison. ... *From the Press of Angier March, Newburyport.* [1800.] 8vo, pp. 32. ba., c. 50721

Each has a title, but the pagination is continuous.

Morisot (C. B.) Clavdii | Bartholomæi | Morisoti. | Pervviana. | ... *Divione,* | *Guido-Annam Gvyot, Typographum.* | m.dc.xliv–xlvi. 4to, pp. (14), 345, 4; (1); (4), 35. + [*Ibid.*] m.dc.xlv–xlvi. h.

This book contains no Peruvian history whatever; it relates, under Peruvian names, the disputes of Cardinal Richelieu with Marie de Médicis and Gaston d'Orléans.

Morisot. Orbis | Maritimi | sive | rervm in Mari | et Littoribvs gestarvm generalis Historia: ... Authore | Clavdio Barthol. Morisoto Diuionensi | *Divione apud Petrvm Pallyot* mdcxliii Folio, pp. (24), including Engraved and Printed Titles, and folded Plate, Text, 725, Index, (19). 50723

A kind of encyclopædia of everything relating to maritime affairs. Pages 592–612 contain a description of America, with three maps. The cuts are copied from De Bry. There are copies on fine paper.

[Morisot.] Relations | veritables | et cvrievses | de l'isle | de Madagascar, | et dv Bresil. | Auec l'Histoire de la derniere Guerre faite au Bresil, | entre les Portugais & les Hollandois. | Trois relations d'Egypte, | & vne du Royaume de Perse. | *A Paris,* | *Chez Avgvstin Cvrbé', au Palais, en la Gallerie | des Merciers, à la Palme.* | m.dc.li. | *Avec privilege dv roy.* | 4to, pp. (16), the 4th leaf blank, 307, (20), 212, 158. 2 Maps. bm. 50724

This collection, but little known and insufficiently described by bibliographers, is due to Augustin Courbé of Paris, who caused it to be edited by M. Morisot after some material which he had received in part from the celebrated brothers Dupuy, to whom the work is dedicated. We have described the part relative to Brasil, under Moreau (P.), No. 50579, *supra.*

Moritz (Johann). *See* Vol. ii., No. 7531.

Morley (J.) Edmund Burke: A Historical Study. By John Morley ... . *London: Macmillan and Co.* 1867. 8vo, pp. xv, 312. c., h. 50725

Mormonism. An Address by a Minister of the Church of Jesus Christ of Latter-day Saints to the People of the United States. [n. p. n. d.] 12mo, pp. 4. 50726

Printed while the Mormons were at Nauvoo.

An Appeal to the American People: being an Account of the Persecutions of the Church of Latter Day Saints; and of the Barbarities inflicted on them by the Inhabitants of the State of Missouri. By Authority of said Church. Second Edition, Revised. *Cincinnati: Shepard & Stearns.* 1840. 12mo, pp. 60.

An Authentic History of Remarkable Persons, who have attracted public attention in various parts of the World; Including a full Exposure of the Iniquities of the Pretended Prophet Joe Smith, and of the Seven Degrees of the Mormon Temple; also an account of the frauds practised by Matthias the Prophet, and other religious impostors. *New York.* 1849. 8vo, pp. 64.

A Book of Commandments, for the government of the Church of Christ, organized according to law, on the 6th of April, 1830. *Zion: W. W. Phelps & Co.* 1833. 32mo, pp. 160. 50729

"Zion" was at Independence, Mo. This book was never published nor even completed. Only two copies are known. The sheets were destroyed by a Missouri mob.

Book of Covenants.
Book of Doctrine. } *See* [Smith (Joseph), *Jun.*]
Book of Mormon.

Brighamism: Its Promises and their Failures. *Plano, Ill.* [n. d.] 8vo, pp. 8. 50730

Catechism for Children, exhibiting the Prominent Doctrines of the Church of Jesus Christ of Latter-Day Saints; By Elder John Jaques. ... Fifteenth Thousand. *Salt Lake City.* 1870. 16mo, pp. 81. 50731

Concordance and Reference Guide to the Book of Doctrine and Covenants, Published by the Reorganized Church of Jesus Christ of Latter Day Saints. *Plano, Ill.* 1870. 24mo, pp. 23.

The Demoralizing Doctrines and Disloyal Teachings of the Mormon Hierarchy. The Condition of Woman in Polygamy. *New York.* 1866. 8vo, pp. 18. 50733

Document containing the Correspondence, Orders, &c. in relation to the disturbances with the Mormons: and the Evidence given before the Hon. Austin A. King, Judge of ... Missouri ... November 12, 1838. ... *Fayette, Missouri.* 1841. 8vo, pp. (4), 163. 50734

A very rare piece. I have seen only one copy.

Elders Journal of the Church of Latter Day Saints. Vol. i. No. i. *Kirtland.* 1837. 8vo, pp. 16. 50735

The Ensign of Liberty of the Church of Christ. Vol. i. No. i. *Kirtland.* 1847. 8vo, pp. 16. 50736

Edited by Dr. W. E. McLellin.

Epitome of the Faith and Doctrines of the Reorganized Church of Jesus Christ of Latter Day Saints. *Plano.* [n. d.] Folio, 1 leaf. 50737

The Gospel. *Plano.* [n. d.] 8vo, pp. 2. 50738

The Gospel Reflector, in which the Doctrine of the Church of Jesus Christ of Latter-Day Saints is set forth ... . Edited by Elder B. Winchester ... . *Philadelphia: Brown, Bicking & Guilbert, Printers.* 1841. 8vo, pp. (4), 316. 50739

The Harp of Zion, A Collection of [Mormon] Poems, &c. By John Lyon. With Notes ... . *Liverpool: Published for the Benefit of the Perpetual Emigrating Fund.* 1853. 16mo, pp. xi, 223. 50740

Idolatry. [On Mormonism.] *Plano.* [n. d] 12mo, pp. 4.

Keep it constantly before the Public, that Eternal Life, is the Knowledge of God, by Direct Revelation. Published by John E. Page, Elder of the Church of Jesus Christ, of Latter Day Saints, a. d. 1843. [n. p. n. d.] Folio, 1 leaf. 50742

"Designed to be put into a frame, or otherwise suspended in some conspicuous place for the convenience of visitors to read."

Latter Day Saints' Messenger and Advocate. Vol. i. No. i. *Kirtland, Ohio, October,* 1834. 8vo. 50743

A monthly. Vols. i. and ii. are paged continuously, and number 384 pages. Afterward continued as "Messenger and Advocate of the Church of Christ."

Latter Day Saints' Millennial Star. Volume i. *Liverpool.* 1839. 8vo. 50744

Law Case [of Pascal B. Smith]. *See* Vol. ix., No. 39340.

Listen to the Voice of [Mormon] Truth. Vol. i. No. i. *New York: Printed by S. Brannan & Co.* 1844. 12mo, pp. 4.

Memorial to Congress from a Committee of the Reorganized Church of Jesus Christ of Latter Day Saints, on the Claims and Faith of the Church. *Plano, Illinois.* [1870.] Imp. 8vo, pp. 8.

Mormon Expositor. No. i. *Salt Lake.* [n. d.] 8vo, pp. 4.

The Mormon Imposture; an Exposure of the Fraudulent Origin of the "Book of Mormon." [*Newbury.*] 1840. 12mo, pp. 12. + Second Edition. *London: G. Hall.* [n. d.] 12mo, pp. 16. 50748

The Mormon Question. Being a Speech of Vice-President Colfax at Salt Lake City, a Reply thereto by Elder John Taylor, ... *Salt Lake City.* 1870. 8vo. 50749

The Mormon Trip, Life Scenes in Utah. [n. p. n. d.] 8vo.

Om Mormonerne. Brev fra Suebfersvend J..... D.... i America, til hans Faber, Boelsmand D. P........ ... *Bjorring .. M. Petersen.* [n. d.] 12mo, pp. 16. 50751

Mormonerne, eblu De fidste Dages Hellige. *Slesvig.* 1853. 12mo, pp. 31. 50752

Mormoniad. [A Poem.] *Boston: A. Williams & Co.* 1858. 8vo, pp. 100. h. 50753

Mormonism. [By W. J. Conybeare.] Reprinted from the Edinburgh Review, No. 202, April 1854. *London: John Murray.* 1854. 12mo, pp. 112. b. 50754

Mormonism: Embracing the Origin, Rise and Progress of the Sect ... . also, their troubles in Missouri ... . By James H. Hunt. With an Appendix, giving ... the late disturbances in Illinois ... . By G. W. Westbrook. *St. Louis: Printed by Ustick & Davies.* 1844. 12mo, pp. 304, 36. 50755

Mormonism Exposed! An Epistle of Demetrius, Junior, the Silversmith, To the Workmen of like occupation and all others whom it may concern—Greeting. Showing the best way to preserve our Craft and put down the Latter Day Saints. [*Pittsburgh, about* 1842.] Folio, 1 leaf. 50756

Mormonism or the Bible? A Question for the Times. By a Cambridge Clergyman. Second Edition. *Cambridge: J. Dixon.* mdccclii. 12mo, pp. (2), 32. 50757

Mormonism Unveiled; or, a History of Mormonism from its Rise to the Present Time. *London: C. H. Clarke.* [1855.] Post 8vo, pp. 250. 50758

Mormonismen och Swedenborgianismen. *Upsala: Warlstrom & C.* 1854. 8vo, pp. 27. 50759

Mormonismen wederlagd of Den Heliga Skrifts och Historiens Wittnesbörd. *Stockholm.* 1858. 18mo, pp. 68. 50760

The Mormons; or, Knavery Exposed. Giving an Account of the Discovery of the Golden Plates, building a Temple, establishment of a Bank ... . *Frankfort, Pa.: E. G. Lee.* 1841. 8vo, pp. 24. c. 50761

The Mormons. The Dream and the Reality; or Leaves from the Sketch Book of Experience of one who left England to join the Mormons in the City of Zion, and awoke to a consciousness of its Hienous Wickedness and Abominations. Edited by a Clergyman. [W. B. F.] *London: J. Masters.* 1857. 16mo, pp. viii, 92. 50762

See [Mayhew (H.)], Vol. xi., No. 47126, [Sunderland (Leroy)], *and* [Van Dusen (I. and M.)]. *See also* "Dublin Univ. Mag.," xxi., "Edinb. Rev.," xcix., "Westminster Rev.," New Series, iii., "Revue des Deux Mondes," Sept. 1, 1853. For other anonymous works, *see* under the first word (particles excepted) of the title.

Mornand (F.) *and* Vilbort (J.) Voyage illustré dans les deux Mondes d'après les relations authentiques les plus nouvelles. Par Félix Mornand et Joseph Vilbort. *Paris: Le Chevalier.* 1862. 4to, pp. (4), 404. 775 Engravings. c. 50763

The engravings are from "L'illustration."

Mornay (E. de). Report on the Proposed Railway in the Province of Pernambuco, Brazil. By Edward de Mornay. [*London.* 1855.] 8vo, pp. 20. 2 Maps. 50764

The Morning and Evening Prayer. The Litany, and Church Catechism. Ne Orhoengene neoni Yogaraskhagh Yondereanayendaghkwa, Ne Ene Niyoh Raodeweyena, neoni Onoghsadogeaghtige Yondadderighwanondoenthia. *Boston, New-England: Printed by Richard and Samuel Draper.* 1763. 18mo, pp. (2), 24.

See also Claesse (L.), iv. 13180. Thomas quotes an edition, *Philadelphia, Printed by Andrew Bradford,* 1715, which is, I think, a mistake.

[Mornington (*Earl of*).] Letters of Themistocles, with Appendix, containing the Character of Dr. Franklin ... . *London.* 1795. 12mo. 50766

Moro (G.) Abstract of a Report on the Practicability of forming a Communication between the Atlantic and Pacific Oceans, by means of a Ship Canal across the Isthmus of Tehuantepec. By Gaetano Moro. [*London:*] *Clay Smith & Co.* [*about* 1845]. 8vo, pp. (2), 16. Map. c. 50767

[Moro.] An Account. *See* Vol. vii., No. 26546, etc., *and* Vol. xi., No. 47520.

Moro. Communication between the Atlantic and Pacific Oceans through the Isthmus of Tehuantepec. Additional Observations to the Report lately given on this subject by the Engineer Signor Gaetano Moro ... . *Ackermann and Co., London.* 1854. 8vo, pp. 16. b. 50768

Moro. L'Isthme de Tehuantepec et L'Isthme de Panama. Exámen des projets de communication maritime proposés Pour ces deux Isthmes. Par G. Moro. *Mexico:* 1848. *Imprimerie de I. Cumplido.* 8vo, pp. 12. 50769

Moro. Observations in Relation to a Communication between the Atlantic and Pacific Oceans, through the Isthmus of Tehuantepec, founded on a report ... by Señor Gaetano Moro ... . *New York: R. Craighead, Printer.* 1849. 8vo, pp. v, 48. 3 Maps. c., h. 50770

Moro. Reconocimiento del Istmo de Tehuantepec, practicado en los años 1842 y 1843, con el objeto de una Comunicacion Oceánica. ... *Mexico: Imprenta de Vicente Garcia Torres.* 1844. Folio, pp. (2), 40. 2 Maps. 50771

Moro (G.) Informe en derecho, sobre que la compañia de el real assiento de la Gran Bretaña, establecida para la introduccion de esclavos negros, en estas Indias, debe declararse libre, y exempta de la paga de los reales derechos ... . Y sobre que aunque esto no procediera assi, deben declararse libres de su contribucion los efectos de repressalia, sin que ni en el vno, ni en el otro caso deba su magestad hazer rebaja, ni descuento à los assentistas indianos, de la renta annual. Por Gerardo Moro, natural de la ciudad de Dingle, en el reyno de Irlanda. *Mexico: J. F. de Ortega.* 1724. Folio, (2) and 127 leaves. c. 50772

A very rare and curious work.

Moro-Mastix : | Mr Iohn Goodwin | whipt with his own Rod. | Or | The dissecting of the sixteenth Section of | his book truly nam'd by himself | Hagio-Mastix : | So far as it falsly and frivolously mentions a | late disputation in Christ-Church Parish, con- | cer- | ning the lawfulness of paying Tythes. | By a diligent observer of the said Disputation. | *London,* | *Printed for Tho. Underhill* ... . 1647. | 4to, pp. 15. 50773

Morote (L.) Despertador Republicano, que por las Letras del A. B. C. Por Luis Morote, Padre de la Provincia de Yucatan. *Mexico.* 1700. 4to. 50774

Morpeth (*Lord*). *See* [Howard (G. W. F.)], viii. 33248–9.

Morphy (P.) The Exploits and Triumphs, in Europe, of Paul Morphy, The Chess Champion; including an Historical Account of Clubs, Biographical Sketches of Famous Players ... . By Paul Morphy's Late Secretary. *New York: D. Appleton and Company.* M.DCCC.LIX. 12mo, pp. viii, 203. Portraits. c.

Morrell (A. J.) Narrative of a Voyage to the Ethiopic and South Atlantic Ocean, Indian Ocean, Chinese Sea, North and South Pacific Ocean, in the years 1829, 1830, and 1831. By Abby Jane Morrell, who accompanied her husband, Capt. Benjamin Morrell, Jr., on the Schooner Antarctic. ... *New-York: J. and J. Harper.* 1833. 12mo, pp. 230. Portrait. H. 50776

The scenes and adventures of which Mrs. Morrell was a witness were highly interesting.

Morrell (A.) ... Morrell's Miscellany for Travelers and the Fireside. ... *New York: Arthur Morrell.* 1852. 6 vols., 16mo. 50777

Morrell (B.), *Jr.* A Narrative of Four Voyages, to the South Sea, North and South Pacific Ocean, Chinese Sea, Ethiopic and Southern Atlantic Ocean, Indian and Antarctic Ocean. From ... 1822 to 1831. Comprising Critical Surveys of Coasts and Islands, with Sailing Directions. And an Account of New and Valuable Discoveries, including the Massacre Islands, &c. To which is prefixed A Brief Sketch of the Author's early Life. By Captain Benjamin Morrell, Jun. *New-York: J. & J. Harper.* 1832. 8vo, pp. (6), 492. Portrait. + *New York: Harper & Brothers.* 1853. 8vo. A. 50778

See "Monthly Review," cxxxii. 193, *and* "American Quarterly Review," xiii. 314.

Morrell (D. J.) Letter from Daniel J. Morrell, Esq. ... Showing the amount of direct and indirect Taxes on American Iron, as compared with the Import Duties levied upon Foreign Iron, &c. *Philadelphia: Sherman & Co., Printers.* 1865. 12mo, pp. 12. H. 50779

Morrell. The Protective Policy and the Warehousing System: A Report submitted ... June, 1868. By Mr. Morrell ... . *Washington.* 1868. 8vo, pp. 45. H. 50780

Also: Financial Condition of the Country. Speech ... January 25, 1868. *Washington: F. & J. Rives ... Printers.* 1868. 8vo, pp. 16. H.—The National Finances. Speech ... March 10, 1870. *Johnstown, Pa.: Geo. T. Swank, ... Printer.* 1870. 8vo, pp. 15.—Review of the Last Report of Commissioner Wells. ... May 19, 1870 ... . *Washington.* 1870. 8vo, pp. (2), 65. H.

Morrell (L. A.) The American Shepherd: being a History of ... Sheep, with their Breeds, Management, and Diseases. Illustrated ... . With an Appendix, embracing ... Letters from Eminent Woolgrowers ... . By L. A. Morrell. *New York: Harper & Brothers.* 1845. 12mo, pp. xxii, 13–437. B. 50781

Morrell (T.) A Sermon on the Death of General George Washington. By Thomas Morrell ... . Delivered on the 22d of February, 1800, in the City of Baltimore ... . *Baltimore: Printed by Warner & Hanna.* [1800.] 12mo, pp. 29. BA. 50782

Morrell (T. H.) Catalogue of the ... Library of T. H. Morrell, comprising ... Works on America, its History and Antiquities. ... *New York: Bradstreet.* 1866. 8vo, pp. (2), 137.

Twelve copies printed on large paper, in quarto.

Morrell. Catalogue of a Valuable Collection of Books on America, ... belonging to T. H. Morrell, ... sold ... Jan. ...

1869 ... . *New York: Bergen & Tripp, Printers.* 1869. 8vo, pp. 176. BA. 50784

Six copies printed on large paper, in quarto.

[Morrell.] A Sketch of the Life of James Wallack [Sen.], late Actor and Manager. *New York: T. H. Morrell.* 1865. 8vo, pp. 63, (1). c. 50785

Two hundred and fifty copies printed, of which fifty are on large paper.

[Morrell (William).] New-England. | Or | A Briefe | Enarration | of the Ayre, | Earth, Water, Fish, and | Fowles of that Country. | With | A Description | of the Natures, Orders, Habits, | and Religion of the Natiues; | in | Latine and English Verse. | ... | *London,* | *Imprinted by I. D.* | 1625. | 4to, Title and Dedications, pp. (6), Text, 24, Postscript, (2). BM. 50786

Reprinted in the "Collections of the Massachusetts Historical Society," Vol. i. The English portion is included in "American Notes and Queries," Part 4, *Philadelphia,* 1857 The only copy I have seen is in the British Museum.

Morrill (D. L.) Sermon delivered next Lord's Day after the Interment of Lieut. Thomas R. Roby. By David L. Morrill. *Concord, N. H.* 1812. 8vo. 50787

Morrill (I.) ... A Sermon, ... at Lexington, April 19, 1780. In Memory of the Commencement of the unnatural War between Great Britain and America; which took place in said Town April 19, 1775. By Isaac Morrill, A.M. ... *Boston, New-England: Printed by John Gill.* M,DCC,LXXX. 8vo, pp. 30.

Morrill. The Soldier exhorted to Courage ... . A Sermon preach'd at Wilmington, April 3. 1775. To Capt. Phinehas Osgood, and His Company of Soldiers: ... . By Isaac Morrill, A.M. ... *Boston; New-England: Printed ... by J. Draper.* 1755. 8vo, pp. 23. B., H., M., W. 50789

Morrill (J. S.) Cabinet Officers in Congress. Speech of Hon. Justin S. Morrill, January 25, 1865. [n. p. n. d.] 8vo, pp. 8. H. 50790

Morrill. Tariff. Speech of Hon. Justin S. Morrill, ... February 6, 1857 ... . [n. p. n. d.] 8vo, pp. 8. + April 23, 1860. [n. p. n. d.] 8vo, pp. 8. + June 28, 1866. [n. p. n. d.] 8vo, pp. 8. 50791

Also: The Currency. Speech ... December 11, 1867. *Washington.* 1867. 8vo, pp. 16.—Eight-Hour Law. Speech ... December 15, 1869. *Washington: F. & J. Rives ... Printers ... .* 1869. 8vo, pp. 16.—An exclusively Paper Currency Inconsistent with Permanent Prosperity. Speech ... January 24, 1867. *Washington.* 1867. 8vo,

pp. 14.—Explanation of the Internal Tax Bill. Speech ... March 12, 1862. [n. p. n. d.] 8vo, pp. 8.—The Funding Bill. Speech ... March 3, 1868. *Washington: F. & J. Rives ... Printers ... .* 1868. 8vo, pp. 14.—Impeachment of the President. Opinion ... May 11, 1868. [n. p. n. d.] 8vo, pp. 14.—The Impolicy of Making Paper a Legal Tender. Speech ... February 4, 1862. [n. p. n. d.] 8vo, pp. 8.—Letter on the Knit Goods Manufacture ... . *Boston.* 1866. 8vo.—Modern Democracy. The Extension of Slavery ... . Speech ... June 6, 1860. ... [n. p. n. d.] 8vo, pp. 8.—A Protective Tariff or Free Trade. Speech ... May 9, 1870. *Washington: F. & J. Rives ... Printers ... .* 1870. 8vo, pp. 20.—Public Debt and Currency. Speech ... February 11, 1869. [n. p. n. d.] 8vo, pp. 7.—Remarks ... in reply to Mr. Voorhees, of Indiana, ... May 21, 1862. [n. p. n. d.] 8vo, pp. 8.—Speech ... on the Loan Bill; ... February 21, 1866. *Washington.* 1866. 8vo, pp. 8.—Speech ... in favor of terminating the Reciprocity Treaty with Great Britain, ... January 27, 1864. *Washington, D. C.: McGill & Witherow, Printers.* 1864. 8vo, pp. 14. —Tax Bill. Speech ... April 19, 1864. ... [n. p. n. d.] 8vo, pp. 7. H.

Morrill (L. M.) Speech of Hon. L. M. Morrill ... . on the Confiscation of Property. ... March 5, 1862. [n. p. n. d.] 8vo, pp. 16. H. 50792

Another speech on the same subject, May 1, 1862. 8vo, pp. 8.—Speech ... on Unmanufactured Cotton. ... April 25, 1866. [n. p. n. d.] 8vo.

Morrill (N.) The Lord's Voice in the Earthquake ... . A Sermon Preach'd in ... New-Castle, ... New-Hampshire, ... Novemb. 16. 1727. ... A Day of ... Fasting ... occasioned by the late awful and terrible Earthquake. ... By Nathaniel Morrill, A.M. & V.D.M. ... *Boston in New-England: Richard Jenness and Joseph Lock.* 1728. 16mo, pp. (2), iv, 32. H. 50793

The preacher "looked upon it to be very unseemly and unbecoming, for Persons to dress themselves up in their forlorn *Hoop'd-Coats,* to appear before God in his House."—*Page* 27. Also: Memento Mori. A Plain Discourse to a Plain People. ... *Boston.* 1730. 12mo, pp. (2), iv, 68.

Morrin (J.) Inaugural Address at the opening of the Quebec School of Medicine. By Joseph Morrin, M.D. *Quebec.* 1849. 8vo, pp. 31. 50794

Morris (A.) ... Canada and her Resources: An Essay, to which, ... was awarded, by ... Sir Edmund Walker Head, Bart., ... The Second Prize. By Alexander Morris, A.M. ... *Montreal: Printed by John Lovell.* 1855. 8vo, pp. 156. + Second Edition. *Montreal: B. Dawson.* 1855. 8vo, pp. 119, (1). 2 Maps. B.

Morris. Nova Britannia; or, British North America, its Extent and Future. A Lecture. By Alexander Morris, A.M. ... *Montreal: Printed by John Lovell.* 1858. 8vo, pp. 67. H.

Also: The Hudson's Bay and Pacific Territories. A Lecture. ... *Montreal.* 1859. 8vo, pp. 57.

[Morris (Anthony Saunders).] Memoranda of the Descendants of Amos Morris, of East Haven, Conn. *New York: A. S. Barnes & Company.* 1853. 12mo, pp. 103. B. 50797

Mr. Whitmore names E. L. Hart and O. Street as the compilers. Reproduced in 1861 as a chart, 8x6 feet.

[Morris (Apollos).] *See* M. (A.), Vol. x., No. 42900.

Morris (B. F.) Christian Life and Character of the Civil Institutions of the United States, developed in the Official and Historical Annals of the Republic. By B. F. Morris. ... *Philadelphia: George W. Childs.* 1864. 8vo, pp. 831. H. 50798

Morris. The Life of Thomas Morris: Pioneer and long a legislator of Ohio, and U. S. Senator from 1833 to 1839. Edited by his son, B. F. Morris. ... *Cincinnati: Printed by Moore, Wilstach ... .* 1856. 12mo, pp. 408. H. 50799

Morris. Memorial Record of the Nation's Tribute to Abraham Lincoln. ... Compiled by B. F. Morris. *Washington, D. C.: W. H. & O. H. Morrison.* 1865. 8vo, pp. 272. Portrait and 5 Plates. H. 50800

Also: Historical Sketch of Rising Sun, Indiana. A Discourse. ... *Cincinnati.* 1858. 8vo.—Our Country. Three Discourses, on National Subjects. ... *Lawrenceburgh (Ind.)* 1848. 12mo, pp. 63. H.

Morris (B. W.) The Opportunities of Life. The Sermon ... at the Forty-Eighth Anniversary of the Society ... for the Advancement of Christianity in Pennsylvania, ... 1860. *Philadelphia: King & Baird, Printers.* 1860. 8vo, pp. 27. H. 50801

Also: The Work done, ... by the Society for the Advancement of Christianity in Pennsylvania. A Sermon ... . *Philadelphia: King & Baird, Printers.* 1856. 12mo, pp. 12. H.

Morris (C.) Memoir of Miss Margaret Mercer, by Caspar Morris, M.D. Second Edition, with Additions. *Philadelphia: Lindsay & Blakiston.* 1848. 12mo, pp. 268. Portrait. A.

Morris [Charles]. A Collection of Songs, by the Inimitable Captain Morris. Part the First. *London: James Ridgway.* MDCCLXXXVI. 8vo, pp. 33. 50803

Morris. A Complete Collection of Songs, by Captain Morris. The Twelfth Edition, Revised, Corrected and Enlarged. *London.* 1790. 8vo, pp. 38, 22. Portrait. 50804

Among the poems contained in this collection occurs the famous one entitled "Billy Pitt and the Farmer," narrating the adventures which befell "Billy," "Brittania's Prime Ruler," and "Harry, a staunch friend to Boston," as they were returning on a

dark night from a cabinet meeting, with their "Skins full of wine." The poem ends with this oft-quoted stanza:

"Solid Men of Boston Make no long orations;
Solid men of Boston Banish strong Potations;
Solid men of Boston Go to bed at sundown,
And never lose your way, Like the loggerheads of London."

Another edition is entitled "The Festival of Ancareon (*sic*) ... The Ninth Edition. ... *Dublin: C. Jackson.* 178–. 8vo, pp. 40. *See* "Historical Magazine," Vol. i. pp. 39 and 216–217. This song is also included in Morris's "Lyra Urbanica," *London.* 1840. 2 vols., 12mo.

Morris. Quashy; or, the Coal-Black Maid. A Tale relative to the Slave Trade. ... *London.* 1796. 8vo. 50805

Morris (C.) Brief Notice of the late Commodore Charles Morris. [n. p. 1856.] 8vo, pp. 15. H. 50806

From the Providence Journal. Possibly by William Gammell.

Morris (C.) Remarks upon Mr. Mills's Proposals for publishing a Survey of the Trade of Great Britain and Ireland, and the British Colonies. By Corbyn Morris. *London.* 1771. Folio.

Morris (D.) Speech of Hon. Daniel Morris, ... on the Confiscation Bill. ... Jan. 21, 1864. [n. p. n. d.] 8vo, pp. 8. BA.

Morris (D.) An Interesting Narrative of the Voyage, Shipwreck, and ... Adventures of Mr. Drake Morris ... . *London: John Abraham.* 1797. 12mo, pp. xi, (4), 198. 50809

Morris. The Travels, Sufferings, and Distresses of Mr. Drake Morris in Several Voyages at Sea ... . *London.* 1755. Post 8vo. 50810

Rare and curious account of the buccaneers, by a captive who was forced to join them in the Island of Tortuga.

Morris (E.) The Tennessee Gazetteer, or Topographical Dictionary; containing a Description of the several Counties, Towns, Villages, Post Offices, Rivers, Creeks, Mountains, Valleys, &c. in the State ... . To which is prefixed a general Description of the State ... And a condensed History from the earliest Settlements down to ... 1834. With an Appendix ... . By Eastin Morris. *Nashville: W. Hassell Hunt & Co.* 1834. 8vo, pp. (4), cxvi, 178, (18). c. 50811

[Morris (Edmund).] Derrick and Drill, or an Insight into the Discovery, Development, and Present Condition and Future Prospects of Petroleum, in New York, Pennsylvania, Ohio, West Virginia, &c. Arranged and Edited from Numerous

Sources ... . *New York: James Miller.* 1865. 12mo, pp. 227. Map. B. + [*Ibid.*] 1866. 50812

[Morris.] Farming for Boys. ... *Boston: Ticknor and Fields.* 1868. 16mo, pp. ix, (2), 286. H. 50813

[Morris.] How to get a Farm, and where to find One. ... With the Public Law on the Subject of Free Homes, and Suggestions from Practical Farmers; ... . *New York: James Miller.* 1864. 12mo, pp. 345. B., C. 50814

[Morris.] Ten Acres Enough. A Practical Experience, showing how a very small Farm may ... keep a very large Family. *New York.* 1864. 12mo. + Third Edition. [*Ibid.*] 50815

Morris (E. D.) Historical Discourse delivered December 3, 1865, at ... Columbus, Ohio, on the Tenth Anniversary of his Pastorate. By Rev. Edward D. Morris. With an Appendix. *Columbus.* 1866. 8vo. 50816

Morris (E. J.) Speech of Hon. Edward Joy Morris, ... in Defence of the American Navy, ... December 28, 1843. *Washington: Printed by Jno. T. Towers.* 1844. 8vo, pp. 8. H. 50817

Also: Admission of Kansas. ... Speech ... March 26, 1858. [*Washington.* 1858.] 8vo, pp. 8. B.—Speech ... in Defence of the Tariff of 1842, ... April 24, 1844. *Washington.* 1844. 8vo, pp. 16.—Speech ... on the Revision of the Tariff, and in defence of the protective policy. ... February 2, 1859. [n. p. n. d.] 8vo, pp. 16.—Speech ... on the Election of Speaker ... December 8, 1859. *Washington.* 1859. 8vo, pp. 6.— ... Speech ... on the Tariff Question. ... April 24th, 1860. [n. p. n. d.] 8vo, pp. 16.—Union—Peace—Popular Rights. Speech ... January 30, 1861. [n. p. n. d.] 8vo, pp. 16. H.

Morris (E. S.) Second Address to the People of Color of Pennsylvania, With ... Remarks for my own Race. By Edward S. Morris. *Philadelphia: James H. Bryson, Printer.* 1863. 8vo, pp. 24. H. 50818

Morris (E.) On the Improvement of the Ohio River. By Ellwood Morris, Civil Engineer. [n. p. n. d.] 8vo, pp. 34. 2 Plates. + *Pottsville: Printed by Benjamin Bannan.* 1857. 8vo, pp. 32. 2 Plates. H. 50819

Morris (G. P.) American Melodies; containing a ... Selection from the Productions of Two Hundred Writers. Compiled by George P. Morris. ... *Philadelphia.* 1840. 12mo. + *New York.* 1841. 18mo, pp. 286. BA. 50820

Reproduced as "The Gift Book of American Melodies" ... . *Philadelphia.* 1854 12mo.

Morris. The Deserted Bride; and other Poems. By George P. Morris. *New-York: Adlard & Saunders.* MDCCCXXXVIII. 8vo, pp. 80. BA. + *New York: D. Appleton & Co.* 1843. 8vo, pp. 172. P. 50821

Includes many pieces on American topics. The illustrations are from paintings by Weir and Darley.

Morris. The Little Frenchman and his Water Lots, with Other Sketches of the Times. By George P. Morris. ... *Philadelphia.* 1839. 12mo. + [n. p. n. d.] 8vo, pp. 16. B.

With twenty-eight illustrations by D. C. Johnston, the "American Cruikshank."

Morris. Poems of George P. Morris: with a Memoir of the Author. *New York: Charles Scribner.* [1860.] 16mo, pp. 336. H. 50823

Morris. ... Songs and Ballads: By George P. Morris. [n. p. n. d.] 8vo, pp. 16. B. + *New York.* 1852. 8vo. A.

Morris. The Prose and Poetry of Europe and America: consisting of Literary Gems and Curiosities ... . Compiled by G. P. Morris and N. P. Willis. ... Seventh Edition. *New York: Leavitt, Trow & Co.* 1848. 8vo, pp. 600. 50825

Morris (G.) The Advantages of the Proposed Canal from Lake Erie, to Hudson's River, fully illustrated in a Correspondence between The Hon. Gouverneur Morris, and Robert Fulton, Esq. [n. p. 1814.] 8vo, pp. 13. B. 50826

[Morris.] An Answer to War in Disguise; or, Remarks upon The New Doctrine of England, concerning Neutral Trade. ... *New York: Printed by Hopkins and Seymour, for I. Riley & Co.* 1806. 8vo, pp. 76. + *London: Johnson.* 1806. 8vo. 50827

See "Monthly Review," L. 216.

Morris. An Inaugural Discourse, ... before the New-York Historical Society, by the Hon. Gouverneur Morris, ... 4th September, 1816; the 206th Anniversary of the Discovery of New-York, by Hudson. *New York: T. & W. Mercein.* 1816. 8vo, pp. 24. H. 50828

[Morris.] Notes on the United States of America. *Philadelphia.* 1816. 8vo, pp. 48. 50829

First written in a letter to a friend, and afterwards printed for circulation.

[Morris.] Observations on the American Revolution. Published according to a Resolution of Congress, by their Committee.

For the Consideration of those who are desirous of comparing The Conduct of the opposed Parties, and The several Consequences which have flowed from it. *Philadelphia: Printed by Styner & Cist.* M DCC LXXIX. 8vo, pp. (4), 122. C., H., P. + ... *Providence, Reprinted.* 1780. 8vo, pp. 126. 50830

A skillful and official résumé of the American view of the question. Reprinted the same year, in the "Remembrancer."

MORRIS. An Oration, upon The Death of General Washington, By Gouverneur Morris. Delivered at ... New-York, on the 31st day of December, 1799. ... *New-York: Printed by John Furnam* ... . 1800. 8vo, pp. 24. BA., N. 50831

MORRIS. An Oration in Honor of the Memory of George Clinton, Late Vice-President ... May 19, 1812. By the Hon. Gouverneur Morris. *New York: Printed by Hardcastle & Van Pelt.* 1812. 8vo, pp. 18. 50832

Also: Discourse ... before the New-York Historical Society, ... 6th December, 1812. ... *New-York: James Eastburn.* 1813. 8vo, pp. 40.—An Oration, ... July 5th, 1813, before the Washington Benevolent Society of ... New-York, in Commemoration of American Independence. ... *New-York: The Society.* 1813. 8vo, pp. 27. BA.—An Oration, ... June 29, 1814, ... in celebration of the ... Deliverance of Europe from ... Military Despotism. ... *New-York: Van Winkle and Wiley.* 1814. 8vo, pp. 23. + *Salem.* 1814. 8vo, pp. 16.—Speech ... on the Free Navigation of the Mississippi. *Philadelphia.* 1803. 8vo. The authorship of our Nos. 8126–7, has been attributed to Morris. *See* New York Historical Society, Sparks (J.), *and* Williston (E. B.)

[MORRIS.] Report of the Commissioners, appointed by an Act of the Legislature of ... New-York, entitled "An Act ... for the Improvement of the Internal Navigation of the State," ... *New-York: Prior and Dunning.* 1811. 8vo, pp. 38. BA. + *Albany: Printed by S. Southwick.* 1812. 8vo, pp. 40. B. 50833

MORRIS (I.) A | Narrative | of the | Dangers and Distresses | Which befel | Isaac Morris, | and | Seven more of the Crew, | Belonging to | The Wager Store-Ship, | Which attended | Commodore Anson, | In his Voyage to the South Sea: | Containing | An Account of their Adventures, | after they were left by Bulkeley and Cummins, | on an Uninhabited Part of Patagonia, ... where they remained ... 'till they were | seized by a Party of Indians, and carried | ... into the Inland Country, ... | After which they were carried to | Buenos-Ayres, and ransomed by the Governor, | ... Interspersed with | A Description of the Manners and | Customs of the Indians in that Part of the | World ... . The Whole | Serving as a Supplement to Mr. Bulkeley's Journal, | Campbell's

Narrative, and Ld. Anson's Voyage. | By I. Morris, late Midshipman of the Wager. | *London:* | *S. Birt.* [1751.] 8vo, pp. 87. H.

"This narrative appears to be genuine, and is well and methodically written," etc.—*Monthly Review*, v. 156.

MORRIS (I. N.) ... Abstracted Indian Trust Bonds. ... Mr. Isaac N. Morris, ... submitted the following Report. [*Washington.* 1861.] 8vo, pp. 365. 50835

MORRIS. Grant: and why he should be elected President. Speech of the Hon. Isaac N. Morris. [n. p. n. d.] 8vo, pp. (2), 17. H. 50836

Also: Argument ... on Indian Affairs, against the Bill proposing to establish a Territorial Government over the Indians. ... Feb. 2, 1870. *Washington.* 1870. 8vo, pp. 15.—Argument ... involving the question of the power of the Government to collect Taxes in the Indian Territory ... . Made ... June 6, 1870. *Washington.* 1870. 8vo, pp. 18.—Speech ... on the Status of the States and Questions ... connected therewith, ... in Springfield, Ill., Jan. 11th, 1867 ... . [n. p. n. d.] 8vo, pp. 23. H.

MORRIS (J.) Address of Gen. Jacob Morris, President of the Otsego County Agricultural Society, ... at Cooperstown, Oct. 14, 1817. Together with the Address of Elkanah Watson, Esq. ... *Cooperstown: Printed by H. and E. Phinney.* 1817. 8vo, pp. 16. B., N. 50837

MORRIS (J.) An Oration, delivered in South-Farms, in Litchfield, February 22, 1800, Commemorative of the Death of General George Washington, who died December 14th, 1799 ... . By James Morris, Esq. *Printed at Litchfield, by T. Collins.* [1800.] 8vo, pp. 29. 50838

MORRIS. A Statistical Account of several Towns in the County of Litchfield. By James Morris ... . Published by the Connecticut Academy of Arts and Sciences. *New Haven: Oliver Steele.* 1815. 8vo, pp. 124. N., S. 50839

MORRIS (J. P.) Valedictory Oration, Senior Class, Philadelphia Academy, July 27, 1809. By James P. Morris. *Philadelphia.* 1809. 8vo. 50840

MORRIS (J. B.) Memorial to the Legislature of Maryland. By John B. Morris. *Baltimore: Printed by Lucas & Deaver.* 1836. 8vo, pp. 21. 50841

The title of another edition reads: "Memorial of John B. Morris to the Legislature of Maryland." *Annapolis: William M'Neir, Printer.* 1836. 8vo, pp. 21. *See also* Maryland, our Vol. x., No. 45078, etc.

MORRIS (J. G.) ... Catalogue of the Described Lepidoptera of North America. Prepared for the Smithsonian Institution by John G. Morris. *Washington: Smithsonian Institution.* 1860. 8vo, pp. viii, 68. C., H. 50842

Included in the Smithsonian "Miscellaneous Collections," Vol. III.

MORRIS. Life of John Arndt. By John G. Morris ... . *Baltimore: T. N. Kurtz.* 1853. 18mo, pp. 237. Portrait. C.

MORRIS. Martin Behaim, the German Astronomer and Cosmographer, of the Times of Columbus: ... Annual Discourse before the Maryland Historical Society ... January 25, 1855. By John G. Morris, D.D. *Baltimore: Maryland Historical Society.* 1855. 8vo, pp. 48. C., H. 50844

MORRIS. ... Synopsis of the Described Lepidoptera of North America. Part I. Diurnal and Crepuscular Lepidoptera. Compiled ... by John G. Morris. *Washington: Smithsonian Institution.* 1862. 8vo, pp. xxvii, 376. B., C. 50845

Included in the Smithsonian "Miscellaneous Collections," Vol. IV. Also: Alphabetical Catalogue of Books proposed to be purchased for the Peabody Institute, Baltimore. *Baltimore.* 1861. 8vo, pp. 415. H.

MORRIS (J. H.) Patchwork; or, Holy Men engaged in Unholy Work. A Controversial, Moral and Political Essay. By John H. Morris. *Leavenworth: Insley & Wright, ... Printers.* 1868. 8vo, pp. 46, (1). H. 50846

MORRIS (L.) The Case of Lewis Morris, Esq; late Chief Justice of the Province of New York, who was removed from the said office by H. E. William Cosby, Governor of said Province. *London.* 1735. Folio, pp. 8. S. 50847

Signed, J. Willes. We know of one copy only—in the New York State Library, at Albany.

MORRIS. Observations on the Reasons given by Mr. [John] Hamilton's Advisers, for his detaining the Seals of the Province of New Jersie, after the demand made of them by Lewis Morris, President of the Council and Commander-in-Chief of the Province of New Jersie. [*New York.* 1736?] Folio, pp. 11.. C.

Probably printed by J. P. Zenger, and possibly unique.

[MORRIS.] The Opinion and Argument of the Chief Justice of the Province of New York, concerning the Jurisdiction of the Supream Court of the said Province, to determine Causes in

a Court of Equity. *New York: J. Peter Zenger.* 1733. Folio, pp. 15. C. + The Second Edition. [*Ibid.*] S. 50849

Relates to the case of Van Dam.

MORRIS. The Papers of Lewis Morris, Governor of the Province of New Jersey, From 1738 to 1746. ... *New York: George P. Putnam.* 1852. 8vo, pp. xxxii, 336. C., H. 50850

With an introductory memoir by William A. Whitehead. Forms Vol. IV. of the "Collections of the New Jersey Historical Society."

MORRIS. The Speeches of His Excellency Lewis Morris, Esq; Governor of New-Jersey &c. To the House of Assembly of the said Province met in General Assembly at Burlington on the 22d of June, 1744. . With the Assembly's Address and Message to His Excellency. To which is Added, An Abstract of the Bill, entitled An Act for Settling and better Regulation of the Militia of the Province of New-Jersey, and for making Provision in cases of Rebellion, Insurrection or Invasion; as sent down from the Council to the House of Assembly, upon the 20th of June. And some Observations from the Votes of the Assembly. *Philadelphia: Printed by B. Franklin.* 1744. 4to, pp. 36.

Thomas' "History of Printing" quotes the following: "Speech ... to the Assembly of the Province of New Jersey, Dissolving them, Nov. 29, 1742." *Philadelphia.* 1743. Of course, the title is incorrect.

MORRIS (M.) Private Journal kept during a portion of the Revolutionary War, for the Amusement of a Sister. By Margaret Morris, of Burlington, N. J. [Edited by John J. Smith, Jr.] *Philadelphia: Privately Printed.* 1836. Sm. 4to, pp. 31. + *New York: Privately Re-printed.* 1865. 4to, pp. (4), 36. C.

Fifty copies reprinted, of which twelve copies only have the new title-page and preface, edited by J. G. Shea.

MORRIS (M. O'C.) Rambles in the Rocky Mountains: with a Visit to the Gold Fields of Colorado. By Maurice O'Connor Morris ... . *London: Smith, Elder and Co.* 1864. 8vo, pp. viii, 264. BA. 50853

MORRIS (M.) Morris Morris's Reasons for his Conduct in the Present Assembly, in the year 1728. 8vo. 50854

I find this title in a Philadelphia catalogue. There was a squabble that year in the House of Representatives of Pennsylvania.

MORRIS (M. N.) Discourses at West Hartford, Conn., March 8 and 15, 1863, on the One Hundred and Fiftieth Anniversary. By Myron N. Morris. *West Hartford.* 1863. 8vo.

MORRIS (O. W.) Remarks on the Quantity of Rain at different heights, New York. Read Sept. 17, 1855. [n. p. n. d.] 8vo, pp. 4. S. 50856

MORRIS (P.) Arguments to prove the Policy and Necessity of granting to Newfoundland a Constitutional Government; being a Letter to the Right Hon. W. Huskisson, Esq. By Hon. Patrick Morris. *London.* 1828. 8vo. 50857

MORRIS. Remarks on the State of Society, Religion, Morals, and Education, at Newfoundland. By Patrick Morris. *London.* 1827. 8vo. 50858

[MORRIS.] A Short Reply to the Speech of Earl Aberdeen, and also a Letter to the ... Marquis of Normanby, on the State of Newfoundland. By a Member of the House of Assembly of Newfoundland. *Liverpool.* 1839. 8vo, pp. 19. 50859

Also: A Short Review of the History, Government, Constitution, Fishery and Agriculture, of Newfoundland, In a Series of Letters addressed to ... Earl Grey. ... *St. Johns, ... I. Woods, Printer.* MDCCCXLVII. 8vo, pp. xvii, 136.

MORRIS (P.) Pete Morris' American Comic Melodist. ... *New York: Robert M. DeWitt.* [1857.] 18mo, pp. 72. 50860

MORRIS (P. P.) Mining Rights in Pennsylvania. A Lecture, ... November 10th, 1860. Before The Law Academy of Philadelphia. By P. Pemberton Morris, Esq. ... *Philadelphia: 300 copies only printed for the Law Academy.* 1860. 8vo, pp. 48. H.

MORRIS [Richard V.] A Defence of the Conduct of Commodore Morris during his Command in the Mediterranean. With Strictures on the Report of the Court of Enquiry held at Washington. *New-York: I. Riley & Co.* 1804. 8vo, pp. 98, (1). Map. B., C., N., S. 50862

[MORRIS (Robert).] Morris, Arnold, and Battersby. [*London.* 1782.] 8vo, pp. 32. P. 50863

Very rare. By Mr. R. Morris of Wales. It consists of an attack on Gen. Arnold by Mr. Morris, and a defense by Capt. Battersby of the 29th regiment.

MORRIS (R.) A Short Account of the Slave Trade ... . By Robert Morris. *London.* 1789. 8vo. 50864

[MORRIS (Robert).] An Historical Account of the ... Canal Navigation in Pennsylvania. With an Appendix, containing Abstracts of the Acts of the Legislature since ... 1790 ... . *Philadelphia: Printed by Zachariah Poulson, Junior.* M DCC XCV. 4to, pp. (2), xvi, 80. BA. 50865

MORRIS. Plan for Establishing a National Bank for the United States ... . To which is annexed, a Resolution of Congress, of the 26th of May, 1781, acceding thereto; And a Particular Explanation of the Use of said Bank, By Robert Morris, Esquire, Superintendant [*sic*] of the Finance of America. *Providence: ... Bennett Wheeler.* [1781.] 8vo, pp. 11. 50866

[MORRIS.] A Statement of the Accounts of the United States ... during the administration of the Superintendent of Finance, Commencing with his Appointment, on the 20th ... of February, 1781, and Ending with his Resignation, on the 1st ... of November, 1784. *Philadelphia: Printed by Robert Aitken.* M.DCC.LXXXV. Folio. C., H., P., W. 50867

MORRIS. Statements of the Receipts and Expenditures of Public Monies, during the Administration of the Finances by Robert Morris, Esquire, ... with other Extracts and Accounts from the Public Records, made out by the Register of the Treasury, by Direction of the Committee of the House of Representatives, Appointed ... the 19th March 1790, upon the Memorial of the said late Superintendant of Finance. [*Philadelphia.* 1790.] Folio, pp. 36, 4, 14. W. 50868

MORRIS. To the Citizens of Philadelphia ... Robert Morris. Philadelphia, July 7. 1779. *Philadelphia: Printed by Hall & Sellers.* [n. d.] Folio, pp. 2. P. 50869

An exposition of his conduct, in reply to the attacks of Paine and others. The following relate to Morris: Account of Robert Morris' Property. [*Philadelphia:*] *King & Baird, Printers.* [n. d.] 8vo, pp. 74.—Deeds. Heirs of Robert Morris to Robert S. Paschall; and Robert S. Paschall to John Moss. *Philadelphia: Printed by Quinn & Swan.* 1854. 8vo, pp. 18.—Life of Robert Morris, the Great Financier; ... *Desilver, Publisher.* 1841. Impl. 8vo, pp. 8. Plate.—Robert Morris' Property. *Philadelphia: King & Baird, Prs.* [n. d.] 8vo, pp. 45. BA. *See also* J. Sanderson's "Biography of the Signers."

MORRIS (Robert), *pseudon.* The Organization of the Public Debt and a Plan for the Relief of the Treasury. By Robert Morris [*i. e.* James S. Gibbons]. *James Miller, New York.* 1863. 8vo, pp. 22. H. 50870

MORRIS (R.) The History of Freemasonry in Kentucky ... and brief Historical Abstracts, an American Masonic Bibliography; A Current History of Cotemporaneous Events in other States and Countries; Historical and Statistical Tables, and the entire Catalogue of the Masons of Kentucky. By Rob. Morris, ... *Louisville, Ky.: Rob. Morris.* 1859. 8vo, pp. 592. 50871

MORRIS. The Masonic Martyr. The Biography of Eli Bruce, Sheriff of Niagara County, New York, who ... was imprisoned twenty-eight months in the Canandaigua Jail. By Rob. Morris ... . *Louisville, Ky.: Morris & Monsarrat.* 1861. 12mo, pp. 314. S. 50872

Also: Circular ... to the Freemasons of Michigan, July, 1863. [n. p. n. d.] 8vo, pp. 4.—The Dictionary of Freemasonry: ... *Chicago, Illinois: John C. W. Bailey.* 1867. 12mo, pp. 518, (1).—Life in the Triangle, or Freemasonry at the Present Time. ... *Louisville: Printed by J. F. Brennan & Co.* 1854. 16mo, pp. 284.—The Lights and Shadows of Free Masonry. ... *Louisville, Ky.: J. F. Brennan.* 1852. 8vo, pp. 390, ii. B. + Sixth Edition. [*Ibid.*]—Solemn Protest, directed to the Masonic Brethren of Missouri, ... concerning the Society of Conservators in May, 1863 ... . [n. p. n. d.] 8vo, pp. 4.

MORRIS (R. D.) Slavery its Nature, Evils, and Remedy. A Sermon ... [at] Newtown, Pennsylvania. ... July 27, 1845. By Rev. Robert D. Morris ... . *Philadelphia: Printed by William S. Martien.* 1845. 8vo, pp. 31. BA. 50873

MORRIS (R. H.) By the Honourable Robert Hunter Morris, Esq; Lieutenant-Governor and Commander in Chief of the Province of Pennsylvania, and Counties of New-Castle, Kent, and Sussex, on Delaware, A Proclamation. ... *Philadelphia: Printed by B. Franklin and D. Hall.* 1756. Folio, 1 leaf. P. 50874

Relates to the suspension of hostilities against the Delawares on the Susquehannah. Dated 23d June.

MORRIS (R. H.) Obituary Addresses on the ... Death of the Hon. Robert H. Morris, Justice of the Supreme Court of ... New-York. ... *New-York: W. E. & J. Sibell.* 1855. 8vo, pp. 115. 50875

Also: The Opinion of the Attorney-General, on the legality of The Conduct of Robert H. Morris, Recorder of ... New-York, in going to the house of one Pierce in the night time, and seizing certain private papers. ... *Albany: Printed by Hoffman, White and Visscher.* 1841. 8vo, pp. 12.

MORRIS (T.) Miscellanies in Prose and Verse. By Captain Thomas Morris. *London: James Ridgway.* 1791. 8vo, pp. 181. Portrait. 50876

Very rare. The author served as Captain under General Bradstreet, and his journal gives an interesting account of his experience during the campaign against Pontiac, in which he was made a captive by the Indians. Other particulars can be found in Parkman's "Conspiracy of Pontiac." *See* "Hist. Mag.," I. 84. One "J. O. W.," who compiled the catalogue of Mr. J. H. V. Arnold's library, New York, 1879, mistakes *this* Captain Morris for Captain Charles Morris—a *very* different person.

MORRIS (T. A.) A Discourse on Methodist Church Polity. By Thomas A. Morris, D.D. *Cincinnati: L. Swormstedt & A. Poe.* 1859. 16mo, pp. 93. Portrait. C. 50877

MORRIS. Miscellany: Consisting of Essays, Biographical Sketches, and Notes of Travel. By Rev. T. A. Morris, D.D., one of the Bishops of the Methodist Episcopal Church. *Cincinnati: L. Swormstedt & A. Poe.* 1853. 12mo, pp. 390. Portrait.

Also: Discourse Commemorative of B. Waugh, D.D. ... *New York.* 1860. 12mo.

MORRIS (V.) A Narrative | Of the Official Conduct of | Valentine Morris, Esq. | Late Captain General, Governor in Chief, &c. &c. | of the | Island of St. Vincent and its Dependencies. | Written by himself. | Supported by his Official Correspondence with the Secretary of | State, Lords of the Treasury, and other of his Majesty's | Servants, Admirals, Governors, &c. | The Originals to be found in the respective Offices, and the | Duplicates now in his Possession. | Also by other Documents equally Authentic. | *London:* | *Printed* | ... *by J. Walter* ... . | MDCCLXXXVII. 8vo, pp. (4), xvii, (3), 467. 50879

J. Walter was the founder of the Times newspaper. "Relates principally to the war with America."—RICH, I. 488.

MORRIS (W.) An Address to the People of the United States, and particularly of the Slave States. By Walker Morris. *Louisville: Printed by Bradley & Gilbert.* 1862. 8vo, pp. 50.

MORRIS (W.) Reply to Six Letters of Archdeacon Strachan, ... on the Clergy Reserves Question. By The Hon. William Morris. *Toronto.* 1838. 8vo, pp. 54. 50881

Also: A Letter on the subject of the Clergy Reserves and Rectories, addressed to the Very Rev. Principal Macfarlan and the Revd. R. Burns, D.D. ... *Toronto.* 1838. 8vo, pp. 74.

MORRIS (W.) Ancient Slavery Disapproved of God. The Substance of A Lecture. By William Morris, M.D. *Philadelphia: Scriptural Knowledge Society.* 1862. 12mo, pp. 20. H.

MORRIS. Whence came the Oil? A Popular Essay on the Palæophytic Origin of Petroleum. By William Morris, M.D. *New-York: American News Company.* 1865. 8vo, pp. 24.

MORRIS (W. G.) Address ... before the Society of California Volunteers, at ... San Francisco, April 25th, 1866, By Wm. Gouverneur Morris ... . *San Francisco.* 1866. 8vo, pp. 33, (1).

MORRIS. The Record of William Governeur [*sic*] Morris nominated for U. S. Marshall for California. ... [n. p.:] *Gibson Brothers, Printers.* [1870?] 8vo, pp. 36. H. 50885

MORRIS (W. S.) Sketch of the Union Library Company, Philadelphia. By William S. Morris. *Philadelphia.* 1858. 8vo.

MORRIS, *Conn.* The Chronicle of Sirrom. Translated from the Original Manuscript by Professor Poakphunn, of the University of Shippog ... . *Shippog.* 1869. 8vo, pp. 7. 50887

"A burlesque on the action of the town of Morris, Litchfield County, in refusing the credit of the town for the erection of the Shepaug Valley Railroad. Printed in the Litchfield Sentinel originally, and reprinted at the same office, 1869."

MORRIS CANAL. Charter of the Morris Canal and Banking Company, and the Several Acts of the Legislature in relation thereto. *New York: J. Narine, Printer.* 1836. 8vo, pp. 31.

Reports and Documents relative to the Morris Canal, in New Jersey. *Morristown.* 1823. 8vo. Continued. N. 50889

To the Stockholders of the Morris Canal and Banking Company, April 2, 1860. *New-York: Latimer Rros.* [sic] *& Seymour.* 1860. 8vo, pp. 19, (2). + [*Ibid.*] 1864. H. 50890

Also: Documents relative to the Negotiation of a Loan to the Morris Canal Company. June, 1833. [n. p. n. d.] 8vo. P.

MORRISON (Charles R.) *See* New Hampshire.

[MORRISON (E.)] A Letter from the Worthy Patriarch of Howard Division, No. 26, to the Grand Worthy Patriarch, S. of T. of Nova Scotia. *Halifax: Printed by James Bowes & Sons.* 1867. 12mo, pp. 10. H. 50891

MORRISON (J. M.) Clarsach Albin, and other Poems. By James M. Morrison. Including his Correspondence with Clark, McCammon and Douglass. *Philadelphia: G. B. Zieber & Co.* 1847. 8vo, pp. 108. Plate. C. 50892

MORRISON (J. H.) Our Common Schools. A Discourse ... at Milton, January 30, 1853, By Rev. J. H. Morrison, and An Address ... at the Dedication of a School House, January 24th, 1853, By Rev. A. K. Teele. ... *Dedham: Printed by H. A. Mann.* 1853. 8vo, pp. 24. B. 50893

MORRISON (M.) A History of the Ninth Regiment Illinois Volunteer Infantry. By the Chaplain, Marion Morrison. *Monmouth, Ills:* [sic] *John S. Clark, Printer.* 1864. 8vo, pp. 95.

MORRISON (N. J.) A Memorial Address at Laying the Corner-Stone of the South Hall of Olivet College. By Rev. N. J

Morrison, President ... . *Lansing: J. A. Kerr & Co., Printers.* 1866. 8vo, pp. 34. 50895

MORRISON (R. N.) Eulogy on Daniel Webster, ... at the New England Festival, at San Francisco, December 22d, 1852. By Hon. Rodk. N. Morrison ... . *San Francisco.* 1853. 8vo, pp. 12. 50896

Also: Speech ... on the Constitutional Amendments, ... 1845. *Albany.* 1845. 8vo.

MORRISON (W.) A Sermon, ... at Newburyport, July 20, 1803, at the Installation of ... Rev. John Giles ... . By William Morrison, A.M. ... *Newburyport: E. W. Allen.* 1803. 8vo, pp. 27.

MORRISON (W. M.) Morrison's Strangers' Guide to the City of Washington, and its vicinity. ... *William M. Morrison, Washington City.* 1842. 24mo, pp. (2), 108. H. + Second Edition. [*Ibid.*] 18mo, pp. 108. Plates. + [*Ibid.*] 1852. 24mo, pp. vi, 144. 18 Plates. + [*Ibid.*] 1855. + *Washington, D. C.: W. H. & O. H. Morrison.* 1868. 18mo, pp. 58. Plates. C., H.

Also: 25 Views of the Statues and Public Buildings of Washington. ... *Washington: McGill.* 1860. 12mo.

MORRISON (W. R.) Speech of Col. W. R. Morrison, ... at Edwardsville, Ill., Oct. 13, 1863. *St. Louis: George Knapp & Co.* 1863. 8vo, pp. 19. 50899

Against the administration of Mr. Lincoln.

MORRISTOWN, *N. J.* Bill of Mortality: Being a Register of all the Deaths which have occurred in the Presbyterian and Baptist Congregations of Morris-town, New Jersey, for thirty-eight years past, containing (with but few exceptions), The cause of every decease. This Register, for the first twenty-two years was kept by the Rev. Doctor Johnes, since which time, by William Cherry, the present Sexton of the Presbyterian Church at Morristown ... . *Morris-town: Printed by Jacob Mann.* 1806. 8vo.

The title explains the purpose of this book, and it is to be regretted that so few church records have since been published.

[MORROW (John).] A Voice from the Newsboys. [*New York:*] *The Author.* 1860. 12mo, pp. 135. C., H. 50901

MORSE (A.) Further Traces of the ancient Northmen in America, with Geological Evidences of the location of their Vineland. By Rev. Abner Morse, A.M. ... *Boston: Printed by H. W. Dutton & Son.* 1861. 16mo, pp. 20. H. 50902

MORSE. A Genealogical Record of several families bearing the name of Cutler: in the United States. By Rev. Abner Morse, A.M. *Boston: Samuel G. Drake.* 1867. 8vo, pp. (4), 80.

MORSE. Genealogy of the Descendants of Several Ancient Puritans by the names of Adams, Bullard, Holbrook, Rockwood, Sanger, Grout, Goulding and Twitchell. By Rev. Abner Morse, A.M. *Boston: Damrell & Moore.* 1855. 8vo, pp. (4), 214. 15 Portraits and Plate. BA. + *Boston: The Author.* 1857. 8vo, pp. (4), 358. 19 Portraits, 2 Plates. C. 50904

The first volume of a series. Whitmore says "this work was published again in 1856, with a new title-page, and additions pp. 265–340. Pages 53–7 were also remodeled, and seven pages of new matter inserted between pp. 57–8, all relating to the Bullards. The illustrations also are very different." Vols. II., etc., are entitled:

MORSE. A Genealogical Register of the Descendants of several Ancient Puritans. Volume II. By Rev. Abner Morse ... . [Brigham, Hapgood, Willis and Cutler.] *Boston: Press of H. W. Dutton & Son.* 1859. 8vo, pp. (4), 96, (2). 11 Portraits and Plate. C. + Volume III. ... [Richards. *Ibid.*] 1861. 8vo, pp. (4), 243. Portraits and Plate. H. + Volume IV. ... [Harding. *Ibid.*] 1864. 8vo, pp. 96, (2). Portrait. 50905

MORSE. A Genealogical Register of the Descendants of the Early Planters of Sherborn, Holliston, and Medway, Massachusetts. By Rev. Abner Morse ... . *Boston: Press of Damrell & Moore.* 1855. 8vo, pp. 264. Portraits. 50906

MORSE. A Genealogical Register of the Inhabitants and History of the Towns of Sherborn and Holliston, By Rev. Abner Morse ... . *Boston: Damrell & Moore.* 1856. 8vo, pp. (8), 342. 2 Plates, 6 Portraits and Plan. H. 50907

MORSE. The Genealogy of the Descendants of Capt. John Grout. By Rev. Abner Morse ... . *Boston: The Author.* 1857. 8vo, pp. (2), 86. Plate and 7 Portraits. H. 50908

MORSE. Genealogy of the Descendants of Lawrence Litchfield, the Puritan. By Rev. Abner Morse ... . *Boston: The Author.* 1855. 8vo, pp. 18. 3 Portraits. BA. 50909

Reprinted from the "New England Historical and Genealogical Register" for April, 1855.

MORSE. Genealogy of the Descendants of Richard Sanger, the Puritan. By Rev. Abner Morse ... . *Boston: George Coolidge.* 1851. 8vo, pp. 12. 2 Portraits. 50910

MORSE. Memorial of the Morses; containing the History of Seven Persons of the Name, who settled in America in the seventeenth century. With a catalogue of ten thousand of their descendants ... . To which are added Biographical Sketches of many of their Number. By Rev. Abner Morse ... . *Boston: William Veazie.* 1850. 8vo, pp. viii, 171, (136). 4 Plates and 19 Portraits. H. 50911

Also: Willis Genealogy ... Printed for the Family. *Boston.* 1863. 8vo, pp. 8.

MORSE (C. W.) Morse's General Atlas of the World. Containing Seventy Maps, drawn ... By Charles W. Morse. With Descriptions and Statistics ... to ... 1856, By Charles Colby, A.M. ... *New York: D. Appleton and Company.* 1856. 4to. B.

MORSE (E.) An Ancient Promise improved, in a Sermon preached at the Instalment of the Rev. Mr. James Wellman, at Cornish, N. H., Sept. 29, 1768. By Ebenezer Morse, M.A. *Boston: Printed ... by Kneeland and Adams.* 1769. 8vo, pp. 21.

MORSE (E. B.) An Oration, ... at Westborough (Mass.) ... July 4th, 1804. In Commemoration of American Independence. By Ebenezer Belknap Morse, A.B. *Printed at Worcester, By Sewall Goodridge.* 1804. 12mo, pp. 12. B., H., W. 50914

This oration created an unusual tempest in the Westborough teapot.

MORSE (E. S.) Observations on the Terrestrial Pulmonifera of Maine, including a Catalogue of all the Species of Terrestrial and Fluviatile Mollusca known to Inhabit the State, By Edward S. Morse. *Portland: Stephen Berry, Printer.* 1864. 8vo, pp. 63. 10 Plates. H. 50915

Also: The Brachiopoda, a Division of Annelida. ... [n. p.] 1870. 8vo, pp. 5. Diagrams. — A Classification of Mollusca, based on the Principle of Céphalization. ... [*Salem.*] 1865. 8vo, pp. 17. Plate. — Descriptions of New Species of Pupadæ. ... [n. p.] 1865. 8vo, pp. 6. Diagrams. H.

[MORSE (F. H.)] ... American Seamen. ... Letter from the American Consul at London. ... [n. p. 1869.] 8vo, pp. 8. H.

MORSE (F. W.) Personal Experiences in the War of the Great Rebellion, from December, 1862, to July, 1865. By F. W. Morse ... . *Albany, N. Y.* 1866. 8vo, pp. 152. B. 50917

MORSE (H. B.) A Brief Memoir of Horace Bassett Morse. ... *Portsmouth, N. H.* 1830. 18mo, pp. 96. 50918

MORSE (H. J.) *See* Connecticut, Vol. IV., Nos. 15784–5.

MORSE (I. E.) The War with Mexico. Speech of Hon. Isaac E. Morse, of Louisiana, February 1, 1848. ... [n. p. 1848.] 8vo, pp. 7. H. 50919

Also: Speech ... in defence of the Mexican War. ... December 22, 1846. *Washington: Ritchie and Heiss, Printers.* 1846. 8vo, pp. 16. — Speech ... on the Territorial Bill. ... February 24, 1849. *Washington: John T. Towers, Printer.* 1849. 8vo, pp. 8. — Speech, ... in relation to California, March 4, 1850. [n. p. n. d.] 8vo. S.

MORSE (J.) A Narrative Of the Proceedings Of the Baptist Church in Medfield, against James Morse. Copied from their Records. Together with Mr. Morse's Remarks ... . By James Morse. ... *Boston: Printed by Benjamin Edes and Son.* M,DCC,-LXXXV. 8vo, pp. 34. H., M. 50920

[MORSE (Jason).] Annals of the Church in Brimfield. By the Pastor ... . *Springfield: Samuel Bowles & Company, Printers.* 1856. 8vo, pp. 83, (1). Map. B. 50921

MORSE (J.) An Abridgment of the American Gazetteer. Exhibiting, ... a Compendious Account of the ... American Continent, and its appendant Islands; Particularly the West-Indies. ... By Jedidiah Morse, D.D. ... Abridged by the Author. ... *Printed at Boston, By Thomas and Andrews.* 1798. 12mo, pp. 388. Map. H. + Second Edition. *Troy.* 1816. 12mo. S. 50922

MORSE. The American Gazetteer, exhibiting, ... a Much more full and accurate Account, than has been given, of the States, Provinces, Counties, Cities, &c. on the American Continent, also Of the West-India Islands ... . Collected and compiled ... by ... Jedidiah Morse, D.D. ... *Boston: Printed ... [by] S. Hall.* 1797. 8vo, pp. viii, (619). 7 Maps. + *Boston: Thomas & Andrews.* 1798. 12mo. Map. + The Second Edition ... . *London: J. Stockdale.* 1798. 8vo, pp. viii, 634. 7 Maps. + Second Edition, revised, corrected and enlarged. ... *Charlestown: Samuel Etheridge.* 1804. 8vo, unpaged. 6 Maps. B., H. + Third Edition, revised and corrected. *Boston: Thomas & Andrews.* 1810. 8vo, unpaged. 2 Maps H., S. 50923

An abridgment of the copious title. "Mr. John Lendrum had a considerable share in the compilation of this work."—RICH, I. 403. "Celebrated for its exact description of the fine old quaint and portly inhabitants of Albany. 'This city and suburbs, by enumeration in 1797, contained 1263 buildings, of which 863 were dwellinghouses, and 6021 inhabitants. Many of them are in the Gothic style, with the gable end to the street, which custom the first settlers brought from Holland.' Just fancy in our days an Albany Dutchman standing with his gable end to the street, and without a pipe in his mouth!"—STEVENS.

MORSE. The American Geography; or, A View of the Present Situation of the United States of America. ... By Jedidiah Morse. *Elizabeth Town: Printed by Shepard Kollock, for the Author.* M,DCC,LXXXIX. 8vo, pp. xii, 534, (4). 2 Maps. + Second Edition. *London: John Stockdale.* M.DCC.XCII. 8vo, pp. xvi, 536. 2 Maps. + Third Edition. *Dublin: John Jones.* 1792. 8vo. + A New Edition, Revised, Corrected, and Greatly Enlarged, by the Author ... . *London: John Stockdale.* 1794. 4to, pp. vi, (6), 715. 25 Maps. + *Edinburgh.* 1795. 8vo. Maps.

The following is a Dutch translation:

MORSE. Tegenwoordige Staat der Vereënigde Staaten van Amerika; Behelzende: een algemeen verslag van derzelver grenzen, meiren, baaijen, rivieren, bergen, voortbrengzelen, bevolkinge, regeeringsform, landbouw, koophandel, fabrieken, nevens de historie van den laatsten oorlog. ... *Amsterdam. By Pieter den Hengst.* 1793–1796. 4 vols., 8vo, pp. viii, 263; 240; 272, Map; 300, and Index. J.C.B. 50925

There are also versions in other European languages. *See* Bigland's "Geographical and Historical View," No. 5338.

MORSE. The American Universal Geography, or, A View of the Present State of all the Empires, Kingdoms, States, and Republics in the Known World, and of the United States of America in particular. ... By Jedidiah Morse, A.M. ... Part I. Being a New Edition of the American Geography ... . *Boston: Isaiah Thomas and Ebenezer T. Andrews.* MDCCXCIII. 2 vols., 8vo, pp. 5–696; (4), 552. Maps. H. + Second Edition. [*Ibid.*] 1795. 2 vols., 8vo. + Third Edition, corrected and ... enlarged. The Introduction revised and amended by Samuel Webber, A.M. ... Part I. Part II. ... Second Edition of this Volume. [*Ibid.*] 1796. 2 vols., 8vo, pp. 808; iv, 692. Maps. + Part II. Third Edition of this Volume. [*Ibid.*] 1801. 8vo, pp. iv, 692. Maps. + Fourth Edition, ... enlarged. ... [*Ibid.*] 1802–1805. 2 vols., 8vo, pp. 831, (1); 664. Maps. + Part First. ... Fifth Edition Corrected ... . Part Second. ... Fourth Edition of this Volume. *Boston: Printed by J. T. Buckingham.* 1805. 2 vols., 8vo, pp. 6, (2), 17–864; 664. Maps. + Sixth Edition. ... *Boston: Thomas & Andrews.* 1812. 2 vols., 8vo, pp. 872; 8–831, (1). Maps. + Seventh Edition. ... *Charlestown: Lincoln & Edmands.* 1819. 2 vols., 8vo, pp. 898, (1); 859. Maps. + Eighth Edition. *Boston: I. Thomas.* 1802. 8vo. + Eleventh Edition ... . *Boston: Thomas & Andrews.* 1807. 12mo, pp. 432. 2 Maps. C. 50926

For an adverse criticism, *see* F[reeman] (J.), Vol. VII., No. 25764.

MORSE. Annals of the American Revolution; or a Record of the Causes and Events which produced, and terminated in the Establishment and Independence of the American Republic. Interspersed with numerous appropriate Documents and Anecdotes. To which is prefixed a summary Account of the First Settlement of the Country, and some of the principal Indian Wars ... and a Biography of the principal Military Officers, who were instrumental in achieving our Independence. ... By Jedidiah Morse, D.D. ... *Hartford.* 1824. 8vo, pp. (4), 400, Appendix, 50. 5 Plates. B., P. 50927

MORSE. An Appeal to the Public, on the controversy respecting the Revolution in Harvard College, and the events which have followed it; occasioned by the use which has been made of certain complaints and accusations of Miss Hannah Adams, against the author. By Jedidiah Morse, D.D. *Charlestown: The Author.* 1814. 8vo, pp. viii, 190, (2). B., H. 50928

The most remarkable quarrel in American literary annals, occasioned by both parties being simultaneously engaged in a "History of New England." For a review, *see* [Lowell (John)], Vol. X., No. 42461.

MORSE. A Compendious and Complete History of Modern Geography. ... By Jedidiah Morse, D.D. ... *Boston: Thomas and Andrews.* 1814. 8vo, pp. 670, (1). 7 Maps. H. 50929

MORSE. A Compendious History of New England, designed for Schools and Private Families. By Jedidiah Morse, DD. and Rev. Elijah Parish, A.M. ... *Charlestown: Printed ... by Samuel Etheridge.* 1804. 12mo, pp. 388. Map. B. 50930

MORSE. A Compendious History of New England, exhibiting an interesting view of the first settlers of that Country, their Character, their Sufferings, and their Ultimate Prosperity. Collected and arranged, from authentic sources of information, By Jedidiah Morse, D.D. and Rev. Elijah Parish, A.M. ... *London: Printed by William Burton ... for C. Taylor.* 1808. 8vo, pp. (16), 207. 50931

Of this edition there are copies on large paper.

MORSE. A Compendious History of New England, designed for Schools and Private Families. By Jedidiah Morse, D.D. and Elijah Parish, D.D. Second Edition, with Improvements by the Authors. *Published at Newburyport by Thomas and Whipple. Joseph Cushing, Printer, Amherst, N. H.* [1809.] 12mo, pp. 8, 9, 336. Map. 50932

MORSE. A Compendious History of New-England: to which is added, a Short Abstract of the History of New-York, and New Jersey. ... By Jedidiah Morse, D.D. and Elijah Parish, D.D. Third Edition, Enlarged and Improved. *Charlestown: Printed by S. Etheridge.* 1820. 12mo, pp. 324. H. 50933

MORSE. A Description of the Soil, Productions, Commercial, Agricultural and Local Advantages of the Georgia Western Territory: Together with a ... View of the Claims of Georgia and of the United States to this Territory ... . Extracted, ... from Rev. Dr. Morse's American Gazetteer ... . *Boston: Printed by Thomas & Andrews.* 1797. 12mo, pp. 24. Map. H. 50934

MORSE. Elements of Geography. ... On a new Plan. ... By Jedidiah Morse, D.D. ... *Printed at Boston, By I. Thomas and E. T. Andrews.* 1795. 24mo, pp. 143. 2 Maps. H. + [*Ibid.*] 1796. + Third Edition Improved. [*Ibid.*] 1798. 12mo, pp. 143. Maps. + Fifth Edition Improved. *Boston: Thomas & Andrews.* 1804. 18mo, pp. 143, (1). 2 Maps. + Sixth Edition. *New-Haven: H. Howe.* 1825. 18mo, pp. 162. 4 Maps.

MORSE. Geography made Easy. Being a short, but Comprehensive System of that Science, &c. ... for the use ... of Schools in the United States. By Jedidiah Morse, A.B. ... *New-Haven: Printed by Meigs, Bowen and Dana.* [1784.] 12mo, pp. 214, (1). 2 Maps. C., H. + Second Edition ... . *Printed at Boston, by Isaiah Thomas* ... . MDCCXC. 12mo, pp. 322. 2 Maps. + Fourth Edition, abridged, corrected and enlarged ... . *Printed at Boston, By I. Thomas & E. T. Andrews.* 1794. 12mo, pp. 432. 9 Maps. + Fifth Edition, corrected ... . [*Ibid.*] 1796. 12mo, pp. 432. Maps. + Seventh Edition, corrected ... . [*Ibid.*] 1800. 12mo, pp. 432. 2 Maps. + *Boston: I. Thomas.* 1802. 12mo. + Tenth Edition, corrected ... . *Boston: Printed by J. T. Buckingham.* 1806. 12mo, pp. 432. 2 Maps. + Eleventh Edition, ... *Boston: Thomas & Andrews.* 1807. 12mo, pp. 432. 2 Maps. + Fourteenth Edition, and Second of this New Abridgment. [*Ibid.*] 1811. 12mo, pp. 362, (1). 2 Maps. + Fifteenth Edition ... . [*Ibid.*] 1812. 12mo, pp. 360. 2 Maps. + Sixteenth Edition ... . [*Ibid.*] 1813. 12mo, pp. 364. 2 Maps. + From the Sixteenth ... Edition. *Troy: Printed by Parker and Bliss.* 1814. 12mo, pp. 360. 2 Maps. + Eighteenth Edition ... . *Boston: Thomas & Andrews.* 1816. 12mo, pp. 364. 2 Maps. + Nineteenth Edition ... . [*Ibid.*] 1818. + Second Troy, ... Edition. *Troy: Parker & Bliss.* 1816. 12mo, pp. 364. 2 Maps.

+ Twentieth Edition. *Utica: William Williams.* 1819. 12mo, pp. 364. 2 Maps. H. + By Jedidiah Morse, D.D. and Sidney Edwards Morse, A.M. Twenty-Second Edition. *Boston: Richardson & Lord.* 1820. 12mo, pp. 368. H. 50936

The precursor of the "American Geography." *See also* "A New System of Geography," No. 50940, *infra.*

[MORSE.] The History of America. In Two Books. Containing, I. A General History of America. II. A Concise History of the late Revolution. Extracted from the American Edition of the Encyclopædia. *Philadelphia: Thomas Dobson.* MDCCXC. 12mo. + The Second Edition. [*Ibid.*] MDCCXCV. 12mo. + The Third Edition. [*Ibid.*] M,DCC,XCVIII. 12mo, pp. viii, 356. + New Edition. *Philadelphia: J. Webster.* 1819. 12mo, pp. 455. Map. C. 50937

Reprinted from the "Encyclopaedia; or Dictionary of Arts and Sciences, and Miscellaneous Literature. Published by Thomas Dobson." 1798–1803. 21 vols.

MORSE. Modern Atlas, adapted to Morse's School Geography. *Boston: Richardson & Lord.* 1828. 4to. 10 Maps. H. 50938

MORSE. A New ... General Atlas. Comprising all the New Discoveries to the Present Time. Containing ... Maps, Drawn by Arrowsmith and Lewis. Intended to accompany the New ... Edition of Morse's Geography ... . *Boston: Thomas & Andrews.* 1812. 4to, pp. (4). 63 Maps. B., C. 50939

MORSE. A New System of Geography, Ancient and Modern ... with an Atlas ... . By Jedidiah Morse, D.D. and Sidney Edwards Morse, A.M. Twenty-Third Edition. *Boston: Richardson & Lord.* 1822. 12mo, pp. viii, 13–278, (2), 100. B. + Twenty-Fifth Edition. [*Ibid.*] 1826. 16mo, pp. 342. C.

See "Geography made Easy," No. 50936, *supra*, for earlier editions.

MORSE. A New Universal Gazetteer, ... By Jedidiah Morse, D.D. ... and Richard C. Morse, A.M. Fourth Edition, Revised and Corrected. *New-Haven: S. Converse.* 1823. 8vo, pp. 856.

MORSE. A Prayer and Sermon, Delivered at Charlestown, December 31, 1799; On the Death of George Washington; Late President; and Commander in Chief of the Armies of the United States ... . With an additional Sketch of his Life. By Jedidiah Morse, D.D. ... To which is prefixed, an account of the Proceedings of the Town on the melancholy occasion; written by Josiah Bartlett, Esq. Annexed is the "Veledictory [*sic*] Ad-

dress of the Deceased" ... . *Charlestown: Printed by Samuel Etheridge.* 1800. 8vo, pp. 46, 36, 24. H. + To which is prefixed The Proceedings of the Town in Respectful Testimony of the Distinguished Talents & Pre-eminent Virtues of the Deceased. Written by Josiah Bartlett, Esq. *London: Printed by J. Bateson.* 1800. 8vo, pp. 44, 36. + *Bristol: J. Cottle.* 1800. 8vo.

For another edition, *see* our Vol. III., No. 12114.

MORSE. Proposals, for Printing by Subscription, A Gazetteer of America. ... By ... Jedidiah Morse, D.D. ... [n. p. n. d.] 8vo, pp. (2), 32. H. 50943

[MORSE.] Remarks on the Review of Inchiquin's Letters, published in the Quarterly Review; addressed to the Right Honourable George Canning, Esquire. By an Inhabitant of New-England. *Boston: Samuel T. Armstrong.* 1815. 8vo, pp. 176.

This is also attributed to Timothy Dwight. *See* Vol. VI., No. 21555.

MORSE. A Report to the Secretary of War of the United States, on Indian Affairs, comprising a Narrative of a Tour performed in the Summer of 1820, under a Commission from the President of the United States, for the purpose of ascertaining, for the use of the Government, the actual State of the Indian Tribes in our Country: ... By the Rev. Jedidiah Morse, D.D. ... *New-Haven: ... Printed by S. Converse.* 1822. 8vo, pp. 400, (1). Map and Portrait. P. 50945

The most complete and exhaustive report of the condition, numbers, names, territory, and general affairs of the Indians, ever made. *See* "North Amer. Review," XVI. 30.

[MORSE.] ... Review of American Unitarianism. ... *Boston: Samuel T. Armstrong.* [1815.] 8vo, pp. 31. H. 50946

[MORSE.] ... Review of the Unitarian Controversy. ... *Boston: David J. Burr.* [1815.] 8vo, pp. 56. H. 50947

MORSE. Sacred Performances at the Dedication of the Baptist Meeting-House in Charlestown, May 12, 1801. ... Introductory Address, by Jedidiah Morse, D.D. A Sermon, ... By Samuel Stillman, D.D. and an Address ... by Thomas Baldwin, A.M. *Boston: Printed by Manning & Loring.* [n. d.] 8vo, pp. 30, (1).

MORSE. A Sermon, Preached at Charlestown, November 29, 1798, on the Anniversary Thanksgiving in Massachusetts. With an Appendix ... . By Jedidiah Morse, D.D. ... *Printed by Samuel Hall, Boston.* 1798. 8vo, pp. 74, (6). H. + Second Edition.

[*Ibid.*] 1799. 8vo, pp. 79. H. + Third Edition. [*Ibid.*] + *Worcester: D. Greenleaf.* 1799. 8vo, pp. 88. C. 50949

A remarkable discourse, with an Appendix, giving an account of a French Revolutionary Society, called the "Lodge of Wisdom," with lists of its members in various parts of America.

MORSE. A Sermon, exhibiting the present Dangers, and consequent Duties of the Citizens of the United States of America. Delivered at Charlestown, April 25, 1799. The day of the National Fast. By Jedidiah Morse, D.D. ... *Charlestown: Printed ... by Samuel Etheridge.* 1799. 8vo, pp. 50. + *New York.* 1799. 8vo, pp. 36. + *Hartford.* 1799. 8vo. 50950

MORSE. Signs of the Times. A Sermon, ... before the Society for Propagating the Gospel among the Indians and others in North America, at their Anniversary, Nov. 1, 1810. By Jedidiah Morse, D.D. ... *Printed ... by Samuel T. Armstrong, Charlestown.* 1810. 8vo, pp. 72. B., H. 50951

MORSE. The True Reasons on which the Election of a Hollis Professor ... in Harvard College, was opposed ... Feb. 14, 1805. By Jedidiah Morse ... . *Charlestown: The Author.* 1805. 8vo, pp. 28. B., H. 50952

MORSE. Universal Gazetteer of the Eastern and Western Continents. By Jedidiah Morse, D.D. ... *Boston.* 1810. 2 vols., 8vo. + Third Edition. *New Haven.* 1821. 8vo, pp. 832.

Also: An Address, To the Students at Phillips Academy, in Andover. ... July 9, 1799. ... *Charlestown: Printed by Samuel Etheridge.* 1799. 8vo, pp. 16.—The Character ... of a Good and Faithful Servant. A Sermon ... at Charlestown, April 29, 1798, ... [after] the Death and Interment of the Honorable James Russell, Esq. ... *Printed by Samuel Hall, Boston.* 1798. 8vo, pp. 21.—A Discourse ... in Boston, July 14, 1808, in ... Celebration of the Abolition of the African Slave Trade ... . *Boston: Printed by Lincoln & Edmands.* 1808. 8vo, pp. 28. + Second Edition. [*Ibid.*]—The Duty of Resignation ... illustrated ... in a Sermon ... at Charlestown, April 17, 1796. Occasioned by the Death of the Honorable Thomas Russell, Esquire ... . *Printed by Samuel Hall, Boston.* MDCCXCVI. 4to, pp. 31.—The Gospel Harvest, illustrated in a Sermon at Boston, Jan. 2, 1815, before the Society for Foreign Missions of Boston and Vicinity, at their Annual Meeting. ... *Boston: Printed by Nathaniel Willis.* 1815. 8vo, pp. 28.—The present situation of other Nations of the World, contrasted with our own. A Sermon ... At Charlestown, ... February 19, 1795; ... the day ... for ... Thanksgiving, ... *Printed by Samuel Hall, Boston.* 1795. 8vo, pp. 37. H., M.—A Sermon ... February 28, 1790, upon the Death of Richard Cary, Esq. ... *Printed by Samuel Hall, Boston.* MDCCXC. 4to, pp. 27.—Sermon ... Day of National Fast. ... *Charlestown.* 1797. 8vo.—A Sermon, ... at Boston, ... and ... Charlestown, May 9th, 1798 ... . *Printed by Samuel Hall, Boston.* 1798. 8vo, pp. 29.—A Sermon ... before the Grand Lodge of Free ... Masons of ... Massachusetts, ... at Concord, ... June 25th, 1798. ... *Leominster, Massachusetts: Printed by Brother Charles and John Prentiss.* 1798. 8vo, pp. 24.—A Sermon ... before the Humane Society of ... Massachusetts, ... June 9th, 1801. ... *Boston: Printed by John & Thomas Fleet.* MDCCCI. 8vo, pp. 53.—A Sermon,

... at the Ordination of ... Rev. Hezekiah May, ... in Marblehead, June 23, 1803. ... *Charlestown: Printed ... by Samuel Etheridge.* 1803. 8vo, pp. 27.—A Sermon, ... before the Ancient & Honourable Artillery Company, In Boston, June 6, 1803, being the Anniversary of their Election of Officers. ... *Charlestown: Samuel Etheridge.* 1803. 8vo, pp. 32.—A Sermon, ... at Charlestown, ... after the Interment of Miss Mary Russell, who died, July 24, 1806; ... [n. p.:] *Printed by J. Howe.* 1806. 8vo, pp. 18.—A Sermon, ... in ... Boston, September 25, 1807, before the Managers of the Boston Female Asylum ... . [*Boston:*] *Russell & Cutler, Printers.* 1807. 8vo, pp. 23, (1).—A Sermon, ... May 18th, 1808, at the Ordination of the Rev. Joshua Huntington, ... in ... Boston. ... *Boston: Printed by Belcher and Armstrong.* 1808. 8vo, pp. 32.—A Sermon, ... before the Convention of Congregational Ministers in Boston, ... May 28, 1812. ... *Boston: Samuel T. Armstrong.* 1812. 8vo, pp. 28.—A Sermon ... at Charlestown, July 23, 1812. The Day appointed ... to be observed in Fasting ... throughout the Commonwealth; in consequence of a Declaration of War with Great Britain. ... *Charlestown: Printed by Samuel Etheridge, Jun'r.* 1812. 8vo, pp. 32. — ... A Sermon ... Ordination of Rev. Eliakim Phelps, ... Brookfield, October 23, 1816. ... *Brookfield: Printed by E. Merriam & Co.* 1817. 8vo, pp. 24.—A Sermon, delivered before the American Board of Commissioners for Foreign Missions, at ... Springfield, Massachusetts, September 19, 1821. ... *Boston: Printed ... by George Clark.* 1821. 8vo, pp. 36. + Second Edition. *Washington, D. C.: Davis and Force.* 1822. 8vo, pp. 31.—Tableau de la Situation actuelle des États-Unis d'Amérique, d'après Jedidiah Morse et les meilleurs auteurs Américains. Traduit par C. Pictet. *Paris.* 1795. 2 vols., 8vo. Maps.—The Traveller's Guide; or, Pocket Gazetteer of the United States. ... *New Haven.* 1823. 18mo. S. + Second Edition. [*Ibid.*] 1826. 12mo. *See also* Vol. III., No. 12121, Vol. VIII., No. 31751, *and* Vol. IX. No. 40517.

MORSE (J. T.) A Treatise on the Law relating to Banks and Banking; with an Appendix containing the National Banking Act of ... 1864, and Amendments ... . By John T. Morse, Jr. ... *Boston: Little, Brown, and Company.* 1870. 8vo, pp. xxxviii, (2), 542. B. 50954

MORSE (O. A.) The President's ... Message on the Lecompton Constitution. Speech of Hon. Oliver A. Morse ... . March 20, 1858. [n. p. n. d.] 8vo, pp. 8. 50955

Also: Slavery and Civilization. An Address ... at Cherry Valley, July 4, 1856 ... . *Cooperstown, N. Y.: Hendryx & Wood, Printers.* 1856. 8vo, pp. 12.—A Vindication of the Claim of Alexander M. W. Ball, of Elizabeth, N. J., to the Authorship of the Poem, Rock me to Sleep Mother. ... *New York: M. W. Dodd.* 1867. 8vo, pp. 72.

MORSE (Richard C.) A New ... Gazetteer. *See* Morse (J.)

MORSE (R. M.) Memoir of Hon. Stephen Minot Weld. By Robert M. Morse, Jr. Esq. ... *Boston: David Clapp & Son.* 1868. 8vo, pp. 11. Portrait. H. 50956

MORSE (S. F. B.) Academies of Arts. A Discourse ... May 3, 1827, ... before the National Academy of Design ... . By Samuel F. B. Morse ... . *G. and C. Carvill, New-York.* 1827. 8vo. pp. 60. W. 5095-

MORSE. ... The Constitution. Addresses of Prof. Morse, Mr. Geo. Ticknor Curtis, and Mr. S. J. Tilden ... . *New-York.* [1863?] 8vo, pp. 16. B. 50958

MORSE. Examination of Col. Trumbull's Address, in opposition to the projected Union of the American Academy of Fine Arts, and the National Academy of Design. By Samuel F. B. Morse ... . *New York.* 1833. 8vo, pp. 20. 50959

MORSE. Fine Arts. A Reply to Article X, No. LVIII, in the North American Review, entitled "Academies of Arts," &c. By Samuel F. B. Morse ... . *New-York: G. & C. Carvill.* 1828. 8vo, pp. 45. B. 50960

[MORSE.] Foreign Conspiracy against the Liberties of The United States. The Numbers of Brutus, originally published in the New-York Observer, revised and corrected, with notes, by the author. *New-York: Leavitt, Lord & Co.* 1835. 12mo, pp. xxx, 15–208. + [*Ibid.*] 1835. 12mo, pp. 188. B. + Fourth Edition. *New York: Van Nostrand & Dwight.* 1836. 12mo, pp. 191. H. + Fifth Edition. *New-York: H. A. Chapin & Co.* 1841. 18mo, pp. 191. + Sixth Edition. *New York: American Protestant Society.* 1844. 18mo, pp. 191. BA. + Seventh Edition. *New York.* 1852. 12mo. 50961

The author's name appears on the later editions, in which the title is slightly changed.

[MORSE.] Imminent Dangers to the Free Institutions of the United States through Foreign Immigration, and the Present State of the Naturalization Laws. ... By an American. *New York.* 1835. 8vo. N. + Newly revised and corrected, ... by the Author. ... *New York: John F. Trow, Printer.* 1854. 8vo, pp. 32. H. 50962

[MORSE.] The Present Attempt to dissolve the American Union. A British Aristocratic Plot. By B. *New York: The Author.* 1862. 8vo, pp. 42. B., H. 50963

Also: Confessions of a French Catholic Priest. To which are added, Warnings to the People of the United States. By the Same Author. Edited by Samuel F. B. Morse. *New York: John S. Taylor.* 1837. 12mo, pp. xiv, 255. C.—Descriptive Catalogue of the Pictures, ... from the most celebrated Masters, ... Painted, in Paris, by Samuel F. B. Morse. *New York.* 1833. 8vo.— ... Electro Magnetic Telegraphs. ... Dec. 30, 1842. ... [A letter from Prof. Morse. *Washington.* n. d.] 8vo, pp. 13. Examination of the Telegraphic Apparatus and the Processes in Telegraphy. ... *Washington: Government Printing Office.* 1869. 8vo, pp. 166.—Key to Morse's Picture of the House of Representatives. [*New-Haven?* 1823.] 8vo, pp. 4.— ... Magnetic Telegraph. ... A letter from Professor Morse ... . Dec. 23, 1844. ... [n. p. n. d.] 8vo, pp. 18—Lord Campbell and Professor Morse. Statement of the ... refusal to grant a Patent for Morse's Telegraph in Great Britain in 1838 ... . [n. p. n. d.] 8vo,

pp. 8.— ... The Memorial of Samuel F. B. Morse, Alfred Vail, and Amos Kendall, to the Senate and House of Representatives ... . [n. p. 1849.] 8vo, pp. 7.—Mémoire de Sam. F. B. Morse, Inventeur de la Télégraphie électrique présenté aux Gouvernements Européens. [*Paris.* 1857.] 8vo, pp. 10.—Report of the Dinner given by the Americans in Paris, August the 17th, ... to Professor S. F. B. Morse, in honor of his Invention of the Telegraph, and on the occasion of its completion under the Atlantic Ocean. *Paris: Printed by E. Brière.* 1858. 16mo, pp. 70. BA. *See also* [Harding (G.)], Vol. VIII., No. 30334.

MORSE (S. E.) An Atlas of the United States ... . By Sidney E. Morse, A.M. *New-Haven: N. & S. S. Jocelyn.* 1823. 4to, pp. (24). BA. 50964

MORSE. The Bible and Slavery. By Sidney E. Morse, A.M. ... [n. p. n. d.] 8vo, pp. 8. B. 50965

MORSE. A Geographical, Statistical and Ethical View of the American Slaveholders' Rebellion. By Sidney E. Morse, A.M. Illustrated with a Cerographic Map. *New York: Anson D. F. Randolph.* 1863. 8vo, pp. 19. Map. B. 50966

[MORSE.] Letter on American Slavery. Addressed to the Editor of the "Edinburgh Witness," 8th July, 1846. By An American. From the Edinburgh Edition, Revised ... by the Author. *New-York: Printed by John Henry.* 1847. 8vo, pp. 8.

MORSE. Memorabilia in the Life of Jedidiah Morse, D.D. ... By his Son, Sidney E. Morse ... . *Boston: Arthur W. Locke and Company.* 1867. 12mo, pp. 24. Portrait. B. 50968

MORSE. Morse's North American Atlas. ... *New-York: Harper & Brothers.* 1842. Folio, Title and 46 colored Maps. + [*Ibid.*] 1845. 4to. A. 50969

MORSE. A New System of Modern Geography, or a View of the Present State of the World. With an Appendix, containing Statistical Tables of ... Commerce, ... and various Institutions of the United States ... . By Sidney E. Morse, A.M. ... Accompanied with an Atlas. ... *George Clark, Boston;* ... 1822. 8vo, pp. vi, 9–676. C., H. 50970

See "North American Review," XVI. 176.

[MORSE.] Remarks on the Controversy between Doctor Morse and Miss Adams, ... with some Notice of the Review of Dr. Morse's Appeal. *Boston: Printed by Samuel T. Armstrong.* 1814. 8vo, pp. 33. BA. + Second Edition, with Additions. [*Ibid.*] 1814. 8vo, pp. 35. B. 50971

See No. 50928, *supra*, and [Lowell (John)], Vol. X., No. 42461. Also: Premium Questions on Slavery, each admitting of a Yes or No Answer; addressed to the

Editors of the New York Independent and New York Evangelist ... . *New York: Harper & Brothers.* 1860. 8vo, pp. 30.—A System of Geography, for ... Schools. ... *New-York: Harper & Brothers.* 1844. 4to, pp. 72. Maps and Plates. B. *See also* Morse (J.), No. 50940, *supra.*

MORSE (T.) A Brief Account of the singular circumstances attending the death of Mr. Joseph Morse, of East-Haverhill, Mass. ... By his Brother, Mr. Thomas Morse. *Haverhill.* 1832. 8vo, pp. 7. H. 50972

MORSE (V.) ... An Address by Verranus Morse, M.D. Before the ... Young Men's Christian Associations ... at Albany, June 5th, 1866. ... *Cincinnati.* 1866. 16mo, pp. 16. H. 50973

MORSE (W.) An Oration ... Nantucket, July 4, 1829 ... . By William Morse ... . *Boston: Press of Putnam & Hunt.* 1829. 8vo, pp. 16. 50974

MORSELL (J.) Teachings of the Past. A Discourse ... January, 1859. By the Rev. Joshua Morsell ... . *Washington: Thomas McGill, Printer.* 1859. 8vo, pp. 16. H. 50975

MORSMAN (O.) A History of Breed's (commonly called) Bunker's Hill Battle, fought between the Provincial Troops and the British, June 17, 1775. By Oliver Morsman. *Sackets Harbor (N. Y.): T. W. Haskell.* 1830. 8vo, pp. 17. C. 50976

MORSS (J.) An Account of the Origin, Progress and Present State of the Episcopal Church, in this Town and Vicinity; in a Sermon ... in ... Newburyport, January 6th, 1811, at the ... close of a Century, since the First Establishment of an Episcopal Church in this Place. By James Morss, Rector. ... *Newburyport: E. Little and Co.* [n. d.] 8vo, pp. 32. B., S. 50977

MORSS. Benefits of the Gospel. A Sermon preached in ... Newburyport, ... Dec. 25, 1837. To which is added ... two Discourses on ... the close of a Century since the First Church Edifice was erected in Newburyport. By James Morss, D.D. *Newburyport: Printed by Morss & Brewster.* 1838. 8vo, pp. 44.

MORSS. A Discourse ... in ... Portsmouth, May 29th, 1808; on ... opening the New Church. By James Morss ... . *Newburyport: Edmund M. Blunt—Printer.* 1808. 8vo, pp. 19, (4).

In the appendix is a brief historical account of the church. Also: A Discourse before the Merrimac Bible Society, ... in ... Newburyport, July 31, 1816. ... *Newburyport: Printed by William B. Allen & Co.* 1816. 8vo, pp. 20.— ... A Sermon ... at ... Newburyport, Dec. 25th, 1812. ... *Exeter: Printed by Charles Norris & Co.* 1813. 8vo, pp. 32. H.

[MORSS (James).] Ocean Mail Steamers. The Sloo Contract. Shall it be cancelled? [n. p. 1852?] 8vo, pp. 14. H.

La Mort de Lincoln. *See* Vol. X., No. 41217.

Mortality Statistics. *See* Vol. III., No. 11672.

El Mortero principeño, por el rayo fulminante. *Puerto-Príncipe, imprenta de Minuese.* 1822. 8vo. 50981

MORTGAT (G.) Felix y Adela, Novela Cubana. Original de D. Guillermo Mortgat. *Madrid.* 1850. 2 vols., 16mo, pp. 198, (1); (2), 5–166, (1). 50982

MORTIMER (C. B.) Bethlehem and Bethlehem School. By C. B. Mortimer ... . *New York: Stanford & Delisser.* 1858. 12mo, pp. 208. BA. 50983

Also: Marrying by Lot. A Tale of the Primitive Moravians. ... *New York: G. P. Putnam & Son.* 1868. 12mo, pp. 405. C.—Morton Montagu; ... a Narrative ... in the early history of a ... Moravian ... Clergyman. ... *New-York: D. Appleton & Company.* 1850. 12mo, pp. 255.

[MORTIMER (*Mrs.* Favell Lee).] Far Off; or, Africa and America described: with Anecdotes ... . *London: Hatchard & Co.* 1853. Fcap 8vo, pp. 323. + New Edition. [*Ibid.*] 1856. 12mo, pp. 334. + [*Ibid.*] 1860. 12mo, pp. xv, 416. Map. + *New York: Carter & Brothers.* [n. d.] 18mo. 50984

MORTIMER (G.) Observations and Remarks made during a Voyage to the Islands of Teneriffe, ... Otaheite, Sandwich Islands; Owhyhee, the Fox Islands on the North West Coast of America, Tinian, and from thence to Canton, in the brig Mercury, Commanded by John Henry Cox, Esq. Illustrated ... . By Lieut. George Mortimer ... . *London: T. Cadell.* M.DCC.XCI. 4to, pp. viii, (8), 71, (1). J.C.B. + *Dublin: Printed for P. Byrne.* M.DCC.XCI. 8vo, pp. xiii, 118, (1). P. 50985

See "Monthly Review," v. 422.

MORTIMER. Waarneemingen en Aanmerkingen geduurende eene Reize naar Teneriffe, Van Diemensland, Sandwich-Eiland, de Noord-West-Kust van Amerika, ... onder Bevel van J. H. Cox. Uit het Engelsch vertaald door J. D. Pasteur. *Leyden: A. en J. Honkoop.* 1793. 8vo. 50986

Corrected title of our Vol. V., No. 17258.

MORTIMER (G. F. W.) The Immediate Abolition of Slavery compatible with the Safety and Prosperity of the Colonies. A

Letter ... . By Rev. G. F. W. Mortimer. *Newcastle-upon-Tyne.* 1833. 8vo, pp. 24. S. 50987

MORTIMER (J.) A Collection of Fugitive Poems. By J. Mortimer. *Philadelphia.* 1824. 18mo, pp. 74. 50988

M[ORTIMER] (J.) La Secession aux États-Unis et son origine. Par J. M. *Paris.* 1861. 8vo. 50989

MORTIMER (J.) The Mail Robbers.. *See* Mellon (M.), XI.

MORTIMER (T.) A General Dictionary of Commerce, Trade, and Manufactures; exhibiting their Present State in every part of the World; ... By Thomas Mortimer, Esq. *London: Richard Phillips.* 1810. 8vo, unpaged. H. + The Second Edition, with Additions ... By William Dickinson, Esq. *London: Longman.* 1819. 8vo. + The Third Edition. [*Ibid.*] 1823. 8vo.

MORTIMER. A New and Complete Dictionary of Trade and Commerce: ... By Thomas Mortimer, Esq; ... *London: The Author.* MDCCLXVI–MDCCLXVII. 2 vols., folio. Plate, Plans and Maps. H. 50991

Also: The Elements of Commerce, Politics and Finances ... . *London: The Author.* MDCCLXXII. 4to, pp. (2), xv, (1), 464. H. + [*Ibid.*] 1780. 4to.

MORTON (A.) Oration at Hampden, Me. July 4, 1803. By Andrew Morton. *Hampden.* 1803. 8vo. 50992

MORTON (A. C.) Report on the Survey of the Bangor, Orono and Oldtown Rail-Road. With Remarks on its Advantages ... . By A. C. Morton ... . *Portland: Harmon and Williams, Printers.* 1850. 8vo, pp. 29. Map. H. 50993

Also: Report on the Survey of the European and North American Railway, made under the Authority of the State of Maine ... . *Portland.* 1851. 8vo. Map.

MORTON (C.) The | Spirit | of | Man: | or, | Some Meditations (by way of Essay) on | the Sense of that Scripture. | 1 Thes. 5. 23. ... | By Charles Morton, Minister of the Gospel | at Charlestown in New-England. | *Boston: Printed by B. Harris, for Duncan | Campbell.* 1693. 16mo, pp. (8), 100. B. 50994

At the end is an advertisement of "some little Treatises formerly published by this Author" (2 pages).

MORTON (D. O.) Memoir of Rev. Levi Parsons, late Missionary ... by Rev. Daniel O. Morton, A.M. ... *Poultney (Vt.) Smith & Shute.* 1824. 12mo, pp. (8), 13–431. Portrait. H. + Second Edition: ... *Burlington: Chauncy Goodrich.* 1830. 12mo,

pp. 408. + Second Edition, with Additions. *Hartford: Cooke & Co.* 1830. 12mo, pp. 408. C. + Edited and Abridged by William Innes ... . *Edinburgh: Waugh & Innes.* MDCCCXXXII. 24mo, pp. 283. 50995

Also: ... A Discourse, ... October 16, 1828. On the formation of the Vermont Temperance Society. ... *Montpelier: Printed by E. P. Walton.* 1828. 8vo, pp. 16.—Mrs. Abigal Bayley: a Pilgrim of Ninety Years. ... *Boston: Massachusetts Sabbath School Society.* 1849. 18mo, pp. 288.—A Sermon, ... Shoreham, December 2, 1824, ... Thanksgiving ... . *Smith & Shute, Printers, Poultney.* 1825. 8vo, pp. 14.

MORTON (E.) More last Words to these Churches. In Answer To a Pamphlet published by the Rev. Mr. John Cotton, of Hallifax, entitled, Seasonable Warnings to these Churches. By Ebenezer Morton, One of the Committee of that Precinct in Middleborough which is taken to Task in said Pamphlet. *Boston: Thomas Fleet.* 1746. 8vo, pp. 35. W. 50996

Some copies have the imprint, *Boston: Printed by Edes & Gill.* 1746.

MORTON (E. W.) An Oration ... before the City Authorities of Boston, ... Fifth of July, 1869, ... By Hon. Ellis W. Morton. *Boston: Alfred Mudge & Son, ... Printers.* 1869. 8vo, pp. 32.

MORTON (H. J.) ... A Sermon Preached on the Sunday succeeding the Death of the Hon. Daniel Webster, In ... Philadelphia. By Rev. Henry J. Morton, D.D. ... *Philadelphia: B. F. Jackson, Printer.* 1852. 8vo, pp. 15. H. 50998

MORTON (J.) Comparative Statement of the number of Deaths in the City of New York, during the years 1804, 5, 6, 7, 8, 9. By Jacob Morton. *New York.* 1810. 8vo. 50999

MORTON (J.) The School Boy's Oration on the State of the Country. New York, March 24, 1863. By Rev. James Morton. [n. p. n. d.] 8vo, pp. 4. 51000

[MORTON (Jeremiah).] Eulogy upon the late Gov. Barbour, of Virginia. [*Richmond.* 1842.] 8vo, pp. 19. BA. 51001

MORTON. Jeremiah Morton's Letter, with a Letter of Mr. Madison Appended, on Secession, &c. [*Washington.* n. d.] 8vo, pp. 16. 51002

MORTON (J. St. C.) Letter to the Hon. J. B. Floyd, ... presenting for his consideration a new Plan for the Fortification of certain Points of the Sea-Coast of the United States. By James St. C. Morton. *Washington.* 1858. 8vo. A. 51003

MORTON. Memoir on the Dangers and Defences of New York City. By James St. C. Morton. ... *Washington: William A. Harris, Printer.* 1858. 8vo, pp. 93. 51004

Also: Memoir on American Fortification. ... *Washington.* 1859. 8vo.

MORTON (J.) The Slave Question. Speech of Hon. J. Morton, ... Feb. 6, 1850 ... . [n. p. n. d.] 8vo, pp. 8. H.

MORTON (J. C.) Memoirs of the Life and Services of John Sanders. By J. C. Morton. *Pittsburgh.* 1861. 8vo. 51006

MORTON (J. W.) Vindication of the True Sabbath; in Two Parts: Part First, A Narrative of Recent Events. Part Second, Divine Appointment of the Seventh Day. By J. W. Morton, ... *Battle Creek, Mich.* 1860. 16mo, pp. 72. + *Battle Creek, Mich.: Seventh-Day Adventist Publishing Association.* 1868. 16mo, pp. 68. B. 51007

MORTON (L.) Report on the Physical Condition of the Rhode Island Regiments, now in the field, in Virginia, and in the vicinity of Washington, D. C., also on the condition of the Hospitals in and around Washington ... . By Lloyd Morton, M.D. ... *Providence: Alfred Anthony.* 1863. 8vo, pp. 21. 51008

MORTON (M.) Address to the Citizens of Taunton on the Proposed Constitution. By Marcus Morton. *Boston: Little, Brown and Company.* 1854. 8vo, pp. 49. 51009

MORTON. Address of ... Marcus Morton to the ... Legislature ... 1840. [n. p. n. d.] 8vo, pp. 16. BA. 51010

MORTON. An Oration, on American Independence; ... at Taunton, July Fourth, 1809. By Marcus Morton, Esq. *New-Bedford: Printed by Elijah Billings.* 1809. 8vo, pp. 20. BA.

Also: A Refutation of the Charge of Abolitionism, brought by David Henshaw, and his Partizans, against ... Hon. Marcus Morton. *Boston: Felch.* 1845. 8vo, pp. 32. BA. *See also* [Hildreth (R.)], Vol. VIII., No. 31784, *and* [Pitman (J.)]

MORTON (N.) New-England's | Memoriall: | or | A brief Relation of the most Memorable and Remarkable | Passages of the Providence of God, manifested to the | Planters | of | New-England in America; | With special Reference to the first Colony thereof, Called | New-Plimouth. | As also a Nomination of divers of the most Eminent Instruments | deceased, both of Church and Common-wealth, improved in the | first beginning and after-progress of sundry of the respective | Jurisdictions in those Parts; in reference unto sundry | Exemplary Passages of their Lives, and | the time of

their Death. | Published for the Use and Benefit of present and future Generations, | By Nathaniel Morton, | Secretary to the Court for the Jurisdiction of New-Plymouth. | ... | *Cambridge: Printed by S[amuel] G[reen] and M[armaduke] J[ohnson], for John Vsher of Boston.* 1669. 4to, pp. (12), 198, (10). B. 51012

The Address "To the Reader," is signed "John Higginson. Thomas Thacher." Concerning the extreme rarity of the first edition of this important work, it will be sufficient to remark, that we know of but three perfect copies in the United States, the last five leaves, "A Brief Chronological Table," are often wanting. "Morton's Memorial is a work of high authority and is confined chiefly to Plymouth Colony. It was compiled principally from manuscripts of his uncle William Bradford, and comprises the period between 1620 and 1646. The journals of Edward Winslow also furnished materials for the work."—J. R. BARTLETT.

MORTON. New-England's | Memorial; | Or, | A brief Relation of the most Memorable and | Remarkable Passages of the Providence of | God, manifested to the | Planters | of | New-England in America: | With special Reference to the first Colony | thereof, Called | New-Plimouth. | ... | Published for the Use and Benefit of | present and future Generations. | By Nathaniel Morton ... . | *Boston: Reprinted for Daniel Henchman.* 1721. 16mo, pp. (10), 248, (2). H. 51013

This edition contains a supplement by Josiah Cotton, register of deeds for the county of Plymouth. Some copies have the imprint, *Boston: Reprinted for Nicholas Boone, at the Sign of the Bible in Cornhill.*

MORTON. New-England's Memorial: or, A brief Relation of the most Memorable and Remarkable Passages of the Providence of God, manifested to the Planters of New-England, in America: With special Reference to the first Colony thereof, Called New-Plimouth. ... Published for the Use and Benefit of present and future Generations. By Nathaniel Morton ... . *Newport: Reprinted and Sold by Solomon Southwick.* M,DCC,LXXII. 8vo, pp. viii, 208, (8). 51014

MORTON. The New England's Memorial: [as before]. By Nathaniel Morton ... . *Plymouth, Mass.: Reprinted by Allen Danforth.* 1826. 12mo, pp. 204. A., B. 51015

MORTON. New England's Memorial. By Nathaniel Morton, Secretary to the Court for the Jurisdiction of New-Plimouth. Fifth Edition. Containing besides the Original Work and the Supplement annexed to the Second Edition, Large Additions in Marginal Notes, and an Appendix; with a Lithographic Copy of an Ancient Map. By John Davis ... . *Boston: Printed by Crocker and Brewster.* 1826. 8vo, pp. 481, (2). H. 50916

MORTON. New England's Memorial. By Nathaniel Morton, ... Sixth Edition. Also Governor Bradford's History of Plymouth Colony; portions of Prince's Chronology; Governor Bradford's Dialogue; Gov. Winslow's Visits to Massasoit; with ... Notes and an Appendix ... . [By Sewall Harding.] *Boston: Congregational Board of Publication.* 1855. 8vo, pp. xxii, (2), 515. 2 Plates. B. 51017

See "N. A. Rev.," III. 145–150; XXV. 204–218. Morton also wrote a brief history of the Church of Plymouth, which may be found in Hazard's "Historical Collections."

MORTON (O. P.) Indiana as a Home for Emigrants. By Oliver P. Morton. *Indianapolis.* 1864. 8vo, pp. 42. 51018

MORTON. Oration of Hon. O. P. Morton, Address of Major General George G. Meade, and Poem of Bayard Taylor, ... with other Exercises at the Dedication of the Monument ... at Gettysburg, July 1st, 1869. ... *Gettysburg: J. E. Wible, Printer.* 1870. 8vo, pp. 47, (1). H. 51019

MORTON. ... Peace or War. The Democratic Position illustrated by Frank P. Blair, Jr. Speeches of Senators Morton, ... Stewart and Nye ... July 9th and 10th, 1868 ... . [n. p. n. d.] 8vo, pp. 8. H. 51020

Also: Laws of Neutrality. Speech ... February 9, 1870. *Washington: F. & J. Rives ...* 1870. 8vo, pp. 8.—Letter ... to James Winslow, Esq., of New York, touching the Payment of Interest on the Funded Debt of Indiana. *Indianapolis.* 1863. 8vo, pp. 14.—Reconstruction and Negro Suffrage. Speech ... at Richmond, Indiana, September 29th, 1865. [n. p. n. d.] 8vo, pp. 23.—Speech ... at Masonic Hall, ... New Albany, ... July 18, 1866. [n. p. n. d.] 8vo, pp. 11.—Speech ... at the Union Meeting at June 20, 1866. [n. p. n. d.] 8vo, pp. 8.—Speech ... Before the Soldiers' and Sailors' Union, of Washington, D. C., ... Jan. 6, 1868. *Washington, D. C.* [n. d.] 8vo, pp. 8.—Reconstruction. Speech ... January 24, 1868 ... [n. p. n. d.] 8vo, pp. 8.—Speech ... at ... Indianapolis, ... Feb. 22, 1870. [n. p. n. d.] 8vo, pp. 8.—Speech ... at ... Terre Haute, Ind., ... July 18, 1870. [n. p. n. d.] 8vo.—Speech ... on the Resumption of Specie Payments, ... December 16, 1868. [n. p. n. d.] 8vo, pp. 14.—Speech ... on the ... Admission of Georgia, ... April 14, 1870. *Washington.* 1870. 8vo, pp. 15. H.

MORTON (P.) An Oration ... at ... King's-Chapel in Boston, April 8, 1776, On the Re-Interment of the Remains of the late Most Worshipful Grand-Master Joseph Warren, Esquire; President of the late Congress of this Colony, and Major-General of the Massachusetts Forces; Who was slain in the Battle of Bunker's-Hill, June 17, 1775. By Perez Morton, M.M. *Boston: Printed ... by J. Gill.* 1776. 4to, pp. 13. + The Second Edition. [*Ibid.*] H. + ... *New-York: Re-printed, by John Holt.* M DCC LXXVI. 12mo, pp. 11. BA. + ... *Philadelphia, Re-printed by John Dunlap.* M,DCC,LXXVI. 4to, pp. 16. P. 51021

MORTON (S. G.) Crania Americana; or, A Comparative View of the Skulls of Various Aboriginal Nations of North and South America: To which is prefixed an Essay on the Varieties of the Human Species. Illustrated by Seventy-Eight Plates and a Colored Map. By Samuel George Morton, M.D. ... *Philadelphia: J. Dobson.* 1839. Folio, pp. (4), v, 296, (1). H. 51022

This valuable work gives accurate delineations of more than forty Indian nations, Peruvian, Brazilian, and Mexican, with a particularly extended series from North America, from the Pacific Ocean to the Atlantic, and from Florida to the regions of the Polar tribes. Concerning the value of this work, *see* "Smithsonian Contributions to Knowledge," VIII. 76, "North American Review," LI., *and* Prichard's "Natural History of Man," 4th ed. II. 502. A "Review," by George Combe, Esq., will be found in the "American Journal of Science and Arts," XXXVIII. The author's "Crania Ægyptiaca," is included in the "Transactions of the American Philosophical Society," IX., of which some copies were issued separately, *Philadelphia*, 1844. 4to, pp. 68. 14 Plates.

MORTON. An Inquiry into the Distinctive Characteristics of the Aboriginal Race of America. By Samuel George Morton, M.D. ... *Philadelphia.* 1840. 8vo. + *Boston: Tuttle & Dennett, Printers.* 1842. 8vo, pp. 37. H. + Second Edition. *Philadelphia: John Penington.* 1844. 8vo, pp. 48. 51023

MORTON. A Memoir of William Maclure, Esq. ... By Samuel George Morton, M.D. ... Read July 1, 1841 ... . *Philadelphia: Printed by T. K. & P. G. Collins.* 1841. 8vo, pp. 37, (1). Portrait. + Second Edition. *Philadelphia: Merrihew and Thompson, Printers.* 1844. 8vo, pp. 33, (1). Portrait. H.

Also: Catalogue of Skulls of Man, and the Inferior Animals, in the Collection of Samuel George Morton, M.D. ... *Philadelphia: Printed by Turner & Fisher.* 1840. 8vo, pp. 48. + Third Edition. *Philadelphia.* 1849. 8vo, pp. x, 37 leaves.—Description of some New Species of Organic Remains of the Cretaceous Group of the United States. ... *Philadelphia.* 1852. 8vo.—Description of Two New Species of Fossil Shells of the Genera Scaphites and Crepidula ... . [n. p. n. d.] 8vo.—Hybridity in Animals and Plants, considered in reference to the question of the Unity of the Human Species. ... *New Haven: Printed by B. L. Hamlen.* 1847. 8vo, pp. 23.—Letter to the Rev. John Bachman, D.D., on the question of Hybridity in Animals, considered in Reference to the Unity of the Human Species. ... *Charleston, S. C.: Walker & James.* 1850. 8vo, pp. 19.—Additional Observations on Hybridity in Animals, and on some Collateral Subjects; being A Reply to the Objections of the Rev. John Bachman, D.D. ... *Charleston, S. C.: Walker & James.* 1850. 8vo, pp. 53.—Observations on the Size of the Brain in Various Races and Families of Man. ... [n. p. n. d.] 8vo, pp. 4.—On the Analogy which exists between the Marl of New Jersey, ... and the Chalk Formation of Europe. ... [n. p.] 1832. 8vo.—Remarks on the Diversities of the Human Species. An Introductory Lecture ... . *Philadelphia.* 1842. 8vo.—Remarks on the so-called Pigmy Race of the Valley of the Mississippi. ... [n. p. n. d.] 8vo.—Some Observations on the Ethnography and Archæology of the American Aborigines. ... *New Haven: Printed by B. L. Hamlen.* 1846. 8vo, pp. 19.—Synopsis of the Organic Remains of the Cretaceous Group of the United States, ... *Philadelphia.* 1834. 8vo. 19 Plates. P. *See also* Nutt (J. C.)

[MORTON (Sarah Wentworth Apthorp).] Beacon Hill. A Local Poem, Historic and Descriptive. Book I. ... *Boston: Printed by Manning & Loring.* 1797. 4to, pp. 56. H. 51025

All that was printed.

[MORTON.] Ouâbi: or the Virtues of Nature. An Indian Tale. In Four Cantos. By Philenia, a Lady of Boston. ... *Printed at Boston, by I. Thomas and E. T. Andrews.* MDCCXC. 8vo, pp. 51, (1). Frontispiece. H. 51026

See "Monthly Review," XII. 72, *and* Bacon (James), I. 2654.

[MORTON.] The Virtues of Society. A Tale, founded on Fact. ... *Boston: Printed by Manning & Loring.* 1799. 4to, pp. 46. BA. 51027

Also: My Mind and its Thoughts, in Sketches, Fragments, and Essays; ... *Boston: Wells and Lilly.* 1823. 8vo, pp. xx, 295. H.

MORTON (T.) New English Canaan | or | New Canaan. | Containing an Abstract of New England, | Composed in three Bookes. | The first Booke setting forth the originall of the Natives, their | Manners and Customes, together with their tractable Nature and | Love towards the English. | The second Booke setting forth the naturall Indowments of the | Country, and what staple Commodities it | yealdeth. | The third Booke setting forth, what people are planted there, | their prosperity, what remarkable accidents have happened since the first | planting of it, together with their Tenents and practise | of their Church. | Written by Thomas Morton, of Clifford's Inne gent, upon tenne | yeares knowledge and experiment of the | Country. | *Printed at Amsterdam,* | *By Jacob Frederick Stam.* | *In the yeare* 1637. | 4to, pp. 188, (3). 51028

A book of such rarity that Mr. Frederik Muller, the eminent bookseller of Amsterdam, remarks: "Although this book is printed in my native place, Amsterdam, I have never seen nor heard of it here." It is interspersed with poems by various authors, including one by Ben Jonson not published in his works. Its author, who appears to have possessed a jovial, and somewhat roystering temperament, found himself ill associated with the puritanical founders of New England. There is more than a little bibliographical uncertainty about this book. In the first place, the catalogue of the so-called Mondidier collection gives the imprint, *Printed by W. S. Stansby for Rob. Blount,* 1625, while Peter Force's reprint gives the imprint, *Printed by Charles Green,* 1632; whereas the book itself relates events sequent to that date (1632); and never having met the book except with the Amsterdam imprint, I content myself with the remark that I suppose that the other titles are erroneous, and a careful examination of the work inclines me to coincide with Mr. Duyckinck, in his remark, "that although the book professes to have been printed at Amsterdam, it was probably executed in London." Peter Force has probably copied White Kennett's catalogue, and the Mondidier copy had a MS. title, which may have been incorrectly copied. Allen remarks that Morton "fell into great licentiousness, and became the lord of misrule;" he supplied the Indians with arms, that they might hunt for him, and was by this means, perhaps, an

instrument in endangering the safety of the colonists. On the occasion of giving to Pasonagessit the name of Maremont, under his auspices, a pine-tree eighty feet in height, with buck's horns at the top, was planted in the ground, around which the company danced with such hilarity, as the good cheer they had not failed to provide inspired; much to the dissatisfaction of the stricter colonists, by whom he was for this offense sent out of the colony as a prisoner. The following is the sentence of the Court of Massachusetts, 7th of September, 1630: "It is ordered by this Court that Thomas Morton at Mount Wollaston should presently be sett into the bilbowes & after sent prisoner unto England by the ship called the Gift now returning thither, that all his goods shall be seized upon to defray the charges of his transportation, payment of his debts, or to give satisfaction to the Indians for a canoe he unjustly took away from them, and that his house, after the goods are taken out, shall be burnt down to the ground." Morton returned to the colonies after the publication of this book and was imprisoned in Boston for a year, ostensibly on account of the libel it promulgated against the colonies. For a reprint, *see* Force's "Tracts," II. 5.

MORTON (T.) Columbus; or, A World Discovered, an Historical Play. As it is performed at the Theatre-Royal, Covent Garden. By Thomas Morton ... . *London: W. Miller.* 1792. 8vo, pp. (8), 66, (2). + Second Edition. [*Ibid.*] + [*Ibid.*] M,DCC,XCVI. 12mo, pp. 61. 51029

See "Monthly Review," X. 93.

MORTON. The Slave; a Musical Drama ... . By Thomas Morton, Esq. ... *London: John Miller.* 1816. 8vo, pp. (4), 72. + Second Edition ... . [*Ibid.*] 1818. 8vo, pp. (8), 72. 51030

The scene is in Surinam. Reprinted in "Cumberland's Theatre."

MORTON (William Thomas Green). Mémoire sur la découverte du nouvel emploi de l'Éther Sulfurique Par W.-T.-G. Morton ... . *Paris: Imprimerie d'Edouard Bautruche.* 1847. 8vo, pp. 60. B. 51031

MORTON. ... Minority Report [of the Committee on the Memorial of] W. T. G. Morton. February 28, 1849. [n. p. n. d.] 8vo, pp. 99. H. 51032

Also: Appeal to the Patrons of Science and the Friends of Humanity in raising a Fund for Dr. W. T. G. Morton. [n. p. n. d.] 8vo.—Proceedings in behalf of the Morton Testimonial. *Boston.* 1866. 8vo, pp. 122.—Report of a Select Committee of the House of Representatives, on his Memorial for remuneration as discoverer of the pain-subduing properties of sulphuric-ether. [n. p. 1849.] 8vo, pp. 46. + [n. p. 1852.] 8vo, pp. 110. 2 Plates. + [Second Edition. *Ibid.*] 8vo, pp. 128. Facsimile.—Statements supported by Evidence, of Wm. T. G. Morton, M.D. on his Claim to the Discovery of the Anæsthetic Properties of Ether: submitted to the ... Select Committee ... of the United States. ... *Washington.* 1853. 8vo, pp. 582, Appendix, (4), 135.—Testimonial of Members of the Medical Profession of Philadelphia, &c. in behalf of Wm. T. G. Morton, M.D. *Philadelphia: Collins, Printer.* 1860. 8vo, pp. 48, folded leaf. H.

Morton's Hope. *See* [Motley (J. L.)]

Morus (G.) Regina Maria, Aloysa, Gabriela, Sabaudiæ Princeps, vel Umbra Hispaniarum Tutela. Ex Mandato, et Auspicio Excmi. Ducis de Linares, Novæ Hispaniæ Pro Regis, cecinet Gerardus Morus, Dingliensis Hibernus, juris utriusque in consultissime jurium facultate Parisiensi Licentiatus, in Regio Mexicano Senatu causarum patronus, et Excellentissimi Ducis aulicis, Anno D. 1715. Superiorum Permissu. *Mexici, apud Hæredes Viduæ Michaelis de Ribera Calderon.* [1715.] Sm. 4to, 13 leaves.

A Latin elegiac poem, in hexameter verse. Excessively rare.

[Moryson (Francis).] *See* Virginia.

The Mosaic Book of the American Adoptive Rite. ... Second Edition. ... *New York: J. B. Taylor.* 1857. 8vo, pp. (4), 64.

El Mosaico Mexicano y Coleccion de Amenidades Curiosos é Instructivos. *Mexico: I. Cumplido.* 1840–42. 7 vols., rl. 8vo.

This journal is of importance to the student of Mexican History and Archæology, as it contains contributions of the most celebrated Mexican authors.

Le Mosaïque. Nouveau Magazin pittoresque ... livre de tout le monde et de tous les pays. *Paris.* 1835–37. 3 vols., 4to. A.

Mosblech (B.) Vocabulaire océanien-français et français-océanien des dialectes parlés aux Iles Marquises, Sandwich, Gambier, etc. D'après les documens recueillis sur les lieux, par les missionaires ... et particulièrement d'après les manuscrits du R. P. Mathias, auteur des Lettres sur l'Oceanie. Par l'Abbe Boniface Mosblech. ... *Paris: Jules Renouard et Cie.* M.DCCC.XLIII. 12mo, pp. (4), vii–xiv, 318. C. 51037

The only vocabulary, in a separate form, of the different Polynesian dialects.

Mosby (C. L.) Congressional Test Act Examined ... . By Chas. L. Mosby ... . *Lynchburg.* 1865. 8vo, pp. 23. 51038

Mosby (J.) Jack Mosby, the Guerilla Chief. By Lieut. Col. ——. *New York: T. R. Dawley.* 1864. 12mo, pp. (4), 15–98. 51039

Mosby (M. W.) Pocahontas; a Legend, with Historical and Traditionary Notes, by Mrs. M. M. Webster [Mosby]. *Philadelphia.* 1840. 12mo. C. 51040

Moscoso y Cordoua (C.) Alegacion | en derecho en competencia | de jurisdicion, entre el Consejo Real y de las | Ordenes. Por el Licenciado don Chris- | toual de Moscoso y Cordoua, Fis- | cal de Consejo. [*Madrid.* 1635.] Folio, 7 leaves. 51041

Moscoso y Cordoua. Discvrso | Legal Militar por el | Licenciado don Christoual de Moscoso y Cordoua, | ... Contra | Francisco Diez Pimienta, Almirante de la Flota | de Nueva España. | Sobre | Auer desamparado las naos faliádo a la obligacion de | su oficio, y causado cogieran vna los enemigos, y otros | graues daños, condenado por el Licenciado Don Miguel de Luna y Arellano ... . [*Madrid.* n. d.] Folio, 18 leaves. J.C.B. 51042

Moscoso y Cordoua. El Licenciado don Christoual de Moscoso y Cordoua, ... Con Don Iuan de Meneses, Gouernador que sue de la Prouincia de Veneçuela. [*Madrid.* 1634.] Folio, 13 leaves. BM. 51043

Also: El Licenciado ... Con El Consulado ... en la Prouincia de Tabasca. [*Madrid.* 1634.] Folio, 22 leaves. + Con Doña Francisca Arce de Otalora, ... Caxamarca. [*Madrid.* 1634. Folio, 42 leaves. + Con El Duque del Infantado. Sobre La Encomienda de Indios. [*Madrid.* 1634.] Folio, 22 leaves. + Con Alonso de Carrion, ... Lima. [*Madrid.* 1634.] Folio, 13 leaves. + Con Don Juan de Amassa. [*Madrid.* 1634.] Folio, 18 leaves. + Con Don Martin Carrillo de Aldrete ... Visitador de la Nueua-España y Obispo de Ouiedo. [*Madrid.* 1634.] Folio, 6 leaves. BM.

[Moscoso y Cordoua. Begins:] Señor. La Resolucion de V Magestad. [*Madrid.* 1635.] Folio, 16 leaves. 51044

Relates to ecclesiastical affairs in Curaçoa.

Moscoso y Peralta (Juan Manuel de). Aranzel de derechos eclesiasticos, parroquiales, de hospitales, Curia eclesiàstica, y secretarià de Càmara del Obispado del Cuzco. ... *Lima.* 1782. Folio, pp. 155. 51045

Mose's Letters—Life as it is, or the Writings of "Our Mose." *Raleigh.* 1858. 12mo. 51046

Moseley (B.) Observations on the Dysentery of the West Indies; with a new and successful manner of treating it. By Benjamin Moseley, Surgeon, at Kingston, in Jamaica. *Jamaica.* 1781. 8vo. + *London: T. Beckett.* 178–. 8vo. 51047

Moseley. A Treatise concerning the Properties and Effects of Coffee. The Second Edition. By Benjamin Moseley, M.D. ... *London: The Author.* M DCC LXXXV. 8vo, pp. (2), xxxi, 69. + The Third Edition: [*Ibid.*] + The Fourth Edition. [*Ibid.*] MDCCLXXXIX. 8vo, pp. (2), xxxi, 69. H. + The Fifth Edition, with ... Additions. ... [*Ibid.*] MDCCXCII. 8vo, pp. (4), xxvii, 80.

See McCulloch's "Literature of Political Economy," 91.

Moseley. A Treatise on Sugar. With Miscellaneous Medical Observations. By Benjamin Moseley, M.D. ... *London.*

1799. 8vo. + Second Edition, with considerable Additions. *London: Printed by John Nichols.* M DCCC. 8vo, pp. iv, 276. H.

Moseley. A Treatise on Tropical Diseases; and on the Climate of the West-Indies. By Benjamin Moseley ... . *London: T. Cadell.* M DCC LXXXVII. 8vo, pp. (4), xix, 544. H. + Second Edition, with ... Additions. [*Ibid.*] MDCCLXXXIX. 8vo, pp. xv, 556. + [*Ibid.*] MDCCXCII. 8vo, pp. xv, 568. + Third Edition, with ... Additions. *London: C. G. and J. Robinson.* 1795. 8vo, pp. xv, 568. + Fourth Edition ... . *London: Printed by Nichols and Son.* 1803. 8vo, pp. xvi, 670. B. + *London: Nichols, Longman* 1806. 8vo. 51050

See "Monthly Review," XLIX. 433.

Moseley (E.) An Oration ... at Newburyport, July 4, 1808 ... at the request of the Federal Republicans. By Ebenezer Moseley. *Newburyport.* 1808. 8vo, pp. 20. + Second Edition. [*Ibid.*] 1808. 8vo, pp. 20. H., W. 51051

Also: An Address to the Essex County Agricultural Society, ... September 25, 1834; ... *Salem: Printed by Foote and Chisholm.* 1835. 8vo, pp. 23. H.

Moseley (E.) A Sermon, occasioned by the Death of ... Rev. Samuel Foxcroft, A.M. ... in New Gloucester; who died March 2d, 1807 ... . By Elisha Moseley, A.M. ... *Portland: Printed ... [by] J. M'Kown.* 1807. 8vo, pp. 16. BA. 51052

Moseley (J. O.) An Oration [Occasioned by the Death of Gen. Washington], delivered at East-Haddam, ... at the request of the Inhabitants of the First Society in that Town, on the 22d of Feb. A.D. 1800. By Jonathan Ogden Moseley. *Hartford: Hudson and Goodwin.* 1800. 8vo, pp. 18. 51053

Also: ... Speech ... On the ... Bill for enforcing the Embargo. . [*Baltimore.* 1809.] 8vo, pp. 10. BA.

Moseley (J.) What is Contraband of War and what is not. Comprising all the American and English authorities on the subject. By Joseph Moseley, Esq., B.C.L. ... *London: Butterworths.* 1861. 12mo, pp. xi, 114. B. 51054

Moser (J. J.) Nord-America | nach den | Friedensschlüssen | vom Jahr 1783. | Nebst | 1. Einem Vorbericht von America überhaupt, | 2. einigen Charten, und 3. einem hinlänglichen | Register. | Von | Johann Jacob Moser, | ... | *Leipzig, | bey Johann Friedrich Junius.* 1784–85. 3 vols., 8vo, pp. xvi, 840; (4), 682; (2), 598, Register, (24). Map. J.C.B. 51055

Moses (F. J.) Remarks of the Hon. F. J. Moses, Jr., at the recent Adjournment of the General Assembly. [n. p. n. d.] 8vo, pp. 7. 51056

Moses (J.) A Few Remarks in Reply to an Anonymous Scribbler [on Mormonism] styling himself "One who hates Imposture," but found to be an impostor himself ... . By Julian Moses. *Philadelphia.* 1841. 8vo, pp. 16. 51057

Moses (M.) The Commercial Directory, and a Digest of the Laws of the United States, relating to Commerce; including a Tariff, or Rates of Duties; ... By Myer Moses. *New-York: Printed by Ludwig & Tolefree.* 1830. 8vo, pp. 280. B. 51058

Moses. Full Annals of the Revolution in France, 1830. To which is added, a Full Account of the Celebration of said Revolution in the City of New-York, on the 25th November, 1830: ... By Myer Moses. *New-York: Printed by J. & J. Harper.* 1830. 12mo, pp. 255. B., C. 51059

An extremely curious volume. Among the guests present on the occasion, was Mr. David Williams, the only surviving captor of Major André. "When the Orator of the day alluded to Williams, his services, and incorruptible integrity at that trying period, the venerable old gentleman involuntarily arose from his seat and burst into tears, which were mingled with those of many present!" The "Full Account" was printed separately [*New-York.* n. d.]. 12mo, pp. 151.

Moses. Oration, ... at Tammany-Hall, on the Twefth May, 1831, being the Forty-Second Anniversary, of the Tammany Society, or, Columbian Order, By Myer Moses ... . *New-York: P. Van Pelt, Printer.* 1831. 8vo, pp. 31. H., N. 51060

Moses b. Mendel. Ample History of the Discovery of America. ... *Altona.* 1807. 8vo, pp. 175. 51061

A very rare volume, printed in Hebrew type.

Mosier (H. A.) Appeal of Hugh A. Mosier to the ... Conference of the Methodist Episcopal Church. *Albany.* 1852. 8vo, pp. 17. 51062

Mosquera de Figueroa (C.) Commentario en | breve compendio de | Disciplina militar, en | que se escriue la jornada de las islas | de los Açores | Por el Licenciado Chris | toual Mosquera de Figueroa, ... | *En Madrid, Por Luis Sanchez: Año* 1596. | Small 4to, 4 prel., Text, 184, and Tabla, 2 leaves. BM. 51063

At the end is the "Elogio del Marques de Santa Cruz," the leader of the Spanish expedition, with a separate title-page. This rare work is not mentioned by Brunet.

Mosquera y Figueroa (Manuel). Compendio de la Bulla de Cena para los Confessores de las Indias Occidentales ... . *Lima.* 1718. 4to. 51064

Mosquera (M. J.) Documentos para la biografiá é historia del episcopado del ... D. Manuel José Mosquera, arzobispo de Santafé de Bogotá. *Paris: Tipografia de Adriano le Clere.* 1858. 3 vols., rl. 8vo, pp. (4), ii, v, 715, (1); (4), xiii, 744, (1); (4), xii, 753, (1). BM. 51065

Mosquera. Mémorial del ilustrisimo y reverendisimo senor Manuel José Mosquera Arzobispo de Santafé de Bogotá, confesor de la fé. ... *Paris.* 1858. Folio, pp. 190, (10). Portrait.

[Mosquera.] Representacion del M. R. Arzobispo de Bogota sobre separacion del Seminario concilar y su arreglo. *Bogotá: Impr. por Jose Ayarza.* 1840. 8vo, pp. 22. BM. 51067

Also: Apologie de J. de Mosquera, archevêque de Santa-Fé de Bogota. *Paris.* 1856. 8vo. The British Museum contains many other works by Mosquera—mostly religious.

Mosquera (T. C. de). Exámen crítico del libelo publicado en la imprenta del comercio en Lima, por el reo profugo José Maria Obando. Escrito por T. C. de Mosquera. *Valparaiso.* 1842. 2 vols., 8vo, pp. x, 653; 459. Map. 51068

Contains the life of Obando, and an account of the battles between the Spaniards and the Republicans, 1819–30.

Mosquera. Memoria sobre la Geografia, Física y Política de la Nueva Granada. ... Por el General T. C. de Mosquera ... . *Nueva York: Imprenta de S. W. Benedict.* 1852. 8vo, pp. 104.

Mosquera. Memoir on the Physical and Political Geography of New Grenada. By General T. C. de Mosquera. Translated from the Spanish, by Theodore Dwight. *New York: T. Dwight.* 1853. 8vo, pp. 105. Map. A. 51070

Mosquera. Memorias sobre la Vida del Libertador Simon Bolivar. Por el General Tomas C. de Mosquera ... . Segunda Entrega. [n. p. n. d.] 8vo, pp. 107, (8). 51071

[Mosquera.] New Grenada and the United States. [n. p. 1856.] 8vo, pp. 19. H. 51072

Also in Spanish.

Mosquera. Proceso contra el Presidente de los Estados Unidos de Colombia, Ciudadano Gran Jeneral Tomas C. de Mosquera, i

otros altos funcionarios nacionales. Edicion oficial. *Bogota: Imprenta de la Nacion.* 1867. Folio, pp. (2), 814, ii. C. 51073

Mosquera. Résumen histórico de los Acontecimientos que han tenido lugar en la Republica, extractado de los Diarios y Noticias que ha podido obtener el General Gefe del Estado Mayor General. ... *Bogota: Imprenta del Neo-Granadino.* 1855. Folio, pp. 226, lxvii, (6). 2 Tables. C. 51074

Mosquera. Schets van de natuur- en staatkundige Aardrijksbeschrijving van Nieuw Grenada. Uit het Engelsch onder toezigt van A. Goldberg. *Amsterdam.* 1856. 8vo. Map.

Sketch of the physical and political geography of New Grenada. From the English. Also: Causa de responsabilidad, contra el ciudadano presidente de la republica i los secretarios del despacho. ... *Bogotá.* 1855. 4to.—Correspondencia entre el Jeneral Tomas Cipriani de Mosquera i el Doctor Mariano Ospina. *Bogota.* 1860. 8vo, pp. 36.—El General Mosquera al Publico de la Nueva Granada. [n. p.] 1856. 8vo, pp. 15.—Manifestacion del Senador Tomas C. de Mosquera a la Nacion. *Bogota.* 1858. 8vo, pp. 36.

Mosquito. Bericht über die im höchsten Auftrage ... bewirkte Untersuchung einiger Theile des Mosquito Landes, erstattet von der dazu ernannten Commission. *Berlin: Alex. Duncker.* 1845. 8vo, pp. iv, 274, 1. 2 Maps and 3 Plates. 51076

Includes on pages 269–274 a Musquito Vocabulary.

The Case of his Majesty's Subjects having Property in and lately established upon the Mosquito Shore in America. ... Humbly submitted to the King's Most Excellent Majesty in Council, the Lords and Commons in Parliament, and the Nation of Great-Britain at Large. 1789. *London: T. Cadell.* M.DCC.-LXXXIX. 4to, pp. (4), 72, 17, (1). H. 51077

See our Vol. III., No. 11313.

Catalogue of Objects in illustration of Natural History composing the Guiana Expedition. *London.* 1840. 8vo. 51078

Convencion relativa a la Mosquita entre Nicaragua y S. M. B. [n. p. n. d.] 8vo, pp. 8. 51079

Documentos Relativos a la Cuestion de Mosquitos [por Castellon]. *San Salvador.* 1852. Folio, pp. 30. 51080

Correspondence of the Department of State. [n. p.] 1856. 8vo, pp. 95. 51081

Correspondence respecting the Mosquito Territory. Presented to the House of Commons, July 3, 1848. *London: Printed by T. R. Harrison.* [1848.] Folio, pp. (ii), 133, ix. 51082

Convenio celebrado entre S.S. M.M. los Reyes de España é Inglaterrá ... en Londres a 14 de Julio de 1786. *Comayagua: Impresor de Orden del Sopremo Gobierno de Honduras.* 1846. 8vo, pp. 7. 51083

Documentos interesantes sobre el atentado cometido por algunos ingleses residentes in Blewfields ... . *San Salvador.* [1848.] 8vo, pp. 17. 51084

Message of the President, May 21, 1865. *Washington.* 1865. 8vo, pp. 8. 51085

Mosquito, Nicaragua, and Costa-Rica. Second Edition. *London: Effingham Wilson.* [1850.] 8vo, pp. (2), ii, 28. 51086

Die Mosquito-Küste und Texas. ... *Charlottenburg: Egbert Bauer.* 1846. 12mo, pp. vi, 70. Map. 51087

[Moss] (C.) A Sermon ... before the Incorporated Society for the Propagation of the Gospel in Foreign Parts; ... February 21, 1772. By the Right Reverend Charles Lord Bishop of St. David's. *London: Printed by T. Harrison* ... . MDCCLXXII. 4to, pp. xxx, 58, (1). H. 51088

Moss (J.) An Almanack for 1720. By Joseph Moss, M.A. *New London: Printed ... by T. Green.* [n. d.] 8vo. 51089

Moss. An Election Sermon, ... at Hartford, May ... 12th, 1715. By Joseph Moss, A.M. ... *New-London: Printed ... by Timothy Green.* 1715. Sm. 8vo, pp. (2), 40. H. 51090

Moss (L.) Annals of the United States Christian Commission By Rev. Lemuel Moss ... *Philadelphia: J. B. Lippincott & Co.* 1868. 8vo, pp. 752. Portrait and 10 Plates. H. 51091

Mossman (S.) Heroes of Discovery. Magellan, Cook, Park, Franklin, Livingstone. By Samuel Mossman. *Edinburgh: Edmondson and Douglas.* 1868. Cr. 8vo, pp. xi, (1), 347. 51092

A | Most Exact and Accurate | Map | of the | Whole World: | Or the | Orb Terrestrial described in Four plain Maps, | (viz.) | Asia, Evrope, Africa, America. | Containing all the known and most Remarkable | Capes, Ports, Bayes and Isles, Rocks, Rivers, Towns, | and Cities; together with their Scituation, Commodities, | History, Customes, Government; and a new and exact Geography, | ... | A Work, as well useful as delightful, for all Scholars, | Merchants, Mariners ... . | D. L. M.A. | *London: Printed for John Garrett* ... . [n. d.] 4to, pp. 192. 51093

A Most friendly farewell given by a wel-willer, to the right worshipful sir Francis Drake knight ... and to all the gentlemen his followers, and captaines in this exploite, who sat sale from Woolwich, the xv day of July, 1585. *London: Printed by Walter Mantel.* [n. d.] 4to. 51094

Sold for £10 15s. at B. H. Bright's sale, in 1854. Title from Brunet, II. 832.

A Most humble Proposal to the Lords Regents, &c., of Great Britain, for an effectual method to prevent Piracy, and make the Trade of America more secure. *London.* 1723. 4to. 51095

Most Important Extra, for the Present and Future Generations. *Baltimore.* [1862.] 8vo. 51096

A Most Remarkable Prophecy, concerning Wars and Political Events; Especially the Glorious King of Prussia. Taken from an ancient Latin Manuscript said to be deposited in the Bodleyan Library. With an Essay towards an Explanation. *Philadelphia: Henry Miller.* MDCCLX. 4to, pp. 8. P. 51097

Mota (J. J. de la). Panegyrico á la Vida y Martyrio de la inclita virgen Catharina, sagrado honor de Alexandria y unica maravilla de Egypto. ... *Mexico.* 1716. 4to, 12 leaves. 51098

The British Museum contains other pieces by this author.

Mota (M. de la). Manifestacion que Manuel de la Mota hace al publico de la conducta que observá como gobernador de la provincia de Tunja ... 1860. [n. p. n. d.] 4to, pp. 40.

Mota Padilla (M. de la). Historia de la Conquista de la Provincia de la Nueva-Galicia, escrita por El Lic D. Matias de la Mota Padilla en 1742. ... *Guadalajara.* 1855–56. 3 vols., sm. 8vo. + *Mexico: Imprenta del Gobierno, ... á cargo de Jose Maria Sandoval.* 1870. Impl. 8vo, pp. xix, 523, (20). 51100

Contains an interesting account of the discovery of Nueva-Galicia, with notices of its military and political progress, ancient rites and ceremonies of the Indians. The author was a canon in the cathedral of Guadalaxara.

Mothe le Vayer. *See* [La Peyrère (Isaac de)], x. 38973.

[Motier (Gilbert de).] Pictorial Life of General Lafayette; containing Anecdotes illustrative of his Character. ... *Philadelphia: Lindsay and Blakiston.* 1846. 16mo, pp. 208. 51101

Also: Lafayette, or Disinterested Benevolence. *Boston.* 1825. 18mo, pp. 35. *See also* Lafayette (M.-P.-J. R.-I.-G. de M.), Vol. x., Nos. 38568–83, *and* Vol. VI. No. 23952, and add [Another Edition. *Ibid.*] 8vo, pp. 40.

Motifs qui doivent, etc. *See* Vol. IV., No. 15915, *note.*

Motions made in the House, etc. *See* [Hartley (D.)], 30690.

Motiven,|Die de Officiers der Militie en de|Hooge Raden in|Brasil,|hebben bewoogen met de Portugee-|sen te Contracteren.|*Gedruckt in 't Iaer ons Heeren* 1654.| 4to, pp. 4. 51102

Motives which induced the officers of the militia and the Counselors in Brazil to treat with the Portuguese. *See also* Vol. II., No. 7605.

Motley (J. L.) Causes of the Civil War in America. By John Lothrop Motley, LL.D. ... Reprinted ... from "The [London] Times." *London: George Manwaring.* MDCCCLXI. 8vo, pp. 30. H. + Second Edition. [*Ibid.*] + *New York: James G. Gregory.* 1861. 12mo, pp. 36. + [*Ibid.*] 12mo, pp. 40. + *New York: D. Appleton & Co.* 1861. 8vo, pp. 24. + *New York: G. P. Putnam.* 1861. 12mo, pp. 23. 51103

Included in "Pulpit and Rostrum," No. 20.

Motley. Oorzaken van den Burgeroorlog in Amerika. ... *'s Hage.* 1861. 8vo. 51104

Motley. Democracy, the Climax of Political Progress. ... An Historical Essay. By J. Lothrop Motley. *Glasgow: Cameron & Ferguson.* [n. d.] 8vo, pp. 32. 51105

Motley. Four Questions for the People, at the Presidential Election. Address of John Lothrop Motley, ... October 20, 1868. *Boston.* 1868. 8vo, pp. 76. 51106

Motley. Historic Progress and American Democracy: an Address ... before the New York Historical Society, ... December 16, 1868, By John Lothrop Motley. ... *New York: Charles Scribner and Co.* 1869. 8vo, pp. (4), 74. 51107

[Motley.] Merry-Mount; A Romance of the Massachusetts Colony. ... *Boston and Cambridge: James Munroe & Co.* M DCCC XLVIII. 2 vols., 12mo, pp. (8), 222; (4) 252. + [*Ibid.*] M DCCC XLIX. 2 vols., 12mo, pp. (8), 222; (4), 252. 51108

[Motley.] Morton's Hope; or the Memoirs of a Provincial. ... *New-York: Harper & Brothers.* 1839. 2 vols., 12mo, pp. 247; 298. A., B. 51109

Reprinted as "Morton of Morton's Hope; an Autobiography." ... *London: Henry Colburn.* 1839. 3 vols., 12mo, pp. viii, 287; (4), 322; (4), 300. Also: The Constitution and Mr. Motley. [By R. E. Evans.] *Philadelphia: The Author.* 1861. 12mo, pp. 36. H. The author's "Rise of the Dutch Republic" and "History of the United Netherlands" treat only incidentally on some American topics.

The Motley Assembly, a Farce. Published for the Entertainment of the Curious. *Boston: Nathaniel Coverly.* M,DCC,LXXIX. 8vo, pp. 15. M., W. 51110

A local satire on some who after attending the British balls in Boston, took part in those given after the Americans had resumed possession. Esq. Runt is Mr. Inman; Turncoat, is Dan. Hubb—d; Bubble, Jas. Sw—n; Mrs. Flourish, Mrs. D—bs; Mrs. Taxall, Mrs. S—h—fe; Miss Flourish, Miss B—y D—bs; Miss Taxall, Miss S—f—e; Miss Doggrel, Perez Morton's wife; Tab, Sally S—f—e.

The Motley Book. *See* [Mathews (C.)], XI. 46835–6.

Mott (A.) Biographical Sketches and Interesting Anecdotes of Persons of Color ... . Compiled by A. Mott. *New York: Mahlon Day.* 1826. 12mo, pp. 192. + *York: W. Alexander & Son.* 1826. 12mo, pp. xi, (1), 240. + Second Edition. [*Ibid.*] 1828. 12mo. + Second Edition ... . *New York: Mahlon Day.* 1837. 12mo, pp. 260. + [*Ibid.* 1839.] 12mo, pp. 408. + *New York: ... D. Fanshaw, Printer.* 1854. 12mo, pp. 408. B.

The pieces of poetry are omitted in the English editions.

Mott (J.) The Lawfulness of War for Christians, examined. By James Mott. ... *New-York: Printed ... by Samuel Wood.* 1814. 12mo, pp. 33. BA. 51112

Also: On Education, and the Duties of Civil Life. ... *New-York.* 18—. 12mo. + *London: A. W. Bennett.* [1863.] 12mo, pp. 112.

[Mott (Jordan (L.)] Report to the Inventors of the United States, of Proceedings, ... from the Convention of 1845, 1846, 1847 ... . By a Member of the Executive Committee. ... *Morrisania, N. Y.: Henry S. Hill, Printer.* 1854. 8vo, pp. 70. H.

Mott (L.) Discourse on Woman, By Lucretia Mott. *Philadelphia: T. B. Peterson.* 1850. 8vo, pp. 20. H. 51114

Also: A Sermon to ... Medical Students, ... by Lucretia Mott, at ... Philadelphia, ... 1849. ... *Philadelphia: W. B. Zeiber.* 1849. 12mo, pp. 21. H.

[Mott (Lydia P.)] A Brief Account of The Life, Last Sickness, and Death of Robert Mott. *New York.* 1815. 12mo. + [With] An Account of ... Jennett B. Mott. *York: W. Alexander.* 1815. 12mo, pp. 38. 51115

[Mott (R. *and* A.)] A Short Account of the Last Sickness and Death of Maria Mott ... of Mamaroneck ... . *New-York: Samuel Wood & Sons.* 1817. 12mo, pp. 28. + *London: Darton, Harvey and Darton.* 1817. Post 8vo, pp. 24. 51116

Mott (V.) A Biographical Memoir of the late John Revere, M.D. ... By Valentine Mott, M.D. ... *New York: Joseph H. Jennings, Printer.* 1847. 8vo, pp. 40. H. 51117

Mott. A Biographical Memoir of Wright Post, M.D. ... By Valentine Mott ... . *New York: Printed by E. Conrad.* 1829. 8vo, pp. 32. B. 51118

Mott. Eulogy on the late John W. Francis, M.D., LL.D. ... By Valentine Mott, ... May 29, 1861. ... *New York: Samuel S. & William Wood.* 1861. 8vo, pp. 33. B. 51119

Mott. Reminiscences of Medical Teaching and Teachers in New York. An Address ... . By Valentine Mott ... . *New York: Joseph H. Jennings, Printer.* 1850. 8vo, pp. 32. BA.

Also: Address of Valentine Mott, M.D. ... before the Graduates of 1860, of the University Medical College of New York. ... *New York: Miller, Mathews & Clasback.* 1860. 8vo, pp. 25.—An Inaugural Address ... New-York Academy of Medicine, February 7, 1849. ... *New-York: Printed by H. Ludwig & Co.* 1849. 8vo, pp. 24. And many other pieces chiefly medical.

Mott (W.) Consolation under Affliction; in a Letter addressed to Clements Willetts, of Bethphage, in Long Island, North America; By William Mott of Marrineck. *Leeds: Printed by Christopher Pickard.* 1824. 12mo. 51121

Motta (V. P. da). Documentos que acompanham o relatorio que O Ill.mo E Ex.mo S.r Conselheiro Doutor Vicente Pires da Motta Apresentou á Assembléa Legislativa Provincial No Anno de 1863. *S. Paulo: Typographia Imparcial de Joaquim Roberto de Azevedo Marques.* 1863. 8vo, pp. 14. 51122

Motte (*M.*) *See* Douin de la Motte (*M.*), v. 20731.

Motte (M. I.) An Address ... at the Funeral of Mrs. Martha Freme ... . By Rev. M. I. Motte. *Brattleboro: Printed by B. D. Harris & Company.* 1849. 12mo, pp. 12. H. 51123

Also: The Christian Patriot. A Sermon ... at ... Boston, July 5th, 1840. ... *Cambridge: Folsom, Wells, and Thurston.* 1840. 8vo, pp. 16. B.

Motte (S.) Outline of a System of Legislation, for securing Protection to the Aboriginal Inhabitants of all Countries colonized by Great Britain ... . Drawn up at the Request of the Committee of "The Aborigines Protection Society" ... . By Standish Motte ... . *London: John Murray.* 1840. 8vo, pp. 32.

Mottey (J.) An Address, occasioned by the Peace between America and Great Britain, established Feb. 17, 1815. ... At

Lynnfield, on the Anniversary Birth-Day of George Washington. By Joseph Mottey ... . *Cambridge: Printed by Hilliard and Metcalf.* 1815. 8vo, pp. 12. B. 51125

Also: Two Sermons, ... at Lynn, ... after the Interment of ... Rev. Joseph Roby, A.M. ... *Boston: Printed by Munroe and Francis.* 1803. 8vo, pp. 16.

Motto's of the Wanderers; in Latin and English: Several of which are paraphras'd in Hewick Verse. *London: Printed by H. Meere.* 1718. 8vo, pp. (xii), 37. P. 51126

Dedicated to William Byrd, Esq., and said to have been written by a Virginian. Of no other interest, however.

Moulton (H.) The Young Pastor's Wife. Memoir of Elizabeth Ann Moulton: containing her Biography, Diary, Letters, etc. By Rev. Horace Moulton. *Boston: Waite, Peirce & Co.* 1845. 18mo, pp. x, 5–275. C. 51127

Moulton (J. W.) An Address, ... at ... Buffalo, on the Anniversary ... of the Niagara and Erie Society for Promoting Agriculture and Domestic Manufactures, the 30th ... of October, 1821. By Joseph W. Moulton, Esq. ... *Buffalo: Printed by D. M. Day* ... . 1821. 8vo, pp. 36. H. 51128

[Moulton.] Dialogue on Democracy, in which the Democratic Principle is defined and applied as a Touchstone to Party-Men ... . *New York.* 1844. 8vo, pp. 28. H. 51129

[Moulton.] History of the State of New-York including its Aboriginal and Colonial Annals. By John V. N. Yates, ... and Joseph W. Moulton ... . Vol. I. Part I. *New-York: A. T. Goodrich.* 1824. 8vo, pp. 325, Notes, xi. + History of the State of New-York. By Joseph W. Moulton. Part II. Novum Belgium. *New-York: E. Bliss & E. White.* 1826. 8vo, pp. viii, 333–418. 7 Maps. H. 51130

"The aboriginal history of New York is very ably treated, these divisions of the work being almost entirely devoted to an examination of the various questions, which have so vexed ethnologists regarding the 'origin of the savages,' the pre-Columbian history, and discovery of America, and a narrative of events connected with Indian history, to the year 1633."—Field. Mr. Moulton is, in fact, the sole author of this scarce book.

Moulton. New York 170 Years Ago; with A View, and Explanatory Notes. By Joseph W. Moulton. *New York: Wm. G. Boggs, Printer.* 1843. 8vo, pp. 24. Plate. BA. 51131

Moulton. View of the City of New-Orange, (now New-York,) as it was in the Year 1673. With Explanatory Notes.

By Joseph W. Moulton, Esq. *New-York: Printed by C. S. Van Winkle.* 1825. 8vo, pp. 40. Plate of New York in 1673. B.

Also: Analysis of American Law, presented in a Chart, with explanatory Comments. ... *New York: John S. Voorhies.* 1859. 12mo, pp. (2), 68. H.

Moulton (R. K.) The Constitutional Guide; comprising The Constitution of the United States; with Notes and Commentaries from the writings of Judge Story, Chancellor Kent, James Madison, and other Distinguished American Citizens. Compiled by R. K. Moulton. *New-York: G. & C. Carvill & Co.* 1834. 8vo, pp. v, 147, 227. C. 51133

Moulton. Legislative and Documentary History of the Banks of the United States, from ... 1781, to ... 1834. ... By R. K. Moulton. *New-York: G. & C. Carvill.* 1834. 18mo, pp. v, 227, (1). C. 51134

Moulton (T. C.) ... A Sermon ... at the Dedication of the Christian Church, at Portsmouth, R. I., ... January 9th, 1866. By Rev. T. C. Moulton ... . *New Bedford: Fessenden & Baker.* 1866. 8vo, pp. 22. H. 51135

Moulton (W.) A Concise Extract, from the Sea Journal of William Moulton; written on Board of the Onico, in a Voyage from the Port of New-London in Connecticut, to Staten-Island in the South Sea; ... with ... Remarks ... Matters ... on the Coast of South America, and at ... [the] Islands in the South Sea and Pacific Ocean, in ... 1799, 1800, 1801, 1802, 1803 and 1804. ... *Printed at Utica for the Author.* 1804. 8vo, pp. 158, (1).

Moultrie (A.) An Appeal to the People on the Conduct of a certain Public Body in South-Carolina, respecting Col. Drayton and Col. Moultrie. *Charleston: Printed by Markland, M'Iver & Co.* 1794. 8vo, pp. 28. 51137

Moultrie. An Oration, ... Fourth of July, 1822, before the Cincinnati and Revolution Societies. By Alexander Moultrie ... . *Charleston: Printed by A. E. Miller.* 1822. 8vo, pp. 16.

Moultrie (J.) An Eulogium on Stephen Elliott, M.D. & L.L.D. ... Professor ... in the Medical College of South-Carolina: ... 8th November, 1830; ... By James Moultrie, Jun. M.D. *Charleston: Printed by A. E. Miller.* 1830. 8vo, pp. 46. H.

Moultrie (J.) Ioannis Movltrie ... Dissertatio Medica de Febre Maligna Biliosa Americae, Anglice the Yellow Fever,

Habita olini die x Martie 1749. In Academia Edinbvrgensi pro Gradv Doctoris. Edidit Itervm et praefatvs est E. G. Baldinger. ... *Longosalissae Impensis I. C. Martini.* MDCCLXVIII. 4to, pp. (6), 26, Ephemerides, (8). 51140

Moultrie. Dissertatio Medica Inauguralis, de Febre maligna biliosa Americæ; quam. Annuente deo ter opt. max. Ex auctoritate reverendi admodum Viri. D. Gulielmi Wishart S. T. D. Academiae Edinburgensæ præfecti, nec non Amplissimi Senatus Academici consensu, et nobilissimae Facultatis Medicinae decreto; pro gradu doctoratus, summisque in Medicina honoribus ac priviligiis rite et legitime consequendis, Eruditorum Examini Subjicit Joannes Moultrie ex Meridionali Carolinæ provincia, A et R. *Ex officina Roberti Flaminii.* M.DCCXLIX. 4to, pp. (4), 24, 8.

Moultrie (W.) Memoirs of the American Revolution, so far as it related to the States of North and South Carolina, and Georgia. Compiled from the most Authentic Materials, the Author's Personal Knowledge of the various events, and including an Epistolary Correspondence on Public Affairs, with Civil and Military Officers at that period. By William Moultrie ... . *New York: Printed by David Longworth, for the Author.* 1802. 2 vols., 8vo, pp. 506; 446. Portrait. A., H. 51142

The author's position as Governor of South Carolina, afforded him ample facilities to consult original authorities, and the result of his researches is a good book.

Mound City, *Pulaski County, Illinois.* Report of Jesse E. Peyton, Esq., to the Eastern Stockholders of the "Emporium Real Estate and Manufacturing Company" of Mound City. *Philadelphia.* 1860. 8vo, pp. 34. Map. 51143

Mount (T.) The Confession ... of Thomas Mount, Who was executed at Little-Rest, ... Rhode-Island, ... 27th of May, 1791, for Burglary. [n. p. n. d.] 8vo, pp. 21. H. 51144

Catalogue of the Mount Airy Agricultural Institute, Germantown, Pa. *Philadelphia: T. K. and P. G. Collins, Printers.* 1849. 8vo, pp. 7, (1). Continued. H. 51145

See also our Vol. VII., No. 27161.

Annual Statement of the Trustees of Mount Auburn Cemetery. 1853. [n. p. n. d.] 8vo, pp. 4. Continued. 51146

Also: Alphabetical and Numerical Lists of Proprietors of Lots in the Cemetery of Mount Auburn, ... 1834 ... . *Boston: Printed by J. T. Buckingham.* 1834. 8vo, pp. 20.—Catalogue of Lots from which Proprietors may make Selections. ... *Boston: John H. Eastburn, Printer.* 1836. 8vo, pp. 8.—Catalogue of the Lots in Mount Auburn

Cemetery, with the Names of the Proprietors ... . *Boston: Geo. C. Rand & Avery.* 1857. 12mo, pp. ix, (2), folded leaf, 159. Continued.—Catalogue of Lots laid out in the Cemetery ... . *Boston: John H. Eastburn, Printer.* 1839. 8vo, pp. 10.—Catalogue of Proprietors in the Cemetery of Mount Auburn ... 21st April, 1835. *Boston: Nathan Hale.* 1835. 8vo, pp. 25. Continued. H.

Guide through Mount Auburn Cemetery. *Boston.* 1839. 8vo.

See Vol. III., Nos. 10145–6, *also* Dearborn (N.), Vol. V., No. 19079.

Mount Auburn Cemetery ... . [n. p.] 1856. 8vo, pp. 108. Plan. 51148

Mount Auburn Illustrated, in a series of highly finished Line Engravings, from Drawings taken on the Spot, by James Smillie; with Descriptive Notices, by Cornelia W. Walter. *New York: Martin & Johnson.* [1848.] 4to, pp. 119. 18 Plates. 51149

There are copies on large paper, in quarto, with proof impressions of the plates.

The Mount Auburn Memorial. ... Volume I. June, 1859–June, 1860. *Mount Auburn: T. H. & D. F. Safford.* 1860. Folio, pp. iv, 412. Continued. B. 51150

Notes on Mount Auburn Cemetery, Edited by an Officer of the Corporation; intended to serve as a Stranger's Guide Book. ... *Boston: James Munroe and Company.* [n. d.] 18mo, pp. 146. Plan. B. 51151

The Picturesque Pocket Companion, and Visitor's Guide, through Mount Auburn: ... with ... Engravings on Wood. *Boston: Otis, Broaders and Company.* MDCCCXXXIX. 18mo, pp. 252. BA. 51152

This cemetery is on the plan of the celebrated one of Pere La Chaise, near Paris. Also: Schedule of Lots laid out in the Cemetery ... . [n. p. 1832.] 8vo, pp. 12.—Sketches in Mount Auburn Cemetery. *Boston: Pendleton.* 1834. 4to. *See also* [Mann (J.)], Vol. XI., No. 44331.

First Annual Catalogue of the Mount Auburn Young Ladies' Institute. ... 1856–1857. *Cincinnati: Moore, Wilstach* ... . 1857. 8vo, pp. 12. Plate. H. 51153

Exhibit of the Value and Importance of the Coal Mines of the Mount Carbon Coal Company, in Jackson County, Illinois. *Washington: Henry Polkinhorn, Printer.* 1854. 8vo, pp. 43. B.

Mount Desert, on the Coast of Maine. *Portland: B. Thurston & Co., Printers.* 1867. 16mo, pp. 36. 51155

First Annual Catalogue of ... Mount Holyoke Female Seminary, South Hadley, Mass. 1837–8. [n. p. 1838.] 12mo, pp. 12. Continued. B. 51156

Also: Catalogue of the Memorandum Society in the Mount Holyoke Female Seminary, for Five Years, ending 1842. *Amherst: J. S. & C. Adams, Printers.* 1843. 4to, pp. 17, (1). Continued.

Female Education. Tendencies of the Principles ... and System ... in the Mount Hope Female Seminary. [n. p. 1839?] 8vo, pp. 26. H. 51157

General View of the Principles and Design of the Mount Holyoke Female Seminary. ... *Boston: Printed by Perkins and Marvin.* 1837. 8vo, pp. 22. H. 51158

Memorial. Twenty-Fifth Anniversary of the Mt. Holyoke Female Seminary. ... *South Hadley, Mass.* 1862. 12mo, pp. 174. Plate. H. 51159

See also Eden (J.), VI. 21825.

Mount Hope Cemetery in Dorchester and West Roxbury. With the Exercises at the Consecration, ... June 24, 1852. *Boston: Crosby, Nichols and Company.* 1852. 8vo, pp. 40. H.

See also Vol. II., No. 6476.

The Fourth Annual Report of the Mount-Hope Institution, for ... 1846. By William H. Stokes, M.D. ... *Baltimore: Metropolitan Press.* 1847. 8vo, pp. 35, (10). Continued. B. 51161

See also Stokes (W. H.)

Mount Moriah Cemetery. [*Philadelphia, about* 1855.] 8vo, pp. 12. P. 51162

Mount Olivet Cemetery. ... [Rules, Regulations, etc. n. p.] 1851. 8vo, pp. 42. Plan. H. 51163

See also Vol. I., No. 3032.

Mount Pleasant, May 5, 1766. ... John M'Pherson. [n. p. n. d.] Folio, 1 leaf. P. 51164

This and the following broadside relate to a quarrel between M'Pherson and Samuel Garrigue: "Philadelphia, May 19. 1766. To the Printers of the Pennsylvania Gazette," etc. [n. p. n. d.] 4to, 1 leaf. P.

Constitution of the Farmer's Association at Mount Pleasant in the State of New York. *New York.* 1803. 12mo. N. 51165

Minutes of the Baptist Convention met at Mount Pleasant, May 31 and June 1, 1791. *New York.* 1791. 12mo. 51166

Circular of the Mount Pleasant Academy, a Military School, at Sing Sing, ... N. Y. 1864–'65. [*New York: G. A. Whitehorne, Printer.* 1865.] 18mo, pp. 39. Continued. H. 51167

First Annual Catalogue of the Mt. Pleasant Boarding School for Boys. Amherst, Mass. 1846–7. *Amherst: J. S. & C. Adams, Printers.* [n. d.] 12mo, pp. 12. Continued. H. 51168

Previously "Mount Pleasant Classical Institution," later, "Mount Pleasant Institute."

Catalogue of the Mount-Pleasant Classical Institution, Amherst, Mass. January, 1828. *Amherst: John S. and C. Adams, Printers.* 1828. 8vo, pp. 16. Plate. Continued. H. 51169

Catalogue of the Officers & Students of Mount St. Mary's College, Emmitsburg, Md. ... 1855–56. *Baltimore: Printed by John Murphy & Co.* 1856. 8vo, pp. 28. Plate. Continued.

The Catholic Mirror's Account of the Fifty-Year Jubilee, ... the 6th and 7th ... of October, 1858, in Commemoration of the founding of the Mount St. Mary's College. *Baltimore: Printed by P. J. Hedian.* 1858. 8vo, pp. 15. H. 51171

First Annual Report of the Physician [W. H. Stokes] of Mount St. Vincent's Hospital, Baltimore. *Baltimore.* 1843. 8vo, pp. 20. M. 51172

Annual Report of the Directors of Mount Sinai Hospital, ... 1867. *New York.* 1867. 8vo. Continued. 51173

Also: Proceedings ... laying of the Corner Stone, ... 1870. *New York.* 1870. 8vo.

Catalogue and Circular of the Mount Union, Ohio, College and Normal Seminary, for 1862–3. *Cleveland.* 1863. 8vo.

Mount Vernon, July 15, 1773. The subscriber, having obtained patents for upwards of 20,000 acres of land, on the Ohio and Great Kanhawa, &c. ... George Washington. [n. p. n. d.] 4to, pp. 1. 51175

Proposals to lease Western lands.

Mount Vernon: A Letter. *See* [Cooper (S. F.)], IV. 16604.

Mount Vernon Record. Vol. I. *Philadelphia.* 1858–9. 4to.

To the Daughters of Washington! An Appeal for Mount Vernon. By the "Mount Vernon Association of the Union." *Philadelphia.* 1855. Rl. 8vo, pp. 8. 51177

By-Laws and Regulations of the Mount Vernon Cemetery Company, at Laurel Hill, ... Philadelphia; and the Act of Incorporation ... . *Philadelphia: Sherman & Co., Printers.* 1864. 8vo, pp. 20. Plan. H. 51178

History, Confession of Faith, etc., of the Mount Vernon Congregational Church in Boston. *Boston.* 1844. 12mo, pp. 28.

See also Vol. II., No. 6658.

By-Laws for the Regulation and Government of Mount Vernon Lodge, Boston. With an Appendix. [By Thomas S. Waterman.] *Boston.* 1867. 12mo, pp. 96. 51180

A Description of the Mount Vernon School in 1832. *Boston: Printed by Pierce and Parker.* [n. d.] 18mo, pp. 72. 51181

By Jacob Abbott. Not published. Also: Catalogue of the Mount Vernon Classical School, January, 1831. *Boston.* 1831. 12mo, pp. 12.

Catalogue of Mount-Washington Collegiate Institute, New York City, ... 1852. [n. p. n. d.] 8vo. 51182

Mount Washington in Winter; or, the Experiences of a Scientific Expedition upon the Highest Mountain in New England —1870–71. *Boston.* 1871. 12mo, pp. vii, 363. Map, Plate.

Mountain (A. S. H.) Memoirs and Letters of ... Colonel Armine S. H. Mountain, C.B. ... Edited by Mrs. Armine S. H. Mountain. *London: Longman, Brown ... .* 1857. 8vo, pp. 319, (1). Portrait. B. 51184

Mountain (A. W.) A Memoir of George Jehoshaphat Mountain, D.D. ... Late Bishop of Quebec. Compiled ... by his Son, Armine W. Mountain, M.A. ... *Montreal.* 1866. 8vo, pp. 477. 51185

[Mountain (George Jehoshaphat).] Journal of the Bishop of Montreal during a Visit to the Church Missionary Society's North-West American Mission [Red River]. To which is added, by the Secretaries, an Appendix, giving an Account of the Formation of the Mission, and its Progress to the present time. *London.* 1845. 12mo, pp. 236. + Second Edition. *London.* 1849. 12mo, pp. 245. C. 51186

Mountain. Songs of the Wilderness: Being a Collection of Poems, Written in some different Parts of the Territory of the Hudson's Bay Company, and in the Wilds of Canada, on the Route to that Territory in the Spring and Summer of 1844: Interspersed with some Illustrative Notes. By George J. Mountain, Bishop of Montreal. *London: F. & J. Rivington.* 1846. 12mo, pp. xxix, 153. 4 Plates. C. 51187

Also: A Charge ... to the Clergy of the Diocese of Quebec. ... 1838. *Quebec, Printed.* 1839. *London: Reprinted for J. G. F. & J. Rivington.* 1839. 8vo, pp. 57. + A Charge ... at the Triennial Visitation ... 1845. *Quebec: Printed by T. Cary & Co.* 1845. 8vo, pp. 40. + A Charge ... 1854. *Quebec.* 1854. 8vo, pp. 46.—The Duty of the Christian Minister ... . The Sermon ... at an Ordination ... held by the Provisional Bishop of New-York ... . *New-York.* 1854. 8vo, pp. 32.—The Education of the Poor ... . A Sermon ... . *Quebec.* 1822. 8vo, pp. 28.—Letter respecting Synodical Action in his Diocese; together with Considerations relative to certain Interruptions of the Peace of the Church in the Parish of Quebec. *Quebec.* 1858. 8vo, pp. 27.— ... Ordination Sermon preached in ... Quebec ... 30th July, 1826 ... . *Quebec: Neilson & Cowan.* 1826. 8vo, pp. 39.—A Pastoral Letter to the Clergy and Laity of the Diocese of Quebec, in connection with the subject of the Bill introduced into the Imperial Parliament, ... for the conveyance of certain Privileges to the Colonial Churches ... . *Quebec.* 1853. 8vo, pp. 14.—A Retrospect of the Summer and Autumn of 1832. A Sermon ... at Quebec, Dec. 30, 1832. With an Appendix of Facts concerning the late awful visitation of the Cholera Morbus. *Quebec.* 1833. 8vo, pp. 33.—A Sermon, ... in ... Fredericton, ... 14th January, 1816; upon ... a Collection ... in aid of the Waterloo Subscriptions. ... *Fredericton: Printed by Geo. K. Lugrin.* [n. d.] 12mo, pp. 15.—A Sermon ... in ... Quebec, ... 12th September, 1819, after the ... Death of ... the Duke of Richmond, Governor in Chief. ... *Quebec: J. Neilson.* 1819. 8vo, pp. 17. —Sermon on the Responsibilities of Englishmen in the Colonies of the British Empire. Preached before the St. George's Society. ... *Quebec.* 1847. 8vo, pp. 18.—Thoughts on "Annexation," in connection with the Duty and the Interest of Members of the Church of England, and as affecting some particular Religious Questions. ... *Quebec.* 1849. 8vo, pp. 28. *See also* Vol. IV., Nos. 13304–07.

[Mountain] (J.) A Sermon ... at Quebec, ... January 10th, 1799: being ... Thanksgiving. By Jacob, Lord Bishop of Quebec. ... *Quebec: Printed by John Neilson.* 1799. 8vo, pp. xi, 35.

Also: Letter ... on the Clergy Reserves. ... *Boston.* 1827. 8vo. S.

Mountain (J.) Sketches of the Life of Joseph Mountain, a Negro, Who was executed at New-Haven, on the 20th day of October, 1790 ... . *New Haven.* [1790.] 8vo. + *Sag-Harbour, (L. I.): For the Purchasers.* 1808. 8vo, pp. 15. H. 51189

Mountain Meadows. *See* Message, Vol. XII., No. 48135.

The Mountain of the [Mormon] Lord's House. Revised Edition. *Plano.* [n. d.] 8vo, pp. 8. 51190

Mountaineer, *pseudon.* *See* [Wright (Charles)].

Mounteney (B.) Selections from the various Authors who have written concerning Brazil; more particularly respecting the Captaincy of Minas Geraës, and the Gold Mines of that Province. By Barclay Mounteney. ... *London: Effingham Wilson.* MDCCCXXV. 8vo, pp. xii, 182. Map. C., H. 51191

Mountford (W.) An Address on behalf of the Seamen's Widow and Orphans' Association in Salem, ... Jan. 26, 1851.

By Rev. William Mountford. ... *Boston: Wm. Crosby and H. P. Nichols.* 1851. 8vo, pp. 15. H. 51192

Mountgomery (*Sir* Robert). Azilia: a Historical Legend of Georgia, from 1717. (From original papers published at the time.) Compiled by George W. Shaffer. *Savannah (Ga.): E. J. Purse.* 1870. 12mo, pp. 36. C. 51193

Proposals for encouraging the settlement of lands in Georgia, in 1717.

Mountgomery. A | Discourse | Concerning the design'd | Establishment | Of a New | Colony | to the | South of Carolina, | in the | Most delightful Country of the Universe. | By Sir Robert Mountgomery, Baronet. | *London: | Printed in the Year.* 1717. | 8vo, pp. (2), 30, Appendix, 3. Plan. BA., C. 51194

Contains a folded plan, "representing the Form of Setling [*sic*] the Districts, or County Divisions in the Margravate of Azilia." A very curious tract. "Sir Robert Mountgomery having obtained a grant of all the land between the rivers Alatamaha and Savanna, now part of Georgia, which he called Azilia, issued these proposals for settling the colony."—Rich. *See* our Vol. V., No. 19719. Reprinted in Peter Force's collection of "Tracts," Vol. I.

Moura e Limos (L. A. I. de). Elogio Funebre do Ser.mo Sr. D. José, Principe do Brasil. Por Luis Antonio Innocencio de Moura e Lemos. *Lisboa, na Typographia Rollandiana.* 1788. 8vo. 51195

Moure (A.) Les Indiens de la Province de Mato-Grosso [Bresil]. Observations par le Docteur Amedee Moure. [Extrait du Nouv. Ann. des Voy.] *Paris.* [1862.] 8vo, pp. 56.

Moure. La Rivière Paraguay, depuis ses sources jusqu'à son ambouchure dans le Parana (1851 à 1854). *Paris.* 1861. 8vo, pp. 90. 51197

A Mournful Lamentation. *See* [Green (Joseph)], VII. 28549.

[Mourt (G.)] A | Relation or | Iournall of the beginning and proceedings | of the English Plantation setled at Plimoth in New | England, by certaine English Adventurers both | Merchants and others. | With their difficult passage, their safe ariuall, their | ioyfull building of, and comfortable planting them- | selves in the now well defended Towne | of New Plimoth. | As also a Relation of Fovre | seuerall discoueries since made by some of the | same English Planters there resident. | I. In a iourney to Pvckanokick the habitation of the Indians great- | est King Massasoyt: as also their message, the answer and entertainment | they had of him. | II. In a voyage made by ten of them to the Kingdome of Naw-

set, to seeke | a boy that had lost himselfe in the woods: with such accidents as befell them | in that voyage. | III. In their iourney to the Kingdome of Namaschet, in defence of their | greatest King Massasoyt, against the Narrohiggonsets, and to reuenge the | supposed death of their Interpreter Tisquantum. | IIII. Their voyage to the Massachusets, and their entertainment there. | With an answer to all such obiections as are any way made | against the lawfulnesse of English plantations | in those parts. | *London, | Printed for Iohn Bellamie, and are to be sold at his shop at the two | Greyhounds in Cornhill neere the Royall Exchange.* 1622. 4to, pp. (12), 72.

The fourth part is signed "R. C." Mourt's "Relation" is the chief corner-stone of a New England library. It had become so rare that the reprint made for the Massachusetts Historical Society was made from a transcript not quite perfect.

[Mourt.] The Journal of the Pilgrims at Plymouth, in New England, in 1620: Reprinted from the Original Volume. With Historical and Local Illustrations of Providences, Principles, and Persons: By George B. Cheever, D.D. *New York: John Wiley.* 1847. 12mo. + Second Edition. [*Ibid.*] 1848. 12mo, pp. ix, iii–v, 3–369. B. + [*Ibid.*] 1849. 51199

Mourt. Mourt's Relation or Journal of the Plantation at Plymouth With an Introduction and Notes By Henry Martyn Dexter *Boston: John Kimball Wiggin.* M DCCC LXV. 4to, pp. xlvii, 176. B. 51200

Two hundred and fifty copies printed on small paper, thirty-five copies on large paper, four on India paper, two on Holland paper, and two on drawing paper. Bishop Kennett and Dr. Allibone each describe an edition which probably does not exist.

[Mourt.] The Pilgrim Fathers: or, The Journal of the Pilgrims at Plymouth, New England, in 1620. ... By George B. Cheever ... . *William Collins, Glasgow.* [1849.] Post 8vo, pp. 309. 51201

See also Young's "Chronicles," Massachusetts Historical Society "Collections," 1st Series, Vol. VIII., pp. 203–239; 2d Series, Vol. IX., pp. 26–73, Purchas's "Pilgrims," Book X., pp. 1842–1852. In the MS. catalogue of the British Museum library it is suggested that the real name of the author is George Morton.

Moussy (V. M. de). L'Industrie dans le bassin de la Plata à l'époque de la découverte et de l'état de la population à cette époque, par M. Martin de Moussy ... . *Paris.* 1866. 8vo, pp. (38)

See also Martin De Moussy (V.), Vol. XI., No. 44923.

Mouttet (E.) Saint-Domingue devant l'Europe, Nécessité, Légitimité, Facilité de son Occupation par la France, dans les circonstances présentes. Par M. Étienne Mouttet ... . *Paris.* 1843. 8vo, pp. 80. N. 51203

Movila (F. de la). Relacion de la sorprecha hecha por los Franceses de la Movila en el Castillo de San Carlos, y punta de Siguenza; y su restauracion por las armas de S. M. el dia 7 de Agosto deste año de 1719. *Mexico.* 1719. Sm. 4to, pp. 8.

Movilla (G. de). Explicacion de la Doctrina que compuso el Cardenal Belarmino, por mandado del Señor Papa Clemente 8. Traducida en Lengua Floridana: por el Padre Fr. Gregorio de Mouilla Diffinidor de la Prouincia de santa Elena ... . Corregida, enmendada y añadida en esta segunda impression por el mesmo Autor. *En Mexico Impressa con licencia en la Imprenta de Iuan Ruyz. Año de* 1635. [Colophon:] *Acabose à 9. de Enero de* 1636. *con licencia en Mexico, por Juan Ruyz.* 8vo, (12), 197, and (2), leaves. [Followed by:] Forma breve de administrar los Sacramentos a los Indios, y Españoles que viuen entre ellos ... . en lêgua Mexicana traducido en lengua Floridana. ... *Impresso en Mexico. Por Iuan Ruyz. Año de* 1635. 8vo, 32 leaves. 51205

The first edition was printed at Madrid in 1631.

Movimento general de aduana. *See* Buenos Aires, III. 9025.

Mowatt (A. C.) Autobiography of an Actress; or, Eight Years on the Stage. By Anna Cora Mowatt. *Boston: Ticknor and Fields.* M DCCC LIV. 16mo, pp. 448. Portrait. + [*Ibid.*] 1859. 51206

Also: Fashion, or Life in New-York. ... *New York: Samuel French.* [n. d.] 12mo, pp. (4), 62. + *London: W. Newbery.* 1850. 8vo, pp. (8), 62.—Mimic Life; or, Before and Behind the Curtain. ... *Boston.* 1856. 16mo.

Mowatt (J. A.) Maguire's "Irish in America." ... A Review. By J. A. Mowatt ... . *London: Heywood & Co.* [n. d.] 8vo, pp. 30. 51207

Mowrey (James D.) Love and Arsenic, the Great Piqua Murder. *Tippecanoe, O.* 18—: 8vo, pp. 16. 51208

Mowris (J.) A History of the One Hundred and Seventeenth Regiment, N. Y. Volunteers, (Fourth Oneida,) from ... its Organization, August, 1862, till ... June, 1865. By J. A. Mowris, M.D. ... *Hartford, Conn.: Case, Lockwood and Company, Printers.* 1866. 8vo, pp. 315. C., H. 51209

Mowry (S.) Arizona and Sonora: The Geography, History, and Resources of the Silver Regions of North America. By Sylvester Mowry, of Arizona ... . Third Edition, Revised and Enlarged. *New York: Harper & Brothers.* 1864. 12mo, pp. 251. Plate. H. 51210

Mowry. The Geography and Resources of Arizona and Sonora; An Address before the American Geographical and Statistical Society, By Sylvester Mowry, ... New York, February 3, 1859. *Washington.* 1859. 8vo, pp. 47. C. + A New Edition, with an Appendix. *San Francisco: A. Romane & Co.* 1863. 8vo, pp. (6), 124, (2). Map. 51211

Mowry. Memoir of the Proposed Territory of Arizona. By Sylvester Mowry ... . *Washington: Henry Polkinhorn, Printer.* 1857. 8vo, pp. 30. Map. H. 51212

Probably the earliest historical document published in relation to this territory.

Moxó (B. M. de). Cartas Méjicanas, escritas por D. Benito Maria de Moxó, año de 1805. Segunda Edicion Correjida y Enmendada. *Genova: Tipografia de Louis Pellas.* [1839.] 8vo, pp. (8), 415, (1). 6 Plates. 51213

"By the prologue to this work we learn, that its author, a native of Cervera, died young, immediately after a revolution (in South America), in which this work came near being buried in 'eternal oblivion':—that it was brought to Europe and printed, but so hastily, that it could hardly be read for the many orthographic errors with which it was stained. In consequence of which, it was thought proper to prepare the present edition, which is indeed, handsomely, but not very correctly printed.—Rich, II. 332.

Moxo. Coleccion de varios papeles relativos a los sucesos de Buenos-Ayres. Escritos por El Illmo S. D. D. Benito Maria de Moxo ... *Lima.* 1808. 4to, pp. (4), 181. BM. 51214

[Moxo.] Entretenimientos de un Prisionero en las Provincias del Rio de la Plata: Por el Baron de Juras Reales, Siendo Fiscal de S. M. en el Reino de Chile. *Barcelona: En la Imprenta de José Torner.* 1828. 2 vols., 8vo, Engraved Titles, pp. (6), viii, 334; (4), 391, 16. 3 Plates. C. 51215

Also on large and thick paper. A valuable set of dissertations upon the natives and history of the New World, written by Don Benito Maria de Moxó, Archbishop of Charcas, whose papers fell into the hands of his nephew, and were printed by the latter under his own name without sufficient acknowledgment. Juras Reales was a Spanish official who fell into the hands of the Patriots, and underwent six years imprisonment in South America after the Revolution. "All the Baron's dissertations are made up *verbatim* from Moxó's 'Cartas Méjicanas,' with a few notes added, and the omission of the passages which shew that they were written in Mexico."—Rich, II. 332.

Moxo. Poesias y Oracion con que la Real Universidad de Cervera aplaudia el arribo del Rey Don Carlos III. y de la Reyna, su autor Don Benito Maria de Moxo y de Francoli. *Cervera.* 1802. Folio. P. 51216

Moxo. Secunda Parte de las Obras patrioticas y doctrinales con que ha accreditado su zelo por la religion y monarquia. D.

Benito, M. de Moxo, Arzobispo de La Plata. *Lima.* 1809. 4to, pp. 211, (2). 51217

Also: Discurso que pronunció ... el dia 27 de Setiembre de 1808 ... *Buenos Ayres.* 1808. 4to.—Homilia que pronunció ... el dia 12 de Octubre de 1808 ... *Buenos Ayres.* 1809. 4to.

Moxo Language. Arte, | y Vocabulario | de la | Lengua | Morocosi. | Compvesto | por vn Padre de la | Compañia de Jesvs, | Misionero de las | Provincias de los Moxos. | ... | *En Madrid. Año de* 1699. 4to, pp. (4), 379. BM. 51218

Moxon (J.) A Brief | Discourse | of a | Passage | by the | North-Pole | to | Japan, China, &c. | Pleaded by Three Experiments. | ... | By Joseph Moxon, Hydrographer ... . *London: Joseph Moxon.* 1674. 4to, pp. (2), 6. Map. + The Second Edition. *London: Printed by J. Moxon.* 1697. 4to, pp. (2), 6. Map. 51219

Moya (J. de). Reglamento para los alcaldes de cuarteles y comisarios de barrio, formado por el Sr. Gobernador interino brigadier D. Juan de Moya. *Impreso en Santiago de Cuba por D. Loreto Espinal.* [n. d.] 4to. 51220

Moyamensing. *See* Philadelphia.

Moyen pour prévenir les inondations de la ville et la vallée de Mexico. *Mexico.* 1858. 8vo. 51221

Des moyens de conserver. *See* [Bertin (A. de)], II. 5011.

[Moyers & Dedrick.] To the ... Senate and House of Representatives ... . [n. p. 1870?] 8vo, pp. 11. H. 51222

On a report relating to the collection and payment of bounties to colored soldiers.

Moyes (R.) The working Classes of the United States in a False Position; or, Error Exposed and Truth Upheld. By Robert Moyes, a Workman. *Boston: Printed by Alfred Mudge & Son.* 1860. 12mo, pp. 14. B. 51223

Moyne (J. de). *See* (Bry T. de), Vol. III., p. 30.

Moziño (J. M.) Tratado del Xiquilite y añil de Guatemala ... Por D. Jose Mariano Moziño ... Con notas puestas por el socio mencionado Dr. Fr. Jose Antonio Goycoechea. *Año de* 1799. 4to, pp. 44, (2). 51224

Mozis Addums' New Letters. Number One. Leave Richmond—Supper at Ashland—The Potomac Boat—Washington Early in the Morning—The Chicago Zouaves— ... Description of Baltimore and its People—Trip from Old Point to Annapolis in the Great Eastern—Incidents of the Voyage, &c., &c. *Richmond: Macfarlane & Fergusson, Printers.* 1860. 8vo, pp. 16.

Mr. Dunn Browne's Experiences. *See* [Fiske (S.)], 24555.

Mr. Madison's War. *See* [Lowell (J.)], x. 42452.

Mr. Merryman's Monthly. ... *New York.* 1863. 4to. Cont'd

Mucius to the Freemen of America. November, 1773. [*Philadelphia.* n. d.] Folio, 1 leaf. P. 51227

Mucury. Berichte, betreffend die Mucury-Colonie in der brasilianischen Provinz Minas Geraes. Erstes Heft. ... *Hamburg: Wilh. Jowien.* 1859. *Druck von Ackermann & Wulff.* 8vo, pp. 29. 51228

Relatorio apresentado aos Accionistas da Companhia do Mucury no dia 10 de Maio de 1860 Pelo Director da Companhia Theophilo Benedicto Ottoni *Rio de Janeiro Typ. do Correio Mercantil* 1860 8vo, pp. 40, 91. Table. 51229

Mudge (A.) Memorials: being a Genealogical, Biographical and Historical Account of the name of Mudge in America, from 1638 to 1868. By Alfred Mudge ... . *Boston: Printed by Alfred Mudge & Son.* 1868. 8vo, pp. xiv, (2), 443. 13 Portraits and Facsimiles. H. 51230

Preceded by a preliminary essay calling attention to a proposed history of the family.

The Mudge Family. [n. p.] 1865. 8vo, pp. 8. 51231

Mudge (B. F.) Geology of Kansas. *See* Vol. ix. 37023.

Mudge (C. R.) In Memoriam Charles Redington Mudge Lieut.-Col. Second Mass. Infantry ... *Cambridge: Privately Printed.* 1863. 8vo, pp. 31. H. 51232

[Mudge (Enoch).] An Address to Sailors. [n. p. n. d.] 8vo, pp. 8. 51233

Mudge. An Oration, ... at Orrington, July 4th 1808. ... By Enoch Mudge. *Boston: Printed by B. Parks.* 1808. 8vo, pp. 14, (1). 51234

Also other pieces, mostly for sailors.

Mudge (E. R.) *and* Hayes (J. L.) Paris Universal Exposition, 1867. Reports of the United States Commissioners ... upon Wool and Manufactures of Wool, By E. R. Mudge, ... [and] John L. Hayes ... . *Washington.* 1868. 8vo, pp. (2), 143.

Mudge. ... Reports of the United States Commissioners. Report upon Cotton, By E. R. Mudge ... with a Supplemental Report, by B. F. Nourse ... . *Washington.* 1869. 8vo, pp. (2), 115. B. 51236

Mudge (Z. A.) Foot-prints of Roger Williams: a Biography, with Sketches of Important Events in early New England History, with which he was connected. By Rev. Z. A. Mudge. *New York: Carlton & Lanahan.* [1871.] 16mo, pp. 285. 4 Plates. C. 51237

Mudge. The Forest Boy: a Sketch of the Life of Abraham Lincoln. For Young People. By Z. A. Mudge. *New York: Carlton & Porter.* [1867.] 16mo, pp. 321. 4 Plates. C. 51238

Mudge. Views from Plymouth Rock; a Sketch of the Early History of the Plymouth Colony. Designed for Young People. By Z. A. Mudge ... *New York: Carlton & Lanahan.* [1869.] 16mo, pp. 451. 5 Plates and Map. B. 51239

Mudge. Witch Hill: a History of Salem Witchcraft. ... By Rev. Z. A. Mudge ... . *New York: Carlton & Lanahan.* [1870.] 16mo, pp. 322. 3 Plates. B. 51240

Also: The Christian Statesman; A Portraiture of Sir Thomas Fowell Buxton; with Sketches of British Antislavery Reform. ... *New York: Carlton & Porter.* [1865.] 16mo, pp. 268. 4 Plates. B., C.

Mudie (R.) The Emigrant's Pocket Companion; containing ... a Description of British North America, especially the Canadas; ... By Robert Mudie ... . *London: James Cochrane and Co.* MDCCCXXXII. 12mo, pp. xvi, 276. H. 51241

Muenscher (Joseph). The Claims of the Episcopal Church. A Sermon preached in ... Boston, June 17, 1829, before the Annual Convention of the Protestant Episcopal Church, in the State of Massachusetts. *Boston.* 1829. 12mo, pp. 24. W.

Muenster (Sebastian). *See* Munster (S.)

Mverte de Pie de Palo. | Segvnda | Relacion, y mvy co-|piosa de vna carta que embiò el| señor Duque de Medina|a la contrastacion de|Seuilla.|Dase cuenta de la batalla que han tenido los Galeones con|40 Nauios de Olandeses, siendo General de ellos Pie de|Palo. Assi mismo se da cuenta de su muerte, con|perdida de siete nauios, en el cabo de S. Anton. [Colophon:] *Con licencia, en Madrid, por Antonio Duplastre,| Año* 1638. 4to, 4 leaves

Muerte politica de la Republica Mexicana, deducida del Articulo que con respecto à ella se ha estampado en el Redactor de Nueva-York del diu 30 de enero de 1829. *Mexico.* 1829. 4to, 40 or more Numbers. 51244

The publication of this periodical was called forth by an article which appeared in a New York paper on Mexico, and in which the political state of that country was portrayed in the darkest colors.

Mühlbach (L.) Henry viii. and His Court, or Catherine Parr. A Historical Novel, By L. Mühlbach. From the German, By H. N. Pierce, D.D. *Mobile: S. H. Goetzel.* 1865. 2 vols., 8vo, pp. 142; 143. 51245

This and the following are quoted as Confederate publications.

Mühlbach. Joseph ii. and his Court. By L. Mühlbach. *Mobile.* 1864. 4 vols., 8vo. 51246

Muhle (C. A.) Om Emancipationen af Færoerne og Gronland ved Carl Adolf Muhle ... . *Kiöbenhavn.* 1835. 8vo, pp. 70. Map. 51247

Muhlenberg [G.] H. [E.] Catalogus Plantarum Americæ Septentrionalis, huc usque cognitarum indigenarum et cicurum: or, A Catalogue of the hitherto known Native and Naturalized Plants of North America ... . By Henry Muhlenberg, D.D. ... *Lancaster: Printed by William Hamilton.* 1813. 8vo, pp. iv, 112. + Second Edition, corrected and enlarged. *Philadelphia: Solomon W. Conrad.* 1818. 8vo, pp. iv, 122. A., C., H. 51248

Muhlenberg. Descriptio Uberior Graminum et Plantarum Calamariarum Americæ Septentrionalis indigenarum et cicurum. Auctore D. Henrico Muhlenberg ... . *Philadelphiæ: ... Solomon W. Conrad.* 1817. 8vo, pp. (2), ii, 295. A., B. 51249

Also: Reduction of all the Genera of Plants contained in the Catalogus Plantarum Americæ Septentrionalis of the late Dr. Muhlenberg, to the natural families of Mr. de Jussieu's System. *Philadelphia: Solomon W. Conrad.* 1815. 8vo, pp. 16. P.

Muhlenberg (H. A.) The Life of Major-General Peter Muhlenberg of the Revolutionary Army. By Henry A. Muhlenberg. *Philadelphia: Carey and Hart.* 1849. 12mo, pp. 456.

Muhlenberg. Political Duplicity, The Revilers of H. A. Muhlenberg. [n. p. 1847.] 8vo, pp. 8. 51251

[Muhlenberg (W. A.)] An Exposition of the Memorial of Sundry Presbyters of the Protestant Episcopal Church; ... By one of the Memorialists. *New York: Stanford and Swords.* 1854. 8vo, pp. (2), 84, (1). H. 51252

Muhlenberg. A Plea for a Church Hospital, in the City of New-York. In Two Lectures, ... in ... New York and ... in ... Brooklyn. By W. A. Muhlenberg, D.D. ... With an Appendix, ... *New-York: Stanford and Swords.* 1850. 8vo, pp. 55, (1).

Muhlenberg. The Rebuke of the Lord; a Sermon preached in the Chapel of the Institute at Flushing, L. I., ... after the Great Fire in New York, 16th & 17 December, 1835. By William Augustus Muhlenberg. *Jamaica.* 1835. 8vo, pp. 16.

[Muhlenberg.] St. Johnland [Long Island]: ... Part 1, 2. [*New York.* 1867?] 8vo, pp. 54. B. 51255

Part 1 describes an imaginary community for the benefit of the working classes. Part 2 gives the realization of this ideal in the establishment of such an institution on Long Island.

Muhlenberg. The Testimony ... . A Sermon preached at the Re-opening of the Church of Augustus ... Trappe, Montgomery Co., Pennsylvania, September 5, 1860. By William Augustus Muhlenberg. ... *New York: Robert Craighead, Printer.* 1861. 8vo, pp. 46. 51256

Also: College of St. James. Address, by the Rev. W. A. Muhlenberg, D.D., at the laying of the Corner Stone of Kemp Hall, ... July 31, 1851. ... *Fountain Rock, Maryland.* 1851. 18mo, pp. 28.—[Plan of] St. Paul's College [near Flushing, L. I. n. p. 1835.] 8vo, pp. 20.—A Sermon in memory of The Rev. Samuel Bacon, and John P. Bankson, agents of the ... American Colonization Society, ... November 5th ... . [*Philadelphia:*] *Clark & Raser, Printers.* 1820. 8vo, pp. 26.—The Studies and Discipline of the Institute at Flushing, L. I. August, 1830. [n. p. n. d.] 8vo, pp. 15.—Two Protestant Sisterhoods. ... *New York.* 1856. 8vo.

Muhlenberg College, *Allentown, Pa.* Catalogue of the Officers and Students with the Charter ... . 1868–9. *Allentown, Pa.: E. D. Leisenring & Co., ... Printers.* 1868. 8vo, pp. 40. Continued. 51257

Mühlenpfordt (E.) Versuch einer getreuen Schilderung der Republik Mejico besonders in Beziehung auf Geographie, Ethnographie und Statistik. ... Von Eduard Mühlenpfordt ... . *Hannover: C. F. Kius.* 1844. 2 vols., 8vo, pp. (12), 472; vi, 552. B., C. 51258

Muilkerk (W. E. J. B. v. D.) *See* Berg van Dussen Muilkerk (W. E. J.), ii. 4843.

Muir (J.) Death Abolished: A Sermon. Occasioned by the Sickness ... at Alexandria ... . With an Appendix ... . By James Muir, D.D. ... *Alexandria: Printed by Cottom and Stewart.* 1803. 12mo, pp. 16, Appendix, (7). BA. 51259

Muir. A Sermon ... at Alexandria, ... 9th of May, 1798, being the Day appointed for ... Fast. By the Revd. ... James Muir. *Philadelphia: William Cobbett.* 1798. 12mo, pp. 14. BA.

Muir. Sermons, by James Muir, A.M. Minister of the Presbyterian Church, Bermuda. *Printed for the Author, by James Tod.* M.DCC.LXXXVII. 8vo, pp. 228. 51261

Also: An Address, ... [before] the Bible Society of the District of Columbia, ... 17th of April 1814. ... *New-York: Griffin and Rudd.* 1814. 12mo, pp. 22.—Instruction from the Grave: ... [on] the Death of Oliver Deming Welman, ... August, 1802. ... *Alexandria: Printed by John Westcott.* 1803. 8vo, pp. 20.—Observations on the Importance of the Present Life, ... From the Funeral Sermon ... in memory of Mrs. Mary Patten. ... *Alexandria: Printed by Cottom & Stewart.* 1808. 12mo, pp. 17. BA.

Mulchahey (J.) Review of the Rev. J. W. Cooke's Pamphlet, entitled "A Statement of Facts relating to the Ordination at Grace Church," in Two Letters addressed to the Bishop of the Diocese. By the Rev. James Mulchahey, ... Portsmouth, R. I. *Providence: C. Burnett, Jr.* 1847. 8vo. 51262

Mulchinock (W. P.) The Ballads and Songs of William Pembroke Mulchinock. ... *New York: T. W. Strong.* 1851. 12mo, pp. 262. A., B. 51263

Mulford (E.) The Nation: the Foundations of Civil Order and Political Life in the United States. By E. Mulford. *New York: Hurd and Houghton.* 1870. 8vo, pp. xiv, 418. BA., C.

Mulford (I. S.) Civil and Political History of New Jersey. By Isaac S. Mulford, M.D. *Camden: P. Keen and E. Chandler.* 1848. 8vo, pp. 500. BA. 51265

Reprinted with the following title:

Mulford. A Civil and Political History of New Jersey: Embracing a Compendious History of the State, from its Early Discovery, ... and Settlement by Europeans, brought down to the Present Time. By Isaac S. Mulford, M.D. *Philadelphia: C. A. Brown & Co.* 1851. 8vo, pp. 500. B. 51266

Mulgrave (*Baron* Constantine John). *See* Phipps (C. J.)

Mulhall (M. G.) The Cotton Fields of Paraguay and Corrientes: being an Account of a Tour through these Countries, preceded by Annals of Cotton-Planting in the River Plate Territories from 1862 to 1864. By Michael G. Mulhall. ... *Buenos Aires: M. G. and E. T. Mulhall.* 1864. 4to, pp. 120. BA. + [*Ibid.*] 1866. 51267

Mulhall. Handbook of the River Plate; comprising Buenos Ayres, the Upper Provinces, Banda Oriental, and Paraguay. By M. G. & E. T. Mulhall ... . Vol. i. *Buenos Ayres.* 1869. 8vo, pp. viii, 176, 48, 129–160. + [Another Edition. *Ibid.*] 1869. Vol. i. 8vo, pp. xvi, 192, 160, 200. B. 51268

Reproduced as "Hand Book of the River Plate Republics." *London: Edward Stanford.* 1875. 8vo, pp. viii, 432.

Mulhall. The Rural Code of the Province of Buenos Ayres. Translated ... by M. G. & E. T. Mulhall. ... *Buenos Ayres.* 1866. 8vo, pp. xv, (2), 49, 3. B. 51269

Mulkins (H.) Report to the Canada Temperance Society on the working and effects of Prohibitory Legislation to suppress Intemperance in the New England States. By Rev. Hannibal Mulkins. *Kingston.* 1855. 8vo, pp. 28. 51270

Mullaly (J.) The Laying of the Cable, or the Ocean Telegraph; being a complete and authentic Narrative of the Attempt to lay the Cable across the Entrance to the Gulf of St. Lawrence in 1855, and of the Three Atlantic Telegraph Expeditions of 1857 and 1858: with ... Biographical Sketches of Messrs. Cyrus W. Field, William E. Everett, and other prominent Persons connected with the Enterprise. ... By John Mullaly, Historian of the Enterprise. *New York: D. Appleton and Company.* 1858. 8vo, pp. 7–329. 2 Maps, 2 Portraits, etc. B., C. 51271

Mullaly. The Milk Trade in New York and Vicinity, giving an Account of the Sale of Pure and Adulterated Milk ... . By John Mullaly. *New York: Fowlers and Wells.* 1853. 12mo, pp. 118. B., C. 51272

Mullaly. A Trip to Newfoundland; its Scenery and Fisheries; With an Account of the Laying of the Submarine Telegraph Cable. By John Mullaly. *New York: T. W. Strong.* 1855. 12mo, pp. 108. + [*Ibid.*] 1856. C. 51273

Mullan (J.) Miners and Travelers' Guide to Oregon, Washington, Idaho, Montana, Wyoming, and Colorado. Via the Missouri and Columbia Rivers. ... By Captain John Mullan ... . *New York: Wm. M. Franklin.* 1865. 12mo, pp. 153. Map.

Mullan. Report on the Construction of a Military Road from Fort Walla-Walla, to Fort Benton. By Captain John Mullan ... . *Washington.* 1863. 8vo, pp. 363. C. 51275

Mullane (A. J.) Exhaustive Argument of A. J. Mullane, Esq. ... on ... a Railroad Connection between the Depots of the Ohio and Mississippi Railway Company and Little Miami Railroad Company ... . *Cincinnati.* 1867. 12mo, pp. 7. H.

Muller (A. A.) Address on laying the Corner Stone of the Masonic Hall, Tuscaloosa. By Albert A. Muller. *Tuscaloosa.* 1831. 8vo. B. 51277

Also: Statement of Facts and Circumstances of the Trial of Dr. A. A. Muller, Late Rector of Trinity Church, Clarksville, Tenn. *Nashville, Tenn.* 1841. 8vo.

Muller (A. P.) De Admiraal Piet Hein te Delftshaven. ... *Amsterdam.* 1832. 8vo. Portrait. 51278

There are copies on thick paper.

Müller (F.) The Case of Franz Müller. Extradition Proceedings in case of Franz Müller, charged with the Murder of Thomas Briggs, on the North London Railway. [*New York.* 1864.] 8vo, pp. 30. S. 51279

Muller (F.) Catalogue of Books relating to America including a large number of rare Works Printed before 1700 amongst which a nearly complete collection of the Dutch Publications on New-Netherland from 1612 to 1820. On Sale ... by Fr. Muller, ... [*Amsterdam.* 1850.] 12mo, pp. (2), 102. 51280

Also on large paper, in quarto.

Muller. Catalogue of Books, Maps, Plates on America, and of a remarkable collection of Early Voyages, offered for sale by Frederik Muller, at Amsterdam, ... with Bibliographical and Historical Notes and presenting an essay towards a Dutch-American Bibliography. ... *Amsterdam: Frederik Muller.* 1872. 8vo, pp. viii, 288. 3 Plates. + Part ii. 1875. 8vo, pp. (2), 289–420. + Part iii. 8vo, pp. (2), 173. 51281

Twenty-five copies on large, thick Dutch paper. "Much more than a catalogue, it is, in fact, a tolerably complete Bibliography of Dutch Books relating to America, contains translations of the titles, with critical and other notes concerning the books, and is a most desirable addition to a bibliographical collection."—Sabin's *American Bibliopolist.* *See also* Tiele (P. A.)

Muller. Catalogus van Boeken, Plaatwerken en Kaarten, over de Nederlandsche Bezittingen ... in Azie, Afrika en Amerika, ... verkrijgbaar bij Frederick Muller te Amsterdam. [*Amsterdam.*] 1854. Rl. 8vo, pp. (2), 103. + Tweede Catalogus. [*Ibid.*] 1858. 4to, pp. (2), 28. 51282

Müller (F.) Der grammatische Bau der Algonkin-Sprachen. Von Dr. Friedrich Müller. *Wien.* 1867. 8vo, pp. 23. 51283

Müller. Reise der österreichischen Fregatte Novara um die Erde in den Jahren 1857, 1858, 1859, unter den Befehlen des Commodore B. von Wütterstorf-Urbair. — Linguistischer Theil von Dr. Friedrich Müller ... . *Wien.* 1867. 4to, pp. vi, (2), 357, (1). BA. 51284

Müller [Gerhard Friedrich]. Voyages|from|Asia to America,|For Completing the Discoveries of the|North West Coast of America.|To which is prefixed,|A Summary of the Voyages|Made by the Russians on the|Frozen Sea,|In Search of a North East Passage.|...|Translated from the High Dutch of|S. [*sic*] Muller, of the Royal Academy of Petersburgh.|With the Addition of three new maps;|1. A Copy of Part of the Japanese Map of the World.|2. A Copy of Delisle's and Buache's fictitious Map. And|3. A large Map of Canada, extending to the Pacific Ocean, containing|the New Discoveries made by the Russians and French.|By Thomas Jefferys Geographer to his Majesty.|*London: T. Jefferys.* 1761. 4to, pp. viii, xliii, 76. 3 Maps. B. + The Second Edition. [*Ibid.*] M.DCC.-LXIV. 4to, pp. viii, 120. 4 Maps. J.C.B., H., N. 51285

Contains the original account of Captain Behring's Polar Expedition, and discovery of the strait which bears his name, and the western limits of North America. Taken from the third volume of Müller's "Sammlung Russischer Geschichte," *Petropol.* 1758. Since the rapid developments of British Columbia and Alaska this important book is becoming indispensable for the history of discovery and exploration in the Northern Pacific.

Müller. Voyages|et|Découvertes|Faites par les Russes le long|des côtes de la Mer Glaciale & sur|l'Océan Oriental, tant vers le Japon|que vers l'Amérique.|On y a joint|l'Histoire|du|Fleuve Amur|Et des pays adjacens, depuis la con|quête des Russes;|...|Ouvrages traduits de l'Allemand de|M. G. P. [*sic*] Muller,|Par C. G. F. Dumas.|...|*Amsterdam:|Marc-Michel Rey.*|MDCCLXVI. 2 vols., 12mo, pp. x, (2), 388; iv, 207, (22). Map. C., H. + *A Amsterdam Et se vend a Paris Chez Roret.* M. DCC. LXVIII. 2 vols., 12mo, pp. (2), x, 388, iv; (2), 207, (22).

Müller (J.) Ueber die fossilen Reste der Zeuglodonten von Nordamerika, mit Rücksicht auf die europäischen Reste aus dieser Familie. ... *Berlin.* 1819. Imp. folio. 27 Plates. 51287

Muller (J.) Leerrede bij Gelegenheid der gelukkige Hereeniging van Curaçao met de Nederlanden. ... *Curaçao.* 1816. Sm. 8vo. 51288

Sermon in commemoration of the fortunate reunion of Caraçao with the Netherlands

MULLER (J.) A Treatise of Artillery: ... By John Muller, ... *Philadelphia: Printed by Styner & Cist.* 1779. 8vo. S. 51289

MÜLLER (J. G.) Geschichte der Amerikanischen Urreligionen. Von J. G. Müller ... . *Basel: Schweighauser.* 1855. 8vo, pp. vii, 706. c. + Zweite unveränderte Auflage. *Basel: Hugo Richter.* 1867. 8vo, pp. vii, (1), 706, (1). BA. 51290

MULLER. Der mexikanische National Gott Huitzilopochtli, von Prof. Dr. J. G. Müller. *Basel.* 1847. 4to, pp. 48.

MÜLLER (J. J.) Extract|aus|Unsers Conferenz-Schreibers| Jahann Jacob Müllers|Geführten Protocoll|Bey der|Fünften Versammlung|der|Gemeine Gottes im Geist,|Gehalten in Germantown 1742. den 6ten April und folgende Tage;|Nebst einer Vorrede an die ehrwürdige Conferenz aller|Arbeiter bey der Kirche Jesu Christi in Pennsylvania.|*Philadelphia: Gedruckt und zu haben bey B. Franklin.*| 4to, pp. (2), 93–102. C. 51292

A scarce specimen of Franklin's typography. It is followed by:

MÜLLER. Extract aus des Conferenz-Schreibers Johann Jacob Müllers Registratur von der Sechsten Versammlung der Evangelischen Arbeiter In Pennsylvania. Und der Gemeine Gottes im Geist Siebender Generals Synodus zu Philadelphia am 2 und 3te Juni, 1742, st. v. *Daselbst gedruckt und zu haben bey B. Franklin.* 4to, pp. 105–120. 51293

MULLER (Niclas). Zehn gepanzerte Sonnette. Mit einer Widmung an Ferdinand Freiligrath, und einem Nachklang, "Die Union wie sie sein soll." Im November, 1862. *New York: Nic. Muller.* 1862. 8vo, pp. 15. 51294

[MULLER (Peter).] A Dissertation on Mans Fall, Translated from the High-German Original. ... *Printed: Ephrata Anno* MDCCLXV. *Sold at Philadelphia by Messieurs Christoph Marshal and William Dunlap.* 8vo, pp. 37. P. 51295

The author was a dunkard of Ephrata. It is of extreme rarity.

MULLER (P. N.) Eene waarschuwende stem uit Californië. ... [n. p. n. d.] 8vo. 51296

MULLER (S.) *See* Muller [Gerhard Friedrich], No. 51285.

MULLIN (J.) Speech of Mr. Joseph Mullin, ... on ... Government for the Territory of California: ... February 26, 1849. *Washington: Printed by J. & G. S. Gideon.* 1849. 8vo, pp. 14.

[MULOCH (*Miss*).] Silas Marner, the Weaver of Raveloe. *Mobile.* 1863. 8vo. 51298

A Confederate publication, with a cover printed on wall paper.

MULLOCK (J. T.) Two Lectures on Newfoundland, delivered at St. Bonaventure's College, January 25, and February , 1860. By Rt. Rev. John Thomas Mullock. *New York.* 1860. 8vo, pp. 60. 51299

Also: A Sermon ... in the Cathedral, St. John's. ... *St. John's.* 1861. 8vo, pp. 15.

MULVANY (D. H.) *See* Brooke (C. W.), II. 8239.

MUMFORD (J. I.) An Oration delivered February 22d, 1812, before the Hamilton Society of the City of New York. By John I. Mumford, A.B. *New York.* 1812. 8vo, pp. 14. 51300

MUMFORD (P. M.) An Oration, delivered ... at Newport, on the 4th of July, 1801 ... . By Paul M. Mumford. *Newport: O. Farnsworth.* 1801. 12mo, pp. 23. W. 51301

MUNCASTER (*Lord*). Historical Sketches of the Slave Trade, ... By the Right Hon. Lord Muncaster. *London: John Stockdale.* M.DCCXCII. 8vo, pp. (2), 100. 51302

See "Monthly Review," VIII. 215.

MÜNCH (E.) Geschichte von Brasilien. Von Dr. Ernst Münch. ... *Dresden: P. G. Hilschersche Buchhandlung.* 1829. 2 vols., 18mo, pp. viii, 103; vi, 114. 51303

MÜNCH. Die Geschichte von Columbia. Durch Dr. Ernst Münch ... . *Dresden: P. G. Hilschersche Buchhandlung.* 1828. 2 vols., 18mo, pp. vi, 113; viii, 111. 51304

MÜNCH (F.) Amerikanische Weinbauschule. Kurze doch hinreichend ausführliche Anleitung zur Anlegung des Weinberges, zur Behandlung der Reben und zur Gewinnung des Weines in Nordamerika. Von Friedrich Münch. *St. Louis: Conrad Witter.* 1864. 16mo, pp. 112. + Zweite Auflage. [*Ibid.*] 1867. 16mo, pp. 142. 51305

MÜNCH. School for American Grape Culture: ... By Frederick Münch ... . Translated ... by Elizabeth H. Cutter. *St. Louis.* 1866. 16mo, pp. 129. 51306

MÜNCH. Der Staat Missouri, geschildert mit besonderer Rücksicht auf teutsche Einwanderung, von Fredrich Münch ... . *New York: L. Hauser.* 1859. 12mo, pp. 237. 2 Maps. BA.

Munchausen at the Pole; or, the Surprising and Wonderful Adventures of a Voyage of Discovery. By Capt. Munchausen. *London: J. Johnston.* 1819. 12mo, pp. (10), 164. Plate. C.

MÜNCKEN (J.) *See* Hulsius—Schiff-Fahrt: VIII. 33679.

MUNDAY (E. H.) Historical Sketch of the Public Ledger of Philadelphia. By Eugene H. Munday. ... [*Philadelphia.* 1870.] 8vo, pp. 7. H. 51309

MUNDAY (W.) Christendom in Confusion; or the Source of Discord, Persecution and Oppression Demonstrated. To which is added, The Baseless Fabric. By William Munday. *Baltimore.* 1818. 12mo, pp. 269. 51310

MUNDE (C.) The Bancroft Naturalization Treaties with the German States; the United States' Constitution and the Rights and Privileges of Citizens of Foreign Birth. ... An Appeal to the German-American Citizens, to the Government, Congress, ... By Charles Munde ... . *Würzburg: A. Stuber.* 1868. 8vo, pp. (4), 163, (1). H. 51311

MUNDELL (Marque B.) Miscellaneous Thoughts, in Prose and Verse. *Cincinnati.* 1855. 12mo, pp. 94. 51312

En Mundsmag vaa Mormonismen i Utah. ... *Kjobenhavn.* 1864. 8vo, pp. 15. 51313

Mundus Novus. *See* [Vespuccius (A.)]

MUNDY [Godfrey Basil]. The Life and Correspondence of the late Admiral Lord Rodney. By Major-General Mundy. ... *London: John Murray.* MDCCCXXX. 2 vols., 8vo, pp. xxiii, 472; xvi, 436. Portrait. 51314

Details his services in North America, the taking of St. Eusthacia, etc.

MUNFORD (G. W.) The Jewels of Virginia. A Lecture delivered by Invitation of the "Hollywood Memorial Association" in Richmond, January 18, 1867. By Col. George Wythe Munford, of Gloucester, Va. ... *Richmond: Gary & Clemmitt, Printers.* 1867. 8vo, pp. 50. C. 51315

MUNFORD (W.) Poems and Compositions in Prose on Several Occasions. By William Munford, of the County of Mechlenburg, and State of Virginia. *Richmond: Printed by Samuel Pleasants, Junr.* 1798. 8vo, pp. (2), 189, (1). 51316

Contains a poem on the defeat of General St. Clair, November 4, 1791, or a lam-

entation for the deaths of the patriots who fell on that unfortunate day. Written when the author was sixteen years old.

MUNGEN (W.) Impeachment of the President. Speech of Hon. William Mungen, ... February 22, 1868. *Washington: F. & J. Rives* ... . 1868. 8vo, pp. 8. H. 51317

Also: President's Message and Repudiation. Speech ... January 27, 1869. *Washington: F. & J. Rives* ... . 1869. 8vo, pp. 15.—Recognition of Cuba. Remarks ... February 19, 1870. *Washington: F. & J. Rives* ... . 1870. 8vo, pp. 13.—United States Debt. Speech ... December 16, 1869. *Washington: F. & J. Rives* ... . 1869. 8vo, pp. 16. H.

MUNGER (T. T.) A Sermon, introductory to the Pastorate over the Centre Church, Haverhill, Mas January 10, 1864. By Rev. T. T. Munger. ... *Boston: Pres f T. R. Marvin & Son.* 1864. 8vo, pp. 23. B. 51318

MUNGNIER (S. A.) Du Climat de Pe ambuco, par S. A. Mungnier, de Brésil. *Paris.* 1820. 4to. 51319

MUNGUIA (C. de J.) Coleccion de las Cartas Pastorales que el Excelentisimo e illustrisimo Señor Licenciado Don Clemente de Jesus Munguia Obispo de Michoacan ha dirigido a los fieles de su Diocesis. *Mexico. Imprenta de Tomas S. Gardida.* 1855. Impl. 8vo, pp. (4), 548, (3). 51320

Beginning with his consecration in 1852, and ending in 1855.

MUNGUIA. Defensa eclesiastica en el Obispado de Michoacan desde fines de 1855 hasta principios de 1858, ó sea Coleccion de representaciones y protestas, comunicaciones oficiales, circulares y decretos diocesanos, con motivo de las leyes, decretos y circulares del gobierno general, constitucion federal de 1857, decretos y providencias de los gobiernos de los estados de Michoacan, y Guanajuato, contra la soberania, independencia, ... y derechos de la santa iglesia, por el Lic. Clemente de Jesus Munguia. *Mexico: Vicente Segura.* 1858. 2 vols., 8vo, pp. viii, 642, (6); (4), 657, (5)

Of great interest on account of the modern ecclesiastical history of Mexico.

MUNGUIA. Manifesto del Obispo electo de Michoacan el Lic. Clemente Munguia, explicando su conducta con motivo de su negativa del dia 6 de enero al juramento civil segun la fórmula que se le presentó, y de su allananamiento posterior a jurar bajo la misma en el sentido del art. 50, atribucion xii. de la constitucion federal. *Morelia.* 1851. 8vo, pp. xvi, 322, xii. 51322

MUNGUIA. Manifiesto que Clemente Munguia, Obispo de Michoacan, dirige á la nacion Mexicana. *Mexico.* 1852. Folio, pp. 105. 51323

M[UNGUIA]. Del Tolerancia, o sea, del culto publico en sus relaciones con el gobierno por el Lic. C. M. *Morelia.* 1847. 8vo, pp. 108. 51324

MUNGUIA. Sermones y Escritos sueltos. ... *Mexico.* 1864. Folio. 51325

Contains the answer of the Archbishop of Michoacan to Captain Aldham, the representative of the British Court.

Also: Decreto del Illmo. Sr. Obispo de Michoacan, Normando la conducta de los Sres. Curas, Sacristanes mayores y vicarios de su Diocesis, con motivo de la ley de 11 Abril de 1857 sobre derechos y obvenciones parroquiales. [*Coyoacan.* 1857.] 8vo, pp. 28.—Exposicion dirigida al Supremo Gobierno de la Nacion, pidiendo la derogacion de varios articulos de la lei orgánica del registro civil, espedida el 27 de enero de 1857. [*Mexico.* 1857.] 8vo, pp. 8.—Opusculo escrito por el Illmo. Sr. Obispo de Michoacan Lic. D. Clemente de Jesus Munguia en defensa de la Soberania, derechos y libertades de la Iglesia, atacadas en la constitucion civil de 1857 y en otros decretos expedidos por el actual Supremo Gobierno de la Nacion. *Morelia.* 1857. 8vo, pp. 42.—Representacion del Illmo. Sr. Obispo de Michoacan al Supremo Gobierno, pidiendo la revocacion de la ley de 11 de Abril de 1857 sobre derechos y obvenciones parroquiales y en caso de no ser derogada, protestando contra sus efectos. *Coyoacan.* 1857. 8vo, pp. 18.—Representacion del Illmo. Sr. Obispo de Michoacan al Supremo Gobierno, protestando contra varios articulos de la Constitucion Federal de los Estados-Unidos Mexicanos, decretada en 1857, manifestando las razones que tuvo para declarar no ser licito jurarla y suplicando sean restituidos á sus destinos los empleados destituidos en consecuencia de lo dispuesto en el decreto de 17 de Marzo de 1857, por no haber prestado el juramento prevenido en el articulo transitorio de la Constitucion. *Mexico.* 1857. 8vo, pp. 24. *See also* Jesus Munguia (C.), Vol. IX., No. 36092.

MUNIBE (José Maria de). Carta edificante que descubre la vida religiosa de la R. M. Ines Josefa del sagrado, Corazon de Jesus, Carmelita descalza en el Convento de Santa Teresa, de la nueva fundacion de esta Corte. ... *Mexico.* 1805. 4to, 18 leaves.

The Municipal Government Examined by its own Records. [n. p. n. d.] 8vo, pp. 7. 51327

Relates to Philadelphia.

Municipal Ordinances for the Government and Regulation of the City and Port of Grey-Tòwn, in the Kingdom of Mosquito. *Kingston, Jamaica.* 1851. 8vo, pp. 12. 51328

Municipal Register. *See* Boston, No. 6749, *and* No. 42842.

Municipalida y Vecindario de la Ciudad Leal de Cojutepequa, a los Centro-Americana. *San Salvador.* 1863. 8vo. 51329

The Municipalist. In Two Parts. ... *New York: George Savage.* 1858. 12mo, pp. 302. Portrait. + Addenda. [n. p. n. d.] 12mo, pp. 303–348, (1). H. 51330

See also Vol. IX., No. 34908.

Die Munition des Loyalisten. *Philadelphia.* 1863. 8vo, pp. 16

MUNIZ (P.) Carta de D. Fedro Muniz al caritativo defensor de P. Aparicio Vidaurrazaga. [En versos.] *Lima.* 1814. 8vo.

MUNK (J.) Beskrivelse of Seigland og resa til Nova Dania. *Kiopenhavn.* 1619. 51333

Title from Ternaux, No. 418.

MUNK. Drie Voyagien | Gedaen na | Groenlandt, | Om te ondersoecken of men door de | Naeuwte Hudsons soude konnen Seylen; om alsoo een Door- | vaert na Oost-Indien te vinden. | Alle ten versoecke van Christianus de IIII. Ko- | ningh van Denemarcken, &c. de eerste door Ioan Monnick, de tweede | door Marten Forbisser, ende de derde door Gotske Lindenau. Als mede een | Beschryvinghe, | Hoe, en op wat wijse men de Walvisschen vanght. | Item, een korte Beschryvingh van Groenlandt, met de manieren en | hoedanicheden der Inwoonderen aldaer. | *t'Amsterdam, Gedruckt* | *By Gillis Joosten Saeghman, in de Nieuwestraet, Ordinaris Drucker van de Journalen der Zee- en Landt Reysen* [*about* 1660]. 4to, pp. 32. 51334

These three voyages to Greenland, to investigate whether there is a passage to the East Indies through the Hudson Straits, and containing a short description of Greenland, the manners and condition of the inhabitants, etc., were made in 1577, 1605, and 1619. Corrected title of our No. 28641, Vol. VII. *See* Tiele, No. 256.

MUNK. Navigatio Septentrionalis paa dansk. ... *Kiopenhavn: H. Valdkirck.* 1624. 12mo. 51335

Title from Ternaux, No. 475.

MUNK. Navigatio Septentrionalis | Det er | Relation Eller Beskrivelse om Seiglads og | Reyse paa denne Nordvestiske Passage, som | nu kaldes Nova Dania; igiennem fretum | Christian at opsöge, | Hvilken Reyse den Stormægtigste | Herre og Konge, Kong Christian den fierde, | udi det Aar 1619 allernaadigst berammet, og til dets Experientz | afferdiget håver Hans Majestets Skibs-Capitain Jens Munk | og hans med havendes Folk, som overalt vare 64 Personer, | med tvende Hans Majestets Skibe Enhiörningen | og Lamprenen | Samme Seiglads efter medgiven naadigste Instruction udi | underdanigst Gehorsomhed saa meget mueligt være kunde, er ten | teret, men Captainen efter höy Perikel udstanden med Jagten | er ikkun uden selv tredie igien til Norge hiem | kommen. | Med Bemeldning ... Jens Munk. | ... | *Kiobenhavn:* | *Trykt udi Kongl. Majestets privilegerede Bogtrykkerie.* | 1723. 12mo, pp. 72, 24. Map. J.C.B., H. 51336

An account of a voyage to Greenland in 1619 and 1620, by John Monck, for the discovery of a passage between Greenland and the main land of America to the West Indies. With a description of Old and New Greenland. It was first printed at Frank-

fort, in Dutch, in 1650. An English translation may be seen in Churchill (A.), "Collection of Voyages," Vol. I. *See also* Hulsius, "Die XXVI. Schiff-Fahrt."

MUNN (L. C.) The American Orator; with an Appendix, ... By Lewis C. Munn. *Boston: Tappan and Whittemore.* 1853. 12mo, pp. 436. H. 51337

Pages 409–436 contain facsimiles of the autographs of eminent persons.

MUNN. Autographs. The American Orator Appendix, containing the Declaration of Independence, with the Fac-Similes of the Autographs of the Signers; the Constitution of the United States; Washington's Farewell Address; and Fac-Similes of the Autographs of a large Number of Distinguished Individuals. By Lewis C. Munn. Sixth Edition. *Worcester: Z. Baker & Co.* 1856. 12mo, pp. xii, 318–454. BA., H. 51338

MUNN [Orson D.] & Co. Hints to Inventors, concerning the Procuring of Patents, either American or Foreign, with Suggestions and ... Information to Patentees. *New York: Munn & Co.* 1861. 32mo, pp. 16. H. 51339

MUNN & Co. The United States Patent Law. Instructions How to Obtain Letters Patent for New Inventions, ... with a Variety of Useful Information concerning the Patent Law. By Munn & Co. ... *New York: John A. Gray, Printer.* 1863. 24mo, pp. 35. + Third Edition. *New York.* 1865. 24mo, pp. 107, (1). + *New York: Munn & Co.* 1866. 24mo, pp. 107, (1). + [*Ibid.*] 1867. H. 51340

Also in German, "Das Patent-Gesetz der Vereinigten Staaten," etc.

MUNOZ (B.) Relacion verdadera Carta Nueva de un traslado enviado del Brasil por un Artillero, llamado Bernardo Muñoz à un hijo suyo dandole cuenta de una grande victoria que las Armas Catolicas han tenido sin pensar en el sitio del Brazil à 29 de Nov^{re} del año 1638. *Madrid.* 1639. 4to. 51341

MUÑOZ (J. F.) Manifiesto de los verdaderos motivos del arresto de D. Fernando del Valle, por D. José Fernando Muñoz. *Habana: Imprenta de Arazoza y Soler.* 1813. 4to, pp. 8.

MUÑOZ (J. B.) Historia del Nuevo-Mundo escribíala D. Juan Baut. Muñoz. Tomo I. *en Madrid por la Viuda de Ibarra.* MDCCXCIII. 8vo, pp. (6), xxx, 364. Map, and Portrait of Columbus.

Also on large paper, in folio. "Undertaken by the especial order of Charles the Third, who demanded of its author a complete history of the Spanish discoveries and conquests in America."—TICKNOR'S *History of Spanish Literature*, III. 305. This volume only reaches to the year 1500. The continuation never appeared in print, as it was

prohibited by the Spanish government, being too enlightened and truthful. The work is principally compiled from original mss. in the archives of Spain and Portugal, and is preceded by a valuable critical review of the various writers on the subject. The manuscript of the second volume is in the library of the late Mr. George Brinley.

MUÑOZ. Don Juan Baptista Muñoz Geschichte der Neuen Welt aus dem Spanischen übersetzt, und mit erläuternden Anmerkungen herausgegeben von M. C. Sprengel. Erster Band. Mit Kupfern und Charten. *Weimar.* 1795. 8vo, pp. xvi, 493. 3 Maps. H. 51344

MUÑOZ. The | History | of | the New World, | by | Don Juan Baptista Munoz. | Translated from the Spanish, | with | Notes | by | the Translator ... . Vol. I. | *London: G. G. and J. Robinson.* 1797. 8vo, pp. xv, lvii, 59–552. Portrait and Map. 51345

MUÑOZ. Carta Segunda en que se continua la Critica de la Historia del Nuevo-Mundo de Don J. B. Munoz, por M. A. R. F. *Madrid.* 1798. 8vo. 51346

Very rare. Not mentioned by Rich or Brunet. *See also* Iturri (F.), IX. 35298.

MUÑOZ. Memoria sobre las Apariciones y el Culto de Nuestra Señora de Guadalupe de Mejico, leida en la Real Academia de la Historia por su individuo supermerario Don Juan Bautista Muñoz. *Madrid.* 1794. 4to. 51347

The history of this patron saint is a most important part of the history of Mexico. It has been believed that the Virgin appeared several times to the Indian, Juan Diego, in 1531, on the barren hill of Tepeyac, with the object of convincing him and the Archbishop Zumarraga of the reality of her presence, and the necessity of having a sanctuary built for her worship. She at last prevailed, by sending to the archbishop, Juan Diego, with his *ayate* full of roses, and her own image stamped on this same cloth. The temples and cloister which were built are famous for their immense treasure. But the historian, Muñoz, declares in this paper that he has had access to a multitude of letters of Zumarraga, and other documents, from which it is certain that these miraculous appearances were not mentioned until a century or two afterwards; although the image is referred to, but not as having any special merit. Only in 1737 was this saint declared *patrona principal* of the city of Mexico; and in 1747, of the whole of New Spain. Muñoz begins as follows, which sounds like Martin Luther: "With the death of the Apostles and Evangelists, the canon of the Sacred Scriptures, and the deposit of the dogmas of our holy religion was closed. No subsequent deed or doctrine, since this was not contained nor announced in the divine books, nor in the apostolic traditions, can ever augment the number of the articles of the Christian faith—of that faith and belief without which it is impossible to please God." The high reputation of the royal historian, and his declaration that the miraculous origin of Guadalupe was a pious fraud, when it was first known in Mexico, in 1818, roused a terrible storm. It first appeared in the "Academia de la Historia." For a reply, *see* Guridi Alcocer (J. M.), VII. 29289.

MUÑOZ (J. R.) Vida y escritos de D. Bernardo Monteagudo, o sea Rasgo biográfico de uno de los mas altos Personajes del Dramo revolucionario de Sud-America. Por Juan R. Muñoz. *Valparaiso: S. Tornero y Ca.* 1859. 8vo, pp. 127, (2). BM.

MUÑOZ (M.) Defensa de las Slaves de san Pedro en la autoridad diosesana y breves noticas de los cismas del Arzobispado de Guatemala y del de la Iglesia Sufraganea de Honduras: por el Presbítero Miguel Muñoz de obispado de Nicaragua. *Nueva York.* 1834. 8vo, pp. vi, 100. 51349

MUÑOZ LEDO (O.) Exposicion que Octaviano Muñoz Ledo dirige a sus conciudadanos sobre la conducta politica que observo en el gobierno del Estado de Guanajuato durante la ultima revolucion. *Mexico.* 1853. 8vo, pp. 84, Apendice, 34. 51350

[MUNOZ LEDO Y BURGUIZA (P.)] Verdadera Idea sobre el Impreso titulado: "Donativo de Medio Millon de Pesos." *Mexico: Imprenta de Cumplido.* 1845. 8vo, pp. 30. 51351

MUNOZ DE CASTRO (Pedro). Exaltacion magnifica de la Betlemitica Rosa de Mejor Americana Jericho, y accion gratulatoria por su plausible plantacion dichosa por la Santidad de Inocenzio XI, que celebra en esta nobilidad ciudad de Mexico el venerable Dean de esta iglesia metropolitana. ... *Mexico, Maria de Benavides.* 1697. 4to, 96 leaves. Portrait. 51352

A piece of great rarity, with the portrait of Betancourt, the founder of the order of the Rose of Jericho.

MUÑOZ (P.) Sermon en la fungion sol. celebrada en accion de gracias por el Feliz restablecim. de la constitucion. ... *Puebla.* 1820. 4to, 12 leaves. 51353

MUÑOZ (T.) Diccionario bibliográfico-histórico de los Antiguos Reinos, Provincias, Ciudades, Villas, Iglesias y Santuarios de España, por Tomas Muñoz y Romero. Obra premiada por la Biblioteca nacional en el concurso público de enero de 1858, é impresa á expensas del Gobierno. *Madrid: Impr. de Rivadeneyra.* 1858. Rl. 8vo, pp. vii, 329. 51354

MUNRO (R.) A Description of the Genesee Country, in the State of New York: ... By Robert Munro. *New-York: The Author.* 1804. 8vo, pp. 16. Map. BA. 51355

MUNSELL (C.) A Collection of Songs of the American Press, and Other Poems relating to the Art of Printing. Compiled by Charles Munsell. *Albany, N. Y.* 1868. 8vo, pp. viii, 206, (1). 51356

A few copies printed "for gratuitous circulation."

MUNSELL (J.) The Albany Annual Register, for 1849: ... By Joel Munsell. *Albany: E. H. Pease & Co.* ... 1849. 12mo, pp. 182. BA. + Part II. *Albany.* 1850. 12mo, pp. 184. N.

This failing to get patronage, two years were united, with a portion of new matter, and omission of some ephemeral articles, and formed the first volume of the "Annals of Albany."

MUNSELL. Albany Minerva. *Albany.* 1828. 8vo, pp. 64.

"Printed while I was a clerk in a bookstore, and less than twenty years of age."—J. MUNSELL.

MUNSELL. The Annals of Albany. By Joel Munsell. ... *Albany: J. Munsell.* 1850–59. 10 vols., 12mo, pp. 377; (2), 312; 380; 3–405; 359; 359; vi, 8–458; vii, (1), 376; 389; xii, 9–497. Plates. H. 51359

MUNSELL. Bibliotheca Munselliana. A Catalogue of the Books and Pamphlets issued from the Press of Joel Munsell, from ... 1828 to 1870. *Albany: Privately Printed.* 1872. 8vo, pp. 191. H. 51360

The only work of its kind issued in the United States. The notes are characteristic, amusing and humorous.

[MUNSELL.] Cases of Personal Identity. *Albany: J. Munsell.* 1854. 8vo. 51361

MUNSELL. Catalogue of a Bibliographical Library, ... for sale ... . Collected by Joel Munsell, Albany. *Albany: Joel Munsell.* 1856. 8vo, pp. 36. C. 51362

MUNSELL. Catalogue of American and Foreign Books in Bibliography and other Departments of Literature. Offered ... by J. Munsell ... . Consisting of Rare Works relating to Printing, Voyages and Travels, &c. *Albany: J. Munsell.* 1857. 12mo, pp. (2), 74. H. 51363

Also on large paper.

MUNSELL. A Chronology of Paper and Paper Making. ... By Joel Munsell. *Albany.* 1856. 8vo, pp. 58. 3 Specimens. + *Albany: Joel Munsell.* 1857. 8vo, pp. vii, 110. + Third Edition. [*Ibid.*] 1864. 8vo, pp. vii, 174. Plate. + Fourth Edition. [*Ibid.*] 1870. 8vo, pp. vii, 226. Plate. B. 51364

The first edition was privately printed for presentation only.

[MUNSELL.] Collections on the History of Albany, from its Discovery to the Present Time. With Notices of its Public Institutions, and Biographical Sketches of Citizens Deceased. ...

Albany, N. Y.: J. Munsell. 1865–71. 4 vols., 8vo, pp. vi, (2), 529; 507; viii, 498; (2), iv, 556. Plates and Portraits.

Fifty copies printed on large paper. A continuation of the "Annals of Albany," containing new matter and upwards of eighty portraits, views, maps, etc. The fourth volume contains, besides the usual variety, the baptisms and marriages recorded in the Dutch church, arranged alphabetically by families, and embrace nearly every family from 1630 to 1800, also a street directory, showing the location of first settlers and transfers of lots from about 1650, onward; compiled by Prof. J. Pearson.

[MUNSELL.] Directory to the Trades in Albany, for ... 1852. *Albany: J. Munsell.* 1852. 12mo, pp. 8, 64. B. 51366

MUNSELL. The Every Day Book of History and Chronology: embracing the Anniversaries of Memorable Persons and Events, in every Period and State of the World, from the Creation to the Present Time. By Joel Munsell. ... *New York: D. Appleton & Co.* 1858. Rl. 8vo, pp. iv, 9–537. BA. 51367

An immense collection of memorable events, arranged under every day of the year, as they occurred; consisting of deaths of eminent men, battles, and occurrences of every kind, with full indexes.

MUNSELL. Munsell's Albany Directory and City Register, for 1852–53. ... *Albany: J. Munsell.* 1852. 12mo, pp. 492. Continued. B. 51368

MUNSELL. Munsell's Guide to the Hudson River by Railroad and Steamboat. ... *Albany: J. Munsell.* [1859?] 16mo, pp. 56. 9 Maps. H. + [*Ibid.*] 1863, 1864, 1865. 51369

MUNSELL. Munsell's Historical Series. *Albany: J. Munsell.* 1857–61. 10 vols., 4to. BA. 51370

This is a general half title to nine books, which in this Dictionary are described under the authors names. *See* Nos. 1311, 9253, 19788, 21694, 33148, *also* "Orderly Book," Ruttenber (E. M.), Shea (J. G.), *and* Stansbury (J.) Ten sets were reprinted on large and one hundred on small paper.

MUNSELL. Munsell's Series of Local American History. *Albany.* 1863–68. 9 vols., 8vo. 51371

Thirty sets were printed on large paper. The various works are described in this Dictionary under the names of the respective authors.

MUNSELL. Outline of the History of Printing, and Sketches of the Early Printers. By Joel Munsell. *Albany: Printed by J. Munsell.* 1839. 8vo, pp. 32. B. 51372

[MUNSELL.] Prynne's Almanac for 1841, adapted ... for the Meridian of Albany, but will answer for any part of the State of New York. *Albany.* 1840. 12mo, pp. 24. 51373

[MUNSELL.] Reminiscences of Men and Things in Northfield as I knew them from 1812 to 1825. [n. p. n. d.] 8vo, pp. 26. B. 51374

MUNSELL. The Typographical Miscellany. By J. Munsell. *Albany: Joel Munsell.* 1850. 8vo, pp. (6), 267, (1). BA.

Two hundred copies printed. Begun with the view of collecting the history of printing in the State of New York by counties.

[MUNSELL.] ... Webster's Calendar or the Albany Almanac, for ... 1844: ... *Albany.* 1843. 12mo, pp. 36. Continued.

Also: Catalogue of a Collection of Books, consisting principally of Local American History ... . *Albany, N. Y.: J. Munsell.* [n. d.] 8vo, pp. 18.— ... Catalogue of ... Books Principally Relating to America, comprising a portion of the Private Library of Joel Munsell, of Albany, N. Y., ... sold at Auction, April 11, 1865 ... . *New York.* [1865.] 8vo, pp. (4), 123. Also on large paper.—Catalogue ... of Books relating to America ... . *Albany, N. Y.: J. Munsell.* [n. d.] 8vo, pp. 16.—Catalogue of Books on Printing and the Kindred Arts: embracing also Works on Copyright, Liberty of the Press, Libel, Literary Property, Bibliography, etc. *Albany: Joel Munsell.* 1868. 8vo, pp. (4), 47. B.

MUNSELL (W. A.) The Bee. By Wm. Augustus Munsell. ... *Albany.* 1844. 8vo, pp. 36. 51377

A serial publication, conducted by the youngest of known editors, who wrote his valedictory, and closed his editorial labors, at the mature age of nine years.

MUNSON (M.) The Gordian Knot Untied; or, a Series of Familiar Letters ... on the right of a State to Secede from the Union. By Merritt Munson. *Geneseo, Ill.* 1861. 8vo.

MUNSTER (S.) Cosmo|graphiae|uniuersalis Lib. VI. in|quibus, iuxta certioris fidei scriptorum|traditionem describuntur,|Omniũ habitabilis orbis partiũ situs, ꝓpriæ 'qꝫ dotes.|Regionum Topographicæ effigies.|Terræ ingenia, quibus fit ut tam differẽtes & uarias|specie res, & animatas & inanimatas, ferat.|Animalium peregrinorum naturæ & picturæ.|Nobiliorum ciuitatum icones & descriptiones.|Regnorum initia, incrementa & translationes.|Omnium gentiũ mores, leges, religio, res gestæ, mu-|tationes: Item regum & principum genealogiæ.|Autore Sebast. Munstero.| [Colophon:] *Basileae apvd Henrichvm Petri,|Mense Martio Anno Salvtis* M. D. L.| Folio. A., C. 51379

Collation: Title, one leaf, on reverse of which is a portrait of Munster, pp. 9, Catalogue of Authors, (1), Index, (12), 14 Maps, Text, pp. 1162, (2).

Pages 1099–1113 contain "De novis insvlis, quomodo, quando & per quem illæ inuentæ sint." Mr. Leahy, in Quaritch's catalogue, erroneously calls this the *first* Latin edition. It is the first which gave large plans of cities. The last map is "Tabula novarum Insularum quas diversis respectibus Occidentales et Indianas vocant." It occupies the entire face of two pages, and contains a respectable delineation of the Continent (although Yucatan becomes an island) from Francisca (or Canada) on the

North to the Tierra del Fuego on the South. Page 33 has a chapter on the recent great voyages of discovery. The woodcuts were engraved by R. Manuel Deutsch, an artist of considerable merit; *see* Strutt's "Dictionary of Engravers." The "Athenae Rauricae" (p. 24) mentions two other Latin editions, 1543 and 1545.

MUNSTER. Cosmographiae universalis Lib. VI. ... [Colophon:] *Basileae, apvd Henrichvm Petri* ... M. D. LII. Folio, pp. (24), 14 Maps, Text, pp. 1162, (2). 51380

This and the following are reprints of the preceding edition.

MUNSTER. Cosmo|graphiae|uniuersalis Lib. VI. in|quibus, iuxta certioris fidei scriptorum|traditionem describuntur,|Omniũ habitabilis orbis partiũ situs, pro|priæ'qꝫ dotes.|Regionum Topographicæ effigies.|Terræ ingenia, quibus fit ut tam differentes & uarias|specieres, & animatas, & inanimatas, ferat.| [as in No. 51379. Colophon:] *Basileae apvd Henrichvm Petri,|mense Septemb. Anno sa|lvtis* M. D. LIIII.| Folio, Engraved Title, pp. (22), 14 Maps, Text, pp. 1162, (2). B., J.C.B., H. 51381

The fourteenth map is entitled "Tabula nouarum Insnlarum [*sic*] quas diuersis respectibus Occidentales & Indianas uocant." On the South American Continent, the words "Die Nüw Welt" appear in large type—the only German on the map, an indication of its use in the editions in that language.

MUNSTER. Cosmographiae Universalis ... . *Basileae.* 1559. Folio. 51382

"This Latin edition differs considerably from the German editions of 1553 and 1564. The description of America (pp. 1099–1113) is quite different, and more ample, embracing for instance the voyages of Vespucius, Magallanes, etc.; the woodcuts of this part are partly different. The maps are the same."—F. MULLER.

MUNSTER. Cosmogra|phiæ Vniversa|lis Lib. VI. in qvibvs ivxta|certioris fidei scriptores, sine|omni cuiuscunque molestia, uel læ|sione, describuntur,|Omnium habitabilis Orbis partium situs propriæque dotes.|Regionum Topographicæ picturæ.|Terrarum ingenia, quibus fit ut tam differentes & uarias specie res, tam animatas|quam inanimatas, producat.|Animalium peregrinorum naturæ & effigies.|Nobiliorum Ciuitatum icones & descriptiones: ac cerciter XX. de nouo additæ.|Regnorum initia, incrementa & translationes.|Cunctarum Gentium mores, leges, religio, res gestæ, & mutationes usque ad an|num Christi M.D.LXXII. Item Regum ac Principum genealogiæ.|Avthore Sebastiano Mvnstero.|Cum Gratia & Priuilegio Cæs. Maiest.|*Basileae, ex officina Henricpetrina.*| [Colophon:] *Basileae,|ex officina Henricpetrina,|mense Martio, anno salvtis*|M.D.LXXII.| Folio. J.C.B.

Collation: Title, Dedication, (5) leaves, Index, (88) leaves, 19 Maps, Text, pp. 1333, Colophon, 1 leaf. Some copies have 22 Maps.

The last map, in some copies, is the same as that in the edition of 1554, with a few

additional names. The plan of Cuzco, in Peru, and the map of Cuba, appear for the first time in this edition. Some passages which had been objected to by the Catholics, are omitted. *See* "Crenii Animadver.," VIII. 94.

MUNSTER. Cosmographia. Beschreibung aller Lender. *Basel* [*durch Henrichum Petri?*] M.DXLI. Folio. 51384

Title from the Labanoff catalogue as cited by Harrisse. Ebert conjectures that the date should be 1544. *See* the following.

MUNSTER. Cosmographia.|Beschreibũg|aller Lender Dürch| Sebastianum Munsterum in welcher begriffen/|Aller völcker, Herrschafften/|Stetten, vnd namhafftiger flecken herkomen:| Sitten gebreüch/ ordnung/ glauben/ secten/ vnd hantie-|rung/ durch die gantze welt/ vnd fürnem-|lich Teütscher nation.|Was auch besunders in iedem landt gefunden/|vnnd darin beschensey.| Alles mit figuren vnd schönen landt taflen erklert/|vnd für augen gestelt.|*Getruckt zü Basel durch Henrichum*|*Petri. Anno* M. D. xliiij.| Folio, pp. (14), 24 Maps, Text, pp. dclix. L. 51385

The mappemund has the words "America seu insula Brasilij," and map xxiiij, with the following inscription on the verso: "Die newe|weldt der grossen|und vilen Inse-|len von den Spa|niern gefunden."| America is described under the heading "Von den neüwen inseln," leaves DCXXVI to DCXLIJ.

MUNSTER. Cosmographia.|Beschreibũg|aller Länder Durch| Sebastianum Munsterum|in wölcher begriffen.|Aller völcker/ Herrschafften/|Stetten/|vnd namhafftiger flecken/ härkõmen:| Sitten/ gebreüch/ ordnung/ glauben/ secten/ vñ han-|tierung/ durch die gantze welt/ vnd für-|nemlich Teütscher nation.|Was auch besunders in iedem landt gefunden/|vnd darin beschehen sey. Alles mit figuren vnd schö-|nen landttafeln erklärt/ vñ für augẽ gestellt.|Weiter ist dise Cosmographei durch gemelten Sebast. Munst.|allenthalben fast seer gemeert vnd gebessert/ auch mit eim züge-|legten Register vil breüchlicher gemacht.| *Getruckt zu Basel durch Henrichum*|*Petri. Anno* M. D. XLV.| Folio, pp. (27), 28 Maps, Text, pp. dcccxviij. BM. 51386

Sometimes the maps and plates to this edition are colored. The "Athenae Rauricae" notices a German edition, 1546.

MUNSTER. Cosmographei|oder Beschreibung aller län|der, herrschafften für nemsten|stetten, geschichten, gebreüche, handierungen etc. ietz|zum dritten Mal trefflich sere durch Sebastianum|Munsterũ vnd gebessert, in weldtlichẽ vnd|naturlichen historien, [illegible] vff ein neuws mit hübschen figuren vnnd landtaflen geziert, sunderlichen|aber werden dar in contrafhetet sechs vnnd viertzig|stett, vnder welchẽ bey dreiszig ausz Teutscher nation| nach irer gelegenheit dar zũ kommẽ, vnd von|der stetten oberkeiten do hin sampt|jrenn beschreibungen|verordnet.|*Getruckt*

zũ Basel.| [Colophon:] *Getruckt zu Basel durch Henricum Petri*| *Anno* M. D. L.| Folio, pp. (22), 14 Maps, Text, pp. MCCXXXIIj.

Ebert, No. 14500, says "This edition is the best for the admirers of ancient good woodcuts, on account of the views of towns being added to it for the first time. That of 1541, mentioned in Aretin's 'Litt. Handb. für die baier. Gesch.' I. 142, is, perhaps, only a typographical error, instead of 1544, as the author says, in his dedication of 1544, that he had been for two years before occupied with this work." "The Munich Royal Library contains three copies in German of the present, all dated 1550, with the same number of leaves, yet evidently different editions."—[HARRISSE] *Bib. Am. Vet.—Additions,* No. 179.

MUNSTER. Cosmographei oder Beschreibung aller länder ... . *Basel, Henrichum Petri.* 1553. Folio. 26 Maps. 51388

The part relating to America fills pp. 1183–92: "Von den neüwen inseln," etc. Title from a European catalogue.

MUNSTER. Cosmographei|oder beschreibung aller län|der herschafften fürnemsten|stetten, geschichten, gebreüchen, hantierun|gen etc. züm offtere mal trefflich seer durch Sebastanũ Munsterũ ... . *Getruckt zu Basel.*| [Colophon:] *Getruckt zu Basel durch Henrichum Petri*|*Anno* M. D. LVj.| Folio, pp. (20), 14 Maps, Text, pp. Mccxxxiij, (1). BM. 51389

The "Athenae Rauricae" quotes an edition of 1559.

MUNSTER. Cosmographey|oder beschreibung aller län|der herrschafften, fürnemsten|stetten, geschichten, gebreüchẽ, hantierun|gen etc. Erstmals beschriben durch Seba|stianum Munsterum,|auch durch in selbst gebessert, an welt vnd natürlichẽ historiẽ,|jetzunder aber bisz auff das M.D.LXIIII.|jar ... . *Getruckt zü Basel.*| [Colophon:] *Getruckt zü Basel durch Henrichum*|*Petri, Im Jar* M. D. LXIIII.| Folio, pp. (12), 14 Maps, Register, pp. (20), Text, pp. Mccccl xxv, (1). J.C.B., C. 51390

The description of America is the same as in the preceding and fills pp. 1424–1433. The maps and woodcuts are also the same. Ebert mentions a Basel edition of 1569, with woodcuts much worn.

MUNSTER. Cosmographey|oder beschreibung aller Län|der, Herrschafften, fürneñsten Stet|ten, geschichten, gebreüchen, handthierungen, &c.|Beschrieben durch Sebastianum Munsterum,|und durch ihn selbst gebessert, an Welt und Na|türlichen Historien, jetztunder aber bis auff das|M.D.LXXIIII jar, nach innhalt nechst|folgends blats verzeichnung, gemehret, darzu mit| etlich neüwen Landtaflen, auch ein unnd viertzig|Stetten neüwen Contrafacturen, welche| uber die alten auff dies mal her|zukommen seind,|beziercet|Mit Röm. Kay. May. Gnad und Freyhet| nicht nach zu Trucken.|*Getruckt zu Basel.*| [1574.] Folio, Title, Preface, Register and Maps, pp. (127), Text, pp. Mccccxvi.

MUNSTER. Cosmographey.|Oder beschreibung|Aller Länder herzschafften|und fürnembstenn Stetten des gantzen|Erdbodens, samptihren Gelegenheiten, Eygenschafften,|Religion, Gebreüchen, Geschichten vnnd Hand|thierungen, &c.|Erstlich durch Herrn Sebastian Munster ... verfasset: ... *Getruckt zu Basel.*| [1578. Colophon:] *Getruckt zu Basel, in der Officin Henricpetrina, im Jar nach Christi geburt*|M. D lxxviij.| Folio, pp. (24), 26 Maps, Text, pp. Mccccxiiij, Colophon, 1 leaf. BM. 51392

Map 26 is of the New World.

MUNSTER. Cosmographey.|Oder beschreibung|Aller Länder herrschafften|und fürnemesten Stetten des gantzen|Erdbodens, samptihren Gelegenheiten, Eygenschaff|ten, Religion, Gebreuchen, Geschichten vnnd|Handthierungen, &c.|Erstlich durch Herrn Sebastian Munster mit grosser Arbeit in sechs Bü|cher verfasset. Demnach an Welt und Natürlichen Historien durch ihne selbs gebes|sert: Jetzt aber mit allerley Gedechtnuswirdigen Sachen bis in das M. D. LXXXVIII. Jar|gemehret, mit newen Landtaflen, vieler Stetten und fürnemmen Männern|Contrafacturen und Wuapen, so uber die Alten herzu|kommen, gezieret.|...| *Getruckt zu Basel.*| [1588.] Folio, Title, Preface, Register, pp. (28), 26 Maps, Text, pp. Mccccxix, (2), Colophon, dated M.D.-LXXXVIII, 1 leaf. S. 51393

Munster's portrait is on the title-page of this and most of the German versions.

MUNSTER. Cosmographey.|Oder beschreibung|Aller Länder herzschafftenn|und fürnemesten Stetten des gantzen|Erdbodens, samptihren Gelegenheiten, Eygenschaff|ten, Religion, Gebreuchen, Geschichten vnnd|Handthierungen, &c.|Erstlich durch Herrn Sebastian Munster ... verfasset: ... *Getruckt zu Basel.*| [Colophon:] *Getruckt zu Basel,|Durch|Sebastianum Henricpetri,* ... M. D. XCII.| Folio, pp. (24), 26 Maps, Text, pp. Mccccxxj, (1), Colophon, 1 leaf. BA., BM. 51394

MUNSTER. Cosmographey:|das ist,|Beschreibung aller Länder, Herrschafften und für-|nemesten Stetten des gantzen Erdbodens, sampt ihren|Gelegenheiten, Eygenschafften, Religion, Gebräuchen|Geschichten und Handtierungten, &c.|Erstlich durch Herrn Sebastian Munster mit grosser Arbeit in sechs| Bücher verfasset: ... *Getruckt zu Basel.*| [1598. Colophon:] *Getruckt zu Basel,|Durch|Sebastianum Henricpetri,* ... M.D.XCIIX.| Folio, pp. (27), 26 Maps, Text, pp. Mccccl xj, Colophon, 1 leaf.

With likeness of Munster on the title, "seins alters LX. jar." America is shown in the general map of the world, and in No. XXVI., "Die Newe Welt." The "Athenae Rauricae" mentions an edition, 1621.

Munster. Cosmographia,|das ist|Beschreibung der gantzen Welt,| ... Erstlichen durch Herrn Sebastanvm Mvnstervm ... . Jetzund ... mit vielerley ... fürstlichen Stammbäumen, Figuren und Stätten|Sonderlich aber|Einer vollkommenen Beschreibung der unbekanndten Länder Asiae, Africae, Americae ... bis auf dies 1628. Jahr kundt gemacht worden,|trefflich vermehrt, und mit newen Indianischen Figu|ren geziehrt. | ... *Basel, Bey den Henricpetrinischen : Im Jahr* | M. DC. XXIIX [*i. e.* 1628]. Folio, Engraved and Printed Titles, pp. (20), 17 Maps, Text, pp. 1752.

Munster. La Cos|mogra|phie vniver|selle contenant | la situation de toutes les parties du monde|auec leurs proprietez & appartenances.|La description des pays & regions d'icelluy|La grande varieté & diuersenature de la terre|Le vray pourtraict des animaux estranges & incogneuz, auec le nature d'iceulx|Les figures & pourtraictz des villes & citez plus notables.|L'origine, accroissement & transport des Royaumes, ensemble les Cou-| tumes, Loix, Religions, Faictz & Changemẽs de toutes nations auec les genealogies des Roys, Ducz, & autres princes de la toute la terre.|Par Sebast. Mvnstere.|Auec privilege du Roy|pour six ans.| [Colophon:] *Cy finist la chronicque universelle ... nouuellement translatee et achevee d'imprimer aux despens de Henry Pierre* [*à Basle*], *en l'an de grâce Mille cinq centz & cinquante deux* [1552]. Folio, pp. (11), 14 Maps, Text, pp. 1429. 51397

The first edition in French; of much rarity. Map 14 has the words "Die Nüw Welt," as in the German versions.

Munster. La Cosmographie universelle contenant la situation de toutes les parties du monde, auec leurs proprietez & appartenances. La description des pays & regions d'icelluy. ... Le vray pourtraict d'aucuns animaulx estranges ... . Les figures & pourtraictz des villes & citez plus notables. ... [Colophon:] ... *Achevée d'imprimer* [*à Basle*] *aux despens de Henry Pierre*, ... 1556. Folio. Maps. 51398

The part relating to America (pp. 1353–1374) is entitled "des novvelles isles: comment, quand et par qui elles ont esté trouvées." Of greater rarity than the foregoing.

Munster. La Cos|mogra|phie Vniver|selle, contenant|la situation de toutes les parties du monde,|auec leurs proprietez & appartenances.|La Description des pays & regions d'iceluy.|La grande variété & diuerse nature de la terre.|Le vray pourtraict d'aucuns animaulx estranges, auec le natural d'iceulx. | Les figures & pourtraictz des villes & citez plus notables.|Les coustumes, loix, et religions, de toutes nations, auec l'origine, accroisse-

ment|& transport des Royaumes & Seigneuries, et les genealogies et faictz des Roys,|Ducz & autres Princes de toute la terre, continuant iusques à nostre temps. | Par Sebast. Monstere. | Auec priuilege du Roy.| [Colophon:] *Cy finist la Cosmographie vniverselle de Monsieur Sebastien Munstere, comprinse en six|liures, nouuellement corrigée & augmenté: laquelle a este acheuée d'impri|mer aux despens de Henry Pierre, en l'an de grace Mille|cinq centz & soixante huict.*| [1568.] Folio. J.C.B. 51399

Collation: Title, To the reader, 4 leaves, Portrait of Munster, 1 leaf, Table, 11 leaves, 12 Maps, the first of which embraces America, Text, pp. 1402.

Munster. La|Cosmographie|Vniverselle de|Tovt le Monde. |En laquelle, suiuant les auteurs plus dignes de foy, sont au vray descriptes toutes les|parties habitables, & non habitables de la Terre, & de la Mer, leurs assiettes & choses|qu'elles produisent: ... Auteur en partie Mvnster, mais beaucoup plus augmentée, ornée & enrichie, par François de Belle-Forest ... . *A Paris, Chez Michel Sonnius* ... . M. D. LXXV. 2 vols., folio, in 3, pp. (38), 390 columns; Second volume du premier Tome, Title, (1), columns, 393–1838, Table, (44) leaves; Vol. II. pp. (12), columns, 2235, Table, (87) leaves. + *A Paris, Chez Nicolas Chesneau, au Chesne Verd.* M.D.LXXV. 2 vols., folio, in 3. 51400

One hundred and one pages are devoted to America. It is a beautifully printed and elaborately illustrated edition, with many maps. Belle-Forest, the French translator, made considerable additions both of his own and from other writers, which occupy volumes II. and III. *See* Belle-Forest (F. de), Vol. II., No. 4506.

Munster. Kozmograffia Czieská. To gest wypsanij opolozienij Kragin neb Zemij yobycziegich Naroduw wsseho Swieta a Hystorij podle pocztu, Leth naniem z biehlych, prwe nikda tak pospolku w Ziadnem. *Jazyku ne wydana. w Praze, Ján Kosorsky z Skosore*, 1554. Folio. 51401

This Bohemian translation, made by Jan z Puchowa, is very rare. It contains the views of towns.

Munster. Sei Libri | Della | Cosmografia Vni | uersale, ne quali secondo che n'hanno|parlato i piu ueraci scrittori son disegnati,|I siti de tutte le parti del mondo habitabile & le proprie doti: |Le Tauole topographice delle Regioni.|Le naturali qualita del terreno, on de nascono tante diferenze, & uarieta|discose, & animate & non animate.|Le natvre, & le dipinture degli animati pellegrini.|L'imagini, & descrittioni della cita piu nobili:|I principij de Regni, gli accrescimenti, é tramutamenti. | I costumi di tutte le genti, le leggi, la Religione, i fatti.|Le mutationi: le genealogie altresi de Re, é de principi.|Avtore Sebastiano Mvnstero.| [Colophon:] *Stampato a Spese di Henrigo Pietro Basi-|liense l'Anno* M. D. LVIII. *nel|Mese di Marzo.*| Folio, Title, 1 leaf, Epistola, etc., pp. (13), (1), Index, (8), 14 Maps, Text, pp. 1237, (1). A.

Produces the old plates of the German, Latin, and French editions. Pages 1178–1192, of this and the edition of 1575 contain under the title "Delle Nvove Isole in qual modo et quando furono trouate," a description of America. Both editions contain the views of cities.

Munster. Cosmographia | Vniversale, | Nella quale secondo che n'hanno parlato i piu|veraci Scrittori, son designati di tutti gli paësi.|...|Raccolta primo da diuersi autori per Sebastiano Munstero, & dapoi corretta & repur-|gata, per gli Censori Ecclesiastici, & quei del Re Catholico nelli pæsi|basi, & per l'Inquisitore di Venetia.|*In Colonia,*|*Appresso gli heredi d'Arnoldo Bryckmanno.*| M. D. LXXV. Folio, Title, Index, etc., pp. (12), 14 Maps, Text, pp. 1237. A. 51403

The fourteenth map in both of the Italian versions has the words "Die Nüw Welt."

Munster. A treatyse of|the newe India, with other new| founde landes and Ilandes, aswell|eastwarde as westwarde, as they|are knowen and found in these oure|dayes, after the descripcion of Se-|bastian Munster in his boke of vni-|uersall Cosmographie: wherin the|diligent reader may see the good|successe and rewarde of noble|and honeste enterpryses,|by the which not only world-|ly ryches are obtayned,|but also God is glo-|rified, & the Chri-|stian fayth en-|larged.|Translated out of Latin into Englishe. By|Rycharde Eden.|...| [Colophon:] *Thus endeth this fyfth boke|of Sebastian Munster, of the lãdes of Asia the greater, and of the|newefounde landes, and|Ilandes.*|1553.|*Imprinted at London, in Lom|barde streete, By Edward|Sutton.*| Sm. 8vo. J.C.B.

Collation: Title, 1 leaf, Dedication, (7) pages, Richard Eden to the reader, (21) pages, Table, 1 leaf, Text, (87) leaves. Corrected title of our No. 21826, Vol. VI. A volume of extreme rarity. It appeared again under the title of:

Munster. A Briefe|Collection and compendious|Extract of straũge and me|morable thinges gathered oute|of the Cosmograupye of | Sebastian Munster. | Where in is made a playne des|crypsion of diuerse and straunge lavves|Rites, Manners, and properties of|sundry nations, and a short re|porte of straunge histories|of diuerse men, and|of the nature and properties of cer-| tayne|Fovvles|Fishes, Beastes, Mon|sters, and sundrie Countries |and places. | *Imprinted at London in Fleet | streete ... by Thomas| Marshe|Anno Domini.* 1572. Sm. 8vo, 4 leaves, one of which is blank, Text, 102 leaves. BM. 51405

Munster. A Briefe|Collection and com|pendious extract of straunge|and memorable thinges, gathered|out of the Cosmographeye of|Sebastian Munster.|Wherein is made a plaine de|scription of diuers and straunge|Lawes, Rites, Manners and pro|perties of sondrye nations, and a short report of straunge histo|ries of diuers men, and of the nature and pro|perties of cer|taine| Fovvles, Fishes, Beastes, Mon|sters, and sondry Countryes|and places. | *Imprinted at London* | ... *by Thomas Marshe. Anno* 1574. Sm. 8vo, 4 leaves, one of which is blank, Text, 102 leaves. BM.

In black letter, and of extreme rarity. Munster's Cosmography is interesting as well for the text as for the profusion of curious and spirited woodcuts by which it is illustrated; as an exhibition of the progress of geographical discovery it is indispensable. *See also* Ptolemy.

Mur (J. F.) Memorial que eleva al Soberano congreso Chileno Juan Francisco Mur accompanado de algunos documentos i reflexiones que prueban el justo titulo con que pido a la nacion Chilene lo indemnizacion de todos i perjuicios que ha sufrido a consecuencia del importante servicio que le hizo el ano de 1836. *Santiago.* 1847. 8vo. 51407

Also: Discurso que dirige los Elejidos del Pueblo Chileno. ... *Santiago.* 1847. 4to, pp. 18.

Muraour (E.) Le Mexique Conquête du Mexique par Fernand Cortez Guerre de l'Indépendance et République Expédition française ... 1861–1863 Par E. Muraour *Paris.* 1863. Sm. 16mo, pp. 415. Plates. B. 51408

Murat (A.) America and The Americans. By the late Achille Murat ... . Translated from the French [by H. J. Bradfield]. *New York: William H. Graham.* 1849. 12mo, pp. (4), 260. H., S. 51409

Murat. Briefe über den moralischen und politischen Zustand der Vereinigten Staaten von Nord-Amerika. *Braunschweig.* 1833. 8vo. 51410

Murat. Brieven over de Zeden en Staatkunde der Vereenigde Staten van Noord-Amerika. Uit het Fransch. *Zalt-Bommel.* 1834. 2 vols., 8vo. S. 51411

Murat. Darstellung der Grundsätze der republikanischen Regierung wie dieselbe in Amerika vervollkommnet worden ist. Aus dem Französischen. ... *Braunschweig und Leipzig.* 1833. 12mo. 51412

Murat. Esquisse morale et politique des États-Unis de L'Amérique du Nord, Par Achille Murat ... . *Paris: Crochard.* 1832. 18mo, pp. (2), xvij, 389. BA. 51413

This work consists of ten letters of Achille Murat to Count Thibaudeau, the first four of which were separately published in the year 1830. For an extract, *see* Rich, II. 243.

Murat. Exposition des Principes du Gouvernement Républicain, tel qu'il a été perfectionné en Amérique. Par Achille Murat. *Paris: Paulin.* 1833. 8vo, pp. (4), 414, Table, (1).

Murat. Karakteristik öfver Förente Staterna. Öfversattn af G. Loederus. *Stockholm.* 1831. 8vo. 51415

Murat. Lettres sur les États-Unis, Par le Prince Achille Murat ... à un de ses Amis d'Europe. *Paris: Hector Bossange.* 1830. 12mo, pp. (4), 155. H. 51416

Murat. A Moral and Political Sketch of the United States of North America. By Achille Murat ... . With a Note on Negro Slavery, by Junius Redivivus. *London: Effingham Wilson.* 1833. 12mo, pp. xxxix, (1), 402. Map. + Second Edition. [*Ibid.*] 51417

"In this purple book the 'nephew of my uncle' defends and upholds negro slavery *in America*, though perhaps, were it brought nearer home to his own business and bosom, like many other philosophers, he would have sung a different tune. Lest these sentiments, so repugnant to British feeling, might give to the book a baleful influence, a neutralizing appendage by another hand is added, combating the Prince's facts, inferences and opinions."—Stevens. In some copies the title reads "The United States of North America."

Muratori (L. A.) Il Christianesimo Felice nelle Missioni de' Padre della Compagnia di Gesù nel Paraguai, descritto da Lodovico Antonio Muratori Bibliotecario del Sereniss. Sig. Duca di Modena. *In Venezia*, MDCCXLIII–MDCCXLIX. *Presso Giambatista Pasquali.* 4to, pp. (8), 196; xii, 180. Map. + [*Ibid.*] MDCCLII. 51418

The history of the Missions of the Jesuits in Paraguay, where they exerted an extraordinary influence and obtained almost supreme power, is full of interest. Most books on the subject are written by members of the order; but the fact that Muratori was not a Jesuit, has given his history a character for impartiality, not claimed for other authors. It was composed in great part from documents written by various Jesuit missionaries and travelers, furnished to Muratori by Father Gaetan Cattanio, a missionary in Paraguay. *See* "Monthly Review," XXIII. 328.

Muratori. Relation des Missions du Paraguai, Traduite de l'Italien de M. Muratori [par le P. de Lourmel]. *Paris: Bordelet.* M.DCC.LIV. 16mo, pp. (2), xxiv, 402, (4). Map. B. + [*Ibid.*] MDCCLVII. + [*Ibid.*] MDCCLXVII. 51419

Muratori. Relation des Missions du Paraguay, traduite de l'Italien de M. Muratori. Edition de la Société catholique de la Belgique. *Louvain.* 1822. 8vo, pp. 218. 51420

Other editions, *Paris*, 1826, 1827, and 1837. The following is a German version:

Muratori. Das glückliche Christenthum in Paraguay, unter den Missionarien der Gesellschaft Jesu; vorhin in welscher Sprache beschrieben von dem Hochwürdigen und berühmten Herrn Lvdovico Antonio Mvratori, seiner Durchlaucht des Herzogens von Modena Bibliothecario; ... *Wien ... Johann Thomas Trattnern.* 1758. 2 vols., 8vo, pp. (16), 255, 83; (16), 266, 84.

Muratori. A Relation of the Missions of Paraguay. Wrote Originally in Italian, by Mr. Muratori, And now done into English from the French Translation [of F. E. de Lourmel]. *London: J. Marmaduke.* M. DCC. LIX. 16mo, pp. xvi, 294, (2). Map. B,. C., H. 51422

Another edition is entitled:

Muratori. The Jesuit's Travels in South-America, Paraguay, Chili, &c. Wrote Originally in Italian, by Mr. Muratori, With the Relations of Father Cagetan Cattaneo. *London: Jeffery and Sael.* 1788. 16mo, pp. xvi, 294, Table, (2). Map.

[Muratori.] Descrizione Geografica, Politica, Istorica del Regno del Paraguay, formatosi da i PP. Gesuiti. *Venezia.* 1767. 12mo, pp. xxx. J.C.B. 51424

[Muratori.] Neue Nachrichten von den Missionen der Jesuiten in Paraguay ... . Aus dem Spanischen. *Hamburg.* 1768. 12mo, pp. xxiii, (1), 307. 2 Tables and Plate. H. 51425

[Muratori.] Die Republick der Jesuiten des umgestürzten Paraguay, welches eine richtige Erzehlung des Krieges enthält, den diese Geistliche gegen die Monarchen Espaniens und Portugalls in America zu führen gewaget ... *Amsterdam.* 1758. 12mo, pp. 307, Auszug aus dem Criminal-Process wider die Jesuiten in Spanien, pp. 56. 2 Maps. 51426

[Muratori.] La Republique des Jesuites, ou Paraguay Renversee, Contenant Une Relation authentique de la Guerre que ces Religieux ont osé soutenir contre ... d'Espagne & de Portugal en Amerique ... . *Amsterdam.* M. D. CC. LIX. 12mo, pp. 64.

[Muratori.] Sammlung der neuesten Schriften, welche die Jesuiten in Portugal betreffen. Aus dem italienischen. *Leipzig.* 1760–62. 4to. 51428

Murcia de la Llana (F.) Canciones funebres a la muerte de D. Christoval de Oñate, capitan general de las conquistas del Nuevo Mexico, por D. Francisco Murcia de la Llana. *Mexico.* 1622. 4to. 51429

Title from Ternaux, No. 444.

[Murden (*Mrs.* Eliza).] Miscellaneous Poems. By a Lady of Charleston, S. C. *Charleston, S. C.* 1826. 12mo, pp. 216. + Second Edition. *New-York: The Author.* 1827. 12mo, pp. 179. C. 51430

The Murder of the Christian Indians in North-America, in the year 1782. A Narrative of Facts. *Dublin: Printed by Bentham & Hardy.* 1826. 12mo, pp. 16. 51431

Murder will out. *See* [De Beck (W. L.)], v. 19107.

Murdin (C.) Three Sermons, entitled I. Liberty when used as a Cloke of Maliciousness, the worst of Evils. II. The Evil of Rebellion, as applicable to American Conduct, considered. III. Great Britain oppressing America, A groundless Charge. Preached on the Three ... Fast Days appointed ... on Account of the American Rebellion; ... By Cornelius Murdin ... . *Southampton: Printed ... by T. Baker* ... . [n. d.] 8vo, pp. (4), 52.

Murdoch (B.) A History of Nova Scotia, or Acadie. By Beamish Murdoch, Esq. ... *Halifax, N. S.: James Barnes.* 1865–67. 3 vols., 8vo, pp. xv, 543; xiv, 624; xxiii, 613. B.

Also: Celebration of the Centenary Anniversary of the Settlement of the City of Halifax: Oration by Beamish Murdoch; Poem by Joseph Howe. *Halifax.* 1849. 8vo.—Epitome of the Laws of Nova Scotia. ... *Halifax.* 1832–33. 4 vols., 8vo.—A Narrative of the Late Fires at Miramichi, New Brunswick; with an Appendix containing the Statements of many of the Sufferers, ... together with a Poem entitled "The Conflagration." *Halifax.* 1825. 8vo, pp. 48.

Murdoch (D.) Death of Abraham Lincoln. A Sermon, ... in ... New Milford, Conn., April 23, 1865. By Rev. David Murdoch. ... *Milford.* 1865. 8vo, pp. 16. B. 51434

Murdoch. The Dutch Dominie of the Catskills; or, the Times of the "Bloody Brandt." By Rev. David Murdoch, D.D. *New York: Derby & Jackson.* 1861. 12mo, pp. 471. C. 51435

Reprinted as "The Royalist's Daughter and the Rebels. Or the Dutch Dominie of the Catskills. A Tale of the Revolution" ... . *Philadelphia: J. E. Potter.* 1865. 12mo, pp. 471. Also: ... A Sermon, ... in ... Elmira on the ... death of Milton Partridge, ... *Elmira: Fairman Brothers, ... Printers.* MDCCCLIV. 12mo, pp. 34.

Murdock (J.) A Sermon, ... at the Installation of ... Rev. William Bascom, ... in Leominster, May 10, 1815. By James

Murdock ... . *Leicester: Printed by Hori Brown.* [n. d.] 8vo, pp. 31. B., W. 51436

Murdock (J. E.) Patriotism in Poetry and Prose: being Selected Passages from Lectures and Patriotic Readings by James E. Murdock. Also, Poems by Thomas Buchanan Read, George H. Boker, Francis de Haes Janvier, and other American Authors, commemorative of the Gallant Deeds of our Noble Defenders on Land and Sea. *Philadelphia: J. B. Lippincott.* 1864. 12mo, pp. 172. Plate. C. + [*Ibid.*] 1865. B. 51437

Murdock (J. N.) Our Civil War: its Causes and its Issues. A Discourse ... in ... Brookline, on ... Thanksgiving, August 6, 1863. By John N. Murdock, D.D. *Boston: Wright & Potter, Printers.* 1863. 12mo, pp. 23. B. 51438

Murdock. Peacemakers and Peacemaking. A Discourse, ... in ... Hartford, ... November 20, 1856. It being ... Thanksgiving. By John N. Murdock, D.D. ... *Hartford: Lyman Webster.* 1856. 8vo, pp. 24. H. 51439

Also: Building the Tombs of the Prophets. A Discourse ... in ... Boston, ... July 4, 1858. ... *Boston: John P. Jewett and Company.* 1858. 12mo, pp. 23.— ... A Sermon ... before the Conn. Baptist Education Society, ... in New London, Conn., ... June 10, 1857. ... *Hartford: Case, Tiffany and Company.* 1857. 12mo, pp. 39. H.—The True Basis and Ends of Civil Government. A Discourse, ... Thanksgiving Day, Nov. 25, 1858, ... in ... Boston. ... *Boston: Printed by McIntire & Moulton.* 1858. 12mo, pp. 32. H.

Murdock (W. D. C.) Address on the Free-Soil Question. By William D. C. Murdock. [*Georgetown.* 1848?] 16mo, pp. 43. BA., M. 51440

[Murdock.] Our True Title to Oregon. *Georgetown: John T. Crow, Printer.* 1845. 8vo, pp. 12. BA. 51441

Also: An Address to the Democratic Party, on the Present Crisis and the next Presidential Election. ... *Washington, D. C.* 1864. 8vo, pp. 28. H.

Murel (J. A.) *See* Murrell (J. A.)

Muret (Pierre). Ceremonies Funebres de toutes les Nations. Par le Sr. Muret ... . *A Paris, chez Estienne Michallet* ... . M. DC. LXXVII. Sm. 8vo, pp. (12), 257, (19). 51442

Muret. Rites of Funeral, Ancient and Modern, in use through the Known World. Written originally in French, by M. Muret. Translated into English by Paul Lorrain. *London: R. Royston.* 1683. 18mo, pp. (12), 308. + [*Ibid.*] 1695.

The seventh and eighth chapters are devoted to the description of the funerals of the Americans and Islanders, with the Caribbes, some of which are very curious.

MURGIRA Y GALARDI (J.) Memoria estadistica de Oaxaca y descripcion del valle de misma nombre, estractado de la que en grande trabajo el Sr. Don José Murguira y Galardi. ... Publicala el Licenciado D. Carlos Maria de Bustamente. *Vera Cruz: En la Imprenta Constitucional.* 1821. 4to, pp. 26, (8). 51444

MURHARD (F.) *See* Martens (G. F. de), 44845 *and* 44847.

[MURIEL (Domingo).] Fasti Novi Orbis et Ordinationum Apostolicarum ad Indias pertinentium breviarium cum Adnotationibus. Opera D. Cyriaci Morelli ... . *Venetiis*, MDCCLXXVI. ... *Antonium Zatta* ... . 4to, pp. viii, 642, (2). C., H. 51445

"Cyriaci Morelli is the pseudonyme of Don Domingo Muriel, a Spanish Jesuit, for many years a professor in the college of his order at Tucuman. When the Jesuits were expelled from the Spanish dominions he retired to Italy, where he prepared the present work, which is a collection of all the orders, decrees, etc., given by the Popes, and by the Kings of Spain, relative to the spiritual concerns of America, from its first discovery."—RICH, I. 197.

MURIETA (J.) The Life and Adventures of Joaquin Murieta, the celebrated California Bandit. By Yellow Bird. *San Francisco.* 1854. 8vo, pp. 91. S. 51446

MURILLO Y GORDILLO (Antonio). Oracion Funebre que en Solemne Anniversariô dotado por el Exmo. Señor Virrey Marqués de Casafuerte á Beneficio de las Benditas Animas. ... *Mexico.* 1792. 8vo. 51447

MURILLO VELARDE (P.) Geographia historica, donde se describen los reynos, provincias, ciudades, fortalezas, mares, montes etc. y se refieren las guerras, las batallas, los frutos, los animales, los concilios, las lenguas ... . *Madrid.* 1752. 10 vols., 4to. 51448

One volume of this important work relates to America.

MURILLO VELARDE. Historia de la Provincia de Philipinas de la Compañia de Jesus. Segvnda parte, que comprehende los progresos de esta provincia desde el año de 1616 hasta el de 1716. Por el P. Pedro Mvrillo Velarde de la Compañia de Jesus, Chronista de dicha Provincia. ... *Manilla, en la Imprenta de Compañia de Iesus. Año de* 1741. Folio, 12 prel. leaves, Text, 419 leaves, and Catalogue, 5 leaves. Map and Plate. J.C.B. 51449

At this period, the Philippines were under the jurisdiction of the Archbishop of Mexico. "Ce volume est intitulé seconde partie parce qu'il forme la continuation du père Chirino."—SALVA. Chirino's work was published at Madrid in 1663, folio.

[MURK VAN FHELGUM.] Brieve van den Heer ... aan den Heer ... betreffende de wijsgeerige Bespiegelingen over Amerika. *Utrecht.* 1772. 8vo. 51450

MURO (J.) Utilidades y medios de que los Indios y Ladinos vistan y calzen a la Español ... Por El R. P. Fr. Antonio de S. Jose Muro. ... *N. Guatemala: Por D. Ignacio Beteta.* 1798. 4to, pp. 73. BM. 41451

MURPHEY (A. D.) Oration ... [at] Chapel Hill [N. C.], ... 27th June, 1827, ... under the Appointment of the Dialectic Society, By the Hon. Archibald D. Murphey. *Raleigh.* 1827. 8vo, pp. 18. + Second Edition. *Raleigh: Printed by Weston R. Gales.* 1843. 8vo, pp. 23. H. 51452

MURPHY (A.) Appendix to Mr. Samuel Vaughan's Appeal. By Arthur Murphy. *London* [*Privately Printed*]. 1770. 8vo.

MURPHY (B. P.) Parties and Politics. Speech of Hon. B. P. Murphy, ... on the Governor's Message. ... March 6, 1860. *Albany: Weed, Parsons & Co.* 1860. 8vo, pp. 8. 51454

MURPHY (D.) Emogene: a Legend of Lookout Mountain. A Poem. By Dave Murphy. *Cincinnati: Applegate & Co.* 1866. Folio, 1 leaf. 51455

MURPHY (D. F.) The Jeff. Davis Piracy Cases. Full Report of the Trial of William Smith for Piracy, as one of the Crew of the Confederate Privateer, the Jeff Davis. ... By D. F. Murphy ... . *Philadelphia: King & Baird, Printers.* 1861. 8vo, pp. 5–100. H. 51456

MURPHY. Presidential Election, 1864. Proceedings of the National Union Convention held in Baltimore, Md., June 7th and 8th, 1864. Reported by D. F. Murphy ... . *New York: Baker & Godwin, Printers.* 1864. 8vo, pp. 94. H. 51457

[MURPHY (George Mollett).] The Slave among Pirates, or, "Uncle Tom's" many Editors; A Satire, By an Unknown. ... dedicated to Mrs. Harriet Beecher Stowe ... . *London: W. Horsell.* 1852. 16mo, pp. 15. H. 51458

MURPHY (H.) The Conquest of Quebec. An Epic Poem. In Eight Books. By Henry Murphy. *Dublin: The Author.* M.DCC.XC. 12mo, pp. (4), xix, 308. H. + *New York,* 1790. 12mo. 51459

MURPHY (H. Cruse). Anthology of New Netherland, or, Translations from the Early Dutch Poets of New York, with

Memoirs of their Lives. By Henry C. Murphy. *New York.* 1865. Rl. 8vo, pp. 209. Portrait, Facsimiles, etc. 51460

Seventy-five copies printed for the Bradford Club Series, No. 4, and seventy-five more for subscribers. A supplement of four pages was subsequently printed.

[MURPHY.] A Catalogue of an American Library, Chronologically Arranged. 1480–1800. [*Brooklyn.* 1850?] 8vo, pp. 57, (1). 51461

A few copies only printed for presentation. Prepared for his own amusement, by its owner, a quarter of a century ago, it falls short of even an approximate description of his almost unrivalled collection of books relating to the history, geography, etc., of America.

MURPHY. Dry Dock—New York Harbor. February 28, 1844. Mr. Murphy, ... made the following Report. [n. p. n. d.] 8vo, pp. 15. 51462

28th Cong., 1st Session, Report No. 198, House of Representatives.

MURPHY. The First Minister. *See* Michaelius (J.), 48688.

[MURPHY.] Henry Hudson in Holland. An Inquiry into the Origin and Objects of the Voyage which led to the Discovery of the Hudson River. With Bibliographical Notes. *The Hague: The Brothers Giunta D'Albani.* 1859. 8vo, pp. 72. Portrait. S.

[MURPHY.] Jacob Steendam, Noch Vaster. A Memoir of the First Poet in New Netherland with his Poems Descriptive of the Colony. *The Hague: The Brothers Giunta D'Albani.* 1861. 8vo, pp. 59. Portrait. 51464

Printed for private distribution, and scarce. It was reprinted with additions in the "Anthology of New Netherland."

[MURPHY.] Monument to the Victims of Prison Ships. Report from the Committee on Military Affairs, presented by G. A. Black to the House of Representatives, 28th Congress, 2d Session. [n. p. n. d.] 8vo, pp. 6. 51465

[MURPHY.] Poetry of Nieuw-Neder-Landt: comprising Translations of Early Dutch Poems Relating to New York, &c. With Memoirs of the Authors, by the Translator. *Williamstadt.* MDCCCLXVI. 8vo, pp. 9–206. Portrait and Plate. 51466

Also: Remarks ... 24th of February, 1849. ... [On] our Duties as a Nation towards our Territories ... in regard to ... Slavery; ... [n. p. n. d.] 8vo, pp. 8.—Remarks upon that portion of the Message of Gov. Seymour, relating to Military Arrests, delivered ... March 6, 1863. *Albany: Comstock & Cassidy.* 1863. 8vo, pp. 25.—Speech ... on the Tariff. ... May 3, 1844. [n. p. n. d.] 8vo, pp. 7.—Speech ... on Slavery in the Territories. ... May 17, 1848. *Washington.* 1848. 8vo, pp. 8.—Speeches, ... on Harbor and River Bill, 1845; ... [n. p. n. d.] 8vo. *See* "Representation of New Netherland," "Vertough," Vries (D. P. de), *also* Vol. II. 8311, *and* Morford (H.)

MURPHY (J. A.) Reference Book and Directory of the Architects, Civil Engineers, Surveyors, Carpenters, Builders ... . Compiled by J. Arthurs Murphy and Co. *New York.* 18—. 4to, pp. 235. 51467

MURPHY (J. McL.) American Ships and Ship-Builders. By Hon. John McLeod Murphy. *New York: Charles W. Baker, Printer.* 1860. 8vo, pp. 23. C., H. 51468

MURPHY. Oration delivered before the Military of the City of Albany, Washington's Birthday, 1860. By Hon. John McLeod Murphy. *New York: Baker & Godwin, Printers.* 1860. 8vo. 51469

MURPHY. Speech of Senator J. McLeod Murphy, ... in relation to the Southern Treason and Rebellion, ... January 25, 1861. [n. p. n. d.] 8vo, pp. 4. H. 51470

[MURPHY (John S.)] Interesting Documents. Containing an Account of the Federal Procession on the Adoption of the Constitution of the United States, July 23, 1788 ... *New York.* 1819. 12mo, pp. 128, (1). N. 51471

MURPHY (J. W.) The Confederate Soldier's Prayer Book: ... By Rev. Joseph W. Murphy ... . *Petersburg, Va.: St. Paul's Congregation.* [n. d.] 32mo, pp. 34. H. 51472

MURPHY (P. P.) Speech ... Senate, March 6, 1860. [n. p. n. d.] 8vo. 51473

MURPHY (T.) Life and Adventures of Timothy Murphy the benefactor of Schoharie, including his History from the commencement of the Revolution—His rencontres with the Indians—The Siege of the three Forts, and the preservation by his unparalleled Courage of all their inmates— ... and Anecdotes of his Adventures with the Indians, etc. *Schoharie C. H., N. Y.: Printed by W. H. Gallup.* 1839. 8vo, pp. 32. 51474

[MURPHY (Th.)] Documentos oficiales relativos a la conversion de la deuda Mexicana Exterior verificada en 1846. *Londres.* [1846.] 8vo, pp. 41. 51475

MURPHY (T.) Memoria sobre la deuda esterior de la Republica Mexicana desde su creacion hasta fines de 1847. Por el C. Tomas Murphy. ... *Paris: Imprenta de Ad. Blondeau.* 1848. 8vo, pp. 174, (1). 51476

MURPHY (W. D.) Biographical Sketches of the State Officers and Members of the Legislature of the State of New York, In 1858. By Wm. D. Murphy. *Albany: J. Munsell.* 1858. 8vo, pp. 244, (2). Continued. 51477

Also: Address of Hon. William D. Murphy, ... before the Albany Co. Agricultural Society, ... Oct. 14, 1870. *Albany: Charles Van Benthuysen & Sons.* 1870. 8vo, pp. 16

MURR (C. G. von). Diplomatische Geschichte des portugiesischen berühmten Ritters Martin Behaims. Aus Originalurkunden, von Christoph Gottlieb von Murr. ... *Nürnberg: Johann Eberhard Zeh.* 1788. Sm. 8vo, pp. 144. Map. J.C.B. + Zweite Ausgabe. *Gotha: Justus Perthes.* 1801. 8vo, pp. 144, (2). Map and Plate. C. 51478

This volume relates to the claim of Martin Behaim to the discovery of America. The author was one of the most learned geographers, and the very best chart-maker, of his age (1430–1506). But these, his real and great merits, have not satisfied certain writers, who, moved by the prejudices of country, or a love of contradiction and paradox, insist that Behaim, and not Columbus, was the discoverer of America. Cellarius and Riccioli both say that he visited the American continent and the Strait of Magelhaens, but Stuvenius appears to have been the first to give great importance to this statement; asserting in his treatise, "De vero Novi Orbis Inventore," that Behaim had accurately traced on his globe preserved at Nürnberg the islands of America, and even the Strait of Magelhaens. Prof. Tozen combated this assertion as far back as 1761, and for a quarter of a century the theory was laid aside as untenable.

MURR. Histoire diplomatique du Chevalier Portugais Martin Behaim de Nuremberg. Avec la description de son globe terrestre par M. Christophe Theophile de Murr. Traduite de l'allemand par ... H. J. Jansen. Troisième Édition ... . *Strasbourg et Paris: Chez Treuttel et Würtz. An* x. [1802.] 8vo, pp. viii, (2), 156, (1). Map and Plate. B. 51479

MURR. Christoph Gottlieb von Murr's Journal zur Kunstgeschichte und zur allgemeiner Litteratur. *Nürnberg: Johann Eberhard Zeh.* 1775–99. 17 vols., 12mo., and Neues Journal, 2 vols. 51480

The editor was not only a ripe scholar, but an accomplished linguist. In regard to matters connected with the Indian languages, and among them of the Amaran, the Chilian, the Brazilian, the Paraguyan, Californian, Quichen, and Yungan tribes, spread at the time chiefly over South and Western America, from which the German Jesuit Fathers had just been expelled on the suppression of their Order in 1773 by Pope Ganganelli. The editor gives besides much curious and interesting matter connected with those portions of America, derived from authentic sources.

MURR. Nachrichten von verschiedenen Ländern des Spanischen Amerika. Aus eigenhändigen Aufsätzen einiger Missionare der Gesellschaft Jesu herausgegeben von Christoph Gottlieb

von Murr. ... *Halle: Joh. Christian Hendel.* 1809–11. 2 vols., 8vo, pp. xxxii, 387, (1); (4), 389–616. Map. A. 51481

Contains a Tarahumarish dictionary, with a profusion of interesting ethnographical and linguistic details.

MURR. Reisen einiger Missionarien der Gesellschaft Jesu in Amerika. Aus ihren eigenen Aufsätzen herausgegeben von Christoph Gottlieb von Murr. ... *Nürnberg: Johann Eberhard Zeh.* 1785. 8vo, pp. (8), 614, (1). Map and 2 Plates. H.

Relates chiefly to the nations on the banks of the Maranon or Amazon, and Orinoco rivers, with copious dissertations on the dialects of South America, and vocabularies of their language.

MURRAY (A.) The True Interest of Great Britain, Ireland and our Plantations: or, a Proposal for Making such an Union between Great Britain, Ireland, and all our Plantations, as that already made betwixt Scotland and England. ... By Sir Alexander Murray. ... *London: The Author.* M.DCC.XL. Folio, pp. viii, 52.

MURRAY (A.) Report of the Committee of Claims, on the Memorial of Alexander Murray, late Commander of the United States Frigate Constellation ... . [n. p.] 1805. 8vo, pp. 11. B.

Also: Opinion of the Supreme Court of Pennsylvania in the case of Alexander Murray, vs. the Schooner Charming Betsy. *Philadelphia.* 1799. 8vo.

MURRAY (A.) Geology. *See* Canada, Vol. III., No. 10460, *also* Newfoundland.

MURRAY (A.) Memoirs of the Life and Services of Admiral Sir P. C. H. C. Durham. By his Nephew, Capt. A. Murray. *London.* 1846. 8vo. P. 51485

Durham served under Lords Howe and Rodney in the American Rebellion.

MURRAY (A. M.) Letters from the United States, Cuba and Canada By the Hon. Amelia M. Murray ... *London: John W. Parker and Son.* 1856. 2 vols., post 8vo, pp. (2), viii, (2), 320; viii, (2), 317. Map. + *New York: G. P. Putnam & Company.* 1856. 12mo, pp. 402. H. 51486

See "Fraser's Magazine," LIII, 522, *also* "Atheneum," January, 1856.

MURRAY (A.) The Geographical Distribution of Mammals. By Andrew Murray. *London: Day and Son.* 1866. 4to, pp. xvi, 420. 101 Maps and Plates. B. 51487

Shows the geographical distribution of each family, and includes American animals. Also "Notes upon Californian Trees" and "Synonymy of various Conifers."

MURRAY (B. B.) A Sermon, ... in ... Norway Village, (Me.) on the Annual Thanksgiving, ... November 29, 1827. By Benjamin B. Murray ... . *Norway.* 1827. 8vo, pp. 12. H. 51488

MURRAY (C. A.) The Prairie-Bird. By the Hon. Charles Augustus Murray ... . *London: Richard Bentley.* 1844. 3 vols., 12mo, pp. iv, 336; (2), 352; (2), 372. + [*Ibid.*] 1845. Fcap 8vo, pp. vii, 581. + *New-York: Harper & Brothers.* 1844. 8vo, pp. 207. + [*Ibid.*] 1847. + *London: G. Routledge & Co.* 1857. Fcap 8vo, pp. viii, 431. + [*Ibid.* n. d.] Post 8vo, pp. vii, 581.

A novel, descriptive of Indian life.

MURRAY. Travels in North America during the years 1834, 1835, & 1836. Including a Summer Residence with the Pawnee Tribe of Indians, in the Remote Prairies of Missouri, and a Visit to Cuba and the Azore Islands. By the Hon. Charles Augustus Murray ... . *London: Richard Bentley.* 1839. 2 vols., 8vo, pp. xvi, 473; x, 372. 2 Plates. C. 51490

This is the first and best edition of a most interesting work, by an intelligent observer of the peculiarities of the Pawnees, before they had been modified by contact with the whites. His departure from St. Louis, and first encounter with the Pawnees, is narrated in chap. xii. of vol. I., and through the remainder of the volume (pp. 235 to 460, and pp. 1 to 96 of vol. II.,) we follow him with unabated interest in his narration of his adventures during a three months' tour in the Indian territory. There is little of scientific value in his narrative, but it possesses a more than common charm in the vividness of his relation.

MURRAY. Travels [as before]. Third Edition Revised: with a new Introduction. *London: Richard Bentley.* 1854. 2 vols., post 8vo, pp. xi, 343; xi, 338. + *New York: Harper & Brothers.* 1839. 2 vols., 12mo, pp. 324; vii, 13–247. H.

Also: The Trapper's Bride; or Spirit of Adventure. ... *Cincinnati.* 1848. 8vo. + *Philadelphia.* 1848. 8vo.

[MURRAY (Daniel).] Extract from a Letter written by a Pious Lawyer, late Lieutenant in the American Navy. [n. p. n. d.] 8vo, pp. 8. 51492

MURRAY (D.) ... Petroleum, its History and Properties: by David Murray. ... [n. p. 1862.] 8vo, pp. 18. H. 51493

MURRAY. A Plan for a Park for the City of Albany. By David Murray, A.M. *Albany: J. Munsell.* 1863. 8vo, pp. (2), 16. Plan. H. 51494

MURRAY (G.) Letter to Sir George Murray, Secretary for the Colonies, relative to the deportation of Lecesne and Escoffery, from Jamaica. *London* [*Privately Printed*]. 1829. 8vo.

MURRAY (G. W.) Incidents in the Life of George W. Murray, during four years of service in the War for the Union, and his long confinement and sufferings in Libby Prison. ... *Cleveland, O.: Printed by Fairbanks, Benedict & Co.* 1865. 18mo, pp. 28. + [*Hartford.* n. d.] 18mo. 51496

MURRAY (H. A.) Lands of the Slave and the Free: or, Cuba, the United States, and Canada. By Captain the Hon. Henry A. Murray, R.N. ... *London: John W. Parker & Son.* 1855. 2 vols., post 8vo, pp. 980. Maps and Plates. + New Edition. *London: G. Routledge & Co.* 1857. Post 8vo, pp. xxiii, 480. Maps and Plates. B. 51497

M[URRAY] (H. L.) Florence Murray: a Narrative of Facts. By her Mother, H. L. M. ... *Boston.* 1849. 18mo, pp. 71.

MURRAY (H.) An Encyclopædia of Geography: comprising a complete Description of the Earth, Physical, Statistical, Civil, and Political; exhibiting ... its Physical Structure, the Natural History of each Country, and the Industry, Commerce, Political Institutions, and Civil and Social State of all Nations. By Hugh Murray, F.R.S.E. [and others.] *London: Longman* ... . 1834. 8vo, pp. xii, 1567, (1). Maps. + Revised, with Additions, by Thomas G. Bradford. *Philadelphia.* 1837. 3 vols., 8vo, pp. 596; 592; 624. + [*Ibid.*] 1840 and 1841. + Second Edition, ... revised and brought down to the Present Time. *London: Longman* ... . 1840. 8vo, pp. xiv, 1576. Maps. H. + [*Ibid.*] 1844. C. + *Philadelphia: Lea and Blanchard.* 1843. 3 vols., 8vo, pp. 597; 592; 648. Maps. + [*Ibid.*] 1846, 1847, 1852.

MURRAY. Historical Account of Discoveries and Travels in North America: including the United States, Canada, the Shores of the Polar Sea, and the Voyages in Search of a North West Passage; with Observations on Emigration. By Hugh Murray, Esq. ... *London: Longman* ... . 1829. 2 vols., 8vo, pp. xi, (2), 530; ix, (2), 556, Errata, 9 lines. Map. H. 51500

Contains a vast amount of information regarding the condition of the aborigines, and a bibliography of voyages and travels in America.

MURRAY. An Historical and Descriptive Account of British America; comprehending Canada Upper and Lower, Nova Scotia, New Brunswick, Newfoundland, Prince Edward Island, the Bermudas, and the Fur Countries: their History from the earliest Settlement; ... also an Account of the Manners and Present State of the Aboriginal Tribes; ... By Hugh Murray,

... With Illustrations of the Natural History, by James Wilson, R. K. Greville, LL.D., and Prof. Traill. ... *Edinburgh: Oliver & Boyd.* MDCCCXXXIX. 3 vols., fcap 8vo. pp. 352; 356; 388. 16 Maps and Plates. + Second Edition. [*Ibid.*] + *New-York: Harper & Brothers.* 1840. 2 vols., 18mo, pp. v–312; 290. + [*Ibid.* 1842] and 1848. 51501

MURRAY. Pictorial History of the United States of America, from the earliest Period to the close of President Taylor's Administration. ... With Anecdotes and Sketches of distinguished leading Men. By Hugh Murray, Esq. ... With additions and corrections, by Henry C. Watson. Illustrated ... . *Boston: Phillips, Samson and Company.* 1851. 8vo, pp. 500. + [*Ibid.*] 1857. B.

MURRAY. The United States of America; their History from the earliest period; ... By Hugh Murray ... . With Illustrations of the Natural History, by James Nichol. *Edinburgh: Oliver & Boyd.* MDCCCXLIV. 3 vols., fcap 8vo, pp. 400; 380; 379. Portraits and Plates. BA. 51503

Also: Adventures of British Seamen in the Southern Ocean. ... *Edinburgh: Constable and Co.* 1827. 12mo, pp. xi, 353. — Enquiries Historical and Moral respecting the Character of Nations. ... *Edinburgh.* 1808. 8vo, pp. viii, 424.

[MURRAY (James).] The Finishing Stroke to Mr. Wesley's Calm Address to the People of England. *New-Castle-upon-Tyne.* 1778. 12mo, pp. 22. S. 51504

MURRAY. An Impartial | History | of the Present | War in America; | containing | An Account of its Rise and Progress, | The Political Springs thereof, | with its various | Successes and Disappointments, | on Both Sides. | By the Rev. James Murray, of Newcastle. | ... | *Newcastle upon Tyne:* | *Printed for T. Robson.* [1778–1780.] 3 vols., 8vo, pp. iv, 573; 576; 332. 31 Portraits, Plates and Map. 51505

This first edition was published in numbers, in blue wrappers. The title of Vol. II. differs. The title of Vol. III., after "The Political Springs," reads: "Of the War now carrying on between Great Britain And the United Powers of France, Spain, and America." This third volume ends abruptly at page 332, and is of extreme scarcity.

MURRAY. An Impartial History of the Present War in America [as before]. *Newcastle upon Tyne: T. Robson.* [1780.] 3 vols., 8vo, pp. iv, 573; 576; 332. 23 Portraits, 25 Plates, 3 Maps and Plan. 51506

There is no date on the title of this edition, but the dedication to the king is dated December 12, 1780. The third volume terminates with the word "enjoying," without finishing the chapter or even the sentence.

The bibliography of this work is somewhat complicated. Some copies have no mention of more than one volume on the title, and for an imprint, *London: R. Baldwin.* [1778.] 8vo, pp. iv, 573. Copies with the Newcastle imprint exist, dated 1779, 1781, 1782, 1784. Our No. 34376 is, perhaps, the same work. The edition which most frequently appears has the following title:

MURRAY. An Impartial History of the War in America; From its first Commencement, to the present Time; Together With the Charters of the several Colonies, and other Authentic Information. Likewise, The Rise, Progress, and Political Springs of the War now carrying on between Great-Britain, And the United Powers of France, Spain, Holland, and America; With a particular Account of the several Engagements both by Sea and Land. By the Rev. James Murray, of Newcastle, Assisted by several Gentlemen of Eminence in Europe, and the Continent of America. *Newcastle upon Tyne: T. Robson.* [n. d.] 2 vols., 8vo, pp. iv, 573; 576. 24 Portraits and Map. 51507

The author's political principles were democratic in sentiment, and it is a little doubtful whether his history *is* "impartial." It is mainly sought for on account of the portraits, the quality of which differs in the different editions to a very great degree.

[MURRAY.] The New Maid of the Oaks. A Tragedy as lately Acted near Saratoga, by a company of Tragedians; under the Direction of the Author of the Maid of the Oaks, a Comedy. By Ahab Salem. *London: Printed for the Author.* 1778. 8vo, pp. 64. J.C.B. 51508

[MURRAY.] Sermons to Asses. [*London.*] 1768. 12mo, pp. vi, 212. + Second Edition. *London.* 1768. 12mo, pp. 261. + Third Edition. [*Ibid.*] + The Third Edition. *Philadelphia: Re-printed by John Dunlap.* MDCCLXIX. 12mo, pp. 114. + Fourth Edition. [*Ibid.*] 12mo, pp. 63. + Fifth Edition. [*Ibid.*] 1770. 18mo, pp. 63. C. + *Boston: Reprinted.* [17—.] 12mo.

Dedicated to G[eo]rg[e] Wh[i]tf[ie]ld, J[o]hn W[e]sl[e]y, W[i]ll[ia]m R[o]m[ai]n, and M. M[i]dd[leto]n.

MURRAY. Sermons to Asses, to Doctors in Divinity, to Lords Spiritual, and to Ministers of State. By the late Rev. James Murray ... . With an Original Sketch of his Life. ... *London: William Hone.* 1819. 8vo, pp. xvi, (2), 58, (4), 70, (2), 97, (4), 63, (2), 72. B. 51510

[MURRAY.] Sermons to Ministers of State. By the Author of Sermons to Asses. Dedicated to Lord North, Prime Minister of England, for the use of Religious, Political, and Philosophical

Rationalists in Europe and America. ... *Philadelphia: Robert Bell.* MDCC,LXXXIII. 8vo, pp. 79. P. 51511

Appended to this edition is "The humble confession, declaration, recantation, and apology of Benjamin Towne, Printer of Philadelphia." This laughable composition is said to have been written by the Rev. John Witherspoon, D.D.

MURRAY [James]. Corporal Murray, of the Fifth Regiment, United States Infantry. *New York: American Tract Society.* [n. d.] 32mo, pp. 64. H. 51512

MURRAY (J. O.) A Discourse, ... in ... South Danvers, on Thanksgiving Day, November 27, 1856. By James O. Murray. ... *Boston: Henry W. Dutton and Son, Printers.* 1856. 8vo, pp. 28

MURRAY. Loyalty to Country and its Duties. A Sermon ... By Rev. James O. Murray, in .. Cambridge, ... September 15, and repeated, ... September 22. ... *Cambridge: Printed by Allen & Farnham.* 1861. 8vo, pp. 23. 51514

Also: ... A Sermon commemorative of Rev. William Ward Merriam ... . *Cambridge: Printed ... by H. O. Houghton.* 1862. 8vo, pp. 28. B.

MURRAY (J.) A Farewell Sermon ... in the Unitarian Church, Rockford, Ill., ... March 29, 1857, By John Murray ... . *Rockford.* 1857. 8vo, pp. 19. B. 51515

MURRAY (J.) An Appeal to the Impartial Public, In Behalf of the Oppressed: Being an Answer to their Call, from the Massachusetts Gazette, or Boston Weekly News-Paper of ... June 16th, respecting a Piece in that Paper of May 12th. 1768. Signed by eleven Ministers in Boston; with some Remarks on that Singular Publication. By John Murray, A.M. Pastor of the Church at Boothbay, in the ... Province of the Massachusetts-Bay. ... *Portsmouth, New-Hampshire: Printed ..] by D. and R. Fowle.* 1768. 8vo, pp. 37. W. + *Salem: Printed ... by Samuel Hall.* 1770. 8vo, pp. 39. H. 51516

MURRAY. The Diligent Servant excited. A Sermon, ... in ... Newburyport, January 23, 1791, ... [before] the Funeral of ... Rev. Joseph Prince ... , *Newburyport: Printed ... by John Mycall.* MDCCXCI. 8vo, pp. 42, Appendix, (10). H. 51517

MURRAY. Jerubbaal ... . A Discourse on America's Duty and Danger, Delivered ... at Newbury-Port, December 11, 1783, on ... Thanksgiving for Peace. ... By John Murray. *Newbury-Port: Printed by John Mycall.* MDCCLXXXIV. 8vo, pp. 75. + *Newburyport: Printed by M. Blunt.* 1801. 8vo, pp. 70. H., W.

Also: Grace and Glory, or Heaven given only to Saints. A Sermon ... at ... Newbury-Port, Jan. 26, 1788, ... [on] the Death of Ralph Cross ... . *Newbury-Port: Printed by John Mycall.* 1788. 8vo, pp. 66. — The Happy Voyage Compleated, and the Sure Anchor cast. A Sermon, occasioned by the ... Death of Capt. Jonathan Parsons, ... Preached ... in Newbury-Port, February 27, 1785. ... *Newbury-Port: Printed ... by John Mycall.* [n. d.] 8vo, pp. 96. + *Reprinted. Newburyport: E. W. Allen.* 1806. 8vo, pp. 50. H. — Justification of Believers ... . Three Sermons ... in Newbury-Port, August, 1788 ... . *Newburyport: Printed by John Mycall.* MDCCLXXXIX. 8vo, pp. 136. — The last Solemn Scene! A Sermon ... in ... Boston, May 22, 1768. ... *Boston: W. M'Alpine.* 1768. 8vo. + *Salem.* 1769. 8vo, pp. 47. + Second Edition. *Newburyport: Printed ... by G. J. Osborne.* MDCCXCIII. 8vo, pp. 69. — Nehemiah, Or the Struggle for Liberty never in vain ... . A Discourse ... at ... Newbury-Port, Nov. 4th, 1779. ... The day ... of ... Fasting and Prayer ... . *Newbury: Printed by John Mycall.* 1779. 8vo, pp. 56. H. — ... A Sermon ... at ... Newbury-Port: occasioned by the Death of Mrs. Phebe Lane, ... who ... [died] Nov. 12th, 1781 ... . *Newbury-Port: Printed by J. Mycall.* 1781. 8vo, pp. 90. H.

MURRAY. The Character of the Reverend John Murray, Formerly of Ireland, But now Minister in Booth-Bay, ... Massachusetts, Set in a Fair and Impartial Light, And well Attested, By Gentlemen of Note, in Europe and America. *Salem: Printed ... by Samuel Hall.* [1769.] 8vo, pp. 15. B. 51519

MURRAY (J.) Letters, and Sketches of Sermons. ... By John Murray ... . *Boston: Joshua Belcher.* 1812–13. 3 vols., 8vo, pp. vii, (1), 17–404; 429; 418, Note and Errata, (2). Portrait. H.

MURRAY. Messages from the Superior State; communicated by John Murray, through John M. Spear in ... 1852. Containing ... a Sketch of the Author's Earthly Life ... by S. C. Hewitt. *Boston: Bela Marsh.* 1852. 12mo, pp. 167. Portrait. 51521

MURRAY. The Substance of a Thanksgiving Sermon, ... in Boston, February 19, 1795. ... By John Murray ... . *Boston: Printed ... by John W. Folsom.* 1795. 8vo, pp. 32. BA. 51522

MURRAY. Universalism Vindicated: Being the Substance of some Observations on the Revelation of the Unbounded Love of God, made to the Patriarch, in the Field of Padanaram. ... And confirmed by the joint Suffrages of the Prophets and Apostles. Delivered ... to the people who ... worship ... in the meeting house in Middle Street ... . *Charlestown: Printed by J. Lamson, for the Author.* [1810?] 8vo, pp. xvi, 96, (1). H. 51523

This, in all probability, is the first book written and published in America advocating the doctrine of universal salvation.

MURRAY. Records of the Life of the Rev. John Murray; late ... Senior Pastor of the Universalists, ... in Boston. Written by Himself. ... To which is added, a Brief Continuation, ...

by a Friend. ... *Boston: Munroe and Francis.* 1816. 8vo, pp. 250. Portrait. + New Edition. *Providence: Z. Baker.* [1816.] 16mo, pp. iv, 360 [*i. e.* 352]. + Second Edition. *Boston: Bowen and Cushing.* 1827. 12mo, pp. 348. Portrait. + Third Edition, with Notes and Remarks, By Rev. L. S. Everett. *Boston: Marsh, Capen & Lyon* ... . 1831. 12mo, pp. 328. Portrait. + With Notes and an Appendix, By Thomas Whittemore. *Boston.* 1833. 12mo, pp. 276. H. + Fifth Edition, with Notes and Appendix, By Rev. L. S. Everett. *Boston: Marsh, Capen & Lyon.* 1833. 12mo, pp. 324. Portrait. + Seventh Edition ... . *Utica, N. Y.: Orren Hutchinson.* 1840. 12mo, pp. 324. B. + Eighth Edition ... . *Boston: A. Tompkins.* 1844. 12mo, pp. 324. Portrait. + With a Continuation, by Mrs. Judith Sargent Murray. A New Edition, with an Introduction and Notes, By Rev. G. L. Demarest. *Boston: Universalist Publishing House.* 1869. 12mo, pp. 408. 4 Plates and Portrait. C. + [*Ibid.*] 1870. 8vo, pp. 408. 2 Plates and Portrait. H. 51524

MURRAY (J.) The Emigrant and Traveller's Guide to and through Canada ... . By John Murray. ... *London: Smith, Elder and Co.* 1835. Fcap 8vo, pp. 63, (1). 51525

MURRAY. A Letter ... On Colonial Slavery. ... By John Murray. ... *London: Holdsworth and Ball.* 1832. 8vo, pp. 19, (1)

MURRAY. Murray's Official Handbook of Church and State; containing the Names, Duties, and Powers of the Principal ... Authorities of the United Kingdom and Colonies ... . *London: John Murray.* 1852. 12mo, pp. xix, (1), 419. + A New ... Edition [by Samuel Redgrave. *Ibid.*] 1855. 12mo, pp. xvi, 283, (1), (4). A. 51527

MURRAY (J.) The Tides and Currents in ... the Polar Sea indicative of the Probability of a North-East Passage to the Pacific; with reasons for persevering in the Search for Sir J. Franklin ... . By John Murray, Civil Engineer ... . *London: E. Wilson.* 1854. 8vo, pp. (2), iii, 54. Map. 51528

MURRAY (J. W. B.) Eulogy on the late Edward Post, Esq. ... The 17th of February, 1816, before the ... College of Physicians ... New-York. By John W. B. Murray, A.M. ... *New-York: Printed by Van Winkle & Wiley.* 1816. 8vo, pp. 15. B.

MURRAY (J.) Opinion of Joseph Murray, relating to the Courts of Justice in the Colony of New York. *New York.* 1734. 4to, pp. 44. N. 51530

MURRAY (Mrs. Judith Sargent). The Gleaner. A Miscellaneous Production. ... By Constantia. ... *Printed at Boston, by I. Thomas and E. T. Andrews.* 1798. 3 vols., 12mo, pp. 348; 321; 328. C., H., P. 51531

A collection of papers, in part originally published in the "Massachusetts Monthly Museum," by the wife of the Rev. John Murray. It contains some curious information on the condition of the stage at Boston and elsewhere; and some dramatic compositions.

MURRAY (*Lieut.*) Red Rupert, the American Buccaneer. ... By Lieutenant Murray. *Boston: Elliott, Thomes & Talbot.* [1867.] 16mo, pp. 5–99. 51532

Also: The Scarlet Flag; or, The Carribbean Rover. A Story of the Early Buccaneers. ... *Boston: Elliott, Thomes & Talbot.* 1864. 4to, pp. 50.

MURRAY (L.) A Biographical Sketch of Henry Tuke. By Lindley Murray. *Burlington, N. J.* 1816. 12mo. P. 51533

MURRAY. Memoirs of the Life and Writings of Lindley Murray: in a series of Letters, written by Himself. With a Preface, and a Continuation ... by Elizabeth Frank. *York: Printed by Thomas Wilson and Sons.* 1826. 8vo, pp. xiv, (1), 280. Portrait and Facsimile. + Second Edition. [*Ibid.*] 1827. + *New York: Samuel Wood and Sons.* 1827. 8vo, pp. viii, 280. Facsimile. H. 51534

Murray, an American by birth, is also the author of an English Grammar, which has enjoyed great popularity on both sides of the Atlantic.

MURRAY (M.) History of the United States of America. Written in accordance with the Principles of Peace. By M. Murray. *Boston: Benjamin B. Mussey & Co.* 1852. 12mo, pp. 441. C. 51535

MURRAY (N.) American Principles on National Prosperity. A Thanksgiving Sermon ... in ... Elizabethtown, November 28, 1854. By Nicholas Murray, D.D. ... *New York: Harper & Brothers.* 1854. 8vo, pp. 32. B. 51536

[MURRAY.] Letters to the Rt. Rev. John Hughes ... . By "Kirwan." *New York: Leavitt, Trow & Co.* 1847. 18mo, pp. 103. B. + [The same] And Bishop Hughes confuted. ... [*Ibid.*] 1849. 12mo, pp. 103; 105; 105. + First Series. *Philadelphia: Presbyterian Board of Publication.* [1851.] 18mo, pp. 105.

MURRAY. Notes, Historical and Biographical, concerning Elizabeth-Town, its Eminent Men, Churches and Ministers.

By Nicholas Murray. *Elizabeth-Town: Printed ... by E. Sanderson.* 1844. 12mo, pp. 166. H., S. 51538

[MURRAY.] Parish and other Pencillings. By Kirwan. *New York.* 1854. 12mo, pp. 272. + *London: Sampson Low.* 1855. 12mo. C. 51539

Also: The Decline of Popery and its Causes. An Address ... in ... [New York] January 15, 1851. ... *New York: Harper & Brothers.* 1851. 8vo, pp. 32. — ... A Discourse ... at the Funeral of the Rev. D. M. Miller, ... Bridgehampton, Long Island, July 1, 1855. ... *New York: John F. Trow, Printer.* 1855. 8vo, pp. 26. — Dying Legacy to the People of His Beloved Charge. ... *New York.* 1861. 8vo. — Preachers and Preaching. ... *New York: Harper & Brothers.* 1860. 12mo, pp. 303. — A Sermon ... Nov. 30, 1837, in ... Elizabeth-Town: Being ... Thanksgiving ... . *Elizabethtown, N. J.: H. H. Hassey, Printer.* 1838. 8vo, pp. 17. B.

MURRAY (O. S.) The Struggle of the Hour; a Discourse ... at the Paine Celebration in Cincinnati, January 29, 1861. By Orson S. Murray. ... *Foster's Crossings, Warren County, Ohio.* 1861. 8vo, pp. 68. H. 51540

[MURRAY (Thomas Boyles).] The Home of the Mutineers. *Philadelphia: American Sunday School Union.* 1854. 16mo, pp. 342. 9 Plates. C. 51541

MURRAY. Kalli, the Esquimaux Christian. A Memoir. By the Rev. T. B. Murray. ... *London.* [n. d.] 16mo, pp. 64. Map. + *New York.* [n. d.] 16mo, pp. 70. 51542

MURRAY. Pitcairn: the Island, the People, and the Pastor; ... By the Rev. Thos. Boyles Murray ... . *London.* [n. d.] Fcap 8vo, pp. (2), 414. Portrait. + Second Edition. [*Ibid.*] 1853. 16mo, pp. 315. 51543

[MURRAY (William), Lord Mansfield.] An Address to The Right Honourable L—d M—sf—d; in which The Measures of Government, respecting America, are considered in a new light; with a view To his Lordship's Interposition therein. *London: J. Almon.* 1775. 8vo, pp. 35. J.C.B. 51544

"The author endeavours, by expatiating on the grievous nature and ruinous consequences of the measures adopted with regard to America, to persuade Lord Mansfield to interpose his influence in favour of the Colonies."—*Monthly Review*, LII. 182. The British Museum catalogue attributes this to James Mansfield—an error, I think.

[MURRAY.] The Genuine Speech of Lord Mansfield, ... In the Cause ... for raising A Duty of Four and an Half per Cent. On all the Exports from the Island of Grenada. ... *London: G. Kearsly.* MDCCLXXIV. 8vo, pp. (4), 24. 51545

See "Monthly Review," LII. 89.

[MURRAY.] Lord Mansfield's Speech ... In the Cause ... for raising a Duty of Four and an Half per Cent. On all the Exports from the Island of Grenada. ... A New Edition Corrected. *London: G. Kearsly.* M.DCC.LXXV. 8vo, pp. (2), 23. 51546

See also Vol. IV., Nos. 15990, 15998, Vol. X., Nos. 40490, 40523, 40574, *and* "Plea of the Colonies."

MURRAY (W.) Case relating to the Southern Boundary of the Massachusetts Bay, &c., 1754. [n. p. n. d.] 8vo, pp. 12.

See also Massachusetts, Vol. XI., No. 45665.

MURRAY (W. H. H.) Address ... the Sabbath following the Assassination of President Lincoln, in ... Greenwich, Conn. ... *New York.* 1865. 8vo, pp. 15. H. 51548

MURRAY. Adventures in the Wilderness; or, Camp-Life in the Adirondacks. By W. H. H. Murray. ... *Boston: Fields, Osgood, & Co.* 1869. 16mo, pp. 236. 8 Plates. H. 51549

Also: Music-Hall Sermons. ... *Boston: Fields, Osgood, & Co.* 1870. 8vo, pp. vi, 276. — Park-Street Pulpit; Sermons. ... *Boston: J. R. Osgood & Co.* 1871. 12mo, pp. v, 372

[MURRAY (William Vans).] Political Sketches, inscribed to ... John Adams, Minister Plenipotentiary, from the United States to the Court of Great Britain. By a Citizen of the United States. ... *London: C. Dilly.* MDCCLXXXVII. 8vo, pp. (8), 96. H.

"These sketches are written with much spirit, and that zeal for America and its cause which has animated her numerous authors and defenders."—*Critical Review.* *See also* "Monthly Review," LXXVII. 72. Corrected title of our Vol. I., No. 257.

MURRAY (W. W.) Isadore or the Captives of the Norridgewocks. By W. W. Murray. [n. p. n. d.] 8vo, pp. 37.

MURRELL (J. A.) A History of the Detection, Conviction, Life and Designs of John A. Murel [*sic*], the Great Western Land Pirate; ... With his System of Villany, and Plan of Exciting a Negro Rebellion. And a Catalogue of the names of Four Hundred and Forty-five of his Mystic Clan Fellows and Followers; and their efforts for the destruction of Mr. Virgil A. Stewart, the young man who detected him. To which is added a Biographical Sketch of Mr. V. A. Stewart. By Augustus Q. Walton, Esq. *Athens, Tennessee.* 1835. 8vo, pp. 75. H. + [n. p. 1836.] 8vo, pp. 71. 51552

MURRELL. The Life and Adventures of John A. Murrell, the Great Western Land Pirate ... . *New York: H. Long & Brother.* 1847. 8vo, pp. 126. + [*Ibid.*] 1848. 51553

See also Howard (H. R.), Vol. VIII., No. 33250.

Murrell (W. M.) Cruise of the Frigate Columbia around the World, under the Command of Commodore George C. Read, in 1838, 1839 and 1840. By William Meacham Murrell. ... *Boston: Benjamin B. Mussey.* 1840. 16mo, pp. 230, (2).

Mursinna (Friedrich Samuel). Geschichte der Entdekkung von Amerika. ... *Halle: Renger.* 1795. 12mo, pp. (8), 400. Plate. c. 51555

Murto (A. L.) Sermon panegirico del glorioso apostol y evangelico S. Mateo patrono principal de la Santa iglesia catedral de Durango. *Mexico.* 1795. 4to, 18 leaves. 51556

Murtola (G.) La Marineide risate e le Strigliate del S. Robusto Pogommega (Andrea Borbazza). *Norimbergh.* 1642. 12mo

The "Strigliate" are sonnets in ridicule of T. Stigliano's poem on America, entitled "Mondo Nuovo." From Libri's catalogue.

Musa Americana. Poema, que en verso heroico latino escribió un erudito Americano, sobre los soberanos atributos de Dios, y traduce en Castellano en octava rima el br. d. Diego Bringas de Manzaneda y Enzinas ... . *México, por D. F. Zúñiga y Ontiveros.* 1783. 18mo, pp. (6), 151. c. 51558

A very scarce work, not mentioned by Rich or Stevens.

Musa Americana, seu de Deo Carmina ad usum Scholarum Congregationis S. Philipi Nerii. *Guanajuato.* 1847. 8vo.

Muscogee. *See* Muskogee Language.

Muse (J. H.) Argument in the Supreme Court of Louisiana, upon the Liability of Debtors to pay the unpaid Price of Slaves. By J. H. Muse ... . Revised Edition. [n. p. n. d.] 8vo, pp. 22.

Muse (J. E.) Oration upon ... Agriculture, delivered November 10th, 1825, before the Dorchester Agricultural Society, Cambridge, Md. By Joseph E. Muse. *Baltimore.* 1825. 8vo, pp. 22. 51561

Also: An Address ... Agriculture of Maryland ... Oct. 29, 1827. *Baltimore.* 1828. 8vo.

The Muse's Pocket Campanion; a Collection of Poems. *Carlisle.* 1785. 8vo. 51562

Includes Seward's Monody on Major André.

Museo Americano: Historia, Viages, Historia natural, Historia religiosa, Biografia, Miscelanea. Tomo I. *Buenos Ayres.* 1835–1836. 4to. 51563

El Museo de ambas Americas. *Valparaiso.* 1842. 3 vols., 8vo. 51564

Contains articles on the geography, history, statistics and politics of America.

Museo de Cuadros de Costumbres. [*Bogota.*] 1866. Rl. 8vo.

El Museo Mexicano, ó Miscelanea Pintoresca de Amenidades Curiosas é Instructivas. *Mexico.* 1843–1845. 5 vols., sm. 4to, pp. 576; 576; 587; 572; 570. 51566

Contains curious and important notices on the ancient and modern history of Mexico, its literature, etc. Profusely illustrated with lithographs.

Museo Pintoresco Mejicano: Historia Natural al alcance de todos. 820 Laminas Sacadas de los trés Reinos de la Naturaleza. Por el Houbloup. *Paris: Rosa.* 1838. 4tó. 51 Plates.

Museo Venezolana. Literatura—ciencias—artes—historia—industria—comercio—agricultura. Ano 1. *Carácas.* 1865.

Twenty-four numbers published.

Museo Yucateco, Periodico Cientifico y Literario. [*Campeche.* 1841–42.] 2 vols., sm. 4to. 51569

All printed. Contains many articles on the history of Yucatan.

Muses de la Novvelle France. *See* [Lescarbot (M.)], 40174.

Museu Pittoresco, ou livro recreativo das familias ... . *Rio de Janeiro: Typographia Universidade de Laemmert.* 18—. 2 vols.

The Museum; a [weekly] Miscellaneous Repository of Instruction and Amusement. Vol. I. *Hartford: Geo. W. Kappel.* 1825. 8vo. 51571

No more published.

Memoirs of the Museum of Comparative Zoölogy, at Harvard College. Vol. I. *Cambridge: University Press.* 1864–65. 4to, pp. (4), vi, (2), 200, xiv, 234. 2 colored Plates. Continued.

Also: ... Report of the Trustees of the Museum of Comparative Zoölogy, 1861. *Boston: William White, Printer ...* 1861. 8vo, pp. 50. Continued. H.

Museum of History: or Narratives of Wonderful Adventures. *New Haven.* [n. d.] 2 vols., 12mo. 51573

The Museum of Remarkable and Interesting Events, containing ... a full Account of the Captivity and truly wonderful Escape of Thomas Andros from the Old Jersey Prison Ship during the Revolutionary War, written recently by himself. Compiled principally by J. Watts. *Cleveland, Ohio.* 1844. 12mo. + *New York: J. Watts.* 1857. 12mo. 51574

The Museum: or, the Literary and Historical Register. ... *London: R. Dodsley.* M.DCC.XLVI. 8vo, pp. 538. Continued.

Musgrave (G. W.) The Polity of the Methodist Episcopal Church, being an exposure of the spurious origin of Methodist Episcopacy. The tyrannical nature of the Government and Discipline of the ... Church. ... By the Rev. G. W. Musgrave, ... of Baltimore. *Baltimore.* 1843. 8vo, pp. 344. 51576

Musgrave. A Sermon occasioned by the Death of Major James Owen Law. By the Rev. G. W. Musgrave, D.D. ... *Baltimore.* 1847. 8vo, pp. 32. s. 51577

Also: A Vindication of Religious Liberty. ... *Baltimore.* 1834. 8vo, pp. 32.

Music in Commemoration of the Death of George Washington. *Boston.* 1800. 8vo. w. 51578

The Musical Advertiser and Masonic Journal. *New Sharon, Maine.* 1854. 4to. 51579

Continued as the "Masonic Journal" to vol. VI. of the title, and was then changed to "The Crystal and Masonic Journal."

The Musical Reporter. *Boston: Saxton & Peirce.* 1841. 8vo, pp. 432. H. 51580

No more published.

The Musical Review, and Record of Musical Science, Literature and Intelligence. Edited ... by E. Ives, Jun. Vol. I. For 1838–9. *New York: Printed by William Osborn.* 1839. 8vo, pp. (2), v, (1), 422. Continued. A. 51581

Muskingum. *See* Message, Vol. XII., No. 48082.

Muskogee Language. The Gospel according to Matthew. Translated into the Muskokee Language. *Park Hill Mission Press.* 1855. 24mo, pp. 153, 7. 51582

For "The Gospel according to John," *see* Vol. V., No. 17460.

In the Court of Claims. The Muscogee or Creek Nation of Indians *versus* the United States. Petition. [n. p. n. d.] 8vo, pp. 16. 51583

Muskogee Hymn Book. Collected and Revised ... . By Daniel B. Asbury. *Baptist Mission Press, C. N.* 1855. 24mo, pp. 82, (2). 51584

Muskokee Hymns ... . By H. F. Buckner, ... and G. Herrod, ... *Marion, Ala.: Mission Board.* 1860. 32mo, pp. 160. 51585

Mvskoke mopunvkv, nakchokv setempohetv. Translation of Introduction to the Shorter [Presbyterian] Catechism into the Creek Language, by R. M. Loughridge [with alphabet]. *Park Hill.* 1846. 8vo, pp. 31. c. 51586

For a second edition, *see* Vol. V., No. 17461.

Muskogee or Creek First Reader. By W. S. Robertson and David Winslett. *New York.* 1856. 12mo, pp. 48. Plates.

Muskoki Imvnaitsv. The Muskokee (Creek) Assistant. *Boston.* 1834. 16mo. M. 51588

Narcokv Esyvhiketv. Muskogee Hymns. Collected and revised by Rev. R. M. Loughridge of the Presbyterian Mission, and Rev. David Winslett, Interpreter. Third Edition. *New York.* 1859. 24mo. + Fourth Edition, Revised and Enlarged. By Rev. W. S. Robertson. *New York: Mission House.* 1868. 24mo, pp. 221. 51589

Mussani (C.) Compendio histórico (de las misiones) en el Perú. Van en seguida noticias historicas sobre las misiones en la Republica de Bolivia por C. Mussani. *Paris.* 1854. 12mo.

Musselman (H. K.) Trial of Henry Kobler Musselman and Lewis Willman for the Murder of Lazarus Zellerback. *Lancaster.* 1839. 8vo. 51591

[Mussey (Benj. B.)] Letter to Rev. Frederick T. Gray: being Strictures on Two Sermons, preached by him on Sunday, November 29, 1841, at the "Bulfinch Street Church." By a Proprietor of said Church. ... *Boston: Benjamin B. Mussey.* 1842. 8vo, pp. 62. BA. 51592

Mussey (O.) Review of Ellwood Fisher's Lecture, on The North and the South. By Osgood Mussey. *Cincinnati: Wright, Fisher & Co., Printers.* 1849. 8vo, pp. 98, (2). H. 51593

Mussey (R. D.) An Address on Ardent Spirit, read before the New Hampshire Medical Society ... June 5, 1827 ... . By R. D. Mussey, M.D. ... *Hanover.* 1824. 8vo, pp. 24. + *Boston: Perkins & Marvin.* 1829. 16mo, pp. 16. H. 51594

Mussey. An Oration, with an Address, on the 4th of July, 1807, to the Ipswich Light Infantry, at Ipswich. By Reuben D. Mussey, M.D. *Salem.* [1807.] 8vo. 51595

Also: An Essay on the Influence of Tobacco upon Life and Health. ... *Boston: Perkins & Marvin.* 1836. 16mo, pp. 48. + Second Edition. [*Ibid.*] 1839. + A New Edition, enlarged ... . *New York: American Tract Society.* [n. d.] 16mo, pp. 64.

[Musson (Eugène).] Lettre à Napoléon III sur l'esclavage aux États du Sud Par un Créole de la Louisiane *Paris: Chez Dentu.* 1862. 8vo, pp. vii, 160. B. 51596

The dedication is signed "E. M."

Musson (J. P.) A Letter to Ministers, suggesting Improvements in the Trade of the West Indies and the Canadas; ... and a ... Plan of forwarding Slave-Emancipation. By John P. Musson, Esq. ... *London: J. M. Richardson.* 1825. 8vo, pp. (4), 109. H. 51597

Muster Roll of Captain —— Company of the —— Class Philadelphia Militia, now in the Service of the United States, Commanded by ——. [*Philadelphia, about* 1777.] Folio, 1 leaf.

Muster-Roll of Citizen Soldiers at North Point and Fort McHenry, September 12 & 13, 1814. *Baltimore.* [n. d.] 16mo, pp. 96. 51599

Musters (G. C.) At Home with the Patagonians. A Year's Wanderings over Untrodden Ground from the Straits of Magellan to the Rio Negro. By George Chaworth Musters. *London: J. Murray.* 1871. 8vo, pp. xx, 323. Map and 9 Plates. c.

Mute's Almanac, for ... 1840 ... calculated for the Meridian of Albany, by L. S. Backus. ... *Canajoharie, N. Y.* [n. d.] 12mo, pp. 36. s. 51601

Mutiny on board the Lady Shore with the Journey through Brazil. *London?* 1798. 8vo. 51602

Title from one of Quaritch's catalogues—probably incorrect.

Mutius, *pseudon.* The Letters of Mutius, ... to the President of the United States. *Washington: Printed by Edward Carter Stanard.* 1810. 8vo, pp. 28. B. 51603

Mütter (T. D.) The Salt Sulphur Springs, Monroe Co., Virginia. By Thomas D. Mütter. *Philadelphia: T. K. and P. G. Collins, Printers.* 1840. 8vo, pp. 42. + *Richmond.* 1850. 8vo

The Deed of Settlement of the Mutual Assurance Company, for Insuring Houses from Loss by Fire in New York. *New York: Printed by William Morton.* MDCCLXXXVII. Sm. 4to, pp. 17

With curious frontispiece of a fire-engine, and a company of firemen playing upon a burning building. Excessively rare.

Mutual Banking. ... *West Brookfield, Mass.: O. S. Cooke & Co.* 1850. 12mo, pp. 94. H. 51606

Prospectus of the Mutual Benefit Life Insurance Company: with Tables of Rates ... . 1846. *New York: Narine & Co., Printers.* [n. d.] 12mo, pp. 34, (1). Continued. H. 51607

Also: Statement of the ... Co. ... 1858. ... [n. p. n. d.] 12mo, pp. 32, (4). Continued. — ... Twenty-Third Annual Report of the President to the ... Directors. ... 1868. [*New-York: John A. Gray & Green, Printers.* n. d.] 24mo, pp. 32. Cont'd.

Mutual Benefit Building and Loan Associations: their History, Principles, and Plan of Operation; together with a Statement of the Benefits attending them, and of the Distinction between American and English Societies; also, a mode by which life insurance may be adapted to the requirements of their members; a form of constitution, etc. *Charleston: Walker and James.* 1852. 12mo, pp. 96. 51608

Second Report of the Mutual Insurance Association of Nassau, Schodack and Chatham. *Albany.* 1858. 12mo. s. 51609

Mutual Interest of Great Britain, 1765. *See* [Bollan (W.)]

The Advantages of Life Insurance ... [as set forth by the] Mutual Life Insurance Company of New York. *New York.* 1853. 8vo. 51610

Also: Correspondence laid before the Board of Examiners, to examine the Affairs of the ... Company ... . *New York.* 1856. 8vo, pp. 63.—Memorial ... to the Supervisors, for relief from unjust Taxation ... . *New York.* 1854. 8vo.—Report of the Board of Examiners appointed April 15, 1856, to examine the Affairs of the ... Company ... . *New York.* 1856. 8vo, pp. 64.—Report exhibiting the Experience of the ... Company ... for Fifteen Years, ending February 1, 1858. ... *New York.* 1859[8?]. 4to, pp. vi, 34. s.

The Constitution of the Mutual Marine Insurance Company, incorporated by the Legislature of Massachusetts, March 24, 1843. *New Bedford: Printed by Benj. Lindsey.* 1852. 12mo, pp. 16. 51611

The Mutual Rights of the Ministers and Members of the Methodist Episcopal Church; published monthly. Edited by a Committee of Ministers and Laymen. *Baltimore.* 1824–28. 4 vols., 8vo. 51612

[Muys van Holy (D.)] Middelen en Motiven om het kopen en verkopen van Oost- en West-Indische Actien ... te beswaren met een impost. *Amsterdam.* 1687. 4to, pp. 4. 51613

Means and motives to tax the buying and selling of the East and West India shares.

Muzzey (Artemas B.) A Discourse ... in Cambridge, August 1, 1847, ... after the ... Death of Lowell M. Stone, Esq.

By A. B. Muzzey ... *Boston: Wm. Crosby and H. P. Nichols.* 1847. 8vo, pp. 16. 51614

Also: Artillery-Election Sermon, 1837. ... *Boston.* 1837. 8vo, pp. 32.—Brotherhood in the Sanctuary. A Sermon ... at the Dedication of the Lee-Street Church, Cambridge, March 25, 1847. ... *Boston: Leonard C. Bowles.* 1847. 8vo, pp. 16.— ... A Discourse ... at the Dedication of the New Meeting House ... [in] Cambridgeport ... October 29, 1834. ... *Boston: Dutton and Wentworth, Printers.* 1834. 8vo, pp. 36.—A Plea for the Christian Spirit. A Sermon preached February 2, 1845, ... [at] Cambridgeport ... . *Boston: Wm. Crosby & H. P. Nichols.* 1845. 8vo, pp. 12. B.

Muzzey (H. W.) The Application to the Legislature of the Haverhill Aqueduct Company. Argument of Henry W. Muzzey, Esq. ... [n. p. n. d.] 8vo, pp. 8. H. 51615

Also: Report ... of expense of maintaining the West Boston and Canal Bridges, ... with the Argument of Henry W. Muzzey ... . [*Cambridge.*] 1870. 8vo, pp. 9. H.

Muzzy (H.) Poems, Moral and Sentimental. By Mrs. Harriet Muzzy. Collected and arranged by Caroline Matilda Thayer. *New York.* 1821. 16mo, pp. ix, 196. s. 51616

My Cave Life in Vicksburg. With Letters of Trial and Travel. By a Lady. *New York: D. Appleton and Company.* 1864. 12mo, pp. 196. 51617

My Conscience! *See* Vol. III., No. 9633.

My Farm of Edgewood. *See* [Mitchell (D. G.)], No. 49675

My First Campaign. Twelfth Regiment R. I. Volunteers. *Boston: Wright & Potter.* 1863. 18mo, pp. 152. 51618

My Native Land. A Poem. *Lynchburg, Va.* 1827. 8vo.

My New Home. By the Author of "Win and Wear" ... . *New York: R. Carter & Bros.* 1865. 16mo, pp. 383. 6 Plates.

My Own Experience. Dedicated to the "Suffolk Board of Trade." *Boston.* 1846. 12mo, pp. 36. H. 51621

A temperance sketch.

My Ride to the Barbecue. or, Revolutionary Reminiscences of the Old Dominion. By an ex-Member of Congress. ... *New York: S. A. Rollo.* 1860. 12mo, pp. 72. 51622

My Southern Friends. [n. p. n. d.] 12mo. 51623

My Vineyard at Lakeview. By a Western Grape Grower. *New York.* 1866. 12mo, pp. 143. 51624

Mycall (J.) A Funereal Address, on the Death of the Late General George Washington; Interspersed with Sketches of, and Observations on, his Life and Character. Delivered in ... Harvard, February 22, 1800. By John Mycall. ... *Boston: Manning & Loring, Printers ...* [1800.] 8vo, pp. (4), 27. W.

Myer (A. J.) A Manual of Signals: for the Use of Signal Officers in the Field. By Col. Albert J. Myer ... . *Washington, D. C.* 1864. 8vo, pp. (2), 148. + *New York: D. Van Nostrand.* 1866. 8vo, pp. xiv, 398. Plates and Diagrams. H. 51626

Also: ... Memorial of Albert J. Myer, ... to the ... Senate ... . [n. p. 1866?] 8vo, pp. 11, Supplement, 12, Appendix, 12, 19. H.

[Myer (I.)] Presidential Power. *See* Binney (H.)], 5484.

Myers (A.) Speech of the Hon. Amos Myers, of Pennsylvania, ... February 3d, 1864, On the Constitutionality and Necessity of a Draft. *Washington, D. C.: H. Polkinhorn, ... Printer.* [n. d.] 8vo, pp. 8. H. 51627

Myers (B.) Miraculous Cure of Sister Beatrix Myers, a Nun of the Visitation in Georgetown, D. C. Obtained by the intercession of Prince Hohenlohe, on the 10th February, 1825. *Washington: Henri Guegan.* 1825. 12mo, pp. 12. 51628

Myers (F.) Lectures on Great Men. By the late Frederic Myers, M.A. Second Edition. *London.* 1856. Post 8vo. c. + Third Edition. *London: James Nisbet and Co.* MDCCCLVII. Post 8vo, pp. xii, 472. 51629

Includes Christopher Columbus and Washington.

Myers (*Gen.*) Copy of General Myers' Affidavit. *London.* 1795. Folio. 51630

Respecting the conquest of the Island of Martinique.

Myers (J.) The Life, Voyages and Travels of Capt. John Myers, detailing his Adventures during Four Voyages round the World; his various Enterprises on the Coast of South America, and Exhibiting a most instructive Description of the North-West Trade. *London: Longman ...* . 1817. 8vo, pp. 410, (8). H.

Myers (J. C.) A Daily Journal of the 192d Regiment Pennsylvania Volunteers, commanded by Colonel William B. Thomas, in the Service of the United States for One Hundred Days. By John C. Myers. *Philadelphia: Crissy & Markley.* 1864. 12mo, pp. 203. Portrait. c. + [*Ibid.*] 1865 and 1866. 51632

Myers (L.) Abraham Lincoln. A Memorial Address ... by Hon. Leonard Myers, June 15th, 1865, before the Union League .... *Philadelphia: King & Baird.* 1865. 8vo, pp. 15.

Myers. Impeachment of the President. Speech of Hon. Leonard Myers, ... February 29, 1868. *Washington: F. & J. Rives, ... Printers.* 1868. 8vo, pp. 8. H. 51634

Also: League Island Navy-Yard. Speech ... June 7, 1866. [n. p. n. d.] 8vo, pp. 8.—Speech ... February 28th, 1865. Compensation to American Ship-Builders. Our Navy. Necessity for a Navy Yard for Iron Clads. *Philadelphia.* 1865. 8vo, pp. 8.—Speech ... March 24, 1866. The Responsibilities of Congress .... *Washington.* 1866. 8vo, pp. 16. H.

Myers (P. H.) The Emigrant Squire. By P. Hamilton Myers. *Philadelphia: T. B. Peterson.* 1853. 8vo, pp. 109. C.

Myers. The First of the Knickerbockers: a Tale of 1673. By P. Hamilton Myers. Second Edition. *New York: George P. Putnam.* 1849. 12mo, pp. 222. + [*Ibid.*] 1850. + *New York: Chapman & Co.* 1866. 12mo, pp. 119. 51636

Myers. The Prisoner of the Border. A Tale of 1838. By P. Hamilton Myers. *New York: Derby & Jackson.* 1857. 12mo, pp. viii, 378. 51637

[Myers.] The Young Patroon; or, Christmas in 1690. A Tale of New York. *New York: George P. Putnam.* 1849. 12mo, pp. (2), 142. C. 51638

Also: The King of the Hurons. ... [n. p.] 1849. 12mo.—Miser's Heir; or, the Young Millionaire. ... *Philadelphia.* 1854. 12mo. C.

Myers (S. A.) Self-Sacrifice, or the Pioneers of Fuegia. By Sarah Ann Myers. *Philadelphia: Presbyterian Board of Publication.* [1861.] 18mo, pp. 300. Portrait. C. 51639

Also "Hunters of the World," and other pieces.

[Myers (Theodorus Bailey).] Some Facts connected with the History of Professor Morse's Picture now in the Corcoran Gallery at Washington. *New York.* 1875. 12mo, pp. 12.

Mr. Myers edited "In Memoriam. Abraham Lincoln. Proceedings at the Athenæum Club. New York, April, 1865." *New York.* 1865. Folio, pp. 37. Portrait.

Myers-Mason (Theodorus Bailey). Naval Light Artillery Tactics, &c., adopted by the Department. By T. B. M. Mason, Lieut. U. S. N. ... *Washington.* 1876. 12mo, pp. 70. 51641

Also: Occasional Papers. "Two Lessons from the Future." ... [*Annapolis.*] 1876. 12mo, pp. 32.—The Preservation of Life at Sea. Read before the American Geographical Society. [n. p. n. d.] 12mo, pp. 38. + *New York.* 1879.

Myers (T.) A New and Comprehensive System of Modern Geography, ... comprising a Perspicuous Delineation of the Present State of the Globe, with its Inhabitants and Productions; ... By Thomas Myers, A.M. *London.* 1822. 2 vols., 4to. P.

Myers (V.) The Letters and Correspondence of Mrs. Virginia Myers, (which have never before been published or even read in Court,) to Dudley Marvin Hoyt, who was murdered at Richmond, Sept. 28th, 1846, by Wm. R. Myers, and two others. Together with a denial of the truth of Mrs. Myers' letter of explanation .... Likewise a short Biography of D. M. Hoyt, by a relative .... *Philadelphia, January* 1847. 8vo, pp. 63. 51643

Mygatt (F. T.) A Historical Notice of Joseph Mygatt, one of the Early Colonists of Cambridge, Mass., and afterward one of the First Settlers of Hartford, Conn.; with a Record of his Descendants. By Frederick T. Mygatt, ... of the Ninth Generation. *Brooklyn, N. Y.: Printed by the Harmonial Association.* 1853. 8vo, pp. 116. 51644

This book contains a well written sketch of Joseph Mygatt, the progenitor of all bearing the name in this country.

Myles (W.) A Chronological History of the People called Methodists, of the Connexion of the late Rev. John Wesley, from ... 1729 to 1802. By William Myles. Third Edition. *London: Jacques & Co.* 1803. 16mo, pp. xii, 357. + Fourth Edition. [*Ibid.*] 1813. C. 51645

Contains an account of Methodism in America.

Mylius (Abraham). *See* Milius (A.), No. 48982.

Mylius *or* Myle (Arnold van der). De Rebvs Hispanicis, Lvsitanicis, Aragonicis, Indicis et Aethiopicis. Damiani a Goes, Hieronymi Pauli, Hieronymi Blanci, Iacobi Tevij, opera. Partim ex manuscriptis nunc primum eruta, partim auctiora edita. ... *Coloniae Agrippinae, in Officina Birckmannica.* 1602. 16mo, pp. (24), 443. Portrait. C. 51646

Corrected title of our No. 27691, Vol. vii.

Mylius (C.) Beschreibung einer neuen Grönlandischen Thierpflanze. ... *London.* 1753. 4to. Plate. 51647

Myrand (D. P.) Mémoires sur le Canada. Études sur l'instruction publique chez les Canadiens Français; par M. Dominique Prosper Myrand. *Québec.* 1857. 8vo, pp. 24. 51648

Myrick (J.) Life of J. Myrick, executed 1755. *Philadelphia.* 1755. Sm. 4to. 51649

Myritius (J.) Opvscvlvm Geographicvm rarvm, totivs eivs negotii rationem, mira indvstria et brevitate complectens, iam recens ex diversorvm libris ac chartis, summa cura ac diligentia collectum & publicatum, per Ioannem Myritivm Melitensem, Ordinis Hospitalis Sancti Ioannis Hierosolymitani, Commendatorem Alemanni Monasterij, ac Domus Ratisponensis. *Ingoldstadii. Ex Officina Typographica Wolfgangi Ederi. Anno* MD.LXXXX. Folio. J.C.B., C. 51650

Collation: Title, Dedication, and Preface, 3 leaves, Text, pp. 136, Colophon, 1 page; 4 diagrams with moving figures, in the text. Preceding Part II., which begins at page 61, is a folded map.

The author was a Maltese by birth, but resided at Ratisbon as a commander of the order of St. John. He seems to have been one of the latest geographers who, in order to reconcile the new discoveries with the original theories, calls the northwestern portion of America, India Orientalis, and places no ocean between the continents of Asia and America. Chapters XX. and XXI. relate to the New World. At the end of the volume is a poem addressed to the author by Edmund Hollyng, M.D., an Englishman at Ingoldstadt. There are copies on large paper.

Myrthe (A. T.) Ambrosio de Letinez; or, the first Texian Novel. Embracing a Description of the Countries bordering on the Rio Bravo. By A. T. Myrthe. *New York.* 1842. 2 vols., 12mo. 51651

Myrtle (Minnie), *pseud.* *See* [Johnson (A. C.)], IX. 36183.

Myself: a Romance of New England Life. *Philadelphia: J. B. Lippincott & Co.* 1872. 12mo, pp. 488. 51652

The Mysteries and Miseries of Philadelphia; as exhibited and illustrated by a late presentment to the Grand Jury, and by a Sketch of the Condition of the most Degraded Classes in the City. *Philadelphia.* 1853. 8vo, pp. 20. 51653

Contains a fund of startling information and frightful facts.

Mysteries of California. *See* Vol. III., No. 10035.

Mysteries of Crime, as shown in remarkable Capital Trials. By a Member of the Massachusetts Bar. *Boston: Samuel Walker and Company.* 1870. 12mo, pp. 431, (1). 6 Plates. BA., C.

Mysteries of Greene Street. *New York.* [1867?] 18mo.

Some of the "mysteries" are revealed or invented in this *liber prohibitus.*

Mysteries of New York: and Eva Labree; or, The Rescued Chief. *London.* 1847. 18mo. 51656

Mysteries of Washington City, during ... the Session of the 28th Congress. By a Citizen of Ohio [Caleb Atwater]. *Washington, D. C.: Printed by G. A. Sage.* 1844. 16mo, pp. 218, (1).

Copyrighted by Caleb Atwater; from an examination I think he is the author. He speaks of this as the first of a series of three works on Washington City, the second "Humbugs of Washington City," the third "The Crimes of Washington City." I have seen only the "Mysteries."

The Mysterious Messenger. Founded on Fact. By A Member of the Georgia Conference. *Nashville, Tenn.: J. B. M'Ferrin.* 1860. 8vo, pp. 22. BA. 51658

The Mystery Finished. The Negro has a Soul. His Normal Relation is that of a Servant of Tribute to Shem and Japheth. The Negro is not a Citizen of the State, but a Member of the Church by Divine Appointment .... *Memphis.* 1868. 12mo, pp. 144. C. 51659

The Mystery Revealed; or, The Way of Peace. [*Richmond.* 186–.] 12mo, pp. 49. BA. 51660

Signed "A Lover of the Truth."

The Mystery Reveal'd; or, Truth brought to Light. Being a Discovery of some Facts, in Relation to the Conduct of the late M——y, which however Extraordinary they may appear, are yet supported by such Testimonies of Authentick Papers and Memoirs as neither Confidence, can, out-brave; nor Cunning invalidate. By a Patriot. Monstrum Horrendum! *London: W. Cater.* 1759. 8vo, pp. (2), 319. 51661

Very scarce. "The title conveys no adequate idea of the contents of this very interesting book. The first part is a statement of affairs, and an analysis of them, from the Peace of Utrecht, till some months after Braddock's Defeat. The second part contains the Original Documents or Vouchers for the Narratives. These comprise the memorials and letters that passed between the English and French officers in Canada and Nova Scotia, and other English colonies, especially on the Ohio, from 1751 to 1755, including the chief papers that fell into the hands of the French after the surrender of Fort Necessity, and Braddock's Defeat, such as Washington's Journal and Letters, Stobo's Letter to Washington, Braddock's Letters, etc., etc., some of which papers are re-translations from the French."—Stevens. For other editions, *see* "The Conduct of the late Ministry," Vol. IV., No. 15205, "Mémoire contenant le Précis des Faits," Vol. XI., No. 47511 *and* "A Memorial containing a Summary View," No. 47512. *See also* "Monthly Review," XVI. 468; XX. 379.

Manual of the Mystic Church, and Historical Sketch from its formation in 1713. *Boston.* 1860. 8vo, pp. 24. 51662

First Catalogue of the Mystic-Hall Seminary, ... West Medford, Mass. ... *Boston: Printed by John Wilson and Son.* 1857. 8vo, pp. 24. Plate. H. 51663

Mystic River. Application of John C. Tucker and others for a Charter for the Mystic River Railroad, to run from the Boston and Maine Railroad across Chelsea Bridge over the Flats to deep water. ... Phonographic Report by Dr. James W. Stone. *Boston.* 1851. 8vo. 51664

By-Laws of the Mystic River Works. ... 1853. *Boston: James French and Company.* 1853. 24mo, pp. 10. H. 51665

See also Vol. II., No. 6726, and Vol. XI., No. 46015, *add* 4 Maps.

The Mystic Star; A Monthly Magazine, Devoted to Freemasonry and its Literature. Rev. W. J. Chaplin, Rev. Jos. Billings, and Sol. D. Bayless, P. G. M., Editors. Vol. I. *Chicago.* 1864. 8vo. Continued. 51666

The Mystic Temple; Devoted to the Interests and Development of the Principles of Freemasonry. Vol. I. *New York.* 1868. 4to, pp. 90. 51667

No more published.

The Mystic Tie: or, Facts illustrative of Freemasonry. *Charleston, S. C.: Miller & Browne.* 1849. 12mo, pp. viii, 220.

The Mystical Craft, the most Crafty of all Crafts, and the most delusive of all delusions, as exemplified by our modern Mercuries, ... engaged in ... proselyting the World, and for hastening on the Glorious Millennium .... *New York: G. Vale.* 1844. 8vo.

Mythen und Sagen der Indianer America's. Deutsch von A. George. *Düsseldorf.* 1856. 4to. 51670

N. (E. D.) *See* N[eill] (E. D.)

N. (F. J.) Barnum's Baby Show; A Satire, Written with a view to prove the Wickedness and Immorality of that Ungracious Exposition of Humanity ... also showing that the ... degeneracy of the present Rulers of the Country ... prepare[s] the People to ... patronize Barnum's Climax of Folly and Iniquity. By F. J. N. *Boston: Damrell & Moore, Printers.* [n. d.] 12mo, pp. 12. B. 51671

N. (S. von). Mein Besuch Americas, im Sommer 1824. Ein Flug durch die Vereinigten Staaten .... Von S. v. N. *Aarau: Sauerländer.* 1827. 12mo. 51672

N. (J.) Indice de las Materias que comprende la Ley de Administracion de Justicia, publicada en 29. de Noviembre de 1858. Por J. N. *Mexico.* 1859. 8vo. 51673

[N. (J.)] A Letter on the Present State. *See* Vol. x. 40369.

N. (J.) The Liberty and Property. *See* Vol. x., No. 40937.

N. (J.) Observations upon Mr. Fauquier's Essay on Ways and Means for raising Money to support the present War .... By J. N. *London: Thomas Payne.* MDCCLVI. 8vo, pp. (4), 67.

Includes references to American topics.

[N. (J.)] Revolutionary Claims. [n. p. n. d.] 8vo, pp. 6.

N—— (J—— A.) *See* Vol. x., No. 41023.

N. (J. C.) Naauwkeurige Beschryving van Noord-America, door J. C. N. *Amsterdam: C. Groenwood.* 1783. 8vo. 51675

N. (J. H.) *See* N[agel] (J. H.)

N—— (K.) The History of Miss Katty N——. Containing a faithful and particular Relation of her Amours, Adventures, and various Turns of Fortune, in Scotland, ... Jamaica, and England. Written by Herself. *London: Noble.* [n. d.] 12mo.

See "Monthly Review," XVI. 178.

N*** (*M.*) Voyages aux Côtes de Guinée et en Amérique. Par Mr. N***. *Amsterdam: Etienne Roger.* MDCCXIX. 12mo, pp. 416. Frontispiece, Maps and 32 Plates. 51677

The plates are mostly illustrations of natural history. *See also* [Bourgeois (A. A.)]

N. (N.) America:|or|An exact Description|of the|West-Indies:|More especially of those|Provinces which are under|the Dominion of the|King of Spain.|Faithfully represented by N. N. Gent.| *London: ... Edw. Dod ....* 1655. Sm. 8vo, pp. (14), 484, (2). Map. C. 51678

Treats of the first discovery of America, by Columbus, and Americus Vesputius; with the adventures of Sir Francis Drake, Sir Thomas Cavendish, the Lord Admiral Clifford, and other Englishmen, and was "apparently written with the view of instigating the English to the conquest of the Spanish dominions in America."—Rich's *Catalogue*, No. 301. Ternaux quotes an edition, *London*, 1665.

N. (N.) Brief van NN. aan zijnen Vriend A. te Amsterdam betreffend de Verbetering van den West-Indischen Handel. *Amsterdam.* 1765. 8vo. 51679

Letter on the improvement of the West India traffic.

N. (N.) Cort verhael,|Vande ordre die sijne Co-|nincklicke Majesteyt van Spa-|gnien aen sijn Generalissimo den Graef de la Torre|inde Bay de todos los Sanctos gegeven heeft, om int|werck te stellen al 'tghene hy tot recuparatie van|Brasil noodigh achten soude.|Mitsgaders 't remarcabelste dat op de Custe van|deselve Capitania, soo int ghevecht vande Spaensche Vlote|sterck 87 zeylen, ende 41 Hollandtsche Schepen, als mede|by de gene die hy te Lande vande Bahia door de Bos-|schen in 't Lant gebracht hadde, voorgevallen is, van|den 19 November tot den 28 February 1640. toe.|Beschreven door den Eerw. N. N.| *Tot Amsterdam, by Ian van Hilten.*| [1640.] 4to, 8 leaves. 51680

Account of the order given by the King of Spain to Count de la Torre in the Bay of Todos los Santos, concerning the recapture of Brazil; and of what happened there between the Dutch and Spaniards. Corrected title of our No. 45404, Vol. XI. *See* Asher, No. 153.

N. (N.) Che la Platina Americana era un Metallo conosciuto dagli Antichi, Dissertazione .... *Bassano.* 1790. 8vo. 51681

[N. (N.)] The Examiner examin'd. *See* [Brown (J.)], 8505

N. (N.) Some Reflections on the Law of Bankruptcy, by N. N. *New Haven.* 1755. 4to, pp. 11. 51682

N. (S.) *See* N[owell] (S[amuel]).

Naamrol der Predikanten in de Gemeenten, de onveranderde Augsburgische Geloofsbelijdenisse toegedaan in de zeven vereenigden Nederlandschen Provintien, de Generaliteit, Portugal, America, Azia, enz. sedert 1518 tot heeden. *Amsterdam: Ch. v. Essen.* 1777. 4to. 51683

Naarder Reglement of het subject van de vrye Vart op de Kust van Africa. *s'Gravenhage.* 1734. 4to. 51684

Includes articles relative to Essequebo, Demerary, etc.

Naaukeurige versameling. *See* [Aa (P. v. d.)], Vol. I., No. 3.

Naauwkeurig|Verhaal|Van de zeer schrikkelykе|Aardbeving,|Voorgevallen op het Eyland|Jamaica,|In Westindien: Vervat in 2 Brieven van|den Predikant van Port Royal, geschreven den 2.|en 8. July 1692. op't schip de Granada leggende|in de Haven van Port Royal, alwaar de|Aardbeeving de grootste schade|heeft gedaan.|Uyt het Engelsch vertaald de 10 October 1692.|*'t Amsterdam,*|*By Johannes Broers ....* 1692. 4to, pp. 7. C. 51685

Relates to the earthquake in Jamaica, etc.

De naauwkeurige Hollandsche Almanach ... 1779. *Amsterdam: A. Meyer.* [1778.] 16mo. Plates. Continued. 51686

Contains a description of the British colonies in North America.

[Nabuco de Araujo (José Paulo de Figueiroa).] Dialogo constitucional brasileiro. Por J. P. F. N. A. *Rio de Janeiro: Typographia de P. Plancher-Seignot.* 1827. 8vo. + Segunda Edição, revista, augmentada e annotada com toda a legislação respectiva á practica da Constituição politica do imperio, e sanccionada até á sessão de 1827 .... *Rio de Janeiro: Typographia de R. Ogier.* 1829. 8vo, pp. viii, 294. Taboa. 51687

Also: Appendix ao Dialogo constitucional, contendo a demais legislação practica da Constituição, e a tabella geral chronologica de toda a obra. *Rio de Janeiro: Typographia de R. Ogier.* 1829. 8vo, pp. 95, 10.

Nabuco de Araujo. Legislação brasileira, ou Collecção chronologica das leis, decretos, resoluções, provisões, ... do imperio do Brasil, desde 1808 até 1831 inclusivé, contendo além do que se acha publicado nas melhores collecções, para mais de duas mil peças ineditas. ... *Rio de Janeiro: Typographia de J. Villeneuve & C.a* 1836-44. 7 vols., folio. 51688

Nach den gegenwärtigen Zuständen. *See* Vol. III. 11682.

Nachklang zum Gesäng der einsamen Turtel Taube/ Enthaltend eine neue Sammlung Geistlicher Lieder. *Ephrata Druck der Brüderschafft Im Jahr* 1755. 4to, pp. 112. P. 51689

A small volume of so much rarity that I have seen only this copy.

Nachricht von den neuesten Entdeckungen. *See* [Cook (J.)]

Nachricht von der Provinz Virginien; nebst einer geographischen Beschreibung der Provinz Pensylvanien. *Frankfurt.* 1772. 8vo. 51690

Title from Meusel, III. I. p. 390.

Nachricht von einer Hochteutschen ... Colonie. *See* No. 27160

Nachricht von Surinam und seine Einwohner sonderlich der Arawacken, Waranen und Karaïben. *Görlitz.* 1808. 8vo. Map and Plate. 51691

Eine Nachricht wegen ... Pennsilvania. *See* [Penn (W).]

Nachrichten aus der Brüder-Gemeinde. *Gnadau.* 1819. 8vo. Continued. 51692

Contains interesting notices and letters from the various missions of the Moravian Brethren in all parts of the world. The accounts from the American settlements are of especial value and very numerous.

Nachrichten und Erinnerungen an verschiedene deutsche Völker die von ihren Fürsten nach America geschickt worden sind. [n. p.] 1778. 12mo, pp. 16. J.C.B. 51693

Nachrichten von den ... Naturforschern. *See* Vol. II. 7607.

Nachrichten von den vereinigten deutschen Evangelisch-Lutherischen Gemeinen in Nord-Amerika, absonderlich in Pensylvanien. Mit einer Vorrede von Johann Ludewig Schulze. *Halle: Waisenhaus.* 1787. 2 vols., 4to, pp. 1518, (20). C. 51694

Continuation of the "Kurtze Nachricht von einigen Evangelischen Gemeinen in America, absonderlich in Pensylvanien." *Halle.* 1850. 4to.

Nachrichten von der Amerikanischen Halbinsel Californien. *See* [Begert (J.)], Vol. II., No. 4363, for collation say pp. (16), 358. Map and 2 Plates.

La Nacion. Periodico general é independiente. *Mejico.* 1856–1857. Folio. 51695

La Nacion. Periódico politico, cientifico y literario. *Mexico.* 1865–66. Folio. 51696

Las Naciones no pueden despojar á la Iglesia de sus bienes. *Mexico.* 1842. 4to, pp. 48. 51697

NACK (J.) Earl Rupert, and other Tales and Poems, By James Nack. With a Memoir of the Author by P. M. Wetmore. *New York: George Adlard.* 1839. 16mo, pp. xx, 220.

NACK. The Legend of the Rocks, and other Poems, By James Nack. ... *New York: E. Conrad.* 1827. 16mo, pp. (2), 204. 51699

NACK. Poems. By James Nack. With an Introduction by George P. Morris. *New York.* 1852. 12mo. 51700

"The Minstrel Boy" is autobiographical. Also: The Immortal; a ... Romance; and other Poems. ... With a Memoir of the Author by George P. Morris. *New York: Stringer & Townsend.* 1850. 16mo, pp. vi, 172.—An Ode on the Proclamation of President Jackson. ... *New York: Monson Bancroft.* MDCCCXXXIII. 8vo, pp. 23.—The Romance of the Ring, and other Poems. ... *New York: Delisser & Proctor.* 1859. 12mo, pp. (4), 282. Portrait. C.

Nacoochee Hydraulic Mining Company. ... [n. p. 1866?] 8vo, pp. 31, (1). Map and Plate. H. 51701

Contains an account of the gold-fields of Georgia and reports of the geologist and engineer, etc.

NADAL (B. H.) A Funeral Discourse on the Death of Rev. James Reid ... . June 23, 1850. By Rev. Bernard H. Nadal, A.M. *New-York: Joseph Longking, Printer.* 1851. 8vo, pp. 20.

NADAL. National Reconstruction. A Discourse ... at ... Washington, D. C. on the 1st day of June, 1865. By ... B. H. Nadal, D.D. *Washington, D. C.: Wm. H. Moore, Printer.* 1865. 8vo, pp. 15. 51703

Also: The War in the Light of Divine Providence. A Fast Day Sermon. ... *New Haven: Tuttle, Morehouse & Co.* 1863. 8vo, pp. 20.

NADAL DE SAINTRAC (Louis). Aux Haitiens. *Port au Prince.* [n. d.] Sm. 4to. 51704

Nader Aanteekening. *See* [Jones (Paul)], IX. 36563.

Nader Ordre, | ende Reglement, | Vande Hooghe Moghende Heeren Staten Generael der Vereenighde | Nederlanden, gearresteert by advijs ende deliberatie vande Bewint-hebberen vande Generale geoctroyeerde West-Indische | Compagnie, ter Vergaderinghe vande Negenthiene, waer nae alle ende een yder der Ingesetenen vande Geunieerde | Provintien, sullen vermogen te halen Hout, Tabacq, Cottoen, ende allerhande Waren ende

Koopman- | schappen, vallende in seeckere ghedeelte vande Limiten van 'tOctroy der voornoemde | Compagnie hier nae gheexprimeert. | [n. p. 1635.] Folio, 1 leaf. 51705

Order and regulation of the Netherland West India Company, relative to trade in tobacco, cotton, etc.

Nader Ordre | Ende Reglement vande Ho: | Mo: Heeren Staten Generael der Vereenighde | Nederlanden, ghearresteert by advijs ende deliberatie vande | Bewindt-hebberen vande Generale Gheoctroyeerde West- | Indische Compagnie, ter Vergaderinge vande Negenthiene, | waer na alle ende een yder der Ingesetenen vande Geunieer- | de Provintien, sullen vermoghen te halen Hout, Tabacq, | Cattoen, ende allerhande Waren ende Koopmanschappen, | vallende in seeckere gedeelte vande Limiten van 't Octroy der | voornoemde Compagnie hier nae geexprimeert. | *In 's Gravenhage,* | *By de Weduwe ende Erfgenamen van wijlen Hillebrandt Iacobssz* | *van Wouw ... . Anno* 1637. ... 4to, 3 leaves. 51706

Second order and regulation relative to commerce with Brazil. *See* Asher's "Bibliographical Essay," No. 163.

Nader Prolongatie van het Octroy voor de Westindische Compagnie, en van de eerste prolongatie van dien, voor den tyd van nog dertig jaaren. Gearresteert den 8 Augusty 1730. *In 's Gravenhage, By Jacobus Scheltus, Anno* 1730. 4to, pp. 20. + Gearresteert den 31 December 1761. *'sGravenhage, By Isaac Scheltus.* 1761. 4to, pp. 38. C. 51707

Further prolongation of the patent of the West India Company.

Nadere trouwhartige | Waarschouwinge, | tegen de Verleindüngen der | Herrnhuthers; | door den | Kerkenraad | van Amsterdam | voorgesteld, | Aan de Gemeente in die Stad, | En aan allen, die hunne zaligheit, naar Gods | Word, met vrezen en beven, in den | Heere Jesus Christus, zoeken. | *Herdrukt te Nieuw-Jork.* 1763. 4to, pp. vii, 56. P. 51708

Het Naderste ... Journalier Verhael. *See* Vol. II., No. 7608.

NADIR (W.) Almanac ... . By William Nadir [*i. e.* Dr. Douglass.] *Boston.* 1743. 12mo. 51709

Continued to 1747 or later.

Naerder Accoort | tusschen den | Koninck van Portugal | aen | D' Hoog: Mogende Heeren | Staten Generael | den 10 Augusty 1661. [n. p. n. d.] Sm. folio sheet. 51710

Further agreement between the King of Portugal and the States General. In French and Dutch. *See* Asher, No. 298.

Naerder | Aenwysin- | ghe | Der | Bewinthebbers Regieringe. | [n. p. 1622.] 4to, 6 leaves. 51711

Further account of the government of directors. *See* Asher, No. 88.

Naerder Bedenckingen. *See* [Usselincx (W.)]

Naerder Klagh-Vertoogh | Aende | Ho: Mo: Heeren Staten Generael, | Wegens | De Bewinthebberen vande Generale geoctro- | yeerde West-Indische Compagnie, ter sake vande onwettelijc- | ke, ende grouwelijcke proceduren der Engelsche in Nieu- | Nederlant, met versoeck van hulp, ende assistentie vande | macht van 't lant, tegens de selve. | ... | Nae de Copye, Anno 1664. 4to, pp. 8. 51712

This further address of complaint to the States General, on the part of the governors of the West India Company, respecting the unlawful and scandalous proceedings of the English in New Netherland, is "one of the most interesting pamphlets that has come down to us, in which the reciprocal position of the East and West India Companies are marked with great precision. It says, that the Dutch government, in which the directors of the East India Company fill the most important places, will feel thankful to England for having 'disembarrassed it of the rival company,'" etc. A complete English translation of the part relating to New Netherland may be found in Asher's "Bibliographical Essay," No. 341, pp. 210–213.

Naerdere Klagten | Van den Heer Resident | Carisius, | Omtrent de | Deensche Africaensche | Compagnie, | Die de Nederlandtsche | West-Indische Compagnie | Aldaer niet wilt gedoghen/ ende alle schade | aen doet. | *t'Heuckelom* [i. e. *Gravenhage*], *voor Adrianus Poortslot* 1660. 4to, pp. 8. 51713

Further complaints of the resident Carisius against the Danish African Company, which will not tolerate the Dutch West India Company. *See* Asher, No. 317.

N[AGEL] (J. H.) Suriname in losse tafereelen en schetsen door J. H. N. *Rotterdam: Locke.* 1840. 8vo. 51714

Surinam represented in loose pictures and sketches.

NAGEL (R.) Geschichtliche Entwickelung der Nord-Amerikanischen Union. Vorlesungen ... . Von Rudolf Nagel. *Leipzig: O. Wigand.* 1854. 8vo, pp. vi, 130. 51715

NAGERA (A. G. de). *See* Gonçalez de Nagera (A.), 27785.

NAGERA (P. de). *See* Castañeda de Nagera (P. de), Vol. III., No. 11379, and for 1840 *read* 1540.

NAGERA YANGUAS (D. de). Doctrina, | y | Enseñança | en la lengua Maçahua | de cosas muy utiles, y pro- | uechosas para los Ministros de Doctrina, | y para los naturales que hablan la | lengua Maçahua | + | Dirigido | Al illustrissimo señor | Don Francisco Manso, | y Çuniga, Arçobispo de Me- | xico, del Consejo de su

Magestad | y de el Real de las Indias. | Por el Licenciado Diego | De Nagera Yanguas, Beneficiado | del partido de Xocotitlan: Comissario del santo | Officio de la Inquisicion, y examinador | en la dicha lengua maçahua | Con licencia | *Impresso en Mexico por Juan Ruyz. Año de* 1637. Sm. 8vo, Title, and (4) leaves, Text, 177 leaves, and Table, (2) leaves. 51716

A book of such excessive rarity that even Señor J. G. Icazbalceta is only able to describe an imperfect copy. Pimentel, in his "Cuadro descriptivo y comparativo de las Lenguas Indigenas de Mexico," remarks: "Ha sido tan pobre de escritores el idioma mazahua que, segun creo, no se ha escrito sobre él mas que una doctrina, precedida de algunas breves notícias gramaticales, por el Lic. Diego de Nájera Yanguas. Esta obrita es tan ezcasa que no he logrado ver mas que un solo ejemplar, trunco, faltándlole una hoja de la parte mas importante, que son las noticias gramaticales. Despues de algunos años de poseer ese ejemplar, y habiendo perdido las esperanza de encontrar otro, me veo obligado à sacar de él las pocas notícias que pongo á Continuacion." Not included in Adelung's "Mithridates." Trübner prices a copy £25.

NAGLEE (H. M.) The Love Life of Brig. Gen. Henry M. Naglee, consisting of a Correspondence on Love, War and Politics [with Mary L. Schell. *San Francisco.*] 1857. 12mo, pp. 182. Portrait. B. + [*New York: Hilton & Co.*] 1867. 12mo, pp. 182. Portrait. C. 51717

NAGLEE. Report of Brig. Gen. Henry M. Naglee, Commanding First Brigade, Casey's Division, Army of the Potomac, of the part taken by his Brigade in the Battle of Seven Pines, May 31, 1862. With ... the Official Report of Gen. Casey. *Philadelphia: Collins, Printer.* 1862. 8vo, pp. 11. 51718

NAGLEE. Report of Henry M. Naglee, ... of the part taken by his Brigade ... from June 26 to July 2, 1862. Army of Potomac. *Philadelphia: Collins, Printer.* 1863. 8vo, pp. 15.

NAGLEE. Report of the Conduct of the Advance of the Column for the Relief of Little Washington, N. C., April 18th–19th, 1863. By Br. Gen. Henry M. Naglee. Also an Appendix consisting of Gen. Foster's Report of the Siege of the same place, from March 30 to April 18, 1863. *Philadelphia: Collins, Printer.* 1863. 8vo, pp. 16. 51720

Very rare. Also: A Chapter from the Secret History of the War. [Signed Henry M. Naglee. n. p. 1864.] 8vo, pp. 4.—Second Chapter from the Secret History of the War. [n. p. n. d.] 8vo, pp. 4.—Correspondence ... with the Mayor and Common Council of the City of Portsmouth. *Philadelphia: J. B. Lippincott & Co.* 1863. 8vo, pp. 20.—Letter to Wm. A. Atkinson, Esq. ... Dover. [n. p. n. d.] 8vo, pp. 4.—Report of ... [his] Command of the District of Virginia: with the Correspondence between Gen. Naglee and the Mayor and Common Council of the City of Portsmouth, referred to in the Report. *Philadelphia: J. B. Lippincott & Co.* 1863. 8vo, pp. 39.—... Two Letters of Gen. H. M. Naglee about Gen. McClellan. [n. p. 1862.] 8vo, pp. 8. B.

NAHANT, *Mass.* First Annual Report of ... the Receipts and Expenditures of the Town of Nahant, For ... 1854. *Lynn: E. Lawrence.* 1854. 8vo, pp. 8. Continued. B. 51721

First Annual Report of the School Committee of ... Nahant, for ... 1854. *Lynn: W. W. Kellogg, Printer.* 1854. 8vo, pp. 8. Continued. B. 51722

Letters from Nahant. *See* [Wheildon (W. W.)]

Nahant, and other Places. *See* [Homer (J. L.)], VIII. 32723.

Nahant, and What is to be Seen there. *Boston: Adams & Co.* 1866. 12mo, pp. 43. 51723

Nahant, or "The Floure of Souvenance." *Philadelphia.* 1827. 8vo, pp. 31. 51724

Things to be seen by the Sea at Nahant ... . *Boston: Press of John Wilson and Son.* 1862. 8vo, pp. 12. C. 51725

A Visit to Nahant ... . By a Lady. *New-York.* 1839. 18mo, pp. 196. + [*Ibid.*] 1846. C. 51726

NAHMEONITAH. Biography of Nahmeonitah, The Spirit of Peace and Silence, afterwards Mrs. M. N. Gardner, ... the wonderful Indian Doctress. *Boston: Weeks & Potter.* [1856?] 12mo, pp. 24. H. 51727

Nails Fastened. *See* [Mather (C.)], Vol. XI., No. 46424.

NAIRN (Thomas). Letter from South Carolina, giving an Account of that Province. ... *London.* 1710. 8vo. + [*Ibid.*] 1732

Title from Allibone's "Dictionary." *See* South Carolina.

NAIRNE (C. M.) ... A Lecture ... before the Young Men's Association for Mutual Improvement in ... Albany, ... March 10, 1848. By Charles Murray Nairne, M.A. ... *Albany: E. H. Pease & Co.* 1848. 8vo, pp. 54. H. 51729

[NAISH (William).] The Negro Slave. A Tale. Addressed to the Women of Great Britain. *London: Harvey & Darton.* 1830. 12mo, pp. 80. 51730

[NAISH.] Reasons for using East India Sugar. *London: Howlett and Brimmer.* 1828. 12mo. 51731

Repeatedly reprinted.

[NAISH.] Sketches from the History of Pennsylvania, &c. intended for the information of that numerous class of Christians who denounce War in general as a great evil; but who consider Defensive War as allowable and unavoidable. *London: Charles Gilpin.* 1845. 12mo, pp. 36. 51732

[NAISH.] The Slave Taker, &c; or, an Appeal to all who in any way promote the Traffic in ... their Fellow-creatures. *London.* 1828. 12mo, pp. 8. 51733

Also: A Brief Description of the Toil and Sufferings of Slaves in the British Sugar Colonies, at the present time, by several Eye-Witnesses. ... [*London.* n. d.] 12mo, pp. 16.—The Negro's Friend; consisting of Anecdotes, designed to exemplify the moral, intellectual, and religious attainments of the African Race, and the cruelties and oppressions to which they have been subjected by Europeans. ... Second Edition. [*London:*] *Harvey & Darton.* [n. d.] 12mo.—Scripture Evidence ... in behalf of the much-injured Africans. *London: Harvey & Darton.* 1828. 12mo, pp. 28.—A Short History of the Poor Black Slaves who are employed in cultivating Sugar, Cotton, Coffee, &c. [*London.* n. d.] 12mo, pp. 12. For a long list of this author's pamphlets, *see* Smith's "Catalogue of Friends' Books," pp. 210–14.

NÁJERA (E.) Observations critiques sur le chapitre XIII. du dernier volume de l'ouvrage intitulé: "Exploration du territoire de l'Orégon, des Californies, et de la mer Vermeille exécutée pendant les années 1840, 1841 et 1842, par M. Duflot de Mofras, attaché à légation de France à Mexico." Par le Père Emmanuel Nájera, Mexicain. *Mexico.* 1845. 8vo, pp. 16. 51734

Nakcokv Setempohetv. *See* Vol. V., No. 17461.

NAKSKOW (P. S.) The | Articles of Faith, | of | The Holy Evangelical Church, | According to | The Word of God, | and | the Augsburg Confession. | Set forth in | Forty Sermons. | By Magist. Petrus Sachariæ Nakskow, ... | Translated from the Original into English, | By Jochum Melchior Magens. *New York: J. Parker and W. Weyman.* MDCCLIV. 4to, pp. (2), ii, ii, (2), 314; The Confession, MDCCLV, pp. 30, (1). 51735

Dedicated "To the Honourable Vestry of the Evangelical Church in New-York." An excessively rare volume, with a translation of the Augsburg Confession at the end.

Naleganta Jesusil Kristusim. *See* Vol. VI., No. 22861.

Nalegapta Jesusib Kristusib Piulijipta Pinniarningit Anialervinga Nellintingmet okantsinnik Tussarnertunnik Aglengniartut sittamaet Katissimavut attantsimut. *Barbine.* 1800. Sm. 8vo.

A rare piece in the Esquimaux language. *See also* Vol. VI., No. 22872.

NALL (R.) A Voice from Twenty Graves: A Sermon, ... December 4th, 1853, By Robert Nall, ... Mobile. ... *Mobile: Dade, Thompson & Co., Printers.* 1854. 8vo, pp. 31. 51737

Names of Addressers to the late Gov. Hutchinson and Protesters against the Solemn League and Covenant ... . [n. p. n. d.] Folio, 1 leaf. 51738

Names of Battles to be placed on Colors. General Orders, No. 20, of the Army of the Potomac, directing the names of the Battles, which the Regiments named may inscribe upon their colors or guidons for meritorious services performed by them. March 7, 1865. [n. p. n. d.] 12mo, pp. 26. 51739

Names of Persons for whom Marriage Licenses were issued by the Secretary of the Province of New York, previous to 1784. ... *Albany: Weed, Parsons & Co., Printers.* 1860. 8vo, pp. ix, 480. B., S. 51740

Names of Persons who have died in New York of the Yellow Fever, ... 1795. [n. p. n. d.] 8vo, pp. 26. 51741

Names of Persons who took the Oath of Allegiance to the State of Pennsylvania between the Years 1777 and 1789, with a History of the "Test Laws" of Pennsylvania. By Thompson Westcott. *Philadelphia: John Campbell.* 1865. 8vo, pp. xlii, 145

Some copies were printed in quarto and folio.

Names of Petty Officers and Seamen in the United States Naval Service to whom Medals have been awarded, who have distinguished themselves by their gallantry in action, or by extraordinary heroism. Navy Department, December 31, 1864. General Order No. 45. [n. p. n. d.] 12mo, pp. 18. 51743

Names of Subscribers. *See* Vol. III., No. 9179.

Names of Voters in Fayette Co., Ky., 1822. [n. p. 1822.] 8vo. 51744

A doubtful title from an auctioneer's catalogue.

Names of the Officers. *See* Vol. VII., No. 27238.

Names of the Officers and Members of the Union League of Philadelphia, 1866. *Philadelphia.* 1866. 8vo, pp. 29. 51745

The Names of the Proprietors of the Unclaimed Dividends of the South Sea Company. [n. p. *to* 1780.] 8vo, pp. 186.

NANCREDE (J. G.) An Address delivered before the New England Society of Philadelphia, May 1, 1820. By Joseph G. Nancrede, M.D. *Philadelphia.* 1820. 8vo, pp. 35. 51747

Nancy Blake Letters to a Western Cousin. *New York: John Bradburn.* 1864. 8vo, pp. 36. H. 51748

Perhaps by Ruth N. Cromwell.

NANTASKET. *See* [Lincoln (S.)], Vol. x., No. 41266.

NANTES (Bernardo de). Katecismo Indico da Lingua Kariris, accrescentado de varias Practicas Doutrinaes e Moraes, adaptadas ao genio e capacidade dos Indios do Brazil. *Lisboa, por Valentim da Costa Deslandes.* 1709. 8vo, pp. xxiv, 363. 51749

Very rare. Langles' copy sold in 1825 for 40 fr. Priced by B. Quaritch, whose books are always dear, in 1866, £4, 14s. 6d. *See* Silva, I. 382.

NANTES (M. de). Relation|succinte|et|sincère|de la mission du Père Martin|de Nantes, prédicateur|ca|pucin, missionnaire apostoli|que dans le Brezil parmy les|Indiens appellés Cariris.| *A Quimper,|chés Jean Perier, imprimeur|du Roy, du Clergé et du College.*| Sm. 12mo, pp. (16), 233, (3). 51750

A volume of extreme rarity, and important for the history of Brazil. Improved title of our No. 44906, Vol. XI.

NANTICOKE INDIANS. *See* Maryland, XI. 45343.

NANTUCKET, *Mass.* Catalogue of the Library of the Nantucket Athenæum. *Nantucket.* 1835. 12mo. + [*Ibid.*] 1841. 8vo. 51751

Copy of a Relation, or Substance of the Pleas made Use of by two Parties Claiming a Right in Half a Share of Land on the Island of Nantucket. [n. p.] 1770. 4to. W. 51752

Papers relating to ... Nantucket. *See* Hough (F. B.), VIII.

Report of ... Teachers, appointed by the School Committee of Nantucket, to consider the Subject of systematizing a Course of Studies ... . *Nantucket: Printed by Authority of the School Committee.* 1855. 8vo, pp. 16, folded leaf. H. 51753

Also: Report of the School Committee of Nantucket, ... February, 1857. [n. p. n. d.] 8vo, pp. 4.—Rules and Regulations of the Public Schools of ... Nantucket. ... 1857. *Nantucket.* 1857. 8vo, pp. 12. H.

Report on a Light House off Nantucket. *Washington.* 1852. 8vo. P. 51754

Seaweeds from ... Nantucket. *See* [Starbuck (L. C.)]

Transactions of the Nantucket Agricultural Society, for 1856. ... *New York: John F. Trow, Printer.* 1857. 8vo, pp. 96. Continued. H. 51755

See also [Hopkins (S.)], Vol. VIII., No. 32964.

NAPHEGYI (Gabor). The Album of Language. Illustrated by The Lord's Prayer in One Hundred Languages ... . By G. Naphegyi, M.D. A.M. ... *Philadelphia: J. B. Lippincott & Co.* 1869. 4to, pp. 323, (1). Colored Plate, and Vignettes. B.

Some of these are American Indian languages. Also: The Grand Review of the Dead. Written for the ... Decorating of the Soldier's Graves, May 30th, 1869 ... . *New York: The Author.* 1869. 8vo, pp. 23. H.

NAPIER (C. J.) Colonization; ... with some remarks on Small Farms and Over Population. By Colonel Charles James Napier ... . *London: T. & W. Boone.* 1835. 8vo, pp. xxxii, 268.

[NAPIONE DE COCCONATO (Gian Francesco Galeani).] Della patria di Cristoforo Colombo Dissertazione pubblicata nelle Memorie dell' Academia imperiale dell scienze di Torino Ristampata con giunte, documenti, lettere diverse ed una dissertazione epistolare intorno all' autor del libro de Imitatione Christi. ... *Firenze Presso Molini, Landi e Comp.* MDCCCVIII. 8vo, pp. xxi, (3), 400, (2). Portrait of Columbus, and folded leaf. A. 51758

There are copies on thick and blue paper. *See* "Edinburgh Review," XXVII. 492, where a translation of Columbus's first letter is given.

[NAPIONE.] Del Primo Scopritore del continente del Nuovo Mondo e dei più antichi storici che ne scrissero ragionamento che serve di supplemento alle due lettere su la scoperta del nuovo mondo pubblicate nel libro intitolato Della patria di Cristoforo Colombo stampato in Firenze nell' anno MDCCCVIII. *Firenze Presso Molini, Landi e Comp.* MDCCCIX. 8vo, pp. x, (1), 115. S.

This and the following are supplementary to the foregoing.

[NAPIONE.] Esame Critico del primo viaggio Di Amerigo Vespucci al Nuovo Mondo ... . Opuscoli pubblicati nelle Memorie dell' Accademia Imperiale dell scienze di Torino e ristampato per servire di nuove aggiunte al contenuto nel libro intitolato Della Patria di Colombo stampato in Firenze nell' anno MDCCCVIII. ... *Firenze Presso Molini, Landi e Compagno* MDCCCXI. 8vo, pp. xxiv, (4), 146. A., C. 51760

One hundred and fifty copies only printed. Extracted from No. 51758, *supra.* This elicited, "Osservazione sul ragionamiento del primo'scopritore." *Firenze.* 1809. 8vo.

NAPIONE. Patria e biografia Del Grande Ammiraglio D. Cristoforo Colombo de' Conti e Signori di Cuccaro castello della Liguria nel Monferrato Scopritor dell' America Rischiarita e comprovata dai celebri scrittori Gio. Francesco Conte Napione di Coconato e Vincenzo de- Conti ... coll' aggiunta di nuovi documenti e schiarimenti di Mons.r Luigi Colombo *Roma: Tipografia*

forense. 1853. 8vo, pp. x, 456, (1). Geneal. Table and Portrait of Columbus. 51761

[NAPIONE.] Discorso intorno ad alcune regole principali dell' arte critica relativament alle due dissertazioni della patria di Cristoforo Colombo publicate ne' volumi dell' Academia Reale della scienze de Torini *Torini coi tipi Allianci* MDCCCXXIV. 8vo, pp. 60. 51762

NAPOLEON I. Manifestacion communicada por el Emperador de los Franceses a sus emissarios a intentar la subversion de las Americas. *Puebla.* 18—. 4to. 51763

NAPOLEON III. Canal of Nicaragua, or a Project to connect the Atlantic and Pacific by a Canal, By N. L. B. *Privately Printed.* 1846. 8vo. 51764

Written while the author was a prisoner in Ham, and printed soon after his arrival in England as a refugee.

NAPOLEON. El Emperador Napoleon III. y la Inglaterra. *Mexico.* 1858. 8vo. 51765

NARAMORE (G. H.) Poems. By Gay H. Naramore. *Cambridge: Riverside Press.* 1865. 16mo, pp. 104. 51766

NARANJO (J.) Analisis que ofrece á este público D. José Naranjo, Alcaide de la Cárcel, de su conducta vulnerada. *Habana: Imprenta de D. Antonio Gil.* 1812. 4to, pp. 32. 51767

NARANJO (Pedro). Venezuela y España. ... *Carácas.* 1860. 8vo, pp. 22. 51768

NARBOROUGH (*Sir* John). *See* [Robinson (Tancred)], *Editor.*

Narcokv Esyvhiketv. *See* Muskogee, No. 51589.

NARDI (F.) Visita dell' Imperatore e Imperatrice del Messico al S. Padre. Narrata da M. F. Nardi. *Roma.* 1864. 4to, pp. 22. 51769

NARES (E.) Memoirs of the Life and Administration of the Right Honourable William Cecil, Lord Burghley, ... containing an Historical View of the times in which he lived, and of the many eminent and illustrious persons with whom he was connected; with extracts from his private and official correspondence, and other papers, now first published from the originals. By the Rev. Edward Nares, D.D. ... *London: Saunders and Otley.*

MDCCCXXVIII–XXXI. 3 vols., 4to, pp. xxxvi, 792; x, 632; xii, 518, (2). 3 Portraits and Facsimile. A., B. 51770

In Chap. XIII. (1586) of the third volume, pp. 261 and 262, Francis Drake's voyage "to attack the Spanish possessions in America and the West Indies," is mentioned. Vols. II. and III. have the imprint, *Colburn and Bentley.*

Narracion. *See* Lima, Vol. XI., No. 41120.

The Narraganset Chief; or, the Adventures of a Wanderer. Written by Himself. *New York: J. K. Porter.* 1832. 12mo, pp. 195. 51771

Purports to be a veritable narration of incidents in the life of an Indian.

Minutes of the First Annual Meeting of the Narragansett Association, held with the Second Baptist Church in Hopkinton, R. I., Oct. 2 and 3, 1860. *Westerly: Starr & Farnham, Printers.* 1860. 8vo, pp. 22. Continued. 51772

Publications of the Narragansett Club. (First Series.) ... *Providence, R. I.* MDCCCLXVI–LXXIV. 6 vols., 4to. BA. 51773

Twenty-five copies printed on large paper, excepting Vol. VI., of which one hundred and fifty copies were struck off. The series embraces the following works:

I. Bibliographical Introduction to the Writings of Roger Williams. By Reuben Aldridge Guild, A.M. A Key into the Language of America. Edited by James Hammond Trumbull, A.M. Letter of John Cotton. Mr. Cotton's Letter Examined and Answered. Edited by Reuben Aldridge Guild, A.M. MDCCCLXVI. pp. vi, (2), 60, 219, (3), 112. II. John Cotton's Answer to Roger Williams. Edited by Rev. J. Lewis Diman. Queries of Highest Consideration. Edited by Reuben Aldridge Guild, A.M. MDCCCLXVII. pp. (12), 240, 36. III. The Bloudy Tenent of Persecution. Edited by Samuel L. Caldwell. MDCCCLXVII. pp. (4), xiv, 425, (3). IV. The Bloody Tenent yet more Bloody. Edited by Samuel L. Caldwell. MDCCCLXX. pp. (4), ix, 547, (1). V. George Fox Digg'd out of his Burrowes. Edited by Rev. J. Lewis Diman. MDCCCLXXII. pp. (6), lviii, (10), 503. VI. Letters of Roger Williams, 1632 to 1682. Now first collected. Edited by John Russell Bartlett. MDCCCLXXIV. pp. xviii, (2), 420.

NARRAGANSETT INDIANS A|Declaration of Former|Passages and Proceedings betwixt the English|and the Narrowgansets, with their confederates, Wherin|the grounds and iustice of the ensuing warre are opened|and cleared.|Published, by order of the Commissioners for the united Colonies:|At Boston the 11 of the sixth month|1645. [*Cambridge: Stephen Daye.* 1645.] 4to, pp. 7. 51774

One of the earliest productions of the Cambridge press; the third, in order of time, of which any copy is extant—preceded only by the Bay Psalm Book and the list of theses at the commencement of Harvard College, in 1643. This Declaration of War against the Narragansets is subscribed by "Jo: Winthrop President, In the name of all the Commissioners," etc. Hutchinson, who printed it, in his "Collection of Papers" (138–146) from a manuscript copy, had "never met with it in print." It was again printed, from the MS. Records of the Commissioners (with many errors), in Hazard's "Collection," II. 45–48. The following entry, in an "Account of Expenses layd out

for the County," Aug. 1645 to Oct. 1646 ("Mass. Archives," XXX. doc. 9), shows the number of copies printed: "First, for ye printing of five hundred Declarations, 4*l.* 00. 00." Of the five hundred, Mr. Brinley's was the only known copy, and that sold for $215. Corrected title of our No. 45706, Vol. XI.

NARRAGANSETT, *pseudon.* *See* Vol. VI., No. 23623.

Narratio Historica, 1650. *See* [Raguenau (Paul)].

Narration of the Practices of the Churches in New England, in their Solemne Worship of God, written by one that desired information therein, by an Inhabitant there. *London.* 1645. 4to.

Title from an English catalogue. Another gives the date 1647.

Narrative and Correspondence. *See* [Duane (W.)], v. 21001.

Narrative and Defence of Proceedings of the Methodist Episcopal Church in Baltimore against certain Local Preachers. *Baltimore.* 1842. 8vo. 51776

Narrative and Discoveries, including the Discovery of a Nation of Welshmen in the Interior of America. *London.* 1817. 8vo.

Narrative and Writings of Andrew Jackson, of Kentucky; containing an account of his Birth, and Twenty-Six Years of his Life while a Slave; his Escape; Five Years of Freedom, together with Anecdotes relating to Slavery, Journal ... Sketches, etc. Narrated by Himself; Written by a Friend. *Syracuse.* 1847. 12mo, pp. 120. B., S. 51778

Narrative concerning the Promises Made to Officers of the Continental Army for Services in the Revolutionary War. *Elizabethtown, N. J.* 1826. 8vo. 51779

Narrative of a late Expedition. *See* Knight, Vol. IX. 38189.

A Narrative of a New ... Imprisonment. *See* Makemie (F.), XI. 44079–80, and add to No. 44079, *London, Reprinted.* 1708.

Narrative of a Private Soldier in the 92d Regiment. Written by Himself. *Philadelphia.* 1822. 16mo. 51781

A Narrative of a Tour. *See* Vol. XII., No. 50023.

Narrative of A Voyage to the Spanish Main, in the Ship "Two Friends;" The occupation of Amelia Island, by M'Gregor, &c. —Sketches of the Province of East Florida; and Anecdotes illustrative of the Habits and Manners of the Seminole Indians: with an Appendix, containing a Detail of the Seminole War, and

the Execution of Arbuthnot and Ambrister. ... *London: John Miller.* 1819. 8vo, pp. ix, (7), 328. A., B., H. 51782

Most of the volume is devoted to the Seminole Indians; the barbarous character of the war of the Americans with them; and anecdotes respecting the Seminoles. Dr. Brinton calls this a rare book—he is mistaken. *See* Rafter (M.)

A Narrative of Affairs. *See* Vol. VIII., No. 35633.

Narrative of an African Prince. Written by Himself. *Newport.* 1774. 8vo, pp. 48. 51783

Narrative of an Attempt to reach the North Pole, in boats attached to his Majesty's Ship Hecla, in the Year 1827, under the Command of Captain William Edward Parry, R. N. *London.* 1828. 8vo. Plates. 51784

Narrative of an Expedition of Five Americans into a Country of Wild Animals. *London: J. Blackwood.* 1853. 12mo, pp. 120

Narrative of certain Events. *See* Vol. IX., No. 35634.

Narrative of Certain Occurrences at the late Special Convention of the Diocese of New-York. *New-York: John R. Winser, Printer.* 1851. 8vo, pp. 13. S. 51786

Relates to the election of a provincial bishop. Signed "T. H. Taylor," etc.

Narrative of Discovery and Adventure in the Polar Seas and Regions; ... Second Edition Enlarged. *Edinburgh: Oliver & Boyd.* MDCCCXXXI. Post 8vo, pp. 468. 51787

A Narrative of Events which occurred in Baltimore Town during the Revolutionary War. To which are appended, various Documents and Letters, the greater part of which have never been heretofore published. *Baltimore: Printed by Jos. Robinson.* 1849. 12mo, pp. 231. 51788

Narrative of Facts and Circumstances that have tended to produce a Secession from the Society of Friends, in New-England Yearly Meeting. *Providence: Printed by Knowles and Vose.* 1845. 8vo, pp. 43. + To which is added, A Declaration of New-England Yearly Meeting of Friends, upon various ... Doctrines ... . *London: Charles Gilpin.* 1845. 8vo, pp. 76. 51789

It elicited: "Notes on a work entitled, 'A Narrative of Facts,' ... With Observations on the Separation in Swanzey Monthly Meeting: ... Also, Remarks on a Letter from Joseph John Gurney." *London: Simpkin, Marshall & Co.* 1848. 12mo, pp. 36. + "Strictures on a Pamphlet purporting to be a 'Narrative of Facts and Circumstances,'" ... [n. p. n. d.] 8vo, pp. 13. H.

A Narrative of Five Youth from the Sandwich Islands, now receiving an Education in this Country ... *New York.* 1816. 8vo, pp. 44. S. 51790

A Narrative of Occurrences. *See* [Douglas (T.)], v. 20699.

In J. R. Smith's catalogue of Americana, this is attributed to Simon McGillivray.

Narrative of Privations and Sufferings of United States Officers and Soldiers while Prisoners of War in the Hands of the Rebel Authorities. Being the Report of a Commission of Inquiry, Appointed by the United States Sanitary Commission. With an Appendix containing the Testimony. *U. S. Sanitary Commission, by King & Baird, Prs. Philad'a.* 1864. 8vo, pp. 283. 4 Plates and Map. B. + *Boston: Office of "Littell's Living Age."* [1864.] 8vo, pp. 86, (1). 4 Plates. + [*Ibid.*] 1864. 5 Plates. + *London: Alfred William Bennett.* 1865. 16mo, pp. 52. 4 Plates. B. 51791

Narrative of Recent Occurrences in the Eastern Subordinate Synod of the Reformed Presbyterian Church. *New York.* 1834. 8vo. 51792

Narrative of recent Proceedings of the Committee, appointed by the Yearly Meeting of Friends of New York, in relation to the Indians in that State. Published for the Information of Friends. *New York: Mercein & Post's Press.* 1839. 8vo, pp. 23, (1). N. 51793

A Narrative of some of the Adventures, Dangers and Sufferings of a Revolutionary Soldier; interspersed with Anecdotes of Incidents that occurred within his Own Observation. Written by Himself. *Hallowell: Printed by Glazier, Masters & Co.* 1830. 12mo, pp. 213. C. 51794

Perhaps by James Sullivan Martin.

Narrative of some ... Occurrences. *See* [Hurlbut (H. A.)]

Narrative of the Adventures of an American Navy Officer, who served during part of the American Revolution under the command of Com. John Paul Jones, Esq. ... *New-York: Printed for the Author.* 1806. 12mo, pp. 270. 51795

This is a corrected title of our No. 23783, Vol. VI.

Narrative of the Barbarous Treatment experienced by American Prisoners in England and the West Indies. *Danville.* 1816. 12mo. P. 51796

Narrative of the Barbarous Treatment. *See* [Harrington (*Miss*)]

Narrative of the Battle of Bladensburg. *See* Vol. II. 5710.

Narrative of the Campaign. *See* [Gleig (G. R.)], VII. 27568–9

Narrative of the Canadian Rebellion. *See* Vol. III. 10527.

Narrative of the Capture, Arrival and Examination of Sixteen Pirates, Taken on the Coast of Africa; with Captain Butman's account of the Robbery and Piracy on board the Mexican. Also, a Description of Don Pedro Hibbert, Commander ... and Antonio Farrer, the Tattoed Guinea Boy. [n. p. 1833.] 8vo, pp. 8.

The "Mexican" was an American vessel, and set sail from Salem, Mass., bound for Rio Janeiro.

A Narrative Of the Capture Of certain Americans at Westmoreland, By Savages; And the perilous Escape which they effected, by surprizing Specimens of Policy and Heroism. To which is subjoined, Some Account of the Religion, Government, Customs, and Manners of the Aborigines of North-America. *New-London: Printed by T. Green.* 1784. 8vo, pp. 16. M.

A Narrative of the Celebrated Dyde Supper. By the Editor and Proprietor of the New-York Morning Post and Morning Star. *New York: Printed for the Author.* 1811. 8vo, pp. (6), 61.

Descriptive of a political squabble between Aaron Burr and DeWitt Clinton, in which the friends of Aaron Burr made an unsuccessful attempt to bring him again before the public as a political leader. Corrected title of our No. 21577, Vol. VI.

Narrative of the Claim and Title of Samuel Allen to New Hampshire. *Boston.* 1728. 4to, pp. 13. M. 51800

Narrative of the Conduct of Members of the Legislature of Pennsylvania, on the Election of a Senator. *Philadelphia.* 1807. 8vo. C., P. 51801

Narrative of the Cruise. *See* Vol. I., No. 577.

Narrative of the Cultivating the Clove Tree in Dominica, one of the Caribbee Islands. *London.* 1797. 8vo. 51802

Narrative of the Deportation. *See* Vol. III., No. 11621.

A Narrative of the Difficulties. *See* Vol. II., No. 8306.

Narrative ... of the Division among the Members of the Associate Body in the United States: By a Ruling Elder. *Philadelphia.* 1789. 8vo. S. 51803

A Narrative of the Dispute. *See* Taylor (John).

A Narrative of the Early Days ... of Oceola. *See* Oceola.

A Narrative of the Excursion and Ravages of the King's Troops, Under the Command of General Gage, On the nineteenth of April, 1775, Together with the Depositions Taken by Order of Congress, To support the Truth of it. Published by Authority. ... *Worcester: Printed by Isaiah Thomas.* [1775.] 8vo, pp. 23. H., W. 51804

Thomas says "The first book printed in Worcester." Very scarce. Corrected title of our No. 26318, Vol. VII. Another edition, with Gage's Protestation, *Boston*, 1779. 8vo. *See also* Massachusetts Historical "Collections," XIV. 204-19.

A Narrative of The Expedition to, and the Storming of Buenos Ayres, by the British Army, Commanded by Lieutenant-General Whitelocke, by an Officer ... . *Bath: Printed by William Meyler.* 1807. 8vo, pp. 33. Plate. 51805

A corrected title of our No. 9026, Vol. II.

Narrative of the Expedition of the Marquis de Nonville against the Senecas in 1687. Translated from the French with Notes by Orsamus H. Marshall. *New York.* 1848. 8vo, pp. 48. Map. 51806

A Narrative of the Facts. *See* [Morgan (W.)], XII. 50684.

Narrative of the Fall ... Campaign. *See* [McClenthen (C. S.)]

Narrative of the General Course of History, from the Earliest Periods to the Establishment of the American Constitution. ... *New York: Harper & Brothers.* 1857. Sq. 12mo, pp. 450. 150 Maps and Plates. 51807

Narrative of the Grand ... Demonstration. *See* No. 50024.

A Narrative of the Great Success God had been pleased to give his Highness Forces in Jamaica, against the King of Spain's Forces ... as it was communicated in a Letter from the Governor of Jamaica. *London: Henry Hills.* 1658. 4to, pp. 6. J.C.B.

A Narrative of the Horrid Massacre by the Indians, of the Wife and Children of the Christian Hermit, a resident of Missouri, with a full Account of his Life and Sufferings, never before published. ... *St. Louis: Leander W. Whiting & Co.* 1840. 8vo, pp. 24. 51809

A Narrative of the Indian and Civil Wars in Virginia, In the Years 1675 and 1676. Published from the original manuscript, ... *Boston: Printed by John Eliot.* 1814. 8vo, pp. 47. B. 51810

Reprinted in Force's "Tracts and other Papers," Vol. I., No. 2.

A Narrative of the late Awful and Calamitous Earthquake in the West India Islands of Antigua, Montserrat, Nevis, St. Christopher, Guadalupe, etc., on Feb. 8, 1843. Written by an Eye Witness. *London.* 1843. 8vo, pp. 32. 51811

Narrative of the Late Massacres. *See* [Franklin (B.)], 25557

A Narrative of the Late Revivals ... within the Bounds of Geneva Presbytery. ... *Geneva: Printed by J. C. Merrell & Co.* 1832. 8vo, pp. 30, (1). H. 51812

Narrative of the late Riotous Proceedings. *See* Vol. IV. 13098

Narrative of the Loss of the Ship Hercules commanded by Capt. Benj. Stout on the Coast of Caffraria, the 16th June, 1796; ... With an Introductory Address to the Right Hon. John Adams, President of the Continental Congress ... . *New York: James Chevalier.* 1797. Sm. 8vo, pp. liii, 113. + [*Ibid.*] 179-. + *London, Printed: New Bedford, Re-printed by Abraham Shearman, Jun.* 1800. 12mo, pp. 124. H. 51813

Narrative of the Loss of the Steam Packet Home, Carleton White, Master, on a voyage from New York to Charleston, with affidavits disproving the Charge of Misconduct against the Master. *New York.* 1838. 8vo, pp. 36. 51814

Narrative of the Loss of the Wager, Man of War. *Dublin.* 1822. 18mo. 51815

A Narrative of the Manner. *See* St. Clair (A.)

Narrative of the Martyrdom. *See* Boston, II. 6532.

Narrative of the Massacre. *See* [Kinzie (*Mrs.* J. H.)]

Narrative of the Measures. *See* Vol. III., No. 8945.

A Narrative of the Miseries. *See* [Mather (I.)], XI. 46708-9.

Narrative of the Missions. *See* Vol. IV., No. 15807.

Narrative of the Modes and Measures pursued at the Anniversary Election, for Representatives, of the Freemen of the Province of Pennsylvania, held at Newtown, in and for the

County of Bucks, on Monday the first Day of October, ... 1770. By a Bucks County Man. ... *Philadelphia: Printed by William Goddard* ... . 1771. 8vo, pp. 7. P. 51816

Narrative of the Mutiny on board the Ship Globe of Nantucket in the Pacific Ocean, January, 1824. *New London.* 1828. 12mo. 51817

Narrative of the Negotiations Occasioned by the Dispute between England and Spain, in ... 1790. [*London.* 1791.] 8vo, pp. vii, 307. 51818

Relative to Nootka Sound, and the title to the north-west coast of America. Contains all the instructions, statements, narratives, etc., relating to the voyages of Capt. Meares (and seizure of his ship by Spain), Capt. Colnett, etc.

A Narrative of the Operations of a Small British Force, under the Command of Brigadier-General Sir Samuel Auchmuty, employed in the Reduction of Monte-Video, on the River Plate, A.D. 1807. By a Field Officer on the Staff. Illustrated with a Plan of the Operations. *London: John Joseph Stockdale.* 1807. 4to, pp. 60. Plan. H. 51819

Narrative of the Oppressive Law Proceedings resorted to by the British Government and numerous private individuals to overpower the Earl of Stirling. Also, a Genealogical Account of the Family of Alexander, Earls of Stirling, etc. Followed by an Historical View of their Possessions in Nova Scotia, Canada, etc. By Ephraim Lockhart, Esq. ... *Edinburgh: J. Walker.* 1836. 4to, pp. vi, viii, 176, 8, vi, 77. Folded Pedigree. C.

Narrative of the Origin and Progess. *See* Vol. V., No. 18621

Narrative of the Origin and Progress of the Church of the United Brethren, or Moravians. *London.* 1842. 8vo. 51821

A Narrative of the Planting, 1694. *See* [Scottow (Joshua)].

Narrative of the Presentation to Sovereigns and those in Authority of the Address on the Slave Trade and Slavery. [n. p.] 1854. 8vo, pp. 64. 51822

Narrative of the Proceedings of a Meeting of the Inhabitants of Buckram, Mill-Neck, The Gut, Yellow Coats, Oak-Neck, Cove-Neck, Pine-Hollow, East Woods, Poverty-Hollow and Hog Island, held June 22, 1848, to determine upon the propriety of Restoring the Name of Oyster Bay. *Snarlingtown.* 1848. 8vo, pp. 15. 51823

A Narrative of the Proceedings. *See* [Thaxter (Thomas)].

A Narrative of the Proceedings. *See* [Stoughton (A.)]

A Narrative of the Proceedings of the Committee appointed by the Adventurers to Prosecute the Discovery of the Passage to the Western Ocean of America, and Extend the Trade, and Settle the Countries beyond Hudson's Bay. *London.* 1749. 8vo.

Narrative of the Proceedings. *See* Vol. II., Nos. 7660-61, Vol. VII., No. 28759, Vol. VIII., No. 30752.

Narrative of the Proceedings of the People. *See* [Yonge (F.)]

A | Narrative | of the | Proceedings | Subsequent to the | Royal Adjudication, | Concerning the | Lands | To the Westward of Connecticut River, lately usurped by | New-Hampshire, | With | Remarks | On the | Claim, Behaviour, and Misrepresentations, | of the | Intruders under that Government: Intended as an Appendix to the General Assembly's State of the Right of the Co- | lony of New-York (with Respect to its Eastern Boundary, on Connecticut | River, so far as Concerns the late Encroachments under the Government of | New-Hampshire) Published at their Sessions 1773. | *New-York:* | *Printed by John Holt*, ... | M,DCC,LXXIII. | Folio, pp. 28, Appendix, 34 leaves. C. 51825

Very scarce. Usually found with "A State of the Right of the Colony of New York," *infra.* It was reprinted in the Brattleboro "Semi-Weekly Eagle," Nos. 44-56, 1851 It is usually followed by:

Appendix containing Grants, Acts of Government, and other Proofs concerning the Encroachments of the Colony of New Hampshire, and the Conduct, Claims, and Misrepresentations of its Grantees, referred to in the preceding "State of the Right of the Colony of New York with respect to its Eastern Boundary on Connecticut River, so far as concerns the late Encroachments under the Government of New Hampshire," and also in the "Narrative of the Proceedings subsequent to the Royal Adjudication concerning the Lands to the Westward of Connecticut River, lately occupied by New Hampshire." [n. p. about 1773.] Folio, pp. 66. 51826

Narrative of the Rebellion. *See* Canada, Vol. III. 10528.

Narrative of the Religious Controversy. *See* Vol. VI. 24600.

Narrative of the Religious Fracas. *See* Baltimore, I. 3050.

A Narrative of the Revival of Religion, in the County of Oneida, particularly in the Bounds of the Presbytery of Oneida, in the Year 1826. *Utica: Printed by Hastings & Tracy.* 1826. 8vo, pp. 88. H. 51827

Signed by John Frost and two others.

A Narrative of the Revival of Religion, ... [in] the Presbytery of Albany, in ... 1820. ... [By Thomas McAuley.] *Schenectady: Printed by Isaac Riggs.* 1821. 8vo, pp. 51. BA. 51828

Narrative of the Revival of Religion in Virginia, in a Letter to a Friend. *London.* 1778. 8vo, pp. 26. 51829

Narrative of the Revolt. *See* [Trumbull (*Mr.*)]

A Narrative of The Rise and Progress of Eben-Ezer Baptist Church, in the City of New-York. ... *New-York: Printed ... by Smith & Forman.* 1808. 8vo, pp. 100. 51830

Narrative of the Scenes and Events. *See* Vol. IV., No. 13099.

Narrative of the Shipwreck of the Transport "Premier," near the mouth of the River St. Lawrence, 4th November, 1843. *London.* 1845. 4to. Plates. 51831

A Narrative of the State of Religion, Within the bounds of the General Assembly of the Presbyterian Church; and of the General Associations of Connecticut and Massachusetts, and the General Convention of Vermont ... . [*Philadelphia: William Bradford.* 1822.] 8vo, pp. 8. B., W. 51832

A Narrative of the Sufferings and Surprising Deliverance of William and Elizabeth Fleming, Who were taken captive by Captain Jacob, Commander of the Indians Who lately made the Incursions on the Frontiers of Pennsylvania. *Boston.* 1750. 8vo, pp. 20. + Second Edition. *Lancaster, Pa.* 1750. 8vo. + *Philadelphia.* 1755. + *Lancaster, Pa.* 1755. 51833

For two other editions, *see* Vol. VI., No. 24708.

Narrative of the Suppression. *See* [Cheetham (J.)] III. 12380.

Narrative of the Surprising Work. *See* [Edwards (J.)], Vol. V., No. 21955, and add an edition of 1737.

Narrative of the Surprize and Capture of M. Gen. Richard Prescott of the British Army, in his Head-Quarters, together with his Aide-de-Camp, Major Barrington, by a party of American Soldiers under Maj. Gen. Wm. Barton, July 9, 1777. To

which is added a Statement of General Barton's Lawsuit in Vermont and his subsequent sufferings. *Windsor, Vt.: W. Spooner.* 1821. 8vo. 51834

A tract with a somewhat similar title was printed in *Philadelphia*, 1817. 8vo, pp. 8. The capture of Gen. Prescott on Rhode Island was one of the boldest incidents of the American Revolution. The town of Barton in Vermont was named after our hero.

Narrative of the Surveying Voyages. *See* [King (P. P.)]

Narrative of the Tragical Death of Mr. Darius Barber and his Seven Children, who were inhumanly butchered by the Indians in Camden County, Georgia, January 26, 1816. To which is added an account of the Captivity and Sufferings of Mrs. Barber, who was carried away a Captive by the Savages, and from whom she fortunately made her escape six weeks afterwards. ... *Boston: David Hazen.* [n. d.] 12mo, pp. 24.

A Narrative of the Uncommon Suffering and Surprizing Deliverance of Briton Hammon, a Negro Man,—Servant to General Winslow, Of Marshfield, Who returned to Boston, after having been absent almost Thirteen Years. Containing An Account of the many Hardships he underwent ... how he was Cast away in the Capes of Florida ... Inhuman barbarity of the Indians ... . *Boston: Green & Russell.* 1760. 16mo, pp. 14.

Narrative of the U. S. Exploring Expedition. *See* Wilkes (C.)

Narrative of the various steps which led to the Unhappy Division which hath taken place among the Members of the Associate Body in the United States. *Philadelphia: Zachariah Poulson, Jun.* 1789. 8vo. 51837

Narrative of Two Months Residence in the Confederate States, including a Visit to New Orleans, under the Domination of General Butler. By an English Merchant. *London.* 1863. 8vo. 51838

Narrative of Two Wonderful Cures, ... in the Monastery of the Visitation at Georgetown, ... District of Columbia, in ... January, 1831. Published with the Approbation of the ... Archbishop of Baltimore, by James Myers ... . *Baltimore: Printed by William A. Francis.* MDCCCXXXI. 8vo, pp. 24, (1). H.

Narrative on the Subject. *See* Vol. IV., No. 15812.

Narrative Shewing. *See* [Hill (M. L.)], Vol. VIII., No. 31848.

Narratives of Calamitous and Interesting Shipwrecks, &c. *Philadelphia.* 1810. 12mo. W. 51840

... Narratives of Reformation, in Canton and Norfolk, Con. in four letters ... . [*Providence: Barnum, Field & Co., Printers.* 1800.] 8vo, pp. 20. BA. 51841

NARRAWAY (J. R.) Sermon on the occasion of the death of Charles F. Allison, founder of Mount Allison Academy. By Rev. J. R. Narraway. *Halifax.* 1859. 8vo, pp. 19. 51842

[NARSH (William).] *See* Vol. VI., No. 23524.

NARVAEZ (F.) Dos años de gobierno en América, ó sean antecedentes del mariscal de campo Francisco Narvaez. *Valencia.* 1839. Sm. 8vo. 51843

NASBY (P. V.), *pseudon.* *See* [Locke (D. R.)], X. 41718-22.

NASCENTES (J. B.) Relatorio que o exm. Presidente da Provincia do Espirito Santo o Bacharel José Bonifacio Nascentes d'Azambuja dirigiu á Assemblea Legislativa da mesma Provincia na Sessão Ordinaria de 24 de Maio de 1852. *Victorio Typographia Capitaniense de P. A. de Azeredo.* 1852. 8vo, pp. 78, Tables, 15. 51844

NASH (A.) Memoir of Edward Dorr Griffin. By Ansell Nash. *New York.* 1842. 18mo, pp. 72. 51845

NASH [Daniel]. A Portrait of Father Nash, Late Missionary in Otsego and adjacent Counties in ... New York. With A Few Fragments ... Taken chiefly from the Genealogy of the Nash Family ... . [n. p. n. d.] 8vo, pp. 8. H. 51846

NASH (J. A.) Memoir of Seth Burroughs, of Williamsburgh, Mass. ... By J. A. Nash. *Boston: T. R. Marvin.* 1829. 18mo, pp. 108. C. 51847

NASH (J.) A Sermon, ... in Chester, May 21, 1814, at the Funeral of the Rev. Aaron Bascom. By Jonathan Nash, A.M. ... *Springfield: Printed by Thomas Dickman.* 1814. 8vo, pp. 19.

Also: Sermon at the Funeral of Mrs. A. Kendall, New Salem, 22 April, 1790 ... . *Springfield.* 1793. 8vo.—A Sermon at Middlefield [Mass.], Oct. 31, 1813, on the Completion of the Twenty-first Year of his Ministry. ... *Springfield.* 1815. 8vo. W.

NASH (Melaliah). The Columbian Ephemeris and Astronomical Diary, for ... 1812; ... . By M. Nash ... . *New-York: Printed by Largin & Thompson.* 1812. 4to, pp. 112. Cont'd.

Also: The Ladies' and Gentlemen's Diary, or United States Almanac ... . For ... 1820. *New-York: J. Seymour, Printer.* 1819. 12mo, pp. 96. H.

NASH (N. C.) The Sunday Law Unconstitutional and Unscriptural. An Argument ... in the Massachusetts Legislature. By Nathaniel C. Nash. *Boston: The Author.* 1868. 8vo, pp. 23

NASH (S.) Morality and the State. By Simeon Nash. ... *Columbus, Ohio: Follett, Foster and Company.* 1859. 8vo, pp. xviii, 442. B. 51851

NASH (S.) Journal of Soloman Nash, a Soldier of the Revolution. 1776-1777. Now first printed from the Original Manuscript. With an Introduction and Notes, by Charles I. Bushnell. *New York: Privately Printed.* 1861. 8vo, pp. 65. 3 Plates. C.

Forms No. 3 of Bushnell's "Crumbs for Antiquarians," Vol. I.

NASH (S.) The Nash Family, in part, traced down from Thomas Nash, an Emigrant from England, in 1638. Compiled by the Rev. Sylvester Nash, ... with Additions by Herman S. Noble, ... 1850. *Watertown: Printed by Herman S. Noble.* [n. d.] 8vo, pp. 17. 51853

NASH. The Nash Family; or Records of the Descendants of Thomas Nash of New Haven, Connecticut, 1640. Collected and compiled by the Rev. Sylvester Nash, A.M. ... *Hartford: Case, Tiffany and Company.* 1853. 8vo, pp. 304. 3 Portraits. C.

NASHOTAH, *Wis.* Annual Letter of the Nashotah Mission, for 1854-5. [n. p. n. d.] 8vo. 51855

Catalogue of the Officers and Students of the Nashotah Theological Seminary, ... 1853-54. ... *Milwaukee.* 1853. 16mo, pp. 7, (1). Continued. B. 51856

See also [Kip (W. I.)], Vol. IX., No. 37950.

NASHUA, *N. H.* Annual Report of Schools, in ... Nashua. *Nashua: Moore & Langley, ... Printers.* 1869. 8vo, pp. 32. B. Continued. 51857

The First Report of the Receipts and Expenditures of ... Nashua, ... 1854, ... [with] Reports of the Selectmen and ... School Committee ... . *Nashua: Printed by Albin Beard.* 1854. 8vo, pp. 6, (2), 27. Continued. B. 51858

The "Report of the Selectmen" has a separate title-page. The titles of the reports vary with the different years.

The Charters granted to the Nashua and Lowell Rail Road Corporation ... with the By-Laws ... . *Nashua, N. H.: Printed by A. and A. Beard.* 1836. 8vo, pp. 32. H. 51859

Also: Report of the Committee of Investigation of the Nashua and Lowell Railroad Company; ... May 29, 1850. [And counter report.] *Boston: Eastburn's Press.* 1851. 8vo, pp. 128, 61. B. — Report of the Directors of the Nashua and Lowell Rail Road Corporation, ... August, 1839. *Nashua: Printed by P. Morrill.* 1839. 8vo, pp. 12. Continued. — Report of the Grantees ... with the Report of the Engineer ... 1836. *Nashua.* 1836. 8vo, pp. 20. B.

The Nashua Directory; containing the City Register ... . By W. A. Greenough, Jr. *Nashua: N. P. Greene.* 1864. 12mo, pp. (4), 120. B. + With the Roll of Nashua Volunteers in the Army and Navy. ... [*Ibid.*] 12mo, pp. 130, 32. Continued.

Catalogue of the ... Nashua Literary Institution, For ... 1846. *Nashua: Wm. H. Gilmore, Printer.* 1846. 12mo, pp. 11. H.

First Annual Report of the Nashua Young Men's Christian Association, for 1869. *Nashua.* 1870. 8vo. Continued.

Ordinances of the City of Nashua, ... [with] the names of the Members of the City Government, and the Officers ... 1854. *Nashua: Printed by Albin Beard.* 1854. 8vo, pp. 32. Cont'd.

Proceedings of a meeting of Citizens of Nashua ... March 10, 1842, upon ... certain grievances; with a Report and Resolutions ... *Nashua: Printed by A. Beard.* 1842. 8vo, pp. 15. H. 51864

Report of the ... School Committee of ... Nashua, for 1838–9. *Nashua: A. and A. Beard, Printers.* [n. d.] 8vo, pp. 12. Cont'd

Also: A Church Memorial, consisting of the History of the First Unitarian Congregational Society in ... Nashua, N. H., ... [and] Letters from Past and Present Pastors. *Nashua: Printed by Albin Beard.* 1859. 12mo, pp. 39. B.

NASHVILLE, *Tenn.* Annual Report for the Municipal Year, ending Sept. 31, 1854, of the Recorder, ... of Fire Department, Superintendent of Water-Works, and the School Department. *Nashville.* 1855. 8vo. S. 51866

Reports of the Board of Education and ... Superintendent of the Public Schools of Nashville. *Nashville: W. F. Bang & Co.*, ... *Printers.* 1855. 8vo, pp. 15. H. 51867

Also: Fourth Annual Report of the Public Schools of the City of Nashville ... . *Nashville: Smith, Camp & Co., Printers.* 1858. 8vo, pp. 20, (1). Continued. H.

City and Business Directory of Nashville for 1860–61. *Nashville.* 1860. 8vo. Continued. C. 51868

Communication from ... the Mayor to the City Council of Nashville, Tenn. With ... Documents ... 1859. *Nashville: Printed by A. S. Camp & Co.* 1859. 12mo, pp. 24. H. 51869

Compilation of the General Laws of the City of Nashville; together with the Charters of the City, granted by the States of North Carolina and Tennessee, from 1806 to 1860. By James E. Rains. *Nashville.* 1860. 8vo. 51870

Description of the Tennessee State Capitol. *Nashville.* 1854. 24mo. S. 51871

Also: Verses on the ... Capitol. [n. p. n. d.] 4to, 1 page.

King's Nashville Directory, for 1867. *Nashville: E. D. King.* 1867. 8vo, pp. 316, 109. Continued. 51872

Letter and Documents in relation to the Location of the Railroad Bridge across the Cumberland River at Nashville. ... *Nashville: W. F. Bang & Co., Printers.* 1856. 8vo, pp. 32. H.

Report of the First Exhibition of the Mechanics' Institute and Library Association of Nashville, October, 1855 [with Address by Turner H. Foster]. *Nashville.* 1855. 8vo, pp. 87, 16. M.

... Names of Soldiers who died in Defense of the American Union, interred in the National Cemetery at Nashville, Tennessee. ... *Washington.* 1869. 8vo, pp. 524. BA. 51875

Report of the Commissioners of the Nashville and Chattanooga Rail Road. *Nashville: J. G. Shepard*, ... *Pr.* 1847. 8vo, pp. 12. H. 51876

Report of the Committee of the City Council of Nashville, upon the Affairs of the Nashville and Northwestern Railroad Company. [*Nashville.* 1859.] 8vo, pp. 16. H. 51877

Nashville Journal of Medicine and Surgery. Edited by W. K. Bowling, M.D. ... Vol. I. February, 1851. ... *Nashville, Tenn.: John S. T. Fall ... Pr.* 1851. 8vo. Continued. H.

The Nashville, State of Tennessee, and General Commercial Directory. ... Volume I. *Nashville.* 1853. 8vo, pp. 352.

Catalogue of the ... University of Nashville. With an Appendix ... . *Nashville: A. Nelson & Co., Printers.* 1850. 8vo, pp. 35. Continued. H. 51880

Also: An Address, ... before the Alumni Society of the University of Nashville, October 7, 1846, By Nathaniel Cross ... . With an Appendix, containing a Catalogue of the Alumni ... . *Nashville: Burton & Billings, Printers.* 1846. 8vo, pp. 45. H. — Annual Announcement of the Law, Literary, and Medical Departments, of the University of Nashville. ... 1854–5. *Nashville, Tenn.* 1854. 8vo, pp. 32. H. — ... Catalogue for the Session of 1856–7, and Announcement for ... 1857–8. *Nashville, Tenn.* 1857. 8vo, pp. 25. Continued. — First Annual Announcement of the Medical Department of the University ... . *Nashville, Ten.: J. T. S. Fall, Pr.* 1851.

8vo, pp. 8. — Important Report by Chancellor Lindsley. The Present Condition and Prospects of the University. [n. p. 1870.] 8vo, pp. 8. — Laws of the University ... . New Edition. *Nashville, T.: Printed by S. Nye and Co.* 1835. 8vo, pp. 28. Continued. — Register of the Collegiate Department, Western Military Institute ... . 1856. [n. p. n. d.] 8vo. *See also* Vol. IX., No. 35373.

[NASON (Daniel).] A Journal of a Tour from Boston to Savannah, thence to Havana, ... New Orleans and several Western Cities ... . By a Citizen of Cambridgeport. *Cambridge: The Author.* 1849. 12mo, pp. 114. H. 51881

NASON (E.) A Brief Record of Events in Exeter, N. H., during ... 1861; ... with the Names of the Soldiers of this Town in the War. By Rev. Elias Nason. ... *Exeter: Printed by Samuel Hall.* 1862. 16mo, pp. 16. + A Brief Record ... during ... 1862; ... *Exeter: Fogg and Fellowes.* 1863. 16mo, pp. 20. B. + A Brief Record ... during ... 1863; ... [*Ibid.*] 1864. 18mo, pp. 24. B. 51882

NASON. Discourse ... before the New-England Historic-Genealogical Society, ... April 2, 1868, on the Life and Character of the Hon. John Albion Andrew, LL.D. ... With Proceedings and Appendix. By ... Rev. Elias Nason, M.A. ... *Boston: New-England Historic-Genealogical Society.* 1868. 8vo, pp. 76. Port.

NASON. Eulogy on Abraham Lincoln, ... before the New England Historic-Genealogical Society, Boston, May 3, 1865, By Rev. Elias Nason ... . *Boston: William V. Spencer.* 1865. 8vo, pp. 28. B. 51884

First delivered in the Rev. Mr. Plumber's Church, Chelsea, afterwards before the citizens of Exeter, N. H.

NASON. A Memoir of Mrs. Susanna Rowson, with Elegant and Illustrative Extracts from her Writings in Prose and Poetry. By Elias Nason, M.A. ... *Albany, N. Y.: Joel Munsell.* 1870. 8vo, pp. 212. Portrait. BA. 51885

Mrs. Rowson performed on the Boston stage in 1796–97

NASON. A Monogram [*sic*] on our National Song. By ... Rev. Elias Nason, M.A. ... *Albany: Joel Munsell.* 1869. 8vo, pp. 69. + [*Ibid.*] 1870. B. 51886

The author should have called this a *monograph.*

NASON. Sir Charles Henry Frankland, Baronet: or Boston in the Colonial Times. By Elias Nason, M.A. *Albany, N. Y.: J. Munsell.* 1865. 8vo, pp. 129. BA. 51887

Three hundred copies printed, of which fifty are on large paper. Forms No. 2 of Munsell's "Series of Local American History."

NASON. ... A Sermon ... at the Dedication of the First Congregational Church in Natick, Massachusetts. November 15, 1854. By Rev. Elias Nason ... . *Boston: S. K. Whipple & Co.* 1855. 8vo, pp. 24. BA. 51888

Contains an historical sketch of the church. Also: The Congregational Tune Book: ... *Boston: John P. Jewett and Company.* 1858. Obl. 16mo, pp. 208. — Our Obligation to defend the Government of the Country. A Discourse on the War ... at Exeter, N. H., April 21, 1861. [n. p. n. d.] 8vo, pp. 6. — A Sermon on the War, ... to the Soldiers at Exeter, N. H., May 19, 1861. [n. p. n. d.] 4to, pp. 4. — Songs for the School Room ... . *Newburyport: John G. Tilton and Company.* [1855.] 12mo, pp. 126. H.

NASON (R.) An Address delivered at Gorham [Me.], on Opening the Academy in that place, September 8, 1806. By Reuben Nason, A.M. ... *Portland: Printed ... by J. M'Kown.* 1806. 8vo, pp. 15. H. 51889

Also: Sermon preached at Gorham, on Thanksgiving Day, November 27th, 1806. ... *Portland.* [1806.] 8vo, pp. 15. — A Valedictory Address, on relinquishing the charge of Gorham Academy, August 19, 1834. ... *Portland.* 1834. 8vo, pp. 14. H.

NASSAU (Guillaume de). Entretiens [etc.]. *See* No. 22672.

NASSAU LA LECK (L. Th. Grave van). Brieven over de Noord-Americaansche onlusten, den waarschijnlijken uitslag dier oorlog, en den invloed die deze gebeurtenisse zoude kunnen hebben op de belangens van Europa. *Utrecht.* 1777–79. 6 parts, 8vo. 51890

Letters on the North American troubles, their probable result and influence.

NASSAU-HALL. *See* New Jersey.

NASSAU ISLAND. Constitution and By-Laws of the St. Nicholas Society, of Nassau Island. ... *Brooklyn: I. Van Anden's Print.* 1848. 12mo, pp. 12, (3). H. 51891

The Nassau Rake, Edited and Published by the Sophomore Class of the College of New Jersey. *Princeton.* 1858. 8vo, pp. 96. 51892

NASSAU WATER COMPANY. *See* Brooklyn, Vol. II. 8322.

NASSY (D.) Observations on the Cause, Nature, and Treatment of the Epidemic Disorder, prevalent in Philadelphia. By D. Nassy, M.D. ... *Philadelphia: M. Carey.* 1793. 8vo, pp. 48. + [*Ibid.*] 8vo, pp. 26. H. 51893

In French and English.

[NASSY (D. de la)]. Essai historique sur la Colonie de Surinam, sa fondation, ses révolutions, ses progrès, depuis son origine

jusqu'à nos jours, ainsi que les causes qui depuis quelques années ont arrêté le cours de sa prosperité; avec la description et l'état actuel de la Colonie et l'histoire de la nation juive portugaise et allemande y établie, leurs privilèges, immunités et franchises, etc. Le tout rédigé sur des pièces authentiques y jointes, et mis en ordre par les régens et représentans de ladite nation juive portugaise. *A Paramaribo.* 1788. 2 vols., 8vo, pp. xxxviii, 192; 197.

An interesting work for the history of the colony of Surinam, and at the same time, the earliest known work printed at Paramaribo.. Should have been under La Nassy.

NAST (W.) Der hundertjährige Bestand des amerikanischen Methodismus. Ein Vortrag, gehalten bei der Eröffnung des Jubiläumjahres. Von Wilhelm Nast, D.D. *Cincinnati.* 1866. 16mo, pp. 128. 51895

NAST. Das Leben und Wirken des Johannes Wesley und seiner Haupt-Mitarbeiter. Bearbeitet ... von Wilhelm Nast. ... *Cincinnati: Verlegt von L. Swormstedt & A. Poe.* 1852. 12mo, pp. 300. Portrait. 51896

NATCHEZ, *Miss.* Annual Reports of the ... Natchez Institute. 1858. *Natchez.* 1858. 8vo, pp. 24. Continued. H. 51897

Also: Course of Instruction and Government of the Natchez Institute ... . *Natchez.* 1858. 8vo, pp. 24. H.

Pastoral Letter, of [William Henry] the ... Bishop of Natchez, on occasion of the Diocesan Synod, ... 1858. *New-Orleans.* 1858. 8vo, pp. 22. H. 51898

Nathan to Lord North. ... *London: G. Wilkie.* MDCCLXXX. 8vo, pp. (4), 59. H. 51899

Censures Lord North with great severity. The writer calls himself "a native of that unhappy country which his Lordship has ruined, and one of the wretches which his Lordship's politics have cursed beyond the power of salvation." "To shew the arch-fiend in his proper diabolical shape," adds the writer, "to procure your removal from the ear of Majesty, where you have been too long squat like a toad, inspiring venom, would give me the greatest pleasure."

NATHAN (J.) An Almanac for 1747. ... By John Nathan. *New York.* 1747. 12mo. 51900

Continued to 1749 or later.

NATICK, *Mass.* An Account of the Expenditures of ... Natick, from ... 1842, to ... 1843. *Dedham, Mass.* 1843. 8vo, pp. 8. H. 51901

Annual Report of the School Committee of ... Natick. ... 1846. *Boston: Printed by Andrews & Prentiss.* 1846. 8vo, pp. 8. Continued. H. 51902

Also: Annual Report of the Selectmen and Town Clerk of ... Natick, ... 1850. *Boston: Damrell & Moore, Printers.* 1850. 8vo, pp. 8. Continued. H.

Catalogue of the Natick Town Library. ... *Boston: S. Chism.* 1866. 12mo, pp. 50, 4. B. 51903

Localities, Streets and their Lengths, in the Town of Natick. And List of Tax-Payers, 1746–7. By Austin Bacon. *Boston.* 1859. 8vo, pp. 16. 51904

Order of Exercises at the Celebration of the Two Hundredth Anniversary of the Settlement of the Town of Natick, 8th October, 1851. *Boston.* 1851. Folio, 1 leaf. M. 51905

Psalm C to be sung at the Tea Party given in the Town Hall at Natick, Oct. 28, 1846, for the purpose of raising means to purchase a copy of Eliot's Indian Bible to be preserved in the Archives of the Town. [n. p.] 1846. 4to, 1 page. 51906

In Natick and English.

Report of the Receipts and Expenditures of ... Natick, for ... 1853. *Boston: J. B. Chisholm.* 1853. 8vo, pp. 15. Continued

Also: First Annual Report ... with the Constitution and By-Laws of the Young Men's Christian Association, of Natick ... . *Natick, Mass.: Geo. W. Ryder & Co., Printers.* 1859. 16mo, pp. 20. H. *See also* Badger (Sarah), Vol. I., Nos. 2701–2.

NATICK, *R. I.* Constitution and By-Laws of the May Queen Union, No. 2, Daughters of Temperance, Natick, R. I. Instituted May 10, 1851. *Providence: A. C. Greene.* 1852. 12mo, pp. 24. 51908

The Nation: A Weekly Journal devoted to Politics, Literature, Science and Art. Volume I. *New York: Joseph H. Richards.* 1865. 4to, pp. (2), ii, 828. Continued. H. 51909

A Nation to become Rich and Prosperous, must protect its Producing Classes. Reasons for Taxing High Wines. *Chicago: Beach & Barnard.* [n. d.] Folio, pp. 11. 51910

The Nation Weeping for the Dead. *See* Springfield, *Mass.*

The National. Volume I. December, 1869. Number I. *Washington, D. C.* 1869. 4to, pp. 8. Continued. H. 51911

Catalogue of the First Winter Exhibition of the National Academy of Design, (1867–8.) ... *New-York: Sackett & Mackay*, ... *Printers.* MDCCCLXVIII. 8vo, pp. 48. Continued. H. 51912

The National Academy of Design. Ceremonies on ... Laying the Corner-Stone, October 21st, 1863. And the Inauguration of the Building, April 27th, 1865. *New York: Miller and Mathews.* M DCCC LXV. Rl. 8vo, pp. 91. BA. 51913

Two hundred copies privately printed. Also: ... Catalogue of the Tenth Annual Exhibition. 1835. ... *New-York: Printed by Edwin B. Clayton.* M DCCC XXXV. 8vo, pp. 16. Continued. — Constitution and By-Laws of the National Academy of Design. ... *New-York: Printed by D. Fanshaw.* 1826. 8vo, pp. 11, (1). + *New-York: E. B. Clayton, Printer.* MDCCCXXXIX. 8vo, pp. 18. + *New York.* 1846. 8vo, pp. 20. — The Exhibition of the National Academy of Design. 1831. The Sixth. ... *New-York: Printed by Clayton & Van Norden.* [1831.] 8vo, pp. 15. H.

Memoirs of the National Academy of Sciences. Volume I. *Washington.* 1866. 4to, pp. (4), 261, 24, 4, 22, 31. Diagrams. Continued. H. 51914

Report of the National Academy of Sciences for ... 1863. *Washington.* 1864. 8vo, pp. (2), 118. Plates. H. 51915

Also: Annual of the National Academy of Sciences, for 1863–64. *Cambridge: Welch, Bigelow, and Company.* 1865. 12mo, pp. 112. Continued. — Annual Report of the Proceedings ... during ... 1864, 1866, [and] 1867. *Washington.* 1865–68. 3 vols., 8vo. — Rules governing The National Academy of Sciences. ... [n. p. 1863?] 8vo, pp. 13. H.

The National Agriculturist and Pennsylvania Farm Journal, ... Volume I. ... *Pittsburgh, Pa.* 1868. Folio, pp. iv, 188. B.

The National Almanac and Annual Record for ... 1863 [and 1864]. *Philadelphia: George W. Childs.* 1863–64. 12mo, pp. 698; 641. H. 51917

No more published.

National and Jackson ... Association. *See* Vol. III. 11357.

The National and Private Advantages of the African Trade Considered, being an Enquiry how far it concerns the Trading Interests of Great Britain to maintain the Forts and Settlements in Africa belonging to the Royal African Company of England, with a correct Map ... . *London: John and Paul Knapton.* 1746. 8vo, pp. 128. Map. 51918

The object of this book is to induce Parliament to grant a subsidy of £30,000 per annum to the Royal African Company to carry on its trade in negroes to the plantations in America. "This trade is the most nationally beneficial of any we carry on. It is also allowed on all hands, that the trade to Africa is the branch which renders our American Colonies and Plantations so advantageous to Great Britain." *See our* Vol. I., No. 501.

National and State Rights, considered, by "One of the People," in Reply to the "Trio." *Charleston: Printed by A. E. Miller.* 1821. 8vo, pp. iv, 28. BA., 51919

National and State Taxation; their Operation and Results as affecting Life Insurance. *New York: John A. Gray, Printer.* 1862. 8vo, pp. 20. 51920

National Anti-Masonic Convention. *See* Vol. XI., No. 45492

Document III.–VIII. ... [Monthly Circular of the] National Anti-Monopoly Cheap Freight Railway League ... . *New York.* 1867. 8vo, pp. 4, (2), 170. H. 51921

Report of the Twenty-First National Anti-Slavery Bazaar. *Boston: J. B. Yerrington & Son, Printers.* 1855. 12mo, pp. 36. Continued. BA. 51922

National Anti-Slavery Standard. Volume I. *New York.* 184–. Folio. 51923

National Arithmetick. *See* [Swan (James)].

The National Armories. A Review of the Systems of Superintendency, Civil and Military, particularly with Reference to Economy and General Management, at the Springfield Armory. ... January, 1853. Third Edition. *Springfield, Mass.* 1853. 8vo, pp. 82, (1). 51924

National Armory. An Appeal To Congress by the Citizens of Rock Island and Moline, Illinois, and Davenport, Iowa, in favor of a National Armory on the site of Fort Armstrong, on the Island of Rock Island, in ... Illinois. *Printed at ... Rock Island* ... . 1861. 8vo, pp. 14, (1). Map. 51925

Also: National Armory. Memorial of Burlington Island Association. [n. p. n. d.] 8vo, pp. 4. *See also* Vol. I., No. 968, *and* Vol. XII., No. 47721.

Proceedings of Annual Conventions of the National Art Association ... at Washington ... From 1858 to 1860 ... . *Washington, D. C.: William H. Moore, Printer.* 1860. 8vo, pp. 11, (1), 19, 21. H. 51926

Constitution and Addresses of the National Association for the Amendment of the Constitution of the United States. ... *Philadelphia: Jas. B. Rodgers, Printer.* 1864. 8vo. 51927

Also: To the voting Citizens of the United States, and to all ... [illegible]ve their Country. [n. p. 1866?] 8vo, pp. 7, (1). H.

Sessional Proceedings of the National Association for t[illegible] motion of Social Science ... . Vol. I. No. 8. ... January 1868. ... [*London.* 1868.] 8vo. Continued. H. 519[illegible]

This number relates to America.

National Association for the Protection of Industry and Capital throughout the British Empire.—The Case of the Free-Labour British Colonies. *London.* 1852. 8vo, pp. 155. S. 51929

First Annual Report of the National Association for the Relief of Destitute Colored Women and Children. *Washington, D. C.: McGill & Witherow, Printers.* 1864. 8vo, pp. 16, (2). Continued. B. 51930

Proceedings of a Convention, held in ... New York, ... April 29, 1868, for ... organizing the National Association of Cotton Manufacturers and Planters; ... with Correspondence and Statistics .... *Boston: Prentiss & Deland, Printers.* 1868. 8vo, pp. 92

Also: Proceedings of the First Annual Meeting of the National Association of Cotton Manufacturers and Planters, ... 1869. *Boston: W. L. Deland & Co.* 1869. 8vo, pp. 52. H.

Proceedings of the National Association of Knit Goods Manufacturers, ... 1866. *Albany: C. Van Benthuysen's ... Printing House.* 1866. 8vo, pp. 17. H. 51932

Proceedings of the National Association of School Superintendents, ... at Washington, D. C. March, 1870. *New York: For the Association, by A. S. Barnes & Co.* [n. d.] 8vo, pp. 19.

Bulletin of the National Association of Wool Manufacturers, ... for ... 1869. [Quarterly.] Edited by John L. Hayes, Secretary. *Boston.* 1869. 8vo, pp. vi, ix, 419. Continued. H.

Third Annual Report of the National Association of Wool Manufacturers, 1867. By John L. Hayes, Secretary. *Boston: John Wilson and Son.* 1867. 8vo, pp. 42, (1). H. 51935

Also: Catalogue of Wool Manufacturers, ... of the National Association of Wool Manufacturers; ... 1869. *New-York: S. W. Green, Printer.* 1869. 8vo, pp. 34.—Considerations ... respecting the Duties on Wool and the Manufacturers of Wool, ... in behalf of the ... National Association of Wool Manufacturers ... . 1867. *Washington, D. C.: Philp & Solomons.* 1867. 8vo, pp. 10.—Objects and Plan of the National Association of Wool Manufacturers: ... *Boston: John Wilson and Sons.* 1866. 8vo, pp. 20.—Report of the Committee ... of the Convention of Wool Manufacturers, ... 1864. *Boston: Printed by John Wilson and Son.* 1864. 8vo, pp. 10.—Report of the Proceedings of the Convention of Delegates from the National Association of Wool Manufacturers, and from the several Organizations of the Wool Growers of the United States, at Syracuse, New York, Dec. 13, 1865. *Boston: Press of John Wilson.* 1866. 8vo, pp. 99.—Statement of Facts relative to Canada Wools and the Manufactures of Worsted. *Boston: John Wilson and Sons.* 1866. 8vo, pp. 21.—Statement of the Executive Committee of the National Association of Wool Manufacturers, ... relative to proposed Duties on Wool and Woollens ... . *Boston: John Wilson and Sons.* 1866. 8vo, pp. 42, folded leaf.—Transactions of the National Association of Wool Manufacturers. 1865–66. *Boston: John Wilson and Son.* 1866. 8vo. H.

National Ballads of Canada. *See* [Lanigan (G. F.)], Vol. x.

The National Bank Amendment Bill. ... [n. p. 1866.] 8vo, pp. 8. H. 51936

Also: Proceedings of the National Bank Convention held in New York City, ... 1869. *Syracuse.* 1869. 8vo, pp. 35.—National Bank Currency Act. Report on its Defects and its Effects. *New York: C. S. Westcott & Co.* 1863. 8vo, pp. 18. *See also* Vol. I., No. 3181–2.

National Bankrupt Law. [n. p. 1800.] 12mo, pp. 32.

The National Bankruptcy Register. A [semi-monthly] Record of Law Reports and Proceedings in Bankruptcy in all the States. Audley W. Gazzam, Editor. *New York: G. T. Deller.* 1870. 4to. Continued. C. 51937

... The National Banks. The System Unmasked, Greenbacks Forever. ... [*Cincinnati, Ohio.* 1869.] 8vo, pp. 32. H. 51938

Also: Report of the Union Committee in Relation to National Banks. *New York.* 1834. 8vo.

Proceedings of the National Baptist Educational Convention, held ... 1870. ... [*New York: Lange & Hillman, Printers.* 1870.] 8vo, pp. 255, (1). H. 51939

Journal of the ... First Annual Meeting of the National Board of Fire Underwriters, held in New York, ... 1867, ... with Proceedings of the Executive Committee ... . *New York.* [n. d.] 8vo, pp. 67. H. 51940

Also: Report of ... the National Board of Fire Underwriters. ... 1869. [n. p. n. d.] 8vo, pp. 23. H.

Proceedings of the First Meeting of the National Board of Trade, held in Philadelphia, June, 1868. ... *Boston: J. H. Eastburn.* 1868. 8vo, pp. ix, (2), 188, 7. B. 51941

Also: Debate on Direct Importations to the Interior. *Boston.* 1870. 8vo.—Proceedings of the First Annual Meeting ... held in Cincinnati, December, 1868. *Boston: J. H. Eastburn's Press.* 1869. 8vo, pp. xi, (5), 371. Continued.—Report ... on a Continuous Water Line of Transportation through Virginia. *Richmond: Gary, Clemmitt, & Jones, Printers.* 1869. 8vo, pp. 42.—Resolutions ... adopted, at the First Annual Meeting ... held in ... Cincinnati, ... 1868. [n. p. n. d.] 4to, pp. 6. H.

The National Calendar. *See* Force (P.), Vol. VI., No. 25056.

National Celebration of Union Victories. ... Mass Meeting at Union Square, New York, March 6th, 1865. *New York: Geo. F. Nesbitt & Co., Printers.* 1865. 8vo, pp. 72. 51942

A National Change in Morals, in Measures, and in Politics, necessary to National Prosperity. *London: T. Cadell.* 1780. 8vo. 51943

"Partly relates to the American Revolution."—*Monthly Review*, LXII. 333.

Minutes of the National Christian Convention, Opposed to Secret Societies, held at Pittsburg, May ... 1868 ... . *Chicago: Ezra A. Cook.* 1868. 12mo, pp. 90. H. 51944

National Circular. Address to the Head of each Family in the United States. [n. p. n. d.] 12mo, pp. 12. H. 51945

An address on temperance, about the year 1831.

The National Clay Melodist, a collection of Popular and Patriotic Songs. Second Edition ... . *Boston: Benj. Adams.* 1844. 16mo, pp. 108. Portrait. BA. 51946

The National Club on the Reconstruction of the Union. February 4, 1864. *New York: G. B. Teubner.* 1864. 8vo, pp. 16. Map. 51947

... The National Colors of the United States and of Great Britain fully explained. *New York.* 1822. 8vo. 51948

National Comic Almanac, 1852. *Philadelphia.* [n. d.] 12mo.

The Memorial to Congress of the National Commercial Convention. [*Boston: Rockwell & Rollins, Printers.* 1868.] 8vo, pp. 15. 51950

Also: Proceedings of the ... Convention, held in Boston, February, 1868. ... *Boston: J. H. Eastburn.* 1868. 8vo, pp. viii, 251.—Report of the Committee on Foreign and Domestic Commerce, ... 1868 ... . [*Boston: Rockwell & Rollins, Printers.* 1868.] 8vo, pp. 13. H.

National Committee. *See* Vol. II., No. 8101.

Address of the National Compensation Emancipation Society. [n. p. n. d.] 4to, pp. 4. 51951

Report of the Third Meeting of the National Conference of Unitarian and other Christian Churches, held in New York, October 7, 8, 9, 1868 ... . *Boston.* 1868. 8vo. Continued.

National Congress on Penitentiary and Reformatory Discipline, ... held in Cincinnati, Ohio, October ... 1870. [n. p. 1870.] 8vo, pp. 6, 8. H. 51953

National Considerations upon Importing Iron in Bars from America, &c. [n. p. about 1716?] Folio, 1 leaf. 51954

National Convention. Circular of the National Committee of the Pittsburgh Convention, appointed February 22, 1856. [n. p. n. d.] 8vo, pp. 6. 51955

Proceedings of the National Convention of the Friends of Public Education, held in Philadelphia, October 17, 18 & 19, 1849. *Philadelphia: E. C. & J. Biddle.* 1849. 8vo, pp. 40.

Debates and Proceedings of the National Council of Congregational Churches, held at Boston ... June 14–24, 1865. ... *Boston.* 1866. 8vo, pp. xiv, (2), 530. B. 51957

The National Crisis. ... May 15, 1860. Vol. I. No. I. ... Theophilus Fiske, Editor ... . [*Washington.* 1860.] 8vo, pp. 16.

The National Crisis. A Letter to the Hon. Milton S. Latham, Senator from California in Washington. By Anglo-Californian. *San Francisco: Towne & Bacon.* 1861. 8vo, pp. 21. 51959

The National Currency. ... [n. p. n. d.] 8vo, pp. 8. H.

Signed "Common Sense."

The National Currency. [Dated] New York, March 28, 1864. [n. p. n. d.] 8vo, pp. 19. 51961

Signed "L. B."

National Currency. An Act proposed by a New York State Banker. [n. p. n. d.] 8vo, pp. 3. 51962

... The National Currency. July 15, 1862. ... A Bill to provide a national currency ... . [*Washington.* 1862.] 8vo, pp. 22.

National Currency. An Act ... 1863. [n. p. n. d.] 8vo.

For "Some Strictures," *see* [Flint (Wlado)], VI. 24796.

An Act to Provide a National Currency, secured by a pledge of United States Bonds, and to Provide for the circulation and redemption thereof. Approved June 3, 1864. *Washington.* 1864. 8vo, pp. 28. + *New York: Jno. S. Voorhies.* 1864. 8vo, pp. 40. + With the Amendments of 1865–70. ... *New York.* 1870. 8vo, pp. 100, 20, 63. C. 51965

National Currency and Banking Association Bill passed the Senate, February 12, 1863. [n. p. n. d.] 8vo. 51966

National Currency and Government Credit. [n. p. 1868.] 8vo, pp. 16. H. 51967

A National Currency. What is Needed. Suggestions by A Practical Banker. *Philadelphia: William S. & Alfred Martien.* 1863. 8vo, pp. 48 or 68. 51968

National Dangers, and Means of Escape. [n. p. n. d] 8vo, pp. 7. H. 51969

National Deaf Mute Gazette. ... Vol. I. September, 1867. No. 9. ... Wm. Martin Chamberlain, Editor. *Boston, Mass.: Packard & Holmes.* 1867. Folio, pp. 16. Continued. H.

National Debt. *See* [Butterfield (C.)], Vol. III., No. 9667.

Address of the National Democratic Executive Committee to the Democracy and the People of the United States. [n. p.] 1860. 8vo. 51971

National Democratic Quarterly Review. Thomas B. Florence and Isaac Lawrence, Editors. Volume I. *Washington City: Little, Morris & Co.* 1860. 8vo, pp. (2), ii, (2), 802. B. 51972

Journal of the Proceedings of the National Division of the Sons of Temperance of North America. Twenty-Second Annual Session, Montreal, C. E., June 21, 1866. *Boston.* 1866. 8vo, pp. 71. 51973

National Educational Associations—1866. Proceedings and Lectures of the National Teachers' Association, the National Association of School Superintendents, and the American Normal School Association, ... held in Indianapolis, Ind., August, 1866, *Albany.* 1867. 8vo, pp. 139, 16. B. 51974

A National Exchange, in A Series of Essays, addressed to Congress on the Question of a Fiscal Agent. ... *Philadelphia: C. Alexander, Printer.* 1842. 8vo, pp. 36. H., S. 51975

National Finance. *See* W[alley (S. H.)]

The National Finances and a National Bank. *New-York.* 1861. 8vo, pp. 20. B. 51976

The National Finances. Letter to Congress. [Dated Washington, January 15, 1862.] 8vo, pp. 6, (1). H. 51977

The National Finances: A Letter ... to the ... Secretary of the Treasury ... on the Subject of the New York Financiers, their Modesty, Wisdom, Patriotism, and Intentions ... . By a Patriot. ... *New York: Baker & Godwin, Printers.* 1862. 8vo,

pp. 8. H. + The Second Letter ... on the Subjects of Cheap Money, the Proposed War Tax, Demand Treasury Notes, etc. ... [*Ibid.*] 1862. 8vo, pp. 8. 51978

The National Finances and the Public Faith. By Adirondack. [n. p. n. d.] 8vo. 51979

National Foundry—Deep River, N. C. Special Report of Dr. E. Emmons, Geologist to the State of North Carolina, concerning the Advantages of the Valley of the Deep River as a site for the Establishment of a National Foundry. *Raleigh.* 1857. 8vo, pp. 14. 51980

The National Freedman, A Monthly Journal of the National Freedmen's Relief Association. Vol. I. February 1, 1865. No. I. *New York.* 1865. 8vo, pp. 40. Continued. H. 51981

The Final Report of the National Freedmen's-Aid Union of Great Britain and Ireland. With the names of the ... Committee of Correspondence with American ... Associations; and ... Proceedings on the Presentation of Addresses to ... Hon. C. F. Adams and ... Hon. R. Johnson ... . *London: R. Barrett & Sons, Printers.* 1868. 8vo, pp. 39. B. 51982

Also: Presentation of an Address to ... Honorable Charles Francis Adams ... . *Birmingham: White and Pike, Printers.* 1868. 8vo, pp. 12. B.—Presentation of an Address to ... Honorable Reverdy Johnson ... . *London: Richard Barrett and Sons, Printers.* 1868. 8vo, pp. 12. B.

National Freedmen's Relief Association, ... in the City of New York. *New York: Wm. C. Bryant & Co., Printers.* 1862. 8vo, pp. 8. B. 51983

Contains Organization, By-Laws and Officers. Also: First Annual Report of the ... Association. New York, February 19, 1863. [n. p. n. d.] 4to, pp. 3.—Monthly Report of the ... Association. No. 2. [n. p. n. d.] 4to, pp. 4.—Fourth Annual Report of the National Freedmen's Relief Association, of the District of Columbia. *Washington, D. C.: McGill & Witherow, Printers.* 1866. 8vo, pp. 21, (1). B.

The National Freemason ... . By Bro. Robert McMurdy. *Washington.* 1863–68. 11 vols., 4to. 51984

National Free Soil Convention. *See* Dyer (O.), VI. 21599.

Exhibition Catalogue of Paintings of the National Gallery. *New York.* 1830. 8vo. S. 51985

National Government Journal. *See* Force (P.), VI. 25057.

The National Guard. [Dated] Camp Pennsylvania, Baltimore, Md. July 4, 1861. 8vo, 4 leaves. 51986

The National Handbook of Facts and Figures, Historical, Documentary, Statistical, Political, from the Formation of the Government to the Present Time. With a full Chronology of the Rebellion. *New York: E. B. Treat & Co.* 1868. 12mo, pp. 409. Plates. 51987

Catalogue of the Extraordinary Curiosities in the National Institute. *Washington.* 1859. 8vo. 51988

Also: Proceedings of the National Institute, Washington, D. C. New Series. Vol. I. No. I. March, 1855. *Washington.* 1855. 8vo. Continued.—Report of the Recording Secretary ... for ... 1850 ... . *Washington.* 1850. 8vo, pp. 10. Cont'd.

Constitution of the National Institute of Letters, Arts and Sciences. ... *New York: Moorhead, Bond & Co.* 1868. 8vo, pp. 14. + *New York: Wm. C. Bryant & Co., Printers.* 1868. 8vo, pp. 15. H. 51989

Bulletin of the Proceedings of the National Institution for the Promotion of Science. ... 1840. *Washington: Printed by Gales and Seaton.* 1841. 8vo, pp. 65. Continued. H. 51990

Also: Constitution and By-Laws of the National Institution for the Promotion of Science ... . *Washington: Printed by Gales and Seaton.* 1840. 8vo, pp. 14.—Constitution of the National Institution for the Promotion of Science ... . Amended ... April, 1841. *Washington: Printed by Peter Force.* 1841. 8vo, pp. 19.—Third Circular of the Committee, March 5, 1844. [n. p. n. d.] Folio, pp. 4.

Circular and Address of the National Institution for Promoting Industry in the United States, to their Fellow-Citizens. *New-York: Printed by J. Seymour.* 1820. 8vo, pp. 28. H. 51991

Also: An Address to the People of the United States ... . *New-York: Printed by J. Seymour.* 1820. 8vo, pp. (2), 22. B. + *Concord (N. H.)* 1821. 8vo. C.

National Interests and Domestic Manufactures: Address of the Philadelphia Society for the Promotion of Domestic Industry, to the Citizens of the United States. *Boston: W. W. Clapp.* 1819. 8vo, pp. 116. N. 51992

... National Johnson Club. I.—Address of the ... Club. 2.—Testimony of Alexander H. Stephens. ... [n. p. 1866.] 8vo, pp. 16. BA. 51993

The National Law; embracing the Appeal in its behalf, and the Laws authorizing it. *Washington.* 1862. 8vo. 51994

The National Life: containing Biographical Sketches of the Presidents of the United States, ... with ... Portraits ... . *Boston: H. R. Stevens.* 1870. 16mo, pp. 36. H. 51995

The National Life Insurance Company of the United States. Office—Montpelier, Vt. *Montpelier: Press of Eastman and Danforth.* 1850. 12mo, pp. 35, (1). B. 51996

Also: Abstract of the Third Annual Report ... 1852. ... *Montpelier: J. M. Stevens, Printer.* [n. d.] 16mo, pp. 56.—Statement, July, 1860. [n. p. n. d.] 8vo, pp. 8.

National Life and Travellers' Insurance Co. of New-York. ... [Statement.] *New York: John A. Gray & Green, Printers.* 1865. 24mo, pp. 48. H. 51997

Abstract of the Proceedings of the National Lord's Day Convention. Held in ... Baltimore, ... 1844. *Baltimore.* 1845. 8vo, pp. 82. H. 51998

The National Magazine and Industrial Record. Edited by Redwood Fisher. June, 1845. Vol. I. No. I. ... *New York: J. W. Bell, Printer.* [1845.] 8vo, pp. (2), 96. Continued. H.

National Magazine and Republican Review. Edited by H. J. Brent. *City of Washington.* 1839. 8vo. 52000

The National Magazine: Devoted to Literature, Art, and Religion. Abel Stevens, Editor. Volume I. ... *New York: Carlton & Phillips.* 1852. 8vo, pp. iv, 572. Portraits. Cont'd.

National Magazine: or a Political, Biographical, Historical and Literary Repository. [Edited by James Lyon.] Vol. I. [*Richmond.*] 1799. 8vo. Continued. C., S. 52002

The National Magazine, or Cabinet of the United States. ... *Washington.* 1801. 8vo. Continued to Part VIII. 52003

Edited by Richard Dinsmore; James Lyon, manager.

National Magazine, or Ladies' Emporium. Edited by Mary Barney ... . Vol. I. November, 1830. No. I. *Baltimore: Printed by Sands & Neilson.* [1830.] 8vo, pp. (2), 78, (2). Plate.

... The National Medical Almanac for 1848. ... By L. Thompson. *Philadelphia: Lindsay & Blakiston.* [n. d.] 8vo, pp. (32). H. 52005

Annual Announcement of the National Medical College, Washington, D. C., 1848. *Washington: Printed by J. and G. Gideon.* 1848. 8vo, pp. 7. 52006

Also: Circular of the ... College ... . *Georgetown.* 1850. 8vo. B.

Minutes of the Proceedings of the National Medical Convention, held ... May, 1846. ... *New-York:* ... *H. Ludwig.* 1846. 8vo, pp. 16. H. 52007

... National Medical Journal edited by Chris. C. Cox, M.D., LL.D. ... Vol. I. No. I. April, 1870. *Washington, D. C.: Judd & Detweiler.* [1870.] 8vo, pp. 128. H. 52008

The National Melodist. A Repository of the Songs of the Day. *Chicago: John R. Walsh.* [n. d.] 18mo, pp. 72. 52009

National Money, or a Simple System of Finance; ... in three Letters, Addressed by a Citizen of Washington to the Congress of the United States. *Georgetown, Ga.: Printed by W. A. Rind and Co.* 1816. 8vo, pp. 18. BA. 52010

Proceedings of the National Musical Convention, held at ... Boston, ... 1841 ... . *Boston: Manning & Hallworth, Printers.* 1841. 8vo, pp. 12. H. 52011

Also: Constitution of the National Musical Convention, with a List of Names comprising the ... Convention and Teachers' Class, 1845. *Boston: Wright's ... Press.* 1845. 24mo, pp. 12. Continued.

The National Normal ... . Volume I. October, 1868. Number I. [*Cincinnati: R. H. Holbrook.* 1868.] 8vo, pp. 42. Continued. H. 52012

See also Lebanon, O., Vol. x., No. 39575.

National Observatory. *See* [Maury (M. F.)], XI. 46966–7.

National Plan for an Atlantic and Pacific Rail Road. [n. p.] 1849. 8vo. 52013

The National Policy. Tracts for the Times. Number One. Conducted by John Williams, Editor of "The Iron Age." ... *New York.* 1865. 8vo, pp. (14). BA. 52014

National Popular Education. *See* Vol. II., No. 6054.

The National Portrait Gallery. *See* Herring (J.), VIII. 31577

There is an edition "Four Volumes in Three." *Philadelphia: D. Rice & A. N. Hart.* 1853–54. 8vo.

National Portrait Gallery. *See* Duyckinck (E. A.), VI. 21504

National Prejudice opposed to National Interest, candidly considered in the detention or yielding up Gibraltar and Cape Breton by the ensuing Treaty of Peace: With some Observations on the Natural Jealousy of the Spanish Nation, and how far it may

operate to the Prejudice of British Commerce if not removed at this Crisis. ... *London: W. Owen.* 1748. 8vo, pp. 50. J.C.B.

The National Problem solved! *See* [Meyer (A.)], XII. 48670

... The National Protestant. ... Edited by Rev. C. Sparry. Vol. I. November. No. I. *New-York: Pudney, Hooker & Russell, Printers.* [1844.] 8vo, pp. 32. Plates. Continued. H.

Minutes and Proceedings of the National Quarantine and Sanitary Convention, held at Philadelphia, ... May 13th, 14th, 15th, 16th, and 17th, 1857. ... *Philadelphia.* 1857. 8vo, pp. 60. S.

Continued annually. Also: Regulations as approved by the National Quarantine and Sanitary Association of the United States. 1860. *Boston: Rand & Avery, ... Printers.* 1860. 8vo, pp. 39. B.

The National Quarterly Review. [Edited by Edward I. Sears.] Vol. I. ... *New York: Pudney & Russell.* 1860. 8vo, pp. (2), ii, 557. Continued. BA. 52018

The National Record of Education: containing Current News and Statistics of Colleges and Schools in the United States. Vol. I. May, 1866. No. I. *New York.* [n. d.] 8vo, pp. 38. H.

The National Recorder. Jan. 1819, to July, 1821. *Philadelphia: Littell & Henry.* [1819–21.] 5 vols., 8vo. B., S.

Vol. I. was issued under the title, "The Philadelphia Register and National Recorder." A second series, consisting of two volumes, July, 1821, to July, 1822, was issued under the title, "The Saturday Magazine."

The National Register. ... No. I Vol. I. *Washington: Joel K. Mead.* 1816. 8vo, pp. 16. C., H. 52021

Continued to nine or more volumes.

National Register. 1865. *New York.* 1865. 8vo. 52022

... National Reform Almanac, for 1849. ... *New-York.* [n. d.] 12mo, pp. 48. H. 52023

National Republican Convention. *See* Vol. IX., Nos. 36729, 36741, *and* Proceedings.

National Republicans. *See* Vol. XI., Nos. 45050 *and* 45102.

National Rights, 1841. *See* [Pickering (John)].

Circular and Address of the National Society for Promoting Industry in the United States, to their Fellow-Citizens. *New York.* 182–. 8vo, pp. 28. 52024

The Fifth National Sunday-School Convention, held at Indianapolis, April 16–19, 1872. With an Historical Introduction, by the Rev. H. Clay Trumbull. *New York:* ... *A. O. Van Lennep.* 1872. 8vo, pp. 159, xxviii. C. 52025

National Sunday School Teacher. *See* Sunday School Teacher.

A National System of Finance suited to a War or Peace Establishment regulating Exchanges, and making Specie Plenty. *Fond du Lac, Wisconsin.* 1862. 8vo, pp. 14. 52026

The National Tax-Law, (complete:) ... *New York: Beadle and Company.* [1861.] 16mo, pp. vii, 130. B. + [*Ibid.*] 1863. 12mo, pp. 124. + *New York: Tribune Office.* 1863. 12mo. + *New York City: O. S. Felt.* 1863. 12mo. 52027

The National Tax Law, as Amended. ... Arranged by Edward H. Hall, Washington, D. C. *New York: Carleton.* 1863. 12mo, pp. 136. 52028

Journal of Proceedings of the National Teachers' Association, at the First Anniversary, held in Cincinnati, O., Aug. ... 1858, with the Constitution ... . *Albany, N. Y.: James Cruikshank.* 1858. 8vo, pp. 62. Continued. H. 52029

The National Temperance Advocate. The Organ of the National Temperance Society and Publication House. ... *New York: J. N. Stearns.* 1866. Folio. Continued. C. 52030

The National Temperance Almanac, for ... 1836; ... [n. p. n. d.] 12mo, pp. (36.) Continued. H. 52031

Also: First Quarterly Report of the National Temperance Society. *New-York.* 1850. 12mo. — Second Annual Report of the National Temperance Society ... May 8th, 1867. With an Appendix, containing the Constitution ... . *New-York: National Temperance Society.* 1867. 8vo, pp. 28, 44. Continued. B.

National Thanksgiving Services held December 7, 1865, in the Hall of United States House of Representatives. Discourse by Rev. Dr. C. B. Boynton, and Historic References to former Thanksgiving Occasions. *Washington.* 1865. 8vo. 52032

The National Union. Vol. I. No. I. *Nashville.* 1860. 8vo.

Loyal Publications of National Union Association of Ohio. No. 3. ... Dayton Speech of Hon. John Brough. President Lincoln's Response relative to the arrest of Vallandigham. *Cincinnati: Moore, Wilstach ... & Co., Printers.* 1863. 8vo, pp. 31. Continued. H. 52034

Articles of Association and Constitution of the National Union Club, Philadelphia. *Philadelphia: King & Baird.* 1863. 12mo, pp. 12. 52035

A Nation's Manhood; or, Stories of Washington and the American War of Independence. ... *London: J. F. Shaw & Co.* 1861. 12mo, pp. viii, 358. 4 Plates. C. 52036

The Nation's Sin and Punishment; or, the Hand of God Visible in the Overthrow of Slavery. By [S. A. Hodgman?] A Chaplain of the U. S. Army, who has been, thirty years, a resident of the Slave States. *New York: M. Doolady.* 1864. 12mo, pp. 274. BA. 52037

A corrected title of our No. 32355, Vol. VIII.

The Nation's Success. *See* [Breckenridge (R. J.)], II. 7681.

The Native American. A Gift for the People. *Philadelphia: Hector Orr.* 1845. Rl. 8vo, pp. 199. 52038

Printed with red ink, in blue borders, on white paper. Edited by the printer, Hector Orr, and contains Washington's Farewell Address, Declaration of Independence, Constitution of the United States, Address of the Native American Conventions, and Address of the Pennsylvania Convention, 1845.

Native American Review. No. I. March, 1855. ... *Philadelphia: J. W. Moore.* [n. d.] 8vo, pp. 112. H. 52039

Native-Americanism. *See* [Hildreth (R.)], Vol. VIII. 31781.

Native Canadian, *pseudon.* *See* [Denison (G. F.)], V. 19565.

Nativism; or the Office Hunter under a Religious Cloak. By a Friend to Equal Rights. *Philadelphia.* 1844. 8vo, pp. 12.

Natural History of Coffie, Thee, Chocolate, and Tobacco. *London: Christopher Wilkinson.* 1682. 4to, pp. 39. 52041

Very rare. Reprinted in the "Harleian Miscellany," Vol. XII. *See also* No. 12861

The Natural History of the Ordinary Cetacea or Whales ... . *Edinburgh: W. H. Lizars.* 1837. Fcap 8vo. 32 Plates.

Natural History of the State of New York. *See* New York.

The Natural Principles of Liberty, Moral Virtue, Learning, Society, Good Manners and Human Happiness; ... Offered ... to the Legislature of ... Massachusetts, in New-England, With all others ... Whom it may concern to promote Peace and Union, Harmony and Concord. ... *Boston: Printed by Benjamin Edes and Sons.* MDCCLXXXII. 8vo, pp. (2), ii, 12. BA. 52043

Natural Resources of Arkansas. *Little Rock.* 1869. 8vo.

La Naturaleza. Periódico Científico de la Sociedad Mexicana de Historia Natural. *Mexico.* 1869. 9 parts, folio, pp. 200. Plates. 52045

The Naturalist. Edited by Daniel Jay Browne ... . Vol. I. December, 1830. No. I. ... *Boston: Peirce & Parker.* 1830. 8vo, pp. 32. Plate. Continued. H. 52046

The Naturalist and Journal of Natural History, Agriculture, Education and Literature, conducted by I. N. Loomis [and others]. *Nashville.* 1846. 8vo. 52047

Eight or more numbers published.

The Naturalist's Directory. North America and the West Indies. *Salem: Essex Institute.* 1865. 12mo, pp. 31, iv.

Le Naturaliste Canadien. Bulletin de recherches, observations et découvertes se rapportant à l'histoire naturelle du Canada. L'Abbé L. Provancher, rédacteur-propriétaire. *Québec: D. Darveau.* 1868–71. 3 vols., 8vo. C. 52049

Naturalization in the American Colonies. [n. p.] 1859. 8vo.

Naturalization Laws of the United States; containing also, the Alien Laws of the State of New-York, a Synopsis of the Alien Laws of other States, with the Forms ... . *Rochester.* 1855. 8vo. C. 52051

See also Vol. x., No. 39426.

The Nature and Extent of Parliamentary Power Considered, in some Remarks upon Mr. Pitt's Speech in the House of Commons, previous to the Repeal of the Stamp Act. With an Introduction. Applicable to the present situation of the Colonies. September, 1767. ... *New-York: Re-Printed from the Pennsylvania Journal, by John Holt.* 1768. 12mo, pp. 40. P. 52052

Impugnes the omnipotency of Government.

The Nature and Fruits of Political Antimasonry, practically exhibited. *Northampton: Printed by Wm. A. Hawley.* 1835. 8vo, pp. 18. B. 52053

Nature and Human Nature. *See* [Haliburton (T. C.)], VIII.

Nature, Design and General Rules of the Methodist Society, with John Wesley's Advice ... . *New York.* 1809. 8vo, pp. 24.

The Nature of the Government in its Relation to Theology. [n. p.] 1870. 12mo, pp. 13. 52055

Nature: on Freedom of Mind: and other Poems. *Boston: Dutton & Wentworth.* 1839. 12mo, pp. 36. H. 52056

NAU (É.) Histoire des Caciques d'Haiti par Le Baron Émile Nau. *Port-au-Prince: T. Bouchereau.* 1855. 8vo, pp. (2), vi, 364. B. 52057

NAUDAIN (A.) Speech of Arnold Naudain ... on the Delaware Jackson Delegates. [n. p.] 1831. 8vo. S. 52058

Naufrage d'Isabelle. *See* [La Condamine (C. M. de)], 38489

Naufragio del bergantin de guerra Almirante. *Habana: Imprenta de Campe.* [n. d.] 4to. 52059

Second Annual Report of the ... Directors to the Stockholders of the Naugatuck Railroad Company, ... 1850. *New Haven: Printed by J. H. Benham.* 1850. 8vo, pp. 12. Continued. B.

Naukeerige Beschriving. *See* Vol. VII., No. 28654.

NAUMANN (Jacob). Nordamerika, sein Volksthum und seine Institutionen. Nach mehrjährigen Erfahrungen, insbesondere zur Belehrung für Ansiedler geschildert. Mit Vorwort herausgegeben von Fr. Bülau. *Leipzig: Hinrichs.* 1848. 8vo, pp. viii, 414. 52061

NAUMANN. Reise nach den Vereinigten Staaten von Nord-Amerika, siebenjähriger Aufenthalt in denselben und Rückkehr nach Deutschland. Mittheilungen für Auswanderungslustige, mit besonderer Beziehung auf Ackerbau, Handel und Gewerbe. Herausgegeben von Prof. Fr. Bülau. *Leipzig: Hinrichs.* 1850. 8vo, pp. vi, 390. C. 52062

Nautahala Land and Mineral Co. [n. p.] 1858. 8vo.

The Nautical Almanac and Astronomical Ephemeris for ... 1812. ... Tenth American Impression ... . *New-Brunswick, New-Jersey: Printed by Elliot & Crissy.* [1811.] 8vo, pp. (8), 168. Continued. H. 52063

Nautical Education. Letter from a Friend to a Young Gentleman of Maryland, on his entrance into the United States Navy. [n. p.] 1841. 8vo. N. 52064

The Nautical Magazine and Naval Chronicle. Volume No. I. 1832. A Journal of Papers on Subjects connected with Maritime Affairs ... . [*London:*] *Fisher, Son & Co.* 1832. 8vo, pp. (2), 616, (7). Plates and Map. B. 52065

Contains accounts of voyages and discoveries in all parts of the world. Continued to 1867 or later.

Nautical Magazine and Naval Journal. *New York.* 1854–57. 6 vols., 8vo. C. 52066

Nautical Remarks and Observations for the Chart of the Harbour of Boston. ... *London: The Author.* M,DCC,LXXV. 4to, pp. 11. H. 52067

Nautical Songster | or | Seaman's Companion. | To Encrease the Joys of | Saturday Night: | A Collection of the Newest | and Most Approved | Songs. | Interspersed with many Originals. | *Baltimore:* | *Printed for Henry S. Keatinge.* | 1798. | 12mo, pp. 64. Plate.

NAUTICUS, *pseudon.* Remarks on Lord Howe's Extraordinary Gazette. By Nauticus. As published in a Morning Paper of Nov. 11, 1782. *London: Sibthorp.* 1782. 8vo, pp. 20. 52069

NAUTICUS, *Junior.* Naval Atalantis; or, A Display of the Characters of such Flag Officers as were distinguished during the last War. By Nauticus, Junior. *London: J. Ridgway.* MDCCLXXXVIII. 8vo, pp. (4), iv, 195. H. 52070

Nautilus Submarine Company. ... [Prospectus.] *New-York: Nesbitt and Co., Printers.* 1854. 8vo, pp. 8. 2 Plates. H.

NAUVOO. Célébration à Nauvoo. *See* [Cabet É.], III. 9778.

Nauwkeurige Beschrijving, 1678. *See* [La Peyrère (I. de)].

Naval Academy. *See* Annapolis, Vol. I., No. 1594*a*.

Naval Achievements. *See* [Jenkins (James)], IX. 35994.

Naval and Marine Laws of the United States. [n. p.] 1843. 8vo. 52072

Naval Battles of the United States in the different Wars with Foreign Nations, from the ... Revolution to the Present Time: including Privateering. ... *Boston: Higgins, Bradley and Dayton.* 1857. 8vo, pp. 278, (1). 20 Plates. B. 52073

Naval Biography; or, the History and Lives of Distinguished Characters in the British Navy from the earliest period to the

present time. *London: John Scott.* 1815. 2 vols., 8vo, pp. (2), 478; 529, (5). 38 Portraits. 52074

The portraits include Sir Walter Raleigh, Sir Francis Drake, Sir Charles Hardy (Governor of New York), Admiral Vernon, Sir Peter Warren, and others.

The Naval Chronicle; or Voyages, Travels, Expeditions, Remarkable Exploits and Atchievements, Of the most Celebrated English Navigators, Travellers, and Sea-Commanders, From the Earliest Accounts to ... 1759; ... thro Asia, Africa, and America; The many Conquests they obtained over the Spaniards, French, and other Nations; ... Including The Lives of the most Eminent British Admirals and Seamen, who have distinguished themselves by their Bravery and Love of Liberty. ... Adorned with Cuts. *London: J. Fuller.* M.DCC.LX. 3 vols., 8vo, pp. vi, (4), 480; 480; 474. 30 Plates. P. 52075

Contains accounts of the voyages of Sir Walter Raleigh, Sir Francis Drake, the Cabots, the first attempts for the discovery of New England, etc.

The Naval Chronicle. Vol. I. From January to June. MDCCXCIX. ... *London: Bunney & Gold.* [1799.] 8vo, pp. (2), iv, iv, 544, (43). Plates. H. 52076

Continued to 40 volumes. Contains full and generally accurate reports of the various conflicts between the English and American Navy in the War of 1812, not to be found elsewhere; also biographies of Earl Howe, Vancouver, Lord Cornwallis, Hood, Anson, and other explorers.

... The Naval Defence of the Great Lakes. Mr. F. A. Conkling, ... submitted the following Report. ... [*Washington.* 1863.] 8vo, pp. 16. 52077

The Naval History of Great Britain with the Lives of the most Illustrious Admirals and Commanders from The Reign of Queen Elizabeth. Interspersed with Accounts of the most important Discoveries made ... *London: James Rivington.* [n. d.] 4 vols., 12mo, pp. xlviii, 271; xii, 336; xi, 339; xi, 370. Portraits, 4 Maps. 52078

Includes Sir Francis Drake, Sir Martin Forbisher, Sir Walter Raleigh, Lord Anson, Admiral Blake, Peter Warren, Admiral Vernon, etc.

The Naval Magazine. ... Edited by ... Rev. C. S. Stewart, M.A. ... *New-York: John S. Taylor.* 1836–37. 2 vols., 8vo, pp. 608, (2), Appendix, 71; 612, Appendix, (2), 87. 2 Vignettes, Map and 2 Plates. BA. 52079

Naval Monitor, containing ... some Observations on the Naval Actions with America. By an Officer. *London.* 1815. 12mo.

The Naval Monument. *See* [Bowen (Abel)], II. 7045.

Naval Rank. A Statement of the Title Question. ... [*Washington?* n. d.] 12mo, pp. 7. H. 52081

Naval Register. ... 1815. [n. p. n. d.] 8vo, pp. 45. B.

Naval Regulations issued by Command of the President of the United States, January 25, 1802. *City of Washington.* 1802. 12mo. C. 52083

Naval Sketch Book. *See* [Glascock (Wm. N.)], Vol. VII., No. 27547, and add, + Second Edition. [*Ibid.*] 1826. 2 vols., post 8vo, pp. xxiv, 284; iv, 304. + [*Ibid.*] 1831. 52084

The Naval Songster, being a Collection of Naval Victories, and other Excellent Songs. *Charlestown.* 1815. 16mo, pp. 16.

The Naval Songster. Songs of the Sea, National, Patriotic, Satirical, and Comic. Original and Selected. *Philadelphia: A. Winch.* [1862.] 18mo, pp. 72. 52086

Naval Staff Rank. By a Naval Staff Officer. ... [n. p. n. d.] 8vo, pp. 11. H. 52087

Naval Temple. *See* Vol. I., Nos. 1165 and 2696.

The Naval Triumph. A Poem. *London: J. Kearsley.* 1783. 4to. 52088

Compliments Lord Rodney. *See* "Monthly Review," LXVIII. 356.

NAVARA (J. I. Maria de). Elogio funebre que en las Honras de D. Juan Joseph Yandiola y el Campo celebrados en la iglesia de S. Antonio de la Ciudad Durango, 20 Feb. 1802. ... *Mexico.* 1802. 4to, 46 leaves. 52089

NAVARES (C. de). *See* Cabrera de Navares (M.), III. 9819.

NAVARIJO (I. R.) Elogios funebres, que la Pontificia y Rl. Universidad de Mexico dedicó á la buena memoria de su Cancelario el Sr. D. Francisco Rodriguez Navarijo, los saca á luz su hermano el Dr. D. Ignacio Rodriguez Navarijo. *Mexico.* 1758. 4to, pp. (14), 14, 21. 52090

[NAVARRE (P.)] Amusements géographiques et historiques, ou les Mémoires de M***, contenant ses voyages et ses aventures dans les quatre parties du monde. *Meaux: Courtois.* 1786.

2 vols., 8vo. + *Paris: Méquignon le jeune.* 1788. 2 vols., 8vo, pp. (2), iv, 346; (4), 318, (2). 5 Maps, 2 Plates. C. 52091

Republished with the following title:

[NAVARRE.] Voyages d'un Étudiant dans les cinq parties du monde ... . Par M. Depping. *Paris: Méquignon le jeune.* 1821. 2 vols., 8vo. 8 Maps. + [*Ibid.*] 1822. + *Paris: F. Delamarche. Lyon: Périsse frères.* 1822 [1825]. 8vo. + Nouvelle édition. *Paris: Delamarche.* 1835. 2 vols., 8vo. 8 Maps and 2 Plates. 52092

Some copies retain the title "Amusements géographiques ... ou Voyages dans les cinq parties du monde."

NAVARRETE (A.) Relacion peregrina de la Agua Corriente, que para beber, y vivir goza la muy noble, leal, y florida Ciudad de Santiago de Queretaro. ... *Mexico: J. B. de Hogal.* 1739. 4to, pp. 164. 52093

In prose and verse.

NAVARRETE (Eustaquio Fernandez de). Noticias para la Vida de D. Hernando Colon; y noticias de D. Bartolomé Colon, hermano del almirante. *Madrid: Calero.* 1850. 8vo, pp. 285. C.

Also includes a Life of Garcilasso de la Vega.

NAVARRETE (Fernandez). Tratados historicos, politicos, ethicos, y religiosos de la Monarchia de China; de los Viages y Navigaciones que hizo el Autor, a la Nueua España, a Mexico, las Philipinas, Macasar, Charamandel, Golocondar ... . *Madrid.* 1676. Folio. 52095

"Ouvrage intéressant."—BRUNET. Also: Synodo Diocesana del Arzobispado de Santo Domingo, celebrada por Fernandez Navarrette Año de 1683 ... . *Madrid.* [n. d.] 4to.

NAVARRETE (Juan Gomez). Esposicion que dirige al Congreso general, como albacea de D. Agustin de Iturbide, promoviendo el cumplimiento del decreto de la Junta soberana gubernativa de 21 de Febrero de 1822. ... *Mexico.* 1832. 4to, pp. 19.

NAVARRETE (M. F. de). Biblioteca Marítima Española, Obra póstuma del Don Martin Fernandez de Navarrete. ... *Madrid: Impr. de la Viuda de Calero.* 1851. 2 vols., 8vo, pp. xxxvii, 671; (4), 784. 52097

A posthumous work, with biographical notices, concerning which *see* Petzholdt's "Bibliotheca Bibliographica," p. 749.

NAVARRETE. Coleccion de los Viages y Descubrimientos, que hicieron por Mar los Españoles desde fines del siglo XV, con

varios Documentos inéditos concernientes á la Historia de la Marina Castellana y de los establecimientos Españoles en Indias, Coordinada é ilustrada por Don Martin Fernandez de Navarrete, ... *Madrid: En la Imprenta Real.* 1825–37. 5 vols., 8vo, pp. (4), cli, (2), 455, Map; (2), 455; (2), xv, 642; xc, 416, Plate; (2), 501. A., B., C. 52098

There are copies on large paper. Vols. I. and II. were reprinted in 1858. Mr. Rich (Vol. II., p. 179,) devotes almost a page of encomium to this valuable work. Brunet characterizes it as an "importante collection," and Washington Irving drew from it most of the material which forms the basis of his "Life of Columbus." It contains the original diary of the voyages of Columbus, compiled by B. de las Casas, the expeditions of Amerigo Vespucci, and the subsequent voyages of the Spaniards, taken from inedited manuscripts or reprinted from rare printed works; also many singular and curious documents concerning the history and manners of the period. It may safely be asserted that the enterprise of this laborious compiler has rescued from oblivion the earliest and rarest records of American discovery. For a list of the contents, *see* Leclerc's Catalogue.

NAVARRETE. Coleccion de Documentos Inéditos para la Historia de España; por Don Martin Fernandez Navarrete, Don Miguel Salvá y Don Pedro Sainz de Baranda. *Madrid: Viuda de Calero.* 1842–73. 59 vols., sm. 4to. Portraits and Facsimiles.

Vols. VI.–LIX. were edited by M. Salvá and other members of the "Academia de la Historia." This very valuable collection of documents is of much importance for the history of the Spanish-American possessions, as they contain many valuable papers relative to Columbus, Cortez, Pizarro, etc., which have not been printed elsewhere.

NAVARRETE. Coleccion de Opúsculos. ... *Madrid.* 1848. 8vo. 52100

Contains historical memoirs of great importance, part of which relate to the history of America.

NAVARRETE. Discurso historico sobre los progresos que ha tenido en España el arte de Navegar. Leido en la Academia de la Historia por Don Martin Fernandez de Navarrete. *Madrid: Imprenta Real.* 1802. 8vo, pp. 61. 52101

NAVARRETE. Disertacion sobre la Historia de la Náutica, y de las ciencias matemáticas que han contribuido á sus progresos entre los Españoles. Obra póstuma: ... *Madrid: Imprenta de la Viuda de Calero.* 1846. 4to, pp. 421. 52102

Important for the history of the Spanish navigators.

NAVARRETE. Narrazione dei quatro viaggi intrapresi da Cristoforo Colombo per la scoperta del nuovo continente dal 1492 al 1504. ... Pubblicati ... da Don M. F. Navarrette ... . *Prato: Tipografia Giachetti.* 1840–41. 2 vols., 8vo, pp. 551; 456, (2). Portraits, Maps and Plates. BA. 52103

NAVARRETE. Relaciones, Cartas, y otros Documentos, concernientes á los Cuatro Viages que hizo el Almirante D. Cristobal Colon, para el Descubrimiento de las Indias Occidentales ... . *Madrid.* 1825. 2 vols., folio. 52104

NAVARRETE. Relations des Quatre Voyages entrepris par Christophe Colomb pour la Découverte du Nouveau-Monde de 1492 à 1504; suivies de diverses Lettres et Pièces inédites Extraites des Archives de la Monarchie Espagnole, et publiées pour la première fois ... par Don M. F. de Navarrete ... . Traduite de l'Espagnol, par MM. F. T. A. Chalumeau de Verneuil ... et De la Roquette ... . *Paris: Treuttel et Würtz.* 1828. 3 vols., 8vo, pp. xxxvij, (3), 400; (4), 489; (4), 444. Portrait, Maps and Plates. BA. 52105

The translators had the advantage of having their labor revised by the original compiler. The chief members of the Geographical Society of Paris took an active interest in it, and Messieurs Rémusat, Balbi, le baron Cuvier, Jomard, Labouderie, Letronne, de Rossel, Saint-Martin, Walckenaer, Humboldt, etc., added notes and explanations, so that, on the whole, the work is a most valuable companion for the student of the original Spanish. *See* "North American Review," XXIV. 265, *and* Rich, II. 197.

NAVARRETE (P.) Chronica de la Provincia de N. S. P. S. Francisco de Zacatecas; compuesta por M. R. P. Fr. Joseph Arlegui ... la que dedica ... S. Francisco ... Joseph de Erreparaz ... en nombre de ... Pedro Navarrete ... . *En Mexico, por Joseph Bernardo de Hogal* ... *año de* 1737. 4to, pp. (30), 412, (18).

Corrected title of our No. 1998, Vol. I.

NAVARRETE. Directorio para informaciones de los Pretendientes de Santo Habito de N. Seraphico P. S. Francisco ... . *Mexico, por D. Maria de Ribera.* 1737. 4to. 52107

NAVARRETE (P. F.) Conservacion | De Monarqvias | y Discvrsos Politicos | sobre la gran Consulta que el Consejo hizo | al Señor Rey Don Filipe | tercero | Al Presidente, y | Consejo Supremo de | Castilla. | Por el Licenciado | Pedro Fernandez Nauarrete ... . *Madrid: Imprenta Real.* M.DC.XXVI. Folio, Title, pp. (8), 344.

Contains incidentally many allusions to America and its influence upon Spain: the new discoveries and colonies in America, etc.

NAVARRO (D.) Auto del Gobierno y Capitanía General de 11 de .... de 1779, por el cual el Sr. D. Diego Navarro establece las reglas necesarias para el arreglo del Foro. [n. p. 1779.] Folio, pp. 16. 52109

NAVARRO Y NORIEGA (Fernando). Catalogo de los Curatos y Misiones que tiene la Nueva España en cada una de sus Dio-

cesis, o sea la division eclesiastica de este Reyno. ... *Mexico.* 1813. 4to, pp. 40. 52110

NAVARRO. Memoria sobre la Poblacion del Reino de Nueva España. Escrita por Don Fernand Navarro y Noriega. *Mexico.* 1820. 4to, pp. 23. 52111

With a statistical table of the population of Mexico.

NAVARRO (Joannis). Liber in quo quatuor passiones Christi Domini continentur, octo lamentatione. Oratio ... . *México.* 1604. Folio. 52112

NAVARRO É IBARRA (Joaquin). Discurso pronunciado el 27 de Setiembre de 1845, solemne aniversario del la entrada de ejercito trigarante en Mexico, el año de 1821. *Mexico.* 1845. 8vo.

NAVARRO (J. M.) Documentos justificativos de la conducta que ha observado en Centro-America el presbíter José Maria Navarro, reimpresso de nuevos atestados. *Guatemala: Imprenta de la Paz.* 1869. 4to. 52114

NAVARRO. Memoria del estado actual de la parroquia de S. Martin Xilotepeque formado por su cura encargado Presbítero José Maria Navarro ... . Comprende los años de 1857 á 1859. *Guatemala: Imprenta de Lima.* 1861. 4to, pp. 72. Map.

Includes geographical, topographical and statistical details of the diocese of Guatemala.

NAVARRO. Memoria del estado de la parroquia de Concepcion de Villa Nueva, formada por su cura encargado presbítero José Maria Navarro. ... *Guatemala.* 1868. 4to. 2 Maps.

NAVARRO (Juan Suarez). Informe sobre las frecuentes revoluciones ocurridas en Yucatan, y medios de evitarlas, asi como la venta de indigenas. ... *México: Cumplido.* 1861. 4to, pp. 189, Table, (2). Map. 52117

NAVARRO (Louis Diez). Extracto de una relacion sobre el Antiguo Reyno de Guatemala hecho en 1745. *Guatemala: S. Suna.* 1859. 8vo, pp. 32. 52118

NAVASCA (*Island of*). *See* Vol. XII., No. 48131.

Navassa Phosphate Company. ... [Report.] September, 1864. [*Baltimore.* 1864.] 8vo, pp. 15, (1). 4 Plates. B. 52119

Navigantium atque Itinerantium Bibliotheca. *See* Harris (J.)

La Navigation du Capitaine Frobisher, Anglois, ez régions d'Oest et Nord-West en l'année 1577. [*Genève*] *par André Chuppin.* 1578. 8vo. 52120

Title from Ternaux, No. 131.

The Navigator. *See* [Cramer (Zadok)], Vol. V. 17364–6.

Navolging van een engelsch Gedigt, op de Vervolgingen tegen America, getrokken uyt het laatste London Magazyn, en geplaatst in de Courant van Providence, Rhode Eyland, den 4. Maart 1775. *Paramaribo.* [n. d.] 8vo, 4 leaves. 52121

NAVY. *See also* Secretary of the Navy, United States, U. S. Naval Observatory, *and* Vol. IV., No. 15059.

A Bill for the Government of the Navy of the United States, 23d January, 1799. [*Philadelphia.* 1799.] 8vo. P. 52122

The Discipline, Harmony and Efficiency of the Navy. [*Washington.*] 1870. 8vo, pp. 32. H. 52123

Signed "A Senior Surgeon, U. S. Navy."

Facts concerning the Navy. *Philadelphia.* 1863. 8vo, pp. 14

A Glance at the Reorganization of the Navy of the United States ... . Compiled in the busy moments of a Late Lieutenant. *Washington, D. C.: F. H. Sage, Printer.* 1855. 8vo, pp. iv, 17.

The Navy a Quarter of a Century behind the Army. [n. p. n. d.] 12mo, pp. 6. 52126

From the "American Journal of Medical Sciences," April, 1849.

The Navy in Congress. Being Speeches of the Hon. Messrs. Grimes, Doolittle, and Nye, of the Senate. And the Hon. Messrs. Rice, Pike, Griswold, and Blow; of the House of Representatives. *Washington: Franck Taylor.* 1865. 8vo, pp. 53, (1). 52127

The Navy of the United States, from 1775 to 1853, with a Brief History of Each Vessel's Service. *Washington.* 1853. 4to.

Navy Register. *See* United States, Navy Department.

Navy's Friend, or Reminiscences of the Navy; containing Memoirs of a Cruise, in the U. S. Schooner Enterprise. By Tiphys Ægyptus. *Baltimore: The Author.* 1843. 12mo, pp. 46

NAXERA (M. C.) Disertacion sobre la Lengua Othomí, leida en latin en la Sociedad Filosófica Americana de Filadelfia, y publicada de su órden en el tomo 5º de la nueva série de sus actas; traducida al castellano por su autor F. Manuel Crisóstomo Náxera, ... *México: En la Imprenta del Aguila.* 1845. 8vo, pp. (2), xiii, 145. C. 52130

In Latin and Spanish. *See* Brasseur de Bourbourg "Bibliothèque," p. 108.

NAXERA. De Lingua Othomitorum dissertatio. Auctore Emmanuel Naxera. *Philadelphiæ: Ex Prelis James Kay, Jun. ac. Fratris.* MDCCCXXXV. 4to, pp. (2), (48). 52131

From the "Transactions of the American Philosophical Society," New Series, Vol. V., pp. 249–296. *See* "Göttinger Gelehrte Anzeigen," 1836, p. 321, *and* "Journal of the Royal Geographical Society," Vol. V., p. 355.

NAXERA. De Othomitorum lingua, dissertatio ... nunc correcta et aucta, utque, praeside R. P. Mexicanae jubente, iterum typis mandata. *Mexico.* 1845. 4to, pp. 116. 52132

See also Najera (E.), No. 51734.

NAXERA (M. de). Oracion funebre por los militares Españoles difuntos. ... *Mexico.* 1767. 4to, 26 leaves. 52133

NAYARITAS. Relacion de la Conquista de la Provincia de los Nayaritas, en el Reyno de la Nueva España, que consiguieron las Armas de su Magestad à principios de este año de 1722. [Colophon:] *Madrid: Imprenta de Phelipe Alonso.* 1722. Sm. 4to, pp. 30. H. 52134

NAYLOR (B.) Naylor's System of teaching Geography, adapted to Pelton's Outline Maps: ... By Benjamin Naylor. *Philadelphia.* 1848. 12mo, pp. 120. H. 52135

NAYLOR (C.) Speech of Charles Naylor ... on the Bill imposing Additional Duties as Depositaries, in certain cases on Public Officers. ... October 13, 1837. *Washington: Printed at the Office of the National Register.* 1837. 8vo, pp. 27. + *Philadelphia: King & Baird, Printers.* 1862. 8vo, pp. 31. H. 52136

Also: Reeside Case. ... Answer of Charles Naylor to the Charges of J. B. Stewart. ... *Washington, D. C.: Buell & Blanchard, Printers.* 1859. 8vo, pp. 29. H.

[NAYLOR & COMPANY.] Letter to the Secretary of the Treasury on Importations of Scrap Iron. *Boston.* 1869. 8vo, pp. 8. H. 52137

NAZARENO, *pseudon.* *See* Vol. IV., No. 16987.

Nazarite Documents: comprising the Obligations, ... of the Nazarite Union, of the Genesee Conference of the M. E. Church. *Brockport, N. Y.: Wm. Haswell, Printer.* 1856. 8vo, pp. 40. H. 52138

NEAL (A. Bradley). The Gossips of Rivertown, with Sketches in Prose and Verse. By Alice B. Neal. *Philadelphia.* 1850. 12mo. P. + Third Edition. [*Ibid.*] 1859. 12mo.

NEAL (D.) The History of New-England Containing an Impartial Account of the Civil and Ecclesiastical Affairs Of the Country To the Year of our Lord, 1700. To which is added The Present State of New-England. With a ... Map. And an Appendix Containing their Present Charter, their Ecclesiastical Discipline, and their Municipal-Laws. ... By Daniel Neal. ... *London: J. Clark.* M DCC XX. 2 vols., 8vo, pp. (2), vi, x, (2), 330; (4), 331–712, Index, xv. Map. C., H. 52140

Gov. Hutchinson says this is little more than an abridgment of Mather's "Magnalia." Thomas Prince thus speaks of this work: "In 1720 came out Mr. Neal's 'History of New-England,' which I was glad to see, and pleased with both his spirit, style and method. And though he has fallen into many mistakes which are commonly known to us, some of which he seems to derive from Mr. Oldmixon's New England; ... yet considering the materials this worthy writer was confined to, and that he was never here; it seems to me scarce possible, that any under his disadvantages should form a better."—*Chronology of New England, Pref.* p. iii.

NEAL. The History of New-England [as before]. The Second Edition. With many Additions by the Author. By Daniel Neal, A.M. *London: A. Ward.* MDCCXLVII. 2 vols., 8vo, pp. (16), 392; (4), 380, Index, 15. 52141

NEAL. The History of the Puritans or Protestant Non-Conformists, from the Reformation to the Death of Queen Elizabeth: with An Account of their Principles; their Attempts for a further Reformation ... their Sufferings; and the Lives and Characters of their Principal Divines. By Daniel Neal, M.A. ... *London: Richard Hett.* M.DCC.XXXII. 4 vols., 8vo, pp. xvi, 649; xii, 658; xvi, 628; xii, 664. C., H. 52142

Written with much ability but a strong bias. It elicited from Dr. Madox a reply to the first volume (our No. 43700). The remaining volumes were reviewed by Dr. Zachary Gray (our No. 28792), to which Toulmin replied.

NEAL. The History of the Puritans ... . From the Reformation under King Henry VIII, to the Act of Toleration, under King William and Queen Mary ... . The Second Edition, Corrected. *London: J. Buckland.* MDCCLIV. 2 vols., 4to, pp. xxiii, 900, Index, (31); xx, 883, (28). Portrait. H. + *Dublin.* 1755.

4 vols., 8vo. + *Dublin*. 1759. 4 vols., 8vo. + A New Edition, Revised, Corrected and Enlarged. By Joshua Toulmin, A.M. To which are prefixed, Some Memoirs of the Life and Writings of the Author. *Bath: C. Dilly*. MDCCXCIII. 5 vols., 8vo, pp. lxiii, 524; xxxii, 574; xxx, 534; xxxii, 652; xiv, 218. Portraits. + *London*. [1811.] 2 vols., rl. 8vo. + *Charles Ewer, Portsmouth, N. H.* 1816–17. 5 vols., 8vo, pp. 572; 600; 560; 552; 488, (4). H. 52143

Vol. I. alone of the last-mentioned edition is published at Portsmouth by Charles Ewer, the other four are published by him at Boston.

NEAL. The History of the Puritans .... A New Edition, ... Reprinted from the Text of Dr. Toulmin's Edition, with his Life of the Author and Account of his Writings. Revised, Corrected and Enlarged. *London*. 1822. 5 vols., 8vo. + *London: Thomas Tegg and Son*. 1837. 3 vols., 8vo. + Edited by John O. Choules, M.A. ... *New-York: Harper & Brothers*. 1843. 2 vols., 8vo, pp. 534; 564. Portraits. + [*Ibid.*] 1844. + [*Ibid.*] 1848. + Corrected and Enlarged with Additional Notes by John O. Choules, M.A. *New York*. 1856. 2 vols., 8vo. 9 Portraits.

NEAL. Neal's History of the Puritans .... Abridged, in two volumes, by Edward Parsons. With a Life of the Author, by Joshua Toulmin, D.D. Second Edition. *London*. [1812.] 2 vols., 12mo. 52145

NEAL. Lotgevallen der Protestanten in Engelandt en Schotlandt. (1530–1689.) Uit het Engelsch vertaald door J. Ross. *Rotterdam*. 1752–54. 3 vols., 4to. 52146

NEAL. A Review of the Principal Facts Objected to [in] the first Volume of the History of the Puritans, By the Author of the Vindication of the Government, Doctrine and Worship, of the Church of England, established in the Reign of Queen Elizabeth. By Daniel Neal, M.A. ... *London: Richard Hett*. M.DCC.XXXIV. 8vo, pp. 87, (1). H. 52147

NEAL (J.) Account of the Great Conflagration in Portland, July 4th & 5th, 1866, By John Neal; and a New Business Guide .... *Portland: Starbird & Twitchell*. 1866. 8vo, pp. 64, viii. H. 52148

[NEAL.] Authorship, a Tale. By a New Englander Over-Sea. *Boston: Gray and Bowen*. 1830. 12mo, pp. iv, 267. C.

[NEAL.] Battle of Niagara. A Poem, without Notes; and Goldau; or the Maniac Harper. ... By Jehu O'Cataract .... *Baltimore: N. G. Maxwell*. 1818. 16mo, pp. 143. + Second Edition—Enlarged: with Other Poems. ... [*Ibid.*] 1819. 18mo, pp. 272. B. 52150

The second edition is not anonymous.

[NEAL.] Brother Jonathan: or, The New Englanders. ... *Edinburgh: William Blackwood*. MDCCCXXV. 3 vols., 8vo, pp. (2), 421, (1); (4), 451, (1); (4), 452. H. 52151

NEAL. The Down-Easters, &c. &c. &c. By John Neal ... *New-York: Harper & Brothers*. 1833. 2 vols., 12mo, pp. vii, (1), 206; 204. H. 52152

[NEAL.] Errata; or, The Works of Will. Adams. A Tale ... *New-York: For the Proprietors*. 1823. 2 vols., 12mo, pp. 325; 364, (1). H. 52153

NEAL. Little Moccasin; or, Along the Madawaska. A Story of Life ... in the Lumber Region. By John Neal .... *London: George Routledge & Sons*. [n. d.] 16mo, pp. 122. Plate. B.

[NEAL.] Logan, a Family History. *Philadelphia: H. C. Carey & I. Lea*. 1822. 2 vols., 12mo, pp. 317; 342. C. 52155

NEAL. Rachel Dyer: A North American Story. By John Neal. *Portland: Shirley and Hyde*. 1828. 12mo, pp. 276. Portrait. B. 52456

This rare American historical tale is founded on the "Trials of Witchcraft, in New England," in 1696, etc.

[NEAL.] Seventy-Six. ... *Baltimore: J. Robinson*. 1823. 2 vols., 12mo, pp. (6), 13–268; (2), 13–260, (2). C. + *London*. 18—. 3 vols., post 8vo. 52157

[NEAL.] Sketch of Old England. By a New-England Man. *New-York*. 1822. 2 vols., 12mo. + *London: Sir Richard Phillips and Co.* 1822. 8vo. 52158

NEAL. True Womanhood: A Tale: By John Neal ... *Boston: Ticknor and Fields*. M DCCC LIX. 8vo, pp. 487. H.

NEAL. Wandering Recollections of a Somewhat Busy Life. An Autobiography. ... By John Neal. *Boston: Roberts Brothers*. 1869. 16mo, pp. viii, 431. H. 52160

NEAL. The Yankee. A Weekly Miscellany. *Portland?* 1828–29. 2 vols., 4to. 52161

Merged in the "New England Galaxy." Also: Address delivered before the Portland Association, for the promoting of Temperance, February 11th, 1829. ... *Portland*. 1829. 8vo, pp. 18.—Appeal From the American Press to the American People. In behalf of John Bratish Eliovich .... *Portland, Maine*. 1840. 8vo, pp. 48.—Banks and Banking. A Letter to the Bank-Directors of Portland: ... *Portland*. 1837. 18mo, pp. 8. H.—Man. A Discourse before the United Brothers' Society of Brown University, September 4, 1838. ... *Providence: Knowles, Vose & Company*. 1838. 8vo, pp. 25.—The Moose-Hunter; or, Life in the Maine Woods. ... *New York: Beadle and Company*. [1864.] 16mo, pp. 7–125. Plate. H.—Oration: ... Portland, July 4, 1838. ... *Portland: Arthur Shirley, Printer*. 1838. 8vo, pp. 25.—Our Country. An Address ... before the Alumni of Waterville College, July 29, 1830. ... *Portland: S. Colman*. 1830. 8vo, pp. 36. H.—The White-Faced Pacer; or, before and after the Battle. ... *New York: Beadle and Company*. 1864. 16mo, pp. 100.

NEAL (J. C.) Charcoal Sketches; or, Scenes in a Metropolis. By Joseph C. Neal. With Illustrations by David C. Johnston. *Philadelphia*. 1838. 12mo. + Second Edition. *Philadelphia: E. L. Carey and A. Hart*. 1838. 12mo. + Sixth Edition. *Philadelphia*. 1841. 12mo. + [*Ibid.*] 1843. + [*Ibid.*] 1844. + [*Ibid.*] 1845. 52162

Reprinted without acknowledgment in the "Pic Nic Papers" edited by Charles Dickens, *London*, 12mo.

NEAL. Charcoal Sketches. Second Series. By the late Joseph C. Neal .... *New York: Burgess, Stringer & Company*. 1848. 8vo, pp. 192. 9 Plates. B. 52163

NEAL. Neal's Charcoal Sketches. Three Books complete in One. Containing the whole of his ... Charcoal Sketches; Peter Faber's Misfortunes; Peter Ploddy's Dream; ... Olympus Pump; and Music Mad. To which is added Forty-one other Sketches by Joseph C. Neal. Illustrative of his own Observations and Experience. ... With Twenty-one Illustrations. ... By Felix O. C. Darley. *Philadelphia: T. B. Peterson & Brothers*. 1865. 16mo, pp. 222, 192, 181. B. 52164

NEAL. Peter Ploddy and other Oddities. ... By Joseph C. Neal. *Philadelphia*. 1844. 12mo. P. 52165

NEAL (T. A.) The Neal Record: being a List of the Descendants of John Neal, one of the early Settlers of Salem, Mass. Compiled by Theodore Augustus Neal. ... *Boston: Henry W. Dutton & Son, Printers*. 1856. 8vo, pp. 30. Geneal. Table. BA. 52166

NEALE (M.) Some Account of the Life and Religious Exercises of Mary Neale, formerly Mary Peisley. Principally Com-

piled from her own Writings. *Dublin: Printed by John Gough*. 1795. 12mo. + Second Edition. [*Ibid.*] 18mo. + *Philadelphia*. 1796. 18mo. 52167

Reprinted in Vol. XI. of "The Friends' Library." Contains ample accounts of her services both in England and America.

NEALE (R. H.) An Address ... Two Hundredth Anniversary of the ... First Baptist Church, Boston, June 7, 1865, By Rollin Heber Neale, D.D. ... *Boston: Gould and Lincoln*. 1865. 8vo, pp. 80. H. 52168

NEALE. The Pastor and Preacher; a Memorial of the late Rev. Baron Stow, D.D. By Rollin H. Neale .... *Boston: Gould and Lincoln*. 1870. 16mo, pp. 96. B. 52169

NEALE. ... A Sermon ... at the Annual Election, January 8, 1852. By Rev. Rollin H. Neale, D.D. ... *Boston: Dutton & Wentworth, ... Printers*. 1852. 8vo, pp. 48. H. 52170

Also: ... A Discourse before the American Baptist Publication Society, at the Thirty-First Anniversary ... in ... Chicago, Ill., May 13, 1855. ... *Philadelphia*. [n. d.] 24mo, pp. 49.— ... A Discourse ... before the Conference of Baptist Ministers, May 25, 1841 .... *Boston: James Loring*. 1841. 32mo, pp. 42. B.

NEALE (S.) Some Account of the Life and Religious Labours of Samuel Neale. *Dublin: Printed by Robert Napper*. 1805. 12mo. + *Philadelphia: James P. Parke*. 1806. 12mo.

Reprinted in Vol. XI. of "The Friends' Library."

NEALE. Some Account of the Lives and Religious Labours of Samuel Neale, and Mary Neale, formerly Mary Peisley .... *Philadelphia*. 1860. 12mo, pp. iv, 11–267, vii–179. H. 52172

NEANDER (J.) Tabacologia: | hoc est | Tabaci, seu Nicotianæ | descriptio | Medico-Chirurgico-Pharmaceutica | vel | Ejus præparatio et usus in | omnibus ferme corporis | humani incŏmodis. | Per | Johannem Neandrum Bremanum .... *Lugduni Batavorum*, | *Ex Officina Isaaci Elzeviri* | ... *Anno* 1626. 4to, Portrait, Engraved Title, Dedication, etc., pp. (2), 36, 256, Tabacks, (3). 9 Plates

NEANDER (M.) Orbis terræ divisio in partes suas, veteres et novus. Acc. chronicorum omnium ætatum, gentium et temporum compendium. *Lipsiae*. 1586. 8vo. + *Lipsiæ: Apel*. 1594. 8vo. 52174

Contains a short description of America.

NEANDER. Orbis Terræ Partium succincta explicatio, seu Simplex Enumeratio distributa in singularum partium regiones.

Lipsiæ, Abrahami Lambergi. 1589. 8vo. + *Wittebergæ*. 1597. 8vo. 52175

The prologomena contains a long and interesting list of authors consulted in its compilation, among whom are fifty works pertaining to geography and America, some of which are hardly known.

Near Home. A Poem. *Boston: James Munroe and Company*. 1858. 16mo, pp. 52. BA. 52176

NEBEL (C.) Voyage Pittoresque et Archéologique dans la partie la plus intéressante du Méxique, par C. Nebel. *Paris*. 1836. Folio. 50 Plates. 52177

A beautiful volume, now scarce. Some copies have a title-page in Spanish as below:

NEBEL. Viaje Pintoresco y Arqueolojico sobre la parte mas interesante de la Republica Mejicana, en los años transcurridos desde 1829 hasta 1834. *Paris, e Mejico* [*P. Renouard*]. 1839. Folio, 30 leaves. 50 colored Plates. C. 52178

For "The War between the United States and Mexico Illustrated," *see* Kendall (G. W.), Vol. XI., No. 37362.

NEBRASKA. ... An Act prohibiting Slavery. [n. p. 1861.] 8vo, pp. 8. H. 52179

... An Act to organize the Territories of Nebraska and Kansas. [n. p. 1854.] 8vo, pp. 16. BA. 52180

Also: A Bill to organize the Territories of Nebraska and Kansas, and the report of the Committee on Territories. In the Senate ... January 4, 1854. Mr. Douglas made the following Report. [n. p. n. d.] 8vo, pp. 8.

Annual Message ... to the Legislative Assembly of ... Nebraska .... *Omaha City, Nebraska: Taylor & M'Clure, ... Printers*. 1865. 8vo, pp. 82. Continued. H. 52181

Appeal of the Independent Democrats in Congress, to the People of the United States. Shall Slavery be permitted in Nebraska? [*Washington: Towers Printers*. 1854.] 8vo, pp. 8.

Third Annual Report of the Nebraska State Board of Agriculture, 1871. *Des Moines*. 1871. 8vo. Continued. 52183

Comments on the Nebraska Bill. *See* Vol. IV., No. 14964.

A Complete Guide. *See* Vol. IV., No. 15054.

Constitution of the State of Nebraska. ... [n. p.] 1866. 8vo, pp. 16. H. 52184

Die Constitution des Staates Nebraska, und Erste Botschaft von Gouverneur David Butler .... *Nebraska City, Nebraska*. [1867.] 8vo, pp. 17, 16. H. 52185

Discourse on the Nebraska Bill, preached in ... Clinton, June 4th, 1854. [n. p. n. d.] 8vo, pp. 17. H. 52186

First and Second Annual Report of the Commissioner of Common Schools of the Territory of Nebraska. *Omaha City*. 1860. 8vo. C. 52187

House Journal of the State Legislature of the State of Nebraska. First, Second, and Third Sessions, 1866–67. *Omaha: State Printer*. 1867. 8vo. 52188

... In the Senate of the United States, July 21, 1854. ... An Act to organize the Territories of Nebraska and Kansas. [*Washington*. 1854.] 8vo, pp. 16. H. 52189

Journal of the Council at the First Regular Session of the General Assembly of the Territory of Nebraska. *Omaha City*. 1855. 8vo. 52190

Journal of the House of Representatives: First Session of the General Assembly of the Territory of Nebraska. *Omaha City*. 1855. 8vo. 52191

Laws ... of the Territory of Nebraska for 1857. December Session, 1857. *Brownville*. 1857. 8vo. Continued. 52192

Laws, Joint Resolutions, and Memorials passed at the First General Assembly of the Territory of Nebraska, at Omaha City, January, 1855. *Omaha City*. 1855. 8vo. Continued.

Laws of the State of Nebraska, ... 1869. *Omaha*. 1869. 8vo. 52194

Message of ... Governor of Nebraska, to the Legislative Assembly; delivered December 18, 1855. [n. p. n. d.] 8vo. Continued. 52195

Nebraska: A Poem, Personal and Political. *Boston: John P. Jewett and Company*. 1854. 12mo, pp. 42. A., B., BA. 52196

By S. R. Phillips of Fitchburg?

Nebraska; a Sketch of its History, Resources and Advantages it offers to Settlers. ... *Nebraska City*. 1870. 8vo, pp. 31. B.

Nebraska and Kansas. Report of the Committee of the Massachusetts Emigrant Aid Company, with the Act of Incorporation, and other Documents. *Boston: Massachusetts Emigrant Aid Co.* 1854. 12mo, pp. 33. B., H. 52198

Nebraska Legislature. ... Report of the Standing Committee on Mines and Minerals. ... 1865. [n. p. n. d.] 8vo, pp. 16.

The Nebraska Question comprising Speeches in the United States Senate by Mr. Douglas, Mr. Chase, Mr. Smith, Mr. Everett, Mr. Wade, Mr. Badger, Mr. Seward and Mr. Sumner ... with the History of the Missouri Compromise—Daniel Webster's Memorial in regard to it—History of the Annexation of Texas—the organization of Oregon Territory—and the Compromises of 1850. *Redfield, New York*. 1854. 8vo, pp. 119. H. + *Chicago*. 1854. 8vo. 52200

Report of the U. S. Senate on the Nebraska Bill. [n. p. 1854.] 8vo, pp. 19. BA. 52201

The Revised Statutes of the Territory of Nebraska, in force July 1, 1866. Revised by A. Estabrook. *Omaha: E. B. Taylor*. 1866. 8vo, pp. 814. C. 52202

Senate Journal of the State Legislature of Nebraska. First, Second, and Third Sessions, 1866–67. *Omaha: State Printer*. 1867. 8vo. S. 52203

[NEBRIJA (Antonio).] Advertencias y Preceptos para la Classe de Menores. *Mexico*. 1721. 12mo. 52204

Also: Explicacion de los libros Quarto, y Quinto, de la Grammatica, conforme al Arte de Antonio de Nebrija, para el uso de los Estudiantes de los Reales Collegios de San Juan, y San Pedro. *En la Puebla de los Angeles: Imprimiólas á sú Costa Bartholomè del Rivero, y se hallaràn en sú Libreria, en la esquina de la Plaza, frontero de la Cathedral bieja*. 1695. 4to.—Explicacion del libro Quarto conforme á las Reglas de el Arte de Antonio de Nebrija. Con un Suplemento singular à las Reglas Generales. *Mexico*. 1717. 8vo.

NEBRIJA (Elio Antonio de). Aelij Antonij nebrissensis grãmatici in cosmographiæ | libros introductoriũ incipitur foeliciter ad lectorem. [*Salmantice*. 1498.] 4to, 14 leaves. 52205

NEBRIJA. Ælii Antonii Nebrissensis Grammatici in Cosmographiæ libros introductorium, multo quæ antea castigatus. *Paris, ex Officina S. Colinæi*. 1533. 4to. 52206

Necesidad de la union de todos los Mexicanos contra las Asechanzas de la nacion española, comprobada con la historia de la

antigua republica de Tlaxcalla, publícala C. M. de Bustamente. *México: Imprenta del Aguila*. 1826. 8vo, pp. (4), 44. 52207

Necesidad Urjente de la Reorganizacion de Centro América bajo un Pacto Federal. *Filadelfia*. 1848. 8vo, pp. 15. + *Paris: Ad. Blondeau*. 1848. 8vo. 52208

Necessaries; Best Product of Land; Best Staple of Commerce. *Philadelphia: Printed by James Humphreys, junr*. M,DCC,-LXXVI. 8vo, pp. 17, (1). P. 52209

Necessary Admonitions. *See* [Mather (C.)], Vol. XI. 46425.

Necessary Truth. *See* [Franklin (B.)], Vol. VII., No. 25558.

The Necessity and Divine Excellency. *See* [Fothergill (S.)]

The Necessity for Improved Military Defences considered. ... *Charleston: Press of Walker, Evans & Co.* 1859. 8vo, pp. 28. Vignette and Portrait. H. 52210

The Necessity of a Ship-Canal between the East and the West. Report of the Committee on Statistics, for the City of Chicago, submitted to the National Convention, assembled at Chicago, June 2, 1863. *Chicago: Tribune Company's Office*. 1863. 8vo, pp. 45. 52211

See also Vol. IV., No. 12636.

The Necessity of Brotherly Love: A Discourse ... delivered ... on a Special Occasion; ... *Boston: Printed by Fowle and Draper*. 1762. 8vo, pp. 36. B. 52212

See also "Great Difficulty," Vol. VII., No. 28443.

The Necessity of Reformation. *See* [Mather (I.)], XI. 46710.

The | Necessity | of | Repealing | the | American Stamp-Act | Demonstrated: | or, | A Proof that Great-Britain must be | injured by that Act. | In a Letter to a Member of the British | House of Commons. *London: J. Almon*. M DCCLXVI. 8vo, pp. 46. + ... *Boston: Re-Printed by Edes and Gill* .... 1766. 8vo, pp. 31.

"One of the most considerable publications on the present disagreeable situation of our affairs in our North American colonies; and contains, indeed, more information than all the rest put together."—*Monthly Review*, XXXIII. 485. "The author is warm in defense of the colonies, and gives good reasons why they should not be taxed by the mother country."—RICH, I. 148.

NECK (J. van). Waerachtigh Verhael | Van de Schip-vaert op | Oost-Indien, | Ghedaen | By de acht Schepen, onder den Heer Admi- | rael Jacob van Neck, en de Vice-Admirael Wybrand van

| Warwijck, van Amsterdam gezeylt in den jare 1598. | Hier achter is aen-ghevoeght | De Voyagie van Sebald de Weert, naer de Strate | Magalanes. | *'t Amstelredam | Voor Ioost Hartgerts, Boeckverkooper in de Gast-huys-steegh*, | ... *Anno* 1648. 4to, pp. (2), 92. Plate

NECK. Waerachtigh Verhael | Vande Schip-vaert op | Oost-Indien, | Gedaen by de acht schepen, onder den Heer Admirael | Jacob van Neck .... Hier achter is by-ghevoegt | De Voyagie van Sebald de Weert, naer de Straet Magalanes, | met noch een Vocabulaer van Duyts en Maleys, 't welck door | geheel Indien gesproken wort. | *'t Amstelredam*, | *Voor Joost Hartgers, Boeckverkooper op den Dam*, ... *Anno* 1650. 4to, pp. 76, (4). c. 52215

NECK (Van der), *pseudon. See* [Burgh (J.)], Vol. III. 9245.

NECKAR, *pseudon. See* [Fisher (R.)], Vol. VI., No. 24484.

NECKER (Jacques). Réponse au Mémoire de l'Abbé Morellet, sur la Compagnie des Indes .... *Paris.* 1769. 8vo, pp. 50.

Also forms part of Vol. xv. of his "Ouvres," *Paris*, 1820–21. *See also* [Morellet (A.)], Vol. XII., No. 50595.

Necrologia de Hilario Maximiano Antunes Gurjão ... Morto em Humaytá em 17 de Janeiro de 1869, do honroso ferimento que recebeo no combate de Dezembro de 1868. Precedida de um Prologo ou Elogio Historico Por seu Tio e Amigo Antonio Agostinho de Andrade Figueira. *S. Luiz do Maranhao.* 1869. 8vo, pp. 59. 52217

Ned Buntline. *See* [Judson (E. Z. C.)], Vol. IX. 36860–62.

NEDERBURGH (S. C.) Verhandeling over het brengen der Ost Indische Bezittingen op den voet der West Indische, en over het voordeelige van eene uitsluitende Compagnie. *'s Hage.* 1802. 8vo. 52218

NEDERLAND. Aan het Volk van Nederland. [Signed:] *Ostende*, 3 Sept. 1781. 8vo, pp. 76. 52219

This violent pamphlet against the house of Orange caused such scandal, that by the States General a reward of 14,000 florins was offered to the discoverer of the author, but in vain. Most probably it is written by the advocate F. A. v. d. Kemp. It is highly interesting for the history of that time and of the American war.

Aan 't Volk van Nederland, of bewijzen en consideratien over de voordeelen der Negotie met de Noord-Americanen. [n. p. 1781.] 8vo, pp. 16. 52220

Address to the people of Netherland, or considerations on the profits of the commerce with North America.

Almanak voor de Nederlandsche West-Indische Bezittingen en de kust van Guinea van 1856. ... *'s Hage.* 1856. 8vo. Continued. 52221

Antwoort-Brief | Van een onpartydigh Coopman uyt Zeelant, | Aen syn vrient in Engelant geschreven, op 't gene den sel- | ven onlanckx wiert toegesonden, rakende de pretensien | der Engelsche, van de Nederlandsche ingesetenen | ende besonderlick d'Engelsche seer onrechtmatige | bekentmakinge vol injurien, ende illatien, korts | door den Engelschen Mercurius publicus, de | werelt genotificeert, ende hier te lande door | de post-tijdinge getranslateert, | gereleveert, ende over al gedistribueert, | dienende tot wederlegginge van de | Engelsche seer ongefondeerde | pretensien, ende lasteringen, | ende tot justificatie van | de goede sake, ende e- | quiteyt der Neder- | landers. | [n. p.:] *Gedruckt voor Simoen Simoensz.* 1662. 4to, pp. 8. 52222

Answer by an impartial merchant from Zeeland to his friend in England, concerning what has been recently sent to him on the complaints of the English against the inhabitants of the Netherlands, etc. *See* Asher, No. 321.

Articulen | En | Conditien | van den | Eeuwigen Vrede | Gesloten tusschen den Groot-mach- | tigen Koninck van Hispaignen, elc ter een- | der, ende de Hoog-mogende Heeren Staten | Generael der Vereenigde Nederlanden, ter | ander zijde, | onderteyckent ende bezegelt den | dertigsten Januarij 1648. | *Tot Munster.* | *Tot Rotterdan.* | *By Haest van Voortganck, Boeckdrucker van de Articulen* | *van der Vrede*, 1648. 4to, pp. 16. 52223

Articles and conditions of the peace concluded between the King of Spain and the States General of the United Netherlands. *See* Asher, No. 269.

Articulen | Van | Vrede | Ende | Confederatie | Tusschen den | Koning van Portugael | Ende de | Staten Generael | Van de Vereenighde Nederlanden, | Gesloten en ondertekent den 6 Aug. 1661. | Getranslateert uyt het Latijn, na de | rechte Copye. | [n. p.] M. DC. LXI. 4to, pp. 16. 52224

Articles of peace between the King of Portugal and the States General of the United Netherlands. *See* Asher, No. 297, *also* our Vol. I., p. 287.

END OF VOLUME TWELVE.

A DICTIONARY OF BOOKS

RELATING TO AMERICA.

NEDERLAND. Besoignes en Communicatien | over de | Ligue Garentie | van de Heeren | Hare Hoog Mogende | de Staten Generael | Den 2, 4 en 5 Julij 1647. | *In 's Graven-Hage*, | *voor de Weduwe van Hillebrant Jacobsz van Wouw, Ordinaris* | *Drucker van Hare Hog: Mog:* 1647. | 4to, pp. 8. 52225

Communications on the league guarantee. *See* Asher's "Bibliographical Essay," No. 268.

Nederlandsche Jaarboeken, inhoudende een verhaal van de merkwaardigste geschiedenissen voorgevallen binnen de Vereenigde Provintiën sedert 1747–65. *Amsterdam.* 1748–66. 41 vols., 8vo. + Nieuwe Nederlandsche Jaarboeken. 1766–98. *Amsterdam.* 1767–99. 79 vols., 8vo. 52226

The second series contains material for the history of America in general, and of the war of independence in particular.

De Nederlandsche Post-Ryder. *Utrecht.* 1772. 18mo. Continued. 52227

This Dutch Postillion brings reports of the affairs of State and War, in Europe and America, and of other remarkable occurrences.

Nederlandsche Reizen tot bevordering van den koophandel na de meest afgelegene Gewesten des Aardkloots. *Amsterdam: P. Conradi.* 1784–87. 7 vols., 8vo. Maps and Plates. 52228

Collection of Dutch voyages to the most remote parts of the globe, containing extracts from original narrations of voyages of which the editions are very rare.

Nederlandsche Zeereizen in het laatst der 16de, 17de en het begin der 18de eeuw. Naar de oorspronkelijke journalen of gelijktijden berigten uitgegeven door R. G. Bennet en J. van Wijk. *Dordrecht.* 1828–30. 5 vols., 8vo. Maps. 52229

Contains the early Dutch voyages of Linschoten, Hudson (to New Netherland), W. Barendsz, etc.

Den Nederlandtschen Bye-korf. *See* [Usselincx (Willem)].

NEDERMEYER V. ROSENTHAL (J. Th. H.) De servorum Afrorum commercio eoque recte sublato, nec non de Afrorum servitute penitus tollenda. *Lugduni Batavorum.* 1816. 8vo, pp. 222. 52230

Also on large paper.

Needful Caution. *See* [Mather (I.)], Vol. XI., No. 47611.

NEEDHAM (D.) Address of Hon. Daniel Needham, ... at the Wool Growers' Convention, at Rutland, September 9th, 1862. ... *Windsor, Vt.: L. J. McIndoe, Printer.* [n. d.] 8vo, pp. 14.

NEEDHAM (J. R.) The Pleasures of Poverty. A Poem, adapted to the Present Hard Times .... By John Rainsford Needham. ... Third Edition. *New-York: For the Proprietor.* 1837. 12mo, pp. 12. B. 52232

NEEDHAM, *Mass.* Constitution and ... Members of the Needham Temperance Society. *Dedham, Mass.* 1831. 16mo, pp. 7. H. 52233

... Report of the ... School Committee of ... Needham, for ... 1854. *Dedham: Printed by Cox & Hutchins.* 1854. 8vo, pp. 17. Continued. H. 52234

Also: Catalogue of the ... Library of the Sabbath School ... [of] the First Parish Church, Needham. ... *Boston: Printed by Alfred Mudge & Son.* 1857. 24mo, pp. 12.

NEEDLES (E.) An Historical Memoir of the Pennsylvania Society, for pomoting [*sic*] the Abolition of Slavery; the relief of free Negroes unlawfully held in bondage, and for improving the condition of the African Race. ... By Edward Needles .... *Philadelphia: Merrihew and Thompson, Printers.* 1848. 12mo, pp. 116. BA., H. 52235

[NEEDLES, *and others*.] A Review of a Pamphlet, entitled An Appeal to the Public on behalf of a House of Refuge for Colored Juvenile Delinquents. *Philadelphia: W. H. Brisbane, Printer.* 1847. 12mo, pp. 15. H. 52236

Signed by Edward Needles and five others, committee.

NEELY (P. P.) A Young Poetess; or A ... review of ... Fugitive Poems of Miss Amanda A. R. Capers, (Holly Springs, Miss.) By Rev. P. P. Neely, D.D. ... [n. p. n. d.] 8vo, pp. 9.

Also: Sermons .... *Mobile: S. H. Goetzel & Co.* [n. d.] 12mo.

NEERINCKX (C.) Nagelaten Brief van ... Carolus Nerinckx, in Leven Missionaris in Kentucky; aan zijne ... Vrienden in Nederland. *Te 's Gravenhage.* MDCCCXXV. 8vo, pp. x, 66.

This letter treats of the state of the Catholic faith in Kentucky, the order of the nuns of Loretto, founded by Neerinckx, etc.

NEERINCKX. De Zegepraal van het Katholvke Geloof, ter beschaming van ongeloof en dwaling, ... of Verhaal van de uitbreiding der H. Kerk in Kentucky. Uit eenen eigenhandigen Brief van den eerw. Heer Neerinckx R. C. Priester in Zendeling, met eene Voorrede van J. G. Lesage Ten Broek, Notaris te Naaldwijk. *Amsterdam: A. Schievenbus.* 1819. 8vo, pp. vi, 48.

With an account of Neerinckx's missionary labors in Kentucky, etc.

NEES VON ESENBECK (C. G.), *and* MARTIUS (C. Ph. F. de). Fraxinellae plantarum familiæ naturalis, definita et secundum genera desposita, adj. specier. Brasiliens. description. *Bonn.* 1823. 4to. 14 Tables. 52240

NEFF (J. K.) The Army and Navy of America: Containing A View of the Heroic Adventures, Battles, Naval Engagements, Remarkable Incidents, and Glorious Achievements in the Cause of Freedom, from the Period of the French and Indian Wars to the close of the Florida Wars .... By Jacob K. Neff, M.D. ... *Philadelphia: J. H. Pearsol & Co.* 1845. 8vo, pp. 624. 2 Maps. + *Philadelphia: John S. Gable.* 1845. 8vo, pp. 624. Plate and Diagrams. H. + To the Close of the Mexican War. *Lancaster, Pa.: G. Hills.* 1849. 8vo, pp. 684. 6 Plates. C. + *Philadelphia: John H. Pearsol.* 1857. 12mo, pp. 687. 2 Plates, and Diagrams. BA. 52241

[NEFF.] Thrilling Incidents of the Wars of the United States; comprising the most striking Events of the Revolution, the French War, the Second War with Great-Britain, and the Mexican War. ... *Philadelphia: Carey & Hart.* 1848. 8vo, pp. xii, 600. C. 52242

Prospectus of the Neff Petroleum Company, with the Geological Reports of A. Winchell, J. S. Newberry, H. L. Smith, [etc.] and a Map .... *Gambier (Ohio).* 1866. 8vo, pp. 46. Map and Plate. C. 52243

Negbauer's Comic Almanac. *San Francisco, Cal.* 1855. 12mo

De Negerstaat van Hayti of Sint Domingo, geschetst in zijne geschiedenis en in zijnen tegenwoordigen Toestand; naar het Engelsche der Quarterly Review, en naar het Fransche geschrift des Negers, Baron de Vastey, Minister des gewezen Konings Christophe [Henri I.]. *Amsterdam.* 1821. 8vo. Map. 52245

The state of the negroes in Hayti sketched in its history and present condition.

NEGLEY (J. S.) Speech of James S. Negley ... May 11, 1870, on Commercial and Shipping Interests. [n. p. n. d.] 8vo.

Negociacion pena. Coleccion de todos los documentos de su referencia. Publicacion oficial. Marzo de 1856. Segunda edicion. *Buenos Aires.* [1856.] 8vo, pp. iv, 98. 52247

Negociations pendantes entre le Mexique et l'Espagne. *Poissy.* 1857. 8vo. 52248

Negotiation for Cherokee Lands .... Report of the Commissioners appointed to negotiate with the Cherokee Indians, for a Certain Portion of their Country, January 30, 1828. ... *Washington: Printed by Gales & Seaton.* 1828. 8vo, pp. 40. 52249

Le Nègre. *See* [La Vallée (*Abbé*)], Vol. X., No. 39281.

NEGREDE (Agustin Lopez) *and* ROLDAN (Francisco Pasqual). Relacion de las demonstraciones con que la Ciudad de Durango explicó su jubilo por las plausibles noticias de haberse alarmato la España antigua, oponiendose á la dominacion de los Franceses, y conseguido la derrota de sus tropas. Con un sermon que predicó el Fr. Pedro Cortina. *Mexico.* 1809. 4to, pp. 8, 21, (10).

NEGREIROS (Antonio Thomás de). Tractado de Operações do Banco, ou Directorio de Banqueiros, extrahido dos melhores auctores. ... *Bahia.* 1817. 8vo, pp. 155. S. 52251

NEGRETE (M. C.) Instituta Criminal Teorica-Practica. Compuesto por D. Modesto Cacho Negrete. *Habana.* 1833. 8vo, pp. 214, (1). 52252

NEGRETE (P. C.) Defensa Legal ... Coronel Cirilo Gomez y Anaya .... *Mexico.* 1828. 8vo. 52253

NEGRI (G.) Istoria degli Fiorent. Scrittori. *Ferrara.* 1722. Folio. 52254

Contains some particulars relating to Vespucius. Title from [Harrisse].

[NEGRIN (J. J.)] The Free-Mason's Vocal Assistant. And Register of the Lodges of Masons in South-Carolina and Carolina. *Charleston (S. C.): Printed by Brother J. J. Negrin.* 1807. 12mo, pp. 255, (1). 52255

NEGRO. The Ancient Story of the Negro Race. March 28, 1863. [n. p. n. d.] 8vo, pp. 24. 52256

The Assiento. *See* Vol. I., No. 2227.

The Gospels written in the Negro Patois of English, with Arabic Characters, by a Mandingo Slave in Georgia. [n. p. n. d.] 12mo, pp. 12. 52257

Negro and Aborigines Fund. Report of the Meeting for Sufferings. [n. p.] 1848. Folio, 1 sheet. Continued. 52258

Negro Apprenticeship in the British Colonies. *London: Office of the Anti-Slavery Society.* 1838. 8vo, pp. 160. H. 52259

Negro Apprenticeship in the Colonies. A Review of the Report of the Select Committee of the House of Commons .... *London: John Hatchard and Son.* 1837. 8vo, pp. 44. H. 52260

The Negro Christianized. *See* [Mather (C.)], XI. 46426.

The Negro Conspiracy. *See* [Horsmanden (D.)], VIII. 33061.

Negro Emancipation: a Dialogue between Mr. Ebenezer Eastlove and Giles Homespun. *London: Thomas and George Underwood.* 1824. 8vo, pp. 28, (8). C. 52261

The last eight pages give a list of pamphlets on the "West Indies, and State of the Negro Population."

Negro Emancipation made Easy; and Reflections on The African Institution, and Slave Registry Bill. By a British Planter. [*London:*] *Edmund Lloyd.* 1816. 8vo, pp. 94. S. 52262

The Negro equalled. *See* [La Vallée (*Abbé*)], X. 39282.

Negro Forget me not Songster. *Philadelphia.* 18—. 16mo.

Also: Negro Melodies. ... Published by A. Winch. *Philadelphia.* 18—. 16mo.—Negro Singer's Own Book.

The Negro Labor Question. By a New-York Merchant. *New-York: John A. Gray, Printer.* 1858. 12mo, pp. 55. BA.

The "Negro Pew:" Being an Inquiry concerning the propriety of Distinctions in the House of God, on account of Color. *Boston: Isaac Knapp.* 1837. 12mo, pp. 108. C., H. 52265

The Negro Servant; an Authentic Narrative of a Young Negro; shewing How he was made a Slave in Africa, carried to Jamaica ... where he became a Christian .... *Edinburgh.* [1817.] 12mo, pp. 24. 52266

A religious chap-book. Reproduced as "The Negro Servant; an Authentic and Interesting Narrative in Three Parts" .... *Newcastle.* [1817.] 12mo, pp. 24.

The Negro Slave. *See* [Naish (William)], XII. 51730.

Negro Slavery. ... *London.* [n. d.] 8vo. 52267

A series of sixteen or more tracts with this general title.

Negro Slavery in the United States. *See* [Cooper (T.)]

Negro Slavery. Observations, in answer to an "Address to the Clergy of the Established Church, and to Christian Ministers of every Denomination. *London: Smith, Elder & Co.* 1826. 8vo, pp. 16, (12). C. 52268

With a list of pamphlets on the "West Indies and State of the Negro Population."

Negro Slavery; or, a View of some of the more prominent features of that State of Society, as it exists in the United States ... and in the ... West Indies, especially in Jamaica. *London: Hatchard.* 1823. 8vo, pp. 118. A. + Third Edition. *London: Printed by Richard Taylor* .... 1824. 8vo, pp. vi, (2), 92. B. + Fourth Edition. [*Ibid.*] 1824. 8vo, pp. vi, (2), 92. B. 52269

"A most interesting and important tract."—*Edinburgh Review.*

The Negro: What is his Ethnological Status; Is he the Progeny of Ham? ... what is his Relation to the White Race? By Ariel. *Cincinnati.* 1867. 12mo, pp. 48. 52270

An anti-negro Tennessean view of the subject.

The Negroes and Africans as Freedmen and Soldiers. *London: Ladies' Emancipation Society.* 1864. 8vo, pp. 30. 52271

Negroes and Religion. The Episcopal Church at the South. Memorial to the General Convention of the Protestant Episcopal Church in the United States .... [n. p. 1863.] 12mo, pp. 4.

Satirical and anti-slavery. Dated Charleston, S. C., Oct. 1, 1856. Reprinted in 8vo, pp. 8, with additions "To Churchmen."

... The Negro's Flight from American Slavery to British Freedom. The Brothers, Fugitive and Free. Prefatory Remarks by George Thompson, Esq., M.P. *London: John Snow.* 1849. 16mo, pp. 16. H. 52273

... The Negro's Friend; consisting of Anecdotes, designed to exemplify the Moral, Intellectual, and Religious Attainments of the African Race, and the Cruelties and Oppressions to which they have been subjected by Europeans. [By J. Capper. *London, about* 1832.] 12mo, pp. 12. Continued. B. 52274

Corrected title of our No. 10763, Vol. III.

The Negro's Memorial, or, Abolitionist's Catechism; By an Abolitionist. ... *London: The Author.* 1825. 8vo, pp. iv, (2), 127. + *Bristol.* 1830. 8vo. 52275

See also [Keith (G.)], Vol. IX., Nos. 37193, 34856, *and* [Kolb (J. E.)], No. 38226.

Negroleum, formerly known as Petroleum. A Treatise on the Nature, Source, and Probability of a Permanent Supply of this valuable commodity, with some remarks on the working and developments of the United States Negroleum Co., by Horrible Greasy. *New York.* [n. d.] 8vo, pp. 8. B. 52276

Nehiro-Iriniui. *See* Vol. V., No. 19378.

NEIDHARD (Charles). Diphtheria, as it prevailed in the United States from 1860–1866 ... . By C. Neidhard, M.D. ... *New York: William Radde.* 1867. 8vo, pp. 176. C. 52277

NEIGHBOR SMITH, *pseudon.* The Cracked Jug, or Five Answers to my Neighbor Parley's Five Letters, cracking his "Fifteen Gallon Jug," with a Preface, and a Congratulation, by Neighbor Smith. *Boston.* 1838. 12mo, pp. 24. + Second Edition. [*Ibid.*] 52278

NEILL (A.) Semi-Centennial Discourse. *Philadelphia.* 1857. 8vo. 52279

NEILL (E. D.) Biographical Sketch of Doctor Jonathan Potts, ... with Extracts from his Correspondence. By Rev. Edward D. Neill. ... *Albany: J. Munsell.* 1863. 8vo, pp. 18.

NEILL. Dahkotah Land and Dahkotah Life, with the History of the Fur Traders of the extreme Northwest during the French and British Dominions. By Edward D. Neill ... . *Philadelphia.* 1859. 8vo. 52281

NEILL. The English Colonization of America during the Seventeenth Century. By Edward Duffield Neill ... . *London: Strahan & Co.* 1871. 8vo, pp. xi, 352. 52282

NEILL. The Fairfaxes of England and America in the Seventeenth and Eighteenth Centuries, including Letters from and to Hon. William Fairfax, ... and his Sons, Col. George William Fairfax and Rev. Bryan, Eighth Lord Fairfax, the Neighbors and Friends of George Washington. By Edward D. Neill ... . *Albany, N. Y.: Joel Munsell.* 1868. 8vo, pp. 234. BA. 52283

NEILL. The History of Minnesota: from the Earliest French Explorations to the Present Time. By Edward Duffield Neill, ... *Philadelphia: J. B. Lippincott & Co.* 1858. 4to, pp. 628. 3 Maps. + Second Edition. [*Ibid.*] 1873. 8vo, pp. lii, 50–758. 3 Portraits and 4 Maps. BA. 52284

Only of the first edition one hundred copies were printed on large paper. *See* "Historical Magazine," III. 28, for a review.

NEILL. History of the Virginia Company of London, with Letters to and from the First Colony never before printed. By Edward D. Neill. ... *Albany, N. Y.: Joel Munsell.* 1869. 4to, pp. xvi, 432. Plate. BA. 52285

N[EILL.] Maryland not a Roman Catholic Colony, Stated in Three Letters, by E. D. N. ... *Minneapolis: Johnson & Smith.* 1875. 8vo, pp. (2), 10. 52286

[NEILL.] Materials for the ... History. *See* Vol. XII. 49264

NEILL. Pocahontas and her Companions; a Chapter from the History of the Virginia Company of London. By Rev. Edward D. Neill. *Albany, N. Y.: Joel Munsell.* 1869. 4to, pp. 32. Portrait of Pocahontas. BA. 52287

Mr. Neill's monogram on Pocahontas would hardly have been printed had he given credit to the letters written by Sir Thomas Dale and Alex. Whittaker, announcing the marriage of Pocahontas to John Rolfe, and the long one by the latter gentleman himself, minutely relating his alternate qualms of conscience, and paroxysms of love, the latter finally victoriously compelling him to lead the Indian princess to the altar.

NEILL. Terra Mariæ; or Threads of Maryland Colonial History. By Edward D. Neill ... . *Philadelphia: J. B. Lippincott & Co.* 1867. 12mo, pp. 260. 52288

Also: Effort and Failure to civilize the Aborigines. Letter to Hon. N. G. Taylor, Commissioner of Indian Affairs ... . *Washington.* 1868. 8vo, pp. 15. H.—Memoir of Rev. Patrick Copland, Rector elect of the first projected College in the United States. A Chapter of the English Colonization of America. ... *New York: C. Scribner & Co.* 1871. 8vo, pp. 96.—The Relation of the Government to the Indian Tribes. Letter to Hon. James Doolittle ... 1863. [n. p. 1863.] 8vo.—Sir George Calvert, created Baron of Baltimore, In the County of Longford, Ireland; and Projector of Province of Maryland ... . *Baltimore: Cushings & Bailey.* 1869. 12mo, pp. 24.—Virginia Company of London. Extracts from their Manuscript Transactions: with Notes ... . *Washington: Government Printing Office.* 1868. 8vo, pp. 17. B., C.

NEILL (H.) A Letter to the Editors of the American Presbyterian, [on Slavery] ... . By Rev. Henry Neill ... . *Philadelphia: King & Baird, Printers.* 1858. 8vo, pp. 21. BA. 52289

NEILL (J.) ... A Sermon ... in ... Philadelphia, ... September 26, 1861, on ... the National Fast ... . By Rev. James Neill. ... *Philadelphia: Collins, Printer.* 1861. 8vo, pp. 23. H. 52290

NEILL (P.) The Fruit, Flower, and Kitchen Garden; adapted to the United States. From the Fourth Edition, revised and improved by the Author. *Philadelphia: H. C. Baird.* 1851. 12mo, pp. xii, 427. Plate. + Edited by G. Emerson; with Notes and Additions, by R. G. Pardee. *New-York.* 1855. 8vo, pp. 408. C. 52291

NEILL (W.) Autobiography of William Neill, D.D. With a Selection from his Sermons. By the Rev. J. H. Jones, D.D. *Philadelphia.* 1861. 12mo, pp. (4), 272. Portrait. C. 52292

NEILL. The Unity of the Spirit ... A Discourse ... at the Organization of the Second Presbytery of Philadelphia, November 27th, 1833, By Rev. William Neill, D.D. ... *Philadelphia: Russell and Martien, Printers.* 1833. 8vo, pp. 18. H. 52293

Also: A Discourse reviewing A Ministry of Fifty Years. ... With An Appendix of Anecdotes and Reminiscences. *Philadelphia: Joseph M. Wilson.* 1857. 8vo, pp. 63.—Farewell Sermon ... at Cooperstown, N. Y., Sept. 3, 1809. ... *Cooperstown.* 1809. 8vo, pp. 13.

NEILSON (C.) An Original, Compiled and Corrected Account of Burgoyne's Campaign, and the Memorable Battles of Bemis's Heights, Sept. 19, and Oct. 7, 1777, from the most Authentic Sources of Information; including many Interesting Incidents connected with the same: and a Map of the Battle Ground. By Charles Neilson, Esq. ... *Albany: Printed by Joel Munsell.* 1844. 12mo, pp. 291, (1). Map. BA. 52294

Got up to aid in selling the author's farm—the battle was *not* fought near his house.

NEILSON (J.) Second Series of The Present and Future Prospects of Jamaica considered, Pointing out the Advantages which may be derived from the Extinction of Slavery, and Shewing the causes which oppose themselves to the successful Working of the Apprenticeship system, in accelerating that object, and proposing a remedy, Suggesting the means for establishing a Bank, on a solid basis, By John Neilson. *Kingston-Jamaica.* 1834. 8vo, pp. 20.

NEILSON (J.) Observations upon Emigration to Upper Canada, being the Prize Essay for which was awarded a Gold Medal,

from the Upper Canada Celtic Society. By Joseph Neilson. *Kingston.* 1837. 16mo, pp. 74. H. 52296

NEILSON (Peter). Recollections of a Six Years Residence in the United States of America. ... *Glasgow: David Robertson.* MDCCCXXX. Post 8vo, pp. viii, 358, (4). 52297

NEILSON (S.) Sketch of the Life of Samuel Neilson. By Hibernicus. *New York.* 1804. 8vo. 52298

NEIMEYER BELLEGARDE (H. L. de). Resumo da Historia do Brasil. Por Henrique Luis de Neimeyer Bellegarde. *Rio de Janeiro, na Typographia de Gueffier.* 1831. Rl. 8vo. + Segunda edição. *Rio de Janeiro, Typographia de Ogier.* 1834. 8vo, pp. 276. 52299

Ne Kagh-ya-dough-se-ra. *See* Mohawk, Vol. XII., No. 49847.

Nek Nechenenawachgissitschik. *See* Vol. IV., No. 19377.

Prospectus of the Nekoosa Lumbering Company; ... with the Charter and By-Laws. *Milwaukee.* 1856. 8vo, pp. 23, (1).

NELL (William C.) The Coloured Patriots of the American Revolution, with Sketches of several distinguished Coloured Persons: ... added, a brief Survey of the Condition and Prospects of Coloured Americans. By Wm. C. Nell. With an Introduction by Harriet Beecher Stowe. *Boston: Robert F. Wallcut.* 1855. 12mo, pp. 396. 2 Plates, and Facsimile. B., C., H.

NELL. ... Property Qualification or no Property Qualification: A Few Facts from the Record of Patriotic Services of the Colored Men of New York, during the Wars of 1776 and 1812, ... Compiled by William C. Nell ... . *New York: Thomas Hamilton.* 1860. 12mo, pp. 24. H. 52302

NELL. Services of Colored Americans, in the Wars of 1776 and 1812. By William C. Nell. *Boston: Printed by Prentiss & Sawyer.* 1851. 8vo, pp. 24. + Second Edition. *Boston: Robert C. Wallcut.* 1852. 8vo, pp. 40. + *Toronto.* 1854. 12mo, pp. 32

NELLES (A.), *pseudon?* Annie Nelles; or, the Life of a Book Agent. An Autobiography. *Cincinnati: The Author.* 1868. 8vo, pp. 385. 4 Plates. C. 52304

Nelly's Hospital. ... [By L. M. Alcott. The Busy Bees; A "Comfort Bag in the Army," by J. T. Higgins. n. p. n. d.] 8vo, pp. 8. B. 52305

NELSON (D.) An Appeal to the Church, in behalf of a Dying Race, By David Nelson ... . *New York: John S. Taylor.* 1838. 12mo, pp. 23. BA. 52306

[NELSON (D.)] *See* Vol. IX., No. 34960.

NELSON (E.) ... A Discourse ... before the Temperance Society in Woburn, December 14, 1829. By E. Nelson ... . *Boston: Peirce and Williams.* 1830. 12mo, pp. 12. H. 52307

NELSON (H.) The Sugar Duties Discussed. By Henry Nelson. *London.* 1863. 8vo. 52308

NELSON (H. A.) A Discourse commemorative of Rev. Frederick Starr, Jr. ... St. Louis. By Rev. Henry A. Nelson. *St. Louis.* 1867. 8vo. 52309

NELSON. ... Two Discourses ... at ... Springfield, Illinois, ... on the Sabbath following the Burial of President Lincoln, May 7, 1865, By Rev. Henry A. Nelson ... . *Springfield, Ills.: Baker & Phillips.* 1865. 8vo, pp. 39. B. 52310

Also: ... Discourse before the American Board of Commissioners for Foreign Missions ... in Norwich, Conn., October 6, 1868. ... *Boston: Missionary House.* 1868. 8vo, pp. 20.—National Blessings; Sources of National Obligations. Thanksgiving Discourse ... at Auburn, 1847. ... *Auburn.* 1848. 8vo.—Our National Religion. Thanksgiving Sermon, preached Nov. 24, 1853. ... *Auburn, N. Y.* 1853. 8vo.

NELSON (H.) Nelson's Northern Lancet, and American Journal of Medical Jurisprudence. Editor ... Horace Nelson, M.D. ... Vol. I. New Series. ... *Plattsburgh, New York.* 1852. 8vo, pp. (8), 318. Continued. H. 52311

NELSON [Horatio]. Memoirs of the Life and Achievements of Lord Viscount Nelson. By a Captain of the British Navy. ... *London.* 1806. 8vo, pp. 124. 52312

Also: Life of Lord Horatio Nelson, containing a correct Account of all his Naval Engagements. ... *London.* [n. d.] 12mo.—Memoirs of the Life and Gallant Services of Admiral Lord Nelson ... *Angus & Son, Newcastle.* [1817.] 12mo, pp. 24. Nelson assisted in the reduction of Fort Juan in the Gulf of Mexico, etc.

NELSON (J.) Address ... in Leicester, Jan. 26, 1827, before ... Delegates from Several "Lyceums for Mutual Instruction" in Worcester. By John Nelson ... . *Worcester: William Manning, Printer.* [1827.] 8vo, pp. 23. BA. 52313

NELSON. [Memorial of] Mrs. Elizabeth Sargent ... . *Worcester.* [1862.] 8vo, pp. 7. H. 52314

NELSON. Sermon, Proceedings and Addresses in commemoration of the Fiftieth Anniversary of the Settlement of ... Rev. John Nelson, D.D. ... in Leicester, Mass. And ... his Golden Wedding. *Boston: Mudge & Son, Printers.* 1862. 12mo, pp. (2), 116. Plate. H. 52315

Also: A Discourse on the Proposed Repeal of the Missouri Compromise; ... Fast Day, April 6, 1854, ... in Leicester, Mass. ... *Worcester, Mass.: Printed by Edward R. Fiske.* [1854.] 8vo, pp. 14. H.—Gatherings from a Pastor's Drawer. ... *Worcester.* 1852. 12mo.—An Oration ... [at] Williams College July 11, 1810; in commemoration of the Death of William D. Hornell, a member of the Sophomore Class, who was drowned in Deerfield River. ... *Northampton: Printed by William Butler.* [n. d.] 8vo, pp. 14.—Oration ... at Leicester, July 5, 1824. ... *Leicester.* 1824. 8vo. W.—Oration, ... before the Adelphic Union Society of Williams College ... Sept. 5, 1826. ... *Worcester: Printed by William Manning.* [n. d.] 8vo, pp. 24.—Sermon ... at Leicester, on the Death of Col. Thomas Denny, Dec. 8, 1814. ... [n. p. n. d.] 8vo.—Sermon ... at the Funeral of Col. Edwards Whipple, at Shrewsbury, Sept., 1822. ... *Worcester.* [n. d.] 8vo.—A Sermon, ... on ... Thanksgiving; Leicester, December 5, 1822. ... *Leicester: Hori Brown, Printer.* 1822. 8vo, pp. 23.—A Sermon ... at The Funeral of the Rev. Arætius B. Hull, ... in Worcester, May, 1826. ... *Worcester: Printed by William Manning.* [n. d.] 8vo, pp. 19.— ... A Sermon ... before the Pastoral Association of Massachusetts, in ... Boston, May 30, 1837. ... *Boston: Printed by Crocker & Brewster.* 1837. 8vo, pp. 24.—A Thanksgiving Sermon, ... November 28, 1839. ... *Worcester.* 1840. 8vo, pp. 14. H.

NELSON (J.) Political and Commercial Importance of Completing the Line of Railway from Halifax to Quebec. By Joseph Nelson. *London.* 1860. 8vo. Map. 52316

NELSON (L.) A Half Century Sermon, delivered in the First Society in Lisbon, December 5th, A. D. 1854. By the Rev. Levi Nelson ... . *Norwich: Andrew Stark, Printer.* 1854. 8vo, pp. 23

NELSON (R.) Asiatic Cholera: ... in Asia, Africa, and Europe, introduction into America through Canada; ... . By R. Nelson, M.D. ... *New York: William A. Townsend.* 1866. 12mo, pp. 206. B. 52318

NELSON. Sketch of the History and Progress of the ... Cholera Epidemic, as it occurred in Montreal. By Robert Nelson, M.D. ... *Montreal: Printed by Thomas A. Starke.* 1832. 12mo, pp. 48. B. 52319

NELSON (T.) & SONS. The Falls of Niagara: ... A Complete Guide ... . *London ... T. Nelson & Sons.* MDCCCLIX. 24mo, pp. 64. Map. B. 52320

Nelson's British Library. ... *London.* [n. d.] 12mo. 52321

Includes Todd's "Lost Sister of Wyoming," "Portrait Painting among the Indians," "Discovery of the Polar Regions," etc.

NELSON & SONS. Our Summer Retreats. A Handbook To all the ... Resorts, and other Places of Interest in the United States. ... *New York: T. Wilson and Sons.* MDCCCLIX. 24mo, pp. 64. B. 52322

Also: Nelson's Guide to Lake George and Lake Champlain ... . *London: T. Nelson and Sons.* MDCCCLVIII. 16mo, pp. 48. Map and 10 Plates. + [*Ibid.*] MDCCCLIX.—Nelson's Guide to the City of New York and its Neighborhood. *London ... T. Nelson & Sons.* MDCCCLVIII. 24mo, pp. 64. 2 Maps.—Nelson's Illustrated Guide to the Hudson and its Tributaries. *New York: T. Nelson & Sons.* MDCCCLX. 16mo, pp. 202. 12 Plates.—Views on the Hudson. *London and New York: Nelson.* [n. d.] 16mo, pp. 15. 12 Plates.—Views on the St. Lawrence. Toronto to Quebec. *London ... T. Nelson and Sons.* [n. d.] 16mo, pp. 15. 12 Plates. H.

NELSON (T. A. R.) The Position of Parties. Speech of Hon. Thomas A. R. Nelson ... December 6, 1859. [n. p. n. d.] 8vo, pp. 8. H. 52323

Also: Speech on the Disturbed Condition of the Country. ... *Washington: R. Polkinborn.* [n. d.] 8vo, pp. 16.

NEMAR (R. M.) The Kentucky Revival; or, A Short History of the extraordinary outpouring of the Spirit of God in the Western States. By R. M. Nemar. *New York.* 1846. 12mo.

NEMBHARD (J. F.) Treatise on the Nature and Cure of the Yaws. By J. F. Nembhard. *Jamaica, Kingston.* 1793. 4to.

NEMO, *pseudon.* A Few Thoughts on the Confiscation Act. By Nemo. *Augusta, Ga.* 1861. 8vo, pp. 16. 52326

NEMO, *pseudon.* Remarks on the Policy of Recognizing the Independence of the Southern States. By Nemo. *London: William Brown & Co., Printers.* 1863. 24mo, pp. 48. + *London: Effingham Wilson.* 1863. 8vo, pp. 31, (1). BA. 52327

NEMO, *pseudon.* Reveries in Rhyme. By "Nemo," of Louisiana. *New York.* 1846. 12mo, pp. 88. 52328

NEMO, *pseudon.* Straws by Nemo. ... *Cambridge: Metcalf and Company.* 1859. 16mo, pp. 160. H. 52329

NEMO (*Mrs.*), *pseudon.* A Series of Appeals; or Lectures addressed not behind a Curtain to One Unfortunate Man, but to all Men and their Families. By Mrs. Nemo. ... *Albany: J. Munsell.* 1863. 12mo, pp. 2, (4), 27, 32, 60, 39. B. 52330

The last "Appeal" is entitled, "Our Present War: Woman's Relation to it."

NEMO NOBODY, *pseudon.* Something. Edited by Nemo Nobody, Esq. ... *Boston.* 1810. 8vo. 52331

Nene karighwiyoston. *See* Vol. XII., No. 49846.

Nepenthes Evangelicum. *See* [Mather (C.)], XI. 46428.

NEPOMUCENO ALMONTE (Juan), *and others.* Refutacion en la parte histórica del artículo de fondo publicado en el num. 305 del periodico titulado "El Universal," el 16 del pasado septiembre. Por una Comision de la Junta Civica. *México: J. Cumplido.* 1849. 8vo, pp. 32. Table and Portrait. C. 52332

See also Almonte (J. N.), Vol. I., No. 956.

NEPOMUCENO ROSAINS (J.) Relacion historica de lo acontecido al Lic. Don Juan Nepomuceno Rosains como insurgente. *Puebla.* 1823. Folio, pp. 21. 52333

NEPOMUCENO TRONCOSO (J.) Fabulas politicas de Juan Nepomuceno Troncoso. [n. p. n. d.] Sm. 8vo, pp. 124. 52334

NEPOMUCENO (M. J.) Vida de Sor Mariana Juana Nepomuceno, fundadora y abadesa del Monasterio de religiosas capuchinas, titulado N. Sra. de Guadalupe y Sta. Coleta. *Mexico.* 1808. 4to, pp. 30. 52335

NEPONSET. Acts of Incorporation, and Rules and Regulations of the Proprietors of Neponset Bridge. *Boston.* [n. d.] 8vo, pp. 16. BA. 52336

Neptune Americo-Septentrional; contenant les côtes, isles et bancs, les baies, ports et mouillages, et les sondes des mers de cette partie du monde, depuis le Groenland inclusivement jusques et compris le Golfe du Mexique avec les isles de sous-le-vent et du vent, accompagnés de plans particuliers des ports les plus frequentés, ou recueil de cartes hydrographiques, à l'usage des vaisseaux du Roi, redigé d'après les cartes françoises et étrangères les plus estimées. Rectifié d'après des plans manuscrits authentiques, et assujetti aux observations astronomiques. Dressé au depôt général des cartes, plans, et journaux de la marine, et publié par ordre du Roi. *Paris.* [n. d.] Atlas folio. 52337

"A collection of very beautiful charts of the coast of North America, with plans of the ports, harbours, &c. published on separate sheets, between 1778 and 1780, for the use of the French navy."—RICH.

NEREUS, *pseudon.* *See* [Croker (J. Wilson)], Vol. V. 17595.

NESBIT (J. C.) On Peruvian Guano; its History, Composition, and Fertilising Qualities; with the best Mode of Application to the Soil. By J. C. Nesbit. *London.* 1852. 8vo, pp. 40. + [*Ibid.*] 1856. 8vo. 52338

NESMITH (J.) Reasons why the Measure of Value Established by Law, should be used as Currency .... By Hon. John Nesmith. *Lowell: Stone & Huse, Printers.* 1868. 8vo, pp. 10.

[NESMITH.] Thoughts on The Currency. By an old Merchant. *Lowell: Knapp & Morey, Printers.* 1866. 8vo, pp. 12.

NESMITH (J. W.) Branch Mint of the United States. ... Speech of Hon. J. W. Nesmith ... April 1, 1864. *[Washington.* n. d.] 8vo, pp. 16. H. 52341

Also: Remarks ... upon the Indian Appropriation Bill, ... May 13th and 14th, 1862. [n. p.:] *McGill, Witherow & Co., Printers.* [n. d.] 8vo, pp. 16.—Speech ... on Reconstruction; ... January 18, 1866. *Washington.* 1866. 8vo, pp. 14. H.

NESS (C.) Wonderful Signs of Wonderful Times, a faithful Collection of Signs, Wonders and Prodigies in the Heavens, Earth, and Waters, in this last year 1680. By Christopher Ness. *London: The Author.* 1681. 4to. 52342

Includes some notices of New England.

A Nest of Love disturbed; or the Farmer's Dialogue, for Nantucket .... *Boston: Printed by J. Belcher.* 1811. 8vo, pp. 15.

Nestor's Address to the Pennsylvania Militia. *Philadelphia: Printed by J. Humphreys.* 1778. Folio, 1 leaf. 52344

The Nests at Washington. *See* [Piatt (J. J., *and* S. M. B.)]

The Net in the Bay; or Journal of a Visit to Moose and Albany. By the Bishop of Rupert's Land. *London.* 1854. 8vo.

NETHERCLIFT (F. G.) The Autograph Miscellany A Collection of Autograph Letters ... in Fac-Simile Lithography By Frederick Netherclift. First Series. Containing Sixty Examples. *London: Netherclift & Durlacher.* 1855. Folio. B. 52346

Contains a letter from William Penn and George Washington. Also: The Hand-Book to Autographs: ... A ... Guide to the Handwriting of Distinguished Men and Women of every Nation. ... *London: John Russell Smith.* M.DCCC.LXII. Sm. 4to. B.

The | Netherland-Historian, | Containing | A true & exact Relation of what hath | passed in the late Warrs between the King of | Great Britain, and the French King with their Allyes, | against the States-Generall of the United Provinces; | from the beginning thereof Anno 1671. to the con- | clusion of Peace .... With the continuation | of what hath since happened between France | and his Alleyes, against the said States, and | their Confederates, to the end of | the Year 1674. | Illustrated with above 60 Sculptures, | ...

of the ... | Fortifications ... . *Amsterdam: Printed by Stephen Smart.* 1675. 12mo, pp. (6), 2, 15–16, 560. 70 Plates. A., B.

Refers incidentally to the West Indies, Surinam, etc. *See also* Vol. XI., No. 43921.

Ne totyerenhton kahyatonhsera. *See* Mohawk, XII. 49851.

The Nets of Salvation. *See* [Mather (C.)], Vol. XI. 46429.

NETSCHER (A. D. van der Gon). Bijdrage ter Aanwijzing van der Grondslagen, waarop de Afschaffing der Slavernij in Suriname dient gevestigd te worden. April 1858. *'sHage.* 1858. 8vo. 52348

Also: Beschouwing van het op 25 Oct. 1858 voorgesteld Ontwerp van wet ter Afschaffing der Slavernij in Suriname. *'sHage.* 1859. 8vo.—De Quaestie van vrijen Arbeid en Immigratie in de West-Indie toegelicht. Nov. 1859. *'sHage.* 1860. 8vo.

[NETSCHER (P. M.)] Gedachten ten Gunste der Planters en Lands-Ambtenaren te Suriname. *'sHage.* 1848. 8vo. 52349

NETSCHER. Les Hollandais au Brésil, Notice historique sur les pays-bas et le Brésil au XVIIe siècle, Par P. M. Netscher .... *La Haye: Belinfante Frères.* 1853. Rl. 8vo, pp. xxxii, 209, (1). Plate, Portrait and Map. 52350

Ne tsinihhoweyea-nenda-onh. *See* Mohawk, Vol. XII. 49850.

NETTLE (R.) The Salmon Fisheries of the River St. Lawrence and its Tributaries. By Richard Nettle. *Montreal: Printed by John Lovell.* 1857. 12mo, pp. 144. H. 52351

NETTLES (J.), *and* CANNON (E.) *See* Vol. III., No. 11005.

NETTLESHIP (Henry). Quibusnam precipue de causis exortum sit bellum civile Americanum. *Oxon.* 1863. 8vo. 52352

An Oxford prize essay on the Causes of the Civil War.

NETTLETON (A.) Remains and Sermons of Rev. Asahel Nettleton. Edited by Rev. R. Tyler. *Hartford.* 18—. 12mo.

NETTLETON. Temperance and Revivals. By ... Rev. Asahel Nettleton. [*Boston.* n. d.] 8vo, pp. 7, (1). B. 52354

NETTLETON (C.) Mining and Manufacturing Laws of Pennsylvania now in force ... . Compiled by Charles Nettleton ... . *New York: Owens & Agar.* 1865. 8vo, pp. 38. 52355

NETTO (A. da S.) 'Estudios sobre a Emancipaçao dos Escravos no Brasil por A. da Silva Netto. *Rio de Janeiro.* 1866. 8vo, pp. 46. 52356

NETTO (L.) Apontamentos relativos á botanica applicada no Brasil pelo Dr. Ladislau Netto. *Rio de Janeiro.* 1871. 8vo, pp. v, 78. 52357

NETTO. Investigacões historicas e scientificas sobre o Museu imperial e nacional do Rio de Janeiro, acompanhadas de uma breve noticia de suas collecções e publicadas por ordem do Ministerio da Agricultura pelo Dr. Ladisláu Netto. *Rio de Janeiro.* 1870. 8vo, pp. iv, 310, x. 52358

Also: Remarque sur la destruction des plantes indigènes au Brésil .... *Paris: A. Parent, Imprimeur* .... 1865. 8vo, pp. 16. H.

Netum Ewh Oomahzenahegun. *See* Jones (P.), IX. 36593.

Neu Jahrs Geschenk. *See* Vol. IX., No. 35635.

Neu-Entdecktes Norden oder gründliche und wahrhaffte Reise-Beschreibung aller mitternächtigen und Nordwärts-gelegenen Länder, Städte, Vestungen und Insulen, samt der darinnen sich befindlichen Nationen, Lebensart, Sitten und Religion. Ingleichen was allda für Handlung und Gewerb getrieben und auf was Art aus diesen Nord-Ländern uns Teutschen Nutzen geschafft werden könnte. Von F. M. *Franckfurt und Leipzig, Verlegts Johann Albrecht, Buchhändler in Nürnberg.* 1728. 12mo, folded Title, pp. (8), 302. J.C.B. 52359

Contains a translation of Hessel Gerritsz' rare collection on the arctic voyages, besides D. Blefkenius' "Description of Iceland and Greenland," the voyages of Zeno, 1370, P. Quirinus, etc.

Neu-Eröffnetes Amphitheatrvm, Worinnen Nach dem uns bekanten gantzen Welt-Creisz, Alle Nationen Nach ihrem Habit, in saubern Figuren repräsentiret. Anbey die Länder nach ihrer Situation, Climate, Fruchtbarkeit, Inclination und Beschaffenheit der Einwohner, Religion, vornehmsten Städten ... und Mappen aufgeführet sind, Und welches, mit Zuziehung der Land-Charten, zu vieler Belustigung, ... als ein sehr nützliches ... Compendium Geographicum ... kan gebrauchet werden. *Erffurth, Gedruckt und verlegt von Johann Michael Funcken.* 1723. 5 parts, folio, pp. (2), (132); (4), 96; (4), 124; (2), 142; 172; Register, (4). 52360

The third part contains thirty-three half-page illustrations, portraits of Columbus, Vespucius, Magellanes, and representations of American Indians.

Neu-Eröffnetes Raritäten-Cabinet, Ost- und West-Indianischer und ausländischer Sachen, so sich in China, Japan, Choromandel, Peru, Guina, etc. und andern Ländern finden. *Hamburg.* 1707. 8vo. 52361

Neu-Gefundenes Eden. Oder ausszführlicher Bericht von Süd und Nord Carolina, Pensilphania, Mary Land & Virginia. Entworffen durch zwey in diese Provintzen gemachten Reisen, Reiss-Journal, und ville Brieffen, dadurch der gegenwärtige Zustand diser Ländern warhafftig entdecket und dem Nebenmenschen zu gutem an Tag gelegt wird. Samt beygefügtem Anhang, oder Freye Unterweisung zu dem verlohrnen, nun aber wieder gefundenen Lapide Philosophorum, dadurch man bald zur Vergnügung und wahrer Reichthum gelangen kan. *In Truck verfertiget durch Befelch der Helvetischen Societät.* 1737. 12mo, pp. (16), 288. Map. J.C.B. 52362

This new-found Eden, or a detailed account of South and North Carolina, Pennsylvania, Maryland, and Virginia is the result of two journeys made through these provinces, and includes considerable correspondence which bears on the condition of the country, contains also full information concerning its resources, evidently intended to influence emigration.

Neu-polirter Geschichte- ... Spiegel. *See* [Franciscus (E.)]

Neu-vermehrt- und vollständiges Gesang-Buch, Vorinnen sowohl die Psalmen Davids ... . *Germanton: Gedruckt und zu finden bey Christof Saur.* 1753. 8vo, Wood-cut Frontispiece, Title, pp. 562, (10), 223. 52363

Der Neue Americanische Landwirthschafts Calender. *Reading, Pa.* 1820. 4to. Continued. S. 52364

Neue Entdeckung. *See* Vol. VIII., No. 31367.

Neue Erdbeschreibung von ganz Amerika. Aus dem Englischen. Herausgegeben von A. L. Schlözer. *Göttingen: Weygand.* 1777. 2 vols., 8vo. Maps and Plates. 52365

Der Neue Hoch Deutsche Americanische Calender. *Baltimore: S. Savr.* 1802. 4to. Continued. S. 52366

Neue Nachricht alter ... Merkwürdigkeiten. *See* No. 10974.

Neue Nachrichten von den Missionen. *See* [Muratori (L. A.)]

Neue Nachrichten von denen neuentdekten Insuln in der See zwischen Asien und Amerika; aus mitgetheilten Urkunden und Auszügen verfasset von J. L. S.** *Hamburg und Leipzig, bey Friedrich Lugo Ludwig Gleditsch.* 1776. 8vo, pp. (2), 173.

Der Neue Pennsylvanische Stadt und Land Calender. *Allentown.* 1823. 4to. Continued. S. 52368

Neue Reise. *See* [La Martinière (P. M. de)], X. 38715.

Neue Reise nach Cayenne. *See* Vol. III., Nos. 11622–3.

Neue Reise Beschreibung. *See* Vol. VIII., No. 31368.

Neue Reisen | nach | Guiana, Peru | und durch das | südliche America, | ... *Göttingen: | Verlegts Abram Vandenhöecks seel., Wittwe,* 1751. | 8vo, pp, (14), 380, Register, (12). Map and Plates. H.

Neue Sammlung der merkwürdigen Reisegeschichten, und Nachricht von den Ländern und Völkern des ganzen Erdkreises, in geographischen und historischen Zusammenhang. *Frankfurt.* 1748–1780. 22 vols., 4to. Maps and Plates. 52370

Perhaps a translation of the Abbé Prevost's collection.

Das Neue Testament | unsers | HErrn | und Heylandes | JEsu CHristi | Verteutscht | Von | D. Martin Luther | Mit | Jedes Capitels Kurtzen | Sumarien. | Auch beygefügten vielen richtigen | Parallelen. | *Gedruckt und zu finden bey Christoph Saur.* 1745. 8vo, rubricated Title, Vorrede, etc., pp. 2, 592, Register, 3. 52371

The first New Testament (except Eliot's Indian version) printed in this country. The printer was the son of the printer of the Bible, 1743.

Das Neue Testament ... . [Second Edition]. *Germantaun: Gedruckt und zu finden bey Christoph Saur.* 1755. 8vo, rubricated Title, Vorrede, etc., pp. (2), 562. + [*Ibid.*] 1760. 12mo. + [Fourth Edition. *Ibid.*] 1763. 12mo, pp. ii, 679, Register, 4. + [Sixth Edition. *Ibid.*] 1769. 8vo, pp. 529, Register, 3.

Das Neue Testament ... . *Germantaun: Chr. Saur.* 1775. 8vo, pp. 529, Register, 3. 52373

There appear to be two editions of this date, or at all events variations in the title. Dr. O'Callaghan (pp. 28–29) observes that *this* is represented as the sixth edition, when it is actually the seventh, and reiterates the remark under the notice of an edition with a different title printed the same year. On page 28 of Dr. O'Callaghan's book, "Das Neue Testament," 1775, is stated to be the *seventh* edition, etc., and on page 29, same date, but a *different* title, the same remark occurs—that is, that too is said to be the *seventh* editon. Is it to be inferred that the *seventh* edition has *variations* in the *title* as well as the *preface?*

Das Neue Testament ... . *Germantaun: Michael Billmeyer.* 1795. 12mo, pp. 537, Anweisung, 5. 52374

This edition was reproduced in 1803 and 1807.

Das Neue Testament ... . *Philadelphia, bey Carl Cist.* 1796. 8vo. 52375

Not noticed by Dr. E. B. O'Callaghan.

Der Neue Welt-Bott. Allerhand so lehr- als geist-reiche Brief-Schrifften und Reis-Beschreibungen, welche von denen

Missionariis der Gesellschafft Jesu in aus beyden Indien, und andern über Meer gelegenen Ländern [1642–1745], in Europa angelangt seynd. *Augspurg und Grätz* [etc.], *P., M. & J. Veith seel. Erben,* [etc.] 1726–58. 36 Parts, in 5 vols., folio. Maps and Plates.

This highly valuable collection of missionary reports relating to America, etc., is mostly taken from unpublished manuscripts. Only the smaller part has been translated from the "Lettres Édifiantes."

Neuer Gemeinnütziger Pennsylvanischer Calender. *Lancaster.* 1835. 4to. Continued. S. 52377

Neuer Hausswirthschafts Calender. *Reading, Pa.* 1799. 12mo

Neuer praktischer Wegweiser für Auswanderer nach Nord Amerika ... mit Karten, Plänen und Ansichten. Dritte Abtheilung enthält: die Beschreibung des Staats- oder Congress-Landes in Iowa .... *Worms,* 1848. *Druck von Steinkühl und Smith.* 8vo, pp. 106. 52379

Neuer Weltbot mit sich bringend eine wahrhaffte Historie einiger von denen Patribus der Gesellschaft Jesu in Paraquaria neubekehrten Völcker: samt ausführlichen Bericht vom Amazonenstrom und der Landschafft Guiana. Aus dem Spanisch und Französischen übersetzet. *Wienn: P. Straub.* 1733. 8vo, pp. (14), 784, 14. Plate. 52380

A German translation of three rare works, viz.: Fernandez's "Relacion," Madrid, 1726, 4to (our No. 24135), Acuna's "Nuevo descubrimiento" (our No. 150), Grillet's "Voyage en Gujane" (our No. 152).

Neueste Kunde von America. ... *Weimar.* 1815–16. 2 vols., 8vo, pp. 610; 648. H. 52381

Neueste Länder- und Völkerkunde. Ein geographisches Lesebuch für alle Stände. *Prag.* 1820. 8vo, pp. 642. Maps and Plates. 52382

Neueste Staats-Akten. *See* Diplomatisches Archiv, v. 20216.

Neueste und richtigste Nachricht. *See* [Oglethorpe (J.)]

Neuester Zustand der Engländischen Schiffarth. Mit einem Anhang von dem Wegnehmen der Englischen Schiffe in West-Indien, und dem grausamen Verfahren mit dem Schiffsvolck derselben. Aus dem Englischen übersetzt. [n. p.] 1731. 4to, pp. 44. 52383

NEUFCHATEAU (Nicholas Louis François de, *Comte de*). Mémoire en forme de discours sur la disette du numéraire à St.

Domingue, et sur les moyens d'y remédier. ... *Cap François.* 1784. 8vo. + *Metz.* 1788. 8vo. + *Paris.* 1788. 8vo.

NEUFFER (M.) Dissertatio de modo probabiliori quo primæ in Americam Septentrionalem immigrationes sunt factæ. Quam sub auspiciis divini numinis præside Ottone Christiano de Lohenschiold. Placidæ eruditorum disquisitioni submittunt. F. Martinus Neuffer, Backnangensis, J. Davides Klett, Untertenningensis. *Tübingae: Litteris Schrammianis.* [1754.] 4to, pp. 24. J.C.B.

A dissertation on the more probable manner in which North America was first peopled. The authors contend that the continent received its earliest inhabitants from the Greenlanders, and nations or tribes who dwelt in the northern regions of Europe before Odin and his followers reached there. They also maintain that no emigration was made from northern Asia; and that the Esquimaux are not the most ancient people of America. The tract is evidently the introduction to a fuller treatise on the same subject.

NEUFVILLE (J.), *and* FRANKLIN (B.) Letters to the Merchant's Committee of Philadelphia, May 14, 1770. *Philadelphia.* 1770. Folio, 1 page. P. 52386

NEUFVILLE (J. de). De iis, quae ad tollendum servorum Afrorum commercium inde a Congressu Viennensi, inter populos gesta sunt. ... *Amsterdam.* 1840. 8vo, pp. 130. 52387

NEUFVILLE. De Vrijlating der Slaven in hare Gevolgen beschouwd, en op de Nederlandsche Volkplantingen toegepast. ... *Amsterdam.* 1841. 8vo. 52388

NEUMANN (B.) Kurzgefasste Geographie für deutsche Schulen Nord Amerika's. ... Zweite Auflage. *St. Louis* (*Mo.*): *Bernard Neumann.* 1865. 16mo, pp. iv, 174. C. 52389

NEUMANN (J.) Memorial relative to the American Flag presented to the State of California. By Joseph Neumann. *Sacramento.* 1870. 8vo. 52390

NEUMANN (K. F.) Geschichte der Vereinigten Staaten von America. Von Karl Friedrich Neumann. ... *Berlin: Carl Heymann.* 1863–66. 3 vols., 8vo, pp. xxviii, 607, (1); xxiv, 592; xxxvi, 559, (1). BA., C. 52391

Contents: I. Die Gründung der Kolonien bis zur Präsidentschaft des Thomas Jefferson. II. Von der ersten Präsidentschaft des Thomas Jefferson bis zum Ende der zweiten Präsidentschaft des Andrew Jackson. III. Von der Präsidentschaft des Martin Van Buren bis zur Inauguration des Abraham Lincoln.

Neutral Rights. The Numbers of Phocion, ... originally published in the Charleston Courier, in 1806. *Charleston.* [n. d.] 8vo

See also Vol. XI., Nos. 47538 and 47735.

De Neutraliteit of onpartijdige Verhandelingen der staat-, geschied- en historiekundige Voorvallen van 't Jaar 1781 [van 20 Dec. 1780] ... tot 5 August. *Amsterdam.* 1781. 8vo, pp. 402. Table and 2 Portraits. 52393

This is a chronicle in the form of the "Annual Register," specially relating to America, after the treaty of armed neutrality.

Neutrality. The United States against Henry Hertz. A Letter to Caleb Cushing, Esquire ... . By a Lawyer and Citizen. ... *Philadelphia: J. W. Moore.* [1855.] 8vo, pp. 34. H. 52394

Neuvitas Copper Mining Company. ... *New-York: John C. Beale.* 1853. 8vo, pp. 11. H. 52395

Statement, incorporation and by-laws.

NEVADA. Annual Report of the State Mineralogist of ... Nevada for 1866. *Carson City: Joseph E. Eckley, State Printer.* 1867. 8vo, pp. 151, folded leaf. Continued. H. 52396

Annual Report of the Surveyor-General of ... Nevada, for ... 1865. [*Virginia City:*] *John Church, State Printer.* 1865. 8vo, pp. 83. Continued. H. 52397

Catalogue of the Nevada State Library, for 1865. [n. p. n. d.] 8vo. 52398

Also: Reports of the Directors of the State Library. [With] The Report of the State Librarian of Nevada, for 1865. *Virginia City.* 1866. 8vo.

The Compiled Laws of the State of Nevada, embracing Statutes of 1861–1873, inclusive. Compiled by M. S. Bonnifield and T. W. Healy. *San Francisco.* 187–. 2 vols., 8vo. 52399

First Biennial Report of the Superintendent of Public Instruction of ... Nevada, for ... 1866. *Carson City: Joseph E. Eckley,* ... *Printer.* 1867. 8vo, pp. 45, folded leaf. H. 52400

This is really the "Second Annual" Report, it is so stated in the pamphlet, and the reports following this have the latter title.

First Directory of Nevada. *See* Kelly (J. W.)], IX. 37309.

Journal of the Assembly of the First Session of the State of Nevada. *Carson City.* 1865. 8vo. Continued. 52401

Journal of the Senate of the First Session of the State of Nevada. *Carson City.* 1865. 8vo. Continued. 52402

Laws of the Territory of Nevada, passed at the First regular Session of the Legislative Assembly, 1861. *San Francisco.* 1862. 8vo. Continued. 52403

Official Report of the Debates and Proceedings in the Constitutional Convention of ... Nevada, ... at Carson City, July 4th, 1864 ... . *San Francisco: Frank Eastman, Printer.* 1866. 8vo, pp. xvi, 943, (1). H. 52404

Report for the Hattie Silver Mining Company of Nevada ... . With Documents, Letters, Estimates, etc. *Boston: Printed by Chandler & Co.* 1866. 8vo, pp. 28. H. 52405

Report of Butler Ives, Commissioner, etc. on the Nevada and California Boundary. 1863. *Carson City.* 1864. 8vo. 52406

Report of the Senate Committee on Mines and Mining Interests, on ... "An Act concerning the Location and Possession of Mining Claims." [*Virginia City:*] *John Church, State Printer.* [1866.] 8vo, pp. 10. H. 52407

Report of the Adjutant-General of ... Nevada, for 1865. [*Virginia City: John Church, State Printer.* n. d.] 8vo, pp. 46. Continued. H. 52408

Reports of Cases determined in the Supreme Court of ... Nevada, reported by the Judges of the Court during ... 1865. Volume I. ... *Sacramento: James Anthony & Co., Printers.* 1866. 8vo, pp. 667. Continued. H., S. 52409

The preface describes the organization of the Territory, adoption of the State Government, etc.

United States of America. Joint Memorial and Resolutions of the Nevada Legislature, asking Government Aid in the Construction of the Sutro Tunnel. ... *San-Francisco: Towne & Bacon, ... Printers.* 1867. 4to, pp. 32. H. 52410

Also: Report of the Committee on Federal Relations of Congress, in regard to the Sutro Tunnel. *Carson City.* 1867. 8vo. — Report of the Controller for ... 1865. *Carson City.* 1866. 8vo. Continued. — Report of the State Treasurer, for ... 1867. *Carson City.* 1869. 8vo. Continued. — Report of the Territorial Secretary, Auditor, etc., for ... 1863. *Carson City.* 1864. 8vo.

[Neve y Molina (Luis de).] Éléments de la Grammaire Othomi, traduits de l'Espagnol, accompagnés d'une notice d'Adelung sur cette langue, traduite de l'Allemand, et suivis d'un Vocabulaire comparé Othomi-Chinois. *Paris: Maisonneuve et Cie.* 1863. 8vo, pp. 39, (1). 52411

From the "Revue orientale et américaine." Fifty copies printed on Holland paper.

Neve y Molina. Grammatica della Lingua Otomi esposta in Italiano dal Conte Enea Silvio Vicenzo Piccolomini, ... Secondo la traccia del Licenziato Luis de Neve y Molina, col Vocabulario

Spagnuolo-Otomì spiegato in Italiano. *Roma, nella Tipografia di Propaganda Fide.* 1841. 8vo, pp. 82, (2). A. 52412

This is an Italian extract of the following.

Neve y Molina. Reglas de Orthographia, Diccionario, y Arte del Idioma Othomi, breve instruccion para los principiantes, qve dictó el L. D. Lvis de Neve, y Molina, Cathedratico Proprietario de dicho Idioma ... . Dedicalo al Gloriosissimo Señor San Joseph ... . *Impressas en Mexico, con las licencias necessarias, en la Imprenta de la Bibliotheca Mexicana, en el Puente del Espiritu Santo. Año de* 1767. 8vo, pp. (24), 160. J.C.B., C. 52413

The Othomi language differs in structure from those spoken in Mexico, having more resemblance to the languages of Eastern Asia than any other. The author was the first to establish a proper system of characters, which has been since retained.

Neve y Molina. Reglas de Ortografía ... . *México: Tipografía de Mariano Villanueva* ... 1863. 24mo, pp. 254, (2). C.

Neves (A. J. S.) Homenagem aos Heroes Brasileiros no Guerra contra o Governo do Paraguay sob o commaudo em chefe dos marechaes de exercito S. A. R. o Sr. Conde d'Eu e Duque de Caxias. ... Por A. J. Santos Neves. *Rio de Janeiro.* 1870. 8vo, pp. xiv, 254. Portraits. 52415

Neves e Mello (Antonio José das). Memoria sobre as Quinas, e Ensaio da Brasiliense, remettida pelo Principe Nosso Senhor para o uso dos Hospitaes do Reino de Portugal. ... *Rio de Janeiro, na Imprensa Regia.* 1812? 8vo. 52416

Nevill (V.) The Reduction of Louisbourgh, a Poem, wrote on board His Majesty's Ship Oxford, in Louisbourgh Harbour. By Valentine Nevill, Esq. *London: J. Owen.* 1859. Folio.

Neville (E.) Rebellion and Witchcraft. A Thanksgiving Sermon ... in ... Newark, N. J. By the Rev. Edmund Neville, D.D. ... *Newark, N. J.* 1861. 8vo, pp. 16. 52418

[Neville (H.)] The Isle of Pines. *See* Vol. IX. 35255.

Neville (S.) Edith Allen; or, Sketches of a Life in Virginia. By Samuel Neville. *Richmond.* 1855. 12mo, pp. 336.

Nevin (A.) Churches of the Valley: or, An Historical Sketch of the Old Presbyterian Congregations of Cumberland and Franklin Counties, in Pennsylvania. By Rev. Alfred Nevin, ... *Philadelphia: Joseph M. Wilson.* 1852. 12mo, pp. xix, 13–338. BA. 52420

Nevin (J. W.) An Address in behalf of ... Temperance ... Newville, Pa., August 8, 1829 ... . By John W. Nevin. *Carlisle.* 1829. 8vo, pp. 34. 52421

Nevin. A Funeral Sermon ... [on] the Death of James Edgar Moore. ... June 23, 1844, By J. W. Nevin, D.D. ... *Mercersburg.* 1844. 8vo, pp. 18. BA. 52422

Also: ... An Address ... before the Goethean Literary Society, of Marshall College, ... August 29, 1842. ... *Chambersburg, Pa.* 1842. 12mo, pp. 22. — Address on Sacred Music ... Princeton, N. J. Dec. 5, 1827. ... *Princeton, N. J.: Printed by D. A. Borrenstein.* 1827. 8vo, pp. 24. — Eulogy on ... Rev. Dr. Frederick A. Rauch. President of Marshall College, Pa. ... *Chambersburg, Pa.* 1841. 8vo, pp. 23. — Life and Character of Frederick Augustus Rauch, ... A Eulogy on ... the re-interment of his Remains at Lancaster, Pa., March 7th, 1859. ... *Chambersburg: Printed by M. Kieffer & Co.* 1859. 8vo, pp. 29. B.

Nevin (W. M.) ... An Address ... before the Goethean Literary Society of Marshall College ... August 28, 1844. By William M. Nevin, Esq. ... *Chambersburg, Pa.* 1844. 8vo, pp. 20. H. 52423

Nevins (W.) Select Remains of the Rev. William Nevins, D.D. With a Memoir. *New York: John S. Taylor.* 1836. 12mo, pp. 398. + Third Edition, revised and corrected. [*Ibid.*] 1837. 12mo, pp. 398. Portrait. B. 52424

Nevis (*Island of*). Acts of Assembly, Passed in the Island of Nevis, From 1664, to 1739, inclusive. *London: Printed by John Baskett.* MDCCXL. Folio, pp. viii, 168. B., C. 52425

Also on large paper.

Addresses ... to Sir Arthur Rumbold, principally with respect to his Administration of the Government of the Island of Nevis. *London: Privately Printed.* 1862. 8vo. 52426

The Case of the Poor Distressed Planters, and other Inhabitants of the Islands of Nevis and St. Christopher's, in America, by the French Invasion, with Grant made by this Country for their Relief. [n. p. 1709.] Folio, 1 leaf. M. 52427

Description of the Island of Nevis, 1775. *See* [Rymer (J.)]

To the Honourable the Knights, Citizens, and Burgesses in Parliament Assembled. The humble Petition of several Proprietors of Plantations in the Islands of Nevis and St. Christophers in America, and Merchants Trading to the same; on behalf of

themselves and other Inhabitants and Traders to the aforesaid Islands. [*London.* n. d.] Folio, 1 leaf. 52428

Corrected title of our No. 33697, Vol. VIII.

Nevome Language. See Pima, *and* Smith (Buckingham).

New Albany, *Ind.* The Commercial and Manufacturing Advantages of New Albany, Ind. ... *New Albany, Ind.* 1857. 8vo, pp. 32. H. 52429

New Albany City Directory, for 1856–7. *New Albany.* 1856. 8vo. 52430

Williams' New Albany Directory, City Guide and Business Mirror, for 1863–4: ... appended a United States Post Office Directory. ... [*New Albany.* 1863?] 8vo, pp. 106, P. O. Directory, 106. H. 52431

Edwards' Annual Director to the Inhabitants, etc., in the Cities of New Albany and Jeffersonville, for 1865–6. *New Albany: Edwards, Greenough & Devee.* 1866. 8vo, pp. 115–695, 61–222. Continued. 52432

The Constitution and By-Laws of New-Albany Lodge, No. 1, I.O.O.F. *New Albany, Ia.* 1836. 16mo, pp. 27. M.

New Albion. Earl of Albion's Proclamation appointing Charles Varlo, Esq., his Agent for New Albion. [n. p. n. d.] Folio, 1 leaf. C. 52434

See also our Vol. V., No. 19724.

New Almaden. Correspondence in relation to the New Almaden Quicksilver Mine, between Counsel for the Proprietors and the Government. *Washington: G. S. Gideon, Printer.* 1856. 4to, pp. 77. + Further Correspondence ... . [*Ibid.* 1859.] 8vo, pp. 42. H. 52435

The New Almaden Mines. Letters from the San Francisco Daily Herald, ... the 15th ... December, 1858. *San Francisco.* 1858. 8vo, pp. 8. + December 31, 1858, and January 1, 1859. [*Ibid.*] 1859. 8vo, pp. 11. H. 52436

New Almaden Mine. Statement ... Arguments ... and Opinion of the Supreme Court ... in the case of the United States *vs.* Andres Castillero. ... December Term, 1862. ... *Philadelphia: King & Baird, Printers.* 1863. 8vo, pp. 15–209. B.

A New American Atlas, designed principally to illustrate the Geography of the United States of North America ... . *Philadelphia: A. Finley.* 1826. Folio. 15 Maps. 52438

The New American Cyclopædia: A Popular Dictionary of General Knowledge. Edited by George Ripley and Charles A. Dana. ... *New York: D. Appleton and Company.* M.DCCC.LVIII–LXIII. 16 vols., rl. 8vo. BA. 52439

For a continuation, *see* our Vol. I., No. 1044.

The New American Magazine: No. I. For January, 1758. Containing I. The History of North-America, Continued. II. The Traveller, Continued. III. The Monthly Miscellany. IV. Poetical Essays. V. The Chronological Diary. VI. The Historical Chronicle. VII. Naval Engagements. ... To be continued Monthly. ... By Sylvanus Americanus. *Woodbridge, in New-Jersey: Printed and Sold by James Parker. Sold also by Parker and Weyman in New-York, and by Thomas Coombe in Front-Street, Philadelphia.* [n. d.] 8vo, pp. 24. N., P. 52440

Continued to March, 1760. Contains a wood-cut plan of the siege of Louisburgh, and a copperplate of Nassau Hall, N. J. It was preceded by the "American Magazine." *See* our No. 1133.

The New American Tariff. *See* Tariff.

New and Accurate Account. *See* [Oglethorpe (J.)]

New and Complete American Encyclopædia: ... *New York.* 1805–11. 7 vols., 4to. B. 52441

A New and Complete | Collection | of | Voyages and Travels; | comprising | Whatever is valuable of this Kind in the most Celebrated | ... Writers; ... | *London:* | ... *J. Coote* ... | MDCCLX. Folio, pp. (4), xvi, 851. 52 Plates. 52442

A New and Complete History of the British Empire in America. [*London.* 1756.] 3 vols., 8vo, pp. xlvi, 402; 496; 272. Maps and Plates. J.C.B., H. 52443

Contains an account of Hudson's Bay, Newfoundland, Nova Scotia, New England, New York, New Jersey, Pennsylvania, Maryland, Virginia and North Carolina, ending abruptly at page 272 of volume III.

The New and Complete Tax-Payer's Manual: ... *New York: D. Appleton and Company.* 1863. 8vo, pp. iv, 148, 36. B., H.

A New and Exact Account. *See* [Leslie (C.)], X. 40190.

A | New and Further Narrative | Of the State of | New-England, | being | A Continued Account of the Bloudy | Indian-War, | From March till August, 1676. | Giving a Perfect Relation of the Several Devasta | tions, Engagements, and Transactions there; As also the | Great Successes Lately obtained against the Barbarous In | dians, The Reducing of King Philip, and the Killing of | one of the Queens, &c. | Together with a Catalogue of the Losses in the whole, sustain- | ed on either Side, since the said War began, as near as can be collected. | ... | *London: Printed by J. B. for Dorman Newman, at the King's Arms* | *in the Poultry.* 1676. Folio, pp. (2), 14. H. 52445

A volume of equal rarity and interest. It is reprinted in Drake's "Old Indian Chronicle," the first in the series, but should be the third in order of time. This is probably the Narrative mentioned by Increase Mather (War with the Indians—Address to the Reader) as having been written by a "Quaker in Road-Island." *See* "Present State of New England." Of this work, there is another edition with the same title-page, but with the woodcut of the Royal Arms on the title.

A | New and Impartial | Collection | of | Interesting Letters, | from the | Public Papers; | many of them | Written by Persons of Eminence, | On a great Variety of Important Subjects, which | have occasionally engaged the Public Attention: | From the Accession of his present Majesty, in September | 1765, to May 1767. | ... | *London:* | *Printed for J. Almon* ... . MDCCLXVII. 2 vols., 8vo.

Contains numerous articles on America, and is a useful addition to Almon's "Remembrancer."

New and Most Exact Account. *See* [Crafford (J.)], V. 17334

New and Old. ... [n. p.] M.DCCC.LI. 8vo, pp. v, 151. B.

Poems by Walter Channing.

New and Popular Songs, ... comprising Sentimental, Comic, Negro, Irish, National, Patriotic ... . *Philadelphia: Simpson & Co.* 1865. 12mo, pp. 120. BA. 52448

A New and Universal History of the United States ... to the Present Time. *New-Haven.* 1827. 12mo. S. 52449

The New Annual Register, or General Repository of History, Politics, and Literature, For ... 1780. ... *London.* 1781. 8vo. + Third Edition, Corrected. *London: G. G. J. and J. Robinson.* 1793. 8vo, pp. (16), xlvii, 184, 191, 224. Continued. C., H.

See Vol. I., No. 1614.

New-Ark Land and Cash Lottery, In New-Castle County on Delaware, &c. [*Philadelphia, about March,* 1770.] Folio, 1 leaf.

The object was to dispose of an iron furnace, etc., in Lancaster County, Pennsylvania. *See also* Newark, *and* our Vol. X., No. 41438.

New Army List of the United States. *Albany.* 1815. 12mo

A New Arrangement. *See* Vol. XI., No. 45268.

A New Atlas; containing a Geographical and Historical Account of all the ... World; with the Natural History and Trade of each Country. Taken from the best Authors. *London.* 1721. Folio. P. 52453

A New Atlas; or, Travels and Voyages in Europe, Asia, Africa, and America, through the most renowned parts of the World, performed by an English Gentleman in nine years. *London.* 1698. 8vo. 52454

A New Authentic and Complete Collection of Voyages round the World, including Captain Cook's Three Voyages, Byron, Carteret, Wallis, ... Lord Anson, and others. Edited by G. W. Anderson. *London.* [n. d.] 2 vols., folio. 52455

A New Ballad On the Taking of Porto-Bello, By Admiral Vernon. *London: R. Dodsley.* 1740. Folio, pp. 7. 52456

New Bedford, *Mass.* ... An Act, in addition to an Act, to establish the City of New Bedford. [April 28, 1857.] 8vo, pp. 8. B. 52457

Also: The Act establishing the New Bedford Fire Department, with the By-Laws and Regulations of the Board of Firewards ... . *New Bedford: Benjamin Lindsey, ... Printer.* 1848. 12mo, pp. 14. — By-Laws and Regulations of the Firewards of New Bedford, ... 1835. *New Bedford: Benjamin T. Congdon, Printer.* 1835. 24mo, pp. 7. Continued. — Law Establishing the New-Bedford Fire Department, ... 1837. *New Bedford: J. C. Parmenter, Printer.* 1837. 12mo, pp. 11, (1). Continued. — Report of the Board of Firewards. [n. p.] 1842. 12mo, pp. 4. — Report of the Board of Firewards of ... New-Bedford. 1846. *New Bedford: Tilden's ... Press.* 1846. 8vo, pp. 4. Continued. B.

... An Act to incorporate the New Bedford and Fairhaven Railway Company. [n. p. 1866.] 12mo, pp. 6. H. 52458

Amended Ordinances of the City of New Bedford. [n. p. 1856.] 8vo, pp. 12. B. 52459

Annual Meeting of the Ladies' Tract and City Missionary Society; with the ... Report ... . *New Bedford: Printed by E. Anthony.* 1857. 8vo, pp. 8. Continued. 52460

Articles of Association of the New Bedford and California Joint Stock Mining and Trading Company. [*New Bedford.*] 1849. 12mo, pp. 10. 52461

Articles of Faith and Government, of the First Baptist Church, ... New Bedford, Mass. With a Sketch of its History, and a Catalogue of its Members ... . *New Bedford: Printed by Benjamin Lindsey.* 184[illegible]. 12mo, pp. 60. 52462

Articles of the New Bedford Reform and Relief Association. Adopted Dec. 15, 1845; ... *New Bedford: Printed by E. Anthony.* 1859. 8vo, pp. 12. 52463

By-Laws for the Town of New Bedford; proposed ... May 21, 1822. [n. p. n. d.] Folio, 1 leaf. 52464

Also: By-Laws ... Passed ... May 6, 1822. [n. p. n. d.] Folio, 1 leaf. + By-Laws and Ordinances ... . *New Bedford: Printed by Benjamin T. Congdon.* 1835. 12mo, pp. 12. Continued. B.

By-Laws and Regulations of the New Bedford Athenæum ... . *New Bedford: Printed by Canfield & Andros.* 1841. 12mo, pp. 12

Catalogue of the Free Public Library, New Bedford, Mass. *New Bedford. B. Lindsey, Printer.* 1858. 8vo, pp. vii, 354, (1). + Supplement. *New Bedford.* 1869. 8vo, pp. (4), 313, (1). + Second Supplement. *New Bedford. E. Anthony & Sons, Printers.* 8vo, pp. (3), 476. 52466

The catalogue, the supplements, and 15 bulletins were edited by R. C. Ingraham.

... First Annual Report of the Trustees of the New-Bedford City Library. *New Bedford: Press of Benjamin Lindsey.* 1853. 8vo, pp. 31. Continued. B. 52467

Also: Proceedings on ... laying the Corner Stone of the Library Edifice, for the Free Public Library, of the City of New Bedford, August 28, 1856. *New Bedford: E. Anthony, Printer.* 1856. 12mo, pp. 64. — Catalogue of Books belonging to the New Bedford [Social] Library, 1821. *New Bedford.* 1821. 12mo, pp. 13. + *New Bedford: Printed by Benj. Lindsey & Co.* 1827. 12mo, pp. 24. + Supplement to ... 1836. [n. p.] 1836. 12mo, pp. 17. + *New Bedford: Printed by Benj. Lindsey.* 1839. 12mo, pp. 48. + [*Ibid.*] 1847. 8vo, pp. iv, 198. + Regulations ... 1824. *New Bedford.* 1826. 12mo, pp. 10. — Catalogue of Books belonging to the ... Library of the North Congregational Church. *New Bedford: Printed by Benj. Lindsey.* 1840. 8vo, pp. 11. — Catalogue ... the Library of the ... First Universalist Society, of New Bedford. *New Bedford. Printed by E. Anthony.* 1856. 12mo, pp. 20. — Catalogue of the Fourth Street ... School Library, August, 1843. *New Bedford: Printed by Wm. Canfield.* 1843. 8vo, pp. 11. — Catalogue of the ... Library of the South Christian Church, April, 1859. *New Bedford. Printed by E. Anthony.* 1859. 12mo, pp. 18. — Catalogue of the ... Library of the First Congregational Church ... . *New Bedford: Printed by Benjamin Lindsey.* 1851. 12mo, pp. 16.

Catalogue of the New Bedford Art Exhibition, ... 1858. ... [*New Bedford.* 1858.] 8vo, pp. 8. H. 52468

Catalogue of the Officers and Students of Friends' Academy, New Bedford, Mass., for ... 1838–9. *New Bedford: Printed by Benjamin Lindsey.* 1839. 12mo, pp. 16. 52469

Also: Catalogue of the Friend's Academy, New Bedford, April, 1859. *New Bedford: Printed by Benjamin Lindsey.* 1859. 12mo, pp. 16. H.

Centennial Celebration. *See* Vol. v., No. 18610.

Charter and By-Laws of the New Bedford Horticultural Society, incorporated March 12, 1847. *New Bedford: Printed by Benjamin Lindsey.* 1847. 12mo, pp. 22. 52470

City Charter. ... An Act to Establish the City of New-Bedford. [*New Bedford.* 1847.] 8vo, pp. 16. B. 52471

Also: City Charter, Rules and Orders of the City Council, List of the Officers, and Ordinances of the City of New-Bedford, for 1847–48. *New-Bedford: Benjamin Lindsey, ... Printer.* 1847. 12mo, pp. 103. B.

City Document—No. 1. Address of the ... Mayor, to the City Council of New Bedford: ... April 28th, 1847. ... *New Bedford: Benjamin Lindsey, Printer.* 1847. 8vo, pp. 14. Continued. H. 52472

The Confession of Faith and Covenant, adopted and used by the Congregational Church in New Bedford. ... *New Bedford: Printed by Benjamin Lindsey.* 1823. 12mo, pp. 11. + [*Ibid.*] 1844. 12mo, pp. 12. 52473

Constitution and By-Laws of the New-Bedford Lyceum. Adopted November 27, 1828. *New Bedford: Printed by Benjamin T. Congdon.* 1829. 8vo, pp. 6. 52474

Also: Constitution and By-Laws of the Lyceum of the Town of New Bedford, as adopted May 29, 1860. ... [Also a Sketch of the Origin and Progress of the Lyceum, by Jas. B. Congdon.] *New Bedford: Printed by E. Anthony.* 1860. 12mo, pp. 20.

Constitution of the New Bedford Auxiliary Society, for the Suppression of Intemperance; ... *New Bedford: Printed by Benjamin Lindsey.* 1815. 8vo, pp. 30. W. 52475

Also: Constitution and By-Laws of the New Bedford Martha Washington ... Abstinence Society. *New Bedford: Printed by Benjamin Lindsey.* 1843. 12mo, pp. 8.—The Constitution and By-Laws of the Protecting Society, for New Bedford, ... October 26, 1829. [*New Bedford.* 1829?] 8vo, 1 page. + April, 1844. *New Bedford: Printed by H. Tilden.* 1844. 12mo, pp. 7.—Constitution and By-Laws of the United Trade Society of Journeymen Sailmakers, of the City of New Bedford. Adopted September 26, 1851. *New Bedford: Press of Benjamin Lindsey.* 1851. 16mo, pp. 16.

Constitution of the New Bedford Mechanics' Association. Incorporated ... 1833. *New Bedford: [J. G.] Harris, Printer.* 1833. 12mo, pp. 12. 52476

Constitution of the New Bedford Rural Cemetery. ... *New Bedford: Printed by J. C. Parmenter.* 1837. 12mo, pp. 12.

Constitution of the New Bedford Young Men's Temperance Society, adopted July, 1834. ... *New Bedford: Printed by Benjamin T. Congdon.* 1834. 12mo, pp. 24. + Adopted February 27, 1836. ... [*Ibid.*] 1836. 16mo, pp. 9, (2). H. 52478

A Copy of the Valuation of Taxable Property in ... New Bedford, and the Tax ... 1849. ... *New Bedford: Printed by E. Anthony.* 1850. 8vo, pp. 48. 52479

The Day! The Hour, and the Man! [*New Bedford.* 1856.] Folio, 1 leaf. 52480

Campaign document, advocating the election of Rodney French to the office of Mayor of New Bedford.

Department of Massachusetts. *See* Vol. xi., No. 45758.

Descriptive Catalogue of Fruit and Ornamental Trees, ... at the Wachusett Nurseries, in New Bedford, Mass. *New Bedford: Printed by Benjamin Lindsey.* 1853. 8vo, pp. 32. 52481

Draft of a City Charter, prepared by a Committee of the Citizens, ... January 23d, 1847; ... *New Bedford: Press of Benjamin Lindsey.* 1847. 8vo, pp. 16. B. 52482

Education. Graded Course of Instruction for the Public Schools of New Bedford ... . Adopted ... Dec. 30, 1867. *New Bedford: E. Anthony & Sons, Printers.* 1868. 8vo, pp. 36. H.

Also: Address to Parents and the Public by the School Committee. *New Bedford: Printed by Benjamin Lindsey.* 1826. Folio, 1 leaf.—[Annual Report of] the New-Bedford School Committee ... [for 1836–37. *New Bedford: J. C. Parmenter, Printer.* 1837.] 12mo, pp. 7, (1). Continued.—Catalogue of Text, Reference and Reading Books, ... Furnished to the New Bedford, Mass., Public Schools. [n. p. n. d.] 8vo, pp. 10.—Correspondence between the School Committee and the City Solicitor. [n. p. n. d.] 8vo, pp. 10.—Laws of New Bedford South School, 5th mo., 1808. [*New Bedford.* 1808.] 12mo, pp. 8.—Regulations of the School Committee of New Bedford. [*New Bedford: B. Lindsey, Printer.* 1837.] 8vo, pp. 8.—Report of the School Committee of the Town of New Bedford, for the year 1843–44. *New Bedford: H. Tilden's Press.* 1844. 8vo, pp. 8. Continued.—Rules of the School Committee, and Regulations of the Public Schools of the Town of New Bedford. [*New-Bedford.* 1845.] 8vo, pp. 16. Continued. B.

First Annual Report of the New Bedford Women's Reform and Relief Association. *New Bedford: Printed by E. Anthony.* 1860. 8vo, pp. 12. 52484

Also: Articles of the ... Association. Adopted Dec. 15, 1845; ... *New Bedford: Printed by E. Anthony.* 1859. 8vo, pp. 12.

First Annual Report of the Board of Managers of the New Bedford Port Society for the Moral Improvement of Seamen, Presented ... June 7, 1831. *New Bedford: Printed by Benjamin T. Congdon.* 1831. 8vo, pp. 23, (1). Continued. H. 52485

First Annual Report of the Managers of the "Orphans' Home." *New Bedford.* 1844. 12mo. Continued. 52486

First Report of the Auditor of the Washington Total Abstinence Society, ... 1841 ... . *New Bedford: Printed by Benjamin Lindsey.* 1848. 8vo, pp. 8. 52487

History of the New Bedford Churches. *See* [Kelley (J. F.)]

Is the Harbor of New Bedford of any Importance to its Inhabitants? *New Bedford: Printed by E. Anthony.* [1854?] 8vo, pp. 8. 52488

Reprint of the Survey of New Bedford Harbor, 1853.

The Lectures delivered before the American Institute of Instruction, at New Bedford, August 17, 1842. Including ... a List of Officers. ... *Boston.* 1843. 12mo, pp. xvi, 166.

List of Voters in the Town of New Bedford, qualified to vote ... [*New Bedford:*] *B. T. Congdon, Printer.* 1835. 4to, pp. 14. Continued. 52490

The New Bedford Directory, ... added the By-Laws and Ordinances of said Town. By Henry H. Crapo. Also, A List of Whale Ships, belonging to the United States. *New Bedford: J. C. Parmenter, Printer.* 1836. 12mo, pp. 125. + *New Bedford.* 1838. 12mo, pp. 156. + *New Bedford: Printed by Benjamin Lindsey, Sept.* 1839. 12mo, pp. 169. B. + *New Bedford.* 1841. 12mo, pp. 166. + *New Bedford: Press of Benjamin Lindsey, October,* 1845. 12mo, pp. 190. + *New Bedford: C. & A. Taber. Press of Benjamin Lindsey.* 1849. 12mo, pp. 198. + *New Bedford: Charles Taber & Co. Benjamin Lindsey, Printer.* 1852. 12mo, pp. 194. + [*Ibid.:*] *E. Anthony, Printer.* 1856. 12mo, pp. 192. + [*Ibid.:*] *Benjamin Lindsey, Printer.* 1859. 12mo, pp. 182. + [With] a List of Citizens who have served or are

serving in the Army and Navy. January, 1865. *New Bedford: Abraham Taber & Brother.* [n. d.] 12mo, pp. 223. Continued.

New Bedford Harbor Signal Book. *See* [Lindsey (H.)]

New Bedford Money Matters. *See* [Congdon (J. B.)]

New Bedford Town Accounts. *New Bedford.* 1826. Folio, 1 leaf. 52492

New Bedford Traders in Rhyme. *See* [Kelley (J. F.)]

New Bedford Water-Works. Contract and Specifications for Storing Reservoir, Brick Conduit, and Receiving Reservoir. [n. p. 1866.] 4to, pp. 65. B. 52493

Also: Distributing Reservoir. New Bedford Water Works. [n. p. 1867.] 8vo, pp. 26.—Report of the ... Committee ... of New Bedford, on the Introduction of Fresh Water, with the Report of Wm. J. McAlpine ... . *New Bedford: Fessenden and Baker, ... Printers.* 1865. 8vo, pp. 96.—Specifications for ... an Engine House ... . *New Bedford: E. Anthony & Sons, Printers.* 1868. 8vo, pp. 12. B.

New Bedford Young Men's Christian Association. List of Officers. *New Bedford: Printed by E. Anthony.* 1853. 8vo, 1 p.

Order of the Procession of "The Invincibles," July, 4, 1860. [*New Bedford.*] 1860. 8vo, 1 page. 52495

Ordinances of the City of New Bedford, with the City Charter, and Rules and Orders, of the City Council. *New Bedford: Benjamin Lindsey, ... Printer.* 1853. 8vo, pp. 149. Continued.

Petition of George Howland, Jr., and others, to widen the Draw of the New Bedford Bridge ... . *Boston.* 1851. 8vo, pp. 16

Regulations for the Government of Social School, near the Head of the River, in New Bedford, ... November 28th, 1798. *Printed by J. Spooner, New Bedford, Jan.* 1799. 12mo, pp. 14.

Regulations for the Government of the New Bedford Alms-House. Feb. 23, 1829. [n. p. n. d.] Folio, 1 leaf. 52499

Report and Resolutions adopted at a Meeting of the Friends of Temperance, held at ... New Bedford, May 30, 1840. *New Bedford: Printed by Benjamin Lindsey.* 1840. 12mo, pp. 12.

Report of the Board of Overseers of the Town of New Bedford, for ... 1843–44. *New Bedford: Tilden's Press.* 1844. 8vo, pp. 4. 52501

Report of the Committee on Finance ... for ... 1848. [n. p. n. d.] 8vo, pp. 38. 52502

Also: Report of the Committee on Elections. [n. p. n. d.] 12mo, pp. 8.—Report ... to ascertain the Lines of the Streets and Highways, of ... New-Bedford. ... *New-Bedford: Printed by Benjamin T. Congdon.* 1830. 8vo, pp. 20.—Report ... on Side Walks, ... 1833. ... *New Bedford: Printed by Benjamin T. Congdon.* 1833. 8vo, pp. 23.—Report ... on the City Charter, ... 1843 ... . [*New Bedford:*] *William Canfield, Printer.* 1843. 8vo, pp. 18. B.

Report of the Overseers of the Poor of ... New Bedford, 1843. *New Bedford.* 1843. 8vo, pp. 4. Continued. 52503

Report of the Selectmen, 1830. [n. p.:] *B. T. Congdon, Printer.* [n. d.] Folio, 1 leaf. Continued. 52504

Report of the Town Temperance Committee. [*New Bedford.* 1842.] 12mo, pp. 12. Continued. B. 52505

Signed by Samuel Rodman.

Roll of Company "C," [New Bedford Home and Coast Guard,] ... 1861. *New Bedford.* 1861. 8vo, 1 page. 52506

Services at the Public Recognition of the Rev. Rufus Babcock, D.D., as Pastor of the First Baptist Church, New Bedford, Mass., ... 29th January, 1846. ... *New York.* 1846. 12mo, pp. 70. 52507

Shipping List and Town Register for 1835. [n. p. n. d.] 4to

Sketches of the Members. *See* [Kelley (J. F.)], IX. 37266.

Sunday School Picnic. First Congregational Society, New Bedford, July 28, 1853. *New Bedford: Printed by Benjamin Lindsey.* 1853. 12mo, pp. 4. 52509

Town of New-Bedford in Account with the Overseers of the Poor. ... 1836. [n. p. n. d.] Folio, 1 leaf. Continued. B.

The New Bond of Love. ... *New-York: The Author.* 1853. 12mo, pp. 110. H., S. 52511

New Book of a Thousand. Songs for the Million ... . Collected ... by an Amateur. *New-York: Richard Marsh.* [n. d.] 32mo, pp. 9–256, (2). B. 52512

The New Book of Knowledge. *Boston.* 1764. 12mo, pp. 172. 52513

Printed, and the cuts engraved, by Isaiah Thomas, then 15 years old. Reproduced in 1772.

The New Book of Nonsense. A Contribution to the Great Central Fair in Aid of the Sanitary Commission. [*Philadelphia:*] *Ashmead & Evans.* 1864. Obl. 16mo, pp. (2), 53. B. 52514

NEW BRIGHTON. Charter and Ordinances of the Village of New Brighton, with Rules of Order of the ... Trustees, 1866. *New York: De Vries & Wood, Printers.* [n. d.] 8vo, pp. 28.

Also: Articles ... of The New Brighton Association. [n. p. 1836.] 8vo, pp. 42.

Documents relating to the case of Christ Church, New-Brighton. *New-York: Van Norden & Amerman, Printers.* 1850. 8vo, pp. 33. H. 52516

Also: Reply of the Vestry of St. Paul's Church, Castleton, to a pamphlet entitled the "Case of the Protestant Episcopal Church, at New Brighton, Staten Island." *New York.* 1849. 8vo. —Standing Committee of the Diocese of New-York. In the matter of Christ Church, New-Brighton. Statement of the Churchwardens and Vestrymen. *New-York: Van Norden & Amerman, Printers.* 1850. 8vo. *See* [Ward (George A.)], *and* [Witherspoon (G.)]

NEW BRITAIN, *Conn.* The New Britain Directory for 1870. *Hartford.* 1870. 12mo. Continued. 52517

NEW BRITTAINE. The | Discovery | of | Nevv Brittaine. | Began August 27. Anno Dom. 1650. |
By { Edward Bland, Merchant. | Abraham Woode, Captaine. | Sackford Brewster, } Gentlemen. | Elias Pennant, }
From Fort Henry, at the head of Appa- | mattuck River in Virginia, to the Fals | of Blandina, first River in New Brit- | taine, which runneth West, being | 120. Mile South-west, between 35. | & 37 degrees, (a pleasant Country,) | of temperate Ayre, and fertile Soyle. | *London,* | *Printed by Thomas Harper for John Stephenson, at the* | *Sun below Ludgate.* M.DC.LI. | 4to, pp. (8), 16. Map and Plate. 52518

Plate of Indian wheat and an Indian jay. Reprinted with the following title:

The Discovery of New Brittaine. Began August 27, Anno Dom. 1650. By Edward Bland, Abraham Woode, Sackford Brewster, and Elias Pennant. *New York: Reprinted by J. Sabin and Sons.* 1873. 8vo, pp. (8), 16. 52519

NEW BRUNSWICK, *N. J.* The Charter of Queen's College, in New Jersey. *New Brunswick: Press of J. Terhune & Son.* MDCCCL. 8vo, pp. 14, (1). B. 52520

A Directory of the City of New Brunswick, for 1855 and 1856, with a Preface giving an Historical Account of the City ... *New Brunswick, N. J.* 1855. 12mo, pp. 96. Continued. N.

A Letter from a Gentleman of New-Brunswick to his Friend in Elizabeth-Town; On the first Point in Controversy between the Proprietors and Elizabeth-Town, Aug. 31, 1752. [n. p. n. d.] 8vo, pp. 4. 52522

The New-Brunswick Review. Vol. I. ... *New York.* 1855. 8vo. H., S. 52523

Pastoral Letter of the Presbytery of New Brunswick to the Churches under their Care. *New Brunswick.* 1801. 8vo, pp. 16

See also Rutgers College *and* Theological Seminary.

NEW BRUNSWICK, *N. S.* Abstract of the Proceedings of the Church Society of the Archdeaconry of New-Brunswick. *St. John, N. B.: Printed by Lewis W. Durant & Co.* 1837. 8vo, pp. 37. Continued. H. 52525

The titles of the later reports vary somewhat.

Acts of the General Assembly, of His Majesty's Province, of New-Brunswick, Passed in the Year 1786. *St. John: Printed by Christopher Sower, Printer to the King's Most Excellent Majesty.* MDCCLXXXVI. Sm. folio, pp. (8), 126. W. 52526

Acts of the General Assembly of ... New Brunswick, passed ... 1823. *Fredericton.* 1823. 8vo, pp. 67. Continued. 52527

Annual Report of the Natural History Society of New Brunswick, 1863. [n. p. n. d.] 8vo, pp. 3. Continued. 52528

Second Annual Report of the Board of Agriculture of ... New Brunswick. ... *Fredericton: J. Simpson, Printer.* 1862. 8vo, pp. 176. Continued. H. 52529

Annual Returns of Trade and Navigation for the Province of New Brunswick for ... 1860. *Fredericton: J. Simpson, Printer.* 1861. 8vo, pp. 103. Continued. H. 52530

... Auditor General's Report on Public Accounts, 1857. ... [*Fredericton.* n. d.] Folio, pp. 149. Continued. H. 52531

Calendar of the University of New Brunswick, Fredericton. ... 1870–71. *Fredericton: G. E. Fenety, Printer.* 1870. 8vo, pp. 24. B. 52532

See also Vol. XI., No. 43752.

Copy of the Report made to ... the Lieutenant-Governor of ... New-Brunswick, by the Commissioners appointed to Inquire into the Judicial Institutions of the Province. 2d. January, 1833. *Fredericton, New-Brunswick: Printed by John Simpson.* [1833.] 4to, pp. (2), 43, Supplement, (4), 82, (1), Appendix, (4), xxx, (1).

Hand Book for Emigrants. *See* Vol. VIII., No. 30205.

Hutchinson's New Brunswick Directory for 1867–8. Containing Alphabetical Directories of each Place in the Province, with Business Directories of Montreal, Quebec, and Halifax. *St. John, N. B.: J. A. T. Bird.* 1867. 8vo, pp. 877. 52534

Journal of the Legislative Council of the Province of New Brunswick, from the First Session of the First General Assembly, in ... 1786, to the Fourth Session of the Ninth General Assembly, in ... 1830. *Fredericton.* 1831. 4to. Continued. 52535

Journal of the New Brunswick Society, for the Encouragement of Agriculture, Home Manufactures and Commerce, throughout the Province, instituted ... 1849. ... *Fredericton, N. B.: Printed by James Hogg.* 1850. 8vo, pp. 95. Continued.

Journal of the Votes and Proceedings of the House of Assembly of ... New Brunswick; from ... February ... to ... March, ... 1787. *St. John.* 1787. Folio, pp. 75–100. M., W. 52537

Law Commission. Queries and Answers published by order of the Legislative Council of New Brunswick. *Fredericton: J. Simpson, Printer.* 1854. 8vo, pp. 69, (1). H. 52538

Laws of the Province of New Brunswick. *St. John.* 1816. 8vo. 52539

Local and Private Statutes of New Brunswick. Volume III. ... *Fredericton, N. B.: J. Simpson, Printer.* 1855. 8vo, pp. xxxii, 1045, lxxxi. H. 52540

Minutes of the Eastern New-Brunswick Baptist Association, ... 1856. *St. John, N. B.* 1856. 8vo. S. 52541

The New Brunswick Almanac, and Register, for ... 1849; ... *Saint John: Printed ... by Henry Chubb & Co.* 1848. 8vo, pp. 144, Index, (2). B. 52542

New Brunswick and Nova Scotia ... . *London: Buckingham.* 1843. 8vo. 52543

New Brunswick and Nova Scotia Land Company. Practical information respecting New Brunswick, ... Soil, Climate, Productions, and Agriculture ... . *London: Printed by Arthur Taylor.* 1834. 8vo, pp. 19. Map. H. 52544

New Brunswick for the Emigrant, Australia a Mistake. *London: Stanford.* 1855. 8vo. 52545

New Brunswick Post Office Directory, ... also a List of the Post and Way Offices. Compiled by I. K. Leavitt ... . *Fredericton, N. B.: J. Simpson, Printer.* 1857. 8vo, pp. 69. H.

New Brunswick Society for the encouragement of Agriculture, Home Manufactures and Commerce ... . [Provincial Exhibition. n. p. 1852.] 8vo, pp. (4), 27. H. 52547

New Brunswick. With Notes for Emigrants. *London: Simmons.* 1847. 8vo. 52548

Population and other Statistics of the Province of New Brunswick, for ... 1851. ... *Fredericton, N. B.: J. Simpson.* 1852. Rl. 8vo. C. 52549

Post Office Department, New Brunswick. The Fourth Annual Report, For ... 1859. ... *Fredericton.* 1860. 8vo, pp. 90, (1), lxii. Continued. H. 52550

Preliminary Report on the Geology. *See* Vol. VIII. 31935.

Provincial Board of Agriculture. ... Abstract of the Proceedings of the First Annual Session, ... 1860. With an Appendix. ... *Fredericton.* 1860. 8vo, pp. 23. H. 52551

Report of the Chief Commissioner of Public Works, For ... 1855. *Fredericton: J. Simpson, Printer.* 1856. 8vo, pp. 63. Continued. 52552

Report of the Commission ... relating to the Public Encouragement of Agriculture. ... 1856. *Fredericton: J. Simpson, Printer.* 1857. 4to, pp. 12, Appendix, (9). H. 52553

Report of the Joint Committee ... of the Province of New-Brunswick, Appointed ... 1828, upon the subject of a Penitentiary. [n. p. 1829.] 8vo, pp. 12. BA. 52554

Report of the Medical Superintendent of the Provincial Lunatic Asylum, ... 1866. ... *Saint John, N. B.: Printed by Barnes and Company.* 1867. 8vo, pp. 10. H. 52555

The Thirty-First Report of the New-Brunswick Auxiliary Bible Society, Formed ... M.DCCC.XIX. ... *Saint John: Printed by D. A. Cameron.* 1851. 8vo, pp. 63, (1). Continued. H.

Report of the New Brunswick Society for the Encouragement of Agriculture, Home Manufactures and Commerce. By James Robb ... . *Fredericton.* 1851. 8vo. 52557

Report of the Railway Commissioners of ... New Brunswick, for ... 1859. *Saint John, N. B.: Printed by Barnes and Company.* 1860. 8vo, pp. 59. Continued. H. 52558

Report on the Geological Survey. *See* Vol. VII., No. 27226.

Report on the Parish Schools of New Brunswick for part of the year 1852 ... . *Fredericton: J. Simpson, Printer.* 1853. 8vo, pp. 72. Continued. H. 52559

Reports of the Debates of the House of Assembly, of the Province of New Brunswick, during the First and Second Sessions of 1866. By John March and T. P. Dixon, Reporters. *St. John.* 1866. Folio, pp. 126, 86. 52560

The Revised Statutes of New Brunswick. Volume I. ... *Fredericton, N. B.: J. Simpson, Printer.* 1854. 8vo, pp. xxiv, 496, lxxvi, (1). H., S. 52561

See also Vol. IV., No. 16852, *and* Vol. XII., Nos. 48105–06.

NEW-CASTLE, *Del.* An Address from the Presbytery of New-Castle to the Congregations under their Care: Setting forth the Declining State of Religion in their Bounds; and exciting them to the Duties necessary for a Revival of Decayed Piety amongst them. Published by Order of the Presbytery, convened at Upper Octorara, August 11, 1784. William Smith, Moderator. *Wilmington: James Adams.* 1785. 8vo, pp. 62. N. 52562

Address of the Democratic Republican Committee of New Castle County, Delaware. [n. p. 1803.] 8vo. C. 52563

Address of the Representatives of the Counties of New-Castle, Kent, and Sussex, upon Delaware, in General Assembly met at Newcastle, the 13th day of June, A. D. 1717, to the Honourable William Keith, Esq; Lieut. Governour ... . [*Philadelphia: Andrew Bradford.* 1717.] Folio, pp. 3. 52564

Asking for a confirmation of their titles to lands, etc. Extremely rare.

A Catalogue of Books of the New Castle Library Company, [with] the Act of Incorporation, and the By-Laws of the Company. *New Castle: J. C. Clark.* 1840. 12mo, pp. 114. C.

Considerations relating to the exclusive Grant of Rail-Road Privileges within certain Limits, to the New Castle and Frenchtown Turnpike and Rail-Road Company ... . [*New Castle.* 1834.] 12mo, pp. 11. H. 52566

Signed "A Stockholder." Also: Report of the President of the ... Company, Dec. 31, 1849. *New Castle, Jan.* 1850. 8vo. S.

The Honest Man's Interest, As he Claims any Lands in the Counties of New-Castle, Kent, or Sussex, on Delaware. [*Philadelphia: Andrew Bradford.* 1726.] Folio, pp. 4. 52567

The Humble Address of the Representatives of the Counties of New-Castle, Kent, and Sussex, upon Delaware, in the Province of Penn, in General Assembly met at New-Castle the 13th June, 1717. *Philadelphia: Andrew Bradford.* 1717. Folio, pp. 3

Signed "Jasper Yeates, Speaker." An important historical document. At the end is this note: "In the present Situation of affairs it is Judg'd to be of Service, to make the foregoing Address more Publick—That the Inhabitants of these Counties may review their own Case so justly exhibited by their Representatives at that Time—which continues the same notwithstanding any Reports or Informations to the contrary." These lands having been in the possession of the Dutch as part of New Netherland, afterwards as part of New York, again under the Dutch, and lastly under William Penn, were in an unsettled state as to title, jurisdiction, and boundary.

In Convention, at New-Castle, For the Delaware State, A Declaration of Rights and Fundamental Rules of the Delaware State. George Read, President. Extract from the Journal. Attest. James Booth, Clk. *Wilmington: Printed by James Adams.* 1776. Folio, pp. 11. 52569

Laws of ... New-Castle. *See* Vol. X., No. 39415.

New-Castle, June 15, 1771. A Scheme of a Lottery, &c. [n. p. n. d.] Folio, 1 leaf. P. 52570

Printed at Philadelphia; a Methodist affair.

New-Castle. February 6. 1772. Scheme of a Lottery for raising the Sum of Three Hundred and Seventy-five Pounds, towards the building a Methodist Preaching-House in New-Castle County; and to discharge a debt upon the Preaching-House in Philadelphia. [n. p. 1772.] Folio, 1 leaf. P. 52571

See also Newcastle.

The New Church Herald, and Monthly Repository. Sabin Hough, Editor. ... May, 1857. ... *Philadelphia: Sabin Hough.* [n. d.] 8vo. Continued. H. 52572

... New Church Magazine for Children. September, 1846. ... *Boston: Otis Clapp.* 1846. 16mo. H. 52573

The New Church Messenger. ... Vol. II. April 16, 1854. No. IV. *Cincinnati.* 1854. 8vo. H. 52574

The New Church Repository and Monthly Review. ... Conducted by George Bush, A.M. Vol. I. No. I.—January, 1848. *New York: John Allen.* [1848.] 8vo. Continued. H. 52575

A Swedenborgian publication. Also: The Book of Publick Worship, prepared for the ... Boston Society of the New Jerusalem. *Boston: Hilliard, Gray ....* 1829. 24mo, pp. 16, xcii, 170. + *Boston: Otis Clapp.* 1836. 12mo, pp. 396.—Constitution and By-Laws of the New Church Tract Society. *New York.* 1869. 12mo, pp. 12. B.—Journal of ... the Thirty-Sixth General Convention of the New Church in the United States. ... *Boston: Otis Clapp.* 1854. 12mo, pp. 68.—The Liturgy of the New Church, signified by the New-Jerusalem in the Revelation. ... With the Forms for the Administration of Baptism ... and A Catechism ... . Also Hymns ... by the Rev. Mr. Joseph Proud. The Fourth Edition. ... *Baltimore: Printed and Sold by Samuel and John Adams.* 1792. 18mo, pp. 342.—Liturgy, or Book of Worship, for the use of the New Church signified by the New Jerusalem. ... *New York.* 1862. 12mo, pp. 254, Hymns, 3–60.—New Churchman, devoted to disseminating the Doctrines of the New Jerusalem Church. ... 1841. *Philadelphia.* 1841. 8vo. Continued.

New Code of Laws. *See* Vol. IX., No. 35627.

A New Collection of Verses applied to the First of November, A. D. 1765, &c. Including a Prediction that the St—p-A–t shall not take place in North-America. Together with A poetical Dream, Concerning Stamped Papers. ... *New-Haven: Printed ... by B. Mecom.* [1765.] 8vo, pp. 24. P. 52576

A New Collection of Voyages, 1708. *See* [Stevens (John)].

A New Collection of Voyages and Travels, never before published in English. *London: J. Smith.* 1721. 2 vols., 8vo. Plates. 52577

A New Collection of Voyages, 1767. *See* [Knox (John)].

The New Comic Almanack. 1842. *New York: S. Colman.* [n. d.] 16mo, pp. 32. H. 52578

New Commission of the Governor of Quebec; and other Instruments of Authority derived from the Crown, Relative to America. [*London.* 1779?] 8vo, pp. (2), 82. C. 52579

A New, Complete, and Universal Collection of Authentic and Entertaining Voyages and Travels to all the various parts of The World. ... *London.* 1790? Folio. 52580

A New Conductor Generalis: ... a summary of the Law relative to ... Justices of the Peace, Sheriffs, Coroners, ... Overseers of the Poor, &c. &c. ... carefully collated with the revised Laws of ... New-York; ... By a Gentleman of the Law. *Albany: D. & S. Whiting.* 1803. 8vo, pp. 479, (1). H. 52581

The New Constitution and the Christian Church. An Address to the Ministers and Members of the Presbyterian Church in the State of Missouri. *St. Louis: George Knapp & Co.* 1865. 8vo, pp. 32. 52582

See also Maryland, Vol. XI., No. 45269, *and* Missouri, Vol. XII., No. 49626.

The New Crisis. By an Old Whig. *New-York: The Author.* 1810. 8vo, pp. 96. B. 52583

The New Crisis of American Independence. [*Philadelphia.* 1808.] 8vo, pp. 8. 52584

Signed "Paul Cox. Philadelphia, Sep. 7, 1808."

A New Critical Pronouncing Dictionary of the English Language. By an American Gentleman. *Burlington, N. J.: D. Allinson & Co.* 1813. 8vo. 52585

The New Custom House. Strictures on an Article in the North American Review, for April, 1844, entitled "Architecture in the United States." *Boston: W. D. Ticknor & Co.* 1844. 12mo, pp. 23. Plate. H. 52586

Corrected title of our No. 6533, Vol. II.

A New Darien Artifice. *See* Darien, Vol. V., No. 18562.

The New Democratic Doctrine. Slavery not to be confined to the Negro Race. ... *New York.* 1856. 8vo, pp. 4. S. 52587

Also the same in German, *New York.* 1856. 8vo, pp. 4. S.

The New Dido; An Honest Laugh at "Honest" People. ... *New York: Henry Kernot.* MDCCCLI. 12mo, pp. 24. H. 52588

In verse. The title is taken from the cover.

By-Laws, Rules and Regulations of the New Diggings and Shullsburg Mining Co., Wis. *Milwaukee.* 1855. 12mo.

New Directions for Sailing along the Coast of North America, from Halifax to Florida; into its several Harbors, with a particu-

lar description of the Coast from New York to St. Augustine. *London.* 1806. 8vo. 52590

New Discoveries concerning the World, and its Inhabitants. ... Part I. Containing a circumstantial Account of all the Islands in the South Sea that have been lately discovered or explored; ... Comprehending all the discoveries made in the several voyages of Commodore (now Admiral) Byron, Captains Wallace, Carteret and Cook. Part II. Containing a summary account of Captain Cook's attempts to discover a Southern Continent, in 1773, 1774, and 1775 ... . *London: J. Johnston.* 1778. 8vo, pp. xviii, 408. 2 Maps and 2 Plates. 52591

See "Monthly Review," LVIII. 309.

A New Discovery. *See* Vol. V. 20247, *and* Vol. VIII. 31372.

New Division of Wards, a particular Description of the Town of Boston, 17th June, 1805. [n. p. n. d.] Folio, 1 leaf.

New Dominion Monthly. *Montreal.* 1870. 8vo. Continued

The New Eclectic Magazine. Volume V. July–December, 1869. *Baltimore: Trumbull & Murdoch.* [n. d.] 8vo, pp. iv, 768

NEW ENGLAND.

An|Abstract|or [*sic*] the|Lawes|of|New England,|As they are novv established.|*London,*|*Printed for F. Coules, and W. Ley at Paules Chain,*|1641.| 4to, pp. (2), 15, 2. B. 52595

The first printed collection of the Laws of New England. The laws are very concise, and each is based upon some passage from the Bible, to which reference is made in the margin. These laws were never "established," or in force, in New England. The code was drawn up by Mr. Cotton for Massachusetts, and "presented to the General Court," but was *not adopted*. Corrected title of our No. 17042, which *see* for a note. A reprint forms No. 9 of Force's "Tracts," Vol. III.

Account of New England Agents. *London.* 1691. 4to.

Title from an English catalogue; certainly incorrect.

An Account of the Late Revolution in New England. Together with the Declaration of the Gentlemen, Merchants, and Inhabitants of Boston, and the Country adjacent. April 18, 1689. *London; Reprinted.* [n. d.] 8vo. 52597

An Account of the Late Revolution in New-England; In a Letter. [n. p. n. d.] 4to, pp. 7. 52598

Signed, "A. B. Boston June 6. 1689." *See* "Andros Tracts," II. 189.

Accurate Journal. *See* [Pepperell (W.)]

An Act for charging of Tobacco brought from New-England with Custom and Excise. ... [n. p.] 1650. Folio, 1 leaf.

An Act for propagating the Gospel in New England. 27 Julii. *London.* 1649. Folio. B. 52600

The Charter of the Society for the Propagation of the Gospel in New England.

An Act of the General Assembly of the Governour, Council and Representatives of New-England, toward promoting the Expedition now on foot against Quebec: With the Governour's Proclamation of it, dated at Boston the 20th July, 1711. [n. p. n. d.] Folio, 1 leaf. 52601

Action of the several Yearly Meeting of Friends, relative to the Secession from New England Yearly Meeting. ... *Philadelphia.* 1846. 8vo, pp. 16. 52602

Acts and Laws passed in New England. *Boston.* 1716. Folio

Title from Rich; probably incorrect, inasmuch as New England had no corporate powers.

An Address from the Yearly Meeting of New-England to the General Assembly of the State of Rhode-Island. [n. p.] 1787. Folio, 1 leaf. 52604

Respecting the slave-trade.

Address of a Minister to the Church under his care on the Subject of Confession of Misdemeanors in the Churches of New England. *Boston.* 1784. 8vo. W. 52605

Address of the Yearly Meeting of Friends for New England, held on Rhode Island, in the Sixth Month, 1837 ... . *New-Bedford: Printed by J. C. Parmenter.* 1837. 8vo, pp. 7. H. 52606

An Address on Peace. Issued by the Yearly Meeting of Friends for New England, 1854. [n. p. n. d.] 8vo, pp. 8.

An Address to the people of New-England: occasioned by the preaching and publishing of certain doctrines, destructive of their rights and liberties, both religious and civil (by James Macsparran) in a sermon, entituled, The Sacred Dignity of the Christian Priesthood. Vindicated. By a Native of New-England. ... *Newport: Printed and Sold by J. Franklin, at the Printing-Office under the Town-School-House.* 1753. 12mo, pp. 31.

By John Aplin. A corrected title of our No. 1758, Vol. I. *See* Vol. XI., No. 43664.

Answer of the Elders and other Messengers of the Churches assembled at Boston in the year 1662 to the Questions pro-

pounded to them by Order of the Honoured General Court. *Cambridge: Printed by Sam'l Green.* [1662.] 4to, pp. 60. M.

An Answer to several New Laws. *See* F[ox] (G[eorge]).

An Apologie of the Churches in New England for Church Covenant, sent over in Answer to Master Bernard, in the Year 1639. *London.* 1643. 4to, pp. 66. 52610

Title from Colonel Aspinwall's catalogue, No. 183.

An Appeal|To the Men|of New-England, with a short Account of|Mr. Randolph's Papers.| [*Boston:*] *Printed in the Year* 1689. 4to, pp. 15. 52611

Reprinted in the third volume of "The Andros Tracts," edited for the Prince Society by Mr. Wm. H. Whitmore. In his introduction, Mr. Whitmore observes that this pamphlet "is of considerable bibliographical importance, as being heretofore unknown, and as being the precursor of 'Further Quæries,'" our No. 21610. On p. 208, he gives good reason for believing "that Cotton Mather was intimately connected with the preparation of this tract," which may have been written by the Rev. Charles Morton, of Charlestown.

An Appeal to the Professors of Christianity in the Southern States and elsewhere, on the subject of Slavery; by the Representatives of the Yearly Meeting of Friends for New England. *Providence: Knowles & Vose.* 1842. 8vo, pp. 24. 52612

The Book of Discipline agreed on by the Yearly Meeting of Friends for New-England. ... [n. p.] 1785. 12mo. + With Alterations, Reprinted. [n. p.] 1809. 8vo. 52613

A Brief Account. *See* [Mather (I.)], Vol. XI., No. 46637.

A brief Account of Meetings [of Friends] in New England. *Providence.* 1836. 8vo. 52614

A Brief Account of the Rise, Progress and Present State of the Paper Currency of New-England, And of the Measures taken by the Massachusetts Province, for establishing a Silver Currency for the Future. ... *Boston: Printed by J. Bushell and J. Green.* 1749. 8vo, pp. 15. BA. 52615

Corrected title of our No. 7851, Vol. II. *See also* No. 7847.

A Brief and True|Narration|Of the Late|Wars|risen in|New-England:|Occasioned by the Quarrelsome disposition,|and Perfidious Carriage|of the|Barbarous, Savage and Heathenish|Natives|There.|*London: Printed for J. S.* 1675. Sm. 4to, pp. 8.

A piece of extreme rarity. *See* "A Farther Brief," No. 52638, *infra*.

Brief Animadversions. *See* [Willard (S.)]

A Brief | Narration | of the | Practices | of the | Churches in New-England. | Written in private to one that desired | information therein; by an Inhabitant there, | a Friend to Truth and Peace. | Published according to Order. | *London,* | *Printed by Matth. Simmons for John Rothwell, and* | *are to be sold at his Shop, at the signe of the Sunne* | *in Pauls Churchyard,* 1645. | Sm. 4to, pp. (2), 18.

A Brief | Narration | of the | Practices | of the | Churches in New-England, in | their solemne Worship of God. | Written to one that desired infor- | mation therein; by an Inhabitant there; | a Friend to Truth and Peace. | Published according to Order. | *London; Printed by Matthew Simmons, and are to be sold by* | *John Pounset at the lower end of Budge-Row* | *neere Canning-streete.* 1647. | 4to, pp. (2), 18. 52618

Differs only from the preceding in the title. A reprint forms No. 11 of Force's "Tracts," Vol. iv.

A Brief Narrative of the Sufferings. *See* [Gould (D.)]

A briefe Relation | of the | Discovery | and Plantation | of | New England: | and | of svndry accidents | therein occvrring, from | the yeere of our Lord M.DC.VII. to this | present M.DC.XXII. | Together with the state thereof as now it standeth; | the generall forme of gouernment intended: and the | diuision of the whole Territorie into Coun- | ties, Baronries [*sic*], &c. | *London,* | *Printed by John Haviland, and are to be* | *sold by William Bladen,* | M.DC.XXII. 4to, pp. (35). P. 52619

The dedication to the Prince his Highness [Charles] is signed by the President and Councell of New England. It is, if not the rarest, certainly one of the most important of all the early books on New England. It is reprinted in the Massachusetts Historical Society "Collections," 2d Series, Vol. VIII.

A Brief Relation. *See* [Mather (I.)], Vol. XI., No. 46642.

Add to "A Brief Review," our No. 7896, Vol. II., *Norwich: Robertsons and Trumbull.* 1774. 8vo, pp. 16.

Collection of the Testimonies of the Fathers of the New England Churches respecting Baptism. *Cambridge: Printed by Sam'l Green.* 1668. 4to, pp. 32. 52620

Congregational Order. The Ancient Platforms of the Congregational Churches of New England; with a digest of Rules and Usages in Connecticut, and an Appendix, containing notices of Congregational Bodies in other States. ... *Middletown: Edwin Hunt.* 1843. 18mo, pp. 361. 52621

Considerations on the Bills of Credit now passing in New England. *Boston: Printed by Benj. Harris and John Allen.* 1691. 12mo, pp. 24. 52622

A Continuation | Of the State of | New-England; | Being a Farther Account of the | Indian Warr, | And of the Engagement betwixt the Joynt Forces | of the United English Collonies and the Indians, | on the 19th. of December 1675. With the true Number of the | Slain and Wounded, and the Transactions of the English | Army since the said Fight. With all other Passages that | have there Hapned from the 10th. of November, 1675. to the | 8th. of February. 167⅚. | Together with an Account of the intended Rebellion of the Negroes in the Barbadoes. | ... | *London: Printed by T. M. for Dorman Newman* ... . 1676. Folio, pp. 20.

Reprinted in Drake's "Old Indian Chronicle," pp. 39–69.

Copy of the Charter for Propagation of the Gospel in New England, &c., 7 Feb. 1662. [n. p. n. d.] 8vo. 52624

Doubtful title from J. R. Smith's catalogue.

The Council for New England. Records. Reprinted from the Proceedings of the American Antiquarian Society, for April, 1867. *Cambridge: J. Wilson & Sons.* 1867. 8vo, pp. 83.

The Day-Breaking. *See* [Shepard (T.)]

A Declaration of New-England Yearly Meeting of Friends, upon Various Christian Doctrines ... . *Providence: Printed by Knowles and Vose.* 1845. 8vo, pp. 23. H. 52626

A Defence of the Clergy of New England against the charges of Interfering in our Political Affairs, and condemning the Policy of the Present War. *Concord: George Hough.* 1814. 8vo, pp. 48

Reprinted from the Concord "Gazette."

A Description of Christ's Navy in New England; ... proved by God's Revealed Word, and shown by Isaac Hillard. [n. p.:] *Printed for the Author.* 1814. 12mo, pp. 23. 52628

Title at length in C. L. Woodward's catalogue, 1879.

A Description of New England in general; with a Description of the Town of Boston in particular. *London: John Sellers.* 1682. 4to. 52629

Dialogues, or Third Conference, between some Young Men, born in New England, and some Ancient Men which came out of Holland and Old England, concerning the Church and Gov-

ernment thereof. With ... Notes, by Charles Deane. *Boston.* 1870. 8vo. 52630

Ten copies printed on Holland paper.

The Diocesan Register and New-England Calendar for the Year 1812. *Dedham.* [n. d.] 12mo. 52631

The Discipline practised in the Churches of New England, containing a Platform of Discipline, Cambridge, 1649 ... . *Whitchurch Salop.* [n. d.] 12mo. 52632

An Epistolary Declaration ... of Friends, for New England, respecting the Proceedings of those who have effected a Schism therein; ... *Providence: B. F. Moore.* 1845. 8vo, pp. 53. H.

An Epistle from the Yearly Meeting of Friends, for New-England; held on Rhode-Island, ... 1828. To our ... Meetings, and the Members thereto belonging. [n. p. n. d.] 8vo.

Signed by "Abraham Shearman, Junr., and Ruth Rodman, Clerks." Also: Epistle to the Quarterly and Monthly Meetings, within the Limits of New-England Yearly Meeting ... . [n. p. 1845.] 8vo, pp. 7. H.

Essay on the Administration of Church Government, as it may be serviceable to the Provincial Churches in New England. *Boston.* 1732. 8vo. 52635

Extracts from the Minutes of New England Yearly Meeting of Women Friends, ... 1854. ... *New Bedford: Press of Benj. Lindsey.* 1854. 8vo, pp. 18. 52636

Extracts from the Records of New-England Yearly Meeting Boarding School. Published by the Trustees of Obadiah Brown's Benevolent Fund. *Providence: Knowles, Anthony, and Co., Printers.* 1854. Folio. 52637

A Farther Brief and True Narrative of The Late Wars risen in New-England, Occasioned by the quarrelsome Disposition and perfidious Carriage of the barbarous and savage Indian Natives there; with an Account of the Fight, the 19th of December last 1675. London February 17th 167⅚. Licensed Henry Oldenburgh. *London, Printed by J. D. for M. K. and are to be sold by the Booksellers.* 1676. 8vo. 52638

Reprinted in Drake's "Old Indian Chronicle," 1868. *See* "A Brief and True Narration," No. 52616, *supra.*

From the Meeting for Sufferings for New-England, to the several Quarterly and Monthly Meetings, belonging to the Yearly

Meeting. *Providence: Printed by John Carter.* [1782.] 4to, pp. 20. 52639

On the institution of schools.

Further Quæries | Upon the Present State of the | New-English Affairs. | [*Boston.* 1689.] 4to, pp. 11. 52640

Apparently a privately printed tract, having no title, signed "S. E." Our No. 21610 gives the collation erroneously.

Historical Relation. *See* [Johnson (Edward)], Vol. IX. 36204.

A Letter from New England, concerning their Customs, Manners, and Religion. Written upon occasion of a Report about a Quo Warranto brought against that Government. *London: Randolph Taylor.* 1682. Folio, pp. (9). 52641

This remarkable letter, written with a free, flowing and gossiping pen, is signed "J. W." "It is a most extraordinary production, both for the matter it contains and its extreme rarity. The tone of it is anything but complimentary to the Bostonians, especially those belonging to the Independent Church. The writer remarks 'For lying and cheating they outvie Judas, and all the false merchants in Hell; and the worst of Drunkards may here find pot-companions enough for all their pretence to sobriety. They make a sport of cheating and look upon it as a commendable piece of ingenuity, and brag of those vile actions which others are ashamed of, commending him that has the most skill to commit a piece of roguery.' Many of the stories related of particular persons, whose initials the author gives, are not such as could be quoted. His account on the last page of the origin of a famous Boston proverb is curious, if not amusing."—BRINLEY *Catalogue.*

A Memorial of the present ... State. *See* Philopolites, *pseudon.*

Memorial to the General Assembly of Rhode Island in relation to bearing Arms, 1863. Record of a Special Meeting of Sufferings, held in Boston, 30th 7th month, 1863, relative to the Conscription Law. Proceedings of a Meeting for Sufferings, held in Providence, R. I., 24th of 3d month, 1863. [n. p. n. d.] 4to.

Minutes of the New England Annual Conference, of the African Methodist Episcopal Church, held in ... New Bedford, Mass., ... 1852. *New Bedford: Printed by Benjamin Lindsey.* 1852. 8vo, pp. 15. 52643

Minutes of the New England Annual Conference of the Methodist Episcopal Church, held in ... Lynn ... 1847. *Boston.* 1847. 12mo, pp. 23. Continued. S. 52644

New England A Degenerate Plant. *See* [Rous (J.)]

New England Agricultural Society. Second Annual Report. 1865. *Boston: J. E. Tilton and Company.* 1866. 8vo, pp. (4), 268. 45 Plates. Continued. B., C. 52645

Also: Premium List of the N. E. Agricultural Society, for their Seventh Annual Exhibition ... held in ... Manchester, N. H., ... September ... 1870. ... *Boston: Press of the Massachusetts Ploughman* ... . 1870. 8vo, pp. 17.—Transactions of the New England Agricultural Society. First Annual Exhibition, at Springfield, September ... 1864. Address of ... John A. Andrew. *Boston: Wright & Potter, Printers.* 1864. 8vo, pp. 267. B.

The New-England Almanack for the Year of our Lord, 1686. And of the World, 5635. Since the Planting of Massachusetts Colony in New-England, 58. Since the Found. of Harv. Coll. 44. ... By S. D. [Samuel Danforth?] *Cambridge: Samuel Green, sen., Printer to Harvard Colledg.* 1686. 8vo. 52646

The author has two pages of verse "Ad Librum," and at the foot of the calendar pages gives a useful "Memorial of some Remarkable Occurrences in N. E. since 1678." In his verses, he alludes to himself as a "Harvardine." *See* our Vol. v., No. 18473.

The New-England Almanack, For the Year 1700 ... . By Samuel Clough, A Lover of the Mathematicks. *Boston: Printed by B. Green & J. Allen.* [1699.] 8vo. 52647

In 1705 the imprint reads "B. Green for Benj. Eliot," and in 1706 and 1707, "B. Green for Benj. Eliot and Nich. Boone." Continued to 1708.

The New England Almanack, 1772, by Benjamin Wirt, A.M. *Newport: Printed by Ebenezer Campbell.* [n. d.] 12mo. 52648

New-England Almanack. E. Freebetter. *New-London: T. Green.* 1780. 12mo. 52649

Continued to 1786 or later

New England Almanac for 1781. [By Isaac Bickerstaff, Esq., Philom.] *Providence: ... John Carter* ... . [n. d.] 12mo.

Continued to the present time. *See also* our Vol. II., No. 5220.

The New England Almanac and Masonic Calendar, for ... 1828 ... . *Boston: Marsh & Capen.* [n. d.] 8vo, pp. (58). Continued. H. 52651

New-England Almanac for 1835: ... Prepared by J. N. Palmer. *New-Haven: Durrie & Peck.* [n. d.] 12mo, pp. (24).

For other New England Almanacs, *see* Ames (N.), Bickerstaff (I.), Thomas (I.), Thornton (E.), *and* West (B.)

New England and her Institutions. *See* [Abbott (J.)], No. 33

Articles of Association of the New England and Michigan Mining Company. [n. p. 1845.] 8vo, pp. 11. H. 52653

The New England Anti-Masonic Almanac, for ... 1829. By Edward Giddins ... . *Boston.* [n. d.] 12mo, pp. 24. Continued.

The New England Anti-Slavery Almanac, for 1841. ... *Boston: J. A. Collins.* 1841. 12mo, pp. 36. H. 52655

Also: The Abolitionist: or Record of the New England Anti-Slavery Society. Edited by a Committee. *Boston: Printed by Garrison & Knapp.* 1833. 8vo, pp. (2), 192. Portrait.—Address to the People of the United States, by a Committee of the New England Anti-Slavery Convention, held in Boston ... May, 1834. *Boston: Printed by Garrison & Knapp.* 1834. 8vo, pp. 16.—Address of the New England Anti-Slavery Convention, to the Slaves of the United States; with an Address to President Tyler, adopted in Faneuil Hall, May 31, 1843. [n. p. n. d.] 8vo, pp. 16.—Constitution of the New England Anti-Slavery Society: with an Address to the Public. *Boston: Printed by Garrison and Knapp.* 1832. 8vo, pp. 16.—First Annual Report of the Board of Managers of the New-England Anti-Slavery Society ... Jan. 9, 1833. With an Appendix. *Boston: Printed by Garrison and Knapp.* 1833. 8vo, pp. 54. BA. Continued to 1835, when the title was changed to Massachusetts Anti-Slavery Society.—Hymns to be sung at the N. E. Anti-Slavery Convention. May 24th and 25th, 1836. [n. p. n. d.] 8vo, pp. (8).—Proceedings of the New-England Anti-Slavery Convention, held in Boston ... May, 1834. *Boston: Garrison & Knapp.* 1834. 8vo, pp. 72. Continued. BA.

New England Antislavery Tract Association. Tracts. *Boston.* [n. d.] 12mo. M. 52656

New England Art Union. ... Catalogue of Paintings ... . *Boston: Dutton and Wentworth.* 1851. 8vo, pp. 8. H. 52657

Also: New England Art Union, ... Boston. [Object and Plan. *Boston:*] *Dutton & Wentworth, Printers.* [1851.] 8vo, pp. 4. H.—Bulletin of the New England Art Union. Number One. *Boston: Dutton & Wentworth, Printers.* 1852. 4to, pp. 12. Plate. H.

The New-England Asylum for the Blind, instituted in February, 1829. [n. p. n. d.] 24mo, pp. 12. BA. 52658

History of its origin and formation. Also: Catalogue of Articles ... offered ... at the Ladies' Fair, Salem, April 10, 1833, for the Benefit of the New-England Asylum for the Blind. [*Salem.* 1833.] 8vo, pp. 7. M.

New England Botanic Medical and Surgical Journal. Calvin Newton, M.D., Editor ... . Vol. III. ... *Worcester, Mass.* 1849. 8vo. Continued. H. 52659

Annual Report of the New England Branch of the American Tract Society. ... [n. p. n. d.] 8vo, pp. 16. Continued. H.

The New England Business Directory ... . By George Adams, ... *Boston: George Adams.* 1856. 8vo, pp. x, 7–752, Advertisements, 104. Continued. H. 52661

New England Callendar, for 1795. 12mo. 52662

The New England Calendar and Ephemeris, 1800. The Astronomical Calculations by Eliab Wilkinson, of Smithfield, Philom. *Newport: Printed for Jacob Richardson.* [n. d.] 12mo.

New England Cities Business Directory ... . Giving a complete index to the Mercantile, Manufacturing and Professional Interests of these Cities, together with Lists of Banks, Savings Banks, Manufacturing Companies, &c. ... *Boston: Briggs & Co.* 1867. 8vo, pp. xxi, 18–544, Advertisements, 376. Continued.

New England Coal Mining Co. [Circular. n. p. 1852.] 16mo, pp. 8. H. 52665

Also: Act of Incorporation and By-Laws of the New England Coal Mining Company, Report of the Directors, January 14, 1852. *Worcester: Printed by Henry J. Howland.* [n. d.] 12mo, pp. 24. H. *See* Report of the Company, *infra.*

New England Conservatory of Music, Boston ... . 1870. *Boston: Alfred Mudge & Son, Printers.* 1870. 16mo, pp. 30.

Also: Annual Catalogue and Circular of the New England Conservatory of Music, ... Boston, Mass. ... 1869. *Boston: Printed by Edward L. Balch.* 1869. 8vo, pp. 40.

New England Copper Company. ... Incorporated under the General Mining Laws of ... Michigan. *Boston.* [1864.] 8vo, pp. 8. H. 52667

New England Coquette, a Tragic Drama. *Salem.* 1797. 8vo.

... N. E. Cotton Manufacturers' Association. Proceedings of the Semi-Annual Meeting, ... at Boston, July 18, 1866. ... *Boston: Printed by Thomas W. Ripley.* 1866. 8vo, pp. 15. Plate. Continued. BA. 52669

M DCC XXV. | The New-England Diary, Or, | Almanack | For ... 1725. ... By a Native of New-England. | *Boston. Printed and Sold by B. Green.* | 1725. 16mo, pp. 16. B. 52670

By Nathan Bowen. Thomas quotes 1721 as the first issue. Continued to 1729.

New England Directory, for 1860. *Boston.* 1860. 8vo. Continued. 52671

Ninth Annual Report of the ... New-England Education Society. ... 1865. *Boston: Press of Geo. C. Rand & Avery.* 1865. 8vo, pp. 24. Continued. B. 52672

New England Emigrant Aid Company. Form of Constitution and By-Laws, for Auxiliary Societies. [n. p. n. d.] 12mo, pp. 4

Also: An Act to incorporate the New England Emigrant Aid Company. [*Boston.*] 1855. 8vo. Relates chiefly to Kansas and Nebraska. *See* Vol. VIII., No. 32188, Vol. XIII., No. 52198, Stringfellow (B. F.), *and* Webb (T. H.)

The New England Family Circle. ... 1859. *Worcester, Mass.: J. A. Spalding.* [n. d.] 8vo, pp. 72. Plate. H. 52674

... The New England Farm Advertiser. Published monthly by Geo. H. Chapin ... . Vol. 4. ... *Boston: Printed by J. A. Cummings & Co.* [n. d.] 8vo. Continued. H. 52675

The New England Farmer. Containing Essays, Original and Selected, relating to Agriculture and Domestic Economy, with Engravings, and the Prices of Country Produce. By Thomas G. Fessenden. Vol. I. *Boston: Thomas W. Shepard.* 1823. 4to, pp. vii, 416. Continued. BA. 52676

The second series commencing with Vol. X., is entitled "The New-England Farmer and Gardener's Journal."

The New England Farmer; A Semi-Monthly Journal, devoted to Agriculture, Horticulture, and their kindred Arts and Sciences; ... S. W. Cole, Editor ... . Volume I. *Boston: J. Nourse.* 1849. 8vo, pp. viii, 408. Continued. BA. 52677

There is a change of editors with the different years.

New England Farmer. Devoted to Agriculture and all its various kindred Arts and Sciences. Vol. I. ... 1849. *Boston.* 1849. 4to. Continued. H. 52678

NEW ENGLAND FARMER, *pseudon.* *See* Vol. VI., No. 22941, [Lowell (J.)], Vol. X., Nos. 42452 and 42456.

The New England Farmer's Almanack, for ... 1828. By Thomas Green Fessenden ... . *Boston: John B. Russell.* [n. d.] 8vo, pp. (40). Continued. H. 52679

The New-England Farmers' and Mechanics' Journal. Conducted by E. Holmes, M.D. ... 1828. Vol. I. *Gardiner, Me.: P. Shelden.* [n. d.] 8vo, pp. 24. Plate. H. 52680

The New-England Farmer's Diary and Almanac, ... 1821. ... By Truman Abell, Philom. ... *Windsor, Vt.: ... Ebenezer Hutchinson.* [n. d.] 12mo, pp. (48). Continued. H. 52681

New England Female Medical College. Circular to the Members of the Massachusetts Legislature. *Boston: Printed by Alfred Mudge & Son.* 1866. 8vo, pp. 16. H. 52682

Seventh Annual Report of the New-England Female Medical College. ... *Boston: The Trustees.* 1856. 8vo, pp. 24. Cont'd.

For previous reports, *see* "Female Medical Education Society," Vol. VI., No. 24049. The college was chartered and carried on in connection with the above, from 1850 until 1856, when the society was reorganized, and the name changed, consolidating the two organization under the name of the New England Female Medical College. Also: First Annual Report of the Chemical Department of the ... College ... 1860. *Boston: Prentiss & Deland, Printers.* 1860. 12mo, pp. 11, (1).—Sixth Annual Advertisement of the ... College, ... 1853. *Boston.* 1853. 8vo, pp. 8.—Circular to the ... House of Representatives. ... [From the] Directors of the Female Medical Education Society, ... pray[ing] to be incorporated as the New England Female Medical College. [n. p. 1853.] 8vo, pp. 7, (1).— ... Statement to its Patrons and Friends. ... [n. p. 1866.] 8vo, pp. 8. H.

Fourteenth Annual Report of the New England Female Moral Reform Society, for ... 1852. ... *Boston: Bazin & Chandler, Printers.* 1852. 8vo, pp. 22, (1). Continued. H. 52684

First Annual Report of the Educational Commission for Freedmen. May, 1863. ... *Boston: Prentiss & Deland, ... Printers.* 1863. 8vo, pp. 22. Continued. B. 52685

With the second report the name is changed to "New England Freedmen's Aid Society." Also: Extracts from Letters of Teachers and Superintendents. Fourth Series. *Boston.* 1864. 8vo, pp. 14. B.

Constitution of the New England Guards. ... Third Edition. *Boston: Printed by Bannister and Marvin.* 1824. 12mo, pp. 94, (1). + Revised, March, 1834. Fourth Edition. *Boston: Printed by Samuel Condon.* 1834. 12mo, pp. 23. + Revised, January, 1839. Fifth Edition. *Boston.* 1839. 16mo, pp. 14. H.

Also: ... By-Laws of Company B (New England Guards) Second Battalion of Infantry, M. V. M. *Boston.* 1860. 32mo, pp. 16.—Proceedings at the Fiftieth Anniversary of the New England Guards, October 15, 1862. ... *Boston: Press of T. R. Marvin & Son.* 1863. 8vo, pp. 92. H.

The New England Historic-Genealogical Society to the Members of the General Court of Massachusetts: being a Counter Remonstrance of said Society to a Remonstrance or "Memorial of the Massachusetts Historical Society" ... . *Boston: Printed by David Knapp.* 1858. 8vo, pp. 8. + Second Edition. [*Ibid.*]

Also: Circular Number Two of the New England Historic-Genealogical Society. April, 1846. [*Boston:*] *Hewes and Watson's Print.* [n. d.] 8vo, pp. 15. Continued.—Constitution and By-Laws of the New England Historic-Genealogical Society. Circular Number Four. January, 1858. *Boston: Henry W. Dutton and Son, Printers.* M.DCCC.LVIII. 8vo, pp. 8 BA.

The New England Historical & Genealogical Register: published quarterly under the direction of the New England Historic, Genealogical Society. Rev. William Cogswell, D.D., Editor. Volume I. *Boston: Samuel G. Drake.* 1847. 8vo, pp. 399, (1). Plate and 5 Portraits. Continued. BA. 52688

A storehouse of New England family history. Vols. XXXI., XXXII. and XXXIII. are scarce, a smaller number than usual having been printed. Also: Proceedings of the ... Society. *Boston.* 1874. 8vo. Continued.—Report of a Committee of the ... Society, respecting the date of Sudbury Fight, and Death of Capt. Wadsworth. *Boston.* 18—. 8vo.— ... Quarter-Century Anniversary Discourse, March 18, 1870. *Boston.* 1870. 8vo. Many other publications by the society are in this Dictionary described under the authors names. *See* Vol. VI., No. 23278.

[Second] Annual Report of the New-England Hospital for Women and Children, For ... 1863. *Boston: Prentiss & Deland, ... Printers.* 1864. 8vo, pp. 23. Continued. B. 52689

The New England illustrated Almanac, for ... 1867. ... *Boston.* [n. d.] 24mo, pp. 24. H. 52690

Annual Report of the Trustees of the New England Institution for the Education of the Blind ... . *Boston: Printed by J. T. Buckingham.* 1834. 8vo, pp. 14, (2). Continued. BA. 52691

The corporate name is "New England Asylum for the Blind," which *see* also. Afterwards (from 1840) the "Perkins Institution." Also: Address of the Trustees of the New-England Institution for the Education of the Blind to the Public. *Boston: Carter, Hendee and Co.* 1833. 8vo, pp. 20. 2 Plates.

New England Insurance Gazette and Monthly Financial Record. William Hadden, Editor. January, 1869. *Boston: W. Hadden.* 1869. 4to. Continued. C. 52692

New England Inventors' and Mechanics' Association. Report of the Investigating Committee, appointed by the Exhibitors of the "Industrial Exhibition," held ... 1855. *Boston: Evans & Plumer, Printers.* 1856. 12mo, pp. 12. H. 52693

The New England Journal of Medicine and Surgery, and Collateral Branches ... . *Boston.* 1812. 8vo. Continued. 52694

The New England Kalendar, for 1703. *Boston: Printed by B. Green.* 1703. 16mo. Continued. M. 52695

The New England Loyal Publication Society. ... Boston. [n. p. 1864.] 4to, pp. (3). 52696

The issues of this society are in the form of broadsides, circulars, etc., many of which occupying four or five closely printed columns. The regular edition has numbered fifteen hundred copies, though, in some instances, it has been much greater. Also: Report of the Executive Committee ... May 1, 1865. *Boston.* 1865. 8vo, pp. 27. *See also* [Hooker (J.)], Vol. VIII., No. 32820.

The New England Magazine for August, 1758. By Urbanus Filter. *Boston: ... Benjamin Mecom ...* . [1758.] 8vo, pp. 60.

The first magazine published in New England. Contains an account of the monument, then just erected, by Benjamin Franklin, to the memory of his parents.

The New-England Magazine. Volume I. [to Vol. IX.] ... By J. T. & E. Buckingham. *Boston: J. T. and E. Buckingham.* 1831–[35]. 8vo, pp. iv, (3), 548. BA. 52698

An interesting periodical containing valuable biographies, historical and literary notices, original communications, etc. After Vol. IX. it became the "American Monthly Magazine."

New-England Magazine of Industry and Trade: ... . July, 1859. *Boston: Dexter & Co.* [n. d.] 8vo. Continued. H.

NEW-ENGLAND MAN, *pseudon.* An Attempt to demonstrate the Practicability of Emancipating the Slaves of the United States ... and of removing them ... without ... subjecting the Nation to a Tax. By a New-England Man. *New-York: G. & C. Carvill.* 1825. 8vo, pp. 75. 52700

See also our Vol. X., Nos. 40474, *and* 40487.

The New England Medical Gazette. ... Edited by I. T. Talbot, M.D. *Boston.* 1865. 8vo. Continued. 52701

The New England Medical Review and Journal. ... *Boston.* 1827. 8vo. 52702

New England Memorandum Book. *Boston.* 1765. 8vo.

The New-England Mercantile Union Business Directory, Six Parts in One. ... *New York: Pratt & Co.* 1849. 8vo, pp. 324, (9)

Also issued in six volumes, 12mo.

New England Meridian. *Boston: J. B. Mansfield.* [n. d.] 8vo

Charter and By-Laws of the New England Mining and Quarrying Company. ... *New York: Hall, Clayton & Co., Printers.* 1855. 8vo. 52706

New England Missionary Intelligencer and General Repository, Vol. I. ... 1819. *Concord.* 1819. 8vo. M. 52707

Articles of Association and Agreement, constituting the New England Mississippi Land Company, as amended, March 12 1798. [n. p. n. d.] 8vo, pp. 9. + [n. p. 1814.] 8vo, pp. 11.

Also: The Claim of Ebenezer Oliver and others, Directors of an Association called the New England Mississippi Land Company. [n. p. n. d.] 8vo, pp. 11.—Memorial of the Agents of the ... Company to Congress, with a Vindication of their Title at Law annexed. [*Washington: A. & G. Way, Printers.* 1804.] 8vo, pp. (4), 7, 109.— ... The Memorial of the Directors of the ... Company, Citizens of ... Massachusetts. [n. p. 1814.] 8vo, pp. 15.—A Vindication of the Rights of the ... Company, by the Agents of said Company. ... *City of Washington: A. & G. Way, Printers.* 1804. 8vo, pp. 109. B.

Annual Reports of the New England Mutual Life Insurance Company of Boston. 1844 to 1862. *Boston: Nathan Sawyer, Printer.* 1863. 8vo, pp. (2), iv, 158. BA. 52709

Also: Exposition of the Objects of the Institution of the New England Mutual Life Insurance Company: ... *Boston: Printed by Freeman and Bolles.* 1844. 12mo, pp. 36. + *Boston: Printed by Samuel N. Dickinson.* 1845. 12mo, pp. 32.—The Objects,

Principles and Regulations of the ... Company ... . *Boston: Printed by Samuel N. Dickinson & Co.* 1846. 12mo, pp. 34. Continued.—Report of the Directors ... Dec. 2, 1844. [n. p. n. d.] 8vo, pp. 4. Continued.

Principles of the [New England] Non-Resistance Society. *Boston: New England Non-Resistance Society.* 1839. 12mo, pp. 15, (1). H. 52710

Also: National Organizations. Prepared for the N. E. Non-Resistance Society. ... *Boston: Isaac Knapp.* 1830. 16mo, pp. 32. H.

New England Offering. Harriet Farley, Editor ... . *Lowell: C. C. P. Moody, Printer.* 1849. 8vo, pp. (2), 278. Plates. H.

For previous years, *see* "Lowell Offering," Vol. X., No. 42491.

New-England. *See* [Morrell (W.)], Vol. XII., No. 50786.

New England Patriot. *See* [Lowell (J.)], Vol. X., No. 42453

New England Persecutors. *See* [Maule (T.)], Vol. XI. 46934

New England Pocket Songster; a choice collection of Popular Songs ... . *Claremont.* 1835. 24mo. 52712

New England Primer.

There is some doubt as to the date of the *first edition* of this "little compendium which, for upwards of a century, was to almost every man born in New England the *first book* in religion, and to thousands has stood in the same office in literature." The earliest account is gathered from the following *Advertisement* copied from a reprint: "There is now in the press, and will suddenly be extant, A Second Impression of the *New England Primer, Enlarged*, to which is added, more *Directions for Spelling*: The Prayer of King Edward 6th, and *Verses made by* Mr. Rogers, *the Martyr, left as a Legacy to his children.* Sold by *B. Harris* at the *London Coffee-House in Boston.*" It is also announced in H. Newman's "News from the Stars," *Boston*, 1691. The following list is chronological:

The New England Primer Enlarged. For the more easy attaining the true Reading of English. To which is added, The Assembly of Divines' Catechism. *Boston.* 1737. 24mo, pp. 79.

The New England Primer improved for the more easy attaining the true reading of English. To which is added the Assembly of Divines, and Mr. Cotton's Catechism. *Providence: ... John Waterman.* 1775. 24mo. 52714

This edition was reprinted in facsimile, *Boston: Printed by Edward Draper, at his Printing-Office, in Newbury-Street, and Sold by John Boyle, in Marlborough-Street.* 1777.

The New England Primer; Or, an easy and pleasant Guide to the Art of Reading. Adorned with Cuts. To which is added, the Catechism. *New-England: Printed for the Booksellers.* [n. d.] 24mo, pp. (62). H. 52715

The | New England | Primer, Improved | For the more easy attaining the true reading of English. | To which is added, | The Assembly of Divines | Catechism. | *Glasgow: Printed by Robert Duncan.* 1784. Sq. 16mo. 52716

Not paged; one leaf precedes the title.

New England Primer, much Improved. *Philadelphia.* 1797. Sq. 24mo. 52717

The New England Primer enlarged and Improved; ... *Newburyport: ... John Mycall ...* . [n. d.] 24mo, pp. 76. 52718

A New and Improved Edition. The New England Primer, improved ... . *New York: Published for the Booksellers. M. Day, Printer.* [n. d.] 24mo, pp. 71. Plate. 52719

The New England Primer, improved ... . *New Haven: S. Babcock.* [n. d.] 24mo, pp. 72. Plate. + *Boston: Printed by James Loring.* [n. d.] 24mo. 52720

New England Primer, Improved ... . *Albany.* 181–. 24mo. 15 Plates. 52721

The New England Primer. *Worcester: William Allen.* [n. d.] 24mo. 52722

The New England Primer; ... with a Historical Introduction by Rev. H. Humphrey ... . *Worcester: ... S. A. Howland.* [n. d.] 24mo, pp. 64. Portrait. 52723

The New England Primer; ... *Massachusetts Sabbath School Society, Boston.* [1810?] 24mo, pp. 64. + *Concord, N. H.* 1813. 24mo. 52724

The New England Primer; ... *Walpole, N. H.: Printed by I. Thomas & Co.* 1814. 32mo, pp. (62). H. 52725

The New England Primer improved; ... Added the Assembly's Shorter Catechism. *Philadelphia: F. Scott.* [n. d.] 24mo, pp. 36. B. 52726

The New England Primer, Improved ... . *Hartford: George Goodwin.* 1820. 32mo, pp. 62. + *Newark.* 1824. 24mo. + *John Punchard, and James Gay, Boston.* 1831. 24mo, pp. 62. Plate. + *Providence.* 1835. 52727

The New England Primer improved ... . *New York: Charles G. Dean.* 1842. 24mo, pp. 64. Plate. 52728

The Improved New-England Primer. ... *Concord, N. H.: Roby, Kimball & Merrill.* 1841. Sq. 16mo, pp. 48. H. 52729

The New-England Primer Improved For the more easy attaining the true reading of English. To which is added The Assembly of Divines, and Mr. Cotton's Catechism. *Boston: Printed by Edward Draper.* 1777. 24mo, pp. (82). + *Hartford, Conn.: Ira Webster.* 1843. 24mo, pp. (82). Portrait. + [*Ibid.*] 1844. 24mo, pp. (84). Portrait. H. 52730

Edited by George Livermore. Contains Mr. John Cotton's exhilarating "Spiritual Milk for American Babes, Drawn out of the Breasts of both Testaments, for their Souls Nourishment." "The edition of the New England Primer, published in 1843, by Mr. Ira Webster, of Hartford, is a correct reprint of the oldest copy of that remarkable book, of which I have any knowledge. All other reprints I have seen, have been considerably altered."—GEORGE LIVERMORE.

The New England Primer. ... *Cambridge.* 1844. Sq. 24mo. + *Boston.* 1844. + *Philadelphia: Thomas Cowperthwait & Co.* [n. d.] 52731

The New-England Primer, Restored ... . *Trenton: Printed for Rev. Eli F. Cooley.* 1846. 18mo, pp. 62. + [*Ibid.*] 1853. Sq. 16mo, pp. 62. 52732

The New England Primer; ... *Concord, N. H.: Rufus Merrill.* 1849. 24mo, pp. 64. + [*Ibid.*] 1850. 24mo. 52733

New England Primer, improved ... . *Albany.* 1875. 24mo.

See [Livermore (G.)], Vol. X., No. 41568.

New England Psalm Book. *Boston: Printed for B. Eliot and N. Buttolph.* 1707. 12mo. 52735

Other editions, *Boston.* 1729. 12mo. + Twenty-Fifth Edition. *Boston.* 1742. 12mo, pp. 348. + Twenty-Sixth Edition. *Boston.* 1744. 12mo.

The New England Psalm-Book; being the New England Psalm-Book revised and improved. By an endeavor after a yet nearer approach to the inspired Original, as well as to the Rules of Poetry, with an addition of fifty other Hymns ... . *Boston, N. E.: D. Henchman.* 1758. 12mo, pp. 350. 52736

This is the revised edition of the Bay Psalm Book of 1640, by Thomas Prince. Also: New England Psalm Book. With Prince's Amendments. *Boston.* 1762. 12mo. + [*Ibid.*] 1764. 12mo.

The New England Psalter, Or, Psalms of David. ... [Twenty-Third Edition?] *Boston.* 1730. 12mo. + *Philadelphia.* 1745. 12mo, pp. 116. + *Boston: Printed by David Kneeland.* 1764. Sm. 8vo. + *Boston: Printed by Edes and Gill.* 1768. 12mo. +

Boston: Printed by D. Kneeland. 1770. 12mo. + *Boston: William McAlpine.* MDCCLXXI. 12mo. + *Boston: Printed by J. Perkins.* 1771. 12mo, pp. 160. + *Boston.* 1774. 8vo, pp. 157. + *Boston.* 1784. 12mo. 52737

The New England Quarterly Journal of Medicine and Surgery. Edited by Charles E. Ware, M.D. and Samuel Parkman, M.D. ... Vol. I. *Boston: D. Clapp, Jr.* 1843. 8vo. Continued. C.

The New England Quarterly Magazine; comprehending Literature, Morals, and Amusement. ... Number I. [to] III. ... *Boston: Printed for the Proprietors, by Hosea Sprague.* 1802–[3]. 3 nos., 8vo, pp. (8), 288; (8), 288; (4), 288. BA. 52739

No more published.

The New England Sabbath School Minstrel ... . *Boston.* 1844. Sq. 16mo, pp. 63, (1). BA. 52740

Constitution of the New England Sabbath School Union, ... with the Proceedings of the First Annual Meeting ... Held ... 1836; ... *Boston: Printed for the ... Union, by J. Howe.* 1836. 8vo, pp. 16. H. 52741

Also: Second Annual Report of the ... Sabbath School Union, ... 1837. *Boston.* 1837. 8vo, pp. 32. Continued. H.

New England Scenery, from Nature. ... *Boston.* 1852. 4 parts, obl. 4to. 52742

New England Scenes, or ... Events which have taken place since the First Settlement. *New Haven: L. H. Young.* 1833. 12mo, pp. 106. 10 Plates. C. 52743

Principally of a religious nature.

First Annual Report of the New-England Society for the Improvement of Domestic Poultry. *Boston.* 1849. 8vo. Cont'd.

Act of Incorporation, and By-Laws of the New England Society for the Promotion of Manufactures and the Mechanic Arts. ... *Boston: Printed by Beals and Homer.* 1826. 8vo, pp. 16. BA.

Constitution of the New-England Society, in the City and State of New-York ... . *New-York: Printed by Sage and Thompson.* 1806. 8vo, pp. 8. + *New-York.* 1832. 8vo. pp. 27. H.

Also: Fifty-Eighth Anniversary Celebration of the New England Society, In ... New York, ... December 22, 1863, with the Constitution, By-Laws, Charities, List of Members, etc., etc. *New York: Wm. C. Bryant & Co., Printers.* 1864. 8vo, pp. 76. Plan. Continued.—Fifty-Sixth Annual Report of the New England Society In the City of New York. With the Constitution ... . *New York: The Society.* 1861. 8vo, pp. 28.

Plan. Continued.—Dinner of the New England Society, with the Speeches of Messrs. Grinnell, Bellows, J. P. Hall, Webster, Bulwer, Bethune, Draper, J. W. Webster, &c. Celebrated at the Astor House, Dec. 23, 1850. *New York.* 1851. 8vo, pp. 62.—Report of the Annual Dinner of the New England Society in the City of New-York; ... Dec. 23, 1851. *New-York.* 1852. 8vo, pp. 45. Continued.—Report, Constitution and By-Laws of the New England Society in the City of New York, December 5, 1843. *New York: J. M. Elliott, Printer.* 1843. 8vo, pp. 40.—Semi-Centennial Celebration of the New England Society, in the City of New York, December, 1855. Oration: By Oliver Wendell Holmes, M.D. Poem: By John Pierpont, D.D. And a Report of the Festival. *New York: Wm. C. Bryant & Co., Printers.* 1856. 8vo, pp. 116. *See also* Vol. III., No. 12086, Vol. IV., Nos. 13063, 14896, *and* Vol. X., No. 42181

Minutes of the Organization and Proceedings of the New England Soldiers' Relief Association. ... New York. ... *New York: John F. Trow, Printer.* 1862. 8vo, pp. 31. + *New York: Root, Anthony & Co.* 1862. 8vo, pp. 62. BA. 52747

Also: Report of the Superintendent ... December, 1862. Founded ... April 3, 1862. ... *New York: Francis & Loutrel, ... Printers.* 1862. 18mo, pp. 18, (2). Continued to 1866.

Constitution and By-Laws of the New England Spiritualists' Association. *Boston: George K. Snow, Printer.* 1854. 8vo, pp. 15

A New England Tale. *See* [Sedgwick (C. M.)]

The New-England Telegraph, and Eclectic Review; for ... 1836. Moses Thacher, Editor. Volume II. *North Wrentham, Mass.* 1836. 8vo, pp. 572, (4). Plate. BA. 52749

Constitution of the New England Tract Society. *Andover, Mass.* 1816. 12mo. 52750

Also: Second Annual Report of the ... New England Tract Society, May 27, 1816. [*Andover: Printed ... by Flagg and Gould.* 1816.] 12mo, pp. 24. Continued. H.

The New England Tour of His Royal Highness the Prince of Wales, (Baron Renfrew), From the Reception at the Massachusetts Line to the Embarkation at Portland. ... *Boston.* 1860. 8vo, pp. 52. BA. 52751

The New England Town and County Almanac, 1769. By Abraham Weatherwise, Gent. *Providence: ... Josiah Goddard & John Carter.* [1769.] 12mo. 52752

Annual Report of the New England Unitarian Book Society; with the Rules of the Society, and Catalogue of the Library. *New York.* 1823. 12mo, pp. 43. M. 52753

New-England Vindicated. *See* [Mather (I.)], Vol. XI. 46712.

New England Women's Association. *See* United States.

Minutes of New-England Yearly Meeting of Friends, 1849. *Providence.* 1849. 8vo, pp. 27. Continued. 52754

See also "Memorials of Deceased Friends," Vol. XII., No. 47739, and add *Providence: Knowles, Anthony & Co.* 1856. 8vo, pp. 32.

New-Englands Advice. *See* [Lechford (T.)], Vol. x. 39641.

New England's Chattels: or Life in the Northern Poor House. *New-York.* 1858. 12mo, pp. 484. 52755

New-England's Crisis [1676]. *See* [Thompson (B.)]

New England's Ensigne; it being the account of Cruelty, the Professor's Pride, and the articles of their faith; signified in characters written in blood, wickedly begun, barbarously continued, and inhumanly finished, (so far as they have gone,) by the present power of a darkness possest in the priests and rulers in New England, with the Dutch also, inhabiting the same land; in a bloody and cruel birth, which the husband to the Whore of Babylon hath brought forth, by ravishing and torturing the seed of the Virgin of Israel. ... This being an account of the sufferings sustained by us in New England, (with the Dutch,) the most part of it in these two last yeers, 1657, 1658. With a letter to John Indicot, and Iohn Norton, Governor, and the Chief Priest of Boston, and another to the town of Boston. Also, the several late Conditions of a friend upon Road, Island, before, in, and after distraction; With some quæries unto all sorts of people, who want that which we have, &c. Written at Sea, by us whom the Wicked, in scorn, call Quakers, in the second month of the yeer 1659. This being a Confirmation of so much as Francis Howgill truly published in his Book, titled, The Popish Inquisition newly erected in (New) England, &c. *London: Printed by T. L. for G. Calvert* ... . 1659. 4to, pp. 120. J.C.B. 52756

Relates to the sufferings of the Quakers in New England. Smith's "Catalogue of Friends' Books" says this is by Humphry Norton, John Rous and John Copeland. *See* our Vol. VIII., No. 33363, *and* Bartlett's "Bibliography of Rhode Island," p. 191.

New-England's Faction Discovered; | Or, | A Brief and True Account of their Persecution of the Church | of England; the Beginning and Progress of the War | with the Indians; and other Late Proceedings there, in | a Letter from a Gentleman of that Country, to a Person | of Quality. | Being, an Answer to a most false and scandalous Pamphlet late- | ly Published; Intituled, News from New-England, &c. | [Colophon:] *London,* | *Printed*

for J. Hindmarsh, at the Sign of the Golden Ball, over against | *the Royal Exchange in Cornhill.* 1690. | 4to, pp. 8. 52757

Signed C. D[ove]. Corrected title of our No. 18229, Vol. v. Extremely rare.

Nevv | Englands | First Fruits; | in respect, | First of the { Conversion of some, | Conviction of divers, | Preparation of sundry } of the Indians. 2. Of the progresse of Learning, in the Colledge at | Cambridge in Massacusets Bay. | With | Divers other speciall Matters concerning that Countrey. | Published by the instant request of sundry Friends, who desire | to be satisfied in these points by many New-England Men | who are here present, and were eye or eare- | witnesses of the same. | ... | *London,* | *Printed by R. O. and G. D. for Henry Overton, and are to be* | *sold at his Shop in Popes-head Alley.* 1643. | 4to, pp. (2), 26, (1). B. 52758

The first and one of the rarest of the series of reports from New England relative to the conversion of the aborigines. Pages 18–20 contain the Commencement Theses at the graduation of the first class, in 1642. It was reprinted *verbatim* with the following title:

New England's First Fruits: with Divers other Special Matters Concerning that Country. *New York: Joseph Sabin.* 1865. 4to, pp. (4), 47. BA. 52759

"This reprint of the first of that series of reports to the Corporation for Propagating the Gospel among the Indians of New England, known as the Eliot *Tracts*, has the great *defect* of being published without note, comment, or biographical sketch. Indeed, the whole of Mr. Sabin's reprints are *unedited*, and thus an excellent opportunity of adding to the common stock of knowledge regarding their bibliographical history as well as that of their author, editors, and the venerable society which printed them, was lost." —T. W. FIELD. I was unkind enough not to avail myself of Mr. Field's offer to do something of the kind here suggested, and I think the above specimen of Mr. Field's indifferent English will be a sufficient reason for my declination.

New England's Lamentations. *See* [Shepard (Thomas)], *and* White (John)].

New-England's | Misery, | The procuring Cause, | And A Remedy | proposed. | [A Poem.] Composed October, 1758. | *Boston: Printed by Z. Fowle and S. Draper.* M,DCC,LVIII. 8vo, pp. 15, (1) 52760

New-Englands Plantation. *See* [Higginson (F.)], No. 31739.

New England's present Sufferings. *See* [Wharton (Edward)].

New-England's Spirit of Persecution. *See* [Keith (G.)], IX.

New England's Tears for her present miseries; or, a late and true relation of the calamities of New England since April last past. With an account of the Battel between the English and Indeans upon Seaconk Plain, and of the Indians burning and destroying Marlbury, Rehoboth, Chelmsford, Sudbury and Providence; with the death of Antononies, the Grand Indian Sachem, and a relation of a Fortification began by women on Boston Neck. Together with an Elegy on the Death of John Winthrop, Esq., late Governor of Connecticott, and Fellow of the Royal Society. Written by an Inhabitant of Boston, in New England, to his friend in London. ... *London: Printed for N. S.* 1676. Sm. 4to.

A volume of extreme rarity. *See also* Vol. VIII., No. 32810–11. For other anonymous books relating to New England, *see* the Index to this Dictionary, or the first word of the title, particles excepted.

The New Englander. ... Volume I. 1843. *New Haven: Printed by B. L. Hamlen.* [1843.] 8vo, pp. vii, 608. 2 Portraits, Plate and Plan. Continued. BA. 52762

New-Englandism not the Religion of the Bible, being an Examination of a Review of Bishop Brownell's fourth Charge to the Clergy. *Hartford.* 1844. 8vo, pp. 60. 52763

A New Essay. *See* [Dickinson (J.)], Vol. v., No. 20046.

New Exercise of Firelocks and Bayonets. Published by a Lover of the Art Military. *New London: T. Green.* 1717. 12mo. 52764

New English Version of the Psalms of David, Suited to the Tunes used in the Reformed Protestant Dutch Churches; together with their Catechism, Confession of Faith, Liturgy, &c., &c. *New York.* 1768. 8vo. 52765

A New Financial Project; together with Some Remarks upon the Currency and Credit System of the United States. *New-York: G. & C. Carvill & Co.* 1837. 8vo, pp. 29. 52766

New Game of Cards; or, A Pack of Cards changed into a Perpetual Almanack. *New-London.* [n. d.] 12mo. + *Boston, Reprinted.* 1761. 8vo, pp. 8. M. 52767

Proceedings of the New General Association, September, 1809. *Charlestown.* 1809. 8vo, pp. 8. N. 52768

A New General Atlas, containing a Geographical and Historical Account of all the ... World: with the Natural History

and Trade of each Country. ... *London: D. Browne* ... . 1721. Folio, pp. (8), 272, 141–261, (10). 32 Maps. C. 52769

A New General Collection of Voyages. *See* [Green (John)].

The New Genesee Farmer and Gardener. ... *Rochester.* 1840. 4to. Continued. S. 52770

Edited by J. J. Thomas, M. B. Bateham, and others.

A New Geographical, Historical, and Commercial History of Canada, and the United States ... Nova Scotia, Hudson's Bay, Newfoundland, St. John's, &c. &c. to the Present Period. ... and the Manners and Customs of the Savage and Civilized Inhabitants. *London: Dean & Munday.* [n. d.] 12mo, pp. (2), 9–68. Plate of Washington City, 1813. 52771

New Gospel of Peace. *See* [White (Richard Grant)].

New Government Colony. British Columbia and Vancouver's Island. [n. p.] 1858. 8vo. 52772

NEW GRANADA. *See also* Nueva Granada.

An Appeal to the British Nation on the Affairs of South America; particularly as regards those of New Granada. *Printed for the Author.* 1819. 8vo. + *London: Effingham Wilson.* 1825. 8vo, pp. 57. 52773

Chiriqui Improvement Company. *New York: W. W. Rose.* 1855. 8vo, pp. 53. Map. 52774

Contract between the Republic of New Granada and The Panama Rail Road Company ... 1850. *New York.* 1856. 8vo, pp. 28. S. 52775

General Treaty of Peace, Amity, &c., between the United States ... and the Republic of New Granada, concluded at Bogota, 12 Decbr. 1846. [And] Message from the President of the United States transmitting the same. [*Washington.* 1847.] 8vo, pp. 78. 52776

New Granada and Costa Rica. The Boundary Question. *London.* 1852. 8vo. Map. 52777

New Granada, and the United States ... final Diplomatic Controversy relating to the Occurrences that took place at Panama on the 15th April, 1856. *Liverpool.* 1856. 8vo. 52778

See also [Mosquera (T. C. de)], Vol. XII., No. 51072.

A New Guide to Geography; ... . Second Edition, improved and corrected. *London: Richard Ware.* MDCCLVI. 12mo, pp. 217. Map. B. 52779

The New Guide. *See* Montreal, Vol. XII., No. 50272.

NEW HAMPSHIRE.

Account of ... the Proceedings. *See* Kentucky, Vol. IX. 37486

An Account of the Numbers. *See* [Fitch (Jabez)], Vol. VI.

An Act Passed, Nov. 19, 1778. To Prevent the Return to this State, of certain Persons ... who have left, or shall leave this State, or either of the United States of America, and have joined, or shall join the Enemies thereof. [n. p. n. d.] 8vo, pp. 16.

Also: ... An Act establishing County Courts. ... June 27, 1860. [n. p. n. d.] 8vo, pp. 14.— ... An Act establishing Town Courts ... . [n. p. 1859.] 8vo, pp. 7. —An Act for the Preservation of White and other Pine Trees Growing in her Majesties Colonies of New Hampshire, Massachusetts Bay, Province of Main, etc., for the Masting her Majesties Navy. *London.* 1711. Folio.—The Act of Incorporation, and Bye Laws of the Proprietors of The Second Turnpike Road in New-Hampshire. ... *Amherst, N. H.: Printed by Joseph Cushing.* 1804. 8vo, pp. 14.— ... An Act relating to Insurance Companies. ... June 30, 1860. [n. p. n. d.] 8vo, pp. 4.— ... An Act reörganizing the Judiciary. [n. p. 1859.] 8vo, pp. 8.— ... An Act to establish a new proportion for the assessment of public taxes. ... June 28, 1860. [n. p. n. d.] 8vo, pp. 16.— ... An Act to establish the office of Superintendent of Public Instruction. June 27, 1860. [n. p. n. d.] 8vo, pp. 8.—Act to Facilitate the Raising of Troops. 1864. [n. p. n. d.] 8vo.—Act to Prohibit all Trade and Intercourse with the Colonies of New Hampshire and other revolting States during the present Rebellion, 1776. [n. p. n. d.] Folio.

Acts and Laws Passed by the General Court or Assembly of His Majesties Province of New-Hampshire ... . *Boston: B. Green.* 1716. Folio, pp. 7, 60. C. 52781

Royal Arms on the title-page. In some copies there are Additional Laws, with a continuous paging beyond page 60.

Acts and Laws of His Majesty's Province of New-Hampshire. In New-England. With Sundry Acts of Parliament. By Order of the General Assembly. To which is prefix'd the Commissions of President John Cuttss, Esq; And His Excellency John Wentworth, Esq; *Portsmouth: Printed by Daniel and Robert Fowle.* 1771. Folio, pp. (2), 6, 8, iv, 272, Temporary Laws, 51, Table, xiii. C., H., S. 52782

Thomas says pp. 6, 8, 5, 5, 8, xiii, 286.

Acts and Laws of the Colony of New-Hampshire. [1776–80. n. p. 1780.] Folio, pp. 182. H. 52783

Acts and Laws of the State of New Hampshire, in America. By order of the General Assembly. To which is prefixed, the Resolution of the American Congress for establishing a Form of Government in New Hampshire; and the Resolve of the Provincial Congress for taking up Government in Form, with the Declaration of Independence. *America: Printed at Exeter, in the State of New Hampshire.* 1780. Folio, pp. vi, 180. S. 52784

The Acts of the Legislature of New-Hampshire incorporating the Dover Manufacturing Company, and the By-Laws ... . *Dover: Printed ... by John Mann.* 1824. 24mo, pp. 26. BA. 52785

Address of ... the Governor, to ... the General Court of New Hampshire. June Session, 1844. *Concord: Carroll & Baker, ... Printers.* 1844. 8vo, pp. 10. Continued. H. 52786

An Address of the Convention For Framing a New Constitution of Government For the State of New-Hampshire to the Inhabitants of said State. *New-Hampshire: Printed, and to be Sold, at the Printing-Offices in Portsmouth and Exeter.* M,DCC,LXXXI. 8vo, pp. 63, (1). H. 52787

Rejected—probably because it was too good.

An Address of the Convention For framing a New Constitution or Form of Government For the State of New-Hampshire, to the Inhabitants of said State. *Exeter, New-Hampshire: Printed in the Year* M,DCC,LXXII. 8vo, pp. 63. H. 52788

An Address of the Convention for framing a Constitution of Government for the people of New-Hampshire, To the Freemen thereof, Voted at their last Meeting, viz., on the First Tuesday of June 1783. *Printed at Portsmouth.* M,DCC,LXXXIII. 8vo, pp. 8.

Address of the Great State Convention of Friends of the Administration, assembled at the Capitol in Concord, June 12, 1828, with the Speech of Mr. Bartlett, in reply to the Charges which have been made against Mr. Adams. *Concord.* 1828. 12mo, pp. 24. H. 52790

An Address of the Inhabitants of the Towns of Plainfield, Lebanon, Enfield (alias Relhan), Canaan, Cardigan, Hanover, Lime, Oxford, Haverhill, Bath, and Landaff to the Inhabitants of the several Towns in the Colony of New Hampshire. *Norwich: Printed by John Trumbull.* MDCCLXXVI. 12mo, pp. 16. 52791

Opposes the legislation at that time about to be adopted in New Hampshire, and was probably written by persons interested in Dartmouth College.

Address, Resolution, and Proceedings of the County Law Reform and Working Men's Convention, holden in Keene, New Hampshire, October 8, 1833, and January 1, 1834. *Concord.* 1834. 8vo. W. 52792

An Address to the Citizens of New Hampshire; By the Author [Hon. Thomas Cogswell]. *Printed in New-Hampshire.* 1805. 12mo, pp. 31. 52793

See also [Plumer (William)].

An Address to the Citizens of New Hampshire, on the approaching Election of State Officers. [n. p.] 1804. 12mo, pp. 11. 52794

An Address to the Citizens of New Hampshire upon a subject of the greatest importance. By a Citizen. [n. p. 1808.] 8vo, pp. 8. BA. 52795

An Address to the Inhabitants of the Towns and Parishes in the State of New Hampshire, particularly those which are vacant: from the Convention of Ministers, ... at Concord, ... June, 1791. *Concord: Printed by George Hough.* M. DCC. XCI. 8vo, pp. 13.

The word *vacant* is supposed to mean that there is no Congregational minister settled in that town.

Address to the Soldiers of New Hampshire, from the Granite State Lincoln Club of Washington, D. C. *Washington: Printed by Lemuel Towers.* 1864. 8vo, pp. (7), 1. 52797

The Administration and the Opposition, addressed to the Citizens of New Hampshire. *Concord.* 1826. 8vo. C. 52798

The Amended Constitution of the State of New Hampshire; with the Resolutions for submitting the Amendments to the People. *Concord: Butterfield and Hill, ... Printers.* 1851. 8vo, pp. 16

First Annual Report of the Board of Agriculture, May 1, 1871. *Nashua.* 1871. 8vo. Continued. 52800

An Appeal to the Old Whigs of New-Hampshire. [n. p.: *February,* 1805.] 8vo, pp. 16. H. 52801

Appendix containing Grants. *See* "A State of the Right," etc.

Articles in addition to, and amendment of, the Constitution of the State of New Hampshire, agreed to by the Convention of Said State and Submitted to the People thereof for their Approbation. *Printed at Exeter, New-Hampshire, by Henry Ranlet.* 1792.

8vo, pp. 33, (1). + *Dover: Printed by E. Ladd, for the State.* 1792. 8vo, pp. 31. 52802

Book for New Hampshire. *See* [Hildreth (H.)], VIII. 31765.

The Case of His Majesty's Province of New Hampshire upon two Appeals Relating to that Province and the Province of the Massachusetts Bay. To be heard before the ... Lords of the Committee of his Majesty's ... Privy-Council for hearing Appeals from the Plantations, at ... Whitehall. [*London.* 1739.] Folio, pp. 8. 52803

Catalogue of the Books, ... in the State Library of New Hampshire. *Concord.* 1850. 8vo. + [*Ibid.*] 1857. 8vo, pp. 48.

Catalogue of the Fraternity of Phi Beta Kappa, Alpha of New Hampshire, Dartmouth College, 1832. *Hanover.* 1832. 8vo, pp. 23. + *Concord.* 1836. 8vo, pp. 23. 52805

Also: Catalogue of the Members of the Φ B K Society, Alpha of New Hampshire. *Hanover.* 1806. 12mo, pp. 15.

A Catechism of the History. *See* [Farmer (J.)], VI. 23819.

Census of New Hampshire ... . *Concord.* 1850. 8vo.

The Christian Reporter, devoted to the interests of the Congregational and Presbyterian Churches of New Hampshire. Benj. P. Stone, D.D., Editor ... . *Concord, N. H.: General Association.* 1865. 8vo, pp. (2), 326. Continued. B. 52807

Collections, Topographical, Historical. *See* Vol. IV. 23837.

Closing Message of ... Nathaniel S. Berry, to the Legislature of New-Hampshire, June Session, 1863. *Concord: Henry McFarland, ... Printer.* 1863. 8vo, pp. 8. H. 52808

Communication from the Governor [S. Bell], covering the Report of the Justices of the Superior Court, on the Question of granting New Trials. [n. p. n. d.] 8vo, pp. 35. 52809

The Compiled Statutes of the State of New Hampshire, to which are prefixed the Constitutions of the United States and ... New Hampshire. ... *Concord.* 1853. 8vo, pp. 760. + Second Edition. [*Ibid.*] 1854. 8vo. A. 52810

By Ralph Metcalf, Calvin Ainsworth and Samuel H. Ayer, Commissioners.

The Complete New-Hampshire Register; containing ... an Almanack for ... 1797. ... *Printed at Exeter by H. Ranlet.* 1796. 8vo, pp. (32). BA. 52811

Constitution and Laws of ... New-Hampshire. ... *Printed at Dover, by Samuel Bragg, jun.* 1805. 8vo, pp. (4), 531. H.

A Constitution, Containing a Bill of Rights, and Form of Government, Agreed upon by the Delegates of the people of New-Hampshire, in Convention, Held at Concord, ... June 1783 ... . *Printed at Portsmouth, in the State of New-Hampshire.* 1783. 8vo, pp. 47. B., N., W. 52813

The Constitution of New Hampshire. [n. p. 1792.] 16mo, pp. 70, (1). H. 52814

The Constitution of New Hampshire, as Altered and Amended by a Convention of Delegates held at Concord, in said State, by adjournment, On the second Wednesday of February, M.DCC.-XCVI. *Printed at Concord by George Hough, for the Convention.* [179-.] 12mo, pp. 59. 52815

The Constitution of New Hampshire and ... Constitution of Vermont ... . *Montpelier.* 1811. 8vo. 52816

Constitution of New Hampshire since it became an Independent State. *Concord.* 1824. 8vo. C. 52817

Also included in the "Collections," Vol. IV.

Constitutional Convention. Report of the Committee on the Judicial Department, made Nov. 19, 1850. ... *Concord: Butterfield and Hill, ... Printers.* 1850. 12mo, pp. 15. H. 52818

Convention of New-Hampshire Publishers, Editors, and Printers, held at Wolfeborough, July 24 and 25, 1868. *Concord: Printed by McFarland & Jenks.* 1868. 8vo, pp. 28. H. 52819

Dartmouth College and the State of New Hampshire. [n. p.] 1828. 8vo. 52820

See also Vol. V., Nos. 18613–18633.

Democratic General Committee of ... New-Hampshire: Nomination of Gen. Houston, Oct. 11. *Concord, N. H.* 1854. 8vo, pp. 11. S. 52821

A Digest of the Laws of New-Hampshire pertaining to Common Schools ... . By Samuel N. Bell ... . *Concord: G. Parker Lyon.* 1853. 12mo, pp. 72. + By Charles R. Morrison ... . *Concord: B. W. Sanborn.* 1869. 8vo, pp. 57. H. 52822

Extracts from the Minutes of the General Association of New Hampshire, at their Session in Exeter in Sept. A. D., 1810. *Charlestown, Mass.* 1810. 8vo, pp. 8. Continued. 52823

Extracts from the Proceedings of the General Association of New-Hampshire, at ... Keene, Sept. 19, 1815. *Concord: George Hough, Printer.* 1815. 8vo, pp. 14. H. 52824

After 1826 the title reads: "Minutes of the Proceedings," etc., until 1829; after which it is simply "Minutes of the General Association," etc.

Facilitated Carriage: A Short Statement of the Proceedings at Concord, N. H. ... 3d June, 1825, on the Subject of Internal Improvements, and some Remarks thereon. *Boston.* 1825. 8vo.

Festival of the Sons of New Hampshire: with the Speeches of Messrs. Webster, ... and others, ... together with ... Letters from Distinguished Individuals. Celebrated in Boston, November 7, 1849. ... *Boston: James French.* 1850. 8vo, pp. 178. 3 Portraits. H. 52826

The First Constitution of New Hampshire, with an Original Letter from Major-General Sullivan to President Ware. *Concord.* 1822. 8vo. + [*Ibid.*] 1831. 52827

The General Statutes of ... New Hampshire; ... *Manchester: J. B. Clarke.* 1867. 8vo, pp. xvii, 676. C. 52828

A Geography of New-Hampshire. Embracing 1. A short Topographical and Historical Sketch of every Town. 2. A General View of each County. 3. A General View of the State. 4. A Glossary. By James Gordon Carter. *Portsmouth, N. H.: N. March.* 1831. 18mo, pp. (2), x, 246. 52829

Geology. First Annual Report on the Geology of ... New-Hampshire. By Charles T. Jackson ... . *Concord: Cyrus Barton, State Printer.* 1841. 8vo, pp. 164. + Second Annual Report. *Concord.* 1842. 12mo, pp. 8. 52830

Final Report on the Geology and Mineralogy of ... New Hampshire; with Contributions towards the Improvement of Agriculture and Metallurgy. By Charles T. Jackson, M.D. Published by order of the Legislature. *Concord, N. H.: Carroll & Baker, State Printers.* 1844. 4to, pp. viii, 376. 2 Maps and 8 Plates. B., BA. 52831

First Annual Report upon the Geology and Mineralogy of ... New Hampshire, By C. H. Hitchcock ... . *Manchester: John B. Clarke, ... Printer.* 1869. 8vo, pp. 36. Map. Continued. H.

From 1870 to 1873, the titles read "Report of the Geological Survey of the State."

The Geology of New Hampshire. A Report comprising the Results of Explorations ordered by the Legislature. C. H. Hitchcock, State Geologist. Part I. Physical Geography. *Concord: E. A. Jenks.* 1874. 8vo, pp. xi, 668. 29 Plates, 20 Maps. Part II. *Concord.* 1877. 8vo, pp. xii, 684. 40 Maps, etc. Part III. [*Ibid.*] 1878. 8vo, pp. viii, 386, 262, 103. 30 Plates, and Atlas, 16 Plates. 52833

Views and Map, illustrative of the Scenery and Geology of ... New Hampshire. By Charles T. Jackson. *Boston: Thurston, Torry, and Company.* 1845. 4to, pp. 20. BA. 52834

Journal of the Proceedings of the Grand Lodge of New Hampshire, at ... Concord, June ... A. L. 5825. *Concord: Printed by Isaac Hill.* 5825. 8vo, pp. 37. Continued. H. 52835

Also: Constitution and By-Laws of the Grand Lodge, I. O. O. F. *Concord.* 1845. 12mo. — Constitution and General Regulations ... . *Manchester.* 1869 8vo. — Proceedings of the Grand Lodge of New Hampshire, at its Annual Meeting in Concord, ... A. L. 5821. *Concord.* 1821. 8vo, pp. 24. — Proceedings of the Grand Lodge of New-Hampshire, from July 8, 5789, to June, 5856, inclusive. *Concord: Printed by McFarland & Jenks.* 1860–1869. 2 vols., 8vo, pp. vii, (1), 474, (4), Appendix, 58, (1); viii, 566. Continued. — ... [Proceedings] of the Grand Royal Arch Chapter of New-Hampshire, ... holden ... in Portsmouth, ... July, A. L. 5822. [n. p. 1822.] 12mo, pp. 6. Continued. H. — Regulations of the Grand Lodge of New Hampshire. *Portsmouth.* 1803. 4to, pp. 27. — Summary of the Proceedings of the Grand Lodge of New Hampshire, at ... Concord, ... June ... A. L. 5818. *Keene, N. H.: Printed by John Prentiss.* 1818. 12mo, pp. 12. Continued. H.

Inquiries occasioned by the Address of the General Association of New Hampshire. *Boston.* 1812. 12mo, pp. 12. M.

Journal of the House of Representatives of the Province of New Hampshire, 1744–1745. [*Boston.* n. d.] Folio, pp. 42. Continued. M. 52837

A Journal of the House of Representatives of the State of New Hampshire, June Session, 1784. *Portsmouth.* 1784. Folio. Continued. C. 52838

A Journal of the Proceedings of the Hon. House of Representatives of the State of New Hampshire, At their Session ... at Concord, June 1799. *Portsmouth.* 1799. 12mo, pp. 78. W.

Journal of the Senate of the State of New Hampshire, October 20, 1784 to February 25, 1785. [*Portsmouth: Melcher and Osborne, Print.* 1785.] Folio, pp. 67. H. 52840

A Journal of the Proceedings of the Honorable Senate, of the State of New-Hampshire ... at Portsmouth, ... December 5th,

1787. *Portsmouth: Printed by J. Melcher.* M,DCC,LXXXVIII. 8vo, pp. 16. Continued. B. 52841

Journal of the Proceedings of the Twenty-Ninth Convention of the Protestant Episcopal Church in ... New Hampshire, ... at Portsmouth, Sept. 23, 1829. *Portsmouth.* 1829. 8vo, pp. 16. Continued. W. 52842

The Laws of the State of New-Hampshire, together with the Declaration of Independence: the Definitive Treaty of Peace between the United States of America and His Britannic Majesty: the Constitution of New-Hampshire, and ... the United States, ... *Portsmouth: Printed by John Melcher.* 1792. 8vo, pp. 396. + [*Ibid.*] 1797. 8vo, pp. 492. H. + *Exeter.* 1815. 8vo, pp. 636, 28. + *Hopkinton.* 1830. 8vo, pp. 623. C. 52843

Laws of the State of New-Hampshire, passed from December ... 1805, to June ... 1810, inclusive. ... *Concord: Printed by Isaac Hill.* 1811. 8vo, pp. 136. H. 52844

Laws enacted since June 1815 ... added an Appendix, containing the Articles of Confederation ... . *Concord.* 1824. 8vo.

Litigation Statistics: furnished by Clerks of several Counties, ... upon the subject of Town or Local Courts ... . June 14, 1860. *Concord: Asa McFarland, ... Printer.* 1860. 8vo, pp. 15.

Massachusetts Bay and New Hampshire. The Case of his Majesty's Province of the Massachusetts Bay touching the Dispute between that Province and his Majesty's Province of New Hampshire, in relation to their Boundaries on the Settlement thereof made by Commissioners appointed for that Purpose; and on Cross-Appeals therefrom. To be heard before the ... Lords of the Committee of his Majesty's ... Privy Council, at the Cock-pit Whitehall, ... the 18th day of February 1739 ... . [*London.* 1739.] Folio, pp. 8. 52847

Message from ... the Governor of New-Hampshire, ... June 4, 1818. [n. p. n. d.] 12mo, pp. 12. Continued. H. 52848

Militia Law. State of New-Hampshire. ... [n. p. 1808.] 8vo, pp. 36. B. + December 22, 1820. [*Concord.* 1821.] 8vo, pp. 46. M. 52849

Minority Report of the Examining Committee on the ... N. H. State Prison, June Session, 1856. *Concord: Amos Hadley, ... Printer.* 1856. 8vo, pp. 32. H. 52850

Minutes of the General Association of New Hampshire, at their Meeting, at Keene, Sept. 1833. ... *Worcester, Mass.* 1833. 8vo, pp. 27. Continued. W. 52851

The first was 1826. *See* No. 52824, *supra.*

Minutes of the New Hampshire Association, held at Boston, June 13, 14, 1804. *Portsmouth.* 1804. 8vo, pp. 11. Cont'd.

Minutes of the New Hampshire Annual Conference of the Methodist Episcopal Church, for ... 1841. ... *Dover: William Burr, Printer.* 1841. 12mo, pp. 23. Continued. B. 52853

A Narrative of the Proceedings. *See* Vol. XII., No. 51825.

New Hampshire. The (late) House of Representatives there Complainants. Jonathan Belcher, Esq. the Governour there, Respondent. The Complainants' Case. To be heard before the ... Lords of the Committee of his Majesty's ... Privy Council for hearing Appeals, Complaints, &c. from the Plantations, at the Cock-pit at Whitehall, on —— day the —— of 1739 ... . [*London.* 1739.] Sm. folio, pp. 4. C. 52854

Case before the Privy-Council, Nov. 12th, 1739. Cause, the action of Governor Belcher with regard to the boundary commission to settle the limits of New Hampshire and Massachusetts, 1737–8.

... The New-Hampshire Agricultural Repository. Published by the State Board of Agriculture ... . *Concord: Printed by Hill and Moore.* 1822. 8vo, pp. 135. H. 52855

Proceedings of the N. H. Anti-Slavery Convention, held in Concord, ... November, 1834. *Concord, N. H.: Eastman, Webster & Co.—Printers.* 1834. 8vo, pp. 36, (1). BA. 52856

Also: First Annual Report of the New Hampshire Antislavery Society, presented June 4, 1835. *Concord.* 1835. 12mo, pp. 48. *See also* our Vol. VI., No. 15149.

Report of the Trustees of the New Hampshire Asylum for the Insane. ... 1840. [*Concord:*] *Cyrus Barton, State Printer.* [1840.] 8vo, pp. 22. Plate. Continued. H. 52857

Also: Reports of the Board of Visitors, ... Trustees, and ... Superintendent ... June Session, 1844. *Concord: Carroll & Baker, ... Printers.* 1844. 8vo, pp. 32. Plate.

Annual Report of the New-Hampshire Auxiliary Colonization Society ... . *Concord.* 1824. 8vo. Continued. 52858

Minutes of the New Hampshire Baptist Convention, at its Thirty-Eighth Anniversary, held at East Jaffrey, ... 1864. *Concord: Fogg, Hadley & Co., Printers.* 1864. 8vo, pp. 24. Cont'd.

Also: Proceedings of the Baptist Convention of ... New-Hampshire, ... June ... 1831. *Concord: Printed by Fisk & Chase.* 1831. 8vo, pp. 32. Continued. — Annual Report of the New Hampshire Baptist Domestick Mission Society. *Concord.* 1819. 8vo. Continued.

Report of the New Hampshire Bible Society, communicated Sept. 16, 1812. *Concord.* 1812. 8vo, pp. 20. Continued.

The New Hampshire Book. Being Specimens of the Literature of the Granite State. ... *Nashua: David Marshall.* 1842. 12mo, pp. 391. + *Nashua: Charles T. Gill.* 1844. 12mo, pp. 391. C. 52861

Selected by C. J. Fox and S. Osgood.

Constitution of the New-Hampshire Branch of the American Education Society, with an Address of the Directors. [*Concord, N. H.* 1827.] 12mo, pp. 11, (1). H. 52862

Also: First Annual Report of the New Hampshire Branch of the American Education Society, ... 1827. *Hanover: Printed by Thomas Mann.* 1827. 8vo, pp. 23, (1). Continued. H.

The New Hampshire Business Directory for ... 1868; a complete Index to the Mercantile, Manufacturing, and Professional Interests of the State. *Boston: Briggs & Co.* 1868. 8vo. C.

The New-Hampshire Calendar: or an Almanack, For ... 1795. ... By Abraham Weatherwise. *Newburyport: Printed by Blunt & March.* [n. d.] 8vo, pp. (24). BA. 52864

Report on the concerns of the New-Hampshire Cent Institution, For ... 1817. ... *Concord: Printed by George Hough.* 1817. 8vo, pp. 15. Continued. H. 52865

Report of the ... Trustees of the New Hampshire College of Agriculture and the Mechanic Arts, ... 1868. *Manchester: John B. Clarke, ... Printer.* 1868. 8vo, pp. 19. Continued. B.

Report of the Board of Managers of the N. H. Colonization Society, ... 1835. *Concord, N. H.: Chadwick & Kimball.* 1835. 8vo, pp. 34. H. 52867

The Ninth Annual Catalogue of the V. A. S. Association, of the N. H. Conference Seminary, Northfield, N. H., 1854–55. ... *Concord: Mower & Nye, Printers.* 1855. 16mo, pp. 16. H.

The New Hampshire Confession Revised. [n. p.:] *Baptist Publishing Society.* 1853. 18mo. 52869

The New-Hampshire Diary; or Almanack; For ... 1797. ... *Printed at Exeter, by H. Ranlet.* [n. d.] 12mo, pp. (52). BA.

The New-Hampshire Gazette, With the Freshest Advices Foreign and Domestick. Thursday, October 7. 1756. Numb. 1. *Portsmouth, in New-Hampshire: Printed by Daniel Fowle* ... . [n. d.] 4to, pp. 4. H. 52871

The first newspaper printed in New Hampshire. Reprinted in "The Celebration of the Centennial Anniversary," our Vol. III., No. 11653.

Collections of the New-Hampshire Historical Society, for ... 1824. Volume I. *Concord: Jacob B. Moore.* 1824. 8vo, pp. 336. Continued. BA. 52872

This collection includes Penhallow's "History of the Indian Wars, from 1703 to 1725," a great variety of ancient documents from manuscripts relating to the Indians, to the colonial history, witchcraft, the Quakers, etc.; Wheeler's "Narrative of an Expedition into the Nipmuch Country," in 1675; Bartlett's "Remarks on the Preservation of the Public Archives," original letters of distinguished men, biographical sketches, histories of the older towns in the State, etc. Vol. VIII. was published in 1866. *See* "North American Review," XVIII. 32–40. Also: The Act of Incorporation, Constitution, and By-Laws of the New-Hampshire Historical Society. ... *Concord: Printed by Jacob B. Moore.* 1823. 8vo, pp. 21, (2). H. — Constitution and By-Laws of the New-Hampshire Historical Society, with the names of Members and Officers. *Concord, N. H.* 1833 18mo, pp. 18. H.

An Act to incorporate ... the New Hampshire Iron Factory Company, ... with the Additional Acts, and the Bye-Laws ... . *Salem: Printed by Chapman and Palfray.* 1842. 24mo, pp. 21.

Also: A Report of the affairs of the New-Hampshire Iron Factory Co. and the Present State of its Works; with a view of its Future Prospects; ... . *Salem: Printed by Thomas C. Cushing.* 1810. 16mo, pp. 27. — Report to the Stockholders of the N. H. Iron Factory Company. [*Salem: Printed by W. Palfray, Jr.* 1816.] 8vo, pp. 8. B.

... The New Hampshire Journal of Education. ... Rev. Wm. L. Gage, A.M., Editor. ... Vol. I. No. 1. January, 1857. *Manchester, N. H.: B. F. Wallace.* 1857. 8vo. Continued. H.

The New-Hampshire Journal of Medicine. Edited by Edward H. Parker ... . Volume I. August, 1850, to ... 1851. *Concord, N. H.: G. Parker Lyon.* 1851. 8vo, pp. iv, 342. Continued. B. 52875

New Hampshire Mechanics and Art Association. First Exhibition at Concord, N. H. October 6, 1868. [n. p. n. d.] 8vo, pp. 11. H. 52876

Annual Circular of the New-Hampshire Medical Institution, 1840. [n. p. n. d.] 8vo. S. 52877

The Charter of the New-Hampshire Medical Society. ... With the By-Laws. ... Prefixed, A List of the Fellows ... Honorary Members, and ... Officers for ... 1816. ... *Concord:*

Printed by George Hough. 1816. 8vo, pp. 32. + For ... 1822. ... [*Ibid.*] 1822. 8vo, pp. 35, (1). B. 52878

Also: The By-Laws, Regulations and Police of the Centre-District New-Hampshire Medical Society. ... *Concord: Printed by Chase & Crosby.* 1840. 12mo, pp. 24. Continued. — The Charter, By-Laws, Regulations and Code of Ethics of the New-Hampshire Medical Society ... . *Concord: McFarland & Jenks, ... Printers.* 1860. 8vo, pp. 40. — Laws of the Eastern District of the New Hampshire Medical Society. *Exeter.* 1799. 8vo. — The Transactions of the New-Hampshire Medical Society, ... Held at Concord June 6th and 7th, 1854. *Concord: McFarland & Jenks.* 1854. 8vo, pp. 65. Continued. H.

Constitution of the New Hampshire Missionary Society, with an Address to all Christian People. *Concord.* 1801. 8vo, pp. 10.

Also: Annual Report of the Trustees of the New Hampshire Missionary Society. ... *Concord.* 1800. 8vo. Continued. — Seventeenth Annual Report on the ... Female Cent Institution, ... 1830. ... *Concord.* 1830. 12mo, pp. 12. Continued. H. — Statement of the Affairs of the ... Society, with an Address to the Public. *Concord.* 1803. 8vo, pp. 18. N.

The New Hampshire, New Jerusalem, and Primitive Religious Intelligencer. *Portsmouth.* 1805. 8vo. W. 52880

The New Hampshire Probate Directory ... . By Charles R. Morrison. *Concord: B. W. Sanborn & Co.* 1870. 12mo, pp. (4), 205. C. 52881

Proceedings of the New Hampshire Publishers, Editors and Printers' Association. ... 1868 ... [and] 1869. *Manchester: Printed by C. F. Livingston.* 1869. 8vo, pp. 35. H. 52882

New Hampshire Rambles. *New York.* 1809. 12mo. W.

Osborne's New-Hampshire Register; with an Almanack, for ... 1788. ... *Portsmouth: Printed ... by George Jerry Osborne.* [n. d.] 24mo, pp. (48). H. 52884

The earliest I have seen. The first was published in 1772, then in 1787, '88, '89, '94, '95, '96, '97, '98, and 1800, and annually thereafter. *See* Concord, No. 15143, *and* Curtis, No. 18062, in this Dictionary. From 1825 to 1838, it was edited by John Farmer; from 1838 to 1840, by Jacob B. Moore; 1841 to 1844, by Asa Fowler; from 1845 to 1872, or later, by G. Parker Lyon, as "The New Hampshire Annual Register, and United States Calendar." *See also* United States Repository.

Hill and Moore's Improved Edition of the New-Hampshire Register, and United States' Calendar, for ... 1822 ... . *Concord: Printed by Hill and Moore.* [n. d.] 24mo, pp. 144. H. 52885

Compiled by John Farmer.

The New-Hampshire Repository; ... . Conducted by Rev. William Cogswell, D.D. Volume I.–II. *Gilmanton: Printed by Alfred Prescott.* 1846–47. 8vo, pp. 292; iv, 9–152. H. 52886

Contains many historical sketches. Discontinued after the publication of Vol. II., No. 2, January, 1847. It was merged into the "New England Historical and Genealogical Register."

First Annual Report of the New-Hampshire Society for the Promotion of Temperance, ... June 2, 1830, ... with the Address of Rev. President Lord ... . *Concord: Printed by Asa M'Farland.* 1830. 8vo, pp. 16. Continued. 52887

Transactions of the New Hampshire State Agricultural Society, for 1850, 1851 and 1852. ... *Concord: Butterfield and Hill, ... Printers.* 1853. 8vo, pp. 400. Plates. Continued. B., C., H.

New Hampshire Statistical Almanac, and Political Manual for 1866. *Concord.* 1866. 18mo. + Second Edition. [*Ibid.*] C.

Third Annual Report to the New-Hampshire Unitarian Association ... 1835. *Concord, N. H.: Amos Head.* 1835. 16mo, pp. 16. H. 52890

Opinions of the ... Justices of the Superior Court of Judicature, on the Act ... "Establishing a Supreme Judicial Court, and Circuit Court of Common Pleas." *Concord: Printed by J. and W. R. Hill, Oct.* 1813. 8vo, pp. 24. H. 52891

The Perpetual Laws of ... New-Hampshire, from the Session of the General-Court, July 1776, to ... December 1788, continued into the ... Year 1789 ... . Printed from attested copies of the Original Acts. ... *Portsmouth: New-Hampshire, Printed by John Melcher.* M,DCC,LXXXIX. 8vo, pp. 256. B., H. 52892

The Political Manual for ... New-Hampshire. For ... 1866–67. *Concord: McFarland and Jenks.* [n. d.] 24mo, pp. 196. Continued. 52893

The above is the cover title; the inside title differs; it reads: "Rules of the Senate and House of Representatives, ... To which is added The Political Manual of New-Hampshire," etc. *See also* Vol. IX., No. 36028.

A Printed Copy of the Humble Address of Her Majesty's Council and Representatives of Her Majesty's Province of New-Hampshire in New-England, convened in General Assembly, this 25th day of July, 1706. to the Queen's most Excellent Majesty.

Title from Kennett's "Bibliothecæ Americanæ Primordia," page 194.

The Proceedings of the General Association of New-Hampshire. [*Charlestown: Samuel T. Armstrong, print.* 1809.] 8vo, pp. 8. B. 52895

Proceedings of the Grand Commandery of Knights Templar in ... New-Hampshire, ... 1867. *Manchester: Charles F. Livingston, Printer.* 1868. 12mo, pp. 117–211.

Proceedings of the Legislature of New Hampshire on the Important Subjects [the Conduct of Richard Evans and Clifton Clagett, late Justices of the Supreme Court,] referred to in the Governor's [John Taylor Gilman's] Speech, at the Opening of the Special Session, October 27, 1813: with the Yeas and Nays in both Branches, on accepting the Reports of the several Committees to whom the Subjects were referred. *Concord: Printed by George Hough, Nov.* 1813. 12mo, pp. 40. H. 52896

Proclamation for Thanksgiving, December, 1778. *Exeter: Zech. Fowle.* 1778. Folio, 1 leaf. 52897

M. Weare, President, John Langdon, Speaker.

Provincial Papers. *See* [Bouton (N.)], Vol. II., No. 6965.

The Public Laws of ... New-Hampshire, passed at a Session of the General Court, ... June, 1808. ... *Concord: Printed for the State.* 1809. 8vo, pp. 77, (2). Continued. BA. 52898

Report made to the Legislature of New Hampshire on the ... Insane. ... 1836. ... *Concord: Cyrus Barton, Printer.* 1836. 8vo, pp. 28. Continued. H. 52899

Report of Commissioners appointed to settle the Line between New-Hampshire and Maine. [November 13, 1828. *Concord, N. H.: A. M'Farland, Printer.* 1828.] 8vo, pp. 18. H. 52900

Corrected title of our No. 44014, Vol. XI. Also: Report of the Commissioners, on the Boundary Line between New-Hampshire and Massachusetts. [*Concord: June* 16, 1826.] 8vo, pp. 7. H. *See also* Vol. IX., No. 37471.

... Report of George C. Williams, W. A. Sanborn and John M. Whipple, commissioned ... to make Examination of the Public Lands ... . A. D. 1859. *Concord: Asa McFarland, ... Printer.* 1859. 8vo, pp. 23. H. 52901

Report of Hon. William Haile, upon an Act for the Suppression of Intemperance, ... in ... New-Hampshire. *Concord: Asa McFarland, ... Printer.* 1859. 8vo, pp. 23. H. 52902

Also: Report of Hon. Ichabod Goodwin, upon An Act for the Suppression of Intemperance, ... in ... New-Hampshire. *Concord: Asa McFarland, ... Printer.* 1860. 8vo, pp. 20. H.

Report of the Adjutant-General, ... June Session, 1859. *Concord: George G. Fogg, ... Printer.* 1859. 8vo, pp. 16. + June, 1860. *Concord.* 1860. 8vo. + May 20, 1862. *Concord: Henry McFarland, ... Printer.* 1862. 8vo, pp. 24. + 1863. *Concord.* 1863. 8vo, pp. 52. + June 1, 1866. *Concord: George E. Jencks, ... Printer.* 1866. 2 vols., 8vo, pp. xxxii, 716; xxviii, (2), 958. H. 52903

Report of the Auditor of Accounts of ... New Hampshire for ... 1865. *Concord: Amos Hadley, ... Printer.* 1865. 8vo, pp. xxiii, 111. Continued. 52904

Report of the Board of Trustees of the House of Reformation for Juvenile and Female Offenders, June, 1858. *Concord: George G. Fogg, ... Printer.* 1858. 8vo, pp. 13. Continued. H.

Also: First Annual Report of the Commissioners for locating and building House of Reformation ... June 11, 1856. *Concord: Amos Hadley, ... Printer.* 1856. 8vo, pp. 23. Folded Plate and Plans. B.

Report of the Commissioner of Common Schools ... of New Hampshire, ... 1847. ... *Hanover.* 1847. 8vo, pp. 95. Cont'd

Continued after 1850 as the "Annual Report of the Board of Education," and subsequently to 1865 as the "Annual Report of the Superintendent of Public Instruction." Also: Report of the Commissioners on the State Reform School, to ... the Governor of New-Hampshire, ... 1852. *Concord: Butterfield & Hill, ... Printers.* 1852. 8vo, pp. 21. Plate and 2 Plans. Continued. H.

Report of the Commissioners appointed to settle the line between New Hampshire and Maine. *Concord: Asa McFarland,* ... [1828.] 8vo, pp. 18. 52907

Report of the Commissioners appointed ... under a Resolution of the House, June 23, 1859, in regard to Town Courts. *Concord: Asa McFarland, ... Printer.* 1860. 8vo, pp. 24. H.

Report of the Commissioners on Fisheries, ... 1866. *Concord: George E. Jenks, ... Printer.* 1866. 8vo, pp. 16. H. 52909

Also: Report of the Select Committee on Fisheries. June Session, 1865. *Concord: George E. Jenks, ... Printer.* 1865. 8vo, pp. 8. B.

Report of the Commissioners to Indian Stream [Territory]. Nov. 1836. [*Concord, N. H.* 1836.] 8vo, pp. 72. Plan. B.

"On the 18 June, 1836, the Legislature of New Hampshire resolved to continue possession of the Indian Stream Territory, and maintain its jurisdiction, until the question of boundaries in dispute between the United States and Great Britain affecting the limits of said territory should be settled. Commissioners were appointed to visit that country and collect such information as they could find, and report in print. This is their report."—H. STEVENS.

Report of the Commissioners to revise, codify and amend, the Statute Laws of New-Hampshire, appointed ... June 30, 1865: with Notes and Citations. *Concord: George E. Jenks, Printer.* 1867. 8vo, pp. xv, 752. H. 52911

Report of the Commissioners upon the War Expenditures of the Towns and Cities in New-Hampshire. *Concord: George E. Jenks, ... Printer.* 1866. 8vo, pp. 32. H. 52912

Report of the Committee appointed by the Directors of the Winnipiseogee Canal to prepare a Statement ... *Dover, N. H.: ... J. Dickinson.* 1826. 8vo, pp. 24. 52913

Report of the Committee appointed to secure a survey of the Canal Route from the ... Piscataqua River by Alton Bay ... to Pemigewasset River near Plymouth. [n. p.:] *John Mann, Printer.* [1825.] 8vo, pp. 13. B. 52914

Report of the Committee ... upon the subject of an Agricultural College, with the Proposition of Hon. David Culver, ... and a Bill to establish the New Hampshire Agricultural College. *Concord: Amos Hadley, ... Printer.* 1864. 8vo, pp. 19. B.

... Report of the Committee on Banks, an Abstract of Bank Returns, and the Reports of the Bank Commissioners: ... 1846. *Concord: Asa McFarland, Printer.* 1846. 8vo, pp. 29. 52916

Report of the Committee on Claims, relative to the ... State National Bank. *Concord: Asa McFarland, State Printer.* 1860. 8vo, pp. 7. H. 52917

Report of the Insurance Commissioners ... 1852. *Concord: Butterfield and Hill, ... Printers.* 1852. 8vo, pp. 123. Cont'd.

Report of the Quartermaster General ... 1862. *Concord: Henry McFarland, ... Printer.* 1862. 8vo, pp. 12. Continued.

Report of the Select Committee of the House of Representatives on the Subject of building an Insane Hospital. ... *Concord: ... Hill & Barton, ... Printers.* 1832. 8vo, pp. 10. 52920

Report of the State Librarian to the New Hampshire Legislature; June Session, 1870. *Manchester: John B. Clarke, State Printer.* 1870. 8vo, pp. 16. B. 52921

Also: Report of the Trustees of the State Library. *Concord: George E. Jenks, ... Printer.* 1867. 8vo, pp. 8. 3 folded Plans. B.

Report of the State Treasurer, for the Fiscal Year ending June 1, 1859. *Concord.* 1859. 8vo, pp. 13. Continued. M.

Also: Reports of the Bank Commissioners, and the Quarterly Returns of the Banks: June Session, 1844. *Concord: Carroll & Baker, ... Printers.* 1844. 8vo, pp. 30. Continued. H.

The First Annual Report of the ... Trustees of the House of Reformation ... . June, 1857. *Concord: Amos Hadley, State Printer.* 1857. 8vo, pp. 11. Continued. B. 52923

Report of the Warden of the State Prison, June, 1835. ... *Concord: Cyrus Barton, Printer.* 1835. 8vo, pp. 15. Cont'd.

Reports of the Cases, the State *vs.* Samuel Small, ... and Andrew Pierce, Jr. & a. tried in the County of Strafford, January Term, 1842. *Concord: Asa McFarland.* 1842. 8vo, pp. 48.

Reports of the Railroad Commissioners, of ... New-Hampshire, June Session, 1849. *Concord: Butterfield & Hill, State Printers.* 1849. 8vo, pp. 16. Continued. H. 52926

Republican Address to the Electors of New Hampshire. *Walpole (N. H.).* 1804. 8vo, pp. 16. N. 52927

... Resolutions on National Affairs ... . June 24, 1859. [*Concord.* 1859.] 8vo, pp. 4. + June Session, 1860. [n. p. n. d.] 8vo, pp. 4. H. 52928

Revised Militia Law ... 1867. *Manchester.* 1868. 12mo.

The Revised Statutes of ... New Hampshire, passed December 23, 1842. ... *Concord: Carroll & Baker.* 1843. 8vo, pp. xv, 555. B., S. 52930

Samuel D. Bell and Charles J. Fox, revisers. Also: Supplementary Report of the Commissioners on the Revision of the Statutes. [n. p. 1867.] 8vo, pp. 16. H.

Rules and Orders of the Senate and House of Representatives of ... New-Hampshire ... . To which are added the Constitution of New-Hampshire and of the United States. *Concord: Printed by Cyrus Barton.* 1839. 24mo, pp. 46. Continued. H. 52931

The Speech of ... Governor Langdon to the Legislature of New-Hampshire, the Answer ... and the Protest ... June Session, 1811. [n. p.] 1811. 8vo, pp. 22. M. 52932

Strictures upon the Observations of a 'Member of Convention;' in answer to the "Author of some Remarks, &c." By a Freeman. ... *New-Hampshire: Printed—Seventeen Hundred, Ninety-two.* 8vo, pp. 15. B. 52933

Strike but Hear me. [n. p. 1817.] Folio, 1 leaf. 52934

Petition of Estwicke Evans to the Legislature of New Hampshire in relation to Salary of Richard Evans, Judge. June Session, 1817.

Sundry Acts and Laws ... passed from June 17 to Nov. 10, 1785. [n. p.] 1785. Folio. M. 52935

Temporary Laws of the Province of New Hampshire. [n. p. 1773.] Folio. M. 52936

To the Republican Electors of ... New Hampshire. [Signed "A Voter." n. p. 1827.] 8vo, pp. 7. 52937

Valedictory Address of ... Frederick Smyth, Governor of ... New-Hampshire, to the ... Legislature, June Session, 1867. *Concord: George E. Jenks, ... Printer.* 1867. 8vo, pp. 15. H.

Warden's Estimate of the Affairs of the State Prison. ... 1840. [n. p. n. d.] 8vo, pp. 3. B. 52939

Proceedings of the Second Annual State Convention of the Young Men's Christian Association, held at Nashua, October, 1869. *Concord.* 1870. 8vo. 52940

Since going to press with the New Hampshire list, the following additions and corrections have been furnished by MR. CHARLES H. BELL, *of Exeter, N. H., who has also assisted me with other titles.*

Acts and Laws, No. 52783, is a duplicate of No. 52784, the collation should read pp. vi, (4), 182.

An Address of the Convention, No. 52788, the date should read M,DCC,LXXXII.

An Address to the Electors of New Hampshire on the choice of Representatives to Congress. [Signed "Gracchus." n. p. 1814.] 12mo, pp. 24. 52941

An Appeal to the Citizens of New Hampshire in behalf of the Suffering Insane. ... *Portsmouth: C. W. Brewster* ... 1838. 8vo, pp. 12. 52942

Eastern Boundary of New Hampshire. Report of Henry O. Kent ... 1859. ... *Concord. George G. Fogg* ... 1859. 8vo, pp. 24

Facilitated Carriage, No. 52825, should read Facilitated Carrying.

Facts and Suggestions in relation to the present state of the Times, addressed to the People of New Hampshire by a Citizen. *Portsmouth.* 1838. 8vo, pp. 20. 52944

General Address to the Freemen of New Hampshire ... . [n. p. 1816.] 12mo, pp. 35. 52945

Letter to the Moderator of the New Hampshire Association, by Timothy. ... *Boston: ... Watson & Bangs.* 1812. 12mo, pp. 15. 52946

The Memorial of the Society of People of Canterbury ... and Enfield ... commonly called Shakers. [n. p. 1818.] 8vo, pp. 13

The Charter of the New Hampshire Medical Society, ... their Laws and Regulations ... a List of the present Fellows and of their Officers. ... *Printed at Exeter by Henry Ranlet,* MDCCXCII. 12mo, pp. 35. 52948

The Protest of the Minority of the House of Representatives against the Answer of the House to his Excellency's Speech, November Session, 1812. [n. p. 1812.] 12mo, pp. 8. 52949

Public Lands in New Hampshire. Report of George C. Williams ... commissioned ... to make examination ... 1859. *Concord: Asa McFarland* ... 1859. 8vo, pp. 23. 52950

For other anonymous books relating to New Hampshire, *see* Index.

NEW HAMPTON, *N. H.* Catalogue of the ... Academical and Theological Institution, New-Hampton, N. H. For ... 1831. *Concord: Printed by Fisk & Chase.* 1831. 12mo, pp. 21, (1). H. Continued. 52951

Also: Catalogue of the Literary Adelphi of the Academical and Theological Institution, at New Hampton, N. H. ... *Concord: Printed by Morrill, Silsby, & Co.* [n. d.] 12mo, pp. 22, (1). Continued.—Catalogue of the ... Literary and Theological Institution, Fairfax, Vt. 1859. *Burlington.* 1859. 8vo, pp. 32. Continued.—Catalogue of the ... Theological School at New Hampton, N. H., 1867. *Concord, N. H.: Printed by A. G. Jones.* 1867. 8vo, pp. 8.—Fifth Annual Report of the Young Ladies' Association of the New-Hampton Female Seminary, ... with the Constitution, etc. 1838–9. *Boston: Press of John Putnam.* 1839. 8vo, pp. 71. Continued. H.

NEW HANOVER COUNTY, *N. C.* Report [of the Committee appointed by the Citizens of New Hanover County, on the improvement of the Cape Fear Bar. n. p. 1854.] 8vo, pp. 8, (1)

The New-Harmony Gazette. ... *New-Harmony (Ind.).* 1826–1828. 3 vols., 4to. BA., C. 52953

Continued after 1828 in "The Free Enquirer." *See* Vol. VII., No. 25708.

NEW HAVEN, *Conn.* An Account of the Farmington ... Hampshire and Hampden ... and ... New Haven and Northampton [Canal] Compan[ies] ... . *New Haven: Thomas J. Stafford, Printer.* 1850. 8vo, pp. 24. B. 52954

An Act to Incorporate the City Bank of New Haven. [*New Haven:*] *Printed by S. Babcock.* MDCCCXXXV. 12mo, pp. 12.

An Address to the Episcopalians of the United States: considering the propriety of supporting the Episcopal Theological Seminary at New-Haven. [n. p. about 1818.] 8vo, pp. 12.

... Address of the Mayor, and Annual Reports of the City Auditor, ... Treasurer, Committee on Sinking Fund, Finance Committee ... . Also, the City Government for 1863–4, and Biographical Sketches of Mayors ... from 1784 to 1830 ... . *New Haven: Printed by Tuttle, Morehouse & Taylor.* 1863. 12mo, pp. 102. B. 52957

The American Mutual Life Insurance Company, of New Haven, Connecticut. ... *New Haven: T. J. Stafford, Printer.* 1852. 12mo, pp. xii, 69, (3). B. 52958

Ancient Waymarks. A Profession of Faith, By John Davenport, at the Institution of the First Church in New Haven, and the New Haven Catechism originally prepared for that Church, By John Davenport, Pastor, and William Hooke, Teacher. With a Preface, by Leonard Bacon, Pastor. *New Haven: Printed by B. L. Hamlen.* 1853. 12mo, pp. 72. 52959

Annual Report of the Board of Education of the New Haven City School District, For ... 1857. *New Haven: T. J. Stafford, Printer.* 1857. 8vo, pp. 24. Continued. B. 52960

Blue Laws of New Haven. *See* Vol. II., No. 6010.

Bye Laws of the City of New Haven, in Connecticut. As revised ... since the Ninth Day of May, ... One Thousand, Seven Hundred, and Eighty-Seven. *New-Haven: Printed by Thomas and Samuel Green.* M.DCC.XC. 4to, pp. 16. H. 52961

Also: By-Laws of the City of New-Haven, January, 1822. *New-Haven, (Conn.): Printed by Gray & Hewit.* 1822. 8vo, pp. 31.—By-Laws, Rules of Procedure, and Catalogue of Churches, with their Pastors, of the New Haven East Consociation. 1854. *New Haven: Printed by J. H. Benham.* 1854. 12mo, pp. 28.

Cases and Observations; by the Medical Society of New-Haven County, in ... Connecticut. ... *New-Haven: Printed by J. Meigs.* 1788. 8vo, pp. 86. H., N. 52962

Catalogue of Books in the New Haven Social Library; with the Constitution and By-Laws of the Company. *New Haven.* 1833. 8vo. 52963

Catalogue of the Members of the Church in the United Society in New Haven, formed by the Union of the White-Haven and

Fair-Haven Churches ... 1742, to ... 1855. ... *New Haven: Printed by Ezekiel Hayes.* 1855. 12mo, pp. 116. H. 52964

Also: Catalogue of the Members of the First Church in New Haven, from ... 1758, to ... 1847. ... *New Haven: Printed by B. L. Hamlen.* 1847. 12mo, pp. 126. + Supplement ... . From ... 1847, to ... 1853. To which is appended a Catalogue of the Persons admitted during the Ministry of Rev. James Pierpont and Rev. Joseph Noyes. *New Haven: Printed by B. L. Hamlen.* 1854. 12mo, pp. 47.—Catalogue of the Persons admitted to the First Church in New Haven, during the Ministry of the Rev. James Pierpont and the Rev. Joseph Noyes, From 1685 to 1757. ... *New Haven: Printed by B. L. Hamlen.* 1854. 12mo, pp. 37.

Catalogue of the New Haven Gymnasium. February, 1830. [n. p. n. d.] 8vo, pp. 8. H. 52965

Catalogue of the Officers and Students in the Collegiate and Commercial Institute, New Haven, Conn. For ... 1857. *New Haven: T. J. Stafford, Printer.* 1857. 8vo, pp. 51. Cont'd.

Charter, Constitution, and By-Laws of the Merchants' Exchange, of New Haven, Conn., ... with the Opening Address, By James Brewster, Esq. *New Haven: T. J. Stafford, Printer.* 1866. 8vo, pp. 38. B. 52967

The Charter of the City of New-Haven; Granted by the General Assembly of the State of Connecticut, holden at New-Haven, on the eighth Day of January, 1784. *New-Haven: Thomas and Samuel Green.* 1784. 4to, pp. 16. 52968

Also: Charter and By-Laws of ... New Haven, June, 1865. *New Haven: J. H. Benham, Printer.* 1865. 8vo, pp. 152. H.

The Church Knaviad, or Horace in West Haven. A Slight Touch of the Serio-Comic, touching Church Knavery. By Horatius Flaccus. *New Haven.* 1864. 12mo, pp. 91. 52969

College [proposed] for Colored Youth. An Account of the New-Haven City Meeting and Resolutions, with Recommendations of the College, and Strictures upon the Doings of New-Haven. *New-York: The Committee.* 1831. 8vo, pp. 24. H.

The Connecticut Diary: or, Almanack for the Year ... 1756 ... for the Meridian of New-Haven. *New Haven: J. Parker.* [n. d.] 12mo. 52971

The Constitution and Rules of the Associated Pastors of New Haven Center. *New Haven: Printed by Ezekiel Hayes.* 1856. 18mo, pp. 12. 52972

The Constitution, Profession of Faith, and Covenant, of the ... United Congregational Society in ... New-Haven: ... with ...

the Officers and Members, From ... 1796, to ... 1823. *New-Haven: Printed by A. H. Maltby and Co.* 1822. 24mo, pp. 34, (1)

Also: The Constitution, Confession of Faith, & Covenant, of the Third Congregational Church in New Haven. *New Haven.* 1831. 12mo, pp. 14. W.

Constitution of the Mechanic Library Society, and Catalogue of Books. *New Haven.* 1792. 8vo. 52974

The Declaration of the Association of the County of New Haven, in Connecticut, Feb. 19, 1744–5, concerning the Conduct of the Rev. George Whitefield. *Boston.* 1745. 8vo, pp. 8

Defence of the Doings of the Consociation. *See* [Todd (J.)]

A Dissertation at the Public Commencement at New Haven. [n. p.] 1772. 8vo. 52976

See also Yale College.

Engineer's Report on the Survey from New Haven City up the Canal to Plainville, and thence to Collinsville, in the Farmington Valley. *New Haven: Hitchcock & Stafford, Printers.* 1845. 8vo, pp. 24. B. 52977

Female Education Society. *See* Vol. IV., No. 15723.

Outline of the Franklin Institution of New-Haven. [*New Haven.* n. d.] 8vo, pp. (2), 10. B. 52978

Second Annual Report of the Home for the Friendless, New Haven, Dec. 2, 1868. *New Haven: J. H. Benham & Son, Printers.* 1869. 8vo, pp. 18. Continued. B. 52979

French Spoliations. [*New Haven.* 1843.] 8vo. 52980

This is a petition of the inhabitants of New Haven on this subject. *See also* Vol. VII., No. 25889.

History of the City Burial Ground, in New Haven, together with the Names of Owners of Lots therein. ... *New Haven: Printed ... by J. H. Benham.* 1863. 8vo, pp. 56. Plan. B.

Journal of the Proceedings of the Convention held in New Haven, May, 1811. *New York.* 1811. 8vo, pp. 36. 52982

The Lectures delivered before the American Institute of Instruction, at New Haven, Conn., August, 1853; including the Journal of Proceedings, and a List of the Officers. *Boston.* 1854. 8vo, pp. xv, 77. 52983

A Letter from the Association, of the County of New-Haven, to the Reverend Elders in the Colonies of Rhode-Island and Massachusetts-Bay who assisted in the Ordination of the Rev. Mr. John Hubbard at Meriden, June 22, 1769. To which are annexed, Remarks ... . *New-Haven: T. & S. Green.* [n. d.] 8vo, pp. 24. S. 52984

Corrected title of our No. 33431, Vol. VIII. For a reply, *see* [Breck (R.)], II. 7655.

Manual of the First Church in New Haven, 1860; including ... catalogues of the present Members, and of those admitted during the Ministry of Rev. James Davenport. *New Haven: Printed by E. Hayes.* 1860. 12mo, pp. 60. 52985

Also: Manual ... and Catalogue of the United Congregational Society. *New Haven.* 1842. 8vo.

Memorial of the Merchants of New Haven, in the State of Connecticut. ... *Washington: A. and G. Way, Printers.* 1811. 8vo, pp. 6. BA. 52986

New Haven as it Is ... . *New Haven.* 1845. 12mo. Map and Plates. B. 52987

Papers of the New Haven Colony Historical Society. Vol. I. *New Haven: The Society.* 1865. 8vo, pp. (4), 15, 170; (2), iv, 192. 52988

Annual Report of the New-Haven County Bible Society, auxiliary to the American Bible Society. [n. p.:] *August* 20, 1829. 12mo, pp. 12. Continued. B. 52989

Charter and By-Laws of the New Haven County Horticultural Society. *New Haven: Printed by J. H. Benham.* 1847. 18mo, pp. 11. B. 52990

Also: Transactions of the New-Haven County Horticultural Society, for ... 1847. *New Haven.* 1847. 8vo, pp. 20. S.

Patten's New Haven Directory, for ... 1840. ... *New Haven: James M. Patten.* 1840. 12mo, pp. 136, Supplement, 12. Map. Continued. H., S. 52991

The New-Haven Gazette, and the Connecticut Magazine, For ... M.DCC.LXXXVI. ... *New-Haven: Printed by Meigs & Dana.* [n. d.] 4to, pp. 360, Index, (2). B., S. 52992

Two or more volumes published. Edited by J. Meigs.

Annual Catalogue of the ... New Haven Hopkins Grammar School, ... July, 1856. *New Haven: Printed by S. Babcock.* 1856. 16mo, pp. 16. H. 52993

Transactions of the New Haven Horticultural and the New Haven County Agricultural Societies, for 1841. Vol. I. *New Haven.* 1842. 8vo. S. 52994

Also: Report of the Managers of the Horticultural Fair, held September 25th, 1838. At ... New-Haven. *New-Haven: Babcock & Galpin, Printers.* 1838. 8vo, pp. 11, (1).—By-Laws ... . Oct. 1837. 8vo, pp. 4. S.

First Annual Report of the New Haven Ladies' Greek Association. *New-Haven: Printed by Nathan Whiting.* 1831. 8vo, pp. 64. B. 52995

Also: Report of the Proceedings of the New Haven Ladies' Greek Association, ... August 19, 1833. [n. p. n. d.] 8vo, pp. 8. H.

Constitution and By-Laws of the New Haven Medical Association. ... *New Haven: Hitchcock & Stafford, Printers.* MDCCCXLII. 8vo, pp. 12. B. 52996

Also: A Report of the New Haven County Medical Society, on ... Repealing ... the Medical Laws ... [excluding] Irregular Practitioners from the ... Collection of Fees. *New Haven: Printed by B. L. Hamlen.* 1837. 8vo, pp. 16. B.

The New-Haven Memorial to the President protesting against the Use of the United States Army to enfore the Bogus Laws of Kansas; the Answer of President Buchanan; and the Reply of the Memorialists. [*Boston.* 1857.] 8vo, pp. 12. BA. 52997

The New Haven Remonstrance. *See* [Coleman (W.)], Vol. VI., No. 23365, *and* Vol. XI., No. 40117.

Charter of the New Haven Water Company, with Amendments. *New Haven: Printed by J. H. Benham.* 1860. 12mo, pp. 19. B. 52998

Also: The Second Annual Report of the ... Directors of the ... Company, ... 1864. *New Haven: Printed by J. H. Benham.* 1864. 12mo, pp. 12. Continued. B.

Catalogue of the Instructors and Pupils, in the New Haven Young Ladies' Institute, during its first Year. November, 1830. [n. p.] 1830. 8vo, pp. 12. B. 52999

See Yale College.

Annual Report of the ... New Haven Young Men's Institute. August 3, 1842. *New Haven: Hitchcock & Stafford, Printers.* MDCCCXLII. 8vo, pp. 6, (2). Continued. H. 53000

Also: Catalogue of the Library of the ... Institute. ... *New-Haven.* 1841. 8vo.

A Plan for Insurance. *See* [Boardman (W. W.)], II. 6092.

Proceedings of the Citizens of New Haven, in relation to the United States Branch Bank. *New Haven.* 1816. 8vo. 53001

Proceedings of the City of New-Haven, in the Removal of Monuments from its Ancient Burying-Ground, and in the Opening of a New Ground for Burial. *New-Haven, (Conn.): Gray & Hewit, Printers. January,* 1822. 8vo, pp. 32. Plan. B.

Contains lists of the early settlers.

The Proceedings of the Union Meeting, ... October 24, 1850, ... *New Haven: Printed by William H. Stanley.* 1851. 8vo, pp. 48. BA. 53003

Records of the Colony and Plantation of New Haven, from 1638 to 1649. Transcribed and Edited ... with occasional Notes and an Appendix. By Charles J. Hoadly, M.A. ... *Hartford: Printed by Case, Tiffany and Company.* 1857. 8vo, pp. vii, 547. BA. 53004

Records of the Colony or Jurisdiction of New Haven, from May, 1653 to the Union. Together with the New Haven Code of 1856. Transcribed and Edited ... By Charles J. Hoadly, M.A. ... *Hartford: Printed by Case, Lockwood and Company.* 1858. 8vo, pp. iv, 626. BA. 53005

See also Vol. IV., No. 15797.

Report and Resolutions in favor of a loan of credit by the City, in aid of a Canal. *New Haven: Hitchcock & Stafford, Printers.* 1839. 8vo, pp. 8. B. 53006

Report of a Committee of the First Ecclesiastical Society of New Haven, on ... ventilating their Meeting House. *New Haven: Printed by B. L. Hamlen.* 1840. 8vo, pp. 12. 53007

Report of the Committee, appointed to Inquire into the Condition of the New Haven Burying Ground, and to Propose a Plan for its Improvement. *New Haven: Printed by B. L. Hamlen.* 1839. 8vo, pp. 28. Plan. B. 53008

Report of the Committee ... in New Haven, to aid in furnishing Supplies to the Sick and Wounded Soldiers of our Army, October, 1861. [n. p. n. d.] 8vo, pp. 7. 53009

Report of the Committee on supplying Water, for the City of New Haven. *New Haven: T. J. Stafford, Printer.* 1853. 8vo, pp. 72, (1). H. 53010

Report of the Committee ... [on the] Bill ... to divide the City of New Haven into Wards; ... . *Hartford.* 1843. 8vo, pp. 11. 53011

Report of the ... School Visitors of the First School Society of New Haven, ... 1850. *New-Haven: Printed by Thomas J. Stafford.* 1850. 8vo, pp. 16. Continued. B. 53012

Report to the Stockholders in the New Haven County Bank, at their ... Meeting, held ... 1858 ... . *New Haven: Printed by Thomas J. Stafford.* 1858. 8vo, pp. 68. 53013

Also: Report of the Special Committee concerning the City Bank of New Haven. *Hartford.* 1830. 8vo.

Sketch of the Rise and Progress of the First Baptist Church in New Haven. [n. p. 1823.] 12mo. W. 53014

Third Anniversary of St. Paul's Missionary Society. *New Haven.* 1855. 8vo. 53015

The First Annual Report of the Washington Temperance Society of New Haven: ... 1842. *New Haven: Printed by William Storer, Jun.* 1842. 8vo, pp. 15. Continued. B.

Name afterwards changed to "Martha Washington Temperance Society."

New-Haven's | Settling in | New-England. | And some | Lawes | for Government: | Published for the Use of that Colony. | Though some of the Orders intended for | present convenience, may probably | be hereafter altered, | and as need requireth other | Lawes added. | *London, Printed by M. S. for Livewell Chapman.* 1656. Sm. 4to, pp. (2), 81. BA., W. 53017

Four copies only known on this side of the Atlantic.

New Havens Settling in New England. And some Lawes for Government, etc. 1656. *Reprinted Hartford: Case, Lockwood & Company.* 1858. 4to. 53018

This accurate and beautiful reprint was made by Mr. Charles J. Hoadly, State Librarian, and an edition of only twenty copies was separately printed, on thick paper.

New Hieroglyphical Bible, &c. *Boston: W. Norman.* [1794.] 12mo, pp. 144. 53019

"A Mr. Thompson was the author of this volume."—Dr. O'Callaghan.

A New History of Jamaica. *See* Vol. IX., No. 35636.

New Hope; Or, the Rescue. A Tale of the Great Kanawha. *New York.* 1855. 2 vols., 12mo. 53020

A spirited and graphic picture of Western life.

The New Icon; or, a Portrait and its Companion, exhibiting the Triumph of T——: with an Expostulary Address to the

Abbé Mably, Author of Letters to the United States of America. *London.* [1784.] 8vo, pp. 24. J.C.B. 53021

A privately printed tract against Arnold the traitor.

In the Matter of the Panoche Grande Rancho. ... Memorial of the New Idria Mining Co. of California. *San Francisco: Printed by Mullin, Mahon & Co.* 1867. 8vo, pp. 16. H. 53022

A new interlude and a mery of the | nature of the. iiij. elements declarynge many pro | per poynts of phylosophy natural, and of dyuers | straunge landys, and of dyuers straunge effects & | causis, whiche interlude yf ȳ hale matter be played | wyl conteyne the space of an hour and a halfe, but yf ye lyst ye may leue out muche of the sad mater | as the messengers p̄te, and some of naturys parte | and some of experyens p̄te & yet the matter wyl de | pend conuenyently, and than it wyll not be paste | thre quarters of a hour of length. | [n. p. n. d.] 8vo. BM. 53023

"Treats, among other things, 'Of certeyn poynts of cosmography, as how and where the see covereth the yerth, and of dyvers straunge regyons and landys, and whiche wey they lye, and of the new found landys, and the maner of the people.'" Mr. Collier quotes this passage:

"But this newe lands founde lately
Ben callyd America, by cause only
Americus dyd furst them fynde."

"First impression dated 25 Oct., 11 Henry VIII."—MS. note on the Garrick copy. The interlude will be found described in Collier's "Annals of the British Stage," II. 319, Ames's "Typographical Antiquities" (edited by Dibdin), III. 105, and Beloe's "Anecdotes," I. 338–341. *See* [Harrisse] "Bib. Am. Vet., Additions," p. 50.

The New Internal Revenue Law of June 30, 1864, with the Amendment of March, 1865, Index and Table of Taxation. *New York: Banker's Magazine Office.* 1865. 8vo, pp. 150. + [Another Edition] with copious Marginal References ... . *New York: D. Appleton & Company.* 1864. 8vo, pp. (4), 122.

A New Introduction to the Knowledge and Use of Maps; to which is added, an Appendix, containing Remarks on Dr. Solander and Mr. Banks's Voyage to the Southern Hemisphere, and also some late Discoveries near the North Pole. *London.* 1774. 12mo. Maps. 53025

New Ipswich, *N. H.* Annual Reports of the Selectmen ... of ... New Ipswich, for ... 1867–8. *Groton Junction, Mass.: Printed by John H. Turner.* 1868. 8vo, pp. 23. H. 53026

Catalogue of ... New Ipswich Academy, at New Ipswich, N. H., ... 1845. *Fitchburg: W. J. Merriam, Printer.* 1845. 12mo, pp. 12. Continued. H. 53027

With the catalogue for 1853–4 the name changes to "New Ipswich Appleton Academy." *See also* Vol. VII., No. 28090.

Report of the ... School Committee, of New Ipswich, N. H., for ... 1855–6. *Groton Junction: Printed by George H. Brown.* 1856. 8vo, pp. 18, (2). Continued. H. 53028

New Ireland. Considerations on the Sovereignty, Independence, Trade and Fisheries of New-Ireland (formerly known by the name of Nova-Scotia) and the Adjacent Islands. [n. p. 1782.] 18mo, pp. 24. C., N., P. 53029

Corrected title of our No. 16009, Vol. IV. *See also* No. 16073, and add pp. 45.

New Jamaica. *See* Vol. IX., Nos. 35637–8.

New Jersey.

Abstract of the Population and Statistics of New Jersey, according to the Census of 1850. *Somerville.* 1852. 8vo.

An | Abstract, | or | Abbreviation | Of some Few of the | Many (Later and Former) Testimonys | from the | Inhabitants of | New-Jersey, | And Other | Eminent Persons, | Who have Wrote particularly concerning | That Place. | *London, Printed by Thomas Milbourn, in the Year,* 1681. | 4to, pp. 32. 53031

An Account of the College of New-Jersey. In which are described the methods of government, modes of instruction, manner and expences of living in the same, &c. With a Prospect of the College neatly engraved. Published, by order of the Trustees, for the information of the Public; particularly of the friends and benefactors of the institution, in Europe and America. *Woodbridge, in New-Jersey: Printed by James Parker.* 1704. 8vo, pp. 47. Plate. BA., P. 53032

An interesting sketch of the early history of this college, including all the minor details of its management, even to the fact that at the Commons table there was meat every day "and sometimes pyes." A note, referring to the plate, says "the Court-yard is represented as inclosed by a pall-fence, in like manner with that of the president's house: But this is done only from the fancy of the engraver." The engraving referred to is frequently lacking.

An Account of the Remains of a Fossil Extinct Reptile; recently discovered at Haddonfield, New Jersey. *Philadelphia.* 1859. 8vo. 53033

An Act for better Settling and Regulating the Militia of this Colony, of New-Jersey; for the repelling Invasions ... . [n. p. n. d.] 4to, pp. 14. P. 53034

An Act for establishing six State Banks in the State of New Jersey, passed at Trenton, January 28th, 1812. *Morristown, February*, 1812. 8vo, pp. 14. N. 53035

An Act of Incorporating of the New Jersey Navigation Company. *Trenton.* 1804. 8vo. 53036

An Act of the Legislature of New Jersey, relative to the unincorporated Society of Friends in that State. ... *London: J. Masters, Printer.* 1836. 8vo, pp. 8. 53037

An Act to establish A System of Public Instruction for ... New Jersey, ... By the State Superintendent ... . *Trenton, N. J.* 1867. 8vo, pp. 47. H. 53038

An Act to Restrain the Trade and Commerce of New Jersey, Maryland, &c. [n. p.] 1775. Folio. 53039

An Act upon that Solemn Affirmation and Declaration of the People called Quakers etc. Passed in the Province of New Jersey in the 13th Year of the Reign of Queen Anne. *William Bradford, Printer, New York.* 1716. Folio. 53040

This is one of the Session Acts of 1716. Mr. Trumbull, in his Catalogue of the Brinley Library, No. 4296, describes others with a query as to the printer—this seems to settle the question.

Acts and Laws of the Province of New Jersey, as they were enacted at the last Session of Assembly held at Perth Amboy, beginning the 7th of May, 1730. *New York: Printed by William Bradford.* 1730. Folio. 53041

Acts Incorporating the Delaware and Raritan Railway Company, the Camden and Amboy Railroad ... and the New Jersey Railroad ... . *Trenton.* 1849. 8vo. 53042

The Acts Of the General Assembly Of the Province of New-Jersey, From the Time of the Surrender of the Government of the said Province, to the Fourth Year of the Reign of King George the Second. Collected and Published by Order of the said Assembly. With a Table of the Principal Matters therein contained. *Philadelphia: Printed and Sold by William and Andrew Bradford, Printers to the King's Most Excellent Majesty, for the Province of New-Jersey,* MDCCXXXII. Folio, pp. (14), 332 and over. 53043

The Acts of the General Assembly of the Province of New-Jersey, From the Time of the Surrender of the Government in the Second Year of the Reign of Queen Anne, to this present

Time, being the Twenty-fifth Year of the Reign of King George the Second. Collected .... With Proper Tables; and an Alphabetical Index containing all the Principal Matters .... By Samuel Nevill, Esq; Second Justice of the Supreme Court of Judicature of the said Province. [n. p.:] *Printed by William Bradford, Printer to the King's Most Excellent Majesty for the Province of New-Jersey,* MDCCLII. Folio, pp. (4), 507. N., P. 53044

Thomas ("History of Printing," II. 121) says this edition was printed at Woodbridge by James Parker.

The Acts of the General Assembly of the Province of New-Jersey, From the Year 1753, being the Twenty-sixth of the Reign of King George the Second, where the First Volume ends, to the Year 1761, being the First of King George the Third. With proper Tables; and an alphabetical Index; containing all the principal Matters ... Together with an Appendix; containing the several Acts of Parliament now in Force in America, relating to his Majesty's Forces, and the Articles of War. Collected .... By Samuel Nevill, Esq; ... . Volume the Second. *Woodbridge, in New-Jersey: Printed by James Parker, Printer to the King's Most Excellent Majesty, for the Province.* M.DCC.LXI. Folio, pp. x, (2), 401. N., P. 53045

The appendix (pp. 64) was printed separately in the preceding year, but is usually bound with this work.

Acts of the General Assembly of the Province of New-Jersey, from the Surrender of the Government to Queen Anne, on the 17th day of April, in the Year of our Lord 1702, to the 14th day of January 1776. To which is annexed, The Ordinance for regulating and establishing the Fees of the Court of Chancery of the said Province. With three Alphabetical Tables and an Index. Compiled ... By Samuel Allinson. ... *Burlington: Printed by Isaac Collins* ... . M.DCC.LXXVI. Folio, pp. viii, 493, Appendix, 6, Ordinance, 6, Tables, 4, 4, 3, Index, 15. BA., P., S. 53046

Acts of the General Assembly of the State of New Jersey. *Trenton.* 1777. Folio. N. 53047

Continued to 1787 in folio, afterwards in 8vo.

Acts of the Council and General Assembly of the State of New-Jersey from the Establishment of the present Government ... to ... 1783; With the Constitution prefixed. ... Compiled under the Appointment of the Legislature, By Peter Wilson, A.M. *Trenton: Printed by Isaac Collins* ... . M.DCC.LXXXIV. Folio, pp. x, 389, 28, 4, 30. N. 53048

Address and Suppressed Report of the Minority of the Committee on Elections on the New Jersey Case. ... March 10, 1840, ... with the Remarks of Mr. Fillmore. ... *Washington.* 1840. 8vo, pp. 16. H. 53049

Address of a Convention of Delegates of the People of New-Jersey ... held by public appointment ... Trenton, 4 July, 1812. *Canandaigua, N. Y.* 1812. 8vo, pp. 8. S. 53050

Also: Address of the Convention to the Free Electors of New Jersey. [n. p.] 1814. 8vo. C.

Address of the Officers and Standing Committee of the New Jersey Monument Association. ... *Trenton, N. J.: Murphy & Bechtel, Printers.* 1859. 8vo, pp. 15. Plate and Map. 53051

Address of the Presbytery of New Jersey, to the Churches under their Care. *Elizabeth-Town, N. J.* [1811.] 8vo, pp. 8.

Address, Resolutions & Proceedings of the Anti-Monopoly State Convention, held at Trenton, N. J., Jan. 22d, 1868, to oppose The Extension of the Monopoly Privileges of the Camden & Amboy Railroad Co. ... [n. p. n. d.] 8vo, pp. 24. H.

Address to the Federal Republicans of the State of New Jersey, recommending the choice of Aaron Ogden, and others, for Representatives in the Seventh Congress, United States. *Trenton.* 1800. 8vo, pp. 16. N. 53054

An Address to the Freeholders of New-Jersey, on the subject of Public Salaries. *Philadelphia: ... Andrew Stewart* ... . MDCCLXIII. 8vo, pp. 24. P. 53055

Subscribed "J. W." Dated "H——n, March 16, 1763," and very rare.

Address to the People of New Jersey on the Present Crisis. Reported to the Democratic State Convention, by the Central Committee, September 11, 1834. [n. p. n. d.] 8vo, pp. 16.

See also [Doane (G. W.)], Vol. v., No. 20383.

Addresses Delivered at the Presentation of the Portrait of Abraham Lincoln, by the Committee of the House of Assembly, February 12, 1867. *Trenton, N. J.* 1867. 8vo, pp. 26.

An Analytical Index to the Colonial Documents of New Jersey, in the State Paper Offices of England, Compiled by Henry Stevens. Edited with Notes, and References to Printed Works and Manuscripts in other Depositories, By William A. White-

head. *New York: D. Appleton and Company.* 1858. 8vo, pp. xxix, 499. 53058

Forms Vol. v. of the "Collections of the New Jersey Historical Society."

Anno Regni Georgii Regis Magnæ Britanniæ ... . At a Session of the General Assembly of the Colony of New-Jersey, begun the twenty fourth day of September, Anno Domini 1723, and continued by Adjournments to the 30th Day of November following, at which time the following Acts were Published. *Printed by William Bradford in the City of Perth-Amboy.* 1723. Folio, pp. 30. S. 53059

One of the Session Laws, which was followed by others with the same general title. The next we have seen is for Session May 25 to August 23, 1725. *Printed and sold by William Bradford in New York and by Andrew Bradford in Philadelphia.* 1725. Folio, pp. 115–132, 19–24. S.

Anno Regni Georgii II. Regis Magnæ Britanniæ ... . At a Session of the General Assembly of the Province of New-Jersey, held at Elizabeth-Town, the 24th of May, 1757 ... . A Supplementary Act to the Act, ... Regulating the Militia ... . *Woodbridge: Printed by James Parker* ... . [1757.] 12mo, pp. 18.

Anno Regni Georgii III. Regis Magnæ Britanniæ ... . At a Session began at Burlington, ... November 10, 1773, and continued until the 11th day of March following. Being the second Session of the Twenty-second Assembly of New-Jersey. *Burlington: Printed by Isaac Collins, Printer to the King, for the Province of New-Jersey.* M.DCC.LXXIV. Folio, pp. 109. P. 53061

A handsome and extremely rare volume.

Annual Report of the Agricultural Society of ... New Jersey, for ... 1860. *Trenton, N. J.* 1861. 8vo, pp. 107. B. 53062

Also: Report of the Committee of Agriculture of the Legislative Council of New Jersey. *Trenton.* 1839. 8vo, pp. 8. — Report of the House Committee on Agriculture of ... New Jersey, for ... 1866. *Trenton, N. J.* 1866. 8vo, pp. 11. — Report of the State Agricultural Society of New Jersey, for ... 1855 and 1856. *Trenton.* 1857. 8vo, pp. 147. Continued. S.

Annual Report of the Condition of the New Jersey State Prison ... . *Trenton.* 1856. 8vo, pp. 37. Continued. S. 53063

Annual Report of the Superintendent of Public Schools ... for ... 1847. ... *Trenton: Printed by Sherman and Harron.* 1848. 12mo, pp. 60, (1). Continued. BA. 53064

Also: Annual Report of the Trustees of the School Fund of ... New Jersey. ... *Trenton: Printed by Sherman and Harron.* 1842. 8vo, pp. 53. Continued. H.

Annual Reports of the State Directors of the Joint Companies, and the several Railroad and Canal Companies of the State of New Jersey, for ... 1868. *Trenton, N. J.: True American Office.* 1869. 8vo, pp. 84. Continued. 53065

An Answer to a Bill in the Chancery of New-Jersey, at the Suit of John Earl of Stair, and others, Commonly called Proprietors of the Eastern Division of New-Jersey, Against Benjamin Bond, and others claiming under the original Proprietors and Associates of Elizabeth-Town. To which is added; Nothing either of The Publications of The Council of Proprietors of East New-Jersey, or of the Pretences of the Rioters, and their Seducers; except so far as the Persons meant by Rioters, Pretend Title against the Parties to the above Answer; But a great Deal of the Controversy, though Much Less of the History and Constitution of New-Jersey, than the said Bill. ... Published by Subscription. *New-York: Printed and Sold by James Parker, at the New Printing-Office, in Beaver-Street.* 1752. Folio, pp. 48. P.

Signed by William Livingston and William Smith, Jr., as Counsel for the 452 defendants, whose names appear in this answer. For the "Bill," *see* Vol. II. 5378.

An Answer to the Council of Proprietors two Publications; Sett forth at Perth-Amboy the 25th of March 1746, and the 25th of March 1747. As also some Observations on Mr. Nevil's Speech to the House of Assembly, in Relation to a Petition presented to the House of Assembly, met at Trentown in the Province of New-Jersey in May 1746. *New-York: Printed and Sold by the Widow Catherine Zenger at the Printing-Office in Stone-Street.* 1747. Folio, pp. 13. 53067

The only book I have seen with this imprint. Excessively rare.

An Answer to the Notes and Observations upon the Votes of the Assembly of New Jersey. *Woodbridge, N. J.* 1743. 4to.

Answer To what has been offer'd as Argument against the Validity and Force of an Act of Assembly, Entituled, An Act upon that Solemn Affirmation and Declaration of the People called Quakers etc. Passed in the Province of New Jersey in the 13th Year of the Reign of Queen Anne. *Printed and Sold by William Bradford in New York; sold also by Andrew Bradford in Philadelphia.* 1716. Folio, pp. 8. 53069

An Appeal to the Congress of the United States on the subject of Bank Tax and Bank Currency, By a Committee of New

Jersey State Bank Officers. *Trenton, N. J.: Printed at the "True American" Office.* 1864. 8vo, pp. 18. 53070

Corrected title of our No. 3176, Vol. I.

An Appeal to the Legislative Council and General Assembly of ... New-Jersey, on behalf of the Religious Society of Friends, commonly called Quakers. *Philadelphia: Printed by Joseph Rakestraw.* 1836. 8vo, pp. 72. H., M., S. 53071

An Appendix, Containing, Abstracts of Such Parts of the Acts of Parliament relating to the Army, as concern the Colonies of North-America. *Woodbridge: Reprinted by Order of the General Assembly of the Province of New-Jersey, by James Parker, Printer to the Province.* MDCCLX. Folio, pp. 64. P. 53072

Designed as an Appendix to the Laws of New Jersey, published in 1752, but when in 1761, Vol. II. of the Laws appeared, it was substituted as an Appendix to that volume, and is always so found.

Beauties of the ... Monopoly System. *See* [Carey (H.)]

Bericht des Boards der Commissäre für Versorgung Invalider New Jersey Soldaten. *Newark.* 1865. 8vo. 53073

Bill in the Chancery of New Jersey at the Suit of Robert Barclay against William, Earl of Stirling, and others, Proprietors of the Eastern Division of the Province of New Jersey. *Burlington.* 1773. Folio. 53074

See also our Vol. II., Nos. 5378–79, *and* Stirling (*Earl of*).

The Bill of Complaint in the Chancery of New Jersey, brought by Thomas Clarke, and others, against James Alexander Esq., and others, commonly called the Proprietors of East New Jersey, etc. *New-York.* 1760. Folio. N. 53075

Body of the Laws of the Province of New Jersey. *Philadelphia.* 1742. Folio. 53076

Boyd's Business Directory of ... New Jersey, ... with a General Directory of the Citizens of Newark, ... and an Appendix ... 1860. *Philadelphia, Pa.: William H. Boyd.* [n. d.] 8vo, pp. xi, 50–410. H. 53077

A Brief Account of the Province of East-Jersey, in America, published by the present proprietors, for information of all such persons who are or may be inclined to settle themselves, families, and servants in that country. *London.* 1682. 4to, pp. 8.

Title as quoted by Rich, No. 397—perhaps intended for the following work:

A | Brief Account of the | Province | of | East: New: Jarsey | in | America: | Published by the | Scots Proprietors | Having Interest there. | For the Information of such, as may have a Desire to Transport them- | selves, or their Families thither. | Wherein | The Nature and Advantage of, and Interest in a Forraign Plantation | to this Country is Demonstrated. | *Edinburgh,* | *Printed by John Reid, Anno Dom.* 1683. Sm. 4to. 53079

Mr. S. L. M. Barlow, of New York, possesses the only known copy. It was reprinted in the "Historical Magazine," Vol. I., Second Series, and twenty-five copies were issued separately, 16mo, pp. (3), 28.

Brief History of the New Jersey Congressional Election of 1838. [n. p. n. d.] 8vo, pp. 16. 53080

A Brief of the Claim. *See* Vol. II., No. 7884.

A Brief State of the Controversy. *See* Vol. II., No. 7902.

A Brief Vindication. *See* Vol. II., No. 7919.

This excessively rare piece "is addressed 'to the Inhabitants of *Newark* and the rest of the American Brethren,' and is subscribed by the author (Griffin Jenkin), p. 32. The Preface (pp. iii–vi) is followed by 'some few Verses, presented with an Intention to soften the Heart' of the reader, before coming to 'the main Intention of the Letter' (pp. vii–xi), and a few pious 'Ejaculations' fill the last five pages (33–37) of the tract."—BRINLEY *Catalogue*, No. 3440.

The Case of Richard Budge, late Commander of the Ship Hope ... . [*London, about* 1709.] Folio, pp. 3. 53081

"Richard Budge, bound for Holland, with a cargo of logwood from the Bay of Campeachy, was compelled by stress of weather to put in to the port of Amboy, N. J., for provisions and other necessaries. By order of Lord Cornbury the *Hope* was seized, and the ship and cargo were condemned by a Court of Vice-Admiralty held at New Jersey, and sold. On Budge's appeal to England, the High Court of Admiralty reversed the condemnation and decreed restitution of the ship and cargo ... Before satisfaction was had, Cornbury was removed from his government. Budge petitioned the House of Commons for redress."—BRINLEY *Catalogue*.

The Case of the Proprietors of East New-Jersey, with the Opinions of Counsel on the same. *Newark: Printed by W. Tuttle & Co.* 1825. 8vo, pp. 14, 21, 7. 53082

Contains the Opinions of Elias Van Arsdale and James Kent.

The Case put & Decided by George Fox, George Whitehead, Stephen Crisp, and other the most Antient & Eminent Quakers, between Edward Billing on the one part, and some West-Jersians, headed by Samuel Jenings on the other Part, In an Award relating to the Government of their Province, wherein, because [illegible] moulded to the Pallate of the said Samuell, the Light, the Truth, the Justice and Infallibility of these great Friends are arreigned

by him, and his Accomplices. Also several Remarks and Animadversions on the same Award, setting forth the Premises. With some Reflections on the Senseless Opposition of these Men against the present Governour, and their daring Audatiousness in their presumptuous asserting an Authority here over the Parliament of England. [*Philadelphia?* 1698–9?] 4to. 53083

Cases adjudged in the Supreme Court of New-Jersey; relative to the Manumission of Negroes and others Holden in Bondage. ... *Burlington: New-Jersey Society for promoting the Abolition of Slavery.* MDCCXCIV. 8vo, pp. 32. H., P. 53084

Catalogue of Books belonging to the State Library. *Trenton.* 1853. 12mo. 53085

Code of Criminal Law, prepared for the Legislature of New Jersey, ... 1833. *Bridgeton: Printed by Fayette Pierson.* 1834. Folio, pp. vii, 72. H. 53086

College of New Jersey. Address of the Trustees of the College of New-Jersey, to the Inhabitants of the United States. *Philadelphia: Printed by W. W. Woodward.* [1802.] 8vo, pp. 8.

A Catalogue of Books in the Library of the College of New Jersey, January 29, 1760. *Woodbridge: Printed by James Parker.* MDCCLX. 8vo, pp. 36. BA. 53088

Thomas ("Hist. of Printing") says there was a New York edition. I have not seen it. Also: Catalogue of the American Whig Society, instituted in the College of New Jersey, 1769. *Princeton, N. J.: The Society.* 1845. 8vo, pp. 63. + [*Ibid.*] 1857. 8vo, pp. 84. Plate. — Catalogue of the Cliosophic Society, instituted in the College of New Jersey, 1765. *Princeton: Printed by John Bogart.* 1840. 8vo. pp. 39, (1). Cont'd. — Catalogue of the Officers and Students of the College of New-Jersey; for 1834 & 1835. *Princeton: Printed by Robert E. Hornor.* 1835. 8vo, pp. 16. Continued. — Catalogus Collegii Neo-Cæsariensis. Rerumpublicarum Fœderatarum Americæ Summæ potestatis. *Princetoniæ: J. Tod.* 1786. 8vo. Continued — Catalogus Eorum qui in Collegio Novæ Cæsareæ Laurea ... donati sunt ab Anno 1748, ad Annum 1770. [*Philadelphia: W. & T. Bradford.* 1770.] Folio. Continued in 8vo. — College of New-Jersey. Catalogue of the Officers and Students of Nassau Hall. [n. p.] 1818. Folio. + [n. p.] 1819. 12mo, pp. 8, (3). — The Decennial Record; or, Digest No. II. of the Class of 1859, of the College of New Jersey. 1859–1869. ... [n. p.] 1869. 8vo, pp. 131. Photographs. — The First Centennial Anniversary of the College of New Jersey, Celebrated June, 1847. *Princeton, N. J.* 1848. 8vo, pp. 36. — An Historical Sketch of the College of New-Jersey ... *Philadelphia: James M. Wilson.* 1859. 8vo, pp. 66. — Inauguration of James McCosh, D.D., LL.D., as President of the College of New Jersey, ... October 27, 1868. *New York: Robert Carter and Brothers.* 1868. 8vo, pp. 96. — Laws of the College of New-Jersey. Reviewed, Amended and ... Adopted ... April, 1794. ... *Trenton: Printed by Isaac Collins.* M.DCC.XCIV. 8vo, pp. 38. Continued. — Proceedings and Address at the Celebration of the One Hundredth Anniversary of the Founding of the Cliosophic Society of the College of New Jersey, Princeton, N. J., June 27th, 1865. *Philadelphia: Sherman & Co., Printers.* 1865. 8vo, pp. 188. — Regulations of the College of New Jersey, April 10th, 1807.

[n. p. n. d.] Folio, pp. 2.—Triennial Report of the Secretary of the Class of 1856, College of New Jersey. ... By Alfred Alexander Woodhull, M.D. ... *Newark, N. J.: Printed ... by A. Stephen Holbrook.* 1860. 8vo, pp. 80. *See also* Vol. v., No. 19397, Vol. XII., No. 51892, *and* Theological Seminary.

Charter of the Jersey Bank; and ... Charter of the Associates of the Jersey Company of Powles Hook. *New York.* 1805. 8vo

A Compilation of the Public Laws of ... New Jersey, passed since the Revision in 1820. Arranged by Josiah Harrison. *Camden.* 1833. 8vo, pp. 644. C. 53090

A | Concise View | of the | Controversy | between the | Proprietors | of | East and West-Jersey | being | An Explanation of the Bill | .... *Philadelphia: Printed by Hall & Sellers.* 1785. 12mo, pp. vi, 18.

A Constitution, Agreed upon by the delegates of the people of New Jersey, ... in the year ... one thousand eight hundred and forty-four. [n. p. n. d.] 8vo, pp. 18. H. 53092

Constitution of the New Jersey Abolition Society. [n. p.] 1793. 8vo. 53093

Constitution of the United States and of ... New Jersey. *Newark.* 1798. 8vo. 53094

Debates in the Eighty-Ninth General Assembly of ... New Jersey, on the Bill to Ratify an Amendment to the Constitution of the United States. ... *Trenton, N. J.: Printed by J. R. Freese.* 1865. 8vo. 53095

Also in German as: "Debatten in der 89en Generalversammlung des Staates New Jersey, über den Gesetzentwurf für Ratifizirung eines Amendements zur Constitution der Vereinigten Staaten." *Newark: Prietb.* 1865. 8vo.

Debates in the General Assembly of ... New Jersey, on the South Jersey Central and Air Line Railroad Bill, and the extension of the Charter of the Camden and Amboy Railroad Company; ... *Trenton.* 1854. 8vo, pp. 80. H. 53096

The cover title reads: "The War with the Monopoly," etc.

Decision in Chancery of New Jersey respecting Friends' Meeting Houses. [n. p.] 1832. 8vo, pp. 88. 53097

The Decision of the Circuit Court of the United States for ... New Jersey, on the Rights of the Proprietors of the Eastern Division of ... New Jersey ... . *New York: James Van Norden.* 1837. 8vo, pp. 64. 53098

A Defence of New Jersey. *See* Vol. v. 19240 *and* 19250.

First Annual Report of the Delaware and Raritan Canal Company, May 10, 1831. *Princeton, N. J.* 1831. 8vo, pp. 31. S.

Our title, No. 19408, is incomplete.

Department of New Jersey, Proceedings of the ... Grand Army of the Republic, ... at New Brunswick, ... 1870. ... *Newark.* 1870. 8vo. 53100

A Digest of the Laws ... containing the Rules and Decisions of the Courts, by Lucius Q. C. Elmer. *Bridgeton.* 1838. 8vo. + Third Edition. ... By John T. Nixon. ... *Bridgeton and Trenton.* 1861. 8vo. + Fourth Edition. ... By John T. Nixon. *Newark: Martin R. Dennis & Co.* 1868. 8vo, pp. xxxii, 1152.

Digest of the Statutory and Constitutional Constructions delivered in the Superior Court and Court of Errors and Appeals, alphabetically arranged by A. Gifford. *Newark.* 1852. 8vo.

Documents of the Ninety-Second Legislature ... . *Jersey City: J. H. Lyon.* 1868. 8vo. Continued. C. 53103

Enquiry into Public Abuses, for want of a Due Execution of Laws for the Suppression of Vice, in New Jersey. *Philadelphia: Hall and Sellers.* 1784. 12mo, pp. 22. 53104

An Examination into the Validity of the New Jersey Senatorial Election of March 15, 1865. [n. p. n. d.] 8vo, pp. 52.

Extracts from the Journal of Proceedings of the Provincial Congress of New-Jersey, held at Trenton, in ... 1775. ... *Burlington: Printed ... by Isaac Collins.* M.DCC.LXXV. 8vo. BA. + *Woodbury, N. J.: Reprinted by ... Joseph Sailer.* 1835. 8vo, pp. 241, (1). 53106

Contains also, "Journal of the Votes and Proceedings," "Ordinances for regulating the Militia," and "Journal of the Votes and Proceedings ... of the Committee of Safety"—all paged continuously, but with separate title-pages.

Extracts from the Minutes and Proceedings of the Assembly of New Jersey relative to the Robbery of the Eastern Treasury, at the Session held at Perth-Amboy in September, 1772. *Burlington.* 1772. 4to. 53107

Extracts from the Minutes and Votes of the House of Assembly of the Colony of New-Jersey; met in General Assembly at Burlington, on Saturday the 16th of October 1742. Printed by Benjamin Franklin, by Order of Andrew Johnston, Esq; their Speaker. To which are added some Notes and Observations

upon the said Votes. Also the Governor's Speech to the Assembly on his Dissolving of them; and the Letters and Orders mentioned and referred to in the Governor's Speech. [n. p.:] *Printed in the Year* M,DCC,XLIII. 4to, pp. 56. P. 53108

Facts for the Shore Owners of ... New Jersey. Issued by the New Jersey Riparian Association. ... *New York: J. O. Seymour,* ... 1870. 8vo, pp. 24. B. 53109

Form of Prayer and Thanksgiving for the Blessings of Civil Liberty; to be used yearly in the Diocese of New Jersey. [n. p.] 1834. 8vo. 53110

General Instructions to the Surveyor General ... . [n. p. n. d.] Folio, pp. 6. Plate. 53111

General Tax Laws. [n. p.] 1862. 8vo. 53112

Geology. Report on the Geological Survey of ... New Jersey. By Henry D. Rogers ... . *Freehold, N. J.* 1836. 8vo, pp. 157. + Second Edition. *Philadelphia: Desilver, Thomas & Co.* 1836. 8vo, pp. 188. Map. BA. 53113

Description of the Geology of ... New Jersey, being a final Report, by Henry D. Rogers ... . *Philadelphia: C. Sherman & Co., Printers.* 1840. 8vo, pp. 301. Map and Plate. BA. + *Trenton, N. J.* 1865. 8vo, pp. 226. 53114

First Annual Report of the Geological Survey of ... New Jersey for ... 1854. [By William Kitchell.] *Trenton.* 1855. 8vo, pp. 103. Plates. + Second Report. [*Ibid.*] 1856. 8vo, pp. viii, 248. 2 Maps and 17 Plates. + Third Report. [*Ibid.*] 1857. 8vo, pp. 79. BA. 53115

Geology of the County of Cape May ... . *Trenton.* 1857. 8vo, pp. 208. Map and Plates. 53116

Report of the Committee of the General Assembly in Relation to the Geological Survey of the State, March 11, 1857. *Trenton.* 1857. 8vo, pp. 13. S. 53117

Report of George H. Cook upon the Geology and Agricultural Resources of the Southern Division of the State. *Trenton.* 1857. 8vo. 53118

Report of George H. Cook upon the Geological Survey of New Jersey and its progress during ... 1863. *Trenton.* 1864. 8vo, pp. 13. 53119

The Annual Report of Geo. H. Cook, State Geologist ... for ... 1864. *Trenton.* 1865. 8vo, pp. 24. + For ... 1865. [*Ibid.*] 1866. 8vo, pp. 12. 53120

Third Annual Report on the Geological Survey of ... New Jersey, for ... 1866. *Trenton.* 1867. 8vo, pp. 27. 53121

Report of the State Geologist, Geo. H. Cook, for ... 1867. *Trenton.* 1868. 8vo, pp. 28. 53122

Geology of New Jersey. By Authority of the Legislature, George H. Cook, State Geologist. ... *Newark: Printed at the Daily Advertiser Office.* 1868. 8vo, pp. xxiv, 899, (1). Atlas of 8 Maps, folded in 4to. BA., C. 53123

Annual Report of the State Geologist of New Jersey, for 1869. *Trenton, N. J.* 1870. 8vo, pp. 57. 3 Maps and Plan. Cont'd.

Governor's Message, transmitting the Report of the Commissioners respecting the Eastern Boundary of New Jersey. *Albany.* 1808. Folio. 53125

General Regulations for the Government of the Grand Lodge of New Jersey. [n. p.] 1790. 8vo, pp. 24. N. 53126

Also: Proceedings at the Annual Commencement ... at Trenton, January 11, 5854. *Trenton.* [n. d.] 8vo, pp. 175–224. S.

The Grants, Concessions, etc. *See* Leaming (A.), No. 39527.

The Hermit of New Jersey; a Collection of Political Essays, and a Dialogue between Lorenzo and the Hermit, on Human Happiness. *Philadelphia.* 1769. 8vo. 53127

A History of the Railroad Conflict in New Jersey. *Trenton.* 1860. 8vo, pp. 80. 53128

Inaugural Address of Rodman M. Price, Governor of New Jersey. ... January, 17, 1854. ... *Trenton.* 1854. 12mo, pp. 10. Continued. H. 53129

Inauguration of Governor M. L. Ward, January 16, 1866. *Trenton.* 1866. 8vo. 53130

An Index to the Statutes at Large, and a Synopsis of the Constitution adopted June, 1844. Alphabetically Arranged by A. Gifford. *Newark.* 1852. 8vo. A. 53131

Instructions to Town Superintendents and others, relative to

the Normal School. By John H. Phillips ... . *Trenton.* 1855. 8vo, pp. 14. H. 53132

Also: Instructions for the use of Public Schools. *Trenton.* 1856. 8vo.

The | Interest | of | New-Jersey | considered, | With Regard to | Trade and Navigation, | By laying of | Duties, &c. | *Philadelphia: W. Bradford* [*about* 1744]. 4to, pp. 20. 53133

An extremely rare piece.

Joint Resolutions Withdrawing the Consent of ... New Jersey, to the proposed Fourteenth Amendment. *Trenton.* 1868. 8vo. 53134

Journal of the General Assembly of His Majesty's Province of New Jersey, in America, 1727. [n. p.:] *Printed by William Bradford.* [1727.] Folio, pp. 14. 53135

Journal of the Proceedings of the Convention to form A Constitution for the Government of ... New Jersey; ... 1844 ... . *Trenton: Printed by Franklin S. Mills.* 1844. 12mo, pp. 297.

Journal of the Proceedings of the First Senate of ... New Jersey, ... at Trenton ... January, One Thousand Eight Hundred and Forty-Five ... . *Morris-Town, N. J.* 1845. 8vo, pp. 900. S. 53137

Followed by: "Journal of the Executive Proceedings of the Senate" ... 1845, pp. 15, [and] "Minutes of the Proceedings of the Joint Meeting of the Senate and General Assembly of ... New Jersey," 1845, pp. 46. Continued. S.

Journal of the Proceedings of the Legislative Council of ... New Jersey ... . *Trenton.* 1777. Folio. Continued. N. 53138

Journal of the Votes and Proceedings, as well of the Committee of Safety, At a Sitting in January, 1776, As the Provincial Congress of New Jersey, at a sitting at New Brunswick, began January 31, and continued to the Second Day of March following. ... *New York: Printed by John Anderson.* M,DCC,LXXVI. 8vo, pp. 146, (2). 53139

Reprinted in "Extracts from the Journal of Proceedings," *Woodbury,* 1835.

Journal of the Votes & Proceedings of the Convention of New-Jersey. Begun at Burlington the tenth of June 1776, and thence continued by adjournment at Trenton and New-Brunswick, to the twenty-first of August following. To which is annexed, sundry Ordinances, and the Constitution. ... *Burlington: Printed ... by Isaac Collins.* M.DCC.LXXVI. 8vo, pp. 150. + *Trenton: Reprinted by ... Joseph Justice.* 1831. 8vo, pp. 100.

Kirkbride's New Jersey Business Directory ... . Collected ... by Stacy B. Kirkbride, Jr. For 1850 & 1851. ... *Trenton, N. J.* 1850. 8vo, pp. 348. 53141

Law of New Jersey for purchasing Clothes for New Jersey Regiments, Nov. 27, 1777. [n. p. n. d.] Folio. 53142

Fifty copies only printed.

The Laws and Acts of the General Assembly of His Majesties Province of Nova Cæsarea or New Jersey, as they were enacted by the Governour, Council and General Assembly, for the time being, in divers sessions, the first of which began in November, 1703. *Printed ... by William Bradford, Printer to the Kings Most Excellent Majesty for the Province of New Jersey.* 1717. Folio, pp. iv, 115. S. 53143

Thomas places this under 1709; probably some of the Laws were issued at that date.

Laws and Votes of the Last Session of the General Assembly of the Province of New Jersey. *Burlington, N. J.* 1772. 8vo.

Laws of New Jersey, regulating Fisheries in the River Delaware, and the Agreement between Pennsylvania and New Jersey, settling the Jurisdiction of the Delaware and its Islands. *Camden: Printed by Josiah Harrison.* 1833. 8vo, pp. 12. P. 53145

Laws of the Province of New Jersey, from 1708 to 1751. *Woodbridge, N. J.* 1750. Folio. 53146

Laws of ... New-Jersey; revised and published ... by William Paterson. *New Brunswick: Printed by Abraham Blauvelt.* 1800. Folio, pp. 509. + *Newark: Printed by Matthias Day.* M.DCCC. Folio, pp. (2), 455, xxi, (1), 46, (1). B., C. 53147

Laws of ... New Jersey, compiled and published ... by Joseph Bloomfield. *Trenton.* 1811. 8vo. 53148

Laws of ... New-Jersey. Revised ... . *Trenton: Printed ... by Joseph Justice.* 1821. 8vo, pp. 900. + *Trenton.* 1847. 8vo, pp. 1155. 53149

Laws Relating to Public Schools ... . *Trenton, N. J.: Printed at the "True American" Office.* 1860. 8vo. 53150

Majority and Minority Report of the Special Committee of the House of Assembly, to whom was referred that portion of the Governor's Message relating to Slavery. ... *Trenton.* 1858. 8vo, pp. 71. H. 53151

Medical Society of New-Jersey. Transactions, 1864. Ninety-Eighth Annual Meeting. *New York: John A. Gray & Green, Printers.* 1864. 8vo, pp. 172. H. 53152

The Memorial of the Council of Proprietors of the Eastern Division of New Jersey, To His Excellency, Jonathan Belcher, ... Governor of the Province of New Jersey, Nov. 20, 1753: with documents annexed (in Support of their title to the lands in controversy between the two Provinces of New York and New Jersey): and the Report made to the General Assembly of New Jersey, Aug. 20, 1755, by David Ogden, Chairman of the Committee upon the subject of the New York Line. [*New York: J. Parker and W. Weyman.* 1755.] Folio, pp. 118. S. 53153

The Memorial of the Publick Creditors, Citizens of ... New-Jersey. *Trenton: Printed by Isaac Collins.* M.DCC.XC. 8vo, pp. 16. BA. 53154

... The Memorial of the Subscribers, Owners, and Insurers of the Ship New Jersey, and her Cargo. [*Washington.* 1806?] 8vo, pp. 66. BA. 53155

See also Vol. VI., No. 23361, *and* Vol. XII., No. 47682.

Message of ... the Governor ... with the Report of the Commissioners ... to settle the Question of Territory ... in Dispute with the State of New-York, &c., &c., February, 1828. *Trenton.* 1828. 8vo, pp. 60. 53156

Message of ... the Governor of New Jersey, to the Senate and House of Assembly ... . January 10, 1856 ... . *Trenton.* 1856. 8vo, pp. 21. Continued. H. 53157

Minutes and Proceedings of the Joint Meeting of the Council and General Assembly of ... New Jersey, ... 1826. [n. p. n. d.] 8vo, pp. 40. S. 53158

The previous "Minutes" had no specific title-page.

Minutes of the Convention of ... New-Jersey, Holden at Trenton the 11th Day of December, 1787. *Trenton: Printed by Isaac Collins,* ... M,DCC,LXXXVIII. 4to, pp. 31. 53159

The convention assembled for the purpose of ratifying the Federal Constitution.

Minutes of the Proceedings of the Joint Meeting of the Council and General Assembly, of ... New Jersey, 1827. [n. p.] 1827. 8vo, pp. 36. Continued. H. 53160

Minutes of the Proceedings of the Legislative Council of New-Jersey, sitting as a High Court of Impeachment (in 1830 and 1837). [n. p. n. d.] 8vo. S. 53161

Minutes of the Votes and Proceedings of the Sixty-Sixth General Assembly of ... New Jersey ... . *Trenton: Printed by Phillips and Boswell.* 1842. 12mo, pp. 675. Continued. B. 53162

Constitution of the Missionary Society of New-Jersey. Instituted December 8, 1801. *Morris-Town: Printed by Henry P. Russell.* 1802. 8vo, pp. 4. BA. 53163

New Jersey Almanack. By William Ball. *Philadelphia.* 1742. 12mo. 53164

Continued to 1743 or later.

New Jersey. The Burlington Almanack for ... 1776. By Timothy Trueman. ... *Burlington: Printed by Isaac Collins.* [n. d.] 12mo, pp. (40). 53165

Afterwards called the "New-Jersey Almanack." The almanac for 1788 is by William Waring, and was continued to 1798 or later. The almanac for 1795 is by Abraham Shoemaker.

New Jersey and New York Almanack for 1800. *New York.* 1800. 8vo. 53166

New Jersey and Pennsylvania Almanack for ... 1800. ... *Trenton.* [n. d.] 12mo. 53167

Continued to 1822 or later.

New Jersey Annual Register, 1846. *See* Lloyd (S.), x. 41695

Minutes of the Twenty-First Anniversary of the New Jersey Baptist State Convention, and of the Thirteenth Annual Meeting of the New Jersey Baptist Education Society, ... at Camden, N. J. ... *New-York: Printed by Holman & Gray* ... 1850. 8vo. Continued. 53168

First Report of the Managers of the New Jersey Bible Society, at their Annual Meeting, Princeton, October 2, 1810. *Trenton.* 1810. 8vo, pp. 24. Continued. N. 53169

New Jersey Business Directory, with Commercial Register of New York City and Philadelphia. By J. F. Howell, Martin & Co. *New York: Bradstreet Press.* 1868. 8vo, pp. 527. 53170

Circular & Catalogue of the New Jersey Classical and Scientific Institute ... Hightstown, N. J. for ... 1865. *Philadelphia: Jas. B. Rodgers, Printer.* 1865. 8vo, pp. 24. H. 53171

Proceedings of the First Annual Meeting of the New Jersey Colonization Society. *Princeton.* 1825. 8vo. 53172

Also: Proceedings of a Meeting held at Princeton, N. J., July 14th, 1824, to form a Society in ... New Jersey to co-operate with the American Colonization Society. *Princeton.* 1824. 8vo, pp. 46.

The New Jersey Conference Memorial. Containing Biographical Sketches of all its Deceased Members, including those who have Died in the Newark Conference. *Philadelphia: Perkinpine & Higgins.* 1865. 12mo, pp. 512. 53173

The New Jersey Farmer. Editors, O. Pharo and D. Pettit, and D. Naar. ... *Freehold* [*Pharo & Bartleson, and D. Naar.* 1855–61]. 6 vols., 8vo. C. 53174

Report to Stockholders of New Jersey Franklinite Company: containing also Charter, By-Laws, ... &c. August, 1855. *New York: J. D. Torrey, Printer.* 1855. 8vo, pp. 47. 3 Maps. H.

Collections of the New Jersey Historical Society. Volume I. [n. p.:] *New Jersey Historical Society.* 1846. 8vo, pp. viii, (2), 341. Maps. Continued. BA. + Second Series. Volume I. *Newark.* 1867. 8vo. Continued. 53176

See Analytical Index, No. 53058, *supra*, Duer (W. A.), Vol. v., No. 21113, Field (R. S.), Vol. vi., No. 24291, Morris (L.), Vol. xii., No. 50849, *and* Whitehead (W. A.) Also: Constitution and By-Laws of the New Jersey Historical Society, with the Circular of the Executive Committee. *Newark.* 1818. 8vo, pp. 16. N.

Proceedings of the New Jersey Historical Society. Vol. I. 1845–1846. *Newark, N. J.* 1847. 8vo, pp. (4), 203. Cont'd

Second Annual Report of the New Jersey Howard Society. *Trenton.* 1834. 8vo, pp. 56. P. 53178

New Jersey Lyceum. Paper No. I. Circular of the Executive Committee. *Princeton, N. J.* 1834. 8vo, pp. 16. 53179

The New Jersey Magazine. Vol. I. No. I. May, 1867. *Newark: New Jersey State Literary Union.* 1867. 8vo, pp. 96.

Continued as the "Northern Monthly."

The New Jersey Magazine and Monthly Advertiser. *New Brunswick, N. J.* 1786–7. 8vo. N., P. 53181

... The New Jersey Medical Reporter; ... *Burlington.* 1850. 8vo. Continued. 53182

New Jersey Monthly Magazine ... . Edited by Thomas S. Wiggins. ... *Belvidere.* 1825. 8vo, pp. 32. Continued. S.

Report to the Stockholders of the New Jersey Mining Company, April 30, 1848. [n. p. 1848.] 8vo, pp. 5. S. 53184

Report of the ... N. J. Railroad and Trans. Co., ... By John P. Jackson ... . *Newark.* 1853. 8vo, pp. 16. Continued. B.

First Annual Report of the New Jersey Prison Reform Association, ... with the Proceedings of the First Annual Meeting, ... in ... Trenton, ... January, 1850. *Trenton: Printed by Phillips & Boswell.* 1850. 12mo, pp. 45. H. 53186

Alden's New-Jersey Register ... for ... 1811, with an Ephemeris ... . *Newark: Printed by William Tuttle.* [1810.] 18mo, pp. 160, (4). H. 53187

Continued by various editors to 1837 or later.

Constitution of the New Jersey Riparian Association ... . *Jersey City, N. J.* 1869. 24mo, pp. 24. B. 53188

New Jersey Senatorial Election. A Reply to the Arguments submitted to the Judiciary Committee in favor of the Protest. [n. p. 1866.] 8vo, pp. 20. H. 53189

Also: The New Jersey Senatorial Question. [n. p. 1866.] 8vo, pp. 8. H.

Constitution of the New Jersey Society for the Abolition of Slavery. *Burlington.* 1793. 8vo, pp. 14. N. 53190

Constitution of the New Jersey Society for the Suppression of Vice and Immorality ... adopted November 11, 1817. [n. p. n. d.] 8vo. 53191

Annual Report of the New Jersey State Board of Education, ... for ... 1866. *Trenton, N. J.* 1867. 8vo, pp. 196. H.

New Jersey State Business Directory for 1866. Talbott and Blood, ... Compilers. ... *New York: Printed by C. A. Alvord.* 1866. 8vo, pp. 244, 187. 53193

Annual Report of the Officers of the New Jersey State Lunatic Asylum at Trenton, for ... MDCCCXLVIII. *Trenton: Printed by Phillips & Boswell.* 1849. 12mo, pp. 45. Continued. H.

Also: By-Laws adopted by the Managers of the New-Jersey State Lunatic Asylum at Trenton. *Trenton.* 1848. 8vo, pp. 46. M.

First Annual Report ... of the ... Trustees of the New Jersey State Normal School, ... for ... 1855. ... *Philadelphia: King & Baird, Printers.* 1856. 8vo, pp. 104. Plate and 3 Plans. Continued. BA. 53195

Also: Annual Reports concerning the State Normal School, to the New Jersey Legislature, for ... 1855. ... *Trenton.* 1856. 8vo, pp. 84, (1). Plate and 3 Plans.—First Triennial Register of the ... State Normal School, including the Farnum Preparatory School, ... 1858. *Trenton.* 1858. 8vo, pp. 55. Plate and Plans.— ... The Induction of Professor John S. Hart as Principal of the Model School. August 26, 1862. *Trenton, N. J.* 1862. 8vo, pp. 48. H.

Statistics of the New Jersey State Prison, from 1799 to 1845, inclusive ... . *Trenton: Printed by Sherman & Harron.* 1846. 8vo, pp. 28. H. 53196

Also: Report on the Condition of the State Prison ... . 1843 ... . *Trenton: Printed by Franklin S. Mills.* 1843. 8vo, pp. 34.—Annual Report of the New Jersey State Prison. *Trenton.* 1849. 8vo. Continued.—Report of the Special Committee of the House of Assembly, on Prison Discipline. *Trenton.* 1857. 8vo. S.

New Jersey State Society. *See* Vol. IV., Nos. 13116 & 13127

Reports of the New Jersey Zinc Company, 1852. Financial ... Geological ... Historical and Mineralogical. ... *New York: Baker, Godwin and Co., ... Printers.* 1852. 8vo, pp. 32. H.

Also: To the President and Directors of the New Jersey Zinc Company. [Dated New York, Dec. 15th, 1852.] 8vo, pp. 7. H.

Order for a Second Evening Service in the Churches in the Diocese of New Jersey, set forth by the Bishop. *New York.* 1857. 12mo, pp. 84. 53198

An Ordinance for Regulating and Establishing Fees within this his Majesty's Province of New Jersey. By his Excellency William Burnet, Esq; ... this 26th day of November ... One Thousand Seven Hundred and Twenty-Three. [n. p.:] *Printed and Sold by William Bradford.* 1724. Folio, pp. 14. S. 53199

An Ordinance for Regulating and Establishing the Fees to be hereafter Taken by the Officers of the Court of Chancery of the Province of New Jersey. ... First day of May ... 1724. [n. p. n. d.] Folio, pp. 7. S. 53200

Also: An Ordinance for Regulating and Establishing the Fees hereafter to be Taken by the Officers of the Courts of Chancery of the Province of New Jersey: By His Excellency Jonathan Belcher, Captain-General and Governor-in-Chief in Council, November 23, 1753. *Woodbridge, New Jersey.* 1755. Folio, pp. 6. S.

An Ordinance for Regulating Courts of Judicature in the Province of New Jersey. *Printed and Sold by William Bradford, in New York.* 1725. Folio, pp. 9. S. 53201

Organization and By-Laws of the State Board of Education, of New Jersey. *Trenton, N. J.: Murphy & Bechtel, Printers.* 1866. 8vo, pp. 12. H. + [*Ibid.*] 1867. 53202

The Petitions and Memorials of the Proprietors of West and East Jersey, to the Legislature of New Jersey, together with a Map of the State of New Jersey and the Country adjacent; and also an Appendix ... The whole ... respecting ... four hundred thousand acres in the heart of New Jersey ... *New York.* [1783.] 8vo, pp. 96. Map. S. 53203

The petition was dated 1775, but Kollock, the printer, was not in business in New York till 1783.

Proceedings and Address of the Convention of Delegates to the People of New Jersey. *Trenton, 4 July,* 1812. 8vo, pp. 20

Proceedings and Address of the ... Democratic Convention, February 22, 1828. *Trenton.* 1828. 8vo, pp. 28. C. 53205

Proceedings of the Congress of New Jersey, January–March, 1776. 53206

Noticed in Sedgwick's "Life of Livingston," p. 183. Also: Proceedings of the Congress of New Jersey, July–August, 1776. Republished by the New Jersey Legislature, 1831.

Proceedings attending the Inauguration of Hon. William A. Newell, as Governor of New Jersey, Jan. 20, 1857. *Trenton.* 1857. 8vo, pp. 13. 53207

Journal of the Proceedings of a Convention of the Protestant Episcopal Church in ... New Jersey, ... June, 1801. *Newark.* 1801. 8vo, pp. 10. Continued. 53208

Also: A Full Report of the Proceedings of the Special Convention ... in Burlington, March 17th, 1851. ... *Philadelphia: King & Baird, Printers.* 1852. 16mo, pp. 63.—Journal of the Special Convention ... 17th ... March, 1852. *Burlington.* 1852. 8vo.

Register of the Commissioned Officers and Privates of the New Jersey Volunteers, in the Service of the United States. ... [n. p.] 1862–63. 8vo, pp. 21, 42, 44. + *Jersey City: Printed by John H. Lyon.* 1863. 8vo, pp. 584. H. 53209

Remarks on The School Law, By the Superintendent of Public Schools of ... New Jersey. *Trenton, N. J.: Printed by David Naar.* 1863. 8vo. 53210

Report of Commissioners, &c. Executive Department, February 7, 1835. To the General Assembly of the State of New Jersey. ... [*Camden.* 1835.] 8vo, pp. 23. P. 53211

Relates to the River Delaware.

Report of the Adjutant-General ... for ... 1861. *Trenton.* 1862. 8vo, pp. 58. Continued. BA. 53212

Report of the Commissioners Appointed by the Legislature of ... New-Jersey, for the Purpose of Exploring the Route of A Canal to Unite the River Delaware, near Easton, with the Passaic near Newark ... . *Morris-Town: Printed by Jacob Mann.* 1823. 8vo, pp. 82, 2. 2 Figures, 1 page, and 2 Plates.

Report of the Commissioners Appointed by the Legislature of New Jersey to meet Commissioners of Virginia and other States, at Washington, February 4, 1861. ... *Trenton.* 1861. 8vo, pp. 7.

Report of the Commissioners appointed to ascertain the number of Lunatics and Idiots in the State. *Trenton.* 1841. 8vo.

Report of the Commissioners appointed to investigate Charges made against the Directors of the Delaware and Raritan Canal, and Camden and Amboy Railroad and Transportation Companies. ... 1850. *Trenton.* 1850. 8vo, pp. 102, 187. S. 53216

Report of the Commissioners appointed to Investigate the Wreck off the Monmouth Coast. *Trenton.* 1846. 8vo, pp. 166.

Report of the Commissioners to Codify the School Law. ... *Trenton.* 1856. 8vo, pp. 24. S. 53218

The Report of the Committee ... of the Friends of Education, ... at ... Trenton, ... 1828; exhibiting a succinct account of the State of Common Schools in New-Jersey. ... *Trenton, N. J.: D. Fenton.* 1828. 8vo, pp. 46. 53219

Report of the Committee of Assembly relative to the creation of a Sinking Fund for the extinguishment of the exclusive privelege [*sic*] of the Camden and Amboy Railroad and Transportation Company. ... *Trenton.* 1853. 8vo, pp. 15. H. 53220

Report of the Committee on the Petition of Peter Soumans, of New Jersey, and Jos. Ormstone, relating to Shares of Land in the Eastern and Western Divisions of New Jersey. *London.* 1718. Folio, 2 leaves. 53221

Report of the Inspectors of the State Prison relative to a Reduction of the Expenses of that Institution. *Trenton.* 1858. 8vo, pp. 58. S. 53222

Also: Report of the Joint Committee on the State Prison Accounts; with the Inspectors' and Physician's Reports. ... 1846 ... . *Trenton: Printed by Sherman & Harron.* 1846. 12mo, pp. 26. H.

Report of the Joint Committee on Treasurer's Accounts, ... with the Treasurer's Report to the Governor ... . *Trenton, N. J.: Jacob R. Freese, Printer.* 1866. 8vo, pp. 216. Continued.

Report of the Judiciary Committee on the subject of the Colonial Records of New Jersey. *Trenton: Franklin S. Mills.* 1844. 8vo, pp. 11. 53224

Report of the Law Commissioners, made to the New Jersey Legislature, January, 1855. *Trenton.* 1855. 8vo, pp. 29. H.

Report of the Majority and Minority of the Committee of the Legislative Council on the Petition of Israel Stratton, claiming a Seat as a Member of that Body, from the County of Cumberland. *Trenton.* 1838. 8vo. 53226

Report of the New Jersey Commissioners upon ... a Canal, from the Delaware to the Raritan ... . *Trenton.* 1824. 8vo, pp. 20

Report of the Registry and Return of Births, Marriages and Deaths in ... New Jersey. ... *New Brunswick.* 1855. 8vo, pp. 53. Continued. S. 53228

Report of the Select Committee of the Legislative Council on the subject of the State of the Lunatic Asylum. *Trenton.* 1839. 8vo, pp. 8. 53229

Report of the Special Committee of the Assembly, on the subject of our Colonial Documents in England. *Trenton.* 1846. 8vo. N. 53230

Report of the Special Committee on Quarantine, relative to the Memorial of the New York Commissioners. *Trenton, N. J.* [n. d.] 8vo, pp. 80. S. 53231

Relative to removing Quarantine to Sandy Hook.

Report of the State Directors of the Delaware and Raritan Canal and Camden and Amboy Railroad Companies ... . *Trenton.* 1856. 8vo, pp. 23. S. 53232

Reports of the Commissioners, appointed by ... the Legislature of New-Jersey, For ascertaining the ... route for, and ... expense of, a Canal to connect the tide waters of the Delaware with those of the Raritan. ... *New-York: Printed by Van Winkle, Wiley & Co.* 1817. 8vo, pp. 40. BA. + *Trenton.* 1817. 8vo.

See also our Vol. v., p. 328.

Reports of the Commissioners on the Controversy with the State of New-York, respecting the Eastern Boundary of ... New Jersey. Published by Order of Council. *Trenton: Printed by Wilson & Halsey.* 1807. 8vo, pp. 67. + *Trenton.* 1826–28. 8vo. C. 53234

Selections from the Correspondence of the Executive of New Jersey, from 1776 to 1786. ... *Newark, N. J.* 1848. 8vo, pp. (4), xvi, 368. BA. 53235

Forms Vol. v. of the "Collections of the New Jersey Historical Society."

A Short State of the Proceedings of the Proprietors of East and West Jersey, relative to the Line of Division between them. *New York: Printed by James Rivington.* 1775. 8vo, pp. 23.

Annual Report of the Soldiers' Children's Home of ... New Jersey, for ... 1869. *Trenton, N. J.* 1870. 8vo, pp. 7. H.

Speeches and Addresses during the Sitting of the Assembly, begun at Burlington, the 28th day of February, 1721, with the Acts and Laws of that Session. [n. p.:] *Printed by Andrew Bradford.* 1721. Folio, pp. 32. 53238

State of New Jersey. An Act to Regulate Elections. [n. p. n. d.] 8vo, pp. 32. 53239

Statutes of ... New Jersey. Revised and Published under the Authority of the Legislature. *Trenton: Printed by Phillips & Boswell.* 1847. 12mo, pp. l, 1155. + Second Edition, containing all the Laws of General Application, now in force, from 1709 to 1855, by John T. Nixon. *Philadelphia.* 1855. 8vo.

Treasurer's Report to the Legislature of New Jersey. ... 1842, ... *Trenton: Printed by Sherman and Harron.* 1842. 8vo, pp. 10.

A Treaty between the Government of New Jersey and the Indians inhabiting the several Parts of said Province, held at Croswicks, In the County of Burlington, on Thursday and Friday, the eighth and ninth Day of January, 1756. *Philadelphia: Printed by William Bradford, Printer to the Province of New Jersey.* 1756. Folio, pp. 11. P. 53242

Vindication of the late New Jersey Assembly. *Woodbridge, N. J.* 1743. 4to. 53243

Votes and Proceedings of the General Assembly of the Province of New-Jersey. At a Sitting at Burlington ... July 25,

1758. *Woodbridge, N. J.: James Parker.* 1758. Folio, pp. 38. Continued. 53244

Parker's was the first press established in New Jersey. He began to print at Woodbridge, about 1751.

Votes and Proceedings of the Twenty-Sixth General Assembly of ... New Jersey ... . *Newark.* 1801. 8vo, pp. 148. Continued. S. 53245

Votes of the General Assembly of New-Jersey, from October 28, 1777, to March 21, 1780. *Trenton.* 1779–80. 8vo. P.

The New Jerusalem Magazine, for 1827–8. Vol. I. *Boston: A. Howard.* 1828. 8vo, pp. iv, 384. Continued. BA. 53247

Constitution of the First New Jerusalem Society of Cincinnati, and Laws of the Church. *Cin.: Bradley & Power, Print.* [1868.] 18mo, pp. 15. 53248

Also: Journal of the Proceedings of the Eighth General Convention, of the receivers of the Doctrines of the New Jerusalem, held in ... New-York, June ... 1826–70. ... *Boston: Cummings, Hilliard & Co.* 1826–70. 8vo, pp. 24.—New Jerusalem Church. Principle of the New Church: signified by the New Jerusalem, Revelation xxi. A Report submitted to the Executive Committee of the General Convention of the New Church in the United States, June, 1860; ... approved June, 1863. *New York.* 1863. 12mo, pp. 201. C.

The | New Life | of Virginea: | Declaring the | former svccesse and pre- | sent estate of that plantation, being the second | part of Noua Britannia. | Published by the authoritie of his Maiesties | Counsell of Virginea. | *London,* | *Imprinted by Felix Kyngston for William Welby, dwelling at the* | *signe of the Swan in Pauls Church-yard.* 1612. | 4to, 27 leaves. H. 53249

Corrected title of our No. 36286, Vol. IX. This very rare tract is dedicated to Sir Thomas Smith. The author (Robert Johnson), in his preface, complains that nothing in his day, except it be the name of God, was so depraved, traduced, and derided, as the name of Virginia. It was reprinted in the "Collections of the Massachusetts Historical Society," Vol. VIII., Second Series, pp. 199–228, and in Force's "Tracts," Vol. I., No. 7.

NEW LONDON, *Conn.* Annual Report of the ... School Visitors, of ... New London. ... 1866. *New London: Starr & Farnham, ... Printers.* 1866. 12mo, pp. 12. H. 53250

An Astronomical Diary. *See* Sherman (Roger).

A Brief Review of the Navy Yard Question, showing that New London has the Advantage of Defensibility, Fresh Water, Iron, Coal, Freedom from Ice, &c. &c. *New London: Starr & Farnham, Printers.* 1863. 8vo, pp. 32. 53251

A Concise Statement of the Action of Congress, in relation to a Navy Yard ... with extracts from Reports ... And the comparative Expense of a Navy Yard at League Island and New London. *New London.* 1866. 8vo, pp. 32. H. 53252

A | Dialogue, | or, | Representation of Matters | of Fact. | Done in a plain and easy Dress. | By Way of Question and Answer. | Occasioned by some Mismanagements which | happen'd in respect of a Gentleman, whose | Affairs lay under the Consideration of an | Ecclesiastical Council. | ... | [n. p.:] *Printed in the Year*, 1736. 8vo, pp. (4), 35. 53253

The half-title reads: "Remarks | On the Result of an | Ecclesiastical Council | At New-London North Parish." | Corrected title of our No. 19946.

Disfranchisement of the Inhabitants of New London. *New London.* 1817. 8vo. 53254

Funeral Observances at New London, Connecticut, in Honor of Abraham Lincoln, ... April 19, 1865, Including the Public Addresses of Rev. G. B. Willcox and Rev. Thomas P. Field, D.D. *New London: C. Prince.* 1865. 8vo, pp. 34. B. 53255

History of the Baptist Association of New London. *New London.* 1851. 8vo. 53256

New London Almanack for ... 1769. *New London.* [n. d.] 12mo. 53257

Also: New London Almanack for 1773. By Freebetter. *New London.* [n. d.] 12mo. Continued. + [Another] for 1773. By Daboll. Continued. Titles from Thomas' "History of Printing," Vol. II.

Minutes of the New-London Baptist Association, held at Lebanon, ... October, 1820. [n. p. n. d.] 8vo, pp. 8. Cont'd

Turner's New-London Directory, for 1853–4. ... *New-London: Williams & Bacon, Printers.* 1853. 16mo, pp. 96. Cont'd

New London City Directory, for 1865–66; with a ... List of New London Volunteers, and other Valuable Local Information for Citizens and Strangers. *New London: Christopher Prince.* 1866. 16mo, pp. 191. 53260

Report of New London, Willimantic & Palmer Railroad Company. ... 1860. *Boston: Wright & Potter, Printers.* 1860. 8vo, pp. 7. H. 53261

Engineer's Report and Charter of the New-London, Willimantic and Springfield Railroad Company. *New-London.* 1847. 8vo. S. 53262

Profession of Faith and Covenant of the Second Congregational Church ... in New-London: with a List of its Members. *New-London: E. Williams, Printer.* 1836. 12mo, pp. 6. H.

Thirty-First Annual Report of the Sabbath School of the Second Congregational Church of New London, Conn. 1865. *New London: D. S. Ruddock, ... Printer.* 1866. 8vo, pp. 19.

Catalogue of the New-London Academy, Chester County, Pa. ... 1850. [n. p. n. d.] 8vo. S. 53265

NEW LONDON, *Wis.* Sketches of the Early History and Present Advantages of New London, Wis. *New London, Wis.* 1857. 12mo, pp. 31. M. 53266

NEW LOTTS, *N. Y.* List of Persons Enrolled in the Town of New Lotts, Kings County, N. Y. [n. p. 1863.] 8vo, pp. 18

... New Louisiana. ... No. 2. August, 1869. [*New Orleans, La.*] 1869. Folio. H. 53268

New Manual, and Platoon Exercise: With an Exercise. Published by Authority. *New York.* 1769. 8vo. 53269

New Manual Exercise to be observed by his Majesty's Troops in the Establishment of Great Britain and Ireland. *New York.* [n. d.] 8vo. 53270

New Manual Exercises, by General Blakeney; and the Evolutions of the Foot, by General Bland. *Philadelphia.* 1746. 8vo. + [*Ibid.*] 1747. 53271

NEW MARLBORO', *Mass.* Report of the Committee on Accounts, of ... New Marlboro', ... for ... 1869. *Great Barrington, Mass.: Marcus H. Rogers, ... Printer.* 1869. 8vo, pp. 7.

New Memorandum, Addressed to all real Lovers of Liberty, either Britons or Americans. *New York.* 1768. 8vo. 53273

New Memorandum Book. ... Third Edition. *New York.* 1750. 8vo, pp. (104). 53274

NEW MEXICO. Address to the Inhabitants of New Mexico and California on Territorial Governments, and on the Social and Political Evils of Slavery. *New York.* 1849. 8vo. 53275

The Second Annual Message of Acting Governor Arny to the Legislative Assembly of New Mexico, ... 1866. *Santa Fé, N. M.: Manderfield & Tucker, ... Printers.* [n. d.] 8vo, pp. 40. Continued. H. 53276

Executive Message of ... William F. M. Arny, Acting Governor of New Mexico, to the Legislative Assembly of the Territory ... the 2d ... of December, 1862. *Printed at the Office of the Santa Fe Gazette.* 1862. 8vo, pp. 26. H. 53277

Relates to the Rebellion. *See also* Nos. 10188 and 48117.

Journal of the Honorable Council of the Territory of N. Mexico; being the First Session of the First Legislative Assembly, ... in the City of Santa Fe, June 3, 1851. *Printed in the Santa Fe Gazette Office.* 1855. 8vo, pp. 120. Continued. S.

Also in Spanish.

Journal of the House of Representatives of the Territory of New Mexico; being the Second Session of the First Legislative Assembly, ... at ... Santa Fé, December 1st, 1851. *Santa Fé.* 1852. 8vo, pp. 235, xxix. Continued. S. 53279

Also in Spanish.

Journal of the Legislative Council of the Territory of New Mexico, ... held in ... Santa Fé, ... December, A. D. One Thousand Eight Hundred and Sixty-six. ... *Santa Fé, N. M.: Manderfield & Tucker, ... Printers.* [n. d.] 8vo, pp. 208, Appendix, pp. 40. H. 53280

Laws of the Territory of New Mexico, passed by the First Legislative Assembly at the Session ... 1851. *Santa Fe.* 1852. 12mo. Continued. S. 53281

Also in Spanish.

... The New Mexico, Arizona and Colorado Missionary Association. *New York: Anson D. F. Randolph & Co.* 1869. 8vo, pp. 16. B. 53282

Also: First Annual Report ... with Constitution ... Officers and Members. ... [n. p.:] *The Society.* 1869. 12mo, pp. 23, (1). Continued. B.

New-Mexico, otherwise the voyage of Antonio de Espejo who in the yeare 1583 with his company, discovered a land of 15 provinces, replenished with townes and villages, with houses of four or five stories height. It lieth northward, and some suppose that the same way men may, by places inhabited, go to the land tearmed the Labrador, translated out of the Spanish. *London: T. Cadman.* [1587.] 12mo. 53283

Extremely rare; not known to Lowndes or bibliographers in general. This voyage (in Spanish) is included in Hakluyt's Collection.

Revised Statutes of the Territory of New Mexico. ... prefixed ... the Organic Law of the Territory. Revised ... by James J. Davenport, Chief Justice of the Territory. *Santa Fé.* 1856. 8vo. C. 53284

The Seymour and Blair Democratic Platform of New Mexico. [N. p. 1868.] 8vo, pp. 2. H. 53285

A New Military Dictionary; or, the Field of War. Containing A Particular and Circumstantial Account of the most Remarkable Battles, Sieges, Bombardments, and Expeditions, Whether by Sea, or Land. Such as relate to Great Britain and her Dependencies. ... By a Military Gentleman. ... *London: Printed for J. Cooke ...* MDCC.L.X. Folio. 53286

Contains Plates, Portraits, Maps, and Plans of Ontario, Crown Point, etc.

... New-Milk Cheese. *See* [Sargeant (L. M.)]

A New Ministry: The very Important Debate of the House of Commons, on Mr. Coke's Motion for an Address to his Majesty "Requesting that he would be graciously pleased to take into his royal Consideration, the distressed Situation of the Country from the Calamities of a long and ruinous War, and that he would choose such an Administration as may deserve the Confidence of the People." ... March 24, 1783. *London: S. Bladon.* MDCCLXXXIII. 8vo, pp. (4), 35. 53287

The New Mirror of Literature ... . Edited by G. P. Morris [and N. P. Willis]. *New-York.* 1843–44. 3 vols., sm. folio.

The New Mirror for Travellers; and Guide to the Springs. By an Amateur [J. K. Paulding?]. ... *New-York: G. & C. Carvill.* 1828. 12mo, pp. 292. B., C. 53289

... The New Monthly Gazette of the Union and Literary Review: ... . Edited by Rev. Aug. C. L. Arnold. Vol. I. ... *New York: A. Skillman.* 1850. 8vo. H. 53290

New Monthly Magazine of Literature, Fashion and the Fine Arts. Edited by E. Sargent. Vol. I. *New York.* 1843. 8vo.

A New Mystery in Physick Discovered, by Curing of Fevers and Agues, by Quinquina, or Jesuite's Powder. *London.* 1681. 12mo. 53292

A most curious account of the bark of a tree which grows in Peru, and by the Indians named *Kipa*.

The New Nation. A Political, Military, and Literary Journal. Vol. I. ... *New York.* 1864. Folio. Continued. BA.

The New National Song Book, containing Songs, Odes, and other Poems, on National Subjects. ... *New York: Leavitt and Allen.* [n. d.] 24mo, pp. 156. 53294

The New National Tax Law as approved June 30, 1864. *New York: Beadle & Co.* 1864. 16mo, pp. 126. 53295

The New Naval Station at League Island. [n. p. 1862.] 8vo, pp. 32. H. 53296

New News from Robinson Cruso's Island, in a Letter to a Gentleman at Portsmouth. *Cruso's Island* [*Boston*], *Printed in the Year* 1720. 16mo, pp. 8. B. 53297

"Dated at the end, Dec. 19th, 1720. Written by an advocate of a larger emission of bills of credit, and against the majority in the Council and the supporters of Gov. Shute in his contest with the popular party. It abounds in allusions, serious and satirical, to prominent men and measures of the time. A hit at 'the great Don Dago, the *Primate-woo'd-be* of our Island (like the famous Dr. S——l [Sacheverel])' and his 'old Itch of Scribbling,' seems intended for Cotton Mather, and so, perhaps, is one at a 'Clergy-man who (*Commedian-like*) will stand *belabouring his Cushion* and intermixing his Harrangue with Thunder-Bolts, while he is entertaining his *peaceable Congregation* with things whereof he is almost as *Ignorant* as I am of the *Saddle* Balaam *rode on* when his Ass spoke,' etc. When Gov. Shute, in his speech at the opening of the session, March 15, 1721, recommeaded measures to punish the authors of factious and seditious papers, the House answered that few or none would dare to publish such papers, 'if proper measures had been taken to discover and punish the authors of a libel, called, *News from Robinson Cruso's Island*, wherein the members of the *House* are grossly reflected upon' (Hutchinson, ii. 223). To that libel, the '*New News*,' etc., was perhaps a rejoinder."—J. H. TRUMBULL.

The New North American Spelling Book ... . *Baltimore: Murphy & Co.* 1856. 12mo, pp. 120. B. 53298

A New Offer to the Lovers. *See* [Mather (C.)], XI. 46430.

New Official Manual for United States Consuls: containing full Regulations and Directions ... . *Washington.* 1837. 8vo.

NEW ORLEANS, *La.* An Act to incorporate the Commercial Bank of New-Orleans. *New-Orleans: Printed by E. Johns & Co.* 1833. 16mo, pp. 32, (1). H. 53300

Also: Report of the Commercial Bank of New Orleans. *New Orleans: L. Dillard & Co. printers.* 1853. 12mo, pp. 8. Continued.—Act to Incorporate the Mechanics' and Traders' Bank of New Orleans. *New Orleans.* 1833. 8vo. S.

Actes du Conseil Législatif du Territoire d'Orléans, 1804 et 1805. *A la Nouvelle-Orléans, de l'Imprimerie du Moniteur, chez J. B. Fontaine.* 1805. 12mo. 53301

An early specimen of printing in New Orleans.

... Acts passed at the First Session of the First Legislature of the Territory of Orleans ... . *New-Orleans: Press of Bradford & Anderson.* 1806. 8vo, pp. ix, 221. C., H. 53302

In French and English.

Adresse au Conseil Législatif du Territoire d'Orléans. *Nouvelle-Orléans, de l'Imprimerie du Telegraphe.* 1808. 12mo, pp. 15

Signed "Probus" at the end. In French and English on opposite pages.

An Address To the Citizens of New Orleans, on ... Temperance. Published by order of the New Orleans Temperance Society. *New Orleans: Toy, Printer.* 1841. 12mo, pp. 22. H.

Addresses delivered at the Celebration of the Thirteenth Anniversary of the Victory of New Orleans. *Philadelphia: Printed by William Stavely.* 1828. 8vo, pp. 16. 53305

Almanach de Commerce pour la Nouvelle-Orléans. The New Orleans Directory and Register. [Fourth Issue.] With the Tariff of June, 1824. By John Adams Paxton. *New Orleans: The Author.* 1827. 18mo, 165 leaves. Continued. C.

Fifth Annual Report of the Association for the relief of Jewish Widows & Orphans of New-Orleans: ... March 25, 1860. *New-Orleans: Lathrop & Co., Printers.* 1860. 8vo, pp. 27, (1).

Annual Report of the Board of Health of ... New-Orleans, for 1849. *New-Orleans.* 1850. 8vo, pp. 16. Plan and 2 folded leaves. Continued. B. 53308

Annual Report of the Council of Municipality Number Two, on the Condition of its Public Schools. *New-Orleans.* 1843. 8vo, pp. 16. Continued. H. 53309

Also: Annual Report of the ... Directors of the Public Schools, ... New Orleans, For ... 1868. *New Orleans: Isaac T. Hinton, ... Printer.* 1868. 8vo, pp. 141, ii. H.

Annual Report of the ... Commissioners and Officers of the Houses of Refuge, ... of New Orleans, for ... 1859. *New Orleans.* 1859. 8vo, pp. 23, (1). H. 53310

Annual Report of the President of the Commercial Bank of New-Orleans, January, 1838. *New-Orleans: Printed by Benjamin Levy.* 1838. 8vo, pp. 53. H., S. 53311

This bank furnished the means for the water-works of the city. Also: Documents relating to Dividend, by the Commercial Bank of New-Orleans. 1847. [*New Orleans: Toy, Printer.* n. d.] 8vo, pp. 14, (4). H.

Boston Board of Trade, 1856. Report o. .. Committee to whom was referred the subject of Steam Communication between

Boston and New Orleans ... . *Boston: Moore & Crosby, Printers.* 1856. 8vo, pp. 18. BA. 53312

Also: Appeal to the Capitalists and others, on Steam Communication between Boston and New Orleans. *Boston.* 1860. 8vo. *See also* Vol. II., No. 6587.

Catalogue of the Library of the Lyceum and Library Society, First District, ... New Orleans. *New Orleans: Printed by R. C. Kerr.* 1858. 8vo, pp. 124. BA., C. 53313

Also: Catalogue of the Public School Library of Municipality No. Two. *New Orleans.* 1848. 8vo, pp. viii, 155. B.

Charter of the City of New Orleans ... . *New Orleans.* 1852. 8vo. S. 53314

City Celebration of the Anniversary of the National Independence, at ... New Orleans, La. July 4th, 1864. *New Orleans.* 1864. 8vo, pp. 24. 53315

Comptroller's Report, ... of ... Receipts and Expenditures of ... New-Orleans, from April 12th, 1852, to January 1st, 1853. ... *New-Orleans: Printed by Cook, Young & Co.* 1853. 8vo, pp. 144. Continued. B. 53316

Constitution and By-Laws of the Battalion of Washington Artillery, adopted Feb. 11, 1861. [With the] Roll of the Battalion. *New Orleans.* 1861. 32mo, pp. 64. 53317

Known as the New Orleans "Tigers."

Constitution and By-Laws of the John Brown Pioneer Radical Republican Club ... of New Orleans ... . Adopted, May 16th, 1870. [n. p. n. d.] 12mo, pp. 13, (1). H. 53318

Constitution and By-Laws of the Unitarian Home Mission, of New Orleans. Organized ... Jan. 13, 1861. *New Orleans: Clark & Brisbin, Printers.* 1860 [*sic*]. 24mo, pp. 10. H. 53319

Correspondence between the Mayor and Federal Authorities relative to the Occupation of New Orleans ... . *New Orleans.* 1862. 8vo, pp. 29. B. 53320

Debate in the House of Representatives of the Territory of Orleans, on a Memorial to Congress, respecting the Illegal Conduct of General Wilkinson. *New Orleans.* 1807. 8vo. S.

Defaite de l'Armée Anglaise, commandée par S. Edw. Packenham, á l'attaque du 8 Janvier 1815 de la ligne de rétranchements de l'Armée Américaine par le Général Jackson. *Nouvelle-Orléans.* 1815. 8vo. Plate. 53322

Digest of the Ordinances and Resolutions of the Second Municipality of New-Orleans, in force May 1, 1840. ... By John Calhoun ... . *New-Orleans: Printed by F. Cook & A. Levy.* 1840. 8vo, pp. (2), 392. B. 53323

A Digest of the Ordinances, Resolutions, By-Laws and Regulations of the Corporation of New Orleans ... . *New Orleans. G. Brusle.* 1836. 8vo, pp. 620. C. 53324

In English and French.

A Faithful Picture of the Political Situation of New Orleans, at the Close of the Last and the Beginning of the Present Year, 1807. [*New Orleans.*] 1807. 8vo, pp. 40. + *Boston: Reprinted ...* 1808. 8vo, pp. 48. B. 53325

Grand Jury Report, and the Evidence taken by them in reference to the Great Riot In New Orleans, Louisiana, July 30th, 1866. [n. p. n. d.] 8vo, pp. 16. H. 53326

A History of the Proceedings in ... New Orleans, on the occasion of the Funeral Ceremonies in honor of Calhoun, Clay and Webster, Dec. 9, 1852. *New Orleans.* 1852. 8vo.

History of the Yellow Fever in New Orleans, during the Summer of 1853. With Sketches of the Scenes of Horror which occurred during the Epidemic: Descriptions and Illustrations of Charity Hospital, and the public Cemeteries ... . By a Physician of New Orleans. ... *Philadelphia: C. W. Kenworthy.* 1854. 8vo, pp. 115. 53328

First Anniversary of the Home for Jewish Widows and Orphans of New Orleans, January 8th, 1857 ... . *New Orleans: Printed by E. C. Wharton.* 1857. 8vo, pp. 28. H. 53329

Report of the Howard Association of New Orleans. Epidemic of 1853. *New Orleans: Printed by Sherman & Wharton.* 1853. 12mo, pp. 32, 36. B., H. 53330

Also: ... Epidemic of 1858. [*New Orleans:*] *Printed at the Office of the Louisiana Courier.* [n. d.] 12mo, pp. 7.—Report ... 1867. *New Orleans.* [n. d.] 8vo, pp. 41. B.—Supplemental Report ... 1870. *New Orleans: Stetson & Armstrong, Printers.* 1870. 12mo, pp. 12.

Instructions from the Inhabitants of the Territory of Orleans to their Representatives in the Legislature. [n. p. 1804.] 8vo, pp. 14. M., P. 53331

Annual Report of the Managers of the Ladies' Benevolent Society, New Orleans. ... *New Orleans: Printed by Sherman, Wharton & Co.* 1855. 24mo, pp. 11. H. 53332

The Laws and General Ordinances of ... New-Orleans ... . By Henry J. Leovy ... . New Edition. *New-Orleans: Bloomfield & Steel.* 1866. 8vo, pp. 614. B. + *New Orleans: Simmons & Co.* 1870. 8vo, pp. 685. C. 53333

Memorial of the ... Inhabitants, of New Orleans, December 31, 1827. Referred to the Committee on Land Claims. *Washington: Printed by Gales & Seaton.* 1828. 8vo, pp. 25. Map.

Constitution and By-Laws of the Mercantile Library Association of New-Orleans. ... [n. p.:] *Wm. Bloomfield, Jr., Printer.* 1857. 24mo, pp. 24. B. 53335

Also: First Annual Report of the Mercantile Library Association of New-Orleans. *New Orleans.* 1858. 8vo. Continued. S.

Message of ... [the] Mayor of ... New Orleans, in relation to the New Orleans, Jackson & Great Northern Railroad Company, ... 1858. *New Orleans.* 1858. 8vo, pp. 36, (2). H.

Minority Report of the Select Committee ... on the New Orleans Riots. [*Washington.* 1867.] 8vo. 53337

Constitution and By-Laws of the New Orleans Academy of Sciences. *New Orleans.* 1859. 8vo. 53338

Also: Report of the Special Committee ... upon the subject of a Geological and Scientific Survey of ... Louisiana ... . *New-Orleans.* 1858. 8vo. S.

First Report of the New Orleans and Nashville Railroad Company. *New Orleans.* 1836. 12mo. Map. 53339

New Orleans as I found it. By H. Didimus. Part I. *New York.* 1845. 8vo. A., C. 53340

New Orleans as it is: Its Manners and Customs ... . By a Resident. [n. p.:] *Printed for the Publisher.* 1850. 8vo, pp. 79.

Report of the New Orleans Canal, ... 1835. [n. p. 1835.] 8vo, pp. 8. 53342

Also: Report ... of the New Orleans Canal and Banking Company. ... 1835. *New Orleans.* 1835. 8vo, pp. 23, 6, 3. + [n. p. 1835.] Folio, pp. (2). H.

New Orleans Chamber of Commerce. 1856. Report of the Committee on Ocean Steamers in reference to ... Steam Communication between New Orleans and Boston ... . *New Orleans: Printed by Edward C. Wharton.* 1856. 12mo, pp. 12. 53343

New-Orleans Directory, for 1841; ... Published by Michel & Co. *New-Orleans: Printed by J. L. Sollée.* 1840. 12mo, pp. vii, 366. C. 53344

New-Orleans Directory for 1842 ... . With Historical Notices of the State of Louisiana, and the City of New-Orleans ... . *New-Orleans: Pitts & Clarke.* 1842. 8vo. Plates. C. 53345

New Orleans Annual Directory and Commercial Register for 1846. Published by Michel & Co. *New Orleans: E. A. Michel & Co.* [n. d.] 16mo, pp. 668. C. 53346

Cohen's New Orleans Directory, including Jefferson City, Carrollton, Gretna, Algiers and McDonough, for 1854. *New Orleans: Office of the Picayune.* 1854. 8vo. Continued. C.

The directory for 1855 contains biographies and directory of the planters of Louisiana and Mississippi, with twenty-seven portraits.

Kerr's General Advertiser and City Directory for 1856. *New Orleans.* 1856. 8vo. C. 53348

Hellier's New Orleans Business Directory, for 1860 and '61, with Commercial Register of Business Men of New York City. Published Annually.—July, 1860. *New-York: Hellier & Company.* 1860. 8vo, pp. 52. 53349

Gardner's New Orleans Directory, for ... 1859; embracing the City Record, a general Directory ... and a Business ... Directory. Compiled ... by Charles Gardner ... . *New Orleans.* 1858. 8vo, pp. 380. Portrait. Continued. B. 53350

Graham's Crescent City Directory for 1867. ... *New Orleans: L. Graham.* 1867. 8vo, pp. 607, iii. 53351

Graham & Madden's Crescent City Directory, 1870. *New Orleans.* 1870. 8vo. C. 53352

[Correspondence relating to] the New-Orleans Free Library. [*New Orleans.* 1847.] 8vo, pp. 14. H. 53353

Also: An Address on the subject of a Free Library. *New Orleans.* 1852. 8vo.

New Orleans Medical Journal ... Edited by E. D. Fenner and A. Hester. *New Orleans.* 1844. 8vo. A. 53354

Continued as the "New Orleans Medical and Surgical Journal," from 1849; edited by A. Hester.

... New Orleans Medical News and Hospital Gazette. A Semi-Monthly Journal, edited by Samuel Choppin, M.D. ... Vol. I. ... 1854. *N[ew] O[rleans.* n. d.] 8vo. Continued. H.

The New Orleans Miscellany. ... February, 1848. Volume I. ... D. Macaulay, LL.D. Editor ... . *New Orleans: Ferguson & Crosby, Printers.* [n. d.] 8vo. H. 53356

New Orleans Riot. Its Official History. *Washington.* 1866. 8vo. 53357

Annual Report and Circular of the New Orleans School of Medicine ... . *New Orleans.* 1857. 8vo, pp. 8. Continued.

New-Orleans Sketch Book. Edited by G. M. Wharton. *Philadelphia.* 1853. 12mo. 53359

Norman's New Orleans and Environs: containing a brief historical sketch of the Territory and State of Louisiana, and the City of New Orleans, from the earliest period to the present time: ... *New Orleans: B. M. Norman.* 1845. 24mo, pp. 223.

Proceedings of the Physico-Medical Society of New-Orleans, on the Expulsion of C. A. Luzenberg. [n. p.] 1838. 8vo. S.

... Removal of City Council of New Orleans. Letter from The General of the Army, in answer to a resolution of the House of 9th instant, relative to the removal of the city council of New Orleans and of Jefferson City, Louisiana. March 10, 1868. ... [*Washington.* 1868.] 8vo, pp. 25. W. 53362

Report of the Board of Administrators of the Charity Hospital. *N. O.* [1851.] 8vo, pp. 19. Continued. H. 53363

Report of the Directors of the Public Schools of the First District ... 1858. *New-Orleans.* 1859. 8vo, pp. 41. S.

Report of the Joint Committee of Finance of the Senate and House of Representatives on the Banking Situation of the Monied Institutions of New Orleans. ... *New Orleans: J. Bayon ... Printer.* 1837. 12mo, pp. 23, 3 folded leaves. H. 53365

Report of the Sanitary Commission of New Orleans on the Epidemic Yellow Fever of 1853; ... *New Orleans.* 1854. 8vo, pp. xx, 542. S. 53366

... Report ... of the Select Committee appointed to investigate Matters connected with the New Orleans Massacre of July 30, 1866, and to report such Legislative Action as the Condition of Affairs in the State of Louisiana required. [*Washington.* 1867.] 8vo, pp. 61. H. 53367

Report of the Select Committee on the New Orleans Riots. *Washington.* 1867. 8vo, pp. (2), 596. B. 53368

Report of the Water Works Committee of the Commercial Bank of New-Orleans. Presented ... 1836 ... . *New-Orleans: Printed by Gaston Brusle.* 1836. 12mo, pp. 14. Continued. H.

Report on the McDonogh Estate, by the Special Committee of the Common Council of New Orleans. [n. p. 1856.] 8vo, pp. 14. H. 53370

See also Vol. XI., Nos. 43175–7.

Report upon the Wealth, Internal Resources, and Commercial Prosperity of ... New Orleans. *New Orleans.* 1855. 8vo, pp. 16

Reports of the Minority and Majority of the Financial Commission of New Orleans, under Special Orders No. 69, issued by General Banks, March 18, 1864. *New Orleans: Era Office.* 1864. 8vo, pp. 21. Tables. 53372

Reports of the Naval Engagements on the Mississippi River, resulting in the Capture of Forts Jackson and St. Philip and the City of New Orleans. *Washington: Government Printing Office.* 1862. 8vo, pp. 107. 53373

Rules and Regulations for the Government of the High School for Boys of the Second Municipality ... . *New Orleans.* 1843. 8vo

Also: Rules and Regulations for the Government of the Public Schools within the Second Municipality of ... New Orleans. *New Orleans.* 1843. 16mo, pp. 8. Continued. H.

Seventh Annual Report of the St. Anna's Asylum, for the Relief of Destitute Females and their ... Children ... . *New Orleans: Isaac T. Hinton, Printer.* 1860. 12mo, pp. 12. H.

Seventh Report of the Southwestern Bible Society of New-Orleans, ... 1856. *New-Orleans.* 1856. 12mo. Continued.

Statement of the Consolidated Debt of New-Orleans, La. ... *New-Orleans.* 1852. 8vo, pp. 17. S. 53377

See also Vol. I., No. 3573, Vol. V., No. 20481, Vol. VI., No 28256, Vol. X., No. 42231, *and* Vol. XI., No. 44519.

Constitution and By-Laws of the Association and Board of Trustees of the New Orphan Asylum. *Cincinnati: Dumas & Lawyer.* 1853. 12mo, pp. 8. 53378

The New Pantheon; or the Age of Black. A Poem. *New York: S. A. Rollo.* 1860. 12mo, pp. 47. 53379

The New Path. Published by the Society for the Advancement of Truth in Art. ... *New York.* 1863–5. 2 vols., 8vo, pp. 163, (1), 4; 200. B. 53380

Edited by Clarence Cook and Russell Sturgis, Jr.

A New Phase in Ecclesiastical Law and Presbyterian Church Government, as recently administered in the Session of the Madison Square Church, and in the Fourth Presbytery of New York, being also an Explanation and Appeal to Members of said Church. *New York.* 1863. 8vo, pp. 62. 53381

New Philadelphia Coal Mining Company. ... *Boston: Wright & Potter, Printers.* 1864. 8vo, pp. 26. 3 Plates. B. 53382

The New Pictorial and Illustrated Family Magazine ... . Edited by Robert Sears. Vol. III. *New York: Robert Sears.* MDCCCXLVI. 8vo, pp. 530. 53383

Contains many articles on America.

NEW PLIMOUTH. The | Book of the General Laws | Of the Inhabitants of the Jurisdiction of | New-Plimouth; | Collected out of the Records of the | General Court | And lately revised, and with some Emendations and Additions, Established | and Disposed into such Order as they may readily conduce to ge- | neral use and benefit, | And published by the Authority of the General Court for that | Jurisdiction, held at Plimouth, the sixth of June, | Anno Dom. 1671. | *Cambridge: Printed by Samuel Green.* 1672. Folio.

Collation: Title; "To our Beloved Brethren and Neighbours, the Inhabitants of New-Plimouth," by the General Court, signed, Nathaniel Morton, Secr., 2 pp.; The Generall Laws and Liberties, pp. 47; The Table, pp. 8. An excessively rare volume. Brinley's copy (No. 843) sold for $130. *See also* Plymouth.

The Book of the General Laws [as before]. *Boston In New-England: Printed by Samuel Green.* 1685. Folio, pp. (6), 75, (9).

Compact, with ... Colony of New Plymouth. *See* No. 7962.

A Declaration of the Warrantable Grounds and Proceedings of the First Associates of the Government of New-Plymouth; In their Laying the First Foundations of this Government, and in their Making Laws, and Disposing of the Lands within the Same. Together With the General Fundamentals of their Laws. Enacted, Ordained, and Constituted, by the Authority of the Associates of New-Plymouth. *Boston: Printed ... at Greenleaf's.* M,DCC,LXXIII. 8vo, pp. 24. C., H., N. 53386

Great Rising and Breaking of a Bubble. *Boston, Reprinted.* 1767. 12mo. 53387

Relates to the Plymouth Company Patent.

Records of the Colony of New Plymouth, in New England, printed [from the original Documents] by order of the Legislature of Massachusetts, Edited by N. B. Shurtleff, M.D., and D. Pulsifer. ... *Boston.* 1855–61. 10 vols., rl. 4to. 53388

These volumes possess uncommon interest as containing the earliest extant records of the oldest English colony in New England. The able manner in which the volumes are edited, and the very handsome manner in which they are printed, reflect high honor on the intelligence, public spirit, and liberality of all concerned in their production.

New Post-Office Directory. Alphabetical List of Post-Offices in the United States ... . *New York: American News Company.* 18—. Rl. 8vo, pp. 238. 53389

The New Priest. *See* [Lowell (R. T. S.)], Vol. X. 42467.

The New Quarterly Review; and British Colonial Register. *London: J. M. Richardson.* 1812. 8vo. 53390

The New Quarterly Review, and Digest of Current Literature, British, American, French, and German. For ... 1852. Vol. I. [*London:*] *Hookham and Sons.* [1852.] 8vo, pp. (2), 442. Continued. B. 53391

New Reasons for Abolition. *See* [Stephen (G.)]

... The New "Reign of Terror" in the Slaveholding States, for 1859–60. *New York: American Anti-Slavery Society.* 1860. 12mo, pp. iv, 144. H. 53392

Anti-Slavery Tracts, No. 4.

New River Guide, or a Gazetteer of all the Towns on the Western Waters. *Cincinnati: J. A. & U. P. James.* 1848. 8vo

A Guide to New Rochelle. *See* [Bolton (R.)], Vol. II. 6246.

New Route to California, and Union of the Atlantic and Pacific, By Road, Railway or Canal. [*London.* 1852.] 8vo, pp. 16. 53394

NEW SALEM, *Mass.* Catalogue of the Trustees, Instructors and Students of New-Salem Academy, October, 1827. *Wendell, Mass.: J. Metcalf, Printer.* [n. d.] Folio, 1 leaf. Continued. H. 53395

Report of the School Committee of ... New Salem, for ... 1855–6. *Athol Depot: Printed by R. Putnam.* 1856. 8vo, pp. 20. Continued. H. 53396

A New Scene interesting to the Citizens of the United States of America, additional to the Historical Play of Columbus, By a Senator of the United States. ... [*Philadelphia:*] *Printed by Benj. Franklin Bach.* M,DCCXCVIII. 8vo, pp. 12. BA. 53397

Supposed to have been written by A. Martin, Governor of North Carolina.

A New Series of the Evangelical Intelligencer. *Philadelphia.* 1808. 8vo. 53398

New Settlement. *See* [Cole (A.)], Vol. IV., No. 14283.

New, Sharp Threshing Instrument, Having Teeth. ... [*New-York.* 1868.] 8vo. H. 53399

A sort of thrust at American customs, institutions, laws, etc.

A New Society, for the Benefit of Indians, organized at the City of Washington, February, 1822. [n. p. n. d.] 8vo, pp. 12

Corrected title of our No. 34597, Vol. IX.

The New South. *Port Royal, S. C.* 1862. 4to. 53401

NEW SPAIN. An Account of the Cruelties exercised by the Inquisition in Portugal: To which is added a Relation of the Detention of Mr. Lovis Ramé in the Prisons of the Inquisition in the Kingdom of Mexico in New Spain, in the Years 1679, 1680, 1681, 1682. and of his happy Deliverance. Written by one of the Secretaries of the Inquisition. *London, for R. Burrough and J. Baker.* 1708. 8vo, pp. 164. 53402

An Account of the Rise and Present State of the Inquisitions, to which is added, the remarkable Tryal and Sufferings of a Protestant by the Inquisition in New Spain. *London.* 1730. 8vo.

See also Nueva Espana.

New Spain; an Opera. *See* [Scawen (John)].

New System of Fortification, constructed with Standing Timber, &c., or the Sentiments of a West India Savage on the Art of War. *London.* 1770. 8vo. 53404

A New System of Military Discipline, Founded upon Principle. By General Officer. *Philadelphia: Printed ... by R. Aitken ...* . M. DCC. LXXVI. 8vo, pp. viii, 267. P. 53405

A New System of Paper Money, by a Citizen of Boston. *Boston: Printed ... by I. R. Butts.* 1837. 8vo, pp. 20. H.

A New System of Philosophy; or The Newtonian Hypothesis examined. By an American. *Poughkeepsie: For the Author.* M,DCC,LXXXIII. 8vo, pp. (3), 19. BA. 53407

New System of Politics, or Sons against Fathers. ... *London.* 1808. 8vo. 53408

Relates to the War of 1812.

The New Tariff. Articles on which Duties will be levied after August 1, 1862. The Rates of Duty, General Provisions and Regulations. Compiled by Horace E. Dresser, Naval Office, New York Custom House. [n. p. n. d.] 8vo, pp. 15.

See also [Hickman (G. H.)], Vol. VIII., No. 31700.

The New | Testament | Of our Lord and Saviour | Jesus Christ; | Newly Translated out of the Original Greek: | And with the former Translations | Diligently compared and revised. | Appointed to be read in Churches. | *Philadelphia: Printed and Sold by R. Aitken* ... . 1777. | 12mo, pp. 353. 53410

The first edition of the New Testament (in English) printed in America with an American imprint.

The New Testament ... . *Philadelphia: R. Aitken.* 1778. 12mo. + [*Ibid.*] 1779. 12mo. + *Philadelphia: F. Bailey.* 1780. 12mo. + *Philadelphia: Hall & Sellers.* 1780. 12mo. + *Philadelphia: For J. Cruikshank* ... . 1786. 12mo. + *Trenton: Isaac Collins.* 1788. 8vo. + *Elizabeth-town: S. Kollock.* 1788. 12mo. + *New York: Hugh Gaine.* 1790. 12mo. + *New Haven: Printed by A. Morse.* 1790. 12mo. 53411

For a list of the numerous errors in the New Haven edition, *see* O'Callaghan, p. 37.

The New Testament ... . *Philadelphia: John McCulloch* [*about* 1791]. 12mo. + *Newbury-port: John Mycall.* [1791.] 8vo. + *Philadelphia: Wm. Young.* 1792. 18mo. + *Boston: For J. Boyle* ... . 1794. 12mo. W. + *Trenton: Isaac Collins.* 1794. 12mo. + ... with Practical Observations ... . By William Burkitt, M.A. ... *New-Haven: Printed by Abel Morse.* M,DCC,XCIV. 4to, pp. 1168. + *New Haven: Ed. O'Brien.* 1797. 12mo. + *Lancaster: J. Bailey and W. & R. Dickson.* 1797. 12mo. + *Philadelphia: Charles Cist.* 1799. 12mo. 53412

The New Testament ... . Appointed to be read by Children. *Hartford: Printed by John Babcock.* 1798. 24mo, pp. 69.

"An ill-written paraphrase; illustrated by coarse wood-cuts."—E. B. O'CALLAGHAN.

The New Testament ... . *Nashville, Tenn.: Graves, Marks & Co.* 1861. 18mo, pp. 225. + *Augusta, Ga.: Confederate States Bible Society.* 1862. 48mo. + [*Ibid.*] 1863. 18mo, pp. 300, 80.

See also Vol. IV., No. 12875, *and* Vol. VI., No. 22875.

New Themes. *See* [Colwell (S.)], Vol. IV., No. 14911.

New Theological Seminary. [*Bangor.* n. d.] 8vo, pp. 24.

This is the Maine Charity School.

A New Trade laid open from the Islands of Tobago, Granados, and others of the Leeward Islands, to the Spanish Main, in the Kingdom of Peru; and from Cape Florida to the Havanna and Santa Cruz in the Kingdom of Mexico. By a Gentleman who resided many years in both Kingdoms. *London: J. Huxman.* [n. d.] 8vo. 53416

New Universal Collection of Voyages and Travels, containing everything Remarkable in the various parts of the Known World. *London: W. Owen.* 1755. 3 vols., 12mo. Maps and Plates. 53417

NEW UTRECHT, *N. Y.* List of Persons Enrolled in the Town of New Utrecht, Kings County, N. Y. [n. p. 1863.] 8vo, pp. 13. 53418

A New Version of the Psalms of David. By Thomas Cradock. *Annapolis, Md.* 1756. 8vo, pp. 160. 53419

See also Vol. II., No. 7315

New Voyage. *See* [La Martinière (P. M. de)], X. 38713–14.

A New Voyage. *See* [Defoe (D.)], Vol. V., No. 19291.

A New Voyage to Georgia. *See* Vol. VII., No. 27079.

New Voyages and Travels. *See* Phillips (R.)

A New Way to carry a Presidential Election. The U. S. Grand Jury as a Political Engine. [n. p. n. d.] 8vo, pp. 16.

Die New Welt. *See* [Huttich (J.)], Vol. IX., No. 34106.

The New World in 1859, being the United States and Canada, Illustrated and Described. In Five Parts. ... *London: H. Baillière.* 1859. 8vo, pp. viii, 114, 87, 78, 96, 80. 53421

These are odd parts of "Putnam's Magazine," with a title as above.

The New Yankee Doodle, by Dan (not Bev.) Tucker. Dedicated to the United States Volunteers. *Washington: O. H. Morrison.* 1861. 12mo, pp. 23. 53422

The New-Year Verses of the Printers Lads, who carry the Pennsylvania Gazette to the Customers, for 1756. [n. p. n. d.] Folio, 1 page. P. 53423

Printed by Franklin and Hall. The Philadelphia Library has a series from 1757 to 1776.

A New-Year Well-begun. *See* [Mather (C.)], XI. 46431.

A New-Years-Day; Dedicated to the Patrons of Liberty Hall, and Cincinnati Gazette. *Cincinnati, January* 1, 1817. 12mo, pp. 7. 53424

A New-Years-Day, For 1820; Dedicated to the Patrons of the Inquisitor and Cincinnati Advertiser. By the Carrier. *Cincinnati, January* 1, 1820. 12mo, pp. 11. 53425

The New Year's Day. By the Author of "Sophia Morton," and "Esther." *Boston: Wait, Greene & Co.* 1830. 24mo, pp. 34

A New Year's Gift to Virginia. *See* Virginia.

New-Year's Reflections, for January 1, 1808. ... *Lansinburgh: Printed by Tracy & Bliss.* [n. d.] 12mo, pp. 19. BA. 53427

New Year's Verses, Addressed to the Kind Customers of the Pennsylvania Evening Post, by the Printer's Lads who carry about the same. ... January 1, 1778. [n. p. n. d.] Folio, 1 leaf.

New-Year's Verses of those who deliver the Pennsylvania Ledger to the Subscribers. *Philadelphia, January* 1, 1778. Folio, 1 leaf. P. 53429

NEW YORK COLONY AND STATE.

In arranging the numerous titles under this head, it has been thought most convenient to put them in alphabetical order. The publications of societies and of departments being under the name of said society or department.

An Abstract of Exports ... from New York, for one year, ending September 30th, 1793. [n. p. n. d.] 8vo. 53430

An Abstract of Manufacturing Establishments and Manufactories in the State of New York. [n. p.] 1810. 8vo. 53431

An Abstract of the ... Revised Statutes of ... New York. ... *Canandaigua.* 1830. 8vo. + [*Ibid.*] 1839. 8vo. 53432

An Abstract of the Quarantine Laws for the use of Pilots attending at the Narrows. [n. p.] 1804. 8vo, pp. 93. 53433

An Abstract of the Returns of Meteorological Observations made to the Regents of the University by sundry Academies in the State. Prepared by T. Romeyn Beck and Joseph Henry. [n. p. n. d.] 8vo. 53434

Account of several Passages and Letters between Benj. Fletcher, Governour of New-York, Pennsylvania, New Castle, etc., and the Administrators of the Laws in the Colony of Connecticut. *New-York.* 1693. Folio. 53435

See our Nos. 24712–14. This tract may perhaps dispute with No. 24714 the priority of printing.

An Account of the | Commitment, | Arraignment, | Tryal | and | Condemnation | of | Nicholas Bayard, Esq; | for | High Treason, | in | Endeavouring to subvert the Government of the Province of | New York, in America, by his signing and procuring others to sign Scandalous Libels, call'd Petitions or Addresses to his | Late Majesty King William, the Parliament of England, | and the Lord Cornbury, now Governour of that Province. ... Together with a true copy of the Libels or Addresses themselves. *Printed at New York by order of his Excellency the Lord Cornbury, and reprinted at London,* 1703. Folio, pp. 31, (1). 53436

Corrected title of our No. 4033, Vol. I.

An Account of the Soil, growing Timber, and other Productions, of the Lands in the ... back Parts of the States of New-York and Pennsylvania ... . And particularly the Lands in the County of Ontario, known by the name of The Genesee Tract ... . [n. p.:] *Printed in the Year* 1791. 4to, pp. (2), 37. 2 Maps. BM.

Very rare. The copy at Worcester is imperfect, the British Museum copy has manuscript notes.

Account of the Treaty. *See* Vol. VI. 24712, Vol. IX. 34601.

The Account stated in respect to the Province, for the Costs and Profits in the Building 100 Sail of Vessels, etc. By order of the Gov.: F. Morris, Sec. *New York: Printed by William Bradford.* 1734. Folio, pp. 4. S. 53438

The Act authorizing the Formation of Corporations for Manufacturing, Mining, Mechanical, and Chemical Purposes. Passed Feb. 17, 1848. ... *New York: John S. Voorhies.* 1864. 12mo, pp. 40. + *New York: Baker, Voorhies & Co.* 1866. 12mo, pp. 40, 2. 53439

An Act for ascertaining ... the Citizens who shall be entitled to the right of Suffrage, and to Prevent Fraudulent Voting. ... *Albany: Printed by C. Van Benthuysen.* 1859. 8vo, pp. 14. H.

An Act for Granting to their Majesties the Rate of One Penny per Pound upon all the Real and Personal Estates within the Province of New-York, and to be allowed unto his Excellency the Governor for the care of the Province, Nov. 12, 1692. [n. p. n. d.] Folio. 53441

Title from H. A. Brady's Catalogue.

An Act for Laying an Excise on all Liquors retailed in this Colony. *New York.* 1709. Folio. 53442

From H. A. Brady's Catalogue.

An Act for raising Six Thousand Pounds for the Payment of Three Hundred Volunteers and Officer, to be employed in the Reinforcement of the Frontiers of the Province at Albany in 1694, in the Reign of William and Mary, the 10th April, 1694. *New York: Printed by William Bradford.* 1693. Folio. 53443

An Act for Restraining and Punishing Privateers and Pyrates, passed at New-York in the Reign of William and Mary. [n. p. n. d.] Folio. 53444

Title from H. A. Brady's Catalogue.

An Act for Regulating the Fees of the several Officers and Ministers of the Courts of Justice within this State, passed 18th of April 1785. *New York: S. Loudon.* 1785. 8vo. 53445

Act for Regulating Elections. Together with an Act for the Regulating of Town-Meetings, passed ... 1787. *New York: S. Loudon.* [1787.] 8vo, pp. 22.

Act for the Formation of Corporations of 1848, with the Amendments to and including 1868. *New York.* 1868. 16mo, pp. 52. 53446

Act for the Support of Common Schools; Assembly, Feb. 25, 1819. [n. p.] 1819. Folio, pp. 19. M. 53447

An Act in relation to the Monies levied by Law on Masters, Mates, Mariners, and Seamen, arriving at ... New York ... . *New-York: John M. Elliott, Printer.* 1854. 8vo, pp. 16. H.

... An Act of Parliament For Ascertaining the Rates of Foreign Coyns in Her Majesties Plantations in America. [Colophon:] *Re-printed by William Bradford in New-York,* 1709. Folio, pp. 4. 53449

Act of the Legislature of New York to provide for the Indigent Deaf and Dumb; with Letters of the Deaf and Dumb. *New York.* 1822. 8vo. W. 53450

Act passed March 12 1805, making further provision for the Effectual Performance of Quarantine, also an Order in Council. *New York.* 1809. 8vo. 53451

An Act regulating the Militia of the State of New York, passed at Poughkeepsie, April 3d, 1778, in the Second Session of Assembly. *Poughkeepsie: John Holt.* 1778. 8vo. N. 53452

An Act to amend ... "An Act to establish a Metropolitan Police District" ... . *New-York: Geo. F. Nesbitt & Co., ... Printers.* 1860. 8vo, pp. 31, (1). H. 53453

The Act to amend the Act for the Support of Common Schools, passed April 17, 1822. ... *Albany: Printed by Packard & Van Benthuysen.* 1822. 8vo, pp. 16. B. 53454

... An Act to authorize Life Insurance Companies to make Special Deposits of Securities in the Insurance Department. ... Passed May 18, 1869. *New York: Kennard & Hay.* 1872. 8vo, pp. 12. B. 53455

An Act to authorize the Formation of a Corporation in Place of the Northern Railroad Company ... . [n. p. 1864.] 8vo, pp. 8

An Act to create a Metropolitan Sanitary District and Board of Health ... . *New York: Bergen & Tripp, Printers.* 1866. 8vo, pp. 46. H. 53457

An Act to Incorporate Medical Societies ... in this State ... with the Bye Laws of the Medical Society of the County of New-York ... . *New-York: Printed by James Cheetham.* 1806. 8vo, pp. 23. B. 53458

An Act to Organize the Militia of ... New York. *Albany.* 1793. 12mo. + *Hudson.* 1810. 8vo. + *Albany: Printed by I. W. Clarke.* 1818. 8vo, pp. 12, 9–46. + *Albany: Printed by Websters and Skinners.* 1821. 8vo, pp. 26. + *Albany.* 1823. 8vo

Act to Prevent Frauds and Perjuries at Elections, and to Prevent Slaves from Voting, April 9, 1811. [n. p. n. d.] 8vo, pp. 4. N. 53460

Act to Provide against Infectious and Pestilential Diseases, passed ... April 8, 1811. [n. p. n. d.] 8vo, pp. 27, ix. + March 26, 1813. [n. p. n. d.] 8vo, pp. 26, vi. 53461

Act to Provide for the Enrolment of the Militia, ... passed May 18, 1847; amended ... December 15, 1847; ... *Albany.* 1848. 8vo. S. 53462

An Act to Provide for the Improvement of the Internal Navigation of this State ... April 17, 1816. [n. p. 1816.] 8vo, pp. 12. BA. 53463

Act to Regulate the Militia of ... New-York; passed the 4th of April, 1786. *New-York.* 1786. 8vo. C. 53464

An Act to Regulate the Sale of Intoxicating Liquors, within the Metropolitan Police District ... *New York: Printed by Bergen & Tripp.* 1866. 16mo, pp. 8. 53465

Acts of Assembly of ... New York ... Fifth Assembly, Fourth Session. *New York.* 1697. Folio. Continued. 53466

Acts of Assembly, passed in the Province of New-York, from 1691, to 1718. ... *London: Printed by John Baskett, Printer to the King's Most Excellent Majesty.* MDCCXIX. Folio, pp. xv, 292. H.

"Probably copied from Bradford's edition ("Laws of His Majesty's Colony," 1719, *infra*), and, according to Trott, was printed by order of the Lords Commissioners of Trade and Plantations."—RICH, I. 26.

Acts | of | Assembly | Passed in the | Province of New-York, | From 1691, to 1725. | Examined and Compared with the Originals in the | Secretary's Office. | *Printed and Sold by William Bradford, Printer to the King's Most Excellent | Majesty for the Province of New-York.* | 1726. Sm. folio, pp. (10), 319. N., S. 53468

The Acts passed from 1726 to 1736 are included in some copies, with continuous paging, to 454 inclusive.

Acts of the Legislature ... respecting Navigable Communications between the Great Western and Northern Lakes and the Hudson River. *Albany: Printed by Websters and Skinners.* 1819. 8vo, pp. 20. BA. 53469

Acts passed ... [by] the Legislature ... respecting the Canals From Lake Erie to the Hudson River, and from Lake Champlain to the same. *Albany: Printed by Websters and Skinners.* 1820. 8vo, pp. 20. B. 53470

The Address and Draft of a proposed Constitution submitted to the People of ... New York. Held at Utica, September, 1837. *New York.* 1837. 8vo, pp. 8. 53471

Address and Proceedings of the Democratic State Convention, Held at Rome, August, 1849. *Albany: Printed by Charles Van Benthuysen.* 1849. 8vo, pp. 24. + *Albany Argus Extra.* 1849. 8vo, pp. 24. S. 53472

An Address from the Committee appointed at Mrs. Vandewater's On the 13th Day of September, 1784. To the People of the State of New-York. *New-York: Printed by Shepard Kollock* ... . M,DCC,LXXXIV. 8vo, pp. 16. 53473

Signed by Melancthon Smith and eight others. Relates to the case of Rutgers *vs.* Waddington, and is the defendant's side of the case in this famous trial, which caused much excitement at the time, and is rare.

An Address from the Legislature of the State of New-York to their Constituents. *Fish-kill: Printed by Samuel Loudon.* M.DCC.-LXXXI. 12mo, pp. 12. BA., P. 53474

Address from the Presbytery of New York to the Churches under their Care, on the subject of Educating Poor and Pious Youth for the Gospel Ministry. *New York.* 1805. 8vo.

Address of a Part of the Democratic Delegation in Congress, from ... New York, to their Constituents. *Washington.* 1854. 8vo. S. 53476

The Address of Epaminondas to the Citizens of ... New York. *T. Hoskins, Caldwell, N. Y.* 1820. 8vo. 53477

Setting forth the merits of DeWitt Clinton and his claims to a re-election as Governor. For another edition, *see our* Vol. VI., No. 22679.

Address of Republican Members of the Senate and Assembly, adopted at ... Albany, April 4, 1820. *Albany.* 1820. 8vo, pp. 16

Address of the Committee of Safety. *New York: Printed by John Holt.* 1776. 8vo. 53479

An Address of the Convention of the Representatives of the State of New-York to their Constituents. *Fish-kill: Printed by S. Loudon.* [1776.] 12mo, pp. 19. B. + [*Ibid.*] M.DCC.LXXVI. 12mo, pp. 19. H. + *Norwich: Reprinted by Green and Spooner.* [1776.] 12mo, pp. 16. + *Philadelphia: Printed by John Dunlap.* M.DCC.LXXVII. 12mo, pp. 12. + *Baltimore: Printed by Mary Katharine Goddard.* MDCCLXXVII. 12mo, pp. 15. 53480

Signed "Abraham Ten Broeck, President."

Address of the Convention to the Legislature of ... New-York, on the subject of the Great State Road, held at Newburgh, October 19, 1825 [1826]. *New-York.* 1827. 8vo, pp. 20. S.

Address of the Delegates in Convention to their Constituents. ... with the Constitution of the State ... as amended. And the Resolutions ... . [n. p. 1821.] 16mo, pp. (2), 12, (2). B.

Address of the Democratic Republican Young Men's General Committee. *New York.* 1838. 8vo. 53483

Address of the Democratic State Convention, ... at Utica, June 22, 1848 to the People of the State, and of the United States, and Mr. Van Buren's Letter. *Buffalo Republic Extra.* [n. d.] 8vo, pp. 16. S. 53484

Address of the Friends. *See* Vol. I., No. 398.

Address of the Loyal National League of ... New York, to the People of ... New York, in Convention Assembled at Utica, Oct. 20, 1863. *New York: Loyal Publication Society, No.* 31, 1863. 8vo, pp. 4. + [n. p. n. d.] Rl. 8vo, pp. 8. + [n. p. n. d.] 8vo, pp. 20. 53485

See also Vol. X., No. 42552.

Address of the National Democratic Volunteers. *New York.* 1860. 8vo. 53486

Address of the National Union Executive Committee of ... New York, November 30, 1860. [n. p. n. d.] 8vo. 53487

Address of the Republican and Union Democratic Members of the Legislature. ... *New York: Isaac J. Oliver, Printer.* 1862. 8vo, pp. 15. 53488

Address of the Republican General Committee of the Republican Electors of the State. *New York.* 1807. 8vo. N. 53489

Address of the Republican Members of the Legislature to the Electors of ... New York. *New York.* 1809. 8vo. N.

Address of the State Convention of Delegates from the Several Counties of ... New-York To the People, on the subject of the approaching Presidential Election. *Albany: Beach.* 1828. 8vo, pp. 16. 53491

Address of the State Convention of Teachers and Friends of Education, held at Utica, January ... 1831. With an Abstract of the Proceedings ... . *Utica: Northway and Porter, Printers.* M DCCC XXXI. 8vo, pp. 16. B. 53492

Address of the Union Electoral Committee to the Union Men of New York. [n. p. 1860.] 8vo, pp. 11. B. 53493

Address of the "United Whig Club." *See* [Macomb (R.)]

An Address to his Fellow-Citizens. By a Citizen of New York. [n. p. n. d.] 8vo. N. 53494

An Address to Major-General Tryon, Written in Consequence of his late Expedition into Connecticut. *Printed* MDCCLXXIX. 8vo, pp. 15. 53495

Address to the Electors of ... New York in favor of Judge Yates's Election as Governor. [n. p. n. d.] 8vo. 53496

See also [Hamilton (Alexander)], Vol. VIII., No. 29947.

Address to the Electors of ... New York. Published by Order of the Republican General Committee. *New York.* 1803. 8vo. + [*Ibid.*] 1808. 8vo, pp. 8. 53497

Address to the Electors of ... New York on the ensuing Charter Election. By a Member of the Washington Society. *New York.* 1809. 8vo. 53498

Address to the Electors of ... New York. *New York.* 1812. 8vo. N. 53499

An Address to the Electors of ... New York, by the Republican Members of the Legislature. *Albany: Printed by J. Buel.* 1814. 8vo, pp. 13. + April 10, 1815. [*Ibid.* 1815.] 8vo, pp. 16. B. 53500

Address to the Federal Electors of New York on the Election of Governor and Lt.-Governor ... . *Albany.* 1820. 8vo. 53501

An Address to the Freeholders of ... New York. By Brutus. Trembling for the Liberties of his Country. *New York: The Author.* 1804. 8vo, pp. 9. BA., N. 53502

Address to the Freemen, Freeholders and Inhabitants of the Colony of New York. [*New York.*] 1774. 8vo. W. 53503

Address to the Independent Electors of ... New York, on the present State of Public Affairs, and on the ensuing General Election. *Albany: Websters & Skinners.* [1810.] 8vo, pp. 14. S.

An Address to the Mechanics and Working Men of New York. By a Committee of Mechanics. [n. p. n. d.] 8vo.

An Address to the Negroes in ... New York. By a Negro, ... [n. p. n. d.] 12mo. 53506

An Address to the People of ... New York, by the Federal Republican Members of the Legislature. *Albany: Printed by Websters and Skinners.* 1815. 8vo, pp. 8. [Another.] 1817. P.

An Address to the People. *See* [Jay (John)], Vol. IX. 35830.

An Address to the People of ... New-York; shewing the Necessity of Making Amendments to the Constitution, proposed by the United States, previous to its Adoption. By a Plebian. *Printed in the State of New-York.* M,DCC,LXXX,VIII. 8vo, pp. 26.

An Address to the Public on the African School, lately established under the Care of the Synod of New York and New Jersey. *New York.* 1816. 8vo. 53509

... Address, to the Republican Citizens, of ... New York. *Albany: Printed by H. C. Southwick.* 1813. 8vo, pp. 15. B.

Supplement to the "Albany Register."

Address to the Republican Citizens of ... New-York. *Albany.* 1828. 8vo, pp. 8. 53511

Address to the Republican Electors of the Southern District, by the General Committee friendly to the General Government and State Administration. ... March 25, 1819. *New-York.* 1819. 8vo, pp. 16. S. 53512

An Address to the Republicans and People of New York, Pennsylvania, and Virginia, upon the State of Presidential Parties. By a Citizen of New York. *New York.* 1824. 8vo, pp. 23. + *Philadelphia.* 1824. 8vo. 53513

An Address to the Young Men of the United States on the Subject of Temperance, by the New York Young Men's Society for the Promotion of Temperance. *New York.* 1830. 12mo, pp. 22. W. 53514

Addresses of the City of New York to George Washington, with his Replies. *New York.* 1867. Impl. 8vo, pp. viii, 14. Facsimile. 53515

Seventy-five copies printed on large paper and five on Whatman's drawing paper.

Annual Report of the ADJUTANT GENERAL ... *Albany.* 1827. Folio. 53516

Continued in octavo. The reports for 1861–5 are important for the history of the Rebellion. Also: Opinion of the Adjutant-General of ... New-York, on two questions of Alienism. *Albany: Printed by Packard and Van Benthuysen.* 1833. 8vo, pp. 15. — General Orders from the Office of the Adjutant General. [n. p.] 1862. 12mo. — Official Digest of the General, Division and Special Orders ... received at or issued from the Adjutant General's Office, Northern Division ... 1815–18. *Sacket's Harbor.* 1818. 8vo, pp. 66.

The Advantages. *See* Vol. VI., No. 22740.

Agreement between the Albany and Schenectady Rail Road Company [and eight other roads], ... whereby the said Companies are consolidated into one Corporation, under the Name of the New York Central Rail Road Company ... . *Albany.* 1853. 8vo, pp. 36. 53517

An Alarm to the Legislature. *See* [Wilkins (I.)]

The Albany Zouave Cadets to the Rochester Union Blues. *Albany, N. Y.: Munsell.* 1866. 4to, pp. 35. 53518

An Almanac for 1697. By J. Clapp. *New York: Printed by William Bradford.* 1697. 8vo. 53519

The first New York almanac. Title from Thomas' "History of Printing."

Alphabetical List of Applicants for the Benefit of the Bankrupt Act, passed August 19, 1841, within the Southern District of New York. *New York.* 1843. 8vo. N. 53520

... The Amended Constitution of ... New York, adopted by the Convention of 1867–1868 ... . *Albany: Weed, Parsons & Co.* 1868. 8vo, pp. 83. C. 53521

Amendments to Acts in regard to Passengers in Vessels coming to ... New York, passed July 11, 1851. [n. p. n. d.] 8vo, pp. 8

The American Party of New York. Address adopted at the Annual Meeting of the State Council at Troy, Feb. 24th & 25th, 1857. [n. p. n. d.] 8vo, pp. 8. S. 53523

American Quarterly Review, and ... New-York, on the Bank System: from the Albany Argus, 1832. [n. p. n. d.] 8vo. S.

Anno Regni Annæ Reginæ ... *London, Printed: ... Re-printed by William Bradford.* 1705. Folio, pp. 10, 7–72, 6 leaves not paged, pp. 73–114, 13. 53525

These are, in fact, the laws of New York.

Anno Regni Georgii II. Regis ... . At a Session of the General Assembly of the Colony of New York, ... in New York; begun ... October, 1751, and continued ... to ... November ... . *New York, James Parker.* 1751. Folio, pp. 31. S. 53526

The titles for each year to 1759 are similar. For the twenty-sixth year, pp. 12; twenty-seventh, pp. 19; Second Session, pp. 48, 4; twenty-eighth, pp. 101; twenty-ninth, pp. 66; thirtieth, pp. 42, 15; thirty-first, pp. 23, 42; thirty-second, pp. 43–67; thirty-third, pp. 23–101; thirty-fourth, pp. 32; George III., pp. 7; Second Year, pp. 36, 17.

Anno Regni Georgii II. Regis ... . At a Session of the General Assembly of the Colony of New-York, held at ... New-York; ... August, 1754, and continued ... to ... February, 1755, ... The several Acts that have been passed, since the above mentioned Session, respecting the Militia of the Colony of New-York, are added to this Edition. *New-York: Printed by J. Parker, and W. Weyman* ... . MDCCLVIII. 8vo, pp. 56. P.

Annual Message of the Governor [John A. King] ... . January 6, 1857. *Albany: C. Van Benthuysen, Printer.* 1857. 8vo, pp. 26. Continued. H. 53528

Annual Report, Fifth Regiment, N. Y. S. M. Jefferson Guard, Col. Louis Burger, for 1861. *New York, December* 21, 1861. 8vo, pp. 8. 53529

Answer of the Senate to the Governor's Speech. *Albany.* 1812. Folio. 53530

Anti-Masonic Republican State Convention. Proceedings. Utica, June 21, 1832. [n. p.:] *Evening Journal Extra.* [n. d.] 8vo, pp. 8. S. 53531

Appeal of the People of ... New York, on the expediency of Abolishing the Council of Appointment. *New York.* 1819. 8vo.

An Appeal to the Honorable the Members of the Senate and House of Assembly of ... New York. By Civis. *New York.* 1816. 8vo. N. 53533

Appeal to the People. *See* Vol. VII., No. 26927.

An Argument Delivered. *See* Vol. I., No. 1967.

Arguments offered to the Right Honorable the Lords Commissioners for Trade and Plantation. *New York: Printed by William Bradford.* 1701. 4to. 53534

Relates to an act of the Assembly of New York.

Asylum for Insane Convicts. First Annual Report, 1860. *Albany.* 1861. 8vo. 53535

Communication from the ATTORNEY GENERAL, ... relative to the Constitutionality of the Law abolishing Tolls on Railroads. Transmitted ... April 2, 1860. *Albany: Charles Van Benthuysen, Printer.* 1860. 8vo, pp. 13. H. 53536

Also: Remarks on the Attorney-General's Report to the Senate. *Albany: J. Munsell.* 1849. 12mo, pp. 7. — Report of the Attorney-General on the Constitutionality of erecting the new Counties of Patterson and Unadilla ... . [*Albany.* n. d.] 8vo, pp. 4.

Authentic Account of the Proceedings of the Congress held at New-York In MDCCLXV On the Subject of the American Stamp Act. [*London.*] MDCCLXVII. 8vo, pp. (2), 37. + *Philadelphia, Reprinted.* 1813. 8vo, pp. 29. 53537

Thomas notes an edition, *Philadelphia*, 1767. *See* "Monthly Review," XXXVII. 73.

The Balloting-Book, and other Documents, relating to Military Bounty Lands in ... New-York. *Albany.* 1825. Folio, pp. 189. S. 53538

Chiefly names of the soldiers and their share of land.

... Annual Report of the BANK COMMISSIONERS, February 1, 1834. [n. p. 1834.] 8vo, pp. 31. Continued. H. 53539

Also: ... Report of the Bank Commissioners ... . *Albany.* 1838. 8vo, pp 7. — Report of the Committee on Banks on ... an Act in relation to the Engraving of Bank Notes. ... *Albany: Printed by C. Van Benthuysen.* 1860. 8vo, pp. 7. BA.

Baptist Education Society of ... New York, Thirty-Ninth Annual Meeting, held at Hamilton, Madison Co., N. Y. Aug. 17, 1856 ... . *Press of Waldron & James, Hamilton, N. Y.* 1856. 8vo, pp. 32. S. 53540

Also: The Baptist Educational Commission ... . *New York: Lange, Hillman & Lange.* 1868. 8vo, pp. 28. — Proceedings of the ... Baptist Missionary Convention. ... [n. p.] 1821. 8vo. Continued.

A Bill for the Incorporation of Companies formed to navigate the Lakes, Rivers and Canals of the State ... . [n. p. n. d.] 8vo, pp. 12. H. 53541

Bill in the Chancery of New York at the Suit of Priscilla Bland, John Mann and Mercy, his Wife, against Redford Ashfield and others. [n. p.] 1771. Folio. 53542

Address of the General Committee of the BOARD OF AGRICULTURE of ... New-York, to the County Agricultural Societies, For 1820. ... *Albany: S. Southwick.* 1820. 8vo, pp. 31, (1). B.

Memoirs of the Board of Agriculture of ... New-York. ... *Albany: Printed by S. Southwick.* 1821–26. 3 vols., 8vo, pp. (8), xlviii, (18), 364, (2), 109, Index, (10); (10), 532, (10); (10), 558, (15). Plates. BA., S. 53544

Also: Report of the Board of Agriculture. *Albany.* 1822. 8vo.

... Annual Report of the BOARD OF INSPECTORS of the Mount-Pleasant State Prison. ... for ... 1846 ... . [n. p. 1847.] 8vo, pp. 155, 5 folded leaves. B. 53545

Second Annual Report of the BOARD OF STATE COMMISSIONERS of Public Charities ... March 22, 1869. *Albany.* 1869. 8vo, pp. cx, 220, (1). B. 53546

Boyd's Business Directory of over One Hundred Cities and Villages in New York State ... . 1869–70. *Albany: C. H. Van Benthuysen & Sons.* 1869. 8vo, pp. 884. C. 53547

Brief Observations on the Militia; respectfully addressed to the Legislature and Commander-in-Chief. By an Officer. *New York.* 1804. 8vo. 53548

A Brief State of the Controversy between the Colonies of New-York and New-Jersey, Respecting the Boundary-Line. [*London.* 1770.] 4to, pp. 8. Map by Bernard Ratzer. 53549

A Brief Topographical and Statistical Manual of ... New York ... . Second Edition, Enlarged and Improved. Containing also an Account of the Grand Canals. *New York: E. Bliss and E. White.* 1822. 8vo, pp. 88. 53550

By Sterling Goodenow. Corrected title of No. 27855, Vol. VII. *See also* No. 27854.

Brief van de Wel Eerwarde Classis van Amsterdam, aan de E. Heeren Predikanten en Ouderlingen in de Provincien van Nieuw-York en Nieuw-Jersie die zigh de Coetus Noemer. *Nieuw-York.* 1765. 8vo. 53551

See also our Vol. II., No. 7909.

... By Authority of the BUREAU OF MILITARY RECORD. The State Military Record, devoted to the Interests of New York Soldiers. *New York and Albany: J. P. Robens.* 1866. 8vo, pp. (2), 26. BA. 53552

First Annual Report of [L. L. Doty] Chief of the BUREAU OF MILITARY STATISTICS, January 26, 1864. *Albany: Comstock & Cassidy.* 1864. 8vo, pp. 212. Continued. 53553

Calendar of Historical Manuscripts in the Office of the Secretary of State, Albany, N. Y. Edited by E. B. O'Callaghan. *Albany: Weed, Parsons and Company, Printers.* 1865–66. 2 parts, 4to, pp. xi, 423; xiv, 893. B., C. 53554

Part I. Dutch Manuscripts, 1630–1664; Part II. English Manuscripts, 1664–1776.

Calendar of Historical Manuscripts relating to the War of the Revolution, in the Office of the Secretary of State, Albany, N. Y. ... *Albany: Weed, Parsons and Company, Printers.* 1868. 2 vols., 4to, pp. (6), 682; (2), 495. 4 Plans and Plate. B., S.

Not a mere calendar, but the publication of the manuscripts themselves.

Calendar of New York Colonial Manuscripts indorsed Land Papers, in the Office of the Secretary of State ... . 1643–1803. *Albany: Weed, Parsons and Company, Printers.* 1864. 8vo, pp. 1087. C. 53556

Annual Financial Report of the Auditor of the CANAL DEPARTMENT of ... New York. [n. p.] 1862. 8vo. S. 53557

Annual Report of the Canal Appraisers of the State ... . February 4, 1861. *Albany: Charles Van Benthuysen, Printer.* 1861. 8vo, pp. 110. Continued. H. 53558

Annual Report of the Canal Commissioners ... 1819. *Albany: Printed by J. Buel.* 1819. 8vo, pp. 46. Continued. B.

Annual Report of the Commissioners of the Canal Fund of ... New-York. ... *Albany: Printed by Croswell and Van Benthuysen.* 1830. 8vo. Continued. 53560

Also: Annual Report of the Commissioners of the Canal Fund, with the Annual Report of the Auditor of the Canal Department, ... January 8, 1855. *Albany: C. Van Benthuysen, Printer.* 1855. 8vo, pp. 160, 2 folded leaves. Continued. — Annual Report of Tolls, Trade and Tonnage, of the New-York Canals, 1843. Made ... April 4, 1844. *Albany: E. Mack, Printer.* 1844. 8vo, pp. 50, (2), 15 folded leaves, (4). Continued. H.

Canal Laws and Regulations. June, 1841. [n. p. n. d.] 8vo. + May, 1850. [n. p. n. d.] 8vo. S. 53561

Canal Policy of the State ... . [n. p. 1845?] 8vo, pp. 8. B.

The Canal Policy of the State ... one of progressive enlargement, Vindicated as the Traditional Policy of Clinton, Morris, and Fulton. Address ... by Carlos Cobb ... [and others]. *New York: Wm. H. Trafton ... Printer.* 1869. 8vo, pp. 19. B.

Canal Regulations, Rates of Toll, and Names of the Principal Places, ... on the New York State Canals; ... *Albany.* 1843. 8vo, pp. 60. — A Certified Copy from the

Register of Canal Boats, kept in the Canal Department, showing the Names of the Boats Registered, ... for 1843, 1845, 1851. [*Albany.* 1843–51.] 3 vols., sm. folio. — Copy of the Register of Canal Boats, in the Comptroller's Office. *Albany.* 1830. Folio. — Digest of Canal Claims presented to the Legislature since the year 1843. *Albany.* 1850. 8vo. — Digest of Claims presented to the Canal Board from its Organization to March 1, 1851. *Albany.* 1851. 8vo. — Extracts from the Reports of the Canal Commissioners and the State Engineers, and from the Proceedings of the Legislature, relating to the State Canals. *Rochester.* 1855. 8vo, pp. 74. — Laws, Regulations, Rates of Toll, and Names of the Principal Places ... . *Albany.* 1850. 8vo, pp. 157. S.

The Official Reports of the Canal Commissioners of ... New-York, and the Acts of the Legislature respecting Navigable Communications between the Great Western and Northern Lakes, and the Atlantic Ocean; with ... Maps and Profiles. ... *New-York: T. & W. Mercein, Printers.* 1817. 8vo, pp. 174, 12. Map

Papers accompanying the Annual Report of the Canal Commissioners. *Albany.* 1828. Folio. — Proceedings of the Canal Board, held at ... Albany, ... March, 1866, ... [n. p. n. d.] 8vo, pp. 15. — Rates of Toll, Canal Regulations, and Distances on the New-York State Canals; ... *Albany: Printed by Croswell* ... . 1835. 8vo, pp. (2), viii, 45. H. — Register of Canal Boats, kept in the Canal Department during the Year 1847–8. [n. p. n. d.] 8vo. — Regulations of the Canal Board in relation to Engineers and Superintendents of Canal Repairs. *Albany.* 1847. 8vo, pp. 16. — Regulations respecting the Issue and Transfer of Certificates of Stock ... . By the Commissioners of the Canal Fund, July 27, 1840. *Albany: Thurlow Weed, Printer.* 1840. 8vo, pp. 16. + August 19, 1851. *Albany: Weed, Parsons and Company.* 1851. 8vo, pp. 28. — Report of the Auditor of the Canal Department, of Claims for Damages, &c. ... made ... 1854. *Albany.* 1854. 8vo, pp. 47. — Report of the Canal Commissioners as to Supply of Water between Tonawanda and Montezuma. ... *Albany.* 1850. 8vo, pp. 13. 10 Plans. — ... Report of the Canal Commissioners on a Resolution of the Assembly of the 23d February, relative to the Cost of Canals and Railroads. [n. p. 1835.] 8vo, pp. 44, 5 folded leaves. H.

... Report of the Canal Commissioners. ... [*Albany.* 1820.] 8vo, pp. 26. B., S. 53565

A report on certain special canal surveys.

Report of the Commissioners ... on the Canals from Lake Erie to the Hudson River, and from Lake Champlain to the same, ... February 17, 1817. *Albany.* 1817. 8vo, pp. 90. M. + January 31st, 1818. *Albany: Printed by J. Buel.* 1818. 8vo, pp. 45, folded leaf. B. 53566

The commissioners of the last-mentioned report were DeWitt Clinton, S. Van Rensselaer, Samuel Young and Myron Holley. *See also* Vol. VI., No. 22758.

Report Of the Commissioners of the Canal Fund, relative to the Amount of Tolls collected and Property transported on the Canals in 1835, &c. &c. ... March 8, 1836. *Albany: Printed by Croswell, Van Benthuysen and Burt.* 1836. 8vo. Continued. H. — Report of the Committee on Canals. March 14, 1820. *Albany: Printed by J. Buel.* 1820. 8vo, pp. 33. — Report of the Committee on Canals, on so much of the Governor's Message as relates to the Completion of the State Canals. ... March 13, 1851. *Albany: Charles Van Benthuysen, Printer.* 1851. 8vo, pp. 63. — ... Report Of the Committee on Canals, on the Bill to authorize the United States to construct the

Niagara Ship Canal. [*Albany*. 1839.] 8vo, pp. 14.—Report of the Committee on Canals, on ... the Sale of the Surplus Waters ... . *Albany*. 1826. 8vo, pp. 88. s.— ... Report of the Committee on Canals, on the Bill to provide for the enlargement of the Erie, Oswego and Champlain Canals ... . *Albany: Charles Van Benthuysen, Printer*. 1862. 8vo, pp. 5.—Report of the Committee on Canals on the Petition of David E. Evans and others. *Albany*. 1827. 8vo.—Report of Committee on Canals on Bill relative to Repairs and Superintendence of Canals, 1856. *Albany*. 1856. 8vo.

Report of the Joint Committee. *See* Vol. VI., No. 22759.

Report of the Minority of the Committee on Canals, on Petitions for Tolls on Railroads of the State of New York, made ... March 24, 1858. *Albany*. 1858. 8vo. 53567

Report of the Select Committee Appointed ... to investigate into the Management of the Canals of the State ... . *Albany: ... Charles Van Benthuysen & Sons*. 1868. 8vo, pp. (2), 1018. B.

... Reports of the Majority and Minority of the Joint Select Committee on Canal Lettings, March 15, 1852. [n. p. n. d.] 8vo, pp. 955, 168. S. 53569

Capitulation by the Dutch to the English subscribed at the Governor's Bowery, August 27, o. s. 1664. [n. p. n. d.] 8vo.

Title from H. A. Brady's Catalogue. *See* "Historical Magazine," III. 174.

The Case of the Provinces. *See* [Hutchinson (T.)], Vol. IX.

Catalogue of Fees established by the Governor and Council at the humble request of the Assembly of New-York. *Printed and Sold by William Bradford, Printer to their Majesties King William and Queen Mary, at the Bible in New York*, 1693. Folio. S.

Catalogue of Maps and Surveys, in the Offices of the Secretary of State, of the State Engineer and Surveyor, and in the New-York State Library. ... *Albany, N. Y.: Weed, Parsons and Company*. 1851. 8vo, pp. (4), 288, (1). Continued. H. 53572

Catalogue of Plants indigenous to ... New York. *Albany*. 1814. 8vo. 53573

A Catalogue of Plants, growing spontaneously within Thirty Miles of ... New-York. Published by the Lyceum of Natural History ... . *Albany: Printed by Websters and Skinners*. 1819. 8vo, pp. 100, (1). B. 53574

Catalogue of the Cabinet of Natural History of ... New-York, and of the Historical and Antiquarian Collection annexed thereto. ... *Albany: C. Van Benthuysen, Printer*. 1853. 8vo. H. 53575

Intended as an accompaniment to the "Natural History of New York." Also: Catalogue of the Natural Productions and Curiosities which compose the Collection of the Cabinet of Natural History. *New York*. 1804. 8vo, pp. 87.

Census of the State of New York, for 1800 ... . [n. p. n. d.] Folio. + [Feb. 21, 1815. *Albany*. n. d.] Folio, pp. 41. S.

Also: Communication from the Secretary of State, transmitting the Census of the State. *Albany* 1822. Folio.—Census of the Electors and other Inhabitants of the State of New-York, for the Years 1825 and 1830. *Albany*. 1831. 8vo. S.

Census ... for 1835; ... *Albany: Croswell, Van Benthuysen & Burt*. 1836. Folio. + For 1845 ... . *Albany*. 1846. Folio. + For 1855. Prepared by F. B. Hough. *Albany*. 1857. Folio, pp. lxvi, 525. + For 1865 ... . Prepared ... by F. B. Hough, ... *Albany: C. Van Benthuysen*. 1867. Folio, pp. (4), cxxvi, 743. + For 1875. Compiled ... by C. W. Seaton ... . *Albany*. 1877. Folio, pp. xxxiv, 465. S. 53577

Fourth Annual Report of the Directors of the CENTRAL ASYLUM, at Canojoharie, for the Instruction of the Deaf and Dumb, made ... 1828. ... *Albany*. 1828. 8vo, pp. 23. S. 53578

Annual Report of the CHAMBER OF COMMERCE of ... New-York, For the Year 1858. ... *New-York: Wheeler and Williams*. 1859. 8vo, pp. (4), 405, (1). Maps. Continued. BA. 53579

Bye-Laws, Resolutions and Orders, adopted by the New-York Chamber of Commerce, September 18, 1787. *New York: H. Gaine*. 1787. 8vo, pp. 14. W. 53580

Also: Bye-Laws, Resolutions and Orders, adopted by The New-York Chamber of Commerce, at a Special Meeting held May 10th, 1796. *New-York: Printed by Archibald M'Lean*. M,DCC,XCVI. 12mo, pp. 12.

Catalogue of the Library of the Chamber of Commerce ... . *New-York: John W. Amerman, Printer*. 1862. 8vo, pp. 25.

Centennial Celebration of the Chamber of Commerce of ... New York, at Irving Hall, April 6, 1868. Report of Proceedings. *New York: John W. Amerman, Printer*. 1868. 8vo, pp. 44. S.

Chamber of Commerce ... . The Committee appointed to consider the Condition of the Lighthouses of the United States ... Report. [n. p. 1852.] 8vo, pp. 8. H. 53583

Chamber of Commerce. Report of Select Committee on Quarantine. ... 1859. *New York: D. Van Nostrand*. 1859. 8vo, pp. 48. B.

The Charter and By-Laws of the Chamber of Commerce of ... New York; Instituted 5th April, 1768; Incorporated 13th

March, 1770. *New-York*. 1818. 8vo, pp. 28. + [*Ibid.*] 1828. 8vo. 53584

Also: Charter, By-Laws, and Organization of the Chamber of Commerce ... . Instituted, April 5, 1768; Incorporated March 13, 1770; Re-incorporated April 13, 1784. *New York*. 1844. 8vo, pp. 35.—The Charter and By-Laws, with a History of the Chamber of Commerce ... By Charles King. *New York*. 1849. 8vo, pp. 104. *See also* King (C.), Vol. IX., No. 37784, and add pp. 160.

Colonial Records. *See* [Stevens (John Austin), *Jr.*]

In Relation to Collisions at Sea. Chamber of Commerce of New-York, December, 1858. *New-York: John W. Amerman, Printer*. 1858. 8vo, pp. 49. H. 53585

International Relations with Brazil. Proceedings on the Reception of H. E. Senhor D'Azambuja ... by the Chamber of Commerce. ... November 2d, 1865 ... . *New-York: John W. Amerman, Printer*. 1865. 8vo, pp. 15. H. 53586

Memorial of the Chamber of Commerce of ... New York. *Washington City: Printed by William Duane & Son*. 1803. 8vo, pp. 7. BA. 53587

Memorial ... to show the Present Rate of Duties, and the Rate of Duties proposed by the Tariff Bill, now before Congress. ... *New-York: Printed by Daniel Fanshaw*. 1824. 8vo, pp. 23.

See also Vol. XI., No. 47710.

Memorial ... [on Ocean Steam Navigation]. Prepared by John Austin Stevens, Jr. ... *New-York: John W. Amerman, Printer*. 1864. 8vo, pp. 80. Map. B. 53589

Proceedings of the Chamber of Commerce ... at the Opening of their New Rooms. June 10, 1858. *New York: Printed by John A. Douglas & Co*. 1858. 8vo, pp. 36. H. 53590

Also: Proceedings of the Chamber of Commerce of ... New York for ... 1862, together with the By-Laws and List of Members. *New York: John W. Amerman, Printer*. 1863. 8vo, pp. iii, 99.—Proceedings ... on the continued Piracies of Vessels fitted out in Great Britain upon American Commerce. ... February 21, 1863. *New-York: John W. Amerman, Printer*. 1863. 8vo, pp. 27. C.—Proceedings ... on the Enlargement of the Canals, February 29, 1864. *New York*. 1864. 8vo, pp. 15.—Proceedings ... March 11, 1864, on ... the Death of its late President, Petatiah Perit. *New-York: John W. Amerman, Printer*. 1864. 8vo, pp. 15.—Proceedings ... Oct. 20, 1864, on ... the Death of Mr. Joshua Bates, American Partner in the House of Messrs. Baring, Brothers & Co., of London. *New York: John W. Amerman, Printer*. 1864. 8vo, pp. 19.—Proceedings ... on occasion of the Reception of their Excellencies, Senor Joaquim Maria Nascentes De Azambuja, Minister of Brazil, and Senor Domingo Faustino Sarmiento, Minister of the Argentine Republic, to the United States, ... November 1, 1866. Including the Speeches delivered by them ... . *New-York: John W. Amerman, Printer*. 1867. 8vo, pp. 26. H. *See also* our Vol. I., No. 578.

Report of a Committee ... on Canal Navigation by Steam. ... *New-York: John W. Amerman, Printer*. 1858. 8vo, pp. 24.

Report of the Committee ... to prepare Memorial to Congress [on Taxation], April 24, 1862. [n. p. n. d.] 8vo, pp. 4.

Also: Report of a Select Committee ... on the Subject of a Return to Specie Payments. November, 1867. *New-York: John W. Amerman, Printer*. 1867. 8vo, pp. 11.—Report of a Special Committee ... February 10, 1860. On Maritime Intercourse in time of War. *New-York: John W. Amerman, Printer*. 1860. 8vo, pp. 8.—Report of a Special Committee ... on the Decline of American Commerce ... *New-York: John W. Amerman, Printer*. 1869. 8vo, pp. 8.—Report of the Committee ... on the Charges at Quarantine for Lighterage, etc. *N. Y.: G. F. Nesbitt & Co., Printers*. [1858]. 8vo, pp. 16.— ... Report of the Executive Committee ... on Subjects of National Importance ... [n. p. 1865.] 8vo, pp. 4.—Report of the Select Committee ... on the Reciprocity Treaty, as to Trade between the British North American Provinces and the United States ... . *New-York: John W. Amerman, Printer*. 1865. 8vo, pp. 72.— ... Report ... on the Coasting and Lake Trade and Registration of Ships. *New-York: John W. Amerman, Printer*. 1861. 8vo, pp. 4.—Report of the Special Committee ... to which was referred the Memorial of Officers of the U. S. Navy to Congress for an increase of pay. *New-York: John W. Amerman, Printer*. 1866, 8vo, pp. 7.—Report ... on the Universal Exposition at Paris, of 1867. ... January 12. 1866. ... *New-York: John W. Amerman, Printer*. 1866. 8vo, pp. 26, (1).— ... Report ... on Relief of the Family of the Late Lieutenant Edmond Templer Shubrick, U. S. N., ... February 1, 1866 ... . [n. p. n. d.] 8vo, pp. 4.—Report ... November 7, 1867, to consider the Subject of Obstructions and Encroachments in the Harbor ... . *New-York: John W. Amerman, Printer*. 1867. 8vo, pp. 80. *See also* Vol. V., No. 17130, *and* Vol. VI., No. 22506.

... Resolutions ... on National Affairs. [*New York*. 1862.] 8vo, pp. 4. H. 53593

The Seizure of the Bark Maury. Report of the ... New York Chamber of Commerce. November 27, 1855. *New York: Wm. C. Bryant & Co., Printers*. 1855. 8vo, pp. 30. B.

Tribute of the Chamber of Commerce ... to the memory of Anson Burlingame, ... March 3d, 1870. Eulogy by Elliot C. Cowdin. *New-York: Press of the Chamber of Commerce*. 1870. 8vo, pp. 11. B. 53595

Chapter I. of the Fourth Part of the proposed Revision of the Statute Laws ... . *Albany: Printed by Croswell & Van Benthuysen*. 1828. 8vo, pp. vi, 95. B. 53596

The Charge Given. *See* Vol. III., No. 12024.

The Charge of ... James De Lancey. *See* Vol. V. 19340–42.

Charter of the First Company of the Great Western Turnpike Road, granted by the Legislature ... . *Albany*. 1802. 12mo, pp. 40. 53597

Fifty copies reprinted, *Albany: Joel Munsell*. 1851. 12mo, pp. 40.

Cholera at the Military Posts in the Harbor of New York, in ... 1867. ... *New York: C. S. Westcott & Co., Printers*. 1868. 8vo, pp. 7. H. 53598

Reprinted from the "Second Annual Report of the Metropolitan Board of Health."

Civil List and Forms of Government of the Colony and State of New York. Compiled ... by Stephen C. Hutchins. *Albany: Weed, Parsons and Company*. 1864. 16mo, pp. 542. 6 Plates.

Continued annually. The first was issued in 1855.

Claims On the United-States, by the Late Contractor for the State of New-York, &c. For Services during the Late War. *New-York*. 1824. 8vo, pp. (2), 179, (1), 24. 53600

By Elbert Anderson, who first applied the term "Uncle Sam" to the United States.

Classified Index to Bills Introduced into the Assembly During ... 1870 ... . *Albany*. 1870. 8vo, pp. 127. H. 53601

The Clerk's Manual of Rules, ... for the Regulation of Business in the Assembly of the State of New York ... . *Albany: Weed, Parsons & Company, Printers*. 1864. 8vo, pp. 92. 53602

... Annual Report of the Agent of the CLINTON STATE PRISON. [n. p. 1846.] 8vo, pp. 32. Continued. S. 53603

Code of Public Instruction of the State ... . *Albany*. 1856. 8vo, pp. iv, 492. S. 53604

Circular and Catalogue of the Faculty and Students of the COLLEGE OF PHYSICIANS ... of the Western District of ... New-York, in Fairfield (Herkimer County.) *Albany: Printed by Websters and Skinners*. 1822. 8vo, pp. 8. Continued. S. 53605

Afterwards the "Albany Medical School."—Also: Ordinances of the College ... . [n. p.] 1813. 8vo, pp. 8. W.

Commemoration of the Conquest of New Netherland, on its Two Hundredth Anniversary, by the New York Historical Society. The Oration by John Romeyn Brodhead. *New York: ... The Society*. M DCCC LXIV. Rl. 8vo, pp. 87. Map, 2 Plates.

Consists principally of Brodhead's Oration.

Comments on the Report of the Select Committee appointed ... March 27, 1832, to examine into the State of the Prisons at Mount Pleasant and Auburn. *Mount Pleasant*. 1833. 8vo, pp. 20

The Commercial Conduct. *See* Vol. IV., No. 14971.

Annual Report of the COMMISSARY GENERAL ... . Made ... 1850. *Albany: Weed, Parsons & Co., ... Printers*. 1850. 8vo, pp. 34, 4 folded leaves. Continued. B. 53608

Commissioners' Office, 19th February, 1799. [n. p. n. d.] 4to, pp. 63. 53609

Very rare. Consists of the Minutes of the Commissioners for settling demands between British Subjects and American Citizens. The case of Bishop Inglis of Nova Scotia is the most important.

Annual Reports of the COMMISSIONERS OF EMIGRATION of ... New York, from the Organization of the Commission, May 5, 1847, to 1860, inclusive: ... *New York*. 1861. 8vo, pp. viii, 428, (1), iii, 63. B., C. 53610

Also: Report of the ... Committee ... to investigate Certain Charges against the Commissioners of Emigration. ... January 18, 1859. *Albany: Charles Van Benthuysen, Printer*. 1859. 8vo, pp. 177. H.—Rules of the Commissioners of Emigration of the State ... . *New York: Casper C. Childs, Printer*. 1847. 8vo, pp. 7. B.

Report of the COMMISSIONERS OF FISHERIES of ... New York. March 9, 1869. *Albany*. 1869. 8vo, pp. 56. Continued. B.

Common School Law and Regulations, June, 1841. [n. p. n. d.] 8vo. + *Albany*. 1864. 8vo. 53612

The Common School System of ... New-York, comprising ... General Laws ... Prepared ... by Samuel J. Randall ... . *Troy, N. Y.: Johnson and Davis, ... Printers*. 1851. 8vo, pp. 408. B.

Communication from Major General Dix, relative to the Arrest of Hawley D. Clapp, April 11, 1864. [n. p. n. d.] 8vo, pp. 22. 53614

Clapp was charged with frauds in bounties to recruits.

Communication from the Auditor transmitting a Report from the State Engineer and Surveyor relative to a Survey of the Hudson River to Fort Edward, and of the Champlain Canal Enlargement ... . *Albany*. [1867.] 8vo, pp. 117. S. 53615

Communication from the Governor relative to the Boundary Line between this State and the State of New Jersey; with the Report of Attorney General Bronson, on the subject. [n. p.] 1831. 8vo. 53616

Also: Communication ... in answer to a resolution relative to the Abduction or Enslavement of Citizens of this State. ... January 31, 1857. *Albany: C. Van Benthuysen, Printer*. 1857. 8vo, pp. 8.— ... Communication ... and Report of the Commission appointed ... to determine and ascertain the Quota of this State, under the different calls for Troops. ... *Albany: Comstock & Cassidy, Printers*. 1864. 8vo, pp. 18.—Communication ... relative to Alleged Abuses. *New York*. 1854. 8vo.—Communi-

cation ... transmitting a Memorial ... on the subject of a Geographical Survey of the State. Feb. 28. *Albany*. 1852. 8vo, pp. 24.—Communication ... transmitting the Report of Alexander Vattemare on the Universal Exhibition at Paris. ... *Albany: C. Van Benthuysen, Printer*. 1856. 8vo, pp. 32.—Communication ... transmitting Report of Commissioners appointed to secure the Establishment, Government, &c., &c., of Common Schools in the City of New York. ... Feb. 11, 1858. *Albany*. 1858. 8vo.—Communication ... transmitting certain Proceedings of the Seneca Nation of Indians. *Albany*. 1849. 8vo, pp. 30.— ... Communication ... transmitting the Report of the Commissioners ... relative to Protecting the Harbors and Frontiers against Ivasion, and to Provide for their Defence. ... February 3, 1864. *Albany: Comstock & Cassidy, Printers*. 1864. 8vo, pp. 50. 2 Plates.—Communication ... transmitting the Report of State Officers concerning the Volunteer Militia ... . *Albany*. 1862. 8vo.—Communication ... transmitting the Report of the Commissioners appointed to locate the Hudson River Asylum for the Insane of the State ... . *Albany: Charles Van Benthuysen & Sons, Printers*. 1867. 8vo, pp. 8. H. *See also* Vol. II., No. 8176, New York Geology *and* Quarantine.

A Comparative View and Exhibition of Reasons, opposed to the Adoption of the New Constitution, of ... New-York. By an Old Citizen. *New-York*. 1822. 8vo, pp. 20. B. 53617

Annual Report of the COMPTROLLER of the State ... . *Albany*. 1812. Folio. 53618

Continued after 1836 in octavo. Also: Report ... relative to the Sale of Lands for Taxes ... April 21, 1835. [n. p. n. d.] 8vo, pp. 715.—Report ... giving the Name of all Stock Corporations doing Business in the State. *Albany*. 1868. 8vo.—Annual Report of the Comptroller, of the Condition of the several Insurance Companies doing Business in this State. ... 1855. *Albany: C. Van Benthuysen, Printer* ... . 1855. 8vo.—Statement of all the Lands Sold by the Comptroller ... Prior to ... 1848, (not heretofore reported,) and which have been or are liable to be conveyed, to wit: at the Sales of 1834, 1839, & 1843. ... *Albany: Printed by Weed, Parsons & Co*. 1850. 8vo, pp. 1024. B.

Conditions for New Planters in the Territories of His Royal Highness the Duke of York. *Cambridge: Printed by S. Green*. 1665. Folio, 1 leaf. 53619

Title from Thomas' "History of Printing."

The Conduct of the Province of New York Considered, and the True Interest of the Colony Attempted to be Shewn. In a Letter to the Society of Arts, Agriculture and Economy. [n. p.] 1767. 4to, pp. 20. N. 53620

A Conference [etc.]. *See* Vol. XI., No. 45689.

Constable's Guide, being a Concise Treatise on the Powers and Duties of a Constable and Collector in the State of New York. *Binghampton*. 1832. 8vo. S. 53621

Constitution amended; or, Items submitted to the consideration of the People of ... New-York ... . Written by an Observer. ... *Albany: The Author* ... . 1821. 8vo, pp. 8. B.

Constitution and By-Laws of Company "A," 23d Regiment, N. C. S. N. Y. ... *New York: Baker & Godwin, Printers*. 1868. Sm. 16mo, pp. 37. 53623

Constitution and Regulations of the Grand Royal Arch Chapter of ... New York ... . *Albany: Printed by ... H. C. Southwick*. 1815. 16mo, pp. 51, (1). Plate. 53624

Constitution, By-Laws and Rules of Order of the ... Grand Encampment of Patriarchs, Independent Order of Odd Fellows of ... New York ... . *Albany: J. Munsell*. 1848. 18mo, pp. 64

The Constitution of the State of New-York. *Fish-kill: Printed by Samuel Loudon*. M.DCC.LXXVII. 8vo, pp. 33. + *Philadelphia: Printed ... by Styner and Cist* ... . MDCCLXXVII. 8vo, pp. 32. + *New York: ... Samuel Loudon*. 1783. 8vo, pp. 43. + *New York*. 1785. 8vo, pp. 48. + As amended. *Albany: Printed by Cantine and Leake*. 1821. 8vo, pp. 24, 4. + *New York*. 1822. 8vo. + *Albany*. 1825. 8vo. + *New-York: Printed by P. & H. Van Pelt*. 1826. 8vo, pp. 74. + *Albany: Printed by Croswell & Van Benthuysen*. 1827. 16mo, pp. 117, (1). 2 Plates. + *New-York: Printed by P. Van Pelt*. 1828. 8vo, pp. 38. + As Revised by the Convention of 1846. *Albany: Gould, Banks & Gould*. 1846. 8vo, pp. 16. H. 53626

See also Hough (F. B.), Vol. VIII., No. 33137, *note*, and "State of New York," *infra*.

The Constitutions of the Ancient ... Fraternity of Free ... Masons in the State of New York ... . *New York: Printed by Francis Childs*. 1789. 8vo, pp. 76. S. + *New York*. 1794. 8vo, pp. 56. N. + [*Ibid.* 1801.] 8vo, pp. 64. N. + [*Ibid.*] 1820. 8vo. + [*Ibid.*] 1827. 8vo, pp. 87. 53627

Convention Manual. A Constitutional Guide to the objects of the New York State Convention: consisting of the Constitution of the State ... . *New York: Printed by Joseph Kingsland & Co*. 1821. 12mo, pp. 39. S. 53628

Convention of Delegates of Insurance Companies. *New York*. 1849. 8vo. 53629

Copy of the Address left with His Excellency, Gov. Tryon, The 3d of July, 1775, by the Worshipful Whitehead Hicks, Esq; Mayor of ... New-York, With the Governor's Answer, Deliver'd to the Mayor ... . To be laid before the Corporation. [n. p. n. d.] 8vo, pp. 8. N. 53630

Charter and Fundamental Laws of the CORPORATION for the Relief of Widows and Children of Clergymen of the Protestant Episcopal Church in ... New York. *New York.* 1807. 8vo, pp. 20. N. 53631

Correspondence between the Commissioners of New York appointed to revise the Laws of that State and Ant. Hammond of the Inner Temple ... . *London: Privately Printed.* 1826. 8vo.

Correspondence between the Governor of New York and Virginia. [n. p.] 1839. 8vo. 53633

The Debates and Proceedings of the Convention of the State of New York, assembled at Poughkeepsie, on the 17th June, 1788, to decide on the Form of Federal Government recommended by the Convention at Philadelphia, 17th September, 1787. ... *New York: Francis Childs.* 1788. 8vo, pp. 144. C. 53634

Debates and Proceedings in the New-York State Convention, for the Revision of the Constitution. By S. Croswell and R. Sutton, Reporters ... . *Printed at the Office of the Albany Argus.* 1846. 8vo, pp. viii, 948. C. 53635

... Decision of the Supreme Court, ... sustaining the Constitutionality of Legal Tender Notes. ... *Rochester: A. Strong & Co., Printers.* 1863. 8vo, pp. 42. H. 53636

Decision of the Vice Chancellor, (William T. M'Coun,) on the application of the Orthodox Party [of Friends] to appoint a Receiver, &c. *New-York: Isaac T. Hopper.* 1835. 8vo, pp. 8.

Decisions of the Superintendent of Common Schools of the State; ... By John A. Dix, Superintendent. ... with the Laws, ... *Albany: Printed by Croswell, Van Benthuysen & Burt.* 1837. 8vo, pp. vi, (2), 479. A. 53638

Democratic Address in opposition to the Special Deposite Schemes ... . *New York.* 1838. 8vo. 53639

Democratic Anti-Abolition State Right Association of New York. [n. p.] 1863. 8vo. 53640

... Democratic State Convention. [Assembled in Syracuse, N. Y., Sept. 14, 1836. *Albany.* 1836.] 8vo, pp. 11. H.

Description of a Prison on the Plan of the N. Wing of the Auburn State Prison. [n. p. n. d.] 4to, pp. 2. M. 53642

Description of the Genesee Country, its rapidly progressive Population and Improvements: in a series of Letters from a Gentleman to his Friend. *Albany.* 1798. 8vo. 2 Maps and Plate. 53643

Description of the Settlement. *See* [Williamson (Charles)].

Descriptive Catalogue of Flags, Trophies and Relics belonging to the New York Bureau of Military Statistics. *Albany.* 1864. 8vo. 53644

A Digest of the Common School System of ... New York; ... with ... Decisions of the Superintendent ... . *Albany.* 1844. 12mo, pp. 335. A., S. 53645

District School Journal of Education of ... New-York. Vol. I. *Geneva.* 1839. 8vo. Continued. S. 53646

The Documentary History of ... New-York; Arranged under Direction of the Hon. Christopher Morgan ... . By E. B. O'Callaghan, M.D. *Albany: Weed, Parsons & Co., Printers.* 1849–51. 4 vols., 8vo, pp. vi, (2), 786, (1); (8), 1211, (1); iv, (4), 1215; xxii, (4), *5, 1144. Maps, Plates and Portraits. B. + [*Ibid.*] 1850–51. 4 vols., 4to, pp. 536; (8), 711; (8), 748; xvii, (3), *3, 700. Maps, Plates and Portraits. 53647

"A most valuable collection, consisting of Documents connected with the early history of the colony, the Indian Aborigines, and its affairs down to the year 1800; reprints of historical manuscripts, rare memoirs, accounts of early settlers; Indian biography, history, difficulties; biographical and genealogical accounts of families; early tours into various parts of the country; statistical accounts; land titles; the Leisler papers; Sir William Johnson's papers; the Rumsey and Fitch steam-boat controversy; churches, wars, disputes, &c., all taken from the manuscript archives of the State. The maps, seals, and coins are particularly worthy of attention." Some volumes have the name of Charles Van Benthuysen as printer.

Documents, Papers and Proofs relating to the Canal Frauds in ... New-York. *Albany.* 1847. 8vo, pp. 867. 53648

Documents in Relation [etc.]. *See* [Squier (E. G.)]

Documents of the Assembly ... Fifty-Fourth Session, 1831. Vol. I. ... *Albany: Printed by E. Croswell.* 1831. 8vo. Continued. 53649

Documents of the Convention of ... New-York, 1846. ... *Albany: Carroll & Cook, Printers.* 1846. 2 vols., 8vo. C., S.

Documents of the Convention of ... New York, 1867–68 Vol. I. ... *Albany: Weed, Parsons and Company.* 1868. 8vo. H.

Documents of the Senate of ... New-York, Fifty-Fourth Session, 1831. *Albany: Printed by E. Croswell.* 1831. 8vo. Continued. 53652

Documents Relating to the N. Y. Contest. *See* Vol. v. 20473.

Documents Relative to the Colonial History of ... New-York; Procured in Holland, England and France, by John Romeyn Brodhead, Esq., Agent. ... Edited by E. B. O'Callaghan, M.D. With a General Introduction by the Agent. *Albany: Weed, Parsons and Company.* 1856–1877. 12 vols., 4to. 53653

Collation: Vol. I. pp. lxx, 646, (1), Map; II. pp. xix, 770, (1); III. pp. xxxv, 861, (2); IV. pp. xix, 1192, (2); V. pp. xix, 985, (1); VI. pp. xx, 1028, (1); VII. pp. xvi, 1006, (2); VIII. pp. xix, 817, (1); IX. pp. xxi, 1112, (1); X. pp. xxi, 1167, (1), General Index; XI. pp. (2), 686; XII. Title differs, pp. l, 669. Vols. III.–VI. are dated 1853, 1854 and 1855.

"These Public Records are, chiefly, in the office of the Secretary of State at Albany, and are as various in their character, as they are voluminous in their extent. Most of them relate to, and illustrate the History of the State; and without them no accurate or detailed knowledge of that history can be gained." They include translations of all the early Dutch records, besides a mass of documents bringing the history of the State down to its political existence as a member of an independent federation.

Drafting; being the Complete Militia Law of ... New York. *New York: Christopher, Morse, & Skippon, Printers.* 1862. 16mo, pp. 72. 53654

Transactions of the ECLECTIC MEDICAL SOCIETY of ... New York, For ... 1866. *Albany: Van Benthuysen & Sons' ... Printing House.* 1867. 8vo, pp. 397, (1). Portraits. Continued. B.

Election Law of New York of 1842, as amended in 1847. [n. p. n. d.] 8vo, pp. 101. + *Albany.* 1856. 8vo. S. 53656

Engravings of Plans, Profiles and Maps illustrating the Standard Models from which are built the Important Structures on the New-York Canals, accompanying the Annual Report of the State Engineer and Surveyor on the Canals for 1859. *Albany.* 1860. 8vo. 18 Plans. S. 53657

An Essay. *See* [Grim (C. F.)], Vol. VII., No. 28847.

The Constitution of the EVANGELICAL LUTHERAN MINISTERIUM of ... New York and Adjacent States and Countries; ... 1816. *Philadelphia: Printed by Conrad Zeutler.* 1816. 12mo, pp. 32. H. 53658

Also: Extracts from the Minutes of the Synod of the Evangelical Lutheran Ministerium ... . Convened at Schoharie, August, 1822. *New York.* 1822. 8vo, pp. 16. Continued. — Extracts from the Minutes of Third Session of the Hartwick Synod and

Ministerium of the Evangelical Lutheran Church ... of New York, convened ... Dansville ... September 21, 1833. *Troy: Norman Tuttle.* 1833. 8vo, pp. 29. — Minutes of the ... Synod of the Evangelical Lutheran Ministerium ... of New York ... . Convened in ... Albany, October 13, ... 1832. *Hudson: Printed by Ashbel Stoddard.* 1832. 8vo, pp. 20. Continued. S.

Constitution and Rules of Order of the EVANGELICAL LUTHERAN SYNOD of the State of New York. *Albany.* 1868. 8vo, pp. 14. S. 53659

Also: Historical Statement of the Evangelical Lutheran Synod of New York ... . *New York: Cutter, Tower & Co.* 1867. 8vo, pp. 16. — Proceedings of the Convention of the First Session of the Evangelical Lutheran Synod ... held in ... Red Hook, ... 1867. *Albany: J. Munsell.* 1867. 8vo, pp. 23. S.

Evening Post Extra. History of the Canal Policy of ... New-York, in Review of a Letter Written by S. B. Ruggles to some Citizens of Rochester. [n. p. 1849.] 8vo, pp. 16. S. 53660

An Examination into the expediency of establishing a Board of Agriculture in ... New-York. Published by the New-York Corresponding Association for the promotion of Internal Improvements. *Brooklyn: E. Worthington, Printer.* 1819. 8vo, pp. 64. B. 53661

Extract from a Report made to the Yearly Meeting of Friends held in Philadelphia, in the 4th mo. 1815—and a Report to the Yearly Meeting of Friends for ... New York, 5th mo. 28th. 1815, made by their respective Committees. *London: Printed by William Phillips.* [n. d.] 8vo, pp. 8. 53662

Extract of an Act of the General Assembly for raising £100,000 for an Army of 20,000 Men to invade Canada, in Conjunction with the King's Troops. *New York.* 1759. 8vo, pp. 19.

Extracts from the Act of the Legislature of New York, entitled "An Act for suppressing Immorality," &c.; with an Ordinance of the Corporation "for the Due Observance of the Lord's Day." *New York.* 1812. 8vo, pp. 12. + [*Ibid.*] 1814. 8vo, pp. 8. 53664

Extracts from the Minutes of the Council of the Province of New-York, containing Petitions and Memorials from various parties belonging to the French Reformed Protestant Church in New-York, and the Proceedings of the Council thereon. [n. p.:] *Printed by William Bradford.* 1725? 4to, pp. 34. 53665

Extracts from the Minutes of the Synod of New-York and New-Jersey. A. D. 1811. *Elizabeth-Town, N. J.: Printed by Shepard Kollock.* [n. d.] 8vo, pp. 33–48. BA. 53666

Extracts from the Minutes of the Yearly Meeting of Friends, held in New York, 5th month, 1857; and Memorials concerning deceased Friends. *New York: B. F. Corlies.* 1857. 12mo.

Facts and Considerations for the Democracy of the Empire State. ... *New-York: Angell, Engel & Hewitt, Printers.* 1852. 8vo, pp. 16. B., S. 53668

Relates to the election of J. L. Curtis.

The Final Report of John Romeyn Brodhead, Agent of the State of New-York, to procure and transcribe Documents in Europe, relative to the Colonial History of said State. Made ... February, 1845. *Albany: E. Mack, Printer.* 1845. 8vo, pp. (2), 374, (1). B. 53669

Corrected title of No. 8176, Vol. II.

First Organization of Colored Troops in ... New York, to aid in Suppressing the Rebellion. *New York.* 1864. 8vo.

Benjamin Fletcher Captain General and Governour of the Province of New-York, Province of Pennsilvanie, and Country of New-Castle, and the Territories and Tracts of Land depending thereon in America. To all Officers and Ministers Ecclesiastical and Civil throughout the Provinces and Territories under my Government. June 8. 1693. *Printed by William Bradford, Printer to King William and Queen Mary, at the City of New York, Anno,* 1693. Folio, 1 leaf. S. 53671

Asking for collections by the clergy and constables of money to redeem Christians of New York City from slavery in Morocco. The earliest known specimen of Bradford's printing in New York. Reprinted in Wallace's "Commemorative Address," p. 66. The note appended to our No. 24714 properly belongs here.

By his Excellency, Benjamin Fletcher, Captain General and Governor in Chief ... and Vice-Admiral ... . A Proclamation. Province of New York, ss. Whereas ... . Fort William Henry, the 25th day of August, 1693. *Printed and sold by William Bradford, Printer to their Majesties King William and Queen Mary, at the City of New York.* 1693. Folio, 1 leaf. S. 53672

Warning the inhabitants to arm against the French. Supposed to be the second piece printed in New York. *See* Wallace's "Commemorative Address."

A Form of Prayer, ... to be used In the Churches throughout the Province of New York, on ... the Thirteenth of July, being the Day appointed ... for a General Fast and Humiliation: To implore the ... Divine Blessing on his Majesty's Arms, by Sea and Land, especially those employed more immediately for the

Security of these Colonies. *New-York: Printed and Sold by J. Parker and W. Weyman* ... . MDCCLVII. 4to, pp. 12. 53673

Also: A Form of Prayer to be used in the Diocese of New York, November 26, 1863, National Thanksgiving. [n. p. 1863.] 8vo, pp. 16. — A Form of Prayer to be used ... November 30, 1863, National Fast Day. [n. p. 1863.] 8vo, pp. 15. *See also* Vol. VI., No. 25091.

Freeman's New York Almanack for 1767. *New York.* [n. d.] 12mo. 53674

Continued to 1770 or later. Also: Freeman's New York Royal Sheet Almanack. *New York.* 1768. 12mo. — Freeman's New York Pocket Almanack. *New York.* 1768. 12mo. — Freeman's Dutch Almanack. *New York.* 1768. 12mo.

... Address of the FRIENDS OF DOMESTIC INDUSTRY, assembled in Convention, at New York, October 26, 1831. [Also] Reports of Committees. *Baltimore.* 1831. 8vo, pp. 44, 174.

Gazetteer of the New York Central Railroad and General Railway Index. ... *Buffalo: E. A. Thomas.* [1863.] 12mo, pp. 106, Railway Index, 37. H. 53676

A Gazetteer of ... New York: comprising its Topography, Geology, Mineralogical Resources, Civil Divisions, Canals, Railroads and Public Institutions. ... The whole Alphabetically Arranged. Also Statistical Tables including the Census of 1840. ... *Albany: J. Disturnell.* 1842. 8vo, pp. 475. Map and Plate. + [*Ibid.*] 1848. N. 53677

Corrected title of our No. 32534, Vol. VIII.

A General Account of the Number of Electors in ... New-York, certified by Thomas Tillotson, Secretary of State, March 10, 1802. [n. p. n. d.] Folio. + *Albany.* 1808. Folio.

General Association of ... New York, ... at Paris, Oneida County, August, 1835. *Syracuse.* 1836. 8vo, pp. 24. Cont'd.

Also: Minutes of the General Association of New York, ... August 26th, 1841; with an Appendix ... . *Utica: Bennett, Backus, and Hawley.* 1841. 8vo, pp. 31. H.

Proceedings of the GENERAL GRAND CHAPTER, at a Meeting held in the City of New-York, Sept. 9, A. L. 5819. [n. p. n. d.] 12mo, pp. 24. BA. 53680

Also: Constitution of the General Grand Chapter, of Royal Arch Masons, for the United States. *New York.* 1829. 8vo, pp. 18.

General Index to the Documents and Laws of the State ... . *Albany.* 1842. 8vo. N. 53681

Also: General Index to the Documents of the State ... from 1777 to 1865 ... . Prepared ... by Ornon Archer ... . *Albany: Weed, Parsons and Company, Printers.* 1866. 8vo, pp 544. B.

General Index to the Documents relative to the Colonial History of ... New York, ... By E. B. O'Callaghan ... . *Albany: Weed, Parsons and Company, Printers.* 1861. 4to, pp. (2), 686.

General Index to the Laws of the State ... from 1777 to 1850. ... *New York.* 1850. 8vo, pp. 665. A. 53683

General Index of the Laws ... . Vol. I. 1777–1857 inclusive. Vol. II. 1858–1865 ... . Prepared ... By T. S. Gillett and Henry H. Havens. *Albany: Weed, Parsons and Company, Printers.* 1866. 8vo, pp. 755; 335. 53684

General Regulations for the Military Forces of ... New York. *Albany: Weed, Parsons and Company, Printers.* 1858. 12mo, pp. 352. S. 53685

General School Law of ... New York. ... *Albany: Weed, Parsons and Company, Printers.* 1867. 8vo, pp. 106. H. 53686

... Communication From the Governor, relative to the GEOLOGICAL SURVEY of the State. ... 1837. [*Albany.* 1837.] 8vo, pp. 212. + [*Ibid.* 1838.] 8vo, pp. 384. 14 Plates. + [*Ibid.* 1839.] 8vo, pp. 351. + [*Ibid.* 1840.] Rl. 8vo, pp. 484. + [*Ibid.* 1841.] 8vo, pp. 184. 53687

See also "Natural History" of New York.

A Geological and Agricultural Survey of the District adjoining the Erie Canal, taken under the Direction of the Hon. Step. Van Rensselaer. Part I. Rock Formations. *Albany.* 1824. 8vo.

Report of the Secretary of State [John A. Dix], in relation to a Geological Survey of ... New-York. Made ... 1836. *Albany: Printed by Croswell, Van Benthuysen and Burt.* 1836. 8vo, pp. (2), 60. H. 53689

See also [Mather *and* Conrad (T. A.)], Vol. XI., No. 46816.

Constitution of the GRAND CHAPTER of ... New York. [n. p. n. d.] 8vo, pp. 16. H. 53690

Also: Extracts from the Proceedings of the Grand Chapter of ... New York, at its Annual Meeting, February, 5824. *Albany: Printed by Packard & Van Benthuysen.* 1824. 12mo, pp. 24. B.

Extract from the Minutes of the GRAND CONSISTORY, at its Session the 28th day of the 12th Month, Anno Lucis 5813. *New York.* 1813. 8vo. 53691

An Abstract of the Proceedings of the GRAND LODGE in June, A. L. 5827. *New York.* 1827. 8vo, pp. 47, and Circular.

Also: Abstract of Transactions of the Grand Lodge of Free ... Masons of the State of New York ... . *New York.* 1853. 8vo, pp. 42. — First Annual Report of the Masonic Board of Relief, presented to the M. W. Grand Lodge, June 6, 1857. *New York.* [1857.] 12mo, pp. 24. — Annual Session of the R. W. Grand Encampment of Northern New York. [n. p.] 1849. 8vo. — Circular addressed to the several Lodges of Free ... Masons in ... New York, By the Committee appointed at Geneva, August 9, A. L. 5848. [n. p. n. d.] 8vo, pp. 12. — Circular Letter of the Grand Lodge of ... New York. *New York.* 1825. 8vo, pp. 66. — Communication from the Grand Lodge of ... New York, in the case of Br. J. Wark [signed E. Hicks. n. p.] 1815. 8vo. — Exercises had at the Celebration of the Sixth Anniversary of the Independent Order of Odd Fellows, Albany, March 21, 1843. *Albany.* 1843. 8vo, pp. 27. — Extracts from the Proceedings of the Grand Lodge, of ... New-York. ... 5825. *Albany: Printed ... by Brothers R. Martin, J. Hunter* ... . 1825. 8vo, pp. 40. Cont'd. — Extraordinary Assembly of the Grand Lodge of ... New York. [n. p. n. d.] 8vo. — Historical Narrative: Explanation and Vindication of the course pursued by the Grand Lodge of New York ... . *New York.* 1849. 8vo, pp. 80. — Proceedings of a Special Grand Communication of the M. W. Grand Lodge ... of ... New York, to Consummate the Union of the Brethren hitherto under the Jurisdiction of St. John's Grand Lodge, with the Grand Lodge of ... New York, December 27th, ... 1850 ... . Also, a Brief Narrative of the Origin, History, and Dissolution of St. John's Grand Lodge; ... . *New York: Bro. Narine, Printer.* 1851. 8vo, pp. 59. — Proceedings of the R. W. G. Lodge of the Independent Order of Odd Fellows at the Annual Meeting, 1835. [n. p. n. d.] 8vo, pp. 8. — Proceedings of the ... Grand Lodge of ... New-York, and of the ... Grand Stewards' Lodge, From ... July, A. L. 5837, to ... September, A. L. 5837 ... . *New-York: J. M. Marsh, Printer.* 1837. 8vo. — Regulations of the Grand Royal Arch Chapter of ... New York. *Albany.* 1799. 8vo. — Report of the District Grand Committee of the District of Albany, relative to District Grand Committees. *Albany.* 1851. 8vo. — Report of the Special Committee of the Grand Lodge of ... New York on the Riotous Proceedings in the presence of that Body on the evening of the 5th of June, 1849. *New York.* [1849.] 8vo, pp. 32. — Transactions of the Grand Lodge ... of Free ... Masons of ... New-York, From ... 5847, to ... 5848. *New-York: Br. J. M. Marsh, Printer.* 1848. 8vo. Continued annually.

Head of Articles of Complaint by Rip Van Dam, Esquire, against Governor Cosby, etc. *Boston.* 1734. Folio, pp. 28.

His Majesty's Royal Commission to William Cosby, Esq; for the Government of the Province of New York. [Colophon:] *Printed by John Peter Zenger, Printer to the King's Most Excellent Majesty, for the Province of New York.* M,DCC,XXXVI. Folio, pp. 8

Historical Review. *See* [Lord (E.)], Vol. X., No. 42023.

An Historical Sketch of the 162d Regiment N. Y. Vol. Infantry ... . *Albany: Weed, Parsons and Company, Printers.* 1867. 8vo, pp. 45. Portrait. BA. 53694

Proceedings of the HOMŒOPATHIC MEDICAL SOCIETY of the State ... . *Albany: Printed by Joel Munsell.* 1851. 8vo, pp. 29.

Also: Transactions of the Homœopathic Medical Society of the State ... . *Albany: Comstock & Cassidy, Printers.* 1863. 8vo, pp. 188. Portrait. Continued. BA.

Constitution of the HUMANE SOCIETY of the State ... . *New York.* 1795. 8vo. 53696

Also: Report of a Committee of the Humane Society of New York, appointed to Inquire into the Number of Tavern Licences .... *New York.* 1810. 8vo.—Sketch of the Origin and Progress of the ... Society. *New York.* 1814. 8vo.

Immigration and the Commissioners of Immigration of ... New York. *New York.* 1870. 8vo. 53697

Impartial Statement. *See* Vol. IX., No. 34385.

Add to the collation "An Appendix," pp. 22 (our No. 1795); to the note add, *see* "Reasons," etc.

In Convention of the Representatives of ... New-York, October 2, 1776. [n. p. n. d.] 8vo, pp. 12. 53698

Index of Awards on Claims of the Soldiers of the War of 1812, as ... allowed by the Adjutant and Inspector Generals .... *Albany: Weed, Parsons and Company.* 1860. 4to, pp. 576. S.

Index to the Documents. *See* Vol. II., No. 6128.

Indexes to the Journals of the House of Assembly of ... New-York; ... 1777, ... [to] 1795. *Albany: Printed by H. C. Southwick.* 1814. Folio, pp. 178. BA., S. 53700

Indexes to the Journals of the Senate of ... New-York; ... 1777, ... [to] 1799, inclusive. *Albany: Printed by H. C. Southwick.* 1814. Folio, pp. 143. BA., S. 53701

Annual Report of the INSPECTOR GENERAL of ... New York, ... *Albany: Van Benthuysen's ... Printing House.* 1864. 8vo, pp. lxxxviii, 76. Continued. BA. 53702

Instructions for taking the Census of the State ... in ... 1855; ... *Albany: Weed, Parsons & Co., Printers.* 1855. 8vo, pp. 47. + For ... 1865. ... *Albany.* 1865. 8vo, pp. 56. S. 53703

Instructions for the Better Government and Organization of Common Schools. ... *Albany: Printed by Websters and Skinners.* 1819. 8vo, pp. 16. 53704

In the Administration of His Excellency, The Honourable Robert Monckton, Captain General, and Governor in Chief, in and over the Province New-York, &c. &c. [*New York, about* 1763.] Folio, 1 leaf. P. 53705

List of the Corporation of New York City; Cruger, Mayor. Headed with Royal Arms, and printed entirely in red.

Is the Diocese of New York vacant? [n. p. n. d.] 8vo, pp. 58. 53706

Relative to Bishop Onderdonk.

A Journal of the Actes of the General Assembly of her Majesty's Colony of New-York in America in 1702, under the Administration of his Excellency, Edward, Lord Cornbury. [*New York: Printed by William Bradford.* 1702.] Folio. 53707

Continued to 1709 or later. Title from Brady's catalogue, probably incorrect.

Journal of the Assembly of the State of New York, ... 1777. *Poughkeepsie.* 1777. Folio. 53708

Continued in folio to 1829, afterwards issued in octavo.

Journal of the Convention of the State of New-York; held at Poughkeepsie, in Dutchess County, the 17th of June, 1788. *Poughkeepsie: Printed by Nicholas Power, a few rods East from the Court-House.* [1788.] 4to, pp. 86. 53709

This convention met for the ratification of the Constitution of the United States as recommended by the Federal Convention at Philadelphia.

Journal of the Convention, of ... New-York. Began and held at the City of Albany, on the Thirteenth Day of October, 1801. *Albany.* 1801. 4to, pp. 42. + *Albany: Re-printed by Cantine & Leake.* 1821. 8vo, pp. 52. B. 53710

Journal of the Convention ... held ... in ... Albany, on the twenty-eighth ... August, 1821. *Albany: Printed by Cantine & Leake* .... 1821. 8vo, pp. 565, xii. S. 53711

Journal of the Convention ... held at ... Albany, ... June, 1846. *Albany: Carroll and Cook, Printers.* 1846. 8vo, pp. 1648.

Journal of the Convention ... begun ... the 4th ... of June, 1867. *Albany: Weed, Parsons & Company.* 1867. 8vo, pp. 1547.

Journal of the Convention of Young Men, of ... New-York, ... at Utica, ... August, 1828. *Utica: Northway & Porter, Printers.* 1828. 8vo, pp. 29. B. 53714

Journal of the Legislative Council Of the Colony of New-York. Began the 9th Day of April, 1691; and Ended the 27 of September, 1743. Published by Order of the Senate of ... New-York. *Albany: Weed, Parsons & Company, Printers.* 1861. 2 vols., folio, pp. xxx, (1), 814; (2), 819–2078, (1). B.

The greater part of the edition was destroyed by fire. Vol. II. is entitled "Journal of the Legislative Council of the Colony of New York. Began the 8th day of December, 1743, and ended the 3d of April, 1775." These volumes, with the Journals of the Assembly, printed by Hugh Gaine, and the supplementary volume issued from the State press, in 1821, make up a complete series of the Legislative Journals of the Colony, from 1691 down to the Revolution. The value of the Index in this volume is the greater, as that of the Assembly Journals is of little use.

Journal of the Proceedings. *See* Vol. IX., No. 36738.

Journal of the Senate of the State of New York, at their Tenth Session. *New York: Printed by Samuel and John Loudon.* M.DCC.LXXX.VII. Folio. 53716

Continued to 1829 in folio, afterwards issued in octavo.

Journal of the Votes and Proceedings of the General Assembly of the Colony of New York. [From March 24, to Sept. 22, 1747. Colophon:] *New York: Printed by James Parker, at the New Printing Office in Beaver Street.* 1747. Folio, pp. 58.

A Journal of the Votes and Proceedings of the General Assembly of the Colony of New York. Begun the twelfth day of February, 1747–8. *New York: Printed and Sold by James Parker,* ... 1747–8. Folio, pp. 96. S. 53718

Journal | of the | Votes and Proceedings | of the | General Assembly | of the Colony of | New-York. | Began the 9th Day of April, 1691, and | Ended the 27th of September, 1743. | Vol. I. Published by order of the General Assembly. | *New-York: Printed by Hugh Gaine* .... M,DCC,LXIV. Folio, pp. iv, 840, (2). + Vol. II. Began the 8th Day of November, 1743; | and Ended the 23d of December, 1765. ... [*Ibid.*] M,DCC,LXVI. pp. 811, viii, (2).

Edited by Abraham Lott. Some copies have a leaf containing the Act of Parliament for reversing the Attainder of Jacob Leisler, Jacob Milbourne, and Abraham Governeur, who were executed for not delivering the Fort at New York to Richard Ingoldsby, 1690.

Journal of the Votes and Proceedings of the General Assembly of the Colony of New-York, from 1766 to 1776, inclusive. Reprinted in pursuance of a joint resolution of the Legislature of ... New-York, passed 30th April, 1820. *Albany: Printed by J. Buell.* 1820. Folio. 53720

Collation: pp. 4, 92, iii; 76, iii; 82, iii; 106, iii; 82, (1), iii; 113, iii; 120, iii (pp. 119 and 120 are more recently printed and inserted); 105, iv (p. 105 is also more recently printed); 117 (pp. 11–14, and 99–102 are repeated, being additions).

A perfect copy should contain six leaves subsequently printed, in the following order: one leaf following page 118, 13th Geo. III.; one leaf following page 104, 14th Geo. III.; two leaves following page 10, 15th Geo. III.; two leaves following page 90, 15th Geo. III. "In March, 1820, on finding that only one copy of the original Journals, from 1766 to 1776, was known to exist, the General Assembly of New York voted to reprint a small edition of fifty copies only. The volume has now become excessively rare."—STEVENS. This volume does not include the Journal of 1766, as stated in the title, for the period between 23d December, 1765, and 17th November, 1767 there is no Journal.

Journal of the Votes and Proceedings of the General Assembly of the Colony of New-York. Began the 17th of November,

1767, and ended, ... 1768. *New-York: Printed by William Weyman.* 1768. Folio. + ... 1768 ... 1769. *New-York: Printed by Hugh Gaine* ... 1769. Folio. + 1769 .... [*Ibid.*] 1769. + ... 1769 ... 1770. [*Ibid.*] 1770. + 1770 ... 1771. [*Ibid.*] M.DCC.LXXI. + 1772 .... [*Ibid.*] 1772. + 1773 .... [*Ibid.*] M,DCC,LXXIII. + 1774 .... [*Ibid.*] M,DCC,LXXIV. + 1775 .... M,DCC,LXXV. Folio. S. 53721

Journal of the Votes of the General Assembly of the Colony of New-York, beginning October 20, 1702, to November 27, 1708. *New-York: Printed by William Bradford.* 1709. Folio.

This series of Session Laws was continued in folio to 1741 or later, being printed successively by William Bradford and John Peter Zenger.

A Journal of what passed. *See* Vol. VI., No. 24713.

Journals of the Provincial Congress, Provincial Convention, Committee of Safety and Council of Safety of ... New-York. 1775–1776–1777. *Albany: Printed by Thurlow Weed* .... 1842. 2 vols., folio, pp. (6), 1196; (4), 543. C., S. 53723

Two hundred and fifty copies printed. These volumes contain documents and records of proceedings which shed great light upon the question of the New Hampshire Grants and the Government of New York, during the first three years of the Revolution.

Report of the JUDGE ADVOCATE GENERAL, upon the Errors and Frauds of the Enrollment. *Albany: Comstock & Cassidy.* 1863. 8vo, pp. 27. 53724

Also: Annual Report of the Judge Advocate General, December 13, 1861. [n. p. n. d.] 8vo, pp. 11.

Een korte Handleiding. *See* Vol. IX., No. 38258.

Law for the due Observance of the Lord's Day, ... 29th March, 1813. *New York.* 1813. 12mo, pp. 6. M. 53725

The | Laws & Acts | of the | General Assembly | for | Their Majesties Province | of | New-York, | As they were Enacted in divers Sessions, the first of | which began April, the 9th, Annoq; Domini, | 1691. | — | *At New-York,* | *Printed and Sold by William Bradford, Printer to their Majesties, King* | *William & Queen Mary,* | 1694. Folio, pp. 92, as first issued. 53726

In describing this *excessively rare* book, the first book printed in New York and the first Collection of the Laws of New York, I have followed, with a few variations, Mr. Trumbull's description of Mr. Brinley's copy (which sold for $1,600). The fortunate possessor of a copy of this work may, perhaps, find other variations. "The irregularity of the pagination and signatures—with the occasional omission of a law which had ceased to be of force, and the substitution of another in its place—renders the giving of an accurate and intelligible collation of the volume almost impossible. The printed

Table of Contents prefixed to the volume shows that, as first made up, it ended with the 'Catalogue of Fees' established in September, 1693, at the end of which is the colophon: 'Printed and Sold by *William Bradford,* Printer to Their Majesties, | King *William* and Queen *Mary,* at the Bible in *New-York,* 1693.' The three following leaves, containing Acts passed in 1694, seem to have been added after the Table of Contents was printed. For so much of the volume, the collation is tolerably plain: Title, 1 leaf; Table of Contents, 1 leaf; Acts, pp. 92; between pp. 68 and 69, An Act granting a Rate, &c. (Nov. 1692) 1 sheet (pp. 4) is inserted; after page 84 is 'A Catalogue of Fees,' &c., pp. 11, with the colophon, as above. The additions to Mr. Brinley's copy, irregularly paged, are as follows: Acts of 4th Assembly, 2d Session (Oct. 1694), pp. 4; 5th Ass. 1st Sess. (June, 1695), pp. 101–106, with colophon; 2d Sess. (Oct. 1695, misnamed '6th Assembly, 1st Session,') pp. 107–113; 3d Sess. (Mch. 1696), pp. 10, with colophon; 4th Sess. (Oct. 1696), pp. 6; 5th Sess. (Mch. 1697), pp. 5; 7th Ass., 1st Sess. [misprinted, 7th Sess.] Mch. 1699 to end of 4th [misprinted, 3d] Sess., Aug. 1701, pp. 119–176, with 10 pp. irregularly numbered, between pp. 156 and 157 (bis); 1st to 5th Sessions (Regno Annæ), Oct. 1702, to June, 1705, pp. 177–238 (and 233–238 repeated); and Sessions of June and Sept. 1706, and Sept. and Oct. 1708, pp. 30." The additions are the so-called Session Laws, which were paged continuously but issued separately. *See also* "Hist. Mag.," III. 174.

Laws and Ordinances of New Netherlands, 1638–74. Compiled and Translated from the Original Dutch Records in the Office of the Secretary of State, Albany, N. Y. By E. B. O'Callaghan. *Albany: Weed, Parsons and Company, Printers.* 1868. 8vo, pp. xxxii, 602. C., S. 53727

The | Laws | of Her Majesties | Colony of New-York, | As they were Enacted, by the Governour, Council and | General Assembly, for the time being, in divers Sessions, | the first of which began April the 9th, Annoq; Dom. 1691. | ... | *Printed by William Bradford, Printer to the Queens most Excellent* | *Majesty for the Colony of New-York.* 1709. Folio, pp. iv, 114, 78, 40. S. 53728

The | Laws, | of Her Majesties | Colony of New-York, | as they were enacted by the Governour, Council and Ge- | neral Assembly, for the time being, in divers Sessions, the first of | which began April the 9th; Annoq; Dom. 1691. | To which is Added, | His Excellency's Speeches and Messages to the General | Assembly, and a Journal of the Votes and | Addresses of the House | during the Administrations | of the Rt. Honorable the Lord Cornbury, | Lord Lovelace, and the honourable Coll. Richard Ingoldsby, Esq. | Governors of said Colony, to the 12th of November, 1709. | *Printed by William Bradford, Printer to the Queens most Excellent* | *Majesty for the Colony of New-York,* 1710. Folio, pp. (4), 6, 114, 78, 40. P., S. 53729

Laws | of | New-York, | from | The Year 1691, to 1751, inclusive. | ... | *New-York:* | *Printed by James Parker* ... | MDCCLII. Folio, pp. (8), iii, 488, (1), An Ordinance, (8). BA., C., N.

Digested by William Livingston and William Smith, Jr. The catalogue of the New York Historical Society claims to have a large paper copy; the earliest instance within our knowledge of a large paper copy of any work printed in New York.

The | Laws | Of His Majesties | Colony of New-York, | As they were Enacted by the Governour, Council | and General Assembly (for the time being), in divers | Sessions, the first of which began April 9th, 1691. | *Printed by William Bradford, Printer to the Kings most Excellent* | *Majesty for the Colony of New-York.* 1719. Folio.

Collation: pp. (12); 88; 155–194; 239–290; 207–253; 246–324; "An Ordinance for Regulating Fees," pp. 20.

The irregular collation of this volume is suggestive of there being a series of Session Laws. This is the edition which was reprinted in London in 1719. *See* "Acts of Assembly," No. 53467, *supra.*

Laws | of | New-York, | from | The 11th November, 1752, to 22d May, 1762. | Published according to an Order of the General Assembly. | The | Second Volume, | with | a Table to both Volumes. | ... Digested by William Livingston, And | William Smith, Jun. | *New-York:* | *Printed by William Weyman.* MDCCLXII. Folio, pp. (8), 268. H., N. 53732

Laws | of | New-York, | from | The Year 1691, to 1773 inclusive. | ... Volume the First. ... *New-York: Printed by Hugh Gaine,* | MDCCLXXIV. Folio, pp. iv, 835. N. 53733

Edited by Peter Van Schaack. The New York Historical Society claims to have this on large paper; all the copies I have seen have a large margin.

Laws of the State of New-York, commencing with the First Session of the Senate and Assembly, after the Declaration of Independence, and the Organization of the New Government of the State: Anno 1777. ... *Poughkeepsie: Printed by John Holt, Printer to the State.* 1782. Folio, pp. 300. N., S. 53734

This paging includes the Sixth Session, A. D. 1780. These laws were printed in folio to the Nineteenth Session, 1796, after that date they were issued in octavo.

Laws | of the | State of New-York, | comprising | The Constitution, | and | The Acts of the Legislature since the Revolution, | from | The First to the Twelfth Session, inclusive. | ... *New-York: Printed by Hugh Gaine.* M,DCC,LXXXIX. 2 vols., folio, pp. (4), 336, (11), xii, (1); (2), 471, (17). 53735

Edited by Samuel Jones and Richard Varick. The laws of the Thirteenth Session were issued with the title as:

Laws | of the | State | of | New-York. | Volume the Third. *New-York: Printed by Francis Childs.* 1790. Folio, pp. (2), 48.

The sequent sessions were continued in the same form.

Laws of the State of New-York, ... from the First to the Fifteenth Session, inclusive. ... *New-York: Printed by Thomas Greenleaf.* M,DCC,XC,II. 2 vols., 8vo, pp. (4), 511; (2), 521, (14).

Laws of the State of New-York, ... from the First to the Twentieth Session, inclusive. ... *New-York: Printed by Thomas Greenleaf.* MDCCXCII–MDCCXCVII. 3 vols., 8vo. N. + Second Edition. [*Ibid.*] 53738

Laws ... relating to the Assessment and Collection of Taxes, ... *Albany: Weed, Parsons and Company.* 1856. 8vo, pp. (8), 228, (1). B. 53739

Laws ... respecting Navigable Communications between the Great Western and Northern Lakes and the Atlantic Ocean. *New York.* 1817. 8vo. 53740

Laws ... relating to Common Schools, with the Instructions of the Department, concerning the Duties of the various ... Officers .... *Albany.* 1843. 8vo. + Prepared by ... Victor M. Rice. *Albany: Weed, Parsons & Co.* 1868. 8vo, pp. xvi, 720.

Laws of ... New York. *See* Vol. VI., No. 22745.

Laws ... in Relation to Banking Associations .... *New-York: John S. Voorhies.* 1850. 8vo, pp. 48. B. 53742

Laws of the Legislature of the State of New York in force against the Loyalists, and affecting the Trade of Great Britain, and British Merchants, and others having Property in that State. *London: Printed by H. Reynell.* MDCCLXXXVI. 8vo, pp. xv, 9–186

For another edition, *see* Vol. XI., No. 39417.

Laws of ... New-York, revised and passed at the Thirty-Sixth Session of the Legislature. With Marginal Notes and References, furnished by the Revisors, William P. Van Ness and John Woodworth .... *Albany: Printed by H. C. Southwick & Co.* 1813. 2 vols., 8vo, pp. 592; 570, (1), Appendix, xiv, Index, l. Continued. C., H. 53744

Laws of the State .... Revision of 1801, by James Kent and Jacob Radcliff. *Albany: Printed by Charles R. and George Webster.* 1802. 2 vols., 8vo. + Second Edition. *Albany.* 1807. 2 vols., 8vo. + Continued by Websters and Skinners, Vol. III., 1804; Vol. IV., 1806; Vol. V., 1809; Vol. VI., 1812. *Albany.* 1804–12. 8vo. C. 53745

Laws of ... New York, of a general nature, passed from 1828 to 1841 inclusive. Selected and Arranged [by E. Perkins Smith]. *Rochester: T. H. Hyatt.* 1841. 8vo, pp. 560. C. 53746

Legislative Documents of the Senate and Assembly of ... New York ... 1824–30. *Albany.* 1824–30. 10 vols., folio. S.

Anterior to 1824, the principal documents were incorporated in the Journals; after 1829, they were issued in octavo.

Legislative Honors to The Memory of President Lincoln. ... *Albany: Weed, Parsons and Company, Printers.* 1865. 8vo, pp. 118. BA. 53748

A Letter from some of the Representatives in the late General Assembly of the Colony of New-York, to his Excellency Governor C——n. Principally in answer to his Message of the 13th of October last, and his Dissolution Speech. [n. p.:] *Printed in the Year* 1747. Folio, pp. 30. S. 53749

Letter from the President of the Senate ... of ... New-York, inclosing certain resolutions ... relative to the protection of the Port .... *City of Washington: A. & G. Way, Printers.* 1807. 8vo, pp. 4. BA. 53750

A Letter to ... Daniel D. Tompkins. *See* [M'Intyre (A.)]

List of Books and Papers in the Office of the Secretary of State .... Albany, N. Y. *Albany.* 1866. 4to, pp. 8. S.

List of Convicts discharged by Expiration of Sentence or Pardon, from the Mount Pleasant, Auburn and Clinton Prisons, during 1819 .... *Albany.* 1819. 4to. Continued. S. 53752

List of Lands to be sold in November, 1815, for Arrears of Taxes. *Albany: Printed by J. Buel.* 1815. 8vo, pp. viii, 140. Continued. S. 53753

List of Patents of Lands, &c. to be sold in November, 1815, for Arrears of Quit Rent. *Albany: Printed by J. Buel.* [1815.] 4to, pp. iv, 20. Continued. S. 53754

List of Representatives in the Assembly of ... New York, ... 1777 to 1852 .... *Albany.* 1852. 8vo, pp. 95. 53755

Manual for the Use of the Convention to revise the Constitution of ... New-York, convened at Albany, June 1, 1846. ... *New York: Walker & Craighead.* 1846. 12mo, pp. 371. BA.

Manual for the Use of the Legislature of ... New York, for ... 1838. ... *Albany*. 1838. 16mo. Continued. 53757

Manual of the Constitutional Convention ... . *New York*. 1821. 12mo. 53758

Manual of the Legislature ... 1827. *Albany*. 1827. 12mo. Continued. 53759

Manual of the Revised Statutes of ... New York ... . *Glen's Falls: Printed by Abial Smith*. 1831. 8vo, pp. 412. S. 53760

Constitutions of the Annual Convention of MECHANICS' MUTUAL PROTECTIONS of ... New York ... . *Albany*. 1847. 12mo, pp. 32. 53761

Transactions of the MEDICAL ASSOCIATION. *See* No. 47312

Bye-Laws of the MEDICAL SOCIETY of ... New York. [n. p. n. d.] 8vo. B. + *Albany*. 1839. 8vo, pp. 23. + With the Rules of Order, Medical Ethics, etc. ... *Albany: Printed by J. Munsell*. 1846. 8vo, pp. 40. + [*Ibid.*] 1853. 8vo, pp. 42. + [*Ibid.*] 1857. 8vo. S. 53762

Also: Proposed By-Laws of the ... Society ... . *Albany, N. Y.: J. Munsell*. 1868. 8vo, pp. 17. B.

Report of the Committee, appointed by the Medical Society, of ... New-York, to enquire into the Symptoms, Origin, Cause, and Prevention of the Pestilential Disease, that prevailed in New York during ... 1798. *New-York*. 1799. 12mo, pp. (2), 47.

A System of Medical Ethics, adopted by the Medical Society ... *New York*. 1823. 8vo. + *Albany: Printed by J. Munsell*. 1846. 8vo, pp. 16. B. 53764

Transactions of the Medical Society ... From its Organization in 1807, ... to ... 1831. *Albany: Charles Van Benthuysen & Sons*. 1868. 8vo, pp. 620. Continued. BA. 53765

Also: Report of a Committee of the Medical Society ... on ... Medical Education. *Albany: Printed by J. Munsell*. 1840. 8vo, pp. 22.—Report on the Epidemic Small Pox and Chicken Pox, which prevailed in New-York during [1815] ... . By the Medical Society of the City and County ... at their Quarterly Meeting, January, 1816. *New-York: Printed by G. Forman*. 1816. 8vo, pp. 28.— ... Semi-Centennial Supper ... February 4, 1857. *Albany*. 1857. 8vo, pp. 7. B.—Transactions of the Medical Society ... for ... 1808. ... With the Bye-Laws ... . *New York: Printed by Collins and Perkins*. 1809. 8vo, pp. 28. Continued.

A Memoir. *See* Vol. XI., Nos. 47502 and 47506.

Memorial concerning a Canal Navigation, &c. [n. p. n. d.] 8vo, pp. 18. BA. 53766

Memorial in Behalf of ... New York, in respect to Adapting its Canals to the Defense of the Lakes. [*Washington*. 1862.] Folio, pp. (10). H. + *Washington, June*, 1862. 8vo, pp. 16.

Memorial of the Canal Board & Canal Commissioners of ... New-York, asking for the Improvement of the Lake Harbors. ... *Albany, N. Y.* 1858. 8vo, pp. 30. H., S. 53768

Memorial [etc.]. *See* Vol. VI., No. 22747, Vol. XII., Nos. 47620, 47624, 47648, 47666.

Memorial of the New-York Convention ... of Friends of Domestic Industry ... . [n. p. 1832.] 8vo, pp. 48. + *Baltimore*. 1832. 8vo. + *Boston*. 1832. 8vo, pp. 48. 53769

Memorial of the New York Convention of the Friends of Domestic Industry, to the Congress of the United States. Presented March 26, 1832. [n. p. 1832.] 8vo, pp. 18–39. + [n. p. 1833.] 8vo. 53770

See also No. 53675, *supra*.

Memorial on the Obstructions at the Head of Navigation of Hudson River. [n. p.] 1818. 8vo. 53771

Mercantile Laws of the State of New York, collected and arranged for the convenience of Merchants and others concerned in Trade. *New York*. 1788. 8vo. N. 53772

The first work of the kind put forth in New York.

Message From Governor Jay, of the 12th January, 1799, accompanying Resolutions from Virginia and Kentucky. ... [*Albany*. 1799.] 8vo. + [Reprinted: n. p. 1833.] 8vo, pp. 79.

The reprint includes Mr. Madison's Report and Letter to the "North American Review."

Message ... enclosing the Report of Commissioners relative to the Eastern Boundary of ... New York. *Albany*. 1808. Folio.

Also: Message ... [in relation to the defence of New York]. *Albany: S. Southwick*. 1812. 8vo, pp. 53.— ... Message ... with the Report of the Commissioners of Fortifications. [*Albany*. 1814.] 8vo, pp. 7.— ... Message ... relative to the Invasion of the Western Frontier of this State. [*Albany*. 1814.] 8vo, pp. 28. B.

Message of His Excellency Governor Clinton, To the House of Assembly, January 18th, 1821. [n. p. n. d.] 8vo, pp. 45.

Communicating the evidence of the interference of the officers of the General Government in the local concerns of the State.

The Message of ... Governor Van Buren, on the subject of Banks; with the Plan suggested. ... January 26, 1829. *Albany*. 1829. 8vo. S.

Message of Governor Morgan, January 7, 1862. *Albany: C. Van Benthuysen*. 1862. 8vo, pp. 74. 53776

Relates chiefly to the Rebellion.

The Military Code of ... New York. 1866. *Albany: Weed, Parsons and Company, Printers*. 1866. 8vo, pp. 213. H. 53777

The Militia Act: being a Law, to organize the Militia of the State of New York. To which are added all the amendatory Acts to the said Law ... . *Albany: Printed by Webster and Skinner*. 1808. 8vo, pp. 38. S. 53778

Also: The New Militia Act ... passed April 23, 1823. ... *Albany: Printed by C. R. and G. Webster* ... . 1823. 8vo, pp. 32.—The Militia Law. *Pougbkeepsie*. 1780. 8vo. + Amendments to the Militia Law. Passed March 13, 1821. [n. p. 1821.] 8vo, pp. 12. + *Albany*. 1835. 8vo. + April 17, 1854. *Albany*. 1854. 8vo, pp. 132. + Passed April 23, 1862. *Albany: Weed, Parsons & Co*. 1862. 8vo, pp. 110.

Minutes of the Meeting for Sufferings of New York, and the Testimony against Elias Hicks. *New York: Printed by Mahlon Day*. 1829. Folio, pp. 2. 53779

Reprinted in "The Annual Monitor," for 1830, p. 109.

Minutes of the Proceedings. *See* Vol. XII., Nos. 49376–7.

Minutes of the State Conventions of Colored Citizens, held at Albany, on the 18th, 19th, and 20th of August, 1840. ... *New York*. 1840. 8vo. N. 53780

Muster Rolls of the New York State Volunteers, First to One-hundred-and-thirty-seventh Regiment. *Albany*. 1864–65. 4 vols., 4to. 53781

Names of Persons. *See* Vol. XII., Nos. 51740–41.

Natural History of the State of New York. *Albany*. 1842–1867. 22 vols., 4to. 53782

This work, published by authority of the State, is usually arranged under divisions or parts as: Zoology, 6 parts in 4 volumes, Botany, 2 volumes, Mineralogy, 1 volume, Geology, 4 volumes, and a large Geological Map, Agriculture, 5 volumes, and Palæontology, 6 volumes, each of which are described below:

[*Engraved Title*:] Natural History of New York. By Authority ... . *Albany: Carroll & Cook, Printers*. 1842. [*Printed Title*:] Zoology of New-York, or the New-York Fauna; comprising detailed descriptions of all the Animals hitherto observed within the State of New-York, with brief notices of those occa-

sionally found near its borders, and accompanied by appropriate Illustrations. By James E. De Kay. Part I. Mammalia. *Albany: Printed by W. & A. White & J. Visscher*. 1842. 4to, Engraved Title, pp. (4), 188, xiii, (1), 146. 33 Plates, 2 Plans.

The introduction (pp. 188) was written by William H. Seward, and the *printed* title is sometimes found after page 188.

Part II. Birds. *Albany: Carroll and Cook, Printers*. 1844. Engraved Title, pp. xii, 380. 141 Plates. 53784

Part III. Reptiles and Amphibia. *Albany: Printed by W. & A. White and J. Visscher*. 1842. pp. vi, 98. 23 Plates. 53785

Part IV. Fishes. *Albany: Printed by W. & A. White and J. Visscher*. 1842. pp. ix, 415. 79 Plates. 53786

The letter-press of this Part IV. is usually bound up with Part III. The plates generally form a separate volume.

Part V. Mollusca. *Albany: Carroll and Cook, Printers*. 1843. Engraved Title, pp. (4), iv, (iv), 271; followed by Part VI. Crustacea, pp. (viii), 70, (1), 40 Plates of Mollusca, (1), 13 Plates of Crustacea. 53787

These six parts are usually bound in 4 volumes, and form the first division.

A Flora of the State of New-York, comprising full Descriptions of all the Indigenous and Naturalized Plants hitherto discovered in the State; with Remarks on their Economical and Medicinal Properties. By John Torrey, M.D., F.L.S. *Albany: Carroll and Cook, Printers*. 1843. 2 vols., 4to, Engraved Title, pp. (4), ix, ix–xii, 484, 72 Plates; Vol. II. [*Ibid.*] pp. (4), 572, 88 Plates. 53788

This part embraces full descriptions of all the plants of the State, with remarks upon their habits, modes of growth, the means of cultivating and improving valuable plants, and of destroying the noxious or troublesome. The work is illustrated by figures of about 100 of the most important and interesting species. Of this a few copies were issued with the plates colored by hand. It is scarcely necessary to add that they are greatly superior to the plain copies.

Mineralogy of New York. ... By Lewis C. Beck. *Albany*. 1842. 4to, pp. xxiv, (2), 536, (4). 8 Plates. 53789

The Mineralogical Department gives a full account of the minerals and ores of the State, their analysis, important uses, etc., together with an interesting account of the Saline and other Mineral Springs of the State, many of which have obtained so much celebrity. The work contains a large amount of practical information on every part of the subject.

Geology of New-York. Part I. Comprising the Geology of the First Geological District. By William W. Mather ... . *Al-*

bany: Printed by Carroll & Cook. 1843. 4to, pp. xxxvii, 653, (18). 46 Plates and Maps. B. 53790

Geology ... . Part II. Comprising the Survey of the Second Geological District. By Ebenezer Emmons, M.D. ... *Albany: Printed by W. & A. White & J. Visscher*. 1842. 4to, pp. x, 437. 17 Plates. BA. 53791

Geology ... . Part III. Comprising the Survey of the Third Geological District. By Lardner Vanuxem. *Albany: Printed by W. & A. White & J. Visscher*. 1842. 4to, Engraved Title, pp. (6), 5–306, (1). 53792

Geology ... . Part IV. Comprising the Survey of the Fourth Geological District. By James Hall. *Albany: Carroll and Cook, Printers*. 1843. 4to, pp. xxii, 683, (1). 34 Woodcuts, 20 Plates and Maps. 53793

The Geological Department embraces a full account of the Primary and New York Systems, or of those from the oldest-known rocks to the carboniferous or coal-bearing period, together with the new red sand-stone and tertiary. It is illustrated by numerous interesting sections, views of scenery, etc., with woodcuts of more than 300 species of fossils characteristic of the strata. The rocks here described, together with their fossils, being little known in this country, and far more complete than the same formations in Europe, will render these volumes exceedingly interesting and important. It is the earliest work in this country where any systematic description of the older stratified rocks is given; and from the circumstance that these are better developed, and the series more complete, in New York than in any part of the known world, it forms the most interesting work yet published upon the popular science of Geology.

Agriculture of New-York: comprising an Account of the Classification, Composition and Distribution of the Soils and Rocks ... the Climate and the Agricultural Productions of the State. By Ebenezer Emmons, M.D. ... *Albany: Printed by C. Van Benthuysen & Co*. 1846–54. 5 vols., 4to. 53794

Vol. I. 1846, Engraved Title, pp. xi, 371. 21 Plates and colored Map.
Vol. II. 1849, pp. viii, 343, 50. 42 Plates.
Vol. III. 1851, Part 1, Text, pp. v, 340.
Vol. IV. or Part 2 of Vol. III., pp. vii. 99 Plates.
Vol. V. 1854, pp. viii, 272. 50 Plates.

Vol. I. contains a general account of the soils of the State, their composition and distribution, and their relations to the underlying formations. Vol II. is devoted mainly to the composition of the inorganic parts of vegetables. Vol. III. is devoted partly to the description and illustration of the fruits of the State, and partly to the principles of Practical Agriculture. Vol. IV. contains beautifully colored Plates of the fruits of the State. Vol. V. forms the entomological portion of the work, together with descriptions of the more common and injurious species of insects.

Palæontology of New York. Volume I. [and II.] Containing Descriptions of the Organic Remains of the Lower Division of the New York System (Equivalent of the Silurian Rocks of Europe). ... By James Hall. *Albany: Printed by C. Van Benthuysen*. 1847. 2 vols., 4to, pp. xxiii, 338, 87 Plates, and Plate 33* with descriptive letter-press. Vol. II. [*Ibid.*] 1852. Engraved Title, pp. (6), 362, (1). 85 Plates and letter-press.

Geological Survey of New York. Palæontology. Volume III. Containing Descriptions and Figures of the Organic Remains of the Lower Helderberg Group and the Oriskany Sandstone. 1855–1859. By James Hall. *Albany: Printed by C. Van Benthuysen*. 1859. Part 1. Text, pp. xii, 532, (1). Part 2. [*Ibid.*] 1861. 120 Plates and letter-press. 53796

Geological Survey ... . Palæontology. Volume IV. Part I. Containing Descriptions and Figures of the Fossil Brachiopoda of the Upper Helderberg, Hamilton, Portage and Chemung Groups. 1862–1866. By James Hall. *Albany, N. Y.: Printed by C. Van Benthuysen & Sons*. 1867. 4to, pp. xi, (1), 428. 63 Plates and descriptive letter-press. 53797

Followed by Vol. IV., Part 2. Illustrations of Devonian Fossils: Corals of the Upper Helderberg and Hamilton Groups, *Albany*, 1876, 4to, 43 Plates, and another volume, pp. 7, 126 Plates.

The volumes on Palæontology contain full descriptions, with engraved figures, of more than 500 species of fossils, principally those found in the rocks intervening between the Primary and the Coal formation. The fossils of each particular rock or group are figured collectively, in the order of the series which they illustrate. The importance and interest in this portion of the Geological Department is, if possible, superior to all the others; giving a large number of entirely new forms of these ancient denizens of our globe, with their geographical distribution and geological range.

"The preparation of this splendid work by the ablest scientific men of the country has cost the State of New York more than 200,000 dollars, and is a good example of enlightened legislative liberality. As a work embracing every department of Natural History, it should find a place in all great libraries."

Report of the Select Committee to the Legislature of 1849, on the Publication of the Natural History of the State ... . January 2, 1850. *Albany: Weed, Parsons & Co. ... Printers*. 1850. 8vo, pp. 178, (1), 12 folded leaves. 53798

Also: Report of the Select Committee [of the Legislature of 1855–56] on the Completion of the Natural History of the State ... . *Albany*. 1856. 8vo, pp. 16. C.

The New-York Annual Register ... 1830. ... with Political, Statistical, and other Information respecting ... New-York and the United States. By Edwin Williams. *New-York: J. Leavitt*. 1830. 12mo, pp. vi, 348. Plate. B. 53799

Continued to 1837, resumed in 1840, then discontinued till 1843, after that date, and up to 1846, it was edited by Skinner and Williams. Fourteen volumes constitute a set. *See also* "New York State Register," No. 53836, *infra*.

Proceedings of the NEW-YORK ANTI-SECRET SOCIETY Convention held at Syracuse, ... 1870. ... [n. p. n. d.] 8vo, pp. 16.

Proceedings of the First Annual Meeting of the NEW-YORK STATE ANTI-SLAVERY SOCIETY ... 1836. *Utica, New York: The Society*. 1836. 8vo, pp. 60. B. 53801

Also: First Annual Report of the Proceedings of the ... Society. *Utica*. 1835. 8vo.

Account of the Ceremonies at the Laying of the Corner-stone of the NEW-YORK ASYLUM for Idiots at Syracuse, Sept. 8, 1854. *Albany*. 1854. 8vo, pp. 42. Plate. S. 53802

Also: ... First Annual Report Of the Trustees of the New-York State Asylum for Idiots. [*Albany*.] 1852. 8vo, pp. 23. Continued.

Fifth Annual Report. NEW-YORK BRANCH FREEDMAN'S UNION COMMISSION ... . *New-York*. 1867. 8vo. 53803

Formerly the "National Freedman's Relief Association."

Catalogue of the ... NEW-YORK CENTRAL COLLEGE. For ... 1853–4. McCrawville, Cortland County, N. Y. *Homer, N. Y.: Printed by Dixon & Gould*. 1854. 8vo, pp. 24. Continued.

New York Civil List. *See* Vol. VIII., No. 33143.

New York Convention. *See* Vol. V., No. 17127.

New York Convention Manual. Prepared ... by F. B. Hough. Part I.—Constitutions. Part II.—Statistics. *Albany: Weed, Parsons & Co*. 1868. 2 vols., 8vo, pp. x, 586; xxii, 462. 53805

Reports of the NEW YORK HARBOR COMMISSION, of 1856 and 1857. Republished by ... the Chamber of Commerce ... . *New York: C. S. Westcott & Co., Printers*. 1864. 8vo, pp. vi, 316. Maps, Diagrams and Plan. H. 53806

New-York Legal Register; containing a Sketch of all the principal Courts of the State; a List of the Senators, Judges, Surrogates, Sheriffs ... . *New-York*. 1850. 8vo. S. 53807

The New-York Liquor Law, as contradistinguished from the Maine Liquor Law ... . *New-York: Crampton & Clarke*. 1853. 8vo, pp. 7. H. 53808

The New York Political Manual, containing the Official Election Returns for 1840–42. Also, the Census of the State ... in 1840. ... *Albany*. 1843. 8vo, pp. 72. 53809

NEW-YORK STATE AGRICULTURAL COLLEGE. Charter, Ordinances and Regulations, 1853. *Albany: Printed by Charles Van Benthuysen*. 1853. 8vo, pp. (2), 21. Continued. H. 53810

Dedication of the New-York State Agricultural Rooms. Albany, February 12, 1857. [n. p.] 1857. 8vo, pp. 91.—Proceedings of the State Agricultural Convention ... at ... Albany ... February, 1832: with the Constitution of a State Agricultural Society ... *Albany: Printed by Websters and Skinners*. 1832. 8vo, pp. 40. Continued. BA., S.

Transactions of the NEW-YORK STATE AGRICULTURAL SOCIETY, for ... MDCCCXLI. Vol. I. *Albany: Printed by T. Weed*. 1842. 8vo, pp. iv, (2), 411. Plates. Continued. B. 53811

Also: 1844, New-York State Agricultural Society. Arrangements for diffusing Agricultural Knowledge through the Instrumentality of Common Schools and Public Libraries ... . *Albany: Press of C. Van Benthuysen & Co*. 1844. 8vo, pp. 24.—The Journal of the New-York State Agricultural Society. Vol. I. ... May, 1850. No. 1, *Albany*. 1850. 8vo, pp. 8. Continued.— ... List of Premiums and Regulations, for the Fourteenth Annual Exhibition, ... October ... 1854. ... [n. p. n. d.] 8vo, pp. 6. 17. Continued.—Proceedings of the ... Society, ... with the Act of Incorporation ... . *Albany: Printed by Webster and Skinners*. 1833. 8vo, pp. 70. B.

By-Laws for the Regulation of the Officers of the Second Regiment NEW YORK STATE ARTILLERY. Passed February 26th, 1825. *New-York*. 1825. 8vo. S. 53812

Address of the NEW-YORK STATE AUXILIARY CLAY MONUMENT ASSOCIATION, to the People of ... New-York. *New-York: Van Norden & King*. 1853. 8vo, pp. 16. H. 53813

An eloquent sketch of Henry Clay. *See also* "Historical Magazine," II. 232, 241.

The New York State Business Directory. ... By Adams, Sampson & Co. *New York: John F. Trow*. 1859. 8vo, pp. 675, Advertisements, 144. Continued. BA. 53814

Minutes of the NEW YORK STATE CHRISTIAN CONVENTION, held at Newark, Wayne Co., N. Y., September ... 1866. ... *Syracuse*. 1866. 12mo, pp. 24. H. 53815

African Colonization. Proceedings, on the Formation of the NEW-YORK STATE COLONIZATION SOCIETY; ... *Albany: Printed by Websters and Skinners*. 1829. 8vo, pp. 24. B. 53816

Also: ... Proceedings ... on its first Anniversary; ... with an Address to the Public, ... *Albany: Printed by Websters and Skinners*. 1830. 8vo, pp. 27. Continued. B.

Second Annual Report of the NEW YORK STATE COMMISSIONER to the Paris Exposition of 1867. *Albany: Charles Van Benthuysen & Sons.* 1868. 8vo, pp. 125. 23 Plates. 53817

The New-York State Guide; ... *Albany: J. Disturnell.* 1843. Sm. 8vo, pp. 96. Map. BA. 53818

Constitution of the NEW YORK STATE HORTICULTURAL SOCIETY. [n. p. 1824.] 8vo, pp. 15. H. 53819

New York State Illustrated: or, The Tourist's Guide ... . Edited and Published by Mrs. S. S. Colt. *Albany, N. Y.* 1872. 8vo, pp. 196. 53820

Fourth Annual Report of the NEW YORK STATE INEBRIATE ASYLUM. ... April 20, 1866. *Albany: C. Wendell, Printer.* 1866. 8vo, pp. 45. Continued. B. 53821

Also: Ceremonies, ... New York State Inebriate Asylum. Binghamton, New York. *New York: Wynkoop, Hallenbeck, & Thomas, Printers.* 1859. 8vo, pp. 184. Plates. — The Charter and By-Laws of the ... Asylum. ... *New York: Press of Wynkoop & Hallenbeck.* 1866. 8vo, pp. 27, (1). — A Letter from the Corresponding Secretary of the ... Asylum to the Governor ... on the Subject of Appropriation. ... *New York: Wynkoop, Hallenbeck & Thomas, Printers.* 1858. 8vo, pp. 21. — A Letter ... to the Governor, ... December 30, 1858. [n. p. n. d.] 8vo. S.

First Annual Report of the ... NEW YORK STATE INSTITUTION FOR THE BLIND at Batavia. For ... 1869. *Albany.* 1870. 8vo, pp. (4), 24. Continued. B. 53822

Transactions of the NEW-YORK STATE INSTITUTION OF CIVIL ENGINEERS. ... Volume First. No. 1. *Albany: Charles Van Benthuysen, Printer.* 1849. 4to, pp. 22, (2). BA. 53823

... Annual Report Of the Trustees of the [NEW YORK] STATE LIBRARY. [n. p.] 1830. 8vo, pp. 34. Continued. B.

Catalogue of Historical Papers ... deposited in the New-York State Library. ... *Albany: Weed, Parsons & Co., ... Printers.* 1849. 8vo, pp. 55. B. 53825

Also: Catalogue of Manuscripts ... deposited in the New York State Library, December 15, 1847. *Albany.* 1849. 8vo. — Catalogue of the Books on Bibliography, Typography and Engravings, in the New-York State Library. *Albany: Charles Van Benthuysen, Printer.* 1858. 8vo, pp. 143. B.

Catalogue of the New-York State Library, January 1, 1846. ... *Albany: C. Wendell, Printer.* 1846. 8vo, pp. iv, 5–252, 294. + January 1, 1850. *Albany: Charles Van Benthuysen, Printer.* 1850. 8vo, pp. 1058, (1). H. 53826

Catalogue of the New-York State Library: 1855. General Library. *Albany: Charles Van Benthuysen, Printer.* 1856. 8vo, pp. x, (2), 987. + First Supplement. I. Titles. II. Index of Subjects. [*Ibid.*] 1861. 8vo, pp. x, (2), 1084. B. 53827

Catalogue of New-York State Library: 1856. Maps, Manuscripts, Engraving, Coins, &c. *Albany: Charles Van Benthuysen, Printer.* 1857. Rl. 8vo, pp. xii, 274. B., C. 53828

Catalogue of the New-York State Library: 1855. Law Library. *Albany: Charles Van Benthuysen, Printer.* 1856. 8vo, pp. x, 402. + Catalogue: 1865. Law Library: First Supplement. [*Ibid.*] 1865. 8vo, pp. 180. B. 53829

Catalogue of the New York State Library, 1872. Subject-Index of the General Library. *Albany: Van Benthuysen Printing House.* 1872. 8vo, pp. xvii, (1), 651. C. 53830

An admirably digested work by Dr. H. A. Homes, the librarian.

Report of the Physician of the NEW-YORK LUNATIC ASYLUM ... *New-York: Printed by Samuel Wood & Sons.* 1818. 8vo, pp. 20. Continued. BA. 53831

Also: Annual Report of the Managers of the State Lunatic Asylum. ... January 18, 1844. *Albany.* 1844. 8vo. Continued. + *Utica: Reprinted at the Asylum.* 1861. 8vo, pp. 56. — ... Report of the Trustees of the ... Asylum, with the documents accompanying the same, pursuant to the act of the Legislature passed May 26th, 1841. [*Albany.* 1842.] 8vo. — Rules, Regulations and By-Laws of the ... Asylum, Utica. *Utica, N. Y.: D. P. White, ... Printer.* 1866. 8vo, pp. 32. B.

Proceedings of the First Annual Meeting of the NEW-YORK STATE LYCEUM, ... at Utica, 1831. ... *Utica: Northway & Porter, Printers.* 1831. 8vo, pp. 40. B. 53832

New York State Mechanic. A Journal of the Manual Arts, Trades and Manufactures. ... *Albany.* 1842.. Folio. Continued.

Edited by E. G. Squier.

Circular of the NEW YORK STATE MECHANICS' ASSOCIATION. *Albany.* 1841. 8vo, pp. 24. 53834

Report and Speeches on the State of the NEW YORK STATE PRISON ASSOCIATION Bill, in the House of Assembly, March, 1844. *Albany.* 1844. 8vo, pp. 41. M. 53835

The New-York State Register, for ... 1830, ... with a concise United States Calendar. By Roger Sherman Skinner. ... *New-York: The Author.* 1830. 12mo, pp. 408. B. 53836

See also "New York Annual Register," No. 53799, *supra*.

The New-York State Register, for 1843. ... Edited by O. L. Holley. *Albany: J. Disturnell.* 1843. 12mo, pp. 432. B.

Continued to 1859 or later.

Proceedings of the NEW-YORK STATE SABBATH CONVENTION ... Saratoga Springs, 1844. *Albany.* 1844. 8vo, pp. 36.

Constitution of the NEW YORK STATE SOCIETY for the Improvement of Education in Common Schools. [n. p. n. d.] 8vo, pp. 4. 53839

First Annual Report of the NEW-YORK STATE SOCIETY for the Promotion of Temperance. ... *New York.* 1830. 8vo, pp. 48. + *Albany: The Society.* 1830. 8vo, pp. 48. Continued.

The title was afterwards changed to "New York State Temperance Society."

New York State Society of the Cincinnati. *See* Nos. 13119–26.

Report of the ... Managers of the NEW YORK STATE SOLDIERS' DEPOT ... . *Albany: Van Benthuysen's ... Printing House.* 1864. 8vo, pp. 160. 5 Maps. 53841

Proceedings of the NEW YORK STATE SUNDAY SCHOOL TEACHERS' ASSOCIATION, Seventeenth Annual Convention, held at Norwich, 1872. *Syracuse.* 1872. 8vo. Continued. 53842

Address of the ... NEW-YORK STATE TEMPERANCE SOCIETY. The Maine Law in New-York. [April 10, 1855. n. p. n. d.] 8vo, 15, (1). H. 53843

Also: Draft of a Bill for the Suppression of the Traffic in Intoxicating Liquors, reported by a Committee appointed by the N. Y. State Temperance Convention, January, 1853. *Albany: H. H. Van Dyck, Printer.* 1853. 8vo, pp. 15. H.

The New York State Tourist. Descriptive of the Scenery of the Hudson, Mohawk, & St. Lawrence Rivers. ... *New-York: A. T. Goodrich.* 1842. 24mo, pp. 234. 5 Plates and 5 Maps.

Notes on the Revised Statutes of ... New York. *Albany.* 1830. 8vo. 53845

... Official Proceedings of the Democratic State Convention, held at Rome, August ... 1849, for the purpose of Forming a Union of the Democratic Masses, in favor of a ... Single Ticket. *Albany: H. H. Van Dyck, Printer.* 1849. Impl. 8vo, pp. 16.

Official Reports, relating to the Militia of the State ... with the Laws ... relating thereto; Organization of the ... Veterans

of the War of 1812 ... . *New York: A. Baptist, Jr., Printer.* 1853. 8vo, pp. 23. H. 53847

Opinion and Argument. *See* [Morris (L.)], Vol. XII. 50849.

An Ordinance of his Excellency and Council for Establishing Courts of Judicature within the Province of New-York, done at New-York 15th May, 1691, in the Reign of William 3d. [n. p. n. d.] Folio. 53848

Title from Henry A. Brady's catalogue.

An Ordinance of ... Edward Viscount Cornbury, Capt. Gen'l and Governor in Chief in and over the Provinces of New-York, New Jersey, &c.; done at Fort Anne in New-York, 7th November, 1704. [*New-York: Printed by William Bradford.*] 1704. Folio, pp. 5. 53849

Also: An Ordinance for the further establishing the Supreme Court of Judicature for the Province of New-York. *Printed by William Bradford in New York.* 1704. Folio, pp. 4. S.

An Ordinance for Regulating and Establishing Fees.|By his Excellency Robert Hunter Esq; Capt. General and Go|vernour in Chief in and over the Province of New-York, New Jersey, and|of all the Territories and Tracts of Land depending thereon in America,|and Vice Admiral of the same, &c. in Council, the 19th Day of|October,|in the ninth year of her Majesty's Reign, Annoq. Domini 1710. [n. p. 1710.] Folio, pp. (12). BM.

This Ordinance is also appended to the "Laws," MDCCLII.

An Ordinance for Regulating and Establishing the Fees|to be hereafter taken by the Officers of the Court of Chancery in the Province of New-York. [n. p. 1723.] Folio, pp. (4). BM.

Also: An Ordinance for Regulating and Establishing Fees ... . 1722. [n. p. n. d.] Folio, pp. (4). — An Ordinance for Regulating the Recording of Deeds ... . [n. p. 1723.] Folio, pp. (2).

An Ordinance of the Convention of the State of New York, for organizing and establishing the Government, agreed to by the said Convention. *Fish-Kill: Printed by Samuel Loudon.* M.DCC.LXXVII. 12mo, pp. 12. J.C.B., S. 53852

Papers relating to an Act. *See* Vol. IV., No. 14272.

Papers relating to the Canal Frauds in New-York. *Albany.* 1847. 8vo. 53853

Acts of the PARTICULAR SYNOD of New York, 1812. *New York.* 1812. 12mo, pp. 28. 53854

One hundred copies only printed. Also: Minutes of the Particular Synod of New-York. May, 1819. [n. p.:] *G. Forman, Printer.* [n. d.] 8vo, pp. 30. Continued.

The Ninth Annual Report of the PASTORAL AID SOCIETY of the Protestant Episcopal Church in the Diocese of New-York. ... *New-York: John A. Gray, Printer.* 1859. 12mo. 53855

Annual Report of the PAYMASTER GENERAL, ... December 31, 1862. *Albany.* 1862. 8vo, pp. 28. Continued. 53856

... The Political Code ... . Reported ... by the Commissioners of the Code. ... *Albany: Weed, Parsons & Company, Printers.* 1860. 8vo, pp. xlvii, 607. B. 53857

Poor-Laws of ... New York, 1832. *Albany.* [n. d.] 8vo.

Preliminary Report on the Census of ... New-York, for the Year 1855. ... *Albany: Weed, Parsons and Company, Printers.* 1856. 8vo, pp. 46. Continued. H. 53859

... Presentation of Regimental Colors to the Legislature. [n. p.] 1863. 8vo, pp. 52. Plate. H. 53860

Two hundred thousand copies ordered published by joint resolution of the Legislature.

First Report of the PRISON ASSOCIATION of New York. December, 1844. *New York: Jared W. Bell, Printer.* 1844. 8vo, pp. 63. Continued. B. 53861

Also: Memorial of the Prison Association to the Governor of ... New York. *New York.* 1870. 8vo, pp. 46. H.

Proceedings and Address, of the Democratic State Convention, held at Syracuse, January ... 1856. *Albany.* 1856. 8vo, pp. 31. H. 53862

Proceedings and Debates of the Constitutional Convention ... held in 1867 and 1868 ... . Reported by Edward F. Underhill, ... Volume I. ... *Albany: Weed, Parsons and Company, Printers.* 1868. 8vo, pp. 15–800, Index, ccxlvi. C. 53863

Proceedings of a Convention of Ministers and Delegates from Evangelical Lutheran Churches, in ... New York. Convened in ... Fordsbush, ... May 24, 1837. *Albany: Hoffman & White.* 1837. 8vo, pp. 24. S. 53864

Proceedings of the Convention of ... New-York ... On the Seventeenth and Eighteenth of September, 1812. *Albany: Printed by Webster and Skinners.* [n. d.] 8vo, pp. 24. B. 53865

Proceedings of the Democratic Convention, held at the Capitol, January 26th and 27th, 1848. [n. p. n. d.] 8vo. N.

Proceedings of the Democratic and Free Democratic Conventions. Held at Rome, ... 1849. Including Addresses ... . *Rome: A. J. Rowley & Co.* 1849. 8vo, pp. 96. 53867

Proceedings of the Democratic State Convention, ... Albany, ... 1861. *Albany.* 1861. 8vo. 53868

... Proceedings of the State Convention, held at Rochester, January 19th, 1870, to consider measures for reforming the Management and improving the Trade of the ... Canals. ... *New-York: George F. Nesbitt & Co., Printers.* 1870. 8vo, pp. (2), 111.

Proceedings of the State Convention of Colored People held at Albany ... 22–24 July, 1851. *Albany.* 1851. 8vo, pp. 36.

Proceedings of the Whig Convention ... . [n. p.] 1838. 8vo.

Proclamation by the Governor, to discover the author of Seditious Papers in Zenger's New York Weekly Journal, 1734. [n. p. n. d.] Folio, 1 leaf. 53872

Proclamation by George Clinton, relative to Controverted Lands [now Vermont], dated Oct. 31, 1778. [n. p.:] *John Holt, Printer.* [n. d.] Folio. 53873

The Constitution and Canons of the PROTESTANT-EPISCOPAL CHURCH in ... New York. *New York.* 1812. 8vo, pp. 15. + [*Ibid.*] 1845. 8vo. + [*Ibid.*] 1851. 8vo, pp. 63. + *New-York: James Pott.* 1860. 8vo, pp. 80. + [*Ibid.*] 1864.

Also: The Constitution of the Protestant-Episcopal Church in the Diocese of New York; with the Canons adopted Oct. 2, 1834. *New York.* 1834. 8vo, pp. 16. M.

Journal of the Annual Convention of the Diocese of Central New York, 1869. *Utica.* 1869. 8vo. Continued. 53875

Journal of the Convention of the Protestant Episcopal Church ... of New York, from ... 1787, to ... 1791. *New York.* 1792. 8vo. 53876

Continued annually since 1804.

Journal of the Primary Convention of the Diocese of Albany, ... at Albany, December 2, 1868. *Albany, N. Y.* 1868. 8vo.

Journal of the Proceedings of the Annual Convention of the Protestant Episcopal Church ... of New York, September, 1804. *New York.* 1804. 8vo, pp. 47. Continued. M. 53878

Journal of the Proceedings of the Primary Convention of the Protestant Episcopal Church in the Diocese of Western New York: held in ... Genesee, ... A. D. 1838. ... *Utica: Press of Eli Maynard.* M.DCCCXXXVIII. 8vo, pp. 41. Continued. S.

Also: Proposed Canons, reported by a Committee of the Convention. *Utica.* 1840. 8vo. S.

Journals of the Conventions of the Protestant Episcopal Church, in the Diocese of New-York, from 1785 to 1819. ... *New York: Henry M. Onderdonk.* 1844. 8vo, pp. 480. C.

Proceedings of the Convention of the Protestant Episcopal Church in the State ... held in ... New York, on 22nd of June, 1785. *New York.* 1787. 8vo. Continued. N. 53881

Also: Records of the Proceedings and Debates at the Sixty-first Annual Convention of the Protestant Episcopal Church in ... New-York, held in ... September ... . By Robert A. West. *New York: Stanford and Swords.* 1845. 8vo, pp. 148. B.

Constitution of the PROTESTANT EPISCOPAL SOCIETY for promoting Religion and Learning in the State ... . *New-York: Printed by T. & J. Swords.* 1802. 16mo, pp. 8. H. 53882

Also: Constitution, &c. of the Auxiliary Protestant Episcopal Society ... . *New-York: John R. Winser, Printer.* 1848. 8vo, pp. 16. B.

Historical Collections of the Protestant Episcopal Society ... for 1851. Containing, ... George Keith's Journal of Travels from New Hampshire to Caratuck. *New York.* 1851. 8vo, pp. 230. 53883

Documents respecting the PROTESTANT EPISCOPAL THEOLOGICAL EDUCATION SOCIETY in the State ... . For the purpose of Founding ... Theological Seminaries ... . *New-York: Printed by T. and J. Swords.* 1820. 8vo, pp. 16. 53884

... Communication from the Governor transmitting the Report of the COMMISSIONERS OF QUARANTINE. ... February 16, 1865. *Albany: C. Wendell.* 1865. 8vo, pp. 102, folded leaf. Cont'd.

Also: Report of a Special Committee ... on the present Quarantine Laws, 1846. ... *Albany: Carroll and Cook, Printers.* 1846. 8vo, pp. 317. 2 Maps and folded leaf. — Report of the Legislative Committee of 1848, on the Removal of the Quarantine. [n. p. 1848.] 8vo, pp. 16. H. — ... Report of the Commissioners for the Removal of the Quarantine Station. [n. p. *February* 12, 1858.] 8vo, pp. 35. + [Another] Report ... . [n. p. *March* 10, 1858.] 8vo, pp. 92. S.

Annual Report of the QUARTERMASTER GENERAL of ... New York, ... 1862, with ... Documents. *Albany: Comstock & Cassidy, Printers.* 1863. 8vo, pp. 188. BA. + December 31, 1863. *Albany* 1864. 8vo, pp. 106. Continued. 53886

Annual Report of the RAILROAD COMMISSIONERS ... for ... 1855. Part First. *Albany: C. Van Benthuysen, Printer.* 1856. 2 vols., 8vo, pp. (22), lxix, 380; xvii, 890. Maps, Plans and 27 Profiles. Continued. BA., S. 53887

A Record of the Commissioned Officers, Non-Commissioned Officers and Privates, of the Regiments which were organized in ... New York and called into the Service of the United States to assist in Suppressing the Rebellion ... as taken from the Muster-in Rolls ... . Vol. I. *Albany, N. Y.: Comstock & Cassidy, Printers.* 1864. 4to, pp. 887. H. 53888

Continued to eight or more volumes.

Regulations for the Interior Police and Discipline. *Newburgh.* 1829. 8vo. S. 53889

Regulations for the Uniform of the Militia ... . *Albany.* 1851. 12mo. S. 53890

Report in the Senate, of the Committee appointed to ... Report relative to the Accounts of Daniel D. Tompkins with this State. *Albany.* 1820. 8vo, pp. 24. S. 53891

Report from the Commissioners appointed to Revise the Statute Laws ... . Communicated March 15, 1826. *Albany: Printed by Croswell* ... . 1826. 8vo, pp. 112. Continued. BA. 53892

Report of Committee on Indian Affairs, on Petitions for an Orphan Asylum and Certain Schools on Indian Reservations ... . January 31, 1855. *Albany: C. Van Benthuysen, Printer.* 1855. 8vo, pp. 31. H. 53893

Report of H. Franklin ... from the Committee appointed to Examine the Public Accounts ... . *New York.* 1857. 8vo, pp. 80

... Report of Samuel B. Ruggles, Commissioner, appointed by the Governor ... in respect to the Enlargement of the Canals for National Purposes. ... *Albany: Printed by Comstock & Cassidy.* 1863. 8vo, pp. 105. 53895

Report of S. M. Stilwell, ... appointed to inquire into the Expediency of a Total Abolition of Capital Punishment. *Albany.* 1832. 8vo. W. 53896

... Report of the Agent of the New State Prison. [n. p. 1845.] 8vo, pp. 12. S. 53897

Report of the Commissioner for embodying in a single Act a Common School Code, for the State ... . Transmitted ... January 7, 1852. *Albany: Charles Van Benthuysen, Printer.* 1852. 8vo, pp. 87. H. 53898

Report of the Commissioners appointed ... April 21, 1825, to revise the Statute Laws ... . Made to the Senate ... 1827. *Albany: Printed by Croswell and Van Benthuysen.* 1827. 8vo. S.

Report of the Commissioners appointed ... March, 1810, to explore The Route of an Inland Navigation, from Hudson's River to Lake Ontario and Lake Erie. *Albany.* 1811. 8vo, pp. 35. + *New York: Prior and Dunning.* 1811. 8vo, pp. 38.

For other reports, *see* our Vol. VI., Nos. 22754-22765.

... Report of the Commissioners ... relative to the Construction of a Rail-Road from ... Boston to the Hudson River. [n. p. 1829.] 8vo, pp. 64. S. 53901

Relative to an organization of what became the "Western Railroad." *See also* note to our No. 6768.

Report of the Commissioners. *See* [Morris (G.)], No. 50833

Report of the Commissioners appointed to ascertain and settle the Boundary Line between the States of New York and Connecticut. ... February 8, 1861. *Albany: Charles Van Benthuysen, Printer.* 1861. 8vo, pp. 63. Map. H. 53902

See also our Vol. IV., Nos. 15686-7.

Report of the Commissioners appointed to investigate the Pecuniary Affairs of the Several State Prisons of New York. ... Jan. 29, 1855. *Albany.* 1855. 8vo. M. 53903

... Report of the Commissioners, ... for Internal Improvement ... [*Albany.* 1814.] 8vo, pp. 8. B. 53904

Relative to the Erie Canal.

Report of the Commissioners ... for the Consideration of all matters relating to ... Inland Navigation. *Albany: Printed by S. Southwick.* 1812. 8vo, pp. 40. 53905

... Report of the Commissioners of the Land Office relative to New York Harbor Encroachments. [n. p.] 1862. 8vo, pp. 80, folded leaf and 2 Maps. B. 53906

Report of the Commissioners ... on the Canals from Lake Erie to the Hudson River and from Lake Champlain to the same. ... *Albany: Printed by J. Buel.* 1817. 8vo, pp. 90, 52. 53907

... First Report of the Commissioners on Practice and Pleadings. ... *Albany: Charles Van Benthuysen, ... Printer.* 1848. 8vo, pp. xxiv, 275, (1), Amendments, 31. Continued. B. 53908

Report of the Committee of His Majesty's Council for the Province of New-York, relating to the Controverted Line between that Province and New Jersey. *New-York.* 1754. Fol.

Title from one of Thomas Thorpe's catalogues. *See also* [Harison F.], VIII. 30378.

Report of the Committee of the Bar, appointed December 12, 1846, on the Judiciary System, proposed by the New Constitution of the State ... . [n. p. n. d.] 8vo, pp. 52. S. 53910

Report of the Committee of the Senate on Banks and Insurance Companies. *Albany.* 1826. 8vo. Continued. 53911

... Report of the Committee of Ways and Means on the ... Accounts of Daniel D. Tompkins, Esquire, late Governor ... . [n. p. 1820.] 8vo, pp. 18, xxxv. S. 53912

Also: Report ... upon the Bills relating to the Manufacture and Duty upon Salt. *Albany.* 1864. 8vo, pp. 196. S.

Report of the Committee on Commerce of the State ... in relation to the Reciprocity Treaty with Great Britain. [*Washington.* 1862.] 8vo, pp. 36. 53913

... Report of the Committee on Federal Relations relative to Condition of Barracks on Riker's Island. ... February 5, 1864. *Albany: Comstock & Cassidy, Printers.* 1864. 8vo, pp. 7. 53914

Report of the Committee. *See* Vol. VI., Nos. 22764-5.

A Report of the Debates and Proceedings of The Convention of the State of New-York; held at ... Albany, ... August, 1821. By L. H. Clarke. *New-York: Printed by J. Seymour.* 1821. 8vo, pp. 367, (1). 53915

Report of the Debates and Proceedings of the Convention for the Revision of the Constitution of the State of New York, 1846. Reported by William G. Bishop and William H. Attree. *Albany: Printed at the Office of the Evening Atlas.* 1846. 8vo, pp. 1143. S. 53916

Report of the General Agent for the Relief of Sick, Wounded, Furloughed and Discharged Soldiers of the State ... . *Albany.* 1864. 8vo. + [*Ibid.*] 1865. 8vo. 53917

Report of the General Committee to the Board of Agriculture; ... January 23d, 1822. *Albany: Printed by Packard & Van Benthuysen.* 1822. 8vo, pp. 10. B. 53918

Report of the Joint Committee of the Legislature on the Petition of the Securities of Robert McClallen, late Treasurer of the State. *Albany.* 1804. 8vo. 53919

See also Erie Canal, Vol. VI., No. 22758.

Report of the Joint Committee of the Senate and Assembly, relative to Governor Clinton's Charge of Interference of Officers of the General Government in the Elections of the State. *Albany.* 1821. 8vo. 53920

Report of the Joint Committee of the Senate and Assembly, relative to the Internal Improvements of the State; to whom was referred the Annual Report of the Canal Commissioners. *Albany: Printed by J. Buel.* 1819. 8vo, pp. 14. B. 53921

Also: Report ... on Canals and Internal Improvements. *Albany: Printed by Croswell & Van Benthuysen.* 1825. 8vo, pp. 33.

Report ... on so much of the Governor's Message as Relates to the Investment and Distribution of the Surplus Revenue. ... [n. p. 1837.] 8vo, pp. 15. 53922

Report ... on the subject of Lands patented to Officers and Soldiers of the late Army of the United States. *Albany.* 1801. Folio. 53923

Report of the Joint Library Committee of the Legislature ... on the subject of International Exchanges. 1847. *Albany: C. Van Benthuysen, ... Printer.* 1847. 8vo, pp. (2), 110. B. 53924

Report of the Majority of the Committee on Banks, ... April 1st, 1864. ... *Albany: Printed by C. Van Benthuysen.* 1864. 8vo, pp. 13. H. 53925

Report of the Select Committee appointed by the Legislature ... to examine into Frauds upon Emigrants. 1847. *Albany: C. Van Benthuysen, ... Printer.* 1847. 8vo, pp. (2), 148, (1). B.

Report of ... Committee appointed to visit Charitable Institutions supported by the State and all City and County Poor and Work Houses and Jails ... . *Albany: C. Van Benthuysen, Printer.* 1857. 8vo, pp. 217, (4). B. 53927

... Report ... in Relation to Passage of Certain Railroad Bills. *Albany, N. Y.* 1869. 8vo, pp. 155, (1). H. 53928

Report of ... Committee of the Senate, appointed pursuant to the Communication of the Hon. Jasper Ward, ... made the third January 1826 ... . To which is annexed the Testimony ... . *Albany: Printed by Croswell ... .* 1826. 8vo, pp. 36, 143. B.

Report ... on ... Wm. Morgan. *See* Vol. XII., No. 50685.

Report ... upon the Investigation of Frauds in the Expenditure of Public Monies upon the Canals of ... New York. ... *Albany: C. Van Benthuysen and Co., ... Printers.* 1847. 8vo, pp. 866.

Report ... showing the Frauds and Peculations of Edwin Croswell, Theodore Olcott, John L. Crew and others, by which the Canal Bank was ruined. *Albany: H. H. Van Dyck, Printer.* 1849. 8vo, pp. 64. H. 53931

Report of ... Committee to which was referred ... the Governor's Message relative to our National Difficulties. ... *Albany: Charles Van Benthuysen, Printer.* 1861. 8vo, pp. 28. H. 53932

Report of ... Committee of the Senate on the Electoral Law, February 24, 1824. [n. p. n. d.] 8vo. 53933

Report ... on Capital Punishment. Made ... March 14, 1851. *Albany: Charles Van Benthuysen, Printer.* 1851. 8vo, pp. 22, (1).

Report ... on Report & Memorial of County Superintendents of the Poor on Lunacy and its Relation to Pauperism ... March 5, 1856. *Albany: C. Van Benthuysen, Printer.* 1856. 8vo, pp. 32.

... Report ... on the Colonial Agency. [n. p. 1845.] 8vo, pp. 16. BA. 53936

Report ... on the Petitions to prevent Slave Hunting in ... New York. ... February 11, 1860. *Albany: Printed by C. Van Benthuysen.* 1860. 8vo, pp. 11. H. 53937

Report ... on ... the Natural History. *See* No. 53798, *supra.*

... Report ... [on] the Practicability and Expediency of establishing a University of active Instruction. ... April 21, 1857. [n. p. n. d.] 8vo, pp. 28. S. 53938

Report ... [on] "That Part of the Speech of ... the Governor, which relates to Lotteries. Made in Assembly," April 6, 1819. *Albany: Printed by Jesse Buel.* 1819. 8vo, pp. 39, Minutes, 149, Appendix, lxiv. BA. 53939

Report of the Special Committee of the Chamber of Commerce of ... New York, on the Confiscation of Cotton in the Southern States by the Government. *New York: J. W. Amerman.* 1865. 8vo, pp. 12. 53940

Report on the Finances & Internal Improvements of ... New York, by the Committee of Ways and Means, ... March 12, 1838. *Albany: Printed by Croswell, Van Benthuysen and Burt.* 1838. 8vo, pp. 37. + *Boston.* [1838.] 8vo, pp. 41, 6. + *Reprinted at New-York By John S. Taylor.* [n. d.] 8vo, pp. (2), 65, 6. + *Reprinted at Boston, By Dutton and Wentworth.* [1839.] 8vo, pp. 65, 6. B. 53941

Reports of the Commissioners appointed to prepare the Revised Statutes of ... New York. *Albany.* 1827-28. 4 vols., 8vo.

A general title to a series of twenty-five pamphlets.

Reports of the Committee on the Sing Sing and Auburn Prisons. [*Albany.* 1843.] 8vo, pp. 18. 53943

Reports of the Majority and Minority of the Select Committee on ... Intemperance and the Sale of Intoxicating Drinks. ... January 25, 1854. *Albany: C. Van Benthuysen, Printer.* 1854. 8vo, pp. 40. H. 53944

Reports of the Proceedings and Debates of the Convention of 1821, ... for the purpose of amending the Constitution ... . By Nathaniel H. Carter and William L. Stone, Reporters; and Marcus T. C. Gould ... . *Albany: E. and E. Hosford.* 1821. 8vo, pp. 703. Plates. B. 53945

Resolutions of the Legislature of New York, relative to the Proclamation of the President of the United States, for the Extinction of Slavery. [*Washington.*] 1864. 8vo. 53946

Resolutions of the Provincial Congress, September 1, 1775. *New York.* 1775. 8vo. N. 53947

Resolutions of the Provincial Congress of the Colony of New York for the Encouragement of Manufactories of Gunpowder, Musket Barrels, Musket Locks and Salt. *New York.* 1776. 8vo. N. 53948

Revised Laws concerning Passengers in Vessels coming to the City of New York ... . *New York: Casper C. Childs, Printer.* 1850. 8vo, pp. 34, (1). H. 53949

The Revised Statutes of the State ... passed during the Years One Thousand Eight Hundred and Twenty-Seven, and One Thousand Eight Hundred and Twenty-Eight. ... *Albany: Printed by Packard and Van Benthuysen.* 1829. 3 vols., 8vo, pp. xviii, 788; x, 860; x, 666, Appendix, 163, xviii. BA. 53950

The Revised Statutes ... from 1828, to 1835, inclusive ... prepared ... under the Superintendence of the late Revisers [John Duer, B. F. Butler and J. C. Spencer. Second Edition.] *Albany: Printed ... by Packard and Van Benthuysen.* 1836. 3 vols., 8vo, pp. xxv, 832; xi, 775; (5), 871. C. + Third Edition. *Albany: Weare C. Little and Co.* 1846–MDCCCXLVIII. 3 vols., 8vo, pp. xviii, 898; (2), xi, 975; ix, 879. + [Fourth Edition.] Prepared by Hiram Denio and William Tracy. *Albany: Gould, Banks & Co.* 1852. 2 vols., 8vo, pp. xxii, (1), 1293; viii, 1126.

The Revised Statutes ... as Altered by subsequent Legislation. ... 1858 ... . Prepared by Amasa J. Parker, Geo. Wolford, and Edward Wade ... . *Albany.* 1859. 3 vols., 8vo. A. 53952

Revision Documents of the Constitutional Convention ... 1867-'68. *Albany, N. Y.: Weed, Parsons & Co., Printers.* 1868. Folio. B. 53953

Rules and Regulations of the Assembly of New York. *Albany.* 1829. 18mo. Map. 53954

Circular to SCHOOL COMMISSIONERS and Supervisors. [n. p. 1867.] 8vo, pp. 27. H. 53955

Annual Report of the SECRETARY OF STATE, giving an Abstract of the County Superintendents of the Poor. [*Albany.*] 1833. 8vo, pp. 39. Continued. S. 53956

Also: ... Annual Report ... on Criminal Statistics of ... New-York. ... March 25, 1850. [*Albany.* 1850.] 8vo, pp. 251, (1), 4 folded leaves. Continued. — Documents accompanying the Report of the Secretary of State on Pauperism. *Albany.* 1824. Folio. — Report ... of Plank-Road Statistics of ... New York, February 8, 1850. *Albany.* 1850. 8vo, pp. 10. — Report ... on Convictions for Criminal Offences, Feb. 1, 1839. [n. p.] 1839. 8vo, pp. 80. M. — Report ... relative to Pardons, ... February 20, 1857. *Albany: C. Van Benthuysen, Printer.* 1857. 8vo, pp. 54. — ... Report ... upon Memorials from the City of New York, respecting the distribution of the Common School Moneys in that City ... . [n. p. 1841.] 8vo, pp. 23. S.

Short Advice To the Counties of New-York. ... By a Country Gentleman. *New-York: Printed by James Rivington.* 1774. 8vo, pp. 15. 53957

Journal of the Provision of the SONS OF TEMPERANCE of ... New York, for 1842-5. *New York.* 1845. 8vo. 53958

Speech of Governor Clinton, to the Legislature of ... New-York on the sixth day of January, 1819. *Albany.* 1819. 8vo, pp. 16. BA. 53959

The Speeches of the different Governors, to the Legislature of the State ... commencing with those of George Clinton, and continued ... [to 1824]. *Albany: J. B. Van Steenbergh.* 1825. 8vo, pp. 247. 53960

Catalogue and Circular of the STATE & NATIONAL LAW SCHOOL, at Ballston Spa, N. Y. *Troy.* 1850. 8vo, pp. 24. H.

First Annual Report of the STATE ASSESSORS ... January 6, 1860. *Albany: Charles Van Benthuysen, Printer.* 1860. 8vo, pp. 33. Continued. B. 53962

Also: Individual Reports of the State Assessors ... . January 7, 1864. *Albany: Comstock & Cassidy, Printers.* 1864. 8vo, pp. vii, 221, (1). Maps. B.

Third Annual Report of the ... STATE COMMISSIONERS of Public Charities ... . 1870. *Albany.* 1870. 8vo, pp. xxvi, 229, (1). Continued. H. 53963

An Account of the Proceedings at the Laying of the Corner-Stone of the STATE EMIGRANT HOSPITAL, ... August 10th, ... 1864. *New York: John F. Trow, Printer.* 1865. 8vo, pp. 43, (1). Plate and Plan. H. 53964

Annual Report of the STATE ENGINEER AND SURVEYOR of Railroad Statistics of ... New York. ... Feb. 20, 1850. *Albany: Weed, Parsons & Co., ... Printers.* 1850. 8vo, pp. 118, 2 folded leaves. Continued. B. 53965

Also: Report of the State Engineer and Surveyor on the Canals of the State. Made ... February, 1851. *Albany: Charles Van Benthuysen, Printer.* 1851. 8vo, pp. 200. Plans. Continued. B.

Annual Register and Circular of the STATE NORMAL SCHOOL, Albany, N. Y. For ... 1846. *Albany: Printed by C. Van Benthuysen and Co.* 1846. 8vo, pp. 22. Continued. B. 53966

State Normal School. *Albany.* 184-. 4to, 2 leaves. 53967

Also: Annual Report of the Executive Committee of the State Normal School. ... December 16th, 1847. [*Albany.*] 1848. 8vo, pp. 32. Continued. — Catalogue of the Officers and Students of the New York State Normal School ... . *Albany: J. Munsell.* 1871. 8vo. Continued. — First Quinquennial Register and Circular ... 1849. *Albany: Printed by Charles Van Benthuysen.* 1849. 8vo, pp. 40. — Annual Report of the State Normal and Training School at Cortland, For ... 1869. *Albany.* 1870. 8vo, pp. 22. Continued. H. — Annual Report of the State Normal and Training School at Oswego, For ... 1869. *Albany.* 1870. 8vo, pp. 55. Continued. — Annual Report of the State Normal and Training School at Potsdam, For ... 1869. *Albany.* 1870. 8vo, pp. 21. Continued.

State of New York. Communication ... transmitting the Report of the Board of State Officers ... Entitled ... the Embodying and Equipment of a Volunteer Militia, and to Provide for the Public Defence. *Albany: Charles Van Benthuysen, Printer.* 1862. 8vo, pp. 214. 53968

State of New York. ... In Senate, Jan. 6, 1847. Constitution of ... New York, adopted Nov. 3, 1846. [n. p. n. d.] Folio, pp. 34. S. 53969

State of New York. ... In Senate, Jan. 16, 1847. Index to the Constitution of ... New York. [n. p. n. d.] Folio, pp. 18.

State of New York. Presentation of Flags of the New York Volunteer Regiments, and other Organizations, to ... Governor Fenton, ... July 4, 1865. ... *Albany: Weed, Parsons and Company, Printers.* 1865. Impl. 8vo, pp. 249. Plate. 53971

Also: ... Proceedings attending the presentation of Regimental Colors to the Legislature, April 20, 1864. *Albany: Van Benthuysen's ... Printing House.* 1864. 8vo, pp. (2), 82. Plate.

State of New York. Report of the State Assessment Laws, by the Joint Select Committee, appointed by the Legislature of 1862. Transmitted Feb. 2, 1863. *Albany: Weed, Parsons and Company, Printers.* 1863. 8vo, pp. 273. S. 53972

At page 25 there is another title-page: "A Digest of Taxation in the States" ... . By Alfred B. Street. ... *Albany.* 1863.

State of New York. Republican Legislative Address and Resolutions. 1836. [n. p. 1836.] 8vo, pp. (2), 8. H. 53973

State of the Case in Dispute between the Queen and the late Assemblies, of the Province of New York arising from the refusal of the latter to admit of any amendments from the Council, to Money Bills. *New York: W. Bradford.* 1713. Folio, pp. 8. C. 53974

Robert Hunter was the royal Governor of New York at that time.

State Papers, on the Negotiation and Peace with America, 1814. With a Preface and Notes. ... *London.* 1815. 8vo, pp. 86. S. 53975

Reprint of the United States documents.

Report of Gershom Powers, Agent and Keeper of the STATE PRISON at Auburn. ... Jan. 7, 1828. *Albany: Printed by Croswell and Van Benthuysen.* 1828. 8vo, pp. 126. 3 Plans. B.

Report of the Inspectors of the State-Prison. *Albany: Printed by Loring Andrews.* [1799.] 8vo, pp. 8, 2 folded leaves. Cont'd.

Also: Annual Report of the Inspectors of the Auburn State Prison. *Albany.* 1829. 8vo. Continued.—An Examination of the Remarks on the Report of the Commissioners, appointed ... April, 1824, to visit the State-Prisons ... . *New-York: Printed by John C. Totten.* 1826. 8vo, pp. 20.—Report of the Committee appointed to visit the State Prisons, made to the Legislature ... January 15, 1825. *Albany.* 1825. 8vo. Continued.—Report of the Select Committee of the Assembly of 1851, appointed to examine ... the State Prisons ... . *Albany: Charles Van Benthuysen, Printer.* 1852. 8vo, pp. 256. H.

An Act to found a STATE WOMAN'S HOSPITAL ... Passed April 18, 1857. *New York: Miller & Company, Printers.* 1857. 8vo, pp. 4. H. 53978

Also: First Report of the ... Hospital. *New-York: Printed by Daniel Fanshaw.* 1856. 8vo, pp. 23, (1). Continued.—First Anniversary of the ... Hospital, New York, February 9, 1856. *New York.* 1856. 8vo, pp. 32.—Memorial to the ... Legislature ... for founding a State Woman's Hospital. 1857. *New York: Miller & Holman, Printers.* 1857. 8vo, pp. 12. H.—Petition of Mrs. C. M. Thompson in aid of the ... Hospital. *New York.* 1857. 8vo.

Statement of an Argument on the Memorials from the County of Allegany in favor of a Survey, by the State, of the New York and Erie Railroad ... . *Albany.* 1834. 8vo. 53979

Statement of Facts in Relation to the Appointment of the Democratic Delegation from the State of New York to the National Democratic Convention. *Albany: Atlas & Argus Print.* 1860. 8vo, pp. 15. H. 53980

Statistical List of the Members and Officers of the Assembly of ... New-York, at the Session of 1853. Prepared by C. H. Maxson, Librarian. *Albany: C. Van Benthuysen, Printer.* 1853. 8vo, pp. 10. 53981

Statistical Tables of ... New-York. Containing ... Lists of the Counties, Towns, ... Population, &c. ... *New-York: Printed by J. Seymour.* 1828. 12mo, pp. 24. 53982

Statutes at Large of ... New York ... . Edited by John W. Edmonds. ... *Weare C. Little ... Albany.* 1863. 5 vols., 8vo, pp. xlii, 814; xxii, 908; xl, 950; xxxvi, 782; lvii, 656. + Second Edition. *Albany.* 1869–72. 7 vols., 8vo. C. 53983

Statutes of ... New York ... from 1829 to 1850 inclusive. With Notes ... . By Samuel Blatchford. *Auburn.* 1852. 2 vols., 8vo, pp. 560; 605. 53984

The Statutes of New York, in relation to Highways, Bridges and Ferries ... By a Counsellor-at-Law. *Rochester.* 1845. 8vo

Statutes ... relating to Common Schools ... . Prepared ... by the Superintendent of Common Schools. *Albany: Printed by Thurlow Weed.* 1841. 8vo, pp. (1), 216. A., B. 53986

Statutes regulating the Practice of Physic and Surgery in the State ... and ... By-Laws of the Medical Society of the County ... *New-York: Printed by J. Seymour.* 1828. 8vo, pp. 63. B.

Statutes Relating to Elections other than for Militia and Town Officers. ... *New-York.* 1839. 8vo, pp. 80. + [*Ibid.*] 1842. 8vo, pp. 56. 53988

... Annual Report of the SUPERINTENDENT AND INSPECTOR OF SALT in Onondaga County, ... Jan. 9, 1841. [n. p. 1841.] 8vo, pp. 30. BA. 53989

Report of the SUPERINTENDENT OF PUBLIC INSTRUCTION, of ... New York. Transmitted to the Legislature, January 9, 1855. *Albany: C. Van Benthuysen, Printer.* 1855. 8vo, pp. 126. Continued. H. 53990

Also: Annual Report of the Acting Superintendent of Common Schools; ... March 13, 1826. [n. p. 1826.] Folio, pp. 37. Continued.—Annual Report of the Superintendent of Common Schools, Jan. 8, 1824. *Albany.* [1824.] 8vo. Continued.—Circular of the Superintendent of Common Schools, ... containing "An Act to amend ... the ... Statutes, relating to Common Schools." ... *Albany: Alfred Southwick, Printer.* 1839. 8vo, pp. 30. BA.

Annual Report of the SUPERINTENDENT OF THE BANKING DEPARTMENT of ... New-York. Transmitted to the Legislature, January 4, 1853. *Albany: C. Van Benthuysen, Printer.* 1853. 8vo, pp. 83. Continued. H. 53991

Report of the Superintendent of the Banking Department relative to Savings Banks. Transmitted ... February 18, 1864. *Albany: Comstock & Cassidy, Printers.* 1864. 8vo, pp. 64. Continued. B. 53992

First Annual Report of the SUPERINTENDENT OF THE INSURANCE DEPARTMENT ... . *Albany: Charles Van Benthuysen, Printer.* 1860. 8vo, pp. (2), 415, (5). Continued. 53993

Also: Circular (No. 27) of the Superintendent of the Insurance Department, relating to Life Valuations; ... *Albany: C. Wendell, ... Printer.* 1866. 8vo, pp. 37, 1 folded leaf.— ... Report of George W. Miller, Superintendent of the Insurance Department of the State of New-York: of his Examination of the Special Charges against the ... Mutual Life Insurance Company of New-York. [n. p. n. d.] 8vo, pp. 14. B.

Annual Report of the SURGEON GENERAL for 1861. *Albany.* 1862. 8vo, pp. 56. Continued. 53994

Also: Letter to the Surgeon General of the State of New York, March 11, 1862. [n. p. n. d.] 8vo.

Annual Report of the TREASURER of the State ... . *Albany.* 1847. 8vo. Continued. 53995

Annual Report of the Regents of the UNIVERSITY to the Legislature of ... New York. ... April 13th, 1827. *Albany.* 1827. 8vo, pp. 5, Meteorological Tables for 1825–27. Continued.

The first report printed separate from the Journals of the Assembly. The title was changed in 1848, and reads thus:

Annual Report of the Regents of the University, on the Condition of the State Cabinet of Natural History. With Catalogues of the same. ... April 11, 1848. *Albany: C. Van Benthuysen, Printer.* 1848. 8vo, pp. 33, Catalogue, 39, 15. Continued. B.

These annual reports include much valuable matter relative to the Indians, and are also the annual reports of the Geology of the State, and form, in fact, a continuation of the "Natural History of New York."

Twentieth Annual Report of the Regents of the University ... on the Condition of the State Cabinet of Natural History, and the Historical and Antiquarian Collection annexed thereto. Transmitted ... April 15, 1867. *Albany: Charles Van Benthuysen & Sons.* 1867. 8vo, pp. 411. 23 Plates, and one leaf of explanatory letter-press to each plate. S. + Revised Edition. [*Ibid.*] 1868 [for 1870]. 4to, pp. 447, (1). 25 Plates, and one leaf of explanatory letter-press to each plate. S. 53998

The twenty-first report is dated 1871, the twenty-second 1869. Continued.

Annual Circular of the COLLEGE OF PHYSICIANS & SURGEONS ... . *New-York: W. Dean, Printer.* 1843. 8vo, pp. 7. Continued. B. 53999

Catalogue of the Alumni, Officers and Fellows of the College of Physicians and Surgeons ... from ... 1807 to ... 1859. *New York: Baker & Godwin, Printers.* 1859. 8vo, pp. 66. H.

Also: Catalogue of the Faculty and Students of the College of Physicians and Surgeons ... . *New-York: Printed by H. Wallis & Co.* 1823. 8vo, pp. 8. Continued.—Catalogue of the Regents of the University and Faculty and Fellows of the College of Physicians and Surgeons ... for 1825-27. *New York.* 1825-27. 8vo.—Catalogue of the Regents of the University, and ... Trustees and Graduates of the College of Physicians ... . *New York.* 1829. 8vo.—Charter, By-Laws and Regulations, of the College of Physicians and Surgeons, in the City of New-York. *New-York: Wm. Jennings, Printer.* 1845. 8vo, pp. (2), 16.—College of Physicians and Surgeons ... . Catalogue ... and Annual Announcement of Lectures ... 1850-51. *New-York: Daniel Adee, Printer.* 1850. 12mo, pp. 12. Continued.—The Duties of the Regents of the University ... . *New York.* 1858. 8vo, pp. 7.—Eighth Annual Report of the Medico-Chirurgical Society of the University ... . *New York.* 1815. 8vo. Continued.—Exposition

of the Transactions relative to the College of Physicians & Surgeons in the City of New-York, from its Establishment until the Assumption of the Charter, by the Regents of the University. ... *New-York: Printed by Collins & Co.* 1812. 8vo, pp. 44.—Historical Sketch of the Origin, Progress, and Present State of the College of Physicians ... of the University ... . *New-York: Printed by C. S. Van Winkle.* 1813. 8vo, pp. 52. Plate.—Instructions from the Regents of the University to the several Academies subject to their Visitation, ... Revised Edition ... . *Albany: Printed by E. Croswell.* 1834. 8vo, pp. 39. Continued.—Memorial of the College of Physicians & Surgeons of the University ... *New-York: Printed by C. S. Van Winkle.* 1814. 8vo, pp. 11, (1). H.—Memorial of the Trustees ... in reply to the "Memorial of the Professors of Rutgers' Medical Faculty." *New-York: Printed by J. & J. Harper.* 1830. 8vo, pp. 24.—... Minutes of the Regents of the University. 1853–1859. *Albany: Printed by C. Van Benthuysen.* 1860. 8vo, pp. 418, Appendices, 8, 26.—Report of a Committee of the Regents of the University, appointed to visit the College of Physicians and Surgeons ... *Albany: Printed by Croswell* ... . 1826. 8vo, pp. 37.—Report of a Committee of the Regents of the University ... on the Education of Common School Teachers, ... Presented ... January, 1835 ... . *Albany: Printed by Croswell* ... . 1835. 8vo, pp. (4), 51.—Report of the Proceedings of the Medical and Surgical Society of the University of ... New York during the Winter of 1809–10 ... *New York: Printed by George Long.* 1810. 8vo, pp. 16. + [The same for] 1810–11. *New York.* 1811. 8vo.—Report of the Regents of the University, ... January, 1835 ... . on the Education of Common School Teachers ... . *Albany: Printed by Croswell* ... 1835. 8vo, pp. 15, (1).—... Report Of the Regents of the University, pursuant to a resolution of the Senate of the 20th March, 1830. [n. p. n. d.] 8vo, pp. 4.—Report of the Regents of the University ... on Military Instruction in Colleges ... . *New York.* 1862. 8vo.—Supplementary Charter of the College of Physicians and Surgeons, with other Ordinances relative to that Institution. *New-York: Printed by C. S. Van Winkle.* 1811. 8vo, pp. 14. B.—Syllabus of the Several Courses of Medical Lectures ... . *New York.* 1814. 8vo, pp. 20.—To the Honorable the Legislature of the State of New-York, ... Memorial of the College of Physicians and Surgeons ... . [n. p. n. d.] 12mo, pp. (2), 9.—Transactions of the Medical and Surgical Society of the University of ... New York. *New York.* 1810. 8vo.

Veto Messages of Governor Hoffman. *New York.* 1870. 8vo, pp. 147. H. 54001

View of certain Proceedings in the Legislature respecting the Incorporation of the New State Bank ... . *Albany.* 1803. 8vo. 54002

Votes of the General Assembly of the Colony of New York. [From June 25, 1745, to May 3, 1746. Colophon:] *New York: Printed by James Parker.* 1746. Folio, pp. 101. S. 54003

Votes and Proceedings of the General Assembly of the Colony of New York. [From June 3, 1746, to July 15, 1746. Colophon:] *New York: Printed by James Parker.* 1746. Folio, pp. 28. S. 54004

Votes and Proceedings of the General Assembly of the Colony of New York. [From July 29, 1746, to Dec. 6, 1746. n. p. n. d.] Folio, pp. 41. S. 54005

Votes and Proceedings of the General Assembly of the Colony of New York. [From Sept. 29, 1747, to Nov. 25, 1747. n. p. n. d.] Folio, pp. 64. S. 54006

Votes and Proceedings of the General Assembly of the Colony of New York. [From June 27, 1749, to Aug. 4, 1749. n. p. n. d.] Folio, pp. 28. S. 54007

Votes and Proceedings of the General Assembly of the Colony of New York, Feb. 15–26, 1757. [*New York:*] *James Parker.* 1757. Folio, pp. 14. C. 54008

This session was held at Flatbush, in King's County, on Nassau [Long] Island, the small-pox being then prevalent in New York.

The | Votes and Proceedings | of the | Assembly | of the | State of New-York, At their first Session, begun and holden ... at | Kingston, in Ulster County, ... 10th Day of September, 1777. | *Kingston: Printed by John Holt.* M,DCC,LXXVII. Folio, pp. 125. Continued. 54009

The Votes and Proceedings of the Assembly of the State of New-York; at the First Meeting of the Fourth Session, ... at Poughkeepsie, In Dutchess County, ... September 7th, 1780. *Albany: Reprinted by Munsell & Rowland.* M,DCCC,LIX. Folio, pp. 59. BA. 54010

At the Seventh Session the title was changed to "Journal of the Assembly." Up to the Fifty-Second Session they were published in folio, afterwards in octavo. All subsequent to the Twentieth Session were printed at Albany.

Votes and Proceedings | of the | Senate | of the | State of New-York, | at their First | Session, | held at | Kingston, ... September 9th, 1777. | *Kingston: Printed by John Holt.* M,DCC,LXXVII. Folio, pp. 216. + *Fish-kill: Printed by Samuel Loudon.* M,DCC,-LXXVII. Folio, pp. 216. Continued annually. 54011

At the Seventh Session the title was changed to "Journal of the Senate." Up to the Fifty-Second Session they were published in folio, afterwards in octavo. All subsequent to the Seventeenth Session were printed at Albany.

The Ordinances and By-Laws of the WESTERN HOUSE OF REFUGE for Juvenile Delinquents, in the State ... adopted ... January 6, 1852 ... . *Rochester.* 1852. 8vo, pp. 29. S. 54012

Fourth Annual Report of the Managers of the Western House of Refuge. Made to the Legislature January 17, 1853. [n. p.:] *C. Van Benthuysen, Printer.* 1853. 8vo, pp. 40. Continued.

NEW YORK CITY.

An Abstract of Laws relating to the Assessment and Collection of Taxes in the City of New York. ... *New York.* 1840. 8vo, pp. 80. 54014

Account of a Political Meeting held at the Circus, April 24, 1809. [n. p. n. d.] Folio, 1 leaf. 54015

Account of Statues, Busts, etc., in the Collection of the ACADEMY OF ARTS ... . *New York.* 1803. 16mo, pp. 16. N.

Catalogue of Paintings ... exhibited by the American Academy of Fine Arts. *New York.* 1816. 4to. Continued. 54017

Also: Charter and By-Laws ... with an Account of the Statues, Busts, and Paintings belonging to the Academy. *New-York: Printed ... by Van Winkle and Wiley.* 1815. 8vo, pp. 32. Continued. N.

Account of the Epidemic Fever which prevailed in New York in 1795. *New York.* 1796. 8vo. 54018

Account of the Great Fire in Broad Street in 1821. *New York.* 1821. 8vo. 54019

Account of the Great Fire in New York, 16th and 17th December, 1835. [n. p. n. d.] 8vo. M. 54020

An Account of the Interment of the Remains of 11,500 American Seamen, Soldiers and Citizens, who fell Victims to the Cruelties of the British, on Board their Prison Ships at the Wallabout, During the American Revolution. With a Particular Description of the Grand & Solemn Funeral Procession, which took place on the 26 May, 1808. And an Oration, Delivered at the Tomb of the Patriots, by Benjamin De Witt, M.D. ... Compiled by the Wallabout Committee. *New York: Printed by Frank, White and Co.* 1808. 12mo, pp. 96. 54021

Account of the Proceedings of the Corporation of ... New York, in regard to the existence of Cemeteries in that City. [n. p.] 1823. 8vo. W. 54022

Account of the Procession, Dinner, and Ball, given in Honour of the Emancipation of Holland, in the City of New York. With Notes, Illustrative and Explanatory, By Nick. Hallabout. *Communipaw* (i. e. *New York*): *Printed for the Publisher by Hons Stufflefunk.* 1814. 8vo, pp. 12. Plate. 54023

A clever satirical tract of great rarity. Contains a plate of Washington Hall, a MS. key, and notes by Mr. Allan.

An Account of the Procession, together with Copious Extracts from the Oration, delivered at the Walla-Bout; (L. I.), April 6, 1808. Upon laying the Corner-stone of the Vault, which is to contain the Relics of that Portion of American Seamen, Soldiers, and Citizens, who perished in the Cause of Liberty and their Country, on board the Prison Ships of the British, at the Wallabout during the Revolutionary War. Also, the Letter addressed to Thomas Jefferson, President of the United States, by the Tammany Society, and his Answer. [*New York.* 1808.] 12mo.

A little tract of much rarity. *See also* Romaine (B.) *and* [Taylor (George)].

An Account of the Reception ... by ... Citizens of New-York to the Survivors of the Officers and Crews of the United States Frigates Cumberland and Congress ... . *New-York: John A. Gray & Green, Printers.* [1862.] 12mo, pp. 37, (2). BA. 54025

An Account of the State Prison or Penitentiary House, in the City of New York. By one of the Inspectors of the Prison. ... *New-York: Printed by Isaac Collins and Son.* 1801. 8vo, pp. 97. 2 folded Plates. BA., C. 54026

By John Murray, Jr., or Thomas Eddy?

Account of the Terrific and Fatal Riot at the New-York Astor Place Opera House, ... May 10th, 1849. With the Quarrels of Forrest and Macready, including all the causes which led to that Awful Tragedy! ... *New-York: H. M. Ranney.* 1849. 8vo, pp. 32. Plate. B. 54027

An Act further to Amend the Charter of the City of New York, Passed ... April 12, 1853. *New York: McSpedon & Baker, Printers.* 1853. 8vo, pp. 12. H. 54028

An Act Supplementary to the Act entitled An Act for the Establishment of Common Schools. *New York.* 1814. 8vo, pp. 6. M. 54029

An Act to alter the Organization of the Common Council of ... New-York. *New York.* 1823. 12mo. 54030

An Act to amend an Act to Improve the New York Police, ... *New York.* 1812. 8vo, pp. 8. N. 54031

An Act to amend the Charter of ... New York. ... With the amendments ... passed ... 1851. *New York: McSpedon & Baker, Printers.* 1852. 8vo, pp. 18. H. 54032

An Act to establish Regulations for the Port of New York, with proposed Amendments. [n. p. 1855?] 8vo, pp. 8. S.

An Act to incorporate the ... Fulton Bank ... New York. [*New York.* 1824.] 12mo, pp. 12. 54034

An Act to provide for the ... Department of Alms and Penitentiary in the City and County of New-York. Passed April 6, 1849 ... . [n. p. n. d.] 8vo, pp. 14. H. 54035

Acts of the Legislature ... and Ordinances of the Common Council ... in relation to the ... introduction of Water into ... New York ... [n. p.:] *C. Dingley, Printer.* 1842. 8vo, pp. 72.

Address and Proceedings of Masters and Past Masters belonging to the ... Fraternity of Free ... Masons in ... New York and its vicinity ... . *New York.* 1848. 8vo, pp. 23. 54037

Address and Resolutions of the Great National Republican Meeting in ... New-York, Dec. 13, 1830. *New York: Printed by Elliott and Palmer.* 1831. 8vo, pp. 15. + Second Edition. [*Ibid.*] 54038

Address by the General Committee of the Federal Republicans in the City of New York, to the People of the State of New York. *New York.* 1810. 8vo. N. 54039

Address, Constitution and By-Laws of the Unconditional Union Central Committee, for the City and County of New York. ... *New York: Wm. C. Bryant & Co., Printers.* 1864. 8vo, pp. 13. H. 54040

Address from one of the Secretaries to the Stockholders of the Fire Insurance Companies of New York. *New York: Wm. C. Bryant & Co., Printers.* 1858. 8vo, pp. 12. H. 54041

Address from the Committee appointed at Mrs. Vandewater's On the 13th Day of September, 1784. To the People of the State of New-York. *New-York: Printed by Shepard Kollock,* ... M,DCC,LXXXIV. 8vo, pp. 16. 54042

Signed "Melancton Smith, Peter Ricker, Jonathan Lawrence, Anthony Rutgers, Peter T. Curtenius, Thomas Tucker, Daniel Shaw, Adam Gilchrist, jun. John Wiley."

Address of Members of the Constitutional Convention of 1846 [on the $9,000,000 Canal Bill. n. p. n. d.] 8vo, pp. 8. S.

Address of the Committee of Mechanics ... . *New York.* 1860. 8vo. 54044

Address of the Committee. *See* Vol. IV., No. 13725.

Address of the Committee of the Greek Fund, of the City of New York, to their Fellow Citizens ... . *New York.* 1823. 8vo, pp. 14. W. 54045

Address of the Committee of Vigilance of the City of New York, to the People of the State of New York. *New York: Printed by G. F. Hopkins.* 1824. 8vo, pp. 18. S. 54046

Address of the Committee to promote the Passage of A Metropolitan Health Bill. ... *New-York: John W. Amerman, Printer.* 1865. 8vo, pp. 68. H. 54047

Address of the Democratic Republican Association. [*New York.* 1838.] 12mo, pp. 9. 54048

Address of the Democratic Young Men's General Committee, to the Democratic Young Men of New York, and their Fellow Citizens generally. *New York: Printed by Peter Van Pelt.* 1835. 8vo, pp. 12. S. 54049

Address of the General Committee of Republican Young Men of ... New York ... to the Republican Young Men of the State ... *New York.* 1808. 8vo, pp. 16. 54050

Address of the General Committee of the Federal Republicans in the City ... to the People of the State ... . *New York.* 1810. 8vo. N. 54051

Address of the General Committee of Whig Young Men of ... New York to the Young Men of the State. *New York.* [n. d.] 8vo, pp. 8. 54052

Address of the General Executive Committee of the American Republican Party of ... New York ... . *New York.* 1845. 8vo, pp. 15. S. 54053

An Address of the General Executive Committee of the Mechanics and other Workingmen of ... New York, June 21st, 1830. *New York.* 1830. 8vo, pp. 7. 54054

Also: Proceedings ... . *New York.* 1830. 8vo, pp. 16.

Address of the Liquor Dealers and Brewers of the Metropolitan Police District to the People of New York. *New York.* 1868. 8vo. 54055

The Address of the Mayor, ... of ... New York. To the People of the State ... [on Legislation. n. p. 1857?] 8vo, pp. 8. S. 54056

Address of the National Democratic ... Committee of ... New York, to the Electors of the State ... who supported ... Breckinridge and Lane. November 14, 1860. *New York: Printed by J. W. Bell.* 1860. 8vo, pp. 15. 54057

Address of the Republican ... Committee. *See* No. 35391, *note*

Address of the Republicans of ... New York, to their Republican Fellow-Citizens ... . *New York: Printed by Frank, White, and Co.* 1808. 8vo, pp. 20. 54058

Address of the Roman Catholics to their Fellow-Citizens of the City and State of New York. *New York.* 1840. 8vo. N.

Address of the Yearly Meeting of the Society of Friends in ... New York, 6th month, 1852, to the Professors of Christianity in the United States, on Slavery. *New York.* 1852. 12mo, pp. 10. M. 54060

Address on the Subject of a Mariner's Church. [*New York.* 1818.] 8vo, pp. 12. C. 54061

An Address to the Citizens. *See* Vol. IV., No. 14803.

An Address to the Committee acting under the Authority of the Meeting at Mechanic-Hall, on the subject of the Memorial lately presented by them to the Vestry of Trinity Church. *New York.* 1812. 8vo, pp. 14. M. 54062

An Address to the Electors of the Ninth Ward. *New-York: J. M. Danforth.* 1828. 8vo, pp. 8. BA. 54063

Address to the Independent Federal Electors of ... New York. *Albany.* 1820. 8vo. 54064

An Address to the Mechanics and Laboring Classes. By a Mechanic. *New York.* 1840. 8vo, pp. 48. N. 54065

Address to the Public, on the occasion of the late disastrous Conflagration of the Crystal Palace, November 4, 1858. [n. p. n. d.] 8vo, pp. 8. S. 54066

Address to the Stockholders of the City Library, on the Management and actual Condition of that Institution. *New-York: G. P. Scott & Co.* 1833. 8vo, pp. 16. H. 54067

Address to Workingmen on the Low Prices of Wages. New York, October, 1840. By a Mechanic. [*New York.* 1840.] 8vo. N. 54068

Addresses of the City of New York to George Washington, with his Replies. *New York.* 1867. Imp. 8vo, pp. viii, 14. Facsimile. 54069

Seventy-five copies only printed for private distribution.

Advertisement ... to Supply the City of New-York with Rock Water, &c. By Levi Disbrow & J. L. Sullivan. *New-York: Printed by Clayton & Van Norden.* 1832. 8vo, pp. 16, (1). H.

Alderman Rooney at the Cable Banquet. The Aitin and Dhrinkin and Spaykin and Toasts, Edited by D. O'C. T. *New York.* 1867. 8vo. 54071

All the Proceedings in relation to the New South Ferry, between the Cities of New York and Brooklyn, from Dec. 1825, to Jan. 1835. *New York.* 1835. 8vo, pp. 12, 100. H., S.

Annual Report of the ALMS HOUSE COMMISSIONER, for the year 1843. *New York.* 1844. 8vo. Continued. 54073

Also: Acts of the Legislature of New York relating to the Alms House of the City and County of New York. [n. p. n. d.] 8vo, pp. 14. M.—City of New-York. ... Representation of the Commissioners of the Alms-House ... . [n. p. 1798.] Folio, 1 leaf.—First Annual Report of the Governors of the Alms House, ... for ... 1849. *New York: George F. Nesbitt, ... Printer.* 1850. 8vo, pp. iv, 199, 6 folded leaves. 9 Plates. Continued.—Report of the Select Committee (Majority) of the Board of Governors ... December 29, 1857. [n. p. n. d.] 8vo, pp. 55. B.—Report of the Special Committee of the Board of Ten Governors ... to the Board, relative to Accounts with the Commissioners of Emigration, made ... 1855. *New-York: J. W. Harrison.* 1855. 8vo, pp. 36.—Rules and Regulations of the Governors of the Alms House. *New York.* 1851. 8vo.—Rules for the Government of the Alms-House ... approved ... the sixth day of October. *New York: Printed by Furman and Loudon.* 1801. 12mo, pp. 22. Continued.—Statement of the President of the Board of Governors of the Alms House ... 1854, on ... Emigrant Paupers ... . *New-York: J. W. Harrison, ... Printer.* 1854. 8vo, pp. 28. H.

Amendments to the Charter of ... New York, ... October, 1846. *New York: Jared W. Bell, Printer.* [n. d.] 8vo, pp. 38.

Constitution of the AMERICAN BIBLE SOCIETY, formed ... in ... New-York, May, 1816. ... With their Address to the People of the United States; ... and a List of their Officers. *New-York: Printed ... by G. F. Hopkins.* 1816. 8vo, pp. 20. B.

Fifteenth Annual Report of the AMERICAN FEMALE GUARDIAN SOCIETY, and Home for the Friendless, for ... 1849. ... *New York.* 1849. 8vo, pp. 24. S. 54076

Journal of the AMERICAN GEOGRAPHICAL and Statistical Society. Vol. I. January, 1859. No. I. ... *New York: John H. Schultz & Co.* [n. d.] 4to, pp. 32. 2 Maps and Plate. Cont'd.

See also Vol. I., Nos. 1091–92.

Constitution of the AMERICAN HOME MISSIONARY SOCIETY, 1826. With Fourth Report of the United Domestic Missionary Society. *New York.* 1826. 8vo, pp. 94. M. 54078

Charter of "THE AMERICAN INSTITUTE of ... New-York." Incorporated May 2, 1829. Accompanied with the By-Laws. ... *New-York: Printed by John M. Danforth.* 1830. 8vo, pp. 8.

Report of the Third Annual Fair of the American Institute, held in ... New York. [n. p.] 1830. 8vo. Continued.

See also Vol. I., Nos. 1105–8.

The American Popular Life Insurance Company of New York. ... 2d Edition. [n. p. 1866.] 24mo, pp. 36, (14).

American Rejected Addresses on the Opening of the Park Theatre, New York, by Woodworth, McDonald, Clarke, Sprague, M. Y. Scott and others. *New York.* 1822. 18mo.

First Annual Report of the AMERICAN WIDOWS' RELIEF ASSOCIATION, ... November 22, 1855, by Solon Robinson, Secretary ... . *New York: W. H. Tinson.* 1855. 8vo, pp. 32. S.

Constitution of the ANCIENT BRITON'S BENEFIT SOCIETY. *New York.* 1805. 8vo. N. 54084

Annals of the Empire City, from its Colonial Days to the present. By a New Yorker. *New York: John F. Trow.* 1852. 12mo, pp. 238. 54085

Annual Report of Deaths in the City and County of New-York, for ... 1820. ... *New-York: Printed by G. L. Birch & Co.* 1821. 12mo, pp. 11, (1). Continued. B. 54086

Some Account of God's Dealings with the ANTIOCH BAPTIST CHURCH, New York, being the Third Annual Report. ... *New York: Holman, Printer.* 1862. 8vo, pp. 15. H. 54087

Appeal in behalf of the Proposed Church and Hospital for British Emigrants arriving at ... New York. [n. p. n. d.] 8vo, pp. 6. 54088

Appeal to the Merchants of New York in behalf of the Mercantile Library Association: to which is appended a List of the Stockholders of the Clinton Hall Association. *New York: Baker & Godwin.* 1855. 12mo, pp. 12. S. 54089

Appeal to the People of the State of New York, adopted by The Executive Committee of Citizens and Taxpayers for ... Financial Reform of the City ... of New York. *New York.* 1871. 8vo. 54090

An Appeal to the People of ... New-York, on the Proposed Alteration of the Charter of the City. By a Poor Citizen. ... *New-York: Printed by J. Seymour.* 1821. 8vo, pp. 24. B.

An Appeal to the Public on the Conduct of the Banks in ... New York. By a Citizen. *New York.* 1815. 8vo. N. 54092

Catalogue of the APPRENTICES' LIBRARY ... . Added, An Address ... By Thomas R. Mercein ... . *New-York: Printed by William A. Mercein.* 1820. 8vo, pp. 48, 22. 54093

A Catalogue of the Books in the Apprentices' Library. April, 1839. ... *New York: Printed by William E. Dean.* 1839. 12mo, pp. 126. + *New York: J. W. Amerman.* 1855. 12mo, pp. xi, 248. C. 54094

Arguments of Counsel. *See* Blundell (J. L.), Vol. II. 6021.

The Aristocracy of New York: Who they are, and what they were: ... By an Old Resident. ... Part I. *New York.* 1848. 8vo, pp. 32. B. 54095

Asmodeus; or The Iniquities of New York; being a complete Expose of the Crimes, ... and Vices ... both in High and Low Life ... . *New York.* 1849. 8vo, pp. 96. 54096

Asmodeus in New York. *New York: Longchamp & Co.* 1868. 12mo, pp. 378. C. 54097

Asmodée à New-York Revue critique des institutions politiques et civiles de l'Amérique vie publique et privée, moeurs coutumes, anecdotes romanesques ... . *Paris: Henri-Plon.* MDCCCLXVIII. 8vo, pp. (4), 503. B. 54098

Association for Improving the Condition of the Poor. First Report of a Committee on the Sanitary Condition of the Laboring Classes of ... New-York ... . *New-York: John F. Trow, Printer.* 1853. 12mo, pp. 32. H., S. 54099

Also: Address to the Public; Constitution and By-Laws; and Visitor's Manual, of the Association ... . *New-York, January,* 1844. 12mo, pp. 34.

Second Annual Report of the ASSOCIATION FOR THE BENEFIT OF COLORED ORPHANS, New York, ... 1838. *New York.* 1838. 12mo, pp. 24. 54100

Association for the Improved Instruction of Deaf Mutes. First Annual Report, ... 1868. *New York: J. Davis Printer.* 1868. 12mo, pp. 24. Continued. B. 54101

Report of the ASSOCIATION FOR THE RELIEF of Respectable Indigent Aged Females. *New York.* 1814. 16mo. Continued.

Constitution and Third Annual Report of the ASSOCIATION FOR THE RELIEF of the Industrious Poor. ... *New-York: Daniel Adee, Printer.* 1849. 24mo, pp. 13, (2). Continued. H.

First Report of the ASSOCIATION OF THE GIRLS' INDUSTRIAL SCHOOL. *New-York.* 1854. 12mo. S. 54104

Commemorative Proceedings of the ATHENÆUM CLUB, on the Death of Abraham Lincoln, President of the United States. April, 1865. [*New York: C. S. Westcott & Co., Printers.* n. d.] 8vo, pp. 36, (1). Portrait. B. 54105

Edited by Theodorus Bailey Myers.

Auctions Inconsistent with regular Trade, and Injurious to the City. Addressed to the People of New-York. *New-York: Printed by Van Winkle ... .* 1817. 8vo, pp. 16. B., N. 54106

Memorial from the AUCTIONEERS, of ... New-York. [n. p. 1824.] 12mo, pp. 12.—Memorial of the Auctioneers of New York to Congress. [n. p. n. d.] 8vo, pp. 17.

Minutes of the ... BANK CONVENTION, held in ... New York, ... 1837. *New York: Bowne & Co.* [n. d.] 8vo, pp. 24. B.

Also: Report of the Delegates of the Banks of ... New-York, to the Bank Convention, held ... 1837. ... *New-York: A. De Camp & Co.* 1837. 8vo, pp. 14. B.

Charter and Bye-Laws of the BANK FOR SAVINGS in ... New York. *New York.* 1819. 12mo, pp. 12. N. 54108

Also: Report of the Trustees ... for ... 1820. *New York: Printed by Clayton & Kingsland.* 1820. 8vo, pp. 13. Continued. H.

Petition for the BANK OF AMERICA, in ... New York. *New York.* 1812. Folio. 54109

Annual Statement to the Shareholders of the BANK OF COMMERCE ... May 14, 1849. [n. p. n. d.] 8vo, pp. 13. Continued. H.—Articles of Association ... of the Bank of Commerce. *New York.* 1839. 8vo. B.—Fifteenth Report of the BOWERY SAVINGS BANK ... . *New York: J. M. Marsh, Printer.* 1849. 8vo, pp. 8. H.

Banks in Danger, or New York in an Uproar from a Greenwich Horse Race: a Poem. *New York.* 1811. 24mo. 54110

Minutes of the BAPTIST ASSOCIATION held at New-York, October, 1787. *New York: John Patterson.* [1787.] 8vo, pp. 8

See also Vol. XII., No. 49376.

Annual Report of the BELLEVUE HOSPITAL, for 1848. ... *New York: McSpedon & Baker.* 1849. 8vo. 54112

Also: Majority and Minority Reports of the Select Committee of the Board of Ten Governors, to whom was referred the Subject of introducing Homœopathy into Bellevue Hospital ... January 19th, 1858. [n. p.:] *Republished by J. T. P. Smith.* [n. d.] 8vo, pp. 28. H.

First Annual Announcement ... of the Bellevue Hospital Medical College, 1861–'62. *New York: Baker & Godwin, Printers.* 1861. 8vo, pp. 14. Continued. H. 54113

Account of the BENEVOLENT CHRISTIAN SOCIETY in ... New York. *New York.* 1815. 8vo, pp. 8. B. 54114

Constitution of the Benevolent Society in ... New York. *New York.* 1804. 12mo.

Remonstrance and Answer of the BETHEL FREE SCHOOL to the Memorial and Observations of the Trustees of the New York Free School. *New York.* 1824. 8vo, pp. 27. 54115

Also: Reply to the Remonstrance ... . *Albany.* 1824. 8vo.

An Address and the Constitution of the BIBLE AND COMMON PRAYER-BOOK SOCIETY established in ... New York. [*New York.* 1809.] 8vo, pp. 4. + [*Ibid.*] 1811. 8vo, pp. 16.

Also: First Report of the Bible and Common-Prayer-Book Society; with an Address, ... *New York.* 1811. 8vo.

Twenty-Fourth Annual Report of the BLOOMINGDALE ASYLUM FOR THE INSANE. By Pliny Earle, M.D. ... *New-York: Egbert, Hovey & King.* 1845. 8vo, pp. 55. Continued. S.

Memorial of the BOARD OF COMMISSIONERS OF HEALTH of ... New York, on the subject of Compulsory Vaccination with a view to Exterminate the Small-Pox. ... *New York: Wm. H. Trafton & Co.* 1862. 8vo, pp. 12. 54118

Annual Report of the BOARD OF COMMISSIONERS OF PUBLIC CHARITIES and Correction. New York, for 1860. *New York.* 1861. 8vo. Continued. S. 54119

Annual Report of the BOARD OF EDUCATION of the City and County of New York ... . *New York.* 1843. 8vo. Continued.

Annual Report of the Condition and Operations of The Free Academy. ... *New York: Printed by McSpedon & Baker.* 1850. 8vo. Continued. 54121

The reports of the Free Academy are contained in the annual reports of the State Board of Education.

Also: An Act authorizing the Board of Education ... to establish a Free Academy, ... *New-York: George F. Nesbitt, Printer.* 1847. 8vo, pp. 8.—Annual Report of the City Superintendent of Schools of the Board of Education of ... New York, for 1866. *New York.* 1867. 8vo. Continued.—Annual Report of the Executive Committee on Normal Schools of the Board of Education ... of New York. ... *New York.* 1854. 8vo. Continued.—By-Laws and General Rules and Regulations of the Board of Education of ... New-York. Amended December 29, 1858. ... *New-York: Pudney & Russell, Printers.* 1859. 12mo, pp. 102.—Documents of the Board of Education ... for ... 1853. *New York.* 1853. 8vo. Continued.—Journal of the Board of Education ... 1854. *New York: Wm. C. Bryant & Co., Printers.* 1854. 8vo, pp. 366, Index, xx. Continued.—Manual of the Board of Education ... . *New York.* 1849. 18mo, pp. 191. Continued.—Report of the Committee ... on the Annual Apportionment; [and] on the ... use of the Bible in the Public Schools ... . *New-York.* 1844. 4to, pp. 8.—Report of the County Superintendent of Common Schools to the Board of Education. May, 1816. *New York.* 1816. 8vo.—Report of the Executive Committee for the ... Free Academy. ... 1849. *New-York: Wm. C. Bryant & Co., Printers.* 1849. 8vo, pp. 8. Continued.—Report of the Select Committee ... [on] establishing a Free Academy for Females. *New-York: Wm. C. Bryant & Co., Printers.* 1849. 8vo, pp. 26.—Report of the Select Committee of the Board ... to which was referred a Communication from the Trustees of the Fourth Ward, in relation to the Sectarian Character of ... Books in use in the Schools of that Ward. *New-York: Printed by Levi D. Slamm.* 1843. 8vo, pp. 21.—Report of the Special Committee of the Board of Education, on the Claims of the Public School Society. February, 1846. *New York.* 1846. 8vo.—Report ... on Evening Schools. 1854. [n. p. n. d.] 8vo. S.

Report of the BOARD OF EXCISE in and for the Metropolitan District of ... New York, from April 20, 1866 to March 30, 1867. *New York.* 1867. 8vo. Continued. 54122

Report of the BOARD OF FIRE UNDERWRITERS concerning Foreign Insurance Companies. *New York.* 1870. 8vo. S.

Address of the BOARD OF HEALTH to their Fellow Citizens. *New York.* 1818. 8vo. + [*Ibid.*] 1824. 8vo. 54124

Also: Address of the Committee of Health, 4th November [1795]. With Names of Persons who died of the Yellow Fever. [n. p. n. d.] 8vo, pp. 24.—Documents relating to the Board of Health. *New-York: Printed by John Cheetham.* 1806. 8vo, pp. 99. Continued. B.—First Annual Report of the Board of Health of the Health Department ... . April 11, 1870 ... . *New York: New York Printing Co.* 1871. 8vo, pp. 628. 9 Plates, 3 Maps and Table.—A History of the Proceedings of the Board of Health ... of New-York, in ... 1822; ... with ... the Rise and Progress of the Yellow Fever ... . *New-York: P. & H. Van Pelt, Printers.* 1823. 8vo, pp. 270.—Letter of Hon. S. Allen on the Yellow Fever, 1821. [*New York.*] 1822. 8vo.—Majority and Minority Reports of the Select Committee of the Board of Health ... [on] the Sources from which Cows' Milk is derived ... . With the Testimony and ... Analyses ... . *New York: Charles W. Baker, Printer.* 1858. 8vo, pp. 305.—Proceedings ... with account of Yellow Fever, 1822. *New York.* 1823. 8vo.—Report of the Proceedings of the Sanatory Committee ... in relation to the Cholera ... in New York in 1849. *New York: McSpedon & Baker, Printers.* 1849. 8vo, pp. 106. — Report of the ... Sanatory Committee ... on the ... Asiatic Cholera ... at ... Staten Island. *New York: McSpedon & Baker, Printers.* 1848. 8vo, pp. 24. B.

Eighth Annual Report of the BOARD OF MANAGEMENT of the Veterans of the National Guard. *New York.* 1867. 8vo.

Fifth Annual Report of the BOARD OF MANAGERS of the Education and Missionary Society. *New York.* 1834. 8vo.

Proceedings of the BOARD OF SCHOOL OFFICERS of the Seventh Ward in the Enlargement ... of Ward School No. 2. *New York.* 1855. 8vo. 54127

Proceedings of the BOARD OF SUPERVISORS of ... New York for ... 1850. *New York.* 1850. 8vo. Continued. 54128

Also: ... Report of the Committee on Substitutes and Relief of the Board of Supervisors. ... Document No. 11. ... *New York: Wm. L. S. Harrison, Printer.* 1863. 8vo, pp. 91. Continued. B.

Bourne's Views in ... New York. *New York.* 1831. 4to. 35 Plates. 54129

Of the many public buildings shown in these illustrations, but two now remain; viz., St. Paul's Church and St. Luke's Church. There are copies with proofs on India Paper.

Breckinridge and Lane ... Documents No. 6. ... Immense Gathering [of] ... Ten Thousand Democrats ... Speech of Daniel S. Dickinson ... . [n. p. n. d.] 8vo, pp. 16. 54130

A Brief Investigation of the causes which created The Late Controversy on the Election of Mayor. By a Democratic Member of the Common Council. ... *New-York.* 1834. 8vo, pp. 24.

A Brief Statement of Facts, as connected with ... St. Jude's Protestant Episcopal Free Church, to ... Trinity Church, N. Y., ... for an Appropriation toward the Support of said Church ... . *New York: Joseph H. Jennings, Printer.* 1846. 8vo, pp. 27.

A Brief Treatise, on the Police of ... New-York. ... By a Citizen. *New-York: Printed by Southwick & Pelsue.* 1812. 8vo, pp. 32, (1). B. 54133

The Broadway Journal. Edited by Charles F. Briggs, Edgar A. Poe and Henry C. Watson. *New York.* 1845. 2 vols., 4to.

"Contains many pieces by Poe not included in the collected editions of his works"

Address in Favor of the BROADWAY RAILROAD. *New York.* [n. d.] 8vo, pp. 8. M. 54135

Also: Facts which were presented by Citizens of New York ... relative to the Broadway Railway Association. [n. p. n. d.] 8vo, pp. 4. — Petition and Remonstrance of Jacob Sharp on behalf of the ... Association. Jan. 1853. [n. p. n. d.] 8vo, pp. 43.

History of the BROADWAY TABERNACLE CHURCH, with the Articles of Faith and Covenant. *New York.* 1846. 8vo, pp. 46.

Also: Manual of the Broadway Tabernacle Church, with a Concise History of the Building, and the Events connected with it. *New York: John Gray.* 1842. 8vo, pp. 22. + *New York: Baker & Godwin, Printers.* 1860. 16mo, pp. 84. — Proceedings of the Session of Broadway Tabernacle, Against Lewis Tappan. With the action of the Presbytery and General Assembly. *New York.* 1839. 8vo, pp. 64.

The Bryant Festival at "The Century," November 5, M.DCCC.-LXIV. *New York: D. Appleton and Company.* M.DCCC.LXV. Sm. 4to, pp. 88. B. 54137

The Bulls and the Bears. Or, Wall St. Squib. No. I. ... *New York.* 1854. 18mo. 54138

By-Laws and Ordinances of the Mayor ... of ... New York. Revised A. D. 1838–1839. ... *New York: Printed by William B. Townsend.* 1839. 8vo, pp. xviii, (1), 394. + Revised A. D. 1845. [By David Graham, Jr.] ... *New-York: John S. Voorhies.* 1845. 8vo, pp. xx, (1), 668. 54139

The Calvary Pastoral ... A Tract for the Times [against Southard]. *New York.* 1849. 4to. 54140

Case of the Manufacturers. *See* [Mitchill (S. L.)], XII. 49737

The Case of the Scotch Presbyterians, of ... New-York. *New-York: Printed in the Year* M.DCC.LXXIII. 8vo, pp. 36.

Catalogue of Articles contained in the Museum and Curiosity Shop. *New York: Baker & Godwin, Printers.* 1864. 8vo, pp. 18

Catalogue of Paintings and other Works of Art, to be sold at auction in New York, for the benefit of the Sanitary Commission. *New York: G. F. Nesbitt & Co.* 1864. 8vo, pp. 13. 54143

Catalogue of the Art Exhibition at the Metropolitan Fair, in aid of the U. S. Sanitary Commission. *New York.* 1864. 4to, pp. 18. 54144

... Catalogue of the Museum of Flags, Trophies and Relics relating to the Revolution, the War of 1812, the Mexican War, and the ... Rebellion; ... exhibited at New York, April 4, 1864, ... for the benefit of the U. S. Sanitary Commission. *New York: Charles O. Jones, ... Printer.* 1864. 8vo, pp. 109, (1). H.

Catalogue of the Natural Productions and Curiosities which comprise the Collections of the Cabinet of Natural History, opened for Public Exhibition, at 38 William St., New York. *New York.* [n. d.] 8vo, pp. 87. 54146

Catalogue of the Pictures ... exhibited at the Gallery of the Lyceum Building ... . Second Edition. *New-York: George F. Nesbitt, ... Printer.* 1849. 8vo, pp. 63. 54147

Celebration of the Birth Day of Linnæus, by the New York Branch of the Linnæan Society of Paris. *New York.* 1824. 8vo. W. 54148

Celebration of the Centennial Anniversary of the Birth of George Washington. *New-York.* 1832. 8vo. 54149

Also: Celebration of Washington's Birth-Day, at New-York, 22d of February, 1851. *New-York: Van Norden & Amerman, Printers.* 1851. 8vo, pp. 113. H.

Census of the Electors, and Total Population of the City and County of New York. [n. p.] 1807. 8vo. 54150

Centenary Memorial of the Dedication of John-Street Church, New York. 1768–1868. [n. p. n. d.] 8vo, pp. (2), 40. B.

First Annual Report of the ... CENTRAL DISPENSARY, ... 1869. *New-York: S. W. Green, Printer.* 1869. 8vo, pp. 26.

Central Park Album. 1862. Twelve Plates, drawn from Nature by G. W. Fasel. *New York: Birchett Bros.* [1862.] Oblong 4to. 54153

The Central Park. Photographed by W. H. Guild, Jr., with Descriptions and a Historical Sketch, by Fred. B. Perkins, *New York: Carleton.* 18—. 4to, pp. 78, 52. Views. 54154

A Description of the New York Central Park. *New York: F. J. Huntington & Co.* 1869. 4to, pp. x, (4), 9–206. 5 Plates.

... Description of Designs for the Central Park. [n. p. n. d.] 8vo, pp. 28, 6. H.

First Annual Report of the Board of Commissioners of the Central Park, January, 1858. *New York: Wm. C. Bryant & Co., Printers.* 1858. 8vo, pp. 9. Continued. 54156

The later volumes are copiously illustrated, and a complete set is valuable as illustrative of the art of landscape gardening.

First Annual Report on the Improvement of the Central Park, New York. January 1, 1857. *New York: Chas. W. Baker, Printer.* 1857. 8vo, pp. (2), 192. Map and 2 Plates. Cont'd.

First Annual Report to the Commissioners of the Central Park, by Egbert L. Viele, Engineer-in-chief. Accompanied by Maps and Plans. *New York.* 1857. 8vo. 54158

Also: A Guide to the Central Park. ... *New York: C. M. Saxton* ... . 1859. 12mo, pp. (2), 30. Map. — A Guide Book to the Central Park; containing a Description ... . *New York: C. M. Saxton and Barker.* 1860. 12mo, pp. 50. Maps. — Memorial of the City Council ... to the Legislature. Approved June 11th, 1853. Jacob A. Westervelt, Mayor. Act of the Legislature, July 21, 1853; Order of Supreme Court, appointing Commissioners. [*New York.* 1854.] Folio. 110 Plans. — Ordinances for the Government and Regulation of the Central Park. *New York: Wm. C. Bryant & Co., Printers.* 1860. 24mo, pp. 8. — ... Particulars of Construction and Estimate for a Plan of the Central Park. [n. p. n. d.] 8vo, pp. 32. H. — Report of Special Committee ... of the New York Central Park. ... *Albany: Charles Van Benthuysen, Printer.* 1861. 8vo, pp. 56. — To the ... Senate of ... New York: [Report of] The ... Commissioners of the Central Park ... . [*New York.* 1860.] 8vo, pp. 50.

Proceedings of the CENTURY ASSOCIATION in honor of the Memory of Brig.-Gen. James S. Wadsworth and Colonel Peter A. Porter; with the Eulogies ... . *New York: D. Van Nostrand.* M.DCCC.LXV. 8vo, pp. 88. H. 54159

Also: Proceedings of the Century Association in honor of the Memory of Gulian C. Verplanck. April 9, 1870. *New York: D. Appleton & Company.* 1870. 8vo, pp. 100. Portrait. H.

Twelfth-Night at the CENTURY CLUB, January 6, 1858. *New York: D. Appleton & Company.* 1858. Sm. 4to, pp. 93. H.

Memorial of the CHAMBER OF COMMERCE of the City of New York. In relation to a discriminating Tariff of Duties. 1842. [n. p. n. d.] 8vo, pp. 11. B. 54161

See also Nos. 53579–53592, *supra.*

Chap. XIV. of the Revised Statutes. Of the Public Health, relating to the Port, Harbour, and State of New York. *New York.* 1836. 8vo, pp. 48. M. 54162

Charter for Establishing a Hospital in ... New York, granted by the Rt. Hon. John, Earl of Dunmore, June 13, 1771. *New York.* 1794. 4to. 54163

The Charter of the City of New York. *New York: Printed by William Bradford* [*about* 1720]. Folio, pp. 11. N. + [n. p. 1730?] 8vo, pp. 96. B. 54164

The | Charter | of the | City | of | New-York; | Printed by Order of the Mayor, Recor- | der, Aldermen and Commonalty of | the City aforesaid. | To which is annexed, | The Act of the General Assembly Confirming the | same. | *New-York: Printed by John Peter Zenger.* 1735. Folio, pp. 52. BA. 54165

The Charter of ... New-York ... . To which is annexed the Act of the Governor confirming the same. *New-York.* 1763. Folio, pp. 125. 54166

The Charter of ... New-York ... . *New-York: Printed by W. Weyman.* 1765. Folio, pp. 50. 54167

The Charter of ... New-York, granted January 15, 1730, by Governor Montgomerie; with the Laws and Ordinances of the Mayor, Aldermen and Commonalty: James Duane, Mayor. *New-York: Printed by Samuel Loudon.* 1776. Folio. S. 54168

The Charter of ... New-York ... . *New-York: Printed by Samuel and John Loudon* ... . M,DCC,LXXXVI. Folio, pp. 44. S.

The Charter of ... New-York. John Montgomerie, Esq. Governor. *New-York: John Tiebout.* 1801. 8vo, pp. 63, (1).

The Charter of ... New York, Together with the Acts of the Legislature in relation thereto, or which have Vested Additional Powers in the Mayor, Aldermen, and Commonalty ... . *New York.* 1805. 8vo, pp. 240. A. 54171

The Charter of ... New-York. ... *New-York: Printed by Grattan and Banks.* 1819. 8vo, pp. (2), 114, xxi. A. 54172

The Charter of ... New York. Published pursuant to an Order of the Common Council. [With Act to Amend, ... April 7, 1830.] *New-York: Gould, Banks & Co.* 1832. 8vo, pp. 114, Index, xxi, Act, 7, (1). H. 54173

The Charter of ... New-York, with Notes ... . Also, ... the Journal of the City Convention. Prepared ... By Chancellor Kent ... . *New-York: Printed by Childs and Devoe.* 1836. 8vo, pp. vii, 370, (1). H. 54174

The Charter of ... New York, with Notes ... . *New York.* 1851. 8vo, pp. 320. N. 54175

The Charter of the City ... with Notes ... . With the amended Charters of 1851, '52, '53. *New York.* 1854. 8vo, pp. 336.

Charter of the Corporation of Trinity Church. *See* No. 32293

First Annual Report of the CHILDREN'S AID SOCIETY. February, 1854. ... *New York: Printed by C. W. Benedict.* 1854. 8vo, pp. 32. Continued. BA. 54177

Also: Annual Report by the Teacher of the Italian School, to the Trustees of the Children's Aid Society ... 1858. *New York: Wynkoop, Hallenbeck & Thomas, Printers.* 1858. 16mo, pp. 8. — A Statement to the Public of ... the Work of the Children's Aid Society. [n. p. n. d.] 8vo, pp. 11. H.

Regulations of the CHILDREN'S ASYLUM. *New York.* 1820. 8vo. 54178

The Anniversary Celebration of the CHRIST CHURCH PARISH School Association ... and ... Ladies' Charitable Association ... . 1863. *New York: Francis Hart & Company, Printers.* [n. d.] 8vo, pp. 34. Continued. H. 54179

Report of Committee of the Vestry of CHRIST PROTESTANT EPISCOPAL CHURCH in ... New York. 1845. *New York.* 1845. 8vo. S. 54180

Also: Constitution of Christ Protestant Episcopal Church, ... New-York; ... and By-Laws of the Vestry ... 1864. *New-York: Francis Hart & Co., Printers.* [n. d.] 8vo, pp. 24, (2). H.

The Christian Alliance; its Constitution, ... Officers, and Address. *New-York: Printed by Daniel Fanshaw.* 1843. 8vo, pp. 16. H. 54181

Also: First Annual Report of the Christian Alliance of ... New York, for ... 1861. *New York: James Egbert, Printer.* [n. d.] 8vo, pp. 21. H.

Chronicles of the City of Gotham, from the Papers of a Retired Common Councilman. *New York.* 1830. 12mo. 54182

Proceedings in the Constitution of the CHURCH OF CHRIST in Fair-Street, New York, under the Pastoral Care of John Stanford, M.A. May 31, 1795. *New York: T. & J. Swords.* 1795. 12mo, pp. 12. 54183

Proceedings of a Council of Congregational Churches, relative to the Privileges of the Members of the CHURCH OF THE PURITANS. *New York.* 1859. 8vo, pp. 92. 54184

Also: Narrative of some recent Occurrences in the Church of the Puritans. *New York.* 1857. 8vo. — Reply of the Church of the Puritans to the Protest of their Late Deacons, also to a "Letter" ... by sundry Individuals ... . *New York: Wm. C. Bryant & Co., Printers.* 1857. 8vo, pp. 76.

A Circular Letter to the Practitioners of Physic and Surgery in the State of New-York, from the Practitioners of Physic and Surgery in the County and City ... with a Memorial ... submitted to the Legislature ... . *New York: Printed by James Smith.* 1829. 8vo, pp. 22. B. 54185

See also [Bloodgood (S. A.)], Vol. II., No. 5982.

Citizens' Association of New York. An Appeal ... against the Abuses in the Local Government ... . *New York: G. F. Nesbitt & Co., Printers.* 1866. 8vo, pp. 32. 54186

Report of the Citizens' Association ... upon the Institutions under the charge of the Commissioners of Public Charities and Correction. *New York.* 1868. 8vo. 54187

Report of the Council of Hygiene and Public Health of the Citizens' Association ... upon the Sanitary Condition of the City. ... *New York: D. Appleton and Company.* 1865. 8vo, pp. cxliii, 360. Plates and Maps. + Second Edition. [*Ibid.*] 1866. 8vo.

Also: ... Analysis of the Proposed Tax Levy, for the City and County ... for 1866. *New York.* 1866. 8vo, pp. 35. — The Citizens' Association of New-York ... . Peter Cooper, Chairman. May 20th, 1868. [Circular. n. p. n. d.] 8vo. — ... Items of Abuse in the Government of the City of New York ... . *New York.* 1866. 8vo, pp. 21. — ... The Public Health. The Basis of Sanitary Reform. The Metropolitan Board of Health. Sketch of the Organization and Powers of the Board. ... *New York.* 1866. 8vo, pp. 28. — Report by the Council of Hygiene and Public Health, of the Citizen's Association of New York, upon Epidemic Cholera and Preventive Measures. ... *New York: Sanford, Harroun & Co.* 1865. 8vo, pp. 48. — ... Report ... . Our Taxes, Markets, Streets and Sanitary Condition ... . What New York might be with a Good Government. *New York.* 1865. 12mo, pp. 20. — Report of the Executive Council to the Honorary Council of the Citizens' Association of New-York. Sept. 10, 1866. *New-York.* 1866. 8vo, pp. 64. — To the Honorary Council of the Citizens' Association of New York. *New York.* 1866. 8vo, pp. 16. S.

City Crimes; or, Life after Dark in New-York; embracing Scenes with Soaplocks, Rowdies, and other Notorious Characters. By a Reformed Bowery Boy. ... *New-York: Anti-Soaplock Society.* 1840. 12mo, pp. 24. B. 54189

"City Evangelization." Papers from the Records of the New York ... Mission and Tract Society. *New York City Mission.* 1866. 12mo, pp. 93. 54190

The City of New York and its Neighbourhood ... . *London and New York: T. Nelson & Son.* [1858.] 18mo, pp. 64. 12 Views. 54191

Annual Report of the CITY INSPECTOR OF FIREWOOD, ... in the City and County of New York ... 1835. ... *New York: Printed by Childs and Devoe.* 1836. 8vo, pp. 7. B. 54192

Annual Report from the CITY INSPECTOR, of the Interments in ... New-York ... for ... 1837. ... *New York.* 1838. 8vo. Continued. B. 54193

Annual Report of the CITY SUPERINTENDENT OF SCHOOLS, of ... New York. For ... 1856. *New York: Wm. C. Bryant & Co., Printers.* 1856. 8vo. Continued. 54194

Claims of the Catholics to a Portion of the Common School Fund, a Debate in the Common Council. *New York.* 1840. 4to. 54195

A Clear and Concise Statement of New-York and the Surrounding Country, containing a faithful account of ... Base Impositions ... upon ... Emigrants. ... *New-York: The Author.* 1819. 12mo. 54196

Proceedings and Report at the Opening of CLINTON HALL, on ... November 2, 1830. *New York: Printed by Elliott and Palmer.* 1830. 8vo, pp. 16. 54197

See also Vol. II., No. 8175.

The Additional Charter Granted to the Governors of the COLLEGE OF NEW-YORK, in America. Published by Order of His Honour the Lieutenant Governor, in Council. ... *New-York: Printed and Sold by J. Parker and W. Weyman* ... . MDCCLV. Folio, pp. 4. P. 54198

Amplified title of our No. 14818, *note*, Vol. IV. Also: ... Address of the ... Alumni to the ... Trustees. *New York.* 1869. 8vo, pp. 11. — Catalogue of the Library of the College ... . *New York: Wm. C. Bryant & Co.* 1860. 8vo, pp. lxxxviii, 367. — Manual of the Board of Trustees of the College ... . May, 1866. *New York.* 1866. 18mo, pp. 51. Continued. S. *See also* Vol. IV., Nos. 14801–14844.

College of Physicians ... . *See* University, pp. 209–210.

Collegiate Institution for the Education of Young Ladies. ... 1853–54. *New York: S. W. Benedict.* 1854. 8vo, pp. 44, (3).

Colonization Society. *See* "N. Y. City Colonization Soc'ty."

Report of the Resident Physician of the COLORED HOME. ... 1848, to ... 1849. *New York: Printed by Charles Vinten.* [n. d.] 16mo, pp. 13, (1). Continued. H. 54200

Columbia College. *See* Vol. IV., Nos. 14801–14844, add to No. 18482, *New York.* 1843. 8vo, pp. 28.

The Commercial Metropolis and American and Foreign Statistician. *New York: Solon Horn.* 1858. 18mo. 54202

Reports, Resolutions, and Proceedings of the COMMISSIONERS OF HEALTH ... 1856 ... [to] 1859. ... *New York: Geo. H. Clark, Printer.* 1860. 8vo, pp. 552, Index, 33. B. 54203

First Annual Report of the COMMISSIONERS OF PUBLIC CHARITIES and Correction, New York. For ... 1860. *New York.* 1861. 8vo, pp. xl, 239, 12 folded leaves. H. 54204

Communication from ... the Mayor in relation to the Precautionary Measures adopted by him to secure the Public Peace at the Recent Election. *New York.* 1839. 8vo, pp. 125–186.

The Mayor's Communications form part of the "Documents" of the City for each year.

A Comparative Statement of the Number of Deaths in ... New-York, during ... 1804, 1805, 1806, 1807, 1808 and 1809. ... *New-York: Printed by Southwick & Pelsue.* 1810. 8vo, pp. 14.

A Comparison of the Taxes of ... New York, during ... 1836 and 1837, showing the difference between the Expenses of a Democratic and Federal Corporation. By a Tax Payer. *New York.* 1838. 8vo, pp. 7. 54207

A Compilation of the existing Ferry Leases and Railroad Grants made by ... New York .... Compiled by David T. Valentine. *New York: E. Jones & Co., Printers.* 1866. 8vo, pp. 503. 54208

A Compilation of the Laws of the State ... relating ... to the City .... Prepared ... by David T. Valentine ... . *New York: Edmund Jones & Co., Printers.* 1862. 8vo, pp. iii, 1396.

Complete and Accurate Description of the Procession which took place in the City, on the Commemoration of the Triumph of Liberty in France. *New York.* 1830. 16mo. 54210

Communication from the COMPTROLLER, relative to Expenditures and Receipts of the County ... on account of the Damage by Riots of 1863. Vol. I. ... *New York: New York Printing Company* .... 1868. 8vo, pp. 1215. 54211

Report of the Comptroller of ... New York, on the Water Right belonging to the Corporation. *New York.* 1806. 8vo.

Also: Annual Report of the Comptroller, and the Report of the Commissioners of the Sinking Fund. *New York.* 1814. 8vo. Continued.—Annual Report of the Comptroller, with the Accounts of the Corporation ... also, ... of the Commissioners of the Sinking Fund .... *New-York: Printed by P. & H. Van Pelt.* 1826. 4to, pp. 7, 2 folded leaves. Continued. H.—Annual Report of the Comptroller ... of the ... Receipts and Expenditures of the Corporation, For ... 1852. *New York: McSpedon & Baker, Printers.* 1853. 8vo, pp. 104. H.— ... Annual Report of the Comptroller, exhibiting the Revenues ... of the County Government For ... 1859. ... *New York.* 1860. 8vo, pp. 75.—Annual Statement of the Funds of the Corporation of the City ... for ... 1840. ... *New-York.* 1840. 8vo.—Communication from the Comptroller,

in reply to a resolution relative to the Market Property of the City. *New York.* 1854. 8vo.—Communication of the Comptroller in relation to revision of Ordinances; also, Contracts with Russ & Reid, and with William B. Reynolds, and Claims for unpaid Assessments and Taxes. *New York.* 1854. 8vo.— ... Communication from the Comptroller to the Commissioners of the Sinking Funds, transmitting Maps and Lists of Real Estate belonging to the Corporation ... 1860. ... *New-York.* 1860. 4to, pp. (4), 12. 12 Plans.—Communication from the Comptroller, transmitting a List of all Bills paid by the Auditor during the preceding Ninety Days. ... July 16, 1855. *New York: McSpedon & Baker, Printers.* 1855. 8vo, pp. 195.— ... Communication from the Comptroller, transmitting his Financial Estimates, or Budget for 1860 ... . *New York: Chas. W. Baker, Printer.* 1859. 8vo, pp. 135.—Comptroller's Annual Report of the Revenues and Expenditures of the City ... for ... 1851 ... . *New York: McSpedon & Baker, Printers.* 1852. 8vo.—Report of the Comptroller, to the Commissioners of the Sinking Fund, in relation to the sale of City Property. *New-York: Collins, Bowne & Co., Printers.* 1853. 8vo, pp. 56. Plan. H.

A Concise Description. *See* [Stanford (T. N.)]

By-Laws of the First CONGREGATIONAL CHURCH ... . *New-York: Printed by Broderick and Ritter.* 1820. 16mo, pp. 16.

Act of Incorporation and By-Laws of the Second CONGREGATIONAL UNITARIAN Church, worshipping in the Church of the Messiah, Broadway, New York. *New York.* 1839. 8vo.

Considerations respecting the Commerce of New York City, and the Construction of the New York, Newburgh and Syracuse Railroad. February, 1854. *Syracuse.* 1854. 12mo, pp. 24.

Considerations upon the Expediency and the Means of establishing a University in ... New-York. Addressed to the Citizens. *New-York: Grattan, Printer.* 1830. 8vo, pp. 29. B. 54216

Constitution and By-Laws of the Democratic Constitutional Union Party, of ... New York. *New York: Hilton ... Printer.* [n. d.] 32mo, pp. 15. B. 54217

Constitution and By-Laws of the Everett Literary Union of ... New York. *New York: W. H. Trafton & Co., ... Printers.* 1860. 32mo, pp. 11. B. 54218

The Constitution and Nominations of the Subscribers to the Tontine Coffee-House. *New-York: Printed in the Year* 1796. 4to, pp. (2), 47. 54219

The Constitution of the Associated Body of House Carpenters of ... New York. *New York.* 1792. 12mo. 54220

Constitution of the New York Friars Tontine, instituted in ... New York, 3 March, 1792. *New York: A. McLean.* 1792. 8vo, pp. 15. 54221

Contracts for the Cleaning of the Streets, and ... Removal of Offal ... from ... New York & Brooklyn. *New York: Bergen & Tripp, Printers.* 1866. 8vo, pp. 20. H. 54222

The Controversy on the Sunday Police ... . [n. p. n. d.] 8vo, pp. 56. 54223

Charter, Trust Deed, and By-Laws of the COOPER UNION ... with the Letter of Peter Cooper ... . *New York: Wm. C. Bryant & Co., Printers.* 1859. 8vo, pp. 61. B. 54224

Also: The First Annual Report of the Cooper Union, ... 1860. *New York: John F. Trow, Printer.* 1860. 8vo, pp. 39. Continued. B.

Copy of Remonstrance against the Monopoly of the Ships and Piers of New York by Floating and Dry Docks. [n. p. 1857?] 8vo, pp. 10. S. 54225

A Copy of the Poll-List, of the Election for Representatives for the City and County of New-York; Which Election began on Monday the 23d Day of January, and ended on Friday the 27th, of the same Month, in the Year of our Lord, MDCCLXIX. Alphabetically Made. [n. p. n. d.] 4to, pp. (4), 43. N., P.

The "Poll List" is curious as showing the politics of almost every citizen of New York of that day.

Correspondence between the Committee appointed by the Monthly Meeting of Friends in ... New York, and a Committee of those called Orthodox who seceded from the Society in 1828, ... *New York: Printed for Isaac T. Hopper.* 1838. 8vo, pp. 81.

Correspondence on the Importance and Practicability of a Rail Road, from New York to New Orleans, ... [with] a Report ... by DeWitt Clinton, Esq., Engineer. *New York: Vanderpool & Cole.* 1830. 8vo, pp. 23. 54228

Correspondence passed between the Conference Committee appointed by the General Committee of the German Democratic Union Party of New York, and the Special Committee appointed by the German Democratic Central Club upon the subject of a Union. *New York.* 1863. 8vo, pp. 15. 54229

Correspondence with the Comptroller of the City of New York, relative to the Reports of the City Treasurer to the Military Commandant, during its occupation by the British. 1776–1783. [n. p. n. d.] 8vo. 54230

Corruption of the City Government. Reprint from the New-York Journal of Commerce, of a series of ... Editorials, showing deep Abuses in the ... City Government. ... *New York: Wm. C. Bryant & Co., Printers.* 1853. 12mo, pp. 54. H. 54231

Report of the CROTON AQUEDUCT DEPARTMENT, made to the Common Council of ... New York. ... 1849. *New York: McSpedon & Baker, Printers.* 1850. 8vo, pp. 35. Map. Cont'd.

Also: Acts of the Legislature ... and Ordinances ... of the Common Council, with the Rules ... of the Croton Aqueduct Board ... 1833 to 1856. *New York.* 1856. 8vo.—Petition of the Croton Aqueduct Department [on water for Sing Sing], to the Legislature. [n. p.] 1856. 8vo. Continued.—Report of the Croton Aqueduct Board in relation to the Ways and Means paying the Croton Water Debt. December 27, 1842. *New York.* 1842. 8vo.—Report of Col. De Witt Clinton, ... on the Route for an Aqueduct to supply the City with Water, December, 1832. [n. p. n. d.] 8vo, pp. 120.—Report of the Special Committee to whom was referred the Communication from the Water Commissioners, with a Report of the Croton Aqueduct Committee .... *New York.* 1840. 8vo.—Report of the Minority of the Special Committee on the subject of the Ordinance creating the Aqueduct Department. *New York.* 1840. 8vo.—Supplement to Col. Clinton's Report on Water, demonstrating the Advantages of a Rock Water Company. *New York.* 185-. 8vo, pp. 46.

Debates at the Robin-Hood Society, in the City of New-York, ... 19th of July, 1774. *New-York: Printed by Order of the Robin-Hood Society [by J. Rivington.* 1774]. 8vo, pp. 14, (1). B.

Debates in the Board of Aldermen, of ... New York, ... 1862. ... By order of the Common Council. *New York: Edmund Jones & Co., Printers.* 1863. 8vo, pp. 1010, Index, 29. Continued.

Declaration of the Objects and Measures of the Farmers, ... and other Working Men, of the City and County of New York; ... *New York.* 1831. 12mo, pp. 19, (4). BA. 54235

First Annual Report of the DEMILT DISPENSARY, in ... New-York. *New-York.* 1852. 8vo, pp. 12. Continued. S. 54236

Also: Act of Incorporation and By-Laws of the Demilt Dispensary .... *New York: Wm. C. Bryant & Co., Printers.* 1854. 12mo, pp. 24. H.

The Democratic Anti-Abolition State Rights Association, of ... New York. *New York.* 1863. 8vo, pp. 32. 54237

Democratic Convention, held at the Cooper Institute, New York, November 1, 1862. *Iron Platform Extra.* [n. d.] 4to, pp. 24. 54238

Democratic Meeting in the Park, New-York City, Sept. 26, 1853. *New-York.* [n. d.] 8vo, pp. 16. S. 54239

Circular [of the DEMOCRATIC SOCIETY. *New York.* 1704]. 16mo, pp. 11. S. 54240

Also: Constitution of the Democratic Society of the City of New York. *New York.* 1794. 24mo, pp. 15.

First Annual Report of the Board of Commissioners of the DEPARTMENT OF PUBLIC PARKS, for the Year ending May 1st, 1871. *New York: Wm. C. Bryant.* 1871. 8vo, pp. 427. 35 Plates, 2 Maps. Continued. C. 54241

Description of a View of ... New York, now exhibiting at the Panorama ... Painted by Robert Burford ... . *London: T. Brettell.* 1834. 8vo, pp. 12. Plate. 54242

Description of Fulton Market House, intended to be built on the Block of Ground bounded by Fulton, Front, Crane-Wharf, and South-Street. [n. p.:] *Printed by George L. Birch.* 1821. 8vo, pp. 8. B. 54243

A Description of the Cities, Townships, ... and Settlements, within thirty miles of the City of New-York: ... *New-York: Colton & Disturnell.* M DCCC XXXIX. 18mo, pp. 77. 54244

Dialogue between an Episcopalian and a Presbyterian, on the late Meeting of Episcopalians at Mechanic Hall. *New York.* 1812. 8vo, pp. 8. M. 54245

Digest of all the Laws and Ordinances ... up to 1st of January, 1830. By a Student at Law. *New York.* 1830. 8vo, pp. 128, 8. 54246

Discipline of the Society of Friends of New-York Yearly Meeting. Revised and adopted by the Meeting held in New York in 1859. *New York: Samuel S. & William Wood.* 1859. 8vo, pp. 134. 54246*a*

Documents and Proceedings. *See* Vol. v., No. 20457.

Documents ... for a Charter for Manhattan College. *New-York: Printed by J. Seymour.* 1829. 8vo, pp. 33. 54247

Documents of the Board of Aldermen, and Board of Assistants, ... New York. Volume I. ... [n. p. n. d.] 8vo. Cont'd.

This is a general title-page to collections published.

Documents of the Board of Councilmen, of ... New York. ... Volume I. *New York: McSpedon & Baker, Printers.* 1854. 8vo, pp. xlvi, 1518, and folded leaves. Map. Continued. H.

Documents of the City Convention, 1846, for forming a ... Charter of the City ... June, 1846. *New York: Printed by Jared W. Bell.* 1846. 8vo, pp. 414. A., B. 54250

An Act to Incorporate ... the EAGLE FIRE COMPANY. *New York.* 1806. 8vo, pp. 12. 54251

An Earnest Plea of Laymen of the New School Presbyterian and Congregational Churches of New York and Brooklyn ... . *New York: E. O. Jenkins, Printer.* 1856. 8vo, pp. 14. B.

An Act to incorporate the EAST RIVER FIRE Insurance Company of ... New-York. [*New-York:*] *G. P. Scott & Co., Printers.* 1835. 12mo, pp. 11. H. 54253

Second Annual Report of the EAST RIVER INDUSTRIAL SCHOOL for Girls. June, 1856. *New York: D. Fanshaw.* 1856. 12mo, pp. 12. S. 54254

Annual Report of the EASTERN DISPENSARY of ... New York ... 1834. *New-York.* 1835. 8vo. Continued. 54255

Also: Act of Incorporation and By-Laws of the Eastern Dispensary .... *New York: James Egbert, Printer.* 1865. 24mo, pp. (2), 50. H.

Annual Announcement of the ECLECTIC MEDICAL COLLEGE of ... New York. ... *New York.* 1867. 8vo, pp. 7. Cont'd.

Regulations of the ECONOMICAL SCHOOL in ... New York. *New York.* 1810. 8vo, pp. 8. 54257

Einige Worte über die Industrie-Austellung in New-York ... Herausgegeben von einem Bewohner Sachsens. *Leipzig: G. L. Fritsche.* [1854.] 12mo, pp. 44. 54258

Endeavours used by the Society for the Propagation of the Gospel in Foreign Parts, to Instruct the Negro Slaves in New York. [n. p.] 1730. 4to. 54259

Episcopal Mission to Seamen in the Port of New-York. ... August, 1845. [n. p. n. d.] 8vo, pp. 8. B. 54260

First Annual Report of the EPISCOPAL SUNDAY SCHOOL SOCIETY, with Sermon by Bishop Hobart. *New York.* 1818. 8vo.

An Epistle and Testimony from the Yearly Meeting of Friends, held in New-York ... 1828. *New-York: Printed by Mahlon Day.* 1828. 8vo, pp. 24. Continued. H. 54262

Essay towards an Improved Register. *See* [Grim (C. F.)]

Constitution and Regulations of the EVANGELICAL LUTHERAN Sunday School Society, of ... New-York. *New-York: Printed ... by A. Paul.* 1817. 16mo, pp. 9. H. 54263

Address to the Churches of Jesus Christ by the EVANGELICAL UNION ANTI-SLAVERY SOCIETY of ... New York. *New York.* 1839. 8vo, pp. 54. 54264

Constitution, By-Laws, and Rules ... of the EVERETT CLUB of ... New-York. ... *New-York: Theo. H. Gray, Printer.* 1854. 16mo, pp. 15. H. 54265

Everett Literary Union. *See* No. 54218, *supra*.

Examination of the Charges of the Board of Trade against the Phenix Bank. ... *New-York: Printed by M. B. Long* ... . [1838.] 8vo, pp. (2), 30. B. 54266

Examination of the Pretended Charters of ... New York ... . By B. S. *New York.* 1852. 8vo, pp. 27. 54267

Extracts from Ordinances relative to the Interment of the Dead. *New-York: William Bowne & Co., Printers.* 1851. 8vo, pp. 7. H. 54268

Familiar Conversational History. *See* Vol. vi., No. 23761.

The Charter ... of the FARMERS' FIRE INSURANCE and Loan Company. ... *New York: Printed by J. Booth & Son.* 1835. 8vo, pp. 34. B., S. 54269

Constitution and Address of the FEMALE ANTI-SLAVERY Society of Chatham-Street Chapel. *New-York: Printed by William S. Dorr.* 1834. 12mo, pp. 16. H. 54270

Annual Report of the FEMALE ASSOCIATION ... . *New York.* 1815. 16mo. 54271

... First Annual Report of the FEMALE BENEVOLENT Society of ... New-York: ... 1834. ... *New-York: West & Trow, Printers.* 1834. 8vo, pp. 32. H. 54272

First Report of The FEMALE DEPARTMENT of the Prison Association of New York. *New York: W. E. Dean, Printer.* 1845. 8vo, pp. 27. Continued. H. 54273

Rules of the FEMALE HIGH SCHOOL .... *New York.* 1826. 8vo.

New Missionary Field. A Report to the FEMALE MISSIONARY SOCIETY for the Poor of ... New York ... . By Ward Staf-

ford, A.M. *New York.* 1817. 8vo. + Second Edition. *New York: Printed by Clayton and Kingsland.* 1817. 8vo, pp. 55.

The Fourth Annual Report ... of the FEMALE SOCIETY of ... New York. *New York.* 1838. 8vo, pp. 14. 54275

First Annual Report of the Female Society of the Presbyterian Congregation in Cedar Street for the Support of Theological Students. *New York.* 1814. 12mo. 54276

A Few Remarks about Sick Children in New York, and the Necessity of a Hospital for them. By Philopedos ... . *New York: William C. Bryant & Co., Printers.* 1852. 8vo, pp. 13.

Annual Report of the Chief Engineer of the FIRE DEPARTMENT. ... *New York: Edmund Jones & Co., Printers.* 1861. 8vo.

Also: Annual Report of the Board of Commissioners of the Metropolitan Fire Department, for 1865. *New York.* 1866. 8vo. Continued.—Ordinances for Regulation of Firemen. *New York.* 1865. 8vo.—Annual Report of ... Firewood, Anthracite, Virginia and Charcoal ... inspected in the City and County ... 1836. ... *New York: Printed by William Denman.* 1837. 8vo, pp. 7. B.

First Five Years of the Sabbath Reform, 1857–62. With ... Documents of the New York Sabbath Committee. *New-York: Edward O. Jenkins, Printer.* 1862. 8vo. B. 54279

Annual Report of the Trustees of the FIVE POINTS HOUSE OF INDUSTRY. ... 1855. ... *New York.* 1855. 8vo, pp. 31. Continued. H. 54280

Also: Incorporation of the Five Points House of Industry: Articles of Incorporation, By-Laws, and Addresses of the Trustees and Superintendent. *New York.* 1854. 8vo, pp. 16.—Annual Report of the Board of Managers of the Five Points Mission, ... New York ... . *James F. Warner ... Printer, Middletown Point, N. J.* 1864. 8vo.—Monthly Record ... . Edited by L. M. Pease. Vol. I. ... [*New York.*] 1858. 8vo, pp. 312. Continued. B. *See also* Vol. vi., No. 24634.

The Fourth Ward Industrial School for Girls. First Annual Report. ... *New-York: Printed by J. P. Prall.* 1854. 12mo, pp. 14, (1). H. 54281

Francis' New Guide to ... New York and Brooklyn, and the Vicinity. *New York: C. C. Francis & Co.* 1853. 18mo.

An Address ... before the FRANKLIN TYPOGRAPHICAL ASSOCIATION of New York, ... on the Fifth of July, 1802. *New York.* 1802. 8vo, pp. 22. 54283

The Frauds ... Exposed. *See* [Genung (A. P.)], VII. 26965.

Addresses ... [at] the Opening of the FREE ACADEMY, January 27, 1849. ... *New-York: Wm. C. Bryant & Co., Printers.* 1849. 8vo, pp. 39. Plate. B. 54284

Also: Catalogue of the Free Academy of ... New York. ... 1851. *New York: Wm. C. Bryant & Co., Printers.* 1851. 8vo, pp. 27, (1). Continued.—Catalogue of the Library of the New York Free Academy. ... *New York: Wm. C. Bryant & Co., Printers.* 1860. 8vo, pp. (2), lxxxviii, 368.—Examination Papers of the New York Free Academy. July, 1853. *New York: Wm. C. Bryant & Co., Printers.* 1853. 8vo, pp. 51. Continued.—Merit Roll of the New York Free Academy, ... 1863. *New York: George H. Clark, Printer.* 1863. 8vo, pp. 22. H. *See also* "Board of Education."

An Account of the FREE SCHOOL SOCIETY of New-York. *New-York: Collins and Co.* 1814. 8vo, pp. 70, (2). B. 54285

Also: Addresses before the ... Society at their Fifth Anniversary, May, 1810. *New York.* 1810. Folio.—Tenth Annual Report of the Trustees of the ... Society .... [n. p.] 1815. Folio, pp. 2.—By-Laws of the ... Society .... *New York.* 1819. 8vo.—List of Members of the ... Society .... *New York.* 1822. 12mo.—Manual of the Lancastrian System, of Teaching ... as Practised in the Schools of the Free School Society .... *New-York: Samuel Wood and Sons, Printers.* 1820. 8vo, pp. 63. 4 Plates. B.—Report of a Committee of the Trustees of the ... Society ... on the Distribution of the Common School Fund. *New York.* 1825. 8vo, pp. 16.—Report of the Committee on the State of the ... Society .... [n. p. n. d.] 8vo, pp. 8. N.

First Annual Report of the FRIENDS' ASSOCIATION for the Relief of the Freedman. *New York: B. F. Corlies & Macy.* 1864. 16mo, pp. 8. 54286

Gay Life in New-York! or, Fast Men and Grass Widows. By an old Traveler. *New York: Robert M. DeWitt.* [1870.] 8vo, pp. 5–100. 54287

The Gem, or Fashionable Business Directory, for ... New York. 1844. *New York: George Shidell.* MDCCCXLIV. 12mo, pp. 108. 54288

First Annual Report [of] The Executive Committee of the "GENERAL PROTESTANT EPISCOPAL Sunday School Union" .... [*New-York.* 1827.] 8vo, pp. 27. Continued. B. 54289

The Charter and By-Laws of the GENERAL SOCIETY OF MECHANICS AND TRADESMEN .... *New-York: John W. Amerman, Printer.* 1866. 12mo, pp. 83. B. 54290

Also: ... Annual Report of the Library Committee, ... also, abstracts from the Annual Reports of the School Committee .... [n. p.:] *The Society.* 1865. 8vo, pp. 14, (1).— ... Report from the Treasurer, Nov. 5, 1845. *New York.* [n. d.] 8vo, pp. 7. Continued. S.—[Report of the Finance Committee of the] General Society .... [n. p. 1848.] 8vo, pp. 8. Continued. B.

Proceedings relating to the Organization ... of the GENERAL THEOLOGICAL SEMINARY of the Protestant Episcopal Church ...

with ... Proceedings of the ... Trustees, from ... 1821 until 1838. *New-York: Daniel Dana, Jr.* 1854. 8vo, pp. x, 668.

Also: The Constitution and By-Laws of the Associate Alumni of the General Theological Seminary .... *New York: Daniel Dana, Jr.* 1850. 16mo, pp. 16. Continued.—Minutes of the Annual Meeting, 1841, of the Associate Alumni .... *New-York.* 1841. 16mo, pp. 12. Continued.—Minutes of the Triennial Meeting, 1841, of the Associate Alumni .... *New-York.* 1841. 16mo, pp. 16.—Publication of the Associate Alumni ... for ... MDCCCXXXIII. ... *New-York: Protestant Episcopal Press, Print.* MDCCCXXXIII. 12mo, pp. 54. Continued. B.

Charter and By-Laws of the GERMAN SOCIETY of the City of New York, with List of Members. *New York.* 1808. 8vo.

Also: Rules and Orders of the German Society ... established 9 October, 1784. *New York.* 1799: 8vo.

... A Glance at New York. A Local Drama .... *New York: Samuel French.* [1869.] 12mo, pp. 32. 54293

A Glance at New York: embracing the City Government, Theatres, Hotels, Churches, Mobs, Monopolies, Learned Professions, Newspapers, Rogues, Dandies, Fires and Firemen, Water and other Liquids, &c. &c. ... [By Asa Greene?] *New-York: A. Greene.* 1837. 18mo, pp. vi, 264. BA., C. 54294

First Annual Report of the GRACE CHURCH EDUCATION SOCIETY. ... April 15, 1834. *New-York: Protestant Episcopal Press.* 1834. 12mo, pp. 12. 54295

Also: A Report of the State of Grace-Church Charity School, 1824. *New York.* 1824. 8vo, pp. 7. M.—Second Annual Reports of the ... Parish Work of Grace Parish, New York. 1870. [n. p. n. d.] 12mo, pp. 44, (2). Plan. H.

Grand Miscellaneous Concert, for the Benefit of the Orphan Asylum, to be performed at Washington Hall, 6th January, 1844. *New York.* 1844. 8vo. N. 54296

The Great Metropolis. Tracts for Cities, No. 1. *New York.* 1848. 12mo, pp. 36. 54297

The Great Metropolis: or New York in 1845. *John Doggett, Jr. ... New-York.* [n. d.] 18mo. 54298

The following year the title reads: "The Great Metropolis; or Guide to New-York for 1846. Second Publication." *New-York: John Doggett, Jr.* [n. d.] 16mo, pp. 165. Map. In 1850, the title was changed to: "The Great Metropolis: or New-York Almanac for 1850. ... Sixth Publication." *New-York: H. Wilson.* [n. d.] 18mo, pp. 141, (1). Continued.

Die grosse Feuersbrunst zu New-York ... 19. Juli 1845. ... *Hamburgh: B. C. Berendsohn.* 1845. 12mo, pp. 27. Plate.

The Growth of New York. *See* Vol. VII., No. 28998.

Guia de Nueva York, para Uso de los Españoles é Hispano-americanos. ... Por R. Alvarez é I. G. Grediaga. *Nueva York: John A. Gray, Printer.* 1863. 12mo, pp. 165. Map. 54300

Corrected title of our No. 981, Vol. I. *See also* Vol. VII., No. 29152.

A Guide for the distributing Reservoir ... together with a General Description of the Croton Aqueduct. *New York: Walter Spinney.* 1853. 12mo, pp. 10, (1). H. 54301

A Guide to ... New York, containing a List of all the Streets, Places .... *New York.* 1842. 18mo. N. 54302

Guide to New York, its Public Buildings .... *New York: John Dainty.* 1867. 12mo, pp. 13–161. Map and Plates. H.

Guide to New York; its Public Buildings, Places of Amusements, Churches, Hotels .... *New York* [*T. Elwood Zell & Co.*]. 1868. 12mo. Map. 54304

Guide to the Environs of ... New York. *New York.* 1836. 12mo. A. 54305

A Hand Book of Streets and Distances .... By Arthur Tayler. *New York.* 1851. 18mo. 54306

Harbour Regulations, relating to Wardens, Harbour Masters and Pilots. *New York.* 1819. 8vo. W. 54307

Report of Committee in relation to the official conduct of the Harbor Masters .... *Albany.* 1857. 8vo, pp. 34. S.

Health Laws of the City of New York. *New York.* 1805. 8vo. 54308

Rules and Orders to be observed by the HEART-IN-HAND FIRE COMPANY. Instituted New York, January, 1781. *New York.* 1805. 12mo, pp. 18. 54309

Constitution and By-Laws of the HEBREW BENEVOLENT SOCIETY, of ... New-York. ... *New-York: Printed by L. H. Frank* 1859. 8vo, pp. 22, (1). Continued. B. 54310

Constitution and By-Laws of the HEBREW YOUNG MEN'S Literary Association. *New York.* 1852. 18mo. S.

Constitution of the HIBERNIAN PROVIDENT SOCIETY in New York. *New York.* 1802. 8vo. 54311

First Annual Report of the Trustees of the HIGH-SCHOOL SOCIETY, in ... New-York. *New-York: Printed by Mahlon Day.* 1825. 8vo, pp. 12. Continued. B. 54312

Also: Report of a Committee of the High School Society ... appointed to prepare a Plan of Instruction and Articles of Subscription. *New York.* 1824. 12mo.—Report on the Plan of Instruction .... [n. p.] 1824. S.

Hints towards Promoting the Health and Cleanliness of ... New-York. *New-York: Printed by T. & J. Swords.* 1802. 8vo, pp. 16. Plate. B., N. 54313

Historical, Geographical and Statistical View of New York City. *New York.* 1836. 18mo. 54314

Historical Sketch of the Board of Supervisors of ... New York; with the Names of its Members from its Creation to the Present Time. ... *New York: William L. S. Harrison.* 1862. 8vo, pp. 39. 54315

Historical Summary. *See* [Mitchill (S. L.)], Vol. XII. 49743.

History of New Amsterdam, or, New York as it was. *London.* 1854. 12mo. 54316

History of the Evangelical Churches .... *See* [French (B.)]

A History of the Mercantile, Political, and Official Career of our "Model" Mayor! the Bark John W. Cater; the Ship Joseph Walker. Fernando Wood masked! ... [n. p. 1856.] 8vo, pp. 32

History of the National Guard. *See* Vol. VIII., No. 32190.

Documents relative to the HOUSE OF REFUGE. *See* Hart (N. C.), Vol. VIII., No. 30640, *and* "Society for the Reformation of Juvenile Delinquents," *infra.*

Prospectus of the HOUSEHOLDERS' MUTUAL Insurance Company .... *New-York: Lane.* 1841. 8vo, pp. 8. H. 54318

How to see The New York Crystal Palace: ... A Concise Guide .... *New York: G. P. Putnam & Co.* 1854. 12mo, pp. 50, (35). B. + [*Ibid.*] 12mo, pp. 85. H. 54319

Illustrated Description. *See* Vol. IX., No. 34333.

In Ejectment. *See* [Miller (R. B.)], Vol. XII., No. 49046.

In the Court for the Correction of Errors. Robert H. Morris, Mayor of ... New York, Plaintiff in Error *vs.* The People ... on the Relation of Edward Williams, Defendant .... [n. p. n. d.] 8vo, pp. 52. 54320

The Income Record: a List giving the Taxable Income For ... 1863, of every Resident of New York. *New York: American News Company.* 1865. 8vo, pp. vi, 5–157. H. 54321

The Constitution and By-Laws of the INFANT SCHOOL SOCIETY of ... New York .... Instituted May 23d, 1827 .... *New York.* 1828. 8vo, pp. 18. 54322

Special Report of the INSURANCE COMMISSIONER .... *Albany: C. Van Benthuysen.* 1857. 8vo, pp. 446. 54323

Aid to Ireland. Report of the IRISH RELIEF COMMITTEE of ... New York. *New York.* 1848. 8vo, pp. 186. 54324

Jahres-Bericht und Mitglieder-Verzeichniss der Deutschen Gesellschaft der Stadt New-York für 1866. *New-York.* 1867. 8vo, pp. 58. H. 54325

Journal of Proceedings. *See* [Horsmanden (D.)], VIII. 33058.

Journal of the Convention in relation to the Charter of ... New York. ... July, 1846. *New York: Printed by Jared W. Bell* .... 1846. 8vo, pp. 762. A. 54326

Journal of the Stated Preacher. *See* [Ely (E. S.)], No. 22383

The Inauguration of the LADIES' HOME FOR SICK AND WOUNDED SOLDIERS ... New-York, May 2, 1862; ... *New-York: John H. Duyckinck, ... Printer.* 1862. 8vo, pp. 10. B.

Second Annual Report of the LADIES' NEW-YORK CITY ANTI-SLAVERY SOCIETY. *New-York: William S. Dorr, Printer.* 1837. 8vo, pp. 14. Continued. B., H. 54328

Constitution of the LADIES' SOCIETY. Established in New York for the Relief of Poor Widows with Small Children. The Second Edition. *New York.* 1800. 12mo, pp. 44. 54329

A Law for Preventing and Extinguishing Fires, in ... New York. *New York.* 1806. 8vo, pp. 21. N. 54330

Law to regulate Public Markets. *New York.* 1814. 8vo, pp. 15. 54331

Laws, Orders, and Ordinances of ... New York. *New York: Printed by William Bradford* [*about* 1720]. Folio, pp. 24. N.

Laws, Orders, and Ordinances, established by the Mayor, Recorder, Aldermen, and Assistants of the City, convened in Com-

mon Council. For the Good Rule and Government of the Inhabitants of the said City. ... *New York: Printed by William Bradford.* 1731. Folio, pp. 37. N. 54333

Laws, Statutes, Ordinances and Constitutions, Ordained, Made and Established .... Published ... 1748. In the Mayoralty of Edward Holland, Esq. ... *New York: Printed by J. Parker.* 1749. Folio, pp. 80. N. 54334

Laws, Statutes, Ordinances and Constitutions, Ordained, Made and Established, by the Mayor, Aldermen, and Commonalty, Of the City of New-York, Convened in Common-Council .... Published ... 1762. And in the Mayoralty of John Cruger, Esq; To which is added, An Appendix, containing Extracts of sundry Acts of the General Assembly of the Colony of New-York, immediately relating to the good government of the said City and Corporation. [*New-York:*] *Printed and Sold, by John Holt* .... 1763. Folio, pp. (4), 3–108, (2). N., P. 54335

Laws and Ordinances, Ordained and Established by the Mayor, Aldermen and Commonalty of the City of New-York, In Common Council convened; ... Published ... 1786, in the Tenth Year of our Independence, And in the Mayoralty of James Duane, Esq. *New-York: Printed by Samuel and John Loudon, Printers.* M,DCC,LXXXVI. Folio, pp. 29. S. 54336

Laws and Ordinances, Ordained and Established ... in the ... Mayoralty of Richard Varick, Esq. *New-York: Printed by Hugh Gaine.* 1793. 8vo, pp. 53, Appendix, 79, Charter, 96. + Passed ... 1797. ... *New-York: George Furman.* 1797. 8vo, pp. 68. + Passed ... 1799 .... [*New York:*] *John Furman.* 1799. 8vo.

Laws and Ordinances .... Passed ... 1803. In the Mayoralty of Edward Livingston. *New York: George F. Hopkins.* 1803. 8vo, pp. 120, ii. N. 54338

Laws and Ordinances .... Passed ... 1805. In the Mayoralty of De Witt Clinton. *New York.* 1805. 8vo, pp. 160, liv. N.

Laws and Ordinances .... Passed ... 1808. In the Mayoralty of Marinus Willett. *New-York: Printed by Frank, White & Co.* 1808. 8vo, pp. 189, lxv. BA. 54340

Laws and Ordinances ... passed during the Mayoralty of De Witt Clinton; to which are added, the Health Laws .... *New-York: Printed by Pelsue and Gould.* 1812. 8vo, pp. 282.

Laws and Ordinances ... during the Mayoralty of Jacob Radcliff, passed ... 1817. ... *New York: T. & J. Swords.* 1817. 8vo, pp. 172. N. 54342

Laws and Ordinances ... during the Mayoralties of Cadwallader D. Colden, and of Stephen Allen, Esqrs. *New-York: Printed by G. L. Birch.* 1821. 8vo, pp. 167. 54343

Laws and Ordinances ... 1823. [Stephen Allen, Mayor.] *New York: P. & H. Van Pelt.* 1823. 8vo, pp. 175. 54344

Laws and Ordinances ... 1827. [William Paulding, Mayor.] *New-York: Printed by E. Conrad.* 1827. 8vo, pp. 208. H.

Laws and Ordinances ... A.D. 1833–1834. [Gideon Lee, Mayor.] *New-York: Printed by Peter Van Pelt.* 1834. 8vo, pp. 280. B., N. 54346

Other editions 1837, 1839, 1841, 1845, etc.

Laws and Ordinances relative to the ... Public Health of ... New York: compiled ... by Geo. W. Morton .... *New York: Edmund Jones & Co., Printers.* 1860. 8vo, pp. (4), 226. B.

Laws of the State .... Relating particularly to the City .... *New-York: Gould and Banks.* 1833. 8vo, pp. xi, 811, 51. B.

Laws of ... New York relating to the Metropolitan Board of Health, and to the Metropolitan Board of Excise, passed in 1866 & 1867. *New York: Bergen & Tripp, ... Printers.* 1867. 8vo, pp. 92. H. 54349

Laws of the Legislature ... for the Government of the New York Prisons. *New York.* 1819. 8vo. 54350

Laws relating to the City and County of New York. A Digest of the Charter. ... By Murray Hoffman. *New York.* 1865. 2 vols., 8vo. 54351

Laws relative to Quarantine and to the Public Health of ... New-York. [n. p. 1858.] 24mo, pp. 67, (1). H. 54352

Also: Laws relative to Quarantine in the Port of New York. Compiled under the direction of the Commissioners of Quarantine. *New York: Francis & Loutrel, ... Printers.* 1867. Sm. 16mo, pp. 79, (1). H.

Letter addressed to the Republicans of the City ... of New York. *New York.* 1807. 8vo. N. 54353

The Letter-List Advertising. *See* [Beach (M. S.)], I. 9047.

Letters concerning the General Health. *See* [Hopkins (S. M.)], VIII. 32961, *and* [Romayne (Nicholas)].

Letters from Superintendents of the Public Schools of New York City: with Correspondence on ... Education .... *New York.* 1868. 8vo, pp. 26. H. 54354

Letters on the Use and Abuse of Incorporations, addressed to the Delegation from the City of New York. *New York.* 1827. 8vo, pp. 59. 54355

Life in New York. *See* Vol. X., Nos. 41014–15.

The Life of Slavery. *See* Vol. X., No. 41029.

Lightfoot Western Currying Oil Company. ... New York. ... [Prospectus.] *New York.* 1865. 12mo, pp. 9. 54356

List of Burials in the City ... in 1798. *New York.* 1798. 8vo. 54357

A List of Inn-Keepers, on the Road from Augusta, Ga. to New-York, and also, from Boston to New-York, with the Distances .... *New-York: Printed by S. Woodworth & Co.* 1814. 12mo, pp. 12. 54358

Corrected title of our No. 41435, Vol. X.

List of Jurors, in the City of New York. Taken in 1825. *New York.* 1827. 8vo, pp. 139. 54359

A List of Real Estate belonging to the Corporation of the City of New York, Prepared by the Comptroller .... *New York.* 1838. 4to, 15 leaves. Plans. 54360

The Charter, Laws, and Regulations of the LITERARY AND PHILOSOPHICAL SOCIETY of New-York; with ... Officers and Members. *New-York: Printed by C. S. Van Winkle.* 1818. 8vo, pp. 19, (1). B. 53761

Circular Letter of the Literary and Philosophical Society of New York; on the subject of a Statistical Account of ... New-York. *New-York: Printed by T. and W. Mercein.* 1815. 8vo, pp. 8. B.

Transactions of the Literary and Philosophical Society of New York: ... Volume I. *New-York: ... Van Winkle and Wiley.* 1815. 4to, pp. (6), 570. H. 54362

Contains Dr. Mitchell's account of the Fishes of New York, and papers by Dr. Hosack, Dr. Francis, Dr. Williamson, Prof. Griscom, and De Witt Clinton.

Report of the Loan Committee of the Associated Banks of ... New York. ... June 12th, 1862. *New York: Hall, Clayton & Medole, Printers.* 1862. 8vo, pp. 45, 2 folded leaves. H.

Loyal Meeting of the People. *See* Vol. x., No. 42551.

... Pamphlets issued by the Loyal Publication Society. From Feb. 1, 1863, to ... 1866. Nos. 1 to 89. *New York: The ... Society.* 1864–66. 3 vols., 8vo. B. 54364

A series of tracts relative to the Rebellion.

Annals of the Lyceum of Natural History of New-York. Vol. I. ... *New-York: Printed ... by J. Seymour.* 1824. 8vo, pp. iv, 192, 12, iv, 410. 29 Plates. Continued. B.

Complete sets are scarce. This valuable work is published at irregular intervals. It is exclusively devoted to the consideration of American subjects. A table of contents will be found in "Trübner's Guide," pp. 147–151. Also: Catalogue of Books in the Library of the Lyceum of Natural History. ... [n. p.] 1825. 8vo. + [n. p.] 1830. 8vo. B. — Charter, Constitution and By-Laws of the Lyceum of Natural History ... . *New-York: Printed by E. Conrad.* 1823. 8vo, pp. 22. + *New-York: The Lyceum.* 1826. 8vo, pp. 17. + [*Ibid.*] 1837. 8vo, pp. 28. + [*Ibid.*] 1867. 8vo, pp. 38. — The Constitution of the Lyceum of Natural History. ... *New York: The Society.* 1817. 8vo, pp. 15. — Index to the Library of the Lyceum of Natural History, ... 1830. [*New York.* 1830.] 8vo, pp. 72.

Madison Square. *New York.* 1852. 8vo, pp. 25. 54366

A report adverse to the Crystal Palace being erected thereon.

Constitution, Report and Directory of the Young Men's Association of the Madison-Square Presbyterian Church. Organized Nov. 4th, 1857. *New York.* 1859. 12mo, pp. 20. S.

First Annual Report of the Magdalen Society of New York. *New York: Printed ... by J. Seymour.* 1813. 8vo, pp. 26.

Magdalen Facts. No. 1. *New York.* 1832. 8vo. *See also* "New York Magdalen Society," *infra.*

The Managers on the Part of New-York ... . John Cruger, Henry Holland, Benjamin Kissam, John Morris Scott. [*New York.* 1769.] Folio, 1 leaf. P. 54368

Supplementary to "To the Honourable," *infra.*

Manual of the Corporation of the City of New York, for ... 1841–2. *New York.* 1842. 18mo. Map. + For ... 1842 & 3. By D. T. Valentine. *New-York: Thomas Snowden, Printer.* [1843.] 18mo, pp. 253,(1). Map and 2 Plates. H. 54369

A set collates as follows: 1843, 24mo, pp. 312; 1844–5, 18mo, pp. 330, 3 Maps; 1845–6, 16mo, pp. 371, Map, 2 Plates; 1847, 18mo, pp. 386, 2 Maps, Facsimile, 6 Plates; 1848, 16mo, pp. 406; 1849, 12mo, pp. 434, 3 Maps, 5 Plates, Facsimile; 1850, 12mo, pp. 552, 8 Plates, 6 Maps, 2 Facsimiles; 1851, 12mo, pp. 480, 8 Plates,

5 Maps, 3 Facsimiles; 1852, 12mo, pp. 504, 7 Plates, 5 Maps, 2 Facsimiles; 1853, 12mo, pp. 505, 13 Plates, 4 Maps; 1854, 12mo, pp. 560, 15 Plates, 6 Maps, 3 Facsimiles; 1855, 12mo, pp. 601, 15 Plates, 7 Maps, 2 Facsimiles; 1856, 12mo, pp. 600; 1857, 12mo; 1858, 12mo, pp. 646; 1859, 12mo, pp. 610; 1860, 12mo, pp. 630; 1861, 12mo, pp. 699; 1862, 12mo, pp. 775; 1863, 12mo, pp. 852; 1864, 12mo, pp. 856. After 1868, it was edited by Joseph Shannon.

The Manual of the Seventh Regiment, National Guard, S. N. Y. [n. p.] 1868. 8vo, pp. 236, (3). 3 Plates. B. 54370

Manual of the System of Discipline and Instruction for the Schools of the Public School Society of New York, instituted in ... 1805. *New York.* 1854. 8vo, pp. 134. 54371

Charter of the Marine Society of the City of New-York, in the Province of New-York, in America. *New-York: Printed by H. Gaine ... .* M,DCC,LXXXI. Folio, pp. 30. S. + With the By-Laws, and a List of the Members. *New York.* 1788. 4to. + [*Ibid.*] 1796. 54372

Also: Report of the Marine Society, of ... New-York. January 13th, 1845. *New-York: William Minns, Printer.* [n. d.] 16mo, pp. 8. H.

Constitution of the Marine Bible Society of New-York, ... with an Address to ... Seamen. *New-York: Printed by J. Seymour.* 1817. 8vo, pp. 16. BA. 54373

Also: Report of the Marine Bible Society of New-York; at their First ... Meeting, April 21, 1817. *New-York: Printed by J. Seymour.* 1817. 8vo, pp. 16. Cont'd.

First Annual Report of the Mariner's Family Industrial Soc'y. of the Port of New York, for ... 1844. *New-York: Tobitt's Print.* 1845. 8vo, pp. 15. Continued. B., H. 54374

Report on a Plan for extending & more perfectly establishing the Mechanic and Scientific Institution of New-York. [*New York:*] *Printed by D. Fanshaw.* 1824. 12mo, pp. 28.

Memorial of the Medical Society of the City ... of New York, remonstrating against a Repeal, of the Statute, Regulating the Practice of Physic and Surgery ... . *New-York: Joseph C. Spear, Printer.* 1830. 8vo, pp. 8. B. 54376

Also: Remarks on the Report of the Committee of the Medical Society ... on the Epidemic Fever of Bancker Street ... in 1820. [n. p. n. d.] 8vo, pp. 16. — Report and Address, delivered by the President [Nicholas Romayne], to the Medical Society ... together with the Charter of the College of Physicians and Surgeons in ... New-York. ... *New-York: Printed by James Cheetham.* 1807. 8vo, pp. 22. — Report of the Committee of the Medical Society ... explanatory of the Causes and Character of the Epidemic Fever ... in Bancker-Street ... in ... 1820. ... *New-York: James V. Seaman.* 1820. 8vo, pp. 38. — Report of the Committee of the Medical Society ... to enquire into the ... Pestilential Disease, ... in New-York during the Summer and Autumn of 1798. *New-York.* 1799. 8vo, pp. (4), 47. — Report of the Committee

of the Medical Society ... appointed to investigate the subject of a secret Medical Association. *New York: Wm. A. Mercein, Printer.* 1831. 8vo, pp. 12. B.

... Memorial Church of The Rev. Henry Anthon, D.D., New-York. 1864. ... *New-York: John A. Gray & Green, Printers.* 1864. 12mo, pp. 12, (8). 54377

Memorial of Merchants and Traders of New York, having Claims upon France for Spoliations. *New York.* 1827. 8vo, pp. 18. 54378

Memorial of the Corporation ... March 26, 1853. *New-York.* 1855. 8vo, pp. 35. 54379

Memorial of the Fire of 1835; being a Collection of Sermons preached on that occasion. [n. p.] 1835. 8vo. N. 54380

The | Memorial | of the | Merchants of the City of New-York, | In the Colony of New-York, | In America; | To the Honourable | The Knights, Citizens, and Burgesses, | in Parliament assembled. | Read in the General Assembly of said | Colony, the 20th of April, 1764. | *New-York:* | *Printed by Hugh Gaine ... .* M,DCC,LXV. 12mo, pp. 14. 54381

Memorial of the Merchants of ... New-York. *New-York: Hopkins & Seymour, Printers.* 1806. 8vo, pp. 38. 54382

Memorial of the Merchants of New York, Jan. 6, 1806. [To the President, etc.] *Washington.* 1806. 8vo. 54383

Memorial of the Pier and Warehouse Company to the Commissioners of the Sinking Fund, and the Commissioners of the Land Office of New York ... 1865. [n. p. n. d.] 8vo. S.

Memorial Record of the New York Branch of the United States Christian Commission. *New York.* 1866. 8vo. 54385

Memorial to the Legislature ... from Citizens of New York ... against Taxing Banks. [n. p.] 1822. 8vo. 54386

Memorial to the Mayor and Commonalty of ... New York, (together with other documents,) relative to the establishment of the New York Passenger and Baggage Line. *New York.* 1856. 12mo, pp. 34. S. 54387

Memorials, presented to the Legislature ... 1823, praying a Repeal of ... a Law granting peculiar Privileges to the Trustees of the Bethel Baptist Church, in the appropriation of the Com-

mon School Fund. ... *New York: Free School Society.* [n. d.] 8vo, pp. 48. H. 54388

Corrected title of our No. 47746, Vol. XII.

Men Furnished and Public Funds Expended. *New York.* 1865. 8vo. 54389

Annual Report of the Board of Directors of the Mercantile Library Association ... . 1820. *New York.* 1820. 8vo. Continued. 54390

Also: Annual Reports of the Board of Direction of the Mercantile Library Association ... from 1821 to 1838. *New York: Reprinted for the Association.* 1868. 8vo, pp. 128. B.

Catalogue of the Books belonging to the Mercantile Library Association of ... New-York: ... prefixed, the Constitution ... . *New York.* 1825. 16mo. 54391

Continued: *New-York.* 1828. 12mo. + *New-York: Printed by J. & J. Harper.* 1830. 8vo, pp. 160. Plate. + *New York.* 1834. 8vo, pp. 199. + Systematic Catalogue ... . *New-York: Printed by Harper & Brothers.* 1837. 8vo, pp. xii, 385, (1). + *New York: Printed by Edward O. Jenkins.* 1844. 8vo, pp. (4), 300. + *New-York: Baker, Godwin & Company, Printers.* 1850. 8vo, pp. 376, 48, 34, (2). + First Supplement ... . *New York: The Association.* 1852. 8vo, pp. 48. + *New York: Baker & Godwin, Printers.* 1856. 8vo, pp. 376, Supplement, (2), 214. + *New York: F. F. Taylor & Co.* 1860. 8vo, pp. 699. + *New York: F. F. Taylor, Printer ... .* 1866. 8vo, pp. (4), 699. + Supplement ... . *New York: John Medale, Printer.* 1869. 8vo, pp. 250, 15. + Catalogue of Novels, Tales, ... in the ... Library, ... 1861. *New York: Baker & Godwin, Printers.* 1861. 8vo, pp. 92. — ... Address of the Board of Direction of the ... Association, ... setting forth the Condition and Advantages of that Institution. September, 1858. ... [n. p.] 1858. 12mo, pp. 12. — Constitution, By-Laws and Regulations of the ... Association. ... *New-York: Baker, Crane & Co.* 1842. 12mo, pp. 10, (1). + *New York.* 1844. 12mo, pp. 12. + [*Ibid.*] 1851. 16mo, pp. 14. + [*Ibid.*] 1852. 12mo, pp. 14. + *New York: M. B. Wynkoop, Printer.* 1855. 8vo, pp. 16. + *New York: Baker, Godwin & Co., Printers.* 1855. 8vo, pp. 16. + *New York.* 1856. 8vo. + [*Ibid.*] 1858. 8vo, pp. 16. H. + *New York: John F. Trow, Printer.* 1859. 16mo, pp. 24. + *New York.* 1866. 16mo, pp. 31. — Constitution ... with the Act of Incorporation ... . *New York: Jordan, Comes & Seymour, Printers.* 1870. 16mo, pp. 27. — Fiftieth Anniversary Celebration of the ... Association ... November 9, 1870. And the Fifth Anniversary of the Ex-Officers Union ... November 10th, 1870. *New York.* 1871. 8vo, pp. 77. S. — The Mercantile Library ... Accession List. ... December 15, 1869, to March 8, 1870. [*New York.* 1870.] 8vo, pp. 20. Continued. B. — Twentieth Annual Report of the ... Directors of the ... Association ... New York, January, 1841. *New York.* 1841. 8vo, pp. 16. S.

Charter and Constitution of the Merchants' and Clerks' Library Association of ... New-York. Founded, 1853. *New York.* 1854. 8vo. S. 54392

Also: Annual Report ... November, 1855. *New York.* 1856. 8vo. Continued.

The Merchants' and Mechanics' Mutual Life Insurance Company, of ... New-York. [n. p. 1850.] 12mo, pp. 45. H.

Message from ... the Mayor ... May 22, 1837. ... [*New York:*] *Printed by T. Snowden.* 1837. 8vo, pp. 15, folded leaf. Cont'd.

Messages ... to the Common Council, during the Mayoralty of ... Gideon Lee. ... 1833, to ... 1834. [*New York.* n. d.] 8vo, pp. 191. B. 54395

The Annual Register of the ... Metropolitan Academy and Gymnasium ... . *New-York: George F. Nesbitt & Co., Printers.* 1853. 8vo, pp. 34. H. 54396

A Metropolitan Art Museum in ... New York. Proceedings of a Meeting held ... November 23, 1869. ... *New York: The Committee.* 1869. 8vo, pp. 39, (1). B. 54397

Second Annual Report of the Metropolitan Board of Excise, 1867. *New-York: W. C. Rogers & Co., Printers.* 1868. 8vo, pp. 36. Continued. B. 54398

Annual Report of the Metropolitan Board of Health. 1866. *New York: C. S. Westcott & Co.'s ... Printing-House.* 1867. 8vo, pp. 453, (2). Diagrams. Continued. H. 54399

Also: An Act to Create a Metropolitan Sanitary District and Board of Health. *New York: Bergen & Co., Printers.* 1866. 8vo, pp. 32. — ... Code of Health Ordinances, and Rules ... 1866 ... . *New York: John W. Amerman, Printer.* 1866. 8vo, pp. 68. H.

Communication from the Metropolitan Board of Police and Board of Health in ... relation to Prostitution in ... New York. ... February 9, 1867. *Albany: Van Benthuysen & Sons, ... Printers.* 1867. 8vo, pp. 11. H. 54400

Also: Communication from the Governor, transmitting the Annual Report of the Metropolitan Police. ... January 3, 1861. *Albany: Charles Van Benthuysen, Printer.* 1861. 8vo, pp. 119. Continued. — Quarterly Reports of the General and Deputy Superintendents of the Metropolitan Police, ending January 31, 1858. *New York: Thomas Holman, Printer.* 1858. 8vo, pp. 48. Continued. — Report of the ... Metropolitan Police of ... New York. ... Transmitted ... 1858. *Albany: C. Van Benthuysen, Printer.* 1858. 8vo, pp. 62. H. — Rules and Regulations for the Government and Guidance of the Metropolitan Police Force ... . *New York.* 1858. 18mo, pp. 125.

Metropolitan Fair in aid of the United States Sanitary Commission. [*New York.*] 1864. 8vo, pp. 22. B. 54401

Also: Report of the Treasurer of the Metropolitan Fair, in aid of the United States Sanitary Commission, ... to August 1st, 1864. *New York: John F. Trow, Printer.* 1864. 8vo, pp. 93. + Final Report ... . [*Ibid.*] 1864. 8vo, pp. 12, (1). B.

The Metropolitan Guide: ... Vol. I. April, 1867. No. I. Third Edition. *New York: Thos. E. Bartow.* [n. d.] 8vo, pp. 44. Map. Continued. B. 54402

Annual Announcement of the Metropolitan Medical College, New-York. ... 1854. *New-York: Eckler, Printer.* 1853. 8vo, pp. 8. H. 54403

Report of the Executive Committee of the Metropolitan Museum of Art ... . *New York.* 1870. 16mo, pp. 30. B.

Also: Address of the Officers of the Metropolitan Museum of Art, to the People of New York. *New York: Francis & Loutrel, Printers.* 1871. 8vo.

The Third Annual Report of The Midnight Mission, for ... 1870. *New York.* 1870. 24mo, pp. 33, (2). 54405

Miller's Guide to Central Park and Mercantile Directory. *New York: James Miller.* 1865. 16mo, pp. 15, (17), 16. H.

Miller's New York as it is, or Stranger's Guide Book to ... New York, Brooklyn, and Adjacent Places ... . *New York.* 1859. 24mo, pp. 128. + [*Ibid.*] 1863, 1864 and 1865, pp. 141; 1870, pp. 134. 54407

Constitution of the Musical Institute. *New York.* 1828. 12mo. 54408

Rules and Regulations of the Mutual Assistance Bag Company. *New York.* 1803. 8vo, pp. 16. N. 54409

Act to Incorporate the Mutual Assurance Company of ... New York ... . *New York.* 1798. 8vo, pp. 24. N. 54410

See also Vol. XII., No. 51605.

Mutual Life Insurance Co. *See* Vol. XII. 51610, and *note.*

Constitution of the Mutual Relief Society of ... New York. *New York.* 1807. 12mo, pp. 14. N. 54411

Narrative of some Recent Occurrences. *See* [Hurlbut (H. A.)]

The Exhibition of the National Academy of Design. M.DCCC.XXX. The Fifth. ... *New York.* [n. d.] 4to, pp. 12. Continued. S. 54412

See also Vol. XII., No. 51913.

Second Annual Statement to the ... National Bank of Commerce in New York, May 14, 1866. [n. p. n. d.] 8vo, pp. 11. Continued. H. 54413

National Freedmen's Relief Association. *See* Vol. XII. 51983.

Minutes of the Proceedings of the National Medical Convention ... New-York, ... May, 1846. ... *New-York.* 1846. 8vo, pp. 16. B. 54414

Constitution and By-Laws of the National Minute Men of ... New York. ... *New-York: Wilbur & Hastings, ... Printers.* 1860. 24mo, pp. 21. B. 54415

An Act to incorporate the National Safe Deposit Company of ... New York. [n. p. 186–.] 24mo, pp. 8. 54416

Constitution and By-Laws of the National Telegraphic Union, 1865. *New York: Francis & Loutrel, Printers.* 1865. 32mo, pp. 29. B. 54417

... Reports of the National War Committee of the Citizens of New-York. [*New-York.* 1862.] 8vo. BA. 54418

A general title to a series of sixteen or more tracts relating to the Rebellion.

The New Charitable Monthly; or, "What is done for the Poor." First Series, 1854. *New York.* 1854. 8vo. 54419

New-York, February 15, 1773. Proposals for publishing Rivington's New-York Gazetteer. [n. p. n. d.] Folio, 1 leaf.

New-York, March 24, 1735–6. ... [Signed] James Alexander. [n. p. n. d.] Folio, 1 leaf. P. 54421

A disavowal of all connection with Hon. Geo. Clarke.

New-York: a Historical Sketch of the Rise and Progress of the Metropolitan City of America. By a New-Yorker. ... *New-York: Carlton & Phillips.* 1853. 8vo, pp. 339. 2 Maps and 15 Plates. S. 54422

Constitution and By-Laws of the New-York Academy of Medicine. ... *New York.* 1848. 8vo, pp. 20. + *New York: G. A. C. Van Beuren, Printer.* 1852. 8vo, pp. 16. H. 54423

Also: Report of Committee on Military Surgery to ... the New York Academy of Medicine. ... *New-York: S. S. & W. Wood.* 1861. 12mo, pp. 31. — ... Report of the Standing Committee on Public Health and Legal Medicine of the New York Academy of Medicine. ... *New York: G. A. C. Van Beuren, Printer.* 1852. 8vo, pp. 15. — The Transactions ... . Vol. I.—Part. I. ... *New-York: S. S. & W. Wood.* 1851. 8vo, pp. xii, 9–165. Continued. H., N., S.

Constitution and Bye-Laws of the New York Academy of Sacred Music. *New York.* 1838. 8vo. 54424

New York and the City Travel. *See* [Benedict (D.)], Vol. II.

First Annual Report presented to the New York Anti-Slavery Society, ... 1854. ... *New York.* 1854. 12mo, pp. 24.

Annual Report of the New York Anti-Tobacco Society, ... for ... 1834. *New-York: Printed by Howe and Bates.* 1834. 12mo, pp. 10, (2). H. 54426

Statements of the Secretary of the New York Association for Colored Volunteers, on the Origin, Difficulties, etc. of the Movement. *New York.* 1864. 8vo. 54427

Communication of the New York Association for Restoration of American Shipping Interests, to John Lynch, with a Reply to John Codman. Also, a Second Communication in Answer to the same. *New York.* 1870. 8vo. 54428

The First Annual Report of the New-York Association for the Improvement of the Condition of the Poor, for ... 1845 ... . *New York: Printed by John F. Trow & Company.* 1845. 12mo, pp. 45. Continued. B. 54429

See also No. 54099, *supra.*

Constitution and Bye-Laws of the New York Association for the Suppression of Gambling ... . *New York: Printed by William S. Dorr.* 1851. 12mo, pp. 12. H. 54430

Also: First Annual Report of the New York Association for the Suppression of Gambling. ... 1851. *New York: The Association.* 1851. 8vo, pp. 40. Continued.

Fifteenth Annual Report of the Managers of the New York Asylum for Lying-In Women; presented March 10, 1838. *New York.* 1838. 8vo, pp. 16. M. 54431

An Address from the Committee of the New-York Athenæum, to the Public. *New-York: Printed by J. W. Palmer & Co.* 1824. 8vo, pp. 8. H. 54432

Also: Charter and By-Laws of the Athenæum, with a List of the Members. [*New-York.*] 1860. 12mo, pp. 22. — Charter and Constitution of the Athenæum Association ... . *New York.* 1865. 16mo, pp. 52. — Charter, and Remarks of the Committee on Amending the Charter ... . *New York.* 1825. 8vo. — Constitution and By-Laws of the New-York Athenæum. *New-York: J. W. Palmer & Co., Printers.* 1825. 8vo, pp. 24. + [*New York.*] 1859. 18mo, pp. 19. — New-York Athenæum. [Prospectus, Constitution, etc. n. p.:] *J. W. Palmer & Co., Printers.* [1824.] 8vo, pp. 20. N. — Report of the Committee appointed to Amend the Constitution of the New-York Athenæum. [n. p.:] *Printed by D. Fanshaw.* 1825. 12mo, pp. 12. H.

Annual Report of the New York Bible Society. *New York.* 1810. 8vo. Continued. 54433

Also: An Address to the Episcopalians in the United States ... . *New York.* 1824. 8vo, pp. 8. — The First Annual Report of the ... Auxiliary New-York Bible and Common Prayer Book Society. *New-York: Printed by T. and J. Swords.* 1817. 8vo, pp. 15. Continued.—The Bible in the Army; a statement of the distribution of the Scriptures among the Military and Naval Forces of the Union, by the New York Bible Society. 1861. *New York Bible Society.* 1862. 8vo, pp. 31. *See also* "An Address," No. 54115, *supra.*

New York Book Society. Constitution, By-Laws, etc. Instituted in the Year 1823. [n. p. n. d.] 18mo, pp. 8.

Also: First Report of the New-York Book Society, for the Year ending November 1, 1823. [n. p. n. d.] 18mo, pp. 7. Continued.

First Annual Report of the New York Central Homœopathic Dispensary. *New York.* 1855. 8vo. s. 54435

New York Central Park. *See* Central Park, Nos. 54153–58.

Address of the New-York City Anti-Slavery Society, to the People of ... New-York. *New-York: Printed by West & Trow.* 1833. 8vo, pp. 46. B. 54436

Address of the New York ... Colonization Society, to the Public. ... *New York: Wm. A. Mercein, Printer.* 1834. 8vo, pp. 18, (1). BA. 54437

Also: First Report of the New-York Colonization Society. ... October 29, 1823. *New York: Printed by J. Seymour.* 1823. 8vo, pp. 31, (1). Continued.— ... Proceedings of the Colonization Society of ... New York at their Third Annual Meeting ... 14th of May, 1835. ... *New York.* 1835. 8vo, pp. 24.

Statement and Plea of the New York City Council, of Political Reform. *New-York: John P. Prall, ... Printer.* 1870. 24mo, pp. 40. B. 54438

New York City During the American Revolution. Being a Collection of Original Papers (now first published) from the Manuscripts in the possession of the Mercantile Library Association, of New York City. [*New York:*] *Privately Printed for the Association.* 1861. 4to, pp. 194, (1). 2 Maps. B. 54439

The New York City Hall Recorder. Vol. I. *New York.* 1816. 8vo. N. 54440

Continued to Vol. VI. or more.

New York City Hall Reporter, and New York General Law Magazine. Edited by John Lomas. Vol. I. *New York.* 1833. 12mo. S. 54441

New York City Library Association. *New York.* 1859. 12mo, pp. 11. S. 54442

Annual Meeting of the New York ... Maternal Association. *New York.* 1838. 12mo. 54443

Thirty-Ninth Annual Report of the New York City Mission and Tract Society. *New York.* 1866. 8vo. Continued.

Also: City Mission Document, No. 9. A Church Directory for New York City. *New York City Mission.* 1867. 12mo, pp. 96. s.

Constitution of the New York City Mission Society. *New York.* [n. d.] 12mo. 54445

New-York City Tax-Book. *See* [Boyd (W. H.)], No. 7123.

New York ... Taxes. Examination of the Levy for 1864. *Albany.* 1864. 8vo, pp. 29. 54446

Fifth Annual Report of the New York ... Temperance Alliance. *New York.* 1855. 8vo, pp. 16. s. 54447

An Address to the Inhabitants ... by the ... Managers of the New-York ... Temperance Society ... . *New-York: Printed by J. Seymour.* 1829. 8vo, pp. 16. 54448

By E. Lord and others. Also: An Address to Physicians, by the Executive Committee of the Board of Managers of the New-York City Temperance Society. *New-York: Printed by J. & J. Harper.* 1829. 8vo, pp. 22.—Address of the ... Society, ... *New York.* 1848. 12mo, pp. 23. s.—First Annual Report of the ... Temperance Society. ... *New York: Printed by Sleight and Robinson.* 1830. 8vo, pp. 51, (4), Appendix, 24. Continued.

Sixth Annual Report of the New York ... Tract Society, Auxiliary to the American Tract Society; ... 1832. *New York.* 1833. 8vo. Continued. 54449

In December, 1864, the name was changed to "New York City Mission and Tract Society."

Address of the New-York City Young Men's Moral Reform Society; with their Constitution, By-Laws, &c. *New-York: J. N. Bolles.* 1834. 24mo, pp. 12. B. 54450

List of Members of the New York Club. April, 1867. ... *New York: Charles O. Jones, ... Printer.* 1867. 24mo, pp. 37, Constitution, 18, (11). B. 54451

The First Annual Report of the New York Committee of Vigilance for ... 1837 ... . *New York: Piercy & Reed, Printers.* 1837. 8vo, pp. 83, (1). B., H. 54452

See also "Address," No. 54046, *supra.*

The New-York Cries in Rhyme. *New-York: Mahlon Day.* 1834. 12mo, pp. 23. 54453

A description of New York occupies page 2.

New York Daily Transcript Extra, containing the Names of all Persons liable to the Draft, Dec. 10, 1864, to Jan. 23, 1865. [n. p. n. d.] Folio. 54454

This is an enrollment of the names of citizens liable to the draft in the Fall of 1864.

New York Democratic Anti-Lecompton Meeting. ... February 17, 1858. *New York: John F. Trow, Printer.* 1858. 8vo, pp. 31. H. 54455

The | New-York Directory, Containing, | A Valuable and well Calculated Almanack; | Tables of the different Coins, suitable for any | State, and digested in such order, as to render an | Exchange between any of the United States plain | and easy. | Likewise, | The names of all the Ci- | tizens, their occupations and places of abode. | ... | By David Franks. | *New York: Printed by Shepard Kollock, corner of Wall | and Water Streets,* M,DCC,LXXX,VI. 12mo, pp. 82. N. 54456

Extremely scarce. Reissued in 1851 with the imprint: *New-York: Printed by Shepard Kollock.* M,DCC,LXXX,VI. *Republished by John Doggett, Jr.* 1851. 12mo, pp. 82. Map. + [Another] Directory. *Printed for the Editor.* 1787. 8vo, pp. 58.

The New-York Directory and Register, for ... 1789. ... *New-York: Hodge, Allen, and Campbell.* M,DCCLXXXIX. 12mo, pp. 144. + [*Ibid.*] 1790. 54457

The New-York Directory ... for ... 1792. By William Duncan. *New-York: Printed ... by T. & J. Swords.* 1793. 12mo, pp. xi, 252. Map. + [*Ibid.*] 1794 and 1795. 54458

New-York Directory ... for 1796. ... To which is added the Names of the Inhabitants of Brooklyn. ... By John Low. *New-York.* 1796. 12mo. N. 54459

Longworth's American Almanack, ... and City Directory ... . *New York: T. & J. Swords.* 1797. 16mo, pp. 340. + [*Ibid.*] 1798. 16mo, pp. (2), 86, 112 leaves. + [*Ibid.*] 1799. + *New York: D. Longworth.* 1800. 18mo, pp. (2), 390. + [*Ibid.*] 1804. *See also* Vol. x., No. 41939.

John Langdon and Son's ... Directory ... . *New York: William W. Vermilye.* 1804. 12mo.

Jones's New York ... Directory. *New York.* 1805. 12mo.

Longworth's ... Directory, for 1805, '6, '7, '10, '11. 12mo.

Elliot & Crissy's ... Directory, for ... 1811 ... . *New York.* 1811. 18mo.—Elliot's Improved New York Double Directory ... . *New York: W. Elliot.* 1812. 8vo.

Longworth's ... Directory, 1813, '14, '15, '16, '17, '18, '19, '20. 12mo.

The Citizen's Directory and Stranger's Guide ... . *New York.* 1814. 12mo.

Mercein's Directory for 1820–21. *New York.* 1820. 12mo.

Longworth's ... Directory for 1821, '22, '23, '25, '26–'43. 12mo.

New-York as it is, in 1833; ... Edited by Edwin Williams. *New-York: J. Disturnell.* 1833. 24mo. Map. + In 1834. ... [*Ibid.*] 1834. 18mo. Map. + [*Ibid.*] 1835. 16mo. Plate and 3 Maps. + 1837. [*Ibid.*] M DCCC XXXVII. 18mo. + *New York: Colton & Disturnell.* 1839. 18mo. Map. *See also* [Beldon (E. P.)], No. 4409.

The Classified Mercantile Directory for ... New-York and Brooklyn. ... *New-York: J. Disturnell.* 1837. 18mo. Map.

The New-York Business Directory, for 1840 and 1841. *New York.* 1840. 16mo. + Second Edition. [*Ibid.*] + For 1841 and 1842. *New York: J. Doggett, Jr.* [1841.] 12mo. + Second Edition. [*Ibid.*] + For 1844–1845. [*Ibid.* n. d.] 12mo. + Supplement ... containing the Removals ... occasioned by the Great Fire, July 19th, 1845. ... [*Ibid.*] 1845. 8vo. + For 1846 and 1847. [*Ibid.* n. d.] 12mo.

Doggett's New York City Directory, for 1842. [*New York.* n. d.] 8vo. Continued to 1849.

The New-York City and Co-Partnership Directory, for 1843 & 1844. *New York: J. Doggett, Jr.* [1843]–48. 8vo.

The Citizen's Directory ... . *New York.* 1844. 12mo.

Doggett's United States Railroad and Ocean Steam Navigation Guide, for 1848. *New-York.* [n. d.] Sm. 4to.

Wilson's Business Directory ... . *New-York: H. Wilson.* 1848. 18mo. + *New-York: John F. Trow.* 1849. 18mo.

New York City Partnership Directory for 1849 and 1850. *New York: J. Doggett.* 1849. 8vo.

New-York Mercantile Register, containing the ... Principal Business Establishments, ... in New-York. *New-York.* 1848. Rl. 8vo.

Doggett's New York City Street Directory for 1851. First Publication. *New York: John Doggett, Jr.* [n. d.] 8vo.

New-York Mercantile Union Business Directory ... 1850–51. *New-York: S. French ...* 1850. 8vo.

New York Pictorial Directory. By Jones, Newman and J. S. Ewbank. *New York.* 1851. 5 vols., 4to.

Rode's New York City Directory for 1850–51. *New York: Charles R. Rode.* [n. d.] 8vo. + [*Ibid.*] 1852–'53.

The New York City Directory for 1851–52. ... *New York: Doggett & Rode.* [n. d.] 8vo.

Wilson's Business Directory ... . *New York.* 1852. 18mo.

Trow's New York City Directory, for 1852–3. ... Compiled by Henry Wilson. *New York: John F. Trow.* [n. d.] 8vo. Map.

Citizen and Strangers' Pictorial ... Directory for the City ... and Vicinity, 1853. Solyman Brown, Editor. *New York: C. Spalding & Co.* 1853. 8vo.

Trow's ... Directory, for 1853–4. ... By Henry Wilson. *New York: John F. Trow.* 1853. 8vo.

The New-York ... Directory, for 1853–1854. ... *New York: Charles R. Rode.* [n. d.] 8vo. + [*Ibid.*] 1854–55. 8vo.

Wilson's Business Directory ... . *New York: John F. Trow.* 1855. 12mo.

Trow's ... Directory, 1855–6. Compiled by Henry Wilson. *New York: John F. Trow.* 1855. 8vo. + [*Ibid.*] 1856, '57.

Wilson's ... Copartnership Directory, for 1856–57. *New York.* [n. d.] 8vo.

New York ... Mercantile ... Business Directory. For ... 1856–57. *New York: Mason Brothers.* 1856. 8vo. + [*Ibid.*] 1857. 8vo.

The New York Merchants' ... Advertising ... Directory for 1857–8. *New York: T. W. Barnum.* 1857. 4to. + [*Ibid.*] 1858. 4to.

Boyd's Pictorial Directory of Broadway ... . 1859. *New-York: William H. Boyd.* [n. d.] 8vo.

Carroll's New York City Directory ... . By G. Danielson Carroll. *New York: Carroll & Company.* 1859. 12mo.

Trow's ... Directory ... 1859–60. ... *New York: John F. Trow.* 1859. 8vo.

Wilson's ... Copartnership Directory, for 1860–61. *New York: John F. Trow.* 1860. 8vo. + For 1863–64. [*Ibid.*] 1863.

Trow's New York ... Directory, ... By Henry Wilson. For ... 1864. *New York: John F. Trow.* 1864. 8vo.

New York ... Directory for 1865–66. ... By Henry Wilson. *New York: John F. Trow.* 1865. 8vo.

The Merchants' Directory for 1866 and 1867, containing a list of the principal Manufacturers ... in and adjoining New York; ... *New York.* 1866. 24mo. Map.

The Metropolitan Merchants' and Manufacturers' Business Directory, for 1867 and '68. ... *New York: Fitzpatrick & Hunter.* 1867. 4to.

Wilson's Business Directory ... 1867–8. *New York.* 1867. 18mo.

Trow's ... Directory. ... By Henry Wilson. For ... 1868. *New York: John F. Trow.* 1867. 8vo. Map.

The Merchants' Directory, 1868–69 ... . By J. Harford & Co. *New York.* 1868. 24mo. Map. + For 1869 and 1870. [*Ibid.* 1869.] 18mo. Map.

Trow's ... Directory, ... By Henry Wilson. For ... 1869. *New York: John F. Trow.* 1868. 8vo. Map.

Wilson's Business Directory ... 1868–9. *New York.* 1868. 16mo.

Trow's ... Directory, ... By Henry Wilson. For ... 1870. *New York: John F. Trow.* [n. d.] 8vo.

Wilson's Business Directory. *New York: John F. Trow.* 1869. 18mo. Map.

Wilson's ... Co-Partnership Directory ... for 1869–70. *New York: John F. Trow.* 1869. 8vo.

Business Directory of ... New York, Philadelphia, Boston, and Baltimore; and a Business Register of the Principal Manufacturers in the Eastern States. 1869. *New York: William P. Cleary & Co.* [n. d.] 4to.

Charter and Ordinance of the New-York Dispensary. *New-York: Printed by Hopkins, Webb & Co.* 1797. 8vo, pp. 30, (1). N. 54460

Also: Annual Report of the Board of Trustees of the ... Dispensary, January, 1830. *New York.* 1831. 8vo. Continued. B.—The By-Laws of the ... Dispensary ... *New York: Printed by William Osborn.* 1848. 12mo, pp. 24. + *New York: Holman, Gray & Co., Printers.* 1854. 12mo, pp. 21.—Charter, By-Laws, &c., of the New York Dispensary. *New York.* 1795. 16mo. + [*Ibid.*] 1805. + *New York: Printed by C. S. Van Winkle.* 1810. 8vo, pp. 23. + *New York.* 1811. 8vo, pp. 24. + [*Ibid.*] 1813. + *New York: Printed by Van Winkle & Wiley.* 1814. 8vo, pp. 15. Cont'd. —Rules ... for the Medical Relief of the Poor. *New York.* [1795.] 8vo, pp. 16.

New York Enrollment Lists. Names of Persons Enrolled in the Third Congressional District, New York. First Ward. 8vo, pp. 29. + Second Ward. 8vo, pp. 48. + Third Ward. 8vo, pp. 46. + Fourth Ward. 8vo, pp. 56. + Fifth Ward. 8vo, pp. 90. + Fifth Ward, 4th Congressional District. 8vo, pp. 64. + Seventh Ward. 8vo, pp. 58. + Seventh Ward, 1st Sub-District. 8vo, pp. 181. + Ninth Ward. 4to, pp. 51. + Tenth Ward, 2d Sub-District. 8vo, pp. 152. + Eleventh Ward. 8vo, pp. 143. + 7th Congressional District, Embracing the 11th and 17th Wards. Impl. 8vo, pp. 199, 120. + 9th Congressional District, Embracing the 12th, 19th, 22d Wards. Impl. 8vo, pp. 450. + 3d Congressional District, Thirteenth Ward. 8vo, pp. 86. + Thirteenth Ward, 3d Sub-District, 5th Congressional District. 8vo, pp. 113. + Fourteenth Ward. 8vo, pp. 134. + Fifteenth Ward. 4to, pp. 37. + Eighteenth Ward. 4to,

pp. 37. + Nineteenth Ward. 8vo, pp. 29. + Twentieth Ward, December 20, 1863. 4to, pp. 38. + Twenty-First Ward, December 20, 1863. 4to, pp. 27. 54461

These are the names of citizens enrolled as subject to being drafted into the army during the Rebellion of 1861–5. They are issued without any imprint and are very rare.

Second Annual Report of the New-York Eye Infirmary ... 1823. *New-York: Printed by Mahlon Day.* 1823. 8vo, pp. 23. Continued. B. 54462

Sixth Annual Report of the New York Female Auxiliary Bible Society [etc.]. *New York.* 1822. 8vo, pp. 32. 54463

Constitution and Circular of the New York Female Bethel Union. June, 1835. [n. p. n. d.] 8vo. 54464

First Report of the New York Female Union Society, April 9, 1817. *New York.* 1817. 8vo, pp. 32. Continued.

New York Free Academy. *See* No. 54284, *note.*

Circular of the New York Freedman's Savings & Trust Co. *Brooklyn.* 1866. 8vo. 54466

Catalogue of the Exhibition of the New York Gallery of Fine Arts for 1844. *New York.* 1844. 8vo. 54467

New York Hibernian Provident Society; or, the Danish Inquisition under Nine Directors. To the People of the State of New York. [n. p.] 1809. 8vo. N. 54468

Anniversary Discourse delivered before the New York Historical Society, December 6th, 1828. *New York.* 1829. 8vo. Continued. 54469

Catalogue of the Books, Tracts, Newspapers, Maps, Charts Views, Portraits, and Manuscripts, in the Library of the ... Historical Society. *New-York: Press of J. Seymour.* 1813. 8vo, pp. 139. 54470

By Timothy Alden. Also: Catalogue of Books ... added to the Library ... since January, 1839. ... *New York: Joseph W. Harrison, Printer.* 1840. 8vo, pp. 32. H.

Catalogue of Printed Books in the Library of the ... Historical Society. *New-York: The Society.* M DCCC LIX. 8vo, pp. viii, 653.

This forms Vol. IV. of the Second Series of the "Collections." Also: Catalogue of the Museum and Gallery of Art of the ... Historical Society. 1862. *New York: The Society.* M.DCCC.LXII. 8vo, pp. 72, 39. + [*Ibid.*] M.DCCC.LXVI. 8vo, pp. viii, 72, 61, (1).—The Charter and By-Laws of the ... Historical Society. Revised March, 1846. *New York: Press of the ... Society.* 1846. 8vo, pp. 47. + Second Edition, with

Amendments ... . [*Ibid.*] M DCCC LIII. 8vo, pp. 22. + With a List of Members. [*Ibid.*] M DCCC LXII. 8vo, pp. 73, (1). B., H.

Collections of the ... Historical Society, for ... 1809. ... *New-York: I. Riley.* 1811–1829. 5 vols., 8vo, pp. vi, (2), 428; xxiv, 358; 129, 404, Portrait; xvi, 320; (4), 390. B. 54472

Vol. IV. was first published in 1826 [pp. (8), 308], and reissued in 1829, it contains the matter reprinted in Vol. V., *i. e.* the continuation of Smith's "History of New York."

Collections of the ... Historical Society. Second Series. *New-York: The Society.* 1841–M DCCC LIX. 4 vols., 8vo, pp. 486, (1), Map and Plate; 493, 2 Maps; Vol. III. Pt. I. pp. iv, (4), 358, (1); viii, 653. H. 54473

Collections of the ... Historical Society for ... 1868. Publication Fund Series. Vol. I. *New York: The Society.* MDCCCLXVIII. 8vo, pp. xviii, 458. Continued. H. 54474

Printed for the subscribers to the fund, and not for sale.

The Constitution and Bye-Laws of the ... Historical Society, founded ... 1804. *New-York: Printed by T. & J. Swords.* 1805. 8vo, pp. 15. + [*Ibid.*] 1829. + *New-York: W. B. & T. Smith, Printers.* 1839. 8vo, pp. 23. + *New York: The Society.* 1844. 12mo, pp. 33. H. 54475

Debate in the Historical Society on "Columbia," as the new name of this country, instead of "America," May 15, 1845. *New York.* 1845. 8vo.—A Letter to the Trustees of the Building Fund of the ... Society. *New York.* 1851. 8vo, pp. 21.—Memorial of the ... Historical Society to the ... Legislature of ... New York. *New York: Printed by C. S. Van Winkle.* 1814. 8vo, pp. 11. B.

Proceedings, of the ... Historical Society. For ... 1843. *New York: The Society.* 1844–49. 7 vols., 8vo. H. 54476

Among the numerous papers read before the Society, and published in these volumes, are many of more than ordinary interest, among which may be mentioned Mr. Bartlett's "Progress of Ethnology;" Schoolcraft's "Aboriginal Names of New York;" Thompson's "Indian Names of Long Island;" Schoolcraft's "Siege and Defence of Fort Stanwix;" "Employment of the Indians by the English in the Revolutionary War;" Van Rensselaer's "Memoir on the French and Indian Expedition against New York, and the burning of Schenectady, 1689;" Schoolcraft's "Notices of Tumuli in Florida, and burial places of Indian Tribes;" Gilman's "Defeat of Gen. St. Clair;" Morgan's "Territorial Limits of the Iroquois;" Peter Wilson's "Address on the Iroquois;" O'Callaghan's "Jesuit Relations, with a Bibliographical Sketch of each;" "Champlain in the Onondaga Valley;" Long's "Ancient Architecture in America," etc.

Proceedings of the ... Society at the Dedication of the Library, November 3, 1857. *New York: The Society.* M DCCC LVII. 8vo, pp. 27.—Proceedings ... on the Announcement of the Death of William Hickling Prescott, February, M DCCC LIX. [n. p. n. d.] 8vo, pp. (2), 16.—Proceedings ... on the ... Death of Thomas J. Bryan. June, 1870. *New York.* M DCCC LXX. 4to, pp. 10.—Proceedings ... on the ... Death of Luther Bradish, President ... October, 1863. *New York.* M DCCC LXV. 8vo, pp. 24. (2). Portrait.—Report ... on a National Name, March 31, 1845. [n. p. n. d.] 8vo, pp. 8.

Semi-Centennial Celebration. Fiftieth Anniversary of the Founding of the ... Historical Society. ... November 20, 1854. *New York: The Society.* M DCCC LIV. 8vo, pp. 96. B. 54477

See also Vol. I., No. 3136, *and* [Verplanck (G. C.)]

An Address from the Trustees of the New-York Homœopathic Dispensary Association. *New-York.* 1852. 8vo. S.

Constitution and By-Laws of the New York Horticultural Society. *New York.* 1824. 8vo. 54479

Also: Charter, Constitution and By-Laws of the ... Society. *New York.* 1833. 8vo.—Proceedings of the ... Society, at the Celebration of its Tenth Anniversary. New York, Aug. 26, 1828. [n. p. n. d.] 8vo.

An Account of the New-York Hospital. *New-York: Printed by Collins & Co.* 1811. 8vo, pp. 65. 2 Plates. + *New York: Printed by Mahlon Day.* 1820. 8vo, pp. 62. 2 Plates.

An Account of Patients in the ... Hospital in 1811. [n. p. n. d.] 8vo.—Address of the Governors of the ... Hospital to the Public, relative to the Asylum of the Insane at Bloomingdale. *New York.* 1821. 8vo.—Address of the Governors of the ... Hospital, to their Fellow Citizens. *New York: Wm. C. Bryant & Co., Printers.* 1852. 8vo, pp. 24. H.

A Brief Account of the New-York Hospital. *New-York: Printed by Isaac Collins and Son.* 1804. 8vo, pp. (4), 72. H.

By John Murray, Jr., or Thomas Eddy. Also: By-Laws and Regulations of the ... Hospital. *New York.* 1820. 8vo.

Catalogue of the Books belonging to the ... Hospital Library. *New York: Collins & Co.* 1811. 8vo, pp. 74. + [n. p. n. d.] 8vo, pp. 125. + *New-York: Printed by G. F. Hopkins & Son.* 1829. 8vo, pp. 132. + *New York.* 1845. 8vo. A. + Supplementary ... Catalogue ... . *New-York: Press of Mahlon Day & Co.* 1839. 8vo, pp. 50. + No. II. Supplementary Catalogue, ... *New York: Robert Craighead, Printer.* 1865. 8vo, pp. 23.

A Catalogue of the Pathological Cabinet of the ... Hospital, ... by Robert Ray, Jr., M.D. ... With a Memoir of the Author. *New York: S. S. & W. Wood.* 1860. 8vo, pp. 364. Portrait.

Charter of the Society of The New-York Hospital, and the Laws relating thereto; ... with ... those of the Bloomingdale Asylum ... . *New-York: Press of G. P. Scott & Co.* 1833. 8vo, pp. 85. + *New-York: Mahlon Day, Printer.* 1838. 8vo, pp. 89. + *New-York.* 1845. 8vo, pp. 148. + [*Ibid.*] 1856. 8vo, pp. 140. N. 54484

See also "Charter," No. 54163, *supra.* Also: The Financial Condition and Restricted Charitable Operations of the ... New York Hospital. Majority and Minority

Reports ... of the Board of Governors. ... *New York: Wm. C. Bryant & Co., Printers.* 1866. 8vo, pp. 22. — State of the New-York Hospital for the Year 1803. [n. p. 1804.] Folio, pp. 4. Continued.

Annual Report of the NEW YORK HOUSE OF MERCY. *New York.* 1860. 12mo. 54485

Act of Incorporation and Laws relative to the NEW-YORK HOUSE OF REFUGE. *New-York: Egbert, Hovey & King, Printers.* 1849. 8vo, pp. 14. H. 54486

See also Hart (N. C.), Vol. VIII., No. 30640, *and* "Society for the Reformation of Juvenile Delinquents," *infra.*

Fourth Annual Report of the NEW YORK HOUSE AND SCHOOL of Industry. *New York: Printed ... by Thomas Wood.* 1855. 8vo, pp. 20. Continued. H. 54487

Catalogue of the NEW YORK HYDROPATHIC and Physiological School, for 1854–5. With the Opening Address of Mrs. L. F. Fowler .... *New York.* 1855. 12mo, pp. 48. S. 54488

New York Illustrated. With a Map of the City .... *New York.* 1870. 8vo, pp. 52. + New Edition with Revisions and New Illustrations. *New York: D. Appleton & Co.* [n. d.] Rl. 8vo, pp. 56. 54489

New-York in a Nutshell; or, Visitor's Hand-Book to the City. [By F. Saunders.] *New York: T. W. Strong.* 1853. 8vo, pp. 144. 54490

New York in 1828. Strangers' Guide to the Commercial Metropolis of the United States. Illustrated .... *New York.* 1828. 16mo. Maps and Plates. 54491

New York in 1845. [n. p. n. d.] 32mo. 54492

New York in Slices. *See* [Foster (G. G.)], Vol. v. 25227.

New York Industrial Exhibition; its Plans, Purposes and Prospects. [n. p. n. d.] 8vo. 54493

New York Industrial Exhibition. Special Report of Professor Wilson. Presented to the House of Commons .... *London: Harrison and Sons.* 1854. 8vo, pp. (2), 133, (1). Plates. B.

Also: New York Industrial Exhibition. General Report of the British Commissioners. Presented to Parliament .. 1854. *London: Thomas Harrison.* 1854. 8vo, pp. 12. — ... Special Report of Sir Charles Lyell. ... *London: Thomas Harrison.* 1854. 8vo, pp. 103. — ... Special Report of Mr. George Wallis. ... *London: Thomas Harrison.* [n. d.] 8vo, pp. (2), 160. 2 Plans. — ... Special Report of Mr. Joseph Whitworth. ... *London: Thomas Harrison.* [n. d.] 8vo, pp. vi, 74. B.

Abstract of the Title of John Stevens, to Lands in East Chester, on behalf of the NEW YORK INDUSTRIAL HOME Association, No. 1. *New York: Privately Printed.* 1851. 12mo, pp. 143. 54495

Appeal in Behalf of the NEW YORK INFANT Asylum .... *New York: C. H. Clayton & Co., Printers.* [n. d.] 24mo, pp. 16.

Seventeenth Annual Report of the NEW YORK INFIRMARY for Women and Children. *New York.* 1871. 8vo. 54497

New York Institution. Companion to American Museum. Catalogue of Fine Arts. *New York.* 1823. 8vo. 54498

An Account of the NEW YORK INSTITUTION FOR THE BLIND. With a Brief Statement ... of the Institutions for the Blind in this and other Countries. To which is added, Biographical Notices of some of the most Illustrious Blind. *New York.* 1833. 8vo, pp. 56. S. 54499

Also: First Annual Report of the Managers of the ... Institution ... 1st of February, 1837. *New York.* 1837. 8vo, pp. 56.

An Act to Incorporate the Members of the NEW-YORK INSTITUTION FOR THE INSTRUCTION of the Deaf and Dumb .... *New York.* 1817. 8vo. + To which is added, the By-Laws, ... Names of ... Officers ... And a List of the Pupils. *New-York: Printed by E. Conrad.* 1819. 8vo, pp. 23. BA. 54500

Also: Acts and By-Laws, and Reports of the Directors of the ... Institution ... [n. p.] 1831. 8vo. — Address, delivered at the ... Institution ... December 2d, 1846. ... With an Appendix, containing the Proceedings at the Dedication of the Chapel. *New York.* 1847. 8vo. — Address of the Directors ... to their Fellow-Citizens. *New York.* 1821. 8vo. — Ceremonies ... [on laying the Corner-Stone of the] Institution, ... *New-York: George F. Nesbitt & Co., Printers.* 1853. 8vo, pp. 34. B. + [*Ibid.*] 8vo, pp. 46, (2). — Circular of the ... Institution .... *New-York: Printed by E. Conrad.* 1818. 8vo, pp. 15, (1). — Sixth Annual Report of the Directors of the ... Institution ... 1825. *New-York: Printed by E. Conrad.* 1825. 8vo, pp. 40. Cont'd.

Constitution of the NEW-YORK IRISH Emigrant Association, ... *New-York: Printed by William A. Mercein.* 1817. 12mo, pp. 12. BA. 54501

Constitution of the NEW YORK JOURNEYMEN Shipwrights' Society. January 5, 1814. *New York.* 1804. 12mo, pp. 12.

Act of Incorporation of the NEW YORK JUVENILE Asylum: ... *New York: Wm. L. S. Harrison, Printer.* 1851. 8vo, pp. (2), 28. B. 54503

Also: Charter and By-Laws of the ... Juvenile Asylum. ... With ... Amendments, & the By-Laws .... *New-York: Printed by A. J. Brady.* 1859. 8vo, pp. 34. H. —

First Report of the ... Juvenile Asylum .... *New York: William H. White, Printer.* 1853. 8vo, pp. 22, (1). Continued. B.

Eleventh Annual Report of the NEW-YORK LADIES' Home Missionary Society .... *New-York.* 1855. 8vo. H. 54504

Catalogue of the Library of the NEW-YORK LAW Institute, July 1, 1842. *New-York.* 1843. 8vo, pp. 111. 54505

Transactions of the NEW YORK LIFE-SAVING Benevolent Association in 1856. *New York: R. C. Root ....* 1857. 8vo, pp. 14. Continued. H., S. 54506

Second Annual Report of the ... NEW YORK LYCEUM, ... 1841. *New York: Narine & Co's Print.* 1841. 12mo, pp. 11, (1)

Constitution of the NEW-YORK LYING-IN Hospital. [n. p.:] *Printed by John Furman.* M,DCC,XCIX. 12mo, pp. 13. H.

Also: Act relating to the Society of the Lying-In Hospital ... with the Bye Laws, Rules and Regulations .... *New York.* [n. d.] 12mo. — Act to Incorporate the Society ... with the Bye Laws .... *Brooklyn.* [n. d.] 12mo. pp. 23. N.

Annual Report of the NEW-YORK MAGDALEN FEMALE Benevolent Society. *New York.* 1833. 8vo. Continued.

First Annual Report of the Executive Committee of the NEW-YORK MAGDALEN Society. Instituted, January 1, 1830. *New-York.* 1831. 8vo, pp. 18. + *Philadelphia.* 1831. 8vo, pp. 8.

See also "Magdalen Society," No. 54367, *infra.*

Report of the NEW YORK MATERNAL Association, ... 1837. *New York.* 1837. 8vo. 54511

Charter, Constitution, and By-Laws of the NEW-YORK MECHANIC and Scientific Institution. ... *New-York: W. A. Mercein, Printer.* 1822. 8vo. 54512

See also No. 54375, *supra.*

Charter and By-Laws of the NEW YORK MECHANICS' and Tradesmen's General Society. *New York.* 1839. 8vo. + [*Ibid.*] 1847. N. 54513

New York Medical College .... Catalogue ... and Announcement of ... Lectures. ... 1850–1. *New York: R. Craighead, Printer.* 1850. 8vo, pp. 16. Continued. H. 54514

Constitution and By-Laws of the NEW YORK MINING Stock Board. *New York: L. H. Biglow & Co., Printers.* 1866. 8vo, pp. 18, (2). H. 54515

The Address and Constitution of the NEW YORK MISSIONARY Society. *New York.* 1796. 8vo, pp. 19. N. 54516

Also: Report of the Directors ... at their Annual Meeting, April 1, 1805. *New York.* 1805. 8vo.

The New York Municipal Gazette. ... Vol. I. ... Edited by E. Meriam. *New York.* 1841. 4to. Continued. B. 54517

Prospectus and Programmes of the NEW YORK MUSICAL Congress. 1854. ... *New York: John Darcie.* [1854.] 8vo, pp. (8), 36. 54518

Constitution of the NEW YORK MUSICAL FUND. *New York.* 1830. 12mo.

First Annual Report of the NEW YORK OPTHALMIC and Aural Institute .... For ... 1870. ... *New York: Francis & Loutrel, ... Printers.* 1870. 8vo, pp. 16. H. 54519

First Report of the Surgeons of the NEW-YORK OPTHALMIC HOSPITAL .... *New-York: D. Fanshaw, Printer.* 1853. 8vo, pp. 16. H. 54520

Also: First Annual Report .... For ... 1853. *New-York: D. Fanshaw, Printer.* 1854. 8vo, pp. 16. Continued. H.

New-York, Past, [etc.]. *See* [Belden (E. P.)], Vol. II. 4410.

First Anniversary of the NEW YORK PEACE Society. *New York: Craighead and Allen, Printers.* 1838. 8vo, pp. 23. H.

Also: Report, ... December 25, 1818. *New York.* [n. d.] 8vo, pp. 7. The Society was afterwards merged in the "American Peace Society," and a new one (with the same name) was formed in 1837.

New York Pension Roll. [n. p. about 1835.] 8vo, pp. 459.

Fourth Annual Report of the NEW YORK PHILHARMONIC Society. *New York.* 1846. 8vo. 54523

Also: Constitution, By-Laws and Regulations of the Philharmonic Society of New York. *New York.* 1824. 8vo.

New York Pictorial Directory. ... *New York.* 1853–4. 12mo.

Includes illustrations of the Astor House, St. Paul's Church, etc.

First Annual Report of the NEW YORK PROTESTANT Church Missionary Society for Seamen .... 1845. *New York.* 1845. 12mo, pp. 24. H. 54525

Account of the Origin and Formation of the NEW-YORK PROTESTANT EPISCOPAL CITY-MISSION Society, with the Constitution, and a List of the Officers and Managers. ... *New-York: Protestant Episcopal Press.* M DCCC XXXI. 8vo, pp. 8. H. 54526

Also: Address of the New-York Protestant Episcopal City-Mission Society. *New-York: Protestant Episcopal Press.* M DCCC XXXIII. 8vo, pp. 13, (1). — Constitution of the ... Society; with the By-Laws of the Managers. *New-York.* M DCCC XXXI. 8vo, pp. 8. — The First Annual Report of the Managers ... Jan. 12, 1832. *New-York.* M DCCC XXXII. 8vo, pp. 16. Continued. H.

The Second Annual Report of the NEW-YORK PROTESTANT EPISCOPAL MISSIONARY Society ... Dec. 1, 1818. ... *New-York: Printed ... by T. & J. Swords.* 1818. 8vo, pp. 15. Continued. BA., M. 54527

First Annual Report of the Board of Trustees of the NEW-YORK PROTESTANT EPISCOPAL PRESS. With the Constitution, ... *New-York.* 1829. 8vo, pp. 11, (1). Continued. H. 54528

By-Laws of the Corporation of the NEW-YORK PROTESTANT EPISCOPAL PUBLIC SCHOOL; ... with the Acts of Incorporation, the Plan of Trinity School .... *New-York: Protestant Episcopal Press.* MDCCCXXXI. 12mo, pp. 18. + *New-York.* 1841. 12mo, pp. 28. H. 54529

Constitution of the NEW YORK PROTESTANT EPISCOPAL SUNDAY-SCHOOL Society. *New York.* 1817. 8vo, pp. 7. 54530

Also: Fourth Annual Report of the Board of Managers .... *New York.* 1821. 8vo, pp. 8. Continued. M.

Report of the NEW-YORK PROTESTANT EPISCOPAL TRACT Society .... *New York.* 1829. 8vo. 54531

First Report of the NEW YORK RELIGIOUS Tract Society; with the Constitution. *New York.* 1813. 12mo. 54532

New-York Sabbath Committee. No. 1. [*New York.* 1858.] 8vo, pp. 8. Continued. B. 54533

The First Annual Report of the N. Y. SACRED Harmonic Society. ... *New-York: Printed by W. H. Dayas.* 1853. 16mo, pp. 8, (2), Constitution, v, (1). H. 54534

Report of the Meteorologist of the NEW YORK SKATING Club, for the Season 1863–64. *New York: Henry Croker, Jr., Printer.* [n. d.] 16mo, pp. 30. 54535

Constitution of the NEW YORK SOCIETY FOR PROMOTING Christian Knowledge and Piety. *New York.* 1794. 8vo.

Second Annual Report of the NEW YORK SOCIETY FOR THE ENCOURAGEMENT of Faithful Domestic Servants. *New York.* 1827. 8vo. 54537

Constitution of the NEW YORK SOCIETY FOR THE INFORMATION and Assistance of Persons Emigrating from Foreign Countries .... *New York.* 1794. Folio, 1 leaf. 54538

First Annual Report of the NEW YORK SOCIETY FOR THE PROMOTION of Knowledge and Industry. *New York.* 1834. 8vo

First Annual Report of the NEW YORK SOCIETY FOR THE RELIEF OF THE RUPTURED and Crippled. ... *New York: John F. Trow, Printer.* 1864. 8vo, pp. 35. Continued. B. 54540

Laws of the NEW-YORK SOCIETY FOR THE RELIEF OF THE WIDOWS and Orphans of Medical Men. ... *New-York: H. Ludwig and Co.* 1849. 24mo, pp. 24. H. 54541

Address of the Trustees of the NEW YORK SOCIETY LIBRARY, to the Members .... *New-York: J. M. Elliott, Printer.* 1833. 8vo, pp. 12. B. 54542

Address to the Stockholders of the ... Library, on the Management and ... Condition of that Institution. *New-York: G. P. Scott & Co.* 1833. 8vo, pp. 16. B.

Catalogue of the Books of the New York Society Library; with the Charter, By-Laws, and Names of the Members. *New York.* 1793. 8vo. + *New-York: Printed by C. S. Van Winkle.* 1813. 8vo, pp. 210, 16. + Supplement. *New York: Library Association.* 1813. 8vo, pp. 135. + *New-York: Printed by C. S. Van Winkle.* 1825. 8vo, pp. 119. + Supplementary Catalogue, ... *New-York: J. Van Norden & Co., Printers.* 1841. 8vo, pp. vii, 72. H. 54543

Also: Alphabetical and Analytical Catalogue of The New-York Society Library: with a brief historical notice of the Institution; ... *New-York: Printed by James Van Norden.* 1838. 8vo, pp. xxvii, 9–328. + *New York: R. Craighead, Printer.* 1850. 8vo, pp. xlviii, 621. B. + *New York.* 1856. 8vo, pp. 348.

Annual Report of the Trustees of the ... Society Library, March 31, 1856. *New York: John F. Trow, Printer.* 1856. 8vo, pp. 16. Continued. B. 54544

The Charter, and Bye-Laws of the ... Society Library; with A Catalogue of the ... Library. *New-York: Printed by H. Gaine.* M,DCC,LXXIII. 12mo, pp. 35. + *New-York: Printed by T. & J. Swords.* 1795. 8vo, pp. 99. 54545

Also: List of the Members of the ... Society Library, and of Books added from April, 1860, to April, 1861. *New York.* 1861. 8vo, pp. 36.

Constitution and By-Laws of the NEW YORK STOCK and Exchange Board. *New York: J. Narine, Printer.* 1837. 8vo, pp. 12

New York Stock Exchange Directory for 1866–7. *New York.* 1866. 8vo.

Proceedings of the NEW YORK SUNDAY-SCHOOL INSTITUTE ... March 17–22, 1867. *New York: The Institute.* 1867. 8vo, pp. 136. Continued. 54547

First Report of the NEW-YORK SUNDAY SCHOOL UNION Society .... *New York: Printed ... by J. Seymour.* 1817. 8vo, pp. 31. Continued. H. 54548

Also: Constitution of the New York Sunday School Union Society. *New York.* 1816. 8vo.

The New York Tax Book. ... *New York.* 1850. 8vo, pp. 99.

Address of the NEW YORK TEMPERANCE Society to the Inhabitants of the City. *New York.* 1829. 12mo. W. 54550

Also: An Address to Physicians .... *New-York: Printed by J. & J. Harper.* 1829. 8vo, pp. 22. B.

Catalogue of the ... NEW-YORK THEOLOGICAL Seminary, January, 1840. *New-York: Printed by William Osborn.* 1840. 8vo, pp. 15. Continued. H. 54551

Constitution and By-Laws of the NEW YORK TYPOGRAPHICAL Society, with a list of the Members. ... *New-York: George F. Nesbitt and Co., Printers.* 1850. 16mo, pp. 39. H. 54552

Annual Report of the NEW-YORK UNITARIAN Book Society; with the Rules ... 1823. *New-York: Joseph C. Spear, Printer.* 1823. 12mo, pp. 43. H. 54553

First Annual Report of the NEW YORK WASHING and Bathing Association. *New York.* 1853. 8vo. 54554

The Constitution and Bye-Laws of the NEW-YORK WASHINGTON MILITARY Society. ... *New York.* 1796. 12mo, pp. 12. + *New-York: Printed by John Tiebout.* 1798. 12mo, pp. 14.

The Constitution of the NEW-YORK WESLEYAN Methodist Relief Society, Established, January, 1818. [n. p. n. d.] 18mo, pp. 8. 54556

Report of the Corresponding Committee of the NEW YORK WHIG CLUB, on the Communication of the "United Whig Club;" Referred to them Together with the Resolution of the New York Club, thereon. *New York: Printed by Frank, White & Co.* 1809. 8vo, pp. 12. 54557

The Annual Regattas of the NEW YORK YACHT CLUB, from its Organization to ... 1862, inclusive. *New York.* 1863. 8vo.

Address of the NEW YORK YEARLY MEETING of Friends upon the Subject of Slavery. *New York.* 1844. 8vo. C.

Also: Minutes of the New-York Yearly Meeting of Friends, 1856. *New York: James Egbert, Printer.* 1856. 12mo, pp. 28. — Report of a Committee of the Representatives ... upon the Condition and Wants of the Colored Refugees. [n. p. 1862.] 8vo, pp. 30. BA.

Address of the NEW-YORK YOUNG MEN'S ANTI-SLAVERY Society, to their Fellow-Citizens. *New-York: W. T. Coolidge & Co.* 1834. 8vo, pp. 38, (2). Continued. H. 54560

Also: Preamble and Constitution of the ... Society. Formed May 2, 1834. *New York.* 1834. 16mo, pp. 11. S.

Constitution of the NEW-YORK YOUNG MEN'S CHRISTIAN Association. ... *New-York: Theo. H. Gray, Printer.* 1852. 12mo, pp. 22. + With the Names of Officers ... for 1854. *New York.* 1854. 24mo, pp. 10, (2). B. 54561

Also: First Annual Report of the New-York Young Men's Christian Association, ... 1853 .... *New York.* 1853. 8vo, pp. 36. Continued. H.

First Annual Report of the NEW YORK YOUNG MEN'S SOCIETY, with the Constitution, By-Laws, and Standing Rules. Instituted May, 1831. *New York.* 1832. 8vo, pp. 26. N. 54562

See also No. 53514, *supra.*

Observations on supplying the City of New-York with Pure Water: ... *New-York: Printed by George P. Scott and Co.* 1832. 12mo, pp. 11. B. 54563

Observations on the Improvements. *See* [Hunn (John S.)]

Official Report of the Great Union Meeting, ... at the Academy of Music, ... December 19th, 1859. ... *New York: Davis & Kent, Printers.* 1859. 8vo, pp. 176. H. 54564

See "Report of Proceedings," No. 54626, *infra.*

On the expediency and practicability of a Time and Weather Observatory in ... New-York, By a Committee of the Chamber of Commerce. *New York.* 1857. 8vo, pp. 8. H. 54565

One Job of the Conspirators who govern our City. [*New York.* 1864.] 8vo, pp. 16. B. 54566

An Ordinance organizing the Departments of the Municipal Government of the City of New York, and Prescribing their Powers and Duties. *New York: McSpedon & Baker, Printers.* 1849. 8vo, pp. 208. B. 54567

Of this there are *two* editions, distinguished only by the type of the imprint differing

Ordinance to Divide the City ... into Convenient Election Districts. *New York.* 1859. 8vo. 54568

Ordinances of the Mayor, Aldermen and Commonalty of ... New York. Revised A. D. 1859, By D. P. Valentine. ... *New York: Chas. W. Baker, Printer.* 1859. 8vo, pp. xv, (1), 9–611.

The Annual Report of the ... ORPHAN ASYLUM SOCIETY, of New-York, for ... 1812. ... *New-York: Printed by Samuel Wood.* 1812. 12mo, pp. 12. Continued. H. 54570

Constitution of the Orphan Asylum Society, established in New York, March, 1806. *New York.* 1806. 12mo, pp. 42.

Also: The Constitution and Laws of the Orphan Asylum of ... New-York. ... *New-York: David Longworth.* 1808. 12mo, pp. 92. H. + [*Ibid.*] 1810. 12mo, pp. 71, (1). BA. + *New York.* 1815. 16mo.

Second Annual Report of the ORPHAN'S HOME of the Protestant Episcopal Church in New-York. ... 1853. *New-York: Van Norden & King.* 1854. 16mo, pp. 16. Continued. 54572

Also: Constitution and By-Laws of the Orphan's Home ... . *New-York: Van Norden & King.* 1854. 12mo, pp. 12. H.

Petition of the Inhabitants of New York on the subject of Common Schools. [n. p. n. d.] 8vo. 54573

Phelps' New York City Guide ... for Strangers and Citizens to the ... Objects of Interest ... . *New York.* 1852. 16mo. + *New York: T. C. Fanning.* 1853. 16mo, pp. 96. Map.

Phelps' Strangers and Citizens Guide to New York City. With Maps and Engravings. *New York: Phelps & Watson.* [1857.] 12mo. 54575

The Constitution of the PHILOLOGICAL SOCIETY in New-York. Instituted April 7, 1788. *New-York: Printed by Harrison and Purdy.* M.DCC.LXXXVIII. 8vo, pp. 7. 54576

Transactions of the PHYSICO-MEDICAL SOCIETY of New-York. Vol. I. ... *New-York: Printed ... by Collins & Co.* 1817. 8vo, pp. xxiii, (1), 446. H. 54577

Pictorial Business Directory of Wall Street, 1850. The Views Engraved by Michelin. *New York.* [1850.] Obl. 4to.

Picture of New York. *See* [Mitchill (S. L.)], XII. 49746.

The Picture of New-York, and Stranger's Guide to the Commercial Metropolis of the United States. *New-York: A. T. Goodrich.* [1828.] 18mo, pp. viii, 492. Plates and Map. BA.

This guide is valuable for the "Historical and Chronological Account of the Origin and Progress of the City." The Plan is dated 1817.

A Picture of New-York. *See* [Ruggles (Edward)].

A Plain Statement, addressed to the Proprietors of Real Estate, in the City and County of New-York. By a Landholder. ... *New-York: J. Eastburn and Co.* 1818. 8vo, pp. 62. B. 54580

Plan for Supplying the City ... with Fuel. By the New-York Coal Company. *New-York: Printed by T. & J. Swords.* 1814. 8vo, pp. 16. B. 54581

Plan of New York City, from the Battery to Spuyten Duyvil Creek. Showing every Lot and Building thereon, Old Farm Lines, Street Numbers, etc. etc. Based on the Surveys of Randall and Blackwell, and on the Special Survey of J. F. Harrison. *New York: M. Dripps.* 18—. Folio. 19 Maps. 54582

A Pocket Map & Visitor's Guide to the Central Park, in ... New-York ... . *New-York: P. Burger & Co.* 1859. 24mo, pp. 24. Map. 54583

Rules and Regulations for The Government of The POLICE DEPARTMENT of ... New-York: ... *New-York: Bowne & Co., ... Printers.* 1848. 12mo, pp. 90. 54584

Also: Municipal Police, or Day and Night Watch. Rules and Regulations prescribed by the Mayor, November 27, 1844. *New York.* 184–. 8vo. — Report of the Special Committee of the Common Council in relation to the Reorganization of the Police Department, May, 1843. *New York.* 1843. 8vo, pp. 381. 2 Maps. + [*Ibid.*] 1844.

Practical Directions for the holding of Elections; and the canvassing of Votes, under the New ... Law, principally applicable to the City of New-York; ... *New-York: Collins, Bowne & Co. Printers.* 1852. 8vo, pp. 54. H. 54585

Manual of the Seventh PRESBYTERIAN CHURCH ... New-York. [n. p. n. d.] 24mo, pp. 36. H. 54586

Manual for the Use of the First Free Presbyterian Church in ... New York. No. 3. *New York.* 1834. 32mo, pp. 72. + Second ... Church ... . [*Ibid.*] 16mo, pp. 47. + Third ... Church ... . No. 2. [*Ibid.*] 32mo, pp. 32.

First and Second Annual Reports of the PRESBYTERIAN HOSPITAL, in ... New York. ... *New York: Trow & Smith.* 1870. 8vo, pp. 47. Plate and Plan. Continued. B. 54587

Proceedings at a Numerous Meeting of the Citizens of New York [to oppose the Collection of the Duty on Tea]. *New York.* 1773. Folio, 1 leaf. 54588

Proceedings at the Mass Meeting of Loyal Citizens, Union Square, New-York, 15th ... July, 1862 ... . *New-York: George F. Nesbitt & Co., Printers.* 1862. 8vo, pp. 116. H. 54589

Proceedings at the Printers' Banquet, at Niblo's, Broadway. *New York.* 1850. 8vo, pp. 64. 54590

Proceedings of a Convention on the Location of the Post Office in New York. [n. p.] 1836. 8vo. 54591

Proceedings of a Meeting in favor of Municipal Reform, ... March 22d, 1844. *New York: Printed by W. B. & T. Smith.* 1844. 12mo, pp. 24. H. 54592

Proceedings of a Meeting of Citizens of New York and others, convened at the Request of the Board of Managers of the American Bible Society, May 13, 1816; with Speeches of George Griffin, and Peter A. Jay, Esq. *New York.* 1816. 8vo, pp. 12. + [n. p.] 1816. 8vo, pp. 16. S. 54593

Proceedings of a Meeting of Citizens of New-York, to express sympathy and respect for the Mexican Republican Exiles. ... July 19, 1865. ... containing the Speeches of the Hon. Matias Romero ... . *New-York: John A. Gray & Green, Printers.* 1865. 8vo, pp. 60. 54594

Proceedings of a Meeting of the Whig Young Men of ... New York, ... August 5th, 1834. ... *New York.* 1834. 8vo, pp. 23. 54595

Proceedings of an Union Meeting held in New York [December 15, 1860]. An Appeal to the South. *New York: John H. Duyckinck.* 1860. 8vo, pp. 36. 54596

Proceedings of the Boards of Aldermen and Assistant Aldermen ... . From ... 1831, to ... 1833. Vol. I. *New-York.* 1835. 8vo, pp. 586. Continued. H. 54597

Proceedings of the Board of Assistants, ... May 10, 1831, to May 8, 1832. Vol. I. *New York.* 1837. 8vo, pp. 476. Cont'd

Proceedings of the Board of Councilmen, of ... New York. ... April 7 to June 11, 1856 ... . Volume LXII. *New York: McSpedon & Baker, Printers.* 1856. 8vo, pp. 920, Index, 223.

Proceedings of the Board of Supervisors ... 1850. *New York: McSpedon & Baker, Printers.* 1850. 8vo, pp. 402, 59.

Proceedings of the Corporation ... in regard to Cemeteries in the City. [*New York.*] 1823. 8vo, pp. 18. 54601

Proceedings of the Corporation of New-York, on Supplying the City with Pure ... Water; with a Memoir by Joseph Browne, M.D. ... [*New York:*] *Printed by John Furman.* M,DCC,-XCIX. 8vo, pp. 29. B. 54602

Proceedings of the Democratic Republican General Committee of ... New York relative to the Death of Colonel William D. Kennedy. [n. p. n. d.] 8vo, pp. 6. 54603

The Proceedings of the Grand Reception extended By the Pupils of the Puplic Grammar Schools ... to Peter Cooper ... . *New-York: Pudney & Russell, Printers.* 1858. 12mo, pp. 9.

Proceedings of the Great Democratic Republican Meeting, in ... New York, January 2, 1838. *Washington: Madisonian Office.* 1838. 8vo, pp. 15. 54605

Proceedings of the Joint Meetings of the Board of Aldermen and Assistant Aldermen, from July 13th, 1831, to April 11th, 1836. *New York.* 1836. 8vo. S. 54606

Proceedings of the Loyal Mass Meeting ... at Cooper Institute, March 6, 1863. [n. p. n. d.] 8vo. 54607

Proceedings of the Meeting in relation to the Establishment of a Large National Bank in this City. *New York.* 1863. 8vo, pp. 8. 54608

Proceedings of the Merchants Great Democratic Meeting at the New York Exchange, ... 2d October, 1856. Correspondence of the Committees, and Speech of Governor Floyd of Virginia. *New York: Printed by John F. Trow.* 1856. 8vo, pp. 32

Proceedings of the Union Meeting, held at Castle Garden, October 30, 1850. ... *New-York: Union Safety Committee.* 1850. 8vo, pp. 62. 54610

Constitution of the PROTESTANT EPISCOPAL Clerical Association of ... New-York; and Forms of Prayer used by the Association. *New-York: Printed by E. Conrad.* 1828. 8vo, pp. 16. + *New-York: G. & C. & H. Carvill.* 1829. 8vo, pp. 16. H.

Also: Account of the True Nature and Object of the Late Protestant Episcopal Clerical Association of ... New-York, together with a Defense of the Association ... By the Members of the Association. ... *New-York: G. & C. & H. Carvill.* 1829. 8vo, pp. 48. — Brief Notice of an "Account of the True Nature and Object of the Late Protestant Episcopal Clerical Association of ... New-York" ... . *New York: T. & J. Swords.* 1829. 8vo, pp. 16. B.

Constitution of the PROVIDENT SOCIETY of New York. *New York.* 1801. 12mo. 54612

Public Documents of the City of New York, 1868. ... *New York.* 1869. 10 vols., 8vo. B. 54613

Public Education in ... New York. Its History, Condition and Statistics. An Official Report to the Board of Education. By Thomas Boese, Clerk of the Board. *New York: Harper & Brothers.* 1869. 8vo. B. 54614

An Address of the Trustees of the PUBLIC SCHOOL SOCIETY in ... New-York, to Their Fellow-Citizens, respecting the Extension of their Public Schools. *New-York: Printed by J. Seymour.* 1828. 8vo, pp. 18, (1). 54615

Also: By-Laws of the Trustees of the Public School Society of New York ... *New York.* 1826. 8vo. + *New-York: Mahlon Day, Printer.* 1836. 8vo, pp. 64. B. + [*Ibid.*] 1841. + [*Ibid.*] 1846. 8vo, pp. 60. — Dissolution of the ... Society ... . *New-York.* 1853. 8vo, pp. 8. — Journal of the ... Society. *New York.* 1854. 8vo. — Reply of the Trustees of the ... Society to the Address of the Roman Catholics. *New York.* 1840. 8vo, pp. 7. — Twenty-Eighth Annual Report of the Trustees of the ... Society ... *New-York: Printed by Mahlon Day.* 1833. 24mo, pp. 24. B.

Catalogue of the Officers and Members of the (Collegiate) REFORMED PROT. DUTCH CHURCH ... . 1841. *New-York: W. E. Dean, Printer.* [n. d.] Sm. 12mo, pp. 67. H. 54616

Also: Standing Rules for the Government of the ... Minister, Elders, & Deacons, of the Reformed Protestant Dutch Church ... . *New-York: Printed by J. Booth & Son.* 1837. 8vo, pp. 24. H.

Constitution of the RELIEF SOCIETY of New York. *New York.* 1800. 8vo. W. 54617

Remonstrance of the City Inspector, against the proposed Bill entitled "An Act to Improve the Public Health" ... . *New York.* 1858. 8vo, pp. 24. 54618

Reply to the Manifesto of the Trustees of the City Library. By a Plebian. ... [n. p. n. d.] 8vo, pp. 8. B. 54619

Report concerning the Woman's Central Association of Relief, at New York, October 12, 1861. [n. p. n. d.] 8vo, pp. 44.

Report in the Common Council, on the "Act for Suppressing Immorality" ... . *New York.* 1812. 8vo. 54621

Report of a Committee appointed by the Common Council of ... New York for devising Measures to Suppress Gaming and Drunkenness. *New York.* 1812. 8vo. 54622

Report of a Committee on the Subject of Pauperism. *New York.* 1818. 8vo. 54623

Report of Commissioners relative to Encroachments and Preservation of the Harbor of New-York. Transmitted ... January 8, 1856. *Albany: C. Van Benthuysen, Printer* ... . 1856. 8vo, pp. 163, (1). + January 29, 1857. [*Ibid.*] 1857. 8vo, pp. 335. Map and 8 Diagrams. B. 54624

Report of Committee on Commerce and Navigation, in relation to establishing Water Lines for part of the Harbor of New York. *Albany.* 1856. 8vo, pp. 8. Map. 54625

Report of New Buildings erected. *See* Leavitt (E.), Vol. X.

Report of Proceedings connected with The Great Union Meeting held at the Academy of Music, in ... New-York, December 19, 1859. *New-York: Davies & Roberts.* 1859. 8vo, pp. 97.

Relates chiefly to the "John Brown" invasion of Virginia. *See also* "Official Report," No. 54564, *supra.*

... Report of Special Committee on Volunteering, embracing a complete Statement of Operations in Filling the Quota of the County of New York under the Call of the President, Dated July 18, 1864, for 500,000 Men. *New York.* 1864. 8vo, pp. 962. 54627

... Report of Special Committee on Volunteering ... *New York: Wm. L. S. Harrison, Printer* ... . 1864. 8vo, pp. 340. + With ... a complete List of all Volunteers ... from August 1, 1863, to May 31, 1864. ... [*Ibid.*] 1864. 8vo, pp. 427. B.

Report of the Commissioners of Common Schools in ... New York. *Albany.* 1858. 8vo. Continued. 54629

Report of the Commissioners ... relative to supplying the City ... with Pure ... Water. November, 1833. *New-York: Printed by Peter Van Pelt.* 1833. 8vo, pp. 357–410. Maps. 54630

There are several other reports on this subject.

Report of the Committee appointed by the Inhabitants to consider of the Expediency of entering into Measures to encourage Industry and Frugality, and employ the Poor. *New York.* 1760. Folio, 1 leaf. 54631

Report of the Committee of Arrangements of the Common Council of ... New York, upon the Funeral Ceremonies in Commemoration of the Death of Gen. Andrew Jackson ... . *New-York.* 1845. 8vo, pp. 133–303. H. 54632

Report of the Committee of Merchants for the Relief of Colored People Suffering from the late Riots in ... New York. *New York: George A. Whitehorne, Printer.* 1863. 8vo, pp. 48. H.

Report of the Committee of the Common Council of New York on Public Schools. *New York.* 1825. 8vo. 54634

Report of the Committee of the Common Council upon the subject of New Streets ... . *New York.* [n. d.] 8vo. 54635

Report of the Committee of the Corporation, on the subject of Fortifying the Harbor of New York. *New York.* 1807. 8vo.

Report of the Committee on Laws, to the Corporation of ... New-York, on the subject of Interment ... . Adopted ... 9th of June, 1825 ... . *New-York: Printed by Mahlon Day.* 1825. 8vo, 75, (1). BA. 54637

... Report of the Committee on Substitutes and Relief of the Board of Supervisors. ... *New York: Wm. L. S. Harrison, Printer.* 1863. 8vo, pp. 91. B. 54638

Report of the Committee on Wharves, relative to the erection of a great Pier in the North River. ... *New York: Printed by William B. Townsend.* [n. d.] 8vo, pp. 421–513. 54639

Contains plans and a fac-simile of "A Plan of the City of New York from an actual survey made by James Lyne 1728. Printed by William Bradford."

Report of the Committee who presented the Report on Ambulance and Camp-Hospital Corps to the authorities in Washington. September 30, 1862. [n. p. n. d.] 8vo, pp. 3. 54640

A series of thirteen or more tracts. A detailed list is included in the "Literature of the Rebellion."

Report of the Joint Committee on Accounts, in relation to unreclaimed Warrants and Checks ... . *New York: Chas. W. Baker, Printer.* 1858. 8vo, pp. 46. H. 54641

Report of the Joint Committee on the subject of the Fire in New Street, which occurred July 19th, 1845. *New York.* 1845. 8vo, pp. 359. A. 54642

Report of the Joint Special Committee of the Chamber of Commerce and American Geographical and Statistical Society on the ... Decimal System ... . *New York: Wm. C. Bryant & Co., Printers.* 1857. 8vo, pp 22. H. 54643

Report of the Jury on Musical Instruments at the Crystal Palace ... . *New York: Baker, Godwin & Co., Printers.* 1853. 8vo, pp. 16. H. 54644

Report of the Majority of the Committee on Cities and Villages in relation to the Bill authorizing the Construction of a Railroad in New-York City. *Albany.* 1859. 8vo, pp. 11. M.

Report of the Select Committee. *See* Trinity Church.

Report of the Select Committee ... to inquire into the Application of that part of the Literature Fund, which is apportioned by the Regents of the University ... . *New-York: G. F. Nesbitt, ... Printer.* 1847. 8vo, pp. 24. H. 54646

Report of the Select Committee of the Senate, appointed to investigate the Health Department of ... New York. [By S. Ely, Jr.] *Albany.* 1859. 8vo, pp. 210. A., S. 54647

Report of the Special Committee appointed by the Common Council ... relative to the Catastrophe in Hague Street, ... February 4th, 1850. ... *New York: McSpedon & Baker, Printers.* 1850. 8vo, pp. 116. 54648

Report of the Special Committee of the Board of Councilmen ... on the use of Castle Garden as an Emigrant Depot. *New York.* 1856. 8vo. S. 54649

... Report of the Special Committee on County Volunteers of the Board of Supervisors ... . *New York: Wm. L. S. Harrison, Printer* ... . 1864. 8vo, pp. 60. B. 54650

Report of the Special Committee on the Subject of Railroads, with a Supplementary Communication, by Alderman Shaw. *New York.* 1850. 8vo. 54651

Report of the Special Committee Relative to Laying Out a New Park in the Upper Part of the City. [n. p. *Jan.* 2, 1852.] 8vo, pp. 83. Map and Table. 54652

Report of the "Union Committee" appointed by the Meeting ... held ... February, 1834, ... in ... New-York. *New-York: Harper & Brothers.* 1834. 8vo, pp. 34, (1). B. 54653

On the removal of the deposits.

Report of William Weston, Esq. on the Practicability of Introducing the Water of the River Bronx into ... New-York. [*New York:*] *Printed by John Furman.* M,DCC,XIX [for 1799]. 8vo, pp. 16. 54654

Report ... on the Encroachments upon the Bay and Harbor of New York, with the Report of E. L. Viele. *Trenton.* 1855. 8vo. 54655

Report on the Subject of Paying Interest on Current Deposits, presented to the Banks in New-York. *New-York: W. H. Arthur & Co., Printers.* 1858. 8vo, pp. 23. B. 54656

Report on the System of Popular Education in the City of New York; ... *New York: Wm. C. Bryant & Co., Printers.* 1851. 8vo, pp. 32. 2 Tables. 54657

Reports and Documents of the Union Defense Committee of the Citizens of New York. ... *New York.* 1861. 8vo, pp. 71.

Reports of the Majority and Minority of Special Committee on the Subject of Widening West Street. *New York.* 1851. 8vo.

Reports of the Special Committee appointed to make suitable Arrangements for bringing on from Mexico the Bodies of the Officers of the New York Regiment of Volunteers. And to prepare and present Medals to the New York Regiment of Volunteers. ... *New York.* 1850. 8vo, pp. 145. S. 54660

Republican Union Festival, New York, Feb. 22, 1862. Liberty and Union, One and Inseparable. Speeches on the occasion. *New York: G. P. Putnam.* 1862. 8vo, pp. 27. 54661

Report of the RESIDENT PHYSICIAN of the Lunatic Asylum, Blackwell's Island. [n. p. 1849.] 8vo, pp. 28. Continued.

Also: Annual Report of the Resident Physician of ... New York, for 1865. ... To the Board of Commissioners of Health .... *New York: Edmund Jones & Co., Printers.* 1866. 8vo, pp. 39. H.

Resolutions adopted at the Mass Meeting of the Loyal National League, in Union Square, New York, on the Anniversary of the Assault on Fort Sumter, April 11, 1863. [n. p. n. d.] 8vo, pp. 3. 54663

Return of Deaths in ... New York for ... 1804, 1805, 1806, 1807, and 1808. *New York.* 1809. 8vo, pp. 8. Continued.

Revenues and Expenditures for the year 1860. *New York.* 1861. 8vo, pp. 139. 54665

"A History of Taxation in New York."

Revised Ordinances of the Mayor, Aldermen, and Commonalty. [By William Kent.] *New York.* 1856. 8vo, pp. xii, 549.

Reports of the SANITARY ASSOCIATION of the City ... in relation to the Public Health. ... [*New York:*] *The Association.* 1859. 8vo, pp. 40. B. 54667

Shadows of the Metropolis. *See* [Laurence (I.)], IX. 39256.

Sketch of the Resources. *See* [Blunt (J.)], *also* Dix (J. A.)]

Annual Report of the SOCIETY FOR PROMOTING THE GOSPEL among Seamen in the Port of New York. *New York.* 1818. 8vo. Continued. 54668

Constitution and Fourth Annual Report of the SOCIETY FOR THE EMPLOYMENT and Relief of the Poor. *New York: G. & C. Van Beuren, Printer.* 1848. 12mo, pp. 15, (1). H. 54669

The First Annual Report of ... The SOCIETY FOR THE PREVENTION of Pauperism in ... New-York .... *New-York: Printed by J. Seymour.* 1818. 8vo, pp. 26, (1). Continued. B. 54670

Also: Documents relative to Savings Banks, Intemperance, and Lotteries. Published by ... the Society for the Prevention of Pauperism .... [n. p.:] *Printed by E. Conrad.* 1819. 8vo, pp. 26.—Report ... on Idleness and Sources of Employment. ... *New-York: Printed by Clayton & Kingsland.* 1819. 8vo, pp. 13.—Report of a Committee appointed by the Society ... on ... Erecting an Institution for the Reformation of Juvenile Delinquents. *New-York: Printed by Mahlon Day.* 1823. 8vo, pp. 56. + *New-York.* 1824. 8vo, pp. 64.

First Annual Report of the ... SOCIETY FOR THE REFORMATION of Juvenile Delinquents, in ... New-York. *New-York: Printed by Mahlon Day.* 1825. 8vo, pp. 52. Plate. Cont'd.

Also: Report of the Committee ... for erecting an Institution for the House of Refuge. *New York.* 1824. 8vo.—Rules and Regulations for the Government of the House of Refuge, as adopted by the Managers of the Society for the Reformation of Juvenile Delinquents in the City of New York, June 3d, 1825. *New York.* 1825. 8vo, pp. 20. S.

Fourth Annual Report of the SOCIETY FOR THE RELIEF of Half-Orphan and Destitute Children, New York. *New York.* 1840. 12mo, pp. 23. M. 54672

Constitution of the SOCIETY FOR THE RELIEF of Poor Widows. *New York.* 1799. 12mo. 54673

Constitution of the SOCIETY FOR THE RELIEF of the Destitute ... in ... New York, with an Address recommending the Society to Public Patronage. *New York: Printed ... by William A. Mercein.* 1827. 12mo, pp. 23. H. 54674

Report of the SOCIETY FOR THE SUPPORT of the Gospel among the Poor in ... New-York. *New-York: Printed by J. Seymour.* 1816. 8vo, pp. 16. Continued. 54675

An Act to Incorporate the SOCIETY OF MECHANICS AND TRADESMEN of the City ... for Charitable Purposes, passed the 14 of March, 1792. *New York: Saml. Loudon, Jr.* [n. d.] 12mo, pp. 11. 54676

An Act to Incorporate the SOCIETY OF TEACHERS of ... New York for Benevolent and Literary Purposes. Passed April 4, 1811. *New York.* 1811. 12mo, pp. 11. N. 54677

Constitution of the Society of Teachers of the City and County of New York. *New York.* 1811. 12mo, pp. 12. N.

Specification and Description of the Work and Materials ... for ... a Library Edifice, ... for the Trustees of the Astor Library. [*New York.* n. d.] 4to, pp. 37. B. 54679

Spring Water Versus River Water for Supplying the City of New York. *New York.* [n. d.] 8vo. Geological Chart.

The Stranger's Guide and Complete Handbook to ... New York. *New York: T. R. Foster.* 1863. 16mo, pp. 94. Map.

The Stranger's Guide through ... New-York. *New-York.* 1828. 18mo. Map and Plates. 54682

The Stranger's Hand-Book. For ... New-York; or, what to see, and how to see it. *New York.* 1854. 18mo, pp. 148. Map. + [n. p.:] *C. S. Francis & Co.* [n. d.] 18mo, pp. 172, (4).

Communication from the STREET COMMISSIONER, transmitting his Fourth Quarterly Report for ... 1859 .... *New York: Edmund Jones & Co., Printers.* 1860. 8vo, pp. 159, 2 folded leaves. Continued. H. 54684

Charter and By-Laws of the STUYVESANT INSTITUTE .... *New York: J. Narine, Printer.* 1837. 24mo, pp. 7. H. 54685

Articles of Association of the STUYVESANT SQUARE Home Guard, and Rules for its Government. Its Officers and Members. *New York.* 1864. 16mo, pp. 10.

A Summary Historical, Geographical, and Statistical View of ... New York; together with some notices of Brooklyn, Williamsburgh, &c., in its Environs. ... *New York: J. H. Colton & Co.* 1836. 18mo, pp. 46. Plate. B. 54686

... Annual Report of the SUPERINTENDENT OF BUILDINGS, For ... 1868. ... *New York.* 1869. 8vo, pp. 489. H. 54687

Also: Communication from the Superintendent of Buildings, transmitting his Semi-Annual Report for ... 1862. ... *New York: Edmund Jones & Co.* 1863. 8vo.

The System of Public Instruction in the State and City of New York. A Memorial, ... to the Legislature and the School Authorities by the German-American Citizens ... May, 1869. *New York: E. Steiger, Printer.* 8vo, pp. 15. H. 54688

Table of the Semi-Centennial Mortality of the City ... from the Records of the City Inspector's Department, from January 1, 1804, to December 31, 1853. [n. p. n. d.] Folio, 1 leaf. + 1804–1855. [n. p. n. d.] Folio, 1 leaf. H. 54689

Tables of Leading Statistics of the Five Dispensaries of New-York, for ... 1854, 1855, 1856 and 1857, with a History of the same .... *New-York: James Egbert, Printer.* [n. d.] 8vo, pp. 21. Plan. H. 54690

Tallis' New York Street Views. Drawn and Engraved on Steel by A. Tallis. *New York.* [1863.] Oblong 8vo. 54691

Report of the President of the THIRD AVENUE RAILROAD COMPANY to the Directors ... November, 1856. *New-York.* 1856. 8vo, pp. 16. S. 54692

Thirty Miles around New York by Railroad, Stage, Steamboat; or how to get in and out of the Metropolis. Compiled and Edited by T. Towndrow. *New York.* 1858. 16mo. A. 54693

Constitution of the THISTLE SOCIETY of ... New York. *New York.* 1806. 12mo, pp. 14. N. 54694

Three Days Reign of Terror, or the July Riots in 1863, in New York. ... [n. p. n. d.] 8vo, pp. 25. BA. 54695

To the Banks of ... New York. A Circular Letter relating to the Vulnerability of New York, and the Cost of Security. November, 1861. [n. p. n. d.] 8vo. 54696

To the Citizens of the Twenty-First Ward, New York, Oct. 29, 1861. [n. p. n. d.] 8vo. 54697

To the Electors of the City of New-York. [n. p. n. d.] 12mo, pp. 34. BA. 54698

To the Free Electors of the State. W. G. Gilbert, Chairman. *New York.* 1795. Folio. 54699

To the Memory of the Martyrs; Abraham Franklin, Peter Hueston, Wm. Jones, James Costello, and others, Slain in the Riots of July, in New York. Funeral Services, New York, September 20, 1863. [n. p. n. d.] 8vo, pp. 8. 54700

Tontine Coffee-House. *See* No. 54219, *supra.*

Trinity Church Title. *See* Trinity Church.

Trustees of the Leake and Watts Orphan House *v.* Lawrence et al. In the Court of Errors of New York, 1844. Case. *New York.* 1844. 8vo. 54701

Reports and Documents of the UNION DEFENSE COMMITTEE of the Citizens of New York. ... *New York: Edmund Jones & Co., Printers.* 1861. 8vo, pp. 71. BA. 54702

The Union of the Democracy .... Proceedings of the ... Mass Meeting, held at Tammany Hall, ... March 2, 1850, by the Democratic Republican Citizens of New York, opposed to the Wilmot Proviso .... *New York: Jared W. Bell, Printer.* 1850. Impl. 8vo, pp. 16. 54703

Catalogue of the Officers, Alumni, and Students, of the UNIVERSITY of the City of New-York. 1839–40. *New-York: Printed by Hopkins & Jennings.* 1840. 8vo, pp. 19. Continued.

Catalogue of the Students of the University of the City of New York. *New York.* 1842. 8vo. Continued.—Catalogue of the Psi Upsilon Fraternity. *New York.* 1847. 12mo, pp. 49.—Circular of the ... University of the City of New York. July, 1852. *New York: J. H. Jennings, Printer.* 1852. 12mo, pp. 12. B. Continued.—The Constitution and Statutes ... of the University .... *New York: William A. Mercein, Printer.* 1831. 8vo, pp. 21. B.

An Exposition by the Council of the University of ... New-York, respecting the late Measures of Retrenchment adopted ... which led to the Dismissal of some of the Professors. *New-York: ... University Press.* 1838. 8vo, pp. 96. B., S. 54705

An Exposition of the Reasons for the resignation of some of the Professors in the University .... *New-York: Printed by Jas. Van Norden.* 1833. 8vo, pp. 24. BA.

History of the Controversy in the University ... with ... Documents and Appendix. By the Professors of the Faculty of Science and Letters. *New-York: John S. Taylor.* 1838. 8vo, pp. 50, Appendix, xxviii. B., S. 54706

Inaugural Addresses, ... in the University ... at the opening of the Law School of that Institution. ... *New-York: E. B. Clayton, Printer.* M DCCC XXXVIII. 8vo, pp. 68. B., S. 54707

Addresses by B. F. Butler, W. Kent, and D. Graham, Jr.

Law Department of the University of ... New York. Annual Announcement ... 1858–9. *New-York: Hosford & Co., ... Printers.* [n. d.] 8vo, pp. 13, (1). H. 54708

A Letter to the Councillors [*sic*] of the University of ... New-York: from the Professors of the Faculty of Science and Letters. *New-York: ... University Press.* 1838. 8vo, pp. 16. B.

... Medical Department. Annual Announcement of Lectures ... MDCCCXLI–XLII. *New-York: Hopkins & Jennings, Printers.* 1841. 8vo, pp. 14, (1). Continued. B. 54710

Also: ... Catalogue of the Spring Course of Lectures, M.DCCC.XLIII. *New York.* 1843. 8vo, pp. 8.—Petition of the Medical Faculty of the University ... for the Legalization of Anatomy. Also, an Introductory Lecture .... By John W. Draper, M.D. ... *New-York: The Faculty.* 1853. 8vo, pp. 26.—University of the City of New-York. *New-York.* 1835. 8vo, pp. 16. Continued. S.

A View of the New York State Prison in the City of New York. By a Member of the Institution. *New York.* 1815. 8vo, pp. 89. S. 54711

Views in New-York, and its Environs, from Accurate, Characteristic and Picturesque Drawings, Taken on the Spot, expressly for this work, by Dakin, Architect; with Historical, Topographical and Critical Illustrations, by Theodore S. Fay, assisted by several Distinguished Literary Gentlemen. *New York.* 1831. 4to. 38 Plates and Map. 54712

Better known as "Peabody's Views." Davis's copy sold for $80. There are copies with proofs on India paper.

Visitor's Guide to the City of New York. *New York.* 18—. 18mo, pp. 36. 54713

Semi-Annual Report of the WATER COMMISSIONERS, for ... 1837. [n. p.:] *Printed by Order of the Common Council.* 1837. 8vo. 54714

Welcome to Charles Dickens. The Boz Ball. To be Given under the Direction of a Committee of Citizens of New York, at the Park Theatre, on the Evening of the Fourteenth of February next. *New York.* 1842. 8vo. 54715

West Side Association, relating to New York City Improvements, Parks [etc.]. *New York.* 1871. 8vo. 54716

The Wharves, Piers and Slips, belonging to the Corporation. 1868. East River. *New York: New York Printing Company.* 1868. Obl. 4to, pp. (6), 15, 68 leaves, 68 Plates. + North River. [*Ibid.*] 1868. Obl. 4to, pp. (4), 8, 67 leaves, 66 Plates.

NEW YORK—MISCELLANEOUS LIST.

Constitution of the NEW YORK AFRICAN SOCIETY for Mutual Relief. *New York.* 1808. 8vo, pp. 8. N. 54718

New-York Almanac, for ... 1833 .... By David Young, Philom. ... *New-York: Daniel D. Smith.* [n. d.] 12mo, pp. (36).

The New York Almanac and Weather Book for ... 1857 .... *New York: Mason Brothers.* 1857. 16mo, pp. 226. B. 54720

Prepared by E. Meriam. Continued as "The New York Almanac and Yearly Record for ... 1858" .... *New York: Mason Brothers.* 1858. 16mo, pp. 226. BA.

The New York Almanac for 1870. Edited by Julius Wilcox. ... *New-York: Francis Hart and Company.* [n. d.] 4to, pp. 60.

By-Laws of the NEW YORK AND AFRICAN Exchange Company. ... *New York: E. S. Dodge & Co., Printers.* 1866. 16mo, pp. 11. H. 54722

Also: Prospectus of the New York and African Exchange Company. ... *New York: E. S. Dodge & Co., ... Printers.* 1866. 8vo, pp. 8. H.

New York and Albany Rail-Road. [*New York.* 1833.] 8vo, pp. 40. Map. 54723

Also: Facts and Suggestions relating to the New-York and Albany Railroad. With the Act of Incorporation. *Albany: Printed by Packard ....* 1832. 8vo, pp. 32. B.—Memorial ... to the Legislature, March 6th, 1841. *New York.* 1841. 8vo.—Opinion of D. B. Ogden, ... Nov. 1840. [n. p. n. d.] 8vo.—Opinions of Charles McVean, John Anthon, and J. Prescott Hall, on the Subject of the New York and Albany R. R. Co. [n. p. 1840.] 8vo, pp. 6.—Report of E. F. Johnson, Esq., Chief Engineer. January, 1839. *New York.* 1839. 8vo, pp. 24.—Report of Joint Special Committee relative to the New York and Albany Railroad. July 24, 1840. [n. p. n. d.] 8vo.—Report of Joseph D. Allen, Esq., to the Commissioners ... November 15, 1836. *New York.* 1836. 12mo, pp. 16.— ... Sketch of the Remarks made by the President of the Company ... November 10, 1840. *New York.* [1840.] 8vo, pp. 15.—Statement in relation to certain Rights and Privileges Claimed by the said Company, and Remonstrating against Permission to the New York and Albany Railroad Company

to cross Harlem River opposite the Sixth or Seventh Avenue. *New York.* 1840. 8vo.—Statistical Facts ... showing the Importance of this Work to the City of New York and the Interior. *New York: Printed by William G. Boggs.* 1838. 8vo, pp. 7 S.

New York and Boston Oil Company. ... *Boston: Press of Geo. C. Rand & Avery.* 1864. 8vo, pp. 8. B. 54724

New York and Boston Railroad. [n. p. 1849?] 8vo, pp. 14. Map. B. 54725

Also: Engineer's Report .... 1847. *Middlebury.* 1847. 8vo.—Message of the Governor to the Legislature [of Connecticut] returning the Bill Chartering the New York and Boston Railroad Company. [*New Haven.*] 1846. 8vo.

Charter of the NEW YORK AND BOSTON STEAM-BOAT COMPANY, with the Report ... of the Stockholders, November 16, 1829. *New Bedford: Printed by Benjamin T. Congdon.* 1829. 8vo, pp. 11. 54726

Fifth Annual Report of the NEW YORK AND BROOKLYN AUXILIARY SOCIETY. *New York.* 1832. 8vo. 54727

The New-York and Brooklyn Coal Company. ... *New-York.* 1837. 8vo, pp. 22. 54728

Address of The Directors of the NEW YORK AND ERIE Railroad Company, To the Stockholders. February 1st, 1850. *New York: Snowden's Printing Establishment.* [n. d.] 8vo, pp. 13.

Also: Address ... October, 1844. *New York.* 1844. 8vo.—The Decision of ... the Lieutenant Governor, together with the Opinion of Mr. W. H. Seward, on the Question whether the Bill in relation to the New York and Erie Rail Road Company is a Majority Bill. *Albany.* 1843. 8vo, pp. 27.—The Impolicy ... of transferring the Terminus of the Erie Railroad from Piermont ... to Hoboken ... *Albany.* 1851. 8vo, pp. 24.—Inquiry into the Causes which have affected the Prospects and Condition of the New York and Erie Rail Road. *New York.* 1843. 8vo.—Memorial of the New-York and Erie Rail-Road Company, to the Legislature .... *New-York: G. P. Scott avd* [sic] *Co., Printers.* 1837. 8vo, pp. 20.—A Memorial to the ... New York & Erie Railroad Company, against changing the location of the Road through the Canisteo Valley. *Corning.* 1849. 8vo, pp. 15.—Report of the Committee on Railroads, on the Petitions of ... the New York & Erie Railroad Company. *New York.* 1838. 8vo, pp. 35.—Report of the Survey of the Route of the New-York and Erie Railroad, by Benjamin Wright; with Report of a Committee of the Common Council of New York. *New York.* 1835. 8vo, pp. 16.—Second Report of the Directors of the New York and Erie Railroad Company, to the Stockholders. February 3d, 1841. *New-York: Printed by Egbert Hedge.* 1841. 8vo, pp. 33, 15, (1). Continued. *See also* Vol. VIII., No. 30449, *and* Vol. IX., No. 42023.

The New-York and Farmer's Almanack, for ... 1830. ... By Thomas Spofford. *New York: David Felt.* [n. d.] 12mo, pp. 36. S. 54730

Steamers to Ireland. NEW YORK AND GALWAY Steam Ship Company .... *New York.* 1851. 8vo, pp. 10. S. 54731

... Copy of the Agreement of the NEW YORK AND HARLEM R. R. Co. with said City. Opinion of Wm. M. Evarts, Esq., Section of Charter ... . *New York.* 1858. 8vo, pp. 16. s.

Also: Case of the New York and Harlem Rail Road Company. *New York.* 1840. 8vo.—Memorial ... to the Mayor, Aldermen and Commonalty of the City of New York. *New York.* 1855. 8vo, pp. 24.—Office of the New York and Harlem Rail Road Company. New York, June 19th, 1840. [n. p. n. d.] 8vo, pp. 14. s.—A Statement of Facts in relation to the Origin, Progress, and Prospects of the ... Company. *New York.* 1833. 8vo.—Reply to a Pamphlet entitled "A Statement of Facts in relation to the Origin [etc.] ... of the ... Company." *New York.* 1833. 8vo.

Report of the Executive Committee upon the Statistics of Business, and of the Engineer of the Survey of the several Routes for the contemplated NEW YORK AND HARTFORD Railroad via Danbury. *Hartford.* 1845. 8vo, pp. 119. s. 54733

... Memorial and Petition of the Proprietors of the NEW YORK AND HAVRE Mail Steamers ... . [n. p.] 1852. 8vo, pp. 10. H.

First Annual Report of the Trustees of the NEW-YORK AND LAKE SUPERIOR Mining Company. ... February 24, 1846. *Albany.* 1846. 8vo, pp. 9. Map. B., s. 54735

Also: Amended Articles of Association ... April 24, 1846. *New York.* 1846. 8vo, pp. 14. s.—First Annual Report of the New York and Lake Superior Mining Company. ... February 24, 1846. *Albany.* 1846. 8vo, pp. 21. s.—Outlines of the Geological Structure of Lake Superior Mineral Region, belonging to the New York and Lake Superior Mining Company. Communicated by James Eights ... . *Albany.* 1846. 8vo, pp. 21. B.

Declaration of Trust and Articles of Agreement of the NEW YORK AND MICHIGAN COMPANY. January 30, 1837. [n. p. n. d.] 12mo, pp. 15. H. 54736

First Report of the Trustees of the NEW-YORK AND MICHIGAN MINING COMPANY. Detroit, 1 Dec. 1845. [n. p. n. d.] 8vo, pp. 10. 54737

The Report of the ... Directors ... of the NEW-YORK AND NEW-HAVEN Railroad Co., 22 August, 1849. *New-York: H. Cogswell & Co., Printers.* 1849. 8vo, pp. 47. Continued. B.

New-York and New-Jersey Almanac, for ... 1828 ... . By David Young, Philom. *New York: ... John C. Totten.* 1827. 12mo, pp. 34. s. 54739

... New York and Nicaragua Colonization Association. [n. p. 1862.] 8vo, pp. 8. H. 54740

An Act to Incorporate the NEW YORK AND STONINGTON Railroad Company, passed May, 1832. [*New York.* 1832.] 8vo, pp. 9. 54741

New York and Taconic Systems. [n. p. n. d.] 8vo, pp. 11.

First Annual Report of the NEW YORK AND TEXAS LAND and Emigration Association. New York, June, 1847. *New York.* 1847. 8vo, pp. 7. 54743

New York and The Five Cotton States, or Remarks on the Social and Economical Aspects of the Southern Political Crisis. *New York.* 1861. 8vo. 54744

By-Laws, etc., of the NEW YORK ASSOCIATION for the Advancement of Science and Art. ... *New York.* 1865. 8vo, pp. 12

Articles and Rules of the NEW-YORK ASSOCIATION for the Improvement of the Breed of Horses. *New-York: James Seymour.* 1823. 12mo, pp. 8. 54746

... New York Baptist Annual For 1870. ... *New York: James French.* [n. d.] 8vo, pp. 90. 54747

Minutes of the NEW YORK BAPTIST ASSOCIATION, held in New York, May ... 1793 ... [*New York.* 1793.] 4to. Cont'd.

Fifth Annual Report of the ... Trustees of the NEW-YORK BAPTIST UNION for the Ministerial Education, with the Proceedings ... together with the Constitution and By-Laws. *Rochester: Press of Curtis & Butts.* 1854. 8vo, pp. 56. Continued. H.

Report of Committee appointed by the NEW-YORK BOARD OF UNDERWRITERS to investigate the Causes of Loss of the ... Steamer Central America ... . *New-York: George F. Nesbitt & Co., Printers.* 1857. 8vo, pp. 7. + Second Part. [*Ibid.*] 1858. 8vo, pp. 16. H. 54750

Also: Report of the Committee on Gas Machines, Carburetters, ... to the New York Board of Fire Underwriters, ... 1869. *New York: Wm. H. Woglam & Reading, Printers.* 1869. 8vo, pp. 14, (1). B.

The New-York Book of Poetry. ... *New-York: George Dearborn.* 1837. 8vo, Engraved Title, pp. x, 253, (1). B. 54751

New York Cabinet. By J. N. Maffit, for September, 1830. *New York.* [n. d.] 8vo. 54752

The New York Catholic Register for 1863. ... *New York: D. & J. Sadlier & Co.* 1863. 12mo, pp. 24. Continued.

First and Second Annual Report of the NEW YORK CENTRAL COLLEGE ASSOCIATION, held ... July 4, 1849 and 1850. *Utica.* 1850. 8vo, pp. 12. s. 54754

Also: Catalogue of the Officers and Students for 1851–2. ... *Homer.* 1852. 8vo, pp. 16. Continued.—Minutes of the Fifth Annual Meeting, 1852 ... . *McGrawville, Cortland Co.* ... 1852. 8vo, pp. 16. Continued.—Origin, Design and Operation of New York Central College. [n. p. 1856.] 8vo, pp. 8. *See also* No. 53804, *supra*, and for McCrawville *read* McGrawville.

Annual Report of The NEW-YORK CENTRAL RAILROAD Company, for ... 1854. [n. p. 1854.] 8vo, pp. 8. Continued.

Also: ... Rates of Fare and Distances ... on the New-York Central Railroad. *Albany.* 1853. 8vo, pp. 102.—Report of a Committee appointed Jan. 4, 1855, on the "Acts and Doings of the Directors and Treasurer" ... Oct. 24, 1855. *Boston.* 1855. 8vo, pp. 47.—Report of the Committee of the Board of Directors ... October, 1855. *Albany.* 1855. 8vo, pp. 26.—Report of the New-York Central Rail-Road Company ... for ... 1854. *Albany: Weed, Parsons & Company.* 1854. Folio, pp. 12. Continued.—Review of the New-York Central Road's Official Exposé of the Causes which led to the Termination of the St. Nicholas Compact. April 11, 1859. [n. p. n. d.] 1859. 8vo, pp. 16. s.

An Address of the Directors of the NEW YORK CHEAP POSTAGE ASSOCIATION ... . *New York.* 1850. 8vo. + Second Edition. [*Ibid.*] 16mo, pp. 16. H. 54756

The New York Chronicle ... . Vol. II.—1850. Edited by Rev. Orrin B. Judd. ... *New York: Holman & Gray.* 1850. 8vo, pp. 387. 6 Portraits. B. 54757

First Annual Announcement of the NEW YORK COLLEGE of Dental Surgery at Syracuse, N. Y. *Syracuse.* 1851. 8vo, pp. 12

New York Colonial Tracts. *See* Vol. IV., No. 13402, Vol. IX., No. 36748, *and* Voyages.

New York Comic Almanack for 1847. [*New York:*] *T. W. Strong.* [n. d.] 12mo, pp. 24. s. 54759

Catalogue of the Officers and Students of the NEW YORK CONFERENCE SEMINARY, Charlotteville, Schoharie County, N. Y., ... First Term, 1850–51. *Albany.* 1851. 8vo, pp. 23. s.

New York Conspiracy Trials. *New York.* 1827. 8vo.

Address of the NEW YORK DEMOCRATIC ASSOCIATION of Washington, on the Presidential Question. [n. p. 1856.] 8vo, pp. 8. s. 54762

... The New York Dental Journal. Edited by W. B. Roberts and Frank H. Norton. July, 1861. Vol. IV. ... *New York: W. B. Roberts.* 1861. 8vo. Continued. 54763

Constitution of the NEW-YORK DENTAL Protective Union. *New-York: Chatterton & Parker, Printers.* 1862. 12mo, pp. 6, (1)

New York Dental Recorder. Edited by Charles W. Ballard, D.D.S. Vol. I. ... *New York.* 1847. 8vo. Continued.

Minutes of the NEW YORK EAST CONFERENCE, Eleventh Session. April, 1859. *New Haven, Conn.* [1859.] 8vo, pp. 32.

Address at the Thirty-Ninth Annual Session of the NEW YORK EASTERN Christian Conference ... . *Irvington, N. J.* 1857. 18mo, pp. 24. s. 54767

The New-York Ecclesiologist ... No. I.—October, MDCCCXLVIII. ... *New-York: H. M. Onderdonk.* [n. d.] 8vo, pp. 48. Continued. H. 54768

The Laws of the NEW-YORK ECCLESIOLOGICAL Society, ... with a Statement of the Object and Intended Operations of the Society. ... *New-York.* 1848. 24mo, pp. 7, (1). H. 54769

Also: Transactions of the New York Ecclesiological Society. 1855. ... *New-York: Daniel Dana, Jr.* 1857. 4to, pp. 90. Plates. H.

Constitution, By-Laws and Rules ... of NEW YORK ENCAMPMENT of Patriarchs, No. 1. of Northern New York. *Albany.* 1852. 18mo, pp. 36. s. 54770

New York Farmer and American Gardener's Magazine. Samuel Fleet, Editor. D. K. Minor, Proprietor. Vol. VI. *New York.* [1833.] 4to. Continued. s. 54771

The New-York Farmer, and Horticultural Repository. ... Under the Patronage of the New-York Horticultural Society. S. Fleet, Editor. ... Vol. I. *New-York.* 1828. 8vo. Continued. 54772

The New York Farmer and Mechanic ... S. Fleet, Editor. ... *New York.* 1843. 8vo. Continued. 54773

The New York Farmer's Almanac, for ... 1821. ... By David Young, Philom. *New York: Printed by Charles N. Baldwin.* [n. d.] 12mo, pp. 36. s. 54774

The New York Fraud. The Conspiracy of the Officeholders Unmasked. ... [*Boston:*] *Boston Harrison Club.* [1840.] 12mo, pp. 24. B. 54775

The New-York Gardener ... . By P. Agricola. *Albany: Daniel Steele & Son.* 1824. 18mo, pp. 214, (2). 54776

Circular of the NEW-YORK GAS REGULATOR Company. ... *New-York.* [n. d.] 8vo, pp. 16. H. 54777

The New York Genealogical and Biographical Record. Devoted to the Interests of American Genealogy and Biography. Issued Quarterly. Volume I., 1870. *New York City: The Society.* [n. d.] 8vo, pp. (4), 8, 52. Continued. H. 54778

Bulletin of the New York Genealogical and Biographical Society. Vol. I. No. I. *New York.* 1869. 8vo, pp. 8. Cont'd.

Also: By-Laws Certificate of Incorporation and Officers ... . *New York: George F. Nesbitt & Co., Printers.* 1869. 8vo, pp. 16.—A Form for Genealogical Records. [*New York.* 1870.] 4to, 2 leaves. C.

New York Hards and Softs: Which is the True Democracy? A Brief Statement of Facts for the Consideration of the Democracy of the Union ... . By a National Democrat. *New York.* 1856. 8vo, pp. 80. B. 54780

A Brief Exposition of the Claims of the NEW-YORK INDIANS to certain Lands at Green Bay, ... Michigan ... . [n. p. 1829.] 8vo, pp. 40. B. 54781

Also: ... Documents approving Of the Treaty made with the New York Indians. April 23, 1838. Presented by Mr. White ... . [n. p. n. d.] 8vo, pp. 5.—... Message of the President of the United States, transmitting Treaties with the Indians in the State of New York, ... [etc.] and ... Documents relating thereto. April 23, 1838. ... [n. p. n. d.] 8vo, pp. 103.— ... Message from the President of the United States, transmitting The amended Treaty with the New York Indians, and certain documents relating thereto ... 1840. ... [n. p. n. d.] 8vo, pp. 296. B.

Act to Incorporate the Stockholders of the NEW YORK INSURANCE Company, 2d April, 1798. *New York.* 1798. 8vo, pp. 15.

The New York Journal. ... An Illustrated Literary Periodical. ... *New York: P. D. Orvis.* 1854. 2 vols., 4to, pp. 376; 258.

New York Journal of Medicine, Edited by J. S. Purple, M.D., Stephen Smith, M.D., and D. H. Bulkley, M.D. ... *New York.* 1843. 8vo. Continued. 54784

New York Journal of Medicine and Surgery. Vol. I. *New York.* 1839. 8vo. Continued. 54785

The New York Journal of Medicine, and the Collateral Sciences. Edited by Samuel Forry, M.D. Vol. I. *New York: J. & H. G. Langley.* 1843. 8vo, pp. 431. Plates. Continued.

New York Journal of Pharmacy, ... Edited by Benjamin W. McReady, M.D. ... Vol. I. No. I. January, 1852. *New York: Joseph W. Harrison, Printer.* [n. d.] 8vo. Continued. H.

New York Judicial Repository. Edited by D. Bacon. ... Vol. I. *New York.* 1818. 8vo. Continued. s. 54788

A History of the NEW-YORK KAPPA Lambda Conspiracy. ... *New-York: William Stuart.* MDCCCXXXIX. 8vo, pp. 32. B.

The New York Lancet. Vol. I. No. I. Jan., 1842. *New York.* [n. d.] 8vo, pp. 16. H. 54790

The New-York Legal Observer, containing Reports of Cases ... Remarkable Trials, Sketches of the Bench and the Bar, Anecdotes ... . Edited by Samuel Owen. October, 1842–April, 1843. Vol. I. *New York: S. Owen.* 1843. 8vo, pp (2), viii, 423. Continued. C. 54791

January 1st, 1863. Eighteenth Annual Report of the NEW-YORK LIFE Insurance Company. ... *New-York: Francis Hart & Co., Printers.* [n. d.] Sm. 16mo, pp. 69, (3). B. 54792

Prospectus of the NEW-YORK LIFE Insurance and Trust Company. *New-York: Printed by Bryant & Co.* 1846. 12mo, pp. 36. + *New-York: Bowne & Co., Printers.* 1851. 24mo, pp. 36. H. 54793

Also: In Chancery. Before the Chancellor. In the matter of the New-York Life Insurance and Trust Company. Order, Answer, and Report. April, 1832. *New York.* 1832. 8vo, pp. 68. + Answer and Report. *New York.* 1835. 8vo, pp. 64. + Answer and Report. 1838. *New York: J. Van Norden.* 1839. 8vo, pp. 71. + Order and Report. May, 1843. *New York: Wm. G. Boggs, Printer.* [n. d.] 8vo, pp. 68.—Rates and Proposals of the New York Life Insurance and Trust Company. Incorporated March 9, 1830. *New York.* 1830. 8vo, pp. 40.—Report ... March 19, 1831. *Albany.* 1831. 8vo. C.

New-York Literary and Scientific Repository. *New York.* 1820–1822. 4 vols., 8vo. 54794

The New York Literary Gazette, and Phi Beta Kappa Repository. Vol. I. No. 8. [James G. Brooks, Editor.] *New York.* 1825. 8vo. Continued. BA. 54795

The New-York Literary Journal, and Belles Lettres Repository. Volume I. ... *New York: A. T. Goodrich & Co.* 1819. 8vo, pp. (2), 480, vi. Continued. B. 54796

Previously "The Belles-Lettres Repository."

The New York Magazine: a Rochester New Monthly. January, 1853. *Rochester, N. Y.: James E. Duryee.* [n. d.] 8vo. Portrait. H. 54797

New York Magazine and General Repository of Useful Knowledge. By James Hardie. Vol. I. ... *New York.* 1814. 8vo. 54798

The New-York Magazine; or, Literary Repository. ... *New-York: Printed by T. and J. Swords.* 1790–97. 6 vols., and New Series, 2 vols., 8vo. 54799

Memorial of the NEW YORK MAIL Steamship Company, ... to the Senate and House ... on Ocean Steam Navigation. ... *New York: Latimer Bros. & Seymour.* 1864. 8vo, pp. 12. Map. H.

New York Marine Register: a Standard of Classification of American Vessels, and of such other Vessels as visit American Ports. *New York: Root & Anthony.* 1857. 4to. C. 54801

The New-York Medical and Philosophical Journal and Review. Vol. I. *New-York: Printed ... by T. & J. Swords.* 1809. 8vo, pp. 316, iv. Continued. B. 54802

The New-York Medical and Physical Journal. Edited by John W. Francis, M.D. ... Vol. I. *New-York: E. Bliss and E. White.* 1822. 8vo, pp. vii, 528. BA. 54803

Continued to nine or more volumes.

The New-York Medical and Surgical Reporter. Edited by Clarkson T. Collins, M.D. ... Vol. I. No. I. October 18, 1845. *New York: Wiley & Putnam.* [n. d.] 8vo, pp. 20. Continued.

Final Report of the NEW YORK MEDICAL ASSOCIATION for the supply of Lint, Bandages, etc. to the United States Army. ... *New York: The Association.* 1861. 8vo, pp. 32. H. 54805

Fifth Annual Announcement of the NEW YORK MEDICAL COLLEGE for Women, 1867–8. *New York.* 1867. 8vo.

The New York Medical Gazette. Volume I. *New York: Uriah Turner, M.D.* 1842. 8vo, pp. iv, 416. Continued. B.

The New-York Medical Gazette, and Journal of Health. ... Edited by D. Meredith Reese, M.D. ... Vol. I. ... July 6, 1850. No. I. [n. p. n. d.] Folio, pp. 15. Continued. H. 54808

The New York Medical Independent, and Pharmaceutical Reporter. ... Vol. I. ... *New York.* 1864. 8vo. H. 54809

The New York Medical Journal. Volume I. *New York: Miller & Mathews.* 1865. 8vo, pp. viii, 480. Diagrams. Continued. B. 54810

The New-York Medical Magazine; ... Edited by Valentine Mott, M.D. ... and Henry U. Onderdonk, M.D. ... Vol. I. *New-York: Printed by H. Van Riper.* 1815. 8vo, pp. (8), 364. Continued. BA. 54811

The New-York Medical Press: ... Edited by J. L. Kiernan, ... M.D., and W. O'Meagher, M.D. ... *New York.* 1860. 8vo.

The New York Medical Times. J. G. Adams, M.D., Editor, ... Vol. I. *New York: Printed ... by Baker, Godwin & Co.* 1852. 8vo, pp. vi, 4, 384. Continued. B. 54813

New-York Medico-Chirurgical Bulletin. ... Edited by George Bushe, M.D. Vol. I. May 1, 1831. No. I. [n. p. n. d.] 8vo, pp. 156. Plates. Continued. H. 54814

The New York Mercury Extraordinary. April 9, 1783. *New York.* 1783. Folio. 54815

New York Messenger. *New York: S. Brannan.* 1845. 8vo.

A Mormon journal, in continuation of the "Prophet." Edited by P. P. Pratt.

The New-York Military Magazine; ... . Volume I. *New York: Labree & Stockton.* 1841. 8vo, pp. viii, 410. BA. 54817

The New York Mirror: A Weekly Journal, devoted to Literature and the Fine Arts. Embellished with ... Engravings, and Music ... . *New-York.* 1831. Folio. Continued. B. 54818

The New-York Mirror, and Ladies' Literary Gazette. ... Edited by Samuel Woodworth and George P. Morris. ... Volume I. *New-York: George P. Morris.* 1824. 4to. 54819

Woodworth's name is omitted in Vol. II. *et seq.* This periodical was commenced August 2, 1823, and terminated with the twentieth volume, December 24, 1842. During its career almost every writer in America, whether celebrated or obscure, contributed to its columns. Complete sets with all the plates of the series are very scarce.

The New-York Missionary Magazine, and Repository of Religious Intelligence; for ... 1800. Vol. I. *New-York: Printed by T. & J. Swords.* 1800. 8vo, pp. vii, (1), 400. Continued.

The New York Monthly. Vol. I. ... [n. p. 1854.] 8vo.

New York Monthly, and Working Women's Advocate. Vol. I. ... *New York.* [1864.] 4to. H. 54822

The New York Monthly Register and United States Complete Bankrupt's Gazette. By Edward Tremayne. ... *New-York: The Proprietor.* 1842. 8vo. H. 54823

New York Musical Pioneer ... . I. B. Woodbury, Editor. Vol. I. ... *New York: F. J. Huntington.* [1856.] 8vo. H.

The New York Musical World. ... July 4, 1857. ... *New York.* [n. d.] 4to. H. 54825

The New York Mutual Life Insurance Company. Examination of Witnesses before George W. Miller, Superintendent of the Insurance Department of the State of New York, in relation to certain Charges against the Officers and Trustees of the Mutual Life Insurance Company ... . [*New York.* 1870.] 8vo, pp. 263. C. 54826

Also: Explanation to the Policy-Holders of the ... Mutual Life Insurance Company of New-York, for ... 1858–'62 ... . *New-York: John A. Gray & Green, Printers.* [n. d.] 8vo, pp. 18.—Matured, Paid-up, and Single Payment Endowments in the ... Company ... . *New-York: John A. Gray & Green, Printers.* 1869. 12mo, pp. 28.—The Mutual Life Insurance Company of New York ... . *New York: W. E. Dean, Printer.* 1845. 8vo, pp. 16.—A Treatise on Life Insurance: ... . *New York: W. E. Dean, Printer.* 1844. 12mo, pp. 36. H. *See also* Vol. XII., No. 51610.

Annual Report of the NEW YORK NATIONAL FREEDMAN'S Relief Association ... with a Sketch of its early History. ... *New York: Holman, Printer.* 1866. 8vo, pp. 30. H. 54827

See also Vol. XII., No. 51983.

The New York Navigation and Colonization Company. Olancho. An Account of the Resources of the State of Honduras, in Central America: especially of the Department of Olancho. *New York: Wynkoop & Hallenbeck.* 1865. 8vo, pp. 65. C. 54828

The New York Needlewoman; or, Elsie's Stars. By the Author of "The Shoebinders of New York," etc. *Philadelphia.* 1868. 16mo, pp. 204. 54829

Continuance of Correspondence between the International Ocean Telegraph Company and the NEW YORK, NEWFOUNDLAND, and London Telegraph Co. *New York: R. C. Root, Anthony & Co.* 1870. 8vo, pp. 14. H. 54830

The New-York News-Letter. A Journal of Instructive and Entertaining Literature. Julius Wilcox, Editor. ... *New York: Francis Hart & Company.* [1868.] 4to. Continued. C. 54831

The New York Observer Year Book. 1871. [*New York:*] *S. E. Morse & Co.* [1871.] 8vo. Continued. C. 54832

New York Organ Pictorial Temperance Almanac for 1852. Adapted for use throughout the Country. *New York: American Temperance Repository.* [n. d.] 12mo, pp. 48, and covers. S.

New York Pathfinder. *New York.* 1853. Folio. C. 54834

Continued to Vol. III. or more.

Circular to the Members of the New York Φ B K Society, in relation to Literary and Scientific Transactions. *Schenectady: S. S. Riggs, Printer.* 1833. 8vo, pp. 8. B. 54835

The New-York Phonographic Journal, ... edited by Augustus F. Boyle, and Oliver Dyer. Vol. I. January, 1851. No. I. ... [n. p. n. d.] 12mo, pp. 24. Continued. B. 54836

New-York Pocket Almanack. *See* Gaine (H.), *and* Moore (T.), add to No. 50441, For ... 1760. 16mo, pp. 48.

New-York Price-Current, Published ... by James Oram ... . August 16, 1800. [n. p. n. d.] 4to. Continued. BA. 54838

An Act to Incorporate the NEW YORK, PROVIDENCE and Boston Railroad Company ... 1832. *Providence: B. Cranston & Co.* 1832. 8vo, pp. 10. 54839

Also: Acts of the Legislatures of Rhode Island and Connecticut, relating to the New York, Providence and Boston Railroad Company, and the New York and Stonington Railroad Company. *New York: James Van Norden.* 1837. 8vo, pp. 39. Map.—Report of the Directors of the New York, Providence and Boston Railroad Company, to the Stockholders, at their Annual Meeting, Providence, September 26, 1844. *New York: Francis Hart.* 1844. 8vo, pp. 8.—Some Remarks shewing the Advantages of the Proposed Railroad from Providence to Stonington, with the Acts of Incorporation. *Providence.* 1833. 8vo, pp. 14, 12, 9. Map.

The New York Pulpit in the Revival of 1858. A Memorial Volume of Sermons. [By Twenty-Five Preachers.] *New York: Sheldon, Blakeman & Co.* 1858. 12mo, pp. 395. C.

The New York Quarterly. Edited by A. G. Remington. Vol. I. ... 1852. *New York: Cornish, Lamport & Co.* [n. d.] 8vo. Continued. H. 54841

New-York Quarterly Magazine ... . [n. p.] 1836. 8vo, pp. (4), 119. BA. 54842

New York Railroads in 1858. [n. p. n. d.] 8vo, pp. 312. Map. 54843

New York Register and Antimasonic Review. ... Vol. I. No. I. ... *New York.* 1831. 8vo, pp. 16. Continued. H. 54844

The New-York Register of Medicine and Pharmacy. Vol. I. No. I. October, 1850. [n. p. n. d.] 8vo, pp. 16. Cont'd.

The New-York Review. Vol. I. *New-York: George Dearborn & Co.* 1837. 8vo, pp. iv, 510. Continued. BA. 54846

Published quarterly. Edited successively by C. S. Henry, and J. G. Cogswell.

The New-York Review and Atheneum Magazine. ... *New York: E. Bliss & E. White.* 1825–6. 2 vols., 8vo, pp. iv, 492; 484. 54847

Edited by William C. Bryant. No more published.

The New York Review and Quarterly Church Journal. ... *New York: Hosley.* 1837–1842. 10 vols., 8vo. 54848

The New-York Review; or, Critical Journal. ... March, 1809. ... *New-York: Inskeep & Bradford.* [n. d.] 8vo. BA.

The New York Sanitary and Chemical Compost Manufacturing Company. ... *New York.* 1865. 8vo, pp. 32. H. 54850

The Act of Incorporation and Constitution of the NEW YORK SOCIETY, for Promoting the Manumission of Slaves ... . *New-York: Printed by Samuel Wood.* 1810. 8vo, pp. 23. BA. + Revised and adopted April 28, 1835. *New York.* 1835. 8vo, pp. 15

Also: A Discourse to the ... Society for Promoting the Manumission of Slaves ... . *New York.* 1797. 8vo.

New York Shipping and Commercial List and Price Current. *New York.* 1815. 4to. Continued. C. 54852

The New York Social Science Review: devoted to Political Economy and Statistics. Edited by Alex. Delmar and Simon Stern. ... *New York.* 1866. 2 vols., 8vo. C. 54853

New York Songster; a Choice Collection of the most New and Popular American, English, Irish, Scotch, Comic, Hunting, Love, Bacchanalian, and Sea Songs, for 1836. *New York.* 1836. 12mo, pp. 124. Portraits. 54854

Transactions of the NEW YORK SOUTHERN CENTRAL Medical Association. ... *Binghampton: The Association.* 1851. 8vo, pp. 121, (1), 8. Continued. B. 54855

The First Annual Report of the NEW YORK SOUTHERN SUNDAY School Union, auxiliary to the American Sunday School Union, for ... 1830. *New-York: The Society.* 1830. 8vo, pp. 23. Continued. H. 54856

The New-York Sporting Magazine, and Annals of the American ... Turf. *New-York: C. R. Colden.* 1833. 8vo, pp. 346. Colored Plates. 54857

The New-York Teacher. Published ... [by] the New-York State Teachers' Association. ... Vol. I. ... *Albany: Joel Munsell.* [1853.] 8vo. Continued. H. 54858

The New York Teacher, and American Educational Monthly: devoted to Popular Instruction and Literature. January, 1868. *J. W. Schermerhorn & Co., New York.* [n. d.] 8vo. Continued.

New York Theological Magazine, or Synopsis of Modern Religious Sentiment ... . *New York: T. and J. Edwards.* 1726–7. 2 vols., 8vo. 54860

The reviews of contemporary religious discussions and books are interesting. It also contains copies of republished letters of John Elliot, the Indian Missionary. Title from J. C. Hotten's catalogue.

Index to the NEW YORK TIMES for 1865. Including the Second Inauguration of President Lincoln, ... and the Close of the War of Secession. *New York: Henry J. Raymond & Co.* 1866. 8vo, pp. 182. 54861

New York Tract Magazine and Christian Miscellany. Vol. I. No. I. [n. p. n. d.] 8vo. 54862

The New York Traveller ... through the State. ... *New York: J. Disturnell.* 1845. 18mo, pp. 48. S. 54863

New York Visiter [*sic*] and Parlor Companion. *New York.* 1838–40. 2 vols., 8vo. Plates. S. 54864

The illustrations include scarce portraits of J. W. Wallack, Ellen Tree, Mrs. Keeley, the Steamer Lexington, etc.

Act to Incorporate the NEW YORK WASHINGTON MUTUAL Assurance Company. Instituted 1801. *New York.* 1802. 8vo, pp. 20. N. 54865

Also: Charter, By-Laws, Rates of Insurance ... . *New York.* 1809. 8vo, pp. 22.

The New-York Weekly Magazine; or, Miscellaneous Repository; forming an interesting Collection of Original and Select Literary Productions in Prose and Verse. Edited by John Bull. Vol. I. ... *New York: John Bull.* 1796. 4to, pp. viii, 408. Frontispiece. C., S. 54866

New York Weekly Museum, or Polite Repository of Amusement and Instruction, dedicated to the American Fair. *New York.* 1814–17. 4 vols., 8vo. A. 54867

Proceedings of the NEW YORK YOUNG MEN'S State Convention, assembled 4th July, 1838, at Utica. [n. p. n. d.] 8vo.

New Yorker, *pseudon.* *See* [Hoffman (C. F.)], VIII. 32389.

New-Yorker Volks-Kalender, 1850. *Druck und Verlag von Magnus u. Bach, in New York.* [n. d.] Sm. 4to, pp. 36. S.

NEWARK, *Del.* Catalogue of the Officers and Students of Newark Academy, the Preparatory Department of Delaware College, 1847–'8. *Philadelphia.* 1848. 8vo, pp. 19. S. 54870

Also: By-Laws of Newark College ... . [n. p. n. d.] 12mo, pp. 8.—Catalogue of the Officers and Students of Newark College, Newark, Del., 1839–40. *Philadelphia.* 1840. 8vo, pp. 17. Continued.—Laws of Newark College. ... 1841. *Philadelphia.* 1841. 8vo, pp. 24. *See also* Vol. XII., No. 52451.

NEWARK, *N. J.* The City Charter and Ordinances of ... Newark ... . With an Appendix. ... *Newark, N. J.* 1858. 8vo, pp. xv, 400. B. 54871

The Clayonian Lectures. Seventh Season. Newark, N. J. *New York: James Sutton & Co.* 1870. 24mo, pp. 13, (4). H.

Constitution of the Female Society for the Relief of Poor and Distressed Persons in Newark. *Newark, N. J.* 1803. 8vo, pp. 8. 54873

Directory of Newark, for 1835–6. With an Historical Sketch of Newark. *Newark, N. J.* 1835. 12mo, pp. 24, 102.

Pierson's Directory of the City of Newark, for 1836–7. By B. T. Pierson. *Newark.* 1836. 12mo, pp. 168, Charter, 34. + For 1845–46. ... *Newark, N. J.: Aaron Guest, Printer.* 1845. 12mo, pp. 244. + [*Ibid.*] 1852. + For 1855–56. Twenty-First Edition. ... *Newark, N. J.: A. Stephen Holbrook, Printer.* 1855. 12mo, pp. 432

Boyd's Newark Business Directory, ... with An Appendix ... . 1857. Compiled by

William H. Boyd ... . *Newark, N. J.: A. L. Dennis & Bro.* [n. d.] 12mo, pp. xi, 160.

Pierson's Newark City Directory for 1863–4. ... By Charles H. Folwell. *Newark.* 1863. 8vo.

Newark City Directory for 1864–5. By Chas. H. Folwell & Co. *Newark.* [n. d.] 12mo, pp. 419, 72.

Newark City Directory for 1865–6. *Newark: James Gopsill.* [n. d.] 12mo, pp. viii, xxxiv, 49–616. + For ... 1868. *Newark: James Gopsill.* [n. d.] 8vo, pp. 698.

Holbrook's Newark City Directory, for 1867–8. *Newark: A. S. Holbrook.* [n. d.] 8vo, pp. 639, xli.

Gopsill's Newark City Directory, for ... 1869. *Jersey City: James Gopsill.* [n. d.] 8vo, pp. xlvii, 641.

Holbrook's Newark City Directory, for ... 1872. *Newark: A. S. Holbrook.* 1871. 8vo.

Message of Moses Bigelow, Mayor of ... Newark, N. J. ... 1857. *Newark: Jacksonian Office.* 1857. 8vo, pp. 8. H.

Newark Academy, New-Jersey. Young Ladies' Department, ... *Newark: Printed by William Tuttle.* MDCCCVIIII. 12mo, pp. 12. H. 54876

Also: Key to the Quarterly Catalogues of the ... Young Ladies, at the Newark Academy, ... with a Historical Sketch of the Academy. *Newark: Printed by William Tuttle.* MDCCCX. 12mo, pp. 12.—Quarterly Catalogue of the Young Ladies' Department ... . *Newark.* 1809. 16mo, pp. 32. M.

Report to the Board of Directors of the NEWARK AND NEW YORK RAILROAD COMPANY. By Alfred F. Sears. *Newark.* 1866. 8vo. 54877

Constitution of the NEWARK BIBLE SOCIETY with the First Annual Report. *Newark.* 1815. 8vo, pp. 16. 54878

Articles of Association and Systems of Organization and Regulations ... of the NEWARK FIRE ASSOCIATION. *Newark.* 1797. 12mo, pp. 24. + [*Ibid.*] 1807. 8vo, pp. 20. 54879

The Charter and By-Laws of the NEWARK LIBRARY ASSOCIATION. *Newark, N. J.* 1856. 12mo, pp. 17. S. 54880

Also: Catalogue of the Library of the Newark Library Association. ... [By F. W. Ricord.] *Newark: Douglass & Starbuck, Printers.* 1857. 8vo, pp. 148. B.

First Jubilee of the NEWARK MECHANICS' ASSOCIATION ... American Independence, and Tribute to Adams and Jefferson. Including an Address by Wm. S. Pennington. *Newark.* 1826. 8vo. 54881

Obsequies of Abraham Lincoln. *See* Vol. VII., No. 25828.

Proceedings Commemorative of the Settlement of Newark, New Jersey, on its Two Hundredth Anniversary, May 17th,

1866. *Newark: New Jersey Historical Society.* 1866. 8vo, pp. 182. B. 54882

This constitutes the supplement to Vol. VI. of the New Jersey Historical Society "Collections."

Records of The Town of Newark, New Jersey, from its Settlement in 1660, to its Incorporation as a City in 1836. *Newark, N. J.* 1864. 8vo, pp. xi, 294. Map. 54883

Tenth Anniversary of the North Reformed Dutch Church, Newark, N. J. *Newark: Daily Advertiser Office.* 1867. 8vo, pp. 38. 54884

NEWARK, *N. Y.* Catalogue of the Officers and Students of New Union Free School and Academy, 1864–65. *Newark, N. Y.* 1865. 8vo, pp. 35. S. 54885

NEWBERN, *N. C.* By-Laws of the Newbern Guards, ... with Their Articles of Association ... . 1822. *Newbern: Printed by Pasteur & Watson.* 1823. 8vo, pp. 32. H. 54886

Constitution and By Laws of the Board of Trade of ... Newbern, N. C. *Newbern, N. C.* 1866. 12mo, pp. 24. 54887

New Bern Mercantile and Manufacturers' Business Directory, ... By Capt. R. A. Shotwell. *New Bern, N. C.: W. I. Vestal.* 1866. 8vo, pp. 56. Map. H. 54888

NEWBERRY (J. S.) Catalogue of the Flowering Plants and Ferns, of Ohio. By J. S. Newberry, M.D. *Columbus: Richard Nevins, Printer.* 1860. 8vo, pp. 41. B. 54889

NEWBERRY. Fossil Fishes from the Devonian Rocks of Ohio. By J. S. Newberry, M.D. ... [n. p. 1857.] 8vo, pp. 8. H.

NEWBERRY. Notes on the later extinct Floras of North America, with Descriptions of some new Species of Fossil Plants from the Cretaceous and Tertiary Strata. By J. S. Newberry, ... *New York.* 1868. 8vo, pp. 76. 54891

NEWBERRY. ... Report on the Condition of the Troops, and the Operations of the Sanitary Commission in the Valley of the Mississippi, for the Three Months ending November 30th, 1861. By J. S. Newberry, M.D. ... *Cleveland: Fairbanks, Benedict & Co.* 1861. 8vo, pp. 48. 54892

NEWBERRY. ... Report on the Operations of the U. S. Sanitary Commission in the Valley of the Mississippi, For the Quar-

ter ending Oct. 1st, 1864. By Dr. J. S. Newberry ... . [n. p. n. d.] 8vo, pp. 29, (1.) H. 54893

NEWBERRY. Report on the Progress of the Geological Survey of Ohio in 1869. By John S. Newberry ... . *Columbus.* 1870. 8vo. C. 54894

NEWBERRY. The Rock Oils of Ohio, By J. S. Newberry. ... [n. p. n. d.] 8vo, pp. 16. H. 54895

NEWBERRY. The United States Sanitary Commission in the Valley of the Mississippi, during the War of the Rebellion, 1861–1866. *Cleveland.* 1871. 8vo. 54896

Also: ... An Address ... before the American Association for the Advancement of Science, August, 1867. ... *Salem, Mass.: Essex Institute Press.* 1867. 8vo, pp. 23.—... Brief Report Of the Operations of the Sanitary Commission in Tennessee, May, 1862. ... [n. p. n. d.] 8vo, pp. 12.—Report on the ... Geology of the ... Ashtabula and New Lisbon Rail Road ... . *Cleveland.* 1857. 8vo, pp. 47. Plate.—... Report on the Sanitary Condition of the United States Troops in the Mississippi Valley, August, 1861. ... [n. p. n. d.] 8vo, pp. 11.—... A Visit to Fort Donelson for the Relief of the Wounded. ... February 15, 1862. [n. p. n. d] 8vo, pp. 10.—... What the U. S. Sanitary Commission is doing in the Valley of the Mississippi. Letter from Dr. J. S. Newberry to Hon. W. P. Sprague. [*New York.* 1863.] 8vo, pp. 31. + [n. p. n. d.] 8vo, pp. 23. *See also* Vol. IX., No. 35308, *note.*

NEWBERY (F.) An Historical Account of all the Voyages round the World, performed by English Navigators ... . *London: F. Newbery.* 1773–4. 4 vols., sm. 8vo. 50 Maps, etc.

Reissued with an additional volume or Appendix, containing Phipps' and Capt. Lutwidge's Journal of a Voyage to the North Pole.

[NEWBERY (J.)] A Curious Collection of Travels, Selected from the Writers of all Nations. In which the Conjectures and Interpolations of Several vain Editors and Translators are expunged, Every Relation is made concise and plain, and The Divisions of Countries and Kingdoms are clearly and distinctly noted. Illustrated ... . *London: J. Newbery.* MDCCLXI. 7 vols., 8vo, pp. (12), 208; (4), 211; (10), 191; (14), 214; (14), 203; (10), 205; (14), 220. 54898

NEWBOLD (E. L.) Fight for the Flag, and Live by the Cross. By Miss E. L. Newbold, Bellevue, Ohio. [n. p.:] *Am. Tract Society.* [n. d.] 8vo. 54899

NEWBURGH, *N. Y.* Catalogue of Manuscripts and Revolutionary Relics deposited in Washington's Headquarters, Newburgh. *Newburgh.* 1858. 8vo, pp. 52. + [*Ibid.*] 1874. 8vo, pp. 74. Plates. 54900

Catalogue of ... the Mechanics' Library Association of Newburgh; ... with the Act of Incorporation ... . *Newburgh: S. T. Callahan, Printer.* 1843. 8vo, pp. 16. H. 54901

Catalogue of ... the Library ... of the First Presbyterian Church, Newburgh, N. Y. ... 1858. *Newburgh: Gray & Lawson, Printers.* [n. d.] 8vo, pp. 16. H.

Charter of the Bank of Newburgh. *Newburgh.* 1811. 12mo, pp. 11. N. 54902

Fifth Annual Report of the Commissioners of the Alms House of ... Newburgh. ... 1857 ... . *Newburgh, N. Y.* 1857. 8vo. 54903

Also: Newburgh Poor System. Report of Committee and Proposed Law. [n. p. 1852.] 8vo, pp. 8. S.

A Correct Copy of the Charter of the Glebe Lands, in the Village of Newburgh. [*Newburgh, December,* 1809.] 8vo, pp. 8

Wilson's Newburgh Directory for 1856–'57. Containing a General Directory, a Business Directory, or Classification of the various Professions, Trades, etc., a Street Directory, and an Appendix containing much useful and interesting information, By H. Wilson. *Newburgh: H. S. Banks.* 1856. 8vo, pp. 114.

Hutchinson's Newburgh Directory, for 1860–61, and an Appendix. By Thomas Hutchinson. *Newburgh: D. Smith.* [1860.] 12mo.
Newburgh Directory for 1864–65; with a Business Directory of Fishkill Landing and Mattewan, and an Appendix ... . By J. H. Lant & Co. *Newburgh: Charles Estabrook.* [n. d.] 12mo, pp. iv, 120.
Newburgh General and Business Directory, for 1868. Compiled by E. Carter. *Newburgh: E. M. Ruttenber & Co.* 1867. 8vo, pp. 158.
Carter's Newburgh City Directory, with a Complete Business Directory attached, for ... 1869. Published by Carter & Minty. *Newburgh: C. Jannicky.* 1868. 8vo. + For ... 1870. *Newburgh (N. Y.): C. Jannicky.* 1869. 12mo, pp. 192. Map. + For ... 1871. *Newburgh (N. Y.): E. Carter.* 1870. 8vo. C.

Annual Report of the Water Commissioners, for 1868–9. *Newburgh.* 1869. 8vo. Continued. 54906

Newbury, *Mass.* Annual Report of the Receipts and Expenditures of ... Newbury, for ... 1860. *Newburyport: William H. Huse & Co., Printers.* 1860. 8vo, pp. 14. Continued. B.

Expenses of the Town of Newbury, ... with the School Report, for ... 1850. *Newburyport: Moses H. Sargent.* 1850. 12mo, pp. 60, 14. H. 54908

Report of the School Committee of ... Newbury, for ... 1859–60. *Newburyport: William H. Huse & Co., Printers.* 1860. 8vo, pp. 8. Continued. B. 54909

Newbury, *Vt.* Catalogue of the Officers and Students of Newbury Seminary, Vt., for ... 1846. *Newbury, Vt.* 1846. 8vo, pp. 23. S. 54910

Newburyport, *Mass.* The Addresses and other Proceedings, at the Laying of the Corner Stone, of the New Town Hall, in Newburyport, July 4th, 1850. *Newburyport: Huse & Bragdon.* 1850. 8vo, pp. 24. H. 54911

Centennial Commemoration of the Death of George Whitefield, in Newburyport, 1870. [n. p. n. d.] 8vo, pp. 58.

City of Newburyport. The Mayor's Address, at the Organization of the City Council; and the Treasurer's Annual Report, for ... 1863. ... *Newburyport: William H. Huse & Co., Printers.* 1864. 8vo, pp. 78, (1). Continued. H. 54913

City Treasurer's Statement of the Receipts, Expenditures, &c., of ... Newburyport, For ... 1852. ... *Newburyport: William H. Huse, Printer.* 1853. 8vo, pp. 56. Continued. H. 54914

The Directory of Newburyport. ... 1849. ... Published Annually by Wooster Smith. *Newburyport: C. Nason, Printer.* 1848. 18mo, pp. 119. Map. Continued. H. 54915

Edited successively by C. A. Dockham and N. P. Brown, John E. Tilton, Caleb Niles Haskell, and Sampson, Davenport & Co.

History of the Founders of the Federal Street Church, Newburyport, from 1745 to 1862. *Newburyport.* 1862. 8vo.

Communication addressed to the First Religious Society in Newburyport, at a Meeting ... the Seventh of May, 1823 ... . [n. p. n. d.] 8vo, pp. 8. H. 54917

Also: Constitution of the Sunday School Association ... of the First Religious Society ... April, 1832. *Newburyport: Printed by E. W. Allen & Co.* 1832. 12mo, pp. 11.

The Ladies' Friendly Society. ... Report of the Committee on Organization. ... May 6, 1869. [n. p. n. d.] 12mo, pp. 6. H.

Acts of Incorporation, and By-Laws of the Marine Society of Newburyport ... . *Newburyport: Printed by Whitton & Hale.* 1846. 16mo, pp. 48. B. 54919

The Municipal Register containing the City Charter and Ordinances, ... of ... Newburyport. *Newburyport: William H. Huse & Company, Printers.* 1869. 8vo, pp. 257. B. 54920

Music performed at Newburyport, Mass., Jan. 2, 1800. Hymns adapted and set to Music by Samuel Holyoke. *Exeter, N. H.* [n. d.] Obl. 8vo, pp. 12. 54921

In respectful memory of George Washington.

Catalogue of the ... Newburyport Female High School, from Dec. 19, 1843 to Dec. 19, 1856. *Newburyport: M. O. Hall.* 1856. 12mo, pp. 24. Continued. H.

A Statement of the Proceedings resulting in the purchase of the Newburyport Public Library Building. With ... the History of the Library. ... *Newburyport: Wm. H. Huse & Co., Printers.* 1866. 8vo, pp. 43. Plate. B. 54922

Also: Catalogue of the Public Library of the City of Newburyport. *Newburyport: William H. Huse & Co.* 1857. 8vo, pp. 207. — First Annual Report of the ... Public Library, of ... Newburyport. *Newburyport.* 1857. 8vo, pp. 11. Continued. — The Rules and Regulations of the Public Library, of ... Newburyport, ... 1854. *Newburyport.* 1855. 12mo, pp. 12. H.

Annual Report of the ... Newburyport Railroad Company, for ... 1853. *Newburyport: Wm. H. Huse, Printer.* 1853. 12mo, pp. 12. Continued. B. 54923

Newburyport Resolutions, &c. [*Newburyport: E. W. Allen, Printer.* 1809.] 8vo, pp. 14. B. 54924

On an act of Congress, laying the embargo, etc.

Particular Account of the Great Fire, at Newburyport, May 31, 1811. ... [*Newburyport.* 1811.] 8vo, pp. 8. H. + An Account ... . Second Edition, Improved. *Newburyport: Printed by W. & J. Gilman.* 1811. 12mo, pp. 23, (1). B. 54925

Catalogue of the Putnam Free School, Newburyport, Mass. [n. p.] 1848. 8vo.

Articles and Regulations of the Relief Fire Society, 1775. [n. p. n. d.] 16mo, pp. 8. M. 54926

A Report of the Proceedings. *See* Bragdon (J. H.), II. 7320.

[Report of] the School Committee of Newburyport, for ... 1841–42 ... . [n. p. n. d.] 8vo, pp. 15, (1). Continued. H.

Address by the Washington Benevolent Society in Newburyport, Feb. 22, 1816. *Newburyport.* 1816. 8vo. 54928

Newcastle, *Del.* Proceedings of the Newcastle County Agricultural Society and Institute, ... at Wilmington, ... Sept., 1843, with the Address ... by William Darlington, M.D. *Wilmington: Allderdice, Jeandell & Miles—Printers.* 1843. 8vo, pp. 58, (1). H., P. 54929

Transactions of the Agricultural Society and Institute of Newcastle County, Delaware, at the Ninth Annual Meeting, 1844. ... *Wilmington.* 1844. 8vo. P. 54930

See also New-Castle, Vol. XII., Nos. 52562–71.

Newcomb (H.) A Cyclopedia of Missions; containing a Comprehensive View of Missionary Operations throughout the World; with Geographical Descriptions, and Accounts of ... the People. By Rev. Harvey Newcomb. *New York: Charles Scribner.* 1854. 8vo, pp. 784. Plates and Maps. + Revised Edition. ... [*Ibid.*] 1855. 8vo, pp. 792. Plates and Map. H. + Second Revised Edition. [*Ibid.*] MDCCCLX. 8vo, pp. 792.

Newcomb. The Harvest and the Reapers; Homework for All, and how to do it. By Rev. Harvey Newcomb ... . *Boston: Gould and Lincoln.* 1859. 12mo, pp. (2), 270. B. 54932

Newcomb. The North American Indians: ... By Harvey Newcomb. *Pittsburgh: Luke Loomis.* [1835.] 2 vols., 18mo, pp. 169; 169. 54933

Also: The Faded Flower: or, History of Charles P. ... Third Edition. *Boston: Massachusetts Sabbath School Society.* 1850. 24mo, pp. 54. — Memoir of Phebe Bartlett, of Northampton, Mass. ... *Philadelphia: American Sunday School Union.* [1831?] 24mo, pp. 35. — The Wyandot Chief: or the History of Barnet, a converted Indian, and his Two Sons. ... *Boston: Massachusetts Sabbath School Society.* 1835. 18mo, pp. vi, 9–92. + Second Edition, Revised. [*Ibid.*] 1839. 24mo, pp. 81. H.

[Newcomb (John B.)] The Bearss Family. [*Elgin, Ill.* 1852.] 8vo, pp. 2. 54934

Newcomb (Richard E.) ... An Address, ... before the Temperance Society at Ashfield, Mass., in 1838. By R. E. Newcomb ... . *Greenfield: L. Merriam, Printer.* 1845. 8vo, pp. 14.

Also: Oration at Greenfield, Mass., July 4, 1799. *Greenfield.* 1799. 8vo.

Newcomb (S.) A Critical Examination of our Financial Policy during the Southern Rebellion. By Simon Newcomb. *New York: D. Appleton and Company.* 1865. 12mo, pp. 222.

Newcomb. On the Latitude and Longitude of the U. S. Naval Observatory, Washington ... . By ... Simon Newcomb, U. S. N. [n. p.] 1864. 4to, pp. 9. H. 54937

[Newcome] (R.) A Sermon ... before the ... Society for the Propagation of the Gospel in Foreign Parts, ... February 20, 1761. By the Right Rev. ... Richard Lord Bishop of Landaff. *London: E. Owen.* MDCCLXI. 4to, pp. 88. M. 54938

Newcome (T.) Original State Epigrams and minor Odes. By Thomas Newcome. *London.* 1760. 8vo. 54939

Includes several poems on the British conquests in America.

Newcomer (C.) The Life and Journal of the Rev'd Christian Newcomer, Late Bishop of the Church of the United Brethren in Christ. Written by Himself ... Transcribed by John Hildt ... . *Hagers-Town: Printed by F. G. W. Kuph.* 1834. 12mo, pp. (4), 330. 54940

Newdegate (C. N.) A Collection of the Customs' Tariffs of all Nations; based upon a Translation of the work of M. Hübner, augmented by Additional Information, brought down to ... 1854. By C. N. Newdegate, M.P. ... *London: John Murray.* 1855. 4to, pp. (2), iii, (4), 368, Errata, (3). 54941

Newe and strange Newes from S. Christopher of a tempestuous Spirit, which is called by the Indians a Hurrycano or Whirlwind ... . *London.* 1638. 12mo. 54942

Partly in verse.

Drey newe Relationes Erste auss Japon, was sich darinn, so wol in Geist- als Weltlichen Sachen im Jahr Christi 1606, denckwürdigs zugetragen. Andere von Missionibus oder Reisen, so etliche Priester der Societet Jesu, im Jahr 1607, in das Königreich Mexico angestelt. Dritte von Ableiben des mächtigen Königs Mogor und wienach selbigem in seinem Reich das Religion und Politisch Wesen beschaffen. Aus underschidlichen der Societet Jesu Lateinischen Italianischen und Portugesischen Schreiben verteutscht. *Augspurg, C. Dabertzhofen.* 1611. 4to.

Newe Schwarmgeister-Bruit, oder Historische Erzählung. I. Von den Quäkern. II. Der Ranter. III. Dess Robins Sect. IV. Der Wiedereinnehmung der Juden in Engeland. V. Der Indianer in New-Engeland. *Im Jahr* 1661. 12mo. 54944

Newe vnbekanthe landte. *See* [Montalboddo (F.)], XII. 50056

Newe Welt. *See* [Abelin (Jean-Philippe)], Vol. I., No. 50.

Der Newe Welt-Bott. *See* Stöcklein (Josephus).

Newe Zeytung | aus Hispanien und | Italien. | Mense Februario. | 1534. | [n. p.] 4to, 4 leaves. L. 54945

Essentially the same as the "Copia delle Lettere," Vol. IV., No. 16669, but more succint. "Of excessive rarity, and appears to have been printed at Nuremberg. It contains the first tidings of the discovery of Peru, and remains unknown to all the bibliographers which we have consulted."—Libri. *See* [Harrisse] "Bib. Am. Vet.," No. 195.

Newe zeittung . von dem lande . das die | Sponier funden haben ym 1521. iare genant Jucatan. | Newe zeittung vô Pruszla/ vô Kay: Ma: hofe 18 Martze. 1522. | Newe zceyt von des Turcken halben von Offen geschrieben. | [n. p. n. d.] 4to, Title, 1 leaf, Text, 5 leaves. 54946

The only known copy is in the Royal Library at Berlin, from which a few copies were reproduced in facsimile, about 1850. *See* [Harrisse] "Bib. Am. Vet.—Additions," No. 70.

Newell (A.) Good Men, under God, the Strength and Defence of a People: a Discourse, ... at Goshen, January 17th, A. D. 1768: occasioned by the ... Death of Deacon Moses Lyman ... . By Abel Newell. *Hartford.* 1768. 12mo, pp. 49.

Newell (C.) History of the Revolution in Texas, particularly of the War of 1835 and '36; together with the latest Geographical, Topographical, and Statistical Accounts of the Country. By Chester Newell. *New York: Wiley & Putnam.* 1838. 12mo, pp. xii, 215. Map. 54948

Newell (D.) The Life of Rev. George Whitefield. By Rev. D. Newell. *New York: D. Newell.* [1846.] 12mo, pp. (4), viii, 7–218. Portrait. S. 54949

Newell (Ebenezer F.) Life and Observations of Rev. E. F. Newell, ... Forty Years an Itinerant Minister in the Methodist ... Church ... *Worcester: C. W. Ainsworth.* 1847. 24mo, pp. 288. Portrait. 54950

Newell (F.) Diary of Fanny Newell; with a Sketch of her Life ... . Fourth Edition ... . *Boston: Charles H. Peirce.* 1848. 18mo, pp. 252. 54951

Newell. Memoirs of Fanny Newell; Written by Herself, ... Second Edition, With Corrections and Improvements. ... *New-York: Francis S. Wiggins.* 1833. 12mo, pp. 216. + Third Edition ... . *Springfield: G. and C. Merriam, Printers.* 1833. 12mo, pp. 216. H. 54952

The statement on the title of the so-called third edition, that it has "Corrections and Improvements," is, on the part of the publishers, a pious fiction. It is simply a reprint of the second edition.

Newell (F. R.) ... A Sermon ... in Littleton, at the Funeral of Jacob Gault Elliot, M.D. ... Nov. 26, 1854. By Frederick R. Newell. *Boston: Crosby, Nichols, and Company.* 1855. 8vo, pp. 14. H. 54953

Newell [Fred. S.] Newell's Notes on the Licentious Treatment of the American Female Slaves. *London: W. Tweedie.* [1864.] Sm. 8vo, pp. 15. 54954

For an explanatory letter, by the author, *see* "Newell's Notes on Tar and Feathers" ... *London: W. Tweedie.* [1864.] 8vo, pp. 15, (1). Also: Newell's Notes on Abraham Lincoln. ... *London: W. Tweedie.* [1864.] 8vo, pp. 15.

Newell (H.) The Life and Writings of Mrs. Harriet Newell. Revised Edition. [By Leonard Woods.] *Philadelphia: American Sunday-School Union.* 1831. 12mo, pp. 267. Portrait. C. + [*Ibid.*] 1832. 54955

Newell. Memoirs of Mrs. Harriet Newell, wife of the Rev. S. Newell, American Missionary ... Added a Sermon on her Death, ... by Leonard Woods, D.D. ... [Edited by William Jaques.] *London: Booth & Co.* 1815. 12mo, pp. 266. + The Fourth Edition. With an Appendix, containing, A Sermon on ... her Death, An Account of the American Missions ... . *Edinburgh: J. Ogle.* 1816. 12mo, pp. 216. + *Edinburgh: Ogle, Allardice, & Thomson.* 1817. 12mo, pp. 228. Portrait. + *Utica, N. Y.* 1818. 12mo. + A New Edition. *Glasgow: Printed by W. Falconer.* 1823. 12mo, pp. 228. Portrait. 54956

Newell (J.) An Aged Minister's Review of the Events and Duties of Fifty Years: A Sermon, Preached at Stow, Oct. 11, 1824. By Jonathan Newell ... . *Concord: Allen & Lamson, Printers.* 1825. 8vo, pp. 20. W. 54957

Newell. A Sermon ... at Stow, on the 16th of May, 1783, By Jonathan Newell ... . *Boston: Printed by John Gill.* M.DCC.LXXXIV. 8vo, pp. 27. H., M. 54958

Contains much local history.

[Newell (Robert Hasell).] The Martyr President. [A Poem.] *New York: Carleton.* M DCCC LXV. 8vo, pp. 43. H.

Five hundred copies printed. "Written in a single evening."—Manuscript note by the author on my copy.

[Newell.] The Orpheus C. Kerr Papers. *New York: Blakeman & Mason.* 1862. 12mo, pp. 382. + Second Series. *New York: Carleton.* M DCCC LXIII. 12mo, pp. 267. + Third Series. [*Ibid.*] M DCCC LXV. 12mo, pp. 300. B. 54960

Also: Avery Glibun; or, Between Two Fires. A Romance. ... *New York: G. W. Carleton & Co.* M DCCC LXVII. 8vo, pp. 301. — The Cloven Foot: being an adaption of ... "The Mystery of Edwin Drood" ... to American Scenes, Characters, Customs, and Nomenclature. ... *New York: Carleton.* M DCCC LXX. 12mo, pp. 279. — The Palace Beautiful, and Other Poems. ... *New York: Carleton.* M DCCC LXV. 12mo, pp. 178, (1).

Portrait and Plates. — Smoked Glass. ... With Illustrative Anachronisms by Thomas Worth. *New York: G. W. Carleton.* M DCCC LXVIII. 12mo, pp. 277.

Newell [Samuel]. A Correction of erroneous Statements concerning the Embarkation of the Rev. Messrs. Judson and Newell, at Salem, February 18, 1812. ... *Boston: Press of T. R. Marvin.* 1849. 8vo, pp. 24. B. 54961

Newell (S.) Sermon in Remembrance of Mrs. Harriet Newell, By S. Newell, with Life ... by L. Woods. *Boston.* 1814. 8vo. Portrait. 54962

Newell (T. M.) Proceedings of a Naval General Court Martial, held at Norfolk, Va., Sept. 1834. On board the U. S. Frigate Java, in the case of Master Commandant Thomas M. Newell, of the U. S. Navy. *Washington City: B. Homans.* 1835. 8vo, pp. 77, 29. C. 54963

Newell (W.) A Discourse on the Cambridge Church-Gathering in 1636; Delivered ... February 22, 1846. By William Newell ... . *Boston: James Munroe and Company.* 1846. 8vo, pp. 65. H. 54964

Newell. Memoir of the Rev. Convers Francis, D.D. By Rev. William Newell, D.D. ... *Cambridge.* 1866. 8vo, pp. 23.

Reprinted from the "Proceedings of the Massachusetts Historical Society."

Newell. The Pastor's Remembrances. A Discourse ... in Cambridge, ... May 27, 1855, By ... William Newell, on the completion of the twenty-fifth year of his ministry. ... *Cambridge: John Bartlett.* 1855. 8vo, pp. 36. H. 54966

Newell. Two Discourses ... before the First Parish in Cambridge; one, upon leaving the Old Meeting House, and the other, at the Dedication of the New. By William Newell. *Cambridge: James Munroe and Company.* 1834. 8vo, pp. 56. H. 54967

Also: ... A Discourse ... before the First Parish in Cambridge, ... January 22, 1854. ... *Cambridge: John Bartlett.* 1854. 8vo, pp. 21. — ... A Discourse ... in Cambridge, ... after the Death of Mrs. Harriet F. Webster, October 16, 1853. ... *Cambridge: John Bartlett.* 1853. 8vo, pp. 16. — ... A Discourse ... in Cambridge, ... [after] the Death of Mr. Andrews Norton, September 25, 1853. ... *Cambridge: John Bartlett.* 1853. 8vo, pp. 32. — ... Discourse occasioned by the Death of Jared Sparks, LL.D. ... March 18, 1866, ... in Cambridge ... . *Cambridge: Sever and Francis.* 1866. 8vo, pp. 23. — A Discourse occasioned by the Death of the Hon. Joseph Story, LL.D., ... Sept. 14, 1845. ... *Cambridge: Metcalf and Company.* 1845. 8vo, pp. 23. — ... A Discourse occasioned by the Death of Charles Beck ... . *Cambridge: Sever and Francis.* 1866. 8vo, pp. 17. — Notice of the Life and Character of Mr. Andrews Norton. ... *Cambridge: Metcalf and Company.* 1853. 12mo, pp. 30. — Our National Legislature. A Discourse

... in Cambridge, on the ... Annual Fast, ... April 7, 1842. ... *Cambridge: John Owen.* 1842. 8vo, pp. 20. — Two Discourses occasioned by the Death of Jared Sparks, LL.D. and Charles Beck, LL.D. ... *Cambridge.* 1866. 8vo, pp. 23, 17. — The Year's Remembrances. A Discourse ... in Cambridge, ... December 31, 1848. ... *Cambridge: Metcalf and Company.* 1849. 8vo, pp. 16. H.

NEWELL (W. A.) Proceedings attending the Inauguration of Hon. William A. Newell, as Governor of New Jersey, ... January 20, 1857. ... *Trenton.* 1857. 8vo, pp. 13. H. 54968

Also: Reconstruction. Speech ... February 15, 1866. [n. p. n. d.] 8vo, pp. 15. — Remarks ... February 17, 1849, On a Proposition to make an Appropriation for the better Preservation of Life and Property from Shipwreck along the Coast of New Jersey, ... [n. p. n. d.] 8vo, pp. 8. — Remarks ... on a Proposition to devise means for the Preservation of Life and Property from Wrecks of the New Jersey Coast. ... *Washington: Printed by John T. Towers.* 1848. 8vo, pp. 15. — Remarks ... on the Death of Senator Wright. ... December 18, 1866. [n. p. n. d.] 8vo, pp. 4. — Restoration of the Rebellious States. Speech ... January 4, 1867. [n. p. n. d.] 8vo, pp. 8.

NEWELL (W. W.) ... A Discourse ... before The Unitarian Society of Germantown, By William W. Newell ... . January 28, 1866. *Philadelphia: Sherman & Co., Printers.* 1866. 8vo, pp. 16. H. 54969

Also: ... A Discourse, ... at Liverpool, N. Y., October 19th, 1852, at the Ordination of Mr. Samuel B. Bell, ... with a Farewell Address to Missionaries ... for California. ... *Syracuse.* 1853. 8vo, pp. 33. S.

Der Newen Weldt. *See* [Benzoni (G.)], Vol. II., Nos. 4797–8

Newes | from New-England: | of | A most strange and prodigious Birth, brought to Boston in New- | England, October the 17. being a true and exact Relation, brought over | April 19. 1642. by a Gentleman of good worth, now resident | in London. ... | [Colophon:] *London:* | *Printed for John G. Smith*, | 1642. 4to, 4 leaves. BM. 54970

Newes from Virginia. *See* [Rich (R.)]

Nevves | Of Sr. Walter Rauleigh. | With | The true Description of Gviana: | As also a Relation of the excellent Gouernment, | and | much hope of the prosperity of the Voyage. | Sent from a Gentleman of his Fleet, to a most | especiall Friend of his in London. | From the Riuer of Caliana, on the Coast of Guiana, Nouemb. 17. 1617. | *London,* | *Printed for H. G. and are to be sold by I. Wright, at the signe of the* | *Bible without New-gate.* 1618. | 4to, pp. (2), 45. 54971

Reprinted in Force's "Tracts," Vol. III., No. 4.

Newes, | True Newes, Laudable | Newes, Citie Newes, Court Newes, | Countrey Newes: The World is mad, or it is | a mad

World my Masters, especially now | when in the Antipodes these things | are come to passe. | *London,* | *for F. Cowles, T. Bates, and T. Banks.* | MDCXLII. 4to, pp. 8. BM., C. 54972

Chiefly about the antipodes, of which there is a most ridiculous woodcut on the title-page. Thomas Thorpe catalogues this work under Americana, but it can only be so by assuming that the author is satirizing the first settlers in New England. It is a very amusing performance.

The Newest Keep-Sake for Eighteen Hundred Thirty-Nine; Containing the Speeches, Circumstances, and Doings of a ... Benevolent Convention at the Chapel of the Marlboro' House, Boston. Embellished with [metaphorical] Cuts ... . *Boston.* 1839. 16mo, pp. 121. H. 54973

NEWFOUNDLAND. Abstract of the Fifth Annual Report of the Newfoundland School Society. ... May 14th, 1828 ... . [n. p. n. d.] 8vo, pp. 8. H. 54974

Act for establishing a Court of Civil Jurisdiction in the Island of Newfoundland. [n. p.] 1791. 8vo. 54975

Also: The Establishing of Courts of Judicature in the Island of Newfoundland, and parts adjacent. [n. p. 1792.] 8vo.

By Captain Joseph Taylour, Commander in Chief of all Her Majesty's Forces in Newfoundland ... . [n. p. 1711.] Folio, 1 leaf. BM. 54976

Indorsed "The Case of John Collins, Esq. Governor of Newfoundland, Jan. 21. 1711."

Case of J. Degrave, Francis Minshall, and others, owners of the Seven Sail of Transports taken up to carry Provisions to Newfoundland. [n. p. 1698.] Folio, 1 leaf. 54977

A Chapter on the History of Newfoundland for the Year 1861. *St. John's, Newfoundland.* 1861. 8vo. 54978

Considerations on the Trade to Newfoundland. [n. p. about 1748.] Folio, pp. 3. 54979

Perhaps by Thomas Whately?

The Constitution of the Government of Newfoundland in its Legislative and Executive Departments. With Appendix ... By John Little. [*St. Johns:*] *Hazard & Owen.* 1855. 18mo, pp. 20, 88. C. 54980

Copy of a Representation of the Lords Commissioners for Trade and Plantations to his Majesty, relating to the Newfoundland Trade and Fishery. *London.* 1718. 4to, pp. 23. + [*Ibid.*]

1766. 4to, pp. 15. 2 Tables. + [*Ibid.*] 1786. 4to, pp. 15. + [*Ibid.*] 1790. 4to, pp. 45. 54981

Journal of the House of Assembly of Newfoundland. ... Sixth Session of the First General Assembly. *St. Johns, Newfoundland.* 1836. Folio, pp. 254, xi. Continued. S. 54982

Newfoundland. List of Contributions ... for Ecclesiastical Purposes in the Diocese of Newfoundland ... . *London: Printed by R. Clay.* 1845. 12mo, pp. 35, (2). BM. 54983

The Newfoundland Almanack, For ... 1845; ... Compiled by Joseph Templeman. ... [*St. Johns, Newfoundland:*] *Printed ... by Ryan & Withers.* [1845.] 8vo, pp. 50. Continued. 54984

Newfoundland and Quebec. Copies or Extracts of Correspondence respecting the Fire at Saint John's, Newfoundland, and the Fire at Quebec. [n. p.] 1847. Folio, pp. 73. 54985

Official Copy of Orders from Governor Palliser for the Protection of the Fishery and Trade of Newfoundland, on the Coast of Labrador ... . [n. p.] 1765. 8vo. 54986

The fourth article is on the especial caution of breaking the peace he had made with the Esquimaux savages.

Proceedings of The Society for Educating the Poor of Newfoundland. Second Year, 1824–5, containing the Anniversary Sermon by the Rev. Henry Budd, the Second Report of the Committee ... . *London: Printed by R. G. Gunnell and Co.* 1825. 8vo, pp. 92. Continued. 54987

Corrected title of No. 8950, Vol. III.

Report on the Geology of Newfoundland for 1865. By Alex. Murray, Esq. with a Prefatory Report and an Appendix, By Sir W. E. Logan ... . *Montreal: John Lovell, Printer.* 1866. 8vo, pp. 46. Plate. H. 54988

Also: Report upon the Geological Survey of Newfoundland, for the year 1870. By A. Murray. *St. John's (N. F.): "Courier" Print.* 1870. 8vo, pp. 51. Plate and Map.

Reports from the Committee appointed to enquire into the State of Trade to Newfoundland. Ordered to be Printed April 24, 1793. [*London.* 1793.] Folio, pp. 230. 2 Tables. 54989

"With several other parliamentary reports, and papers on the same subject." — RICH, I. 496.

Select Cases from the Records of the Supreme Court of Newfoundland; With a Table of the Names of Cases and an Appendix. *St. Johns, Newfoundland.* 1829. 8vo, pp. viii, 604. S.

Summary of the Laws of Commerce and Navigation, adapted to the present State, Government and Trade of the Island of Newfoundland. By Rev. Lewis Amadeus Anspach ... . *London.* 1809. 8vo. 54991

See also Vol. VIII., No. 30001, *and* Vol. X., No. 40319.

NEWHALL (E.) ... A Sermon ... at the Dedication of the New Meeting House, ... Oxford, Mass. November 3, 1829. By Ebenezer Newhall ... . *Boston: T. R. Marvin.* 1830. 8vo, pp. 16. 54992

NEWHALL (F. H.) ... A Funeral Discourse occasioned by the Death of John Brown of Ossawattomie, who entered into rest, From the Gallows, at Charlestown, Virginia, Dec. 2, 1859. Preached ... at Roxbury, Dec. 4, By Rev. Fales Henry Newhall, ... *Boston: J. M. Hewes.* 1859. 8vo, pp. 22. H. 54993

Also: National Exaltation ... . A Discourse ... at ... Roxbury, January 4th, 1861, on ... the National Fast. ... *Boston: John M. Hewes.* 1861. 8vo, pp. 16. — ... The Life-Work of Theodore Parker; A Discourse preached at ... Roxbury, June 10, ... 1860. ... *Boston: J. M. Hewes.* 1860. 8vo, pp. 24. — The Theater; A Discourse ... at the Bromfield Street M. E. Church, March 15, 1863. ... *Boston: J. P. Magee.* 1863. 8vo, pp. 27. B.

NEWHALL (J. R.) The Essex Memorial, for 1836; embracing a Register of the County. By James R. Newhall. *Salem: Henry Whipple.* 1836. 16mo, pp. 281, (2). Map. C. 54994

[NEWHALL.] Lin: or, Jewels of the Third Plantation. ... By Obadiah Oldpath. *Lynn: Thomas Herbert and James M. Munroe.* 1862. 12mo, pp. 400. H. 54995

Also: A Lecture on the Occult Sciences: embracing some account of the New England Witchcraft ... . *Salem: G. W. & E. Crafts.* 1845. 8vo, pp. 36. B.

NEWHALL (J. B.) The British Emigrant's "Hand Book," and Guide to the New States of America, particularly Illinois, Iowa, and Wisconsin; ... By J. B. Newhall ... . *London: T. Stutter.* 1844. 12mo, pp. 99, (1). H. 54996

NEWHALL. A Glimpse of Iowa in 1846; or, the Emigrant's Guide, and State Directory; with a Description of the New Purchase: ... By J. B. Newhall ... . *Burlington.* 1846. 12mo. + Second Edition. *Burlington, Iowa: W. D. Skillman.* 1846. 12mo, pp. 106. H. 54997

NEWHALL. Sketches of Iowa; or the Emigrant's Guide: containing a correct Description of the Agricultural and Mineral Resources, Geological Features and Statistics of the Territory of

Iowa ... By John B. Newhall ... . *New York: J. H. Colton.* 1841. 18mo, pp. 252. Map. C. 54998

NEWHALL (W. S.) Walter S. Newhall. A Memoir. ... *Philadelphia: Sanitary Commission.* 1864. 8vo, pp. 140. Port.

NEWHOUSE (S.) The Trapper's Guide: A Manual of Instructions for Capturing all kinds of Fur-bearing Animals, ... Observations on the Fur Trade, Hints on Life in the Woods, and Narratives of Trapping and Hunting Excursions: By S. Newhouse ... . Edited by J. H. Noyes. *Published by the Oneida Community. Wallingford, Conn.* 1865. 8vo, pp. 118. Portrait. + Second Edition ... . [*Ibid.*] 1867. 8vo, pp. 215. + Third Edition. *New York: Oakley, Mason & Co.* 1869. 8vo. Portrait and Plates. B. 55000

A curious and interesting little work, giving facts in Natural History and entertaining adventures of experienced trappers.

NEWLAND (Jeremiah). Verses occasioned by the Earthquakes in November, 1755. [n. p. n. d.] Folio, 1 leaf. 55001

NEWLAND (S. W.) Memorial of S. W. Newland, of Saratoga. [n. p. n. d.] 8vo. Portrait. 55002

NEWLANDS (J.) A Dream ... . By John Newlands. *Albany.* 1835. 18mo, pp. 12. S. 55003

NEWLIGHT (Aristarchus). *See* [Whately (Richard)].

NEWLIN (W. H.) An Account of the Escape of Six Federal Soldiers from Prison at Danville, Va.: their Travels by Night through the Enemy's Country to the Union Pickets at Gauley Bridge, West Virginia, in the Winter of 1863–64. *Cincinnati: Western Methodist Book Concern, Printers.* 1870. 8vo, pp. 112.

NEWMAN (A.) Ups and Downs In America; ... An Autobiography by Alfred Newman. ... *Nicholls and Son, London.* 1868. 12mo, pp. 83. 55005

NEWMAN (B. J.) The Eagle of Washington: A Story of the American Revolution. A Poem in Three Cantos. By Burkitt J. Newman. *Louisville.* 1859. 12mo. 55006

NEWMAN (F. W.) Character of the Southern States of America. Letter to a Friend who had joined the Southern Independence Association, By F. W. Newman ... . *Manchester (Eng.): Union and Emancipation Society.* 1863. 8vo, pp. 14, (1). H.

[NEWMAN.] Foreign Affairs: A Series of Articles re-printed from the Sheffield Free Press. ... *Sheffield: Eaton, Blenkin and Co.* 1852. 8vo, pp. (2), 50. B. 55008

Also: The Good Cause of President Lincoln. A Lecture ... . [*London:*] *Emancipation Society.* [1863.] 12mo, pp. 24. C. — Hiawatha: Rendered into Latin, With Abridgment. ... *London: Walton and Maberly.* 1862. 12mo, pp. vii, 110. BM.

NEWMAN (H.) Harvard's Ephemeris. Or Almanack ... for ... 1690. By H. Newman. *Cambridge: Printed by Samuel Green.* 1690. 12mo. 55009

NEWMAN. News from the Stars. An Almanack ... For the Year of the Christian Empire, 1691 ... Respecting the Meridian of Boston, in New-England. By Henry Newman, Philomath. *Boston: Printed by R. Pierce for Benj. Harris.* 1691. 12mo.

NEWMAN (J.) Eulogy, ... at the Funeral of ... Horace Clark, Esq., at West Poultney, Vt., ... the 25th day of February, 1852, By Rev. John Newman. *Rutland.* [n. d.] 12mo, pp. 19. H.

NEWMAN (J. B.) Ancient History and Discovery of America before the Time of Columbus. By John B. Newman. *New York.* 1848. 8vo, pp. 48. 55012

Reproduced as: "The Early Peopling of America and its Discovery before the Time of Columbus," *New York*, 1848, 8vo, pp. 48; also as "Origin of the Red Men; an Authentic History of the Peopling of America by the Atlantians and Tyrians; ... Legend of Quetzalcoatl, a Reformer and Divine of the Early Ages of Mexico; the Aztec City of Sumai, etc." ... *New York.* 1849. 8vo, pp. 48. Plate. + *New York: John C. Wells.* 1852. 8vo, pp. 48. Plate.

NEWMAN. Texas and Mexico, in 1846; ... with an Account of the Soil, Climate, and Productions of Each. By John B. Newman ... . *New-York: J. K. Wellman.* 1846. 8vo, pp. 32. Map. H. 55013

Also: Wawawanda. A Legend of Old Orange. *New York.* 1860. 12mo.

NEWMAN (L. C.) The Bible View of Slavery Reconsidered. Letter to the Rt. Rev. Bishop Hopkins, By Louis C. Newman. *New York: C. S. Westcott & Co.* 1863. 8vo, pp. 14. + Second Edition. *Philadelphia.* 1863. 8vo. 55014

NEWMAN (M. H.) Mark H. Newman's Almanac, for ... 1844. ... *New York: Mark H. Newman.* [n. d.] 32mo, pp. (24)

[NEWMAN (S. C.)] An Address ... at the Formation of the Blackstone Monument Association, together with the Preliminaries, and Proceedings at Study Hill, July 4, 1855. ... *Pawtucket, R. I.: Printed by James L. Estey.* 1855. 8vo, pp. 39. Plate.

+ *Pawtucket, R. I.: Printed by Pearce and Estey.* 1855. 8vo, pp. 39. Plate. 55016

NEWMAN. 1610. Dexter [Genealogy]. 1857. Prepared and Compiled by S. C. Newman ... . *Providence: Knowles, Anthony & Co., Printers.* 1857. Folio, 1 leaf. 55017

NEWMAN. The Dexter Genealogy: being a Record of the Families descended from Rev. Gregory Dexter; with Notes and Biographical Sketches of each Parent. ... By S. C. Newman, ... *Providence: Printed by A. Crawford Greene.* 1859. 12mo, pp. 108

NEWMAN. A Numbering of the Inhabitants: together with Statistical and other Information, relative to Woonsocket, R. I. ... By S. C. Newman. *Woonsocket: Printed by S. S. Foss.* 1846. 12mo, pp. 45. 55019

NEWMAN. Rehoboth in the Past. An Historical Oration ... Fourth of July, 1860, By Sylvanus Chace Newman, A.M. ... Also an Account of the Proceedings in Seekonk, (the Ancient Rehoboth) at the Celebration of the Day, Completing two Hundred and sixteen Years of its History. *Pawtucket: Printed by Robert Sherman.* 1860. 8vo, pp. 112. B., S. 55020

Also: 1628–1858. Descendants of Jonathan Padelford. ... *Providence: A. C. Greene & Brother.* 1859. Folio, 1 leaf. — Descendants of John Read [from 1598 to 1859]. ... *Providence: A. Crawford Greene.* 1859. Folio, 1 leaf.

NEWMAN (S. P.) Address ... before the Benevolent Society of Bowdoin College, ... Sept. 5, 1826, By Samuel P. Newman. *Portland: Printed at the Mirror Office.* 1826. 8vo, pp. 29.

NEWMAN (T. F.) ... Character and Labours of ... William Knibb, Twenty-one Years a Missionary in Jamaica. A Sermon ... By Thomas Fox Newman ... . *London: Houlston and Stoneman.* 1846. 8vo, pp. (4), 36. 55022

NEWMAN (U.) Brief Summary of some of the ... Incidents relative to the Life of Ursula Newman, and the Intercourse between her and Richard Johnson. *New York.* 1829. 8vo.

NEWMARCH (W.) ... The New Supplies of Gold: ... By William Newmarch. *London: Pelham Richardson.* 1853. 8vo, pp. vii, 122. 55024

Production of gold in California is one of the subjects.

NEWPORT, *Ky.* Facts relating to the Bridge Question. ... Opinions of Eminent Bridge Builders. ... [n. p.:] *Bradley & Power, Printers.* 1868. 8vo, pp. 31. H. 55025

NEWPORT, *Pa.* Charter and By-Laws of the Newport Coal Company. Incorporated by ... the Legislature of ... Pennsylvania, ... 1864. ... *Boston: Alfred Mudge & Son, Printers.* 1865. 8vo, pp. 15. H. 55026

NEWPORT, *R. I.* An Account of the Pirates, with divers of their Speeches, Letters, &c. And a Poem made by one of them: Who were executed at Newport, on Rhode Island, July 19th, 1723. *Reprinted in the Year* 1769. 12mo, pp. 16. 55027

I have not seen the original edition. *See* Bartlett's "Bibliog. of Rhode Island," p. 6

... Addresses of George H. Calvert, Mayor of ... Newport; and Reports of Committees; comprising the Finance, Overseers of the Poor, Firewards and School Reports, for ... 1853–54. *Newport, R. I.: Coggeshall & Pratt, ... Printers.* 1854. 8vo, pp. 61. Continued. B. 55028

Anderson Improved: Being an Almanack ... Calculated for Newport, Rhode Island. But may well serve throughout all the Northern Colonies. By John Anderson. *Newport: Solomon Southwick.* 1772. 12mo. 55029

Annual Report of the School Committee of ... Newport, R. I., for ... 1865–66. [n. p. n. d.] 8vo, pp. 22. Continued.

Answer to a printed Letter said to be wrote by a Gentleman in Newport to his Friend in Boston ... . *Boston.* 1739. 8vo.

Catalogue of the Books in the People's Library, Newport, R. I. *Providence: Hammond, Angell & Co., Printers.* 1870. 8vo, pp. iv, 338. B. 55032

Catalogue for the Library belonging to Spring Street Church Sabbath School, Newport, R. I. [n. p. n. d.] 24mo, pp. 23. B.

The Charter of ... Newport, R. I., and the special Laws relating thereto, ... with the Ordinances ... . *Newport, R. I.: Coggeshall & Pratt, ... Printers.* 1858. 8vo, pp. 164. H. 55033

... The Charter and By-Laws of the Artillery Company of ... Newport ... Rhode Island. Also a List of its Commanders and Members from ... 1741 to the Present Time ... . *Newport, R. I.: Charles E. Hammett, Jun.* 1857. 24mo, pp. 44. H. 55034

Also: The Charter and Regulations of the Artillery Company of Newport, R. I., ... *New York.* 1860. 18mo, pp. 24.

The Controversy. *See* [Brooks (C. T.)], Vol. II., No. 8342.

Foggy Night at Newport. *St. Louis.* 1860. 8vo. 55035

A Hand-Book of Newport. *See* [Dix (J. R.)], v. 20343.

First Report of the ... HOME FOR FRIENDLESS CHILDREN, ... Newport, R. I. *Newport: Fred. A. Pratt, Printer.* 1868. 8vo, pp. 16. Continued. H. 55036

Also: Constitution and By-Laws of the Home for Friendless Children, ... Newport, R. I. ... *Newport, R. I.: Davis & Pitman's Press.* 1867. 12mo, pp. 14. H.

Manual of the United Congregational Church, 1834. [n. p. n. d.] 8vo. 55037

Charter and By-Laws of the MARINE SOCIETY of Newport. *Newport.* 1786. 8vo. N. 55038

Also: Charter of the Marine Society of ... Newport, ... added the Bye-Laws ... . *Newport.* M.DCCC.VI. 8vo, pp. (4), 25.

The Newport Almanac, 1800. *Newport: Printed by Oliver Farnsworth, Printer to the State of Rhode Island.* [1800.] 12mo.

Newport and Environs. *See* [Mason (G. C.)], XI. 45442.

The Newport and Fall River Route between New York and Boston. A Descriptive Guide ... . *Taintor Brothers, New York.* [1869.] 18mo, pp. 61. 55040

Newport and Narraganset Bay. A Guide to the Principal Places of Interest in Newport, and to the Summer Resorts of Narragansett Bay ... . *Providence: Tillinghast & Mason.* 1870. 12mo, pp. 29. H. 55041

The Charter, Constitution and By-Laws of the NEWPORT ASSOCIATION OF MECHANICS AND MANUFACTURERS, with List of Officers and Committee ... . *Newport: Henry Barber.* 1792. 18mo, pp. vi, 24. 55042

Also: Catalogue of the Library ... . *Newport: Cranston & Norman.* 1850. 8vo, pp. 43.

The Newport Business Directory and Advertiser. *Newport.* 1870. 12mo, pp. 82, (1). B. 55043

The Newport Directory, containing the Names of the Citizens ... also a reprint of the Centenary Discourse of the Rev. John Callendar, A.M. being a History of Rhode Island to 1738, ... printed ... 1856–57. William H. Boyd, Compiler ... . *Newport, R. I.: Charles E. Hammett, Jr.* [n. d.] 24mo, pp. 121. Continued. H. 55044

This is the first Newport Directory.

Newport Female Evangelical Miscellany. No. 1. *Newport.* [1806.] 8vo, pp. 16. Continued. 55045

Newport Free Library. Directors' Report. 1867–'68. [n. p. n. d.] 8vo, pp. (4). Continued. B. 55046

Newport Illustrated. *See* [Mason (G. C.)], Vol. XI. 45443.

Constitution, By-Laws, &c. and ... Members, of the NEWPORT READING ROOM. ... *Newport, R. I.: Printed by James Atkinson.* 1855. 16mo, pp. 15. H. 55047

Also: Catalogue of the Newport Reading Room. [n. p. 1858.] 12mo, pp. 24.

The Newport Tide Almanac ... 1864. ... *Newport: Charles E. Hammett, Jr.* 1863. 12mo. Continued. 55048

Argument for the Extension of the OLD COLONY AND FALL RIVER RAILROAD to Newport, before a Committee of the Legislature of Massachusetts. By Hon. Josiah G. Abbott. *Boston: G. C. Rand & Avery.* 1861. 8vo, pp. 36. 55049

Ordinances of the City of Newport, Revised ... by Charles C. Van Zandt ... . 1856. *Newport, R. I.: Coggeshall and Pratt, Printers.* 1856. 8vo, pp. 64. B. 55050

... Petition of Inhabitants of Newport, R. Island, Distillers of Rum and Importers of Molasses, against an Increase of Duty on Molasses. ... *Washington: Printed by Gales & Seaton.* 1828. 8vo, pp. 3. H. 55051

Annual Report of the Directors of the REDWOOD LIBRARY and Athenæum ... . September 26, 1860. *Boston: Printed by John Wilson & Sons.* 1860. 8vo, pp. 23. Continued. B.

Catalogue of the Books belonging to the Redwood Library Company in Newport, ... Rhode Island, April, A.D. 1816. *Newport: Rousmaniere & Barber.* 1816. 8vo. 55053

Also: Appendix to the Catalogue of Books belonging to the Redwood Library Company, ... September, 1829. *Newport: W. & J. H. Barber.* 1829. 8vo, pp. 14.—A Catalogue ... to which is prefixed a short Account of the Institution; with the Charter, Laws and Regulations. *Providence: Knowles and Vose, Printers.* 1843. 8vo, pp. xix, 95. B.—Catalogue of the Redwood Library ... . *Boston: Printed by John Wilson and Son.* 1860. 8vo, pp. liii, (2), 383.—Charter of the Redwood Library Company, granted A.D. 1747. *Newport.* 1816. 8vo, pp. 36.—Proposals for improving the Redwood Library ... . *Newport.* 1856. 8vo, pp. 8.

The Laws of the Redwood Library Company ... . *Newport: Samuel Hall.* 1764. 8vo, pp. 28. 54054

The preface to the catalogue is by Ezra Stiles. Also: Laws and Regulations ... as revised and adopted, September 26, 1810. *Newport: Rousmaniere & Barber.* 1816. 8vo, pp. 25.

Report of the Minority of the Committee upon the Memorial of Samuel T. Hopkins, against the Validity of the Election of the Fourth Representative from the City of Newport, the Hon. Charles C. Van Zandt. *Providence: H. L. Tillinghast.* 1859. 8vo, pp. 14. 55055

Constitution and By-Laws of the SAINT ALOYSIUS JUVENILE SOCIETY, Newport, R. I. ... *Newport, R. I.: F. A. Pratt, Printer.* 1863. 24mo, pp. 12. B. 55055*a*

Services at the Dedication of the School House erected by the Trustees of the Long Wharf, at Newport, R. I., May 20th, 1863, With an Appendix. *Newport: Printed by Pratt & Messer.* 1863. 8vo, pp. 106. H. 55055*b*

The Charter of TRINITY CHURCH, Newport, in ... Rhode Island. ... *Newport: Wm. & J. H. Barber.* 1823. 8vo, pp. 8.

Annual Report of the Board of Managers of ... Trinity Church ... . *Boston: James B. Dow.* 1842. 8vo, pp. 11.

See also Bours (John), Vol. II., No. 6935.

News for this Week from Norimberg ... with something from Brazil ... . *London: Nathaniel Butter, Ap.* 23, 1640. 4to.

News from Africa. A Collection of Facts, relating to the Colony of Liberia, for the Information of the Free People of Color in Maryland. ... *Baltimore: J. D. Toy, Printer.* 1832. 24mo, pp. 36. H. 55059

News from | New-England, | Being | A True and last Account of the present Bloody Wars | carried on betwixt the Infidels, Natives, and the | English Christians, and Converted Indians of | New-England, declaring the many Dreadful | Battles Fought betwixt them: As also the many | Towns and Villages burnt by the merciless Hea- | thens. And also the true Number of all the Chri- | stians slain since the beginning of that War, as it | was sent over by a Factor of New-England to a | Merchant in London. | Licensed by Roger L'Estrange. | *London,* | *Printed for J. Coniers at the Sign of the Black-Raven* | *in Duck-Lane,* 1676. 4to, pp. (2), 6. 55060

First edition, of extreme rarity. The only copy I know belongs to Mr. C. H. Kalbfleisch. Reprinted with a variation in the title as:

News from | New-England, | Being | A True and last Account of the present Bloody Wars | carried on betwixt the Infidels, Natives, and the | English Christians, and Converted Indians of | New-England, declaring the many Dreadful | Battles Fought betwixt them: As also the many | Towns and Villages burnt by the merciless Hea- | thens. And also the true Number of all the Chri- | stians slain since the beginning of that War, as it | was sent over by a Factor of New-England to a | Merchant in London. | Licensed Aug. 1. Roger L'Estrange. | *London,* | *Printed for J. Coniers, at the Sign of the Black Raven* | *in Duck-Lane,* 1676. 4to, pp. (2), 6. J.C.B., BM. 55061

This edition has an additional paragraph on the last page, stating "There has been a treaty," etc. Of such excessive rarity that when, in 1850, Mr. Drake reprinted it, he supposed that Mr. J. C. Brown's was the only copy. It was reprinted as below:

News from New-England [as before]. *Boston, N. E.: Reprinted for Samuel G. Drake.* 1850. Sm. 4to, pp. 20. 55062

News from New England. *Albany: Reprinted by Joel Munsell for W. E. Woodward.* 1865. 4to, pp. 22. 55063

Sixty-four copies printed on one side of the paper only, of which four were printed on Whatman's drawing paper. Of this reprint there are *two* issues, the publisher—a druggist in Roxbury Mass.—thus explains the matter: "By permission of Mr. Drake 75 copies of this pamphlet were reprinted in quarto. So far as the printing was concerned the work was fairly done, and in a manner tolerably satisfactory, with the single exception of an error in the paging; but the sheets being entrusted for binding to a firm in Boston, the work was done in a manner so entirely unworkmanlike as to induce or rather compel me to destroy the entire edition with the exception of 15 copies, which are preserved to show how unfaithfully and shabbily a job can be done. Sixty copies are already destroyed, so that the two editions consist of 75 copies only." For a reply, *see* Vol. XIII., No. 52757.

News | from | Newcastle. | *London, Printed in the Year* 1651. | *By William Ellis.* | 4to, Title, pp. 5. BM. 55064

A most rare and curious poem "Upon the Coale-pits about New Castle upon Tine," which appears to have been privately printed, by William Ellis, who was probably the author. It commences thus:

"England's a perfect World; has Indies too—
Correct your Maps: New Castle is Peru.
Let th' haughty Spanyard triumph, till, 'tis told,
Our sootie Min'rals purifie his Gold."

News from Pensilvania. *See* [Bugg (F.)], Vol. III., No. 9071.

News from the Moon. A Review of the State of the British Nation, Vol. 7. Numb. 14. Page 53.—Tuesday, May 2, 1710. [*Boston: J. Franklin.* 1721?] 16mo, pp. 8. + *Boston.* 1772. 12mo. 55065

A satire aimed, apparently, at the House of Representatives, for their proceedings against the publisher and printer of "New News from Robinson Cruso's Island."

The News-Gong: A Literary Intelligencer ... . Vol. I. No. 2. *New-York: Geo. L. Curry & Co.* 1841. 8vo. H. 55066

NEWSAM (A.) Albert Newsam, the Deaf and Dumb Artist. [*Philadelphia?* 1862.] 4to, pp. (4). B. 55067

Newsboy. *See* [Smith (E. O.)]

The Newsman's Interpreter, or A Description of Several Spanish Territories in America; Particularly of those Places against which, it is supposed, the English have a Design, with their Situation, Limits, Extent, Division, Chief Towns, Commodities, &c. by the help of which any Paragraph in News Papers &c. Relating to those Places may be better understood. To which are added The Trade-Winds explained, and an Account of the Spanish Trade to and from America; as also a short Account of the English Navy, with Plans of Porto Bello Carthagena and the Havanna, and an Explanation of those Plans. The Second Edition. *Manchester: J. Berry.* 1741. 18mo, pp. 67. 3 folded Plates. H. 55068

The Newsman's New Years Address. ... 1865. [*New York.* 1865.] 4to, pp. 8. H. 55069

[NEWTON (A.)] The Conspiracy Exposed, and the Rev. S. S. Lattimore Unmasked. *Carrollton (Miss.): G. W. H. Brown.* 1841. 8vo. 55070

NEWTON (A.) Sketch of the Life and Character of Ebenezer Lane, LL.D. (Late Judge of the Supreme Court of Ohio.) By Rev. A. Newton ... . [n. p. 1866?] 4to, pp. 12. Portrait.

NEWTON (Alonzo E.) A Review of the Criticisms of the Congregationalist on the "Letter to the Edwards Church," including the Reply, rejected by that Journal ... . By A. E. Newton. ... *Boston: The Author.* 1853. 12mo, pp. 28. H.

This writer and his wife were Spiritualists, and printed other pieces on the subject.

NEWTON (C.) ... A Sermon ... before the Officers and Students of Waterville College, February 28, 1833 ... . By Calvin Newton, A.M. ... *Augusta: Eaton & Severance, Printers.* 1833. 8vo, pp. 19. H. 55073

NEWTON (*Dr.*) Dr. Newton's Columns on the Position of the Old School Presbyterian Assembly on the Subject of Slavery. First published ... in the "Eagle of the South," Jackson, Miss. ... *Jackson, Miss.: Purdom & Brother.* 1859. 8vo, pp. 112.

NEWTON (Eben). Address ... by Hon. E. Newton, ... before the Highland Union Agricultural Association, ... in Garrettsville, ... O., October ... 1862. *Ravenna, Ohio: Lyman W. Hall, Printer.* 1862. 8vo, pp. 12. 55075

Also: ... Speech ... April 20, 1852, in Favor of the Establishment of an Agricultural Bureau. [n. p. n. d.] 8vo, pp. 8. H.

NEWTON (J.) Thoughts upon the African Slave Trade. By John Newton ... . *London: J. Buckland.* M.DCC.LXXXVIII. 8vo, pp. (4), 41. C. + The Third Edition. ... *Edinburgh: Reprinted* M.DCC.LXXXVIII. 8vo, pp. 24. P. 55076

See "Monthly Review," LXXVIII. 160.

NEWTON, *and* FALCONBRIDGE (A.) Gedachten over den Afrikaanschen Slaavenhandel. Uit het Engelsch door M. van Werkhoven. *Amsterdam.* 1788. 8vo. 55077

NEWTON (J. H.) An Appeal to the Latter-Day Saints. By Joseph H. Newton, William Richards, and William Stanly. *Philadelphia: The Author.* 1863. 12mo, pp. 72. 55078

NEWTON (*Mr.*) Speech of Mr. Newton, of Virginia, in support of the Apportionment Act, ... February 8th, 1844. *Washington.* 1844. 8vo, pp. 14. 55079

NEWTON (O. E.) An Essay on Asiatic Cholera, as it appeared in Cincinnati, O., in ... 1849, 1850, and 1866 ... . By Orin E. Newton, M.D. ... *New York and Cincinnati.* 1867. 8vo, pp. 30.

NEWTON (R.) An Oration, ... at Worcester, Mass. On the Fourth of July, 1814. By Rejoice Newton, Esq. *Printed at Worcester, by Isaac Sturtevant.* 1814. 8vo, pp. 24. H. 55081

NEWTON (R.) The English and American Rebellion compared and contrasted. An Address delivered at the University of Pennsylvania, December 4, 1865. By Rev. Richard Newton, D.D. *Philadelphia: King & Baird.* 1866. 8vo, pp. 37. 55082

[NEWTON.] Pleasant Memories of a Happy Day; or, A Pastoral Letter to the Sunday School Children of St. Paul's Church, ... January 7th, 1855. *Philada: King & Baird, Prs.* [n. d.] 16mo, pp. 14. Plate. H. 55083

Also: Anniversary Oration. ... Before the Faculty and Students of the University of Pennsylvania, February 22, 1836. ... *Philadelphia: Printed by William F. Geddes.* 1836. 8vo, pp. 16.—God's Interest in the Death of his People: A Tribute to the Memory of Rev. Robert J. Parvin and Rev. Franklin S. Rising. ... *Philadelphia.* 1869. 8vo, pp. 48.—God's Marvellous Doing for the Nation. A Sermon ... on ... Thanksgiving

... In ... Philadelphia; ... August 6th, 1863. *Philadelphia: William F. Murphy & Sons.* 1863. 8vo, pp. 16.—A Sermon, ... in ... Philadelphia, ... April 9th, 1854, on the ... Death of the Rev. James H. Fowles ... . *Philadelphia: King and Baird, Printers.* 1854. 8vo, pp. 32. B.

NEWTON (T.) ... A Sermon ... before the ... Society for the Propagation of the Gospel in Foreign Parts, ... February 17, 1769. By Thomas Newton, D.D., Lord Bishop of Bristol. *London: Printed by E. Owen.* MDCCLXIX. 4to, pp. 29, 62. M.

NEWTON (W. W.) "Carpe Viam." A Poem, ... before the ... University of Pennsylvania, ... By Wm. Wilberforce Newton. ... *Philadelphia: Lineaweaver & Wallace, Printers.* 1865. 8vo, pp. 14. H. 55085

NEWTON, *Mass.* Account of the Formation of the Eliot Church in Newton, Mass., with the ... Confession of Faith and Covenant ... . *Boston: Printed by Dow and Jackson.* 1846. 12mo, pp. 12. H. 55086

Articles of Faith submitted ... to the Eliot Orthodox Congregational Church, At Newton Corner, Mass. [n. p. n. d.] 16mo, pp. 7.—The Confession of Faith, Covenant and By-Laws of the Eliot Church, in Newton, Mass. With the Names of its Officers and Members. *Boston: Printed by Tuttle & Dennet.* 1852. 12mo, pp. 12.—Articles of Christian Doctrine and Church Covenant, adopted by the Baptist Church ... in Newton, (Mass.) ... 1832. *Boston: Printed by Lincoln and Edmands.* 1832. 24mo, pp. 7.—Catalogue of ... the Eliot Sabbath School Library, Newton. ... *Boston.* 1854. 16mo, pp. 20. Continued.—Catalogue of the Sunday School Library, belonging to the Second Unitarian Society, in Newton. *Boston: Press of J. Howe.* 1854. 16mo, pp. 16.—Catalogue of the Sunday School Library, of Grace Church, Newton. 1857. *Boston: Printed by Alfred Mudge & Son.* [n. d.] 24mo, pp. 20. Continued. H.

An Account of the Receipts and Expenditures of the Town of Newton, from ... 1851, to ... 1852. *Boston: Stacy & Richardson, Printers.* 1852. 8vo, pp. 24. Map. Continued. H.

A Brief Notice. *See* [Jackson (W.)], Vol. IX., No. 35475.

By-Laws of Dalhousie Lodge, of Newton, Mass. A.L. 5861. *Boston: Printed by Stacy & Richardson.* 1861. 12mo, pp. 11.

Ceremonies at the Dedication of the Soldiers' Monument, in Newton, Mass. *Boston: S. Chism.* 1864. 12mo, pp. 48. Plate.

History, Standing Rules, Articles of Faith, and Covenant of the Second Congregational Church, in Newton, Mass. With a Catalogue of the Members. 1852. *Boston: Printed by Damrell & Moore.* 1852. 12mo, pp. 14. 55090

Also: Record of Past and Present Members of the Second Congregational Church, of Newton, Mass. ... *Boston: Wright & Potter, Printers.* 1868. 12mo, pp. 38. H.

Catalogue of ... the NEWTON ATHENÆUM; with a Sketch of the Origin and Object of the Institution. *Boston: Printed by Bazin & Chandler.* 1856. 12mo, pp. 41. Continued. H.

The Newton Directory; containing a General Directory ... a Business Directory, and the Town Record. ... C. C. Drew, Publisher. *Newton: H. N. Hyde.* 1868. 8vo, pp. 216, 200. Cont'd

Order of Exercises, at the Dedication of the NEWTON FREE LIBRARY, ... June 17th, 1870 ... . *Newton.* [n. d.] 12mo, pp. 8.

Quarter-Centennial Celebration of the NEWTON SABBATH SCHOOL UNION, ... October 16th, 1863. *Boston: Sam'l Chism.* 1863. 12mo, pp. 35, (1). H. 55094

Newton Theological Institution: A Sketch of its History, and an Account of ... the Dedication of the New Building, September 10, 1866. By a Committee of the Board of Trustees. *Boston: Gould and Lincoln.* 1866. 8vo, pp. 54. 2 Plates. B.

Also: ... The Act of Incorporation, with the Rules and Regulations. *Boston: Gould and Lincoln.* 1868. 18mo, pp. 18.—Catalogue of the Officers and Students of the Newton Theological Institution, December, 1831. ... *Boston: Lincoln and Edmands.* 1831. 8vo, pp. 12. Continued.—A General Catalogue of the Newton Theological Institution: ... with the Annual Catalogue for 1853–54. *Boston: Gould and Lincoln.* 1854. 12mo, pp. 36. Continued.—Laws of the Newton Theological Institution. *Boston: Gould, Kendall & Lincoln.* 1849. 12mo, pp. 12. Continued.—Report of the Professors of the Newton Theological Institution, to the Trustees, Sept. 9, 1830. ... *Boston: Lincoln and Edmands.* [n. d.] 8vo, pp. 22.—Rules and Regulations of the Newton Theological Institution. *Boston: Printed by Lincoln & Edmands.* 1826. 12mo, pp. 12.

Constitution of the NEWTON UNION LEAGUE organized May 23, 1863. [n. p. n. d.] 12mo, pp. (3). H. 55096

First Annual Report of the ... Directors of the NEWTON YOUNG MEN'S CHRISTIAN ASSOCIATION. With Constitution and ... Members. ... 1857. *Boston: Printed by B. F. Allen.* 1857. 8vo, pp. 15. H. 55097

[First Annual] Report of the School Committee of ... Newton. For 1838. [n. p. n. d.] 8vo, pp. 8. Continued. H.

Statement of Christian Faith held by the Channing Congregational Church, Newton, Massachusetts, 1858. [n. p. n. d.] 24mo, pp. 14. B. 55099

The Newton Mining Company, Canada East, organized under the General Statutes of Massachusetts. *Boston: Printed by Alfred Mudge & Son.* 1864. 8vo, pp. 13. B. 55100

Newtonian Reflector; or New England Almanack for ... 1825. ... Calculated for Hartford. By Anson Allen. *Hartford.* [n. d.] 12mo. 55101

Newtonville, *Mass.* Revised Catalogue of ... the Sunday School Library of the Central Congregational Church, Newtonville, Mass. *Boston: Printed by Chas. T. Valentine.* 1870. 12mo, pp. 12. H. 55102

Newtown, *N. H.* A Confession of Faith and Church Order: adopted by the Baptist Church of Christ in Newtown, New Hampshire. Constituted February 17, 1796. *Exeter.* 1796. 12mo, pp. 16. W. 55103

Newtown, *Pa.* A True and Faithful Narrative of the Modes and Measures pursued at the Anniversary Election, for Representatives, of the Freemen of the Province of Pennsylvania, held at Newtown, in and for the County of Bucks, on ... the first day of October, Anno Domini 1770. By a Bucks County Man. *Philadelphia.* 1771. 8vo, pp. 7. W. 55104

Newzeit wie vnnsers allergnadigistn hern des Romischn vnd hyspaenischn Konigs leut Ain Costliche Newe Lanndschafft habn gefundn. [n. p. 1520.] 8vo. 55105

"News how the men of our most gracious Sovereign King of Rome and Spain have found a costly new country. A conscientious reproduction of the text of a manuscript in Yucatan, with a translation in modern German and French, printed with old Gothic characters of the fifteenth century."—Muller.

The Next Administration to be Crippled! "A Board of Survey of the Navy." [n. p. 1865?] 8vo, pp. 23. H. 55106

The cover title reads: "What is it?"

The Next Presidency, The Chicago Convention. Shall the People or "The Politicians," Decide the Issue? By one of the Democratic People of Jackson's Day. [n. p. n. d.] 8vo, pp. 8.

The Next Presidential Election. Mr. Lincoln—The Presidency—Action of Legislatures ... [n. p. 1864?] 8vo, pp. 8.

Neyn (P. de). Lust-hoff der Huwelyken, Behelsende Verschyde seldsame Ceremonien ... soo in Asia, Europa, Africa els America In gebruyck zyn [*i. e.* zeyn] ... Door P. de Neyn. *Amsterdam: Jan. Bouman.* 1681. 12mo, pp. (30), 265, (6). 8 Plates. + *'T Amsterdam, by Willem Lamsveld.* 1697. 12mo, pp. (30), 265, (6). 55109

The pleasant matrimonial garden. Pages 231–265 treat of the American tribes: Apalachians, Brazilians, Inhabitants of Guiana, Florida, Ingas, New-Netherland, New-

France, Virginia, etc. Two plates relate to America. The errata of the edition of 1681 is corrected in that of 1697. Another edition, *Rotterdam,* 1730, 12mo.

Nez-percés' First Book. Designed for Children and New Beginners. *Clear Water Mission Press.* 1839. 18mo, pp. 20.

Niagara. An Account of a Journey to Niagara, Montreal, and Quebec, in 1766; or, "Tis Eighty Years Since." *New York: Printed by William Osborn.* 1846. 8vo, pp. 30. 55111

An Act to construct a Ship Canal or Marine Railway around the Falls of Niagara. [n. p. 1865.] 12mo, pp. 18. 55112

A Concise View of Black Rock, ... and ... property, belonging to the Niagara City Association, ... and the Black Rock Land and Railroad Company. *Black Rock.* 1836. 18mo, pp. 92

Description of a View of the Falls of Niagara ... *Boston: Printed by Perkins and Marvin.* 1837. 8vo, pp. 12. Plate. B.

Engineers' Report on the Niagara Ship Canal, made to the Commissioners ... of New York, by C. B. Stuart & Edward W. Serrell ... *New York.* 1854. 8vo, pp. 26. Map. S. 55115

See also Vol. vi., No. 22585.

The Falls of Niagara and the Vicinity. A Complete Guide ... *T. Nelson & Sons, London.* [1858.] 12mo, pp. 64. 12 Plates. + [*Ibid.*] MDCCCLX. 55116

Falls of Niagara, as seen from the Table Rock, October, 1834. A Poem. ... *Jacksonville: Printed by Calvin Goudy.* 1835. 8vo, pp. 16. B. 55117

Falls of Niagara, Sketches by the Way; a Poem. By an Author for the first time. *New York.* 1829. 8vo, pp. 30. 55118

A Guide to Travelers visiting the Falls of Niagara. By a Resident at the Falls. [*Buffalo, N. Y.: C. Faxon, Printer.* n. d.] 12mo, pp. 12. B. 55119

Niagara; A Poem. By a Member of the Ohio Bar. *New-York: Edward O. Jenkins.* 1848. 12mo, pp. 11. H. 55120

Sundry Documents referring to the Niagara and Detroit Rivers Railroad ... Albany, 12th July, 1845. [n. p. n. d.] 8vo, pp. 8. S. 55121

The Niagara Falls Companion, and Fashionable Miscellany. ... Opinions and Remarks of Capt. Basil Hall, Don Jose Maria

Meredia, and ... other Persons. ... First [and last] Edition. [n. p.] 1834. 16mo, pp. 16. H. 55122

... The Niagara Falls Guide With Full Instructions to direct the Traveller To all the Points of Interest at the Falls and Vicinity. ... *Buffalo: A. Burke.* 1848. 18mo, pp. 100. Map. + [*Ibid.*] 1850. 18mo, pp. 112. Map. + *Buffalo: James Faxon.* 1851. 18mo. + [*Ibid.*] 1852. 55123

Niagara Falls the Great Manufacturing Village of the West: ... a Statement of the ... Niagara Falls Hydraulic Company. With ... the Charter and By-Laws ... *Boston: Printed by Dutton and Wentworth.* 1853. 8vo, pp. 33. 2 Maps. H., S. 55124

Final Report of John A. Roebling, Civil Engineer, to the Presidents ... of the Niagara Falls Suspension ... and ... International Bridge Companies, May 1, 1855. *Rochester, N. Y.* 1855. 8vo, pp. 47. S. 55125

The Niagara Ship Canal: its Military and Commercial Necessity. *New York.* 1863. 8vo, pp. 15. 2 Maps. H. 55126

Niagara Steamer, chartered for the Banks Expedition in 1862. Letter of the Secretary of War, with information relative thereto. [n. p. 1864.] 8vo, pp. 8. 55127

Pecks' Tourist's Companion to Niagara Falls, Saratoga Springs, the Lakes, Canada, etc. ... *Buffalo: William B. & Charles E. Peck.* 1845. 18mo, pp. 194. 55128

Pictorial Guide to the Falls of Niagara: A Manual for Visiters [*sic*]. Illustrated ... by ... J. W. Orr. *Buffalo: Salisbury & Clapp.* 1842. 16mo, pp. 232. 4 Plates, 3 Charts. C. 55129

... Report of the Committee on Commerce and Navigation [of the Senate of the State of New York] on the Bill for the Incorporation of the Niagara Ship Canal Company. Transmitted ... January 22, 1864. *Albany: Comstock & Cassidy, Printers.* 1864. 8vo, pp. 16. B. 55130

Report on the Location and Expenses of the Niagara Falls Ship Canal. *New York.* 1834. 8vo, pp. 16. Map. 55131

Also: Report of a Select Committee on a Ship Canal around the Falls of Niagara. *Columbus.* 1836. 12mo.

Tunis's Topographical and Pictorial Guide. *Niagara Falls.* 1865. 16mo. Map and Engravings. 55132

Visit to the Falls. *See* [Maude (J.)], Vol. xii., No. 46913.

Niblack (W. E.) Public Revenue and the Tariff. Speech of Hon. William E. Niblack, ... January 27, 1869. [n. p. n. d.] 8vo, pp. 8. H. 55133

Also: State of the Union. Speech ... January 31, 1861. [n. p. n. d.] 8vo, pp. 7.

Niboyet (P.) Les Mondes Nouveaux. Voyages ... dans l'Océan Pacifique. ... *Paris.* 1855. 8vo. 55134

Includes Chili, Peru, Califonia, etc.

Nicaise (A.) Les Flibustiers américains; Walker et l'Amérique Centrale; le Tueur de Jaguars. Par A. Nicaise. *Paris.* 1861. 12mo. 55135

Nican y cuiliuhtica ynin Xitlapoualcatea Mexica ca nauhtetl y niuh quitova ce acatl quitlamia 13 acatl, ... 1576. 8vo, pp. 158.

These are Mexican pictographic plates from the collection of Mr. Aubin.

Nicaragua. America del Centro Memoria dirijida por el Ministerio de Estado á la Asambléa Constituyente ... en Diciembre de 1847 ... *Léon de Nicaragua.* [1847.] 8vo, pp. 28.

The Atlantic and Pacific International Ship-Canal Company (limited). Isthmus of Nicaragua, Central America. *Paris.* [n. d.] Folio, pp. 34. 55138

For private circulation only. In English, French, and Spanish.

Charter and Act of Incorporation of The American Atlantic & Pacific Ship Canal Company, as amended: ... and Charter granted by the State of Nicaragua ... *New York: Wm. C. Bryant & Co., Printers.* 1852. 8vo, pp. 28. 55139

Constitucion Politica del Estádo de Nicaragua, 1826. *Guatemala.* [1826.] 4to, pp. 27. M. 55140

Constitucion Politica del Estádo Soberano Libre é Independiente de Nicaragua Reformada y Sancionada por su Asambléa Constituyente en 12 de Noviembre de 1838. [*Leon.* 1848.] Sm. 4to, pp. (2), 89. 55141

Cuadro Estadistico del Departamente de Gracias precedido de un Compendio elemental de Estadistica. *Paris.* 1857. 8vo, pp. 38. 2 Maps. 55142

Defensa del Padre Legislativo del Estado de Nicaragua. [Por T. Maria Estrado.] *Granada.* 1851. 8vo, pp. 23. 55143

El Defensor del Pueblo. [*Granada.*] 1851. 8vo. 55144

Defenza de los Directios del Pais en las Cuestiones promovidas por el Consul de S. M. Britanica, F. Chatfield. [*Leon.* 1843.] 13 leaves. 55145

The Destiny of Nicaragua: Central America as it was, is, and may be. ... By an Officer in the service of Walker. *S. A. Bent & Co., Boston.* 1856. 8vo, pp. 72. Plate. B. 55146

Documentos Creados sobre platicas de paz. *Granada: Impresone de orden del Gobierno de la Republica de Nicaragua.* 1854. 4to, pp. 16. 55147

Documentos interesantes. *See* Vol. xii., No. 51084.

Documentos relativos á la Legacion de los Estados de Nicaragua y Honduras cerca del Gabinete Británico, sobre el Territorio de Mosquitos y Puerto de San Juan del Norte. Los publica el Sor Don Francisco Castellon, Ministro ... *Granada.* 1851. Folio, pp. (4), 124. 55148

Documentos relativos al armisticio preliminar celebrado el dia 7. del corriente Marzo en la pequeña isla de Cuba del gran lago de Nicaragua ... *Leon de Nicaragua, Año de* 1848. 8vo, 4 leaves.

On the Mosquito Question.

Informe del Ministro de Relaciones interiores. *Granada.* 1853. 8vo, pp. 39. 55150

Informe presentada por el Ministro Interimo de Relaciones interiores y exteriores á las Cameras legislativas de Nicaragua. *Granada.* 1853. 8vo. 55151

Interposicion de la R. N. de C. A. Contestacion del Gobierno Provisorio. *Leon.* 1851. 8vo, 6 leaves. 55152

Ley reglamentaria de la administracion de justicia del estado de Nicaragua decretada por el poder legislativo y sancionada por el ejecutivo en 15 de Junio de 1841. *Impresa en Leon en la Imprenta del Gobierno, año* 1841. 4to, 16 leaves. 55153

Manifiesto que el Supremo Director del Estado de Nicaragua hall a los Gobiernos de América ... *Leon, Año de* 1848. 8vo, 8 l.

On the Mosquito Question.

Mensage [del] Director Supremo del Estado ... á la Asambléa Legislativa 16 del corriente [*sic*] en la Ciudad de Managua. *Granada.* 1853. 8vo, 6 leaves. 55155

Also: Mensage del Supreme Director de Nicaragua. *Managua.* 1854. 8vo, pp. 10. *See also* Vol. xii., No. 48121.

El Ministro de Nicaragua á sus Conciudadanos. [n. p. 1851.] 4to, pp. 19. H. 55156

Nicaragua. *See* [Sampson (M. B.)]

The Nicaragua Canal Contract, etc. [n. p. n. d.] 12mo.

Nueva Discusion entre el ajiente de S. M. B. y el Gobierno Supremo de Nicaragua ... Octubre de 1849. *Leon: Imprenta de Minerva.* [1849.] 8vo, pp. 44. 55158

Des Orden del Director Supremo del Estado de Nicaragua se dan al publico los documentos ... *Leon, Nov.* 20 *de* 1847. 4to, 12 leaves. 55159

A los Pueblos de Centro-América. [Por Feo Castellon. *Comayagua.* 1851.] 8vo, pp. 16. 55160

Reglamentos para la Organizacion ... del Ejérceto del Estado de Nicaragua. *Leon.* 1850. 8vo, pp. (2), 40, Additions, pp. 6, 15 and 4, (1). 55161

Terms of Contract between the State of Nicaragua, and the Atlantic & Pacific Ship Canal Company, ... August, 1849. *New-York: Wm. C. Bryant & Co., Printers.* 1849. 8vo, pp. 18.

Niccolls (S. J.) In Memoriam. A Discourse on the assassination of Abraham Lincoln, ... delivered in ... St. Louis, April 23, 1865, By Rev. Samuel J. Niccolls. ... *St. Louis: Sherman Spencer, Printer.* 1865. 8vo, pp. 16. B. 55163

Also: Thanksgiving. A Sermon preached in Chambersburg, November 28, 1861. ... *Chambersburg: Repository Office.* 1861. 8vo, pp. 8.

Nicely (W. S.) Facts for Emigrants. A Description of Twenty-Six Counties of South-West Missouri; showing the Climate, Soil, Timber, Prairie, Minerals, and Water of each County; ... By W. S. Nicely. *St. Louis: George Knapp & Co.* 1867. 12mo, pp. 72. 55164

Nicely (W.) The Great Southwest or Plain Guide for Emigrants and Capitalists; embracing a Description of the States of Missouri and Kansas ... By Wilson Nicely. *St. Louis: R. P. Studley & Co., Printers.* 1867. 12mo, pp. 115, (1). Map. C.

Nicholas (G.) Correspondence between George Nicholas, Esq. of Kentucky, and the Hon. Robert G. Harper, Member of Congress from ... South Carolina. *Lexington: Printed by John Bradford.* 1799. 8vo, pp. 26, viii. C. 55166

Nicholas. A Letter from George Nicholas, of Kentucky, to his Friend, in Virginia. Justifying the Conduct of the Citizens of Kentucky, as to some of the late Measures of the General Government, and Correcting Certain False Statements. *Lexington: Printed by John Bradford.* 1798. 8vo, pp. 42. BA. + ... *Philadelphia: Reprinted, by James Carey.* 1799. 8vo, pp. 39. H.

This elicited: "Observations, on a Letter from George Nicholas, ... to his Friend in Virginia: in which, some of the Errors, ... in that Letter are corrected ... By an Inhabitant of the North-Western Territory." *Cincinnati: Printed ... by Edmund Freeman,* Feb. 14, M,DCC,XCIX. 8vo, pp. 46. BA.

Nicholas (J.) Address ... before the Ontario Agricultural Society, at its First Annual Meeting, Oct. 13, 1819, by the Hon. John Nicholas ... *Canandaigua.* [n. d.] 8vo, pp. 23. S.

[Nicholas.] Decius's Letters, on the opposition to the Federal Constitution, in Virginia: written in 1788 and 1789. The Third Edition. With ... additional Pieces ... on the Principles and Operation of Party Spirit Since. ... [And] Letters, &c. from Washington, Jefferson ... and other High Characters ... Written in 1818. *Richmond: The Author.* 1818. 8vo, pp. (2), 36. BA.

Also: Speech ... on the Alien and Sedition Laws. *Philadelphia.* 1799. 8vo.

Nicholas (R. C.) Considerations on the Present State of Virginia Examined, by Robert Carter Nicholas. [n. p.:] *Printed in the Year* M,DCC,LXXIV. 8vo, pp. 43. 55170

See Jefferson's "Notes on Virginia," Query xxii., *and our* Vol. viii., No. 31346.

Nicholas. Letter of Hon. Robert Carter Nicholas, to The Governor of Louisiana, on The Resolutions of the General Assembly. *Washington: Blair and Rives, Printers.* 1839. 8vo, pp. 14. 55171

Nicholas (S. S.) Conservative Essays Legal and Political. By S. S. Nicholas ... *Philadelphia: J. B. Lippincott & Co.* 1863. 8vo, pp. 551. + Second Series. *Philadelphia.* 1865. 8vo, pp. 232. + Vol. iii. *Louisville: Bradley & Gilbert.* 1867. 8vo, pp. 155. + Vol. iv. *Louisville: J. P. Morton & Co.* 1869. 8vo.

Nicholas. Habeas Corpus. A Response to Mr. Binney. By S. S. Nicholas. *Louisville: Printed by Bradley & Gilbert.* 1862. 8vo, pp. 20. 55173

Nicholas. Habeas Corpus, The Law of War, and Confiscation. By S. S. Nicholas. *Louisville: Printed by Bradley & Gilbert.* 1862. 8vo, pp. 29. H. 55174

[Nicholas.] Letters on the Presidency. First published in 1840. [n. p. n. d.] 8vo, pp. 57. H. 55175

[Nicholas.] Martial Law: By a Kentuckian. ... [n. p. about 1842.] 8vo, pp. 14. 55176

Nicholas. Martial Law. By S. S. Nicholas. Part of a Pamphlet First Published in 1842, over the Signature of a Kentuckian. [*Louisville:*] *Bradley & Gilbert, Printers.* [1861.] 8vo, pp. 16. + *Reprinted, Philadelphia: John Campbell.* 1862. 8vo, pp. 32. B. 55177

Of the last edition forty-nine copies were printed in quarto.

[Nicholas.] A Plan for obtaining our Presidents without the intervention of Political Parties. [n. p. n. d.] 8vo, pp. 7. H.

Nicholas. A Review of the Argument of President Lincoln and Attorney General Bates, in favor of Presidential Power to suspend the Privilege of the Writ of Habeas Corpus. ... *Louisville, Ky.: Printed by Bradley & Gilbert.* 1861. 8vo, pp. 38. B.

Nicholas (Wilson Cary, *Gov. of Virginia*). Letter to his Constituents, 1809. [n. p. n. d.] 8vo. 55180

Nicholas. Case of the Ship Nicholas. [*London.* 1786.] 8vo, pp. 43. H. 55181

Nicholds (——). Report of the Case, Nicholds, ... against Wells, being that of a Treasury Warrant, opposed to a County Court Pre-emption. *Frankfort, Ky.* 1803. 8vo. 55182

Nicholl (J.) An|Houre Glasse of In-|dian News.|Or|A true and tragicall discourse, shewing the|most lamentable miseries, and distressed Calami-|ties indured by 67 Englishmen, which were sent|for a supply to the planting in Guiana in|the yeare. 1605.|Who not finding the saide place, were for want of vic-|tuall, left a shore in Saint Lucia, an Island of Caniballs,|or Meneaters in the West-Indyes, vnder the Con-|duct of Captain-Sen-Iohns, of all which said|number, onely a 11. are supposed to be|still liuing, whereof 4. are lately|returned into Eng-|land.|Written by John Nicholl, one of the aforesaid|Company.|...|*London|Printed for Nathaniell Butter, and are to be|Solde at his Shop neere Saint Austens Gate.*|1607.| Sm. 4to, Half-Title, Title, 20 leaves.

A work of the greatest rarity, printed in black letter. The only copy I have seen, except one in the British Museum, belongs to Mr. C. H. Kalbfleisch, of New York. The half-title has a large woodcut of a ship.

NICHOLL (T. S.) Perspicuous Compendium of Invaluable Advice for American Emigrants. By T. S. Nicholl, of Carlisle. *Newcastle*. 1839. 8vo. 55184

NICHOLLS (J. F.) The Remarkable Life, Adventures and Discoveries of Sebastian Cabot, of Bristol, the Founder of Great Britain's Maritime Power, Discoverer of America, and its first Colonizer. By J. F. Nicholls. ... *London: Sampson Low, Son, and Marston*. 1869. Sq. 8vo, pp. xv, 190, (1). Map and Portrait. C., H. 55185

For a long, and appreciative note on this work, *see* Stevens' "Bibliotheca Historica."

NICHOLLS (J.) Recollections and Reflections, Personal and Political, as Connected with Public Affairs, during the Reign of George III. By John Nicholls, Esq. *London: James Ridgway*. 1820. 2 vols., 8vo, pp. viii, 408; Vol. II., 1822, pp. (2), 250. + Second Edition. *London: Longman* .... 1822. 2 vols., 8vo, pp. viii, 408; (2), 250. C. + *Philadelphia: H. C. Carey*. 1822. 12mo, pp. iii, 302. P., S. 55186

Some chapters relate to American affairs.

NICHOLS (——). Jefferson and Liberty; or Celebration of the Fourth of March. A Patriotic Tragedy: A Picture of the Perfidy of Corrupt Administration. In Five Acts. Written by Nichols. [n. p.:] *Sold at the Printing-Office, Temple Street*. 1801. 8vo, pp. 28, (1). BA. 55187

NICHOLS (A.), *Jr.* Address ... before ... Jordan Lodge, ... Danvers: December 25, A. L. 5811. By Andrew Nichols, Jun. *Salem: Printed by Thomas C. Cushing*. 1812. 8vo, pp. 16.

[NICHOLS.] Address of the Health Committee of Danvers, May, 1849. *Danvers: G. R. Carlton*. 1849. 8vo, pp. 12. H.

NICHOLS. Danvers: a Poem, written for the Centennial Celebration, June 16, 1852. ... *Boston*. 1852. 8vo, pp. 40. S.

Included in our No. 18513. Also: Address, ... in Danvers, before the Society ... for Suppressing Intemperance, ..: April 27, 1819. ... *Salem: Printed by John D. Cushing*. 1819. 8vo, pp. 24.—The Spirit of Free-Masonry; A Poem. ... *Boston: John Punchard*. 1831. 8vo, pp. 24.

NICHOLS (Beach). Atlas of Herkimer County, New York, from Actual Surveys, by and under the Direction of B. Nichols,

assisted by [eight others]. *New York: Stranahan & Nichols*. 1868. Folio, pp. (2), 32 leaves. Colored Maps. C. 55191

Also: Atlas of Montgomery and Fulton Counties, New York, from Actual Surveys. *New York: Stranahan & Nichols*. 1868. 4to, pp. (4). 28 maps.

NICHOLS (B. R.) An Oration, ... Fifth of July, 1813, in ... Salem .... By Benjamin R. Nichols. *Salem: Printed by Joshua Cushing*. 1813. 8vo, pp. 24. H. 55192

NICHOLS (C. B.) ... Part I. ... Nichols' Illustrated New York: a Series of Views of the Empire City and its Environs; ... with Explanatory Descriptions. *New York: C. B. & F. B. Nichols*. 1847. 8vo, Engraved Title, pp. 24. 4 Plates. H.

Complete in twelve numbers.

NICHOLS (C. I. H.) On the Responsibilities of Woman. A Speech by Mrs. C. I. H. Nichols, Worcester, Oct. 15, 1851. [n. p. n. d.] 8vo, pp. 16. H. 55194

NICHOLS (E. H.) Argument before the Hon. J. D. Cox, ... in support of the ... Central Branch Union Pacific Railroad Company ... By Effingham H. Nichols ... . *Washington: Gibson Brothers, Printers*. 1869. 8vo, pp. 44. + [*Ibid.*] 1870. 8vo, pp. 43. H. 55195

NICHOLS. A Letter to the Rt. Rev. H. Potter, Bishop of New York, as to the Proceedings against Rev. S. H. Tyng, Jr. ... *Washington: Gibson Brothers, Printers*. 1868. 8vo, pp. 15.

Also: Argument ... relating to the ... Central Branch Union Pacific R. R. Co. [n. p. n. d.] 8vo, pp. 8, (2).—The Law relating to the rights of the Central Branch Union Pacific R. R. Co. [n. p. 1868.] 8vo, pp. 7. B.

NICHOLS (G. W.) Reconstruction: a Poem: By G. W. Nichols ... . *Beloit: Guernsey, Printer*. 1868. 16mo, pp. 7. H.

NICHOLS. The Sanctuary: a Story of the Civil War. By George Ward Nichols. *New York*. 1866. 12mo, pp. 286.

NICHOLS. The Story of the Great March. From the Diary of a Staff-Officer. By Brevet-Major George Ward Nichols ... . *London: Sampson Low, Son & Marston*. 1865. 12mo, pp. xii, 288. Map. + *New York: Harper & Brothers*. 1865. 12mo, pp. 394. Map and Plates. + Sixteenth Edition. [*Ibid.*] 12mo, pp. 408. 14 Plates and Map. + Twenty-Sixth Edition. [*Ibid.*] 1866.

NICHOLS (G. Warner). Fragments from the Study of a Pastor. By George W. Nichols, A.M. *New York: Henry B. Price*. 1860. 16mo, pp. 252. Plate. H. 55200

NICHOLS (Ichabod). A Discourse ... at the Dedication of the Stone Church of the First Parish in Portland, February 9th, 1826. By I. Nichols. With an Appendix containing a Memoir of the Parish. [By Wm. P. Preble.] *Portland: James Adams, Jr.* 1862. 8vo, pp. (2), 24, (1). H. 55201

NICHOLS. An Oration, ... on the Fourth of July, 1805, at ... Salem, Massachusetts. By Ichabod Nichols, Ter. *Salem: Printed by Joshua Cushing*. 1805. 8vo, pp. 24. H., S. 55202

Also: Address ... before the Portland Association for the Promotion of Temperance. February 22, 1828. ... *Portland: Hill and Edwards, Printers*. 1828. 8vo, pp. 32.—A Sermon ... at Biddeford, at the Ordination of Rev. Thomas Tracy, January 15, 1824. ... *Portland*. 1824. 8vo, pp. 30. H.

NICHOLS (J.) ... A Discourse ... at the Funeral of Mrs. Cornelia Higinbotham, ... Oneida, N. Y., May 16, 1850. By James Nichols ... . *Utica, N. Y.: R. Northway, Printer*. 1850. 8vo, pp. 23. H. 55203

NICHOLS (J. R.) Address ... before the Essex Agricultural Society, By James R. Nichols. ... 1855. *Newburyport: Morse, Brewster & Huse, Printers*. 1855. 8vo, pp. 20. H. 55204

NICHOLS. Poem, ... at the Semi-Centennial Celebration of Bradford Academy, July 6, 1853. By J. R. Nichols. *Boston*. 1853. 16mo, pp. 10. H. 55205

Also: ... A Lecture ... before the State Board of Agriculture, Salem, December 11, 1866. ... *Boston: Wright & Potter, Printers*. 1867. 8vo, pp. 25. H.

NICHOLS (J.) ... A Sermon occasioned by the Death of Daniel Hildreth, ... in Beverly, Mass., August 19, 1860. By Rev. John Nichols ... . *Boston: Wright & Potter, Printers*. 1860. 8vo, pp. 16. BA. 55206

NICHOLS (J. H.) The Future. A Poem: delivered before the ... Alumni of Washington College, ... Hartford, August 3d, 1842. By J. H. Nichols. *New Haven*. 1842. 8vo. N.

NICHOLS (J. M.) Tom Wiley, the Scout of the Northwest. By J. M. Nichols. *New York: American News Company*. 1866. 8vo, pp. 44. 55208

NICHOLS (J. T. G.) A Discourse on the Twentieth Anniversary of his Ordination, ... April 12, 1863. ... By John T. Gilman Nichols. ... *Saco: William Noyes, Printer*. 1863. 8vo, pp. 19. H. 55209

Also: A Sermon, ... at Saco, Maine, May 16, 1852, on the Sabbath following the

Decease of Samuel Pierson, Esq. ... *Boston: T. R. Marvin*. 1852. 8vo, pp. 28. Portrait. B.

[NICHOLS (Mary Grove).] Mary Lyndon; or, Revelations of a Life. An Autobiography. *New York: Stringer & Townsend*. 1855. 12mo, pp. 388. + [*Ibid.*] 1860. 12mo. C.

NICHOLS (Philip). *See* Drake (*Sir* F.), Vol. V. 20838–40.

NICHOLS (R. S.) Bernice; or the Curse of Minna, and other Poems. By Rebecca S. Nichols. *Cincinnati*. 1844. 12mo.

NICHOLS (T. L.) A Biography of the Brothers Davenport. With some Account of the Physical and Psychical Phenomena which have occurred in their Presence, in America and Europe. By T. L. Nichols, M.D. ... *London: Saunders, Otley and Co.* 1864. 8vo, pp. viii, 360. + Second Edition. [*Ibid.*] 55212

NICHOLS. Phénomenes des Frères Davenport ... Par Le Docteur Nichols ... . *Paris: Didier et Cie.* 1865. 12mo, pp. xvi, 376. 55213

NICHOLS. Forty Years of American Life By Dr. Thomas L. Nichols ... *London: John Maxwell and Company*. M DCCC LXIV. 2 vols., 8vo, pp. xii, 408; xi, 368. H. + Second Edition ... . *London: Longman* .... 1874. Post 8vo, pp. xvi, 509. 55214

NICHOLS. Journal in Jail, kept during a Four Months' Imprisonment for Libel, in the Jail of Erie County. By Thomas L. Nichols. *Buffalo: A. Dinsmore*. 1840. 12mo, pp. 248. C.

Also: Father Larkin's Mission in Jonesville; a Tale of the Times. ... *Baltimore: Kelly, Hedian & Piet*. 1860. 18mo, pp. iv, 3–64.—An Introduction to the Water-Cure: ... *New York: Fowlers and Wells*. 1850. 16mo, pp. 46.—The Lady in Black: a Story of New York Life, Morals, and Manners. ... *New York*. 1844. 8vo, pp. 44.—Religions of the World: Impartial History of Religious Creeds. ... *Cincinnati*. 1855. 8vo.—Woman, in all Ages and Nations. ... *New-York: H. Long & Brother*. 1849. 12mo, pp. 237. S. + With a Preface by S. P. Andrews. *New York*. 1854. 12mo.

NICHOLS (W.), *Jr.* Oration at West Cambridge, July 4, 1808, in Commemoration of the Anniversary of American Independence. By William Nichols, Jr. ... *Boston*. 1808. 8vo.

NICHOLS (W. T.) Eulogy ... at the Funeral of the Late Silas Bowen, M.D., at Clarendon, Vt., ... May, 1858. By W. T. Nichols, Esq. ... *Rutland: Geo. A. Tuttle & Co., Printers*. 1858. 8vo, pp. 16. H. 55217

NICHOLS & GORMAN. Hand-Book for County Officers: ... with Approved Forms and Precedents. ... Second Edition. *Raleigh: Nichols & Gorman, Printers*. [n. d.] 16mo, pp. cccvi.

NICHOLSON (A. O. P.) Address ... before the Two Literary Societies of the University of North-Carolina, June 1, 1853, By Hon. A. O. P. Nicholson .... *Raleigh: Printed by W. W. Holden*. 1853. 8vo, pp. 31. H. 55219

NICHOLSON (E. G.) The Votaries of Twilight. A Poem. ... Jan. 6, 1840. By E. G. Nicholson. [n. p.] 1840. 8vo.

NICHOLSON (F.) An Apology or Vindication of Francis Nicholson, Esq; His Majesty's Governor of South-Carolina, From the Unjust Aspersions cast on Him by some of the Members of the Bahama-Company. *London: T. Payne*. 1724. 8vo, pp. 62. BM. 55221

[NICHOLSON.] A Modest Answer To a Malicious Libel Against his Excellency Francis Nicholson, Esq; &c. Or An Examination of that Part of Mr. Blair's Affidavit, relating to the School-Boys of the Grammar-School, in her Majesty's Royal College of William and Mary in Virginia. Written in Virginia, in the Year 1704. [*London*. 1706.] 8vo, pp. 55. BM. 55222

The imputation was that Mr. Nicholson encouraged an insurrection in the school, and found the insurgents powder and shot *See also* Vol. IX., No. 36703.

[NICHOLSON.] Papers Relating to An Affidavit Made by His Reverence James Blair, Clerk, pretended President of William and Mary College, and supposed Commissary to the Bishop of London in Virginia, against Francis Nicholson, Esq; Governour of the said Province. Wherein his Reverence's great Respect to Government ... will plainly appear; ... [*London*:] *Printed in the Year* 1727. 8vo, pp. (4), 104. BM. 55223

[NICHOLSON (J. W. A.)] Reports of the Trial Trip of the United States Steamer Wampanoag, ... February 7 to ... 17, 1868. [n. p. n. d.] 8vo, pp. 8. H. 55224

NICHOLSON (J.) An Account of the Impeachment, Trial, and Acquittal of John Nicholson, Esquire, Comptroller General of the State of Pennsylvania. *Philadelphia: Frances Bailey*. M.DCC.XCIX. 8vo, pp. (2), 62–776. 55225

NICHOLSON. Address to the People of Pennsylvania; containing a Narrative of the Proceedings against John Nicholson, Comptroller-General of the said Commonwealth. *Philadelphia: Printed by Frances Bailey*. M.DCC.XC. 8vo, pp. 56. 55226

See also [Hogan (E.)], Vol. VIII., No. 32418, *and* [Huidekoper (H. J.)], Vol. VIII., No. 33625.

NICHOLSON (J.) The Farmer's Assistant; ... By John Nicholson, Esq. ... *Albany*. 1814. 8vo, pp. 327. + Second Edition, ... Enlarged. *Philadelphia: Benjamin Warner*. 1820. 8vo, pp. 468. BA. 55227

NICHOLSON (J. A.) Impeachment of the President. Speech of Hon. John A. Nicholson, ... February 24, 1868. *Washington: F. & J. Rives, ... Printers*. 1868. 8vo, pp. 7. H. 55228

NICHOLSON (J. J.) ... A Funeral Sermon, ... [on] the Death of Henry Clay, ... in ... Waterford, N. Y. ... 4th of July, ... 1852. By the Rev. J. J. Nicholson ... . *Waterford: Andrew Hoffman, Printer*. 1852. 12mo, pp. 14. H. 55229

NICHOLSON (J.) The | Standard | Of the Lord lifted up in New-England, | In opposition to the | Man of Sin: | or, | The Trumpet of the Lord sounding there, with a Visitation to the suffering seed of | God in New-England, or elsewhere. With a Warning from the Lord, to the Rulers | and Magistrates, Priests and People of New-Eng- | land; but more especially to the Rulers and | Magistrates of the Bloody Town of Boston, who | have put the Servants of the Living God to Death. | ... | Written (in the Prison at Boston in New-England, in America,) | By a Friend of Israels Commonwealth, known to the | world by name, Joseph Nicholson. | *London, Printed for Robert Wilson, at the Signe of the Black-spread-Eagle, and Winde-mil in Martins Le grand*, 1660. 4to, pp. 24, 2 additional pages signed James Naylor. BM.

A volume of excessive rarity.

NICHOLSON (Joseph H.) Mr. Nicholson's Motion, Feb. 10, 1806. *Washington*. 1806. 8vo. 55231

Relative to the Commerce of Great Britain with the United States. Also: Speech ... on the Organization of the Judiciary. *Washington*. 1802. 8vo.—Speech ... on the Bank Bill, January 23, 1811. [n. p. n. d.] 8vo, pp. 13.

NICHOLSON (T.) An Affecting Narrative of the Captivity and Sufferings of Thomas Nicholson (a Native of New Jersey), ... Six Years a Prisoner among the Algerines, ... and some Particulars of Commodore Decatur's Expedition against the Barbary Powers. *Boston: G. Walker*. [n. d.] 12mo, pp. 24. Portrait.

NICHOLSON (T.) An Essay on Yellow Fever, comprising the History of that Disease as it appeared in ... Antigua in ... 1835–1842, with ... the History to 1853. By Thomas Nicholson ... . Second Edition. *London: John Churchill and Sons*. MDCCCLXVI. 16mo, pp. vi, 62. 55233

NICHOLSON (T.) An Epistle to Friends in Great Britain, To whom is the Salutation of my Love, in the unchangeable Truth. [Little River in North Carolina, the 15th of the ninth Month, 1762.] 8vo, pp. 4. BM. 55234

NICHOLSON (W. R.) The Missionary at Work ... . A Sermon ... at the opening of the ... Meeting of the Board of Missions in ... Cincinnati, O., April 25, 1869. By Rev. Wm. R. Nicholson, D.D. *Cincinnati: Robert Clapp & Co.* 1869. 8vo, pp. 31. H. 55235

Nick of the Woods. *See* [Bird (R. M.)], Vol. II., 5554.

NICKERSON (F.) *See* Parsons (Tyler).

[NICKLIN (Philip Houlbrooke).] Letters Descriptive of the Virginia Springs; and the Roads leading thereto, and the Doings thereat. Collected, Corrected, Annotated and Edited, By Peregrine Prolix. ... *Philadelphia: H. S. Tanner*. 1835. 18mo, pp. 99, (4). Map. + Second Edition, containing Eight more Letters. [*Ibid.*] 1837. 12mo, pp. 248. Plate and Map. 55236

See "North American Review," XLV. 256.

[NICKLIN.] A Pleasant Peregrination through the Prettiest Parts of Pennsylvania. Performed by Peregrine Prolix. *Philadelphia: Gregg & Elliott*. 1836. 8vo, pp. 148. B., BA. 55237

"In spite of its affected title, this little book is both amusing and instructive. It presents, in a series of playful letters, a great many important facts in relation to the internal improvements of Pennsylvania."—*North American Review*, XLIII. 272. Also: Remarks on Literary Property. ... *Philadelphia: P. H. Nicklin and T. Johnson*. 1838. 18mo, pp. 144.—A Report ... to the ... Trustees of the University of Pennsylvania, ... concerning the Universities of Oxford and Cambridge, in England. ... *Philadelphia: Joseph and William Kite, Printers*. 1834. 8vo, pp. 40. B. Mr. Allibone refers to "Papers on Free Trade," which I have not seen.

NICKOLLS (J.), *pseudon.* *See* [Plumard de Dangeul].

NICKOLLS (R. B.) A Letter to the Treasurer of the Society instituted for the purpose of effecting the Abolition of the Slave Trade. From The Rev. Robert Boucher Nickolls ... . *London: Printed by James Phillips*. MDCCLXXXVII. 12mo, pp. 16. + A New Edition with ... Additions. [*Ibid.*] MDCCLXXXVIII. 16mo, pp. 58, (2). BA. 55238

See "Monthly Review," LXXVIII. 68 and 344. For a reply, *see* Vol. VI., No. 25479.

NICLUTSCH (F.) Amerikanische Nachrichten von Quito und den wilden Indianern in Maragnon. Verfasset von Francisco

Niclutsch ... . [*Leipzig*:] *Gedruckt im Jahr* 1781. Sm. 8vo, pp. 158, (1). BM. 55239

An account of Quito and the savages of Maragnon.

NICOL (J.) Copy of Three Letters, the first written by Dr. John Nicol at New York ... the second, by a Dissenting Minister in England ... the third, from a Minister at Boston ... giving an Account of the Progress ... of the Gospel in Foreign Parts, ... *Edinburgh*. 1740. 12mo, pp. 8. S. 55240

NICOL (J.) The Life and Adventures of John Nicol, Mariner. *William Blackwood, Edinburgh*. MDCCCXXII. 12mo, pp. ix, 215. Portrait. C., S. 55241

Edited by J. H. Relates to Canada, the Indians, etc.

NICOLAI (E.) Newe vnd warhaffte relation, von de | me was sich in beederley, | Dass ist, | In den West- vnd Ost- | Indien, von der zeit an zugetragen, dass | sich die Nauigationes der Holl- vnnd Engelländi | schen compagnien daselbsthin angefangen | abzuschneiden. | ... | Sambt einer newen description des Erdtbodens in | welchem die rechte beschaffenheit der Septentrionalischen Landt | so wol gegen Auff- als gegen Nidergang der Soñen jetzt erstreckt | an tag gebracht hingegen der falsche wohn den man biss | hero von dem freto Anian ... gehabt men | niglich benommen wirdt. Alles aus gewissen Castiglianischen vnnd Portugesischen | relationen colligiert, | Mit einer introduction in die bey | gefügte neue description dess Erdbodens | Durch | Elivd Nicolai | an tag geben. | *Getruckt zu München, durch Nicolaum Hen* | *ricum im Jahr* | M.DC.XIX. 4to, pp. (23), 158. Map. BM., H. 55242

This very scarce and highly interesting treatise, relating many circumstances now entirely lost, gives an account of the English and Dutch voyages of discovery. The map delineates the latest information concerning America.

NICOLAO PLUMBENSI. Opusculum vitæ, virtutum et miraculorum ven. servi dei fr. Sebastiani ab Apparitio ordinis min. de obseruantia laici professi Prouinciæ Mexicanæ. Por Nicolao Plumbensi, fratre, diacovensi, sev bosnensi episcopo, ord. minorum. *Romæ, ex officina Reverendæ Cameræ Apostolicæ*. 1696. 4to, pp. (30), 207, (4). 55243

NICOLAS (——). Emancipation—White and Black. [n. p. n. d.] 8vo, pp. 13. 55244

NICOLAS I. De Jesuit op den Throon; of de gevallen van Nicolaus de I., Koning van Paraguai en Keizer der Mamelukken. *Leeuw*. 1758. 8vo, pp. 54. 55245

The Jesuit on the throne; or the life of Nicolaus I., King of Paraguay, and Emperor of the Mamelucs. Also: Nicolas premier jésuite et Roi du Paraguai. *Buenos Aires.* 1761. 8vo. *See also* our Vol. VIII., No. 32020.

NICOLAS DE CASTRO. *See* Castro (N. de), Vol. III. 11466.

NICOLAS DE JESUS MARIA. La Cathedra en concurso de opositores Conjuncion publica a la del Adorado Principe de los Apostoles San Pedro. Sermon que el R. P. F. Nicolas de Jesus Maria predicò en la Ciudad de S. Luis Potosi el 22 de Febrero de 1749. *Mexico.* 1749. 4to, pp. 20. 55246

See also Jesus Maria (Nicolas de), Vol. IX., No. 36091.

[NICOLÁS (A.)] Esplicacion de la doctrina cristiana acomodada á la capacidad de los negros bozales. ... *Habana: En la imprenta de D. Esteban Boloña, año de* 1797. 8vo. 55247

By Antonio Nicolás, Duque de Estrada. The "Explicaciones" are in a broken negro dialect.

NICOLAS (D.) Relacion | summario de la | Vida, y Dichosa mverte | del U. P. Cypriano Baraze de la | Compañia de Iesus, muerto á ma- | rios de Barbaros en la Mission | de los Moxos de la Provin- | cia del Perù. | Sacala a lvz | el Yllmo S.or D.or D. Nicolas | Vrbano de Mata Obispo de la Paz. | ... | *En Lima en la Imprenta Real de Joseph de Contreras, Año de* 1704. 4to. Portrait.

NICOLAS (N. H.) The Privy Purse Expenses of King Henry the Eighth, ... with ... notes by Nicholas Harris Nicolas ... . *London: William Pickering.* MDCCCXXVII. 8vo, pp. (4), xlvi, 372

Narrates the rewards given for discoveries, and among them those given for the early English discoveries in America.

NICOLAS (P. H.) Historical Record of the Royal Marine Forces. By Paul Harris Nicolas. *London: Thomas and William Boone.* 1845. 2 vols., 8vo, pp. xii, ix–xxxix, 384; (iv), 390.

NICOLAY (Charles Grenfell). The Oregon Territory: a Geographical and Physical Account of that Country and its Inhabitants with Outlines of its History and Discovery. By the Rev. C. G. Nicolay ... . *London: Charles Knight & Co.* 1846. 24mo, pp. 226. Map and Plate. + Second Edition. With Supplement. *London: Hodson & Son.* 1862. 18mo. 55251

NICOLAY. A Proposal to Establish a Missionary College on the North-West Coast of British America, ... From the Reverend Charles Grenfell Nicolay ... . *London: Saunders and Stanford.* 1853. 8vo, pp. 28. BM. 55252

NICOLAY (E.) Du perfectionnement de l'Industrie sucrière aux Antilles, seul moyen de lutter contre a betterave et l'étranger. ... *Paris.* 1844. 8vo, pp. 56. 55253

NICOLET. Geological Surveys and Reports on the Property of the Nicolet Mining Co. Township of South Ham, Canada East. ... *Boston: Geo. C. Rand & Avery.* 1864. 8vo, pp. 23. 2 Maps. H. 55254

NICOLIN (J. R.) La Division de Territorio en Yucatan: Coleccion de los Editoriales, dados á luz en "La Censura;" Periodico publicado en Campeche en los Años de 1849 y 1850, y Redactado Por ... Jose Raimundo Nicolin ... . *Mexico: Imprenta de vicente Garcia Torres.* 1861. 4to, pp. (2), iii, 41. 55255

NICOLL (H.) Early History of Suffolk County, L. I. ... By Hon. Henry Nicoll. *Brooklyn: The Society.* 1866. 8vo, pp. 18.

Also: An Address, ... before the Alumni Association of Columbia College, ... Sept. 29, 1843. ... *New-York: Henry Austice.* M DCCC XLIII. 8vo, pp. 20.—The Loan Bill. Speech ... February 15, 1848 ... . [n. p. n. d.] 8vo, pp. 7. H.

NICOLLET (Joseph Nicolas). ... Report intended to illustrate a Map of the Hydrographical Basin of the Upper Mississippi River, made by J. N. Nicollet ... February 16, 1841. ... *Washington: Blair and Rives, Printers.* 1843. 8vo, pp. 170. Map.

Also: Essay on Meteorological Observations. ... [*Washington.* 1839.] 8vo. S.

NICOLOSIUS (J. B.) Dell' Hercole | E Stvdio | Geografico | Di Gio. Battista Nicolosi | Dottore di Sacra Teologia | Tomo Primo. | ... | *In Roma, Nella Stamperia di Vitale Mascardi,* M. DC. LX. | *A Spese Dell' Avtore.* | *Con Licenza de' Svperiori, e Privilegio.* | 2 vols., folio, pp. (22), 414, Index, 38; Vol. II., pp. (8), 22 Maps. A. + *Romæ.* 1660–71. 2 vols., folio. 55258

The second volume contains, among others, eight grand geographical maps of America (Canada, United States, Mexico, Antilles, Peru, etc.).

[NICOLSON (P.)] Essai sur l'Histoire Naturelle de l'Isle de Saint-Domingue. Avec des figures en taille-douce. *A Paris, Chez Gobreau* ... . M.DCC.LXXVI. 8vo, Engraved and Printed Titles, pp. xxxi, 374, (2). 10 Plates. S. 55259

A valuable supplement to Charlevoix. *See* Vol. III., No. 12127.

NICOLSON (S.) The Nicolson Pavement, Invented by Samuel Nicolson ... . *Boston: Printed by Dutton and Wentworth.* 1855. 8vo, pp. 24. + Second Edition ... . *Boston: Printed by Henry W. Dutton and Son.* 1859. 8vo, pp. 32. H. 55260

NICOLSON (W.) An Apology for the Discipline of the Ancient Church, ... especially for that of our Mother the Church of England: ... By William Nicolson. ... *London: William Leake.* 1659 [*i. e.* 1658]. 4to, pp. (12), 241, (6). 55261

Among other references to New England he states that Robinson arrived at Plymouth, N. E., and established the form of church government there, which John Cotton continued.

NICOSELLI (A.) Relacion historica de la admirable Aparácion de la Virgen Santíssima Madre de Dios Baxo el título de Nrâ. Srâ. de Guadalupe Acaecida en México, el año de 1531. Traducida del Latin en Italiano ... . Por Anastasio Nicoseli ... . *Impresa en Roma, a expensas del Tinassi* ... . 1681. 4to. + Ultimamente traducida en nuestro idioma Castellano, por un Presbítero de este Arzobispado, devoto suyo. *Mexico.* 1781. 4to, prelim. leaves, pp. 26. 55262

Also in the "Coleccion" published by Luis Antonio and Cayetano Torres Tuñon. *See* Bartolache's "Manifiesto," pp. 14–17, 55.

NICOSELLI. Vita di S. Toribio Alfonso Mogrovesio Arcivescovo di Lima, Capitale del Regno del Perù, Raccolta di Anastacio Nicoselli, e di nuovo data alla luce Dall' Illustrissimo, e Revmo. Signore Mons. D. Gregorio de Molleda, Vescovo di Isauria. ... *Roma. Nella Stamperia di Antonio de' Rossi nella Strada del Seminario Romano.* 1726. 4to, Engraved and Printed Titles, pp. (18), 332. Portraits of Benedict and Mogrovesius. J.C.B.

A compilation from Cipriano Herrera. *See* our Vol. VIII., No. 31561. Antonio mentions an edition printed at Rome in Latin in 1670.

NICOT (J.) ... Juan Nicot cumple su promesa contraida con el público. *Habana: Oficina de Arazoza y Soler.* 1812. Folio.

"En una defensa justificada de D. Francisco de Arango contra quien se dirigieron alusiones inmotivadas hasta de falta puntualidad y malversacion."

NIEMCEWICZ (Julian Ursyn). [Life of Washington in the Polish Language.] 55265

The author accompanied Kosciusko, and married a daughter of Gov. Livingston. I have not seen the book. It is not in the British Museum.

NIEREMBERG (J. E.) De la Devocion y Patrocinio de San Miguel, Principe de los Angeles Antiquo Tutelar de los Godos, y Protector de España. ... *Mexico, por la Viuda de B. Calderon.* 1643. 4to. 55266

NIEREMBERG. Ioannis Evsebii Nierembergii ... De arte volvntatis libri sex: ... Accedit ad calcem Historia Panegyrica de tribus Martyribus eiusdem Societatis, in Vrugai pro fide occisis.

Lugduni, J. Cardon. 1631. 8vo, pp. (16), 572, 45. + *Parisiis Sumptibus Natalis Caroli* ... M. D. C. XXXIX. 8vo, pp. (16), 543, (16). BM. 55267

Contains a relation of the martyrdom of Fathers Roque Gonzalez de Santa Cruz, Alonso Rodriguez, and Juan del Castillo, massacred in Portugal.

NIEREMBERG. Ioannis Evsebii Nierembergii ... Historia Naturæ, Maxime Peregrinæ, Libris XVI. distincta. In quibus rarissima Naturæ arcana, etiam astronomica, & ignota Indiarum animalia ... describuntur; ... *Antverpiæ: Ex Officina Plantiniana Balthasaris Moreti.* M.DC.XXXV. Folio, pp. (8), 502, (104). H.

The greater part of this work relates to the natural history of Mexico, or New Spain. It also contains some particulars relative to Mexico before its conquest. Compare with Hernandez, our Vol. VIII., Nos. 31514–18.

NIEREMBERG. Ideas de Virtud en Algvnos Claros Varones de la Compañia de Iesus. Para los Religiosos della. Recopilados Por el Padre Iuan Eusebio Nieremberg ... . *En Madrid, Por Maria de Quiñones.* M.DC.XLIII. Folio, Frontispiece, pp. (12), 804. BM. 55269

This is usually followed by:

NIEREMBERG. Firmamento Religioso de Lvzidos astros, en algvnos Claros Varones de la Compañia de Iesus. Cumplense en este Tomo, y en el antecedente vna Centuria entera. Por el P. Iuan Eusebio Nieremberg ... . *En Madrid, Por Maria de Quiñones.* M.DC.XLIIII. Folio, pp. (12), 808. BM. 55270

NIEREMBERG. Honor del Gran Patriarca San Ignacio de Loyola, fvndador de la Compañia de Iesvs, En que se propone su vida y la de su Discipulo el Apostol de las Indias S. Francisco Xavier. Con la milagrosa Historia del admirable Padre Marcelo Mastrilli, y las noticias de grand multitud de Hijos del mismo S. Ignacio, varones clarissimos en santidad, dotrina, trabajos, y obras marauillosas en seruicio de la Iglesia. ... Por el Padre Ivan Evsebio Nieremberg ... . *Año* 1645. *En Madrid, Por Maria de Quiñones.* Folio, pp. (12), 784, (12). BM. 55271

NIEREMBERG. Vidas Exemplares, y Venerables Memorias De algunos Claros Varones de la Compañia de Iesvs, de los quales es este, tomo qvarto. ... Por el Padre Ivan Evsebio Nieremberg ... . *Año* 1647. *Madrid, Alõso de Paredes* ... . Folio, pp. (12), 787, (9), Carta, 4 leaves. BM. 55272

For the completion of this rare series of books, *see* Andrade (A. de), Vol. I., No. 1447, and Cassani (J.), Vol. III., No. 11360. This work having been published at different periods during the space of almost a century, complete sets are excessively

rare. The interest of the work, excluding some "jesuitical chaff," is not inferior to its rarity, as it contains accounts of many early voyages to the Indies, not elsewhere to be found. *See* Leclerc's catalogue, No. 408, for a descriptive note.

NIESS (J.) Ioannis | Niess | Societatis Iesv | Adolescens | Evropaevs | ab | Indo Moribvs Chri | stianis | Informatus. | *Dilingæ* | *sumptu* | *Caspari Sutoris.* CIƆIƆCXXIX. 12mo, Engraved Title, pp. (22), 450, (15). BM. 55273

An interesting volume, relating to "Michael Ayatumus, Gemma Indiæ Occidentalis."

NIETO (A. M. S.) Declaracion legal de la Inocencia del Ciudano A. Olarte acusado calumniasamente de Conspiracion contra la Patria. ... *Mexico.* 1826. 4to, pp. viii, 38. 55274

NIETO (J. J.) El Ciudano Juan Jose Nieto, Gobernador suspenso de la Provincia de Cartajena, ante los hombres honrados e imparciales de todos los partidos. *Bogota.* 1855. Imp. 8vo, pp. 62. 55275

NIETO. Geografia histórica, estadistica y local de la Provincia de Cartagena, por Juan Jose Nieto. *Cartagena.* 1839. 16mo.

NIETO DE ALMIRON (M.) Sermon ... Predicò en las Exequias del Illustrissimo Señor D. Pedro Nogales Davila, Dignissimo Obispo de dicha Ciudad de la Puebla en su Iglesia Cathedral. El Sr. Doct. D. Miguel Nieto de Almiron ... . *Puebla, en la Imprenta de la Viuda de Miguel de Ortega. Año de* 1721. 4to, 6 p. l., Text, 14 leaves. BM. 55277

Nieu Spagnien. *See* Mexico *and* Nueva España.

NIEUHOF (J.) Joan Nieuhofs | Gedenkwaerdige Zee en Landreize | Door de voornaemste Landschappen van | West en Oostindien. | *t'Amsterdam* | *By de Weduwe van Iacob van Meurs* 1682. | [Followed by] Johan Nieuhofs | Gedenkweerdige | Brasiliaense | Zee- en Lant- | Reize. | ... | *t'Amsterdam,* | *Voor de Weduwe van Jacob van Meurs, op de Keizers-gracht.* 1682. | Folio, pp. (12), 240, (2). Map, 49 Plates. [Followed by] Joan Nieuhofs | Zee en Lant- | Reize | door verscheide Gewesten van | Oostindien, | Behelzende | veele zeltzaame en wonderlijcke voorvallen | en geschiedenissen. | ... | *t'Amsterdam,* | *Voor de Weduwe van Jacob van Meurs, op de Keizers-gracht.* 1682. | Folio, pp. (4), 308, (4). 2 Maps.

Also on large paper. The author lived nine years (1640–49) in Brazil in the service of the Dutch West India Company. The account of Brazil contains many precious documents, and includes the history of Brazil from its first discovery by the Portuguese, both civil and ecclesiastical. *See* Trömel's "Bibliothèque Américaine," No. 385. The second work contains also a small poem of Jacob Steendam, the first poet of New

Netherland "Op de stad Batavia" dated: "Batavia den 24. van Wijnmaand 1670." For a translation of a portion of this work, *see* Churchill's "Voyages," II., *also* "Collection of Voyages," II., *and* Pinkerton's "Collection," VII. and XIV.

Een Nieuw Lied over dezen Oorlog van Engeland met de Staaten ... . [n. p. 1780.] 4to, pp. (2), 4. 55279

Popular songs, referring to the war in America, Paul Jones, etc. *See also* our Vol. IX., No. 36564.

NIEUW-NEDERLANDT. Conditien, | Die door de Heeren Bvrgermeesteren | der Stadt Amstelredam, | volgens 't gemaeckte | Accoordt met de West-Indische Compagnie, | ende d'Approbatie van hare Hog. Mog. de | Heeren Staten Generael der Ver- | eenighde Nederlanden, daer op gevolght, ge- | presenteert werden aen alle de gene, die als | Coloniers na Nieuw-Nederlandt willen ver- | trecken, &c. | *t'Amsterdam,* | *By Jan Banning, Ordinaris Drucker* | *deser Stede, in 't jaer* 1656. | 4to, 7 leaves. C. 55280

Conditions offered by the Burgomasters of Amsterdam, according to the agreement with the West India Company, to all those who will go as colonists to New Netherland. A very rare and most important document, translated by O'Callaghan, II. 328. Our No. 15186, Vol. IV., is the same work with a few variations, which forms, in fact, the appendix to Donck (A. v. d.), Vol. V., No. 20594.

Conditien [as No. 55280]. *t'Amsterdam,* | *By de Weduwe van Jan Banning, Boek-* | *verkoopster aen de Beurs, in 't jaer* 1659. | 4to, 7 leaves. C. 55281

A new edition of the preceding with very considerable changes, and of equal, if not greater, rarity. A comparison of both may be found in Asher's "Essay," Nos. 337–8.

Decreet van den Directeur en Raden van Nieuw-Nederlandt over 't stelen van Beesten. [n. p. 1654.] Folio, 1 leaf.

This ordinance of the Director and Councilors of New Netherland on the stealing of beasts is not mentioned by Asher.

Kort Verhael Van Nieuw Nederlants. *See* Vol. IX. 38253.

Nieuw Plan van accomodement, waardoor de vaart en handel op Essequebo en Demarary vry en open zou worden gesteld. [n. p. 1775.] 8vo, pp. 16. 55283

See also our Vol. VI., No. 22995.

Nieuwe Beschryving der Walvischvangst en Haringsvisschery. *Amsterdam.* 1791. 4 vols., 4to. 21 Maps and Plates. 55284

This description of the whale and herring-fishery is the same as "De Walvischvangst," reissued with a new title.

De Nieuwe Engelsche Robinson, of de overzeldzame gevallen van Capit. Rob. Boyle, ... en eindelyk de reize, schipbreuk en behouden van Rich. Castelman, met een Beschrijvinge van Pen-

silvania en Philadelphia. Uit het Engelsch. Tweede vermeerde druk. *Amsterdam.* 1761. 2 vols., 8vo. Plates. 55285

This new English Robinson, or adventures of Capt. R. Boyle, is a translation of [Chetwood (W. R.)], Vol. IV., No. 12553.

Nieuwe In-teykeninge ende verhoog. der Capitalen van de West-Indische Compagnie. [n. p. 1636.] Folio, 1 leaf.

New subscriptions and increase of the capital of the West India Company. Not described by Asher.

Nieuwe Nederlandsche Jaerboeken of merkwaerdige geschiedenissen voorgevallen in de Vereenigde Provincien en de Volkplantingen. *Amsterdam.* 1747–95. 117 vols., 8vo. 55287

New Dutch annals or the memorable events which took place in the United Provinces and the colonies. The volumes embracing the years of the American war, are full of valuable materials for the American historian.

Het Nieuwe Nederlandsche, Fransche, Americaansche en Engelsche Kolfspel, vertoond in drie bedryven. *Amsterdam.* 1782. 8vo, pp. 77. Allegorical Title-plate. 55288

The new Dutch, French, American and English play at golf, represented in three acts. *See also* New York State.

Nieuwe Ontdekkinge. *See* [Hennepin (L.)], VIII. 31360.

Nieuwe Tijdinge uyt | Oost-Indien | Van den 1 February, 1673. [n. p. 1673.] Folio, 1 leaf. 55289

This news from East India contains an account of the "Great victory obtained in Virginia" by the Dutch over the English.

De Nieuwe Vermeerde Groenlantse Walvisch-Vangst, ofte Amsterdamse Y-Stroom, vervult met veelderhande nieuwe en aengename liederen ... . *t'Amsterdam, Erven Gijsbert de Groot en A. van Dam.* 1719. Small square 8vo, pp. 94, Index, 1 leaf.

This newly augmented whale-fishery of Greenland or the Amsterdam Y-River, with various new and agreeable songs, etc., is very rare.

Nieuwe Werelt, 1622. *See* [Herrera (A.)], Vol. VIII. 31542.

Nieuwe Weerelt. *See* [Colyn (M.)], Vol. IV., No. 14348, *and* [Huttich (J.)], Vol. IX., No. 34107.

NIEWINDT (J.) Catechismo pa uso di Catolicanan di Curaçao. Catechismus ten gebruike der Katholyken van Curaçao, door M. Joh. Niewindt. *Curaçao.* [1840?] 8vo, pp. 157. 55291

Text in the language of Curaçao and in Dutch.

NIEVES (J. M.) Imposturas del Dr. Felix Maria Alfonzo. Por J. M. Nieves. *Carácas.* 1837. 8vo, pp. 12. BM. 55292

NIFO (M. D.) Noticia de los Caudales, Frutos, y Efectos, que han entrado en España de la America en el feliz reynado de nuestro Católico Monarca Don Cárlos III. (que Dios guarde). Por D. Manuel Deogracias Nifo. *Madrid: D. Antonio Espinosa.* 1788. 16mo, pp. (4), 122. J.C.B., H. 55293

"Contains a monthly report of the importations into Spain from America from 1759 to 1788. It appears that the amount of money alone, during that period, exclusive of merchandise, precious stones, etc., was $447,571,737."—RICH, I. 353.

NIGER, *pseudon.* Short Statement of Facts in Reply to the Attacks on the Policy of the present Government towards the Colonies, in a Letter to Lord John Russell. By Niger. *London.* 18—. 8vo, pp. 22. 55294

The Nigger Melodist; a Choice Collection of all the Original Songs, as sung in America. *London.* 1846. 8vo. 55295

A Night in Buenos Ayres; A Drama. *Georgetown.* 1854. 12mo. C. 55296

The Night Side of New York, a Picture of the Great Metropolis after Nightfall. By Members of the New York Press. *New York: J. C. Harvey & Co.* 1866. 12mo, pp. 121. C.

The Night Watch; or, Tales of the Sea. *London: Henry Colburn.* 1828. 2 vols., 12mo, pp. vi, xi, 13–328; viii, 340.

By W. N. Glascock or C. Crewe? Includes the "Boatswain's Spell at Washington."

NIGHTINGALE (C.) A Discourse ... at the Funeral of Caleb Butler, ... By Crawford Nightingale ... . *Boston: Printed by C. C. P. Moody.* [n. d.] 8vo, pp. 14. B. 55299

Also: A Sermon at the Funeral of Mr. Warren Fay Stone ... . February 7, 1858. ... *Groton Junction: Printed by Brown Brothers.* 1858. 8vo, pp. 24. B.

NIGHTINGALE (F.) A Woman's Example: and A Nation's Work. A Tribute to Florence Nightingale. *London: William Ridgway.* 1864. 16mo, pp. 90. BA. 55300

By F. M. Edge. Contains chiefly Americana.

[NIGHTINGALE (J.)] The Scriptural Deacon; an inquiry into the Distinct Rights of the Officers and People, in the Management of the Temporal Concerns of the Church. By a Committee Man. *New-York: Printed by William Osborn.* 1845. 8vo, pp. 48. 55301

NIGHTINGALE (J.) The Religions and Religious Ceremonies of all Nations: ... By the Rev. J. Nightingale. *London: Sir Richard Phillips and Co.* 1821. 12mo, pp. xx, 647. Map.

Nightingale (T.) Oceanic Sketches: By Thomas Nightingale, Esq. ... With a Botanical Appendix by Dr. Hooker. *London: Cochrane.* 1835. Sm. 8vo. Plates. 55303

The Nightingale. *See* [Mather (C.)], Vol. xi., No. 46432.

The Nightingale, or Mélange de Littérature; a periodical publication. Edited by J. Lathrop, Jun. Vol. i. *Boston: Printed by John Russell & Co.* 1796. 12mo, pp. 108. s. 55304

A *belles-lettres* periodical. No. i. appeared May 10th, No. ix. (the latest I meet), May 28th, 1796.

Nigon de Berty (L.) Histoire abrégée de la liberté individuelle chez les principaux peuples anciens et modernes, Par L. Nigon de Berty ... . *Paris: Moutardier.* 1834. 8vo, pp. (4), 602. B., C. 55305

A chapter (about 30 pages) relates to America.

Nigrinus *or* Schwartz (Franz). Schauplatz der gantzen Welt; oder, summarische Voorstellung aller Königreiche, Länder, [etc.] in Europa, Asia, Africa, und America; auch eine kurtze Lebensbeschreibung aller Kaiser, Könige und Regenten. *Neustadt an der Aysch: C. Redelhamer.* 1679. 18mo, pp. (4), 520

Nihima Ayamie-Mazinahigan. Kanachchatageng. *Montréal: Imprimé par Duvernay.* 1830. 18mo, pp. 100. 55307

An Iroquois catechism, with prayer and hymns.

Nijenhuis (Jan Tiberius Bodel). Jonas Michaëlius, eerste Predikant der Nederlandschen Hervormde Gemeente op Manhattans of Nieuw-Amsterdam. [*Amsterdam.* 1857.] 8vo, pp. 24. 55308

Michaelius was the first minister of the Dutch Reformed Church in New York, and this very interesting letter, written from New Amsterdam in 1628, gives an account of his arrival and adventures in his new home. For a translation, *see* our Vol. xii. 48686.

Nijhoff (M.) ... Livres Anciens et Modernes en vente aux prix marqués chez Martinus Nijhoff à la Haye .... Ouvrages sur L'Amérique. *New York: B. Westerman & Co.* 1868. 8vo, pp. 65, cover, 2 leaves. B. 55309

Also: Ouvrages sur L'Amérique: L'Asie et L'Afrique ... . *La Haye: Martinus Nijhoff.* 1869. 8vo, pp. 42.—Ouvrages de Linguistique et de Littérature Orientales, des Langues de L'Amérique ... . *La Haye: Martinus Nijhoff.* 1869. 8vo, pp. 32.

Nikkanochee (Oceola). *See* Oceola (Nikkanochee).

Niles (H. E.) Address of Rev. H. E. Niles on the Occasion of President Lincoln's Funeral Obsequies in York, Pa.

Printed by Hiram Young, York, Pa. [1865.] 8vo, pp. 8, cover, 2 leaves. B. 55310

Also: A Discourse ... at the Funeral of Rev. Samuel N. Steele, ... Spencertown on ... March 12, 1854; ... *Volatie: H. N. Hopkins, Printer.* 1854. 8vo, pp. 23. BM.

Niles (H.) Politics for Working Men. An Essay on Labor and Subsistence; addressed to the Free Productive People of the U. States. By Hezekiah Niles. ... July 4, 1831. [n. p. 1831.] 8vo, pp. 15. B. 55311

Niles. Principles and Acts of the Revolution in America: or, an Attempt to Collect and Preserve some of the Speeches, Orations & Proceedings, with Sketches and Remarks on Men and Things, and other fugitive or neglected pieces, belonging to the Revolutionary Period in the United States; ... By H. Niles. *Baltimore: ... William Ogden Niles.* 1822. Rl. 8vo, pp. viii, 495.

[Niles.] Things as they are, or Federalism turned Inside Out! being a Collection of Extracts from Federal Papers, &c. and Remarks upon them, originally written for and published in the Evening Post. By the Editor. *Baltimore: Printed at the Office of the Evening Post. By H. Niles.* [1809.] 8vo, pp. 75.

Also: Agriculture of the United States, or an Essay concerning ... Domestic Manufactures, showing their inseparable connection with Agriculture, &c. From Niles' Register, March 24, 1827, with additions. ... [n. p. n. d.] 8vo, pp. 16.—Journal of the Proceedings of the Friends of Domestic Industry; in General Convention met at ... New York, October 26, 1831. *Baltimore.* 1831. 8vo, pp. 16. C.

Niles. The Weekly Register: Containing Political, Historical, Geographical, Scientifical, Astronomical, Statistical, and Biographical Documents, Essays and Facts; ... with Notices of the Arts and Manufactures, and a Record of the Events of the Times. H. Niles, Editor. ... September 1811 to March 1812. —Vol. i. *Baltimore: The Editor.* [n. d.] Large 8vo, pp. (4), 480. Continued. B., C., P. 55314

This work was edited successively by H. Niles (Vols. i. to l.), Wm. Ogden Niles (l. to lvi.), Jeremiah Hughes (lvii. to lxxv.), and George Beatty. After Vol. vi. the title is "Niles' Weekly Register" to Vol. l.; Vols. li. and lii. are entitled "Niles' Weekly Register," W. O. Niles, editor; Vols. liii. to lxxv. are entitled "Niles' National Register," W. O. Niles, editor. Vols. i. to li., to which there are nine supplements, are printed in double columns. The remaining volumes are printed in triple columns in quarto, and these volumes are rarer than the preceding. There was a suspension of the work, from February, 1848, to July, 1848 [*i. e.* for March, April, May, and June, 1848]. Vols. lxxiv. and lxxv. were edited by George Beatty, and published at Philadelphia, from July 1st, 1848, to June 27th, 1849, when the work was discontinued. This valuable series covers a period of American political history which is nowhere else recorded with so much minuteness. A complete set is rarely to be found. Of Vol. i. there were three editions, the last is entitled:

Niles. The Weekly Register. Containing Documents, Essays, and Facts; together with Notices of the Arts and Manufactures, and a Record of the Events of the Times. Vol. i. *Baltimore.* 1816. 8vo. 55315

Niles. General Index to the First Twelve Volumes, ... of Niles' Weekly Register ... September, 1811, to September, 1817. ... *Baltimore: The Editor.* 1818. 8vo, pp. (2), 232, 22.

Niles (J. B.) Address before the Officers and Students of the Indiana Medical College. By John B. Niles. *Indianapolis.* 1846. 8vo. 55317

Niles (J. M.) The Connecticut Civil Officer. ... By Hon. John M. Niles ... . *Hartford.* 1855. 8vo. 55318

Niles. History of South America and Mexico; comprising their Discovery, Geography, Politics, Commerce and Revolutions. By Hon. John M. Niles ... . To which is annexed, a Geographical and Historical View of Texas, with a detailed account of the Texian Revolution and War. By Hon. L. T. Pease. ... *Hartford: H. Huntington, Jun.* 1837. 2 vols., 8vo, pp. 370; 230. Plate and Map. B. + [*Ibid.*] 1838. + [*Ibid.*] 1839. + [*Ibid.*] 1844. 55319

Niles. The Life of Oliver Hazard Perry. With an Appendix, comprising Biographical Sketches of ... General Pike and Captain Lawrence, and a View of the Present Condition and Future Prospects of the Navy of the United States. ... By John M. Niles, Esq. *Hartford: William S. Marsh.* 1820. 12mo, pp. 376. Portraits. + Second Edition, Enlarged and Improved. *Hartford: Oliver D. Cooke.* 1821. 12mo, pp. 384. 4 Portraits and Plate. 55320

Niles. Remarks ... on the Erection of a Monument to the Memory of Captain Nathan Hale. *Washington.* 1836. 8vo.

Niles. Speeches of Mr. Niles of Connecticut, and Mr. Stewart of Pennsylvania, on the Tariff. ... July 20, 1846. [*Washington.*] 1846. 8vo, pp. 32. H. 55322

Also: Speech ... on the Bill imposing Additional Duties ... February 13, 1838. *Washington.* 1838. 8vo.—Speech ... January 5, 1839 ... relative to the Transactions between the Government and the Bank of the United States ... . [n. p. n. d.] 8vo, pp. 16.—Speech ... on the Abolition of Slavery. [n. p. 1836.] 8vo.—Speech ... on the Oregon Question. [n. p. 1846.] 8vo.—Speech ... on the Treasury Order. [n. p. 1837.] 8vo.—Speech ... on the Compromise Bill. ... July 25, 1848. *Washington.* 1848. 8vo, pp. 13.—Speech ... on Slavery in the Territories, delivered ... June 2, 1848. *Washington.* 1848. 8vo, pp. 8.

Niles (*Mr.*) Mr. Niles's Resolution, calling on the Governor for Evidence relative to Impressment; together with his Excellency's Answer. *Montpelier.* 1813. 8vo, pp. 8. 55323

Niles (M. A. H.) The Distinctive Characteristics of the Pilgrims. A Sermon ... in Lowell, Mass., July 12th, 1846. By M. A. H. Niles ... . *Lowell: A. L. Dayton.* 1846. 8vo, pp. 16. H. 55324

Also: Address before the ... Alumni of Hanover College, ... Sept. 25th, 1836. *Hanover, Ind.: James Morrow, Printer.* 1836. 8vo, pp. 23.—The Moral Aspect of our Country. A Sermon ... at Marblehead, ... 5th of April, 1838. A Day of ... Fasting ... and Prayer. ... *Newburyport: Hiram Tozer.* 1838. 8vo, pp. 22.—The Sin of Duelling. A Sermon, ... at Marblehead, on the Fifth of April, 1838:—A Day of ... Fasting and Prayer. ... *Newburyport: Hiram Tozer.* 1838. 8vo, pp. 18. BA.

Niles (N.) A Sermon ... at Medway, West Parish, Oct. 31, 1771. By Nathaniel Niles. *Boston.* 1771. 8vo, pp. 42.

Niles. Two | Discourses | on | Liberty, | ... at the | North Church, in Newbury-Port, | ... June 5th, 1774 ... . By Nathaniel Niles, M.A. | ... | *Newbury-Port:* | *Printed by I. Thomas and H. W. Tinges.* MDCCLXXIV. 8vo, pp. 60. BA. 55326

Probably the second issue of the Newburyport press. There are several printed sermons by this author. *See also* Case (W), Vol. iii., No. 11304.

Niles (N.), *Jr.* Medical Statistics; or a Comparative View of the Mortality in New-York, Philadelphia, Baltimore, and Boston, for a series of years ... . By Nathaniel Niles, Jun., M.D. and John D. Russ, M.D. *New-York: Elam Bliss.* 1827. 8vo, pp. 10, (1). B., N. 55327

Niles (N.) Letter to the Secretary of State on the Construction of a Ship Canal—Central America. *New York.* 1849. 8vo. 55328

Also: Mr. Niles' Plan for the Construction of a Ship Canal between the Atlantic and Pacific Oceans, Central America. *New York.* 1868. 8vo, pp. 8.

Niles (P.) The Writings of Peter Niles. *Walpole, N. H.* 1811. 8vo. W. 55329

Niles (S.) A Brief and Plain | Essay | on | God's Wonder-working Providence | for | New-England, | In the Reduction of Louisbourg, and Fortresses | thereto belonging on Cape Breton. | With | A short hint in the Beginning, on the French | Taking & Plundering the People of Canso, | which led the several Governments to Unite | and Pursue that Expedition. | With the Names of the Leading Officers in | the Army and the several Regiments to |

which they belonged. | By Samuel Niles. ... *N. London,* | *Printed and Sold by T. Green.* 1747. 8vo, pp. (6), 34. BA., M. 55330

[Niles.] The | Sentiments and Resolution | of an | Association of Ministers | (Convened at Weymouth, Jan. 15th. 1744, 5.) | Concerning the Reverend | Mr. George Whitefield. | To which is added, | The like Opinion of the venerable | Mr. Nehemiah Walter of Roxbury, and | others. | As Also, | The solemn Advice of the venerable Mr. Natha | nael Stone ... . *Boston: Printed and sold by T. Fleet* ... . 1745. 8vo, pp. 15. B. 55331

Niles. Tristitiæ Ecclesiarum | or, A brief and sorrowful Account | of the | Present State of the Churches | in | New-England; | in a | Letter | from a | Minister in the Country | to the | Publick. | ... [With] Some healing Measures. | ... [And] an Appendix. | By Samuel Niles, | A mournful Spectator and Sharer in the present Calamities. | And | Pastor of a Church ... in Braintree. | ... | *Boston: N. E.* | *Printed and Sold by J. Draper.* 1745. 4to, pp. 8, 21, Appendix, 4 [5]. BA., C. 55332

Also: The True Scripture-Doctrine of Original Sin stated and defended. ... *Boston, N. E. Printed ... by S. Kneeland.* 1757. 8vo, pp. (6), 320. H.—A Vindication of Divers Important Gospel-Doctrines, ... against ... a ... Discourse of ... Rev. Lemuel Briant's ... [With] Remarks ... on ... John Bass's ... Narrative. ... *Boston: Printed ... by S. Kneeland.* 1752. 8vo, pp. 120. C., M.

Niles (S.) Remarks on a Sermon ... before the Plymouth Association of Ministers in ... Middleborough, Sept. 26, 1810, By John Reed, D.D. ... By Samuel Niles, A.M. ... *Boston: Printed ... by Lincoln & Edmands.* 1813. 8vo, pp. 62. BA. 55333

Niles. A Sermon, ... before the Massachusetts Missionary Society, ... May 26, 1801. By Samuel Niles ... . *Cambridge: Printed ... by William Hilliard.* 1801. 8vo, pp. 38, Appendix, 14.

Niles. The Vanity of Man considered in A Sermon delivered February 22d, 1800, commemorating the Death of George Washington ... . By Samuel Niles ... . *Boston: Printed by John & Thomas Fleet.* MDCCC. 8vo, pp. 23, and Errata. B. 55335

Niles (W. A.) Our Country's Peril and Hope. A Sermon ... January 4th, 1861, at Corning, N. Y. By Rev. William A. Niles. *Corning (N. Y.): E. E. Robinson.* 1861. 8vo, pp. 30.

Niles (W. H.) Geological Formations of the Burlington Limestone. By W. H. Niles, ... and Charles Wachsmuth ... . [n. p. 1866.] 8vo, pp. 7. H. 55337

From the "American Journal of Science and Arts," July, 1866.

Niles (W. O.) The Tippecanoe Text-Book, compiled from Niles' Register and other Authentic Records, By William Ogden Niles, and respectfully dedicated to the young men of the United States. *Baltimore: Duff Green.* 1840. 8vo, pp. 95. 4 Plates.

The great Harrison campaign text-book.

Nimble-Chops (A.) *See* [Livingston (Brockholst)], Vol. x.

Nimni (N.), *pseudon.* A Letter to Hull Barton, an Excommunicated Member from the Society of Friends; now a New Light Preacher:— ... By his Friend Notus Nimni. [n. p. 1823.] 8vo, pp. 12. H. 55339

Nimmo (J.), *Jr.* Report to the Secretary of the Treasury in relation to the Foreign Commerce of the United States and the Decadence of American Shipping, by Joseph Nimmo, Jr. ... *Washington.* 1870. 8vo, pp. 62. 23 Charts. H. 55340

Nimrod (H.), *pseudon.* The Fudge Family in Washington. Edited by Harry Nimrod. ... *Baltimore: Joseph Robinson.* 1820. 12mo, pp. 109. B. 55341

Ninde (W. W.) Oration ... Gouverneur Wesleyan Seminary, January 27, 1841. By W. W. Ninde. *Lowville.* 1841. 8vo. 55342

Nine Grants in Fee Simple, of Eleven Leagues ... located on the Rio Nueces. [n. p. 1833.] 8vo, pp. 20. H. 55343

Nine Years of Democratic Rule in Mississippi; being Notes upon the Political History of the State, from the beginning of the year 1838, to the present time. *Jackson.* 1847. 12mo. C.

The Nineteenth Century. A Quarterly Miscellany. Vol. i. *Philadelphia: G. B. Zieber & Co.* 1848. 8vo, pp. 400. Portraits. Continued. H. 55345

Full of strange, Utopian notions. Edited by C. C. Burr.

The XIX Century. [A Monthly Magazine.] Volume First, ... 1869. *Charleston, S. C.* [n. d.] 8vo, pp. vii, 496. Cont'd.

The Nineteenth Century; or the New Dispensation: ... Examination of the Claims and Assertions of Emanuel Swedenborg. By a Layman. *New York: John Allen.* 1852. 8vo, pp. xi, 425. Engraved Title and Plate. B., C. 55347

Niño Jesus (P. A. del). Sermon predicado en la ... Ciudad de Cholula del Imperio el dia 16 de Agosto de 1863, en accion de gracias por la proclamacion y llamamiento al trono de Mexico

de su ... Fernando Maximiliano i. por el R. P. Fr. Pablo Antonio del Niño Jesus. *Mexico.* 1864. 8vo, pp. 16. 55348

Also: Oracion Funebre ... 28 de Setiembre de 1859 en sufragio del Almo Del E. S. benemerito de la Patria ... Don Agustin de Iturbide ... *Puebla.* 1859. 4to, pp. 14. —Sermon con motivo del regresso a la republica y de la presidencia del ex. General ... D. Antonio L. de Santa-Anna. ... *Guadalajara.* 1853. 8vo, pp. 16. BM.

Nipho y Cagigal (F. M.) Dialogo, Metrico-Heroyco, entre la España y America, intitulado: Amorosas Respiraciones y Alegres Regocijos, que plausiblemente gozosa, y placentera respira la gran monarchia de las dos Españas, por la venturosa, feliz, y justa aclamacion de su natural dueño y sacro catholico monarca Don Fernando vi. ... por la amable direccion del excelentissimo Señor Conde Altamira el mas humilde Español. D. Francisco Mariano Nipho y Cagigal. [*Lima?* n. d.] 4to, pp. (12), 51.

A metrical-heroic dialogue between Spain and America, entitled "Sighs and Blissful Satisfaction with which the great Empire of the Two Spains regards her natural lord and holy Catholic Monarch, Don Fernando vi."

Nips (Jack), *pseudon.* The Yankee Spy. By Jack Nips. *Boston.* [n. d.] 12mo. 55350

Nisbet (C.) An Address to the Students of Dickinson College, By the Rev. Charles Nisbet, D.D. On his Re-election to the Office of Principal ... . *Carlisle: Printed by Kline & Reynolds.* [1786.] 8vo, pp. 16. + *Edinburgh: W. Martin.* MDCCLXXXVI. 8vo, pp. 12. BM. 55351

Also: Monody to the Memory of the Rev. Dr. Charles Nisbet, many years first Minister of Montrose, and late President of the College of Carlisle in Pennsylvania. *Edinburgh: James Ballantyne.* 1805. 8vo, pp. 23.

Nisbet (J.) The Annals of San Francisco. *See* Soulé (F.)

Nisbet (J. H.) An Address, ... by Bro. Joseph Henry Nisbet, before the Garmany Division, ... S. of T. ... Milledgeville, Ga., February 22, 1850. *Milledgeville, Ga.* 1850. 8vo, pp. 11.

Nisbet (R.) The Capacity of Negroes for Religious and Moral Improvement Considered: with Cursory Hints to Proprietors and to Government, for the immediate Melioration of the Condition of Slaves in the Sugar Colonies; ... By Richard Nisbet, of the Island of Nevis. *London: J. Phillips.* 1789. 8vo, pp. xii, 207. C. 55353

See "Monthly Review," ii. 120.

[Nisbet.] Slavery Not Forbidden by Scripture: A Defence of the West India Planters. By a West Indian. *Philadelphia.* 1773. 8vo. C. 55354

Nispen (A. v.) Voyagien ende Beschryvinge van Siam, Moscovien, Yslandt ende Groenlandt. *Dordrecht.* 1652. 12mo, pp. 48. 55355

Voyages and descriptions of Iceland and Greenland. Rare, forms part of A. v. Nispen's "Collection of Voyages."

Nissen (J. P.) Reminiscences of a 46 Years' Residence in the Island of St. Thomas, in the West Indies. By Johan Peter Nissen. *Nazareth, Pa.: Printed by Senseman & Co.* 1838. 12mo, pp. 228. 55356

Le Niveau de l'Europe et de l'Amérique Septentrionale, ou le Guide l'Observateur. [A Periodical.] *Philadelphie.* 1794–95. 4to. 55357

Niven (A. C.) The Centennial Memorial, ... of ... the One Hundredth Anniversary of the A. R. Presbyterian Church, of Little Britain, N. Y. ... With a Sketch of the Clinton Family, Biographical Notes, &c. Edited by Archibald C. Niven. *New York: Robert Carter & Brothers.* 1859. 12mo, pp. xxii, 35–251. Portrait. B., S. 55358

Nix's Mate. *See* [Dawes (Rufus)], Vol. v., No. 18920.

Nixon (B.) Extracts from the Manuscript Writings of Barnaby Nixon ... . With "An Introduction, by the Meeting for Sufferings, Virginia," dated, 5th month, 1814. *Richmond: J. Warrock, Printer.* 1814. Sm. 8vo, pp. 54. 55359

A reprint is entitled "Biographical and other Extracts from The Manuscript Writings of Barnaby Nixon." *York: Printed ... by W. Alexander and Son.* 1822. Sm. 8vo, pp. 72.

Nixon. A Serious Address to the Rulers of America and Virginia. *Richmond.* 1806. 8vo. C. 55360

Nixon (J. T.) Endurance, Individual and National: An Address at Princeton. By Hon. John F. Nixon. *Philadelphia.* 1863. 8vo. C. 55361

Also: The Rebellion: Its Origin, and the Means of Suppressing it. Speech ... April 11, 1862. *Washington, D. C.* 1862. 8vo, pp. 14. + [Another Edition.] 8vo, pp. 8. —The Tariff, its Constitutionality, Necessity, and Advantages. Speech ... May 24, 1860. [n. p. n. d.] 8vo, pp. 7. *See also* No. 53101, and add *Philadelphia.* 1855.

Da Njoe va wi Masra en Helpiman Jesus Christus. Translated into the Negro-English Language, by the Missionaries of the Unitas Fratrum, or United Brethren. *London: W. McDowall, Printer.* 1829. 8vo, pp. 484, (4). + *Bautzen: E. Moritz Monse.* 1846. 8vo, pp. 592. 55362

Edited by C. A. Austen and C. J. Latrobe. Printed for the use of the negroes in Surinam. *See* "Historical Magazine," II. 241, 282.

No Abolition of Slavery; or the Universal Empire of Love. A Poem. *London: R. Faulder.* 1791. 4to, pp. 24. 55363

See "Monthly Review," IV. 467.

No Abolition; or, an Attempt to prove ... that the Abolition of the British Trade with Africa, for Negroes, would be ... fatal to the Interests of this Nation, ruinous to its Sugar Colonies, and ... pernicious in its Consequences ... . *London: J. Debrett.* MDCC-LXXXIX. 4to, pp. (4), 52. 55364

See "Monthly Review," LXXX. 559.

No Church without a Bishop. *See* [Potter (A.)]

No Colonies no Funds, proving that the present certain destruction of the West India Colonies will yet involve the National Debt, addressed to the Abettors of Injustice. *London.* 1826. 12mo. A. 55365

No Compensation for Slaves. [*Baltimore.* 1864?] 8vo, pp. 4.

Issued by the Unconditional Union State Central Committee.

... No Failure for the North. From the "Atlantic Monthly." ... *New York: Wm. C. Bryant & Co., Printers.* 1863. 8vo, pp. 23. BA. 55367

No Party Now. *See* Lieber (F.), Vol. X., No. 40985, *note.*

No Rum, No Sugar, ... being half an hour's Conversation between a Negro and an English Gentleman, shewing the horrible nature of the Slave Trade. *London.* 1792. 8vo. 55368

No Slave-Hunting in the Old Bay State. An Appeal to the People and Legislature of Massachusetts. [By W. H. Burleigh.] *New York: American Anti-Slavery Society.* 1860. 12mo, pp. 23. 55369

No Slur, Else-Slur. *See* [Richmond (*Dr.*)]

No Song No Supper: An Opera, in Two Acts. With Additional Songs. ... Second Philadelphia Edition. *Philadelphia: Mathew Carey.* M.DCC.XCIII. 12mo, pp. 32. B. 55370

No standing Army in the British Colonies; Or an Address to the Inhabitants of the Colony of New York. Against unlawful Standing Armies. *New York: Printed by John Holt* ... . M DCC-LXXV. 8vo, pp. 18. P. 55371

No Throughfare. By C——s D——s, Bellamy Brownjohn, and Domby. Second Edition ... . *Boston: Loring.* 1868. 8vo, pp. 15. B. 55372

A burlesque on Dickens' story "No Thoroughfare," by Robert Carr Dunham; the scenes are laid in Boston and vicinity, and it contains numerous local hits.

No Union of Church and State; or a Letter containing a brief Reply to the Rev. James R. Wilson's Pamphlet. By a Citizen of Albany. *Albany.* 1832. 8vo. S. 55373

NOAH (Mordecai Manuel). Discourse on the Evidences of The American Indians being the Descendants of the Lost Tribes of Israel. ... By M. M. Noah. *New-York: James Van Norden.* 1837. 8vo, pp. 40. B. 55374

NOAH. Beweis, dass die Amerikanischen Indianer ... . Aus dem Englischen des M. M. Noah ... . *Altona, bei Johann Friedrick Hammerich.* 1838. 18mo, pp. (2), 53, (1). 55375

Also: An Address ... before the General Society of Mechanics and Tradesmen of the City of New-York, on the opening of the Mechanic Institution ... . *New-York: William A. Mercein, Printer.* 1822. 8vo, pp. 28. — Correspondence and Documents relative to the Attempt to Negotiate for the Release of the American Captives at Algiers. ... *Washington.* 1816. 8vo, pp. 128. — Discourse, delivered at the Consecration of the Synagogue ... in ... New-York, on ... 17th of April, 1818. *New-York: Printed by C. S. Van Winkle.* 1818. 8vo, pp. 47. — Gleanings from a Gathered Harvest. ... *New York.* 1845. 8vo, pp. 216. + [*Ibid.*] 1847. 8vo. S. — A Letter addressed to the Southern Delegates of the Baltimore Democratic Convention, on the Claims of the "Barn-Burners" to be admitted to Seats in that Convention. ... *New York.* 1848. 8vo, pp. 13. — Marion; or, The Hero of Lake George. A Drama in three Acts. Founded on the Events of the Revolutionary War. ... *New York: E. Murden.* 1822. 18mo, pp. 70. — Report of the Trial an action on the Case brought by Silvanus Miller, Esq., against Mordecai M. Noah, Esq., for an alleged Libel. By L. H. Clark. *New York.* 1823. 8vo, pp. 72. — A Statement of Facts relative to the Conduct of Henry Eckford, Esq., as connected with the National Advocate. ... *New-York: Printed by J. W. Bell & Co.* 1824. 8vo, pp. 12. BA.

NOBBE (C. F. A.) C. F. A. Nobbii Litteratura Geographiæ Ptolemaeæ. *Lipsiæ: Typis Tauchnitii.* 1838. 8vo, pp. (10), 36.

Interesting to the student of early geography.

Nobiliario de el Valle de Valdorba, illustrada con los escudos de armas de sus Palacios y Casas nobles con el extracto de la Conquista de el Ytza en la Nueva Espana. *Pamplona.* 1714. 4to. 55377

NOBLE (F. A.) ... A Thanksgiving Discourse. Delivered ... November 27, 1862. By Rev. Frederic A. Noble ... . *Saint Paul.* 1862. 8vo, pp. 21. H. 55378

Also: Address ... before the Minnesota State Bible Society. [n. p. n. d.] 8vo, pp. 10. — ... A Thanksgiving Discourse, delivered ... November 24, 1864. ... *St. Paul: David Ramaley, Printer.* 1864. 8vo, pp. 28. H.

NOBLE (John). Noble's Instructions to Emigrants: an Attempt to give a correct account of the United States ... and offer some Information ... to those who have a wish to Emigrate to that Republic ... . *Boston [England]: John Noble.* 1819. 8vo, pp. vi, 112. Map and Errata, folded leaf. BM. 55379

NOBLE (L. L.) After Icebergs with a Painter: A Summer Voyage to Labrador and around Newfoundland. By Rev. Louis L. Noble ... . *New York: D. Appleton and Company.* M.DCCC.LXI. 12mo, pp. xiv, (2), 336. 6 Plates. B. 55380

NOBLE. The Course of Empire, Voyage of Life, and other Pictures by Thomas Cole, N.A. With Selections from his Letters and Miscellaneous Writings ... . By Rev. Louis N. Noble. *New York: Cornish, Lamport & Company.* MDCCCLIII. 8vo, pp. 415.

NOBLE. The Life and Works of Thomas Cole, N.A. by Rev. Louis L. Noble. *New York.* 1853. 12mo. + Third Edition. *New-York: Sheldon, Blakeman and Company.* 1856. 12mo, pp. 415. H. 55382

See "North American Review," LXXVII. 302. Also: Church's Painting. The Heart of the Andes. ... *New York: D. Appleton and Company.* 1857. 8vo, pp. 24. — The Lady Angeline; a Lay of the Apalachians. The Hours, etc. ... *New York: Sheldon, Blakeman & Company.* M.DCCC.LVI. 12mo, pp. 148, (1). — Poem ... to House of Convocation, 1856. *New York.* 1857. 8vo.

NOBLE (M.) Centennial Discourse, ... in Williamstown, Mass., November 19, 1865, By Mason Noble. *North Adams, Mass.: James T. Robinson & Co., Printers.* [n. d.] 8vo, pp. 60.

NOBLE. Sermon ... in the United States Naval Academy, on the Day of the Funeral of ... Abraham Lincoln, By Mason Noble ... . *Newport: George S. Hammond, Printer.* 1865. 8vo, pp. 16. B. 55384

Also: Sermon delivered Nov. 22, 1832, at Washington. ... *Washington.* 1832. 8vo.

NOBLE (*Mr.*) Speech of Mr. Noble, of Michigan, on the Plan to levy Tonnage Duties for the Improvement of Rivers and Harbors. ... Feb. 20, 1854. *Washington.* 1854. 8vo, pp. 13.

NOBLE (O.) Regular and skilful Music in the | Worship of God, | Founded in the Law of Nature, ... shewn in a Sermon, | ... at the | North Meeting-House, Newbury-Port | ... February 8th,

1774. | By Oliver Noble, A.M. | ... Printed at the Desire of the Musical Society, | In Newbury-Port. | ... | *Boston: Printed by Mills and Hicks, for Daniel Bayley in | Newbury-Port.* 1774. 8vo, pp. 46

NOBLE. Some | Strictures | upon the | Sacred Story recorded in the | Book of Esther, | Showing | The Power and Oppression of State Ministers, tend- | ing to the Ruin and Destruction of God's People:— | And the remarkable Interpositions of Divine Providence, | in Favour Of the Oppressed; | in a | Discourse, | delivered at | Newbury-Port, North Meeting House, | March 8th, 1775. | In Commemoration of the Massacre at Boston, | March the Fifth, 1770. | By Oliver Noble, M.A. ... *Newbury-Port, New England: | Printed by E. Lunt and H. W. Tinges.* | MDCCLXXV. 8vo, pp. 31, (1). B., M. 55387

Also: ... Sermon ... at Arundel, at the Ordination of ... Reverend Mr. Silas Moody, ... January 9, 1771. ... *Salem: Printed and sold by Samuel Hall.* MDCCLXXI. 8vo, pp. 32. — ... Two Sermons ... in Newbury, June 3d. 1781. ... [on] the Death of his Amiable Consort ... . *Newbury-Port: Printed by John Mycall.* 1781. 8vo, pp. 40. H.

NOBLE (S.) Two Sermons ... at Westhampton, June 26, 1802. By the Rev. Seth Noble ... . *Northampton: Printed ... by Thomas M. Pomroy.* 1804. 8vo, pp. 22. S. 55388

NOBLE (W. P.) Speech of Warren P. Noble on the Causes of the Rebellion. ... June 6, 1862. [n. p. n. d.] 8vo, pp. 8.

Noble Deeds of American Women. *See* Clement (J.), Vol. IV

NOBLES (W. H.) Speech of the Hon. Wm. H. Nobles, ... relative to an Emigrant Route to California and Oregon, through Minnesota Territory. *Saint Paul: Olmsted and Brown.* 1854. 8vo, pp. 13. 55390

Los Nobles de Guatemala. *San Salvador.* 1863. 8vo, pp. 11.

NOBODY (N.), *pseudon.* "Simon Snapping Turtle," Esq., The Paradise of Fools; or, the wonderful Adventures of Beelzebub Bubble. A Satire on Somebody. By Nathan Nobody. With a Critique. *Baltimore.* 1841. 8vo. 55392

NOBREGA (*P.*) Copia de unas Cartas embiadas del Brasil, por el Padre Nobrega, de la Compañia de Jesus, y otros padres que estan debaxo de su obediēcia: al Padre Maestre Simon, preposito de la dicha Compañia en Portugal, y a los padres y hermanos de Jesus de Coimbra. Tresladadas de portugues en castellano. Recebidas el año de 1551. [n. p. n. d.] 4to, pp. (27). 55393

NODAL (B. G. de). Relacion | del viaje qve por | orden de sv Mag^d^. | y acverdo del real Consejo | de Indias. Hizieron los Capitanes | Bartolome Garcia de Nodal, y Gonçalo | de Nodal hermanos, naturales de Ponte | Vedra, al descubrimiento del Estrecho | nuebo de S. Vicente y reconosimj^o^. | del de Magallanes. | A Don Fernando Carrillo | Caballero del abito de Santiago, Presidente | en el mismo Consejo. | *Con Privilegio | En Madrid. Por Fernando Correa | de Montenegro. Año* 1621. 4to, Engraved Title, 11 p. l., Text, 65 and 15 leaves. Map. 55394

The original edition of the voyage for the discovery of the Magellan Straits, etc., performed by the two brothers Captains Nodal, with the original map, is one of the rarest books of its class. The map is almost always wanting, and is sometimes supplied by the reprint in a smaller form, from the second edition. In order that a purchaser may be certain as to the completeness of a copy, we append a more minute collation: 12 prel. leaves, viz.: engraved title with portraits of the two brothers Nodal; 'Fee de aprouacion,' 3 pp.; 'Suma del priuilegio,' 1 p.; 'Tassa,' 1 p.; 'Erratas,' 1 p.; 'A Don Fernando Carrillo,' 3 pp.; 'Al Lector,' 5 pp.; 'Advertencias,' 3 pp.; 'Variacion de la aguja,' 3 pp.; 'Reglas,' 2 pp.; Text, 65 numb. leaves; 'Tabla para saber las Horas,' etc., 1 leaf; 'Relacion ... de los Servicios de los Capitanes Bartolome Garcia de Nodal, y Gonçalo de Nodal hermanos,' leaves numb. 2–15. At fol. 35 there is a copperplate Map entitled 'Reconocimiento de los Estrechos de Magellanes,' etc., "I. de Courbes sculpsit," 13⅓ by 15⅓ inches. The strait of San Vincente had been traversed by Le Maire shortly before the brothers Nodal, and his name has remained to designate it. But the Spanish map has a special value of its own, and is more detailed than Le Maire's. Colonel Stanley's copy sold for £3 10s. *See* Trömel, No. 80, Rich, 158, Ternaux, 431.

NODAL. Relacion | del viage, | que por orden de su Magestad, | y acuerdo de el Real Consejo | de Indias, | Hicieron los Capitanes | Bartholome Garcia de Nodal, | y Gonzalo de Nodal, Hermanos, naturales | de Pontevedra, | Al Descubrimiento | Del estrecho Nuevo de San | Vicente, que hoy es nombrado de Maire, y | Reconocimiento del de Magellanes. | Reimpresso de Orden | del Sr. D. Joachin Manuel de Villena | y Guadalfaxara, Marquès del Real Thesoro, Cavallero | del Orden de S. Juan, del Consejo de S. M. Gefe de Esqua- | dra de la Real Armada, y Presidente de la Real | Audiencia, y Casa de la Contratacion | a las Indias: | En Utilidad del Hospicio de la Santa | Charidad de la Ciudad de Cadiz. | Lleva Añadido | Las Derrotas de la America Occiden- | tal de unos Puertos á otros, que diò á luz el Theniente | de Navio, de la Real Armada Don Manuel | de Echavelar. | *Con Licencia en Madrid: | Y Reimpresso en Cadiz por Don Manuèl Espinosa de los Monteros, | Impressor de la Real Marina, Calle de S. Francisco. | Donde se hallara.* [1766 or 1769.] 4to, pp. (18), 164. Map.

Usually followed by:

... | Instruccion | exacta, y util | de las derrotas, | y navegaciones, | que se executan en todos | tiempos en la | America septentrional, |

de unos Puertos à otros: | con las advertencias de | Sondas, y Notas, para ponerlas | en pràctica. Sacala a luz | D. Manuel de Echevelar, | ... | *Con licencia; | En Cadiz en la Real Imprenta de Marina, | Calle de San Francisco.* [1753.] 4to, pp. 41, (2).

NODAL (J. F.) Elementos de Gramática Quichua, ó idioma de los Yncas. Bajo los auspicios de La Redentora, Sociedad de Filántropos para mejorar la suerte de los Aboríjenes Peruanos. Por el Dr. José Fernandez Nodal ... . *Cuzco [impreso por Watson & Hazell, Londres]: En el depósito del Autor.* [1872.] Rl. 8vo, pp. xvi, 441, 9. B. 55397

The best work on the Quichuan Grammar that has appeared. The old Ynca cipher-language is explained in a special section; and the text of a famous Quichuan drama is given entire from manuscript sources.

NODAL. Los Vinculos de Ollanta y Cusi-Kcuyllor. Drama en Quichua. Obra compilada y expurgada con la Version Castellana al frante de su Testo por el Dr. José Fernandez Nodal. ... *Ayacucho.* [n. d.] Rl. 8vo, pp. 70. 55398

In Quichua and Spanish.

NODIER (——), *and others.* *See* Vol. III., No. 10754.

NOEL (B. W.) Freedom and Slavery in the United States of America. By Baptist Wriothesley Noel. ... *London: James Nisbet & Co.* M.DCCC.LXIII. 16mo, pp. iv, 242. BA. 55399

NOEL. The Rebellion in America. By Baptist Wriothesley Noel, M.A. ... *London: James Nisbet & Co.* M.DCCC.LXIII. Post 8vo, pp. xviii, (2), 494. BA., C. 55400

NOEL. De Opstand in Noord-Amerika. ... *Kampen.* 1864. 2 vols., 8vo. 55401

NOEL (E.) The Labour Question in the West Indies. Three Letters from Ernest Noel, Esq. ... also Extracts from the Correspondent of the New York Times. *Buckingham: Ladies Negro's Friend Society.* [n. d.] 16mo, pp. 39. H. 55402

NOEL (G.) A Catalogue of Books in History, Divinity, Law, Arts and Sciences, ... To be Sold By Garrat Noel ... . *New-York: Printed by H. Gaine.* 1755. 8vo, pp. 24. B. 55403

Also: Catalogue of Books sold by Garrat Noel & Co. *New York.* 1759. 18mo. — Catalogue of Books, &c., sold by Garrat Noel, Bookseller ... from London, at his store next door to the Merchants Coffee House, New York. *Printed by Hugh Gaine in the Year* 1762. 8vo.

NOËL (Jacques), *de St. Malo.* Deux Lettres sur la découverte des Saults en Canada; publiées sous la direction de la Société littéraire et historique de Québec. *Québec.* 1843. 8vo.

For his letter written in 1587, touching the discoveries of Jacques Cartier, *see* Hakluyt, Vol. III.

NOËL DE LA MORINIÈRE (Simon Barthélemi Joseph). L'Amérique Espagnole, ou Lettres civiques à M. de Pradt. Par S. B. J. Noël, Inspecteur des Pêches Maritimes ... . *Paris: E. Gide fils.* 1817. 8vo, pp. (2), iv, 187. 55405

NOËL. Histoire générale des Pêches anciennes et modernes dans les mers et les fleuves des deux continens. ... Vol. I. *Paris: Imprimerie Royale.* 1816. 4to. 55406

At the author's death two hundred and fifty pages only of Vol. II. were printed. "The two volumes only form the introduction to the work, giving the history of fisheries from antiquity to the present day."—QUÉRARD.

Noel Hill Mining and Smelting Company, Township of Ascot, Canada East ... . Geological Surveys and Reports, ... with a Statement of the Condition and Prospects of the Company. *Boston: Geo. C. Rand & Avery, Printers.* 1864. 8vo, pp. 14, (1). Map. H. 55407

NOELL (J. W.) Speech of Hon. John W. Noell, ... on Federal Relations, and the Question of Secession. ... January 20, 1860. *Washington: Thomas McGill, Printer.* 1860. 8vo, pp. 16. B. 55408

Noetica. *See* [Johnson (S.)], Vol. IX., No. 36292.

NOGUEIRA VALLE DA GAMA. *See* Gama (N. A. N. V. da).

NOIR (Jean le). *See* Vol. V., No. 19493.

NOIR (L.) Campagne de Mexique. Puebla, par Louis Noir. *Paris: Achille Faure.* 1867. 8vo. + Mexico. [*Ibid.*] 1867.

Les Noirs [etc.]. *See* [Gilmore (J. R.)], Vol. V., No. 27451

NOLL (H. R.) The Botanical Class-Book, and Flora of Pennsylvania. By Henry R. Noll. *Lewisburg (Pa.): O. N. Worden.* 1852. 16mo, pp. 158, 452. C. 55410

NOLTE (V.) Fünfzig Jahre in beiden Hemisphären. Reminiscenzen aus dem Leben eines ehemaligen Kaufmannes, Von Vincent Nolte ... *Hamburg.* 1854. 2 vols., 8vo, pp. xvii, 323; xiv, 360. 55411

NOLTE. Fifty Years in Both Hemispheres or, Reminiscences of the Life of a Former Merchant. By Vincent Nolte. ... Translated from the German ... . *New York: Redfield.* 1854. 12mo, pp. xxii, 11–484. H. 55412

Nomenclatura Brevis Anglo-Latino in usum Scholarum. Together with Examples of the Five Declensions of Nouns: With the Words in Propria quæ Maribus and Quæ Genus reduced to each Declension. Per F. G. *Boston, in New-England: Printed by J. Draper, for J. Edwards and H. Foster in Cornhil.* 1735. 12mo, pp. (4), 88. 55413

Thomas remarks "There were several editions of this."

Nomination of Candidates for Governor and Lieutenant Governor of the State of New York; with an Address, reported by Mr. Van Buren. *Albany.* 1813. 12mo. 55414

Nomination of President & Vice President of the United States. [*Jefferson County, O., Dec.* 22, 1823.] 12mo, pp. 12.

The Nomination of U. S. Grant. Mass Meeting, Cooper Institute. *New York.* 1867. 8vo. 55416

NOMONY, *Va.* Minutes of the Meeting at Nomony, Westmorland County, Virginia, Oct. 9, 1802. *Richmond, Virginia, Printed by J. Dixon and J. Courtney, Jun.* 1803. 8vo. 55417

Noms | Svrnoms | et Qualitez | des Associez | En la Compagnie de la Nouuelle France, | suyuant les iours & dates de leurs signatures. | [n. p. n. d.] 4to, pp. 8. 55418

A corrected title of No. 10529, Vol. III.

NOMSZ (J.) Bartholomeus Las Casas. Treurspel, door Johannis Nomsz. *Amsterdam: W. Holtrop.* 1785. 8vo. Plate.

Also: Cora, of de Peruanen. Treurspel. *Amsterdam: P. T. Uilenbroek.* 1784. 8vo, pp. 58. Plate.

The Nonconformist's Plea for Uniformity. Being the Judgment of ... a ... Provincial Assembly of Ministers and Elders, in and about London; and of several eminent Preachers, English, Scottish, and New-English, concerning Toleration and Uniformity in matters of Religion. *London.* 1674. 4to. 55420

NONNIUS (Pedro). *See* Nunez (P.)

NONVILLE (*Marquis de*). Narrative of the Expedition of the Marquis Denonville against the Senecas in 1687; translated from the French by O. H. Marshall. *New York.* 1848. 8vo.

Noodle (*Mr.*) ... Speech of the Hon. Mr. Noodle against the Assembly Bill empowering Members of Benevolent and other Societies to vote by Proxy. ... *New York: Roe Lockwood & Son.* 1859. 8vo, pp. 19. H. 55422

Het Noodlot van Amerika, of klaer-afmaelende samenspraeck, waer in de oorzaek ontzwachteld werd der hedendagsche gebeurtenissen, ... toepasselijk op dezen oorlog, als ook de gevolgen die hy zou moeten hebben. Uit het Engelsch. *Gend.* [1780?] Sm. 8vo. 55423

A Dutch translation of [Cerisier's] "Destin del l'Amérique." *See* Vol. III. 11702.

Nooley (B.) Enquiry into Mr. B. Nooley's Conduct, and his being Stationed by the South Sea Company, First Factor at Porto Bello and Panama. *London.* 1735. 8vo. 55424

Noon (D.) Facts relative to the Campaign on the Niagara. By Major Darby Noon. *Boston.* 1815. 8vo. 55425

[Noonan & McNab.] Repeal of the Paper Duty. *Milwaukee.* 1865. 8vo, pp. 7. H. 55426

Noord Amerika. Drietal van uitmuntende Dichtstukjes op het Onafhangelyk verklaaren van Noord Amerika ... . [n. p. 1781.] 8vo, pp. 4. 55427

Three poems on the declaration of Independence of North America, etc.

Declaratie door de Gemagt. der Vereenigden Colonien van Noord-Amerika, te Philadelphia vergadert, de Oorzaaken en de Noodwendigheid van het opvatten der Wapenen, betoogende, 1775. *Gedruckt te Paramaribo.* [1776.] 4to, pp. 8. 55428

Declaration of the Plenipotentiaries of the United Colonies of America, on the necessity of taking up arms.

Extract uit de Dag-Registers van het Noord-Amerikaansche Congrês, Betrekkelyk tot het neemen en verbeurdverklaaren van Scheeps-Pryzen en het uitrusten van Kaapers; ... *Philadelphia: Printed by J. Dunlap.* MDCCLXXV. 8vo, pp. 48. 55429

Naauwkeurige Beschryving | van | Noord-America, | zynde thans het Toneel des | Oorlogs, | En in dat Werelddeel de Bezittengen der | Spanjaarden, | ... En andere Europiaansche Natien, de byzon- | dere Eilanden ... . *Dordrecht: | Gedrukt by Adriaan Walpot.* MDCCLXXX. 16mo, pp. 207. H. 55430

De Noordsche Weereld. *See* [La Martinière], Vol. x. 38712.

Noordtsche Landen. Beschrijvinghe | Van de Noordtsche | Landen, | Die gelegen zijn onder den Koude | Noordt-pool, | Als Denemarcken, Sweden, ... en | Groenlandt: Waer in verhaelt wert de verscheydenheyt der Coop- | manschappen en Kleedinge der Inwoonderen. | Midtsgaders: | Eenighe Vreemdicheden die men aldaer te Lande vindt, | soo van Beesten, Voghelen, Vissen, en Zee-Monsters, &c. | *t'Amsterdam, Gedruckt | By Gillis Joosten Saeghman* ... . [166-.] 4to, pp. 40. 55431

Description of Northern countries, which are situated under the North Pole.

Noort (O. van). Extract | oft | Kort Verhael wt het groote Journael | vande wonderlijcke ende groote reyse/ ghedaen door de strate Ma- | gellana eñ andere vremde Koninckrycken eñ Landen/ by den E. Olivier van Noort, | Admirael eñ General vande vier Schepen/ toegerust tot Rotterdam/ A°. 1598. | *Tot Rotterdam/ by Jan van Waesberghe/ ande Merct inde Fame.* | *Anno* M. CCCCCC. I. Sm. obl. 4to, (16) leaves. 55432

"Not mentioned by any bibliographer."—James Lenox.

Noort. Neuwe Schiffart | Warhafftige | vnd eygentliche | Be- | schreibung der langwirigen, sörglichen vnd | gefährlichen Reyse, so Olivier van Noort, | General Oberster vber vier Schiffe, auff welchen 248 Mañ, | mit Kriegszrüstung vnd Prouiant nach Notturfft wol verse | hen gewesen, durch das gefehrliche Fretum Magellanum, vñ | die gantze Kugel der Welt in dregen Jaren, nemlich vom Ju | lio desz 1598 Jares, da er von Roterdam abgefahren, bisz | auff den Augustum desz 1601. Jares wunderbarlich gethan, | vnd verrichtet hat, sampt Erzehlung allerhandt Abendtheuwer, | Mühe, Nocht vnd Gefahr, so jm in der Zeit begegnet, | auffgestossen, vnd zuhanden | gangen. | Ausz Niderländischer Verzeichnusz in hochteut | scher Sprach beschrieben | Durch | M. Gothardt Arthes von Dantzigk. | Auch mit schönen Kupfferstucken gezieret, vnd an Tag ge | ben durch Dieterichs de Bry S. ... | *Gedruckt zu Franckfurt, durch Matthæum Becker.* 1602. | 4to, pp. 119. Map and 6 Plates. J.C.B. 55433

Mr. Tiele, in describing the French edition of this voyage ("Mémoire Bibliographique," pp. 31–32), says he never saw the German version, which is abridged; and Camus, although he mentions several Dutch and French editions, does not speak of it; nor is it mentioned in the "Bib. Grenvilliana" (Vol. I., p. 192,) in the list of separate editions of portions of the "Great and Small Voyages" of De Bry. The Latin edition of the brothers De Bry ("Great Voyages," Part IX.) is said by Mr. Tiele to have been translated from this German version.

Noort. Beschryvinghe vande Voyagie om den geheelen | Werelt Cloot, ghedaen door Olivier van Noort van Vtrecht,

Generael over vier | Schepen, te weten: het Schip Mauritius als Admirael, dat wederom ghecomen is, Hendrick Fredrick Vice-Ad- | mirael, het Schip de Eendracht, midtsgaders de Hope, wel ghemonteert van alle Ammonitie van Oorloghe | ende Victualie, op hebbende 248. man, om te gaen door de Strate Magellanes, te handelen langhs de Custen | van Cica Cili ende Peru, om den gantschen Aerden Cloot om te zeylen, ende door de Moluckes we- | derom thuys te comen. Te zeyl ghegaen van Rotterdam, den tweeden July 1598. | Ende den Generael met het Schip Mauritius is alleen weder ghe- | keert inde Maent van Augusti, Anno 1601. | Daer in dat vertelt wort zyne wonderlijcke avontueren, ende in verscheyden Figueren afghebeelt, vele Vrem- | digheden dat hem is bejegent, 't welck hy ghesien, ende dat hem wedervaren is. | *Men vintse te coop tot Rotterdam, by Ian van Waesberghen, op de Marct inde Fame. Ende tot* | [*Amstelredam, by Cornelis Claesz opt Water, int Schrijfboeck.* n. d.] Obl. 4to, pp. (2), 92, (1). 25 Maps and Plates. A. 55434

"A reprint, with some differences in orthography, of the first edition of 1601, which is so rare that I have had and met with it only *once*. This reprint is rare, but not to an equal degree. De Bry has given in his "Great Voyages," IX., 3, a Latin translation, much abridged, in which the twenty-five plates and maps of the original are reduced to twelve and two imaginary prints."—Muller.

Noort. Beschryvinghe van de Voyagie om den geheelen | Werelt Cloot/ ghedaen door Olivier van Noort van Vtrecht, Generael over vier | Schepen/ te weten: Mauritius als Admirael/ Hendrick Fredrick Vice-Admirael/ de Eendracht, | midtsgaders de Hope, op hebbende tsamen 248. man/ om te zeylen door de Strate Magellanes, te handelen langs de | Custen van Cica, Chili eñ Peru, om den gantschen Aerden Cloot/ ende door de Molucques wederom thuys te | comen. Te zeyl gegaen van Rotterdam/ den tweeden July 1598. Ende de Generael met | het Schip Mauritius is alleen weder ghekeert in Augusto/ Anno 1601. | Daer in dat vertelt wort zyne wonderlijcke avontueren, ende vremdigheden hem bejegent, by hem | ghesien, ende die hem wedervaren zijn, Met vele Copere Caerten ende Figueren afgebeelt, by | hemlieden nieulicx gheteeckent ende mede ghebracht | *Tot Rotterdam.* | *By Ian van Waesberghen, ende by Cornelis Claesz tot Amstelredam, op 't Water.* | *int Schryfboeck, Anno* 1602. | Obl. 4to, pp. (8), 92. 25 Maps and Plates. 55435

Noort. Description | dv penible Voya- | ge faict entovr de l'Vnivers | ov Globe terrestre, par Sr. Olivier dv Nort d'Vtrecht, | General de quattre Navires, ascavoir: de celle dicte Mauritius

avecq laquelle il est retour- | ne comme Admiral, l'aultre de Henrij filz, de Fredericq Vice-Admiral, la troisiesme dicte la | Concorde, avecq la quatriesme nomme l'Esperance, bien montees dequipage de guerre & | Vivres, ayant 248. Hommes en icelles, pour traversant le destroict de Magellanes, des- | couvrir les Costes de Cica, Chili & Peru, & y traffiquer & puis passant le Mo- | lucques, & circumnavigant le Globe du Monde retourner a la Pa- | trie. Elles singlerent de Rotterdame le 2. Iuillet 1598. Et | l'An 1601. d'Aougst y tourna tant seulement la | susdicte navire Mauritius. | Ou sont deduictes ses estranges adventures, & pourtraict au vif en diverses Figures, plu- | sieurs cas estranges a luy advenus, qu'il y a rencontrez & veus. | Le tout translaté du Flamand en Franchois, a service de ceulx qui sont curieux & | se delectent de nouvelles remarquables & dignes de memoire. | *Imprimé à Amstelredame, chez Cornille Claessz sur l'Eau au Livre* | *a Escrire, l'An* 1602. Folio, pp. (2), 61, (1). J.C.B., C., BM. 55436

This first French edition, of the utmost rarity, is reprinted in De Bry, Vol. IX. and in Hulsius, Vol. XI. Mr. Tiele quotes this edition only from Camus, and a copy at the National Library at Paris.

Noort. Eigentliche und warhafftige Beschreibung | der wunderbärlichen Schiffarth (der Holländer) rundtumbher dem gantzen | Kreitz der Erden gethan durch Olivier von Nort, geburtig von Utrecht, General Obersten über vier Schiffen ... 1598–1601. Ausz der Niederländischen Sprach in die Hochteutsche vertolmetschet durch Joannem Schäffer. | *Gedruckt zu Amsterdam durch Cornelium Nicolaum Anno* 1602. Obl. 4to, pp. (4), 92. 25 Maps and Plates. 55437

This German edition is among the rarest of all, and differs from the German translation by G. Artus, in De Bry's "Collection of Voyages." Mr. Tiele knew only one copy, in possession of Mr. J. Lenox of New York.

Noort. Description | dv penible voya- | ge fait entovr de l'Vnivers | ov Globe terrestre, par Sr. Olivier Dv | Nort d'Vtrecht, General de qvatre navires, | assavoir: de celle dite Mauritius, avec laquelle il est retourné comme Admiral, l'autre de | Henry fils de Frederic Vice-Admiral, la troisiesme dite la Concorde avec la quatriesme | nommé l'Esperance, bien montees d'equipage de guerre & vivres, ayant 248 hommes en | icelles, pour traversant le Destroict de Magellanes, descouvrir les Costes de Cica, Chili & | Peru, & y trafiquer, & puis passant les Molucques, & circomnavigant le Globe | du Monde retourner à la Patrie. Elles singlerent de Rotterdame le 2 | Iuillet 1598. Et l'an 1601 d'Aoust y tourna tant seu- | lement la susdite navire Mauritius. | Où sont deduites

ses estranges adventures, & pourtrait au vif en diverses Figures, plu- | sieurs cas estranges à luy advenuz, qu'il y a rencontrez & veuz. | Le tout translaté du Flamand en François, & à service de ceux qui sont curieux | se delectent de nouvelles remarquables & dignes de memoire. | *Imprimé à Amsterdam, chez la Vefve de Cornille Nicolas, Marchand Librai- | re, demeurant sur l'eauë, au Livre à escrire. L'an* 1610. Folio, pp. (2), 62. 25 Maps and Plates.

This second French edition is also printed in De Bry's "Great Voyages," Part IX., Third Part, "Additamentum," 1602.

Noort. Beschrijvinge van de Voyagie om den geheelen | Werelt-Kloot, ghedaen door Olivier van Noordt van Vtrecht, Generael over vier Sche- | pen, te weten: Mauritius als Admirael, Hendrick Frederick Vice-Admirael, de Eendracht, midtsgaders | de Hope, op hebbende t'samen 248. Man, om te zeylen door de Strate Magellanes, te handelen | langhs de Custen van Cica, Chili ende Peru, om den gantschen Aerden-Cloot, ende door | de Molucques weder 'thuys te komen. Te zeyl gegaen van Rotterdam den tweeden Julij 1598. Ende den Generael met het Schip Mauritius is alleen weder | ghekeert in Augusto, in 't jaer onses Heeren, 1601. | Daer in dat vertelt wordt sijne wonderlijcke avonturen. ende vreemdicheden hem bejegent, by hem | ghesien, ende die hem wedervaren zijn. Met veel Copere Caerten ende Figueren af ghebeeldt by hen | lieden nieulijcks gheteeckent ende mede ghebracht. | *t'Amsterdam,* | *By Michiel Colijn, Boeckverkooper op 't Water, aen de Koorn-Marckt, in 't Huys-boeck. A°* 1618. Obl. 4to, pp. 132. 25 Maps and Plates. 55439

A reprint of the original edition. *See* Tiele, page 33.

Noort. Wonderlijcke Voyagie, | By de Hollanders gedaen, | Door de Strate | Magalanes, | Ende voorts den gantschen kloot des Aert- | bodems om, met vier Schepen: onder den Admirael | Olivier van Noort, uytghevaren Anno 1598. | Hier achter is bygevoeght | De tweede Voyagie van Iacob van Neck, naer | Oost-Indien. | *t'Amstelredam,* | *Voor Ioost Hartgers, Boeck-verkooper in de Gast-huys-steegh,* | *in de Boeck-winckel, bezijden 't Stadt-huys, Anno* 1648. 4to, pp. 88. C. 55440

Pages 59–88 contain the second voyage by Van Neck, much abridged.

Noort. Wonderlijcke Voyagie, | By de Hollanders ghedaen, | Door de Strate | Magalanes, | Ende voorts den gantschen Kloot des Aerdt- | bodems om, met vier Schepen: onder den Admirael | Olivier van Noort, van Utrecht, Uyt- | gevaren Anno 1598. |

t'Utrecht. | *By Lucas de Vries, Boeck-verkooper in de Snippe-vlucht,* 1649. | 4to, pp. 67. BM. 55441

Reprint of Hartgers' edition, with two additional pages, Van Neck's voyage being omitted.

Noort. Wonderlijcke Voyagie ... ghedaen ... des Aerdt- | bodems om, ... by-ghevoeght [as No. 55440]. *t'Amstelredam,* | *Voor Joost Hartgers, Boeck-verkooper op den Dam, bezijden* | *'t Stadthuys in de Boeck-winckel, Anno* 1650. | 4to, pp. 88. C. 55442

This edition is inserted in Hartgers' "Collection" published in 1648.

Noort. Wonderlijcke Voyagie [as No. 55441]. *t'Utrecht,* | *By Lucas de Vries.* 1652. 4to, pp. 64. 55443

Noort. Journael | Van de wonderlijcke Voyagie | Door de Straet | Magalanes, | Ende voorts den | Gantschen Kloot des Aerdtbodems om, | Gedaen met vier Scheepen, onder het beleydt van | Olivier van Noordt, | Uytgevaren in 't Jaer 1598. Verhalende de bysonderste Vreemdicheden, haer op de Reyse voor gevallen, als mede de zeden en manieren der Inwoonderen, | vreemde aerdt van Vogelen, en Beesten, &c. die zy daer te Lande gesien hebben. | *t'Amsterdam, Gedruckt* | *By Gillis Joosten Saeghman, in de Nieuwe-straet,* | *Ordinaris Drucker van de Journalen ter Zee, ende Landt-Reysen* [*about* 1663]. 4to, pp. (2), 48. BM. 55444

Noort. Wonderlijcke Voyagie, | By de Hollanders ghedaen, | Door de Strate | Magalanes, | Ende voorts den gantschen Kloot des Aerdtbodems om, met vier Schepen: onder den Admirael Olivier van | Noort, van Utrecht, Uytgevaren Anno 1598. | *t'Amsterdam,* | *By Michiel de Groot, Boeckverkooper op den Nieuwen dijck,* | *tusschen de twee Haerlemmer sluysen, inden grooten Bibel.* 1664. 4to, pp. 64

Noort. Journael van de Wonderlijcke Voyagie, | By de Hollanders gedaen/ | Door de Straet of Enghte van | Magallanes, | Ende voorts den gantschen Kloot des Aerdbodems om/ | Met vier Schepen, onder het Beleydt van | Olivier van Noord, | Uytgevaren Anno 1598. | Vermeerdert met noodige In-Werpen; en in desen | laetsten Druck op nieuws Verrijckt met verscheydene aenmerckelijcke | Byvoeghselen. | *Tot Utrecht,* | *Gedruckt by Jurriaen van Poolsum, Boeckdrucker en* | *Boeckverkoper* | *wonende op de Plaets* | *recht tegen over het Stadthuys. Anno.* 1684. 4to, pp. 72.

Noort. Journael vande Wonderlijcke Voyagie | [as No. 55446]. *T' Utrecht,* | *Gedruckt by Weduwe: J: Van Poolsum, Boeckdruckster,* | *wonende op de Plaets, recht tegenover het Stadthuys. Anno* 1708. 4to, pp. 72. 55447

Noort. Wonderlyke Reyze, | By de Hollanders gedaan, | Door de Strate | Magalanes, | Ende voorts den gantschen Kloot des | Aardbodems om, met Vier Scheepen: onder den Ad- | miraal Olivier van Noort, van | Utrecht, Uitgevaren Anno 1589 [*sic*]. | *Gedrukt,* | *Voor Abraham Cornelis Boekverkooper aen den Over- | toom* [*te Amsterdam*]. 1764. 4to, pp. 64. C. 55448

This is a reimpression of the edition of 1664. *See also* [Commelin (I.)], Vol. IV., Nos. 14958–9, "Recueil des Voyages de la Compagnie des Indes," III. An abstract in English is given in Burney's "Discoveries in the South Sea," II., Purchas's "Pilgrims," I., "Voyage round the World," 1598, Moore's "Collection of Voyages," I., Kerr's "Collection of Voyages," X., Harris' "Navigantium," I., and Renneville (R. A.)

Nootka Sound. *See* [Etches (J.)], Vol. VI., *and* Official Papers

Nootwendich | Discovrs | Oft | Vertooch aan de Hooch-Mogende Heeren | Staten Generaal van de Participan- | ten der Oost-Indische Compag- | nie tegens Bewinthebbers. | *In't Iaar onses Heeren* 1622. 4to, 20 leaves. 55449

"Relates chiefly to the foundation of the West India Company."—Muller, 155. There is another edition in black letter, folio, 1 leaf. *See also* "Tweede Noot-wendiger."

Nor-Peruano. Codigo Santa Cruz, de procedimientos judiciales del estado Nor-Peruano. ... *Lima: E. Aranda.* 1836. 4to, pp. viii, 166. 55450

Norberto (F.) Memorie Storiche intorno alle Missioni dell' Indie Orientali dal R. P. Norberto Cappucino, presentate al somme Pontefice Benedetto XIV. *Lucca.* 1774. 2 vols., 4to.

Describes the proceedings of the Jesuits in the Malabar Mission, where they authorized the most blasphemous mixture of the Christian and Pagan rites. The author, who was appointed Procurator General of these Missions, was, by the intrigues of this order, removed to the West Indies, thence he returned for the purpose of laying open these practices in the Papal courts. The author's real name is Pierre Parisot.

Norberto de Souza. Historia da Conjuração Mineira, estudios sobre as primeiras tentativas para a Independencia Nacional. *Rio de Janeiro.* [1865.] 8vo. 55452

Nord Amerika. Abbildung Nordamericanischer Länder und Eingebohrner Wilden, dabey die Erd-Beschreibung und Natur Seltenheiten der dortigen Gegenden, auch die sonderbahren Gebräuche des Landes Einwohner, die Handlung, Policey and Regiments Verfassung ... *Erfurt, J. H. Nonnens.* 1787. 12mo, pp. xii, 360. Plate. 55453

A picture of North America and the aboriginal savages inhabiting it.

Das | Nord-Amerika | Historisch | und | Geographisch | beschrieben. | ... | *Hamburg:* | *Friederich Christian Ritter.* 1777. 4 vols.,

16mo, pp. xxxii, 160; 192; viii, 179; (2), 126. Map and Portrait. H. 55454

Unfavorably criticised in the "Allgemeine deutsche Bibliothek."

Nord-Amerika in Bildern oder eine Auswahl von Ansichten der interessantesten Gegenden, hauptsächlich am Missouri, Abbildungen der dort lebenden Völkerstämme, ihrer Häuptlinge, Spiele, Waffen, &c. [n. p. n. d.] 8vo. BM. 55455

This is a reissue of thirty-six plates of Maximilian's "Travels." *See* our Vol. XI., No. 47017, with a brief letter-press description.

Nord-Amerika oder Neuestes Gemälde der Nord-Amerikanischen Freistaaten. Von einem Würtemberger, der sich dort befindet, seinen deutschen Landsleuten gewidmet. Mit einer Ansicht von Philadelphia. *Tübingen.* 1818. 16mo, pp. x, 166.

Die Nord-Polarländer, nach ältern und neuesten Reisebeschreibungen. *Pesth.* 1822. 2 vols., 8vo. Map and Plates. 55457

Nordenflycht (T.), *Baron of.* Part II. Catalogue of ... Metallick Fossils, collected between Buenos Ayres, on the River of Plate, and the Mines of Chota, in the Northern Part of Peru, By Timothy, Baron of Nordenflycht ... . *Boston: Printed by Joseph W. Ingraham.* 1822. 8vo, pp. 15. H. 55458

Nordhoff (C.) America for Free Working Men! ... How Slavery injures the Free Working Man. The Slave-Labor System and Free Working-Man's worst Enemy. By Charles Nordhoff. *New York: Harper & Brothers.* 1865. 8vo, pp. iv, 39.

Reprinted by the Loyal Publication Society, No. 80.

Nordhoff. Cape Cod and All Along Shore. Stories, by Charles Nordhoff. *New York: Harper & Brothers.* 1868. 12mo, pp. 235. 55460

[Nordhoff.] Man-of-War Life; a Boy's Experience in the United States Navy. *New York.* 1845. 12mo. + Sixth Edition. [*Ibid.*] 1856. 12mo. 55461

Nordhoff. ... The Freedmen of South Carolina; Some Account of their Appearance, Character, Condition, and Peculiar Customs. By Charles Nordhoff. *New-York: Charles T. Evans.* 1863. 8vo, pp. 27. H. 55462

Nordhoff. Nine Years a Sailor; being Sketches of Personal Experience in the United States Naval Service, the American and British Merchant Marine, and the Whaling Service. *Cincinnati*. 1857. 8vo. C. 55463

Also: The Merchant Vessel: A Sailor Boy's Voyage to see the World. ... *New York*. 1855. 8vo. + Sixth Edition. [*Ibid.*] 1866. 8vo.—Secession is Rebellion. Rebellion cannot succeed. The Union is Indissoluble, except by consent of all the States. An open Letter to the Rev. A. A. Lipscomb, of Alabama. ... *New York: Baker & Godwin*. 1860. 8vo, pp. 20.—Stories of the Island World. ... *New York: Harper & Brothers*. 1857. 16mo, pp. 315. 3 Plates.—Whaling and Fishing. ... *Cincinnati: Moore, Wilstach, Keys & Co.* 1856. 16mo, pp. 383. 4 Plates.

NORDISKE OLDSKRIFT-SELSKAB. Antiquarisk Tidsskrift, udgivet af det Kong. Nordiske Oldskrift-Selskab, 1843. *Kjøbenhavn*. 1845. 8vo. Continued. 55464

This valuable journal, published by the Antiquarian Society of the North, contains many very interesting articles (by Rafn and others) on the history, mythology, antiquities, etc. of America.

NORES (Giasone di). Breve Trattato | del mondo, | et delle sve parti, | semplici, et miste: di Jason De Nores ... *In Venetia, Appresso Andrea Muschio*. 1571. 8vo, 3 p. l., Text, 74 leaves, Capitoli, 2 leaves. BM. 55465

Chapter 17 of this very rare work relates to America.

NORES. Discorso di Jason Denores intorno alla Geographia All' Illvstre Signor Andrea Rosa ... *In Padoa, Appresso Paolo Meiett*. M.D.LXXIX. 4to, 13 leaves. BM. 55466

NORFOLK CO., *Mass.* Address to the Citizens. *See* [Ruggles (Nathaniel)].

Transactions of the NORFOLK AGRICULTURAL SOCIETY. For ... 1849. ... [*Boston*. 1849.] 8vo, pp. 15, (4), 145, (1). H.

Norfolk Convention ... [of] Republican Delegates from ... the County of Norfolk assembled at ... Dedham ... . [n. p. 1812.] 8vo, pp. 20. H. 55468

First Annual Report of the ... NORFOLK COUNTY BIBLE SOCIETY. ... January 7, 1829. *Boston: T. R. Marvin, Printer*. 1829. 8vo, pp. 32. B. 55469

The Fifth Annual Report of the Directors of the ... NORFOLK COUNTY SUNDAY SCHOOL ASSOCIATION. ... June 13th. 1860. *Boston: Printed by ... the Association*. 1860. 18mo, pp. 26. H. 55470

By-Laws of the NORFOLK DISTRICT MEDICAL SOCIETY ... . *Boston: Printed by David Clapp*. 1851. 12mo, pp. 12. + [*Ibid.*] 1859. 8vo, pp. 6, (1). H. 55471

Proceedings of the Grand Caucus, composed of Delegates from the Several Towns in the County of N[orfolk]. Assembled at Mr. H****'s Inn, in D*****, ... February 9—1809 ... . *Printed—Massachusetts, February—*1809. 8vo, pp. 8. H.

Proceedings of the Norfolk County Anti-Slavery Convention ... at Dedham, January 26, 1838. *Quincy: John A. Green, Printer*. 1838. 8vo, pp. 12. H. 55473

Rules and Regulations of the Bar in the County of Norfolk, ... *Dedham: Printed by H. Mann*. 1811. 8vo, pp. 8. BA.

To the Electors of the County of Norfolk. By a Republican [John Lowell?]. ... *Printed at Boston*. 1812. 8vo, pp. 8. H.

NORFOLK, *Va.* ... Address from the Colored Citizens of Norfolk, Va., to the People of the United States. Also an account of the Agitation among the Colored People of Virginia for Equal Rights. ... *New Bedford, Mass.: E. Anthony & Sons, Printers*. 1865. 8vo, pp. 26, (2). H. 55476

Address of the Merchants of the City of Norfolk, Va., to General Naglee; and his Reply. October, 1863. *Philadelphia*. [n. d.] 8vo, pp. 8. 55477

The Norfolk Directory: *Norfolk: Printed by A. C. Jordan and Co.* 1806. 12mo, pp. 82. 55478

The Norfolk Directory for 1851–1852: ... Also, Information relative to Portsmouth: ... By Wm. S. Forrest. *Norfolk*. 1851. 8vo, pp. iv, 132. H. Norfolk City and Business Directory for 1866. To which is added a Business Directory of Portsmouth. *Baltimore: Webb & Fitzgerald*. 1866. 8vo, pp. 128, 72. Norfolk City Directory for 1869. [With] a History of the City. *Norfolk, Va.* [n. d.] 8vo. Norfolk City Directory for 1870. *Norfolk: J. F. Milligan & Co.* 1870. 8vo.

Ordinances of the Borough of Norfolk; to which are prefixed the Charter ... and ... Acts of Assembly ... *Norfolk: Printed by T. G. Broughton* ... . [1829.] 8vo, pp. 281, (1). B. 55479

Proceedings of the Citizens ... of Norfolk, on the Boston Outrage, in the Case of the Runaway Slave George Latimer. *Norfolk: T. G. Broughton & Son, Printers*. 1843. 8vo, pp. 20.

Receipts and Expenditures of the County of Norfolk, ... 1868 to ... 1869. *Dedham, Mass: John Cox, Jr.* 1870. 8vo, pp. 8.

Report of the Philadelphia Relief Committee to collect Funds for the Sufferers by Yellow Fever, at Norfolk and Portsmouth, Va. *Philadelphia*. 1855. 8vo. P. 55482

Report of the Howard Association ... to all Contributors ... in Behalf of the Sufferers from ... Yellow Fever, ... 1855. *Philadelphia*. 1857. 8vo, pp. 113. BA. 55483

Report on the Origin of the Yellow Fever in Norfolk, during the Summer of 1855, made to the City Councils, by a Committee of Physicians. *Richmond, Va.: Ritchie and Dunnavant*. 1857. 8vo, pp. 44. 55484

NORGATE (E.) Mr. John Dunn Hunter Defended; Or, some Remarks on an Article in the North American Review, in which that Gentleman is branded as an Impostor. By E. Norgate. *London: John Miller*. 1826. 8vo, pp. 38. 55485

Scarce. Mr. J. Neale wrote an article on this pamphlet against J. D. Hunter, which was published in some magazine of July of this year, occupying twenty-seven pages.

Norge og Amerika. Et maanedligt Flyveblad. [Udgivet af Chr. S. Reiersen og E. Tvede.] *Christiania*. 1845. 8vo. Continued. 55486

NORIE (John William). New Sailing Directions for the East Coast of North America. Revised and Augmented by J. S. Hobbs. *London*. 1849. 8vo. C. 55487

Also: Norie's New South American Pilot, exhibiting the Coast from the River Plate to Cape Horn, Valparaiso, Lima, Truxillo, and Panama. *London*. 1823. Folio. 7 Charts.

NORIE. West India Directory, containing Instructions for Navigating the Caribbee ... Islands, Porto Rico, Hayti, or St. Domingo, Jamaica, Cuba, and the ... Harbours and Coasts of America, from the River Maranon to Florida; ... By J. W. Norie ... . A New Edition ... . *London: Charles Wilson*. 1845, '42, '44. 4 parts, 8vo, pp. iv, 76; vii, 143; iv, (2), 90; iv, 156.

NORIEGA (J. M. D.) *See* Diaz Noriega (José Maria), Vol. v.

[NORIEGA Y GUERRA (José Servando Santa Teresa Mier).] Historia de la Revolucion de Nueva España, antiguamente Anáhuac, ó verdadero Origen y Causas de ella con la Relacion de sus Progresos hasta el presente año de 1813. *Londra: E. Glindon*. 1813. 2 vols., 8vo, pp. liii, 364, Documentos, xiv, Errata, 2; (2), 365–777, Documentos, xlvi, Errata, 6. A., C. 55489

Privately printed in London, to be circulated in Mexico, but the vessel in which nearly the whole of the impression was sent out, was lost, and the work is extremely scarce. The author was several times imprisoned by the Inquisition.

NORIEGA (M.) Maximiliano y los ultimos sucesos del imperio en Queretaro y Mexico. Opusculo en que se refutan las memorias redactadas por Felix de Salm-Salm, escrito por el ex-coronel de artilleria Ignacio de la Peza y el ex-teniente coronel Agustino Pradillo, único oficial de órdenes del Emperador en Queretaro, con un apendice sobre los sucesos de Pueblo y contestacion al mismo principe de Salm, por D. Manuel Noriega, general en gefe de las fuerzas que defendieron aquella plaza. *Mexico*. 1870. 8vo, pp. 79. 55490

Normal School Advocate. Devoted to Education, Literature, and Science. Vol. I. ... 1856. *Lebanon*. 1856. 8vo. Continued. 55491

Normal School for Colored Girls, Washington, D. C. [Circular. n. p. 1857.] 8vo, pp. 7. H. 55492

NORMAN (B. M.) Rambles by Land and Water, or Notes of Travel in Cuba and Mexico; including a Canoe Voyage up the River Panuco, and Researches among the Ruins of Tamaulipas, &c. By B. M. Norman ... . *New-York: Paine & Burgess*. 1845. 12mo, pp. 216. 16 Plates. A., C. 55493

NORMAN. Rambles in Yucatan; or, Notes of Travel through the Peninsula, including a Visit to the Remarkable Ruins of Chichen, Kabah, Zayi, and Uxmal. With numerous Illustrations. By B. M. Norman. *New York: J. & H. G. Langley*. MDCCCXLIII. 8vo, pp. 304. Plates. BA. + Second Edition. [*Ibid.*] + Third Edition. *New York: Henry G. Langley*. MDCCCXLIII. 8vo, pp. 304. Plates and Map. C. + Fourth Edition. [*Ibid.*] 1844. H. + Seventh Edition. *New York*. 1849. 8vo.

Including a valuable ethnological disquisition, and a vocabulary of the Maya tongue, with a sketch of the grammar. This work will serve as a companion or complementary volume to those by J. L. Stephens. Indeed, it is said that Mr. Norman was hurriedly sent to Yucatan, to anticipate the researches of Mr. Stephens. For "Norman's New Orleans and Environs," *see* New Orleans, No. 53360.

NORMAN (L.) A Youth's History of California from the Earliest Period of its Discovery to the Present Time. By Lucia Norman. *San Francisco: A. Roman & Company*. 1867. 12mo, pp. x, 187. Plate. B., C. 55495

NORMAN (R.) The New Attractive; containing a short Discovrse of the Magnes or Loadstone, and amongst other his vertues, of a new discovered secret and subtill Propertie, concerning the Declining of the Needle, ... now first found out by

Robert Norman, Hydrographer; with certaine Necessarie Rules for the Art of Navigation. *London, T. East for R. Ballard*. 1585. 4to. 55496

Usually followed by "A Discourse of the Variation of the Cumpas, or Magneticall Needle, made by W. B[urroughs] and is to be annexed to The New Attractive of R. N." *London*. 1585. 4to. Diagrams. Robert Norman, in "The New Attractive," announced his discovery of the dip of the magnetic needle; and Burroughs's important observations of the *declination* of the needle, followed up by Gunter, led to the discovery (by Gillebrand?) of the cycle or change of the variation in declination.

NORMAN (W.) The American Pilot. By William Norman. *Boston: W. Norman*. 1798. Folio, pp. (6). 9 Maps. C.

NORONHA FREIRE (João de). Istoria delle Gverre del Regno del Brasile accadvte tra la Corona di Portogallo, e la Repvblica di Olanda. [1626–54,] da Giovanni Giuseppe di S. Teresa. ... *Roma, eredi del Corbelletti*. 1698. 2 vols., folio, pp. (12), 232, (16), 12 Maps and Portrait; 211, (20), 6 Plates. C. 55498

NORONHA (J. M. de). La Revolucion de mayo 1810. Drama historico, por Juana Manso de Noronha. *Buenos Aires*. 1864. 8vo, pp. 72. 55499

[NORRIEGA Y GUERRA (J. S.)] *See* [NORIEGA], No. 55489.

NORRIS (Isaac). Friendly Advice to the Inhabitants of Pensilvania. [*Philadelphia: Andrew Bradford, about* 1710.] Folio, pp. 3. 55500

NORRIS. The Journal of Isaac Norris (afterwards Speaker of the Assembly) during a Trip to Albany in 1745, and an Account of a Treaty held there in October of that year. *Philadelphia: Hawthorne Press*. 1867. 4to, pp. iii, 31. C., S. 55501

Only eighty copies printed. With a biographical sketch by J. P. Norris.

[NORRIS (John).] Profitable | Advice | for Rich and Poor. | In a | Dialogue, or Discourse | between | James Freeman, a Carolina Planter, | and | Simon Question, a West-Country Farmer, | containing | A Description, | or true Relation | of | South Carolina, | an | English Plantation, or Colony, in America: | with | Propositions for the Advantageous Set- | tlement of People, in General, but espe- | cially the Laborious Poor, in that Fruit- | ful, Pleasant, and Profitable Country, | for its Inhabitants. | Entered in the Hall-Book, according to Law. | *London, Printed by J. How, in Grace-Church-street* | 1712; *and Sold in Parcels by Robert Davis*, | *Bookseller, in Bridgewater, Somersetshire, and by* | *in* | *with Gilt Forrels, Price* 1*s.* 6*d.* | 12mo, pp. 110, Advertisement, 1 leaf.

The author appears to have been a native of Somersetshire, and very desirous to encourage emigrants to South Carolina, where he was settled. Priced by J. R. Smith at £5 5s. *See also* the "South Carolina Calendar," Vol. III., No. 10962.

NORRIS (J. S.) Biographical Notice of the late Moses Sheppard. By John Saurin Norris. *Utica, N. Y.* 1857. 8vo. + *Albany*. 1857. 8vo. 55503

NORRIS. The Early Friends (or Quakers) in Maryland, ... By J. Saurin Norris. [n. p.:] *Printed for the Maryland Historical Society, by John D. Toy*. [1862.] 8vo, pp. 30. H. 55504

NORRIS. A Sketch of the Life of Benjamin Banneker; from Notes taken in 1836. Read by J. Saurin Norris, before the Maryland Historical Society, October 5th, 1854. [n. p.:] *Printed for the ... Society, by John D. Toy*. [1854.] 8vo, pp. 20. B.

NORRIS (Moses). Speech of Hon. M. Norris, ... July 2, 1846. ... On the Bill ... amendatory of the Tariff Law of 1842. [n. p. n. d.] 8vo, pp. 16. BA. 55506

Also: Speech ... on the Right of Members [elected by New Hampshire, Georgia, Mississippi and Missouri] to their Seats in the House of Representatives: ... February 10, 1844 ... . [n. p. n. d.] 8vo, pp. 8.—Speech ... on the Annexation of Texas. January 24, 1845. *Washington*. 1845. 8vo.—Speech ... March 3, 1854, on the Kansas and Nebraska Bill. *Washington*. 1854. 8vo.

NORRIS (R.) A Short Account of the African Slave-Trade. By Robert Norris. A New Edition, Corrected. *London: W. Lowndes*. M.DCC.LXXXIX. 8vo, pp. 41. 55507

First appeared in "Memoirs of the Reign of Bossa Ahadee, King of Dahomy." By Robert Morris. *London*. 1789. 8vo. Map.

NORRIS (T.) The American Angler's Book: embracing the Natural History of Sporting Fish, and the Art of taking them. ... By Thad. Norris ... . *Philadelphia: E. H. Butler & Co.* 1864. 8vo, pp. 604. 8 Plates. + New Edition, with a Supplement. [*Ibid.*] 1865. 8vo, pp. 701. 8 Plates. B. 55508

Also: American Fish-Culture, embracing all the details of Artificial Breeding and Rearing of Trout; the Culture of Salmon, Shad and other Fishes. ... *Philadelphia: Porter & Coates*. 1868. 12mo, pp. 304. 9 Plates. B.

NORRIS (W. H.) ... Sermon, before the Convention of the Diocese of New Jersey, in ... Newark, ... 1858: By the Rev. William Herbert Norris, M.A. ... *Burlington: Franklin Ferguson, Printer*. 1858. 8vo, pp. 22. B. 55509

[NORRIS *vs.* NEWTON.] The South Bend Fugitive Slave Case, involving the right to a Writ of Habeas Corpus. *New York*. 1851. 12mo, pp. 24. H. 55510

The Norristown and Bridgeport Directory for 1867–68. With a Business Directory. *Norristown: J. H. Lant*. 1867. 16mo, pp. 119. 55511

NORT (Olivier du). *See* Noort (O. van), Nos. 55432–48.

NORTES (J. de M.) Nortes Josephinas de Mirtilo Sobre a Infausta Morte do Serenissimo Senhor D. Joze Principe do Brazil. [In Verse.] *Lisboa*. 1790. 8vo. Plates and Portraits.

NORTH (E.) The Uses of Music: An Address ... Utica Musical Academy, Feb. 5, 1858. By Prof. Edward North. With ... a Historical Sketch of the Academy. ... *Utica*. 1858. 8vo. S. 55513

NORTH (E.) A Treatise on a Malignant Epidemic, commonly called Spotted Fever ... . By Elisha North. *New-York: Printed by T. & J. Swords* ... . 1811. 12mo, pp. xi, 249. H.

NORTH (*Lord*). The History of Lord North's Administration, to the Dissolution of the Thirteenth Parliament of Great-Britain. ... [Part I.] *London: J. Wilkie*. 1781. 8vo. + *Dublin: P. Byrne*. M DCC LXXXII. 8vo, pp. vii, 183. 55515

See "Monthly Review," LXIV. 431, *and* "A View of the History," etc.

NORTH. Lord N—th condemned, and Lord S—ld—ne vindicated: by General Observations on their respective Administrations. By a Gentleman ... . *London: T. Cooper*. 1784. 8vo.

See "Monthly Review," LXXII. 309.

NORTH. Het Oor in het Kabinet, of geheime zamenspraken van Lord North, Lord Weymouth, de Hertog van Richmond etc. betreffend den Toestand van America ... . *London: J. Bew*. [1780?] 8vo. 55517

The ear in the cabinet, or secret intercourses of Lord North, Lord Weymouth, etc., on the state of America, was apparently printed in Holland. It is a translation of Cerisier's "Destin de l'Amérique." *See also* "Het Noodlot," No. 55423.

NORTH. The Speech of The Right Hon. Lord North, in the ... House of Commons, ... 17th of February, 1778, with Draughts of two Bills, pacific and conciliatory, moved for by his Lordship, and ordered to be brought in. To which are annexed, A Copy of the same noble Lord's conciliatory Propositions of the 20th of February, 1775, and an Extract from the celebrated Mr. Burke's prophetic Oration in March, 1775. *Baltimore: M. K. Goddard*. [n. d.] 8vo, pp. 16. P. 55518

See also Vol. v., No. 19254, [Hilliard d'Auberteuil], Vol. VIII., Nos. 31901–3, Vol. IX., No. 40524, *and* Vol. XII., No. 51899.

NORTH (J. *and* M.) Fiftieth Anniversary of the Marriage of James and Mary North, Middletown, Conn., Oct. 24, 1860. *Hartford: Press of Case, Lockwood and Company*. 1860. 12mo, pp. 30. 55519

NORTH (J. W.) The History of Augusta, from the earliest settlement to the present time: with Notices of the Plymouth Company, and Settlements on the Kennebec; together with Biographical Sketches and Genealogical Register. By James W. North. ... *Augusta: Clapp and North*. 1869. 8vo, pp. xii, 990. Plates, Portraits, and Map. + [*Ibid.*] 1870. C., H. 55520

NORTH (M. F. D.) Memorial of Mrs. Mary F. Dexter North, and her Father, Hon. S. Newton Dexter. *Utica, N. Y.: Curtiss & Childs*. 1869. 8vo, pp. 15. H. 55521

NORTH (M. L.) North's Guide for Invalids. Analysis of Saratoga Waters; also of Sharon, Avon, Virginia, and other mineral waters of the United States ... . By M. L. North ... . Fourth Edition. *New York: Saxton & Miles*. 1846. 16mo, pp. 72. + Sixth Edition; with an Appendix. *Saratoga Springs: B. Huling*. 1855. 16mo, pp. 72. + Seventh Edition ... . [*Ibid.*] 1858. 16mo. B. 55522

The seventh edition is entitled: "Book of the Spring."

NORTH. Saratoga Waters, or the Invalid at Saratoga. By M. L. North ... . *New York: M. W. Dodd*. 1840. 16mo, pp. 70. + Second Edition ... . *New York: Saxton & Mills*. 1843. 16mo, pp. 72. H. 55523

NORTH (S.) The College System of Education. A Discourse ... before the Trustees of Hamilton College, May 8, 1839, By Simon North. *Utica: Printed by Bennett & Bright*. M DCCC XXXIX. 8vo, pp. 20. B. 55524

Also: ... A Discourse ... in ... Hamilton College, June 25, 1849, before the ... Candidates for the Baccalaureate Degree. ... *Utica*. 1849. 8vo, pp. 22.— ... A Discourse ... in the Chapel of Hamilton College, June 23, 1850, before the ... Candidates for the Baccalaureate Degree. ... *Utica*. 1850. 8vo, pp. 22.— ... A Discourse ... in ... Hamilton College, March 10, 1852, at the Funeral of Rev. Henry Davis, D.D. ... *Syracuse*. 1852. 8vo, pp. 25.—Obedience in Death. A Discourse ... in ... Hamilton College, Sept. 13th, 1849, at the Funeral of Professor Marcus Catlin. ... *Clinton, N. Y.* 1850. 8vo, pp. 19.— ... An Oration, ... before the Connecticut Alpha of the Phi, Beta, Kappa, at New Haven, August 18th, 1847. ... *Utica: Roberts, Sherman & Colston, Printers*. 1847. 8vo, pp. 31.— ... A Sermon, ... January 13, 1842, before the Oneida County Bible Society, at Vernon, New York. ... *Utica*. 1842. 8vo, pp. 24. S.

NORTH AMERICA. An Historical Review of North America ... By a Gentleman immediately returned from a Tour of that Continent. ... *Dublin: C. Brown.* MDCCLXXXIX. 2 vols., 18mo, pp. xxviii, 268, 2 folded leaves; ix, 377. BA. 55525

For another edition, *see* Vol. VIII., No. 32079.

North America; a Descriptive Poem, representing the Voyage to America, a Sketch of that beautiful Country; with Remarks upon the political Humour and singular Conduct of its Inhabitants. To which are subjoined, Notes critical and explanatory. *London: Shepheard.* 1757. 8vo. 55526

Very scarce. *See* "Monthly Review," XVI. 460.

North America. No. 2. Extract of a Despatch from Her Majesty's Minister at Washington ... 1861, including Papers relating to Foreign Affairs; laid before the Congress of the United States ... 1861. ... *London: Printed by Harrison and Sons.* [1862.] Rl. 8vo, pp. xii, 367. 55527

North America. No. 3. Correspondence respecting International Maritime Law. *London.* [1862.] Folio, pp. v, 37.

North America. (No. 4.) 1864. Communications between the Collector of Customs at Liverpool and Messrs. Klingender and Co. respecting Shipment of Guns on Board the "Gibraltar." ... *London: Printed by Harrison and Sons.* [n. d.] Folio, pp. (2), 3, (1). BA. 55529

Corrected title of our No. 15003, Vol. IV.

North America. No. 5. Correspondence respecting the Seizure of Messrs. Mason, Slidell, McFarland, and Eustis, from ... the ... "Trent." ... *London.* [1862.] Folio, pp. (4), 37.

Also: ... Correspondence respecting Instructions given to Naval Officers of the United States in regard to Neutral Vessels and Mails. ... 1863. *London: Printed by Harrison and Sons.* [1863.] Folio, pp. (2), 7, (1).— ... Correspondence respecting the Assassination of the Late President of the United States. Presented to both Houses of Parliament by Command of Her Majesty. 1865. *London: Printed by Harrison and Sons.* [1865.] Folio, pp. (2), 3, (1). BA.

North America. No. 6. 1863. Correspondence with Mr. Adams respecting Neutral Rights and Duties. ... 1863. *London: Printed by Harrison and Sons.* [n. d.] Folio, pp. (2), 6, (1). BA.

North America. No. 8. Papers relating to the Blockade of the Ports of the Confederate States. *London.* [1862.] Folio, pp. vi, 126. 55532

North America. No. 10. Memorial from certain Shipowners at Liverpool, suggesting an alleviation in the Foreign Enlistment Act. *London.* 1862. Folio, pp. 2. 55533

North America. Correspondence relating to the Steamers "Nashville" and "Tuscarora" at Southampton. *London: Printed by Harrison and Sons.* [n. d.] Folio, pp. 30. 55534

North America. Correspondence respecting the Negotiations with the United States' Government on the Questions of the "Alabama," British Claims, Naturalization, and San Juan Water Boundary. *London.* 1869. 2 parts, folio. 55535

See also Vol. II., No. 5943, Vol. III., No. 9159, Vol. IV., No. 16887, *note*, and Vol. IX., Nos. 37130–1.

NORTH AMERICAN, *pseudon.* *See* [Dickinson (J.)], V. 20037.

North American Almanac and Massachusetts Register. *Boston.* 1770. 12mo. + [*Ibid.*] 1771. 55536

The North-American and the West-Indian Gazetteer. Containing An Authentic Description of the Colonies and Islands in that part of the Globe, Shewing their Situation, Climate, Soil, Produce, and Trade: With their Former and Present Condition. Also an exact Account of the Cities, Towns, Harbours, Ports, Bays, Rivers, Lakes, Mountains, Number of Inhabitants, &c. ... *London: G. Robinson.* MDCCLXXVI. 12mo, pp. (6), xxiv, Text, 119 leaves, Addenda, pp. (2). 2 Maps. + The Second Edition. [*Ibid.*] MDCCLXXVIII. 12mo, pp. (6), xxiv, Text, 109 leaves. 2 Maps. C. 55537

"A compilation from other similar works."—*Monthly Review*, LVI. 70. "This compact little book was a second time printed for the use of officers going over during the American War. If all the book is as reliable as the information given under the heading BRISTOL in Rhode Island, it might have afforded more amusement than instruction: 'Bristol is remarkable for the King of Spain's having a palace in it, and being killed there.' Shade of King Philip of Pokonoket and Mount Hope!"—STEVENS.

North American Atlas, 1777. *See* [Faden (W.)], VI. 23643.

North American Boundary. A Correspondence relating to the Boundary between the British Possessions in North America and the United States of America, under the Treaty of 1783. ... *London: Printed by J. Harrison and Son.* [1838.] Folio, pp. 100, 13. Map. S. 55538

Followed by: ... Proceedings and Correspondence relating to the Pretensions of the States of Maine, Massachusetts and New Hampshire, and to the Question of Jurisdiction within the disputed Territory from 1831 to 1837. ... *London.* [1838.] Folio, pp. 192. — ... [No. III.] Part I. Correspondence relating to the Boundary between the British

Possessions in North America and the United States of America under the Treaty of 1783. ... *London.* [1840.] Folio, pp. 6, 168. + Part II. Correspondence [as before]. *London.* [1840.] Folio, pp. 57, Appendix, pp. 37. 2 Maps. [For another edition, *see* Vol. IV., No. 16885.]— ... [No. V.] Supplementary Reports relating to the Boundary between the British Possessions in North America and the United States of America under the Treaty of 1783. ... *London.* [1842.] Folio, pp. 120. 2 Maps.— ... [No. VI.] Correspondence relating to the Boundary between the British Possessions in North America and the United States of North America under the Treaty of 1783. ... *London.* [1843.] Folio, pp. iv, 167. S. *See also* Vol. IV., No. 16899.

North American Calendar. By Samuel Stearns. *Boston.* 1772. 12mo. Continued to 1775. 55539

The North American Calendar, or An Almanac, for 1780. [By John Anderson, A.M.] *Providence: ... Bennett Wheeler.* [n. d.] 12mo. 55540

The North American Calendar, and Rhode Island Register, for 1782. The Astronomical Calculations by the ingenious Benjamin West, A.M. ... *Providence: Printed by Bennett Wheeler.* [n. d.] 12mo. Continued to 1785. 55541

The North American Calendar ... for 1786. [By Copernicius Partridge, A.M.] *Providence: Printed by Bennett Wheeler.* [n. d.] 12mo. 55542

The North American Calendar ... for 1786. By Benjamin West, Professor of Mathematics and Astronomy in the College of Rhode Island. *Providence: Printed by Bennett Wheeler.* [n. d.] 12mo. Continued to 1798. 55543

Afterwards "Wheeler's North American Calendar."

The North American Calendar, or the Columbian Almanac for ... 1829 ... . By W. Collom. *Wilmington, Del.* [n. d.] 8vo, pp. 36. S. 55544

A Brief Sketch of the Property belonging to the NORTH AMERICAN COAL COMPANY; with some general Remarks on the Subject of Coal and Coal Mines. *New York.* 1827. 8vo, pp. 23. 2 Maps. P. 55545

Corrected title of our No. 7901, Vol. II. Also: Memorial of the North American Coal and Mining Company, to the Legislature of ... New York ... . *Albany.* 1814. 8vo, pp. 16. N.—Observations on the intended Application of the North-American Coal & Mining Company, to the Legislature of ... New-York. February, 1814. [n. p. n. d.] 8vo, pp. 23. B.

North American Fauna. [Insects.] *Norwich, Eng.* 1837. 8vo. Plates. 55546

North American Indians. *See* Vol. IX., No. 34600, etc.

... The North American Homœopathic Journal, A Quarterly Magazine of Medicine and the Auxiliary Sciences. Conducted by Constantine Hering, M.D., ... E. E. Marcy, M.D., ... J. W. Metcalf, M.D. ... No. I. February, 1851. *New-York: William Radde.* 1851. 8vo, pp. 5–148. Continued. H. 55547

Plan of Association of the NORTH AMERICAN LAND COMPANY. Established February, 1795. *Philadelphia: Printed by R. Aitken and Son.* M,DCC,XCV. 8vo, pp. 25, folded leaf. BA., C.

See also Vol. VIII., Nos. 30436–38.

The North American Magazine. ... Volume I. Edited by Sumner Lincoln Fairfield. *Philadelphia: C. Sherman & Co.* 1833. 8vo, pp. iv, 392. BA., S. 55549

Continued as the "North American Quarterly Magazine."

The North American Medical and Surgical Journal. Conducted by Hugh L. Hodge, ... [and others]. No. I. January, 1826. ... *Philadelphia: J. Dobson.* 1826. 8vo, pp. (3), 244. H. Continued. 55550

... The North American Medical Reporter. Edited by W. Elmer, M.D. Vol. I. No. I. October, 1858. ... *New York: W. A. Townsend & Co.* 1858. 8vo, pp. 30. Continued. H.

The North American Medico-Chirurgical Review: ... Edited by S. D. Gross, ... and T. G. Richardson ... . Vol. I. *Philadelphia: J. B. Lippincott and Co.* [1857.] 8vo, pp. iv, 968. Continued. 55552

The North American Miscellany: A Weekly Magazine ... . Vol. I. *Boston: Albert Palmer and Company.* 1851. 8vo, pp. 4, 620. Continued. B. 55553

An Act, to incorporate the NORTH AMERICAN MINING COMPANY, (Passed 1st March, 1822,) ... . [n. p. n. d.] 8vo, pp. 21.

North American Mining Company for Gold & Silver Mining in Nevada, and other sections of the United States. Charter ... *Philadelphia.* [1865.] 8vo, pp. 16. H. 55555

Statement concerning the Property of the NORTH AMERICAN PETROLEUM Co. of the City of New York. ... *New York: J. O. Seymour & Co.* 1864. 8vo, pp. 24. B. 55556

The North-American Pilot for Newfoundland, Labradore, the Gulf and River St. Lawrence: being a Collection of Sixty accu-

rate Charts and Plans, drawn from Original Surveys: taken by Captain James Cook and Michael Lane, Surveyors, and Joseph Gilbert, and other Officers in the King's Service. ... Chiefly engraved by the late Thomas Jeffreys, ... on Thirty-six large Copper-Plates. *London: Printed and sold by R. Sayer and J. Bennett.* M.DCC.LXXV. Folio. [Part II.] The North-American Pilot for New England, New York, Pennsylvania, Maryland, and Virginia; Also, the two Carolinas, and Florida. Drawn from Original Surveys, taken by Capt. John Cascoigne, Joshua Fisher, Jacob Blamey, and other Officers ... . [*Ibid.*] MDCCLXXV. Folio. + [*Ibid.*] MDCCLXXIX. 2 vols., folio. + *London.* 1783, '84, '89. + A New Edition. *London: Robert Laurie and James Whittle.* 1799–1800. 2 vols., folio. + *London.* 1806, '09.

Corrected titles of our Nos. 16277–78, Vol. IV.

Exposé of the Condition and Progress of the NORTH AMERICAN PHALANX: in reply to the inquiries of Horace Greeley, and ... the Criticisms of Friends and Foes ... . *New York: De Witt & Davenport.* 1853. 8vo, pp. 28. B. 55558

Proceedings of the NORTH AMERICAN POMOLOGICAL CONVENTION. Held at Syracuse, Sept. 14, 1849. [*Syracuse:*] *Printed by V. W. Smith & Co.* [1849.] 8vo, pp. 64. Plate. S. 55559

The North American Protestant Magazine or the Anti Jesuit. Edited by Rev. C. Sparry. April, 1846. (New Series.) Vol. I. No. I. *New-York.* [n. d.] 8vo, pp. 16. Plate. H. 55560

The North American Quarterly Magazine. Edited by Sumner Lincoln Fairfield. Vol. I. *Philadelphia.* 183–. 8vo. 55561

The North-American Review and Miscellaneous Journal. Volume First. *Boston: Wells and Lilly.* 1815. 8vo, pp. iv, 448. Continued. B. 55562

After vol. XIII. the words "and Miscellaneous Journal," on the title are omitted. Vols. I.–IV. were edited by W. Tudor; V., VI., XVIII., XIX., XXII.–XXX. by J. Sparks; VII.–IX. by E. T. Channing; X.–XVII. by E. Everett; XX.–XXI. by E. Everett and J. G. Palfrey; XXXI.–XLI. by A. H. Everett; XLII.–LV. by J. G. Palfrey; LVI.–LXXVII. by F. Bowen; LXXVIII.–XCVII. by A. P. Peabody; XCVIII.–CVI., CVII., No. 220, by J. R. Lowell and C. E. Norton; CVII., No. 221, by J. R. Lowell; CVIII.–CXI. by J. R. Lowell and E. W. Gurrey; CXII.–CXV. by J. R. Lowell and H. Adams; CXVI.–CXVIII., No. 242, by T. S. Perry; CXVIII., No. 243, CXIX.–CXXIII. by H. Adams and H. C. Lodge; CXXIV. by A. T. Rice.

Extracts from the North American Review for Jan. 1824, on the subject of Colonization. *Princeton, N. J.* 1824. 8vo.

General Index to the North American Review, from its Commencement in 1815 to the End of the Twenty-Fifth Volume. ... *Boston: Gray & Bowen.* 1829. 8vo, pp. (8), 442. BA. 55564

The North American Tourist. *New-York: A. T. Goodrich.* [1839.] 12mo, pp. ix, 506. Maps and Plates. + [*Ibid.*] 1840.

Articles of Association and By-Laws of the NORTH AMERICAN TRUST AND BANKING COMPANY: also, the General Banking Law ... . *New-York: Printed by J. Booth & Son.* 1838. 8vo, pp. 40. B. 55566

The North American's Almanack, ... For 1770. By Samuel Stearns. *Boston: Edes and Gill.* [n. d.] 12mo. Continued.

North and South. *See* [Fuller (H.)], Vol. VII., No. 26163.

North and South. Impressions of Northern Society upon a Southerner, from the New York Daily Times. *New York.* MDCCCLIII. 12mo, pp. 35. 55568

The North and South. A Statistical Comparison, showing the Progress, Prosperity, &c., of the different Sections; what Slavery has done for the South and Freedom for the North. *Boston.* [n. d.] 12mo. 55569

The North and South; or, Slavery and its Contrasts. A Tale of Real Life. ... *Philadelphia: The Author.* 1852. 12mo, pp. 350. 6 colored Plates. C. 55570

North and South, Reason why Coleman Yellott, State Senator of Baltimore, would not have voted to censure H. W. Davis, for voting for Wm. Pennington for Speaker of the United States House of Representatives. [n. p. n. d.] 8vo, pp. 12. 55571

The North and the South. The Crisis before us, for Reading and Reflecting Men. [n. p. n. d.] 8vo, pp. 8. 55572

The North and the South. Reprinted from the New York Tribune. *New York.* 1854. 8vo, pp. 48. B. + [*Ibid.*] 1854. 8vo, pp. 40. B. 55573

See also [Carey (H. C.)], Vol. III., No. 10842.

The North and the South: the Crisis before us. From the N. Y. Herald, September 24. [n. p. n. d.] 8vo, pp. 15. B.

The North and the South Misrepresented and Misjudged: or, a Candid View of our Present Difficulties and Danger, and their

Causes and Remedy. *Philadelphia: The Author.* 1861. 8vo, pp. 48. H. 55575

The North Atlantic Telegraph via the Færöe Isles, Iceland, and Greenland. ... Reports of the Surveying Expeditions, etc. ... *London: Edward Stanford.* 1861. 8vo, pp. 94. Maps. 55576

The Declaration of Faith, ... with Rules ... and ... Members of the NORTH-ATTLEBOROUGH BAPTIST CHURCH. ... *Providence: H. H. Brown, Printer.* 1840. 18mo, pp. 12. H. 55577

Report of the Superintendent of the NORTH BRANCH CANAL, ... For ... 1855. [n. p.: *A. Boyd Hamilton, State Printer.* 1856.] 8vo, pp. 22. H. 55578

Also: Report of Wm. B. Foster, Jr., Engineer on the North Branch Canal. [*Towanda, Penn.* 1851.] 8vo, pp. 14. H.

History of NORTH BRIDGEWATER, *Mass.* *See* Kingman (B.)

NORTH BROOKFIELD, *Mass.* Account of the Receipts and Expenditures ... of North Brookfield, for ... 1844. *West Brookfield: Merriam and Cooke, Printers.* 1844. 12mo, pp. 16. Continued. H. 55579

Copy of the Valuation and Taxes ... of North Brookfield. For ... 1850. *West Brookfield: O. S. Cooke & Co.* 1851. 8vo, pp. 36. Continued. H. 55580

Report of the School Committee of ... North Brookfield, for ... 1852–3. *West Brookfield: O. S. & G. W. Cooke.* 1853. 8vo, pp. 14. Continued. H. 55581

NORTH CAROLINA.

Acts and Laws of his Majesty's Colony of North Carolina; with the Acts of such as are expired. *Newbern.* [n. d.] Folio, pp. 580. 55582

The Acts of the General Assembly of the State of North Carolina, passed during the Sessions held in the Years 1791, 1792, 1793 and 1794. *Newbern: Francois X. Martin.* 1795. 4to, pp. (4), 182, Table, (6). S. 55583

Acts and Resolutions of the General Assembly of ... North Carolina, passed in December, 1799. *Charleston.* 1800. Folio.

Acts of the General Assembly of North Carolina, from 1715 to 1803. *Newbern: Francois X. Martin.* 1804. 2 vols., 4to. + *Raleigh.* 1830. 8vo. Continued. C. 55585

Acts of Assembly in relation to Common-Schools in North-Carolina: with a Plain Digest of the Same, ... prepared ... By Calvin H. Wiley ... . *Raleigh: Holden & Wilson, Printers* ... . 1857. 8vo, pp. 32. H. 55586

Address from the Yearly Meeting of Friends in North Carolina, ... 1826, to the ... Meetings which constitute it; on the subject of removing the People of Colour under Friends' care to free Governments. [n. p. 1826.] Folio, 1 leaf. 55587

Address of the Administration Convention, held ... at Raleigh, Dec. 20, 1827. To the Freemen of North Carolina. [n. p. n. d.] 8vo, pp. 8. H. 55588

Address of the Executive Committee of the Democratic Party of North Carolina, on the Objections to an Ad Valorem System of Taxation. [n. p. 1861.] 8vo, pp. 32. H. 55589

Address to the Inhabitants of North Carolina on the Want of a Medium in lieu of Money. *Williamsburgh, Va.* 1746. 4to, pp. 26. M. 55590

An Address to the People of North Carolina, on the Evils of Slavery. By the Friends of Liberty and Equality. ... *Wallace Swain, Printer, Greensborough, N. C.* 1830. 16mo, pp. (2), 68, (1)

Agriculture of North Carolina. Part I. [and Part II.] ... By E. Emmons. *Raleigh.* 1860. 8vo. 55592

Annual Report of the Board of Public Improvements of North-Carolina, to the General Assembly, November 26, 1821; ... With Mr. [Hamilton] Fulton's Reports to the Board ... . *Raleigh: Printed by J. Gales.* 1821. 8vo, pp. xxviii, 68. Continued. BA. 55593

... The Answer of ... [Gov.] William W. Holden ... to the Articles of Impeachment ... against him by the House of Representatives of ... North Carolina. [*Raleigh.* 1870.] 8vo, pp. 45. H. 55594

Auszug der Totalsummen aus den Seelenlisten von Nordcarolina ...folge der an den Marschall dieses Distrikts von seinen Assistenten abgestatteten Berichte. [n. p. 17—.] Folio, 1 leaf.

Report of the BIBLE SOCIETY of North-Carolina, with their Constitution ... . *Raleigh: Printed at J. Gales's Office.* 1816. 8vo, pp. 24. BA. 55596

... A Bill to provide for the establishment of a State Hospital for the Insane in North Carolina. *Raleigh: Seaton Gales, Printer.* 1848. 8vo, pp. 12. H. 55597

First Annual Report of the BOARD OF PUBLIC CHARITIES, of North Carolina. February, 1870. *Raleigh.* 1870. 8vo, pp. 126, folded leaf. H. 55598

Branson's North Carolina Business Directory, for 1867–8. ... *Raleigh: Branson & Jones.* [1868.] 8vo, pp. 168, Advertisements interleaved, xcv. B. 55599

The Claim of the North Carolina Indians to a Participation in Proportion to Numbers in all the Lands and Moneys of the Cherokee Nations. *Washington.* 1869. 8vo, pp. 16. H.

See Vol. III., No. 12464, for the cover title.

A Collection of all the Acts of Assembly, of The Province of North Carolina, In Force and Use Since the Revisal of the Laws in the Year 1751. Together with the Titles of all such Laws as are Obsolete, had their Effect, Expir'd or Repeal'd. With an exact Table. ... *Newbern: Printed by James Davis.* M,DCC,LXIV. 4to. 55601

A Collection of the Private Acts of the General Assembly of the State of North-Carolina, from ... 1715, to ... 1790, Inclusive. Now in Force and Use. *Newbern: Francois-Xavier Martin.* 1794. 4to, pp. (4), 249, Table, etc., 3, Subscribers, 1 leaf.

A Collection of the Statutes. *See* Martin (F. X.), Vol. XI.

A Complete Revisal of all the Acts of Assembly of the Province of North-Carolina, now in force and use ... With Marginal Notes and References ... *Newbern: James Davis.* 1773. Folio, pp. (4), x, 566, (9). 55603

This is the second edition of a revisal of the laws, "the Sale of the whole [of the first] Impression being very rapid."

The Constitution, or Form of Government Agreed to, and Resolved upon By the Representatives of the Freemen of the State of North-Carolina. ... In Congress assembled, at Halifax. ... *Philadelphia: Printed by Francis Bailey.* 1779. 8vo, pp. 16.

The Constitution of North Carolina, adopted ... 1776; and the Amendments ... 1835; ... with an Ordinance for carrying the same into Effect. *Raleigh: Printed by J. Gales & Son.* 1835. 12mo, pp. 24. BA. 55605

Constitution of ... North-Carolina, ... with the Ordinances and Resolutions of the Constitutional Convention, ... 1868. *Raleigh: Joseph W. Holden, ... Printer.* 1868. 8vo, pp. 129, iv.

Constitution of North Carolina. [With Preliminary Address. *Raleigh.* 1868.] 8vo, pp. 46, 2. C. 55607

The Declaration of Independence. *See* Vol. XI., No. 47286.

An Epistle from the Yearly Meeting of Friends, held at New-Garden, Guilford County, North Carolina, by adjournments, from the 5th of the 11th month, to the 9th of the same, inclusive, 1827, to the Quarterly, Monthly and Preparative Meetings, within its limits, and to all its Members. *Printed by T. E. Strange, Greensborough, N. C.* [n. d.] 8vo. 55608

Executive and Legislative Documents, Extra Session, 1863 and 1864. *Raleigh.* 1864. 8vo. 55609

Exposé de la situation politique et militaire aux États-Unis. Protestation des habitants de la Caroline du Nord contre la continuation de la guerre. *Paris.* 1863. 8vo, pp. 32. Map.

A Fan for Fanning, and a Touchstone for Tryon. Being an Account of the Rise and Progress of the Regulators in North-Carolina, which ended in Civil War. *Boston.* 1771. 8vo, pp. 64.

First Annual Message of Gov. W. W. Holden, to the Legislature of North Carolina. 1868. [n. p. n. d.] 8vo, pp. 16.

Geology. Annual Report on the Geology of North Carolina. By Denison Olmsted. Part I. 1824. [n. p.] 1825. 8vo, pp. 84. + Second Report. 1825. 55613

Reports were also made in 1826 and 1827, by Dr. Mitchell, which I have not seen. Dr. C. E. Rothe made a report on the mineralogy of the State.

... Report of Professor Emmons, on his Geological Survey of North Carolina. *Raleigh: Seaton Gales, Printer ...* 1852. 8vo, pp. 181, (1). BA. 55614

Report of the Progress and Present State of the Geological and Agricultural Survey of North Carolina. By Ebenezer Emmons. *Raleigh.* 1855. 12mo, pp. 20. 55615

Geological Report of the Midland Counties of North Carolina. By Ebenezer Emmons. Illustrated with Engravings. *New York: George P. Putnam & Co.* 1856. 8vo, pp. xx, 351, (1). 9 Plates, 7 Maps and Sections. B. 55616

Report of the North-Carolina Geological Survey. Agriculture of the Eastern Counties; ... with Descriptions of the Fossils of the Marl Beds. Illustrated by Engravings. By Ebenezer Emmons. *Raleigh: Henry D. Turner.* 1858. 8vo, pp. xvi, 314, (2). B., C. 55617

Special Report on the Swamp Lands belonging to the Literary Board. By Ebenezer Emmons. *Raleigh.* 1860. 8vo. 55618

North-Carolina Geological ... Survey. Part II., Agriculture. Containing Descriptions, with many Analyses, of the Soils of the Swamp Lands. By Ebenezer Emmons ... *Raleigh: W. W. Holden, Printer ...* 1860. 8vo, pp. 95. H. 55619

Geological and Natural History Survey of North Carolina. Part III. Botany; ... By Rev. M. A. Curtis ... *Raleigh.* 1867. 8vo, pp. 156, (2). B. 55620

Report of the Progress of the Geological Survey of North Carolina, 1866. By Prof. W. C. Kerr. *Raleigh: W. E. Pell.* 1867. 8vo, pp. 66. C., S. 55621

Also appendix to the report for 1873, and report for 1875.

Constitution of the GRAND LODGE of York Masons of North Carolina. *Raleigh.* 1821. 8vo. 55622

Also: Proceedings of the Grand Lodge of Ancient York Masons of North Carolina. A. L. 5829. *Raleigh: Lawrence & Lemay.* 1830. 8vo, pp. 15. Continued. H.

Proceedings of the Grand Lodge of North Carolina and Tennessee, for 1802. *Raleigh.* 1803. 8vo. Continued. W.

Indexes to Documents relative to North Carolina during the Colonial Existence of the said State: now on file in ... London. ... *Raleigh: T. Loring.* 1843. 12mo, pp. (2), 120. 55624

Information concerning the Province. *See* Vol. IX., 34708.

Report of Directors [of the INSANE ASYLUM of North-Carolina, For ... 1858. *Raleigh: Holden & Wilson, Printers ...* n. d.] 8vo, pp. 50. Continued. B. 55625

... Report of the ... Directors and ... Principal of the INSTITUTION FOR THE DEAF AND DUMB and the Blind. [*Raleigh:*] *Holden & Wilson, Printers ...* [n. d.] 8vo, pp. 27. Continued.

Journal of the Constitutional Convention. *Raleigh.* 1868. 8vo. 55627

Journal of the Convention of the People of North Carolina, held on the 20th day of May, ... 1861 [to enact the Ordinance of Secession]. *Raleigh: Jno. W. Syme.* 1862. 8vo, pp. 193. + Second Session, ... November and December, 1861. [*Ibid.*] 8vo, pp. 86. + Third Session, ... January and February, 1862. [*Ibid.*] 8vo, pp. 119. + Fourth Session, ... April and May, 1862. [*Ibid.*] 8vo, pp. 109, iii, ii, ii, iii. BA., C. 55628

Journal of the Convention at its Session of 1865. *Raleigh: Cannon & Holden.* 1865. 8vo, pp. 94, iii. Continued. C.

Journal of the House of Commons of the General Assembly of ... North Carolina. [n. p.] 1786. Folio, pp. 56. C. 55630

The Journal of the Proceedings of the Provincial Congress of North-Carolina, held at Halifax, on the 4th day of April, 1776. ... *Newbern: Printed by James Davis ...* 1776. 8vo, pp. 46. + Reprinted ... *Raleigh: Lawrence and Lemay, Printers.* 1831. 8vo, pp. 66. C., S. 55631

The Journal of the Proceedings of the Provincial Congress of North-Carolina, held at Halifax the 12th day of November, 1776. Together with the Declaration of Rights, Constitution, and Ordinances of Congress. ... *Newbern: Printed by James Davis ...* 1777. Sm. 4to, pp. 84. C. 55632

Journal of the Senate of the General Assembly of ... North Carolina. [*Raleigh.*] 1786. Folio, pp. 44. 55633

Journal of the Senate of the General Assembly of ... North Carolina at its Session 1860–'61, Extra Session, 1861, and Journal of the House of Commons of the General Assembly ... at its Extra Session, 1861. *Raleigh.* 1861. 8vo. + ... Second Extra Session, 1861, and Journal of the House of Commons ... at its Second Extra Session, 1861. [*Ibid.*] 1862. 8vo. + ... First and Second Session, 1862–'63, and Journal of the House of Commons ... at its Session, 1862–'63. [*Ibid.*] 1862–63. 8vo.

These are the Confederate journals.

Laws and Resolutions of a Public Nature ... Adjourned Session, ... 1863. *Raleigh.* 1863. 8vo. C. 55635

Laws and Resolutions passed by the General Assembly of ... North Carolina, at the Special Session ... 1868. ... *Raleigh: N. Paige, Printer ...* 1868. 8vo, pp. ix, 116. H. 55636

Laws of the State of North-Carolina. [Passed 1715–1790.] Published, according to Act of Assembly, by James Iredell ... *Edenton: Hodge & Wills.* M,DCC,XCI. Folio, pp. (4), iv, 732.

Laws of North-Carolina. At a General Assembly, begun and held at Newbern ... November ... One Thousand Seven Hundred and Ninety-Two ... [n. p. n. d.] Folio. Continued.

The Laws of ... North-Carolina, Passed in 1801. ... [n. p. n. d.] Folio, pp. (2), 56. H. 55639

Laws of ... North Carolina ... 1805. *Raleigh.* 1806. Folio.

Continued in octavo.

Laws of ... North Carolina, including the titles of such Statutes and parts of Statutes of Great Britain as are in force in said State; together with the second Charter granted by Charles II. to the Proprietors of Carolina: the great Deed of Grant from the Lords Proprietors, the Grant from George II. to John, Lord Granville: the Bill of Rights and Constitution of the State ... *Raleigh.* 1821. 2 vols., 8vo, pp. 803; 858. 55641

Revised, under the authority of the General Assembly, by H. Potter, J. L. Taylor, and B. Yancey.

Laws of ... North Carolina, ... 1822–1831. *Raleigh.* 1831. 8vo. Continued. 55642

Laws of ... North Carolina, ... 1860–'61, also for Extra Session, ... 1861. *Raleigh.* 1861. 8vo. 55643

These Confederate laws were continued to 1864.

... Legislature of North Carolina, ... Dec. 16, 1840. Message of the Governor in relation to the University of North Carolina. *Raleigh: Thos. J. Lemay, Printer.* 1840. 8vo, pp. 8, (1)

A Manual of the Laws of North Carolina. Arranged under distinct heads in alphabetical order ... By John Haywood. Third Edition. *Raleigh.* 1814. 8vo. C. 55645

For another edition, *see* Vol. VIII., No. 31086.

Minutes of the Tenth Annual Meeting of The MEDICAL SOCIETY of ... North Carolina ... May, 1859. *Wilmington, N. C.: Fulton & Price, ... Printers.* 1859. 8vo, pp. 27, (1). H. 55646

Memoir on the Internal Improvement contemplated by the State; and on its Resources and Finances. *Raleigh.* 1819. 8vo.

Message of Governor James Iredell to the General Assembly of North Carolina. 1828. *Raleigh.* 1828. 8vo, pp. 14. Continued. W. 55648

Narrative of the Proceedings of the House of Burgesses. *Williamsburgh.* [n. d.] 8vo. 55649

North Carolina Almanac. *See* Virginia.

North Carolina Gazetteer ... *Raleigh.* 1856. 8vo. 55650

Account of the NORTH CAROLINA GOLD MINE COMPANY. [n. p. n. d.] 4to, pp. 8. N. 55651

Also: Charters, Rules, and Regulations of the North Carolina Gold-Mining Company. *Washington.* 1806. 8vo. C.

... The North Carolina Journal of Education. November, 1861. ... *Greensborough: Printed ... by James W. Albright.* 1861. 8vo. Continued. H. 55652

The North Carolina Land Company. A Guide to Capitalists and Emigrants; being a Statistical ... Account of the Several Counties of the State ... together with Letters of Prominent Citizens of the State in relation to the Soil, Climate, Productions, Minerals, ... and an Account of the Swamp Lands of the State. *Raleigh: Nichols & Gorman.* 1869. 8vo, pp. 136. Map. C.

North Carolina Law Repository; containing Biographical Sketches of Eminent Judges ... *Raleigh.* 1814–16. 2 vols., 8vo

North Carolina School.—A Circular soliciting Subscriptions,—dated, London, 6th mo. 27th, 1851. [n. p. n. d.] 4to, 1 leaf.

Signed by "Samuel Gurney, Josiah Forster, John Pease, and Thomas Norton, Junr."

The North Carolina University Magazine. By a Committee of the Senior Class. ... November, 1844. *Raleigh, N. C.: Thomas Loring.* 1844. 8vo. Continued. H. 55656

Ordinances and Resolutions passed by the State Convention of North Carolina, to dissolve the Union between the State of North Carolina and the other States, June, 1861. *Raleigh.* 1861. 8vo.

Ordinances [First to Fourth Sessions] of the State Convention, published in pursuance of a Resolution of the General Assembly, ratified 11th Feb., 1863. *Raleigh: W. W. Holden, Printer.* 1863. 8vo, pp. 93, (8). BA., C. 55658

These are the Confederate ordinances. Also: Ordinances and Resolutions passed by the North Carolina State Convention, 1866. *Raleigh.* 1866. 8vo.

Private Laws of ... North-Carolina, passed by the General Assembly, at its Session of 1858–'9. *Raleigh: Holden and Wilson, Printers.* 1859. 8vo, pp. xi, 407, (1). Continued. H.

Private Laws [Confederate] ... 1862–'63. *Raleigh: W. W. Holden.* 1863. 8vo. + Adjourned Session of 1862–'63. [*Ibid.*] 1863. 8vo, pp. 84, (1), Index, v. + Called Session of 1863. [*Ibid.*] 1863. 8vo, pp. 13, (2). + Adjourned Session of 1863. [*Ibid.*] 1863. 8vo, pp. 32, (2), iii, ii. + Adjourned Session of 1864. [*Ibid.*] 1864. 8vo, pp. 42, (2), iv. C. 55660

Private Laws passed by the General Assembly of ... North Carolina, at the Special Session, ... July, 1868. ... *Raleigh: N. Paige, Printer.* 1868. 8vo, pp. iv, 46, (1). H. 55661

Proceedings and Debates of the Convention of North-Carolina, Convened at Hillsborough, ... the 21st Day of July, 1788, for the purpose of deliberating and determining on the Constitution recommended by the General Convention at Philadelphia, the 17th Day of September, 1787. To which is prefixed the said Constitution. *Edenton: Hodge & Wills.* M.DCC.LXXXIX. 8vo, pp. 280. 55662

Proceedings and Debates of the Convention of North-Carolina, called to amend the Constitution of the State, which assembled at Raleigh, June 4, 1835. To which are subjoined the Convention Act and the Amendments to the Constitution ... *Raleigh: Printed by Joseph Gales and Son.* 1836. 8vo, pp. 424, (2), Index, 7. B. 55663

Proceedings of the Convention of Freedmen of North Carolina, ... Raleigh, September, 1865. [n. p. n. d.] 12mo, pp. 23.

Proceedings of the General Assembly of North Carolina of the Subject of International Exchanges. Session 1848–'49. *Raleigh.* 1849. 8vo, pp. 118. S. 55665

Proceedings of the North Carolina Lodge. *Raleigh.* 1807. 12mo. 55666

Proceedings of the Tenth Annual Meeting of the Baptist State Convention of North Carolina, Oct. 2–5, 1840. *Raleigh.* 1841. 8vo. BM. 55667

Proclamation By the Governor of North Carolina: ... with the Opinion of Chief-Justice Pearson, and the Reply of the Governor. *Raleigh.* 1870. 8vo, pp. 36. H. 55668

Prospectus of the Episcopal School of North-Carolina, near ... Raleigh. *Raleigh: Printed by Joseph Gales & Son.* 1834. 8vo, pp. 24. H. 55669

The Public Acts of the General Assembly of North Carolina. Vol. I. Containing the Acts from 1715 to 1790; revised and published, ... by the Hon. James Iredell. And now revised by François-Xavier Martin. *Newbern: Martin & Ogden.* 1804. 2 vols., 4to, pp. 500, (2); Vol. II. 1790–1803, pp. 226, (18).

Public Laws of ... North-Carolina, passed by the General Assembly, at its Session of 1856–'57: ... with the Comptroller's Statement ... *Raleigh: Holden and Wilson, Printers.* 1857. 8vo, pp. 174, Index, iv. Continued. H. 55671

Public Laws of ... North-Carolina, passed by the General Assembly, at its Second Extra Session, 1861. *Raleigh: John Spelman, Printer.* 1861. 8vo, pp. 140, iv. B. 55672

This and the following are Confederate laws.

Public Laws of ... North-Carolina, passed by the General Assembly, at its Adjourned Session of 1862–'63. *Raleigh: W. W. Holden, Printer.* 1863. 8vo, pp. 82, iv. + Called Session of 1863. [*Ibid.*] 1863. 8vo, pp. 22, (1), ii. + Adjourned Session of 1863. [*Ibid.*] 1863. 8vo, pp. 36. + Adjourned Session of 1864. [*Ibid.*] 1864. 8vo, pp. 31. BA. 55673

Public Laws of ... North Carolina, passed by the General Assembly ... 1866–'67. *Raleigh.* 1867. 8vo. Continued.

Register of North Carolina Troops. 1861. *Raleigh.* 1861. 8vo, pp. 26, (1). Continued. H. 55675

Report of Hon. David L. Swain, LL.D., on the Historical Agency for procuring Documentary Evidence of the History of North-Carolina. [n. p. n. d.] 8vo, pp. 18. + *Raleigh: Holden & Wilson, Printers.* 1857. 8vo, pp. 20. H. 55676

Report of the Comptroller of Public Accounts. [n. p. n. d.] 8vo. C. 55677

... Report of the Joint Select Committee appointed ... to inquire into the Causes why Soldiers were paid in Confederate Treasury Notes instead of North-Carolina Treasury Notes. [*Raleigh:*] *W. W. Holden, Printer.* [n. d.] 8vo, pp. 31. BA.

... Report of the Joint Select Committee of the Legislature of ... North Carolina, on the alteration of the Tariff, contemplated by the Woolens Bill. ... *Washington: Printed by Duff Green.* 1828. 8vo, pp. 5. H. 55679

... Report of the Joint Select Committee on Federal Relations. [*Raleigh:*] *John Spelman, Printer.* [n. d.] 8vo, pp. 8. BA.

Report of the Public Treasurer, to the Legislature of North Carolina, at the Session of 1850–'51. *Raleigh.* 1850. 8vo, pp. 40. Continued. C. 55681

Report of the Special Committee to inquire into certain outrages of the Enemy. [n. p. n. d.] 8vo, pp. 3. BA. 55682

Report of the Trustees, and Speech of J. M. Lovejoy, Esq., on the subject of Masonic Seminary, Grand Lodge of North Carolina. *Raleigh, Dec.* 7, 1848. 12mo, pp. 16. 55683

Report on the Subject of Cotton and Woolen Manufactories, and on the growing of Wool in North Carolina. 1828. *Raleigh: Printed by Lawrence and Lemay, Philadelphia—Reprinted by William Brown.* 1828. 8vo, pp. 16. B., BA. 55684

... Resolution of the Legislature of North Carolina, against an increase of Duties on Imports. ... *Washington: Printed by Gales & Seaton.* 1828. 8vo, pp. 5. H. 55685

... Response of Public Treasurer to Resolutions of the House of Commons. [*Raleigh:*] *W. W. Holden, Printer* ... . [n. d.] 8vo, pp. 48. BA. 55686

Revisal of the Laws of ... North Carolina, passed from 1821 to 1825 ... . Revised by John L. Taylor. *Raleigh.* 1827. 8vo.

Revised Code of North Carolina, ... 1854; ... By Bartholomew F. Moore and Asa Biggs. *Boston.* 1855. 8vo, pp. 728.

The Revised Statutes of ... North Carolina, ... 1836–'7 ... by Frederick Nash, James Iredell and William H. Battle. ... *Raleigh: Turner and Hughes.* 1837. 2 vols., 8vo, pp. xx, 712; vi, 558. B. 55689

Revolutionary History. *See* Hawks (F. L.), VIII., 30969.

Rules of Order for the ... Senate and House of Commons of North-Carolina, and Joint Rules for both Houses. 1822. *Raleigh: Printed by Thomas Henderson.* [n. d.] 24mo, pp. 20. H.

School Laws of North Carolina, as Ratified April 12th, ... 1869, with Instructions, Forms, Plans of School-Houses ... . *Raleigh: M. S. Littlefield, ... Printer.* 1869. 8vo, pp. 98. H.

... Special Message of Gov. Vance and accompanying Documents. [*Raleigh:*] *W. W. Holden, Printer* ... . [n. d.] 8vo, pp. 16. BA. 55692

Statements of the Comptroller of Public Accounts, for ... 1861 and 1862. [n. p. n. d.] 8vo, pp. 214. BA. 55693

Fifth Annual Report of the Superintendent of Common Schools of North Carolina. [*Raleigh: Holden & Wilson, Printers* ... . n. d.] 8vo, pp. 92, Index, ii, folded Table and Map. Continued. B. 55694

The Swamp Lands of ... North-Carolina: Facts for Emigrants and Capitalists. ... *Raleigh, N. C.: Printed by W. E. Pell.* 1867. 8vo, pp. 31. 55695

To the honorable Albert Gallatin, Esq. ... Sir, The commissioners for surveying the coast of North Carolina, have the honor to report: ... [n. p. n. d.] 8vo, pp. 8. P. 55696

To the Individual Members of the General Assembly of North Carolina. [n. p. 1832.] Folio, 1 leaf. 55697

A Quaker anti-slavery address.

To the People of North-Carolina. [Report of] the Convention which met ... to form a Constitution "republican in form," ... [n. p. 1868.] 8vo, pp. 46, 2. H. 55698

... Treasurer's Report. ... November 19th, 1860. [*Raleigh:*] *W. W. Holden, Printer* ... . [n. d.] 8vo, pp. 56, folded Table. Continued. B. 55699

Acts of the General Assembly, and Ordinances of the Trustees ... of the University of North Carolina. *Raleigh.* 1838. 12mo, pp. 21. 55700

Also: Acts of the General Assembly and Ordinances of the Trustees, for the Organization and Government of the University of North Carolina. *Raleigh.* 1852. 12mo, pp. 24. B.

Catalogue of the Faculty and Students of the University, ... October 1, 1826. *Hillsborough: Printed by D. Heartt.* 1826. 8vo, pp. 13. Continued. H. 55701

Also: A Catalogue of the Members of the Dialectic Society, ... in the University, ... *Raleigh.* 1841. 8vo, pp. 22. Continued.—Catalogue of the Philanthropic Society,

instituted in the University ... 1795. *Raleigh: Printed by Thomas J. Lemay.* 1841. 8vo, pp. 15.—Catalogus Senatus Academici et eorum Qui Munera et Officia Academica Gesserunt, quique aliquovis gradu exornati sunt, in Universitate Carolinæ-Borealis. *Ralegæ: Gulielmus-Dewey Cooke, Typographo.* MDCCCLII. 8vo, pp. 43. H.— ... Catalogus Universitati Carolinæ Septentrionalis. *Raleigh.* 1812. 12mo.—First Report of the Historical Society of the University of North Carolina. *Hillsborough.* 1844. 8vo, pp. 8

Verrichtungen der Evangelisch-Lutherischen Synode für Nord-Carolina und angränzende Staaten, gehalten in Guilford-County, ... May, 1825. *Philadelphia.* 1825. 8vo. 55702

See also "North American Review," XII. 16, XXIV. 365, 468.

North Chelsea, *Mass.* School Committee's Report; North Chelsea, 1851–52. [n. p. n. d] 12mo, pp. 12. S. 55703

See also Vol. VII., No. 26161.

North Clear Creek Gold and Silver Mining Company, Gilpin Co., Colorado Territory. ... [n. p. 1864.] 8vo, pp. 17. B.

North Coventry, *Conn.* The Celebration at North Coventry, March 10, 1859, of the Settlement of Rev. George A. Calhoun, D.D., over the Church and Society in that place, March 10, 1819. ... *Hartford: Case, Lockwood and Company.* 1859. 8vo, pp. 40. B. 55705

North Danvers, *Mass.* *See* [Osgood (G.)]

... Proceedings at the Centennial Anniversary of the Dedication of the North Dutch Church, ... and also, at the laying of the Corner-Stone of the New Church ... . *New York.* 1869. 8vo, pp. 76. 3 Plates. B. 55706

By-Laws and Rules ... of the North-Eastern Agricultural Society, with the ... Officers and List of Premiums ... 1860, ... *Paris, Missouri.* 1860. 16mo, pp. 16. H. 55707

North-Eastern Boundary. Documents relating to the North Eastern Boundary of ... Maine. *Boston: Dutton & Wentworth—Printers* ... . 1828. 8vo, pp. 14, (2). B. 55708

... Message from the President ... communicating Additional Correspondence in relation to the ... Northeastern Boundary ... . March 26, 1840. ... [n. p. n. d.] 8vo, pp. 7. BA. 55709

... Message from the President ... communicating ... Copies of Correspondence in relation to the Northeastern Boundary ... of Maine. January 23, 1840. ... [n. p. n. d.] 8vo, pp. 66.

... Message from the President ... transmitting A Copy of the Report of the Commissioners ... [on] the Northeastern Boundary. February 9, 1841. ... [n. p. n. d.] 8vo, pp. 13. BA.

... Message from the President ... communicating the Correspondence ... between the Government of Great Britain and ... the United States between ... June, 1840, and ... March, 1841, relative to the Northeastern Boundary. April 3, 1846. ... [n. p. n. d.] 8vo, pp. 22. 2 Maps. BA. 55712

See also Vol. XII., No. 48107.

The North-Eastern Boundary of the United States. *Boston: Peirce & Parker.* 1832. 16mo, pp. 100. C. 55713

Extract from the "North American Review," No. 75. Perhaps by Peter Thacher Vose. Corrected title of our No. 29649, Vol. VIII. *See also* [Bliss (H.)], Vol. II., No. 5924, Gallatin (A.), Vol. VII., No. 26390, Vol. XI., Nos 43900, 43928, *and* "North American Review," XXVI. 421; XXXIII. 262; XXXIV. 514; XLIII. 413; LII. 424; LIII. 439; "Frasers' Magazine," XXII. 346.

The North Georgia Gazette and Winter Chronicle. Edited by Edward Sabine. *London: John Murray.* MDCCCXXI. 4to, pp. xii, 132. A. + Second Edition. [*Ibid.*] MDCCCXXII. 4to.

A weekly newspaper established by Parry's crew in 1819–20, "to enliven the tedious and inactive months of winter" in the Arctic region. It is an amusing collection of poems, songs, humorous essays, etc.

Report of the First Annual Examination at North Granville Female Seminary, ... 1856. *North Granville: Weed, Parsons and Co., Printers.* 1856. 8vo, pp. 23, (1). Plate. Cont'd.

Also: Third Annual Catalogue of the ... North Granville Ladies' Seminary. For ... 1858. ... *North Granville, N. Y.: Geo. A. Tuttle & Co., Printers.* 1858. 8vo, pp. 23, (1). Plate.—A Quinquennial Catalogue of the ... North Granville Ladies' Seminary, For ... 1860. ... *North Granville, N. Y.: George A. Tuttle & Co., Printers.* 1860. 8vo, pp. 32. Plate. H.

Manual of the Baptist Church at North Haven, 1846. *New Haven.* 1846. 12mo. 55716

Town of North Hempstead *vs.* Town of Hempstead. In the Court for the Trial of Impeachments ... between the Town of North Hempstead and the Town of Hempstead. Case on the part of the Appellants. *New York: W. Grattan.* 1825. 8vo, pp. 400, 152, (2). C. 55717

Improved title of our No. 31300, Vol. VIII.

Annual Catalogue of the Academic Department of North Illinois University for ... 1859. *Henry, Ill.: Henry Courier.* 1859. 8vo, pp. 15. H. 55718

Also: Report of the Board of Trustees of the North Illinois University, Henry, Illinois, for ... 1857–8. *Boston: Printed by John Wilson and Son.* 1858. 8vo, pp. 7, (1).

Prospectus of the North-Martinsburg Lead-Mining Company, with ... Reports ... . *New-York.* 1865. 8vo, pp. 16. H.

Catalogue of North Middlesex Circulating Library, ... Groton Centre, Mass. *Groton Junction: John H. Turner, ... Printer.* 1866. 12mo, pp. 16, 4. H. 55720

First Annual Report of the North-Middlesex Sunday-School Society; presented Oct. 8, 1856. By Augustus Woodbury. *Lowell.* 1856. 8vo, pp. 16. 55721

North Missouri and Eastern Kansas Business Directory for 1867–8. *Quincy (Ill.): S. B. Wyckoff.* 1867. 8vo, pp. 455. C.

Facts for Emigrants. Northern Missouri. A New and Important Region! ... Description of the Counties and Towns along the ... North Missouri Railroad and Branches. *St. Louis.* 1870. 8vo, pp. 64. H. 55723

Also: Report of the ... Directors of the North Missouri Railroad Company to the Stockholders, ... 1865. *St. Louis: George Knapp & Co., Printers.* 1865. 8vo, pp. 54. Continued.—Special Report of Directors ... to the Governor and Legislature. *St. Louis.* 1865. 8vo. *See also* Vol. VIII., No. 32739, *and* Vol. XII., No. 49554.

A Guide on the North Pennsylvania Rail Road, between Philad'a & Fort Washington. Illustrated. *Philadelphia: Printed by Ringwalt & Co.* 1859. 12mo, pp. 16. H. 55724

Also: A Memorial to the Councils of the City of Philadelphia ... . *Philadelphia.* 1854. 8vo.

Act of Parliament, offering Rewards of £20,000 for the North Passage, and £5000 for approaching the North Pole. *London.* 1775. Folio. 55725

Manual of the North Presbyterian Church, in the City of New-York. ... *New-York: John A. Gray, Printer.* 1858. 18mo, pp. 36. 55726

North Providence Centennial. A Report of the Celebration at Pawtucket, North Providence, of the One Hundredth Anniversary of the Incorporation of the Town, June 24th, 1865. With an Address containing Historical Matter of Local Interest. ... *Pawtucket: Robert Sherman, Printer.* 1865. 8vo, pp. 91, (1).

Fifty copies printed on large paper, for Albert V. Jenks.

The By-Laws of the North Randolph Church ... . *Lynn: Printed by Lewis Josselyn.* 1850. 16mo, pp. 16. H. 55728

Financial Report of ... North Reading, for ... 1866, with the Annual Report of the School Committee. *Boston: J. C. French, Printer.* 1866. 8vo, pp. 16. Continued. B. 55729

Also: Receipts and Expenditures of ... North Reading, from ... 1861 ... to ... 1862. *Boston: Geo. C. Rand & Avery.* 1862. 8vo, pp. 8. Continued.—Report of the Superintending School Committee of ... North Reading, for ... 1861–62. *Boston: Geo. C. Rand & Avery.* 1862. 8vo, pp. 8. Continued. B.

North River. *See* Hudson River, Vol. VIII., No. 33524.

The North Star: The Poetry of Freedom, by her Friends. ... *Philadelphia: Printed by Merrihew and Thompson.* 1840. 24mo, pp. 117, (1). H. 55730

Annual Report of the North Street Union Mission. *Boston.* 1862. 8vo, pp. 3. Continued. B. 55731

Reports on the Property of the North Sutton Mining & Smelting Co. ... Canada East. [n. p. 1863.] 8vo, pp. 19. B.

North-West Mining Company of Michigan. Proceedings of the Stockholders, ... 1852: ... with the Report of the ... Directors ... . *Philadelphia: Printed by John C. Clark.* 1852. 8vo, pp. 26. Continued. H. 55733

Also: North-West Mining Company. Report ... of a Visit to the Locations and an Examination of the Works, in June, 1847. With a more recent Letter from the Agent ... . New-York, Aug. 10, 1847. [n. p.:] *J. A. Fraetas & Co., Printers.* [n. d.] 8vo, pp. 15, (1). H.

North-West Passage. Atlas of the North West Passage. *London.* 1853. 8vo. 55734

See also [Drage (Theodore Swaine)], Vol. V., No. 20808, *and* [Pickersgill (R.)]

Memoranda and Prospectus of the North-West Transportation and Land Company. *Toronto.* 1858. 8vo, pp. 12. S.

North-Western American Boundary. Notice respecting the Boundary between His Majesty's Possessions in North America and the United States; with a Map ... . *London.* 1817. 8vo.

The Constitution of the North-Western Branch of the American Society for educating Pious Youth for the Gospel Ministry; with ... An Address ... . *Middlebury: Printed by Copeland and Allen.* 1820. 8vo, pp. 31. H. 55737

North-Western Christian Magazine, John Boggs, Editor ... . Vol. IV. January. No. 7. ... *Cincinnati.* 1858. 8vo. Cont'd.

Catalogue of ... North-Western Christian University, for ... 1856–1857. Indianapolis, June 1, 1857. *Indianapolis.* 1857. 8vo, pp. 15. Plate. Continued. H. 55739

First Annual Report of the ... North-Western Dispensary, ... 1853. *New-York: Oliver & Brother, ... Printers.* 1853. 8vo, pp. 21. Continued. H. 55740

North Western Farmer. A Monthly Magazine of Agriculture, Horticulture, Home Improvement, and Family Literature. T. A. Bland, Editor. ... *Indianapolis: Downey & Brouse.* 1866. 4to. Continued. C. 55741

Catalogue of the ... North-Western Female College at Evanston, Ill., for ... 1858–9. ... *Chicago: Dunlop, Sewell & Spalding, ... Printers.* 1859. 8vo, pp. 15, (1). Plate. H.

Minutes of the First Annual Meeting of the North Western Freedmen's Aid Commission, Chicago, 1864. *Chicago.* 1864. 8vo. 55743

Also: Second Annual Report of the Northwestern Freedmen's Aid Commission, presented at Chicago, April 13, 1865. *Chicago: James Barnet.* 1865. 8vo, pp. 24.

Transactions of the North-Western Fruit Growers Association, at their Second Annual Meeting, held in the Court House at Dixon, Ill., Sept. 29th and 30th, 1852. [n. p. n. d.] 8vo, pp. 40. S. 55744

The North-Western Journal of Education, Science and ... Literature. O. M. Conover, Editor. Vol. I. No. I. March, 1850. *Madison, Wis.: Beriah Brown, Printer.* 1850. 8vo, pp. 60. Continued to No. 3. H. 55745

... The North-Western Journal of Homœopathia. ... No. I. Oct. 1, 1848. Edited by Geo. E. Shipman, M.D. *Chicago: H. K. Davis.* 1848. 8vo, pp. 16. Continued. H. 55746

Constitution and By-Laws of the North-Western Medical Society ... with the Proceedings of the First Annual Meeting ... January 11th, 1853 ... . *Dubuque: Mahony, Stanton, & Dorr.* 1853. 8vo, pp. 20. B. 55747

... The North-Western Medical and Surgical Journal, edited by W. B. Henick, M.D., and A. Johnston, M.D. *Chicago.* 1848. 8vo. Continued. 55748

Report of the ... North Western Mining Company of Detroit ... June, 1852. *Pittsburgh: Printed by Kennedy & Brother.* [n. d.] 8vo, pp. 12. Plan. H. 55749

North-Western Pennsylvania Oil and Coal Company. Reports by P. W. Sheafer, ... Dr. Charles T. Jackson, ... William F. Roberts ... . January, 1865. [n. p. n. d.] 8vo, pp. 36. Map

Second Report of the President and Directors of the North-Western Railroad Company, with the Report of the Chief Engineer. *Philadelphia: T. K. and P. G. Collins, Printers.* 1855. 8vo, pp. 26. P. 55751

North-Western Soldiers' Fair. *See* Vol. IV., No. 12656.

The Constitution of the North-Western Union Missionary Society. Formed in ... 1819. *Cincinnati: Looker, Reynold & Co.* [n. d.] 12mo, pp. 8. 55752

Circular of the ... North Western University; Evanston, Illinois. 1856. *Chicago.* [n. d.] 8vo, pp. 15. H. 55753

Also: Catalogue ... . 1858–9. *Chicago: Dunlop, Sewell & Spalding, Printers.* 1859. 8vo, pp. 19. Continued. H.

Catalogue of the North-Western University, Watertown, for 1869–70. *Watertown.* 1870. 8vo. 55754

See also "Northwestern," Nos. 55849–55856, *infra.*

North Wood's Walton Club. *Utica.* 1858. 12mo, pp. 16.

North-Yarmouth, *Me.* Catalogue of ... North-Yarmouth Academy, ... for ... 1837. *Portland: Arthur Shirley, Printer.* 1837. 24mo, pp. 12. Continued. H. 55756

Confession of Faith and Covenant, of the First Church in North Yarmouth, Me. With a Catalogue of its Members, and Brief Historical Notices. ... *Portland.* 1848. 8vo, pp. 64, 8.

The author was Rev. David Shepley, pastor of the church. *See also* Vol. IX. 40635

Northall (W. K.) Before and Behind the Curtain; or, Fifteen Years' Observations among the Theatres of New York. By William Knight Northall ... . *New York: W. F. Burgess.* 1851. 12mo, pp. 229. B., C. 55758

Contains an account of the Astor Place Opera House Riot, reminiscences of the Olympic Theatre, and of Mary Taylor, George Holland, and other actors.

Northall. Life and Recollections of Yankee Hill: together with Anecdotes and Incidents of his Travels. Edited by Dr. W. K. Northall. *New York.* 1850. 12mo, pp. 203. Portrait.

[NORTHAMPTON, *pseudon.*] To George Bancroft, Secretary of the Navy, the Traducer and Eulogist of General Andrew Jackson. *Washington.* 1846. 8vo, pp. 15. BA. 55760

NORTHAMPTON, *Mass.* Annual Report of the Selectmen of Northampton, ... 1855. *Northampton.* 1855. 8vo. Cont'd.

Catalogue of ... the Library of the Northampton Book Club. [n. p. n. d.] 12mo, pp. (12). B. 55762

Printed on one side only.

Catalogue of the Library of the Young Men's Institute. ... *Northampton: Hopkins, Bridgman & Co., Printers.* 1857. 8vo, pp. 133. H. 55763

Catalogue of the Northampton Public Library, including the Agricultural Library. *Northampton: Trumbull & Gere, Printers.* 1862. 8vo, pp. iv, 75. + First Supplement, ... [n. p. n. d.] 8vo, pp. 8. + Second Supplement ... . [n. p. n. d.] 8vo, pp. 13. + Catalogue ... . With Supplements. *Northampton: Trumbull & Gere, Printers.* 1868. 8vo, pp. 75, 8, 13. B.

First Church in Northampton. Confession of Faith, and Catalogue of Members. ... 1843. *Northampton: Metcalf, Printer.* [n. d.] 12mo, pp. 35, (1). H. 55764

The Lectures delivered before the American Institute of Instruction, at Northampton, Mass., August, 1850; including the Journal of Proceedings ... . *Boston.* 1851. 8vo, pp. xvi, 159.

Manual of the First Church in Northampton, Mass. *Northampton.* 1832. 18mo. 55766

Memorial to the Twenty-Seventh Congress, from Inhabitants of Northampton, Massachusetts. March, 1842. [n. p. 1842.] 8vo, pp. 23. H. 55767

Northampton Business Directory and General Advertiser. 1860-61. ... *Northampton: Trumbull & Gere.* 1860. 18mo, pp. 154, (2). H. 55768

Register of the Deaths in Northampton, from the First settlement of the town in 1653, to August 1824. ... *Northampton: Printed by T. Watson Shepard.* 1824. 12mo, pp. 80. BA.

Report of the School Committee of Northampton, ... 1837. [n. p. n. d.] 8vo, pp. 16. Continued. H. 55770

The Result Of a Council of Nine Churches Met at Northampton, June 22. 1750. With A Protest against the same, By

a Member [Jonathan Edwards] of the said Council. [*Boston.* 1750.] 8vo, pp. 8. B. 55771

Names of Pupils of the ROUND HILL SCHOOL, Northampton, Mass., from its commencement until June, 1831. *Newport, R. I.: Printed by James Atkinson.* 1862. 8vo, pp. 8. B. 55772

Also: Outline of the System of Education at the Round Hill School. Present Instructors and ... Pupils from its Commencement until ... June—1831. *Boston: N. Hale's ... Press.* MDCCCXXXI. 8vo, pp. (2), 24.—Prospectus ... 1823. [n. p. n. d.] 8vo. *See also* [Breck (R.)], Vol. II., No. 7663, *and* [Tucker (Mark)].

NORTHAMPTON COUNTY, *Pa.* ... Petition of Inhabitants of Northampton County, ... Pennsylvania, praying for an additional ... Duty On imported ... Slate. ... *Washington: Printed by Gales & Seaton.* 1828. 8vo, pp. 3. H. 55773

State of the Accounts of the late Lieutenant and Sub-Lieutenants of Northampton County, ... from March 1777 to September 4, 1779; with Lists, shewing the Names of the Persons from whom received, and the Sums paid by them respectively; likewise the Appropriation and Disbursement of the Monies thus collected. [n. p. n. d.] 8vo, pp. 40. P. 55774

Title printed from bottom to top, by Hall and Sellers, Philadelphia; probably in 1783. Also: State of the Accounts of the Collectors of Excise for Northampton County. *Philadelphia: Printed by John Dunlap.* M,DCC,LXXXIII. 8vo, pp. 12.—State of the Accounts of Jesse Jones, Esq. State Collector of Excise for Northampton County. *Philadelphia: Printed by F. Bailey.* M,DCC,LXXXIV. 8vo, pp. 4. P.—State of the Accounts of George Graff, Esq. Collector of Excise, Northampton County. ... 1782 to ... 1784. *Philadelphia: Printed by John Steele.* M,DCC,LXXXV. 8vo, pp. 7.—State of the Accounts of George Graff, Esquire, Collector of Excise, Northampton County; ... 1784, to ... 1785. *Philadelphia: Printed by Robert Aitken.* M,DCC,LXXXVI. 8vo, pp. 5.

... Memorial of the NORTHAMPTON SLATE QUARRY COMPANY, in Pennsylvania, praying that further Protecting Duty be laid on Imported Slate for Roofing. ... *Washington: Printed by Duff Green.* 1828. 8vo, pp. 3. H. 55775

NORTHBOROUGH, *Mass.* Annual Report of Selectmen ... for ... 1863–4. *Worcester: Printed by Chas. Hamilton.* [n. d.] 8vo, pp. 16. Continued. H. 55776

Annual Report of the School Committee of Northborough, March, 1845. [n. p. n. d.] 8vo, pp. 8. Continued. 55777

Also: Regulations of the Free Schools of ... Northborough, adopted November 4th, 1831. ... *Worcester: Moses W. Grout, Printer.* 1831. 12mo, pp. 11. H.

The Centennial Celebration of the Town of Northborough, Mass., August 22, 1866. ... [*Boston.*] 1866. 8vo, pp. 47, (1).

Reports and Statistics of ... Northborough, for ... 1850–51. *Worcester: Printed by Henry J. Howland.* [n. d.] 8vo, pp. 24. Continued. H. 55779

NORTHBRIDGE, *Mass.* The Confession of Faith and Covenant of the Congregational Church, in Northbridge (Centre) Mass. ... *Boston: Wright & Potter, Printers.* 1867. 12mo, pp. 22

Report of the School Committee of ... Northbridge, for ... 1854–55. ... *Worcester: Printed by Henry J. Howland.* [n. d.] 8vo, pp. 14. H. 55781

NORTHEND (C.) Obstacles to the Greater Success of Common Schools. An Address ... before the American Institute of Instruction, at Portland, Me., August 30, 1844. By Charles Northend ... . *Boston: William D. Ticknor & Co.* 1844. 12mo, pp. 42. B., H. 55782

This is the cover title, the title-page reads: "Obstacles to the Greater Success of Common Schools. By Charles Northend," etc.

NORTHEND. The Teacher and the Parent; a Treatise upon Common-School Education; ... . By Charles Northend, A.M. ... *New York.* 1853. 12mo. + Second Edition. *Boston: Jenks, Hickling, & Swan.* 1853. 12mo, pp. 327. B. + Fifth Edition. *New York.* 1856. 12mo. 55783

NORTHEND (W. D.) ... Abstract of Remarks of Hon. William D. Northend, ... on the Bill concerning the Troy and Greenfield Railroad, ... April 17, 1862. *Boston: Wright & Potter, Printers.* 1862. 8vo, pp. 15. B. 55784

Also: An Oration ... before the Citizens of Salem, ... July 4th, 1862. [n. p. n. d.] 8vo, pp. 8.—Speech ... before the Constitutional Democratic Club of Boston. November 4, 1863. *Boston.* 1863. 8vo, pp. 6.—Speeches and Essays upon Political Subjects, from 1860 to 1869. *Salem: H. P. Ives.* 1869. 8vo, pp. 268. B.

Constitution and By-Laws of the NORTHERN ACADEMY of Arts and Sciences; and First Annual Report ... . *Hanover: Printed by W. A. Patten.* 1842. 8vo, pp. 28. H. 55785

Northern and Western Traveler. *New York.* 1834. 12mo.

Northern Archives for History, Statistics, etc. *St. Petersburg.* 1826. 55787

In the Russian language. Contains notices of the languages of the aborigines of Russian America.

The Northern Association. *See* Vol. VIII., No. 30142.

Annual Report of the NORTHERN BAPTIST EDUCATION SOCIETY; ... 1815. *Boston.* 1815. 8vo. Continued. 55788

Northern Baptist Society. *See* Vol. I., No. 3236.

Northern Boundary between New Brunswick and Canada. ... Communicated by ... the Lieutenant Governor ... . February, 1844. [*Fredericton:*] *John Simpson, ... Printer.* [n. d.] 8vo, pp. 34. Map. H. 55789

Northern Boundary of Ohio, and admission of Michigan into the Union, March 2, 1836. Mr. Thomas, ... made the following Report: ... [*Washington.* 1836.] 8vo, pp. 131. Map.

Northern California. *See* [Metlar (G. W.)], Vol. XII. 48209.

First Annual Report of the President and Directors of the NORTHERN CENTRAL RAILWAY COMPANY ... 1855. *Baltimore: Printed by James Lucas & Son.* 1856. 8vo, pp. 35. Folded Table. Continued. H. 55791

The Northern Coasts of America, and the Hudson's Bay Territories. A Narrative of Discovery and Adventure. *London: T. Nelson and Sons.* MDCCCLIII. 16mo, pp. vi, 409. Map, Portrait and Plates. H. 55792

Northern Democrats. What Traitors Say. [n. p. n. d.] 8vo

Act of Incorporation and By-Laws of the NORTHERN DISPENSARY of ... New York. *New York.* 1838. 8vo, pp. 16. + *New York: Printed by John A. Gray.* 1852. 12mo, pp. 24. + *New York: Hall, Clayton & Co., Printers.* 1858. 8vo, pp. 23.

Also: Twenty-Fourth Annual Report of the Northern Dispensary ... . *New York.* 1851. 8vo, pp. 49. B.

The Northern Farmer and Practical Horticulturist. ... Volume I. *Newport, N. H.: H. & C. H. E. Newton.* 1833. 4to, pp. iiii, 208. H. 55795

The Northern Farmers' Almanac for 1851. Calculated for ... New York City ... . Edited by Solon Robinson ... . *New York: A. B. Allen & Co.* 1851. 8vo. 55796

Northern Grievances, set forth in a Letter to James Madison. By a North American. *New-York: The Author.* 1814. 8vo, pp. 16. BA. 55797

First Annual Report of the NORTHERN HOME for Friendless Children. ... Read at the Anniversary May 9, 1854. *Philadel-*

phia: T. K. and P. G. Collins, Printers. 1854. 8vo, pp. 32. P. Continued. 55798

Transactions of the NORTHERN ILLINOIS HORTICULTURAL SOCIETY ... . With the Proceedings and Essays at the First Annual Meeting ... 1868. *Chicago.* 1868. 8vo, pp. 120. H.

History of the Regulators of NORTHERN INDIANA. Published by Order of the Central Committee. *Indianapolis: Indianapolis Journal Co., Printers.* 1859. 8vo, pp. 67. 55800

Circular Statement of the Condition and Prospects of the NORTHERN INDIANA RAIL-ROAD COMPANY. ... *New-York: Van Norden & Amerman, Printers.* 1851. 8vo, pp. 18. Map.

Corrected title of our No. 34571, Vol. IX.

Northern Indicator. Devoted to Literature, Historical Research, Biography ... &c. Rev. Daniel Lancaster, Co-Editor. Vol. I. No. I. *Concord, N. H.* 1853. Folio, pp. 8. H.

Northern Inland Lock Navigation Co. *See* Vol. VIII. 33523.

The Northern Invasion. *See* Hough (F. B.), Vol. VIII. 33144

Northern Iowa. *See* Vol. IX., No. 35029.

The Northern Iowa Sanitary Fair, held in Dubuque, June, 1864. Donations and Treasurer's Report ... . *Dubuque: Marsh & Bro., ... Printers.* 1864. 8vo, pp. 64. H. 55803

The Northern Lancet and Gazette of Legal Medicine: ... Edited by Horace Nelson, M.D., and Francis J. D. Avignon, M.D. [n. p. n. d.] 8vo. 55804

Substantial Facts relating to the great richness of the Coal Hill and Union Mines about to be extensively worked by the NORTHERN LEAD COMPANY of New-York. *New-York.* 1852. 8vo, pp. 29. S. 55805

The Northern Light, devoted to Free Discussion ... . *Albany.* 1842–1844. 4 vols., 8vo. 55806

... Northern Lights An Illustrated Magazine of Tales, Travels ... Vol. I. No. I. January, 1867. ... *New York: American News Company.* [n. d.] 4to, pp. 36. Continued. H.

Proceedings of the Convention of the NORTHERN LINES OF RAILWAY, held at Boston, in December, 1850, and January, 1851. *Boston: J. B. Yerrinton & Son.* 1851. 8vo, pp. 128. S.

NORTHERN MAN, *pseudon.* *See* [Reed (W. B.)]

A NORTHERN MAN, *pseudon.* Abolition and Sedition. By a Northern Man. *Philadelphia.* 1839. 12mo. 55809

The Northern Man with Southern Principles, and the Southern Man with American Principles; or, a View of the Comparative Claims of W. H. Harrison, and M. Van Buren, ... to the Support of Citizens of the Southern States. *Washington.* 1840. 8vo. N. 55810

Minutes of Proceedings of the Supreme Grand Council ... for the NORTHERN MASONIC Jurisdiction of the United States ... . *Boston: Printed by Tuttle & Dennett.* 1851. 8vo, pp. 30. Continued. B. 55811

The Constitution of the NORTHERN MISSIONARY SOCIETY in the State of New-York. ... *Schenectady: Printed by C. P. Wyckoff.* 1797. 8vo, pp. 19. H. 55812

Also: Report of the Directors of the Northern Missionary Society, at their Annual Meeting, ... 1816. ... With the Speech of Schenando, ... Treasurer's Accounts, &c. *Albany: Printed by E. & E. Hosford.* 1816. 8vo, pp. 15. Continued. BA.

... The Northern Monthly: A Magazine of Literature, Civil and Military Affairs. No. I, March, 1864. *Portland: Bailey & Noyes.* [n. d.] 8vo, pp. 74. Continued. H. 55813

The Northern Monthly. A Magazine of General Literature. Allen L. Bassett, Editor. May, 1867, to June, 1868. *New York and Newark: New Jersey State Literary Union and A. L. Bassett.* 1867–68. 3 vols., 8vo. C. 55814

First styled the "New Jersey Magazine." *See* No. 53180.

The Northern Monthly Advertiser for January, 1865. ... *Portland: Brown Thurston.* [n. d.] 8vo, pp. 16. H. 55815

A Northern No! Addressed to the Delegates from the Free States to the Whig National Convention. At Philadelphia, 1848. [n. p. n. d.] 8vo, pp. 16. H. 55816

Signed "A Whig of the Free States."

First Annual Report of the ... Trustees ... of the NORTHERN OHIO LUNATIC ASYLUM for ... 1855. *Columbus.* 1856. 8vo. Continued. C. 55817

Northern Pacific Railroad. Explanation of the Bill now before Congress, with a Statement Showing the amount of

Money which the Government will receive from the Company from sales of Lands ... . [n. p. 1866.] 8vo, pp. 32. H. 55818

Northern Pacific Railroad. Memorial of the Board of Direction of the Company. ... November, 1867. *Hartford: Case, Lockwood and Company, Printers.* 1867. 8vo, pp. 16, 56. Continued. 55819

Petition ... praying for a Charter, by the Name of "The Northern Pacific Railway Company" ... . *Quebec: Printed by Lovell and Lamoureux.* [n. d.] 8vo, pp. 7. + *Reprinted by Ira Berry, Portland.* [1854.] 8vo, pp. 7. 55820

United States of America. Northern Pacific Railroad Company, Charter, Organization, and Proceedings. *Boston: Printed by Alfred Mudge & Son.* 1865. 8vo, pp. 62, (2). H. 55821

Also: The Charter and Amendments. The General Mortgage ... . [n. p. 1865?] 8vo, pp. 29, (4).— ... Policy for the Management of its Affairs, Adopted ... January 11, 1865. [n. p. n. d.] 8vo, pp. 4. H.— ... Report ... to the Board of Directors, November, 1867. *Hartford.* 1867. 8vo, pp. 56. Map. H.— ... Statement of its Resources and Merits, March, 1868. *Washington.* 1868. 8vo. *See also* Vol. II., No. 6586.

Guide to the NORTHERN PACIFIC RAILROAD LANDS in Minnesota. *New York.* [1872.] 8vo, pp. 48. 2 Maps. B. 55822

Also: The Land Grant of the Northern Pacific R. R. Company. *Cambridge.* [n. d.] 8vo.

Memorial of ... the Citizens of NORTHERN PENNSYLVANIA, to the Senate and House ... for the admission of the New-York & Erie Railroad into the Northern Counties of Pennsylvania. *Harrisburg.* 1845. 8vo, pp. 8. H. 55823

The Second Annual Report of the NORTHERN PENNSYLVANIA RAILROAD CORPORATION, ... May 19, 1847. [n. p.] 1847. 8vo, pp. 16. Continued. H. 55824

Act of Incorporation and By-Laws of the NORTHERN RAILROAD. *Concord: Printed by Asa McFarland.* 1845. 24mo, pp. 16

Address of the Northern Rail-Road Company to the Friends of Internal Improvement in New-Hampshire. *Hanover.* 1845. 8vo, pp. 15. Map. BA. 55826

Also: Report of the Committee of Investigation ... to the Stockholders, May, 1850. *Concord: Asa McFarland.* [n. d.] 8vo, pp. 32, Appendix, 64, folded leaf.—Report of the Engineer [T. J. Carter] on the Route surveyed for the Northern Railroad ... 1844. *Manchester: Wetmore & Wallace, Printers.* 1844. 8vo, pp. 16. Map. H.—The Second Annual Report of the Directors ... 1847. [n. p. 1847.] 8vo, pp. 16. Continued. B.

Northern (Ogdensburgh) Railroad. Mr. Chandler's Statement in relation to the Location of Machine Shops at Malone. [n. p. 1852.] 8vo, pp. 20. H. 55827

This elicited: Reply to Mr. Chandler's Statement, in relation to ... Machine Shops of the Northern (Ogdensburgh) Rail Road at Malone. *Ogdensburgh: Stillman Foote, Printer.* 1853. 8vo, pp. 36. H.

The Northern Railroad in New York. With Remarks on the Western Trade. *Boston: Freeman and Bolles.* 1845. 8vo, pp. 36. H. + [*Ibid.*] 1847. 8vo, pp. 32. M. 55828

Also: Northern Rail Road of New York, Ogdensburg to Rouse's Point. Report of the Sub-Committee on Consolidation of Bonds and Stock. With accompanying Documents. *Boston: Brown, Bazin & Co.* 1856. 8vo, pp. 47. H.—Report of the Directors ... . June 5th, 1848. *Ogdensburgh: Printed by Hitchcock & Smith.* 1848. 12mo, pp. 12, folded leaf. Continued.—Report of the Examining Committee on the Management ... of the Northern (N. Y.) Rail Road. ... 1851. *Ogdensburgh: Smith & Orwell.* 1851. 8vo, pp. 48.—Report of the Special Committee in the Matter of the Application of the Northern R. R. Co. for Relief ... . *Albany: J. Munsell.* 1854. 8vo, pp. 32. B.—Report of the Trustees of the Second Mortgage Bond Holders ... January 17, 1857. *Ogdensburgh, N. Y.: Hitchcock, Tillotson, ... Printers.* 1857. 8vo, pp. 37. H. *See also* Vol. VIII., No. 31064, *note*.

Northern Regions; or, Uncle Richard's Relation of Captain Parry's Voyages for the Discovery of a North-West Passage, and Franklin's and Cochrane's Overland Journeys to the other parts of the World. *New York: O. A. Roorback.* 1827. 12mo, pp. 256. 8 Plates. + *Boston: Munroe and Francis.* [1829.] 12mo, pp. 256. 14 Plates. H. + *New York: William Burgess.* 1832. 12mo, pp. 228. + *New York.* 1855. 16mo, pp. 302. 24 Plates. + [*Ibid.*] 1856. 55829

The Northern Star and Freemen's Advocate. Edited by John G. Stewart and Charles S. Morton. [n. p. n. d.] Folio.

A weekly paper published in the interest of the Africo-American race.

A Northern Tour: Being a Guide to Saratoga, Lake George, Niagara, Canada, Boston, &c. &c. Through the States of Pennsylvania, New Jersey, New York, Vermont, New Hampshire, Massachusetts, Rhode Island, and Connecticut; embracing an account of the Canals, Colleges, Public Institutions, Natural Curiosities, and interesting Objects therein. [By Thomas Gilpin.] *Philadelphia: H. C. Carey & I. Lea.* 1825. 12mo, pp. (8), 279. 55831

Corrected title of our No. 27457, Vol. VII.

The Northern Traveller. *See* Disturnell (J.), No. 20325, *note*, add, pp. 84.

The Northern Traveller; containing the Routes to Niagara, Quebec, and the Springs; with Descriptions of the Principal Scenes, and useful Hints to Strangers: ... *New-York: Wilder & Campbell.* 1825. 12mo, pp. (2), 222. 4 Plates, 16 Maps. + Second Edition. [*Ibid.*] 1826. 18mo, pp. (2), 8, 382. Maps and Plates. B. + Third Edition. *New York: G. & C. Carvill.* 1828. 18mo, pp. 403. 19 Maps, 11 Plates. 55832

The Northern Traveller, and Northern Tour: with the routes to the Springs, Niagara, and Quebec, and the Coal Mines of Pennsylvania; also, the Tour of New-England. Fourth Edition. *New York.* 1830. 18mo. Maps and Plates. + New Edition; ... *New-York: Printed by J. & J. Harper.* 1831. 18mo, pp. viii, 444. Maps and Plates. + With an Appendix, containing the Western Traveller, and Emigrant's or Stranger's Guide to the Valley of the Mississippi. ... Fifth Edition ... . *New York: Goodrich & Wiley.* [1834.] 18mo, pp. 432. Maps and Plates. B.

The sixth edition has the name of Theodore Dwight as the author. *See* No. 21536.

... Northern True Men and Southern Traitors. Address and Resolutions of the Connecticut Soldiers. Extracts from Richmond Journals. *New York: Loyal Publication Society.* [No. 6.] 1863. 8vo, pp. 8. H. 55834

A Northern Voice for the Dissolution of the Union. [n. p.] 1860. [1861?] 8vo. 55835

Third Annual Catalogue of the ... NORTHFIELD INSTITUTE, for ... 1853. *Fitchburg: Printed by E. & J. F. D. Garfield.* 1853. 8vo, pp. 12. H. 55836

The Northfield Slate-Quarry Company. ... *Boston: Printed by J. B. Chisholm.* 1865. 8vo, pp. 15. H. 55837

NORTHMORE (T.) Washington, or Liberty Restored: A Poem, In Ten Books, By Thomas Northmore, Esq. ... *London: Printed by Richard Taylor and Co.* 1809. 12mo, pp. viii, 253. + *Baltimore: John Vance and Co.* 1809. 12mo, pp. viii, 253. B. + [*Ibid.*] 1812. 12mo, pp. viii, 253. BA. 55838

See "Quarterly Review," II. 265, for a severe notice.

NORTHROP (B. G.) Supervision of Schools. A Lecture ... before the American Institute of Instruction, ... August 26, 1863, By Rev. Birdsey Grant Northrop ... . *Boston: Ticknor and Fields.* 1864. 12mo, pp. 32. H. 55839

NORTHROP (G.), *and* KELLEY (W. D.) The Joint Debates between George Northrop, Esq., Democratic, and Hon. Wm. D. Kelley, Republican, Nominees for Congress in the Fourth Congressional District of Pennsylvania. *Philadelphia: John Campbell.* [1864.] 8vo, pp. 12. 55840

The subsequent debates are as follows: The Second Joint Debate ... September 26, 1864. *Philadelphia.* [n. d.] 8vo, pp. 12.—The Third ... Debate ... . September 28, 1864. *Philadelphia.* [n. d.] 8vo, pp. 12.—The Fourth ... Debate. Mr. Northrop's Reply. Sept. 29, 1864. *Philadelphia.* [n. d.] 8vo.—The Fifth ... Debate ... October 3, 1864. Opening of George Northrop. *Philadelphia.* [n. d.] 8vo, pp. 16.—The Sixth ... Debate, Oct. 4, 1864. Reply of George Northrop. *Philadelphia.* [n. d.] 8vo, pp. 13.—The Seventh ... Debate, Oct. 6, 1864. Opening of George Northrop, Esq. *Philadelphia.* [n. d.] 8vo, pp. 16.—The Eighth ... Debate. Mr. Northrop's Reply, October 7, 1864. *Philadelphia.* [n. d.] 8vo, pp. 12.

NORTHROP (N. B.) Pioneer History of Medina County. By N. B. Northrop. *Medina, Ohio: Geo. Redway, Printer.* 1861. Sm. 8vo, pp. 224. B. 55841

[NORTHRUP (C. B.)] Political Remarks by "N." *Charleston: Evans & Cogswell.* 1861. 8vo, pp. 31. B. 55842

[NORTHRUP.] Southern Odes, by the Outcast, a Gentleman of South Carolina. ... *Charleston: Harper & Calvo.* 1861. 8vo, pp. 40. B. 55843

NORTHRUP (G. W.) ... Sermon and Address on the Death of Dea. Oren Sage, by Rev. G. W. Northrup, D.D., and M. B. Anderson, LL.D., ... September 16, 1866, with other Memorial Papers. *Rochester, N. Y.* 1866. 8vo, pp. 49, (4). H. 55844

NORTHUMBERLAND Co., *Pa.* ... Memorial of sundry Citizens of Northumberland County, Pennsylvania, in favor of an increase of Duties for the Protection of Domestic Manufactures. ... *Washington: Printed by Duff Green.* 1828. 8vo, pp. 3. H.

State of the Accounts of Col. Samuel Hunter, Lieutenant of Northumberland County. From ... March 1777, to March 1784. *Philadelphia: Printed by F. Bailey.* M,DCC,LXXXIV. 8vo, pp. 13. P. 55846

Also: State of the Accounts of Walter Clarke & William Murray, Esqrs. Sub-Lieutenants of Northumberland County. ... *Philadelphia: Printed by Robert Aitken.* M,DCC,-LXXXV. 8vo, pp. 4.—State of the Account of William Wilson, Esquire, Collector of Excise, Northumberland County; From 21st Nov. 1783, until the Appointment of Mr. Hunter his Successor. *Philadelphia: Printed by Robert Aitken.* M.DCC.LXXXVI 8vo, pp. 3. P.

NORTHUP (S.) Twelve Years a Slave. Narrative of Solomon Northup, a Citizen of New York, kidnapped in Washington City in 1841, and rescued in 1853 ... . *Auburn.* 1853. 12mo. + [*Ibid.*] 1854. + New Edition. [*Ibid.*] 1855. 12mo, pp. 336. + *New York: C. M. Saxton.* 1859. 12mo, pp. 336. Portrait and Plates. H. 55847

... Exploration of the NORTHWEST COAST. January 16, 1826. Mr. Baylies, ... made the following Report. [n. p. n. d.] 8vo, pp. 26. 55848

See also Vol. I., No. 4067, *and* "North American Review," XV. 370; XLVIII. 109, 558; L. 75; LXII. 214.

Northwest Company. *See* M'Tavish, Vol. IX., No. 43666.

Report of the Fifth Anniversary Meeting of the NORTHWESTERN DAIRYMEN'S ASSOCIATION, held in 1871. *Elgin.* 1871. 8vo. 55849

The Northwestern Educator and Magazine of Literature & Science. Chicago, Illinois. [*Chicago.* n. d.] 8vo. 55850

... The Northwestern Medical and Surgical Journal. Alexander J. Stone, M.D., Editor. Vol. I. No. I. ... *St. Paul: The Editor.* 1870. 8vo, pp. 24. Continued. H. 55851

... Northwestern Quarterly Magazine. Vol. I. No. I. October, 1858. *Chicago, Ill.: Rufus Blanchard.* [n. d.] 8vo, pp. 104. H. 55852

The Northwestern Review, and Commercial and Real Estate Reporter. ... H. H. Belding, Editor. [*Keokuk, Iowa.*] 1857–58. 12mo, 11 Nos. C. 55853

Report of the NORTHWESTERN SANITARY COMMISSION for ... 1863. *Chicago: Dunlop, Sewell & Spalding.* [n. d.] 8vo, pp. 33. 55854

Northwestern Sanitary Fair. 1865. Catalogue of the Department of Arms and Trophies. *Chicago.* 1865. 8vo.

Northwestern Ship Canal Convention. Memorial to Congress from the Convention at Dubuque, Iowa, May 4, 1864. [n. p. n. d.] 8vo. 55855

First Annual Report of the President and Directors to the Stockholders of the NORTHWESTERN VIRGINIA RAILROAD COMPANY ... 1852. *Parkersburg: Printed by M'Creary & Sterrett.* 1852. 8vo, pp. 26. H. 55856

Also: Charter ... of the ... Company. *Parkersburg.* 1851. 8vo. *See also* "North Western," Nos. 55735–55754, *supra.*

NORTMANN (Robert Comtæus). *See* Comtæus, IV. 15079.

NORTON (A. B.) Descendants of Chas. Norton, of Guilford, Conn. By Albert B. Norton. Part I. *Washington.* 1856 8vo. 55857

NORTON (A. B.) A History of Knox County, Ohio, from 1779 to 1862 inclusive: comprising Biographical Sketches, Anecdotes and Incidents of Men connected with the County from its first Settlement: ... Also a Sketch of Kenyon College, and other Institutions of Learning and Religion within the County. By A. Banning Norton. *Columbus: Richard Nevins, Printer.* 1862. 8vo, pp. 424. Plates and Portraits. BA. 55858

Also: Speech ... in Vindication of History and the Constitution and the Union, in the Texas Legislature, January 24, 1860. [n. p. n. d.] 8vo, pp. 16.

NORTON (A. S.) A Sermon, ... in Clinton, on ... Thanksgiving, December 6, 1820. By A. S. Norton, D.D. ... *Utica: Printed by William Williams.* 1821. 8vo, pp. 19. H. 55859

NORTON (A.) An Address, ... before the Mercantile Library Association, January 19, 1836. By Alfred Norton. *Boston: N. Southard, Printer.* 1836. 8vo, pp. 23. BA. 55860

NORTON (A.) Address ... at the Interment of Professor Frisbie. July XII. MDCCCXXII. By Andrews Norton ... . *Cambridge: Printed ... by Hilliard and Metcalf.* 1822. 12mo, pp. 24.

[NORTON.] Review of a Sermon delivered at New York, December 7, 1826. By William Ellory Channing. *Boston: Printed by Isaac R. Butts and Co.* 1826. 8vo, pp. 8. 55862

[NORTON.] A Review of "Men and Manners in America," by ... [T. Hamilton. n. p. n. d.] 8vo, pp. 21. H. 55863

[NORTON.] Review of Prof. Frisbie's Inaugural Address. ... *Cambridge: Printed by Hilliard and Metcalf.* 1823. 8vo, pp. 35.

NORTON. Verses by Andrews Norton. [n. p.] 1853. 8vo, 33, (2). B. 55865

Also: A Discourse ... at Hingham, May 20, 1818. Before the Trustees of the Derby Academy; ... *Boston: Printed by Wells and Lilly.* 1818. 8vo, pp. 27.—Inaugural Discourse, delivered before the University in Cambridge, August 10, 1819. ... *Cambridge: Printed by Hilliard and Metcalf.* 1819. 8vo, pp. 48.—Letter to Mr. Ticknor on the Origin and Progress of Liberal Views of Christianity in New England, and on Mr. Buckminster's Relations to them. [n. p. n. d.] 8vo, pp. 8.—Letter to Andrews Norton, July 19, 1839, by an Alumnus. *Boston.* 1839. 8vo.—Speech ... before the Overseers of Harvard College, February 3, 1825, in behalf of the Resident

Instructers of the College. ... *Boston: Cummings, Hilliard, & Co.* 1825. 8vo, pp. xxiii, 35. *See also* No. 30757.

NORTON (C. B.) ... Catalogue of ... Works relating to ... America ... . *New York: Charles B. Norton.* 1860. 8vo, pp. 48.

NORTON. Norton's Literary Advertiser. Vol. I. May–Dec., 1851. *New-York.* 1851. Folio, pp. 108. BA. 55867

Continued as "Norton's Literary Gazette," "Norton's Literary Gazette and Publisher's Circular," and "American Publisher's Circular."

NORTON. Norton's Literary Almanac for 1852; ... containing ... accounts of American Libraries ... . *New York: Charles B. Norton.* 1851. 12mo, pp. 52. H. 55868

Continued to 1854.

NORTON. Norton's Literary and Educational Register for 1854. *New York.* 1854. 4to. 55869

NORTON. Norton's Literary Letter ... . No. I. *New York.* 1857. 4to, pp. 41, (7). BA. 55870

No. 4 includes "The Bibliography of the State of Maine." This was followed by a "New Series," of which No. 1 includes the "Bibliography of the State of New Hampshire," No. 2 "The Bibliography of the State of Vermont." Vermont excepted, the bibliography is crude, imperfect, and badly arranged. No more published.

NORTON. Norton's Literary Register and Bookbuyer's Almanac, for 1853. *New York: Charles B. Norton.* 1853. 12mo, pp. 132. 55871

Continued as "Norton's Literary Register; or, Annual Book-List for 1856. [Compiled by Reuben A. Guild.] *New York: Charles B. Norton.* 1856. 8vo, pp. 138. Also: Bibliotheca Americana. *New York.* 1857. 8vo, pp. 24.—A Catalogue of Valuable Works relating to America ... . [*New York.* 1856.] 8vo, pp. 1[illegible].—Catalogue ... of Books, relating chiefly to America; ... *New York: John A. Gray, Printer.* 1862. 8vo, pp. (2), 138. B.

NORTON, *and* VALENTINE (W. J.) Report to the Government of the United States on the Munitions of War exhibited at the Paris Universal Exhibition, 1867. With Eighty Illustrations. By Charles B. Norton, ... and W. J. Valentine, ... United States Commissioners. ... *New York.* 1868. Rl. 8vo, pp. 268. B. + *Washington.* 1868. 8vo, pp. 213. 8 Plates. C. 55872

NORTON (C. D.) The Old Ferry at the Black Rock ... Dec. 14, 1863. By Charles D. Norton. [n. p. n. d.] 8vo.

[NORTON (C. E.)] Dwellings and Schools for the Poor. ... *Cambridge: Printed by Houghton & Haywood.* 1852. 8vo, pp. 28. Plan. B. 55874

NORTON. ... The Soldier of the Good Cause. By Charles Eliot Norton. *Boston: American Unitarian Association.* 1861. 16mo, pp. 14. 55875

This is No. 2 of the "Army Series." There are copies on large paper.

NORTON (E. H.) Speech of Hon. E. H. Norton, ... on the State of the Country. ... January 9, 1863. [n. p. n. d.] 8vo, pp. 8. 55876

Also: Speech ... on Confiscation and Emancipation. ... April 24, 1862. [n. p. n. d.] 8vo, pp. 8. B.

[NORTON (E. L.), *and* SMITH (F. W.)] Correspondence concerning the Purchase of Naval Supplies. [*Boston.* 1864.] 8vo, pp. (2), 14. H. 55877

NORTON (H.) Record of Facts concerning the Persecutions at Madeira in 1843 and 1846: the Flight of a Thousand Converts to the West India Islands: and also, the Sufferings of those who arrived in the United States. By Rev. Herman Norton ... . *New-York: American Protestant Society.* 1849. 18mo, pp. 228. 2 Portraits. H. 55878

Also: Startling Facts for American Protestants! Progress of Romanism since the Revolutionary War; ... *New York: Amer. Protestant Society.* 1844. 12mo, pp. 23. Map. BA.

NORTON (H.) New England's Ensigne. *See* No. 52756.

NORTON (J.) ... Discourse ... Weymouth, Feb. 3, 1811 [on the Death of his Wife] ... . By Jacob Norton, A.M. ... *Boston: Printed by Lincoln & Edmands.* 1811. 8vo, pp. 27. BA. 55879

Also: ... A Sermon ... before the Massachusetts Missionary Society, ... May 29, 1810. ... *Boston: Printed by Lincoln & Edmands.* 1810. 8vo, pp. 40.—A Sermon ... December 1, 1814, on ... Thanksgiving in Massachusetts. ... *Boston: Printed by Lincoln & Edmands.* [n. d.] 8vo, pp. 23.—A Sermon delivered partly, ... Dec. 11, 1815, at the Interment of the Hon. Cotton Tufts, M.D. ... And partly on the Sabbath [following] ... . *Boston: Printed by Lincoln & Edmands.* 1816. 8vo, pp. 24.—A Sermon ... July 27, 1815, at the Interment of the Rev. Joseph Barker ... . *Boston: Printed by Lincoln & Edmands.* 1815. 8vo, pp. 24.— ... A Sermon ... in Weymouth, Nov. 8, 1821 ... . *Boston: Printed by John Cotton, Jr.* 1822. 8vo, pp. 28.—A Valedictory Discourse, ... [in] Weymouth, ... July 4, 1824. ... *Boston: Nathaniel Balch, Jr., Printer.* 1824. 8vo, pp. 52. H.

NORTON (J. O.) Nebraska and Kansas. Speech of Hon. Jesse O. Norton ... March 29, 1854 ... . [n. p. n. d.] 8vo, pp. 8. B. 55880

NORTON (J.) Abel being Dead yet speaketh; | or, the | Life & Death | Of that deservedly Famous Man of God, | Mr John Cotton, | Late Teacher of the Church of | Christ, at Boston in | New-England. | By John Norton, Teacher | of the same Church. | ... | *London,* | *Printed by Tho. Newcomb for Lodowick Lloyd* ... . 1658. 4to, pp. 51, (5). B., BA., W. 55881

Extremely scarce. The last five pages contain a catalogue of books printed for L. Lloyd, including several works by New England divines. For the first edition, *see* "Life and Death," No. 55885, *infra.*

NORTON. Copy of the Letter. *See* "Three Choice," etc.

NORTON. A | Discussion | of that Great Point in | Divinity, | the | Sufferings of Christ; | And the Questions about his | Righteousnesse Active, Passive: | and the Imputation thereof. | Being an Answer to a Dialogue | [by Wm. Pynchon] Intituled | The Meritorious Price of our Redemption, | Justification, &c. | By John Norton, Teacher of the Church | at Ipswich in New-England. | Who was appointed to draw up this Answer by the Generall Court. | *London, Printed by A. M. for Geo. Calvert* ... . 1653. 8vo, pp. (16), 270, (4). B., W. 55882

There is an error in the pagination, page 243 following 240. "Drawn up by the appointment of the General Court of Massachusetts, at a time when theological hair-splitting in the legislature held the place of modern log-rolling. Pynchon's book was forbidden to enter New England under penalty, and this censure was backed, in a long letter at the end, by five of the chiefest of the ruling Elders of Boston, rebuking the English Ministers who had recommended Pynchon's book. Nothing daunted two years later Pynchon hurled at the heads of the General Court, and Boston Elders, another book under a similar title."—STEVENS.

NORTON. The | Heart of N-England | rent at the | Blasphemies | of the Present | Generation. | Or | A brief Tractate concerning the Doctrine of | the Quakers, demonstrating the destructive nature | thereof, to Religion, the Churches, and the State, | with consideration of the Remedy against it. | Occasional Satisfaction to Objections, and Confir | mation of the contrary Trueth. | By John Norton, Teacher of the | Church of Christ at Boston. | Who was appointed thereunto by the Order of the | General Court. | ... | *Printed by Samuel Green, at Cambridge in New-England.* 1659. 4to, pp. (2), 58. H. 55883

NORTON. The | Heart of New England | Rent at the | Blasphemies | of the present Generation. | Or a brief | Tractate, | Concerning the | Doctrine of the Quakers, | Demonstrating the destructive nature | thereof, to Religion, the Churches, | and the State; with consideration of the Re- | medy against it. | Occasional Satisfaction to Objections, and Confirmation of the contrary Truth. | By John Norton, Teacher of the Church of | Christ at Boston. | Who was appointed thereunto by the Order of

the | General Court. | ... | *London, Printed by J. H. for John Allen* ... 1660. Sm. 8vo, pp. (4), 96 (pp. 81–82 repeated). 55884

To be complete, this should have "the Copie of a Letter sent from New-England, to a Friend in London, by way of Defence, for their dealing with the Quakers" (pp. 81–83, and one blank page), and the important appendix (pp. 81–96) which is wanting in some copies, of "Matter coming from New-England since this Book was printed." Scarcely less rare than the original Cambridge edition. Rice's copy sold for $67.50.

NORTON. The Life and Death of that deservedly Famous Mr. John Cotton, the late Reverend Teacher of the Church of Christ at Boston in New England. Collected out of the Writings and Information of the Rev. Mr. John Davenport of New-haven, the Rev. Mr. Samuel Whiting, at Lynne, the pious Widow of the Deceased, and others: and compiled by his unworthy Successor, John Norton. *Cambridge: Printed by S. Green.* 1657. 4to, pp. 56. 55885

NORTON. Memoir of John Cotton, By John Norton. With a Preface and Notes, by Enoch Pond ... . *Boston: Perkins & Marvin.* 1834. 18mo, pp. 108. + *New-York: Saxton & Miles.* 1842. 18mo, pp. 108. B. 55886

NORTON. The | Orthodox Evangelist. | Or a | Treatise | Wherein many Great | Evangelical Truths | (Not a few whereof are much opposed and Eclipsed | in this perillous hour of the Passion of the Gospel) | Are briefly Discussed, cleared, and con- | firmed: As a further help, for the Begeting, and Establishing of the Faith which is in Jesus. | As also the State of the Blessed, Where; | Of the condition of their Souls from the | instant of their Dissolution: and of their | Persons after their Resurrection. | By John Norton, Teacher of the Church | at Ipswich in New England. | ... | *London,* | *Printed by John Macock, for Henry Cripps, and Lodowick Lloyd,* | ... 1654. 4to, pp. (16), 356, Table, (14). + *London,* | *Printed by John Macock, for Lodowick Lloyd* ... . 1657. 4to, pp. (16), 355, (15). B. 55887

NORTON. Responsio | ad | Totam Quæstionum Syl- | logen à clarissimo Viro | Domino Guilielmo | Apollonio, Ecclesiæ | Middleburgensis Pasto- | re, propositam. | Ad componendas Controversias | quasdam circa Politiam Ecclesiasticam | in Anglia nunc temporis | agitatas spectantem. | Per Johannem Nortonum ... . *Londini,* | *Typis R. B. impensis Andreæ Crook* ... . 1648. 16mo, pp. (44), 170, (14). B., BA., M., W. 55888

The address, headed "Lector Benevole," pp. 4, is signed "Tho. Goodwin. Phil. Nye. Sidr. Simpson." The "Præfatio Apologetica," pp. 22, is signed "Johannes

Cotton," and is followed by a letter of Apollonij, pp. 6, dated "Medioburgi Zelandorum 31. die Maii. 1644. This is said to be the first Latin book written in New England, and the rarest of all the author's works.

Norton. Three Choice and Profitable | Sermons | Upon Severall Texts of Scripture; | ... | By that Reverend Servant of Christ, | Mr. John Norton | Late Teacher of the Church of Christ at Boston in N. E. | The First of them being the Last Sermon which | he Preached at the Court of Election at Boston. | The Second was the Last which he Preached on the Lord's-day. | The Third was the Last which he Preached on his Weekly-Lecture-Day. | Wherein | (Beside many other excellent and seasonable Truths) is shewed, | the Lords Sovereignty over, and Care for his Church and People, | in order to both their Militant and Triumphant condition; | and their Fidelity and good affection towards himself. | *Cambridge*: | *Printed by S. G. and M. I. for Hezekiah Usher of Boston*. 1664. 4to, pp. (6), 38. [Followed by:] A Copy | of the | Letter | Returned by the | Ministers of New-England | to | Mr. John Dury | about his | Pacification. | Faithfully Translated out of the Original Manuscript written in | Latine, by the Reverend Author of the Three | former Sermons. | ... | By a Lover of Truth and Peace. | *Published in the Year* 1664. 4to, pp. (6), 12. B. 55889

An excessively rare tract. The letter to Mr. John Dury is a translation from the original manuscript written in Latin by Mr. Norton, and signed by the clergy of New England, in reply to a letter from Mr. Dury on the subject of "Pacification of the Churches." Also: Selections from the New-England Fathers. No. 1, John Norton, 1652. J. B. Felt, Editor. *Boston*. 1851. 8vo. s.

Norton (J.), *of Hingham*. An Essay | Tending to Promote | Reformation, | By a brief Sermon. | Preached before His Excellency the | Governour, the Honourable | Council, & Representatives, of the | Province of the Massachusetts-Bay in N. E. | On May 26. 1708. | Which was the Anniversary Day for | Election of Her Majesties Council | for this Province. | By John Norton, | Pastor of the Church of Christ in Hingham. | *Boston*. 1708. 16mo, pp. 29. M. 55890

Norton (J.) The Redeemed Captive, | Being a | Narrative | Of the Taking and carrying into Captivity | The Reverend Mr. John Norton, | When Fort-Massachusetts Surrendered to a large Body | of French and Indians, August 20th, 1746. | With a particular Account of the Defence made before the | Surrender of that Fort, and the Articles of Capitula- | tion, &c. | Together with an Account, both entertaining and affecting, | of what Mr. Norton met with, and took Notice of, | in his travelling to, and while in

Captivity at Canada, | and 'till his Arrival at Boston, on August 16. 1747. | Written by himself. | ... | *Boston: Printed & Sold opposite the Prison*. 1748. 8vo, pp. 40. B. 55891

Norton. Narrative of the Capture and Burning of Fort Massachusetts by the French and Indians, in the time of the War of 1744–1749, and the captivity of all those stationed there, to the number of thirty persons. Written at the time by one of the Captives, the Rev. Mr. John Norton, Chaplain of the Fort. Now first published with Notes, by Samuel G. Drake. *Albany: Printed for S. G. Drake of Boston, by Joel Munsell*. 1870. 4to, pp. 51. B. 55892

Mr. Drake has added a biography, and many notes, explanatory of the very minute relations of the captive. One hundred copies only printed.

[Norton (*Capt.* John).] *See* Vol. xii., Nos. 49846, 49849.

Norton (J. F.) The Home of the Ancient Dead restored. An Address at Athol, Mass., July 4, 1859, By Rev. John F. Norton, at the Re-consecration of the ... Cemetery, and the erection of a Monument ... . *Athol Depot: Rufus Putnam*. 1859. 8vo, pp. 24. H. 55893

Norton (J. N.) Life of Bishop Bass, of Massachusetts. By John N. Norton, A.M. ... *New York*. 1859. 18mo, pp. 192. Portrait. C. 55894

Norton. The Life of Bishop Bowen, of South Carolina. By John N. Norton ... . *New York*. 1859. 18mo. 55895

Norton. Life of Bishop Claggett, of Maryland. By John N. Norton ... . *New York: F. D. Harriman*. 1859. 18mo, pp. 135. 55896

Norton. Life of Bishop [Geo. W.] Freeman, of Arkansas. By John N. Norton ... . *New York*. 1867. 18mo, pp. 203. Portrait. C. 55897

Norton. The Life of Bishop Henshaw, of Rhode Island. By John N. Norton ... . *New York: F. D. Harriman*. 1859. 18mo. 55898

Norton. Life of Bishop Provoost, of New York. By John N. Norton ... . *New York*. 18—. 18mo. 55899

Norton. Life of Bishop Stewart, of Quebec. By John N. Norton ... . *New York*. 1859. 12mo, pp. 137. 55900

Norton. The Life of the Rt. Rev. William White, Bishop of Pennsylvania. By John N. Norton ... . *New York*. 1856. 18mo, pp. 103. Portrait. C. 55901

Norton. Life of Bishop Wainwright. By John N. Norton, ... *New York*. 1858. 18mo, pp. 184. Portrait. 55902

Norton. Life of General Washington By John N. Norton, ... *New York: Pudney & Russell*. 1860. 12mo, pp. 400. Portrait and 4 Plates. BA. 55903

Norton. Pioneer Missionaries, or the Lives of Phelps and Nash. By John N. Norton ... . *New York*. 1859. 16mo, pp. 193. 55904

Gives many particulars of the early life of Brant, the Mohawk Chief. Also: Rockford Parish; or, the Fortunes of Mr. Mason's Successors. ... *New York: Dana & Co.* 1856. 12mo, pp. 216. C.

Norton (J. P.) Address ... at the Annual Meeting of the N. Y. State Agricultural Society ... . By John P. Norton ... . *Albany: Printed by Charles Van Benthuysen*. 1848. 8vo, pp. 23.

Also: Address before the Hampshire, Franklin, and Hampden Agricultural Society, at Northampton, Mass. October, 1849. ... *Northampton*. 1849. 8vo, pp. 18. H.—Address ... before the Ontario Co. Agricultural Society ... . *Canandaigua, N. Y.: Printed by J. J. Mattison*. 1850. 8vo, pp. 25. H.—Notes for American Farmers. ... *New York*. 1851. 8vo. C.

Norton. Memorials of John Pitkin Norton, late Professor ... in Yale College, ... New Haven, Conn. *Albany: J. Munsell*. 1853. 4to. Portrait. 55906

Published for private distribution.

Norton (Joseph), *Jr.* Norton's Improved Calendar, from 1501 to 1900. ... *Boston*. 1858. 4to, pp. 36. B., M. 55907

Norton (L.) Auto-Biography of Lemuel Norton. ... Also his ... Labors in the Gospel Ministry. *Portland: H. C. Little*. 1861. 16mo, pp. 192. C. 55908

Norton (R.) God's Discipline of Nations. A Sermon on the Death of President Lincoln, preached at St. Catherines, Canada West, April 23, 1865. By Rev. Robert Norton ... . *St. Catherines: Leavenworth*. 1865. 8vo, pp. 17. 55909

Also included in "Maple Leaves," our No. 44452, Vol. xi.

Norton (S. H.) Memorial of Isaac Hayes. By Rev. S. H. Norton. *New York*. 1857. 12mo. 55910

Norton (S. S.) Circular of the ... School, at Vernon, Oneida County, N. Y. S. Sheldon Norton, A.M., Principal ... *Utica: R. Northway & Co., Printers*. 1852. 12mo, pp. 12. H.

Norton (W.) Honduras: A Record of Facts, and Reply to a Pamphlet entitled "Belize." By William Norton ... and Frederick Crowe ... . For Private Circulation. *London: Printed by Stewart and Murray*. 1849. 8vo, pp. iv, 143. 55912

[Norton and Russell's] Connecticut Register. *See* Vol. iv., Nos. 15666–67, and 15829.

Norton Family. Genealogy. *See* [Whittemore (W. H.)]

Norton, *Mass.* Report of the School Committee of Norton ... 1846. ... *Taunton: E. Anthony, Printer*. 1846. 8vo, pp. 8.

Later reports include those of selectmen and treasurer.

Norval (J.) The Generous Chief: A Tragedy. By James Norval. *Montreal*. 1792. 8vo. 55914

Norvell (——). Speech of Mr. Norvell, of Michigan, on the Bill Imposing Additional Duties as Depositaries ... . March 6, 1838. *Washington*. 1838. 8vo, pp. 14. 55915

Norvell (L. C.) Address by L. C. Norvell, Esq., ... to the Old Line Whigs of the South. [n. p. 1868?] 8vo, pp. 7. H.

Norwich (*Bishop of*). Letter from the Bishop of Norwich to the Clergy of his Diocese. *London*. 1741. 4to. 55917

Relates to the great good done by the missionaries in America to the Negroes and Indians. *See also* Vol. i., No. 2715, Vol. viii., No. 31062, [Leng (J.)], Vol. x., No. 40025, *and* [Trimmel (*Dr.*)]

Norwich, *Conn.* By-Laws of ... Norwich, Conn. *Norwich*. 1837. 8vo. 55918

A Catalogue of Books belonging to Norwich Library Company. *Norwich: Henry Trumbull*. [n. d.] 12mo, pp. 12.

Catalogue of ... the Otis Library, of the City of Norwich. *Norwich*. 1867. 8vo, pp. (6), 173. B.

The Charter of the City of Norwich. Granted by the General Assembly of ... Connecticutt, holden ... the second ... of May, 1784. *Norwich*. 1784. 4to, pp. 16. BA. 55920

Journal of the Proceedings of the Court of Common Council of ... Norwich, 1868. *Norwich*. 1869. 8vo, pp. 124. + For 1869. [*Ibid.*] 1870. 8vo, pp. 153. B. 55921

Manual of the First Congregational Church, of Norwich, Conn., ... with Historical Notes, and ... Officers and Members from December, 1699, to January 1, 1868. *Norwich*. 1868. 12mo, pp. 78. H. 55922

The Norwich Almanac, Directory, and Business Advertiser, for 1846. *Norwich: L. & E. Edwards*. [n. d.] 16mo, pp. 108.

Norwich and Worcester Rail Road. [Act of Incorporation.] *New-York: Coolidge & Lambert*. 1839. 12mo, pp. 22. + *Norwich: J. Dunham*. 1842. 8vo, pp. 27. H. 55924

Also: Report of a Committee of the Stockholders ... 1842. *Worcester: Printed by Henry J. Howland*. 1842. 8vo, pp. 8.—Statement of Facts in relation to the ... Company. *New York*. 1840. 8vo, pp. 15. + *New York: R. Craighead, Printer*. 1841. 8vo, pp. 17. H.

Norwich City Directory; containing the Names of the Inhabitants of Norwich, Norwich Town, Bean Hill, Yantic, Greenville, and part of Preston [etc.], 1857. Compiled by William H. Boyd. *Norwich: J. W. Stedman*. 1857. 8vo, pp. viii, 157. Plate. C., S. 55925

Stedman's Directory of ... Norwich and ... part of Preston ... . *Norwich: J. W. Stedman*. 1865. 12mo, pp. lii, 156. Map. Continued.

The Norwich Jubilee. A Report of the Celebration at Norwich, Connecticut, on the Two Hundredth Anniversary of the Settlement of the Town, September 7th and 8th, 1859. With ... Historical Documents ... . Compiled ... by John W. Stedman. *Norwich, Conn.* 1859. 8vo, pp. 304. Map. 55926

Catalogue of the Corporation, Officers and Cadets of the Norwich University, For ... 1843–4. *Woodstock*. 1844. 12mo, pp. 30. Continued. H. 55927

Proposals of the Norwich Water Power Company. *Norwich*. 1831. 8vo. 55928

Norwich Mine. [Prospectus. n. p.] 1854. 8vo, pp. 16.

Also: A Statement of the Condition and Prospects of the Norwich Mine, Lake Superior; with ... Diagrams and Maps. ... *New York: Narine & Co., Printers*. 1853. 8vo, pp. 8.—Second Annual Report of the ... Norwich Mining Company, and Report of the Treasurer. ... 1857. *New-York: Sackett & Cobb, ... Printers*. 1857. 8vo, pp. 7.—A Statement to the Stockholders of the Norwich Mining Company, with Report of Israel Coe, Esq., and By-Laws ... . *New York: Narine & Co., Printers*. 1855. 8vo, pp. 12. Plan. H.

Norwich, *Vt.* Charter of Norwich, Vt., and Names of Original Proprietors; with Historical Notes. *Boston*. 1869. 8vo. 55930

Catalogue of Officers & Cadets of the American Literary, Scientific, and Military Academy, ... with the Prospectus and ... Regulations ... . Norwich, Vt. November, 1822. *Woodstock, Vt.: David Watson, Printer*. 1822. 8vo, pp. 20. H. 55931

See also Vol. ix., No. 36701.

[Norwood (Abraham)?] The Acts of the Elders. *See* Vol. i., No. 148, and add, New Edition. *Boston*. 1846. 12mo. + Eighth Edition. *Boston*. 1847. Sq. 16mo, pp. 160. Plate.

Norwood (J. G.) *See* Vol. ix., No. 34252.

Norwood (*Col.*) A Voyage to Virginia. By Colonel Norwood. [n. p. n. d.] 8vo, pp. 50. 55933

Forms No. 10 of Force's "Tracts," Vol. iii. *See also* "Virginia Historical Register," ii., *and* Churchill's "Voyages," vi.

Nos D. Francisco Antonio Lorenzana ... arzobispo de México ... A las Reverendas Madres Preladas, á cada una de todas las Religiosas de nuestra Filiacion, y á sus Confesores, y Directores Espirituales: Salud en nuestro Señor Jesu-Christo. *Mexico à 22 dias de septiembre* 1768. 8vo, pp. viii. 55934

Nos los Inquisidores. *See* Vol. ix., No. 34817, and add, *Mexico*. 1738. Folio, 6 leaves.

Nostradamus (M.) Explication d'une Prophétie de Nostradamus faite en 1545. Dans laquelle il prédit la grande révolution en Angleterre et dans les Colonies Angloises de l'Amérique que seront victorieuses. *London*. 1775. 12mo. 55935

Nostradamus. The true Prophecies or Prognostications of Mich. de Nostradamus. Translated and Commented by Theophilus de Garensieres. *London*. 1672. Folio. + [*Ibid.*] 1685. Folio. 55936

Nostradamus. Les Vrayes Centuries et Propheties de Maistre Michel Nostradamus. *Amsterdam, chez Iean Lauser*. 1688. 16mo, pp. (32), 158. Portrait. + *Leyde*. 1650. 8vo.

Not Careful but Prayerful. *Cincinnati: American Reform Tract Society*. 1861. 8vo. 55938

Not Impossible. [*Philadelphia: W. F. Geddes*. 1862.] 12mo, pp. 4. H. 55939

Subject: the practicability of removing from the United States its entire colored population.

Not Published. *See* [De Kay (N.)], Vol. v., No. 19321.

Notable Women of Olden Time. *Philadelphia*. 1852. 16mo, pp. 301. 9 Plates. C. 55940

Notaris (J. de). Jungermanniearum Americanarum pugillus. ... [n. p.: *Aug. Taurin*. 1857.] 4to, pp. 28. 55941

Notas diplomaticas, ultimas cambiadas entre Ministerio de relaciones esteriores de la republica Mexicana, y las legaciones estrangeras. *Mexico*. 1862. 4to, pp. 43. 55942

Notas Estadisticas del Departamento de Querétaro, formados por la Asemblea Constitucional del mismo, y remitidas al supremo Gobierno año de 1845. *Mexico*. 1848. 8vo, pp. (6), 128, (1).

Note explicative. *See* [Laffitte (J.) & Co.], Vol. ix. 38590.

Note, in addition to that of 1845, on the Jesuits' Estates, after the Suppression and since the Revival of the Order, and on the Uses to which they have been Applied. With Tables. *Quebec*. 1847. 8vo, pp. 21. 55944

The Note-Maker noted, and the Observer observed upon; Or, a Full Answer to some Notes and Observations Upon the Votes of the House of Assembly of the Colony of New-Jersey; Met in General Assembly at Burlington, on Saturday the 16th of October 1742. Being a Vindication of the present, and some former Governors, Councils and Assemblies of the said Colony, against the unreasonable Cavils of the said Observer or Note-maker. By a Lover of True English Liberty. [n. p.:] *Printed in the Year* M,DCC,XLIII. Sm. 4to, pp. 31. P. 55945

Probably printed by Benjamin Franklin *See* No. 55952.

A Note of the Shipping, Men, and Provisions, sent to Virginia ... . *London*. 1619. 4to, pp. 8. 55946

A Note of the Ship- | ping, Men, and Provisions, sent | and Prouided for Virginia, by the Right Hono- | rable, the Earle of Sovthampton, and the Company; | this yeare 1620. [*London*. 1620.] Folio, pp. (3). BM. 55947

Note Officielle. *See* Vol. iii., No. 9027, *note*.

Note sur la Compagnie Belge de Colonisation (en Amérique). *Paris*. 1843. 8vo, pp. 20. 4 Maps. 55948

Note sur la fondation. *See* [Lechevalier (J.)], Vol. x. 39637.

Note sur les biens que les Jésuites possédaient en Canada et sure l'affectation que ces biens doivent recevoir aujourd'hui. *Québec*. 1845. 12mo. 55949

Note sur les Botecudos. *See* [Jomard (E. F.)], Vol. ix.

Notelijke Consideratien die alle goede Liefhebbers des Vaderlandts behooven rypelye te overweghen op den vorgheslagen Tractate van Pays met den Spagniarden. [n. p.] 1608. 4to, pp. 16. 55950

Relates to the commerce of the West Indies.

Notes and Letters. *See* [Bayman (R.)], Vol. i., No. 4080.

Notes and Observations on the Bill supplementary to the "Act for the final adjustment of Land Titles in ... Louisiana and ... Missouri," Approved April 12th, 1814. *Washington: Printed by William A. Davis*. 1816. 8vo, pp. 22. BA. 55951

Notes and Observations upon the Votes of the House of Assembly of the Colony of New-Jersey; Met in ... Burlington, on Saturday the 16th of October, 1742. *Woodbridge, N. J.* 1743. 4to. P. 55952

Notes and Queries: a Medium of Intercommunication for Literary Men, Artists, Antiquaries, Genealogists, etc. Volume First. November, 1849–May, 1850. *London: George Bell*. 1850. Sm. 4to, pp. (2), 510. Continued. + General Index to Series the First. Vols. i.–xii. *London: Bell and Daldy*. 1856. Sm. 4to, pp. iv, 146. Continued. BA. 55953

A work of constantly increasing value and importance. The earlier series and the indexes are out of print. Many of the articles relate to American topics. To each series of twelve volumes there is an index.

Notes and Statistics. *See* Vol. iii., No. 10426.

Notes bibliographiques. *See* [Boimare (A. L.)], Vol. ii. 6152

Notes d'un Voyage dans l'Amérique Centrale. Lettres á M. Alfred Maury. [n. p. n. d.] 8vo, pp. 30. 55954

Extrait des "Nouvelles Annales des Voyages," Août, 1835.

Notes for an Essay. *See* Vol. xi., No. 45270.

Notes made during an Excursion. *See* [Hale (N.)], Vol. vii.

Notes of a Short ... Tour. *See* [Harden (E. J.)], Vol. viii.

Notes of a Traveller through the Middle and Northern States of America. *London*. 1834. Post 8vo. 55955

Notes of Conversations with a Volunteer Officer in the United States Navy [G. C. Taylor] on the Passage of the Forts below New Orleans, April 26th, 1864. ... *New York.* 1868. 4to, pp. 29. 55956

One hundred copies printed for private circulation.

Notes of Hospital Life from November, 1861, to August, 1863. ... *Philadelphia: J. B. Lippincott & Co.* 1864. 12mo, pp. 210. B., C. 55957

Notes of Reference. *See* Vol. XI., No. 45271.

Notes of Travel. *See* [Barney (J.)], Vol. I., No. 3538.

Notes of Travel and Life. By Two Young Ladies. *New York.* 1854. 12mo. 55958

Notes on a Work entitled "A Narrative of Facts," ... with Observations on the Separation in Swanzey Monthy Meeting: ... *Manchester: The Author.* 1848. 8vo, pp. 23. B. + *Boston, Reprinted.* 1850. 8vo. 55959

For another edition, *see* No. 51789, Vol. XII.

Notes on California. *See* Vol. III., No. 10036.

Notes on Colorado Territory. [n. p. 1865.] 8vo, pp. 19.

Notes on Colored Troops and Military Colonies on Southern Soil. By an Officer of the 9th Army Corps. *New-York.* 1863. 8vo, pp. 16. BA. 55961

Notes on Columbia. *See* [Bache (R.)], Vol. I., No. 2593.

Notes on Columbus. *See* [Harrisse (H.)], Vol. VIII. 30603.

Notes on Cuba. *See* [Wurdman (*Dr.*)]

Notes on Farming. *New-York: Printed in the Year* M,DCC,-LXXXVII. 8vo, pp. 38. BA. 55962

Notes on Mexico. *See* [Poinsett (Joel (R.)]

Notes on Mount Auburn Cemetery. *See* Vol. XII. 51151.

Notes on Political Economy, as Applicable to the United States. By a Southern Planter. *New-York: Leavitt, Trow, and Co.* 1844. 8vo, pp. viii, 304. B. 55963

Notes on Some ... Questions. *See* [Kane (J. K.)], X. 37006.

Notes on "Southern Wealth and Northern Profits." *Philadelphia: C. Sherman & Son, Printers.* 1861. 8vo, pp. 31. H.

In reply to T. P. Kettell. *See* Vol. IX., No. 37658.

Notes on the American Mining Companies, 1825. ... *London.* 1825. 8vo. 55965

Notes on the Colors of the National Guard, with some incidental passages of the History of the Regiment. Prepared at the Request of "the Veterans of the National Guard." *New York, from an Amateur Press.* 1864. Imp. 8vo, pp. 55. 55966

A few copies only were printed for private distribution. Contains information relative to military matters in New York. The work was set up in type by a young lady.

Notes on the Constitution of the United States. *New York.* 1864. 8vo. 55967

Notes on the ... Death, of a ... Friend. *See* [Magaw (S.)]

Notes on the Establishment of a Money Unit, and of a Coinage for the United States. [*Annapolis.* 1784.] 12mo, pp. 14.

Notes on the Finances of the State of South Carolina. By a Member of the House of Representatives. *Charleston.* [n. d.] 8vo. W. 55969

Notes on the Navigation of the Mississippi; taken by a Gentleman of Talents ... and corrected after several voyages, in all stages of the Water. *State of Kentucky: Frankfort, Printed by James M. Bradford* ... . 1803. 12mo, pp. 56. 55970

Notes on the North-Eastern Boundary. *Quebec.* 1830. 8vo.

Notes on the Origin and Necessity of Slavery. *Charleston: Printed by A. E. Miller:* 1826. 8vo, pp. 48. 55972

The dedication is signed "Edward Brown."

Notes on the Process of Amalgamation at the Hacienda of La Sanceda, Veta Granade, Zacatecas. [n. p. about 1840.] 12mo, pp. (21). 55973

Notes on the Sea-Shore. *See* [Homer (J. L.)], Vol. VIII., No. 32722, and No. 33648.

Notes on the Slave Trade. *See* [Benezet (A.)], Vol. II. 4675

Notes on the State of Virginia. *See* [Jefferson (T.)], Vol. IX.

Notes on the Two Reports. *See* Vol. IX., No. 35640.

Notes on the United States *See* [Morris (G.)], XII. 50829.

Notes on the Vice-Royalty. *See* Vol. X., No. 38999.

Notes pour servir à l'histoire. *See* [Harrisse (H.)], Vol. VIII.

Notes respecting ... Waldo. *See* [Jones (M. C.)], Vol. X.

Notes respecting the United States of North-America, in relation to their Constitution, Progress, and the Stocks of the different States. *London.* 1839. 8vo, pp. 24. 55974

Notes sur le Chili. *See* Vol. IV., No. 12790.

Notes sur les Colonies. *See* Vol. VII., No. 29181.

Notes upon Canada. *See* Todd (H. C.)

Notes upon Copper and Copper Ores, and upon the Legislation proper to promote the increase of the Trade in Copper. [n. p. 1869.] 8vo, pp. 12, folded Table. H. 55975

Notes upon the South Western Boundary Line of the British Provinces of Lower Canada and New Brunswick and the United States of America. *Montreal.* 1839. 8vo, pp. 63. 55976

Nothing to Do: a Tilt at our Best Society. [By Horatio Alger, Jr.] ... *Boston: James French & Co.* 1857. 16mo, pp. 45. Plate. H. 55977

Nothing to Wear. *See* [Butler (W. A.)], Vol. III. 9663.

Notice. To be Sold, by Public Vendue ... . *Wilmington: Printed by Jacob A. Killen & Co.* [n. d.] 4to, 1 leaf. 55978

"The Executors will also at the same time dispose of a likely Negro Wench, about twenty-five years of age, ... August 3, 1786."

Notice of a Reply to the Review of a Memoir on the U. S: Artillery. [n. p. 1852?] 8vo, pp. 32. H. 55979

Notice of Societies. *See* [Carey (M.)], Vol. III., p. 341, *note.*

Notice of the Silver Mines of Fresnillo in the State of Zacatecas, Mexico, now working for account of that State, and of their present Condition and Prospects. With the Basis of the Conditions on which the Government of Zacatecas offers to grant the Rights of Possession, and of working these Mines for a term of Years. *London.* 1834. 8vo, pp. 46. View and Plan.

Improved title of our No. 25911, Vol. VI..

Notice of Tertiary Fossils, from Labrador, Maine, &c., and Remarks on the Climate of Canada ... . [By J. W. Dawson. *Montreal.* n. d.] 8vo, pp. 13. 55981

Notice respecting the Boundary between his Majesty's Possessions in North America and the United States; with a Map of America ... exhibiting the principal Trading Stations of the North-West Company; and intended to accompany the Narrative of Occurrences in the Indian Countries of North America, ... *London: Printed by B. McMillan.* 1817. Rl. 8vo, pp. 12. Folded Map. C., H. 55982

Not printed for sale. *See* our Vol. V., No. 20699.

Notice Statistique et Commerciale sur la Republique Orientale de l'Uruguay. *Havre.* 1836. 8vo, pp. 40. 55983

An extract from the "Archives de Commerce."

Notice Statistique sur le Chili. [*Monteran.* n. d.] 8vo, pp. 32

See also Vol. IV., No. 12791, Vol. VII., No. 29183, *and* [Ternaux (H.)]

Notice sur Alpina. Terres situées dans les Comtés de Jefferson et de Lewis, État de New-York. *Neuchatel: H. Wolfrath.* 1847. 8vo, pp. 64. S. 55985

Notice sur le Chili, par un Voyageur Français. [Eugène Duflot de Mofras.] *Paris: Imprimerie A. Francois et Compagnie.* 1844. 8vo, pp. 43. H. 55986

Notice sur l'État Actuel de la Mission de la Louisiane. *Paris: Adrien Le Clere.* 1820. 8vo, pp. 58. + Nouvelle Édition a laquelle on a ajouté de nouveaux détails. *Lyon, chez Rusaud.* 1822. 8vo, pp. 67. + *Turin.* 1822. 8vo. + *Avignon.* 1824. 12mo. 55987

Notice sur Haiti. *See* Vol. X., No. 38378.

Notice sur le port de Cobija. *See* Vol. IV., No. 14042.

Notice sur le territoire et sur la mission de l'Oregon. [n. p. 1858?] 8vo, pp. 39. H. 55988

Notice sur la transportation. *See* Vol. VII., No. 29184.

Notice sur la Vie. *See* [Dupont de Nemours], Vol. VI. 21390

Notice sur les chemins de fer de l'État de New-York ... 1858. [n. p. n. d.] Folio, pp. 31. Map. B. 55989

Notice sur les Indiens Ioways. *See* Vol. XI., No. 47467.

Notice sur les Mœurs et Coutûmes. *See* Vol. VI. 22863.

Notice sur les Nouveaux Établissements Agricole fondes au Venezuela. Extrait ... 1841. [n. p. n. d.] 8vo, pp. 17. Map.

Notice sur les troubles survenus. *See* [Clair Roy], Vol. IV.

Notices, 1837–40. *See* [Saint Hilaire].

Notices and Journals. *See* Vol. XI., No. 45307.

Notices biographiques de Messire C. Gauvreau, V. G., Ancien Supérieur du Collège de Saint Anne, et de Messire Ths. B. Pelletier, Ancien Préfet des Études. *Ste. Anne de la Pocatière.* 1865. 8vo, pp. 46. Portraits. 55991

Notices of East Florida. *See* Vol. VI., No. 24889.

Notices of Parkersburg, Virginia, as it is in July, 1860. *Baltimore: John W. Woods, ... Printer.* [n. d.] 8vo, pp. 12. Plate.

Notices of St. Mary's Hall. [*Burlington.* 1837?] 8vo.

Notices of Sullivan's Campaign. *See* [O'Reilly (H.)]

Notices of the Early History. *See* [Miller (A. E.)], Vol. XII.

Notices of the Harbor. *See* Vol. IV., No. 14850.

Notices of the Life of ... Lincoln. *See* [Kirkland (J. F.)]

Notices of the Press. *See* Vol. IX., No. 37518.

Notices of the Rideau Canal; by a Friend to Justice and Merit. With a Sketch of the Chaudière Bridge. *Kingston, U. C.* 1832. 8vo, pp. 22. C. 55994

Notices on the Claims. *See* Vol. VIII., No. 33545.

Notices on the Slave Trade. *See* [Harrison (G.)], Vol. VIII.

Notices Statistiques. *See* [Tiby (P. A.)]

Notices sur les colonies françaises. *See* Vol. IV., No. 14718.

Noticia annalica y Estado, qve tiene el pverto del Callao, y la ciudad de Lima, à el año cumplido de su desolacion, y ruyna, que lo hace en este mes de Octubre de 1747. [*Lima.* 1747.] 4to, 11 leaves. 55995

Noticia breve de la expedicion Militar de Sonora y Cinaloa, su exito feliz, y ventajoso estado en que por consecuencia de ella se han puesto ambas provincias. [*Mexico.*] 1771. Folio, pp. 12.

Noticia breve de la Solemne. *See* Vol. XII., No. 48596.

Noticia de la Causa seguida al Senador Diego Jose Benevente. *Santiago de Chile.* 1837. 8vo. 55997

Noticia de la Compania formado en la Provincia de Guipuzcoa, para embiar dos Navios cada Ano, con Registro, a la Provincia de Benezuela, y conducir Carga de Cacao y otros Frutos de ella a estos Reynos. [n. p. about 1740.] 12mo. 55998

Noticia de las cosas notables. *See* Vol. X., No. 41121.

Noticia de los premios aplicados. *See* Vol. VII., No. 29090.

Noticia del editor sobre el establecimiento del oficio de escribano ... . [n. p. n. d.] 8vo, pp. 15–34. 55999

Relates to Pueblo.

Noticia descriptiva da Provincia do Rio-Grande de S. Pedro do Sul, contendo além da topographia physica e politica, e de um ensaio de estatistica local, informações sobre o estado actual da população, suas subdivisões, e sobre o caracter e costumes dos habitantes. Com um mappa reduzido do theatro da guerra presente. *Rio de Janeiro: ... J. Villeneuve & C.a* 1839. 4to, pp. xi, 216. 56000

Noticia, e Justificaçam do titulo, e boa fee com que se obrou a Nova Colonia do Sacramento nas terras da capitania de S. Vicente no sitio chamado de S. Gabriel nas margens do rio da Prata. E tratado provisional sobre o novo Incidente cauzado pelo governador de Buenos Ayres, ajustado nesta corte de Lisboa pelo Duque de Jovenaso, Embaxador de el rey catholico, com os Plenipotenciarios de sua Alteza: approvado, y ratificado, et confirmado por ambos os Principes. *Lisboa: A. Craesbeeck de Mello.* 1681. Folio, pp. 34, (12). 56001

Contains the official acts and the treaty concluded between the two kingdoms, relative to the establishment of the colony of Sacramento.

Noticia Historica de los Cuerpos de Infanteria permanente y activa que actualmente existen en la República. *México.* 1841. 8vo. C. 56002

Noticia Individual de los Derechos, que, segun lo Reglado en el ultimo Real Proyecto de 5 de Abril de 1720, deven contribuir á sú Magestad de Salida de España, Flete, y conduccion á los Reynos de las Indias ... . *Barcelona.* 1732. 4to. 56003

Noticia que se da' ao publico para consolacao dos Portuguezes, dos successos, que acontecaraõ no estado da nossa India desde o maz de Janeiro de 1759, até o de 1760. *Lisboa.* 1760. 4to, 15 leaves. 56004

Noticia sobre. *See* No. 14614, *and* [Gutierrez (J. M.)], VII.

Noticia verdadeira da Guerra. *See* Vol. X., No. 38660.

Noticia verdadera de los tres dias de ministerio. *Mexico.* 1839. 12mo, pp. 32. 56005

Noticia y justificacion del titulo. *See* Vol. X., No. 38998.

Noticias biográficas del exmo. Señor Don Lúcas Alaman, secretario de estado y del despacho de relaciones esteriores ... . *México: R. Rafael.* 1853. Folio, pp. 59. Portrait. C. 56006

Noticias curiosas. *See* Vol. II., No. 7609.

Noticias de la Provincia de Californias en tres cartas de un sacerdote religioso hijo del real convento de predicadores del Valencia a un amigo suyo. ... *Valencia, por los Hermanos de Orga.* M.DCC.XCIV. 3 vols., sm. 8vo, pp. (2), 104; 96; 104, 2 folded leaves. H. 56007

Signed F. L. S. The author, who was a missionary, gives an apparently truthful account of California, wherein he attempts to correct some of the errors into which Venegas has fallen.

Noticias de la Vida y Escritos de Fray Toribio de Benavente, ó Motolinia uno de los primeros Misioneros Catolicos y Fundadores de la provincia Franciscana del Sto. Evangelio de Mexico. Acompañadas de investigaciones sobre el origin y motivos de sus discidencias con el Illmo. Don Fr. B. de las Casas Obispo de Chiapas por Don José Fernando Ramirez. *Mexico, para el Autor.* 1859. 4to, pp. (4), 109. 56008

Published originally in Vol. I. of Señor Icazbalceta's "Documentos para la Historia de Mexico," and of this separate edition only fifty copies were printed.

Noticias del Sur. Despacho. *See* Vol. IV., No. 12792.

Noticias Estadisticas de la Huasteca, y de una parte de la Sierra Alta, formadas en el año de 1853, por Manuel Férndo. Soto. *Mexico: Imprenta del Gobierno.* 1869. 8vo, pp. v, 207. 56009

Noticias geográficas y estadísticas del departemento de Zalisco, reunidas y coordinadas de orden del gobierno del mismo. *Guadalajara: Imprenta del Gobierno.* 1843. 8vo, pp. (8), 154.

Noticias históricas. *See* [Nunez (Ignacio)].

Noticias muy importantes y recientes de los Estados-Unides del Norte. *Queretara.* [1848.] 12mo, pp. 12. 56011

Noticias para la Historia de Nuestra Señora de los Remedios, desde el año de 1808, hasta el comente de 1812. *Mexico.* 1812. 8vo. 56012

Noticias relativas à el primer plan de Independencia, formado por los Hijos de los Conquistadores. [n. p. n. d.] 8vo. 56013

Noticias Sagradas que á Major Honra y Gloria Dios y de sú S. M. Maria S.ra Nuestra Retorna la Ciudad de la Puebla de los Angeles, en esta Nueva España en obsequiosa gratitud regraciando la fervorosa devoccion de la Ciudad de Sevilla ... [*Mexico:*] *D. F. de Leon.* [n. d.] 4to. 56014

Noticias sobre el Temporal de Octubre. *San Salvador.* 1853. 8vo, pp. 24. 56015

Relates to Central American affairs.

Noticias sobre los dos sitios de la colonia del Sacramento, en 1762 y 1777, escrita por testigos oculares, y publicadas por primera vez. *Montevideo.* 1849. 4to, pp. 72. 56016

Noticioso de Ambos Mundos. Ano I. ... 1836. *Nueva York.* 1836. Folio. Continued. H. 56017

Notificatie. De Bewinthebberen van de Generale Geoctroyeerde West-Indische Compagnie ... maken bekent, dat sy goetgevonden hebben op het Eylant Curaçao aan te stellen eene opene Marckt van Swarte-Slaven, soo wel Pieces d'Indias als Manquerons, voor "elk en een yder die deselve sal willen kopen," etc. *Middelburg: B. de Later.* 1689. Folio, 1 leaf. 56018

Notification by the directors of the West India Company that they have resolved to establish at the island of Curaçao, a free market for black slaves.

Notifications, Orders, and Instructions, relating to Prize Subjects, during the Present War. *London: Printed by A. Strahan.* 1807. 8vo, pp. (4), 83, (4). BA. + *London.* 1813. 8vo. C.

Notions of the Americans. *See* [Cooper (J. F.)], IV. 16486.

Notitia de los premios aplicados a las mejores hilanderas al torno ... en la Escuela de la Nueva Guatemala. *Nueva Guatemala.* 1796. 4to. 56020

Notitia dignitatum et administrationum omnium tam civilium quam militarium in partibus Orientis et Occidentis. Ad codd. Mss. editiorumque fidem recensuit commentariisque illustravit Ed. Böcking. *Bonn.* 1839–53. 2 vols., 8vo. 92 Plates.

There are copies with the engravings colored.

Notitia of New-Brunswick, for 1836, and extending into 1837; comprising Historical, Geographical, Statistical, and Commercial Notices of the Province. By an Inhabitant. ... *Saint John: The Author.* 1838. 8vo, pp. 136. H. 56022

Notitia vtraqve cvm Orientis tvm Occidentis vltra Arcadii Honoriiqve Caesarvm Tempora, illustre Uetustatis Monumentum, imò Thesaurus prorsum incomparabilis. ... *Basileae: Froben.* 1552. Folio. Vignette and 106 Woodcuts. 56023

Edited by Sigismund Ghelen, and reprinted in 1593.

Notitiæ Parochiales. Parish Statistics of the Church of the Ascension, New-York. Prepared by the Rector ... . *New-York: Baker, Godwin & Co., Printers.* 1851. 12mo, pp. 24. + *New-York: John A. Gray, Printer.* 1860. 12mo, pp. 62. B. 56024

Notiz der grossbrit. Colonien. *See* [Schirach (G. B. von)].

NOTMAN (W.) Portraits of British Americans, by W. Notman ... . With Biographical Sketches by Fennings Taylor ... . *Montreal: William Notman.* 1865–68. 3 vols., 8vo, pp. (4), vi, 425, 30 Portraits; (4), 350, 30 Portraits; (4), 280, 24 Portraits.

Notoriedades del Plata. Album de fotografias de Emilio Mangel du Mesnil. ... *Buenos Aires.* 1862. 18mo, pp. 90. 7 Plates. 56026

Notre Cable Transatlantique (France aux États-Unis). *Paris.* 1867. Imp. 8vo, pp. 40. 56027

NOTT (A. K.) Memoir of Abner Kingman Nott, Late Pastor of the First Baptist Church in ... New York; with ... Extracts from his Correspondence by his Brother. *New York.* 1860. 12mo, pp. 395. Portrait. 56028

NOTT (B.) Constitutional Ethics. ... By Benjamin Nott. *Albany.* 1857. 8vo. S. 56029

[NOTT (Charles C.)] The Coming Contraband; a Reason against the Emancipation Proclamation, not given by Mr. Justice

Curtis, to whom it is addressed, by an Officer in the Field. *New York: G. P. Putnam.* 1862. 12mo, pp. 21. 56030

This is also attributed to Charles P. Kirkland.

NOTT. Sketches in Prison Camps: a Continuation of Sketches of the War. By Charles C. Nott ... . *New York.* 1865. 12mo. + Second Edition. *New York: Anson D. F. Randolph.* 1865. 12mo, pp. 204. H. 56031

NOTT. Sketches of the War: a Series of Letters ... . By Charles C. Nott, Captain in the Fifth Iowa Cavalry ... . *New York: Charles T. Evans.* 1863. 12mo, pp. 174. + Second Edition. *New-York: Anson D. F. Randolph.* 1865. 12mo, pp. 174.

NOTT (E.) The Addresses, delivered to the Candidates for the Baccalaureate, at ... Union College. By Eliphalet Nott, D.D. ... *Schenectady: Printed by Riggs and Stevens.* 1814. 12mo, pp. 240. BA. 56033

NOTT. A Discourse ... in ... Albany, before the Ladies' Society, for the Relief of Distressed Women and Children, March 18th, 1804. By Eliphalet Nott ... . *Albany: Printed by Charles R. and George Webster.* 1804. 8vo, pp. 39, (1). BA. 56034

The appendix contains an obituary notice of Mrs. Sally Nott, "the amiable consort of Rev. Eliphalet Nott."

NOTT. A Discourse ... in ... Albany, occasioned by the ... Death of General Alexander Hamilton, July 29, 1804. By Eliphalet Nott, A.M. ... *Albany: Printed by Charles R. and George Webster.* 1804. 8vo, pp. 40. + The Second Edition. [*Ibid.*] 1804. 8vo, pp. 32. + The Third Edition. [*Ibid.*] 1806. 8vo, pp. 22. + [Another] Third Edition. *Salem: Printed by Joshua Cushing.* 1804. 8vo, pp. 40. + ... *Stockbridge—Re-printed by Heman Willard.* 1804. 8vo, pp. 31. + Fourth Edition. *Boston: Printed by David Carlisle.* 1805. 8vo, pp. 24. H. + To which is added, A Paper, written by Gen. Hamilton ... . *Printed at Greenfield—Mass. By John Denio.* 1805. 8vo, pp. 30. BA. + *Schenectady.* 1810. 8vo. + *Schenectady: Re-published by G. Y. Van Debogart.* 1853. 8vo, pp. 46. B. 56035

Reprinted in Dr. Nott's "Miscellaneous Works," No. 56036, *infra.*

NOTT. Miscellaneous Works. By Eliphalet Nott, D.D. With an Appendix. *Schenectady: Wm. J. M'Cartee.* 1810. 8vo, pp. 280. B., C. 56036

Also: Address delivered to the Candidates for the Baccalaureate in Union College, at the Anniversary Commencement, May 18th, 1805. ... *Albany.* 1805. 8vo. + July 30th, 1806. ... *Schenectady: Printed by John L. Stevenson.* [1806.] 8vo, pp. 18. B. + *Cambridge: Printed by W. Hilliard.* 1806. 8vo, pp. 16. BA. + July 29, 1807. ... *Albany: Printed by Websters and Skinners.* 1807. 8vo, pp. 24. + July 24, 1811. ... [*Ibid.*] 1811. 8vo, pp. 21. BA.—A Discourse ... in ... Albany, the Fourth of July, 1801 ... . [n. p. n. d.] 8vo, pp. 35. + *Albany.* 1801. 8vo, pp. 24. + *Schenectady.* 1810. 8vo.—Lectures on Temperance ... . With an Introduction by Taylor Lewis, LL.D. ... Edited by Amasa M'Coy ... . *New-York: Sheldon, Blakeman & Co.* 1857. 12mo, pp. xxx, 341.—Lijkrede ... Dood van A. Hamilton: uit het Engelsch vertaald ... *Amsterdam.* 1836. 8vo S.—A Sermon ... before the General Assembly of the Presbyterian Church ... May 19, 1806. ... *Philadelphia: Printed by Jane Aitken.* 1806. 8vo, pp. 39.—Tribute to the Memory of Mrs. Mary L. Sprague, Wife of W. B. Sprague ... . *Albany: Packard and Van Benthuysen, Printers.* 1837. 8vo, pp. 16. B.—Trust Deed, from Eliphalet Nott and Wife, to the Trustees of Union College. [*Albany.* 1854.] 8vo, pp. 24. B., S.

[NOTT (Henry Junius).] Novellettes of a Traveller; or, Odds and Ends from the Knapsack of Thomas Singularity, Journeyman Printer. *New York: Harper & Brothers.* 1834. 2 vols., 12mo, pp. 228; 203. C. 56037

NOTT (J. C.) ... Indigenous Races of the Earth; or, New Chapters of Ethnological Inquiry; including Monographs on Special Departments of Philology, Iconography, Cranioscopy, Palæontology, Pathology, Archæology, Comparative Geography, and Natural History: contributed by Alfred Maury, ... Francis Pulszky, and J. Aitken Meigs, M.D. ... presenting fresh Investigations, Documents, and Materials; by J. C. Nott, M.D., and Geo. R. Gliddon ... . *Philadelphia: J. B. Lippincott & Co.* 1857. 4to, pp. 656. Plates and Maps. BA. 56038

[NOTT.] The Negro Race. Its Ethnology and History. ... *Mobile, Ala.* 1866. 12mo, pp. 28. H. 56039

NOTT. Types of Mankind: or, Ethnological Researches, based upon the Ancient Monuments ... . Illustrated ... from the inedited Papers of Samuel George Morton, ... [and others]. By J. C. Nott, M.D., and Geo. R. Gliddon ... . *Philadelphia: Lippincott, Grambo & Co.* 1854. 4to, pp. lxxvi, (2), 49–738. Map and Plates. + Second Edition. [*Ibid.*] Rl. 8vo, pp. 738. + Seventh Edition. [*Ibid.*] 1855. 56040

Also on large paper in quarto. It elicited: "Review of Gliddon and Nott's 'Types of Mankind.'" [n. p.:] *Printed by Isaac Ashmead.* [1854.] 8vo, pp. 41. Reprinted from the "Presbyterian Quarterly Review," Sept. 1854. Also: An Essay on the Natural History of Mankind, viewed in Connection with Negro Slavery ... . *Mobile.* 1851. 8vo, pp. 26.—The Physical History of the Jewish Race ... . *Charleston.* 1850. 8vo.—Two Lectures on the Connection between the Biblical and Physical History of Man. ... *New York: Bartlett and Welford.* 1849. 8vo, pp. 146. Map.—Two Lectures on the Natural History of the Caucasian and Negro Races. ... *Mobile: Printed by Dade and Thompson.* 1844. 12mo, pp. 53. H.

NOTT (S.) Prayer, ... the Duty of Rulers ... . A Sermon, ... at Hartford, in Connecticut, on the General Election, May 11th, 1809. By Samuel Nott, A.M. ... *Hartford: Hudson and Goodwin.* 1809. 8vo, pp. 36. S. 56041

NOTT. Reasons for Ministerial Fidelity. A Half-Century Sermon: ... at Franklin, March 13, 1832. By Rev. Samuel Nott, D.D. ... *Norwich: J. Dunham.* 1832. 8vo, pp. 28. + Second Edition. [*Ibid.*] B. 56042

NOTT. The Sixtieth Anniversary Sermon, preached at Franklin, March 13, 1842. By Rev. Samuel Nott, D.D. ... *Norwich: J. Cooley, Printer.* 1842. 8vo, pp. 16. BA. 56043

Also: Funeral Oration on the Death of Samuel Gurley ... . *Hartford.* 1778. 8vo. —Ministers ... are Earthen Vessels ... Sermon ... at ... the Funeral of A. Lee, D.D. *Norwich.* 1832. 8vo.—Sermon at the Interment of Deacon J. Hunt, 1786. ... [n. p. n. d.] 8vo.—Sermon at the Ordination of the Rev. Oliver Ayer, West Stockbridge, May 29th, 1793. ... *Stockbridge.* 1793. 8vo.— ... A Sermon ... at the Funeral of the Rev. Moses C. Welch, D.D. ... April 28, 1824. ... *Hartford: Printed by Goodwin & Co.* 1824. 8vo, pp. 18. H.

NOTT (S.), *Jr.* A Discourse on the Death of President Harrison, ... at Wareham, May 14, 1841. With an Appendix, on the Principles and Character of Washington. By Samuel Nott, Jr. ... *Boston: Whipple & Damrell.* 1841. 8vo, pp. 48.

NOTT. The Freedom of the Mind, demanded of American Freemen; being Lectures to the Lyceum, on the Improvement of the People. By Samuel Nott, Jun. *Boston: Crocker & Brewster.* 1830. 12mo, pp. 131. B. 56045

NOTT. Lessons of Piety and Patriotism, from Harrison and Washington. By Samuel Nott, Jr. ... *Boston: Whipple & Damrell.* 1841. 8vo, pp. 48. 56046

NOTT. The Necessities and Wisdom of 1861. A Supplement to ... Slavery and the Remedy. By Samuel Nott. *Boston: Crocker and Brewster.* 1861. 8vo, pp. 12. BA. 56047

NOTT. The Present Crisis: with a Reply and Appeal to European Advisers, from ... Slavery and the Remedy. By Samuel Nott. *Boston: Crocker and Brewster.* 1860. 8vo, pp. xliii. + [*Ibid.*] 1861. B. 56048

NOTT. Sixteen Years' Preaching and Procedure, at Wareham, Ms., By Rev. Samuel Nott, Jr. With a reprint of the ... result of Ex Parte Council ... . *Boston: Charles Tappan.* 1845. 8vo, pp. 192. B. 56049

NOTT. Slavery, and The Remedy; or, Principles and Suggestions for a Remedial Code. By Samuel Nott. *Boston: Crocker and Brewster.* 1856. 8vo, pp. 118. + Second Edition. [*Ibid.*] + Third Edition. [*Ibid.*] + Fourth Edition. [*Ibid.*] 8vo, pp. 120. + Fifth Edition; with a Review of the Decision of ... the Case of Dred Scott. *New York: D. Appleton and Company.* 1857. 8vo, pp. (2), 137. + Sixth Edition; with a Reply and Appeal to European Advisers. *Boston: Crocker and Brewster.* 1859. 8vo, pp. xliii, 137. BA. 56050

Also; An Appeal to the Temperate ... . *Albany.* 1828. 12mo. + *Hartford: D. F. Robinson & Co.* 1828. 18mo, pp. 120.— ... Education for an Agricultural People. ... Before the American Institute ... August, 1835. ... [*Boston.* 1835.] 8vo, pp. 27. —Nott's Testimony in favour of Judson. A Letter ... to Rev. Enoch Pond ... . *Boston: Lincoln & Edmands.* 1819. 8vo, pp. 16.—The "Preaching and Procedure," of Rev. Samuel Nott, Jr. [For distribution among the People at Wareham, Mass.] *Boston.* 1839. 8vo, pp. 22.—Sermons on Public Worship, suited to the Times. ... *Boston.* 1841. 12mo.

[NOTT (Samuel), *Civil Engineer.*] Report on Surveys for the Extension of the Hartford, Providence and Fishkill Railroad, from Waterbury to Fishkill. *Hartford: Case, Tiffany and Company.* 1853. 8vo, pp. 62. 2 Maps. H. 56051

NOTUS NIMINI, *pseudon.* *See* [Ogden (G. W.)]

Noua Francia. *See* [Lescarbot (M.)], Vol. x., No. 40177.

Noue de le Isole & Terra fer | ma Nouamente trouate | In India per el Capi | taneo de larmata de la Cesarea | Maiestate. | [Colophon:] *Cautum est a principe ne quis preter Caluum intra annum | Imprimat: sub pena ducatorum centum.* | [Verso of title-page:] Andrea caluo ad Paulo uerrano | & Abramo Tassio/ | ... *Mediolani decimosexto calē. Decembris* M.D.XXII. 4to, 6 leaves. BM. 56052

A brief abstract of Cortes' second account.

NOUETTE-DELORME (É.) Les États-Unis et l'Europe ... Par Émile Nouette-Delorme *Paris: E. Dentu.* 1863. 8vo, pp. 30.

NOUETTE-DELORME. Un Européen au Président Abraham Lincoln Réponse a son dernier message Par Émile Nouette-Delorme *Paris: E. Dentu.* 1863. 8vo, pp. 16. B., BA.

NOUGARET (P.-J.-B.) Beautés de L'Histoire des États-Unis de l'Amérique Septentrionale ... . Publié par P.-J.-B. Nougaret. *A Paris, Chez Brunot-Labbe* ... . 1817. 12mo, pp. (4), 509. 9 Plates. H. + [*Ibid.*] 1824. 56055

Curious for blunders in place, time, and costume. *See also* [Bourgeois (A. A.)], II.

[NOURSE (B. F.), *and* HILTON (W.)] Report of the Boston Committee of Policy-Holders upon the Conduct and Management of the Mutual Life Insurance Co. of New York. *Boston: Printed by Rockwell & Churchill.* 1870. 8vo, pp. 12. H. 56056

NOURSE (J.) Views of Colonization. By Rev. James Nourse, A.M. ... *Philadelphia: Merribew and Gunn, Printers.* 1837. 12mo, pp. 52. H. 56057

NOURSE (J. D.) Remarks on the Past and its Legacies to American Society. ... By J. D. Nourse. *Louisville, Ky.: Morton & Griswold.* 1847. 12mo, pp. 223. BA., P. 56058

NOURSE (Joseph E.) The Maritime Canal of Suez: ... and comparison of its Probable Results with those of a Ship Canal across Darien. By J. E. Nourse, U.S.N. *Washington City: Philp & Solomons.* 1869. 8vo, pp. (4), 57. Plate, Portrait, 3 Maps.

[NOURSE (*Mr.*)] A Letter to the Rev. Dr. Price. By the Author of the Defence of the American Congress, in Reply to Taxation no Tyranny. *London: J. Williams.* MDCCLXXVI. 8vo, pp. 31. 56060

"The spirited writer of this letter applauds Dr. Price's late publication, but dissents from the part of it where, treating of the colonists, the Doctor says, 'They are not our subjects, but our fellow-subjects.' It appears to him, he says, that they are 'neither the one nor the other,' and his reasoning on this point is worthy of attention."—*Monthly Review*, LIV. 407.

Le nouueau monde. *See* [Montalboddo (F.)], XII. 50062.

Nouuelles certaines, 1534. *See* [Pizarro (F.)]

Le Nouveau Mississippi. *See* [Jacquemart (Fr.)], IX. 35512.

Le nouveau Nabuchodonosor ou Raynal parmi les quadrupèdes, par M. Bontems. *Liouville.* 1782. 12mo. 56061

Nouveau Recueil Traitez, d'Alliance, de Treve, de Paix, et de Commerce; conclus entre les Rois, Princes, et États de l'Europe, de 1647 à 1709. Par J. du Mont. *Amsterdam.* 1710. 2 vols., 12mo. C. 56062

Nouveau Voyage à la Mer du Sud. *See* [Rochon (Alexis)].

Nouveau Voyage autour de Monde en 1838, 1839 et 1840, par les Corvettes l'Astrolabe et la Zelée. Publication du Journal d'un matelot parisien abord de l'Astrolabe, et du Journal d'un matelot provençal abord de la Zelée. *Toulon.* 1841. 8vo, pp. 252

See also Vol. v., No. 21210.

Nouveau Voyage. *See* [La Barbinais (L. G. de)], Vol. IX., No. 38397, [Labat (J. B.)], Nos. 38409–12, *and* [La Martinière (P. M.)], Vol. x., No. 38716.

Nouvel Examen. *See* [Millet (Th.)], Vol. XII., No. 49083.

Nouvelle Bibliothèque des Voyages anciens et modernes, contenant la relation complète ou analysée des voyages de Christophe Colomb, Fernand Cortez, Pizarre, Anson, Byron, Bougainville, Cook, La Pérouse, ... Levaillant, ... Basile-Hall, ... Ross, ... Duperrey, Freycinet, ... Dumont-d'Urville, etc. etc. Ouvrage illustré de 100 magnifiques planches gravées sur acier, représentant les scènes les plus variées de la vie des différents peuples, telles que leurs combats, jeux, divertissements, cérémonies religieuses, etc., et accompagnié de 5 belles cartes géographiques coloriées. *Paris, chez P. Dumenil, éditeur.* 1842. 12 vols., 8vo, pp. (4), lxxvi, 363 (3); (4), 393, (3); (4), 403, (3); (4), 396, (3); (4), 396, (8); (4), 388, (3); (4), 412, (2); (4), 441, (1); (4), 438, (4); (4), 439, (1); (4), 412; (4), 400. 56064

Nouvelle de Saint Domingue du 9 au 14 Mars 1790. [n. p. 1790.] 8vo, pp. 8. J.C.B. 56065

Novvelle Decovverte de l'Isle Pinés située au delà de la ligne Œquinoctiale. Faite par vn Nauire Hollandois l'an 1667. [Colophon:] *Paris, Sebastien Mabre Cramoisy.* 1668. 4to, pp. 4.

This rare piece is a translation of our No. 35255, Vol. IX.

NOUVELLE ECOSSE. *See* Nova Scotia.

NOUVELLE ESPAGNE. Bref du Pape sur le différend d'entre l'Eveque d'Angelopolis, ou colonie dite Anges, à la Nouvelle Espagne, et les PP. Jésuites. [n. p.] 1659. 4to. 56067

See also New Spain *and* Nueva España.

NOUVELLE FRANCE. Arrest | du Conseil d'Estat: | qvi permet aux habitans | de Canada, d'apporter en France des | Morues de la pesche dudit Païs, & du | Charbon de Terre. | [Colophon:] *A Paris,* | *Par Sebastien Mabre-Cramoisy, Imprimeur* | *du Roy* 1670. | 4to, pp. 4. 56068

Arrest | du Conseil d'Estat | du Roy. | Du douzième Aoust 1671. | Qui Ordonne que les Marchandises venant des Isles | Françoises de l'Amérique & Canada, joüiront du benefice porté par l'Edit du mois de Feurier 1670. | Et en consequence, qu'elles pouront sortir hors du | Roïaume, sans païer aucuns Droits; Et que ceux

qui | auront esté païez à l'Entrée, seront rendus & resti- | tuez, à l'exception neantmoins des Sucres Bruts, | dont les droits seront restituez seulement après qu'ils | auront esté rafinez. | [Colophon:] *A Paris,* | *chez Guillaume Saugrain, à l'entrée du Quay de Gévres,* | *du costé du Pont au Change, au Paradis.* | [1671]. 4to, pp. 4.

Arrest | du Conseil | d'estat: | pour faire rendre compte | à ceux qui ont levé le droit de dix pour | cent au Païs de Canada. | Du 12 Juin 1675. | *A Paris.* | *Par Sebastien Mabre-Cramoisy, Impri-* | *meur du Roy.* | M.DC.LXXV. | *de l'expres comandment de Sa Majesté.* | 4to, pp. 4. 56070

Arrest | du Conseil d'estat | du Roy, | Qui exempte de tous droits de sortie, & autres | generalement quelconques, les Marchandises qui seront | chargées dans le Royaume, pour estre portées en Canada | à la charge par ceux qui les feront sortir, de faire leurs | soumissions de raporter | six mois après, un certificat de la | decharge d'icelles au dit Païs, etc. 10 May 1677. [Colophon:] *A Paris,* | *Chez Joseph Saugrain, au milieu du Quay de* | *Gêvres, à la Croix Blanche.* | [1677]. 4to, 2 leaves. 56071

Arrest | du Conseil d'Estat du Roy, | Du Dixhuitième Juillet 1682. | Portant que faute par les Marchands Negocians, | qui feront porter des Marchandises ès Isles de l'Ame- | rique & du Canada, pour y estre consommées, de | raporter dans huit mois, Certificats de la Descente d'icelles, au bas de Acquits à Caution que leur seront | fournis, & de faire decharger leurs Soumissions sur | les Registres; Ils demeureront exclus de la décharge | des Droits d'Entrée, & contraints au payement du | Quatruple. | [n. p. 1682.] 4to, pp. 4. 56072

Arrest | du Conseil | d'Estat, | Sa Majesté y estant, | pour le rétablissement de la fabrique | des purs Castors de Canada. | Du 8 Fevrier 1685. | *A Paris.* | *Chez Sebastien Mabre-Cramoisy, Imprimeur* | *du Roy.* | M.DC.LXXXV. | *De l'expres commandement de Sa Majesté.* | 4to, 2 leaves. 56073

Arrest | du Conseil | d'Estat, | Sa Majesté y estant, | pour le rétablissement de la fabrique | des purs Castors de Canada. | Du 12 Avril 1685. | *A Paris,* | *Par Sebastien Mabre-Cramoisy, Imprimeur* | *du Roy.* | M.DC.LXXXV. | *De l'expres commandement de Sa Majesté.* | 4to, pp. 8. 56074

Arrest | du Conseil d'Estat | du Roy, | Qui ordonne que les Droits seront levez & perceus | sur les Castors en Peau & en Poil qui viendront des | Pays Estrangers dans les Ports du Royaume, permis | par les Arrests des 24 Mars 1685. & 25 Janvier 1687. | même dans les vaisseaux qui seront pris par les | Armateurs François. | Du treizième Décembre 1689. | [Colophon:] *De l'imprimerie de Frederic Leonard, Premier Imprimeur du | Roy, & seul pour les Finances* | 1689. | 4to, pp. 4. 56075

Arrest | du Conseil d'Etat | du Roy. | Du 9 Fevrier 1700. | Qui permet à la Colonie du Canada de vendre, trafiquer | & negocier librement tant en France que dans les Païs | Etrangers, tous les Castors provenans | des Traites dudit Païs, | à commencer par ceux de l'année 1699, le tout en payant le quart en espèce de tous lesdits Castors au Fermier du | Domaine d'Occident. | [n. p. 1700.] 4to, pp. 8. 56076

Arrest du Conseil d'Estat du Roy, qui permet aux sieurs Bergier, Boucher, Gautier et de Mantes, d'établir une pêche le long de la côte de l'Acadie et de la Rivière Saint-Jean, et leur accorde plusieurs privilèges. Du dernier jour de Fevrier 1682 *Paris, veuve Saugrain et P. Praust.* 1720. 4to, pp. 3. 56077

Arrêt du Conseil d'Etat du Roi, portant suppression des 24 paquebots établis pour la correspondance avec les colonies françoises et les États-Unis de l'Amérique. Du 5 Juillet 1788. *Paris, Imp. Royale.* 1788. 4to, pp. 6. 56078

See also Vol. I., No. 2103, *and* Vol. III., Nos. 10356–57.

Articles | accordez par | le Roy. | A la Compagnie de la | Nouuelle France. | [n. p. 1628.] 4to, pp. 23. 56079

Au Roy | Raisons qui font voir combien il est important | au Roy & à son Estat, de deffendre ses sujets de la nouuelle France, | dite Canada, contre les inuasions des Iroquois & d'esten- | dre sa protection sur ce nouueau Monde. | [n. p. 1640.] Folio, pp. 3.

See also Vol. III., Nos. 10362–3, *and* [Laval de Montmorency (F. de)], Vol. X.

Av Roy | svr | la Novvelle | France. | [n. p.] 1626. Sm. 8vo, pp. (4), 23. 56081

Avis au Roi sur les Affaires de la Nouvelle France en 1620. [n. p. 1620.] 8vo. 56082

Coppie d'une lettre envoyée de Nouvelle France ou Canada, par le Sier Côbes, gentilhomme poictevin, à un sien amy, en laquelle sont briefvement descrites les merveilles, excellences et richesses du pays, ensemble la façon et mœurs de ceux qui l'habitent, la gloire des François et l'esperance qu'il y a de rendre l'Amerique Chretienne. *Lyon, Leon Savine.* 1609. 8vo, pp. 15.

Declaration | au Roy. | Du vingt-un May 1696. | Qui supprime et declare nuls tous les | Congez et Permissions qui ont esté et seront expediez pour aller en traite chez les | Sauuages au Canada, ... [n. p. 1696.] 4to, pp. 4. 56084

De par le Roy. | Extrait des Registres du Conseil d'Estat. | *Paris, le 2. Iour de Iuin l'an de grace* 1670. Folio, 1 leaf.

Edict | du Roy | pour | l'estabissement | de la Compagnie de la | Nouuelle France | Auec l'Arrest de verification de la Cour | des Aydes de Rouën. | *A Paris.* | *Chez Sebastien Cramoisy Imprimeur* | *ordinaire de la Marine, ruë sainct Iacques aux Cicognes.* | M.DC.XXXIII. | *Auec priuilege dv Roy.* | 8vo, pp. (2), 26. Plate. 56086

Estat General | des debtes passives | de la Compagnie generale | de la Nouuelle France. | [n. p. 1642.] Folio, 32 leaves.

Extraict des Registres | du Conseil Priué du Roy. | [n. p. 1655.] 4to, pp. 4. 56088

Extrait des Registres du Conseil d'Estat. | Sur la Requeste presentée au Roy en son Conseil par les Directeurs et Associez de la Compagnie de la Nouvelle France ... . [Colophon:] *Le Quinzieme Iour de Mars* 1656. [n. p. 1656.] Folio, 2 leaves.

Extrait des Registres du Conseil d'Estat. | "Le Roy ayant par son Arrest du dernier Fevrier 1682, concédé aux Sieurs Bergier, Gaultier, Boucher et autres les terres qu'ils trouveroient propres le long de la coste de l'Acadie et de la Riviere St. Jean" ... . Versailles 3 Mars 1684. [At page 3:] Lettres Patentes Pour la confirmation de l'Establissement de la Pesche sedentaire | de l'Acadie, & extention de la Concession. | Versailles, Avril 1684. 4to, pp. 4. + [*Ibid.*] Folio, pp. 4. 56090

Extrait des Registres | du Conseil d'Estat. | [n. p. 1684.] Folio, 2 leaves. 56091

Le Roy Estant informé par les remonstrances des Directeurs de la Compagnie generalle de la Nouuelle France ... . [n. p. 1653.] 4to, pp. 4. 56092

Nouvelles Annales des Voyages, de la Géographie et de l'Histoire, ou Recueil des Relations originales inédites, communiquées par des voyageurs Français et Étrangers; des Voyages nouveaux traduits de toutes les langues Européennes; ... Publiées par MM.

J. B. Eyriès et Malte-Brun ... . *Paris: Gide Fils.* 1819–70. 208 vols., 8vo. Maps and Plates. BA. 56093

There are six series up to 1866, when the title changes to "Annales des Voyages."

Nouvelles | de | l'Amérique, | ou | le Mercure | Ameriquain. | Où sont contenües trois Histoires véritables | arrivées de nostre Temps. | *A Rouen:* | *Chez François Vaultier.* | M.DC.LXXVIII. 24mo, pp. 267, (1). + *Cologne, chés Jean l'Ingenu.* 1678. 12mo, pp. 248.

A collection of three love-tales. The heroes are buccaneers and filibusters.

Nouvelles des Missions d'Amérique. *See* Vol. X., No. 40710

Nouvelles Idées. *See* [Everett (A. H.)], Vol. VI., No. 23234

Nouvelles Lettres. *See* Vol. X., No. 40704.

Nouvelles Observations sur la Seconde Lettre de Mr. de Pinto, à l'occasion des troubles de l'Amérique Septentrionale. Pour servir de suite aux observations d'un homme impartial sur la première lettre de Mr. *****. *Londres (Holland?)* 1776. 8vo, pp. 60. N. 56095

See "Observations d'un Homme Impartial," *and* Pinto (M.)

Nouvelles Officielles extrêmement importantes arrivées hier a Paris. Extrait d'une Lettre de l'Assemblée Générale de la partie Françoise de Saint Domingue, a l'Assemblée Nationale. *Paris: l'Imprimerie Nationale.* 1790. 8vo, pp. 4. J.C.B. 56096

Nouvelles Questions. *See* Vol. IV., No. 15915, *note.*

NOUVION (Victor de). Extraits des auteurs et voyageurs qui ont écrit sur la Guyane, suivis du catalogue bibliographique de la Guyane. *Paris: Béthune et Plon.* 1844. 8vo, pp. (4), xcii, 616.

The catalogue occupies pp. 579–616, and contains a list and description of 240 works on Guiana.

Nova Britannia: | Offering most | Excellent fruites by Planting in | Virginia. | Exciting all such as be well affected | to further the same. | *London* | *Printed for Samvel Macham, and are to besold* [sic] *at* | *his Shop in Pauls Church-yard, at the* | *Signe of the Bul-head,* | 1609. | 4to, 18 leaves. 56098

Black letter. This title varies slightly from our No. 36284. A reprint forms No. 6 of Force's "Tracts," Vol. I. *See also* No. 36285.

By-Laws of NOVA CESAREA HARMONY LODGE ... . With a History of its Organization ... . *Cincinnati: Printed by J. Ernst.* 1853. 12mo, pp. 184. 56099

Nova Francia. *See* [Lescarbot (M.)], Vol. X., No. 40175.

NOVA SCOTIA (*Bishop of*). Sermon ... before the Governor, Council, and House of Assembly of the Province of Nova Scotia, on the 25th of November, 1787. With an Appendix. *Halifax.* 1787. 4to, pp. 32. N. 56100

See also [Inglis (C.)], Vol. IX., Nos. 34765–69.

NOVA SCOTIA. Abstract of the Scheme of Government so far as it relates to the Grantees for settling the Land lying between Nova Scotia and the Province of Maine. *London.* 1721. Folio.

An Account of the Aborigines of Nova Scotia, called the Micmac Indians. *London: Printed by Luke Howard & Sons.* 1822. 12mo, pp. 11. 56102

An Account of the Colony of Nova Scotia. [n. p. 1751?] 8vo, Half Title, pp. (2), 21. J.C.B. 56103

An Account of the Present State of Nova-Scotia: In Two Letters to a Noble Lord: One from a Gentleman in the Navy lately arrived from thence. The other from a Gentleman who long resided there. Made publick by his Lordship's Desire. *London Printed,* 1756. 8vo, pp. 11, 31. B., J.C.B. 56104

The letters are signed respectively "J. B." and "W. M." *See also* [Hollingsworth (S.)], Vol. VIII., No. 32543.

Account of the Wreck of the Transport Premier, on the Coast of Nova Scotia, and Sufferings of the Crew ... . *London.* 1845. 4to. Plates. 56105

Act for the Relief of Debtors with respect to the Imprisonment of their Persons. *Halifax.* 1752. Folio. 56106

An Act to Amend the Act relating to the Gold Fields. [n. p. 1863.] 8vo, pp. 14. H. 56107

[Acts passed by] the General Assembly of the Province of Nova-Scotia, begun and holden at Halifax, ... June, 1770 ... . [n. p. n. d.] Folio, paging irregular. Continued. H. 56108

Additional Papers on the Nova Scotia Gold Fields, including Messrs. Poole and Campbell's Reports. [n. p. 1861.] Folio, pp. 36. H. 56109

Address, Petition, and Memorial of the Representatives of the Freeholders of Nova Scotia, to the King, on the Tax ... . *Halifax.* 1775. Sm. folio. 56110

Agricultural Exhibition of Nova Scotia. ... At Halifax ... October 5th and 6th, 1853. *Halifax, N. S.* [1853.] 8vo, pp. 24.

Annexation to the United States: is it Desirable? and is it Possible? By "One of the People." *Halifax (N. S.): J. Bowes & Son.* 1868. 8vo, pp. 64. C. 56112

Annual Report of the Common, Superior, Academic, and Normal and Model Schools in Nova Scotia ... 1866. ... *Halifax, N. S.: Printed by A. Grant.* 1867. 8vo, pp. lix, 86. H.

Appendix No. 14. Crown Lands. Crown Land Office, 10th February, 1863. [n. p. n. d.] Folio, pp. 7. H. 56114

Board of Works Report. [*Halifax.* 1864.] Folio, pp. 11.

Comparative Statement of the Value of Merchandize imported at different Ports of Nova Scotia, ... 1854 and 1855. [n. p. n. d.] Folio, pp. 111. H. 56116

Correspondence and Returns relating to the Provincial Railway Expenditure. [n. p. 1857.] Folio, pp. 24. H. 56117

Correspondence On Constitutional Questions. Laid before the Legislature 1860. [n. p. n. d.] Folio, pp. 27. H. 56118

Correspondence relating to the Reciprocity Treaty and Coasting Trade. [n. p. 1864.] Folio, pp. 10, 2. H. 56119

Debate on Resolutions relative to Repeal of the "British North American Act," in the House of Assembly of Nova Scotia, ... 1868. [n. p. n. d.] 8vo, pp. 126. BA. 56120

Debates and Proceedings of the Legislative Council, ... of the Province of Nova Scotia. 1858. ... *Halifax.* 1858. Folio, pp. 108. S. 56121

Delegation to Washington. [n. p. 1865.] Folio, pp. 8. H.

Descriptive Catalogue of Books in the Iron Safe of the Provincial Secretary's Office. Nova Scotia. *Halifax.* 1859. Folio, pp. 17. H. 56123

Descriptive Catalogue of the Nova Scotia Department for the International Exhibition. *Halifax.* 1862. 8vo, pp. 51.

An Essay On the Present State Of the Province of Nova-Scotia, With some Strictures on the Measures pursued by Gov-

ernment from its first Settlement by the English in the Year 1749. [*Halifax.* 1774.] 8vo, pp. 24. J.C.B. 56125

Signed "A Member of Assembly."

Estimate Of Revenue and Expenditure of the Province of Nova Scotia for 1862. [n. p. n. d.] Folio, pp. 23. Continued.

Explanation for the New Map. *See* Nos. 28537 and 35963.

Exposition Universelle de 1867. Catalogue of the Nova Scotian Department with Introduction and Appendices. *Paris.* 1867. 8vo, pp. 66. Plate. 56127

Extract from the Votes of the House of Assembly of the Province of Nova-Scotia. Containing, An Address, Petition and Memorial, To the King's Most Excellent Majesty, The Lords Spiritual and Temporal and The Commons of Great-Britain, In Parliament, assembled. *Boston: Printed and Sold at Draper's Printing Office* ... MDDCCLXXV [*sic* for 1775]. 8vo, pp. 13. M.

A Fair | Representation | of | His Majesty's Right | to | Nova-Scotia or Acadie. | Briefly stated from the | Memorials of the English | Commissaries; | with an | Answer to the Objections | Contained | In the French Memorials, | and | In a Treatise, Entitled, | Discussion Sommaires sur les anciennes | Limites de l'Acadie. | *London: Printed by Edward Owen.* MDCCLVI. 8vo, pp. 64. + *Dublin: Re-printed by Richard James.* M,DCCLVI. 8vo, pp. 48.

"The French Commissioners having, besides their voluminous 'Mémoires,' published a pamphlet, 'in order to prejudice all the courts of Europe in favour of their unjustifiable pretensions,' the English Commissioners thought proper, 'to obviate the wrong impressions that these might create, briefly to recapitulate what had been offered in support of H. M.'s claim, collected from the English memorials.'"—*Monthly Review,* XIV. 365.

Financial Returns. ... 1867. [n. p. n. d.] Folio, pp. 21.

A Form of Prayer, to be used in all the Churches, on May 10, 1793, for a General Fast in the Province of Nova Scotia. *Halifax.* [n. d.] 4to, pp. 6. N. 56131

Form of Prayer, for Fast Day, Nova Scotia, February 23, 1810. *Halifax.* 1810. 4to. N. 56132

A General Description of Nova Scotia, Illustrated by a New and Correct Map. ... *Halifax: Printed at the Royal Acadian School.* 1823. 8vo, pp. (2), 208, (1). + *Halifax: Reprinted for and sold by Clement H. Belcher.* 1825. 8vo, pp. 200. Map. + A New

Edition, printed at the Royal Acadian School. *Halifax: E. Ward.* 1825. 8vo. 56133

A Genuine Account of Nova Scotia: Containing a Description of its Situation, Air, Climate, Soil and its Produce; also Rivers, Bays, Harbours, and Fish, with which they abound in very great Plenty. To which is Added His Majesty's Proposals, as an Encouragement to those who are willing to settle there. *London Printed: And Dublin, Re-printed for Philip Bowes,* MDCCL. 8vo, pp. 16. 56134

A Geographical History of Nova Scotia. Containing an Account of the Situation, Extent and Limits thereof. As also Of the various Struggles between the Two Crowns of England and France for the Possession of that Province. Wherein is shewn, The Importance of it, as well with Regard to our Trade, as to the securing of other Settlements in North America. To which is added, An Accurate Description of the Bays, Harbours, Lakes, and Rivers, the Nature of the Soil, and the Produce of the Country. Together with the Manners and Customs of the Indian Inhabitants. *London: Paul Vaillant.* 1749. 8vo, pp. 110, (1).

Geology of Nova Scotia. *See* Gesner (A.), Nos. 27225–6.

The Gold Seeker's Guide. A Practical Directory in the search for Gold, especially in Nova Scotia; ... *Yarmouth, N. S.: R. Huntington, Printer.* 1862. Sm. 8vo, pp. 48. B. 56136

Histoire géographique de la Nouvelle Ecosse; contenant le détail de sa situation, de son étendue & de ses limites; ainsi que des différens démélés entre l'Angleterre & la France, au sujet de la possession de cette Province. Où l'on en démontre l'importance, tant par rapport à notre commerce, que pour la sûreté de nos autres établissemens dans l'Amérique Septentrionale; avec une exacte Description des Bayes, Portes, Lacs & Rivières; de la Nature & des Productions du Pays, & des Mœurs et Usages des Indiens. *Londres (Paris?)* M.DCC.XLIX. 12mo, pp. vi, 144.

Mr. Rich, quoting from Meusel, suggests that the copies of this work dated 1749, 1754 and 1755, are all the same. It is probably a translation of the "Geographical History," 1749.

Historische und Geographische Beschreibung von Neu-Schottland, darinnen von der Lage, Grösse, Beschaffenheit, Fruchtbarkeit und besondern Eigenschaften des Landes, wie auch von den Sitten und Gewohnheiten der Indianer, und von merckwürdigsten Begebenheiten, so sich zwischen denen Cronen

Franckreich und England seit deren Besitznehmung zugetragen hinlängliche Nachricht ertheilet wird. ... *Franckfurt und Leipzig; bey Heinrich Ludwig Brönner,* 1750. 12mo, pp. (4), 216. Map.

A translation of our No. 56135, *supra.*

The Humble Petition of the House of Representatives of the Province of Nova Scotia, of the Session of ... 1790, to the King's ... Majesty; ... [n. p. n. d.] 4to, pp. iv, 16. BA.

Immigration Report. [n. p. 1866.] Folio, pp. 30. H.

The Importance of Settling and Fortifying Nova Scotia; with a particular Account of the Climate, Soil, and Native Inhabitants of the Country. By a Gentleman lately arrived from that Colony. *London: Scott.* 1751. 8vo. 56141

"We find very little, if any thing, worth notice in this piece."—*Monthly Review,* V. 397.

Index to Journals of the House of Assembly of Nova Scotia. 1758–1830. *Halifax.* [n. d.] 4to. 56142

Journal, and Proceedings of the General Assembly, Of the Province of Nova Scotia. [n. p. 1786.] Folio, pp. 37. Cont'd

Journal and Proceedings of the House of Assembly [of the Province of Nova Scotia. n. p. 1793.] Folio, pp. (2), 68. Continued. H. 56144

Journal and Proceedings of Her Majesty's Legislative Council of the Province of Nova-Scotia. 1839–40. [*Halifax.* 1840.] 4to, pp. 137, Appendices, 80, Index, xv. Continued. H., S.

Journal and Votes of the House of Assembly, For the Province of Nova-Scotia. [n. p. 1779.] Folio, pp. 23. Continued

The Law concerning Public Schools in Nova Scotia. As Amended ... 1866. ... With the Comments and Regulations of the Council of Public Instruction. ... *Halifax, N. S.: Printed by A. Grant.* 1866. 8vo, pp. iv, 64. H. 56147

Laws of the Province of Nova Scotia, from 1758 to 1776. [n. p. n. d.] Folio, pp. (8), 320. B. 56148

Manual of Preliminary Drill, for Nova Scotia Volunteers. *Halifax: Printed by A. Grant.* 1860. 8vo, pp. (6), 36. Plate.

Message of the Lieutenant-Governor [Sir C. Campbell] to the Legislative Council. *Halifax.* 1838. 8vo. 56150

Mines and Minerals. *Halifax.* 1864. Folio, pp. 31. Table.

Minutes of the First Session of the Western Baptist Association of Nova Scotia. Held ... June, 1851. ... *Halifax.* MDCCCLI. 12mo, pp. 23, (1). Continued. H. 56152

Minutes of the Nova Scotia and New Brunswick Baptist Association in Upper Granville. *Halifax.* 1812. 8vo. 56153

See also Vol. I., No. 3239.

Missionaries of Nova Scotia and its Dependencies. *Halifax, N. S.* 1804. 8vo. 56154

The Nova-Scotia Calendar, or an Almanack, For ... 1783 ... . By Metonicus. ... *Halifax, Printed, and Sold by A. Henry and J. Howe.* [n. d.] 8vo, pp. (32). + For 1788. [*Ibid.* n. d.] 8vo, pp. (24). H. 56155

Nova Scotia Gold Fields. *Halifax.* 1861. Folio, pp. 23. + [n. p.] 1861. Folio, pp. 7. H. 56156

Transactions of the NOVA-SCOTIA LITERARY AND SCIENTIFIC SOCIETY, ... 1859. *Halifax, N. S.: The Society.* 1859. 8vo, pp. 49. H. 56157

The Nova-Scotia Magazine and Comprehensive Review of Literature, Politics, and News. Volume I. ... 1789. ... *Halifax: Printed ... by John Howe.* M.DCC.LXXXIX. 8vo, pp. viii, 480, (5). BA. 56158

The first magazine published in Nova Scotia. Edited by John Howe, and continued to five or more volumes.

Proceedings and Transactions of the NOVA SCOTIAN INSTITUTE OF NATURAL SCIENCES of Halifax, Nova Scotia. ... *Halifax.* 1863. 8vo. Continued. 56159

The | Perpetual Acts | of the | General Assemblies | of | His Majesty's Province of | Nova Scotia. | *Halifax, in Nova Scotia:* | *Printed by Robert Fletcher.* M. DCC. LXVII. Folio, pp. (26), 217, (1). + Revised, ... 1783. *Halifax: Printed ... by Anthony Henry.* M. DCC. LXXXIV. Folio, pp. (34), 245. C. 56160

Private and Local Acts of Nova-Scotia. Prepared by William Young, John W. Ritchie, Jonathan M'Cully and Joseph Whidden, Commissioners ... . *Halifax.* 1851. 8vo. S. 56161

Prize List and ... Proceedings of the Provincial Agricultural and Industrial Exhibition of Nova Scotia. 1868. ... *Halifax: Printed by James Bowes & Sons.* 1869. 8vo, pp. 104. B. 56162

Province of N. Scotia. Proceedings ... upon the Convention, ... between his Majesty and the United States ... . *Halifax, Nova-Scotia.* 1819. 8vo, pp. (12), 29, (41). 56163

Railway Extension. Mr. Laurie's Report as to Extension of the Railway from Truro to Pictou. [*Halifax.*] 1859. Folio, pp. 40. BA., S. 56164

Railways. Extension Correspondence. 1864. [n. p. n. d.] Folio, pp. 16. H. 56165

Record Commission. Report of Thomas B. Akins ... . February 24th, 1864. [n. p. n. d.] Folio, pp. 8. H. 56166

Registration Report. ... 1st February, 1867. [n. p. n. d.] Folio, pp. 40. H. 56167

Regulations relating to Public Health. ... 1866. [n. p. n. d.] Folio, pp. 24. 56168

The Report and Statistical Tables of the Superintendent of Education, and Principal of the Normal School, for 1857. *Halifax: Printed by William A. Penny.* [n. d.] 4to, pp. 33 H., S.

Report from Committee on Strait of Canso. [n. p. 1842?] 8vo, pp. 7. H. 56170

Report of an Inspection of the Nova Scotia Railway, 1863. [n. p. n. d.] Folio, pp. 18. 56171

Report of Inspector of Mines. ... 24th January, 1862. [n. p. n. d.] Folio, pp. 8. 56172

Also: Appendix No. 15. Mines. ... 10th February, 1863. [n. p. n. d. Folio, pp. 15.

Report of Nova Scotia Commissioner for the International Exhibition. *Halifax: Printed by T. Chamberlain.* 1864. 8vo, pp. (4), 27, 11. 56173

These reports were edited by Robert G. Haliburton.

Report of Postmaster General, 1866. [n. p. n. d.] Folio, pp. 46. Continued. H. 56174

Report of the Chairman of the Board of Works, for ... 1866. [n. p. n. d.] Folio, pp. 32. 56175

Report of the Chief Commissioner of Mines for the Province of Nova Scotia, for ... 1866. *Halifax, N. S.: Printed by A. Grant.* 1867. 8vo, pp. 88. Continued. H. 56176

Report of the Chief Gold Commissioner for the Province of Nova Scotia, for ... 1862. *Halifax, N. S.: Printed by E. M. McDonald.* 1863. 8vo, pp. 38, (1). H. 56177

Report of the Commissioner of Indian Affairs of Nova Scotia. [n. p.] 1863. Folio. 56178

Also: Appendix No. 16 Indian Affairs. Crown Land Office, 9th February, 1863. [n. p. n. d.] Folio, pp. 7.

Report of the Delegates from the Legislative Council appointed to proceed to England, 25th January, 1835. [n. p. n. d.] 4to, pp. 18. M. 56179

Report of the Department of Mines, ... Province of Nova Scotia, for ... 1872. *Halifax, N. S.* 1873. 8vo, pp. (2), vii, 92.

Report of the International Show Committee of Nova-Scotia. *Halifax, N. S.: Printed by Ritchie & Bulger.* 1863. 8vo, pp. 36

Report of the Secretary of the Board of Statistics on the Census of Nova Scotia, 1861. ... *Halifax, N. S.* 1862. Folio, pp. 298, (1). 56182

Report of the Superintendent of Education on the Schools of Nova Scotia, for 1850. *Halifax.* 1851. 8vo, pp. 128. Continued. 56183

Report of Thomas B. Akins, Commissioner of Public Records. Nova Scotia. *Halifax.* 1858. 4to, pp. 8. Continued. H., S.

Report on the Nova-Scotia Railway; ... . By James Laurie, Civil Engineer. ... 1858. *Halifax: Printed by A. Grant.* 1858. Folio, pp. 53. 56185

Return of Post Routes. [n. p. 1864.] Folio, pp. 8. H.

Rev. Dr. Honeyman's Geological Survey in Nova Scotia and Cape Breton. [n. p. 1864.] Folio, pp. 6. H. 56187

The Revised Statutes of Nova-Scotia. Prepared by William Young, John W. Ritchie, Jonathan McCully, [and] Joseph Whidden. *Halifax: R. Nugent.* 1851. 8vo, pp. xxi, 578. C.

The Revised Statutes of Nova-Scotia. Second Series. Prepared by J. Wilkins, W. A. Henry, J. R. Smith. *Halifax: J. & W. Compton.* 1859. 8vo, pp. xx, 815, (1). + Third Series. [*Ibid.*] 1864. 8vo, pp. xii, 869. B. 56189

Selections from the Public Documents of the Province of Nova Scotia. ... Edited by Thomas B. Akins ... . The Translations from the French by Benj. Curren ... . *Halifax, N. S.: Charles Annaud.* 1869. 8vo, pp. (2), ii, 755, folded leaf. 2 Facsimiles. BA., S. 56190

Standing Orders of the Legislative Council of the Province of Nova-Scotia. *Halifax.* 1847. 12mo. S. 56191

Statutes at Large passed in the several General Assemblies held in Nova Scotia from the First Assembly in 1758 to 1804, inclusive, with complete Index and Abridgment, by R. J. Uniacke. *Halifax.* 1805. 4to. Continued. 56192

The Statutes of Nova Scotia passed in the First and Second Sessions of the General Assembly, ... held ... November 2, 1851, and January 29, 1852. *Halifax.* [1852.] 8vo. Continued.

The Temporary Acts of the General Assemblies of His Majesty's Province of Nova Scotia. *Halifax, in Nova Scotia: Printed ... by Robert Fletcher.* M.DCC.LXVII. Folio, pp. 65. H. + Revised in ... 1783. *Halifax: Printed ... by Anthony Henry.* M.DCC.LXXXIV. Folio, paging irregular. H. 56194

Tenure of Office. ... Government House, Halifax, N. S. 17th September, 1863. [n. p. n. d.] Folio, pp. 12. H. 56195

Various Statements connected with the Trade and Commerce of the Province of Nova Scotia, for ... 1858. [n. p. 1858.] Folio, pp. 139, (1). Continued. 56196

NOVA SCOTIAN, *pseudon.* Remarks upon the Proposed Federation of the Provinces. By a Nova Scotian. [n. p. n. d.] 8vo.

For a reply, see Wetherby (——). *See also* Vol. IV., No. 15426, [Frame (Eliza)], Vol. VI., No. 25420, *and* Vol. X., No. 40604.

NOVANGLUS, *pseudon.* *See* [Adams (J.)], Vol. I., No. 263.

Novellettes of a Traveller. *See* [Nott (Henry Junius)].

Novellista Brasileiro, ou Armazem de Novellas escolhidas, contendo as composições mais afamadas dos melhores auctores modernos da escola romantica sobre novellas, assumptos e recordações dos mais brilhantes factos da historia dos provos, viagens, memorias, anecdotas e charadas; poesias, revista das ultimas modas, theatros, etc. Ornado com 26 finissimas gravuras historicas, de modas e de bordados. *Rio de Janeiro.* 1851. 4to, pp. 208. 56198

Novenas a la Santisima Virgen Maria Madre de Dios, para en sus Milagrosos Santuarios de los Remedios y Guadalupe de Mexico: ... *Madrid.* 1785. 4to. 56199

"Contains the entire history, bibliography, and theology, of the miraculous Guadaloupana of Mexico, from the first appearance of the vision to Juan Diego, the Indian, in 1531. This subject has become one of the stock institutions of Mexico, and its history and influence seem to pervade all others."—STEVENS. *See also* Stevens' "Bibliotheca Historica," Nos. 1295–6.

Novi Avisi di piv lo | chi de l'India et Massime | de Brasil riceuuti quest' anno del MDLIII. | doue chiaramente si puo intendere la con | uersione di molte persone etiam moito | principali nelle terre gia sco | perte & nõ minor s'aspetta | nell' altre che si han | de scoprir & | la mutatione grande che fanno de la lor vita dil che | n'han conseguito oltra la ciuilta & politia di | costumi che Dio operi al presenti euidenti segni & miracoli | in loro. | [Colophon:] *In Roma, per Antonio Blado stampatori Apostolice* MDLIII. *Ad instancia de Messer Battista Genouese de Rossi.* 12mo, 22 leaves. J.C.B.

Contains letters and reports from missionaries in Brazil. For the contents, *see* Leclerc's catalogue, No. 1625.

NOVION (*Citoyen de*). *See* [Sullivan (James)].

Novissima Recopilacion de las Leyes de España, en que se reforma la recopilacion publicada por el Señor Don Felipe II. en al año de 1567: y se incorporan las fragmáticas cédulas, decretos, ordenes y resoluciones y expedidas hasta el de 1804. *Madrid.* 1805–7. 6 vols., folio. C. 56201

Novoe Snstětatneskoe Opnsanie Mineralbnago Kavineta Imperatorskago Volbnago Ekonomiouskago Obchtchestva. [n. p.] 1815. 8vo, pp. 54. M. 56202

Novos Impostos. Lei N. 1507 de 26 de Setembro de 1867 fixa a despeza e orça a receita geral do Imperio para os exercicios de 1867 a 1868 e 1868 a 1869 e dá outras providencias annotada com todos os regulamentos, avisos e circulares publicados até o fim do mez de Abril de 1868. *Rio de Janeiro.* 1868. 8vo, pp. 68.

Ἡ Καινὴ Διαθήκη. Novum Testamentum, juxta exemplar Joannis Millii accuratissime impressum. Editio Prima Americana [curâ Caleb Alexander]. *Wigorniæ, Massachusettensis: Excudebat Isaias Thomas Jun. Singulatim et numerose eo vendita officinæ suæ, April*–1800. 8vo. 56204

"The first edition of the New Testament printed in Greek in this country."—O'CALLAGHAN. Prefixed is a chronological table of the books of the New Testament, by Caleb Alexander. Very rare.

Novvs Orbis Regionvm. *See* [Huttich (J.)], IX. 34100–5.

Now in the Press, And next Week will be Published, &c. [*Philadelphia, about August* 8, 1771.] 4to, 1 leaf. P. 56205

A clever bit of satire on I. Wikoff. *See also* Tim Trimmer.

N[OWEL] (S.) Abraham in Arms, | or, | The First Religious | General | with his | Army, | Engaging in | a War, | for which he had wisely prepared, and by | which not only an eminent | Victory | was obtained, but | a Blessing | gained also. | Delivered in an Artillery-Election-Sermon, June 3, 1678. | By S. N. | *Boston: Printed by John Foster.* 1678. 4to, pp. (4), 19. B., M. 56206

A rare tract. The only published work of "excellent Samuel Nowel, never to be forgotten," the "fighting chaplain" of the Massachusetts troops in Philip's War.

NOWELL (A.) An Almanack of Coelestial Motions for the year of the Christian Epoch 1665. By Alex. Nowell φιλόμουσος. *Cambridge: Printed by Samuel Green.* 1665. 12mo. 56207

NOXON (B. D.) In Memoriam, B. Davis Noxon. [*Syracuse.* 1869.] 8vo, pp. 43. H. 56208

NOXON (J.) Speech of the Hon. James Noxon, of Onondaga, on the Trinity Church Bill. ... *Albany: Weed, Parsons & Company, Printers.* 1857. 8vo, pp. 47. H. 56209

Also: Speech ... against the Repeal of the Metropolitan Police Act. *Albany.* 1858. 8vo, pp. 18. S.

NOYER (*M.*) Forêts Vierges de la Guiane Française, considérées sous le rapport des Produits qu'on peut en retirer pour les Chantiers maritimes de la France, les constructions civiles et les arts, par M. Noyer ... . *Paris: Madame Huzard.* 1827. 8vo, pp. (8), 104. C. 56210

NOYER. Mémoire sur la Guiane Française. Par M. Noyer, Ancien Ingénieur-Géographe, Habitant Propriétaire et Deputé de cette Colonie en France. *Cayenne.* 1824. 8vo, pp. 121.

NOYES (D. J.) A Discourse ... at the Funeral of Rev. Abraham Burnham, D.D., Pembroke, N. H., Sept. 23, 1852. By Rev. Daniel J. Noyes ... . *Concord: McFarland & Jenks.* [1852.] 8vo, pp. 27. B. 56212

NOYES (D.) The History of Norway: comprising a Minute Account of its First Settlement, Town Officers, the Annual Expenditures of the Town, with other Statistical Matters; interspersed with Historical Sketches, Narrative and Anecdote, and

occasional Remarks by the Author. By David Noyes. *Norway: The Author.* 1852. 8vo, pp. 215, (1). BA. 56213

Written, printed and manufactured in the little village of Norway.

NOYES (G. F.) The Bivouac and the Battle-Field; or, Campaign Sketches in Virginia and Maryland. By George F. Noyes, Capt. U. S. Volunteers. *New York: Harper & Brothers.* 1863. 12mo, pp. 339. B. 56214

Also: Oration at the Celebration of the National Independence, by Doubleday's Brigade, at Camp opposite Fredericksburg, Virginia, July 4, 1862. ... *Philadelphia: Crissy & Markley.* 1862. 8vo, pp. 16.

NOYES (G. R.) An Address in support of the ... Temperance Reformation, ... in Brookfield, February 26, 1833. By George R. Noyes. ... *Brookfield: E. Merriam and Co., Printers.* 1833. 12mo, pp. 24. BA. 56215

NOYES (J.) A Genealogical Account of the Noyes Family, together with the Dike Family, and the Fuller and Edson Families. Compiled by Jacob Noyes ... . *Abington: C. G. Easterbrook, Pr.* 1861. 8vo, pp. 13. + *East Abington.* 1869. 8vo, pp. 12.

NOYES (J.) The Federal Arithmetic; ... adapted to the Currency of the United States. By James Noyes. *Exeter: H. Raulet.* 1797. 16mo, pp. 128. C. 56217

NOYES (J.) Moses and Aaron: | Or, The Rights of | Church and State; | Containing two | Disputations. | The former concerning the Church ... . The latter asserts the Sacredness of the persons and autho- | rity of Kings against Sacrilegious Usurpation ... . | By that judicious and faithful Minister of Christ, Mr. | James Noyes, sometimes of Newbury in | New England. | Published by Benj. Woodbridge ... . *London,* | *Printed by T. R. for Edmund Paxton, in Pauls-chain, over* | *against the Castle-Tavern, near Doctors Commons.* 1661. 4to, pp. (14), 96, 24. B. 56218

The "Epistles Dedicatory" to King Charles and "To the Reader" are by Thomas Parker, dated "Newbury, New England, August 6, 1660."

NOYES. A Short Catechism, composed by James Noyes. Late Teacher of the Church of Christ, in Newbury, in New-England. For the use of the Children there. *Boston.* 1694. 16mo. W. + *Boston: Bartholomew Green.* 1714. 16mo. + *Newburyport: Printed by Barrett & March.* 1797. 12mo, pp. 13

NOYES. The Temple Measured: | or, | A brief Survey of the Temple Mystical, | which is the Instituted | Church of Christ. |

Wherein are solidly and modestly discussed, | Most of the material Questions touching the | Constitution and Government of the Visible | Church-Militant here on Earth. | Together with | The Solution of all sorts of Objections ... . By James Noyes ... . *London:* | *Edmund Paxton, and are to be sold at his Shop in Pauls* | *chain* ... . 1647. 4to, pp. (6), 95. B. 56220

Published on occasion of the disputes about the settlement of the church government in New England.

[NOYES (James O.)] A Few Considerations for Reflecting Voters. [*New York.* 1855.] 8vo, pp. 16. H. 56221

[NOYES.] The Mississippi & Mexican Gulf Ship Canal. Connecting the Mississippi River with Lake Borgne, Ten Miles below New Orleans. ... *New Orleans.* 1869. 8vo, pp. 16. Map.

NOYES. Noyes' Illustrated National Guide. Containing Early History of New York, Butler's Poem of "Nothing to Wear," etc., with ... Illustrations ... of old New York Buildings ... . *New York.* 1865. 8vo, pp. 96. 56223

Also: ... Noyes's Illustrated National Railway and Steam Navigation Guide ... *N. Y.: James O. Noyes.* [1857.] 8vo, pp. 16. H.

NOYES (J.) A Discourse, ... in Norfield, May 29th, 1836, By John Noyes, at the close of the Fiftieth Year of his Ministry. *New Haven: Hitchcock & Stafford, Printers.* 1839. 8vo.

NOYES. An Oration delivered in Brattleborough, July 4, 1811. By John Noyes. *Brattleborough.* 1811. 8vo, pp. 13.

NOYES (J. H.) History of American Socialisms. By John Humphrey Noyes. *Philadelphia: J. B. Lippincott & Co.* 1870. 8vo, pp. vi, 678. 56226

NOYES (N.) A Sermon ... at South-Hampton, December 2, 1784. Being ... Thanksgiving throughout the State of New-Hampshire. By Nathaniel Noyes, A.M. ... *Newbury-Port: Printed and sold by John Mycall.* 1785. 8vo, pp. 23. BA. 56227

NOYES (N.) The Temperature of the Weather, at the Summit of Mt. Washington, New Hampshire. ... By Nathaniel Noyes. *Summit House, Mount Washington.* 1854. 12mo, pp. 43. B. + *Portland.* 1854. 12mo. C. 56228

NOYES (N.) New-Englands | Duty and Interest, | To be an | Habitation of Justice, | and | Mountain of Holiness. | Containing |

Doctrine, Caution & Comfort | with | Something relating to the Restaurations, | Reformations and Benedictions, | Promised to the Church and World in | the latter dayes; With grounds of Hope, | that America in General, & New-England | in Particular, may have a Part therein. | Preached to the General Assembly of the Province | of the Massachusetts-Bay, at the | Anniversary Election. | May, 25. 1698. | By Nicholas Noyes, Teacher | of the Church at Salem. | ... | *Boston in New-England.* | *Printed by Bartholomew Green, and John Allen.* | *Printers to the Governour & Council.* 1698. | Sm. 8vo, pp. (12), 99. B., C. 56229

Dedicated to Richard Earl of Bellomont, by John Higginson. Pages 89-99 contain an account of the visit of the Rev. Grindal Rawson and the Rev. Samuel Danforth, in 1698, to the "Plantations of the Indians, within this Province."

Noyes. Poem on the Death of Joseph Green. By Nicholas Noyes ... . *Boston.* 1715. 8vo. 56230

Noyes (*Rev. Mr.*) Letter to a Friend, on the subject of Rev. Mr. Noyes's proposed Examination by the Corporation of Yale College ... . *New-Haven.* 1757. 8vo, pp. 32. M. 56231

Noyes. Sermon delivered by the Rev. Mr. N-O-Y-E-S in 1707, and taken down in Short Hand. [n. p.] 1785. 12mo.

See also Vol. x., No. 40282.

Noyes (T.) An Address ... at ... Needham, before the Military Company of Exempts, ... at their Disbanding, ... April 19, 1815. By Thomas Noyes ... . *Dedham.* 1815. 8vo, pp. 16.

Noyes. Discourse delivered at Fitchburg on the Death of Captain Joseph Fox, February 28, 1797. By Thomas Noyes. *Leominster.* 1797. 8vo. 56234

Noyes. Review of a Pamphlet entitled "A Report of the Evidence in the Case, John Atkins, Appellant, *vs.* Calvin Sanger *& al.* Executors, relative to the Will of the Late Mrs. Badger, of Natick. Also, the Affidavit of the Appellant." ... By Thomas Noyes. ... *Dedham: Printed by H. & W. H. Mann.* [1825.] 8vo, pp. 71. H., M. 56235

Noyes. A Sermon preached at Barrington, R. I. January 29, 1817, at the Installation of the Rev. Luther Wright, over the Church and Congregational Society in that Town. By Thomas Noyes, A.M. ... *Providence, R. I.: Printed by Miller & Hutchens.* 1817. 8vo, pp. 32. BA. 56236

Also: Mr. Noyes' Address, and Mr. Palmer's Sermon, at the Dedication of the New Meeting House, in Dover. [*Dedham.* 1811.] 8vo, pp. 30, (1).—A Sermon, ... in Weymouth, before the Norfolk Auxiliary Society for the Education of Pious Youth ... June 12, 1822. ... *Dedham: B. Field—Printer.* [n. d.] 8vo, pp. 30, (1).—A Sermon ... at Needham, March 12, 1815, ... after the Decease of Mrs. Clarissa Allen ... . *Dedham.* 1815. 8vo, pp. 24.—Two Sermons, delivered in Needham, on the Annual Fast, April 6, 1809. ... *Dedham.* 1809. 8vo, pp. 34. *See also* Vol. I., No. 2701.

Noyes (W. C.) An Address ... before the Graduating Class of the Law Department of Hamilton College, July 16, 1856, By William Curtis Noyes. ... *New York: Baker & Godwin, Printers.* 1856. 8vo, pp. 36. BA. + *Utica, N. Y.* 1856. 8vo. 56237

Noyes. "One Country! One Constitution! One Destiny!" Speeches of William Curtis Noyes, ... and ... [others], at the Great Union War Ratification Meeting held ... in ... New York, October 8th, 1862. Also, the Speech ... of Gen. James S. Wadsworth. [n. p. n. d.] 8vo, pp. 19. 56238

Also: The Argument on the ... Constitutionality of the General Banking Law of ... New-York, ... February 23d and 24th, 1840. ... *New-York.* 1840. 8vo. S.—The Argument ... March 14th, 1854, in the Matter of extending Albany Street to Broadway. ... *New York: Hall, Clayton & Co., ... Printers.* 1854. 8vo, pp. 33.—The "Senator" Case. Argument ... November 17th, 1863 ... . *New York: Wm. C. Bryant & Co., Printers.* 1863. 8vo, pp. 25.—To the Committee on Post-Offices and Post-Roads of the ... Senate of the United States. [n. p. 1864.] 8vo, pp. 6. H.—... United States Treasury Notes a Legal Tender. Argument ... . *New York: Wm. C. Bryant & Co., Printers.* 1863. 8vo, pp. 41. H.

Noyle (I.) An Historical Memoir of the Boston Episcopal Charitable Society. By Isaac Noyle. *Boston: Printed for the Society.* 1840. 8vo, pp. 31. 56239

Conquista de la Nueva Castilla, Poema Eroico, publicado por la primera vez, por Don J. A. Sprecher de Bernegy. *Paris.* 1848. 12mo, pp. (16), 210. 56240

Printed from a manuscript of a contemporary of Pizarro.

Nueva division de la isla de Cuba, en provincias marítimas. [*Habana.*] 1829. 8vo, pp. (1), 24. Map. C. 56241

Nueva España. *See also* Mexico and Nouvelle Espagne.

Aranzel, de los derechos, que deben precibir los Escribanos Mayores de la Gobernacion, y Guerra de esta Nueva-España, y sus Oficiales. *Mexico.* 1746. Folio, pp. 39. 56242

Arreglamento mandado observar con los dos Fragatas que Su Mag. Christianissima suple para passar a la Nueva España. [n. p.] 1707. 4to. 56243

Of this there are three editions.

Carta escrita á un americano sobre la forma de gobierno que conviene establecer en Nueva España. *Madrid: Ibarra.* 1821. 8vo, pp. 12. 56244

Catalogo de los Curatos y Missiones que tiene la Nueva España en cada una de sus Diocesis. *Mexico.* 1813. 4to, pp. 20

Cedula sobre el remate del asiento de la Real Fabrica y Estampa de Naypes de esta Nueva-España. *Mexico.* 1760. Folio, pp. 16. 56246

Comission, Cedulas Reales, y Arancel, despachado para la fundacion, administracion y cobranza del derecho de la Media Anata, perteneciente á Su Magestad, de los Cargos, Plazas Officios de Paz y Guerra, y otras cosas; y los que se proveyeren en su Real Consejo de las Indias etc. Fundose, gobernando el Marques de Cerralvo, Virrey en estos Reynos de la Nueva-España, en 23. de Octubre de 1631. *Mexico.* 1766. Folio, pp. 33, 40, (4), (6). 56247

Conducta del excelentisimo Señor D. Jose Iturrigaray durante su gobierno en Nueva España. Se contesta a la vindicacion que publicó Facundo Lizarza. *Cadiz: Imprenta del Estado mayor.* 1812. 8vo, pp. 135. Portrait. 56248

Constituciones y Ordenanzas para el regimen de la botica del Hospital de los Indios de esta Nueva-España. *Mexico.* 1778. Folio, pp. 6. 56249

Constituciones y Ordenanzas para el regimen, y govierno del Hospital Real y general de los Indios de esta Nueva-España. *Mexico: F. de Zuñiga.* 1778. Folio, pp. (34), 64. 56250

Documentos relativos á las ultimas ocurrencias de Nueva España. *Madrid: Ibarra.* 1821. 4to, pp. 19, 20, 26. 56251

Instruccion para formar una linea ó cordon de quince Presidios sobre las fronteras de las Provincias Internas de este Reino de Nueva-España. *Mexico.* 1771. Folio, pp. 80. 56252

Lamentacion Juridica. *See* Vol. x., No. 38754.

El Lutero. *See* [Martin de Valencia], Vol. XI., No. 44930.

Manifiesto á todas las Naciones, por el Superior Gobierno de Nueva España. *Mexico.* 1820. 4to. 56253

Ordenanza para la formacion de los Autos de visitas y padrones, y tasas de tributarios de N. E. hecha por el Conde de Revilla Gigedo. *Mexico.* 1809. 4to, 21 leaves. 56254

Ordenanzas de la Real Renta de los Naypes, para esta Reyno de Nueva-España, y Provincias de sú comprehension: que se administra de cuenta de S. M. *Mexico, J. A. de Hogal.* 1768. Folio, pp. 35. + *Reimpresas en Mexico.* 1787. 4to, pp. 30, 11.

Ordenanzas de la Real Renta de la Polvora, para este Reyno de Nueva España. *Mexico.* 1787. Folio, pp. 73. 56256

Ordenanzas de la Real Renta del Tabaco, para este Reyno de Nueva-España: que se administra de cuenta de S. M. *Mexico: J. A. de Hogal.* 1768. Folio, pp. 86. 56257

Ordenanzas del Consulado de la Universidad de los Mercaderes de esta Nueva-España, impressas ... año de 1636, y reimpressas ... en el de 1772. *Mexico.* 1772. Folio, pp. 66. 56258

Real Ordenanza para el establecimiento é instruccion de Intendentes de exército y provincia en el reino de la Nueva-España. De Orden de su Magestad. *Madrid. Año de* 1786. Folio, pp. (2), lx, 410. 56259

Usually followed by our No. 26482. This body of laws, relating to the government of Mexico and its provinces, is of the highest importance to the student of Mexican colonial history.

Reales Ordenanzas para la direccion, Régimen y Gobierno del Importante cuerpo de la Mineria de Nueva-España, y de su Real Tribunal General. De Orden de su Magestad. *Madrid. Año de* 1783. Folio, pp. (4), xlvi, 214. Frontispiece. C. + *Lima, casa Real de los niños huerfanos.* 1786. 4to, pp. lxxix, vii, 269. + *Reimpresa en Santiago de Chile.* 1833. Folio. 56260

A rare and valuable compendium of the old mining laws and mineral customs, printed only for the use of the parties concerned, and prepared by Josef de Galvez. A fine engraving of the Spanish arms precedes the title-page of the Madrid edition.

Recopilacion Sumaria de todos los Autos accordados de la Real Audiencia y Sala del Crimen de esta Nueva España, y Providencias de superior Gobierno; de varias Reales Cédulas y Ordenes que despues de publiesda la Recopilacion de Indias han podido recogerse asi de las dirigidas á la misma Audiencia ó Gobierno ... Por Eusebio Bentura Belleña. *Mexico, Don Felipe de Zuñiga y Ontiveros.* 1787. 2 vols., folio. 56261

Of the highest rarity.

Reglamento, e instruccion para los Presidios que se han de formar en la linea de frontera de la Nueva España. Resuelto por el Rey N. S. en cedula de 10 de Septiembre de 1772. *Madrid.* 1772. 4to, pp. 122. + *Reimpresso en Mexico.* 1773. Folio. + *Madrid.* 1822. 4to. + *Mexico.* 1834. Folio, pp. 30. 56262

Reglamento para el gobierno del Monte-Pio de viudas, y pupilos de ministros de audiencias, del virreynato de Nueva España, resuelto el 20. de Febrero de 1765. *Mexico.* 1781. 4to.

Reglamento y Ordenanzas que con Adiciones que se expressan, manda sú Magestad observar para el Govierno y Administracion del Ramo de Reales Tributos, en las Provincias Virreynato de Nueva-España. *Mexico.* 1771. Folio, pp. 66. 56264

Al Rey Nuestro Senor. Satisfacion al memorial de los Religiosos de la Compañia del nombre de Jesus de la Nueva España. Por la Dignidad Episcopal de la Puebla de los Angeles ... . [n. p.] 1652. Folio. 56265

Nueva Granada. *See also* New Granada.

Almanacque nacional o Guia de forasteros de la Nueva Granada, para el año de MDCCCXXXVIII. *Bogota.* 1837. 16mo, pp. 198. 56266

Catalogo de las Obras ... existentes en la biblioteca nacional, ... *Bogotá: Imprenta del Estado.* 1855-57. 5 parts, 8vo. C.

Codigo de Comercio (de 1° de junio de 1853). [*Bogotá.* 1853.] 8vo, pp. clxxx, (28). C. 56268

Comentario o anotacion de las leyes que contiene el libro titulado "Recopilacion de leyes de la Nueva Granada," i de las sancionadas despues desde 1845 a 1852, inclusives. Por M. E. A[cevedo]. *Bogota: Imprenta del Neo-Granadino.* 1853. 12mo, pp. (2), 112. C. 56269

Comission y poder general del Rey ... dado al Señor Dotor Antonio Gonzalez ... para la visita de la Audiencia y distrito del Nueuo Reyno de Granada, cõ algunas de las cedulas ẽ instruciones, assi para ella, como para arbitrios q̃ se assentaron ... . [*Madrid.* 16—.] Folio, 10 leaves. 56270

Los Conservadores quieren perder la Republica. [*Bogota:*] *Imprenta del Neo-Granadino.* 1852. 8vo, pp. 24. H. 56271

Constitucion Politica de la Nueva Granada. Sancionada El Año de 1853. Segunda edicion. *Bogota. Imprenta de Echeverria Hermanos.* 1853. 12mo, pp. 48. 56272

Disertacion sobre el decreto de Tuicion ... en la Republica de la Nueva Granada ... *Paris.* 1861. 8vo, pp. (2), 24. 56273

Esposicion que el Ministro Secretario de Estado en el despacho del interior y justicia del Gobierno de la Republica presenta a la Convencion Granadina de 1831, sobre los negocios de su departamento. *Bogota.* 1831. Sm. 4to, pp. 42. 56274

Also: Esposicion del Secretario de Estado, en el despacho del interior y relaciones esteriores del Gobierno de la Nueva Granada, al Congreso Constitucional del año de 1838, sobre el curso i estado de los negocios de su departamento. *Bogota.* 1838. Sm. 4to, pp. 74 7 Tables.—Esposicion del Secretario de relaciones esteriores de la Nueva Granada al Congreso de 1858. *Bogota.* 1858. 4to.—Esposicion que el Ministro Secretario de Estado en el despacho de relaciones esteriores del Gobierno de la Republica, presenta a la Convencion Granadina de 1831, sobre los negocios de su departamento. *Bogota.* 1831. Sm. 4to, pp. 12.—Esposicion que el Secretario del Interior i relaciones esteriores del Gobierno de la Nueva Granada, hace al Congreso Constitucional del año de 1833, sobre los negocios de su departamento. *Bogota.* 1833. 8vo, pp. 83.—Esposicion que presenta a las camaras legislativas de la Nueva Granada en 1836, el Secretario de Guerra i Marina. *Bogota.* 1836. 8vo, pp. 26.

Estadística Jeneral de la Nueva Granada, que conforme al decreto ejecutivo de 18 de Diciembre de 1846. ... Parte primera: poblacion e instituciones. [*Bogota:*] *Imprenta de J. A. Cualla.* 1848. Folio, pp. 231, (1). B. 56275

El General Simon Bolivar en la campaña de la Nueva Granada de 1819. Relacion escrita por un Granadino, que en calidad de aventurero y unido al Estado Mayor del Exercito Libertador, tubo el honor de presenciarla hasta su conclusion. *Santafé.* 1820. 8vo, pp. 21. 56276

Informe del Secretario de Relaciones esteriores [Eusebio Borrero] y mejoras internas de la Nueva Granada, al Congreso Constitucional de 1846. *Bogota: Jose A. Cualla.* 1846. Rl. 8vo, pp. 15. 17 Tables. 56277

Also: Informe que el Secretario de Estado del despacho de Gobierno de la Nueva Granada dirije al Congreso de 1858. *Bogota.* 1858. 4to, pp. 32.—Informe que el Secretario de Guerra de la Nueva Granada dirija al Congreso de 1858. *Bogota.* 1858. 4to, pp. 52.

Jeografia fisica i politica de las provincias de la Nueva Granada. Por la Comision Corografica. Provincias del Socorro, Velez, Tunja i Tundama. *Bogotá: Imprenta del Estado.* 1856. 8vo, pp. (2), 363. C. 56278

Lei sobre policia jeneral, espedida por el Congreso de la Nueva Granada en sus sesiones de 1841. *Bogota: Imprenta del Estado.* 1841. 8vo, pp. 24, (2). C. 56279

Leyes de la Republica de Colombia. *Bogotá.* 1821. 4to. Continued. 56280

After the year 1827 the title was changed to "Coleccion de las leyes i decretos de la Nueva Granada."

Leyes i Decretos espedidos por el Congreso Constitucional de la Nueva Granada en 1849, 1853-1857. Edicio oficial. *Bogota: Imprenta de Estado.* 1857. 6 vols., 8vo. C. 56281

El maestro fr. Martin de Cañizares de la orden de S. Agustin, difinidor, y procurador general de la Prouincia del Nuevo Reyno en Indias, con fr. Franc. de la Resurreccion, Descalzo de la dicha orden. Excepciones para no dever admitir a fr. Franc. de la Resurreciõ, en el pleito que pretende introduzir ante su M. en su Real consejo de Indias, contra la Prouincia del Nueuo Reyno de Granada. [*Madrid, about* 1643.] Folio, 4 leaves. 56282

La Nueva Granada al empezar el año de 1836. *Bogota.* 1835. 8vo, pp. 20. 56283

Nueva Granada i los Estados-Unidos de America. Final controversia diplomatica con relacion á los sucesos de Panama, del dia 15 de abril de 1856. *Bogota: Imprenta del Estado.* 1857. Sm. folio, pp. 87. C. 56284

Proyecto de Codigo de Instruccion Publica para el estado de la Nueva-Granada. *Bogotá: Ayarza.* [1834.] 4to. 56285

Recopilacion de Leyes de la Nueva Granada. Formada i publicada en cumplimiento de la lei de 4 de mayo de 1843, i por comision del poder ejecutivo por Lino de Pombo ... . *Bogotá: V. Martinez.* 1845. Folio, pp. (4), xxvi, 541. C. 56286

Relaciones exteriores de la Nueva Granada. *Bogota.* 1838. 8vo. 56287

Nueva Recopilacion. Las Leyes de Recopilacion; y los autos acordados, por el orden de titulos de las leyes de recopilacion. *Madrid.* 1772. 3 vols., folio. + Que contiene el Indice general de ellas ... . *Madrid.* 1776-7. 7 vols., 8vo. C. 56288

Nueva York. *See* Vol. VII. 29152, *and* Vol. XIII. 54300.

Nuevas Reflexiones sobre la Cuestion Franco-Mexicana. Folleto publicado en Paris, el 30 de setiembre de 1862, por suplemento al Correo de ultramar por Justus Strictus Veritas. *Mexico: V. G. Torres.* 1862. 16mo, pp. 192. C. 56289

Nuevitas. Cuestion de utilidad del ferro-carril de Nuevitas a Puerto-Principe por el lugareño. *Puerto-Principe: Imprenta de Gobierno.* 1845. 8vo, pp. 13. B. 56290

Also: Informe de la comision del camino de Nuevitas. *Puerto-Principe.* 1836. *Imprenta de Gobierno.* 8vo, pp. 38. B.

Nuevo Almaden. Algunas Declaraciones en el asunto de Nuevo Almaden en la Alta California. *Mexico.* 1859. 8vo, pp. 36. 56291

Nuevo Arancel de capturas aprobado por S. M. en Real Orden expedida en S. Lorenzo con fecha 21 de Diciembre de 1796. *Habana: Imprenta de la Capitania general.* [1797.] 8vo, pp. 18.

Nuevo Assiento, que de orden de el rey, ha celebrado el Señor Don Geronimo de Sola y Fuente, con el gremio de mineros administradores de la real mina de la Villa Rica de Oropeza de Guancanelica. *Lima.* 1745. Folio. C. 56293

Nuevo donativo [para la persecucion de los piratas. *Habana.*] 1814. 8vo, pp. 3. B. 56294

Nuevo Escribano Instruido. 3ª edicion, aumentada y corregida con arreglo á las ultimas disposiciones patrias. *Méjico.* 1852. 4to. C. 56295

Nuevo Febrero Méxicano. Obra completa de jurisprudencia teorico-practica. *México.* 1851-2. 4 vols., 4to. C. 56296

Nuevo Leon. Constitucion Politica del Estado Libre de Nuevo Leon, sancionada en 5 de Marzo de 1825. [n. p.:] *Imprenta de D. Mariano Ontiveros.* [n. d.] 8vo, pp. 88. 56297

La Contre-Guerilla française sur les hauts plateaux et dans l'État de Nuevo-Leon [1865]. *Versailles.* 1871. 8vo. 56298

El Nuevo Mundo Pintoresco. Edicion de tres obras clasicas en tomos separados con un sinnúmero de grabados en cobre y madera, letras de adorno y marmosetes alusivos. *Madrid.* 186–. 8vo. 56299

The three works are Antonio de Solis' "Historia de la conquista," etc., Marmontel's "Incas," and Ercilla's "Araucana."

Nuevo reglamento, que su magestad se ha servido expedir parva gobierno del monte pio militar en España é Indias. *Buenos Aires.* 1800. 4to, pp. viii, 46. + *Mexico.* 1804. 4to, pp. xv, 115. 56300

Nuevo Vocabulario Filosofico Democratico. Indispensable para todos los que deseen entender la Nueva Lengua Revolucionaria. *Mexico.* 1834. 12mo. 56301

"The dry sarcasm of this book is something delightful, when applied to the Mexicans just after their great struggle for independence. These are some of the new words taught and explained to the new-fledged Republicans just emerged from the ignorance and barbarism of the Old Empire into the broad light of the Revolution: ... all explained in a Pickwickian manner."—STEVENS.

NUGATOR, *pseudon.* Nugæ. By Nugator. *Baltimore.* 1844. 24mo. 56302

Poems and prose on Old Virginia, by St. L. L. Carter.

NUGENT (H. P.) A Letter to his Excellency William C. C. Claiborne, Governor of the Territory of Orleans. A Letter to James Brown, Esq. A Defence of the Hon. John Rowan and Daniel Clark against the Slanders of the Tergiversant Redacteur of the Courier. By H. P. Nugent. *New Orleans.* 1808. 4to, pp. 52. C., N. 56303

Also: An Account of the Proceedings had in the Superior Court of ... Orleans, against Thierry & Nugent for Libels and Contempt of Court; with an Account of Nugent's Trial .... *Philadelphia.* 1810. 8vo, pp. 14. BA.

NUGENT (M.) A Journal of a Voyage to, and Residence in the Island of Jamaica, from 1801 to 1805; and of subsequent events in England from 1805 to 1811. By Maria Lady Nugent. *London.* 1839. 2 vols., 8vo, pp. 20, xx, 500, 4 Plates; xx, 515.

Nugent's Nova-Scotia People's Almanac for ... 1856. *Halifax.* [n. d.] 8vo, pp. 107. S. 56305

Nugumouinum Genunugumouat igiu Anishinabeg Anumiajig. *Boston.* 1836. 12mo. 56306

An Ojibwa hymn book.

Les Nuits Peruviennes, ou le Dictionnaire a la mode, dans lequel ou trouve des Anecdotes Curieuses. *A Lima.* 1771. 12mo. 56307

NUIX (G.) Riflessioni | Imparziali | Sopra l'Umanita degli Spagnuoli | nell' Indie | Contr' i pretesi Filosofi e politici | per servire di lume alle storie | de' Signori Raynal e Robertson | del Sig

Abbate | D. Giovanni Nuix. | *In Venezia.* MDCCLXXX. 12mo, pp. 346. 56308

"The author would have rendered a more important and honorable service to the Spaniards, if, instead of endeavouring to disculpate them from calumnies, not entirely without foundation, he had manifested to foreigners the useful measures which the Spanish Ministry were taking to remedy the abuses of their colonial government."—*Sempere Biblioteca.*

NUIX. Reflexîones | Imparciales | sobre la humanidad de los Españoles | en las Indias, | contra los pretendidos filósofos y politicos. | Para ilustrar las historias de MM. Raynal y Robertson. | Escritas en Italiano | por el Abate Don Juan Nuix, | y traducidas con algunos notas Por D. Pedro Varela y Ulloa ... . *Madrid.* MDCCLXXXII. *Por D. Joachin Ibarra.* 4to, pp. (4), lii, 315. C.

A Spanish translation of the previous work. Also on large paper.

NUIX. Reflexiones Imparciales [as before]. Para servir de luz à las historias de los Sres. Raynal y Robertson: de D. Juan de Nuix y de Perpiná, añadidas por el mismo autor y traducidas del idioma Italiano al Español por su hermano D. Josef de Nuix y de Perpiná. *Cervera.* 1783. Sm. 4to, pp. 523. 56310

This second translation was made by the brother of the author, from a copy sent to him for the purpose, with considerable additions.

NULLI (N.), *pseudon.* Microcosmus Philadelphicus. In Two Epistles to My Cousin Tom, in New York. By Notus Nulli, Esq., M.R.I.A. And other Poems. *Philadelphia: The Author.* 1825. 12mo, pp. 60. P. 56311

Nullification. An Appeal to the People on the Question, What shall we do next? *Columbia.* 1832. 12mo, pp. 12. M.

The Book of Nullification. By a Spectator of the Past [C. G. Memminger]. *Charleston.* 1830. 8vo, pp. 31. 56313

A Genuine Book of Nullification, being a True History of Examples of the Recognition ... of that Sovereign State Remedy, from 1798 to the present day. *Charleston.* 1831. 12mo.

Nullification. Should the Nullifiers succeed in their views of Separation, and the Union be in consequence dissolved, the following will be an Appropriate Epitaph. *Philadelphia, Feb.* 22, 1832. 8vo, pp. 4. 56315

Nummi Britannici Historia: or an Historical Account of English Money, from the Conquest to the Uniting of the Kingdoms. *London: W. Meadows.* 1726. 8vo. 56316

Describes New England and Maryland coins.

Nunc Dimittis. *See* [Mather (C.)], Vol. XI., No. 46433.

Catalogue of ... NUNDA LITERARY INSTITUTE, Nunda, N. Y. for ... 1845. *Buffalo: Clement & Faxon.* 1846. 8vo, pp. 16.

NUNES (J. A.) Speech of Col. Joseph A. Nunes, ... before the Union League, of Philadelphia, August 31st, 1869. ... [n. p. n. d.] 8vo, pp. 15. H. 56318

Also: Fast Folks; or, The Early Days of California. A Comedy .... *Philadelphia: Barnard & Jones, Printers.* 1861. 12mo, pp. 95.—"Let us have Peace." A Poem, ... *Philadelphia: King & Baird, Printers.* 1869. 8vo, pp. 9. H.

[NUNES (Joseph Q.)] A Diplomat on Diplomacy. A Reply to Wm. B. Reed. *Philadelphia.* 1863. 8vo. 56319

NUNES (P.) Tratado da Sphera com a Theorica do Sol e da Lua. E ho primeiro liuro da Geographia de Claudio Ptolomeu Alexãdrino. Tirados nouamente de latim em lingoagem pello Doutor Pero Nunes Cosmographo del Rey dõ João ho terceyro deste nome nosso senhor. E acrecẽtados de muitas annotações e figuras perque mays facilmente se podem entender. Item dous tratados q̃ o mesmo Doutor fez sobre a carta de marear. Em os quaes se decrarão todas as principaes duuidas da nauegação. Cõ as tauoas do mouimento do Sol e sua declinação. E o Regimento da altura assi ao meyo dia: como nos outros tempos. Com preuilegio Real. [Colophon:] *Acabouse de emprimir a presente obra na muyto nobre e leal cidade de Lixboa per Germão Galharde emprimidor. Ao primeiro dia do mes de Dezembro. De* 1537 *annos.* Folio, 90 leaves. 56320

NUÑEZ DE CASTRO (A.) Historia Ecclesiastica, y seglar de ... Gvadalaxara. Por Alonzo Nuñez de Castro. *Madrid. P. de Val.* 1653. Folio, pp. (7), 406, (10). 56321

Salazar y Castro ("Bib. Gen. Española") states that this was written by Hernando Pecha. This statement is accepted by Muñoz y Romero, Ferrer del Rio, and Backer.

NUÑEZ DE HARO Y PERALTA (A.) Contestaciones que para el mejor govierno y direccion de la real casa de S. Joseph de Niños Expositos de Mexico formó D. Alonso Nuñez de Haro, Arzobispo. . *Mexico.* 1774. Folio, pp. 56, (10). 56322

NUÑEZ DE HARO Y PERALTA. Nos el Dr. D. Alonso Nuñez de Haro, y Peralta, por la Gracia de Dios, y de la Santa Sede Apóstolica, Arzobispo de Mégico, del Consejo de su Magestad ... [*Mexico.* n. d.] Folio, broadside in 2 sheets. 56323

NUÑEZ DE HARO Y PERALTA. Al Rector, ... y directores del Real Colegio Seminario de Instruccion, de retiro voluntario, y

correccion de Tepotzotlan ... . [*Mexico.* 1776.] Sm. 4to, pp. 266, (2). C. 56324

Also: Carta Pastoral dirige a todos sus Amados Diocesanos ... . *Mexico.* 17—. 8vo, pp. (2), 186.—Constituciones que Don Alonso Nuñez de Haro y Peralta, Arzobispo de Mexico, formò para el mejor régimen y govierno del Real Colegio Seminario de Instruccion, fundado en el pueblo de Tepotzotlan. *En Mexico, Zuñiga y Ontiveros.* 1777. 4to, pp. (6), 87.—Oracion Fúnebre del Señor D. Alonso Nuñez de Haro y Peralta del Consejo de S. M. Arzobispo de México ... . *México.* 1800. 4to. *See also* Vol. IV., No. 16064, *and* Haro y Peralta, Vol. VIII., No. 30411.

NUÑEZ (Alvar). *See* Cabeça de Vaca, Vol. III. 9767–71.

NUNEZ (Antonio). Distribucion de las Obras ordinarias y extraordinarias del Dia, para hazerlas perfectamente conforme al Estado de las Señoras Religiosas, instruida con doze maximas substanciales, para la Vida Regular y Espiritual, que deben seguir. Sale a luz a expensas de la Señoras Religiosas del Convento Real de Jesus Maria. *En Mexico, por la Viuda de Miguel de Ribera Calderon.* 1712. 4to, pp. (12), 160, (1). 56325

NUÑEZ CASTANO (Diego). Breve compendivm | Hostivm Haere- | ticorvm Olandensivm | aduentum in Valdiuian, explorato- | rem missum, & narrationem eius, | fugam illorum cum pacto rede- | un | di: prouidas dispositiones Prorregis: | Classim expeditam ad conditum e- | ius cum rebus necessarijs, | & alia continens. | Gvbernante Exc. D.D. | Petro à Toleto & Ley va Prorrege. | Regnante Philippo IIII. | Hispaniarum Rege. | Stvdio, et Labore | Didaci Nuñes Castaño Presbyteri. | *Limæ, Anno* 1645. | 12mo, 36 leaves

NUÑEZ DE LA VEGA (F.) Cartas pastorales del illmo. fray Francisco Nuñez de la Vega, del orden de Predicadores, obispo de Chiapa, y Soconusco, del consejo de su Magestad ... . *Mexico, doña Maria de Benavides.* 1694. 4to, 46 and 55 leaves. 56327

NUÑEZ DE LA VEGA. Constituciones diaecesanas del obispado de Chiapa, hechas y ordenadas por Sa. Ill. el Sr. Maestro D. Fr. Francisco Nuñez de la Vega, ... obispo de Ciudad Real de Chiapa y Soconusco, ... año de 1692. *En Roma, año de* 1702, *En la Nueva Imprenta ... de Caietano Zenobi. En la Curia Innocenciana.* Folio, pp. (8), 164, 142, (30). 56328

A volume of great rarity, relating chiefly to the country of the Chiapas. *See* Brasseur de Bourbourg, Bibliothèque, 110. Nuñez was born in Carthagena, West Indies, became Bishop of Chiapas in 1683, and died in 1703. *See* Leclerc, No. 1218.

NUÑEZ (F.) Oracion Fúnebre que con motivo de las Solemnes Exequias celebradas por la buena Memorial de Sr. D. Juan de Antonio del Castillo y Llata, Conde de Sierragorda. Por

Francisco Nuñez, Padre de la Santa Provincia de Michoacan. *Mexico.* 1818. 4to. 56329

Also: Oracion Funebre que en las Solemnes Exéquias celebradas en el Convento de Santa Clara de Queretaro, por las almas de los Valerosos Españoles 5 Jan. 1809. *Mexico.* [1809.] 4to.

[NUÑEZ (Ignacio).] An Account, Historical, Political, and Statistical, of the United Provinces of Rio de la Plata: with an Appendix, concerning the Usurpation of Monte Video by the Portuguese and Brazilian Governments. Translated from the Spanish. *London: R. Ackerman.* 1825. 8vo, pp. x, (1), 345, (1). Map and Plan. B., S. 56330

NUÑEZ. Efemérides Americanas desde el descubrimiento del Rio de la Plata, por D. Juan Diaz de Solis. Escritas por D. Ignacio Nuñez. *Buenos Aires.* 1857. 4to, pp. 82. 56331

NUÑEZ. Esquisses Historiques, Politiques et Statistiques de Buenos-Ayres, des autres Provinces Unies du Rio de la Plata, et de la République de Bolivar, avec un appendice sur l'usurpation de Montévidéo par les gouvernemens portugais et brésilien, et sur la guerre qui l'a suivie. Par M. Ignacio Nuñez ... . Traduit de l'Espagnol, avec des Notes et des Additions, par M. Varaigne. *Paris: Ponthieu.* 1826. 8vo, pp. viii, 556. Map. H. 56332

[NUÑEZ.] Noticias Historicas, Politicas, y Estadisticas, de las Provincias Unidas del Rio de la Plata, con un Apendice sobre la usurpacion de Montevideo por los gobiernos Portugues y Brasilero. *Londres: R. Ackerman.* 1825. 8vo, pp. xi, 323. Map and Plan.

NUÑEZ. Noticias Historicas de la Republica Argentina. Obra postuma de D. Ignacio Nuñez. Dedicado al Sr. Dr. Valentin Alsina, por el hijo del autor, D. Julio Nuñez. *Buenos-Aires.* 1857. 4to, pp. viii, 198. 56334

NUÑEZ (Jos. Philippus de Villavicencio). Oratio en Honras de D. P. Alvarez de Abreu ... . *Mexico.* 1765. 4to. Plate.

[NUÑEZ (Juan).] Chronica del muy esclavescido principe y Rey don Alfonso el Onzeno. *Valladolid.* 1551. Folio.

NUÑEZ DE LA PEÑA (Juan). Conqvista y antigvedades de las Islas de la Gran Canaria, y sv descripcion. Con mvchas advertencias de sus Priuilegios, Conquistadores, Pobladores, y otras particularidades en la muy poderosa Isla de Thenerife. Dirigido a la milagrosa imagen de nuestra Señora de Candelaria. ...

Madrid: Imprenta real, acosta de Florian Anisson. 1676. 4to, pp. (16), 560, Table, (4). 56337

Viera blames this author, a native of Teneriffe, for having written his history before making acquaintance with the MS. of Abreu, and the French account of Bethencourt, but admits that it is a "rico tesoro de noticias para la historia de Canarias," and describes it as "el libro en que dejó asegurada su memoria." He also says, "The islands are indebted to the immense labours of Nuñez de la Peña for different notices which already perhaps would have been forgotten."

NUNEZ (Pedro). *See* Nunes (P.), No. 56320, *supra.*

NUNEZ DE BALBOA (Vasco). Carta del Rey Catholico a Pedra Arias Davila Governador de Castilla del Oro, por la qual se conocera si pudo cortar la cabeça a su yerno el Adelantado Basco Nunez de Balboa, o a lo menos sy como lo dize la Historia Pontifical deuiera otorgalle apelacion. [*Madrid, about* 1600.] Folio, pp. 3. 56338

Of the highest rarity and interest. A letter, dated the 27th September, 1514, from Valladolid, appointing Vasco Nunez de Balboa, the discoverer of the Pacific, Adelantado of the Coast of the South Sea, which he discovered, and to the government of Panama and Coyba. After this letter there are notices of several other letters of the king, in which he speaks highly of the services of the said Vasco Nunez, and also respecting his residencia. *See also* Vol. X., No. 41604.

Der nunmehro in der Neuen Welt. *See* Vol. III., No. 10975.

NUNN (J.) Narrative of the Wreck of the Favourite on the Island of Desolation, with the Adventures, Sufferings, &c., of John Nunn, and an Account of the Island and its Whale and Seal Fisheries. *London: W. E. Painter.* 1850. 12mo. Chart.

Nuove lirichi. *See* [Colombo (C.)], Vol. IV., No. 14660.

Nuovi Avisi | dell' Indie di | Portogallo, | Riceuuti dalli Reuerendi Padri della compa | gnia di Giesu, tradotti dalla lingua | Spagnuola nell' Italiana. | Terza parte. | Con priuilegio del sommo Pontefice, & dell' Il- | lustrissimo Senato Veneto per anni XX. | [Colophon:] *In Venetia per Michele Tramezzino.* MD.LXII. 12mo, 7 prel. leaves, Text, 316 leaves. J.C.B. 56340

A portion of these letters relate to Brazil. The dedication is signed by the publisher. A work with a similar title was published, *Venetia, Tramezzino,* 1556–1565, 4 vols., small 8vo, of which Vol. I. relates to Brazil.

Second Annual Report of the NURSERY for the Children of Poor Women in New York. *New-York: Henry Ludwig, Printer.* 1856. 18mo, pp. 18. Continued. H. 56341

[NUSDORFERS (B.)] Beytrag zur Geschichte von Paraguay, und den Missionen der Jesuiten daselbst, in einem Sendschreiben

des P. Bernhard Nusdorfers ... . *Frankfurt und Leipzig.* 1768. 16mo, pp. 72. H. 56342

Nutak, eller det Nye Testamente, oversat i det Grönlandske Sprog, med Forklaringer, Paralleler, og udförlige Summarier, af Paul Egede. *Kiöbenhavn: Trykt paa Missionens Bekostning, af Gerhard Giese Salikath.* 1766. 8vo, pp. (24), 1000, (8) + *Kiöbenhavnime: C. F. Schubart.* 1799. 8vo, pp. 1072. 56343

The first and second editions of the New Testament in the Esquimau tongue. *See also* Vol. VI., Nos. 22032 and 22875.

Nuts for Future Historians. *See* Smith (H. W.)

... The Nutshell. The System of American Slavery "Tested by Scripture" ... . By a Layman ... . *New York: The Author.* 1862. 16mo, pp. 72. B., H. 56344

NUTT (——). History of Commodore Nutt. *New York.* 1862. 16mo. 56345

NUTT (C.) Baccalaureate Sermon [at] ... Indiana State University ... June 29, 1862. By Rev. Cyrus Nutt, D.D. ... *Cincinnati: R. P. Thompson, Printer.* 1862. 8vo, pp. 20. B.

NUTTALL (T.) The Genera of North American Plants, and A Catalogue of the Species, to the Year 1817. By Thomas Nuttall, F.L.S. ... *Philadelphia: Printed for the Author by D. Heartt.* 1818. 2 vols., 12mo, pp. viii, 312; 254, 10, (4.) H.

NUTTALL. A Journal of Travels into the Arkansa Territory, during the year 1819. With occasional Observations on the Manners of the Aborigines. ... Illustrated by a Map and other Engravings. By Thomas Nuttall ... . *Philadelphia: Thos. H. Palmer.* 1821. 8vo, pp. xii, 9–296. 5 Plates and Map. C., H.

The naturalist records in almost every chapter some incidents of his personal intercourse with the Chickasaw, Cherokee, and Osage Indians, then inhabiting the territory he explored. "Mr. Nuttall's knowledge of natural history, renders his travels highly interesting to scientific readers."—RICH. Ludewig says "Reprinted Boston, 1834, 12mo," which edition I have not seen, and I do not think it exists. *See also* "North American Review," XVI. 59.

NUTTALL. A Manual of the Ornithology of the United States and of Canada. By Thomas Nuttall ... . The Land Birds. *Cambridge.* M DCCC XXXII. 12mo, pp. viii, 683. H. + Second Edition, with Additions. ... *Boston: Hilliard, Gray and Company.* MDCCCXL. 12mo, pp. vi, 683. H. 56349

NUTTALL. A Manual of the Ornithology of the United States and of Canada. By Thomas Nuttall ... . The Water

Birds. *Boston: Hilliard, Gray and Company.* M DCCC XXXIV. 12mo, pp. vii, 627. C., H. 56350

Mr. Nuttall is styled by Mr. Audubon ("Ornithological Biography," II. 427,) "The learned Nuttall, who has been able to make new discoveries by his indefatigable and enthusiastic devotion to a science, in a country where Wilson, Bonaparte, Bachman, Pickering, Cooper, Say, and others had already exerted themselves to the utmost to complete its diversified and interesting Fauna." *See also* "N A. Rev.," XVI. 59-76.

NUTTALL. The North American Sylva; or, A Description of the Forest Trees of the United States, Canada, and Nova Scotia, not described in the work of F. Andrew Michaux, and containing all the Forest Trees discovered in the Rocky Mountains, the Territory of Oregon, down to the shores of the Pacific, and into the confines of California, as well as in various parts of the United States. ... By Thomas Nuttall, F.L.S. ... *Philadelphia: T. Dobson.* 1842–1849. 3 vols., imp. 8vo, pp. (4), xii, 19*–24*, 136; (4), 123; (4), 148, (4). 122 Plates. B. 56351

This is the first and best edition. It has been frequently reprinted: *Philadelphia,* 1852, 1853, 1857, 1859, 1865, and more recently with other dates. It is now issued only as a part of Michaux's "Sylva." *See also* Michaux (F. A.), Vol. XII., No. 48695. Also: An Introduction to Systematic Physiological Botany. ... *Boston.* 1827. 8vo. + *Cambridge: Hilliard and Brown.* 1827. 8vo, pp. xi, 360. Plates. + Second Edition, with Additions. [*Ibid.*] 1830. 12mo, pp. xi, 363. Plates. H.

NUTTING (R.) Memoirs of Mrs. Emily Egerton. By Rufus Nutting. *Boston: Perkins & Marvin.* 1832. 18mo, pp. 180. Plate. C. 56352

Nützliche Anweisung oder Beyhülfe vor die Teutschen um Englisch zu lernen. Nebst einer Grammatic vor diejenigen. *Germantaun: C. Saur.* 1751. 8vo, pp. (4), 288. 56353

An English vocabulary and grammar, in the German language. Apparently compiled by (the younger) Saur. The preface (pp. 2) is signed "C. S." A noteworthy and a very scarce book.

Nya Sverige. *See* Vol. II., No. 8103.

[NYE (G.)] Some casual Papers upon the "Alabama" and her Commander. [n. p. 1864.] Folio, pp. 6. 56354

NYE (J. W.) ... Speech of Hon. James W. Nye ... Feb. 28, 1866 [on Reconstruction]. [n. p. n. d.] 8vo, pp. 24. B. + [*Ibid.*] Jan. 24, 1868. 56355

Also: Speech ... on Executive Appointments and Removals; ... May 9 and 10, 1866. *Washington.* 1866. 8vo, pp. 16. H.

NYE (J.) The Law of God, against all Irreligious Associations; ... A Sermon Preached in Windsor (Vt.), October 8th, A. L. 5811; before the Grand Lodge of the State. By Reverend Brother Jonathan Nye, A.M. ... *Keene.* 1811. 8vo, pp. 15. W.

Nye (Philip). The Lawfulnes of Hearing the Publick Ministers of the Church of England Proved. ... *London: Printed for Jonathan Robinson.* 1683. 4to, pp. (4), 40. 56357

The second treatise (pp. 13–40) is by the Rev. John Robinson; reprinted from the first (Leyden) edition, of 1634.

Nye (W. F.) La Sonora, étendue, population, climat, produits du sol, mines, tribus indiennes, etc. Ouvrage traduit de l'anglais et accompagné de notes, suivie d'une notice sanitaire et géographique sur la ville et le port de Panama, par A. de Zeltner. *Paris.* 1864. 8vo, pp. 90. 56358

Nye unbekande Lande. *See* [Montalboddo (F.)], xii. 50057.

Nyenborgh (Johan van). Hof-Stede met desselfs andere Bedenckingen, Gedichten en Historien. ... *Groningen.* 1659. 4to, pp. 192, 29, and Register. Plate and Portrait. 56359

Relates partly to the West India Company.

Nyenborgh. Weeckwercken der ghedenckwaerdighe Historien, Leerghedichten en Spreucken, enz. ... *Groningen.* 1657. 4to. Plates and Portrait. 56360

Among the histories is that of the discovery of New Netherland.

Nylant (P.), *and* Hextor (J. van). Het Schouwtooneel der aertsche Schepselen, afbeeldende allerhande Menschen, Beesten, Vogelen ... . *Amsterdam: W. Doornick.* 1672. 3 vols., 4to. 160 Woodcuts. 56361

This theatre of the earthly creatures contains (pp. 26–41) a description of the inhabitants of America.

Nystrom (J. G.) Informe al Supremo Gobierno, sobre la Expedicion de Chanchamayo. Por Juan Guillermo Nystrom. ... *Lima.* 1869. 4to, pp. 18. 3 Plates. 56362

Nystrom (J. W.) Project for a Tonal System. ... *Philadelphia.* 1862. 8vo. 56363

Die Nywe Testament van ons Herr Jesus Christus ka set over in die Creols Tael en ka giev na die ligt tot dienst van die deen Mission in America. *Copenhagen, van Godiche.* 1781. 8vo, pp. (16), 1,166, (2). + *Barby.* 1802. 8vo, pp. 812, (10). + *Copenhagen: Schultz.* 1818. 8vo, pp. (20), 1,166. 56364

The New Testament in the creole-dutch jargon (often erroneously called creole-danish) spoken by the negroes in the islands of St. Thomas, St. Croix, and St. Jean; not unlike, in its expressions and constructions, to the corrupted English spoken by the negroes in the United States. The edition dated 1818 is erroneously called the second.

O. (A.) *See* Vol. vi., No. 23470.

O. (B. V.) Greto de alarma en los Indios contra los Blancos y Cartas. ... *Mexico.* 1829. 8vo, pp. 4. 56365

O. (D. J. E.) Manuel del abogado americano. ... *Paris: J. Renouard.* 1827. 2 vols., 12mo. 56366

[O. (F.)] The Government is an Effect, not a Cause, of the Situation of Every Country. *Boston.* 1819. 8vo, pp. 31. M.

O. (M. N.) The Canadian Crisis, and Lord Durham's Mission to the North American Colonies: with Remarks, the result of Personal Observation in the Colonies and the United States, on the Remedial Measures to be adopted in the North American Provinces. By M. N. O. *London: Rodwell.* 1838. 8vo, pp. 56. 56368

O. (N.) *See* [Cuoq (A.)], Vol. v., Nos. 17980–1.

O*** (T.) De la nécessité de différer l'expédition de Saint-Domingue. Par Mr. T. O***. *A Paris: Chez L. G. Michaud.* 1814. 16mo, pp. 62. H. 56369

O Auxiliador da Industria Nacional periodico da sociedade auxiliadora dA [*sic*] Industria Nacional sob a redacção e direcção do Dr. F. L. C. Burlamaque ... . *Rio de Janeiro: Typographia de N. Lobo Vianna & Filhos.* 1863. 12mo. 56370

O Brasil visto por Cima. Carta a huma senhora sobre as questões do tempo. *Rio de Janeiro: Typographia do Diario.* 1822. 8vo, pp. 46, (2). 56371

O Brazil agricola, industrial, commercial, scientifico, litterario, e noticioso. *Pernambuco.* 1863. 8vo. Continued. 56372

O. P. Q. *See* [Worth (Gorham A.)]

O Parlamentar. Publica-se nas quartas-feiras e Sabbados. Anno 1. *Rio de Janeiro.* [n. d.] 8vo. 56373

O Patriota Brasileiro. *See* Vol. ii., No. 7613.

O se hace la Guerra de Tejas, o se pierde la Nacion. [A las camaras del congreso nacional.] *Mexico: Lara.* 1845. 12mo, pp. 7. C. 56374

O Tempora. [A Poem.] *Philadelphia: J. B. Lippincott & Co.* 1863. 8vo, pp. 24. 56375

Constitution of the O U A Laws of Arch-Chancery, and Constitution of the Chancery, of the State of New York. ... *New York: Douglass & Colt, Printers.* 1851. Sm. 8vo, pp. 67.

Oajaca. *See* Oaxaca.

Report of the Trustees of Oak Dale Cemetery, to the Mayor and Trustees of the Corporation of Urbana [Ohio] ... and the Address of Rev. James F. Chalfant. *Urbana: Printed by C. B. Flood.* 1856. 8vo, pp. 40. Plan. H. 56377

Oak Hall, or the Glory of Boston. A Poem ... . *Boston.* 1844. 8vo, pp. 45. 56378

Also: Oak Hall Pictorial. ... *Boston.* [1854.] Sq. 8vo, pp. 16. H.

History and Analysis of ... Oak Orchard Acid Mineral Springs ... . *Buffalo: Jewett, Thomas & Co.* 1850. 16mo, pp. 23.

Oakes (J.) Matters of Josiah Oakes, Sen'r: Four Years wrongfully imprisoned in the McLean Asylum, through an Illegal Guardianship ... containing a full Account of the Hearing before the Supreme Court of Lowell ... . *Boston.* [1860?] 8vo, pp. 24.

[Oakes (U.)] Astronomical Calculations. *See* Vol. xi. 47210

[Oakes.] En Elegie | upon | The Death of the Reverend | Mr. Thomas Shepard, | Late Teacher of the Church at | Charlestown in New-England: | By a grêat Admirer of his Worth, and true Mourner for | his Death. | *Cambridge: Printed by Samuel Green.* 1677. 4to, pp. 16. M. 56381

Oakes. New-England | Pleaded with, | And pressed to consider the things which | concern her | Peace, | at least in this her Day: | Or, | A Seasonable and Serious Word of faithful Advice to the Churches | and People of God (primarily those) in the Massachusets Colony; | musingly to Ponder, and bethink themselves, what is the Tendency, | and will certainly be the sad Issue, of sundry unchristian and crooked | wayes, which too too many have been turning aside unto, if persisted | and gone on in. | Delivered in a Sermon Preached at Boston in New-England, | May. 7. 1763.

being the Day of Election there. | By Urian Oakes Pastor of the Church of Christ in Cambridge. | ... | *Cambridge, Printed by Samuel Green.* 1673. | 4to, pp. (6), 64. H., M. 56382

This very rare sermon was the first published work of President Oakes. An address, headed "Christian Reader" (pp. 4) is signed "John Sherman. Thomas Shepard."

Oakes. A | Seasonable Discourse | Wherein | Sincerity & Delight | in the Service of God | is earnestly pressed upon | Professors of Religion. | Delivered on a Publick Fast, at Cambridge in | New-England. | By the Reverend, and Learned | Urian Oakes Late Pastor of the Church there and Præsident of | Harvard Colledge. | ... | *Cambridge,* | *Printed by Samuel Green* 1682. 4to, pp. (6), 33. B. 56383

An address "To the Reader" (pp. 4) is signed "Increase Mather."

Oakes. The Soveraign Efficacy of Divine | Providence; | Over-ruling and Omnipotently Disposing and Ordering all | Humane Counsels and Affairs, Asserted, Demonstrated | and Improved, in a Discourse Evincing, | That (not any Arm of Flesh, but) the right Hand of the | Most High is it, that Swayeth the Universal Scepter ... . As Delivered in a | Sermon | in Cambridge, on Sept. 10. 1677. | Being the Day of | Artillery-Election there. | By Mr. Urian Oakes ... . *Boston in New-England:* | *Printed for Samuel Sewall.* 1682. 4to, pp. (6), 40, (1). H. 56384

The address "To the Reader" (pp. 3) is signed "John Sherman."

Oakes. The Unconquerable, All Conquering, & more than Conquering Souldier; ... a Sermon preached at Boston in New England, on the day of the Artillery Election there, June 3d, 1672. By Urian Oakes ... . *Cambridge: Printed by Samuel Green.* 1674. 4to, pp. (6), 40. B. 56385

An address to the "Christian Reader" (pp. 4) is signed "Thomas Shepard." *See also* [Mather (C.)], Vol. xi., No. 46462.

Oakes (W.) Catalogue of Vermont Plants. As published in Thompson's History of Vermont. By William Oakes. [*Burlington.* 1842.] 8vo. 56386

Oakes. Scenery of the White Mountains: with Sixteen Plates, from the Drawings of Isaac Sprague. By William Oakes. ... *Boston: Little & Brown.* 1848. Folio. B., C. 56387

Oakesmith (E.) *See* Smith (Elizabeth Oakes).

Oakey (P. D.) The War: its Origin ... . A Sermon ... in ... Jamaica, L. I., ... July First, 1861. By Rev. P. D. Oakey, ... *New-York: John A. Gray, Printer.* 1861. 8vo, pp. 23.

Oakham (John), *pseudon.* *See* [Phillips (Walter (P.)]

Oakland, *Cal.* Manual of the First Independent Presbyterian Church, Cal. [n. p. 1869.] 24mo, pp. (4). 56389

Description ... of the Oakland and Ottawa Railroad, from Detroit to Grand Haven. *Detroit.* 1854. 8vo. S. 56390

Prospectus of the Oakland Coal and Iron Co. of Baltimore. *Baltimore: Wiley, Printer.* 1865. 8vo, pp. 8. 56391

Catalogue of Oakland College [Claiborne County, Miss.] ... 1852. *New-Orleans.* 1853. 8vo. S. 56392

Catalogue of Oakland Female Seminary, Hillsborough, Ohio, ... 1848. [n. p. n. d.] 8vo. S. 56393

[Oakley (Charles).] Report of the State Trustee of the Illinois & Michigan Canal, made in relation to certain Charges which were preferred by him against the Chief Engineer ... . *Chicago.* 1848. 8vo, pp. 41. H. 56394

Oakwood Cemetery. *See* Syracuse.

The Oath of Allegiance. *See* [Palmer (B. M.)]

Oath to be administered to all such Persons as enter into the King's Service, in the Pay of the Government of Pennsylvania. [n. p. about 1756.] 4to, 1 leaf. P. 56395

The Oaths, Signs [etc.]. *See* Vol. ix., No. 38343.

Oaxaca. Alegato por el Dean y Cavillo Sedevacante de la Santa Yglesia Cathedral de Antequera Valle de Oaxaca, sobre haver admitido à la opposicion de su Canongia Magistral vacante al Doctor Juan de Cara, Presbytero Colegial Mayor de el Colegio viejo de Santos de Mexico, despues de cumplido el termino de los Edictos ... . [n. p. n. d.] Folio, 16 leaves. 56396

Coleccion de Decretos y Ordenes del Estado Libre de Oajaca. Vol. 1. *Oajaca.* 1829. 16mo. C. 56397

Constitucion Politica del Estado Libre de Oajaca. *Mexico: Imprenta de la Aquila.* 1825. 12mo, pp. (2), xiii, 104. 56398

Constituciones formadas par la Junta Tridentina y sancionadas por el Illmo. Señor Obispo diocesano para el Seminario conciliar de esta capital. *Oaxaca.* 1843. 12mo, pp. 64, (2).

Contestacion del Obispo y Cabildo de la Santa Iglesia Catedral de Oajaca, al Oficio del Ministro de Justicia sobre instrucciones al Enviado á Roma. *Oajaca.* 1826. 4to, pp. 55. + *Guadalajara.* 1827. 4to. 56399

Esposicion que el Gobernador del Obispado de Oaxaca dirije al Supremo Gobierno en defensa de los bienes eclesiasticos. *Mexico.* 1834. 4to, pp. 21. 56400

Esposicion que en cumplimiento del articulo 83 de la Constitucion del Estado hace el Gobernador del mismo al soberano congreso al abrir sus sesiones el 2 de Julio de año de 1848. *Oaxaca.* 1848. Folio, 35 and 36 leaves.

Guerra de Religion anunciada por el R. Obispo y Cabildo de Oajaca. *Mexico.* 1827. 8vo. 56401

Memoria del Ejecutivo de Oaxaca del periodo de la Administracion publica de 1868–1869. *Oaxaca.* 1869. Folio. 56402

Ordenanza para el establecimiento é instruccion de los Alcaldes de Barrio de la Ciudad de Oaxaca. *Mexico.* 1796. Folio, pp. 26. Plan. 56403

Por la Provincia de S. Hipolyto Martyr del Sagrado de Predicadores de Oaxaca. En los autros sobre que no imponga principal alguno en fincas del Obispado de la Puebla sin consentimiento y licencia de la jurisdicion ordinaria Eclesiastica. *Mexico.* 1771. Folio. *See also* [Guerrero (V.)], Vol. vii., No. 29135.

Obando (J. M.) Apuntamientos para la Historia por el General José Maria Obando. *Lima.* 1842. 8vo. 56404

Obando. Apuntamientos para manifestacion de la persecucion que ha sufrido, 1837 ... . *Lima.* 1842. 8vo. 56405

For a reply to this, *see* Mosquera (T. C. de), Vol. xii., No. 51068.

Obedience the best Charter, or, Law the only Sanction of Liberty. In a Letter to Rev. Dr. Price. *London: Richardson & Urquhart.* 1776. 8vo, pp. 103. 56406

This author adopts the exploded notions of despotism and passive obedience—retails the common topics on the dispute with America—and deals plentifully in vague surmises, uncharitable censures, and opprobrious names.

Obedientia Potentissimi Emanuelis Lusitaniæ | Regis zc. per clarissimum Iuris. v. cõsultum Die- | ghum Pacettum Oratorem ad Iulium. ii. Ponti. | Max. Anno Dñi. M. D. V. Pridie No. Iunii. | [n. p. n. d.] 4to, 4 leaves. 56407

Contains vague indications concerning America.

O'Beirne (Thomas Lewis), *Bishop of Meath.* An Excellent Sermon preached in St. Paul's Church, New-York, Before the

Right Hon. Lord and General Howe, the Commodores, Generals, Colonels, and all the other inferior Officers belonging to the British Army, there residing. By the Reverend Mr. O'Beirne, Chaplain to the Hon. Lord Howe. Upon The first Sunday after the attempt to burn New-York, being the 22d of Sept. last. ... In which you have an Account in a Note, of the Damages done to the Churches, and other public buildings, in this flourishing City. Printed at the Desire of the Congregation. [n. p. 1776.] 12mo, pp. 12. 56408

Another edition is entitled:

O'Beirne. A | Sermon | ... at | St. Paul's, New-York, | The first Sunday after the English Churches | opened, on | General Howe's | Taking Possession of the Town, and the Day subsequent | to the attempt to destroy | New-York by Fire: | By the Rev. Mr. O'Beirne, | Chaplain to the Right Hon. Lord Viscount Howe. | ... | *Southampton:* | *Printed and Sold by T. Baker.* [1776.] 4to, pp. 16. H. 56409

Obelisco que en la Ciudad de la Puebla de los Angeles celebrando la Jura de D. Carlos iii. *Imprenta en el Real Colegio de S. Ignacio de dicha Ciudad.* 1763. 4to, pp. (5). Plate. 56410

[Obelitz (——).] En kort Beskrivelse over den Jamaica. *Kiobenhavn: Trukt hos M. Hallager.* 1782. 16mo, pp. 38. H.

Ober (B.) Slavery: a Lecture ... before the Lyceum in Attleborough, Jan. 4th. 1838. By Rev. Benjamin Ober. ... *Pawtucket, Mass.: Robert Sherman, Printer.* 1838. 8vo, pp. 28.

Oberea, *pseudon.* *See* Vol. i., Nos. 3204–5.

Oberbauer (J. C.) Amerika und die Sklaverei. Von Julius C. Oberbauer. ... *New York: Verlag von Helmich & Stark.* 1854. 8vo, pp. 32. C. 56413

Oberlin (Jacob). Orbis antiqui monumentis suis illustrati primæ lineæ. ... *Argentorati, typis Lorenzii et Schuleri.* 1790. Sm. 8vo, pp. (2), viii, 280, (140). 56414

America occupies the last two pages.

Oberlin, *O.* Catalogue of the Trustees, Officers and Students, of the Oberlin Collegiate Institute. 1838. *Allison & Mariner, Printers, Cuyahoga Falls.* [1838.] 8vo, pp. 32. Continued.

Also: Laws and Regulations of the Female Department ... 1867. *Oberlin.* 1867. 12mo.—Triennial Catalogue of the ... College, for ... 1851–52. ... *Oberlin, Ohio: James M. Fitch.* MDCCCLI. 8vo, pp. 40. Continued. B.

Oberlin Quarterly Review. Edited by A. Mahan and W. Cockran ... . *Oberlin.* 1845. 8vo, pp. 510. 56416

Oberlin Students' Monthly. Vol. 1. No. 1. November, 1858. *Oberlin, O.* 1858. 8vo. Continued. S. 56417

Report of a Public Meeting of the Colored Citizens of Oberlin, Lorain Co., O.; ... with ... Resolutions ... and an Address to the Colored Citizens of Ohio. [n. p. 1848.] 8vo, pp. 8.

[Obert (*M.*)] Mémoire contenant un Aperçu Statistique de l'État de Guatémala, ainsi que des renseignements précis sur son commerce, son industrie, son sol, sa température, son climat, et tout ce qui est relatif à cet État: Indiquant les avantages qu'il présente pour la Colonisation du département de Vera Paz et du district de Santo Thomas, dont la territoire a étè cédé en propriété perpetuelle, avec des privilèges à la Compagnie Commerciale et Agricole des Côtes orientales de l'Amérique Centrale, pour la fondation d'Établissements coloniaux. Accompagnée de cartes. *Bruxelles: Lesigne et Cie.* 1840. 8vo, pp. vii, viii, 157, 34, xii. 4 Maps. 56419

Obi; or, the History of Threefingered Jack. In a Series of Letters from a resident in Jamaica [William Earle, Jr.] ... . *Worcester: Printed by Isaiah Thomas, Jun.* 1804. 12mo, pp. 168. + *Boston: N. H. Whitaker.* 1830. 18mo, pp. 140. 56420

Obiter Dictum, *pseudon.* The Union of the British North American Provinces considered, in a Letter addressed to the Citizens of British America, By Obiter Dictum. *Montreal.* 1859. 8vo. 56421

Obituary Addresses; namely, address of Col. Crittendon, upon ... Gen. Chas. Scott; ... Col. O'Hara, upon ... Hon. W. T. Barry; ... Col. Marshall, upon ... Capt. Ballard ... in the Cemetery at Frankfort, November 8, 1854. ... *Frankfort, Ky.* 1855. 8vo. 56422

Obituary Addresses. *See* Nos. 9956, 13562, 13577, 28410, 37858, 42077, *and* 50690.

See also under the names of the persons whose deaths are noticed.

The Objections to African Colonization. *See* [Hopkins (E.)]

Objections To An Act to quiet land titles in the State of California, ... April 25, 1862 ... . [*Washington.* 1862.] 8vo, pp. 5.

Objections to Exemption. *See* Vol. IV., No. 15322.

Objections to the Ballot, answered from the Writings and Speeches of Mill, Grote, &c. ... *London: Henry Hooper.* MDCCC-XXXVII. 8vo, pp. 20. H. 56424

Contains references to America.

Objections to the Bank of Credit. *See* [Dudley (P.)], Vol. V.

Objections to the Taxation. *See* [Jenyns (S.)], Vol. IX. 36053

Objections to Yielding. *See* Vol. I., No. 2992, *note.*

Objects and Plan. *See* Vol. XI. 45867, XII. 51935, *notes.*

Objects of the Institute for Colored Youth, with a List of the Officers and Students ... for ... 1864. *Philadelphia: Sherman & Co., Printers.* 1864. 12mo, pp. 11. B. 56425

... Objects of the Rebellion, and Effects of its Success upon Free Laborers and Civilization. By a Member of the Cincinnati Bar. *Cincinnati: Wrightson & Co.* 1863. 8vo, pp. 32.

Oblação do Instituto Historico e Geographico Brasileiro á memoria do seu presidente honorario, o senhor D. Affonso, augusto primogenito de Suas Magestades Imperiaes. *Rio de Janeiro: Typographia Universal de Laemmert.* 1847. 4to, pp. viii, 88. 56427

Corrected title of our No. 7610. Contains poems by Sanctiago Nunes Ribeiro, Joaquim Norberto de Sousa Silva, Rodrigo de S. José, and Francisco de Paula Menezes.

Obligatiën ten laste der Zuid-Amerikaansche Republieken Venezuela en Nieuw-Grenada, in betrekking to Geldbelegging. *Rotterdam: M. Wijt en Zonen.* 1846. 8vo. 56428

OBOOKIAH (H.) Memoirs of Henry Obookiah, a Native of Owhyhee and a Member of the Foreign Mission School; who died at Cornwall, Conn., Feb. 17, 1818. ... *New Haven: Nathan Whiting.* 1819. 18mo, pp. 129. BM. + *Elizabethtown, N. J.: Edson Hart.* 1819. 12mo. + *Philadelphia.* 1830. 12mo.

OBREEN (J. A.) De Noord-Amerikaansche Oorlog van 1861–1865. ... *Leiden: A. W. Sijthoff.* 1867. 8vo, pp. x, 629. 8 Maps. 56430

Also: Opwekking tot Landverhuizing naar de Republiek der Vereenigde Staten van Noord-Amerika. ... *Leiden: A. W. Sijthoff.* 1871. 8vo, pp. 31.

O'BRIEN (G. S.) The Tourist's Guide to Quebec. By Godfrey S. O'Brien ... *Quebec.* 1864. 12mo, pp. 70. 56431

O'BRIEN (J.) A Treatise on American Military Laws, and the Practice of Courts Martial; with Suggestions for their Improvement. By John O'Brien. *Philadelphia.* 1846. 8vo, pp. 570. C. 56432

[O'BRIEN (J. W.)] Excursion aux Provinces Maritimes. Impressions de Voyage. Par le Correspondant du Canadien. *Québec.* 1864. 4to, pp. 52. 56433

O'BRIEN (R.) Message from the President ... communicating the copy of a letter from Richard O'Brien, Late Consul of the United States, at Algiers, giving some detail of transactions before Tripoli. ... *Washington City: Printed by William Duane & Son.* 1804. 8vo, pp. 8. BA. 56434

O'BRIEN (T. M.) General Orders of the War Department, embracing the Years 1861, 1862, & 1863. ... Chronologically Arranged ... By Thos. M. O'Brien & Oliver Diefendorf ... . *New York: Derby & Miller.* 1864. 2 vols., 8vo, pp. (4), xxiv, (2), 472; xxxi, 711. B., C. 56435

O'BRYAN (W.) A Narrative of Travels in the United States of America, with advice to Travellers. By William O'Bryan. *London: The Author.* 1836. Sm. 8vo. 56436

The author was the founder of the singular religious sect, known as the "Bryanites."

[O'BRYEN (Denis).] A Defence of the Right Honorable the Earl of Shelburne, from the Reproaches of his numerous Enemies; ... added a Postscript ... . Fourth Edition. *London.* 1782. 8vo, pp. 96. S. + Sixth Edition. [*Ibid.*] 56437

Ascribed to Denis O'Bryen. The Shelburne here satirized was John Fitzmaurice

Obsequies of Abraham Lincoln in Union Square, New York, April 25, 1865. Printed for the Citizens Committee. *New York: D. Van Nostrand.* 1865. Impl. 8vo, pp. 30, (2). Portrait.

Fifty copies printed on large paper.

Obsequies of Abraham Lincoln, in the City of New York, under the Auspices of the Common Council. By David T. Valentine, Clerk of the Common Council. *New York: Edmund Jones & Co.* 1866. Rl. 8vo, pp. (10), 254. Plates. 56439

See Vol. VII., No. 25828, *see also* Vol. V., No. 18320.

Obsequio que dedica un vecino de esta ciudad por su feliz arribo al Sr. Mariscal de Campo D. Francisco Dionisio Vives, Capitan General y Gefe superior político de esta plaza. *Imprenta de la Marina por el ciudadano José Boloña.* 1823. 4to, pp. 6.

Observacion crítico-legal. *See* Vol. IV., No. 12848.

Observaciones á la carta que en 25 del ultimo julio dirigio D. Pedro Celestino Negrete al Ciudadano Gobernador del Estado libre de Xalisco Luis Quintanar. *Guadalajara.* 1823. 4to, pp. 113. 56441

Observaciones a un parrafo de la esposicion que hizo el Exmo. Sr. Ministro de hacienda a la Camaras, titulado: Aranceles.—Prohibiciones. *Guadalajara.* 1850. 8vo, pp. 18. 56442

Observaciones al Dictamen, que la Comision de negocios eclesiasticos presentó al Congreso de Guatemala en 29 de Abril de 1845, consultando la derogatoria del Decreto de 3 de Julio de 1843, que permitia establecerse en dicho Estado á los Padres Jesuitas. *Mexico.* 1845. 8vo, pp. 112. 56443

Observaciones de Regon contra los Tratados de Paz. *Queretaro.* 1848. 8vo. 56444

Observaciones del Obispo y Cabildo de la Puebla de los Angeles sobre las instrucciones que deben darse al Enviado de la Republica Mexicana á Roma. *Mexico.* 1827. 4to, pp. 84.

Observaciones Generales sobre el Establecimiento de caminos de hierro en los Estados Unidos Mejicanos ... *Nueva-York.* 1838. 8vo, pp. 17. 2 Maps. S. 56446

Observaciones | Historico-Canonicas, | del Procurador General | de la ordende Santiago, | sobre | un Manifesto | Politico-Legal, | en que se procura | persuadir justa, y necessaria la violencia, | con que el Obispo de Cartagena declarò | incursos en censuras reservadas, al Vica- | rio interino, y al Alcade mayor de | Cararaca, ambos Ministros de la | misma Orden. | [n. p. 1730?] Folio, pp. 3, 404, (12). B. 56447

Observaciones Politico-Legales, que en abono de sús impresos hace el Pensador Mejicano. *Mexico: Imprento de Mariano Ontiveros, Año de* 1821. 8vo, pp. 14. 56448

Observaciones por un oficial del egercito Norte-Americano, á los habitantes de la Republica Megicana. [n. p. n. d.] Sm. 8vo, pp. 16. 56449

For a reply, *see* "Carta de un Ciudadano Mexicano," Vol. XII., No. 48318.

Observaciones que el Arzobispo de Carácas hace el Ejecutivo Nacional sobre Código Civil. Refutacion que el Dr. Antonio

José Sucre hace á las objecciones del Señor Doctor Julian Viso. *Carácas.* 1868. 8vo, pp. 22, 42. 56450

Observaciones que hace el ejecutivo. *See* Vol. XII. 48605.

Observaciones que hace la Iglesia Catedral del Estado de Chiapis acerca del dictamen y articulos de las instrucciones que deben darse al Enviado á Roma, y que se mandaron imprimir y circular por el Senado de la Republica Mexicana. *Mexico.* 1826. 4to, pp. 30. 56451

Observaciones que hace un Patriota a la Carta de un Mazon ... *Bogota.* 1823. 8vo, pp. 32. 56452

Observaciones que hizo un Yucatano a la iniciativa que dirig. al congreso la leg. de Queretaro y de Jalisco relat. a la pacificacion de Yucatan. *Mejico.* 1831. Sm. 4to. 56453

Observaciones que sobre el proyecto de bases organicas hacen á la Junta legislativa el Obispo y Cabildo de Guadalajara. *Guadalajara.* 1843. 8vo, pp. 16. 56454

Observaciones sobre el Comercio de la Nueva Granada, con un apendice relativo al de Bogota. *Bogota.* 1831. 8vo, pp. 78.

Observaciones sobre la Mineria de la Nueva Granada. *Bogota.* 1837. 8vo, pp. (20). Table. Documento Numero Segundo, pp. (8). 56456

Signed "Powles, Illingworth, i compania."

Observações sobre a carta. *See* Vol. II., No. 7611.

OBSERVADOR, *pseudon.* *See* Vol. III., No. 9016.

El Observador Católico. Periódico religioso, social y literario. *Mexico.* 1848–49. 3 vols., 4to. 56457

El Observador de la República Mexicana, Periódico Semanario. *Mexico.* 1827–30. 6 vols., 4to. 56458

Observador Ecclesiastico en Chile. *Santiago de Chile.* 1823. 4to. + Reimpreso en Cordoba y aumentado por il D. Pedro Ignacio de Castro. *Cordoba.* 1824. 4to. 56459

El Observador Judicial. *See* Vol. XII., No. 48606.

Observador Portuguez historico e politico de Lisboa, desde o dia 27 de Novembro de 1807, em que embarcou para o Brasil o Príncipe regente e toda a real familia, por motivo da invasão dos

francezes n'este reino, até o dia 15 de Septembro de 1808, em que foram expulsos ... . *Lisboa, na Imprensa Regia.* 1809. 4to, pp. 528. 56460

Observanda. *See* [Mather (C.)], Vol. XI., No. 46436.

L'Observateur. *See* Vol. II., No. 5207, Vol. IX., No. 33986

Observations and Annotations upon the Apologetical Narration, submitted to Parliament, the learned Divines of the Assembly, and all Protestant Churches here and abroad. *London: Christopher Meredith.* 1644. 4to. 56461

"The key-note of this conservative production is found in its last sentence, 'And finally, as for the *latitude* and *tolerance*, ye sue for, it is unjust and most pernicious, both to Christ's Church and the Kingdom.' The tenets, practices and apologies of the five authors of the 'Narration' are herein handled without gloves by the author who signs his preface 'A. S.' Throughout the book a great deal of theological mustard and vinegar is poured out against the New England Men, their inconsistencies and divisions. It was written while Roger Williams was in London, and no doubt the pungent passage on page 64 alludes to his expulsion by the Saints of Massachusetts, and Settlement in Rhode Island. 'If they [the New England Men] had the upper hand over us here, as there, they should send us all to some Isle of Dogs, as they have done others.'"—STEVENS.

Observations | and | Reflections, | On an Act, passed in the Year, | 1774, | For the Settlement, | Of the Province of Quebec. | ... | By a Country Gentleman, | *London: | J. Stockdale* ... | 1782. 8vo, pp. 30. J.C.B., C. 56462

Observations and Remarks upon the state of our Controversy with Great Britain, and on the Proceedings of the Continental Congress, By a Moderate Whig. *America.* 1775. 8vo. 56463

See also [Jackson (Hall)], Vol. IX., No. 35412.

Observations arising from the Declaration of War against Spain, and the Future Management ... . In a Letter to ——. *London.* 1739. 8vo, pp. 56. N. 56464

For a response, *see* "Reply to a Pamphlet," etc.

Observations at the Magnetic and Meteorological Observatory, at the Girard College, Philadelphia, made under the direction of A. D. Bache, 1840–1845. *Washington.* 1847. 3 vols., 8vo.

Observations concerning Indigo and Cochineal, (dedicated to the Planters of South Carolina,) 1746. ... *London.* 1746. 12mo.

Relates entirely to the cultivation of the above drugs, silk, etc., in the plantations, and contains several letters from planters and gentlemen in Carolina. Some of the letters are addressed to "J. C." who appears to have been the editor, and was probably "James Crokatt." *See* our Vol. V., No. 17593.

Observations concerning the Canal Bridge. *See* Vol. II. 6601.

Observations concerning the Funding System of Pennsylvania. ... To which is prefixed a Petition of the Public Creditors to the House of Assembly. *Philadelphia.* 1789. 8vo, pp. 16. W.

Observations Critiques et Politiques, sur le Commerce Maritime; dans lesquelles on discute quelques points relatifs à l'Industrie et au Commerce des Colonies Françoises. *Amsterdam.* 1755. 12mo. 56468

See also [Brignoles (M. de)], Vol. II., No. 7980.

Observations d'un Américain. *See* [Maillet Duclairon (A.)]

Observations d'un Citoyen de la Plata sur le traité du 29 Octobre avec le Gouverneur Rosas. *Paris.* 1841. 8vo, pp. 24.

Signed "B. Ey. O. Citizen of Montevideo."

Observations d'un Homme Impartial sur la Lettre de Mr. ***** à Mr. S. B. Docteur en Médécine a Kingston dans la Jamaique ... . *Londres.* 1776. 8vo, pp. 65. J.C.B. 56470

Probably printed in Holland. The writer exposes the false reasoning of Mr. Pinto, and shows himself a zealous defender of the colonies. *See* Pinto (M.), *also* "Nouvelles Observations," No. 56095, *supra.*

Observations des Commissaires du Commerce de la Martinique, sur les procès-verbal de l'Assemblée Coloniale de cette isle. Du 14 janvier 1788. *Saint-Pierre-Martinique: Pierre Richard.* 1788. 4to, pp. 98. Table between pp. 68–69. 56471

The commissioners for France were Ruste and Fortier, and for the colony, L. Joyau and Terrien.

Observations des Négocians de Bordeaux sur l'Arrest du Conseil du 30 Août 1784, qui a été connu à Bordeaux le 20 Nov. *A Paris.* 1784. 8vo, pp. 71. 56472

"On the commerce of the colonies."—RICH.

Observations des Syndics de la Chambre de Commerce de Normandie, servant de réponse à un Mémoire intitulé: sur l'étendue et les bornes des loix prohibitives du commerce étranger dans nos colonies. *Rouen.* 1765. 8vo. 56473

Observations et Détails, 1742. *See* [Rothelin (*l'Abbé*)].

Observations from a Gentleman in Town to his Friend in the Country, relative to the Sugar Colonies, proving their importance to England. ... *London: T. Becket* ... 1781. 8vo. 56474

See "Monthly Review," LXV. 237.

Observations from the Law of Nature and Nations, and the Civil Law; shewing that the British Nation have an undoubted right, during the present War, to seize on all French property in Neutral Bottoms, and particularly everything brought from the French Settlements in America, or carried to them; ... and shewing that the Treaty between England and Holland in 1647, does not entitle the Dutch to any right to trade to the French settlements in America. *London: J. & R. Dodsley.* 1759. 4to, pp. 12. 56475

Observations Générales et impartiales sur l'Affaire du Scioto. *A Paris: Didot le jeune.* 1790. 8vo, pp. 25. J.C.B. 56476

Relative to a colony established on the banks of the River Scioto. *See also* [Jacquemart (F.)], Vol. IX., No. 35512.

Observations Générales sur les maladies des climats chauds, leurs causes, leur traitement, et les moyens de les prévenir. Par Dazille, Médecin à St-Domingue, ancien chirurgien-major des troupes de Cayenne ... . *Paris.* 1785. 8vo. 56477

Observations | Impartiales | d'un | vrai Hollandois, | Pour servir de Réponse au Discours d'un | soi-disant | bon Hollandois | à ses compatriotes. | [Par A. M. Cérisier. Avec la suite.] *Arnhem: Nyhof.* [1778–79.] 2 parts, 8vo, pp. (4), 60; (4), 74. H.

On the revolution in the North American colonies.

Observations in answer to an "Address to the Clergy of the Established Church" ... [on Slavery]. *London.* 1826. 8vo.

Observations leading to a Fair Examination. *See* [Lee (R. H.)]

Observations made upon the Virginian Nutts imported from the Indies. *London.* 1682. 4to. 56480

Observations Occasion'd by reading a Pamphlet, intitled a Discourse concerning The Currencies of the British Plantations in America. In a Letter to *****. *London: T. Cooper.* 1741. 8vo, pp. 23. 56481

In speaking of the pamphlet referred to in the title, the author says, "It is written with great judgment, and seems the production of a very wise and honest man. He has so thoroughly exposed the depredations of their Paper Emissaries on the Trade of this Kingdom, that I had almost said they were equal to those of the Spaniards." For the "Discourse," *see* Vol. V., No. 20721.

Observations occasioned by the Stamp Act. [*Philadelphia?*] 1768. 8vo. P. 56482

Observations occasioned by writings against alterations, proposed in the Convention, to be made in the Judiciary System *Portsmouth (N. H.): Printed by George and John Osborne.* M,DCC,-XCII. Sm. 8vo, pp. 23. B. 56483

Observations of a Person. *See* [Patterson (J.)]

Observations of the Merchants. *See* Vol. II., No. 6536.

Observations on a Direct Exportation of Sugar from the British Islands, with Mr. Toriano's Objections to it. *London.* 1735. Sm. 4to. 56484

Observations on a late Epitaph. In a Letter from a Gentleman in the Country. To his Friend in Philadelphia, Chester Co. Sept. 3. 1764. *Philadelphia: Printed by Anthony Armbruster.* [1764.] 12mo. P. 56485

Observations on a late Pamphlet, entituled, "Considerations upon the Society or Order of the Cincinnati," clearly evincing the Innocence and Propriety Of that Honourable and Respectable Institution. In Answer to Vague Conjectures, False Insinuations, and Ill-Founded Objections. By an Obscure Individual. ... *Philadelphia: Printed and Sold by Robert Bell.* M,DCC,LXXXIII. 8vo, pp. 28. + *Hartford: Hudson & Goodwin.* MDCCLXXXIV. 8vo, pp. 22. 56486

In reply to Ædanus Burke. *See also* Vol. III., No. 9279.

Observations on a late publication, intituled, Thoughts on Executive Justice ... added, A Letter containing remarks on the same work. ... *London: T. Cadell.* M.DCC.LXXXVI. 16mo, pp. (4), 162. H., N. 56487

Observations on a late State of the Nation. [By Ed. Burke.] *London: J. Dodsley.* MDCCLXIX. 4to, pp. (2), 97. + The Second Edition. [*Ibid.*] 8vo, pp. (4), 155. + The Third Edition. [*Ibid.*] + The Fourth Edition. [*Ibid.*] 56488

This title varies from our No. 9294. *See* "Monthly Review," XL. 143, 149, 191.

Observations, on a Letter. *See* No. 55167, *note.*

Observations on a Letter from Noah Webster, Jun. Esq. published in the Panoplist ... . By an Old-Fashioned Clergyman. *New-Haven: Printed by Oliver Steele and Co.* 1809. 8vo, pp. 24

Observations | on | A Pamphlet, Entitled, | A Short History of Opposition, | During the last Session of Parliament. | With | A

Postscript to the Author.|...|By a Member of Parliament.|*London:|Printed for W. Davis.*|M DCC LXXIX. 8vo, pp. x, 121.

See "Monthly Review," LXI. 227.

Observations on a Pamphlet, entitled A State of the Present Form of Government of the Province of Quebec; circulated in London, during the last summer. With an Appendix, containing information on the subject. By a Citizen of Quebec. *London: J. Stockdale.* MDCCXC. 8vo, pp. (2), 78. 56491

See also Vol. VI., No. 21578, *note*.

Observations on a Proposal. *See* [Selkirk (*Earl of*)].

Observations on a Variety of Subjects. *See* [Duché (Jacob)].

Observations on American Independency. *Edinburgh.* 1779. 8vo, pp. 16. 56492

"A North British publication in favor of American Independency; which the writer supposes, on commercial principles, to be the most advantageous ground on which we can settle our differences with the colonies."—*Monthly Review*, LXII. 89.

Observations on, and Reasons against. *See* Vol. IX. 35641.

Observations on Church Government, by the Presbytery of Springfield, Ky. To which is added the Last Will and Testament of that Reverend Body. *Albany: E. & E. Hosford.* 1808. 16mo, pp. 23. C. + *Pittsfield.* 1808. 12mo, pp. 28. 56493

Observations on Conventions. *See* [Smith (William Pitt)].

Observations on Dr. Price's Theory. *See* [Goodricke (H.)]

Observations on Dr. Stevens's History. *See* [Jones (G. W.)]

Observations on Extracts taken out of the Report from the Lords Commissioners for Trade and Plantations. *London.* 1708. Folio, pp. 4. 56494

On the number of negroes yearly imported into America.

Observations on Facts. *See* Vol. V., No. 18622.

Observations on Free Masonry .... Addressed, By a Lady in Worcester, to her Female Friend. ... *Printed at Worcester*, 1798. 8vo, pp. 14. H. 56495

Observations on Government. *See* [Livingston (W.)], Vol. X.

I have seen a catalogue in which John Stevens is said to be the author.

Observations on History. *St. Christopher.* [n. d.] 12mo. C.

Observations on Incorporating New Banks. *See* Vol. I. 3180.

Observations on Mr. Buckminster's Sermon. *See* Vol. III. 8931

Observations on Mr. Burke's Bill, for the better Regulation of the Independence of Parliament, and Economical Reformation ... By a Lady. Addressed to Lord North. *London.* 1780. 8vo, pp. 28. 56497

Observations on Mr. Madison's Message. [n. p.] 1814. 8vo.

See Vol. XII., No. 48071.

Observations on Mr. Wesley's ... Address. *See* [Lofft (C.)]

Observations on National Defence, drawn from Capt. Partridge's Lecture ... and from Gen. Sumner's Letter ... on the Importance of the Militia System. *Boston.* 1824. 8vo, pp. 46.

Observations on Rail Roads, in the Western & Southern States, and of the ... Pioneer System ... with Remarks on the Importation of Foreign Iron. *Cincinnati.* 1850. 12mo, pp. 28.

Observations on Senator Douglas. *See* Vol. V., No. 20693.

Observations|on|Several Acts of Parliament,|Passed|In the 4th, 6th and 7th Years of his present Majesty's Reign:|And Also,|on|The Conduct of the Officers of the Customs,|since|Those Acts were passed,|and|The Board of Commissioners appointed|to|Reside in America.|Published by the Merchants of Boston.|[*Boston:*] *Printed by Edes & Gill.* M,DCC,LXIX. 8vo, pp. 24. + *London: G. Kearsly.* M. DCC. LXX. 8vo, pp. (2), 37. P.

In addition to the duties against which the colonists complained, their trade was greatly embarrassed by the multiplicity of bonds required in exporting and importing goods. The unlimited power given to officers of the customs, and of the advantage taken by these officials of their position, proved another serious injury to commerce. It was for these grievances that the merchants of Boston endeavored to obtain redress. *See* "Monthly Review," LXII. 155, *and* our Vol. II., No. 6536.

Observations on that part of the late Treaty of Peace with France, which relates to the African Slave Trade. *London: Ellerton and Henderson, Printers.* [1814.] 8vo, pp. 12. B. 56502

Observations on the Act for Granting Excise on Wine ... . *Boston* [*about* 1720]. 12mo. 56503

Observations on the Agriculture, Manufactures and Commerce of the United States. In a Letter to a Member of Congress. By a Citizen of the United States [Tench Coxe]. *New York:*

Printed by Francis Childs and John Swaine. M,DCC,LXXXIX. 8vo, pp. 102. 56504

Corrected title of our No. 17301, Vol. V.

Observations on the American Revolution. *See* [Morris (G.)]

Observations on the American Treaty. *See* [Courtenay (T. P.)]

Observations on the Answer of the King of Great Britain to the Manifesto, &c. of the Court of Versailles. By an Independent Whig. *London: Fielding.* 1779. 4to. 56505

"The Independent Whig is a vehement advocate for the cause of the revolted colonies; whose independency he treats as a matter of *establishment* as *just* as it is *certain*."—*Monthly Review*, LXII. 83.

Observations on the Application which the West India Planters intend to make for a Law to prohibit the Importation of Foreign Molasses into the British Colonies of America. *London.* 1786. 8vo. 56506

Observations on the Articles of Confederation of the Thirteen United States of America, entered into July 1778 and ratified March 1, 1781. *New York.* 1781. 8vo, pp. (2), 16. P. 56507

Observations on ... "A Dialogue on the actual State of Parliament," and also on ... "Free Parliaments." *London.* 1783. 8vo, pp. 20. 56508

In response to our No. 19941, Vol. V.

Observations on the Bank of the U. S. *See* Vol. I. 3189, *note.*

Observations on The Bill introduced ... by Mr. Wilberforce, for ... preventing the Unlawful Importation of Slaves, and ... Slavery in the British Colonies. *London: J. M. Richardson.* 1816. 8vo, pp. 28. C. 56509

Observations on the Canada Thistle. *See* Vol. III. 10530.

Observations on the Case of the Northern Colonies. *London: J. Roberts.* 1731. 8vo, pp. 31. B. 56510

A vindication of the Sugar Act, then pending in Parliament. This act prohibited the Northern Colonies from trading for sugar, etc., with the French West Indies, and required them to obtain these articles from the British West Indies or from England.

Observations on the Case of the Whig Merchants indebted to Great Britain at the Commencement of the late War. By a Citizen. *New York.* 1785. 8vo. 56511

Observations on the Climate. *See* Vol. II., No. 8104.

Observations on the Commerce of Spain with her Colonies, in Time of War. By a Spaniard, in Philadelphia [the Marquis d'Irujo]. Translated from the original Manuscript, by another Spaniard. *Philadelphia: Printed by James Carey.* 1800. 8vo, pp. 63, (1). N. 56512

Observations on the Commerce. *See* [Holroyd (J. B.)], VIII.

Observations on the Conduct of Great Britain in respect to Foreign Affairs. *London.* 1743. 8vo. S. 56513

Observations on the Conduct of Great-Britain, with Regard to the Negociations and other Transactions Abroad. *London, Printed: And Sold by J. Roberts.* 1729. 8vo, pp. 61. BA.

Relates to Admiral Hosier's, and other British expeditions to the West Indies against the Spaniards, and defends the government in its relations with foreign States, especially with Spain after the Treaty of Hanover.

Observations On the Crisis. 1836–37. By a Merchant. [n. p. n. d.] 8vo. P. 56515

Observations on the Demerara Memorial. *See* Vol. V. 19468

Observations on the Diseases. *See* [Rollo (John)].

Observations on the Doctrines. *See* [Tucker (John)].

Observations on the Dutch Manifesto, addressed to the Earl of Shelburn. *London: G. Kearsly.* [1781.] 8vo, pp. iv, 27.

Observations on the Effect of the Californian and Australian Gold. *London.* 1852. 8vo. C. 56517

Observations on the Emigration. *See* [Cobbett (W.)], Vol. IV

Observations on the Evidence. *See* [Ranby (J.)]

Observations on the Excise Bill. *Boston.* 1754. 18mo.

Observations on the existing Difficulties between Spain and the United States, By Verus? *Philadelphia.* 1817. 8vo.

Observations on the Fift [*sic*] Article. *See* [Galloway (J.)]

Observations on the Finances. *See* Vol. XII., No. 45927.

Observations on the Geology. *See* Bailey (L. W.), I. 2743.

Observations on the Government, Trade, Fisheries, and Agriculture of Newfoundland; in a Series of Letters to Earl Bathurst.

By an Inhabitant of that Colony. *London: Simpkin & Co.* 1824. 8vo, pp. 64. 56520

Observations on the Importance of Improving the Navigation of the River Schuylkill for the purpose of connecting it with the Susquehanna and ... to the Genesee Lakes and the Ohio. [*Philadelphia.* 1821.] 8vo, pp. 21. P. 56521

Observations on the Importance. *See* [Kennedy (A.)], 37393

Observations on the Impressment of American Seamen by ... Great Britain, with ... Remarks on ... Non-Expatriation ... added a correct list of Impressed Seamen taken from Documents laid before Congress. By a Citizen of Baltimore. *Baltimore: C. Dobbin & Murphy.* 1806. 8vo, pp. 59, (1). 56522

Observations on the Improvements. *See* [Hunn (J. S.)], VIII.

Observations on the Increase of Mankind. *Boston.* 1755. 4to, pp. 15. M. 56523

Observations on the Inslaving. *See* [Benezet (A.)], II. 4676.

Observations on the Instructions given by the President of the United States of America to the Representatives of the Republic at Panama, in 1826, on the Conduct of Mr. Poinsett, Minister of the United States in Mexico. *London.* 1829. 8vo. 56524

Observations on the intended Application. *See* No. 55545, *note*

Observations on the intended Establishment of a Naval Arsenal on the waters of the Chesapeake Bay. *Annapolis: Printed by J. Chandler.* 1818. 8vo, pp. 15. 56525

Observations on the Isthmus of Panama. *London.* 1844. 8vo, pp. 31. Map. 56526

Observations on the Justificative Memorial. *See* [Rayneval (J. M. G. de)].

Observations on the Kingdom of Peace .... *New-York: Printed by J. Seymour.* 1816. 8vo, pp. 11. B., W. 56527

Address before the New York Peace Society.

Observations on the Late ... Conduct. *See* [Clarke (Wm.)]

Observations on the late Popular Measures, Offered to the serious Consideration of the sober Inhabitants of Pennsylvania,

by a Tradesman of Philadelphia. *Philadelphia: Printed for a Tradesman.* MDCCLXXIV. 8vo, pp. 26. 56528

By John Drinker. Correct title of our No. 20950, Vol. V.

Observations on the late Presidential Veto, together with a Plan for a change of the Constitution relative to this Power. *Boston: James Munroe and Company.* 1842. 8vo, pp. 78. BA. 56529

Observations on the late Treaty of Peace with France; so far as it relates to the Slave Trade: ... *London: J. Butterworth and Son.* 1814. 8vo, pp. 23. B. 56530

Signed "Liber." *See* "Monthly Review," LXXIV. 329.

Observations on the Letters of the Honorable William B. Giles, to the People of Virginia. ... [n. p. n. d.] 12mo, pp. 46.

Observations on the Means. *See* [Rollo (John)].

Observations on the Militia. By an Officer of the Brigade of New York. *New York.* 1804. 8vo. C. 56532

Observations on the Mineral Waters of the South Western Part of Virginia. In a Series of Letters. By a Physician of Philadelphia. ... *Philadelphia: Printed by J. Thompson.* 1834. 8vo, pp. 30. BA. 56533

Observations on the Natural and Constitutional Rights of Conscience in relation to Military Requisitions on the People called Shakers. *Albany.* 1816. 8vo, pp. 24. N. 56534

Observations on the Nature of the Claims of American Citizens to Lands in the States of Louisiana and Mississippi, Derived from Grants under the former British Province of West Florida, ... *London.* 1818. 8vo, pp. 23. 56535

Observations on the Nature and Use of Paper-Credit ... including Proposals for founding a National Bank. *Philadelphia: Printed and Sold by R. Aitken.* M. DCC. LXXXI. 8vo, pp. 40. BA.

Observations on the Navy Pension Laws. By an Officer of the U. S. Navy. *Washington.* 1840. 8vo. N. 56537

Observations on the Necessity of Introducing ... Clergymen into our Colonies in the West Indies ... *London: F. C. and J. Rivington.* 1807. 8vo, pp. 12. 56538

Observations on the New Constitution, and on the Federal and State Conventions. By a Columbian Patriot. ... [n. p.

1786.] 8vo, pp. 19. W. + *Boston printed, New-York re-printed,* M,DCC,LXXXVIII. 8vo, pp. 22. BA., W. 56539

Observations on the Opinion of Mr. George Rous, lately delivered in the House of Commons, that the Crown can give Independence to America without the assent of Parliament. *London: J. Kearsley.* 1780. 8vo. 56540

See "Monthly Review," LXIII. 146.

Observations on the Origin and Conduct of the War with Mexico. ... *New York.* 1847. 8vo, pp. 11. N., S. 56541

Observations on the Papers. *See* [Wilkes (John)].

Observations on the Part of the United States, by their agent, to the Reply of Daniel Dulany, under the Sixth Article of the Treaty of Amity, Commerce and Navigation, between his Britannic Majesty and the United States of America. [*Philadelphia.* 1798.] 4to, pp. 17. BA., P. 56542

Observations On the Peculiar Case. *See* [Trumbull (John)].

Observations on the pending Question. *See* [Koster (T.)], Vol. IX., No. 38275.

Observations on the Pestilential Fever which prevailed in Philadelphia, in 1793, 7, and 8. *Philadelphia.* 1799. 8vo. 56543

Observations on the Petitions from various Merchants of Rhode-Island, to the Congress of the United States, Praying to be relieved from the Penalties of certain Exportation Bonds. With an Appendix. [By William Hunter.] *Printed at Newport,* (*R. I.*) 1803. 4to, pp. 34. H. 56544

Observations on the Petitions of Grievance, addressed to the Imperial Parliament, from the Districts of Quebec, Montreal and Three-Rivers. *Quebec.* 1828. 8vo, pp. (2), 54. H.

Observations on the Petitions to Congress of the Inhabitants of Mackinaw, Brown and Crawford Counties in the Territory of Michigan. [Dated Michigan, Nov. 5, 1821.] 8vo, pp. 7. W.

Observations on the Plan. *See* Vol. III., No. 10531.

Observations on the Political Character and Services of President Tyler and Cabinet. By a Native of Maryland. *Washington.* 1841. 8vo. 56547

Observations on the Power of Climate over the Policy, Strength, and Manners of Nations. *London: J. Almon.* 1774. 8vo. 56548

The writer in his "Observations" has the comparison "As Carthage was to Tyre, so is America to Britain."

Observations on the Preliminary and Provisional Articles. Attempting to prove from a Comparative View of the Situation of this Country now, and at the close of the late War, that they are equally, if not more beneficial to the true Interest of this Country than the Terms procured by the Treaty of Paris in 1763. *London: J. Debrett.* MDCCLXXXIII. 8vo, pp. 33. N.

See "Monthly Review," LXVIII. 179.

Observations on the Present Condition. *See* Vol. X. 42272.

Observations on the Present Convention with Spain. *London: T. Cooper.* M.DCC.XXXIX. 8vo, pp. (4), 60. 56550

Observations on the Present State of Newfoundland in reference to its Courts of Justice, Local Government, and Trade. By an Inhabitant of the Colony. *London.* 1823. 8vo. 56551

Observations on the Present. *See* Vol. VIII., No. 30148, Vol. XI., No. 45272, *and* [Young (Arthur)].

Observations on the Project for Abolishing the Slave Trade ... *London: J. Debrett.* M.DCC.XC. 8vo, pp. (2), 62. 56552

Observations on the Propos'd American Tax, So far as relates to the Continent [*sic*] Colonies. [n. p. 1750.] Folio, pp. 3.

Relates to Massachusetts equipping one-fourth of her people to fight the French in Canada.

Observations on the Proposed Bill, Entitled, "An Act to Declare and Explain the Law in certain Cases therein mentioned." *Easton: Printed by James Cowan.* M,DCC,XCIV. 12mo, pp. 43. 56554

The earliest imprint at this place I have seen.

Observations on the proposed Constitution for the United States of America, Clearly shewing it to be a complete System of Aristocracy and Tyranny, and destructive of the Rights and Liberties of the People. *Printed in the State of New-York,* M,DCC,LXXXVIII. 8vo, pp. 126. B., S. 56555

Signed "Centinel." Originally addressed to the Inhabitants of Pennsylvania.

Observations on the Proposed Patriotic Bank. [*Washington:*] *Gales & Seaton, May*, 1815. 8vo, pp. 40. 56556

Observations on the proposed State Road. *See* [Williamson (Hugh)?]

Observations on the Proposed Union. *See* Vol. III. 10532.

Observations on the Proposition. *See* Vol. VIII. 30765, *note*.

Observations on the Propriety. *See* [Hartley T.)], Vol. VIII.

Observations on the Public Fast, Dec. 12, 1765. *Newport.* 1766. 4to. 56557

Observations: | on the | Reconciliation | of | Great-Britain, | and the | Colonies; | In which are exhibited, Arguments | for, and against, that Measure. | By a Friend of American Liberty. | ... | *Philadelphia;* | *Printed, by Robert Bell* ... | MDCCLXXVI. 8vo, pp. 40. H. 56558

Perhaps by Rev. Jacob Green of New Jersey. *See* "Life of Ashbel Green," p. 46. At the end (pp. 33–40) is "The Plan of an American Compact, with Great-Britain. First published at New-York."

Observations on the Remarks. *See* Vol. II., No. 6702.

Observations on the Report of the Committee of Ways and Means, made at Washington, March 12th, 1828. *Philadelphia.* 1828. 8vo. P. 56559

Observations on the Report ... of the House of Lords relative to the Timber Trade. By a British Merchant [Simon Cock]. *London: J. M. Richardson.* 1821. 8vo, pp. viii, 118. 56560

This and the following are probably by Simon Cock.

Observations on the Reports of ... the Timber Trade ... . Also Some Remarks on Canada and the United States, and the Trade between those Countries and the West India Colonies. *London: J. M. Richardson.* 1820. 8vo, pp. (1), 72. 56561

Observations on the Rev. Dr. Gannett's Sermon. *See* [Curtis (G. T.)], Vol. v., No. 18042.

Observations on the Rev. Pastor. *See* [Gordon (W.)]

Observations | on the | Review of the Controversy | between | Great-Britain | and | her Colonies. | *London,* | *T. Becket and P. A. De Hondt.* M DCC LXIX. 8vo, pp. (2), 43. H. 56562

See [Bancroft (E.)], Vol. I., No. 3111, *and* "Monthly Review," XL. 433.

Observations on the Rhode Island Coal, and Certificates with regard to its Qualities, Value, and ... uses. [n. p. 1814.] 8vo, pp. 16. H. 56563

Observations on the Right of Jurisdiction claimed by the States of New York and New Hampshire over the New-Hampshire Grants (so-called) lying on both Sides of Connecticut River, in a letter to the Inhabitants of those Grants. *Danvers: Printed by E. Russell.* MDCCLXXVIII. 12mo, pp. 15. 56564

See Belknap's "New Hampshire," II., 441, *and* William's "Vermont," II. 179.

Observations on the River Potomack. *See* [Lear (Tobias)].

Observations on the Slave Trade, ... during a Voyage made in 1787 and 1788, in company with Dr. Sparrman and Capt. Arrehenius ... . *London.* 1789. 8vo. 56565

Observations on the Slavery of the Africans and their Descendants, and on the use of the Produce of their Labour. *New York.* 1814. 12mo, pp. 23. W. 56566

Observations on the Speech. *See* [Stephen (James)].

Observations on the State of the Controversy with America, 1775. [n. p. n. d.] 8vo. 56567

Observations on the State of the Currency with suggestions for equalizing its Value and reducing to Uniformity the Banking System in the United States. *Boston, Jan.* 1, 1829. 8vo.

Observations on the System. *See* Vol. IX., No. 35642.

Observations on the Treaty with America ... . *London.* 1780. 8vo. 56569

Observations on the Trial by Jury. Addressed to the Citizens of Pennsylvania, By an American. *Strasbourg.* 1803. 8vo.

Observations on the Union of the Canadas. *See* Vol. III. 10533

Observations on the War, the projected Invasion, and a Decree of the National Convention for the Emancipation of the Slaves in the French Colonies. *London: J. Baldwin.* 1794. 12mo.

Observations on the West India Company Bill as printed and read a Second Time. *London.* 1825. 8vo. 56572

Observations on the Whale-Fishery. [*New York.* 1788.] 12mo, pp. 13. BA. 56573

Observations on the Wisconsin Territory. *See* [Smith (W. R.)]

Observations on Two Campaigns. *See* Vol. III., No. 12469.

Observations par le Corsaire l'Espérance. *Havre.* 1797. 8vo

Observations personnelles. *See* [Barbé-Marbois], No. 3311*a*.

Observations relatives au plan de l'Établissement d'une Colonie sur les bords de l'Ohio et du Scioto dans l'Amérique Septentrionale. *Paris.* 1790. 8vo, pp. 13. Map. 56575

Against the Scioto Company.

Observations respecting the Propriety of fixing a Central and Inland Situation for the Permanent Residence of Congress. [By Phocion. n. p.] 1789. 8vo. P. 56576

Observations, showing the great esteem had for the Royal African Company; with Petitions of Robert Heysham (in 1693 and 1695) in behalf of his brothers, Giles and William Heysham, Merchants in the Island of Barbadoes. [n. p.] 1712. Folio, 1 leaf. 56577

Observations Sommaires et Preuves sur le Navire le New-Jersey, et ses Propriétaires. *Paris.* 1803. 4to. C. 56578

See also "Conseil de Liquidation," Vol. IV., No. 15915.

Observations Sommaires sur le "Pour et le Contre." *Paris.* [1785.] 4to. C. 56579

Relates to the French colonies. *See* Vol. v., No. 21034.

Observations sur la multiplication. *See* Vol. VII., No. 29185.

Observations sur la prise. *See* [Le Picquier (——)], Vol. x.

Observations sur la réponse. *See* Vol. III., No. 10535.

Observations sur le deuxième Mémoire. *See* [Balfour (J.)]

Observations sur le Mémoire Justificatif de la Cour de Londres. *Paris.* 1780. 4to, pp. 84. 56580

These "Observations" are in answer to the "Mémoire Justificatif" written by Gibbon, our No. 27283, Vol. VII.

Observations sur le Plan. *See* Vol. III., No. 10534.

Observations sur le Rapport fait à l'Assemblée Nationale, avant le Décret sur la Marine, du 26 Juin 1790; & doutes proposés sur se Décret par M. Bory, Officier Général de la Marine,

Auteur des Mémoires sur l'Administration de la Marine. [*Paris.* 1790.] 8vo, pp. 20. 56581

Observations sur le Traité de Paix conclu a Paris le 10 février 1763 entre la France, l'Espagne et l'Angleterre. *Amsterdam.* 1780. 12mo. 56582

Relates to the disputes between France and England in North America.

Observations sur les Sauvages du Nord de l'Amérique. *Paris.* 1795. 12mo, pp. 28. 56583

By Benjamin Franklin. A translation of our No. 25578, Vol. VII.

Observations sur tout. *See* [Legal (G.)], Vol. x., No. 39848.

Observations sur un pamphlet. *See* [Grégoire (H.)], Vol. VII.

Observations tending to illustrate the Views of the Irish Emigrant Association. [n. p.] 1817. 8vo, pp. 12. N. 56584

Observations Topographiques. *See* Vol. x., No. 39000.

Observations upon a late Pamphlet. *See* Vol. III., No. 9280.

Observations upon certain passages. *See* [Moore (C. C.)]

Observations upon the African Slave Trade, and on the Situation of Negroes in the West Indies; with some proposed Regulations for a more mild and humane Treatment of them ... . By a Jamaica Planter. *London: The Author.* M.DCC.LXXXVIII. 8vo, pp. 56. 56585

See "Monthly Review," LXXVIII. 429.

Observations upon the Conduct. *See* [Mauduit (I.)], Vol. XI.

Observations | Upon the Congregational Plan of | Church Government, | Particularly as it Respects the Choice and Removal of | Church-Officers, | Supported by the Testimony of the Fathers of | New-England, | And Unanimously offered to the Consideration of the | Churches, | by the | Convention of Ministers | Of the Province of the Massachusetts-Bay ... 1773 ... . *Boston: Printed ... by John Boyle.* 1773. 8vo, pp. 21. H., N. 56586

Observations upon the Doctrine, lately advanced, that his Majesty's Council have no Constitutional Power to controul Individual Appropriations, or to amend or alter Money Bills; ... *Halifax: Printed at the Nova Scotian Office.* 1828. 8vo, pp. 40.

Observations upon the Duties and Emoluments of certain Public Offices. *New York.* 1826. 8vo, pp. 26. S. 56588

Observations upon the Effects. *See* [Walton (George)].

Observations upon the Importance. *See* [Halliburton (B.)]

Observations upon the Liturgy. *See* [Knox (W.)], Vol. IX.

Observations upon the Manifesto of His Catholic Majesty [Philip v.]; with an Answer to his Reasons for not Paying the Ninety-Five Thousand Pounds. In Vindication of the Honour of Great Britain. *London: T. Cooper.* 1739. 8vo, pp. 42.

Observations upon the Memorial and Report of the Citizens of Boston, opposed to a Further Increase of Duties on Importations. ... *Providence: Printed by F. Y. Carlile & Co.* 1828. 8vo, pp. 8.

Observations upon the Oligarch, or Committee of Soi-Disant Saints ... . By an Hereditary Planter. *London: Edmund Lloyd.* 1816. 8vo, pp. (2), 67. 56591

Relative to slavery in the West Indies.

Observations | upon the present | Government | of | Pennsylvania. | In | Four Letters | to the | People of Pennsylvania. | ... | *Philadelphia:* | *Printed and Sold by Styner and Cist* ... . M DCC LXXVII. 8vo, pp. 24. H. 56592

Observations upon the Report. *See* Vol. VII., No. 28760.

Observations upon the State of Negro Slavery in the Island of Santa Cruz, the principal of the Danish West India Colonies. *London.* 1829. 8vo. 56593

Observations upon the Treaty. *See* [Walpole (Robert)].

OBSERVATOR, *pseudon.* Thoughts on the increasing Wealth and National Economy of the United States of America. *Washington.* 1801. 8vo. 56594

The Observator Observed: Or some few Remarks on the Observations published in the Gazette on the 20th of November last. Addressed to any Man that shall chance to read it. In a Letter to the Author. *Boston.* 1735. 8vo. 56595

This elicited: "The Observer Observed." ... *Boston.* 1735. 8vo.

The Observator's Trip to America, in a Dialogue between the Observator, and his Countryman Roger. [*Philadelphia.*] 1726. 12mo. BM. 56596

Observatorio fisico-meteorico. *See* Vol. VII., No. 29445.

OBSERVER, *pseudon.* The Case of Dr. Bullions Fairly Stated by an Observer. *New York.* 1835. 8vo. 56597

OBSERVER, *pseudon.* "Greenbacks;" or, The Evils and the Remedy of using "Promise to Pay the Bearer on Demand" ... . By Observer. *New York: Dion Thomas.* 1864. 8vo, pp. 29.

OBSERVER, *pseudon.* An Inquiry into the Necessity and General Principles of Reorganization in the United States Navy, with an Examination of the True Sources of Subordination. By an Observer. *Baltimore.* 1842. 8vo. BM. 56599

OBSERVER, *pseudon.* Observations on Canal Navigation. By an Observer. [n. p. about 1811.] 8vo, pp. 15. Plan.

Relates to the Erie Canal.

OBSERVER, *pseudon.* Remarks on the Moral and Religious Character of the United States of America, supported by numerous extracts from the best authorities; addressed to the Author of "A Reply to the Charge lately delivered by the Archdeacon of Colchester." By Observer. *Colchester.* 1831. 8vo, pp. 64.

The object of this pamphlet is to show that there is "no moral and religious character in the United States." *See also* Vol. XIII., No. 53622.

OBSERVER, *pseudon.* Review of Address in respect to a late Ordination. By Observer. *New York.* 1843. 8vo, pp. 23.

OBSERVER, *pseudon.* The Two concluding Articles of an Observer. [n. p. n. d.] 8vo, pp. 16. BA. 56603

The Observer and Repository of Original and Select Essays ... By Beatrice Ironside. *Baltimore.* 1806–7. 2 vols., 12mo.

Obstacles and Objections to the Cause of Permanent and Universal Peace Considered. By a Layman. *Boston.* 1837. 8vo. 56605

O'BYRNE (J.) Speech of John O'Byrne, Esq. ... before the Democratic Association of Pennsylvania, on January 23d, 1868. ... *Philadelphia: John Campbell.* 1868. 8vo, pp. 4. H. 56606

O'BYRNE (W. R.) A Naval Biographical Dictionary; comprising the Life and Services of every Living Officer in Her Majesty's Navy, from the Rank of Admiral of the Fleet to that of Lieutenant inclusive: compiled from Authentic Family Documents. By William R. O'Byrne. *London.* 1849. Rl. 8vo, pp. 1408. C., P. 56607

OCA (Ignacio Montes de). Fiesco, Poema Historico. ... *Mexico.* 1859. 16mo. 56608

O'CALLAGHAN (E. B.) A Few Notes on the Jesuit Relations, Compiled for Private Circulation, by E. B. O'Callaghan, M.D. *New York.* 1850. Folio, 1 leaf. 56609

O'CALLAGHAN. History of New Netherland, or, New-York under the Dutch. By E. B. O'Callaghan ... . *New York: D. Appleton & Company.* 1846–1848. 2 vols., 8vo, pp. 493; 608. Maps, Plate, and 2 Sheets of Facsimiles. BA. + Second Edition. [*Ibid.*] 1855. 2 vols., 8vo. S. 56610

See "North American Review," LXII. 447.

O'CALLAGHAN. Jesuit Relations of discoveries and other occurrences in Canada and the Northern and Western States of the Union. 1632–1672. By E. B. O'Callaghan, M.D. ... *New York: Press of the Historical Society.* MDCCCXLVII. 8vo, pp. 22.

Most valuable to the collector of Jesuit "Relations," as it contains a list of the "Relations" and names of the owners of collections in this country.

O'CALLAGHAN. Relations des Jésuites sur les Découvertes et les autres évènements arrivés en Canada, et au Nord et à l'Ouest des États-Unis (1611–1672). Par le Dr. E. B. O'Callaghan. Traduit de l'Anglais [par Father Felix Martin] avec quelques notes, corrections et additions. *Montréal, pres de l'Évêché.* 1850. 8vo, pp. 70. 56612

O'CALLAGHAN. A List of editions of the Holy Scriptures and parts thereof, Printed in America previous to 1860: with Introduction and Bibliographical Notes. By E. B. O'Callaghan. *Albany: Munsell & Rowland.* 1861. Rl. 8vo, pp. liv, (10), 415.

A carefully executed work. One hundred and fifty copies only printed. It contains facsimiles of the title-pages to Eliot's Indian Bible.

O'CALLAGHAN. Origin of Legislative Assemblies in the State of New York, including titles of the Laws passed previous to 1691. *Albany.* 1861. 4to, pp. 39. 56614

O'CALLAGHAN. The Register of New Netherland; 1626 to 1674. By E. B. O'Callaghan, LL.D. ... *Albany, N. Y.: J. Munsell.* MDCCCLXV. 8vo, pp. xx, 198. BA. 56615

Compiled from the Dutch records in the Secretary of State's office, and from other sources. It contains the names of all who held office, either civil or ecclesiastical, in the Province of New Netherland. For other works edited by Dr. O'Callaghan, *see* our Nos. 7856, 13402, 20597, 36748, 53554, 53647, 53682, *and* 53727.

O'CALLAGHAN (J.) Usury, Funds, and Banks; also forestalling Traffick & Monopoly; likewise Pew Rent, and Grave Tax; ... To which is prefixed A Narrative of the Author's Controversy with Bishop Coppinger, and of his Sufferings for Justice Sake. By the Rev. Jeremiah O'Callaghan ... . *Burlington: The Author.* 1834. 12mo, pp. (4), 380. + Fifth Edition. *New York.* 1866. 12mo. C. 56616

Also: Usury, or Interest proved to be repugnant to the Divine and Ecclesiastical Laws, and Destructive to Civil Society. ... *New York: J. O'Callaghan.* 1824. 12mo, pp. 206. C.

OCAMPO (D. G. de). [Begins] Señor, El Sargento Major D. Diego Gomez de Ocampo, Primer Castellano del Fuerte y Puerto de la Concepcion, Rio de S. Joan, Provincia de Nicaragua dize. [*Guatemala.* 1676.] Folio, 2 leaves. 56617

A petition to the king, setting forth his services and praying for further employment and rewards, followed by a certificate from el Capitan Don Lorenço de Montufar, Secretario de Camara, etc. recounting Ocampo's services.

OCAMPO (Florian de). Las quatro partes enteras de la Cronica de España, que mando componer el rey Don Alonso llamado el Sabio: donde se contienen los acontescimientos y hazañas mayores y mas señaladas que suçedieron en España: desde su primera poblaçion, hasta casi los tiempos del dicho señor rey. *Zamora.* 1541. Folio. 56618

"Édition très rare de cet ouvrage."—BRUNET'S *Nouvelles Recherches*, II. 499. *See also* "Bibliotheca Grenvilliana." "It is among the rarest of the Spanish chronicles, and to any collector or public library it is indispensably necessary. See a full account in Mr. Southey's preface to the 'Chronicle of the Cid.'" Title and note from Thomas Thorpe's catalogue.

OCAMPO. Los quatro Libros Primeros de la Cronica General de España ... . [n. p. n. d.] 4to. 56619

Excessively rare. "Of this edition (probably the first) of Ocampo's valuable Chronicle of the History of Spain, I know of no other copy."—THOMAS THORPE.

OCAMPO. Los quatro libros primeros de la Cro | nica general de España que recopila el mae- | stro Florian do campo [*sic*] criado y cronista del | Emperador Rey nuestro señor por man- | dado de su magestad çesarea. | *Ençamora.* *Anno* . M . D . xliij. | [Colophon:] *Fuerõ impressos estos quatro libros | primeros de la Cronica de España que recopila el Maestro Flo | rian do campo, Cronista de la Magestad Cesarea, en la magni- | fica, noble, y antiquissima ciudad de Zamora por el honrra | do varon Iuan picardo impressor de libros, vezino de la | dicha ciudad. A costa y espensas del virtuoso varon | Iuan pedro mussetti mercader de libros vezino d' Medina del campo. Acabaronse a quinze* |

dias del mes de Deziembre. Año del nasci| miēto de nuestro saluador Iesu christo| de mil y quinientos y quarenta y| tres años. Reynando en Espa-|ña el Emperador don Car-|los nuestro señor y| Re natural.:.| Folio, ccxxxv leaves, Tabla, 10 leaves. B., L. 56620

Contains an interesting chapter (xxth on fol. clv) devoted to the discovery of the islands of Hispaniola, Cuba, etc.

OCAMPO. Los Cinco Libros Primeros de la Coronica General de España ... . *Impresso en Medina del Campo, por Guillermo de Millis, Año* 1553. Folio. + *Alcala, I. Iñiguez de Lequerica.* 1578. Folio, 222 and 8 leaves. C. 56621

For a continuation, *see* Vol. XII., No. 50498.

OCANE (F.) The Government and Laws of every Country, are the Effect, not the Cause of the Condition of the People. By Francis Ocane. *Charleston, S. C.* 1819. 8vo. P., W.

Ocangra Aramee Wa wa Ka Ka ra. Ocangra Prayer-Book. *Detroit: George L. Whitney, Printer.* 1833. 12mo, pp. 18.

A Catholic prayer-book in the Winnebago dialect.

OCARIZ (J. F. de). Libro primero [y segvndo] de las Genealogias del Nvevo reyno de Granada. Por Jvan Florez de Ocariz. *Madrid: J. Fernandez de Buendia.* 1674–76. 2 vols., folio, pp. (44), 492; (40), 488. 56624

This very rare work contains the most complete history of the colonization of New Granada at the epoch of the conquest, and gives the most exact details of the foundation of various colonies and the *personnel* of the first colonists. It is full of genealogical details of but little interest.

O'CATARACT (J.), *pseudon.* *See* [Neal (J.)], Vol. XII. 52150.

The Occasional. *Cincinnati, Ohio: American Reform Tract and Book Society.* [v. d.] 56625

A series of ten tracts.

Occasional Essays. *See* [Maseres (Francis)], Vol. XI. 45417.

Occasional Letters on Taxation; on the Means of raising the Supplies within the Year, to answer the Expenses of a necessary War; and on such Means as would probably tend to secure Great Britain and its natural Dependencies, the Blessings of Peace, on a durable System. By an Independent Man. *London: J. Dodsley.* 1780. 8vo, pp. 80. 56626

See "Monthly Review," LXII. 83.

Occasional Offices of the Protestant Episcopal Church in the United States. *Philadelphia.* 1790. 12mo. 56627

The Occasional Pamphlet. ... The Mistakes and Failures of the Temperance Reformation. *New York: Mason Brothers.* 1864. 8vo, pp. 48. H. 56628

Occasional Papers. *See* [Wood (W.)]

Occasional Reflections. *See* [Williamson (Peter)].

The Occasional Reverberator. ... [*New-York: Printed by J. Parker.* 1753.] Folio, pp. 8. BA. 56629

Occasional Reviews. No. I. ... *Charleston: J. S. Burges.* 1832. 12mo, pp. 35, (1). Continued. BA. 56630

Occasional Thoughts of a Free Briton. *London: J. Almon.* 1766. 8vo. 56631

The author "seems to have the American taxations in view." *See* "Monthly Review," XXXIV. 239.

Occasional Thoughts on the Present German War. *London.* 1761. 8vo. 56632

Relates to the island of Martinico, and the hiring of Hessian soldiers.

The Occident, and American Jewish Advocate ... . [Edited by] Isaac Leeser. ... Vol. I. No. I. *Philadelphia.* 5603. 8vo, pp. 60. Continued. H. 56633

OCCOM (S.) A Choice Collection of Hymns and Spiritual Songs; intended for the Edification of Sincere Christians of all Denominations. By Samson Occom ... . *New London: Printed and Sold by Timothy Green* ... 1774. 12mo, pp. 119. + Second Edition. [*Ibid.*] 1784. 12mo, pp. 111. + Third Edition, with additions. *New-London: Printed by Timothy Green & Son.* 1792. 12mo, pp. 112. 56634

The first and second editions have a preface of two pages, which is omitted in the third.

OCCOM. A| Sermon,| Preached at the Execution of| Moses Paul,| An Indian,| Who was executed at New-Haven, on the 2d of| September, 1772, for the| Murder of Mr. Moses Cook,| Late of Waterbury, on the 7th of December, 1771.| Preached at the Desire of said Paul.| By Samson Occom,| Minister of the Gospel, and Missionary to the Indians.| *New London: ... Timothy Green* ... [1772.] 8vo, pp. 24. + *New Haven.* [1772.] 8vo, pp. 32. + Third Edition. *New London.* 1772. 8vo. + Fourth Edition. [*Ibid.*] + *Hartford.* 1772. 4to. + *Boston: ... John Boyles,* ... 1773. 8vo, pp. 32. + [Another Edition.] *Boston.* 1773. 8vo,

pp. 22, (2). + *Salem.* 1773. 8vo, pp. 31. + The Ninth Edition. *Boston: Printed for and Sold by Eldad Hunter.* MDCCLXXIV. 8vo, pp. 24. + [*London.* 1789.] 8vo, pp. 32. + *Bennington: William Watson.* [178–.] 8vo, pp. 14, (1). H. + [n. p. 178–.] 8vo, pp. 24. + *Northampton.* 1801. 8vo. + *Exeter: Printed for Josiah Richardson, the Lord's Messenger to the People.* 1819. 12mo, pp. 22. + *Springfield: Henry Brewer, Printer.* [n. d.] 8vo, pp. 26. 56635

Occom was the first Indian pupil of the celebrated Eleazer Wheelock, at his school in Lebanon, 1742, where he remained four years. He established a school among the Montauk Indians on Long Island, 1755, which he continued for ten years. Reprinted in England with the following title:

OCCOM. A| Sermon| at the Execution of| Moses Paul, an Indian;| Who had been guilty of Murder,| Preached at New Haven in America.| By Samson Occom,| A native Indian, and Missionary to the Indians, who was in England| in 1776 [1766] and 1777, [1767] collecting for the Indian Charity Schools.| To which is added| A Short Account of the| Late Spread of the Gospel,| among the Indians.| Also| Observations on the Language of the| Muhhekaneew Indians;| Communicated to the Connecticut Society of Arts and Sciences,| By Jonathan Edwards, D.D.| *New Haven,* ... *Printed* 1788.| *London: Reprinted,* 1788, *and Sold by Buckland,* ...| 8vo, pp. 24, 15, (1). B. + *London: Reprinted,* 1789. 8vo, pp. 24, 16. 56636

In the last-mentioned edition the dates are correctly given.

The Ocean Harp: a Poem; in Two Cantos: with some smaller Pieces; and a Monody on the Death of John Syng Dorsey, M.D. .... [By John Agg.] *Philadelphia: M. Thomas.* 1819. 18mo, pp. 182. C. 56637

Ocean Mail Steamers. *See* [Morss (James)], XII. 50980.

The Ocean Plague: or, A Voyage to Quebec in an Irish Emigrant Vessel. ... *Boston: Coolidge and Wiley.* 1848. 12mo, pp. 127. H. 56638

Ocean Scenes, or, the Perils and Beauties of the Deep: being an Account of the most popular Voyages ... remarkable Shipwrecks, &c. *New York.* 1848. 12mo. + *New York: Leavitt & Allen.* 1855. 12mo, pp. 492. H. 56639

Ocean to Ocean. The Pacific Railroad and Adjoining Territories, with Distances and Fares of Travel from American Cities. ... [By M. J. Carrington.] *Philadelphia: J. B. Lippincott & Co.* 1869. 18mo, pp. 31. Map. 56640

Ocean Waves. *See* [Schadd (J. C.)]

Report of the OCEANIC Oil and Guano Company, ... and the By-Laws ... . *Boston: Wright & Potter, Printers.* 1859. 8vo, pp. 28. B. 56641

OCEOLA (N.) A Narrative of the Early Days and Reminiscences of Oceola Nikkanochee, Prince of Econchatti, a young Seminole Indian; Son of Econchatti-Mico, King of the Red Hills, in Florida; with a Brief History of his Nation, and his Renowned Uncle, Oceola, and his Parents; And Amusing Tales illustrative of Indian life in Florida. ... Written by his Guardian. *London: Hatchard and Son.* 1841. 8vo, pp. x, 228. 3 Plates.

Exceedingly interesting. "An imbecile old chief, called Enematkla, was the first to declare himself a traitor to the tribe, by affixing his sign-manual; he was followed by a few others of inferior grade, until it was submitted to Oceola, who, with all the pride of offended dignity thus offered to himself and his countrymen, with indignation sparkling in his eye, and a contemptuous curl of the lip, drew from his bosom a dagger, and with a countenance that seemed to strike terror into all by whom he was opposed, he hurled the trusty steel with such force into the hateful document, that it passed fairly through the table, exclaiming at the same time, 'There is my mark.'"

OCHOA (D. de). *See* Durama de Ochoa, Vol. VI. 21402–04.

OCHOA (E. de). Miscelánea de literatura viajes y novelas. ... *Madrid: C. Bailly-Bailliere.* 1867. 16mo, pp. viii, 407, (1).

Contains "Un Paseo por América" and "El Emigrado."

OCHOA (Eugene de). Cataloga Razonado de los Manuscritos Españoles, existentes en la Biblioteca Real de Paris, seguido de un suplemento que contiene los otras tres Bibliotecas publicas (del Arsenal de Santa Genoveva y Mazarina). ... *Paris: er la Imprenta Real.* 1844. 4to, pp. (16), 703. 56644

Contains numerous important documents relating to the Indies, etc.

OCHOA (J.) Vida y muerte de el P. Pablo de Salceda, religioso professo (de la compañia de Jesus), en la Puebla de los Angelos. ... *Mexico.* 1689. 4to, pp. (12), 63, (2). 56645

OCHOA (J. I. de). Exprecion panegirica solemne demonstracion de las Festivas Reales, y Magestuosas pompas con que solemniço el Maestre de Campo D. Thomas de Endaya, con sus Sargento mayor, Capitanes, y Real Tercio, de estas Islas Philipinas. El feliz nacimiento de nuestro principe D. Luis Phelipe Fernando, y las alegres noticias de los Triumphos, y victorias conseguidas por Philippo v. Por el Capitan Juan Ignacio de Ochoa, Uezino de

Manila. *Mexico: Franc. de Ribero Calderon.* 1710. 4to, 3 prel. and 71 leaves. 56646

A sermon by Nicolas de San Pedro occupies leaves 53–71.

OCHS (Joh. Rudolff). Americanischer Wegweiser oder Kurtze und eigentliche Beschreibung der Engelischen Provintzen in Nord America, sonderlich aber der Landschafft Carolina. Mit grössern Fleisz zusammen getragen und an Tag gegeben. ... *Bern. Anno* MDCCXI. 12mo, pp. 102. J.C.B. 56647

Ocios de Espanoles Emigrados. Periodico mensual. 7 vols., 8vo. [Followed by] El Emigrado observador. Periodico mensual por una Sociedad de Espanoles refugiados en Inglaterra y Francia. *Londres.* 1824–28. 8vo. 56648

A large proportion of this valuable periodical is devoted to America.

Ocios de un Mexicano empleados en estudiar las instituciones que convendrian a su patria. O sea ensayo de una constitucion. *Mexico.* 1840. Sm. 8vo, pp. 91. 56649

OCKANICKON. A True| Account| of the| Dying Words| of| Ockanickon, | an | Indian King. | Spoken to | Jahkursoe, | His Brother's Son, whom he appointed | King | after him. | *London,| Benjamin Clark*| ... . 1682. 8vo, pp. 8. H. + [*London:*] *Printed in the Year* 1683. 4to, pp. 6. 56650

On the reverse of the title, "A Letter," etc., dated "Burlington the 12th, of the 5th. Month, 1682," signed "John Cripps." The signatures or marks of the Indian witnesses are inserted with the pen, there being no type for their characters. Only a few copies were printed. The history of the book is this: John Cripps, a Quaker in Burlington, New Jersey, 1682, wrote to a friend in London, enclosing the "Dying Words of the Indian King," and requesting him that, if they were printed, a few copies might be sent over to him. His curious letter is on the back of the title-page. Many tears, it is said, were shed over the King's grave, both by the Indians and English in the Quakers' church-yard at Burlington. Corrected title of our No. 17510, Vol. v.

Charter and By-Laws of the OCOEE MINING COMPANY ... . *New York: Douglass & Hempstead, Printers.* 1852. 16mo, pp. 16

O'CONNELL (D.) ... Daniel O'Connell upon American Slavery: with other Irish Testimonies. *New York: American Anti-Slavery Society.* 1860. 12mo, pp. 48. B. 56652

O'CONNELL. The Irish Patriot. Daniel O'Connell's [*sic*] Legacy to Irish Americans. *Philadelphia.* [1847.] 8vo, pp. 32.

Also: Address from the People of Ireland to their Countrymen in America. [n. p. n. d.] 8vo. — Address of the Irish Liberator to the Irish Repeal Association of Cincinnati, with the Pope's Bull on Slavery and the Slave-Trade. *New York.* 1843. 8vo. To Daniel O'Connell, the Great Agitator: the Repealers in General, and the Abolitionists in Particular ... . Showing the fallacious doctrine of the Fanatics in regard to ... Slavery in America. ... By an American Citizen. *New-York.* 1843. 12mo, pp. 29.

Preamble, Constitution, and By-Laws of the O'CONNELL CLUB. *New York: ... Casserly & Sons.* 1845. 12mo, pp. 12.

O'CONNOR (F. J.) The Heroine of the Confederacy; or, Truth and Justice. By Miss Florence J. O'Connor. *New Orleans: A. Eyrich.* 1869. 8vo, pp. 408. 56655

O'CONNOR (J. D.) Speech of Hon. J. D. O'Connor, ... February 28, 1863, on the Conduct of the Administration. [n. p. n. d.] 8vo, pp. 8. 56656

O'CONNOR (*Mr.*) Considerations on the Trade to Africa. ... For Fixing ... the Capital Stock of the Royal African Company. ... By Mr. O'Connor. *London: J. Barnes.* M.DCC.XLIX. 8vo, pp. 53. 56657

Relates in part to the West Indies, South America, etc.

[O'CONNOR (Thomas).] An Impartial and Correct History of the War between the United States of America, and Great Britain; Declared ... June 18, 1812, and concluded ... Feb. 17, 1815. Comprising a particular detail of the Naval and Military Operations, and a faithful Record of the Events produced during the Contest. And including, ... Important Documents: ... *New-York: ... John Low,* ... 1815. 12mo, pp. 304. Plate. + Second Edition, revised and corrected. ... [*Ibid.*] 12mo, pp. 312. Plate. + Third Edition. [*Ibid.*] 1816. 12mo. + Fourth Edition ... . [*Ibid.*] 1817. 12mo, pp. 336. 56658

[O'CONNOR (William Douglas).] The Good Gray Poet. [Walt Whitman.] A Vindication. *New York: Bunce & Huntington.* 1866. 8vo, pp. 46. 56659

O'CONOR (C.) Negro Slavery Not Unjust. Speech of Charles O'Conor, Esq. ... Dec. 19, 1859. *New York: Van Evrie, Horton & Co.* [n. d.] 8vo, pp. 14. C. 56660

Also: Opinion of Charles O'Conor on the Treasury Agent System of Cotton Seizure in the South. *New York.* 1866. 8vo. — The Real Question Stated; a Letter to the Merchants of New York. Conflicting Authorities. [n. p. n. d.] 8vo. — The Status of Slavery. ... [n. p. n. d.] 8vo.

La Octava maravilla y sin segundo Milagro de Mexico, perpetuado en las Rosas de Guadalupe. [n. p.] 1729. 4to. 56661

OCTOGENARIAN, *pseudon.* The Origin and End of the Irrepressible Conflict. By "Octogenarian." [n. p. 1861.] 8vo, pp. 12. 56662

See also [Halliburton (B.)], Vol. VIII., No. 29898.

OCTOGENARIAN LADY, *pseudon.* *See* Vol. III., No. 10976.

OCTOGENARY, *pseudon.* *See* [Huntington (D.)], Vol. VIII.

Octroi of Fondamenteele Condition, onder dewelke Haar Hoog Mog. ten besten en voordeele van de Ingezeetenen deeser Landen de Colonie van Suriname, hebben doen vallen in handen en onder directie van de Bewindhebberen van de generale Neederlandsche Geoctroyeerde Westindische Compagnie. *'s Gravenhage.* 1682. 4to. + *'s Gravenhage: J. Scheltus.* 1752. 4to, pp. 22. C.

Conditions by which the States General have committed the colony of Surinam to the West India Company.

Octrooy of Condition, waar by ... de Stat.-Gen. aan de directeuren van de Colonie de Berbice hebben toegestaan de vrije vaart en navigatie op dezelve colonie, voor alle Ingezetenen dezer landen open te stellen. *Amsterdam: G. en J. de Broen.* [1732.] 4to. 56664

Privileges allowing governors of the colony of Berbice to open free navigation.

Octroy,| By de Hooghe Mogende| Heeren Staten Generael/ verleent aende West-| Indische Compagnie/ in date den derden Junij 1621.| *In s'Graven-Haghe,*| *By Hillebrant Iacobssz, Ordinaris ende Ghesworen*| *Drucker vande Ed: Mo: Heeren Staten van Hol-*| *landt en VVest-Vrieslandt. Anno* 1621.| 4to, 11 leaves. C.

Patent granted to the West India Company. The original edition; rare. A translation of this is in O'Callaghan's "Documentary History of ... New York," I. 399–407.

Octroy,| [as No. 56665]. Mette Ampliatien van dien,| ende| Het accoort tusschen de Bevvint-hebberen ende Hooft-partici-| panten vande selve Compaignie, met approbatie vande Hoog:| ende Moog: Heeren Staten Generael ghemaeckt.| *In 's Graven-Haghe,| By de VVeduwe, eñ Erfghenamen van wijlen Hillebrant Iacobssz| van Wouw, Ordinaris Druckers vande Hog: Mog: Heeren| Staten Generael. Anno* 1623.| *Met Privilegie.* 4to, 16 leaves.

A translation of this agreement is in O'Callaghan's "Documentary History of ... New York," I. 408–410.

Octroy,| [as No. 56666]. Mette ... Het accord tusschen de Bewinthebberen ende Hooft-partici-| panten ... . *In s'Graven-Haghe,| By de Weduwe, en Erfghenamen van wijlen Hillebrant Iacobsz| van Wouw ... . Anno* 1623.| ...| 4to, 16 leaves. 56667

This and the seven following (Nos. 56668–56674) are reprints.

Octroy| [as No. 56666]. Mette ... Het accourt tusschen de Bevvint-hebberen ende Hooft-partici-| panten ... . *In 's Graven-Haghe,*| ... *Anno* 1623.| ...| 4to, 16 leaves. 56668

Octroy,| By de Hooghe/ Moghende| Heeren Staten Generael/ verleent aende| West-Indische Compagnie/ in date| den derden Junij 1621.| Mette Ampliatien van dien,| Ende:| Het Accoordt tusschen de Bewint-hebberen ende| Hooft-participanten vande selve Compagnie: Met| approbatie vande Ho: Mo: Heeren Staten| Generael ghemaeckt.| *In 's Graven-Haghe, By de VVeduvve, ende Erfghenamen van vvijlen Hillebrant| Iacobssz van VVouw* ... . *Anno* 1624.| 4to, 18 leaves. 56669

Octroy| ... in date den| derden Junij 1621.| [as No. 56669]. *In 'sGraven-Haghe, Byde Weduwe, eñ Erfgenamen van wijlen Hillebrant Iacobssz van Wouw*,| ...| *Anno* 1629. ... 4to, 18 leaves.

Octroy,| [as No. 56670]. Ende| Het Accoordt ... Met| approbatie vande Ho. Mo. Heeren Staten| Generaal ghemaeckt.| *In 'sGraven-Haghe,| By de Weduwe, en Erfgenamen van wijlen Hillebrant Iacobssz van Wouw*| ...| *Anno* 1629. ... 4to, 16 leaves.

Octroy,| [as No. 56666]. *In 's Graven-Haghe,| By de Weduwe ende Erfgenamen van wijlen Hillebrant Iacobssz| van Wouw ...* . *Anno* 1637. ... 4to, 16 leaves. 56672

Octroy,| By de Hooge Moghende| Heeren Staten General/ verleent aende West-| Indische Compagnie/ in date den derden Junij 1621.| Mette ...| Het accoort tusschen de Bewint-hebberen ...[as No. 56666]. *In 's Graven-Haghe,| Byde Weduwe, ende Erffgenamen van wijlen Hillebrant Iacobssz| van Wouw ... . Anno* 1642. ... 4to, 16 leaves. C. 56673

Octroy,| By de Hooge Mog: Heeren| Staten Generael/ verleent aende West-Indische| Compagnie/ in date den derden Junij 1621.| Mette Ampliatien van dien.| Ende| Het Accoort tusschen de Bewinthebberen ende Hooft-| participanten vande selve Compagnie, met approbatie van| de Ho: Mo: Heeren Staten Generael gemaeckt.| *In 's Graven-Hage,| By de Weduwe, ende Erfgenamen van wylen Hillebrandt Iacobsz| van Wouw* ... . *Anno* 1642. ... 4to, 16 leaves. C. 56674

Octroy| Concédé—Par les Haults et| Pvissants Seigneurs les| Estats Generaulx, de la| Compagnie des| Indes| Occidentales.| En date du troisième jour du mois| de Juin 1621.| Ensemble la premiere et la seconde ampliation.| *A Amstredam| Pour Jaques de Wachter, demeurant sur le Dam,| à l'enseigne du Guet. Anno* 1623. 4to, 12 leaves. 56675

A French translation of the patent to the West India Company, with the first and second amplifications.

Octroy, | By de Hoogh Mog: Hee-|ren Staten Generael, verleent aen de | West-Indische Compagnie, in date | den twintighsten September sesthien | hondert vier en tseventigh. | *In 's Graven-Hage, | By Jacobus Scheltus, Ordinaris Drucker van de | Hoogh Mogende Heeren Staten Generael der Ver-| eenighde Nederlanden, woonende op het | Binnen-Hoff. Anno* 1674. | 4to, pp. 36. c. 56676

First edition of this second patent, quite different from that of 1621, published after the definitive cession of New Netherland to England. The following (Nos. 56677–78) are reimpressions:

Octroy, | By de Hoogh-Mog: Hee-|ren Staten Generael, verleent aen de | West-Indische Compagnie, in date | den twintighsten September sesthien | hondert vier-en-tseventigh. | *t' Amsterdam, by Marcus Doornick, Gedruckt voor | de Heeren Bewinthebberen van de Geoctroyeer-| de West-Indische Compagnie.* 1675. | 4to, pp. 34, (6). + *Middleburg.* 1675. 4to. 56677

Octroy, | By de Hoog Mogende Heeren | Staten Generael, verleent aen de West-| Indische Compagnie. | In date den twintighsten September sestien | hondert vier en tseventigh. | *In 's Graven-Hage, | By Jacobus Scheltus, ... Anno* 1681. | ... | 4to, pp. 39.

Octroy, by de ... Staten General, verleent aen de West-Indische Compagnie. In dato den 20. September 1674. Mitsgaders de prolongatie van het selve Octroy voor den tydt van dertigh jaren. In dato den 30. November 1700. *In 's Gravenhage: Paulus Scheltus.* 1701. 4to, pp. 50. c. 56679

The same patent, with the prolongation for thirty years.

Octroy der Staten Generael der Vereenigde Nederlanden, gegeven aan Jan Reeps c. s., om een colonie op te rechten aan de westzijde van Rio de las Amasones tot aen Cabo d'Orange, midtsgaders een korte beschryvinge van die landen ... . *'s Gravenhage.* 1689. 4to. 56680

Octroy door d' Ed: Geoctr: Societeit van Suriname verleent aan de Heer Wilhelm Hack, omme, met syne mede-Ingeteresseer dens, over de Colonie van Suriname ondersoeck te mogen doen naar Mineraal, off andere handelbaare Stoffen, en Producten, soo als deselve boven en onder d'aarde in gem ... . *Amsterdam: Salomon Schouten.* 1743. 4to, pp. 25. J.C.B. 56681

Octroy ofte Privilegie. *See* [Usselincx (W.)]

Octroy, | Van de Hoog: Moog: Heeren | Staten Generael, aengaende de | Colonie op de Wilde Kust | Van | America. | Onder het

beleyt van den Ridder | Balthazar Gerbier Baron Douvily. | [n. p.:] *Gedruckt in 't Iaer ons Heeren,* 1659. | 4to, 4 leaves. c.

The first Dutch patent for the colonization of Surinam.

Oculus, *pseudon.* The Home of the Badgers, or a Sketch of the Early History of Wisconsin. With a Series of Familiar Letters and Remarks on Territorial Character and Characteristics, ... By Oculus. *Milwaukie: Wilshire & Co.* 1845. 12mo, pp. 36

Oculus (I), *pseudon.* Picolilly; or, the Critical Chronicle of Ichabod Oculus, Esq. and others. ... *Boston: Phelps and Farnham, Printers.* 1823. 12mo, pp. 20. BA. 56684

Oda [al Iturbide. Colophon:] *En la imprenta Imperial.* [n. p. n. d.] 4to, pp. 4. BM. 56685

Oda al Jeneral Flores, Vencedor en Miñarica. [Signed "J. J. O." *Guayaquil: Imprenta de M. I. Murillo.* 1835.] 4to, pp. 8. H. 56686

O'Daniels (D. C.) A Discourse ... in Westminster, Mass., October 14, 1855, By D. C. O'Daniels, on ... resigning the Pastoral Charge ... . *Boston: Printed by John Wilson and Son.* 1855. 8vo, pp. 16. B. 56687

Also: ... A Discourse ... before the Universalist Societies, in Ilion and Frankfort, N. Y., March 23, 1856 ... . *Ilion, N. Y.: Geo. W. Bungay, Printer.* 1856. 8vo, pp. 24. B. — Letter to the Mohawk Association of Universalists. [*Ilion, N. Y.* 1856.] 8vo, pp. 19. B.

Odd Fellows. Celebration of the Semi-Centennial Anniversary of the I. O. of O. F., New York, April 26, 1869. *New York: J. Medole, Printer.* 1869. 8vo, pp. 24. 56688

The Covenant and Official Magazine of the Grand Lodge of the United States, I. O. O. F. ... Edited by P. G. M. James L. Ridgely. Vol. I. 1842. [n. p. n. d.] 8vo, pp. iv, 608. Continued. H. 56689

A General History of the ... Independent Odd Fellows Society, with an Expose of their Secret Signs, Grips, &c. &c. showing the bearing which Secret Societies have upon our Republican Institutions ... . [Second Edition.] *New York.* 1842. 8vo, pp. 30, (1). B. 56690

Journal of Proceedings of the Right Worthy Grand Lodge of the Independent Order of Odd Fellows of the United States of America, and the Jurisdiction thereunto belonging ... . From ...

1821, to ... 1843; together with Statistical Tables, showing the progress of the order; and Notes. ... [By Charles McGowen and John G. Treadwell.] *New York: McGowen & Treadwell.* 1844. 8vo, pp. xxxi, 601. Plate and Portrait. c. + To ... 1851. ... *Baltimore: Printed by P. G. James Young.* 1852. 8vo, pp. 734. Portraits. H. + To ... 1862. ... *Baltimore: Jas. L. Ridgely ...* . 1863. 8vo, pp. (2), 824. Portraits. Continued.

Journal of Proceedings of the ... Grand Lodge of ... Massachusetts. From ... 1823, to 1847. ... Vol. I. *Boston: Bro. P. G. Alfred Mudge.* 1847. 8vo, pp. 414. Continued, B. 56692

... Odd-Fellows' Casket & Review. Vol. I. *Cincinnati, O.: Longley Brothers.* [1859.] 8vo. 56693

Odd-Fellows' Literary Magazine. Edited by W. K. Cole. No. 1. July, 1848. *Albany.* 1848. 8vo. s. 56694

The Odd-Fellows' Offering, for MDCCCXLIV. Edited by Paschal Donaldson. *New York: Henry D. Loomis.* MDCCCXLIV. 18mo, pp. 288. Engraved Title and 5 Plates. Continued.

Odd-Fellowship—What is it? [n. p. 1867.] 8vo, pp. 8. B.

Also: An Account of the Grand Celebration of the Independent Order of Odd-Fellows, for the Dedication of the New Hall in ... Baltimore ... 26th ... of April, 1831 ... . *Baltimore: Sands & Neilson.* 1831. 8vo, pp. 52. — Digest of the Laws of ... Odd-Fellows, and Compend of the Legislation of the Grand Lodge of the United States ... . *Baltimore: James L. Ridgely.* 1853. 8vo, pp. 454. — Proceedings of the ... Grand Lodge of the United States ... held at Baltimore. *Baltimore.* 1827. 8vo. Portrait.

Oddi (Longaro degli). Della vita del Ven. servo di Dio P. Guiseppe Anchieta della Compagnia di Gesú detto l'Apostolo del Brasile libri due, cavati dai Processi authentici formati per la sua Beatificazione. Da un sacerdote della medesima Compagnia. *Roma: stamperia Romaresca.* MDCCXXXVIII. 8vo, pp. (16), 307. Plate. + Segonda edizione. *Roma: stamperia di Arcangelo Cataletti.* 1771. 12mo. + Dal P. Longaro degli Oddi della medesima Compagnia. *Torino: Giacinto Marietti.* 1824. 18mo, pp. 313. 56697

Ode for the Federal Procession, upon the Adoption of the New Government. [*New York.* n. d.] Folio, 1 leaf. 56698

Struck off in the streets of New York, and thrown among the people from the press.

Ode for the New Year, 1776. *London: J. Almon.* 1776. 4to.

Against the ministry. *See* "Monthly Review," LIV. 340.

An Ode, for the Thanksgiving Day. By Titus Antigallicus, Esq. *Boston.* 1749. 8vo. 56700

Ode in Commemoration of the first Settlement of a Congregation of the United Brethren at Newport, Rhode Island, November 10, 1758, for the Jubilee in 1808. ... *Newport.* 1808. 8vo, pp. 10. 56701

An Ode in honor of the Pennsylvania Militia, and a small band of Regular Troops under the Command of General George Washington, who in the depth of winter in the year 1776 turned the tide of fortune against Britain, and repulsed her Forces to the banks of the river Delaware. *Albany.* 1800. 12mo, pp. 10.

Ode on the Bones. *See* [Marshall (J.)], Vol. XI., No. 44803.

Ode on the late Glorious Successes. *See* [Evans (N.)], Vol. VI

An Ode on the Prospect of Peace. *Philadelphia.* 1761. 8vo.

Ode, on the Surrender at York-Town. To the Honourable W. Pitt. *London: Bowen.* 1782. 4to. 56704

See "Monthly Review," LXVI. 473.

An Ode, set to Music, consecrated to the Memory of the Rev. George Whitefield, A.M. [n. p. n. d.] Folio, 1 sheet. 56705

Ode suggested by Rembrandt Peale's National Portrait of Washington. [By John D. Godman.] *Philadelphia: Printed by Jesper Harding.* 1824. 8vo. 56706

Ode to a Friend, on our leaving, together, South Carolina. Written in June, 1780. *London: J. Dodsley.* 1783. 4to, pp. 15.

An Ode to Peace, occasioned by the present Crisis of the British Empire. *London: J. Almon.* 1778. 4to. 56708

See "Monthly Review," LVIII. 237.

Ode to Science read before the Western Museum Society at its Second Anniversary, June 10, 1820. *Cincinnati.* 1820. 12mo

Ode sung at the Thirty-First Anniversary of the Independence of the United States. [n. p. n. d.] 8vo, pp. 3. 56710

Odell (J.), *Jr.* Odell's Dayton Directory and Business Advertiser. To which is prefixed a sketch of the History of the City [by M. C. Curwen]. *Dayton: James Odell, Jr.* 1850. 12mo, pp. 120. 56711

This "sketch" was also issued separately. *See* our No. 18074, Vol. V.

[Odell (Margaretta Matilda).] Memoir and Poems of Phillis Wheatley, a Native African and a Slave. ... *Boston: Geo. W. Light.* 1834. 16mo, pp. 103. Portrait. BA. + Third Edition. *Boston: Isaac Knapp.* 1838. 24mo, pp. 155. Portrait. BA.

Odell (*Rev. Mr.*) The Times, a Satirical Poem, written during the American Revolution, by the Rev. Mr. Odell. *New-Jersey: Printed but not Published.* [n. d.] 8vo, pp. 26. 56713

Scarce and furious.

"Strike up Hell's music, roar infernal drums
Discharge the cannon—Lo! the warrior comes—
He comes not such as on Ohio's banks,
But rampant, at the head of ragged ranks,
Hunger and itch are with him, Gates and Wayne,
And all the lice of Egypt in his train.
Sure these are Falstaff's soldiers, poor and bare,
Or else the rotten regiment of Rag Fair."—*Page* 7.

Odenheimer (W. H.) The Origin and Compilation of the Prayer Book, with an Appendix containing various historical facts and documents connected with our Liturgy. By W. H. Odenheimer. *Philadelphia.* 1844. 18mo. 56714

Odérahi, histoire américaine; contenant une peinture fidelle des moeurs des habitants de l'intérieur de l'Amérique Septentrionale. *Paris.* [1800.] 8vo. 56715

Oderay, usos, trages, ritos, costumbres y leyes de los habitantes de la America septentrional, traducidas del Francés é illustradas con varias notas criticas, ... por Don Gaspar Zavala y Zamora. *Madrid: Gomez Fuentenebro y Compania.* 1804. 16mo, pp. 288. C., H. 56716

Odes of Horace. *See* [Peirce (Thomas)].

Odes, suivies d'une lettre. *See* [Cornillon (Ch. de)], Vol. IV.

Odes, to be performed at the Commencement of Union College, in the City of Schenectady. May 5, 1802. *Albany.* 1802. 8vo, pp. 8. 56717

Odes to be sung at the Juvenile Patriotic Festival, July 4, 1839. [n. p. n. d.] 8vo. 56718

Odescalchi (C.) Memorias edificantes sobre la vida religiosa del P. Carlos Odescalchi, de la Compañia de Jesus. *Mexico.* 1846. 8vo, pp. 98. 56719

Odet-Julien Leboucher. *See* Leboucher (O.-J.), Vol. X.

Odet-Pellion. Reconnaissance Hydrographique des Côtes occidentales de Centre-Amérique exécutée par la Corvette la Brillante. *Paris.* 1854. 8vo, pp. 80. Maps and Plates.

Odin. Pedigree of the Odin Family. ... [*Boston.*] 1858. 8vo, pp. 4. 56721

Odiorne (T.) The Progress of Refinement, A Poem, in Three Books. To which are added, A Poem on Fame, and Miscellanies. By Thomas Odiorne. *Boston: Printed by Young and Etheridge.* MDCCXCII. 12mo, pp. 176. B. 56722

Also: Ethic Strains; and other Minor Poems. ... *Boston.* 1821. 8vo. — Poems ... . *Boston: The Author.* 1821. 8vo, pp. 48. B.

Odizhijigeuiniua igiu Gaanoninjig. Anishinabe enuet Anikunotabiung, au Sherman Hall, gaie au George Copway. *Boston.* 1838. 12mo, pp. 108. 56723

Acts of the Apostles in the Ojibwa language.

Odlin (J.) Christian Courage necessary for a Gospel Minister. Sermon ... At Kingston, Sept. 29. 1725. When Mr. Ward Clark Was Ordained ... . By John Odlin, A.M. ... *Boston: Printed by B. Green.* 1727. 8vo, pp. (2), ii, 22. B., BA. 56724

[Odlin (Woodbridge), *and others.*] *See* Vol. VI., No. 23393.

Odlum (J.) A Memoir on the Cultivation of the Vine in America ... . By John Odlum. *Washington.* 1828. 8vo.

O'Doherty (*Sir* Morgan), *pseudon.* A Reply to the Libel of James Gordon Bennett on Daniel O'Connell. By Sir Morgan O'Doherty. *New York.* 1838. 8vo, pp. 12. 56726

O'Donnel (K.) The Song of Iron and the Song of Slaves; with other Poems. By Kane O'Donnel. *Philadelphia: King & Baird, Printers.* 1863. 18mo, pp. 72. H. 56727

O'Donnell (——). Speech of Senator O'Donnell on National Affairs. ... March 1st, 1866. *Albany: Weed, Parsons and Company, Printers.* 1866. 8vo, pp. 15. BA. 56728

O'Donoju (J.) Correspondencia entre el General D. Juan O-Donoju, y el Brigadier D. Francisco Lemaur, Y las últimas cartas de aquel al general Dávila, con las respuestas de éste. [Colophon:] *Habana.* 1821. *Diaz de Castro.* 8vo, pp. 25.

O'Donoju. Refutacion, con notas interestantes, al parte que dirigio a Superior Gobierno el Teniente General Don Juan

O-Donoju sobre el Tratado que Firmó en Córdoba. *Habana.*—1822. *Pedro Nolásce Boloña.* 8vo, pp. (2), 15. 56730

Odriozola (M. de). Terremotos. Coleccion de las Relaciones de los mas notables que ha sufrido esta Capital y que la han arruinado ... . Colectadas y arregladas por D. Manuel de Odriozola. *Lima.* 1863. Sm. 4to, pp. 205. Plate and folded sheet.

Oehler (A.) The Life, Adventures, and unparalleled Sufferings of Andrew Oehler; containing an Account of his Travels through ... the East and West Indies, and part of the United States ... . Written by Himself. [*Trenton, N. J.:*] *The Author.* 1811. 12mo, pp. 226. C., P. 56732

Oelen (A. Jsz. van). Kort en opregt verhaal van het droevig en avontuurlijk wedervaren van A. Jsz. van Oelen, schipper van Nieu Vosmeer ... in 1682 op 26 Jan. En hoe hij op 7 October van het selve jaar, op een wonderlijke ... wijs, bij St. Annaland een (sogenaemde) Walvis gevangen heeft enz. Waar agter ... eenige voorvallen, van sommige commandeurs en gasten in Groenland uytgestaan. [n. p.] 1683. 4to. 56733

Oelsner-Monmerqué, der Kreole. Vorlesung. *Berlin.* 1848. 8vo. 56734

Oersted (Anders Sandöe). L'Amérique Centrale. Recherches sur sa flora et sa géographie physique. ... Liv. I. *Copenhague: F. S. Muhle.* 1863. 4to, pp. (6), 18. 22 Plates.

Also: Det Centralamerikanske Ambatrae. ... [n. p.] 1870. 8vo. 2 Plates. — Copalme de l'Amérique centrale. ... [n. p. n. d.] 8vo. — Mexicos og Centralamerikas Acanthaceer. ... [n. p.] 1854. 8vo. 3 Plates. — Myrsineae Centro-americanae et Mexicanae. ... [n. p.] 1861. 8vo. Plate.

[Oertel (Philipp Friedrich).] Benjamin Franklin. Lebensbild eines Ehrenmannes in Amerika. ... Von W. O. von Horn. *New York: E. Steiger.* 1865. 18mo, pp. 77. + Zweite Auflage. *Wiesbaden: Julius Niedner.* 1869. 16mo, pp. 116. Portrait and 3 Plates. B. 56736

[Oertel.] Der Lebensgang Georg Washingtons, des Begründers der Freiheit der Vereinigten Staaten Nordamerika's. ... Von W. O. Von Horn ... . *Wiesbaden: Julius Niedner.* [n. d.] 16mo, pp. 136. Portrait and 3 Plates. B. 56737

[Oertel.] Les Trappeurs du Kansas. Histoire américaine racontée a la jeunesse; ... traduit de l'allemand [par Mlle El. Dufour]. *Lausanne: Delafontaine et Rouge.* 1862. 16mo. 56738

Also: Johann Jacob Astor. Lebensbild eines Ehrenmannes in Amerika. ... *New York: E. Steiger.* 1865. 18mo, pp. 76. + *Wiesbaden: Verlag von Kreidel und Niedner.* [n. d.] 16mo, pp. 102. Portrait and 3 Plates.

Oettinger (E. M.) Bibliographie biographique universelle. Dictionnaire des ouvrages relatifs à l'Histoire de la Vie publique et privée des Personnages célèbres de tous les temps et de toutes les nations ... . Par Édouard Marie Oettinger. *Leipzig.* 1850. Impl. 8vo, pp. (8), 788. + *Bruxelles: Stienon.* 1854. 2 vols., impl. 8vo, pp. (4), iv, 1264 columns; pp. (4), 1265–2192 columns

This laborious work indicates under the name of each remarkable person, all the biographies that have been written concerning him.

Oexmelin (A. O.) *See* Exquemelin (A. O.), Nos. 23475–8.

Of Negro Slavery as it exists in our West India Colonies ... . *Hull.* 1824. 12mo, pp. 12. 56740

Of Sturbridge. *See* Vol. VI., No. 23710.

Of the Birth and Death of Nations. A Thought for the Crisis. *New York: G. P. Putnam.* 1862. 12mo, pp. 32.

Of the Circumference of the Earth. *See* [Howe (E.)], VIII.

Of the Conversion of Five Thousand and Nine Hundred East Indians, In the Isle Formose, ... by means of M. Ro: Junius ... Related by his friend M. C. Sibellius in a Latine Letter, Translated by H. Jessei. With a Post-script of the Gospel's good Successe amongst the West-Indians, in New England. *London: Printed by Iohn Hammond ...* 1650. 4to, pp. (8), 38, (2).

The postscript of this rare volume is compiled from three tracts: "Good News of the Day-Breaking," "Of the Sunshine," "Of the Glorious Progress of the Gospel," etc., and from letters by John Eliot (the Indian Apostle), dated, Roxbury, 1648–49, about ten years before the publication of his *Bible.*

Of the Nature and Effects of Negro Slavery. *London.* 1823. 8vo, pp. 3. 56743

Of the newe lādes. *See* [Emanuel], Vol. VI., No. 22406.

Of the Ten Tribes of Israel, and the Aborigines of America, ... By a Bible Professor ... . *New Albany, Indiana: Printed by Collins & Green.* 1831. 8vo, pp. 32. 56744

Of the VVood called Gvaiacvm. *See* [Hutten (Ulrich)].

O'Fallon Polytechnic Institute; its Objects and Present Condition. *St. Louis, Mo.* 1858. 8vo, pp. 27. H. 56745

O'Farill (Joseph R.) En la junta de sociedad patriotica de 24 de Noviembre de 1796, se leyó un oficio de la clase de agricultura, remitiendo el informe pedido à D. J. Ricardo O-Farill sobre las ideas que en la memoria de la conservacion de los montes del Padre Manuel Gil halle adaptables à este pais. [Colophon:] *Havana 22 de Octubre de 1796.—Joseph Ricardo O-Farill.* 4to, pp. 24. 56746

[O'Farill.] Gracia concedida por S. M. á los habitantes de la Isla para la introduccion de caballos frisones de ambos sexos desde las provincias del Norte de América, en Real órden de 9 de Junio de 1798. *Habana.* [1799.] 4to. 56747

Contains a "Memoria sobre la cria de ganado mular y caballar y mejora de sus castas, por los Sres. D. José Ricardo O-Farill y D. J. B. Lanz." Also: Discurso que se leyó en Junta ordinaria de la Sociedad Patriótica por D. Juan Manuel O-Farill. *Habana.* 1796. 4to, pp. 17.

Ofensa, y Defensa de la Libertad Eclesiastica. La primera en veinte y qvatro capitulos, que mandò publicar el Duque de la Palata, Virrey del Perú, en despacho de 20. de Febrero de 1684. Y la Segvnda Armada con los escudos Catolicos de la ley, y la razon, que establecen los dominios de su Majestad, y dictò su propria Obligacion, al Señor Dr. D. Melchor de Liñan y Cisneros, Arçobispo de Lima. [n. p. n. d.] Folio, 104 leaves. 56748

This important volume was intended for private distribution only, but without doubt was printed in Lima, 1684–5.

Off Hand Sketches; a Companion for the Tourist, ... over the Philadelphia ... and Reading Railroad. *Philadelphia: J. W. Moore.* 1854. 12mo, pp. 194. c. 56749

The Offering, for 1829. *Cambridge: Hilliard and Brown.* 1829. 12mo, pp. ix, (2), 252. 4 Plates. B. 56750

Office and Duty of Sheriffs, Under-Sheriffs, and Coroners. *Philadelphia: Andrew Bradford.* 1721. 4to. 56751

Office of Institution of Ministers into Parishes or Churches prescribed by the Protestant-Episcopal Church in the United States. *New York.* 1808. 8vo, pp. 19. M. 56752

The Office of the Supervising Architect. What it was, is, and ought to be. *New York.* 1867. 8vo. 56753

Office of the Western Kansas. *See* Vol. ix., No. 37073.

Officer, *pseudon.* *See* Nos. 1024, 18170, 19622, 24585–7, 40324, 53548, *and* 55961.

The Officers' Manual. Napoleon's Maxims of War. *Richmond, Va.: West & Johnston.* 1862. 16mo, pp. 159. 56754

Officers of our Union Army and Navy. [Biographical.] *Boston.* 1862. 12mo. 56755

Officia Propria foederatis provinciis Americæ Septentrionalis Concessa. Pars Hiemalis. *Mechliniæ: P. J. Hanicq.* MDCCCXLVII. 12mo. 56756

Official Account of Naval Victories, during the Present War between the United States and Great Britain. *Boston.* 1813. 8vo

An Official Account of the Trial and Execution of Arbuthnot & Ambrister; ... containing the whole Proceedings of the Court Martial, as ordered by Major-General Jackson .... Together with some remarks on the conduct of the two Chiefs, Francis and Bull Head .... [n. p.:] *P. M. Davis.* 1825. 12mo, pp. 45. 56758

Official Army List of the Western States for August, 1862, including Volunteers of Illinois, Indiana, Wisconsin, Minnesota, Michigan, Iowa, Missouri, Kansas, Nebraska, and Colorado. Compiled ... by George B. Smith. *Chicago: John R. Walsh.* 1862. 12mo, pp. (2), 176. c. 56759

Official Army Register ... 1802. *Washington.* 1802. 12mo. Continued. c. 56760

See also Vol. i., No. 2053.

Official Army Register of the Volunteer Force of the United States Army, for ... 1861 ... 1865. *Washington.* 1865–67. 8 vols., 8vo. c. 56761

Official Arrangements for the Funeral Solemnities of the late Secretary of State, Abel P. Upshur; the late Secretary of the Navy, Thomas W. Gilmer; the late Captain B. Kennon; the late Virgil Maxcy; and of the late Hon. D. Gardiner. *Washington.* 1844. 12mo. c. 56762

Official Catalogue of the N. Y. Exhibition. *See* Vol. i. 2239.

Also: Official Awards of the Juries. *New York.* 1853. 8vo.—Official Catalogue of the Pictures ... in the ... Gallery of the Crystal Palace. *New York: G. P. Putnam & Co.* 1853. 12mo, pp. 23. H.

Official Catalogue of the Products of the United States of America, exhibited at Paris, 1867, with Statistical Notices. Catalogue in English. Catalogue Français. Deutscher Catalog.

Third Edition. *Paris: A. Chaix et Cie.* 1867. 16mo, pp. (4), 160. c. 56763

Official Copy of Orders. *See* No. 54986.

Official Correspondence between the Agents. *See* No. 15323.

Official Correspondence between the United States and Mexico, from May 12 to September 10, 1842. [n. p. about 1843.] 8vo, pp. (2), 38. c. 56764

The Official Correspondence on the Claims of the United States in respect to the 'Alabama.' *London: Longmans* ... . 1866. 8vo, pp. 279. 56765

Official Correspondence on the Fisheries. *Halifax.* 1852. 4to

Official Correspondence. *See* Vol. ix., No. 35321.

Official Despatches. *See* Bartlett (J. R.), Vol. i., No. 3745.

Official Documents relative to the Operations of the British Army employed in the Reduction of the Canadas under Majors-General Wolfe, Amherst, &c., in 1759–'60. *Philadelphia.* 1813. 8vo. 2 Maps. c., s. 56767

See D. W. Smith's "Gazetteer of the Province of Upper Canada." *See also* Nos. 9618, 12536, *and* 27080.

Official Draft of Instructions for the Dispatch of an Expedition to the Spanish Territories, and for reducing New Orleans, protecting West Florida, &c. [n. p. n. d.] 8vo. 56768

Title from one of Thomas Thorpe's catalogues. Endorsed "Most Secret."

Official Extracts from the Resolutions of the States General of the United Provinces, Reports, Requests, Memorials, etc., concerning Curaçao. [n. p.] 1739. 8vo. 56769

Mostly on the capturing of Dutch vessels by the English.

Official Journal of the Conference Convention. *See* No. 15433

Official Journal of the Constitutional Convention, held in Montgomery, commencing Nov. 5th, 1867. *Montgomery: Barrett & Brown.* 1868. 8vo, pp. iii, 291. c. 56770

Official Letter. *See* Vol. i., No. 2719.

Official Letters. *See* Brannan (J.), Vol. ii., No. 7411.

Official List of Officers who marched with the Army, under Command of Major-General Winfield Scott, from Puebla upon the City of Mexico, the 7th, 8th, 9th and 10th of August, 1847, and who were engaged in the Battles of Mexico. *Mexico: American Star Print.* 1848. 4to, 14 leaves. Plan. s. 56771

Among the names omitted and put in the errata, was that of George B. McClellan.

Official Monthly Bulletin of the great National Peace Jubilee and Musical Festival, ... in Boston, ... June ... 1869 .... *Boston: George Coolidge.* [n. d.] 5 Nos., 8vo. B. 56772

Official Note from the Consul. *See* Vol. iii., No. 9028.

Official Notes from the Minister of the French Republic to the Secretary of State of the United States; with a Replication to the First Note. *Philadelphia.* [1796.] 8vo, pp. 42. P.

Official Opinions of the Attorneys-General of the United States, advising the President and Heads of Departments in relation to their Official Duties; and expounding the Constitution, subsisting Treaties with Foreign Governments and with Indian Tribes, and the Public Laws of the Country. Compiled, with Notes and References, by Benjamin F. Hall. ... *Washington.* 1852–58. 8 vols., 8vo. Continued. c. 56774

Official Papers relating to the Conduct of the United States Legation. *Paris.* 1867. 8vo. 56775

Official Papers relative to the Dispute between the Courts of Great Britain and Spain, on the subject of the Ships captured in Nootka Sound, and the negotiation that followed thereon; together with The Proceedings in both Houses of Parliament on the King's Message ... [With] The Report of M. de Mirabeau, and the subsequent decrees of the National Assembly of France on the Family Compact. *London: J. Debrett.* [1790.] 8vo, pp. vii, (1), 100. H. 56776

See also [Etches (John)], Vol. vi., No. 23087.

Official Papers. *See* Nos. 6537, 32625, *and* Vermont.

Official Proceedings of the Democratic National Convention, held in 1860, at Charleston and Baltimore. Proceedings at Charleston, April 23–May 3; Prepared and Published under the Direction of John G. Parkhurst, Recording Secretary. *Cleveland: Nevins' Print.* 1860. 8vo, pp. 188. 56777

See also Nos. 13100, 49530, 49554, *and* 53846.

Official Record from the War Department, of the Proceedings of the Court Martial which tried, and the Orders of General Jackson for Shooting the Six Militia Men ... showing that these American Citizens were Inhumanly & Illegally Massacred. *Washington: Jonathan Elliot.* 1828. 8vo, pp. 32. + *Concord: Printed by Jacob B. Moore.* 1828. 8vo, pp. 52. + *Albany.* 1828. 8vo. + Fourth Edition. *Washington.* 1828. 8vo. 56778

Official Record of Rhode Island in the United States Army and Navy, during the Rebellion of the Southern States. *Providence.* MDCCCLXVI. Rl. 8vo, pp. (4), 819. Portraits. 56779

Twenty-four copies printed on tinted paper, with rubricated title.

Official Record of the National ... Council. *See* No. 15484.

Official Register ... of Officers and Agents in the Service of the United States, Sept. 30, 1816. *Washington.* 1816. 8vo. Continued. 56780

Official Register of Missouri Troops. *See* Vol. xii. 49627.

Official Register of the Army for 1867. *Washington.* 1867. 12mo, pp. 178. 2 Tables. Continued. c. 56781

Official Register of the United States Naval Academy. *Newport.* 1862. 8vo. 56782

Official Report of Generals Johnston and Beauregard of the Battle of Manassas, July 21, 1861; also, Official Report of the Battle of September 10 and 11; Bombardment of Forts Walker and Beauregard, Nov. 7; Engagement of Piketon, Ky., Dec. 13; Battle in the Alleghany Mountains, Dec. 13; Battle of Chustenahlah, Dec. 26; Battle of Belmont, Nov. 7. ... *Richmond.* 1862. 8vo. 56783

Official Report of the Debates and Proceedings of the Southern Commercial Convention, ... at Knoxville, Tennessee, August 10, 1857. *Knoxville: Kinsloe & Rice.* 1857. 8vo, pp. 96.

See also Nos. 2840, 12674, 15324, 21036, 49627, *note, and* 54564.

Official Reports from the Executive Departments to the House of Representatives of the United States, 1790 to 1793. *New-York and Philadelphia.* 1790–1793. Folio. c. 56785

Official Reports of Battles. Published by Order of [the Confederate] Congress at Richmond; Being a Southern History of

the War. *New York: Chas. B. Richardson.* 1863. 8vo, pp. 578. Portrait. c. 56786

Official Reports of Engagements on the Mississippi River and Capture of Forts Jackson and St. Philip and the City of New Orleans. *Washington.* 1862. 8vo. 56787

... Official Reports ... of the Battle of Bethel, on the 10th of June, 1861 .... *Richmond.* 1862. 8vo, pp. 31. B. 56788

See also Nos. 15325–15330, 22749, *and* 53564.

Offley (G. W.) A Narrative of the Life and Labors of Rev. G. W. Offley, A Colored Man, and Local Preacher, Who lived twenty-seven years at the South and twenty-four at the North; who never went to school a day in his life, and only commenced to learn his letters when nineteen years and eight months old; ... *Hartford, Conn.* 1860. 12mo, pp. 52. 56789

Oficio de Difuntos Para sufragio de los serviles que por nuestra diligencia, patriotismo y misericordia decansan en la paz del olvido. *Mexico:* 1822. *Imprenta de Dona Herculano del Villar y socios.* 4to, pp. 8. 56790

Oficio del Consul. *See* Vol. iii., No. 9027.

Oficios del Consulado de Veracruz al Escmo. Ayuntamiento referentes al estado de la Plaza y disposiciones del Gobierno; con otras contestaciones ocurridas posteriormente. *Veracruz.* 1821. 4to, pp. 28. 56791

O'Flaherty (T.) Civilization; A Lecture, ... in ... Buffalo, N. Y., February the 14th, 1855, By Rev. Thomas O'Flaherty .... *Auburn: Knapp & Peck, Printers.* 1855. 8vo, pp. 24.

O'Flanaghan (J.) The Continuation of a Government of Fraud. By J. O'Flanaghan. *New York.* 1862. 8vo, pp. 20.

Ofrenda a Muchachas Calaberas que les dan los Arrancados. *Mexico.* 1835. Sm. 8vo, 2 leaves. 56794

Ofrenda al Bazar de la Real Casa de Beneficencia. *Habana.* 1864. 8vo, pp. 206. 56795

[Ogden (Aaron).] Concerning Steam Boats. Documents without Comments. [n. p. 1818.] 8vo, pp. 25. BA. 56796

Ogden. Memorial of Aaron Ogden, of Elizabeth Town .... *Washington City: Printed by R. C. Weightman.* 1811. 8vo, pp. 4.

[Ogden.] A Statement of the Case of the surviving Officers of the Revolution, who continued in the Service to the Termination of the War. [n. p. n. d.] 8vo, pp. 10, Appendix, 6. B.

Also: Report of the Committee ... [on the] Memorial and Petition of Aaron Ogden, a Citizen of ... New-Jersey. [*Albany.*] 1814. 8vo, pp. 13, (1). B. *See also* Vol. xiii., No. 53054.

Ogden (C. R.) Petition of Charles Richard Ogden, Esq., late Attorney-General of Canada, to Her Majesty. *Liverpool.* [1860.] 8vo. 56799

[Ogden (D.)] The Claim of the Inhabitants of the Town of Newark; In virtue of The Indian Purchase made by the first Settlers of Newark, in 1667, Stated and Considered. *Woodbridge, in New-Jersey: Printed by Samuel F. Parker.* M.DCC.LXVI. 8vo, pp. 12, and over. 56800

A very rare piece. I have never seen a perfect copy.

[Ogden.] To the several Persons claiming under the Indian Purchases, called the Mountain, Horsneck and Van Gieson Purchases. [n. p. n. d.] 8vo, pp. 7. P. 56801

Subscribed "David Ogden, Newark, February 20, 1767." It relates to some disputed land-titles in New Jersey, and is most rare.

Ogden *vs.* Folliott (G.) In Error. House of Lords. Between David Ogden, Plaintiff in Error, and George Folliott, Defendant in Error. The Case for the Plaintiff in Error. To be heard, 18th May, 1791. [*London.* 1791.] Folio, pp. 11. c.

Relative to large sums of money due by Ogden to Folliott in 1769. Ogden was a loyalist, and urged the confiscation of his property in New Jersey. Also: Case of the Defendant in Error. [*London.* 1791.] Folio, pp. 11. c.

Ogden (D. B.) Oration at Newark, 4th July, 1798. By David B. Ogden. *Newark.* 1798. 12mo. N. 56803

Ogden (D. L.) ... A Sermon ... before the Auxiliary Foreign Mission Society, of Farmington and Vicinity, Oct. 22, 1828. By David L. Ogden, A.M. ... *New Haven: Printed by Hezekiah Howe.* 1828. 8vo, pp. 20. B. 56804

Ogden (E. D.) *See* Tariff.

[Ogden (G. W.)] A Letter to Hull Barton, an Excommunicated Member from the Society of Friends; now a New Light Preacher: ... By his Friend Notus Nimini. [*New Bedford.*] 1823. 8vo, pp. 12. 56805

Ogden. Letters from the West, Comprising a Tour through the Western Country, and a Residence of two Summers in the States of Ohio and Kentucky ... . By George W. Ogden. ... *New-Bedford: Melcher & Rogers.* 1823. 12mo, pp. 126. B.

Ogden (G. M.) A Defence of Columbia College from The Attack of Samuel B. Ruggles. By Gouverneur M. Ogden, a Trustee. *New-York: J. P. Wright, Printer.* 1854. 8vo, pp. 43

Also: Lecture on National Character. ... *New York.* 1843. 8vo.

Ogden (J.) The British Lion Rous'd; or Acts of the British Worthies, a Poem in Nine Books. By James Ogden. *Manchester: Printed by R. Whitworth.* M,DCC,LX,II. Rl. 8vo, pp. (20). 56808

France disturbs the peace of British settlements in America. Her encroachments there form part of the contents.

Ogden (J. De P.) An Address delivered October 5, 1842, at the Celebration of the Fiftieth Anniversary of Union Hall, Jamaica, Long Island, By James De Peyster Ogden .... *Jamaica: Printed by Charles S. Watrous.* 1842. 8vo, pp. 19. H. 56809

Ogden. The Founders of New York; being the Anniversary Address ... at the Lyceum, 5th December, 1845, before the St. Nicholas Society. By J. De Peyster Ogden. *New York.* 1846. 8vo, pp. 19. 56810

[Ogden.] Remarks on the Currency of the United States and the Present State and Future Prospects of the Country. By Publius. 1840. [*New York.* 1840.] 8vo, pp. 59. B., N. 56811

[Ogden.] Additional Remarks on the Currency of the United States. By Publius. *New-York: Wiley and Putnam.* 1841. 8vo, pp. iv, 3–45. B., N. 56812

Also: Lecture on National Character, ... at the Jamaica Lyceum, L. I., April 25th, 1843 .... *New-York: Jas. P. Wright, Printer.* 1843. 8vo, pp. 32. H.

Ogden (J. C.) An Address ... at the Opening of Portsmouth Academy, ... 1791. By the Reverend John Cosens Ogden .... *Printed by George Jerry Osborne, Portsmouth.* M.DCC.XCI. 8vo, pp. 35. 56813

Ogden. An Epistolary Correspondence between the Rev. John C. Ogden ... of ... Portsmouth, New-Hampshire; and the Rev. Samuel Macclintock ... of ... Greenland, on a Variety of Subjects .... *Portsmouth: Printed ... by J. Melcher.* M,DCC,XCI. 8vo, pp. 38. BA., H. 56814

Ogden. An Excursion into Bethlehem & Nazareth, in Pennsylvania, in ... 1799; with a Succinct History of the Society of United Brethren, commonly called Moravians. By John C. Ogden, Presbyter in the Protestant Episcopal Church, in the United States. *Philadelphia: Printed by Charles Cist* ... M,DCCC. 12mo, pp. (2), 167, (1). + [*Ibid.*] 1805. 12mo, pp. (2), 167.

Includes a short narration of the massacre of Christian Indians at Salem and Gnadenhutten.

Ogden. Letters, occasioned by the Publication of a Private Epistolary Correspondence, begun by Mr. Samuel Macclintock, Preacher ... In Greenland, New-Hampshire. By John Cosens Ogden ... . *Printed at Boston, By I. Thomas and E. T. Andrews.* MDCCXCI. 8vo, pp. 60. H., N. 56816

Ogden. A Sermon, ... at the Annual Election, Holden at Concord, ... June, M.DCC.XC. By John C. Ogden, A.M. ... *Printed at Concord, by George Hough* ... M.DCC.XC. 12mo, pp. 24

[Ogden.] A Tour through Upper and Lower Canada, By a Citizen of the United States. *Litchfield.* 1799. 12mo, pp. 119

Scarce. The author was son-in-law of Gen. David Wooster, and resided in New Haven, 1771–1785; afterwards, Episcopal minister in Portsmouth, N. H.

Ogden. A Tour through Upper and Lower Canada. Containing a View of the Present State of Religion, Commerce, Agriculture [etc.], among the English, French, and Indian Settlements. By John C. Ogden ... . The Second Edition. *Wilmington: Printed by Bonsal and Niles.* 1800. 12mo, pp. 117. C.

Also: Sermon ... before the Columbian Lodge, at Nottingham, N. H., September 7th, 1790. ... *Portsmouth.* 1791. 8vo, pp. 35. N.

Ogden (L. M.) Oration ... 4th July, 1803, at Newark. By Lewis M. Ogden. *Newark.* 1803. 8vo. N. 56820

Ogden (O. N.) Eulogy on the Life and Character of Lafayette, delivered ... [at] Philadelphia, By O. N. Ogden, of Louisiana. July 28, 1834. *Published by the Institute.* 1834. 12mo, pp. 21. 56821

Also: An Anniversary Oration, ... 13th of April 1836, ... [before] the Jefferson Society, of the University of Virginia. ... *Charlottesville: Printed by James Alexander.* 1836. 8vo, pp. 35.—Oration Eulogistic of O. N. Ogden, before the Jefferson Society of the University of Virginia. *Charlotte.* 1836. 8vo. N.

Ogden (U.) An Address To those persons at Elizabeth-Town, and Newark, and in their Vicinity, In ... New-Jersey, Who have lately been seriously impressed with a Desire to obtain

Salvation. ... By the Reverend Uzal Ogden. ... *New-York: J. M'Lean, and Co.* M.DCC.LXXXV. 8vo, pp. 43. BA. 56822

Ogden. A Sermon ... at Morris-Town, ... December 27, 1784, ... Before the ... Masons, Of Lodge No. 10, in ... New-Jersey. By the Reverend Uzal Ogden. ... *New-York: Printed by J. M'Lean, and Co.* M.DCC.LXXXV. 8vo, pp. 47. N. 56823

Ogden. The Theological Preceptor; or Youth's Religious Instructor. Containing a Summary of the Principles, Rise, and Progress of Religion ... . In a Series of Dialogues. By Uzal Ogden, Jun. ... *New York: Printed by John Holt.* M,DCC,LXXII. 12mo, pp. xii, 259. 56824

Ogden. Two Discourses, Occasioned by the Death of General George Washington, ... December 14, 1799. By the Rev. Uzal Ogden, D.D. Rector of Trinity Church, Newark, in ... New-Jersey. Delivered in that Church, and in the Church in union with it, At Belleville, December 29th, 1799, and January 5th, 1800. ... *Newark: Printed ... by Matthias Day.* MDCCC. 8vo, pp. 46. Portrait. BA. + Second Edition. *Philadelphia: ... A. Dickins* ... 1800. 8vo, pp. 40. 56825

Also: Antidote to Deism. The Deist Unmasked; or, an ample Refutation of all the Objections of Thomas Paine, against the Christian Religion; ... *Newark: John Woods.* M,DCC,XCV. 2 vols., 12mo, pp. xxiv, 327; xxii, 342.—A Circular Letter to the several Congregations of the Episcopal Church of New Jersey. [n. p.] 1798. 8vo. —Four Sermons on Important Subjects delivered in St. George's and St. Paul's Chapels, in the City of New York ... . *Elizabethtown.* 1788. 8vo, pp. 78.—A Sermon ... at Roxbury, in Morris County, March 19, 1781, at the Funeral of Mrs. Elizabeth Hackett ... . *Chatham: Printed by Shepard Kollock.* M,DCC,LXXXI. 4to, pp. 17. BA.—A Sermon ... in ... Perth-Amboy, May 16, 1786. Before A Convention of Clerical ... Delegates, of the Protestant Episcopal Church, in ... New-Jersey. ... *New-York: Printed by Samuel & John Loudon.* M,DCC,LXXXVI. 8vo, pp. 31. H.

Ogdensburgh, *N. Y.* Act in Relation to Schools ... in Ogdensburgh, New York, passed April 13, 1857. With the Rules and Regulations ... . *Ogdensburgh.* 1857. 8vo. S. 56826

Carrier's Address, to the Patrons of the Ogdensburgh Sentinel. [Also, a Directory. n. p. 1852.] 8vo, pp. 8. H. 56827

Handbook, Descriptive of the Route to Ogdensburgh, Montreal, Quebec, White Mountains, Ticonderoga, Saratoga Springs and Boston ... . *Niagara Falls: W. E. Tunis.* 1856. 24mo, pp. 10. Map. H. 56828

See also Vol. VIII., No. 30207.

Third Annual Report of the ... Ogdensburgh and Lake Champlain Railroad. *Boston: Henry W. Dutton & Son, Printers.* 1868. 8vo, pp. 16. Continued. H. 56829

Articles of Association of the Ogdensburgh, Clayton and Rome Railroad Company. *Rome.* 1853. 8vo. S. 56830

Also: Report of the Chief-Engineer, and of the President and Directors ... and Letter of John B. Jervis, Esq., Civil Engineer, April 20, 1854. *Rome.* 1854. 8vo.

The Ogdensburgh Directory for 1867–68. *Ogdensburgh: C. J. Hynes, Printer.* [n. d.] 12mo, pp. 94. 56831

Ogdensburgh Rail Road. Reasons for New Organization and Extension of First Mortgage. *Malone, N. Y.: Printed by J. K. Seaver.* 1857. 8vo, pp. 14. H. 56832

Report of Dr. Peters on the Longitude and Latitude of Ogdensburgh. *Albany.* 1865. 8vo.

Ogee (Q.), *pseudon.* Extracts from Humbuggiana: or, the World's Convention. A Satire ... . By Quirk Ogee, LL.D. *Gotham* [i. e. *New York*]: *Gas, Green & Ginger.* XVIII. XLVII. 12mo, pp. 24. H. 56833

Ogilby (F.) The Sermon ... Sunday ... after the Death of Bishop Doane. By the Rev. F. Ogilby, D.D. ... *New York: Pudney & Russell, Printers.* 1859. 8vo, pp. 23. B. 56834

Ogilby (John). *See* Vol. I. 1427, *and* Vol. XII. 50088–9.

Ogilby (J. D.) ... Annual Sermon, ... before the ... Diocese of New Jersey, ... May, ... 1843: By Rev. John D. Ogilby, M.A. ... *New-York.* 1843. 8vo, pp. 24. H. 56835

Ogilby. The Catholic Church in England and America: Three Lectures ... . By John D. Ogilby, D.D. *New York.* 1844. 16mo, pp. 208. C. 56836

Also: An Address ... before the Philoclean Society of Rutgers College, ... December 8, 1832. ∴ *New-Brunswick: Printed by Terhune and Letson.* 1833. 8vo, pp. 24. —... Address ... [before] the General Theological Seminary ... December, 1847. ... *New-York: Daniel Dana, Jr.* 1847. 8vo, pp. 27. B.

Ogilvie (J.) Speech delivered in Essex County [Va.], in support of a Memorial on the subject of the Alien and Sedition Laws. By James Ogilvie. *Richmond.* 1798. 8vo. C. 56837

Also: Cursory Reflexions on Government, Philosophy, and Education. ... *Alexandria.* 1802. 8vo. C.

Ogilvie (J. G.) The Religious Principles, and Forms of Government, of the following ... [fifteen] Denominations ... .

Collected ... By the Rev. J. G. Ogilvie ... . *Auburn: Printed ... by U. F. Doubleday.* 1820. 16mo, pp. 227, (1). 56838

Ogilvie. A Sermon delivered in The Baptist Meeting House, in the Village of Troy, ... March 10, 1816. By the Rev. James G. Ogilvie ... . *Hudson: Press of William L. Stone.* 1816. 8vo, pp. 26. 56839

Ogilvie (J.) Providence, an Allegorical Poem. In Three Books. By John Ogilvie, A.M. ... *Boston: ... J. Mein* ... . M DCC LXVI. 12mo, pp. 180. B., P. + *London.* 1764. 4to.

Ogle (A. J.) Remarks of Mr. Ogle, of Pennsylvania, On the Civil and Diplomatic Appropriation Bill. ... April 14, 1840. [n. p. n. d.] 8vo, pp. 32. B. 56841

Also: The pretended Democracy of Martin Van Buren. Being the Second Part of Mr. Ogle's Speech. [n. p. n. d.] 8vo, pp. 24.—Speech ... on the Life and Character of W. H. Harrison, April 16, 1840. [n. p. n. d.] 8vo.

Ogle (C.) True and Genuine Copy of the Trial of Sir Chaloner Ogle, Knt., Rear Admiral of the Blue, before the Chief Justice of Jamaica, for an Assault on the person of His Excellency Edward Trelawney, Esq., Captain-General, General and Commander in Chief of the said island. *London.* 1743. 12mo. C. 56842

Ogle. The Tryal of Sir Chaloner Ogle, Kt. Rear-Admiral of the Blue, before the Chief Justice of Jamaica, For an Assault on the Person of his Excellency Mr. Trelawney the Governor, committed in his own House in Spanish Town on the 22d Day of July last. With Authentic Copies of the several Letters that passed on that Occasion, between Mr. Concanen, now Attorney-General of the Island, Sir Chaloner Ogle, the Governor, and A—l V—. [Admiral Vernon.] *London Printed: Dublin Reprinted* MDCCXLII. 8vo, pp. 16. + *London: W. Webb.* M,DCCXLIII. 8vo, pp. 32. B. 56843

See also Vol. V., No. 21101.

Ogle (Charles). Speech of Mr. Ogle, of Pennsylvania, on the Regal Splendor of the President's Palace. Delivered ... April 14, 1849. [n. p. n. d.] 8vo, pp. 32. BA. 56844

See also Vol. XI., No. 45366.

[Oglethorpe (James).] A Full Reply to Lieut. Cadogan's Spanish Hireling ... and Lieut. Mackay's Letter, concerning the action at Moosa: wherein the Impartial Account of the late Ex-

pedition to St. Augustine is clearly vindicated, by plain facts and evidence. By the Author of the Impartial Account. *London.* 1743. 8vo, pp. 63. 56845

[Oglethorpe.] An Impartial Account Of the late Expedition Against St. Augustine Under General Oglethorpe. Occasioned by The Suppression of the Report, made by a Committee of the General Assembly in South-Carolina, transmitted, under the Great Seal of that Province, to their Agent in England, in order to be printed. With an Exact Plan of the Town, Castle and Harbour of St. Augustine, and the adjacent Coast of Florida; shewing the Disposition of our Forces on that Enterprize. ... *London: J. Huggonson.* 1742. 8vo, pp. 68. Plan. BA. 56846

See South Carolina—Report of the Committee.

[Oglethorpe.] A | New and Accurate Account | of the | Provinces | of South-Carolina | and | Georgia: | With many curious and useful Observati- | ons on the Trade, Navigation and Plantations of Great-Britain, compared with her | most powerful maritime Neighbours in an- | tient and modern Times. | *London:* | ... *J. Worrall* ... . 1732. 8vo, pp. (2), 76. + [*Ibid.*] 1733. S.

Mostly from Salmon's "Modern History," fourth edition, III. 770. Reprinted in the "Collections of the Georgia Historical Society," Vol. I. *See also* pp. 311–322 in Harris' "Biographical Memorials of James Oglethorpe," *and* Tailfer (P.)

[Oglethorpe.] Neueste und richtigste Nachricht von der Landschaft Georgien; mit Anmerkungen, die der Uebersetzer bey seinem vieljährigen Aufenthalt in America angestellet hat, begleitet von J. M. K. *Goettingen.* 1746. 8vo. 56848

See "Both Sides of the Question," Vol. II., No. 6814, of which there is a second edition.

Oglethorpe, *pseudon.* The Doctrine of Nullification examined: An Essay ... under the Signature of Oglethorpe. To which is annexed, The Proceedings of the Meeting of the Union & State Rights Party of Charleston, ... June 12, 1832. *Charleston: Printed by J. S. Burges.* 1832. 12mo, pp. 24. H. 56849

Improved title of No. 20423, Vol. V.

Appeal in behalf of Oglethorpe University. *Augusta, Geo.* 1835. 8vo. 56850

Also: Catalogue of the Officers, Alumni & Students of Oglethorpe University, ... Georgia, 1857–1858. *Macon, Georgia: Lewis H. Andrews, ... Printer.* 1858. 8vo, pp. 27. Continued. H.

... Oglethorpe University Magazine. March, 1855. Vol. I. ... *Talmage, Ga.* [n. d.] 8vo. H. 56851

O'Gorman (D.) Chronological Record: containing ... the Presidents of America; ... Third Edition. *Manchester: Alcock.* 1866. Rl. 8vo, pp. 482. 56852

O'Gorman (E.) Trials and Persecutions of Miss Edith O'Gorman, otherwise Sister Teresa de Chantal, of St. Joseph's Convent, Hudson City, N. J. Written by Herself. With an Appendix ... . *Hartford: Connecticut Publishing Company.* [1871.] 12mo, pp. 264. Portrait. C. 56853

O'Gorman (R.) Address before the Democratic Central Club, Philadelphia, on the War, 1863. By Richard O'Gorman. [n. p. n. d.] 8vo. 56854

O'Halloran (*Capt.*) Speech delivered by Captain O'Halloran, at a Temperance Society Meeting. *St. John, N. B.* 1840. 8vo. 56855

[O'Héguerty (*Comte de Magnières*).] Essai sur les Intérêts du Commerce Maritime, par M. D. *La Haye.* 1754. 8vo.

"Reprinted, in 1761, in the so-called 'Discours de David Hume,' trad. de l'anglais par M. de M."—Quérard.

[O'Higgins (Ambrosio).] La Dictadura de O'Higgins. Por Miguel Luis Amunátegui ... . *Santiago: Imprenta de Julio Belin i Ca.* 1855. 8vo, pp. (4), iii, 495. B. 56857

O'Higgins was of English or Irish origin.

O'Higgins. Elogio del Exc. Señor D. Ambrosio O. Higgins, Marques de Osorno, Virey del Perú. [*Lima.* 1800.] 4to.

Also: Auto de buen gobierno. [*Lima.* 1796.] Folio, pp. (19). B.

Ohio.

Abstract of Laws regulating State and Municipal Elections. ... *Cincinnati: Block & Co.* 1869. 8vo, pp. 65. 56859

Abstract of the Valuation of Real Property in ... Ohio, as assessed ... and equalized by the Boards of Equalization ... 1853. *Columbus: Osgood & Blake, Printers.* 1853. 8vo, pp. 117. Cont'd

An Account of the Coal Bank Disaster at Blue Rock, Ohio, in which four men were buried beneath the hill for two weeks; ... *Malta, Ohio: E. Ballou.* 1856. 12mo, pp. 32. 56861

An Account of the Controversy between the Warrantees and Actual Settlers on the Ohio and Allegheny Rivers and Conewango Creek, Pa. *Lancaster.* 1810. 8vo. 56862

An Account of the Organization. *See* Vol. II., No. 3967.

An Act Establishing an Equitable Mode of Levying the Taxes ... and ... to provide for the Internal Improvement of ... Ohio, by Navigable Canals. ... *Columbus: Printed by P. H. Olmsted.* 1825. 8vo, pp. 27. 56863

An Act to Incorporate Medical Societies, ... regulating the Practice of Physic and Surgery in Ohio ... *Columbus.* 1829. 8vo

An Act to incorporate the Bank of Ohio and other Banks. Passed April 11, 1856; ... *Columbus.* 1856. 8vo, pp. 31. H.

An Act to incorporate the State Bank of Ohio and other Banking Companies, February 24, 1845. *Columbus.* 1845. 8vo.

Acts and Proceedings of the Government of ... Ohio, relating to the ... Muskinghum River and ... the Ohio and Erie Canal. *Zanesville.* 1828. 8vo, pp. 30. 56867

Acts of A General Nature, ... ordered to be Re-printed, ... 1819 ... . *Columbus: Printed ... By P. H. Olmsted.* 1820. 8vo, pp. 488. Continued. B. 56868

Acts of the State of Ohio ... 1803 ... . *Chillicothe.* [1803.] 8vo. Continued. C. 56869

Address of the Ohio Soldiers. *See* [Connell (J. M.)], Vol. IV.

Address of the Union Members of the Legislature of ... Ohio, to the Soldiers ... . [n. p. 1863.] 8vo, pp. 4. 56870

Address to the Citizens of ... Ohio, concerning ... the Black Laws. *Cincinnati: A. Pugh.* 1848. 12mo, pp. 15. 56871

An Address to the People of Ohio, on the Important Subject of the next Presidency; ... *Cincinnati: Looker & Reynolds, Printers.* [1824.] 8vo, pp. 16. H. 56872

Addresses and Proceedings of the State Independent Free Territory Convention of the People of Ohio, held ... June ... 1848. *Cincinnati.* 1848. 8vo, pp. 14. H. 56873

Annual Report of the Adjutant General, ... for the Year 1861. [*Columbus.*] 1861. 8vo, pp. 98. Continued. BA.

The Advantages of a Settlement upon the Ohio in North America. [*London:*] *J. Ridley.* M DCC LXIII. 8vo, pp. (2), 44.

Extremely scarce. *See* "Monthly Review," XLVIII, 63.

Advice of Ohio Yearly Meeting, ... held at Mount-Pleasant, ... 1823; ... [n. p.] 1824. 8vo, pp. 4. 56876

Annual Message of Governor Medary. [n. p. 1860.] 8vo, pp. 13. Continued. 56877

Appeal in behalf of the Diocese of Ohio, in the Western Territory of the United States. [*London.* 1824.] 8vo, pp. 15.

Army Register of Ohio Volunteers in the Service of the United States; ... from the Official Records ... *Columbus.* 1862. 8vo, pp. 74. + July, 1862. By Charles A. Poland. [*Ibid.*] 8vo, pp. 85. B. 56879

Annual Report of the Attorney General ... for ... 1848. *Columbus: S. Medary, Printer.* 1848. 8vo, pp. 7. Table. Continued. B. 56880

Report of the Auditor of State, December, 1834. [n. p. n. d.] 8vo, pp. 15. 2 folded Tables. B. 56881

Also: Annual Report of the Auditor of State, ... for 1841. *Columbus: Samuel Medary, Printer.* 1841. 8vo, pp. 34. 2 folded Tables. Continued.—Report of the Auditor ... upon certain inquiries presented to the Banks of Ohio, January 27, 1838. [n. p. n. d.] 8vo, pp. 110. Folded Table.—Special Report of the Auditor ... in reply to a Resolution of the Senate, calling for a List of the Officers, Agents, and others, in ... the State ... . January 27, 1843. [n. p. n. d.] 8vo, pp. 11.—Special Report of the Auditor ... containing Abstracts of Real Property ... as equalized by the State Board of Equalization ... . *Columbus: Osgood, Blake & Knapp, Printers.* 1854. 8vo, pp. 111.—State Liabilities. Annual Report of the Auditor ... . 1841. [n. p. n. d.] 8vo, pp. 11. H.

First Annual Report of the Bank Commissioners of Ohio ... 1839. *Columbus: Samuel Medary, Printer.* 1839. 8vo, pp. 104. Continued. H. 56882

Ein Blick in's Thal des Ohio, oder Briefe über den Kampf und das Wiederaufleben der Katholischen Kirche im fernen Westen. *München.* 1836. 8vo. 56883

Annual Report of the Board of Agriculture of ... Ohio, made ... 1845. *Columbus.* 1846. 8vo. Continued. 56884

Also: Premiums awarded at the Second Annual Fair of the Ohio State Board of Agriculture. *Columbus.* 1851 8vo.

First Annual Report of the General Agent of the Board of National Popular Education; with the Constitution of the Board. *Cincinnati.* 1848. 8vo, pp. 32. Continued. 56885

Eleventh Report of the Board of Public Works, Jan. 10, 1848. *Columbus.* 1848. 8vo. Continued. S. 56886

First Annual Report of the BOARD OF STATE CHARITIES ... for ... 1867. *Columbus: L. D. Myers & Bro.* 1868. 8vo, pp. 40. Continued. B. 56887

A Brief Sketch. *See* [Ward (Nahum)].

Report of the CANAL COMMISSIONERS. *Columbus.* 1823. 8vo. Continued. 56888

Also: Report of the Canal Commissioners ... in relation to the Ohio Canal. *Columbus.* 1828. 8vo.

Catalogue of the Unios, Alasmodontas and Anodontas of the Ohio River and its Northern Tributaries. Adopted by the Western Academy of Natural Sciences of Cincinnati, ... 1849. *Cincinnati: J. A. & U. P. James.* [1849.] 18mo, pp. 19.

Celebration of the Forty-Seventh Anniversary of the First Settlement of ... Ohio. By Native Citizens. *Cincinnati: Printed by Lodge, L'Hommedieu and Co.* 1835. 8vo, pp. 74. BA.

Commercial Reference Book for ... Ohio. *Cincinnati.* 1851. 4to. C. 56891

Report of the COMMISSARY GENERAL for 1861. [n. p. n. d.] 8vo, pp. 28. 56892

Annual Report of the COMMISSIONER OF RAILROADS and Telegraphs ... of Ohio, for ... 1867. Prepared by George B. Wright, Commissioner. *Columbus: L. D. Myers & Bro. ... Printers.* 1868. 8vo, pp. 388, (1). Continued. H. 56893

Annual Report of the COMMISSIONER OF STATISTICS ... for ... 1857. *Columbus: Richard Nevins, ... Printer.* 1858. 8vo, pp. 112. Continued. B. 56894

Report of the COMMISSIONERS OF COMMON SCHOOLS of Ohio. *Columbus.* 1823. 8vo. Continued. 56895

Also: Report of the Committee to whom was referred the Report of the Commissioners of Common Schools. *Columbus.* 1826. 8vo.

Circular of the COMMISSIONERS OF THE OHIO CANAL FUND, to the Stockholders of the State. 1843. *New-York: Chatterton & Crist, Printers.* 1843. 12mo, pp. 12. Statistical Table. H.

Report of the COMMISSIONERS OF THE SINKING FUND. *Washington.* 1809. 8vo. Continued. 56897

Also: Semi-Annual Reports of the Commissioners of Sinking Fund, ... for ... 1864. *Columbus: Richard Nevins, ... Printer.* 1865. 8vo, pp. 8. Continued. B.

A Compilation of Laws, Treaties, Resolutions, and Ordinances, of the General and State Governments, which relate to Lands in ... Ohio; ... *Columbus: Printed by Geo. Nashee* ... 1825. 8vo, pp. 534. B., C. 56898

The Complicity of the Ohio Democracy with Treason. Its Record for Ohio. [n. p. August, 1865.] 8vo, pp. 16. 56899

Annual Report of the COMPTROLLER OF THE TREASURY ... for ... 1865. *Columbus: Richard Nevins, ... Printer.* 1866. 8vo, pp. 49. Continued. B. 56900

A Concise View of ... Ohio, ... Exhibiting The unexampled Increase and Success of its Population, and its present flourishing Condition; ... *London.* 1825. 8vo, pp. 30. 56901

A Condensed History of Mount Union College: ... *Mt. Union, Ohio.* 1866. 8vo, pp. 16. 56902

Condition of the People of Color in ... Ohio. With Interesting Anecdotes. *Boston: Isaac Knapp.* 1839. 12mo, pp. 48.

Constitution of ... Ohio; done in Convention ... in Chillicothe, ... [1802]. ... *Chillicothe: Press of N. Willis.* 1802. 8vo, pp. 32. M. 56904

Constitution of ... Ohio, passed in Convention, March 10, 1851. *Columbus.* 1852. 8vo. 56905

The Contract of the Ohio Company. *See* [Cutler (M.)]

Sixteenth Annual Report of the ... DEAF AND DUMB ASYLUM of ... Ohio for ... 1842. *Columbus.* 1843. 8vo, pp. 29. Continued. S. 56906

A Declaration of Ohio Yearly Meeting, held at Mount-Pleasant and Short-Creek ... 1828. *Ohio, Printed: Philadelphia, Re-printed: Joseph Rakestraw.* 1829. 8vo, pp. 24. + *New York: Mahlon Day.* 1829. 8vo. 56907

Description abrégée Du Territoire & Gouvernement des États-Unis de l'Amérique au sud de l'Ohio. [Colophon:] *De l'Imprimerie de L. Potier.* [n. d.] 8vo, pp. 28. 56908

Description du Sol. *See* [Cutler (M.)], Vol. v., No. 18176.

Detailed Statement of the Receipts and Disbursements of the Public Money at the State Treasury during ... 1854 and '55. *Columbus.* 1855. 8vo. Continued. A. 56909

Directory of the Fifty-Eighth General Assembly, 1868. *Columbus.* 1868. 8vo. Continued. 56910

The Discipline of the Society of Friends, of Ohio Yearly Meeting; ... held at Mountpleasant, in ... 1819. *Mountpleasant, Ohio: Printed by Elisha Bates.* [1819.] 12mo, pp. 102. + *Mountpleasant, Ohio: Printed by Enoch Harris, Jun.* 1839. 12mo, pp. 116. 56911

Documents relative to the Separation that took place in the Ohio Yearly Meeting, ... 1854. [n. p. 1854.] 12mo, pp. 48.

Édit du Congrès des États-Unis de l'Amérique, Traduite de l'Anglois. Pour les Terres dépendantes des dits États, situées au Nord Ouest de la revière de l'Ohio, dans lesquelles se trouvent celles de la Compagnie du Scioto. [*Paris:*] *De l'Imprimerie de Prault* ... 1789. Sm. 8vo, pp. 16. H. 56913

Very rare. Corrected title of our No. 21837, Vol. VI.

Extracts from the [Ohio] Yearly Meeting Minutes about Indian Concerns, Slave Trade ... [n. p.] 1820. Folio, 1 leaf.

Annual Report of the FUND COMMISSIONERS of ... Ohio, for ... 1849. [*Columbus.* 1850.] 8vo, pp. 7. Continued. H.

General Description of ... Ohio. [n. p. n. d.] 12mo, pp. 35.

General Regulations for the Military Forces of Ohio ... Compiled by H. B. Carrington ... *Columbus.* 1859. 8vo, pp. 294. + [*Ibid.*] 1861. 8vo. 56917

Geology. Report of the Special Committee, ... on the best method of obtaining a complete Geological Survey of ... Ohio. *Columbus: James B. Gardiner, Printer.* 1836. 8vo, pp. 18. Plan and Plate. BA. 56918

Report of John L. Riddell on ... a ... Geological Survey of this State. [n. p.] 1837. 8vo, pp. 34. 56919

First Annual Report on the Geological Survey of ... Ohio. By W. W. Mather ... *Columbus: Samuel Medary, Printer.* 1838. 8vo, pp. 134. Folded Plate. + Second Annual Report. [*Ibid.*] 8vo, pp. 286. 16 folded Maps, and Diagrams. 56920

Catalogue of the Geological Specimens, collected on the late Survey of ... Ohio. By W. W. Mather ... [*Columbus.*] 1842. 8vo, pp. 7. 56921

Report of the Select Committee ... on so much of the Governor's Message as relates to a Mineralogical and Geological Survey of ... Ohio. *Columbus.* [1854.] 8vo, pp. 18. S. 56922

Report to the Purchasers of Coal and Salt Lands, on Federal Creek and Marietta Run, ... Ohio. By E. B. Andrews ... *Marietta.* [1854.] 8vo, pp. 12. 56923

Report on the Economical Geology of Southern Ohio ... By E. B. Andrews ... *Cincinnati.* 1865. 8vo, pp. 26. Map.

The Geological Survey of Ohio, its Progress in 1869. Report of an Address delivered ... Feb. 7th, 1870, by J. S. Newberry, Chief Geologist. *New York.* 1870. 8vo, pp. 60.

Geological Survey of Ohio. Part I. Report of Progress in 1869, By J. S. Newberry ... Part II. Report of Progress in the Second District, by E. B. Andrews ... Part III. Report on Geology of Montgomery County, by Edward Orton ... *Columbus: Nevins & Myers, ... Printers.* 1871. 8vo, pp. 176. 3 Maps, 1 Chart, and Plans. B., C. 56926

Geological Survey of Ohio. Report of Progress in 1870. ... *Columbus: Nevins & Myers, ... Printers.* 1871. 8vo, pp. 568. 7 Plates. C. 56927

Report of the Geological Survey of Ohio. Volume I. Geology and Palæontology. Part I. Geology. *Columbus, Ohio: Nevins & Myers, ... Printers.* 1873. Rl. 8vo, pp. v, (1), 680. 18 Maps and Plans, 5 Sections. + Volume I. ... Part II. Palæontology. [*Ibid.*] 1873. Rl. 8vo, pp. xiii, 399, (2). 49 Plates, 3 Diagrams. + Volume II. ... Part I. Geology. [*Ibid.*] 1874. Rl. 8vo, pp. xv, 701. 24 Maps and Plates, 8 Sheets of Sections. + Vol. II. ... Part II. Palæontology. [*Ibid.*] 1875. Rl. 8vo, pp. viii, 435. 59 Plates, 2 Sheets. + Vol. III. ... Part I. Geology. [*Ibid.*] 1878. Rl. 8vo, pp. viii, 958. 20 Maps and Plates. 56928

Governor's Message, transmitting the Report of the Canal Engineer on the subject of a Canal at the Falls of Ohio. *Columbus.* 1824. 8vo. 56929

The Great Convention. Description of the Convention of the People of Ohio, held at Columbus, ... February, 1840. By John G. Miller ... *Columbus: Cutler & Wright.* [1840.] 8vo, pp. 40. 56930

First published in the "Ohio Confederate" and known as the "Harrison Convention."

Historical Account of the Expedition. *See* [Smith (Wm.)]

Journal of the HISTORICAL AND PHILOSOPHICAL SOCIETY of Ohio. [Part I. Vol. I.] *Columbus: Printed for the Society, by Cutler and Pilsbury.* 1838. 8vo, pp. 111. Plan. + *Reprinted, Cincinnati: Robert Clarke & Co.* 1872. 12mo, pp. viii, 131.

Transactions of the Historical and Philosophical Society of Ohio. Part Second. Vol. I. ... *Cincinnati: Geo. W. Bradbury & Co., Printers.* 1839. 8vo, pp. 334. Map and Errata. BA.

Part I. consists of the "Journal," No. 56931, *ante.* *See* "N. A. Rev.," LIII. 320.

Historical Sketch of the Synod of Ohio, (N. S.) From 1838 to 1868. ... *Cincinnati.* 1870. 8vo, pp. 40. 56933

A History of the Eleventh Regiment Ohio Volunteer Infantry, ... Compiled from the Official Records. *Dayton, Ohio: W. J. Shuey.* 1866. 8vo, pp. xv, 287. 56934

History of the Ohio Canals. *Columbus.* 1832. 8vo. 56935

Inaugural Address of James D. Cox, Governor of Ohio, January 8, 1866. [n. p. n. d.] 8vo, pp. 10. Continued. 56936

An Index to all the Laws and Resolutions of ... Ohio ... from the Commencement of the Territorial Government, to the Year 1844–45 ... Prepared by Zechariah Mills. *Columbus: Scott and Co's ... Press.* 1846. 8vo, pp. 181. H. 56937

See also Coggeshall (William T.), Vol. IV., No. 14204, *note.*

The Joint Resolutions and Report to the Ohio Legislature, against Federal Consolidation. *Columbus.* 1859. 8vo, pp. 50.

Journal of the ... Annual Convention of the Protestant Episcopal Church in the Diocese of Ohio. [n. p.] 1818. 8vo. Continued. 56939

Also: Journals of the Annual Conventions ... 1818–1821. *Columbus: Reprinted by Scott & Bascom.* 1853. 8vo, pp. 64. C.

Journal of the House of Representatives of the Territory of the United States, North West of the River Ohio, at the Second Session of the First Assembly of Ohio. *Chillicothe.* 1800. 8vo.

Continued as the "Journal of the House of Representatives of the State of Ohio." *Columbus.* [v. d.]

Journal of the Proceedings of the Grand Royal Arch Chapter of ... Ohio, at the Annual Communication held at Worthington, A. L. 5829. *Columbus.* 1829. 12mo, pp. 34. Continued. B.

Journal of the Proceedings of the Medical Convention of Ohio, at its Third Session, Cleveland, May ... 1839. *Cleveland.* 1839. 8vo. Continued. 56942

Journal of the Senate of the State of Ohio, being the Sixth General Assembly, ... 1808. ... *Chillicothe: Printed ... By Nashee & Denny.* 1808. 8vo, pp. 271. Continued. H. 56943

Journal of the Senate ... in Cases of Impeachments. December 24, 1808. ... *Chillicothe: Printed ... By Nashee & Denny.* 1809. 8vo, pp. 100. H. 56944

Law of Ohio relative to Soldiers' Voting. *Columbus: Richard Nevins.* 1863. 8vo, pp. 12. 56945

Laws for the Protection of the Canals of Ohio. *Columbus.* 1849. 8vo. 56946

The Laws of Ohio in respect to the Colored People, shown to be Unequal ... By Rev. S. C. Aiken ... Address on Thanksgiving Day, November 20, 1845. ... *Cleveland.* 1845. 8vo, pp. 8. 56947

Laws of the Northwest Territory. *See* Vol. x., No. 39420.

Laws passed by the Ohio Legislature establishing the Miami University ... added an Address to the Inhabitants of the Miami County Lands ... *Hamilton: Printed by Keen & Stewart.* 1814. 8vo, pp. 66. 56948

See also Vol. XII., No. 48682.

Laws passed in the Territory of the United States, North-west of the Ohio River, from the Commencement of the Government to the 31st of December, 1791. ... *Philadelphia: Printed by Francis Childs and John Swaine.* 1792. 8vo, pp. 70. 56949

Laws passed in the Territory of the United States, North-west of the Ohio River, from July to December, [1792] inclusive. ... *Philadelphia: Printed by Francis Childs and John Swaine* ... 1794. 8vo, pp. 77. 56950

Laws of the Territory of the United States, North-west of the Ohio, ... [1795]. ... *Cincinnati: Printed by W. Maxwell.* 1796. 8vo, pp. 225. 56951

The first book printed in Cincinnati.

Laws of the Territory of the United States, Northwest of the River Ohio, ... 1798 ... *Cincinnati: Edmund Freeman.* 1798. 8vo, pp. 32. 56952

Laws of the Territory of the United States, Northwest of the Ohio River, passed ... 1799; also Certain Laws enacted by the Governor and Judges of the Territory ... to December, 1792. With an Appendix ... Vol. I. ... *Cincinnati: From the Press of Carpenter and Findley* ... 1800. 8vo, pp. 280. + Vol. II. ... *Chillicothe: Printed by Windship & Willis* ... 1801. 8vo, pp. 112. + Vol. III. ... *Chillicothe: From the Press of N. Willis* ... 1802. 8vo, pp. 253. 56953

A Letter to a Friend. *See* Nos. 12320 and 40382.

Letter to the Committee of the Third-District Medical Society of Ohio, from the Trustees of the Commercial Hospital and Lunatic Asylum of Ohio, 1833. [n. p. n. d.] 8vo, pp. 8. M.

Report of the Directors of the LUNATIC ASYLUM of Ohio, ... Dec. 10, 1835. *Columbus.* [1836.] 8vo, pp. 7. Continued.

Also: Annual Report of the Directors of the Ohio Lunatic Asylum, ... 1839. *Columbus: Samuel Medary, Printer.* 1839. 8vo, pp. 31. Continued. H.

An Inquiry into the Causes that have retarded the Prosperity of the MEDICAL COLLEGE OF OHIO. [*Cincinnati.* 1838.] 8vo, pp. 42. 56956

Also: Catalogue of the Officers and Students in the Medical College of Ohio, ... 1829–30. *Cincinnati.* 1830. 8vo, pp. 8. Continued. B

The Memorial of the Religious Society of Friends, composing Ohio Yearly Meeting ... On behalf of the Free People of Colour. [n. p.] 1837. 4to, 1 leaf. 56957

Message of the Governor of Ohio ... *Columbus.* 1821. 8vo. Continued. 56958

Message of the President ... [on] Making a Road from Cumberland ... Maryland, to the State of Ohio. *Washington City: Printed by R. C. Weightman.* 1812. 8vo, pp. 16. 56959

See also our Nos. 48082, 48100, Vol. XII.

Militia Law of Ohio, being an act to organize and discipline the Militia and Volunteer Militia: passed March 28, 1857: ... *Columbus: Richard Nevins, ... Printer.* 1857. 8vo, pp. 48, and folded leaf. C., H. 56960

Minutes and Address of the State Convention of the Colored Citizens of Ohio, convened at Columbus, January ... 1849. *Oberlin: J. M. Fitch.* MDCCCXLIX. 8vo, pp. 28. H. 56961

Minutes of the State-Education Convention, Columbus, O., December, 1837. With Address by William Slocomb. *Columbus.* 1837. 8vo, pp. 24. M. 56962

Second Annual Report of the ... NORTHERN OHIO LUNATIC ASYLUM, ... for ... 1856. *Columbus: Richard Nevins, ... Printer.* 1856. 8vo, pp. 23. Continued. B. 56963

Notices of the House of Representatives of ... Ohio, in the Fifty-Second General Assembly, ... 1856. *Columbus, Ohio.* 1857. 8vo, pp. 48. BA. 56964

The Ohio Almanac for ... 1810. By Robert Stubbs ... *Cincinnati: Carney & Morgan.* [n. d.] 12mo, pp. (68). 56965

Continued to 1815 or later. Peter G. Thomson erroneously states that the one for 1814 was the first printed in Cincinnati.

First Annual Report ... of the OHIO AND INDIANA RAILROAD COMPANY. Bucyrus, January 30, 1852. *Pittsburgh.* [n. d.] 8vo, pp. 17. Continued. S. 56966

The Ohio and Mississippi Navigator: ... A New and Corrected Edition. *Pittsburgh: Zadock Cramer.* 1804. 12mo, pp. 62

... Annual Reports ... of the OHIO & MISSISSIPPI RAILROAD Co. ... For ... 1857–8 and 1858–9. *Cincinnati.* 1859. 8vo, pp. 76. 4 folded Tables. Continued. B. 56968

Also: Report of the Committee [of] the City Council of Cincinnati on the Ohio and Mississippi Railroad Company. *Cincinnati.* 1855. 8vo, pp. 46. S.

The Ohio Annual Register. *See* Vol. III., No. 8796.

Memorial of the OHIO ANTI-SLAVERY SOCIETY to the General Assembly of Ohio. *Cincinnati.* 1838. 8vo, pp. 34. M.

Also: Report of the [second] Anniversary of the Ohio Anti-Slavery Society. *Cincinnati.* 1837. 8vo.

First Annual Report of the ... OHIO ASYLUM for ... Idiotic and Imbecile Youth, ... for ... 1857. *Columbus: Richard Nevins, ... Printer.* 1858. 8vo, pp. 33. Continued. B. 56970

Claims of the OHIO BAPTIST Book and Tract Society, presented in an Address, ... September, 1845. *Zanesville.* 1845. 8vo. 56971

Report of the ... "OHIO BIBLE SOCIETY," from its formation, to November, 1815:—By a Committee appointed for the purpose. *Marietta,* (*O.*) 1816. 12mo, pp. 12. BA. 56972

Ohio Boys in Dixie: the adventures of Twenty-two Scouts sent by Gen. O. M. Mitchell to destroy a railroad; with a narrative of their barbarous treatment by the rebels, and Judge Holt's Report. *New York: Miller & Mathews.* 1863. 8vo, pp. 47.

Commencement of the OHIO CANAL, at the Licking Summit, July 4th, 1825. *Lancaster, Ohio: Printed by John Herman.* [1825.] 8vo, pp. 8. + [Another Edition. *Ibid.*] 8vo, pp. 22.

Contains an address by Thomas Erving, speeches by Governor Clinton, etc. Also: The Ohio Canal. By the Voice of New York. [n. p.] 1823. 8vo.

Ohio Common School Director. Vol. I. ... *Columbus.* 1838. 8vo. H. 56975

Articles of an Association by the name of the OHIO COMPANY. *Printed at Worcester, Massachusetts, by Isaiah Thomas.* MDCCLXXXVI. 12mo, pp. 12. W. 56976

The last six pages left blank for "Subscriber's Names." Perhaps the first publication by the Ohio Company.

Articles|of an|Association|by the|name|of the|Ohio Company.|*New-York, Printed by|Samuel and John Loudon,* ...|MDCCLXXXVII. Sm. 8vo, pp. 45. H., P. 56977

Contains all the proceedings of the company since their former publication, No. 56976, *ante.* Both editions are rare.

At a meeting of the Directors and Agents of the Ohio Company, at Mr. Bracket's Tavern, the 21st of November, and continued by adjournment to the twenty-second ... . At a meeting of the Directors of the Ohio Company at Mr. Bracket's Tavern, in Boston, November 23, 1787—For the purpose of carrying into effect the Surveys, and other business, of the Ohio Company; as agreed upon by the Directors and Agents, at their meetings of the 29th of August last, and the 21st instant. [n. p. n. d.] 8vo, pp. 4. P. 56978

This and the following are equally rare.

At a meeting of the Directors and Agents of the Ohio Company, at Mr. Rice's Tavern, in Providence, State of Rhode-Island, Wednesday, March 5, 1788. [n. p. n. d.] 8vo, pp. 4.

Ohio Contested Election. Vallandigham *vs.* Campbell. Memorandum of Points submitted by the Sitting Member. [n. p. 1858.] 8vo, pp. 10. B. 56980

History, Organization and Transactions of the OHIO EDITORIAL ASSOCIATION, during the years 1853, 1854 and 1855. ...

Columbus. 1855. 8vo, pp. 112. + During ... 1856 and 1857. [*Ibid.*] 1857. 8vo. S. 56981

Ohio Educational Monthly. *See* Ohio Journal of Education.

Catalogue of OHIO FEMALE COLLEGE, Hamilton County, ... 1858. [n. p. n. d.] 8vo. S. 56982

Also: The Ohio Female College ... with the Plan, Reasons, and Encouragement for its Permanent Endowment ... . *New York: Edward O. Jenkins, Printer.* 1862. 8vo, pp. 32. Plate. H.

The Ohio Hunter: Or a Brief Sketch of the Frontier Life of Samuel E. Edwards, the Great ... Hunter of ... Ohio. *Battle Creek, Mich.* 1866. 16mo, pp. 240. 56983

Annual Reports of the ... OHIO INSTITUTION FOR THE EDUCATION OF THE DEAF AND DUMB ... from 1827 to 1851. *Columbus.* 1870. 8vo, pp. (2), 256. Plate. B. 56984

Fifth Annual Report of the ... OHIO INSTITUTION FOR THE INSTRUCTION OF THE BLIND. January 10, 1842. *Columbus: Samuel Medary, Printer.* 1842. 8vo, pp. 22, (1). Facsimile. Continued. H. 56985

The Ohio Journal of Education. ... Editors: A. D. Lord, ... H. H. Barney, ... [and others]. Vol. I.—1852. *Columbus: Printed by Scott & Bascom.* 1852. 8vo, pp. v, (3), 400. Cont'd.

The Ohio Legislature. Biographical Notices of the Members of the Fifty-fifth General Assembly of ... Ohio. *Columbus.* 1862. 8vo, pp. 132. 56987

Constitution, Rules, Regulations and By-Laws, of OHIO LODGE, No. 1: of the American Protestant Association of Ohio. *Cincinnati: W. H. Ongley, Printer.* 1854. 16mo, pp. 32. H.

Annual Report of the Board of Directors of the OHIO MECHANICS' INSTITUTE. *Cincinnati.* 1829. 8vo. Continued.

Also: A Catalogue of the Library and Reading Room of the Ohio Mechanics Institute. *Cincinnati.* 1841. 12mo, pp. 48.—Charter, Constitution and By-Laws of the ... Institute. *Cincinnati.* 1850. 12mo. Continued. S.—Report of the First Annual Fair of the ... Institute, held ... May and ... June ... . *Cincinnati.* 1838. 8vo, pp. 51. Continued. H.

The Ohio Medical and Surgical Journal. Edited by Richard L. Howard, M.D. ... *Columbus.* [n. d.] 8vo. 56990

Annual Report of the ... OHIO PENITENTIARY ... January 4, 1842. *Columbus: Samuel Medary, ... Printer.* 1843. 8vo, pp. 34. Continued. H. 56991

Prospectus of the OHIO PETROLEUM COMPANY. ... *New York: E. S. Dodge & Co., Printers.* 1864. 8vo, pp. 11. B.

The Ohio Railroad Guide ... Containing Topographical, Biographical and Statistical Notices ... . *Cincinnati.* 1852. 12mo, pp. 132, (4). Map. 56993

The Ohio Railroad Guide Illustrated. Cincinnati to Erie via Columbus & Cleveland. *Columbus.* 1854. 12mo, pp. (6), 135. 28 Plates. 56994

Redfield's Ohio Railway Gazetteer, Traveler's Guide, and Express and Shippers' Directory. *Indianapolis.* 1865. 8vo.

Report of the Commissioners of the OHIO REFORM SCHOOL. December 11, 1836. [n. p. n. d.] 8vo. Continued. 56996

Also: Fifth Annual Report of the Reform School Commissioners. *Columbus.* 1861. 8vo. Continued.

Ohio School Laws ... prepared by the State School Commissioner ... . *Columbus.* 1858. 8vo. + Second Edition. [*Ibid.*] 8vo, pp. 168. B. + Third Edition. [*Ibid.*] 1862. 8vo. + Fourth Edition. [*Ibid.*] 1865. 8vo. 56997

Ohio School Library [at Cincinnati]. Catalogue ... . *Cincinnati.* 1860. 8vo. C. 56998

See also Vol. IV., No. 13094.

Ohio Southern Boundary Line. ... John Sebastian *vs.* Covington and Cincinnati Bridge Company. *Cincinnati.* [n. d.] 8vo.

First Annual Catalogue of the OHIO SOUTHWESTERN STATE NORMAL SCHOOL, Lebanon, for 1856. *Lebanon.* 1856. 8vo.

Circular and Catalogue of the OHIO STATE AND UNION LAW COLLEGE, for ... 1857–'8. ... *Cleveland, O.: Fairbanks, Benedict & Co., Printers.* 1858. 8vo, pp. 15. Continued. B. 57001

W. W. Reilly & Co.'s Ohio State Business Directory: ... for 1853–4. *Cincinnati: Morgan & Overend, Printers.* 1853. 8vo, pp. xxxi, 424, 328. Map and Plan. H. 57002

Proceedings of the OHIO STATE CHRISTIAN ANTI-SLAVERY CONVENTION, at Columbus, August, 1859. *Columbus.* 1859. 8vo

Williams' Ohio State Directory and Shippers' Guide. ... Vol. I. For 1866. *Cincinnati: Williams & Co.* [n. d.] 8vo, pp. 870. Continued. 57004

George W. Hawes' Ohio State Gazetteer and Business Directory, for 1859 and 1860. ... To be Revised and Continued. *George W. Hawes, ... Cincinnati, Ohio.* [n. d.] 8vo, pp. xxxii, 717. 57005

Annual Report of the OHIO STATE HORTICULTURAL SOCIETY ... . For ... 1867. *Columbus: L. D. Myers & Bro.* 1868. 8vo, pp. 84. 57006

Report of the Commissioners of the OHIO STATE LIBRARY, ... For ... 1856. *Columbus: Richard Nevins, ... Printer.* 1857. 8vo, pp. 8. Continued. 57007

Also: Catalogue of the Ohio State Library, December, 1834. *Columbus.* [n. d.] 12mo. + *Columbus: Printed by Thrall and Reed.* 1848. 8vo, pp. 91. H.

Transactions of the OHIO STATE MEDICAL SOCIETY. *Cincinnati.* 1854. 8vo. Continued. 57008

Proceedings of the Third Annual Meeting of the OHIO STATE PHONETIC ASSOCIATION. ... 1854. [n. p. n. d.] 8vo, pp. 22, (2)

Williams' Ohio State Register and Business Mirror, for 1857. First Issue. *Cincinnati: C. S. Williams.* 1857. 8vo, pp. 311. Map and Plate. Continued. C. 57010

Minutes of the Meeting of the OHIO STATE SUNDAY SCHOOL CONVENTION, at Delaware, May, 1865. *Cincinnati.* 1865. 8vo.

The Ohio Teacher. Edited by Thomas Rainey. Vol. I. *Columbus and Cincinnati.* 1850. 12mo, pp. 602. Continued.

Memorial of OHIO TEACHERS' ASSOCIATION. [n. p. 1864.] 8vo, pp. 8. 57013

Facts ... relating to the Endowments of the OHIO THEOLOGICAL SEMINARY. *Gambier.* 1849. 8vo. 57014

Addresses delivered at the Inauguration of the Rev. Robert G. Wilson, D.D., President ... OHIO UNIVERSITY, Aug. 11, 1824. Together with a Short Account of that Institution. *Zanesville: Printed by Ezekiel T. Cox & Co.* 1824. 8vo, pp. 27. 57015

Also: Catalogue of the Officers and Students of the Ohio University, at Athens. 1843. *Columbus: Printed by Wright & Legg.* 1843. 8vo. Continued.—Catalogue of the Officers and of those who have received any Degree in the Ohio University, at Athens. 1848. *Athens, Ohio: N. H. & A. J. Van Vorhes—Printers.* 1849. 8vo.—General Catalogue of the Ohio University from the Date of its Charter in 1804 to 1857. *Athens, Ohio: Printed by N. H. Van Vorhes.* 1857. 8vo, pp. 41.—Memorial of the Lessees ... to the Trustees of the Ohio University. [*Athens, O.* 1842.] 8vo, pp. 14.

Ohio Valley Historical Series. ... [*Cincinnati: Robert Clarke & Co.* 1868.] 8vo, pp. xxiii, 162. Maps and Plates. Cont'd.

First Annual Catalogue of the OHIO WESLEYAN FEMALE COLLEGE, for ... 1854. Delaware, O. *Columbus.* 1854. 8vo, pp. 19. Continued. H. 57017

Catalogue ... of the OHIO WESLEYAN UNIVERSITY, for ... 1844–5. Delaware, Ohio. *Columbus: S. Medary, Printer.* 1845. 8vo, pp. 20. Continued. H. 57018

Proceedings of the OHIO WOMEN'S RIGHTS CONVENTION, at Akron, Ohio, May 28 and 29, 1851. *Cincinnati.* 1851. 8vo.

Post-Office Directory of Ohio; ... *Cincinnati.* 1864. 12mo.

Proceedings of the ... Colored Freemen. *See* Vol. IV. 13106.

Proceedings of the Democratic State Convention, ... at Columbus, Ohio, ... July 4, 1862. Containing the Speeches ... . *Dayton.* 1862. 8vo, pp. 22. 57021

Proceedings of the Grand Commandery of Knights Templars, of ... Ohio ... . *Cincinnati: John Tanner & Co.* 1867. 8vo, pp. 72. 57022

Proceedings of the Grand Encampment, of ... Ohio, at its Organization, at Lancaster, October, A. D. 1843. ... *Massillon: Luce & Worstell, Printers.* 1843. 12mo, pp. 8. H. 57023

Proceedings of the Grand Lodge of ... Ohio, ... from 1808 to 1847 inclusive. ... *Cincinnati.* 1857. 8vo. Plates. 57024

Also: Proceedings of the Grand Lodge of Free and Accepted Masons, of ... Ohio, at its several Grand Communications, from 1848 to 1857 inclusive. *Columbus.* 1858. 8vo. Continued.

Proceedings of the Medical Convention of Ohio, held ... May, 1842; ... *Cincinnati: Printed by R. P. Brooks.* 1842. 8vo, pp. 51. Continued. H. 57025

Proceedings of the several State Boards of Equalization, assembled ... previous to ... 1853, to which is appended a Special Report of the Auditor of State, exhibiting the valuation of the real property of each City, Town, and Township in Ohio ... . *Columbus: Franklin Printing Company.* 1854. 8vo, pp. (2), 139. Table. Continued. B. 57026

Proceedings of the State Convention at Canton, 21st July. [n. p. 1830.] 12mo. 57027

Proceedings of the State U. C. of Ohio. [n. p. 1862.] 8vo, pp. 16. H. 57028

Public Documents. *See* Kilbourn (J.), Vol. IX., No. 37731, and add, *Columbus: John Kilbourn.* 1828. 8vo, pp. (4), 403, (1).

Public Statutes at Large of ... Ohio; from the close of Chase's Statutes, February, 1833, to the present time. ... Edited by Maskell E. Curwen. *Cincinnati.* 1853–54. 3 vols., 8vo. A.

Report of the QUARTERMASTER GENERAL for 1861. [n. p. n. d.] 8vo, pp. 34. Continued. 57031

First Annual Report of the REFORM SCHOOL for Girls ... for ... 1869. *Columbus.* 1870. 8vo, pp. 8. Continued. 57032

First Semi-Annual Report of the REFUGEE RELIEF COMMISSION of Ohio. ... 1864. ... *Cincinnati.* 1864. 8vo, pp. 14.

Report of the Commissioners of Morgan Raid Claims ... Dec. 15, 1864. *Columbus: Richard Nevins.* 1865. 8vo, pp. 453

Report of the Debates and Proceedings of the Convention for the Revision of the Constitution of the State ... 1850–51. J. V. Smith, Official Reporter ... . *Columbus: S. Medary, Printer.* 1851. 2 vols., 8vo, pp. 751; (2), 897. A., B., C. 56935

Report of the Investigation Commission appointed to enquire into the causes of the Defalcation in the State Treasury ... 1858. [*Columbus.* 1859.] 8vo, pp. 909, 4 folded leaves. H. 57036

Report of the Joint Committee of the General Assembly on Finance. ... *Columbus: Richard Nevins, ... Printer.* 1857. 8vo, pp. 59. 57037

Report of the Joint Committee. *See* Vol. I., No. 3189, *note*, add, *Columbus: Printed ... By P. H. Olmsted.* 1820. 8vo, pp. 37. + *Columbus.* 1821. 8vo, pp. 36.

Report of the Joint Committee of the General Assembly upon Public Institutions and Buildings. *Columbus.* 1857. 8vo.

Report of the Joint Select Committee, to whom was referred the Governor's Message ... on the subject of the Northern Boundary. ... *Columbus: James B. Gardiner.* 1835. 8vo, pp. 18.

Report of the Select Committee of the Ohio Senate, on giving the Right of Suffrage to Females. [n. p. n. d.] 8vo, pp. 10.

Report of the Standing Committee on the Currency. Presented ... January 16, 1838. *Columbus: Samuel Medary, Printer.* 1838. 8vo, pp. 22. 57041

Report of the Yearly Meeting of Ohio, on Indian Concerns, ... [n. p.] 1819. 8vo, pp. 4. 57042

Report on the Condition of the People of Color in ... Ohio. [n. p. 1835.] 8vo, pp. 24. 57043

From the "Proceedings of the Ohio Anti-Slavery Convention ... 1835."

Reports, including Messages, and other Communications, made to the Thirty-Fifth General Assembly of ... Ohio. ... *Columbus: James B. Gardiner, Printer.* 1836. 8vo, paging not continuous. Plan and Tables. 57044

... Resolutions and Report of a Committee of the General Assembly of Ohio, favorable to the exercise ... of the Power to protect Domestic Manufactures. ... *Washington: Printed by Duff Green.* 1828. 8vo, pp. 12. 57045

Resolutions of Thanks to Major General Rosecrans, with ... [his] reply; and the Address of the Ohio Soldiers ... with the Correspondence connected therewith. *Columbus: Richard Nevins, ... Printer.* 1863. 8vo, pp. 8. 57046

A Revising Index to the Statute Law of ... Ohio ... . With References to the Ohio Reports ... . By M. E. Curwen ... . *Dayton: Wilson & Decker, Printers.* 1849. 8vo, pp. 90, (1).

School Law of Ohio accompanied by Blank Forms prepared by the Secretary of State ... . *Columbus: Osgood & Blake, Printers.* 1853. 8vo, pp. 71, folded leaf. 57048

Annual Report of the SECRETARY OF STATE to the Governor ... including the Statistical Report ... for ... 1869. *Columbus: Columbus Printing Company.* 1870. 8vo. 57049

Statistical Report of the Secretary of State, ... for ... 1868. *Columbus.* 1869. 8vo, pp. 147. 57050

Reprinted from the annual report of the Secretary of State. Also: Report of the Secretary of State, on the ... Common Schools ... of Ohio [for 1842]. *Columbus: Samuel Medary, ... Printer.* 1842. 12mo, pp. 11. 2 folding Tables. Continued.

Special Message of Governor [Robert] Lucas to ... the General Assembly of Ohio ... in regard to the Northern Boundary Line ... December 8th, 1835. *Columbus: James B. Gardiner, Printer.* [n. d.] 8vo, pp. 31, 64. 57051

Annual Report of the STATE COMMISSIONERS of Common Schools, ... for ... 1854. *Columbus, Ohio.* 1855. 8vo, pp. 123. Continued. 57052

Amended By-Laws, Rules and Regulations for the STATE REFORM FARM, near Lancaster, Ohio: ... *Columbus: Richard Nevins, ... Printer.* 1858. 8vo, pp. 33. 57053

State Rights and Joint Resolutions and Report to the Ohio Legislature against Federal Consolidation. Session 1859. *Columbus: Richard Nevins.* 1859. 8vo, pp. 51. 57054

Statement of the Condition of the Banks of Ohio ... . 1842. [n. p. n. d.] 8vo, pp. 41, folded leaf. 57055

Statement relative to an intended Theological Seminary in the Diocese of Ohio. [*London.* 1824.] 8vo, pp. 9. 57056

Statutes of ... Ohio ... in force, December 7, 1840; ... Collated ... by J. R. Swan. ... *Columbus: Samuel Medary, ... Printer.* 1841. 8vo, pp. xv, (1), 1111. + In Force, January 1st, 1854; with References to prior Repealed Laws. ... *Cincinnati.* 1854. 8vo. + In Force, August, 1854: ... [*Ibid.*] 8vo, pp. 1114. + In Force at the Present Time; with Notes and References to the Judicial Decisions. By M. E. Curwen. [*Ibid.*] 8vo. C.

See also Chase (S. P.), Vol. III., No. 12199.

Report of the SUPERINTENDENT OF COMMON SCHOOLS on State Institutions for Teachers and others, in answer to sundry resolutions passed March 19, 1838. February 16, 1839. [n. p. n. d.] 8vo, pp. 20. 57058

Also: First Annual Report of the Superintendent of Common Schools, ... January, 1838. ... *Columbus: Samuel Medary, Printer.* 1838. 8vo, pp. 65. Continued.—Report on the Condition of Common Schools, for 1853. *Columbus.* 1854. 8vo.

Report of the SURGEON GENERAL, November 5, 1864. *Columbus.* 1864. 8vo. Continued. 57059

The Tax Law of Ohio, ... so far as ... relates to the Assessment of Personal Property ... . *Columbus.* 1855. 8vo, pp. 47. + *Columbus: Richard Nevins, ... Printer.* 1857. 8vo, pp. 27.

Thanksgiving for Victory. *See* Vol. I., No. 1388.

Annual Report of the TREASURER OF STATE, ... December 7, 1842. [*Columbus:*] *Samuel Medary, ... Printer.* [n. d.] 8vo, pp. 14. Continued. 57061

Treasury Report. Report of the Special Commissioner and the Auditor of State ... June, 1857 ... . *Columbus: Richard Nevins, ... Printer.* 1857. 8vo, pp. 59. 57062

Veto Message of Governor Medary, on the Bill prohibiting Slavery in Kansas. [n. p. 1860.] 8vo, pp. 16. 57063

View of the Ohio State Fair Grounds, 1854. [n. p. n. d.] Folio, 1 leaf. 57064

Ohio River. Central-Water Line. *See* [Lorraine (E.)]

Commercial Gazetteer and Business Directory of the Ohio River ... . By G. W. Hawes. *Indianapolis, Ind.: G. W. Hawes.* 1861. 8vo, pp. 446. Map and Plates. 57065

Memorials relative to the Navigation of the Ohio River, 1870–71. [n. p. n. d.] 8vo. 57066

See also Vol. XII., No. 47662.

Proceedings of a Meeting ... [at] Cincinnati, held ... January 22, 1846, Expressing the Sense of the Citizens on ... improving the Navigation around the Falls of the Ohio River. *Cincinnati.* 1846. 8vo, pp. 16. BA. 57067

Report ... on a Survey and Examination of the various Plans for Canals around the Falls of the Ohio River. *Washington.* 1853. 8vo. S. 57068

Review of the Report of the Board of Engineers, on the Improvement of the Falls of the Ohio. [By George Graham and others.] *Washington: Printed by John T. and Lem. Towers.* 1854. 8vo, pp. 65. H. *See also* Vol IV., No. 13072.

An Act to incorporate the OHIO RIVER IMPROVEMENT COMPANY. *Philadelphia: T. K. and P. G. Collins, Printers.* 1855. 8vo, pp. 31. 57069

The Ohio River Land and Marble Company ... . *New York.* 1853. 16mo, pp. 14. Map. H. 57070

OHIO VOLUNTEER, *pseudon.* The Capitulation, or, a History of the Expedition conducted by William Hull, Brigadier-General of the North-Western Army. By an Ohio Volunteer [James Foster]. *Chillicothe: Printed by James Barnes.* 1812. 12mo, pp. 78, iv, (2). 57071

The author was captured at Detroit, and criticises General Hull severely.

OHSSON (*M.* D'). Oriental Antiquities, and General View of the Othoman Customs, Laws and Ceremonies, exhibiting

many curious pieces of the Eastern Hemisphere relative to the Christian and Jewish Dispensations, with various Rites and Mysteries of the Oriental Free Masons. From the French of M. D'Ohsson ... . *Philadelphia: "Printed for the Select Committee and Grand Lodge of Inquiry."* 1788. 4to, pp. 593. Plates.

A curious work, inquiring into the Oriental and sacred origin of Freemasonry, traces of the order in Mexico, etc.

Prospectus of the OIL CREEK and Allegany [*sic*] Oil Co. ... *Boston: Wright & Potter, Printers.* 1865. 8vo, pp. 12. B.

Oil Creek [Pa.] Business Directory for 1865: ... By J. H. Lamb. *New York: Chapin, Bromell & Co., Printers.* 1865. 8vo, pp. 72. 57074

Oil Districts of Canada. *See* Vol. III., No. 10536.

The Oil-Dorado of West Virginia. A Full Description of the Great Mineral Resources of West Virginia, the Kanawha Valley, and the Country between the Ohio, the Hughes, and the Kanawha River. *New York: American News Company.* 1865. 16mo, pp. 86. 57075

Oil on the Waters [right and wrong of the North and South]. *Boston: J. E. Tilton and Company.* 1867. 16mo, pp. 436. BA.

Ojeadá al Proyecto. *See* G[uzman] (A. L.), Vol. VII. 29369.

Ojeada histórica sobre el Paraguay, seguida del vapuleo de un traidor, vividida en varias azotainas administradas al estraviad autor de las producciones contra el Paraguay, conocido vulgarmente por el nombre de Luciano el sonso. Obrita en verso y prosa por el ciudadano Paraguayo Juan J. Brizuela. *Buenos Aires.* 1857. 8vo, pp. 86. 57077

Ojeada sobre la campaña que hizo el General Santa-Anna en el estado de Coahuila el mes de Febrero proximo pasado. Por G. A. y N. *Mexico.* 1847. 4to, pp. 19, 11. Plan. 57078

Ojeada sobre la cuestion Española, 1864. *Lima.* 1865. 8vo, pp. 142, (2). 57079

Ojibwa Language. Abinoji aki Tibajimouin. ... [n. p.] 1840. 12mo. 57080

Catechism, in the Ojibwa Language. *Toronto.* 1834. 8vo.

The Gospel of St. Matthew; translated into the Ojibwa Language. By Peter Jones. *Toronto.* 1829. 12mo. 57081

The Gospels of St. Matthew and St. John in the Language of the Ojibwa Indians. [n. p.] 1850. 12mo. Plates. *See also* Vol. IV., No. 12832.

A Hymn Book for the use of Ojibwa Indian Congregations of the Church of England. Translated by Rev. Frederick A. O'Meara and Rev. Peter Jacobs. *Toronto.* 18—. 12mo.

Minuajimouin au St. Mathiu. The Gospel according to Matthew in the Ojibwa Language. *Boston: Printed ... by Crocker & Brewster.* 1839. 12mo, pp. 112. + [*Ibid.*] 1844. A. 57083

Minuajimouin Gainajoinot au St. Luke, Anishinabe enuet Giizhianikunotabiung au S. Hall, Mekvdeuikonaie: Gaie au George Copway, Anishinable Gugikueuinini. *Boston.* 1837. 12mo, pp. 112. 57084

St. Luke in the Ojibwa language.

New Testament Stories and Reading Book, in the Ojibwa Language. [n. p.] 1835. 8vo. 57085

Ojibue Nugumouinun. Geaiouajin igiu Anishinabeg Enumiajig. [Hymns.] *Boston.* 1836. 18mo. + *Boston: American Board of ... Foreign Missions.* 1844. 18mo, pp. xii, 10–212. B.

O-jib-ue Spelling Book, designed for the use of Native Learners. Second Edition ... . *Boston: American Board of ... Foreign Missions.* 1835. 12mo, pp. 107. B. + Third Edition. *Boston: Printed ... by Crocker & Brewster.* 1846. 12mo, pp. 96. H.

See also Bingham (A.), Vol. II., No. 5429.

Ojibwa Nugumoshäng. Ojibwa Hymns. *New-York: American Bible Society.* [n. d.] 18mo, pp. 95. 57088

Old Testament Bible Stories ... in O-jib-ue. *Boston.* 1835. 12mo. 57089

Ju Otoshki-kikindiuin au Kitogimaminan gaie bemajiinvng Jesus Krist: ima Ojibue inueuining guzhitong. The New Testament ... . *New York: American Bible Society.* 1844. 12mo, pp. (4), 643. 57090

Ju Otoshki-kikindiuin au Tebeniminvng gaie bemajiinvng Jesus Christ: ima Ojibue Inueuining giizhitong. The New Testament ... . *New-York: American Bible Society.* 1856. 12mo, pp. iv, 717. 57091

See also Vol. IV., No. 12833.

Peep of Day in the Language of the Ojibwa Indians. *Boston.* 1844. 12mo. 57092

A Translation of the Book of Common Prayer, in the Ojibwa Language. By Rev. Frederick A. O'Meara ... . *Toronto.* 1853. 12mo, pp. 628. 57093

A Translation of the Five Books of Moses, commonly called the Pentateuch, into the Ojibwa Language. By Rev. Frederick A. O'Meara and Rev. Peter Jacobs. *Toronto.* 18—. 12mo.

A Translation of the New Testament in the Ojibwa Language. By Rev. Frederick A. O'Meara ... . *Toronto.* 1854. 12mo, pp. 766. 57095

OKAH TUBBEE. A Sketch of the Life of Okah Tubbee, alias William Chubbee, son of the Head Chief, Mosholeh Tubbee, of the Choctaw Nation of Indians. *Springfield, Mass.* 1848. 12mo. 57096

Okalluktuaet [etc.]. *See* Esquimau, Vol. VI., No. 22864.

O'KELLY (J.) Essay on Negro Slavery. By James O'Kelly. *Philadelphia.* 1784. 8vo. 57097

OKES (T. V.) An Account of the Providential Preservation of Eliz. Woodcock, who survived a confinement under the Snow of nearly eight days and nights, in Feb. 1799. By Thomas Verney Okes. *Cambridge: F. Hodson.* [1799.] 12mo, pp. 33. C.

OKES (W.) Scenery of the White Mountains. By W. Okes. *Boston.* [n. d.] Folio. 57099

OKIE (A. H.) An Address delivered before the Rhode Island Homœopathic Society. By A. Howard Okie, M.D. ... *Providence: George H. Whitney.* [n. d.] 8vo, pp. 28. B. 57100

Okikinoadi-mezinaigan. *See* Vol. IV., No. 12834.

OLABARRIETA MEDRANO (Miguel de). Recuerdo de las Obligaciones del Ministerio Apostolico en la cura de las almas. Manual Moral ordenado primariamente á los Señores Parachos, ò curas, de este Nuevo Mondo, en este Reino del Perù, y los demas de las Indias; segun los Decretos del Santo Concilio Tridentino, y del Sagrado Concilio Tercera Limense ... . *Lima, por D. de Lyra.* 1717. 4to. 57101

OLAGUIBEL (M. de). Discurso patriotico, pronunciado en Puebla en la festividad nacional del 16. de Setiembre de 1832, aniversario del grito de Dolores [año de 1810]. ... *Mexico.* 1841. 8vo. 57102

OLARTE (A.) Declaracion legal de la inocencia del Ciudadano Antonio Olarte, acusado calumnosamente de conspiracion contra la patria por Andres Maria Segismundo Nieto. *Mexico.* 1826. 4to, pp. 38. 57103

OLARTE (R.), *and others.* Cuestion de Tehuantepec y representacion que dirigen al Gobierno Ramon Olarte, Manuel Payno y José Pesado. *Mexico.* 1852. 8vo, pp. 66, 13. 57104

OLASAGARRE (M.) Informe que por orden de Su Alt. Ser. presento al Supremo Gobierno sobre el Estado de la Hacienda Publica; por M. Olasagarre. *Mexico.* 1855. 8vo. 57105

OLAUS MAGNUS. De wonderlijcke Historie van de Noordersche Landen. ... Bij ghevoecht zyn verscheyden warachtige Navigatien tegent Noorden, als op Nova-Sembla, Groenlant en door de Strate van Nassouwen, anders Weygats ghenoemt. *Amsterdam: C. Claesz.* [1599.] Sm. 8vo. Maps. 57106

The Northern Lands described; to which are added various voyages to Greenland and through the Straits of Nassau. The appendix of fourteen leaves is the first collection of voyages to the North, and contains the voyages of St. Burrough, Frobisher, Pette and Jackman. Extremely scarce. *See also* Vol. XI., Nos. 43830–35.

OLCOTT (B.) Brotherly Love ... a Sermon Preached before a Society of ... Free ... Masons, in Charlestown, ... 27th of December, 1781. By Rev. Bulkley Olcott, A.M. ... *Westminster.* 1782. 4to, pp. 15. W. 57107

[OLCOTT (Henry S.)] A Letter on the Taxation of Loans as Capital ... in behalf of the Bankers and Brokers of New York. [n. p.] 1869. 8vo, pp. 8. B. 57108

Genealogy of the OLCOTT FAMILY. *Hartford.* 1845. 8vo.

OLD (R. O.) Colorado: ... its History, Geography, and Mining. Including a ... Catalogue of ... Ores. By R. O. Old. *London.* [1869.] 8vo, pp. 64. Map. H. 57110

Old Abe, the Miller; or, the Campaigns of Richmond. A Story in Verse. [n. p. n. d.] 8vo, pp. 8. 57111

Relates to Abraham Lincoln. *See also* [Lincoln (A.)], Vol. IX., No. 41218.

Old and New. Volume I. January to July 1870 ... . *Boston: H. O. Houghton and Company.* 1870. 8vo, pp. iv, 852. Continued. 57112

A monthly magazine. Edited by Edward Everett Hale and F. B. Perkins.

Old and New Tariffs compared. With Observations on the Effect of High Duties, on Revenue and Consumption. By a Citizen. *Boston: Wells and Lilly.* 1820. Folio, pp. 31. H.

Old and New Unitarian Church. *Charleston, S. C.* 1854. 8vo. 57114

The Old Bachelor. *See* [Wirt (W.)]

The Old Brewery, and the New Mission House at the Five Points; By the Ladies of the Mission. *New York: Stringer & Townsend.* 1854. 12mo, pp. 304. C. 57115

The Old Capitol and its Inmates. By a Lady, who enjoyed the hospitalities of the Government for a "season." *New York: E. J. Hale & Son.* 1867. 12mo, pp. 226. B. 57116

"Old Central School" Re-Union. ... with the Oration and Addresses ... on that Occasion. *Cincinnati: Longley Brothers.* 1856. 8vo, pp. 36. 57117

OLD CITIZEN, *pseudon.* *See* Nos. 19107, 50289, *and* 53617.

The Old City, and its Highways and Byways ... By "Aleph." *London: W. H. Collingridge.* M.DCCC.LXV. Crown 8vo, pp. viii, 387, (16). 57118

London is the "Old City." It contains an account of the South Sea Bubble, Sir Walter Raleigh, etc.

Acts of Incorporation and By-Laws of the OLD COLONY AND FALL RIVER RAILROAD COMPANY. *Boston: Crocker and Brewster.* 1855. 12mo, pp. 40. B. 57119

Also: First Annual Report of the ... Old Colony and Fall River Rail Road Company .... 1855. *Boston: Crocker and Brewster.* 1855. 8vo, pp. 10. Continued.—The Old Colony and Fall River Rail Road Company *vs.* the Broadway Rail Road Company. ... *Boston.* 1858. 8vo. *See also* No. 55049.

First Annual Report of the Directors of the OLD COLONY AND NEWPORT RAILWAY COMPANY ... 1864. *Boston: Geo. C. Rand & Avery, Printers.* 1864. 8vo, pp. 9. Continued. B.

First Report of the OLD COLONY RAILROAD COMPANY ... *Boston.* 1845. 8vo. Continued. 57121

Also: Report of the Committee for investigating the Affairs of the Old-Colony Railroad Company, 1850. *Boston.* 1850. 8vo.

Old Continental, and the New Greenback Dollar. Uncle Sam's Debts, and his ability to pay them. [n. p. n. d.] 8vo, pp. 8. 57122

The Old Continental. *See* [Paulding (J. K.)]

OLD COVENANTING ... LAYMAN, *pseudon.* *See* No. 47276, *note*

Old Dartmouth Centennial Celebration, 1864. *New Bedford, Mass.* 1865. 8vo, pp. 129. 57123

Old Days of the Second [Presbyterian] Church. [*Philadelphia.* n. d.] 8vo, pp. 24, Cover Title, (2). 57124

OLD DEMOCRAT, *pseudon.* *See* [Moore (Jacob B.)]

First Celebration by the OLD DOMINION SOCIETY, of the City of New-York, of the Anniversary of the Settlement at Jamestown, Va., on the 13th of May, 1607. Hon. Geo. W. Summers, Orator. *New York: Pudney & Russell, Printers.* 1860. 8vo, pp. 109. BA. 57125

Improved title of No. 35738, Vol. IX.

Old England for Ever, or, Spanish Cruelty display'd; Wherein the Spaniards' Right to America is impartially Examined and found Defective, their Pretensions founded in Blood, supported by Cruelty, and continued by Oppression. ... With an Account of their Intolerable Oppression and Barbarous Treatment of the poor Indians, and the Shocking and Tragical Methods used to deprive them of their Countrey, and obtain Possession of their rich Mines, etc. ... *London.* 1740. Sm. 8vo, pp. 320. 57126

The title at length can be found in Mr. Bartlett's catalogue of J. Carter Brown's library. It is partly a translation of B. de las Casas.

Old-Fashioned 'lection and the Cake. [Poetry.] *Hartford: Brown & Gross.* 1869. 12mo, pp. 12. B. 57127

The Old Flag. *Philadelphia: American Sunday School Union.* 1864. 16mo, pp. 368. 3 Plates. C. 57128

The Old Flag, First Published by Union Prisoners at Camp Ford, Tyler, Texas. Vol. I. ... *Bridgeport.* [1864.] 4to. BA.

Only one hundred copies printed. *See also* May (W. H.), Vol. XI., No. 47085.

Old Fort Duquesne; a Tale of the Early Toils, Struggles and Adventures of the First Settlers at the Forks of the Ohio, in 1754. *Pittsburgh.* 1844. 8vo. S. 57130

An Old Fox Tarr'd [1755]. *See* [Toplady (Augustus M.)]

The Old Franklin Almanac ... for 1861. ... *Philadelphia: Haslett & Wince.* [n. d.] 8vo. Continued. H. 57131

Contains a diary of the rebellion.

Old Friends. A Remembrancer of Beloved Companions: and Years Bygone. *New-York: Bliss, Wadsworth and Co.* 1835. 12mo, pp. 327, (1). C. 57132

The Old Guard, A Monthly Journal, devoted to the principles of 1776 and 1787. Vol. I. ... *New York: C. Chauncey Burr & Co.* [1863.] 8vo, pp. (4), 288. Portrait. Continued. B.

Old Haun, the Pawnbroker, or the Orphan's Legacy. A Tale of New York, founded on Facts. *New York: Livermore & Rudd.* 1857. 12mo, pp. 463. Plate. C. 57134

The Old House. *See* [Prime (W. C.)]

OLD HUMPHREY, *pseudon.* *See* [Mogridge (G.)], XII. 49835.

Old Indian Chronicle. *See* Drake (Samuel G.), V. 20879.

"Old Jack" and his Foot-Cavalry; or a Virginian Boy's Progress to Renown. A Story of the War in the Old Dominion. ... *New York: John Bradburn.* 1864. 12mo, pp. 300. 4 Plates.

Relates to "Stonewall" Jackson.

Old Jersey Captive. *See* Andros (Thomas), Vol. I. 1527.

Old John Uncas. *See* Vol. IV., Nos. 15749–52.

The Old Judge. *See* [Haliburton (T. C.)], Vol. VII. 29692.

The Old Man's Story of Old Times. Related by Himself. *Adrian: Jermain's Steam Press.* 1855. 8vo, pp. 38. Portrait.

Old Men's Tears | For their own | Declensions, | Mixed with | Fears | Of their and Posterities further falling off | from New England's | Primitive Constitution. | Published by some of Boston's old | Planters | And some others. | *Boston: Printed in the Year* 17—. *Reprinted for B. Gray.* 1732. 12mo, pp. 20. 57137

I have not met with the first edition.

OLD MERCHANT, *pseudon.* *See* [Nesmith (J.)], No. 52340.

OLD MORTALITY, *pseudon.* The Song of the Sexton, addressed to his Shovel, after the Dedication of the Albany Cemetery, By Old Mortality. [*Albany.* n. d.] 8vo, pp. (8). B. 57138

Old Nick of the Swamp; ... A Story of Texas. By an Old Hunter. *New-York: George Munro & Co.* [1867.] 12mo, pp. (2), 9–99. 57139

The Old Path. [Sandemanian.] *Portsmouth, N. H.* 1765. 8vo, pp. 4. M. 57140

The Old Paths Restored. *See* [Mather (C.)], XI. 46438.

OLD PIONEER, *pseudon.* *See* [Peck (J. M.)]

OLD PLANTER, *pseudon.* *See* Vol. VI., No. 22946.

The Old Principles. *See* [Mather (C.)], Vol. XI. 46439.

OLD RESIDENT, *pseudon.* *See* Vol. XIII., No. 54095.

The Old Roll of Fame. The Patriots of the Revolution of 1776. Sketches of the Survivors. *Boston.* 1864. 8vo.

Old Rough and Ready Almanac. *Philadelphia: Turner & Fisher.* 1849. 12mo. S. 57142

The Old Settler: Devoted to the Early History ... of Northern New York. *Keeseville.* 1847. Folio. Continued. S.

Old Settler's Festival ... in Buffalo ... 1867 ... *Buffalo.* 1867. 8vo, pp. 20. 57144

The Old South Church, in Boston, Mass, with List of the Founders, the Pastors, the Ruling Elders and Deacons, and the Surviving Members. *Boston.* 1826. 12mo, pp. 24. 57145

Also: Account of the Poor Fund ... held in Trust by the Old South Society, ... Boston, with Copies of Original Papers ... By Joseph Ballard. *Boston.* 1868. 8vo. — Act of Incorporation and By Laws of the Old South Society in Boston. *Boston: Printed by Alfred Mudge and Son.* 1861. 18mo, pp. 18. + *Boston: M. Stevens.* 1870. 18mo, pp. 18. — Extracts from the Information of the Concerned. [Relating to the Old South Church. *Boston.* 1807.] 16mo, pp. 15. — List of Pastors, Officers, and Members of Old South Church, ... June 1, 1870. ... *Boston: J. Frank. Farmer, Printer.* 1870. 12mo, pp. 34. — Members of the ... Church, January 1, 1863. *Boston: Alfred Mudge & Son, Printers.* 1862 [*sic*]. 12mo, pp. 21. B. *See also* Vol. II., Nos. 6662–67.

The Old Stone Farm House. *Philadelphia.* [1864.] 16mo, pp. 214. 8 Plates. C. 57146

Old Testament ... into Greenlandish. *See* Vol. VI. 22865.

Old Truths and Established Facts: Being an Answer to A Very New Pamphlet Indeed! [*London.* 1793.] 8vo, pp. 15.

On the slave-trade. Signed "Vindex."

Old Woman's Loyalty: ... Also A Poem on the Taking of the Havannah and the Re-taking of Newfoundland. *London.* 1762. 8vo, pp. 16. 57148

Old Zeke: or, The Wild Hunter of the Rocky Mountains. ... *New York: George Munro & Co.* 1867. 18mo, pp. 98.

OLDBUCK (A.), *pseudon.* A Legend of Boston, By Anthony Oldbuck. *Boston.* 1837. 12mo. 57150

OLDBUG (J.), *pseudon.* *See* [Withington (Leonard)].

The Olden Time. *See* Craig (N. B.), Vol. IV., No. 17365.

Olden Time in New-York. *See* [De Forest (T. R.)], Vol. V.

OLDENDORP (C. G. A.) Fuldstaendigt Udtog af Christian Georg Andreas Oldendorp's Missions-Historie om de Evangeliske Broeders Mission paa de Caraibiske der St. Thomas, St. Cruz, og St. Jan. *Kjöbenhavn: J. R. Thiele.* 1784. 16mo. C.

OLDENDORP. C. G. A. Oldendorp's Geschichte der Mission der Evangelischen Brüder auf den caraibischen Inseln S. Thomas, S. Croix und S. Jan. Herausgegeben durch Johann Jakob Bossart. ... *Barby: Christian Friedrich Laux.* 1777. 2 vols., 16mo, pp. (16), 444, (4); (4), 447–1068, (46). 3 Maps, 4 Plates. H.

Bossart made large additions to the materials collected by Oldendorp, and reduced the whole to order. The designs for the plates are by Oldendorp.

OLDEST INHABITANT, *pseudon.* *See* Vol. X., No. 42821.

OLDFIELD (J.) A Few Observations upon the Value and Importance of our North American Colonies. By Lieut. Col. John Oldfield. *London: F. Pinkney.* 1838. 8vo, pp. 17. C.

OLDFIELD (J.) "'Tother side of Ohio," or a Review of a "Poem in Three Cantos." By J. Oldfield. *Hartford: S. G. Goodrich.* 1863. 16mo, pp. 40. 57154

OLDHAM (W. S.) Rights of the South in opposition to "Squatter Sovereignty." Speech of Hon. W. S. Oldham, ... 27th ... August, 1856, and Letter of Hon. William R. Scurry. *Austin: Marshall & Oldham ... Printers.* 1856. 8vo, pp. 36.

Also: Speech ... in the [Confederate] Senate, September 4, 1862, on ... the Conscript Law ... [*Richmond.* 1862.] 8vo. — Speech ... on the subject of the Finances, December 23, 1863. [n. p. n. d.] 8vo. — Speech ... On the Resolutions of ... Texas, concerning Peace, Reconstruction and Independence. ... January 30, 1865. [n. p. n. d.] 8vo, pp. 13. BA. *See* Texas.

[OLDMIXON (John).] The British Empire | in | America, | Containing | The History of the Discovery, | Settle | ment, Progress and present State of all the | British Colonies, | on the | Continent and Islands of America. | ... | Being an Account of the Country, Soil, Cli | mate, Product and Trade of them ... . With curious Maps of the several Places, done from | the newest Surveys. By Herman Moll, Geographer. | *London: John Nicholson.* | 1708. 2 vols., 8vo, pp. xxxviii, (2), 412; (2), 382, Index, (32). 8 Maps. BA.

The dedication is signed by J. Oldmixon; but the work is often attributed to Herman Moll, who prepared the maps. It was reprinted in 1741, with considerable additions as below:

[OLDMIXON.] The British Empire | in | America, | containing | The History of the Discovery, | Settlement, Progress and State of the | British Colonies | on the | Continent and Islands of America. | ... | Second Edition, Corrected and Amended. | With the Continuation of the History, and the Variation in | the State and Trade of those Colonies, from the Year 1710 | to the present Time. ... | *London:* | ... *J. Brotherton* ... MDCCXLI. 2 vols., 8vo, pp. xxxiv, 567; (2), 478. 8 Maps. BA. 57157

Oldmixon's name is omitted in the dedication to this second edition, and the text differs in many particulars, and as both are frequently referred to, it often happens that the passages cited from one are not to be found in the other. In the first edition there is much relative to Pennsylvania, apparently derived from personal communication with William Penn, but it is omitted or abridged in the edition of 1741; while on the other hand, the history is continued in the latter down to the date of its publication. The story of William Penn and the Indian princess, as related by himself to the author, is first given in the second edition. So much as relates to Carolina is reprinted in Carroll's "Collections," Vol. II.

[OLDMIXON.] Gross-Brittannisches America nach seiner Erfindung, Bevölckerung und allerneuestem Zustand. ... Aus dem Englischen übersetzet durch M. Vischer. *Hamburg: ... Zacharias Hertels* ... 1710. 12mo, pp. xvi, 879. 57158

In volume VII. we have referred this book to [Oldmixon (John)], but we now believe it to be a German translation of Robert Blome's "English Empire in America."

OLDMIXON. Das | Gross-Britannische Scepter | in der | Neuen Welt, | Oder | ... Beschrei- | bung aller Engellandischen Plantingen, so | wohl auf dem vesten Lande, als denen | in America gelegenen | Insuln. | Durch Mons. Oldmixon. | ... | *Hamburg: Philip Hertel.* 1715. Sm. 8vo, pp. (28), 879. H. 57159

[OLDMIXON.] Het | Britannische Ryk | in | Amerika, | Zynde eene Beschryving van de Ontdekking, Be- | volking, Innwooders, het Klimaat, den Koop- | handel, en tegenwoordigen Staat van | alle de Britannische Coloniën, | In dat gedeelte der Wereldt. ... *Te Amsterdam,* | *By Rudolf en Gerard Wetstein.* | MDCCXXI. | 2 vols., 4to, pp. (26), 300; (2), 327, (14). Maps and Plates. BA. + *Te Amsterdam: H. Bosch.* 1727. 2 vols., 4to, pp. (26), 300; (2), 327, (14). Maps and Plates. 57160

To this Dutch translation is added "an Account of Coffee and the Coffee Plantations."

[OLDMIXON.] Das Britische Reich in America worinnen enthalten die Geschichte der Entdeckung der Aufrichtung des Anwachses und Zustandes der Englischen Colonien auf dem festen Lande und den Insuln von America. ... Aus dem Englischen ins Teutsche übersetzet von Theodor Arnold. *Lemgo: Bey Johann Heinrich Meyer.* 1744. 2 vols., 4to, pp. (36), 706; (2), 709–1254, (22). 8 Maps and 13 Plates. J.C.B. 57161

[OLDMIXON.] Das Brittische Reich in America sammt dem eroberten Canada, mit ... Inseln Gadaloupe, Martinique, und andern See-Plätzen, oder: ... Beschreibung der Engländischen Pflanzstädte ... in Nord-America. Nebst ... Nachricht von denen Gränzstreitigkeiten ... mit denen Franzosen, durch drey ... Landkarten ... erläutert. Dritter ... Druck. *Sorau: Bey Gottlob Hebold.* 1761. 4to. P. 57162

See also "Memoirs of North Britain," Vol. XII., No. 47571.

OLDMIXON (J.) Gleanings from Piccadilly to Pera. By John Oldmixon, R.N. *London: Longman* ... . 1854. Post 8vo, pp. 409. C. 57163

OLDMIXON. Transatlantic Wanderings; or, A Last Look at the United States. By Capt. Oldmixon, R.N. ... *London: George Routledge & Co.* 1855. 16mo, pp. iv, 189. B. 57164

OLDPATH (O.), *pseudon.* *See* [Newhall (J. R.)], No. 54995.

OLDS (E. B.) Arbitrary Arrests; Speech of Hon. Edson B. Olds, for which he was arrested, and his Reception Speeches on his return from the Bastile. [n. p. 1862.] 8vo, pp. 48.

Also: Speech ... on the Appropriation for the Collins Ocean Steamers; delivered ... Feb. 15, 1855. *Washington.* [n. d.] 8vo, pp. 16. — Speech ... on the Collins Line of Steamers. ... February 15, 1855. ... *Washington: Printed by J. T. & Lem. Towers.* 1855. 8vo, pp. 56. — Speech ... January 23 and 28, 1863, on the Cause and Conduct of the War. [n. p. 1863.] 8vo, pp. 14. — Speech ... on the Presidency ... 1852. [n. p. n. d.] 8vo. — Speech ... [on the Ocean Mail Steamers Appropriation Bill. n. p. 185–?] 8vo, pp. 51. H.

OLDS (G. S.) An Inaugural Oration, delivered in the Chapel of Williams College, October 14th, 1806. By Gamaliel S. Olds, A.M. ... *Stockbridge: Printed by H. Willard.* 1806. 8vo, pp. 16.

Also: Statement of Facts, relative to the Appointment of the Author to the Office of Professor of Chemistry, in Middlebury College, and the Termination of his connexion with that College. ... *Greenfield: Printed by Denio and Phelps.* [1818.] 8vo, pp. 20.

OLDS, *and* CORNING (Richard S.) Review of a Narrative by Rev. John Keep. *Syracuse.* 1833. 8vo, pp. 12. M. 57167

OLDSCHOOL (O.) *See* Oliver Oldschool, *pseudon.*, No. 57215

OLDSTYLE (J.) *See* [Irving (W.)], Vol. IX., No. 35188.

OLDYS (F.) The Life of Thomas Pain, the Author of the Rights of Man, with a Defence of his Writings. By Francis Oldys, A.M. of the University of Pennsylvania. The Second Edition. *London: John Stockdale.* 1791. 8vo, pp. 35. Portrait. + The Third Edition. [*Ibid.*] M DCC XCI. 8vo, pp. (2), 129. + With a Review of his Writings; Particularly of Rights of Man, Part First and Second. ... The Fifth Edition, corrected and enlarged. [*Ibid.*] M DCC XCII. 8vo, pp. viii, 166. + Tenth Edition. [*Ibid.*] 1793. 8vo, pp. 172. + The First Boston, from the Second London Edition. *Boston: Printed by Manning & Loring.* 1796. 8vo, pp. 40. + *Dublin.* 17—. 8vo. 57168

This work is usually attributed to G. Chalmers; but, in the year 1864, I sold a letter, written by Chalmers, in which he indignantly denies the statement.

OLDYS. The Abridged Life of Thomas Pain. By Francis Oldys, A.M. The Second Edition. *London: John Stockdale.* 1791. 8vo, pp. 34. + The Eighth Edition, corrected. [*Ibid.*] 1793. 8vo, pp. (2), 32. 57169

OLEA (Nicolao de). Svmma Tripartita Scholasticæ Philosophiæ; ... *Sumptibus Iosephi de Contreras Regio Limani Typographi.* 1694. 4to, pp. (14), 727, (14). 57170

An early Peruvian imprint.

O'LEARY (Arthur). An Essay on Toleration: or, Mr. O'Leary's Plea for Liberty of Conscience. *Philadelphia.* 1785. 8vo. 57171

Notices William Penn and Pennsylvania.

OLIER (M.) *See* [Faillon (l'Abbé)], Vol. VI., No. 23652.

OLIN (S). College Life: Its Theory and Practice. By Rev. Stephen Olin, D.D. ... *New York: Harper & Brothers.* 1867. 12mo, pp. (2), 239. 57172

OLIN. The Life and Letters of Stephen Olin, D.D. ... *New York: Harper & Brothers.* 1854. 2 vols., 12mo, pp. vi, 361; xiii, 486. Portrait. B. 57173

OLIN. The Works of Stephen Olin, D.D. ... *New York: Harper & Brothers.* 1852. 2 vols., 12mo, pp. viii, 422; (2), 475. Portrait. 57174

Also: An Address, ... at the opening of the Genesee Wesleyan Seminary, January 13, 1843: By Rev. Dr. Olin ... . *Rochester: Printed by David Hoyt.* MDCCCXLIII. 8vo, pp. 24. — Early Piety the Basis of Elevated Character. A Discourse to the Graduating Class of Wesleyan University, August, 1850. *New York.* 1851. 16mo.

The Olio; being a Collection of Poems, Fables, Epigrams, &c., including Tributes to the Memory of Lieut. Allen, The Hon. Wm. W. Van Ness, and The Hon. Brockholst Livingston. By the Author of "Patriotic Effusions." *New York: The Author.* 1823. 18mo, pp. iv, 104. 57175

The Olio; collected by a Literary Traveller. *Boston.* 1833. 16mo, pp. (4), 310. C. 57176

Olio; or Satirical Poetic-Hodge-Podge. With an illustration or explanatory Dialogue in vindication of the Motive. ... *Philadelphia.* 1801. 12mo, pp. 46. BM. 57177

OLIPHANT (——). Appel de la capitale de l'Écosse aux États-Unis d'Amérique au sujet de l'esclavage, tiré d'une brochure publiée en Mai 1836, par Oliphant. *Paris.* 1836. 8vo, pp. 43. 57178

[OLIPHANT (Andrew).] A | Letter | from | New-England, concerning | The State of Religion there. | *Edinburgh: Printed in the Year* MDCCXLII. 12mo, pp. 7. H. 57179

OLIPHANT (D.) ... A Sermon ... at Beverly, Nov. 24, 1825, being ... Thanksgiving. By David Oliphant ... . *Salem: Printed by Warwick Palfray, Jun.* 1825. 8vo, pp. 22. 57180

OLIPHANT (E.) The History of North America and its United States. Including also, A Distinct History of each Individual State; its Manners and Customs, Trade, Commerce, Religion, and Government; Manufactures and Agriculture, Climate, Soil, and Produce; with new Tables of the whole of their Imports and Exports, Revenue, Debt, Expenditure, Currency of Coins, etc. To which is Annexed, An Account of New Discoveries. By Edward Oliphant, Esq. *Edinburgh: Printed by J. Johnstone.* 1800. 8vo, pp. 408. Map. + Second Edition. [*Ibid.*] 1801. BA. 57181

Extracted from Jedidiah Morse's "History of America," without acknowledgment.

OLIPHANT (J.) Memoirs and Remains of John Oliphant, of Auburn, New-York. ... Added his Funeral Sermon, By Rev. J. Hopkins. ... *Auburn: H. Ivison & Co.* 1835. 12mo, pp. 212. Portrait. B. 57182

OLIPHANT (L.) Minnesota and the Far West. By Laurence Oliphant ... . *William Blackwood and Sons, Edinburgh.* MDCCCLV. 8vo, pp. xiii, (1), 306. 17 Plates. BA. 57183

See "New Quarterly Review," January, 1856, *and* "Blackwood's Magazine," Vols. LXXVII. and LXXVIII.

OLIPHANT. Patriots and Filibusters or Incidents of Political and Exploratory Travel By Laurence Oliphant ... . *William Blackwood and Sons, Edinburgh.* MDCCCLX. Post 8vo, pp. viii, 242

Relates Walker's adventures in Nicaragua. Also: On the Present State of Political Parties in America. ... *William Blackwood and Sons, Edinburgh.* MDCCCLXVI. 8vo, pp. 30. C.

OLIPHANT (M. O. W.) Caleb Field. A Tale of the Puritans. By Margaret O. Wilson Oliphant. *New York: Harper & Brother.* 1851. 12mo, pp. 136. C. 57185

OLIVA (A.) Histoire du Pérou Par le P. Anello Oliva Traduite de l'espagnol sur le manuscrit inédit par M. H. Ternaux Compans. *Paris: P. Jannet.* MDCCCLVII. 16mo, pp. 128

The author died at Lima in 1642. Also: Catalogo de alguno varones illustres en santidad de la provincia del Peru de la compania de Jesus. ... *Sevilla, F. de Lyra.* 1632. 8vo.

OLIVAN (Alejandro). Discurso que pronunció en la sesion del 9. de diciembre, y diferentes documentos concernientes al relevo y partida de D. Miguel Tacon, Capitan General que fue de esta isla. ... *Habcna.* 1838. 4to, pp. 54. 57187

OLIVAN. Informe á la junta de gobierno del real consulado de agricultura y comercio de la isla de Cuba. Por A. Olivan ... *Habana:* 1831. *Imprenta fraternal.* Sm. 4to, pp. (1), 50. B.

Also: Informe á la junta de gobierno, sobre el nuevo tren de elaborar azúcar. ... *Habana.* 1831. 8vo, pp. (1), 36. B.

OLIVARES (Ignacio Gonzalez). Observaciones sobre la esclavitud en la Isla de Cuba. ... *Madrid: Durán.* 1865. 8vo.

Olive and the Pine. *See* [Lowe (*Mrs.* M. A. P.)], Vol. X.

The Olive Branch: or, Herald of Peace and Truth to All Saints. *Kirtland, Ohio: Hazen Aldrich.* 1848–50. 2 vols., 8vo, pp. 208; 192. BA. 57190

A Mormon monthly magazine. Vol. II. was published at Springfield, Ill., in 1849. I have seen a catalogue purporting to have a volume dated 1860, but have only met with Vols. I. and II. Vol. I. was edited by A. Cowles, who was succeeded by James C. Brewster.

The Olive-Branch; or, White Oak Farm. A Tale of Life in the Old Dominion. *Philadelphia: J. B. Lippincott & Co.* 1857. 12mo, pp. 329. C. 57191

The Olive-Leaf. No. 1. May 8, 1869. [*Waltham, Mass.: George Phinney.* 1869.] 4to, pp. 8. Continued. B. 57192

OLIVEIRA (Candido Baptista de). Systema financial do Brasil. ... *Rio de Janeiro.* 1842? 8vo. + *S. Petersburgo.* 1842. 8vo, pp. iii, 181, 47. 57193

OLIVEIRA (Francisco Manuel de). Ecloga pastoril, consagrada á memoria do serenissimo sr. D. José, principe do Brasil. ... *Lisboa, na Officina Nunesiana.* 1778. 4to. 57194

OLIVEIRA (H. V. D'). Systema de materia medica vegetal brasileira contendo o catalogo e classificação de todas as plantas brasileiras conhecidas os seus nomes em lingua nacional com individuação do modo porque são chamadas nas diversas localidades; ... Obra extrahida e traduzida das obras de C. F. Ph. de Martius. *Rio de Janeiro.* 1854. 8vo. 57195

OLIVEIRA E DAUN (João Carlos de Saldanha de). Observações sobre a Carta que os membros da Junta do Porto dirigiram a S. M. o Imperador do Brasil em 5 de Agosto de 1828. *Paris: Typographia de J. Tastu.* 1829. 8vo. 57196

OLIVEIRA (José Alvares de). Historia do districto do Rio das Mortes, sua descripção, descobrimento de suas minas, casos nelle acontecidos entre Paulistas e Imboabas, e erecção de suas villas. Offerecida ao Dr. Thomás Roby de Barros, ouvidor e corregedor da comarca do Rio das Mortes, juiz dos Feitos do Corôa ... . [n. p. n. d.] Folio, 13 leaves. 57197

OLIVEIRA BASTOS (Manuel José de). Roteiro da cidade de Sancta Maria de Belem do Grão-Pará, pelo rio Tocantins acima, até o porto-real do Pontal. *Rio de Janeiro, na Imprensa Regia.* 1811. 8vo, pp. 19. 57198

OLIVER (A.) An Essay on Comets, In Two Parts. Part I. Containing an Attempt to explain the Phænomena of the Tails of Comets, and to account for their perpetual Opposition to the Sun, upon Philosophical Principles. Part II. Pointing out some important Ends for which these Tails were probably designed: Wherein it is shewn, that, in consequence of these curious Appendages, Comets may be inhabited Worlds, and even Comfortable Habitations; notwithstanding the vast Excentricities of their Orbits. The Whole interspersed with Observations and Reflections on the Sun and primary Planets. ... By Andrew Oliver, Jun. Esq. *Salem, New-England: ... Samuel Hall ...* MDCCLXXII. 8vo, pp. (4), vi, 87. Folded Plate. BA., N., P. 57199

The earliest American work on the subject. For a reprint, *see* Winthrop (J.) *See also* Vol. XI., No. 45940.

OLIVER (B. L.) The Rights of American Citizens; with a Commentary on State Rights, and on the Constitution and Policy of the United States. By Benjamin L. Oliver ... . *Boston: Marsh, Capen & Lyon.* 1832. 8vo, pp. 411. BA. 57200

Also: An Address .. before the ... Royal Arch Masons, ... January 27, A.L. 5820. ... *Salem: Henry Whipple.* 1820. 8vo, pp. 15. Mr. Oliver was also the author of several legal works.

OLIVER (Daniel). An Address ... Dartmouth College upon the Induction of the Author into the Professorship. ... *Concord.* 1825. 8vo, pp. 24. 57201

[OLIVER.] Remarks on a Pamphlet entitled "Prof. Hale and Dartmouth College." [n. p. 1846.] 12mo, pp. 34. 57202

Also: An Address ... before the Temperance Society of the Medical Class in Dartmouth College, Oct. 31, 1832. ... *Windsor, Vt.* [1832.] 8vo, pp. 16.—An Address, ... before the New-Hampshire Medical Society, at Concord, June 4, 1833. ... *Concord: Marsh, Capen & Lyon.* 1833. 12mo, pp. 23.

OLIVER (G.) History of Freemasonry from the Year 1829 to 1841. By George Oliver, D.D. *New York.* 1855. 8vo, pp. 125. S. 57203

Also: History of Masonic Persecutions in different quarters of the Globe ... . *New York.* 1866. 12mo, pp. 429.

OLIVER (H. K.) An Address delivered at the Dedication of the School-House ... in Salem, March 18, 1856 ... . By Henry K. Oliver. ... *Salem: Wm. Ives and Geo. W. Pease, Printers.* 1856. 8vo, pp. 38. H. 57204

Also: Genealogy of Descendants of Thomas Oliver, Of ... Boston, New England, ... [n. p. 1868.] 8vo, pp. 7.

OLIVER (I.) Poems on Various Subjects. ... By Isabella Oliver, of Cumberland County, Pennsylvania. *Carlisle: From the Press of A. Loudon, Whitehall.* 1805. 12mo, pp. 220. 57205

A list of subscribers fills sixteen pages.

OLIVER (J. McC.) The Battle of Franklin, the Little Girl at Spanish Fort, and other Poems. By James McCarty Oliver. *Philadelphia: J. B. Lippincott & Co.* 1870. 12mo, pp. 118. C.

OLIVER (Jerusha). *See* [Mather (C.)], Vol. XI., No. 46410.

OLIVER (J.) A Present to be given to Teeming Women by their Husbands and Friends. By John Oliver. *Boston: Reprinted by Benj. Harris.* 1694. 8vo. 57207

OLIVER (M.) Ancestry of Mary Oliver, who lived 1640–1698, and was the wife of Samuel Appleton, of Ipswich. By William S. Appleton. *Cambridge: Press of John Wilson & Son.* 1867. Rl. 8vo, pp. 29. 3 Tables. C. 57208

OLIVER (M.) Speech of Hon. M. Oliver ... January 24, 1854, on Tonnage Duties. [n. p. n. d.] 8vo. S. 57209

OLIVER Y BRAVO (P.) Memoria histórica, geográfica y estadistica de Cienfuegos y su jurisdiccion redactada por Pedro Oliver y Bravo. *Cienfuegos.* 1846. 8vo, pp. 54. 57210

[OLIVER (Peter).] A | Poem | Sacred to the Memory of the | Honorable | Josiah Willard, Esq; | Late Secretary of the Province of the | Massachusetts-Bay, | in | New England; | Who Deceased December 6th, 1756. | ... | *Boston: | Printed by Green and Russell ...* | M. DCC. LVII. 4to, pp. 16. B., BA. 57211

Also: A Speech ... in Plymouth, May 15. 1750. ... After the Death of Isaac Lothrop, Esq; ... *Boston: Printed by D. Fowle.* 1750. Sm. 4to, pp. (2), 12. BA.

OLIVER (P.) The Puritan Commonwealth. An Historical Review of the Puritan Government in Massachusetts in its Civil and Ecclesiastical Relations from its Rise to the Abrogation of the First Charter. Together with some general Reflections on the English Colonial Policy, and on the Character of Puritanism. By the late Peter Oliver ... . *Boston: Little, Brown and Company.* M.DCCC.LVI. 8vo, pp. xii, 502. BA., C. 57212

"Written in a style of unsurpassed beauty. Uniformly correct and classic in diction, pointed and terse in its emphatic passages, exact and chastened in its rhetoric."—*North American Review.* For a scathing review, *see* Thornton (J. W.), *and* "Historical Magazine," II. 286.

OLIVER (T. F.) [Masonic] Discourse at Providence, Jan. 1, 1784. By Thomas F. Oliver. *Providence.* [n. d.] 4to. W.

OLIVER (W.) Eight Months in Illinois; with Information to Emigrants, By William Oliver. *Newcastle upon Tyne: William Andrew Mitchell.* MDCCCXLIII. 12mo, pp. (6), iv, 141. 57214

OLIVER OLDSCHOOL, *pseudon.* The Poetry of the Port Folio. By Oliver Oldschool [*i. e.* Joseph Dennie]. *Philadelphia: Harrison Hall.* 1818. 32mo, pp. 144. 57215

OLIVER OPTIC, *pseudon.* Our Standard Bearer; or, the Life of General Ulysses S. Grant. ... By Oliver Optic. *Boston: Lee & Shepard.* 1868. 16mo, pp. 348. 6 Plates. C. 57216

Also: Haste and Waste; or, the Young Pilot of Lake Champlain. ... *Boston: Lee & Shepard.* 1867. 16mo, pp. 313. 4 Plates.—Hope and Have; or, Fanny Grant among the Indians. ... *Boston: Lee & Shepard.* 1867. 16mo, pp. 283. 4 Plates.—On Time; or, The Young Captain of the Ucayga Steamer. ... *Boston: Lee and Shepard.* 1870. 16mo, pp. 282. Plates.—Outward Bound; or, Young America Afloat. ... *Boston: Lee & Shepard.* 1867. 16mo, pp. 336. 4 Plates.—The Sailor Boy; or Jack Somers in the Navy. A Story of the Great Rebellion. ... *Boston: Lee & Shepard.* 1865. 12mo, pp. 336.—The Soldier Boy; or Tom Somers in the Army. A Story of the Great Rebellion. ... *Boston: Lee and Shepard.* 1864. 12mo, pp. 333.—The Starry Flag; or, the Young Fisherman of Cape Ann. ... *Boston: Lee & Shepard.* 1868. 16mo, pp. 312. 8 Plates.—The Young Lieutenant, or the Adventures of an Army Officer. A Story of the Great Rebellion. ... *Boston: Lee & Shepard.* 186–. 16mo, pp. 373. *See also* [Adams (W. T.)], Vol. I., No. 357–9.

Oliver's Magazine. Oct. 1841. [*Boston.* 1841.] 8vo, pp. 54, Music, (2). H. 57217

OLIVERS (T.) A Full Defence of the Rev. John Wesley, in answer to the several Personal Reflections cast on that Gentleman by the Rev. Caleb Evans, in his Observations on Mr. Wesley's late Reply prefixed to his "Calm Address:" By Thomas Olivers. *London: Printed in the Year* 1776. 12mo, pp. 24.

Manual of the OLIVET BAPTIST CHURCH. ... *Philadelphia: Barnard & Jones, Printers.* 1858. 12mo, pp. 36. 57219

Annual Catalogue of ... OLIVET INSTITUTE, Olivet, Eaton County, Mich. 1847–8. *Marshall.* 1848. 12mo, pp. 12. Continued. 57220

OLIVEYRA (Francis Xavier d'). Mémoires historiques, politiques et littéraires concernant le Portugal, et toutes ses dependances ... Par D'Oliveyra. *La Haye: A. Moetjens.* 1743. 2 vols., 12mo, pp. (16), 384; (8), 384. 57221

Relates partly to Brazil. The first edition, with a variation in the title, was printed in Amsterdam, 1741.

[OLIVIER DE CORANCEZ (Louis Alexandre).] Histoire des Wahabis, depuis leur origine jusqu'à la fin de 1809; par L. A. *Paris: Crapart.* 1810. 8vo, pp. (4), viii, 222, (2). C. 57222

Ollanta, ó sea La Sevéridad de un padre y la clemencia de un Rey. Drama dividido en tres actos. Traducido del Quichua al Castellano; con notas diversas, por José S. Barranca. *Lima.* 1868. 8vo, pp. xvi, 71, (1). 57223

Ollanta. An Ancient Ynca Drama. Translated from the original Quichua. By Clements R. Markham. *London: Trübner & Co.* 1871. 12mo, pp. (2), 128. 57224

This remnant of the literature of the Incas was preserved until about 1770, by the quipus, or knotted calendar; when Dr. Valdez, who had often witnessed the representation of the drama by Indian actors, before the ill-fated Inca, Tupac Amaru, reduced it to writing. From this copy, written in pure Quichua, Mr. Markham has made this translation. Also: Ollantai. Texte quichua, traduction française, notes, glossaire, etc., publié par Pacheco Zégarra. *Paris: Maisonneuve et Cie.* [n. d.] 8vo.—Ollanta. Ein altperuanisches Drama, aus der Kechuasprache. Uebersetzt und Commentirt von J. J. von Tschudi. *Wien: Gerold's Sohn.* 1875. 4to, pp. 220.

OLLIFFE (C.) Scènes Américaines Dix-huit Mois dans le Nouveau Monde Par Charles Olliffe ... . *Paris: Amyot.* 1852. 8vo. Portrait of Washington. + Deuxième Édition ... . [*Ibid.*] 1853. 12mo, pp. xvi, 344. Portrait. H. 57225

There are copies on *papier vélin.*

OLLIVANT (J. E.) A Breeze from the Great Salt Lake; or, New Zealand to New York ... By J. E. Ollivant, M.A. *London.* 1871. 8vo, pp. 176. Map. 57226

OLMEDO Y TORRE (A. de). Arte de lengua mexicana, corregido segun l'original por el Fr. D. Antonio de Olmedo y Torre. *Puebla, por Fernandez de Leon en la imprenta de F. X. de Morales.* 1726. 4to, (2) and 54 leaves. 57227

OLMEDO (J. J. de). Discurso sobre las Mitas de America. Por J. J. de Olmedo ... . *London.* 1812. 8vo, pp. 46. 57228

OLMEDO. Obras Poeticas ... Edicion aumentada con algunas poesías inéditas por M. N. Corpancha. ... *Mexico.* 1862. 8vo.

[OLMEDO.] Oda al Jeneral Flores. *See* No. 56686.

Also: La Victoria de Tunin, Canto á Bolivar. ... Nueva Edicion. *Carácas.* 1842. Sm. 8vo, pp. xviii, 46.

OLMO (J. V. del). Nueva Descripcion del orbe de la tierra. En que se trata de todas sus partes interiores y exteriores y circulos de la Esphera y de la inteligencia, uso y fabrica de los mapas y tablas geographicas, assi universales y generales como particulares. Explicanse sus diferencias, se corrigen los errores y imperfecciones de las Antiguas y se añaden otras modernas. Con la fabrica y uso del globo terrestre artificial y de las cartas de Navegar ... Por Joseph Vicente del Olmo. *Valencia.* 1681. Folio

OLMOZ (Andres de). Ars et Vocabularium Mexicanum. *Mexico.* 1555. 4to. 57231

Quoted by Brunet from Equiara; perhaps the MS. from which the following is printed.

OLMOS. Arte de la lengua mexicana. Grammaire de la langue nahuatl ou mexicaine, composée, en 1547. Publiée avec notes, éclaircissements, etc. par Rémi Siméon. *Paris: Imprimerie Nationale.* 1875. 8vo, pp. (2), xv, 273, (1). B. 57232

In Spanish. The introduction and notes are in French.

OLMOZ. Grammatica et Lexicon Linguæ Mexicanæ, Totonaquæ et Huastecæ. *Mexici.* 1560. 2 vols., 4to. 57233

Vater gives the date 1565. Concerning this rare book, *see* Ludewig's "Literature of American Aboriginal Languages," p. 113. Neither Rich, Ternaux, or Brunet, give the title of this book.

OLMOS (Didac. de). Gramatica de la Lengua Indica. ... *Lima.* 1633. 4to. 57234

Tschudi gives 1634 as the date; Ludewig, 1633.

OLMOS (Juan Manuel). Informes dados al supremo Gobierno de la Republica por las Autoridades superiores del Departamento de Michoacan, acerca de la solicitud del Ayuntamiento de Colima y Subprefectura de Alonoloyan, dirigida a que aquel districto sea declarado nuevamente Territorio. *Morelia.* 1845. 4to, pp. 28.

OLMSTEAD (G.) Sundry Documents (copied from the original) relative to the Claim of Gideon Olmstead, against the Commonwealth of Pennsylvania. ... *Philadelphia: E. Olmstead.* 1811. 8vo, pp. 120. C., N. 57236

Also: Debates in the Legislature of Pennsylvania, ... 1809–10 [relating to the case of G. Olmstead] ... . [n. p. n. d.] 8vo, pp. 278.—Letter and Statement, in the Case of Olmstead, From the Auditor-General, ... 1810. [n. p.:] *William Greer, Printer.* [n. d.] 8vo, pp. 7.—Message of the Governor, ... with Documents, relative to The Case of Gideon Olmstead and others. [*Lancaster?*] 1809. 8vo, pp. 17. + *Washington City: Printed by Roger C. Weightman.* 1809. 8vo, pp. 26.—Report on the Governor's Message, relative To the Mandamus ... in the Case of Gideon Olmstead. [*Lancaster, Pa.:*] *Benjamin Grimler, Printer.* [1809.] 8vo, pp. 16. + [n. p. n. d.] 8vo, pp. 12.—The Whole of the Proceedings in the Case of Olmstead and others *versus* Rittenhouse's Executrices ... . Collected ... by Richard Peters, Jun. *Philadelphia: William P. Farrand and Co.* 1809. 8vo, pp. vi, 108. BA.

OLMSTEAD (J. W.) ... A Discourse ... on ... Fast [Day], in ... Chelsea, April 4, 1844. By J. W. Olmstead ... . *Boston: Printed by Tuttle and Dennett.* 1844. 8vo, pp. 18. B. 57237

OLMSTED [Denison]. Memoir of John Treadwell, LL.D., late Governor of Connecticut. By Professor Olmsted, of Yale College. *Boston: T. R. Marvin.* 1843. 8vo, pp. 31. Portrait.

Also: An Address on the Scientific Life and Labors of William C. Redfield, A.M. ... [To which is added a list of the Books and Papers of the late William C. Redfield.] *New Haven: Printed by E. Hayes.* 1857. 8vo, pp. 28. Portrait.—Memoir of Eli Whitney, Esq. ... *New-Haven: Durrie & Peck.* 1846. 8vo, pp. 80. Plate

and Portrait.—An Oration ... at New Haven, before the Connecticut Alpha of the Phi Beta Kappa, September 11, 1827. ... *New Haven: Printed by Hezekiah Howe.* 1827. 8vo, pp. 24. *See also* Vol. XI., Nos. 45433 *and* 55613.

OLMSTED (F. A.) Incidents of a Whaling Voyage. To which are added Observations on the Scenery, Manners, and Customs, and Missionary Stations of the Sandwich and Society Islands, accompanied by numerous Lithographic Prints. By Francis Allyn Olmsted. *New York.* 1841. 12mo, pp. 360.

OLMSTED (F. L.) The Cotton Kingdom: a Traveller's Observations on Cotton and Slavery in the American Slave States. ... By Frederick Law Olmsted. ... *New York: Mason Brothers.* 1861. 2 vols., 12mo, pp. viii, 376; iv, 404. Map. + [*Ibid.*] 862. 2 vols., 12mo, pp. viii, 376; iv, 404. Map. B. 572401

Based on three former volumes of Journeys and Investigations, by the same author. Reproduced in England as "Journeys and Explorations in the Cotton Kingdom. A Traveler's Observations on Cotton and Slavery in the American States." ... *London: Sampson Low* ... . 1861. 2 vols., 12mo, pp. viii, 376; iv, 404. Map. BA.

OLMSTED. A Journey in the Back Country. By Frederick Law Olmsted ... . *New York: Mason Brothers.* 1860. 12mo, pp. xvi, 11–492. BA. + [*Ibid.*] 1861. 57241

OLMSTED. A Journey in the Seabord Slave States ... . By Frederick Law Olmsted ... . *New York: Dix & Edwards.* 1856. 12mo, pp. xv, (1), 723, (1). Map and Plate. B. 57242

OLMSTED. A Journey through Texas; or, a Saddle-Trip on the South-Western Frontier; with a Statistical Appendix. By Frederick Law Olmsted ... . *New York: Dix, Edwards & Co.* 1857. 12mo, pp. xxxiv, 516. Map and Plate. + *New York: Mason Brothers.* 1860. 12mo, pp. xxxiv, 516. Map and Plate.

See "New Quarterly Review," May, 1857, p. 153.

OLMSTED. Our Slave States. By Frederick Law Olmsted, ... *New York.* 1856–60. 3 vols., 12mo. 57244

New title only to our Nos. 57241–43, *supra.*

OLMSTED. Wanderungen durch Texas. Aus dem Englischen ... . *Leipzig.* 1857. 8vo. 57245

Also: ... A Brief Outline of ... [the Work of] the U. S. Sanitary Commission ... [n. p. 1861.] 8vo, pp. 24.—A Few Things to be thought of before proceeding to plan Buildings for the National Agricultural Colleges. *New York.* 1866. 8vo, pp. 23.— ... Public Parks and the Enlargement of Towns. ... *Cambridge, Mass.: American Social Science Association.* 1870. 8vo, pp. 36.—A Report to the Secretary of War ... upon the Sanitary Condition of the Volunteer Army, its Medical Staff, Hospitals and Hospital Supplies. ... December, 1861. *Washington, D. C.* 1861. 8vo, pp. 107.

See also Vol. VIII., No. 33118, *and* Vol. x., No. 42018, which has also been attributed to Olmsted.

OLMSTED, VAUX & Co. Report on the Proposed City Park [at Albany]. By Olmsted, Vaux & Co. *Albany, N. Y.: J. Munsell.* 1868. 8vo, pp. 14. 57246

Also: Report upon a Projected Improvement of the Estate of the College of California, at Berkeley ... . *San Francisco: Towne and Bacon, Printers.* 1866. 8vo, pp. 28.

OLMSTED (W. N.) The Universal Pathfinder ... Being a Guide ... to all Subjects and to all Lands. By W. N. Olmsted. *New York: Jas. Miller.* 1866. 16mo, pp. 186. 57247

OLNEY (J.) A History of the United States, on a new Plan; ... By Jeremiah Olney. *New-Haven: Durrie & Peck.* 1836. 16mo, pp. 287. C. 57248

OLNEY (J.) *and* BARBER (J. W.) The Family Book of History; comprising ... Events in the History of all the Civilized Nations ... . By Jesse Olney and John W. Barber. *Philadelphia: G. N. Loomis.* [1839.] 8vo, pp. 720. C., S. 57249

OLNEY (L. W.) Discourse ... "Politics in the Pulpit." ... August 31, 1856. By Lafayette W. Olney. *New York.* [n. d.] 8vo. 57250

OLNEY (W. T.) Report of a Joint Special Committee, relative to Wm. T. Olney, Feb. 1843. [n. p. 1843.] 8vo, pp. 10.

OLNEYVILLE, *R. I.* Constitution and By-Laws of Olneyville Division, No. 10, of the Sons of Temperance ... . *Providence: M. B. Young.* 1848. 12mo, pp. 16. 57252

OLSEN (G.) Testimony before Coroner's Jury holding an Inquisition on the bodies of Gabriel Olsen, ... and Simon O'Breadance, or Britton, ... killed ... May 14, 1867, in ... Mobile, Ala. [*Mobile.* 1867.] 8vo, pp. 49. 57253

OLSEN (*Mrs.*) Mrs. Olsen's Narrative of her One Year's Imprisonment at Jacksonville Insane Asylum. *Chicago: A. B. Case.* 1868. 12mo, pp. 144. C. 57254

OLSHAUSEN (T.) Geschichte der Mormonen oder Jüngsten-Tages-Heiligen in Nordamerika. ... *Göttingen: Bandenhoeck u. Ruprecht.* 1856. 8vo, pp. iv, 244. 57255

OLSHAUSEN. Die Vereinigten Staaten von Amerika geographisch und statistisch beschrieben von Theodor Olshausen ... .

Kiel. 1853–55. 2 vols. in 3 parts., 8vo, pp. viii, 426, (1); x, (8), 190; x, 201. 7 Maps. 57256

With the second title-pages: Vol. I. Das Mississippi-Thal; Vol. II. Part 1. Der Staat Missouri; Part 2. Der Staat Iowa. No more published.

OLTMANNS (Jabbo). Untersuchungen über die Geographie Amerika's südwärts vom Aequator, gegründet auf die Beobachtungen des Don. Alex. Malaspina. ... *Berlin.* 1827. 4to.

See also Humboldt (A. de), Vol. VIII., No. 33747.

OLYPHANT (J.) The Privileges of Jamaica Vindicated: with An Impartial Narrative of the Dispute ... Upon the Case of John Olyphant, Esq. ... A New Edition ... . *Jamaica: Printed by Alex. Aikman, jun. Printer.* 1810. 8vo, pp. (2), xviii, 122. B. 57258

For another edition, *see* Vol. IX., No. 35650.

Om Amerika samt om Emigrant-Föreningen i Stockholm. *Stockholm.* 1841. Map. 57259

Intended to furnish Swedish emigrants with the necessary information about the United States. It contains, besides, a short historical introduction in which the fate of the Swedish settlements in North America is related. In this part of the book some new particulars about "Nova Suecia" are to be found.

OMAHA, *Neb.* Charter and Ordinances of the City of Omaha, Nebraska. *Omaha.* 1857. 8vo, pp. 74. 57260

Collins' Omaha Directory, June, 1866. With an Appendix, containing a Great Variety of Historical Data, Statistics, and Facts. By Charles Collins. *Omaha: Charles Collins.* 1866. 12mo, pp. 204. 57261

Directory for 1870. Compiled and published by J. M. Wolfe. *Omaha.* 1870. 8vo.

Omahaw Language. Alphabet of Omahaw Syllables. [n. p. n. d.] 12mo, pp. 8. 57262

O'MAHONY (*le Comte*). *See* Vol. x., No. 40721.

OMAI (——). Narrations d'Omai, insulaire de la mer du sud, ami et compagnon de voyage du Captain Cook, traduite de l'O-Taïtien. *Rouen.* 1790. 8vo. Portrait. 57263

END OF VOLUME THIRTEEN.

A Dictionary of Books

RELATING TO AMERICA.

MAÑA Y SOTOMAYOR (Gregorio). Obras de Eloquencia y Poesia premiadas por la Real Universidad de México, en el Certamen Literario que celebró el dia 28 de Diciembre de 1790. ... *Mexico: Zuñiga y Ontiveros.* 1791. 4to, pp. (6), Preface, xxii, 14 Odes, all separately paged, 73 l.

Also: Oracion Funebre, que en las anniversarias Honras de los difuntos Militares de España celebradôs de orden de S. M. en la S. Iglesia Cathedral de Mexico, dixo, el dia 22 de Nov. 1769. *Mexico.* 1770. 4to.

O'MEARA (F. A.) Ewh Oomenwahjemoowin owh Tawanemenuung Jesus Christ, kahenahjemoowand egewh newin Manwahjemoojig owh St. Mathew owh St. Mark owh St. Luke kuyha owh St. John ... *Toronto.* 1850. 8vo, pp. 338. 57265

The Gospels in Chippewa. *See also* Nos. 12831-4, *and* Ojibwa, Nos. 57080-95.

O'MEARA. A Short Account of the Missions of the Church of England, among the Ojibwa and Ottawah Indians of Lakes Huron and Superior. By Rev. Frederick A. O'Meara ... . *London.* [n. d.] 8vo. 57266

Title from Morgan's "Bibliotheca Canadensis," p. 298.

OMEGA, *pseudon.* Popery, a Craft, and Popish Priests, the Chief Craftsmen. ... Added Another Voice from the Watchtower, to American Citizens. By Omega. ... *Cambridge, Mass.* 1855. 8vo, pp. 46, (1). H. 57267

OMNIUM (J.), *pseudon.* Is Cheap Sugar the Triumph of Free Trade? ... By Jacob Omnium. Second Edition. *London: Printed by James Ridgway.* 1847. 8vo, pp. 19. P. + [*Ibid.*] 1848. 8vo, pp. 64. P. 57268

Omnium Gatherum, for November, 1809. Vol. I. No. I. *Boston: T. Kennard.* 1809. 8vo, pp. 48. 2 Plates. Continued

Omstandigh Verhael van de Fransche rodomontade voor het Fort Curassau. [n. p. 1673.] 4to, pp. 4. 57270

Circumstantial account of the French rodomontade before Fort Curaçao.

On Monday, The Sixteenth Instant ... . [*Philadelphia: J. Humphreys.* 1778.] Folio, 1 leaf. P. 57271

Notice of dramatic performances by the British officers at Philadelphia, Feb., 1778.

On Monday, the Second Day of March, at the Theatre in Southwark ... . [*Philadelphia: J. Humphreys, March,* 1778.] Folio, 1 leaf. P. 57272

Poster of the dramatic performances of the British officers.

On Monday, the Ninth Day of March, at the Theatre in Southwark ... . [*Philadelphia: J. Humphreys.* 1778.] Folio, 1 leaf. P. 57273

Poster of the Officers' theatre.

On Monday, the Sixteenth Day of March ... . [n. p. n. d.] Folio, 1 leaf. 57274

Poster, etc. as before, 1778. Another poster for the same night occurs, however, in which *Lethe* is substituted for the *Mock Doctor.*

On Monday next, the Thirteenth Day of April ... . [*Philadelphia: J. Humphreys.* 1778.] Folio, 1 leaf. — On Wednesday, the Twenty-Fifth Day of March, at the Theatre in Southwark ... . [*Philadelphia: J. Humphreys.* 1778.] Folio, 1 leaf. — On Wednesday next, the Sixth Day of May, 1778. ... [n. p. n. d.] Folio, 1 leaf. — On Friday next, the Tenth Day of April ... . [*Philadelphia: J. Humphreys.* 1778.] Folio, 1 leaf. — On Friday next, the Twenty-Fourth Day of April ... . [n. p. n. d.] Folio, 1 leaf. — On Friday next, the First Day of May ... . [n. p. n. d.] Folio, 1 leaf. P.

On Monies, Coins, Weights, and Measures, proposed for the United States ... . *Philadelphia: Printed by Daniel Humphreys.* M.DCC.LXXXIX. 8vo, pp. 25, (1), 6. BA. 57275

On Paper Money. *See* [Heath (L.)], Vol. VIII., No. 31190.

On Political Economy. Read and Ponder. [n. p. about 1862.] 8vo, pp. 9. 57276

On Protection to West India Sugar. *See* [Larpent (G.)]

On Receiving Donations from Holders of Slaves. *Boston: Perkins & Marvin.* [n. d.] 12mo, pp. 20. 57277

On Recent Occurrences at Litchfield, on Slavery ... . *London.* 1826. 8vo, pp. 52. 57278

On recent Proceedings. *See* Vol. I., No. 3279.

On Self-Government; ... with ... Plans of a State Constitution, and a Constitution for a Confederation of States, ... also, ... the New Constitution of the State of New York, examined ... *Boston: Crosby & Nichols.* 1847. 12mo, pp. vi, 65. B.

On Slavery. [n. p.:] *American Reform Tract Society.* [n. d.] 12mo, pp. 22. 57280

On Sugar Cultivation in Louisiana, Cuba, and the British Possessions, By an European and Colonial Sugar Manufacturer. *London.* 1848. 2 parts, 8vo. 57281

On the Abolition of the Slave Trade, ... the African Institution, &c. *London.* 1816. 8vo, pp. 235. 57282

On the Beauties [etc.]. *See* [Bucke (C.)], Vol. III. 8887.

On the British African Colonization Society. *See* Vol. IV., No. 14732, *note.*

On the Conservative Elements. *See* [Douglas (*Mrs.* R.)]

On the Continental Money. [n. p.:] *Privately Printed.* 1863. 8vo. 57283

On the Course of College Education adapted to the Circumstances of British America. *Montreal.* 1855. 8vo. 57284

On the Debt of the Nation, compared with its Revenues; and the Impossibility of carrying on the War without Public Oeconomy. *London: J. Debrett.* 1781. 8vo. 57285

On the Disturbances in South America. *London.* 1830. 8vo, pp. 63. S. 57286

On the Establishment of Public Schools in the City of New York. *New York.* 1825. 8vo, pp. 18. M. 57287

On the Exploration of the North Polar Region. *London.* 1863. 8vo. 57288

On the Formal Recognition of Chile. *See* Vol. IV. 12793.

On the Frontier, or Scenes in the West. *Boston.* [1864.] 18mo, pp. 320. C. 57289

On the Growth and Trade of Timber, in America. *London.* 1769. 4to. 57290

On the Inconsistency of Man, particularly exemplified in the practice of Slavery in the United States. *New York.* 1795. 8vo

On the Mischief of Usury Laws: ... . *Cincinnati: Lorenzo Stratton.* 1852. 8vo, pp. 26. H. 57292

On the Mode [etc.]. *See* [Dix (J. A.)], Vol. V., No. 20339.

On the Nomination of Agents. *See* [Falconer (T.)], Vol. VI.

On the Origin and Progress. *See* Vol. III., No. 10537.

On the past Relations between Great Britain and the United States. *London: G. Sidney.* 1813. 8vo, pp. 59. 57293

On the Plains; or, The Race for Life. A Story of Adventure among the Black Hills. *New York: S. Tousey.* 1863. 8vo, pp. 62. 57294

On the present Distressed State of the British West India Colonies; their Claims for Relief, &c. *London.* 1823. 8vo, pp. 63. 57295

On the Relations of Slavery to the War, and on the treatment of it necessary to Permanent Peace. [n. p. n. d.] 8vo.

On the Representation of Minorities. *See* [Gilpin (Thos.)]

On the Rights and Powers of Corporations. A Notice of the Pamphlet by a Citizen of Boston. *Boston.* 1837. 8vo, pp. 17

On the Rock Salt. *See* Vol. X., No. 42280.

On the Ten Tribes of Israel, and the Aborigines of America, &c., &c. By a Bible Professor. ... *Providence, Indiana, May 2d,* 1831. *Printed by Collins and Green, New Albany, Indiana.* 1831. 8vo, pp. 32. 57298

"The real or fancied points of resemblance between the customs, language, and physical appearance of the American Indians and the Jews, has many believers, and the author of this rhapsody adds one more to the list."—FIELD.

On Thursday last, ... Mr. Cornelius Bradford, returned express from Philadelphia, with the following interesting Intelligence ... . [*New York: Printed by J. Holt, January* 1, 1774.] Folio, 1 l.

OÑA (P. de). Primera parte | de Aravco | Domado, | compvesto por el licen | ciado Pedro de Oña, Natural de los Infantes de | Engol en Chili. Collegial del Real Co | legio mayor de Sant Felipe, y S. | Marcos, fundado en la Ciu | dad de Lima. Dirigido

a don Hvrtado de Men- | doça, Primogenito de don Garcia Hurtado de Mendoça, Marques | de Cañete, Señor de las Villas de Argete, y su Partido, Visorrey | de los Reynos del Piru, Tierra Firme, y Chilé, y de la Mar- | quesa doña Teresa de Castro, y de la Cueua. | Hijo, Nieto, y Biznieto | de Virreyes. | Con previlegio. | *Impresso en la Civdad de los | Reyes, por Antonio Ricardo de Turin. Primero | Impressor en estos Reynos.* | *Año de* 1596. *Esta tassado a tres quartillas el pliego, | en papel.* | 4to, Title, 10 prel. leaves, on the third of which is a woodcut Portrait of Oña; Text, 335 leaves, Table, 1 leaf. J.C.B. 57300

A work of the greatest rarity, and the first great poem written in South America, by a native poet: on the same subject and in continuation of Ercilla's celebrated epic, "La Araucana," compared with which it is rather dull. It opens with the departure of D. G. H. de Mendoza for Chili, and concludes with the great naval combat of Callas between D. Beltram de Castro and the English Admiral Hawkins. Drake and his followers are called pirates. Its historical value is greater than its literary merit; and the student must refer to the stanzas of "Arauco Domado" (fortunately unembellished by a brilliant imagination) for many details of the conquest and settlement of Chili, not to be found in Ovalle or elsewhere. A second part, which the author promised at the end of this work, never appeared. *See* Ticknor's "History of Spanish Literature," II. 465.

OÑA. Aravco | domado. | Compvesto por el | Licenciado Pedro de Oña, natural de los | Infantes de Engol en Chile, Colegial del | Real Colegio Mayor de San Felipe, y | San Marcos fundado en la Ciu- | dad de Lima. | Dirigido a Don Hvrtado | de Mendoça, Primogenito de don Garcia Hur- | tado de Mendoça, Marques de | Cañete ... . *Año,* 1605. | *Con privilegio;* | *En Madrid, por Ivan de la Cuesta.* | *Vendese en casa de Francisco Lopez.* | 8vo, 16 prel. leaves, Text, 342 leaves, Table, pp. (3). 57301

A reprint of the foregoing.

OÑA. El Arauco Domado, compuesto por el Licenciado Pedro de Oña ... . Dirijido á D. Hurtado de Mendoza ... . Nueva edicion arreglada á la Madrid del año 1605. *Valparaiso.* 1849. 18mo, pp. vi, 524. 57302

Another edition is included in the "Biblioteca de Autores Españoles," Madrid, 1854. Nicolas Antonio, who never saw the original, mentions two other Madrid editions, one printed in 1595, quarto, the other in 1608, octavo, which I have not seen.

OÑA. Tremblor de Lima del año 1599. Poema. *Lima.* 1599. 57303

Title from Ternaux, No. 230.

OÑA. El tremblor de tierra de Lima. Poema. *Lima.* 1609. 8vo. 57304

Title from Ternaux, No. 320.

OÑATE (A. de). Parecer de vn hombre docto en la facvltad de Theologia y Canones, y Lector de la misma facultad, y de muchos años de experiencia en las cosas de las Indias, cerca del seruicio personal de los Indios del Piru y Nueva España, sobre el qual ha auido estos dias tantas y tan graues juntas, y consultas de varones eminentissimos. Presentado a la Magestad Catolica del Rey don Felipe nuestro señor, Tercero deste nombre, y à su Real Consejo de las Indias, por don Alonso de Oñate, Procurador general de los Mineros de la Nueva España. [n. p. 1600.] Folio, 11 leaves. J.C.B. 57305

Relates to the personal service of the Indians of Peru and New Spain, about which there have lately been so many grave assemblies and conferences of most eminent men.

Onbezwekene Gehechtheid en Trouw, of de edele Negerslaaf, eene merkw. Geschiedenis uit den Opstand der Zwarten op St. Domingo, gevolgd door een kort Overzigt van St. Domingo en deszelfs Geschiedenis. *s'Hage: A. Kloots.* 1833. 8vo. 57306

Once a Month; a Magazine of Miscellaneous Selections. ... *Springfield (Mass.): W. J. Holland & Co.* [1867–68.] 8vo. C.

No more published. Also: Once a Month. ... 1869. ... *Philadelphia: T. S. Arthur & Sons.* [n. d.] Sm. 4to. Continued.

ONDERDONK (B. T.) The Church—the Faith—Tradition. A Sermon, by Benjamin T. Onderdonk, D.D. ... *New-York: Onderdonk & Forrest.* 1844. 8vo, pp. 23. B. 57308

Also: An Address, ... before the ... General Theological Seminary. ... *New York.* 1825. 8vo, pp. 28. — ... A Sermon ... at the Funeral of the Right Reverend John Henry Hobart, D.D. ... September 16th, 1830. ... *New-York.* MDCCCXXX. 8vo, pp. 87. — ... A Sermon ... in Geneva, ... at the ... Primary Convention of the Diocese of Western New-York, ... November 1, 1838. ... *New-York: Swords, Stanford, & Co.* 1839. 8vo, pp. 18. — ... A Sermon ... in New York, ... October 20, 1840, at the Funeral of the Rev. Peter Williams ... . *New York.* 1840. 8vo, pp. 16. — Sermon ... at the Funeral of Rev. Lewis P. Bayard. ... *New York.* 1841. 8vo.

The following works relate to Bishop B. T. Onderdonk:

ONDERDONK. The Proceedings of the Court ... December 16, 1844, for the Trial of the Right Rev. Benjamin T. Onderdonk, D.D. ... on a presentment made by the Bishops of Virginia, Tennessee, and Georgia. ... *New York: D. Appleton & Co.* MDCCCXLV. 8vo, pp. 333. B. 57309

Also: An Appeal from the Sentence of the Bishop of New York; In behalf of his Diocese. ... *New York: James A. Sparks.* 1845. 8vo, pp. 32. B. — A Letter to the Rev. James C. Richmond, Principal Agent in the recent combination to destroy the Bishop of New York. *New York.* 1845. 8vo. — Opinions of the Minority of the Court on the Trial of Bishop Onderdonk. *New York.* 1845. 8vo. — A Reply to a Communication signed by Three Hundred and Twenty-Eight Laymen ... . *New-York: H. M. Onderdonk.* 1844. 8vo, pp. 8. B. — Report of the Committee appointed to

consider the Sentence upon The Right Reverend Benjamin T. Onderdonk ... . *New York: Stanford & Swords.* [n. d.] 8vo, pp. 13. — Ein scandalöser Prozess. Bischof Benjamin Onderdonk von New York und seine Verurtheilung vor dem dortigen Bischofshofe, wegen gewaltsamer Verletzung weiblicher Ehre. Mit einem Auszuge des Zeugenverhörs. Nach amerikanischen Blättern ... . *Hamburg.* 1844. 8vo. — ... A Statement of Facts and Circumstances connected with the recent Trial of the Bishop of New-York. *New-York: Henry M. Onderdonk.* 1845. 8vo, pp. 31. *See also* Jay (John), Vol. IX., No. 35842, Vol. X., Nos. 38651 *and* 40623, Vol. XIII., No. 53706, Richmond (J. C.), Spectator, *pseudon.,* "The Verdict," *and* "Voice of Truth."

ONDERDONK. Obsequies and Obituary Notices of the Late Right Rev. Benj. Tredwell Onderdonk, D.D. ... By a New-York Churchman. *New-York: H. B. Price.* 1862. 8vo, pp. 191. Portrait. B. 57310

ONDERDONK (H.) A History of Maryland upon the basis of McSherry, for the use of Schools. By Henry Onderdonk. *Baltimore: John Murphy & Co.* 1868. 16mo, pp. 251. + Second Revised Enlarged Edition. [*Ibid.*] 1870. 18mo, pp. 288. Plate

ONDERDONK (H.), *Jr.* The Barbarous Capture and Death of Gen. Nathaniel Woodhull, in a series of Letters addressed to J. Fenimore Cooper, by Henry Onderdonk, Jr. *New York.* 1848. 12mo, pp. 52. BA. 57312

ONDERDONK. Documents and Letters Intended to Illustrate the Revolutionary Incidents of Queens County; with Connecting Narratives, Explanatory Notes, and Additions. By Henry Onderdonk, Jr. ... *New-York: Leavitt, Trow and Company.* 1846. 12mo, pp. 264. BA. 57313

ONDERDONK. Queen's County in Olden Times: Being A Supplement to the Histories thereof. By Henry Onderdonk, Jr., A.M. ... *Jamaica, N. Y.: Charles Welling.* 1865. 4to, pp. (2), 122. BA. 57314

ONDERDONK. Revolutionary Incidents of Suffolk and Kings Counties; with an Account of the Battle of Long Island, and the British Prisons and Prison-Ships at New-York. By Henry Onderdonk, Jr. *New-York: Leavitt & Company.* 1849. 12mo, pp. 268. Map. BA. 57315

Also: An Historical Sketch, of Ancient Agriculture, Stock Breeding and Manufactures, in Hempstead ... . *Jamaica.* 1867. 8vo, pp. 41–63. Plate. — Long Island and New-York in Olden Times; being Newspaper Extracts and Historical Sketches, compiled by Henry Onderdonk, Jr. *Jamaica.* 1851. 8vo. S.

ONDERDONK (H. M.) A History of the Protestant Episcopal Churches in the City of New-York. By Henry M. Onderdonk, ... Embellished with ... Engraving of each Church ... executed

by J. N. Gimbrede. *New-York: Onderdonk & Gimbrede.* 1843. Rl. 8vo. 57316

ONDERDONK (H. U.) Address of the Right Rev. Henry U. Onderdonk, D.D. at the Anniversary ... of the Society ... for the Advancement of Christianity in Pennsylvania, ... 1829. *Philadelphia: Jesper Harding, Printer.* 1829. 8vo, pp. 11. 57317

Also: An Answer to the Letter addressed to the Author by the Wardens ... of Christ Church, Cincinnati ... . *New York: Printed by T. & J. Swords.* 1824. 8vo, pp. 16. H. — An Appeal ... in behalf of the Protestant Episcopal Church, against the Slanders and Sophistry Printed under the name of the Rev. W. Bacon: ... *Canandaigua: Printed by J. D. Bemis.* 1818. 8vo, pp. 70, (2). B. — A Discourse ... at the Funeral of the Right Rev. William White, D.D. ... July 20th, 1836. ... *Philadelphia: Jesper Harding, Printer.* 1836. 8vo, pp. 28. — A Sermon, on General Education; ... Canandaigua, Sept. 8th, 1816. ... *Canandaigua: Printed by J. D. Bemis.* 1816. 8vo, pp. 16. — Sermon in ... New-York, on the ... Consecration of ... John H. Hopkins, D.D. Bishop of Vermont. ... Benjamin B. Smith, D.D. Bishop of Kentucky. ... Charles P. McIlvaine, D.D. Bishop of ... Ohio. And ... George W. Doane, A.M. Bishop of ... New-Jersey. ... *New-York.* 1832. 8vo, pp. 17. H. — A Sermon April 20, 1841, ... at the Funeral Solemnities in honour of [W. H. Harrison,] the Late President of the United States. ... *Philadelphia: J. Crissy, Printer.* 1841. 8vo, pp. 16. B.

The following works relate to Bishop Henry U. Onderdonk:

ONDERDONK. Narrative of the Consecration of the Rev. Henry U. Onderdonk, D.D. with the Address of the Presiding Bishop. ... *Philadelphia: Jesper Harding, Printer.* 1827. 8vo, pp. 20. BA. 57318

Also: The Case of the Right Rev. Henry U. Onderdonk, D.D. stated and considered with reference to his continued Suspension. By a Member of the Church. *Philadelphia: T. K. and P. G. Collins, Printers.* 1853. 8vo, pp. 52. B. — The Decision of the Bishops who united in the Consecration of the Rev. Henry U. Onderdonk, D.D., on the Reasons presented to them Against the ... Act ... . *Philadelphia: Jesper Harding, Printer.* 1827. 8vo, pp. 16. *See also* Observer, *pseudon.,* No. 56602, Presbyter, *pseudon.,* "A Reply," *and* "Statement."

ONDERDONK (J.) An Inaugural Address delivered before the Medical Society of the County of New-York, on the 8th ... of August, 1825. By John Onderdonk ... . *New-York: Printed by J. Seymour.* 1825. 8vo, pp. 23. H. 57319

Ondersoeck der | Amsterdamsche Requesten/ | Tot | Verdedigingh | Der Onschuldighe, | ende | onder-rechtingh | Der misleyde. | [n. p.:] *Ghedruckt in't Jaer ons Heeren/* M. DC. XXVIII. 4to, pp. 36

This pamphlet affords an interesting insight into the position of the leading parties of Amsterdam, who played such an important part in the history of the West India Company.

De Onderwijs der Negerslaven in Suriname. [n. p.] 1841. 4to. 57321

Onderzoek ten gevolge der circulaire van Otto Tank, hoofdvoorstander van de zending der Evang. Broedergemeente in Suriname aan de eigenaren en administrateuren van plantaadjen in die kolonie Paramaribo. [n. p. 1848.] 8vo. 57322

Onderzoek van Groot-Brittanjes Gedrag, ten opzichte van Holland zedert de opkomste der Republicq tot nu toe. Door een welmeenend Hollander. Dienende tot opmaking van het Nationale Character der Engelschen, in haar gedrag met de Americaanen. [n. p.] MDCCLXXVIII. 8vo, pp. xxx, 148.

Inquiry into the conduct of Great Britain in regard to Holland, serving for an analysis of the national character of the English in their conflict with the Americans.

One Hundred and Fifty Stories. *See* [Merrill (R.)], Vol. XII.

One Hundred and Fifty Years of the General Association of Connecticut Commemoration, 1859. *New Haven.* 1861. 8vo, pp. 559. 57324

One Hundred Years' Progress of the United States. ... *Hartford: L. Stebbins.* 1870. 8vo, pp. 546. 122 Plates and 2 Maps.

One Job of the Conspirators. *See* Vol. XIII., No. 54566.

One more Letter to the People of England, by their Old Friend. *London.* 1762. 8vo. 57326

On American affairs.

ONE OF THE PEOPLE, *pseudon.* An Address to the Legislature of Indiana, ... December 6th, 1847. Upon Popular Education. By One of the People. *Indianapolis: Printed by John D. Defrees.* 1848. 12mo, pp. 45, (1). H. 57327

See also [Burges (T.)], Vol. III., No. 9233.

One Week at Amer, an American City of the Nineteenth Century. ... *Boston and Cambridge: James Munroe and Company.* M DCCC LVIII. 12mo, pp. 119. BA., C. 57328

O'NEAL (H.) Report in the Case of Henry O'Neal, Esq., a Justice of the Peace in the County of Philadelphia. *Harrisburgh.* 1833. 8vo. P. 57329

O'NEALL (J. B.) The Annals of Newberry, Historical, Biographical and Anecdotical: By John Belton O'Neall, LL.D. *Charleston, S. C.: S. G. Courtenay & Co.* 1859. 12mo, pp. 413, viii. Portrait. B. 57330

O'NEALL. Biographical Sketches of the Bench and Bar of South Carolina. By John Belton O'Neall, LL.D. ... *Charleston, S. C.: S. G. Courtenay & Co.* 1859. 2 vols., 8vo, pp. xxxii, 431, Table and 3 Facsimiles; iv, 614, (1). BA. 57331

O'NEALL. The Negro Law of South Carolina, collected and digested by John Belton O'Neall ... . *Columbia: Printed by John G. Bowman.* 1848. 8vo, pp. 56. BA. 57332

ONEBY (J.) Narrative of the Life and Actions of John Oneby, Esq., commonly called Major Oneby, who was to have been Executed for the Murder of William Gower, Esq., giving an Account of his ... Killing ... Lieutenant Tooley, in Jamaica, ... *London.* 1726. 8vo. 57333

ONEIDA. Confession of Faith and Covenant, adopted by the Presbytery of Oneida, February, 1831. ... *Utica: Printed by R. Northway, Jr.* 1837. 12mo, pp. 12. BA. 57334

Journal of the Proceedings of the Board of Supervisors of the County of Oneida, for 1859. *Utica.* 1860. 8vo. Continued.

Oneida and Genesee Conference Seminary, Cazenovia, 1828–29. [n. p. n. d.] 8vo. 57336

First Annual Report of the ONEIDA ASSOCIATION, 1849. *Oneida Reserve: Leonard & Co.* 1849. 8vo. Continued. H.

Also: ... Bible Communism; a Compilation from the Annual Reports and other Publications of the Oneida Association ... presenting, in connection with their History, a Summary View of their Religious and Social Theories. ... *Brooklyn, N. Y.* 1853. 12mo, pp. 128. Plate. — The Circular. Published weekly by the Oneida and Wallingford Communities. ... *Oneida Community.* 1864. Folio. *See also* Vol. VIII., No. 30208

Minutes of the ONEIDA BAPTIST ASSOCIATION. *Peterborough, N. Y.* 1821. 8vo. Continued. S. 57338

Also: Minutes of the Jubilee Anniversary of the Oneida Baptist Association, ... Whitesboro, N. Y., Sept. ... 1870. *Utica.* 1870. 8vo.

The Oneida Community: a familiar exposition of its Ideas and Practical Life, in a Conversation with a Visitor. *Wallingford, Conn.* 1865. 8vo, pp. 32. Plate. 57339

Thirty-Fourth Catalogue of ONEIDA CONFERENCE SEMINARY. 1859. Cazenovia, N. Y. *Cazenovia.* 1859. 8vo, pp. 23, (1).

Award of Premiums at the Annual Fair of the ONEIDA COUNTY AGRICULTURAL SOCIETY, Utica, 1853. *Utica.* 1853. 8vo. Continued. S. 57341

Second Report of the Trustees of the ONEIDA INSTITUTE of Science and Industry. ... *Utica: William Williams.* MDCCCXXX. 8vo, pp. 28. Continued. B. — By-Laws of the ONEIDA MEDICAL SOCIETY, with a System of Medical Ethics ... . *Utica.* 1833. 8vo

The Report of the Trustees, ... to the Female Oneida Missionary Society, ... September 3, 1816. *Utica: Printed by Seward & Williams.* 1816. 12mo, pp. 24. BA. 57342

Report of the Surveyor-General on the Oneida Purchases. *Albany.* 1801. Folio. *See also* Vol. XII., No. 51827.

O'NEIL (C.) The Military Adventures of Charles O'Neil. *Worcester.* 1851. 12mo, pp. 259. 57343

[O'NEIL (Elizabeth).] Opposition Mornings; with Betty's Remarks. ... *London: J. Wilkie.* MDCCLXXIX. 8vo, pp. viii, 67. + *Dublin.* 1779. 8vo. C. 57344

A satire on the ministry. *See* "Monthly Review," LX. 473.

O'NEIL (J. T.) Cuba and Porto Rico: Geographical, Political, and Industrial. By J. T. O'Neil. *London.* 18—. 8vo.

O'NEIL (*Lieut.*) Account of the Proceedings of the Squadron under Admiral Sir Sydney Smith in effecting the Escape of the Royal Family of Portugal to the Brazils. *London.* 1810. 8vo. 57346

O'NEILL (H.) Traveller's Hand-Book of ... Quebec and its environs. ... [By] H. O'Neill ... . *Quebec: St. Michel & Darveau, ... Printers.* 1859. 12mo, pp. 12. H. 57347

O'NEILL (J.) Official Report of Gen. John O'Neill, President of the Fenian Brotherhood; on the attempt to Invade Canada, May 25th, 1870. ... also a Report of the Battle of Ridgeway, Canada West ... . *New York: John J. Foster.* 1870. 8vo, pp. 62. B., C. 57348

Also: Address ... to ... the Fenian Brotherhood, on ... its attempted Disruption. *New York: Baker & Godwin, Printers.* 1868. 8vo, pp. 24. H.

O'NEILL (N. J.) The Guide to Texas ... with an Appendix containing ... the Constitution of Mexico and of the States of Coahuila and Texas. With Observations on Mexico. By Neal John O'Neill. *Dublin.* 1834. 8vo, pp. 176. S. 57349

Also: Observations, Historical, Geographical, ... on Texas. ... *London.* 1834. 8vo.

ONESIMUS, *pseudon.* The Doctrine of the New Birth, ... also, the Visions ... concerning the City of Philadelphia in the days when George Washington was President of the United States ... . *Philadelphia.* 1839. 8vo. 57350

ONESIMUS SECUNDUS, *pseudon.* The True Interpretation of the American Civil War, and of England's Cotton Difficulty or Slavery, from a different point of View, shewing the relative Responsibilities of America and Great Britain. By Onesimus Secundus. Second Edition. *London: Trübner & Co.* 1863. 8vo, pp. 47. BA. 57351

ONFFROY DE THORON (Enrique), *Vicomte.* Amérique Équatoriale; son histoire pittoresque et politique; sa géographie et ses richesses naturelles; son état présent et son avenir. ... *Paris: Renouard.* 1866. 8vo. 57352

ONFFROY DE THORON. Voyages des flottes de Salomon et d'Hiram en Amérique. Position géographique de Parvaïm, Ophir et Farschisch. *Paris: Maisonneuve et Cie.* 1869. 4to.

Contains comparisons of the Hebrew and Quichua languages. Only a few copies printed.

ON-HI (Hart). *See* Drake (*Mrs.*), Vol. v., No. 20864.

ONION (S. B.) Narrative of the Mutiny on Board the Schooner Plattsburgh ... . By Stephen B. Onion ... . *Boston: Printed by Sylvester T. Goss.* 1819. 8vo, pp. 13. BA. 57354

ONIS (L. de). Memoria sobre las negociaciones entre España y los Estados-Unidos de América, que dieron motivo al Tratado de 1819. con una noticia sobre la estadistica de aquel pais. Acompaña un Apéndice, que contiene documentos importantes para mayor ilustracion del asunto. Por D. Luis de Onis ... . *Madrid* 1820. *Imprenta de D. M. de Burgos.* 2 parts, rl. 8vo, pp. (2), vi, 108, (2), 70, (1); 213. Map. H. + *Madrid* 1820, *Mexico* 1826 *reimpresa, a cargo del C. Martin Rivera.* 4to, pp. (6), 60, Appendix, 72. 57355

For a reply, *see* Forsyth (J.), Vol. VI., No. 25149.

ONIS. Memoir upon the Negotiations between Spain and the United States of America, which led to the Treaty of 1819. With a Statistical Notice of that Country [Florida], Accompanied with an Appendix, containing important Documents ... . By D. Luis de Onis ... . Translated from the Spanish, with Notes, by Tobias Watkins. [*Washington:*] *E. De Krafft, Printer.* 1821. 8vo, pp. 152. + *Baltimore: Fielding Lucas, Junr.* 1821. 8vo, pp. 152. H. 57356

Also: Official Correspondence between Don Louis de Onis, Minister from Spain ... and John Quincy Adams, ... in relation to the Floridas and the Boundaries of Louisiana, with other matters in dispute between the two governments. *London.* 1818. 8vo, pp. 130. C.

The only Correct Account of the Life, Trial, and Confession of John Banks, executed July 11, for the Murder of his Wife. *New York.* 1806. 8vo, pp. 21. N. 57357

ONONDAGA, *N. Y.* Journal of the Board of Supervisors of Onondaga, for 1859. *Syracuse.* 1859. 8vo. Continued. S.

Minutes of the ONONDAGA BAPTIST ASSOCIATION, ... 1825. *Onondaga.* 1825. 8vo. S. 57359

Transactions of the ONONDAGA COUNTY AGRICULTURAL SOCIETY, ... 1854. *Syracuse.* 1855. 8vo. S. 57360

History of the ONONDAGA HISTORICAL ASSOCIATION. *Syracuse.* 1865. 12mo. 57361

Proceedings of the ONONDAGA TEACHERS' INSTITUTE; Spring Term, 1845. *Syracuse: Tucker & Kinney, Printers.* 1845. 12mo, pp. (1), 34. 57362

Also: Catalogue of the Onondaga Teachers' Institute, ... 1851. *Syracuse.* 1851. 8vo. Continued. — Proceedings of the Onondaga Whig Convention. *Syracuse, July* 4, 1834. 8vo. — Report ... from the Commissioners for Settling the Titles to Land in the County of Onondaga, New York. *Albany, February,* 1800. 8vo. — Report of the Commissioners ... relative to the Salt Springs in ... Onondaga; ... *Albany.* 1825. 8vo. — Annual Report of the Superintendent of the Onondaga Salt Springs, ... 1798. [n. p. n. d.] 8vo. Continued.

Onpartydich Discours. *See* [Usselincx (Willem)].

Onpartijdige raadgevinge. *See* [Heuvell (H. H. v. d.)], VIII.

ONSLOW (——). Onslow in Reply to Patrick Henry. [n. p. n. d.] 12mo, pp. 28. 57363

ONTARIO, *Canada.* The Province of Ontario Gazetteer and Directory, containing Concise Descriptions of Cities, Towns and Villages in the Province ... . H. McEvoy, Editor ... . *Toronto: Robertson & Cook.* 1869. 8vo, pp. 718. H. 57364

Report of the Commissioner of Public Works for the Province of Ontario, for ... 1869. ... *Toronto: Printed by Hunter, Rose & Co.* 1869. 8vo, pp. (4), 58. Plans and Plates. H.

Statutes of Ontario. 1867–68. *Toronto: H. J. Hartney.* 1868. 8vo. Continued. C. 57365

Annual Report and Minutes of the ... TEACHERS' ASSOCIATION of Ontario, held ... August, 1867. ... *Toronto: Printed by Thomas Cuttell & Son.* 1868. 12mo, pp. 28. H. 57366

See also Vol. III., No. 10347, *and* Vol. IX., No. 36709.

ONTARIO, *N. Y.* Information relating to the Proposed Charter of the Ontario and Erie Ship Canal Co. *Niagara.* 1869. 8vo. 57367

... The Ontario and St. Lawrence Steamboat Company's Hand-Book for Travelers to Niagara Falls, Montreal, and Quebec, and through Lake Champlain to Saratoga Springs. ... *Buffalo: Jewett, Thomas & Co.* 1852. 12mo, pp. 158. Map and 21 Plates. + [*Ibid.*] 1853. 12mo, pp. 174. Map and 25 Plates.

Report of the Committee appointed on the subject of the Ontario and Champlain Canal. *Potsdam, N. Y.* 1823. 8vo.

Address ... before the ONTARIO AGRICULTURAL SOCIETY ... 1819. [n. p. n. d.] 8vo. Continued. — Minutes of the ONTARIO BAPTIST ASSOCIATION ... 1815. *Canandaigua.* 1815. 8vo. — Catalogue of the ONTARIO FEMALE SEMINARY, Canandaigua, N. Y. ... 1851. [n. p. n. d.] 8vo.

Ontdeckinge van 't Eyland van Pines, sijnde een waerachtige beschrijvinge ... . Uit het Engels vertaelt. *Amsterdam: Jac. Stichter.* 1668. 4to, pp. 8. Map on the title. 57370

A romance like that of Swift and Defoe, but shorter and less spirited. An account by the discoverer, Joris Pines, shipwrecked at the island in 1589. This edition of the discovery of the island of Pines is the one referred to in the note to our No. 35257. It is not mentioned in Muller's and Meulman's "Bibliotheek van Pamfletten."

Ontdeckinghe van Rijcke Mijnen. *See* Vol. II., No. 7612.

Ontdekking van 't Geheel ... Deel. *See* [Kimyser (A.)], IX.

ONTONAGON, *Mich.* Prospectus for the Formation of a Mining Company ... in the County of Ontonagon, Michigan. ... *Pittsburgh: Printed by W. S. Haven.* 1863. 8vo, pp. 28. Map.

By-Laws of the ONTONAGON COPPER COMPANY ... with Forest Shepherd's Report. ... *Boston: Dutton and Wentworth, Printers.* 1846. 12mo, pp. 12. Plan.

Ontwa, the Son of the Forest. *See* [Whiting (Henry)].

Ontwerp eener Nederlandsche West-Indische Ontginning- en Handel-Maatschappij, met een Kapitaal van 50 Millioen Guldens. [*Amsterdam.* 1857.] 8vo. + *In 's Gravenhage.* 1857. 8vo.

Ontworp, en Voor-stel | Tot | Remedie, van twee swarigheden | Inde West-Indische | Compagnie. | [n. p.:] *Gedruckt, in 't Iaar* 1644. 4to, pp. 8. 57373

Plan and proposal as a remedy for difficulties in the West India Company.

Onward: A Magazine for the Young Manhood of America. Conducted by Captain Mayne Reid. ... *New York.* [1869–70.] 3 vols., 8vo, pp. viii, 534; (2), 546; (2), 184, xxxii. Plates.

Les Onze Indiens O-jib-be-was. [*Paris.* 1845.] 8vo, pp. 8. 2 Plates. 57375

This is a pendant to the French translation of the "Catalogue of Catlin's Gallery." *See* Catlin (G.)

Ooghen-Salve | Tot verlichtinghe, van alle Participanten, so | vande Oost, | Ende | West-Indische | Compaignien, | Mitsgaders | Verscheyden notabele Consideratien, aengaende de | Vereeninghe van de Oost-ende-West- | Indische Compaignien, met malkanderen. | Leest zonder voor-oordeel totten eynde. | *In 'sGraven-Haghe,* | *By Lieven de Lange, in April. An.* 1644. | Sm. 4to, pp. 35. H.

Eye-salve for clearing the eyes of the shareholders of the East and West India Co.

Oost- en West-Indische Warande. *See* [Hoorn (Jan ten)], Vol. VIII. 32884, and add *Amsterdam: J. Hayman.* 1729. 8vo.

OOST-INDISCHE COMPAIGNIE. Copye | Van eenen Brieff van eenen vrient aen den | anderen geschreven | nopende het Redres van de | Oost-Indische | Compaignie. [n. p. 1622.] 4to, pp. 8.

Copy of a letter by a friend to a friend on the reformation of the East India Co.

Oost-Indische ende Vvest Ind. voyagien. *See* [Colijn], 14349

Oost-Indische Voyagien. *See* [Hartgerts (J.)], VIII. 30680.

Ootmoedighe | Beklagh- | Redenen | Aan de Hoogh-Mogende Heeren Staten Ge- | neraal vande geunieerde Provincien, ge- | daen door d'onderdanige Deel-heb | bers in de Oost-Indische han- | delinge tegens de schadelijcke Disordren. | [n. p.:] *Int Iaar onses Heeren* 1622. | 4to, pp. 33. 57379

Humble complaint to the States General of the United Provinces, by the shareholders of the East India Company.

Oowa Wowapi. Dakota Iapi En (Reading-Book). John P. Williamson Owa. *New York.* 18—. 12mo, pp. 80. 57380

Op de Onafhankelykheid van Noord-America. Door Amstelophilus. [n. p. 1783.] 8vo, pp. 4. 57381

On the independence of North America.

Op de verschrikkelyke Aardbevinge ... in Essequebo en Demerary, 21. Octob. 1766. *Middelburg.* 1767. 4to, pp. 9.

Verses on the frightful earthquake at Essequebo and Demerary.

Op het Inneemen van St. Eustatius, St. Martin en Saba, door de Engelschen, 1781. *Amsterdam.* [1781.] 8vo, pp. 8. 57383

On the capture of St. Eustatius, St. Martin and Saba, by the English. In verse.

Op het ontset van Piet Heyns buyt. *See* [Vondel (J. v.)]

The Opal: ... . Edited by Mrs. Sarah J. Hale. *New York: J. C. Riker.* [n. d.] 8vo, pp. 320. Engraved Title and 5 Plates

The Opal: Published by the Patients in the State Lunatic Asylum, Utica. Vol. I. *Utica.* 1852. 4to. Continued in 8vo.

Opata Language. Doctrina Christiana y Platicas Doctrinales, traducidas en lengua Opata por el P. Rector Manuel Aguirre, de la Compañia de Jesus. ... Con las licencias necessarias. *Impressas en la Imprenta del Real, y mas antiguo Colegio de San Ildefonso de Mexico, año de* 1765. 4to, pp. (6), 162, (2). 57386

Extremely rare. The Opata is the dialect spoken by the Indians of Bacadeguachi, Mochopa and Nacori, in the province of Sonora. The author, who was a Jesuit, labored zealously for a number of years in the Sonora missions, and died in 1768.

Doctrina cristiana en lengua Opata. [n. p. n. d.] 8vo, 11 l.

OPDYKE (G.) The Great Libel Case. Opdyke *vs.* Weed. A full Report of Proceedings including Speeches of Counsel, Testimony and the Result. *New York.* 1865. 8vo, pp. 156.

OPDYKE. Official Documents, Addresses, etc., of George Opdyke, Mayor ... during ... 1862 and 1863. *New York: Hurd & Houghton.* 1866. 8vo, pp. xi, 368. 57389

[OPDYKE.] A Report on the Currency. *New York: John F. Trow, Printer.* 1858. 8vo, pp. 31. BA. 57390

Also: Letter on National Finances, from George Opdyke to Hon. Roscoe Conkling. *New York.* 1869. 8vo, pp. 23. — The Opdyke Libel Suit. A Full Metrical, Juridical, and Analytical Report of the Extraordinary Suit for Libel of George Opdyke "verses" Thurlow Weed ... . *New York.* 1865. 8vo, pp. 62. — A Treatise on Political Economy. ... *New York.* 1851. 16mo, pp. viii, 339, (2). C.

An Open Church. An Appeal for a Free Episcopal Church in ... Boston. [n. p. n. d.] 12mo, pp. 12. 57391

Opene Brieven of Octroy onder 't Groot Zegel van Schotland. [n. p. 1697.] 4to, pp. 12. 57392

Contains articles on America.

Opening of the Atlantic and Pacific Railroad, and completion of South Pacific Railroad to Springfield, Mo., May 3, 1870. *Springfield.* 1870. 8vo, pp. 41. 57393

Opening of the Mississippi; or Two Years Campaigns in the South West. A Record of the Campaigns, Sieges, etc., of the 8th Wisconsin Volunteers. *Madison.* 1860. 8vo. 57394

Operations of the War for the first Twelve Months, Examined and Accounted for. *London.* 1740. 8vo. 57395

Included in J. R. Smith's "Bibliotheca Americana."

The First Report of the OPHIR MINING Co. ... at Renfrew, Nova Scotia. ... *Boston,* ... *Printed by J. B. Chisholm.* 1866. 8vo, pp. 48. 2 Sections and Map. 57396

OPIE (A.) The Negro Boy's Tale, a Poem ... . By Amelia Opie. *London: Harvey and Darton.* 1824. 8vo. Plate. + *New York.* [n. d.] Sq. 12mo. Plate. 57397

Also: The Black Man's Lament; or how to make Sugar. ... *London: Harvey and Darton.* 1826. 12mo. In verse.

La Opinion. *Tegucigalpa.* 1852. Folio, 1 leaf. 57398

Opinion and Argument. *See* [Morris (L.)], Vol. XII. 50849.

Opinion de la Presse du Canada sur deux Albums prépares par M. Viger, et adressés le 4 Juin 1854, par les Pères du Concile tenu à Québec à cette époque ... . *Montréal.* 1854. 8vo, pp. 8.

The Opinion of Congress on a resolution of the House of Commons of Great Britain, of the 20th of February, 1775. *Philadelphia.* 1775. 8vo. P. 57400

Opinion of the Adjutant-General of ... New-York, on two questions of Alienism. *Albany: Printed by Packard and Van Benthuysen.* 1833. 8vo, pp. 15. 57401

Opinion of the Solicitor of the Treasury on the Question of the Liability of Manufacturers to Taxation ... . *Washington.* 1862. 8vo, pp. 16. 57402

Opinion sobre si conviene ó nó la diputacion provincial que se proyecta para la eleccion de regidores en América, con una letrilla á los regidores del actual sistema. El de las décimas en elogio de Piñeres. *Habana: Imprenta de Juan Pablo.* 1812. 8vo.

Opinions delivered by the Judges. *See* Vol. x., No. 39852.

Opinions of Loyalists concerning the Great Questions of the Times. *New York.* 1863. 8vo. B. 57404

Opinions of the Attorneys General of the United States, from the beginning of the Government to March 1st, 1841: ... Henry D. Gilpin [Editor]. *Washington City: Blair and Rives, Printers.* 1841. 8vo, pp. xi, 1495. B. + To July 19, 1850. *Washington.*

1852. 2 vols., 8vo. C. + Compiled by Benjamin F. Hall, and completed to March 4, 1857, by C. C. Andrews. *Washington.* 1852–58. 8 vols., 8vo. Continued. C. 57405

... Opinions of the Early Presidents, and of the Fathers of the Republic, upon Slavery, and upon Negroes as Men and Soldiers. *New York: Wm. C. Bryant & Co., Printers.* 1863. 8vo, pp. 19. BA., C. 57406

Opinions of the Judges of the Supreme Court of Pennsylvania, on the Constitutionality of the Act ... "For Enrolling and Calling out the National Forces ... . *Philadelphia.* 1864. 8vo.

Opinions of the Press and of eminent Public Men on the Importance of our Mineral Resources and the Advantages ... of a National School of Mines. *Washington, D. C.: Wm. H. Moore, Printer.* 1868. 8vo, pp. 32. H. 57408

Opinions of the United States Courts ... involving the Construction of the Non-Intercourse and Captured Property Acts, and their relation to the Prize Acts. *Washington.* 1866. 8vo, pp. 78. C. 57409

See also Nos. 6538, 7015, 12031, 24890 and 52891.

Opmerkingen omtrent den Afrikaanschen Slavenhandel en de Emancipatie in de Brittische Koloniën ... . *'s Hage: Gebr. Belinfante.* 1848. 8vo. 57410

Oposicion hecha al Progresso en las Causas y Processos de la Beatificacion y Canonizacion del D. Juan de Palafox y Mendoza. *Mexico.* 1699. Folio. 57411

A rare work, relating to the difficulties between the Jesuits and the Bishop of Puebla, and Viceroy of Mexico, whose canonization met with opposition from the Jesuits. This treatise gives the reasons on which they founded their opposition.

De Opper-Admiraal van Holland, waar in te vinden zijn veel fraaije oorlogs- en andere Liederen, alle op de tegenwoordige tijdsomstandigheid toepasselijk. *Amsterdam: B. Koene.* [1781?] Sm. 8vo, pp. 92. 57412

Contains a song in honor of Paul Jones, on his arrival in Texel with two captured English vessels, in 1779, etc.

The Opportunity; or, Reasons for an Immediate Alliance with St. Domingo. ... *London: J. Hatchard.* 1804. 8vo, pp. viii, 156

See also Vol. v., No. 17530.

Opposition Mornings. *See* [O'Neil (Elizabeth)], No. 57344.

Opposition Politics, Exemplified. ... *London: John Stockdale.* M,DCC,LXXXVI. 8vo, pp. 64. 57414

The Opposition to the Late Minister [Lord Bute] Vindicated from the Aspersions of a Pamphlet, intitled, Considerations on the Present Dangerous Crisis. *London.* 1763. 8vo, pp. 45.

Oppression. A Poem: By an American. With Notes, by a North Briton. *London: C. Moran.* [1765.] 4to, pp. 34. P. + *London: Printed. Boston: Re-printed and Sold opposite the Probate Office* ... . 1765. 8vo, pp. (2), 21. + *New York.* 1765. 8vo.

See page 10 for a Portsmouth "Yankey." No earlier use of the term within my knowledge. *See* "Monthly Review," XXXII. 392.

Oprecht verhaal [etc.]. *See* Vol. IX., No. 35257.

OPTIC (O.), *pseudon.* *See* [Adams (W. T.)], *and* Oliver Optic.

Opusculo sobre la hacienda publica de Chile. *Santiago.* 1842. Sm. 4to. 57417

Opuscules philosophiques. *See* [Suard et Bourlet].

Opusculo en defensa del clero en la iglesia mejicana, por la oposicion que ha manifestado á algunas disposiciones legislativas. *Mejico.* 1857. 8vo, pp. 36. 57418

Opusculos ácerca do Sebastianismo. Carta em resposta a um amigo, na qual se dá noticia da ilha Antilia, ou de S. Borondon, ou Sancta Cruz, vulgarmente denominada a ilha Encoberta. *Lisboa, na Officina de Simão Thaddeo Ferreira.* 1815. 8vo, pp. 40.

De Ora Antarctica. *See* [Vespuccius (A.)]

Oracion fúnebre de las exequias que se hicieron á la difunta inquisicion en el templo del fanatismo por un ministro de la misma, año de 1820. [*Habana:*] *Reimpreso por D. Pedro Nolasco Palmer é hijo.* 1821. 8vo. 57420

Oracion funebre. Qve en honras del immortal valor de los soldados espanoles difuntos celebradas de orden de su Magestad en la Santa Iglesia Metropolitana de Lima el dia de 15. de Noviembre de 1692. *Lima: Joseph de Contreras.* 1693. 4to, 30 prel. leaves, Text, 12 leaves. 57421

Oracion funebre, que en las Exequias que celebradas los Señores D. J. M. Castaños, D. Juan Jos. Yandiola, D. Jos. Revilla, y D. Andres de Ibarra, á la Digna Memoria de sú Padre D. Jos. de el Campo Soberon y Larrea, Primer Conde del Valle del Suchil, dixo el D. F. Gabriel de Olivares. *Mexico.* 1783. 4to. — Oracion fúnebre ... pronunciada

en la iglesia del convento de San Agustin por el M. R. P. presentado fray Juan Gonzalez, del orden de predicadores. *Havana: Imprenta de la Capitania General.* [n. d.] Folio, pp. 23. — Oracion funebre que en las solemnas ecsequias que el Jeneral de Division y Presidente de la Republica Peruana, D. Luis Jose Orbegoso Mando, se hicieran con asistencia de todas las corporaciones en honor de los valientes Guerreros muertos en el Campo de Yanacocha. Pronuncio en la Santa Iglysia Catedral de Arequipa. *Arequipa.* 1835. Sm. 4to. *See also* Vol. IV., No. 14615, *and* Vol. VII., No. 29446.

Oracion panegirica que à la felix llegada del D. A. de Gorrichategui, Obispo del Cuzco, dixo Ign. de Castro, cura en la provincia de Tinta. *Lima.* 1771. 4to, pp. 30. 57422

Oracion Panegyrica dixo Diciembre 12, 1777, el P. D. Juan Greg. de Campos. *Mexico: Zuñiga.* 1778. 4to, pp. (2), 20. S.

Oracion que el Illmo. Señor D. Manuel de Alday y Aspee, del consejo de S. M. Obispo de Chile, dixo en esta Santa Iglesia Metropolitana de la Ciudad de los Reyes, 12 de Enero de 1772, Sacala a Luz el D. E. J. Gallegos. *Lima.* 1772. 4to. 57423

The Oracle of Liberty. *See* [Hermes, *pseudon.*], No. 31500.

Oracles of Reason: as formed by the Deists, are Husks for Deistical and Heathen Swine; but the Truths of the Gospel are Bread for God's Children. A Concise, but plain Answer, to Gen. Allen's Oracles of Reason: ... By Common Sense. *Litchfield: Printed by T. Collier.* [n. d.] 12mo, pp. 40. 57424

L'Oraison dominicale et autres prières traduites en langage des montagnards du Canada. Par le R. P. Massé. *Orléans: Herluison.* 1865. 12mo, pp. 12, (2). 57425

Reprinted from Champlain's "Voyages," edition of 1632.

Oramaika. An Indian Story. *New York: E. Dunigan & Brothers.* 1854. 18mo, pp. 366. C. 57426

ORANGE, *N. J.* The First Church, Orange, N. J. One Hundred and Fiftieth Anniversary, November 24 and 25, 1869. Memorial. ... *Newark, N. J.: Jennings Bros.* 1870. Sq. 8vo, pp. 174. BA. 57427

Catalogue of the ORANGE LIBRARY ASSOCIATION, Orange, New Jersey, February, 1866. *New York: John F. Trow & Co., Printers.* 1866. 8vo, pp. 19. 57428

The library died for want of nourishment.

ORANGE, *N. Y.* Constitution of the Benevolent Society of the County of Orange. [n. p. n. d.] 8vo, pp. 8. C. 57429

Constitution and By-Laws of the New England Society of Orange, ... 1870. Second Edition ... . *New York.* 1870. 24mo, pp. 22, (2). H.

Proceedings of the Board of Supervisors of the County of Orange, for 1869. *Goshen.* 1870. 8vo. Continued. 57430

ORANGEBURGH, *S. C.* ... Memorial of sundry Citizens of Orangeburgh District, S. C. adverse to the increase of Duties on ... Imports. ... 1828. ... *Washington: Printed by Duff Green.* 1828. 8vo, pp. 4. H. 57431

Catalogue of the ... ORANGEBURGH FEMALE COLLEGE ... . *Charleston, S. C.: Walker, Evans & Co., Printers.* 1858. 8vo, pp. 20, (2). Plate. H. 57432

ORANTES (Segundico). Esposicion del gobierno del estado de Chiapas contra la desmembracion de una parte considerable de su territorio, intentada por el Exmo. Sr. Gobernador de Tabascas. *Imprenta del Gobierno del Chiapas, dirigida par Manuel Maria Truquillo; año de* 1856. 4to. 57433

Oratio Dominica ... nimirum plus Centum Linguis, Versionibus aut Characteribus, reddita & expressa. *Londini.* 1700. 4to. + Editio novissima, Specimenibus variis quam priores auctior. ... *Johann Ulrich Kraussen ... Augspurg.* [1712.] 4to, pp. (4), 22. + *Londini.* 1713. 4to, pp. (4), 71. + [*Ibid.*] 1736. 4to.

Includes the Mexican, Poconchi, and Virginian versions.

Oratio Dominica ... Editore Johanne Chamberlaynio ... . *Amstelædami: Typis Guilielmi & Davidis Goerei.* MDCCXV. 4to, pp. (44), 94, (6), 256. BA. 57435

Also on large paper.

Oratio Dominica CL Linguis versa, ... Edente J. J. Marcel, ... *Parisiis.* 1805. 4to, pp. (16), 150, (1). BA. 57436

By far the most splendid edition of the Lord's Prayer in different languages, and forms a most elegant volume, as well as an unrivaled specimen of typography.

Oratio Dominica in CLV. Linguas versa et Exoticis characteribus plerumque expressa. ... *Parmæ: Typis Bodonianus.* 1806. Folio. 57437

Oratio Dominica Polyglotta, DCCCXVI. Linguis et Dialectis, studio et labore Aloysii Auer. *Viennæ e Typographia Imp.* 1851. Rl. 8vo. 57438

Oratio Dominica in CCL. Linguas Versa ... *Romæ: Typographia S. C. Propoganda Fide.* 1870. 4to.

Oration [by Beverley R. Wellford, Jr.] and Poem [by John R. Thompson] delivered before the Convention of the Delta

Kappa Epsilon ... Washington, January 3, 1856. *Richmond: Macfarlane & Fergusson.* 1856. 8vo, pp. 40. 57439

An Oration Commemorative of the Declaration of American Independence; delivered before the Ciceronian Society, ... Fourth of July, M,DCC,XCIV: ... *Philadelphia: William Young.* M,DCC,XCIV. 8vo, pp. 16. 57440

An Oration, delivered ... on Board the Nassau Prison Ship, at Chatham, England, on the Fourth of July, 1814. By an American Seaman, Prisoner of War. *Boston.* 1815. 8vo, pp. 8.

An Oration, in Memory of ... Gen. George Washington. Delivered at Lovett's Hotel on the Evening of the 22d February, 1800, before a Literary Society; and published by their Order. By a Member. *New-York: T. S. Arden.* 1800. 12mo, pp. 23. M., N. 57442

Oration on the Beauties of Liberty. *See* [Skillman (Isaac)].

Oration, Poem, and Chronicles, ... before the Alumni of New Ipswich Appleton Academy, ... September 18, 1861; ... *New York: John N. Stearns.* 1861. 8vo, pp. 76. Plate and Portrait.

Oration, Poem, and Speeches. *See* Nos. 9996 *and* 44101.

An Oration, pronounced at Hanover, New Hampshire, January 9, 1800, at the request of Franklin Lodge, No. 6, in Memory of their Illustrious Brother the beloved Washington, who died at Mount Vernon, Dec. 14, 1799. ... *Hanover.* 1800. 8vo, pp. 17

An Oration, which might have been delivered to the Students in Anatomy, on the late Rupture between the two Schools in this city. *Philadelphia: Printed by T. Dobson and T. Lang.* 1789. 4to, pp. 19. P. 57445

An ironical poem, on the dispute between Shippen and Foulke.

An Oration written for the Fourth of July, 1863 ... . By an American Citizen. *Philadelphia.* 1863. 12mo, pp. 20. 57446

Orationes Viennae Austriae ad divum Maximilianum Caes. Aug. aliosque illustrissimos principes habitae; in celeberrimo trium Regum ad Caes. Conventu; anno. 1515. *Impressum Viennae, expensis L. et L. Atlansee.* 1516. 4to, 88 leaves.

A reference to the New World will be found on the verso of E 5.

Orationis dominicae versiones fere centum editae a Th. Ludekenio [And. Müller]. *Berolinae.* 1680. 4to. 57448

Orations delivered. *See* Vol. II., No. 6737.

The Orator. ... No. 1. Original and Selected. Edited by D. T. Stiles. *Buffalo.* 1856. 8vo. S. 57449

Orazione in lode di Christoforo Colombo. *See* Vol. IV. 14667.

ORBEGOSO Y NIETO. Contestacion que da Trinidad Moran a los Manifiestos de los Jenerales Orbegoso y Nieto en la parte que se ocupan de el. *Valparaiso.* 1840. 4to. 57450

ORBIGNY (A. d'). Coquilles et Echinodermes Fossiles de Columbie (Nouvelle Grenade), recueillis de 1821 à 1833 par M. Boussingault et décrits par Alcide d'Orbigny. *Paris: A. Bertrand.* 1843. 4to, pp. 72. 6 Plates. 57451

ORBIGNY. Descripcion Geografica, Historica, y Estadistica de Bolivia. ... Tome. I. *Paris: Gide et Cia.* 1846. 8vo, pp. xiv, 402. 57452

Announced to be complete in eleven volumes, with an atlas.

ORBIGNY. Foraminifères de l'Île de Cuba, par M. Alcide d'Orbigny. *Paris.* 1838. 8vo. 12 colored Plates, folio.

ORBIGNY. Fragment d'un voyage au Centre de l'Amérique Méridionale; Contenant des Considérations sur la Navigation de l'Amazone et de la Plata et sur les anciennes missions des Provinces de Chiquitos et de Moxos (Bolivia). Par Alcide d'Orbigny. *Paris: A. Bertrand.* 1845. 8vo, pp. (4), 584. Map.

ORBIGNY. L'Homme Américain (de l'Amérique Méridionale), considéré sous ses rapports physiologiques et moraux; par Alcide D'Orbigny ... . *Paris: Pitois-Levrault et C.ᵉ* 1839. 2 vols., 8vo, pp. (4), xxviij, 423, 2 folded Tables, Map; 372, 2 folded Tables and Map. Atlas in 4to, pp. (4). 15 Plates and Map. B., H.

The author made a personal examination of the natives and their locality, and accomplished as much as any one man can of the labors which will require the toil and thought of many to perfect.

ORBIGNY. Malerische Reise in Süd- und Nord-Amerika, übersetzt von Diezmann. *Leipzig.* 1839. 4to. + [*Ibid.*] 1841. 4to. 57456

ORBIGNY. Voyage dans l'Amérique Méridionale (le Brésil, la République Orientale de l'Uruguay, la République Argentine, la Patagonie, la République du Chili, la République de Bolivia, la République du Pérou,) exécuté pendant les Années 1826, 1827,

1828, 1829, 1830, 1831, 1832, et 1833, Par Alcide d'Orbigny, ... *Paris: Pitois-Levrault et C.ᵉ* 1835–49. 7 vols., 4to, and 2 vols. of Plates. 415 Plates and 18 Maps. B. 57457

Contents: Vol. I.–III. Partie Historique. III. Géographie; Part 2. Géologie, Paléontologie. IV. L'Homme américain; Mammifères; Oiseaux. V. Reptiles, Poissons, Mollusques, Zoophytes, et Foraminifères. VI. Crustacés; Insectes. VII. Cryptogamie; Palmiers. VIII. Atlas historique, géographique, géologique, paléontologique, et botanique. IX. Atlas zoologique; mammifères, oiseaux, reptiles, poissons, mollusques, polypiers, foraminifères, crustacés, et insectes; Cartes géologiques; Carte d'une partie de la république Argentine, comprenant les provinces de Corrientes et des Missions; Deux cartes générales de la république de Bolivia.

ORBIGNY. Voyage pittoresque dans les Deux Amériques résumé général de tous les Voyages de Colomb, Las-Casas, Oviedo, Gomara, Garcilazo de la Vega, Acosta, Dutertre, Labat, Stedman, La Condamine, Ulloa, Humboldt, ... par les Rédacteurs du Voyage Pittoresque autour du Monde; Publié sous la direction de M. Alcide D'Orbigny ... Accompagné de Cartes et de nombreuse Gravures, en taille douce sur acier ... . *A Paris: L. Tenré.* M DCCC XXXVI. Rl. 8vo, pp. (2), xvi, 568. 268 Plates. + *Paris.* 1841. 4 vols., 8vo. 2 Maps and 300 Plates. C. + Nouvelle Édition, par Vanderauwera. *Bruxelles.* 1854. 4 vols., 12mo. 57458

Comprises a résumé of the principal facts gleaned from the relations of the authors enumerated on the title-page, but has but little other value than is derived from the steel and copperplate engravings, of which there are two on each page. More than one-half of these are illustrative of some phase in the life, customs, and history of the numerous tribes of Indians of South America and Mexico. Brief descriptions are found in the text.

ORBIGNY. Viaje pintoresco a las dos Américas, Asia y Africa. Resumen jeneral de todos los viajes y descubrimientos de Colon, Magallanes, Las Casas, Gomara, La Condamine, Ulloa, Jorge Juan, Humboldt, Molina, Cabot ... . Publicada en francais hujo la direccion de MM. A. D'Orbigny y J. B. Eyries. ... *Barcelona: Juan Olivares.* 1842. 3 vols., 4to, pp. (6), xvii, 312, 92 Plates; (6), 180, 80 Plates, 2 Maps; (6), 239, 156, 98 Plates and Map. 57459

Also: List of the Shells of South America in the Collection of the British Museum. Collected and described by M. Alcide D'Orbigny, in the "Voyage dans l'Amérique Méridionale." *London.* 1854. 12mo, pp. (2), 89. *See also* Vol. V., No. 17786

Orbis | Habitabilis | Oppida et Vestitus, | Centenario Numero Complexa, | Summo Studio Collecta, | Atque in lucem edita | à | Carolo Allard. | ... | *Tot Amsterdam,* | *By Carel Allard,* ... | [n. d.] Folio, pp. (14). 100 Plates. 57460

In Latin and Dutch.

Orbis lumen et Atlantis juga tecta retecta: das ist: Newe auszführliche Entdeckung und Beschreibung der gantzen Welt. *Franckfurt am Main.* 1658. 4to. 57461

Pages 1352–1403 treat on America and the West Indies.

De Orbis Situ, ac descri|ptione, ad Reverendiss.|D. Archiepiscopum Panormitanum, Fran|cisci, Monachi ordinis Franciscani, Epistola,|sane quam luculenta. In qua Ptolemæi, cæ|terorumq; superiorum geographorum hal|lucinatio refellitur, aliaque præterea de re|cens inuentis, terris, mari, insulis. De ditio|ne Papæ Ioannis, de situ Paradisi, & di|mensione miliarium ad propor|tionem graduum cœli, præ|clara & memoratu|digna recen-|sentur. | *Antverpiae,* | *Excudebat Ioannes Withagius. Anno* 1565. 12mo, Title, and 18 leaves. J.C.B. 57462

Orbis terræ. *See* [Neander (M.)], Vol. XII., Nos. 52174–5.

Orçamento da receita e despeza do imperio para o anno financeiro de 1832–33. *Rio de Janeiro.* 1831. 4to. 57463

Orçamenta da receita e despeza do imperio para o exercicio de 1862–63. *Rio de Janeiro.* 1861. Folio.

Orchardist's Companion; devoted to the Fruits of the United States. *Philadelphia.* 1841. 4to. C. 57464

ORCOLAGA (Diego Ambrosio de). La Luz del Pharo mas pura fixo norte de la juventud en las incultas sendas de la noche, que sobre el fuerte de la razon ... . Discurso metrico, moral y politico. ... *Mexico.* 1718. 4to, 10 and 22 leaves. 57465

ORD (G.) Sketch of the Life of Alexander Wilson, Author of the American Ornithology. By George Ord, F.L.S. ... *Philadelphia: Harrison Hall.* 1828. 8vo, pp. cxcix. B., H., P.

[ORD.] Supplement to the American Ornithology of Alexander Wilson. Containing a Sketch of the Author's Life, with a Selection from his Letters; some Remarks upon his Writings; and a History of those Birds which were intended to compose Part of his Ninth Volume. Illustrated with Plates, engraved from Wilson's original Drawings. *Philadelphia: J. Laval and S. F. Bradford.* 1825. 4to, pp. 298, Index, (4). 4 Plates. H.

Published separately, but forms Vol. IX. of the 4to edition of Wilson.

The Ordeal: A Critical Journal of Politicks and Literature. ... Vol. I. *Boston: Printed by J. T. Buckingham.* 1809. 8vo, pp. iv, 412. Discontinued. C., H. 57468

ORDEN DE NUESTRO SERAPHICO. Estatutos Generales de Barcelona para la Familia Cismontana, de la orden de nuestro Seraphico Padre S. Francisco; los quales por mandado de nuestro R. P. F. Francisco Gonzaga, Ministro General ... . [*Mexico:*] *En Casa de Pedro Ocharte.* 1585. 4to, pp. 125, Table, etc., 31 and over. 57469

This excessively rare production of Ocharte's press appears to be unknown to Mexican bibliographers. It is not found in the lists given by Salva, Harrisse, and Icazbalceta.

Ordenácas y copilacion de Leyes. *Mexico.* 1548. Folio.

Organizing the courts of law, regulating the lawyers, attorneys, constables, etc., enacted in April, 1528. Title and note from [Harrisse's] "Bib. Amer. Vetus."

Ordenanças, Recopilacion de Leies, para el Govierno de la Audiencia de Mexico. *Mexico.* 1545. Folio. 57471

Title from Pinelo as quoted by Harrisse, concerning which *see* his "Bib. Amer. Vetus," No. 288.

Ordenanza General formada de órden de su Magestad, y mandada imprimir y publicar para el gobierno é instruccion de Intendentes, Subdelegados y demas empleados en Indias. *Madrid: Viuda de Harro.* 1803. Folio, pp. xxxvi, 194, Instrucciones, Cédulas y Ordenes, pp. (100). C. 57472

Ordenanza por el Real Compañia de Comercio para las Islas de Santo-Domingo, Puerto-Rico, y la Margarita. *Madrid.* 1775. Folio. 57473

See also Nos. 12794–5, 26483, 29447, *and* 48609–11.

Ordenanzas de la Junta de Guerra de Indias. *Madrid.* 1634. Folio. 57474

Ordenanzas de Marina, para los Navios del Rey, de las Islas Philipinas que en Guerra, y con Reales Permissos hacen Viages al Reyno de la Nueva España, ù otro destino del Real Servicio. [*Madrid.*] 1757. Folio. Maps. A. 57475

Ordenanzas de Mineria, y coleccion de las ordenes y decretos de esta materia posteriores á su publicacion. Reimpresas por orden del supremo gobierno del Estado. *Ures: J. Covarrubias.* 1852. 4to, pp. 359. + Con un apéndice concerniente las minas del Péru, y dos laminas para explicar los metodos mas economicos de disfrutar las vetas. Nueva edicion, dispuesta por C. N. *Paris.* 1854. 8vo. C. 57476

Ordenanzas del Consejo Real de las Indias. Nvevamente recopiladas, y por el Rey Felipe quarto, para su govierno, establecidas Año de 1636. *Madrid: Julian de Paredes.* 1681.

Folio, pp. 206, (14). C. + Nuevamente recopiladas, y por el Rey D. Phelipe IV. N. S. para su govierno, establecidas año de M.DC.XXXVI. *Madrid: A. Marin.* 1747. Folio, pp. 208, (12).

Ordenanzas del Juzgado general privativo de bebidas prohibidas. *Mexico.* 1782. Folio, pp. 45. 57478

Ordenanzas del Noblissimo Arte de la Plateria, hechas y mandadas observar por el Excel. Señor Marques de Cadereyta, Vi-Rey de esta Nueva-España. *Mexico.* 1715. Folio. + *Mexico.* 1746. Folio, pp. 22. 57479

Ordenanzas del tribunal del consulado de esta ciudad de los Reyes, y Reynos del Peru, Tierra firme, y Chile. Confirmadas por D. Felipe IV 1627. Imprimierõse, siẽdo Prior y Consules ... Franc. Saenz de Vidaurre, Iñigo de Olaerrota, y Juan de Aguilar. *Lima: Manuel de los Olivos.* 1680. Folio, 47 leaves. 57480

Ordenanzas para el Archivo General de Indias. *Madrid: En la Imprenta de la Viuda de Ibarra.* 1790. Rl. 8vo, pp. 66. J.C.B.

Ordenanças para Remedio de los daños e inconvenientes, que se siguen de los descaminos y arribadas maliciosas de las Navios, que navegan a las Indias Ocidentales (fecha en San Lorenço 10 de Junio año 1589). *Con Licencia, en Madrid, por Pedro Madrigal, Año de* 1591. Folio, Title and 24 leaves. + *Madrid: Viuda de Alonso Martin.* 1619. Folio. 57482

Ordenanzas Reales del Consejo de las Indias (hechas por el Rey en Consejo, Sept. 24, el año 1571). *Valladolid del Licen. Varez de Castro.* 1603. Folio, Title and 22 leaves, Summario, 5 leaves. 57483

Ordenanzas Reales para el Govierno de los Tribunales de la Contaduria mayor, que en los Reynos de las Indias y Ciudades de los Reyes en el Piru, Mexico en la Nueva España, Santafe, en el Nuevo Reyno de Granada ha mandado fundar el Rey nuestro Señor (dada en Burgos 24 de Agosto el año 1605). *En Valladolid, impressas por Luys Sanchez.* 1606. Folio, Title and 11 leaves.

Ordenanzas Reales para la Casa de la Contratacion de Sevilla, y para otras cosas de las Indias, y de la navegacion y contratacion dellas (dada en Valladolid 14 de Julio, año 1556). *En Valladolid por los herederos de Juan Iñiguez de Leguerica.* 1604. Folio, Title and 84 leaves. 57485

A reprint of the first edition, with the additional decrees issued by Philip II., down to 1583. This royal code, by which the Spanish West-India House was established and

regulated, is of considerable importance to any one desiring to comprehend the relations between Spain and the colonies. Very rare. It was again reprinted at *Sevilla, Francisco de Lyra.* 1647. Folio, 86 leaves.

Ordenanzas sobre alcabalas. *Mexico.* 1574. Folio. 57486

This brief title is from [Harrisse's] "Bib. Amer. Vetus."

Order for Daily Morning and Evening Prayer, ... of the Protestant Episcopal Church in the Confederate States of America, ... *Atlanta, Georgia: R. J. Maynard.* 1863. 8vo, pp. 47.

The Order|For Morning and Evening Prayer,|and Administration of the|Sacraments,|and some other|Offices of the Church,|Together with|A Collection of Prayers, and some Sentences of|the Holy Scriptures, necessary for Knowledge|Practice.| ... Collected, and translated into the Mohawk|Language, under the direction of the late Rev.|Mr. William Andrews, the late Rev. Dr. Henry|Barclay, and the Rev. Mr. John Oglivie:|Formerly Missionaries from the venerable Society|for the Propagation of the Gospel in Foreign|Parts, to the Mohawk Indians.| [*New York:*] *Printed* [*by Weyman and Gaine*] *in the Year,* M,DCC,-LXIX. 8vo, pp. (2), 204. 57488

Of this work four hundred copies were printed, of which twenty were on fine paper. The printing was commenced by Weyman, who died in 1768; at his death, Hugh Gaine completed it. *See* "Documentary History of New York," IV. 321, 326, 330, 340, 343, 364, 414, *and* "Historical Magazine," I. 15.

The Order|For Morning and Evening Prayer,|and Administration of the|Sacraments,|and some other|Offices of the Church|of England,|Together with|A Collection of Prayers,|and some Sentences of the Holy|Scriptures, necessary for Knowledge and Practice.| ... The Third Edition,|Formerly collected and translated into the Mohawk or Iroquois Lan-|guage, under the direction of the Missionaries from the Venerable|Society for the Propagation of the Gospel in Foreign Parts, to the|Mohawk Indians.|Published|By Order of His Excellency Frederick Haldimand,|Captain-General and Commander in Chief of all his Majesty's|Forces in the Province of Quebec ...|Revised with Corrections and Additions by|Daniel Claus, Esq; P.T. Agent|For the six Nation Indians in the Province of Quebec.|*Printed in the Year* M,DCC,LXXX. 8vo, pp. (2), iii, 208. 57489

Order for the Levy of 5000 Blankets for the Army now raising for the Defence of the American Colonies, Jan. 20, 1777. [n. p. n. d.] Folio, 1 leaf. 57490

Order of American Knights; or Sons of Liberty. A Report from the Judge Advocate General. *Washington.* 1864. 8vo.

An Order of Council. *See* Vol. XI., No. 45929.

Order of Exercises. *See* Nos. 6539, 31913, 50025, 51905, *and* 55093.

Order of Service at the Consecration of the New Synagogue, Greene Street, ... 25th September, 5611. The ... Sermon by the Rev. Dr. Raphall ... . *New-York: Printed by John M. Jackson.* 5611. 8vo. 57492

See also Vol. IV., No. 13415.

The Order of the Churches. *See* [Mather (C.)], XI. 46441.

Order of the General Court of April 29, 1668, for the banishment of Thomas Gold, Wm. Turner, and John Farnham, Senior, being Obstinate and Turbulent Anabaptists. [n. p. n. d.] Folio. W. 57493

Order of the King in Council, on Report of the Lords of the Committee for Hearing of Appeals, etc., on the Petitions of Peter Sonmans, of New Jersey, and of Joseph Ormstone, relating to several Proprietes or undivided Shares of Land in the Eastern and Western Divisions of New Jersey, purchased heretofore by Arent Sonmans, Father to said Peter ... . [*London: J. Baskett.* 1718.] Folio, pp. 3. 57494

Constitution of the ORDER OF UNITED AMERICANS, and Laws of Archchancery; together with By-Laws of Star-spangled Banner Chapter, No. 56. *Albany.* 1855. 18mo. S. 57495

Constitution of the O. U. A. and Sub-Constitution of the O. U. A. for Massachusetts. *Boston: Bros. Edw. W. Hinks & Co.* 1855. 16mo, pp. 16.

Orderly Book of that portion [etc.]. *See* Vol. X., No. 40785

Orderly Book of the Northern Army, at Ticonderoga and Mt. Independence, from October 17th, 1776, to January 8th, 1778, with Biographical and Explanatory Notes [by Joel Munsell], and an Appendix. *Albany: J. Munsell.* 1859. 4to, pp. viii, 224. Map, and Portrait of Gates. C. 57496

"Munsell's Historical Series," No. III. One hundred and ten copies printed, of which ten are on large paper.

Orderly Book of the Siege of Yorktown; from September 26th, 1781, to November 2nd, 1781. Now First Printed from the Original MSS. *Philadelphia: Horace W. Smith.* MDCCCLXV. 4to, pp. (4), 66. 57497

Sixty copies printed, of which ten are on plate paper.

Orders|and|Articles|granted by the|High and Mightie Lords|the States Generals of|the Vnited Provinces,|Concerning the erecting of a West India|Companie:|Together with the priviledges and rights|given unto the same.| [*London:*] *Printed Anno Dom.*|M.DC.XXI.| Sm. 4to, pp. 18. H. 57498

Orders and Constitvtions, partly collected out of his Majesties Letters Patents; and partly by Authority, and in Virtue of the said Letters Patents: Ordained upon mature deliberation, by the Gouvernour and Company of the City of London, for the Plantation of the Svmmer Islands; for the better gouerning of the Actions and Affaires of the said Company and Plantation, 6 February, 1621. *London: Felix Kyngston.* 1622. Sm. 4to, pp. 83.

Orders for Governing His Majesty's Forces in America. In Two Letters to a Friend. 1755. 57500

Title quoted by George Bancroft, Vol. IV., p. 170.

Orders in Council and Instructions for Blockade, &c. issued between 10th Nov. 1807, and 1st Jan. 1808; and a View of the several Provisions thereof. *London.* 1808. 8vo. 57501

Orders in Council; or, an Examination of the Justice, Legality, and Policy of the New System of Commercial Regulations. With an Appendix ... . *London: Longman.* 1808. 8vo, pp. 144. + The Second Edition. [*Ibid.*] 1808. 8vo, pp. (4), 120. BA.

The Orders of Council, and Instructions for imposing the Restrictions of Blockade, ... *London.* 1807. 8vo, pp. 53.—The Orders of Council for Blockade, and for regulating Navigation, Importation and Exportation. *London.* 1808. 8vo, pp. 51.

Orders, Regulations, and Instructions for the Administration of Law and Justice in the United States Navy. *Washington.* 1870. 8vo, pp. 61. C. 57503

ORDERSON (J. W.) Creoleana: or, Social and Domestic Scenes and Incidents in Barbados in days of yore. By J. W. Orderson ... . *London: Saunders and Otley.* 1842. 16mo, pp. viii, 246. BA. 57504

Also: Colonial Register for 1802, being a correct List of all Public Officers in Barbados ... *Bridge Town, Barbados.* [1802.] 8vo.

ORDINAIRE [Claude Nicolas]. Histoire naturelle des Volcans ... . *Paris.* 1802. 8vo. A. 57505

ORDINAIRE. The Natural History of Volcanoes: ... By the Abbé Ordinaire ... . Translated ... by R. C. Dallas. *London: T. Cadell.* MDCCCI. 8vo. P. 57506

An Ordinance, ascertaining what Captures on Water shall be lawful. Done in Congress, the Fourth Day of Dec., 1781. [*Philadelphia: Printed by David C. Claypoole.* n. d.] Folio, 1 leaf.

Also: An Ordinance, for amending the Ordinance ascertaining what Captures on Water shall be lawful. Done ... January, 1782. [n. p. n. d.] Folio, 1 leaf.

Ordinance for establishing a Board to Liquidate and Settle all Accounts between the United States and Individual States. [n. p.] 1786. Folio, 1 leaf. 57508

An Ordinance for the Establishment of the Mint of the United States of America; and for Regulating the Value and Alloy of Coin. [*Philadelphia.*] 1786. Folio, 1 leaf. C. 57509

An Ordinance of the Lords and Commons assembled in Parliament, whereby Robert Earl of Warwick is made Governour in Chief and Lord High Admirall of all the Islands and Plantations within the Bounds or Coasts of America, &c. *London.* 1643. 4to. 57510

Ordinance of the State Convention which convened at Little Rock, May 6, 1861. *Little Rock.* 1861. 8vo. S. 57511

An Ordinance organizing ... Patrols for the Police of Slaves in the Parish of St. Landry. *Opelousas.* 1863. 8vo, pp. 29.

See also Nos. 53199, 53200–53201, 53848–53852, *and* 54567–68.

Ordinances and By-Laws of ... Cincinnati ... February, 1857. *Cincinnati.* 1857. 8vo, pp. 383. 57513

Ordinances and Constitution of Alabama, with the Constitution of the Confederate States. *Montgomery.* 1861. 8vo.

Ordinances of the City Council of Charleston, S. C., passed in the First Year of the Incorporation of the City. ... *Charleston: J. Miller.* 1784. Sm. 4to, pp. x, 57. C. 57515

The Ordinances of the Mines of New Spain; translated from the ... Spanish. With Observations upon the Mines and Mining Associations. By Charles Thomson, Esq. ... *London: Booth.* 1825. 8vo, pp. 27–76–196. C. 57516

Ordinarium Sacri Ordinis heremitarũ sancti Augustini episcopi et regularis Observãtie, nũc denuò correctũ, sic q nõ secũdum morẽ antiquũ ceremonie fiant, sed secũdũ choros altos. *Mexici anno dñi* 1556 *idibus julii.* 4to, 40 leaves. 57517

The musical lines are printed in red, the notes in black. Probably printed by Juan Pablos. It is an excessively rare specimen of early Mexican typography.

Ordinationes legumque collectiones pro conventu juridico mexicano. *Mexici, per Joannem Paulum Brissensem,* 1549. Folio.

"The question in regard to this title is not so much whether it represents the first book printed in Mexico, as whether it ever was printed at all, anywhere." Title and note from [Harrisse's] "Bib. Am. Vet.," No. 288, which *see* for a long note.

Constitutiones ORDINIS FRATRUM EREMITARUM Sancti Augustini, nuper recognitae, et in ampliorem formam ac ordinem redactæ. *Mexici Excudebat Petrus Ocharte.* 1587. 12mo, 8 leaves, Text, 225 leaves, and Index, 42 leaves. 57519

An excessively rare production of the Mexican press of the sixteenth century.

The Ordnance Manual for the use of the Officers of the United States Army. Second Edition. *Washington: Gideon & Co., Printers.* 1850. 8vo. 57520

See also Vol. IV., Nos. 15332–33.

ORDOÑEZ (J.) Opusculo sobre ascensos militares, ... por el Coronel Juan Ordoñez. *Mexico.* 1849. 4to, pp. 12. 57521

ORDOÑEZ. Reflecsiones militares sobre la organizacion del ejercito permanente ... . *Mexico.* 1853. 8vo, pp. 68. 57522

Also: Opusculo sobre la estincion de las comandancias generales, por el Teniente Coronel retirado Juan Ordoñez ... . *Mexico.* 1849. 8vo, pp. 11.—Refutacion al cuaderno titulado: Ojeada sobre la campaña que hizo el General Santa-Anna en el estado de Coahuila el mes de Febrero proximo pasado, ... *Mexico.* 1847. 2 parts, 4to, pp. 27, 24.

ORDOÑEZ DE CEVALLOS (P.) Tratado|de las|relaciones|verdaderas de|los reynos de la China,|Cochinchina, Champa, y otras cosas|notables, y varios sucessos, sacadas|de sus originales. ... *Iaen, por Pedro de la Cuesta, Año de* 1628. Sm. 4to, (4), 52, (4) leaves. B. 57523

ORDOÑEZ DE CEVALLOS. Viage del Mvndo. Contiene tres libros. Hecho y compuesto por Pedro Ordoñez de Cevallos. *En Madrid, por Luis Sanchez,* M.DC.XIIII. 4to, 10 leaves, Text, 290 leaves, Table, 4 leaves. Portrait. C. 57524

By far the greater part of this work is occupied with an account of the author's voyages in Spanish South America. Rare. *See* Boucher de la Richarderie, I. 116.

ORDOÑEZ DE CEVALLOS. Historia, y Viage del Mvndo, contiene tres libros: Itinerario à las cinco partes de la Europa, Africa, Asia, America, y Magalanica. ... *Madrid, por Juan Garcia Infanzon.* 1691. 4to, pp. (12), 432, (8). C. 57525

In a concise article by E[yriy]s in the "Biographie Universelle," LII., it is stated, "Zevallos est un homme qui a vu ce qu'il rapporte." *See also* Vol. IV., No. 14352, *and* Vol. VIII., Nos. 31540, 31542–43.

Ordonnance de nos Seigneurs les Commissaires du Conseil deputez par le Roy pour la Regie de la Compagnie des Indes. En faveur des habitans de la colonie de la Loüisiane. Du 2 septembre 1721. *Paris, Veuve Saugrain et Pierre Prault.* 1721. 8vo, pp. 4. 57526

Ordonnance du Roy. Au sujet des Engagez. Du 15 fèvrier 1724. *Paris: Imprimerie Royale.* 1724. 4to, pp. 4. 57527

"Pièce relative aux engagés ou plutôt aux émigrants français qui vont aux iles françaises de l'Amérique et au Canada."—LECLERC.

Ordonnance du Roy, Concernant les Convois pour les Isles françoises de l'Amérique. Du 14 Mai 1745. *A Paris, de l'Imprimerie Royale.* 1745. 4to, pp. 4. 57528

Ordonnance du Roi concernant le gouvernement de l'Ile de la Martinique et celui de l'Ile de la Guadeloupe et de ses dépendances. *Paris: Imprimerie Royale.* 1827. 4to, pp. 83. 57529

Ordonnance ... concernant l'organisation de la conversation des hypothèques à la Martinique, à la Guadaloupe et dans ses dépendances et à la Guyane française. *Paris.* 1829. 4to.

Ordonnance du Roy, qui renouvelle pour six années l'exemption accordée aux navires marchands destinez pour la Louisiane d'y porter des engagés et des fusils, du 25 novembre 1748. *Paris, de l'Imprimerie Royale.* 1748. 4to, pp. 4. 57531

Ordonnance du Roi, concernant les procureurs et économes-gérans des habitations situées aux isles sous le vent. Du 3 décembre 1784. *Paris: Imprimerie Royale.* 1784. 4to, pp. 20.—Ordonnance du Roi, portant défenses aux capitaines de navires de laisser débarquer aucun noir, mulâtre ou autres gens de couleur, avant d'avoir fait leur rapport à l'Amirauté. Du 23 février 1778. *Paris: Imprimerie Royale.* 1778. 4to, pp. 3.—Ordonnance du Roy, Portant défenses des Jeux de hazard aux Colonies. Du 4 Novembre 1744. ... *Paris: Imprimerie Royale.* M.DCC.XLIV. 4to, pp. 2.—Ordonnance du Roy portant que les Capitaines et Maistres qui vont à la pesche de la Morue à la Coste de Labrador ... . *Paris: Imprimerie Royale.* 1718. 4to, pp. 4.—Ordonnance du Roy, Pour la Défense des Jeux aux Colonies Françoises de l'Amérique. *A Versailles le quinziéme Decembre* 1722. 4to, pp. 3.—Ordonnance du Roi pour l'incorporation des différens Corps employés au département des Colonies, dans les régiments de la Martinique et Guadeloupe pour y former un troisième Bataillon. [n. p.] 1784. 4to, pp. 8.—Ordonnance du Roy, qui dispense les vaisseaux marchands qui seront armez et destinez pour la colonie de la Louisiane, d'y porter des engagez et fusils ... . Du 4 août 1731. *A Paris, de l'Imprimerie Royale.* 1731. 4to, pp. 4.—Ordonnance du Roy, qui proroge pour six années, à compter du 4 aoust 1737, l'exemption accordée aux navires marchands destinez pour la Loüisiane, d'y porter des engagez et fusils. Du 15 Juillet 1738. *Paris: Imprimerie Royale.* 1738. 4to, pp. 4.—Ordonnance du Roy, Qui règle le payement des équipages des navires expédiez pour les Isles de l'Amérique sous l'escorte des vaisseaux de la Majesté, pendant le tems qu'ils auront été retenus dans les Rades pour attendre le depart des convois. Du 21 Avril 1746. ... *A Paris, de l'Imprimerie Royale.* 1746. 4to, pp. 3.

Ordonnantien | ende | articvlen | Beraemt by de Hoogh Mo: | Heeren Staten Generael, der Geunieerde | Provintien, op het toerusten ende toe-stellen, van eene | West-Indische Compagnie. Mitsgaders alle privi- | legien ende gherechticheden, de zelve ghe- | gheven ende vergundt. | *Ghedruckt in het Iaer onses Heeren*, | *Anno* 1621. 4to, 8 leaves. C. 57532

Regulations and articles for the establishment of a West India Company.

Ordonnantien | ende | Articvlen | Beraemt by de Ho: Mo: | Heeren Statē Generael der Geunieer- | de Provintien/ op het toerusten ende toestellen | van eene West-Indische Compagnie. Mits- | gaders alle privilegien ende gerecht | tigheden, de selve ghegeven | ende vergunt. | *Gedruckt in het Iaer onses Heeren* | *Anno* 1621. 4to, 8 leaves. 57533

The same as the foregoing pamphlet.

Ordonnantien | ende | Articvlen | Voor desen beraemt/ by de | Hoogh Mogh: Heeren Staten Generael der | geunierde Provintien/ op het toerusten van eene | West-Indische Compagnie. | Midtsgaders | De laeste ampliatie van de selve/ ghearresteert | op den 21 Junij laestleden/ met alle privilegien ende gerecht- | tigheden daer toe gegeven ende vergunt. | *t'Arnhem*, | *by Jansen, Boeckverkooper, anno* 1623. 4to, pp. 24. 57534

ORDONNEZ DE CEVALLOS (P. van). *See* Ordoñez de Cevallos

Ordre by de ... Staten Generael ghemaeckt op het bevaren vande Middellantsche Zee ende het Southalen in West-Indien. *Amsterdam: M. Colijn.* 1621. 4to, pp. 20. 57535

Order by the States General relative to the salt-trade of the West-Indies.

Ordre ende Reglement, | Byde Heeren Staten Gene- | rael der Vereenighde Nederlanden ghearresteert, | Waer op, ende waer naer alle gemonteerde Sche- | pen uyt dese respective Provincien, sullen vermo- | gen te varen in seecker gedeelte vande Limiten van | 't Octroy vande West-Indische Compaignie, | hier nae gheexprimeert. | *In 's Graven-Haghe.* | *Byde Weduwe, eñ Erfgenamen van wijlen Hillebrandt Jacobssz van* | *Wouw, Ordinaris Druckers vande Ho: Mo: Heeren Staten* | *Generael. Anno* 1633. *Met Privilegie.* | 4to, 4 leaves. 57536

Order and regulations, according to which armed vessels from the respective provinces shall be able to trade within certain limits of the patent of the West India Company.

Ordre ende Reglement: vande H. M. Heeren Staten Generael der Vereenighde Nederlanden gearresteert by advijs ende deli-

beratie vande Bewint-hebberen vande generale gheoctroyeerde West-Indische Compagnie ter Vergaderinge vande Negenthiene over het bewoonen ende cultiveren der Landen ende Plaetsen by die vande voor-ghemelte Compagnie in Brasil gheconquesteert. *In 's Gravenhage, Weduwe van Hillebrandt Jacobssz van Wouw.* 1634. 4to, 8 leaves. C. 57537

Ordre et Progrez du Triomphant et Magnifique Advenement du Roy [Henry II.] et de la Royne de France en leur bonne ville de Rouen. *Rouen.* 1551. 4to. 57538

One of the many entertainments given by the city of Rouen, at the entry of Henry II. and Catharine of Medici, was a show of three hundred American Indians, representing them in their sports, pastimes, fights, and mode of living, in a place got up in imitation of the localities and general appearance of their native land. To make the show approach reality as near as possible, fifty wild Indians had been actually imported from Brasil.

ORDRONAUX (J.) Eulogy on the Life and Character of Rev. Zachariah Greene, a Patriot of the Revolution, and Late Senior Pastor of the First Presbyterian Church, Setauket, N. Y. Delivered at ... Hempstead, February 10th, 1859. By John Ordronaux. ... *New York: Baker & Godwin, Printers.* 1859. 8vo, pp. 50. Portrait. H. 57539

Mr. Greene fought in the battles of White Plains, Germantown, etc. Three hundred copies only printed. Also: ... Proposed Scheme for the Relief of Disabled Soldiers, ... *New York: Wm. C. Bryant & Co., Printers.* 1863. 8vo, pp. 8.—Report ... . On a System for the ... Relief of Disabled Soldiers ... . *New York: Stafford, Harrison & Co., Printers.* 1864. 8vo, pp. 163. B.

ORDUÑA (L. de). Informe zeloso discvrsivo, que en servicio de ambas Magestades (divina y humana) para manifestacion de la verdad, se opone a todo rebozo, que pretende simularla; en ordena que se impida la justicia, en su operacion; dexando de dar, lo que es suyo a cada vno. Por Fray Luis de Orduña ... . *Con Licencia* [*en Mexico*] *Año* 1642. 4to, 30 leaves. 57540

A memorial against the pastoral letter of Palafox y Mendoza, bishop of Puebla.

ORE (L. G. de). Relacion de los martyres que ha havido en la Florida, por Luis Geronimo de Ore, franciscano. *Lima.* 1612. 4to. 57541

Title from Ternaux, No. 346. Noticed in Barcia's "Ensayo Cronologico," p. 173. *See also* Finotti, p. 13.

ORE. Ritvale, sev Manvale Pervanvm, et forma brevis administrandi apud Indos sacrosancta Baptismi, Pœnitentiæ, Eucharistiæ, Matrimonij, et Extremæ vnctionis Sacramenta. ... Et qvæ indigent versione, vvlgaribus Idiomatibus Indicis, secun-

dum diuersos situs omnium Prouinciarum noui orbis Perù, aut per ipsum translata, aut eius industria elaborata. Per P. F. Lvdovicvm Hieronymvm Ore ... . *Neapoli, apud Jo. Jacobum Carlinum, et Constantinum Vitalem.* 1607. 4to, pp. 418, (2). 57542

In Latin and Spanish, with a translation in Quichua and Aymara. It contains the bull of Alexandre VI., dated Rome, 1493, fixing the limits of the possessions of the Spaniards and Portuguese in the New World.

ORE. Symbolo Catholico Indiano. ... *Mexico.* 1598. 57543

Title from Ternaux, No. 224.

OREGON. ... An Account and History of the Oregon Territory; together with a Journal of an Emigrating Party ... . Second Edition. *London: William Lott.* 1846. 16mo, pp. (2), 159, (1), viii. BA. 57544

By J. Bryant. Corrected title of No. 8807, Vol. III.

Acts and Resolutions of the Legislative Assembly of the State of Oregon, ... 1866. *Salem: W. A. McPherson.* 1866. 8vo, pp. 110. Continued. C. 57545

Code of the Civil Procedure and other General Statutes of Oregon, enacted ... 1862. ... *Oregon.* 1863. 8vo. 57546

The Constitution of the Oregon Republic. [n. p. n. d.] 8vo, pp. 8. B. 57547

The Constitution; together with the Session Laws of Oregon, enacted during the First Regular Session of the Legislative Assembly, 1860. *Salem: State Printer.* 1860. 8vo. C. 57548

Correspondence relative to the Negotiation of the Question of Disputed Right to the Oregon Territory ... subsequent to the Treaty of Washington, August 9, 1842. Presented in the year 1846. *London: Printed by T. B. Harrison.* 1846. Folio, pp. iv, 71. S. 57549

The Decision of the Supreme Court, in ... the Territory of Oregon, upon the Location Law, ... with the Oregon Land Law. *Portland: Printed by Thos. J. Dryer.* 1852. 8vo, pp. 39, (1).

A General Circular to all ... who wish to emigrate to the Oregon Territory ... and ... directions for becoming an Emigrant. ... *Charlestown: Printed by William W. Wheildon.* 1831. 8vo, pp. 27, (1). B. 57551

Improved title of No. 26871, Vol. VII.

Journal of the Council of the First Session of the Legislative Assembly of the Territory of Oregon ... 1849. *Salem.* 1849. 8vo. Continued. 57552

Journal of the House of Representatives ... December 4, 1854. *Corvallis.* 1855. 8vo. Continued. 57553

Journal of the Senate and House ... for 1866. *Salem: W. A. McPherson.* 1866. 2 vols., 8vo. C. 57554

Laws ... passed by the Legislative Committee and Legislative Assembly, ... from ... 1843 ... to ... 1849 ... . *Salem, Oregon.* 1853. 8vo. Continued. 57555

Message of the Governor to the Legislature ... 1856. *Salem.* 1856. 8vo. Continued. 57556

Minutes of the Congregational Association of Oregon, ... held at Salem, 1864. *Salem, Oregon.* 1864. 8vo, pp. 14. H.

The Oregon Archives: including the Journals, Governors' Messages and Public Papers of Oregon, from the earliest attempt on the Part of the People to form a Government, down to, and inclusive of the Session of the Territorial Legislature, held in ... 1849. ... By La Fayette Grover ... . *Salem: Asahel Bush, ... Printer.* 1853. 8vo, pp. 333, (2). C., H. 57558

Supposed to be the first book printed in Oregon.

The Oregon Controversy Reviewed, In Four Letters. By a Friend of the Anglo-Saxons. *New-York: Leavitt, Trow & Co.* 1846. 8vo, pp. 54. 57559

Das Oregon-Gebiet. ... Officielle Correspondenz des brittischen bevollmächtigten Ministers in Washington und des Staatssecretärs der Vereinigten Staaten. ... *Bremen.* 1846. 8vo, pp. 114

Oregon: its Resources, Soil, Climate and Productions. *Jacksonville.* 1871. 8vo. 57561

The Oregon Medical and Surgical Reporter, edited by E. R. Fiske, A.M., M.D., ... and H. Carpenter, M.D. ... Vol. I. 1870. *Salem, Oregon.* [n. d.] 8vo, pp. viii, 384. B. 57562

The Oregon Question. Comparative Chronological Statement of Events Connected with the Rights of Great Britain and the Claims of the United States. [n. p. n. d.] 16mo. 57563

See "North Amer. Rev.," LXII. 214, "Edinb. Rev.," LXXXII. 238, "Quart. Rev.," LXXVII. 564, "Fraser's Mag.," XXVII. 484, "Dublin Univ. Mag.," XXI. 377.

Oregon Territory. Report of the Committee. [*Washington.* 1844.] 8vo. 57564

Relates to the extension of jurisdiction of the courts of Iowa to Oregon.

Oregon: the Claim of the United States to Oregon, as stated in the Letters of the Hon. J. C. Calhoun and the Hon. J. Buchanan ... . With an Appendix, containing the Counter Statement of Mr. Pakenham to the American Secretaries of State. And a Map ... . *London: Wiley and Putnam.* 1846. 8vo, pp. iv, 55, 16. S. 57565

All the material is official, and had already been published.

Oregon. The Cost and the Consequences. ... By a Disciple of the Washington School. *Philadelphia: John C. Clark.* 1846. 8vo, pp. 12. B. 57566

... The Organic and other General Laws of Oregon, ... 1845–1864. Compiled ... by M. P. Deady. ... *Portland, Oregon: H. L. Pittock, State Printer.* 1866. 8vo, pp. 1107. S. + 1843–1872. ... [n. p.:] *Eugene Semple, State Printer.* 1874. Rl. 8vo, pp. iv, 923. S. 57567

Proceedings of the ... Grand Lodge of ... Masons, of ... Oregon ... . *Portland: ... R. D. Austin.* [n. d.] 8vo, pp. 75, (1).

Report of the Adjutant-General of ... Oregon, for 1863–4, ... *Portland, Oregon: Henry L. Pittock, ... Printer.* 1865. 8vo, pp. 66. Continued. BA. 57569

Report of the Sup't Penitentiary of the State of Oregon, for ... 1865–6. *Salem, Oregon: Henry L. Pittock, ... Printer.* 1866. 8vo, pp. 31. 57570

Statistics of the State of Oregon. Published by the State Agricultural Society. *Salem.* 1869. 8vo. 57571

Statutes ... of the Territory of Oregon: ... December 2, 1850. ... *Oregon City: Asahel Bush, ... Printer.* 1851. 8vo, pp. 301. + *Oregon,* 1855. 8vo. C. 57572

Tracts [VII] on the Oregon Question. By an American. *New York: W. Taylor.* 1846. 12mo, pp. 52. 57573

The Wealth and Resources of the State of Oregon. *Salem, Oregon.* 1864. 8vo, pp. 66. 57574

See also Nos. 19712, 47716, 55988, *and* Twiss (Travers).

... The Oregonian, and Indian's Advocate. Our Object, the Elevation of the Indian Race—Our Means, a Christian Settlement in Oregon. October, 1838. ... *Boston: David H. Ela.* 1838. 8vo, pp. 32. 57575

Continued to eleven (or more) parts.

L'Oréide. *See* [Le Blond (F. F.)], Vol. X., No. 39601.

O'REILLY (B.) Greenland, the Adjacent Seas, and the North-West Passage to The Pacific Ocean, illustrated in a Voyage to Davis's Strait, During the Summer of 1817. With Charts and numerous Plates, from Drawings of the Author taken on the Spot. By Bernard O'Reilly, Esq. *London: Baldwin, Cradock, and Joy.* 1818. 4to, pp. vi, (2), 293. 3 Maps and 18 Plates. B. + *New-York: James Eastman and Co.* 1818. 8vo, pp. vi, (2), 251. Maps and Plates. S. 57576

"Made up principally from information derived from Prof. Giesecke's lectures."—*Dublin University Magazine,* III. 300. The "Quarterly Review" calls it "a barefaced imposition." *See* "Monthly Review," LXXXVIII. 62.

O'REILLY (Miles), *pseudon.* *See* [Halpine (C. G.)], 29918–20

ORELLANA (Antonio de). Compendio de la vida del V. Padre Cypriano Baraze, natural de la villa de Issaba, del Valle de Roncal, y Reyno de Navarra, ... Muerto à manos de los Barbaros Moxos, en la Provincia del Peru. ... *Madrid: Blas de Villanueva.* 1711. 8vo, pp. (16), 118, (10). J.C.B. 57577

This narrative includes very important historical information about the Indians of this part of Peru.

ORELLANA (Estevan de). Instruccion de la Lengua Latina, o Arte de adquirirla por la traduccion de los Autores. [Segunda Edicion Mexicana.] ... *Mexico, en la Imprenta nueva Madrileña de Zuñiga y Ontiveros.* 1781. 12mo, pp. 84. 57578

ORELLANA (F. J.) Cristobal Colon, Historia Popular, por Francisco José Orellana. *Barcelona.* 1858. 4to. 57579

ORELLANA (Manuel). Manifestacion al publico de los actos practicados por el en Junta liquidataria de la deuda española, de las acusaciones formuladas contra el ... . *Mexico.* 1859. 8vo, pp. 43, 15. 57580

ORFORD (R.) A Further Report from the Committee of Secrecy, Appointed to Enquire into the Conduct of Robert, Earl of Orford; During the last Ten Years of his being First Commissioner of the Treasury, and Chancellor and Under-Treasurer

of his Majesty's Exchequer. Delivered the 30th of June, 1742. *London: T. Leech.* 1742. 8vo, pp. 132. 57581

"No. 13" a folded sheet between pages 128 and 129. Corrected title of No. 26260.

ORFORD, *N. H.* Centennial Celebration of ... Orford, N. H., containing the Oration, Poems and Speeches, delivered ... September 7, 1865. With some additional matters relating to the History of the place. [*Manchester.* 1865.] 8vo, pp. 145.

Organic Laws of Illinois. The Act and Deed of Cession from Virginia; Ordinance of 1787; Constitutions of 1818, 1848 and 1870 ... . [n. p. n. d.] Rl. 8vo, pp. 64. 57583

A Organisação dos Poderes Constitucionaes nas Monarchias Representativas Pelo Academico José Pedreira Franca Junior. *Bahia: Typ. Constitucional de França Guerra.* 1865. 8vo, pp. 94.

The Organization and Constitution of The Boston Light Artillery: with the ... Members ... . *Charlestown: Caleb Rand, Printer.* 1854. 12mo, pp. 96. H. 57585

Organization and Proceedings of the First Annual Festival of the Sons of Penn, in Chicago, Illinois. Washington's Birthday, 22d February, 1850. *Chicago.* 1850. 8vo, pp. 20. Portrait.

Organization, Objects, and Plan. *See* Vol. IX., No. 37054.

Organization of the Military Peace Establishment of the United States. ... *Washington City: Gales & Seaton, Print.* 1815. 12mo, pp. iv, 62. 57587

Organization of the Service of the Baltimore and Ohio Rail Road ... . *Baltimore.* 1847. 8vo, pp. 30. 57588

ORIBE (M.) Manifiesto sobre la infamia, alevosia y perfidia con que el Contra-Almirante Frances M.r Leblanc, ... Fructuoso Rivera, al Estado Oriental del Uruguay, que, conforme a su constitucion, se hallaba bajo la presidencia legal del Brigadier General D. Manuel Oribe. *Buenos-Aires: Imprenta del Estado.* 1838. 8vo, pp. viii, 89. 57589

For a French version, *see* Leblanc, Vol. IX., No. 39596.

O'RIELLY (H.) ... Memorial of Henry O'Rielly, proposing a System of Telegraphic & Letter-Mail Communication Between the Atlantic & Pacific, including the Protection of Emigrants, the Formation of Settlements and Promotion of amicable Relations with the Indians, through Nebraska, Deserета ... . [n. p. 1852.] 8vo, pp. 13, (1). H. 57590

[O'RIELLY.] Notices of Sullivan's Campaign, in the Revolutionary Warfare in Western New York: embodied in the Addresses and Documents connected with the Funeral Honors rendered to those who fell with the gallant Boyd in the Genesee Valley, including the Remarks of Gov. Seward at Mount Hope. *Rochester: William Alling.* 1842. 12mo, pp. 192. Plate.

"Published ... to preserve a record of the honors paid to the soldiers whose blood first consecrated to freedom the soil of the Genesee Valley." The plate represents the "Hill of the Revolutionary Patriots at Mt. Hope, Rochester."

O'RIELLY. Origin and Objects of the Slaveholders' Conspiracy against Democratic Principles, as well as against the National Union. ... [Edited] by Henry O'Rielly. *New York: Baker & Godwin, Printers.* 1862. 8vo, pp. 16. B. 57592

See also Sherwood (L.)

O'RIELLY. Rochester in 1835. Brief Sketches of the present Condition of the City of Rochester. ... By Henry O'Reilly [*sic*]. *Rochester: Luther Tucker, Printer.* 1835. 8vo, pp. 14.

O'RIELLY. Settlement in the West. Sketches of Rochester; with incidental Notices of Western New-York. A collection of matters designed to illustrate the progress of Rochester during the first quarter-century of its existence. ... Arranged by Henry O'Reilly [*sic*]. ... *Rochester: William Alling.* 1838. 12mo, pp. 416. Map, Plates and Portrait. B. 57594

Also: American Anthems, on the Triumph of Liberty and Union, over Slavery and Treason. ... [n. p. n. d.] 8vo, pp. 3. — First Organization of Colored Troops in the State of New York, to aid in Suppressing the Slaveholders' Rebellion. ... *New York: Baker and Godwin, Printers.* 1864. 8vo, pp. 24. — The Real Motives of the Rebellion. ... [n. p. n. d.] 8vo, pp. 16.

O'RIELLY (H. B.) A Brief Memento of Captain Henry Brooks O'Rielly, of the First Excelsior Regiment, who fell in the Battle of Williamsburg, ... May 5, 1862. [n. p. n. d.] 8vo, pp. 7. B. 57595

Orientalisch- und Occident. Sprachmeister. *See* [Schulke (B.)]

ORIGEN, *pseudon.* Words for the People. Part I. Civil Government. Part II. Government of the United States. Part III. Social Duties. By Origen. *Hartford: Case, Lockwood & Co.* 1865. 18mo, pp. 295. C. 57596

Origen de la guerra del Paraguay con la potentias aliadas del Rio de la Plata et Brasil. Elementos de los beligerantes organizacion de sus ejercitos y puntos estrategicos que ocupan. *Barcelona.* 1865. 8vo, pp. 32. 57597

Origen, verdadero, carácter, causas, resortes, fines y progressos de la revolucion de Nueva España. *Mexico.* 1820. Folio, pp. xvii, 114, 66, (2). 57598

Origen y estado de la causa formada sobre la Real orden de 17 de Mayo de 1810, que trata del comercio de América. *Cadiz: Vicente Lema.* 1811. 4to, pp. 122, Appendix, 80, 8, 81–120.

The author of this book, D. Manuel de Albuerne, was the first secretary to the "Ministero de Hacienda" of the Indies.

Origin and Characteristics. Also a Catalogue of Officers and Students. By the Senior and Junior Professors, as ordered 2nd November, 1830, by the Presidential Committee. *Troy.* 1831. 8vo, pp. 24. S. 57600

[Origin and Progress of] British Colonial Slavery. [*London.* 1833.] 8vo, pp. 16. B. 57601

Origin and Progress. *See* [Boulanger (N. A.)], Vol. II. 6885.

Origin and Progress of The Late Difficulties in the First Church in Worcester, Mass. Containing all the documents relating to the subject. To which is added The Result of a ... Council, ... May, 1820, to investigate ... charges ... against Rev. Charles A. Goodrich ... . *Worcester: Printed by Manning & Trumbull, July,* 1820. 8vo, pp. 88. H. 57602

Origin and Progress of the Present Difficulties between the United States and Great Britain considered, etc. By a Citizen of Otsego County. *Utica.* 1809. 12mo. N. 57603

The Origin and True Causes of the Texas Insurrection commenced in ... 1835. [*Philadelphia.* n. d.] 8vo, pp. 32.

Origin, History, and Character. *See* [Livermore (G.)], Vol. X.

Origin of the Narrative of the Onondaga Tradition of Hia-a-wat-ha; and Correspondence relative thereto. *Syracuse and New York.* 1856. 4to. 57605

The Origin of the Whale bone-petticoat. A Satyr. [In Verse.] *Boston, August 2d.* 1714. 8vo, pp. 8. 57606

Origin, Principles, and Objects of the Contest in which Texas is at present engaged. *New York.* 1836. 8vo, pp. 56. 57607

Origin, Progress, and History of the Tammany Society. *New York.* 1838. 12mo, pp. 32. 57608

Origin, Provisions and Effect of the Safety Fund Law of the State of New-York. *Albany.* 1834. 8vo, pp. 15. S. 57609

Origin, Struggles and Principles of the U. S. Sanitary Commission. ... [n. p. n. d.] 8vo, pp. 42. B. 57610

See also No. 22750, [Heard (J. M.)], No. 31179, *and* [Leonard (D.)], No. 40098.

The Original Constitution, Order and Faith of the New-England Churches. Comprising the Platform of Church Discipline Adopted in 1648. Propositions respecting Baptism and Consociation of Churches Answered by the Synod of 1662. A Confession of Faith, Adopted by the New-England Churches 1680, with an Appendix ... . *Boston, Printed: Reprinted for A. Lyman & Co.* 1812. 12mo, pp. (2), 118, 12. A., H. 57611

Original Contracts for the Survey of the Coast. [*Washington?* 1842.] 8vo. 57612

Original Letters of Ferdinand and Elizabeth. *New York.* 1798. 18mo, pp. 144. 57613

The story of two lovers who committed suicide in the Bowery in 1797 or 1798.

Original | Letters | to an | Honest Sailor. | *London: R. Thomas.* [1746.] 8vo, pp. 94. BA. 57614

These interesting letters were addressed to Admiral Vernon by Admiral Sir Charles Wager, W. Pulteney, Lord Cathcart, Speaker Onslow, Holles Duke of Newcastle, Lord Chancellor Hardwicke, Lord Vere, Beauclerk, and Admiral Byng, and contain some interesting particulars relative to the expedition to the West Indies, Peru, Mexico, etc., from 1730 to 1745.

Original Papers. *See* Nos. 11134, 17794, 18563, 40541, *and* [Vernon (Edward)].

Original Poem, written and dedicated to Post 15, Grand Army of the Republic, By High Private. *Boston: Rockwell & Rollins, Printers.* 1868. 8vo, pp. 7. H. 57615

Original Poems, By a Citizen of Baltimore. *Baltimore: Samuel Jefferis.* 1809. 12mo, pp. x, 139, (2). B. C., 57616

Original Rights. *See* M[ather] (I), Vol. XI., No. 46715.

The Original Steam-Boat. *See* Fitch (J.), Vol. VI. 24582.

Origine, et progress. *See* [Badin (S. T.)], Vol. I., No. 2710.

Origines transatlantiques. *See* [Margry (P.)], Vol. XI. 44533.

ORIHUELA (E. Jose Calixto de). Carta Pastoral que sobre las Obligaciones del Cristianismo y la Oposicion de este al espi-

ritu Revolucionario de estos ultimos Tiempos ... . *Lima.* 1820. 4to. + [*Ibid.*] 1833. 4to. 57617

Relates to emancipation in Peru.

The Orion: a Monthly Magazine of Literature, Science, and Art. Edited by William C. Richards. Vol. I. *Penfield (Ga.): W. C. Richards.* 1842. 8vo. Continued. C. 57618

ORIZAVA. Contrato de Tabacos para la siembra que ha de hacerse en los cantones de Orizava, Córdova y Jalapa el presente año de 1826 ... . [n. p. n. d.] Folio, pp. 4. 57619

Fastos Militares de iniquitad, barbarie y despotismo del gobierno espanol, ejecutados en las villas de Orizava y Cordoba en la guerra de once anos ... por D. J. Maria Fornel. *Mexico.* 1843. 8vo, pp. 78. 57620

Representacion dirijida al Soberano Congreso General por el ilustre Ayuntamiento y venerable clero secular y regular de la Ciudad de Orizava, pidiendo el retablecimiento de la Sagrada Compañia de Jesus. *Orizava.* 1841. 8vo, pp. 31. 57621

ORLANDOS (J.) Report of the Evidence and Reasons of the Award between Johannis Orlandos & Andreas Luriottis, Greek Deputies, of the one part, and Le Roy, Bayard & Co., & G. G. & S. Howland, of the other part. By the Arbitrators. *New-York: Printed by W. E. Dean.* 1826. 8vo, pp. 72. BA., N., S.

ORLEANS (F. F. P. L. M. d'). *See* [Joinville], IX. 36406–8.

ORLEANS (W.) The Travels of Father William Orleans, A Jesuit, Who being banished from France, ... travelled through Asia, Africa and America ... . *London: J. Mackenzie.* [n. d.] 8vo, pp. 31. Plate. H. 57623

ORLEANS (*l'Évêque d'*). Lettre de Mgr. L'Évêque d'Orleans au clergé de sons diocése sur l'Esclavage. *Paris.* 1862. 8vo, pp. 16. 57624

ORLEANS CO., *N. Y.* Proceedings of the Board of Supervisors of the County of Orleans, for 1869. *Albion.* 1869. 8vo.

Archives of Science and Transactions of the Orleans County Society of Natural Sciences. Vol. I. No. I. *Newport.* 1870. 8vo.

Orleans Territory. ... Memorial of the House of Representatives of the Territory of Orleans, ... respecting the Titles to

Lands: ... *Washington City: Printed by William Duane and Son.* 1806. 8vo, pp. 14. BA. 57626

Message ... transmitting the Constitution ... of the Territory of Orleans. ... under the Title of the State of Louisiana. March 5th, 1812. *Washington City: Printed by R. C. Weightman.* 1812. 8vo, pp. 32. 57627

See also Vol. XII., No. 42227, Vol. XIII., Nos. 53301–3, *and* 53331.

ORLENDIUS (F.) Orbis sacer et profanus illustratus. ... *Florentina.* 1728–32. 3 vols., folio. 57628

The American provinces are included.

Orllie-Antoine Ier Roi d'Araucanie et de Patagonie Son Avénement au Trône et Sa Captivité au Chili Relation écrite par lui-même *Paris Libraire de Thevelin* 1863 8vo, pp. iv, 174. Portrait. 57629

A sequel to the poems of Ercilla and Pedro de Oña. Also: Manifeste d'Orlie-Antoine Ier, roi d'Araucanie et de Patagonie. *Paris.* 1863. 8vo, pp. 16.

ORMAECHEA (J. B.) Oracion Funebre en Honras del J. M. Santiago 28 Sept. 1845 ... . *Mexico.* 1845. 4to. Plate.

ORMOND (——). The Lay of the Last Pilgrim. *Charleston, S. C.* 1832. 12mo. 57631

ORMOND (J. J.) Code of Alabama; prepared by J. J. Ormond, A. P. Bagby, and G. Goldthwaite, 1852. *Montgomery.* 1852. 8vo. C. 57632

ORMSBY (R. McK.) A History of the Whig Party, or some of its main features; with a ... glance at the formation of parties in the United States, and outlines of the history ... . By R. McKinley Ormsby. ... *Boston: Crosby, Nichols & Company.* 1859. 12mo, pp. 377. + Second Edition. [*Ibid.*] 1860. 12mo. B.

ORMSBY (W. L.) Cycloidal Configurations, or the Harvest of Counterfeiters. Containing matter of ... importance concerning Paper Money. ... By W. L. Ormsby ... . *New York: W. L. Ormsby.* [n. d.] 8vo, pp. 45. H. 57634

Also: A Description of the present System of Bank Note Engraving, showing its tendency to facilitate Counterfeiting; ... *New York.* 1852. 4to, pp. 104. Plates.

ORNE (C. F.) Sweet Auburn and Mount Auburn, with other Poems. By Caroline F. Orne. *Cambridge: John Owen.* 1844. 16mo, pp. viii, (4), 196. H. 57635

ORNE (H.) An Oration, pronounced at Boston, 4th July, 1820 ... . By Henry Orne. ... *Boston: Printed by Elisha Bellamy.* 1820. 8vo, pp. 23. BA. 57636

ORNE. Reply of Colonel Orne to the attacks of Mr. Nathaniel Greene, and David Henshaw, and others, in the Boston Statesman. *Boston: Putnam & Hunt.* 1829. 8vo, pp. 48. H.

Orondalee. A Tale by Byron Whippoorwill, Esq., and other Poems. *Hudson.* 1825. 8vo. 57638

OROÑO (N.) Consideraciones sobre fronteras y colonias. Por Nicasio Oroño ... . *Buenos Aires.* 1869. 4to, pp. 53.

OROZCO (J. M.) Sermon en la funcion titular de la hermandad de Cocheros y Pages del SS. viatico. ... *Guadalajara.* 1853. 8vo, 12 leaves. 57640

OROZCO Y BERRA (M.) Geografía de las lenguas y carta etnográfica de México Precedidas de un Ensayo de clasificacion de las mismas lenguas y de apuntes para las inmigraciones de las Tribus Por El Lic. Manuel Orozco y Berra ... . *México: Imprenta de J. M. Andrade y F. Escalante.* 1864. 4to, pp. xiv, 392. Ethnographical Map. BA., C. 57641

Contents: Primera Parte. Ensayo de clasificacion de las lenguas de México. Segunda Parte. Apuntes para las inmigraciones de las tribus en México. Tercera Parte. Geografia de las lenguas de México.

This is without question not only the best publication about the geography of Mexican idioms, but also a standard for all books on the geography of languages in general.

OROZCO Y BERRA. Materiales para una cartografia mexicana. ... *México: Imprenta del Gobierno.* 1871. Folio, pp. xii, 337, (2).

OROZCO Y BERRA. Memoria para el plano de México, formada de órden del Ministerio de Fomento por el ingeniero topógrafo Manuel Orozco y Berra. *México.* 1867. 12mo, pp. viii, 232. Table in folio. Plan of Mexico 40½ × 28 in. 57643

OROZCO Y BERRA. Memoria para la Carta Hidrografica del Valle de Mexico, formada por acuerdo de la Sociedad Mexicana de Geografia y Estadistica. Por su socio honorario el Sr. Lic. D. Manuel Orozco y Berra. *Mexico: A. Boix, á cargo de M. Zornoza.* 1864. 4to, pp. 185. 2 Illustrations and Map.

The map consists of two sheets in large folio.

OROZCO Y BERRA. Noticia histórica de la Conjuracion del Marques del Valle. Años de 1565–1568. Formada en vista de nuevos documentos originales, y seguida de un estracto de los

mismos documentos por el Licenciado D. Manuel Orozco y Berra. *Mexico: Tipografia de R. Rafael.* 1853. 4to, pp. 72, 502, (2). B. 57645

Alleged conspiracy to cause Mexico to "secede," and place at the head of the government Martin Cortes, son of the *conquistador*.

OROZCO Y BERRA. Posiciones geográficas de varios puntos del Imperio Mexicano Colectadas por los ingenieros Don Manuel Orozco y Berra, Don Francisco Martinez de Chavero y Don Francisco Jimenez. ... *Mexico.* 1866. 4to, pp. 74. 57646

Also: Informes escritos para la memoria del Ministerio de Fomento en 1857. ... *Mexico.* 1857. Folio, pp. 38, 31, 28. Map.

OROZCO (Seb. de Cobarruvias). Tesoro de la Lengua Castellana o Española ... *En Madrid, por L. Sanchez.* 1611. Folio, (10) leaves, text, 507 and 79 leaves. 57647

Several of the articles give particulars relating to New Spain.

Third Report of the ORPHAN'S HOME, Pittsburgh, Pa., and the Orphans' Farm School, Zelienople, Butler Co., Pa. 1861–1862. *Pittsburgh: Printed by W. S. Haven.* 1862. 8vo, pp. 30, 10. H. 57648

General Report of the ORPHANS' HOME OF INDUSTRY, near Iowa City, Iowa, from ... 1854, to ... 1861. *New-York: George Russell, Printer.* 1861. 18mo, pp. 18.

The Orpheus C. Kerr Papers. *See* [Newell (R. H.)], XIII.

ORPHEUS JUNIOR, *pseudon.* *See* [Vaughan (W.)]

Orpheus, Priest of Nature, and Prophet of Infidelity; or, The Eleusinian Mysteries Revived. A Poem, in Three Cantos. *London: J. Stockdale.* 1781. 4to, pp. 41. 57649

A satire on David Williams, Dr. Franklin, Priestley, and other writers on free thought

La Orquesta. Periódico omniscio, de buen humor y con caricaturas. Vol. I. *Mejico.* 1861. Folio. Continued. 57650

The Mexican Punch. The caricatures are curious and have an interest in respect to events occurring during the French intervention, and the reign of the Emperor Maximilian.

ORR (B.) Oration at Belford [Mass.], Feb. 22, 1800, on the Death of George Washington. By Benjamin Orr. *Amherst, N. H.* 1800. 8vo. W. 57651

ORR (G.) The Possession of Louisiana by the French, considered, as it affects the interests of those nations more immediately concerned, viz. Great Britain, America, Spain, and Portu-

gal. By George Orr, Esq. *London: J. Ginger.* 1803. 8vo, pp. 45. BA. 57652

ORR (H.) A History of Freemasonry; ... Discourse ... in Bridgewater, ... June 30th, A. L. 1797. By Hector Orr ... . *Boston: Printed by Samuel Etheridge.* 1798. 8vo, pp. 32. H.

Also: An Oration, ... at Bridgwater [Mass.], October 1, 1801, ... [before] the Columbian Society ... . [*Boston:*] *Printed by Russell and Cutler.* 1801. 8vo, pp. 24. — An Oration, pronounced at Bridgewater, July 4, 1804 ... . *Boston: Printed by Gilbert & Dean.* 1804. 8vo, pp. 19. BA.

[ORR (Hector).] Letter to Hon. James Buchanan, occasioned by his late Speech at Greensburg, Pa. [n. p. 1852.] 8vo, pp. 8. H. 57654

ORR (J. L.) Address ... before the Literary Societies of Erskine College, Abbeville District, S. C. ... September 16, 1846. By James L. Orr. *Greenville, S. C.: Printed by O. H. Wells.* 1846. 8vo, pp. 13. H. 57655

[ORR.] Address of the Confederate Congress to the People of the Confederate States. [n. p. n. d.] 8vo, pp. 16. 57656

Also: Reasons for Joining the Republican Party in South Carolina. ... [n. p.] 1870. 8vo. — ... Report Of the Select Committee to whom was referred that portion of the Message of the President ... relating to the Action of Congress ... . [n. p. 1865.] 8vo, pp. 8. — Speech ... February 24, 1852, on Public Lands. ... [n. p. n. d.] 8vo. — Speech ... June 9, 1852, on the Presidency. ... *Washington.* [n. d.] 8vo, pp. 8. — ... Terms of Treaties hereafter to be made with certain Tribes of Indians. ... [n. p. 1854.] 8vo, pp. 11. B.

ORRANTIA (Tomas de). Oracion Funebre que en las Exequias de la Reyna Madre Señora Doña Isabel Farnesio, dixo el dia xi. de Julio de MDCCLXVII. en la Cathedral de Lima. ... [n. p. 1768.] 4to, pp. xiv, 50. J.C.B. 57657

ORRIO (Francisco Xavier Alexo de). *See* Alexo de Orrio.

ORRUÑO (J. M.) Sermon panegirico en la funcion anual de orden dal supremo consejo de Castilla de las injurias con que fue insultado por las tropas Alemanas. ... *Mexico.* 1814. 4to, 20 leaves. 57658

Also: Para que sirven los frayles en el mundo? Sermon panegyrico con motivo de la celebracion de capitulo provincia de Fr. menores de la provincia de S. Diego de Mexico. ... *Mexico.* 1815. 4to, 22 leaves.

ÖRSTED (A. S.) Grönlands annulata dorsibranchiata. ... *Kjöbenhavn.* 1843. 4to, pp. 64. 8 Plates. 57659

See also Oersted (A. S.), Vol. XIII., No. 56735.

ORSUNA (Bravo de). Opera Medicinalia. *Mexico.* 1549. 4to

ORTA (Fr. de P.) Refutacion de la guarnicion de Veracruz, sobre los sucesos memorables del 5. de Diciembre anter. verific. en aquella plaza. ... *Mexico.* 1839. 8vo, pp. 24. 57661

ORTA (G. de). Coloquios dos simples, e drogas he cousas mediçinais da India, e assi dalgũas frutas achadas nella onde se tratam algũas cousas tocantes a mediçina, pratica, e outras cousas boas, pera saber cõpostos pello Doutor garçia dorta: fisico del Rey nosso senhor, vistos pello muyto Reuerendo senhor, ho liçençiado Alexos diaz: falcam desenbargador da casa da supricaçã inquisidor nestas partes. Com priuilegio do conde viso Rey. *Impresso em Goa, por Ioannes de endem as x. dias de Abril de* 1563 *annos.* 4to, 217 [for 257] leaves. 57662

This was reproduced in facsimile, *Lisboa*, 1872, with a preface by Mr. F. A. de Varnhagen. A few copies only printed, some of which are on large paper. The original edition is of extreme rarity.

ORTA. Aromatvm, et simplicivm aliqvot medicamentorvm apvd Indos nascentivm historia: ... *Antuerpiæ, apud Christophorum Plantinum.* 1567. 8vo. 57663

ORTA. Aromatvm, | et | simplicivm aliqvot | medicamentorvm apvd | Indos nascentivm | historia: | Primùm quidem Lusitanica lingua per Dialogos | conscripta, D. Garcia ab Horto, Pro- | regis Indiæ Medico, auctore. | Nunc verò Latino sermone in Epitomen contracta, & ico- | nibus ad viuum expressis, locupletioribusq[ue] annotatiun- | culis illustrata à Carolo Clvsio Atrebate. | *Antverpiæ*, | *Ex officina Christophori Plantini*, | *Architypographi Regij.* | cIↄ.Iↄ.-LXXIIII. | 8vo, pp. 227, (4). J.C.B. 57664

In this translation are some laudatory verses by Camoens, whom the author met at Goa.

ORTA. Aromatvm, et simplicivm aliqvot medicamentorvm apvd Indos nascentivm historia ... . Tertia editio ... *Antverpiæ, Ex officina Christophori Plantini* ... 1579. 8vo, pp. 217, (6). + [*Ibid.*] 1582. 8vo. + [*Ibid.*] 1584. 8vo. 57665

ORTA. Aromatvm, | et | simplicivm aliqvot | medicamentorvm apvd | Indos nascentivm | historia: | Primùm quidem Lusitanica lingua διαλογικῶς | conscripta, à D. Garçia ab Horto, | Proregis Indiæ Medico: | Deinde Latino sermone in Epitomen contracta, & iconi- | bus ad viuum expressis, locupletioribusq[ue] annotatiun- | culis illustrata à Carolo clvsio Atrebate. | Qvarta editio, | Castigatior, & aliquot locis auctior. | *Antverpiæ*, | *Ex officina Plantiniana*, |

Apud Viduam, & Ioannem Moretum. | M. D. XCIII. | *Cum gracia & priuilegio.* | [Followed by:] Christophori | A costa, medici | et cheirvrgi, | Aromatum & medicamentorum | in Orientali India nascentium | liber: | Plvrimvm lucis adferens iis quæ à Doctore | Garcia de Orta in hoc ge- | nere scripta sunt: | Caroli clvsii atrebatis operâ ex | Hispanico sermone Latinus factus, in Epitomen | contractus, & quibusdam notis illustratus. | Altera editio, | castigatior & auctior. | *Antverpiæ*, | *Ex officina Plantiniana*, | *Apud Viduam, & Ioannem Moretum.* | M. D. XCIII. | [Colophon:] *Antverpiæ*, | *Ex officina plantiniana*, | *apvd Vidvam*, | *et Ioannem Moretvm.* | M. D. XCIII. | 8vo, pp. 456, (6). J.C.B., C. 57666

Barbosa cites other editions, *Lisboa*, 1568 and 1695; and *Lugduni Batavorum*, 1642. 12mo.

ORTA. Dve libri dell' historia de i semplici, aromati, et altre cose, che vengono portate dall' Indie Orientali, pertinente alla Medicina, di Don Garzia dall' Horto, Medico Portughese; con alcune breui annotationi di Carlo Clvsio. Et dve altri libri parimente di qvelle che si portano dall' Indie Occidentali, di Nicolò Monardes ... . Hora tutti tradotti dalle loro lingue nella nostra Italiana da M. Annibale Briganti ... . *In Venetia.* M D LXXVI. 4to, (8) leaves, Text, 92 and 44 leaves. J.C.B. 57667

This Italian translation is also an abridgment.

ORTA. Dve libri dell' historia de i semplici, aromati, et altre cose; ... pertinenti all' vso della medicina di Don Garzia dall' Horto ... . *Venetia, por Francesco Ziletti.* 1582. 8vo, pp. (26), 347; (12), 249, (26). 57668

ORTA. Dve libri dell' historia de i semplici, aromati, et altre cose; ... . *Venetia, appresso gli heredi di Francesco Ziletti.* 1589. 8vo, pp. (28), 347, (5); Monardes, pp. 131, (13). + *Venetia.* 1597. 8vo. 57669

In the second part of the edition of 1589 will be found a long and interesting letter to Monardes, from Pietro di Osma & di Xara & Zegio, dated "Lima nel Peru a 25 di Decemb. l'anno 1568."

ORTA. Dell'historia | de i semplici aromati. | Et altre cose che vengono | portate dall' Indie Orientali pertinenti | all' vso della Medicina. | Di Don Garzia da l'Horto | Medico Portughese, con alcune breui | Annotationi di Carlo Clusio. | Parte Prima diuisa in quattro Libri. | Et dve altri libri parimente | di quelle cose che si portano dall' Indie Occidentali. | Con Vn Trattato della Neue & del beuer fresco. | Di Nicolò Monardes Medico di Siuiglia. | Hora tradotti dalle loro lingue nella nostra Italiana da M. | Annibale Briganti, Marrucino da Ciutta di Chieti, | Dottore & Medico

eccellentissimo. | Con Privilegio. | *In Venetia*, MDCV. | *Appresso l'Herede di Girolamo Scotto.* | 8vo, pp. (32), 525. + *Venetia.* 1616. [Colophon:] *Stampato in Venetia nella Stamperia di Giouanni Salis.* M. DC. XVI. 8vo, pp. (32), 525. 57670

See also Acosto (C.), Clusius (C.), Colin (A.), *and* Monardes (N.)

ORTEAGA (Jos. Joachin de). Nueva Aljaba Apostolica, con varias Canciones y Saètas, para el exercicio de las Missiones ... *Imprenta de la Biblioteca Mexicana.* 1757. 4to. 57671

ORTEGA (C. de). Resumen Historico del primer Viage hecho al rededor del mundo, emprendido por Hernando de Magallanes, &c. Su Autor ... Don Casimiro de Ortega ... . *En Madrid.* 1769. 4to, pp. (12), 55. Plate. H. 57672

See also Byron (J.), Vol. III., No. 9733.

ORTEGA (E. M.) Elogio de Cristobal Colon por Eulalio Maria Ortega, presentado y premiado en el concurso abierto por convocatoria del Ateneo Mexicano de 20 de Julio de 1845. *Mexico.* 1846. 8vo. Portrait. + [*Ibid.*] 1853. 8vo, pp. 32.

Also: Playdoyer sur l'incompetence du conseil de guerre français appelé à statuer sur les faits imputés au Colonel J. S. Facio, fait devant le même conseil. ... *Mexico.* 1864. 8vo, pp. 26.

ORTEGA (F. de). Alegacion Juridica por D. Fernando de Ortega y D. Juan de Larivas en el Pleyto con D. Dom. de la Canal, y D. J. G. de Retana. *Mexico.* 1714. Folio. 57674

ORTEGA (F.) Poesias del Ciudano F. Ortega. *Toluca.* 1834. 18mo, pp. 95. 57675

ORTEGA Y PIMENTEL (Isidro Joseph). Fùnebre Pompa, Magnificas, Exèquias, que a la justa memoria del Illmo. Señor Doct. Juan de Castañeda Valasques y Salazar, Obispo de Panama y el Cuzco; solemnizo en la Metropolitana de la ciudad de los Reyes ... . *Lima: En la Oficina nueva de la Calle de la Coca.* 1763. 4to, pp. (38), 41, (16). J.C.B. 57676

Also: Oracion cominatoria, que, a fin de corregir los excesos de algunos Profesores de las Artes subalternas à la Medecina, dixo el dia 4 de Octubre 1764. ... [*Lima.* 1764.] 4to, (37) leaves. J.C.B.

ORTEGA (Jesus G.) ... General Gonzales Ortega and his Nine Endorsers versus the Mexican Nation and the Constitutional President ... . [n. p. 1866?] 8vo, pp. 8. H. 57677

ORTEGA. Parte general que da al supremo gobierno de la nacion respecto de la defensa de la plaza de Zaragoza. ... *Zacatecas.* 1863. 4to, pp. 185. 57678

ORTEGA. The Presidency of Mexico. Protest of General Jesus Gonzales Ortega, ... against the Decrees of Senor Benito Juarez, Ex-President of the Mexican Republic, issued November 8th, 1865, and his Address to the Mexican Nation ... . *New-York.* 1866. 8vo, pp. 88. H. 57679

[ORTEGA (J. de).] Apostolicos Afanes de la Compañia de Jesus escritos por un Padre de la misma Religion de su Provincia de Mexico. *Barcelona, por P. Nadal.* 1754. 4to, pp. (12), 452, (8), (2). 57680

Beristain assigns this work to Father Joseph Ortega, who was born in Francala in 1700, and became a missionary in the province of Nayarit. The work is a history of the missions in Nayarit and Pimeria alta.

ORTEGA. Doctrina Cristiana, Oraciones, Confesonario, Arte y Vocabulario de la Lengua Cora, por P. Jose Ortega. *Printed by the Bishop of Guadalaxara, Sr. Don Nicolas Gomez de Cervantes.* 1729. 57681

Title from Ludewig. The imprint is probably erroneous.

ORTEGA. Vocabulario en Lengua Castellana, y Cora, dispuesto por el P. Joseph de Ortega, de la Compañia de Jesus ... . Con Licencia. *En Mexico: Por los Herederos de la Viuda de Francisco Rodriguez Lupercio, en la Puente de Palacio. Año de* 1732. 4to, (9) and 43 leaves. 57682

The Cora dialect is that spoken in the mountains of Nayarit, in the State of Jalisco. *See also* Adelung's "Mithridates," Vol. III., part 2, pp. 131–138.

ORTEGA (J. de San Antonio). Parentacion Lugubre de la Sa. Dña. Maria de Llera, y Bayas, Esposa, y Consorte, que fue del D. Joseph de Escandon, Cabellero ... . Quien celebrò à sú Esposa estos solemnes Funerales, Predicado en la Iglesia Colegio de la Santa Cruz de Queretaro ... . *Mexico.* 1764. 4to. 57683

ORTEGA (L.) México Libre. Melodrama heroico en un acto. Por D. Francisco Luis Ortega. *Mexico:* 1821. *En la imprenta de D. Celestino de la Torre.* 4to, pp. 23. 57684

ORTEGA (Manuel). El Trono de Mexico. ... *Mexico.* 1864. 4to, pp. 16. 57685

ORTEGA (T. F.) Memoria sobre los medios de desterrar la Embriaguez. ... *Mejico.* 1847. 8vo. 57686

ORTEL (A.) America seu Novi Orbis descriptio. *Antverpiæ.* 1587. Folio. 57687

Title from Ternaux, No. 172. This is probably the letter-press only to the atlas.

ORTEL. Epitome | dv theatre dv monde | d'Abraham Ortelivs: | Auquel se represente, tant par figures que characteres, la vraye | situation, nature, & proprieté de la terre vniuerselle. | Reueu, corrigé & augmenté de plusieurs Cartes, pour la troisiesme fois. | *A Anvers*, | *de l'Imprimerie de Christofle Plantin, pour Philippe Gallé.* | M.D.LXXXVIII. | Oblong 8vo, (8), 94, and (2) leaves. 94 Maps.

ORTEL. Epitome Theatri Orteliani, praecipuarum Orbis Regionum delineationes, minoribus tabulis expressas, brevioribusque declarationibus illustratas, continens. *Antverpiae, Philippo Gallaeo excudebat Christophorus Plantinus.* 1589. Oblong 8vo, pp. (16), 94 Maps, Table, pp. 3. 57689

ORTEL. Epitome Theatri Orteliani Præcipuarum Orbis Regionum delineationes ... . Nova editio ... . *Antverpiæ, Philippo Gallæo excudebat Arnoldus Coninx.* MDXCV. Oblong 8vo, (6) and 104 leaves. 109 Maps. P. + *Antverpiæ.* 1601. 111 Maps.

ORTEL. L'Epitome du theatre de l'univers d'Abraham Ortelius. Nouvelle recogneu et augmenté par M. Coignet. *Antverpiæ.* 1602. Oblong 8vo. 123 Maps. 57691

ORTEL. Synonyma geographica ... . *Antverpiæ, Ex officina Christophori Plantini* ... . 1578. 4to, pp. 419. P. 57692

[ORTEL.] Thea | trvm | orbis | terra | rvm. | [Colophon:] *Auctoris ære & cura impressum absolutumque* | *apud Ægid. Coppenium Diesth. Antverpiæ* M.D.LXX. Folio, Engraved Title, and (7) leaves. 53 Maps engraved by Hogenberg, Index, 27 leaves. C.

The first and most rare edition of one of the most celebrated geographical works of the fifteenth century, of which there have been many subsequent editions, and in which the number of maps has been much increased. Stevens remarks: "A thorough study of Ortelius is of the last importance to the student of the geography of the western hemisphere. He was a bibliographer, a cartographer, and an antiquarian, as well as a good mathematician and geographer, and what is of infinite importance to us now, he gave his authorities. Many of the rampant errors that disturb and puzzle us can be treed and flayed by the help of Ortelius. It was Ortelius' famous list of authorities that first gave to Humboldt the hint that Hylacomilus and Waldseemuller were one and the same person, the key to his investigations upon the St. Dié fraternity, and the Vespucci voyages."

[ORTEL.] Thea | trvm | orbis | terra | rvm | [Colophon:] *Auctoris ære & cura impressum absolutumque* | *apud Ægid. Coppenium Diesth*, | *Antverpiae* | M. D. LXXI. | [Followed by:] Additamentvm | theatri orbis | terrarvm | Cum Imperatoriæ & Regiæ Maiestatum Priuilegiis. | cIↄ. Iↄ. LXXIII. | *Antuerpiæ Aduaticorum.* | Folio, pp. (16), 53 Maps, (62); Additamentvm, pp. (2), 18 Maps. C., S.

ORTEL. Theatre de l'Univers. *Anvers.* 1574. Folio. 69 Maps. 57695

The text varies considerably, but the sixty-nine maps are just the same as in the German edition of 1572. Some copies have the text in Latin.

ORTEL. Ortelii Theatrum Orbis Terrarum denuo recognitum ... *Antverpiæ.* 1575. Folio. 70 Maps. + [Colophon:] *Auctoris ære & cura impressum, absolutùmque apud Christophorum Plantinum, Antverpiae*, M.D.LXXIX. Folio. 93 Maps. BA. 57696

ORTEL. Ortelii Theatrum Orbis Terrarum, opus nunc tertio ab ipso recognitum, multis locis castigatum et novis tabulis auctum. *Antverpiæ.* 1589. Parergon and Nomenclator, 1584. Folio. 167 Maps on 100 leaves; Parergon, 12 Maps. 57697

This atlas is the first European book in which Chinese characters appeared.

ORTEL. Ortelii Theatrum Orbis Terrarum ... . [*Antverpiæ.*] 1591. Colophon, 1592. Folio. Theatrum, 108 Maps, Parergon, 26 Maps, Nomenclator, 43 leaves. 57698

ORTEL. Ortelii Theatrum Orbis Terrarum, opus nunc denuo ab auctore recognitum ... *Antverpiæ.* 1592. Folio. 201 Maps on 134 sheets. 57699

Of equal importance with the first edition, if it be not indeed more valuable.

ORTEL. Theatrum Orbis Terrarum Abrahami Orteli Antverp ... . Editio vltima. *Antverpiæ, Apud Ioannem Bapt. Vrintivm. Anno* cIↄ. Ic. CIII. Folio. Maps and Plates. + Editio novissima aucta, ed. a Balth. Moreto. *Antverpiæ, ex officina Plantiniana.* 1624. Folio. Maps. A. 57700

ORTEL. Theatro del Mondo ... ridotto in forma piccola, augumentato di molte carte nuove ... . Tradotto in lingua italiana da Giovanni Paulet. *Anversa, nella Stamperia Plantiniana.* 1593. Square 8vo. 107 Maps, with descriptive Text. 57701

ORTEL. Il Teatro del Mondo ... nel qvale distintamente si dimostrano in tauole tutte le Prouincie, Regni, e Paesi del Mondo, al presente conosciuti ... Ridotto dalla forma grande in qvesta piccola [da P. Marie Marchetti]. *Brescia, Appresso la compagnia Bresciana.* 1589. 4to, pp. (8), 215, (12). A. 57702

ORTEL. Teatro del Mondo de Abrahamo Ortelio ... con la vita dell' Autore. Traslato in Lingua Toscana del Sigr. Filippo Pigafetta. *In Anversa, Appresso Giovanni Bapta. Vrintio.* cIↄ.Iↄc.-VIII. Folio, pp. lv, 128. Maps. S. + [*Ibid.*] 1612. 57703

ORTEL. Theatro del Mondo, nel quale si dà notitia distinta di tutte le Provincie, Regni, e Paesi del Mondo. *Venetia.* 1697. Sm. 8vo. Maps. 57704

ORTEL. Theatrvm Orbis Terrarvm. Theatre, ofte Toonnel des Aerdt-bodems waer inne te seine sijn de Landt-tafelen van de geheele Weerelt; met een corte Verdarenge de seluer. *Antverpen.* 1571. Folio. Maps. 57705

First edition, in Dutch. Though the first Latin edition bears the date of 1570, and may have seen the light before this, yet there are evidences that this Dutch edition was the one in which the work was composed. The maps are each the same.

ORTEL. Theatrum Orbis Terrarum. Theatrum oder Schawplatz des erdbodems, warin di Landtafell der gantzen weldt zu sehen ist, ihietz mitt vielen neuwen Landtafflen gemehret. [n. p.] 1573. [Colophon:] *Durch beuelch des Autors hatt diss Buch gedruckt Gielis von Diest tzo Antorff.* 1572. Folio. Portrait and 69 sheets of Maps. 57706

The rarest issue of the atlas of Ortelius. The map of the New World is singularly correct and full of detail.

ORTEL. Theatrum oder Schawbuch des Erdtkreys ... . *Antorff.* 1580. Folio. Portrait and 93 sheets of Maps. 57707

In this second German issue the text is entirely re-written, and the barbarous language of the edition of 1572 is changed. Twenty-four additional maps are added, of which two have a special value for the American collector.

ORTEL. Theatrum Orbis Terrarum: The Theatre of the whole World, set forth by that excellent geographer, Abraham Ortelius, with historical descriptions of the various countries, ... Translated and printed by John Norton. *London.* 1606. Rl. folio. Portrait, Maps and Plates. 57708

The maps are from the Antwerp edition of 1595. There are other editions with the text abridged, in 12mo.

ORTEL. Abrahami Ortelii Antverpiani | Thesavrvs Geographicvs, | recognitvs et avctvs. | In qvo | Omnium totius terræ regionum, | montium, promontoriorum, collium | ... nomina & | appellationes veteres; additis magna | ex parte etiam recentioribus. | ... *Antverpiæ* | *ex Officina Plantiniana.* | M. D. XCVI. Folio, (361) leaves

Other editions, *Antverpiæ*, 1587, folio, and *Hanoviae*, 1611, 4to.

ORTH (G. S.) Our Duty and Destiny. Speech of Hon. Godlove S. Orth, ... January 11th, 1865. *Washington: Printed by Lemuel Towers.* 1865. 8vo, pp. 8. BA. 57710

[ORTH.] Report of the Committee on Foreign Affairs, on the Memorial of Porter C. Bliss and George F. Masterman, in relation to their Imprisonment in Paraguay ... . *Washington.* 1870. 8vo, pp. (2), xxx, 314. H. 57711

Also: The Case of Father McMahon. The Doctrine of Perpetual Allegiance considered. Speech ... . January 8, 1868. *Lafayette, Indiana.* 1868. 8vo, pp. 8. H.—Financial Questions of the Day. Speech ... December 22, 1869. [n. p. n. d.] 8vo, pp. 8.—Independence of Cuba. Speech ... June 14, 1870. *Washington: F. & J. Rives ... Printers.* 1870. 8vo, pp. 8.—The Island Republics of St. Domingo. Speech ... April 5, 1869. [n. p. n. d.] 8vo, pp. 8.—Speech ... on Treason and its Punishment. January 15, 1864. [n. p. n. d.] 8vo.— ... Speech ... on the Resolution to expel Mr. Long. ... April 14, 1864. [n. p. n. d.] 8vo, pp. 8.—The True Basis of Reconstruction. Speech ... March 10, 1866. [n. p. n. d.] 8vo, pp. 8. H.

ORTIGOSA (J.) Sermon con motivo de la jura de independencia en la iglesia de Nuestra Señora de las asuncion. ... *Mexico.* 1822. 4to, 18 leaves. 57712

ORTIGOSA (Vicente). Cuatro Memorias sobre Puntos de Administracion ... *Mexico: Ignacio Cumplido.* 1866. 4to.

ORTIZ (A.) Los tratados del doctor alonso ortis | Tratado dela herida del rey. | Tratado consolatorio ala princesa de portugal. | Item vna oracion alos reyes en latin y en romance | Item dos cartas mésajeras a los reyes. vna que embio | la cibdad la otra el cabildo dela yglesia de toledo | Tratado contra la carta del prothonotario de lucena | [Colophon:] *Fue imprimido enla* | *muy noble & muy leal cibdad de Se* | *uilla por tres Alemanes cõpañerõs.* | *Enel ano del señor.* M.cccc.xciij. | Folio, 100 leaves. B. 57714

"Contains one of the earliest allusions to the discovery of the Western Hemisphere." —[HARRISSE'S] *Bib. Am. Vet.*, No. 10.

ORTIZ (D.) Vida del Padre F. Diego Ortiz, Protomartire del Ordine del Padre S. Agostino nel Regno del Peru, martirizzato 1571, raccolta dal P. Fulgentio Baldani. *Genova.* 1645. 4to.

ORTIZ DE ZUÑIGA (Diego). Annales | Eclesiasticos, | y Secvlares | de la mvy noble y mvy leal Civdad | de Sevilla, Metropoli de la Andaluzia, | qve contienen svs mas principales Memorias. | Desde el Año de 1246. En que emprendio | conquistarla del poder de las Moros, el gloriosissimi Rey S. Fernando | Tercero de Castilla, y Leon, hasta el de 1671. En que la | Catolica Iglesia le concediò el culto, y titulo | de Bienaventurado. Por D. Diego Ortiz de Zvniga ... . *Año* 1677. *La Imprenta Real, Madrid.* Folio, Engraved Title, pp. (21), 817, (14). B., H. 57716

From the constant use made of this excellent work by Irving, Prescott, Ticknor and Bancroft, it is manifest that it should hold high rank among books relating to America, especially as much that we know of Columbus and his sons Diego and Ferdinand, his brother Bartholomew, Las Casas, Cortes, and many others, is found only in this volume.

Ortiz de Zuñiga. Annales | Eclesiásticos y Secvlares | … . Por Don Diego Ortiz de Zuniga … . Ilustrados y corregidos | por D. Antonio Maria Espinosa y Carzel. *Madrid, Imprenta Real.* 1795–96. 5 vols., sm. 4to, pp. (18), 434; (4), 478; (2), 454; (2), 444; 471. B. 57717

Ortiz de Cervantes (J.) Memorial, que presente a Su Magestad el Licenciado Juan Ortiz de Cervantes, Abogado, y Procurador General del Reyno del Piru, y Encomenderos, sobre pedir remedio del daño, y diminucion de los Indios; y propone ser medio eficaz la perpetuydad de Encomiendas. [*Lima.*] *Año* MDCXIX. Folio, 19 leaves. 57718

A very rare piece. Ternaux, Nos. 434 and 490, gives brief titles of two other editions. *See also* Vol. III., No. 11716.

Ortiz (J.) Defensa de la carta del Sagrario de Guadalajara, reimpresa en "La Cruz" el 13. de Agosto, é impugnada en el Apendice que se ha publicado en el "Siglo XIX" el 14. de Noviembre 1857. *Guadalajara.* 1857. 8vo, pp. 71. 57719

Ortiz (L.) Origen, y Institvto de la Compañia de Jesus, en la Vida de San Ignacio de Loyola su Padre, y Fvndador, qve ofrece a las seis mvy Religiosas, y Apostolicas Prouincias de la Compañia de Jesus de las Indias Occidentales, qve comprehende la Assistencia General en Roma, por la Corona de Castilla el Hermano Lorenzo Ortiz. … *Sevilla.* 1679. Folio, pp. (16), 197, (2). H. 57720

Ortiz (L. G.) Poesias de D. Luis G. Ortiz. Edicion del Republicano. *Mexico.* 1866. 12mo, pp. iv, 546. 57721

Ortiz de la Torre (M.) Discurso sobre los medios de fomentar, la poblacion, riqueza e ilustracion de los Estados Unidos Mexicanos, premiado en el certamen literario, con que el colegio de San Ildefonso de Mexico recibio a su alumno el Ciudadano Guadalupe Victoria primer presidente de la Républica: su autor Manuel Ortiz de la Torre. *Mexico.* 1825. Sm. 8vo, pp. 68.

Ortiz (S.) Apuntes biográficos del General de la Nacion Nicanor Caceres, por Severo Ortiz. *Buenos Aires.* 1867. 12mo, pp. 206. 57723

Ortiz (T.) México considerado como Nacion independiente y libre, ó sean algunas indicaciones sobre los deberes mas esenci-

ales de los Mexicanos; Por Tadeo Ortiz. *Burdeos: Imprenta de Carlos Lawalle Sobrino.* 1832. 8vo, pp. 598, (2). BA. 57724

A most valuable contribution towards a history of Mexico.

Ortiz de Ayala (T.) Resumen de la estadistica del imperio mexicano. … *Mexico.* 1822. 12mo. 57725

Orto (Garcia). *See* Orta (Garcia de).

Orton (Edward). *See* Ohio Geological Survey, No. 56926.

Orton (H. S.) The History and Development of Races. An Address before the State Historical Society of Wisconsin … 23 February, 1869. By the Hon. Harlow S. Orton. *Madison.* 1869. 8vo, pp. 32. 57726

Orton (J.) The Andes and the Amazon; or, Across the Continent of South America. By James Orton, M.A. … *New York: Harper & Brothers.* 1870. 12mo, pp. 356. Plates and Map. BA. 57727

Orton (J. R.) Camp Fires of the Red Men; or, a Hundred Years Ago. By J. R. Orton. … *New York: J. C. Derby.* 1855. 12mo, pp. 401. Plates. + [*Ibid.*] 1857 and 1859.

A novel in which the red men appear but seldom.

Orton (W.) Government Telegraphs. Argument of William Orton, President of the Western Union Telegraph Company … . *New York.* 1870. 8vo, pp. 52. B. 57729

Orville (André Guillaume C. d'). Histoire | des | Différens Peuples | du Monde, | contenant | Les Cérémonies | religieuses et civiles, | l'origine des religions, | leurs sectes & superstitions, & les mœurs & | Usages de chaque nation; | dédiée | a Monseigneur | Le Duc de la Vrilliere, | Ministre et Secretaire d'Etat. | Par M. Contant Dorville. | … | *A Paris,* | *Herissant* … [*et*] *J. P. Costard* … . M. DCC. LXX. 6 vols., 8vo. 57730

Orville. Geschichte der verschiedenen Völker … Gebräuche, Ursprung der Religionen, Sekten, Aberglauben, Sitten und Gewohnheiten enthaltend … . Aus dem Französischen des Herrn C. Dorville. *Hof: Vierling.* 1773–1777. 8vo. 57731

Orvis (J. U.) … An Estimate of the Public Services and Personal Character of Joseph U. Orvis, Esq., … of … New York. [By Claudius B. Conant.] *New York: S. W. Green, Printer.* 1870. 8vo, pp. 16. 57732

O'Ryan (M.) A Letter on the Yellow Peruvian Bark, containing an Historical Account of the first Introduction of that Medicine into France, and A Circumstantial Detail of its Efficacy in Diseases. By Michael O'Ryan, M.D. *London.* 1794. 8vo. 57733

Os Coyuntura todas las fiestas, y demàs dias movibles, que corren desde la Septuagesima hasta el fin del Adviento de qualquier año, preterito, presente, y futuro. *Mexico.* 1757. 4to, pp. (6), 30. Table. 57734

Os Garimpeiros. *See* [Cunha Barbosa], Vol. V., No. 17945.

Os Indios Bravos. e O S'r. Lisboa, Timon 3°. pdo auter da "Historia geral de Brazil." Apostilla e nota G aos n°s 11 e 12 de jornal de Timon; contendo 26 cartas ineditos de jornalista, e um extracto de folbeto "Distribe contra a Timonice, etc. (En parte agora de nove reimpressa.) *En Lima.* 1867. 4to, pp. iv, 124. 57735

Os liuros. *See* [Castenheda (F. L. de)], Vol. III., No. 11385

Os Orizes conquistados. *See* [Mascarenhas (J. F. de M.)]

Os Partidos. *Rio de Janeiro.* 1866. 8vo, pp. 32. 57736

Osage Language. Washashe Wageressa Pahugreh Tse. The Osage First Book. *Boston: Printed … by Crocker & Brewster.* 1834. 18mo, pp. 126. BA. 57737

The Osage Treaty. [n. p. n. d.] 8vo, pp. 8. H. 57738

See also Vol. XII., No. 48145.

Osander, *pseudon.* Miscellaneous Poems, on Moral and Religious Subjects: By Osander [*i. e.* Benjamin Allen]. … *Hudson: Printed by Wm E. Norman.* 1811. 12mo, pp. 180. + *New York: Printed by J. Seymour.* 1812. 18mo, pp. 180. BA. 57739

[Osbaldistun] (R.) A Sermon … before the Society for the Propagation of the Gospel in Foreign Parts; … February 21, 1752. By … Richard Lord Bishop of Carlisle. *London: Edward Owen.* MDCCLII. 4to, pp. 71. 57740

Osbon (A. M.) The Duty of America to Her Emigrant Citizens: A Sermon preached … November 25, 1848. By Abiathar M. Osbon … . *New-York: Joseph Longking, Printer.* 1848. 8vo, pp. 32. 57741

Osbon (Bradley S.) Hand Book of the United States Navy: being a compilation of all the principal Events in the History of every vessel in the United States Navy, from April, 1861, to May, 1864. Compiled … by B. S. Osbon. *New York: D. Van Nostrand.* 1864. 8vo, pp. iv, 277. B., C. 57742

Also: Cruise of the United States Flag-Ship, Hartford, 1862–'63. … *New York.* 1863. 8vo.

Osborn (A.) Field Notes of Geology. A. Osborn. … *New-York: Sherman & Co.* 1858. 12mo, pp. 82. H. 57743

Osborn (B.) Farewell Sermon at Tinmouth, Oct. 28, 1787. By Benjamin Osborn. *Bennington, Vermont.* 1788. 8vo.

Also: Truth Displayed; in a Series of Elementary Principles, illustrated and enforced by Practical Observations. … *Rutland, Vt.: Fay and Davidson.* 1816. 8vo, pp. 626.

Osborn (C.) Journal of that Faithful Servant of Christ, Charles Osborn, containing an account of many of his travels and labours in the Work of the Ministry, and his Trials and Exercises in the Service of the Lord, and his defense of Truth, … *Cincinnati: Printed by Achilles Pugh.* 1854. 8vo. 57745

Contains the testimony of Clear Lake Monthly Meeting of Anti-Slavery Friends.

Osborn (D.) An Oration … . Delivered, … February 22nd. 1820. By David Osborn, Esq. … *Albany: Printed by G. J. Loomis.* 1820. 8vo, pp. 14. BA. 57746

Osborn (Elbert). Autobiography of Elder Osborn, an Itinerant Minister of the Methodist Episcopal Church. Sixth Edition. To which is added a brief Memoir of Rev. Hezekiah Calvin Wooster. *New York: Carlton & Porter.* 1865. 16mo, pp. 240.

Osborn. Passages in the Life and Ministry of Elbert Osborn, an Itinerant Minister of the M. E. Church, illustrating the Providence and Grace of God. Written by Himself. *New-York: The Author.* 1847. 18mo, pp. 158. C. 57748

Osborn (E.) The Pastor of the Old Stone Church. Mr. Hotchkins' Memorial, Judge Elmer's Eulogy, and Mr. Burt's Address, Commemorative of Rev. Ethan Osborn, late Pastor of the First Presbyterian Church, Fairfield, N. J. *Philadelphia.* 1858. 12mo, pp. 144. S. 57749

Osborn (H. S.) The Metallurgy of Iron and Steel, … with special reference to American Materials and Processes. By H. S. Osborn … . *Philadelphia: Henry Carey Baird* … . 1869. Rl. 8vo, pp. xx, 17–972. 6 folded Plates. B. 57750

Osborn (J.) A Few Observations regarding the Tariff of Duties upon Foreign Wines & Spirits. By John Osborn … . *New-York: Henry Spear, Printer.* [1866.] 8vo, pp. (2), 8. H.

[Osborn (Laughton).] Arthur Carryl, a Novel, Cantos First and Second. … *New York: D. Appleton and Company.* M.DCCC.-XLI. 8vo, pp. lvii, 357. B., C. 57752

Some of the poems are on historical subjects.

[Osborn.] Confessions of a Poet. *Philadelphia.* 1835. 2 vols., 12mo. 57753

"I do not think that a better book of its kind has been written in America."—E. A. Poe.

[Osborn.] Sixty Years of the Life of Jeremy Levis. *New York.* 1831. 2 vols., 12mo. 57754

[Osborn.] The Vision of Rubeta, an Epic Story of the Island of Manhattan. With Illustrations done on Stone. … *Boston: Weeks, Jordan, and Company.* M DCCC XXXVIII. 8vo, pp. xviii, (2), 424. 4 Plates. BA. 57755

An attack on W. L. Stone, Chas. King, and the "Commercial Advertiser." E. A. Poe is said to have asserted that it was the only American satire ever written. It elicited: "A Critical Examination of the Poem entitled 'The Vision of Rubeta.' With an Inquiry concerning its Author." [*New York,*] *April,* 1839. 8vo, pp. vii, 42. Critique of the Vision of Rubeta. A Dramatic Sketch in One Act. By Autodicus. … [n. p.] 1838. 8vo.

Also: Calvary—Virginia Tragedies … *New York: Doolady.* M DCCC LXVII. 8vo, pp. (8), 200.—Dramatic Works. … Tragedies. *New York: American News Company.* 1870. 12mo, pp. 605.—The Montanini Poetry. … *New York.* 1868. 12mo.

Osborn (S.) The Case and Complaint of Mr. Samuel Osborn, late of Eastham; as it was represented in a Letter to Rev. Dr. Colman, to be communicated by him to the Convention. *Boston.* 1743. 8vo, pp. 29. 57756

The author was dismissed for Arminianism.

Osborn (S.) Familiar Letters, written by Mrs. Sarah Osborn and Miss Susanna Anthony, late of Newport, Rhode-Island. … *Newport (R. I.).* 1807. 12mo, pp. 170. 57757

Osborn (S.) An Oration, delivered at Newburgh … on the 4th of July, 1798. By Selleck Osborn. [n. p. n. d.] 12mo.

Also: An Oration commemorative of American Independence, delivered … at New Bedford, July 4, 1810. … *Boston.* 1810. 8vo.—Poems … . *Boston: J. P. Orcutt, Printer.* [1823.] 12mo, pp. (2), x, (1), 13–200, (2). H.

Osborn (S.) The Discovery of the North-West Passage. *See* M'Clure (R. J. Le M.), Vol. XI., No. 43073.

Osborn. The Polar Region, or a Search after Sir John Franklin's Expedition. By Lieut. Sherard Osborn … . *New York: A. S. Barnes & Co.* 1854. 12mo, pp. 216. 57759

This is the same as the following, with a different title-page only.

Osborn. Stray Leaves from An Arctic Journal; or, Eighteen Months in the Polar Regions, in search of Sir John Franklin's Expedition, in the years 1850–51. By Lieut. Sherard Osborn, commanding H. M. Vessel, "Pioneer." … *London.* 1852. Post 8vo, pp. x, 320. + *New York: George P. Putnam.* M. DCCC. LII. 12mo, pp. 216. + [*Ibid.*] MDCCCLV. + To which is added the Career, Last Voyage, and Fate of Captain Sir John Franklin. New Edition. *William Blackwood and Sons, Edinburgh.* 1864. Sm. cr. 8vo, pp. x, 334. 57760

Also: The Career, Last Voyage, and Fate of Captain Sir John Franklin. *London.* 1860. 18mo, pp. 111, (1). B.—On the Exploration of the North Polar Region. … [*London.* 1865.] 8vo, pp. 31, (1). H.

[Osborne (Cyrus Pearl).] The Catholic Congregational Church, Bristol, R. I. … *Providence: Hammond, Angell & Co., Printers.* 1867. 8vo, pp. 15. 57761

Osborne (G. G.) Poetical Miscellany. By George Gerry Osborne. *Newburyport, Mass.* 1793. 12mo. W. 57762

Osborne (J.) Guide to the … British and Foreign West Indies, Mexico, and Northern South-America. … By John Osborne. *London: Printed by Walton & Mitchell.* [n. d.] Fcap 8vo, pp. viii, slip, 208. Map. + *London.* 1843. Fcap 8vo, pp. 216. + Second Edition, Enlarged. [*Ibid.*] 1844. Fcap 8vo, pp. 332. + Third Edition. [*Ibid.*] 1845. Fcap 8vo, pp. xliv, 310. B.

Osborne (P.) Oration to the People of Color, of New Haven, assembled at Wallingford, to celebrate the Fourth of July. By Peter Osborne. *New Haven.* 1835. 8vo. W.

[Osborne (Thomas).] A | Collection | of | Voyages and Travels, | Consisting of | Authentic Writers in our own Tongue, which have | not before been collected in English, or have only been abridged | … Continued with | Others of Note, that have published Histories, Voyages, | Travels, Journals or Discoveries in other Nations and | Languages, | Relating to | Any Part of the Continent of Asia, Africa, America, | Europe, or the Islands thereof, from the earliest Account to the | present Time. | … | Compiled | From the … valuable Library of the late | Earl of Oxford. | … | Containing, | Either a General Account of the Dis-

covery of those Countries, or an | abstract of their Histories … . *London: Thomas Osborne.* MDCCXLV–XLVII. 2 vols., folio, pp. (4), xii, lxiii, 873, (30); (2), 931. BA. 57765

A necessary accompaniment to Churchill's "Collection," all the works being different. They do, in fact, form Vols. VII. and VIII. of that collection. *See* our Vol. III., No. 13015. They are familiarly known as the "Oxford Collection," but are also sometimes called the "Harleian Collection of Voyages and Travels," and include on America, Galvano's "Discoveries" by Hakluyt, Drake's "World Encompassed," Dunton's "Journal," Le Maire's "Canaries," Castell's "America," De Monts' "Nova Francia," Warren's "Surinam," etc.

Osborne (T. B.) Speech of Mr. Osborne, of Connecticut, on the Sub-Treasury Bill, … June 3, 1840. *Washington: Printed by Gales and Seaton.* 1840. 8vo, pp. 20. B. 57766

Osceola. *See* [Simms (William G.)]

Osculati (G.) Esplorazione delle Regioni Equatoriali lungo il Napo ed il Fume delle Amazzoni Frammento di un Viaggio fatto nelle due Americhe negli anni 1846–47–48 Di Gaetano Osculati … . *Milano: Typographia Bernardino.* 1850. 8vo. B.

Indian vocabularies, pp. 281–300.

Osculati. Note d'un Viaggio nella America Meridionale … negli anni 1834–35–36 Di Gaetano Osculati … *Milano Tipografia e Libreria di Giuseppe Chiusi* 1844. 8vo, pp. 51. A.

Also: Viaggio per il Napo al Pará. *Milano.* 1849. 8vo.

Osés (G. R.) Ministro de la audiencia territorial, satisfaccion al publico. … *Mexico.* 1820. 4to, pp. 16. 57769

Osgood (D.) A Letter on the Yellow Fever of the West Indies. By Daniel Osgood … . *New-York: Elam Bliss.* 1820. 8vo, pp. 72. B., N. 57770

Also: Cautions to Seamen and other Voyagers for Shunning the Yellow Fever. … *Boston: Printed by Sewell Phelps.* 1821. 8vo, pp. 20. B.

[Osgood (David).] The Devil Let Loose … . A Discourse … the Day of the National Fast, April 25, 1799. *Boston: Samuel Hall.* 1799. 8vo, pp. 16. BA. 57771

Osgood. A Discourse delivered February 19, 1795, the Day … for a General Thanksgiving Through the United States. By David Osgood … . *Printed by Samuel Hall,* … *Boston.* 1795. 8vo, pp. 30. BA. + Third Edition. [*Ibid.*] 57772

Osgood. A Discourse … on the Day of … Thanksgiving, November 19, 1795. By David Osgood, A.M. … *Printed by Samuel Hall, Boston.* 1795. 8vo, pp. 32. BA. 57773

Osgood. A Discourse, Delivered December 29, 1799, the Lord's-Day immediately following the Melancholy Tidings of the Loss sustained by the Nation in the Death of its most Eminent Citizen, George Washington … . By David Osgood, D.D. Pastor of the Church in Medford. … *Printed by Samuel Hall,* … *Boston.* 1800. 8vo, pp. 19. BA., H., M., N. 57774

Osgood. A Discourse, Delivered … May 31, 1809, being the Day of General Election. By David Osgood … . [*Boston:*] *Russell & Cutler, Printers.* 1809. 8vo, pp. 28. BA. + Second Edition. [*Ibid.*] 57775

Osgood. … A Sermon … Annual Thanksgiving, November 20, 1794. By David Osgood … . *Printed by Samuel Hall,* … *Boston.* MDCCXCIV. 8vo, pp. 29. + Second Edition. [*Ibid.*] + Third Edition. [*Ibid.*] MDCCXCV. 8vo, pp. 29. + *Philadelphia, reprinted.* M.DCC.XCV. 8vo, pp. 31. + *Newburyport: Printed by Blunt & March.* MDCCXCV. 12mo, pp. 24. H. + *Albany, N. Y.* 1795. 8vo. W. 57776

Osgood. Sermons by … Rev. David Osgood, D.D. … *Boston: Cummings, Hilliard, & Co.* 1824. 8vo, pp. 469. 57777

Osgood. A Solemn Protest against the late Declaration of War, in a Discourse, delivered on the next Lord's Day after the Tidings of it were received. By David Osgood, D.D. … *Cambridge: Printed by Hilliard and Metcalf.* 1812. 8vo, pp. 20. B. + Second Edition. *Exeter: Printed by C. Norris & Co.* 1812. 8vo, pp. 16. B., BA. 57778

Also: … Discourse … before the Annual Convention of … Ministers of Massachusetts, In Boston, May 31, 1798. … *Printed by Samuel Hall,* … *Boston.* 1798. 8vo, pp. 32. N.— … Discourse … at the Ordination of the Rev. Leonard Woods in … Newbury December 5, 1798. … *Newburyport: Printed by Angier March.* 1799. 8vo, pp. 32.—A Discourse … delivered … May 5, 1802, at the [Dudleian] Lecture … . *Cambridge: Printed by William Hilliard.* 1802. 8vo, pp. 36.—A Discourse … February 4, 1803, at the Funeral of the Rev. Joseph Roby, … Lynn … . *Boston: Printed by Munroe and Francis.* 1803. 8vo, pp. 26.—A Discourse … at Cambridge in the hearing of the University April 8, 1810. … *Cambridge: William Hilliard.* 1810. 8vo, pp. 40. + Second Edition. [*Ibid.*]— … A Sermon … Thanksgiving, December 11, 1783 … . *Boston: Printed by T. & J. Fleet.* 1784. 8vo, pp. 35. N.— … A Sermon delivered at the Introduction of the Rev. Peter Thatcher To the Pastoral Care of the Church … in Brattle-street, Boston, January 12th, 1785. … *Boston: Printed by Edward Draper.* M,DCC,LXXXV. 8vo, pp. 28.—A Sermon … at the request of the Ancient and Honourable Artillery Company, in Boston, June 2, 1788 … . *Printed by Benjamin Russell,* … *Boston.* 1788. 8vo, pp. 20.— … A Sermon, … at the Ordination of the Rev. Nathaniel Thayer … Lancaster, on the 9th of October, 1793. … *Printed at Boston by Belknap and Hall.* MDCCXCIII. 8vo, pp. 32.— … Sermon … 9th of May, 1798, the Day … for Solemn Humiliation, Fasting, and Prayer. … *Boston: Printed by Samuel Hall.* 1798. 8vo, pp. 27. M.—A Sermon at the Ordination of the

Reverend Converse Francis ... in Watertown, June 23, 1819. ... *Cambridge: Printed by Hilliard and Metcalf.* 1819. 8vo, pp. 22.— ... Two Discourses ... at Malden, in the beginning of the Year 1804. Occasioned by the Setting up a Baptist Society in that place. ... *Boston: Printed by Munroe and Francis.* 1804. 8vo, pp. 67. + Second Edition. *Charlestown: Printed ... by Samuel Etheridge.* 1804. 8vo, pp. 83. BA.

OSGOOD (F. S.) Poems, By Frances S. Osgood. ... *New York: Clark & Austin.* M DCCC XLVI. 12mo, pp. (2), 252. Plate.

OSGOOD. Poems by Frances Sargent Osgood. ... Illustrated by Huntington, Darley, Rossiter, Cushman, and Osgood. *New York: Riker, Thorne & Co.* [n. d.] 8vo, pp. (2), 466. 57780

OSGOOD. A Wreath of Wild Flowers from New England. By Frances Sargent Osgood. ... *London: Edward Churton.* 1838. 12mo, pp. xv, (1), 364. BA. + Second Edition. [*Ibid.*] 1842. 12mo, pp. (2), xv, (1), 368. B. 57781

See also Hewitt (M. E.), Vol. VIII., No. 31643.

OSGOOD (G.) Historical Sketch of School District Number Thirteen, North Danvers: or, as it is known abroad, Danvers Plains: or, by its ancient name, Porter's Plains ... . By George Osgood. *Salem.* 1855. 8vo, pp. 32. BA. 57782

Also: Address, in Danvers, [on] Intemperance ... April 25, 1820. *Salem.* 1820. 8vo, pp. 16. S.

OSGOOD (J.) Discourse ... in Cohasset ... October 27, 1867. By Joseph Osgood, on the Twenty-fifth Anniversary of his Ordination as Pastor of the First Parish. *Boston.* 1868. 8vo, pp. 18.

OSGOOD (*Mr.*) Speech of Mr. Osgood, of Massachusetts; delivered ... May 5, 1834, On the ... Bank of the United States. *City of Washington: Printed by Francis Preston Blair.* 1834. 8vo, pp. 13. B. 57784

[OSGOOD (Samuel)], *and* [LIVINGSTON (Walter).] Board of Treasury. [n. p. 1786.] 4to, pp. 28. N. 57785

This is a report on the establishment of a mint, dated April 8, 1786. Also: Mr. Osgood's Address to the United Whig Club. ... March 22. 1809. [n. p. n. d.] 8vo, pp. 8.

OSGOOD (S.) A Sermon delivered in ... Springfield, Mass., January 25, ... 1849. By Samuel Osgood, ... on the termination of the Fortieth Year of his Ministry. *Springfield: Geo. W. Wilson, Printer.* 1849. 8vo, pp. 33. B. 57786

OSGOOD (S.) American Leaves: Familiar Notes of Thought and Life. By Samuel Osgood ... . *New York: Harper & Brothers.* 1867. 12mo, pp. 380. B. 57787

OSGOOD. Faith and Freedom in America. Sermon at the Consecration of the Church of the Messiah, ... April 2, 1868. By Rev. Samuel Osgood, D.D. ... *New York: Trow & Smith Book Manufacturing Co.* 1868. 8vo, pp. 57. 57788

OSGOOD. New York in the Nineteenth Century. A Discourse ... before the New York Historical Society, ... November 20, 1866. By Rev. Samuel Osgood, D.D. ... *New York: The Society.* MDCCCLXVII. 8vo, pp. 127. + [*Ibid.*] MDCCCLXVIII.

OSGOOD. Our Patriot Scholar. Discourse in Memory of Edward Everett, at Vespers, in the Church of the Messiah, ... January 22, 1865. By Samuel Osgood, D.D. *New York: James Miller.* 1865. Impl. 8vo, pp. 24. Portrait. BA. 57790

Fifty copies only printed.

OSGOOD. ... Two Sermons preached in ... Providence, September 9, 1849, on closing his Ministry there. By Samuel Osgood. *Providence: Joseph Knowles.* 1849. 8vo, pp. 31. 57791

Contains a history of the Westminster Congregational Church and Society. Also: The Coming Church, and its Clergy. Address, ... June 30, 1858. ... Second Edition. *New-York: John A. Gray, Printer.* 1859. 8vo, pp. 32. B.—Farewell Address to the Unitarian Society in Nashua. ... *Nashua: Albin Beard.* 1841. 12mo, pp. 35.—Farewell: Pastoral Letter to the People of the Church of the Messiah ... . *New York: Trow and Smith Book ... Co.* 1869. 8vo, pp. 16. H.—The Hearth-Stone; Thoughts upon Home-Life in our Cities. ... *New-York: D. Appleton and Company.* 1854. 12mo, pp. 290. + Fourth Edition. [*Ibid.*] + Fifth Edition. [*Ibid.*] 12mo, pp. (4), 318. Plate.—Mile-Stones in our Life-Journey. ... *New York: D. Appleton and Company.* 1854. 12mo, pp. 307.— ... An Oration before the Alumni of Harvard University ... July 19, 1860. ... *Cambridge: Sever and Francis.* 1860. 8vo, pp. 50.—An Oration, ... on the Fourth Day of July, 1839, before the Citizens of Nashua ... . *Nashua: Albin Beard.* 1839. 8vo, pp. 40.—Student-Life: Letters and Recollections ... . *New York: James Miller.* [n. d.] 12mo, pp. 164.—Studies in Christian Biography ... . *New York: C. S. Francis and Co.* 1850. 12mo, pp. xi, 395.—Twenty-Five Years of a Congregation. A Discourse ... in the Church of the Messiah, New York, December 7th, 1851. ... *New-York: Printed by J. A. Gray.* 1852. 18mo, pp. 33. *See also* New Hampshire Book, Vol. XIII., No. 52861.

OSGOOD (S. S.) Alvah: a Poem by S. S. Osgood. ... Sketches from the Life of the Author. *Boston.* 1833. 12mo, pp. 34.

O'SHIELL (B. B.) Réponses aux objections contre le Système Colonial aux Antilles ... . *Paris.* 1825. 8vo. 57793

OSHKOSH, *Wis.* Biographical and Statistical History of the City of Oshkosh, Winnebago Co., Wisconsin ... *Oshkosh.* 1867. 8vo, pp. 76. 57794

Directory of ... Oshkosh ... 1857. *Oshkosh.* 1857. 12mo. Continued. 57795

Also: Annual Report and Rules of the Board of Education of ... Oshkosh. *Oshkosh.* 1873. 8vo.

OSINGA (S.) Dagboek mijner Reizen naar Noord-Amerika's Vereenigde Staten, in den jare 1847 gedaan, gevolgd door eenige aanteekeningen des lands. Eerste stuk. *Franeker: T. Telenga.* 1849. 8vo. 57796

OSLER (E.) The Life of Admiral Viscount Exmouth. By Edward Osler ... . *London: Smith, Elder and Co.* 1835. 8vo, pp. xvi, 448. Portrait, Plates, and folded Plan. + *New York: William Jackson.* 1835. 12mo, pp. xii, 287. Portrait, Plates, and folded Plan. B. + A New and Revised Edition. *London: Geo. Routledge & Co.* 1854. Fcap 8vo, pp. xv, 235. Portrait.

Relates his services in America.

OSLER. The Voyage; a Poem written at Sea, and in the West Indies, and illustrated by Papers on Natural History. ... *London.* 1830. Fcap 8vo. 57798

OSLER (L.) ... A Discourse ... at the Dedication of the Advent Chapel, ... Providence, R. I., December 23, 1857. By Lemuel Osler ... . *Boston: Kneeland Street.* 1858. 12mo, pp. 31

[OSMA (J. I. de).] Peru and the United States on a Plain Point of International Law. *London: Printed by Brettell.* 1860. 8vo, pp. (2), 86. H. 57800

OSORIO (D. de S. E.) Qvarta y qvinta parte de la Aravcana de D. Diego de Santisteuan Osorio. ... *Salamanca: S. Renaut.* 1597. 12mo, (8) leaves, Text, 400 leaves, Tabla, 4 leaves. H.

OSORIO. Qvarta y qvinta parte de la Aravcana. De Don Diego de Santisteuan Osorio. ... *En Barcelona. Con licencia de los Ordinarios Año.* M.D.LXXXXVIIJ. *Acosta de Miguel Menescal, mercader de libros.* [Colophon:] *Fue impressa la presente obra en Barcelona en casa de Ioan Amello any* 1598. 12mo, (6) leaves, Text, 246 leaves, Table, 4 leaves. J.C.B. 57802

OSORIO. La Araucana quarta y quinta parte, en que se prosigue y acaba la historia de D. Alonzo de Ercilla, hasta la reduccion del valle de Arauco en el reyno de Chile. Enmendada, corregida en esta tercera impression, y añadida con algunas notas, y indice copioso. *Madrid: Francisco Martinez Abad.* 1735. Folio, pp. (8), Text, 186 and 167. Index. J.C.B. 57803

"Taken as a whole," says Mr. Ticknor, "it is nearly as dull and chronicling as anything of its class that preceded it."—*History Spanish Literature*, II. 465.

OSORIO (J.) De Rebvs,|Emmanvelis Regis Lv-|sitaniæ Invictissimi Virtvte|et Avspicio gestis libri|dvodecim.|Auctore Hieronymo Osorio|Episcopo Sylvensi.|*Olysippone.*|*Apud Antonium Gondisaluũ Typographum.*|*Anno Domini* M.D.LXXJ.|*Cvm Privilegio Regio.*| Folio, pp. 480, (2). C. + *Coloniæ Agrippinæ, Apud Hæredes Arnoldi Birckmanni.* CIↃ.IↃ.LXXIV. 8vo, (16) leaves, Text, 412 leaves, Index, (16) leaves. C. + [*Ibid.*] M.D.LXXVI. 8vo, pp. (86), 374, (48). + [*Ibid.*] M.D.LXXX. 8vo. + [*Ibid.*] *Anno* M.D.LXXXI. 8vo, 368 and (19) leaves. + *Coloniæ. In officina Birckmannica, sumptibus A. Mylij.* M.D.LXXXVI. 8vo, (52), 368 and (19) leaves. C. + [*Ibid.*] M.D.XCVII. 8vo, 368 and (19) leaves. + *Conimbricæ: Ex Typographia Academico-Regia.* M.DCC.LXXXXI. 3 vols., 8vo, pp. xvi, 204, 261, (1); 557, (1); 583, (1). H. + *Coloniæ.* 1795. 8vo. 57804

This history of Portugal contains an account of the early voyages of discovery of the Portuguese to the East Indies, including their discovery of the eastern shores of South America, now known as Brazil. A considerable portion is taken from Castaneda.

OSORIO. Histoire de Portvgal, contenant les entreprises, nauigations, & gestes mémorables des Portugallois, tant en la conqueste des Indes Orientales par eux descouuertes, qu'ès guerres d'Afrique & autres exploits, depuis l'an mil quatre cens nonãte six, sous Emmanuel premier, Ieã troisiesme, & Sebastiã premier du nom. Comprinse en vingt Liures, dont les douze premiers sont traduits du Latin de Ierosme Osorivs, Evesque de Sylues en Algarve, les huit suivants prins de Lopez Castagneda & d'autres historiens. Nouuellement mise en François par S[imon]. G[oulard]. ... *A Paris, De l'Imprimerie de Pierre Chevillot.* 1581. 8vo, (4) leaves, Text, 680 leaves, Index, 21 leaves. J.C.B. 57805

OSORIO. Leven en Bedrijf van Don Emanuel Koning van Portugal, behelzende d'ontdecking van Oost-Indien, en derwaerts de eerste tochten der Portugezen ... . Uit het Latijn ... door F. v. H[oogstraten]. *Rotterdam: F. v. Hoogstraeten.* 1661–1663. 2 vols., 12mo. 57806

A third volume ("beschreven door Kastagnede"), translated from the French, was printed at Rotterdam, 1670.

OSORIO. The History of the Portuguese, during the Reign of Emmanuel: containing All their Discoveries, from the Coast of Africk to the farthest Parts of China; ... Including also, Their Discovery of the Brazils, and Their Wars with the Moors. ... Now first translated into English by James Gibbs. *London: A. Millar.* MDCCLII. 2 vols., 8vo, pp. (4), 376; (2), 388. B.

OSORIO Y BALCON (Juan Prudencio de). Oracion Funebre. Que a la justa memoria de Illmo. Sr. Doct. Juan de Castañeda Velasquez y Salazar, Dignissimo Obispo de la Santas Iglesias de Panama y el Cuzco ... . *Lima: En la Oficina de la Calle de la Coca.* 1763. 4to, 14 leaves. Plate. J.C.B. 57808

OSPINA (P.) Breve Instruccion para el cultivo del Algodon, en Centro-América, escrita por Don Pastor Ospina ... . *Guatemala.* 1864. 8vo, pp. 42. 57809

OSSAYE (M. F.) Les Veillées Canadiennes; Traité élémentaire d'agriculture à l'usage des habitants Franco-Canadiens ... . Par M. F. Ossaye. *Québec: Augustin Côté et Cie.* 1852. 16mo, pp. 150, ii. S. 57810

Also: Nouveau Système de Comptabilité agricole; ... *Montréal.* 1853. 8vo, pp. 35.

OSSERA Y ESTELLA (Joseph Miguel de). El' Fisico Christiano parte primera de la Entrada a su noble Exercicio obra politica. ... *Impressio en Lima.* 1690. 4to. 57811

Osservazioni sull' esame critico del primo viaggio d'Amerigo Vespucci al Nuovo Mondo. [*Firenze.* 1811.] 8vo, pp. 33.

See also Vol. IV., No. 14661, *and* Napione (G. F. G.), Vol. XII., No. 51760, *note.*

OSSOLI (S. M. F. de). At Home and Abroad, or Things and Thoughts in America and Europe. ... By Margaret Fuller Ossoli ... . Edited by her brother, Arthur B. Fuller. *Boston: Crosby, Nichols, and Company.* 1856. 12mo, pp. x, (2), 466. + Second Edition. [*Ibid.*] + Third Edition. [*Ibid.*] BA. 57813

[OSSOLI.] Life on the Lakes: being Tales and Sketches collected during A Trip to the Pictured Rocks of Lake Superior. ... *New-York: George Dearborn.* 1836. 2 vols., 12mo, pp. (4), 270; (4), 275. 2 Plates. H. 57814

[OSSOLI.] Summer on the Lakes, in 1843. By S. M. Fuller. *Boston: Charles C. Little and James Brown.* M DCCC LXIV. 12mo, pp. (4), 256. 7 Plates. B. 57815

OSSOLI. Memoirs of Margaret Fuller Ossoli. *Boston: Phillips, Sampson and Company.* MDCCCLII. 2 vols., 12mo, pp. 351; (2), 352. B. 57816

Also: Art, Literature and the Drama. ... Edited by ... Arthur B. Fuller. *Boston: Brown, Taggard and Chase.* 1860. 12mo, pp. 449.—Life Without and Life Within; or, Reviews, Narratives, Essays, and Poems. ... Edited by Arthur B. Fuller. *Boston: Brown, Taggard and Chase.* 1859. 12mo, pp. 424. + *New York: Tribune Association.* 1869. 12mo, pp. 424.—Literature and Art ... with Introduction, by Horace Greeley.

New York: Fowlers and Wells. 1852. 12mo, pp. (2), viii, 182. B.—Woman in the Nineteenth Century, and kindred Papers ... Edited by ... Arthur B. Fuller. With an Introduction by Horace Greeley. ... *Boston: John P. Jewett & Company.* 1855. 12mo, pp. 428. Portrait. BA.

OSSORIO ET PERALTA (Didaco). Principia Medicinæ: Epitome et totius humani corporis fabrica, seu ex Microcosmi armonia divinum germen ... *Mexici, apud Heredes Viduæ B. Calderon.* 1685. Sm. 4to. 57817

One of the earliest Mexican books on medicine.

OSSORIO (Diego). Americano Seraphico Llanto de esta Provincia del Santo Evangelio, en la bien sentida Muerte de N. Exc. Fr. Juan de Soto, ex Comissario General de Indias. Exequias Honorarias, que los dias 16 y 17 de Dec. 1736. ... *Mexico.* 1737. 4to. 57818

OSSWALD (A.) Abbildungen zu Assal. Nachrichten über die früheren Einwohner von Nord-Amerika. *Heidelberg, bei August Osswald.* [n. d.] Oblong 4to. 10 Plates. 57819

This is a clear case of theft of both plates and text. *See* "Archæologia Americana," I.

OSSWALD (H.) Californien und seine Verhältnisse. Ein unterrichtendes Handbuch für Alle, welche sich um dieses Land interessiren. ... Nach authentischen Quellen bearbeitet von H. Fr. Osswald. *Leipzig: K. F. Köhler.* 1849. 12mo, pp. 130.

OST (N. C.) Samlinger til Kundskab om Grönland. ... *Kjöbenhavn.* 1830. 2 parts, 8vo. 57821

Ost und West-Indischer ... Lust- ... Garten. *See* Franciscus (E.), Vol. VI., No. 25463.

OSTEN-SACKEN (R.) ... Catalogue of the described Diptera of North America. Prepared ... by R. Osten-Sacken. *Washington.* 1858. 8vo, pp. xx, 92. + [*Ibid.*] 1859. 8vo. B.

OSTEN-SACKEN. Monographs of the Diptera of North America. By R. Osten-Sacken. Part IV. *Washington.* 1869. 8vo, pp. xi, 345. 4 Plates. C. 57823

"Smithsonian Institute Miscellaneous Collections," Vol. VIII.

OSTEN-SACKEN. On the Cynipidæ of the North American Oaks, and their Galls. [*Philadelphia.*] 1861. 8vo, pp. 47–72.

From the proceedings of the Entomological Society of Philadelphia, October, 1861. Also many other scientific tracts reprinted from the pages of scientific journals.

OSTERMAYER (H.) Tagebuch einer Reise nach Texas. ... *Biberach.* 1850. 8vo. 2 Plates. 57825

O'SULLIVAN (J. L.) Union, Disunion, and Reunion: a Letter to General Franklin Pierce, Ex-President of the United States. By John L. O'Sullivan ... . *London: Richard Bentley.* 1862. 8vo, pp. 122. BA. 57826

Also: Peace the Sole Chance now left for Reunion. ... *London: Printed by William Brown & Co.* 1863. 8vo, pp. 25.—Recognition: its International Legality, its Justice and its Policy. ... *London: Waterloo & Sons.* 1863. 8vo, pp. 30. H.

OSUNKHIRHINE (P. P.) Wobanaki kimzowi awighigan, P. P. Wzokhilain, kizitokw. *Boston: Printed by Crocker and Brewster.* 1830. 18mo, pp. 90. Folded Table. BA. 57827

OSWALD (E.) The Case of the Commonwealth against Eleazer Oswald, for Contempt of the Supreme Court of Pennsylvania; with Proceedings of the General Assembly ... . *Philadelphia.* 1788. 8vo, pp. 16. W. 57828

Oswald was the editor of the "Independent Gazetteer."

OSWALD (J.) Memorials of the Public Life and Character of the Right Hon. James Oswald, of Dunnikier. ... Correspondence with ... Distinguished Men of the Last Century. *Edinburgh: Archibald Constable and Co.* 1825. 8vo, pp. 23, 418. Portrait. + [*Ibid.*] 1829. 8vo. 57829

Mr. Oswald was a Lord Commissioner of Trade and Plantations; his correspondence includes much that relates to the North American colonies.

Oswegatchie Lead and Smelting Company, St. Lawrence County, New York. *Boston: Geo. C. Rand & Avery.* 1863. 8vo, pp. 16. 57830

OSWEGO, *N. Y.* Annual Report of the Board of Education of Oswego, for 1854. *Oswego.* 1854. 8vo. 57831

Annual Report of the Finances of Oswego. February 20, 1860. [n. p. n. d.] 8vo.—Annual Statement of the Trade and Commerce of Oswego, for 1856. [n. p. n. d.] 8vo. Continued.—Circular. Oswego Training School for Primary Teachers. 1864. [n. p. n. d.] 8vo, pp. 7. H.

A Communication from ... the Board of Trade of ... Oswego, to a Convention of the Friends of the Hoosic Tunnel ... at Fitchburg, Oct. 11th, 1853. *Oswego, N. Y.: Printed by L. A. Winchester.* 1853. 8vo, pp. 10. B. 57832

Oswego and Utica Rail Road Company. Report of Joseph D. Allen, Esq. Chief Engineer, ... September, 1837. *New-York: T. & C. Wood.* 1837. 8vo, pp. 23. 57833

Oswego Board of Trade. Reciprocity with British North America vindicated. *Oswego: Jas. N. Brown, Printer.* 1860. 8vo, pp. 26. 57834

Oswego Directory for 1852–3. *Oswego.* [n. d.] 8vo. Continued. 57835

Oswego and Fulton Directory and History for 1862–3. By A. D. Brigham. *Oswego.* [n. d.] 8vo.—Oswego Directory for 1864 and 1865, with a Synopsis of Incidents and Events transpiring in the War for the Union. Compiled ... by John Fitzgerald. *Oswego: J. N. Brown, Printer.* 1864. 8vo, pp. 334.

Minutes of Proceedings of the Board of Supervisors of the County of Oswego, for 1856. *Oswego.* 1856. 8vo. Continued

Annual Report of the NORMAL AND TRAINING SCHOOL, with Catalogue. 1866. *Albany.* 1866. 8vo.

Catalogue of the OSWEGO CITY LIBRARY. *Oswego, N. Y.* 1857. 18mo, pp. 46. S. 57837

Also: First Catalogue of the Oswego City Library. Founded by Gerrit Smith, 1855. *New York.* 1858. 8vo, pp. 103. S.

OTEIZA Y VERTIZ (J. M. de). Breve Descripcion de la Lápida de la Constitucion colocado en Querétaro á 14 de Octubre de 1820, y Sermon que antes de descubrirse por su muy ilustre ayuntamiento dijo ... el Dr. y Mtro. D. Joaquin Maria de Oteiza y Vertiz. *Mexico.* 1821. 4to, pp. 51. Plate. 57838

OTERO Y BALDILLO (J. A. E. de). Memoria del D. Jos. Ant. E. de Otero y Baldillo el dia 3 Oct. 1796. *Mexico.* 1796. 4to.

OTERO (M.) Relacion de lo Agaecido con el Sr. D. Mariano Otero y el Baron Alleye de Cyprey. Documentos relativos á lo ocurrido últimamente entre el Sr. Alcalde 3 Constitucional D. Mariano Otero, y el Sr. Baron Alleye de Cyprey. [*Mexico.*] 1845. 8vo, pp. 16. 57840

Also: Ensayo sobre el verdadero estado de la cuestion social politica en la Republica Mexicana. ... *Mexico.* 1842. 8vo, pp. 136.—Replica á la defensa que D. José Ramon Pacheco ha publicado en favor de la politica del Gobierno del General Santa-Anna, por lo relativo á las negociaciones diplomaticas de la casa de Alfaro. ... *Mexico.* 1848. 4to, pp. 46, (4).

OTERO (Miguel A.) Pacific Railroad. Speech of Hon. M. A. Otero, of New Mexico, ... May 25, 1858. *Washington: Henry Polkinhorn, Printer.* 1858. 8vo, pp. 15. H. 57841

OTEY (J. H.) ... A Sermon ... at the Consecration of the Right Rev. William Mercer Green, D.D., ... Jackson, Miss. ...

Feb. 24th, 1850. By James Hervey Otey, D.D. ... *New-York: Stanford and Swords.* 1850. 8vo, pp. 43. + [*Ibid.*] 1856. 8vo, pp. 32. 57842

Also: The Triennial Sermon, before the ... Board of Missions of the Protestant Episcopal Church ... September 6, 1838. ... *Philadelphia: C. Sherman & Co. Printers.* 1838. 8vo, pp. 31. BA.

OTHEMAN (E.) Memoirs and Writings of Mrs. Hannah Maynard Pickard; late Wife of Rev. Humphrey Pickard, A.M. ... By Edward Otheman, A.M. ... *Boston: David H. Ela, Printer.* 1845. 8vo, pp. 311. B. 57843

The Other Side of the Question. *See* [Livingston (P.)], x.

The Other Side of the Question. In three parts. I. An Explanation of the proceedings of Eunice Chapman ... against the ... Shakers ... . II. A refutation of the false statements of Mary Dyer ... . III. An account of the proceedings of Abraham Van Vleet, Esq. ... against the ... United Society at Union Village, Ohio. *Cincinnati: Looker, Reynolds & Co., Printers.* 1818. 16mo, pp. 168, vii. + [*Ibid.*] 1819. 57844

The Other Side; or Notes for the History of the War between Mexico and the United States. ... Translated from the Spanish, and Edited, with Notes, by Albert C. Ramsey. ... *New York: John Wiley.* 1850. 12mo, pp. xv, (1), 458. • 9 Portraits and 14 folded Plans. BA. 57845

The Other Side: or some Reasons against the Removal of an Ancient Landmark. By a Member of the Newark Presbytery. ... *Newark, N. J.* 1850. 8vo, pp. 30. B. + No. II. [*Ibid.*] 8vo, pp. 41. 57846

OTHOA (José Gabriel). Al Congreso nacional. ... *Carácas.* 1865. 8vo, pp. 30. 57847

OTIS (A.) An Account of the Discovery of an Ancient Ship on the Eastern Shore of Cape Cod. By Amos Otis ... . *Albany: J. Munsell.* 1864. 8vo, pp. 10. B. 57848

OTIS (Belle), *pseudon.* *See* [Woods (C. H.)]

OTIS (C.) Oration at Scituate [Mass.], July 4, 1800. By Cushing Otis. *Boston.* [n. d.] 12mo. W. 57849

OTIS (C. N.) Specifications ... for a State Arsenal ... Buffalo, N. Y. ... *Buffalo.* 1858. 8vo. S. 57850

OTIS (F. N.) Illustrated History of the Panama Railroad; ... By F. N. Otis, M.D. *New York: Harper & Brothers.* 1861. 12mo, pp. 263. + Second Edition, Revised and Enlarged. [*Ibid.*] 1862. 8vo, pp. 273. C. 57851

Also: Isthmus of Panama. History of the Panama Railroad; and of the Pacific Mail Steamship Company. ... *New York: Harper & Brothers.* 1867. 16mo, pp. 317. 30 Plates, and Map. C.

OTIS (G.) A Sermon ... at Cambridge, July 30, 1826, on ... Re-opening the Episcopal Church. By George Otis ... . *Cambridge: Printed by Hilliard, Metcalf, and Co.* 1826. 8vo, pp. 13. BA. 57852

OTIS (George A.), *and* WOODWARD (Joseph J.) Reports on the Extent and Nature of the Materials available for the preparation of a Medical and Surgical History of the Rebellion. *Philadelphia.* 1865. 4to. C. 57853

See also our Vol. XI., No. 47307.

OTIS (H. G.) Eulogy on Gen. Alexander Hamilton, pronounced at ... Boston, July 26, 1804. By Hon. Harrison G. Otis, Esq. *Boston: Printed by Manning & Loring.* 1804. 8vo, pp. 24. + Second Edition. [*Ibid.*] + *New York: Isaac Collins & Son.* 1804. 8vo, pp. 23. + *Albany: Printed by Charles R. & George Webster.* 1804. 8vo, pp. 24. B. 57854

OTIS. Letter, from the Hon. Harrison G. Otis, to the Hon. William Heath, ... for Petitioning Congress, against permitting Merchant Vessels to arm. *Boston: Printed by John Russell ...* . 1798. 8vo, pp. 30. BA. 57855

[OTIS.] A Letter to the Hon. Josiah Quincy, ... on the Law of Libel, as laid down by him in the case of Commonwealth *vs.* Buckingham. By a Member of the Suffolk Bar. *Boston: Wells and Lilly.* 1823. 8vo, pp. 62. BA. 57856

Reflections upon the Law of Libel, in a Letter addressed to "a Member of the Suffolk Bar." By a Citizen. *Boston: Wells and Lilly.* 1823. 8vo, pp. 55. B.

[OTIS.] Letters Developing the Character and Views of the Hartford Convention: By "One of the Convention." ... *Washington.* 1820. 12mo, pp. 43. BA. 57857

[OTIS.] Mr. Whipple's Report, and Mr. Otis's Letter. *Boston: Printed by Cassady and March.* 1839. 8vo, pp. 30. B.

The report was to the Rhode Island Legislature on the Atherton Resolutions.

OTIS. An | Oration | delivered July 4, 1788. | At the request of the | Inhabitants of the Town of Boston, | in celebration | of the Anniversary of | American Independence. | By | Harrison-Gray Otis, Esquire. | *Printed by* | *Benjamin Russell* | ... *Boston.* | 1788. 4to, pp. 23. BA. 57859

OTIS. Otis' Letters in Defence of the Hartford Convention, and the People of Massachusetts. *Boston: Simon Gardner.* 1824. 8vo, pp. vii, 103. BA. 57860

Also: An Address to the ... Common Council, of Boston, on the Organization of the City Government, January 5, 1829. ... *Boston: John H. Eastburn, ... Printer.* 1829. 8vo, pp. 15. + January 4, 1830. *Boston.* 1830. 8vo, pp. 11.—An Address ... on the Removal of the Municipal Government, to the Old State House. ... *Boston: John H. Eastburn.* MDCCCXXX. 8vo, pp. 15.— ... Letter ... to ... the Governor. [*Washington.* 1818.] 8vo, pp. 4.—Letter from an aged and retired Citizen of Boston ... on Coercive Measures in aid of Temperance. *Boston: Eastburn's Press.* 1848. 8vo, pp. 11. + Second Edition. [*Ibid.*]—Mr. Otis's Speech ... on the Sedition Law, with Remarks by the "Examiner" on this ... subject. *Boston.* [1818?] 8vo, pp. 35.—Mr. Otis's Speech to the Citizens of Boston [on the American System] ... . *Boston: J. H. Eastburn.* 1830. 8vo, pp. 27.—Speech ... on the Restriction of Slavery in Missouri ... January 25, 1820. [n. p. n. d.] 8vo, pp. 22. BA. *See also* Vol. II., No. 7248, *and* Vol. X., No. 40646.

OTIS (H. G.) The Barclays, of Boston. By Mrs. Harrison Gray Otis. ... *Boston: Ticknor, Reed, and Fields.* M DCCC LIV. 12mo, pp. (4), 419. BA. 57861

OTIS (H. N.) Family Record and Lineage of Isaac Otis, Esq., of New York. By Horatio Nelson Otis. *New York.* 1859. 12mo, pp. 21. M. 57862

OTIS. A Genealogical and Historical Memoir of the Family of Otis; descended from John Otis, an Early Settler at Hingham, in Massachusetts. By Horatio Nelson Otis ... . *Boston: Printed by Coolidge & Wiley.* [n. d.] 8vo, pp. 39. 57863

OTIS. A Genealogical Memoir of the Family of Richard Otis, and collaterally of the Families of Baker, ... &c., &c. Prepared ... by Horatio N. Otis, of New York. *Boston.* 1851. 8vo, pp. (2), 48. B. 57864

[OTIS (James).] Considerations On Behalf of the Colonists. In a Letter to a Noble Lord. *London: J. Almon.* M DCC LXV. 8vo, pp. (2), 52. + Second Edition. [*Ibid.*] B., BA. 57865

Signed "F. A.," and is in reply to "The Objections to the Taxation of our American Colonies," etc. "The author appears to be a staunch North American, fired with the glorious idea of Liberty! and flaming with a patriotic zeal for the rights of his native country; of which he appears to be neither an incompetent judge, nor a weak defender."—*Monthly Review,* XXXIII. 398.

OTIS. The | Rights | of the | British Colonies | Asserted and Proved. | By James Otis, Esq; | ... | *Boston: Printed ... by Edes and Gill* ... . M,DCC,LXIV. 8vo, pp. 80. B. + *London Reprinted, for J. Almon.* [1765.] 8vo, pp. 120. B. + The Second Edition. [*Ibid.*] + Third Edition, corrected. ... *London Reprinted, for J. Williams and J. Almon.* [1766.] 8vo, pp. 120. BA., H. 57866

The writer, a native of Boston, was one of the first and most influential of the controversialists on the popular side. This piece was read in MS. to the Massachusetts House of Representatives, and was published with their knowledge though not by their orders. The Instructions of May, 1764, in the Appendix, were drawn by Samuel Adams. *See* Kennedy's "Memoirs of the Life of Wirt," II. 49. "A very zealous defence of the colonies, tending to prove that ... no part of his Majesty's dominions can constitutionally be taxed without their own consent."—*Monthly Review.*

[OTIS.] The Rudiments of Latin Prosody: with a Dissertation on Letters, and The Principles of Harmony in Poetic and Prosaic Composition. ... *Boston, N E.: Printed by Benj. Mecom.* M,DCC,LX. 12mo, pp. 72. B. 57867

Only a few months after its publication, Otis, "with a tongue of flame and the inspiration of a seer," was arguing the question of Writs of Assistance in the council-chamber in Boston, and "leading the van of American patriots." Very scarce.

[OTIS.] A Vindication | of the | British Colonies, | against | The Aspersions of | The | Halifax Gentleman, | in | His Letter to a Rhode-Island Friend. | ... | *Boston: Printed by Edes & Gill.* 1765. 8vo, pp. 32. + ... *London, reprinted for J. Almon.* 1769. 8vo, pp. (4), 48. BA. + [Another Edition. [*Ibid.*] 1769. 8vo, pp. (4), 158. J.C.B. 57868

See Tudor's "Life of Otis," Chap. XII., Bancroft's "History," IV. 448, V., Chap. XIII, *and* "Monthly Review," XL. 251.

OTIS. A Vindication of the Conduct of the House of Representatives ... . By James Otis ... . *Boston: Printed by Edes & Gill.* 1762. 8vo, pp. 53. BA., C. 57869

[OTIS (James F.)] A Sketch of the Character, ... of William Lloyd Garrison ... . *New-York: Printed by Henry R. Piercy.* 1833. 8vo, pp. 15. B. 57870

OTIS (J. *and* A.) Trial of J. and A. Otis for Murder ... . *Boston.* 1834. 8vo, pp. 44. 57871

OTIS (O. G.) Oration ... on the Centennial Anniversary of the Birth-Day of Washington, in ... Albany, on the twenty-second of February, 1832, by the Hon. Oran G. Otis ... . *Albany: Printed by Croswell, Van Benthuysen and Burt.* 1832. 8vo, pp. 16. BA. 57872

OTIS (W. F.) An Oration ... before the "Young Men of Boston," on the Fourth of July, M.DCCC.XXXI. By William F. Otis. *Boston: Carter, Hendee and Babcock.* M DCCC XXXI. 8vo, pp. 36. B. 57873

This elicited: "A Review of 'An Oration ... before the Young Men of Boston, on the Fourth of July, M.DCCC.XXXI.'" [n. p. n. d.] 8vo, pp. 16. B.

OTIS. The Reviewer Reviewed. A Defence of an Oration ... before the "Young Men of Boston," on the Fourth of July, 1831, By William F. Otis ... . *Boston: Carter, Hendee and Babcock.* M DCCC XXXI. 8vo, pp. 29. BA. 57874

Also: Report of the Trinity Hall Sunday School. ... *Boston.* 1844. 8vo, pp. 11.

Otoe Hymn Book, by Moses Merrill. *Shawanoe Mission: J. Meeker, Printer.* 1834. 12mo. 57875

Iu Otoshki-Kikindiuin. *See* Vol. XIII., Nos. 57090–91.

OTSEGO, *N. Y.* Minutes of the OTSEGO BAPTIST ASSOCIATION, ... 1796. *Cooperstown, N. Y.* [n. d.] 8vo. Continued.

Proceedings of the Board of Supervisors of the County of Otsego, for 1857. *Cooperstown.* 1858. 8vo. Continued. S.

OTT (J. C.) A Crack in the Wall for you to take a Peep in if you please: There are some things in the House. By James Cramer Ott. *Albany.* 1846. 8vo, pp. 20. S. 57878

OTT. Ott Genealogy. Family Register. *Albany.* [n. d.] 8vo, pp. 10. S. 57879

[OTTARSON (F. J.), *and* COLSTON (E. R.)] The Campaign or Scott and Graham Songster. *New York: D. E. Garit.* 1852. 16mo, pp. 64. + Second Edition, enlarged ... . [*Ibid.*] 12mo, pp. 48. H. 57880

Ottawa Language. Abinodjiiag Omasinaiganiwan. *Buffalo: Oliver G. Steele.* 1837. 16mo, pp. 8. BA. + *Detroit: Bagg and Harmon, Printers.* 1845. 16mo, pp. 8. BA. 57881

The Morning and Evening Prayer, translated ... with ... Hymns. *Detroit: Geiger & Christian, Printers.* 1844. 12mo, pp. (2), 59. BA. 57882

The New Testament ... translated into the Ottawa ... by Jotham Meeker ... . *Shawanoe Baptist Mission Press: J. G. Pratt, Printer.* 1841. 16mo, pp. 125. 57883

This comprises only St. Matthew. *See also* Meeker (J.), Vol. XI., Nos. 47375–7.

Otawa Anamie-Misinaigan. ... *Wawiyatanong: Geo. L. Whitney: Ogimisinakisan Manda Misinaigan.* 1832. 16mo, pp. 207.

Otawa Anamie-Misinaigan, Gwaiakossing Anamiewin Ejitwadjig, mi sa Catholique-Enamiadjig Gewabandangig. *Paris: ... E. J. Bailly Ogimisinakisan Manda Misinaigan.* 1837. 12mo, pp. (8), 300. + *Detroit: Eugene T. Smith.* 1842. 12mo, pp. (4), 293. BA. + Troisième édition ... . *Detroit, Wawiiatanong: Bagg & Harmon, Ogi-misinakisanawa Mandan Masinaigan.* 1846. 16mo, pp. 256. BA. 57885

OTTAWA, *Canada.* Ottawa Mining Co. Lands situated in ... Canada East. *Boston: Alfred Mudge & Son, Printers.* 1863. 8vo, pp. 8. B. 57886

Report of Walter Shanly, Esq., on the Ottawa Survey. ... *Toronto.* 1858. 4to, pp. 56. C. 57887

Ottawah, the Last Chief of the Red Indians of Newfoundland. A Romance ... . *London: E. Appleyard.* [n. d.] 8vo, pp. iv, 176. 57888

OTTENS (Reinier en Josua). Atlas van Zeevaert en Koophandel door de geheele Weereldt. ... *Amsterdam.* 1745. Folio.

Contains numerous colored maps relating to America, with text.

OTTER (W.) History of My Own Times. By William Otter. *Emmitsburg (Md.)* 1835. 18mo, pp. 357. C. 57890

OTTMAN (S.) God always Right ... . A Fast Day Sermon, delivered January 4, 1861. By Rev. S. Ottman. *Penn Yan: S. C. Cleveland.* 1861. 8vo, pp. 15. 57891

OTTO (Carolus). Commentatio de Quibusdam Americæ Meridianæ Medicamentis parum cognitis. ... *Hauniæ.* 1841. 4to, pp. 14. M. 57892

OTTO (Ed.) Reiseerinnerungen an Cuba, Nord- und Süd-america ... 1838–41. ... *Berlin.* 1843. 8vo. 57893

OTTO (F.) Diesseits und jenseits des Oceans. ... *Schwerin: Oertzen & Schloepke.* 1852. 12mo, pp. vi, 114. C. 57894

Also: Nordwestliche Bilder. ... *Schwerin: Oertzen & Schloepke.* 1854. 8vo, pp. (2), iv, 172. C.

OTTOLENGHE (J.) Directions for Breeding Silk-Worms, Extracted from a Letter of Joseph Ottolenghe, Esq; late Superin-

tendent of the Public Filature in Georgia. *Philadelphia: Printed by Joseph Crukshank.* M,DCC,LXXI. 8vo, pp. 8. P. 57895

OTTONI (C. B.) Esboço historico das estradas de ferro do Brazil por C. B. Ottoni ... . *Rio de Janeiro: Typ. Imp. e Constit. de J. Villeneuve & C.* 1866. 8vo, pp. 30. H. 57896

OTTONI (J. E.) A suas Altezas reaes o serenissimo Principe Regente, e Princeza do Brasil, por occasião do nascimento de seu augusto neto. *Rio de Janeiro.* 1811. 4to, pp. 3. 57897

OTTONI (T. B.) Circular dedicada aos Srs. Eleitores de Senadores pela provincia de Minas-geraes no quatriennio actual, e especialmente dirigida aos Srs. Eleitores de Deputados pelo 2º districto eleitoral da mesma provincia para a proxima legislatura. Pelo ... Theophilo Benedicto Ottoni. *Rio de Janeiro: Typ. do Correio Mercantil.* 1860. 8vo, pp. (2), 161. + Segunda edição. [*Ibid.*]

OTTONI. Condições para a encorporação de uma Companhia de commercio e navegação do rio Mucury, precedidas de uma exposição das vantagens da empreza por T. B. Ottoni e H. B. Ottoni. *Rio de Janeiro: Typ. Imp. e Const. de J. Villeneuve e Comp.* 1847. 8vo, pp. 51. 57899

OTTONI. Considerações sobre algumas vias de communicação ferreas e fluviaes a entroncar na estrada de ferro de D. Pedro II e no rio de S. Francisco ... . Por Theophile Benedicto Ottoni. *Rio de Janeiro: Typ. do Correio Mercantil.* 1865. 8vo, pp. 39.

Also: Breve resposta, que ao Relatorio da liquidação da Companhia do Mucury por parte do governo ... . *Rio de Janeiro: Typ. de M. Barreto Mendes Campos & C.ª* 1862. 8vo, pp. 96.—A Colonisação do Mucury: Memoria justificativa em que se explica o estado dos colonos estabelecidos no Mucury, e as causas dos recentes acontecimentos n'aquella colonia. ... *Rio de Janeiro: Typographia de Maximiano Gomes Ribeiro.* 1859. 8vo, pp. 58.—Companhia do Mucury. Historia da empreza. Importancia dos seus privilegios. Alcance de seus projectos. ... *Rio de Janeiro: Typ. Imp. e Constit. de J. Villeneuve* ... 1856. 8vo, pp. 47.—Companhia Mucury. Relatorio. [17 de Maio de 1852.] 4to, pp. 4.—Noticia sobre os selvagens do Mucury, em uma carta dirigida pelo sr. Theophilo Benedicto Ottoni ao sr. dr. Joaquim Manuel de Macedo, datada de Philadelphia a 31 de Março de 1858. ... *Rio de Janeiro: Typographia de Maximiano Gomes Ribeiro.* 1858. 8vo, pp. 48.—Relatorio apresentado aos accionistas da Companhia do Mucury ... em 15 de Junho de 1853. *Rio de Janeiro: Typographia Universal de Laemmert.* 1853. 4to, pp. xvi, 37. Table. + Em 7 de Agosto de 1854. [*Ibid.*] 1854. 4to, pp. 37. Table. + Em 8 de Julho de 1855. [*Ibid.*] 1855. 4to, pp. 23. Table. + [23 de Outubro de 1856]. *Rio de Janeiro: Typ. Imp. e Constit. de J. Villeneuve & C.ª* 1856. 8vo, pp. 14. Table. + Em 15 de Outubro de 1857. [*Ibid.*] 1857. 8vo, pp. 33. + Em 1 de Outubro de 1858. [*Ibid.*] 1858. 8vo, pp. 8. Table. + Em 1860. [*Ibid.*] 1860. 8vo.—Relatorio apresentado á assembléa geral dos instituidores do Monte-pio geral ... . *Rio de Janeiro: Typ. Imp. e Constit. de J. Villeneuve & C.ª* 1854. Folio, pp. 16. Table. + [*Ibid.*] 1855. 4to, pp. (6). + [*Ibid.*] 1856. 4to, pp. (6). + [*Ibid.*] 1857. 4to, pp. (5).

OTTSEN (H.) Journael | Oft Daghelijcx-register van de Voyagie na Rio | de Plata, ghedaen met het Schip ghenoemt de Silveren Werelt, het welcke onder | t'Admiraelschap van Laurens Bicker, ende het bevel van Cornelis van Heems-kerck als Commies die | Custen van Guinea versocht hebbende, ende van den Admirael daer na versteken zijnde, alleen voorts seylende | na Rio de Plata, daer in de voorsz. Rieviere by de 60. mijlen opwaerts gekomen wesende, tot Bonas Aeris den Commis (d'welcke op de val- | sche aen-biedinghe van den Gouverneur derselver Plaetsen, om vry te mooghen handelen, aen Landt voer) met noch 8. ander | Personen heeft moeten achter laten, ende van daer wederom wech varende, noch selven seer deyrlijcken na 't af-ster- | ven van bycans all het Volck met die Reste in de Bay Todos los Santos in der Portugijsen handen | ghevallen is, allen Zee-varende Luyden tot eenen Spieghel ende Excempel beschreven | Door den Schipper daer op gheweest zijnde Hendrick Ottsen. | Zeer weerdich om lesen eñ aenmerckelijck om der Spaengiaerden gruwelijcke wreetheyt wille; die trouw, eer ende geloof schandelijck mis-bruycken, | om alle andere Natien, ('tzy met gheweldt oft met schalcheyt) uyt de niewe Werelt te sluyten, daer sy door sulcken middel de verste af werden sullen. | ... | *Gedruckt tot Amstelredam by Cornelis Claesz, op 't Water in 't Schrijf-boeck, Anno* 1603. | Obl. 4to, pp. 49. 5 Plates. + *Tot Amstelredam by Michiel Colijn, Boeck-vercooper op 't Water by de Oude-brugge int Huys-boeck.* 1617. Obl. 4to, pp. 54. 5 Plates. 57901

Concerning this, *see* Tiele, pp. 229–31. In the edition dated 1617, the plates are in the text.

OTUQUIS. Descripcion de la nueva provincia de Otuquis en Bolivia. *Buenos-Ayres.* 1843. 4to. 57902

OUDENARDE (H.) Seven Letters to the Hon. Daniel Horsmanden concerning an unnecessary and cruel Imprisonment. By Hendrick Oudenarde. *New York.* 1766. 8vo. 57903

OUDIETTE (J.) Resultat du Conseil | du 24 May. | Portant adjudication a Maistre Iean Oudiette | des Droits cy-devant appartenant à la Com- | pagnie des Indes d'Occident, & autres. | ... | *St. Germain en laye, le 24 May* 1675. 4to, pp. 10. 57904

Ought Private Vessels to be Exempt from Capture in time of War. The Negative Maintained. *Baltimore.* [n. d.] 8vo, pp. 16. 57905

OULBATH (H. d'). Christophe Colomb. Par M. le Vicomte H. d'Oulbath. *Paris: Cantel et Cie.* 1869. 12mo, pp. 159. Plates

Oultreman (Pierre d'). Tableavx des Personnages signalés de la Compagnie de Jesvs, exposés en la solennité de la canonization des SS. PP. Ignace et François Xavier. ... *A Dovay, chez Balt. Bellère.* 1623. 8vo, pp. (16), 521, (21). 57907

Includes biographies of Jean Carrera, Emmanuel Nobrega, Antoine Sedennio, Joseph Anchieta, Alphonse Barzena, Pierre d'Anasco, and others.

Our Ancestors. *See* [Painter (E. *and* H.)]

Our antient Testimony renewed ... occasioned ... by several unjust charges published against us ... by G. Keith, who hath unfairly ... misrepresented us. Given forth by a Meeting of Publick Friends, and others, at Philadelphia in Pensylvania. *London: ... T. Sowle* ... 1695. 8vo, pp. 10. 57908

Our Book. A Call from Salem's Watch-Towers, in behalf of Destitute Churches of the Unitarian Faith. September 5, 1844. *Salem.* 1844. 12mo, pp. 72. H. 57909

Our Camp Journal. 26th Michigan Infantry. 186–. 4to.

Our Campaign around Gettysburg. *See* Vol. VII., No. 27241

Our Chronicle of '26. *See* [Mellen (G.)], Vol. XI. 47441.

Our City Clubs. *Philadelphia.* 1840. 12mo. 57911

Our Commercial and Political Relations with China, by an American Resident in China. [*Washington.* 1855.] 8vo, pp. 8.

Our Country ... . A National Book, consisting of Original Articles, ... contributed by American Writers. Edited by Mrs. Lincoln Phelps ... . *Baltimore: Printed by John D. Toy.* 1864. 12mo, pp. 423. B. 57913

Our Country; its Capabilities; its Perils, and its Hope. ... A Plea for ... Gospel Institutions in the Destitute Portions of the United States. ... *New York.* 1842. 12mo, pp. 60, cover, (1). + No. 2: A Plea for Home Missions. *New York: American Home Missionary Society.* 1858. 12mo, pp. 144. H. 57914

Our Country's Greatest Danger and true Deliverance. *Cincinnati: American Reform Tract Society.* 186–. 8vo, pp. 8.

Our Cruise in the Confederate States War Steamer Alabama. The Private Journal of an Officer. *Capetown (Africa).* 1863. 8vo, pp. 64. 57916

Our Currency, Some of its Evils, and Remedies for Them. By a Citizen of North Carolina. *Raleigh.* 1861. 8vo, pp. 47.

Our Daily Fare. [*Philadelphia.* 1864.] 4to, pp. 96. BA.

Published under the auspices of the United States Sanitary Commission.

Our First Year. *See* W[alker] (E. A.)

Our Flag. [Patriotic Songs.] *New York.* 1862. 12mo, pp. 41

Our Forefathers; their Homes and their Churches. By [T. A. L.] the Author of "Carolina in the Olden Time." *Charleston (S. C.)* 1860. 12mo, pp. 172. C. 57921

Our Free Trade Policy Examined; ... with an Appendix on the Free Trade and Tariff Question in the United States. Written in 1846. *Toronto.* 1849. 8vo, pp. 14. 57922

Our Globe A Universal Picturesque Album ... . [*Philadelphia.* 184–.] 2 vols., obl. 4to, pp. v, 350. Plates. BA. 57923

Our Great American Horses. No. 1. Hambletonian. *New York: W. Smith.* [1869?] 4to, pp. (2), 12. C. 57924

Our Great Captains. Grant, Sherman, Thomas, Sheridan, and Farragut. *New York: Chas. B. Richardson.* 1865. 12mo, pp. 251. Portraits. 57925

Our Ladys retornes to England, accompanied with S. Frances and the good Jesus of Viana in Portugal who, coming from Brasell, arrived at Clavelly in Devonshire the third of June, 1592. *London.* 1592. 4to, 4 leaves. 57926

Title from Ternaux, No. 188. A volume of excessive rarity; I am unable to trace the sale of a copy.

Our Liberty; The People to the Rescue. [n. p.] 1865 Folio, 1 leaf. 57927

Our Military Experience. *See* [Hassan (A. B.)], VIII. 30809.

Our Mother; a Memorial of Mrs. Susan Charlotte Farley Maxwell. *Boston.* [1860.] 12mo, pp. 312. Portrait, Plate. C.

Our National Finances. Sundry Facts and Divers Figures. *Gardner, Ill.* [n. d.] 8vo, pp. (6). H. 57929

Our National Finances. Three Financial Problems and their Attempted Solution. *Philadelphia.* 1868. 8vo, pp. 16. H.

Our National Finances. What shall be done? *Boston, November* 15, 1862. 8vo, pp. 12. H. 57931

See also [Stetson (A. W.)], [Townsend (S. O.)], *and* [Wolcott (A.)]

Our Navy. Its Offense is rank. [n. p. n. d.] 4to, pp. (4).

Our Navy: what it was. *See* [Woodhull (Maxwell)].

Our Own. Conducted by Fannie Warner. Vol. I. No. 1. April. *Philadelphia: Gillin, M'Guigan & Griffin.* 1869. 8vo, pp. 48. Plates. Continued. B. 57933

Our Pacific Possessions. Railway to the Pacific. Our Future Relations with the Pacific Islands and Mexico. ... *Washington: Henry Polkinhorn, Printer.* 1861. 8vo, pp. 23. H. 57934

Our Pastor. *See* [Weston (Isaac)].

Our Pastors' Offering. A Compilation from the Writings of the Pastors of the Second Church. ... *Boston: Printed by George Coolidge.* M DCCC XLV. 16mo, pp. 126, (2). B. 57935

Our Public Schools. [n. p. n. d.] 8vo, pp. 20. H. 57936

Our Resources. ... *New York: Press of Wynkoop, Hallenbeck & Thomas.* 1864. 8vo, pp. 36. 57937

Our Resources. A Series of Articles on the Financial and Political Condition of the United States. By a Citizen of this State. *Providence: S. S. Rider & Brother.* 186–. 8vo, pp. 32.

Our Stars. [Patriotic Songs.] *Philadelphia.* 1863. 16mo, pp. 120. 57939

Our Summer Retreats. A Hand-Book to all the Chief Waterfalls, Springs, Mountain and Seaside Resorts, ... in the United States. With Views ... . *New York: T. Nelson & Sons.* MDCCCLVIII. 16mo, pp. 64. 12 Plates. 57940

Our True Title to Oregon. *See* [Murdock (W. D. C.)]

Our Village in War Time. *See* [Martyn (S. T.)], No. 45007

Our World: or, The Slaveholder's Daughter. [By F. Colburn Adams.] *New York: Miller, Orton & Mulligan.* 1855. 8vo, pp. (6), 597. Plates. 57941

Our Young Folks: an Illustrated Magazine for Boys and Girls. Edited by T. J. Trowbridge, Gail Hamilton, and Lucy

Larcom. Vol. I. *Boston: Ticknor and Fields.* 1865. 8vo, pp. iv, 808. Plates. Continued. B. 57942

Ouseley (W. G.) Description of Views in South America, from Original Drawings made in Brazil, the River Plate, the Parana, &c. With Notes. By William Gore Ouseley. *London: Thomas M'Lean.* 1852. 8vo, pp. 124. 57943

Ouseley. Mission de M. Ouseley et du Baron Deffaudis a Rio de la Plata, suivi de la Réfutation de la Note collective. *Paris: Imprimé par Plon Frères.* 1846. 8vo, pp. (2), 94. H.

Ouseley. Notes on the Slave-Trade; with Remarks on the Measures adopted for its Suppression. By William Gore Ouseley. *London.* 1850. 8vo, pp. 80. C. 57945

Ouseley. Remarks on the Statistics and Political Institutions of the United States, with some Observations on the Ecclesiastical System of America, her Sources of Revenue, &c. To which are added Statistical Tables, &c. By William Gore Ouseley, Esq. Attaché to His Majesty's Legation at Washington. ... *London: J. Rodwell.* 1832. 8vo, pp. xv, 208. C. + *Philadelphia: Carey & Lea.* 1832. 8vo, pp. 226. B., C. 57946

See "Quarterly Review," 408, p. 307.

Ouseley. Views in South America, from Original Drawings made in Brazil, the River Plate, the Parana, &c. By William Gore Ouseley, Esqr. ... *London: Thomas M'Lean.* [1852.] Folio, pp. (4). 27 Plates. 57947

Out of Prison. *Boston.* 1864. 12mo. 57948

Out on Picket. *See* Vol. XII., No. 48973, *note.*

Out on the Deep; or, the Perils and Beauties of the Ocean. Being Interesting, Instructive and Graphic Accounts of the most Popular Voyages on Record, Remarkable Shipwrecks ... . *New York: Leavitt & Allen Brothers.* [1870.] 12mo, pp. 492. Plate.

This is another edition of "Ocean Scenes," our No. 56639.

Outalissi, A Tale of Dutch Guiana. *London: J. Hatchard.* 1826. 8vo. 57950

Outcroppings: being Selections of California Verse. *San Francisco; A. Roman and Company.* 1866. Sm. 4to, pp. 144.

Outghersz (J.) Nieuwe | Volmaeckte Beschryvinghe der vervaer-|lijcker Strate Magellani, waer in van mijl tot mijl, van Baye tot Baye,|tot nut der Schippers ende Stuerlieden d'opdoe-

ningen vlytighlijck | verthoont, ende de streckingen beschreven worden, door Jan Outghersz. | van Enchuysen. die de selve Strate (Stuerman zijnde op | 't schip 't Geloove genaemt) hen ende weder ge-|zeylt, ende over de 9 maenden daer in | gheleghen heeft. | *t'Amsterdam, by Zacharias Heyns, inde Warmoestraet inde Hooft-dueghden.* | [n. d. Colophon:] *Ghedruckt t'Amsterdam | by Herman de Buck | inde Mol-steegh.* | [n. d.] Obl. 4to, pp. (21).

The ship "Geloof," under the command of Captain Sebald De Weert, was one of the five ships sent to the Indies by the Straits of Magellan, in June, 1598, under Admirals J. Mahn and Simon de Cordes. The expedition was unfortunate. Both admirals perished, and the ship of De Weert alone returned to Holland.

Outhier (Renauld). Journal d'un Voyage au Nord, en 1736, & 1737. Par M. Outhier ... . *A Paris, Chez Piget.* MDCCXLIV. 4to, pp. (6), 238, (2). Maps and Plates. B. + *Amsterdam.* 1746. 16mo. 57953

An English version is included in Pinkerton's "Voyages," Vol. I.

Outlaw (D.) Speech of Mr. David Outlaw of N. C., on the Army Appropriation Bill: delivered ... August 3, 1848. *Washington: Printed by J. and G. S. Gideon.* 1848. 8vo, pp. 14.

An Outline History of an Expedition to California, containing the Fate of The Get All You Can Mining Association. *New York.* 1849. Obl. 18mo. C. 57955

Outline of a Consular Establishment for the United States, in Eastern Asia. *New York.* 1838. 8vo. N. 57956

Outline of a Plan for a National Bank, with Incidental Remarks on the Bank of the United States. *New York: Newcomb & Cropsey.* 1833. 8vo, pp. 18. B. 57957

See also Vol. III., No. 10437, *and* Vol. VII., No. 27703.

Outline of the Revolution. *See* [Palacio (——)].

Outline of the United States, with a Statistical Comparison, showing her progress during thirty years ... . *Philadelphia.* 1826. 8vo. 57958

Outlines Illustrative [etc.]. *See* [Johnston (D. C.)], Vol. IX.

Outlines of a Constitution for United North and South Columbia. *Washington.* 1815. 8vo, pp. 14. 57959

Outlines of a Plan for establishing a State Society of Agriculture in Pennsylvania. *Philadelphia: Printed by Charles Cist* ... . MDCCXCIV. 8vo, pp. 11. P. 57960

Outlines of a Plan for providing a Settlement in South America for the Unemployed Poor of Great Britain and Ireland. *London.* 1824. Folio. 57961

Outlines of American History: from the First Discovery to the Present Time. ... *Philadelphia: Thomas Cowperthwait & Co.* 1845. 16mo, pp. 191. C. 57962

Outlines of the Principal Events in the Life of General Lafayette. From the North American Review. *Boston: Cummings, Hilliard & Co.* 1825. 8vo, pp. 64. 57963

The Outrage in the Senate upon Charles Sumner. Proceedings of a Public Meeting of the Citizens of Providence, held ... June 7th, ... 1856. *Providence: Knowles, Anthony & Co.* 1856. 8vo, pp. 12. 57964

The object was to consider the assault upon Charles Sumner, in the Senate Chamber at Washington, by Preston S. Brooks.

Outram (J.) Hand-book of Information for Emigrants to Nova Scotia. Prepared ... by Joseph Outram. *Halifax: Printed by A. Grant.* 1864. 8vo, pp. 86. 57965

Outram. Nova Scotia, its Condition and Resources ... By Joseph Outram, Esq. ... *William Blackwood and Sons, Edinburgh.* MDCCCL. 16mo, pp. 35. B. 57966

Outward Bound; or, Hints to Emigrant Families. *London.* 1853. 18mo, pp. 54. 57967

Ouviere (F. P.) An Account of the Contagious Epidemic Yellow Fever, which prevailed in Philadelphia in the Summer and Autumn of 1797. By Felix Pascalis Ouviere. *Philadelphia: Snowden & McCorkle.* 1798. 8vo, pp. viii, 180. C., P.

... Les Ouvrièrs des Deux Mondes. Études sur les Travaux, la Vie Domestique et la Condition Morale des Populations Ouvrières des diverses Contrées. ... Publiées ... par la Société Internationale des Études Pratiques d'Économie Sociale. *Paris: La Société.* 1857–62. 4 vols., 8vo, pp. 464; 504; 470; 500. H.

Ouwerkerk de Vries (J. v.) Het Godsdienstig Onderwijs der Negerslaven en de bloei der Kolonie Suriname in groot gevaar. ... *Amsterdam.* 1841. 8vo. 57970

The religious instruction of the negroes and the prosperity of Surinam in danger.

Ovalle (A.) Historica | Relatione | Del Regno di Cile, | E delle missioni, e ministerii che esercita in quelle | la Compagnia di Giesv. | ... Alonso D'Ovaglie Dela Compagnia di Giesv, Natiuo di S. Giacomo di Cile ... . *In Roma, Appresso Francesco Cavalli:* M.DC.XLVI. 4to, pp. (8), 378, (1). Map, 9 Plates, 18 Woodcuts.

Ovalle. Historica | Relacion | Del Reyno de Chile, | Y delos missiones, y ministerios que exercita en el | la Compañia de Iesvs. | ... | Alonso de Ovalle | Dela Compañia de Iesvs ... . *En Roma, por Francisco Cauallo.* M.DC.XLVI. | *Con licencia delos Superiores.* | Folio, pp. (10), 455, (1). Map, 14 Plates, 21 Portraits, and 18 Woodcuts. A., C. 57972

The most complete edition; the highly curious portraits of the principal Spaniards who had conquered or governed in Chile, are not in the Italian edition. The leaf preceding the title is generally wanting, it not being known in more than two or three copies. "There is even yet a doubt which is the original edition, the Italian or Spanish, both having been printed at Rome the same year."—Stevens. A translation into English is in Churchill and Pinkerton's collections of voyages.

Ovalle. Historica [as No. 57972.] *Roma: Francisco Cauallo.* M.DC.XLVIII. Folio, pp. (10), 455, (1). 23 Plates, 12 Portraits, 18 Woodcuts. H. 57973

Ovalle. Carta al general de la Compania de Jesus, en que da cuenta del estado de su religion en la provincia de Chile. *Madrid.* 1652. Folio. 57974

Title from Ternaux, No. 716.

Over de gevangenhuizen. *See* [La Rochefoucauld], X. 39055

Over de hervorming. *See* [Belmonte (B. E. D.)], II. 4586.

Over Volksverhuizingen in het algemeen, en over die naar Noord-Amerika in het bijzonder. *Amsterdam.* 1846. 8vo.

The Overland Monthly Devoted to the Development of the Country. Volume I. *San Francisco: A. Roman & Company.* 1868. 8vo, pp. 4, 9–584. Continued. BA. 57976

Overland Traction Engine Company. Transportation by Steam from Missouri River to the Rocky Mountains, Reports of A. P. Robinson ... and Edw. Warner ... *Boston: Wright & Potter, Printers.* 1865. 8vo, pp. 61. Map. 57977

Overman (F.) Practical Mineralogy, Assaying and Mining, with a Description of the useful Minerals ... . By Frederick Overman ... . *Philadelphia: Lindsay & Blakiston.* 1851. 12mo, pp. x, 13–230. H. + Sixth Edition. [*Ibid.*] 1863. B. 57978

Overman. A Treatise on Metallurgy, comprising Mining, and general and particular Metallurgical Operations ... . By Frederick Overman ... . *New York.* 1852. 8vo. + Sixth Edition. *New York: D. Appleton & Co.* 1865. 8vo, pp. 723. B.

The preface of the edition of 1865 contains a short biographical notice of the author.

The Overseer's Guide; or, a History of the Laws of Massachusetts respecting Paupers. *Brookfield.* 1815. 8vo. 57980

Overton (John). A Vindication of the Measures of the President and his ... Generals, in the commencement and termination of the Seminole War. ... *Washington.* 1819. 8vo.

Oviatt (G. A.) A Memorial Address ... at the Funeral of Captain Samuel S. Hayden, at Windsor Locks, ... June 19, 1863. By Rev. George A. Oviatt ... . *Hartford: Case, Tiffany & Co.* 1863. 8vo, pp. 22. 57982

Also: A Sermon ... at Somers, Conn., Sept. 18, 1859, on the death of Rev. Wm. L. Strong ... who died ... August 31, 1859 ... . *New Haven: Thomas J. Stafford, Printer.* 1859. 8vo, pp. 18. H.

Ovidius Naso (Publius). Ovidii Nasonis, tam de Tristibus quam de Ponto una cum Elegantissimis quibusdam Carminibus divi Gregorii Nazianzeni. *Mexici, In Collegio SS. Petri et Pauli ap. Antonium Ricardum.* 1577. 12mo, 64 leaves. 57983

An excessively rare production of Ricardo's Mexican press. In the archbishop's licence, he is said to be allowed to print the works there mentioned (nearly all of which are Latin classics) "para la frequencia y continuacion de los Estudios de los Collegios adjacentes y annexos à la dicha Compañia (de Jesus) y de los de mas estudiantes desta ciudad."

Ovidius. Ovid's | Metamorphosis | English'd, | Mythologiz'd, | And Represented in Figures. | An Essay to the Translation of Virgil's Æneis. | By G. S. | *Imprinted at Oxford,* | *By Iohn Lichfield,* | *An. Dom.* MDCXXXII. Folio, Frontispiece, engraved and printed Titles, pp. (16), 550. 16 Plates. BA., C. 57984

The first translation of a classic into the English language made on this continent. The translator was George Sandys, who was Secretary to the Colony of Virginia at that time. *See* the dedication. Also on large paper. The translator is better known as a traveler than as a poet. *See* Wood's "Athenæ," II. 46, Brydges' "Censura Liter.," V. 231, *and* Fry's "Bibliog. Mem.," 14. The first edition is dated 1626. The third edition, *London: Imprinted by R. B. for Andrew Hebb* ... MDCXXXVIII. 18mo, pp. (4), 316, (10). Other editions, 1640, 1673, 1678, and 1682.

Oviedo (Ant. de). Los Milagros de la Cruz, y marvillas del Padecer. Sermon en Honras del M. Sor. Maria Ynes de los Dolores. ... *Mexico.* 1728. 4to. 57985

Also: Sermon en Honras del D. Balthasser de Zuñiga y Guzman. ... *Mexico.* 1729.

OVIEDO (D. A. de). Por el licenciado D. Diego Antonio de Oviedo y Baños, Oidor y Alcalde del Crimen en propriedad de la Real Audiencia de Goathemala, con el Dr. G. Carill, sobre Precedencia, en que pretende se declare á sú favor, y deber gozar de la Antiguedad, desde el dia en que se le hizo merced de dicha Placa ... [n. p. n. d.] Folio. 57986

OVIEDO Y VALDES (G. F. de). Ouiedo de la natural hy|storia de las Indias.|Con preuilegio de la|S. C. C. M.| [Colophon:] *El p̄sente tratado in | titulado Ouiedo de la natural hystoria | d' las indias se imprimio a costas del au|tor Gōçalo Fernādez de Ouiedo al's de | Ualdes. Por industria de maestre Re|mō de petras: y se acabo en la cibdad de| Toledo a. xv. dias del mes de Hebrero.|de. M.D.xxvj. años.* Folio, Engraved Title, lij and (2) leaves. C., H. 57987

For an elaborate disquisition on this work, *see* [Harrisse's] "Bib. Am. Vet.," No. 139. *See also* J. R. Bartlett's "Catalogue of John Carter Brown's Library," *and* Ternaux, No. 35. Republished in Barcia's "Historiadores Primitivos," I., and in the "Bib. de Autores Españoles," LV. An Italian version is included in Ramusio, III. 44–74, and a summary in English will be found in Purchas, III. 970, etc.

[OVIEDO.] La historia general|de las Indias.|Con priuilegio imperial.| [Colophon:] ... *La qual se acabo y imprimio enla muy noble y muy leal cibdad de Sevilla| enla empr̄e|ta de Juam Cromberger| el postrero dia del mes de Setiembre. Año de mil y quinientos y treynta y cinco Años* [1535]. Folio, (5) and cxcij leaves. J.C.B. 57988

"Entirely different from the 'Natural Hystoria de las Indias,'" No. 57987, *supra*. "This first part contains nineteen books, and, we think, a portion of the fiftieth (on shipwrecks). These nineteen and a half books were republished at Salamanca, in 1547. In 1557, the twentieth book, which is the first of the second part, was printed separately. No other portion of this work appeared in print until 1851." For further particulars consult [Harrisse], No. 207.

[OVIEDO.] Coronica de las Indias.|La hystoria general de|las Indias agora nueuamente im|pressa corregida y emendada.|1547.| [*Salamanca: Juan de Junta.* 1547.] Folio, (4) and cxcij leaves. + Y con la conquista del Peru| [Colophon:] ... *La qual se acabo et Imprimio en ... Salamanca en casa de Juan de Junta ... Año de mil y quinientos et quarenta et siete* [1547]. Folio, (4) and cxcij leaves; Title, and 21 leaves. J.C.B., C., H. 57989

Second edition of our No. 57988. The title of the edition bound up with Xerez (F. de), "Conquista del Peru," etc., differs slightly.

OVIEDO. Historia General y Natural de las Indias, Islas y Tierra-Firme del Mar Océano Por el Capitan Gonzalo Fernandez de Oviedo y Valdès, primer Cronista del Nuevo Mundo. Publícala la Real Academia de la Historia, cotejada con el códice original, enriquecida con las enmiendas y adiciones del autor, é

ilustrada con la vida y el juicio de las obras del mismo, por D. José Amador de los Rios ... . *Madrid: Imprenta de la Real Academia de la Historia.* 1851–55. 4 vols., 4to, pp. cxii, 632, (2), 5 Plates; vii, 511, (2), 3 Plates; viii, 651, (2), 2 Plates; viii, 619, (2), 5 Plates. B. 57990

The third part of this important history, which comprises the entire of the fourth volume, had never before been published.

OVIEDO. Libro xx. De la segunda parte de la general|historía de las Indías. Escrípta por el Capítan | Gonçalo Fernandez de Ouíedo, y Valdes. Al-|cayde de la fortaleza y puerto de Sācto Domín|go, d'la isla Española. Cronista d' su Magestad. | Que trata del estrecho de Magallans.| *En Valladolid. Por Francisco Fernandez de Cordoua,| Impressor de su Magestad. Año de* M.D.L.vij.| [Colophon:] *Impresso en Valladolid, por frā-|cisco fernandez de Cordoua.| En este año de* M.D.L.vij. Folio, lxiiij leaves. J.C.B.

It is usually bound up with our No. 57988, *supra.*

[OVIEDO.] L'Histoire | Natvrelle et Generalle | des Indes, Isles, et Terre | Ferme de la Grand|Mer Oceane.| Tradvicte de Castillan en Francois.| *A Paris, De l'imprimerie de Michel de Vascosan ...* M.D.LV. Folio, (5) and 134 leaves. H. 57992

[OVIEDO.] L'Histoire | Natvrelle et Generalle | des Indes, Isles, et Terre Ferme de la Grand Mer Oceane. | Traduicte de Castillan|en Francois,|par Jean Poleur.| *A Paris, De l'imprimerie de Michel de Vascosan, demeurant | rue sainct Iaques, à la Fontaine.* M.D.LVI.| *Avec privilege dv Roy.*| Folio, (5) and 134 leaves. J.C.B.

Extremely rare. Comprises the first ten books of Oviedo. It differs from the previous number only in having the translator's name on the title. Ternaux, No. 47, places this under 1536.

[OVIEDO.] L'Histoire de la|Terre Nevve dv|Perù en l'Inde Occidentale, qui|est la principale mine d'or du|monde, naguères descou-|uerte, & conquise, &|nommée la nou-|uelle Castille,| Traduitte de l'Italien en Françoys.| ...| *On les vend à Paris au Palais en la Galerie|par ou on va à la Chancellerie en la|boutique de Vincent Sertenas.*|1545.| *Avec Privilege.*| [Colophon:] *Imprimé à paris par Pierre Gaul-|tier, pour Iehan Barbé & Vincent Sertenas.*| 1545.| Sm. 4to, (4) and (49) leaves. J.C.B. 57994

The last two lines of leaf Bij read: "L'aucteur est Gonzalo Ferdinando del Ouiedo natif de Madril q̄ a faict l'histoire generale, dōt est extraict ce summaire." Corrected title of our No. 32018. The translation is said to be by Jacques Gohory. *See* [Harrisse], No. 264.

"The work of Oviedo, who resided more than twenty years in America, is the fountain head whence most succeeding writers have drawn their accounts of the early

occurrences in the New World."—RICH. "Among the persons who early came to America, and have left important records of their adventures and times, one of the most considerable was Gonzalo F. de Oviedo."—TICKNOR'S *Hist. Spanish Lit.*, I. 561. "With all his obvious defects, Oviedo showed an enlightened curiosity, and a shrewd spirit of observation, which place him far above the ordinary range of chroniclers."—PRESCOTT'S *Hist. of the Conquest of Mexico*, II. 293, note. Las Casas remarks: "Oviedo should have written at the head of his history: This book was written by a conqueror, robber and murderer of the Indians, whole populations of whom he consigned to the mines, where they perished."—*Gen. Hist. de las Yndias*, MS. cap. XXIII. *See also* our Vol. I., No. 1565.

[OVIEDO.] Libro del | muy esforçado y inuencible Cauallero de la Fortuna propria-|mēte llamado don Claribalte q̄ segū su verdadera interpretaciō | quiere dezir don Felix o bienauenturado. Nueuamēte imprimi|do y venido a esta lengua castellana: el qual procede por nueuo|y galan estillo de hablar.| [Colophon:] ... *el qual se a|cabo en valencia a. xxx. de Ma-|yo por Juan viñao.* M.| D. XIX.| Folio, lxxiiii leaves. 57995

"A romance of chivalry written by Gonzalvo Fernandez de Oviedo, which, in the dedicatory epistle to 'Don Fernando de Aragon Duque de Calabria,' contains an interesting sketch of the author."—[HARRISSE'S] *Bib. Am. Vet. Additions*, No. 57.

OVIEDO. Histoire de Nicaragua, (écrite dans le 16e siècle,) par Gonzalo Fernandez de Oviedo y Valdes. ... *Paris: Arthus Bertrand.* MDCCCXL. 8vo, pp. xv, 269. H. 57996

This forms Vol. XIV. of Ternaux-Compans's "Voyages."

OVIEDO Y BAÑOS (J. de). Historia de la Conquista, y Poblacion de la Provincia de Venezuela. Escrita por D. Joseph de Oviedo y Baños ... . Primera Parte. *Madrid: Gregorio Hermosilla.* M.DCC.XXIII. Folio, pp. (16), 380, (7). C., H. + *Carâcas.* 1824. 4to, pp. (20), 615, (14). 57997

The second part is said to have been destroyed by the aristocratic families of Venezuela on account of its containing the history of their beginnings, which were in many cases anything but aristocratic. This story, however, appears rather improbable.

OVIEDO (J.) Galeria de Contemporaneos. Cuarta entrega. El Dr. D. Juan Oviedo. *Lima.* 1862. 12mo, pp. 4. Portrait.

OVIEDO (J. A. de). Carta de la Vida Pedro Spetiali ... *Mexico.* 1727. 4to. 57999

OVIEDO. Elogios de muchos Hermanos Coadjutores de la Compañia de Jesus, que en las Quarto Partes del Mundo han florecido con grandes creditos de santidad ... *Mexico: Viuda de J. B. de Hogal.* 1755. 2 vols., 4to, pp. (16), 512; 612, (10).

Dedicated "A lus carissimos Hermanos coadjutores de toda la compañia, y especialmente à los de esta Nueva España."

OVIEDO. Succus Theologiæ Moralis pro maiori pœnitentium et confessariorum expeditione diligenter expressus. ... *Mexici: Typis Viduæ Josephi de Hogal.* 1754. 18mo, pp. (16), 342, (6).

OVIEDO. Vida Admirable, Apostolicos Ministerios, y Heroicas Virtudes del Venerable Padre Joseph Vidal, Professo de la Compañia de Jesvs en la Provincia de Nueva-España. ... *Mexico: En la Imprenta del Real y mas antiguo Colegio de S. Ildefonso. Año de* 1752. 4to, pp. (18), 282, (4). 58002

The second book details the travels of the Padre in various Mexican provinces, and is of value for the geographical information. Also: Vida exemplar, heroicas virtudes, y Apostolicos Ministerios de el V. P. Antonio Nunes de Miranda de la Compania de Jesus. ... *Mexico.* 1702. Sm. 4to, pp. 14, 214. Portrait.

OVIEDO Y HERRERA (Luis Antonio de). Vida de Sta. Rosa de Santa Maria, Natvral de Lima, y Patrona del Peru. Poema Heroyco. ... *Madrid: Juan Garcia Infançon.* 1711. 4to, pp. (80), 484. J.C.B. + *Mexico.* 1729. 4to. 58003

In the preface to J. A. de Oviedo's life by Lazcano, this poem is described as equalling in beauty but surpassing in its theme the works of Homer and Virgil. Pinelo cites an edition 1713.

OVILO Y OTERO (M.) Enciclopedia popular mejicana. Manual de biografía y de bibliografía de los escritores españoles del siglo XIX. Por D. Manuel Ovilo y Otero. ... *Paris: Rosa y Bouret.* 1859. 2 vols., 16mo, pp. 288; 252. B., C. 58004

OWEGO, *N. Y.* Report of a Committee of ... the Church connected with the Owego Congregational Society. *Owego: B. H. Calhoun.* 1847. 8vo, pp. 16. 58005

OWEN (D. D.) First Report of a Geological Reconnoissance of the Northern Counties of Arkansas, made ... 1857 and 1858, By David Dale Owen ... . *Little Rock: Johnson & Yerkes, State Printers.* 1858. Rl. 8vo, pp. 256. 9 Plates. + Second Report ... of the Southern and Middle Counties of Arkansas. Made ... 1859 and 1860. *Philadelphia: C. Sherman & Son, Printers.* 1860. Rl. 8vo, pp. 433. Map, 6 Plates. 58006

OWEN. Letter of the Secretary of the Treasury, communicating a Report of a Geological Reconnoissance of the Chippewa Land District of Wisconsin, and the Northern Part of Iowa. By David Dale Owen ... . *Washington.* 1848. 8vo, pp. 134. Map, 37 Plates. H., S. 58007

Some copies are entitled: "Report of a Geological Reconnoissance of the Chippewa Land District of Wisconsin, and of a portion of the Kickapoo County, and of a part of Iowa and Minnesota." ... *Washington.* 1848. 8vo, pp. 134. Map, 37 Plates. C.

OWEN. Report of a Geological Exploration of part of Iowa, Wisconsin, and Illinois, made ... 1839 by David Dale Owen ... [n. p. n. d.] 8vo, pp. 161. H. + [*Washington.*] 1844. 8vo, pp. 191. Maps, Plates and Charts. A., H. 58008

OWEN. Report of a Geological Survey of Wisconsin, Iowa, and Minnesota; and incidentally of a portion of Nebraska Territory. Made ... By David Dale Owen ... . *Philadelphia: Lippincott, Grambo & Co.* 1852. 4to, pp. 638, (1). BA. 58009

Maps and plates form a separate volume with the title: "Illustrations to the Geological Report of Wisconsin, Iowa, and Minnesota. By David Dale Owen ... . *Philadelphia: Lippincott, Grambo & Co.* 1852. 4to. 15 Plates, 21 Maps. Also: Geological Reports on the Mineral & Timber Lands of D. Kingsbury, in the Counties of Clearfield, Elk, and Jefferson, ... Pennsylvania. ... *Buffalo.* [n. d.] 8vo, pp. 39. 2 Tables. *See also* Indiana, Vol. IX., No. 34528, *and* Kentucky, Vol. IX., No. 37513.

OWEN (Iohn). *See* H[ayman] (R[obert]), Nos. 31036–7.

OWEN (*Mr.*) Remarks of Mr. Owen, of Georgia. *Washington.* 1789. 8vo. 58010

OWEN (N.) British Remains; ... comprehending: ... The Discovery of America by the Welsh more than 300 years before ... Columbus. ... By Rev. N. Owen, A.M. *London.* 1777. 8vo.

OWEN (R.) Memoir on the Megatherium, or Giant Ground-Sloth of America (Megatherium Americanum Cuvvier). By Richard Owen ... . *London: Williams and Norgate.* 1861. 8vo, pp. (2), 84. 27 Plates. H. 58012

See also Darwin (C.), Vol. V., No. 18649.

OWEN (R.) Nautical Memoir descriptive of the Surveys made in H.M.S.'s "Blossom" and "Flanders," from 1829 to 1837. By Capt. Richard Owen, R.N. *Dublin.* [n. d.] 8vo.

In the West Indies and coasts of the Western Pacific. Not printed for sale.

OWEN (R. E.), *and* COX (E. T.) Report on the Mines of New Mexico. By Prof. Richard E. Owen, ... and E. T. Cox, ... *Washington: John S. Watts.* 1865. 8vo, pp. 59. 58014

OWEN (R.) Life of Robert Owen. Written by himself. With Selections from his Writings and Correspondence. *London: Effingham Wilson.* 1857–58. 2 vols., 8vo, pp. xliv, 390, (1); (15), xxxviii, 358, (1). BA. 58015

OWEN. Two Discourses on a New System of Society; as delivered in ... Washington, ... 1825. By Robert Owen ... .

London: Printed by Whiting & Branston. 1825. 8vo, pp. 36. B. + *Louisville, Ky.* 1825. 12mo. W. 58016

See also [Packard (F. A.)], No. 58110, *infra.*

OWEN (R. D.) A Brief ... Treatise on ... Plank Roads. By Robert Dale Owen. ... *New Albany* [*Ind.*]: *Kent & Norman.* 1850. 12mo, pp. viii, 139. Plate. C. 58017

OWEN. The Conditions of Reconstruction, In a Letter from Robert Dale Owen to the Secretary of State. *New York: W. C. Bryant & Co., Printers.* 1863. 8vo, pp. 24. BA. 58018

OWEN. The Future of the Northwest: in connection with The Scheme of Reconstruction without New England. By Robert Dale Owen. *Philadelphia: Crissy & Markley, Printers.* 1863. 8vo, pp. 15, (1). + *New York: E. O. Jenkins.* 1863. 8vo, pp. 15. C. 58019

OWEN. Hints on Public Architecture, containing, ... Views and Plans of the Smithsonian Institution: ... by Robert Dale Owen ... . *New-York: George P. Putnam.* 1849. 4to, pp. xvii, (2), 119. Plates. BA., H. 58020

[OWEN.] Pocahontas: A Historical Drama, in Five Acts; With an Introductory Essay and Notes. By a Citizen of the West. *New York: George Dearborn.* 1837. 12mo, pp. 240.

OWEN. The Policy of Emancipation: In Three Letters ... By Robert Dale Owen ... . *Philadelphia: J. B. Lippincott & Co.* 1863. 12mo, pp. 48. B., C. 58022

OWEN. ... Report of the American Freedmen's Inquiry Commission. By R. Dale Owen, J. McKayes, and Samuel G. Howe, Commissioners. [*Washington.* 1864.] 8vo, pp. 110.

OWEN. The Wrong of Slavery the Right of Emancipation and the Future of the African Race in the United States. By Robert Dale Owen. ... *Philadelphia: J. B. Lippincott & Co.* 1864. 12mo, pp. 246. BA. 58024

Also: Address before the Young Men's Mercantile Library Association of Cincinnati, Feb. 1, 1848. ... *Cincinnati.* 1848. 8vo.—Democratic Address at Indianapolis, 10 Feb. 1838. [n. p. n. d.] 8vo, pp. 8. B.—... Emancipation is Peace. ... *New York: W. C. Bryant & Co.* 1863. 8vo, pp. 7.—Footfalls on the Boundary of another World. ... *Philadelphia: J. B. Lippincott & Co.* 1865. 12mo, pp. 528.—Labor; its History and Prospects. ... *New York.* 1851. 12mo.—Letter ... to the Hon. Salmon P. Chase. The Cost of Peace. November 10, 1862. [n. p. n. d.] 8vo.—Speech ... on the Bill for the Organization of the Smithsonian Institution, delivered ... April 22, 1846. *Washington.* 1846. 8vo, pp. 8.—Speech ... on Commercial Restrictions. *Washington.* 1846. 8vo, pp. 8.—Village Life in the West. Beyond the Breakers.

A Story of the Present Day. ... *Philadelphia: J. B. Lippincott & Co.* 1870. 8vo, pp. 274. 4 Plates.

OWEN (T.) The Taylor Anecdote Book: Anecdotes and Letters of Zachary Taylor; with a brief Life, by Tom Owen, the Bee-hunter ... *New York.* 1848. 8vo. C., S. 58025

OWENS (G.) General Directory ... of the principal Towns East of the Cascade Mountains, for 1865. Compiled by George Owens. *San Francisco, Cal.* 1865. 8vo, pp. 210. Map. C.

OWENS. A General Directory ... of the principal Towns in the Upper Country, embracing a portion of California; together with Mining and Statistical Information concerning Idaho Territory. Compiled by George Owens. *San Francisco: A. Gensoul.* 1866. 8vo, pp. 171. Map. C. 58027

Owl Creek Letters. *See* [Prime (W. C.)]

OWLS-GLASS, *pseudon.* Rebel Brag and British Bluster; ... By Owls-Glass. *New York: American News Company.* [1865.] 12mo, pp. 111. C. 58028

O[XENBRIDGE] (J[ohn].) New-England Freemen warned and warmed. Election Sermon, 1671. By Rev. J. O. [n. p.] 1673. 16mo, pp. 48. M. 58029

[OXENBRIDGE.] A Quickening Word for the hastening a Sluggish Soul to a seasonable Answer to The Divine Call. Published by a poor Sinner that found it such to him. Being the last Sermon Preached in the First Church of Boston Upon Isaiah 55. 6. By the Pastor there, on the 24th of the fifth Month, 1670. *Cambridge: ... S. G. and M. J.* 1670. 8vo, pp. 21.

"Superlatively rare, if not unique."—J. H. TRUMBULL. Also: A Seasonable Proposition of propagating the Gospel by Christian Colonies in Guiana. ... [n. p. n. d.] 8vo, pp. 12. M.

OXFORD (*Bishop of*). *See* [Hume (J.)], VIII. 33778, [Jackson (W.)], IX. 35471, [Lowth (R.)], X. 42542, [Secker (T.)], *and* [Wilberforce (S.)]

OXFORD (*Earl of*). A Further Report from the Committee of Secrecy, appointed to Enquire into the Conduct of Robert, Earl of Oxford. *London.* 1742. 8vo. 58031

Relates chiefly to the Jamaica currency.

The Oxford Academy Jubilee, held at Oxford, ... N. Y. August 1st and 2d, 1854. *New York: Baker & Godwin, Printers.* 1856. 8vo, pp. 132. 4 Portraits. B. 58032

Miami University and Cincinnati. By the OXFORD COMMITTEE. *Hamilton: Printed by James B. Camron.* 1822. 8vo, pp. 20. 58033

Oxford English Prize Essays ... . *Oxford.* 1836. 5 vols., post 8vo. C. 58034

Denison's essay, Vol. IV., contains a "Brief View of the Political Circumstances of the United States." *See also* Dr. Arnold's essay, in Vol. III.

Dedication Services. OXFORD PRESBYTERIAN CHURCH, ... Philadelphia, ... Dec. 12, 1869. [n. p. n. d.] 8vo, pp. 15.

Oxford Prize Poems. ... *Oxford.* 1810. Post 8vo. 58036

The "Conquest of Quebec," by Middleton Howard, is the subject of the first poem.

OXFORD UNIVERSITY. Address to the Ministers of the Gospel in England and Wales, in favor of propagating the Gospel among the Indians in New England. [n. p.] 1649. Folio, 1 l.

Verses by the University of Oxford, on the Death of the Most Noble and Right Valiant Sir Bevill Grenville, ... with Report of the Truth of the Fight about the Isles of the Azores, the last August, 1591 ... . *Oxford.* 1684. 4to. 58038

OXFORD, *Mass.* Auditor's Report of the Receipts and Expenditures, with the School Committee's Report of the Town of Oxford, for ... 1863. *Webster.* 1863. 8vo, pp. 32. 58039

OXFORD, *N. H.* Centennial Celebration, ... Sept. 7, 1865. *Manchester.* 1865. 8vo. 58040

OXHOLM (J. N.) Bibel voor Kinders of Bibels spreek met Kort Opmuntringen voor opmerksame Kinders set over na die Creols tael van J. N. Oxholm. *Kopenhagen.* 1822. 16mo, pp. 60

OXHOLM (P. L.) De Danske Vestindske Öers Tilstand i Henseende til Population, Cultur og Finance. Forfatning ... *Kiöbenhavn.* 1797. 8vo. 4 Plates. 58042

OXHOLM. Etat des Isles danoises aux Indes occidentales. Traduit en français. *Paris.* 1799. 8vo. 58043

First published in Danish at Copenhagen, 1772.

OYANGUREN DE SANTA INES (M.) Arte|de la lengua Japona, |dividido in quatro libros|segun el Arte de Nebrixa,| ... Hermano Pr. Fr. Melchior Oyanguren de Santa Ines ... . *Mexico, por Jos. Bern. de Hogal.* 1738. 4to, pp. (20), 200, (2). 58044

Oyanguren de Santa Ines. Tagalysmo elucidado, y reducido (en lo possible) â la Latinidad de Nebrija con su Syntaxis, Tropos, Prosodia, Passiones, etc. y con la alusion, que en su uso, y composicion tiene con el Dialecto Chinico Mandarin, ... para alivio de los R.R. Padres Missionerôs Appostolicos, que passan â aquellas Missiones. *En Mexico, en la Imprenta de D. Franc. Xavier Sanchez.* 1742. 4to, pp. (6), 228. 58045

A rare work on the principal language of the Philippine Islands.

Oyanzabal (Juan de). El Espion Serrano ... *Lima.* 1812. 4to, pp. 40. 58046

Oyárvide (Andres de). Memoria geografica de los Viajes practicados desde Buenos Aires hasta el salto grande del Paraná, por las primeras y segundas partidas de la demarcacion de limites en la América Meridional, en conformidad del tratado preliminar de 1777, entre las coronas de España y Portugual. 1ª y 2ª parte. [1784–91.] ... *Paris.* 1865–66. 4 vols., 8vo. c. 58047

A continuation of Calvo. *See* our Vol. III., No. 10087.

Ozaeta y Gallaiztegui (J. H. de). La Cantabria vindicada, y demostrada, segun la extension que tuvo en diferentes tiempos: la variedad del govierno de los romanos ... . Por Don Joseph Hippolito de Ozaeta y Gallaiztegui. *Madrid: P. Marin.* 1779. Sm. 4to, pp. (19), 243. B. 58048

Contains some curious information respecting Columbus and the discovery of America.

Ozanne (T. D.) The South as it is, or Twenty-One Years' Experience in the Southern States of America. By the Rev. T. D. Ozanne ... . *London: Saunders, Otley, and Co.* 1863. 16mo, pp. v, (1), 306. B. 58049

Ozcariz (J.), *translator.* Ceremonial y Rubricas Generales, con la Orden de Celebrar las missas, y avisos para los defectos q acerca dellas pueden acontecer. Sacados del nuevo Missal Tridentino, y traduzido por el muy R. P. Fray Juan Ozcariz. Dirigido al illustriss. Señor Don Pedro Moya y Cõtreras, Arçobispo de Mexico. *Mexico, por Pedro Balli.* 1579. 12mo, 120 leaves.

Excessively rare.

P. (A.) *See* P[ember] (A[rthur].)

P. (A.-D. de). Apuntes para la historia de la Republica oriental del' Uruguay desde el año de 1810, hasta el de 1852; ... Por A.-D. de P. ... *Paris: Th. Duchessoir, Editor.* 1864. 2 vols., 8vo, pp. xii, 367; 512. Map and Portraits. H. 58051

P. (A. S.) The Story of Thomas Ellwood. By A. S. P. *Philadelphia: T. Ellwood Zell.* 1861. 12mo, pp. 48. 58052

P. (C.) *See* P[usey] (C[aleb].)

P. (D. L.) *See* P[ouncy] (D[e] L[onvilliers].)

P. (D. V. A. E.) Historia de la Isla de Santo Domingo, continuada hasta los ultimos acontecimientos durante la insurreccion de los xefes negros, especialmente en el año 1800 (VIII de la republica fiancesa) y siguientes hasta el presente de 1806. Por D. V. A. E. P. *Madrid.* 1806. 12mo, pp. 270. 58053

P. (E.) Aun las cuestiones de límites del Ecuador ó sea Pedro Moncayo y su nuevo folleto, sus absurdos y su malafe &c. panfleto escrito á veces en su estilo, incluyendo curiosos asertos y acompañado de importantes documentos verídicos que por sí solos aclaran todas las cuestiones. Por E. P. *Lima: Tipografía de Aurelio Alfaro.* 1862. 4to, pp. 58, xviii. H. 58054

P. (G.) Lex Parliamentaria: | or, a | Treatise | of the | Law and Custom | of the | Parliaments | of | England. | By G. P. Esq: | *London Printed, and Reprinted in New-York | and Sold by William and Andrew Bradford | in New York and Philadelphia.* 1716. 12mo, pp. (6), 184. 58055

We are unable to trace the sale of any copy (except Mr. W. Menzies') of this most rare book. First printed at London, in 8vo, 1698.

P. (G. C.) Reflections on the Slave-Trade; with Remarks on the Policy of its Abolition. ... By G. C. P. *London.* 1791. 8vo, pp. 56. 58056

P. (H. W.) *See* P[arker] (H[enry] W.)

P****** (J***). The | Life | of | General James Wolfe, | The | Conqueror of Canada; | or, the | Eulogium of that Renowned | Hero, | Attempted according to the | Rules of Eloquence. | With a | Monumental Inscription, | Latin and English, | To perpetuate his Memory. | By J*** P******, A.M. | *London: G. Kearsly.* MDCCLX. 8vo, pp. (4), 24. + ... *Boston: Reprinted and Sold by Fowle and Draper.* M,DCC,LX. 8vo, pp. 36. + *Portsmouth, N. H.* 1760. 8vo, pp. 24. 58057

A book of much rarity. Morrell's copy of the London edition sold for $30.

P. (J.) Glorious Glimmerings of the Life, Love, Unity and pure Joy. Written in Rome Prison of Madmen in the Year 1660, but conserved as in Obscurity until my Arrival at Barbados in the Year 1662. From whence it is sent the second time to the Lord's Lambs. By J. P. *London: Robert Wilson.* 1663. 4to, pp. 15. 58058

P. (J. A.) *See* P[erreau] (J. A.)

P. (J. C.) Insulæ Caraibicæ in America sitæ fatum. Seu brevis & succinta Insulæ hujus descriptio, tribus constans capitibus, quibus Magnitudo, ... à J. C. P. *Groningæ, Apud Jacobum Sipkes.* 1727. 4to, 68 leaves irregularly paged, pp. 33–116.

P. (J.-N.) L'Œuvre d'un grand Peuple. Par J.-N. P. ... *Paris: Dentu.* 1864. 8vo, pp. 63. H. 58060

P. (L.) Two Essays sent in a Letter from Oxford to a Nobleman in London. ... *London.* 1695. 8vo. 58061

Pages 15–28 contain the "Peopling and Planting the New World."

P. (L. J. de la). El Tratado de Paz entre el Director provisorio de la Confederacion Argentina y el Gobierno de Buenos Aires en 9 de Marzo de 1853. Por L. J. de la P. *Buenos Aires.* 1853. 4to, pp. 98. 58062

P*** [*M.* de]. *See* P[auw (Cornelis van)], *and* [Chastellux (F. J.)], Vol. III., No. 12224.

P. (*Mlle.* de). Histoire des Demoiselles de Saint-Janvier les deux seules blanches conservées à Saint-Domingue, par Mademoiselle de P... . *Paris.* 1812. 18mo. Plates. 58063

P. (*Mr.*) *See* P[itt (William)].

P. (M. O. T. des). La Nouvelle-Grenade L'Émigration et les Divers Projets du Canal de Jonction entre les deux océans, par M. O. T. des P. *Paris: Adrien Delahaye.* 1859. 8vo, pp. 30

P. (R. A.) *See* P[aige] (R[hoda] A[nn].), No. 58179, *infra.*

[P. (T. C.)] Kalewala and Hiawatha. [By T. C. P., Lancaster, Pa. n. p. n. d.] 8vo, pp. 21. H. 58065

P. (W.) History of Witches and Wizards, giving a true Account of all their Tryals in England, ... and New England, with their confession and condemnation. By W. P. *London: C. Hitch and L. Haws.* [1669.] 12mo, pp. (10), 144. H. 58066

P. (W.) *See* P[enn] (W[illiam].)

P. (W. S.) *See* P[erry] (W. S.)

P's and Q's. *Boston.* 1828. 18mo. 58067

Pablo de Avecilla. La Conquista del Peru. Novela histórica original. *Carácas.* 1853. 4to, pp. 63. 58068

Pablo de Prado. Directorio Espiritual de la lingua Española, y Quichua general del Inga, compuesto por el Padre Pablo de Prado. *Lima.* 1650. 12mo. 58069

Pabor (W. E.) A Campaign Poem, delivered at ... Harlem, July 4th, 1860. ... By William E. Pabor. *New-York: Callahan & Bloom, Printers.* 1860, 16mo, pp. 16. 58070

Pachecho (A.) Discurso del D. D. Anjel Pachecho, Diputado por la Provincia de Cangallo, en pro de la Insubsistencia de las Providencias para las Mitras de Lima. *Lima.* 1827. 4to, pp. 16. M. 58071

Pacheco (J. F.) Coleccion de Documentos ineditos relativos al descubrimiento, conquista y colonizacion de las posesiones españolas en America y Oceania, sacados en su mayor parte, del real Archivo de Indias, bajo la direccion de ... D. Joaquin F. Pacheco, D. Francisco de Cárdenas, ... y D. Luis Torres de Mendoza, con la cooperacion de otras personas competentes. *Madrid: Imprenta de Manuel Bernaldo de Quirós.* 1864–77. 28 vols., 8vo. B. 58072

Pacheco (José Praxedes Pereira). Breves Noções para se estudar com methodo a geographia do Brasil; Ensaio para, pela primeira vez, indicar os tanques maritimos no Atlantico, as vertentes d'elles, as valladas ou bacias que ellas encerram, accommodando o Brasil ao ultimo plano de estudos para o imperio francez, seguindo a geographia da França. ... *Rio de Janeiro, na Typ. Imp. e Const. de J. Villeneuve & C.ª* 1857. 12mo, pp. 204. 58073

Pacheco (José Ramon). Descripcion de la solemnidad funebre con que se honraron las cenizas del heroe de Iguala D. Agustin de Iturbide en octubre de 1838. ... *México: J. Cumplido.* 1849. 8vo, pp. 66. Portrait, 3 Plates. 58074

Pacheco. La Cuestion de Mexico. Cartas de D. José Ramon Pacheco al Ministro de Negocios Estranjeros de Napoleon III. Mr. Drouyn de Lhuys. *Nueva York: S. Hallett.* 1862. 8vo, pp. 70. + *Mexico: N. Chavez.* 1863. 16mo, pp. 124. C.

Pacheco. Lettres sur le Mexique. Par J. R. Pacheco ... . *Bordeaux.* 1833. 8vo, pp. 52. 58076

Also: Exposicion con motivo de la comunicacion oficial que acerca de las conferencias tenidas en Agosto y Setiembre con el comisionado de los Estados-Unidos, dirigio el Diputado D. Mariano Otero al Sr. Gobernador de Jalisco. ... *Queretaro.* 1847. 4to, pp. 29.

Pacheco (Nicolas). Oracion panegirica, que en la solemne accion de gracias a dios nuestro señor, y a su santisima madre en la advocacion de la merced, por la feliz conclusion de la grada de construccion finalizada en el astillero de la Havana. ... *Havana: E. Joseph Boloña.* 1792. 4to, pp. xxiv. 58077

Pacheco (N.) Demonstracion compendiosa y Evidente de los muchos y graves Males que acarrea la Insurreccion, para el uso y utilidad de los Indios y otras Gentes semejantes ... *Mexico.* 1812. 8vo. 58078

The Pacific Almanac, 1865. Compiled by Wm. H. Knight. *San Francisco: H. H. Bancroft & Co.* 1864. 12mo. 58079

The Pacific Coast Almanac and Year Book of Facts. Compiled by Henry G. Langley, 1868. *San Francisco: H. G. Langley.* 1868. 16mo. *See also* Vol. x. 38893.

Pacific Congregational Church, in Providence, R. I. A Candid Statement of Facts, relative to Difficulties existing between this Church, and those Brethren who withdrew and were formed into a separate Church, with the Documents ... . *Providence: Barnum Field.* 1823. 8vo, pp. 23. 58080

The Pacific Gleaner. No. 1. *Chatham: Printed by Townson and Burrill.* 1826. 8vo, pp. 16. H. 58081

The Pacific Gold Company, of Colorado. Report of Hon. G. R. Mitchell, and Official Statements of Exports, &c. ... *Boston: Printed by A. Mudge & Son.* 1866. 18mo, pp. 19. 58082

"Pacific Mail." A Review of the Report of the President. [n. p. 1868?] 8vo, pp. 36. 58083

The Pacific Mail Steamship Co. Prest. McLane's Report reviewed. [n. p. 1868.] 8vo, pp. 12. 58084

Also: Charter of the ... Company, with its Amendments; also the By-Laws ... . *New York: Slote & Janes.* 1867. 8vo, pp. 21. — Fourth Annual Report ... May 10, 1853. ... *New York: George F. Nesbitt & Co., Printers.* 1858. 8vo, pp. 6. — Report of the President to the Stockholders. February, 1868. [n. p. n. d.] 8vo, pp. 72.

Pacific Medical and Surgical Journal. H. Gibbons, M.D. Editor. June, 1867, to May, 1868. New Series. Vol. I. *San Francisco: Bancroft & Co.* [1867–68.] 8vo. Continued. C.

Second Annual Catalogue of Officers and Students of the Pacific Methodist College, Vacaville, California, 1862–63. *San Francisco: Printed by Towne & Bacon.* 1863. 8vo, pp. 16.

Catalogue of the Pacific Mills Library, Lawrence, Mass. Opened August 21, 1854. *Boston: Printed by Damrell and Moore.* 1855. 8vo, pp. 84. 58087

The Pacific Monthly: devoted to the Arts, Science, Literature, and Life on the Pacific Coast. Editors J. D. Strong, M. D. Strong. Vol. X. ... *San Francisco, Cal.: Charles F. Robbins & Co., Printers.* [1863.] 8vo. 58088

Pacific Railroad. Importance to the United States Government of its early Completion as shown by Extracts from the Annual Report of the Hon. James M. Edmands, ... and others. ... *Detroit.* 1863. 8vo, pp. 6. 58089

Also: The Pacific Railroad. A Defense against its Enemies, with Report of the Supervisors of Placer County, and Report of Mr. Montanya ... Dec. 1864. [n. p. n. d.] 8vo, pp. 35. — Proceedings of a Pacific Railroad Convention, at Lacon, Illinois; with the Address of Col. Samuel R. Curtis. *Cincinnati: Printed by John D. Thorpe.* 1853. 8vo, pp. 16. — Proceedings of the Friends of a Railroad to San Francisco, at their Meeting in Boston, April 19, 1849. *Boston.* 1849. 8vo. + Fourth Edition. *Boston.* 1849. 8vo, pp. 24. *See also* Reports and Explorations.

Pacific Railroad of Missouri. Statement relating to Southwest Branch, Lands, Bonds, &c. *New York.* 1857. 8vo, pp. 22. S.

Also: Ninth Annual Report of the Pacific Railroad, to the Stockholders. *St. Louis.* 1859. 8vo, pp. 34.

Pacificator, *pseudon.* *See* [Hoffman (M.)], VIII. 32401.

Pacificator, *pseudon.* The Nail hit on the head; or, the Two Jonathans agreeing to settle The Slave Question with or without more fighting, as the South pleases. By Pacificator. *New Haven: Thomas H. Pease.* 1862. 8vo, pp. 24. 58091

Pacificus: the Rights and Privileges of the several States in regard to Slavery. A Series of Essays, published in the Western Reserve Chronicle, (Ohio,) after the Election of 1842. By a Whig of Ohio. [n. p. n. d.] 8vo, pp. 16. BA. 58092

Pacificus, *pseudon.* Appeal to American Christians on the Practice of War. By Pacificus. *New York.* 1830. 8vo, pp. 28

Pacificus, *pseudon.* A Serious Expostulation with the Society of Friends, in Pennsylvania and parts adjacent ... . By Pacificus. *Philadelphia.* 1808. 8vo, pp. 16. C., N. 58094

This elicited: "Remarks on a Pamphlet, by 'Pacificus,' addressed to the Society of Friends, together with some other interesting Papers." [n. p.] 1808. 12mo, pp. 32. *See also* Philo Veritas, *and* [Hamilton (A.)], Vol. VIII., Nos. 29967–8.

Pacifique de Provins (*P.*) Briève relation du voyage des isles de l'Amérique, par le père Pacifique de Provins, capucin, missionnaire apostolique, etc. *Paris.* 1636. 8vo, 18 leaves.

Title from Ternaux, No. 573.

Packard (Alpheus S.) History of the Bunker Hill Monument. By Professor Packard, of Bowdoin College. *Portland: Brown Thurston, Printer.* 1853. 8vo, pp. 33. Plate. B. 58096

See also "Collections of the Maine Historical Society," III. Also: Address on the Life and Character of William Smyth, D.D., ... Bowdoin College, July 7, 1868. ... *Brunswick.* 1868. 8vo. — Our Alma Mater. An Address delivered before the Association of the Alumni of Bowdoin College, ... August 5, 1858. *Brunswick: J. Griffin.* 1858. 8vo, pp. 49.

Packard (Alpheus Spring), *Jr.* The American Naturalist, a Popular Illustrated Magazine of Natural History. Edited by A. S. Packard, Jr. [and others]. ... Vol. I. *Salem: Essex Institute.* 1868. 8vo. Continued. C. 58097

Packard. A Guide to the Study of Insects ... . For the use of Colleges ... . By A. S. Packard, Junior, M.D. *Salem.* 1868. 8vo. + Third Edition. [*Ibid.*] 58098

Packard (A.) An Oration, on the means of perpetuating Independence. ... East-Sudbury, July 4, 1815. By Asa Packard, A.M. ... *D. & A. Bowen, Printers, Boston.* [1815.] 8vo, pp. 15.

Packard. A Sermon, ... at Surry, at the Ordination of the Rev. Perley Howe, Sept. 16, 1795. By Asa Packard ... . *Walpole, New Hampshire, By David Carlisle, Jun.* 1796. 8vo, pp. 30

See also "Collections of the Massachusetts Historical Society," IV. 46–50.

Packard (C.) A Discourse ... in Cambridgeport, Thanksgiving Day, November 30, 1854. By Charles Packard. *Cambridge.* 1854. 8vo. S. 58101

Packard (*Mrs.* Clarissa), *pseudon.?* Recollections of a Housekeeper. By Mrs. Clarissa Packard. *New York: Harper & Brothers.* 1834. 16mo, pp. 155. C. + [*Ibid.*] 1838. + [*Ibid.*] 1842. 58102

Packard (D. T.) The Dawn of the Morning. A Sermon, ... Somerville, Dec. 28, 1862. By Rev. David Temple Packard. ... *Boston: Geo. C. Rand & Avery.* 1863. 8vo, pp. 16.

[Packard (*Mrs.* Elizabeth Parsons Ware).] The Exposure on board the Atlantic & Pacific Car of Emancipation for the Slaves of Old Columbia; ... With an Appeal to the Government to emancipate the Slaves of the Marriage Union. Volume I. ... *Chicago: The Authoress.* 1864. 8vo, pp. 157. Portrait, Plate.

[Packard.] Great Disclosure of Spiritual Wickedness!! in High Places. With an Appeal to the Government to protect the inalienable Rights of Married Women. ... Fourth Edition. *Boston: The Authoress.* 1865. 8vo, pp. 158. H. 58105

These titles seem to indicate the propriety of their origin—an insane asylum. Also: Marital Power exemplified in Mrs. Packard's Trial, ... with an Appeal to the Government to change its Laws as to ... Married Women. ... *Hartford: Case, Lockwood & Company.* 1867. 8vo, pp. 137, (1). — Mrs. Packard's Reproof to Dr. McFarland, for his abuse of his Patients ... . Given him in Jacksonville Insane Asylum, Illinois, Nov. 12th, 1860. *Chicago.* 1864. 8vo, pp. 32. — The Prisoners' Hidden Life, or Insane Asylums Unveiled. ... *Chicago: The Author.* 1868. 12mo, pp. 346.

[Packard (Frederic Adolphus).] The Daily Public School in the United States. *Philadelphia: J. B. Lippincott & Co.* 1866. 8vo, pp. 158. C. 58106

[Packard.] Historical Sketch of the American Sunday-School Union and of its Contributions to Popular Education in the United States. [n. p.] 1865. 12mo, pp. 45. H. 58107

[Packard.] An Inquiry into the alleged Tendency of the Separation of Convicts, one from the other, to produce Disease ... By a Citizen of Philadelphia. *Philadelphia: E. C. & J. Biddle.* 1849. 8vo, pp. 160. H. 58108

[Packard.] Letters on the Design and Importance of the Agency of the American Sunday School Union in New England. ... *Philadelphia.* 1838. 8vo, pp. 28. 58109

[PACKARD.] Life of Robert Owen. *Philadelphia: Ashmead & Evans.* 1866. 12mo, pp. 264. H. 58110

[PACKARD.] Memorandum of a late Visit to the Auburn Penitentiary .... *Philadelphia: J. Harding, Printer.* 1842. 8vo, pp. 8

[PACKARD.] Sketch of the principal Transactions of the "Philadelphia Society for Alleviating the Miseries of Public Prisons" .... *Philadelphia: Merrihew & Thompson.* 1859. 8vo, pp. 32. H. 58112

[PACKARD.] Thoughts on the Condition and Prospects of Popular Education in the United States. ... *Philadelphia.* 1836. 8vo. BM. 58113

[PACKARD.] A Vindication of the Separate System of Prison Discipline from the Misrepresentations of the North American Review, July, 1839. *Philadelphia.* [n. d.] 8vo, pp. 56. S.

PACKARD (H. J.) The Choice: a Tragedy; with other Miscellaneous Poems. By Hannah James Packard. [With a Memoir.] *Boston: L. C. Bowles.* 1832. 18mo, pp. 22, 142. Port.

PACKARD (H.) ... Discourse ... June 28th, 1797; at the Ordination of the Rev. Andrew Beattie ... in the West Parish of Salisbury. By Hezekiah Packard. ... *Printed at Newburyport by E. M. Blunt.* 1797. 8vo, pp. 36. BA. 58116

PACKARD. Federal Republicanism Displayed in Two Discourses ... on ... the State Fast at Chelmsford [Mass.], and on ... the National Fast at Concord, in April, 1799. By Hezekiah Packard .... *Boston: Printed by John Russell.* 1799. 8vo, pp. 35

PACKARD. The Plea of Patriotism. A Sermon preached in Chelmsford, on the Day of General Thanksgiving, Feb. 19. 1795. By Hezekiah Packard .... *Boston: Printed by William Greenough.* 1795. 8vo, pp. 23. H. 58118

Also: A Dedicatory Address at the Opening of the Female Academy in Augusta, erected by Hon. Daniel Cony, 1816. ... *Hallowell.* 1816. 8vo, pp. 20. — A Sermon on the Death of Miss Sibyl Richardson, of Chelmsford, who died 12 Dec. 1798 .... *Amherst.* 1799. 8vo, pp. 28. — Sermon ... Nov. 11, 1802; at the Interment of Mrs. Betsey Wood, at Wiscasset. ... *Wiscasset.* 1803. 8vo, pp. 16. — A Short Address, delivered before the sufferers by the late fire in Wiscasset and Alna [Maine], at their meeting, Jan. 18, 1824. ... [n. p. n. d.] 8vo. S.

PACKARD. Memoir of Hezekiah Packard, D.D., chiefly Autobiographical. *Brunswick.* 1850. 8vo, pp. (2), 68. Portrait.

PACKARD (L.) A Sermon, ... in Ware, Mass. October 2, 1838, at the funeral of Rev. Augustus B. Reed .... By Levi Packard .... *Brookfield: E. & L. Merriam, Printers.* 1838. 8vo, pp. 16. 58120

Also: A Sermon ... at the Dedication of the Meeting-House, in Spencer, Mass. November 14, 1838. ... *Brookfield: E. and L. Merriam, Printers.* 1839. 8vo, pp. 24.

PACKARD (T.) Sermon ... on the Occasion of the Fiftieth Anniversary of the Ordination of Rev. Theophilus Packard, D.D., as Pastor of the Congregational Church ... in Shelburne, Mass. Feb. 20, 1849. *Greenfield: Printed by Charles A. Mirick.* MDCCCXLIX. 8vo, pp. 40. B., C. 58121

Also: Life and Death of [his Son] Isaac T. Packard, 1820.

PACKARD (T.), *Jr.* A History of the Churches and Ministers, and of Franklin Association, in Franklin County, Mass. and an Appendix respecting the County. By Rev. Theophilus Packard, Jr. *Boston: S. K. Whipple and Co.* 1854. 8vo, pp. vii, 456.

Also: Thanksgiving Sermon ... in Shelburne, Mass. in 1836. ... *Greenfield.* 1837. 8vo.

Packard's Monthly; an American Magazine, devoted to the Interests ... of the Young Men of the Country. ... 1868. *New York: S. S. Packard.* [1868.] 4to, pp. (2), 128. 58123

PACKER (J. B.) A Journal of the Life and Travels of Joseph-Bill Packer, now under sentence of Death in the City-Hall of Albany, for Counterfeiting the Currency. *Albany.* 177–. 12mo. + *Hartford.* 1773. 12mo, pp. 15. 58124

Packer Collegiate Institute .... *Brooklyn: I. Van Anden's Print.* 1855. 8vo, pp. 54. Continued. 58125

Pacto de la Confederacion Centro-Americana. *Comayagua.* 1842. 8vo, pp. (2), 12. 58126

[PADDENBURG (G. G. van).] Beschrijving van het Eiland Curaçao en onderhoorige Eilanden. Uit onderscheidene stukken, bijdragen en opmerkingen opgemaakt, door een bewoner van dat eiland. *Te Haarlem, Erven F. Bohn.* 1819. 8vo. 58127

A description of Curaçao and the adjacent islands.

PADDOCK (B. H.) Life in Death, ... A Sermon, ... in ... Norwich, ... Sept. 24th, 1854; ... after the funeral of Col. Samuel Tyler, ... By Benj. H. Paddock .... *Norwich: Woodworth and Perry.* 1854. 8vo. 58128

Also: Our Cause, our Confidence, and our Consequent Duty. A Sermon preached May 12, 1861, before Co. A, 1st Regiment Michigan Volunteers. ... [n. p. n. d.] 8vo, pp. 15.

PADDOCK (J. A.) An Historical Discourse, ... in ... Stratford, Conn., ... March 28th, 1855. By the Rev. John A. Paddock, M.A. ... *New York: G. P. Putnam & Co.* 1855. 8vo, pp. 45, (1). 58129

PADDOCK (W. F.) A Great Man Fallen! A Discourse on the Death of Abraham Lincoln. Delivered in ... Philadelphia, ... April 23, 1865. By the Rev. Wilbur F. Paddock. *Philadelphia: Sherman & Co., Printers.* 1865. 8vo, pp. 24. 58130

Also: God's Presence and Purpose in our War. A Thanksgiving Discourse delivered in ... Philadelphia, ... November 26, 1863. ... *Philadelphia: C. Sherman, Son & Co.* 1863. 8vo, pp. 27. + Second Edition. [*Ibid.*] 1864.

PADILLA (Juan de). Memorial del Peru. *Lima.* 1660. 4to.

Title from Ternaux, No. 780.

PADILLA (M.) Apuntamientos para la biografia del señor Licenciado Don José Antonio Larrave y Velazco .... *Guatemala.* [1858.] 4to, pp. 20. 58132

PADILLA. Ensayo historico sobre el origin de la enfermedad venerea ó des Babas y de su antiguedad tanto en Europa, como en America. Escrito por el Sr. Dr. Don Mariano Padilla .... *Guatemala.* 1861. 4to, pp. 20. 58133

PAE (D.) A Popular History of the Discovery, Progress, and Present State of America; .... By David Pae. *Edinburgh: Thomas Grant.* 1852. 18mo, pp. iv, 164. C. 58134

PAES DE ANDRADA. Flores Singelas ... *Pernambuco.* 1861. 8vo. 58135

Paesi Nouamente. *See* [Montalboddo (F.)], XII. 50050–56.

PÁEZ (J. A.) Autobiografia del General José Antonió Páez. *Nueva York.* 1867–9. 2 vols., 8vo, pp. xiii, 576; 488, vii. C.

PAEZ. Carta que el General José A. Paez escribio de la cároil de Carácas á un amigo suyo. *Carácas.* 1850. 8vo, pp. 21.

PAEZ. Documento Curioso sobre los Acontecimientos de Venezuela del 30 de Abril de 1826. Carta Confidencial del Vicepresidente de la Republica [Francisco de Paula Santander] el Jen. J. A. Paez. *Bogota.* 1826. 4to, pp. 10. M. 58138

[PAEZ.] Important Documents in relation to the Present Situation of Venezuela; and the attempt of General Jose Tadeo Monagas to establish a Despotic Government in that country: With a few Introductory Remarks. *New-York.* 1848. 8vo, pp. 27. 58139

Also: Canto Patriotico ... *Carácas.* 1858. 8vo. — Documents relating to the Life of Gen. José A. Paez. *New York.* 1854. 8vo. — Ejecucion del Decreto del Poder Ejecutivo para Alistamiento en las Milicias, que motivó la Acusacion del Jeneral en Jefe José Antonio Paez ante el Senado. *Valencia.* 1826. 12mo, pp. 31. — Guirnalda poética de Paez, Ciudadano Esclarecido de Venezuela, Contiene ademas de las mejores composiciones dedicadas al héroe, su retrato y unos apuntes biográficos. *Carácas.* 1850. 8vo, pp. 47. — Mensaje del Poder Ejecutivo y contestacion de las Cámaras. *Carácas.* 1842. 4to, pp. 15. — Recibimiento del General Paez en Washington, capital federal de los Estados-Unidos. *Nueva York.* 1851. 8vo, pp. 38. *See also* No. 14621.

PAEZ (R.) Travels and Adventures in South and Central America. First Series: Life in the Llanos of Venezuela. By Don Ramon Paez. *New York: Charles Scribner & Co.* 1868. 12mo, pp. xlviii, (2), 473. Map and Plates. 58140

A new edition is entitled: "Wild Scenes in South America: or, Life in the Llanos of Venezuela." ... *New York: Charles Scribner.* 1862. 12mo, pp. x, 502. Plates. + Second Edition. [*Ibid.*] 1863.

PAGAN (Blaise François de). Relation | Historiqve | et Geographiqve, | de la grande Riviere | des Amazones | dans l'Ameriqve | Par Le Comte de Pagan. | Extraicte de diuers Autheurs, & reduitte en | meilleure forme. | Auec la Carte ... . | *A Paris:* | *Chez Cardin Bessongne* | ... | M. DC. LVI. 8vo, pp. (10), 190. Map. 58141

Several chapters of this curious work are devoted to descriptions of the aborigines of the valley of the Amazon; and those treating of the advantages of commerce with them, suggest an odd comparison with the works of our own day, written two centuries later, which do but little more than repeat the same statements. It is composed principally from that of Acuna.

PAGAN. An | Historical & Geographical | Description | of the | Great Country & River | of the Amazones | in | America. | Drawn out of Divers Authors, and reduced | into a better forme; with a Mapp of | the River, and of its Provinces, being | that place which Sr Walter Rawleigh intended | to conquer and plant, when he made his Voy- | age to Guiana. | Written in French by the Count of Pagan, and | dedicated to Cardinall Mazarine, in order | to a Conquest by the Cardinals moti | on to be undertaken. | And now translated into English by William | Hamilton ... | *London: Printed for John Starkey at the Miter in Fleet-* | *Street near Temple-Barre.* 1661. 8vo, pp. (30), 153, (6). Map. H. 58142

The map is usually missing.

PAGAN (W.) The Birthplace and Parentage of William Paterson, Founder of the Bank of England, and Projector of the Darien Scheme: ... By William Pagan. *Edinburgh: W. P. Nimmo.* 1865. 12mo, pp. (6), 146. C. 58143

PAGE (A.) The Banner of Freedom; a Collection of Patriotic Songs, original and selected, designed for the Rhode Island Suffrage Association. Edited by Miss Ann Page. *Providence: S. M. Millard & Co.* 1841. 12mo, pp. 24. 58144

PAGE (C. A.) ... On the Naturalization Question. By Charles A. Page, M.A. ... *Washington: Philp & Solomons.* 1869. 8vo, pp. 19. 58145

PAGE (C. G.) Psychomancy. Spirit-Rappings and Table-Tippings Exposed. By Prof. Charles G. Page, M.D. ... *New-York: D. Appleton and Company.* MDCCCLIII. 12mo, pp. 96. H.

PAGE (D. C.) The Quadrennial Confederacy; ... A Sermon ... on ... Thanksgiving for National Victories. By David Cook Page, D.D. *Pittsburgh: J. M'Millan.* 1865. 8vo. 58147

Also: ... A Lecture ... before the American Institute of Instruction ... at Pittsfield, Ms. ... *Boston.* MDCCCXLIV. 12mo, pp. 38. *See also* Dow (*Jr.*), No. 20760.

PAGE (H. M.) Alumni Address ... at Beloit College, July 10, 1861. By Harlan M. Page. *Madison.* 1861. 8vo. 58148

PAGE (H. F.) The Law of Warrants, Entries, Surveys, and Patents, in the Virginia Military District in Ohio .... By Henry Folsam Page. *Columbus: J. H. Ripley & Co.* 1850. 8vo, pp. viii, 160. 58149

Also: The Laws and Decisions in relation to the Virginia Military Land Titles. ... *Columbus.* 1851. 8vo.

PAGE (J.) Address to the Citizens of the District of York, in Virginia. By ... John Page .... [n. p. 1796.] 8vo, pp. 32.

PAGE (J. E.) An Address to the Inhabitants ... of Washington, to ... the President ... and the World at Large. *Washington.* 1844. Folio, pp. 4. 58151

A Mormon piece.

PAGE. Slander Refuted. By John E. Page, Elder of the Church of Latter-day Saints. [n. p. n. d.] 8vo, pp. 16.

PAGE. The Spaulding Story, concerning the Origin of the Book of Mormon, duly examined, and Exposed ... By John E. Page ... *Pittsburgh.* 1843. 8vo. + *Plano, Ill.* 1866. 8vo, pp. 16

Also: The Bible System. Vol. I. No. I. [and II.]. *De Kalb, Ill.* 1856. John E. Page, Editor. *See also* No. 50742.

PAGE (J. W.) Uncle Robin, in his Cabin in Virginia, and Tom without one in Boston. By J. W. Page. *Richmond: J. W. Randolph.* 1853. 12mo, pp. 299. Plate. + Second Edition. [*Ibid.*] 58154

PAGE (J. R.) ... Historical Sermon before the Presbytery of Ontario, at its Semi-Centennial Celebration in Mount Morris, N. Y., March 12, 1867. By Rev. Jos. R. Page. *Rochester, N. Y.* 1867. 8vo, pp. 54. B. 58155

PAGE (Karl G.) Page's Darstellung der bürgerlichen Verhältnisse in den Freistaaten von Nordamerika; nebst einer merkwürdigen Reise dahin. *Bautzen.* [n. d.] 12mo. 58156

An interesting and curious narrative of a shrewd German handicraftsman, who observed much that other travelers pass over. Printed for subscribers only, and scarce.

PAGE (M.) Deed of Gift to my Dear Son, Capt. Mat. Page, one of His Majesty's Justices for New Kent, Va., 1617. Preface by Bishop Meade. *Philadelphia.* 1856. 16mo. 58157

PAGE (P. F.) Traité d'Economie politique et de Commerce des Colonies. Par P. F. Page. Premiere Partie. *Paris: Brochot. An* IX. [1801.] 8vo, pp. 356. Tables. 58158

Chiefly relating to the West Indies.

PAGE (R.) A Critical Examination of the Twelve Resolutions of Mr. Joseph Hume, respecting the Loan of Fifteen Millions for Slave Compensation; ... By Richard Page. *London: Pelham Richardson.* 1839. 8vo, pp. viii, 278. C. 58159

PAGE (S.) The Representation of Dr. Samuel Page to the South-Sea Company, Shewing that the Author of a late Pamphlet, entitled, "The Trade Granted to the South-Sea Company considered with relation to Jamaica," had advanced nothing material ... but what has been publicly proposed, ... by the said Dr. Page ... before. *Printed in the Year* 1714. 8vo, pp. 16. J.C.B.

PAGE (T. J.) La Plata, the Argentine Confederation and Paraguay. Being a Narrative of the Exploration of the Tributaries of the River La Plata and adjacent countries during ... 1853, '54, '55, and '56, under the orders of the United States Government. By Thomas J. Page .... *New York: Harper & Brothers.* 1859. 8vo, pp. 632. Map and Plates. BA. 58161

Also: Le Paraguay et les Républiques de la Plata. ... *Paris.* 1851. 8vo, pp. 48. —

Report of the Exploration and Survey of the River "La Plata" and Tributaries .... *Washington: Cornelius Wendell, Printer.* 1856. 8vo, pp. 38. Map.

PAGE (W. P.) Common Schools; the Necessity of their Improvement, and School Libraries: ... By Rev. Wm. P. Page. *Geneseo: Printed by S. P. Allen.* 1838. 8vo, pp. 32. H. 58162

[PAGE (——).] Blanchelande, ex-gouverneur de Saint-Domingue, convaincu de trahison par ses propres moyens justificatifs. [*Paris: Imprimerie de L. Potier de Lille.* 1793.] 8vo, pp. 28.

Also: Discours historique sur la cause et les désastres de la partie française de Saint-Domingue. [*Paris:*] *Potier de Lille.* [n. d.] 8vo, pp. 68. — Page, Commissaire de Saint-Domingue, á Paul Alliot, maire de Levroux. [*Paris: L. Potier de Lille.* 179–.] 8vo, pp. 4. — Réflexions sur la déportation des citoyens Verneuil, Ballio, Fournier et Gervais, ordonnée par Sonthonax. [n. p. n. d.] 8vo, pp. 8. — Réflexions sur le despotisme qu'exercent à Saint-Domingue les commissaires Polverel et Sonthonax. [n. p. n. d.] 8vo, pp. 24. — Réflexions sur les colonies. [n. p. n. d.] 8vo, pp. 11.

[PAGE *and* BRULLEY.] Sentinelle, garde à vous! À J. B. Louvet. [n. p. n. d.] 8vo, pp. 16. H. 58164

Also: Conspirations, trahisons et calomnies dévoillées et dénoncées par plus de dix mille Francais réfugiés au continent de l'Amérique (analyse des pièces par Page et Brulley). *Paris: Fonrouge.* [n. d.] 8vo, pp. viii, 78. — Courte réponse que font les commissaires de Saint-Domingue, Page et Brulley, au précis de la justification de P. A. Cambefort, et autres déportés de Saint-Domingue. *Paris, 2 février* 1793. 8vo, pp. 12. — Notes fournies au Comité de Salut public par les commissaires de Saint-Domingue Page et Brulley. [n. p. n. d.] 8vo. — Observations sur le rapport du citoyen Dornier relatif aux lettres de change. [n. p.] 1793. 8vo, pp. 8.

PAGE, BRULLEY, *and* LEGRAND. Défi au factieux. Adresse à la Convention. *Paris: Laurens. An* III. 8vo, pp. 16. 58165

PAGEAN (M.) Extrait de la Relation des aventures et voyages de Mathieu Pagean. *Nouvelle-York.* 1863. 8vo. 58166

PAGÈS (Pierre Marie François). Nouveau Voyage autour du Monde, en Asie, en Amérique et en Afrique, en 1788, 1789 et 1790; précédé d'un voyage en Italie et en Sicile, en 1787. ... *Paris: H. J. Jansen.* 1797. 3 vols., 8vo. C. 58167

PAGÈS. Voyages autour du Monde et vers les deux Poles, par Terre et par Mer pendant les années 1767, 1768, 1769, 1770, 1771, 1773, 1774 & 1776. Par M. de Pagès .... *Paris: Chez Moutard.* M.DCC.LXXXII. 2 vols., 8vo, pp. 432; 272. Maps and 10 Plates. BA. + *Berne: Nouvelle Société Typographique.* 1783. 3 vols., 8vo, pp. viii, 199; 166; 219. J.C.B. 58168

PAGÈS. Herrn De Pagès Reisen um die Welt und nach den beiden Polen zu Lande und zur See in den Jahren 1767, 1768, 1769, 1770, 1771, 1773, 1774 und 1776. Aus dem Französi-

schen übersetzt. *Frankfurt und Leipzig: Johann Georg Fleischer.* 1786. 8vo, pp. (10), 716. 7 Maps. J.C.B. 58169

PAGÈS. Zee- en Land-Reizen rondom de Waereld, en naar derzelver beide Poolen. ... *Rotterdam.* 1784. 4to. 58170

PAGÈS. Travels Round the World, in the Years 1767, 1768, 1769, 1770, 1771. By Monsieur de Pagés .... Translated from the French. *London: J. Murray.* MDCCXCI. 2 vols., 8vo, pp. xiv, 289; iv, 261. + *Dublin: P. Byrne.* 1791. 8vo, pp. xv, 437. + The Second Edition Enlarged. *London: J. Murray.* MDCCXCIII. 3 vols., 8vo, pp. xx, 300; xii, 268; xxii, (1), 303.

Partly reprinted in Mavor's "Voyages," XII. and XV. *See also* Rich, I. 309, 370.

Pages from the Ecclesiastical History. *See* [Burgess (G.)], III.

PAGET (J.) An Inquiry into the Evidence relating to the Charges brought by Lord Macaulay against William Penn. By John Paget, Esq. *William Blackwood & Sons, Edinburgh.* M DCCLVIII. Fcap 8vo, pp. v, 138. C. 58172

PAGET. New "Examen;" ... *Edinburgh.* 1861. 12mo. C.

Includes his "Inquiry" relative to Macaulay's "Penn."

PAGOS (*Gen.* de). Dos Palabras al Escmo. Presidente de la República sobre la Suspension General de Pagos. *Mexico.* 1846. 8vo. 58174

PAIGE (A. C.) Address to the Graduating Class of the State and National Law School. By Alonzo C. Paige. *Albany: Little & Company.* 1852. 8vo, pp. 27. H. 58175

Also: Address to the Graduating Class ... University of Albany, ... February 18, 1858. ... *Albany.* 1858. 8vo, pp. 36.

PAIGE (L. R.) An Address at the Centennial Celebration in Hardwick, Mass., November 15th, 1838. By Lucius R. Paige. *Cambridge: Metcalf, Torrey and Ballou.* 1838. 8vo, pp. 76. C.

Also: Address ... Amicable Lodge, October 18, 1855. ... *Cambridge.* M DCCC LVI. 8vo, pp. 31.

PAIGE (R.) An Oration ... in Hancock, July 4th, 1803 .... By Reed Paige. *Amherst: Printed by Joseph Cushing.* 1804. 8vo, pp. 20. BA. 58177

PAIGE. A Sermon, ... at Concord, before ... the Governor, ... at the Annual Election, June 6th, 1805. By Reed Page, A.M. ... *Concord: Printed by George Hough.* [1805.] 8vo, pp. 24.

P[aige] (R[hoda] A[nn].) Wild Notes from the Back Woods. By R. A. P. *Cobourg.* 1850. 12mo, pp. 62.

See Morgan's "Bibliotheca Canadensis," p. 120, article, Falkner.

Pain (Lewis). Short View of Spanish America. *London.* 1732. 8vo. 58180

A doubtful title from Allibone's "Dictionary." Compare with Campbell (John).

Paine (B.) Unconstitutionality of the Fugitive Act. Argument of Byron Paine, Esq. and Opinion of Hon. A. D. Smith, ... [*Milwaukee.* 185–.] 8vo, pp. 35. H. 58181

Paine (C.) An Oration, pronounced July 4, 1801, at ... Boston ... . By Charles Paine, Esq; ... . *Boston: Manning & Loring.* [1801.] 8vo, pp. 24. B. 58182

Also: An Address ... before the ... Massachusetts Charitable Fire Society, ... May 27, 1808. ... *Boston: The Society.* 1808. 8vo, pp. 25.

Paine (E. H.) In Memoriam—Eliza Hale Paine entered into rest May 31, 1855. *Albany.* 1855. 8vo, pp. 75. 58183

Paine (E.) An Oration ... before the Students of Brown University, ... in Providence, July 5, 1813. In Commemoration of ... American Independence. By Emerson Paine. *Providence: Printed by H. Mann and Co.* 1813. 8vo, pp. 30. B. 58184

With notices of the War of 1812 between England and the United States. The author favors a vigorous prosecution of the war, but protests against the invasion of the Canadas.

Paine. Sermon, ... at Middleborough ... June 9, 1822. By Emerson Paine ... Occasioned by his Dismission. ... Added the Result of the Ecclesiastical Council ... . *Plymouth, Mass.: Printed by Allen Danforth.* 1822. 8vo, pp. 31, (1). B. 58185

Paine (H. E.) Purchase of Alaska. Speech of Hon. Halbert E. Paine, ... March 21, 1868. *Washington.* 1868. 8vo, pp. 15. 58186

Also: Speech ... March 27, 1866, on the Bankrupt Bill. [n. p. n. d.] 8vo.—Payment of Soldiers' Bounties. Speech ... January 6, 1868. [*Washington.* 1868.] 8vo, pp. 8.—Reconstruction. Speech ... January 16, 1868. [*Washington.* 1868.] 8vo, pp. 8.

Paine (H. D.) The Paine Family Register, or, Genealogical Notes and Queries. *Albany, N. Y.: J. Munsell.* 1857–59. 4to.

Paine (J. A.), *Jr.* Catalogue of Plants found in Oneida County and Vicinity. By John A. Paine, Junr. *Albany.* 1865. 8vo, pp. 140. C. 58188

Paine (L. L.) Political Lessons of the Rebellion. A Sermon ... at Farmington, Connecticut, April, 1862. By Levi L. Paine. *Farmington: Samuel S. Cowles.* 1862. 8vo, pp. 19.

Paine (L. W.) Six Years in a Georgia Prison. Narrative of Lewis W. Paine ... . *New York.* 1851. 12mo. Portrait. + *Boston: Bela Marsh.* 1852. 12mo, pp. 187. H. 58190

Paine (M.) Defence of the Medical Profession of the United States: Valedictory Address ... March 11, 1846. By Martyn Paine ... . Seventh Edition. *New York: The Author.* 1846. 8vo, pp. 24. + Eighth Edition. [*Ibid.*] + Tenth Edition. [*Ibid.*]

Paine. Letters on the Cholera Asphyxia ... in New York. ... With other Letters. By Martyn Paine, M.D. *New York: Collins & Hannay.* 1832. 8vo, pp. 160. BA. 58192

Paine. Memoir of Robert Troup Paine. By his Parents. ... Printed for Private Distribution, especially for the Classmates of the Youth. *New York: John F. Trow, Printer.* 1852. 4to, pp. (2), viii, 524, (2). 2 Portraits, 2 Plates. BA. 58193

One copy printed in folio for Harvard University. Also: Defence of an Introductory Lecture on the "Improvement of Medical Education in the United States." ... *Boston.* 1844. 8vo, pp. 4.—A Lecture on the Improvement of Medical Education in the United States; ... *New York.* 1843. 8vo, pp. 16. B.

Paine (N.) Remarks on the Early Paper Currency of Massachusetts. ... April 25, 1866. By Nathaniel Paine. *Cambridge: Press of John Wilson and Sons.* 1866. Imp. 8vo, pp. 66. BA.

Paine (R.) Baccalaureate Address, ... at ... Lagrange College, June 8th, 1837; by Robert Paine, A.M. ... *Nashville, Ten.* 1837. 8vo, pp. 19. H. 58195

Paine (Robert Treat), *Jr.* Resumption of Specie Payments, Enforced Contraction of the Currency will Cause Distress and Panic ... . By R. T. Paine, Jr. *Boston: Little, Brown & Co.* 1869. 8vo, pp. 58. 58196

Paine (R. T.) Resolutions adopted by the Senior Class, March 18, 1851, on the Death of Robert Troup Paine. [n. p.] 1851. 12mo, pp. 12. M. 58197

See also No. 58193, *supra.*

Paine (S.) An Eulogy on General George Washington, pronounced ... in presence of the Grand Lodge of South Carolina, ... 22d of February, 1800 ... . By Seth Paine ... . *Charleston, South Carolina: Printed by Freneau & Paine.* 1800. 8vo, pp. 28.

Paine (T.) An Eulogy on the Life of General George Washington ... . Written At the request of the Citizens of Newburyport, and delivered ... in that town, January 2nd, 1800. By Thomas Paine, A.M. ... *Printed at Newburyport, by Edmund M. Blunt.* 1800. 8vo, pp. 22. C., H. + *London.* 1800. 58199

The author afterward had his name changed to Robert Treat Paine, in order that he might not be confounded with Thomas Paine, author of "Common Sense," etc.

Paine. An Oration, ... Delivered, July 17th, 1799, in Commemoration of the Dissolution of the Treaties, and Consular Convention between France and the United States of America. By Thomas Paine. *Boston: Printed by John Russell.* 1799. 8vo, pp. 30. H. + Second Edition. [*Ibid.*] 58200

Also: Adams and Liberty. [Patriotic Song. n. p. n. d.] Folio, 1 leaf.—The Invention of Letters: a Poem, ... delivered in Cambridge, ... July 15, 1795. ... *Boston: Printed by Alexander Martin.* 1795. 4to, pp. 15. W. + Second Edition. [*Ibid.*] 12mo, pp. 16. + Third Edition. *Boston.* 1819. 8vo.—The Ruling Passion: An occasional Poem. ... *Boston: Printed by Manning & Loring.* 1797. 4to, pp. 32.—Sketch of the Character of the Late Hon. Robert Treat Paine, LL.D. ... [*Boston.* n. d.] 8vo, pp. 4.

Paine. The Works, in Verse and Prose, of the Late Robert Treat Paine, Jun. Esq., with Notes. To which are prefixed Sketches of his Life, Character and Writings. [By Charles Prentiss.] *Boston: J. Belcher.* 1812. 8vo, pp. lxxxviii, (2), 464, (1). Portrait. B. 58201

Paine (T.), *of Weymouth.* An Almanack, for the Year, 1718. By Thomas Paine, B.A. *Boston: T. Crump.* 1718. 12mo. Continued. 58202

[Paine.] A | Discourse | shewing, | That the real first Cause | of the Straits and Diffi | culties of this Province | of the Massachusetts | Bay, | is its Extravagan | cy, & not Paper Money; | and also | What is a safe Foundation to Raise a Bank of Credit on, and what | not ... . By Philopatria. | *Boston: Printed by J. Franklin, for D. Henchman* ... 1721. 8vo, pp. 16. 58203

Paine. The Doctrine of Earthquakes. Two Sermons ... at a particular Fast in Weymouth, Nov. 3, 1727, the Friday after the Earthquake ... . By Thomas Paine. ... *Boston: D. Henchman.* MDCCXXVIII. 8vo, pp. 87. 58204

Paine. The Temporal Safety of the Lord's People ... . Considered with Respect to God's People in New England ... . Preached at Weymouth, July 30, 1732. On the Occasion of

the Treaty with the Indians ... . By Thomas Paine. ... *Boston, N. E.: S. Gerrish.* 1732. 12mo, pp. 19. B. 58205

Also: The Pastoral Charge ... . A Sermon ... at ... Weymouth, August 19, 1719. ... *Boston: Daniel Henchman.* 1720. 8vo, pp. ii, 42.— ... Sermon preached at Braintree ... after the Burial of ... Mrs. Ann Niles, ... who died Oct. 25th, 1732. ... *Boston: Printed by S. Kneeland & T. Green.* M,DCC,XXXII. 8vo, pp. 28.— ... A Sermon at the Gathering of the Church at Biddeford, and ordaining of Rev. Samuel Willard, Sept. 30, 1730. ... *Boston.* M,DCC,XXXI. 8vo, pp. (4), 51. B., M.

[Paine (Thomas).] The American Crisis. Number I. By the Author of Common Sense. [n. p. n. d.] 8vo, pp. 8. No. II. 9–24; No. III. 25–54. H. + *New York.* [n. d.] 8vo.

The original issue of this celebrated work. The first is without date. The second is addressed to Lord Howe, and is dated at Philadelphia, January 13, 1777. The third, April 19, 1777.

[Paine.] The American Crisis. Number III. ... *Philadelphia: Styner and Cist* ... [1777.] 8vo, pp. (1), 27–57. + Number IV. [*Ibid.* n. d.] 8vo, pp. (1), 58–60. 58207

[Paine.] The American Crisis. Number V. Addressed to General Sir William Howe. ... *Lancaster: Printed by John Dunlap.* M,DCC,LXXVIII. 8vo, pp. (2), 63–88. + *Hartford, reprinted.* 1778. 8vo, pp. 32. + *New Haven: Re-printed by T. & S. Green.* 1778. 8vo, pp. 32. BA. 58208

Paine. The American Crisis, and a Letter to Sir Guy Carleton, on the murder of Captain Huddy, and the intended retaliation on Captain Asgill, of the Guards. By Thomas Paine ... . *London: Daniel Isaac Eaton.* [1788?] 8vo, pp. (2), 293. C. + [*Ibid.* 1796.] + *London: W. T. Sherwin.* 1817. 8vo, pp. 196. + *London: R. Carlile.* 1819. 8vo, pp. 196. + *London: James Watson.* 1835. 18mo, pp. (2), 145. + *Granville, N. J.* 1839. 8vo. 58209

[Paine.] La Crise Américaine. ... *Paris.* 1791. 8vo.

[Paine.] Common Sense: Addressed to the Inhabitants of America, on the following interesting Subjects. I. Of the Origin and Design of Government in general, with concise Remarks on the English Constitution. II. Of Monarchy and Hereditary Succession. III. Thoughts on the present State of American Affairs. IV. Of the present Ability of America, with some miscellaneous Reflections. ... *Philadelphia: Printed, and Sold, by R. Bell* ... . MDCCLXXVI. 8vo, pp. (4), 79. P. 58211

The next tract speedily followed this, and the two together constitute the ordinary editions of this work.

[Paine.] Large Additions to Common Sense; Addressed to the Inhabitants of America, on the following interesting Subjects. I. The American Patriot's Prayer. II. American Independancy defended, by Candidus. III. The Propriety of Independancy, by Demophilus. ... IV. A Review of the American Contest, with some Strictures on the King's Speech. Addressed to all Parents in the Thirteen United Colonies, by a Friend to Posterity and Mankind. V. Letter to Lord Dartmouth, by an English American. VI. Observations on Lord North's Conciliatory Plan, by Sincerus. To which is added and given An Appendix to Common Sense: Together with an Address to the People called Quakers, on their Testimony concerning Kings and Government, and the present Commotions in America. *Philadelphia:* ... *R. Bell* ... . MDCCLXXVI. 8vo, pp. (2), 81–147. BA., P. 58212

Original edition. *See* "Monthly Review," LIV. 493.

[Paine.] Large Additions to Common Sense; ... [as in No. 58212]. *Boston:* ... 1776. 8vo, pp. 43, (1). + *Newport, Reprinted.* 1776. 8vo, pp. 70. 58213

[Paine.] Common Sense; addressed to the Inhabitants of America ... . Written by an Englishman. Second Edition. ... *Philadelphia: Printed by R. Bell.* MDCCLXXVI. 8vo, pp. 79. BA.

This famous work passed through several editions as below:
New-York: Reprinted ... by John Anderson. [1776.] 8vo, pp. (4), 56.
Boston: Edes & Gill. MDCCLXXVI. 8vo, pp. (2), 44.
Newport: ... Solomon Southwick. M,DCC,LXX,VI. 8vo, pp. (4), 16, 31. B.
Newbury Port: Reprinted by John Mycall. [1776.] 8vo, pp. 56. BA.
Norwich: Re-printed by Judah P. Spooner. M,DCC,LXXVI. 8vo, pp. 56.
Philadelphia: ... W. & T. Bradford. [1776.] 8vo, pp. (4), 50. B.
The Third Edition. *Salem.* 1776. 8vo, pp. 28.
The Fourth Edition. *Lancaster.* [1776.] 12mo, pp. 63.
The Sixth Edition. *Providence: ... John Carter.* M,DCC,LXXVI. 4to, pp. 33. H.
A New Edition ... . To which is added an Appendix; together with an Address to the People called Quakers. N. B. The New Additions here given increases the Work upwards of One-Third. ... *London: Re-printed for J. Almon.* 1776. 8vo, pp. (6), 54.
Philadelphia: ... W. and T. Bradford. [1776.] 8vo, pp. (6), 56. C.
Edinburgh, reprinted: ... M.DCC.LXXVI. 12mo, pp. (6), 99.
Newcastle upon Tyne, Re-printed: By T. Robson and Co. MDCCLXXVI. 8vo, pp. 131.

[Paine.] Common Sense; with the whole Appendix; the Address to the Quakers; also, the Large Additions, and A Dialogue between the Ghost of General Montgomery just arrived from the Elysian Fields; and an American Delegate in a Wood, near Philadelphia; On the Grand Subject of American Independancy. *Philadelphia: R. Bell.* MDCCLXXVI. 8vo, pp. (8), 147, 16.

[Paine.] Common Sense; addressed to the Inhabitants of America ... . *London: J. Ridgway.* M,DCC,XCI. 8vo, pp. 88. BA.
London: J. S. Jordan. M,DCC,XCI. 8vo, pp. 90, (1).
Philadelphia. 1791. 8vo.
London: H. D. Symonds. 1791. 12mo. + [*Ibid.*] 1792. 12mo, pp. 36. Portrait.

[Paine.] Common Sense ... . *London.* M.DCC.XCII. 12mo, pp. 58. + [*Ibid.*] 1792. 8vo, pp. 120.
Boston: Printed ... by John M. Dunham. 1803. 8vo, pp. 43. B.
London: R. Carlile. 1819. 8vo, pp. 56.
London: Printed by W. T. Sherwin. 1817. 8vo, pp. 56. BA.
London: Benbow, ... 1821. 12mo, pp. 32.
Dedham, Mass.: ... S. Bryant. 1844. 8vo, pp. 39. H.
New York. 1850. 12mo, pp. 48. B.

For replies, *see* Candidus, *pseudon.*, our Vol. III., No. 10671, Plain Truth, Rationalis, *pseudon.*, True Interest, *and* True Merits.

[Paine.] Additions to Common Sense, Addressed to the Inhabitants of America. ... *London: Reprinted for J. Almon.* 1776. 8vo, pp. 47. C. 58215

"With these 'Additions,' Paine had nothing to do. The pamphlet was made up by Robert Bell, the original publisher, after his quarrel with Paine, to be bound with the third edition of 'Common Sense,' with Paine's own Additions and 'Appendix.' The publication was a device to help the sale of Bell's edition against the one printed about the same time by W. and T. Bradford, who had become Paine's publishers."—J. H. Trumbull. For the American edition, *see* "Large Additions," No. 58212, *supra.*

[Paine.] Le Sens Commun, addressé [*sic*] aux habitants de l'Amérique ... . Nouvelle Édition, avec Plusieurs Additions, un Appendix, etc. Traduit de l'Anglois. *Rotterdam.* 1776. 8vo.

[Paine.] Le Sens-Commun. Ouvrage adressé aux Américains, et dans lequel ou traite de l'origine et de l'objet du Gouvernement, de la Constitution Angloise, de la Monarchie héréditaire, et de la situation de l'Amérique Septentrionale. *Paris: Gueffier.* 1791. 8vo, pp. iv, 113. + Traduit sur la dernière édition par l'auteur. *Paris.* 1793. 8vo. C. + [*Ibid.*] 1794.

Paine. The Crisis, a Work written while with the Army of the Revolution, with a view of stimulating that patriotic band to persevere in their Glorious Struggle for the Rights of Man. By Thomas Paine. ... *Granville, Middletown, N. J.: George H. Evans.* 1839. 8vo, pp. 365. 58218

[Paine.] A Crisis Extraordinary. Wednesday, August 9. 1775. [Colophon:] *Philadelphia: William Harris.* [1780.] 8vo, pp. 16. P. 58219

Relates to General Gage's Proclamation.

[Paine.] A Dialogue between the Ghost of General Montgomery just arrived from the Elysian Fields; and an American Delegate in a Wood near Philadelphia. [*Philadelphia: R. Bell.*] 1776. 8vo, pp. 14. M. + [*New York: Reprinted.* 1865.] 8vo, pp. 16. 58220

Of the New York edition, eighty copies only were privately printed.

[Paine.] Dissertations on Government, the Affairs of the Bank, and Paper-Money. ... *Philadelphia: Printed by Charles Cist,* ... M,DCC,LXXXVI. 8vo, pp. (2), 53. B., H., M., P. 58221

[Paine.] Letter addressed to the Abbe Raynal on the Affairs of North-America. In which the Mistakes in the Abbe's Account of the Revolution of America are corrected and cleared up. By Thomas Paine, M.A. ... *Philadelphia: Robert Aitken.* M,DCC,-LXXXII. 8vo, pp. 77. BA. 58222

See "Monthly Review," LXVIII. 324; *see also* Raynal (Abbé). This famous piece was repeatedly reprinted as below:
Boston: Re-Printed by Benjamin Edes & Sons. M,DCC,LXXXII. 12mo, pp. 70. W.
London, reprinted: C. Dilly. M.DCC.LXXXII. 8vo, pp. viii, 76. BA.
Dublin. 1782. 8vo, pp. viii, 76.
London: John Stockdale. MDCCLXXXII. 8vo, pp. (2), 83. P.
Second Edition. *Philadelphia: Printed by Melchior Steiner. London: Reprinted for J. Stockdale.* MDCCLXXXIII. 8vo, pp. (2), 83. P. + Third Edition. [*Ibid.*] J.C.B.
London: J. Ridgway. M,DCC,XCI. 12mo, pp. (2), vi, 67. A. + [*Ibid.*] M,DCC,XCII. 8vo, pp. vi, 81. + [*Ibid.*] 8vo, pp. 46. + [*Ibid.*] M,DCC,XCIII. 8vo, pp. 36. BA.
London. 1795. 8vo. + *London.* 1817. 8vo. + *London: R. Carlile.* 1819. 8vo, pp. 59, (2).

[Paine.] Lettre addressé [*sic*] à M. l'Abbé Raynal, sur les affaires de l'Amérique Septentrionale, où l'on reléve les erreurs dans lesquelles cet auteur est tombé, en rendant compte de la Révolution d'Amérique. Traduite de l'Anglois de M. Thomas Payne, M.A. ... [n. p.] 1783. 8vo, pp. xii, 124. J.C.B. 58223

Paine. A Letter to George Washington, President of the United States ... . On Affairs Public and Private. By Thomas Paine ... . *Philadelphia: Printed by Benj. Franklin Bache.* 1796. 8vo, pp. 76. BA. + *Dublin: Printed by J. Stockdale* ... 1797. 8vo, pp. 48. B. + *London: H. D. Symonds.* 1797. 8vo, pp. (2), 77. + *London: Daniel Isaac Eaton.* 1797. 8vo, pp. (2), 53.

"Mr. Paine complains of Washington for not having interfered for his liberation, when a prisoner in France, in the time of Robespierre; accuses him of wanting gratitude and humanity, and attacks his military skill, which he pronounces inferior to that of Generals Gates and Green."—*Monthly Review*, XXII. 216.

Paine. Letter from Thomas Paine to George Washington, dated Paris, July, 1796. To which is added, Thomas Paine's Letter, dated Federal City, Nov., 1802. ... *Baltimore: Printed by G. Douglas.* 1802. 8vo, pp. 44. 58225

Mr. Paine was no admirer of Washington and thus addresses him: "Elevated to the chair of the presidency, you assumed the merit of everything to yourself; and the natural ingratitude of your constitution began to appear. You commenced your presidential career by encouraging and swallowing the grossest adulation; and you travelled America from one end to the other to put yourself in the way of receiving it. You have as

many addresses in your chest as James the Second. As to what were your views, for you are not great enough to have ambition, though you are little enough to have vanity, they cannot be inferred from expressions of your own; but the partizans of your politics have divulged the secret."

Paine. Thomas Paine's Letter to the Late General George Washington, when President of the United States. Dated, Paris, June 30, 1795 [for July 30, 1796]. A New Edition. *New-York: R. D. Taylor.* 1803. 8vo, pp. 34. H. 58227

Paine. A Letter to George Washington, on ... The Late Treaty concluded between Great Britain and the United States ... including other matters. By Thomas Paine. *London: T. Williams.* 1797. 8vo, pp. 50. + Second Edition, Enlarged. *London.* 1797. 8vo. + *London: ... R. Carlile.* 1819. 8vo, pp. 36, vii. 58228

This elicited: "A Five Minutes' Answer to Paine's Letter to Washington." *London.* 1797. 8vo, pp. 44. M.

Paine. A Letter to the Earl of Shelburne, on his Speech, July 10, 1782, respecting the acknowledgement of American Independence. By Thomas Paine ... . *Philadelphia.* 1782. 8vo. + *London: Reprinted for J. Stockdale.* MDCCLXXXIII. 8vo, pp. (2), 28. + A New Edition. *London: J. Ridgway.* 1791. 8vo, pp. 58. Portrait. + *London: J. S. Jordan.* MDCCXCI. 8vo, pp. 28. + *Dublin: William Wilson.* M.D.CCXCI. 8vo, pp. 48. + Ninth Edition. *London.* 1792. 8vo. W. 58229

Paine. Letters from Thomas Paine to the Citizens of the United States on his arrival from France. *Washington City: Printed by W. Duane & Son.* 1802. 8vo, pp. 34. B. + [*Ibid.*] 8vo, pp. 40. + [*Ibid.*] 8vo, pp. 50. + *New York.* 1802. 8vo, pp. 24. + [*Ibid.*] 8vo, pp. 32. 58230

Paine. Letters from Thomas Paine, to the Citizens of America, after an absence of fifteen years in Europe. To which are subjoined Some Letters, between him and the late General Washington, Mr. Samuel Adams, and the present President of the United States, Mr. Jefferson: ... *London: ... T. C. Rickman.* 1804. 8vo, pp. (2), vii, 70. + *London: W. T. Sherwin.* 1817. 8vo. + *London: R. Carlile.* 1819. 8vo, pp. 44, (2). 58231

Paine. Of the Cause of the Yellow Fever; and the Means of Preventing it in Places not yet infected with it; Addressed to the Board of Health in America. ... By Thomas Paine. *London: T. C. Rickman.* 1807. 8vo, pp. 68. 58232

Paine. The Political and Miscellaneous Works of Thomas Paine. *London: R. Carlile.* 1819. 2 vols., 8vo. H. 58233

Each work separately paged.

Paine. The Political Works of Thomas Paine, ... with Appendix, containing the Author's Life. *London.* 1817. 2 vols., 8vo. Portrait. + *Springfield.* 1824. 12mo. + As approved of by Gen. Washington, ... and ... [others]. *Springfield: Peter Reynolds.* 1826. 12mo, pp. xxx, 425. 58234

Paine. The Political Writings of Thomas Paine ... . To which is prefixed A Brief Sketch of the Author's Life. *Charlestown, Mas.: G. Davidson.* 1824. 2 vols., 8vo, pp. 432; 416. + *New York.* 1830. 2 vols., 8vo. + *New York: Geo. H. Evans.* 1835. 2 vols., 8vo. + *Middletown, N. J.* 1837. 2 vols., 8vo. + A New Edition, with Additions. [*Ibid.*] 1839. 2 vols., 8vo. + *Boston.* 1856. 2 vols., 8vo. 58235

Paine. Die Politischen Werke von Thomas Paine. Erster [–Zweiter] Band. *Philadelphia: Verlag von Maasz und Cursch.* 1852. 12mo. C. 58236

[Paine.] Public Good, being an Examination Into the Claim of Virginia to the Vacant Western Territory, and Of the Right of The United States to the Same. To which is added, Proposals for laying off a new State, to be applied as a Fund for Carrying on the War, or Redeeming the National Debt. By the Author of Common Sense. *Philadelphia: Printed by John Dunlap.* M,DCC,LXXX. 8vo, pp. 38. BA. 58237

Reprinted with the author's name as below:

Paine. Public Good [etc.] ... Written in the year 1780. By Thomas Paine. *London: Printed by W. T. Sherwin.* 1817. 8vo, pp. 35. + *London: R. Carlile.* 1819. 8vo, pp. 25.

Paine. Remarques sur les Erreurs de l'Histoire philosophique et politique de M. G. T. Raynal, par rapport aux Affaires de l'Amérique Septentrionale, par M. Thomas Paine ... . Traduites de l'Anglois et augmentées d'une préface et de quelques notes par A. M. Cerisier. *Amsterdam.* 1783. 8vo, pp. 126. + *Bruxelles.* 1783. 8vo. 58239

Paine. Thomas Paine to the Citizens of Pennsylvania, on the Proposal for calling a Convention. *Philadelphia: Printed by Wm. Duane.* 1805. 12mo, pp. 40. B. 58240

Paine. Thoughts on the Peace, and the Probable Advantages thereof to the United States ... . By Thomas Paine ... . *London: J. Stockdale.* MDCCLXXXIII. 8vo, pp. (4), 18. J.C.B. 58241

Paine. Tom Paine's Jests; being an entirely New and Select Collection of Patriotic Bon Mots, Repartees, Anecdotes, Epigrams, Observations, &c. on Political Subjects. By Thomas Paine ... . To which is added, A Tribute to the Swinish Multitude, Being a Choice Collection of Patriotic Songs. *Philadelphia: Printed for Mathew Carey.* MDCCXCVI. 12mo, pp. 72. H.

It is questionable whether Paine had anything to do with this scarce little tract. It is, however, one of the earliest American jest-books.

Paine. Two Letters to Lord Onslow ... and one to Mr. Henry Dundas ... on the Subject of the Late Excellent Proclamation ... . By Thomas Paine ... . *London: James Ridgway.* 1792. 8vo, pp. 36. + Third Edition. [*Ibid.*] S. 58243

Paine. The Works of Thomas Paine ... . *London.* 1792. 8vo. Portrait. 58244

Paine. The Works of Thomas Paine, Secretary for Foreign Affairs to the Congress of the United States in the late War. *Philadelphia: Printed by James Carey.* 1797. 2 vols., 8vo, pp. vi, (1), 391; vi, 368, 148. C. 58245

Paine. The Works of Thomas Paine. With an Account of his Life. *Philadelphia.* 1854. 3 vols., 12mo. C. 58246

Paine. The Writings of Thomas Paine, Secretary for Foreign Affairs to the Congress of the United States of America, in the Late War. *Albany: State of New York, Charles R. & George Webster.* [1792.] 8vo, pp. 517. 58247

The following numbers (58248–52) relate to Thomas Paine:

Paine. An Impartial Sketch of the Life of Thomas Paine, ... To which is added The Letters ... . *London: T. Browne.* 1792. 8vo, pp. 48. C. 58248

Paine. A Letter to Thomas Paine, in answer to his Scurrilous Epistle ... to Washington. ... By An American Citizen. ... *New-York: Printed ... by John Bull.* 1797. 8vo, pp. 24.

Paine. The Life of Thomas Paine. ... *London.* 1850. 12mo, pp. 54. 58250

For another edition, *see* [Holyoake (G. J.)], Vol. VIII., No. 32665; *see also* [Blanchard (C.)], Vol. II., No. 5819.

Paine. The Paine Festival. Celebration of the 119th Anniversary of the Birth-Day of Thomas Paine, at Cincinnati, January 29, 1856. ... *Cincinnati: Valentine Nicholson & Co.* 1856. 16mo, pp. 35. H. 58251

Paine. Some Account of Thomas Paine, in his last Sickness. *New York: Printed by Mahlon Day.* 1820. 8vo, pp. 8. 58252

Paine (T.) Eulogy on George Washington ... . By Thomas Paine, A.M., not the Author of the Crisis. *Geneva, N. Y.* 1841. 8vo, pp. 16. 58253

Paine (T. O.) History of Fort Halifax, Me. By Timothy O. Paine. [n. p. n. d.] Folio, 1 leaf. M. 58254

Paine (W.) An Address to the ... American Antiquarian Society, ... Boston, Oct. 23, 1815. By William Paine, M.D. ... *Worcester, Mass.: Printed by William Manning.* 1815. 8vo, pp. 27

Paine (W. P.) A Sermon preached by Rev. William P. Paine, D.D. ... Holden, Mass., on the Twenty-fifth Anniversary of his Settlement, October 24, 1858. *Worcester: Printed by Edward R. Fiske.* 1859. 8vo, pp. 16. B. 58256

Also: A Sermon preached ... in Holden, October 25th, 1863; the Sunday following the Thirtieth Anniversary of the Settlement of ... Rev. Wm. P. Paine, D.D. *Worcester.* 1864. 8vo, pp. 27. S.

[Painter (E. *and* H.)] Our Ancestors. [n. p.] 1869. 8vo, pp. 20. 58257

Relates to the Painter family of Lima, Delaware Co., Pa.

Painter (H. M.) Brief Incidents in the War in Missouri; and of the Personal Experience of one who has suffered. *Boston.* 1863. 8vo, pp. 28. 58258

Painter. The Duty of the Southern Patriot and Christian in the Present Crisis. A Sermon ... Boonville, Missouri, January 4, 1861. By Rev. H. M. Painter. *Boonville: Caldwell & Stahl.* 1861. 8vo, pp. 16. 58259

Pairpoint (A.) Uncle Sam and his Country; or, Sketches of America in 1854-55-56. By Alfred Pairpoint. *London: Simpkin, Marshall & Co.* 1857. 12mo, pp. 346. 58260

Paiva. Roteiro da Viagem de Vasco de Gama em MCCCCXCVII. Segunda Edição correcta e augmentada ... por A. Herculano e o Barrão do Castello de Paiva. *Lisboa: Imprensa Nacional.* MDCCCLXI. 8vo, pp. xliii, 180, (1). 2 Portraits, 2 Maps.

La Paix de 1782, ou le Bowl de Punch de Master Oliver Dreamer. Traduit de l'Anglais. *Londres.* 1782. 8vo, pp. 47.

Pajeken (C. A.) Reise-Erinnerungen und Abenteuer aus der neuen Welt ... . Mit Vorwort von F. Ruperti. *Bremen.* 1861. 8vo. 58263

Palacin (Joseph Felix). De la Regular Observancia de N. S. P. S. Francisco, Lector Jubilado, ... a los RR. PP. Guardianes, y demas religiosas de esta nuestra Sobredicha Provincia, Salud, y Paz en el Señor. [*Lima.* 1780?] 4to, (19) leaves.

[Palacio (——).] Outline of The Revolution in Spanish America; or An Account of the Origin, Progress, and Actual State of the War carried on between Spain and Spanish America; containing the Principal Facts which have marked the Struggle. By a South-American. *London: Longman ... .* 1817. 8vo, pp. vii, 362. + *New York: James Eastburn and Co.* 1817. 12mo, pp. 219. B., H., P. 58265

[Palacio.] Esquisse de la Révolution de l'Amérique Espagnole; ou, Récit de l'origine, des progrès et de l'état actuel de la guerre entre l'Espagne et l'Amérique espagnole, contenant les principaux faits et les divers combats ... . Par un Citoyen de l'Amérique méridionale. Traduit de l'anglais. *Paris.* 1817. 8vo, pp. 359. + Seconde Édition ... augmentée ... *Paris.* 1819. 8vo, pp. 430. Map. 58266

[Palacio.] Der Freiheitskampf im Spanischen Amerika oder Bericht von dem Ursprunge, Fortgange und gegenwärtigem Stande des Krieges zwischen Spanien und dem Spanischen Amerika. Von einem Südamerikanischen Offizier. Aus dem Englischen. *Hamburg: Hoffman & Campe.* 1818. 8vo, pp. (2), ii, 254. C. 58267

Palacio (Diego Garcia de). Dialogos Militares de la formacion, é informacion de personas, instrumentos, y cosas necessarias para el buen uso de la guerra ... *Con Licencia, en Mexico en Casa de Pedro Ocharte.* 1583. 4to, (4) and 191 leaves. 58268

An extremely rare production of Ocharte's Mexican press.

Palacio. Instrucion Nauthica, y Vocabulario Nautico para el buen uso, y regimiento de las naos, su traça y gouierno conforme à la altura de Mexico ... *Mexico: Pedro Ocharte.* 1587. 4to. 58269

One of the scarcest productions of the early Mexican press.

Palacio. Collection of Rare and Original Documents and Relations, concerning The Discovery and Conquest of America. Chiefly from the Spanish Archives. Published in the Original, with Translations, Illustrative Notes, Maps and Biographical Sketches. By E. G. Squier. No. 1. Carta dirijida al Rey de España, por el Licenciado Dr. Don Diego Garcia de Palacio, 1576. Spanish and English. *New York: Charles B. Norton.* M DCCC LX. 4to, pp. (2), 129, Map, Errata, (2). 58270

Gives a description of the ancient provinces of Guazacapan, Izalco, Cuscatlan, in the Audiencia of Guatemala; with an account of the languages, customs and religion of their aboriginal inhabitants. One hundred copies printed on small and ten on large paper.

Palacio. San Salvador und Honduras im Jahre 1576. Nützlicher Bericht des Licenciaten Dr. Diego Garcia de Palacio an den König von Spanien über die central amerikanischen Provinzien San Salvador und Honduras im Jahre 1576. Aus dem Spanischen ... von Dr. A. von Frantzius ... *Berlin: Dietrich Reimer.* 1873. 8vo, pp. xv, 70. Map. 58271

[Palacio (F. G.)] Claims of Mexican Citizens against the United States for Indian Depredations, being the Opinion of the Mexican Commissioners in the Joint Claims Commission. *Washington, D. C.: Printed by Judd & Detweiler.* 1871. 8vo, pp. 162

Palacio (M. R.) Memorandum sobre el Proceso del Archiduque Fernando Maximiliano de Austria por los C. C. Mariano Riva Palacio y Lic. Rafael Martinez de la Torre. *Mexico* [*Imprenta de F. Diaz de Leon y S. White*]. 1867. Folio, pp. v, 109, 55. 58273

The appendix is entitled: "Defensa del Archiduque de Austria por los C. C. Lics. Jesus Maria Vazquez y Eulalio Maria Ortega en el proceso que se le fromó en la ciudad de Querétaro." Some copies are on large paper. Corrected title of our No. 47036.

Palacio (V. R.) El Libro Rojo. Obra historica escrita por Vicente Riva Palacio y Manuel Payno. Ilustrada con Retratos, Alegorias y Composiciones históricas, en Litografia, por los mejores artistas de la Capital. *Mexico.* 1870. Folio. 58274

Palácios (B.) Corona fúnebre del malogrado jóven Barcelino Palácios. *Carácas.* 1851. 8vo, pp. 35. 58275

Palacios (E.) Memoria leida en la junta general que celebró la Sociedad Económica de amigos del pais, el 26 de diciembre de 1861, por su Secretario D. Enrique Palacios. *Guatemala: Imprenta de L. Luna.* 1861. 4to, pp. 24. 58276

Palacios. Memoria sobre el cultivo del café en Escuintla, ... por ... D. Enrique Palacios. *Guatemala: Imprenta de L. Luna.* 1862. 4to. 58277

Palacios (J. Garcia de). Constituciones synodales de la iglesia cathedral de Cuba. ... [n. p. 1682.] Folio, (20), 122 leaves.

Palafox y Mendoza (J. de). Al Rey Nuestro Señor por la Provincia de la Compañia de Jesus de la Nueva España. En Satisfacion de un libro de el Visitador Obispo D. Juan de Palafox y Mendoza. Publicado en nombre de el Dean y Cabildo de su Iglesia Catedral de la Puebla de los Angeles. [*Mexico.* 1646?] 4to, pp. 278. 58279

A rabid reply by the Jesuits to the charges made by the Bishop.

[Palafox.] Al | Rey Nvestro Señor. | Satisfacion | al Memorial de los | Religiosos de la Compañia | del nombre de Iesvs de la | Nveva-España. | Por | La Dignidad Episcopal de la Puebla de los Angeles. | Sobre la Execvcion, y Obediencia | del Breue Apostolico de N. Santissimo Padre | Innocencio x. | Expedido en sv favor a XIIII. | de Mayo de M.DC.XLVIII. | Y | Passado repetidamente, y mandado executar por el | Supremo Consejo de las Indias. | En el qual determinó su Santidad veinte y seis Decretos | Sacramentales, y Iurisdiccionales, importantes | al bien de las almas. | [n. p.] *Año de* M.DC.LII. | Folio, Title, and 157 leaves. + *Madrid: Gregorio de Mata.* 1652. Folio, pp. 315. 58280

This is the response of Palafox to the attack.

Palafox. Carta del V. Siervo de Dios D. Juan de Palafox y Mendoza al sumo Pontifice Inocencio x. Traducida del Latin al Castellano por Don Salvador Gonzalez. *Madrid.* 1766. 4to. + [*Ibid.*] 1768. 4to. Portrait. + *Megico.* 1841. 4to, pp. 38.

This is the famous letter against the Jesuits which aroused their bitter attacks upon the good Bishop's character.

[Palafox.] Carta Pastoral a la Venerable Congregacion de San Pedro, de la civdad de los Angeles. Y a los reverendos sacerdotes de todo el obispado. *Mexico.* 1640. 4to, 8 leaves.

[Palafox.] Carta Pastoral | del Illvst.mo y R.mo Señor Obispo | de la Pvebla de los Angeles, | que oy es de osma. | A las Religiosas | de aqvel Obispado, | sir viendo aqvella Santa Iglesia | Año de 1641. | Es muy vtil para el conocimiento de las obligacio- | nes de las Esposas de Jesu Christo bien nuestro, | alteza de su Dignidad, y atencion que | deuen tener a ser- | uirle. | Imprimese por orden de su

Eminencia, y concede cien | dias de Indulgencia à quien leyere, ò oyere esta | Carta Pastoral, tan docta, y espiritual, *En To- | ledo à 25. de Março de 1659. años.* | 4to, 10 leaves. 58283

[Palafox.] Carta Pastoral, previniendo los animos de los Fieles de sv Obispado, a la Consacracion del Real Templo de sv Cathedral, qve los Invictissimos Reyes Nuestros, Señores fvndaron, y con sv orden acavó el dicho Señor Obispo. *Año de* 1649. *En Mexico, por la Viuda de Bernardo Calderon.* 4to, Title, 21 l.

[Palafox.] Carta que escrivió al Padre Oratio Carochi de la Compañia de Jesus, sacada de su original que se halla en el convento de Carmelita de la Puebla. *Lovaina: Egidio Denique.* 1713. 8vo, pp. 202. + [*Ibid.*] *Anno* M. DCCXIII. 4to, pp. 129. 58285

Palafox. Cartas al R. P. Andres de Rada, Provincial de la Compañia de Jesus en Mexico, y otros documentos concernientes que en parte de obsequio á la verdad, y justicia ofrece al publico. Th. Vasconsellos. *Roma.* 1700. 12mo, pp. 117. + *Madrid.* 1768. 4to. 58286

There were many publications respecting the dispute between the Bishop of Puebla and the Jesuits.

Palafox. Constituciones para la Contaduria de la Iglesia Cathedral de la Puebla de los Angeles ... [*Mexico:*] *Imprenta de M. de Ortega, y Bonillá.* 1713. 4to. 58287

Palafox. Decreto pontifico expedido en 13 de diciembre de 1769. En que se aprueban todos los procesos pertenecientes a la causa de beatificacion de D. Juan Palafox y Mendoza ... . Siguese la carta que nuestro santisimo Padre Clemente XIV, escribio con fecha de 14, del mismo més y año al ilmo. Sr. D. Fr. Joaquin de Osma ... . [*Puebla de los Angeles.*] 1770. Folio, 5 leaves. C.

Palafox. Decretum Oxomen. Beatificationis, et Canonizationis Ven. Servi Dei Joannis de Palafox y Mendoza ... . *Angelopoli: C. T. Ortega.* 1767. Folio, pp. xviii, (2). C. 58289

Palafox. Discvrsos espiritvales ... Recogidos por el P. Jvan Antonio Velasquez, Prouincial de la Compañi de Jesus. *Madrid: Francisco Martinez.* 1641. 4to, (7), 126 leaves. Portrait and Frontispiece. 58290

Very rare. Leaves 119–126 contain "Carta Pastoral," our No. 58282, *supra.*

[Palafox.] Dell' Eccellenze di St Pietro, opera publicata ora per la prima volta nell' Italiana Favella. *Roma.* 1788. 3 vols., 4to. 2 Portraits. 58291

Palafox. Estatvtos y Constitvciones hechas con comission particvlar de su Magestad, para ello: Por ... D. Jvan de Palafox, y Mendoza ... . Intimadas en clavstro pleno, por el Señor Doctor D. Andres Sanchez de Ocampo, Oydor de la Real Audiencia de Mexico ... Siendo Rector Fray Marcellino de Solis, y Haro, del orden de San Agustin, prior que ha sido del convento de Mexico ... *En Mexico, por la Viuda de Bernardo Calderon.* 1668. Folio, (20), 84, (11) leaves. 58292

The half-title reads: "Estatvtos, y Constitvciones Reales de la Imperial, y Regia Vniversidad de Mexico."

Palafox. Histoire | de | Dom Jean | de Palafox, | Evêque d'Angelopolis, & de- | puis d'Osme. | Et | Des differens qu'il a eus avec les | P. P. Jesuites. | [n. p.] M. DC. XC. | 12mo, pp. (20), 478, (2).

Corrected title of our No. 2055, Vol. I. The author's name is Arnauld.

Palafox. Historia de las Virtudes del Indio: Por el Illo Don Juan de Palafox y Mendoza, Obispo de la Puebla de los Angeles ... *Zaragoza.* 1661. 16mo. 58294

A reprint of our No. 58307, *infra.*

Palafox. Historia Real Sagrada, luz de Principes y Subditos ... *Puebla de los Angeles.* 1643. Folio. + Segunda Impression. *Brusselas: Fr. Foppens.* 1655. 4to. + *Madrid.* 1688. Folio.

Although this work does not contain anything relating to America, I have placed it in this Dictionary because the first edition is an early Mexican imprint.

Palafox. Inocencia vindicada. *See* Juan de la Anunciacion.

[Palafox.] Lettre au Pape Innocent x., contenant diverses plaintes contre les entreprises et les violences des Jésuites dans les Indes Occidentales. [n. p. n. d.] 4to. 58296

Palafox. Manual de los Sanctos Sacramentos corregido por Alvarez de Abreu. *Madrid.* 1758. 4to. 58297

Pages 25–28 contain the office of the Sacrament of Baptism administered to the Indians in the Mexican language.

Palafox. Obras ... con su Vida. *Madrid.* 1659–1671. 8 vols., folio. Portrait. + [*Ibid.*] 1668–1671. 9 vols., folio.

Palafox. Obras ... con Vida del Autor, por el P. Ant. Gonzalez de Rosende, O.S.F. *Madrid.* 1762. 15 vols., folio. Port.

Best edition. For an account of this learned Bishop, and the persecutions he suffered, *see* Poinder's "History of the Jesuits." The "Virtudes del Indio" is included in this edition.

Palafox. El Pastor de noche bvena. ... *México.* 1644. 16mo. + Van añadidas al fin mas consideraciones, i remedios para conservar la amistad de Dios, del P. Eusebio Nieremberg. *Valencia: C. Macé.* M. DC. XLVI. Sm. 8vo, (22), 95, (3) leaves. + Duodecima Impression. *Madrid: Viuda de J. Muñoz.* 1761. 16mo, pp. (16), 224, (8). c. 58300

Palafox. El Venerable Señor Don Juan de Palafox y Mendoza, ... justificado en el Tribunal de la Razon, por haber remitido a España y separado del vireinato de México al Señor D. Diego Lopez Pacheco, Duque de Escalona. *México: A. Valdés.* 1831. 4to, pp. (2), 79. B. 58301

Palafox. Vida i Virtudes de Majestad en el Real de las Indias, et Arzobispo Electo de Mexico. *Madrid.* 1666. Sm. folio, Portrait. 58302

Palafox. Vida Interior del Excel. Señor Don Juan de Palafox y Mendoza, Obispo antes de la Puebla de los Angeles, Virrey, y Capitan General de la Nueva España ... La qual vida el mismo Señor Obispo dexô escrita. *Brusselas: Franc. Foppens.* 1682. 4to, pp. (16), 404. 58303

Palafox. Vida interior o Confesiones. ... *Madrid.* 1772. 4to. 58304

Palafox. Vie du ... Dom Jean de Palafox. *See* No. 20201.

Palafox. Vita del venerabile servo di Dio Monsignor D. Giovanni di Palafox, Vescovo d'Angelopoli e pio d'Osma, ... e colla lettera da lui scritta al Re di Spagna, Altra del Re Cattolico regnante alla santita' Din. S. Clemente XIII ed il decreto del sacra congregazione de' Riti, 9 Decembre 1760. *Venezia.* 1761. 8vo.

Palafox. Vita Interiore ... . *Venezia.* 1772. 2 vols., 8vo.

[Palafox.] Virtudes | del Indio. | [*Puebla.* 1634?] 4to, pp. (93). 58307

"Palafox was a second Las Casas in representing to the Spanish Government the wretched condition of the Americans, and in advocating its amelioration. His zeal and humanity were most conspicuous in this exposition addressed to the King, in which he has described with much ingenuousness the good dispositions of the natives. The work has thence acquired the title of the 'Virtudes del Indio.' But so true has it always been that *Veritas odium parit*, that secrecy was necessary in printing the book without any title-page, date, or place of publication; and it has become one of the scarcest works relating to the affairs of America." *See* Brunet, IV. 313. Ternaux dates it 1650. *See* Stevens's "Historical Nuggets," No. 2084.

Also: Puntos que el Señor Obispo de la Puebla de los Angeles D. Juan de Palafox y

Mendoza, dexa encargados, y encomendados á las Almas de su Cargo, al Tiempo de Partirse des Provincias, á los Reynos de España, Año de 1649. *Puebla: J. Blanca de Alcazar.* 1649. 4to.—Tercera carta del venerable siervo de dios Don Juan de Palafox y Mendoza, al Snmo. Pontifice Inocencio X. *Megico [reimpresa en la Officina de Vicenta Garcia Torres].* 1841. 4to, pp. 52. *See also* our No. 57540.

Palairet (J.) A | Concise | Description | of the | English and French | Possessions | in | North-America, | For the better explaining of the Map | published with that Title. | By | J. Palairet, Agent of their High Mightinesses | the States General of the United Provinces, &c. | *London: J. Haberkorn.* MDCCLV. 8vo, pp. 71, (1). + The Second Edition Improved. [*Ibid.*] 8vo, pp. 69, (1).

Palairet. Description Abrégée des Possessions Angloises et Françoises du Continent septentrional de l'Amérique, Pour servir d'Explication à la Carte publiée sous ce même Titre, par J. Palairet ... . *A Londres, Chez ... J. Nourse* ... 1755. 8vo, pp. 62. + Troisième Édition. [*Ibid.*] 1756. 8vo, pp. 72. H. 58309

Palairet. Beknopte Beschryving der Engelsche en Fransche Bezittingen, in het vaste-land van Noord-America, dienende tot Verklaaring van de Land-Kaart onder dezelve Tytel uitgegeven. Door J. Palairet. ... Uit het Fransch vertaalt door H. W. Löhner. *Te Amsterdam: R. en J. Ottens.* 1755. 8vo, pp. 72. H.

Paläorama. *See* [Brown (G.)], Vol. II., No. 8478.

Palata (*Duque de la*). Sobre Mitas de Potosi ... *Lima.* 1689. Folio, pp. 7. 58311

Palata was Viceroy of Peru.

[Paleske (Charles G.)] Observations on the application for a Law to Incorporate "The Union Canal Company." ... submitted to the ... Legislature of Pennsylvania. ... [n. p. 1808.] 8vo, pp. 16. BA., P. 58312

Signed "Charles G. Paleske. Pensylvania December 1808." *Duane, printer.*

[Palfray (Warwick).] Remarks on the recent Ordination at Beverly. By "Another Layman." *Salem: Warwick Palfray, Jun. Printer.* 1824. 8vo, pp. 24. BA. 58313

[Palfrey (Francis Winthrop).] The Ambulance System. ... *Boston: Crosby and Nichols.* 1864. 8vo, pp. 16. BA. 58314

[Palfrey.] In Memoriam H[enry] L[ivermore] A[bbott] ob. May VI., A. D. MDCCCLXIV. ... *Boston.* 1864. 8vo, pp. 31.

[Palfrey (J. G.)] Chapter of ... History. *See* No. 12012.

Palfrey. The Claims of Harvard College upon its Sons. A Sermon, ... July 13, 1834. By John G. Palfrey ... . *Cambridge: James Munroe and Co.* 1834. 8vo, pp. 20. B. 58316

This elicited "Review of Professor Palfrey's Sermon, entitled 'The Claims of Harvard College upon its Sons.'" [n. p. n. d.] 8vo, pp. 35. B.

Palfrey. A Discourse ... August 9, 1832, the Day ... for Fasting ... on Account of ... Cholera. By John G. Palfrey ... . *Boston: Gray and Bowen.* 1832. 8vo, pp. 26. + Second Edition. [*Ibid.*] B. 58317

Palfrey. A Discourse ... at Barnstable on the third of September, 1839, at the Celebration of the Second Centennial Anniversary of the Settlement of Cape Cod. By John Gorham Palfrey. *Boston: Ferdinand Andrews.* 1840. 8vo, pp. 50. BA., C.

Palfrey. History of New England during the Stuart Dynasty. By John Gorham Palfrey. *Boston: Little, Brown, and Company.* 1858–65. 3 vols., 8vo, pp. xxxi, (2), 636; xx, 640; xxii, 659. 4 Maps. 58319

One hundred copies were printed on large paper. Our collation is of the first issue, later dates vary slightly.

Palfrey. A History of New England, from the Discovery by Europeans to the Revolution of the Seventeenth Century, being an abridgment of his "History of New England during the Stuart Dynasty." By John Gorham Palfrey. *New York: Hurd & Houghton.* 1866. 2 vols., 12mo, pp. xx, 408; xii, 426. B.

[Palfrey.] A Letter to the Corporation ... of Harvard College on the proposed Change in the Constitution of that Seminary. By an Alumnus. *Boston: Russell, Odiorne, and Metcalf.* 1835. 8vo, pp. 24. 58321

Palfrey. Lowell Lectures ... . By John Gorham Palfrey. With a Discourse on the Life of John Lowell, Jr. By Edward Everett. *Boston: James Munroe and Company.* MDCCCXLIII. 2 vols., 8vo, pp. lxxxviii, 367; 444. B. 58322

[Palfrey.] Notice of Professor Farrar. ... *Boston.* 1853. 8vo, pp. 18. H. 58323

[Palfrey.] Remarks on the Proposed State Constitution. By a Free-soiler from the Start. *Boston: Crosby, Nichols, & Company.* 1853. 8vo, pp. 35. H., s. 58324

[Palfrey.] A Review of Lord Mahon's History of the American Revolution. ... *Boston: Little, Brown and Company.* 1852. 8vo, pp. 86. B. 58325

Also: An Address ... before the Society for Promoting Theological Education, June 5, 1831. ... *Boston.* 1831. 8vo, pp. 18.—An Address to the Society of Middlesex Husbandmen and Manufacturers, ... at Concord, October 7, 1846. ... *Cambridge: Metcalf and Company.* 1846. 8vo, pp. 24.—Discourses on Intemperance, ... April 5, 1827, the Day of ... Fast, and April 8 ... . [*Boston:*] *Nathan Hale.* 1827. 12mo, pp. 111. BA. + Second Edition. *Boston.* 1827.—A Discourse on the Life and Character of the Reverend John Thornton Kirkland, D.D., ... June 5, 1840. ... *Cambridge: John Owen.* 1840. 8vo, pp. 62, (2).—A Discourse on the Life and Character of the Reverend Henry Ware, D.D. ... pronounced in ... Cambridge, September 28, 1845 ... . *Cambridge: John Owen.* 1845. 8vo, pp. 37. + *Boston: Wm. Crosby and H. P. Nichols.* 1846. 12mo, pp. 42.—The Inter-State Slave-Trade. [n. p. n. d.] 8vo, pp. 8.—A Letter to a Friend, ... [July 30th 1850; in vindication of his own course as a politician]. *Cambridge: Metcalf and Company.* 1850. 8vo, pp. 28.—An Oration pronounced before the Citizens of Boston, ... July 4th, 1831. ... *Boston: John H. Eastburn, Printer.* 1831. 8vo, pp. 42.—Papers on the Slave Power, first published in the "Boston Whig." ... *Boston: Merrill, Cobb & Co.* [1846.] 8vo, pp. iv, 91. + Second Edition. [*Ibid.*]—A Plea for the Militia System. In a Discourse ... before the Ancient and Honorable Artillery Company, on its cxcvIIth Anniversary, June 1, 1835. ... *Boston: Dutton and Wentworth, Printers.* 1835. 8vo, pp. 34, (1).—Remarks concerning the late Dr. Bowditch By the Rev. Dr. Palfrey, with the Replies of Dr. Bowditch's Children. *Boston: Charles C. Little & Co.* MDCCCXL. 8vo, pp. 26.— ... Sermon at the Dedication of the Twelfth Congregational Church in Boston, Oct. 13, 1824. ... *Boston: W. W. Clapp, Printer.* 1825. 8vo, pp. 34.—A Sermon preached to the Church in Brattle Square, in two parts, July 18, 1824. ... *Boston: Oliver C. Greenleaf.* 1825. 8vo, pp. 81.—Sermon preached to the Society in Brattle Square, June 8th, 1823; ... after the interment of ... Hon. John Phillips. ... *Boston.* 1823. 8vo, pp. 24.—A Sermon ... December 1, 1833, the Lord's Day after the decease of Miss Elizabeth Bond. ... *Boston: Nathan Hale.* 1833. 8vo, pp. 20.—A Sermon occasioned by the Death of John Gorham, M.D. ... preached at ... Boston, April 9th, 1829. ... *Boston: S. G. Goodrich and Co.* 1829. 8vo, pp. 23.—A Sermon preached ... August 1, 1830, the Lord's Day after the Decease of the Honourable Isaac Parker, Chief Justice of Massachusetts. ... *Boston: Nathan Hale.* 1830. 8vo, pp. 32.—A Sermon, ... at the Installation of Rev. Samuel Kirkland Lothrop, ... as Pastor of the Church in Brattle Square, ... June 18, 1834. ... *Boston: Nathan Hale.* 1834. 8vo, pp. 40.—Speech ... on the Political Aspect of the Slave Question. ... January 26th, 1848. *Washington: Printed by J. & G. S. Gideon.* 1848. 8vo, pp. 16.—Speech ... on Postage Reform; delivered ... February 21, 1849. [*Washington.* 1849.] 8vo, pp. 8.—Speech ... on the Bill creating a Territorial Government for Upper California; delivered ... February 26, 1849. [n. p. n. d.] 8vo, pp. 10.—The Worthy Student of Harvard College. A Sermon ... March 23, 1834. ... *Cambridge: James Munroe and Co.* 1833. 8vo, pp. 29. *See also* Vol. XI., Nos. 46146, *and* 46157.

[Palfrey (Sarah Hammond).] Herman, or Young Knighthood. [A Story of the Civil War.] By E. Foxton. *Boston: Lee and Shepard.* 1866. 2 vols., 8vo. H. 58326

Palisot de Beauvois (Ambroise Marie François Joseph), *Baron.* Insectes recueillis en Afrique et en Amérique, dans les Royaumes d'Oware et de Benin, à Saint-Domingue et dans les

États-Unis pendant les années 1786–97. Par Palisot de Beauvois. *Paris: A. Bertrand.* 1806–19. Folio. Plates. A.

"These Insects," says Quérard, "were promised in thirty *livraisons* but only fifteen appeared, including the part published, in 1821, by Audinet-Serville." Also: Catalogue raisonné du Museum de Mr. C. W. Peale. *Philadelphia.* [1796.] 8vo. There are other works by this author relating to America.

The Palladium of Knowledge; or, The Carolinian and Georgian Almanack, For ... 1788. *Charleston: Wright and Co.* [n. d.] 12mo, pp. 36. 58328

[Pallas (P.-S.), *and others.*] Histoire des Découvertes faites par divers Savans Voyageurs dans plusieurs contrées de la Russie & de la Perse, relativement à l'Histoire civile & naturelle, à l'Économie rurale, au Commerce, &c. Avec Figures (abrégée de l'Allemand par J.-R. Frey de Landres). *A Berne, Chez la nouvelle Société Typographique.* M. DCC. LXXXI–87. 4 vols., 8vo.

Includes Russian America.

Pallen (M. M.) An Address to the Graduates of the Medical Department of the St. Louis University. ... March 1, 1853. By M. M. Pallen, M.D. ... *St. Louis: Printed by Charles & Hammond.* 1853. 8vo, pp. 19. 58330

Palliser (J.) Journals relative to the Exploration of that portion of British North America between Lake Superior and the Pacific Ocean. By Capt. Palliser. *London.* 1863. Folio. Map. 58331

Palliser. Papers relative to the Exploration by Capt. Palliser of that portion of British North America which lies between the Northern Branch of the River Saskatchewan and the Frontier of the United States, and between the Red River and Rocky Mountains. ... *London.* 1859. Folio, pp. 64. Maps and Plates. + Further Papers relative to the [same expedition and region,] and thence to the Pacific Ocean. [*Ibid.*] 1860. Folio, pp. 73. 3 Maps. c. 58332

Palliser. Solitary Rambles and Adventures of a Hunter in the Prairies. By John Palliser, Esq. With Illustrations. *London: John Murray.* 1853. 8vo, pp. xiv, (1), 326. H. + New Edition. *London: George Routledge & Co.* 1856. 12mo, pp. 224.

Also: Index and Maps to Captain Palliser's Reports on the Exploration of British North America. *London.* 1865. Folio.

Pallmer (C. N.) Speech in the House of Commons, on Mr. Wilberforce's Motion for Papers, &c., June 19, 1816. *London.* [n. d.] 8vo, pp. 44. 58334

The Palm-Bearers. *See* [Mather (C.)], Vol. XI., No. 46444.

Palma Faxardo (Francisco). Sermon del Santo Martyr y Pontifice Marcelo, Abogado de los frutos de la Ciudad de los Reyes. ... *Impresso in Lima, por Geronymo de Contreras.* 1633. 4to, 28 leaves. 58335

Palma (M. R.) Poesias de Manuel R. Palma. *Lima.* 1855. 18mo, pp. 118. 58336

Palma (R.) Lira Americana: Coleccion de Poesias de los mejores poetas del Peru, Chile, y Bolivia. Recopiladas por Ricardo Palma. *Paris: Rosa y Bouret.* 1865. 8vo, pp. (8), 656.

Palma. Dos Poetas (Apuntes de mi Cartera) ... *Valparaiso.* 1861. 8vo, pp. 38. 58338

Palmer (A. G.) A Discourse delivered at the One Hundredth Anniversary of the Organization of the First Baptist Church, in North Stonington, September 20, 1843. By A. G. Palmer. With an Appendix. *Boston: Gould, Kendall & Lincoln.* 1844. 18mo, pp. 72. 58339

Palmer (A. H.) Documents and Facts illustrating the Origin of the Mission to Japan, Authorized by ... the United States, May 10th, 1851; and ... the Treaty concluded by ... Perry ... 31st March, 1854. ... By Aaron Haight Palmer. *Washington: Henry Polkinhorn, Printer.* 1857. 8vo, pp. 22. B. 58340

Also: Letter to the Hon. Charles J. Ingersoll ... respecting the Present State ... of the Comoro Islands, ... and recommending ... the United States to make treaties, ... *New York.* [1846.] 8vo, pp. 16. H.—Letter ... submitting a plan for opening, extending, and protecting American Commerce in the East, &c.: ... Revised, and ... republished with an Appendix. *Washington: Gideon & Co., Printers.* 1849. 8vo, pp. 63.—Memoir on the present state ... of Siberia, ... and the Asiatic Islands of the North Pacific Ocean, and on the Importance of opening Commercial Intercourse with them. ... *Washington.* 1848. 8vo, pp. 76, (1). Map.

Palmer (A.) Speech of Hon. Andrew Palmer in the Legislature of Wisconsin, Jan. 23, 1851, on Representation and Taxation. [n. p. n. d.] 8vo. 58341

Palmer (B. F.) A Poem read before the Society of the Sons of New England, in Pennsylvania. ... Delivered ... December 22, 1858. By B. Frank Palmer. *Philadelphia: Crissy & Markley, Printers.* 1859. 8vo, pp. 15. 58342

Palmer (Benjamin Morgan). A Discourse before the General Assembly of South Carolina, on December 10, 1863, ... a

Day of Fasting ... . By B. M. Palmer, D.D. ... *Columbia: Charles P. Pelham, ... Printer.* 1864. 8vo, pp. 24. 58343

[Palmer.] The Oath of Allegiance to the United States. [*Columbia, S. C., Feb.* 10, 1860.] 18mo, pp. 32. 58344

Reprinted with the author's name as below:

Palmer. The Oath of Allegiance to the United States discussed in its moral and political bearings. By Rev. B. M. Palmer, D.D. ... *Richmond: Macfarlane & Fergusson.* 1863. 12mo, pp. 22. H. 58345

Palmer. The South; her Peril and her Duty. A Discourse ... in ... New Orleans, ... November 29, 1860. By Rev. B. M. Palmer, D.D. *New Orleans.* 1860. 8vo, pp. 16. + *Milledgeville, Ga.* 1860. 8vo. + *New York.* 1861. 8vo, pp. 20.

Also: ... Discourse before the Graduating Class of the University of North Carolina, June 4, 1855. ... *Raleigh.* 1855. 8vo, pp. 41.—Mormonism. A Lecture ... January 26, 1853. *Columbia, S. C.: Printed by I. C. Morgan.* 1853. 8vo, pp. 34.—National Responsibility ... . A Discourse, ... on the day of Fasting, ... appointed by the President of the Confederate States of America, June 13, 1861. ... *New Orleans.* 1861. 8vo, pp. 28.—Slavery, a Divine Trust. The Duty of the South ... . *New York: Geo. F. Nesbitt & Co.* 1861. 8vo, pp. 20.—Two Sermons on the Signs of the Times, Charleston, S. C. ... *Charleston, S. C.* 1816. 8vo, pp. 20.—A Vindication of Secession and the South from the Strictures of Rev. R. J. Breckenridge in the Danville Quarterly Review. ... *Columbia, S. C.* 1861. 8vo, pp. 46.

Palmer, *and* Leacock (W. T.) The Rights of the South defended in the Pulpits. By B. M. Palmer, D.D., and W. T. Leacock, D.D. ... *Mobile: Printed by J. Y. Thompson.* 1860. 8vo, pp. (2), 16. H. 58347

Palmer (D.) Anniversary Address to the ... Graduates of the Vermont Medical College, ... 1839. By David Palmer, M.D. ... *Woodstock: Printed by Augustus Palmer.* 1839. 12mo, pp. 12.

Palmer (D. Mc. N.) Four Weeks in The Rebel Army. By Don Mc. N. Palmer. *New London: D. S. Ruddock, Printer.* 1865. 8vo, pp. 40. 58349

Palmer (Edward). Money versus the Higher Law: Two Lectures. *Perth Amboy: Privately Printed.* 1856. 8vo, pp. 29.

Palmer (E.) An Enquiry relative to the Moral & Political Improvement of the Human Species. ... Oration ... in ... New-York on the Fourth of July. ... By Elihu Palmer. *New York: Printed by John Crookes.* 1797. 12mo, pp. 35. 58351

Palmer (H.) Speech of Hon. Harvey Palmer ... March 13, 1863, on the Governor's Message ... . [n. p. n. d.] 8vo.

Palmer (H.) Letters on the Slave-Trade. By Rev. Henry Palmer. *London.* 1846. 8vo. 58353

Palmer (H. G.) Centennial Discourse at the Baptist Church in Stonington. By H. G. Palmer. *Boston.* 1844. 8vo.

Palmer (H. S.) British Columbia. Williams Lake and Cariboo. Report on portions of the Williams Lake and Cariboo Districts, and on the Fraser River, from Fort Alexander to Fort George. By Henry Spencer Palmer. *New Westminster [British Columbia].* 1863. 8vo, pp. (4), 25. c. 58355

Also: Reports of a Journey of Survey from Victoria to Fort Alexander, via North Bentinck Arm. ... *New Westminster.* 1863. 8vo, pp. (4), 33. c.

Palmer (James Croxall). Thulia: a Tale of the Antarctic. By J. C. Palmer, U.S.N. ... *New-York: Samuel Colman.* MDCCCXLIII. 8vo, pp. 72. 58356

Also: Antarctic Mariner's Song. ... *New York: D. Van Nostrand.* 1868. 8vo, pp. 92. c.

Palmer (J. N.) Report of the Engineer upon the ... location for the Hartford and Springfield Railroad; ... . Second Edition. *Hartford.* 1841. 8vo. 58357

Palmer (J.) Journal of Travels over the Rocky Mountains, to the Mouth of the Columbia River; made during the Years 1845 and 1846: containing minute Descriptions of the Valleys of the Williamette, Umpqua, and Clamet; A General Description of Oregon Territory: its Inhabitants, Climate, Soil, Productions ... . Also a Letter from the Rev. H. H. Spalding, resident Missionary, for the last ten years among the Nez Percé Tribe of Indians, on the Koos-koos-kee River; The Organic Laws of Oregon Territory; Tables of about 300 words of the Chinook Jargon, and about 200 words of the Nez Percé Language; a Description of Mount Hood; Incidents of Travel, &c., &c. By Joel Palmer. *Cincinnati: J. A. & U. P. James.* 1847. 12mo, pp. 189. H. + [*Ibid.*] 1852. 12mo. c. 58358

Palmer (J.) An | Impartial Account | of the | State of New England | or, the | Late Government there, Vindicated | In answer to the | Declaration | Which the Faction set forth, when they Over- | turned That Government | With a Relation | Of the horrible Usage they treated the Gover- | nour with, and his Council;

and all that had His Ma|jesty's Commission.|In a Letter to the Clergy there. | By John Palmer. | *London: Printed for Edward Poole at his Shop over against the Royal|Exchange in Cornhill*, 1690. 4to, pp. 40. 58359

A very rare tract, relating to the Andros affair. *See also* Nos. 46731–2. Our No. 46722 is also attributed to Palmer.

Palmer (J.) ... Journal of Travels in the United States of North America, and in Lower Canada, ... in ... 1817; containing ... Remarks on the Country and People, Interesting Anecdotes ... . added, A Description of Ohio, Indiana, Illinois, and Missouri ... . By John Palmer. *London: Sherwood, Neely, and Jones.* 1818. 8vo, pp. vii, 456. Map. C., P. 58360

"Mr. Palmer travelled through all, or the greater part of the country he describes; but he confesses that the outlines of his travels were filled up from other books."—Rich. "A plain man of good sense and slow judgment." *See* "Edinburgh Review," Dec. 18, 1818, *and* "Monthly Review," LXXXVII. 279.

Palmer. Reisebemerkungen über die Vereinigten Staaten und Nieder Canada in 1817–18. Aus dem Englischen. [n. p. n. d.] 8vo. 58361

Palmer. Dagverhaal eener Reize in de Vereenigde Staten van Noord-America, en Neder-Canada, gedaan in 1817. Uit het Engelsch ... . *Haarlem.* 1820. 8vo. Map. 58362

Palmer (J. N.) New England Almanac. *See* No. 52652.

Palmer (J. C. R.) Explanation, or Eighteen Hundred and Thirty. ... A Series of Facts connected with the Life of the Author, from Eighteen Hundred and Twenty-Five to the Present Day. *Boston: The Author.* 1831. 24mo, pp. 191. B.

Palmer was supposed to be implicated in the murder of Capt. White, at Salem.

Palmer (J.) Necrology of Alumni of Harvard College, 1851–52 to 1862–63. By Joseph Palmer. ... *Boston: Printed by John Wilson and Son.* 1864. 8vo, pp. vi, (2), 536. B. 58364

Palmer (J. W.) The New and the Old; or, California and India, in Romantic Aspects. By J. W. Palmer, M.D. ... *New York: Rudd & Carleton.* M DCCC LIX. 12mo, pp. 433. H.

Some copies have the imprint *London.*

Palmer (O.) Obadiah Palmer and others, Complainants, against Jacobus van Cortland and Adolph Philipse, Defendants, In Cancellaria Novæ Eborac. Decree (for the Complainants),

made May 2d, 13th George I. [1727. *New York: Wm. Bradford.* 1727.] Folio, pp. 22. N. 58366

The action was brought to determine the bounds of the "Great Neck" at Mamaroneck, and to establish a partition line between the parties.

Palmer (P. S.) History of Lake Champlain, from its First Exploration by the French in 1609, to the close of the year 1814. By Peter S. Palmer. *Plattsburgh: J. W. Tuttle.* 1853. 8vo, pp. 223. + *Albany, N. Y.: J. Munsell.* 1866. Rl. 8vo, pp. (4), 276. 6 Plans. 58367

Palmer (R.) An Address ... at the Funeral of Daniel Campbell. By Ray Palmer. *Albany.* 1851. 8vo, pp. 14. S.

Palmer. The Highest Civilization a result of Christianity ... a Discourse ... at Norwich, Conn., Nov. 14, 1865, on behalf of the Society for Promoting Collegiate and Theological Education at the West ... . By Ray Palmer ... . *Albany, N. Y.: J. Munsell.* 1866. 8vo, pp. 43. 58369

Palmer. Our Country Must be Saved. The Voice of God to the American Congregational Churches. ... By Ray Palmer, D.D. *New York.* 1867. 8vo, pp. 32. 58370

Palmer. Reminiscences of our Work for Fifteen Years A Discourse delivered in the First Congregational Church, Albany, ... December 24, 1865. By Ray Palmer ... . *Albany: J. Munsell.* 1865. 8vo, pp. 30. B. 58371

Palmer. Two Discourses on our Own Religious Affairs. By Ray Palmer ... . *Albany: J. Munsell.* 1856. 8vo, pp. 61.

Two historical discourses on the First Congregational Church at Albany. Also: Address on the Education of Woman, delivered at ... Pittsfield Young Ladies' Institute, September 30, 1852. ... *Albany: J. Munsell.* 1852. 8vo, pp. 31.—National Sufferings the Result of National Sins. Fast Sermon, ... at Bath, Me., April 6, 1843. ... *Boston.* 1843. 8vo, pp. 33.—Results of the Present War. A Thanksgiving Discourse. ... November 26, 1863. ... *Albany.* 1863. 8vo. M.—Speech ... on behalf of the University of Albany. *Albany.* 1852. 8vo.

Palmer (R. M.) Washington and the Union. Oration ... by Hon. Robert M. Palmer, ... at the Reception of President Lincoln at Harrisburg, ... 22d ... of February, 1861. [n. p. n. d.] 8vo. 58373

Palmer (R.) A Speech ... in the House of Commons, ... on the North American Blockade, March 7, 1862. By Sir Roundell Palmer, M.P. ... *London: James Ridgway.* 1862. 8vo, pp. 29. B. 58374

Palmer (S.) A Journey beyond the Rocky Mountains in 1835, '36, and '37, Corrected and Extended in the Present Edition. *Edinburgh: W. & R. Chambers.* 1841. 8vo. A. 58375

Palmer (S. L.) Six Months among the Secessionists. A Reliable and Thrilling Narrative of the Sufferings and Trials of Miss Sarah L. Palmer, ... who at the opening of the Great Southern Rebellion, was teaching school in Knoxville, the home of Parson Brownlow. ... *Philadelphia: Barclay & Co.* 1862. 8vo, pp. 40. H. + *New York.* 1863. 8vo. 58376

Palmer (S.) A Sermon ... at Mansfield, July 31, 1808; ... after the interment of the Rev. Rowland Green ... who died July 4, 1808. ... By Stephen Palmer, A.M. ... *Dedham: Printed by H. Mann.* 1808. 8vo, pp. 32. H. 58377

Palmer. A Sermon ... in Needham, Nov. 16, 1811, on the Termination of a Century since the Incorporation of the Town. By Stephen Palmer ... . *Dedham: Printed by Herman Mann.* 1811. 8vo, pp. 44. H. 58378

Also: A Sermon, occasioned by the Death of Calvin Whiting of Needham ... who died at Hartford ... October 17, 1795. Æt 25. ... *Boston: Printed by Samuel Etheridge.* 1797. 8vo, pp. 19.—A Sermon ... at Rowley, ... June 7, 1797, at the Ordination of the Rev. I. Braman. ... *Dedham: Nathaniel and Benjamin Heaton.* M,DCC,XCVII. 8vo, pp. 35.—Sermon occasioned by the Death of Mr. Jeremiah Fuller, who died April 19, 1798. ... *Dedham: Printed by Mann and Adams.* 1798. 8vo, pp. 27.—A Sermon occasioned by the death of Mr. Amos Fuller ... and of ... Mrs. Sarah Fuller, who died ... 1810. ... *Dedham: Printed by H. Mann.* 1810. 8vo, pp. 20.—A Sermon ... in Needham, ... March 22, 1812, occasioned by the death of The Rev. Mr. Sears of Natick ... [and others]. ... *Dedham: Printed by Herman Mann.* 1812. 8vo, pp. 24. H.—A Sermon ... October 22d, 1812, at the Interment of the Rev. Thomas Thacher ... . *Boston: J. Belcher, Printer.* 1812. 8vo, pp. 26. H.—A Sermon, preached before the Military Company of Exempts, in Needham, ... November 17, 1814. ... *Dedham.* 1814. 8vo, pp. 15, 4.—A Sermon, delivered in Needham ... after the interment of Mrs. Lydia Fairbanks ... . *Dedham.* 1816. 8vo, pp. 16. H. *See also* No. 56236, *note.*

Palmer (T. H.) The Historical Register of the United States. Part I. From the Declaration of War in 1812 to January 1, 1814. Edited by T. H. Palmer. Second Edition. *Philadelphia: G. Palmer.* 1814–16. 4 vols., 8vo, pp. x, 226; (2), iii, 351; vi, 328; v, 354. 58379

For the first edition, *see* our Vol. VII., No. 32076.

Palmer. Prize Essay. The Teacher's Manual: being an Exposition of an Efficient and Economical System of Education, suited to the Wants of a Free People. By Thomas H. Palmer. *Boston.* 1842. 12mo, pp. 263. 58380

Palmer (V. B.) Palmer's Business Men's Almanac. *New York.* 1849–50. 12mo. S. 58381

Palmer (W. C.) Life and Letters of Leonidas L. Hamline, D.D. By Walter C. Palmer, M.D. ... *New York: Carlton & Porter.* 1866. 12mo, pp. 544. Portrait. C. 58382

Palmer (W. J.) Report of Surveys across the Continent in 1867–'68, ... for a Route extending the Kansas Pacific Railway, ... By Gen. Wm. J. Palmer. ... *Philadelphia: W. B. Selheimer. Printer.* 1869. 8vo, pp. 250. Map and Plan. S. 58383

Palmerston (Henry John Temple). Speech of Viscount Palmerston, ... on the Treaty of Washington, of the 9th of August, 1842. *London: James Ridgway.* 1843. 8vo, pp. 95.

Palmerston. Speech of Viscount Palmerston in the House of Commons, ... July 16, 1844, on the Slave Trade. *London.* 1844. 8vo, pp. 48. 58385

The Palmetto Dictionary; ... New Edition. ... *Richmond, Va.: J. W. Randolph.* 1864. 12mo, pp. (2), xx, 730, (1). Portrait of Walker. 58386

This is really an English edition of Walker's Dictionary, with a new title-page adapted for the Confederate States.

Palmetto Pictures. *New-York: Walter Low.* 1863. 12mo, pp. 67. 58387

Palomino (P.) Cartas historicas a un amigo, o apologia del Pichon Palomino que pario una muger y' se vio el dia 6 de abril 1804, y se las dedica Jose Pastor Larrinaga, protocirujano. *Lima.* 1812. 4to. 58388

Palomo (J. G.) Carta del General de la Merced. Fr. José Garcia Palomo, Maestro en Sagrada Teologia ... . [Colophon:] *Reimpresa en Mexico, año de* 1820. 4to, 2 leaves. 58389

The following notice is printed at the head of the letter: "Por justas consideraciones al estado eclesiastico ha parecido bien á un religioso de esta provincia de la Merced de Mexico hacer que se reimprima la siguiente Carta que ha recibido en este ultimo maritimo."

Palos (J. F. de). Funeraria Moerenti Mexicanæ Minervæ Declamatio in Exequiis N. C. Gomez de Cervantes, Postremo Guadalaxarensis Episcopi ... *Mexici.* 1735. 4to. 58390

Palos. Reflectio supra quintam libri tertij Magist. Sententiarum distinctionem, pro petitione Canonicatus Magistralis Metro-

politanæ Mexicanensis Ecclesiæ assueto viginti quatuor horarum spatio elaborata et die xxii. Nov. 1746. ... *Mexico.* 1747. 4to. Folded Plate. 58391

Palou (F.) Relacion Historica|de la vida|y apostolicas tareas|del venerable Padre|Fray Junipero Serra,|Y de las Misiones que fundó en la California Sep|tentrional, y nuevos establecimientos de Monterey. | Escrita | Por el R. P. L. Fr. Francisco Palou,| Guardian actual del Colegio Apostolico de S.|Fernando de Mexico ... . *Impresa en Mexico, en la Imprenta de Don Felipe de Zúñiga y Ontiveros,* ... *año de* 1787. 4to, pp. (28), 344. Plate and Map.

Fathers Serra and Palou were among the earliest of the Catholic missionaries sent to California; they established the first missions in that country which had so great an influence upon the natives, and brought most of the tribes under their control. The letters from Father Serra to Father Palou, which chiefly make up the volume, give not only an account of the founding of the missions but interesting details of the various Indian tribes, their manners and customs, together with descriptions of the country. Also included in Clavigero ("Historia de la ... California"), our No. 13523, Vol. III.

Paloz (J.) Carta que el señor Doctor. D. Joseph de Antequera y Castro. Cavallero del orden de Alcantara Protector Genl. de Indios en la Real Audiencia de la Plata y Governador que fue de la Provincia de el Paraguay Escrivio al Illmo. y Rmo. Señor Obispo de el Paraguay Doctor. D. Fr. Joseph Paloz ... . [Colophon:] *Typis Missionum Paraquariæ Superiorum permissu In Oppido S. Xaverij Anno* 1727. 4to, 16 leaves. 58393

[Paltock (Robert).] The Life and Adventures of Peter Wilkins, a Cornish Man. Taken from his own Mouth, in his Passage to England, from off Cape Horn in America, in the ship Hector. By R. S. a Passenger in the Hector. *London.* 1750. 2 vols., 12mo. 58394

Other editions: *Dublin: George Faulkner,* 1751; *London,* 1783; *Berwick,* 1784; *London: Allman,* 1816; *London,* 1822; *Boston,* 1828; *Boston,* 1833; *London: Parker,* 1839; *London,* 1844; *Hartford,* 1845.

Pama (P.) Memorie voor Pieter Pama, *cum suis*, alle zoo Eigenaars van Plantagien, geleegen in de Colonie de Berbice als op eenige andere wyze in diverse Plantagien van mitsgaders in de Commercie en Navigatie op dezelve Colonie geinteresseerd: ... [n. p. 1774.] Folio, pp. 143, 41. J.C.B. 58395

Pama. Requeste aan de Staten Generael der Nederlanden, Memorie en Bijlagen voor Pieter Pama c. s., allen, zoo Eigenaars von Plantagien, gelegen in de Colonie de Berbice, als op eenige andere wijze geinteresseerden in dezelve Plantagien, mits-

gaders in de Navigatie en Commertie op de gemelde Colonie. [n. p. 1771.] Folio, pp. 188. 58396

Corrected title of our No. 4813.

Pamphile de Lacroix (*Baron*). Mémoires pour servir à l'histoire de la Révolution de Saint-Domingue, par le Lieut. Général, Baron Pamphile de Lacroix. *Paris.* 1820. 2 vols., 8vo.

A Pamphlet against the Immoral Conduct of many of the Quakers of New Jersey, New Castle, and Pennsylvania, who are represented as "a Cage of Unclean Birds." *New York.* 1701. 8vo. 58398

Perhaps by George Keith.

The Pamphlet, entitled, "Taxation no Tyranny," candidly considered, and it's Arguments, and Pernicious Doctrines, Exposed and Refuted. ... *London: W. Davis and T. Evans.* [1775.] 8vo, pp. (4), 131, (1). H. 58399

In reply to [Johnson (S.)] *See* our No. 36306, *and* "Monthly Review," LII. 449.

A Pamphlet on Equal Rights and Privileges. To the People of the United States. Andrew County, Missouri. *St. Joseph, Mo.* 1856. 8vo, pp. 21. 58400

A Pamphlet Showing how easily the wand of a Magician may be broken, and that, if Amos Kendall can manage the United States Mail well, a female of the United States can manage him better; ... [n. p. n. d.] 8vo, pp. 24. 58401

Against Van Buren. By Lucy Kenney.

The Pamphleteer. Respectfully Dedicated to Both Houses of Parliament. ... *London: A. J. Valpy.* 1813–28. 29 vols., 8vo.

Contains many tracts relating to America, all of which are referred to in this Dictionary.

... Pamphlets ... by the Loyal Pub. Society. *See* No. 54364.

Panama. Description de l'Isthme de Darien, des proprietez du Païs et de la ville de Panama; ... [n. p. 1740.] Folio.

Examen sobre la Franca Comunicacion entre los dos Oceanos por el Istmo de Panama. *Bogota.* 1846. 8vo. 58404

The Executive Proceedings of the Senate of the United States, on the subject of The Mission to the Congress at Panama, together with the Messages and Documents Relating Thereto. March, 22, 1826. ... *Washington: Gales & Seaton.* 1826. 8vo, pp. 160. B., P. 58405

See also our Vol. IV., No. 15489.

Informe en derecho en defensa de la Justicia sobre la declaratoria de la vacante de vn curato en el obispado de Panamà. ... *Impresso en Lima: en la calle de San Ildephonso, año de* 1743. Folio, 156 leaves. 58406

Memoria del Gobernador de Panama a la camara provincial en sus sesiones de 1843. [n. p. n. d.] 8vo, pp. 23. 58407

Original Papers relating to ... Panama. *See* [Vernon (E.)]

The Panama Massacre, a Collection of the Principal Evidence and other Documents, including the Report of Amos B. Corwine, Esq., U. S. Commissioner; the Official Statement of the Governor and the Depositions taken before the Authorities, relative to the Massacre of American Citizens at the Panama Rail-Road Station, on the 15th of April, 1856. ... *Panama.* 1857. Rl. 8vo, pp. 69. 58408

Communication of the ... Directors of the Panama Rail-road Company to the Stockholders. ... with the Report of the Chief Engineer ... . *New York: John F. Trow, Printer.* 1853. 8vo, pp. 19. Map. Continued. P. 58409

Panama Rail-Road Company. ... [Documents.] *New-York: Van Norden & Amerman, Printers.* 1849. 8vo, pp. 62. Map.

Also: Report of the Committee on Naval Affairs, on the Memorial of the Panama Railroad Company. [n. p. 1849.] 8vo, pp. 46. S.

Pancirollus (Guidus). Rerum Memorabilium Libri II. Latine reddidit et notis illustrata ... Henrico Salmuth. *Ambergae: M. Forster.* 1607–8. 2 vols., 8vo. + [*Ibid.*] 1812. 2 vols., 8vo. + *Francofurti.* 1629–31. 2 vols., 4to. 58411

Contains, among other interesting particulars, an account of the discovery of America by Columbus.

Pancirollus. Guidonis Pancirolli Rerum Memorabilium sive Deperditarum Pars prior Commentariis illustrata et locis propé innumeris postremum aucta ab Henrico Salmuth. *Francofurti.* 1646. 2 vols., 4to, pp. viii, 350, xxii; Nova Reperta, pp. 313, xvii. S. + *Joannis Godefridi Schönwetter, Francofurtens.* 1660. 2 vols., 4to, pp. (8), 349, (21); 313, (15). H. + *Ambergensium.* 1660. 2 vols., 4to. 58412

Pancirollus. Nova Reperta sive Rerum Memorabilium recens inventarum et veteribus plane incognitarum. Liber secundus ex Italico Latine redditus et commentariis illustratus ab H.

Salmuth. *Ambergae.* 1602. 8vo. + [*Ibid.*] 1608. 8vo. A. + [*Ibid.*] 1612. 8vo. + *Francofurti.* 1617. 12mo. 58413

This work is not noticed by Rich, Ternaux, Trömel, or Stevens.

Pancirollus. Livre premier des Antiquitez perdues; accompagné d'un second des choses nouvellement inventées at auparavant incogneuës, traduit par Pierre de la Noue. *Lyon: P. Roussin.* 1617. 2 vols., 12mo. 58414

Pancirollus. The History of Many memorable Things lost, Which were in Use among the Ancients, and An Account of many excellent Things found now in Use among the Moderns, both Natural and Artificial. Written Originally in Latin by Guido Pancirollus; and now done into English, and illustrated with a new Commentary ... from Salmuth's large Annotations; ... To this English Edition is added, First, A Supplement to the Chapter on Printing ... . Secondly What the Moderns have found, the Ancients never knew: ... *London: John Nicholson.* 1715. 2 vols., 12mo. BA. 58415

Pages 265 to 279 treat of the New World. This work contains incidentally many interesting allusions to America, especially the early use of the term New World, Novus Orbis, etc., long before Columbus and Vespucci.

Pancoast (Joseph). A Discourse commemorative of ... Professor T. D. Mütter, M.D. ... October 14, 1859. By Professor Pancoast. ... *Philadelphia: Joseph M. Wilson.* 1859. 8vo, pp. 28

Pandectas Hispano-Megicanas ó sea codigo general comprehensivo de las leyes generales, utiles y vivas de las siete partidas, recopilacion novisima, ... autos y providencias conocidas por de Montemayor y Beleña, y cédulas posteriores hasta el año de 1820, con exclusion de las totalmente inútiles de las repetidas, y de las expresamente derogadas. ... Nueva edicion. *Méjico.* 1852. 3 vols., 4to. C. 58417

Pando (José María de). Appendice a la Memoria presentada al Congreso sobre el estado de la hacienda publica del año de 1830. ... *Lima.* 1831. 8vo. 58418

Pando. Elogio patriotico que pronuncio el Ciudadano Jose Maria Pando, el dia 16 de Setiembre del año de 1827, por solemnizar el aniversario del grito de independencia. *Oajaca.* 1827. Sm. 8vo, pp. 32. 58419

Also: Epistola á Próspero. ... *Lima.* 1826. Sm. 8vo, pp. 12, and 2 notes.

Pandosy (M. C.) Grammar and Dictionary of the Yakama Language. By Rev. Mie. Cles. Pandosy. ... Translated by George Gibbs and J. G. Shea. *New York: Cramoisy Press.* 1862. Rl. 8vo, pp. 59. B. 58420

Forms No. 6 of Shea's "Library of American Linguistics."

Panegyrico a A. de A. Ribafria. *See* Vol. iv., No. 16834.

Panet (Jean-Claude). Journal du Siége de Québec en 1759. ... *Montréal.* 1866. 8vo, pp. 24. 58421

Pangloss (P.), *pseudon.* Memoirs of Sylvester Daggerwood, Comedian, etc., deceased; including Many Years of Provincial Vicissitudes, interspersed with Genuine Anecdotes of many Eminent Persons ... . Collected from the Deceased Author's mss., with Notes, ... by Peter Pangloss, Esq., ll.d., and a.s.s. *London.* 1807. 2 vols., 12mo. 58422

Includes an account of adventures in America during the Revolutionary War.

The Pangs of a Patriot, expressed in a Letter to a Nobleman, on the unfortunate Capture of Lord Cornwallis. *London: Walker.* 1782. 8vo. 58423

"If the nobleman to whom this letter is addressed hath received from it no more entertainment or instruction than it hath afforded to us, his lordship will not be violently disposed to encourage a continuance of the correspondence."—*Monthly Review*, lxvi. 227. *See also* our No. 16816.

Panoche Grande Rancho. *See* Vol. xiii., No. 53022.

The Panoplist, for the year ending June, 1806. Volume the First ... . *Boston: Printed by E. Lincoln.* 1806. 8vo, pp. iv, viii, 568, Appendix, 34, References, ii, Index, vii. 58424

Continued as "The Panoplist and Missionary Magazine United for ... 1809. Vol. i. New Series ... . *Boston: Farrand, Mallory, and Co.* 1809. 8vo, pp. viii, 576. In 1818, the title was changed to read: "Panoplist and Missionary Herald for the year 1818." Vol. xiv. *Boston: Samuel T. Armstrong.* 1818. 8vo, pp. x, 576. After 1820, continued as the "Missionary Herald."

The Panorama of Boston. Description of the City of Boston, ... with an outline Key, as represented in the Panorama. *London.* 1846. 8vo, pp. 16. 58425

Panorama of the Hudson River. *See* Vol. viii., No. 33518.

Panorama of the Old World and the New. Comprising a View of the Present State of the Nations of the World, their Names, Customs and Peculiarities, and their Political, Moral, Social, and Industrial Condition. Interspersed with Historical Sketches and Anecdotes. *London.* 18—. 8vo. 58426

Panorama of the River St. Lawrence, being an Illustrated and Descriptive Guide From Niagara to Quebec ... . *Ogdensburgh, N. Y.: Tilley & Brothers.* [n. d.] 8vo, pp. 72. 58427

Panoramic View. *See* Vol. iii. 9181, *and* Vol. viii. 33519.

Panormita (A.) De dictis et factis Alphonse regis Aragonum et Neapolis libri iv. Cum respondentibus principum illius aetatis, dictis et factis similibus, ab A. Sylvio collectis. Editae studio D. Chytraeus. *Witebergae.* 1585. 4to. Map. 58428

See also Chytraeus (N.), Vol. iv., No. 13037.

Pansey (Henrion de). Del Poder Municipal, Obra traducida al castellano por el Dr. Elias Acosta. Comprende tambien 1 una resena histórica de los municipios tanto en el gobierno colonial como desde se independizó Venezuela 2 algunas natas que ponen al corriente la doctrina del autor con la legislacion patria. *Carácas.* 1850. 8vo, pp. xxxi, 195. 58429

Pantaleon (G.) Exposicion que publica Gabriel Pantaleon de Escoyti y Norri. *Habana: Oficina de Arazoza y Soler, impresor del Gobierno Constitucional.* 1821. Folio. 58430

Panthéon Littéraire. *Paris.* 1839. 4 vols., rl. 8vo. 58431

The fourth volume contains a succinct history of the early American explorers.

The Pantheon of the Age; or, Memoirs of Three Thousand Contemporary Public Characters, British and Foreign ... . Second Edition. ... *London: George B. Whittaker* ... 1825. 3 vols., 12mo. Portraits. 58432

El Pantheon Real, Funebro Aparato a las exequias que en la Ciudad de Santiago de los Caballeros de Guatemala ... . *Guatemala.* 1763. 4to. Plate. 58433

Panzacola. *See* Vol. v., No. 19949.

Die Panzerschiffe Merrimac und Monitor und das Seegefecht in den Hampton Roads am 8 und 9 März, 1862. *Darmstadt: Gustav Georg Lange.* 1862. Rl. 8vo, pp. 12. 58434

Papel Sellado. 1. El Contador encargado de los Sellos, al "Curioso." 2. Carta que se dirige al Señor D. Ventura de Arzac. 3. Contestacion Remitida al Piloto el Miércoles de la Semaña pasada. *Buenos Ayres.* [1826.] 4to. M. 58435

Papel sobre el Verdadero y unico modo de beneficiar a los Yndios en los espiritual y temporal (bien necesitados de ello) y de

hacerlos mas utiles a el estado: impugnando un Cura de Mexico cireto dictamen de otro de Puebla. [Colophon:] *Mexico, año de* 1770. 4to, 108 leaves. 58436

Papeles curiosos. *See* Vol. vii., No. 29091.

Papeles Peruanos; ... containing a description of the various ... Bishoprics of Peru ... . *London.* 1768. 12mo. 58437

Paper. The Duty on Paper. Why it should be removed. From the Journal of Commerce. [n. p. 1863.] 8vo, pp. 19.

Manufacture of Paper and Printed Books in Pennsylvania. *Philadelphia.* 1773. 58439

See also Vol. xii., No. 47685.

Paper Bills. Act to regulate and restrain Paper-Bills of Credit, in his Majesties Colonies or Plantations of Rhode-Island, and Providence Plantations, Connecticut, Massachusets-Bay, and New Hampshire, in America. [n. p.] 1751. Folio, pp. 4. 58440

Paper Book: Sharpless John Hebler, and others *vs.* The City of Philadelphia, respecting the Subscription to the Hempfield Railroad. *Philadelphia.* 1853. 8vo. P. 58441

A Paper containing a Statement. *See* [Reed (W. B.)]

A Paper containing Exceptions against some things in the present mode of administring & receiving the Lord's Supper in most of our Presbyterian Societies ... laid before the Synod of Philadelphia in May 1747 ... . Together with a Preface ... by the Presbytery of Newcastle ... . *Lancaster: Printed by James Coulter.* mdccxlvii. 16mo, pp. 17. S. 58442

One of the first books printed in Lancaster.

Paper Money. *See* Nos. 30613, 31190, *and* [Potter (E. R.)]

A Paper of Tobacco: Treating of the Rise, Progress, Pleasures, and Advantages of Smoking ... . By Joseph Fume. ... Second Edition, with Additions. *London: Chapman and Hall.* 1839. 16mo, pp. iv, 174. S. 58443

A Paper | To | William Penn, | at | The Departure of that Gentleman to his Territory, for his Perusal, | in | Pensilvania. | Wherein | Two Points are proposed to him concerning the | Quakers' Religion ... . | The one is their | Belief of an Infallible Guidance; The other is their | Disuse of the Two Holy and Blessed Sacraments. | ... | By a Friend unknown. | *London: Printed by T. M. for H. Mortlock* ... 1700. 4to, pp. (4), 24, (2). C. 58444

Papers and Despatches relating to the Arctic Searching Expeditions of 1850–51. With a few brief Remarks as to the Probable Course pursued by Sir John Franklin. *London: F. & J. Rivington.* 1851. 8vo, pp. 49. Map. C. 58445

For the second edition, *see* Vol. xi., No. 44251.

Papers and Documents. *See* Vol. xii., No. 49854.

Papers and Further Papers relative to British Columbia. *London.* 1859–60–62. Folio. 58446

Papers and Letters on Agriculture, Recommended to the Attention of the Canadian Farmers, By the Agricultural Society in Canada. *Quebec: Printed by Samuel Neilson.* m.dcc.xc. 8vo, (5) leaves, pp. 34, doubly numbered. 58447

In English and French on opposite pages.

Papers and Practical Illustrations of Public Works of Recent Construction, both British and American: supplementary to previous publications. *London: John Weale.* 1856. Rl. 8vo, pp. 104. 50 Engravings. 58448

Papers concerning the Attack on Hatfield and Deerfield by a Party of Indians from Canada, September Nineteenth, 1677. *New York.* 1859. Impl. 8vo, pp. 82. Map. 58449

One hundred copies privately printed for the Bradford Club, being No. 1 of the series. Of the subsequent publications by the club, one hundred and fifty copies were printed, consequently this number commands a large price.

Papers concerning the Capture ... of ... André. *See* No. 18936

Papers for The People. ... Issued weekly ... under the patronage of the ... Democratic Delegation in Congress. ... *Jefferson Union,* ... *New-York.* 1852. 8vo. 58450

Papers from the Society for the Diffusion of Political Knowledge. [*New York.* 1863.] 8vo, 20 or more tracts. 58451

Papers in relation to ... Silas Deane. *See* Vol. v., No. 19065.

Papers in relation to the Official Conduct of Winthrop Sargent, Governor of the Mississippi Territory. [*Boston.*] 1801. 8vo. 58452

Papers laid before the Royal Commission. *See* Vol. ix. 35643.

Papers of the New Haven Col. Hist. Soc. *See* No. 52988.

Papers on the Boundary Line between Massachusetts and the Easterly Line of Rhode Island. First Published, September and October, 1847, in the Boston Atlas. By Plymouth Colony. ... [*Boston.* n. d.] 8vo, pp. 19. B. 58453

Papers on the British Colonies in the West Indies. *London.* [n. d.] 8vo. 58454

Papers on the Colonial Questions, extracted from Fraser's Magazine. *London.* 1830. 8vo. 58455

Papers on the comparative Merits. *See* Vol. x., No. 41047.

Papers on the Defence of Boston and other Places. [*Boston.* 1813.] 8vo, pp. 16. M. 58456

Papers on the Skirmishes at Lexington and Concord. *Poughkeepsie: Abraham Tomlinson.* 1855. 8vo, pp. 128. Plate.

See also Vol. x., No. 42860.

Papers presented by His Majesty's Command to both Houses of Parliament, February, 1808. [*London.*] 1808. Folio, pp. 11.

Papers presented pursuant to Address; viz: Acts of Colonial Legislatures for Registry of Slaves. *London.* 1823. Folio.

Papers presented to Parliament in 1809. *London: A. Strahan.* 1809. 8vo, pp. iv, 999, Index, (20). 58460

Includes correspondence between Great Britain and the United States, and Proceedings of the United States respecting their commerce.

Papers presented to Parliament in 1813. *London: Printed by R. G. Clarke.* [1813.] 8vo. 58461

Papers presented to the Committee appointed to Enquire into the State and Condition of the Countries adjoining to Hudson's Bay, and of the Trade carried on there. *London: Printed in the year* 1749. Folio, pp. 79. 2 Maps. C. 58462

Papers presented to the House of Commons relating to America. *London.* 1810. Folio, pp. 135. 58463

Papers relating chiefly to the Maryland Line. *See* Balch (T.)

Papers relating to America, presented to the House of Commons, 1809. *London: A. Strahan.* 1810. 8vo, pp. viii, 178, (4).

These papers relate to the "Leopard" and "Chesapeake," Correspondence of Canning and Pinkney, Instructions to Erskine, and Correspondence of Erskine and Hon. Robert Smith.

Papers relating to American Loyalists. *London.* 1821. Folio.

Papers relating to an Act. *See* Vol. iv., No. 14272.

Papers relating to an Affidavit. *See* [Nicholson (F.)], 55223.

Papers relating to Boston in New England. *London.* 1755.

Papers relating to Foreign Affairs, ... communicated to Congress, December 1, 1862. *Washington: Government Printing Office.* 1863. 3 parts, 8vo, pp. 910; 439. + December, 1863. [*Ibid.*] 1864. 2 parts, 8vo, pp. 1389. + December, 1864. [*Ibid.*] 1865. 2 parts, 8vo, pp. 896; 814. 58467

These papers, which embrace the correspondence of the Hon. William H. Seward, Secretary of State, accompany the messages of the President of the United States, and relate chiefly to the Rebellion, or matters growing out of that event.

Papers relating to Foreign Affairs, accompanying the Annual Message of the President to the First Session Thirty-Ninth Congress. Part i. *Washington: Government Printing Office.* 1866. 8vo, pp. 671. + Part ii. [*Ibid.*] 1866. 8vo, pp. 584. + Part iii. [*Ibid.*] 1866. 8vo, pp. 850. 58468

Papers relating to Foreign Affairs, accompanying the Annual Message of the President to the Second Session, Fortieth Congress. ... *Washington.* 1868. 2 vols., 8vo, pp. 730; 830.

Papers relating to Free Labour and the Slave-Trade; with A Corrected Report of the Debate in the House of Commons, ... 26th of February, 1861, upon Resolutions reported by Mr. Cave, the Chairman of the West India Committee, for more effectual Suppression of the African Slave-Trade. *London: Robert Barclay.* 1861. 8vo, pp. 64. 58470

Papers relating to Pemaquid. *See* Vol. viii., No. 33146.

Papers relating to the Action between His Majesty's Sloop, Little Belt, ... and the United States Frigate President ... . *London.* 1812. 8vo. 58471

Papers relating to the Arctic. *See* Vol. vii., No. 25633, *note.*

Papers relating to the Canal Frauds. *See* Vol. xiii. 53853.

Papers relating to the Colonization Experiment at A'Vache, Hayti, W. I. [n. p. n. d.] 8vo, pp. 15. H. 58472

Papers relating to the Condemnation of the British Barque "Springbok" and her Cargo, by the District Prize Court of New York. *London.* 1864. 8vo. 58473

Papers relating to the Disturbances. *See* Vol. ix., No. 35645

Papers relating to the illegal Seizure of the British Barque "Springbok," by an American Cruiser, and the wrongful Condemnation of her Cargo, by the Supreme Court of the United States. ... *London.* 1868. 8vo, pp. 70. H. 58474

Papers relating to ... Nantucket. *See* Hough (F. B.), viii.

Papers relating to the Negotiation between the British Plenipotentiaries and the Plenipotentiary on the part of the United States of America, 1824. [n. p. n. d.] Folio. A. 58475

Papers relating to Public Events. *See* Vol. xi., No. 45930.

Papers relating to the Powers of the Corporations of Bowdoin College. *Brunswick.* 1831. 8vo, pp. 14. M. 58476

Papers relating to the ... "Chesapeake." *See* Vol. iii. 12493

Papers relating to the Territory of Kansas. ... *Washington.* 1855–6. 8vo, pp. 822. 58477

Papers relative To French Affairs, communicated by General Armstrong to Mr. Monroe. Accompanying the message of the president ... March 23, 1808. ... *Washington City: A. & G. Way, Printers.* 1808. 8vo, pp. 21. 58478

Corrected title of our No. 2025, Vol. i.

Papers relative to Great-Britain [dated] Philadelphia, Nov. 29. 1791. [n. p. n. d.] 8vo, pp. 116; French originals, pp. 32.

For another edition, *see* [Jefferson (T.)], Vol. ix., No. 35911.

Papers relative to Mexican Affairs. *See* Vol. xii., No. 48620

Papers relative to the Affairs of Jamaica. *See* No. 35644.

Papers relative to the Exploration. *See* Vol. x., No. 38673.

Papers relative to the late Negotiation. *See* [Johnson (Sam.)]

Papers relative to the Negotiation with France, presented by His Majesty's Command to both Houses of Parliament, 22d December, 1806. In French and English. Second Edition. *London: J. Ridgway.* 1807. 8vo, pp. xv, 254. C. 58480

Papers relative to the Origin and Present State of the Questions pending with the United States of America, on the Subject of the Malvinas, (Falkland Islands,) laid before the Legislature

of Buenos Ayres, by the Government of the Province charged with the Direction of the Foreign Relations of the Argentine Republic. *Buenos Ayres: Printed at the Office of the Gaceta Mercantil.* 1832. 8vo, pp. 160. 58481

At the end are five "Papers relating to the occupation of the Malvinas by Great Britain in 1833."

Papers relative to the Recent ... Expedition. *See* No. 25633.

Papers relative to the Restriction of Slavery. Speeches of Mr. King, ... and of Messrs. Taylor and Talmadge, ... on the Bill For Authorising the People of the Territory of Missouri to form a Constitution and State Government, and for the Admission of the same into the Union, ... 1818–19. With a Report of a Committee of the Abolition Society of Delaware. *Philadelphia.* 1819. 8vo, pp. 35. W. 58482

Papers relative to the Rupture with Spain. In French and English. ... *London: Printed by E. Owen and T. Harrison.* 1762. 8vo, pp. (4), 279. C. 58483

See "Monthly Review," xxvi. 228. For replies, *see* our Nos. 1660, 1662, *and* [Wilkes (John)]. *See also* No. 26150.

Papers relative to the Settlement of the Disputed Boundaries between the Provinces of Canada and New Brunswick. Presented to both Houses of Parliament by Command of Her Majesty, 11th July, 1851. *London.* 1851. Folio, pp. iv, 131.

Papers relative to the Tariffs of 1824 and 1828. Presented to the House of Commons. [*London.*] 1828. Folio.

Papers relative to the West Indies. Part i. Circular Instructions—Jamaica—British Guiana. ... 1839. ... Printed, 15 March 1839. Folio. P. 58486

Papers respecting intrusions. *See* Vol. iii., No. 15684.

Papers respecting the "Emily St. Pierre." *See* Vol. vi. 22512.

Papers respecting the Proposed Union. *See* Vol. ii. 8090.

Papers respecting ... The United States, presented to Parliament in 1808. *London: A. Strahan.* 1808. Folio, pp. 617, (17).

Papers respecting the War. *See* Vol. iii., No. 12796.

Papers transmitted to the U. S. Senate. *See* Vol. ix. 37076.

Papiers relatifs à la Rupture avec l'Espagne. *See* No. 58483.

PAPINEAU (L. J.) Discours de ... Louis Joseph Papineau, à l'occasion du 23ème anniversaire de la fondation de l'Institut Canadien, le 17 Dec., 1867. *Montreal.* 1868. 8vo, pp. 20.

PAPINEAU. Histoire de l'Insurrection du Canada, par L. J. Papineau, en réfutation du Rapport de Lord Durham. *Burlington.* 1839. 8vo, pp. 35. 58489

Also: Address ... to the Electors of the Counties of Huntingdon and St. Maurice, December, 1847. [n. p. n. d.] 8vo.—Speech ... at the Meeting of the County of Montreal, on the 15th May, 1837. ... *Montreal.* 1837. 8vo, pp. 20.—Speech ... on the Hustings, at the opening of the Election for the West Ward of ... Montreal, on the 11th August, 1827, and his Reply to Peter M'Gill, Esq. Translated from the French. To which are added, the Speech of ... the Earl of Dalhousie, ... to the ... Assembly ... and the Address of certain Members in consequence ... . *Montreal.* 1827. 12mo, pp. 48. S. *See also* "Procédés de l'Assemblée."

PAPINEAU, *and* NEILSON (John). Letter from J. L. [*sic*] Papineau and J. Neilson, Esqs., addressed to His Majesty's Under Secretary of State on the subject of the proposed Union of ... Upper and Lower Canada. *London.* 1824. 8vo, pp. 81. S.

PAPINIAN, *pseudon.* The Letters of Papinian; in which The Conduct, Present State, and Prospects of the American Congress are examined. *New York: Hugh Gaine.* 1779. 16mo, pp. v, 130. C. 58491

For a note on the work, *see* "Monthly Review," LXII. 89. For other editions, *see* [Inglis (C.)], Vol. IX., No. 34764.

PAPON (*Marquis*). Lola Montez: a Reply to the "Private History and Memoirs" of that Celebrated Lady. By the Marquis Papon. *New York.* 1851. 12mo. Portrait. 58492

See also Vol. XII., No. 50129.

PAPOONAHOAL. An Account of a Visit lately made to the People called Quakers, In Philadelphia, by Papoonahoal, an Indian Chief, and several other Indians, chiefly of the Minisink Tribe. With the Substance of their Conferences on that Occasion. *London: Printed ... by S. Clark.* MDCCLXI. 18mo, pp. 21.

"His speeches are models of good sense and religious conviction; but the most remarkable of all the addresses by American Indians, was made by him to the Governor, who offered him a considerable, and to the chief very valuable amount of goods, as a present. The dignified and noble reply, in which he declined to receive them, on the ground that his visit was entirely for religious instruction, and therefore of too sacred a character to admit of the gross indulgence of personal desires, is worthy of a place on the same page with the most renowned sayings of the heroes of antiquity. The book is rare."—FIELD.

Paquebots. Cinq pièces, de 1783 à 1788. *Paris.* 1788. 4to.

PAQUIN (Messire). Journal historique des évènemens arrivés à St. Eustache pendant la rebellion du Comté du Lac des Deux Montagnes. ... *Montréal.* 1838. 32mo. 58495

Par Perpetua a los Chilenos. *See* Vol. IV., No. 12797.

PARÁ. Almanach administrativo, mercantil, industrial e noticioso da Provincia do Pará para o anno de 1869. Coordenado por Carlos Seidl e Octaviano José de Paiva. Anno Segundo. *Pará.* [1869.] 8vo. Continued. 58496

Catalogo provisorio dos Objectos apresentados na Exposição Paraense de 10 de Junho de 1866. *Pará.* [1866.] Obl. 8vo, pp. 98. H. 58497

Parecer da Commissão Expecial, nomeada pela Assemblea Legislativa da Provincia do Pará. ... *Pará.* 1840. Sm. 4to, pp. 44. 58498

Relatorio apresentado Á Assemblea Legislativa da Provincia do Pará na Segunda Sessão da XIII Legislatura Pelo Excellentissimo Senhor Presidente da Provincia Dr. Francisco Carlos de Araujo Brusque ... *Pará: Imp. na Typ. de Frederico Carlos Rhossard* ... 1863. Folio, pp. 115. 58499

Relatorio Da Commissaõ da Praça do Commercio do Pará apresentado em sessaõ ordinaria da Assemblea Geral em 2 de Janeiro de 1868. *Pará* ... 1868. 8vo, pp. 23, 3. Continued.

Relatorio do Presidente da Provincia do Pará Doutor João Alfredo Corrêa de Oliveira, Passando a Administração da Mesma ao 4.° Vice-Presidente, Doutor Abel Graça. *Pará* ... 1870. 8vo, pp. 54. Table. 58501

Relatorio feito pelo Exm.° Sñr. Conselheiro Jeronimo Francisco Coelho, Presidente desta Provincia, e entregue ao 1.° Vice Presidente em exercicio, o Exm.° Sñr. Dr. Angelo Custodio Corrêa, ... 1850. *Impresso na Typographia de Santos & Filhos*, ... 1850. *Pará.* 8vo, pp. 50. Plan. 58502

O Tocantins e o Anapú. Relatorio do Secretario da Provincia [Domingos Soares Ferreira Penna]. *Para: Impresso na Typ. de Frederico Rhossard.* 1864. 8vo, pp. 87, Appendice, 40, 1 folded leaf. 58503

Para cortar los peligros de nuestra actual division ¿Qué haremos? *Habana.* 1823. 4to, pp. 18. 58504

Para la historia. *See* [Gonzalez (J. V.)], VII. 27817.

PARADA (Antonio). Del Consejo de sa Magestad ... [*Lima.*] 1770. Folio, pp. 8. 58505

PARADA (V. G.) *See* Gomez Parada, Vol. VII., No. 27771.

PARADÈS (R.) Mémoires secrets de Robert Comte de Paradès. Écrites par lui au fortir de la Bastille. Pour servir à l'Histoire de la dernière Guerre. [n. p.] 1789. 8vo, pp. 188. J.C.B.

M. Paradès was employed by the French government as a secret agent in England, from 1778 to 1780.

Paradisisches Wunder-Spiel, Welches sich in diesen letzten Zeiten und Tagen in denen Abendländischen Welt-Theilen, als ein Vorspiel der neuen Welt hervorgethan: Bestehend in einer neuen Sammlung andächtiger [*sic*] ... Lieder. *Ephratæ: Typis & Consensu Societatis A: D:* MDCCLXVI. 4to, pp. 472, (6). P.

A religious treatise, and very rare as are all the productions of the Ephrata press.

The Paradox Solved; or, a Financial Secret worth Knowing: with the means of Dissipating Dearth and Desolation, by the due Encouragement of National Industry, in A Letter to the President of the United States. By the author of Statisticus. *Baltimore: Printed by Joseph Robinson.* 1820. 8vo, pp. 24. B.

PARADYS (N.) Specimen Juridicum inaugurale, de conditione servorum; praesertim in Colonia Surinamensi, quod annuente summo numine ex auctoritate rectoris magnifici Nicolai Paradys, Med. Doct. ... *Lugduni Batavorum: Th. Koet.* MDCCXCIII. 4to, pp. 54. J.C.B. 58509

A | Paraenetick | or | Humble Addresse | to the Parliament | and Assembly | for (not loose, but) | Christian Libertie. | The second Impression. | Perused and allowed according to Order. | *London:* | *Printed by Matthew Simmons, for Henry Overton* | *in Pope's-Head-Alley.* 1644. | Sm. 4to, pp. (2), 14. 58510

Relates to the Puritans and New England. In the catalogue of Mr. John Carter Brown's library this tract is attributed to Roger Williams.

Paragraphs on Banks. *Philadelphia.* 1810. 8vo. 58511

Paragraphs on Judicial Reform in Maryland. *See* [Price (W.)]

PARAGUAY. Beytrag zur Geschichte. *See* [Nusdorfers (B.)]

Cabichui (gaceta humoristica Paraguaya) desde el 3 de Junio hasta 9 de Setiembre 1867. *Paso Pucu.* 1867. 36 Nos., impl. 4to. 1000 or more Wood-cuts. 58512

A very rare and curious newspaper, published during the war, and consisting mainly of satirical attacks upon the Brazilians and their allies, which are written and illustrated with much ability notwithstanding the rudeness of the cuts. Specimens of the native tongue occur in every number. This journal shows clearly the strong national feeling of the Paraguayans and their unshaken attachment to Lopez at that time.

Causa Jesuitica. *See* Vol. III., No. 11576.

Coleccio Regno Jesuitico del Paraguay: Efemerides de la Guerra de los Guaranies, 1754, ó Diario de la Guerra del Paraguay, escrit por el Padre Tadéo Henis, Rigular de la Compania, ... [n. p. 1755?] 4to, pp. 355. 58513

Relates to the Jesuit Missions to these parts, the Guarini and Chiquito Indians, etc. *See also* Vol. VIII., No. 31341.

Coleccion general de Documentos. *See* Cardenas (B. de), III.

Correspondencia diplomatica relativa a la cuestion del Paraguay. Publicada por orden de S. E. el Jefe supremo provisorio para ser presentada al Congreso Constityente. *Lima.* 1867. Impl. 8vo, pp. 158. 58514

Correspondencias Cambiadas entre el Ministerio dr [*sic*] Relaciones Esteriores de la República y el Señor Charles A. Washburn Ministro Residente de los Estados Unidos de América sobre la Conspiracion fraguada contra la Patria y el Gobierno ... y el Atentado de Asesinato a la persona del Éxmo. Señor Mariscal Lopez ... . *Luque: Imp. Nacional.* 1868. 8vo, pp. 124. H.

Description géographique, politique et historique du Royaume de Paraguay, fondé par les Jésuites, imprimés à terræ et traduite en François par Mr. Pingeron ... . *Paris.* 1769. 12mo. 58516

Title as quoted by Rich from Meusel, III. 2, 37.

Descrizione geografica, politica, storica, del Regno del Paraguay, formatosi da i Padri Gesuiti. *Venezia.* 1767. 8vo, pp. xxx.

Erbauliche und angenehme Geschichten. *See* Vol. IV. 12835.

Europeis Magazyn der byzondere Zaken ... . July–December 1754. *Haerlem: Iz. en Joh. Enschedé.* [1754.] 6 parts, 8vo.

Contains essays on the government of the Jesuits in Paraguay; on the earlier or late population of America.

Forfaits des Jésuites. *See* Vol. VI., No. 25089.

Histoire de ce qvi s'est passé. *See* Vol. VIII., No. 32007.

Histoire du Paraguay. *See* [Echavarry (I. de)], VI. 21763.

Historica Relatio. *See* Vol. VIII., No. 31535.

Letters from the Battlefields of Paraguay. By Captain Richard F. Burton ... . With a Map and Illustrations. ... *London: Tinsley Brothers.* 1870. 8vo, pp. xix, 481. BA. 58519

Litteræ Annuæ. *See* Beroa (Diego de), Vol. II., No. 4956.

Manuale ad usum Patrum Societatis Jesu qui in reductionibus Paraguariæ versantur ex Rituali Romano ac Toletano decerptum. *Laure[n]ti: Typis P.P. Societate Jesu.* 1721. 4to, pp. 165.

This excessively rare volume, scarcely indeed known in Europe, is part in Latin and part in the language of Paraguay.

Mémoire touchant l'établissement. *See* Vol. XII., No. 47540.

Memorias sobre los sucesos. *See* Vol. XII., No. 47758.

Messis Paraquariensis. *See* Vol. XII., No. 48157.

Las Misiones del Paraguay. *See* Vol. XII., No. 49456.

Le Paraguai Jésuitique. *See* Bravet, Vol. II., No. 7458.

Paraguay. A Concise History of its Rise, and Progress; and the Causes of the present War with Brazil. ... *London: Effingham Wilson.* 1867. 8vo, pp. 67. Map. 58521

Paraguay and the Alliance against the Tyrant, Francisco Solano Lopez. General Remarks—Reliable Documents. *New York: Hallet & Breen, Printers.* 1869. 8vo, pp. 40. H. 58522

Paraguay and the War in La Plata. *London: Stanford.* 1865. 8vo. 58523

Paraguay, in zijnen vroegeren en tegenwoordigen Toestand, met een Blik op zijne Toekomst. [n. p. n. d.] 8vo, pp. 96.

Le Paraguay, son passé, son présent et son avenir, par un Étranger. *Rio de Janeiro.* 1848. 8vo. + *Paris.* 1851. 8vo, pp. 78. 58525

The Paraguayan Question. The Alliance between Brazil, the Argentine Confederation and Uruguay vs. the Dictator of Paraguay. Claims of Peru and Bolivia in regard to this Alliance. *New York: Hallet & Breen, Printers.* 1866. 8vo, pp. 56. H.

Paraguayo Independiente. *Asuncion.* 1845–6. Folio. 58527

In consequence of the isolation of the republic, its few periodicals are scarce. This gives a history of the revolution and the dictatorship of Francia.

Une Question du Droit des Gens. M. Washburn, ex-Ministre des États-Unis à l'Assomption et la Conspiration paraguayenne. *Paris.* 1868. 8vo, pp. 96. 58528

Recueil des Décrets apostoliques et des Ordonnances du Roi de Portugal, concernant la conduite des Jésuites dans le Paraguay, ... les moyens employés pour un procurer la réforme de la part du S. Siege; l'attentat du 3. Septembre 1758; les suites de cet attentat; la communication qui en a été faite au S. Pere; la punition des coupables ... . *Amsterdam: M. Rey.* 1760–1. 3 vols., 12mo. + *Amsterdam: Pieter Meije.* 1781. 3 vols., 12mo. J.C.B.

Regno Gesuitico del Paraguay dimostrato co' documenti piu classici de' medesimi Padri della Compagnia, i quali confessano, e mostrano ad evidenza la regia sovranità del R. P. Generale con independenza e con odio verso la Spagna anno 1760. *Lisbona: Stamperia Reale.* 1770. 4to, pp. xix, 167. Frontispiece.

Relation abrégée, etc. *See* [Pombal (*Marquis de*)].

Relation von der Blutigen Schlacht, welche den 1. October 1759 in Paraguay zwischen den Jesuiten einer Seits, und den Spaniern und Portugiesen andern Theils, vorgefallen; sammt der Beylage eines Schreibens von einem Spanischen Minister an Pabst Clemens XIII. Aus dem Spanischen. [n. p.] 1760. 4to, pp. 36.

An account of the bloody battle which occurred on the 1st October, 1759, in Paraguay, between the Jesuits on one side and the Spanish and Portuguese on the other; together with a letter from a Spanish Minister to Pope Clement XIII.

Relazione della Battaglia del di Ottobre, 1759, seguita nel Paraguai, fra i Gesuiti e gli Spagnuoli e Portughesi ... . *Napoli.* 1760. 4to. 58532

Remonstrances au Parlement (en vers) avec des Notes relatives au sujet. *Au Paraguay, de l'imprimerie de Nicolas premier.* 1762. 8vo. 58533

This curious tract relates to the proceedings of Lavalette in the Island of Martinique.

Die Republik der Jesuiten, oder das Umgestürzte Paraguay, welches eine richtige Erzählung des Krieges enthält, den diese Geistlichen gegen die Monarchen Spaniens und Portugals in Amerika zu führen gewaget. ... *Amsterdam.* 1758. 8vo, pp. 68. + [*Ibid.*] 4to, pp. 36. J.C.B. 58534

The original of this work is said to have been written in Portuguese by the Marquis de Pombal.

La République des Jésuites, ou Paraguay Renversée, contenant une Relation authentique de la Guerre que ces Religieux ont osé soutenir contre les Monarques d'Espagne & de Portugal en Amérique ... . *Amsterdam, aux dépens de la Compagnie.* 1758. 12mo, pp. 64. J.C.B. + [*Ibid.*] 1759. + *La Haye.* 1758. 12mo.

A very curious and interesting little volume. The translation was made by Pinault.

El Rey ... Previniendo lo que se ha de observar en las Missiones, y Pueblos de Indios de los distritos del Paraguay, y Buenos-Ayres, que estàn à cargo de los PP. de la Compañia de Jesus. *Madrid.* 1746. 4to, 16 leaves. 58536

De Vita et Moribus sex Sacerdotum Paraguaicorum. *Faventiæ: Typis Archii.* 1791. 8vo. 58537

De Vita et Moribus tredecim Virorum Paraguaicorum. *Faventiæ: Typis Archii.* 1793. 8vo. 58538

A Parallel between the Faith and Doctrine Of the Present Quakers, And that of the Chief Hereticks. ... *London.* 1704. 4to, pp. (6), 59. 58539

Directed against the Quakers in Pennsylvania.

A Parallel Drawn between the Administration In the Four last Years of Queen Anne And the Four First of George the Third. By a Country Gentleman. *London: J. Almon.* 1766. 8vo, pp. 25. 58540

PARALTO-BARNUEVO (Pedro de). *See* Peralto.

PARAMARIBO. Catalogus der Surinaamsche Koloniale Bibliotheek te Paramaribo. *'sHage.* 1859. 8vo. + [*Ibid.*] 1862.

Singi-Buku vo da Ningre-Gemeente na Paramaribo. [n. p.] 1820. 12mo, pp. 304. 58542

PARAMUS, *N. J.* Manual and Record of the Church of Paramus. *New York.* 1859. 8vo, pp. 105. 58543

PARANÁ. Revista del Paraná. Periódico de historia, literatura, lejislacion y economia politica. Año I. *Paraná.* 1861. 4to, pp. 120. 58544

Directed by Dr. Vicente G. Quesada. Only eight numbers published, and scarce.

PARANAMARTAGH, *pseudon.* *See* Vol. IX., No. 38391.

PARANHOS (Silva da). La Justification de la Politique brésilienne dans la Plata. ... *Bruxelles.* 1865. 8vo. 58545

Paraphrase de l'Astrolabe, contenant les Principes de Géométrie, La Sphere, L'Astrolabe, ou, déclaracion des choses celestes. Le Miroir du Monde, ou, exposicion des parties de la Terre. Reuue et corrigée par Jaques Bassentin Escossois, auec vne amplification de l'vsage de l'Astrolabe par luimesme aiouteé. *Lyon, Ian de Tovrnes.* MDLV. Sm. 4to, pp. (12), 192. 58546

The second edition of a rare and curious work. The passage relating to the West Indies is found on pages 133–134. For the first edition, *see* [Focard (Jacques)].

A Paraphrase on a Passage. *See* [Maseres (F.)], XI. 45418.

A Paraphrase on Eight Chapters of the Prophet Isaiah; Wherein it is attempted to express the Sense of the Prophet, in proper English Style. *Worcester: Isaiah Thomas.* 1795. 8vo, pp. 41. 58547

PARÄUPÁBA (A.) Twee Verscheyden | Remonstrantien | ofte | Vertogen, | Overgegeven | Aen hare Ho: Mo: de Heeren Staten | Generael der Vereenighde Nederlanden. | Door | Anthonio Paräupába, | In syn leven geweest Regidoor vande Brazilianen | inde Capitania van Rio Grande: Ende met het laetste onge- | luckigh verlies van Brazyl, vande gantsche Braziliaensche | Natie afgesonden; aen hare Ho: Mo: om derselver Natie | erbermelijcken eñ jammerlijcken toestant te vertonen, | ende met eenen hulpe ende bystant te versoecken. | *In 'sGraven-Hage*, | *Gedruckt by Henricus Hondius, woonende* | *inde Hofstraet, inde nieuwe Kunst-en-Boeck-Druckery.* 1657. | 4to, pp. 20. 58548

Antonio Paräupába was Brazilian *regidoor* in Rio Grande, and appears to have been sent as an envoy to the Dutch States General to represent the grievances of his country. An important document for the history of the period.

PARAVEY (Charles Hippolyto). L'Amérique sous le nom de Pays de Fou-Sang, est-elle citée, dès le 5e Siècle de notre ère, dans les grandes annales de la Chine, et, dès lors, ... ce qu'a cru voir le célèbre M. de Guignes, et ce qu'ont nié Gaubil, Klaproth et M. de Humboldt? Discussion ou dissertation abrégée, où l'affirmative est prouvée, Par M. de Paravey. *Paris: Treuttel et Wurtz.* 1844. 8vo, pp. 27. 58549

PARAVEY. Documens hiéroglyphiques, emportés d'Assyrie, et conservés en Chine et en Amérique, sur le Déluge de Noé, les dix générations avant le déluge, l'existence d'un premier homme, et celle du péché originel : ... Par le Cher de Paravey. ... *Paris : Treuttel et Wurtz.* 1838. 8vo, pp. 56, (2). 2 Plates and Table.

Hieroglyphic documents brought from Assyria, and preserved in China and in America, on the Deluge of Noah, the ten generations before the Deluge, etc.

PARAVEY. Mémoire sur l'Origine Japonaise, Arabe et Basque de la civilisation des peuples du Plateau de Bogota, d'après les travaux recens de MM. de Humboldt et Siebold ; par M. de Paravey. *Paris : Dondey-Dupré.* 1835. 8vo, pp. 33. Plate. H.

Memoir on the Japanese, Arab, and Basque origin of the natives of the plains of Bogota, from the recent travels of Messieurs Humboldt and Siebold.

[PARAVEY.] Nouvelles Preuves que le Pays du Fou-Sang mentionné dans les livres Chinois est l'Amérique. [*Paris.* 1847.] 8vo, pp. 12. Plate. 58552

New proofs that the country of Fou-Sang, mentioned in the Chinese books, is America.

PARAVEY. Origine Asiatique d'un Peuple de l'Amérique du Sud. *Paris.* 1830? 8vo. 58553

PARAVEY. Réfutation de l'Opinion émise par Jomard que les Peuples de l'Amérique n'ont jamais eu aucun rapport avec ceux de l'Asie. *Paris.* 1849. 8vo. 58554

PARAYBA. Relacion de la toma de Parayba por los Olandeses el año de 1628 y de la aliança de los Indios con ellos, daños de os moradores y como se apoderaron de Naçaret. [n. p.] 1636. Folio. 58555

Title from Ternaux, No. 567.

PARBURT (G. R.) Oration ... on Board the Ship Sylph, in the Pacific Ocean, July 4, 1849. ... Together with a Brief Account of Her Voyage from Panama to San Francisco. By George R. Parburt, Esq. *Geneva, N. Y.: I. & S. H. Parker.* 1849. 8vo, pp. 31. 58556

PARC D'AVAUGOUR. *See* Du Parc D'Avaugour, No. 21347.

PARCHAPPE (*M.*) Coup d'Œil sur le Voyage de M. Parchappe dans la République Argentine, lu dans la séance mensuelle du comité central de la Société du Bulletin universel tenue le 25 février 1831. *Paris : F. Didot.* [1831.] 8vo, pp. 32.

PARDEE (H. E.) Statistics of the Class of 1856. *See* Yale College.

PARDEE (R. G.) Complete Manual for the Cultivation of the Strawberry ; ... . Also, Notices of the Raspberry, ... and Grape ; with Directions ... . By R. G. Pardee. Third Revised Edition. *New York : G. M. Saxton & Co.* 185–. 12mo, pp. 157. + Sixth Edition. *New York.* 1858. 12mo. C. 58558

PARDEE. The Sabbath-School Index. Pointing out the History and Progress of Sunday-Schools ... . By R. G. Pardee. *Philadelphia : J. C. Garrigues & Co.* 1868. 16mo, pp. 256.

PARDEE (S. J.) The Providences of God in History. A Lecture, delivered through and by S. Judd Pardee, ... Boston, ... July 25th, 1858. ... *Boston : Bela Marsh.* 1859. 12mo, pp. 32.

PARDESSUS (Jean Marie). Collection de Lois maritimes antérieures au XVIIIe Siècle ... . Par J. M. Pardessus ... . *Paris.* 1828–45. 6 vols., 4to. BA., C. 58561

PARDIGON (C. F.) Infantry Sword Exercise. ... By C. F. Pardigon ... illustrated ... by Conrad W. Chapman. *Richmond, Va.: J. W. Randolph.* 1863. 12mo, pp. 38. 58562

PARDIGON. The Practice of War ; Being a Translation of a French Military Work. ... By C. F. Pardigon. *Richmond : West & Johnston.* 1863. 18mo, pp. 216. Plates. 58563

PARDO (F.) Cuentas de D. Felipe Pardo con el Tesoro del Peru Legacion de la Confederacion Peru-Boliviana, en Chile. *Santiago de Chile.* 1837. 8vo. 58564

PARDO. Discurso pronunciado ante el supremo consejo de la guerra por Felipe Pardo defendiendo al Señor Contra-Almirante Don Eugenio Cortes y al Señor General de Brigada Don Jose Maria Egusquiza. *Lima.* 1834. 4to. 58565

PARDO. Proyecto de Constitucion politica escrito por el Sr. D. Felipe Pardo y representado a la Convencion Nacional por los SS. disputados Quiros, Babilon, Terri (D. J.), Terri (D. J. M.), y Tejëda. Con algunas Explicaciones y Comentarios por José A de Lavalle. Segunda Edicion. *Lima : Aurelio Alfaro y Ca.* 1859. 8vo, pp. (2), xxvi, 282. H. 58566

PARDO (F.) Vida de la Madre Mariana de Jesus, religiosa profesa en el Convento de la Concepcion de la Ciudad de la Puebla de los Angeles, por D. Francisco Pardo. *Mexico.* 1676. 4to. 58567

PARDO (F. de P.) Meditaciones sobre el Desastre de Cumaná. Por Francisco de Paulo Pardo. *Carácas.* 1852. 8vo, pp. 23.

[PARDO (Manuel).] Memoria que el Ex-Secretario de Estado en el Despacho de Hacienda y Comercio presenta al Yefe Supremo Provisorio de la Republica. *Lima.* 1867. 8vo, pp. 91.

PARDON (J.) The Soldier's Boy. A Poem. By Jane Pardon. [n. p. n. d.] 8vo. 58570

Parecer da Commissão de fazenda da camara dos deputados da Assemblea Geral Legislativo do Imperio do Brasil ... . *Rio de Janeiro.* 1826. 4to, pp. 256. 58571

Parecer da Commissão Expecial. *See* No. 58498, *supra.*

Parecer de un hombre docto. *See* Oñate (A. de), No. 57305.

PAREDES (A. de). Carta Edificante en que el P. Antonio de Paredes, ... dà Noticia de la Vida de la Hermana Salvadora de los Santos, India Otomi, donado del Beaterio de las Carmelitas de la Ciudad de Queretaro. ... *Mexico.* 1762. 8vo. + Que reimprimen las Parcialidades de S. Juan y de Santiago ... . *Reimpresa en Mexico* [*en la Imprenta nueva Madrileña de los Herederos del Lic. D. Joseph de Jaureguí*]. 1784. 12mo, pp. (12), 112. + *Mexico* [*Don felipe de Zuniga y Ontiveros*]. 1791. 12mo, pp. (12), 112.

Also : Carta Edificante, ... dà noticia à su Provincia Mexicana de las solidas virtudes, religiosos empleos, y santa muerte del P. Francisco Xavier de Solchaga ... . [*Mexico.* 1784.] 4to, pp. 29.

PAREDES (I. de). Catecismo Mexicano. *See* Ripaldi (G.)

PAREDES. Compendio del Arte de la Lengua Mexicana del P. Horacio Carochi de la Compañia de Jesus, ... dispuesto con brevedad, ... por el P. Ignacio de Paredes ... . *En Mexico, en la Imprenta de la Bibliotheca Mexicana, en frente de S. Augustin. Año de* 1759. 4to, pp. (24), 202. Plate. 58573

See Icazbalceta's "Catalogo de Escritores," No. 58, for the title at length.

PAREDES. Doctrina breve sacada del Catecismo Mexicana que dispuso el P. Ignacio de Paredes. *Mexico : Zuñiga.* 1809. 8vo, 8 leaves. 58574

PAREDES. Promptuario Manual Mexicana. Que à la verdad podrá ser utilissimo à los Parrochos para la enseñanza ; à los necessitados Indios para su instruccion ; y à los que aprenden la lengua para la expedicion. Contiene quarenta y seis Platicas con

sus Exemplos, y morales exhortaciones, y seis Sermones morales, ... Añadese por fin un Sermon de Nuestra Santissima Guadalupana Señora ... . *En Mexico, en la Imprenta de la Bibliotheca Mexicana, enfrente de San Augustin. Año de* 1759. 4to, pp. (46), 380, Sermones Mexicanos, xc. Frontispiece. J.C.B. 58575

In Mexican, with Spanish and Latin passages inserted throughout, for the purpose of explaining the more difficult phrases. *See* Icazbalceta, No. 57, for a full title. *See also* Vol. I., No. 996.

PAREDES (José Greg.) Almanaque Peruano y Guia de Forasteros. ... [*Lima :*] *Real Casa de Niños Expositos.* 1810. 12mo, (45) leaves. 58576

See also Vol. X., Nos. 41081*a*, *and* 41111.

PAREDES Y ARRILLAGA (Mariano). Esposicion que hace a sus conciudadanos en manifestacion de su conducta politica, militar y economica de la presente revolucion. ... *Mexico.* 1841. 4to, pp. 28. 58577

PAREDES (Pablo de). Oracion Panegirica que dixo en nombre de la Real Universida de S. Marcos en 21 Diciembre de 1648 ... *Lima.* 1649. 4to. 58578

PAREDES (V. de D.) The Coast of Mosquito and the Boundary Question between New Grenada and Costa Rica, by Victoriano de D. Parédes. *New York.* 1855. 8vo, pp. 62, doubly paged. Map. 58579

In English and Spanish.

PAREJA (F.) Catecismo de la Doctrina Cristiana en Lengua Timuiquana ... *Mexico.* 1617. 8vo. 58580

The author was a native of Toledo, in Spain, and was one of the founders of the Franciscan Order in Santa Elena, in Florida. This is the earliest work in a native Indian language which issued from the press. *See* Finotti's "Bib. Cat. Amer.," p. 14.

PAREJA. Cathecismo en Lengua Castellana, y Timuquana. En el qual se contiene lo que se les puede enseñar a los adultos que han de ser baptizados. Compuesto por el P. F. Francisco Pareja, Religioso de la Orden del seraphico P. S. Francisco, ... y Padre de la Custodia de santa Elena de la Florida. *En Mexico. En la Imprẽta de la Viuda de Pedro Balli. Por C. Adriano Cesar.* M. DC. XII. 8vo, (80) leaves. 58581

PAREJA. Cathecismo y Breve Exposicion de la Doctrina Christiana. Muy util y necessaria, asi para los Españoles, como para los Naturales, en Lengua Castellana, y Timuquana, en modo de preguntas y respuestas. Cõpuesto por el P. F. Fran-

cisco Pareja ... . [Colophon :] *Con licencia de los superiores. en Mexico, en casa de la viuda de Pedro Balli. Año de* 1812. *Por C. A. Cesar.* 8vo, 176 leaves. 58582

PAREJA. Cathecismo y Examen para los que comulgan en Lengua Castellana y Timuquana. Por el Fr. Francisco Pareja, ... *Mexico, en la imprenta de Juan Ruyz.* 1627. 8vo. 58583

PAREJA. Confessionario en Lengua Castellana y Timuquana. Con algunos consejos para animar al penitente. Y assi mismo van declarados algunos effectos y prerrogativas deste sancto sacramento de la Confession. Todo muy vtil y provechoso, assi para que los padres confessores sepan instruyr al penitente como para que ellos aprendan à saberse confessar. Ordenado por el Padre Fr. Francisco Pareja ... . *Impresso con licencia en Mexico, en la Emprenta de la Viuda de Diego Lopez Daualos. Año de* 1613. 12mo, 238 leaves. 58584

PAREJA. Gramatica de la Lengua Timuiquana de Florida, por Fr. Francisco Pareja ... . *Mexico.* 1614. 8vo. 58585

PARENT (Étienne). Discours prononcés à Québec, en 1852, par E. Parent, ecr., sur les [trois] sujets ... . *Québec.* 1853. 8vo, pp. 22, 67, 26. 58586

Parental Wishes. *See* [Mather (C.)], Vol. XI., No. 46445.

Parentator. *See* [Mather (C.)], Vol. XI., No. 46447.

The Parent's Magazine. Edited by Rev. I. Bird and Mrs. Bird. ... *Gilmanton, N. H.* 1841. 8vo. 58587

PARENTE (Filippe Alberto Patroni Martins Maciel). A Prophecia do Novo-Mundo. Primeira collecção dos fragmentos, artigos ou extractos das obras do Doutor Patroni, publicados no Brasil, e agora com a chegada do auctor a Lisboa em 20 de Março de 1851, reimpressos e publicados por J[oão] M[aria] A[ugusto] C[astellar]. *Lisboa : Typ. de Ricarda Pires Marinho.* 1851. 4to, pp. 92. 58588

PARENTE. A Viagem de Patroni pelas Provincias Brasileiras de Ceará, Rio de S. Francisco, Bahia, Minas geraes e Rio de Janeiro, nos annos de 1829 e 1830. ... *Lisboa, na Officina de J. C. A. Vianna.* 1851. 4 parts, 8vo, pp. 134 ; 134. 58589

PARIAN. Coleccion de Documentos oficiales relativos á la Construccion y Demolicion del Parian. *Mexico.* 1843. 4to.

PARIGOT (J.) Memoria sobre as Minas de Carvão de Pedra do Brazil. ... *Rio de Janeiro.* 1841. 4to, pp. 30. 2 Plates.

PARIS (J.) History of the Methodist Protestant Church : ... . By Rev. John Paris ... . *Baltimore : Sherwood & Co.* 1849. 12mo, pp. 411. C. 58592

Also : A Sermon ... before Brig. Gen. Hoke's Brigade, at Kinston, N. C., ... 28th of February, 1864 ... . *Greensborough, N. C. : A. W. Ingold & Co. Printers.* 1864. 8vo, pp. 15.

PARIS (M.) Essai sur la Construction Navale des Peuples Extra-Européens ou Collection des Navires et Pirogues Construits par les Habitants de l'Asie, de la Malasie, du Grand Océan et de l'Amérique Dessinés et mesurés par M. Paris, capitaine de corvette pendant les voyages autour du monde de l'Astrolabe, la Favorite et l'Artémise. *Paris : Arthus Bertrand.* [n. d.] Folio, pp. (6), 156 ; Atlas, pp. (4), 132 Plates. 58593

PARIS (S. B.) The Remains of Samuel B. Paris, M.D., comprising Poems and Essays, with a Biographical Sketch. *Plymouth, Mass.* 1829. 12mo, pp. 312. 58594

Paris, le 10 fructidor. *See* Bonnet (G.-J.), Vol. II., 6322.

Paris Universal Exposition, 1867. Reports of the United States Commissioners. General Survey ... with a Report on the ... United States Section [By N. W. Beckwith]. *Washington : Government Printing Office.* 1868. 8vo, pp. 324, (1). Plate.

Also : Catalogue des Objets exposés dans la Section des États-Unis d'Amérique. *Paris.* 1855. 8vo.—Catalogue of Awards to American Exhibitors at the Paris Universal Exposition of 1867. *Washington.* 1868. 8vo, pp. 15.— ... Official Papers relating to the Conduct of the Legation of the United States at Paris ... 1867. Second Edition. With the Complaint ... *Paris : Printed by E. Brière.* 1867. 8vo, pp. (2), 23.—Report of Samuel B. Ruggles on International Coinage. [n. p.] 1867. 8vo. + Supplementary Report. [n. p.] 1870. 8vo.—Report of Samuel B. Ruggles and George S. Hazard, United States Commissioners, on Cereals. *Washington.* 1869. 8vo. —Report on Civil Engineering and Public Works, by William P. Blake. *Washington.* 1870. 8vo.— ... Reports of the United States Commissioners. Extracts from the Report ... on Weights, Measures, and Coins, with a Notice of the ... Metric System in the United States. ... *Washington.* 1870. 8vo, pp. 47.— ... Reports of the United States Commissioners. Introduction, with Selections from the Correspondence of ... General Beckwith and Others ... . *Washington.* 1870. 8vo, pp. 184.—Reports of the United States Commissioners to the Paris Universal Exposition, 1867. Published under Direction of the Secretary of State. ... Edited by William P. Blake. ... *Washington.* 1870. 6 vols., rl. 8vo. *See also* Vol. XIII., No. 56763.

PARISET (N.) The American Trooper's Pocket Companion : ... for the Cavalry of the United States. By Nicholas Pariset. *Trenton : The Author.* M,DCC,XCIII. 24mo, pp. 45. H. 58596

Dedicated to George Washington.

PARISH (A.) Management of the School-Room. A Lecture ... Worcester, November 24, 1846, at the ... Meeting of the Mass. Teachers' Association. By Ariel Parish ... . *Boston : Printed by George Coolidge.* 1853. 16mo, pp. 49. H. 58597

[PARISH (E.)] A Candid Analytical Review of the "Sketches of the History of Dartmouth College and Moor's Charity School, with a particular Account of some late Remarkable Proceedings of the Board of Trustees, from the year 1779 to the year 1815." [n. p. n. d.] 8vo, pp. 32. C. 58598

PARISH. A Compendious System of Universal Geography, ... By Elijah Parish, D.D. ... *Newburyport.* [1807.] 12mo. Maps. + Second Edition ... . *Newburyport, (Mass.) : Thomas & Whipple.* 1807. 12mo, pp. 212. Maps. B. 58599

PARISH. A Discourse ... at Byfield on the Annual Thanksgiving, in the Commonwealth of Massachusetts, Nov. 29, 1804. By Rev. Elijah Parish, A.M. ... *Salem : Printed by Joshua Cushing.* 1805. 8vo, pp. 24. BA. 58600

PARISH. A Discourse ... at Byfield, on the Public Fast, April 7, 1814. By Elijah Parish, D.D. *Newburyport : William B. Allen and Co.* 1814. 8vo, pp. 24. + Second Edition. [*Ibid.*]

PARISH. An Eulogy on John Hubbard, Professor of Mathematics and Natural Philosophy in Dartmouth College ; ... . Pronounced ... September, 1810. By Elijah Parish ... . *Hanover, N. H.: Printed by C. W. S. & H. Spear.* 1810. 8vo, pp. 27.

PARISH. Memoirs of Eleazer Wheelock. *See* McClure (D.)

PARISH. A New System of Modern Geography ; ... . Compiled by Elijah Parish ... . *Newburyport.* 1810. 8vo. Maps. + Second Edition. [*Ibid.*] 1812. 12mo, pp. 366. Maps.

PARISH. An Oration, ... at Byfield, February 22d, 1800, The Day of National Mourning for the Death of General George Washington. By the Rev. Elijah Parish ... . *Newburyport : From the Press of Angier March.* [1800.] 8vo, pp. 32.

Contains an elegiac poem of four pages.

PARISH. A Protest against the War. A Discourse ... at Byfield, Fast Day, July 23, 1812. By Elijah Parish ... . *Newburyport.* 1812. 8vo, pp. 26. M. + Second Edition. [*Ibid.*] + *Stockbridge : E. Kingsley.* 1812. 8vo, pp. 28. B. 58605

PARISH. A Sermon, ... at the Ordination of the Rev. Ariel Parish, A.M., Pastor of the Church in Manchester, April 4, 1792. By Elijah Parish ... . *Salem : Printed by Thomas C. Cushing.* 1792. 8vo, pp. 40. BA. 58606

PARISH. A Sermon ... at Boston, ... upon the Annual Election, May 30, 1810. By Elijah Parish ... . *Boston.* 1810. 8vo, pp. 24. BA. 58607

PARISH. A Sermon ... at Boston, November 3, 1814, before the Society for Propagating the Gospel among the Indians and others in North-America. By Elijah Parish ... . *Boston : Printed by Nathaniel Willis.* 1814. 8vo, pp. 44. BA. 58608

PARISH. Sermons ... by the late Elijah Parish, D.D. With a Biographical Sketch ... *Boston : Crocker & Brewster.* 1828. 8vo, pp. xvi, 421, (1). 58609

Also : A Discourse, ... at Byfield on the Annual Fast, April 8, 1813. ... *Newburyport : E. W. Allen.* 1813. 8vo, pp. 24.—The Excellence of the Gospel ... . A Discourse ... December 20, 1797, being the Tenth Anniversary of his Ordination. ... *Printed by A. March, Newburyport.* 1798. 8vo, pp. 28.—An Oration ... at Byfield, July 4, 1799. ... *Newburyport : Printed by Angier March.* [1799.] 8vo, pp. 18. + Second Edition. [*Ibid.*] 8vo, pp. 14.—Ruin or Separation from Anti-Christ. A Sermon ... at Byfield, April 7, 1808, on the Annual Fast in the Commonwealth of Massachusetts ... . *Newburyport : E. W. & W. B. Allen, Printers.* 1808. 8vo, pp. 24. + Second Edition. *Portland.* [n. d.] 8vo, pp. 21.—A Sermon ... at the Ordination of the Rev. Mathew Waldo, A.B., in Williamstown, Vermont, February 27, 1806. ... *Hanover, N. H.* 1806. 8vo, pp. 15.—A Sermon ... in the Vicinity of Dartmouth College, on the Sabbath preceding Commencement, 1806 ... . *Hanover, N. H.: Printed by Moses Davis.* 1806. 8vo, pp. 15.—A Sermon ... before the Massachusetts Missionary Society, at their Annual Meeting in Boston, May 26, 1807. ... *Newburyport : Printed by E. W. Allen.* 1807. 8vo, pp. 26.—A Sermon ... at the Ordination of the Rev. David Thurston, ... in Winthrop, February 18, 1807. ... *Augusta : Printed by Peter Edes.* 1807. 8vo, pp. 30.—Sermon ... before the Female Charitable Society of Newburyport, May 17, 1808. ... *Newburyport.* 1808. 8vo, pp. 28.—A Sermon, ... in the Presbyterian Church, Schenectady. ... *Schenectady.* 1808. 8vo.—A Sermon ... at Byfield, on the Annual Fast, April 11, 1811. ... Second Edition. ... *Newburyport : Press of E. W. Allen.* 1811. 8vo, pp. 30. + With Gov. Gerry's Proclamation for a Fast. *Boston : Printed by B. True.* 1811. 8vo, pp. 24.—A Sermon, ... 29th September, 1815, at the Ordination of Rev. D. Smith and Cyrus Kingsbury as Missionaries to the West. ... *Newburyport.* 1815. 8vo.—A Sermon, ... before the Convention of the Congregational Ministers in Massachusetts, ... May 30, 1821. ... *Cambridge : Printed by Hilliard and Metcalf.* 1821. 8vo, pp. 20.—A Sermon, ... at Byfield, and in ... Newburyport. ... *Charles Whipple, Newburyport.* 1823. 8vo, pp. 16. BA.

PARISH (H.) The Last Will and Testament and Three Codicils of Henry Parish, deceased. *New-York : Wm. C. Bryant & Co. Printers.* 1856. 8vo, pp. 12. 58610

PARISH. Surrogate's Court. County of New York. In the Matter of proving the Last Will and Testament of Henry Parish, deceased. [n. p. n. d.] 3 vols., 8vo, pp. 778, 13, 4; 771, 28; xxix, 794. 58611

Vol. III. has the title: "County of New York: Surrogate's Court. Before Hon. Alexander W. Bradford, Surrogate. In the Matter of proving the Will of Henry Parish, deceased. Testimony and Exhibits." Vol. III. *New York: Wm. C. Bryant and Company, Printers.* 1857.

Also: The Parish Will Case before the Surrogate of the City of New York. Medical Opinions upon the Mental Competency of Mr. Parish ... . *New York: John F. Trow, Printer.* 1857. 8vo, pp. 573.—Parish Will Case, in the Court of Appeals. Statement of Facts on Behalf of Daniel Parish and the Heirs of James Parish ... For the Court. John K. Porter, Jacob B. Jewett, of Counsel ... *New York: John F. Trow, Printer.* 1862. 8vo, pp. 123.—The Parish Will Case. Argument of John K. Porter, ... January 10, 1862. *Albany: Comstock & Cassidy, Printers.* 1862. 8vo, pp. 98. + *Albany: J. Munsell.* 1862. 8vo, pp. 72.—The Parish Will Case, in the Court of Appeals. The Opinion of the Court, and of the several Judges. *New York: D. Appleton and Company.* M.DCCC.LXII. 8vo, pp. 43.—The Parish Will Case in the Court of Appeals. The Statement of Facts, and the Opinion of the Court. *New-York: D. Appleton and Company.* 1865. 8vo, pp. 123.—The Parish Will Case. ... *New York: John S. Voorhies.* 1865. 2 vols., 8vo.

PARISH (W.) Buenos Ayres and the Provinces of the Rio de La Plata: their Present State, Trade, and Debt; with some Account from Original Documents of the Progress of Geographical Discovery in those parts of South America during the last Sixty Years. By Sir Woodbine Parish ... . *London: John Murray.* 1839. 8vo. Map and Plates. S. 58612

The author is the discoverer of those extraordinary fossil animals, the megatherium and the glyptodon. Contains information not to be found in the second edition.

PARISH. Buenos Ayres and the Provinces of the Rio de la Plata: from their Discovery and Conquest by the Spaniards to the establishment of their Political Independence. With ... a Description of the Geology and Fossil Monsters of the Pampas. By Sir Woodbine Parish ... . Second Edition, enlarged with a new Map and Illustrations. *London: John Murray.* 1852. 8vo, pp. xlii, 434. BA. 58613

Professing to be a second edition of No. 58612, it is, in reality, almost a new work, from the great quantity of fresh matter it contains.

PARISH. Buenos Aires y las Provincias de la Plata. Version castellana de la edicion inglesa de 1839. *Buenos Aires.* 18—. 8vo. 58614

Parish Statistics. *See* Vol. VI., No. 22193.

Parisian Sights. *See* [Jarves (J. J.)], Vol. IX., No. 35798.

PARISMAS (T.) The History of Captain Thomas Parismas, ... *Medford (Massachusetts).* 1698. 8vo, pp. 34, 21, 5. + [n. p.] 1805. 18mo, pp. 35. C. 58615

PARK (E. Amasa). Addresses of Rev. Drs. Park, Post, & Bacon, at the Anniversary of the American Congregational Union, May, 1854. ... *New York: Clark, Austin & Smith.* 1854. 8vo, pp. 133. 58616

PARK. ... A Discourse ... before the Convention of the Congregational Ministers of Massachusetts, ... May 30, 1850. By Edwards A. Park ... . *Boston: Perkins & Whipple.* 1850. 8vo, pp. 44. B. 58617

PARK. A Discourse ... in Boston before the Pastoral Association of Congregational Ministers in Massachusetts, May 28, 1844. By Edwards A. Park ... . *Andover: Allen, Morrill, & Wardwell.* 1844. 8vo, pp. 44. B. + Second Edition. [*Ibid.*] 8vo, pp. 60. B. 58618

This elicited: "Letter to E. A. Park, touching his late Sermon before the Pastoral Association of Massachusetts." *Boston.* 1844. 8vo, pp. 30.

PARK. The Imprecatory Psalms Viewed in the Light of the Southern Rebellion: An Essay ... . By Edwards A. Park ... . *Andover: Warren F. Draper.* 1862. 8vo, pp. 48. 58619

PARK. The Indebtedness of the State ... . A Sermon ... at the Annual Election, January 2, 1851. By Edwards A. Park, ... *Boston: Dutton & Wentworth, ... Printers.* 1851. 8vo, pp. 59

PARK. Memoir of Nathanael Emmons; with Sketches of his Friends and Pupils. By Edwards A. Park ... . *Boston: Congregational Board of Publication.* 1861. 8vo, pp. xx, 468. Portrait.

PARK. Memoir of the Life and Character of Samuel Hopkins, D.D. By Edwards A. Park ... Second Edition. *Boston: Doctrinal Tract and Book Society.* 1854. 8vo, pp. viii, 264.

PARK. New England Theology; with Comments on a Third Article in the Princeton Review, relating to a Convention Sermon, by Edwards A. Park ... . *Andover: Warren F. Draper.* 1852. 8vo, pp. 53. H. 58623

PARK. Remarks on an Article in the Biblical Repertory and Princeton Review concerning a recent Discourse ... before the Convention of Congregational Ministers of Massachusetts. By Edwards A. Park ... . *Andover: W. F. Draper.* 1851. 8vo, pp. 48. H. 58624

PARK. Unity amid Diversity of Belief ... with Comments on a Second Article in the Princeton Review relating to a Conven-

tion Sermon, by Edwards A. Park ... . *Andover: Warren F. Draper.* 1851. 8vo, pp. 57. H. 58625

Also: A Discourse ... at the Funeral of Professor Moses Stuart. ... *Boston: Tappan & Whittemore.* 1852. 8vo, pp. 56.—A Discourse ... at the Ordination of Rev. Walter S. Alexander over the First Congregational Church in Pomfret, Conn., November 22, 1861. ... *Andover: Printed by Warren F. Draper.* 1862. 8vo, pp. 48.—Duties of a Theologian: an Anniversary Address, ... before the Theological Society of Dartmouth College, July 24, 1839. ... *New-York.* 1839. 8vo, pp. 35.—The Life and Services of Professor B. B. Edwards. Discourse ... Andover, June 25, 1852. ... *Andover: Press of Warren F. Draper.* 1852. 8vo, pp. 41.—Revelation of God ... . A Sermon ... at the installation of the Rev. Jacob M. Manning, as Associate Pastor of the Old South Church in Boston, March 11, 1857. ... *Boston: S. K. Whipple & Company.* 1857. 8vo, pp. 47.—Sermon ... at the Interment of Rev. Charles Backus Storrs, ... who died ... Sept. 15, 1833. ... *Boston: Printed by Perkins & Marvin.* 1833. 8vo, pp. 24.—Theological Education. An Address ... before the American Education Society, ... Boston, May 30, 1865. ... *Boston: Press of T. R. Marvin & Son.* 1865. 8vo, pp. 31.—The Utility of Collegiate and Professional Schools. An Address ... Boston, May 29, 1850. ... Second Edition. *Andover: Warren F. Draper.* 1851. 8vo, pp. 31. B.

PARK (H. G.) ... A Sermon occasioned by the Death of the Rev. George Cowles and Mrs. Elizabeth R. Cowles; ... in Danvers, November 12, 1837. By Harrison G. Park ... . *Salem: Printed by Wm. Ives & Co.* 1837. 8vo, pp. 40. 58626

[PARK (John).] An Address to the Citizens of Massachusetts, on the Causes and Remedy of our National Distresses. By a Fellow-Sufferer. *Boston.* 1808. 8vo, pp. 13. W. 58627

Also: An Address ... before the ... Masters and Brethren of the Lodges of St. Peter and St. John, ... in Newburyport, ... June 24, 5803. ... *Newburyport.* 1803. 4to, pp. 12, (1).

PARK (J. Cochran). Address at a Meeting of the Descendants of Richard Haven, of Lynn, at Framingham, Mass., August 29, 1844. Being the Second Centennial Anniversary of his Landing in New England. By John C. Park, of Boston. ... *Boston: Samuel N. Dickinson, Printer.* 1844. 8vo pp. 27.

[PARK.] A Memorial of Major Edward Granville Park, ... 35th Massachusetts Volunteers. ... *Boston: Press of John Wilson and Son.* 1865. 8vo, pp. 41. Portrait. 58629

[PARK, *and others.*] To the Citizens of Boston [on the New Plan of Public Schools. *Boston.* 1836.] 8vo, pp. 14, (1).

PARK (J. W.) An Address on African Slavery ... 14th July, 1857. By John W. Park. *Atlanta, Geo.: Press of G. P. Eddy & Co.* 1857. 8vo, pp. 26. 58631

PARK (Joseph). Sermon at Westerly, R. I., Feb. 24, 1760. ... With a Narrative, and a Letter from a Gentleman in Connecticut. *New London.* 1761. 8vo, pp. 39, 23. 58632

PARK (R.) Jerusalem; and other Poems ... . With a Brief Memoir of Mrs. Mary Brewster Park. By Roswell Park, D.D. *New York: T. N. Stanford.* 1857. 12mo, pp. 309, xv. Port's.

PARK. A Sketch of the History and Topography of West Point, and the U. S. Military Academy. ... By Roswell Park, A.M. *Philadelphia: Henry Perkins.* 1840. 18mo, pp. 140. Map

PARK (S.) American Antiquities. Read before ... the Pioneer Associations of the Counties of Franklin, Muskingum, and Licking, ... at Pataskala, Ohio, July 4, 1870. By Samuel Park, ... *Terre Haute: O. J. Smith & Co.* 1870. 8vo, pp. 22. 58635

PARK. ... Notes of the Early History of Union Township, Licking County, Ohio. By Samuel Park ... *Terre Haute: O. J. Smith & Co.* 1870. 8vo, pp. 56. 58636

PARK (T.) An Oration: Delivered in the College-Hall, at Providence, August 13, 1788, on the death of Mr. Nathan Merrick. By Thomas Park, a Member of the Junior Class. ... *Providence: Printed by Bennett Wheeler.* [1788.] 8vo, pp. 16.

Mr. Merrick, also of the Junior Class, drowned July 12, 1788.

PARK-STREET CHURCH. *See* Vol. II., Nos. 6668–9.

PARKE (B.) Oration delivered on Rinehart's Island, near Harrisburg, Pa., before the "National Guard" of Harrisburg, "Walker Sharp Shooters" of the City of Washington, and Citizens, ... July 4, 1853. By Benjamin Parke, Esq. *Harrisburg.* [1853.] 8vo, pp. 8. 58638

PARKE (*Col*) Some Instances of the Oppression and Male Administration of Col. Parke, ... with an Account of the Rise and Progress of the Insurrection at Antegoa ... . [n. p. n. d.] Folio, pp. 4. 58639

[PARKE (John).] The Battle of Bunkers Hill. ... By a Gentleman of Maryland. *Philadelphia.* MDCCLXXVI. 8vo, pp. (4), 79. 58640

For a full and correct title of this piece, and "The Death of General Montgomery," *see* [Brackenridge (H. H.)], Vol. II., Nos. 7184–5, to whom it has also been attributed.

PARKE (J. G.) Report of Explorations for that portion of a Railway Route, near the Thirty-Second Parallel of Latitude,

lying between Dona Ana, on the Rio Grande, and Pimas Villages on the Gila. By Lieut. John G. Parke, U.S.A. ... [n. p. n. d.] 8vo, pp. 53. 2 Maps. S. 58641

PARKE (N. G.) The Assassination of the President of the United States overruled for the Good of our Country. A Discourse ... in ... Pittston, Penna., June 1st, 1865. [By] Rev. N. G. Parke, A.M. *Pittston, Pa.* 1865. 8vo, pp. 20. B.

[PARKER (——).] An Argument [etc.]. *See* Vol. I. 1968.

PARKER (A. A.) Trip to the West and Texas. Comprising a Journey of Eight Thousand Miles, through New-York, Michigan, Illinois, Missouri, Louisiana and Texas, in ... 1834–5. Interspersed with Anecdotes ... . With a Brief Sketch of the Texian War. By A. A. Parker, Esq. *Concord, N. H.: White & Fisher.* 1835. 12mo, pp. 276. Map, 3 Plates. + Second Edition. *Concord, N. H.: William White.* ... 1836. 12mo, pp. 380. Map, 3 Plates. B. 58643

PARKER (Adaline Rice). Letters of Ada R. Parker. ... *Boston: Crosby and Nichols.* 1863. 12mo, pp. xv, 302. Plate. B.

PARKER (A.) An Oration ... on the 4th of July, 1829, in Southbridge, Mass. By Rev. Addison Parker. *Southbridge.* 1829. 8vo, pp. 28. 58645

PARKER (*Ald.*) Address of Alderman Parker to the City Council, January 3, 1845. *Boston.* 1845. 8vo, pp. 7. M.

PARKER (A. J.) An Address ... before the Graduating Class of the Albany Medical College, January 21, 1851. By Amasa J. Parker ... . *Albany: E. H. Pease & Co.* 1851. 8vo, pp. 32.

Also: Speech ... on the Amendment ... declaring that Messrs. Prentiss and Wood were not entitled to Seats in the 25th Congress. *Washington.* 1838. 8vo.— ... Speech ... at the Cooper Institute. [n. p. n. d.] 8vo, pp. 8. B.

PARKER (A. X.) Speech of A. X. Parker, of St. Lawrence, in Assembly, 1864, on the Proposition for a Niagara Ship Canal. [*Albany.* 1864.] 8vo, pp. 7. 58648

PARKER (B.) ... Sermon ... in Haverhill, February 20, 1774, ... after the Death ... of the Reverend Mr. Edward Barnard. By Benjamin Parker, M.A. ... *Salem: Printed by Samuel and Ebenezer Hall.* 1774. 8vo, pp. 19. BA. 58649

Also: The Difficulties, ... of Christ's Ministers considered, in a Sermon ... at the Ordination of the Reverend Mr. Jonathan Eames, ... New-Town, in the Province of

New-Hampshire, January 17, 1759. ... *Portsmouth, New-Hampshire; Printed ... by Daniel Fowle.* M,DCC,LIX. 8vo, pp. 33. N.

PARKER (C. C.) The Early History of Waterbury. A Discourse delivered February 10th, 1867. By Rev. C. C. Parker, ... *Waterbury.* 1867. 8vo, pp. 28. 58650

PARKER (C.) Philip Kearny: Soldier and Patriot. An Address ... before the New-Jersey Historical Society, January 17, 1867. By Cortlandt Parker. ... *Newark.* 1868. 8vo, pp. 49.

Also: An Address ... before the Alumni Association of Rutgers College, July 23, 1853 ... . *New-York: Printed by John A. Gray.* 1853. 8vo, pp. 29.—Oration ... Bloomfield, July 4, 1865. ... *Newark.* 1865. 8vo. For his "Sketch of the Life ... of Theodore Frelinghuysen," *see* Vol. VII., No. 25831.

PARKER (D.) A | Perswasive | To make a | Publick Confession of Christ, | and come up to | All his Ordinances, | ... | And Objections answered. | ... | By the late Hon. Daniel Parker, Esq; | of Barnstable. | ... | *Boston, New-England:* | ... *D. Henchman* ... | 1730. 12mo, pp. (4), 19. B. + *Salem: Reprinted ... by Samuel Hall.* 1770. 12mo, pp. 24. B. 58652

PARKER (D.) Church Privilege and Obligation on Congregational Principles: A Discourse, ... in ... Brookfield, Vt., March 9, 1845. By Rev. Daniel Parker, A.M. ... *Montpelier, Vt.: E. P. Walton and Sons, Printers.* 1847. 8vo, pp. 19.

PARKER (D.) A Complete Refutation of the Reply of Mr. Joseph Harvey to Proscription Delineated. By Daniel Parker. ... *New York: Wiley & Halsted.* 1820. 8vo. P. 58654

PARKER. A Discourse, ... at Canaan, March 23, 1815, at the Installation of Meridian Chapter. By Daniel Parker ... . *Hartford: Peter B. Gleason & Co., Printers.* 1815. 8vo, pp. 25.

PARKER. Proscription Delineated; or a Developement [*sic*] of Facts appertaining to the Arbitrary and Oppressive Proceedings of the North Association of Litchfield County, in relation to the author. By Daniel Parker ... . *Hudson: Stone and Corss.* 1819. 12mo, pp. 290. B., S. 58656

Also: A Discourse ... before ... the Literary School in Sharon, Ellsworth Society, ... September 6, 1815. ... *Hartford: Printed by Peter B. Gleason and Co.* 1815. 8vo, pp. 24.—New Year's Discourse, ... before the Literary Institution in Greenville, Greene County, N. Y. ... *Catskill.* 1817. 8vo.

PARKER (D.) ... A Sermon ... in ... Rhinebeck Flats, March 30, 1823. Occasioned by the Death of Mrs. Margaret Tillotson. By David Parker, A.M. [n. p. n. d.] 8vo, pp. 15.

PARKER (D. G.) A Compilation of Startling Facts, or Romanism Against Republicanism ... . By D. G. Parker. *Chicago: Charles Scott, Printer.* 1856. 12mo, pp. 112. BA. 58658

PARKER (E. G.) The Golden Age of American Oratory. By Edward G. Parker. *Boston: Whittemore, Niles and Hall.* 1857. 12mo, pp. vi, (2), 425. 58659

Contains notices of Clay, Webster, Ames, Everett, etc.

PARKER. Reminiscences of Rufus Choate, the great American Advocate. By Edward G. Parker. ... *New York: Mason Brothers.* 1860. 12mo, pp. 522. Portrait. + Fourth Edition. [*Ibid.*] 58660

Also: The Lesson of '76 to the Men of '56. An Oration ... before the Municipal Authorities of the City of Boston, ... July 4, 1856. ... *Boston: Geo. C. Rand & Avery, ... Printers.* 1856. 8vo, pp. 35.—Report ... to the Senate of Massachusetts on the purchase of the Hancock House by the State. [n. p.] 1859. 8vo, pp. 13.

PARKER (E. H.) ... The Annual Address before the Medical Society of the State of New York, and the ... Legislature, ... February 6th, 1862. By Edward H. Parker, M.D. ... *Poughkeepsie, New York.* 1862. 8vo, pp. 23. 58661

PARKER (E. Latwycke). A Century Sermon, ... in the East-Parish Meeting House, Londonderry, New Hampshire, April 22, 1819, in commemoration of the First Settlement of the Town. Containing, A Sketch of the History of the Town from its earliest Settlement. By Edward L. Parker ... . *Concord: Printed by George Hough.* 1819. 8vo, pp. 44. B., W. 58662

PARKER. The History of Londonderry, comprising the Towns of Derry and Londonderry, N. H. By Rev. Edward L. Parker ... . With a Memoir of the Author [by Samuel H. Taylor. Edited by his son Edward P. Parker.] *Boston: Perkins and Whipple.* 1851. 12mo, pp. lv, 358, (1). Map, Plates, and Portraits. H. 58663

Also: A Sermon, ... at Bedford, N. H. March 26, 1822, occasioned by the sudden Death of James Parker, Esq. ... *Amherst: Printed by Richard Boylston.* 1822. 8vo, pp. 16.—A Sermon ... at the Ordination of the Rev. Abijah Cook, ... Salisbury, N. H., March 24, 1824. ... *Plymouth.* 1824. 8vo, pp. 24. W.

PARKER (E. S.) Report on the Dismal Swamp Canal, its cost, condition, and resources. By Ely S. Parker ... . *Washington.* 1867. 8vo, pp. 9. H. 58664

PARKER (F. A.) ... Squadron Tactics under Steam. By Foxhall A. Parker ... . *New York: D. Van Nostrand.* 1864. 8vo, pp. 172. 77 Plates, and 2 folded Plates. B. 58665

PARKER (F.) Centennial Sermon, ... at Boston, November 27, 1814, on the Anniversary of the New North Church. By Rev. Francis Parker. *Boston.* 1814. 8vo. 58666

[PARKER (Francis J.)] The Mexican Empire and the American Union. *Boston: Geo. C. Rand & Avery.* 1865. 8vo, pp. 12.

PARKER (F.) A Masonic Address ... at Wiscasset, ... June 24, A.L. 5813. By Freeman Parker, A.M. ... *Hallowell: Printed by N. Cheever.* 1813. 8vo, pp. 16. BA. 58668

PARKER (G.) The West-India Almanack for the Year 1719. By George Parker. *London.* 1719. 18mo. 58669

Contains an account of America, particularly of "New England or Virginia" (all the English Dominions south of Canada, etc.), and the West-Indies; a Jamaica Chronology from 1494, and list of Governors of the West India Islands.

[PARKER (G. G.)] Piratical Barbarity, or the Female Captive, comprising the Particulars of the Capture of the English Sloop Eliza-Ann, on her passage from St. Johns to Antigua, and the horrid Massacre of the unfortunate Crew, by the Pirates, March 12, 1825, and of the unparalleled Sufferings of Miss Lucretia Parker ... . *New York: Printed by S. Walker for G. G. Parker.* [1825.] 8vo, pp. 36. B., W. 58670

PARKER (Helen F.) Discoverers and Pioneers of America. By H. F. Parker. *New York: Derby & Jackson.* 1856. 12mo, pp. 416. 6 Plates. + [*Ibid.*] 1860. 58671

The same as the following with a new title-page.

PARKER. Morning Stars of the New World: Biographical Sketches. By H. F. Parker. *New York: James C. Derby.* 1854. 12mo, pp. 416. 6 Plates. C. 58672

PARKER (H. E.) A Discourse the day after the Reception of the Tidings of the Assassination of President Lincoln, Preached in ... Concord, N.H., April 16, 1865. By ... Rev. Henry E. Parker. *Concord: Printed by McFarland & Jenks.* 1865. 8vo, pp. 15. B. 58673

Also: An Election Sermon ... before The ... Senate and House ... of ... New-Hampshire, ... June 6, 1861 ... . *Concord: Asa McFarland, State Printer.* 1861 8vo, pp. 32. B.

PARKER (H. G.) Hoosac Tunnel. Speech of Hon. H. G. Parker of Greenfield, ... March 24, 1854. [n. p. 1854.] 8vo, pp. 10. 58674

PARKER (H. M.) Speech of Henry M. Parker, Esq.; ... in the Convention of the Protestant Episcopal Church for the Diocese of Massachusetts; May 19, 1853, on the Admission of the Free Church of St. Mary for Sailors ... . *Boston: Learned, Tompson & Co.* 1853. 8vo, pp. 21. B. 58675

Also "Notes on Mount Auburn Cemetery." *See* Vol. XII., No. 51151.

PARKER (H. W.) The Despised Race. A Discourse, ... in ... New Bedford, December 28, 1862. By Henry W. Parker, ... *New Bedford: Printed by Fessenden & Baker.* 1863. 8vo, pp. 15. 58676

P[ARKER]. Verse. By H. W. P. *Boston: H. W. Dutton and Son.* 1862. 12mo, pp. 144. B. 58677

[PARKER (Isaac).] Address of Chief Justice Parker to the Bar of the County of Suffolk at a Meeting held for the purpose of Testifying their Respect for the Memory of the Hon. Samuel Howe ... . *Boston: Nathan Hale.* 1828. 8vo, pp. 14. BA.

[PARKER.] Letter to Rev. Parsons Cooke. From the Christian Examiner, for July and August, 1828. [n. p. n. d.] 12mo, pp. 12. 58679

PARKER. An Oration on the Sublime Virtues of General George Washington ... . Pronounced before the Inhabitants of Portland, February 22nd, 1800 ... . By Isaac Parker. *Portland: Printed by Elezer Alley Jenks.* [1800.] 8vo, pp. 24 W. + *Boston, reprinted.* 1800. 8vo. 58680

PARKER. Sketch of the Character of the late Chief Justice Parsons, ... Address ... delivered at the Opening of the Supreme Judicial Court at Boston, ... Twenty-Third ... November, 1813. ... By Isaac Parker ... . *Boston: Printed by John Eliot.* 1813. 8vo, pp. 32. B. 58681

Also: A Funeral Discourse delivered in ... Harvard, at the Interment of Mr. Josiah Bowles, who departed this life March 26, 1799, in the 23d year of his age. ... *Boston: Luther Parker.* 1800. 8vo.

PARKER (J.) Conductor Generalis: or, the Office, Duty, and Authority of Justices of the Peace, High Sheriffs, Under Sheriffs, Coroners, Constables, Gaolers, Jurymen, and Overseers of the Poor. As also the Office of Clerks of Assize ... . Compiled by James Parker, a Justice of the Peace for Middlesex County, New Jersey. *Woodbridge, N. J.: James Parker.* 1764.

8vo, pp. xvi, 592. + *New York: J. Patterson.* 1788. 8vo. + *Albany.* 1794. 8vo. + [*Ibid.*] 1819. 58682

See also Vol. IV., No. 15215.

PARKER (J. M.) Under his Banner. By Mrs. J. M. Parker. *New York.* 18—. 16mo, pp. 261. 58683

PARKER (J. W.) Defence of James W. Parker, against Slanderous Accusations preferred against him. *Houston.* 1839. 8vo, pp. 7. 58684

PARKER (J. W.) Narrative of the Perilous Adventures, Miraculous Escapes and Sufferings of Rev. James W. Parker, during a frontier residence in Texas, of fifteen years; with an Impartial Geographical Description of the Climate, Soil, Timber, Water, &c. ... of Texas; Written by Himself. To which is appended a Narrative of the Capture, and subsequent Sufferings, of Mrs. Rachel Plummer (his daughter), during a Captivity of twenty-one months among the Comanche Indians; with a Sketch of their Manners, Customs, Laws, &c. With a short description of the Country over which she travelled whilst with the Indians; Written by Herself. *Printed at Louisville, Ky.* 1844. 12mo, pp. 95. 58685

Mrs. Plummer's narrative has a separate title and pagination (pp. 35), with the date 1839.

PARKER (J.) A Sermon ... at Southborough, July 17, 1827, the day which completed a Century from the Incorporation of the Town, By Jeroboam Parker ... . *Boston: John Marsh.* 1827. 8vo, pp. 39. B. 58686

Also: A Sermon, ... at Southborough, December 17, 1806, at the Dedication of a new Meeting-House. ... [With Address by Peter Whitney.] *Boston: Printed by Manning & Loring.* 1807. 8vo, pp. 23. BA., M.

PARKER (J.) A Sermon, ... Preached to the Orthodox People of Peterborough, March 30, 1823. By Jesse Parker. ... *Amherst.* 1823. 8vo, pp. 22. 58687

PARKER (J.) The Character of the Rebellion, and the Conduct of the War. By Joel Parker. *Cambridge: Welch, Bigelow & Company.* 1862. 8vo, pp. 42. B. 58688

PARKER. A Charge to the Grand Jury upon the Importance of maintaining the Supremacy of the Laws; with a Brief Sketch of the Character of William M. Richardson. By Joel Parker. *Concord, N. H.: Marsh, Capen & Lyon.* 1838. 8vo, pp. 32.

PARKER. A Charge to the Grand Jury, upon the Uncertainty of the Law; ... Delivered on the Circuit, 1841 and 1842. By Chief Justice Parker. ... *Concord, N. H.: Luther Hamilton.* 1842. 8vo, pp. 16. BA., M. 58690

PARKER. Constitutional Law and Unconstitutional Divinity. Letters to Rev. Henry M. Dexter, and to Rev. Leonard Bacon, D.D. By Joel Parker. *Cambridge: Printed by H. O. Houghton.* 1863. 8vo, pp. 63. B. 58691

PARKER. Constitutional Law: with Reference to the Present Condition of the United States. By Joel Parker. *Cambridge: Welch, Bigelow, and Company.* 1862. 8vo, pp. 35. B. 58692

PARKER. Daniel Webster as a Jurist. An Address ... . By Joel Parker, LL.D. ... *Cambridge: John Bartlett.* 1853. 8vo, pp. 71. + Second Edition. [*Ibid.*] B. 58693

PARKER. The Domestic and Foreign Relations of the United States. By Joel Parker. *Cambridge: Welch, Bigelow, and Company, Printers.* 1862. 8vo, pp. 74. B. 58694

Also in the "North American Review" for January, 1862.

PARKER. The First Charter and the Early Religious Legislation of Massachusetts. Lecture ... Feb. 9, 1869. By Joel Parker. *Boston: John Wilson and Son.* 1869. 8vo, pp. 85.

PARKER. Habeas Corpus and Martial Law. A Review of the Opinion of Chief Justice Taney, in the Case of John Merryman. By Joel Parker. *Cambridge: Welch, Bigelow, and Company.* 1861. 8vo, pp. 58. + Second Edition. ... *Philadelphia: John Campbell.* 1862. 8vo, pp. 55. 58696

Of the second edition, twenty-five copies were printed on large paper. It first appeared in the "North American Review" for October, 1861.

PARKER. International Law. Case of the Trent. Capture and Surrender of Mason and Slidell. By Joel Parker. *Cambridge: Welch, Bigelow & Company.* 1862. 8vo, pp. 66. B.

PARKER. Personal Liberty Laws, ... and Slavery in the Territories ... . By Joel Parker. *Boston: Wright & Potter, Printers.* 1861. 8vo, pp. 97. B. 58698

PARKER. Revolution and Reconstruction. Two Lectures ... in the Law School of Harvard College, in January, 1865, and

January, 1866. By Joel Parker, Royall Professor. *New York: Hurd & Houghton.* 1866. 8vo, pp. 89. 58699

An argument for "the admission of the Southern members."

PARKER. The Right of Secession. A Review of the Message of Jefferson Davis to the Congress of the Confederate States. By Joel Parker. *Cambridge: Welch, Bigelow and Company.* 1861. 8vo, pp. 39. B. 58700

PARKER. The Three Powers of Government. The Origin of the United States; and the Status of the Southern States, on the Suppression of the Rebellion. Three Dangers of the Republic. Lectures ... 1867–68, and '69. By Joel Parker. *New York: Hurd and Houghton.* 1869. 8vo, pp. (2), 108. 58701

PARKER. The True Issue, and the Duty of the Whigs. An Address before the Citizens of Cambridge, October 1, 1856. By Joel Parker. *Cambridge: James Munroe and Company.* 1856. 8vo, pp. 92. 58702

The cover-title reads "The Non-Extension of Slavery," etc.

PARKER. The War Powers of Congress, and of the President. An Address ... Salem, March 13, 1863. By Joel Parker. *Cambridge: Printed by H. O. Houghton.* 1863. 8vo, pp. 60.

Also: An Address ... before the Association in Keene, for the Promotion of Temperance, August 5, 1829. ... *Keene, N. H.: Geo. Tilden.* 1830. 12mo, pp. 22.—The Law School of Harvard College. ... *New York: Hurd and Houghton.* 1871. 8vo, pp. 56.—A Letter to the People of Massachusetts. ... *Cambridge: Printed by H. O. Houghton.* 1862. 8vo, pp. (2), 12.—Memorial to the Legislature of Massachusetts, Sept. 13, 1859. ... [*Boston.* 1859.] 8vo, pp. 14.—The Origin, Organization, and Influence of the Towns of New England; a Paper read before the Massachusetts Historical Society, December 14, 1865. ... *Cambridge.* 1867. 8vo, pp. 54.—Progress. An Address before the Phi Beta Kappa Society of Dartmouth College, July 29, 1846. ... *Hanover: Printed at the Dartmouth Press.* ... 1846. 8vo, pp. 26. B.

PARKER (J.) The Beloved Physician: A Tribute to the Memory of James C. Bliss, M.D. A Discourse ... . By Joel Parker, D.D. ... *New York: Samuel S. and William Wood.* 1856. 8vo, pp. 29. 58704

PARKER. The Discussion between Rev. Joel Parker, and Rev. A. Rood, on the Question "What are the Evils Inseparable from Slavery." ... *New York: S. W. Benedict.* 1852. 12mo, pp. 120. B. 58705

PARKER. A Farewell Discourse to the Free Presbyterian Churches, delivered ... October 27th, 1833. By Joel Parker, ... *New York.* 1834. 8vo, pp. 20. S. 58706

Also: A Memorial Discourse. The Beneficent Ministries of an Early Christian Death as illustrated in the decease of George Douglass, Jr. ... *New York: John F. Trow, Printer.* 1859. 8vo, pp. 29. B.—The Signs of the Times; a Sermon, ... in Rochester, December 4, 1822, ... the Day of Publick Thanksgiving. ... *Rochester: Printed by E. Peck, & Co.* 1823. 8vo, pp. 16. B.

PARKER [Joel]. ... Speech of Governor Parker, at Freehold, N. J., Aug. 20, 1864. ... [n. p. 1864.] 8vo, pp. 8. 58707

Also: Oration ... at the Dedication of a Monument to John Hart, one of the Signers of the Declaration of Independence, from New Jersey. *Trenton.* 1865. 8vo, pp. 29. S.

PARKER (J.) Memorial of John Parker, of Boston. [War of 1812.] *Washington City: Printed by R. C. Weightman.* 1812. 8vo, pp. 10. 58708

PARKER (J. A.) Argument upon the Alabama Claims, Addressed to the Commissioners. By John A. Parker. *Washington, D. C.: W. H. Moore, Printer.* [1871.] 8vo, pp. 15. H.

Also: Correspondence ... with Reverdy Johnson and others, on the Alabama Claims. [n. p. 1870.] 8vo, pp. 24.

PARKER (J. L.) The Stoneham, Wakefield, and Reading Directory; embracing ... the Town Records for ... 1869. By John L. Parker. *Woburn (Mass.): J. L. Parker.* 1869. 8vo, pp. 214. C. 58710

PARKER (J. R.) A Musical Biography: or Sketches of the Lives and Writings of Eminent Musical Characters. By John R. Parker. *Boston.* 1825. 8vo, pp. 250. 58711

PARKER (J.) The Extraordinary and Singular Law Case of Joseph Parker, who was Indicted as Thomas Hoag *alias dictus* Joseph Parker for Bigamy. *Baltimore.* 1808. 8vo, pp. 10.

Not only one of the rarest of American trials, but it is perhaps one of the most remarkable cases of mistaken identity.

PARKER (J.) American War and American Slavery. A Speech ... by Rev. Joseph Parker. *Manchester: Union and Emancipation Society.* 1863. 8vo, pp. 8. 58713

PARKER (L. M.) An Oration, ... at Charlestown, Massachusetts, ... Fourth of July, A. D. 1816, by request of the Republican Citizens of Middlesex County ... . By Leonard M. Parker, Esq. *Boston: Printed by Rowe and Hooper.* 1816. 8vo, pp. 16. W. 58714

PARKER (Lucretia). *See* [Parker (G. G.)]

[PARKER (Mary Ann).] A | Voyage | round the | World | in | The Gorgon Man of War: | Captain John Parker. | Performed and written by his widow; | for the advantage of a numerous family. | ... | *London.* 1795. 8vo, pp. xxxii, 149. 58715

PARKER (N.) A Discourse occasioned by the Death of the Rev. Joseph Buckminster, ... Portsmouth, ... June 19, 1812. By Nathan Parker ... . *Printed at Portsmouth by S. Whidden* ... 1812. 8vo, pp. 22. B. 58716

PARKER. A Sermon ... at Concord, before ... the Legislature of ... New-Hampshire, June 3, 1819, being the Anniversary Election. By Nathan Parker ... . *Concord: Printed by Hill & Moore.* 1819. 8vo, pp. 26. 58717

PARKER. Sermons by Nathan Parker, D.D. ... With a Memoir of the Author by Henry Ware, Jr. D.D. ... *Portsmouth: J. W. Foster and J. F. Shares.* 1835. 8vo, pp. xcii, 402. 58718

Also: A Sermon ... February 15, 1826, at the Dedication of a New Church, ... Portsmouth. ... *Portsmouth, N. H.: John W. Foster.* 1826. 8vo, pp. 19. *See also* [Coues (S. E.)], Vol. v., No. 17136, *and* A Teacher, *pseudon.*

PARKER (N. H.) Illustrated Hand-Book of the Great West. A Record of Statistics and Facts, with Practical Suggestions to Immigrants ... . By Nathan H. Parker ... . *New York: American News Company.* 1869. 8vo, pp. 162. 3 Maps. 58719

PARKER. Iowa as it is in 1855: a Gazetteer for Citizens, and a Hand-Book for Immigrants ... . By N. Howe Parker. *Chicago, Ill.: Keen and Lee.* 1855. 12mo, pp. 264. Map. B. Continued. 58720

PARKER. The Iowa Hand Book for 1856. ... By Nathan H. Parker ... . *Boston: John P. Jewett and Company.* MDCCCLVI. 12mo, pp. 187, (1). Map. Continued. B. 58721

PARKER. The Kansas and Nebraska Hand-Book for 1857–8. ... By Nathan H. Parker ... . *Boston: John P. Jewett and Company.* 1857. 12mo, pp. 189. Map. B. 58722

PARKER. The Minnesota Hand Book for 1856–7. ... By Nathan H. Parker ... . *Boston: John P. Jewett and Company.* M.DCCC.LVII. 12mo, pp. 159, (1). Map. B. 58723

PARKER. Missouri as it is in 1867. An Illustrated Historical Gazetteer ... embracing the Geography, History, ... the New Constitution, ... and Important Facts concerning "Free Mis-

souri" ... . By Nathan H. Parker ... . *Philadelphia: J. B. Lippincott & Co.* 1867. 8vo, pp. 458. Plates. 58724

PARKER. The Missouri Hand-Book, embracing a full description of ... Missouri; ... By Nathan H. Parker ... . *Saint Louis: P. M. Pinckard.* 1865. 12mo, pp. 162. Map. 58725

PARKER (P.) A Biographical Memoir of the late Sir Peter Parker, Baronet, Captain ... Killed in Action while storming the American Camp at Bellair, near Baltimore, on the thirty-first of August, 1814. *London: Longman* ... 1815. 4to, pp. (2), 111.

By Sir George Dallas. Corrected title of our No. 18215, Vol. v.

PARKER (R. G.) Outlines of General History, in the form of Question and Answer; designed as the Foundation, and the Review of a Course of Historical Reading. By Richard Green Parker ... . *New York: Harper and Brothers.* 1848. 8vo. N. + A New Edition, with Additions. [*Ibid.*] 8vo, pp. 413. B.

[PARKER.] A Tribute to the Life and Character of Jonas Chickering. "By one who knew him well." ... *Boston: William P. Tewksbury.* M DCCC LIV. 12mo, pp. 162. Portrait. 58728

Also: A Sketch of the History of the Grammar School in the Easterly Part of Roxbury. ... *Roxbury: Printed by Thomas S. Watts.* 1826. 8vo, pp. 32. B.

PARKER (S.) Journal of an Exploring Tour Beyond the Rocky Mountains, under the Direction of the A[merican] B[oard] C[ommissioners] F[oreign] M[issions], Performed in the years 1835, '36, and '37; Containing a Description of the Geography, Geology, Climate, and Productions; and the Number, Manners, and Customs of the Natives. With a Map of Oregon Territory. By Rev. Samuel Parker, A.M. *Ithaca, N. Y.: Mack, Andrus & Woodruff, Printers.* 1838. 12mo, pp. 371. Map. + Second Edition. [*Ibid.*] 1840. 12mo. + Third Edition. [*Ibid.*] 1841. 12mo. + *Ithaca.* 1842. 12mo. + Fourth Edition. *Ithaca, N. Y.: Andrus, Woodruff & Gauntlett.* 1844. 12mo, pp. 416. Map. + Fifth Edition. *Auburn: J. C. Derby & Co.* 1846. 12mo, pp. 422. Map. B. 58729

A leading object of exploration "was to become acquainted with the situation of the remote Indian tribes, and their disposition in regard to teachers of Christianity." *See* "North American Review," L. 129.

PARKER. People's Edition. A Journey Beyond the Rocky Mountains in 1835, 1836, and 1837. By the Rev. Samuel Parker, A.M. Corrected and extended in the present edition. *Edinburgh: William and Robert Chambers.* 1841. Impl. 8vo, pp. 78.

PARKER (S.) Legal Views of the Alabama Case, and Ship-Building for the Confederates. By Samuel Parker. *Manchester: Union and Emancipation Society.* 1863. 8vo, pp. 8. 58731

PARKER (S.) A Sermon, ... before ... the Lieutenant-Governor, the ... Council, and the ... Senate, and House ... of Massachusetts, May 29, 1793; Being the Day of General Election. By Samuel Parker, D.D. ... *Boston: Thomas Adams, Printer.* M,DCC,XCIII. 8vo, pp. 42. B. 58732

Also: Charity to Children enforced, in a Discourse, ... in Trinity Church, Boston, before the Subscribers to the Boston Female Asylum, Sept. 23, 1803, at their third Anniversary. ... *Boston: Printed by Russell and Cutler.* 1803. 8vo, pp. 32. BA., W.

PARKER (S. H.) A Funeral Oration at the Obsequies of ... Thomas Wildey, ... November 24th, 1861, By ... S. H. Parker. ... *San Francisco: Whitton, Waters & Co., Printers.* 1861. 8vo, pp. 20. 58733

PARKER (S. P.) The Catholic Mission of the Protestant Episcopal Church. Unity, Liberty, and Love. An Essay ... By S. P. Parker, D.D. ... Stockbridge, Mass. *Boston: E. P. Dutton and Company.* 1864. 16mo, pp. 60. B. 58734

PARKER. Education in Castleton, Staten Island. By S. P. Parker. *New York.* 1856. 8vo, pp. 8. 58735

Also: ... A Sermon ... at St. Mary's Church, Castleton, Staten Island, and at the Church of the Holy Communion, N. Y. ... *New York.* 1853. 8vo, pp. 16.— ... A Sermon ... before the 70th Convention of the Diocese of New Hampshire, ... May 25, 1870. ... [n. p.] 1870. 12mo, pp. 24. B.—A Sermon in Memory of the Rev. George Champlin Shepard, D.D., preached in ... Amherst, Mass. ... 20th December, 1868. ... *Hartford.* 1869. 8vo, pp. 11, (1). H.

PARKER (S. W.) Kansas and Nebraska—The Deed and its Results. Speech of Hon. S. W. Parker, of Indiana, ... May 18, 1854. [n. p. n. d.] 8vo, pp. 16. B. 58736

PARKER (T.) Additional Speeches, Addresses, and Occasional Sermons. ... By Theodore Parker ... . *Boston: Little, Brown and Company.* 1855. 2 vols., 12mo, pp. xii, 435; iv, 448.

[PARKER.] Answers to Questions contained in Mr. Parker's Letter to the Boston Association of Congregational Ministers. By one not of the Association. *Boston: Wm. Crosby & H. P. Nichols.* 1845. 8vo, pp. 39. B. 58738

PARKER. Beroemde Amerikanen. Uit het Engelsch ... . Met Aanteekeningen van Dr. M. A. N. Rovers. *Utrecht: J. L. Beijers.* 1872. 8vo, pp. (6), 274. 58739

A translation of No. 58747, *infra*.

PARKER. The Boston Kidnapping. A Discourse to commemorate the Rendition of Thomas Simms, delivered before the Committee of Vigilance, Boston, April 12, 1852. By Theodore Parker. *Boston: Crosby, Nichols, & Company.* 1852. 8vo, pp. 72.

PARKER. The Collected Works of Theodore Parker .... Edited by Frances Power Cobbe. ... *London: Trübner & Co.* 1863–65. 12 vols., sm. 8vo. Portrait. B. 58741

PARKER. The Critical and Miscellaneous Writings of Theodore Parker. ... *Boston: James Munroe and Company* .... 1843. 12mo, pp. (8), 360. C. 58742

PARKER. A Discourse occasioned by the Death of John Quincy Adams: ... March 5, 1848. By Theodore Parker .... *Boston: Bela Marsh.* 1848. 8vo, pp. 66. 58743

PARKER. A Discourse occasioned by the Death of Daniel Webster, preached ... October 31, 1852. By Theodore Parker, ... *Milwaukee.* 1852. 8vo, pp. vii, 108. + *Boston: Benjamin B. Mussey & Co.* 1853. 8vo, pp. vii, 108. B. 58744

For "A Review," see Junius Americanus, *pseudon.*, Vol. IX., No. 36924.

PARKER. Elemento Servil. Estudo por Theodoro Parker. *Rio da Janeiro: Typ. da Rua da Ajuda.* 1871. 16mo, pp. 58.

PARKER. The Great Battle between Slavery and Freedom, Considered in two Speeches delivered before the American Anti-slavery Society, at New York, May 7, 1856. By Theodore Parker .... *Boston: Benjamin H. Greene.* 1856. 8vo, pp. 93.

PARKER. Historic Americans. By Theodore Parker. *Boston: Horace B. Fuller.* 1870. 12mo, pp. 312. 58747

"Lectures prepared in 1858 for the Fraternity Course."—*Preface.* Contains biographies of Franklin, Washington, J. Adams, and Jefferson.

PARKER. The Idea of a Christian Church. A Discourse at the Installation of Theodore Parker, as Minister of the Twenty-Eighth Congregational Church in Boston, January 4, 1846. Delivered by Himself. ... *Boston: Benj. H. Greene.* 1846. 8vo, pp. 39. BA. 58748

PARKER. John Brown's Expedition Reviewed in a Letter from Rev. Theodore Parker, at Rome, to Francis Jackson, Boston. *Boston: The Fraternity.* 1860. 12mo, pp. 19. 58749

PARKER. Lectures on the Present Crisis by the late Theodore Parker and the late Hon. Henry Clay, at New York, December

16, 1860. Mrs. C. L. V. Hatch, Medium. *New York.* 1861. 8vo. 58750

PARKER. Letter to the People of the United States touching the Matter of Slavery. By Theodore Parker. *Boston: James Munroe and Company.* MDCCCXLVIII. 12mo, pp. 120. 58751

PARKER. Life and Writings of Theodore Parker. By Albert Reville, D.D. *London: Simpkin.* 1865. 12mo, pp. 201. Port.

PARKER. Life and Correspondence of Theodore Parker .... By John Weiss. *New York: D. Appleton & Company.* 1864. 2 vols., 8vo, pp. 478; 530. 5 Portraits. 58753

PARKER. The Nebraska Question. Some Thoughts on the New Assault upon Freedom in America .... By Theodore Parker ... *Boston: Benjamin B. Mussey & Co.* 1854. 8vo, pp. 72.

PARKER. Occasional Sermons and Speeches, by Theodore Parker. *Boston.* 1852. 2 vols., 12mo. 58755

PARKER. The Present Aspect of Slavery in America and the Immediate Duty of the North: A Speech ... January 29, 1858. By Theodore Parker. *Boston: Bela Marsh.* 1858. 8vo, pp. 44.

[PARKER.] Remarks on an Article from the Christian Examiner, entitled "Mr. Parker and his Views." *Boston: Wm. Crosby and H. P. Nichols.* 1845. 8vo, pp. 15. B. 58757

In answer to "Mr. Parker and his Views. An Article from the Christian Examiner." ... [By Ezra S. Gannett.] *Boston: Crosby & Nichols.* 1845. 8vo, pp. 30.

PARKER. A Reviewer Reviewed. A Few Remarks upon "Four Papers from the Boston Courier," concerning Theodore Parker, Ralph Waldo Emerson, George William Curtis, and the Abolitionists. ... *Boston: William L. Kent and Company.* 1858. 8vo, pp. 35. B. 58758

PARKER. A Sermon of the Dangers which Threaten the Rights of Man In America; ... July 2, 1854, By Theodore Parker .... *Boston: Benjamin B. Mussey & Co.* 1854. 8vo, pp. 56.

PARKER. A Sermon of the Mexican War: Preached ... June 25th, 1848, By Theodore Parker .... *Boston: Coolidge and Wiley.* 1848. 8vo, pp. 56. BA. 58760

PARKER. Speeches, Addresses, and Occasional Sermons. By Theodore Parker .... *Boston: Wm. Crosby and H. P. Nichols.* M DCCC LII. 2 vols., 12mo, pp. vi, 442; iv, 440. + *New York:*

D. Appleton & Co. 1864. 3 vols., 12mo, pp. viii, 420; iv, 398; iv, 410. B. 58761

PARKER. Teodoro Parker ossia Cristianesimo e Patriottismo estratto dalla Riforma del Secolo XIX .... *Milano: A. Lombardi.* 1870. 8vo, pp. 22. 58762

PARKER. Théodore Parker Sa Vie, et ses Oeuvres ... Par Albert Réville *Paris: C. Reinwald.* 1865. 12mo, pp. (4), 330, (1). 58763

PARKER. Theodore Parker's Experience as a Minister, with some Account of his early Life .... *Boston: Rufus Leighton, Jr.* 1859. 8vo, pp. 182. 58764

PARKER. Theodore Parker's Review of Webster. Speech of Theodore Parker ... March 25, 1850. *Boston: R. F. Wallcutt.* 1850. 8vo, pp. 26. BA. 58765

PARKER. Theodor Parker's Sämmtliche Werke. Deutsch von Dr. Johannes Ziethen. ... *Leipzig: Voigt & Günther.* 1854–1861. 5 vols., 16mo, pp. vi, (2), 439; vi, (2), 452; xvi, 330, (1); x, 430, (1); (4), 154. Portrait. B. 58766

PARKER. The Trial of Theodore Parker, for the "Misdemeanor" of A Speech in Faneuil Hall against Kidnapping, before the Circuit Court of the United States, at Boston, April 3, 1855: with the Defence, by Theodore Parker .... *Boston: The Author.* 1855. 8vo, pp. xx, 221, (1). BA. + *New York.* 1864. 8vo.

PARKER. The True Position. *See* [Sargent (J. T.)]

Also: An Address ... before the New York City Anti-Slavery Society, ... May 12, 1854. *New York: American Anti-Slavery Society.* 1854. 12mo, pp. 46.—The Chief Sins of the People: A Sermon ... on Fast-Day, April 10, 1851. ... *Boston: Benjamin H. Greene.* 1851. 8vo, pp. 40.—A Discourse of the Function of a Teacher of Religion in these times, ... at the Ordination of Marshall G. Kimball, ... June 13, 1855. ... *Boston: Benjamin H. Greene.* 1855. 8vo, pp. 56.—A Discourse on the Transient and Permanent in Christianity; ... at the Ordination of Mr. Charles C. Shackford, ... in Boston, May 19, 1841: ... *Boston.* MDCCCXLI. 8vo, pp. 48. + Second Edition. *Boston: The Author.* 1841. 8vo, pp. 39.—The Effect of Slavery on the American People. A Sermon, ... Boston, ... July 4, 1858. ... *Boston: William L. Kent & Company.* 1858. 8vo, pp. 14.—The Function and Place of Conscience, in Relation to the Laws of Men; A Sermon for the Times; ... September 22, 1850. ... *Boston: Crosby & Nichols.* 1850. 8vo, pp. 40.—An Humble Tribute to ... William Ellery Channing, D.D. A Sermon ... October 9th, 1842. ... *Boston: Charles C. Little and James Brown.* 1842. 8vo, pp. 38.—The Law of God and the Statutes of Men. A Sermon, ... at ... Boston, ... June 18, 1854. ... *Boston: Benjamin B. Mussey & Co.* 1854. 8vo, pp. 32.—A Letter to the Boston Association of Congregational Ministers. ... *Boston: Charles C. Little and James Brown.* M DCCC XLV. 8vo, pp. 20. + Second Edition. [*Ibid.*]—The Material Condition of the People of Massachusetts. ... *Boston: The Fraternity.*

1860. 12mo, pp. 52.—The New Crime against Humanity. A Sermon, ... in Boston, ... June 4, 1854. ... *Boston: Benjamin B. Mussey & Co.* 1854. 8vo, pp. 76.—A New Lesson for the Day: a Sermon, ... 25 May, 1856, in ... Boston. ... *Boston.* 1856. 8vo.—The Public Education of the People. An Oration ... before the Onondaga Teachers' Institute, at Syracuse, N. Y., ... 4th of October, 1849. ... *Boston: Wm. Crosby & H. P. Nichols.* 1850. 8vo, pp. 59.—The Relation of Slavery to a Republican Form of Government. A Speech ... at the New England Anti-Slavery Convention, ... May 26, 1858. ... *Boston: William L. Kent & Company.* 1858. 8vo, pp. 21.—The Revival of Religion which we need. A Sermon ... Boston, ... April 11, 1858. ... *Boston: W. L. Kent & Company.* 1858. 8vo, pp. 15.—A Sermon for Midsummer Day. ... July 18, 1855. ... *Boston: The Fraternity.* 1859. 12mo, pp. 24.—A Sermon for the New Year. What Religion may do for a Man. ... Jan. 2, 1859. ... *Boston: The Fraternity.* 1859. 12mo, pp. 23.—A Sermon of Merchants: ... November 22d, 1846. ... *Boston: Printed by George Coolidge.* 1847. 8vo, pp. 47.—A Sermon of Slavery, ... Jan. 31, 1841, repeated June 4, 1843 .... *Boston: Printed by Thurston and Torry.* M DCCC XLIII. 12mo, pp. 24.—A Sermon of the Consequences of an Immoral Principle and False Idea of Life. ... November 26, 1854. ... *Boston: Benjamin H. Greene.* 1855. 8vo, pp. 32.—A Sermon of the Dangerous Classes in Society, ... Jan. 31 .... *Boston: C. & J. M. Spear.* 1847. 8vo, pp. 48.—A Sermon of the Moral Condition of Boston, ... Feb. 11, 1849. ... *Boston: Crosby and Nichols.* 1849. 12mo, pp. 36. [Followed by:] A Sermon of the Spiritual Condition of Boston, Feb. 18, 1849. ... *Boston: Crosby and Nichols.* 1849. 12mo, pp. 37–74.—A Sermon of the Moral Dangers incident to Prosperity, ... November 5, 1854. ... *Boston: Benjamin H. Greene.* 1855. 8vo, pp. 29.—Sermon of the Perishing Classes in Boston; preached ... Aug. 30, 1846. ... *Boston.* 1846. 8vo, pp. 28. B. + Second Edition. *Boston: Benjamin H. Greene.* 1847. 8vo, pp. 28.— ... A Sermon of the Public Function of Woman ... at ... Boston, March 27, 1853. ... *Boston: Robert F. Wallcutt.* 1853. 12mo, pp. 20.—A Sermon of War, preached ... June 7, 1846. ... *Boston: Charles C. Little and James Brown.* 1846. 8vo, pp. 43. + Third Edition. *Boston: Printed by I. R. Butts.* 1846. 12mo, pp. 33.—Some Thoughts on the most Christian Use of the Sunday: A Sermon ... on Sunday, Jan. 30th. ... *Boston: B. H. Greene.* 1848. 8vo, pp. 51.—The State of the Nation, Considered in a Sermon for Thanksgiving Day, ... Nov. 28, 1850. ... *Boston: Wm. Crosby and H. P. Nichols.* M DCCC LI. 8vo, pp. 38.—The Three Chief Safeguards of Society, considered in a Sermon ... July 6, 1851. ... *Boston: Wm. Crosby and H. P. Nichols.* 1851. 8vo, pp. 40.—Two Sermons ... before the Twenty Eighth Congregational Society in Boston, on the 14th and 21st of November, 1852, on leaving their old and entering a new Place of Worship. ... *Boston: Crosby, Nichols, & Company.* 1853. 8vo, pp. 56. + Second Edition. *Boston: Benjamin B. Mussey & Co.* 1853. 8vo, pp. 59. B., BA.

PARKER. Tributes to Theodore Parker, ... at the Music Hall, June 17, 1860, with the Proceedings of the New England Anti-Slavery Convention, ... May 31, and the Resolutions of the Fraternity and the Twenty Eighth Congregational Society. *Boston: The Fraternity.* 1860. 12mo, pp. 60. B. 58768

PARKER (T.) The Copy of a Letter Written by Mr. Thomas Parker, Pastor of the Church of Newbury in New-England, to His Sister, Mrs. Elizabeth Avery, Sometimes of Newbury in the County of Berks, Touching Sundry Opinions by her Professed and Maintained.—Novemb. 22, 1649. Imprimatur John Downame. *London: Printed by John Field.* 1650. 4to, pp. (4), 20. 58769

Extremely rare. It seems to have escaped the search of even Mr. Sibley, who puts Woodbridge's tract on "Justification by Faith," 1652, as first in the brief list of his publications, and remarks that that "is probably the *second* work printed by any Harvard graduate." This little tract refutes some heretical opinions maintained by his "very loving sister" in reference to which, Cotton, Wilson, and Noyes also corresponded with her.

PARKER. The true Copy of a Letter written by Mr. Thomas Parker, a learned and godly Minister in New-England unto a Member of the Assembly of Divines now at Westminster; declaring his Judgment touching the Government practised in the Churches of England. Imprimatur Ja. Cranford. *London: Printed by Richard Cotes.* 1644. 4to, pp. 4. 58770

PARKER. The | Visions and Prophecies | of | Daniel expounded: | ... | By Thomas Parker of Newbery in Berkshire, and now Pastor to the | Church at Newbery in New-England. | *London, Printed by Ruth Raworth and John Field, for Edmund Paxton, dwelling | at Pauls chain neer Doctors Commons.* 1646. | 4to, pp. (4), 156.

"It was with an assiduous conjunction of meditations and supplications that he followed this delightful study till he had written several volumes, a great part of them in Latin; whereof no part was ever published but one upon Daniel, which he wrote in English."—*C. Mather in his Life of Mr. T. Parker.*

PARKER (T.) A History of Farmington, Me. From its First Settlement to 1846. By Thomas Parker. *Farmington, Me.: J. S. Swift.* 1846. Sm. 8vo, pp. 136. 58772

PARKER (T. H.) History of the 51st Regiment of P. V. and V. V. from its Organization, at Camp Curtin, Harrisburg, Pa., in 1861, to its being mustered out of the United States Service, at Alexandria, Va., July 27th, 1865. By Thomas H. Parker .... *Philadelphia: King & Baird, Printers.* 1869. 8vo, pp. xx, 9–703. 4 Portraits. B. 58773

PARKER (T. J.) Tee-Totalism Unmasked! and its Advocates Demonstrated to be Ignorant, Stupid and Degraded. By Thomas J. Parker. *New York.* 1851. 8vo. Portrait. 58774

A curious apology for rumselling.

PARKER (W. B.) Notes taken during the Expedition commanded by Capt. R. B. Marcy, U. S. A., through unexplored Texas, In the Summer and Fall of 1854. By W. B. Parker, Attached to the Expedition. *Philadelphia: Hayes & Zell.* 1856. 12mo, pp. 242. 58775

Contains interesting details of personal intercourse with the Indian tribes of the Southern prairies—the Bedouins of the American desert.

PARKER (W. H.) Instruction for Naval Light Artillery, Afloat and Ashore. Prepared ... for the U. S. Naval Academy, By William H. Parker, ... U. S. N. Second Edition, Revised by Lieut. S. B. Luce, U. S. N. ... *New York: D. Van Nostrand.* 1862. 8vo, pp. 120. Plates. BA. 58776

PARKER. Questions of Practical Seamanship; Together with Harbor Routine and Evolutions Prepared for the Midshipmen of the C. S. Navy. By Wm. H. Parker, Commanding C. S. School-Ship Patrick Henry. *Richmond: Macfarlane and Fergusson, Printers.* 1863. 8vo, pp. 92. 58777

Also: Elements of Seamanship, Prepared as a Text Book for the Midshipmen of the C. S. Navy. ... *Richmond.* 1864. 16mo.

Notices of PARKERSBURG, Va. *See* No. 55992, add 2 Maps.

PARKES (J.) Memoirs of Sir Philip Francis, ... with Correspondence and Journals. ... By Joseph Parkes ... completed and edited by Herman Merivale ... *London: Longman* ... 1867. 2 vols., 8vo, pp. xxxiii, (2), 458; viii, 566. 2 Portraits, 7 Facsimiles. 58778

Relates to the politics of Great Britain from 1740–1818, and indirectly to America.

Parkhill. In the District Court of the United States, for the Eastern District of Pennsylvania, sitting as a Prize Court. Case of the Ship General Parkhill. *Philadelphia.* [1861.] 8vo, pp. 34.

PARKHURST (J.) An | Oration, | ... on the | Fourth of July, 1798, | ... at Newark .... | By Capt. Jabez Parkhurst. | ... | *Newark: Printed by Pennington and Dodge.* M,DCC,XCVIII. 8vo, pp. 12

PARKHURST (J. W.) A Historical Sermon, giving a Concise History of the First Baptist Church in Dedham, ... delivered Aug. 2d, 1846. By Rev. J. W. Parkhurst. ... *Boston: John Putnam, Printer.* 1846. 8vo, pp. 20. H. 58781

Also: Proceedings of the Anti-Sabbath Convention, ... March 23d and 24th. ... *Boston.* 1848. 8vo.

[PARKIN (Miles).] Columba, a Poetical Epistle. Heroic and Satirical, to the Right Honourable Charles, Earl Cornwallis. [*London:*] *J. Debrett.* MDCCLXXXIII. 4to, pp. 36 J.C.B. 58782

PARKINS (J. W.) The Extraordinary Proceedings at ... New York, respecting the Lunacy of Joseph Wilfred Parkins, with his Defence. *New York.* 1833. 8vo. 58783

PARKINSON (R.) The Experienced Farmer, an entire new work, in which the whole System of Agriculture, Husbandry and

Breeding of Cattle, is explained and copiously enlarged upon, and the best methods with the most recent improvements pointed out. By Richard Parkinson ..., *Philadelphia: Printed by Charles Cist.* 1799. 2 vols., 8vo, pp. xx, 16, iii, 275; (2), 292. P. 58784

PARKINSON. The Experienced Farmer's Tour in America: exhibiting, in a copious and familiar view, the American System of Agriculture and Breeding of Cattle, with its recent improvements. By Richard Parkinson .... To which are added Sketches, published by J. B. Bordley, Esq., Philadelphia, an American Cultivator. *London: John Stockdale.* 1805. 8vo, pp. 735.

Another edition has the following title:

PARKINSON. A Tour in America, in 1798, 1799, and 1800. Exhibiting Sketches of Society and Manners, and a particular Account of the American System of Agriculture, with its Recent Improvements. By Richard Parkinson, late of Orange Hill near Baltimore. ... *London: J. Harding.* 1805. 2 vols., 8vo, pp. (8), 319; (8), 320–735. BA. 58786

Parkinson was an English agriculturist, who came to America, recommended by Sir John Sinclair, to superintend the farms of General Washington, respecting whom the book abounds in curious details, that seem to have been generally overlooked by his biographers. *See* "Edinburgh Review," VII. 29.

PARKINSON (S.) A Journal of a Voyage to the South Seas, in his Majesty's Ship, The Endeavour. Faithfully transcribed from the Papers of the late Sydney Parkinson, Draughtsman to Joseph Banks, Esq. on his late Expedition, with Dr. Solander, round the World. Embellished with Views and Designs, delineated by the Author .... *London: Stanfield Parkinson.* M.DCC.-LXXIII. 4to, pp. xxiii, 212, (2). Portrait and 27 Plates. BA.

An account of Capt. Cook's First Voyage, published by the brother of the author. With vocabularies of the South-Sea languages. Large paper. *See* "M. Rev.," L. 410.

PARKINSON. A Journal of a Voyage to the South Seas, in His Majesty's Ship the Endeavour; faithfully transcribed from the Papers of the late Sydney Parkinson .... To which is now added, Remarks on the Preface, by the late John Fothergill, M.D. ... And an Appendix, containing an Account of the Voyages of Commodore Byron, Captain Wallis, Captain Carteret, Monsieur Bougainville, Captain Cook, and Captain Clerke. *London: Charles Dilly.* MDCCLXXXIV. 4to, pp. (2), xxiii, 353, (2). Portrait and 29 Plates. J.C.B., C. 58788

Also on large paper.

PARKINSON. Voyage Autour du Monde, sur le vaisseau de sa Majesté Britannique l'Endeavour, Par Sidney Parkinson .... Pré-

cédé d'un discours ... sur les principaux navigateurs anglais et français qui ont précédé l'Endeavour: ... Ouvrage traduit de l'Anglais. Par le C. Henri. ... *A Paris, De l'Imprimerie de Guillaume* ... *An cinquième*—1797. 2 vols., 8vo, pp. 12, lvj, 344, 5 Plates; (4), 309. N. 58789

PARKINSON (W.) Jubilee: A Sermon, containing a History of the Origin of the First Baptist Church in the City of New York, and its Progress, during the first Fifty Years ... delivered ... Jan. 1, 1813. By Wm. Parkinson, A.M. ... To which are annexed a Narrative of Facts, interspersed with Remarks; and an Appendix; all relating to the reports that have gone abroad, concerning the Pastor of the above named Church; .... By the Accused. *Printed for the Proprietor. New York.* 1813. 8vo, pp. v, 52, 105. S. 58790

PARKINSON. A Jubilee Sermon, containing a History of the Origin of the First Baptist Church in the City of New-York, and its Progress during the first Fifty Years .... Delivered ... Jan. 1, 1813. By William Parkinson, A.M. ... *New York: Republished by a Friend, John Gray, Printer.* 1846. 12mo, pp. 106.

PARKINSON. A Narrative, interspersed with Remarks, and an Appendix; all relating to the Reports which have gone abroad concerning William Parkinson .... By the Accused. ... *New York.* 1813. 8vo, pp. (2), 104, (1). BA. 58792

PARKINSON. A Sermon, ... in ... New-York, August 20th, 1812, ... on account of The Present War. By William Parkinson .... *New York: John Tiebout.* 1812. 8vo, pp. 25, (1).

PARKINSON. Trial of Mr. William Parkinson, ... on an Indictment for Assault and Battery upon Mrs. Eliza Wintringham. Taken in short hand by William Sampson. *New York.* 1811. 8vo, pp. 84. 58794

The two following publications relate to Parkinson:

PARKINSON. Observations on the Trial of William Parkinson, for Assault and Battery, on Mrs. Eliza Wintringham. A Poem. By Epaphroditus. ... *New York: The Author.* 1811. 12mo, pp. 21. N. 58795

PARKINSON. The Proceedings in the First Baptist Church in the City of New York in relation to the Slanderous Charge brought against ... William Parkinson, by Maria Shade, otherwise called Maria Seaman. [*New York.* 1829.] 8vo, pp. 12.

[PARKMAN (Charles McDonogh).] A Statement of Facts in regard to the Proposed Division of the Diocese of Maryland, with some Comments thereon. *Philadelphia: Frank E. Remont.* [1868.] 8vo, pp. 23. 58797

Also: A Valedictory Sermon, preached ... at the Patapsco Female Institute, Ellicott City, Md. ... *Baltimore: William K. Boyle, Printer.* [1867.] 8vo, pp. 11.

PARKMAN (E.) ... A Sermon ... before the Ministers of the Province of the Massachusetts-Bay, ... May 28, 1761, By Ebenezer Parkman, A.M. ... *Boston: ... J. Winter.* M.DCC.LXI. 8vo, pp. 37. BA. 58798

Also: Reformers and Intercessors sought by God; ... Discourse ... at Southborough, May 15, 1757. ... *Boston: Printed by S. Kneeland.* 1757. 8vo, pp. (4), 44. M., W.

PARKMAN (F.) Enquiring of the Fathers ... . Discourses ... in the New North Church, ... December 9th, on the completion of the 124th Year from the Establishment of the Church and of the 25th Year since the settlement of the present Pastor. By Francis Parkman, D.D. ... *Boston: Printed by Samuel N. Dickinson.* 1839. 8vo, pp. 40. BA. 58799

PARKMAN. History of the Humane Society of Massachusetts. *See* Vol. XI., No. 45765, *note.*

PARKMAN. The Providence of God displayed in the Revolutions of the World. A Sermon ... Sept. XIX. Occasioned by the Recent Revolutions in the Government of France. By Francis Parkman ... . *Boston: Printed by Samuel N. Dickinson.* 1830. 8vo, pp. 18. BA. 58800

Also: A Discourse delivered ... May 3, 1840, occasioned by the Death of Rev. John T. Kirkland, D.D. ... *Boston: John H. Eastburn, Printer.* 1840. 8vo, pp. 30, (1).—Extracts from a Discourse on the late Rev. Professor Ware. [n. p. 1843.] 8vo, pp. 8.—A Sermon ... at the Interment of Rev. John Lathrop, D.D. ... who died Jan. 4, 1816. ... *Boston: J. W. Burditt.* 1816. 8vo, pp. 23.—A Sermon ... at the Ordination of Rev. Amos Smith, as Colleague ... of the New North Church, ... Dec. 7, 1842. ... *Boston: William Crosby & Company.* 1843. 8vo, pp. 46, (1).—A Sermon ... in the New North Church, ... Jan. XXVIII. 1849, on resigning his Pastoral Charge. ... *Boston: Printed by John Wilson.* 1849. 8vo, pp. 28.—The Spirit of the Christian Ministry: A Sermon ... at the Ordination of ... Rev. John Parkman, ... in Greenfield, Oct. XI, MDCCCXXXVII. ... *Boston: Printed by Samuel N. Dickinson.* 1837. 8vo, pp. 30.—A Survey of God's Providence ... . A Sermon ... November 27, 1814, on the completion of a century since the settlement of the New-North Church. .. *Boston: Printed by John Eliot.* 1814. 8vo, pp. 25. BA.

PARKMAN (F.), *Jr.* The California and Oregon Trail: being Sketches of Prairie and Rocky Mountain Life. By Francis Parkman, Jr. *New-York: George P. Putnam.* 1849. 12mo, pp. 448. Plate. BA. + Third Edition. [*Ibid.*] 1852. 12mo, pp. 448.

+ Fourth Edition. *Boston: Little, Brown and Company.* 1872. 12mo, pp. xii, 381. 58801

The title-pages of the third and fourth edition differ slightly.

PARKMAN. France and England in North America. A Series of Historical Narratives. Part First. Pioneers of France in the New World. By Francis Parkman ... . *Boston: Little, Brown, and Company.* 1865. 8vo, pp. xxii, (2), 420. Portrait. B. + [*Ibid.*] 1866. + Part Second. The Jesuits in North America in the Seventeenth Century. ... [*Ibid.*] 1867. 8vo, pp. lxxxix, 463. Map. + Part Third. The Discovery of the Great West. ... [*Ibid.*] 1869. 8vo, pp. xxi, (2), 425. Map. + [*Ibid.*] 1870. + Part Fourth. The Old Régime in Canada. ... [*Ibid.*] 1874. 8vo, pp. xvi, 448. Map. + Part Fifth. Count Frontenac and New France under Louis XIV. ... [*Ibid.*] 1877. 8vo, pp. xvi, 463. Map. 58802

Seventy-five copies printed on large paper. "The charm which Mr. Parkman's books assert on the attention of every reader, is not wholly derived from the pleasing style of his writing. His perfect knowledge of Indian life and manners, acquired by personal experience, and his exhaustion of the literature of his subject, as it is found in printed works, unedited manuscripts, and authenticated tradition, give new interest to the subjects of which he treats."—FIELD. We have seen translations of the "Pioneers of France" in French (*Paris*, 1874), and in German (*Stuttgart*, 1875); probably others exist.

PARKMAN. History of the Conspiracy of Pontiac, and the War of the North American Tribes against the English Colonies after the Conquest of Canada. By Francis Parkman, Jr. ... *Boston: Charles C. Little, and James Brown.* 1851. 8vo, pp. xxiv, 630. 4 Maps. + *Boston.* 1855. 8vo. + Third Edition. *Boston.* 1863. 8vo. + *Boston: Little, Brown, and Company.* 1866. 8vo, pp. xxiv, 632. Maps. + Sixth Edition ... . [*Ibid.*] 1870. 2 vols., 8vo, pp. xx, 367; vii, 384. Maps. 58803

See "North American Review," LXXIII.

PARKMAN (G.) Management of Lunatics, with Illustrations of Insanity. By George Parkman, M.D. ... *Boston: Printed by John Eliot.* 1817. 12mo, pp. 36. 58804

Also: Proposals for Establishing a Retreat for the Insane. ... *Boston.* 1814. 8vo, pp. 12.—Remarks on Insanity. ... [n. p. n. d.] 8vo, pp. 13. 2 Plates.

PARKMAN (J.) .... A Sermon occasioned by the Death of Hon. William Hale, ... Dover, Nov. 12, 1848. By John Parkman ... . *Boston: Wm. Crosby and H. P. Nichols.* 1848. 8vo, pp. 18. 58805

PARKMAN (Sarah). Some Notices. *See* [Ware (H.), *Jr.*]

PARKS (G.) Speech of Hon. Gorham Parks ... on the ... Public Deposites ... June 22, 1836. *Washington.* 1836. 8vo.

[PARKS (L. D.)] Correct View of the Controversy between the Congregational Association of South Carolina and the Rev. L. D. Parks. By a Friend to Truth. *Charleston.* 1822. 8vo.

PARKS (M. P.) A Word to Commanders: being a discourse ... in the ... United States Military Academy, June 11th, 1843. Addressed To the Graduating Class, ... By M. P. Parks ... . *New-York: Printed by A. G. Powell.* 1843. 8vo, pp. 16.

PARKS (S.) Troy Conference Miscellany, containing a Historical Sketch of Methodism within the ... Troy Conference ... with Reminiscences of its Deceased, and Contributions by its Living Ministers, with an Appendix by Rev. Stephen Parks. *Albany: J. Lord.* 1854. 12mo, pp. 424. Portrait. S. 58809

The Parks of Colorado. *See* Vol. IV., No. 14748.

Le Parlement de Paris Établi au Scioto, sur les bords de l'Oyo. *Et se trouve à Paris, chez tous les Marchands de Nouveautes,* 1790. 8vo, pp. 60. 58810

PARLEY (Peter). *See* [Goodrich (S. G.)], VII. 27910-15.

Parliamentary Debates in England, from ... 1668 to the present time [1741]. *London.* 1741-42. 21 vols., 8vo. A. 58811

See our Vol. VIII., No. 32112.

Parliamentary Debates on the Subject of the Confederation of the British North American Provinces, 3rd Session, 8th Provincial Parliament of Canada. ... *Quebec: Hunter, Rose & Co. ... Printers.* 1865. 8vo, pp. ix, 1032. H. 58812

See also Vol. VIII, No. 33343.

Parliamentary History of England, from the Norman Conquest in 1066 to ... 1803 ... . *London.* 1806-20. 36 vols., 8vo. A.

See Hansard (T. C.), Vol. VIII., No. 30245.

The Parliamentary or Constitutional History of England ... . *London.* 1762-63. 24 vols., 8vo. A. 58814

Parliamentary Papers; consisting of a Complete Collection ... from the Restoration in 1660 to the Dissolution of the last Parliament, in May, 1796. ... *London.* 1797. 3 vols., 8vo. N.

Parliamentary Papers relating to the West India Colonies and Mauritius. Part I. British Guiana, Jamaica, and Trinidad. *London.* 1859. Folio, pp. 600. 58816

The Parliamentary Register; or, History of the Proceedings and Debates of the House of Commons; containing an account of the most interesting Speeches and Motions; accurate Copies of the most Remarkable Letters and Papers; of the most material Evidence, Petitions, ... laid before and offered to the House. *London: J. Almon.* MDCCLXXV-MDCCLXXX. 14 vols., 8vo. A.

Continued at various periods. *See* "Monthly Review," LVI. 472, *and* Rich, I. 465.

Parliamentary Report from the Select Committee on Sugar and Coffee Planting; together with the Minutes of Evidence, and Appendix. 27th March, 1848. *London.* 1848. 8vo. 58818

Parliamentary Reports of the Correspondence with the British Commissioners at Sierra Leone, the Havana, Rio de Janeiro, and Surinam, relating to the Slave Trade. *London: Printed by William Clowes & Sons.* 1842. 8vo. 58819

Parliamentary Reports on the State of the Colonies, for 1860. Part I. West Indies, Mauritius, and Ceylon. *London.* 1862. 8vo. 58820

The Parlour Song Book. A choice and well-selected Collection of the most Popular, Sentimental, Patriotic, Naval, and Comic Songs. *New York: Leavitt and Allen.* [n. d.] 16mo, pp. 160. H. 58821

PARMELEE (A) ... A Sermon ... at the Interment of Miss Susan Winchester, ... who died Dec. 28, 1814 ... . By Ashbel Parmelee ... . [Followed by:] A Sermon ... at the Funeral of Mrs. Lucy Parmelee, ... who died at Westford, Vt. Feb. 13. 1814. By Josiah Hopkins, A.M. ... *Middlebury, Vt.: Printed by Timothy C. Strong.* 1815. 8vo, pp. 27. 58822

PARMENTER (F. A.) God's Leadership of our Nation. A Discourse delivered Nov. 24, 1864, in Elizabeth, N. J. By Rev. Frederick A. Parmenter. *Providence: R. Manning.* 1864. 8vo, pp. 15. 58823

PARMENTER [William]. Speech of Mr. Parmenter of Massachusetts. ... April 20, 1840. ... on the civil and diplomatic appropriation bill. [n. p. n. d.] 8vo, pp. 16. 58824

PARMENTIER (J.) *and* CRIGNON (P.) Description | Novvelle des Merveilles | de ce mõde, & de la dignite de lhomme, com- | posee en rithme francoyse en maniere de ex- | hortation, par Ian parmentier, faisant sa | derniere nauigation, auec Raoul son frere, en lisle Tapro- | bane, aultrement | dicte Sama | tra. | Item vn champ royal specialement cõpose par ma- | niere de paraphrase sur loraison dominicale. | Item plusieurs chãps royaulx par ledit Ian | Parmentier soubz termes astronomiques & geogra | phiques & maritimes, a lhonneur de la tresheureu- | se vierge Marie mere de Dieu. | Item Moralite treselegante | composee par le susdit | Ian Parmentier, a dix personnaiges, a lhonneur de | lassumption de la vierge Marie. | Deploration sur la mort desditz Parmentiers com- | posee par Pierre crignon, compaignon desditz Par- | mentiers en ladicte nauigation. | [Colophon:] *Imprime a paris, en la rue de Sorbonne. Le | Septiesme iour de Ianuier. Lan | de grace* Mil. D. | XXXI. | 4to, (48) leaves. 58825

See [Harrisse's] "Bib. Am. Vet.—Additions," No. 96.

PARMENTIER (*M.*) Mémoire couronné le 25 Aout 1784, par l'Académie Royale des Sciences de Bordeaux, sur cette question: Quel seroit le meilleur procédé pour conserver, le plus long-temps possible, ou en grain ou en farine, le Maïs ou Blé de Turquie, plus connu dans la Guienne sous le nom de Blé d'Espagne? Et quels seroient les différens moyens d'en tirer parti dans les années abondantes, indépendamment des usages connus & ordinaires dans cette Province? ... *Bordeaux: A. Antoine Pallandre.* 1785. 4to, pp. 164. Plate. J.C.B. 58826

PARMLY (E.) Thoughts in Rhyme, by Eleazar Parmly. *New York: Printed by Thomas Holman.* 1867. 8vo, pp. 600.

Also: Temperance Address ... at Runsom, N. J. ... *New York.* 1844. 8vo.

Parnaso Brasileiro, ou collecção das melhores poesias dos poetas do Brasil, tanto ineditas como já impressas. *Rio de Janeiro, na Typ. Imperial e Nacional.* 1829-30. 4 vols., 4to. 58828

El Parnaso del real collegio de S. Marcos prostrado a los pies del Conde de la Monclava, Virrey del Peru. *Lima.* 1694. 4to.

Title from Ternaux, No. 1072, under 1694, dated 1674.

Parnaso Maranhense: collecção de poesias. [n. p.:] *Typ. do Progresso.* [1861.] 8vo, pp. (7), 285, iv, (1). 58830

El Parnaso Peruano ó Repertorio de Poesias Nacionales antiguas y modernas, precedidas del retrato y biografia de su autor.

Coleccion hecha por Jose Toribio Polo. Tomo I. ... *Lima.* 1862-63. 8vo, pp. xiii, 224. 58831

A Parnassian Shop. *See* [Story (Issac)].

Parnassus in Philadelphia. *See* Pindar (Peter), Jr.

Parochial and Township Subdivisions. *See* Vol. III. 10538.

Parole and Documentary Evidence. *See* [Findley (W.)], VI.

PARQUIN *and* CALART. Les Puits Artésiens en général, et des services qu'ils peuvent rendre en popularisant leur usage aux États-Unis. Rapport fait au conseil municipal de la ville de Broolen, par MM. Parquin et Calart. *Paris: Imprimerie de Boisseau.* 1852. 8vo. 58832

PARR [John]. Vindication of Governor Parr and his Council, against the Complaints of certain Persons Who sought to engross 275,000 Acres of Land in Nova Scotia, at the expense of Government, and to the great prejudice of the Province of Loyalists in general. Founded on various authentic Letters and Papers herein inserted. By a Gentleman of Halifax. ... *London: John Stockdale.* M,DCC,LXXXIV. 8vo, pp. 35. B., J.C.B. 58833

PARR. Remarks on a late Pamphlet, entitled, "A Vindication of Governor Parr, and his Council" .... By a Consistent Loyalist. *London: John Stockdale.* MDCCLXXXIV. 8vo, pp. 52. J.C.B.

See "Notes and Queries," VI. 151, and for a "Reply," *see* Viator (J.)

PARRA (A.) Descripcion de Diferentes Piezas de Historia Natural, las mas del Ramo Maritimo, representadas en setenta y cinco laminas. Su Autor Don Antonio Parra. *En la Havana, año de* 1787. 4to, pp. (4), 195, (5). 75 Plates. 58835

One of the earliest specimens of printing in Havana, and contains the first copper-plates engraved in Cuba.

PARRA. Discurso sobre los medios de connaturalizar y propagar en España los cedros de la Havana, y otros arboles, asi de construccion, como de Maderas curiosas y frutales. Por Don Antonio Parra ... . *Madrid.* MDCCXCIX. *Imprenta de la viuda de Ibarra.* Sm. 4to, pp. 36. H. 58836

PARRA (F. de la). Testamento de D. Francisco de la Parra encontrado en la iglesia de S. Felipe Neri por el mulato Gerónimo. *Havana: Oficina del ciudadano José Boloña.* 1822. 4to.

PARRA (J.) Rosa laureada entre los Santos Epitalamios sacros de la corte, aclamaciones de España, aplausos de Roma, congratulaciones festivas del clero y religiones, al feliz desposorio que celebro en la gloria con Christo la Beata Virgen Rosa de Santa Maria de la tercera orden de Predicadores, Patrona del Perù. Por Fr. Jacinto de la Parra ... . *Madrid: Domingo Garcia Morrás.* 1670. Folio, pp. (20), 651, (88). 58838

PARRA. Vida de Santa Rosa del Peru, por Fr. Jacinto de la Parra ... . *Dominico.* 1668. 4to. 58839

PARRA (J. G. de la). Idea Evangelica en elogio de la milagrosa imagen de N. Señ. del Filar ... por Dr. D. Joseph Gomez de la Parra. *Puebla.* 1691. 4to, 32 leaves. 58840

Also: Importantissimas y verdaderes revoluciones, para Ecclesiasticos que dessean ajustarse á los sagrados Ritos de la Missa, sacadas de los Comentarios sobre las Rubricas del Missal Romano de Pablo Maria Quarti. ... *Puebla.* 1712. 4to, pp. (18), 93. *See also* Gomez de la Parra (J.), Vol. VIII., Nos. 27763-4.

PARRAS (P. J.) Gobierno de los Regulares de la América, ajustado religiosamente á la voluntad del rey: trabajado en obsequio de las paz y tranquilidad conveniente à los Regulares mismos con los Señores Diocesanos, Virreyes, Presidentes, Audiencias, Gobernadores y demas Tribunales subalternos. Arreglado á las Leyes de aquellos Reynos, Reales Cedulas de S. M. Autos-acordados, Decretos, y Providencias de su Real y Supremo Consejo de las Indias. ... Se trata en algunos capitulos de la primera parte de la institucion del Comisario General de Indias de la dependencia que este tiene de su Ministro General ... . Su Autor El P. Fr. Pedro Joseph Parras ... . *Madrid, Por D. Joachin Ibarra.* MDCCLXXXIII. 2 vols., 4to, pp. (4), xliv, 217; (4), xxxvi, 493.

PARRIS (S. B.) Remains of Samuel Bartlett Parris, M.D., comprising Miscellaneous Poems and Essays, ... with a Biographical Sketch of the Author. *Plymouth, Mass.: E. Collier.* 1809. 12mo, pp. 312. C. 58842

PARRISH (I.) Biographical Memoir of John C. Otto, M.D. ... read ... March 4th, 1845; by Isaac Parrish, M.D. ... *Philadelphia: Wm. F. Geddes, Printer.* 1845. 8vo, pp. 20. 58843

PARRISH (J.) Remarks on the Slavery of the Black People; addressed to the Citizens of the United States, particularly to those who are in Legislative or Executive Stations ... . By John Parrish. *Philadelphia: Printed ... by Kimber, Conrad, & Co.* 1806. 8vo, pp. (4), 66. C. 58844

PARRISH (J.) Address of Joseph Parrish, ... Haverford College, Tenth Month, 27th, 1866. ... *Philadelphia: Henry B. Ashmead, Printer.* 1866. 8vo, pp. 14. 58845

[PARRISH.] Bishop Doane's Sermon, "Rev. Mr. Keith" and the Society of Friends; a Series of Essays showing the great similarity between George Keith and his Followers, who dissented from and left the Society in 1692, and that portion which Separated in 1827, and are now styled "Orthodox." *Princeton, N. J.* 1835. 8vo. P. 58846

PARRISH. Outline of a Plan for classifying the Archives and preparing the History of the United States Sanitary Commission. [n. p. n. d.] 4to, pp. 14. 58847

Dated, Centre Harbor, N. H., July 27, 1866. Also: The "Negro Question." ... *Philadelphia: Perkenpine & Higgins.* 1864. 8vo, pp. 11. *See also* Vol. V., No. 20394.

[PARRISH (Robert A.), *Jr.*] Details of an unpaid Claim on France for 24,000,000 Francs, guaranteed by the Parole of Napoleon III. ... *Philadelphia.* 1869. 8vo, pp. iv, (2), 147. 58848

PARRISH. Petition (and accompanying Correspondence) of Robert A. Parrish, Jr., of Philadelphia, to the U. S. House of Representatives, praying for Relief against the Emperor and Government of France who have defrauded him of Fifteen Millions of Francs ... . [n. p. n. d.] 8vo, pp. 40. 3 Facsimiles. H.

PARRODI (Anastasio). Memoria sobre la evacuacion militar, del Puerto de Tampico de Tamaulipas. ... *San Luis Potosi.* 1848. 4to, pp. 53. 58850

PARROTT (M. J.) Admission of Kansas. Speech of Hon. Marcus J. Parrott, ... delivered ... April 10, 1860. *Washington, D. C.: Buell & Blanchard.* 1860. 8vo, pp. 14. 58851

PARROTT. Kansas: a Description of the Country—its Soil—Climate & Resources, by Marcus J. Parrott, Gov. A. H. Reeder, and M. W. Delahay. [n. p. n. d.] 8vo, pp. 8. 58852

PARROTT (W. P.) Back Bay Improvement. Letter of Wm. P. Parrott, Esq. Civil Engineer. [*Boston.* 1860.] 8vo, pp. 4.

PARRY (C. C.) Physiographical Sketch of that Portion of the Rocky Mountain Range, at the head waters of South Clear Creek and East of Middle Park. By Dr. C. C. Parry ... . [n. p.] 1862. 8vo. 58854

PARRY. Preliminary Report of the Physical Geography, and Natural Resources of the Country along the Route of the Kansas Pacific Railway ... . By Dr. C. C. Parry, Geologist to the Survey. *Philadelphia.* 1868. 8vo, pp. 20. Map. H. 58855

PARRY (E.) Memoirs of Rear-Admiral Sir W. Edward Parry, ... By his Son, ... Rev. Edward Parry ... . *London: Longman, ...* 1857. 8vo, pp. xii, 403. Map and Portrait. + Third Edition [*Ibid.*] 58856

PARRY (E. O.) Argument for the Heirs of Stephen Girard, in the Supreme Court of Pennsylvania. By Edward Owen Parry. *Pottsville (Pa.).* 1863. 8vo. 58857

PARRY (J. D.) The Anthology: an Annual Reward Book for Youth. Consisting of amusing and instructive Selections from the best Authors. By Rev. John D. Parry. *London: Whittaker, Treacher & Co.* 1829. 16mo, pp. xii, 275. C. 58858

Contains some accounts of American natural history.

[PARRY] (Thomas). A Charge Delivered in the Cathedral Church of Barbadoes, Aug. 24, 1843, By Thomas Lord, Bishop of Barbadoes, at the Primary Visitation. *London.* 1843. 8vo, pp. 62. 58859

PARRY (W. E.) Journal of a Voyage for the Discovery of a North-West Passage from the Atlantic to the Pacific; performed in the years 1819–20, in His Majesty's Ships Hecla and Griper, under the Orders of William Edward Parry, R.N., F.R.S., and Commander of the Expedition. With an Appendix, containing the Scientific and other Observations. Published by Authority of the Lords Commissioners of the Admiralty. *London: John Murray.* M,DCCC,XXI. 4to, pp. (8), xxix, (2), 310, Appendix, clxxix. 20 Maps and Plates. + The Second Edition. [*Ibid.*] + To which is added, The North Georgia Gazette and Winter Chronicle. *Philadelphia: Abraham Small.* 1821. 8vo, pp. xxiv, 9–278, 78. 58860

See "Monthly Review," XCVI. 140, 276.

PARRY. A Supplement to the Appendix of Captain Parry's Voyage ... in the years 1819–20. Containing an Account of the Subjects of Natural History. *London: John Murray.* MDCCCXXIV. 4to, pp. (8), clxxxiii–cccx. 6 Plates. C. 58861

PARRY. Reise zur Entdeckung einer nordwestlichen Durchfahrt aus dem Atlantischen in das Stille Meer, in den Jahren 1819

und 1820, mit den Schiffen Hekla und Griper, unter Capitain Parry. Aus dem Englischen. *Hamburg.* 1822. 8vo. 58862

PARRY. Reis ter Ontdekking van eene noordwestelijke Doorvaart, uit de Atlantische in de Stille Zee, gedaan in de Jaren 1819 en 1820 door de Schepen The Hecla en The Griper. Uit het Engelsch. *Amsterdam.* 1822. 8vo. Map and 3 Plates.

PARRY. Journal of a Second Voyage for the Discovery of a North-West Passage from the Atlantic to the Pacific; performed in the years 1821–22–23, in His Majesty's Ships Fury and Hecla, under the Orders of Captain William Edward Parry, R.N., F.R.S., and Commander of the Expedition. Illustrated by Numerous Plates. Published by Authority of the Lords Commissioners of the Admiralty. *London: John Murray.* MDCCCXXIV. 4to, pp. (8), xxx, (2), 571, (1). 39 Plates, Maps and Plans. + *New York: E. Duyckinck, G. Long, Collins & Co.* ... 1824. 8vo, pp. vii, xx, 464. Plate. 58864

Throughout the whole of this work, the characteristics of the Esquimaux, and incidents of intercourse with them, absorb the attention of the writer. The work is a treatise on aboriginal life, rather than a narrative of scientific discoveries.

PARRY. Appendix to Captain Parry's Journal of a Second Voyage ... . *London: John Murray.* MDCCCXXV. 4to, pp. (4), 432. 2 Plates. C., S. 58865

PARRY. Zweite Reise zur Entdeckung der nordwestlichen Durchfährt ... 1821–23. Aus dem Englischen. *Jena.* 1824. 8vo. 58866

PARRY. Journal of a Third Voyage for the Discovery of a North-West Passage from the Atlantic to the Pacific; performed in the years 1824–25, in His Majesty's Ship Hecla and Fury, under the Orders of Captain William Edward Parry, R.N., F.R.S. and Commander of the Expedition. Illustrated by Plates and Charts. Published by Authority of the Lords Commissioners of the Admiralty. *London: John Murray.* MDCCCXXVI. 4to, pp. xxvii, (1), 186, (1), Appendix, 151. + *Philadelphia: H. C. Carey and I. Lea.* 1826. 8vo, pp. 232. Map. BA., C. 58867

PARRY. Narrative of an Attempt to reach the North Pole, in boats ... attached to His Majesty's Ship Hecla, in the year MDCCCXXVII., under the Command of Captain William Edward Parry, R.N. ... *London: John Murray.* MDCCCXXVIII. 4to, pp. xxii, (2), 229. Maps and Plates. BA. 58868

This forms the fourth voyage to the North Pole. Improved title of our No. 51784.

PARRY. Journal of a Voyage of Discovery. *See* Vol. IX. 36696

PARRY. Journal of the First, Second, and Third Voyages for the Discovery of A North-West Passage, ... in 1819–20–21–22–23–24–25, in His Majesty's Ships Hecla, Griper and Fury, under the Orders of Capt. W. E. Parry ... . *London: John Murray.* MDCCCXXVIII. 5 vols., 16mo, pp. (2), viii, 283; iv, 270; vii, 312; vii, 295; v, 330. Map and 5 Plates. The Sixth Volume. [*Ibid.*] MDCCCXXIX. pp. xxxv, 211. 58869

PARRY. Entdeckungs Reise nach den nördlichen Polargegenden, ... 1818, in dem Schiffe Alexander, Capitain Parry. Aus dem Englischen. *Hamburg.* 1819. 8vo. Map. 58870

A German translation of No. 36696, Vol. IX.

PARRY. Three Voyages for the Discovery of a Northwest Passage from the Atlantic to the Pacific, and Narrative of an Attempt to reach the North Pole. By Sir W. E. Parry, Capt. R.N. ... *New York: Harper & Brothers.* [1840.] 2 vols., 12mo, pp. 321; 328. Plate and Portrait. + [*Ibid.*] 1844. 58871

See Dennett (F.), Vol. V., No. 19582, Vol. VII., No. 25631, *and* Vol. XIII., No. 55829.

A Parsee's Letters to Sahib Horace Greeley. *New York.* [n. d.] 8vo. 58872

PARSHALL (R. F.) Trial of the Rev. Revilo F. Parshall, late Pastor of the Baptist Church at Sandy Hill, N. Y., on Charges of Licentiousness, Imprudence, and Bad Example; before an Ecclesiastical Council, ... 17th, 18th, 19th and 20th ... January, 1860. *New York.* 1860. 12mo, pp. 69. S. 58873

PARSONS (——). Parsons ... Almanack for 1757. *New York; J. Parker.* [1756.] 12mo. 58874

PARSONS (C. G.) Inside View of Slavery: or a Tour among the Planters. By C. G. Parsons, M.D. With an Introductory Note by Mrs. H. B. Stowe. ... *Boston: John P. Jewett and Company.* 1855. 12mo, pp. 318. H. 38875

PARSONS (C. W.) History of the Population in the State of Rhode Island. [n. p. 1850?] 8vo. 58876

PARSONS. 1788–1868. Memoir of Usher Parsons, M.D., of Providence, R. I. By his Son Charles W. Parsons. *Providence: Hammond, Angell & Co., Printers.* 1870. 12mo, pp. viii, 72. Portrait. 58877

Also: Report on the Medical Topography and Epidemic Diseases of Rhode Island. ... *Philadelphia: Collins, Printer.* 1864. 8vo, pp. 27.

PARSONS (D.) A Sermon, Preached before His Excellency John Hancock, Esq. Governour: ... of the Commonwealth of Massachusetts, May 28, 1788. Being the Day of General Election. By David Parsons, A.M. ... *Boston: Printed by Adams & Nourse* ... . [1788.] 8vo, pp. 46. N., W. 58878

Also: Sermon ... at the Ordination of Jonathan L. Pomeroy. ... *Northampton.* 1795. 8vo.

PARSONS (E.) Address to the Students in the Independent Academy at Idle, June 18, 1823. By Edward Parsons. *Halifax.* 1823. 8vo. 58879

PARSONS (E. B.) Sermon ... at the Funeral of Adoniram Foot. By Rev. E. B. Parsons. With Genealogical Notes on the Foot Family, by Rev. J. B. Foot. *Rome, N. Y.* 1867. 8vo.

PARSONS (E. W.) The Rosary. By E. W. Parsons. *Cambridge: John Wilson & Son.* 1865. 4to. 58881

PARSONS (G. F.) The Life and Adventures of James W. Marshall, the Discoverer of Gold in California. By George Frederic Parsons. *Sacramento: James W. Marshall and W. Burke.* 1870. 12mo, pp. 188. 58882

PARSONS (H. A.) The Book of Niagara Falls. By Horatio A. Parsons, A.M. *Buffalo: Oliver G. Steele.* 1836. 18mo, pp. 111, (1). + Second Edition. [*Ibid.*] + Third Edition. [*Ibid.*] + Fourth Edition. Carefully revised, and enlarged. Accompanied by Maps. [*Ibid.*] + Fifth Edition ... . *Buffalo: Steele & Peck.* 1838. 18mo, pp. 111, (1). Map and Plates. + Sixth Edition. [*Ibid.*] + Thirteenth Edition. *Buffalo: Oliver G. Steele.* 1851. 18mo, pp. 80. Map. 58883

PARSONS (I.) Memoir of the Life and Character of Rev. Joseph Vaill, late Pastor ... in Hadlyme. By Rev. Isaac Parsons ... . *New York: Taylor & Dodd.* 1839. 12mo, pp. viii, 13–236. Plate. B., C. 58884

PARSONS. A Retrospect. Two Sermons, preached ... Oct. 24, 1841, on occasion of the close of the Quarter of a Century in his Ministry. By Isaac Parsons, Pastor ... East Haddam, Ct. With an Appendix. *Hartford: Printed by E. Gleason.* 1841. 8vo, pp. 32. B. 58885

Also: Memoir of Susannah Elizabeth Bingham, of East Haddam, Conn. ... *Phila-*

delphia. [1836.] 18mo, pp. 90.—A Sermon, ... Death of Mrs. Carile Mary Whitmore, East Haddam, Sept. 29th, 1822. ... *Middletown, Conn.: Printed by E. & H. Clarke.* 1822. 8vo, pp. 23. B.

PARSONS (J.) Remains of Japhet: being Historical Enquiries into the Affinity and Origin of the European Languages. By James Parsons, M.D. *London: The Author.* MDCCLXVII. 4to, pp. xxxii, 419. C. 58886

The author refers to Acosta, Mexico, Peru, etc.

PARSONS (J.) Reflections on the Mysterious Fate of Sir John Franklin. By James Parsons. *London: J. F. Hope.* 1857. Post 8vo, pp. iv, 116, (2). 2 Maps. C. 58887

PARSONS (J.) A Consideration of some Unconstitutional Measures, adopted and practiced in this State. In an Address to the Public. By Jonathan Parsons ... . *Newbury-Port: John Mycall.* 1784. 8vo, pp. 24. BA. 58888

PARSONS. Freedom from Civil and Ecclesiastical Slavery ... . A Discourse Offered to a numerous Assembly, On March the Fifth, 1774, At the Presbyterian Meeting-House, in Newbury-Port. By Jonathan Parsons ... . *Newbury-Port, New-England: Printed by J. Thomas and H. W. Tinges.* [1774.] 4to, pp. 19.

On the Boston massacre. The first book printed in Newburyport; a press having been established there late in 1773.

PARSONS. ... A Funeral-Sermon on the Death of the Reverend Mr. George Whitefield, ... who died ... at Newbury Port, ... Sept. 30th, 1770. ... By Jonathan Parsons, A.M. ... *Portsmouth, New-Hampshire: Daniel and Robert Fowle.* [1770.] 8vo, pp. 44. BA. 58890

PARSONS. ... A Funeral Sermon On the Death of the Rev. Mr. George Whitefield, ... Who died ... at Newbury Port, ... Sept. 30th, 1770. ... By Jonathan Parsons, A.M. ... To which are added, An Account of his Interment; The Speech over his Grave, By the Rev. Mr. Jewet; And some Verses to his Memory, By the Rev. Tho. Gibbons, D.D. *Portsmouth, New-Hampshire, Printed, London Reprinted, For James Buckland.* 1771. 8vo, pp. (4), 35, (1). C., H. 58891

PARSONS. Good News From a Far Country. In Seven Discourses From 1 Tim. I. 15. Delivered ... in Newbury: ... By Jonathan Parsons ... . *Portsmouth, in New-Hampshire: Printed, ... by Daniel Fowle.* 1756. 8vo, pp. viii, 168. 58892

"This must be one of the first books printed in New Hampshire, as in that year

(1756) the first press was established in the State, by D. Fowle, at Portsmouth." *See* Thomas' "History of Printing."

These discourses brought forth, "Observations on the Doctrines, and Uncharitableness of Rev. Jonathan Parsons; as exhibited more especially in his late discourses on 1. Tim., I. 15." ... *Boston.* 1757. 8vo, pp. 70. M.

PARSONS. Manna gathered in the Morning; ... A Discourse delivered at ... Newbury. By Jonathan Parsons ... . *Boston: Printed by D. Fowle.* 1751. 8vo, pp. 37. + Second Edition. *Newburyport.* [n. d.] 16mo, pp. 38. M. 58893

PARSONS. A Needful Caution in a Critical Day. ... A Discourse ... at Lyme, Feb. 4th, 1741, 2, By Jonathan Parsons, ... *N. London: Printed by T. Green.* 1742. 8vo, pp. (2), 71.

PARSONS. Sixty Sermons on various Subjects, by ... Jonathan Parsons, A.M. ... To which is prefixed a Funeral Sermon, by the Rev. Mr. Searl. *Newburyport: Edmund Sawyer and Jonathan Parsons.* MDCCLXXIX–LXXX. 2 vols., 8vo, pp. (2), lxvi, 625, vii; 855, ix, (1). H. 58895

"Jonathan Parsons, a graduate of Yale College in 1729, was settled as a Congregational minister at Newburyport, where he continued for thirty years. He was one of the most distinguished preachers of his time, and was also eminent as a scholar. His publications were numerous."—BLAKE, *Biog. Dictionary.*

Also: A Funeral Sermon occasioned by the Death of Mr. Ebenezer Little, one of the Elders of the Presbyterian Church in Newbury ... . *Salem.* 1768. 8vo, pp. 26. Portrait.—Wisdom Justified of her Children. A Sermon ... at the Publick Lecture in Boston ... Sept. 16, 1742. ... *Boston: N. Proctor.* 1742. 8vo, pp. (4), viii, 5–54.

PARSONS, *and* MCGREGORE (D.) A Rejoinder to the Reverend Mr. Robert Abercrombie's late Remarks on a fair Narrative of the Proceedings of the Presbytery of Boston, against himself ... By J. Parsons and D. McGregore ... . *Boston: Printed by Green and Russell.* M. DCC. LVIII. 8vo, pp. 27. BA. 58896

PARSONS. A Letter from A Gentleman in the Country, to His Friend in Boston, Respecting some late Observations upon the Conduct of the Rev. Mr. Jonathan Parsons, while he was Minister at Lyme in Connecticut. ... *Boston: Printed by Z. Fowle.* 1757. 8vo, pp. 11. BA. 58897

PARSONS (J.), *of Lebanon.* The Validity of Presbyterian Ordination. A Sermon ... at New-Castle, in New-Hampshire, Dec. 20. 1732. at the Ordination of Mr. John Blunt. By Joseph Parsons, M.A. ... *Boston, N. E.: Printed by S. Kneeland & T. Green.* M, DCC, XXXIII. 8vo, pp. (4), 27. B. 58898

PARSONS (J.), *of Bradford.* Religion recommended to the Soldier. A Sermon ... to the ancient and honourable Artillery-

Company, June 4. 1744. Being the Day of their Election ... . By Joseph Parsons, A.M. ... *Boston: ... D. Henchman and J. Edwards.* 1744. 8vo, pp. 30. B. 58899

PARSONS. A Sermon ... in the Audience of ... the Governor ... and ... Council and House of Representatives, of the Province of ... Massachusetts-Bay ... May 31st, 1759. ... By Joseph Parsons ... . *Boston in New-England: Printed by John Draper.* 1759. 8vo, pp. 35. BA., M., W. 58900

Also: A Minister's Care about his Life and Doctrine, considered and inforced. A Sermon ... at the Ordination of Mr. Samuel Webster, ... in Salisbury, August 12. 1741. ... *Boston: S. Eliot.* 1741. 8vo, pp. 30. B.—Christians may and ought to be influenced by the Recompence of Reward. The Substance of Two Sermons, ... at Bradford, March 11th and 25th 1743, 4. ... *Boston: S. Eliot.* 1744. 8vo, pp. 30.—Two Discourses concerning the Importance of the Belief and Profession of the Gospel to Eternal Salvation. ... *Boston.* 1759. 8vo, pp. 37. M.

PARSONS (L.) ... A Sermon, ... in ... Boston, ... Oct. 31, 1819, just before the Departure of the Palestine Mission. By Levi Parsons, A.M. ... *Boston: Samuel T. Armstrong.* 1819. 8vo, pp. 20. W. 58901

Also: ... A Sermon at the Funeral of Mr. Samuel Rhoades, ... at Skeneateles, Onondaga County, N. Y., March 31, 1850. ... *Albany: J. Munsell.* 1850. 8vo, pp. 20.

PARSONS (M.) A Sermon preached at Cambridge, Before ... Thomas Hutchinson, Esq; Governor: ... Andrew Oliver, Esq; Lieutenant-Governor, ... his Majesty's Council, and ... House of Representatives, Of the Province of the Massachusetts-Bay in New-England, May 27th 1772. Being the Anniversary for the Election of His Majesty's Council for said Province. By Moses Parsons, A.M. ... Newbury Falls. *Boston: Printed by Edes and Gill* ... . M,DCC,LXXII. 8vo, pp. 43. M., W. 58902

Also: The Character of able Ministers of the New-Testament described. A Sermon ... November 11, 1772, at the Ordination of the Rev. Mr. Obadiah Parsons, ... in Gloucester. ... *Salem: Printed by S. and E. Hall.* MDCCLXXIII. 8vo, pp. 38.— ... A Sermon ... at Ipswich, Nov. 7, 1765. at the Ordination of the Rev. Joseph Dana, M.A. ... *Boston: Printed by Richard and Samuel Draper.* 1766. 8vo, pp. 36. BA.

[PARSONS (Robert).] Elizabethæ Angliæ Reginæ hæresim Calvinianam propugnantis sævissimum in Catholicos sui Regni Edictum, quod in alios quoque reipublicæ Christianæ principes contumelias continet indignissimas. Promulgatum Londini 29 Nov. 1591. Cum Responsione ad singula capita, qua non tantum sævitia et impietas tam iniqui Edicti, sed mendacia quoque et fraudes et imposturæ deteguntur et confutantur per Andream Philopatrum. *Romæ.* 1593. Sm. 4to. + *Lugduni.* 1593. 8vo.

This rare volume was written by Robert Parsons, the Jesuit, on the publication of the edict against the Catholics. It contains some singular notices of Sir Francis Drake and Sir Richard Grenville, described as pirates and robbers, also of Sir Walter Raleigh, etc. One of Thorpe's catalogues describes an edition, *Lugduni*, 1592.

PARSONS (S.) Review of a Pamphlet, entitled, "An Epistle and Testimony, from the Yearly Meeting of Friends, held in New York" ... . Signed by Samuel Parsons and Anne Mott. *New York: Alexander Ming, Jr.* 1828. 8vo, pp. 16. 58904

PARSONS (S. B.) An Address delivered at the Annual Fair of the New Haven Co. Agricultural Society. By S. B. Parsons. *New Haven.* 1849. 8vo. 58905

[PARSONS (Theodore), *and* PEARSON (Eliphalet).] A Forensic Dispute. *See* Vol. VI., No. 25075.

[PARSONS (Theophilus).] Result of the Convention of Delegates Holden at Ipswich in the County of Essex, who were deputed to take into Consideration the Constitution and Form of Government, proposed by the Convention of the State of Massachusetts-Bay. *Newbury-Port: Printed by John Mycall.* 1778. 8vo, pp. 68. 58906

Signed, Peter Coffin. *See* "A Vindication of the Result." Also: Catalogue of the Library of ... Theophilus Parsons. ... March 1st. 1814 ... . *Boston.* 1814. 8vo, pp. 23.

PARSONS (T.) An Address ... before the Phi Beta Kappa Society of Harvard University, 27 August, 1835. On the Duties of Educated Men in a Republic. By Theophilus Parsons. *Boston: Russell, Odiorne & Co.* 1835. 8vo, pp. 28. 58907

PARSONS. Commentaries on American Law. By Theophilus Parsons ... . *New-York.* 1836. 8vo, pp. iv, 396. 58908

PARSONS. Defence of the Third Article of the Massachusetts Declaration of Rights; as delivered by Chief Justice Parsons, as the Opinion of the Supreme Judicial Court, in the Case of Barnes vs. Falmouth ... . *Worcester: Printed by Manning & Trumbull.* 1820. 8vo, pp. 7. 58909

PARSONS. Memoir of Theophilus Parsons, Chief Justice of the Supreme Judicial Court of Massachusetts; with Notices of some of his Contemporaries. By his Son, Theophilus Parsons. *Boston: Ticknor and Fields.* MDCCCLIX. 12mo, pp. viii, 476. Portrait. C. 58910

PARSONS. Slavery. Its Origin, Influence, and Destiny. By Theophilus Parsons. *Boston: William Carter and Brother.* 1863. 12mo, pp. 36. + Second Edition. [*Ibid.*] 58911

[PARSONS.] To the Citizens of Boston. March, 1846. [n. p.] 1846. 8vo, pp. 12. 58912

Also: Address commemorative of Rufus Choate .... *Boston: Little, Brown, and Company.* 1859. 8vo, pp. 40.—The Constitution, its Origin, Function, and Authority. A Lecture ... before the Law School of Harvard University .... March 7, 1861. ... *Boston: Little, Brown and Company.* 1861. 8vo, pp. 30.—Memoir of Charles Greely Loring; ... *Cambridge: Press of John Wilson and Son.* 1870. 8vo, pp. 31.—An Oration ... on the Fourth of July, 1861, before the Municipal Authorities of ... Boston. ... *Boston: J. E. Farwell & Co., ... Printers.* 1861. 8vo, pp. 42. + With an Appendix. [*Ibid.*] 8vo, pp. 59.

PARSONS (T. W.) Poems by Thomas William Parsons. *Boston: Ticknor and Fields.* M DCCC LIV. 8vo, pp. 189. 58913

Also: Twenty-Fourth of October, 1852. [Poem on the Death of Daniel Webster. *Boston.* 1852.] 4to, pp. 4.

[PARSONS (Tyler).] Candid Enquiries, ... relative to the Difficulties which existed in the Town of Manchester, Massachusetts, from ... 1816, to ... 1819. By a Friend to Truth. [n. p. n. d.] 8vo, pp. 8. BA. 58914

PARSONS. Mormon Fanaticism Exposed. A Compendium of the Book of Mormon, or Joseph Smith's Golden Bible. Also, The Examination of its Internal and External Evidences; with the Argument to refute its pretences to a revelation from God: Argued ... in ... Boston, July, 1841, between Elder Freeman Nickerson, a Mormon, and the Author, Tyler Parsons. *Boston: The Author.* 1841. 8vo, pp. 102, (1). + [*Ibid.*] 1842. 58915

"I am not aware that the Mormons claim the privilege of polygamy as yet. I presume they will, when they revise their creed."

[PARSONS.] Truth espoused, relative to the Difficulties ... in the Town of Manchester, Massachusetts, between James Thurston ... and a ... number of the Inhabitants .... By Tyler Parsons. ... *Dedham: Printed by H. & W. H. Mann.* 1823. 8vo, pp. 96. B. 58916

PARSONS (U.) Battle of Lake Erie. A Discourse, delivered before the Rhode-Island Historical Society, ... February 16. 1852. By Usher Parsons. ... *Providence: Benjamin T. Albro. Printer.* 1853. 8vo, pp. 36. + Second Edition. [*Ibid.*] 1854.

A defence of Perry and a refutation of J. F. Cooper.

PARSONS. The Descendants of Peter Hill of York County. Maine, with some Incidents relating to the French and Indian Wars, gleaned from old Manuscripts of the time. By Usher Parsons. ... *Boston: Henry W. Dutton and Son, Printers.* M.DCCC.LVIII. 8vo, pp. 16. S. 58918

[PARSONS.] Genealogy of the Frost Family. Elliot, York County, Maine. [n. p. n. d.] 8vo, pp. 27. 58919

PARSONS. Indian Names of Places in Rhode-Island: collected by Usher Parsons, M.D. ... *Providence: Knowles, Anthony & Co., Printers.* 1861. 8vo, pp. 32. 58920

PARSONS. The Life of Sir William Pepperrell, Bart., the only Native of New England who was created a Baronet during our connection with the Mother Country. By Usher Parsons. *Boston: Little, Brown and Company.* 1855. 8vo, pp. xii, 352. Map. + Second Edition. [*Ibid.*] 1856. + Third Edition. [*Ibid.*] 8vo, pp. xvi, 356. Portrait, Map, and Plate. 58921

Some copies have a London imprint. Also: An Address, ... before the Providence Association for the Promotion of Temperance, May 27, 1831. ... *Providence: Printed by Weeden and Knowles.* 1831. 8vo, pp. 16.—Address ... before the American Medical Association, at St. Louis, Missouri, May 2nd, 1854. ... [n. p. n. d.] 8vo, pp. 4.—Brief Sketches of the Officers who were in the Battle of Lake Erie. ... *Albany: Munsell.* 1862. 8vo, pp. 13. S.—Memoir of Charles Frost. ... [*Boston.* n. d.] 8vo, pp. 15.—Pepperrell Genealogy. ... *Boston.* 1866. 8vo, pp. 6.—Report of the Committee on Medical Sciences, presented at the ... Meeting of the American Medical Association ... 1850 .... *Philadelphia: T. K. & P. G. Collins, Printers.* 1850. 8vo, pp. 53.—Sketches of Rhode Island Physicians, deceased prior to 1850; .... *Providence: Knowles, Anthony & Co., Printers.* 1859. 8vo, pp. 64.—Speech ... at Put-in Bay Island, September 10, 1858, the ... 45th Anniversary of the Battle of Lake Erie. [n. p. n. d.] 8vo, pp. 4. H.

PARSONS (W.) Account of the Life of William Parsons, Esq., Executed at Tyburn, for Returning from Transportation, containing a True Account of his Amours, Forgeries, and other Villanies, a Particular Account of the Robberies he committed while in America .... *London.* 1751. 8vo. 58922

PARSONS (W. B.) Gold Mines of Western Kansas. By Wm. B. Parsons .... *Lawrence.* 1858. 12mo. + New and Enlarged Edition. *Cincinnati, Ohio: Geo. S. Blanchard.* 1859. 8vo, pp. 63. H. 58923

PARSONS (William L.), *Editor.* Reminiscences of the Life and Character of Col. Phineas Staunton ... [and] A Sermon on the Death of Miss Marietta Ingham. ... *Rochester: E. Darrow & Kempshall.* 1867. 8vo, pp. 94. Plate. C. 58924

Parte literaria de "El Porvenir." Año I. *Carácas.* 1866. 4to, pp. 80. 58925

Ten numbers only published. Contains in Nos. 6, 7, 8, "Formas caracteristicas de la Flora Venezolana, Palmas," by A. Ernst, partly translated from Dr. Seeman's "Popular History of Palms," and other valuable articles.

PARTHENIUS GIANNETTASIUS (N.) Nicolai Parthenii Giannettasii Neapolit. Soc. Jesu. Piscatoria, et Nautica. [*Neapoli: Typis Regiis.* MDCLXXXV.] 16mo, engraved title, pp. (14), 7-246, (2). 10 Plates. C. 58926

Pages 236-246 contain a poetical description of the discovery of the New World by Columbus.

The Parthenon, and Academician's Magazine: published by Undergraduates of Union College. ... *Schenectady.* 1832-34. 2 vols., 8vo. S. 58927

The Parthenon, containing Original Characteristic Papers by Living American Authors, illustrated by Darley ... and others. No. 1. *New York: Loomis, Griswold & Co.* [n. d.] 4to, pp. 40.

The Parthenon, or Literary and Scientific Museum. Edited by S. Woodworth. ... *New York.* 1827. 8vo, pp. 256. 58929

Le Parti Républicain, ses Doctrines et ses Hommes. Aux Français. *New York: Club Républicain Français.* 1860. 8vo, pp. 24. 58930

A Particular Account of a Monstrous Sea-Serpent, the largest ever seen in America. Which has lately made its appearance in Gloucester Harbor, Cape Ann, (Mass.) ... *Published at the Brattleboro' Book Store.* 1817. 16mo, pp. 24. Plate. S. 58931

Particular Account of the Battle of Bunker ... Hill. *See* [Bradford (A.)], Vol. II., No. 7228, *also* Vol. III., No. 9180.

A Particular Account of the Commencement and Progress of the Insurrection of the Negroes in St. Domingo, which began in August last. Being a Translation of the Speech made to the National Assembly, The 3d of November, 1791, by the Deputies from the General Assembly of the French Part of St. Domingo. [n. p.:] *Printed by Order of the National Assembly.* M.DCC.XCI. 8vo, pp. 36. + The Second Edition, With Notes and an Appendix, containing Extracts from authentic Papers. *London: J. Sewell.* M.DCC.XCII. 8vo, pp. iv, 47. J.C.B. 58932

Particular Account of the Dreadful Fire at Richmond, Virginia, December 26, 1811. Which destroyed the Theatre and the house adjoining, and in which more than sixty persons were either burnt to Death, or destroyed in attempting to make their escape. To which is added, Some Observations on Theatrical Performances; and, an Essay from the Virginia Argus. ... *Baltimore: J. Kingston.* 1812. 8vo, pp. 46. 58933

Particular Account of the Great Fire. *See* Vol. XIII. 54925.

Particular and Impartial Narrative of the late Mutiny and Running away with the Chesterfield Man of War off the Coast of Guinea. *London.* 1749. 8vo. 58934

The Particular Case. *See* Vol. VII., No. 27082.

PARTICULAR SYNOD. *See* Vol. XIII., No. 53854.

The Particulars and Inventories of the Estates of the late Sub-Governor, Deputy-Governor, and Directors of the South-Sea Company: and of Robert Surman late Deputy-Cashier, and of John Grigsby late Accomptant of said Company. Together with the Abstracts of the same. ... *London: Printed for Jacob Tonson, Bernard Lintot, and Wm. Taylor.* MDCCXXI. 2 vols., folio. C.

The Particulars of an Indian Treaty at Conestogoe. Between his Excellency Sir William Keith, Bart. Governor of Pennsylvania, and the Deputies of the Five Nations. *Dublin: Reprinted by Elizabeth Sadleir, for Samuel Fuller.* 1723. 8vo, pp. 48. P.

Particulars of the dreadful Tragedy in Richmond, on the morning of the 19th July, 1852; being a full account of the awful Murder of the Winston Family by Jane and John Williams. *Richmond.* 1852. 8vo. 58937

The Particulars of the Enquiry into Mr. Benjamin Wooley's Conduct; and his being Stationed by the Court of Directors of the South Sea Company, First Factor at Porto Bello and Panama. Humbly dedicated to Thomas Woodford, Esq. *London: A. Dodd.* 1735. 8vo, pp. 32. J.C.B. 58938

Mr. Wooley was a man of but twenty-one years of age, and it was thought that one so young and inexperienced should not be placed in so responsible a position, in which he was charged with improper acts. Hence this investigation or inquiry.

Particulars of the late Duel. *See* Burr (A.), Vol. III. 9430.

Particulars of the late Melancholy and Shocking Tragedy which happened at Salem, June 17, 1773. *Boston.* 1773. 8vo.

Particulars respecting the Schools for Negro Children, &c., under the Direction of Moravian Missionaries, in the West Indies. No. V. *London.* 1831. 8vo, pp. 12. 58940

El Partido conservador en Mexico. *Mexico.* 1855. 8vo, pp. 44. 58941

Parties in Massachusetts. [n. p. 1850?] 8vo, pp. 16. W.

The Partisan. *See* [Simms (W. G.)]

PARTON (J.) The Danish Islands: Are we bound in honor to pay for them? By James Parton. *Boston: Fields, Osgood, & Co.* 1869. 8vo, pp. 76. 58943

PARTON. Eminent Women of the Age; being Narratives of the Lives and Deeds of the most Prominent Women of the Present Generation. By J. Parton, H. Greeley, ... [and others]. *Hartford: S. M. Betts & Co.* 1868. 8vo, pp. 628. 14 Plates. + [*Ibid.*] 1869. 8vo. 58944

PARTON. Famous Americans of Recent Times. By James Parton .... *Boston: Ticknor and Fields.* 1867. 8vo, pp. (4), 473. Portrait. C. 58945

Contains sketches of Henry Clay, Daniel Webster, John C. Calhoun, John Randolph, Stephen Girard and his College, James Gordon Bennett and the "New York Herald," Charles Goodyear, Henry Ward Beecher and his Church, Commodore Vanderbilt, Theodosia Burr, and John Jacob Astor.

PARTON. General Butler in New Orleans. History of the Administration of the Department of the Gulf in the year 1862; with an Account of the Capture of New Orleans, and a Sketch of the previous Career of the General, Civil and Military. By James Parton .... *New York: Mason Brothers.* 1863. 12mo, pp. 649. Portrait and Plan. + Fourth Edition. [*Ibid.*] 12mo, pp. 661. 2 Portraits. + Fifth Edition. [*Ibid.*] + Tenth Edition. [*Ibid.*] + Fifteenth Edition. [*Ibid.*] H. + People's Edition. [*Ibid.*] 8vo, pp. 174. 58946

PARTON. General Butler in New Orleans. Von James Parton. Nach der Englischen Ausgabe bearbeitet von Hermann Roster und Edmund Remack. *New York: Mason Brothers.* 1864. 8vo, pp. 368. Portrait. 58947

PARTON. How New York City is Governed. By James Parton. *Boston: Ticknor and Fields.* 1866. 16mo, pp. 48. B.

PARTON. The Life and Times of Aaron Burr, Lieutenant-Colonel in the Army of the Revolution, United States Senator, Vice-President of the United States, etc. By J. Parton .... *New York: Mason Brothers.* 1858. 8vo, pp. 706. 2 Portraits and Engravings. + Eleventh Edition. [*Ibid.*] + [*Ibid.*] 1859. + New and Enlarged Edition. [*Ibid.*] 1864. 2 vols., 12mo, pp. xxii, 443; xii, 431. 2 Plates. C. 58949

PARTON. The Life and Times of Benjamin Franklin. By James Parton .... *New York: Mason Brothers.* 1864. 2 vols.,

12mo, pp. 627; 707. 4 Portraits. + [*Ibid.*] 1865. 2 vols., rl. 8vo, pp. 627; 707. 4 Portraits. + *Boston: Ticknor and Fields.* 1867. 2 vols., 12mo, pp. 627; 707. 4 Portraits. H. 58950

Of the edition of 1865 only one hundred copies were printed.

PARTON. Life of Andrew Jackson, By James Parton. *New-York: N. P. Fitzpatrick.* [n. d.] 8vo. 58951

This edition was not completed.

PARTON. Life of Andrew Jackson. ... By James Parton .... *New York: Mason Brothers.* 1860. 3 vols., 8vo. + [*Ibid.*] 1861. 3 vols., 8vo, pp. xxx, (2), 29, 636; 672; 734. Portraits. + *Boston.* 1866. 3 vols., 8vo. 58952

PARTON. Life of Andrew Jackson, condensed from the Author's "Life of Andrew Jackson," in Three Volumes. *New York: Mason Brothers.* 1863. 8vo, pp. 479. Portrait. 58953

PARTON. The Life of Horace Greeley, Editor of the New York Tribune. By J. Parton. ... *New York: Mason Brothers.* 1855. 12mo, pp. 442. 2 Portraits, Plates. + New Edition, brought down to the Present Time. *New York: Derby & Miller.* 1868. 12mo, pp. 598. Portraits and Plates + *Boston: Fields, Osgood & Co.* 1869. 12mo, pp. 598. 2 Portraits, 7 Plates.

PARTON. Das Leben Horace Greeley's. Nach dem Englischen des James Parton von Adolph Nahmen. *Boston.* 1872. 8vo, pp. iv, 126. S. 58955

PARTON. Life of John Jacob Astor. To which is appended, a Copy of his last Will. By James Parton. *New York: American News Company.* 1865. 12mo, pp. vi, 13-121. B. 58956

PARTON. People's Book of Biography; or, Short Lives of the most Interesting Persons of all Ages and Countries. ... By James Parton .... *A. S. Hale & Company, Hartford.* 1868. 8vo, pp. xii, 624. 12 Plates. C. 58957

PARTON. Sketches of Men of Progress. By James Parton, Bayard Taylor, Hon. Amos Kendall, Rev. E. D. Mayo, J. Alexander Patten. . And other writers. ... *New York and Hartford Publishing Co.* 1870-71. 4to. 50 Portraits. C. + [*Ibid.*] 8vo. 58 Portraits. C. 58958

Also: Manual for the Instruction of "Rings," Rail Road and Political; with a History of the Grand Chicago and North-Western "Ring," etc. Edited by James Parton. *New York: A. Brentam.* 1866. 24mo, pp. 76.—Smoking and Drinking ... *Boston: Ticknor & Fields.* 1865. 16mo, pp. viii, 151.

[PARTON (Sarah Payson Willis).] Fern Leaves from Fanny's Port-Folio. With ... Designs by Fred. M. Coffin. *Auburn: Derby and Miller.* 1853. 12mo, pp. (2), 400. 7 Plates. + Second Series. *Auburn: Miller, Orton & Mulligan.* 1854. 12mo, pp. (2), 400. 6 Plates. + *London: Clark, Beeton & Co.* [n. d.] 16mo, pp. xi, 211. S. 58959

[PARTON.] Fresh Leaves. By Fanny Fern. *New York: Mason Brothers.* 1857. 18mo, pp. 336. 58960

[PARTON.] The Life and Beauties of Fanny Fern. ... *New York: H. Long and Brother.* 1855. 12mo, pp. 330. 58961

Also: Folly as it flies; hit at by Fanny Fern. *New York: G. W. Carleton & Co.* 1868. 12mo, pp. 355.—Ginger-Snaps. ... *New York: Carleton.* 1870. 12mo, pp. 312.—Little Ferns for Fanny's Little Friends. ... With Original Designs by Fred. M. Coffin. *Auburn: Derby & Miller.* 1854. 16mo, pp. 298.—Rose Clark. ... *New York: Mason Brothers.* 1856. 12mo, pp. 417.—Ruth Hall; a Domestic Tale of the present time .... *New York.* 1855. 12mo.

PARTRIDGE [Alden]. Capt. Partridge's Lecture on Education. [*Middletown, Conn.* 1828.] 8vo, pp. 12. B. 58962

PARTRIDGE. Capt. Partridge's Lecture on National Defence. [Windsor, Vt., June, 1821. n. p. n. d.] 8vo, pp. 14. B.

PARTRIDGE. Journal of An Excursion. *See* Vol. IX. 36701.

Also: Catalogue of the Officers and Cadets of the American Literary, Scientifick, and Military Academy, Norwich, Vt. ... *Windsor, Vt.* 1828. 8vo, pp. 20.—Prospectus of the American Literary, Scientifick, and Military Academy, Norwich, Vt. ... *Windsor.* [1820.] 8vo.—Prospectus and Internal Regulations of the American Literary, Scientifick, and Military Academy; to be opened at Middletown, ... Connecticut, in ... August, 1825. [n. p. n. d.] 8vo, pp. 23. *See also* Vol. XIII., No. 56497.

PARTRIDGE (A.) The Memory of the Just. A Memorial of the Hon. William Jay, who died October 4, 1858. Preached in Bedford, N. Y., September 18, 1859. By Rev. Alfred Partridge. *New York: R. Lockwood & Sons.* 1860. 8vo, pp. 20.

[PARTRIDGE (Copernicus).] *See* Vol. XIII., No. 55542.

PARTRIDGE (John). Merlinus Liberatus. Almanack for the Year 1705. *London.* 1705. 16mo. M. 58965

Continued to 1836 or later.

PARTRIDGE. Monthly Observations and Predictions for this Present Year. ... *Boston.* 1697. 16mo. 58966

PARTRIDGE (J. A.) The False Nation and its "Bases;" or, why the South can't stand. By J. Arthur Partridge .... *London: Edward Stanford.* 1864. 8vo, pp. xiii, 60. B. 58967

PARTRIDGE. The Making of the American Nation; or, The Rise and Decline of Oligarchy in the West. By J. Arthur Partridge .... *London: Edward Stanford.* 1866. 8vo, pp. (4), xxxvii, 523. + *Philadelphia: J. B. Lippincott & Co.* 1866. 8vo, pp. (4), xxxvii, 523. 58968

PARTRIDGE. On Democracy. By J. Arthur Partridge .... *London: Trübner & Co.* 1866. 8vo, pp. xxiii, (4), 418. + *Philadelphia: J. B. Lippincott and Co.* 1866. 8vo, pp. xxiii, (4), 418.

The Party in Power, and the new Constitution. [Signed A. *Albany.* 1848?] 8vo, pp. 8. S. 58970

Party Satire Satirized, A Poem. *London: S. Bladon.* 1779. 8vo. 58971

A lick at the lashers, who are represented as a pack of seditious libellers.

"For injur'd poor America they bawl,
Rejoic'd to see her rise by England's fall;
Thus politics makes rebels of us all."

See "Monthly Review," LX. 229.

Party Spirit Exposed; or, Remarks on the Times; to which is added some Important Hints to the Ladies. By a Gent. of New York. *New York.* 1799. 12mo, pp. 24. N. 58972

Party-Tyranny. *See* [DeFoe (D.)], Vol. V., No. 19288.

PARVIN (R. J.) Soldier-Life and Every-Day Battles. With Biographical Illustrations, Anecdotes, etc. By Rev. R. J. Parvin. *New York.* 1863. 18mo, pp. 107. 58973

PARVIN (T. S.) An Address, Delivered before the ... Grand Lodge of Iowa ... June 4, 1863. By Theodore S. Parvin .... [n. p. n. d.] 8vo, pp. 16. 58974

PARVIN. The Constitutions of the Free Masons, with the Constitution and By-Laws of the Grand Lodge of Iowa; ... By T. S. Parvin .... Seventh Edition. *Des Moines.* 1866. 8vo, pp. 193. 58975

Also: The Book of Constitutions, and the Constitution, By-Laws, and General Regulations of the Grand Lodge of Iowa. ... *Burlington.* 1850. 12mo, pp. 192.—Catalogue of the Library of the Grand Lodge of Iowa. ... 1873. ... *Iowa City.* 1873. 8vo, pp. 144. (Earlier editions, 1849, 1856, 1858.)—A Catalogue of ... Books, on Masonry ... in the Library of the Grand Lodge of Iowa, June, 1873. ... *Iowa City.* 1873. 8vo, pp. 100.—Constitution, By-Laws, and General Regulations of the Grand Lodge of Iowa. ... *Muscatine, Iowa.* 1854. 8vo, pp. 44.—Masonic Code for Trials and Punishments .... Revised Edition by W. E. Miller. *Davenport.* 18—. 8vo.—Report on Foreign Correspondence ... May 31, 1856 .... [n. p. n. d.] 8vo.

PARVIN (T.) Address on the Life and Character of Andrew Wylie, D.D., late President of the State University of Indiana. Delivered before the Alumni ... by Theophilus Parvin, M.D., ... July 14th, 1858, at Bloomington. *Indianapolis: Cameron & Mc-Neely, Printers.* 1858. 8vo, pp. 42. S. 58976

Pascagoula River. Letters laid before the Senate respecting Obstructions at the Mouth of the Pascagoula River. [*Washington.* 1828.] 8vo. 58977

PASCAL (C.) Abraham Lincoln Sa Vie, son Caractère, son Administration. Par César Pascal. *Paris: Grassart.* 1865. 12mo, pp. (8), 232. B. 58978

PASCAL. A travers l'Atlantique et dans le Nouveau-Monde. Par César Pascal. Deuxième Édition. *Paris: Grassart.* 1870. 12mo, pp. (8), 395. B. 58979

PASCALIS (F.) An Account of the Contagious Epidemic Yellow Fever, which prevailed in Philadelphia in the Summer and Autumn of 1797; comprising the Questions of its Causes and Domestic Origin, Characters, Medical Treatment, and Preventives. By Felix Pascalis Ouviere, M.D. ... *Philadelphia: ... Snowden & McCorkle.* 1798. 8vo, pp. viii, 180. P. 58980

PASCALIS. An Exposition of the Dangers of Interment in Cities ... . With Additions by Felix Pascalis ... . *New-York: W. B. Gilley.* 1823. 8vo, pp. 167. B. 58981

[PASCALIS.] A Statement of the Occurrences during a Malignant Yellow Fever, in ... New York, in ... 1819. ... *New-York: Printed by William A. Mercein.* 1819. 8vo, pp. 52. B.

Also: Directions for Silk-Worm Nurseries, and the Cultivation of the Mulberry Tree. ... *New York.* 1829. 8vo. — Eulogy on the Life and Character of the Hon. Samuel Latham Mitchill, M.D. ... at New-York ... October 15th, 1831. ... *New-York.* 1831. 8vo, pp. 25. S.

PASCHAL (Creuzé). Conspiration contre la République. ... *Imprimé à Paris et réimprimé à New York, chez J. Delafond, ...* [*an III*]. 8vo, pp. 23. + *Philadelphia.* 1795. 8vo. 58983

Also: Quels sont les coupables dans l'affaire de S. Domingue. ... [n. p.] *An III.* 8vo, pp. 18. *See also* Saint Domingo.

PASCHAL (G. W.) Concluding Argument of Hon. George W. Paschal ... in the Case of William McGarrahan ... . *Washington City: M'Gill & Witherow, Printers.* 1870. 8vo, pp. 121.

PASCHAL. The Constitution of the United States Defined and Carefully Annotated. By George W. Paschal ... . *Washington, D. C.: W. H. & O. H. Morrison.* 1868. 12mo, pp. xxviii, 407. B. 58985

Also: Lecture before the American Union Academy of Literature, Science and Art, March 7, 1870. ... *Washington.* 1870. 12mo. — Letter to the President in behalf of Lodovic P. Alford and others. ... *Washington.* 1870. 8vo. — Ninety-Four Years. Agnes Paschal. ... [*Washington.*] 1871. 12mo, pp. 361. 2 Facsimiles. — Speech ... in the Case of William McGarraghan. *Washington.* 1869. 8vo.

PASCHALL (E.) Old Times; or, Tennessee History for Boys and Girls. By Edwin Paschall. *Nashville.* 1869. 18mo.

PASCHOUD (*Mr.*) Historico-Political Geography: Or, A Particular Description Of the Several Countries in the World; in their Situation, ... &c. ... The Second Edition, with Additions. *London: William France.* 1729. 8vo, pp. (2), xiv, 395, (5).

PASCUAL DE ANDAGOYA. *See* Vol. V., No. 18783.

PASCUAL (A. D. de). Um Epeysodio da Historia Patria. As quatro derradeiras noites dos inconfidentes de Minas Geraes [1792] por A. D. de Pascual. *Rio de Janeiro.* 1868. 8vo, pp. x, 138. 58988

Also: Rasgos memoraveis do Senhor Dom Pedro I, imperador de Brasil. ... *Rio de Janeiro.* 1862. 8vo.

Paseo pintoresco por la Isla de Cuba. *See* Vol. V., No. 17795.

PASEVINIUS (A.) Antonii Pasevinii Cultura ingeniorum. Septima edito cui accessit vera narratio fructicis (florum et fructuum novissime in occid. Indies nascentium). *Coloniæ Agrippinæ.* 1610. 8vo. 58989

PASH (M.) The Pasha Papers, Epistles of Mohammed Pash, ... from New York to his Friend Abel Ben Hassen. *New York: Charles Scribner.* MDCCCLIX. 12mo, pp. 312. BA. 58990

PASKELL (T.) Abstract of a Letter from Thomas Paskell of Pennsilvania, to his Friend J. J. of Chippenham. [n. p.] 1683. Folio, 1 leaf. 58991

An interesting paper, full of curious information about the early settling of Pennsylvania.

PASLEY (C. W.) Essay on the Military Policy and Institutions of the British Empire. By C. W. Pasley ... . Third Edition. *London: Edmund Lloyd.* 1811. 8vo, pp. xx, 531, (1).

Includes many references to American topics.

PASQUAL (A. R.) Descubrimiento de la Aguja Náutica, de la Situacion de la América, del arte de navegar, y de un nuevo Método para el adelantamiento en las artes y ciencias: Disertacion En que se manifiesta que el primer Autor de todo lo expuesto es el Beato Raymundo Lulio, ... Con un Apéndice De la enseñanza pública, de los progresos de la literatura, y otros puntos históricos pertenecientes á Mallorca. Su Autor El R. P. Mtro. Don Antonio Raymundo Pasqual ... . *Con Licencia: Madrid: En la Imprenta de Manuel Gonzalez.* MDCCLXXXIX. 8vo, pp. (8), 320. J.C.B. 58993

A discursive work, proving that its author was a learned man, but containing little about the discovery of the mariner's compass. The appendix contains proofs that Father Bernardo Boil, the Benedictine, who accompanied Columbus on his second voyage, and said the first mass in the New World, was not he of the same name who founded the first convent of his order in Spain.

PASQUIER DE DOMMARTIN (H.) *See* Du Pasquier (H.), VI.

PASQUIN, *pseudon.* *See* [Williams (John)].

Pasquin and Marforie on the Peace, but particularly pending the late War and in Negotiating the Present Peace. *London.* 1748. 8vo. 58994

Relates to American and Spanish affairs, etc.

PASQUINO, *pseudon.* *See* [McLaughlin (J. F.)], Vol. XI. 43499

PASSÆUS (C.) Effigies Regvm ac Principium, eorum scilicet quov vic ac potentia in re nautica seu Marina præ cæteris spectabilis est. ... Summa diligentia et artifico depictæ, et tabellis æneis incisæ a Crispiano Passæo Zelando. ... [*Coloniæ Agrippinæ, anno* 1598. *ipso die Theophotiæ Colonienses.*] Folio, pp. (19). 3 Plates, 21 Portraits. 58995

Includes portraits and notices of Columbus, Vespucius and Drake.

PASSÆUS. Hortus Floridus. In quo rariorum & minus vulgarium florum Icones ad vivam veramquæ formam accuratissime delineatæ. ... *Arnhemii.* 1624. Obl. 4to. Plates. 58996

Includes some American plants.

Un Passage de la Cordillère des Andes. Passe de la Cumbre entre Mendoza et Santa-Rosa, sur la route de Buenos-Ayres a Valparaiso en 1860. *Hâvre.* 1862. 8vo. 58997

The Passage of the Isthmus. *See* [Carrington (J. W.)], III.

Passaic. *See* [Ward (Thomas)].

PASSAIC FALLS. Visitors' Guide to Passaic Falls. *Paterson: Van Derhoven.* 1859. 12mo. 58998

The Rights and Privileges of the PASSAICK AND HACKINSACK [*sic*] Bridge Company Examined; ... . By Monitor. With a few Introductory Observations. By Justice. ... *Newark: Printed by W. Tuttle.* 1811. 8vo, pp. 31. 58999

PASSERINI (——). Notizie sulla moltiplicazione dell' Uccello Americano Paroaria Cucullata. ... *Firenze.* 1841. Folio. Plate.

Passing Bell. ... *Boston.* 1789. 8vo. 59001

Passio gloriosi martyris. *See* [Martin de Valencia], Vol. XI.

Passion Flowers. *See* [Howe (Julia Ward)], VIII. 33318.

The Past: a Fragment. *See* [Bent (N. T.)], Vol. II. 4756.

The Past and Present—Freedom National, Slavery Sectional. A Document for the People. ... *Washington: Buell & Blanchard, Printers.* 1853. 8vo, pp. 16, 31. H. 59002

Past and Present. *See* [Carroll (J.)], Vol. III., No. 11076.

Past, Present and Future of Greenbacks, including the National Currency Law. By a Republican Farmer [C. Alvord?]. *Milwaukee: Hanlon & Richardson.* 1868. 8vo, pp. 50. C.

The Past, the Present, and the Future. *See* [Gales (J.)], VII.

The Past, the Present and the Future of our Country. Interesting and Important Correspondence between the Opposition Members of the Legislature of Virginia, and John Minor Botts, Jan. 17, 1860. [n. p. n. d.] 8vo, pp. 16. 59004

PASTEUR (J. D.) Reizen naar den Stillen Oceaan en rondom de Wereld, vertaald door J. D. Pasteur. *Leyden.* 1797–1803. 13 vols., 8vo. Atlas of 133 Plates and Maps in folio. 59005

Voyages to the Pacific Ocean and round the world.

The Pastime. No. 1. ... [*Schenectady.*] 1807. 8vo. Cont'd.

Edited by John Howard Payne, author of "Home, Sweet Home."

PASTO. Memoria del Gobernador de Pasto á la Camara provincial en sus sesiones de 1843. [n. p. n. d.] 8vo, pp. 16.

PASTOR (Antonio). Tony Pastor's New Union Song Book. *New York: Dick and Fitzgerald.* [n. d.] 18mo, pp. 72. 59008

Also: 201 Bowery Songster. ... *New York: Dick & Fitzgerald.* [1867.] 24mo, pp. 72.

PASTOR (The), *pseudon.* Five Years of Ministerial Life: Being a Discourse delivered Dec. 2, 1860, at the Second Presbyterian Church, Columbus, Ohio. By the Pastor [Edward D. Morris]. Together with an Appendix, briefly showing the present condition of the Church. *Columbus: Printed by Harris & Hurd.* 1861. 8vo, pp. 24. 59009

The Pastor; a Poem. *New-York: F. & R. Lockwood.* 1821. 16mo, pp. xvi, 500. C. 59010

A Pastor's Jottings; or, Striking Scenes during a Ministry of Thirty-Five Years. *New-York.* [1864.] 12mo, pp. 348. 6 Plates. C. 59011

The Pastor's Wife; or, Memoirs of [Mrs.] E[liza] M. S[aunders]. *New York: Little, Rennie & Co.* 1867. 18mo, pp. 198. Portrait. C. 59012

A Pastoral Address to the Clergy and Laity of the Protestant Episcopal Church in the United States of America, From the House of Bishops of said Church, Assembled in General Convention, At New-Haven, Connecticut, May, A. D. 1811. *New York.* 1811. 8vo, pp. 13. 59013

PASTORAL AID SOCIETY. *See* Vol. XIII., No. 53855.

Pastoral de illmo. Sr. Obispo de Cuba [D. Santiago Joseph de Hechavarria] para todo el venerable clero secular de su diocesis. *Havana: Imprenta del Compnto* [sic] *Eclesiastico. Año de* 1770. 4to, pp. 11. 59014

Pastoral Desires. *See* [Mather (C.)], Vol. XI., No. 46449.

Pastoral Letter from a Minister to his Flock, who remained in the City during the Pestilence of 1798. *Philadelphia.* 1799. 8vo, pp. 12. 59015

Pastoral Letter from the Bishops of the Protestant Episcopal Church, to the Clergy and Laity of the Church in the Confederate States of America, delivered before the General Council in ... Augusta, ... Nov. 22, 1862. [*Augusta.* 1862.] 8vo, pp. 16. + *Baltimore: W. M. Innes.* [n. d.] 8vo, pp. 15. + [*New York.* n. d.] 8vo, pp. 15. B. 59016

A | Pastoral Letter, | from | The Reverend Synod of | New-York and Philadelphia | convened at New-York, | to | The Churches subject to their | care. | *New-York:* | *Printed by H. Gaine,* ... 1766. 8vo, pp. 8. 59017

Pastoral Letter of the Archbishop and Bishops of the Province of New York, in Provincial Council assembled, to the Clergy and Laity of their Charge. *New York: Dunigan & Bro.* 1854. 8vo, pp. 16. S. 59018

Pastoral Letter of the ... Archbishop of Baltimore, and the ... Prelates of the Roman Catholic Church of the United States ... Oct. 1829, to the Roman Catholic Laity of the United States ... *Baltimore: James Myers.* 1829. 8vo, pp. 29. S. 59019

See also [Mareschal (Ambrose)], Vol. XI., No. 44522, *and* [Spalding (M. J.)]

Pastoral Letter of the Bishops. *See* Nos. 43323 *and* 51898.

Pastoral Letter of the First National Council of the United States, held at Baltimore in May, 1852. *Baltimore: Murphy & Co.* 1852. 8vo, pp. 16. S. 59020

Pastoral Letter of the First Provincial Council of Cincinnati, to the Clergy and Laity. *Cincinnati: John P. Walsh.* 1855. 8vo, pp. 19. 59021

A Pastoral Letter of the House of Bishops, of the Protestant Episcopal Church in the United States ... . *Philadelphia: Bradford and Inskeep.* 1814. 8vo, pp. 14. 59022

... Pastoral Letter of the House of Bishops, to the Clergy and Laity ... 1868. [*New York.* 1868.] 8vo, pp. 7. B. 59023

Pastoral Letter of the Presbytery. *See* Nos. 12063, 52524.

Pastoral Letter of the Synod. *See* Vol. XII., No. 48777.

Pastoral Letter, to Families. *See* [Mather (C.)], XI. 46451.

Pastoral Letter to the Churches. *See* Vol. VIII., No. 30550.

A Pastoral Letter to the Clergy and the Laity of the Protestant Episcopal Church, from the Bishops ... assembled in convention in ... Philadelphia, this 24th day of May, ... one thousand eight hundred and twenty. *Philadelphia: S. Potter, & Co.* 1820. 8vo, pp. 24. P. 59024

Pastoral Letter to the English. *See* [Mather (C.)], No. 46450.

A Pastoral Letter to the Members of the Protestant Episcopal Church in the United States ... from the House of Bishops ... assembled in General Convention at Baltimore, May, 1808. *New York: Printed by T. & J. Swords.* 1808. 8vo, pp. 25.

Pastoral Letter, to the Parishioners. *See* [Jackson (C. D.)]

Pastoral Report. *See* [Clark (S. A.)], Vol. IV., No. 13367.

Pastoral Sketches. From the "American Pastor's Journal." *Springfield: G. & C. Merriam.* 1834. 18mo, pp. 124. 59026

PASTORET (D'Emm.) Motion d'Ordre sur l'état actuel de nos rapports politiques et commerciaux avec les États-Unis de l'Amérique Septentrionale. Séance de 2 Messidor an V. *Paris: De l'Imprimerie Nationale, An* 5 [1797]. 8vo, pp. 26. J.C.B.

PASTORIUS (F. D.) Umständige Geogra- | phische | Beschreibung | Der zu allerletzt erfundenen | Provintz | Pensylva- | niæ, | In denen End-Gräntzen | Americæ | In der West-Welt gelegen, | Durch | Franciscum Danielem | Pastorium, | J. V. Lic. und Friedens Richtern | daselbsten. | Worbey angehencket sind eini- | ge notable Begebenheiten, und | Bericht-Schreiben an dessen Herrn | Vattern | Melchiorem Adamum Pasto- | rium, | Und andere gute Freunde. | *Franckfurt und Leipzig,* | *Zufinden bey Andreas Otto.* 1700. | 8vo, pp. (12), 140. P. 59028

PASTRANA (A. M.) Cancion. Real Histórica á la milagrosa Imagen de María Santísima Señora nuestra de Guadalupe de México que escribia ... Antonio Morales Pastrana ... . Y dá á la Estampa ... Silvestre Florido. *México: Juan Joseph Guillena Carrascoso.* 1697. 8vo, pp. 34. 59029

See Bartolache's "Manifiesto," p. 31.

PATAGONIA. An Account of the Giants lately discovered. In a Letter to a Friend in the Country. *London: F. Noble.* MDCCLXVI. 12mo, pp. 31. 59030

Commodore Byron, on his return from his voyage to the South Sea, reported that he had seen five hundred giants on horseback on the coast of Patagonia, an opinion that prevailed till quite recently. The object of the author of this tract was to ridicule and disprove the statement of Byron. *See* our Vol. III., No. 9732.

... A Brief Explanation Relative to the End of the ... Missionaries of The Patagonian Missionary Society in Terra del Fuego, In ... 1851, ... founded on Capt. Morshead's Despatch. *Bristol.* [1852.] 12mo, pp. 24. 59031

Correspondence respecting the Establishment of a Welsh Colony on the River Chupat. *London.* 1867. 8vo. 59032

PATAVINUS (J. A. M.) Geographiæ Universæ, Veteries et Novæ. ... *Coloniæ.* 1597. 2 vols., 4to. Maps. 59033

Includes a map of America.

A Patent for Plymouth in New-England. To which is annexed, Extracts from the Records of that Colony, &c. &c. *Boston; New-England: Printed by John Draper.* 1751. 4to, pp. (2), 19, (1). 59034

Dated August 14, 1751. Printed to attract settlers.

A Patent Grant by King William for Incorporating a Society for Propagation of the Gospel in Foreign Parts. *London.* 1702. Folio. 59035

Patents. Alphabetical List. *See* [Hunter (A.)], VIII. 33909.

Catalogue of the Library of the Patent Office. *Washington.* 1847. 8vo. C. 59036

A Digest of Patents. *See* Ellsworth (H. L.), VI. 22344.

Exposition of Part of the Patent Law. *See* [Evans (O.)], VI.

Information to Persons having business to transact at the Patent Office ... . *Washington.* 1851. 8vo, pp. 29. 59037

See also Vol. VI., No. 22345.

List of Patents granted by the United States, for the Encouragement of Arts and Sciences, alphabetically arranged from 1790 to 1820. *Washington.* 1820. 8vo. + From 1790 to 1828. *Washington: S. Alfred Elliot.* 1828. 8vo, pp. 118, xxiv, 8.

List of Patents for Inventions and Designs, issued by the United States from 1790 to 1847; with the Patent Laws and Notes of Decisions of the Courts of the United States ... . Compiled ... under the direction of Edmund Burke, Commissioner of Patents. *Washington.* 1847. 8vo, pp. lxxv, 606. S.

The Patent Laws of the United States, together with information to persons having business to transact at the Patent Office. *New York.* 1845. 8vo. 59040

The Patent Laws of the United States, with the Decisions of the Courts of the United States; also, the Opinions of the Hon. William Cranch upon appeals from the decisions of the Commissioners of Patents. *Washington.* 1848. 8vo, pp. 150. 59041

Patent Laws. [*Washington:*] *Gideon & Co. Print.* [1851.] 8vo, pp. 18. + [1861.] 8vo, pp. vi, 26. + 1870. 8vo, pp. 35.

... Patent Office. Report from The Commissioner of Patents, transmitting information, in relation to ... his office for ... 1837. Jan. 17, 1838. [*Washington.* 1838.] 8vo, pp. 52. s. Continued annually. 59043

This first report was made by Commissioner Ellsworth; from 1837 to 1840 inclusive, these reports formed an appendix to the President's message; after this date they were published separately. To the report for 1843 was appended a list of the claims of the patents issued, which was published in the form of an appendix until 1849–50, when it was embodied in the report. By an act of Congress, March 3, 1849, the commissioner was required to add to his report the Agricultural Department. Previous to 1849–50 the Mechanical and Agricultural Departments of the report were published in one volume; since that time the volumes have appeared annually. The report for 1853 was the first in which the patents issued were illustrated by cuts.

The Patent Right Gazette. A Monthly Illustrated Journal of the Industrial Arts ... . *New York.* [1870.] 4to. Continued.

Patent Right Oppression; or, Knavery Detected, in an Address, to unite all good people to obtain a repeal of the Patent Laws. By Patrick N. I. Elisha, Esq. ... To which is added an alarming Law Case: Also, Reflections on the Patent Laws. Illustrated by Notes and Anecdotes by the Editor. *Philadelphia: R. Folwell & G. Allchin.* 1813. 8vo, pp. 189. P. 59045

Corrected title of our No. 22182, Vol. vi.

Patents of Canada. *See* Vol. iii., No. 10539, *add* Vol. ii. from 1849 to 1855. *Toronto.* 1865. 8vo.

A Popular Catalogue. *See* [Hunter (A.)], Vol. viii. 33910.

Proceedings at the Opening of the Patent Office Fair, under the Auspices of the Ladies' Relief Association, District of Columbia, February 22, 1864. *Washington.* 1864. 8vo, pp. 30.

Report of the [Confederate] Commissioner. *See* No. 15376.

Report on the State of the Patent Office. *Washington.* 1831. 8vo. 59047

Rules and Directions for Proceedings in the Patent Office, November 1, 1869. *Washington.* 1869. 8vo, pp. 48. 59048

Pater (A. I.) Een cort ... Verhael. *See* Vol. ii. 7573.

Pater (Ezra). The Book of Knowledge, ... translated by W. Lilly. *Canaan, N. Y.* 1794. 8vo. 59049

Pater (J. R.) Argument of John R. Pater on the Trial of William Landon, acquitted July 21, 1855, on a charge of Violating the Prohibitory Law. *Albany.* 1855. 8vo, pp. 52. 59050

Paterson (D.) A Topographical Description of the Island of Grenada; surveyed by Monsieur Pinel in 1763, ... with the Addition of English Names, Alterations of Property, [etc.] ... By Lieutenant Daniel Paterson ... . *London: W. Faden.* MDCCLXXX. 4to, pp. 13. 59051

Paterson (Paul). *See* Playfair (Hugo).

Paterson (T. J.) Speech of Hon. Thomas J. Paterson on Post-Office Reform, &c.; delivered ... March 1, 1845. *Washington.* 1845. 8vo, pp. 13. 59052

Paterson (W.) Bill for Relief of William Paterson, Esq., as regards his Claim upon the Stock of the African and Indian Company of Scotland, agreeable to the Treaty of Union, and in Consequence of the Reduction of the Coin of Scotland to the English Standard. *London.* 1714. Folio. 59053

Paterson was the celebrated projector of the Bank of England, and of the Scotch Darien Company, etc. *See also* Vol. v., Nos. 18565 *and* 18573.

Paterson. Central America; by William Paterson, the Merchant-Statesman. From a MS. in the British Museum, 1701. ... Edited by S. Bannister, M.A. ... *London: Trübner & Co.* 1857. 8vo, pp. 62, 6. Map. B. 59054

Paterson. A Memorial Addressed to William the Third, on Darien; ... by William Paterson. *London.* 1852. 8vo, pp. (6), 63, (1). Map. 59055

Paterson (W.) The Charge of Judge Paterson To the Jury, in the case of Van Horn's Lessee against Dorrance: Tried at a Circuit Court for the United States, held at Philadelphia, April Term, 1795: Wherein the controverted title to the Wyoming Lands, between the claimants under Pennsylvania and Connecticut received a decision. *Philadelphia: Samuel H. Smith.* 1796. 8vo, pp. 41, (2). + *Philadelphia.* [1801.] 8vo, pp. 24.

Paterson (W. B.) An Oration, ... February 22d, 1815, before the New-Jersey Washington Benevolent Society, in ... New-Brunswick. By William B. Paterson. *New-Brunswick: Printed by L. Deare, & G. L. Austin.* 1815. 8vo, pp. 19. BA.

Paterson, *N. J.* The Charter and Ordinances of the City of Paterson. *Paterson, N. J.: T. Warren, Printer.* 1851. 8vo, pp. 36. 59058

Paterson City Directory ... 1857. Compiled by W. H. Boyd. *Paterson.* [n. d.] 12mo, pp. 168. Continued. S. 59059

Report and Explanation of a Survey for a Railroad from Paterson to New York. *Paterson.* 1829. 16mo, pp. 15. 59060

Report on the Origin and Increase of the Paterson Manufactories, and the intended Diversion of their Waters by the Morris Canal Company; also on Post Rail Roads, as the means of Cheap Conveyance throughout New-Jersey, of bringing Susquehanna Coal to the Iron Mines and Forges, and to supply Paterson and New York; also on a Method of supplying the City of New York with water from the Great Falls of the Passaic. *Paterson: Printed by Day & Burnett.* 1828. 8vo, pp. 60. 59061

A Statement, showing the Condition and Prospects of the Paterson and Hudson River Railroad Co. on First April, 1835. [n. p. n. d.] 8vo, pp. 4. P. 59062

Supplement to Charter, and By-Laws, Standing Resolutions, and Ordinances of the City Council of Paterson. *Paterson: L. R. Steele, Printer.* 1852. 8vo, pp. 28, (1). 59063

Also: Supplement to Charter, and Ordinances ... . *Paterson, N. J.: T. Warren, Printer.* 1854. 8vo, pp. 1416, vii.

Pateshall (R.) Pride Humbled, or, Mr. Hobby chastised: Being some Remarks on said Hobby's Piece, Entitled, A Defence of the Itinerancy and the Conduct of the Rev. Mr. Whitefield in a Letter to the Reverend Mr. William Hobby ... . By Richard Pateshall, A.M. ... *Boston, N. E.: J. Draper.* 1745. 4to, pp. 12.

The Path of the Pilgrim Church, from its Origin in England to its Establishment in New England. An Historical Sketch. *Boston.* [1862.] 16mo, pp. 267. 4 Plates. C. 59065

The Path to Riches. *See* [Sullivan (James)].

A Pathetic History of the Plague in London in ... 1665. To which is here added, an Account of the Surprising Revivals of Religion in a number of Towns in the New England States, and also in Nova Scotia. Extracted chiefly from Letters written by several Gentlemen ... . To which is affixed a very interesting Letter, from a Minister in London, to his Friend in Massachu-

setts. *Printed at Worcester, (Massachusetts,) by Daniel Greenleaf.* 1803. 8vo, pp. 40. W. 59066

The Pathfinder. *See* [Cooper (J. F.)], Vol. iv., No. 16493.

The Pathfinder Railway Guide for the New England States; ... A. E. Newton, Editor. *Boston: Snow & Wilder.* 1850. 16mo. Continued. 59067

Patiño (A.) Derocho Apologetico por la Justicia de el Capitan Don Andres Patiño Castellanos, Albacea y heredero que sué de el D. Juan de Ortega Montañez Arcobispo de esta Metropoli, difunto ... . *Mexico.* 1715. Folio. 59068

Patiño (P. P.) Disertacion Critico-Theo-Filosofica sobre la conservacion de la Santa Imagen de Nuestra Señora de los Angeles, que se venera en extra muros de ésta Ciudad de México, y con motivo de una Novena, que se la dispuesto apropiada á la dicha conservacion, se consideró necesaria para prevenir la sabia critica de las personas doctas. Es Autor de una y otra el R. P. Fr. Pedro Pablo Patiño. *Mexico.* 1801. 8vo, pp. 16, 138.

A very important work as regards the ecclesiastical history of Mexico. "One of the notable Saints of Mexico, not so much for miraculous origin like that of Guadalupe, but for its preservation, being painted on a wall of *adobe* or clay. The manuscript documents accompanying show that although its origin is claimed to have been in 1695, it attracted the attention of the Archbishop and the Inquisition in 1745, and here is the original order to stop such worship, to close the doors and windows of the *oratorio* where it was, and to cover the image. It was also ordered to discontinue the collection of money, and to deliver up the whole property existing. Like the Guadalupe apparition the antiquity of origin is shown by these papers to have been a later idea. But by efforts here shown the image triumphed, and we have the order of the Virey, Feb. 18, 1770, to collect money, and the plan of the *Contador*, Sept. 4, 1785, to give greater splendor to the worship of this 'Imagen Portentosa.'"—Stevens's *Bibliotheca Historica.*

Paton (A.) Narrative of the Loss of the Schooner Clio, of Montrose, Captain George Reid; containing an account of the Massacre of her Crew by the Indians, on the North Coast of Brazil, in October, 1835; with other interesting particulars, relative to the ... Adventures, and miraculous Escape of the Author from the hands of a Savage People. By Alexander Paton, a native of Ferryden, the only Survivor. Second Edition, Enlarged and Improved. *Montrose: Smith & Co.* 1838. 12mo, pp. 60.

This truthful story affords us a new view of the character of the natives of the coast of Brazil.

Paton (A. P.) Wilson the Ornithologist: a new Chapter in his Life. ... By Allan Park Paton. *London: Longman, Green & Company.* 1863. 8vo, pp. 32. 59071

[Patot (T. de).] *See* [Tyssot de Patot].

La Patria en Cadenas. [*Bogota.* 1863.] 8vo, pp. 4. 59072

The Patriarch; or Family Library Magazine. Edited by Rev. R. W. Bailey. Vol. i. 1841. ... *New-York: George A. Peters.* 1841. 8vo, pp. viii, 236. 2 Portraits, Plates. 59073

Patricium (P.), *pseudon.* Apologvs | Vanden Krijch der | Gansen, | Met de | Vossen, | Gepractiseert door Philonem Patricium, | Tot welstant der ver-eenighde Nederlanden/ | ende bevorderinghe vande aen-staende Vloot | op West Indien. | [n. p.:] *Ghedruckt int Iaer ons Heeren/ | Anno* 1622. | 4to, 8 leaves.

Apology of the war between the geese and the foxes ... for the welfare of the United Netherlands and the advancement of the fleet to the West Indies.

[Patrick (J.)] Quebec: A Poetical Essay, in Imitation of the Miltonic style: being a regular Narrative of the Proceedings and Capital Transactions performed by the British Forces under the Command of Vice-Admiral Saunders and Major-General Wolfe, in the glorious Expedition against Canada, in the year 1759. The Performance of a Volunteer on board His Majesty's Ship Somerset, during the Passage Home from Quebec. The whole embellished with entertaining and explanatory notes. *London: T. Whitridge.* MDCCLX. 4to, pp. 30. 59075

Patrick (R. S.) Statement on behalf of R. Shedden Patrick, of Trearne, and W. Cochran Patrick, of Ladyland, his Guardian. May, 1857. [n. p. n. d.] 8vo. 59076

One of the most remarkable cases ever brought before a legal tribunal.

Patrick (W.) Historical Sketches of Canterbury. A Sermon delivered October 27, 1833, at the close of the Thirtieth Year of the Author's Ministry. By William Patrick. *Concord: Marsh, Capen & Lyon.* 1834. 8vo, pp. 39. 59077

See "Collections of the New Hampshire Historical Society," Vol. iv., pp. 174–193.

Patrignani (G. A.) Menologie di pie memorie di alcuni religiosi della Compagni di Gesu, raccolte del P. Giuseppe A. Patrignani, S. J. ... dall' anno 1538 all' anno 1728. *Venezia.* 1730. 4to. 59078

The Patriot. *Boston, N. E.* 1714. Folio, pp. 4. 59079

The Patriot. A Poem. By a Mechanic of Charlestown. *Charlestown.* 1798. 12mo, pp. 24. 59080

The Patriot. Addressed to the Electors. *See* [Johnson (S.)]

The Patriot. Addressed to the People, on the Present State of Affairs in Britain and in France. With Observations on Republican Government, and Discussions of the Principles advanced in the Writings of Thomas Paine. ... *Edinburgh: J. Dickson.* 1793. 8vo. 59081

Against Thomas Paine; with some references to American topics.

A Patriot, *pseudon.* A Political Essay upon the English and French Colonies in Northern and Southern America, Considered in a New Light. By a Patriot. *London: G. Woodfall.* 1760. 8vo, pp. 15. 59082

"A very trifling affair, and very little to the purpose." *See* "M. Rev.," xxii. 434.

A Patriot, *pseudon.* *See* Mystery Reveal'd, Vol. xii., No. 51661, *and* [Townsend (S. O.)]

The Patriot Chief. *See* [Markoe (P.)], Vol. xi., No. 44622.

The Patriot Highwayman. A Tale of the Revolution. By the author of "Leah, the Forsaken." *New York: J. P. Beadle & Co.* 1864. 16mo, pp. 111. Frontispiece. 59083

The Patriot known by Comparison; being a Disquisition of some great Characters. By a Friend to the Prosperity of the British Empire. *London: J. Wilkie.* 1782. 8vo. 59084

"A rhapsodical invective against the opposition."—*Monthly Review*, lxvi. 227.

The Patriot or People's Companion, consisting of Five Essays, on the Laws and Politics of our Country. By One of the People. *Hudson, N. Y.* 1828. 8vo, pp. 24. W. 59085

The Patriot, or Scourge of Aristocracy. Vol. i. ... *Stonington-Port, Conn.* 1801–2. 8vo. 59086

Report of the ... Patriot Orphan Home, May 1, 1866. *New York.* 1866. 8vo. 59087

The Patriot Preachers of the American Revolution. With Biographical Sketches, 1766–1783. ... [*New York.*] MDCCCLX. 12mo, pp. 368. C. 59088

Edited by Frank Moore. Corrected title of our No. 50363, Vol. xii.

O Patriota, Jornal litterario, politico, mercantil, ... do Rio de Janeiro. *Rio de Janeiro: Impressaõ Regia.* 1813–14. 2 vols., 8vo. BM. 59089

Le Patriote Anglois, ou Réflexions sur les Hostilités que la France reproche à l'Angleterre. *Geneve.* 1756. 12mo.

Relates principally to America.

Patriote Voyageur, *pseudon.* *See* [Jacquemart (Fr.)], ix.

Les Patriotes Déportés de la Guadeloupe par les Anglois, aux membres de la Convention Nationale, composant la Commission des Colonies. *Limbourg.* 1795. 8vo, pp. 19. J.C.B. 59091

The Patriots. A Comedy in Five Acts. *Philadelphia.* [n. d.] 8vo. P. 59092

Patriotic and Heroic Eloquence: A Book for the Patriot, Statesman, and Student. *New York: James C. Gregory.* 1861. 12mo, pp. 264. C. 59093

Patriotic Bank. Facts and Elucidations as connected with the Management of the Patriotic Bank. *City of Washington: Printed by Edward De Krafft.* 1829. 16mo, pp. 26. 59094

Patriotic Effusions. *See* Short (Bob), *pseudon.*

The | Patriotic Mirror, | or the | Salvation of Great Britain | in Embryo. | *London: R. Faulder.* MDCCLXXXI. 8vo, pp. 7, 88.

"A violent invective against the Opposition—the diabolical congress—the republicans—the American commanders—lee-shore admirals, etc., all in the usual low, intemperate style of the common run of pamphleteers and newspaper politicians."—*Monthly Review*, lxiv. 379.

Patriotic Perfidy; a Satire. *London: J. Bell.* 1779. 4to.

"A serious invective against some leading men in what is called the opposition party or the patriots." *See* "Monthly Review," lx. 477.

The Patriotic Song Book ... written and composed for the Times, ... during the War ... . *New York: Horace Waters.* [1861.] Obl. 12mo, pp. 64. 59097

Patriotic Songster. *New York: Robert M. De Witt.* [n. d.] 18mo, pp. 64. 59098

The Patriotic Speaker: Extracts from the Oratory of Judge Joseph Holt, Gen. Mitchell, E. Everett and others. *New York.* 1862. 12mo. 59099

Patriótica Iniciativa. *See* Vol. ix., No. 35555.

The Patriotick Proceedings. *See* Vol. xi., No. 45931.

Patriotism at Home; or, the Young Invincibles. ... *Boston: W. V. Spencer.* 1866. 18mo, pp. 320. C. 59100

Patriotism, Government Nationality. [n. p. n. d.] 8vo, pp. 7.

Patriotism, in Poetry. *See* Murdock (J. E.), xii. 51437.

Patriotism ... of the First Settlers of Wyoming. *Washington.* 1842. 8vo. 59102

Le Patriotisme Américain, ou Mémoires sur l'établissement de la partie française de l'isle de Saint-Domingue, sous le vent de l'Amérique. [n. p.] 1750. 12mo. 59103

Patriotismo. De Nirgua y Abuso de los Reyes. *Lima.* 1822. 4to, pp. 22. 59104

Patriot's Memorial. Honor to the Dead. Justice to the Living. [*Haverhill, Mass.* 1862.] 8vo, pp. 4. 59105

Contains tributes to Major H. J. How and Lieut. Thomas T. Salter.

The Patriot's Offering; or the Life, Services and Military Career of the Noble Trio, Ellsworth, Lyon and Baker. *New York: Baker & Godwin, Printers.* 1862. 8vo, pp. 108. 59106

The Patriot's Referee; containing the Declaration of Independence, the Articles of Confederation, the United States Constitution, and Washington's Farewell Address. *New York: Brown & Ryan.* 1861. 8vo. 59107

The Patriots Calendar, for ... 1795. Containing ... the American Constitution, ... with a Collection of Poems in favour of Liberty ... . *London: J. Bew.* 1795. 12mo. 59108

See "Monthly Review," xv. 473.

The Patriots of North-America: A Sketch. With Explanatory Notes. ... *New York: Printed in the Year*, M,DCC,LXXV. 8vo, pp. iv, 47. P. 59109

In this curious revolutionary poem the States are characterized as school-boys, and notwithstanding "a tory here reviles the whigs in verse," it is a clever performance with curious notes. It was probably printed by Rivington.

Patron (F.) Discours sur les causes qui ont fais établier l'esclavage dans les Colonies. Mémoire présente à la Chambre des Députés relatif à l'Emancipation des Esclaves. Par M. Felix Patron. *Guadeloupe.* 1837. 4to. 59110

Patron. De Quelques Questions Relatives aux Colonies Françaises. Par M. Felix Patron. *Paris.* 1832. 8vo, pp. 62.

Patronata en la Nacion. *See* Vol. XII., No. 48621.

El Patronato Analizado contra el Patronato Embrollado por los Novadores para sacar á la Autoridad Civil dueña absoluta de lo Espiritual. *Mejico.* 1833. 4to. 59112

Patronato Dialogo entre un Cura y un Abogado. *Mexico.* 1827. 4to. 59113

Patronato Nacional. *México.* 1821. 4to. 59114

PATTEN (D.) Our Indebtedness to the Fathers. A Centennial Discourse ... before the Providence Annual Conference, in Bristol, R. I., March 22, 1866, By David Patten, D.D. ... *Boston: James P. Magee.* 1866. 8vo, pp. 29. 59115

PATTEN (E.) A Glimpse at the United States and the Northern States of America, with the Canadas, comprising their Rivers, Lakes, and Falls. *London.* 1853. 8vo. Plates. 59116

PATTEN (G. W.) Voices of the Border: comprising Songs of the Field, Songs of the Bower, Indian Melodies, and Promiscuous Poems. By Lt.-Col. G. W. Patten. ... *New York: Hurd and Houghton.* 1867. 12mo, pp. 361. 59117

PATTEN (J. H.) Oration ... on the Fiftieth Anniversary of American Independence, At Newport, R. I. By Joseph H. Patten. *Providence: Carlile & Brown* ... . 1826. 8vo, pp. 28.

PATTEN (M.) Particulars of the late horrid Murder of the accomplished but unfortunate Miss Maria Patten, who was barbarously murdered in Fayette, Georgia, 25 July last, by a rival suitor ... . *Boston: Nathaniel Coverley.* 1815. 8vo. Frontispiece.

PATTEN (Robert). Report of the Locating Survey of the St. Croix and Lake-Superior Railroad. ... *Madison.* 1856. 8vo, pp. 23. M. 59120

PATTEN (W.) A Discourse Delivered at Hallifax In the County of Plymouth, July 24th 1766. On the Day of Thanksgiving ... throughout the Province of the Massachusetts-Bay in New-England, for the Repeal of the Stamp-Act. By William Patten, A.M. *Boston: N. E. Printed by D. Kneeland.* MDCCLXVI. 8vo, pp. 22. B. 59121

Also: Sermon ... on the Death of Capt. Daniel Goodwin. ... *Hartford.* 1772. 8vo, pp. 25.

PATTEN (W.) A Discourse, delivered in the 2d Congregational Church, Newport, December 29th, 1799: occasioned by the Death of General George Washington ... . By William Patten, A.M. ... *Newport: Printed by Henry Barber.* M,DCCC. 8vo, pp. 19. BA., N. 59122

Hough remarks that "It appears ... that two discourses ... were published."

PATTEN. Memoirs of Mrs. Ruth Patten, of Hartford, Conn. with Letters and Incidental Subjects. By William Patten, D.D. ... *Hartford: Printed by P. Canfield.* 1834. 12mo, pp. 148. Portrait. C. 59123

PATTEN. On the Inhumanity of the Slave Trade, and the Importance of correcting it. A Sermon delivered in the Second Congregational Church, Newport, Rhode-Island, August 12, 1792. By William Patten ... . *Printed at Providence, by J. Carter.* M,DCC,XCII. 8vo, pp. 14. M., W. 59124

PATTEN. Reminiscences of the Rev. Samuel Hopkins, D.D., of Newport, R. I. ... *Warren, R. I.* 1795. 12mo. 59125

PATTEN. Reminiscences of the late Rev. Samuel Hopkins, D.D., of Newport, R. I., Illustrative of his Character and Doctrines, with Incidental Subjects ... . By William Patten, D.D. *Isaac H. Cady, Providence, R. I.* 1843. 12mo, pp. 157. 59126

Also: Directions with regard to the Improvement of Temporal Blessings. A Sermon ... in New London, Dec. 2, 1784. ... *New London.* 1784. 8vo.—A Discourse, delivered in the 2d Congregational Church, Newport, ... [after] the Interment of Doctor Isaac Senter, who died, December 20th, M,DCC,XCIX, Aetat. 45. ... *Newport: Printed by Henry Barber.* 1800. 8vo, pp. 12, iv.—A Discourse, Occasioned by the Death of The Rev. President Stiles; delivered in ... Newport. ... *Exeter: Henry Ranlett.* MDCCXCV. 8vo, pp. 16.—Mr. Patten's Sermon The Lord's Day Succeeding his Ordination. [n. p. 1786.] 16mo, pp. 19, (1).—A Sermon delivered at the Request of the African Benevolent Society, ... Newport, 12th April, 1808. ... *Printed at the Office of the Newport Mercury.* [1808.] 4to, pp. 15.—A Sermon in ... Newport, November 9th, 1806; ... [after] the Death of Miss Abigail Potter. ... *Newport: ... Printed at the Office of the Newport Mercury.* 1807. 8vo, pp. 24. B.

Pattern for Governours, Exemplified in the Character of Scroop, late Lord Viscount Howe, the Governour of Barbadoes, is gratefully attempted by several of the most Ingenious Pens of that Island. *London.* 1735. 4to. 59127

PATTERSON (A. J.) Eulogy on Abraham Lincoln, Delivered in Portsmouth, N. H. April 19, 1865. By Adoniram J. Patterson ... . And an Account of the Obsequies observed by the City. *Portsmouth: C. W. Brewster & Son, Printers.* 1865. 8vo, pp. 30.

PATTERSON (Albert Clarke). A View of American Unitarian Missions; with Thoughts on the Missionary Cause ... . By A. C. Patterson. *Boston: James Munroe and Company.* 1838. 12mo, pp. 64. 59129

PATTERSON (A.) A Petition presented by Capt. Alexander Patterson, to the Legislature of Pennsylvania, during The Session of 1803–'4, for Compensation for the Monies he Expended, and the Services he Rendered in Defence of the Pennsylvania Title against Connecticut Claimants, in which is Comprised a Faithful Historical Detail of Important and Interesting Facts and Events that took place at Wyoming, and in the County of Luzerne, &c., in consequence of the dispute which existed between the Pennsylvania Land-Holders and the Connecticut Intruders, Commencing with the year 1763. *Lancaster: Printed by Robert Bailey.* 1804. 8vo, pp. 34. 59130

PATTERSON (A. D.) The Anglo-American. A Journal of Literature, News, Politics, the Drama, Fine Arts, etc. Edited by A. D. Patterson. *New-York: E. J. Garvin & Co.* [1843.] 2 vols., folio. 59131

PATTERSON (A. W.) History of the Backwoods; or, the Region of the Ohio: Authentic, from the Earliest Accounts. Embracing many Events, Notices of Prominent Pioneers, Sketches of Early Settlements, etc., etc. Not heretofore published. ... By A. W. Patterson. *Pittsburgh: The Author.* 1843. 8vo, pp. x, 5–311. Map. B., S. 59132

A good compilation of the narratives, histories, and sketches of western adventure and frontier life, with a considerable proportion of that material described by the author as "Not heretofore published."

PATTERSON (D. W.) John Stoddard of Wethersfield, Conn., and his Descendants, 1662–1872. A Genealogy. ... [n. p.] 1873. 8vo. 59133

PATTERSON (G.) Memoir of the Rev. James McGregor, D.D., Missionary ... to Pictou, Nova Scotia; with Notices of the Colonization of the Lower Provinces of British America, and of the Social and Religious Condition of the Early Settlers. By Rev. George Patterson ... . *Philadelphia.* 1859. 12mo, pp. 548.

Also: A Brief Sketch of the Life and Labors of the late Rev. John Keir, D.D. ... *Pictou.* 1859. 8vo, pp. 43.

PATTERSON (H. Stuart). Oration delivered before the Pennsylvania Literary Institute on the Sixty-Fifth Anniversary of the

Declaration of Independence. By Henry S. Patterson, M.D. *Philadelphia.* 1841. 8vo, pp. 26. 59135

Also: Memoir of the Life and Scientific Labors of Samuel George Morton, M.D. ... *Philadelphia: Lippincott, Grambo & Co.* 1854. 8vo, pp. (2), lvii. Portrait.—Notice of the Life and Professional Services of William R. Grant, M.D. A Discourse at the ... Pennsylvania College, ... 1852–'53. ... *Philadelphia: King & Baird, Printers.* 1852. 8vo, pp. 16. H.

PATTERSON (J.) The Light in which Public Calamities ought to be viewed ... . Sermon ... at Dunkeld, February 9, 1779, the Day appointed for a General Fast. By the Rev. James Patterson. *Edinburgh.* 1779. 8vo. 59136

"Very well written and very loyal. The preacher expresses his abhorrence of the American rebellion in the warmest terms. 'Horrid treason! Ingrateful disloyalty!'" *See* "Monthly Review," LX. 488.

[PATTERSON (J.)] Observations of a Person of Eminence and Worth in Caledonia, written to his Friend in Boston, N. E. on their Scots Settlement, New Edinburgh, at Darien, in America; with an Account of the Nature and Condition of the Country, and good Disposition of the Natives towards them, and of their addressing the President of Panama. Dated at Fort St. Andrews, Feb. 18th, 1698–9. *Boston.* 1699. 8vo, pp. 76. 59137

PATTERSON (J. B.) Life of Ma-ka-tai-me-she-kia-kiak. *See* Vol. II., No. 5675.

PATTERSON (J. Willis). Memorial Address on the Life and Character of Abraham Lincoln, Delivered at Concord, New-Hampshire, June 1, 1865, ... By Hon. James W. Patterson. *Concord: Printed by Cogswell & Sturtevant.* 1865. 8vo, pp. 24.

PATTERSON. Responsibilities of the Founders of Republics: An Address on the Peninsula of Sabino, On the Two-Hundred and Fifty-Eighth Anniversary of the Planting of the Popham Colony, Aug. 29, 1865. By Hon. James W. Patterson. ... *Boston: John K. Wiggin.* 1865. 8vo, pp. 38. B. 59139

Two hundred and fifty copies only printed. Also: Opinion of Hon. J. W. Patterson, of New Hampshire, in the Case of the Impeachment of the President. [n. p. n. d.] 8vo, pp. 12.—Speech ... on a Change in the Consular System establishing Consular Pupils ... May 11, 1864. *Washington, D. C.: Gibson Brothers, Printers.* 1864. 8vo, pp. 16.—Reconstruction. Speech ... in the House ... May 19, 1866. *Washington, D. C.: McGill & Witherow, Printers.* 1866. 8vo, pp. 16.—Reconstruction. Speech ... in the ... Senate, Feb. 25, 1868. [n. p. n. d.] 8vo, pp. 8. H.

PATTERSON (L. B.) Twelve Years in the Mines of California; embracing A General View of the Gold Region, with Practical Observations on Hill, Placer, and Quartz Diggings; ...

By Lawson B. Patterson. *Cambridge: Printed by Miles and Dillingham.* 1862. 12mo, pp. 108. C. 59140

PATTERSON (R.) A Narrative of the Campaign in the Valley of the Shenandoah, in 1861. By Robert Patterson, late Major-General of Volunteers. *Philadelphia: Sherman & Co., Printers.* 1865. 4to, pp. 128. Map. 59141

Six copies printed on thick paper, and one hundred on large paper.

PATTERSON (R. M.) Communication to the Board of Trustees of the University of Pennsylvania, Aug. 4, 1818. By Robert M. Patterson, M.D. *Philadelphia.* 1818. 8vo, pp. 14. M.

PATTERSON. Early History of the American Philosophical Society; a Discourse ... at the Celebration of its Hundredth Anniversary, By Robert M. Patterson, M.D. ... With the Introductory Address of the President ... . *Philadelphia: John C. Clark, Printer.* 1843. 8vo, pp. (2), 36. B. 59143

PATTERSON (R. M.) The Character of Abraham Lincoln. By Robert M. Patterson, Pastor of the Great Valley Presbyterian Church. *Philadelphia: James S. Claxton.* 1865. 8vo, pp. 44.

PATTERSON (S.) Narrative of the Adventures and Sufferings of Samuel Patterson, Experienced in the Pacific Ocean, and many other parts of the World, with an account of the Feegee [*sic*] and Sandwich Islands. *From the Press in Palmer. May* 1, 1817. 12mo, pp. 144. + Second Edition Enlarged. *Providence.* 1825. 18mo, pp. 164. C. 59145

PATTERSON (S.) The Contrast, ... by S. Patterson. *Burlington, N. J.* 1835. 8vo. 59146

PATTERSON (W.) Some Facts stated, relative to the conduct of Walter Patterson, Esq; Late Governor and Lieutenant-Governor of the Island of St. John. Of Edmund Fanning, Esq; The present Lieutenant-Governor; and of Peter Stewart, Esq; Chief Justice of the said Island; Occasioned by some Notes, contained in a Pamphlet, entitled The Criminating Complaint, &c. &c. [n. p. about 1785.] 8vo, pp. (2), 40. 59147

PATTERSON (W. J.) Statements relating to the Home and Foreign Trade of the Dominion of Canada; also, Annual Report of the Commerce of Montreal, for 1869. ... By William J. Patterson ... . *Montreal: Starke & Co., ... Printers.* 1870. 8vo, pp. 146. 59148

See also Vol. XII., Nos. 50282 *and* 50287.

PATTERSON *and* MURGUIENDO. [Alto Velo Island.] Report of the Secretary of State on the Claim of Patterson and Murguiendo, with a further Argument of the Claimants. *Washington: Government Printing Office.* 1868. 8vo. 59149

This valuable publication contains no less than sixteen fac-simile copies of early and late maps of St. Domingo and adjacent parts, taken from the Kohl collection in the Department of State at Washington. These maps render this a book of considerable geographical importance outside of Alto Velo, the subject of the controversy.

PATTIE (J. O.) The Personal Narrative of James O. Pattie, of Kentucky, during an Expedition from St. Louis, through the Vast Regions between that Place and the Pacific Ocean, and thence back through the City of Mexico to Vera Cruz, during Journeyings of Six Years; in which he and his Father, who accompanied him, suffered unheard of Hardships and Dangers, had various Conflicts with the Indians, and were made Captives, in which Captivity his Father died: together with a Description of the Country, and the various Nations through which they passed. Edited by Timothy Flint. *Cincinnati: E. H. Flint.* 1833. 8vo, pp. 300. 5 Plates. BA. 59150

"Possesses more than the ordinary interest and value, which attaches to the stories of adventurers. He crossed the continent of America on a route which his party were the first to pursue. He encountered tribes of Indians who then saw a white man for the first time, and his narrative has the merit of being given in a candid, unexaggerated style, which impresses us with its veracity."—FIELD.

PATTISON (G. S.) An Answer to a Pamphlet, entitled "Strictures on Mr. Pattison's Reply to certain Oral and Written Criticisms, by W. Gibson" ... . By Granville Sharp Pattison, Esq. ... *Baltimore: Printed by Richard J. Matchett.* 1820. 8vo, pp. 52. H. + Second Edition. [*Ibid.*] 8vo, pp. 32. B. 59151

PATTISON. Correspondence between Mr. Granville Sharp Pattison, and Dr. N. Chapman. Second Edition, with Explanatory Remarks. [*Philadelphia.* 1821.] 8vo, pp. 35. B. 59152

PATTISON. A Final Reply to the Numerous Slanders, circulated by Nathaniel Chapman, M.D. ... By Granville Sharp Pattison. Second Edition. *Baltimore: Printed by J. Robinson.* 1821. 8vo, pp. 37. B. 59153

PATTISON. A Refutation of certain Calumnies ... in a Pamphlet, entitled "Correspondence between Mr. Granville Sharp Pattison and Dr. Nathaniel Chapman." By Granville Sharp Pattison. ... *Baltimore: Printed by J. Robinson.* 1820. 8vo, pp. 64.

Also: A Discourse ... on commencing the Lectures in Jefferson Medical College,

Session MDCCCXXXII–III. ... *Philadelphia: French & Perkins.* 1832. 8vo, pp. 39. B.—Jefferson Medical College. ... Introductory Lecture. Session 1838–9. *Philadelphia: A. Waldie.* 1838. 8vo, pp. 19. B.

PATTISON (M. A.) The Emigrant's Vade-Mecum or Guide to the "Price Grant" in Venezuelan Guayana. By Margaret Amanda Pattison. *London.* 1868. 16mo, pp. (6), 150, (2). 2 Plates. C. 59155

PATTISON (Robert Everett). Eulogy on Rev. Jeremiah Chaplin, D.D. First President of Waterville College, Me. ... August 8, 1843. By R. E. Pattison. *Boston: William D. Ticknor & Co.* M DCCC XLIII. 8vo, pp. 32. 59156

Also: Address at the Western Baptist Theological Institution. ... *Covington, Ky.* 1847. 8vo.

PATTON (A. S.) The Hero Missionary; or, a History of the Labors of the Rev. Eugenio Kincaid. By Alfred S. Patton. *New York: H. Dayton.* 1858. 12mo, pp. 312. Portrait. C.

PATTON (B.) The Character of William Penn Vindicated, in an Address, By Hon. Benjamin Patton, ... at Greensburgh, Pa. *Pittsburgh: George Parkin & Co.* 1849. 8vo, pp. 21.

PATTON. Jurisdiction of the Lakes. An Argument, ... in the case of the United States vs. Richard C. Bristol ... . By Benjamin Patton, Jr. *Pittsburgh.* 1842. 8vo, pp. 36. 59159

PATTON (J. H.) The History of the United States of America, from the Discovery of the Continent, to the close of the first Session of the Thirty-fifth Congress. By J. H. Patton, A.M. *New-York: D. Appleton & Company.* 1860. 8vo, pp. xvi, 806. + Fifth Edition. [*Ibid.*] 1865. 8vo, pp. xiv, 812. 59160

PATTON (J. M.) Argument of J. M. Patton in Case of the Commonwealth vs. Garner, et al., on the Boundary between Ohio and Virginia. *Richmond.* 1846. 8vo. 59161

PATTON. The Code of Virginia, with the Declaration of Independence. By John M. Patton. *Richmond.* 1849. 8vo.

PATTON (R. M.) Address of Gov. Robert M. Patton to the People of Alabama. *Montgomery.* 1868. 8vo. 59163

PATTON (W.) Capital Punishment Sustained by Reason and the Word of God. By William Patton, D.D. *New York: Dayton & Newman.* 1842. 18mo, pp. 52. C. 59164

Also: Correspondence between Rev. William Patton, D.D. and the Secretaries of the

Evangelical Alliance on the American War. From the "New Englander," for April, 1863. [n. p. n. d.] 8vo, pp. 27.

PATTON (W. D.) My own Memoir: or, the most Important Incidents in the Life of William Delany Patton. Dedicated to the Servant and the Serf—the Autocrat and the Patriot—the Taxgatherer and the Tax-payer—the Oppressor and the Oppressed. ... [*Columbus, O.* 1850.] 8vo, pp. 16. 59165

A sarcastic attack on the corrupt state of the Government at that time.

PATTON (W. W.) The American Board and Slaveholding. By Rev. William W. Patton. *Hartford.* 1846. 12mo, pp. 47.

PATTON. Slavery—The Bible—Infidelity. An Attempt to prove that Pro-Slavery Interpretations of the Bible are productive of Infidelity. By Rev. Wm. W. Patton. *Hartford: William H. Burleigh.* 1846. 12mo, pp. 20. 59167

Also: The Compensated Agency of the U. S. Sanitary Commission explained and defended. ... *Chicago, Ill.: Dunlop, Sewell & Spalding, Printers.* 1864. 8vo, pp. 8.—The Execution of John Brown; a Discourse delivered at Chicago, December 4th, 1859, ... *Chicago: Church, Goodman & Cushing, Printers.* [1859.] 8vo, pp. 14.—Rev. W. W. Patton's Decennial and Farewell Sermons. ... *Hartford: Press of Case, Tiffany and Co.* 1857. 12mo, pp. 50.—Thoughts for Christians, suggested by the case of Passmore Williamson. A Discourse preached in ... Hartford, Conn., ... October 7, 1855. *Hartford, Conn.: Montague and Co.* 1855. 12mo, pp. 23.

PATTON *and* ISHAM. Report on the Condition of Camps and Hospitals at Cairo and Vicinity, St. Louis, etc. By Drs. Patton and Isham, October, 1861. [n. p. n. d.] 8vo, pp. 12. 59168

PATTRICH (F.) Portraits of Distinguished Indians from Several Tribes, who visited Washington in 1837. Also a faithful Representation of the Indian War Dance. Six large folio tinted lithographs by F. Pattrich. *Baltimore.* [n. d.] 59169

PATY DO ALFERES (B. de). Memoria sobre a fundação e costeio de uma fazenda na Provincia do Rio de Janeiro pelo Barão do Paty do Alferes, e annotada pelo Dr. Luiz Peixoto de Lacerda Werneck. *Rio de Janeiro.* 1863. Sm. 8vo, pp. 252. 59170

PAU (Augusto). Abramo Lincoln e la Guerra fra i Federali ed i Confederati degli Stati-Uniti, narrazione storica trographica. ... *Livorno.* 1866–. 8vo. 59171

[PAUCTON.] Métrologie ou Traité des Mesures, Poids et Monnoies Des Anciens Peuples & des Modernes. *A Paris: Desaint.* M, DCC, LXXX. 4to, pp. xvi, 956. C. 59172

Chap. II., Art. III.: Digression tendant à prouver que l'Amérique a été connue des Anciens.

PAUKE (F.) Pater Florian Pauke's Reise in die Missionen nach Paraguay, und Geschichte der Missionen St. Xaver und St. Peter. Ein Beytrag zur Geschichte der Jesuiten in Paraguay. Aus der Handschrift Pauke's herausgegeben von P. Johann Frast, ... *Wien, Bey Anton Edlem von Schmid.* 1829. 12mo, pp. 164.

PAUL (H.) History of Wells, Vermont, for the First Century after its Settlement; By Hiland Paul, with Biographical Sketches by Robert Parks, Esq. *Rutland: Tuttle & Co., Printers.* 1869. 12mo, pp. 154. 59174

PAUL (H.) The Book of American Songs: with Notes, Biographical and Historical. Edited and arranged by Howard Paul. *London: Ward and Lock.* 1857. 12mo, pp. 128. 59175

PAUL. Dashes of American Humor, By Howard Paul. Illustrated by John Leech. *New-York: Garrett & Co.* 1853. 12mo, pp. viii, 306. 59176

PAUL (J.) A Narrative of the Wonderful Escape and Dreadful Sufferings of Col. James Paul, after the Defeat of Col. Crawford. When that unfortunate Commander and many of his men were burnt at the stake, and others were slaughtered by other modes of torture, known only to Savages. *Cincinnati.* 1869. 8vo, pp. 22. 59177

Paul Jonas. *See* Jones (John Paul), Vol. IX., Nos. 36565-8.

The Paul Jones Pine Tree and Rattle Snake Song Book and Liberty Tree Minstrel. *Philadelphia: Turner & Fisher.* [1850?] 32mo, pp. 128. Plate. 59178

PAUL (M.) Memorias para la Historia de la Revolucion de Centro-America. Por Manuel Paul. *Jalapa: Aburto y Blanco.* 1832. 12mo, pp. 257. 59179

PAUL (N.) An Address ... on the Celebration of the Abolition of Slavery, in the State of New York, July 5, 1827. By Nathaniel Paul, ... in the City of Albany ... . *Albany: J. B. Van Steenberg.* 1827. 8vo, pp. 24. S. 59180

Also: An Address ... at Troy, on the Celebration of the Abolition of Slavery, in ... New York, July 6, 1829. ... *Albany: Printed by John B. Van Steenberg.* 1829. 8vo, pp. 16. B.

Paul Venner; or, the Forge and the Pulpit. Based on Facts. *New York.* [1867.] Sq. 16mo, pp. 371. Plate. 59181

PAUL WILHELM (Friedrich). Erste Reise nach dem nördlichen Amerika in den Jahren 1822 bis 1824, von Paul Wilhelm, Herzog von Würtemberg. *Stuttgart & Tübingen: J. G. Cotta.* 1835. 8vo, pp. vi, 394, (4). Map of Louisiana. C. 59182

PAULA CANDIDO (F.) Relatorio sobre Medidas de Salubridade reclamadas pela Cidade do Rio de Janeiro e acerca da Febre Amarella em Particular, Para subir a Augusta Presença de S. M. O. Imperador, pelo Dr. Francisco de Paula Candido ... . *Rio de Janeiro: na Typographia Nacional.* 1854. 4to, pp. (4), 51, (1). 13 Plates and Tables. 59183

See also Candido (Franc. de Paula), Vol. III., No. 10669.

[PAULDING (——).] *See* Vol. II., No. 8142.

PAULDING (D.) The Brigantine; or Admiral Lowe's Last Cruise. By Decatur Paulding, U. S. N. A Tale of 1763. *New York: Beadle & Co.* 186–. 16mo, pp. 100. 59184

PAULDING (E. E.) Argument of N. P. Chipman in the Trial of Col. Edmund E. Paulding before a Court Martial, June, 1866. *Washington.* 1866. 8vo, pp. 41. 59185

Corrected title of our No. 12825, Vol. IV.

PAULDING (H.) Journal of a Cruise of the United States Schooner Dolphin, among the Islands of the Pacific Ocean; and a Visit to the Mulgrave Islands, in pursuit of the Mutineers of the Whale Ship Globe. ... By Lieut. Hiram Paulding of the U. S. Navy. *New York: G. & C. & H. Carvill.* MDCCCXXXI. 12mo, pp. 258. Map. B., C. 59186

PAULDING (J.) Sybrandt Westbrook eller Hollænderens Arne; nordamerikansk Roman af James Paulding, oversat af O. F. Bræmer. *Kjöbenhavn.* 1838. 8vo. 59187

PAULDING (J. K.) American Comedies. By J. K. Paulding, ... and William Irving Paulding. ... *Philadelphia: Carey & Hart.* 1847. 12mo, pp. (2), v, 17-295. 59188

PAULDING. The Backwoodsman. A Poem. By J. K. Paulding. *Philadelphia: M. Thomas.* 1818. 8vo, pp. (4), 198.

For this production Paulding was mercilessly criticised by Snelling, in "Truths."

PAULDING. The Banks of the Ohio, or Westward Ho! A Tale. By Mr. Paulding, Author of the "Dutchman's Fireside," ... &c. *London: A. K. Newman & Co.* 1833. 3 vols., 12mo, pp. 246; 233; 224. 59190

[PAULDING.] The Book of Saint Nicholas. Translated from the Original Dutch of Dominie Nicholas Ægidius Oudenarde. *New-York: Harper & Brothers.* 1836. 12mo, pp. 237.

PAULDING. A Book of Vagaries; Comprising the New Mirror for Travellers and other Whim-Whams: being Selections from the Papers of a Retired Common-Councilman, erewhile known as Launcelot Langstaff, and, in the Public Records as James K. Paulding. Edited by William I. Paulding. *New York: Charles Scribner and Company.* 1868. 8vo, pp. xiv, (2), 417. Portrait. B. 59192

PAULDING. The Bulls and the Jonathans; comprising John Bull and Brother Jonathan, and John Bull in America. By James K. Paulding. Edited by William I. Paulding. *New York: Charles Scribner and Company.* 1867. 8vo, pp. (2), 378.

[PAULDING.] Chronicles of the City of Gotham, from the Papers of A Retired Common Councilman. Edited by the Author of "The Backwoodsman," ... &c. *New York: G. & C. & H. Carvill.* 1830. 8vo, pp. 270. H., P. 59194

[PAULDING.] The Diverting History of John Bull and Brother Jonathan, by Hector Bull-us. *New York: Inskeep & Bradford.* 1812. 18mo, pp. 153. + Second Edition. [*Ibid.*] 1813. 12mo, pp. 132. + *London: Sherwood, Neely, and Jones.* 1813. 12mo, pp. (2), 135. + *Philadelphia: Robert Desilver.* 1827. 12mo, pp. 114. 4 Plates. + *New-York: Harper & Brothers.* 1835. 12mo, pp. 193. C. + *London.* 1851. 2 vols., 12mo. 59195

[PAULDING.] The Dutchman's Fireside. A Tale. By the Author of "Letters from the South," ... &c. "Somewhere about the Time of the Old French War." ... *New York: J. & J. Harper.* 1831. 2 vols., 12mo, pp. 192; 179. + Fifth Edition. [*Ibid.*] 1837. + [*Ibid.*] 1838. + *New York: Harper & Brothers.* 1845. 2 vols., 12mo, pp. 192; 179. + *London.* 1852. 2 vols., 12mo. 59196

Some editions have the title: The Dutchman's Fireside. A Tale. By James K. Paulding. ... Edited by William I. Paulding. ... *New York: Charles Scribner and Company.* 1868. 8vo, pp. xi, 376. C.

[PAULDING.] The First of the Knickerbockers: a Tale of 1673. *New York.* 1848. 12mo, pp. 236. 59197

[PAULDING.] John Bull in America; or, the New Munchau-

sen. *New-York: Charles Wiley.* 1825. 12mo, pp. xvii, 226. + Second Edition. [*Ibid.*] + *London.* 1825. 12mo. 59198

Written in the extravagant style of Baron Munchausen, purporting to be a foreigner's tour through the United States. The extravaganza is intended to sharply satirize the English tourists who have visited and written on America, the United States particularly.

[PAULDING.] The King of the Hurons. ... *New York: George P. Putnam.* 1850. 12mo, pp. 319. 59199

[PAULDING.] Koningsmarke, the Long Finne, a Story of the New World. ... *New York: Charles Wiley.* 1823. 2 vols., 12mo, pp, 236; 298. C. 59200

[PAULDING.] Koningsmarke, or, Old Times in the New World. ... New Edition revised ... . *New-York: Harper & Brothers.* 1836. 2 vols., 12mo, pp. 228; 215. B., S. 59201

[PAULDING.] The Lay of the Scottish Fiddle: a Tale of Havre de Grace. Supposed to be written by Walter Scott, Esq. First American from Fourth Edinburgh Edition. *New-York: Inskeep & Bradford.* 1813. 18mo, pp. 262. 59202

A satire on the "predatory warfare of the British on Chesapeake Bay."—DUYCKINCK.

[PAULDING.] Letters from the South, written during an Excursion in the Summer of 1816. ... *New York: James Eastburn & Co.* 1817. 2 vols., 12mo, pp. 254; 260. B. 59203

Another edition: Letters from the South. By a Northern Man. *New York: Harper & Brothers.* 1835. 2 vols., 12mo, pp. 224; 212.

[PAULDING.] Letters from Virginia, translated from the French. ... *Baltimore: Fielding Lucas, Jr.* 1816. 12mo, pp. 220

PAULDING. A Life of Washington. By James K. Paulding. ... *New-York: Harper & Brothers.* 1834. 2 vols., 12mo, pp. 267; 233. 4 Plates. + [*Ibid.*] 1835. C. + [*Ibid.*] 1836. + [*Ibid.*] 1840. + [*Ibid.*] 1841. + [*Ibid.*] 1842. + [*Ibid.*] 1858. + *Aberdeen.* 1848. 12mo, pp. 284. BA. 59205

PAULDING. Literary Life of James K. Paulding. Compiled by his Son William I. Paulding. ... *New York: Charles Scribner and Company.* 1867. 8vo, pp. 397. Portrait. BA. 59206

[PAULDING.] The Merry Tales of the Three Wise Men of Gotham. ... *New-York: G. & C. Carvill.* 1826. 12mo, pp. 324. + *New-York: Harper & Brothers.* 1839. 12mo, pp. 236. H.

[PAULDING.] The New Mirror for Travellers; and Guide

to the Springs. By an Amateur. *New-York: G. & C. Carvill.* 1828. 12mo, pp. 292. 59208

A satirical affair—the title having been misunderstood; it was altered to read "The New Pilgrim's Progress."

[PAULDING.] The Old Continental; or, the Price of Liberty. *New York.* 1846. 2 vols., 12mo. S. + Second Edition. *New York: Cady & Burgess.* 1851. 2 vols., 12mo, pp. 191; 192.

PAULDING. The Puritan and his Daughter. By J. K. Paulding ... . *New York.* 1849. 2 vols., 12mo, pp. 216; 270. S.

[PAULDING.] Salmagundi; or, the Whim Whams and Opinions of Launcelot Langstaff, Esq. and others. ... *New York: D. Longworth.* 1808. 2 vols., 12mo, pp. (2), 206; 207-430. + First Series. ... A New Edition corrected by the Authors. *New-York: Harper & Brothers.* 1835. 2 vols., 12mo, pp. 215; 262. + Second Series. ... [*Ibid.*] 2 vols., 12mo, pp. 264; 300. A.

For other editions, *see* Vol. IX., Nos. 35222-25.

[PAULDING.] A Sketch of Old England, by a New-England Man. ... *New-York: Charles Wiley.* 1822. 2 vols., 12mo, pp. viii, 305; iv, 250. + *London: Richard Phillips.* 182–. 59212

Severely handled in the "Quarterly Review," XXX. 519-542.

PAULDING. Slavery in the United States. By J. K. Paulding. *New York: Harper & Brothers.* 1836. 18mo, pp. 312. 59213

[PAULDING.] Tales of the Good Woman. By a Doubtful Gentleman. ... *New York: G. & C. & H. Carvill.* 1829. 12mo, pp. (4), 13-367. BA. + New Edition. *New-York: Harper & Brothers.* 1836. 2 vols., 12mo, pp. 235; 233. C. 59214

Another edition is entitled: Tales of the Good Woman. By a Doubtful Gentleman: otherwise, James K. Paulding. Edited by William I. Paulding. ... *New York: Charles Scribner.* 1867. 12mo, pp. 402.

[PAULDING.] The United States and England: Being a Reply to the Criticism on Inchiquin's Letters. Contained in the Quarterly Review [by Robert Southey] for January, 1814. *New-York: A. H. Inskeep.* 1815. 8vo, pp. 115. BA. 59215

[PAULDING.] Westward Ho! A Tale. By the Author of "The Dutchman's Fireside," &c. ... *New-York: J. & J. Harper.* 1832. 2 vols., 12mo, pp. 203; 196. 59216

See Atlantic Club Book, Vol. I., No. 2298.

PAULDING (J.) Affairs and Men of New Amsterdam, in the time of Governor Peter Stuyvesant. Compiled from Dutch

Manuscript Records of the Period. By J. Paulding. *New York: Casper C. Childs, Printer.* 1843. 12mo, pp. 161, (2). BA.

PAULDING (J.) Report of the Select Committee on Erecting a Monument to the Memory of John Paulding, with an Address by the Mayor of the City of New York. *New York.* 1827. 8vo, pp. 47. 59218

Paulding was one of the captors of Major André.

[PAULDING (W. K.)] History of the City of New York. By David T. Valentine. *New York: G. P. Putnam & Company.* 1853. 8vo. 59219

This work was really compiled by William K. Paulding, although published over the name of Mr. Valentine.

Pauline of the Potomac, or General McClellan's Spy. An Authentic ... Narrative of ... Miss Pauline D'Estraye. *Philadelphia: Barclay & Co.* 186–. 8vo, pp. 100. Plates. 59220

Pauline, the Female Spy. By a Lieutenant-Colonel of the U. S. Army. *New York: T. R. Dawley.* 1865. 18mo, pp. 104.

PAULISON (C. Z.) A Development of Facts and Circumstances justifying a Union with the True Reformed Dutch Church. By Christian Z. Paulison, A.M. ... of Hackensack and English Neighbourhood. *New York: J. T. West & Co.* 1831. 8vo, pp. 48. S. 59222

PAULLI (S.) Simonis Paulli, D. | Medici Regij, ac Prælati Aarhusiensis | Commentarius | De | Abusu Tabaci | Americanorum Veteri, | et | Herbæ Thee | Asiaticorum in Europa Novo, | Quæ ipsissima est Chamæleagnos Dodonæi, | aliàs Myrtus Brabantica, Danicè Porsz/ German. Post/ | Gallicè Piment Royal, Belgicè Gagel dicta; | cum Figuris aneis ... . | M.DC.LXV. *Argentorati,* | *Sumptibus Authoris Filij* | *Simonis Paulli, Bibliop.* | 4to, (10), 56, (2) leaves. Portrait. A., C. + Editio Secunda priori auctior & correctior. [*Ibid.*] M.DC.LXXXI. 4to, (30) leaves, and pp. 88, (4), (7). 2 folded Plates. 59223

PAULLI. Orbis Terraqueus in tabulis geographicis et hydrographicis descriptus, à Simone Paulli Bibliopola Argentinensi. *Argentorati, in Officina Libraria Editoris.* M.DC.LXX. 4to, pp. (8), 12, 16, 132, 40. C. 59224

The maps relating to America are found on pp. 113-118.

PAULLI. A Treatise on Tobacco, Tea, Coffee, and Chocolate. ... Written originally by Simon Pauli; and now Translated

by Dr. James. *London: T. Osborne.* M,DCC,XLVI. 8vo, pp. (4), 171. 2 Plates. 59225

[PAULMYER (J. P.)] Memoires | tovchant | l'Establissement | d'vne | Mission Chrestienne | dans | le Troisieme Monde, | Autrement appellé, | La Terre Australe, Meridionale, | Antartique, & Inconnuë. | Dediez à Nostre S. Pere le Pape | Alexandre VII. | Par vn Ecclesiastique Originaire de cette | mesme Terre. | *A Paris,* | *Chez Claude Cramoisy, ruë Saint* | *Victor* ... | M.DC.LXIII. | *Avec privilege dv Roy.* | 8vo, pp. (36), 216. Map. C. 59226

Corrected title of No. 27790, Vol. VII., which see for a note.

PAULO DO ROSARIO. Relacam breve e verdadeira da Memoravel Victoria que ovve o Capitano môr da Capitania da Paraiva Antonio de Albuquerque dos Rebildes de Olando ... composta pello Rev. F. Paulo do Rosario Commissario Provincial da Provinciado Brazil ... . *Em Lisboa, por Jorge Rodrigues.* 1632. 4to, pp. 32. 59227

PAULO (S.) Chronica Litteraria de S. Paulo. Retrospecto de anno de 1866. *Rio de Janeiro.* 1866. 8vo, pp. 78. 59228

PAULUS (*Dr.*) Magikon. Wunderbare Prophezeihungen über das Pabstthum und dessen baldigen Untergang; nebst Weissagungen über Amerika ... . Von Dr. Paulus. *New York.* 1869. 8vo, pp. 147. 24 Plates. C. 59229

PAULUS. Magicon: Wonderful Prophecies concerning Popery and its impending Overthrow and Fall, together with Predictions relative to America ... . By Dr. Paulus. *New York.* 1869. 12mo, pp. 152. 24 Plates. C. 59230

PAULUS (M.) Marci Pauli Veneti, Historici fidelissimi juxta ac præstantissimi, De Regionibus Orientalibus Libri III. Cum Codice Manuscripto Bibliothecæ Electoralis Brandenburgicæ collati, exq; eo adjectis Notis plurimùm tum suppleti tum illustrati. Accedit, propter cognationem materii, Haithoni Armeni Historia Orientalis; quæ & De Tartaris inscribitur; Itemque, Andreæ Mulleri, Greffenhagii, de Chataja, cujus prædictorum Auctorum uterque mentionem facit, Disquisitio; inque ips m Marcum Paulum Venetum Præfatio & locupletissimi Inices. *Coloniæ Brandenburgicæ, George Schulzii. Anno* MDCLXVI. 4to, pp. (6), 167, Index, 25 leaves. Plate. 59231

Contains a few references to America.

Paulus Epis. Middleburgensis. Paulinae de recta Paschae Celebratione; et de Die Passionis Domini Nostri Jesus Christi. *Impressum Forosempronii per Octavianum Petrucium.* MDXIII. Folio, (495) leaves. 59232

A reference to Columbus and Vesputius will be found on signature F F III.

PAULY (T. de). Description Ethnographique des Peuples de la Russie Par T. de Pauly ... . *Saint-Petersbourg: ... H. Schmitzdorff (Charles Roettger).* MDCCCLXII. Folio. Colored Plates.

Pauperism on a Great Scale, or the Case of the West India Planters. [*London: Bagster and Thoms.* n. d.] 8vo, pp. 6.

Pause and Think before you Vote!! [n. p. n. d.] 8vo, pp. 4.

PAUTA (D'.) Alfandega do Rio de Janeiro. ... *Rio de Janeiro.* 1830. 8vo. 59236

Pauta das Avaliaçoes de todas as mercadorias que se importao ao Imperio do Brasil. *Rio de Janeiro.* 1826. 4to. 59237

Pauta de Comisos. *See* Vol. XII., No. 48622.

PAUTHER (A.) A Surprising Narrative of a Young Woman, Discovered in a Rocky Cave, after having been taken by the Savage Indians of the Wilderness in the year 1777. ... *New York.* [n. d.] 12mo, pp. 9. 59238

P[AUW] (M. [Corneille] de). Defense des Recherches Philosophiques sur les Américains. Par M. de P***. ... *Berlin: George Jacques Decker.* MDCCLXX. Sm. 8vo, pp. 256. + [*Ibid.*] MDCCLXXI. + [*Ibid.*] MDCCLXXII. 59239

De Pauw's reply to Pernety's "Dissertation." It forms Vol. III. of the "Recherches Philosophiques sur les Américains."

PAUW. Œuvres Philosophiques. ... *Paris: Bastien. An* III. 7 vols., 8vo. C. 59240

Includes "Recherches Philosophiques sur les Américains.

P[AUW]. Recherches Philosophiques sur les Américains, ou Mémoires intéressants pour servir à l'Histoire de l'Espèce Humaine. Par Mr. de P***. ... *A Berlin: George Jacques Decker.* MDCCLXVIII. 3 vols., sm. 8vo, pp. (24), 326, Table, (26); (2), 366, Table, (32); 136, Défense, 256. 59241

The second volume was published in 1769; and the third, being a defense of the two first, against the Abbé Pernety, in 1770. Vol. III. has in addition to the above title: "Nouvelle édition augmentée d'une Dissertation Critique par Dom Pernetty; & de la Défense de l'Auteur des Recherches contre cette Dissertation." The author endeavors to show the inferior character of everything American, especially the inhabitants, and his work evoked considerable controversy. It contains a very curious account of the "Hermaphrodites de la Floride," and the custom of "Circoncision" and "Infibulation."

P[AUW]. Recherches Philosophiques sur les Americains [as in No. 59241]. Par Mr. de P***. Avec une Dissertation sur l'Amérique & les Américains, par Dom Pernety. Et la Défense de l'Auteur des Recherches contre cette Dissertation. ... *A Berlin.* M.DCC.LXX. 3 vols., sm. 8vo, pp. xxiv, 326, Table, (26); (2), 366, Table, (32); 136, 256. 59242

P[AUW]. Recherches Philosophiques sur les Americains [as in No. 59241]. Par M. de P***. Avec une Dissertation sur l'Amérique & les Américains, par Dom Pernety. ... *A Londres.* M.D.CC.LXXI. 3 vols., 12mo, pp. xx, 510; (2), 164; x, (2), 479. + [*Ibid.*] 3 vols., 12mo, pp. xviii, (2), 276, Table, (26); (4), 304, Table, (32); Dissertation, 116; iv, 232. BA. 59243

The "Dissertation" and "Défense" have the imprint, *A Berlin* M.DCC.LXX.

P[AUW]. Recherches Philosophiques sur les Americains [as No. 59241]. Par M. de P***. Nouvelle édition, augmentée d'une Dissertation critique par Dom Pernety, & de la Defense de l'Auteur des Recherches contre cette Dissertation. ... *A Berlin.* M.DCC.LXXI. 3 vols., 12mo, pp. xix, 326, Table, (26); 336, Table, (30); 133, Défense, 247. J.C.B. 59244

P[AUW]. Recherches Philosophiques sur les Americains [as No. 59241]. Par Mr. de P***. ... Nouvelle édition, corrigée & considérablement augmentée. *Berlin: George Jacques Decker, Imp. du Roi.* MDCCLXXII. 3 vols., sm. 8vo, pp. xxii, (2), xxii, 384, Table, (30); (4), 416, Table, (32); 256. H. + *Clèves.* MDCCLXXII. ? vols., sm. 8vo. 59245

These editions do not contain the "Dissertation" of Pernetty. Vol. III., the "Défense," has the imprint, *Berlin,* MDCCLXXII.

P[AUW]. Recherches Philosophiques sur les Américains [as No. 59241]. Par M. de P***. Nouvelle édition, augmentée d'une Dissertation critique par Dom Pernety, & de la Défense de l'Auteur des Recherches contre cette Dissertation. ... *A Berlin.* M.DCC.LXXIV. 3 vols., 12mo, pp. xviij, (2), 276, Table, (26); (4), 304, Table, (32), Dissertation, 116; iv, 216. BA. + *A Londres.* M.DCC.LXXIV. 3 vols., 12mo. + *A Berlin.* M.DCC.LXXVII. 3 vols., 12mo, pp. xviii, (2), 276, Table, (26); (4), 304, Table, (32), Dissertation, 116; iv, 231 59246

P[AUW]. Recherches Philosophiques sur les Américains ... . Par M. de P***. ... *Paris.* 1799. 7 vols., 8vo. Maps.

P[AUW]. Philosophische Untersuchungen über die Amerikaner, oder wichtige Beyträge zur Geschichte des menschlichen Geschlechts. Aus dem Französischen des Herrn von P***. *Berlin: George Jacques Decker.* MDCCLXIX. 2 vols., 8vo, pp. (8), 258, (18); 294, (22). J.C.B. 59248

P[AUW]. Wysgeerige Bespiegelingen over Amerika ... . *Deventer.* 1771–72. 3 vols., sm. 8vo. 59249

PAUW. A General History of The Americans, of their Customs, Manners, and Colours. An History of the Patagonians, of the Blafards, and White Negroes. History of Peru. ... Selected from M. Pauw. By Daniel Webb, Esq. *Rochdale: Printed by ... T. Wood.* 1806. 8vo, pp. viii, 235. 59250

PAUW. Selections from les Recherches Philosophiques sur les Americains of M. Pauw. By Mr. W***. [Webb.] ... *Bath: Printed by R. Cruttwell.* MDCCLXXXIX. Sm. 8vo, pp. (4), 211.

Fifty copies printed for presentation. *See* Nichols' "Literary Anecdotes," II. 335.

PAUW. Selections from M. Pauw, with Additions by Daniel Webb, Esq. ... *Bath: Printed by R. Cruttwell.* MDCCXCV. 8vo, pp. vi, 235, "Sequel," 100. BA., C. 59252

In some copies, the "Sequel" is apparently complete in fifty-eight pages.

PAVIE (T.) Fragmens d'un Voyage dans l'Amérique Méridionale, en 1833. Par Théodore Pavie. *Angers.* 1840. 8vo, pp. 237. + [*Ibid.*] 1842. 8vo. 59253

PAVIE. Souvenirs Atlantiques. Voyage aux États-Unis et au Canada. Par Théodore Pavie. *Paris: Roret.* 1833. 2 vols., 8vo, pp. viii, 350, (2); 354, (2). 59254

PAVON (Francisco G.) Manifestacion ... á la Nacion de su conducta militar. *Mexico.* 1841. 4to, pp. 24. 59255

PAVON (M. F.) Informe sobre los Diferentes Ramos de la Administracion publica presentado al Exmo. Señor Presidente. *Guatemala: Imprenta de la Paz.* 1844. Folio, pp. 11. 59256

PAVON. Noticia biografica del Señor D. Manuel Francisco Pavon, Consejero de Estado y Ministro de lo Interior del Gobierno de la Republica de Guatemala. *Guatemala.* 1855. 4to, pp. 24. 59257

PAWCATUCK, *R. I.* Catalogue of the Pawcatuck Library, ... by Rev. Thomas H. Vail. With Forms of Regulations, Hints on Reading, [etc. n. p.] 1848. 8vo, pp. 120. 59258

Prepared at the request of Mr. H. Barnard, intended as a model catalogue and the evident result of labor and research.

Catalogue of Books in the Library of the PAWCATUCK LIBRARY ASSOCIATION, Westerly, R. I.; with a Sketch of the ... Association, a Copy of its Constitution and By-Laws ... . *Providence.* 1849. 8vo, pp. (2), xviii, 92. 59259

PAWLET, *Vt.* Constitution and Catalogue of Pawlet Library. *Bennington: Printed by Anthony Haswell.* MDCCXCIX. 12mo, pp. 6. 59260

PAWTUCKET, *R. I.* Catalogue of the Pawtucket Library, to which are added the Charter, By-Laws, and an Historical Sketch of the Institution. *Pawtucket.* 1860. 12mo. 59261

Constitution and By-Laws of Franklin Section, No. 3, Cadets of Temperance, Pawtucket, R. I. Instituted August, 1848. *Providence: M. B. Young.* 1848. 12mo, pp. 16. — Constitution and By-Laws of William Penn Division, No. 8, of the Sons of Temperance, of ... Rhode Island. Instituted at Pawtucket, June 29, 1848. *Providence: M. B. Young.* 1848. 12mo.

North Providence Centennial. *See* Vol. XIII., No. 55727.

The Pawtucket, Central Falls, and Woonsocket Directory. 1867–8. ... *Providence.* [n. d.] 8vo, pp. 320. 59262

Pawtucket and Woonsocket Directory, for ... 1857. Compiled by W. H. Boyd. *New York.* [1857.] 18mo, pp. 204.

PAXTON (J. A.) The Stranger's Guide. An Alphabetical List of All the Wards, Streets, Roads, Lanes, Alleys, Avenues, Courts, Wharves, Ship Yards, Public Buildings, &c. in the City and Suburbs of Philadelphia, with References for finding their Situations on an Alphabetical Plan. By John Adems [*sic*] Paxton. [*Philadelphia:*] *Edward Parker.* [1810.] 16mo, pp. 56. Map.

PAXTON (J. D.) Letters on Slavery; addressed to the Cumberland Congregation, Virginia. By J. D. Paxton, their former Pastor. *Lexington, Ky.: Abraham T. Skillman.* 1833. 12mo, pp. viii, 207. S. 59264

Also: An Appeal to the American Board of C. F. Missions, from the Unjust and Oppressive Measures of the Secretary and Prudential Committee. ... *New Haven: J. H. Benham.* 1848. 8vo, pp. 40. S.

PAXTON. A Memoir of J. D. Paxton, D.D. late of Princeton, Indiana. *Philadelphia: J. B. Lippincott & Co.* 1870. 12mo, pp. 358. Portrait. C. 59265

Edited by his widow. Composed of an autobiography, a diary, and sketches of travel.

PAXTON (P.), *pseudon.* *See* [Hammitt (S. A.)], VIII. 30083–4.

PAXTON (W. W.) The Nation: Its Relation and Duties to God. A Sermon ... in ... Pittsburgh, Pa. on Thanksgiving Day, Nov. 24, 1859. By Rev. William M. Paxton ... . *Pittsburgh: Printed by W. S. Haven.* 1859. 8vo, pp. 30. 59266

Also: The Nation's Gratitude and Hope. A Sermon ... in Pittsburgh, Penn., on Thanksgiving Day, November 27, 1862. ... *Pittsburgh: W. G. Johnston & Co.* 1862. 8vo, pp. 38.

PAXTON BOYS. The | Cheat Unmask'd: | being | A Reputation | Of that Illegitimate | Letter, | Said to be wrote by | A Clergyman in Town. | In a true Copy of | A Letter | from that | Clergyman to his Friend. | [*Philadelphia:*] *Printed in the Year* M,DCC,LXIV. | Sm. 8vo, pp. 8. P. 59267

Corrected title of our No. 12358, Vol. III.

The | Conduct | of the | Paxton-Men, | Impartially Represented: | with some | Remarks | on the | Narrative. | *Philadelphia:* | *Printed by Andrew Steuart.* MDCCLXXIV. | [Followed by a second title:] The Conduct of | The Paxton-Men, | Impartially represented; | The Distresses of the Frontiers, and the | Complaints and Sufferings of the People fully | stated; ... | With some | Remarks upon the Narrative, | Of the Indian-Massacre, lately publish'd. | Interspers'd with several interesting Anecdotes, relating to the | Military Genius, and Warlike Principles of the | People call'd Quakers: ... | In a Letter from a Gentleman in one of the | Back-Counties, to a Friend in Philadelphia. | ... | *Philadelphia:* | *Printed by A. Steuart,* ... 1764. | 12mo, pp. (2), 34. BA., P. 59268

"An attempt to justify one of the foulest, most cruel, and cowardly massacres of an unoffending people that was ever committed. The Paxton-men were a mob of poltroons, who preferred to murder unarmed men and boys to risking their worthless carcasses on the frontier, fighting the savages who ravaged their homesteads almost unresisted."—FIELD. Written by Rev. Thomas Barton. *See* Sabin's "Dictionary," Vol. IV., No. 15209.

A | Letter, | From a Clergyman in Town; | Vindicating himself against the | Malevolent Aspersions | Of a late Pamphelteer [*sic*] Letter-Writer. | [*Philadelphia:*] *Printed in the Year* M, DCC, LXIV. Sm. 8vo, pp. 8. P. 59269

The | Paxton Boys, | A | Farce. | Translated from the Original | French, | By a Nâtive of Donegall. | The Second Edition. | *Philadelphia:* | *Printed and Sold by Anthony Armbruster,* | ... | 1764. Sm. 8vo, pp. 16. Folded Plate. N., P. 59270

See also Vol. I., Nos. 1663, 3961, Vol. IV., No. 13782, Vol. V., Nos. 19163, 19926, 19938, Vol. VII., No. 25557, Vol. VIII., No. 32053, Vol. X., Nos. 40280, 41946, Philanthropos, *pseudon.*, Plain Dealer, *pseudon.*, Positive, *pseudon.*, Quaker Unmasked, Quakers Vindicated, Remonstrance, A Scene, *and* Serious Address.

PAXTON, *Mass.* Centenary Memorial of Paxton: or the Exercises of the Hundredth Anniversary of the Incorporation of the Town ... June 14, 1865. *Worcester: Printed by Edward R. Fiske & Son.* 1868. 8vo, pp. 78. H. 59271

The | Paxtoniade. | A | Poem. | By Christopher Gymnast, Esq; | With the Prolegomana and Exercitations of | Scriblerus. | The Second Edition. | ... | *Philadelphia: Printed ... by* | *John Morris,* ... [1764.] Sm. 8vo, pp. 8. P. 59272

... Pay as you go! or the Unconstitutionality of the Nine Million Debt Bill demonstrated. ... *New York: Wm. C. Bryant & Co.* 1851. 8vo, pp. 46. B. 59273

Pay Rolls of Militia entitled to Land Bounty under the Act of Congress of September 28, 1850. *Richmond.* 1851. 8vo.

La Paya, Insurgenta y la Mexicana Patriota. [*Mexico.* n. d.] 12mo, pp. 8. 59275

PAYEN DE BOISNEUF. Rapport fait à l'Assemblée Nationale sur les Événements arrivés à Cayenne les 9, et 10 Août 1790. *Paris.* 1790. 4to. 59276

PAYNE (Abraham). Remarks [connected with the Political Contest] at Central Falls, R. I., Nov. 1, 1864. By A. Payne. *Providence: Sidney S. Rider, & Bro.* [1864.] 12mo, pp. 16. B.

PAYNE (A. R. M.) The Geral-Milco; or The Narrative of a Residence in a Brazilian Valley of the Sierra-Paricis. By A. R. Middletoun Payne ... . *New York: Charles B. Norton.* 1852. 16mo, pp. (4), 264. 3 Plates and Map. C. 59278

[PAYNE.] Rambles in Brazil: or, A Peep at the Aztecs, by one who has seen them. Second Edition, with Map and Illustrations. *New York: Charles B. Norton.* 1854. 12mo, pp. (4), 264. B. 59279

PAYNE (D. A.) The Semi-Centenary and the Retrospection of the African Meth. Episcopal Church in the United States of America. By Daniel A. Payne, one of the Bishops ... of the A. M. E. Church. *Baltimore: Printed by Sherwood & Co.* 1866. 8vo, pp. 189. C. 59280

Also: Welcome to the Ransomed; or Duties of the Colored Inhabitants of the District of Columbia. ... *Baltimore: Bull & Tuttle.* 1862. 8vo, pp. 16.

PAYNE (J.) A Short Narrative of the ... Life of Jacob

Payne; ... *Petersburg: Printed by Dickson & Pescud.* 1805. 8vo, pp. 24. 59281

[PAYNE (J.)] French Encroachments Exposed. *See* Vol. VII., No. 25883, *add* "Map" to the collation.

PAYNE (J.) An Epitome of History; or, A Concise View of the most Important Revolutions and Events, ... in the World; ... Forms of Government, &c. By John Payne. Second Edition. *London: J. Johnson.* 1795. 2 vols., 8vo, pp. vi, 429, Plate; (4), 536. C. 59282

PAYNE. Geographical Extracts, forming a General View of Earth and Nature. In Four Parts. ... Illustrated with Maps. By John Payne ... . *London: G. G. and J. Robinson.* 1796. 8vo, pp. xiv, 530. P. 59283

Contains many interesting notifications on the physical and geographical position of North America.

PAYNE. A New and Complete System of Universal Geography; ... To which is added, A View of Astronomy, as connected with Geography; Of the Planetary System ... and of the Universe in General. With a Copious Index ... to each Volume. ... By John Payne. With Additions, ... By James Hardie ... . *New-York: John Low.* 1798–99. 4 vols., 8vo, pp. xiviii [*sic*], 518, (11); 578, (13); 710, (4); 525, Tables, 36, (4), Supplement, 17. BA. 59284

Vol. IV. relates entirely to America, and contains a supplement, "Description of the Genesee Country."

PAYNE (J.) Bishop Payne's First Annual Address to the Philadelphia Annual Conference of the A. M. E. Church, May 16, 1853. *Philadelphia: C. Sherman, Printer.* 1853. 8vo, pp. 23.

PAYNE (J. H.) Juvenile Poems, principally written between the Age of Thirteen and Seventeen Years. By John Howard Payne. ... *Baltimore: Edward J. Coale.* 1813. 18mo, pp. (2), 20.

PAYNE. Lispings of the Muse: A Selection from Juvenile Poems, chiefly written at and before the Age of Sixteen by John Howard Payne. ... *London.* 1815. 8vo, pp. 30. 59287

Excessively scarce, but few copies being known.

PAYNE. Memoirs of John Howard Payne; the American Roscius; With Criticisms on his Acting, In the various Theatres of America, England and Ireland. Compiled from Authentic

Documents. *London: John Miller.* 1815. 8vo, pp. (4), 131. Portrait. 59288

Also: Brutus; or, the Fall of Tarquin: an Historical Tragedy. ... *New York.* 1819. 16mo, pp. 54. — Sketch of the Life of John Howard Payne. *Boston.* 1833. 8vo, pp. 27. — The Thespian Mirror. ... *New York.* 1806. 8vo.

PAYNE (J. J. W.) Masonic Address, By John J. W. Payne, M.D., W. M. of Yorkville Lodge, No. 131, ... at Yorkville, Pickens County, Alabama, December 27, ... 1856. ... *Carrollton.* 1857. 8vo, pp. 16. 59289

PAYNE (L.) Reglamento que se establece para el gobierno de la venducta aprobada por el Excmo. Ayuntamiento de la Habana, bajo la fianza hipotecaria de 4000 ps. á cargo de D. Luis Payne. *Habana.* 1813. 4to. 59290

PAYNE (R. G.) Report to the General Assembly on the Condition of the Railroads in Tennessee. By R. G. Payne. *Nashville.* 1857. 8vo. 59291

PAYNE (R. W.) A Letter of Rice W. Payne, Esq., on Know-Nothingism. *Alexandria, Va.* 1855. 8vo, pp. 10.

PAYNE (W. W.) Speech of William W. Payne on the Proposition to refund the Fine to General Jackson, delivered ... January 28, 1843. [*Washington.* 1843.] 8vo. 59293

Also: Speech ... on the Bill making Appropriations for Certain Rivers and Harbors; ... April 5, 1844. [*Washington.* 1844.] 8vo, pp. 16. — Speeches ... December 28, 1841, and July 7, 1842, on the Tariff. [*Washington.* 1842.] 8vo.

PAYNO (M.) Carta que sobre los Asuntos de Mexico, dirige al Sr. General Forey, Comandante en Gefe de las Tropas Francesas el Ciudadano Manuel Payno. *Mexico.* 1862. 4to, pp. 79. + Edicion del Heraldo. *Mexico: N. Chaves.* 1863. 16mo, pp. 120. C. 59294

Also in French, *Mexico.* 1862. 4to, pp. 67. This elicited: Observaciones y Comentarios á la Carta que D. Manuel Payno ha dirijido al Sr. General Forey. [*Veracruz.* 1863.] 4to, pp. 30.

[PAYNO.] Coleccion de las Leyes, Decretos, Circulares y Providencias relativas á la desamortizacion eclesiástica ... . *México.* 1861. 2 vols., 12mo. 59295

PAYNO. Contestacion á la Memoria sobre la Convencion Española, por Manuel Payno. ... *Mexico.* 1857. 8vo, pp. 74, 24.

PAYNO. Cuentas, Gastos, Acreedores y otros Asuntos del Tiempo de la Intervencion Francesa y del Imperio. Obra escrita

y publicada de orden del Gobierno Constitucional de la Republica, por M. Payno. De 1861 á 1867. *México: Imprenta de Ignacio Cumplido.* 1868. 8vo, pp. 934, (5). B. 59297

PAYNO. Memoria de Hacienda presentada al Exmo. Sr. Presidente de la Republica, por el Ciudadano Manuel Payno. Comprende el Periodo de Diciembre de 1855, á Mayo de 1856, en que esturo á su cargo el Ministerio del Ramo. *Mexico* [*Imprenta de Ignacio Cumplido*]. 1857. 4to, pp. 125. 59298

PAYNO. Memoria sobre el Maguey Mexicano y sus diversos productos, escrita por D. Manuel Payno ... . *Mexico: Imprenta de A. Boix, A Cargo de Miguel Zarnoza.* 1864. 4to, pp. 132. B.

PAYNO. Memoria sobre la Revolucion de Diciembre de 1857 y Enero de 1858 ... . *Mexico.* 1860. 4to, pp. 137. 59300

PAYNO. Mexico y sus Cuestiones Financieras con la Inglaterra, la España y la Francia. Memoria que por órden del Supremo Gobierno Constitucional de la República escribe el C. Manuel Payno. *Mexico: Imprenta de Ignacio Cumplido.* 1862. Folio, pp. 346, 151. C. 59301

The appendix is entitled: "Leyes, Tratados y Documentos justificativos, relativos á la Deuda contraida en Lóndres á las Convenciones diplomáticas y á diversas reclamaciones de súbditos estrangeros."

PAYNO. Mexico and her Financial Questions with England, Spain, and France. Report by order of the Supreme Constitutional Government of the Mexican Republic, by Manuel Payno. *Mexico.* 1862. Folio, pp. 324, 148. 59302

PAYNO. Proyectos de Arreglo de los Gastos de la Hacienda Publica, por M. Payno. *Mexico.* 1848. 8vo. 59303

Relates to Chihuahua.

PAYNO. Tratado de la Propiedad. Ensayo de un Estudio del derecho romano y del derecho público y constitucional en lo relativo a la propiedad, por Manuel Payno. *Mexico.* 1869. 4to, pp. viii, 218. 59304

Also: Bosquejo biografico de los Generales Iturbide y Teran. ... *Mexico.* 1843. 8vo, pp. 35. 2 Portraits. — Cuadro Sinóptico de la Historia Antigua de Mexico, desde los tiempos fabulosos hasta la ocupacion de la Capital por Hernan Cortes. Formado, segun los datos mas auténticos, por el Ciudadano Manuel Payno, quien lo dedica, en demonstracion de aprecio, á la Juventud estudiosa de la República. *Mexico.* 1859. Folio, 1 leaf. — Mexico y el Sr. Embajador D. Joaquin Francisco Pacheco. ... *Mexico.* 1862. 4to, pp. 98. — Presente Amistoso dedicado a las Señoritas Mejicanas. ... [*Mexico.*] 1848. 12mo.

Payo de Ribera (F.) El Maestro D. F. Payo de Ribera, Obispo de Gvatemala y de la Vera Paz, representa al Real Acuerdo destas Provincias de Gvatemala lo que siente acerca de la execucion de la Real Cedula, que manda se tasen los Indios de suerte que no correspondan mas de quatrocientos à una Doctrina. *Gvatemala.* 1664. Folio. 59305

Payot (H.) Payot's California Miners' Almanac for 1864, ... Published by Henry Payot. *San Francisco, December*, 1863. 24mo, pp. 65. 59306

Payson (A. M.) The Poets of Portsmouth. Compiled by Aurin M. Payson and Albert Leighton. ... *Boston: Walker, Wise and Company.* 1865. 8vo, pp. xix, (2), 405. BA. 59307

Payson (E.) Pious Heart-Elations: Being The Substance of a Sermon In Publick On November 29th. in Consideration of present Awful Providences amongst us; and on ... December 3d, 1727. ... By Edward Payson, M.A. ... *Boston: Printed by B. Green, for J. Phillips.* 1728. Sm. 8vo, pp. (4), 23, (1). B.

Payson (E.) God's Praises Sung; ... A Sermon, ... Thanksgiving, November 30, 1820. ... at Portland. By Edward Payson. ... *Portland: Printed by Arthur Shirley.* 1820. 8vo, pp. 20.

Also: An Address to Seamen, ... in Portland, ... October 28, 1821; at the request of the Portland Auxiliary Marine Bible Society. ... *Portland.* [n. d.] 12mo, pp. 12. — A Discourse, ... at Portland, May 5, 1814; before the Bible Society of Maine .... *Portland: Printed by Arthur Shirley.* 1814. 8vo, pp. 24. + Third Edition. *Andover.* 1818. 8vo. — The Oracles of God. A Sermon ... at Boston, Jan. 21, 1824, before the Marine Bible Society ... . *Portland, Me.* 1824. 8vo, pp. 23. — Sermons. ... *Portland: Shirley and Hyde.* 1828. 8vo, pp. 503. + *Boston: William Hyde.* 1831. 12mo, pp. viii, 13-400. + Edited by Asa Cummings, D.D. *Portland: Hyde & Lord.* 1849. 2 vols., 8vo, pp. xvi, 13-608; 608.

Payson. A Memoir of the Rev. Edward Payson, D.D. Late Pastor of the Second Church in Portland. *Portland: Ann L. Payson.* 1830. 12mo, pp. 444. Portrait. C. 59310

Memoir and Select Thoughts, of the late Rev. Edward Payson, D.D. ... By Rev. Asa Cummings, D.D. New Edition ... enlarged. *New York: William H. Hyde.* 1849. 8vo, pp. 606. Portrait. — Memoir, Select Thoughts and Sermons ... . Compiled by Rev. Asa Cummings ... . *Portland: Hyde, Lord & Duren.* 1846. 3 vols., 8vo. + *Philadelphia: J. L. Gibon.* 1858. 3 vols., 8vo, pp. xvi, xiii, 13-606, Portrait; xi, 13-608; x, 11-608. — Selections from Conversations and Unpublished Writings ... . Second Edition. *Boston: Crocker & Brewster.* 1834. 32mo, pp. 192. Plate.

[Payson (Edward).] The Maine Law in the Balance; or, An Inquiry into the Theory and Working Capacities of that Measure. By a Citizen of Maine. ... *Portland, Me.: Merrill and Whitman.* [1855.] 8vo, pp. 56. B. 59311

Payson (P.) A Professing People directed ... to prepare to meet God, in the Way of his Judgments. In Two Sermons Preached Feb. 26. 1740, 1. Upon A Public Fast, Occasion'd by the present War with Spain, and other Judgments. By Phillips Payson, A.M. ... *Boston: Printed by S. Kneeland & T. Green, and Sold by J. Eliot.* 1741. 12mo, pp. (4), ii, 49. B. 59312

Payson (P.) A Memorial of Lexington Battle, and of some signal Interpositions of Providence in the American Revolution. A Sermon Preached at Lexington, on the Nineteenth of April, 1782. The Anniversary of the Commencement of the War between Great-Britain and America, which Opened in a most Tragical Scene, in that Town, on the Nineteenth of April, 1775. By Phillips Payson ... . *Boston: Printed by Benjamin Edes & Sons.* M,DCC,LXXXII. 8vo, pp. 24. BA., W. 59313

Payson. A Sermon delivered at Chelsea, January 14, 1800. ... on the Sorrowful Event of the Death of General Washington. By the Rev. Phillips Payson, A.M. ... *Charlestown: Printed by Samuel Etheridge.* 1800. 8vo, pp. 15. BA. 59314

Payson. A Sermon Preached before the Honorable Council, and ... Representatives of ... Massachusetts-Bay, ... at Boston, May 27, 1778. Being the Anniversary for the Election of the ... Council. By Phillips Payson ... . *Boston: N. E. Printed by John Gill.* M.DCC.LXXVIII. 8vo, pp. 39. BA. 59315

With singular historical remarks upon the American Revolution. Also: A Sermon Preach'd at the Ordination of the Rev. Mr. Samuel Payson, to the Pastoral Care of the Church at Lunenburgh. September 8th 1762. ... *Boston: ... Printed by Thomas and John Fleet.* 1762. 8vo, pp. 27. — A Sermon ... at the Ordination of the Reverend Mr. John Payson, to the ... Church ... in Fitchburg, January 27, 1768. ... *Boston: ... Printed by Richard Draper.* 1768. 8vo, pp. 27. — A Sermon ... at the Ordination of the Rev. Mr. Seth Payson, to the ... Church in Rindge, December 4th, 1782 ... *Boston: ... Printed by T. & J. Fleet.* 1783. 8vo, pp. 30. BA.

Payson (S.) Proofs of the Real Existence and Dangerous Tendency of Illuminism. Containing Parts of what Dr. Robison and the Abbe Barruel have published on this Subject. ... By Seth Payson ... . *Charlestown: The Author.* 1802. 12mo, pp. iv, 290. B. 59316

Payson. A Sermon ... at Concord, June 6th, 1799. Before ... the Governor, the ... Council ... Senate, and Representatives of the State of New-Hampshire. By Seth Payson, A.M. ... *Portsmouth: ... Printed by John Melcher.* 1799. 8vo, pp. 23.

Also: Abridgment of two Discourses preached at Rindge, at the Annual Fast, April 11, 1805. ... *Keene.* 1805. 8vo, pp. 24. W. — Discourse, ... December 16, 1807,

at the Ordination of Rev. Edward Payson, ... in Portland. ... *Portland.* 1808. 8vo, pp. 24. — ... A Sermon ... at the Ordination of the Rev. Ebenezer Hill, to the ... Church in Mason, November 3d MDCCXC. ... *Printed at Worcester, ... by Isaiah Thomas.* MDCCXCI. 8vo, pp. 32. — Sermon ... at the Ordination of the Rev. Joseph Brown ... *Dover.* 1796. 8vo. — A Sermon, at the Consecration of the Social Lodge in Ashby, ... June 24, A. D. 1799. ... *From Preston's Printing-Office, Amherst, N. H.* 1800. 8vo, pp. 16. — Sermon ... Feb. 24, 1802, at the Interment of Mrs. Sibyl, Consort of the Rev. Cornelius Waters, ... in Ashby. ... *Boston.* 1802. 8vo, pp. 23. — A Sermon, ... at Ashburnham, May 22, 1806, at the Interment of Mr. John Cushing, jun. ... *Leominster: Printed by S. & J. Wilder.* 1807. 8vo, pp. 15. — A Sermon, ... at the Ordination of Rev. Joel Wright, ... in Leverett, Mass., December 9, 1812. ... *Greenfield.* 1813. 4to, pp. 18. W. — ... A Sermon, ... at the Funeral of the Rev. Levi Pilsbery, Late Pastor ... in Winchendon, Mass., April 8, 1819. ... *Worcester: Printed by William Manning.* 1819. 8vo, pp. 19. BA., W.

Payson (T.) Address before the Associated Instructers [*sic*] of Boston and its Vicinity, on their Anniversary, Oct. 10, 1816. By Thomas Payne. *Worcester.* 1816. 8vo, pp. 28. W. 59318

Paz (——). Ley, Justicia y Verdad, resplandecen en la Suprema Corte de Justicia de México, por la Inocencia de Regidor Paz. *Mexico.* 1828. 8vo. 59319

Paz (Gil.) Las Palabras del Pueblo. ... *Carácas.* 1867. 16mo, pp. 36. 59320

Paz (J. de). Memorias postumas del Brigadier General D. José de Paz. Comprenden sus Campanas, Servicios y Padecimientos; desde la Guerra de la Independencia, hasta su muerte, con variedad de otros documentos inéditos de alta importancia. *Buenos Aires.* 1855. 4 vols., 8vo, pp. 372; 384; 384; 328.

Paz-Soldan (J. Gregorio). Anales Universitarios del Perú. Redactados y publicados por el D. D. José G. Paz-Soldan. *Lima: Imprenta del Gobierno* ... 1862. 2 vols., 4to, pp. xvi, 392, Portrait; (2), 344, (4). C. 59322

Paz-Soldan. Contestacion al Memorandum del Señor D. Eusebio de Salazar y Mazarredo en los puntos que se refiere a José Gregorio Paz-Soldan. Tercera edicion aumentada con algunas documentas importantes. *Lima.* 1864. 4to, pp. 51, (1).

Paz (J. M. de). Arancel de los Derechos que deben llevar los Corregidores, Alcaldes y Escribanos públicos, por Joseph Manuel de Paz. *México.* 1723. 4to. 59324

Paz Soldan (M. F.) Atlas Geografico del Peru, publicado á expensas del Gobierno Peruano ... . Por Mariano Felipe Paz Soldan. *Paris.* 1865. Folio, pp. 81, 67. Maps and Plates.

Paz Soldan. Atlas Géographique de la République du Pérou, par Mariano Felipe Paz Soldan ... . Publié aux frais du Gouvernement Péruvien ... . Édition française par P. Arsène Mouqueron, ... avec la collaboration de Manuel Rouaud y Paz Soldan ... . *Paris: Librairie de Auguste Durand.* 1865. Folio, pp. 82. Maps and Plates. 59326

Paz Soldan. Ensayo de una Teoria del Magnetismo Terrestre en el Peru. ... *Lima.* 1869. Rl. 8vo, pp. 42. Plate.

Paz Soldan. Examen de las Penitenciarias de los Estados Unidos. ... *Nueva York: S. W. Benedict.* 1853. 8vo, pp. 180.

Paz Soldan. Historia del Perú independiente por Mariano Felipe Paz Soldan. ... *Lima.* MDCCCLXVIII-LXXIV. 3 vols., rl. 8vo, pp. (4), ix, 467, 11, (2), Catalogo, 109, (5); (4), iv, 408, Catalogo, 81; (4), 209, Catalogo, (2), 96. Maps and Portraits.

[Paz Soldan.] Dos Ilustres Sabios Vindicados. *Lima.* 1868. Folio, pp. 28. 59330

Privately printed by the lamented Paz-Soldan, in vindication of Raimondi and Lorente, against the attacks of M. E. Dejardin.

Paz Soldan. Reglamento para el Servicio interior de la Prision Penitenciaria de Lima. ... *Lima.* 1863. 4to. 59331

See also Rouaud y Paz Soldan (Manuel).

Paz (*Marquis de la*). Letters of the Marquis de la Paz and Col. Stanhope on the West Indies and the Dispute with Spain. *London.* 1720. 4to. 59332

Paz Soldan (M.) Compendio de Geografia Matematica, Fisica y Politica. Obra postuma del D. D. Mateo Paz Soldan, corregida y aumentada por su Hermano Mariano Felipe Paz Soldan. *Paris.* 1863. 8vo, pp. 475. 59333

Paz Soldan. Geografia del Peru, Obra postuma del D. D. Mateo Paz Soldan, corregida y aumentada por su Hermano Mariano Felipe Paz Soldan. Publicada a expensas del Gobierno Peruano. Tomo Primero. *Paris: F. Didot Hermanos, Hijos y Ca.* 1862. Rl. 8vo, pp. (4), cxxvii, 745. Portrait. C. 59334

No more published.

Paz Soldan. Géographie Du Pérou, Œuvre posthume de D. D. Mateo Paz Soldan, corrigée et augmentée par son frère Le D. D. Mariano Felipe Paz Soldan ... . Publiée aux frais du Gouvernement Péruvien ... . Traduction française par P. Arsène

Mouqueron, ... avec la collaboration de Manuel Rouaud y Paz Soldan. *Paris: Librairie de M. A. Durand.* 1863. Rl. 8vo, pp. (4), xxxj, 538. Portrait. 59335

Some copies have the imprint, *Paris: Librairie du Firmin Didot Frères.*

Paz (Pedro). Arte Menor de Arithmetica ... . *Megico.* 1623. 12mo. 59336

La Paz es Torrersas porque la Guerra es imposible. *Bogota.* 1860. 8vo, pp. 16. 59337

La Paz i el Congreso. *Bojota.* 1860. 8vo, pp. 17. 59338

La Paz. Periódico politico y literario. *Mexico.* 1858. 8vo.

Pazos (Manuel Antonio de). Sermon Funebre que en el Aniversario de Difuntos, que en sú Capitulo Provincial hace la Provincia de N. S. P. S. Francisco de Zacatecas el dia 11 de Nov. 1782 en el Convento Capitular de San Luis Potosi. ... *Mexico.* 1783. 4to. 59340

Pazos (V.) Letters on the United Provinces of South America, addressed to the Hon. Henry Clay ... . By Don Vincente Pazos. Translated from the Spanish, by Platt H. Crosby, Esq. *New York: Printed by J. Seymour.* 1819. 8vo, pp. xi, 9-259, (1). Map. B., C. 59341

Pazos. Memorias Historico-Politicas de Don Vicinte Pazos. Tomo I. *Londres: Impreso para el Autor.* 1834. 8vo, pp. (4), iij, 412, (2). C. 59342

Contains essays on Columbus, etc.

[Pazos.] Narrative of Facts connected with the Change in the Political Condition and Relations of Paraguay, under the Directions of Dr. Thomas Francia. *London.* 1826. 8vo.

Pazos. Projet de l'Établissement de Navigation à Vapeur entre la Guyane française et les républiques de Pérou, de l'Équateur et de la Bolivie, présenté au Gouvernement de S. M. le Roi des Français. ... [n. p.] 1844. 8vo. 59344

Pazos-Kanki (V.) El Evangelio de Jesu Christo segun San Lucas en Aymará y Español. Traducido de la Vulgata Latina. Al Aymará por Don Vicente Pazos-Kanki, Doctor de la Universidad del Cuzco ... . Al Español por el P. Phelipe Scio de San Miguel, Obispo de Segovia. *Londres: J. Moyes.* 1829. 12mo, pp. (2), 130. 59345

[Peabody (A. P.)] The Baccalaureate Sermon [by Peabody] and the Oration and Poem. Class of 1862. *Cambridge: Welch, Bigelow, and Company.* 1862. 8vo, pp. 50, (1). 59346

Also for 1864, '65, '67, '69, in some of which allusions are made to the Civil War.

Peabody. Lessons from our late Rebellion. An Address at the Anniversary of the American Peace Society, May 19, 1867. By Andrew P. Peabody ... . *Boston: American Peace Society.* 1867. 8vo, pp. 31, (1). BA. 59347

Peabody. Memoir of Rev. Charles Mason, D.D. ... By Rev. A. P. Peabody, D.D. With an Appendix. *Boston: Printed by John Wilson and Son.* 1863. 8vo, pp. 39. Portrait. 59348

Peabody. A Memorial of John W. Foster. Edited by Andrew P. Peabody. *Portsmouth: James F. Shores, Jun.* 1852. 12mo, pp. vi, 400. Portrait. 59349

Peabody. Position and Duties of the North with Regard to Slavery. By Andrew P. Peabody. Reprinted from the Christian Examiner of July, 1843. *Newburyport: Charles Whipple.* 1847. 12mo, pp. 22. H. 59350

[Peabody.] The Power of the Resurrection. Sermon ... at King's Chapel ... Boston, April 21, 1867, on the Dedication of a Monument to the Memory of the Young Men of the Parish who fell during the recent War. *Boston: J. H. Eastman's Press.* 1867. 8vo, pp. 22. H. 59351

Peabody. A Sermon ... at Portsmouth, N. H., by Andrew P. Peabody, ... October 24, 1858, ... the Twenty-Fifth Anniversary of his Ordination. *Portsmouth: Frank W. Miller, Printer.* 1858. 8vo, pp. 13. 59352

Peabody. Sermons connected with the Re-opening of the Church of the South Parish, in Portsmouth, New Hampshire, ... Dec. 25 & 26, 1858, and Jan. 30 and Feb. 6, 1859. By Andrew P. Peabody ... . *Portsmouth: James F. Shores, Jun., & Joseph H. Foster.* 1859. 16mo, pp. 112. B., C. 59353

Peabody. The Wealth, Industry, and Resources of Portsmouth. A Lecture before the Portsmouth Lyceum, Nov. 12, 1844, by Rev. A. P. Peabody. ... [*Portsmouth:*] *C. W. Brewster, Printer.* 1844. 8vo, pp. 11. H. 59354

Also: An Address ... at the Thirty-Third Anniversary of the South Parish Sunday School in Portsmouth, N. H. ... June 29, 1851. ... *Portsmouth.* 1851. 8vo, pp. 16.

— Anti-Supernaturalism. A Sermon ... in Harvard University, July 13, 1845. ... *Cambridge.* 1845. 8vo, pp. 26. — Baccalaureate Sermon [by Peabody] and Oration and Poem. Class of 1870. *Boston.* 1870. 8vo, pp. 42, (3). — ... A Discourse ... at the Ordination of Rev. Amos D. Wheeler, at Standish, Maine, Jan. 14, 1835. ... *Limington.* 1835. 8vo, pp. 15. B. — ... A Discourse ... at the Ordination of Rev. Henry Emmons, ... at Dunstable, N. H. June 10, 1835. ... *Nashua, N. H.* 1835. 8vo, pp. 22. — Eulogy ... at the Funeral of Rear Admiral George Washington Storer, U. S. N. 13, January, 1864. ... *Portsmouth.* 1864. 8vo, pp. 8. — Forgiveness. A Sermon, ... at the Ordination of Mr. Horatio Stebbins, ... in Fitchburg, Mass., November 5, 1851. ... *Fitchburg.* 1851. 8vo, pp. 47. — The Immutable Right: An Oration ... before the Phi Beta Kappa Society of Brown University, Aug. 31, 1858. ... *Boston.* 1858. 8vo, pp. 25. — ... Lectures delivered before the Lowell Institute. ... *Boston.* 1864. 8vo, pp. 256. + Second Edition, Revised. [*Ibid.*] — The Nature and Influence of War. An Address delivered before the American Peace Society, ... May 29, 1843. ... *Boston.* 1843. 8vo, pp. 24. — Old Age. A Sermon ... at Epping, N. H., December 27, 1850, at the Interment of Hon. W. Plumer. ... *Portsmouth.* 1851. 8vo, pp. 18. — Reform and Reformers. A Sermon ... June 11, 1854. ... *Portsmouth.* 1854. 8vo, pp. 14. H. — ... A Sermon ... at the Installation of Rev. Nathaniel S. Folsom, ... in Haverhill, Ms. October 7, 1840. ... *Andover.* 1840. 8vo, pp. 24. — A Sermon ... at Epping, N. H., September 21, 1854, at the Funeral of Hon. William Plumer. ... *Portsmouth.* 1854. 8vo, pp. 91. — ... A Sermon ... at the Installation of Rev. Charles Lowe, ... in Salem, Massachusetts, September 27, 1855. ... *Salem.* 1855. 8vo, pp. 34, (1). — ... A Sermon ... at the Ordination of Edwin M. Wheelock, in Dover, N. H. January 7, 1857. ... *Boston.* 1857. 8vo, pp. 27. — A Sermon, ... at the Closing of the Sunday-School Room in Count Street, prior to its removal ... Feb. 15, 1857. ... *Portsmouth.* 1857. 8vo, pp. 24. — ... A Sermon ... at ... Boston, Jan. 23, 1859, ... after the Death of Mary Lyman Lothrop ... . *Boston.* 1859. 8vo, pp. 14. — A Sermon ... at Portland, Maine, at the Funeral of Rev. Ichabod Nichols, D.D. ... *Boston.* 1859. 8vo, pp. 27. — A Sermon ... March 9, 1862, ... after the Funeral of Cornelius Conway Felton, LL.D., President of Harvard University. ... *Cambridge.* 1862. 8vo, pp. 30. — ... A Sermon ... at the Ordination of Mr. H. F. Jenks, at Fitchburg, Mass., April 10, 1867. ... *Boston.* 1867. 12mo, pp. 17. — ... A Sermon ... at ... Boston, June 2, 1867 ... [after] the Decease of Mr. Thomas Bulfinch. ... *Boston.* 1867. 8vo. — A Sermon ... at the Installation of Rev. Charles E. Grinnell ... in Charlestown, Massachusetts, November 10, 1869. ... *Charlestown.* 1869. 8vo, pp. 64. — ... A Sermon ... at the Installation of A. Judson Rich, ... in Brookfield, Mass. ... *Springfield, Mass.* 1870. 8vo, pp. 38. — The Triumphs of War. A Sermon ... on ... the Annual Fast, April 15, 1847. ... *Portsmouth.* 1847. 8vo, pp. 20. + Second Edition. [*Ibid.*] 12mo, pp. 23. — Two Sermons ... [after] the Interment of John W. Foster, Jan. 18, 1852. ... *Portsmouth.* 1852. 8vo, pp. 21. — ... Two Sermons, ... at Portsmouth, N. H. on the ... Annual Thanksgiving, November 25, and on ... Nov. 28, 1841. ... *Portsmouth.* 1841. 8vo, pp. 28. — Views of Duty adapted to the Times. A Sermon ... May 14, 1837 ... . *Portsmouth.* 1837. 8vo, pp. 16. — The Will and the Affections. A Sermon prepared for the Ordination of Mr. Richard Pike ... in Dorchester, Mass. February 8, 1843. ... *Boston.* 1843. 8vo, pp. 48. — "The Word of God is not bound." A Sermon, preached ... June 4, 1854. ... *Portsmouth.* 1854. 8vo, pp. 15. — The Work of the Ministry. A Sermon ... before the ... Meadville Theological School, June 26, 1850. ... *Boston.* 1850. 8vo, pp. 21.

Peabody (D.) ... A Discourse delivered in ... Worcester, on Fast Day, April 7, 1836. By David Peabody. *Worcester.* 1836. 8vo, pp. 20. W. 59355

Peabody (E. P.) Chronological History of the United States. Arranged with Plates on Bem's Principle. By Miss Elizabeth

Palmer Peabody. *New York: Sheldon, Blakeman & Co.* 1856. 12mo, pp. 312. 4 colored Plates. C., S. 59356

[Peabody.] Record of a School. [A. B. Alcott's.] ... *Boston: James Munroe and Company.* 1835. 12mo, pp. vi, 208. + Second Edition ... . *Boston: Russell, Shattuck & Company.* 1836. 12mo, pp. (8), iii-xliii, (2), 198. B. 59357

Peabody. Universal History: arranged to illustrate Bem's Charts of Chronology. ... *New York: ... Sheldon & Co.* 1859. Obl. folio, pp. (2), cii, 154. C. 59358

Peabody (E.) An Address delivered at the Centennial Celebration in Wilton, N. H., Sept. 25, 1839. By Ephraim Peabody. With an Appendix. *Boston: Benjamin H. Greene.* 1839. 8vo, pp. 103. 59359

Peabody. Discourse occasioned by the Death of the Hon. Samuel Sumner Wilde, LL.D.; delivered ... June 24, 1855. By Ephraim Peabody. ... With the Proceedings of the Suffolk Bar, ... *Boston.* 1855. 8vo, pp. 35. B., M. 59360

Peabody. Eulogy on William Henry Harrison, late President of the United States, delivered before the Citizens of New-Bedford, April 27, 1841. By Ephraim Peabody. *New-Bedford: William Howe.* 1841. 8vo, pp. 39. H. 59361

Peabody. The Object of the Ministry. A Sermon preached at the Installation of Rev. Samuel Osgood, as Pastor ... in Providence, December 29, 1841. By Rev. Ephraim Peabody. *Providence: B. Cranston and Company.* 1842. 8vo, pp. 40. 59362

Peabody. Sermons. By Rev. Ephraim Peabody, D.D. ... With a Memoir. *Boston: Crosby, Nichols and Company.* 1857. 12mo, pp. xliv, 388. Portrait. BA. 59363

[Peabody.] Slavery in The United States: its Evils, Alleviations, and Remedies. Reprinted from the North American Review, Oct. 1851. *Boston: Charles C. Little and James Brown.* 1851. 8vo, pp. 36. H. 59364

Also: A Discourse ... at the First Public Meeting of the New Bedford Orphan's Home, December 7, 1842 ... . *Boston.* 1842. 8vo, pp. 30. — Pauperism in Boston: A Sermon before the Society for the Prevention of Pauperism, March 18, 1849. ... *Boston.* 1849. 8vo, pp. (2), 21. — Sermon on ... the Death of Rev. Frederick T. Gray, ... March 18, 1855. ... *Boston.* 1855. 8vo, pp. 29. B.

Peabody (G.) Address at the Opening of the Eastern Rail

Road, between Boston and Salem. August 27, 1838. By George Peabody .... *Salem.* 1838. 8vo, pp. 19. 59365

PEABODY. Letter from George Peabody, Esq., to the Trustees, for the Establishment of an Institute in the City of Baltimore. *Baltimore: Printed by John D. Toy.* 1857. 8vo, pp. 28.

PEABODY. An Account of the Proceedings at the Dinner given by Mr. George Peabody to the Americans connected with the Great Exhibition at London ... 27th October 1851. *London: William Pickering.* M DCCC LI. 8vo, pp. 114, (1). 59367

Also on large paper.

PEABODY. Mr. George Peabody's Gift for Southern Education. Proceedings of the Trustees. [*Salem.* 1867.] 8vo, pp. (2), 15. 59368

[PEABODY.] The Peabody Donation. Reprinted for Private Distribution only. *London: Printed by E. Couchman and Co.* 1862. 8vo, pp. 76. 59369

Contains the correspondence of Mr. Peabody with the trustees, etc., and extracts from the leading papers of the time.

PEABODY. Welcome to George Peabody, Esq. Songs written for the Dinner, at his Reception by the Citizens of his Native Town, October 9th, 1856. [*Salem.* 1856.] 8vo, pp. 4.

See also Vol. v., Nos. 18513 *and* 18517.

PEABODY (J. R.), *pseudon.* A World of Wonders; or ... Animal Magnetism in New-England. By Joel R. Peabody. *Boston: Robert S. Davis.* 1838. 16mo, pp. 158. 8 Plates. C.

PEABODY (J.) A Memoir of the late Joseph Peabody, Esq. ... *New York: Printed by G. W. Wood.* 1845. 8vo, pp. 19.

PEABODY (M.) Miss Slimmens' Window, and Other Papers. By Mrs. Mark Peabody. *New York: Derby & Jackson.* 1859. 12mo, pp. 312. C. 59373

PEABODY (O.) An Essay to revive and encourage Military Exercises, Skill, and Valour ... in New-England. A Sermon ... before the Honourable Artillery Company, in Boston, June 5th. 1732. ... Day of Election of Officers .... By Oliver Peabody, A.M. ... *Boston: J. Eliot.* 1732. 8vo, pp. 45. H., M. 59374

PEABODY. The Foundations, Effects and distinguishing Properties of a good and bad Hope of Salvation .... Considered in a

Sermon, the Substance of which was delivered at the Evening-Lecture at the New-North Church in Boston, ... June 8th, 1742. ... By Oliver Peabody .... *Boston: Printed by D. Fowle for S. Eliot.* 1742. 8vo, pp. 52. BA., M. 59375

Also: That Ministers are to seperate [*sic*] Men to the ... Ministry, by Laying on their Hands; ... shewn in A Sermon ... at Brimfield, June 9th. 1736. When the Reverend Mr. James Bridgham Was ... Ordained. ... *Boston: Printed by S. Kneeland & T. Green.* MDCCXXXVI. 8vo, pp. (4), ii, 26. B., N.

PEABODY (O. W. B.) A Discourse delivered ... in Burlington, ... December 21, 1845, the Anniversary of the ... Landing of the Pilgrim Fathers at Plymouth. By Oliver W. B. Peabody. *Burlington: University Press.* 1846. 8vo, pp. 22. 59376

Also: An Address ... before the Peace Society, of Exeter, N. H., ... April, 1830. ... *Exeter.* 1830. 8vo, pp. 16.

PEABODY (S.) A Sermon, delivered at Concord, before the ... General Court of the State of New-Hampshire, at the Annual Election, ... June, 1797. By the Rev. Stephen Peabody ... . *Concord: Printed by George Hough.* M.DCC.XCVII. 8vo, pp. 23.

PEABODY. A Sermon, delivered at the Ordination of Rev. Josiah Webster, ... in Ipswich, November 13th, 1799. By Stephen Peabody .... *Haverhill.* [n. d.] 8vo, pp. 35. 59378

Also: A Sermon ... March 18, 1801, at the Ordination of the Rev. Moses Dow, ... in Beverly. ... *Salem: Printed by Joshua Cushing.* 1801. 8vo, pp. 26. H.

PEABODY (W. A.) ... A Sermon, ... before the Auxiliary Education Society of Norfolk County, at their Annual Meeting ... August 3, 1847. By William A. Peabody .... *Boston: Press of T. R. Marvin.* 1847. 8vo, pp. 31, (1). B. 59379

PEABODY (W. B. O.) An Address delivered at Springfield, before the Hampden Colonization Society, July 4th, 1828. By William B. O. Peabody. ... *Springfield.* 1828. 8vo, pp. 16.

PEABODY. The duties and dangers of those who are born free. A Sermon ... at the Annual Election, January 2, 1833, before ... Levi Lincoln, Governor, ... and the Legislature of Massachusetts. By William B. O. Peabody. ... *Boston: Dutton and Wentworth, Printers.* 1833. 8vo, pp. 31. BA. 59381

PEABODY. The Literary Remains of the Late William B. O. Peabody, D.D. Edited by Everett Peabody. *Boston: Benjamin H. Greene.* 1850. 12mo, pp. (2), iv, 448. Portrait. 59382

[PEABODY.] Reports on the Fishes, Reptiles and Birds of Massachusetts. Published ... by the Commissioners on the Zo-

ological and Botanical Survey of the State. *Boston: Dutton and Wentworth, Printers.* 1839. 8vo, pp. xii, (4), 426, 18. 59383

PEABODY. Sermons by ... William B. O. Peabody, D.D. With a Memoir by his [twin] Brother. Second Edition. *Boston: Benjamin H. Greene.* 1849. 12mo, pp. vi, 393. B. 59384

Also: Address ... at the Consecration of the Springfield Cemetery, September 5th, 1841. ... *Springfield.* 1841. 8vo, pp. 16. B. — Discourse in Memory of John Abbot Emery, ... Nov. 6, 1842. ... *Cambridge.* 1842. 8vo, pp. 20. — Sermon ... at the Ordination of Rev. Oliver W. B. Peabody ... in Burlington ... . August 14th, 1845. *Burlington.* 1846. 8vo, pp. 24. — A Sermon ... at the Ordination of the Rev. W. B. Peabody, ... in Burlington, ... Aug. 14th, 1845. *Burlington.* 1846. 8vo, pp. 24. *See also* Vol. vi., No. 22560.

PEABODY ACADEMY OF SCIENCE, *Salem, Mass.* First Annual Report of the Trustees of the Peabody Academy of Science, January, 1869. ... Record of the Proceedings of the Trustees from their organization, March, 1867. *Salem.* 1869. 8vo, pp. (4), 103. Continued. H. 59385

Memoirs of the Peabody Academy of Science. ... *Salem.* 1870. 8vo. S. 59386

PEABODY EDUCATION FUND. Memorial of the Trustees of the Peabody Education Fund. [n. p. n. d.] 8vo, pp. 4. 59387

Addressed to the Senate and House of Representatives of Mississippi.

... Peabody Education Fund. Proceedings of the Trustees at their Meeting in Richmond, January 21 & 22, 1868, together with The Report of the General Agent. [*Staunton, Va.* 1868.] 8vo, pp. (2), 14. Continued. B. 59388

Report of the General Agent [B. Sears] of the Peabody Education Fund, from January 21, 1868, to July 1, 1869, with some Account of the Proceedings of the Trustees relating to ... his Agency. [*Staunton, Va.* 1869.] 8vo. 59389

PEABODY INSTITUTE, *Baltimore.* ... Address of the President [John P. Kennedy] ... on the Organization ... of the Institute. February 12, 1870. [n. p. n. d.] 8vo, pp. 33. B. 59390

Address of the President [John P. Kennedy], and Reports of the Treasurer, and Provost to the Trustees of the Peabody Institute of ... Baltimore. Feb. 12, 1869. [n. p. n. d.] 8vo, pp. 11. B.

The Peabody Institute of ... Baltimore. The Founder's Letters and the Papers relating to its Dedication and its History, up to the 1st January, 1868. *Baltimore: Press of William K. Boyle.* 1868. 8vo, pp. 146. 2 Plates. C. 59391

Proceedings of the ... Trustees of the Peabody Institute of ... Baltimore, on the Announcement of the Death of Hon. John Pendleton Kennedy .... [*Baltimore.* 1870.] 8vo, pp. 4. B.

First Annual Report of the Provost to the Trustees of the Peabody Institute of ... Baltimore, June 4, 1868. *Baltimore: Press of Wm. K. Boyle & Son.* 1876. 8vo, pp. 24. Continued.

Also: Alphabetical Catalogue of Books proposed to be purchased for the Library of the Peabody Institute, Baltimore. *Baltimore: Printed by John D. Toy.* 1861. 8vo, pp. 415. + No. 2. ... [*Ibid.*] 1863. 4to, pp. 218. BA.

PEABODY INSTITUTE, *Danvers, Mass.* Catalogue of the Library. *See* Vol. v., No. 18514, add, "Supplement ... January, 1865." *South Danvers: Printed by Charles D. Howard.* 1865. 8vo, pp. 115. H. 59394

First Annual Report of the Trustees of the Peabody Institute, Danvers. March 1st, 1868. *Salem: George W. Pease & Co., Printers.* 1865. 8vo, pp. 15. Continued. 59395

Rules and Regulations of the ... Trustees, and Lyceum and Library Committee, of the Peabody Institute, Danvers, Mass. *Boston.* 1854. 8vo, pp. 8. + *South Danvers: Charles D. Howard, Printer.* 1866. 12mo, pp. 14. B. 59396

PEABODY MUSEUM. First Annual Report of the ... Peabody Museum of American Archæology and Ethnology, ... 1868. *Cambridge: Press of John Wilson and Son.* 1868. 8vo, pp. 28. Portrait. Continued. BA. 59397

The Peabody Trust for the Promotion of Science and useful Knowledge in the County of Essex. *Salem.* 1867. 8vo, pp. 8.

The Peace Almanac for 1845. *New-York: Collins, Brother, & Co.* [n. d.] 12mo, pp. (32). B., S. 59399

Peace and Harmony restored. Being an Account of the Agreement which took place amongst the Burgher and Antiburgher Seceders, and Reformed Presbytery in North America, in Summer 1782; with A Copy of the Proposals, according to which the Associate-Reformed Synod of North America was erected; and an Act of that Synod for a Fast. ... *Glasgow: Printed by John Bryce.* M,DCC,LXXXIII. 12mo, pp. 16. BA.

"Peace and Unity Recommended." A Sermon delivered at Stockland, Dorset, before the Friendly Society, May 22, 1777. By a Country Clergyman. *Exeter.* 1777. 8vo. 59401

Proceedings of the PEACE CONVENTION held in Boston, Sept. 18, 19, 20, 1838. *Boston.* 1838. 16mo, pp. 32. 59402

The "Peace Convention" at Washington, and the Virginia Convention at Richmond. *New York: Dodge & Grattan.* 1861. 8vo, pp. 18. 59403

Proceedings of the Peace Conference Convention, held at Willard's Hall, February, 1861. *Washington.* 1861. 8vo. — Proceedings of the Peace Convention on the Death of J. C. Wright, one of the Commissioners. February 14, 1861. *Washington: R. A. Waters.* 1861. 8vo, pp. 14.

Report made to the General Assembly of ... Rhode Island, at their January Session, 1861, by the Commissioners on the part of the State to the Convention of Commissioners from the several States, held at the request of Virginia at Washington, on the 4th ... February, 1861. *Providence: Knowles, Anthony & Co.* 1861. 8vo, pp. 9. 59404

The Peace Democracy, alias Copperheads—Their Record. [n. p. n. d.] 8vo, pp. 16. 59405

Peace or War? [*New York: J. B. Smith & Co.* 1862.] 8vo, pp. 8. B. 59406

"Peace! Peace!!" *See* [Spring (Lindley)].

Peace Society of Windham County. Its Institution, Sentiments and Purposes. ... *Brooklyn, Con.: ... John Gray, Jr.* 1827. 8vo, pp. 24. BA. 59407

Peace the Sole Chance now left for Reunion. [n. p. n. d.] 32mo, pp. 30. 59408

Peace, To be Enduring, must be Conquered. [n. p. n. d.] 8vo, pp. 7. 59409

Peace with America. A Poem. To General Conway. *London.* 1782. 8vo. + [*Ibid.*] 4to. 59410

Peace with France! Ships, Colonies, and Commerce; ... . *London: John Murray.* 1810. 8vo. 59411

See "Monthly Review," LXVIII. 101.

PEACHAM, *Vt.* Catalogue of the Officers and Students of the Caledonia-County Grammar School, Peacham, Vt., 1834. *Windsor, Vt.* [1834.] 16mo, pp. 16. 59412

The Peacock at Home. A Sequel to the Butterfly's Ball. *New York.* 1808. 8vo. 59413

PEACOCKE (J. S.) The Creole Orphans; or, Lights and Shadows of Southern Life. A Tale of Louisiana. By James S. Peacocke, M.D. *New York: Derby & Jackson.* 1856. 12mo, pp. 365 + *Philadelphia.* 1865. 12mo. 59414

PEAK (J.) Memoirs of Elder John Peak, Written by Himself. *Boston: J. Howe.* 1832. 12mo, pp. 203. Portrait. + Second Edition, Enlarged. [*Ibid.*] 12mo, pp. 252. Portrait.

Also: Sermon ... [and] Memoirs of Mrs. Gale and ... Mrs. Esther Peak. ... Fourth Edition. *Boston.* 1840. 32mo, pp. 96. Portrait.

PEAKE (R.) Trial of Mrs. Rebecca Peake, Indicted for the Murder of Ephraim Peake, Tried at Orange County Court, December Term, 1835, Embracing the Evidence, Arguments of Counsel, Charge and Sentence. *Montpelier: E. P. Walton & Son.* 1836. 12mo, pp. 88. 59416

PEALE (C. Willson). Address delivered by Charles W. Peale, to the ... Citizens of Philadelphia, ... 18th ... July, 1816 ... . *Philadelphia.* 1816. 8vo, pp. 23. N., P. 59417

PEALE. Discourse Introductory to a Course of Lectures on the Science of Nature; with Original Music, Composed for, and Sung on, the occasion. Delivered in the ... University of Pennsylvania, Nov. 8, 1800. By Charles W. Peale. ... *Philadelphia: Printed by Zachariah Poulson, Junior.* 1800. 8vo, pp. 50. P.

PEALE. A Scientific and Descriptive Catalogue of Peale's Museum, By C. W. Peale, ... and A. M. F. J. Beaurois ... . *Philadelphia: Printed by Samuel H. Smith,* ... M, DCC, XCVI. 8vo, pp. xii, 34. 59419

Also: Introduction to a Course of Lectures on Natural History. Delivered in the University of Pennsylvania, Nov. 16, 1799. ... *Philadelphia: Printed by Francis and Robert Bailey.* 1800. 8vo, pp. 28. BA., P.

PEALE (F.) On the Stone Implements of the Indians of North America ... . By Franklin Peale. ... June 21, 1861. [*Philadelphia.* n. d.] 8vo, pp. 8. B. 59420

[PEALE (Harriet G.), *and others.*] To the ... Senate, and House of Representatives, of the United States. *New York.* 1865. Folio, 1 leaf. 59421

Memorial respecting the purchase of the painting of Washington before Yorktown, by Rembrandt Peale.

PEALE (R.) Account of the Skeleton of The Mammoth, a non-descript Carnivorous Animal of Immense Size, Found in

America. By Rembrandt Peale, the Proprietor. *London: E. Lawrence.* 1802. 8vo, pp. 46. 59422

Contains a narrative of the discovery of nearly an entire skeleton near New York, in the autumn of 1801, together with a comparative description, etc.

PEALE. Catalogue of the National Portrait and Historical Gallery, illustrative of American History, formerly belonging to Peale's Museum, Philadelphia. *Cincinnati.* 1852. 8vo, pp. 26.

PEALE. Catalogue of Valuable Original Paintings by the Late Rembrandt Peale, with Engravings, etc., comprising the Contents of the Studio of this Eminent Artist. To be sold ... November 18th, 1862 .... *Philadelphia.* 1862. 8vo, pp. 32. 59424

PEALE. An Historical Disquisition on the Mammoth, or Great American Incognitum ... whose Fossil Remains have been found in North America. ... By Rembrandt Peale. *London: E. Lawrence.* 1803. 8vo, pp. v, (3), 91. Plate. H. 59425

[PEALE.] Portrait of Washington. [n. p. 1824.] 8vo, pp. 20

Portrait of Washington. [*Philadelphia.* 1846.] 8vo, pp. 14. — Portrait of Washington. [n. p. 1860.] 8vo, pp. 16. *See also* Vol. XIII., No. 56706.

PEALE (R.) Outlines of the Life of Theodore Newell, and History of his Inventions. Compiled by Rubens Peale and Joseph Lancaster .... *Baltimore: Printed by John D. Toy.* 1824. 12mo, pp. 12. 59427

PEALE (T. R.) Mammalia and Ornithology. By Titan R. Peale, one of the Naturalists of the Expedition. *Philadelphia: Printed by C. Sherman.* 1848. 4to, pp. xxv, 17–338. Plates.

This volume was suppressed, and is of the greatest rarity.

PÉAN (M.-J.-H.) Mémoire pour Michel-Jean-Hughes Péan, Chevalier, Capitaine-Aide-Major des Ville & Gouvernement de Quebec ... Accusé. Contre M. le Procureur-Général du Roi en la Commission, Accusateur. *Paris: De l'Imprimerie de Guillaume Desprez.* M.DCC.LXIII. 4to, pp. xii, 318, (1). H. 59429

Signed by M. Dupont and two others.

PEARCE (D. J.) Speech of Mr. Pearce, of Rhode Island, ... in the House ... on the 5th, 6th, and 7th ... April, on the Resolution of The Judiciary Committee, relative to the Collector of Wiscasset. *Washington: Jonathan Elliot.* 1832. 8vo, pp. 34.

PEARCE. Slanders Refuted. Being a Reply to the foul and abusive attacks made on Dutee J. Pearce, and Tristam Burges. [n. p. about 1826.] 8vo, pp. 18. 59431

PEARCE [James Alfred]. Letter from Senator Pearce, of Maryland, on the Politics of the Day. Washington, July 31, 1856. [*Washington.* 1856.] 8vo, pp. 8. 59432

Also: Old Line Whigs for Buchanan and Breckinridge. Letters from Hon. James Alfred Pearce, and Hon. Thomas G. Pratt .... [n. p. 1855.] 8vo, pp. 16. — Speech ... on the ... Coast Survey of the United States, ... in the Senate of the U. S. ... Feb. 17, 1849. Second Edition. *Washington.* 1849. 8vo, pp. 16. B.

PEARCE. Addresses on the Death of the Hon. James A. Pearce, delivered ... January 13th, 1863. *Washington.* 1863. 8vo, pp. 52. 59433

PEARCE (S.) Annals of Luzerne County; a Record of Interesting Events, Traditions, and Anecdotes. From the First Settlement, at Wyoming, to 1860. By Stewart Pearce. Illustrated by a Map and Engravings. *Philadelphia: J. B. Lippincott & Co.* 1860. 8vo, pp. (4), 554. C. + [Another] Edition with Notes, Corrections, and Valuable Additions. [*Ibid.*] 1866. 8vo, pp. 564. Map and Plates. 59434

PEARCE (Z.) A Sermon Preached before the Incorporated Society for the Propagation of the Gospel in Foreign Parts: ... 20th of February, 1729 ... . By Zachary Pearce, D.D. ... *London: Printed by J. Downing.* M.DCC.XXX. 8vo, pp. 63, (3). B.

PEARCE. A Sermon preached ... April the 17th, 1735 ... . By Z. Pearce, D.D. ... To which is annexed An Account of the Origin and Design of the Society for Promoting Christian Knowledge. *London: Printed by M. Downing.* 1735. 4to, pp. 28. S.

The Pearl of Great Price: ... Selection from the Revelations ... and Narratives of Joseph Smith, First Prophet ... to the ... Latter-Day Saints. *Liverpool.* 1851. 8vo, pp. 56. Facsimile.

PEARSE (J.) A Narrative of the Life of James Pearse ... . Part I. Containing a General Account of his early Life, his Five Years Residence in Mississippi, Louisiana, &c. Part II. Containing an Account of his ... Imprisonment at Plattsburgh, &c. Written by Himself. *Rutland: Printed by William Fay* ... 1825. 12mo, pp. 144. C. 59438

PEARSON (C. H.) ... The Cabin on the Prairie. By Rev. C. H. Pearson ... . *Boston: Lee & Shepard.* 1870. 16mo, pp. 299. 4 Plates. C. 59439

[PEARSON.] On the Frontier, or Scenes in the West. ... *Boston.* [1864.] 16mo, pp. (4), 7–320. 2 Plates. H. 59440

Also: The Young Pioneers of the North-West. ... *Boston.* 1871. 16mo, pp. 331. 3 Plates. C.

[PEARSON (*Mrs.* C. H.)] Cousin Franck's Household; or, Scenes in the Old Dominion. By Pocahontas. Second Edition. *Boston: Upham, Ford and Olmstead.* 1853. 12mo, pp. vii, 259. Plate. C. 59441

PEARSON (E.) A Public Lecture, occasioned by the Death of the Rev. Joseph Willard ... . *Printed ... Cambridge by William Hilliard.* MDCCCIV. 8vo, pp. 21. BA. 59442

PEARSON. A Sermon ... in Boston, before the American Society for Educating Pious Youth for the Gospel Ministry, Oct. 26, 1815. By Rev. Eliphalet Pearson ... . *Andover: Printed by Flagg and Gould.* 1815. 8vo, pp. 28. BA. 59443

This elicited: "From the Independent Chronicle. Review of Mr. Pearson's Sermon ... in Boston, before the American Society for Educating Pious Youth for the Gospel Ministry, October, 26, 1815." ... *Charlestown: Printed by Thomas Shepard.* 1816. 12mo, pp. 84. BA.

PEARSON. A Sermon ... in Boston, before the Massachusetts Society for Promoting Christian Knowledge, Nov. 27, 1811. By Rev. Eliphalet Pearson ... . *Cambridge: Printed by Hilliard and Metcalf.* 1811. 8vo, pp. 36. B., W. 59444

Also: A Sermon ... Nov. 3, 1812, at the Funeral of Madam Phebe Phillips, ... of Andover. ... *Boston: Printed by Samuel T. Armstrong.* 1812. 8vo, pp. 24. B. — A Sermon ... at the Ordination of the Rev. Ephraim Abbot, ... Greenland, Oct. 27, 1813. ... *Andover: Flagg and Gould, Printers.* 1813. 8vo, pp. 39. H. *See also* Vol. I., No. 1437.

PEARSON (E. C.) Prince Paul: the Freedman Soldier. By Mrs. Emily C. Pearson. *Boston.* [1867.] 16mo, pp. 359. 2 Plates. 59445

Also: Ruth's Sacrifice; or Life on the Rappahannock. ... *Boston: Graves & Young.* 1863. 12mo, pp. iv, 259.

PEARSON (H. B.) A Discourse delivered ... at Harvard, Worcester Co., Mass., on the Day of the Annual Fast, April 6, 1848. By Henry B. Pearson. ... *Boston: Wm. B. Fowle.* 1848. 8vo, pp. 22. BA. 59446

Also: Freedom versus Slavery. Letters from Henry B. Pearson, ... to Rufus Choate, on his Letter to the Whig Committee of the State of Maine, originally ... published in the Eastern Mail, Waterville, for August and September, ... 1856. *Portland: Daley & Lufkin.* 1856. 8vo, pp. 16. H.

PEARSON (J.) Notes made during a Journey in 1821, to the United States of America, from Philadelphia to the Neighbourhood of Lake Erie: through Lancaster, Harrisburgh, Carlisle &

Pittsburgh, and back to Philadelphia: through Louis Town, Huntingdon, & New Holland: in search of a Settlement. By John Pearson. *London: W. and S. Couchman.* 1822. 12mo, pp. 12. 59447

PEARSON (J.) Contributions for the Genealogies of the Descendants of the First Settlers of the Patent and City of Schenectady, from 1662 to 1800. By Jonathan Pearson. *Albany, N. Y.: J. Munsell.* 1873. 4to, pp. iv, 324. B. 59448

PEARSON. Contributions for the Genealogies of the First Settlers of ... Albany, from 1630 to 1800. By Prof. Jonathan Pearson. *Albany, N. Y.: J. Munsell.* 1872. 4to, pp. (2), 182. B.

PEARSON. Early Records of the City and County of Albany, and Colony of Rensselaerswyck, (1656–1675.) Translated from the original Dutch, with Notes. By Jonathan Pearson ... . *Albany, N. Y.: J. Munsell.* 1869. Imp. 8vo, pp. vii, 528. B.

PEARSON (J.) Speech of the Hon. Joseph Pearson, on the Loan Bill, ... February 16, 1814 ... . *Georgetown: R. Alleson.* 1814. 8vo, pp. 27. 59451

PEARSON (T. S.) Sketch of the Life of the late Rev. David Merrill ... . By Thomas Scott Pearson, A.M. *Windsor, Vt.* 1855. 12mo, pp. 24. 59452

See also Vol. XII., No. 48834.

PEARSON (W.) A Dissertation on the Mixed Fever, ... June 30, 1789, ... before ... the ... President, the Medical Professors, and the Governors of the University at Cambridge in America. By William Pearson. ... [n. p. n. d.] 8vo, pp. (4), 12. BA.

PEASE (A. G.) Christ ... . A Sermon ... at the Funeral of Harry S. Richards, Esq., ... in Norwich, Vt., Wednesday, November 16, 1853. By A. G. Pease. ... *Albany: Joel Munsell.* 1853. 8vo, pp. 33. 59454

PEASE (A. S.) The Early History of the Pease Families in America. By Austin Spencer Pease. *Springfield, Mass.: Samuel Bowles and Company, Printers.* 1869. 8vo, pp. v, (2), 96, (1). 4 Portraits. B., C. 59455

This is often bound up with the "Genealogical and Historical Record," No. 59458.

PEASE (C.) Address, ... before the Graduating Class, in the Medical Department of the University of Vermont, June 4, 1856. By Calvin Pease ... . *Burlington.* 1856. 16mo, pp. 35.

PEASE. Sermon preached before the Graduating Class in the University of Vermont, August 2d, 1857, by Rev. Calvin Pease, D.D. *Burlington.* 1857. 8vo, pp. 40. 59457

Also: ... An Address, ... on the Occasion of his Inauguration as President of the University of Vermont, August 5, 1856, By Rev. Calvin Pease. *Burlington.* 1856. 8vo, pp. 52. BA. — ... A Sermon ... before the Graduating Class in the University of Vermont, July 29, 1869. ... *Burlington.* 1860. 8vo, pp. 36. — ... A Discourse ... before the ... University of Vermont. August 3, 1842. . . *Burlington.* 1842. 8vo, pp. 43. — A Sermon; ... in Burlington, November 17, 1858, at the Funeral of Noble Lovely, Esq. ... *Burlington.* 1858. 8vo, pp. 18. — Sermon ... before the Graduating Class in the University of Vermont, July 31, 1859 ... . *Burlington.* 1859. 8vo, pp. 33. — Sermon, on ... the Death of John G. Gollond and Joshua V. R. Arthur, ... of the University of Vermont, ... November 13, 1859. ... *Burlington.* [n. d.] 8vo, pp. 25. — A Tribute To the Memory of Elizabeth Bloss Buel, from her Pastor, ... Rochester, March 8, 1863. *Rochester, N. Y.* 1863. 12mo, pp. 40.

PEASE (D.) Genealogical and Historical Record of the Descendants of John Pease, Sen., Last of Enfield, Conn. Compiled by Rev. David Pease and Austin Pease ... . *Springfield, Mass.: Samuel Bowles & Company, Printers.* 1869. 8vo, pp. xxiv, 401, (1); v, (2), 96, (1). Portraits. B. 59458

See Pease (A. S.), No. 59455, *supra.*

PEASE (E. H.) In Memoriam. Calvin Pease. ... *New Haven: Thomas H. Pease.* 1865. 8vo, pp. (4), 129. B. 59459

PEASE (F. S.) An Account of the Descendants of John Pease, who landed at Martha's Vineyard in ... 1632. By Frederick S. Pease ... . *Albany: Joel Munsell.* 1847. 12mo, pp. 52.

PEASE. Genealogy of the Ancestors and Posterity of Isaac Lawrence. By Frederick S. Pease of Albany. *Albany: Printed by Joel Munsell.* 1848. 8vo, pp. 20. + [*Ibid.*] 1852. 8vo, pp. 76. + [*Ibid.*] 1853. 8vo. + [*Ibid.*] 1854. 59461

Also: A Family Gathering of the Family of Pease. [n. p. n. d.] 8vo, pp. 4.

[PEASE (Giles).] The Barnstable Conference ... comprising the Constitution of the Conference, ... with a ... Historical Sketch of the Several Churches ... . By a Committee of the Conference. *Boston: Printed by S. N. Dickinson & Co.* 1846. 16mo, pp. 44. B. 59462

[PEASE.] Nineteenth Birth-Day Gathering, of Rev. Charles Cleveland. June 21, 1862. *Boston.* 1862. 16mo, pp. 64. Portrait and Plate. B. 59463

PEASE. "Who is on the Lord's Side?" or, does the Bible sanction Slavery? ... Examination into the Egyptian, Mosaic, and

American Systems of Service and Labor. By Giles Pease. *Boston: Henry Hoyt.* 1864. 12mo, pp. 64. H. 59464

PEASE (J.) The Rifleman's Hand-Book, ... for the use of the Massachusetts Rifle Club. By John Pease ... . *Boston: ... Alfred Mudge & Son.* 1862. 16mo, pp. 46. Plates. 59465

PEASE (J. C.) A Gazetteer of the States of Connecticut and Rhode-Island. ... Consisting of Two Parts. I. A Geographical and Statistical Description of each State: ... II. A General Geographical View of each County, and a Minute and Ample Topographical Description and Statistical View of each Town, ... with succinct Biographical Notices of Eminent Deceased Men. ... By John C. Pease and John M. Niles. *Hartford: William S. Marsh.* 1819. 8vo, pp. vii, (1), 389, (1). Portraits of Wolcott and Knight. 2 Maps. BA. 59466

PEASE (J.) A Letter from Joseph Pease, Sen. ... on the ... Slave Trade and Slavery ... . [*Darlington.* 1862.] Folio, pp. 4.

[PEASE.] On Slavery, and its Remedy. [Signed] Joseph Pease. [*London.* 1841.] 4to, pp. 3. 59468

[PEASE (Richard L.)] Report of the Commissioner appointed to complete the Examination and Determination of all Questions of Title to Land, and of all Boundary Lines between the Individual Owners, at Gay Head, on the Island of Martha's Vineyard. *Boston: Wright & Potter.* 1871. 8vo. 59469

PEASLEE (C. H.) Speech of C. H. Peaslee at the Democratic State Convention at Concord, N. H., June 11, 1851. [n. p. 1851.] 8vo. 59470

PECK (B. D.) *See* Vol. XI., No. 44026.

PECK (G.) Early Methodism within the ... Old Genesee Conference, from 1788 to 1828; or, the First Forty Years of Wesleyan Evangelism in Northern Pennsylvania, Central and Western New York, and Canada. By George Peck, D.D. ... *New York: Carlton & Porter.* 1860. 8vo, pp. 512. Portrait.

PECK. Wyoming; its History, Stirring Incidents, and Romantic Adventures. By George Peck, D.D. ... *New York: Harper & Brothers.* 1858. 12mo, pp. 432. 12 Plates. 59472

The author was familiar with the scenes, as well as many of the actors in the Wyoming tragedy, for a period of forty years. Also: Our Country: Its Trials and its Triumphs. ... suggested by the varying Events of the War for the Union. ... *New*

York: Carlton & Porter. 1865. 16mo, pp. 300. — The Past and the Present. A ... Sermon, ... before the Oneida and Wyoming Conferences, at Ithaca, N. Y., April 16, 1866. ... *New York: Carlton & Porter.* 1866. 12mo, pp. 43. — Slavery and the Episcopacy; being an Examination of Dr. Bascom's Review ... in the Case of Bishop Andrew. ... *New York.* 1845. 8vo, pp. 139. S.

PECK (G. W.) Melbourne, and the Chincha Islands; with Sketches of Lima, and a Voyage round the World. By George W. Peck. *New York: Charles Scribner.* 1854. 12mo, pp. (2), v, 13–294. Plate and Map. B. 59473

PECK (I. B.) A Genealogical History of the Descendants of Joseph Peck, who emigrated with his Family to this Country in 1638: and Records of his Father's and Grandfather's Families in England: with the Pedigree extending back from Son to Father for Twenty Generations; ... . Also, an Appendix, giving an Account of the Boston and Hingham Pecks ... . By Ira B. Peck. *Boston: Printed by Alfred Mudge & Son.* 1868. 8vo, pp. (2), 442. 13 Portraits, folded leaf, 2 Plates. 59474

PECK (J.) A Poem on General Taylor; or A Blow at the Root of War; in "Rough and Ready" Measure. By J. Peck. [n. p.:] *Printed for the Author.* 1848. 8vo, pp. 16. H. 59475

PECK (J. H.) Report of the Trial of James H. Peck, Judge of the United States District Court for the District of Missouri, before the Senate of the United States, on an Impeachment preferred by the House of Representatives against him for high Misdemeanors in Office. By Arthur J. Stansbury. *Boston: Hilliard, Gray & Co.* 1833. 8vo, pp. iv, 591. C. 59476

[PECK (Jedediah).] The Political Wars of Otsego; or Downfall of Jacobinism and Despotism: Being a Collection of Pieces lately published in the Otsego Herald. To which are added, An Address to the Citizens of the United States; and Extracts from Jack Tar's Journals, kept on board the Ship Liberty ... . By the Author of the Plough-jogger. *Cooperstown, N. Y.* 1796. 8vo, pp. 123. S. 59477

PECK (J. T.) The History of the Great Republic, ... considered from a Christian Stand-Point. By Jesse T. Peck, D.D. *New York: Broughton & Wyman.* 1868. 8vo, pp. viii, 710. 10 Portraits. 59478

PECK (John). A | Description | of the | Last Judgment, | with | some Reflections thereon. | The Happiness of being Ready, | and the Misery of being Unready for | such a day; | Also, | a Poem on

Death, | and | on the Resurrection. | *Boston.* 1773. 8vo, pp. 31. 2 Plates. 59479

PECK (J.), *and* LAWTON (J.) An Historical Sketch of the Baptist Missionary Convention of the State of New York, embracing a Narrative of the Origin and Progress of the Baptist Denomination in Central and Western New York: with, 1. History of the Hamiltonian Baptist Missionary Society; 2. Sketch of the Associations in the State; 3. Biographical Notices of the Founders of the Convention. By John Peck and John Lawton. *Utica, N. Y.* 1837. 8vo, pp. 255. 59480

See "North American Review," January, 1838.

PECK (John J.) Andrew Johnson Club. Inaugural Address of the President. [n. p. n. d.] 8vo, pp. 7. 59481

[PECK (J. M.)] "Father Clark;" or The Pioneer Preacher. Sketches and Incidents of Rev. John Clark. By an Old Pioneer. *New York: Sheldon, Lamport & Blakeman.* 1855. 12mo, pp. 287. B. 59482

PECK. A Gazetteer of Illinois, in Three Parts: Containing a General View of the State, a General View of each County, and a Particular Description of each Town ... . By J. M. Peck. *Jacksonville: R. Goudy.* 1834. 12mo, pp. viii, 376. + Second Edition, Revised, Corrected and Enlarged. [*Ibid.*] + Second Edition, Entirely Revised ... . *Philadelphia: Grigg & Elliott.* 1837. 12mo, pp. xi, 328. BA. 59483

PECK. A Guide for Emigrants; containing Sketches of Illinois, Missouri, and the Adjacent Parts. By J. M. Peck ... . *Boston: Lincoln & Edmands.* 1831. 18mo, pp. 336. Map. B.

PECK. A New Guide for Emigrants to the West, containing Sketches of Michigan, Ohio, Indiana, Illinois, Missouri, Arkansas, with the Territory of Wisconsin and the Adjacent Parts. By J. M. Peck, A.M. ... *Boston: Gould, Kendall & Lincoln.* 1836. 12mo, pp. 374. + Second Edition. [*Ibid.*] 1837. 12mo, pp. 381. + New Edition. *Boston.* 1844. 12mo, pp. 394. + *Cincinnati: D. Anderson.* 1848. 12mo, pp. 381. C. 59485

PECK. The Traveler's Directory for Illinois ... . Intended as a Companion to the New Sectional Map of Illinois. *New York: J. H. Colton.* 1839. 8vo, pp. 219. Map. 59486

Also: Death of Eminent Men a Public Calamity. A Discourse in Reference to the Decease of the Late Governor of Illinois, Ninian Edwards, Delivered in ... Belleville,

... December 22, 1833. ... *Rock-Spring, Ill.* 1834. 8vo, pp. 20. — The Duties of American Citizens: A Discourse, ... Springfield, Illinois. ... January 26, 1841. ... *St. Louis.* 1841. 8vo, pp. 24. — The Principles and Tendencies of Democracy: An Address, ... in Belleville, St. Clair County, Illinois, July Fourth, Eighteen Hundred and Thirty-Nine. *Belleville, Illinois.* 1839. 8vo, pp. 11. — A Sermon, ... December 25, 1827, in reference to the Death of Daniel P. Cook. ... *Edwardsville.* 1828. 8vo, pp. 14.

PECK. Forty Years of Pioneer Life. Memoir of John Mason Peck, D.D. Edited from his Journals and Correspondence. By Rufus Babcock. *Philadelphia.* [1864.] 12mo, pp. 360. Portrait. 59487

This volume gives numerous anecdotes of the quaint sayings, originality, and eccentricity of this backwoods preacher.

PECK (Lucius). Slavery in the Territories. Speech of Hon. L. B. Peck, of Vermont in the House ... August 3, 1848. In Committee of the Whole on the State of the Union, on the Army Appropriation Bill. [n. p. n. d.] 8vo, pp. 7. + Slavery in the Territories. Speech ... April 23, 1850, In Committee of the Whole ... on the President's Message transmitting the Constitution of California. [n. p. n. d.] 8vo, pp. 8. 59488

Proceedings of the Washington County Bar, in Relation to the Deaths of Hon. Lucius B. Peck and Luther Henry, Esq., at March Term, 1867. ... *Montpelier.* 1867. 8vo, pp. 20. B.

PECK (Nathaniel), *and* PRICE (Thomas S.) Report of Messrs. Peck and Price, who were appointed at a Meeting of the Free Colored People of Baltimore, held ... 25th November, 1839, Delegates to visit British Guiana, and the Island of Trinidad; for the Purpose of ascertaining the Advantages to be derived by Colored People Migrating to those Places. *Baltimore: Woods & Crane.* 1840. 8vo, pp. 23. BA. 59489

PECK (P. B.) *and* (L. M.) Memoirs of Rev. Philetus B. Peck, and Rev. Linus M. Peck. With a Biographical Sketch of Mrs. Sarah Peck. *Utica: Printed by P. Bennett.* 1848. 16mo, pp. 135, (1). S. 59490

PECK (P.) A Discourse ... on the ... General Election, at Montpelier, October 9, 1817, before ... Jonas Galusha, Esq. Governor; ... of Vermont. By Phinehas Peck ... . *Jesse Cochran ... Windsor, Vt.* 1817. 8vo, pp. 23. 59491

Elder Peck was of the Methodist persuasion, and the first settled minister in Lyndon, Vt., 1812–19.

PECK (T.) Historical Sketch of the Congregational Society ... in Bristol, Conn. By Tracy Peck. *Hartford.* 1852. 8vo.

PECK (W. B.) *and* (C. E.) *See* Vol. XIII., No. 55128.

PECK (W. D.) A Catalogue of American and Foreign Plants cultivated in the Botanic Garden, at Cambridge, Massachusetts. By W. D. Peck. ... *Cambridge: Printed by Hilliard and Metcalf.* 1818. 8vo, pp. iv, 60. BA. 59493

[PECK.] Obituary Notice of Professor Peck. [n. p. 1823.] 8vo, pp. 10. BA. 59494

Also in the "Col. of Mass. Hist. Soc.," Vol. XX.=2d Ser., Vol. X.

PECK (W. H.) The M'Donalds; or, the Ashes of Southern Homes: a Tale of Sherman's March. By William Henry Peck. *New York.* 1867. 12mo, pp. 192. C. 59495

Also: The Confederate Flag on the Ocean. A Tale of the Cruises of the Sumter and Alabama. ... *New York: Van Evrie, Horton & Co.* 1868. 18mo, pp. 96. C.

PECKARD (P.) Justice and Mercy Recommended particularly with reference to the Slave Trade. A Sermon preached before the University of Cambridge, By P. Peckard, D.D. ... *Cambridge: Printed by J. Archdeacon* ... . MDCCLXXXVIII. 8vo, pp. xi, 48. P. 59496

PECKARD. Memoirs of the Life of Mr. Nicholas Ferrar. By P. Peckard, D.D., Master of Magdalen College, Cambridge. *Cambridge: Printed by J. Archdeacon* ... MDCCXC. 8vo, pp. xvi, 316, folded leaf. Portrait. B. 59497

Nicholas Ferrar was Deputy Governor of the Virginia Company while the Earl of Southampton was Governor. He was also one of the managers or council of the company, the third associate being Sir Edward Sandys. Ferrar too, was for a time king's counsel for the company. He was born in 1592 and died in 1637. He is noticed in Wood's "Athenæ Oxonienses" and by Chalmers.

This volume contains many documents and facts pertaining to Virginia no where else to be met with, and is, to the American historian, of the highest value. It contains the only authentic account we have of the royal high-handed dissolution of the Virginia Company through the intrigues of Gondimar, compiled from materials which are now believed to be lost. This work was reprinted with additions from a MS. in the Lambeth library in Wordsworth's "Ecclesiastical Biography." New Edition, abridged, London, 1833, fcap 8vo.

[PECKHAM (*Sir* George).] A Trve Reporte of the late Discoueries, and Possessions, taken in the Right of the Crowne of Englande of the Newfound Landes: By that valiaunt and worthye Gentleman, Sir Humfrey Gilbert, Knight. Wherein is also breefly sette downe her Highnesse lawfull Tytle therevnto ... . *London: Printed by I[ohn] C[harlewood] for Iohn Hinde.* 1583. 4to. 59498

The "Reporte" is reprinted in Hakluyt. *See also* Collier's "Early English Lit."

PECKHAM (J.) Gen. Nathaniel Lyon, and Missouri in 1861. A Monograph of the Great Rebellion. By James Peckham. ... *New York: American News Company.* 1866. 12mo, pp. 447. 2 Plates and Portrait. B. 59499

PECKHAM (R.) Historical Poem, ... Dedication of the Soldiers' Monument, in Westminster, Mass., July 4th, 1868. By Robert Peckham ... . *Fitchburg.* 1868. 8vo, pp. 26. B. 59500

PECKHAM (Rufus W.) Speech of Mr. Peckham, of New York, on the Kansas and Nebraska Question. Delivered ... May 18, 1854. *Washington.* 1854. 8vo, pp. 15. S. 59501

PECKHAM (W. H.) A Review of the Arguments of Counsel in the New York Court of Appeals on the Constitutionality of the Law making United States Treasury Notes a Legal Tender in Payment of Private Debts, and of the Opinion of the Court thereon. By Wheeler H. Peckham. *New York: Banks & Brothers.* 1864. 8vo, pp. 65. S. 59502

PECKOLT (T.) Analyses de Materia Medica Brasileira dos Productos que forão premiados nas Exposições Nacionaes e na Exposição Universal de Parisi em 1867 Pelo Dr. Th. Peckolt, ... *Rio de Janeiro.* 186–. 12mo, pp. 108. 59503

[PECQUET DU BELLET (Paul).] Amérique du Nord. Lettre au Corps Législatif. *Paris: Impr. L. Tinterlin et Cie.* 1864. 8vo, pp. 24. H. 59504

[PECQUET.] La Révolution Américaine dévoilée. ... *Paris: E. Dentu.* 1861. 8vo, pp. 31. BA. 59505

See also Prevost (F.)

The Peculiar Treasure. *See* [Cotton (E.)], Vol. v. 17040.

Peculiarities of the Shakers, Described in ... Letters from Lebanon Springs, in ... 1832. ... By a Visitor. *New York: J. K. Porter.* 1832. 24mo, pp. 116. C. 59506

Peculio do Procurador de segunda instancia ou Collecção Contendo a Lei da creação do Supremo Tribunal de Justiça os Regulamentos das Relações, ... addicionados de notas indicativas das Leis, ... publicados até, 1866 ... . Por um Bacharel. *Bahia.* 1867. 8vo, pp. 114. 59507

The Pedagogiad, or Literary Fracas, a Literary Tale, by Peregrine Pastime. [*New York.* 1801. Colophon:] *G. & R. Waite, Printers.* 4to, pp. 15. S. 59508

PEDDER (J.) Report made to the Beet Sugar Society of Philadelphia, on the Culture in France, of the Beet Root ... . By James Pedder. *Philadelphia.* 1836. 8vo, pp. 40. 59509

A Pedestrian Tour of 2300 Miles in North America, to the Lakes, the Canadas, and the New England States. Performed in the Autumn of 1821. Embellished with Views: by P. Stansbury. *New York.* 1822. 12mo. 59510

See "North American Review," xv. 340.

A Pedestrian's Adventures—Thro' Baltimore in Disguise, in 1861 ... . *New York.* 1862. 8vo. 59511

Pedimento de los Sres. de la Junta de Censura por el abogado de la imprenta. *Habana: Arazoza y Soler.* 1811. 4to, pp. 8.

PEDLEY (C.) The History of Newfoundland from the Earliest Times to ... 1860. By the Rev. Charles Pedley, of St. John's, Newfoundland. *London: Longman* ... . 1863. 8vo, pp. 531. Map. B. 59513

PEDRAÇA (Julien de). *See* Vol. III., No. 10806.

PEDRARIAS DE BENAVIDES. *See* Benavides (P.), II. 4639.

PEDRAZA (M. Gomez). Notas al Manifiesto publicado en Nueva Orleans ... *Méjico.* 1831. 8vo. 59514

PEDRAZA. Revista de los Documentos relativos al llamamiento hecho al Gen. G. Pedraza y sú regreso á la Republica Mexicana. *Méjico.* 1832. 8vo. 59515

See also Gomez Pedraza (M.), Vol. VII., No. 27770.

PEDREIRA DO COUTTO FERRAZ (Luiz). *See* Vol. VI., No. 24165, *and* Vol. IX., No. 38224.

PEDRO I. Correspondance de Dom Pedre Premier, Empereur constitutionnel du Brésil, avec le feu Roi de Portugal Don Jean VI, son Père, durant les troubles du Brésil; traduites sur les lettres originales; précédée de la vie de cet empereur et suivie de pièces justificatives; par Eugène de Monglave. ... *Paris.* 1827. 8vo, pp. v, 360. S. 59516

Also: Eloge funèbre de S. M. Don Pedro. [*Paris: Imprimerie de Dezaucbe.* 1834.] 8vo, pp. 36.—La Statue de l'Empereur Dom Pedro I. par F. A. Burgain, et offert pour l'Auteur et les Éditeurs à la Nation Brésilienne. *Rio de Janeiro.* 1862. 8vo, pp. 32.

PEDRO DE AGURTO. Tratado de que se deben Administrar los Sacramentos à los Indios. *Mexico.* 1573. 8vo. 59517

PEDRO DE GANTE. Catecismo de la Doctrina Cristiana en Lengua Mexicana. *Antuerpiæ.* 1528. 8vo. 59518

Ascribed to Pedro de Gante by Dr. Ramon in "Boletin de la Societ. Mexic. de Geografia," x. 378.

PEDRO DE GANTE. Doctrina Cristiana en Lengua Mexicana. [Colophon:] *A honrra y gloria de nuestra Señor Iesu xpo y de su bēdita madre aqui se acaba la presente doctrina xpiana en lēgua Mexicana. La ql fue recopilada por el R. P. Fray Pedro de Gāte de la ordē de Sant frācisco. Fue impressa en casa de Iuā Pablos impressor de libros. Año. de.* 1553. 8vo, 172 leaves. 59519

PEDRO DE GANTE. Epistola ad Provincialem Flandriæ de rebus ad fidem Christianam in Novo orbe pertinentibus. *Antuerpiæ.* 1528. 8vo. 59520

Concerning this *see* [Harrisse's] "Bib. Am. Vet.—Additions," p. 95, *note.* *See also* our Vol. I., No. 994.

PEDRO DE TOBAR. Verdadera historica relacion del origen manifestacion y prodigiosa y milagros de la imagen de la sacratissima virgen del Rosario de Chiquinquira que esta en el nuevo reyno de Granada de las Indias. *En Madrid.* 1694. 4to.

PEDRO PHELIPE. Primer Synodo Diocesana [de Chile], celebròla el ilmo Señor D. Pedro Phelipe ... en la santa iglesia cathedràl de dicha Ciudad de la Concepcion. [*Concepcion:*] *En la oficina de la Viuda de Peralta impressore de dicho consejo.* 1749. Folio, pp. (16), 191. 59522

PEDROSA (J. de la). Via Lactea, seu Vita candissima S. Philippi Nerii ... *Mexico.* 1698. 4to. 59523

PEDROSO (P. J. R. S. de). *See* Vol. XII., No. 48519.

PEEBLES (C. G.) Exposé of the Atlantic and Pacific Railroad Company. ... By Corns. Glen Peebles. ... *New York.* 1854. 8vo, pp. 16. B. 59524

PEEL (R.) The Speeches of the Late Right Honourable Sir Robert Peel, ... in the House of Commons. ... *London: George Routledge and Co.* 1853. 4 vols., 8vo, pp. 31, 768; iv, 864; iv, 887; iv, 856. BA., C. 59525

PEELE (George). A Farewell entituled to Sir Iohn Norris and Syr Frauncis Drake, Knights, and all their brave and resolute Followers: whereunto is annexed a Tale of Troy. *London: Printed by I[ohn] C[harlewood].* 1589. 4to, pp. 21. 59526

See Brydges' "Censura Literaria."

A Peep at the Pilgrims in Sixteen Hundred and Thirty-Six. A Tale of Olden Times. ... *Boston.* 1824. 2 vols., 12mo, pp. 306; 276. 59527

For another edition, *see* Vol. III., No. 12425.

A Peep behind the Curtain. By a Supernumerary [Tom. Ford]. *Boston: Redding & Co.* [1850.] 12mo, pp. 91. 59528

See also [Moore (J. B.)], Vol. XII., No. 50395.

A Peep into Catharine Street, or the Mysteries of Shopping. By a Late Retailer. *New York.* 1846. 8vo, pp. 25. 59529

A Peep into the Past by an Ancient Lady. *Charleston.* 1853. 12mo. 59530

A Peep into the Sanctuary, being a Succinct Examination of the Right Rev. B. T. Onderdonk, Bishop of New York. *Boston.* 1845. 8vo, pp. 32. 59531

A Peep into Uncle Tom's Cabin, by "Aunt Mary," for her Nephews and Nieces; with an Address from Mrs. Harriet Beecher Stowe to the Children of England and America. *London.* 1853. 12mo, pp. 430. 59532

PEERS (B. Orr). American Education; or, Strictures on the Nature, Necessity & Practicability of A System of National Education, suited to the United States. By Rev. Benjamin O. Peers. *New York: John S. Taylor.* 1838. 12mo, pp. 364.

Also: Inaugural Address at the Opening of Morrison College, Lexington, Ky. ... *Lexington, Ky.* 1833. 8vo.—Obituary: (From the Journal of Christian Education.) [n. p. 1842.] 8vo, pp. 14. B.

PEET (E. W.) A Sermon on the ... Public Thanksgiving. For the happy termination of the late civil Dissensions in Rhode Island; ... in ... Providence, July 21, 1842. By Rev. Edward W. Peet. *Providence: Isaac H. Cady.* 1842. 8vo, pp. 16.

Also: ... A Sermon ... in ... Rahway, ... on the 150th Anniversary of the Society for the Propagation of the Gospel ... . *New York.* 1851. 8vo, pp. 23, (1).

PEET (H. P.) History of the United States of America. By Harvey Prindle Peet, LL.D. *New York: Egbert, Bourne & Co.* 1869. 12mo, pp. 423. C. 59535

Also: Address ... in ... Raleigh, on ... laying the Corner Stone of the North Carolina Institution for the Instruction of the Deaf and Dumb. ... *New York: Egbert, Hovey & King.* 1848. 8vo, pp. 47. C.

PEET. A Biographical Sketch of Harvey Prindle Peet ... . With a Paper on the Notions of the Deaf and Dumb before Instruction. *New York.* 1857. 8vo. 59536

PEET (J.) Memoir, with Sermons, of Rev. Josiah Peet. By Rev. David Shepley. ... *New York: J. F. Trow.* 1854. 8vo, pp. 344. S. 59537

PEET (S.) History of the Presbyterian and Congregational Churches and Ministers in Wisconsin. Including an Account of the Organization of the Convention, and the Plan of Union. By Rev. Stephen Peet. *Milwaukee: Silas Chapman.* 1851. 16mo, pp. 208. BA. 59538

[PEIRCE (Augustus).] The Rebelliad; or Terrible Transactions at the Seat of the Muses; a Poem ... . Edited ... by the Pi Tau. *Boston.* 1842. 12mo, pp. 77, (1). + *Boston: R. B. Muzzey.* 1842. 12mo, pp. 77, (1). H. 59539

PEIRCE (B.) A History of Harvard University, from its Foundation, in ... 1636, to the ... American Revolution. By the late Benjamin Peirce ... . *Cambridge: Brown, Shattuck, and Company.* 1833. 8vo, pp. xix, 316; Appendix, 159. 2 Plates.

Also: An Oration ... at Salem, ... Fourth of July, 1812. ... *Salem: Printed by Thomas C. Cushing.* 1812. 8vo, pp. 24. H.

PEIRCE (B.) Address of Professor Benjamin Peirce, President of the American Association for 1853, on retiring from the Duties of President. [n. p. n. d.] 8vo, pp. 17. H. 59541

PEIRCE (B. M.) United States' State Department: A Report on the Resources of Iceland and Greenland. Compiled by Benjamin Mills Peirce. *Washington.* 1868. 8vo, pp. 72. 2 Maps.

PEIRCE (B. K.) The Eminent Dead; or, Triumphs of Faith. By Bradford K. Peirce. *Boston: Charles H. Peirce.* MDCCCLI. 12mo, pp. 502. 59543

PEIRCE. Life in the Woods; or, the Adventures of Audubon. By Rev. Bradford Kinney Peirce. *New York: Carleton & Porter.* [1864.] 18mo, pp. 252. 59544

Also: A Half Century with Juvenile Delinquents; or, the New York House of Refuge and its Times. ... *New York: D. Appleton and Company.* 1869. 8vo, pp. 384. 17 Plates.—Trials of an Inventor: Life and Discoveries of Charles Goodyear. ... *New York: Carleton & Porter.* [1866.] 18mo, pp. 224. Portrait, 4 Plates. BA.

PEIRCE (C.) Meteorological Account of the Weather in Philadelphia from January 1, 1790, to January 1, 1847. By Charles Peirce. *Philadelphia.* 1847. 12mo. 59545

See also Vol. I., No. 1074.

[PEIRCE (Cyrus).] An Address to the Inhabitants of Nantucket, on Education and Free Schools. *Providence.* 1838. 8vo, pp. 24. H. 59546

PEIRCE (E. W.) The Peirce Family of the Old Colony: or the Lineal Descendants of Abraham Peirce. By Ebenezer Weaver Peirce. *Boston: The Author.* 1870. 8vo, pp. xx, 490. 6 Plates and 5 Portraits. 59547

Also: The Barnaby or Barneby Family. ... [n. p. n. d.] 8vo.

[PEIRCE (I.)] The Narraganset Chief; or, the Adventures of a Wanderer. Written by Himself. *New York: J. K. Porter.* 1832. 12mo, pp. 195. 59548

PEIRCE (I. B.) An Oration, ... before the Newport Moral and Literary Association called the Hycarpedian Society, ... Fourth of July, 1808 ... . By I. B. Peirce. ... *Providence: Printed by Jones & Wheeler.* 1808. 8vo, pp. 20. BA. 59549

PEIRCE [James]. A Tractate on Church Music; being an Extract from the Reverend and Learned Mr. Peirce's Vindication of the Dissenters. ... *London.* MDCCLXXXVI. 8vo, pp. 31.

"Inscribed to the reverend Doctor Chauncy and the reverend Mr. John Clark, the Ministers; and to the several members of the First Congregational Dissenting Church in Boston in America." "The interest of this tract is considerably enhanced by a knowledge of the circumstances which called it forth. It is well known that Mr. Tho. Brande Hollis, one of the benefactors of Harvard College, had acquired widespread reputation for wealth and liberality, and was not unfrequently subjected to calls for considerable sums of money for objects in which he had either no sympathy, or did not feel that *he* should be bled. Among these applications was one from Dr. Charles Chauncy and the pillars of the First Congregational Church of Boston for £500, to buy an Organ. Instead of granting this extraordinary request from a well-to-do Society, Mr. Brande Hollis caused, it is said, 500 copies of this Tractate to be printed and sent over to the Members of the Society, endeavoring thereby to inculcate in them that modesty and simplicity in their public worship, which they seemed for the moment to be outgrowing."—STEVENS.

PEIRCE (J. D.) An Address on the Death of President Lincoln, ... in ... North Attleboro', Mass., April 19, 1865. By J. D. Peirce ... . *Boston: Printed by Davis & Farmer.* 1865. 8vo, pp. 16. B. 59551

PEIRCE (N.) An Account of the Great Dangers and Distresses and the Remarkable Deliverance of Capt. Nathanael Peirce, who sailed from Portsmouth, in New Hampshire, ... and being taken up at Sea, was carried to Oporto. *Boston: Edes and Gill.* 1756. 8vo, pp. 20. H. 59552

PEIRCE (P.) An | Eulogy, | pronounced on the 22d of February, 1800. | Before the Inhabitants of | Greenfield, Massachusetts. | Assembled to commemorate the death of | Gen. George Washington, | ... | By Proctor Peirce, A.M. | ... | *Greenfield: Printed by Thomas Dickman.* 1800. 8vo, pp. 16. 59553

[PEIRCE (Thomas).] Odes of Horace in Cincinnati; as published in the "Western Spy and Literary Cadet," during ... 1821. *Cincinnati: Printed at Harrison's Press.* 1822. 18mo, pp. 117.

The notes are personal and sarcastic.

PEIRCE (W.) An Almanac for New England. By Mr. William Peirce, Mariner. *Cambridge: [Printed by Samuel Daye.]* 1639. 59555

Concerning this, *see* the note to No. 25791. The date to 25791 should read 1639.

PEIRCE (W. L.) The Year: A Poem. By William Leigh Peirce. *New York: D. Longworth.* 1813. 18mo, pp. 191, 75.

Catalogue of the Officers and Students of PEIRCE ACADEMY, ... Nov. 22d, 1850. *Boston.* 1850. 12mo, pp. 20. Continued.

Also: Semi-Centennial Jubilee ... Aug. 6, 1858. [Oration by B. F. Hallett, Poem by G. C. Burgess.] *Boston.* 1858. 8vo, pp. 48. H.

Peirpoint's Pamphlet. From the Norfolk, Va., New Regime of ... June 24th, 1864. [n. p. n. d.] 12mo, pp. 28. 59558

PEIRSON (Abel Lawrence). Address on Temperance, ... Salem, January 14, 1830. By A. L. Peirson, M.D. ... *Boston: Perkins & Marvin.* 1830. 8vo, pp. 32. B. 59559

[PEIRSON.] Memoir of Edward Augustus Holyoke. ... *Boston.* 1829. 8vo, pp. 80. 2 Portraits. 59560

PEIRSON (A.) Some | Helps for the Indians | Shewing them | How to improve their natural Rea- | son, to know the True God, and | the true Christian Religion. | 1. By leading them to see the Di- | vine Authority of the Scriptures. | 2. By the Scriptures the Divine | Truths necessary to Eternal Salvation. | Undertaken | at the Motion, and published by | the Order of the Commission- | ers of the United Colonies. | By Abraham Peirson. | Examined and approved by Thomas | Stanton, Interpreter-General to the U- | nited Colonies for the Indian Language, | and by some others of the most able Interpreters amogst [*sic*] us. | *Cambridg:* [sic] *Printed by Samuel Green.* 1658. Sm. 8vo, pp. 67. L. 59561

A catechism for the use of the Quiripi Indians of New Haven Colony, in English and Indian (interlinear). The only known copy with this, the original title, is in the

Lenox Library. Another copy, in the British Museum, reads, after "Abraham Peirson," | "Pastor of the Church at Branford. | Examined and approved by that | Experienced Gentleman (in the In- | dian language) Captain | John Scot." | and, in the imprint, "*Cambridge: Printed for Samuel Green.*" This alteration was made after the publication of the book, and probably in England. These are the only copies known to be preserved. The first sheet of the catechism was reprinted in London, in 1659, at the end of "A Further Accompt of the Progresse," etc. *See* our Vol. VI., No. 22149. The whole was reprinted, with an introduction, by J. Hammond Trumbull, in an edition of one hundred copies, *Hartford,* 1873. It should be noted that the author wrote his name Pierson, though it is Peirson on the title-page.

PEIRSON (L. J. [Wheeler]). The Forest Minstrel. By Mrs. Lydia Jane Peirson. Edited by Rev. B. S. Schenck. ... *Philadelphia: J. W. Moore.* 1846. 12mo, pp. 264. BA. 59562

Also: Forest Leaves. ... *Philadelphia.* 1845. 12mo, pp. 264.

PEISSNER (E.) The American Question in its National Aspect. Being also an Incidental Reply to Mr. H. R. Helper's "Compendium on the Impending Crisis of the South." By Elias Peissner ... . *New York: H. H. Lloyd & Co.* 1861. 12mo, pp. 164. BA. 59563

Also: The English Address, ... at the Great Turner's Festival, in Albany, June 28th, 1858 ... [n. p. 1858.] 8vo, pp. 8.

PEIXOTO (Ribeiro dos Guimaraens). Dissertation Inaugurale sur les Médicamens Brésiliens ... *Paris.* 1830. 4to. 59564

PEIXOTTO (D. L. M.) Address ... before the Medical Society of ... New-York, ... 25th ... July, 1831. By Daniel L. M. Peixotto, M.D. ... *New-York: J. Seymour, Printer.* 1831. 8vo, pp. 30. 59565

Also: Anniversary Discourse, ... before the Society for the Education of Orphan Children, and the Relief of Indigent Persons of the Jewish Persuasion. ... *New-York.* 1830. 8vo, pp. 47.—Introductory Lecture, ... at the Willoughby Medical College of ... Lake Erie, 1836–7. ... *Cleveland.* 1837. 8vo, pp. 30, (1). B.

PEKIN, *Ill.* Pekin City Directory for ... 1870–71. To which is added a History of Pekin, from its earliest settlement to the present time. *Pekin (Ill.): Sellers & Bates.* 1870. 8vo. C.

PELAEZ (F. de P. G.) Memorias para la Historia del antiguo Reyno de Guatemala, Redactadas por el Ilmo. Señor Dr. D. Francisco de Paula Garcia Pelaez ... . *Guatemala:* ... *L. Luna.* 1851–52. 3 vols., 4to, pp. (4), 310, (3), (4); (4), iii, 311, (4); (4), iii, 299. C. 59567

PÉLAGE (M.) Mémoire pour le Chef de Brigade Magloire Pélage, et pour les habitans de la Guadeloupe, chargés, par cette Colonie, de l'Administration provisoire, après le départ du Capitaine-Général Lacrosse, dans le mois de brumaire an 10. ... *A Paris, Desenne, an* XI.—*Août* 1803. 2 vols., 8vo, pp. (4), 326, xxxix, (1); viii, 358, (2). A. 59568

Corrected title of our No. 29042, Vol. VI.

PELBY (W.) Letters on the Tremont Theatre. ... By William Pelby. ... *Boston: John H. Eastburn.* 1830. 8vo, pp. 44.

PELET DE LA LOZÈRE ([Privat Joseph Claramond], *Comte*). Lafayette en Amérique et en France. Par le Comte Pelet de la Lozère *Paris: Grassart.* 1867. 12mo, pp. (4), 210, (1). B.

PELET DE LA LOZÈRE. Précis de l'Histoire des États-Unis d'Amérique, depuis leur Colonisation jusqu'à ce jour. Par le Cte Pelet de la Lozère ... . *Paris: Firmin Didot Frères.* 1845. 8vo, pp. (4), 550, (1). BA. 59571

PELHAM (C.) The World: or, the Present State of the Universe. Being a ... Collection of Modern Voyages and Travels. ... By Cavendish Pelham. *London: J. Stratford.* 1806–8. 2 vols., 4to, pp. (4), 2, 743, iv; 870, iv, iv. 117 Plates, 7 Maps.

Includes Entrecasteaux, La Pérouse, Portlock, Vancouver, Wilson, and other voyages in America.

PÉLISSOT (F.) Misterios de Buenos Aires. Novela original escrita en frances por Felisberto Pélissot y traducida en castellano para la tribuna, por uno de sus colaboradores. *Buenos Aires.* 1856. 2 vols., 4to, pp. 82; 78. 59573

[PELL (A.)] *See* [Pell (Robert Cruger)].

PELL (A. S.) Address to the ... Electors of the State of New York. By Alfred S. Pell, Esq. *Albany.* 1824. 8vo, pp. 9.

Also: An Address. ... to the Electors of Dutchess County, on the ... Caucus and Anti-Caucus Nominations for Representative Offices. ... [n. p. 1822?] 8vo, pp. 11.

[PELL (Ferris).] Letter to ... Albert Gallatin, Esq., on the Doctrine of Gold and Silver, and the Evils of the Present Banking System in Effect and Tendency. By Publicola. *New York.* 1815. 8vo, pp. 96. W. 59575

PELL. Memorial to the Legislature of New York, on the Adjustment of the Demands of the State against the United States. By Ferris Pell. *Albany.* 1823. 8vo. 59576

Also: A Review of the Administration and Civil Police of the State of New York, from ... 1807 to ... 1819. ... *New York: Printed by E. Conrad.* 1819. 8vo, pp. 184. *See also* Vol. VI., No. 22767.

[PELL (Robert Cruger).] Forward or Backward? *New York: James Miller.* 1863. 8vo, pp. 12. BA. 59577

PELLEPRAT (P.) Relation des Missions des PP. de la Compagnie de Iesvs dans les Isles, & dans la Terre Ferme de l'Amérique Méridionale. Divisée en Devx Parties: Avec vne Introdvction à la Langue des Galibis Sauuages de la Terre Ferme de l'Amérique. Par le Père Pierre Pelleprat ... . *A Paris, Chez Sebastien Cramoisy & Gabriel Cramoisy.* M.DC.LV. 2 parts, 8vo, pp. (16), 93; (2), 121, (4); 30, (1). C., S. 59578

One of the most valuable of the Jesuit "Relations," with an introduction to the language of the Galibis, savages in America. Brunet (Vol. III., p. 664,) says that the introduction is sometimes found separate.

PELLERIN (*M.*) Reflexions sur le Traite des Noirs. Par M. Pellerin. *Paris: Imprimerie Nationale.* 1790. 8vo, pp. 15.

PELLET (E. P.) History of the 114th Regiment, New York Volunteers. ... By Brevet-Major Elias P. Pellet. *Norwich, N. Y.* 1866. 12mo, pp. (2), viii, ii, (2), 406. 59580

PELLETAN ([Pierre Clément] E.) Adresse au Roi Coton. Par Eugène Pelletan, auteur de plusieurs ouvrages sur l'Amérique. ... *Publié par H. de Mareil,* ... *New York.* 1863. 8vo, pp. 19. + *Paris: Pagnerre* ... . 1863. 8vo, pp. (4), 43. B. 59581

PELLETAN. An Address to King Cotton. By Eugene Pelletan ... . Translated by Leander Starr. *H. de Mareil, New York.* 1863. 8vo, pp. 19. B. 59582

PELLETIER (E.) Honduras et ses Ports. Documents officiels sur le chemin de fer interoceanique, par E. Pelletier. [n. p.] 1869. 8vo, pp. 30. 59583

PELLETREAU (F.) Statement of the Demands of the Representatives of F. Pelletreau, on the Parties Interested in the American Vessels, the Hart, Two-Friends, Alpha and Minerva, Destroyed at Sea by a French Squadron, Commanded by Admiral Lallemand. *New York.* 1838. 8vo, pp. 18. 59584

PELLETREAU (William Smith, Jr.) Register of the Pelletreau Family, from their Arrival in this Country to the Present Time, collected from Authentic Sources. ... *Southampton, L. I.* 18—. 12mo. 59585

PELLHAM (E.) Gods Power and Providence: shewed in the Miracvlous Preservation and Deliverance of eight Englishmen

left by Mischance in Green-land, Anno 1630, nine Moneths and twelve Dayes. Faithfully reported by Edward Pellham, one of the eight men aforesaid. *London: Printed by R. G. for Iohn Partridge.* 1631. 4to, pp. (12), 35. 59586

Reprinted in Churchill's "Voyages," IV. Ternaux (No. 533) says "Anno 1629."

PELLICER DE OSSAV Y TOVAR (J.) Annales | de la Monarqvia | De España | depves de su perdida, | qve escrivió | Don Ioseph Pellicer do Ossav y Tovar, | ... | *En Madrid: Por Francisco Sanz, Impressor del Reyno ... Año de* 1681. Folio, pp. (18), 432. A.

PELLICER. Genealogia de la noble, y antigva casa, de Cabeza de Vaca. ... *Madrid: Domingo Garcia i Morràs.* 1652. Folio, (5), 110 leaves. 59588

PELLICER. Memorial de la Calidad, i servicios de don Cristoval Alfonso de Solis i Enriqvez, septimo adelantado de Yvcatan, ... que pone en las reales manos de su M. de la Reyna ... don Alonso de Solis Valderabano i Bracamonte, octavo adelantado de Yvcatan. ... *Madrid.* 1670. Folio, (1) leaf, 114 leaves.

PELLICER (J. A.) Y SAFORCADA. Ensayo de una Bibliotheca de Traductores Españoles donde se da Noticia de las Traducciones que hay en Castellano de la Sagrada Escritura, ... Historiadores, Medicos, Oradores, Poetas, asi Griegos como Latinos; y de otros Autores ... . Por D. Juan Antonio Pellicer y Saforcada ... . *Madrid: Por D. Antonio de Sancha* ... M.DCC.LXXVIII. 8vo, pp. (16), 206, 175. BA. 59590

[PELS (E.)] Lof-Dicht | Des Vermaerde, Wyt-Beroemde, Manhaftige Zee-Heldt | Pieter Pietersen Heyn | Generael: | Der Geoctroyeerde, Vereenighde | West-Indische Compagnie. | Waer in Historischer-Wyse ver haelt wordt | de Loffelycke daet Begaen inde Baya | de Todo los Sanctos, en het Veroueren | vande Silvere-Vloot, aen t Eylant Cuba | Inde Haven van | Matanca. | *t'Amsterdam voor Wyllem Ianssen Wyngaert Boeck ver Coper by 't Stadt huys,* 1629. | 4to, (6) leaves. 59591

Panegyric of the hero P. P. Heyh, wherein is historically narrated the capture of the silver-fleet, etc. *See also* Vol. VIII., No. 31659, *and* Vol. IX., No. 41779.

PELTERIE (T. de). Mémoire sur l'Ile d'Haïti, ... avec l'exposé des avantages et des resources immenses ... . *Paris, Chez l'Auteur.* 1841. 8vo, pp. 32. A. 59592

PELTIER (——). États-Unis de l'Amerique. Pièces officielles, Messages, Instructions, Dépêches, etc. relatives aux dif-

férends avec la France. Traduites de l'Anglois. *Londres: Baylis.* 1798. 8vo, pp. 70. 59593

PELTRIE (*Mme. de la*). Life of Madame de la Peltrie (Magdalein de Chauvigny), Foundress of the Ursuline Convent, Quebec. By a Member of the Community. *New York: E. Dunigan & Brother.* 1859. 12mo. 59594

This lady devoted her life to the civilization of the Indians. *See* "Hist. Mag.," III. 98, and Carne's "Lives of Eminent Missionaries."

PELZ (E.) Briefe aus Nord-Amerika. Von Eduard Pelz. ... Erster Brief: Bremen. *New York.* 1850. 12mo, pp. (2), iv, 71.

Also: Ein Jahresbericht der Emigranten-Commissäre von New York. Mitgetheilt ... von Eduard Pelz. ... *Rudolstadt.* 1852. 8vo, pp. 72. B.—Minnesota in seinen Hauptverhältnissen. Emigrations-Monographie. ... *Hamburg: Hoffman und Tampe.* 1868. 8vo, pp. 60.

PELZELN (A. von). Reise der Österreichischen Fregatte Novara um die Erde in ... 1857, 1858, 1859 unter den Befehlen des Commodore B. von Wüllerstorf-Urbair. Zoologischer Theil. Erster Band Vögel. Von August von Pelzeln. ... *Wien.* 1865. 4to, pp. (2), iv, 176. 6 Plates. BA. 59596

PELZELN. Zur Ornithologie Brasiliens, Resultate von Johann Natterers Reisen ... 1817 bis 1835. Dargestellt von August von Pelzeln. ... *Wien: A. Pichler's Witwe & Sohn.* 1871. 8vo, pp. (6), 462, lix, Zusätze, (18). 2 Maps. B. 59597

P[EMBER] (A[rthur].) Mysteries and Miseries of the Great Metropolis. By "A. P." *New York: D. Appleton & Company.* 1874. 8vo, pp. viii, 462. 12 Plates. 59598

PEMBERTON (E.) A Discourse ... By the late ... Mr. Ebenezer Pemberton, Previous to the Ordination Of the Reverend Mr. Joseph Sewall, At Boston, September 16. 1713. ... *Boston: Printed by J. Franklin, for S. Gerrish* ... 1718. 8vo, pp. (4), 15.

PEMBERTON. The Divine Original and Dignity of Government Asserted; and an Advantageous Prospect of the Rulers Mortality recommended. A Sermon preached before ... the Governor, ... of Massachusetts-Bay, ... May 31, 1710. The Day for the Election of her Majesties Council there. By Ebenezer Pemberton ... . *Boston ... Printed by B. Green* ... 1710. 8vo, pp. (2), 106. B., BA. 59600

PEMBERTON. A Funeral Sermon on the Death of ... The Reverend Mr. Samuel Willard ... . By Ebenezer Pemberton,

A.M. To which is Annexed, A Poem, ... By the Rev. Mr. Benjamin Colman. *Boston: Printed by B. Green, for Benjamin Eliot.* 1707. 16mo, pp. (16), 80, Poem, (2), 14. B. 59601

"By his Printed Works He has Erected himself a Monument that will Endure when the Famed Mausoleum's of the World shall Moulder down, and be buryed in their own Ruines."—*Extract.*

PEMBERTON. Sermons and Discourses on Several Occasions. By the late ... Ebenezer Pemberton, A.M. ... in Boston ... . To which is added, A Sermon after his Funeral ... by ... Mr. Colman ... . *London: Printed for J. Batley; ... and for Sam. Gerrish, in Boston, New England.* MDCCXXVII. 8vo, pp. (2), iv, (2), 310. Portrait. BA., C. 59602

Also: A Christian Fixed in His Post. A Sermon ... at the Boston Lecture, April 20, 1704. ... *Boston ... Printed by B. Green* ... 1704. 12mo, pp. 39.—A Sermon ... in the Audience of the General Assembly at the Publick Lecture in Boston, Nov. 1, 1705. ... *Boston ... Printed by B. Green* ... 1706. 16mo, pp. (2), 35. H.—The Souldier defended & directed: ... a Sermon ... to the Artillery Company in Boston, on the ... Election of Officers, June 2d. 1701. ... *Boston: Printed by B. Green and J. Allen, for Samuel Sewall, Junior.* 1701. 12mo, pp. 42.—A True Servant of his Generation Characterized ... . A Sermon ... on the Death of ... John Walley ... . *Boston ... Printed by Bartholomew Green.* 1712. 4to, pp. (2), 32. B., BA., W.

[PEMBERTON.] Catalogue Of Curious and Valuable Books, belonging to the late ... Mr. Ebenezer Pemberton, Consisting of Divinity, Philosophy, History, Poetry, &c. ... To be Sold by Auction, ... in Boston, the Second Day of July, 1717 ... . Also a valuable Collection of Pamphlets will then be exposed to Sale. The Books may be viewed ... at the House of the late Reverend Mr. Pemberton ... . *Boston: Printed by B. Green* ... . 1717. 8vo, pp. (2), 28. 59603

Very rare. "Perhaps the first instance in New England of a printed catalogue of Books at auction."

PEMBERTON (E.) All Power in Heaven, and in Earth Given unto Jesus Christ. A Sermon preached at the Public Lecture in Boston, ... Jan. 29th 1756. By Ebenezer Pemberton, A.M. ... With a Preface by the Reverend Dr. Sewall, Mr. Prince, and Mr. Foxcroft. *Boston: Printed by D. Fowle.* 1756. 8vo, pp. (2), iv, 30. BA., C. 59604

PEMBERTON. The Duty of Committing our Souls to Christ, explained and improved in a Sermon: the Substance of which was preached at Stratfield ... Connecticut, Sept. 13th. 1742. By Ebenezer Pemberton, A.M. ... *Boston: Printed by Rogers & Fowle.* 1743. 8vo, pp. 41. BA. 59605

PEMBERTON. Heaven the Residence of the Saints. A Sermon Occasioned by the Sudden and much Lamented Death of the Reverend George Whitefield, A.M. ... Delivered at the Thursday Lecture in Boston, Oct. 11. By Ebenezer Pemberton, D.D. ... *Boston: Printed by D. Kneeland, for Joseph Edwards.* MDCCLXX. 8vo, pp. 31. B. + To which is added, An Elegiac Poem on his Death, By Phillis, a Negro Girl, of Seventeen Years of Age, Belonging to Mr. J. Wheatley of Boston. *Boston, Printed: London, Reprinted, For E. and C. Dilly.* M.DCC.LXXI. 8vo, pp. 31. 59606

PEMBERTON. Practical Discourses on various Texts. By E. Pemberton, A.M., Pastor of the Presbyterian Church in the City of New York. *Boston: Printed by T. Fleet, for D. Henchman.* 1741. 12mo, pp. (6), 3–199. 59607

PEMBERTON. A Sermon preached in New-Ark, June 12. 1744, at the Ordination of Mr. David Brainerd, a Missionary among the Indians ... . By E. Pemberton, A.M. ... With an Appendix touching the Indian Affairs. *Boston: Printed by Rogers and Fowle, for J. Pemberton.* 1744. 4to, pp. (4), iv, 39. B. 59608

The appendix contains (pp. 24–39) a narrative by David Brainerd of the commencement and progress of his Mission among the Indians, 1743–4; and an account of the Rev. Azariah Horton's labors among the Indians of Long Island. Reprinted with Edwards's "Life," Edinburgh, 1765.

PEMBERTON. A Sermon, ... May 25th. 1757. Being the Anniversary for the Election of His Majesty's Council for the Province. By Ebenezer Pemberton ... . *Boston: Printed by John Draper.* 1757. 8vo, pp. 32. B. 59609

With historical narrations, a quaint production. Also: The Knowledge of Christ Recommended, in A Sermon ... in New-Haven: April 19th, 1741. ... *New-London: Printed ... by T. Green.* 1741. 8vo, pp. (4), 28, (2).—A Sermon. Preach'd before the Commission of the Synod, at Philadelphia. April 20th, 1735. ... *New York: Printed by John Peter Zenger.* 1735. 8vo, pp. 21.—A Sermon ... at the Ordination of the Reverend Mr. Walter Wilmot at Jamaica on Long-Island. April 12. 1738. ... *Boston ... Printed by J. Draper, for D. Henchman.* 1738. 8vo, pp. (2), 38.—A Sermon ... on ... the Death of John Nicoll, M.D. ... *New York: Printed by James Parker.* 1743. 4to, pp. 32.—Sermon ... to the Ancient and Honourable Artillery Company, ... June 7, 1756. ... *Boston: Printed by Edes and Gill.* M.DCC.LVI. 8vo, pp. 22.—A Sermon ... at the Ordination of the Reverend Mr. Isaac Story, to the ... Care of the Second Church in Marblehead, ... May 1, 1771. ... *Salem: Printed by Samuel Hall.* 1771. 8vo, pp. 27.—Sermons on Several Subjects. Preach'd at the Presbyterian Church in ... New York. ... *Boston: Daniel Henchman.* 1738. 8vo pp. (4), 94.— ... Thanksgiving Sermon ... New York, July 31 ... *New York.* 1746. 4to.

[PEMBERTON (Israel), *and others.*] An | Address | to the | Inhabitants of Pennsylvania, | By | Those Freemen, of the City of Philadelphia, | who are now confined in the | Mason's Lodge, | by

virtue of | A General Warrant. | Signed in Council | by the | Vice President | of the | Council of Pennsylvania. | *Philadelphia: Printed by Robert Bell.* MDCCLXXVII. 8vo, pp. (4), 52. + ... *New York: Reprinted by Mills and Hicks.* MDCCLXXVII. 8vo, pp. 43. BA. + ... *London: Reprinted by James Phillips.* MDCCLXXVII. Post 8vo, pp. 46. + ... *Dublin: Reprinted by Robert Jackson.* 1777. 8vo, pp. 32. 59610

These freemen, principally Quakers, were imprisoned in consequence of their refusal "not to depart from their dwelling-houses and engage to refrain from doing anything injurious to the United States, by speaking, writing, or otherwise, and from giving intelligence to the commander of the British forces, or to any other person, concerning publick affairs." *See* "Monthly Review," LVIII. 81.

PEMBERTON. Remonstrance of Israel Pemberton, John Hunt and Samuel Pleasants, to the President and Council of Pennsylvania. *Philadelphia: Robert Bell.* 1777. Folio, 1 leaf. P.

[PEMBERTON.] Several Conferences Between some of the principal People amongst the Quakers in Pennsylvania, and the Deputies from the Six Indian Nations, In Alliance with Britain; In order to reclaim their Brethren the Delaware Indians from their Defection, and put a Stop to their Barbarities and Hostilities. To which is prefix'd ... Two Addresses from the said Quakers; ... *Newcastle-upon-Tyne: Printed by I. Thompson and Company.* MDCCLVI. 8vo, pp. 28. C. 59612

See also Vol. IX., No. 36337.

[PEMBERTON (James).] An Apology for the People called Quakers, Containing some Reasons, for their not complying with Human Injunctions and Institutions in Matters relative to the Worship of God. Published by the Meeting for Sufferings of the People at Philadelphia, in pursuance of the Directions of their Yearly Meeting, held at Burlington, for Pennsylvania and New-Jersey, ... 1756. [*Philadelphia: James Chattin.* 1756.] Folio, pp. 3. 59613

A defense of the position assumed by the Quakers in regard to the French and Indian War.

[PEMBERTON (J.)] The Ancient Testimony and Principles of the People called Quakers, renewed, with respect to the King and Government; and touching the commotions now prevailing in these and other parts of America, addressed to the People in General.—Signed in and on behalf of a Meeting of the Representatives of our Religious Society, in Pennsylvania and New-Jersey, held at Philadelphia, the 20th day of the 1st month, 1776. —John Pemberton, Clerk. [n. p. n. d.] Folio, 1 leaf. 59614

PEMBERTON. A Testimony of the Monthly Meeting of Friends, at Pyrmont in Westphalia, Germany, concerning John Pemberton, of Philadelphia in North America: With his Epistle to the Inhabitants of Amsterdam. ... *Philadelphia: Printed by Henry Tuckniss.* 1798. 12mo, pp. 36. + ... *London reprinted by James Phillips & Son.* 1798. 12mo, pp. 36. + ... *Dublin, reprinted by John Gough.* 1798. 12mo, pp. 36. 59615

PEMBERTON. The Life and Travels of John Pemberton. Compiled for the "American Friends' Library," by W[illiam] H[odgson], Jun. *London: Charles Gilpin.* 1844. 12mo.

Contains an account of missionary wanderings in settlements of America.

PEMBERTON (J. C.) Report of Affair at Port Royal Ferry on 1st January, 1862, J. C. Pemberton, Brigadier-General Commanding. [n. p. n. d.] 8vo, pp. 21. H. 59617

PEMBERTON (J. D.) Facts and Figures relating to Vancouver Island and British Columbia Showing what to expect and how to get there. ... By J. Despard Pemberton, Surveyor-General V. I. ... *London: Longman* ... . 1860. 8vo, pp. ix, 171. 4 Maps.

PEMBERTON (T.) An Historical Journal of the American War. 1765–1784. By Thomas Pemberton. *Printed by Samuel Hall, ... Boston.* 1793. 8vo, pp. (2), 43–246. + *Boston: Printed* 1793. *By Belknap & Hatt.* 8vo. + *Boston: ... Joseph Belknap.* 1795. 8vo. C. 59619

See "Mass. Hist. Soc. Coll.," 1st. Ser. II. 41; *see also* 1st Ser. III. 241, for "A Topographical and Historical Description of Boston."

PEMBERTON MILL. *See* Vol. X., No. 39392.

PEMBROKE, *Mass.* The Annual Report of the School Committee of the Town of Pembroke, ... 1855–6. *Pembroke.* [n. d.] 8vo, pp. 15. Continued. 59620

A Plan of Union, agreed on, and adopted, by the Presbyterian and Congregational Churches in Pembroke, June—1797. ... *Concord: Printed by George Hough.* 1798. Sm. 8vo, pp. 8. 59621

PEN (W.) Dagboek van het Britisch Ministerie sedert het begin der Noord Amerikaanschen Onlusten. ... *Amsterdam.* 1782. 8vo. 4 Plates. 59622

A political satire on the war with England, with thorough reference to the American affairs.

Peña Montenegro (A. de). Itinerario para Parochos de Indios, su Oficio y Oblicaciones, en que se tratan las Materias mas particulares, tocantes a ellos, para su buena Administracion. Compuesto por ... Señor Doctor Don Alonso de la Peña Montenegro .... *Madrid.* 1668. Folio. 59623

Peña was bishop of Quito. One of the most interesting accounts of the Indies, their laws, privileges, religions, etc.

Peña Montenegro. Itinerario para Parochos de Indios, en que se tratan las materias mas particulares, tocantes a ellos, para su buena Administracion: Compuesto por ... Señor Doctor Don Alonso de la Peña Montenegro, Obispo del Obispado de San Francisco del Quito ... . Nueva Edicion Purgada de muchos Yerros. *En Leon de Francia: Joan. Ant. Huguetan.* 1678. 4to, pp. (64), 848, (112). + *En Amberes. Por Henrico y Cornelio Verdussen. Año* M.DC.XCVIII. *Con Licencia.* 4to, pp. (56), 697, (86). + *En Amberes: Verdussen.* 1726. 4to, pp. (56), 697, (86). + *En Amberes por la Viuda de H. Verdussen.* 1737. 4to, pp. (56), 701, (86). + *En Amberes: A costa de los Hermanos de Tournes.* MDCCLIV. 4to, pp. (56), 701, (86). + *En Madrid: En la Oficina de Pedro Marin. Año de* 1771. ... Folio, pp. (32), 612.

Peña (Andres Saenz de la). Manual de los Santos Sacramentos, conforme al Ritual de Paulo Quinto, formado por mandado del Señor D. Juan de Palafox y Mendoça, Obispo de la Puebla de los Angeles. ... *En Mexico, por Francisco Robledo, Impressor del Secreto del Santo Officio, Año de* 1642. 4to, (8), 194 ll.

Very scarce. In Mexican and Spanish. *See also* No. 58297.

Peña (Ant. de la). Derrotero de la Expedicion en la Provincia de los Texas, nuevo reyno de Philipinas que passar a executar el muy ill. Señor D. Joseph de Azlor, Marques de S. Miguel de Aguayo, Governador de dichas Provincias de Texas. ... *En Mexico: En la Imprenta nueva Plantiniana de Juan Franc. de Ortega Bonilla, año de* 1722. 4to, Title, 29 leaves. 4 Maps. 59626

One of the earliest works on Texas, with maps of the four presidencies into which the country had been divided by the Spaniards.

Peña (D. M. de la). *See* La Peña (D. M. de), x. 38956.

Peña (F. J. de la). *See* La Peña (F. J. de), Vol. x. 38957.

Peña (I. de la). Trono Mexicano, en el Convento de Religiosas Pobres Capuchinas, su construccion y adorno en la insigne Ciudad de Mexico. Dibuxado por el Rev. Padre Fray Ignacio

de la Peña ... . Con Licencia. *En Madrid. Por Francisco de Hierro. Año de* 1728. 4to, pp. (24), 333, (6). 59627

This book contains important notices about the foundation of Mexico. Not mentioned by Brunet, Rich or Stevens.

Peña (J. de la). El Amigo de la Religion, Agricultura, Politica, Comercio ... . *Puebla.* 1839–40. 2 vols., 4to. 59628

Peña (J. A. de la). Oratio pro Carolo iv. Hispaniarum et Indiarum Potentissimo Rege exequiis persolvendis habita in Sancta Ecclesia Cathedrali Dioecesis Michoacanensis, iii. Indus. Novembris. Ann. MDCCCXIX a Josepho Antonio de la Pena el Campuzano ... [*Valladolid de Michoacan.* 1819.] 4to, pp. 48. 59629

Peña y Garcia (J. M. de la). Elogio sepulcral en las solemnas exequias del Señor D. Carlos Ant. de Borbon. ... *Mejico.* 1820. 4to, 15 leaves. 59630

Peña y Peña (M. de la). Coleccion de los Documentos mas Importantes relativos á la Instalacion y Reconocimiento del Govierno provisional del Sr. Presidente de la Suprema Corte de Justicia D. Manuel de la Peña y Peña. *Mexico.* 1847. 4to, pp. 79.

Peña y Peña. Volo fundado en la causa formada contra los [ex-ministros] Lucas Alaman, J. J. Espinosa y J. A. Facio ... . *Mexico.* 1835. 4to. 59632

Peña y Peña, y Jauregui (José Maria). Dictamenes dados al Ministerio de Justicia y Negocios Eclesiasticos, con motivo de la protesta hecha por el Obispo de Michoacan, D. Juan Cayetano Portugal, á la ley de 31 de Agosto de 1843. *Mexico.* 1847. 8vo, pp. 124. 59633

The Penal Code of ... Georgia. *See* Vol. vii., No. 27083.

The Penal Enactment of the Slave Registry Bill Examined ... [By a Mr. Robinson?] *London: J. M. Richardson.* 1816. 8vo, pp. (2), 56. 59634

Peñalosa y Mondragon (B. de). Libro de las cinco excelencias del Español qve despveblan a España para sv mayor potencia y dilatacion. Ponderanse para qve meior se aduiertā las Causas del Despueblo de España: ... Por el M. Fr. Benito de Peñalosa y Mondragon ... . Dedicado al Rey nuestro Señor Filipo iiii. *Año* 1629. *Con Licencia. Impresso en Pamplona por Carlos de Labàyen, Impressor del Reyno de Nauarra.* 4to, (8), 178, (6) leaves.

Leaves 114–189 treat of America, especially of Peru.

Peñalver (Fernando de). Apela de la Sentencia del Jurado del Canton de Caracas al Tribunal de la Opinion ilustrada de sus Conciudadanos. ... *Carácas.* 1825. 8vo, pp. 28. 59636

A defense against certain charges made against him as governor of Carabobo, concerning the murder of Hipólito Cas. Lucena.

Peñalver (N.) Carta de Don Nicolas Peñalver y el Conde de Santa Maria de Loreto, en contestacion á las diversas declamaciones que ha publicado el presbítero Doctor D. Manuel de Echeverria, como albacea fiduciario del Ilmo. Sr. Dr. Don Luis de Peñalver. *Habana: Arazoza y Soler.* 1812. 4to, pp. 23.

Pencil (M.), *pseudon.* The White Sulphur Papers; or, Life at the Springs of Western Virginia. By Mark Pencil. *New York: Samuel Colman.* 1839. 12mo, pp. 166. c. 59638

Penciller (H.), *pseudon.* Rural Life in America; or, Summer and Winter in the Country. By Harry Penciller. *New York: J. C. Derby.* 1856. 12mo, pp. 285. Plate. c. 59639

Pencillings about Ephrata. *See* Vol. vi., No. 22681.

Penc[s]illy Sketches. *See* "York," *pseudon.*

Pender (T.) The | Divinity of the Scriptures, | from | Reason & External Circumstances: | A | Sermon | Preach'd at | Trinity-Church in New-York, | The second Sunday after Trinity, 1728. | By | The Reverend Mr. Thomas Pender, Minister | of Elizabeth-City in the Parish of Hampton, | in Virginia. | *Printed and Sold by William Bradford in the City | of New-York,* 1728. Small 8vo, pp. 32. BM. 59640

Pendleton (E.) An Address of ... Edmund Pendleton, ... to the American Citizens, on the Present State of our Country. *Boston: Printed by Benjamin Edes.* 1799. 12mo, pp. 20. BA.

[Pendleton.] The Crisis: or Nullification Unmasked. [n. p. 1832.] 8vo, pp. 35. B. 59642

[Pendleton.] Letter to Hon. Charles Sumner, dated Jan. 1866, on the annexation of Berkeley and Jefferson Counties to West Virginia. [n. p. n. d.] 8vo, pp. 4. H. 59643

Pendleton (G. H.) George H. Pendleton, the Copperhead Candidate for Vice-President. *Washington, D. C.* 1864. 8vo, pp. 8. 59644

Pendleton. Hear Hon. Geo. H. Pendleton. ... [Speech at New York Hotel, October 24th, 1864. Lincoln the Rebel Candidate. From the Richmond Enquirer, Sept. 5, and Richmond Examiner, October 17. n. p. n. d.] 8vo, pp. 8. 59645

Pendleton. Payment of the Public Debt in Legal Tender Notes!! Speech of Hon. George H. Pendleton, Milwaukee, November 2, 1867. [n. p. n. d.] 8vo, pp. 16. 59646

Also: George H. Pendleton and the Volunteers. [n. p. n. d.] 8vo, pp. 4.—The Power of amending the Constitution. Speech ... January 11, 1865. [n. p. n. d.] 8vo, pp. 8.—Power of the President to Suspend the ... Habeas Corpus. Speech ... December 10, 1861. [n. p. n. d.] 8vo, pp. 8.—The Power to Make Treasury Notes a Legal Tender. Speech ... January 29, 1862. [n. p. n. d.] 8vo, pp. 7.—The Resolution to expel Mr. Long, of Ohio. Speech ... April 11, 1864. [n. p. n. d.] 8vo, pp. 8.— ... Speech ... on the State of the Union. ... January 18, 1861. [n. p. n. d.] 8vo, pp. 8.—Speech ... on the Enlistment of Negro Soldiers. ... January 31, 1863. [n. p. n. d.] 8vo, pp. 8.—Speech ... March 3, 1863, on the Power of the Postmaster General to exclude Newspapers from the Mail. [n. p. n. d.] 8vo.—Speech ... [on the proposed Amendment to the Constitution] June 15, 1864. [n. p. n. d.] 8vo, pp. 8.

[Pendleton (John S.)] Letter written to my Immediate Representative Gov. Smith. [n. p. n. d.] 8vo, pp. 8. 59647

[Pendleton, *and others.*] To the Whig Party of Virginia. [*Washington.* 1848.] 8vo, pp. 15. 59648

Also: An Account of Oregon ... *Washington.* 1842. 8vo.—Speech ... on the Oregon Question: ... January 26, 1846. *Washington.* 1846. 8vo, pp. 16.

Pendleton (Nathaniel G.) Oration, ... Fourth of July, 1831, before the Citizens of Cincinnati. ... By N. G. Pendleton, Esq. ... *Cincinnati: Printed by Lodge and L'Hommedieu.* 1831. 8vo, pp. 28. 59649

Pendleton also wrote a "Letter on our Political Troubles."

Péneveyre (H.) L'Utilité du Ministère Evangélique: Sermon d'Inauguration, prononcé à New-York, ... Decembre 24, 1815. Par le Rev. H. Péneveyre ... . *À New-York: Imprimé par T. et J. Swords.* 1816. 8vo, pp. 21. 59650

[Penfield (A.)] The Dix-Douglas Oration: Argument for Constitutional Guarantees. [n. p. 1867.] 8vo, pp. 3. 59651

[Penfield.] A Tale of the Rebellion. Facts and Figures from the Standpoint of a Departmental Clerk. ... Second Edition. *Washington.* 1867. 8vo, pp. 10. 59652

Penhallow (J.) A Report of the Opinions of the Judges in the ... Cause of Penhallow *et al.* against Doane's Administrators,

... Supreme Court of the United States, at February Term, 1795. ... *Philadelphia: W. W. Woodward.* 1795. 8vo, pp. (2), 69. B.

Relates to privateering in the revolutionary war.

Penhallow (S.) The | History | of the | Wars of New-England, | With the Eastern Indians. | Or, A | Narrative | Of their continued Perfidy and Cruelty, | from the 10th of August, 1703. | To the Peace renewed 13th of July, 1713. | And from the 25th of July, 1722. | To their Submission 15th December, 1725. | Which was Ratified August 5th, 1726. | By Samuel Penhallow, Esqr. | ... | *Boston: Printed by T. Fleet, for S. Gerrish* ... . 1726. Sm. 8vo, pp. (2), iv, (2), 134, (1). C., W. 59654

This work, in any condition, ranks among the rarest of New England imprints, while a perfect copy with good margin, is very difficult to obtain. The author was born in Cornwall, England, July, 1665, and arrived in Portsmouth, New Hampshire, July, 1686. He held many important offices of public trust with great honor, being Chief Justice of the Province, at the period of his death, in December, 1726, at the age of sixty-one. His work on the Indian wars is esteemed as the highest authority on that subject. His design in emigrating was to serve the corporation for the propagation of the gospel among the Indians, as a missionary, after he had made himself acquainted with their language. Whether he ever really performed that service is uncertain.

Penhallow. The History of the Wars of New-England with the Eastern Indians ... . By Samuel Penhallow, Esqr. ... *Cincinnati: Reprinted ... for Wm. Dodge, by J. Harpel.* 1859. 4to, pp. 138, 36. B. 59655

Of this reprint the copies having a rubricated title are most esteemed, as they contain an appendix, with "Lovewell's Fight," Gardener's Account of the "Pequot Warres," and "The Gospel in New-England."

Penhor Mercantil. Questão entre Antonio Francisco de Lacerda e os Representantes do Casal do Commendador José Agostinho de Salles. *Bahia: Typ. de Camillo de Lellis Masson & C.* 1864. 8vo, pp. 56. 59656

P[enington] (E[dward].) Some Brief Observations upon George Keith's Earnest Expostulation ... . Offered to the Perusal of such as the said Expostulation was Recommended to. By E. P. *London: ... T. Sowle* ... 1696. 8vo. 59657

At page 21 is a curious account of some books which Keith sent from Pennsylvania, but which were intercepted, and bought by the Quakers and destroyed.

Penington (I.) Brief Extracts from the Works of Isaac Penington. *Philadelphia: Printed by Joseph Rakestraw.* 1819. 12mo, pp. iv, 62. H. + *Philadelphia.* 1830. 12mo. 59658

Penington. An | Examination | of the | Grounds or Causes, | Which are said to induce the Court of | Boston in New-England

to make that Order or Law | of Banishment upon pain of Death against the Quakers; | As also of the Grounds and Considerations by them pro- | duced to manifest the warrantableness and justness both of | their making and executing the same, which they now stand | deeply engaged to defend, having already thereupon put | two of them to death. | As also of some further Grounds for justifying of | the same, in an Appendix to John Norton's Book (which | was Printed after the Book it self, yet as part thereof) whereto | he is said to be appointed by the General Court. | And likewise of the Arguments briefly hinted in that which | is called, A true Relation of the Proceedings against the Quakers, &c. | ... | By Isaac Penington, the Younger. | *London, Printed for L. Lloyd,* ... 1660. 4to, pp. (4), 99. C. 59659

Penington. Letters of Isaac Penington, written to his Relations and Friends, now first published from manuscript copies. To which are added Letters of Stephen Crisp, William Penn, R. Barclay, William Caton, Josiah Coale, and others. ... *London: James Phillips.* 1796. 8vo. P. 59660

Letters of Isaac Penington, ... Minister of the Gospel in the Society of Friends ... . From the Second London Edition. *Philadelphia: Nathan Kite.* 1842. 12mo, pp. 292. + *Philadelphia.* 1859. 12mo, pp. 125. H.

[Penington.] To Friends in England, ... New-England, Barbado's, or any where else where the Lord God shall order this to come ... . From Alisb. Prison, the 14th of the 5th month, 1666. [n. p. n. d.] 4to. 59661

Penington. The Works of Isaac Penington ... . *Sherwood, N. Y.: David Heston.* 1861–63. 4 vols., 8vo. 59662

The first edition of his works was published, *London: Benjamin Clark.* 1681. Folio.

Penington (J.) An | Apostate | Exposed: | Or, | George Keith | Contradicting himself and his | Brother Bradford. | Wherein | Their Testimony to the Christian | Faith of the People called Qua- | kers, is opposed to G. K.'s late | Pamphlet, Stiled, Gross Error | and Hypocrise detected. | By John Penington. | *London, Printed ... by T. Sowle* ... 1695. Sm. 8vo, pp. 29. 59663

The "Brother Bradford" referred to in the title, is William Bradford, the printer.

Penington. Certain | Certificates | Received from | America, | On behalf of | Samuel Jennings, | Tending to clear him from | Scandals, Cast on him by | George Keith, and others | of his Opposers. | Made publick by John Penington. | *London* ... *T. Sowle,* ... 1695. 16mo, pp. (2), 43. 59664

A spirited account of Quaker quarrels in New England, New Jersey, Philadelphia, etc., with curious bickerings about nick-names and slang terms, such as "Prick-louse Taylor," "Cut me in Collops," etc.

Penington. The People called Quakers cleared by Geo. Keith from the False Doctrines charged upon them by G. Keith, and his Self-Contradictions laid open in the ensuing Citations out of his Books. By John Penington. *London: ... T. Sowle* ... . 1696. 12mo, pp. 47. W. 59665

Penington (J.) Chemical | and | Economical Essays, | designed to illustrate | the connection between ... Chemistry, and the application of | that Science to some of the Arts | and Manufactures of | the | United States of America. | ... | By John Penington. | *Philadelphia: | Printed by Joseph James.* | M.DCC.XC. 8vo, pp. vi, 200. C.

Penington (J.) An Examination of Beauchamp Plantagenet's Description of the Province of New Albion. By John Penington. *Philadelphia.* 1840. 8vo, pp. 33. 59667

Also: Scraps, Osteologic and Archæological, read before the Council of the Historical Society of Pennsylvania ... . *Philadelphia.* 1841. 8vo, pp. 16.—Works connected with American History, Selected from the Stock of John Penington & Son, Philadelphia. [n. p. 1864.] 8vo, pp. 9.

[Penington (Mary).] A Brief Account of my Exercises, from my Childhood; left with my dear Daughter, Gulielma Maria Penn. *Philadelphia: Privately Printed.* 1848. 8vo, pp. 39. C.

The Peninsular Campaign. A Secret Chapter in the History of the War. *Philadelphia.* 1864. 8vo. 59669

Fourth Annual Report of the Directors of the Penitent Females' Refuge ... . *Boston.* 1823. 12mo, pp. 24. Cont'd.

Penitential Tears. *See* [Withington (L.)]

Penn (G.) Memorials of the Professional Life and Times of Sir William Penn, Knt. Admiral and General of the Fleet, during the Interregnum; Admiral, and Commissioner of the Admiralty and Navy, after the Restoration. From 1644 to 1670. By Granville Penn, Esq. ... *London: James Duncan.* MDCCCXXXIII. 2 vols., 8vo, pp. xvi, (2), 580; (4), 619. Plates. B. 59671

Relates the capture of Jamaica.

Penn (H.) The Case of Hannah Penn, the Widow and Executrix of William Penn, Esq. late Proprietor and Governour of Pensilvania [against the pretensions of Lord Sutherland. *London.* 1720.] Folio, 1 leaf. 59672

Penn. Hannah Penn's Letter of Instructions to Sir William Keith, for the Government of Pennsylvania. [*Philadelphia: S. Keimer?* 1724.] Folio, pp. 4. P. 59673

Some copies have eight lines additional at the end.

[Penn (John).] The General Address. *See* Vol. vii., No. 26864, *and* Vol. ix., No. 34416.

Penn (W.) An Account of W. Penn's Travails in Holland and Germany, Anno M.DC.LXXVII. for the Service of the Gospel of Christ: by way of Journal. ... *London: ... T. Sowle* ... . 1694. 8vo. + Second Impression ... . [*Ibid.*] + The Third Impression ... . *London: ... Assigns of J. Sowle* ... . 1714. 12mo, pp. (10), 240, 56. + The Fourth Edition. ... [By John Barclay.] *London: Darton and Harvey.* 1835. 12mo. 59674

Penn. An Address to Protestants upon the Present Conjuncture. ... By a Protestant, William Penn. [n. p.:] *Printed in the Year,* 1679. Sm. 4to, pp. (8), 248. C., H. 59675

Reprinted as: "An Address to Protestants of all Perswasions:" ... By W. P. a Protestant. The Second Edition ... . [*London:*] ... *T. Sowle* ... . 1692. 8vo.

[Penn.] The Allegations Made against Proprietary Governments, considered; and their Merit and Benefit to the Crown Humbly and Briefly Observed. [n. p. n. d.] Folio, pp. 4.

Penn. Argumentum ad Hominem: being an Extract from a Piece entitled, England's Present Interest considered, with Honour to the Prince and Safety to the People. In answer to this one question: What is most Fit, Easy and Safe at this Juncture of Affairs to be done, for quieting of Differences, allaying the Heat of contrary Interests, and making them subservient to the Interest of the Government, and consistent with the Prosperity of the Kingdom. By William Penn, Founder of the Province of Pennsylvania. To which are added, Some Extracts from the Writings of divers Authors, more particularly recommended to the Notice of the People called Quakers. *Philadelphia: Printed in the Year* M,DCC,LXXV. 8vo, pp. 28. J.C.B., P. 59677

Printed with a view of quieting the scruples of the Quakers, and engaging them on the popular side.

Penn. Brief aan den Koning van Poolen. Opgestelt door William Penn uyt de Naam van zijn verdrukte en lydende Vrienden tot Dantzig. Uit het Engelsch vertaald door P. V. M. *Amsterdam: Jacob Claus.* 1701. 4to, pp. 8. J.C.B. 59678

[PENN, *and others.*] A Brief Account of the Province of East Jersey, in America. Published by the present Proprietars [*sic*] thereof, viz., William Penn, Robert West, Thomas Rudyard, [and 9 others,] for information of all such persons who are or may be inclined to settle themselves, Families, and Servants in that Country. *London:* ... *Benjamin Clark* ... . 1682. 4to.

An improved title of our No. 53078, Vol. XIII.

[PENN.] A Brief Account of the Province of Pennsilvania lately Granted by the King, under the Great Seal of England, to William Penn, and his Heirs and Assigns. *London:* ... *Benjamin Clark* ... . 1682. 4to, pp. 8. 59680

[PENN.] A Brief Account of the Province of Pennsylvania in America, lately granted under the Great Seal of England to William Penn, &c. [n. p. n. d.] Folio, 1 leaf. H. 59681

PENN. A Brief Account of the Rise and Progress of the People called Quakers. ... By William Penn. ... *London:* ... *T. Sowle* ... . 1694. 12mo. + [*Ibid.*] 1695. 12mo, pp. (10), 158. + The Sixth Edition. *Philadelphia: Reprinted by Joseph Crukshank.* MDCCLXX. 16mo, pp. (6), 88. BA. + *Wilmington* [*Del.*]: *James Adams.* 1783. 16mo, pp. (6), 88. + *Philadelphia.* 1803. 12mo, pp. 95. + *Philadelphia: Printed by Solomon W. Conrad.* 1807. 12mo, pp. 95. + *Philadelphia: Printed by Joseph Rakestraw.* 1816. 12mo, pp. 95. H. + *Philadelphia.* 1849. 12mo. + [*Ibid.*] 1855. 12mo. 59682

For a fuller list of the many reprints, *see* Smith's "Catalogue of Friends' Books," II. 312–314. For French translations, *see* "Exposition Succincte" and "Histoire Abrégée de l'Origine;" also translated into German, Welsh and Danish.

P[ENN]. A Brief Answer to a False and Foolish Libell, called, The Quaker's Opinions ... . By W. P. [n. p.:] *Printed in the Year*, 1678. 4to, pp. 26. C. 59683

PENN. Een | Brief | Van een zeker Heer | aan | William Penn, | Eygenaar en Gouverneur van | Pensylvania; | Beneffens zyn | Antwoord | daar op. | Uyt het Engelsch vertaald. | *t'Amsterdam, by de Wed: van Steven Swart,* | *bezyde de Beurs,* | 1689. | 4to, pp. 16.

For the English version of this anonymous letter to William Penn, with his reply, from which this Dutch translation was made, *see* No. 59714, *infra.*

[PENN.] The Case of Messieurs Penn, and the People of Pensilvania, and the three lower Counties of Newcastle, Kent and Sussex, on Delaware, in relation to a Series of Injuries and

Hostilities made upon them, for several Years past, by Thomas Cressap, and others, by the Direction and Authority of the Deputy-Governor of Maryland. [*London.* 1737.] Folio, pp. 8.

[PENN.] The Case of William Penn, Esq. as to the Proprietary Government of Pensilvania; which together with Carolina, New York, etc. is intended to be taken away by a Bill in Parliament. [*London.* 1685.] Folio, 1 leaf. 59686

[PENN.] The Case of William Penn, Proprietary, and Governor in Chief of the Province of Pennsylvania, and Territories, against the Lord Baltimore's Pretensions to a Tract of Land in America, Granted to the said William Penn in the year 1682, by his then Royal Highness James Duke of York, adjoyning to the said Province, commonly call'd the Territories thereof. [n. p. 1682 to 1709.] Folio, 1 leaf. 59687

[PENN.] The Case of William Penn, Esq. Proprietary Governor of Pensilvania, and of Joshua Gee, Henry Goulding, Silvanus Grove and other Mortgagees, under the said William Penn. [*London.* 1720.] Folio, 1 leaf. 59688

PENN. The Christian-Quaker, and his Divine Testimony Vindicated by Scripture, ... against The Injurious Attempts, that have been lately made ... . In II Parts. The First ... by William Penn. The Second ... by George Whitehead. [n. p.:] *Printed in the Year*, 1674. Folio, pp. (34), 162, (2); 377. C.

Penn's part was reprinted, *London:* ... *T. Sowle* ... 1699. 8vo. Both parts reprinted, with other pieces, by the same authors, entitled: The Christian Quaker, and his Divine Testimony stated and vindicated, by William Penn & George Whitehead. ... *Philadelphia: Printed* ... *by Joseph Rakestraw.* 1824. 8vo.

PENN. A Collection of the Works of William Penn. ... To which is prefixed A Journal of His Life. With many Original Letters and Papers Not before Published. ... *London:* ... *The Assigns of J. Sowle* ... . 1726. 2 vols., folio, pp. (8), 911; (4), 916, 18. B., J.C.B., C., P. 59690

The catalogue of the library of Congress gives a copious list of contents of these volumes.

PENN. A Defence of a Paper, Entituled, Gospel-Truths, against the Exceptions of the Bishop of Cork's Testimony. By W. Penn. *London:* ... *T. Sowle* ... . 1698. Sm. 8vo, pp. (6), 119. C. + The Second Edition. [n. p.:] *Printed in the Year*, 1698. Sm. 8vo. 59691

Also on large paper. A curious little volume.

[PENN.] The Description of the Province of West-Jersey, in America: as also Proposals to such who desire to have any Propriety therein. [n. p. about 1676.] Folio, 1 leaf. 59692

[PENN.] England's Present Interest discover'd with Honour to the Prince, and Safety to the People. In Answer to this one Question; What is most Fit, Easie and Safe at this Juncture of Affairs to be done, for Composing, at least Quieting of Differences; Allaying the Heat of contrary Interests, & making them Subservient to the Interest of the Government, and Consistent with the Prosperity of the Kingdom? Presented and submitted to the Consideration of Superiours. ... [n. p.:] *Printed in the Year*, 1675. Small 4to, pp. (4), 62. C. + [Second Edition. *Ibid.*] H. + [n. p. n. d.] 4to. + *London:* ... *T. Sowle* 1698. 12mo. 59693

It appears that two editions were printed in 1675. The second may be known by having Penn's name on the title-page, also by having the errata in the first edition corrected in the second. Also reprinted anonymously, entitled: England's True Interest considered, with Honour to the Prince and Safety to the People. The Fifth Edition. *London:* ... *E. Baldwin* ... . 1702. 12mo.

PENN. Exposition Succincte de l'Origine et des Progrès du Peuple qu'on appelle les Quakers ou les Trembleurs: ... . Par Guillaume Penn. A quoi l'on a ajouté un des Temoignages rendus à la Lumière, par George Fox. Le tout traduit de l'Anglois, par Claude Gay. *A Londres: Imprimé par Luc Hinde,* ... 1764. 8vo. 59694

A French translation of "A Brief Account of the Rise," No. 59682, *supra.* For another, *see* "Histoire Abrégée," No. 59705, *infra.*

[PENN.] Extract from the Laws of William Penn; translated into German for the Use of the Germans in Pennsylvania. *Germantown: Printed by Christopher Sower.* 1741. 59695

[PENN.] The Frame of the | Government | of the | Province of Pennsilvania | in | America: | Together with certain | Laws | Agreed upon in England | by the | Governour | and | Divers Free-Men of the aforesaid | Province. | To be further Explained and Confirmed there by the first | Provincial Council and General Assembly that shall | be held, if they see meet. | [n. p.:] *Printed in the Year* MDCLXXXII. Folio, pp. (4), 11. 59696

Some of the laws in this collection are exceedingly curious: *see* No. XXXVII, an act for the preserving of the public morals.

[PENN.] The Frame of the Government of the Province of Pennsilvania in America. [*London:*] *Printed,* ... *by Andrew Sowle* ... 1691. Sm. 8vo. 59697

[PENN.] Fruits of a Father's Love: being the Advice of William Penn to his Children, Relating to their Civil and Religious Conduct. Written occasionally many years ago, and now made Publick for a General Good. By A Lover of his Memory. ... [John Rhodes.] *London:* ... *The Assigns of J. Sowle* ... . 1726. 12mo. + Second Edition. *Philadelphia:* ... *Andrew Bradford,* ... 1727. 12mo. + The Eighth Edition. *Philadelphia: Printed by Benjamin Johnson.* 1792. 12mo. + Ninth Edition. *Philadelphia.* 1794. 16mo, pp. 64. 59698

For a list of the numerous editions, *see* Smith's "Catalogue of Friends' Books," II. 321–322.

PENN. Fruits of Solitude, in Reflections and Maxims relating to the Conduct of Human Life. ... [Tenth Edition.] *Philadelphia: Printed by Benjamin Johnson.* 1792. 12mo. + Eleventh Edition. Also, his Advice to his Children ... . To which are added Extracts from the Writings of William Law and Judge Hale; ... *New Brunswick* (*N. J.*): *R. Eastburn.* 1807. 16mo, pp. viii, 272. C. 59699

For other editions, *see* "Some Fruits," No. 59734, *infra.*

PENN. Früchte der Einsamkeit. Von Wilhelm Penn. ... Aus dem Englischen. *Friedensthal: Ludwig Seebohm.* 1803. 16mo, pp. xii, (4), 224. 59700

[PENN.] A | Further Account | Of the Province of | Pennsylvania | and its | Improvements. | For the Satisfaction of those that are Adventurers, and | enclined to be so. | [n. p. n. d.] Sm. 4to, pp. 20. P. 59701

Signed "William Penn," and dated at the end "Worminghurst Place, 12th of the 10th Month 85." This issue has thirty-four lines to a full page. For a Dutch version, *see* "Tweede Bericht," No. 59738, *infra.*

[PENN.] A Further Account | of the Province | of Pennsylvania, and its Improvements. | For the Satisfaction of those that are Adventurers, and | Inclined to be so. | [n. p. n. d.] Sm. 4to, pp. 16. P. 59702

Signed and dated as No. 59703, but contains thirty-eight lines to a full page.

[PENN.] A General Epistle given forth by the People of the Lord, called, Quakers ... . *Printed and sold by William Bradford at Philadelphia, in Pennsilvania.* 1686. Sm. 8vo. 59703

Part by William Penn and Frances Taylor.

[PENN.] The Great Question to be considered by the King, and this approaching Parliament, briefly proposed, and modestly

discussed: (to wit) How far Religion is concerned in Policy or Civil Government, and Policy in Religion? ... [n. p. about 1681.] Folio. 59704

Signed "Philo-Britannicus."

PENN. Histoire Abrégée | De l'Origine et de la Formation | de la Société | dite des | Quakers, | ... | Par Guillaume Penn. | Nouvellement traduite de l'Anglois | Par Edd P. Bridel. | *Londres:* | *De l'Imprimerie de J. Phillips* ... . M.DCC.XC. 12mo, pp. 199. + *Philadelphia.* 1802. 12mo. + Nouvelle Édition, revue et corrigée. *Londres: De l'Imprimerie de J. Rider* ... . 1839. 16mo, pp. vi, 138. H. 59705

French translation of "A Brief Account of the Rise," No. 59682, *supra.*

[PENN.] An Index to William Penn's Works. [n. p. about 1730.] Folio, pp. 18. C. 59706

Signed "Philalethes," *i. e.* Henry Portsmouth.

[PENN.] Information and Direction | To | Such Persons as are inclined | to | America, | More | Especially Those related to the Province | of | Pennsylvania. | [*London, about* 1684.] Folio, pp. 4.

This tract, written by William Penn, is unknown to Rich. It is of the greatest rarity, and of interest as exhibiting the terms upon which Penn disposed of his lands.

P[ENN]. The Invalidity of John Faldo's Vindication of his Book, called, Quakerism No Christianity. ... By W. P. ... [*London.*] 1673. Sm. 8vo, pp. (8), 439. 59708

[PENN.] A Key opening a way to every common Understanding, How to discern the Difference betwixt the Religion professed by the People called Quakers, and the Perversions, Misrepresentations and Calumnies of their several Adversaries. ... [*London.*] 1692. Sm. 8vo. + The Fifteenth Edition. *London:* ... *T. Sowle Raylton, and Luke Hinde* ... . 1748. 16mo, pp. (12), 48.

The title-pages of the later impressions read somewhat different. For the many reprints, and French, Welsh and Danish editions, *see* Smith's "Catalogue of Friends' Books," II. 306–307.

[PENN.] Een kort Bericht | Van de Provintie ofte Landschap | Penn-Sylvania | genaemt, leggende in | America; | Nu onlangs onder het groote Zegel van Engeland | gegeven aan | William Penn, etc. | Mitsgaders | Van de Privilegien, ende Macht om | het selve wel te Regeeren. | Uyt het Engels overgeset na de Copye tot Londen gedrukt by Benja- | min Clark, Boekverkooper in George Yard Lombardstreet. 1681. | Waer by nu gevoegt is de Notificatie van s'Konings Placcaet, | in date van den 2 April 1681. waar inne de tegenwoordige | Inwooners van Penn-Sylvania,

belast word | Willem Penn en zijn Erfgenamen, als volkomene | Eygenaars en Gouverneurs, te gehoorsamen. | Als mede, | De Copye van een Brief by den selven W. P. geschreven aan | zekere Regeeringe Anno 1675. tegens de Vervolginge | en voor de Vryheyt van Conscientie, aan alle &. | *Tot Rotterdam,* | *Gedrukt by Pieter van Wynbrugge, Boek-Drukker in de* | *Leeuwe-straat, in de Wereld Vol-Druk. Anno* 1681. | 4to, pp. 24. 59710

The first Dutch translation of this extremely rare description of Pennsylvania. For the original English edition, *see* "Some Account," No. 59733, *infra.*

[PENN.] Letter from a Gentleman in the City about the Odiousness of Persecution. *London.* 1687. Sm. 4to. 59711

PENN. A | Letter | from | William Penn | Poprietary [*sic*] and Governour of | Pennsylvania | In America, | to the | Committee | of the | Free Society of Traders | of that Province, residing in London. | Containing | A General Description of the said Province, its Soil, Air, Water, Seasons and Produce, | both Natural and Artificial, and the good Encrease thereof. | Of the Natives or Aborigines, their Language, Customs and Manners, Diet, Houses or Wig- | wams, Liberality, easie way of Living, Physick, Burial, Religion, Sacrifices and Cantico, | Festivals, Government, and their Order in Council upon Treaties for | Land, &c. their Justice upon Evil Doers. | Of the first Planters, the Dutch, &c. and the present Condition and Settlement of the | said Province, and Courts of Justices, &c. | To which is added, an Account of the City of | Philadelphia | newly laid out. | Its Scituation between two Navigable Rivers, Delaware and Skulkill, | with a | Portraiture or Platform thereof, | Wherein the Purchasers Lots are Distinguished by certain Numbers inserted, directing | to a Catalogue of the said Purchasors Names, | And the Prosperous and Advantagious [*sic*] Settlements of the Society aforesaid, within | the said City and Country, &c. | *Printed and Sold by Andrew Sowle, at the Crooked-Billet in Holloway-Lane in* | *Shoreditch, and at the several Stationers in London,* 1683. Folio, pp. 10, Lot Holders, (4). Plan of Philadelphia. B. 59712

One of the first printed accounts of Philadelphia by the founder of the colony, and is of the highest interest to a Pennsylvania collector. There were two editions. In the second, "Poprietary" is corrected to "Proprietary," and the signature varies from "Your Kind Cordial Friend," in the first, to "Your Kind and Cordial Friend" in the second. The plan and list of lot holders are usually deficient. For a Dutch version, *see* "Missive," No. 59716, *infra.*

PENN. A Letter from William Penn to his Wife and Children, written a little before his first voyage to America, and first

published in the London Chronicle, Jan. 1st, 1761, by Philalethes [supposed E. Waring], with his Letter to the Printer, dated, Oxfordshire, Nov. 7, 1760. [n. p. n. d.] 8vo, pp. 8. + *Philadelphia.* 1809. Sm. 8vo, pp. 16. 59713

Dated "Worminghurst, 4th of 6th month, 1682." For other editions, *see* Smith's "Catalogue of Friends' Books," II. 322–23.

PENN. A | Letter | to | Mr. Penn; | with | His Answer. | *London: Printed for Andrew Wilson* ... . 1688. 4to, pp. 10. + *London:* ... *T. Sowle* ... . [*about* 1700.] 8vo. 59714

Dated "Paddington, October, the 24th, 1688." Relates to Pennsylvania. For a Dutch version, *see* "Een Brief," No. 59684, *supra.*

PENN. Memorials of the English Affairs, from the Suppos'd Expedition of Brute to this Island, to the End of the Reign of King James the First. By Sir Bulstrode Whitlocke ... . Publish'd from his Original Manuscript, with Some Account of his Life and Writings by William Penn, Esq., Governour of Pennsylvania. And a Preface by James Wellwood, M.D. *London:* ... *E. Sanger* ... . 1709. Folio. 59715

PENN. Missive | van | William Penn, | Eygenaar en Gouverneur van | Pennsylvania, | In America. | Geschreven aan de Commissarissen van de Vrye Socie- | teyt der Handelaars, op de selve Provintie, | binnen London resideerende. | Behelsende: | Een generale beschrijvinge van de voornoemde Provintie: te weten, van | hare Grond, Lucht, Water, Saisoenen en't Product, soo uyt de natuur als | door het bouwen, neffens de groote vermeerderinge of meenighvuldin- | ge, welke het Land aldaar uytgevende is. | Als mede: van de Naturellen of Inboorlingen des Landts, haer Taal, Gewoontens, en Manieren, haar Spijsen, Huysen of Wigwams, | Mildheyt, gemackelijcke manier van leven, Medicijnen, manieren, van | Begraaffenis, Godsdienst, Offerhanden en Gesangen, haar Hooge- | feesten, Regeeringe, en ordre in hare Raden, wanneer sy met yemandt | handelen over het verkoopen van Landeryen, etc. Nevens hare Justi- | tie, of Recht doen over quaatdoenders. | Mitsgaders een Bericht van de eerste Coloniers de Hollanders, etc. En | van de tegenwoordige toestant en welgesteltheyt van de voornoemde Pro- | vintie en Rechtbanken, etc. aldaar. | Waar by noch gevoeght is een Beschrijving van de Hooft-Stadt | Philadelphia. | Nu onlangs uytgeset, en gelegen tusschen twee Navigable Rivieren, | namentlijk: tusschen Delaware en Schuylkil. | Ende een verhaal van de voorspoedige en voordeelige standt van saken van |

de voornoemde Societeyt binnen de voornoemde Stadt en Provintie, etc. | *Amsterdam,* | *Gedruckt voor Jacob Claus, Boekverkooper in de Prince-straat,* 1684. | 4to, pp. 23. Plan of Philadelphia.

The same plan as in the London edition, but reduced and with slight variations. For the original English edition, *see* "A Letter from William Penn," No. 59712, *supra.*

PENN. Missive | van | William Penn, | ... [as in No. 59716,] Geschreven aan de ... Vrye Societeyt der | Handelaars op deselve Provintie, binnen London residerende. | Behelsende: | Een ... Grondt, ... soo uyt de natuur | als ... haer Taal, | ... xc. En | van de ... weltgesteltheyt ... xc. aldaar. | ... Waar by noch komt een Voor-reden, gevende een korte onderrechtinge van de | Conditien, hoe de Gouverneur sijn Landt nu verkoopt, en verhuurt op een | eeuwige Erf-pacht, als mede van eenige van de voornaamste Wetten, xc. | Den tweeden Druk. | *t'Amsterdam,* | *By Jacob Claus,* ... 1684. | 4to, pp. 28. Plan. 59717

[PENN.] More Work for George Keith; being George Keith's Vindication of the People, called Quakers, with himself, against the Forgeries and Abuses of Thomas Hicks, and William Kiffin, called Anabaptists, with the rest of their confederate Brethren of the Barbican Meeting, held at London the 28th of the 6th Month, 1674. *London:* ... *T. Sowle* ... . 1696. 8vo. + [Another Edition, differing. *Ibid.*] 8vo. 59718

[PENN.] Eine | Nachricht | wegen der Landschaft | Pennsilvania | in | America: | Welche | Jüngstens unter dem Grossen Siegel | in | Engelland | an | William Penn, &c. | Sambt den Freyheiten und der Macht, so zu behöriger | guten Regierung derselben nötig, | übergeben worden, | und | zum Unterricht derer, so etwan bereits bewogen, oder noch | möchten bewogen werden, ümb sich selbsten darhin | zu begeben, oder einige Bediente und Gesinde | an diesen Ort zu senden, hiermit | kund gethan wird. | Aus dem in London gedrucktem und aldar bey Benjamin Clarck, Buchhändlern in George-Yard Lombard-street befindlichem | Englischen übergesetzet. | Nebenst beygefügtem ehemaligem im 1675. Jahr gedrucktem | Schreiben des oberwehnten Will. Penns. | *In Amsterdam, gedruckt bey Christoff Cunraden, Im Jahr* 1681. 4to, pp. 31. P.

This earliest German account of Pennsylvania is of the greatest rarity. For the original English edition, *see* "Some Account," No. 59733, *infra.*

P[ENN]. The New Witnesses proved Old Hereticks: or Information to the Ignorant; in which the Doctrines of John Reeve and Lodowick Muggleton, ... are proved to be mostly

Ancient Whimsies .... By a Living true Witness .... W. P. [n. p.:] *Printed in the Year*, 1672. 4to. 59720

PENN. No Cross, No Crown: or several Sobre Reasons against Hat-Honour, Titular-Respects, ... and Recreations .... With Sixty-Eight Testimonies .... By W. Penn, j. ... [n. p.:] *Printed in the Year*, 1669. 4to. 59721

PENN. No Cross, No Crown. A Discourse shewing the Nature and Discipline of the Holy Cross of Christ: ... To which are added, The ... Testimonies .... By William Penn. The Second Edition, corrected and much enlarged. *London: ... Mark Swaner: ...* 1682. Sm. 8vo. + The Seventh Edition. *Boston.* 1741. Sm. 8vo. + *Boston.* 1751. 8vo, pp. 470. + *Philadelphia: Printed by Benjamin & Jacob Johnson.* 1797. 8vo, pp. (6), 358. H. + *Philadelphia.* 1807. Sm. 8vo. + *Philadelphia.* 1845. 12mo, pp. (6), 408. + *New York: Collins, Brother and Co.* 1845. 12mo. + *Philadelphia: Printed by T. K. & P. G. Collins.* 1853. 16mo, pp. 426. + [*Ibid.*] 1854. 59722

For a list of the various editions, including the German and French translations, *see* Smith's "Catalogue of Friends' Books," II. 299-301.

[PENN.] A Paper to William Penn. *See* No. 58444.

[PENN.] The People's Ancient and Just Liberties Asssrted, [*sic*] in the Tryal of William Penn, and William Mead, ... in London, the first, third, fourth, and fifth of Sept. 70. ... [n. p.:] *Printed in the Year*, 1670. 4to. + [*Ibid.*] 1670. 4to. 59723

There is no doubt that two editions were printed in this year, as one issue has different type and the composition differs as well. + *London: Printed for William Butler.* 1682. 4to, pp. 51. + *London: ... T. Sowle ....* [*about* 1699.] 8vo. + *London: .. The Assigns of J. Sowle ....* [*about* 1725.] 8vo.

P[ENN]. Plain-Dealing with a traducing Anabaptist; or Three Letters Writ upon occasion of some Slanderous Reflections, given and promoted against William Penn by one John Morse. ... By ... W. P. [n. p.:] *Printed in the Year*, 1672. 4to, pp. 19. C.

PENN. Primitive Christianity Revived, in the Faith and Practice of the ... Quakers. ... By William Penn. ... *London: ... T. Sowle ....* 1696. 16mo, pp. (16), 122. H. + *Philadelphia.* 1782. 12mo. + *Philadelphia: Printed ... by Joseph Cruksbank.* MDCCLXXXIII. 8vo, pp. 66. B. + *Salem.* 1844. 12mo, pp. 61. + To which is prefixed a Memoir of Penn, by James Brown of Virginia. *Philadelphia.* 1857. 12mo. C. 59725

Also in German and Welsh. For a list of editions, *see* Smith's "Catalogue of Friends' Books," II. 316.

PENN, EVERET (John), *and* STORY (Thomas). The Quaker a Christian. Being an Answer to John Plimpton's Dis-Ingenuous Paper, Entituled, A Quaker No Christian. *Dublin: Printed in the Year*, 1698. Sm. 4to, pp. 16. 59726

PENN. Quakerism a New Nick-Name for Old Christianity: Being An Answer to a Book, Entituled, Quakerism No Christianity; subscribed by J. Faldo. ... By ... William Penn. [n. p.:] *Printed. Anno* 1672. 8vo. 59727

PENN. Reason against Railing, and Truth against Fiction. Being An Answer to those Two late Pamphlets, Intituled, A Dialogue between a Christian and a Quaker, and the Continuation of the Dialogue, &c. by one Thomas Hicks .... By ... W. Penn. [n. p.:] *Printed. Anno* 1673. 8vo, pp. 236. 59728

PENN. A Reply to a Pretended Answer, By a Nameless Author, to W. P.'s Key, in which the Principles of the People of God, called Quakers are further Explain'd and Confirm'd. By William Penn. *London: Thomas Northcott.* 1695. 8vo.

PENN. The Rise and Progress of the People called Quakers. By William Penn. ... *Philadelphia: Henry Perkins.* 1838. 12mo, pp. 106. + *Philadelphia: T. Ellwood Chapman.* 1855. 12mo, pp. 102. BA. 59730

The same as "A Brief Account of the Rise," No. 59682, *supra.*

PENN. Select Works of William Penn. To which is prefixed a Journal of his Life. *London: Printed in the Year* MDCCLXXI. Folio, pp. (4), lxi, 362. P. + The Third Edition. *London ... James Phillips ....* 1782. 5 vols., 8vo, pp. (4), clvii, 331; (4), 490; (4), 514; (2), 486; (4), 472. BA. + The Fourth Edition. *London: ... William Phillips ....* 1825. 3 vols., 8vo.

PENN. The Skirmisher Defeated and Truth Defended; Being an Answer to a Pamphlet, entituled, A Skirmish made upon Quakerism. By William Penn. [n. p.:] *Printed in the Year*, 1676. 4to. 59732

[PENN.] Some | Account | of the | Province | of | Pennsilvania | in | America; | Lately Granted under the Great Seal | of | England | to | William Penn, &c. | Together with Priviledges and Powers neces- | sary to the well-governing thereof. | Made publick for the Information of such as are or may be | disposed to Transport themselves or Servants | into those parts. | *London: Printed, and Sold by*

Benjamin Clark | Bookseller in George-Yard Lombard Street, 1681. Folio, pp. (2), 10. H. 59733

For the Dutch and German translations of this account, *see* Nos. 59710 and 59719.

[PENN.] Some Fruits of Solitude, in Reflections and Maxims, Relating to the Conduct of Human Life. In Two Parts. The Eighth Edition. *Newport, Rhode-Island: Printed by James Franklin ....* 1749. 12mo, pp. (12), 158, (7). More Fruits of Solitude: ... [*Ibid.*] pp. (6), 106. C. + *New York.* 1813. 12mo.

Repeatedly reprinted. *See* Smith's "Catalogue of Friends' Books," II. 309-310.

[PENN.] Some Proposals for a Second Settlement in the Province of Pennsylvania. [*London:*] *Printed ... by Andrew Sowle ....* 1690. Folio, 1 leaf. C. 59735

P[ENN]. The Spirit of Truth vindicated against That of Error & Envy; Unseasonably Manifested: in a late Malicious Libel, Intituled, The Spirit of the Quakers Tryed, &c. By a Friend ... W. P. [n. p.:] *Printed in the Year* 1672. 4to, pp. 138. C.

[PENN, *and* COOLE (Benjamin).] A Testimony to the Truth of God, as held by the ... Quakers, being a short Vindication of them from the Abuses ... often put upon them by Envious Apostates ... . [n. p.] 1698. 8vo. + The Second Impression. *London: ... T. Sowle ....* 1699. 18mo, pp. 56. C. 59737

In answer to Francis Bugg.

PENN. Tweede | Bericht ofte Relaas | Van | William Penn, Eygenaar en Gouverneur van de Provintie van | Pennsylvania, | In America. | Behelsende een korte Beschrijvinge van den | tegenwoordige toestand en gelegentheid | van die Colonie. | Mitsgaders, een aanwijsinge op wat voor Conditien, die gene die | onmachtig zijn, om haar selven te konnen transporteeren, daar- | heenen souden konnen worden gebracht, met voordeel tot de gene, die | daer Penningen toe souden verschieten. | Uyt het Engels overgeset. | *t'Amsterdam*, | *By Jacob Claus, Boekverkoper in de Prince-straat.* | [1685.] 4to, pp. 20. 59738

This second account of Pennsylvania is as rare as the other Dutch translations of the first account. For the English version, *see* "A Further Account," No. 59701.

PENN. Wilhelm Penn's Kurze Nachricht vom dem Ursprunge ... der ... Quäker .... *London: Edward Marsh.* 1846. 16mo, pp. viii, 105. H. 59739

PENN. Wilhelm Penn's Kurze Nachricht von der Entziehung ... der Freunde .... Aus dem Englischen übersetst ... von Ludwig Seebohm. *Pyrmont.* 1792. 16mo, pp. 176. H. 59740

[PENN.] William Penn and the Quakers. *See* [Young (S.)]

The following are books relating to William Penn:

[PENN.] The Life of William Penn, the Founder of Pennsylvania; with ... Anecdotes and Embellishments. *Philadelphia: Lindsay & Blakiston.* 1848. 16mo. + [*Ibid.*] 1849. 59741

[PENN.] A Memoir of William Penn. *Philadelphia.* 1858. 12mo, pp. 172. 59742

[PENN.] Penn Vindicated and Macaulay Refuted; shewing the Injustice of T. B. Macaulay's Attack upon the Character of William Penn, and the entire absence of any proof by which it can be sustained. *London: ... Aylott & Jones ....* 1850. Rl. 8vo, pp. 20. 59743

[PENN.] Proceedings and Speeches at the Dinner in Celebration of the Landing of William Penn, by the Historical Society of Pennsylvania, Dec. 8, 1852. *Philadelphia.* 1852. 8vo, pp. 42.

[PENN.] Proceedings of a Meeting ... in Philadelphia on the 4th of November, 1824, (24th October, O. S.) to commemorate the Landing of William Penn on the Shore of America, on the 24th of October, 1682, being the 142d Anniversary of that Memorable Event. ... [n. p.] 1824. 8vo, pp. 23. 59745

[PENN.] A Sketch of the Life and Character of William Penn. *Philadelphia.* [n. d.] 24mo, pp. 32. 59746

[PENN.] Some Memoirs of the Religious Life of William Penn, Founder of Pennsylvania .... To which is added Letters, written, by him, on Love and Friendship. *Walpole (N. H.): David Cooledge.* 1806. 16mo, pp. 14. W. 59747

[PENN.] William Penn oder die Zustände Englands, 1644–1718. Aus dem Englischen übertragen von E. Bunsen. *Leipzig.* 1854. 8vo. 59748

[PENN.] William Penn, Proprietary of Pennsylvania, his Ancestry and Descendants. Philadelphia, 1 June, 1852, Thomas Gilpin. 1 sheet. 59749

[PENN.] The Young American's Library. The Life of William Penn; with numerous illustrative Anecdotes. *Philadelphia.* 1848. 12mo, pp. 210. Plates. 59750

PENN (W.), *pseudon.* A Letter to Certain of my Friends in the Legislature of Pennsylvania, and to such of my Fellow Citi-

zens as are alive to the true interests of the Commonwealth ... By William Penn. [n. p. 1834.] 8vo, pp. 45. B. 59751

See also [Colwell (S.)], Vol. IV., No. 14910, *and* [Evarts (J.)], Vol. VI., No. 23206.

First Report of the PENN INDUSTRIAL Reform School with the Act of Incorporation, and Proceedings of the ... Managers since ... May, 1859. *Erie: S. J. Goodrich.* 1859. 8vo, pp. 42.

Penn Medical University; Remarks on the new System of Medical Education, consisting of four ... Courses of Lectures ... 1855-56. *Philadelphia.* 1855. 8vo. 59753

The Penn Monthly, devoted to Literature, Art, Science and Politics. ... Vol. I. *Philadelphia.* [1870.] 8vo. Continued.

The Penn Square Improvement Bill. [Protest of Citizen's Committee. n. p. n. d.] 8vo. 59755

[PENNA (Domingos Soares Ferreira).] *See* No. 58503.

[PENNANT (Thos.)] American Annals; or, Hints and Queries, for Parlement Men .... [*Darlington?* 1778.] 4to, pp. 16.

The object of the author seems rather to comment upon the acts of the generals commanding the British forces in America than to present continuous annals of events. It relates only to events which transpired in the years 1775 to 1778 inclusive. The running title is "Miscellanies."

[PENNANT.] Arctic Zoology. ... *London: Printed by Henry Hughes.* MDCCLXXXIV-LXXXV. 2 vols., 4to, pp. (10), Introduction, CC, (6), 185; 187-586, (14). 23 Plates. + Supplement ... MDCCLXXXVII. pp. 163. 2 Maps. + The Second Edition. *London: Robert Faulder.* M. DCC. XCII. 3 vols., 4to, Introduction, pp. (14), CCCXXXIV, (8); (4), 376; (4), 418, (13). 24 Plates, 2 Maps.

Relates to the Kurile Islands, Alaska, British America, California, the Polar Seas of America, Greenland, Baffin's Bay, Hudson's Bay, Canada, and Nova Scotia.

PENNANT. The Literary Life of Thomas Pennant. By Himself. *London.* 1793. 4to, pp. 144. Portrait and Plates. 59758

Contains an appendix on the Patagonians, and includes notices of Falkner, a Jesuit, with an account of travels in Bolivia, La Plata, and the Straits of Magellan.

[PENNANT.] Le Nord du Globe, ou Tableau de la Nature dans les contrées Septentrionales; qui fait connoître la terre dans ses formes, ses climats, ses qualités; la mer dans ses marées, ses écueils, ses phénomènes; et le ciel dans ses météores; depuis le 60°. degré de latitud, jusqu'aux extrémités les plus voisines du pole. Traduit de l'Anglois. *A Paris: Chez Theophile Barrois le jeune ....* MDCCLXXXIX. 2 vols., 8vo, pp. xii, 376; 375. Plates.

A French translation of Pennant's "Arctic Zoölogy."

[PENNANT.] Thiergeschichte der Nördlichen Polarländer. Aus dem Englischen des Herrn Thom. Pennant, mit Anmerkungen und Zusätzen durch E. A. W. von Zimmerman .... *Leipzig, bey Siegfried Lebrecht Crusius.* 1787. 2 vols., 4to, pp. (14), 256, 180; 181-568. 23 Plates. C. 59760

A German translation of Pennant's "Arctic Zoölogy."

PENNELL (R.) An Inaugural Essay on the Bilious Typhus which prevailed ... in ... New York, ... 1820. By Richard Pennell. ... *New-York: E. Bliss and E. White.* 1821. 8vo, pp. 72.

PENNIMAN (*Major*), *pseudon.* The Tanner-Boy, and How he became Lieutenant-General. By Major Penniman. ... *Boston: Roberts Brothers.* 1864. 16mo, pp. 316. Plate. 59762

Also: Winfield, the Lawyer's Son, and How he became Major-General. ... *Philadelphia: Ashmead & Evans.* [186-.] 12mo, pp. 323.

[PENNIMAN (Purcell).] Questions and Expositions of Slavery, Obtained from those who have experienced it, by the author. [n. p. n. d.] 12mo, pp. (2), 13. BA. 59763

PENNINGTON (J. W. C.) The Fugitive Blacksmith: Or Events in the History of James W. C. Pennington, Formerly a Slave in the State of Maryland .... Third Edition. *London.* 1850. 12mo, pp xix, 84. 59764

PENNINGTON. A Lecture ... before the Glasgow Young Men's Christian Association. ... By Rev. J. W. C. Pennington, D.D. [n. p. n. d.] 8vo, pp. 20. 59765

The colored population of the United States have no destiny separate from the nation of which they form an integral part. Also: Covenants Involving Moral Wrong are not obligatory upon Man: A Sermon ... in ... Hartford, on Thanksgiving Day, Nov. 17th, 1842. ... *Hartford: John C. Wells.* 1842. 8vo, pp. 12. — The Reasonableness of the Abolition of Slavery at the South, a legitimate inference from the Success of British Emancipation: An Address ... 1st August, 1856. *Hartford.* 1856. 8vo. — ... Sermon ... in the Fifth Congregational Church, ... Nov. 2nd, 1845. *Hartford.* 1845. 8vo, pp. 37. — A Text Book of the Origin and History, &c. &c. of the Colored People. ... *Hartford: L. Skinner, Printer.* 1841. 16mo, pp. 96.

PENNINGTON [William]. Opinion of Governor Pennington, of New Jersey; Argument of Mr. Armstrong, ... and Letter of Mr Maxwell; in relation to the Powers and Duty of the Governor and Privy Council, in Canvassing the Votes for Representatives in Congress. *Washington.* [1838.] 8vo, pp. 12. BA.

PENNINK J. J.) Gedachten en Wenken over de Kolonisatie en ter Bevordering van de Cultuur in de Nederlandsche West-Indiën. ... *Arnhem.* 1845. 8vo. 59767

PENNSYLVANIA.

The following list of anonymous books are, with a few exceptions, alphabetical under the first word of the book or the name of the institution or society which puts forth the book. The geology is grouped under that head. In the preparation of this list I am under special obligations to Mr. C. R. Hildeburn of Philadelphia, for his valuable assistance.

An Abridgment of the Laws of Pennsylvania, from 1700 to the second day of April 1811. By John Purdon. *Philadelphia: Farrand, Hopkins, Zantzinger & Co.* 1811. 8vo. C. 59768

An Abridgment of the Laws of Pennsylvania, being a complete Digest of all such Acts ... as concern the Commonwealth at large. To which is added, an Appendix, containing a variety of Precedents (adapted to the several Acts) for the use of Justices of the Peace, Sheriffs, Attornies and Conveyancers. By Collinson Read, Esquire. *Philadelphia: ... The Author.* MDCCCI. 8vo, pp. (2), lvii, (2), 468, (28). 59769

Abstract from the Returns of Banks in the Commonwealth, for Four Periods of the Year 1836. *Harrisburg.* 1837. 4to. Continued. P. 59770

Abstract of the Constitutions of the United States, prepared and published by order of the Convention, assembled at Harrisburg, May 2, 1837, to propose amendments to the Constitution of Pennsylvania. *Harrisburg: Thompson & Clark.* 1837. 8vo, pp. 22. 59771

Abstract of the Laws of Pennsylvania, now in force, relative to Excise. July, 1786. Taken from a Digest of John Nicholson, Esqr. ... *Philadelphia: Printed ... by Robert Aitken.* M.DCC.-LXXXVI. 8vo, pp. 60. H. 59772

Abstract of the Report of the Joint Committee of the Legislature, appointed to examine into the state of the Bank of Pennsylvania. With Remarks and Explanations .... *Philadelphia, November*, 1829. 8vo, pp. (2), 28. 59773

The Accomplished Demagogue: or Patriot's Vade-Mecum. ... Adapted to the Meridian of Pennsylvania. ... *Pennsylvania*, ... 1804. 8vo, pp. 46. BA. 59774

Account of the Great Divisions. *See* Vol. IX., No. 37178.

Account of the Penitentiary and Penal Code of Pennsylvania, from Rees's Cyclopædia. [*Philadelphia.* 1823.] 4to. 59775

Account of the Schuylkill Navigation in the State ... with its Improvements. ... *Philadelphia.* 1840. 8vo, pp. 6. 59776

Accounts of the Treasury of ... Pennsylvania, from the 1st. of January to the 31st. of December, 1796. *Philadelphia: Hall and Sellers.* 1797. 8vo, pp. 10. P. 59777

An Act for establishing an Health Office, and to secure ... Philadelphia from the introduction of pestilential ... diseases .... *Philadelphia: Printed by William Duane*, ... 1803. 12mo, pp. 29. + Supplement .... [*Ibid.*] 1804. 8vo, pp. 5. + [*Ibid.*] 1818. 8vo, pp. 32. + [n. p.] 1823. 8vo, pp. 35, (2). 59778

An Act for Forming and Regulating the Militia of the Province of Pennsylvania; which passed the House of Assembly ... March, 1757, together with the Amendments proposed by the Governor. [n. p. 1757.] Folio, pp. 12. 59779

An Act [passed in Pennsylvania, Nov. 27, 1755] for Granting £60,000 to the Kings Use. [n. p. n. d.] Folio. 59780

An Act for granting His Majesty the sum of one hundred thousand pounds, passed at a General Assembly, begun ... October, 1758, and ... continued ... to the 5th February, 1759. *Philadelphia: Printed ... by B. Franklin ....* MDCCLIX. Folio, pp. (2), 45. 59781

An Act, for Incorporating the Society, formed for the Relief of Poor, Aged, and Infirm Masters of Ships, their Widows and Children. ... *Philadelphia.* 1792. 8vo, pp. 35. + *Philadelphia: Printed by Henry Tuckniss.* 1800. 8vo, pp. 37. 59782

An Act for the better Employment, Relief and Support of the Poor, within the City of Philadelphia, the District of Southwark, the Townships of Moyamensing and Passyunte, and the Northern Liberties. [n. p. about 1766.] Folio, pp. 4. P. 59783

An Act for the Consolidation & Amendment of the Laws, as far as they respect the Poor ... of Philadelphia, the District of Southwark, and the Township of the Northern Liberties, with the Supplements. *Philadelphia.* 1810. 8vo. + [*Ibid.*] 1814. 8vo, pp. 46. S. + *Philadelphia: John Young, Printer*, ... 1828. 8vo, pp. 46. 59784

An Act ... for the Organizing, Arming and Disciplining of the Militia. *Philada: King & Baird, Printers.* [1864?] 8vo, pp. 15. H. 59785

An Act for the Regulation of Banks in ... Pennsylvania, approved, April, 16, 1850. *Harrisburg.* 1850. 8vo, pp. 17.

An Act for the Regulation of the Militia of the Commonwealth of Pennsylvania. Published by order of the General Assembly. [n. p. 1780.] 8vo, pp. 20. + *Philadelphia: Printed by E. Oswald* .... M,DCC,XCIII. 8vo, pp. 16. P. + *Lancaster.* 1807. 16mo. P. 59787

An Act for the Regulation of the Militia of ... Pennsylvania, passed the second day of April, one thousand eight hundred and twenty-two; together with the Several Supplements thereto. *Harrisburg: Holbrook, Henlock, & Bratton, Printers.* 1839. 8vo, pp. 99, viii. 59788

An Act for the Relief of the Insolvent Debtors, residing in ... Philadelphia; and their Creditors: Passed by the Legislature ... on the Thirteenth day of March, One thousand eight hundred and twelve. *Philadelphia: Printed ... by John Bioren* .... 1812. 8vo, pp. 16. 59789

Act Laying Duties on Household Furniture, and on Gold and Silver Watches. *Philadelphia.* 1815. Folio. 59790

An Act of Incorporation, for that Part of the Northern Liberties, lying between the West of Sixth Street and the River Delaware, and between Vine Street and Cohocksink Creek. ... *Philadelphia: Printed by William Duane.* 1807. 8vo, pp. 35.

An Act of Incorporation, for that part of the Northern Liberties, lying between the middle of Sixth Street and the River Delaware, and between Vine Street and Cohocksink Creek. ... *Philadelphia: S. Probasco, Printer.* 1819. 8vo, pp. 106.

An Act of Incorporation for the Kensington District of the Northern Liberties, with Rules and Regulations for the Government of the ... Commissioners. *Philadelphia: Simon Probasco.* 1823. 8vo, pp. 59. + [*Ibid.*] 1828. + *Philadelphia: Printed ... by Joseph Rakestraw* .... 1828. 8vo, pp. 80, (1). 59792

Act of Incorporation of the Northern Liberties Gas Works; ... *Philadelphia.* 1844. 8vo, pp. 30. 59793

An Act of the Legislature ... and a Patent to Incorporate a Company for Erecting a ... Bridge over the River Schuylkill. *Philadelphia: Printed by John Fenno* .... [1798.] 8vo, pp. 21.

Act of William and Mary laying a Tax to be Employ'd in Pennsylvania. [n. p. 1693 or '94.] Folio, 1 leaf. 59795

An Act passed in the General Assembly, Held at Philadelphia for the Province of Pennsilvania The Twenty Fifth Day of April, in the Fifth Year of His Majesties Reign Annoq; Domini 1719. *Philadelphia: Printed ... by Andrew Bradford* .... MDCCXIX. Folio, pp. (10). 59796

An Act pass'd in the General Assembly ... of Pennsylvania ... 1722. *Philadelphia: Printed ... by Andrew Bradford* .... MDCCXXIII. Folio, pp. 6. 59797

An Act providing for the Resumption of Specie Payments by the Banks ... . Approved October 13th, 1857. *Philadelphia.* [n. d.] 8vo, pp. 7. 59798

An Act Relating to Banks, and to provide the better government thereof; accompanied with the Veto Message of the Governor. ... *Harrisburg.* 1841. 8vo, pp. 25. 59799

An Act supplementary to an Act to establish a General System of Education by Common Schools. Reported by Mr. Anderson, of Del. Chairman. ... *Harrisburg.* 1835. 8vo, pp. 6.

An Act to authorize the Governour to Incorporate a Company to make a Lock Navigation, on the River Schuylkill. *Philadelphia.* 1815. 8vo, pp. 28. 59801

Act to enable the Governor ... to Incorporate a Company for making an Artificial Road from ... Philadelphia, ... to the ten mile stone on Chestnut-Hill, and from thence to the ... bridge over Perkimen Creek, in the County of Montgomery. *Germantown, Pa.: Printed by P. R. Freas & Co.* 1840. 12mo, pp. 16.

An Act to establish a General System of Education by Common Schools. *Harrisburg.* 1834. 12mo, pp. 11. 59803

An Act to Incorporate ... a Rail Road through the Northern Section of ... Philadelphia, from the ... Delaware to Schuylkill, ... *Philadelphia.* 1832. 12mo, pp. 11. 59804

... An Act to incorporate the City of Philadelphia. [*Colophon:*] *Printed by Peter Stewart.* 1789. Folio, pp. 11. 59805

The first under the State Government. It consists of thirty-nine articles; it should be orthodox.

An Act to Incorporate the City of Philadelphia, with enlarged boundaries. [n. p. n. d.] 8vo, pp. 22. 59806

See also "A Further Supplement," *infra.*

An Act to Incorporate ... the District of Spring Garden, lying between Vine Street and the Middle of Hickory Lane, and between the Middle of Sixth and the Middle of Broad Streets; ... *Philadelphia: Printed by John Binns.* 1813. 8vo, pp. 27, 7.

An Act to Incorporate the District of Spring Garden, ... extending the bounds of the corporation, with Supplements and Acts ... relating to the District; ... *Philadelphia: Jacob Frick & Co.* 1827. 8vo, pp. 90, xiii.

An Act to promote the more certain and equal assessment of Taxes in Philadelphia. [n. p. 1865.] 8vo, pp. 7. 59808

An Act to Re-Charter Certain Banks. To which are added the Several Acts ... Relative to Banks, and the By-Laws of the Farmers and Mechanics Bank. *Philadelphia: R. Desilver* ... . 1824. 8vo, pp. 68. 59809

An Act to Regulate the General Elections of this Commonwealth, and to prevent Frauds therein. *Philadelphia: Printed by Thomas Bradford* .... MDCCLXXXV. 8vo, pp. 22. P. 59810

An Act to regulate the General Elections, within the Commonwealth .... *Philadelphia: Printed by Francis and Robert Bailey.* 1799. 8vo, pp. 40. 59811

An Act to regulate the Militia of the Common-Wealth of Pennsylvania. *Philadelphia: Printed by John Dunlap* .... M,DCC,-LXXVII. 8vo, pp. 32. P. 59812

An Act to Regulate the Sale of Intoxicating Liquors; ... March 31, 1856. [*Harrisburg.* 1856.] 8vo, pp. 11, (1).

Eine Acte zur Anordnung der Militz der Republik Pennsylvanien. Aus dem Englischen übersetzt. *Philadelphia: Gedruckt bey Steiner und Cist* .... 1777. 8vo, pp. 28. P. 59814

Eine Acte, zur Incorporirung der zur Unterstützung nothleidender Deutschen beysteurenden Deutschen Gesellschaft in Pennsylvanien. *Philadelphia: Gedruckt bey* [illegible] 1782. 8vo, pp. 30. H. + *Philadelphia. Gedruckt* [illegible] *Kämmerer.* 1793. 8vo, pp. 21. H. + *Philadelphia,* [illegible] 8vo, pp. 15, (2). + 1843. 8vo, pp. 15. [illegible]

Acts of the Province of Pennsylvania pass'd in the General Assembly, held at Philadelphia, ... 1720 ... to ... August 1721. *Philadelphia: Printed and sold by Andrew Bradford* .... MDCCXXI. Folio, pp. 12. + [*Ibid.*] pp. (2), 13-30. + [*Ibid.*] MDCCXXII. pp. (2), 33-90. 59816

Acts passed in the General Assembly of the Province of Pennsylvania. Held at Philadelphia, The Fourteenth day of October 1723, and continued by Adjournments till ... December next after ... . *Philadelphia: Printed ... by Andrew Bradford* ... . MDCCXXIII. Folio, pp. 28. 59817

Acts passed in the General Assembly ... . Held at Philadelphia, The Fourteenth Day of October 1724, and continued ... till the Twenty First Day of August 1725. *Philadelphia:* ... *Andrew Bradford* .... MDCCXXV. Folio, pp. 37. 59818

Acts ... of Pennsylvania, ... 1726. *Philadelphia:* ... *Andrew Bradford* .... MDCCXXVI. Folio, pp. 28. 59819

For intermediate dates of acts, etc., *see* "Anno Regni," Nos. 59877-81, *infra.*

The Acts of Assembly of the Province of Pennsylvania, Carefully compared with the Originals. And an Appendix, containing such Acts, and Parts of Acts, relating to Property, as are expired, altered or repealed. Together with The Royal, Proprietary, City and Borough Charters; and the Original Concessions of the Honourable William Penn to the First Settlers of the Province. Published by Order of Assembly. *Philadelphia: Printed ... by Hall and Sellers* .... MDCCLXXV. Folio, pp. xxi, 536, Appendix, 22, Index, (12), Addendum, 3. B., P. 59820

Edited by Joseph Galloway.

The Acts of the General Assembly of the Commonwealth of Pennsylvania, Carefully compared with the Originals. And an Appendix, Containing the Laws now in Force, passed between the 30th Day of September 1775, and the Revolution. Together with The Declaration of Independence; the Constitution of ... Pennsylvania; and the Articles of Confederation of the United States of America. Published by order of the General Assembly. *Philadelphia: Printed and sold by Francis Bailey* ... . M,DCC,LXXXII. Folio, pp. (4), xxxi, 527, Index, viii. B., P.

Edited by Thomas M'Kean.

Acts of Assembly relative to the Board of Wardens of the Port of Philadelphia, and Regulations of Pilots and Pilotages. Also Rules and Regulations of the Board, Relative to Owners, Masters or others .... *Philadelphia: R. Desilver* .... 1829. 8vo, pp. 56. 59822

Acts of the Assembly relative to the Incorporation of the Township of Moyamensing, &c. With the Ordinances passed

by the Commissioners, their ... Regulations for the ... Watch. *T. S. Manning, Printer, Philadelphia.* 1824. 8vo, pp. 38.

Acts of the General Assembly of ... Pennsylvania: Passed at a session, ... begun ... the first day of December, ... one thousand eight hundred and one ... . *Lancaster: Printed by Robert Bailey* ... . 1802. 8vo, pp. 286, xii. Continued annually.

Acts of the General Assembly of Pennsylvania, relating to the Eastern State Penitentiary and to the New Prison of ... Philadelphia. *Philadelphia.* 1831. 8vo, pp. 24. W. 59825

Acts ... relating to the Circuit Courts in Pennsylvania, with the Rules established by the Judges of the Supreme Court. *Philadelphia.* 1826. 8vo, pp. 23. 59826

Additional Report of the Commissioner, on the Subject of the Lien of the Commonwealth upon the Lands of John Nicholson and Peter Baynton, deceased. ... *Harrisburg: Holbrook, Henlock, & Bratton, Printers.* 1840. 8vo, pp. 16, folded leaf 59827

Address [to the Democrats of Pennsylvania. n. p. 1838.] 8vo, pp. 12. 59828

Address and Reasons of Dissent of the Minority of the Convention of ... Pennsylvania, to their Constituents. [n. p. n. d.] 8vo, pp. 22. BA. 59829

An Address from the Inhabitants of Wyoming and others to the People ... of ... Pennsylvania, Sept. 12, 1786. [n. p. n. d.]

An Address from the Trustees and Treasurer of "The Friendly Association for preserving Peace with the Indians," to William Denny, Esq., Governor of Pennsylvania. [n. p. 1757.] Folio, pp. 4. P. 59831

Corrected title of our No. 34589, Vol. IX.

An Address Lately presented to J[oseph] G[alloway] Esq. [n. p. 1764.] 4to, 1 leaf. 59832

Address of a Committee appointed by the Citizens of Pittsburgh, July 20, 1831, on the ... Railroad from the Western Termination of the Pennsylvania Canal to the Ohio Canal. *Pittsburgh: Printed by Johnston & Stockton.* 1832. 8vo, pp. 24.

Address of the Central Committee of Correspondence, to the Democratic Citizens of ... Pennsylvania. *Harrisburg.* 1835. 8vo, pp. 8. P. 59834

Address of the Convention of 27th June, 1827, to their Fellow Citizens of Pennsylvania. [n. p. n. d.] 8vo, pp. 12. 59835

Relates to plans for promoting manufactures.

An Address of the Council of Censors to the Freemen of Pennsylvania. [n. p.:] *Printed by Hall and Sellers.* [1784.] Folio, 1 leaf. 59836

Address of the Democratic Central Committee of Correspondence, to the People of Pennsylvania. *Harrisburg.* 1838. 8vo, pp. 30. P. 59837

Address of the Democratic State Central Committee. *Philadelphia.* 1863. 8vo, pp. 8.— Address of the Democratic State Central Committee. [n. p. 1864.] 8vo, pp. 8.

Address of the General Committee of Correspondence, [appointed at a General Meeting of the Republican Members of the Legislature of ... Pennsylvania,] to the Democratic Citizens of ... Pennsylvania, on the ... Presidential Election, 1812. *Philadelphia: Printed by John Binns.* [n. d.] 8vo, pp. 20. + Second Address ... . [*Ibid.*] 8vo, pp. 8. 59838

The Address of the Members of the General Assembly ... to the Democratic Citizens of Pennsylvania, recommending a new Candidate for the office of Governor. [n. p. 1805.] 12mo, pp. 19. P. 59839

The | Address | of the | People call'd Quakers, | In the Province of Pennsylvania, | To John Penn, Esquire, | Lieutenant-Governor of the said | Province, &c. | *Philadelphia:* | *Printed by Andrew Steuart* .... 1764. Sm. 8vo, pp. 11. P. 59840

Address of the Representatives of the ... Quakers, in Pennsylvania, New Jersey, Delaware, &c. To the Citizens of the United States. *Philadelphia: Joseph & William Kite.* 1837. 8vo, pp. 15. 59841

Address of the Republican Convention, convened at Pittsburgh, ... On the 22d of February, 1656 [*sic*]. *Washington, D. C.:* ... *Buell & Blanchard.* 1856. 8vo, pp. 16. P. 59842

Address of the State Committee of Correspondence, to the Citizens of Pennsylvania. [n. p. 1825.] 8vo. 59843

[illegible] election address. *See also* [Leib (Michael)], Vol. x., No. 39888.

[illegible] of The State Committee of Republicans, appointed [illegible] with the Committees of the Several Counties of

... Pennsylvania, on the ... Election of 1802. [*Philadelphia:*] *Printed by William Duane.* 1802. 8vo, pp. 16. 59844

Address of the Union State Central Committee of Pennsylvania. [Sept. 1863.] 8vo, pp. 15. 59845

An Address to Friends within the Compass of the Yearly Meeting held in Philadelphia. *Philadelphia: Printed ... by D. & S. Neall.* 1827. 16mo, pp. 10. 59846

Address to Governor Gordon by the Assembly. [*Philadelphia: Printed and Sold by Andrew Bradford* ... . 1728.] Folio, pp. 10. P. 59847

Address to Governor Gordon by the Assembly. [*Philadelphia: Printed ... by Andrew Bradford* ... . 1728.] Folio, 1 leaf.

An Address to the Assembly of Pennsylvania, on the Abolition of the Bank of North-America. *Philadelphia: Printed ... by Robert Aitken* .... M. DCC. LXXXV. 12mo, pp. 25. P. 59848

Address to the Citizens of Pennsylvania. *Philadelphia:* ... *Merrihew and Gunn* ... 1837. 8vo, pp. 16. P. 59849

In favor of the formation of a State Anti-Slavery Society.

Address to the Citizens of Pennsylvania on the ... more liberal Encouragement of Agriculture. Accompanied with inquiries ... proposed by the Philadelphia Society for Promoting Agriculture, ... *Philadelphia.* 1818. 8vo, pp. 14. H. 59850

An Address to the Citizens of Pennsylvania, upon ... a Life Insurance Company. [n. p. 1813.] 8vo, pp. 13. 59851

An Address to the Farmers of Pennsylvania. [n. p. 1799.] 8vo, pp. 16. 59852

A Federalist election address.

An | Address | to the | Freeholders | and | Inhabitants | of the | Province | of | Pennsylvania. | In Answer to a Paper called | The Plain Dealer. | *Philadelphia:* | *Printed ... by Anthony Armbruster,* ... | 1764. 8vo, pp. 12. P. 59853

An Address to the House of Representatives from the Meeting for Sufferings, 10 mo. 26. [n. p. 1775.] Folio, 1 leaf.

Address to the Inhabitants. *See* [Pemberton (I.)], No. 59610.

Address to the Members of the Society of Friends in Pennsylvania and elsewhere, 10th month, 18, 1845. *Philadelphia.* 1845. 12mo, pp. 8. 59855

Address to the People of Pennsylvania and the United States, by the Pennsylvanian Society for the Suppression of Lotteries. *Philadelphia: William Brown.* 1834. 8vo, pp. 19. P. 59856

Address to the People of Pennsylvania, issued by authority of Loyal Pennsylvanians of Washington, D. C., Sept. 1864. *Washington.* 1864. 8vo, pp. 15. 59857

An Address to the People of Pennsylvania on the Approaching Election for Governor. [n. p. 1808.] 8vo, pp. 22. 59858

[Address to the People of Pennsylvania over the Signature of Franklin. n. p. n. d.] 8vo, pp. 12. BA. 59859

An Address to the People of Pennsylvania, upon a Great Public Question. By a Meeting of Freeholders from ... the State, ... Philadelphia, March 15, 1817. ... [n. p. n. d.] 8vo, pp. 9.

Address to the People. *See* Nicholson (John), XIII. 55226.

Address to the People of the Commonwealth ... relative to the License Question. [n. p. 1846.] 8vo, pp. 8. P. 59861

Addresse an die democratischen Republickaner in Adams County. [n. p. 1835.] 8vo, pp. 4. P. 59862

Addresses on the Consideration of Resolutions relative to the Death of Abraham Lincoln, ... delivered in the House ... January 23, 1866 ... . *Harrisburg: Singerly & Myers.* 1866. 8vo, pp. 26. P. 59863

Addresses on the ... Death of the Hon. Robert R. Reed, ... Jan. 4, 1865. ... *Harrisburg.* 1865. 4to, pp. 35. Portrait. B.

Annual Report of the ADJUTANT-GENERAL of Pennsylvania. Transmitted to the Governor ... for ... 1861. [*Harrisburg.* 1862.] 8vo, pp. 23. Continued. 59865

Advertisement [of the Commissioners of Property calling for the payment of Quitrents. *Philadelphia: And. Bradford.* 1712.] Folio, 1 leaf. + [1729.] 4to, 1 leaf. 59866

Advertisement | I beg leave to take this Opportunity of informing the Publick | that I have ... in part compiled a Work | ... Proposals | for printing by Subscription | a General History of the Lies | raised & propagated by the Pr——y Faction, since the year 1753; | with Remarks: in Four Volumes, in Folio. | [*Philadelphia. Oct.* 1, 1766.] Folio, 1 leaf. P. 59867

Advice and Information To the Freeholders and Freemen of the Province of Pensilvania. And particularly to those of the County and City of Philadelphia. *Philadelphia, Printed by Andrew Bradford, September* 1727. Folio, pp. 4. 59868

Advice to the Free-holders and Electors of Pennsylvania, &c. [n. p. 1735.] Sm. 4to, pp. 7. 59869

The Ahiman Rezon, containing a View of the History and Policy of Free Masonry, together with the Rules and Regulations of the Grand Lodge, and of the Grand Holy Arch Chapter of Pennsylvania, compiled for the Grand Lodge. *Philadelphia.* 1825. 8vo, pp. 274. 59870

All's Well; or an Address to the Public, occasioned by "Methodism Anatomized;" or the (Unseasonable) "Alarm to Pennsylvania," &c. To which is suffixed A Word or Two for the sole Benefit of the Author of that Alarm. *Philadelphia.* 1763. 59871

Charter and By-Laws of the ALLEGHANY Railroad and Coal Company. ... *Philadelphia.* 1854. 8vo, pp. 30. Map. 59872

Report of the President ... of the ALLEGHANY VALLEY Rail Road ... with the Chief Engineer's Report, and Treasurer's Statement. Read February 7, 1854. *Pittsburgh.* 1854. 8vo, pp. 59. Map. Continued. 59873

Amendments to the Constitution of Pennsylvania proposed by a Convention to the Vote of the People, ... October, 1838: Together with the existing Constitution. *Philadelphia: Printed by John C. Clark.* [n. d.] 8vo, pp. 16. C. 59874

Constitution of the AMERICAN Sunday-School Union; with the By-Laws ... Officers, Managers, and Committees, 1832–3. *Philadelphia.* 1832. 8vo, pp. 8. 59875

Anno Regni Annæ Reginæ Octavo. An Act for Ascertaining the Rates of Money for the Payment of Debts, &c. ... [*Philadelphia:*] *Printed ... by J[acob] Taylor.* [1709.] Folio, pp. (2).

Anno Regni Georgii II. Regis Magnæ Britanniæ, Franciæ, & Hiberniæ, Tertius. At a General Assembly of the Province of Pennsylvania, begun and holden at Philadelphia, the fourteenth day of October, Anno Dom. 1729. In the third year of the reign of our Sovereign Lord George II. ... And from thence continued by adjournment to the twelfth of January, 1729. Being the

second session of this present Assembly. *Philadelphia: Printed and sold by B. Franklin and H. Meredith* ... . M,DCC,XXX–XXXIX. Folio. P. 59877

Collation: M,DCC,XXX, pp. 47; *Ib.* pp. (2), 51–57; *Ib.* pp. (2), 59–90; MDCCXXXI, pp. (2), 93–95; MDCCXXXII, pp. (2), 99–102; MDCCXXXIII, pp. (2), 105–128; MDCCXXXIV, pp. (2), 131–133; *Ib.* pp. (2), 137–154; MDCCXXXVI, pp. (2), 157–169; MDCCXXXVIII, pp. (2), 173–189; MDCCXXXIX, pp. (2), 193–229, (2).

Anno Regni Georgii II. ... At a General Assembly of the Province of Pennsylvania, begun and holden at Philadelphia, the Fourteenth Day of October, Anno Dom. 1734. In the Eighth Year of the Reign of our Sovereign Lord George II. ... And from thence continued by adjournments to the Seventeenth Day of March, 1734. *Philadelphia: Printed and Sold by B. Franklin* ... . M,DCC,XXXIV. 12mo, pp. 24. P. 59878

A synopsis of the poor laws.

Anno Regni Georgii II. ... At a General Assembly of the Province of Pennsylvania, begun and holden at Philadelphia, the Fourteenth Day of October, 1743, ... to ... May, 1744. *Philadelphia: Printed and sold by B. Franklin* ... . M,DCC,XLIV–LIX. Folio. P. 59879

Collation: M,DCC,XLIV, pp. 22; *Ib.* pp. (2), 25–26; MDCCXLVI, pp. (2), 25 [*sic*]–59; *Ib.* pp. (2), 61–69; MDCCXLVII, pp. iv; MDCCXLIX, pp. (2), 73–88; *Ib.* pp. (2), 91–105; MDCCL, pp. (2), 107–119; *Ib.* pp. (2), 123–125; MDCCLI, pp. (2), 129–151; *Ib.* pp. (2), 155–158; *Ib.* pp. (2), lxi; MDCCLII, pp. (2), 161–184; *Ib.* pp. (2), 187–208; MDCCLV, pp. (2), 211–222; *Ib.* pp. (2), 225–235; *Ib.* pp. (2), 239; *Ib.* pp. (2), 243–260; MDCCLVI, pp. (2), 263–266; *Ib.* pp. (2), 269–270; *Ib.* pp. (2), 273–274; *Ib.* pp. (2), 277–316; *Ib.* pp. (2), 319–321; *Ib.* pp. (2), 325–334; MDCCLVII, pp. (2), 337–344; *Ib.* pp. (2), 347–361; *Ib.* pp. (2), 365–372; MDCCLVIII, pp. (2), 375–390; *Ib.* pp. (2), 393–427; *Ib.* pp. (2), 431–436; MDCCLIX, pp. (2), 439–483; *Ib.* pp. (2), 487–513; *Ib.* pp. (2), 517–526; *Ib.* pp. (2), 529–530.

Anno Regni Georgii II. ... At a General Assembly of the Province of Pennsylvania, begun and holden at Philadelphia, the Fifteenth Day of October, ... 1759, ... and ... continued by adjournments to the Eleventh Day of February, 1760. *Philadelphia: Printed ... by B. Franklin* ... . MDCCLX–LXIX. Folio. P.

Collation: MDCCLX, pp. 45; MDCCLXI, pp. (2), 49–98; *Ib.* pp. (2), 101–103; *Ib.* pp. (2), 107–125; MDCCLXII, pp. (2), 129–183; *Ib.* pp. (2), 187–211; *Ib.* pp. (2), 215–220; MDCCLXIII, pp. (2), 223–276; *Ib.* pp. (2), 279–286; *Ib.* pp. (2), 289–296; *Ib.* pp. (2), 299–311; MDCCLXIV, pp. (2), 315–330; *Ib.* pp. (2), 333–358; *Ib.* pp. (2), 361–369; MDCCLXV, pp. (2), 373–410; *Ib.* pp. (2), 413–428; *Ib.* pp. (2), 431–448; *Philadelphia: Printed ... by David Hall* ... . MDCCLXVI, pp. (2), 451–485; *Philadelphia: Printed ... by D. Hall and W. Sellers* ... . MDCCLXVI, pp. (2), 489–498; MDCCLXVII, pp. (2), 501–538; *Philadelphia: Printed ... by William Goddard* ... MDCCLXVII, pp. (2), 541–583; *Philadelphia: Printed ... by D. Hall and W. Sellers* ... MDCCLXVII, pp. (2), 587–593; MDCCLXVIII, pp. (2), 597–636; MDCCLXIX, pp. (2), 639–737; *Ib* pp. (2), 741–744.

Anno Regni Georgii III. ... At a General Assembly of the Province of Pennsylvania, begun and holden at Philadelphia, the Fourteenth Day of October, ... 1769 ... . And from thence continued ... to the Twenty-fourth Day of February, 1770. *Philadelphia: Printed ... by D. Hall, and W. Sellers* ... . MDCCLXX–LXXV. Folio. P. 59881

Collation: MDCCLXX, pp. 34; *Ib.* pp. (2), 37–38; *Ib.* pp. (2), 41–50; MDCCLXXI, pp. (2), 53–153, (1); *Ib.* pp. (2), 157–165; MDCCLXXII, pp. (2), 169–286; *Ib.* pp. (2), 289–290; MDCCLXXIII, pp. (2), 293–355; *Ib.* pp. (2), 359–366; MDCCLXXIV, pp. (2), 369–410; *Ib.* pp. (2), 413–436; MDCCLXXV, pp. (2), 439–464; *Ib.* MDCCLXXV.

Annual Digest of the Laws of Pennsylvania, for ... 1854 and 1855. By Frederick C. Brightly. *Philadelphia.* 1855. 8vo. Continued. 59882

Annual Message of the Governor of Pennsylvania, ... with ... Documents. ... *Harrisburg.* 1845. 8vo, pp. 16. Continued.

Annual Message of the Governor ... January 2, 1850. [n. p. n. d.] 8vo, pp. 16. 59884

Annual Message of the Governor ... Andrew G. Curtin, ... January 7, 1864. *Harrisburg.* 1864. 8vo, pp. (2), 16. + January 30, 1865. [*Ibid.*] 8vo, pp. 18. 59885

Annual Report of the Executive Office, Military Department, of the Commonwealth ... for the year ending December 1, 1864. *Harrisburg: Singerly & Myers.* 1865. 8vo, pp. 263. + ... Report ... for ... 1865. [*Ibid.*] 1866. 8vo, pp. 239. 59886

Answer to an invidious Pamphlet. *See* [Cross], Vol. V. 17666.

Answer to Mr. Franklin's Remarks. *See* Vol. VII. 25577.

The Antidote. [n. p. n. d.] 8vo, pp. 8. 59887

Antwort auf Hrn. Franklins Anmerckungen über ein ohnlängst herausgekommenes Protestations-Schreiben. Uebersetzt aus dem Englischen. *Gedruckt im Jahr* 1765. 8vo, pp. 27.

A German translation of our No. 25577, Vol. VII.

Appeal and Protest of the Loyalists confined in the Mason's Lodge, September 9, 1777. [n. p. 1777.] Folio, pp. 22.

Appeal on Behalf of the Sick [by the Pennsylvania Hospital]. *Philadelphia.* 1851. 8vo, pp. 48. 59890

Appeal to the Citizens. *See* [Kirkbride (T. S.)], IX. 37980

Appeal to the People of Pennsylvania on the ... Asylum for the Insane Poor. *Philadelphia.* 1858. 8vo. 59891

See also "A Second Appeal," *infra.*

An Appeal to the People of Pennsylvania from the Decision of their Representatives in Congress on the Question of Peace or War. Second Edition, Revised and Corrected; with ... Important Documents respecting the Presidential Election. *Philadelphia.* 1812. 12mo, pp. 31. 59892

An Argument addressed to ... the Governor of Pennsylvania, in support of the bill to incorporate the Pennsylvania Fiscal Agency. ... *Philadelphia.* [1859.] 8vo, pp. (2), 32. 59893

An Argument for cleansing the Sanctuary; ... . *Philadelphia.* 1853. 12mo, pp. 147. 59894

Arrangement of the Pennsylvania Line, January 17, 1781. *Philadelphia: ... Francis Bailey.* [1781.] Sm. 8vo, pp. 16. P.

Articles of Agreement ... . [*Philadelphia: B. Franklin.* 1733.] Sm. folio, pp. 7. 59896

Relates to the boundary "Lines between Maryland, and Pensilvania and the Three Lower Counties on Delaware." *See also* Vol. XI., No. 45073.

The | Articles, | Settlement and Offices | Of the Free | Society | of | Traders | in | Pennsilvania: | Agreed upon by divers | Merchants | And Others for the better | Improvement and Government | of | Trade | in that Province. | *London,* | *Printed for Benjamin Clark in George-Yard in Lombard-street,* | *Printer to the Society of Pennsilvania,* M DC LXXXII. Folio, (8) leaves. C., H. 59897

An extremely rare piece.

Declaration and Testimony for the Doctrine and Order of the Church of Christ ... . By the ASSOCIATE PRESBYTERY ... . *Philadelphia.* 1784. 8vo, pp. 59. 59898

For a second edition, *see* Vol. V., No. 19164.

A Solemn | Warning | by the Associated Presbytery, | in | Pennsylvania: | Addressed to | All Persons into whose Hands it may come | in these United States; particularly to the | People under their Inspection. | Wherein | The great Sin, Danger and Duty of | the Inhabitants of the Land, are pointed | out and declared. | ... | *Lancaster: Printed by Francis Bailey.* [1778.] Sm. 8vo, pp. 27.

Also: Act of the Associate Presbytery of Pennsylvania, against Occasional Communion. ... Added, a Justification of the Doctrine ... . *Philadelphia: Printed by David*

Hogan. 1797. 8vo, pp. iv, 55. B.—Display of Religious Principles ... . *Philadelphia* 1794. 12mo. W. + [*Ibid.*] 1814. 8vo. *See also* Vol. IV., No. 15113.

Account of the ASYLUM for the Relief of Persons Deprived of ... Reason, near Frankford, Pennsylvania; with the Statistics ... from its foundation to the 31st. 12th month, 1838. By Charles Evans, M.D. ... *Philadelphia.* 1839. 8vo, pp. 15. + [*Ibid.*] 1846. 8vo, pp. 14. 59900

Also: Account of the ... Asylum, ... Established, near Philadelphia, for the Relief of Persons deprived of ... Reason. ... *Philadelphia.* 1814. 12mo, pp. 76. Plate.—Account of the ... Asylum ... . *Philadelphia.* 1816. 12mo, pp. 24. Plate.—Annual Report of the Asylum ... . *Philadelphia.* 1814. 8vo. Continued. The reports for 1818–27 were published as "State of the Asylum."

At a Meeting of Clergymen and Lay-Delegates from sundry Congregations of the Episcopal Church in the State of Pennsylvania, held ... in Philadelphia, on ... 25th ... May, 1784. [n. p. n. d.] Folio, 1 leaf. P. 59901

This very rare piece was the commencement of the organization of the present Protestant Episcopal Church in the United States.

Annual Report of the ATTORNEY GENERAL of Pennsylvania. For ... 1862. [*Harrisburg.* 1863.] 8vo, pp. 4. Continued.

Also: Opinion of the Attorney General, relative to the Election in the Sixteenth Congressional District. [*Harrisburg.* 1865.] 8vo, pp. 7.

Communication from the AUDITOR GENERAL, ... Accompanied with a Statement of Certain Banks. Read in House ... January 10, 1832. *Harrisburg.* 1832. 8vo, pp. 32. Contin'd.

Report on the Finances of the Commonwealth ... for ... 1810; made to the Legislature, by the Auditor General, agreeably to Law. *Lancaster: Printed by John Burnside.* 1810. 8vo, pp. 29.

Continued until changed in 1851 to "Report of the Auditor General on the Finances," and as such continued to the present time.

Reports of the several Railroad Companies, ... Communicated by the Auditor General, to the Legislature, Jan. 12, 1860. *Harrisburg: A. Boyd Hamilton.* 1860. 8vo; pp. 166. 59905

Continued to 1866, and then changed to "Annual Report of the Auditor General ... and of the Tabulations and Deductions from the Reports of the Rail Road and Canal Companies for ... 1866." *Harrisburg: Singerly & Myers.* [1867.] 8vo, pp. (2), lvi, 530. Continued until 1875, and thenceforth published as Part IV. of the "Report of the Secretary of Internal Affairs." Also: Communication from the Auditor General relative to the Account of John Dungan. [n. p. 1852.] 8vo, pp. 27.—Communication ... relative to Escheats and Alleged Escheats. [*Harrisburg.* 1852.] 8vo, pp. 22.—Communication ... showing the Receipts and Expenditures on the Public Improvements, for the last fiscal year. ... *Harrisburg.* 1845. 8vo, 2 leaves.—Communication ... transmitting Quarterly Statements of the Several Banks and Savings Institutions ... *Harrisburg.* 1849. 8vo, pp. 109.—Jahresbericht des General-Auditors

über die Finanzen des Staats ... . *Harrisburg.* 1850. 8vo.—Letter ... accompanied by the Bank Report. [n. p. 1816.] 8vo, pp. 28. Continued.—Letter ... enclosing ... the condition of the Banks of Pennsylvania. ... *Harrisburg.* 1840. 8vo, pp. 70.—Letter ... transmitting a Statement of the Affairs of certain Banks and Savings Institutions. Read in Senate Jan. 5, 1836. *Harrisburg.* 1835–'36. 12mo, pp. 46.—Letter ... transmitting Tabular Statements of the Condition of the Banks ... 1841. ... *Harrisburg.* 1842. 8vo, pp. (4), folded leaf.—Report ... accompanied with a Statement of Certain Banks and Savings Institutions. ... *Harrisburg.* 1836–7. 8vo, pp. 118. Continued.—Report .. in relation to the Circulation of Paper Currency. *Harrisburg.* 1837. 12mo, pp. 28.—Report ... relative to the Free Banking Law of ... Pennsylvania. [n. p. 1863.] 8vo, pp. 12. + [n. p. 1865.] 8vo, pp. 22.—Reports of the Several Banks ... communicated by the Auditor General, ... January 8, 1863. *Harrisburg: Singerly & Myers.* 1863. 8vo, pp. 380.

Ausführliche Beschreibung. *See* [Höen (M. W.)], VIII. 32377

An Authentic View of the Progress of ... Pennsylvania, since the Establishment of the Independence ... . [Colophon:] *Printed by D. Humphreys, ... Philadelphia, May,* 1799. 8vo, pp. 8.

To the Stock-Holders of the BANK OF NORTH-AMERICA, On the ... Old and New Banks. [Colophon:] *Philadelphia: ... Joseph Crukshank* ... . MDCCXCI. 8vo, pp. 16. 59907

An Act to incorporate the Subscribers to the BANK OF PENNSYLVANIA. [n. p. 1793.] 8vo, pp. 44. 59908

Contains the minutes of the proceedings of the stockholders, Aug. 12 to Sept. 4, 1793 (pp. 27–44).

Bank of Pennsylvania. Philadelphia, November 14, 1829. [n. p. n. d.] 8vo, pp. 28. + Report ... . [n. p. n. d.] 8vo, pp. 14. 59909

Representation and report of the State Directors of the Bank of Pennsylvania, in regard to the refusal of the bank, to subscribe to the State Loan of 1829.

Laws of the Bank of Pennsylvania. *Philadelphia: John Binns, Printer.* 1811. 8vo, pp. 26. 59910

Also: An Address to the Stockholders of the Bank of Pennsylvania. December 22d, 1829. *Philadelphia: Clark & Raser, Printers* ... . 1829. 8vo, pp. 18, (1).—Charters and Laws ... . *Philadelphia.* 1830. 8vo, pp. 28.—Facts in relation to the Bank ... published by the State Directors. [n. p. 1829.] 8vo, pp. 28.—Memorial of the President, Directors, and Company of the Bank ... . [n. p. 1851?] 8vo, pp. 9.—Proceedings of the Stockholders ... at their ... Meeting, held, February 5, 1844. *Philadelphia.* 1844. 8vo, pp. 8.—Report and Documents of the Committee appointed to inquire into the Conduct of the Cashier and Directors of the Bank ... . [n. p. 1815.] 8vo.—Report of a Committee of the Bank ... in relation to the Legislative Investigation ... and the conduct of its Officers. [n. p. 1829.] 8vo, pp. 14.—Report of the Directors ... to the Stockholders, Feb. 1, 1858. *Philadelphia.* 1858. 8vo. Continued.

Report of the ... Directors of the BEAVER Meadow Railroad and Coal Company ... August 15, 1839. Together with the

Proceedings ... and the By-Laws ... . *Philadelphia.* 1839. 8vo, pp. 16. Continued. 59911

Berigt, en Onderrigtinge, nopens en aan de Colonie en Kerke van Pensylvaniën. Opgestelt en uytgegeven door de Gedeputeerden van de E. christelyke Synodus van Zuyd-Holland, benevens de Gecommitteerden van de E. Classis van Delft en Delfsland; en Schieland. [*Amsterdam.* 1730?] 4to, pp. (2), 18. 59912

An historical sketch of Pennsylvania, and very interesting for the history of the Reformed Church in Pennsylvania.

Beschreibung der neuerfundenen pensylvanischen Kamine oder Oefen, 1794. Aus dem Englischen und Holländischen übersetzt. *Gotha: Ettinger.* 1794. 8vo. Plate. 59913

Beschryving van de nieuw uitgevonden Pensilvanische Schoorsteenen. *Leiden: C. Haak.* 1746. 8vo. 59914

Biographical Sketches of the Senators and Representatives of Pennsylvania ... . Published Annually. The ... Sketches being those of the Legislators of 1864. ... [n. p. n. d.] 16mo, pp. 143

Biography, or Memoirs of Eminent Pennsylvanians. *Philadelphia.* 1839. 12mo. 59916

Bioren's Pennsylvania Pocket Remembrancer, for ... 1814. *Philadelphia.* 1813. 18mo. Continued. 59917

The Black Heath Coal Company. *Philadelphia.* 1865. 8vo, pp. 20. 59918

First Annual Report of the BOARD OF COMMISSIONERS of Public Charities of ... Pennsylvania ... . *Harrisburg.* 1871. 8vo, pp. lvi, 290. Continued. 59919

Report of the BOARD OF MILITARY Claims, made to the Legislature ... for ... 1863. *Harrisburg.* 1864. 8vo, pp. 142. Discontinued after 1868. 59920

First Annual Report of the BOARD OF MISSIONS of the Diocese of Pennsylvania ... . *Philadelphia.* 1860. 8vo, pp. 35.

Journal of the BOARD OF REVENUE Commissioners of ... Pennsylvania, ... Feb., 1857. *Harrisburg.* 1857. 8vo. Cont'd.

Boyd's Business Directory of [ten] Counties of ... Pa. Together with a General Directory of all the Inhabitants of Harrisburg, with an Appendix of much useful information. 1860.

William H. Boyd, ... Philadelphia, Pa. [n. d.] 8vo, pp. 246. Continued. 59923

Bribery and Corruption!! Report of the Proceedings of the Williamsport Convention, embracing the Spirited Debates, ... Testimony in relation to the attempt to bribe two of the Delegates; and other interesting particulars of the occasion. ... Reported by W. E. Drake, Reporter to the Legislature. *Philadelphia.* 1850. 8vo, pp. 32. 59924

A Brief Account of the Proceedings. *See* Vol. IX. 34617.

A Brief Account of the Province. *See* [Penn (W.)], 59680.

A Brief Exhibition of the Right of Jurisdiction and Soil of the State of Pennsylvania, and those under Pennsylvania in the 42d Degree of North Latitude from Delaware River to the Western Bounds of that State, where they Join the Tract of Country attempted to be Reserved by Connecticut. [n. p. 1781.] 8vo.

... A Brief History. *See* [McKean (T.)], Vol. XI. 43380.

A Brief History of the Rise. *See* Vol. II., No. 7876.

Brief Sketch of the State Penitentiary for Eastern Pennsylvania, at Philadelphia. *Philadelphia.* 1822. Rl. 8vo. 59926

A Brief State of the Province. *See* [Smith (W.)]

A Brief View of the Accounts of the Treasury of Pennsylvania, from the time of the Commencement of the Revolution to the First of October, 1781: Extracted from the books of the Comptroller-General, ... agreeable to ... the Act ... passed the 13th ... April, 1782. In which is exhibited, The Monies in the Treasury at the commencement, the several receipts and payments during that time, and the balance on hand at the end thereof: Also, the accounts of the State Treasurer, Continued from the said First of October, 1781, to the First of October, 1782: Likewise, the accounts of the several Counties for their taxes to October 1782 ... . Together with, the state of the outstanding debts, due by the Counties for their deficiencies in payment of taxes. *Philadelphia: Printed by Hall and Sellers.* M, DCC, LXXXIV. 8vo, pp. 237. HSP. 59927

A Brief View of the Conduct. *See* [Smith (W.)]

A Brief View of the Province. *See* [Smith (W.)]

By the Honourable Collonel [*sic*] | John Evans, Lieutenant Governour of the Province | of Pensilvania and the Counties annexed. | A Proclamation, | Against Immorality and Prophaneness. | *Printed at Philadelphia by Reynier Jansen* 1704. Folio, 1 l.

By William Keith ... . A Proclamation [for the apprehension of Robert Moore, who had killed John Gee. *Philadelphia:*] *Printed by Andrew Bradford* ... . [1720.] Folio, 1 leaf. 59929

By Sir William Keith ... . A Proclamation [announcing the agreement between the Penns and Lord Baltimore for settling their dispute. *Philadelphia: S. Keimer.* 1724.] Folio, 1 leaf.

By ... Patrick Gordon ... . A Proclamation [against riots in Philadelphia]. *Philadelphia: Printed by Andrew Bradford* ... . 1726. Folio, 1 leaf. 59931

By ... Patrick Gordon ... . A Proclamation [against abusing the Indians]. *Philadelphia: Printed by Andrew Bradford* ... . 2728 [*sic*]. Folio, 1 leaf. 59932

By ... Patrick Gordon ... . A Proclamation [against the murderers of some Indians]. *Philadelphia: Printed by Andrew Bradford* ... . 1728. Folio, 1 leaf. 59933

By ... Patrick Gordon ... . A Proclamation [to enforce the Riot Act]. *Philcdelphia: Printed by Andrew Bradford* ... . 1729. Folio, 1 leaf. 59934

By ... George Thomas, Esq; ... A Proclamation [relative to the Indians in Lancaster County. *Philadelphia.* 1742.] Folio, 1 leaf. 59935

By ... George Thomas, Esq; ... A Proclamation [announcing the declaration of War with France. n. p. 1744.] Folio, 1 l.

By ... George Thomas, Esq; ... A Proclamation [of a day of thanksgiving for the victory at Culloden]. *Philadelphia: Printed by B. Franklin.* [1746.] Folio, 1 leaf. 59937

By the ... President and Counsel of the Province of Pennsylvania. A Proclamation for a General Fast. *Philadelphia: Printed by B. Franklin.* MDCCXLVII. Folio, 1 leaf. 59938

By ... James Hamilton, Esq; ... A Proclamation [against selling liquor to Indians in Philadelphia]. *Philadelphia: Printed by B. Franklin* ... . [1749.] Folio, 1 leaf. 59939

By ... James Hamilton, Esq; ... A Proclamation [against settlers on Indian lands west of the Blue Hills]. *Philadelphia: Printed by B. Franklin* ... . [1749.] Folio, 1 leaf. 59940

... By ... James Hamilton, Esq; ... *Philadelphia: Printed by B. Franklin* ... . MDCCL. Folio, 1 leaf. 59941

A proclamation of the Lieutenant-Governor of Pennsylvania, etc., requiring an account of all iron mills, etc.

By ... James Hamilton, Esquire, Lieutenant Governor ... . [n. p. about 1751.] Folio, 1 leaf. 59942

By ... Robert Hunter Morris, Esq; ... A Proclamation. *Philadelphia: Printed by B. Franklin, and D. Hall.* MDCCLVI. Folio, 1 leaf. 59943

Orders the killing and destroying of the Delaware Indians, and offers a reward for Indian scalps.

By ... John Penn ... . A Proclamation [of a reward for the arrest of two murderers]. *Philadelphia: Printed by D. Hall, and W. Sellers.* 1768. Folio, 1 leaf. 59944

By ... John Penn ... . A Proclamation [relative to the Connecticut Boundary]. *Philadelphia: Printed by Hall and Sellers.* 1774. Folio, 1 leaf. 59945

By ... John Penn, Esquire ... . A Proclamation [relative to the Maryland Boundary]. *Philadelphia: Printed by Hall and Sellers.* 1774. Folio, 1 leaf. 59946

By ... John Penn ... . A Proclamation [revoking the preceding]. *Philadelphia: Printed by Hall and Sellers.* 1774. Folio, 1 l.

By ... John Penn ... . A Proclamation [on the Virginia Boundary]. ... *Philadelphia: Printed by Hall and Sellers.* 1774. Folio, 1 leaf. 59948

By ... John Penn, Esquire ... . Given the Fifteenth Day of September 1774. *Philadelphia: Printed by Hall and Sellers.* 1774. Folio, 1 leaf. 59949

In reference to the boundary between Pennsylvania and Delaware.

By ... John Penn ... . A Proclamation [relative to the murder of an Indian called Joseph Wipey]. *Philadelphia: Printed by Hall and Sellers.* [1774.] Folio, 1 leaf. 59950

By ... John Penn ... . A Proclamation [relative to the Maryland Boundary]. *Philadelphia: Hall and Sellers.* [1775.] Folio, 1 leaf. 59951

Communication from the CANAL Commissioners exhibiting the condition of the Canals and Rail Roads. Read in the House ... March 11, 1839. *Harrisburg: Boas and Coplan—Printers.* 1839. 8vo, pp. 78. 59952

First Report of the Pennsylvania Canal Commissioners, accompanied with Official Documents. *Harrisburg: Printed by Cameron & Krause.* 1827. 8vo, pp. 96. 59953

Continued to 1858 inclusive.

Journal of the Board of Canal Commissioners of Pennsylvania, for ... 1853. [n. p. n. d.] 8vo, pp. 124. 59954

Pennsylvania Canal Regulations and Rates of Toll, as established by the ... Canal Commissioners, and in force on the First of August, 1833: Together with the Acts for the Protection of the Canal. *Harrisburg: Printed by Hugh Hamilton & Son.* 1833. 8vo, pp. 56. 59955

Also: Communication from the Canal Commissioners relative to the Sale of the Main Line of the Public Works of the State. *Harrisburg.* 1856. 8vo, pp. 91.—Jahresbericht der ... Canal Commissioners, mit begleitenden Dokumenten. *Harrisburg.* 1850. 8vo.—Report of the Canal Commissioners ... . Read ... February 7, 1826. *Harrisburg.* 1826. 8vo, pp. 8.—Report of the Canal Commissioners relative to amount paid for repairs upon the Pennsylvania Canal and Rail Road. ... *Harrisburg.* 1832. 8vo, pp. 8.—Report of the Canal Commissioners relative to the Extension of the Pennsylvania Canal. ... *Harrisburg.* 1833. 8vo, pp. 11.—Report of the Canal Commissioners, relative to the number of Officers and Agents, upon the Pennsylvania Canal and Rail Roads. Read in the House ... January 6, 1835. *Harrisburg.* 1834–'35. 8vo, pp. 11.—Report of the Canal Commissioners ... relative to the Pennsylvania Canals and Rail-Roads. Dec. 18, 1830. *Harrisburg.* 1830. 8vo, pp. 38.—Report of the Canal Commissioners relative to the Superintendents, Engineers, &c. in the Employment of the State upon the Pennsylvania Canal and Rail Road. Read in the House ... March 9, 1832. *Harrisburg.* 1832. 8vo, pp. 16, 6 folded leaves. Continued.—Reports of Moncure Robinson, Esq. & Col. Stephen H. Long, Engineers appointed by the Canal Commissioners for examining the different routes for crossing the Alleghany Mountain ... . Read in Senate, March 14, 1831. *Harrisburg.* 1831. 8vo, pp. 32.

Candid Address to Episcopalians. *See* Plain Truth, *pseudon.*

A Candid Examination of the Address of the Minority of the Council of Censors to the People of Pennsylvania: Together with Remarks upon the Danger and Inconveniences of the principal Defects of the Constitution of Pennsylvania. By One of the Majority. *Philadelphia: Printed in the Year* 1784. Sm. 8vo, pp. 40. 59956

An improved title of our No. 10662, Vol. III.

The Case of Isaac Taylor and Elisha Gatchel, Two Officers of Pennsylvania, made Prisoners by the Government of Mary-

land. *Printed at Philadelphia [by Andrew Bradford] in the Year,* 1723. Folio, pp. 2. 59957

The Case of the German Protestant Churches settled in ... Pennsylvania, and in North America. [n. p. about 1751.] Fol. 1 leaf. BM. 59958

The Case of the Heir-at-Law and Executrix of the late Proprietor of Pensilvania, etc. in relation to the removal of Sir William Keith, and the appointing Major Patrick Gordon to succeed him as Deputy Governor there. *London.* 1725. Folio, pp. 4. + *Philadelphia.* 1725. 59959

The Case of the Inhabitants of Pensilvania. [n. p. 1742.] Folio, 1 leaf. 59960

Respecting the paper currency, which is shown to have been highly beneficial, and the proposed bill for doing away with it strongly objected to.

The Case of the People called Quakers In the Province of Pennsylvania, With respect to the Forms of Declaration of Fidelity to the King, and of Affirmation, lately granted to their Friends in Great Britain and Ireland, &c. by Acts of Parliament, briefly stated and humbly offer'd to the Consideration of the Governour and Council of the said Province. [Colophon:] *Philadelphia: Printed by Andrew Bradford.* 1724. 12mo, pp. 7. P.

The Case of the Proprietors of the Province of Pensilvania and the Three Lower Counties ... . To be heard before Privy Council at Whitehall, 23 Feb. 1737. [*London.* 1737.] Folio, pp. 8. 59962

Catalogue of Papers Relating to Pennsylvania and Delaware, deposited at the State Paper Office, London. *Philadelphia: C. Sherman.* 1850. 8vo, pp. 167. 59963

By-Laws of the CATAWISSA Railroad Co., and Organization for Conducting the Business ... . 1860. *Philadelphia.* [n. d.] 8vo, pp. 24. 59964

Also: Lease and Contract of the Catawissa Rail Road to the Western Central Rail Road Company of Pennsylvania, and the Atlantic & Great Western Railway Company of New York, Pennsylvania and Ohio, executed 1st November, 1865. *Philadelphia.* 1865. 8vo, pp. 20.—Report of a Reconnoissance made in April, 1865, by Joseph Lesley, Topographical Geologist, of the Coal Property owned by the Catawissa Railroad Company. *Philadelphia.* 1865. 8vo, pp. 8. 3 Maps.—Second Annual Report of the Catawissa Rail Road Company, for ... 1861. *Philadelphia.* 1862. 8vo, pp. 32. Continued.

Exhibit of the CATAWISSA, WILLIAMSPORT and Erie Railroad Company, ... and the proposed completion of the road to Will-

iamsport, ... in ... Pennsylvania. ... [n. p.] March, 1851. 8vo, pp. (2), 19, xlii, (1). 2 Maps. 59965

Also: The Catawissa Williamsport and Erie Rail Road Company. ... Charter and Supplements thereto. *Philadelphia.* 1856. 8vo, pp. 33.—Report of the ... Company, 1855. ... *Philadelphia.* [n. d.] 8vo, pp. 14. Continued to 1860.

Census of the Eastern and Western Districts of Pennsylvania. 1830. ... *Harrisburg.* 1832. 12mo, pp. 18. 2 folded Tables.

Central Rail Road. Report of the Chief Engineer of the Danville and Pottsville Rail Road Company. With a Report of the President and Managers ... January, 1833. *Philadelphia.* 1833. 8vo, pp. 8. 59967

Continued as "Report of the President and Managers." Also: ... Reports of the Engineers of the Danville and Pottsville Rail Road Company. With the Report of a Committee ... . October 15, 1831. *Philadelphia.* 1831. 8vo, pp. 27. Continued.

Charter granted by Charles II. to William Penn, Esq. Proprietor and Governor of Pennsylvania (4th March 1681). Folio, pp. 4

The Charter of the Province of Pennsylvania. *Philadelphia: Printed ... by William Bradford.* MDCLXXXIX. Folio. 59969

The Charter of Privileges Granted by the Honourable William Penn, Esq; to the Freeholders and Inhabitants of Pennsylvania. October 28. 1701. *Philadelphia: Printed ... by Samuel Keimer,* ... MDCXXV [*sic* for 1725]. Folio, pp. 7. P. 59970

The Charter of Privileges, granted by William Penn, Esq., to the Inhabitants of Pensilvania and Territories. *Philadelphia: Printed ... by B. Franklin.* 1741. Folio, pp. 8. 59971

The Charters and Acts of Assembly of the Province of Pennsylvania. ... Vol. I. Containing the Charters of the said Province, and the City, Boroughs and Towns thereof: The Titles of all the Laws of the said Province, since its first Establishment down to ... 1700; The Acts of ... Assembly from ... 1700 to 1743, now in Force; ... Compared with the Public Records. *Philadelphia: Printed by Peter Miller and Comp.* MDCCLXII. Folio, pp. (2), 164. + Vol. II. Containing the Acts of Assembly ... from ... 1744 to 1759, now in Force: A Collection of all the Laws that have been formerly in Force within this Province, for Regulating of Descents and Transferring the Property of Lands, but are since expired, altered or repealed; from the Establishment of the Province, down to this present Time. ... [*Ibid.*] Folio, pp. (2), iii, 116, (2), 18, 32. + [*Ibid.*] MDCCLXII. 2 vols., 8vo, pp. (2), 653; (2), xii, 464, (2), 71, (2), 127. P. 59972

The appendix has a separate title-page in both editions, and in the octavo the index has also a separate title-page. The octavo edition, except the appendix and index to volume II., is only "A Collection of Laws" published in 1760. *See* No. 59985, *infra.* Horace Binney says of this collection: "I have known it cited as Peter Miller's edition of the laws. A manuscript entry on my copy calls it 'Weiss & Brockden's edition,' and I have so cited it. It is valuable for several old laws not to be found in other editions, and especially for many proceedings in the Privy Council of England, repealing or disallowing certain of the laws of the Province."

The Charters of the Province of Pensilvania and City of Philadelphia. *Philadelphia: Printed ... by B. Franklin.* M DCC XLII. Folio, pp. 30. H., P. 59973

Statement by the President of the CHESTER Valley Railroad Company, ... in reference to the Lease of the Road to the Philadelphia and Reading Railroad Co. ... December 17, 1858. *Philadelphia.* 1859. 8vo, pp. 12. 59974

[Federalist] Circular. Lancaster, May 30th, 1799. Folio.

An Address by the CITIZENS Association of Pennsylvania, to the People; with Act of Incorporation. *Philadelphia.* 1866. 8vo, pp. 15. 59976

Also: Dependent and Criminal Population of Pennsylvania. Report of the Citizens Association ... . 1868. *Philadelphia.* 1868. 8vo, pp. 15.—First Annual Report of the President ... . *Philadelphia.* 1867. 8vo, pp. 30. Folded Plan.

First Annual Report of the CLEARFIELD Coal and Lumber Company. ... *Philadelphia.* 1856. 8vo, pp. 23. Map and Plan.

Clintonian Meeting [in Cumberland Co., Sept. 1812]. Folio, 1 leaf. 59978

Coal Ridge Improvement and Coal Company ... . *Philadelphia.* 1864. 8vo, pp. 16. Map. 59979

Charter and By-Laws of the COAL RUN Improvement and Railroad Company, with Reports on their Coal Lands, together with a Synopsis and Supplementary Remarks. *Philadelphia.* 1853. 8vo, pp. 26, 27, (1). 2 Maps. 59980

Constitution and By-Laws, of the COHOCKSINK Beneficial Society of Pennsylvania. Chartered February 24, 1835. *Philadelphia.* 1842. 12mo, pp. 20. 59981

A Collection of all the Laws of the Province of Pennsylvania, now in force. Published by Order of Assembly. *Philadelphia: Printed ... by B. Franklin.* M,DCC,XLII. Folio, pp. 562. [Followed by:] An Appendix; containing a Summary of such Acts

of Assembly as have been formerly in Force within this Province, for Regulating of Descents, and Transfering [*sic*] the Property of Lands, &c. But since expired, altered or repealed. [*Ibid.*] pp. iv, 24, Index, xi. H., P. 59982

A Collection of Charters and other Publick Acts relating to the Province of Pennsylvania ... . *Philadelphia: Printed ... by B. Franklin.* M,DCC,XL. Folio, pp. (2), 46. P. 59983

A Collection of Hymns for the Use of the Protestant Church of the United Brethren. New and Revised Edition. ... *Philadelphia: Printed by Conrad Zentler.* 1819. 12mo, pp. xxxvi, 348, (52). 59984

A Collection of the Laws of the Province of Pennsylvania, now in Force. ... *Philadelphia, By P. Miller and Company.* MDCCLX. 2 vols., 8vo, pp. (2), 653; (2), xii, 464. P. 59985

Collection of the Penal Laws of the Commonwealth of Pennsylvania. *Philadelphia.* 1801. 8vo, pp. 72. 59986

Catalogus Bibliothecæ COLLEGII ALLEGHANIENSIS. *E Typis Thomas Atkinson et Soc. apud Meadville,* 1823. 8vo, pp. 139.

See also Vol. I., No. 777.

Die Colonie St. Maria in Pennsylvanien, N. Amerika. [n. p. n. d.] 8vo, pp. 15. 59988

Colored School Statistics. To the Board of Education of the Pennsylvania Society for promoting the Abolition of Slavery. [n. p. 1853.] 8vo, pp. 4. 59989

Fourth ... Exhibition of the COLUMBIAN Society of Artists and the Pennsylvania Academy, May 14th, 1814. *Philadelphia.* 1814. 8vo, pp. 32. 59990

The Commercial, Agricultural, Manufacturing and Mining Interests of Pennsylvania: How can they be promoted? [n. p. 1861?] 8vo, pp. (2), 44. 59991

Favoring the repeal of the "tonnage tax."

Report of the COMMISSARY General of ... Pennsylvania, for ... 1861. *Harrisburg.* 1861. 8vo, pp. 11. + Report ... for ... 1862. [*Ibid.*] 1863. 8vo, pp. 7. + Report ... for ... 1863. [*Ibid.*] 1864. 8vo, pp. 4. Discontinued. 59992

The Common School Journal of Pennsylvania. Edited by John S. Hart. Vol. I. *Philadelphia.* 1844. 59993

The Common School Laws ... . *Harrisburg.* 1848. 8vo. + [*Ibid.*] 1853. 8vo. + [*Ibid.*] 1855. 8vo, pp. 103, (1). + By H. C. Hickok. [*Ibid.*] 1857. 8vo, pp. 142. + Revised ... by T. H. Burrowes ... . [*Ibid.*] 1862. 8vo, pp. 119. + Revised and arranged by J. P. Wickersham ... . [*Ibid.*] 1870. 18mo, pp. vi, 276. 59994

Common Schools. Remarks on the School Law of the Last Session of the Legislature; and Information concerning the Common Schools of Massachusetts, New York, South Carolina, &c. &c. *Philadelphia.* 1826. 8vo, pp. 30. 59995

Communication from the Governor, accompanied with a Report of the ... Canal Commissioners of Pennsylvania. And Documents accompanying the said Report. ... January 1, 1827. *Harrisburg.* 1827. 8vo. + No. 2. Read ... February 7, 1827. *Harrisburg: ... John S. Wiestling.* 1827. 8vo, pp. (2), 185, (1).

Communication from the Governor, accompanied with a Communication from the ... Canal Commissioners, transmitting the reports of Charles T. Whippo and Charles De Hass, Principal Engineers for a Rail Road from New Castle to Freeport, from Laughlintown to Pittsburg, from Lewistown to Hollidaysburg, and to avoid the Inclined Plane over the Allegheny Mountain to Pittsburg. ... *Harrisburg.* 1837. 8vo, pp. 40.

Comparative Calculations, and Remarks on Internal Improvements by Roads, Canals, and River Navigation; illustrative of the advantages to be derived from the improvement of the River Lehigh. *Philadelphia: Printed by William Brown.* 1821. 8vo, pp. 12. 59997

Corrected title of our No. 15029, Vol. IV.

Comparative Views of the most important Anthracite Collieries in Pennsylvania; exhibiting their avenues to tide waters; with an Appendix, Map, and Draught of Comparative Heights and Distances. *Pottsville.* 1835. 8vo. 59998

See "North American Review," XLII. 241.

A Compilation and Digest of the Road Laws and the Election Laws; together with certain forms prepared and published under authority of an Act of the Assembly ... February 1, 1827. *Harrisburg.* 1828. 8vo. 59999

A Compilation of the Canal and Railroad Laws of Pennsylvania ... . *Harrisburg.* 1837. 8vo. 60000

A Compilation of the Health Laws of Pennsylvania. *Philadelphia.* 1798. 8vo. 60001

A Compilation of the Laws of ... Pennsylvania, relative to the Poor, from ... 1700 to 1788 ... . *Philadelphia: Printed by Zachariah Poulson, Junior.* 1789. 8vo, pp. 95. + From ... 1700, to 1795 ... . [*Ibid.*] 1796. 8vo, pp. (2), 112, 10. P. 60002

Compilation of the Laws of Pennsylvania, relative to the Internal Improvements; together with the Canal and Railway Regulations ... . *Harrisburg.* 1840. 8vo. 60003

A Compilation of the School Laws of Pennsylvania, with explanatory instructions and forms. Prepared by the Superintendent. *Harrisburg.* 1842. 8vo, pp. 32. 60004

Continued annually; after 1866 in 16mo.

The Conduct, Letters ... Addresses of a Number of Citizens ... appointed to investigate the Evils of Freemasonry, during the Session of the General Assembly ... 1835–36. *Philadelphia.* 1836. 8vo, pp. 26. H. 60005

A Confutation of the Reply to the Speech, &c. [*Philadelphia: Andrew Bradford.* 1727.] Folio, pp. 4. 60006

Isaac Norris's defense of his charge to the Grand Jury.

Report of the CONNEAUT & Beaver, & Beaver & Conneaut Rail Roads; ... from Conneaut Harbor, on Lake Erie, to the Ohio River, ... by W. K. Scott, Esq. Civil Engineer. ... *Beaver.* 1836. 12mo, pp. 20, (2). 60007

Considerations on the Jurisprudence of ... Pennsylvania. No. I. ... *Philadelphia.* 1808. 8vo, pp. 10. 60008

Considerations on the Practicability and Utility of immediately constructing a Central Railway, from Pottsville to Sunbury and Danville, through the Coal Region of Mahanoy and Shamokin, with the proceedings of a Meeting at Sunbury, Dec. 1830, Republished with Additions by the Philadelphia Committee, December 23, 1830. [n. p. n. d.] 8vo, pp. 37. 60009

Considerations upon the present Test-Law of Pennsylvania: Addressed to the Legislature and Freemen of the State. [By B. Rush.] *Philadelphia: Printed by Hall and Sellers.* MDCCLXXXIV. 8vo, pp. 23. BA. + The Second Edition. [*Ibid.*] MDCCLXXXV. 8vo, pp. 23. H. 60010

The Consolidation Bill, as Finally Passed by the Legislature of Pennsylvania, January 31st, 1854. [n. p. 1854.] 8vo, pp. (2), 16. 60011

The Conspiracy of Cataline; Recommended to the Serious Consideration of the Authors of Advise [*sic*] and Information to the Freeholders and Freemen of the Province of Pennsylvania: And Further Information, dated October 2, 1727. But more especially to One who stands impeached in Thirteen Articles, tending to detain the Rights, infringe on the Properties, and oppress the Freemen of this Province. [n. p. n. d.] Folio, 1 l.

Constitution and By-Laws of the First Constitution Club of the State of Pennsylvania. *Philadelphia.* 1866. 12mo, pp. 19.

The Constitution of the Common-Wealth of Pennsylvania, as established by the General Convention elected for that Purpose, and held at Philadelphia, July 15th, 1776, and continued by Adjournments to September 28, 1776. *Philadelphia: Printed by John Dunlap.* M,DCC,LXXVI. 8vo, pp. 32. H. + [*Ibid.*] MDCCLXXVII. 12mo, pp. (4), 18. + To which is prefixed The Confederation of the United States of America. *Philadelphia: Printed by F. Bailey.* M.DCC.LXXXI. 8vo, pp. 67. P. 60014

The Constitution of ... Pennsylvania, as established by the General Convention. To which is added a report of the Committee appointed to enquire "Whether the Constitution has been Preserved Inviolate in Every Part, and whether the Legislative and Executive Branches of Government, have performed their duty as Guardians of the People, or assumed to themselves or exercised other or greater Powers, than they are entitled to by the Constitution." As adopted by the Council of Censors. Published by their Order. *Philadelphia: ... Francis Bailey.* MDCCLXXXIV. 8vo, pp. 64. 60015

The Constitution of ... Pennsylvania, as established by the General Convention. Carefully compared with the Originals. *Philadelphia: Daniel Humphreys.* M.DCC.LXXXVI. 8vo, pp. 16.

The Constitution of ... Pennsylvania, as Altered and Amended by the Convention for that Purpose freely chosen and assembled, and by them proposed for the Consideration of their Constituents. *Philadelphia: Printed by Zachariah Poulson, Junior.* MDCCXC. 8vo, pp. 28. 60017

The Constitution of ... Pennsylvania. *Philadelphia: Printed by Zachariah Poulson, Junior.* MDCCXC. 8vo, pp. 29. + [n. p. n. d.] 12mo, pp. 12. 60018

Constitution of the First Regiment of Volunteer Artillery of Pennsylvania. Adopted November 13, 1837. *Philadelphia.* 1838. 8vo, pp. 16. 60019

Constitution of the First Regiment of Artillery of Pennsylvania. Adopted June 12th, 1843. *Philadelphia.* 1843. 8vo, pp. 16.

Constitutions of Pennsylvania, of 1790 and 1838. ... *Harrisburg: Boas and Coplan.* 1839. 8vo, pp. 28. 60020

The Continental Petroleum Company, of Pennsylvania. *New York.* 1865. 8vo. 60021

Contributions to American History. *See* Vol. IV., No. 16190.

Cool Thoughts on the Subject of the Bank. Addressed to the Representatives of the General Assembly. [n. p. n. d.] 8vo, pp. 16. 60022

Copies of several Public Papers, passed in the Province of Pennsylvania in the month of November 1755. [*London.* 1756.] Folio, pp. 7. 60023

Copies of some Original Papers and other Proceedings, relating to the Difference in the House of Representatives of the Province of Pennsylvania, in General Assembly met the 15th, and continued by Adjournments to the 20th of April, 1728. [n. p.: *Printed by S. Keimer?* 1728.] Folio, pp. 4. 60024

Copies of Sundry Papers which have passed between the Lieut. Governor of Pennsylvania, and the Assembly there, from Oct. 1754 to Jan. 1755. [*London.* 1756.] Folio, pp. 20. 60025

Copy of a Report from Reading Howell, Frederick Antes and William Dean, Esquires, Commissioners appointed to explore the Head-Waters of the Rivers Delaware, Lehigh, and Schuylkill, and the north-east branch of Susquehanna. Also, the Report of the Commissioners appointed to examine the Western Waters of the State of Pennsylvania. *Philadelphia: Printed by Francis Bailey.* MDCCXCI. 8vo, pp. 13, 33. 60026

Corrected title of our No. 33351, Vol. VIII.

Correspondence relating to the Examination of the Structures on the Catawissa, and Elmira and Williamsport Railroads. [n. p. 1862.] 8vo, pp. 12. 60027

Cost, Revenue, and Expenditures of the Public Works ... . [n. p. 1852.] 8vo, pp. 16. + *Harrisburg.* 1854. 8vo, pp. 16.

Counter Report of the Minority of the Committee to whom was referred the Memorials of a number of Citizens of ... Pennsylvania, praying that the same rates of toll may be charged on the Delaware Division of the Pennsylvania Canal as are charged by the Lehigh Coal and Navigation Company for the use of the Lehigh Canal; ... Read in Senate, February 25, 1832 ... . *Harrisburg.* 1832. 8vo, pp. 12. 60029

The Crisis. Think twice ere you speak once: But when you speak—speak the truth, without Fear, Favor or Affection. ... [n. p. 1817?] 8vo, pp. 16. 60030

Election address to Democratic citizens of Pennsylvania.

The Crisis Extraordinary. *See* [Paine (T.)], No. 58219.

Report of William Milnor Roberts, Chief Engineer of the CUMBERLAND Valley Rail Road Company, ... 23d Oct. 1835. *Philadelphia.* 1835. 8vo, pp. 8. 60031

Also: Annual Report of the Cumberland Valley Rail Road Company, with their Receipts and Expenditures from ... January, 1842, to ... 1843. *Carlisle, Pa.* 1843. 8vo, pp. 6. Continued to about 1866.

Daily Chronicle and Convention Journal; containing the Substance and Spirit of the Proceedings of the Convention, which assembled at ... Harrisburg, May 2, 1837, to alter and amend the Constitution of the State ... . By E. Guyer. *Harrisburg.* 1837. 4to. 60032

Daily Legislative Record. Published by Royal & Clyde, Harrisburg, Penn'a. Vol. I. No. I. January 24, 1853. 4to, 2 l. Continued. 60033

Laws and By-Laws of the DANVILLE and Pottsville Rail Road Company. *Philadelphia.* 1832. 8vo, pp. 28. + [*Ibid.*] 1851. 8vo, pp. 40. 60034

Also: Memorial of the President ... of the Danville and Pottsville Rail Road Company, to the City Councils, with the Report of the Chief Engineer. [n. p.] May, 1835. 8vo, pp. 14.—Report of the Acting Manager ... Jan. 28, 1841. *Philadelphia.* 1841. 8vo, pp. 11.—Report of the Superintendent ... . *Philadelphia.* 1838. 8vo, pp. 8.

Report of the DANVILLE, HAZLETON & Wilkesbarre Railroad Company. ... *Philadelphia.* 1868. 8vo, pp. 40. Map. 60035

Report ... of the DAUPHIN and Susquehanna Coal Company. *Philadelphia.* 1848. 8vo, pp. 16. Map. 60036

Debate in the House of Representatives ... on Mr. Holgate's Resolutions relative to the Bank of the United States. January, 1811. Reported by W. Hamilton. ... [n. p. n. d.] 8vo, pp. 54.

Debate in the Legislature ... on inviting Gov. A. Johnson and Ex-Gov. Wright of Indiana, to visit the State Capitol. *Harrisburg.* 1863. 8vo. 60038

Debate in the Senate ... relative to the use of the Senate Chamber for the Reception of A. Johnson. *Harrisburg.* 1863. 8vo.

Debate on the Resolutions to issue Certificates of State Stock, for the Payment of Interest on the Public Debt: in the House ... January 29th and 30th, 1844. *Harrisburg.* 1844. 8vo, pp. 8

Debates and Proceedings. *See* Carey (M.), Vol. III., No. 10864, for M.CC.LXXXVI read M.DCC.XXXVI.

Debates in the Legislature. *See* [Olmstead (G.)], No. 57236.

Debates of the Convention, of the State of Pennsylvania, on the Constitution, proposed for the Government of the United States. In Two Volumes. Vol. I. Taken accurately in Short-Hand, by Thomas Lloyd. ... *Printed by Joseph James, in Philadelphia, A. D.* M.DCC.LXXXVIII. 8vo, pp. 147, (3). BA. 60040

This seems to have been the only volume published.

Debates of the Legislature ... of 1809–10, at Lancaster. Reported by William and Hugh Hamilton. ... [n. p. n. d.] 8vo, pp. 278. B. 60041

Debates of the Legislature ... of 1810–11, at Lancaster. Reported by William Hamilton ... . [n. p. n. d.] 8vo. 60042

On the renewal of the charter of the Bank of the United States.

The Decision of the Supreme Court of Pennsylvania, in the Ejectments brought by the Heirs at Law of the late Stephen Girard against "The Mayor, Aldermen, and Citizens of Philadelphia," stated and considered. Philadelphia, September, 1833. *Philadelphia.* 1833. 8vo, pp. 35. 60043

Decisions of the Superintendent of Common Schools. [n. p. 1852.] 8vo, pp. (2), 7. 60044

Continued annually in connection with "The Common School Laws."

A | Defence | of the | Legislative Constitution | Of the Province of | Pennsylvania. | As it now stands Confirmed and Established, by | Law and Charter. With some Observations, on the Pro-

ceedings published | by Sixteen Members of Assembly, in a Paper, en- | titled, The Votes and Proceedings of the House of Re- | presentatives: Recommended to the Consideration | of all the Free-Men of the Province. [n. p. 1728.] Folio, pp. 11. 60045

Address of the Committee of the DELAWARE and Schuylkill Canal Company, to the Committees of the Senate and House ... on the Memorial of the said Company. *Printed by John Ormrod, Philadelphia.* [1799.] 8vo, pp. 32. 60046

Also: Extracts from the Resolutions of the Stockholders of the Delaware and Schuylkill Canal; and the Procedure of the Managers thereon ... . *Philadelphia, ... 25th January,* 1800. 16mo, pp. 12.

First Annual Report ... of the DELAWARE DIVISION Canal Company of Pennsylvania ... . *Philadelphia.* 1859. 8vo, pp. 13.

Law Authorising the Incorporation of the DELAWARE, LEHIGH, Schuylkill & Susquehanna Railroad Company, with the Supplements, Charter ... and concurrent Act of New Jersey. *Easton, Pa.* 1852. 8vo, pp. 24. 60048

Democratic Fellow Citizens of Western Pennsylvania. [*Pittsburg.* 1840.] Folio, 1 leaf. 60049

A Democratic Peace offered for the Acceptance of Pennsylvania Voters. *Philadelphia.* 1864. 8vo, pp. 13. 60050

Also in the German language.

Report of the Committee of the DEMOCRATIC SOCIETY. *Philadelphia.* 1811. 8vo. 60051

Democratic State Convention, for Nomination of Governor, March 5th, 1866. Full Proceedings ... . [n. p. n. d.] 8vo, pp. 8

Democratic Young Men's Meeting of Montgomery County. [n. p. 1838.] Folio, 1 leaf. 60053

Description du Sol. *See* [Cutler (M.)], Vol. V., No. 18176.

Jahresbericht der DEUTSCHEN GESELLSCHAFT von Pennsylvanien für ... 1866. *Philadelphia: Druck von Grassmann u. Goodman.* [n. d.] 8vo. Continued. 60054

Regeln der incorporirten DEUTSCHEN GESELLSCHAFT zur Unterstützung bedrängter Deutschen im Staat Pennsylvanien. *Philadelphia: Gedruckt bey Steiner und Kämmerer.* 1794. 8vo, pp. 19. + *Philadelphia.* 1843. 8vo, pp. 19, (2). + 1860. 8vo, pp. 31. + 1870. 8vo, pp. 22. 60055

See also No. 59815, *supra.*

A Dialogue between Freeman and Trusty. [n. p. 1728.] Folio. 60056

A | Dialogue, | Containing some Reflections on the late | Declaration and Remonstrance, | Of the Back-Inhabitants of the | Province of Pennsylvania. | With a serious and short Address, to those | Presbyterians, who (to their dishonor) have | too much abetted, and conniv'd at the late | Insurrection. | By a Member of that Community. | ... | *Philadelphia, printed:* | ... | M,DCC,LXIV. Small 8vo, pp. 16. P. 60057

This scarce little tract relates to the disturbances among the Indians in Lancaster county. Corrected title of our No. 19938.

A | Dialogue | shewing, | What's therein to be found. | A Motto being Modish, | for Want of good Latin, are put | English Quotations. | ... | [*Philadelphia:*] *Printed* [*by S. Keimer*] *in the Year* MDCCXXV. | Sm. 8vo, pp. 40, Errata, (1). 60058

An answer to Rawle's "Ways and Means," probably by James Logan.

A Digest of County Laws: Containing the Acts of Assembly relating to Counties and Townships throughout the State, and Local Laws relating to the County of Philadelphia. [*Philadelphia:*] *J. Crissy, Printer.* 1839. 8vo, pp. (6), 531, lxxv.

A Digest of Select British Statutes, comprising those which, ... appear to be in force in Pennsylvania; ... . With Notes and Illustrations. By Samuel Roberts. Second Edition, with additional Notes, ... by Robert E. Wright. *Philadelphia.* 1847. 8vo

A Digest of the Acts of Assembly relative to the Board of Health; with the Rules of the Board. *Philadelphia.* 1836. 8vo, pp. 97. 60061

A Digest of the Acts of Assembly relative to the First School District of ... Pennsylvania. ... *Philadelphia.* 1843. 12mo, pp. 43. + [*Ibid.*] 1852. 8vo, pp. 85. 60062

A Digest of the Acts of the General Assembly ... of a General Nature, from 1700, to 1840, inclusive; containing the Constitution of the United States, the Constitution of Pennsylvania, the Acts of Assembly arranged alphabetically and under various titles, and a Copious Index; by Mordecai M'Kinney. *Harrisburg.* 1841. 8vo. C. 60063

A Digest of the Laws of Pennsylvania from 1700 to 1824; ... By John Purdon. *Philadelphia.* 1824. 8vo. + 1700 to 1840. Sixth Edition. By George M. Stroud. [*Ibid.*] 1841.

8vo. + 1700 to 1846. Seventh Edition. [*Ibid.*] 1847. 8vo. + Brought down to 28th April, 1851, with Index to the entire work, by Frederick C. Brightly. [*Ibid.*] 1852. 8vo. + Eighth Edition. [*Ibid.*] 1853. 8vo. C. 60064

Other editions were published in 1811, 1818, 1831, 1837, 1856, and 1860.

A Digest of the Laws of Pennsylvania from April 7, 1830, to April 15, 1835, with Explanatory Notes showing the Nature, Extent and Operation of the Laws contained in this volume, as far as they alter, amend, repeal and supply the pre-existing Laws ... with Purdon's Digest ... . By Benjamin Parke and Ovid F. Johnson. *Harrisburg.* 1836. 2 vols., 8vo. C. 60065

A Digest of the Laws of Pennsylvania, of a General Nature, relative to Banks and Bankers, Savings Institutions and Loan Companies; to Bank Notes and Paper Currency, embracing References to the Laws incorporating the several Banks; ... by Mordecai M'Kinney. *Harrisburg.* 1854. 8vo. C. 60066

A Digest of the Road Laws and Election Laws. *Harrisburg.* 1828. 8vo. B. 60067

Proceedings connected with the Establishment of the DIOCESAN MISSIONARY SOCIETY of the Protestant Episcopal Church in Pennsylvania, and Charter of the same. *Philadelphia.* 1853. 8vo, pp. 15. 60068

Also: Proceedings of the First Annual Meeting ... and Charter ... with the Reports of the Committees. *Philadelphia.* 1854. 8vo, pp. 37. Continued. S.

Constitution of the DIOCESAN SUNDAY-SCHOOL SOCIETY of Pennsylvania, auxiliary to the General Protestant Episcopal Sunday-School Union. ... *Philadelphia.* 1832. 8vo, pp. 8. 60069

The Dissent of the Minority, of the House of Representatives of the Commonwealth of Pennsylvania, from the Address to the President of the United States, adopted by said House, December, 1798. [n. p. n. d.] 8vo, pp. 8. P. 60070

Documents accompanying the Report of the Committee, on Roads, Bridges and Inland Navigation, read in the Senate ... 23d of March, 1822. *C. Mowry, Printer, Harrisburg.* [1822.] 8vo, pp. 192, iii. 60071

Documents officiels. *See* Eastern Penitentiary, *infra.*

Documents referring to the Controversy between the Canal Commissioners of ... Pennsylvania and the Harrisburg and Lancaster and the Pennsylvania Railroad Companies. … *Philadelphia.* 1852. 8vo, pp. 53. 60072

Documents relating to the Manufacture of Iron in Pennsylvania. Published on behalf of the Convention of Iron Masters, … December, 1849. … *Philadelphia.* 1850. 8vo, pp. (2), 115. 12 folded Tables. 60073

Documents relative to a Communication between Pittsburgh and the Ohio Canal. *Pittsburgh.* 1833. 12mo, pp. 27. 60074

Draft of a Revised Common School Law, and of a Law Relative to … Teachers; with Explanatory Remarks … . Prepared by Thos. H. Burrowes … . Read in Senate, Jan. 15, 1838. *Harrisburg.* 1839. 8vo, pp. 61. 60075

The Duty of Pennsylvania Concerning Slavery. [n. p. 1840?] 8vo, pp. 8. 60076

Early History of Western Pennsylvania. *See* [Rupp (D.)]

Act of the Legislature … Incorporating the EASTERN Market Company … . *Philadelphia.* 1859. 8vo, pp. 7. 60077

A Concise History of the EASTERN PENITENTIARY of Pennsylvania, together with a Detailed Statement of the Proceedings of the Committee, appointed by the Legislature, December 6th, 1834, for the purpose of examining into … that institution … . By a Member of the Legislature. *Philadelphia: Neall & Massey, Printers.* 1835. 8vo, pp. 283, Errata, 1 slip. A. 60078

Documents Officiels sur le Penitencier de l'Est, ou de Cherry Hill à Philadelphie … . Extraits des Rapports Annuels lus au Senat et à la Chambre des Representants … de Pennsylvanie, depuis l'ouverture du Penitencier en 1829, jusqu'au 8 Mars, 1843. Traduits par ordre de M. le Comte Duchatel, Ministre de l'Interieur; par M. Moreau Christophe, Inspecteur Général des Prisons de France. *Paris.* 1844. Rl. 8vo, pp. (2), 130. Plan.

Appears to be the first number of the "Revue Penitenciare."—RICH.

History of the Eastern Penitentiary … . *Philadelphia.* 1852. 8vo. 60080

Also: Address, by a Female Visitor to the Prisoners of the Eastern Penitentiary … . *Philadelphia.* 1844. 8vo.—First and Second Annual Reports of the Inspectors … Made to the Legislature at the Sessions of 1829–30, and 1830–31. *Philadelphia.* 1831. 8vo, pp. 22, (2). Continued.—A View and Description of the … Penitentiary … . *Philadelphia.* 1830. 8vo, pp. (2), 8. 2 Plates.

First Annual Announcement of the ECLECTIC Medical College of Pennsylvania. *Philadelphia.* 1851. 8vo. 60081

Election Law of … Pennsylvania, passed at the Session of 1838–9. *Philadelphia.* 1839. 8vo, pp. 52. 60082

Election Laws of … Pennsylvania, relating to … Philadelphia, with a Copious Index. Compiled by Horn R. Kneass … . *Philadelphia.* 1847. 8vo, pp. 79. + 1852. 8vo, pp. x, 109, 13, (1).

The Election Laws of Pennsylvania: … *Philadelphia.* 1854. 8vo, pp. 77. + *Harrisburg.* 1868. 8vo, pp. 152. 60084.

The Elmira and Williamsport Railroad Co. 1860. … *Philad'a.* [n. d.] 8vo, pp. (2), 45. 60085

Also: First Annual Report of the Managers … . *Philadelphia.* 1861. 8vo, pp. 35. Continued.

Aux Émigres de toutes les Contrées de l'Europe. *Philadelphie.* 1794. 4to. 60086

Official information on Pennsylvania and its physical advantages, its productions, etc., with "Plan de Vente de 300 mille acres de terres, situées dans les Comtés de Northumberland, et de Huntingdon, dans l'État de la Pensylvanie, avec Observations et Notes Instructives," addressed to emigrants at the period of the French Revolution.

An Enquiry into The Political Grade of the Free Coloured Population. By a Member of the Chambersburg Bar. [n. p. n. d.] 8vo. 60087

The Third Annual Report of the … Managers of the EPISCOPAL Education Society of Pennsylvania. … *Philadelphia.* 1832. 8vo, pp. 27. Continued. 60088

An Act to Authorize the Governor to incorporate the ERIE Canal Company. … *Erie, Pa.* 1843. Sm. 4to, pp. 23. 60089

Also: Second Annual Report of the Erie Canal Company, to the Legislature … for … 1844. … *Harrisburg.* 1845. 8vo, pp. 5.

Erläuterung für Herrn Caspar Schwenckfeld … wegen vielen Stücken, beydes aus der Historie und Theologie … durch etliche der ehemaligen gottseeligen Auswanderer aus Schlesien nach Pennsylvanien in Nord Amerika. Zweyte Auflage. *Sumnytaun: Gedruckt bey E. Benner.* 1830. 8vo, pp. xiv, 507, (2). 60090

État Présent de la Pensilvanie. *See* [Smith (W.)]

Evidence taken in the Pennsylvania Contested Election. [n. p.] 1852. 8vo. 60091

An Examination of the Causes & Effects, of the present state of the Circulating Medium, and of the Remedy for its Depreciation. By a Citizen of Pennsylvania. *Doylestown: Printed by Asher Miner.* 1816. 8vo, pp. 53. 60092

Examination of the Connecticut Claim. *See* [Smith (W.)]

… Executive Communication. *See* Vol. XI., No. 45141.

Experience the Test of Government. *See* [Duane (W.)]

Exposition of Sentiments. Adopted by the Pennsylvania Yearly Meeting of Progressive Friends. … [n. p. n. d.] 8vo, pp. 15. B. 60093

An Exposition of the Law, accompanied by Remarks on the Rights and Duties of Master and Apprentice … . By one of the Aldermen of … Philadelphia. *Philadelphia.* 1836. 8vo, pp. 28.

Extract from a Report, made by a Committee of the House of Representatives of Pennsylvania, Mr. Wallace, Chairman, … 11th February, 1833. [n. p. n. d.] 8vo, pp. 8. 60095

Relates to the Union Canal Company.

Extracts from the Votes of the House of Assembly, Of the Province of Pennsylvania; Containing Rules and Regulations for the better Government of the Military Association … the Articles of said Association, and, the Resolutions directing the Mode of levying Taxes on Non-Associators … . Published by order of the Committee of Safety. *Philadelphia: Printed by W. and T. Bradford.* [1776.] 12mo, pp. 20. P. 60096

Facts and Arguments. *See* [Blodget (W.)], Vol. II. 5959.

Address from the … Trustees of the FARMERS' High School to the People of Pennsylvania. *Carlisle, Pa.* 1858. 12mo, pp. 10

Also: Annual Report of the Farmers' High School … . December, 1857. *Harrisburg.* 1858. 8vo. Continued.—Catalogue of the Officers and Students … . 1859. *Philadelphia.* 1859. 8vo, pp. 32., Continued to 1861.—Memorial of the Committee of the … Trustees … . To the … Senate and House … . [n. p. 1856.] 8vo, pp. 5.

A farther Account. *See* Vol. VI., No. 23894.

A Farther Supplement to the Act entitled, "An Act to regulate the Militia of the Common-Wealth of Pennsylvania. *Philadelphia: Printed by John Dunlap.* M,DCC,LXXVIII. 8vo, pp. 8.

Fellow Citizens of Pennsylvania. [n. p. 1828.] 8vo, pp. 12.

Anti-Jackson election address, signed "Franklin."

First Annual Announcement of the FEMALE Medical College … for the session of 1850–51, situated in Philadelphia. *Philadelphia.* 1850. 8vo, pp. 8. Continued. 60100

See also Vol. II., No. 5341.

A Few Plain Facts, addressed to the People of Pennsylvania. By a Citizen of Pennsylvania. Fourth Edition, Enlarged. … *Philadelphia.* 1844. 12mo, pp. 14. 60101

A Few Reasons. *See* "X. X."

A Few Words for Honest Pennsylvania Democrats. [n. p. n. d.] 8vo, pp. 16. 60102

First Report of the Commissioners appointed … 1840 to Settle the Estates of John Nicholson, and Peter Baynton, made … to … the Senate … . [n. p.] 1841. 8vo, pp. 14. 60103

The Frame of Government of the Province of Pennsilvania. [*Philadelphia: William Bradford.* 1689.] Sm. 8vo, pp. 16.

This is the charter for printing which Bradford was summoned before the Governor and Council.

The Frame of the Government. *See* [Penn (W.)], 59696–7.

Mr. Franklin, The absolute and obvious Necessity of Self-Defence, in the present Conjuncture … . [*Philadelphia: Franklin and Hall.* 1748.] Folio, pp. 2. 60105

In support of Tennent's defensive warfare.

Report of the FRANKLIN Institute of … Pennsylvania … on … Paving Highways. … [n. p.] 1843. 8vo, pp. 40. 60106

See also Vol. VII., Nos. 25653–56.

Franklin Rail Road. A Report of the Chief Engineer … with a Report of the President and Managers … . *Chambersburg, Pa.* 1837. 8vo, pp. 8. 60107

Constitution of the FREE Produce Society of Pennsylvania. *Philadelphia.* [1827.] 12mo, pp. 12. 60108

Friendly Advice to the Inhabitants. *See* [Norris (I.)], 55500.

Friends and Countrymen. *See* [Dickinson (J.)], v. 20041.

From the General Committee of Conference, for the Erection of a Monument to the Memory of Washington, to the Inhabitants of … Pennsylvania. [n. p. 1833.] 8vo, pp. 4. 60109

Second Annual Report of the Proceedings of the FRUIT Growers' Society, of Eastern Pennsylvania. *West Chester, Pa.* 1861. 8vo, pp. 48. 60110

A Full and Correct Report of the Testimony given before the Joint Committee … inquiring into the charges of Bribery … by the Banks … . Together with the Proceedings at the Bar of the House of Representatives, in the case of George Handy, one of the Directors of the United States Bank. And copies of the original letters … compiled … by J. Franklin Reigert … . *Harrisburg.* 1842. 8vo, pp. 319, iii. 60111

This is the "Report of the Joint Committee of Investigation … July 12, 1842," with a new title-page.

A Full and True Relation of Count Martini, in Silesia, Who was transformed into a Dog, all but the Head … . *Philadelphia: Printed by Anthony Armbruster.* 1765. Sm. 4to, pp. 4. 60112

An election squib, of which Joseph Galloway was probably the subject.

Fundamental By-Laws and Tables of Rates, for Reversionary Annuities, … by the Corporation for the Relief of the Widows and Children of Clergymen, … of the Protestant Episcopal Church, in … Pennsylvania. … *Philadelphia.* 1851. 8vo. + [*Ibid.*] 1866. 8vo, pp. 64, (4). 60113

Further Account of the Province. *See* [Penn (W.)], 59701–2

A Further Supplement to an Act … to Incorporate … Philadelphia, passed January 31, 1854; … *Philadelphia.* 1854. 8vo, pp. 42, (1). + [*Ibid.*] 1855. 8vo, pp. 55. 60114

General Index to the Colonial Records. *See* Hazard (S.)

General Index to the Laws of Pennsylvania, from … 1700 to March 31, 1812 inclusive. *Philadelphia.* 1812. 5 vols., 8vo.

The General Laws of Pennsylvania, from … 1700, to April 22, 1846, … with Notes and References to all the Decisions of the Supreme Court of Pennsylvania … Compiled by James Dunlop. *Philadelphia.* 1847. 8vo. + From … 1700, to April 18, 1849. Second Edition. [*Ibid.*] 1849. 8vo. + From … 1700, to … 1852. Third Edition. [*Ibid.*] 1853. 8vo. C. 60116

Proceedings of the GENERAL Society of the Cincinnati. *See* Vol. IV., No. 13131.

Constitution and By-Laws of the GEOLOGICAL Society … with a List of Officers and Members. *Philadelphia.* 1834. 8vo.

Also: Transactions of the Geological Society … . Vol. I. Part I. *Philadelphia … W. P. Gibbons.* 1834. 8vo, pp. 179, (1). 6 Plates.

Geology. First Annual Report of the State Geologist. Read in the House of Representatives, December 22, 1836. *Harrisburg: Printed by Samuel D. Patterson.* 1836. 8vo, pp. 22. Plate. + Second … Report of the Geological Exploration of the State … By Henry D. Rogers … . *Harrisburg: Printed by Packer, Barrett and Parke.* 1838. 8vo, pp. 91, (1), folded leaf. + Third … Report of the Geological Survey of … Pennsylvania. By Henry D. Rogers … . *Harrisburg: Printed by E. Guyer.* 1839. 8vo, pp. 119. + Fourth … Report … . *Harrisburg: William D. Boas—Printer.* 1840. 8vo, pp. 215. + Fifth … Report … *Harrisburg: James S. Wallace, Printer.* 1841. 8vo, pp. 179. Folded Plate. + Sixth … Report … . *Harrisburg: Henlock & Brattan, Printers.* 1842. 8vo, pp. 28. 60118

These reports were also published in the German language.

A Few Facts regarding the … Survey. *See* Vol. VI. 24233.

The Geology of Pennsylvania, A Government Survey. By Henry Darwin Rogers, State Geologist … . *Philadelphia: J. B. Lippincott & Co.* MDCCCLVIII. 2 vols., 4to, pp. (2), xxvii, (1), 586, 8 Plates; xxiv, 1045, 42 Plates, 6 Maps. 60119

A second geological survey was made in 1874–5.

Minutes of the 100th Annual Meeting of the GERMAN Evangelical Lutheran Ministerium of Pennsylvania. *Reading.* 1847. 8vo. C. 60120

A Catalogue of the Books belonging to the Incorporated GERMAN Society, … of Pennsylvania. … The Rules enacted by the Society, in relation to the Library. *Philadelphia: Printed by Conrad Zentler.* 1826. 12mo, pp. 28. + Catalogue … . *Philadelphia.* 1839. 8vo. 60121

Also an additional Catalogue. [*Ibid.*] 1850.

Report of the Committee Relative to the GETTYSBURG Rail Road, accompanied with Testimony. … Read in the House … June 15, 1839. *Harrisburg.* 1839. 8vo, pp. 80. Map and 2 folded leaves. 60122

Also: Report of the Majority of the Committee … to examine the route of the Gettysburg Rail Road. … 1838. *Harrisburg.* 1838. 8vo, pp. 19.—Report of the Minority of the Committee … 1838. *Harrisburg.* 1838. 8vo, pp. 15.—Reports of the Majority and Minority of the Select Committee … to view the line of the Gettysburg Extension of the Pennsylvania Railroad … . *Harrisburg.* 1838. 8vo, pp. 26.

Memoirs of the GLOUCESTER Fox Hunting Club. *See* [Milnor (W.)], Vol. XII., No. 49133.

Governor's Speech. [To the Legislature, December 8, 1808. n. p. n. d.] 8vo, pp. 8. 60123

The Governour's Message to the House of Representatives, with the Bill, Entitled, An Act for Emitting Fifty Thousand Pounds in Bills of Credit, &c. [*Philadelphia: Andrew Bradford.* 1729.] Folio, pp. (2). 60124

The Governour's Speech to the Assembly, at Philadelphia | the 15 September 1701. | *Printed at Philadelphia by Reynier Jansen* 1701. | Folio, pp. 22. H.S.P. 60125

Governour Penn's Speech, to the Assembly held at Philadelphia, in Pensylvania; Septr. the 15th, 1701, with their address, and thankful acknowledgments for the same. *London, Printed in the Year* 1701. Folio. 60126

Minutes of the Formation of the GRAND BOARD of Pennsylvania, of the U. A. O. O. Organized June 14, 1847. Held in Philadelphia. Also, Minutes of the … Sessions from June 14th, to October 16th, 1847 … . *Philadelphia.* 1847. 8vo, pp. 16. Continued. 60127

Abstract of the Proceedings of the GRAND LODGE of Pennsylvania for 1853, containing the Ceremonies on Laying of the Corner-Stone of the New Temple. *Harrisburg.* 1854. 8vo, pp. 43. + Abstract … A. D. 1862, A. L. 5862. *Philadelphia.* 1863. 8vo, pp. 74. 60128

An Account of the Proceedings of the Grand Lodge … which led to the establishment of the "M. E. Grand Holy Royal Arch Chapter of … Pennsylvania," Organized … 23d Nov. 1795, … the first Grand Chapter formed in the United States … . Also the latest Constitution of the Grand Chapter … adopted … 1824; and the Rules … adopted … 1828. … *Philadelphia.* 1829. 8vo, pp. 32. 60129

Also: A Brief Statement of the Cost of the New Hall of the Grand Lodge of Pennsylvania … . Harrisburg, 28 January, 1814. 8vo, pp. 6.—Grand Lodge … Extra Quarterly Communication … Philadelphia, December, 1858. 8vo, pp. 24.—Plan of a Loan of Forty Thousand Dollars proposed to be received by the Grand Lodge … . *Philadelphia.* 1809. 8vo.—Proceedings of the Grand Lodge … at Philadelphia, March 6, 1865, on the Death of Geo. M. Dallas. *Philadelphia.* 1865. 8vo.

Samuel Güldins … Zeugnüss über die neue Vereinigung aller Religions-Partheyen in Pensylvanien, wie auch von andern nöthi-

gen Puncten … . *Gedruckt bey Christoph Saur in Germantown* 1743. 8vo, pp. 127, (1). 60130

First Annual Report of the President … of the HARRISBURG & HAMBURG Railroad Co., accompanied by the Report of the Chief Engineer, made November, 1855. *Philadelphia.* 1855. 8vo, pp. 15. 60131

Third Annual Report of W. Milnor Roberts, Chief Engineer of the HARRISBURG AND LANCASTER Rail Road Company, … January 8th, 1838. *Philadelphia.* 1838. 8vo, pp. 14. 60132

Annual Report of the … Directors, … of the HARRISBURG, PORTSMOUTH, Mount Joy and Lancaster Railroad Company, Since … September, 1839. … *Philadelphia.* 1840. 8vo, pp. 36. Continued. 60133

Also: Copy of the Lease of the Harrisburg, Portsmouth, Mountjoy & Lancaster Rail Road to the Pennsylvania Rail Road Company … . *Philadelphia.* 1861. 8vo, pp. 14.—Report of the President … 1851. *Philadelphia.* 1851. 8vo, pp. 24.—Report of the Select Committee appointed to Inquire into the Condition of the Harrisburg, Portsmouth, Mountjoy, and Lancaster Railroad. … March 30, 1840. *Harrisburg.* 1840. 8vo, pp. 15.

Health Laws of the State of Pennsylvania. *Philadelphia.* 1798. 8vo, pp. 56. 60134

Act of Incorporation, … &c. of the HIBERNIAN Society, for the relief of Emigrants from Ireland. *Philadelphia.* 1845. 8vo, pp. 28, (1). 60135

Hints for the Representatives of the Country. [n. p. 1830.] 8vo, pp. 24. 60136

Histoire naturelle et politique. *See* [Kalm et Mittelberger].

An | Historical | Account, | of the late | Disturbance, | between the Inhabitants | Of the Back | Settlements; | Of Pennsylvania, | and the Philadelphians, &c. | Impartially related by a well Wisher. | *Printed at Rome, by A. S.* | [1764.] Sm. 8vo, pp. 8. 60137

Corrected title of our No. 32053, Vol. VIII. For a German translation, *see* No. 60145, *infra.*

An Historical Account [as before]. ☞ The Second Edition, may be called a Piracy. I said Printed at Rome: I meant nothing but + Printed in Second-Street, by Andrew Steuart-Stockfish. *Philadelphia: Anthony Armbruster.* 1764. Sm. 8vo, pp. 8.

An Historical Account. *See* [Smith (W.)]

An Historical Review. *See* [Franklin (B.)], Vol. VII. 25512.

Historical Sketch of the North-Eastern Convocation of the Protestant Episcopal Church, in the Diocese of Pennsylvania, 1849–1859. ... *Wilkes-Barre.* 1860. 8vo, pp. 21. 60139

Annual Report of Samuel L. Taylor, Librarian of the HISTORICAL SOCIETY of Pennsylvania, for ... 1864. *Philadelphia.* 1864. 8vo. 60140

A very singular performance.

The Bulletin of the Historical Society of Pennsylvania. Vol. I. 1845–1847. *Philadelphia.* 1848. 8vo. 60141

One volume was printed, and that was issued in thirteen parts, some of which are paged separately.

Collections of the Historical Society ... . Vol. I. [all published]. *Philadelphia: John Penington.* 1853. 8vo, pp. (2), ii, 426. 60142

Memoirs of the Historical Society ... . *Philadelphia.* 1826–50. 4 vols., 8vo. 60143

Vol. I. was reprinted, *Philadelphia*, 1864, Edward Armstrong being the editor. The Publication Fund Series was published in 8 vols., rl. 8vo, *Philadelphia*, 1864–74.

Proceedings of the Historical Society ... April 24, 1865. [n. p. n. d.] 8vo, pp. 4. 60144

Relates to Abraham Lincoln. Also: Appeal to the Citizens of Pennsylvania on behalf of the Historical Society. *Philadelphia.* 1865. 8vo.—Catalogue of the Library of the Historical Society ... . Part I. History, Biography, and Manuscripts. *Philadelphia.* 1849. 8vo, pp. 36.—Circular respecting the Publication Fund ... . *Philadelphia.* 1855. 8vo, pp. 7.—Constitution of the Historical Society of Pennsylvania. *Philadelphia.* 1856. 8vo, pp. 16.—Historical Society of Pennsylvania. [Preamble and Resolutions signed] Joseph R. Ingersoll, President. [n. p. n. d.] 8vo, pp. 4.—Proceedings and Speeches ... December, 1852. *Philadelphia.* 1853. 8vo, pp. 42.—Publications of the Historical Society ... . Constitution. *Philadelphia.* 1856. 8vo, pp. 16.—Report of the Visit of a Committee of the ... Society to New York, in 1863, in Celebration of the 200th Birthday of William Bradford. *Philadelphia.* 1863. 8vo.—Statement relating to the Publication Fund ... . *Philadelphia.* 1855. 8vo, pp. 7.

Eine Historische Beschreibung von den Letzthin geschehenen Unruhen zwischen den Hintern Einwohnern d. Provintz Pennsylvanien u. denen zu Philadelphia, ... aus dem Englischen ins Hochteutsche übersetzet. *Philadelphia: Anton Armbruster.* 1764. Sm. 8vo, pp. 8. 60145

Relates to the Paxton Boys. A German translation of our No. 60137.

History of Pennsylvania Hall. *See* [Webb (S.)]

History of the 16th Regiment ... Cavalry. *See* No. 32212.

Der Hoch Deutsch Americanische Calender auf das Jahr nach der Gnadenreichen Geburt unsers Herrn und Heylandes Jesu Christi 1739. Eingerichtet von 40 Grad Norder-Breite, sonderlich vor Pensylvanien. ... *Germantown: Gedruckt ... bey Christoph Saur.* [1739.] 4to, pp. 36. 60146

Homœopathic Medical College of Pennsylvania. Professor Morgan's Valedictory: ... March 2, 1867; with Catalogue ... . 1866–67. *Philadelphia.* [n. d.] 8vo, pp. 23, (1). 60147

Also: Charter, By-Laws, &c., of the Homœopathic Medical College ... . *Philadelphia.* 1865. 8vo.—Third Annual Announcement of the ... College ... . 1850–51. *Philadelphia.* 1850. 8vo, pp. 16. Continued.

Constitution and By-Laws of the HORTICULTURAL Society ... *Philadelphia.* 1831. 8vo. 60148

Also: Report of the Committee appointed by the Horticultural Society ... for visiting the Nurseries and Gardens in ... Philadelphia. July 13th, 1830. *Philadelphia.* 1831. 8vo, pp. 16.

Annual Report of the Officers of the HOUSE OF REFUGE, for Western Pennsylvania. ... *Pittsburgh.* 1854. 8vo, pp. 45. Continued. 60149

House of Representatives. Wednesday, Jan. 26, 1820. Report of the Committee on Roads and Inland Navigation. [*Harrisburg.* 1820.] 8vo, pp. 8. 60150

How Unequal and Unjust Taxation Affects the Interest of the Citizens of Pennsylvania. *Philadelphia.* 1861. 8vo, pp. 38.

Report upon the HUNTINGDON and Broad Top Rail Road and Coal Company's Coal Lands. By W. F. Roberts and H. K. Strong, Geologists. *Philadelphia.* 1853. 8vo, pp. 16. Map.

Also: First Annual Report of the Directors of the Huntingdon and Broad Top Mountain Rail Road and Coal Company. With Report of the Chief Engineer, and the Act of Incorporation and Supplements thereto. *Philadelphia.* 1854. 8vo, pp. 20. Continued.

In Chancery. *See* Vol. IX., No. 34416.

In Convention for the State of Pennsylvania. Saturday, August 10. 1776. ... John Morris, jun. Secretary. [n. p. n. d.] Folio, 1 leaf. 60153

Ordering Pennsylvania battalions to New Jersey.

In General Assembly, Saturday, February 13, 1799. ... *Philadelphia: Printed by John Dunlap.* [n. d.] Folio, pp. 3. 60154

An act of Pennsylvania for supplies for 1779.

... In the Name ... . A Proclamation. ... Thomas Mifflin. [n. p. 1794.] Folio, 1 leaf. 60155

Relates to the Whiskey Insurrection.

Inaugural Address of Governor F. R. Shunk, together with his Veto Messages of certain Rail-Road and Coal Companies. ... *Philadelphia.* 1847. 8vo, pp. 12. 60156

The Inaugural Address, of the Rev. Gilbert Morgan, President of the Western University of Pennsylvania. *Pittsburgh.* M DCCC XXXV. 8vo, pp. 15, (1). 60157

Indenture of Agreement. *See* Vol. IX., No. 34439.

Announcement of the INDEPENDENT Medical School of Pennsylvania. ... *Philadelphia.* 1854. 8vo, pp. 8. 60158

Also: The Voluntary System of Medical Education, instituted by the Independent Medical School ... . *Philadelphia.* 1854. 8vo, pp. 20.

A Digest of the Laws of the INDEPENDENT Order of Odd Fellows in Pennsylvania. *Philadelphia.* 18—. 12mo, pp. 300. + [*Ibid.*] 1861. 16mo, pp. 198. 60159

Minutes of the Proceedings of the Grand Encampment of Pennsylvania of the Independent Order of Odd Fellows, from its commencement to the last meeting in December, 1846 ... . *Philadelphia.* 1847. 8vo, pp. 199. Continued. 60160

Also: Constitution of the Grand Lodge of the Independent Order of Odd Fellows ... Revised and Adopted, October 16, 1826. [n. p.:] *J. Bicking, Printer.* [n. d.] 8vo, pp. 11.—Journal of Proceedings of the ... Grand Lodge ... of Pennsylvania; Commencing Dec. 1823, and Ending March, 1847. ... *Philadelphia.* 1847. 8vo, pp. viii, 590. Continued.—Journal of the Grand Encampment ... [1829–1857.] *Philadelphia.* 1857. 8vo, pp. 385. Continued.

Minutes of a General Convention of the INDEPENDENT Order of the Sons of Malta, ... with the Minutes of the Proceedings of the Grand Consistory I. O. S. M. of Columbia, Philadelphia, ... July 20th, 1858. *Philadelphia.* 1858. 8vo, pp. 12. 60161

Also: Proceedings of Convention and Supreme Grand Lodge of I. O. S. M. of ... Pennsylvania, held in Philadelphia, June 13th and 14th, 1860. *Philadelphia.* 1861. 8vo, pp. 14.

Information and Direction. *See* [Penn (W.)], No. 59707.

Annual Report of the INSPECTOR General of ... Pennsylvania, made to the Governor ... for ... 1864. *Harrisburg.* 1865. 8vo, pp. 7. + ... Report ... for ... 1865. [*Ibid.*] 1866. 8vo, pp. 7. Discontinued. 60162

At a meeting of the Stockholders of the INSURANCE Company of ... Pennsylvania ... . [n. p. 1844.] 8vo, pp. 12. 60163

Interesting Debate at the Reception of Gov. Andrew Johnson and Gov. Wright of Indiana, at the State Capital of Pennsylvania. *Harrisburgh.* 1863. 8vo, pp. 32. 60164

Interesting Trial! The Commonwealth of Pennsylvania vs. Lieut. Richard Smith, charged with the late Murder of Captain John Carson, at Philadelphia. *Boston.* 1816. 12mo, pp. 14.

Internal Improvement. Rail Roads, Canals, Bridges, &c. [Philadelphia, March 15th, 1825.] 8vo, pp. 28. 60166

Jahresbericht des Staats Schatzmeisters über die Finanzen des Staats. *Harrisburg.* 1853. 8vo, pp. 46. 60167

January 7, 1778. When the Chimneys ... . [n. p. n. d.] 4to, 1 page. P. 60168

Notice of employment of Christian Apple to sweep the British barrack chimneys. Printed by J. Humphreys, Philadelphia.

Constitution of the Second JEFFERSON Benevolent Institution, of Pennsylvania. ... *Philadelphia.* 1836. 12mo, pp. 36. 60169

Journal of the Convention of the State of Pennsylvania, to propose Amendments to the Constitution, commenced and held ... in Harrisburg, on the second day of May, 1837. *Harrisburg.* 1837. 8vo, pp. 852. Vol. II. *Philadelphia.* 1838. pp. 715.

Journal of the Council of Censors, ... Philadelphia, ... the Tenth Day of November, One Thousand Seven Hundred Eighty and Three. *Philadelphia: Printed by Hall and Sellers.* MDCCLXXXIII. Folio, pp. 179. BA., P. 60171

For the German translation, *see* "Tagebuch des Raths," *infra.*

Journal of the First Session of the House of Representatives of ... Pennsylvania, Which commenced at Philadelphia ... the Seventh Day of December, ... One Thousand Seven Hundred and Ninety. *Philadelphia: Printed by Hall and Sellers.* MDCCXC–[1791]. Folio, pp. 573, 20, 5. Continued. 60172

Journal of the House of Representatives of ... Pennsylvania. Beginning the twenty-eighth Day of November, 1776, and ending the second Day of October, 1781. With the Proceedings of the several Committees and Conventions, before and at the Commencement of the American Revolution. Volume the

First. *Philadelphia: Printed by John Dunlap.* MDCCLXXXII. Folio, pp. 699. Continued. P. 60173

Journal of the Senate ... Anno MDCCXC ... . *Philadelphia: Printed by Zachariah Poulson, Junior.* [1791.] Folio, pp. 355. Continued. 60174

Journal of the Session of the House of Representatives ... which commenced at Lancaster on the third Day of December, 1799, and ended the seventeenth day of March, 1800. *Lancaster.* 1800. Folio. Continued. P. 60175

Journal of the Session of the Senate ... which commenced at Lancaster on the third Day of December, 1799, and ended the seventeenth Day of March, 1800. *Lancaster.* 1800. Folio. Continued. 60176

A Journal of the Votes and Proceedings of the ... Representatives Of the Province of Pensylvania, ... 1724. *Philadelphia: Printed ... by Andrew Bradford.* MDCCXXV. Folio, pp. 42. Continued. + *Philadelphia Printed* [*by S. Keimer*], *and sold by Mary Rose.* [1725.] Folio, pp. 12. 60177

Journals and Proceedings of the General Assembly Of the Commonwealth of Pennsylvania. *Philadelphia: Printed by John Dunlap.* M,DCC,LXXVII. Folio, pp. 64. 60178

Continued until changed in 1781 to "Minutes."

Journals of the Senate, when sitting for the purpose of trying an Impeachment against John Nicholson, Comptroller-General of ... Pennsylvania, commencing ... 8th of January, 1794. *Philadelphia.* 1794. Folio. S. 60179

Judgements [*sic*] in the Admiralty of Pennsylvania in four suits, brought as for Maritime Hypothecations. Also the case of Silas Talbot, against the Brigs Achilles, Patty, and Hibernia, and of the Owners of the Hibernia against their Captain, John Angus. With an Appendix, containing the Testimony ... . The Hon. Francis Hopkinson Judge. *Philadelphia: Printed by T. Dobson and T. Lang.* MDCCLXXXIX. 8vo, pp. 131. 60180

Jurisdiction of the Court of Chancery in Pennsylvania, vindicated and asserted, with some Remarks upon Mr. Freeman's late Performance, in Franklin's Gazette. [1736?] 60181

Advertised in the Philadelphia "American Weekly Mercury," March 2, 1735–6, as "speedily to be published."

A Just Rebuke. *See* [Rawle (Francis)].

Kalendarium Pennsilvaniense,|or,|America's Messinger.|Being an|Almanack|For the Year of Grace, 1686.|Wherein is contained both the English & Forreign|Account, the Motions of the Planets through the Signs ... . By Samuel Atkins.|Student in the Mathamaticks and Astrology.|...|*Printed and Sold by William Bradford, at Philadelphia in Pennsilvania*, 1685. 8vo, (20) leaves.

An improved title of our No. 36981, Vol. IX. The first work of the first printer of Philadelphia and New York, and of superlative rarity. An address "To the Reader," by the Editor, dated "Philadelphia, the 3d of the 10th Month (December) Anno 1685," occupies the second and half the third page, and is followed by one from "The Printer to the Readers," subscribed by "W. Bradford, Philadelphia, the 28th, 10th Month." It begins: "Hereby understand that after great Charge and Trouble, I have brought the great Art and Mystery of *Printing* into this part of America, believing it may be of great service to you in several respects," etc.

Kern alter und neuer ... Geistreicher Lieder welche ... in denen Reformirten Kirchen der Hessisch-Hanauisch-Pfaltzisch-Pensilvanischen ... Landen ... gebraucht werden. ... *Gedruckt zu Germantown bey Christoph Saur.* 1752. 8vo. 60183

Proceedings of the Fourth Annual Session of the Grand Commandery of KNIGHTS Templar of ... Pennsylvania, held at Harrisburg, ... 1857. *Harrisburg.* 1857. 8vo. 60184

Een kort Bericht. *See* [Penn (W.)], No. 59710.

Kurtze Nachricht von einigen evangelischen Gemeinen in America, absonderlich in Pensylvanien. *Halle.* 1750–76. 4to.

Report of the Directors of the LACKAWANNA and Bloomsburg Rail-Road Company ... . *Philadelphia.* 1856. 8vo, pp. 31. Continued. 60186

Also: Report on the Survey, Estimates and Revenues, of the Lackawanna & Bloomsburg Rail-Road. *Carbondale.* 1853. 12mo, pp. 15. Map.

Extracts from the Report on the Survey of the LACKAWANNA and Lanesboro' Railroad. By John C. Trautwine ... . *Philadelphia.* 1856. 8vo, pp. 20, 21. Map. 60187

Constitution of the LAFAYETTE Beneficial Society of Pennsylvania. ... *Philadelphia.* 1836. 12mo, pp. 36. 60188

Memorial to the Legislature of Pennsylvania, for the Incorporation of LA FAYETTE College, at Easton. [n. p.] 1825. 8vo, pp. 11. 60189

Report of the Superintendent of the LANCASTER & Harrisburg Rail Road. Made January 8, 1838. [n. p. n. d.] 8vo, pp. 6.

Law of Evidence. [n. p. 1865?] 8vo, pp. 12. 60191

The|Laws|Of the Province of|Pennsilvania|Collected into|One Volumn, [*sic*]|By Order of the Governour and Assembly of the|said Province.|*Printed & Sold by Andr. Bradford in Philadelphia,*|1714.| Folio, pp. (4), 184. BM., P. 60192

The paging is very erratic.

The Laws of the Province of Pennsylvania: Now in Force, Collected into One Volumn [*sic*]. Publish'd by Order of the General Assembly ... . *Philadelphia: Printed ... by Andrew Bradford*, ... MDCCXXVIII. Folio, pp. (4), 352. P. 60193

At the end is one leaf, paged 280–281, containing an act omitted in its proper place.

Laws enacted in a General Assembly of the ... Commonwealth of Pennsylvania, ... at Philadelphia the Twenty-eighth day of November, One Thousand Seven Hundred and Seventy-six. ... *Philadelphia: Printed by John Dunlap.* M,DCC,LXXVII. Folio, pp. 36. Continued. 60194

Laws of the Commonwealth of Pennsylvania, from the fourteenth day of October, one thousand seven hundred, to the first day of October, one thousand seven hundred and eighty-one. Republished, under the Authority of the Legislature, by Alexander James Dallas. Vol. I. *Philadelphia: Printed by Hall and Sellers.* MDCCXCVII. Folio, pp. (4), 913, 64, iv, (22). P. 60195

Laws ... from the second day of October, one thousand seven hundred and eighty-one, to the second day of October, one thousand seven hundred and ninety. Republished, ... by Alexander James Dallas. Vol. II. *Philadelphia: Printed by Hall and Sellers.* MDCCXCIII. Folio, pp. (2), ix, 817, iii, (33).

Laws ... from the seventh day of December, one thousand seven hundred and ninety, to the twentieth day of April, one thousand seven hundred and ninety-five. Published ... by Alexander James Dallas. Vol. III. *Philadelphia: Printed by Hall and Sellers.* MDCCXCV. Folio, pp. (2), xliii, 793, v, (37). [Contains Constitutions of the United States and Pennsylvania.]

Laws ... from the first day of December, one thousand seven hundred and ninety-five, to the twenty seventh day of February, one thousand eight hundred and one. Published, ... by Alexander James Dallas. Vol. IV. *Lancaster: Printed by Francis Bailey* ... . 1801. Folio, pp. v, 719, (23). [Vols. III. and IV. are the Session Laws, and are usually found with the special title-pages bound in.]

Laws of ... Pennsylvania, from the fourteenth day of October, one thousand seven hundred, to the sixth day of April, one thousand eight hundred and two. Republished under the authority of the Legislature, by M. Carey, and J. Bioren ... . *Philadelphia: Printed by J. Bioren* ... . 1803. 6 vols., 8vo, pp. (4), 528; (4), 520; (4), 457; (4), xxxiii, 429; (4), 426, (1); (4), 332, 95, 63. + Laws ... [Dec. 7, 1802, to April 14, 1804]. Republished,

... by John Bioren. Vol. VII. *Philadelphia: Printed by John Bioren* ... . 1806. 8vo, pp. xvi, 576, (2). + Laws ... [Dec. 3, 1805, to March 28, 1808]. Vol. VIII. [*Ibid.*] 1808. 8vo, pp. xviii, 502, (1). H.S.P. 60196

Laws of ... Pennsylvania, from the fourteenth day of October, 1700, to April 23, 1829. Republished under the authority of the Legislature. With Notes and References. *Philadelphia.* 1810–1844. 10 vols., 8vo. C. 60197

The Laws of Pennsylvania in relation to the Board of Health, and the Health Laws of ... Philadelphia: The Acts of Congress relating to Quarantines, Health Laws, and Passenger Vessels. Arranged Chronologically. ... *Philadelphia.* 1848. 8vo, pp. (6), 133. 60198

Charter of the LEHIGH and Delaware Water Gap Railroad Company, with the Supplements thereto. ... *Philadelphia.* [1863.] 8vo, pp. (2), 4, (2). 60199

Also: Report upon the Condition ... of the Lehigh and Delaware Water Gap Rail Road ... . Made ... by Oliver W. Barnes, Civil Engineer. *Philadelphia.* 1860. 8vo, pp. 10.

Second Annual Report of the ... Directors of the LEHIGH Luzerne Railroad Company, ... with the Engineer's Report ... . *Philadelphia.* 1858. 8vo, pp. 15, (1). Continued. 60200

Seventh Annual Report of the ... Managers of the LEHIGH Valley Rail-Road Company. ... *Mauch Chunk.* 1863. 12mo, pp. 12. 60201

Continued to the present time in 8vo. Also: Charter, Supplements and By-Laws ... *Philadelphia.* 1864. 8vo, pp. 28.

A Letter from a Countryman to his Friend in the City of Philadelphia. 12 mo. 2. 1735. Folio, pp. 2. 60202

Letter from Brev. Brig. Gen. Jos. G. Totten, to the Governor of Pennsylvania, in reference to the Lake and River Defences. [*Harrisburg.* 1861.] 8vo, pp. (4). 60203

A Letter, Occasioned by the Perusal of a Paper lately published, called, A Dialogue between Freeman and Trusty. [*Philadelphia: Andrew Bradford.* 1728.] Folio, pp. 2. 60204

Letter on the subject of raising money for the Canal System of Pennsylvania, originally addressed to a Member of Congress from Pennsylvania, and now submitted to the Legislature … . [n. p. n. d.] 8vo, pp. 8. 60205

Dated "Meadville, Dec. 5, 1828," signed "H." [Huidekooper?]

Letter, Report and Documents, on the Penal Code, from the President and Commissioners appointed to superintend the erection of the Eastern Penitentiary, adapted and modelled to the system of Solitary Confinement. Read in the Senate, January 8, 1828. *Harrisburg.* 1828. 8vo, pp. 51. 60206

A Letter to a Friend. [*Philadelphia: Andrew Bradford.* 1725.] Folio, pp. 4. 60207

In reply to Logan's "Memorial."

A | Letter | to | His Majesty's Justices of the Peace | for the County of | Chester, | With the Governour's | Speech | … Chester the 15th Day of April, 1718. | Published at the Request of the Represen- | tatives of the Free-men of this Province, in | General Assembly met at | Philadelphia | The 5th Day of May, 1718. | *Philadelphia,* | *Printed … by Andrew Bradford.* MDCCXVIII. Small 4to, pp. 12. H.S.P. 60208

Written by Sir William Keith. It has a rubricated title-page.

Letter to the Republican Members of the Legislature of Pennsylvania, on the Principles of Legislation and Executive Conduct, best calculated to insure the Good and Tranquility of the State, and the present Republican Ascendency. [n. p. 1810.] 8vo, pp. 38. 60209

See also Vol. x., Nos. 40261, 40499, 40510, *and* 40620.

Letters and Papers. *See* [Balch (T.)], Vol. I., No. 2871.

Letters to the People of Pennsylvania on the Political Principles of the Free Soil Party. By Jacob Leisler [*pseudonym*]. *Philadelphia.* 1850. 8vo, pp. 21. 60210

Vincent L. Bradford was the author.

Lettres d'un Fermier. *See* [Dickinson (J.)], Vol. v. 20045.

Report of the Survey for the LEWISBURG, Centre and Spruce Creek Railroad. Made June 1, 1857. A. B. Warford, Civil Engineer. *Harrisburg.* 1857. 8vo, pp. 61, (1). 60211

List of Bankrupts in the United States Court for the Eastern District of Pennsylvania. *Pittsburg.* 1844. 8vo, pp. 36.

List of Bankrupts in the United States Court for the Western District of Pennsylvania. *Pittsburg.* 1844. 8vo, pp. 38.

List of Delegates and Officers to the Convention to propose Amendments to the Constitution … . [n. p. 1837.] Folio, 1 l.

List of Members and Officers who served in the Pennsylvania Legislature before 1850. [n. p. n. d.] Folio, 1 sheet. 60215

List of the Justices of the Peace … . *Lancaster.* 1809. 8vo.

List of the Taxable Inhabitants, … of Pennsylvania, … in … 1842–43. … *Harrisburg.* 1843. 8vo, pp. 4. 60217

The Act incorporating the LITTLE Schuylkill and Susquehanna Rail-Road Company. Approved … March, 1831. … *Philadelphia.* 1835. 12mo, pp. 24. + [*Ibid.*] 1838. 12mo, pp. 28.

Also: First Annual Report of S. W. Roberts, Chief Engineer of the Little Schuylkill and Susquehanna Rail Road Company. … *Philadelphia.* 1839. 8vo, pp. 12. Continued. — Report of the President … of the … Company to the Stockholders. *Philadelphia.* 1838. 8vo, pp. 27. Map. Continued.

Abstract of a Report on the Coal and Iron Estate of the LITTLE Schuylkill Navigation Rail Road and Coal Company, from actual survey. Made … October, 1845. By W. F. Roberts, Engineer … . *Philadelphia.* 1846. 8vo, pp. 21. Map.

Also: An Act Incorporating the Little Schuylkill Navigation Rail Road and Coal Company … . *Philadelphia.* 1835. 12mo, pp. 48. — Rejoinder. … [n. p. 1862.] 8vo, pp. 8. — Report of the … Company, January 1, 1853. *Philadelphia.* 1853. 8vo, pp. 19. Continued.

Report of the President of the LOCK-HAVEN and Tyrone Railroad Company and Report of Engineer, with Act of Incorporation … . *Philadelphia.* 1855. 8vo, pp. 36. Map. 60220

Der Lockvögel Warnungsgesang vor den Stossvögeln: oder nöthige Beantwortung der sogenannten getreuen Warnung gegen die Lockvögel … . *Gedruckt … im Jahr* 1764. 4to, pp. 8.

Eleventh Annual Report of the … LOCUST Mountain Coal and Iron Company … . *Philadelphia.* 1864. 8vo, pp. 16.

A Looking-Glass, for Presbyterians. … *Printed in the Year* MDCCXLIV [for 1764]. 8vo, pp. 34. 60223

Differs from our No. 41946, Vol. x.

Lucifer's Decree, After a Fray. Or, A Friendly Warning to all Persons Of whatsoever Station, Nation, or Qualification, In the City of Deceit, and Province of Transylvania. … [*Philadelphia:*] *Printed in the Year* 1765. Sm. 8vo, pp. 7, (1). 60224

Improved title of our No. 42626, Vol. x.

Ludovici a Thurenstein. *See* [Zinzendorf (Nic. Lud. von)].

Act of Incorporation, Supplementary Acts, and By-Laws of the LYKENS Valley Rail-Road and Coal Company. *Philadelphia.* 1846. 8vo, pp. 20. 60225

Also: Report of the Lykens Valley Rail Road and Coal Co. for … 1863. *Philadelphia.* 1864. 8vo, pp. 10 Continued.

Report of Richard B. Osborne, … to John Tucker, Esq., on the MAHONOY Railway, as the Natural Eastern Outlet for the Coal of the Middle Coal Field. *Philadelphia.* 1858. 8vo, pp. 21. Map. 60226

The Main Line of the Pennsylvania State Improvements; its History, Cost, Revenue, … and … Value. *Philadelphia.* 1855. 8vo, pp. 76. 60227

Majority and Minority Reports of the Joint Committee of the Senate and House … relative to an investigation into any corrupt means which may have been employed by the Banks, or their Agents, for the purpose of Influencing the Action of the Legislature, … in regard to any Legislation for their Benefit: Accompanied with Testimony. … July 12, 1842. *Harrisburg: Henlock & Bratton, Printers.* 1842. 8vo, pp. 360, iii. 60228

Manifesto; containing a Plain Statement of Facts relative to the Acts and Doings of the General Assembly. [n. p. n. d.] 8vo, pp. 22. M. 60229

First Annual Report of the … Trustees of the MANUAL Labour Academy of Pennsylvania. November 10, 1829. … *Philadelphia.* 1829. 8vo, pp. 15. Continued. 60230

Manual for the Directors and Teachers of Common Schools. *Philadelphia.* 1840. 12mo. 60231

A Manual for the Government of the Senate and House of Representatives … of Pennsylvania. Compiled by Jacob Ziegler. *Harrisburg.* 1858. 12mo. + Revised Edition. [*Ibid.*] 1864. 16mo, pp. 440. 60232

Manual of Rules for the Government of Both Branches of the Legislature … Preceded by the Constitutions of the United States and of Pennsylvania: With a List of the Members and Officers … . Printed by order of the Legislature. *Harrisburg.* 1858. 8vo, pp. 72. 60233

Manual of Rules of the General Assembly, and Legislative Directory; with the Constitution of the United States and of Pennsylvania. Compiled by J. A. Smull. *Harrisburg: Singerly & Myers.* 1868. 18mo, pp. 332. Map and Plate.

A Mapp of ye Improved Part of Pensilvania in America, divided into Countyes, Townships, and Lotts. Surveyed by Thomas Holme. [n. p. about 1700.] Folio. 60234

Dedicated to W. Penn, Esq., Proprietor and Governor, by John Harris. With references to settlements and the names of owners; also with plan of Philadelphia at top of map said to be "two miles in length and one in breadth."

Proceedings of the Convention of the MEDICAL SOCIETY of … Pennsylvania, … Lancaster, April, 1848, and the Constitution … . *Lancaster.* 1848. 8vo. Continued. s. 60235

Also: Constitution of the Medical Society of … Pennsylvania. With a Catalogue … *Philadelphia.* 1862. 8vo, pp. 12. — Transactions of the … Society … at its Annual Session … 1851. *Philadelphia.* 1851. 8vo. Continued.

Memoirs of a Life. *See* [Graydon (Alexander)], Vol. VII., No. 28418.

Memorial. To … Congress … [by citizens of Pennsylvania in regard to "the unfortunate situation" of the Indians. n. p. 1830.] Folio, 1 leaf. 60236

Memorial of Sundry Farmers of … Pennsylvania. … *Washington.* 1824. 8vo, pp. 6. 60237

In favor of a protective tariff.

A Memorial of the Case. *See* [Franklin (B.)], VII. 25554.

Memorial of the Free Citizens of Color in Pittsburg and its vicinity, relative to the Right of Suffrage. Read in Convention, July 8, 1837. *Harrisburg.* 1837. 8vo, pp. 11. 60238

Memorial of the Inhabitants of Pennsylvania praying further protection of the National Industry. … *Washington.* 1828. 8vo, pp. 11. 60239

Memorial of the Several Incorporated Insurance Companies of the State … . February 6, 1807. [n. p. n. d.] 8vo, pp. 13.

A Memorial presented to the Legislature … relative to the "Sunday Question." [n. p. n. d.] 8vo. 60241

Memorial soliciting a State Hospital for the Insane, submitted to the Legislature … February 3, 1845. *Philadelphia.* 1845. 8vo, pp. 52. 60242

Memorial to the Legislature respecting a Canal on the West Side of the Schuylkill. Read in … Councils, January 29, 1835, and passed. *Philadelphia.* 1835. 8vo, pp. 8. 60243

See also Vol. XII., Nos. 47621, 47653, 47713, *and* Vol. XIII., No. 55823.

Memorials concerning Deceased Friends. *See* No. 47736.

Men and Women Medical Students, and the Woman Movement. [n. p. 1869.] 8vo, pp. 15. + No. 2. [n. p. 1870.] 8vo, pp. (2), 20. 60244

Relates to the Pennsylvania Hospital.

Message from the Governor of Pensilvania to the Indians on the Ohio. [n. p. 1759.] 8vo. 60245

Message of the Governor, … 1809. *See* Vol. XIII. 57236.

Message from the Governor of Pennsylvania, transmitting the Reports of the Joint Commissioners, and of Col. Graham, U. S. Engineers, in relation to the Boundary Lines between the States of Pennsylvania, Delaware and Maryland. *Harrisburg.* 1850. 8vo, pp. 36. 60246

See also Vol. XII., Nos. 45088–9.

Message … transmitting Resolutions relative to Slavery passed by the Legislatures of Virginia and Georgia. *Harrisburg.* 1850. 8vo, pp. 17. P. 60247

Message of … W. F. Packer, to the Legislature, January, 1861. [n. p. n. d.] 8vo, pp. 18. 60248

Message of Andrew G. Curtin, … to the Legislature, January, 1862. [n. p. n. d.] 8vo, pp. 14. + January 7, 1863. 8vo, pp. 14. 60249

Also: Message of Andrew G. Curtin, … relative to Military Arrests. February 12, 1863. [n. p. n. d.] 8vo, pp. 4. — Message of Governor Andrew G. Curtin, relative to the Reserve Corps, Pennsylvania Volunteers. [n. p. 1863.] 8vo, pp. 16.

Message … transmitting … Documents. *See* Vol. XII. 48056

Also: Message … accompanied by the Report of the Canal Commissioners, … Dec. 13, 1828. *Harrisburgh.* 1828. 8vo. Continued. — Message … with a Communication from the Secretary of War, and an extract from the Report of Hartman Bache, United States Engineer, relative to the location of a Railroad from Williamsport, in Pennsylvania, to Elmira, in New York. … *Philadelphia.* 1835. 8vo, pp. 43. Map. Message … relative to the Finances … and recommending a temporary loan … . June 7, 1836. *Harrisburg.* 1836. 8vo, pp. 4. — Message … relative to the Finances … and the Accounting Departments of the Government. Read … Jan. 14, 1836. [n. p. n. d.] 8vo, pp. 4. — Message … transmitting a Communication from the … Canal Commissioners, with a Report and Estimate for avoiding the Inclined Plane at Philadelphia … . *Harrisburg.* 1837. 8vo, pp. 19. — Message … transmitting a Communication from the President … of the West Philadelphia Rail Road Co. … Read … March 4, 1837. *Harrisburg.* 1837. 8vo, pp. 7. — Message … relative to the Condition of the Treasury. Read … Jan. 26, 1839. *Harrisburg.* 1839. 8vo, pp. 14. — Message … vetoing the Local Appropriation Bill. … *Harrisburg.* 1839. 8vo, pp. 11. — Message … to … the Legislature, … January, 1840. *Harrisburg.* 1840. 8vo, pp. 44. — Message … returning with his Objections, the Apportionment Bill, together with the Report of the Select Committee of the House … . *Harrisburg.* 1850. 8vo. — Message of Governor Bigler returning Bill No. 590, with his Objections. [n. p. 1852.] 8vo, pp. 8. — Message of Governor Bigler, in relation to the Franklin Canal Company. … *Harrisburg.* 1854. 8vo, pp. 11. — Message … transmitting a List of the Taxable Inhabitants, with the number of Deaf, Dumb and Blind Persons in this Commonwealth. [n. p. 1857.] 8vo, pp. 54.

Military Laws of … Pennsylvania, Passed at the Sessions of 1861. *Harrisburg.* 1861. 8vo, pp. 35. 60250

Report of President … of the MILL CREEK and Mine Hill Navigation and Railroad Company, for … 1857. *Philadelphia.* 1858. 8vo, pp. 12. 60251

Act of Incorporation of the MINE HILL & Schuylkill Haven Rail Road Company; with the Supplements and By-Laws. *Philadelphia.* 1836. 8vo, pp. 32. + 1854. 8vo, pp. 48. 60252

Also: Memorial of the Mine Hill and Schuylkill Haven Rail Road Company, to the Senate and House … . [n. p. n. d.] 8vo, pp. (2), 7. — Report to the … Company. January 9th, 1837. *Philadelphia.* 1837. 8vo, pp. 6. Continued.

Minority Report of the Committee on Banks of the Senate … in relation to the Issue of Small Notes by the Banks. … *Harrisburg.* 1848. 8vo, pp. 7. 60253

Minority Report of the Select Committee, on … the Consolidation of … Philadelphia, with enlarged Boundaries. [*Harrisburg.* 1851.] 8vo, pp. 32. 60254

The | Minutes | of a | Treaty | held at | Easton, in Pennsylvania, | In October, 1758. | By | The Lieutenant Governor of Pennsylvania, | and | The Governor of New Jersey; | with | The Chief Sachems and Warriors of the | Mohawks, Nanticokes and Conoys, | Oneydos, Chugmits, | Onondagas, Delawares, | Cayugas, Unamies, | Senecas, Mohickons, | Tuscaroras, Minisinks, and | Tuteloes, Wapings. | *Woodbridge, in New Jersey:* | *Printed … by James Parker* … 1758. Folio, pp. 35. 60255

Minutes of the Committee of the Whole of the Convention of the State of Pennsylvania, to propose Amendment to the Constitution, commenced and held … in Harrisburg, on the second day of May, 1837. *Harrisburg.* 1837. 8vo, pp. 289.

Minutes of the Convention of the Commonwealth of Pennsylvania, Which commenced at Philadelphia, … the Twentieth Day of November, One Thousand Seven Hundred and Eighty-Seven, for the purpose of Taking into Consideration the Constitution framed by the late Fœderal Convention for the United States of America. *Philadelphia: Printed by Hall and Sellers* … . M,DCC,LXXXVII. Folio, pp. 28. N. 60257

Minutes of the Convention of the Commonwealth … which commenced at Philadelphia, … the twenty-fourth … November … one thousand seven hundred and eighty-nine, for the purpose of Reviewing, … Altering and Amending, the Constitution of this State. *Philadelphia: Printed by Zachariah Poulson, Jun.* … M DCC LXXXIX. Folio, pp. 146. + Minutes of the Second Session … . [n. p. 1790.] Folio, pp. 147–222. C., N., P. 60258

Minutes of the Grand Committee of the Whole Convention … at Philadelphia, … the twenty-fourth … November, … one thousand seven hundred and eighty-nine, for … Reviewing, … Altering and Amending, the Constitution of this State. *Philadelphia: Printed by Zachariah Poulson, Jun.* … [1790.] Folio, pp. 101. C., N., H.S.P. 60259

Minutes of the Debate in the Legislature of Pennsylvania, on the Bill to Incorporate the American Sunday School Union. *Philadelphia.* 1828. 8vo, pp. 25. 60260

Minutes of the First Session, of the Sixth General Assembly of the Commonwealth of Pennsylvania, … at Philadelphia, … twenty-second … October, one thousand seven hundred and eighty and one. *Philadelphia: Printed by John Dunlap.* MDCCLXXXI. Folio, pp. 498–562. 60261

Continued to 1790. *See* our No. 60178, *supra.*

Minutes of the Provincial Council. *See* Hazard (S.), 31104.

Minutes of the State Convention of the Coloured Citizens of Pennsylvania, … Harrisburg, December 13th and 14th, 1848. *Philadelphia.* 1849. 8vo, pp. 24. 60262

Minutes of the Supreme … Council. *See* Hazard (S.), 31104.

Miscellaneous Documents read in the Legislature … during the Session … of January, 1855. *Harrisburg.* 1855. 8vo, pp. 800. 60263

Fifth Annual Report, of the … MONONGAHELA Navigation Company; … With … Documents. *Pittsburgh.* 1845. 12mo, pp. 24. Continued. 60264

Act of Incorporation and By-Laws of the MOUNT CARBON Rail Road Company. *Philadelphia.* 1830. 8vo, pp. 24.

Muskingum Oil Spring Petroleum Co. Pittsburgh. … *Pittsburgh.* [1864?] 12mo, pp. 9. 60266

"My Lord. However" … being Reasons … why the lands beginning at the termination of the Southern Boundary Line of Pensylvania, and which are bounded by the Allegheny Mountains and the River Ohio, … should be separated from Virginia. [Dated, *London, May* 25, 1770.] 8vo, pp. 26. 60267

Eine Nachricht wegen der Landschaft. *See* [Penn (W.)]

Nachrichten von den Vereinigten … Gemeinen. *See* Vol. XII., No. 51694.

Names of Persons. *See* Vol. XII., No. 51742.

A Narrative of Facts relative to the Conduct of some of the Members of the Legislature of Pennsylvania, professing to be Democrats, at the election of a Senator to represent this State in the Senate of the United States, on the 13th of January, 1807. *Philadelphia, May,* 1807. 8vo, pp. 16. + Second Edition. *Philadelphia, June,* 1807. 8vo, pp. 16. 60268

An improved title of our No. 51801, Vol. XII.

Navigation and Advantages of the River Schuylkill. January, 1829. [n. p. n. d.] 8vo, pp. 8. 60269

First Annual Report of the NESQUEHONING Valley Railroad Company, to the Stockholders, January, 1862 … . *Philadelphia.* 1862. 8vo, pp. 43. 60270

Neu-vermehrt- und vollständiges Gesang-Buch. *See* Vol. XIII., No. 52363, *add* Dritte Auflage. *Germantown: Gedruckt … bey Christoph Saur.* 1772. 8vo, pp. 404, 8, 18, 66. 60271

Fourth Annual Report … of the NEW CREEK Company … . *Philadelphia.* 1858. 8vo, pp. 14. 60272

A New Penal Code for Pennsylvania; or, Mr. Ingersoll's Bill … with Comments by Mr. Samuel Riddle, … and … Notes By the Hon. Jonathan Walker … . *Bedford, Pa.: Charles McDowell.* 1818. 8vo, pp. 64. 60273

New-Year Verses. *See* Vol. XIII., Nos. 53423, 53428–29.

News from Pensilvania. *See* [Bugg (Francis)], Vol. III. 9071.

Report of L. E. Corson, ... of the NORRISTOWN and Freemansburg Rail Road Company: Together with the Supplement to the Act of Assembly, incorporating said Company. ... *Norristown, Penn'a.* 1853. 8vo, pp. 24. 60274

The North Branch Canal Company; its Prospects, and its Laws of Incorporation. *Philadelphia.* 1845. 8vo, pp. (2), 45. Map. 60275

Also: An Address from a Committee ... on the ... North Branch Canal. ... *Harrisburg.* 1840. 12mo, pp. 12. — Circular of a Corresponding Committee on the ... North Branch Canal, ... February 10, 1846. *Towanda, Pa.* 1846. 8vo, pp. 16. — Communication from the Canal Commissioners, relative to the Allotment of Work on the North Branch Canal. *Harrisburg.* 1850. 8vo, pp. 6. — Report of Wm. B. Foster, Jr., Engineer on the ... Canal. [n. p. 1851.] 8vo, pp. 14. — Report of a Late Re-survey and Examination of the ... Canal, showing its ... Condition and ... Revenue: ... By William B. Foster .... With an Appendix. *Philadelphia.* 1847. 8vo, pp. 25. Map. — Report of the Committee of Ways and Means relative to the Completion of the ... Canal; with an Appendix, by a Citizen of Northern Pennsylvania. *Harrisburg.* 1849. 8vo, pp. 24.

North Branch Extension. Reports of the Superintendent and Engineer, for ... 1853. [n. p. n. d.] 8vo, pp. (2), 7, 26. Continued to 1856. 60276

Act of Incorporation of the NORTH PENNSYLVANIA Railroad Company, and the Supplements thereto; with the General Railroad Law of Pennsylvania. *Philadelphia.* 1853. 8vo, pp. 23, (10). 60277

A Guide on the North Penn. R. R. *See* Vol. XIII. 55524.

A Narrative of the Gywnedd Cut-Off on the North Pennsylvania Rail Road. [n. p. 1855?] 8vo, pp. (2), 22. 60278

Also: By-Laws of the ... Directors of the North Pennsylvania Rail Road Company. *Philadelphia.* 1854. 8vo, pp. 12. — Communication [to the Councils of Philadelphia. n. p. 1856.] 8vo, pp. 20. — Correspondence in regard to the Right of Way ... through the "Fair Hill Estate." [n. p. 1854.] 4to, pp. (4). — Facts ... relative to the Negociation of the First Mortgage Loan .... *Philadelphia.* 1857. 8vo, pp. 29. [Signed by Thomas S. Fernon.] — First Annual Report of the ... Directors ... with the Proceedings of the Annual Meeting of Stockholders and the Report of the Chief Engineer. January 9, 1854. *Philadelphia.* 1854. 8vo, pp. 47. Continued. — Memorial ... to the Councils of ... Philadelphia. ... *Philadelphia.* 1854. 8vo, pp. 15. Map. — The North Pennsylvania Railroad. [n. p. 1863.] 8vo, pp. 15. — North Pennsylvania Railroad. ... Mass Meeting at ... [Philadelphia,] January 31, 1854. [n. p. n. d.] 8vo, pp. 15. — ... Coal Depot Site on the Delaware River. ... *Philad'a.* [1855.] 8vo, pp. (2), 19. — ... Correspondence between the President and Chief Engineer. [n. p. 1856?] 8vo, pp. 37. — ... Facts relative to the First Mortgage

Loan. ... *Philadelphia.* [1856.] 12mo, pp. 11. — ... Plan of Organization: adopted by the Road Committee .... *Philadelphia.* 1857. 12mo, pp. 10. — ... Salary of Certain Officers. [n. p. 1855.] 8vo, pp. 8. — ... Six Per Cent. Mortgage Loan. [n. p. 1855.] 8vo, pp. 8. — ... Surveyed Route from Philadelphia to the New York State Line at Waverley. Reports of Edward Miller, Esq., Chief Engineer. *Philadelphia.* 1855. 8vo, pp. (2), 15. — Report of the Committee having in charge the Fund subscribed for the Relief of the Sufferers by the Collision ... at Camp Hill, July 17, 1856. *Philadelphia.* [n. d.] 8vo, pp. (2), 15. — Report of the Testimony in the Case of Harry Ingersoll *versus* the North Pennsylvania Railroad Co. for alleged damages at Green Lane. *Philadelphia.* 1855. 8vo, pp. 40. — Reports of Edward Miller, Chief Engineer, to the ... Directors .... *Philadelphia.* 1854. 8vo, pp. 28. — A Review of the Report of Mr. Edward Miller, ... dated January 11, 1856, &c. To the Stockholders .... [n. p. n. d.] 8vo, pp. 30. — Startling Truths concerning the Management .... *Philadelphia.* 1863. 8vo, pp. 14. [The last two pieces are signed by Thos. S. Fernon.]

Charter, Supplements and By-Laws of the NORTH WESTERN Railroad Company; together with the General Railroad Laws of Pennsylvania and Ohio. *Philadelphia.* 1857. 8vo, pp. 37.

Also: First Report of the ... North Western Railroad Company, with the Report of the Chief Engineer. *Philadelphia.* 1853. 8vo, pp. 28. Map.

Address of the President ... of the NORTHERN CENTRAL Railway Company ... May 17, 1855. *Baltimore.* 1855. 8vo, pp. 47

Also: First Annual Report ... of the Northern Central Railway Company, ... 1855. *Baltimore.* 1856. 8vo, pp. 35, folded leaf. — Laws of Maryland and Pennsylvania and Ordinances of ... Baltimore, relating to the consolidation of the various Rail Road Companies into the Northern Central Railway Company, 1854. *Baltimore.* 1855. 8vo.

Notes on the Penal Laws, from the Seventh Volume of the Appendix of the Laws of Pennsylvania. Published by authority of the Legislature. [n. p. 1822?] 8vo, pp. 58. 60281

O! Justitia. A Complete Trial. God gives, and takes away. Well, Justice Shall Take Place. [*Philadelphia: A. Armbruster.* 1765.] Sm. 8vo, pp. 16. 60282

Observations In a Letter from a Gentleman of the Bar at Harrisburg, on a Bill before the Legislature for abolishing certain titles, &c. [Dated February 2nd. 1813.] 8vo, pp. (2), 38.

Relates to land sold by the State.

Observations | On a late Epitaph, | In a Letter from a Gentleman in the Country, | To his Friend in Philadelphia: | ... | *Philadelphia: | Printed by Anthony Armbruster.* [1764.] Sm. 8vo, pp. 8.

Improved title of No. 56485, Vol. XIII.

Observations on the Revival of Bank Charters. [n. p. 1823.] 8vo, pp. 10. 60285

Observations relative to the Manufacture of Paper and Printed Books in the Province of Pennsylvania. [*Philadelphia: Robert Bell.* 1773.] Folio, 1 leaf. 60286

Opinion of the Supreme Court ... of Pennsylvania ... in the case of the Commonwealth, *ex-relatione* Thomas, *vs.* the Commissioners of Allegheny County. *Philadelphia.* 1858. 8vo, pp. 20. 60287

Opinions of the Supreme Court in the case of Commonwealth *vs.* Bank of Pennsylvania ... *Philadelphia.* 1842. 8vo. 60288

Outlines of a plan for establishing a State Society of Agriculture in Pennsylvania. *Philadelphia: Printed by Charles Cist* .... MDCCXCIV. 8vo, pp. (2), 11. P. 60289

A Pamphlet in relation to the State Debt written by ... John Haney. With an Address to the Voting Classes ... of Philadelphia. [n. p.] August 30, 1842. 12mo, pp. 12. 60290

The Parole and Documentary Evidence. *See* [Findley (W.)]

Report of the PAYMASTER GENERAL ... of Pennsylvania, for ... 1861. *Harrisburg.* 1861. 8vo, pp. 5. 60291

Pennsylvania: a Poem. By a Student of the College of Philadelphia. *Philadelphia: Printed by B. Franklin, and D. Hall.* MDCCLVI. Folio, pp. 11. 60292

Charter, By-Laws, and Standing Resolutions, of the PENNSYLVANIA ACADEMY of the Fine Arts. *Philadelphia.* 1813. 12mo, pp. 22. 60293

Exhibition of the Pennsylvania Academy of the Fine Arts, ... 1838. *Philadelphia.* [n. d.] 8vo, pp. 15. Continued. 60294

This was the catalogue of the permanent exhibition, and is a different publication from the annual exhibition. Also: The Act of Incorporation, and Standing Regulations of the Pennsylvania Academy of the Fine Arts. *Philadelphia.* 1831. 16mo, pp. 24. + [*Ibid.*] 1847. 8vo, pp. 24. — The Act of Incorporation, and By-Laws and Ordinances of the ... Academy .... *Philadelphia.* 1860. 12mo, pp. 24. — Catalogue of Statues, Busts, &c. ... *Philadelphia.* 1807. 8vo, pp. 8. — Catalogue of Paintings, Statues, Prints ... . *Philadelphia.* 1818. 8vo, pp. 19. — Catalogue of the Paintings and Statuary .... *Philadelphia.* 1848. 8vo, pp. 26. Continued. — ... Proceedings of the Annual Meeting of the Stockholders. ... *Philadelphia.* 1855. 8vo, pp. 20. — ... Report of the Board ... to the Stockholders. ... *Philadelphia.* 1851. 8vo, pp. 15. — To the Citizens of Philadelphia. Pennsylvania Academy of the Fine Arts, 23d June, 1845. [n. p. n. d.] Folio, 1 leaf. + [n. p. 1845.] 4to, 1 leaf. — Sixth Annual Exhibition .... *Philadelphia.* 1817. 8vo, pp. 22. [For earlier exhibitions, *see* Society of Artists, *infra*, and Columbian Society of Artists, *supra*.

First Annual Report of the PENNSYLVANIA AGENCY of the American Tract Society; ... Philadelphia, May 1, 1854. ... [n. p. 1854.] 8vo, pp. 48, 28. 60295

Hints for American Husbandmen, with Communications to the PENNSYLVANIA AGRICULTURAL Society. By Order of the Directors. *Philadelphia: Printed by Clark & Raser.* 1827. 8vo, pp. (178). 4 Plates. B. 60296

Improved title of our No. 31972, Vol. VIII.

Memoirs of the Pennsylvania Agricultural Society: with selections from the most approved authors, adapted to the Use of the Practical Farmers of the United States. ... *Baltimore: J. S. Skinner* .... 1824. 8vo, pp. xv, 9–255, (2). 4 Plates. 60297

Also: Pennsylvania Agricultural Society. Strictures upon Arator's Attack. [n. p. 1823.] 8vo, pp. 4. — Proceedings of the ... Society: with the Address of ... Jonathan Roberts, Esq. ... at their First Annual Meeting. *Philadelphia.* 1823. 8vo, pp. 39. Continued.

The Pennsylvania Almanack ... For ... 1733. ... By T. Godfrey. *Philadelphia: ... A. Bradford.* [n. d.] 12mo, pp. (24).

Continued to 1735 or later. Also: The Pennsylvania Almanac, for ... 1796 .... By Joshua Sharp. *Philadelphia: Printed by Jacob Johnson & Co.* [n. d.] 12mo, pp. (36). — The Pennsylvania Almanac ... For ... 1803. By A. Shoemaker. *Philadelphia.* [n. d.] 12mo. Continued to 1823.

Pennsylvania and Ohio Canal Company's Charter. [n. p. 1833.] 8vo, pp. 25. 60299

Also: Annual Report .... In Senate [of Ohio]. February 21, 1846. 8vo, pp. 10. — Minutes of the Proceedings of a Convention, holden at Warren, Ohio, ... 13th of November, 1833; on ... connecting the Pennsylvania and Ohio Canals. ... *Warren, O.* [n. d.] 8vo, pp. 40.

Pennsylvania Annual Almanac, and Reference, for ... 1813. By Josiah S. Kay, J.W.C.L. ... *Philadelphia.* 1813. 18mo, pp. (72). Continued. 60300

Pennsylvania Anti-Masonic Almanac ... *Lancaster.* 1830. 12mo. S. 60301

Pennsylvania Archives. *See* Hazard (S.), Vol. VIII. 31105.

A second series, edited by J. B. Linn and Wm. H. Egle, M.D., was issued *Harrisburg: B. Singerly.* 1874.

Pennsylvania as a Borrower. Some Considerations on her Ancient Credit, her Subsequent Disgrace, her Reviving Prospects and her True Policy in Future. *Philadelphia.* 1863. 8vo, pp. 60. 60302

Minutes of the Third Anniversary of the PENNSYLVANIA BAPTIST Convention, ... held ... Mount Pleasant, Westmoreland Co., ... October 30 and 31, 1839. ... *Philadelphia.* 1840. 8vo, pp. 14. Continued. 60303

Report of the Fourth Anniversary of the PENNSYLVANIA BAPTIST EDUCATION Society, ... *Philadelphia.* 1844. 8vo. Continued. — Origin, and Constitution of the PENNSYLVANIA BAPTIST MISSIONARY Society. ... *Philadelphia.* 1826. 8vo, pp. 11, (1). — Minutes of the Annual Meeting of the PENNSYLVANIA BAPTIST STATE Convention for Missionary Purposes .... *Philadelphia.* [1838.] 8vo, pp. 24. Continued.

Charter and By-Laws of the PENNSYLVANIA BIBLE Society, with ... Officers and Managers from the origin of the Society. ... *Philadelphia.* 1854. 8vo, pp. 22. 60304

Also: The Bible Society: Its Design and Operations. By the Pennsylvania Bible Society. [n. p. n. d.] 8vo, pp. 7. — History of the Charter and By-Laws of the ... Society, with a List of Officers and Managers from the origin of the Society to the present date, May 11, 1866. ... *Philadelphia.* 1866. 8vo, pp. 24. — Thirty-Seventh Annual Report of the ... Society .... *Philadelphia.* 1845. 8vo. [For earlier reports, *see* Philadelphia Bible Society.]

The Proceedings and Constitution of the PENNSYLVANIA BRANCH of the General Union for promoting the observance of the Christian Sabbath. ... *Philadelphia.* 1828. 8vo, pp. 16.

Pennsylvania Bubble. *See* Vol. II., No. 6108.

Ulman's PENNSYLVANIA BUSINESS Directory ... for ... 1854 5. ... By H. C. Ulman. ... *Philadelphia.* 1854. 8vo, pp. 352, 173. 2 Maps. S. 60306

Petition for the Extension of the PENNSYLVANIA CANAL from Columbia to the Maryland Line. *Harrisburg.* 1835. 8vo, pp. 7

Also: Report of a Committee of the House of Representatives, appointed upon the application of James Clarke, Acting Commissioner on the Juniata Division of the Pennsylvania Canal, to investigate his official conduct .... Together with some of the Documents ... in Evidence. ... *Harrisburg.* 1830. 8vo, pp. 14.

An Act to authorize a loan to defray the expenses of the PENNSYLVANIA CANAL AND RAIL ROAD, and to continue for a further time "An Act to incorporate the Subscribers to the Bank of Pennsylvania" .... [n. p. 1830.] 8vo, pp. 8. 60308

Pennsylvania Canals. [n. p. n. d.] 8vo, pp. 3. 60309

Letter on their importance. Signed "Hamilton." Philadelphia, May 15, 1828.

The Pennsylvania Chronicle and Universal Advertiser. Containing the freshest Advices, both Foreign and Domestic; with a Variety of other Matter, useful, instructive, and entertaining. ... *Philadelphia: Printed by William Goddard* .... [n. d.] Folio, pp. 4.

No. 1 appeared Monday, Jan. 26, 1767. The fourth journal in English published at Philadelphia, and the first with four columns to a page in the colonies. Goddard's silent partners were Jos. Galloway and Thos. Wharton. In 1770, Goddard became sole proprietor. The "Chronicle" appeared weekly, and was always edited with ability. In 1768–9, it was printed on a quarto sheet, afterward on a folio, but of a less size than that of 1767. Discontinued, February, 1774.

A Refutation of the Misstatements contained in a Pamphlet recently issued by W. Darrach, M.D., and John Wiltbank, M.D. in reference to the Medical Department of PENNSYLVANIA COLLEGE. *Philadelphia.* 1855. 8vo, pp. 64. 60311

Reply to a Pamphlet entitled "A Statement of the Facts connected with the late re-organization of the Faculty of the Medical Department of Pennsylvania College ..." *Philadelphia.* 1855. 8vo, pp. (2), 68. 60312

A Statement of the Facts connected with the late re-organization of the Faculty of the Medical Department of Pennsylvania College, together with a Documentary History of said Department from its origin to the present time. *Philadelphia.* 1855. 8vo, pp. (2), 64. 60313

Also: Address of Rev. C. P. Krauth, at his Inauguration as President of Pennsylvania College, Gettysburg. *Gettysburg.* 1834. 8vo, pp. 15. — Annual Catalogue, with Officers and Students ... *Gettysburg.* MDCCCXLIV. 8vo, pp. 18. Continued. — The Charter .... With a list of the patrons .... *Gettysburg.* 1834. 8vo, pp. 10. — The Literary Record and Journal of the Linnæan Association .... Conducted by a Committee .... Volume I. *Gettysburg: H. C. Neinstedt.* 1845. 8vo, pp. (2), 274. Continued. — The Medical Department ... at Philadelphia. The Annual Announcement of Lectures, &c., &c., For ... 1840–1, with a Catalogue of the Graduates ... for ... 1840. *Philadelphia.* 1840. 8vo, pp. 7. Continued.

Report of the ... Managers of the PENNSYLVANIA COLONIZATION Society, with an Appendix. *Philadelphia.* 1830. 8vo, pp. 48. Continued. 60314

Also: Constitution of the ... Society. [n. p. n. d.] 4to, 1 leaf.

An Address from The President and Directors of the PENNSYLVANIA COMPANY for Insurances on Lives and granting Annuities. To the Inhabitants of the United States .... *Philadelphia.* 1814. 8vo, pp. 45. B. 60315

Also: The Charter and By-Laws of the Pennsylvania Company for Insurances .... *Philadelphia.* 1836. 8vo, pp. 22. + 1848. 8vo, pp. 26. — Proposals of the ... Company ... Incorporated March 10, 1812, with a perpetual Charter .... *Philadelphia.* 1837. 8vo, pp. 16. Continued.

An Act to Incorporate the PENNSYLVANIA, DELAWARE and Maryland Steam Navigation Company, Passed March 6, 1826. [n. p. n. d.] 16mo, pp. 8. 60316

A Statement of the Origin, Nature and Operations of the PENNSYLVANIA DOMESTIC Missionary Society. ... *Philadelphia.* 1827. 8vo, pp. 15. 60317

The Pennsylvania Evening Post. MDCCLXXV. Volume I. *Philadelphia: Printed by Benjamin Towne.* [n. d.] 4to, pp. (2), 604. Continued to 1782. 60318

Pennsylvania Farm Journal, devoted to Agriculture, Horticulture & Rural Economy. S. S. Haldeman, Editor. Volume I. *Lancaster, Pa.* 1852. 8vo, pp. (8), 380. Continued. 60319

The Pennsylvania Farmer, and Scientific Journal. ... Vol. I. January 15th, 1844. No. 1. [*Lancaster.* 1844.] 8vo, pp. 24.

Constitution of the PENNSYLVANIA FIRE Company: To which is annexed, Bye Laws and Rules .... *Philadelphia.* 1808. 18mo, pp. 18. 60321

An Act to Incorporate the PENNSYLVANIA FIRE Insurance Company. *Philadelphia.* 1838. 8vo, pp. 16. 60322

The Pennsylvania Freedman's Bulletin. Philadelphia, May, 1866. [n. p. n. d.] 8vo, pp. 4. 60323

Issued irregularly in separately paged numbers until 1868.

Report of ... a Meeting [of the PENNSYLVANIA FREEDMEN'S Relief Association], ... Nov. 3, 1863, [on] the Condition of the Freed People of the South. *Philadelphia.* 1863. 8vo, pp. 24.

Also: Annual Report of the ... Association, Philadelphia, March, 1864. *Philadelphia.* 1864. 8vo.

The Pennsylvania Gazette. *See* The Universal Instructor.

Postscript to the Pennsylvania Gazette. Friday Evening, Five O'Clock, Dec. 24. 1773. Folio, 1 leaf. 60325

An account of the destruction of the tea in Boston harbor; the news was brought express from New York by Mr. Cornelius Bradford, and was instantly issued in this form from the printing office. W. and T. Bradford headed the postscript to their paper "A Christmas Box."

Act of Incorporation and By-Laws of the PENNSYLVANIA HORTICULTURAL Society. Instituted 1827. Incorporated 1831. *Philadelphia.* 1861. 8vo, pp. 15. 60326

Also: By-Laws of the Pennsylvania Horticultural Society. ... *Philadelphia.* 1846. 8vo, pp. (2), 48. — Catalogue of the Library of the ... Society. *Philadelphia.* 1840. 8vo, pp. 24. + 1850. 8vo, pp. 48. — Constitution and By-Laws .... *Philadelphia.* 1831. 8vo, pp. 20. + 1836. 8vo, pp. 19. + 1840. 8vo, pp. 24. — The Pennsyl-

vania Horticultural Society, ... offers the following Premiums .... *Philadelphia.* 1839. 8vo, pp. 12. — ... Programme for ... 1862. ... *Philadelphia.* 1862. 12mo, pp. (2), 16. Continued. — Report of the Tenth Exhibition .... To which is added a List of Premiums awarded in ... 1837. *Philadelphia.* 1837. 8vo, pp. 16. — Transactions of the ... Society. ... *Philadelphia.* 1839. 8vo, pp. 40. Continued.

An Account of the Rise, Progress, & Present State, of the PENNSYLVANIA HOSPITAL, December 12, 1801. *Philadelphia: Printed by Robert Carr.* 1801. Sm. 8vo, pp. 8. 60327

A Catalogue of the Medical Library belonging to the Pennsylvania Hospital. Exhibiting the Names of Authors and Editors ... Also, A List of Articles contained in the Anatomical Museum and the Rules of the Museum, and of the Library. *Philadelphia: Arch. Bartram.* 1806. 8vo, pp. 127. 60328

Catalogue of the Medical Library [by W. G. Malin] of the Pennsylvania Hospital. *Philadelphia: T. A. Conrad, Printer.* 1829. 8vo, pp. xiv, (2), 324. Continued. — Catalogue Raisonné of the Medical Library .... By Emil Fischer, M.D. ... *Philadelphia: Printed by T. K. & P. G. Collins.* 1857. 8vo, pp. xxvii, 750. C. + Supplement .... By A. F. Müller. [*Ibid.*] 1867. 8vo, pp. 713–810.

Some Account of the Pennsylvania Hospital; from its first Rise, to the Beginning of the Fifth Month, called May, 1754. *Philadelphia.* 1817. 8vo, pp. 146. C. 60329

For the first edition and the "Continuation," *see* [Franklin (B.)], Vol. VII. 25588.

State of the Accounts of the Pennsylvania Hospital, ... laid before the ... Annual Meeting, ... 1816. [n. p. n. d.] Folio, 1 leaf. 60330

Continued until 1842, and thereafter in 8vo until 1856, when the title was changed to "Report of the Board of Managers," 8vo. — Also: An Address on the Occasion of the Centennial Celebration ... June 10th, 1851, by George B. Wood, M.D. ... *Philadelphia.* 1851. 8vo, pp. 60. — The Charter, Laws and Rules .... *Philadelphia.* 1837. 8vo, pp. 31. + 1848. 8vo, pp. 33. + 1875. 8vo, pp. 32. — ... Proceedings of a Meeting held First Month (January) 15th, 1867. *Philadelphia.* 1867. 8vo, pp. 28. Plate. — Report of the Board of Managers .... *Philadelphia.* 1856. 8vo. Continued. — Report of the Committee on Repairs and Alterations .... *Philadelphia.* 1853. 8vo, pp. 15. Plate. — Rules for the Government of the ... Hospital. *Philadelphia.* [n. d.] 12mo, pp. 20. — Some Account of the Origin, Objects and Present State of the ... Hospital. *Philadelphia.* 1828. 12mo, pp. 24. Plate. + 1831. 8vo, pp. 46. Plate. + 1832. [*Ibid.*] — To the Contributors .... [n. p. 1869.] 8vo, pp. 5. *See also* No. 60244, *supra*.

Pennsylvania Hospital Reports. Volume I. *Philadelphia: Lindsay & Blakiston.* 1867. 8vo, pp. 420. 60331

Report of the PENNSYLVANIA HOSPITAL FOR THE INSANE, for ... 1841. With ... its History, Buildings and Organization. By Thomas S. Kirkbride, M.D. ... *Philadelphia.* 1841. 8vo, pp. 46, (1). 2 Plates. Continued. 60332

Also: Code of Rules and Regulations ... of the Pennsylvania Hospital for the Insane. Second Edition. *Philadelphia.* 1850. 12mo, pp. 51.—Proceedings on ... Laying the Corner Stone ... . Including the address by Geo. B. Wood, M.D. ... *Philadelphia.* 1856. 8vo, pp. 30.—Proceedings on ... Opening the New ... Hospital ... at Philadelphia. ... *Philadelphia.* 1859. 8vo, pp. 26.—Report ... in relation to an Asylum for the Insane Poor. *Philadelphia.* 1839. 8vo. *See also* [Kirkbride (T. S.)], Vol. IX., No. 37980, *and* "Memorial," No. 60242, *supra.*

The First Annual Report of the PENNSYLVANIA INDUSTRIAL Home for Blind Women, ... Philadelphia. *Philadelphia.* 1869. 8vo, pp. 16. Continued. 60333

The Pennsylvania Infirmary, for Diseases of the Eye and Ear Established at Philadelphia. *Philadelphia.* 1822. 8vo, pp. 6.

Constitution and By-Laws of the PENNSYLVANIA INSTITUTE ... Incorporated 1856. *Philadelphia.* 1856. 8vo, pp. 31.

Constitution and By-Laws of the PENNSYLVANIA INSTITUTE OF DESIGN, for the Encouragement of Apprentices and Amateurs, with a list of the Officers. *Philadelphia.* 1855. 12mo, pp. 12. 60336

Also: Report of the First Annual Exhibition of Ingenuity and Design, held in ... Philadelphia, ... May, 1857, ... with the Address of the Rev. Kingston Goddard. *Philadelphia.* 1857. 8vo, pp. 27.

An Account of the Origin and Progress of the PENNSYLVANIA INSTITUTION for the Deaf and Dumb. With ... Contributors, &c. ... *Philadelphia.* 1821. 8vo, pp. 38. 60337

Letters to C. C. Biddle, Wm. M'Ilvaine, Mary Cowgill, and John Bacon: Connected with the Dismissal of David C. Seixas, the Founder ... of the Pennsylvania Institution for the Deaf and Dumb. [n. p.] 1822. 8vo, pp. 28. 60338

Also: Charter, By-Laws, and Act of Assembly ... . *Philadelphia.* 1842. 8vo.—Constitution and By-Laws ... with the Address of the ... Directors, and a List of the Officers. *Philadelphia.* 1820. 8vo, pp. 16.—Documents in relation to the Dismissal of David G. Seixas ... . *Philadelphia.* 1822. 8vo, pp. 48.—Fifth Annual Report of the ... Institution ... to the Legislature. *Philadelphia.* 1826. 8vo. Cont'd.

Pennsylvania Institution for the Instruction of the Blind, ... in Philadelphia. Instituted, February 21, 1833. *Philadelphia.* 1833. 8vo, pp. 8. 60339

Also: Address to the Public on the Home for the Industrious Blind, by the Managers ... . *Philadelphia.* 1861. 8vo, pp. 7.—Constitution, Charter, and By-Laws ... relating to the ... Institution ... . [n. p.] 1837. 8vo.—Constitution, By-Laws and Rules ... . With ... Acts of Assembly, ... Origin of the Institution, and an abstract of the first five reports of the ... Managers. *Philadelphia.* 1856. 8vo, pp. 41. + With an Appendix containing Certain Acts of Assembly. [*Ibid.*] 1862. 8vo, pp. 34, (1).—First Annual Report of the Managers ... . *Philadelphia.* 1834. 8vo.—Publi-

cations relative to the ... Institution for the Instruction of the Blind ... . I. Observations on the Instruction of Blind Persons, in a Letter to Roberts Vaux, John Vaughan, and Robert Walsh: by Julius R. Friedlander. [n. p. 1833.] II. Proceedings of the Association for establishing a School for the Education of the Blind in Philadelphia, for ... Pennsylvania, under J. R. Friedlander. [n. p. n. d.] III. Account of the First Exhibition of the Blind Pupils in the ... Institution, ... 1833. [n. p. n. d.] IV. An Address ... [*see* No. 25938]. V. Statement of the number of Blind in Pennsylvania. *Philadelphia.* 1833. 8vo, pp. (2), 8, 8, 8, 15, (2).— ... Report ... [on] the Subject of A Home, ... for the Adult Blind ... . *Philadelphia.* 1851. 8vo, pp. 16.

The Pennsylvania Journal of Prison Discipline and Philanthropy. Published under the Direction of "The Philadelphia Society for the Alleviation of the Miseries of Public Prisons," instituted 1787. Vol. I. *Philadelphia: Joseph Tatum.* 1845. 8vo, pp. 398. Plates. Continued. 60340

Statement of the Incumbrances at present on the Property of the PENNSYLVANIA LAND Company. [n. p. 1797.] 12mo, pp. 3

Pennsylvania Law Journal, containing Judge Randall's Decisions in Bankruptcy. ... *Philadelphia.* 1842–48. 7 vols., 8vo.

Edited by Henry E. Wallace, E. W. David, David Webster, and S. J. Robbins. Continued as the "American Law Journal."

... Numb. I. The Pennsylvania Ledger: Or the Virginia, Maryland, Pennsylvania, & New Jersey Weekly Advertiser. Saturday, January 28, 1775. *Philadelphia: Printed by James Humphreys, junr.* [n. d.] Folio, pp. (4). 60343

Continued to May 23, 1778.

Report of the Progress of the PENNSYLVANIA LYCEUM. *Philadelphia.* 1836. 8vo, pp. 8. 60344

Address of the Managers of the PENNSYLVANIA LYING-IN and Foundling Hospital, ... with the Charter and By-Laws. *Philadelphia.* 1862. 8vo, pp. 32. 60345

The Pennsylvania Magazine: or, American Monthly Museum. MDCCLXXV. Volume I. *Philadelphia: Printed ... by R. Aitken* ... . 8vo, pp. 625, (5). 15 Plates. P. 60346

Vol. I. from January to December, 1775; Vol. II. from January to July, 1776, pp. 334. No. I. reached a second edition. A periodical of great rarity, owing probably to the troublesome times of its publication. Francis Hopkinson, the Rev. Dr. Witherspoon, and other able writers contributed to this magazine. Paine wrote for it several noticeable articles—his "Ode on Gen. Wolfe," and the "Reflections on Lord Clive." *See* Duyckinck's "Cyclopedia," I. 198.

Pennsylvania Masonic and Civil Almanac for ... 1813. *Philadelphia.* [n. d.] 12mo. 60347

The Pennsylvania, New Jersey, Delaware, Maryland and Virginia Almanac, for ... 1799 ... . *Philadelphia: Printed ... by Peter Stewart.* [n. d.] 12mo, pp. (40). 60348

Pennsylvania Normal School Laws. Passed ... 1857, and ... 1859. *Harrisburg.* 1860. 8vo, pp. 14. 60349

The Pennsylvania Pocket Almanac For ... 1769. ... *Philadelphia: Printed ... by W. and T. Bradford.* [n. d.] 24mo, pp. (28).

Continued to 1810.

Annual Announcement of the PENNSYLVANIA POLYTECHNIC College, 1853–54. *Philadelphia.* [n. d.] 8vo. 60351

Transaction of the PENNSYLVANIA POMOLOGICAL Society. ... *Philadelphia.* 1852. 8vo. 60352

Pennsylvania Population Company. *See* Vol. VIII., No. 33625

Pennsylvania Poultry Society. Report of the Annual Exhibition, held at Philadelphia, ... 1852. *Philadelphia.* 1853. 8vo, pp. 16. 60353

The Pennsylvania Primer, ... for the use of Country Schools; ... *Lancaster: Printed by W. Dunlap.* 1755. 12mo. 60354

Plan of Association of the PENNSYLVANIA PROPERTY Company ... . *Philadelphia.* 1797. 8vo, pp. 16. P. 60355

An Act to Incorporate the PENNSYLVANIA RAILROAD Company. Passed April 13, 1846. With a Supplement. *Philadelphia.* 1846. 8vo, pp. 14. 60356

Letter to the Stockholders of the Pennsylvania Railroad Company. By James Page. *Philadelphia.* 1863. 8vo, pp. 23.

Reasons of the ... Directors of the Pennsylvania Railroad Company, for declining to offer to purchase the Main Line of the State Works; with a copy of the Act of Assembly, authorizing the Sale. *Philadelphia.* 1854. 8vo. C. 60358

Also: By-Laws of the ... Directors, ... with the Charter of the Pennsylvania Railroad Company. *Philadelphia.* 1847. 8vo. + 1853. 8vo, pp. 65.—Charter and Supplements ... with the Acts of Assembly and Municipal Ordinances ... with the By-Laws of the ... Directors. *Philadelphia.* 1859. 8vo, pp. (4), 141.—The Coal Business on the Pennsylvania Railroad. A communication addressed to the President ... of the ... Railroad, on the cost of transportation. *Philadelphia.* 1857. 8vo, pp. 33.—A Few Facts and Considerations for Business Men upon a Delaware Terminus ... *Philadelphia.* 1859. 8vo, pp. 56. Map.—First Annual Report of the Chief Engineer ... 1848. *Philadelphia.* 1848. 8vo, pp. 32. Map.—First Annual Report of the Directors ... to the Stockholders. October 30, 1847. *Philadelphia.* 1847.

12mo, pp. 20. Continued in 8vo.—Guide for the Pennsylvania Railroad, with an Extensive Map ... . *Philadelphia.* 1855. 8vo, pp. 40. Map.—Pennsylvania Rail Road, its Necessity and Advantages to Philadelphia. [n. p. 1846.] Folio, 1 leaf.— ... Address of the Committee of Seven to the Citizens of Philadelphia, and of Pennsylvania, appointed at a Town Meeting, held at Philadelphia, ... 28th of April, 1846. [n. p.] 1846. 8vo, pp. 38.— ... Organization for Conducting the Business of the Road. ... *Philadelphia.* 1852. 8vo, pp. 16.— ... Organization for Conducting the Business and keeping the accounts of the Canal Department ... . *Philadelphia.* 1858. 8vo, pp. 12.—Points for Consideration by the Investigating Committee of the ... Company. [n. p.] 1867. 8vo, pp. 9.—Proceedings of the ... Annual Meeting of the Stockholders ... . April 30th, 1867. *Philadelphia.* 1867. 8vo, pp. 19.—Prohibition of Sunday Travelling ... . *Philadelphia.* 1850. 8vo, pp. 12.—Report of H. Haupt, Chief Engineer of the ... Company, with a Communication from the President of the Ohio & Pennsylvania Rail Road Company ... . *Philadelphia.* 1854. 8vo, pp. 39.—Report of Thomas S. Fernon, to the Pennsylvania Railroad Company, on "Western Connections. [n. p. 1852.] 8vo, pp. 44.—Report on the Eastern Terminus of the Pennsylvania Rail Road. By Strickland Kneass ... . *Philadelphia.* 1859. 8vo, pp. 15.—Reports of the Majority and Minority of the Committee appointed ... 1861, to examine the ... Company. *Philadelphia.* 1862. 8vo, pp. 52.—The West Market Street Meeting. Termination of the Pennsylvania Rail Way. [n. p. 1846?] 8vo, pp. 11.—Will the Interests of Pennsylvania be advanced, or the Revenue increased by continuing the Tonnage Tax upon the Pennsylvania Railroad? Is a Tax on the through tonnage constitutional? [n. p. 1861?] 8vo, pp. 53.

Pennsylvania Railway Gazetteer, Commercial Advertiser, Business and Post-Office Directory, for 1866–7. *Philadelphia: A. O. Loomis & Co.* 1866. 8vo, pp. xxxi, 542. 60359

Pennsylvania Register. *See* Hazard (S.), Vol. VIII. 31106.

Report to the Contributors to the PENNSYLVANIA RELIEF Association for East Tennessee. By a Commission sent by the Executive Committee to visit that region ... . *Philadelphia.* 1864. 8vo, pp. 45. 60360

A Pennsylvania Sailor's Letters. *See* [Macpherson (J.)], XI.

Pennsylvania School Journal, Thomas H. Burrowes, Editor. *Lancaster.* 1852–59. 7 vols., 8vo. 60361

Constitution and By-Laws of the PENNSYLVANIA SEAMEN'S Friend Society; with an Address ... . *Philadelphia.* 1843. 12mo, pp. 11. + 1845. 16mo, pp. 8. 60362

Also: Address of the Pennsylvania Seamen's Friend Society to the Citizens of Philadelphia, with the Constitution and ... Officers, 1845. *Philadelphia.* 1845. 12mo, pp. 16.—The Board of Managers ... . Preamble and Resolutions ... in relation to [the assassination of Lincoln. n. p. 1865.] 12mo, 1 leaf.—Seventh Annual Report of the Pennsylvania Seamen's Friend Society, and the Eighteenth Annual Report of the Female Seamen's Friend Society. *Philadelphia.* 1851. 8vo.

Report of a Committee Appointed by the PENNSYLVANIA SOCIETY FOR DISCOURAGING the Use of Ardent Spirits, to ... report

what amendments ought to be made in the Laws ... for the Suppression of ... Gaming. ... *Philadelphia.* 1828. 8vo, pp. 17.

Also: The Anniversary Report of the Managers of the Pennsylvania Society for Discouraging the Use of Ardent Spirits. Read ... 27th May, 1831. ... *Philadelphia.* 1831. 8vo, pp. 72. + The Fourth Edition. [*Ibid.*] 1833. 8vo.—Report of the ... Managers ... . Read ... May 26th, 1830. [n. p.] 1830. 8vo, pp. 8.

The Constitution of the PENNSYLVANIA SOCIETY FOR PROMOTING the Abolition of Slavery, and the Relief of Free Negroes, unlawfully held in Bondage. ... To which are added Acts of the General Assembly ... for the Gradual Abolition of Slavery. *Philadelphia.* 1781. 8vo. + *Philadelphia: Printed by Joseph James.* M.DCC.LXXXVII. 8vo, pp. 15. + *Philadelphia: Printed by Francis Bailey.* MDCCLXXXVIII. 8vo, pp. 29. + 1800. 8vo, pp. 53. + 1820. 8vo, pp. 31. 60364

Also: Act of Incorporation and Constitution ... . *Philadelphia.* 1860. 8vo, pp. 36.—Celebration of the Ninetieth Anniversary of the organization ... held ... April 14, 1865 ... . *Philadelphia.* 1866. 8vo, pp. 25.—Rules for the Regulation of the ... Society ... . *Philadelphia: Zachariah Poulson, Jun.* 1784. 8vo.

Pennsylvania Society for Promoting the Culture of the Mulberry and the raising of Silkworms ... [*Philadelphia.* 1828.] 8vo.

Annual Report of the PENNSYLVANIA SOCIETY FOR THE ADVANCEMENT of Christianity in Pennsylvania ... 1844. *Philadelphia.* 1845. 8vo. Continued. 60366

Communication of the PENNSYLVANIA SOCIETY FOR THE ENCOURAGEMENT of Manufactures and the Useful Arts, Feb. 7, 1804. *Philadelphia.* 1804. 8vo, pp. 28. M. 60367

Also: Constitution of the ... Society ... adopted Sept. 4, 1819. [n. p. n. d.] 8vo, pp. 3.—Memorial of the Board of Managers ... Agreed to March 10th, 1824. *Philadelphia.* 1824. 12mo, pp. (2), 24.—Memorial of the Board of Manufactures ... . *Washington.* 1822. 8vo, pp. 9.—The Plan of the ... Society ... . *Philadelphia: Printed by R. Aitken & Son.* M.DCC.LXXXVII. 12mo, pp. 12, (1).

Annual Report of the PENNSYLVANIA SOCIETY FOR THE PREVENTION of Cruelty to Animals. *Philadelphia.* 1869. 8vo, pp. 8

Also: Address of the Committee appointed by the ... Society ... . *Philadelphia.* 1867. 8vo, pp. 10.—Charter and By-Laws ... . *Philadelphia.* 1868. 12mo, pp. 12. + [*Ibid.*] 1871. 12mo, pp. 12.

The Memorial of the PENNSYLVANIA SOCIETY FOR THE PROMOTION of American Manufactures to Congress in favor of "Protection." [n. p. 1820.] 8vo, pp. 14. 60369

Address of the Committee of the PENNSYLVANIA SOCIETY FOR THE PROMOTION of Internal Improvement ... in favor of the Union Canal. [n. p. 1826.] 8vo, pp. 7. 60370

Also: The First Annual Report of the Acting Committee of the Society for the Promotion of Internal Improvement in ... Pennsylvania. *Philadelphia.* 1826. 8vo, pp. 45, (2).

Address "of the PENNSYLVANIA SOCIETY FOR THE PROMOTION of Manufactures and the Mechanic Arts," in regard to the depressed state of woolen manufacture. [n. p. 1827.] 8vo, pp. 12. 60371

Also: At a meeting of the ... Society ... held in Philadelphia, ... 14th ... May, 1827. [n. p. n. d.] 8vo, 1 leaf.

Report of the Library Committee of the PENNSYLVANIA SOCIETY FOR THE PROMOTION of Public Economy, containing a summary of the information ... in reply to the ... letter of the Committee of Superintendence of February 21, 1817. *Philadelphia.* 1817. 8vo, pp. 53. 60372

Also: Report of the Committee on Domestic Economy, to the Pennsylvania Society, for the Promotion of Public Economy. ... *Philadelphia.* 1817. 8vo, pp. 27.

The First Report on the State of Education in Pennsylvania, made to the PENNSYLVANIA SOCIETY FOR THE PROMOTION of Public Schools, to which is added the Constitution of the Society. *Philadelphia.* 1828. 8vo, pp. 9. Continued. 60373

Also: Constitution of the ... Society ... . [n. p. 1826?] 8vo, pp. 4.

Address to the People of Pennsylvania and the United States, by the PENNSYLVANIA SOCIETY FOR THE SUPPRESSION of Lotteries. *Philadelphia.* 1834. 8vo, pp. 19. 60374

Pennsylvania Society of the Cincinnati. *See* Vol. IV. 13130.

Report of Col. R. Biddle Roberts, PENNSYLVANIA STATE AGENT at Washington, D. C. *Harrisburg.* 1864. 8vo, pp. 6. + Report of Col. Fr. Jordan, ... Agent ... . [*Ibid.*] 1865. 8vo, pp. 6. + 1866. 8vo, pp. 6. + Annual Report ... for ... 1866. [*Ibid.*] 1867. 8vo, pp. 6. Discontinued. 60375

Report of Col. James Chamberlain, Pennsylvania State Agent at the South West. *Harrisburg.* 1865. 8vo, pp. 7. + Report ... [for 1865. *Ibid.*] 1866. 8vo, pp. 6.

First Annual Report of the Transactions of the PENNSYLVANIA STATE AGRICULTURAL SOCIETY. ... *Harrisburg: A. Boyd Hamilton.* 1854. 8vo, pp. 481, iv. Continued. 60376

Also: Addresses delivered before the Pennsylvania State Agricultural Society, at its Exhibition ... at Williamsport, Lycoming County, September, 1865, by Hon. Edgar Cowan, ... and William H. Allen, LL.D. ... [n. p. n. d.] 8vo, pp. 26.—List of the Premiums of the ... Society, ... 1862. [n. p. n. d.] 8vo, pp. (2), 43.—Officers, Charter, Constitution and Life Members of the ... Society, with the Regulations and Award of Premiums, ... at Pittsburg in 1858, and at Philadelphia in 1857. *Harris-*

burg. 1858. 8vo, pp. 84.—Report of a Committee appointed ... to visit the Farmers' High School of Pennsylvania. ... *Harrisburg.* [1860.] 8vo, pp. 7.—Reports of Judges and Premiums Awarded at Second Annual Exhibition, ... held at Lancaster, ... October, 1852. [n. p.] 1852. 8vo, pp. 32.—To the Members of the ... Society. [n. p. 1860.] 8vo.

Petition, praying for the establishment of "THE PENNSYLVANIA STATE BANK," presented ... in the Senate, March 25, 1834. [n. p. n. d.] Folio, 1 leaf. 60377

Catalogue of the Miscellaneous Books in the PENNSYLVANIA STATE LIBRARY. *Harrisburg.* 1829. 8vo. + *Harrisburg: Royal & Schroyer.* 1853. 16mo, pp. xvi, 124. C. 60378

Catalogue of the ... Library, with Index. *Harrisburg: E. Guyer.* 1839. 8vo.—Catalogue of the Books ... added during ... 1854, '55, '56, '57. *Harrisburg.* 1854–1858. 8vo.—Catalogue of the ... Library. Compiled and Classified by Wallace De Witt. *Harrisburg: A. Boyd Hamilton.* 1859. 8vo, pp. xiv, (2), 440.—Catalogue of the ... Library. *Harrisburg.* 1867. 8vo.

By-Laws of the PENNSYLVANIA STATE LUNATIC Hospital at Harrisburg. *Harrisburg.* 1851. 8vo, pp. 19. 60379

Also: Report of the Trustees and Superintendent of the ... Hospital for 1851. *Harrisburg.* 1852. 8vo. Continued.

Pennsylvania State Normal School. ... An Act ... for the due training of Teachers ... . [n. p. 1857.] 8vo, pp. 8. 60380

The Pennsylvania State Register, for 1831. ... *Philadelphia: John Conrad.* 1831. 12mo, pp. (4), 120, 34. 60381

At a meeting of the PENNSYLVANIA STATE SOCIETY of the Cincinnati, held at the State House, July 5, 1790. [n. p. n. d.] Folio, 1 leaf. 60382

A record of the proceedings of the meeting.

Address of the PENNSYLVANIA STATE TEMPERANCE Society to the Inhabitants of the Commonwealth. [n. p. 1834.] 8vo, pp. 16. 60383

Also: The Anniversary Report of the Managers of the ... Society for 1834. *Philadelphia.* MDCCCXXXIV. 8vo, pp. 40.—Annual Report of the ... Society. *Philadelphia.* 1831. 8vo.—Memorial of the ... Managers of the ... Society to the Convention for revising the Constitution of ... Pennsylvania. *Philadelphia.* 1837. 8vo, pp. 29.

Pennsylvania State Trials. *See* [Hogan (E.)], VIII. 32418.

The Pennsylvania System of Separate Confinement Explained and Defended. *Philadelphia.* 1867. 8vo, pp. 99, iv, 116.

The Pennsylvania System of Prison Discipline Triumphant in France. ... Published by the ... "Philadelphia Society for the Alleviation of the Miseries of Public Prisons." *Philadelphia.* 1847. 8vo, pp. 24.

Appeal of the ... Directors on behalf of the PENNSYLVANIA TRAINING School for Idiotic and Feeble-Minded Children, with the First Annual Reports of the Treasurer and Principal. *Philadelphia.* 1854. 4to, pp. 18, (1). Continued in 8vo. 60385

Also: The Act of Incorporation and By-Laws of the ... Training School ... . *Philadelphia.* 1857. 8vo, pp. 22.—Second Annual Report of the ... Directors ... to the Corporation. *Philadelphia.* 1855. 8vo, pp. 22. Continued.—The Proceedings at the Opening of the New Buildings ... near Media, ... Pennsylvania ... . *Philadelphia.* 1859. 8vo, pp. 38. Plate.

Proceedings of the PENNSYLVANIA YEARLY Meeting of Progressive Friends, ... 1853. *New York.* 1853. 8vo. Contin'd.

Petition from Inhabitants of Beaver County, Pa. for an Increased Tariff. ... *Washington.* 1828. 8vo, pp. 3. 60387

Petition of Sundry Inhabitants of ... Pennsylvania. *Washington.* 1808. 8vo. 60388

Relates to land claims.

Petition to Congress of Inhabitants of Pennsylvania settled on Lands claimed by Connecticut; with Report and Action thereon. *Philadelphia.* [n. d.] 8vo, pp. 8. M. 60389

Addresses ... before the PHILOMATHEAN Society of the University of Pennsylvania, on ... its Semi-Centennial Celebration, October 6th, 1863. *Philadelphia.* 1864. 8vo, pp. 26. 60390

Also: Catalogue of the Library of the Philomathean Society ... . *Philadelphia.* 1870. 8vo, pp. 6.—Catalogue of the Members ... . *Philadelphia.* 1850. 8vo, pp. (24). + 1859. Sm. 4to, pp. 24. + 1867. 4to, pp. 32. + 1878. 4to, pp. 36.

A Plan for encouraging Agriculture, and increasing the Value of Farms in the Midland and more Western Counties of Pennsylvania ... . [n. p. about 1795.] 12mo, pp. 11. 60391

A Plan for Liquidating Certain Debts ... of Pennsylvania, collecting Arrearages with greater Expedition, restoring Confidence in the Government, and providing the Quota of Federal Supplies. [n. p. 1778.] Folio, pp. 6. 60392

A Plan for the Establishment of Public Schools ... in Pennsylvania; to which are added Thoughts upon the Mode of Education, proper in a Republic. ... *Philadelphia: ... Thomas Dobson.* M DCC LXXXVI. 12mo, pp. 36. BA., S. 60393

A Pleasant Peregrination. *See* [Nicklin (P. H.)], XIII. 55237.

Political Anti-Masonry, Abolition, and Amalgamation. [n. p.] 1838. 12mo, pp. 12. 60394

"A brief account of the introduction of political anti-masonry in Pennsylvania."

Political Running, or An Account of a Celebrated Race over the Pennsylvania Course, in ... 1823, for the Governor's Purse. ... [n. p.] 1823. 8vo, pp. 16. 60395

Second Annual Announcement of the POLYTECHNIC College, ... of Pennsylvania. ... *Philadelphia.* 1854. 8vo, pp. 18. Plate. Continued. 60396

The Present State and Condition of the Free People of Color at ... Philadelphia and adjoining Districts, as exhibited by the Report of a Committee of the Pennsylvania Society for Promoting the Abolition of Slavery. *Philadelphia.* 1838. 8vo. 60397

Principles and Articles agreed upon by the Members of the Constitutional Society, in Philadelphia; And Proposed for the Consideration of the Lovers and Supporters of Civil Government in other parts of the State. *Philadelphia: Printed by Francis Bailey* ... . [1780.] Folio, 1 leaf. 60398

Also: To the Citizens of Pennsylvania. [n. p. 1780.] Folio, 1 leaf. [Signed by Richard Bache, Chairman, by order of the Society.]

The Printed Copy of an Act made by Charles Gookin, Esq; by the Queen's Royal Approbation Lieutenant Governour under William Penn, Esq; of the Province of Pensilvania, with the Advice and Consent of the Freemen of the said Province in General Assembly met, directing an Affirmation to Such, who, for Conscience-sake cannot take an Oath, as received in a Letter from Pensilvania, and Publish'd. *London, July* 3. 1711. 60399

Proceedings & Address, of the Committee of the Anti-Jackson Men of Franklin County, Pennsylvania. [n. p. 1832.] 8vo, pp. 48. 60400

Proceedings and Debates of the Convention of the Commonwealth of Pennsylvania, to propose Amendments to the Constitution, commenced and held at Harrisburg, on the second day of May, 1837. Reported by John Agg ... . *Printed by Packer, Barrett, and Parke,* ... *Harrisburg.* 1837–9. 14 vols., 8vo. 60401

For the German translation, *see* "Tagebuch der Convention," *infra.*

Proceedings and Debates of the General Assembly of Pennsylvania. Accurately Taken in short hand, by Thomas Lloyd. ... *Philadelphia: Printed by Daniel Humphreys.* M,DCC,LXXXVII. 4 vols., 8vo, pp. 143; (2), 189, (1); (2), 234; 348. P. 60402

Vol. II. is printed by Joseph James, while vols. III. and IV. have no printer's name on the title-page, and are dated M,DCC,LXXXVIII.

Proceedings of a Convention of Delegates from the Citizens of Pennsylvania, Opposed to Executive Usurpation and Abuse, ... Harrisburg, May 27, 1834. *Harrisburg.* 1834. 8vo, pp. 22.

Proceedings of a Convention of Democratic Young Men, Delegates from the Citizens of Pennsylvania, in favour of the Re-Election of Joseph Ritner, and opposed to Martin Van Buren and the Sub-Treasury. ... Reading, June 4th, 1838. *Reading.* 1838. 8vo, pp. 24. 60404

Proceedings of a Public Meeting ... New Hope, February 14, 1846, in favor of an Out-Let Lock at Wells' Falls, to connect the Delaware Division with the Del. & Raritan Canal. [n. p. n. d.] 8vo, pp. 8. 60405

Proceedings of an Improvement Convention, of Delegates from Luzerne, Susquehanna and Bradford Counties: ... Tunkhannock, May 5, 1840. [n. p. n. d.] 8vo, pp. 8. 60406

Relates to the North Branch Canal.

The Proceedings of some Members of Assembly, at Philadelphia, April, 1728, vindicated from the unfair Reasoning and unjust Insinuations of a certain Remarker. [*Philadelphia: S. Keimer.* 1728.] Folio, 2 leaves. P. 60407

For printing this Keimer was arrested by the Sergeant-at-Arms, and brought before the Assembly. He acknowledged the truth of the charge, but the matter was not pressed against him.

Proceedings of the Agricultural Convention ... at Harrisburg, January 21, 1851. [n. p. n. d.] 8vo, pp. 14. 60408

Proceedings of the Convention ... at Harrisburg, March 4, 1824, for the purpose of forming an Electoral Ticket, to be supported by the Democratic Republicans of Pennsylvania, at the ensuing election for President and Vice-President ... . [n. p. n. d.] 8vo, pp. 8. 60409

Proceedings | of the | Convention, | for the | Province | of | Pennsylvania, | held at | Philadelphia, | January 23, 1775, and continued | by Adjournments, to the 28th. | *Philadelphia:* | *Printed by William and Thomas Bradford,* | ... | M.DCC.LXXV. | 8vo, pp. (2), 10.

Proceedings of the Democratic Antimasonic State Convention, ... Harrisburg, Feb. 22, 1832. *Harrisburg.* 1832. 8vo, pp. 16.

Proceedings of the Democratic Convention, ... at Harrisburg,

January 4, 1828. *Harrisburg.* 1828. 8vo. + March, 5, 1832. *Harrisburg.* 1832. 8vo, pp. 24. 60412

For the German translation, *see* "Verhandlungen," *infra.*

Proceedings of the Democratic Convention of Pennsylvania, ... March, 1835, to nominate a Candidate for Governor and to elect Delegates to the National Convention. ... *Harrisburg.* 1835. 8vo, pp. 16. 60413

Proceedings of the Democratic Republican Convention of Young Men of ... Pennsylvania, ... Harrisburg, July 4, 1836. ... [n. p. n. d.] 8vo, pp. 28. 60414

Proceedings of the Democratic State Convention, ... Harrisburg, Pa., March 16, 1859. ... *Harrisburg.* [n. d.] 8vo, pp. 32

Proceedings of the Democratic Whig National Convention, ... Harrisburg, ... December, 1839, for ... nominating Candidates for President and Vice-President ... . *Harrisburg.* 1839. 8vo, pp. 42. 60416

Proceedings of the Electoral College of ... Pennsylvania, ... Harrisburg, December 7, 1836. *Harrisburg.* 1836. 8vo, pp. 12.

The Proceedings of the Executive of the United States, respecting the Insurgents. 1794. *Philadelphia: Printed by John Fenno.* MDCCXCV. 8vo, pp. 130. 60418

Proceedings of the Legislature ... in Commemoration of the Birth-Day of Washington, ... 1861. *Harrisburg.* 1861. 8vo, pp. 29. 60419

Proceedings of the Military Convention ... Harrisburg, ... January 2, 1832. ... *Harrisburg.* 1832. 8vo, pp. 24. 60420

Proceedings of the National Republican Convention. [n. p. 1832.] 8vo, pp. 4. 60421

Convention of Pennsylvania National Republicans only.

Proceedings of the Native American State Convention, ... Harrisburg, February 22, 1845. ... *Philadelphia* ... . 1845. 8vo, pp. 24. 60422

Proceedings of the Pennsylvania Canal Convention, ... Harrisburg, August 4, 1825. *Harrisburg.* 1825. 8vo, pp. 19.

Proceedings of the Pennsylvania Convention assembled to organize a State Anti-Slavery Society, at Harrisburg, on 31st

January and 1st, 2d and 3d February, 1837. *Philadelphia.* 1837. 8vo, pp. 97. 60424

Proceedings of the Pennsylvania Democratic State Convention, ... Harrisburg, March 4th, 1856. Reported by James B. Sheridan. *Philadelphia.* 1856. 8vo, pp. 90. 60425

Proceedings of the Pennsylvania State Convention, to promote Common School Education, ... Harrisburg, Jan. 16 and 17, 1850. ... *Harrisburg.* 1850. 8vo, pp. 16. 60426

Proceedings of the Provincial Conference of Committees, of the Province of Pennsylvania, Held at the Carpenter's Hall, at Philadelphia. Began June 18th, and continued by adjournments to June 25, 1776. *Philadelphia: Printed by W. & T. Bradford.* [1776.] 8vo, pp. 31. 60427

Proceedings of the Railroad Convention, ... Harrisburg, March 6th, 1838. *Philadelphia.* 1838. 8vo. 60428

Proceedings of the State Convention of the State Rights Democracy ... Harrisburg, ... April 13, 1859. *Harrisburg.* 1859. 8vo, pp. 45. 60429

Proceedings of the State Medical Convention, held in Lancaster, April, 1848: and Constitution of the Medical Society of ... Pennsylvania; ... *Lancaster, Penn.* ... 1848. 8vo, pp. 20.

Proceedings of the State Sabbath Convention, ... Harrisburg, May 30, 31, 1844. *Philadelphia.* 1844. 8vo. 60431

Proceedings of the State Temperance Convention: ... Harrisburg, Penn., January 12 and 13, 1842. *Shiremanstown.* 1842. 8vo, pp. 16. 60432

Proceedings of the Supreme Executive Council of ... Pennsylvania, in the Case of Major General Arnold. [*Philadelphia:*] *Printed by Hall & Sellers.* 1779. 4to, pp. 11. 60433

Proceedings of the Whigs of Chester County, favorable to a distinct organization of the Whig Party. ... West Chester, Nov. 5, 1838. [n. p. n. d.] 8vo, pp. 23. 60434

The Proceedings relative to calling the Conventions of 1776 and 1790. The Minutes of the Convention that formed the present Constitution of Pennsylvania, together with The Charter to William Penn, the Constitutions of 1776 and 1790, and a View of the Proceedings of the Convention of 1776, and The

Council of Censors. *Harrisburg: Printed by John S. Wiestling.* 1825. 8vo, pp. 384, iv. A. 60435

Contains much valuable matter relative to the early history of the State.

Proclamation of the President [B. Franklin] and Executive Council, offering a Reward for the Apprehension of Daniel Shays and others, March 10, 1787. [n. p. n. d.] Folio, 1 leaf.

Proposal for calling a Convention. *Philadelphia: William Duane.* 1805. 12mo, pp. 30. 60437

Proposals relating to the Education. *See* [Franklin (B.)], VII.

An Appeal to the Lay Members of the PROTESTANT EPISCOPAL CHURCH in Pennsylvania. [n. p.] *April,* 1827. 8vo, pp. 19

Also: Constitution, Canons, and Regulations of the Protestant Episcopal Church ... *Philadelphia.* 1829. 8vo, pp. 47. ... 1839. 8vo. — Journal of the Convention of the ... Church, held in Philadelphia, A. D. 1785. *Philadelphia.* 1785. 8vo. Continued. — Journal of the Meetings which led to the Institution of the Convention ... and of the First Six Conventions. *Philadelphia.* 1790. 8vo, pp. 26. — Journal of the Proceedings of the Bishops, Clergy and Laity ... at Philadelphia, May 17 to 24, 1814. *Philadelphia.* 1814. 8vo, pp. 39. — Prayers and Thanksgivings which may be used in this Diocese. A. Potter, Bishop, &c. [n. p. n. d.] 8vo, pp. 8. — Report of the Committee of Seven on the Division of the Diocese, appointed ... in 1863 ... . *Philadelphia.* 1864. 8vo, pp. 16.

Report of a Committee ... of the PROTESTANT EPISCOPAL MISSIONARY SOCIETY of Pennsylvania on the Subject of a General Missionary Society for Foreign and Domestic Missions ... . *Philadelphia.* 1820. 8vo, pp. 16. B. 60439

Public Faith. [n. p. 1833?] 8vo, pp. 15. 60440

Relates to the Union Canal Lottery.

Report of the QUARTERMASTER GENERAL of the Commonwealth ... for ... 1861. *Harrisburg.* 1861. 8vo, pp. 23. + Report ... for ... 1862. [*Ibid.*] 1863. 8vo, pp. 26. + Report ... for ... 1864. [*Ibid.*] 1865. 8vo, pp. 177. Discontinued.

Reasons for Repealing the Act of the Legislature of Pennsylvania, of September 13, 1785, for Repealing their Acts of March 18, and April 1, 1782, For Supporting and Incorporating the Bank of North-America. Humbly offered to the Consideration of the Public. By a Citizen of Philadelphia. *Philadelphia: Printed by Eleazer Oswald.* M,DCC,LXXXVI. 8vo, pp. 8. 60442

Receipts and Expenditures in the Treasury of Pennsylvania, from ... December, ... [1806] to ... November, ... [1807]

inclusive. *Lancaster: Printed by John Burnside.* 1807. 8vo, pp. 142. 60443

Continued to 1818, and thereafter as "Receipts and Payments at the Treasury of Pennsylvania," until changed in 1824 to "Report of the State Treasurer," and so continued until 1850, from which time it has appeared as "Detailed Report of the State Treasurer."

Reception of Gov. Andrew Johnson, of Tennessee, and Ex-Gov. Wright, of Indiana, at the State Capitol of Pennsylvania. Full Proceedings in the Senate. *Harrisburg.* 1863. 8vo, pp. 32

Recüeil | de | Diverses | pieces, | Concernant | la | Pensylvanie. | *A la Haye,* | *Chez Abraham Troyel,* | *Marchand Libraire, dans la Grand Sale* | *de la Cour,* M.DCLXXXIV. | 12mo, pp. 118. 60445

A translation of various tracts by William Penn, Mr. Furley, and Thomas Paskel. One of the rarest books about Pennsylvania. *See* Leclerc, No. 1249.

Reflections upon the Administration of Justice in Pennsylvania. By a Citizen. *Philadelphia: Hopkins and Earle.* 1809. 8vo, pp. 66. 60446

Die | Regierungsverfassung | der | Republik Pennsylvanien, | wie solche von der | General Convention, | die zu dem Zweck erwählet | und | vom 15ten Julii, 1776, bis zum 28sten September, 1776, | in Philadelphia gehalten wurde, | vestgesetzt worden. | Aus dem Englischen übersetzt. | *Philadelphia:* | *Gedruckt bey Melchior Steiner.* 1784. 8vo. 60447

A translation of No. 60014, *supra.*

Report of the REGISTER-GENERAL on the State of the Finances of Pennsylvania, for ... 1794. *Philadelphia: Zachariah Poulson.* 1795. 8vo, pp. 19. Continued until 1809. 60448

The Register of Pennsylvania. *See* Vol. VIII., No. 31106.

Regulations for Common School Districts, in Two Parts. ... Prepared by Thomas H. Burrowes ... . *Harrisburg.* 1838. 8vo, pp. 16. 60449

Reise in Ober-Pensylvanien. *See* [Crevecœur], Vol. v. 17502

The Remainder of the Observation, promised in the Mercury. [n. p. 1735.] Folio, pp. 4. 60450

In answer to the piece against the Governor's acting as Chancellor.

Remarks on a late Protest. *See* [Franklin (B.)], VII. 25576.

Remarks on a late Publication. *See* [Reed (Joseph)].

Remarks on a second Publication of B. Henry Latrobe, Engineer, said to be printed by Order of the Committee of Councils; ... and distributed among the members of the Legislature. [n. p. 1799.] 8vo, pp. 7. 60451

Defense of the Delaware and Schuylkill Canal.

Remarks on Money, and the Bank Paper of the United States: Together with a Review of Governor Snyder's Objections to the Bank Bill, passed by two of the Legislative Branches of ... Pennsylvania, at their Session of 1812–13. *Philadelphia.* 1814. 8vo, pp. 31. 60452

Remarks on Scurrility. *See* [Stanley (J. W.)]

Remarks on the Address. *See* [Webster (P.)]

Remarks on the late Proceedings of some Members of Assembly at Philadelphia, April, 1728. [n. p. 1728.] Folio, 2 l.

See also [Huidekoper (H. J.)], Vol. VIII., No. 33625.

Remarks on the School Law of Pennsylvania. *Philadelphia.* 1826. 8vo. 60454

Remarks upon a Memorial circulated by the Agents of the Forest Improvement Company, designed to produce an unjust prejudice against the Mine Hill and Schuylkill Haven Rail Road Company. *Philadelphia.* 1853. 8vo, pp. 8. 60455

Remarks upon the Advice to the Freeholders ... [n. p. 1727?] Folio, pp. 4. 60456

Reply to "A Spectator." [*Washington.* 1825.] 8vo, 1 leaf.

Dispute of R. R. Keene with R. W. Meade.

Reply to "The Crisis." *Printed by James Peacock,* ... *Harrisburg.* [1817.] 8vo, pp. 14. 60458

Report and Correspondence of the Commissioners for Promoting the Internal Improvement of the State. *Harrisburg.* 1825. 8vo, pp. 71. 60459

Report from the Committee on Inland Navigation, on the Delaware and Raritan Canal. ... February 21, 1825. [n. p. n. d.] 8vo, pp. 8. 60460

Report in relation to the Antietam National Cemetery, made to the Governor ... March 30, 1866. [n. p. 1867.] 8vo, pp. 6.

Report of a Committee appointed to investigate the evils of Lotteries, in ... Pennsylvania, and to suggest A Remedy for the same. *Philadelphia.* 1831. 8vo, pp. 16. 60462

Report of a Committee of the Senate on the Subject of Weights and Measures. *Philadelphia.* 1809. 8vo, pp. 35. P.

Report of a Select Committee of the Senate ... relative to the Navigation of the Ohio River. ... *Harrisburg.* 1842. 8vo, pp. 8, folded leaf. 60464

Report of Col. James Worrall, in relation to the Passage of Fish up the Susquehanna River, made to the Governor ... December 3, 1866. *Harrisburg.* 1867. 8vo, pp. 7. Continued.

Report of Mahlon H. Dickinson, on the Condition and Management of the Prisons and Almshouses ... . [*Harrisburg.* 1868.] 8vo, pp. 17. 60466

Report of Messrs. Benj. Wright and J. L. Sullivan, Engineers, ... Survey of the ... Proposed Canal, from the Hudson, to the ... Lackawaxen River. ... *Philadelphia.* 1824. 8vo, pp. viii, 70. Map. 60467

Report of Messrs. Wright and Buckalew, Commissioners to investigate the Affairs of the Bank of Susquehanna County. ... [n. p. 1849.] 8vo, pp. 40. 60468

Report of Mr. Stevenson, Chairman of the Committee on Domestic Manufactures, ... December 24, 1822. *Harrisburg.* [n. d.] 8vo, pp. 8. 60469

Report of the Case of ... Pennsylvania *v.* John Smith, Marshal of the United States for ... Pennsylvania, ... with the ... Opinion by William Tilghman, Chief Justice of Pennsylvania. By a Member of the Philadelphia Bar. *Philadelphia.* 1809. 8vo, pp. 52. S. 60470

Report of the Case of the Commonwealth, *vs.* Tench Coxe, Esq. on a Motion for a Mandamus, in the Supreme Court of Pennsylvania; Taken from the manuscript of the Fourth Volume of Mr. Dallas's Reports. ... *Philadelphia: Printed by Jane Aitken.* 1803. 8vo, pp. 137. 60471

Corrected title of No. 17303, Vol. v.

Report of the Commission appointed by the Governor ... to investigate the Alleged Army Frauds, August, 1861. *Harrisburg.* 1861. 8vo, pp. 63. 60472

Report of the Commissioners Appointed by an Act of the Legislature ... to ... examine all the contemplated routes for connecting the waters of Lake Erie and French creek by canal and slack water navigation. ... Jan. 30, 1824. [n. p. n. d.] 8vo, pp. 12. 60473

Report of the Commissioners. *See* Connecticut, v. 15685.

Report of the Commissioners appointed by the Governor, to prepare a Revised Revenue Code. ... Approved April 11, 1862. [*Harrisburg.* n. d.] 8vo, pp. 31. 60474

Report of the Commissioners, appointed by the President of the United States ... to confer with the Insurgents in the Western Counties of Pennsylvania. *Philadelphia: Printed by Francis Childs & John Swaine.* M,DCC,XCIV. 8vo, pp. 38. C. 60475

Report of the Commissioners appointed to Examine the Claims upon the Main Line of the Public Improvements. ... *Harrisburg.* [n. d.] 8vo, pp. 11. 60476

Report of the Commissioners appointed to Explore the River Susquehanna. ... Dec. 20, 1823. [n. p. n. d.] 8vo, pp. 7.

Report of the Commissioners appointed ... to prepare a revised Revenue Code, for ... Pennsylvania, ... 1863. [n. p. n. d.] 8vo, pp. 31. 60478

Report of the Commissioners appointed to revise the Civil Code of Pennsylvania. ... *Harrisburg.* 1834–35. 8vo, pp. 252.

Report of the Commissioners appointed to Revise the Code of Pennsylvania. [n. p. 1853.] 8vo, pp. 42. 60480

Report of the Commissioners appointed to Revise the Penal Code ... of Pennsylvania, January, 4, 1860. ... *Harrisburg.* 1860. 8vo, pp. 129. 60481

Report of the Commissioners appointed ... March 23, 1830, relative to a Revised Code of Pennsylvania ... . Read in House ... Feb. 2, 1831. *Harrisburg.* 1831. 8vo, pp. 89. + Second Report ... 1833. [*Ibid.*] 1833. 8vo, pp. 62. + Third Report ... [*Ibid.*] 1833. 8vo, pp. 59. + Fourth Report ... [*Ibid.*] 1834. 8vo, pp. 179. + [Fifth] Report ... March 23, 1834. [*Ibid.*] 1834. 8vo, pp. 87. + [Sixth] Report ... January 16, 1835. [*Ibid.*] 1834–5. 8vo, pp. 252. + [Seventh] Report ... March 18, 1835. 8vo, pp. 61. 60482

Report of the Commissioners on the Internal Improvement Fund ... . February 7, 1831. *Harrisburg.* 1831. 8vo, pp. 8.

Report of the Commissioners ... on the part of ... Pennsylvania ... relative to the use of the Waters of the River Delaware. *Harrisburg.* 1834. 8vo, pp. 28. 60484

Report of the Commissioners relative to the National Cemeteries, made to the Governor ... . *Harrisburg.* 1868. 8vo, pp. 6

Report of the Committee, appointed by the House ... to inquire into the Conduct of the Governor ... . Read February 16, 1820. *Harrisburg.* [1820.] 8vo, pp. 29. 60486

Report of the Committee appointed on the subject of Free-Masonry. ... Read in the House ... . *Harrisburg.* 1834. 8vo, pp. 7. 60487

Report of the Committee appointed to enquire into the ... Disturbances at the Seat of Government, in December, 1838. ... Read ... June 18, 1839. *Harrisburg.* 1839. 8vo, pp. 163. 4 folded leaves. 60488

Report of the Committee appointed to enquire into the expediency of bringing in a bill to enable the people to vote at the next General Election, for or against a Convention, to revise and amend the Constitution ... . Feb. 23, 1824. ... [n. p.] 1824. 8vo, pp. 7. 60489

Report of the Committee appointed to enquire into the Official Conduct of the Governor ... . [n. p. 1807.] 8vo, pp. 79.

Report of the Committee appointed to enquire into the Operation of the Poor Laws ... . *Harrisburg.* 1825. 8vo, pp. 30.

Report of the Committee Appointed to Examine into the state of the Bank of Pennsylvania and Philadelphia Bank. ... February 10, 1829. *Harrisburg.* 1829. 8vo, pp. 118. 60492

Report of the Committee appointed to Inquire into the Organization of the Two Bodies Claiming to be the House of Representatives. ... Read in Senate, Dec. 19, 1839. *Harrisburg.* 1838. 8vo, pp. 31. 60493

Report of the Committee Appointed ... to investigate the cause of an Increased Number of Slaves being returned for that

Commonwealth, by the Census of 1830, over that of 1820. ... *Harrisburg.* 1833. 8vo, pp. 7. 60494

Also published in the German language.

Report of the Committee appointed to investigate the Evils of Freemasonry ... . June, 1836. With an Exposure of Odd-Fellowship. *Harrisburg.* 1836. 8vo. B. 60495

Report of the Committee appointed to Investigate the Official Conduct of the Canal Commissioners. ... March 23, 1832, by Mr. Greenough, Chairman. [n. p. n. d.] 8vo, pp. 4. 60496

Report of the Committee appointed to visit and inquire into the Condition ... of the Eastern Penitentiary and the House of Refuge, in ... Philadelphia, and the Moyamensing Prison, Mr. M'Cleland, Chairman. Read in the House ... February 14, 1837. *Harrisburg.* 1837. 8vo, pp. 10. + Read in Senate, February 14, 1837. [n. p. n. d.] 8vo, pp. 6. 60497

Report of the Committee of Conference, to whom was referred An Act to Reduce the State Debt, and to incorporate the Pennsylvania Canal and Railroad Co. ... *Harrisburg.* 1844. 8vo, pp. 16. 60498

Report of the Committee of Elections, to whom was referred ... the Petition of sundry Citizens of the County of Washington, in ... Pennsylvania, complaining of an undue election and return of John Hoge, ... as one of the Representatives ... . [*Washington.* 1804.] 8vo, pp. 5. 60499

Report of the Committee of Inquiry ... . [n. p. 1819.] 8vo, pp. 26. 60500

In regard to the official conduct of Thos. Sergeant, Secretary of the Commonwealth.

Report Of the Committee of Inquiry relative to the Farmers and Mechanics' Bank, &c. &c. Together with a Statement of the Evidence ... . Jan. 18, 1811. [*Harrisburg.* n. d.] 8vo, pp. 24. 60501

Report of the Committee of Senate, relative to Banks in Philadelphia ... . [n. p. 1816.] 8vo, pp. 15. 60502

Report of the Committee of the House ... to whom were referred the Message of the Governor and sundry memorials relating to the abolition of Lotteries. ... *Harrisburg.* 1832. 8vo, pp. 37. 60503

Report of the Committee of the Senate appointed on the Judiciary System. [n. p. 1810?] 8vo, pp. 11. 60504

Report of the Committee of the Senate appointed to inquire into the Extent and Causes of the Present General Distress. [n. p. 1819.] 8vo, pp. 23. 60505

Report of the Committee of the Senate ... relative to Foreign Corporations. *Harrisburg.* 1825. 8vo, pp. 16. 60506

Report of the Committee of the Senate ... upon the ... Coal Trade. S. J. Packer, Chairman. *Harrisburg.* 18—. 8vo, pp. 126. 60507

Report of the Committee of [*sic*] Vice and Immorality of the Senate ... to whom were referred the Message of the Governor and sundry memorials relating to the Abolition of Lotteries. ... *Philadelphia.* 1832. 8vo, pp. 15. 60508

Also: Report of the Committee of Vice and Immorality of the Senate ... in relation to the Manufacture ... of Spirituous Liquors. ... *Harrisburg.* 1855. 8vo, pp. 8.

Report of the Committee of Ways and Means, relative to the Finances of the Commonwealth. ... Read in the House ... March 7, 1827. *Harrisburg.* 1827. 8vo, pp. 7. Continued.

Also: Report of the Committee of Ways and Means, to whom was referred the message from the Governor and memorial from the auctioneers of Philadelphia, on the ... prohibition, by Congress, of Sales at Auction. Read in the House ... Feb. 20, 1824. [n. p. n. d.] 8vo, pp. 4. — Report of the Committee ... on the Currency and Finances of the Commonwealth. ... March 1, 1834. *Harrisburg.* 1834. 8vo, pp. 40, folded leaf. — Report of the Committee ... in relation to the Revenue to be derived from Banks. ... *Harrisburg.* 1835. 8vo, pp. 6. — Report of the Committee ... relative to the Union Canal Lottery, and to prevent the Sale of Foreign Lottery Tickets. ... *Harrisburg.* 1828. 8vo, pp. 7. — Report of the Committee ... upon that part of the Governor's Message which relates to the Surplus Revenue, the State Debt, &c. ... Read in the House ... January 10, 1837. *Harrisburg.* 1837. 8vo, pp. 8. — Report of the Minority of the Committee ... in relation to the Revenue to be derived from Banks. ... *Harrisburg.* 1835. 8vo, pp. 7.

Report of the Committee on Agriculture, ... March 15, 1823. [n. p. n. d.] 8vo, pp. 3. Continued. 60510

Also: Report of the Committee on Agriculture, in the House ... on the Resolution instructing them to inquire into the influence which the encouragement now given to the Manufacturing Interests of the State, has upon the Interests of Agriculture ... . Read Feb. 2, 1833. *Harrisburg.* 1833. 8vo, pp. 24.

Report of the Committee on Banks, in the House ... in pursuance of a resolution instructing them to present ... a detailed report on the Currency of Pennsylvania ... . *Harrisburg.* 1833. 8vo, pp. 14. 60511

The same in German, *Harrisburg.* 1833. 8vo, pp. 15. Also: Report of the Committee on Banks, to whom was referred the Bill from the House ... entitled "An Act for the better regulation of the several Banking and Savings Institutions and Loan Companies, within this Commonwealth." ... Read in Senate, March 18, 1838. *Harrisburg.* 1838. 8vo, pp. 13. — Report of the Committee on Banks of the House ... relative to Banks and Savings Institutions. ... *Harrisburg.* 1856. 8vo, pp. 6. — Report of the Committee on Banks. Read in the House ... January 26, 1824. [n. p. n. d.] 8vo, pp. 4. — Report of the Minority of the Committee on Banks. ... *Harrisburg.* 1838. 8vo, pp. 7.

Report of the Committee on Claims. ... Dec. 12, 1837. *Harrisburg.* 1837. 8vo, pp. 4. 60512

Report of the Committee on Education. ... January 27, 1831. ... *Harrisburg.* 1831. 8vo, pp. 16. 60513

Also: Report of the Committee on Education to the House ... . *Harrisburg.* 1832. 8vo, pp. 6. — Report of the Committee ... on ... Manual Labor Academies ... . Read in the House ... February 21, 1833. *Harrisburg.* 1833. 8vo, pp. 14. — Report of the Committee ... to whom was referred so much of the Governor's Message as relates to the Improvement of the Moral and Intellectual Condition of the Citizens ... . Read in the House ... February 15, 1833. *Harrisburg.* 1833. 8vo, pp. 16. — Report of the Minority of the Committee ... relative to a General System of Education by Common Schools. By Mr. Reigert. *Harrisburg.* 1835. 8vo, pp. 6.

Report of the Committee on Estimates, to the County Board, in relation to the Finances of ... Philadelphia. ... December 23d, 1851. *Philadelphia.* 1852. 8vo, pp. 11. 60514

Report of the Committee on Finance of the Senate, in relation to Public Credit. ... *Harrisburg.* 1841. 8vo, pp. 7.

Report of the Committee on Inland Navigation, relative to a Water Communication between the Eastern and Western Waters. ... Feb. 28, 1825. ... *Harrisburg.* [n. d.] 8vo, pp. 7.

Also: Report of the Committee on Inland Navigation and Internal Improvement, relative to the further extension of the Pennsylvania Canal ... . Mr. Lehman, Chairman. Read in the House ... February 28, 1827. *Harrisburg.* 1827. 8vo, pp. 18. + [*Ibid.*] 1827. 8vo, pp. 8. — Report of the Committee ... relative to the Danville and Pottsville Rail-Road. By Mr. Keating. Read in the House ... Jan. 29, 1834. *Harrisburg.* 1834. 8vo, pp. 6. — Report of the Committee ... relative to the use of the Railways of the Commonwealth. *Harrisburg.* 1835. 8vo, pp. 20. — Report of the Committee ... relative to the Susquehanna Canal Company. Mr. Reed, Chairman. Read in the House ... February 3, 1836. *Harrisburg.* 1836. 8vo, pp. 9. — Report of the Committee on Inland Navigation, relative to an Aqueduct over the Delaware River, together with the Amendment of Mr. Porter. *Harrisburg.* 1850. 8vo, pp. 9. — Report of the Committee ... . Read in the House, March 15, 1825. [n. p. n. d.] 8vo, pp. 3. — Report of the Minority of the Committee ... . Mr. Baily, Chairman. Read in the House ... March 17, 1840. *Harrisburg.* 1840. 8vo, pp. 8.

Report of the Committee on Internal Improvement relative to the Extension of the Pennsylvania Canal, and the Construc-

tion of a Rail Road. ... Feb. 4, 1828. *Harrisburg.* 1828. 8vo, pp. 7. 60517

Also: Report of the Committee on Internal Improvement and Inland Navigation. Read in the House ... January 11, 1831. Mr. Ingersoll, Chairman. *Harrisburg.* 1831. 8vo, pp. 16.

Report of the Committee on Public Schools to the Pennsylvania Society for the Promotion of Public Economy. ... *Philadelphia.* 1817. 8vo, pp. 13. 60518

Report of the Committee on Revenue Bills, relative to repealing the Tax on Dealers in Foreign Merchandise. ... Read in Senate, March 1, 1837. *Harrisburg.* 1837. 8vo, pp. 7.

Also: Report of the Committee on Revenue Bills, relative to the State Loan, ... [and] A Message from the Governor ... . Mr. A. Miller, Chairman. Read ... March 12, 1839. *Harrisburg.* 1839. 8vo, pp. 13.

Report of the Committee on Roads and Inland Navigation. Read in the House ... January 20, 1823. [n. p. n. d.] 8vo, pp. 8. 60520

Report of the Committee on Roads, Bridges and Inland Navigation, on granting the Baltimore and Susquehanna Rail Road Company the privilege of extending their rail road into Pennsylvania. ... January 17, 1829. *Harrisburg.* 1829. 8vo, pp. 11.

Report of the Committee on the Coal Lands. *See* [Cobb (M. G.)], Vol. IV., No. 13851.

Report of the Committee on the Judiciary relative to the Abolition of Slavery in the District of Columbia and in relation to the Colored Population of this Country. ... June 24, 1839. *Harrisburg.* 1839. 12mo, pp. 14. 60522

Also: Report of the Committee on the Judiciary (General) of the Senate ... relative to Alleged Extortionate Charges by the Railroad Companies ... . *Harrisburg.* 1868. 8vo, pp. 16, 241.

Report of the Committee on the Judiciary System, relative to an Over-issue of Relief Notes by the Berks County Bank ... . *Harrisburg.* 1844. 8vo, pp. 12. 60523

Also: Report of the Committee on the Judiciary System, relative to the Penal Code and Penitentiary Discipline. Read ... January 15, 1829. [n. p. n. d.] 8vo, 1 leaf. — Report of the Majority of the Committee ... relative to ... An Act to provide for the more effectual punishment and prevention of crimes heretofore punishable with death. And the Report of the Minority ... on the said Bill. ... *Harrisburg.* 1842. 8vo, pp. 8. — Report of the Minority of the Committee ... on the resolution to inquire into the expediency of providing by law to supply an alleged vacancy in the Convention to alter and reform the State Constitution, occasioned by the death of Dan Caldwell ... . *Harrisburg.* 1837. 8vc, pp. 14.

Report of the Committee on the Militia System, relative to Military Disbursements and Collections, and against the Abolition of the Militia Law. ... *Harrisburg.* 1844. 8vo, pp. 7.

Report of the Committee on Vice and Immorality, relative to the appointment of a Moral Instructor in the Eastern Penitentiary. *Harrisburg.* 1839. 8vo. 60525

Also: Report of the Committee on Vice and Immorality, relative to Intemperance. ... April 11, 1829. [n. p. n. d.] 8vo, pp. 3.

Report of the Committee relative to the subject of a Board of Commissioners for the purpose of Improving the State. Read in the House ... December 19, 1828. [n. p. n. d.] 8vo, pp. 8.

Report of the Committee to whom was referred the subject of the Juniata and Conemaugh Canal. ... Feb. 10, 1824. ... [n. p.] 1824. 8vo, pp. 13. 60527

Report of the Committee to whom were referred the Message of the Governor, and Documents, relative to the Delaware River ... . *Harrisburg.* 1835. 8vo, pp. 14. 60528

Report of the Discussion at Pottsville, August 10, 1844. Between J. G. Clarkson and F. W. Hughes, on the course of Henry Clay and James K. Polk, Relative to the Protective System, &c. ... *Philadelphia.* 1844. 8vo, pp. 27. 60529

Report of the Grand Committee appointed to investigate the present System of Internal Improvement ... and a Supplementary Report from a Minority of the Committee. ... April 5, 1833. *Harrisburg.* 1833. 8vo, pp. 12. 60530

Report of the Joint Committee of Investigation, appointed by the Legislature ... to investigate whether corrupt means had been used to procure legislation favorable to the Banks from 1836 to 1841. ... July 12, 1842. *Harrisburg: Boas and Patterson.* 1842. 8vo, pp. 319, iii. 60531

See "A Full and Correct Report," No. 60111, *supra.*

Report of the Joint Committee of the Legislature ... relative to the Eastern State Penitentiary, at Philadelphia. By Mr. Penrose of Cumberland. ... March 26, 1835. *Harrisburg.* 1835. 8vo, pp. 64. 60532

Report of the Joint Committee of the Senate and House ... on the publication of the Geological Survey. [n. p. 1852?] 8vo, pp. 16. 60533

Report of the Joint Committee of the Senate and House ... to which was referred so much of the Governor's Message, as relates to the Election of State Printers. ... *Harrisburg.* 1844. 8vo, pp. 64. 60534

Report of the Joint Committee of the two Houses of the ... Legislature, on the ... System of General Education: Together with the bill ... and an appendix ... . *Harrisburg.* 1834. 8vo, pp. 52. 60535

Report of the Joint Committee Relative to Frauds upon Volunteers as made to the Legislature ... April 20, 1864. *Harrisburg.* 1864. 8vo, pp. 47. 60536

Report of the Judges of the Supreme Court of ... Pennsylvania, made [to the] Legislature ... . Passed ... 1807–8. ... *Philadelphia.* 1808. 8vo, pp. 38. 60537

Also: Report of the Judges ... of the English Statutes ... in force in ... Pennsylvania, and of those ... which ... ought to be incorporated into the Statute Law of the ... Commonwealth. *Lancaster.* 1809. 8vo, pp. 28.

Report of the Judiciary Committee of the Senate, in relation to Certain Moneys ... drawn ... by the Governor without authority. *Harrisburg.* 1841. 8vo, pp. 28. 60538

Report of the Majority and Minority of the Select Committee of the Senate ... on the ... Tariff. ... *Harrisburg.* 1844. 8vo, pp. 13. 60539

Report of the Minority of the Committee to whom was Referred the Petition of Andrew Miller and others, praying that Articles of Impeachment may be preferred against David R. Porter, Governor of Pennsylvania, for certain High Crimes and Misdemeanors ... . Read in the House ... March 2, 1843. *Harrisburg.* 1843. 8vo, pp. 15. 60540

Report of the Normal School Committee on Abolishing the Pledge to teach in the Common Schools of Pennsylvania. *Philadelphia.* 1855. 8vo, pp. 16. 60541

Report of the Proceedings upon the late Project of Democratic Union. *Philadelphia.* 1816. 8vo, pp. 12. 60542

Report of the Select Committee appointed to confer with the Authorities of the State of New York, relative to a connection of the Public Works of New York and Pennsylvania. ... May 15, 1839. *Harrisburg.* 1839. 8vo, pp. 15. 60543

Report of the Select Committee, ... to examine the Condition of the Public Schools of the First School District of Pennsylvania. ... *Harrisburg.* 1838. 8vo. 60544

Report of the Select Committee ... to inquire into the authorship of a Speech, purporting to have been delivered [in] Senate by Thomas C. Miller, a Senator from Adams County; ... June 3, 1839. *Harrisburg.* 1839. 8vo, pp. 31. 60545

Report of the Select Committee ... to inquire into the Cause of an Armed Force, being brought to the Capitol of Pennsylvania, whether any disturbance took place in the Senate Chamber on the 4th December, 1838, &c. ... Mr. Barclay, Chairman. ... June 24, 1839. *Harrisburg: Printed by E. Guyer.* 1839. 8vo, pp. 247. 60546

Known as the "Buck-Shot War."

Report of the Select Committee ... to Investigate the Expenditures upon the Canals and Railroads ... . April 16, 1841. *Harrisburg: James S. Wallace.* 1841. 8vo, pp. 200. 3 folded leaves.

Report of the Select Committee ... to investigate the Management on the Columbia and Philadelphia Railroad ... . March 28, 1840. *Harrisburg.* 1840. 8vo, pp. 140. 60548

Report of the Select Committee ... to visit the Pennsylvania Institution for the Deaf and Dumb ... . *Harrisburg.* 1838. 8vo, pp. 5. 60549

Report of the Select Committee [of the Senate] in relation to the Colonial Records. [n. p. 1851.] 8vo, pp. 8. + [Of the House. n. p. 1851.] 8vo, pp. 4. 60550

Report of the Select Committee in relation to the Sunbury and Erie Railroad. [n. p. 1851.] 8vo, pp. 15. 60551

Report of the Select Committee, made in the Senate ... upon the Admission of Kansas, February 24, 1858. [n. p. n. d.] 8vo. 60552

Report of the Select Committee of the House ... on the ... alleged frauds in the Election of United States Senator. *Harrisburg.* 1863. 8vo, pp. 72, 4. 60553

Report of the Select Committee of the House ... relative to the Exemption of certain Persons from ... Military Duty. *Harrisburg.* 1850. 8vo. 60554

Report of the Select Committee of the Senate ... upon the Condition of the Several Institutions Receiving Aid from the Commonwealth. *Harrisburg.* 1864. 8vo, pp. 92, (1). 60555

Report of the Select Committee of the Senate ... in relation to the Bridge across the Ohio River at Wheeling, Virginia, *Harrisburg.* 1850. 8vo, pp. 10. 60556

Report of the Select Committee relative to an Extravagant Expenditure of Public Money on the Delaware Division ... . April 12, 1843. *Harrisburg.* 1843. 8vo, pp. 40. 60557

Report of the Select Committee relative to Frauds upon the Soldiers, the People and Government. *Harrisburg.* 18—. 8vo, pp. 44. 60558

See also Gettysburg, Vol. VII., Nos. 27246–7.

Report of the Senate Committee Relative to the Call of a National Convention to consider Amendments to the Constitution of the United States. *Harrisburg.* 1863. 8vo, pp. 8.

Report of the Senate Commttee relative to the Immigration of Blacks and Mulattoes into ... Pennsylvania. [n. p. 1863.] 8vo, pp. (2), 4. 60560

Report of William E. Morris, Civil Engineer, to Judge Burnside and Others, of the survey for a rail road by the Valley of the Bald Eagle; ... *Philadelphia.* 1839. 8vo, pp. 8. Map.

Report on Liens of the Commonwealth upon the Lands of John Nicholson and Peter Baynton; made by Jos. B. Anthony, Commissioner. *Harrisburg.* 1839. 8vo, pp. 56. M. 60562

Report on Limited Partnerships, ... December 21, 1824. ... *Harrisburg.* 1824. 8vo, pp. 8. 60563

Report on Roads, Bridges and Canals, ... March, 23, 1822. [n. p. 1822.] 8vo, pp. 18. 3 folded leaves. 60564

See also "Documents," No. 60071, *supra.*

Fourth Report on the Common Schools ... . *Harrisburg.* 1838. 8vo, pp. 100. 33 folded leaves. + [Another Edition. *Ibid.*] 8vo, pp. 96. 30 folded leaves. 60565

The next report was entitled: "Report of the Superintendent of Common Schools," and so continued to 1875, thence "Report of Superintendent of Public Instruction."

Report on the continuation of the Little Schuylkill Rail Road, from Port Clinton to Reading, as surveyed by Moncure Robinson, Engineer. *Philadelphia.* 1834. 8vo, pp. 10. 60566

Report on the Governor's Message. *See* Vol. XIII. 57236, *note*

Report on the Penitentiary System. [n. p. 1821.] 8vo, pp. 12

Report on the Proposed Railroads from Phœnixville to Cornwall, and from Cornwall to Pinegrove, by W. H. Wilson ... . *Philadelphia.* 1852. 8vo, pp. 16, (3). Map. 60567

Report on ... Education, Read in the Senate ... March 1, 1822. ... *Harrisburg.* 1822. 8vo, pp. 24. 60568

Report on the Surveys, ... of a Rail Road, from the Coal and Iron Mines near Blossburg or Peters's Camp to the State Line at Lawrenceville, ... and Mineralogical Report on the Coal Region ... of Blossburg. By Richard C. Taylor, Engineer. *Philadelphia.* 1833. 8vo, pp. 56. 2 Maps. 60569

Report relative to Frauds at Elections, in certain Counties of ... Pennsylvania, as made by a Select Committee of the House ... March 13, 1865. *Harrisburg.* 1865. 8vo, pp. 191.

Report relative to the Rail Road Line, from the west end of the Harrisburg bridge, ... to the Borough of York. By W. R. Hopkins, Engineer. ... January 19, 1829. *Harrisburg.* 1829. 8vo, pp. 16. 60571

Report to the Canal Commissioners, in Reply to Strictures passed by Mr. Robinson, on the Views entertained by Lieut. Col. Long in relation to the manner of crossing the Allegheny mountain ... . By S. H. Long ... . *Philadelphia.* 1831. 8vo, pp. 12.

Report to the House ... on the Seventh Day Baptists. *Harrisburg.* 1850. 8vo. 60573

Report upon ... Nullification, in the Senate ... by Mr. Miller. ... December 17, 1832. *Harrisburg.* 1833. 8vo, pp. 8.

Reports and Bills of the Select Committee of the Senate, relative to the Sale of the Public Works of Pennsylvania. ... February 4, 1854. ... *Harrisburg.* 1854. 8vo, pp. 18. 60575

Reports of Sundry Commissioners appointed to view and explore the Rivers Susquehanna and Juniata; ... &c. *Philadelphia: Printed by Francis Bailey.* MDCCXCI. 8vo, pp. 27. 60576

Reports of the Heads of Departments, ... to the Governor in pursuance of law, for ... 1844. *Harrisburg.* 1845. 8vo.

Made up of the reports of the various state officers, and paged separately. Continued to 1873.

Reports of the Majority and Minority of the Select Committee relative to the Estates of J. Nicholson, read in the House ... March 21, 1842. *Harrisburg.* 1842. 8vo. 60578

A Representation on behalf of the People called Quakers, to the President and Executive Council, and the General Assembly of Pennsylvania, &c. *London: Reprinted by James Phillips.* M.DCC.LXXXII. 12mo, pp. 15. + *York: Reprinted by Walker and Pennington.* M.DCC.LXXXII. 12mo, pp. 12. 60579

Representation to the President and Executive Council and General Assembly of Pennsylvania, 1781. *Providence.* [n. d.] 4to, pp. 8. M. 60580

Republican Convention. Carlisle, March 4, 1817. [n. p. n. d.] 8vo, pp. 19. 60581

The Resolution of the High Court of Errors and Appeals for the State of Pennsylvania in the cause of Silas Talbot, quitam, &c. Against the Commanders and Owners of the Brigs Achilles, Patty and Hibernia, January 14, 1785. *Philadelphia: T. Bradford.* MDCCLXXXV. 8vo, pp. viii, 16. 60582

This cause was of great consequence, not only on account of the property depending on its decision, but because the following questions were determined upon solemn argument. First, that the owners of letters of marque are responsible for injuries committed on the high seas, by the commanders of vessels sent out by them. Secondly, that in cases of capture from enemies, persons in other vessels acquire no rights, merely by seeing the capture made. Thirdly, that the judge of admiralty may legally take cognizance in similar cases, and that the appeal in such cases to a higher court is irregular.

Resolution relative to an Amendment of the Constitution [of Pennsylvania. n. p. 1849.] Folio, 3 leaves. 60583

Resolutions in the Senate on ... calling a Convention to alter and amend certain parts of the Constitution of the Commonwealth. *Harrisburg.* 1812. 8vo. 60584

Resolutions of the Union Republican State Convention ... Williamsport, June 26, 1867: ... [n. p. n. d.] 8vo, pp. 16.

Resolutions relative to National Affairs. [n. p. 1861.] 8vo, pp. 56. 60586

Returns of the several Banks and Savings Institutions of Pennsylvania, ... 1855. *Harrisburg.* 1855. 8vo, pp. 185. Cont'd.

Report of the REVENUE COMMISSIONERS, ... to the Governor ... in pursuance of an Act of the 29th ... April, 1844. ... *Harrisburg.* 1845. 8vo, pp. 30. Continued. 60588

Review of the Opinions of the Three Judges of the Supreme Court of Pennsylvania, affirming the Validity of Acts of Assembly authorizing Subscriptions by Municipal Corporations to the Stock of Rail Road Companies. By a Member of the Bar. *Pittsburgh.* 1857. 8vo, pp. (2), iv, 76. 60589

A Review of the Question of the Outlet Lock at Black's Eddy. 1840. [n. p. n. d.] 8vo, pp. 12. Map. 60590

A Revisal of the Intreagues of the Triumvirate, with the rest of the Trustees of the Proprietor of Pennsilvania. And also, Of a Warning To the Inhabitants of the said Province against the Guiles of the Devil and Man. [*Philadelphia: S. Keimer.* 1729.] Folio, pp. 4. 60591

Revised Report made to the Legislature ... relative to the Soldiers' National Cemetery at Gettysburg, embracing an Account of the Origin of the Undertaking; Address of Hon. E. Everett, with the Dedicatory Speech of President Lincoln, and Major-General O. O. Howard, ... July 4, 1866, upon the Dedication of the Monument. *Harrisburg.* 1866. 8vo, pp. 282. Plate and 2 Maps. BA., C. 60592

See also Gettysburg, Vol. VII., No. 27247.

A Riddle. [n. p. 1770.] 4to, 1 leaf. 60593

An election squib, signed "A Whiteoak."

Robbery of the Bank of Pennsylvania in 1798. *See* Lyon (P.)

The Royal Pennsylvania Gazette. Published by James Robertson ... . Philadelphia, Tuesday, March 3, 1778. Number 1. Folio, pp. (4). 60594

Continued twice a week during the British occupation. The last issue was No. XXV, on May 26, 1778.

Rules and Decisions of the General Assembly. Legislative Directory. Together with useful Political Statistics. List of Post Offices, County Officers, etc. by John A. Smull. *Harrisburg.* 1869. 18mo. + [*Ibid.*] 1870. 18mo, pp. (2), 491. Plate and 2 Maps. C. 60595

Rules and Orders for regulating the Practice of the Supreme Court of Pennsylvania. *Philadelphia.* 1787. Sm. 4to.

Rules and Orders for regulating the Practice of the Supreme Court of Pennsylvania, the Circuit Court of the United States for ... Pennsylvania, and the Court of Common Pleas of Phila-

delphia County. *Philadelphia: Printed for T. De Silver.* 1810. 12mo, pp. 58. 60597

Rules for establishing Rank of Precedence amongst the Pennsylvania Associators. ... [*Philadelphia.* 1775.] 8vo, pp. 12, and folded sheet of signals. P. 60598

Rules of Discipline and Christian Advices of the Yearly Meeting of Friends for Pennsylvania, and New Jersey. *Philadelphia.* 1797. 4to, pp. 72. 60599

Rules of Discipline of the Yearly Meeting of Friends, for Pennsylvania, New-Jersey, Delaware, and the Eastern Parts of Maryland: ... 1834. *Philadelphia.* 1834. 8vo, pp. 191. H.

Rules of Equity Practice adopted by the Supreme Court of Pennsylvania, May 27th, 1865, with the Report of the Commissioners. *Philadelphia.* 1867. 8vo, pp. 51. 60601

The Saddle placed on the Right Horse; or a Candid Statement of Facts, showing the cause of, and the Persons who originated the State Tax. Addressed to the People of Pennsylvania. [n. p. 1832?] 8vo, pp. 10. 60602

The School Fund. [n. p. 1854.] 8vo, pp. 8. 60603

Address of the Philadelphia Democratic Committee.

School Laws; with Decisions of the Superintendent. *Harrisburg.* 1853. 8vo. 60604

The Scribler, Being a Letter from a Gentleman in Town To his Friend in the Country, concerning the State of Public Affairs; with a Lapidary Character. ... [*Philadelphia:*] *Printed in the Year* MDCC,LXIV. Sm. 8vo, pp. 24. P. 60605

A Seasonable Advice to the Inhabitants of the Province of Pennsylvania against the Guiles of the Devil and Man. [n. p. 1729.] Folio, pp. 3. 60606

A Second Appeal to the People of Pennsylvania on the ... Asylum for the Insane Poor ... . *Philadelphia.* 1840. 8vo, pp. 35

Second Report of Charles L. Schlatter, Principal Engineer ... of the State ... to the Canal Commissioners, relative to the continuous Railroad from Harrisburg to Pittsburg. ... *Harrisburg.* 1841. 8vo, pp. 60. Map. + Third Report ... . [*Ibid.*] 1842. 8vo, pp. 148. 2 Maps. 60608

Letter from the SECRETARY OF THE COMMONWEALTH of Pennsylvania [A. J. Dallas], by Direction of the Governor, relative to the late malignant fever; and report of the ... Managers of the Marine and City Hospitals, in reply. *Philadelphia: Printed by Thomas and Samuel F. Bradford.* 1798. 12mo, pp. 16.

Also: Communication from the Secretary of the Commonwealth in relation to Census. [*Harrisburg.* 1852.] 8vo, pp. 4.—Communication from the Secretary ... relative to Educating Poor Children, within the Commonwealth. ... *Harrisburg.* 1833. 8vo, pp. 11, folded leaf.—Letter from the Secretary ... and Auditor General, accompanied with a Report on the Expenses of General Education, ... for 1835. Read ... June ... 22, 1837. *Harrisburg.* 1837. 8vo, pp. 23.—Letter from the Secretary ... to the Legislature ... accompanying the report of the Susquehanna Commissioners ... . *Harrisburg.* 1824. 8vo, pp. 8.—Letter from the Secretary ... relative to the Justices of the Peace and Aldermen, in Pennsylvania. ... *Harrisburg.* 1837. 8vo, pp. 102, folded leaf.—Letter from the Secretary ... with ... the number of Institutions for Banking, and for other purposes, incorporated ... since 1776 ... . *Harrisburg.* 1837. 8vo, pp. 160, 5 folded leaves.—Report of the Secretary ... of "The names of all persons holding office under this Commonwealth ... . *Harrisburg.* 1817. 8vo, pp. 69.—Report of the Secretary ... relative to the County Prisons of the State, 1830. *Harrisburg.* 1830. 8vo.—Report of the Secretary ... relative to the publication of the Colonial Records. ... *Harrisburg.* 1838. 8vo, pp. 12.—Report of the Secretary ... and Superintendent of Common Schools. ... March 3, 1835. *Harrisburg.* 1834–35. 8vo, pp. 8.

A Serious Address to the Freeholders and other Inhabitants, of the Province of Pennsylvania. *New-York: Printed in the Year,* M,DCC,LVIII. 8vo, pp. 16. P. 60610

Signed "Philo-Pennsylvania," and dated "Phil. 10 Sept. 1758."

Session of 1863. Pennsylvania Legislature. Names of the Senate and House ... with their Post-Offices. *Harrisburg.* 1863. 12mo, pp. (11). Continued. 60611

The Several Acts of Assembly providing for the Education of Children at Public Expense within ... Philadelphia. *Philadelphia.* 1821. 12mo, pp. 24. + 1825. 12mo, pp. 24. + 1827. 8vo, pp. 40. + 1831. 12mo, pp. 40. 60612

Several Conferences between some ... People. *See* [Pemberton (Israel)], No. 59612.

Sir, In the present state. *See* [Mifflin (Thos.)], XII. 48895.

A Sketch of the further Proceedings of the Committees appointed by the Yearly Meetings of Friends of Pennsylvania, &c. and Maryland, for Promoting the Improvement and Gradual Civilization of the Indian Natives in some parts of North America. *London: W. Phillips.* 1812. 8vo. 60613

A Sketch of the Origin and Progress of the Institutions for the Instruction of the Deaf and Dumb in Pennsylvania. ... [n. p. 1825?] 8vo, pp. 23. 60614

Sketches from the History of Pennsylvania ... intended for the Information of that numerous Class of Christians who denounce War in general as a great evil; but who consider Defensive War as allowable and unavoidable. *London.* 1845. 8vo, pp. 34.

Report of the Committee appointed to examine into the Rise, Progress, and Present State of the SOCIETY OF ARTISTS of the United States. ... *Philadelphia: James W. Palmer.* 1812. 12mo, pp. 24. 60616

Also: Second Annual Exhibition of the Society of Artists of the United States, and the Pennsylvania Academy. 1812. *Philadelphia.* [n. d.] 8vo, pp. 30. + Third ... Exhibition ... . 1813.

Resolutions of the SOCIETY OF PAPER MAKERS ... of Pennsylvania and Delaware, in regard to "want of care in sending papers to market." [n. p. 1816.] 8vo, pp. 3. 60617

The First Report of the ... Trustees of the SOCIETY OF THE PROTESTANT EPISCOPAL CHURCH, for the Advancement of Christianity in Pennsylvania. ... Constitution ... and List of ... Members. *Philadelphia.* 1813. 8vo, pp. 27. P. 60618

Afterward styled "Society for the Advancement of Christianity."

Soldiers Read!! Citizens Read!!! Address of the Democratic State Central Committee, September 19, 1863. Letter of Maj. Geo. A. Woodward. Letter of Judge Woodward. *Philadelphia.* 1863. 8vo, pp. 8. 60619

Catalogue of Oil Paintings on Exhibition ... for the Benefit of the SOLDIERS' AND SAILORS' HOME ... . *Philadelphia.* 1865. 8vo, pp. 6. 60620

Some Account of the Province of Pennsilvania. *See* [Penn (W.)], No. 59733.

Some | Letters | and an | Abstract of Letters | from | Pennsylvania, | Concerning | The State and Improvement of that | Province. | Published to prevent Mis-Reports. | [*London:*] *Printed, and Sola by Andrew Sowe* [*sic*] ... . 1691. Sm. 4to, pp. 12. 60621

Some necessary Precautions, worthy to be considered by all English Subjects, in their Election of Members, to Represent them in General Assembly; wherein, neither Fear, Flatery [*sic*], nor Gain, ought to byass. [n. p. n. d.] Folio, 1 leaf. 60622

Some Objections to a Joint Resolution ... of the Legislature, ... recommending to the People of Pennsylvania an Elective Judiciary. [n. p.] *December*, 1849. 8vo, pp. 61. 60623

Some Proposals for a Second Settlement. *See* [Penn (W.)]

Some Remedies Proposed. *See* [Rawle (Francis)].

Some Transactions between the Indians and Friends in Pennsylvania, in 1791–2. *London.* 1792. 8vo. 60624

Special Message. *See* Curtin (A. G.), Vol. v., No. 18019.

The Speech Delivered from the Bench in the Court of Common Pleas held for the City and County of Philadelphia, the 11 Day of September, 1727. [n. p. 1727.] Folio, pp. 3, (1).

An attack, by Judge Isaac Norris, on the proceedings of Sir William Keith. In some copies the fourth page is headed "A Supplement," and in others "Some Remarks on a Paper directed to all True Patriots." A defense by Sir Wm. Keith is entitled: "A Modest Reply to the Speech of Isaac Norris, Esq; delivered from the Bench, in the Court of Common Pleas, ... Philadelphia, the 11th Day of September, 1727. And afterwards Printed. [n. p. 1727.] Folio, pp. 4.

The Speech of Sir Wm. Keith, Bart. ... To the ... Assembly ... January 5, 1724–5. *Philadelphia: Printed ... by Andrew Bradford.* MDCCXXV. Folio, 1 leaf. 60626

The Speech of ... Patrick Gordon, Esq. Lieutenant-Governour of the Province of Pennsylvania, To the Representatives ... August 2d. 1726. [And their Reply.] *Philadelphia: Andrew Bradford.* [1726.] Folio, pp. 4. + November 22d. 1726. [*Ibid.* 1726.] Folio, pp. 4. + December 17th. 1728. [*Ibid.* 1728.] Folio, pp. (4). + April 2, 1729. [*Ibid.*] 1729. Folio, 1 leaf.

The Speech of ... George Thomas, Esq; Lieutenant Governor of the Province of Pennsylvania, and Counties ... on Delaware. To the Representatives of the Freemen of the said Province, in General Assembly met. *Philadelphia: Printed ... by B. Franklin* ... M,DCC,XXXVIII. Folio, pp. (3). 60628

The Speech, of the Speaker of the House of Commons upon Presenting the Money Bills to His Majesty, April 29, 1740. In Assembly, the 9th. of the 6th Month, 1740. [Resolution of the Pennsylvania Assembly granting £3000 to the King's use, under great restrictions. *Philadelphia: B. Franklin.* 1740.] Folio, pp. (3). 60629

The Speech and Resolutions are printed in parallel columns, and at the end are some lines on "The Contract."

Report of the STATE HISTORIAN, appointed "To prepare a Military History of the Organization of Pennsylvania Volunteers and Militia" ... . [*Harrisburg.* 1867.] 8vo, pp. 7. + [*Ibid.* 1869.] 8vo, pp. 11. 60630

Report of the Commissioners of the STATE HOSPITAL for the Insane, Danville, Penn'a, for ... 1868. ... *Harrisburg, Pa.* [n. d.] 8vo, pp. 11. Continued. 60631

Report of the STATE LIBRARIAN ... for ... 1854. *Harrisburg.* 1855. 8vo, pp. 45. Continued. 60632

First Annual Report of the ... Trustees of the STATE LUNATIC HOSPITAL ... January 14, 1852. *Harrisburg.* 1852. 8vo, pp. 24. Continued. 60633

Also: Annual Report ... of the State Lunatic Hospital .... *Harrisburg.* 1867. 8vo, pp. 32. Continued.

State of Pennsylvania. Important General Laws, passed ... 1864. Embracing the Revenue, Militia, Appropriation and Apportionment Acts. [n. p. n. d.] 8vo, pp. 52. 60634

State of the Accounts of John Nixon, Esquire, from ... 1775, till ... 1776, as Treasurer of the Committee of Safety, State of Pennsylvania. *Philadelphia: Printed by Robert Aitken.* M.DCC.LXXXVI. 8vo, pp. 56. P. 60635

State of the Accounts of William Webb, Esquire, Paymaster of late Navy Board of Pennsylvania, from March to September, 1777. *Philadelphia: Printed by Robert Aitken.* M.DCC.LXXXVI. 8vo, pp. 36. P. 60636

State of the Accounts of the Treasury of Pennsylvania, from the 1st of October 1782, to the 1st of January 1785. Likewise the Accounts of the several Counties for their Taxes ... . View of the Balances due from the Counties ... first of January 1785, ... *Philadelphia: Printed by Robert Aitken.* M.DCC.LXXXV. 8vo, pp. 128. P. 60637

Constitution and By-Laws of the STATE POULTRY SOCIETY ... *Philadelphia.* 1853. 12mo, pp. 12. 60638

Report of the STATE TREASURER, shewing the Receipts and Expenditures at the Treasury of Pennsylvania, ... December, 1823 to ... November, 1824. *Harrisburg.* 1824. 8vo, pp. 479.

Also: Communication from the State Treasurer, showing the Outstanding Temporary Loans, and amount of Money Due by Certain Banks, from January 1, 1854 to January 1, 1855. ... *Harrisburg.* 1855. 8vo, pp. 11.—Report of the State Treasurer on the Finances ... . December 7, 1832. *Harrisburg.* 1832. 8vo, pp. 22. Continued.—Report ... relative to Banks which have declared dividends since the suspension of specie payments. ... *Harrisburg.* 1840. 8vo, pp. 4.—Report ... relative to Monys [*sic*] Received from the Bank of the United States. ... *Harrisburg.* 1840. 8vo, pp. 4. *See* Receipts and Expenditures, No. 60443, *supra.*

A Statement of Facts relating to the late Democratic Militia Bill. 1848. [n. p. n. d.] 8vo, pp. 14. 60640

Statement of the Amount of Internal Duties, imposed by the United States; (excepting those on household furniture, on watches, and on stamps.) Paid by Each Person in the First Collection District, ... during ... 1817. [n. p. n. d.] 8vo, pp. 17.

A Statement of the Measures contemplated against Samuel Bryan, Esquire, Register-General of ... Pennsylvania, ... the evident motive for them, was his Spirited Prosecution of Francis Johnston, Esquire, late Receiver-General, for great abuses in the said office, ... also a summary account of the late disgraceful fracas by the Friends of Good Order and Regular Government in the Chamber of the House of Representatives. ... *Philadelphia: Printed by Francis and Robert Bailey.* 1800. 8vo, pp. 62.

Improved title of No. 8800, Vol. III.

Constitution and By-Laws of the STATISTICAL SOCIETY of Pennsylvania: with ... Officers and Members. *Philadelphia.* 1847. 12mo, pp. 24. 60643

A Statistical View of the Operation of the Penal Code of Pennsylvania. To which is added, a View of the Present State of the Penitentiary and Prison in ... Philadelphia. ... *Philadelphia.* 1817. 8vo, pp. 14. 60644

Stulta est Clementia. [A reply to the "Confutation of the Reply to the Speech" of Isaac Norris, Sept. 11, 1727.] Folio, pp. 4. 60645

The Substance of a Council Held at Lancaster, August the 28th, 1764. By a Committee of Presbyterian Ministers and Elders deputed from all Parts of Pennsylvania, in order to settle the ensuing Election of Members for the Assembly. Published, at the Request of their respective Congregations. ... *Printed in the Year* MDCCLXIV. Sm. 8vo, pp. 19. 60646

Very scarce. A coarse lampoon on the Presbyterians who sustained the Proprietor in his contest with the popular party in the Assembly. The Moderator, "Mr. J..n E...g" [Ewing], is represented as offering, at the end of the Council, a prayer, in which occurs the petition: "Lord! Take the Pistol of thy Vengeance, and the Mortar-Piece of thy Wrath, and pound all our Enemies to Hodge Podge! But for us, thy Children, feed us with the Pruins and Raisins of thy Promises, and give us the Spurs of Confidence, and Boots of Hope," etc. Said to have been written by Franklin.

Motto.

When Gospel Trumpeter surrounded
With long-eared rout to Battle sounded,
And Pulpit Drum ecclesiastic,
Was beat by Fist instead of a Stick
Such Priests deserve to have their A-se Kick'd.

Substitute for the Report of the Committee of the Senate ... on the Memorial of sundry Banks of ... Philadelphia, ... praying for ... the Restoration of the Public Deposits to the United States Bank. ... *Harrisburg.* 1834. 8vo, pp. 11. 60647

[Fifth] Report of the SUPERINTENDENT OF COMMON SCHOOLS, accompanied with Bills relating to the Common School System. ... *Harrisburg.* 1839. 8vo, pp. 61. 60648

See "Report on Common Schools," No. 60565, *supra.* Also: Supplementary Report of the General Superintendent of Common Schools, upon the System of Common School Education. Read in Senate, Feb. 20, 1836. *Harrisburg.* 1835–'36. 8vo, pp. 13, 2 folded leaves.

Annual Report of the SUPERINTENDENT OF SOLDIERS' ORPHANS, made to the Governor ... for ... 1864. [n. p. 1865.] 8vo, pp. 22. Continued. 60649

A Supplement to an Act, Entitled an "Act to Incorporate the District of Spring Garden" ... . Passed ... 1815. *Philadelphia.* 1815. 8vo, pp. 6. 60650

A Supplement to an Act for Amending the several Acts for electing Members of Assembly. [Colophon:] *Printed by Styner and Cist* .... [1777.] 8vo, pp. 8. P. 60651

Supplement to Purdon's Digest of Laws, by F. C. Brightly, 1846–1848. *Philadelphia.* 1848. 8vo. C. 60652

A Supplement to the "Act for Regulating the Militia of Pennsylvania." *Lancaster.* 1778. 8vo. P. 60653

Supreme Court, &c. *See* Vol. IV., No. 15097.

Report of the SURGEON GENERAL ... of Pennsylvania, for ... 1861. *Harrisburg.* 1861. 8vo, pp. 13. Discontinued after 1866. 60654

Report of the SURVEYOR-GENERAL ... on the Surveys of Swamps in Crawford County. *Harrisburg.* 1869. 8vo.

The Swedes Petition to the House of Representatives of the Province of Pennsylvania, The Governor's Letter thereupon to the Commissioners of Property, with their Report in Answer to the same. *Philadelphia: Printed by Andrew Bradford at the Bible, in the Second Street.* MDCCXXII. Folio, pp. 12, (1). 60656

Tabular Statement of the Cost, Revenue and Expenditures, of the several Finished Lines of the Canals and Railroads of the Commonwealth. Prepared by John W. Hammond ... . April 20, 1841. *Harrisburg.* 1841. 8vo, pp. (4), folded leaf.

A Tabular Statement relating to the Tax on Real and Personal Estate, for State Purposes, ... and to the Payments to Common Schools ... . *Harrisburg.* 1846. 8vo, pp. 26. Continued.

A Tabular View of the Financial Affairs of Pennsylvania, from the Commencement of her Public Works to the Present Time: In which are included the Cost, Revenue and Expenditures of the several Lines of Canal and Rail-Roads, &c. ... By J. W. Hammond ... . *Philadelphia: Edward C. Biddle.* 1844. 8vo, pp. 60. 60659

Tagebuch der Convention von dem Staat Pennsylvanien um Verbesserungen vorzuschlagen zu der Constitution. Angefangen und gehalten im Staats Capitol zu Harrisburg, am zweiten May, 1837. *Harrisburg.* 1837–39. 14 vols., 8vo. 60660

Tagebuch des Raths der Censoren, ... den Zenten November, Ein Tausend Sieben Hundert und Drey und Achtzig. ... *Philadelphia: Gedruckt bey Melchior Steiner.* 1784. Folio, pp. 147.

Teucro duce nil desperandum. First Battalion of Pennsylvania Loyalists, Commanded by His Excellency Sir William Howe, K.B. ... [n. p. n. d.] Folio, 1 leaf. P. 60662

A recruiting address, by Lieut.-Col. Allen and Capt. Kearny, October, 1777.

Testimony before the Select Committee to Inquire into the Alleged Frauds in Army Contracts. *Harrisburg.* 1862. 8vo.

The Testimony of Truth. *Philadelphia.* 1830. 12mo, pp. 14

Relates to a quarrel among the Odd Fellows of Pennsylvania.

Testimony taken before the Select Committee appointed to examine into the return of James Hanna, as a Senator from the Second ... District. ... Jan. 26, 1839. *Harrisburg.* 1839. 8vo, pp. 51, 3 folded leaves. 60665

Testimony taken by the Committee appointed by the House of Representatives to Investigate the Evils of Freemasonry. *Harrisburg.* 1836. 8vo, pp. 101. 60666

Der Teutsche Pilgrim: | Mitbringende | Einen Sitten- | Calender, | Auf das Yahr | Nach der ... Geburt unsers | Herrn und Heylandes Jesu Christi | MDCCXXXI. | ... Auf den Pennsylvanischen Meridianum gerichtet, jedoch auch | in denen beyliegenden Orten, ja von Newfoundland an bis Carolina, | ohne mercklichen Unterschied, gar wohl zu gebrauchen. | Zum ersten mahl herauss gegeben. ... *Zu Philadelphia: Gedruckt bey Andreas Bradford.* [n. d.] Sm. 4to. 60667

Continued to 1733 or later.

Things as they have been, are and ought to be. Address'd to the People, upon the ... coming election for Governor ... of Pennsylvania. By One of the People. [n. p.] *August*, 1832. 8vo, pp. 16. 60668

Titles of Acts and Resolutions ... *Harrisburg.* 1865. 8vo.

To all true Patriots and real Lovers of Liberty. [n. p. 1727?] Folio, pp. 3. 60670

To Morris Morris. On the Reasons published for his Conduct in Assembly, in the Year 1728. [*Philadelphia.* 1728.] Folio, pp. 2. 60671

To my Friends. *See* [Veritt (Paul)].

To my respected Friend I[saac] N[orris]. [n. p. 1727.] Folio, pp. 4. 60672

In answer to Norris' speech, No. 60625.

To Robert Jordan, and others the Friends | of the Yearly Meeting for Business, | now conven'd in Philadelphia. [*Philadelphia: B. Franklin.* 1741.] Sm. folio, pp. 4. 60673

James Logan's letter to the Quakers suggesting that they should cease to obstruct the necessary measures for the defense of the Province. Only thirty copies were printed for Logan.

To the Advocates for Ministerial Oppression. [n. p. 1773.] Folio, 1 leaf. 60674

"Clodius" on the tea tax.

To the Citizens of Pennsylvania. [*Philadelphia:*] *Printed by Hall and Sellers.* [1784.] Folio, 1 leaf. 60675

An address, signed by George Grey, Speaker, in behalf of a majority of the Assembly.

To the Citizens of Pennsylvania. [*Pittsburg.* 1808.] Folio.

Federalist election address.

To the Citizens ... of Pennsylvania. [n. p. 1825.] 8vo, pp. 24. 60677

Address on internal improvements.

To the Citizens ... of Pennsylvania. [n. p. 1832.] 8vo, pp. 15. 60678

To the Clergy and Congregations of the Diocese of Pennsylvania. [n. p. 1861.] 8vo, pp. 8. 60679

To the Delegates of the Democratic National Convention ... at Baltimore. [n. p. 1835.] Folio, 1 leaf. 60680

To the Delegates to the Convention of the Democratic Party to assemble at Harrisburg, On June 11th, 1851, for nominating Candidates for the Supreme Court of Pennsylvania. [n. p. n. d.] Folio, pp. (3). 60681

To the Democratic Citizens of Pennsylvania. [n. p. 1844.] 8vo, pp. 8. 60682

A letter in support of the Democratic nominees for President, Vice-President, and Governor. Richard Rush is said to have been the author.

To the Democratic Delegates of Pennsylvania, composing the Convention of the 4th of March, 1835. *Philadelphia.* 1835. 8vo, pp. 33. 60683

To the Democratic Party. *See* [Rush Richard)].

To the Democrats of Pennsylvania. [n. p. 1844.] Folio, 1 l.

Address from the New York Democratic Committee.

To the Electors of Pennsylvania. [n. p. 1799.] 8vo, pp. 8.

Federalist election address.

To the Electors of the Second Congressional District ... of Pennsylvania. [n. p. 1828.] 8vo, pp. 8. 60686

Democratic election address.

To the Electors of ... Pennsylvania. [*Philadelphia.* 1817.] 8vo, pp. 11. 60687

Democratic election circular.

To the Freeholders. *See* [Biddle (J.)], Vol. II., No. 5233.

To the Freeholders and Electors, Of the Province of Pennsylvania. [n. p. 1765.] Folio, 1 leaf. 60688

To the Freeholders and Freemen a Further Information. [n. p. 1727.] Folio, 1 leaf. 60689

To the Freeholders and Freemen, In Pennsylvania. [n. p. n. d.] Folio, 1 leaf. 60690

Address on the tea question, signed "A Countryman," and dated "Chester County, October 14, 1773."

To the Freeholders and other Electors of Assembly-Men, for Pennsylvania. [n. p. n. d.] Folio, 1 leaf. 60691

An anti-proprietary election circular.

To the Free-Holders of the Province of Pennsylvania. [n. p. 1743.] Folio, pp. 4. 60692

Address on the "unhappy differences" concerning the passage of a militia law.

To the Freeholders, to prevent Mistakes. A Short Vindication and Explanation of Part of a late Mysterious printed Sheet, called Advice and Information to the Freeholders and Freemen of the Province of Pennsylvania, but particularly to ... Philadelphia. [n. p. 1727.] Folio, 1 leaf. 60693

To the Freemen of Pennsylvania. [n. p. 1764.] Folio, 1 l.

Against the newly passed militia law.

To the Freemen of Pennsylvania. [n. p. 1772.] Folio, 1 l.

In regard to a proposed extension of the excise laws, signed "Civis." Attributed to Thos. Mifflin.

To the Freemen of Pennsylvania. [n. p. 1772.] Folio, 1 l.

Addressed to Thos. Mifflin. Signed "A. P," and opposes the proposed excise laws.

To the Freemen of Pennsylvania. [n. p. n. d.] Folio, 1 l.

Philadelphia, about Dec. 1, 1773. Signed "Regulus," and denounces the tea tax.

To the Freemen of Pennsylvania. [n. p. 1784.] Folio, pp. 12. 60698

Reasons for dissent of a minority of the council of censors, on a resolution to print the report of a committee appointed to inquire into the conduct of the legislature.

To the Friends of Home Industry. Pennsylvanians, Read, and Assert your own Dignity. [n. p. 1844.] 8vo, pp. 4.

Relates to the tariff and political issues of the time.

To the Good People of Pennsylvania. ... [n. p. n. d.] Folio, pp. 3. 60700

Signed "Publicus," and dated January 5, 1773. In defense of the new excise bill.

To the Honourable Patrick Gordon, Esq; Lieutenant Governor of the Province of Pennsylvania. The Representation of the Assembly of the said Province. *Philadelphia: Printed ... by Andrew Bradford ...* . [1725.] Folio, pp. 10. 60701

To the Honourable the Legislature of ... Pennsylvania: The Petition and Remonstrance ... . [n. p. 1812?] 8vo, pp. 8.

Against an act explanatory of an act for the sale of vacant lands.

To the honourable the Senate and House of Representatives ... of Pennsylvania ... . [n. p. 1811.] 8vo, pp. 35, folded leaf.

The memorial of the Holland Company in regard to their western lands.

To the Honorable the Senate and House of Representatives ... in Congress assembled, The Memorial and Remonstrance of the Public Creditors, who are Citizens of ... Pennsylvania, by their Committee duly appointed, instructed and authorized. [n. p. n. d.] 12mo, pp. 28. s. 60704

To the Independent Electors of Pennsylvania. [n. p. n. d.] 8vo, pp. 11. 60705

Signed "An American."

To the Inhabitants of Pennsylvania. [n. p. 1782.] 4to, pp. 7. 60706

"A Freeholder" on the approaching election.

To the Inhabitants of the Province of Pennsylvania. [n. p. 1748.] Folio, 1 leaf. 60707

In support of the association for the defense of the Province, signed Ebenezer Durham.

To the Merchants and other Inhabitants of Pennsylvania. ... [n. p. n. d.] Folio, 1 leaf. 60708

"A Friend to Trade" advocates a canal from Delaware to Chesapeake bays, etc., dated Philadelphia, Dec. 13, 1771.

To the Militia of Pennsylvania. ... [n. p. n. d.] Folio, 1 l.

Signed "Nestor," and addressed to the Whig militia, persuading them that they are fighting for a few interested schemers. That they are causelessly robbing their fellow-countrymen. That if taken they will be treated not as prisoners of war but as marauders, that consequently they should quit the service and trust to the clemency of the British commanders. Printed by J. Humphreys, Philadelphia, April, 1778.

To the People of Pennsylvania. [n. p. 1844.] Folio, 1 leaf.

Relates to Gov. Schunk's participation in a Catholic procession.

To the People of Pennsylvania, and to the Legislature now in Session. [n. p. 1863.] 8vo, pp. 8. 60711

"Reasons" against the election of F. W. Hughes to the U. S. Senate.

To the People. *See* [Dewees (J.)], Vol. v., No. 19841, *note.*

... To the President and Executive Council, the General Assembly of Pennsylvania, and others whom it may concern: The following Representation on Behalf of the ... Quakers. [n. p. 1781.] Folio, pp. 3. + [Another edition, smaller type. *Ibid.*] 60712

Signed, in and on behalf of a Meeting of the Representatives of the said People, held in Philadelphia, the 22d day of the 11th month, 1781, by John Drinker, Clerk.

To the Privates of the several Battalions of Military Associators in the Province of Pennsylvania. [n. p. 1776.] 4to, pp. 3.

To the Public. [n. p. 1764.] 8vo, pp. 4. 60714

Signed "Cornelius Esten." Against bribery and corruption of electors.

To the Public. [n. p. n. d.] Sm. 8vo, pp. 8. 60715

A tract signed "Pacificus," and dated at Philadelphia, July 16, 1768, ironically congratulating the province on the preservation of the public tranquility, by the lukewarm spirit evinced in opposing the measures of the British ministry. It appeared on Monday, July 18, 1768.

To the Public. *Philadelphia: Printed by William Goddard.* [1768.] 4to, 1 leaf. 60716

Signed "Pacificus," and dated July 25, 1768. An answer to "A Letter from a Gentleman in Virginia."

To the Public. [n. p. 1770.] Folio, 1 leaf. 60717

"Philadelphus" against non-importation agreements.

To the Public. [n. p. n. d.] Folio, 1 leaf. 60718

Address proposing a canal between the Delaware and Chesapeake, dated Philadelphia, January 15, 1772.

To the Public. [n. p. 1776.] Folio, 1 leaf. 60719

Signed by several officers of the Pennsylvania navy, in defense of their conduct.

To the Public. [n. p. 1852.] 8vo, pp. 4. 60720

E. S. Lawrence's account of an election quarrel, and his challenges to two of his assailants.

To the Public, and particularly the kind Customers of the Pennsylvania Chronicle ... . [n. p. n. d.] Folio, 1 leaf. 60721

Signed "Benjamin Towne." He and William Goddard were publishers of the "Chronicle," and fell out.

To the Representatives. *See* Vol. iv., No. 12547.

To the | Representatives | of the | Free-Men | Of This Province of | Pennsylvania, | In Assembly Conven'd at Philadelphia the 10th of | the 3d Moneth, 1692. [*Philadelphia: Wm. Bradford.* 1692.] Folio, pp. 4. 60722

A protest against the first tax law passed in Pennsylvania.

To the Representatives of the Freemen of the Commonwealth of Pennsylvania, in General Assembly met. The Memorial and Remonstrance of Isaac Howell and White Matlack, in behalf of themselves, and others, who have been disowned by the ... Quakers. [n. p. 1781.] Folio, pp. (4). 60723

Also: To the Representatives ... Divers Freemen of the said Commonwealth beg Leave to shew. [n. p. 1781.] Folio, 1 leaf.

To the Republican Citizens of ... Pennsylvania. Lancaster, Sept. 17, 1800. [n. p. n. d.] 16mo, pp. 16. 60724

To the Senate and House of Representatives of ... Pennsylvania. The Memorial of the ... Schuylkill and Susquehanna Navigation, and of the Delaware and Schuylkill Canal Navigation. [n. p. 1810.] 8vo, pp. 3. 60725

Application for an act to consolidate the companies as the Union Canal.

To the Senate and House of Representatives of Pennsylvania. [n. p. 1845.] 8vo. 60726

Memorial in regard to tax on ground rents. *See also* [Baker (J. B.)], Vol. ii. 2827.

To the several Battalions of the Military Associators in the Province of Pennsylvania. [n. p. 1776.] Folio, 1 leaf.

Address from the "Committee of Privates" of Philadelphia, concerning the choice of officers at the coming election for that purpose.

To the Tradesmen, Mechanics, &c. of the Province of Pennsylvania ... [n. p. n. d.] Folio, 1 leaf. 60728

"A Mechanic" against the tea tax, and dated Philadelphia, December 4, 1773.

To William Denny, Esquire, Lieutenant-Governor and Commander in Chief of the Province of Pennsylvania, &c. The Address of the Trustees and Treasurer of the Friendly Association for regaining and preserving Peace with the Indians by Pacific Measures. ... [n. p. n. d.] Folio, pp. 4. 60729

Dated "Philadelphia, the 14th of the Seventh Month, 1757."

A Tradesman's Address to his Countrymen. [n. p. n. d.] 4to, 1 leaf. 60730

Relates to the proposed excise law. Signed "A Tradesman," and dated Philadelphia, March 2, 1772.

Report of the Chief of Transportation and Telegraph Department of the Commonwealth ... for ... 1861. *Harrisburg.* 1861. 8vo, pp. 4. Discontinued after 1867. 60731

A Treatise shewing the Need we have to rely upon God as sole Protector of this Province; and the Reason of Man's degenerating ... and the Means whereby he may be re-established again. ... Together with Something in Answer to a late Performance, intituled, Plain Truth; discovering the Falsity therein contained, with Remarks on the Authors Irreligion. ... By one that wisheth well to all Mankind. *Philadelphia: Printed by Godhard Armbrister, in Arch-Street.* 1748. 8vo, pp. 26. 60732

A | Treaty | Of | Peace and Friendship | Made and Concluded between His Excellency | Sir William Keith, Bart. | Governor of the Province of Pennsylvania, | For and in Behalf of the said Province, | And The | Chiefs of the Indians of the Five Nations, | At Albany, in the Month of September, 1722. | *Philadelphia: Printed by Andrew Bradford ...* . MDCCXXII. Folio, pp. 8.

A Treaty of Friendship held with the Six Nations, at Philadelphia, in September and October, 1736. *Philadelphia: Printed ... by B. Franklin ...* . M,DCC,XXXVI. Folio. 60734

The Treaty Held with the Indians of the Six Nations at Philadelphia, In July, 1742. *Philadelphia: Printed ... by B. Franklin,* ... M,DCC,XLII. Folio, pp. 25. 60735

A | Treaty, | Held at the Town of | Lancaster, in Pennsylvania, | By the Honourable the | Lieutenant-Governor of the Province, | And the Honourable the | Commissioners for the Provinces | of | Virginia and Maryland, | with the | Indians | of the | Six Nations, | In June, 1744. | *Philadelphia: | Printed and sold by B. Franklin, at the New-Printing-Office, | near the Market.* M,DCC,XLIV. | Folio, pp. 39. 60736

Of the greatest rarity.

The Treaty Held with the Indians of the Six Nations, at Lancaster, in Pennsylvania, in June, 1744. To which is prefixed, An Account of the first Confederacy of the Six Nations, their present Tributaries, Dependents, and Allies, and of their Religion, and Form of Government. *Williamsburg: Printed by William Parks.* [1744.] 8vo, pp. xii, 79. c., h. 60737

A Treaty between the President and Council of the Province of Pennsylvania, and the Indians of Ohio. Held at Philadelphia, Nov. 13, 1747. *Philadelphia.* 1747. Folio, pp. 8.

A Treaty held by Commissioners, Members of the Council of the Province of Pennsylvania, at Lancaster, in July, 1748, with some Chiefs of the Six Nations at Ohio, and others, for the admission of the Twightwee Nation into the Alliance of his Majesty, &c. *Philadelphia.* 1748. Folio, pp. 10. 60739

A Treaty held with the Indians at Carlisle, in October, 1753. *Philadelphia: Printed ... by B. Franklin, and D. Hall ...* . MDCCLIII. Folio, pp. 12. 60740

The Trial of Alexander Addison. *See* Vol. i., No. 381.

Tribute to the Principles. *See* [Chambers (G.)], iii. 11795.

The Triumvirate of Pennsylvania. In a Letter to a Friend in the Country. [n. p. 1725.] Folio, pp. 4. 60741

True and Faithful Narrative. *See* Vol. xiii., No. 55104.

A | True and Impartial State | Of the Province of | Pennsylvania. | Containing, | An exact Account of the Nature of its Government; | the Power | of the Proprietaries, and their Governors; ... | The Rights and Privileges of the Assembly, and People ... . With a True Narrative of the Dispute between the Governors and Assemblies ... . The whole being a full Answer to the Pamphlets intitled A | Brief State, and A Brief View, &c. of the Conduct of Pennsylvania. | ... | *Philadelphia: | Printed by W. Dunlap,* ... M,DCC,LIX. 8vo, pp. v, 3–173, 34, (1). 60742

• This rare book completes a series relating to one of the most stirring periods in the provincial history of Pennsylvania. *See* "Monthly Review," xxi. 367. It is rather a heavy defense of the Quakers in the Assembly.

True Copies of i. The Agreement between Lord Baltimore and Messieurs Penn, dated 10 May, 1732. ii. The Commissions given the Commissioners to mark out the Lines between Maryland and Pensilvania and the Three Lower Counties on Delaware. iii. The Return or Report of the Commissioners on both Sides, made 24 Nov. 1733. Shewing for what Reasons the Lines were not mark'd out within the Time appointed for that Purpose. [n. p. n. d.] Folio, pp. 7. p. 60743

This is a reprint of our No. 45073, and is apparently a "paper-book" of one of the parties to the suit in chancery. There was another edition printed in Philadelphia in 1736.

The True Interest of the United States, and particularly of Pennsylvania, considered, &c. [n. p. n. d.] 8vo, pp. 31. j.c.b.

The True Policy of the State of Pennsylvania regarding the Land of her Citizens. By One of the People. ... [n. p.] *February,* 1818. 8vo, pp. 35. n., p. 60745

Twee Missiven | Geschreven uyt Pensilvania, | d'Eene door een Hollander, woonachtig in | Philadelfia, | d'Ander door een Switser, woonachtig in | German Town | Dat is Hoogduytse Stadt. | Van den 16 en 26 Maert 1684. Nieuwe Stijl. | ... | *Tot Rotterdam, by Pieter van Alphen. Anno* 1684. 4to, 2 leaves. c. 60746

Two letters written from Pennsylvania, one by a Dutchman resident in Philadelphia, and the other by a Swiss dwelling in Germantown.

Twelve Views of Churches, ... and Other Buildings, erected by the United Brethren in America; ... *New York.* 1836. Oblong 4to, pp. (16). 12 Plates. 60747

Relates mainly to the Moravians in Pennsylvania.

The Two following Depositions were laid before the House, the ninth day of August, 1728. [n. p. n. d.] Folio, 1 leaf.

Setting forth Sir Wm. Keith's scheme to appeal to the King for a revocation of the proprietary charter.

Two Letters ... . *Se* Tax Payer, *pseudon.*

An Act to Incorporate the Union Canal Company of Pennsylvania, with the Bye-Laws, ... enacted ... 24th July, 1811. *Philadelphia: Printed by John Binns.* 1811. 8vo, pp. 34.

The Union Canal Company of Pennsylvania. *Philadelphia* 1853. 8vo, pp. 47, (1). 2 Maps. 60750

Also: Acts of the Legislature ... relating to the Union Canal Company ... . *Philadelphia.* 1825. 8vo, pp. 72.—Additional Acts of the Legislature ... . [n. p. 1826.] 8vo, pp. 12.—Address of the President and Managers, of the ... Company ... . *Philadelphia.* 1812. 8vo, pp. 11.—Communication from the President ... with a Report of James D. Harris, ... Engineer, relative to enlarging the Union Canal. ... February 9, 1839. *Harrisburg.* 1839. 8vo, pp. 24.—Letter and Documents, in relation to the dissolution of the engagement of Loammi Baldwin, with the ... Company. *Harrisburg.* 1823. 8vo, pp. 23.—Observations on the Application for a Law to incorporate "The Union Canal Company" ... . [n. p. 1808.] 8vo.—Proceedings of the Union Canal Convention, ... Harrisburg, December 4, 1838. *Harrisburg.* 1839. 8vo, pp. 19.—Report [on the financial condition of the company. n. p. 1832.] 8vo, pp. 3.—Report and Memorial ... . Made ... to the Legislature ... at the Session 1812–13. *Philadelphia.* 1812. 8vo, pp. 11.—Report of the Committee of Holders of Union Canal Bonds. ... [n. p. 1857.] 8vo, pp. (2), 46.—Report of the President ... to the Stockholders ... . *Philadelphia.* 1813. 8vo, pp. 18. Continued.—Report relative to the Enlargement of the Union Canal. [n. p. 1845?] Folio, 1 leaf.—Reports of the ... Engineers on the ... Location of the Summit Level ... . Also the Report of Chas. B. Fisk, c.e. ... *Philadelphia.* 1853. 8vo, pp. 68. 2 Maps.—Reports of the Committee of Bondholders ... . *Philadelphia.* 1860. 8vo, pp. (2), 35, (1).—Rules and Regulations for the Government of Superintendents, Lock-Keepers, and Persons navigating the Union Canal: And Acts ... for the protection of said Canal ... . *Philadelphia.* 1834. 8vo, pp. 42.—A Supplement to the Act to Incorporate the Union Canal Company ... and an Extract from the "Act for the Improvement of the State;" together with the By-Laws, adopted ... 22d of May, 1821. *Philadelphia.* 1821. 8vo, pp. 18, (1).—To the President and Managers of the Union Canal Company. [Report of the Engineer. n. p. 1821.] 8vo, pp. 11. Continued.

Address of the Union State Central Committee of Pennsylvania. [n. p. 1863.] 8vo, pp. 15. 60751

Constitution, ... of Covenant Lodge, ... of the United Ancient Order of Druids of Pennsylvania. ... *Philadelphia.* 1848. 16mo, pp. 30. 60752

Also: Constitution, ... of Pride of Oak Lodge ... . *Philadelphia.* 1847. 16mo, pp. (2), 32, (1).

The United Brethren's Missionary Intelligencer, and Religious Miscellany; containing the most recent accounts relating to the United Brethren's Missions among the Heathen; ... [Vol. i.] *Philadelphia.* [1822–24.] 8vo, pp. (2), iii, ii, 576. 60753

Continued to ten volumes.

Numb. i. The Universal Instructor in all Arts and Sciences: and Pennsylvania Gazette. To be continued Weekly. Decemb. 24. 1728. *Philadelphia: Printed by Samuel Keimer ...* . Folio, pp. (4). 60754

Keimer's prospectus, dated October 1, 1728, promises "that each Person who preserves these Papers, will possess the richest Mine of useful Knowledge (of the Kind) ever before discover'd, except of late in Europe." Keimer in No. xiii. states that he printed two hundred and fifty copies, while Franklin says he had never more than ninety subscribers. With the 39th number Keimer's connection with the paper ceased, and No. 40 appeared as "The Pennsylvania Gazette. Containing the freshest Advices Foreign and Domestick. From Thursday, September 25, to Thursday, October 2, 1729." *Philadelphia: Printed by B. Franklin and H. Meredith ...* . With No. 44 the paper became bi-weekly, appearing Mondays and Thursdays. At No. 56 it became weekly, appearing Tuesdays to No. 66, continuing bi-weekly to No. 70, when it settled down to a weekly, appearing on Thursday, with occasional exceptions, until July 29, 1772, when the day was changed to Wednesday. The imprint was changed in No. 180 to *Philadelphia: Printed by B. Franklin, at the New-Printing-Office near the Market.* It remained the same until Oct. 6, 1737 (No. 460), when *Post-Master* was added after Franklin. The paper continued a small folio, generally four pages, until Oct. 6, 1739, when it was reduced to small quarto, double columns, the date transferred to the top of the page in the left corner, and a cut of the provincial arms, which was retained until No. 2533, was added. The sheet was enlarged in February, 1741–2, to three columns, and further enlarged in 1749, to the size it ever after maintained. In January, 1747, D. Hall's name was added to the imprint, and remained until October 31, 1765, thence to February 13, 1766, there is no imprint. From this last date till May 1, 1766, it was *Printed by David Hall;* from May 8, 1766, to Dec. 23, 1772, it was *Printed by D. Hall and W. Sellers,* and afterward *Hall & Sellers.* The paper was suspended from November 27, 1776 (No. 2501), to February 5, 1777 (No. 2502), and the regular issue ceased with September 10, 1777 (No. 2533), which was not resumed till January 5, 1779 (No. 2534), when it appeared as "The Pennsylvania Gazette and Weekly Advertiser." In the interim some twenty-five issues, of various sizes and irregular dates, were printed at York, Pa. The publication was continued with some interruptions until 1830.

Catalogue of the Officers, Teachers and Students of the University of Northern Pennsylvania, from November 3rd, 1851 to September 30th, 1852: Together with the Address of the Hon. George W. Woodward ... . *Honesdale, Penna.* 1852. 8vo, pp. 32. Continued. 60755

Catalogue of Books, belonging to the Library of the University of Pennsylvania. *Philadelphia: Judah Dobson ...* . 1829. 8vo, pp. (4), 103. 60756

Catalogue of the Anatomical Museum ... with a Report by W. E. Horner. Second Edition. *Philadelphia.* 1832. 8vo, pp. 51.—Catalogue of the Medical Graduates ... with an Historical Sketch of the ... Medical Department. ... *Philadelphia.* 1836. 8vo, pp. (2), 97. Continued.—Catalogue of the Members of the Zelosophic Society. Founded MDCCCXXIX. *Philadelphia.* 1854. 8vo, 10 leaves.—Catalogue of the Trustees, Officers, and Students, ... and of the Grammar and Charity Schools, attached ... . *Philadelphia.* 1824. 8vo, pp. 8. Continued.

An Examination of Certain Charges preferred against the Medical Class ... of 1834–5. [n. p. n. d.] 8vo, pp. 24.

Relates to the removal of Dr. J. Redman Coxe from the chair of Materia Medica.

General Catalogue of the Officers and Graduates in the Department of Arts ... . From 1749 until 1849. *Philadelphia.* 1849. 8vo, pp. 56, (1). 60758

Also: Address of the Trustees of the University of Pennsylvania to the Public. [n. p. 1829.] 8vo, pp. 7.—Charters, Statutes, and By-Laws ... . Revised, March, 1826. *Philadelphia.* 1826. 8vo, pp. 42. + 1853. 8vo.—Constitution of the Society of the Alumni ... . *Philadelphia.* 1858. 8vo, pp. 14.—Laws for the Government of the Collegiate and Medical Departments and the Department of Natural Sciences ... . *Philadelphia.* 1820. 8vo.—Laws for the Government of the Collegiate Department ... . *Philadelphia.* 1832. 8vo, pp. 8. + [n. p. n. d.] 8vo, pp. 16.—Laws for the Government of the Medical Department ... . *Philadelphia.* 1826. 8vo.—List of Medical Graduates ... April 7, 1826. *Philadelphia.* 1826. 8vo, pp. 2.—Medical Department of the University ... . [n. p. 1844.] 8vo, pp. 36—Memorial ... to the Trustees ... . *Philadelphia.* 1850. 8vo.—A Morning Prayer for the University ... . *Philadelphia.* 1780. 12mo.—Objections to Re-Organization of the Department of Arts ... Considered by a Trustee. *Philadelphia.* 1853. 8vo, pp. (4), 42.—Proceedings of the Medical Class ... which led to the employment of a distinguished Artist to make a portrait of Dr. Physick ... . Also ... Address ... by the Students; and a ... reply by Dr. Horner and Dr. Hare. [n. p. 1837.] 8vo, pp. 7.—Report of the Committee of the Trustees ... on filling up the vacancies in the Faculty of Natural Science. *Philadelphia.* 1821. 8vo.—Report of the Committee of Ways and Means of the University ... . *Philadelphia.* 1830. 8vo. Continued.—Report on the Medical Department ... 1847–48. *Philadelphia.* 1847–48. 8vo. Continued.—Rules and Statutes of the University ... . [n. p. 1811.] 8vo, pp. 23. + [n. p.] 1820. 8vo, pp. 31.—A Short Introduction to Latin Grammar, for the use of the University ... . *Alexandria.* 1805. 8vo.—Statement of the Funds of the University ... . [n. p.] January 1, 1812. 8vo, pp. 8. Continued.—Testimonials, submitted to the Consideration of the Trustees ... . [n. p. 1818.] 12mo, pp. 24.—University of Pennsylvania, ... Nov. 7, 1854. [Communication from the faculty of arts to the trustees in regard to defects in the course of instruction. n. p. n. d.] 8vo, pp. 9.—University of Pennsylvania. To the Legislature ... . [Petition for a share of the public land script. n. p. 1864.] 8vo, pp. 10.

The University, a Literary Monthly, devoted to the Interests of the University ... . March, 1869. ... *Philadelphia.* [1869.] 8vo, pp. 32. 60759

Only two numbers were issued.

The University Magazine, a Literary and Scientific Periodical, Edited by a Committee of the Philomathean and Zelosophic Societies of the University ... . January, 1843. Vol. I. No. I. *Philadelphia.* [n. d.] 8vo. 60760

Continued monthly to No. VIII.

The University Record. ... University of Pennsylvania, June 25, 1868. [n. p. n. d.] Folio, pp. 4. 60761

Continued in 4to.

Valuation; Taxes assessed and received in the several Counties of Pennsylvania, from 1845 to 1846. *Harrisburg.* 1846. 8vo. 60762

Verhandlungen der Democratischen Convention, gehalten zu Harrisburg, Pennsylvanien, den 5ten März, 1832. [n. p. 1832.] 8vo, pp. 20. 60763

Verschuldigd Dank-Adres aan de Staaten van Holland ... en aan alle Weldoenders, die zich ... der zaak van de Gereformeerden Gemeenten in Pensylvanien ... hebben aangenomen ... met bericht, hoe de giften besteedt zijn. *Amsterdam.* 1758. 4to, pp. 24. 60764

Address of thanks to the States General and to all benefactors of the Reformed Church in Pennsylvania, etc. Very scarce.

Verses, Of the Printers Lads, who carry the Pennsylvania Gazette to the Customers. Ode on the New Year. January 1, 1768. Folio, 1 leaf. 60765

Vierte General Versammlung der Kirche Gottes aus allen Evangelischen Religionen in Pennsylvania, Teutscher Nation; Gehalten zu Germantown am 10, 11, und 12ten Martii im Jahr 174½. An Mr. Ashmeads Hause. *Philadelphia: Gedruckt und zu haben bey B. Franklin.* [1742.] 4to, pp. (2), 59–76. 60766

A continuation of "Zuverlässige Beschreibung," No. 60787, *infra.* For the sequent parts *see* "Gründliche," Vol. VII., No. 29010, and Müller (J. J.), Vol. XII., Nos. 51292–3.

A View of the Calumnies lately spread in some Scurrilous Prints against the Government of Pennsylvania. [n. p. 1729?] Folio, pp. 4. 60767

A View of the Debts and Expenses of the Commonwealth of Pennsylvania, and of the Funds and Revenues of the same. [n. p.] *December*, 1786. 4to, pp. 25. N., P. 60768

Printed and sold by R. Aitken, Philadelphia. A report, signed "John Nicholson, Comptroller General's Office," to the Legislature.

View of the Present State of the Slave Trade in Pennsylvania and New Jersey. *Philadelphia.* 1824. 8vo. W. 60769

A View of the Principles, Operations and Probable Effects of the Funding System of Pennsylvania. *Philadelphia: R. Aitken & Son.* 1788. 8vo, pp. 23. 60770

A View of the Scandals lately spread in some Printed Libels against the Government of Pennsylvania. [*Philadelphia: A. Bradford.* 1729.] Folio, pp. 4. 60771

This is a second edition, with some additions, of "A View of the Calumnies," No. 60767, *supra.*

View of the Whole Ground. A Brief History of the Proposed Impeachment of the Governor of Pennsylvania: To which is added His Excellency's Message of January 28th, 1808, comprising a ... Satisfactory Defence. *Lancaster: Printed by William Hamilton.* 1808. 12mo, pp. 69. 60772

A Vindication of the Legislative Power, Submitted to the Representatives of the Province of Pennsylvania, now sitting in Assembly. [n. p. n. d.] Folio, pp. 4. 60773

Signed by David Lloyd, and dated "the 19th of the Month called March, 1724–5."

Vindication of the Separate System. *See* [Packard (F. A.)]

Mr. Vogdes' Report relative to the Expenses Incurred in prosecuting the Claims of the State ... against the Bank of the United States. Filed March 19th, 1853. [n. p. n. d.] 8vo, pp. (2), 20. 60774

Votes and Proceedings of the House of Representatives of the Province of Pennsylvania. Beginning the Fourth Day of December, 1682. Volume the First in Two Parts. *Philadelphia: Printed and Sold by B. Franklin, and D. Hall* ... . MDCCLII. Folio, pp. xxxviii, 164, Appendix, xxix; Part Second, pp. (2), viii, 187. + Beginning the Fourteenth Day of October, 1707. Volume the Second. [*Ibid.*] MDCCLIII. Folio, pp. (2), 494. + Beginning the Fourteenth Day of October, 1726. Volume the Third. [*Ibid.*] MDCCLIV. Folio, pp. 591. + Beginning the Fifteenth Day of October, 1744. Volume the Fourth. *Philadel-*

phia: Henry Miller. 1774. Folio, pp. 856. + Beginning the Fourteenth Day of October, 1758. Volume the Fifth. [*Ibid.*] 1775. Folio, pp. 560. + Beginning the Fourteenth Day of October, 1767. Volume the Sixth. [*Ibid.*] 1776. Folio, pp. 766. 60775

The sixth volume terminates the Proceedings of the House of Representatives of the Province of Pennsylvania under the crown of Great Britain. A complete series is very scarce.

Votes and Proceedings. *Philadelphia: Printed ... by Andrew Bradford* ... . [1727.] Folio, pp. 30. + [*Ibid.* 1728.] Folio, pp. 22. 60776

Votes and Proceedings of the House of Representatives of the Province of Pennsylvania, met at Philadelphia, on the Fourteenth of October, Anno Dom. 1729, and continued by Adjournments. Published by Order of Assembly. *Philadelphia: Printed and Sold by B. Franklin and H. Meredith* ... . M,DCC,XXIX–LXXV. Folio. 60777

Collation: M,DCC,XXIX, pp. 38; *Philadelphia: Printed ... by B. Franklin,* ... M,DCC,XXXVII, pp. 36; *Ib.* M,DCC,XXXVIII, pp. 60; *Ib.* M,DCC,XXXIX, pp. 131, (1); M,DCC,XLI, pp. 33, (1); *Ib.* pp. 92; *Ib.* M,DCC,XLIII, pp. 73; *Ib.* M,DCC,XLIV, pp. 54; *Ib.* M,DCC,XLV; *Ib.* M,DCC,XLVII, pp. 36, (1); *Ib.* M,DCC,XLVIII; *Ib.* MDCCL, pp. 77, (1); *Ib.* MDCCLIV; *Ib.* MDCCLVIII, pp. 94; *Ib.* MDCCLIX, pp. 111, (1); *Ib.* MDCCLXI, pp. 80; *Ib.* MDCCLXII, pp. 58, (1); MDCCLXIII, pp. 67, (1); *Ib.* MDCCLXIV, pp. 113; *Philadelphia: Printed ... by B. Franklin and D. Hall* ... MDCCLXIV, pp. 16; *Philadelphia: Printed ... by William Goddard* ... MDCCLXIX, pp. 109; *Philadelphia: Printed ... by Henry Miller* ... MDCCLXX, pp. 201; *Ib.* MDCCLXXI, pp. (2), 205–300; *Ib.* MDCCLXXII, pp. (2), 303–412; *Ib.* MDCCLXXIII, pp. (2), 415–498; *Ib.* MDCCLXXIV, pp. (2), 501–578; *Ib.* MDCCLXXV, pp. (2), 581–682.

Voyage dans la Haute Pensylvanie. *See* [Crevecœur], 17501.

Constitution of the WASHINGTON BENEVOLENT SOCIETY of Pennsylvania. [n. p.] ... 1813. 16mo, pp. 59. + Together with Washington's Farewell Address. ... *Philadelphia.* 1817. 12mo, pp. 74. 60778

Also: Plan of A Loan, proposed to be received by the Washington Benevolent Society of Pennsylvania ... . [n. p. 1814.] 12mo, pp. 11.—A Summary Statement of the Origin, Progress, and Present State of the Washington Benevolent Society ... with ... the Opening and Dedication of the Washington Hall, ... 1st of October, 1816; ... the Religious Services by the Right Reverend William White, D.D. and an oration by the Hon. Joseph Hopkinson. To which is added ... the Constitution and By-Laws, ... *Philadelphia.* 1816. 12mo, pp. 104. 2 Plans and Plate.

No. I. The Weekly Advertiser, or Pennsylvania Journal. Thursday, December 2, 1742. *Philadelphia: Printed and Sold by William Bradford* ... . [n. d.] Folio, pp. (4). 60779

The third journal in English published at Philadelphia. Afterward known as "The Pennsylvania Journal and Weekly Advertiser." Continued to about 1797.

A Brief View of the Proceedings of the WESTERN MISSIONARY SOCIETY, Pa. With an Address to the Public by the Trustees. *Washington, Pa.* 1807. 12mo, pp. 24. 60780

Report of the Inspectors of the WESTERN PENITENTIARY of Pennsylvania for ... 1843. ... *Allegheny.* [n. d.] 8vo, pp. 16. Continued. 60781

Also: Report of the Committee appointed to visit the Western Penitentiary. ... *Harrisburg.* 1835. 8vo, pp. 4.

Report of the Managers of the WESTERN PENNSYLVANIA HOSPITAL, together with the ... Documents for ... 1856. ... *Harrisburg.* 1857. 8vo, pp. 16. 60782

Catalogue of the Officers and Students of the WESTERN UNIVERSITY of Pennsylvania. *Pittsburg, May,* 1832. 12mo, pp. 12. Continued. 60783

Why Pennsylvania should become one of the Confederate States. *See* [McHenry (G.)], Vol. XI., No. 43308.

A Word to the Whigs of Pennsylvania. [n. p. 1851.] 8vo, pp. 8. 60784

Young Men's Colonization Society of Pennsylvania. [n. p. n. d.] 4to, 1 leaf. 60785

Zuverlässige Beschreibung der Dritten Conferenz der Evangelischen Religionen Teutscher Nation in Pennsylvania, welche am 9, 10, und 11ten Februarii, 174½, in Oley an Johann de Türcks Hause gehalten worden; Samt denen dieses mahl verfassten Gemein-Schlüssen. *Philadelphia: Gedruckt und zu haben bey B. Franklin.* [n. d.] 4to, pp. (2), 43–56. 60786

A continuation of "Avthentische Nachricht" and Avthentische Relation," Vol. I., No. 2462–3. It was followed by No. 60766, *supra.*

PENNSYLVANIAN, *pseudon.* An Address to the Citizens of Pennsylvania, on the Situation of our Country; connected with the public conduct of James Ross, a Candidate for the Governmental Chair of Pennsylvania. By a Pennsylvanian. *Philadelphia: Printed.* 1808. 8vo, pp. 13. 60787

PENNSYLVANIAN, *pseudon.* Address to the Senate and House of Representatives of the United States, on the ... Tariff. By a Pennsylvanian. *Philadelphia.* 1822. 8vo. 60788

PENNSYLVANIAN, *pseudon.* A Candid View of the Presidential Question, by a Pennsylvanian. *Philadelphia: William Stavely.* 1828. 8vo, pp. 22. 60789

PENNSYLVANIAN, *pseudon.* Causes of the Kensington Riots Explained, in ... letters to the Hon. Daniel O'Connell. By a Pennsylvanian—a Dutchman. ... Number 1. *Philadelphia: A. H. Rowand.* 1845. 8vo, pp. 50. 60790

See also Vol. I., No. 1275, [Carey (M.)], Vol. III., Nos. 10862, 10868–9, 10889, pp. 340 and 342, Vol. IV., No. 15991, Vol. VI., No. 23363, Vol. X., No. 41947.

Pennsylvanish Deitsh. *See* [Rauch (E. H.)]

Pennsylvanischer Calender, auf das 1796ste Jahr Christi ... . *Ephrata.* [n. d.] 4to, pp. 40. S. 60791

PENNY (J.) The Life and Adventures of Joshua Penny, a Native of Southhold, Long Island, Suffolk County, New York, who was Impressed into the British Service. Interspersed with many Hair Breadth Escapes. Also, Account of his being taken out of his bed by Commodore Hardy, on the night of Aug. 21, 1813, and carried to Halifax, where he suffered imprisonment nine months. *New York.* 1815. 8vo, pp. 60. 60792

PENNY (*Miss*). Poems: The Birth-Day, a Dramatic Entertainment, dedicated to Jonas Hanway, Esq. [etc.] *London.* 1771. 4to. 60793

Containing, among others, "Anningait and Ajutt, a Greenland Tale."

PENNY (V.) The Employments of Women: a Cyclopædia of Woman's Work. By Virginia Penny. *Boston.* 1862. + [*Ibid.*] 1863. 8vo. 60794

Also: Think and Act. A Series of Articles on Man and Woman, Work and Wages. ... *Philadelphia.* 1869. 12mo, pp. 372.

PENNYLESS (Peter), *pseudon.* Sentimental Lucubrations: in Twelve Chapters. By Peter Pennyless. *Philadelphia: Printed by William Gibbons.* 1793. 18mo, pp. 168. 60795

PENNYPACKER (S. W.) Annals of Phœnixville and its Vicinity: from the Settlement to ... 1871, ... with Information concerning the adjacent Townships of Chester and Montgomery Counties and the Valley of the Schuylkill. By Samuel Whitaker Pennypacker ... . *Philadelphia: Bavis & Pennypacker.* 1872. 8vo, pp. 295. 4 Plates and Map. C. 60796

The Penokie Mineral Range in Wisconsin. *Boston.* 1863. 8vo. 60797

PENROSE (B.) An Account of the last Expedition to Port Egmont, in Falkland's Islands, in the Year 1772. Together with the Transactions of the Company, of the Penguin Shallop during their stay there. By Bernard Penrose, Surgeon's Mate. *London: J. Johnson.* MDCCLXXV. 12mo, pp. 81. J.C.B. 60798

See "Monthly Review," LII. 188.

PENROSE (C. B.) Address of the Hon. Charles B. Penrose, ... and the Speeches of Messrs. Fraley (City), Williams, Pearson, and Penrose, ... in the Senate of Pennsylvania, on the ... Insurrection at Harrisburg ... . *Harrisburg: Printed by E. Guyer.* 1839. 8vo, pp. 207. 60799

These tracts relate to what is known as the Buck-Shot War. Also: Eulogium upon the Rev. John F. Greer, D.D. ... *Carlisle, Pa.* 1828. 8vo, pp. 16. *See also* No. 60532, *supra.*

[PENROSE (John).] Lives of Vice-Admiral Sir Charles Vinicombe Penrose, and Capt. James Trevenen. By their Nephew. *London: John Murray.* 1850. 8vo, pp. ix, 301. S. 60800

Trevenen sailed with Captain Cook.

PENROSE (L.) The Journal of Llewellen Penrose, a Seaman. *London: Houlston.* 1815. 4 vols., 16mo, pp. (4), xvi, 239; (4), 217; (4), 215; (4), 197. 60801

Contains some particulars relative to the North American Indians.

PENROSE (T.) Public Tranquillity the Object of every Individual's Concern. A Sermon Preached in the Parish-Church of Newbery, Berks, December 13, 1776. Being the Day appointed for a Public Fast On Account of the Troubles in America. By the Rev. Thomas Penrose, Curate of Newbery. *London: T. Davies.* 1776. 4to, pp. (2), 14, Errata, 4 lines.

See "Monthly Review," LVI. 73.

PENSACOLA, *Fla.* Sale of Town Lots at Pensacola, with Descriptions of the Place, Climate, &c. [*New York:*] *T. & C. Wood* [*about* 1836]. 8vo, pp. 8. 2 Maps. 60803

Signed by Wm. H. Chase, trustee. *See also* Vol. XII., No. 48112, *and* "Report on the Circumstances," *infra.*

El Pensador del Peru. *Lima: B. Ruiz.* 1815. 4to, pp. 196, (2). 60804

A very rare document relative to the revolution in Chili in 1814.

Pensador Mexicano. *See* Vol. X., No. 41666.

El Pensamiento nacional. Periodico religioso, politico, literario, artistico y mercantil. *Méjico.* 1855–6. Folio. 60805

Discontinued with No. 46 of the second volume.

Pensées sur la Révolution. *See* [Pownall (T.)]

Pensées sur les transactions. *See* [Johnson (S.)], IX. 36311.

Pensions. A Compilation of Pensions, Pay and Bounty Lands. Together with full Instructions, Forms and Decisions. *Chicago.* 1862. 8vo, pp. 96. 60806

Laws and Abstracts of Laws relating to Army and Navy Pensions. *Washington.* 1869. 8vo. 60807

A Manual of the Pension Laws. *Washington.* 1862. 8vo. 60808

Pension and Bounty Land Laws, 1776–1852. *Washington.* 1852. 8vo. B. 60809

Pension Laws now in force. In a Letter from William L. Marcy, Secretary of War, to the House of Representatives of the United States, January 29, 1846. *Washington.* 1846. 8vo. 60810

Pension Laws of the United States, including sundry Resolutions of Congress, from 1776 to 1833. Compiled by Robert Mayo. *City of Washington.* 1833. 8vo. 60811

Pentecost; or, the Work of God in Philadelphia, A. D. 1858. Prepared by the Young Men's Christian Association. *Philadelphia.* 1859. 12mo, pp. 83. 60812

PEÑUELAS (*P.*) Sermon por la exaltacion al trono de N. Catol. Monarca D. Carlos IV. ... *Mexico.* 1791. 4to, 15 leaves. 60813

PEÑUELAS (P. A.) Breve Noticia de la Prodigiosa Imagen de Nuestra Señora de los Angeles, que por espacio de dos siglos se há conservado pintada en una pared de adove, y se venera en sú Santuario extramuros de México. *México.* 1781. 12mo, pp. (16), 103, Table, 3. 60814

PEOLI (G.) Poesias de Gonzalo Peoli. *Matanzas.* 1858. 18mo, pp. xii, 348. 60815

PEON (J. J.) Cronica Sucinta de Yucatan, escrita por D. Jose Julian Peon il año de 1831. *Merida de Yucatan: Imprenta de Geronimo Castillo.* 1831. 8vo. 60816

The People of the State of New York *ads.* The State of New Jersey. Case in the Supreme Court of the United States. *Albany.* 1832. 8vo. 60817

The People's Almanac. 1834. *Boston: Willard, Felt & Co. and Charles Ellms.* [1833.] 12mo, pp. 48. 60818

The People's Ancient ... Liberties [etc.] *See* [Penn (W.)], No. 59723.

The People's Answer to the Court Pamphlet: Entitled A Short Review of the Political State of Great Britain. ... Second Edition. *London: Printed for J. Debrett.* M DCC LXXXVII. 8vo, pp. (4), 50. 60819

Circular of the PEOPLE'S COLLEGE, of the State of New York. And Act of Incorporation ... . *Buffalo.* 1853. 12mo, pp. 12. Continued. 60820

The People's Democratic Guide. *New York.* 1842. Rl. 8vo, pp. 376. 60821

The People's Doctors. A Review, by "The People's Friend." *Cincinnati, Ohio.* 1830. 8vo, pp. 60. 60822

A severe satire. Dr. D. Drake is supposed to be the author.

Proceedings of the PEOPLE'S LEAGUE of the Old and New World, at Wheeling, September 18, 1852. *Philadelphia.* 1852. 8vo. 60823

The People's Magazine. Vol. I., March 23, 1833–March 8, 1834. [*Boston.* n. d.] 8vo, pp. 208. Continued. 60824

The People's Military Almanac for 1862. *New York: Dexter & Co.* [n. d.] 8vo, pp. 116. 60825

The People's Organ. [Mormon.] ... Religious, ... and Political. Vol. I. *Pittsburg.* 1844. 60826

The People's Own Book. ... Second Edition. ... *Boston.* 1850. 12mo, pp. 24. 60827

Memorial of the PEOPLE'S PACIFIC RAILROAD COMPANY, ... Dec. 18, 1860. [*Washington.* 1860.] 8vo, pp. 8. + March 24, 1862. [*Ibid.* 1862.] 8vo, pp. 6. 60828

Also: ... An Act to Incorporate the People's Pacific Railroad Company. [n. p. 1860.] 8vo, pp. 11.— ... Charter, [etc.] *Boston.* 1860. 8vo, pp. 26.

Circular ... and Prospectus ... of the People's Perpetual Loan Association. ... *Boston.* 1858. 12mo, pp. 44. 60829

The People's Rights Re-claimed; Being an Exposition of the Unconstitutionality of the Law of the State of New York, compelling the Observance of a Religious Sabbath Day ... . *New York: A. Spooner.* 1826. 8vo, pp. 72. 60830

Peoria, *Ill.* A Descriptive Account of the City of Peoria, combining a Sketch of its Early History, ... &c. ... *Peoria, Ill.* 1859. 8vo, pp. 32. 60831

First Annual Report [of the Peoria Board of Trade] of the Trade and Commerce of ... Peoria, for 1870. ... *Peoria, Ill.* [n. d.] 8vo, pp. 73. Continued. 60832

The Peoria Directory for 1844, with a History of the Town. By S. De Witt Drown. *Peoria.* 1844. 12mo. Continued.

Root's Peoria City Directory for 1867-8. *Peoria.* 1866. 8vo, pp. 188.

First Annual Report of the Peoria Eye Infirmary and Orthopaedic Institution. Ending Oct. 1, 1852. [*Peoria.* 1852.] 8vo, pp. 6. 60834

Pepoli (C.) Les Puritains et les Cavaliers, Opera seria. ... paroles de M. C. Pepoli ... . *Paris: Imprimerie Lange Lévy et Comp.* 1844. 8vo, pp. 75. 60835

Pepper (C.) An Oration, ... at Wilbraham [Mass.] on the 4th of July 1810. By Calvin Pepper. ... *Palmer: E. Terry.* [n. d.] 8vo, pp. 13, 1 leaf, numbered 15, containing "Independence," a poem. 60836

Pepper (Calvin), *Jr.* Manor of Rensselaerwyck. By C. Pepper, Jr. ... Published by the Albany and Rensselaer Anti-Rent Associations. *Albany: Munsell.* 1846. 8vo, pp. 34. s.

The author went into the patroon's wood-lot and cut down a tree, informing him of it, hoping to provoke a suit for trespass, that would test his title. Nothing came of it.

Pepper (G. W.) The National Cause: its Sanctity and Grandeur. Oration. By Rev. George W. Pepper ... at Raleigh, North Carolina, on July 4th, 1867. *Raleigh.* 1867. 8vo, pp. 29. 60838

Pepper. Personal Recollections of Sherman's Campaigns, in Georgia and the Carolinas. By George W. Pepper. *Zanesville, O.* 1866. 8vo. 60839

Pepper (H.) Juvenile Essays; or, a Collection of Poems: inscribed to my valued friend Henry Mac-Neale Kennedy. By Henry Pepper. ... *Philadelphia: Printed by Richard Folwell ...* [1800?] 8vo, pp. 75, (1). 60840

Pepperell (W.) An Accurate Journal and Account of the Proceedings of the New-England Land-Forces, During the late Expedition Against the French Settlements on Cape Breton, To the Time of the Surrender of Louisbourg. ... With A Computation of the French Fishery on the Banks of Newfoundland, Acadia, Cape Breton, and neighbouring Shores ... . All sent over, by General Pepperell ... . *Exon: ... A. and S. Brice,* 1746. 8vo, pp. 40. c. 60841

For another edition, *see* our No. 10723, Vol. iii. *See* Rich, i. 82, *and* "Monthly Review," xix. 499. *See also* Vol. iv., No. 15436.

Pepperell, *Mass.* Truth and Character Vindicated: ... Review of Hon. Caleb Butler's History of the Ecclesiastical Affairs of Pepperell. By a Committee ... in that Place. ... *Boston: T. R. Marvin.* 1849. 8vo, pp. 49. 60842

Corrected title of our No. 1492, Vol. i.

Historical Sketch of Pepys' Island in the South Pacific Ocean; from the work on the Rio de la Plata by P. de Angelis. *Buenos-Aires.* 1842. 8vo, pp. 9, xvii. Map. 60843

Report to the Directors of the Pequa Railroad and Improvement Company. *Philadelphia.* 1849. 8vo, pp. 24. Map.

Also: Reports ... on the Coal Properties owned by the Pequa Railroad and Improvement Company, and the Dauphin and Susquehanna Coal Company. *New York.* 1849. 8vo, pp. 10.

The Pequot of a Hundred Years. An Authentic Narrative. *New York: American Tract Society.* [n. d.] 8vo, pp. 4. 60845

Peralta (Antonio de). Dissertationes Scholasticæ de S. Joseph unigeniti filii Dei putativo patri, deique genitricis spouso dignissimo; ... *Mexici: Typis J. B. de Hogal.* 1729. 12mo, pp. (28), 219, (4). 60846

Peralta Calderon (D. Mathias de). El Apostol de las Indias, y nvevas gentes San Francisco Xavier de la Compañia de Jesvs. Epitome de svs apostolicos hechos, virtudes, enseñança, y prodigios antiguos, y nuevos. ... *Mexico: Imprenta de A. de Santistevan y Franc. Lupercio.* 1661. 4to, pp. (20), 101, 112, 100, 96, (14). 60847

A very rare piece. *See* Leclerc, No. 1149.

Peralta Barnuevo Rocha y Benavides (Pedro de). Fvnebre Pompa, demonstracion doliente, magnificencia triste, que en las altas exequias, y tumulo eregido en la Santa Iglesia Metropolitana de la ciudad de Lima ... al ... Señor Francisco Farnese, ... *Lima: Calle de Palacio.* 1728. 4to, 132 leaves. Plate. j.c.b.

Peralta. Historia de España vindicada. en qve se haze sv mas exacta descripcion la de sus excelencias, y antiguas Riquezas, Se prueba su Poblacion, Lengua y Reyes verdaderos primitivos. Se describe la verdadera Cantabria ... . *Lima: Fr. Sobrino.* 1730. Folio, pp. (70), 1646 cols. Frontispiece, 26 Portraits. 60849

The illustrations are curious specimens of South American art.

Peralta. Imagen Politica del Gobierno del Exc.mo. Señor D. Diego Ladron de Guevara, del consejo de S. M., Obispo de Qvito, Virrey, Governador, y Capitan General de los Reynos del Perù, Tierra-firme, y Chile ... . *Lima: Geronimo de Contreras.* 1714. 4to, pp. (10), 96. j.c.b. 60850

Peralta. Jvbilos de Lima y fiestas reales, que hizo esta ciudad ... en celebracion de los casamientos de D. Luis Fernando ... y la Princessa de Orleans. *Lima: Ignacio de Luna.* 1723. 4to, (85) leaves. 60851

Peralta. Lima Fundada. O Conquista del Peru. Poema Heroico en que se decanta toda la historia del descubrimiento, ... Y se Contine [*sic*] la serie de los Reyes, ... y varones ilustres, que la ciudad y reyno han producido. La Qual Dedica ... al ... Señor Don Joseph de Armendariz ... D. Pedro de Peralta Barnueuo Rocha y Benavides ... . *Lima: En la Imprenta de Francisco Sobrino y Bados.* 1732. 2 vols., 4to, pp. (168), 209, (13); (4), 210–648. b. + Reimpreso en 1863. 8vo. 60852

The pagination is exceedingly incorrect. There are 400 leaves in all. This writer proposes that the commerce with America should be carried on by Spaniards only, and that its produce should circulate in Spain alone.

Peralta. Lima inexpugnabile. Discvrso Hercotectonico, o de Defensa por medio de la Fortificacion de este Grande Emporio ... . Representado al Exc. Señor D. Antonio Joseph de Mendoza Sotomayor y Camaño ... Por el Doct. D. Pedro de Peralta Barnueuo y Rocha y Benavidas ... . [*Lima.*] 1740. Folio, pp. 53. h. 60853

Peralta. Lima trivmphante, glorias de la America, jvegos pythios y jubilos de la minerua peruana en la entrada que hizo ... en esta muy leal ciudad ... y en el recibimiento con que fue cele-

brado por la Real Universidad de S. Marcos ... el Dr. D. Isidoro de Olmedo y Sossa, su rector. *Lima: J. de Contreras.* 1708. 4to, (164) leaves. 60854

Peralta. Relacion de la Sacra Festiva Pompa que en el Reverente accion de gracias de la exaltacion à la Cardinalicia Dignidad ... . Solemnizo afectivo y consagro humilde, en nombre de su Augustiniana Religion y Provincia del Peru. ... *Lima.* 1739. 4to, pp. vii, 15. j.c.b. 60855

Peralta. Relacion del Avto de Fé celebrado por el Sagrado Tribunal del Santo Officio de la Inquisicion de estos Reynos en la Civdad de Lima, en el dia 12 de Julio del año de 1733. ... *Lima: F. Sobrino.* 1733. Sm. 4to, 66 leaves. c. 60856

Also: Cartel del certamen. El theatro heroico. Certamen poetico que ofrece ... la Universidad de Lima ... a D. Diego Morcillo Rvbio de Avñon Virrey y Capitan General. *Lima: Diego de Lyra.* 1720. 4to, pp. (2), 124. — El cielo en el parnasso, certamen poetico con que la Real Vniversidad ... celebro el favsto feliz recibimiento de S. E. ... *Lima: Imprenta Real.* 1736. 4to, (136) leaves. — La Galeria de la omnipotencia, cartel del certamen poetico con qve celebra ... la santa iglesia metropolitana de Lima ... . [*Lima.* n. d.] 4to, (62) leaves. — Oracion que dixo ... en que fuè reeligido ... 30 de Junio de 1716. *Lima.* 1716. 4to, (17) leaves. — Oracion qve dixo ... en accion de gracias ... 30. de Junio de 1715. *Lima.* 1715. 4to, (14) leaves. — Passion y trivmpho de Christo ... . *Lima: Imprenta extra muros de Santa Cathalina.* 1738. 4to, pp. (106), 326. — El templo de la fama vindicado. Discurso escrito en honor de Diego Morcillo Rubio de Auñon, Arçobispo de la ciudad de la Plata, Virrey del Peru. ... *Lima: Fr. Sobrino.* 1720. 4to, pp. (14), 55.

Peramas (Joseph Emmanuel). De Vita et Moribus sex Sacerdotum Paraguaycorum. ... *Faventiæ:* mdccxci. *Ex Typographia Archii.* 8vo, pp. xxxix, 299. + Tredecim virorum Paraguaycorum. [*Ibid.*] 1793. 8vo, pp. xxvii, 462, (2). Plate.

Contains an account of the aborigines of South America, of the remains of the ancient Incas of Peru, and of the march of civilization among the nations of Paraguay, forming a supplement to Dobrizhoffer's "History of the Abipones," No. 20412, Vol. v. The first edition contains six and the second thirteen biographies.

Peraza (Joaquin Castillo). Ensayos Poéticos. ... *Merida: Raf. Pedrera.* 1862. 8vo, pp. (8), 152. Portrait. 60858

These poetical pieces have generally a religious subject, but some relate to the history of the author's country.

Perce (E.) The Battle Roll: An Encyclopedia containing Descriptions of the most Famous and Memorable Land Battles and Sieges in all Ages. ... By Albert Perce. *New York: Mason Brothers.* 1858. 8vo, pp. 752. 24 Plates. 60859

Percement de l'Isthme Américain par un Canal Interocéanique. Journal des Voyages, Explorations et Travaux rélatifs à la ligne

du Darien (Nouvelle-Grenade, aujourd'hui États-Unis de Colombie). *Paris.* 1864. 4to, pp. 112. 60860

[Perceval (John).] Remarks upon a Scandalous Piece, entitled A Brief Account of the Causes that have retarded the Progress of the Colony of Georgia. *London.* 1743. 8vo.

"An Examination of the Principles," "Faction Detected," Nos. 23367, 23610, Vol. vi., and "An Impartial Enquiry," No. 45001, Vol. xi., have been attributed to this author. "Faction Detected" is also ascribed to William Pulteney.

[Perceval (J.)] The Memorial of John, Earl of Egmont. [n. p. *Privately printed* 1763.] 8vo. 60862

The Earl wished to have a grant of the whole Island of St. John's, in the Gulf of St. Lawrence. Our No. 40263, Vol. ix., has been ascribed to this author.

Percival (E.) The Golden Gift: a Wreath of Gems from the Prose and Poetical Writers of America. By Emily Percival. *Boston: Phillips, Sampson & Co.* 1850. Sq. 12mo, pp. 252. c.

Percival (J. G.) Clio. By James G. Percival. No. i. ... *Charleston: S. Babcock & Co.* 1822. 12mo, pp. 108. + No. ii. ... *New Haven: S. Converse.* 1822. 18mo, pp. 132. + No. iii. *New York: G. & C. Carvill.* 1827. 18mo, pp. 203.

Percival. The Dream of a Day, and other Poems. By James G. Percival. *New Haven: Printed by S. Babcock.* 1843. 12mo, pp. 264. 60865

Percival. Geological Reports on the Middletown [Ct.] Silver-Lead Mines ... . By James G. Percival, ... and Wm. H. Stevens ... . *New York.* 1853. 8vo, pp. 11. 60866

Percival. Poems. By James G. Percival. *New Haven: Printed for the Author.* 1821. 16mo, pp. 348. + *New York: Charles Wiley.* 1823. 8vo, pp. (4), 396. + *London: John Miller.* 1824. 60867

Percival. The Poetical Works of James Gates Percival. ... With a Biographical Sketch [by L. W. Fitch]. *Boston: Ticknor and Fields.* mdccclix. 2 vols., 16mo, pp. lxii, (2), 402; vii, 517. Portrait. 60868

Percival. Report on the Geology of the State of Connecticut. By James G. Percival. ... *New Haven: Osborn & Baldwin, Printers.* 1842. 8vo, pp. 495. Map. 60869

Also: Geological Report on the Kensington Silver-Lead Mines, Berlin, Conn. ... *New Haven.* 1853. 8vo, pp. 6. — Oration ... before the Φ. B. K. Society, September 10th, 1822, on some of the Moral and Political Truths derivable from the Study of

History. ... *New Haven.* 1822. 8vo, pp. 19. — Poem ... before the Connecticut Alpha ... September 13th, 1825. ... *Boston.* 1826. 8vo, pp. 40. — Prometheus ii. with other Poems. ... *New Haven: A. H. Maltby.* 1822. 18mo, pp. 108. — Report on the Iron of Dodge and Washington Counties, ... Wisconsin. ... *Milwaukee.* 1855. 8vo, pp. 12. Folded Plate. *See also* Wisconsin.

The Percy Anecdotes, Revised Edition. To which is added a Valuable Collection of American Anecdotes. *New York: Harper & Brothers.* 1832. 8vo. 60870

Percy (F.) Forest Buds, from the Woods of Maine. By Florence Percy [*i. e.* Elizabeth Akers Allen]. *Boston: Brown, Bazin & Co.* 1856. 12mo, pp. 207. c. 60871

Percy (W.) The Charge Delivered to the Clergy of the Diocese of Guiana, at the Primary Visitation in April, 1843. By William Percy, Lord Bishop of Guiana. *Demerara.* 1843. 8vo, pp. 44. 60872

Perdigão Malheiro (A.) A Escravidão no Brasil. Ensaio Historico–Juridico–Social, pelo Dr. Agostinho Marques Perdigão Malheiro. Parte I. (juridica). Direito sobre os escravos e libertos. *Rio de Janeiro.* 1866. 8vo, pp. 211, xxx. + Parte 2, Indios. [*Ibid.*] 1867. 8vo, pp. iv, 160, 2. + Parte 3a. Africanos. [*Ibid.*] 1867. 8vo, pp. xii, 248, 216, 4, 2. 60873

Also: Supplemento ao Manual do procurador dos feitos da fazenda nacional ... . *Rio de Janeiro.* 1870. 8vo, pp. viii, 100, 267, 12.

Perdigon Garay (J. G.) Defensa del articulo "El Ministro de la Guerra," que publicó J. Suarez y Navarro. ... *Mejico.* 1849. 8vo. 60874

Perea (Estevan de). Relacion de la Nueva Mexico. ... [n. p.] 1630. 60875

This and the following title from Ternaux, Nos. 516 and 598.

Perea. Relacion del Nuevo Mondo o de la conversion de los Xumanas, embiada al arzobispo de Mexico D. Francisco Manso, por Fray Estevan de Perea, de la Orden de S. Francisco. [n. p.] 1640. 60876

Perea (P. de). Copia de la carta qve el Opispo de Areqvipa fray Don Pedro de Perea, de la orden de San Agustin, escriuiò al Ray nuestro señor Don Felipe iv. deste Nombre, prouando la certeza que tiene, el auer sido la Virgen concebida sin pecado original: y no poderse definir en la Iglesia la opinion contraria.

Impresso en la ciudad de los Reyes, por Geronymo de Contreras. 1629. 4to, pp. (48), 259, (32). 60877

A work of the greatest rarity. *See* Leclerc, No. 1820.

Peredo (J. J.) Discurso Dogmatico sobre la Potestad Eclesiastica por el Sr. Dr. D. Jose Joaquin Peredo. *Puebla.* 1835. 4to, pp. 28, (4). 60878

Pereira de Berredo (B.) *See* Berredo (B. P. de), ii. 4967.

Pereira Coruja (Antonio Alvares). Collecção de Vocabulos e frases usados na provincia de S. Pedro do Rio Grande do Sul no Brazil. ... *Londres: Trübner.* 1856. 4to, pp. 32. 60879

Pereira (João Manso). Memoria sobre o methodo economico de transportar para Portugal a agua-ardente do Brasil ... . *Lisboa: ... Simão Thaddêo Ferreira.* 1798. 8vo, pp. 28. 60880

Pereira da Silva (J. M.) Discursos Parliamentares de J. M. Pereira da Silva ... . *Rio de Janeiro: B. L. Garnier.* 1870. 8vo, pp. (4), 218, (1). 60881

Pereira da Silva. Historia da Fundação do Imperio Brazileiro por J. M. Pereira da Silva ... . *Rio de Janeiro: B. L. Garnier ...* 1864. 7 vols., 8vo, pp. (4), 318, Portrait; (4), 375; (4), 397; (4), 366; (4), 344; (4), 314; (4), 420. 60882

Pereira da Silva. Parnaso Brasileiro, ou Collecção de Poesias dos melhores Poetas brasileiros, desde o descobrimento do Brasil, precedida de uma introducção historica e biographica sobre a litteratura brasileira. ... *Rio de Janeiro: Typ. Univ. de Laemmert.* 1843–48. 2 vols., 8vo, pp. 298; x–324. 60883

Pereira da Silva. Plutarco Brasileiro. ... *Rio de Janeiro: ... Laemmert.* 1847. 2 vols., 8vo, pp. viii, 342, (2); 268, (2).

Pereira da Silva. Situation sociale, politique et economique de l'Empire du Brésil. *Paris: Durand.* 1865. 8vo. 60885

Pereira da Silva. Variedades Litterarias por J. M. Pereira da Silva. *Rio de Janeiro.* 1862. 2 vols., 8vo, pp. (4), 528;

Pereira da Silva. Os Varões Illustres do Brasil durante os tempos coloniáes. ... *Paris: A. Franck.* 1858. 2 vols., 8vo, pp. 391, (2); (4), 369, (2). 60887

Pereira de Alencastre (J. M.) Relatorio com que o Exm. Snr. Dr. Galdino Augusto da Natividade Silva 1o Vice-Presidente

da Provincia das Alagoas ... ao exm. snr. presidente José Martins Pereira de Alencastre. *Mageio: Typ. do Bacharel Felix da Costa Moraes.* 1866. Folio, pp. 74. Table. 60888

Pereira de Vasconcellos (J. M.) Ensaio sobre a Historia e Estatistica da Provincia do Espirito-Sancto, contendo além de muitos documentos curiosos e interessantes ... . *Victoria: Typ. de P. A. d'Azeredo.* 1858. 8vo, pp. 254. Portrait. 60889

Also: Jardim poetico, ou Collecção de Poesias Antigas e Modernas, compostas por Naturaes da Provincia do Espirito-Sancto ... . 1.a Serie. *Victoria: Typ. de Pedro Antonio d'Azeredo.* 1856. 8vo, pp. 177. + 2.a Serie. [*Ibid.*] 1860. 8vo, pp. 239.

Pereira de Barros (José Maurico Fernandes). Apontamentos de Direito Financeiro Brasileiro. ... *Rio de Janeiro: Typ. de E. & H. Laemmert.* 1855. 8vo, pp. 431. 60890

Pereira (J. de Solorzano). *See* Solorzano Pereira (J. de).

Pereira (Nuño Marquez). Compendio Narrativo do Peregrino da America, em que se tratam varios discursos espirituaes, e moraes, com muitas advertencias, e documentos contra os abusos, que se achaõ introduzidos pela malicia diabolica no Estado do Brasil. ... *Lisboa: M. M. da Costa.* 1752. 4to, pp. (24), 436. + *Lisboa: Na Offic. de Antonio Vicente da Silva. Anno* mdcclx. 4to, pp. (30), 475. + *Lisboa: Fr. Borges de Sousa.* 1765. 4to, pp. (30), 474. 60891

Pereira Gamba. Revista de la casa de Pereira Gamba i Compañia. Numero 1. *Bogota.* 1866. 8vo, pp. 32. 60892

Pereire (E.) Considérations sur les Finances de France, et des États-Unis. ... *Paris.* 1832. 8vo. 60893

Perez de Lara (Alon.) Compendio de las Tres Gracias de la Santa Crozada, contra Infideles ... . *Leon de Francia: P. Chevalier.* 1672. 4to. 60894

Contains many dispatches and instructions relating to America.

Perez de Ribas (A.) Historia | de los Trivmphos de Nuestra | Santa Fee entre Gentes las mas Barbaras, | y fieras del nueuo Orbe: | conseguidos por los Soldados, de la | Milicia de la Compañia de Iesvs en las Missiones | de la Prouincia de Nueua- | España. | Refierense assi mismo las costvmbres, | ritos, y supersticiones que vsauan estas Gentes: | sus puestos, y temples: | las vitorias que de algunas dellas alcaçaron con las armas los Ca- | tolicos Españoles, quando les obligaron à tomarlas: ... Dedicada a la ... Rey N. S. Felipe Qvarto. | Escrita por el Padre Andres

Perez de Ribas, | Prouincial en la Nueua España, natural de Cordoua. | *Año* 1645. | *Con Privilegio.* | *En Madrid. Por Alōso de Paredez, jūto a los Estudios de la Cōpañia.* | Folio, pp. (40), 763. c. 60895

The chief interest of this very rare volume lies in its accounts of the Indian tribes of Cinaloa, California, New Mexico, and Florida.

PEREZ (A.) Las Obras y Relaciones de Ant. Perez. *Geneva: Chuet.* 1654. 8vo. + *Geneva.* 1676. 8vo, pp. 1129. 60896

PEREZ (A. J.) Exhortacion Patriotica-Sagrada que hacia su Magistral Don A. Joaquin Perez, en la Santa Iglesia Catedral de la Puebla, Feb. 9, 1810. *En la Puebla.* 1810. 4to, pp. (4), 17.

PEREZ. Oracion Fúnebre del D. S. Biempica y Sotomayor, Obispo de Puebla. Pronunciada en las honras que le hizo, y solemnes sufragios que le aplicó su Santa Iglesia Catedral 16 Dec. de 1802. Por A. J. Perez. *Madrid.* 1802. 4to. 60898

Also: Oracion Funebre que en las Solemnes Exequias en la Iglesia del Espiritu Santo de la Puebla, á devocion y expensas de los hijos y Oriundos de Vizcaya de Navarra, por todos los que murieron en la Gloriosa Defensa de Buenos-Ayres, dixo 24 de Feb. de 1808. ... *Mexico.* 1808. 4to, 20 leaves. Folded Plate.—Sermon ... en la Santa Iglesia Metropolitana de Megico con motivo de la solemna coronacion de Señor D. Augustin de Iturbide. ... *Puebla.* 1839. 4to, 15 leaves.

PEREZ Y LOPEZ (Antonio Xavier). Teatro de la Legislacion Universal de España é Indias, por orden cronológico de sus cuerpos y decisiones no recopilados; y alfabético de sus títulos y principales materias. ... *Madrid.* 1791–98. 28 vols., 4to. C.

PEREZ (F.) Anales de la Revolucion, escritos segun sus propios documentos. Primera Epoca, que comprende desde el 1º de Abril de 1857 hasta el 18 de Julio de 1861. Por Felipe Perez. *Bogotá: Imprenta del Estado de Cundinamarca.* 1862. 8vo, pp. viii, 641, (2). C. 60900

Also: Jeografia fisica i politica del Estado del Cauca. *Bogotá.* 1862. 8vo, pp. 334. + Distrito federal, capital de los Estados Unidos de Colombia; ... [*Ibid.*] 1862. 8vo, pp. 54, (2). + Estados Unidos de Colombia ... . Comprende la jeografia del distrito federal i las de los Estados de Panamá i el Cauca. [*Ibid.*] 1862. 8vo, pp. xi, 494. + Estado de Magdalena. [*Ibid.*] 1862. 8vo, pp. 53. + Estado de Panamá. [*Ibid.*] 1862. 8vo, pp. 107, (2). + Estado de Antioquia ... . [*Ibid.*] 1863. 8vo, pp. (2), 98, (2). + Estado de Bolivar. [*Ibid.*] 1863. 8vo, pp. (2), 40, (2). + Estado de Boyacá. [*Ibid.*] 1863. 8vo, pp. 139, (2). + Estado de Cundinamarca. [*Ibid.*] 1863. 8vo, pp. 117. + Estado de Santander. [*Ibid.*] 1863. 8vo, pp. 94, (2). + Estado de Tolima. [*Ibid.*] 1863. 8vo, pp. 106, (2). 8 Plates.

PEREZ Y COMOTO (Florencio). Beneficios que deben resultar á la monarquia española del exacto cumplimiento de su liberal y sabia constitucion. ... *Mexico: Jauregui.* 1813. 4to, pp. (2), 76.

PEREZ Y COMOTO. Impugnacion de algunos errores politicos que fomentan la insurreccion de Nueva España. ... *Mexico.* 1812. 12mo, pp. (8), 50. 60902

Also: Desengaños que a los insurgentes de Nueva España seducidos por los fracmazones agentes de Napoleon ... . *Mexico.* 1812. 12mo, pp. 162.—Representacion que a favor del libre comercio ... . *Habana.* 1818. 4to, pp. iv, 84.

PEREZ (F.) Catecismo de la Doctrina Cristiana en lengua Otomi, traducida literalmente al Castellano por el Presbitero D. Francisco Perez ... . *Mexico: ... José Maria Gallegos.* 1834. 8vo, pp. (10), 17. [Followed by:] Manualito otomitica para los principiantes por D. Francisco Perez. [*Mexico.* 1834.] pp. 44, (2). 60903

The "Catecismo" may be a translation of the Otomi catechism of J. L. Yepes, Mexico, 1826.

PEREZ (G.) Relatione | Della Missione fatta da Padri | Gio. Perez, et Gio. Battista Zappa Della Compagnia de Giesù nelle tre | Prouincie di Tulancinco, Giustepec, | e Tenancinco, e ne suoi Popoli, e | Poesi circonuicini dall' anno | 1685. fino al 1687. Divisa in dve Parti. | Con l'aggiunta della Relatione d'altra | Missione fatta da Padri, Gio. | Battista Zappa, eà | Antonio Ramirez | della medesima Compagnia | in varie Terræ della | nuoua Spagna dall' anno 1687. sino | al 1688. | Portata dalla Spagnuolo all' Italiana | da Sebastiano Maria Castellini. | *In Milano,* | *Dall Ramellati.* [n. d.] 16mo, pp. 79. 60904

PEREZ GOMAR (G.) Curso elemental de Derecho de Gentes precedido de una introduccion sobre el derecho natural. Por Gregorio Perez Gomar. Tomo I. *Montevideo.* 1864. 8vo, pp. 280. Frontispiece. 60905

PEREZ (Jerónimo). Memorias para la Historia de la Revolucion de Nicaragua, 1854 á 1857. ... 1ª Parte. *Managua.* 1865. Sm. 4to, pp. (2), ii, 173, (4). [Followed by:] Memorias para la Historia de la Campaña Nacional. Contra el Filibusterismo. 1856 y 57. 2ᵈᵃ Parte. *Masayo.* 1873. pp. (6), 215, (4). C.

PEREZ (José). Note sur un ancien Manuscrit Américain. ... *Paris.* 1858. 8vo. 60907

Extract from the "Revue Américaine."

PEREZ (J.) A Correct Report of the Trial of Josef Perez, for Piracy, committed on board the Schooner Bee, of Charleston, S. C. ... Sept 9th, 1823. *New York: J. W. Bell.* 1823. 8vo, pp. 36. C. 60908

PEREZ (J. R.) Defensa de Eugenio Perez de Cerro presentado por José R. Perez. *Buenos-Aires.* 1858. 8vo, pp. 74.

PEREZ (J. P.) Diccionario de la Lengua Maya. Por D. Juan Pio Perez. *Merida de Yucatan: ... Juan F. Molina Solis.* 1866–77. 4to, pp. x, xx, 437. B. 60910

PEREZ (M.) Arte | de el Idioma | Mexicano. | Por el P. Fr. Manuel Perez, | ... Cathedratico de | dicho Idioma en la Real Vniversidad | de Mexico. | ... | *En Mexico, por Francisco de Ribera Calderon ... . Año de* 1713. 4to, pp. (16), 80, (3). C. 60911

A very rare and important work.

PEREZ. Cathecismo | Romano, | Traducido | en Castellano, | y Mexicano, | Por el P. F. Manuel | Perez, | ... *Con Licencia, en Mexico, por Francisco de* | *Rivera Calderon. Año de* 1723. 4to, pp. (28), 248. C. 60912

Of the greatest rarity. Fisher's copy sold for £15, 10s.

PEREZ. Farol | Indiano, | y Gvia de Curas | de Indios. | Summa de los Cinco Sacramen | tos que administran los Ministros Evangelicos en | esta America. Con todos los casos morales que su | ceden entre Indios. Deducidos de los mas clasicos | Authores, y amoldados à las costumbres, y pri | vilegios de los Naturales. | Por el P. Fr. Manuel Perez | ... . | *En Mexico, por Francisco de Rivera Calderon ... . Año de* 1713. 4to, pp. (48), 192, (3). C. 60913

Parts of this rare work are in Mexican and Spanish. A copy sold in 1869 at Puttick's for £8, 5s.

PEREZ DE OLIVA (Manuel). Exhortacion pronunciada en la Iglesia parroquial de Guadalupe el dia 25 de Julio de 1812. ... *Habana: Arazoza y Soler.* [1812.] 4to, pp. 4. 60914

PEREZ DE ANASTARIS (R.) Sermon, que en el dia de la Aparicion de Nra. Señora de Guadalupe dixo en su Santuario, Dec. 1796, por D. Ramon Perez de Anastaris. *Mexico: J. Jauregui.* 1697. 4to, pp. 26. 60915

PEREZ (T. M.) La Industria y el Poder, Drama en tres Actos, por Trinidad Manuel Perez. Segunda Edicion. *Lima.* 1863. 8vo, pp. 52. 60916

PEREZ-ROSALES (V.) Essai sur le Chili. ... *Hambourg.* 1857. 8vo, pp. 455. 2 Maps. 60917

There are copies on thick paper. Also: Manual del Ganadero Chileno, dedicado à las bibliotecas departamentales de Chile. ... *Hamburgo.* 1858. 8vo, pp. 160.

A Perfect Description of | Virginia: | Being, | A full and true Relation of the present State | of the Plantation, their Health, Peace, and Plenty: the number | of people, with their abundance of Cattell, Fowl, Fish, &c. with severall | sorts of rich and good Commodities, which may there be had, either | Naturally, or by Art and Labour. Which we are fain to | procure from Spain, France, Denmark, Swedeland, Germany, | Poland, yea, from the East-Indies. There | having been nothing related of the | true estate of this Planta- | tion these 25 years. | Being sent from Virginia, at the request of a Gentleman of worthy note, who desired to know the true State of Virginia as it now stands. | Also, | A Narration of the Countrey, within a few | dayes journey of Virginia, West and by South, where people come | to trade: being related to the Governour, Sir William Berckley, | who is to go himselfe to discover it with 30 horse, and 50 foot, | and other things needfull for his enterprize. | With the manner how the Emperor Nichotawance | came to Sir William Berckley, attended with five petty Kings, | to doe Homage, and bring Tribute to King Charles. With his solemne Protestation, that the Sun and Moon should lose | their Lights, before he (or his people in that Country), should prove disloyall, but ever to keepe Faith | and Allegiance to King Charles. | *London, Printed for Richard Wodenoth, at the Star under Peters* | *Church in Cornhill.* 1649. | 4to, pp. (4), 19. 60918

Extremely rare. The first leaf contains the royal arms on the verso. Reprinted in the "Collections of the Mass. Hist. Society," Second Series, Vol. IX., pp. 105–122, and in Force's "Tracts," Vol. II., No. 8.

A Perfect List. *See* Vol. v., No. 18504.

Perfection. A Poetical Epistle. Calmly addressed to the greatest Hypocrite in England: ... *London: Printed for J. Bew.* MDCCLXXVIII. 4to, pp. 36. J.C.B. 60919

Seems to be aimed at the Rev. John Wesley, in response to his "Calm Address."

The Perfectionist. J. H. Noyes and J. L. Skinner, Editors. Vol. III. *Putney, Vt.: S. R. Leonard, Printer.* 1843. Folio, pp. 96. Continued. B. 60920

With Vol. IV. the title was changed to "The Perfectionist and Theocratic Watchman."

Perfectionists. The Resolutions and Circular Address of the Convention of Perfectionists, held at New York and New Jersey, May 12th, 1842. *Putney.* [n. d.] 8vo. 60921

PERHAM (J.) Pictorial Voyage, known as The Seven Mile Mirror to Canada, American Frontier, and the Saguenay ... . By Josiah Perham. *New York.* 1854. 8vo, pp. 48. 60922

PERHAM. Gen. Perham's Platform. The most feasible Plan yet offered for suppressing the Rebellion. ... *Boston: Alfred Mudge & Son.* 1862. 8vo, pp. 12. 60923

PERHAM (S.) The Slaveholders' Rebellion and Modern Democracy. Speech of Hon. Sidney Perham, of Maine, ... May 3, 1864. [n. p. n. d.] 8vo, pp. 8. 60924

PERICLES, *pseudon.* New Crisis, or Grand Appeal to the Nation, for its Decision on this Most Important Question, Are Happiness and Freedom consistent with Foreign Commerce at all events, or are they not? Likewise on Necessity or Non-Necessity of a War. By Pericles. *Philadelphia.* 1809. 8vo, pp. 36. 60925

PERIER (*M.* Du). *See* Du Perier (*M.*), Vol. VI. 21349–51.

Perils and Adventures on the Deep. *London: T. Nelson.* 1850. 16mo, pp. (6), 326. 8 Plates. C. 60926

Perils and Captivity: comprising the Sufferings of the Picard Family after the Shipwreck of the Medusa in ... 1816. Narrative of the Captivity of M. de Brisson in ... 1785. Voyage of Madame Godin along the river of the Amazons in the year 1770. *Edinburgh: Constable and Co.* 1827. 18mo, pp. xx, 19–334. + *Boston: T. S. Hill.* 1831. 18mo, pp. 334. B. 60927

The Perils of Pearl Street. *See* [Greene (Asa)], VII. 28584.

Perils, Pastimes, and Pleasures of an Emigrant in ... Vancouver's Island and California. *London: Thomas Cautley Newby.* 1849. Post 8vo, pp. (2), 606. 60928

PÉRIN (R.) L'Incendie du Cap, ou le Règne de Toussaint-Louverture, où l'on développe le caractère de ce chef de révoltés, sa conduite atroce depuis qu'il s'est arrogé le pouvoir ... . Par René Périn ... . *Paris, Chez Marchand.* 1802. 12mo, pp. 256. Plate. H. 60929

PERINCHIEF (Octavius). A Discourse ... on ... Thanksgiving at the Church of the Messiah, in Brooklyn, 18th Nov., 1858. By the Rev. O. Perinchief. ... *Brooklyn: E. Ray, Printer.* 1858. 8vo, pp. 13. H. 60930

Also: Sermons ... . Edited by Charles Lanman. *Washington: W. Ballantyne.* 1869. 8vo, pp. 308, iv.—Sermons ... in Memorial Church, Baltimore. Edited by Charles Lanman. *New York: D. Appleton & Co.* 1870. 8vo, pp. 327. C.

Periodical Account of Baptist Missions within the Indian Territory, for the year ending December 31, 1836. [n. p. n. d.] 8vo, pp. 8. 60931

Periodical Accounts relating to the Missions of the Church of the United Brethren, established among the Heathen. *London.* 1790. 8vo. Continued. 60932

These volumes contain accounts of missions in Greenland, Labrador, and other parts of North America.

Periódico de la Sociedad Económica de Guatemala. (No. 1, 1. mayo 1815.) [n. p. 1815.] 12mo. 60933

Continued to No. 24, April 15, 1816.

El Periquillo Sarmiento. *See* [Lizardi (J. F. de)], x. 41664

PERITSOL (A.) ... Itinera Mundi, sic dicta nempe Cosmographia, autore Abrahamo Peritsol. Latinâ Versione donavit & Notas passim adjecit Thomas Hyde S. T. D. è Coll. Reginæ Oxon. Protobibliothecarius Bodlejanus. Calce exponitur Turcarum Liturgia, Peregrinatio Meccano, ægrotorum visitatio, circumcisio, &c. Accedit Castignatio in Angelum à S. Joseph, al. dictum de la Brosse, Carmelitam discalceatum sui Ordinis in Ispahan Persidis olim Præfectum. *Oxonii. E. Theatro Sheldoniano* MDCXCI. *Impensis Henrici Bonwick Bibliopolæ Londinensis.* 4to, pp. (16), 196. J.C.B. 60934

In Hebrew and Latin. *See* for America, chapt. 20, 21, 26, 29, "De insulis maris Oceani in India, De inventione Mundi Novi," etc. The "Turcarum Liturgia" is often wanting. This work was compiled by Abraham Peritsol or rather Farissol, a learned Jew, at Ferrara in 1525, and first printed in Hebrew at Venice in 1587. The Latin version of 1691 is reprinted in Hyde's "Syntagma Dissertationum," Oxon. 1767, vol. I., and in Ugolino, "Thesaur. Antiq.," vol. VII. *See* Fürst's "Biblioth. Judaica," I. 276.

PERKINS (A. E. P.) A Semi-Centennial Sermon, ... before the Brookfield Associational Conference in West Brookfield, June 15, 1870. By A. E. P. Perkins. *Springfield.* 1871. 8vo, pp. 22. 60935

Also: ... Discourse at the Funeral of Joseph Cummings. ... *Boston.* 1860. 8vo.—Decennial Sermon, ... December 3, 1865, and Thanksgiving Sermon, December 7, 1865. ... *Boston.* 1866. 8vo, pp. 34.

[PERKINS (A. T.)] A Sketch of the Family of Dumaresq, to which are added Reminiscences of James Dumaresq, and an

Appendix of Documents. *Albany: J. Munsell.* 1863. 8vo, pp. 23. 60936

PERKINS (A. T.) A Sketch of the Life and a List of some of the Works of John Singleton Copley. By Augustus Thorndike Perkins, A.M. ... *Privately Printed.* [*T. R. Marvin & Son, Boston.*] 1873. 4to, pp. 144. + Supplement. [*Boston.* 1875.] 4to, pp. 15. 60937

Also: A Sketch of the Life and a List of some of the Works of John Singleton Copley, R.A. Prepared for the Massachusetts Historical Society. *Cambridge: John Wilson & Son.* 1873. 8vo, pp. 13.—Losses to Literature and Art by the Great Fire in Boston. *Boston.* 1873. Sm. 4to.

PERKINS (B.) Nebraska and Kansas. Speech of Hon. Bishop Perkins, of New York, ... May 10, 1854. [*Washington.* 1854.] 8vo, pp. 7. 60938

Also: Speech ... on the Differences existing in the Democratic Party in New York. *Washington.* 1854. 8vo. S.

PERKINS (C.) An Oration ... at ... Norwich, Conn., on the Anniversary of American Independence, July 4th, 1822. By Charles Perkins. *Norwich: Printed by Robinson & Dunham.* 1822. 8vo, pp. 24. BA. 60939

PERKINS (C. C.) American Art Museums. By Charles C. Perkins. *Boston: Fields, Osgood & Co.* 1870. 8vo, pp. 30. H.

Also: Art in Education. ... *New York.* 1870. 8vo, pp. 6.

PERKINS (C.) An Eulogy on the Hon. William H. Woodward, late a member of the Corporation of Dartmouth University, who died August 9, 1818, Pronounced ... at Hanover, N. H. August 26, 1818. By Cyrus Perkins. *Hanover, N. H. Printed by Charles Spear.* 1818. 8vo, pp. 16. BA., W. 60941

PERKINS [Elisha]. Certificates of the Efficacy of Doctor Perkins's Patent Metallic Instruments. *Newburyport.* [1796.] 8vo, pp. 24. M. + *New Haven.* 1796. 8vo. + *New London: S. Green.* 1796. 8vo, pp. 16. + [*Ibid.*] 1797. 8vo, pp. 32.

The "Metallic Tractors," which were invented by Dr. Elisha Perkins of Connecticut, gained an extensive notoriety in 1796, and many cures were attributed to them. The doctor's son, Benjamin Douglas Perkins, went to London, where he established a Perkinsian institute, and published several pamphlets and books concerning them. The "tractors," however, were attacked and ridiculed by the medical profession, and in a few years lost their reputation. For an amusing account of them *see* [Fessenden's] "Terrible Tractoration," *our* vol. VI. 24218. *See also* Thacher's "Am. Medical Biography," p. 422.

PERKINS (E. B.) Address ... before the Peace Society of Windham County at its Annual Meeting in Brooklyn, August

20th, 1828. By Elisha B. Perkins, Esq. *Brooklyn, Con.: Wm. H. Bigelow.* 1828. 8vo, pp. 32. H. + Second Edition. [*Ibid.*]

PERKINS (E.) A "Bunker Hill" Contest, A. D. 1826, Between the "Holy Alliance" for the Establishment of Hierarchy and Ecclesiastical Domination over the Human Mind. ... The Rev. Charles Finney ... . By Ephraim Perkins. *Utica: The Author.* 1826. 12mo, pp. 104. H. 60944

Also: Letter to the Presbytery of Oneida County ... respecting the Late Revival ... *Utica: Printed by Dauby & Maynard.* 1827. 12mo.—A Serious Address to the Presbytery of Oneida, on the Manner of conducting the late Revivals ... [*Utica.* 1831.] 12mo, pp. 12.

[PERKINS (F. Beecher).] The Ermine in the Ring; a History of the Wood Lease Case. *New York: G. P. Putnam & Son.* [1869.] 8vo, pp. 32. B. 60945

PERKINS. Perkins Family of Connecticut. By Fred. B. Perkins of Hartford, Conn. [*Boston.* 1860.] 8vo, pp. 8. 60946

Reprinted from the "N. E. Hist. and Gen. Register," for April, 1860. It gives only descendants of Joseph and Jabez Perkins, who settled in Connecticut.

PERKINS. The Picture and the Men; being Biographical Sketches of President Lincoln and his Cabinet ... . Compiled by Fred. B. Perkins. *New York: A. J. Johnson.* 1867. 16mo, pp. 190. C. 60947

Also: The Station and Duty of American Teachers as Citizens ... Address ... Association of Alumni of Connecticut State Normal School ... . *Hartford.* 1858. 8vo, pp. 27.

PERKINS (G. A.) A Record of Births, Baptisms, Publishments, Marriages and Deaths, in the Perkins Family of Ipswich. Communicated by Geo. A. Perkins, M.D. ... *Salem.* 1872. 8vo, pp. 16. 60948

PERKINS (*Mrs.* G. A.) Early Times on the Susquehanna. By Mrs. George A. Perkins. *Binghampton.* 1870. 12mo.

PERKINS (G. W.) Facts and Duties of the Times. A Sermon [on Slavery] ... by Rev. G. W. Perkins, Chicago, Illinois. [*Chicago:*] *Printed by Hays & Thompson.* 1856. 8vo, pp. 28. + *New York: William S. Dorr, Printer.* 1856. 18mo, pp. 36.

PERKINS. Historical Sketches of Meriden. By G. W. Perkins. *West Meriden: Franklin E. Hinman.* 1849. 12mo, pp. 117. Map. B., P. 60951

PERKINS. Prof. Stuart and Slave Catching. Remarks on Mr. Stuart's book "Conscience and the Constitution," at a Meeting in Guilford, August 1, 1850, commemorative of Emancipation in the West Indies. By G. W. Perkins. *West Meriden, Ct.: Hinman's Print.* 1850. 8vo, pp. (2), 28. 60952

Also: Address to the "Pacific Pioneers," ... March 22, 1849. ... *West Meriden.* 1849. 8vo, pp. 16.—Minority Report of a Committee of the General Association of Connecticut, on ... Slavery, presented June, 1849 ... . [*Meriden.* 1849.] 8vo, pp. 20. —Sermons ... with Memoir. *New York: A. D. F. Randolph.* 1859. 12mo, pp. 331.

PERKINS (James). Report of the Committee of Merchants and others, of Boston; on the Tariff. *Boston: Printed by Wells and Lilly.* 1820. 8vo, pp. 23. BA. 60953

PERKINS (J. H.) Annals of the West: embracing a concise account of Principal Events which have occurred in the Western States and Territories, from the Discovery of the Mississippi Valley to the year Eighteen Hundred and Forty Five. ... By James H. Perkins. *Cincinnati: James R. Albach.* 1846. 8vo, pp. xx, 591, (1). 2 Maps. A., C. + [*Ibid.*] 1847. 8vo, pp. xx, 591, (1). 2 Maps. 60954

PERKINS. Annals of the West: embracing a concise account of Principal Events, which have occurred in the Western States and Territories, from the Discovery of the Mississippi Valley to the year Eighteen Hundred and Fifty. ... First Edition, by James H. Perkins. Second Edition, Revised and Enlarged by J. M. Peck. *St. Louis: James R. Albach.* 1850. 8vo, pp. 808. BA. + [*Ibid.*] 1851. 8vo, pp. 818. 60955

This valuable work of reference was originated by J. R. Albach, who collected the materials and issued a "Prospectus" in 1845. The first edition was restricted to the central portions of the West. The edition of 1850 contains no index. It was again issued, omitting the names of Perkins and Peck, as "Compiled from the most authentic sources and published by James R. Albach," *St. Louis,* 1852, 8vo, pp. 818. An enlarged edition, from which the marginal references were mostly omitted, was published at Pittsburgh in 1856, for which *see* our vol. I., No. 585, and add: + [*Ibid.*] 1857. 8vo, pp. 1016. + [*Ibid.*] 1858. 8vo, pp. 1016.

Also: Christian Civilization. An Address ... before the Athenian Society of the University of Ohio, at Athens, September 16, 1840. ... *Cincinnati.* 1840. 8vo, pp. 26.—A Discourse ... before the First Congregational Society of Cincinnati, ... October 8, 1848. ... *Cincinnati.* 1848. 8vo, pp. 16.

PERKINS. The Memoir and Writings of James Handasyd Perkins. Edited by William Henry Channing. ... *Boston: Wm. Crosby and H. P. Nichols.* 1851. 2 vols., 12mo, pp. xii, 527; (7), 502. B. + *Cincinnati.* 1851. 2 vols., 12mo. 60956

Contains many details of frontier life and Indian warfare, presented in an interesting and scholarly manner.

[PERKINS (John).] The True Nature and Cause of the Tails of Comets elucidated. *Boston.* 1772. 4to, pp. 8. M. 60957

[PERKINS.] Theory of Agency; or, An Essay on the Nature, Source and Extent of Moral Freedom. ... *Boston.* 1771. 8vo, pp. 43. M. 60958

Also: Thoughts on Agency; wherein the Article of Motive (as necessitating Human Action) is particularly examined ... . *New Haven.* 1765. 8vo, pp. 27. W.

PERKINS (J.), *Jr.* Speech of Hon. John Perkins, Jr., on the Diplomatic System of the United States, delivered ... January, 1855. *Washington.* 1855. 8vo, pp. 27. 60959

Also: Speech ... Feb. 6, 1855, on the Consular System of the United States. *Washington.* 1855. 8vo.

PERKINS (J.) A Sermon ... before the Auxiliary Education Society of Norfolk County at their Annual Meeting in Stoughton, June 8, 1831. By Jonas Perkins. *Boston: T. R. Marvin, Printer.* 1831. 8vo, pp. 24. H. 60960

PERKINS (J.) An Oration upon Genius; pronounced at the Anniversary Commencement of Harvard University, ... July 19, 1797. By Joseph Perkins, A.M. *Boston: Printed by Manning & Loring.* 1797. 8vo, pp. 22. H., W. 60961

PERKINS (J. A.) The Female Prisoner. A narrative of the Life and singular adventures of Josephine Amelia Perkins. *New York.* 1839. 8vo, pp. 24. 60962

PERKINS (J.) Our Country's Sin. A Sermon preached to the Members and Families of the Nestorian Mission, at Oroomiah, Persia, July 3, 1853. By Rev. Justin Perkins, D.D. ... *Boston: John P. Jewett and Company.* 1854. 8vo, pp. 24. + *New-York: H. B. Knight.* 1854. 8vo, pp. 24. BA. 60963

Also: A Good Missionary. A Sermon occasioned by the Death of Rev. William Redfield Stocking, Missionary to the Nestorians, preached at Oroomiah, Persia, July 9, 1854. ... *Boston.* 1854. 8vo, pp. 42.

PERKINS (L.) A Poem delivered on the Celebration of Independence ... at Wilton, Maine. By Lafayette Perkins. *Hallowell.* 1828. 8vo. BM. 60964

PERKINS (N.) The Benign Influence of Religion on Civil Government and National Happiness. Illustrated in A Sermon, preached before His Excellency Jonathan Trumbull, Esq. Governor: ... and House of Representatives of the State of Connecticut, on the Anniversary Election, May 12th, 1808. By

Nathan Perkins, D.D. ... *Hartford: Printed by Hudson and Goodwin.* 1808. 8vo, pp. 60. 60965

PERKINS. A Discourse, ... at the Ordination of the Rev. Calvin Chapin, ... [at] Wethersfield, April 30th, 1794. By Nathan Perkins ... . *Hartford: Printed by Hudson & Goodwin.* M,DCC,XCIV. 8vo, pp. 38. BA. 60966

PERKINS. A Half-Century Sermon, delivered at West Hartford, on the 13th day of October, 1822 ... . By Nathan Perkins, D.D. *Hartford: George Goodwin.* 1822. 8vo, pp. 24. 60967

PERKINS. A Sermon, ... June 2, 1775, to Soldiers, who went from West Hartford, in defense of their Country. ... *Hartford.* 1775. 12mo, pp. 15. 60968

Also: Discourse ... in Newington, January 16th, 1805, at the Ordination of the Rev. Joab Brace. ... *Hartford.* 1807. 8vo.—A Discourse, ... October 10, 1810, at the Ordination of the Rev. Nathan Perkins, Jr. ... [at] Amherst ... . *Northampton, Mass.: William Butler, Printer.* 1810. 8vo, pp. 24.—A Sermon at the Installation of the Rev. Mr. Solomon Wolcott, to the Church in Wintonbury, May 24th, 1786. ... *Hartford: Hudson & Goodwin.* 1786. 8vo.—Sermon ... at the Ordination of Rev. Hezekiah N. Woodruff, ... Stonington, July 2, 1789. ... *New London.* 1790. 8vo, pp. 30.—Sermon ... at the Ordination of William F. Miller. ... *Hartford.* 1792. 8vo.—Sermon ... at the Ordination of Oliver Wetmore. ... [n. p.] 1807. 8vo.—Sermon ... at the Ordination of E. G. Welles. [n. p.] 1808. 8vo.—Sermon ... at the Ordination of Elihu Mason. ... [n. p.] 1810. 8vo.—Sermon ... July 23, 1812 [on the State Fast] ... *Hartford.* 1812. 8vo.—Sermon ... at the interment of Rev. Timothy Pitkin. ... *Hartford.* 1812. 8vo, pp. 24.—A Sermon ... at the interment of the Rev. Nathan Strong, D.D. ... *Hartford: George Goodwin and Sons.* 1817. 8vo, pp. 27.—Twenty-four Discourses ... . *Hartford.* 1795. 8vo.

PERKINS (N.), *Jr.* A Discourse ... November 24, 1819, at the Ordination of the Rev. Rufus William Bailey, ... in Norwich, Vermont. By Nathan Perkins, Jr. ... *Woodstock: Printed by David Watson.* 1820. 8vo, pp. 31. H. 60969

Also: A Sermon ... on the Death of Dr. Seth Coleman ... . *Amherst.* 1815. 8vo. —Sermon ... at the Ordination of E. Moody. ... [n. p.] 1818. 8vo.

PERKINS (O. L.) The History of the Buccaniers. *See* [Exquemelin], Vol. VI., No. 23494.

PERKINS (S.) General Jackson's Conduct in the Seminole War, Delineated in a History of that Period, affording conclusive reasons why he should not be the next President. By Samuel Perkins, Esq. *Brooklyn, Con.: John Gray, Jr.* 1828. 8vo, pp. 39. 60970

PERKINS. Historical Sketches of the United States, from the Peace of 1815 to 1830. By Samuel Perkins, Esquire. *New York: S. Converse.* 1830. 12mo, pp. 444. BA. 60971

PERKINS. A History of the Political and Military Events of the Late War between the United States and Great Britain. By Samuel Perkins, Esq. *New Haven: Printed ... by S. Converse.* 1825. 8vo, pp. xi, (1), 9–512. H. 60972

Also: Address ... before the Peace Society of Windham County, at ... Pomfret, February 14, 1827. ... *Brooklyn, Con.* ... *John Gray, Jr.* [n. d.] 8vo, pp. 20.—The World as It Is: containing a View of the Present Condition of the Principal Nations, ... Second Edition. [*New Haven:*] *T. Belknap.* 1837. 12mo, pp. 457. Map. + Fifth Edition. [*Hartford.*] 1840. 8vo, pp. 460.

PERKINS (S.) An Address delivered before the Reading Peace Society, in Minot, Dec. 21, 1825. By Simeon Perkins. *Portland.* 1826. 8vo, pp. 16. 60973

PERKINS (S. K. B.) A Discourse at the Semi-Centennial Celebration of the First Congregational Church, Glover, Vt., July 12, 1867. By Rev. S. K. B. Perkins. *Barton, Vt.* 1867. 8vo, pp. 8. 60974

[PERKINS (Stephen H.), *and others.*] Report on the Expediency of providing better tenements for the Poor. [*Boston.* 1846.] 8vo, pp. 36. B. 60975

PERKINS (Thos. H.) Remarks ... by the Hon. T. H. Perkins at the Laying of the Corner Stone of the Boston Exchange, August 2, 1841. *Boston: Printed by Samuel N. Dickinson.* 1841. 8vo, pp. 24. H. 60976

PERKINS (W. S.) Sermon preached at the Celebration of the One Hundred and Fiftieth Anniversary of the Society for the Propagation of the Gospel in Foreign Parts, containing a Brief History of St. James's Church. By Rev. W. S. Perkins. *Bristol, Pa.* 1851. 8vo, pp. 20. 60977

Eighth Annual Report of ... the PERKINS INSTITUTION and Massachusetts Asylum for the Blind ... . *Boston: John H. Eastburn, Printer.* 1840. 8vo, pp. 31. 5 Plates. Continued. BA.

Formerly known as "The New England Institution for the Education of the Blind," which see for previous reports.

First Annual Report of the ... Directors of the PERKIOMEN CONSOLIDATED MINING COMPANY ... May 5, 1852 ... . *Philadelphia: Crissy & Markley, Printers.* 1852. 8vo, pp. 32. Plates.

PERLEY (I.) Eulogy of the Hon. Ira Perley on ... Daniel Webster, ... before the executive and legislative departments of New Hampshire, Dec. 22, 1852. *Concord: Butterfield & Hill.* 1852. 8vo, pp. 38. 60980

PERLEY (J.) An Anniversary Oration ... before the Federal Republicans of Hallowell ... July Fourth, 1807. By Jeremiah Perley, A.M. ... *Augusta: Printed by Peter Edes.* 1807. 8vo, pp. 24. BA. 60981

PERLEY (M. H.) Descriptive Catalogue (in Part) of the Fishes of New Brunswick and Nova Scotia. By M. H. Perley, ... *Fredericton: J. Simpson, Printer.* 1851. 8vo, pp. 43. B. + Second Edition. [*Ibid.*] 1852. 8vo, pp. 50. 60982

PERLEY. A Handbook of Information for Emigrants to New-Brunswick. ... By M. H. Perley ... . *St. John, N. B.: Printed by H. Chubb & Co.* 1854. 8vo, pp. 88. Map and Plates. + *London: Edward Stanford.* 1857. Post 8vo, pp. (2), 94. Map.

PERLEY. Reports on the Sea and River Fisheries of New Brunswick. By M. H. Perley. *Fredericton.* 1852. 8vo. + Second Edition. ... *Fredericton: J. Simpson, Printer.* 1852. 8vo, pp. xvi, 294. A., BA. 60984

Also: Report on the Fisheries of the Gulf of St. Lawrence. ... *Fredericton.* 1849. 8vo.—Report on the Fisheries of the Bay of Fundy. ... *Fredericton.* 1851. 8vo.

A Permanent and Effectual Remedy suggested for the Evils under which the British West Indies now Labour. In a Letter from a West India Merchant to a West India Planter. *London: J. M. Richardson.* 1807. 8vo, pp. 48. + [*Ibid.*] 1808. 8vo, pp. 48. 60985

Permanent Temperance Documents of the American Temperance Society. Vol. I. *Boston: S. Bliss.* 1835. 8vo, pp. (6), 503. P. 60986

See also our Vol. I., No. 1240.

PERNAMBUCO. Advys | Op de | Presentatie | Van | Portugael. | Het tweede Deel. | Met een Remonstrancie aen sijn Ko- | ninck-lijcke Majesteyt van Portugael by de In- | woonders Portugesen van de Capitanie | van Parnambocq overgelevert. | *Gedruct in't Jaer ons Heeren,* 1648. | Sm. 4to, pp. (2), 37. C. 60987

For the first part, which was probably printed in 1648, *see* our Vol. II., No. 7503.

Description de la Brasil, et de la ville de Pernambuco; aussi de tout les païs, et des moulins de sucre ... . *Anuers: A. Verhoeuen.* [1625.] Sm. 4to, folded sheet. Plate. C. 60988

Falla recitada pelo excellentissimo senhor Antonio Pinto Chichorro da Gama Presidente da Provincia ... de Pernambuco, aos

9 de Março de 1846. *Pernambuco. Typ. Imp. de L. I. R. Roma.* 1846. 8vo, pp. 4. 60989

Projecto e Memoria sobre o encanamento das aguas potaveis para a cidade do Recife, na Provincia de Pernambuco. *Rio de Janeiro.* 1841. 8vo, pp. 28. Map. 60990

Relatorio apresentado á Assembléa Legislativa Provincial em o 1.º de Marco de 1866 Pelo exm. snr. Conselheiro Joaõ Lustosa da Cunha Paranaguá Presidente de Pernambuco *Recife* 1866. Folio. 60991

Relatorio que á Assemblea Legislativa de Pernambuco apresentou na Sessão Ordinaria de 1842 o ex.mo Barão da Boa Vista, Presidente ... . *Pernambuco.* [1842.] 8vo, pp. 23. Table.

Relatorio que á Assembléa Legislativa Provincial de Pernambuco appresentou no dia da abertura de sua sessaõ extraordinaria em 11 de Setembro de 1854. O exm. Conselheiro Dr. José Bento da Cunha e Figueiredo, Presidente ... . *Recife Typographia de M. F. de Faria.* 1854. 8vo. 60993

[PERNETY (Antoine Joseph Dom).] Dissertation sur l'Amérique et les Américains, contre les Recherches Philosophiques de Mr. de P[auw]. *Berlin: G. J. Decker ... Samuel Pitra.* [1769.] Sm. 8vo, pp. (8), 239. J.C.B. + [*Ibid.* 1770.] Sm. 8vo, pp. (8), 239. BA. + [*Ibid.* 1772.] Sm. 8vo. 60994

"In this dissertation the author controverts the sentiment of Mr. de Pauw, that America occupies an inferior position in the scale of Nature, to other parts of the World; and that the degradation of the American Indians, as well as the inferior size, ferocity, and utility of its animals, proves it."—FIELD. Also reprinted in the third volume of "Recherches Philosophiques." *See* Nos. 59241–46. It was replied to by Mr. de Pauw in his "Defense des Recherches Philosophiques," to which Dom Pernety rejoined in the following work:

[PERNETY.] Examen | des | Recherches Philosophiques | sur l'Amérique | et les Américains, | et de la Défense de cet Ouvrage. | *A Berlin, chez G. J. Decker.* 1771. 2 vols., 12mo, pp. xx, 318, (1); xx, 603, (1). BA. 60995

PERNETY. Histoire d'un Voyage aux Isles Malouines, Fait en 1763 & 1764; avec des Observations sur le Detroit de Magellan, et sur les Patagons, Par Dom Pernetty, Abbé de l'Abbaye de Burgel, Membre de l'Académie Royale des Sciences & Belles-Lettres de Prusse; ... Nouvelle Edition. Refondue & augmentée d'un Discours Préliminaire, de Remarques sur l'Histoire

Naturelle, &c. *A Paris, Saillant & Nyon.* M.DCC.LXX. 2 vols., 8vo, pp. iv, 385; (2), 334, (2). 18 Plates and Maps. C. 60996

Bartlett's catalogue of the Brown library gives an edition: "Histoire d'un Voyage aux Isles Malouines," etc., *Paris: Chez Saillant & Nyon.* MDCCLXIX. 2 vols., 8vo. First printed at Berlin with the following title:

PERNETY. Journal Historique d'un Voyage fait aux Isles Malouïnes en 1763 et 1764, pour les reconnoitre, et y former un établissement; et de deux voyages au Détroit de Magellan, avec un relation sur les Patagons. Par Dom Pernetty ... . *Berlin: Et. de Bourdeaux.* 1769. 2 vols., 8vo, pp. xiv, 403; 405–704, (48). 18 Plates and Maps. S. 60997

Leclerc (1867), No. 1155, gives an edition: "Journal Historique [etc., as above]. Nouvelle Edition. Refondue et augmentée d'un discours préliminaire, de remarques sur l'histoire naturelle. *Paris, Saillant.* 1770. 2 vols., 8vo, pp. iv, 385; 334, (2). 18 Plates and Maps. For an English translation, *see our* Vol. II., No. 6870, and add to the collation: 5 Maps and 11 Plates. The "Second Edition" of the same, *London: W. Goldsmith,* 1773, has the same collation. *See* "Monthly Review," XLII. 509.

PÉRON (F.) Voyage de Découvertes aux Terres Australes, exécuté par ordre de Sa Majesté l'Empereur et Roi, sur les Corvettes le Géographe, le Naturaliste, et la Goelette le Casuarina, Pendant les Années 1800, 1801, 1802, 1803 et 1804; Publié par décret impérial, sous le Ministère de M. de Champagny, Et rédigé par M. F. Péron ... . *A Paris, de l'Imprimerie Impériale.* M.DCCC.VII–1816. 2 vols., 4to, pp. (4), xv, 496, (2); xxxi, 471. Portrait and 2 folded Tables. Atlas in 2 parts, folio. A. 60998

The above four volumes are entitled "Partie Historique." Tome Second, "Rédigé en partie par feu F. Péron, et continué Par M. Louis Freycinet," is dated *Paris,* 1816. The atlas to vol. I. is by MM. Lesueur and Petit, [n. p. n. d.] and contains 41 maps and plates. The second part, by M. L. Freycinet, *Paris,* 1811, contains 14 maps.

PÉRON. Voyage de Découvertes aux Terres Australes, fait par ordre du Gouvernement, Sur les corvettes le Géographe, le Naturaliste et la goëlette le Casuarina, pendant les années 1800, 1801, 1802, 1803 et 1804; Historique. Rédigé par Péron, et continué par M. Louis de Freycinet. Seconde Edition, Revue, Corrigée et Augmentée par M. Louis de Freycinet ... . Ouvrage enrichi d'un superbe Atlas composé de 68 planches, dont 27 coloriées ... . *Paris: Arthus Bertrand.* 1824. 4 vols., 8vo, pp. xxiv, 400, Portrait; (4), 532; (4), 432; (4), 353, (4). Atlas in folio. 68 Maps and Plates. A., C. 60999

See also Vol. VII., Nos. 25916–17. For a translation in part, *see* Phillips's "Coll. of Voyages," vol. XI., *and* Pinkerton, vol. XI.

PÉRON. Entdeckungsreise nach den Südländern, ausgeführt auf Befehl des Kaisers von Frankreich in den Jahren 1800 bis

1804. ... Aus dem Französischen von Ph. W. G. Hausleutner. *Tübingen.* 1808–19. 2 vols., 4to. + *Stuttgart.* 1808–19. 2 vols., 4to. Portrait. + *Weimar.* 1808–19. 2 vols., 8vo. Map and 2 Plates. 61000

PÉRON. Mémoires du Capitaine Péron, sur ses Voyages aux côtes d'Afrique, ... à l'Ile d'Amsterdam, ... aux côtes Nord-Ouest de l'Amérique ... . *Paris.* 1824. 2 vols., 8vo. Plates.

PEROU. *See* Peru.

PÉROUSE (J. F. G. de la). *See* La Pérouse (J. F. G. de), X.

A Perpetual Almanac of Spiritual Meditation. *Boston.* 1724. 18mo, pp. 170. 61002

Perpetual War. *See* [Lowell (John)], Vol. IX., No. 42456.

[PERRAULT (*Rev.* Charles Ovide).] L. J. C. & M. J. Prières, Cantiques et Catechisme en langue Montagnaise ou Chipeweyan ... *Montreal: Imprimerie de Louis Perrault.* 1857. 18mo, pp. 144. + *Montreal: Imprimerie de Louis Perrault et Compagnie.* 1865. 18mo, pp. xi, 3–179, 145–180. 61003

Printed in syllabic characters. Also: Prières, Cantiques, Catechisme ... en langue Crise ... . *Montreal: Louis Perrault et Compagnie.* 1866. 18mo, pp. 324. In syllabic characters.

PERRAULT (J.) Relation du cap Breton, dans la Nouvelle France, par Julien Perrault, de Nantes. *Paris.* 1634. 12mo.

See Ternaux, No. 585, *and* [Harrisse's] "Notes," No. 58. Julien Perrault, a native of Nantes, and a member of the Society of Jesus, arrived in Canada in 1634. It is not certain that his "Relation" was ever printed separately. To Le Jeune's "Relation" of 1635 (*Paris,* 1636,) is appended a brief "Relation de qvelqves particvlaritez, dv liev et des habitans de l'isle dv Cap Breton. Enuoyée par le P. Iulien Perrault, de la Compagnie de Iesvs, à son Prouincial, en France, l'an 1634. et 35," comprising pp. 207–219.

PERRAULT (J. F.) Abrégé de l'Histoire du Canada, Première Partie: Depuis sa Découverte jusqu'à sa Conquête par les Anglais, en 1759 et 1760. Rédigé par Jos. Perrault, Protonotaire, à l'usage des Ecoles Elémentaires. *Québec: P. & W. Ruthven.* 1832. 18mo. Second Partie: Depuis sa Conquête par les Anglais, en 1759 et 1760, jusqu'à l'Etablissement d'une Chambre d'Assemblée, en 1792. [*Ibid.*] 1833. 18mo. + Troisième Édition [containing both parts]. *Québec: W. Ruthven.* 1843. 18mo, pp. 162. Troisième Partie: Depuis l'Etablissement d'une Chambre d'Assemblée, jusqu'à l'année 1815. *Québec: P. & W. Ruthven.* 1833. 18mo, pp. 197. Quatrième Partie: Depuis le départ du Général Provost [*sic*] jusqu'à celui du Comte Dalhousie. [*Ibid.*] 1833. 18mo, pp. 164. Cinquième Partie: Depuis le départ du Comte Dalhousie jusqu'à l'arrivée de Lord Gosford et des Commissaires Royaux. [*Ibid.*] 1836. 18mo. 61005

Also: Le Juge de Paix et Officier de Paroisse pour la Province de Québec. ... *Québec.* 1789. 8vo. — Traité d'Agriculture adapté au climat du Bas-Canada. ... *Québec.* 1839. 8vo, pp. 69.

For other works, legal and educational, by Mr. Perrault, who died in 1844, *see* Morgan's "Bibliotheca Canadensis."

PERRAULT (Joseph François). Exploration de Québec au Lac St. Jean. ... *Montréal.* 1864. 8vo, pp. 57. 61006

Also: Compte-rendu d'une Excursion agricole dans les États de l'Ouest. 1860. ... *Montréal.* 1860. 8vo, pp. 36. — Four Years in Parliament. ... *Montréal.* 1867. 8vo. — Histoire du Canada. ... *Montréal.* 1859. 8vo, pp. 50.

P[ERREAU] (J. A.) Lettres Illinoises ... par J. A. P. *Londres et Paris.* 1772. 8vo. 61007

PERREY (A.) ... Documents sur les Tremblements de Terre au Pérou, dans la Colombie et dans la Bassin de l'Amazone ... . Par M. Alexis Perrey ... . [*Bruxelles: Imprimerie de M. Hayez.*] 1857. 8vo, pp. 131. H. 61008

Also: Documents relatifs aux Tremblements de Terre au Chili. ... *Lyon.* 1854. Rl. 8vo. — Documents sur les Tremblements de Terre ... des Isles aleutiennes, de la Péninsule d'Aljaska et de la Côte nord d'Amérique. ... *Dijon.* 1865. 8vo, pp. 131.

PERRIN (Edwin O.) A Plea for the State Canals, and for the Introduction of Steam Towage thereon. By E. O. Perrin. *Albany.* 1870. 8vo, pp. 32. S. 61009

PERRIN (L.) The Claims of Cæsar. A Sermon, preached in ... New Britain, May 19, 1861, and repeated, ... in Goshen, August 18, 1861. By Lavalette Perrin. ... *Hartford: Press of Case, Lockwood and Company.* 1861. 8vo, pp. 27. 61010

PERRIN (W.) The Present State of the British and French Sugar Colonies, and our own Northern Colonies considered. Together with some Remarks on the Decay of our Trade, and the Improvements made of late Years by the French in theirs. By William Perrin. *London: T. Cooper.* M.DCC.XL. 8vo, pp. (4), 63. A. 61011

PERRIN DU LAC (F. M.) Voyage dans les Deux Louisianes, et chez les Nations Sauvages du Missouri, par les États-Unis, l'Ohio et les Provinces qui le bordent, en 1801, 1802 et 1803; Avec un aperçu des Mœurs, des Usages, du Caractère et des Coutumes religieuses et civiles des Peuples de ces diverses Con-

trées. Par M. Perrin du Lac. *A Paris, Chez Capelle et Renand, ... Et à Lyon, chez Bruysset aîné et Buynand.* 1805. 8vo, pp. (6), x, 479. Folded Map and Plate. A., C. + *A Lyon, chez Bruyset aîné et Buynand, An* XIII [1805]. 8vo, pp. (6), x, 479. Folded Map and Plate. 61012

PERRIN DU LAC. Travels through the Two Louisianas, and among the Savage Nations of the Missouri; also, in the United States, along the Ohio, and the adjacent provinces, in 1801, 1802, & 1803. With a sketch of the manners, customs, character, and the civil and religious ceremonies of the people of those countries. By M. Perrin du Lac. Translated from the French. *London: Richard Phillips.* 1807. 8vo, pp. 106, (2).

A translation of the preceding work, very much abridged. Included in Phillips's "Collection of Voyages," VI.

PERRIN DU LAC. Reise in den beyden Louisianen unter die wilden Völkerschaften am Missouri, durch die Vereinigten Staaten und die Provinzen am Ohio, in den Jahren 1801, 1802 und 1803. ... Nach dem Französischen von K. L. M. Müller. *Leipzig: J. C. Hinrichs.* 1807. 2 vols., 8vo, pp. x, 206; vi, 122. Map and Plates. C. + *Wien.* 1807. 8vo. Map and Plates. 61014

PERRINE (C. O.) Perrine's New Topographical War Map of the Southern States ... . With an Introduction and Statistical Appendix by Capt. John S. Bishop. *Indianapolis, Ind.: C. O. Perrine & Co.* 1863. Folded. 61015

Also: Topographical War Map of the United States, with Chronology of the Great Rebellion. *Boston.* 1864. 12mo.

PERRINE (H.) ... Feb. 17, 1838. Mr. Deberry ... made the following Report ... on the Memorial of Dr. Henry Perrine in relation to the culture of Tropical Plants. ... Mar. 8, 1838. *Washington.* [n. d.] 8vo, pp. 99. S. 61016

PERRINE. ... Mr. Linn submitted the following report on Henry Perrine's Memorial for a grant of land in Florida for the cultivation of Tropical Plants. Mar. 12, 1838. *Washington.* 1838. 8vo, pp. 142. 24 Plates. S. 61017

PERRINE (M. la R.) Women have a Work to do ... . Discourse ... May 12, 1817. By Mathew la Rue Perrine. ... *New York: Printed by Edward W. Thomson.* 1817. 8vo, pp. 32. H.

[PERRINON (A. F.)] Statuts et autres Documents concernant la Société des Étangs Salins de St.-Martin (Antilles). ... *La Haye.* 1859. 8vo. 3 colored Plates. 61019

PERRODIN (J. C.) Conversations of a Catholic Missionary with Americans. By Rev. John C. Perrodin. *Milwaukee: Hoffman Brothers.* 1868. 16mo, pp. 345. C. 61020

PERROT (J.) To the Upright in Heart, and Faithful People of God; being an Epistle written in Barbado's the 3d of the 9th Month, 1662. By John Perrot. *London, Printed in the Year,* 1662. 4to, pp. 10. 61021

For other works by Perrot, *see* Smith's "Descriptive Catalogue of Friends' Books," II. 398–404.

PERROT (N.) Mémoire sur les Moeurs, Coustumes et Relligion des Sauvages de l'Amérique Septentrionale, par Nicolas Perrot Publié pour la première fois par le R. P. J. Tailhan de la Compagnie de Jesus. *Leipzig & Paris: Librairie A. Franck.* 1864. 8vo, pp. viii, 341, xliii. BA. 61022

"This work of Perrot had remained in manuscript for more than a century and a half, but not unknown. It had served Charlevoix in the preparation of his great history of New France; as it had long before its governors La Barre, Denonville, and Frontenac, in determining their policy towards the various tribes of Indian allies and foes it describes."—FIELD. *See* "Historical Magazine," IX. 205–208.

PERROTTET (G. S.) Rapport adressé à M. le Ministre de la Marine et des Colonies, sur une Mission dans l'Inde, à Bourbon, à Caïenne, à la Martinique et à la Guadeloupe concernant l'Industrie Sérigène et la Culture du Mûrier. Par M. Perrottet ... . *Paris: Imprimerie Royale.* M DCCC XLII. 8vo, pp. 80. A. 61023

See also "Feuille de la Guyane française," *our* Vol. VII., No. 29173.

PERRY (A. F.) Speech of Aaron F. Perry ... Cincinnati, Sept. 20, 1864. [n. p. n. d.] 8vo, pp. 15, (1). + *Cincinnati: Caleb Clark.* 1864. 8vo, pp. 15. B. 61024

PERRY. Argument ... in the Vallandigham Habeas Corpus Case before U. S. Circuit Court. [*Cincinnati.* 1863.] 8vo.

See Vallandigham (C. L.) Also: An Oration ... before the Literary Societies of the Western Reserve College, ... June 26, 1867. ... [*Cincinnati:*] *Caleb Clark, Printer.* 1867. 8vo, pp. 19. H.

PERRY (B. F.) Address of the Hon. Benj. F. Perry before the South Carolina Institute, at their Annual Fair, November, 1856 ... . *Charleston: Walker Evans & Co., Printers.* [1856.] 8vo, pp. 64. H. 61026

PERRY. Speech of Hon. B. F. Perry, of Greenville District, ... in the House of Representatives of South-Carolina, on the 11th December, 1850, ... on the State and Federal Affairs. *Charleston: J. B. Nixon, Printer.* 1851. 8vo, pp. 40. 61027

PERRY (D.) Recollections of an Old Soldier. The Life of Captain David Perry, a Soldier of the French and Revolutionary Wars. Containing many Extraordinary Occurrences relating to his own private history, and an Account of some Interesting Events in the History of the Times in which he lived, no-where else recorded. Written by Himself. *Windsor, Vt.: Printed ana for sale at the Republican & Yeoman Printing-Office.* 1822. 12mo, pp. 55. C. 61028

PERRY (D. L.) Sermon delivered at the Funeral of the Rev. Cotton Mather Smith, November 27, 1806, at Sharon, Conn. By David L. Perry. *Hartford.* 1806. 8vo. 61029

PERRY (G. B.) A Discourse delivered in ... Bradford, December 22, 1820, two hundred years after the first Settlement in New England. Containing a History of the Town. By Gardner B. Perry, A.M. *Haverhill: Burrill and Hersey.* 1821. 8vo, pp. 72. W. 61030

PERRY. History of Bradford, Mass., from the Earliest Period to the close of 1820, by Gardner B. Perry, A.M. (As contained in his Historical Sermon delivered Dec. 20, 1820.) *Haverhill, Mass.: C. C. Morse & Son, Printers.* 1872. 8vo, pp. 69. 61031

Also: An Address, ... before the Society for Promoting Temperance in Haverhill, ... February 5, 1828 ... . *Haverhill: Printed by A. W. Thayer.* 1828. 8vo, pp. 24.

PERRY (G. H.) The Staple Trade of Canada; a Lecture. By George H. Perry. *Ottawa.* 1862. 8vo, pp. 45. 61032

Also: British North America at the Detroit Convention. ... *Ottawa.* 1865. 8vo. — Lecture on the Ottawa River. ... *Ottawa.* 1861. 8vo. — River Communications of the British North American Provinces. ... *Ottawa.* 1865. 8vo.

PERRY (G. W.) A Treatise on Turpentine Farming, by G. W. Perry, of Craven County. *Newbern, N. C.* 1859. 8vo.

PERRY (G. B.) Two Discourses on ... the death of William Henry Harrison, late President ... . Delivered in ... Alton, Illinois ... April 18; and ... May 14. By Gideon B. Perry ... . *Alton, Ill's.* 1841. 8vo, pp. 19. BA. 61034

PERRY (J.) Plan and Propositions for Organization of Joint Stock Companies. By James Perry. *Brooklyn.* 1867. 8vo, pp. 38. 61035

PERRY (J. H.) The Man for the Times: A Thanksgiving Discourse, preached before the M. E. Churches of ... Brooklyn, November 30, 1854. By James H. Perry ... . *New York: Carlton & Phillips.* 1855. 8vo, pp. 22. 61036

PERRY (J. B.) Queries on the Red Sand Stone of Vermont, and its relation to other rocks. By the Rev. John B. Perry ... . *Boston: Press of Abner A. Kingman.* 1868. 8vo, pp. 16. 61037

Also: Life and Death ... . Discourses preached in Swanton ... . *Burlington.* 1861. 8vo, pp. 80. C.

PERRY (J. J.) Freedom National—Slavery Sectional. Speech of Hon. John J. Perry ... . May 1, 1856 ... . [n. p. n. d.] 8vo, pp. 15. H. + *Washington.* 1856. 8vo, pp. 16. 61038

Also: Defense of Republicanism. Speech ... January 27, 1857. [n. p. n. d.] 8vo, pp. 8. — Platforms and Candidates of 1856. Speech ... August 7, 1856. [n. p. n. d.] 8vo, pp. 8.

PERRY (J.) The Character of Moses Illustrated and Improved: in a Discourse Occasioned by the Death of the Hon. Roger Wolcott, Esq. of Windsor, who for several years was Governor of the Colony of Connecticut; and died May 17, 1767, in the 89th Year of his Age. ... By Joseph Perry, A.M. *Hartford: Printed by Thomas Green.* [1767.] Sm. 4to, pp. 28. BA., W. 61039

PERRY. The Character & Reward of the Faithful & Wise Minister ... . Sermon occasioned by the ... Death of the Reverend Nathanael Hooker, Pastor of the Fourth Church in Hartford, ... delivered ... June 11th. 1770. ... By Joseph Perry. *Hartford: Printed by Green & Watson.* 1770. 4to, pp. 24. BA.

PERRY. A | Sermon, | Preached before the | General Assembly | of the Colony of | Connecticut, at Hartford, | on the Day of their | Anniversary Election, May 11, 1775. | By Joseph Perry, A.M. | Pastor of the first Church of Christ, in East-Windsor. | ... | *Hartford: | Printed by Eben. Watson, near the Great- | Bridge,* M, DCC,-LXXV. | Sm. 4to, pp. 23. BA., W. 61041

PERRY (Marshall S.) Case of C. Sumner; communicated to the Boston Society for Medical Improvement, Dec. 8, 1856. [*Boston.* 1856.] 8vo, pp. 7. B. 61042

PERRY. The Principles and Objects of the Massachusetts Medical Society, Delivered ... June 3, 1857. By M. S. Perry. ... *Boston: Printed by John Wilson and Son.* 1857. 8vo, pp. 28.

PERRY (Matthew C.) A Paper read before the American Geographical and Statistical Society, March 6, 1856. [The Enlargement of Geographical Science]. *New York.* 1856. 8vo, pp. 31. S. 61044

For the "Narrative of the Expedition," etc., *see* Hawks (F. L.), VIII. 30968.

PERRY (N.) The Constitution and the Union. Let them together be Maintained. Speech of Hon. N. Perry ... March 6, 1862. [n. p. n. d.] 8vo, pp. 8. 61045

PERRY. Rebellious States. Speech of Hon. Nehemiah Perry, ... May 3, 1864. [n. p. n. d.] 8vo, pp. 8. H. 61046

Also: The Omissions and Commissions of the Administration. Speech ... Feb. 28, 1863. [n. p. n. d.] 8vo, pp. 8.

PERRY (O. H.) Letter from the Secretary of the Navy, transmitting ... copies of the Proceedings of the Court Martial ordered ... for the trial of Captain Oliver H. Perry; also, for the trial of Captain John Heath of the Marine Corps. *Washington: E. De Kraft.* 1818. 8vo, pp. 34. 61047

See "Documents in Relation to the Differences," etc., and "A Review of a Pamphlet," etc., *our* Vol. VI., No. 22270, note. These "Documents" were transmitted to the Navy Department by Commodore Perry as a means of guarding his character against the aspersions of Captain Jesse D. Elliott, who replied to them in: "Additional Documents, in relation to the Difference between the late Commodore O. H. Perry, and Captain J. D. Elliott: made necessary for the public eye by the recent publication of a pamphlet by the friends of the former." *Norfolk.* 1821. 16mo, pp. 66. *See also* our Vol. IV., No. 13678.

PERRY (P. F.) Poems. By Phil. Frank. Perry. *Winsted.* 1869. 8vo, pp. 52. 61048

PERRY (Thomas). Speech of Mr. T. Perry, of Maryland, on the Tariff. ... July 1, 1846. *Washington: Printed by J. & G. S. Gideon.* 1846. 8vo, pp. 14. 61049

Also: Speech ... Jan. 25, 1847, on Pay of the Army. *Washington.* 1847. 8vo.

PERRY (W. S.) Bishop Seabury and Bishop Provoost; an Historical Fragment. By the Rev. William Stevens Perry, M.A. [n. p.:] *Privately Printed.* 1862. 8vo, pp. 20. H. 61050

This is an ably written essay on the important division in the Episcopal Church, after the Revolution, when Bishop Seabury, consecrated in Scotland and founding the hierarchy here, was ignored on that account and as an ex-loyalist, by Bishop Provoost.

PERRY A Century of Episcopacy in Portland. A Sketch of the History of the Episcopal Church in Portland, Maine, from the Organization of St. Paul's Church, Falmouth, November 4, 1763, to the Present Time. By the Rev. William Stevens Perry, M.A. ... *Portland.* 1863. 8vo, pp. 16. B. 61051

PERRY. A Handbook of the General Convention of the Protestant Episcopal Church ... 1785–1874. By William Stevens Perry, D.D. ... *New York: T. Whittaker.* [1874.] 12mo, pp. xiv, 277. C. 61052

PERRY. Historical Collections relating to the American Colonial Church. Edited by William Stevens Perry, D.D. Vol. I. Virginia. [*Hartford.*] 1870. 4to, pp. xvii, 585. Vol. II. Pennsylvania. 1871. pp. (2), xxi, 607. Vol. III. Massachusetts. 1873. pp. xxv, 720. Vol. IV. Maryland. 1878. pp. xii, 370. Vol. V. Delaware. 1878. pp. vii, 151. 61053

Two hundred and fifty copies printed for subscribers. The series, which relates to the Protestant Episcopal Church, is to be completed in about ten volumes. Also issued separately, with special title-pages, as "Papers," etc. *See* Nos. 61057–59, *infra.*

PERRY. Historical Notes and Documents illustrating the Organization of the Protestant Episcopal Church in the United States of America. By William Stevens Perry, D.D. ... *Claremont, N. H.* 1874. 8vo, pp. viii, 3–524. Plate. A. 61054

PERRY. An Historical Sketch of the Church Missionary Association of the Eastern District of the Diocese of Massachusetts. By the Rev. William Stevens Perry ... . *Boston: E. P. Dutton and Company.* MDCCCLIX. 8vo, pp. 32. S. 61055

P[ERRY]. A Memorial of the Rev. Thomas Mather Smith, D.D. ... By W. S. P. [*Cambridge: H. O. Houghton and Company.*] 1866. 8vo, pp. (2), 68. S. 61056

PERRY. Papers relating to the History of the Church in Virginia, A. D., 1650–1776. Edited by William Stevens Perry, D.D. [*Hartford:*] *Privately Printed.* 1870. 4to, pp. xvii, 585.

A separate edition of Vol. I. "Historical Collections," No. 61053, *supra.*

PERRY. Papers relating to the History of the Church in Pennsylvania, A. D., 1680–1778. Edited by William Stevens Perry, D.D. [*Hartford:*] *Privately Printed.* 1871. 4to, pp. (2), xxi, 607. 61058

A separate edition of Vol. II. "Historical Collections," No. 61053, *supra.*

PERRY. Papers relating to the History of the Church in Massachusetts, A. D., 1676–1785. Edited by William Stevens Perry, D.D. [*Hartford:*] *Privately Printed.* 1873. 4to, pp. xxv, 720.

A separate edition of Vol. III. "Historical Collections," No. 61053, *supra.*

PERRY. Thankfulness for our Past ... . A Sermon preached in ... Litchfield, Conn., on ... Thanksgiving, ... November 26,

1866. By the Rev. William Stevens Perry, M.A. *Philadelphia: Stevens & Chase, Printers.* 1866. 12mo, pp. 9. H. 61060

Also: Anglo-American Sympathy with Continental Reform. A Sermon, ... in Westminster Abbey, October 17th, 1875. ... *London.* [1875.] 8vo, pp. 17. — Bishop Seabury and the "Episcopal Recorder;" a Vindication. ... [n. p.:] *Privately Printed.* 1863. 8vo, pp. 48. — The Churchman's Year Book, with Kalendar, for 1870. ... *Hartford.* 1870. 12mo, pp. vi, 449. Continued. — The Connection of the Church of England with early American Discovery and Colonization. ... *Portland, Me.* 1863. 8vo, pp. 7. *See also* Vol. VIII., No. 30973, *and* Protestant Episcopal Church, *infra.*

PERRY ACADEMY. First Annual Register of the Officers and Students for 1854–5. *Perry, Wyoming Co., N. Y.* [n. d.] 8vo. Continued. S. 61061

PERRY-CENTRE INSTITUTE at Perry-Centre. Catalogue of Officers and Students for 1843–44. [n. p. n. d.] 8vo. Continued. S. 61062

PERRYMAN (S. W. *and* L. C.) Constitution and Laws of the Muskokee or Creek Nation, translated into Muskokee Language, by S. W. & L. C. Perryman, by An Act of the National Council. *Washington City: McGill & Witherow, Printers.* 1868. 8vo, pp. 16. 61063

Perry-Patetic Songs. *See* [Darlington (W.)], Vol. V. 18598.

PERS (J. B. Le). *See* Charlevoix (P. F. X. de), III. 12127.

Persecution in America! Occasioning Suicide!! And the same Persecution continued on others!!! alias, Sangerfield Suicide or Self-Murder!! which took place July 4, 1809, on the Wife of Thomas King; with the subsequent Trials of her Fellow-Sufferers under Oppression, Brought up to this present year, (Aug.) 1811. Including ... The Lamentations of her surviving Partner in a Poem ... . *Utica.* 1811. 12mo, pp. iv, 88. 61064

The Persecution in New York: as shown in an authentic Collection of the Letters already published by the Most Rev. Archbishop Hughes, and the Rev. Fathers Dayman and Camps. ... *New York: Frederic A. Brady.* 1851. 12mo. 61065

PERSON (W.) Life and Letters, together with Poetical and Miscellaneous Pieces of the late William Person, a Student of Harvard University. ... *Cambridge: Printed by Hilliard and Metcalf.* 1820. 12mo, pp. 251. BA., P. 61066

Personal and Historical Recollections of the Baltimore and Ohio Railroad. *Baltimore.* 1869. 8vo. 61067

Personal Liberty. *See* [Ingersoll (E.)], Vol. IX., No. 34741.

Personal Narrative. *See* Vol. IV., No. 14668.

Personal Recollections. *See* [Post (Lydia Minturn)].

Personal Slavery Established, By the Suffrages of Custom and Right Reason. Being a full Answer to the gloomy and visionary Reveries, of all the fanatical and enthusiastical Writers on that Subject. ... *Philadelphia: Printed by John Dunlap* ... . M. DCC. LXXIII. 8vo, pp. 26. P. 61068

Dated "New-Castle Co. Nov. 26, 1773." Rather flat and poor irony.

PERSONEL (F. B.) An | Authentic and Particular | Account | of the Life of | Francis Burdett Personel. | Written by Himself. | Who was executed at New York, Sep- | tember 10th, 1773, in the Twenty- | Sixth Year of his Age, for the Murder | of Robert White. | *New York: | Printed in the Year* M.DCC.LXXIII. | 12mo, pp. 23. N. 61069

PERSONNE, *pseudon.* Marginalia; or, Gleanings from an Army Note-Book. By "Personne" ... . *Columbia, S. C.: F. G. De Fontaine & Co.* 1864. 8vo, pp. (4), iii, 248. BA. 61070

PERSPECTIVE, *pseudon.* *See* Vol. II., No. 6513, *and* Vol. III., No. 11890.

PERTH-AMBOY. An | Act | for | Incorporating | the | Free Port | of | Perth-Amboy. | Passed at Trenton, December | 21, 1784. | *Trenton: Printed by Isaac Collins.* | M.DCC.LXXXV. | 8vo, pp. 24.

The Charter and Project, with a Description of the Situation and Peculiar Advantages of the Perth Amboy Manufacturing Company. *Newark.* 1831. 8vo, pp. 8. 61072

[PERTHES (*M.*)] *See* [Deperthes (J. L. H. S.)], v. 19619–21

PERTHES (J.) *See* Vol. XII., No. 49765.

Pertinente Beschrijvinge. *See* Vol. VII., No. 29186.

PERU. Abolicion de la Esclavitud en el Peru. *Lima.* 1855. 8vo, pp. 50. 61073

Acta Capitvli provincialis Limæ celebrati in conventu S. Mariæ del Rosario sacri ordinis Prædicatorum ciuitatis Regum, anno 1621. Sub admodum R. P. fr. Ludouico Cornejo. *Limæ, Apua Hieronymum de Contreras.* 1621. 4to, (14) leaves. 61074

Also: Acta capitvli provincialis hvivs provinciæ S. Joannis Baptistæ del Perv ... celebrati die 24 Julij Anni Dni 1740. Sub P. Joanne de Gazitua. ... *Limæ.* 1740. 4to, (31) leaves. — Acta capitvli provincialis ... celebrati 24 Julij Anni Dni 1748. Sub Fr. Ferdinando Davila. *Limæ.* 1748. 4to, (34) leaves. — Acta capitvli provincialis celebrati 24 Julij 1760. Sub P. Joanne Menesses. *Limæ.* 1760. 4to, (19) leaves. — Acta capituli provincialis celebrati 24 Julii 1768. Sub P. Antonio de la Cueva. *Limæ.* 1768. 4to, (41) leaves. — Acta capituli provincialis celebrati 24 Julij 1772. Sub P. Emmanuele Muoarra. *Limæ.* 1772. 4to, (29) leaves. — Acta capituli provincialis celebrati die 24 Julii 1776. Sub P. Joseph Rosales. *Limæ.* 1776. 4to, (40) leaves.

Address from the Directors of the Peruvian Mining Company to the Shareholders. *London.* 1825. 8vo. 61075

Almanaque Peruano y guia de forasteros ... de 1799. Por el Doct. D. Gabriel Moreno ... . [*Lima:*] *Imprenta Real.* [n. d.] 12mo, pp. (82). Continued. BA. 61076

By G. Moreno, 1799–1809; by Jose Gregorio Paredes, 1810–11, 15–21; by Francisco Romero, 1812–14. *See also* our Vol. X., No. 41081.

Anales de la dictadura. Coleccion de Documentos oficiales de la jefetura suprema del Coronel Mariano I. Prado. Entregas 1–13. *Lima.* 1866. 4to, pp. 324. 61077

Anti-Argos. [*Lima.*] 1813. 4to, pp. 20. 61078

Three numbers appeared, when it was combined with the "Argos" and published under the name of "Verdadero Peruano."

Arancel de la República del Perú, que debe regir en los annos de 1865 y 66; formado en cumplimiento del reglamento de comercio. *Lima.* 1866. 4to, pp. 72. 61079

Argos Constitucional de Lima. [*Lima: Imprenta B. Ruiz.*] 1813. 4to, pp. (4), 56. 61080

Issued weekly from February 7 to March 23, 1813, forming seven numbers, when it was combined with the "Anti-Argos" and published under the name of "Verdadero Peruano."

Aviendo entendido la materia que se controvierte, sobre si se debē fortificar la boca del Rio de la ensenada del Dariel y el desembarcadero del Playon, en el parage de los Cayos de las Cabeças, para estorvar á los Piratas el poder passar à las Costas del Perù, se debe considerar ... . [*Lima.* 1694?] 4to, 4 leaves. 61081

Also: Aviendo prevenido en el Papel antecedente la mejor forma de assegurar los Puertos, y Poblaciones de todas los Costas de las Indias, y su Comercio Navàl ... . [*Lima.* 1694?] 4to, pp. 15.

Bolivia; or, Upper Peru, its Geographical Position. ... *London.* 1846. 8vo, pp. 29. 61082

Calendario y Guia de Forasteros de la Republica Peruana para el año bisiesto de 1848. Por Don Eduardo Carrasco ... . *Lima.* 1847. 12mo, pp. 388. 61083

See also our Vol. III., No. 11037.

Cedula real sobre lo que por punto general se ha de observar en los Reynos del Perù, y Nueva España, en quanto à la aplicacion del producto de vacantes de Arzobispados, Obispados, dignidades y demàs prebendas eclesiasticas. *Madrid.* 1737. Folio, 7 leaves. 61084

Codigo civil del Perú. *Lima.* 1852. 4to, pp. 328. 61085

Codigo de Comercio de la República del Perú. *Lima.* 1853. 4to, pp. vi, 250. 61086

Codigo de instruccion publica del Perú presentado en proyecto a la camara de diputados por su comision de instruccion. *Lima.* 1862. 4to, pp. iv, 76. 61087

Coleccion de las aplicaciones que se van haciendo de los bienes, casas, y colegios que fueron de los Regulares de la Compañia de Jesus, expatriados de estos Reales dominios. Siguiendo en todo lo adaptable las reglas que prescribe la Real Cedula dada en Madrid, à 9. de Julio de 1769. *Lima, oficina de la Calle de S. Jacinto.* 1772–73. 2 vols., 4to, pp. (54), 207, (4); (158), 306, (4).

Coleccion de las Cartas del Canonista de la Sierra dadas a luz en los numeros del Mercurio Peruano de Lima a fin del año de 1631. *Lima.* 1832. 4to, pp. 40. 61089

Coleccion de Leyes y Decretos Sancionados desde la Jura de la Independencia. *Lima.* 1825–6. 2 vols., 18mo. 61090

Coleccion de Leyes, Decretos y Ordenes publicadas en el Peru desde el ano de 1821 hasta 31 de Diciembre de 1859 Reimpresa por Orden de materias por el Dr. D. Juan Oviedo. *Lima.* 1861–63. 11 vols., 4to, pp. 440; 494; 431; 454; 462; 384; 400; 422; 434; 460; 328. 61091

Coleccion de los Discursos que Pronunciaron los Señores Diputados de America, contra el Articulo 22 del Progecto de Constitucion, Ilustrados con algunas notas. *Lima.* 181[illegible]

Coleccion de los Recursos de los Mag[illegible]dos Despojados por la Revolucion Judicial. *Lima.* 1832. 4to, pp. 112. 61093

Coleccion Diplomatica ó Bennio.ı de los Tratados celebrados por el Perú con la Naciones extranjeras, desde su Independencia hasta la fecha. *Lima.* 1858. Folio. 61094

Conferencias y Comunicaciones tenidas en Quito entre los Ministros Plenipotentiarios del Peru y del Ecuador nombrados para transijir las diferencias que existen entre una y otra republica. *Lima.* 1842. 8vo. 61095

Conflit Hispano-Péruvien. Circulaire adressée par M. T. Pacheco, ... aux agents diplomatiques de la République. *Paris.* 1866. 8vo, pp. 84. 61096

Conqueste van Indien. *See* [Zarate (A. de)].

La conquista del Peru | llamada la nueua Castilla. La q̄l tierra por diuina vo | luntad fue marauillosamente conquistada en la felicis | sima ventura del Emperador y Rey nuestro señor: | y por la prudencia y esfuerzo del muy magnifico y vale | roso cauallero el Capitan Francisco pizarro Gouerna | dor y adelantado de la nueua castilla/ y de su herma | no Hernando pizarro/ y de sus animosos capitanes | & fieles y esforzados compañeros q̄ cō el se hallaron. | [Colophon:] *Esta obra fue impressa | en la muy noble y muy | leal ciudad de Se | uilla/ en casa de Bartolome | perez. en el | mes de | Abril. | Año de mil & quiniētos y treynta y quatro.* | Folio. L.

Collation: Title, 1 leaf, 8 unnumbered leaves; the verso of the seventh leaf contains a portion of the text, followed by a repetition of the large chap-like vignette on the title-page. Recto of the eighth leaf blank.

This narration was evidently composed by one of Pizarro's companions, and seems to be the original of the third part of our No. 1565, but more succinct than the Italian. The "Bibliotheca Grenvilliana" states that it is identical with the "Relatione d'un Capitano Spagnuolo della Conquista del Peru," published by Ramusio, but with "many variations." "Ouvrage rarissime."—TERNAUX.

Constitucion para la Republica Peruana. *Lima: Jose Maria Masias.* 1826. 4to, pp. 24, vi, 25–120. C. 61098

Constitucion Politica de la Republica Peruana Jurada en Lima el 20 de Noviembre de 1823. *Lima,* 1825. *Imprenta del estado por J. Gonzalez.* 16mo, pp. cxii, 52, (2). H. 61099

Constitucion Politica de la Republica Peruana, dada por el Congreso Jeneral Constituyente, el dia 18 de Marzo de 1828. *Lima: J. Fabian Solorzano.* [n. d.] 16mo, pp. 54. — Constitucion Politica de la Republica Peruana dada por el Congreso Jeneral el dia diez de Noviembre de 1839. *Lima.* 1839. 8vo.

La Constitucion y Leyes Organicas de la Republica Peruana dadas ... la Convencion Nacional en 1856. *Lima.* 1856. 4to.

Constitucion y Leyes Organicas ... Dadas por El Congreso de

1860, comparadas con las que sancionó la Convencion Nacional de 1855. *Lima.* 1863. 8vo, pp. 174, (1). 61101

Constituciones desta Provincia de los doze apostoles del Pirv. *Impresso en Lima; Por Geronimo de Contreras* ... . *Año de* 1631. 4to, pp. 58, (2). J.C.B. 61102

Constitvciones Synodales. *See* Vol. IV., Nos. 16065–71.

Constituciones y Ordenanzas. *See* Vol. X., Nos. 41091, '93.

Consulta del auditor general de la gente de mar, i guerra de este reino. Sobre la fuga de 20 soldados que se huyeron del navio San Pedro. *Lima.* 1683. Folio, 8 leaves. 61103

By Juan Luis Lopez.

Consulta, y Representacion Hecha al Exmo Señor Marquès de Villa Garcia, Virrey Governador y Capitan General de los Reynos del Perû, tierra firme, y Chile, &c. Por El Tribunal del Consulado, y Junta General de Comercio de esta Ciudad de los Reyes. Sobre que se sobresca en la Execucion, de la Capitulacion quarta de las concedidas por Su Mag. (Dios le guarde) á los Navios del permiso de Don Lorenzo del Arco, en que se contiene la facultad de poder internar sus ropas desde Buenos Ayres, à todas las Provincias del Perû, y Reyno de Chile, sin Excepcion de alguna, y se sugete à las tres Provincias del Rio de la Plata, Tucuman, y Paraguay, sin passar de las Ciudades de Salta, y Jujui. Siendo Prior y Consules D. Gabriel Bocangel y Vnzueta, D. Thomas de Costa del Orden de Santiago, y D. Pedro Cosio. [n. p. n. d.] Folio, 20 leaves. 61104

Copia de carta escrita a un cavallero de la ciudad de los Reyes, dandole cuenta de la muerte del duque de la Palata, en Portobelo 13 de Abril de 1691. [*Lima.* 1691?] Folio, 2 leaves.

By P. Francisco Lopez.

Corona poetica ofrecida al pueblo Peruano el 28 de julio de 1866. *Lima.* 1866. 8vo, pp. 74. 61106

Cuenta General de la Administracion de las Rentas, de la Republica, en el ano de 1846, y Presupuesto de Gastos, para el bienio de 1847 y 1848. *Lima.* 1847. 4to. 61107

Cuestion Talambo ante la América. *Lima.* 1864. 8vo.

The question was the origin of the last wars of Spain against the Peruvians.

De examine symboli politici ac militaris plus ultra. Apud Bartholomæum Leonardum Epistolica exercitatio. *Limæ.* 1682. Folio, 4 leaves. 61109

By Juan Luis Lopez.

Decision de la Real Audiencia de los Reyes, en favor de la Regalia, i Real Jurisdicion, sobre el articulo, dos vezes remitido, en la causa de Oliberos Belin llamado comunmente D. Carlos Clerque. *Lima.* 1682. Folio, pp. 26, (2). 61110

By Juan Luis Lopez. It relates to the buccaneers.

Los Derechos adquiridos y los actos de la dictadura del Peru en 1866. *Lima.* 1867. 8vo, pp. iii, 260. 61111

Derrotero jeneral de las républicas del Péru, Buenos-Ayres, Colombia y Chile se ha formada circunstantiadamente por carreras con el objeto de dar un conocimiento ecsacto de las comunicaciones para el jiro de diversos intereses. *Lima.* 1825. Sm. 4to, pp. 41. 2 Tables. 61112

See also Vol. V., No. 19680.

Despachos y Cartas de Govierno acerca de la Execucion de la Provision y Ordenanza de XX de febrero, 1684. [*Lima.* 1685.] Folio, pp. 63. J.C.B. 61113

By Juan Luis Lopez. It forms an appendix to No. 61115, *infra.*

The Discoverie and Conqvest. *See* [Zarate (A. de)].

Discurso Jvridico-historico-politico, en defensa de la Jurisdicion Real ilvstracion de la prouision de 20 de febrero del año 1684 ... sobre qve en reciber los Corregidores deste Reyno informaciones secretas de oficio, ò à instancia de parte, en orden à averiguar como observan los Curas, y Doctrineros las Disposiciones Canonicas, Synodales, Cedulas, y Ordenanças de su M., que tratan de las obenciones que deben llevar à los Indios à fin solo de dar cuenta con ellas à sus Prelados, y al Govierno superior destos Reynos, para que lo remedien no se contraviene en cosa alguna à la immunidad de la Iglesia. *Lima.* 1685. Folio, pp. 146.

By Juan Luis Lopez. Improved title of our No. 41987, Vol. X.

Discvrso Legal Theologico-Practico en defensa de la provision y ordenanza de Govierno de XX de febrero de el año M. DC.-LXXXIV ... . Escrito del Orden de el Excelentissimo Señor Don Melchior de Navarra y Rocafull ... Por Don Ivan Lvis Lopez, de el Consejo de su Majestad ... . *Impresso en Lima. Con Licencia de el Govierno. Año* M. DC. LXXXV. Folio, pp. (8), 192. J.C.B.

Division de los Obispados de Guamanga y Arequipa separados del Cuzco, y del Obispado de Truxillo separado del Arzobispado de los Reyes, y del Obispado de Quito. [*Lima.* 167–.] Folio.

Documentos justificativos sobre la espedicion libertadora del Perú. Refutacion de las Memorias de Lord Cochrane en lo concerniente a las relaciones del Vice-Almirante con el gobierno de Chile. *Santiago.* 1861. 8vo, pp. 122. 61117

Documentos Literarios del Peru. Tomo Primero. *Lima.* 1863. 4to. 61118

Documentos relativos a reclamos al Gobierno del Peru sobre Propriedades Britanicas tomadas por autoridades Peruanas saqueadas durante commociones Militares o Civiles o robadas de los Almacenes de la Aduana del Callao. *Lima.* 1840. Sm. 4to.

Documentos sobre el contrato de conversion de la moneda feble, publicados en el "Peruano" y otros periodicos. *Lima.* 1864. 8vo, pp. 198. 61120

Especifico Celestial. Preservativo Singularissimo contra los Tremblores de Tierra, e Inundaciones del Mar: experimentado, y executoriado en las Americas, donde esta pension y congoja se padece mas continuamente. [*Lima.*] 1762. 4to. 61121

Relates to the earthquakes in Peru.

Esposicion de la Tareas Administrativas del Gobierno desde su Instalacion hasta el 15 de Julio de 1822. Presentada al Consejo por ... Bernardo Monteagudo ... . *Lima: Imprenta de Manuel del Rio.* 1822. Sm. 4to, pp. 31. B. 61122

Esposicion que Hace el præcid. provision de la Repub. Peruana Luis Jose Orbegoso de las Razones q. le obligaron a solicit. de la republ. Bonelliviana auxil. para pacificar Peru. *Arequipa.* 1835. 4to. 61123

Title from J. R. Smith's catalogue.

Estado politico del reyno del Perù, govierno sin leyes, ministros relaxados, thesoros con pobreza, fertilidad sin cultivo, sabiduria desestimada, milicia sin honor, ciudades sin amor patricio, la justicia sin templo, huertos por comercios, integridad tenida por locura, rey, el mayor de ricos dominios, pobre de thesores. [*Madrid.* 1747.] Folio, 46 leaves. 61124

A curious and rare work. It has been attributed to D. Vitorino Montero.

Estatuto Provisional dado ... para el Mejor Regimen de los Departamentos Libres interinse establece la Constitution Permanente del Estado. [n. p. n. d.] 4to, pp. 11. H. 61125

Exposé historique du Conflit Péruvien-Espagnol. *Havre.* 1864. 8vo, pp. 44. 61126

Fastos de la Dictadura del Peru, y refutacion a Brandsen y Riva-Agues. *Arequipa.* 1826. 8vo. 61127

El Freno. Dialogo de los editores del Argos. [*Lima.* 1813.] 4to, pp. 10. 61128

Signed "Manuel Salcedo y Hernández."

Gemino luminari Toleto ac Navarræ, utriusque orbis miraculo, primævo altari, altari non secundo Peruviani Imperii proregi, gratulatio. [*Lima.*] 1691. Folio, 6 leaves. 61129

Epitaphs in honor of the viceroy, by P. Francisco Lopez.

Guia politica, eclesiastica y militar del Virreynato del Perú, para el año de 1793. Por Joseph Hipolito Unanue. *Lima: Por la Sociedad Académica de Amantes del Pais de Lima.* [1793.] Sm. 8vo, pp. (20), 352, (10). 4 Tables. Continued. C. 61130

Histoire des Tremblements de Terre. *See* [Lozano (P.)]

The History of the Conquest of Peru. ... *London: T. Newbery.* MDCCLXXXVI. 18mo, pp. 116. Plates. 61131

Impugnacion el articulo inserto contra el Fundador de la Libertad del Peru, y los Jefes de su Ejercitu en el No. 5. de la Abeja Republicana. *Lima.* 1823. 4to. 61132

Investigacion de los Medios. *See* Vol. IX., No. 34956.

Investigaciones Politico-Ecclesiasticas. *See* Vol. IX. 34957.

El Investigador del Peru. *See* Vol. IX., No. 34955.

Juris Allegatio pro Episcopo del Cuzco super solutione decimarum. [*Lima.* 16—.] Folio. 61133

Lealtad Peruana. *See* Vol. IX., No. 39525.

Ley Reglamentaria de Elecciones de diputados a Congreso, Senadores, diputados Departamentales, y de los Individuos de las Municipalidades, Sancionado por el Congreso Constituyente conforme, a la Constitucion Politica de la Republica Peruana. *Lima: J. Gonzalez.* 1825. Sm. 4to, pp. 20. B. 61134

Ley Reglamentaria de Elecciones para los Individuos de las Municipalidades, conforme a la Constitucion Politica de la Republica Peruana. *Lima: J. Gonzalez.* [n. d.] Sm. 4to, pp. 8.

Libro Primo de la Conqvista del Perv. *See* [Xeres (F. de)].

Mandó que se imprimiesse este escrito el ... conde de Alva de Aliste, y de Villaflor, Virrey destos reynos del Perv. En la Jvnta, qve se ha formado, por cedvla de sv Magestad. De 21. de Setiembre de 1660 años. Para conferir Las materias y puntos de la Carta, que con la Cedula referida se remite, cerca de la enseñanza y buen tratamiento de los Indios. [*Lima.* 1660?] Folio. 61135

Manifestacion historica y politica. *See* Vol. XI., No. 44271.

Manifeste des motifs. *See* Vol. XI., No. 44278.

Manifiesto de la Justicia, y fundamentos que assisten à D. Matheo de la Vega, D. Pedro Gutierrez Cosiò, y D. Francisco Martin de Layseca, Prior, y Consules del tribunal del consulado de la ciudad de los Reyes, y Reyno del Peru, en la instancia que tienen pendiente en el Real, y supremo consejo de las Indias, para que se declare por nulo todo lo actuado por el oidor D. Pedro Bravo del Ribero, y aprobado por el Virrey, sobre la eleccion de Prior, y Consul que se celebro para el año de 1748 ... *Madrid.* 1748. 4to, (13) leaves. 61136

Manifiesto sobre los Representantes que corresponden a los Americanos en las immediatas Cortes. *Lima.* 1820. 4to.

Memoria del Despacho de Guerra y Marina que Presenta el Ministro del Ramo al Congreso de 1864. *Lima.* 1864. 8vo, pp. 41, cxxxvi, xv, (1). 4 Tables. A. 61138

Signed "Manuel de la Guarda."

Memoria General del Despacho de Relaciones Exteriores que presenta el Ministro del Ramo al Congreso de 1864. *Lima.* 1864. Rl. 8vo. 61139

Also: Apendice a la Memoria de Relaciones Exteriores. [*Lima.* 1864.] Rl. 8vo, pp. (2), 19, 4, 13, (3), 3–9, 3, 3–6. A.

Memoria presentada a S. E. el Jefe Supremo Provisorio de la Republica por el Director General de Contribuciones. *L...* ... *por J. Enrique del Campo.* 1867. 8vo, pp. 15. 6 Tables.

Signed "M. Felipe Paz Soldan."

Memoria que el Ministro de Gobierno, policia y obras publicas presenta al Congreso nacional de 1862. *Lima.* 1862. 4to, pp. 256. 61141

Memoria que presenta el Ministro de Estado en el Departamento de Justicia, Instruccion Publica, Beneficencia y Culto al Congreso Nacional, de 1864. Edicion Oficial. *Lima: ... por E. Aranda.* 1864. Rl. 8vo, pp. (2), 22, (66). 18 Tables. A.

Memoria que el Ministro de Estado en el Departamento de Gobierno, obras publicas y policia presenta al Congreso ordinario de 1860. *Lima.* 1860. 4to, pp. 212. — Memoria que el Ministro de Hacienda y Comercio presenta al Congreso de 1864. *Lima.* 1864. Sm. folio. — Memoria que el Ministro de Justicia, instruccion publica y beneficencia presenta al Congreso extraordinario reunido en 1858. *Lima.* 1858. 4to, pp. 56. — Memoria que el Ministro de Relaciones Exteriores presenta a la Legislatura Ordinaria de 1864 sobre los Asuntos de España. Edicion Oficial. *Lima. ... Por Eusebio Aranda.* 1864. Rl. 8vo, pp. (2), 34, "Documentos," (85) leaves. — Memoria que el Secretario de Estado en el despacho de relaciones exteriores presenta por orden del gefe supremo provisorio de la republica al congreso constituyente. *Lima.* 1867. Imp. 8vo, pp. 50. — Memoria que presenta el Ministro de Estado en el Departamento de Gobierno, Policia y Obras Publicas al Congreso Nacional de 1864. Edicion oficial. *Lima.* 1864. Folio. — Memoria que presenta el Ministro de Hacienda de Peru al Congreso de 1847. *Lima.* 1847. 4to.

Memoria sobre los Principios Politicos que segui en la Administracion del Perú y acontecimientos posteriores a mi Separacion. *Reimpreso en Santiago de Chile.* 1823. 4to, pp. 40. 61143

See also Vol. XII., No. 47599, *and* Vol. XIV., No. 58569.

Memorial del Ministro de Hacienda J. M. de Pando en 1830 y 1831. *Lima.* 1831–32. 8vo. 61144

Memorial sobre quitar las Doctrinas y Curatos que administran Frayles en Piru. [n. p. n. d.] Folio. 61145

Memorias de los Vireyes. *See* [Fuentes (M. A.)], VII. 26119.

Mensaje de S. E. El Presidente del Peru a la Asamblea Deliberante de los Departamentos del Sud. *Cuzco: P. E. Gonzalez.* 1836. 4to, pp. (2), 8. H. 61146

Mensaje del Presidente provisorio de la Republica Peruana al Congreso. *Lima: Jose Masias.* 1839. 4to, pp. 19. 61147

Signed "Agustin Gamarra."

Mercurio Peruano. *See* Vol. XII., Nos. 47935–7.

El Ministerio de Hacienda del Peru en sus relaciones con los administradores del huano en Europa. *Besanzon: J. Jacquin.* 1859. 8vo, pp. 178. 61148

Noticias del Sur, despacho y felizes sucesos de la Armada del año de 1685, en el govierno del duque de Palata. [*Lima.* 1685.] Folio, 13 leaves. 61149

By P. Francisco Lopez. It relates to the buccaneers. Also: Noticias del Sur continuadas desde 6. de Nouiembre de 1685. hasta Junio de 1688. [*Lima.* 1688.] Folio, 18 leaves. — Ultimas noticias del Sur, y felizes operaciones del navio San Joseph, de la Esquadra de N. Señora de Guia contra Piratas. [*Lima.* n. d.] Folio, 2 leaves.

Nouuelles certaines. *See* [Pizarro (F.)]

Ofensa, y Defensa. *See* Vol. XIII., No. 56748.

Parecer sobre si al vasallo que ofrece descubrir algun arbitrio en beneficio de la causa publica con exorbitanes condiciones, se le podra obligar â que lo manifieste, dandole la recompensa, que se tuviere por justa. *Lima.* 1682. Folio, pp. 12. Portrait.

By Juan Luis Lopez.

El Parnaso del Real Colegio de San Martin postrado a los pies del Exc.mo Señor Conde de la Monclova, Virrey, Gouernador, y Capitan General de estos Reynos &c. Le consagra. Como a su esclarecido, y real Patron vna varia, hermosa, y florida selva de Poesias en aplauso de la heroyca obra del Muelle que en el Puerto de Callao à fabricado su Excelencia, que es la octava Marauilla ... Con Licencia de los Superiores. *En Lima, en la Imprenta de Joseph de Contreras, y Alvarado. Año de* 1694. 4to, 99 leaves. J.C.B. 61151

Improved title of No. 58829.

Le Pérou et ses derniers événements. *Paris.* 1872. 8vo.

Peru and the United States. *See* [Osma (J. I. de)], 57800.

Peru nach seinem gegenwärtigen Zustande dargestellt aus dem Mercurio Peruano von Skinner. Nach dem Englischen von Weyland und Er. A. Schmidt. Herausgegeben von F. J. Bertuch. *Weimar, F. S. pr. Landes-Industrie-Comptoir.* 1808. 2 vols., 8vo, pp. xiv, 574; xxviii, 380. 2 Maps. C. 61153

The first volume is translated from [Skinner's] "Present State of Peru," and the second volume from the "Mercurio Peruano."

El Peru y la influencia Europea. *Paris.* 1862. 8vo, pp. 32.

The Present State of Peru. *See* [Skinner (Joseph)].

Principios politicos en la administracion del Peru. *Quito.* 1823. 8vo. 61155

Proyecto de Ley de Responsabilidad Presentado a la Convencion por la comision respectiva: De Ley Organica de Supremo consejo de la Guerra; De Ley de Municipalidades. *Lima.* 1834. 4to, pp. 18. 61156

Proyecto de Reforma de la Constitucion de 1856. *Lima.* 1860. 4to, pp. 41. 61157

Proyectos de Tratados sobre Principios de Derecho Internacional entre las Republicas aliadas. *Lima.* 1867. Rl. 8vo, pp. 24. 61158

Privately printed. The author was Mr. J. A. Barrenechea, the Peruvian foreign minister in 1867.

Reglamento de Comercio de la República del Perú. *Lima.* 1864. 4to, pp. 46. 61159

Reglamento Provisional dado por el Supremo Delegado del Peru, para el regimen de los Tribunales de Justicia, en los departamentos libros, interim se establece el Código permanente del Estado. *Lima.* 1828. 4to, pp. 25. 61160

Republica Peruana Gobierno Eclesiastico Arequipa Junio 28 de 1834; al señor Ministro de Estados del despacho de Gobierno y Relaciones esteriores. *Lima.* 1834. 8vo. 61161

El Sistema representativo y la cuestion del dia. *Lima.* 1860. 4to, pp. 64. 61162

The Strange and Delectable History. *See* [Zarate (A. de)].

Tomo Primero de las Ordenanzas del Peru, recogidas y coordenadas por el licenciado D. Tomas de Ballesteros. *Con licencia en Lima por Joseph de Contreras.* 1685. Folio, (19) leaves, Text, 320 leaves, Index, 24 leaves. 61163

Improved title of our No. 2962, Vol. I. The first body of laws published in Peru. It was not continued, but was reprinted with additions as follows:

Tomo Primero | de las Ordenanzas | del Peru | Dirigidas | al Rey Nuestro Señor | En su Real, y Supremo Consejo de las Indias. | Por mano | del Excmo. Señor D. Melchor de Navarra | y Rocafull, ... | Recogidas, y Coordinadas. | Por el Lic. D. Thomas De Ballesteros, | ... | Y | Nuevamente añadidas las Ordenanzas, | que para el Nuevo Establecimiento del Tribunal de la Sta. | Cruzada, hà dispuesto, y mandado observar segun la Real | Intencion de S. M. y Bula de N. S. P. Benedicto XIV. | El | Excellentissimo Señor Don Joseph An- | tonio Manso de Velasco, Conde de Super-

Unda ... . | *Reimpressas en Lima: Con Licencia del Superior Govierno.* | *En la Imprenta de Francisco Sobrino y Bados: Año de* 1752. Folio, (23) leaves, Text, 339 leaves, Index, 35 leaves. A.

This important work, of which no more was published, is divided into three parts. The first relates to the Courts of Lima, the second to the Indians, and the third to the mines.

A Voyage to Peru. *See* [Courte de la Blanchardière], 17177.

Wonderlijcke ... Historie ... van Peru. *See* [Zarate (A. de)].

Yo fray Francisco de S. Antonio, del orden de S. Juan de Dios ... certifico, y doy fee, a los que el presente vierẽ, que por las autos de residencia, que fueron remitidos ... por el P. fray Diego de Alfaro, comissario general de la prouincia del archangel San Rafael en los reynos del Pirù, y Chile, de la que tomò al P. fray Juan de Ferriol su antecessor ... consta, y parece que se probeyò auto en que se mandòse notificasse al dicho P. fray Juan de Ferriol ... *Madrid.* 1670. Folio, 4 leaves. 61165

A Peru-Bolivian, *pseudon.* *See* Vol. IV., No. 12772.

El Peruano Liberal. *Lima: Imprenta Peruana.* 1813. 4to, pp. 179. 61166

Twenty-one numbers were issued from October 3 to December 9, 1813, when it was discontinued.

The Peruvian; a Comic Opera. *London.* 1786. 8vo.

Peruvian and Bolivian Guano. Its Nature, Properties and Results. *London.* 1844. 8vo. 61168

Peruvian Guano Trade. Statements and Documents in relation to Imposing a Sliding Scale of Duty on the Importation of Peruvian Guano into the United States; together with a Treatise ... by Daniel Lee, M.D. *Washington.* 1854. 8vo, pp. 32. C.

Peruvian Pamphlet; being an Exposition of the Administrative Labors of the Peruvian Government from the Time of its Formation, till the 15th of July, 1822: ... presented by Don Bernardo Monteagudo. ... *London: Printed by A. Applegath.* ... 1823. 8vo, pp. (2), vi, 99. BA. 61170

Peruvian Tales. *See* [Gueullette (Thomas Simon)], 29143.

PESADO (J. J.) Las Aztecas, Poesias tomadas de los antiguos cantares mexicanos. Por José Joaquin Pesado. *Mexico: V. Segura Argüelles.* 1854. 8vo, pp. 60. 6117[illegible]

PESADO. Poesias Originales y Traducidas de D. José Joaquin Pesado. Segunda edicion, corregida y notablemente aumentada. *Mexico.* 1840. 8vo, pp. vi, 372. Portrait. + [*Ibid.*] 1849. 8vo. Portrait. 61172

PESCHEL (O.) Geschichte des Zeitalters der Entdeckungen. Von Oscar Peschel. *Stuttgart: J. G. Cotta'scher Verlag.* 1858. 8vo, pp. viii, 681. BA. + Zweite Auflage. [*Ibid.*] 1877. 8vo, pp. x, 536. Portrait. A. 61173

Largely relates to the discoveries of the Spaniards in America.

Petaubun. Peep of Day. Vol. I. ... *Sarnia, C. W.* 1861. 4to. 61174

A four-page monthly, in the Chippewa and English languages, "Printed and Published by Rev. Thomas Hurlburt," in 1861–62.

PETAVIUS (D.) The History of the World; or, an Account of Time, Compiled by the Learned Dionisius Petavius. And Continued by Others, To the Year of our Lord, 1659. Together with A Geographicall Description of Europe, Asia, Africa, and America. *London: Humphrey Mosely.* MDCLIX. Folio, pp. (8), 610, Table, (34), Geographicall Description, (2), 154, (5). + *London: Printed by J. Streater.* MDCLIX. Folio, pp. (8), 610, (34), (2), 154, (5). BA. 61175

PETER (R.) A Brief Sketch of the History of Lexington, Ky., and of Transylvania University. By Robert Peter, M.D. *Lexington: The Author.* 1845. 8vo, pp. 21. P. 61176

Also: Summary of Meteorological Observations, made 1836, in Lexington, Ky. [n. p. n. d.] 8vo. — Summary of Meteorological Observations, made July–September, 1837, in Lexington, Ky. [n. p. n. d.] 8vo. B.

PETER PARLEY, *pseudon.* *See* [Goodrich (S. G.)], 27910–15.

Peter Parley's Canada (*London, Darton & Co.*, 1839,) is a spurious production, not by S. G. Goodrich.

Peter Pilgrim: or A Rambler's Recollections. ... *Philadelphia: Lea & Blanchard.* 1838. 2 vols., 12mo, pp. (8), 13–247; (4), 13–256. + *London.* 1839. 2 vols., post 8vo. 61177

By R. M. Bird.

"PETER PINDAR, *Jr.*," *pseudon.* *See* "Pindar (Peter), Jr.," *pseudon.*

PETER PLOUGHSHARE, *pseudon.* *See* Vol. IV., No. 15939.

PETER PORCUPINE, *pseudon.* *See* [Cobbett (W.)], Vol. IV.

Peter Schlemihl in America. *See* [Wood (George)].

Peter Scriber on Protection. [n. p.] 1844. 8vo, pp. 10.

"Peter Scriber" was Charles Augustus Davis.

PETER WILKINS. *See* [Paltock (Robert)], No. 58394.

PETERBOROUGH (*Bishop of*). *See* [Hinchliffe (J.)], Vol. VIII., No. 31927, [Kennett (White)], Vol. IX., No. 37449, [Thomas (John)], *and* [Terrick (Richard)].

PETERHOFF. ... The United States vs. the Steamer Peterhoff and her Cargo. In Prize. Opinion of the Court, By Judge Betts. With an Appendix, containing the Opinions of Judge Marvin, ... in the Cases of the Dolphin and the Pearl. *New-York: John W. Amerman, Printer.* 1864. 8vo, pp. 116. 61179

The Seizure of the "Peterhoff," being a Statement of the Facts, the Reason, the Law, and the Correspondence. *London: Effingham Wilson.* 1863. 8vo. 61180

See also Sherwood (Lorenzo), *and* Smith (E. Delafield).

PETERKIN (Joshua). Treatise on Planting, from the Origin of the Semen to Ebullition; with a Correct Mode of Distillation, and a Melioration on the Whole Process Progressively, dedicated to the Planters of the Leeward Charribbee Islands. ... *St. Christopher's: Printed by Edward Luth and R. Low, Cayon Street, Baseterre.* 1790. 4to. 61181

PETERMANN (A.) Historical Summary of the Five Years' Search for Sir John Franklin. By Augustus Petermann. *London: [J. E. Taylor.* 1853?] 8vo, pp. 30. C. 61182

Printed for private circulation.

PETERMANN. The Search for Franklin: A Suggestion submitted to the British Public. By Augustus Petermann. *London: Longman & Co.* 1852. 8vo, pp. 24. Map. C. 61183

See also Vol. XII., No. 49765.

PETERS (A.) The City of the Silent. A Tribute to the Wood-Lawn Cemetery established for the City of New-York and Westchester County. ... By A. Peters, D.D. *New-York: John A. Gray & Green, Printers.* 1866. 12mo, pp. 12. 61184

PETERS. Colleges Religious Institutions. A Discourse, ... Newark, N. J., Oct. 29, 1851, before the Society for the Promotion of Collegiate and Theological Education in the West.

By Absalom Peters, D.D. ... *New-York: John F. Trow, Printer.* 1851. 8vo, pp. 29. 61185

PETERS. Life and Time. A Birth-Day Memorial of Seventy Years. ... By Absalom Peters, D.D. *New York: Sheldon & Co.* 1866. Sq. 16mo, pp. 80. C. 61186

A poem, with personal reminiscences. Also: Brief Answer to an Official Reply of the Board of Missions of the General Assembly to Six Letters of Rev. Absalom Peters. *New York.* 1831. 8vo. — Reply to the Rev. J. D. Wilson's Four Propositions sustained against the Claims of the American Home Missionary Society. ... *New York.* 1831. 8vo.

PETERS (B. M.) Eine besonders merkwürdige Reise von Amsterdam nach Surinam, und von da zurück nach Bremen, in den Jahren 1783 und 1784. Von Bernhard Michael Peters, einem Jeverländer. Wobei die Reisen und Lebensgeschichte John Thomsons eines Engländers, seines vertrauten Freundes und Reisegefährten auf der See. *Bremen.* 1788–90. 2 vols., 8vo, pp. (8), 214; (12), 188. 61187

PETERS (C.) Two Sermons, preached at Dominica, ... April, 1800 ... . [with] Minutes of Three Trials ... at Roseau ... together with Remarks on the ... Trials; as well as on the Slave Trade, &c. By the Rev. C. Peters, A.M. ... *London: J. Hatchard.* 1802. 8vo, pp. 80. 61188

PETERS (C. H. F.) ... Report of Dr. Peters ... on the Longitude of Elmira. ... *Albany: Comstock & Cassidy, Printers.* 1864. 8vo, pp. 8. H. 61189

Also: ... Report of Dr. Peters ... on the Longitude and Latitude of Ogdensburgh. ... *Albany: C. Wendell, Printer.* 1865. 8vo, pp. 15. H.

PETERS (D. W. C.) The Life and Adventures of Kit Carson, the Nestor of the Rocky Mountains; from facts narrated by himself. By De Witt C. Peters, M.D. ... *New York.* 1858. 8vo, pp. (4), 534. Plates. + *New York: W. R. C. Clark & Meeker.* MDCCCLIX. 8vo, pp. (4), 534. Plates. + [*Ibid.*] 1860. 8vo. + *Hartford, Conn.: Dustin, Gilman & Co.* 1874. 8vo, pp. 604. 30 Plates and 2 Portraits. C. 61190

PETERS (H.) A | Dying Fathers | last | Legacy | to an | Onely Child | or | Mr. Hugh Peter's | Advice | to his | Daughter | Written by his own Hand, during his | late Imprisonment in the Tower of Lon- | don; and given her a little before his | Death. | *London: E. Calvert.* [n. d.] Sm. 12mo, pp. (6), 122. Portrait. 61191

Contains slight reference to New England. In some copies the latter part of the

title reads: Written by his own Hand, during his | late Imprisonment in the Tower of | London: And given her a little | before his Death. | *London: Printed for G. Calvert and T. Brewster.* 1660. 12mo. + [*Ibid.*] 1661. 12mo.

PETERS. A | Dying Fathers | last | Legacy | to an | Only Child: | or, | Mr. Hugh Peter's | Advice | to his | Daughter. | Written by his own Hand, during | his late Imprisonment in the Tower | of London; And given her a little | before his Death. | *Boston; Printed by B. Green, | for Benjamin Eliot, at his Shop on | the North Side of King-Street.* 1717. | 18mo, pp. (2), ii, 92. Portrait. B. 61192

[PETERS.] Good Work for a Good Magistrate, or A Short Cut to Great Quiet ... . *London, by W. Du Gard, Printer* ... . 1651. 12mo. M. 61193

PETERS. An Historical and Critical Account of Hugh Peters. After the Manner of Mr. Bayle. *London: J. Noon.* MDCCLI. 8vo, pp. 72. Portrait. + ... *Reprinted by G. Smeeton.* M.DCCC.-XVIII. 4to, pp. 41. Portrait. 61194

By William Harris, D.D. Hugh Peter or Peters came to New England in 1635, succeeded Roger Williams as pastor of the church in Salem, and assisted in revising the colonial laws of 1638. He returned to England in 1641, and was tried and executed for high treason in 1660.

PETERS. Mr. Peters Last Report of the English Wars, Occasioned by the Importunity of a Friend pressing an Answer to seven Quæres. *London: Printed by M. S. for H. Overton.* 1646. 4to, pp. 15. 61195

PETERS. The Tales and Jests of Mr. Hugh Peters, Collected into one Volume. Published by one that hath formerly been conversant with the Author in his life time. And dedicated to Mr. John Goodwin and Phillip Nye. Together with his Sentence, and the manner of his Execution. *London: Printed by S. D.* ... 1660. 4to, 22 leaves. + ... *Reprinted for J. Caulfield.* 1807. 8vo, pp. xx, (4), 51. Portrait. + [*Ibid.*] 1860. 8vo. Portrait. 61196

Reprinted at least twice in the seventeenth century. Of the 1807 edition there were fifty copies on large paper. Also reprinted in "The American Bibliopolist," vol. IV. *See* Collier's "Bib. Account of Early English Lit.," vol. III., pp. 181-186.

Also: Gods Doings, and Mans Duty. ... Sermon ... before ... Parliament, ... at the last Thanksgiving Day, April 2, 1645. For the recovery of the West ... . *London.* 1646. 4to, pp. (12), 38.—A Sermon by Hugh Peters: Preached before his Death: As it was taken by a faithful hand, And now published for publick Information. *London: John Best.* 1660. 4to, pp. (4), 28.—A Word for the Armie, and Two Words to the Kingdome, to clear the one, and cure the other. ... *London: Printed by M. Simmons, for G. Calvert.* 1647. 4to, pp. 14. *See also* [Ward (Nathaniel)] *and* Yonge (William).

PETERS. The History of the Life and Death of Hugh Peters, that Archtraytor, from the Cradell to the Gallowes. *London.* 1661. 4to. 61197

PETERS (J.), *pseudon.* Chronicles of Turkeytown; or, the works of Jeremy Peters. First Series. Containing the History of a dreadful Catastrophe, the Amours of Dr. Post and Mrs. Peweetle, and the History of a Tatterdemalion. ... *Philadelphia: R. H. Small.* 1829. 12mo, pp. 238. C. 61198

PETERS (P.) An Elegy Sacred to the Memory of that Great Divine the Reverend and Learned Dr. Samuel Cooper, who departed this Life December 29, 1783, Ætatis 59. By Phillis Peters. *Boston: Printed by E. Russell.* M,DCC,LXXXIV. 4to, pp. 8

PETERS. Liberty and Peace, a Poem. By Phillis Peters. *Boston: Printed by Warden and Russell.* MDCCLXXXIV. 8vo, pp. 4

Phillis Peters, better known as Phillis Wheatley, the negro poetess, was married to Dr. John Peters, a colored man. For her earlier poems *see* Wheatley (Phillis).

PETERS (R.) A Sermon on Education. Wherein some Account is given of the Academy, Established in the City of Philadelphia. Preach'd at the Opening thereof, on the Seventh Day of January, 1750-1. By the Reverend Mr. Richard Peters. *Philadelphia: Printed and Sold by B. Franklin, and D. Hall* ... . MDCCLI. 8vo, pp. vii, 48, 8. P. 61201

The last eight pages consist of an "Idea of the English School Sketch'd out for the Consideration of the Trustees of the Philadelphia Academy," signed B. F., and written by Franklin. The Peters' preface is dated Sept. 12. 1751. Very handsomely printed on fine paper.

PETERS. The Two Last | Sermons | Preached at | Christ's-Church | in | Philadelphia | July 3, 1737. | By Richard Peters. | *Philadelphia: | Printed and Sold by B. Franklin.* M,DCC,XXXVII. | Sm. 4to, pp. xxii, 29. C., H. 61202

PETERS, *and others.* A Treaty held with the Ohio Indians. ... Oct. 1753. ... The Report of Richard Peters, Isaac Norris, and Benjamin Franklin, ... Commissioners appointed to treat with ... the ... Indians at Carlisle, ... County of Cumberland, ... 22d Day of September, 1753. [*Philadelphia: Printed by B. Franklin and D. Hall.* 1753.] Folio, pp. 10. BA., M. 61203

PETERS (Richard). Agricultural Enquiries on Plaister of Paris ... . *Philadelphia: C. Cist & J. Markland.* 1797. 8vo, pp. 109. + [With a fac-simile of Washington's handwriting and a

sketch of his character. Second Edition.] *Philadelphia: Jane Aitken.* 1810. 8vo, pp. xvi, 129, ix. C. 61204

[PETERS.] A Statistical Account of the Schuylkill Permanent Bridge, communicated to the Philadelphia Society of Agriculture, 1806. *Philadelphia: J. Aitken.* 1807. 8vo, pp. 84. Plate. C.

Also: A Discourse on Agriculture ... . *Philadelphia: Johnson and Warner.* 1816. 8vo. BA.

PETERS (R.), *Jr.* The Case of the Cherokee Nation against the State of Georgia; argued and determined at the Supreme Court of the United States, January Term, 1831. With an Appendix, Containing the Opinion of Chancellor Kent on the Case; the Treaties between the United States and the Cherokee Indians; the Act of Congress of 1802, entitled "An Act to regulate intercourse with the Indian tribes, &c."; and the Laws of Georgia relative to the country occupied by the Cherokee Indians, within the boundary of that State. By Richard Peters. *Philadelphia: John Grigg.* 1831. 8vo, pp. (8), 286. C. 61206

PETERS. Report of the Case of Edward Prigg against ... Pennsylvania ..., in which it was decided that all the Laws of the several States relative to Fugitive Slaves are Unconstitutional and Void. ... By Richard Peters ... . *Philadelphia: L. Johnson.* 1842. 8vo, pp. 140. BA. 61207

PETERS. ... The Public Statutes at Large of the United States of America, from the Organization of the Government in 1789, to March 3, 1845. Arranged in Chronological Order. With reference to the matter of each Act and to the subsequent Acts on the same subject, and copious Notes of the Decisions of the Courts of the United States construing those Acts, and upon the Subjects of the Laws. With an Index to the Contents of each Volume, and a full General Index to the whole work ... Edited by Richard Peters, Esq., Counsellor at Law. ... *Boston: Charles C. Little and James Brown.* 1845-46. 8 vols., 8vo, pp. lxxii, 777; xxxviii, 856; xxxix, 820, (7); xlv, 850; xxxv, 832; (2), xcix, 1012; (2), viii, 612; xii, 954. 61208

Each volume has been revised and reprinted several times. Later editions differ in the collation. Vols. I.-V. contain the Public Statutes, 1789-1845; Vol. VI. Private Statutes, 1789-1845; Vol. VII. Indian Treaties, 1778-1842; Vol. VIII. Foreign Treaties, 1778-1845, and General Index. Supplemented by: ... The Statutes at Large and Treaties of the United States of America. From December 1, 1845, to March 3, 1851, Arranged in Chronological Order; with references to the matter of each Act and to the subsequent Acts on the same subject. Edited by George Minot, Esq., Counsellor at Law. ... Vol. IX. *Boston: Charles C. Little and James Brown.* 1851. 8vo, pp. xxv, 1065. Continued. Vols. IX. and X. (1851-55) were edited by

George Minot; Vol. XI. (1859) by George Minot and George P. Sanger; Vols. XII.-XVII. (1863-73) by George P. Sanger. These supplementary volumes, which include "Proclamations," were also issued in annual parts, with special titles, as "Public Laws," "Private Laws," and "Treaties." *See also* Vol. XIII., No. 57236, note, *and* "A Synoptical Index."

[PETERS (Samuel A.)] A | General History | of | Connecticut, | from its | First Settlement under George Fenwick, Esq. | To its | Latest Period of Amity with Great Britain; | including | a Description of the Country, | And many curious and interesting Anecdotes. | To which is added, | An Appendix, wherein new and true Sources of the present | Rebellion in America are pointed out; together with the particu- | lar Part taken by the People of Connecticut in its Promotion. | By a Gentleman of the Province. | ... | *London: | Printed for the Author; | And sold by J. Bew,* ... | MDCCLXXXI. | 8vo, pp. x, 2*, 436. BA. + Second Edition. [*Ibid.*] MDCCLXXXII. 8vo, pp. x, 2*, 436. H. + To which is added a Supplement, verifying many important statements made by the Author. Illustrated with Eight Engravings. *New-Haven: ... D. Clark and Co.* 1829. 12mo, pp. 405. 8 Woodcuts. B. 61209

The first edition is very rare. The so-called second edition differs only in the substitution of a new title-page. Reprinted again as follows:

PETERS. The Rev. Samuel Peters' LL.D. General History of Connecticut, from its first settlement under George Fenwick to its latest period of amity with Great Britain prior to the Revolution; including a Description of the Country, and many curious and interesting Anecdotes. With an appendix, pointing out the causes of the Rebellion in America; together with the particular part taken by the people of Connecticut in its promotion. By a Gentleman of the Province. London: 1781. To which are added, Additions to Appendix, Notes, and Extracts from Letters, verifying many important Statements made by the Author. By Samuel Jarvis M'Cormick. *New York: D. Appleton and Company.* 1877. 12mo, pp. 285. 61210

Dr. Peters, the "Parson Peters" of Trumbull's M'Fingal, was born at Hebron, Connecticut, in 1735; graduated at Yale College in 1759, and took charge of the Episcopal church at his native place in 1762. On the breaking out of the American Revolution in 1774, he made himself particularly obnoxious by his prominence and activity as a royalist. He was mobbed and obliged to flee to England, where he remained until 1805, when he returned to America. He died at New York in 1826, and his remains were removed to Hebron for burial. His History of Connecticut, which is a remarkable tissue of misstatements and exaggerations, is very severe in its reflections upon the inhabitants of that State, to whom he attributes some fictitious "Blue Laws." It also contains a curious account of "bundling," and a description of a midnight invasion of Windham by frogs, and the consequent terror and flight of the inhabitants. Speaking of the upper Cohoes Falls, he says: "Here water is consolidated, without frost, by pressure, by swiftness, between the pinching, sturdy rocks, to

such a degree of induration, that no iron crow can be forced into it: here iron, lead, and cork, have one common weight." Dr. Peters also wrote a brief History of Hebron. "That most unscrupulous and malicious of lying narratives, Peters' history of Connecticut."—DR. L. BACON. "The Lying History."—*Anal. Mag.* IV. 49. "That mass of folly and falsehood commonly called Peters's History of Connecticut."—DR. DWIGHT. *See* Professor Kingsley's "Historical Discourse," 38; "Monthly Review," LXVI. 250; Duyckinck, I.; Dwight's "Travels," III. 495; Palfrey's "New England," II.

PETERS. A History of the Rev. Hugh Peters, A.M. ... By the Rev. Samuel Peters, LL.D. *New York: The Author.* 1807. 12mo, pp. vi, 155. Portrait. BA., C. 61211

The appendix contains much interesting matter relating to "William Peters of Boston, in N. E., 1634, and of his Children and Descendants." For two pamphlets, which have been attributed to Samuel Peters, *see* Viator (J.), *pseudon.*

PETERS. A Sermon, preached at Charlotte Chapel, Pimlico, the 25th of March, 1787, on the death of Thomas Moffatt, M.D. Late of New London, in Connecticut ... . By Samuel Peters, A.M. *London: D. & D. Bond.* 1787. 4to, pp. 28. + [*Ibid.*] 1788. 4to. 61212

Dedicated to General Gage, as a mark of the author's gratitude to him "for his generous support of the *Pious*, the Loyal, and Brave." Dr. Moffatt was a reputable physician of New London, and held the office of Controller of the Customs at the beginning of the Revolution, when, says his reverend eulogist "the Libertines 'gnashed on him with their teeth,' as the Cyrenians did on Stephen, because he was loyal to his King, ... and like the deaf Adder, they 'stopped their Ears, ran upon him, and cast him out of the City'" (p. 24).—J. H. TRUMBULL. *See* "Monthly Review," LXXVIII. 446.

PETERS. Review of a History of Connecticut. [n. p. 1781.] 8vo. View of Guard House. 61213

PETERS (T. C.) Report on the Condition of the South in regard to ... a Cotton Crop. ... By Theodore C. Peters. ... *Baltimore: Printed by H. A. Robinson.* 1867. 8vo, pp. 23. 61214

PETERSBURG, *Va.* First Annual Report of the BOARD OF EDUCATION of the City of Petersburg, Va. For ... 1868-'9. *Petersburg: John B. Ege's Printing House.* 1869. 8vo, pp. 37. Continued. B. 61215

Catalogue of the Library of Petersburg. *New York: D. Appleton & Company.* 1854. 8vo, pp. 82. C. 61216

A Guide to the Fortifications and Battlefields around Petersburg. ... *Petersburg, Va.* 1866. 8vo, pp. (2), 27. Map. + [*Ibid.*] 1869. 8vo, pp. (2), 26. Map and Plate. 61217

First Annual Report of the ... LIBRARY ASSOCIATION, for ... 1854. *Petersburg.* 1854. 8vo. 61218

Petersburg City Directory for 1866. To which is added a Business Directory. *Petersburg: Webb & Fitzgerald.* 1866. 8vo, pp. 115, 39. 61219

Report of the PETERSBURG RAILROAD COMPANY to the Board of Public Works of Virginia, September 3, 1846. *Richmond: Shepherd & Co.* 1847. 8vo, pp. 55. S. 61220

Resolution of the Inhabitants of Petersburg. *Washington.* 1806. 8vo. 61221

Relates to the rights of neutrals.

PETERSEN (B. v.) En historisk Beretning om de danske-vestindiske Oer: St. Croix, St. Thomas og St. Jan. *Kjöbenhavn.* 1855. 8vo, pp. 285. 61222

PETERSEN (C.) Erindringer fra Polarlandene optegnede af Carl Petersen, 1850-55. Udgivne af Lieut. L. B. Deichmann. *Kjöbenhavn.* 1857. 12mo. Map. 61223

PETERSEN. Den sidste Franklin-Expedition med "Fox," Capt. M'Clintock, ved Carl Petersen ... . *Kjöbenhavn: Fr. Wöldikes Forlagsboghandel.* 1860. 8vo, pp. (6), 266. 3 Maps, 9 Plates and a Fac-simile. A. 61224

PETERSEN (F. A.) Military Review of the Campaign in Virginia & Maryland, under Generals John C. Fremont, N. P. Banks, Irwin McDowell, Franz Sigel, John Pope, James S. Wadsworth, Wm. H. Halleck and George B. McClellan. In 1862, by Fred'k A. Petersen. ... A Contribution to the Future History of the United States. *New York: Sinclair Tousey* ... . [1862.] 8vo, pp. (2), 55. + Part II. [*Ibid.* 1863.] 8vo, pp. (2), 69. 61225

PETERSEN (J. C. P.) Dissertatio de Cortice Peruviano ... . Johan Christian Peter Petersen. *Upsaliæ: L. M. Höjer.* [1758.] 4to, pp. (2), 38. J.C.B. 61226

PETERSEN (N. M.) Hans Egedes levnet. ... *Kjöbenhavn.* 1839. 8vo. 61227

PETERSON (C. J.) The American Navy: being an Authentic History of the United States Navy, and Biographical Sketches of American Naval Heroes, from the Formation of the Navy to the Close of the Mexican War. By Charles J. Peterson ... . Illustrated ... . *Philadelphia.* 1858. 8vo. + [*Ibid.*] 1859. 8vo,

pp. xiii, 545. + *Philadelphia: James B. Smith & Co.* 1860. 8vo, pp. xiii, 545. A. 61228

First published in 1848.

[PETERSON (C. J.)] The Cabin and Parlor; or Slaves and Masters. By J. Thornton Randolph. ... *Philadelphia: T. B. Peterson.* [1852.] 12mo, pp. 324. P. 61229

PETERSON. Cruising in the last War. By Charles J. Peterson ... . *Philadelphia: T. B. Peterson.* [1850.] 8vo, pp. 114. B.

A naval story of the war of 1812.

PETERSON. Grace Dudley; or, Arnold at Saratoga. An Historical Novel. By Charles J. Peterson. *Philadelphia: T. B. Peterson.* 1849. 8vo, pp. 111. 61231

PETERSON. History of the American Revolution, and Biographical Sketches of the Military Heroes of the War of Independence. By Charles J. Peterson. *Philadelphia.* 1852. 8vo. Plates. + [*Ibid.*] 1856. 8vo. 61232

PETERSON. The History of the Wars of the United States. Containing a History of the Revolution, and of the Wars of 1812 and Mexico, with Biographical Sketches of all the prominent Military Heroes. *Philadelphia.* 1860. 3 vols., 8vo, pp. 487; 208; 282. 61233

PETERSON. Kate Aylesford. A Story of the Refugees. By Charles J. Peterson. *Philadelphia: T. B. Peterson.* [1855.] 12mo, pp. (2), 21-356. C. 61234

Also with the title: "Kate Aylesford. The Heiress of Sweetwater."

PETERSON. The Military Heroes of the Revolution, with a Narrative of the War of Independence. By Charles J. Peterson. *Philadelphia.* 1848. 8vo, pp. 487. + *Philadelphia: James B. Smith & Co.* [n. d.] 8vo, pp. 487. + *New York.* 1859. 8vo, pp. 487. 61235

PETERSON. The Military Heroes of the War of 1812: with a Narrative of the War. By Charles J. Peterson. *Philadelphia: William A. Leary.* 1848. 8vo, pp. 208. 6 Plates. + Third Edition. [*Ibid.*] 1849. 8vo, pp. 208. 6 Plates. + Tenth Edition. *Philadelphia: Jas. B. Smith & Co.* 1856. 8vo, pp. 208. Plates. + [*Ibid.*] 1858. 8vo, pp. 208. Plates. 61236

PETERSON. The Military Heroes of the War with Mexico: with a Narrative of the War. By Charles J. Peterson. *Phila-*

delphia: William A. Leary. 1848. 8vo, pp. 282. Plates. + Third Edition. [*Ibid.*] 1849. 8vo, pp. 282. 14 Plates. + Tenth Edition. *Philadelphia: Jas. B. Smith & Co.* 1856. 8vo, pp. 282. Plates. + [*Ibid.*] 1858. 8vo, pp. 282. Plates.

PETERSON. Monody on Certain Members of the "Press Club." (Believed to bear date about A. D. 1900.) By Chas. J. Peterson. [*Philadelphia:*] *Privately printed for F. J. Dreer.* [n. d.] 4to, 11 leaves. 61238

PETERSON. The Oath of Marion. A Story of the Revolution. By Charles J. Peterson. *Boston: F. Gleason.* 1847. 8vo, pp. 50. 61239

PETERSON (D. H.) The Looking Glass: being a True Report and Narrative of the Life, Travels and Labors of the Rev. Daniel H. Peterson, Colored Clergyman; ... from 1812 to 1854, ... *New York: Wright, Printer.* 1854. 18mo, pp. 151. S.

PETERSON (E.) Facts on Congregational Intolerance and Ecclesiastical Despotism. By Rev. Edward Peterson, Providence, R. I. *Providence: B. F. Moore, Printer.* 1845. 8vo, pp. 16.

PETERSON. History of Rhode Island. By Rev. Edward Peterson ... . *New-York: John S. Taylor.* 1853. 8vo, pp. 370. Lithographed title and 7 Plates. A., BA. 61242

The lithographed title reads: "History of Rhode Island and Newport. In the Past."

PETERSON (H.) An Address ... before the Junior Anti-Slavery Society of ... Philadelphia, December 23, 1836. By Henry Peterson ... . *Philadelphia: Printed by Merrihew and Gunn.* 1837. 8vo, pp. 12. BA. 61243

PETERSON. Address on American Slavery, ... before ... the Junior Anti-Slavery Society of Philadelphia, July 4th, 1838. By Henry Peterson ... . *Philadelphia: Merrihew and Gunn, Printers.* 1838. 8vo, pp. 28. 61244

PETERSON (T. B.) Peterson's Complete Coin-Book, containing ... Fac-simile Impressions of all the various ... Coins throughout the World, with the United States Mint Value of each ... . *Philadelphia: T. B. Peterson.* 1859. 4to. 61245

PETHERAM (J.) Bibliographical Miscellany. Edited by John Petheram. *London.* 1859. 8vo. 61246

Five numbers appeared. The first three contain: "Particulars of the Voyage of Sir

Thomas Button for the Discovery of a North-West Passage, A.D. 1612." Sir Dudley Digges' "Of the Circumference of the Earth; or, a Treatise of the North-East Passage, 1611–13." Letter of Sir Thomas Button on the North-West Passage, in the State-Paper Office.

PETHERICK (T.) *See* Misisquoi, Vol. XII., No. 49458.

PETIGRU (C.) An Oration prepared for Delivery on ... Laying the Corner Stone of a Monument erected to the Memory of Kosciuszko at West Point, By the Corps of Cadets, July 4, 1828. By Cadet Charles Petigru. *Newburgh: W. M. Gazlay.* 1828. 8vo, pp. 15. H. 61247

PETIGRU (J. L.) An Oration ... before the Washington Society, the Fourth July, 1834. By James Louis Petigru. ... *Charleston: Printed by D. J. Dowling.* 1834. 8vo, pp. 18. H.

Also: An Oration ... before the Phi Kappa and Demosthenian Societies of the University of Georgia, August 6, 1846. ... *Athens, Ga.* 1846. 8vo, pp. 24. — Oration ... before the Charleston Library Society, at its First Centennial Anniversary, June 13th, 1848. ... *Charleston, S. C.: J. B. Nixon, Printer.* 1848. 8vo, pp. 21. — Oration ... on the third Anniversary of the South Carolina Historical Society, May 27th, 1858. ... *Charleston.* 1858. 8vo.

PETIGRU. Memorial of the late James L. Petigru. Proceedings of the Bar of Charleston, S. C., March 25, 1863. *New York: Richardson & Company.* 1866. 8vo, pp. 43. 61249

PÉTION [DE VILLENEUVE] (J[érome].) Discours sur les Troubles de Saint-Domingue. Par J. Pétion, Député à l'Assemblée Nationale. *A Paris, Chez Desennes* ... 14 *Octobre* 1790. 8vo, pp. (4), 44. H., P. 61250

[PETIT (Emilien).] Dissertations sur le Droit Public des Colonies Françoises, Espagnoles et Angloises, d'après les loix des trois nations, comparées entr'elles; dans la 1ère on traite de la guerre entre l'Angleterre et ses colonies, et de l'état civil et religieux des Canadiens catholiques. *Genève.* 1778. 8vo, pp. 500. + *Paris: Knapen.* 1778. 8vo. 61251

Contains an account of the origin and the causes of the war between Great Britain and her colonies, and the civil and religious state of the French Canadians.

PETIT. Droit Public,|ou|gouvernement|des|Colonies Françoises.|D'apres les Loix faites pour ces Pays.|Par M. Petit, Député des Conseils Supérieurs des|Colonies Françoises.|*A Paris, Chez Delalain.* M.DCC.LXXI. 2 vols., 8vo, pp. (2), xvi, 474, (2); (4), 521. 61252

PETIT. Traité sur le Gouvernement des Esclaves. Par M. Petit, Député des Conseils Supérieurs des Colonies. ... *A Paris, Chez Knapen.* 1777. 2 vols., 12mo, pp. (2), iv, 466; (2), 330, (2)

This has also been attributed to Jacques Petit, a son of Emilien Petit, and an advocate at Martinique.

PETIT (L.) Household Mysteries; a Romance of Southern Life. By Lizzie Petit. *New York: D. Appleton & Company.* 1856. 12mo, pp. 300. C. 61254

PETIT (Pablo). Breve tratado de la enfermedad venerea o morbo galico, en que se explican sus verdaderas causas, y su perfecta curacion segun los verdaderos principios de la Medicina y Cirurgia moderna ... . *En Lima. En la Imprenta que esta en la Calle Real de Palacio. Año de* 1730. 4to. J.C.B. 61255

PETIT (Pierre). De Amazonibus Dissertatio, qua an vere extiterint, necne, variis ultro citroque conjecturis et argumentis disputatur. Multa etiam ad eam gentem pertinentia, ex antiquis monumentis eruuntur atque illustrantur ... *Lutetiae Parisiorum* 1685. 8vo, pp. 386, and Index. + Editio Secunda, Auctior & Correctior. *Amstelodami: Wolters.* 1687. Sm. 8vo. Map and Plates. 61256

PETIT. De Natura et Moribus Anthropophagorum ... . *Utrecht.* 1688. 8vo. 61257

See cap. VI., "Anthropophagi frequentes in Novo Orbe."

PETIT. Traité historique sur les Amazones; où l'on trouve tout ce que les auteurs, tant Anciens que Modernes, ont écrit pour et contre ces Héroïnes ... . *Leide: Chez J. A. Langerak.* 1718. 2 vols., 8vo. Map. 61258

PETIT-GOAVE, *St Domingo.* Fête civique [donnée au paroisse du Petit-Goave, 4 mai 1790]. *Port-au-Prince: Bourdon.* [n. d.] 4to, pp. 48 or less. 61259

PETIT-THOUARS (Abel du). *See* Du Petit-Thouars (A.), Vol. VI., No. 21354, *and* Arago (D. F. J.), Vol. I., No. 1862.

PETIT-THOUARS (A. A.) Vie, Lettres, Voyages, Memoires et Opuscules d'Aristide-Aubert du Petit-Thouars, Capitaine de vaisseau, commandant le Tonnant, tué à la bataille de Aboukir; précédés d'un precis de la guerre que la France a eue avec l'Angleterre de 1778 à 1783. Appuyé de notes biographiques sur les

principaux personages cités. [*Paris: Dentu.* n. d.] 8vo, pp. xliv, 232. J.C.B. 61260

This volume relates wholly to the war in America, but particularly to the operations of the French fleet and army. At the close it says: "Fin du premier volume," from which it may be inferred that another volume was contemplated.

PETIT DE BARONCOURT (*M.*) De l'Émancipation des Noirs; ou lettres à M. le Duc de Broglie sur les dangers de cette mesure, suivies de considérations sur le droit de visite, par M. Petit de Baroncourt. ... Deuxième édition. *Paris: Amyot.* 1845. 16mo, pp. xv, 321. S. 61261

PETIT DE BARONCOURT. Première Lettre à M. le Duc de Broglie, sur la Decadence de la Civilisation aux Antilles, et sur la ruine de Notre Marine, et de nos Colonies, par suite de l'Émancipation des Noirs. Par M. Petit de Baroncourt. *Paris: Amyot.* 1843. 8vo, pp. 40. + Deuxième Lettre ... . [*Ibid.*] 1843. 8vo, pp. 41–88. + Troisième Lettre ... . [*Ibid.*] 1844. 8vo, pp. 89–132. 61262

[PETIT DE VIEVIGNE.] Code de la Martinique. *Saint-Pierre: Pierre Richard.* 1767. Folio, pp. (4), xx, 552. + Supplément au Code ... . [*Ibid.*] 1772. Folio, pp. viij, 152. + Second Supplément au Code ... . [*Ibid.*] 1786. Folio, pp. xii, 384. 61263

PETITE BUNKUM. The Showman. Autobiography, showing his birth, education, and bringing-up; his Astonishing Adventures; his connection with Tom Thumb, the Woolly Horse, etc. *New York.* 1855. 12mo. Illustrations. 61264

Petition and Memorial of Citizens of the United States to the Senate and House of Representatives in Congress Assembled. ... *New York: Francis & Loutrel.* 1865. 8vo, pp. 20. 61265

In favor of the rights of colored citizens.

The Petition & Memorial of the Towns of Bristol, Nobleborough, New-Castle, Edgcomb, and Boothbay, in the County of Lincoln, to the General Court of Massachusetts, Anno Domini, 1810. *Boston: Printed by J. Belcher.* 1811. 8vo, pp. 32.

Petition des Citoyens de Couleur de St. Domingue à l'Assemblée Nationale. *Paris.* 1791. 8vo. C. 61267

Pétition des Citoyens de Couleur des Colonies, sur la conspiration et la coalition des Colons avec les Anglais. Lue, le 5 Vendémiaire, à la barre de la Convention. ... [*Paris:*] *De l'imprimerie de Pain, Passage-Honoré.* [1791?] 8vo, pp. 12. P. 61268

Petition from the People of Louisiana to Congress for the relief of the New Orleans, Opelousas and Great Western Railroad Company. ... *Washington, D. C.: McGill & Witherow.* 1868. 8vo, pp. 27. 61269

Petition from the West India Planters ... in Scotland, for the protection of their Rights ... respecting Slavery in the West Indies. *Glasgow.* [n. d.] 8vo, pp. 3. 61270

Petition Nouvelle des Citoyens de Couleur des Isles Françoises à l'Assemblée Nationale; précédée d'un avertissement sur les manœuvres employées pour faire échouer cette petition, et suivie de pieces justificatives. *Paris: Desenne.* 1791. 8vo, pp. 19.

Petition of Citizens of New Orleans, Creditors of the Late Republic of Texas, to the Thirty-Second Congress. *New Orleans: Hinton & Bros. Print.* 1852. 8vo, pp. 51, folded leaf.

The Petition of the Heirs of Gen. Thomas Nelson, late Governor of Virginia. [n. p. n. d.] 8vo, pp. 42. BA. 61273

Petition of the Merchants and Shop Owners of Saint John, New Brunswick, ... Respecting the Timber Trade ... *Saint John, N. B.* 1820. 8vo, pp. 14, (1). 61274

Petition of the Proprietors of Plantations in the Islands of St. Nevis and St. Christophers. [n. p. 1706.] Folio, 1 leaf.

Petition of the Receivers and Exporters of American Leaf Tobacco, to Congress. *New York, Dec.* 19, 1863. 8vo, pp. 11.

Petition of the Stockholders of the Spot-Pond Aqueduct Company, August, 1845. [*Boston.* 1845.] 8vo, pp. 8. 61277

Petition respecting Patucket Falls. *Boston, Feb.* 3, 1838. 8vo, pp. 8. 61278

Petition to Congress for Claims of American Citizens against Poland and Russia. *New York.* 1870. 8vo. 61279

A Petition to His Majesty King George the Third [by Grantees of New Hampshire, asking to be continued under the jurisdiction of that Province. n. p. 1766.] Sm. 4to, pp. (2), 5. 61280

Usually followed by a Power of Attorney, dated November, 1766, to Samuel Robinson, Esq. and others, to act for the subscribers, to obtain confirmation of their grants, 1 page.

"The Petition and Power are reprinted in 'Doc. Hist. of New York,' IV. 619, 621, and in 'Vermont Hist. Soc. Collections,' I. 277 and after. Most of the *subscribed*

copies of these instruments were discovered by Mr. Henry Stevens, among the W. S. Johnson Papers, at Stratford, and are now in the Vermont State Library."—J. H. TRUMBULL.

Petition to the Congress. *See* [La Reintrie (H. R. de)], 39026

Petition to th[e] General Assembly. *See* Vol. XI., No. 45276

Petition to the Houses of Parliament for the Abolition of Negro Apprenticeship. [*London.*] 1838. 4to, pp. 2. 61281

Petition to the Legislature of the Catawba Navigation Company. *Charleston.* 1808. 8vo. 61282

The Petition to the Legislature of ... Connecticut against Extra Judicial Oaths ... . [n. p.] 1834. 12mo, pp. 8. 61283

Petitioners Case of certain Inhabitants in the Island of Cape Breton against the Annexation of that Island to the Province of Nova Scotia. *London.* 1843. Folio. 61284

Petitions from Prince Edward Island, addressed to the King representing the Conduct of Lt. Gov. Charles Douglass Smith; the defective state of the administration of Justice; and concluding with a Prayer for his removal ... . *London.* 1824. 8vo.

Published by J. Stewart, appointed by the inhabitants to present the petitions.

Petitions from the Old and New Subjects, Inhabitants of the Province of Quebec, to the ... Lords Spiritual and Temporal. *London: Printed in the Year* 1791. 8vo, pp. (4), 55. 61286

PETITVAL (J. B.) Report of the Survey of the Neenah or Fox River, Wisconsin. ... [*Washington.*] 1839. 8vo. 61287

PETIVER [Jacobo]. Musei Petiveriani: Centuriæ X. Rariora Naturæ, continens, Animalia, Fossilia, Plantas, ex variis Mundi Plagis advectu, ordine digesta, et Nominibus Propriis Signata. *Londini.* 1695–1703. 8vo, pp. 95. 2 Plates. 61288

Many of the articles came from America, and as the names and residences of the donors are given it becomes interesting.

Also: Pterigraphia Americana Icones, continens plusquam 400 filicum variarum specierum. [*London.* 1715?] Folio, 3 leaves. 20 Plates. — Hortus Peruvianus Medicinalis, or the South-Sea Herbal. *London.* 1715. Folio, 2 leaves. 5 Plates. These are all reprinted in: "Opera Historiam Naturalem spectantia." *London.* 1764–67. 2 vols., folio, and 1 vol., 8vo.

PETO (Samuel M.) The Resources and Prospects of America. Ascertained during a Visit to the States in the Autumn of 1865. By Sir S. Morton Peto, Bart. *London and New York: Alexander*

Strahan. 1866. 8vo, pp. xv, 428. 2 Plates. + *New York: A. Strahan & Co.* 1866. 16mo, pp. xii, 404. C. 61289

Also: Speech ... at Bristol, ... November 13th, 1865. *London: Printed by John King and Company.* [1865.] 8vo, pp. 20. H.

PETRARCHA (F.) Chronica delle Vite de Pontefici|et Imperatori Romani compo|sta per. M. Francesco Petrar|cha alla qvale sono state|aggivnte qveile che da|tempi del Petrarcha|insino alla eta no-|stra mancavano.| [Colophon:] *Stampata in Venetia per Mae|stro Iacomo de pinci da Lecco|cō gratia come nel priuilegio|si cōtēne* MDVII. *Adi iii. di|Decembre.*| 4to, 90 leaves, 2 blank leaves. 61290

A reference to Columbus on folio 88.

PETRARCHA. Chroni|ca delle Vite|de Pontefici et|Imperatori Romani composta:|per. M. Francesco Petrar|cha alla quale sono sta|te aggiūte q̄lle che|da tempi del|Petrarcha|isino al|la nostra mācauano.| [Colophon:] *Stampata in Vinegia per Gregorio di Grego-|rii, Nel anno.* M.D.XXVI. *Del|mese de Setembre.*| 4to, 120 leaves, Index, 2 leaves. 61291

PETRARCHA. Chronica|dele Vite di Ponte|fici et Imperadori Ro-|mani Composti per M. Francesco Pe-|trarcha allaquale sono state aggiunte|q̄lle che da tēpi del Petrarcha infino alla eta nostra|mancavano.| [Colophon:] *Stampata in Venegia per Marchio Sessa. Nel|anno* M.D.XXXIIII. *Adi* XV.|*Del Mese di Marzo.*| Sm. 8vo, 120 leaves, Table, pp. (4). 61292

A reference to Columbus on the recto of leaf 116, under the year 1494.

PETRUS ALBINUS. Petri Albini|Nivemontii|Commentatio|de|Lingvis peregrinis|atqve|insvlis ignotis|ex|scripto manv ipsivs exarato|edidit|M. Samvel Cnavthivs|Misenensis|Biblioth. ... Præf.|accedit|Hvgonis Grotii|de|Origine gentivm|Americanarvm|dissertatio.|*Vittembergae in Saxonibus apud Io. Lvdovicvm Meisnerum A.* CIƆIƆCCXIII. 12mo, pp. 47. J.C.B. 61293

PETTENGILL & Co. (S. M.) The Advertiser's Hand-Book, comprising a complete list of all Newspapers, Periodicals, and Magazines published in the United States ... . *New York: S. M. Pettengill & Co* 1870. 8vo, pp. 206, (2), cxliv. C. 61294

PETTES (George W.) Corona; A Poem. ... First Anniversary of the First Light Infantry Veteran Association of Providence. *Cambridge.* 1870. 8vo, pp. 24. 61295

Pettie's-Island Land and Cash Lottery, For Dispensing of Sundry Houses and Lots, in and near the Borough of Lancaster, &c. ... October 9, 1772. [*Philadelphia.* n. d.] Folio, 1 leaf. P.

Also: Pettie's Island Cash Lottery, in Three Classes ... March 1, 1773. [*Philadelphia.* 1773.] Folio, 1 leaf. — Pettie's Island Cash Lottery. [*Philadelphia, June,* 1773.] Folio, 1 leaf. — Philadelphia, September 23, 1773. Pettie's Island Cash Lottery ... . [*Philadelphia.* 1773.] Folio, 1 leaf. — January 17, 1774. Supplement to the American Flint Glass Manufactory, Pettie's Island Cash Lottery. [*Philadelphia.* 1774.] Folio, 1 leaf. P. *See also* Vol. X., No. 41454, *and* Vol. XI., No. 46191–2.

[PETTIGREW (J. J.)] Report of the Minority of the Special Committee of Seven, to whom was referred so much of his Excellency's Message, No. 1, as relates to Slavery and the Slave Trade. *Columbia, S. C.* 1857. 8vo, pp. 40. B. 61297

Signed by J. Johnston Pettigrew.

PETTIGREW (T. J.) A History of Egyptian Mummies, ... with Remarks on the Funeral Ceremonies of different Nations, and Observations on the Mummies of the Canary Islands, of the Ancient Peruvians, ... &c. By Thomas Joseph Pettigrew, F.R.S. ... *London: Longman* ... . MDCCCXXXIV. 4to, pp. xxi, 264, (1). 13 Plates. A. + [*Ibid.*] 1840. 4to. 61298

PETTIGREW. Memoirs of the Life and Writings of the late John Coakley Lettsom. With a Selection from his Correspondence. By Thomas Joseph Pettigrew. *London: Longman.* 1817. 3 vols., 8vo. 61299

Includes letters written by Dr. Franklin, Benj. Rush, and other distinguished Americans.

PETTIGREW. Memoirs of the Life of Vice-Admiral Lord Viscount Nelson, K.B. ... By Thomas Joseph Pettigrew, F.R.S. ... *London: T. & W. Boone.* MDCCCXLIX. 2 vols., 8vo, pp. xxxii, (1), 501; 667. + Second Edition. [*Ibid.*] 1849. 2 vols., 8vo.

PETTIS (F. H.) Letter to the People of the United States, Nov. 30, 1831. By F. H. Pettis. *Washington.* 1831. 8vo, pp. 7. W. 61301

PETTIS (S.) Boston and its Environs; as they appear from the Cupola of the State House. A Poem. By Samuel Pettis. *Boston.* 1832. 12mo, pp. 47. W. 61302

PETTIS (Spencer). Circular to his Constituents. — To the People of the State of Missouri. March 3d, 1831. [n. p. n. d.] 8vo, pp. 16. 61303

PETTIT (J.) Speech of Hon. John Pettit ... Feb. 20, 1854, on the Nebraska and Kansas Bill. *Washington.* 1854. 8vo, pp. 21. B. 61304

PETTIT (T. McK.) An Annual Discourse delivered before the Historical Society of Pennsylvania, November 19, 1828. By Thomas M'Kean Pettit, Esq. *Philadelphia: Carey, Lea & Carey.* 1828. 8vo, pp. 38. P. 61305

PETTIT. Memoir of Roberts Vaux ... . By Thomas M'Kean Pettit. *Philadelphia.* 1840. 8vo, pp. 27. 61306

Also: Annual Discourse before the Philomathean Society of the University of Pennsylvania. ... *Philadelphia.* 1836. 8vo.

PETTIT (W. V.) Addresses [on Colonization] delivered in the hall of the House of Representatives, Harrisburg, Pa. ... April 6, 1852, by William V. Pettit, and Rev. John P. Durbin, D.D. ... *Philadelphia: Printed by W. F. Geddes.* 1852. 8vo, pp. 47

PETTY (W.) Several Essays in Political Arithmetick. By Sir William Petty. *London.* 1699. 8vo. Portrait. + [*Ibid.*] 1711. 8vo. + *Edinburgh.* 1751. 8vo. + The Fourth Edition, corrected, with Memoirs of the Author's Life. *London.* 1755. 8vo.

Contains much statistical matter relating to the American colonies.

PETZHOLDT (Julius). "Das Buch der Wilden" im Lichte Französischer Civilization. Mit Proben aus dem in Paris als "Manuscrit Pictographique Américain" veröffentlichten Schmierbuche eines Deutsch-Amerikanischen Hinterwäldler-Jungen. Von J. Petzholdt. *Dresden: G. Schönfeld's Buchhandlung (C. A. Werner).* 1861. 8vo, pp. 16. 8 Plates. + Zweite unveränderte Auflage. [*Ibid.*] 1861. 8vo. 61309

An exposure of the Abbe Domenech's "Manuscrit Pictographique Américain." For the Abbe's reply see our Vol. V., No. 20551.

[PETZHOLDT.] Le Livre des Sauvages au point de vue de la civilisation française Avec des planches explicatives tirées du prétendu Manuscrit Pictographique Américain Traduction de l'Allemand *Bruxelles* 1861 8vo, pp. 16. 8 Plates. C. 61310

PEUCER (C.) De Dimen|sione Terræ, et|Fontibvs Doctri-|nae Longitvdinis|et Latitvdinis|Locorvm.|Avtore|Casparo Pevcero.|*Wittebergae|Excudebant Haeredes|Petri Seitzii.*|*Anno* 1550.| Sm. 8vo, (64) leaves. 61311

The seventh, eighth and sixty-fourth leaves are blank. It contains a chapter on America in which Peru is said to be an island.

Peucer. De Dimensione Terrae et Geometrice numerandis locorum particularium intervalis ex doctrina triangulorum sphaericorum et canone subtensarum liber auctore C. Peucero. *Wittebergae.* 1554. Sm. 8vo. + *Francofurtae.* 1554. Sm. 8vo.

Peuchet (*M.*) [Jacques]. État des Colonies et du Commerce des Européens dans les Deux Indes, depuis 1783 jusqu'en 1821, pour faire suite a l'Histoire Philosophique et Politique des Établissements et du Commerce des Européens dans les Deux Indes, de Raynal; Par M. Peuchet. ... *Paris: Amable Costes et Cie*, 1821. 2 vols., 8vo, pp. vii, (1), 352; (4), 353–787, (1). A., C.

Peugh (S. A.) Vindication of the District. Speech of Samuel A. Peugh in the Common Council of Washington, D. C., Jan. 2, 1866. [n. p. n. d.] 8vo, pp. 6. 61314

Also: Report to the Common Council [of Washington] by S. A. Peugh, from the Select Committee on the subject of [colored] Suffrage, November 6, 1865. [n. p. n. d.] 8vo, pp. 6.

Peuple Français ... . [Colophon:] *Au Port-au-Prince, de l'Imprimerie Nationale, chez F. Chaidron.* [n. d.] 4to, pp. 7. 61315

Le Peuple instruit. *See* [Shebbeare (John)].

Le Peuple juge. *See* Reasons humbly offered.

Peverelly (C. A.) The Book of American Pastimes, containing a History of the Principal Base Ball, Cricket, Rowing, and Yachting Clubs of the United States. By Charles A. Peverelly. ... *New York: The Author.* 1866. 12mo, pp. (4), 556. 4 Plates. c. 61316

Report of the Pewabic Mining Company. March, 1858. *Boston: Printed by J. P. Plumer.* 1858. 8vo, pp. 13. Continued.

Pewani Ipi Potewatemi Missinoikan, eyowat nemadjik, Catholiques Endjik. *Baltimoinak: John Murphy, Okimissinakisan Ote Missinoikan.* 1846. 24mo, pp. 31. 61318

A primary book of religious instruction, in the Pottawatomie Indian dialect, with translations of the Lord's Prayer, Apostles' Creed, and the Decalogue.

P[eyroux] D[e] L[a] C[oudrenière] (*M.*) Lettres sur l'état primitif de l'homme, jusqu'à la naissance de l'esclavage; sur le désir de l'immortalité, et sur l'héroisme militaire. Par M. P. D. L. C. *Amsterdam, et ... Paris, chez La veuve Ballard & fils; Mérigot, jeune.* 1783. 8vo, pp. 48. + Nouvelle Édition. *Amsterdam, et ... Paris, chez Royez.* 1785. 8vo, pp. (8), 3–48. c.

Peyster. *See* De Peyster, Vol. v.

Peyton (J. L.) The Adventures of my Grandfather [J. R. Peyton, of Stoney Hill, Virginia,] with ... Biographical Sketches of himself and his son, John Howe Peyton, Esq. By John Lewis Peyton ... . *London: John Wilson.* MDCCCLXVII. 8vo, pp. 249. B. 61320

Peyton. The American Crisis; or, Pages from the Note-Book of a State Agent during the Civil War. By John Lewis Peyton ... . *London: Saunders, Otley, and Co.* 1867. 2 vols., 12mo, pp. xii, 340; vi, 329. 61321

Peyton. Memoir of William Madison Peyton, of Roanoke, ... By John Lewis Peyton. *London: John Wilson.* MDCCCLXXIII. 8vo, pp. vii, 392. c. 61322

Peyton. Over the Alleghanies and Across the Prairies. Personal Recollections of the Far West One and Twenty Years Ago. By John Lewis Peyton ... . *London: Simpkin, Marshall and Co.* MDCCCLXIX. 12mo, pp. xvi, 377. + Second Edition. [*Ibid.*] MDCCCLXX. 12mo, pp. xvi, 377. A., B. 61323

Peyton. A Statistical View of the State of Illinois, to which is appended an article upon the City of Chicago. By John Lewis Peyton ... . *Chicago: Spaulding & Tobey, Printers.* 1855. 8vo, pp. 48. H. 61324

Also: Suggestions on Railroad Communication with the Pacific ... . Published in ... the Chicago Daily Democratic Press. ... *Chicago: W. W. Danenhower.* 1853. 8vo, pp. 32. B. *See also* Blundell (B.), Vol. II., No. 6020.

Peyton (R. L. Y.) Proceedings and Speeches on the ... Death of Hon. R. L. Y. Peyton, of Missouri, In the House of Representatives of the Confederate States, December 19th, 1863. *Richmond.* 1864. 8vo, pp. 8. H. 61325

Peyton (Wm. M.) Letter [Jan. 8, 1861] to Hon. Wm. C. Rives on the Crisis. *New York: J. Russell.* 1861. 8vo.

Pezuela (J. de la). Diccionario Geografico, Estadistico, Historico de la Isla de Cuba, Por Don Jacobo de la Pezuela. ... *Madrid: Joaquin Bernat.* 1863–67. 4 vols., 4to, pp. 216, 414, (2); 572; 624; 696. c. 61327

Pezuela. Discursos leidos ante la Real Academica de la historia en la recepcion publica de D. Jacobo de la Pezuela, el dia 21 de Mayo de 1866. *Madrid.* 1866. 8vo, pp. 67. 61328

Pezuela. Ensayo Historico de la Isla de Cuba, por Don Jacobo de la Pezuela. *Nueva York: Imprenta de R. Rafael.* 1842. 8vo, pp. xiii, 631. B. + *Habana.* 1842. 8vo. 61329

Pezuela. Historia de la Isla de Cuba. ... *Madrid: C. Bailly-Baillière.* 1868. 2 vols., 8vo, pp. 463; 606. c. 61330

Pezuela (J. de la). Manifieste en que el Virey del Peru Don Joaquin de la Pezuela refiere el hecho y circunstancias de su separacion del Mando. *Madrid.* 1821. Sm. 4to. 61331

Also: Copia del oficio que los gefes del egército nacional pasaron a D. Joaquin de la Pezuela, Virrey del Peru. *Madrid.* 1821. Sm. 4to, pp. 8.

Pezuela (L. R.) Apuntes sobre las mejoras materiales aplicables á la América latina. Por Luis Robles Pezuela, ingeniero mexicano. *Paris: Brachet.* 1869. 8vo, pp. 240. 7 Plates.

Pezuela. Memoria presentada á S. M. El Emperador por el Ministro de Fomento Luis Robles Pezuela de los trabajos ejecutados en su Ramo el Año de 1865. *Mexico.* 1866. Imp. 8vo, pp. 658. 10 Plates, 4 Maps. 61333

Pfefferkorn (I.) Beschreibung | der | Landschaft | Sonora | samt | andern merkwürdigen Nachrichten | von den inneren Theilen | Neu-Spaniens | und | Reise aus Amerika | bis in | Deutschland, | nebst einer Landcharte von Sonora. | Von Ignaz Pfefferkorn, | eilfjährigen Missionar daselbst. | ... | Mit allergnädigster kaiserlicher Freiheit. | *Auf Kosten des Verfassers* | *gedrukt zu Köln am Rhein in der Langenschen* | *Buchhandlung* 1794–95. | 2 vols., sm. 8vo, pp. (16), 455, (9), Map; (2), 447, (13). A., H. 61334

A work of considerable rarity and importance.

Pfeiffer (G.) An Eulogium to the Memory of General George Washington. By George Pfeiffer, M.D. *Natchez: Printed by B. M. Stokes.* 1800. 12mo, pp. 38. P. 61335

One of the rarest of the Washington eulogies. Dated, March 1st, 1800. Prefixed is a dirge sung at the chapel in Natchez on February 22, when the eulogium was pronounced.

Pfeiffer (Ida). Eine Frauenfahrt um die Welt. Reise von Wien nach Brasilien, Chili, Otaheiti, China, Ost-Indien, Persien und Kleinasien. *Wien: Gerold.* 1850. 3 vols., 8vo. 61336

Pfeiffer. A Lady's Travels Round the World: Travels from Vienna to Brazil, Chili, Otaheite, China, the East Indies, Persia and Asia Minor. Translated by William Hazlitt. *London.* 1852. 16mo. 61337

Pfeiffer. A Lady's Voyage round the World; a selected translation from the German of Ida Pfeiffer. By Mrs. Percy Sinnett. *London: Longman.* 1851. 12mo. + New Edition. *London.* 1852. 12mo. + Third Edition. *London.* 1852. 12mo. + *New York.* 1852. 12mo. 61338

Pfeiffer. A Woman's Journey round the World, from Vienna to Brazil, Chili, Tahiti, China, Hindostan, Persia, and Asia Minor. An Unabridged Translation, from the German of Ida Pfeiffer. *London.* [1852.] 8vo, pp. xii, 338. 12 Plates. + Second Edition. *London.* [1852.] 8vo, pp. xvi, (2), 338. Plates. H. + Fourth Edition. *London: N. Cooke.* 1854. 8vo, pp. xii, 338. Plates. c. + New Edition. *London: Ward & Lock.* 1856. Post 8vo. 61339

Pfeiffer. Voyage d'une femme autour du Monde par Mme Ida Pfeiffer. Traduit de l'Allemand, avec l'autorisation de l'auteur, par W. de Suckau. *Paris: Hachette et Cie.* 1858. 12mo. + [*Ibid.*] 1859. 12mo, pp. xii, 612. Map. + Troisième Edition. [*Ibid.*] 1865. 12mo. 61340

Pfeiffer. Meine Zweite Weltreise. *Wien: Gerold's Sohn.* 1856. 4 vols., 8vo. 61341

Pfeiffer. A Lady's Second Journey round the World: from London to the Cape of Good Hope, Borneo, Java, Sumatra, Celebes, Ceram, the Moluccas, etc., California, Panama, Peru, Ecuador, and the United States. By Ida Pfeiffer ... . *London: Longman* ... . 1855. 2 vols., post 8vo, pp. xii, 451; viii, 423. + *New York: Harper & Brothers.* 1856. 12mo, pp. xii, 500.

Pfeiffer. Mon Second Voyage autour du Monde; traduit de l'allemand par W. de Suckau. *Paris: Hachette et Cie.* 1859. 12mo. 61343

Pfeil (A. R.) The Anglo-French Intervention in the River Plate, considered especially with reference to the Negociations of 1847, under the conduct of Lord Howden. By Adolph R. Pfeil. *London.* 1847. 8vo, pp. 111. 61344

Pfeil. Résumé des Affairs de la Plata. ... *Paris.* 1849. 8vo.

Pfister (F.) Der Nordamerikanische Unabhängigkeits-Krieg. ... Von Ferdinand Pfister. ... *Kassel: J. C. Krieger.* 1864. 8vo, pp. xii, 360. BA. 61346

Die Pflichten der Adoptiv-Bürger in der gegenwärtigen Krise. *Philadelphia: Gedruckt bei King und Baird.* 1863. 8vo, pp. (2), 16

The Phantom. June, 1841, to Feb. 1842. Nos. 1–7. *Cincinnati.* 1841–42. 24mo, pp. 64. c. 61348

A travesty on many well known citizens of Cincinnati, in 1841, '42; the great negro mob in 1841, and the bank mob in 1842.

Pharmacopœia Nosocomii Neo-Eboracensis; or, The Pharmacopœia of the New York Hospital. ... *New York.* 1816. 8vo, pp. 181. 61349

The Pharmacopœia of the Massachusetts Medical Society. *Boston: E. & J. Larkin.* 1808. 12mo, pp. x, (4), 272. A.

The Pharmacopœia of the United States of America. 1820. *Boston.* 1820. 8vo, pp. 272. + *Philadelphia: John Grigg.* 1831. 8vo, pp. xxx, 268. + *Philadelphia: Lippincott, Grambo, & Co.* 1851. 8vo, pp. xxiii, 317. + *Philadelphia: J. B. Lippincott & Co.* 1863. 12mo, pp. xxvii, 399. 61351

Phelan (P.) Life of Right Reverend Patrick Phelan, third Bishop of Kingston, to which is added a synopsis of the lives of the two first Bishops of Kingston. By the Clergyman who served Bishop Phelan's last mass. *Kingston.* 1862. 8vo.

Phelipe v. *See* Philip v.

Phelps (A. H. L.) Familiar Lectures on Botany, practical, elementary, and physiological, with Descriptions of the Plants of the United States ... . By Mrs. Almira H. Lincoln Phelps. ... Fourth Edition ... *Hartford: F. J. Huntington.* 1835. 8vo, pp. 307, 190. + Fifth Edition. [*Ibid.*] 1836. 8vo, pp. 3–246, 186. + New Edition. *New York: Huntington & Savage.* 1845. 12mo, pp. (2), 7–246, 220. 8 Plates. c. 61353

Phelps. Hours with my Pupils: or, Educational Addresses, ... *New York: Charles Scribner.* 1859. 12mo, pp. 363. c.

Phelps. Lectures to Young Ladies ... . Delivered to the Pupils of Troy Female Seminary. ... *Boston.* 1833. 12mo, pp. 308. Plate. + *London.* 1838. 18mo. + *New York.* 1842. 12mo. 61355

Phelps. Our Country, in its Relations to the Past, Present, and Future. A National Book, consisting of Original Articles ... contributed by American Writers. Edited by Mrs. Lincoln

Phelps ... . *Baltimore: Printed by John D. Toy.* 1864. 12mo, pp. xx, 13–423. B. 61356

Phelps. Plea for Cuba: addressed to the Senate and House of Representatives of the United States. *Baltimore.* 1870. 8vo.

[Phelps.] Tribute to the Memory of Jane Porter Lincoln. Printed for Private Circulation. [*John D. Toy, Printer, Baltimore.* 1855.] 8vo, pp. (2), 51. 61358

Mrs. Almira Hart Lincoln Phelps, formerly Mrs. Lincoln, was the sister of Emma Willard, and the author of a large number of educational works. *See also* Vol. x., No. 41241.

Phelps (A.) Confession of Alonzo Phelps, the Rob Roy of the Mississippi. *Jackson.* 1834. 8vo, pp. 50. 61359

Phelps (Amos A.) Address on the Position in regard to Slavery of the American Board of Commissioners for Foreign Missions. With the Proceedings. [n. p. n. d.] 8vo, pp. 12. B.

Phelps. Lectures on Slavery and its Remedy. By Amos A. Phelps ... . *Boston.* 1834. 18mo, pp. 284. B. + *Philadelphia.* 1834. 18mo. 61361

Also: Letters to Dr. Bacon and others ... *New York.* 1848. 12mo, pp. 168. Also other pamphlets on slavery.

Phelps (Ansel). An Oration ... at Gill [Mass.], before the Republican and Harmony Lodges, ... June 24, A. L. 5823. ... *Greenfield.* 1823. 8vo, pp. 14. W. 61362

Phelps (Ansel), *Jr.* Speech ... on the Petition of the Troy and Greenfield Railroad, for State Aid, April 6, 1853. *Boston.* 1853. 8vo. S. 61363

Phelps (A.) The relations of the Bible to the Civilization of the Future. A Sermon delivered before His Excellency ... at the Annual Election, ... January 2, 1861. By Austin Phelps, ... *Boston: William White, Printer.* 1861. 8vo, pp. 61. 61364

Phelps. A Sermon ... at the Ordination of Mr. Lyman Cutler, ... Pepperell, Mass., January 22, 1851. By Austin Phelps, ... *Andover: Warren F. Draper.* 1851. 8vo, pp. 36. 61365

Also: ... A Sermon ... before the Convention of Congregational Ministers of Massachusetts, May 26, 1859. ... *Andover.* 1859. 8vo, pp. 30.

Phelps (A. R.) Circular Letter to the Public. [*Worcester.*] 1831. 12mo, pp. 7. W. 61366

Phelps (B. K.) Meeting of the Society of the Church of the Puritans, May 3, 1860. Argument of Benjamin K. Phelps, Esq., in support of the Resolutions of Mr. Smith, and against the Appeal for British Aid. *New York.* 1860. 8vo, pp. 18. c.

[Phelps (Charles).] Vermonters Unmasked; or, some of their evil conduct made manifest, from facts too glaring to be denied, and many of them too criminal to be justified, as follows, viz. ... [*New York.* 1782.] 8vo, pp. 12. 61368

Very rare. Signed, "A Citizen of the United States. 10th June, 1782." *See* Hall's "History of Eastern Vermont," pp. 449, 685, *et seq.* Also: An Address ... in Townshend, ... 4th July, 1811. ... *Brattleboro.* 1811. 8vo.

Phelps (C. A.) ... Life and Public Services of General Ulysses S. Grant ... And a Biographical Sketch of Hon. Schuyler Colfax. By Charles A. Phelps. ... *Boston: Lee & Shepard.* 1868. 8vo, pp. (2), xvi, 344. 2 Portraits, 4 Plates. + [With] a Biographical Sketch of Hon. Henry Wilson. [*Ibid.*] 1872. 12mo, pp. 371. 61369

Phelps (D.) An Address ... in Haverhill, Feb. 8, 1829, on ... the First Anniversary of the Society for the Promotion of Temperance in Haverhill and Vicinity. By Dudley Phelps. ... *Haverhill: Printed by A. W. Thayer.* 1829. 8vo, pp. 36. H.

Also: Address ... Jan. 24, 1830, preparatory to the organization of the East-Haverhill Temperance Society. ... *Haverhill.* 1830. 8vo, pp. 23. B.

Phelps (E.) Modern Benevolence: A Satire, delivered before The ... Alumni of Union College. July 25th, 1860. By Egbert Phelps. *New-York: Pudney & Russell, Printers.* 1860. 8vo, pp. 37. 61371

Phelps (E.) A Sermon addressed to the First Church in Brookfield, on the Sabbath after the Interment of the Hon. Dwight Foster. By Eliakim Phelps. *Boston.* 1823. 8vo, pp. 23

[Phelps (*Mrs.* Elizabeth Stuart).] The Last Leaf from Sunny Side. By H. Trusta. With a Memorial of the Author by Austin Phelps, D.D. *Boston.* 1853. 12mo. + *New York.* 1864.

[Phelps.] A Peep at Number Five; or, a Chapter in the Life of a City Pastor. *Boston.* 1851. 18mo. + [*Ibid.*] 1864.

[Phelps.] The Sunny Side; or, the Country Minister's Wife. *Philadelphia: American Sunday-School Union.* [1851.] 18mo, pp.

142. 4 Plates. + *Andover.* 1851. 18mo. + Second Edition. *Philadelphia.* 1852. 18mo. + [*Ibid.*] 1865. 18mo. 61375

Reprinted in Edinburgh as "The Manse of Sunnyside." This elicited "The Shady-side."

[Phelps.] The Tell Tale; or, Home Scenes told by Old Travellers. *New York.* 1852. + *New York.* 1864. 61376

Phelps (E. J.) A Sketch of the Life and Character of Charles Linsley, read before the Vermont Historical Society. By E. J. Phelps. *Albany, N. Y.: J. Munsell.* 1866. 8vo, pp. 20.

Phelps (H.) The Lions of New York, being a Guide to Objects of Interest in and around the Great Metropolis. By H. Phelps. ... *New York: Phelps, Fanning & Co.* 1853. 12mo, pp. 50. Map. 61378

Phelps. Phelps' Hundred Cities and Large Towns of America: with Railroad Distances ... Maps of Fourteen Cities ... . *New York: Phelps, Fanning & Co.* 1853. 8vo, pp. 80. 4 Plates. + *New York: Ensign, Bridgman, & Fanning.* 1854. 8vo, pp. 80

Also: Phelps' Traveller's Guide through the United States. ... *New York.* 1847. 18mo. Map.—The Traveller's Steamboat and Railroad Guide to the Hudson River. ... *New York.* [n. d.] 8vo, pp. 50. Maps and Plates.—What to See and How to See it. ... Guide to New York City. *New York.* [n. d.] 18mo, pp. 72. Map and Plates. *See also* Vol. XIII., Nos. 54574–5.

Phelps (J. A.) The Shipper's Guide, containing a complete list of all Railroad Stations ... By James A. Phelps. *Buffalo.* 1859. 12mo, pp. 12. S. 61380

Phelps (J.) The Legal Classic, or Young American's First Book of Rights and Duties. ... By John Phelps, Esq. *Amherst: J. S. & C. Adams.* 1835. 12mo. 61381

Phelps (J. S.) Confiscation of Property and Emancipation of Slaves. Speech of Hon. John S. Phelps, of Missouri, in the House of Representatives, May 22, 1862. [n. p. n. d.] 8vo, pp. 8. 61382

Also: Letter to Citizens of Arkansas in relation to a Pacific Railroad. ... *St. Louis.* 1858. 8vo, pp. 16. + *Washington.* 1858. 8vo.—Speech ... April 16, 1846, on the Oregon Question. *Washington.* 1846. 8vo.—Speech ... June 8, 1850, on the Admission of California. *Washington.* [1850.] 8vo.—Speech ... Feb. 12 and 19, 1852, on the Grant of Land to Missouri. [n. p. n. d.] 8vo, pp. 7.

Phelps (*Mrs.* Lincoln). *See* Phelps (A. H. L.), *supra.*

Phelps (Matthew). *See* Haswell (A.), Vol. VIII., No. 30829

PHELPS (M.) The Excommunication of M. Phelps from the Congregational Church in Chester [Mass.] [n. p.] 1809. 8vo.

PHELPS (N. A.) History of Simsbury, Granby and Canton, from 1642 to 1845. By Noah A. Phelps. *Hartford: Press of Case, Tiffany and Burnham.* 1845. 8vo, pp. (4), 9–176. c.

PHELPS. A History of the Copper Mines, and Newgate Prison, at Granby, Conn. Also, of the Captivity of Daniel Hays, of Granby, by the Indians, in 1707. By Noah A. Phelps. *Hartford: Press of Case, Tiffany & Burnham.* 1845. 8vo, pp. 34.

An extract from the "History of Simsbury." Also: The Vine: Its Culture in the United States, Wine making from Grapes .... *Hartford.* 1855. 12mo, pp. 28.

PHELPS (O. S.) Genealogy of Othniel Phelps, Esq., of Aylmer, Canada West. Prepared ... by ... Oliver Seymour Phelps, Esq. ... *St. Catharines: H. F. Leavenworth's ... Press.* 1862. 8vo, pp. 44. 61386

[PHELPS.] In Memoriam. Orson Phelps. A Brother's Bouquet for a Brother's Burial and Grave. *Geo. H. Himes, Printer, Portland, Oregon.* [1870.] 8vo, pp. 54. s. 61387

Consists of genealogical notes by and letters addressed to Oliver Seymour Phelps. Also: Our Phelps Genealogy. Oliver Seymour Phelps: 'Prospect Place,' St. Catharines, C. W. January 12th, 1860. *Edwin S. Leavenworth, printer.* Folio, 1 leaf.

PHELPS (P.) Soldiers and Soldiers' Homes. By Mrs. Phebe Harris Phelps. *New York: American Tract Society.* 1864. 8vo, pp. 120. 61388

PHELPS (R. H.) Newgate of Connecticut: A History of the Prison, its Insurrections, Massacres, &c. Imprisonment of the Tories, in the Revolution. The Ancient and Recent Working of its Mines, &c., to which is appended a description of the State Prison, at Wethersfield. By Richard H. Phelps. *Hartford: Press of E. Geer.* 1844. 8vo, pp. 24. + Second Edition. [*Ibid.*] 1844. 8vo, pp. 24. + Third Edition. *Hartford: Press of Elihu Geer.* 1844. 8vo, pp. 33. 61389

PHELPS. A History of Newgate of Connecticut, at Simsbury, now East Granby; its Insurrections and Massacres; the Imprisonment of the Tories in the Revolution, and the Working of its Mines. Also, some Account of the State Prison at Wethersfield. By Richard H. Phelps. *Albany, N. Y.: J. Munsell.* 1860. 4to, pp. 151. Portrait. BA. 61390

Ten copies printed on large paper.

PHELPS. Newgate of Connecticut; its Origin and Early History. Being a full description of the famous and wonderful Simsbury Mines and Caverns, and the Prison built over them. To which is added a Relation of all the Incidents, Insurrections, and Massacres, connected with their use as a Prison for the Tories during the Revolution, and otherwise; with interesting sketches of their surroundings, in (now) East Granby. Also an illustrated description of the State Prison at Wethersfield. By Richard H. Phelps. *Hartford, Conn.: American Publishing Company.* 1876. 8vo, pp. (6), 13–117. 4 Plates. 61391

PHELPS (S.) A Treatise on the Importance of extending the British Fisheries, containing a description of the Iceland Fisheries and the Newfoundland Fisheries and Colony, by Samuel Phelps. *London: W. Simpkin & R. Marshall.* 1818. 8vo, pp. (16), 232. 61392

PHELPS (S. S.) Mr. Phelps's Appeal to the People of Vermont, in vindication of himself against the charges made against him [by W. Slade] upon ... his Re-election to the Senate ... in relation to his course as a Senator. *Middlebury.* 1845. 8vo.

PHELPS. Remarks of Mr. Phelps, of Vermont, on the Oregon bill, and the Compromise bill: delivered in the Senate of the United States, June 29 & July 24, 1848. [*Washington:*] *J. & G. S. Gideon, Printers.* [n. d.] 8vo, pp. 32. s. 61394

Also: Address of the Council of Censors. [n. p.] 1827. 8vo.—Speech ... on the War and the Public Finances, ... in the Senate ... January 27, 1848. [*Washington:*] *J. & G. S. Gideon, Printers.* [n. d.] 8vo, pp. 15.—Speech ... on the Subject of Slavery, &c. In Senate, January 23, 1850. [n. p. n. d.] 8vo, pp. 16.—Substance of the Speech ... on the ... Tariff, delivered in the Senate ... Feb. 16 & 19, 1844. *Washington: Gales & Seaton.* 1844. 8vo, pp. 35.—To the Freemen of Vermont. [Signed Samuel S. Phelps.] *Middlebury.* 1848. 8vo, pp. 4.—To the People of Vermont. Mr. Phelps's rejoinder to Mr. Slade's "Reply." [*Washington.* 1844.] 8vo, pp. 40. + *Burlington.* 1846. 8vo. *See* Slade (W.)

PHELPS (S. D.) The Memorial Sermon preached in the House of Worship on Chapel Street, on the last Sabbath of its occupancy by the First Baptist Church, December 10th, 1865. By S. D. Phelps, Pastor. With an Appendix. *New Haven: Printed by Thomas J. Stafford.* 1869. 8vo, pp. 20. 61395

PHELPS. Military Power a Blessing. A Discourse ... in New Haven, November 24, 1864. By Sylvanus Dryden Phelps. *New Haven: Thomas H. Pease.* 1864. 8vo, pp. 16. 61396

PHELPS. National Symptoms. A Discourse ... in the First Baptist Church, New Haven, on ... the Annual State Fast, April 18, 1862. By S. D. Phelps .... *New York: Sheldon & Company.* 1862. 8vo, pp. 16. 61397

PHELPS. A Quarter-Century Sermon, ... in the First Baptist Church in New Haven, 22d January, 1871. By [S.] Dryden Phelps .... *New Haven: Denison & Grenell, Printers.* 1871. 8vo, pp. 22, xii, (1). 61398

Also: Eloquence of Nature, and other Poems. ... *Hartford.* 1842. 12mo, pp. 168.—The Poet's Song for the Heart and the Home. ... *New York: Sheldon & Co.* 1867. 12mo.—Sermon ... at the Re-opening of the First Baptist Church, ... New Haven. *New Haven.* 1850. 8vo.—Sunlight and Heartlight; or, Fidelity, and other Poems. ... *New York: Sheldon, Lamport & Blakeman.* 1856. 12mo, pp. 252. Portrait.

PHELPS (W. D.) Fore and Aft; or, Leaves from the Life of an Old Sailor. *Boston: Nichols & Hall.* 1870. 16mo. + [*Ibid.*] 1871. 16mo. 61399

PHELPS (W. F.) Normal Schools: their Relations to ... Institutions of Learning, and to ... Society, together with their Future in the United States. By William F. Phelps .... *Trenton.* 1857. 8vo, pp. 23. H. 61400

Also: Desultory Thoughts on Educational Science .... An Address ... before the Dialectic and Franklin Societies of the New Jersey State Normal School, January 15th, 1857. ... *Trenton, N. J.: Murphy & Bechtel, Printers.* 1857. 8vo, pp. 29.—The Reform in Geographical Studies in our American Schools, with a Sketch of Prof. A. Guyot. *Chicago.* 1871. 12mo.

[PHELPS (———).] The | Rights | of the | Colonies, | and the extent of the | Legislative Authority | of | Great-Britain, | Briefly Stated and Considered. | *London: J. Nourse.* MDCCLXIX. 8vo, pp. (4), 20. J.C.B. 61401

"The great points of representation and taxation are here decided against the colonies, by a very sensible writer—who holds 'That Constitutional rights cannot, from their very nature, have an existence in any other soil, than that which gave them birth.' ... His ideas of colonization will, we believe, be disputed by our American brethren; the consequence of his grand position being, they will say, obviously nothing less than Slavery."—*Monthly Review*, XL. 173. The author was Under Secretary to Lord Sandwich.

Proposals of the PHENIX MINING COMPANY; with a Statement of the History and Character of their Mines .... *New York.* 1831. 8vo, pp. 30. s. 61402

Relates to the Simsbury copper mines, Connecticut.

A Phew Phelps Phamily Phacts Phigures and Phancies. [n. p.] 1862. 4to. 61403

PHILADELPHIA.

The arrangement of the following list of anonymous books is alphabetical under the names of institutions and societies or the first word of the title. Mr. Charles R. Hildeburn, of Philadelphia, has furnished valuable assistance in its preparation.

Journal of the ACADEMY OF NATURAL SCIENCES of Philadelphia. Vol. I. Part I. *Philadelphia: D. Heartt.* 1817. 8vo, pp. iv, 192. 18 Plates. 61404

Continued to 1842, 8 vols., 8vo; second series, 1847 to 1880, 8 vols., 4to. For a detailed list of the contents, *see* Trübner's "Bibliographical Guide to American Literature."

Proceedings of the Academy of Natural Sciences of Philadelphia. Vol. I. 1841–'42–'43. *Philadelphia.* 1843. 8vo, pp. x, 341. Continued. 61405

First series, 1841–1856, 8 vols.; second series, 1857–1870, 14 vols.; third series, in progress.

Also: Act of Incorporation ... of the Academy of Natural Sciences .... *Philadelphia.* 1818. 8vo, pp. 12. + 1836. 8vo, pp. iv, 8. + 1837. 8vo. + 1840. 8vo, pp. 12. + 1849. 8vo, pp. 12. + 1857. 8vo, pp. 38. + 1866. 8vo, pp. 24. + 1876. 8vo, pp. 24.—Catalogue of the Library .... *Philadelphia.* 1837. 8vo, pp. x, 300.—Notice of the Academy .... Third Edition. *Philadelphia.* 1836. 8vo. + Fourth Edition. [*Ibid.*] 1837. 8vo, pp. 24.

An Account | Of a surprising | Phænomenon, | Which appeared in the Sky at the City of Phi- | ladelphia and different Parts of Pennsylva- | nia, on Saturday the 2d. of February 1765. | ... | *Philadelphia, printed by Anthony Armbruster in Arch-Street* 1765. | 4to, pp. 4. P. 61406

Account of Receipts and Payments at the City Treasury, ... 1836. [n. p. 1837.] 8vo, pp. 29. Continued. 61407

An Account of the Baptisms and Burials in all the Churches and Meetings in Philadelphia, from December 5, 1774 to December 25, 1775. [n. p. n. d.] 4to, 1 leaf. P. 61408

An Account of the Births | and Burials in Christ-Church Parish, | in Philadelphia, from December 24, 1750, | to December 24, 1751. By Caleb Cash, | Clerk, and Samuel Kirke, Sexton. | [n. p. n. d.] Folio, 1 leaf. C. 61409

Continued annually to 1812 or later. After 1762, St. Peter's Parish was included. The "Account" for 1770–71 is misdated "New-Year's Day, 1771, to New-Year's Day, 1772." A nearly complete set is in the Philadelphia Library.

An Account of the Distances from the City of Philadelphia, of all the Places of Note within the Improved Part of the Province of Pennsylvania. ... *Philadelphia: Printed by William Bradford* .... [1755.] 8vo, pp. 15. P. 61410

Account | of the | Grand Federal | Procession, | Philadelphia, July 4, 1788. | To which is added, | a | Letter | on the | Same Subject. | ... | [*Philadelphia:*] *M. Carey, Printer.* [n. d.] 8vo, pp. (2), 22. + To which are added, | Mr. Wlson's [*sic*] Oration, | and a | Letter | on the | Subject of the Procession. | ... | [*Ibid.*] 8vo, pp. (2), 22.

An Account of the Rise, Progress, and Termination, of the Malignant Fever, Lately prevalent in Philadelphia. Briefly stated from Authentic Documents. *Philadelphia: Printed ... by Benjamin Johnson* .... MDCCXCIII. 12mo, pp. 36, 12. 61412

An Account of Two Terrible Fires. Which happened in the City of Brotherly-Love, On Friday the 26th of October. ... [n. p.] *Printed in the Year* MDCCXLIV [for 1764]. 8vo, pp. 7, (1).

Accounts of the Corporation, for ... 1802. ... *Philadelphia: Printed by Robert Cochran.* 1803. 8vo, pp. 16. Continued.

An Act for raising a Fund to pay the Damages, done by Dogs within the City and County of Philadelphia, and the County of Bucks. *Philadelphia: Printed by Hall and Sellers.* 1772. Folio.

ACTS.—For the several "Acts" of Assembly, relative to Philadelphia and its institutions, see Pennsylvania.

Additional | Charter | of the | College, | Academy, | and | Charitable School | of | Philadelphia, in Pennsylvania. | *Philadelphia:* | *Printed by B. Franklin, and D. Hall.* 1755. | Folio, pp. (2), 13.

Additional Facts and Observations. *See* College of Physicians.

An Address adopted at a Meeting of Citizens of Philadelphia, opposed to Secret Societies; held on ... September 14, 1829. Prepared by a Committee .... *Philadelphia.* 1829. 8vo, pp. 44.

The Address and Petition of the Clergy of Various Denominations, in ... Philadelphia, ... relative to ... a law against Vice and Immorality. ... subjoined some Considerations ... [on] the Prohibition of Theatrical Exhibitions. *Philadelphia: Printed by William Young.* M.DCC.XCIII. 8vo, pp. 16. 61418

An Address from the Monthly Meeting of Friends of Philadelphia, to its Members. *Philadelphia: S. W. Conrad, Printer.* 1827. 12mo. + *London: Harvey and Darton.* 1827. 12mo.

Signed by Peter Thomson, Clerk to the Men's Meeting, and Mary Elliott, Clerk to the Women's Meeting, the 29th of 3rd mo. 1827.

An Address Of Thanks to the Wardens of Christ Church and St. Peters, and the Reverend W[illiam] S[mit]h, D.D. Provost of the College, and Tool to the P[roprieto]r, and J[aco]b D[uch]é, A.M. and M.V.D. from F[rancis] A[liso]n, D.D. and J[ohn] E[win]g in our Name and in the Name of all the Presbyterian Ministers in Pennsylvania. [*Philadelphia: Anthony Armbruster.* 1764.] Folio, 1 leaf. P. 61420

Address of the Catholic Lay Citizens, of ... Philadelphia, to their Fellow Citizens, in Reply to the Presentment of the Grand Jury ... May Term, 1844, in regard to the Causes of the late Riots in Philadelphia. *Philadelphia: M. Fithian.* 1844. 8vo, pp. 12. 61421

Address of the Citizens of ... Philadelphia, to the Roman Catholics of Ireland. February 5th, 1828. [n. p. n. d.] 8vo, pp. 4. 61422

Address of the Committee of Correspondence for ... Philadelphia, appointed by the Democratic Convention of ... Pennsylvania, ... March 5, 1832. [n. p. n. d.] 8vo, pp. 8. 61423

Address of the Committee of Democratic Delegates of the several Wards ... of Philadelphia, to the Democratic Citizens of the State .... *Philadelphia.* 1834. 8vo, pp. 20. 61424

Address of the Correspondence Committee for ... Philadelphia, to the Electors of ... Pennsylvania. [n. p. 1817.] 8vo, pp. 16. 61425

Address of the People's Club of Philadelphia, in favor of Gen. Simon Cameron for President. *Philadelphia.* 1859. 8vo.

Address of the Republican Committee of Correspondence of Philadelphia to the People of the United States. *Philadelphia: William Stavely.* 1828. 8vo, pp. 12. 61427

Address of the Young Men of Philadelphia to the Young Men of the United States. *Philadelphia.* 1834. 8vo. 61428

An Address to Friends within the Compass of the Yearly Meetings held in Philadelphia. [n. p. n. d.] 8vo, pp. 7. H. + *Philadelphia.* 1827. 12mo. 61429

Relates to the Hicksite controversy. *See also* No. 59846, *supra.*

An Address to my Fellow Citizens. [n. p. 1771.] Folio, 1 l.

Isaac Wikoff's denial of the charge of selling adulterated wines and liquors.

Address to the Booksellers of the United States, from the Booksellers' Company of Philadelphia. *J. S. Manning, Printer,* ... *Philadelphia.* 1813. 8vo, pp. 12. 61431

Address to the Citizens of Philadelphia, in favor of Texas. [n. p. 1836.] 8vo, pp. 8. 61432

Address to the Citizens of Philadelphia, on the Advantages from the Trade of the Western Country. By Messrs. Tarascon, Jun., James Berthoud and Co. *Philadelphia.* 1806. 8vo.

An Address to the Citizens of Philadelphia on ... Fancy Fairs. *Philadelphia.* 1834. 12mo, pp. 15. 61434

An Address to the Citizens of Philadelphia, on ... Establishing an Asylum for the Cure of Victims of Intemperance. *Philadelphia.* 1841. 8vo, pp. 14. 61435

Address to the Freeholders of Philadelphia, Chester and Bucks. [n. p., about 1765.] Folio. 61436

Address to the Freemen, Citizens of Philadelphia, on the subject of Market-Houses, June 16, 1773. [*Philadelphia.* 1773.] Folio. 61437

Address to the Inhabitants of ... Philadelphia. [n. p. n. d.] Folio, 1 leaf. 61438

Signed "A Friend to Mankind. Philadelphia, September 6th, 1797." Relates to the Yellow Fever.

Address to the Liberal and Humane. [n. p. 1829.] 8vo, pp. 8. 61439

An Address to the Members of the Philadelphia Yearly Meeting. *Philadelphia.* 1862. 8vo. 61440

Relates to the Rebellion.

Address to the Physicians of Philadelphia, on the present decline of the Medical Character, and the means of advancing Professional Respectibility. [n. p. n. d.] 8vo, pp. 39. 61441

Address to the Voters of Philadelphia, Oct. 1, 1764. *Philadelphia.* 1764. 8vo. 61442

Address. Philadelphia, Oct. 1, 1772. [n. p. 1772.] Folio, 1 leaf. P. 61443

Addresses and Remonstrances against Fifth and Sixth Street Railways. [n. p. n. d.] 8vo, pp. 34. 61444

Addresses of the Hon. W. D. Kelley, Miss Anna E. Dickinson, and Mr. Frederic Douglass, at a Mass Meeting, held at National Hall, Philadelphia, July 6, 1863, for the Promotion of Colored Enlistments. [n. p. n. d.] 8vo, pp. 8. 61445

A Sketch of the Origin and Progress of the ADELPHI SCHOOL ... established under the Direction of the Philadelphia Association of Friends for the Instruction of Poor Children. *Philadelphia.* 1810. 8vo, pp. 48. 61446

Advertisement. [*Philadelphia: W. Goddard.* 1770.] 4to, 1 l.

Dated, Philada Aug. 1, 1770, signed by Wm. Goddard, in answer to Towne's "To the Public," and announcing the forthcoming of "The Partnership."

Advertisement. ... *Philadelphia: Printed by B. Towne.* [n. d.] 4to, 1 page. P. 61448

Issued Oct. 13, 1777. Orders a return of the number of horses, carts, etc., to Capt. Beaman.

Advice and Caution from Our Monthly Meeting At Philadelphia. Held the 25th Day of the Sixth Month, 1732, Concerning Children and Servants. [*Philadelphia: Andrew Bradford.* 1732.] Sm. 8vo, pp. 8. 61449

Agreement between the Atlantic and Great Western Railway Company, and the Philadelphia and Reading Railroad Company. January 10, 1866. *Philadelphia.* 1866. 8vo, pp. 20. 61450

Agreements ... between the ... Citizens of Philadelphia, and the Schuylkill Navigation Company, relative to the Water Power, &c. at Fair Mount. *Philadelphia.* 1832. 8vo, pp. 31. + 1854. 8vo, pp. 22. 61451

Constitution ... of the ALBION SOCIETY, of Philadelphia. Established: ... 1855. ... *Philadelphia.* 1858. 12mo, pp. 16.

All Loyal Seamen .... [n. p. 1778.] 4to, 1 page. P. 61453

Recruiting bill for the galley Philadelphia. Fifty copies printed by J. Humphreys.

All Persons having in their Possession any kind of Stores and Provisions, belonging to the Rebel Army, are ... to report the same to the Quarter-Master or Commissary-General, ... Philadelphia, September 29, 1777. [n. p. n. d.] 4to, 1 leaf. 61454

Printed by J. Humphreys. Relates to seizure of rebel stores.

Catalogue of the Medical Library belonging to the Philadelphia ALMSHOUSE. *Philadelphia.* 1824. 12mo. + Prepared by Dr. E. F. Rivinus. [*Ibid.*] 1831. 8vo. 61455

Also: Ordinances, Rules, and By-Laws for the Alms-House and House of Employment. [*Philadelphia.* 1796.] 8vo, pp. 10.—Rules and Regulations ... . *Philadelphia.* 1822. 8vo, pp. 38. *See also* "Plan for the Government," *infra.*

Alphabetical List of the Streets in ... Philadelphia ... . By A. E. Rogerson ... . *Philadelphia.* 1859. 8vo, pp. (2), 12. 61456

Charter, ... of the AMERICA HOSE COMPANY. ... Revised October 11, 1869. *Philadelphia.* 1870. 12mo, pp. 44. 61457

Act of Incorporation of the AMERICAN ACADEMY OF MUSIC, ... *Philadelphia.* 1857. 8vo, pp. 15. 61458

Also: Charter and Prospectus of the Opera House, or American Academy of Music. *Philadelphia.* 1852. 8vo, pp. 16.—Fourteenth Annual Report of the American Academy of Music ... . *Philadelphia.* 1867. 8vo, pp. 7.—To the Building Committee ... of the ... Academy ... . *Philadelphia.* 1854. 8vo, pp. 8.

The Annual Report of the AMERICAN EMIGRANTS' FRIEND SOCIETY, for ... 1852. ... *Philadelphia.* 1852. 8vo, pp. 6. Continued. 61459

The First Annual Report of the ... AMERICAN FEMALE MEDICAL EDUCATION SOCIETY ... . *Philadelphia.* 1854. 8vo, pp. 8.

Reception of the AMERICAN MEDICAL ASSOCIATION ... Philadelphia, May 2, 1855. *Philadelphia.* 1855. 8vo, pp. 11.

Constitution and By-Laws of the AMERICUS CLUB. Incorporated ... 1869. *Philadelphia.* 1870. 12mo, pp. 36. 61462

The Amicable Fire Company are requested to meet at the Cross Keys ... this Evening. [n. p. n. d.] 4to, 1 leaf. 61463

Dated Philadelphia, Jan. 26, 1778. Fifty copies printed by J. Humphreys.

An die Deutschen, vornemlich die zum Wählen berechtigten, in Philadelphia- Bucks- und Berks County. ... [Colophon:] *Philadelphia, Gedruckt bey Henrich Miller* ... . [1765.] Folio, pp. (2).

An election circular, printed about October 1, 1765.

An | Die Freyhalter | und Einwohner | der | Stadt und County | Philadelphia, deutscher Nation. | [n. p.:] *Gedruckt im Jahr* 1764. 4to, 2 leaves. P. 61465

Andrews & Co.'s Stranger's Guide in ... Philadelphia. ... *Philadelphia.* 1851. Square 16mo, pp. (2), 60, (4). 61466

Constitution ... of the ANGLO-AMERICAN BENEFICIAL SOCIETY ... . Incorporated 1854. ... [n. p.] 1859. Square 12mo, pp. 23. 61467

Answers of the Committee ... of "The President, ... and Company for erecting a permanent Bridge over the ... Schuylkill at ... Philadelphia," to the Questions propounded by the Committee of Councils ... . *Philadelphia.* 1833. 12mo, pp. 12.

The Antient Testimony of the ... Quakers, Reviv'd. By the Order and Approbation of the Yearly Meeting ... . *Philadelphia: Printed by Andrew Bradford.* 1723. 16mo, pp. 48. H.S.P. 61469

An Appeal to the Citizens of Philadelphia, for means to Purchase a Lot ... for the Howard Institution for Discharged Female Prisoners. *Philadelphia.* 1858. 16mo, pp. 14, (2). 61470

An Appeal to the Citizens of Philadelphia, in behalf of Domestic Missions ... . [n. p.:] *John Young, Printer.* 1824. 8vo, pp. 16. 61471

An Appeal to the Citizens of ... Philadelphia against the City Councils. [n. p. 1840.] 8vo, pp. 8. 61472

Relates to Girard's Will.

An Appeal to the Freemen, Friends of Liberty and the Rights of Man, in ... Philadelphia. [n. p. n. d.] 8vo, pp. 4. 61473

Appeal to the Public. [n. p. n. d.] 8vo, pp. 8. 61474

On behalf of the Pennsylvania Hospital, dated 10th mo. 31, 1864.

Address of the Managers of the APPRENTICES' LIBRARY COMPANY; ... *Philadelphia.* 1838. 12mo, pp. 12. 61475

Also: Annual Report, ... of the Apprentices Library Company ... . *Philadelphia.* 1831. 8vo, pp. 7, (1.)—Catalogue of Books ... . *Philadelphia.* 1838. 16mo, pp. 126. + *Philadelphia.* 1842. 16mo, pp. 135. + *Philadelphia.* 1845. 16mo, pp. 46. + *Philadelphia.* 1850. 16mo, pp. 159, 23. + [*Ibid.*] 1854. 8vo, pp. 176. + [*Ibid.*] 1863. 16mo, pp. 176.—Charter ... of the ... Company ... . *Philadelphia.* 1856. 16mo, pp. 15.—An Historical Sketch of the ... Company ... . *Philadelphia.* 1869. 24mo, pp. 12.—Report of the Managers of the ... Company ... March 12, 1823 ... . *Philadelphia: Jesper Harding, Printer.* 1823. 12mo, pp. 12.

The Arcade Hotel Guide, ... Philadelphia ... . *Philadelphia.* 1856. 24mo, pp. 28. + [*Ibid.*] 1856. 24mo, pp. 34. + [*Ibid.*] 1857. 16mo, pp. 34. 61476

Charter and By-Laws of the ARCH STREET PRESBYTERIAN CHURCH ... . *Philadelphia.* 1850. 12mo, pp. 22. + [*Ibid.*] 1859. 12mo, pp. 22. 61477

Also: Manual of the Arch Street Presbyterian Church ... . *Philadelphia.* 1860. 12mo, pp. 56.—Treasurer's Statement ... for 1859. ... *Philadelphia.* 1860. 8vo, pp. 13.

Report of the Committee ... to investigate the local causes of Cholera in the ARCH STREET PRISON, in ... Philadelphia ... . *Harrisburg.* 1833. 8vo, pp. 21. 61478

Arrangement of the Music at the Funeral Solemnities in Honor of Gen. Washington, Philadelphia, Dec. 26, 1799. [n. p. 1799.] 8vo, pp. 6. 61479

Transactions of the ART UNION of Philadelphia. For ... 1848. *Philadelphia.* 1848. 8vo, pp. 64. Continued. 61480

Also: Catalogue. Philadelphia Art Union. [n. p. 1849.] 8vo, pp. 4.

Articles of Agreement &c. for Raising a Sum of Money, to purchase A Lot of Ground, and Erecting thereon A Church (Since known by the name of St. Paul's Church) In ... Philadelphia. ... *Philadelphia: John Ormrod.* 1798. 8vo, pp. 16.

Articles of Association "for carrying on the Linen Manufactory" in Philadelphia. [n. p. 1765.] Folio, pp. 2. P. 61482

Articles of Faith and Plan of Church Government, Composed and Adopted by the Churches Believing in the Salvation of All Men, Met in Philadelphia, May 25th, 1790. *Philadelphia.* 1790. 8vo. 61483

Artists' Fund Society of Philadelphia. Catalogue of the First Exhibition. 1835. ... *Philadelphia.* [1835.] 8vo, pp. 12.

Articles, or By-Laws, for the Government of the ASSOCIATED INDEPENDENT Philadelphia Troop of Volunteer Greens, Originally settled ... July, 1794 ... . *Philadelphia: Printed by Henry Tuckniss.* 1798. 8vo, pp. 8, (2). 61485

Constitution and By-Laws of the ASSOCIATED MEMBERS OF THE BAR of Philadelphia. *Philadelphia: Printed ... by T. S. Manning.* 1821. 8vo, pp. 16. 61486

Proceedings of the ASSOCIATION FOR ESTABLISHING a School for the Education of the Blind in Philadelphia and Pennsylvania, under J. R. Friedlander. *Philadelphia.* [1833.] 8vo. 61487

First Report of the ASSOCIATION FOR THE CARE of Colored Orphans ... . *Philadelphia.* 1836. 8vo, pp. 44. Continued.

A Catalogue of Books, Belonging to the ASSOCIATION LIBRARY COMPANY of Philadelphia: ... *Philadelphia: Printed by William Bradford* ... . M.DCC.LXV. 8vo, pp. 68. 61489

The First Annual Report of the Executive Board of the ASSOCIATION OF FRIENDS at Philadelphia and Vicinity, for the Relief of Colored Freedmen. Read at the Annual Meeting ... the 18th of 4th month, 1864. *Birmingham: White & Pike.* [1864.] 8vo, pp. 39. 61490

At a Council held at Philadelphia, May 17th. 1742. [*Philadelphia: B. Franklin.* 1742.] Folio, pp. 12. H.S.P. 61491

At a General Meeting of the Citizens of Philadelphia, and Parts adjacent, at the State-House Yard in this City, on ... 25th of May 1779, General Roberdeau was unanimously requested to take the Chair; who introduced the Business with the following address: ... . *Philadelphia: Printed by Francis Bailey.* [1779.] Folio, 1 leaf. 61492

In regard to appointing a committee to regulate the price of provisions, etc.

At a Meeting of a Number of the Citizens of Philadelphia, ... November the 2d, Samuel Howell, Chairman, Jonathan B. Smith, Secretary, It was unanimously Resolved, to publish the following Address to the Inhabitants of ... Philadelphia. [n. p. 1776.] 4to, 1 leaf. 61493

Protest against the creation of the Council of Censors.

At a Sub-Committee for managing the Donation Fund, containing a Letter from the Trustees of the Negro School in Philadelphia, America, relating to the Negro School. [n. p. n. d.] Folio, 1 leaf. 61494

Dated, London, 30th of 5th month, and 1st of 6th month, 1787.

At a Yearly Meeting at Philadelphia ... . [n. p. 1794.] Folio, 1 leaf. 61495

Minutes relating to the establishment of a boarding-school.

Charter and By-Laws of the ATHENÆUM ... . *Philadelphia: Printed by W. Fry.* 1817. 8vo, pp. 35. + *Philadelphia: Printed by S. Roberts.* 1820. 8vo, pp. 80. 61496

Also: Thirty-Second Annual Report of the Athenæum ... with the Report of the Architect and the Address of ... President, at the laying of the Corner Stone of the New Hall ... 1845. *Philadelphia: John C. Clark, Printer.* 1847. 8vo, pp. 24. Plate. Continued.—Annual Report of the Directors ... . *Philadelphia.* [1856.] 8vo pp. 16.

Authentic Historical Memoir. *See* [Milnor (Wm.)], 49133.

A | Confession | of | Faith, | ... | Adopted by the BAPTIST ASSOCIATION | ... at Philadelphia, Sept 25. 1742. | The Sixth Edition. | To which are added, | Two Articles viz. Of Imposition of Hands,

| and Singing of Psalms in Publick Worship. | Also | A Short Treatise of Church Discipline. | ... | *Philadelphia: Printed by B. Franklin.* | M,DCC,XLIII. | 16mo, pp. 112, (2), 62. + The Seventh Edition. *Philadelphia: Printed by John Dunlap* ... . M,DCC,-LXXIII. 12mo, pp. vii, 56, (2), 31. 61497

Also: The Association Letter. [n. p. 1766.] Folio, pp. (2).—Minutes of the Baptist Association held in Philadelphia, October the 12th, 13th, 14th, 1774. [n. p. n. d.] 4to, pp. 11. Continued. *See also* Philadelphia Baptist Association, No. 61962.

Proceedings of the BAPTIST CONVENTION for Missionary Purposes; held at Philadelphia, in May, 1814. *Philadelphia.* 1814. 8vo, pp. 43. 61498

The | Bill | For the better raising | of Money on the In- | habitants | of Phila- | delphia for Publick | Uses, and for repeal- | ing a former Act | made to like Purpo- | ses; | Together with the Governor's | Reasons for not Passing the same. | [*Philadelphia:*] *Printed* [*by B. Franklin*] 1739. | Folio, pp. (2), 16. H.S.P. 61499

A | Bill | For the better Regulating the | Nightly Watch | Within the City of Philadelphia, and | for raising Money on the Inhabitants | of the said City, for defraying the | necessary Expences thereof. | *Philadelphia:* | *Printed by B. Franklin,* M,DCC,XLIII. | Folio, pp. 11. H.S.P. 61500

Biographies of ... Merchants. *See* [Winslow (S. N.)]

Memorial of the BOARD OF CONTROLLERS of Public Schools of ... Philadelphia, for such a modification of the late Act of Assembly, ... as will restore the Jurisdiction ... of School Directors. ... *Philadelphia.* 1854. 8vo, pp. 14. 61501

Also: Report of the Committee of the Board of Controllers to distribute the Appropriation for Night Schools in the First School District of Pennsylvania, for ... 1855. *Philadelphia.* 1855. 8vo, pp. 7.—Report of the Committee on Revision of Studies, with the graded Course of Instruction, approved March 10th, 1868, by the Board of Controllers ... . *Philadelphia.* 1868. 8vo, pp. 86. *See also* Controllers of the Public Schools, *infra.*

By-Laws of the BOARD OF DIRECTORS of the Public Schools for the First Section of the First School District ... . *Philadelphia.* 1835. 8vo, pp. 8. + [*Ibid.*] 1839. 8vo. + 1848. [n. p. n. d.] 8vo, pp. 6. + 1850. [n. p. n. d.] 8vo, pp. 7.

Also: By-Laws of the Board of Directors ... for the Third Section, Philadelphia ... *Philadelphia.* 1859. 12mo, pp. 23.—Rules for the ... Grammar, Secondary, and Primary Schools ... . Revised and re-adopted ... June 5, 1843. *Philadelphia.* 1843. 8vo, pp. 24. + [*Ibid.*] 1848. 8vo, pp. 32. + 1850. 8vo, pp. 27.

Rules for the Government of the BOARD OF GUARDIANS, its Officers, Business and Affairs; and for regulating ... the Alms-House, Hospital, and House of Employment. ... *Philadelphia: William Brown, Printer.* 1835. 8vo, pp. 64, ii. + *Philadelphia: J. Perry, Printer.* 1844. 8vo, pp. 74. BA. 61503

Also: Report of the Committee appointed by the Board of Guardians of the Poor ... of Philadelphia, to visit the cities of Baltimore, New York, Providence, Boston, and Salem. ... *Philadelphia: Printed by Samuel Parker,* ... 1827. 8vo, pp. 38.—Report of a Committee appointed by the Guardians for the Relief ... of the Poor ... to visit the Almshouses of Baltimore, New York, Boston, and Salem, November, 1833. *Philadelphia: Printed by Wm. F. Geddes,* ... 1834. 8vo, pp. 52.

Report of the BOARD OF HEALTH of Philadelphia, for 1860. *Philadelphia.* 1861. 8vo, pp. 81. Continued annually. 61504

Also: Report of the Sanitary Committee of the Board of Health upon ... Slaughter Houses and Soap Boiling Establishments in Cities ... . August 22, 1854. *Philadelphia.* 1854. 8vo, pp. 15.—Sanitary and Preventive Measures, or what may be done by the Public in anticipation of the Cholera. By the Sanitary Committee of the Board of Health ... . *Philadelphia.* 1866. 12mo, pp. 12.

Board of Trade. *See* Philadelphia Board of Trade, *infra.*

Charter Articles and Bye Laws, of the BRICKLAYERS CORPORATION. Founded ... 1790. Incorporated ... 1797. *Northern Liberties: Printed by B. Scheffler & Co.* M,DCC,LXXXXVII. 12mo, pp. 23. 61505

Bridge Documents, submitted to the Consideration of those who have not before had an Opportunity of investigating the Subject to which they refer. *Philadelphia.* 1821. 8vo, pp. 16.

A Brief Sketch of the Efforts. *See* Vol. IX., No. 34622.

A Brief Sketch of the Origin and Present State of ... Philadelphia. *Philadelphia: Printed by J. H. Oswald.* 1804. 12mo, pp. 10. BA. + *Philadelphia: Printed by Joseph Rakestraw.* 1805. 18mo, pp. 18. 61507

Manual of the BROAD STREET BAPTIST CHURCH, Philadelphia. *Philadelphia.* 1848. 16mo. 61508

Also: Report of the ... Trustees ... Jan. 30, 1854. *Philadelphia* 1854. 8vo.

Calculation, shewing in what time a permanent bridge over the river Schuylkill, ... may be built ... . [*Philadelphia: Z. Poulson, jun.* 1798.] Folio, pp. 3. 61509

Calendrier de Philadelphie, ou le Moraliste Américain, pour tous les jours de l'année. *A Philadelphie* [*Paris*]. 1777. 18mo.

+ Édition augmentée de l'auis de ceux qui veulent passer en Amérique. *A Philadelphie, pour la présente année* [*Paris,* 1785?] 18mo, pp. (12), 15, xli, 118. 61510

Calendrier de Philadelphie, en Pensylvanie. *A Philadelphie.* [*Paris.*] M.DCC.LXXIX. 18mo, pp. xli, 118. C. 61511

By Jacques Barbeu-Dubourg. Contains a description of Philadelphia and of Pennsylvania, with several burlesque poems on Burgoyne's defeat, and highly curious and liberal maxims, composed in the interest of American liberty, under date of each day in the year. For another edition, *see* Vol. I., No. 3335.

Call for a Public Meeting. [Dated, Philadelphia, July 12, 1770.] 1 leaf of 7 lines. 61512

Call for a Public Meeting to instruct the Representatives. [Dated, Philadelphia, July 30, 1768.] Folio, 1 leaf.—Call for a Non-Importation Meeting of Tradesmen, Artificers, &c., of Philadelphia. [Dated, 23d May, 1770.] Folio, 1 leaf.—Call for a Public Meeting. [Dated, Philadelphia, Sept. 27, 1770.] Folio, 1 leaf.—Call for a Public Meeting of Manufacturers and Mechanics. [Dated, Philadelphia, June 8, 1774.] Folio, 1 leaf.

A Calm Address to the Citizens and Voters of Philadelphia. [n. p. n. d.] 8vo, pp. 8. 61513

Calm Address to the Citizens of Philadelphia. [n. p. 1833?] 8vo, pp. 3. 61514

Candid Statement of Facts, relative to the Concert, ... in Grace Church, December 21st, 1835. [n. p. n. d.] 12mo, pp. 12. 61515

A Candid Statement respecting The Philadelphia County Ticket. [n. p. n. d.] 8vo, pp. 32. + [Another Edition. n. p. 1838.] 8vo, pp. 63. 61516

Relates to the election for Governor.

A Card. ... Philadelphia, December 2, 1773. [n. p. n. d.] 12mo, 1 page. P. 61517

"To Messieurs James and Drinker," consignees of the tea-ship.

An Act to incorporate the CARPENTERS' COMPANY of ... Philadelphia; ... . *Philadelphia.* 1857. 8vo, pp. 21, 57. + [*Ibid.*] 1866. 8vo, pp. 153. 61518

Catalogue des Livres Qui se trouvent chez Boinod & Gaillard. ... *Philadelphie.* MDCCLXXXIV. 8vo, pp. (5), 117. H.S.P. 61519

A Catalogue of a large Collection of New and Old Books, ... Now for Sale at ... Bell's Book-Store ... . *Philadelphia: Printed by Robert Bell.* M.DCC.LXXXIII. 8vo, pp. 88. 61520

A Catalogue of Books published by the Philadelphia Company of Printers and Booksellers. *Philadelphia.* 1794. 12mo, pp. 24.

A Catalogue of choice and valuable Books, consisting of near 600 Volumes, ... to be sold, for ready money only, by Benj. Franklin, ... beginning April 11, 1744. [*Philadelphia: B. Franklin.* 1744.] 16mo, pp. 16. 61522

Catalogue of Drugs, Chymical and Galenical Preparations, Shop Furniture, Patent Medicines, and Surgeons' Instruments, sold by John Day, and Co. Druggists and Chymists, in Second-Street, Philadelphia. *Philadelphia: Printed by John Dunlap* ... . M. DCC. LXXI. 8vo, pp. 31. 61523

Catalogue of the Books belonging to the Library of the Three Monthly Meetings of Friends of Philadelphia. To which is prefixed a Brief Account of the Institution, with the Rules and Regulations. *Philadelphia.* 1813. 12mo, pp. 117. 61524

For the "Brief Account," *see* Smith's Catalogue of Friends' Books," I. 385. Also: Catalogue of the ... Library of the Four Monthly Meetings of Friends of Philadelphia. ... *Philadelphia.* 1831. 12mo. + *Philadelphia: Kite & Walton.* 1853. 12mo, pp. 350

Catalogue of the Exhibition of a Private Collection of Works of Art, for the benefit of the United States Christian Commission, held at ... Philadelphia. ... [n. p.] 1864. 8vo, pp. 24.

Catalogue of the National Portraits in Independence Hall ... . *Philadelphia.* 1855. 8vo, pp. 24. Plate. + [*Ibid.*] 1856. 8vo, pp. 24. 61526

Causes of the Kensington Riots Explained. *See* Pennsylvanian, *pseudon*, No. 60790.

... Celebration of the Seventy-Fourth Anniversary of the Signing of the Constitution of the United States ... . Philadelphia, September 17th, 1861. *Philadelphia.* 1861. 8vo, pp. 32.

Constitution and By-Laws of the CENTRAL DEMOCRATIC CLUB, organized ... 1863. *Philadelphia.* 1863. 8vo, pp. 23.

Catalogue of the CENTRAL HIGH SCHOOL of Philadelphia. Eighteenth Term. ... *Philadelphia.* 1847. 8vo, pp. 18. Cont'd.

Also: A General Catalogue of the Central High School ... . *Philadelphia.* 1862. 8vo, pp. 134. Plate.—Reorganization of the Central High-School ... . *Philadelphia.* 1839. 8vo, pp. 12.—Report ... by the Board of Controllers ... of Philadelphia. ... 1862. *Philadelphia.* 1862. 8vo, pp. 16.—Reports of the Committee on Central High School ... . *Philadelphia.* 1866. 8vo, pp. 16, 251, (1).

Ceremonies on the Completion of the Monument, to the Memory of Washington and Lafayette, in the Monument Cemetery of Philadelphia. ... [n. p.] 1869. 8vo, pp. 14. 2 Plates.

Chamber of Commerce. *See* Philadelphia Chamber of Commerce, *infra.*

The Charge. *See* [Logan (J.)], Vol. x., Nos. 41793–94.

First Report of the ... Charity Hospital of Philadelphia. *Philadelphia.* 1858. 8vo. 61531

The Chestnut and Walnut Street Railway. [n. p. n. d.] 8vo, pp. 94. 61532

Eighth Annual Report of the ... Chestnut Hill Railroad Company. *Germantown.* 1862. 8vo, pp. 6, (5). Continued.

Chestnut Street Business Directory. *Philadelphia.* [n. d.] 12mo, pp. 58. 61533

Charter and By-Laws of Christ Church, founded in 1695. *Philadelphia.* 1851. 8vo. P. 61534

Also: Charter of Christ Church, ... and St. Peter's Church, ... Philadelphia ... . *Philadelphia: C. Alexander, Printer.* 1832. 8vo, pp. 26.

Christ Church Hospital. Extracts from the Will of the Founder, Dr. John Kearsley, Acts of Assembly, By-Laws, &c. *Philadelphia.* 1850. 8vo. 61535

Also: ... Proceedings on ... Laying the Corner-Stone of the New Hospital in Belmont, Philadelphia, including the Addresses ... . *Philadelphia.* 1856. 8vo, pp. 23.

The Laying of the Corner-Stone of the Church of the Covenant, in ... Philadelphia. ... *Philadelphia.* 1861. 24mo, pp. 24. 61536

To the Legal Voters of the Church of the Epiphany. [n. p. 1856.] 8vo, pp. 8, (1). 61537

Also: A Statement to the Congregation of the Church of the Epiphany, ... of Facts bearing on the action of the Vestry in requesting the Resignation of the Rector. Second Edition ... . *Philadelphia.* 1856. 8vo, pp. 66.

Constitution, ... of the Church of the Messiah, ... with a Sketch of the Origin of the Society ... . *Philadelphia.* 1852. 18mo, pp. 18. 61538

Circular Letter No. I. To the Republican Committee of Correspondence. [Dated Philadelphia, June 14, 1817.] 8vo, pp. 7. + No. IV. [n. p. 1817?] 8vo, pp. 14. + No. V. pp. 10.

Circular of the Native Americans of Philadelphia to the Voters of the City. [n. p. 1845.] 4to, 2 leaves. 61540

The Citizens Hand Book for Philadelphia. ... Compiled ... by William White Smith. *Philadelphia.* [1867.] 18mo, pp. 70.

City Characters. *See* Vol. IV., No. 13159.

Annual Report of the City Commissioners, For ... 1837. [n. p. 1838.] 8vo, pp. iv, 52. Continued. 61542

Also: Quarterly Report of the City Commissioners, ... April 1st, to June 30th, 1837. [n. p. n. d.] 8vo, pp. 19. Continued.—Statement of the Expenditures of the City Commissioners, for ... 1817. ... *Philadelphia.* 1818. Folio, pp. 19. Continued to 1836.

City of Philadelphia. | By the Mayor, Recorder, and Aldermen, and the | Commissioners for paving and cleaning the Streets, &c. [*Philadelphia: Franklin & Hall.* 1765.] Folio, 1 leaf. P.

Notice that "A Scavenger" had been appointed, and extracts from the act of Assembly.

City Ordinance on cleaning the Streets of Philadelphia, March, 1765. *Philadelphia.* 1765. Folio. 61544

Opinion of the City Solicitor on the Appointment of the Committees ... . *Philadelphia.* 1856. 8vo, pp. 14. 61545

Account of the Commencement in the College of Philadelphia, May 17, 1775. [n. p. n. d.] 8vo, pp. 15. 61546

The Plan of a Performance of Solemn Music, to be sung in the College of Philadelphia. [n. p.] 1765. 8vo. 61547

For commencement "Exercises," *see* Vol. VI., Nos. 23387–9, *add* Continued.

Facts and Observations relative to the Nature and Origin of the Pestilential Fever, which prevailed in this City, in 1793, 1797, and 1798. By the College of Physicians of Philadelphia. *Philadelphia: Thomas Dobson.* 1798. 8vo, pp. 52. + *London: James Phillips & Son.* 1799. 8vo, pp. 40. 61548

Also: Additional Facts and Observations relative to the ... Pestilential Fever. ... *Philadelphia: Printed by A. Bartram, for Thomas Dobson.* 1806. 8vo, pp. (4), 99.—The Charter, Constitution, and By-Laws of the College ... . *Philadelphia.* 1790. 12mo, pp. 15. + [*Ibid.*] 1818. 8vo, pp. 76. + [*Ibid.*] 1834. 8vo.—Proceedings of the College ... relative to the prevention of ... Contagious Diseases. *Philadelphia: Printed by Thomas Dobson.* 1798. 8vo, pp. (4), 37.—Report of the College ... to the Board of Health, on Epidemic Cholera. *Philadelphia.* 1832. 8vo, pp. 36.—Transactions of the College ... . Vol. I. Part I. ... *Philadelphia.* 1793. 8vo, pp. xxxi, 254. Continued.

The Committee appointed to examine into the title of the Corporation to the north east public square, ... and whether any ... encroachments have been made thereupon, Report ... . [n. p. At top of sheet:] *Printed by Zachariah Poulson, Junior, February* 22, 1797. Folio, 1 leaf. H.S.P. 61549

Relates to the use of part of Franklin Square as a burying-ground.

Committee Chamber, Philadelphia, May 18, 1776. [n. p. n. d.] 4to, 1 leaf. 61550

Notice of a public meeting at the state house. *See also* our Vol. IV., No. 14993.

The Committee of Ways and Means ... . [n. p. 1807?] 8vo, pp. 23. 61551

Common Council Documents. New City Buildings. 1860. *Philadelphia.* 1860. 8vo, pp. (2), 85, (1). 61552

Minutes of the Common Council of ... Philadelphia. 1704 to 1776. ... *Philadelphia: Crissy & Markley, Printers.* 1847. 8vo, pp. 811. 61553

Also: Minutes of the Common Council ... for 1835–6. ... *Philadelphia.* 1836. 8vo, pp. (2), 246. Continued.—Report of the Committee of Common Council, on the City Debts and Expenditures, and on City Credits and Resources. [n. p. 1798.] Folio, pp. 12.—Rules for the Government of the Common Council ... . *Philadelphia.* 1835. 8vo, pp. 8.

Communication from a Committee of the Several Banks of ... Philadelphia, exhibiting their condition and inability to meet the requirements of their charters ... . *Harrisburg.* 1840. 8vo, pp. 7

Communication from the Select and Common Councils of ... Philadelphia, in relation to Independence Hall. [*Harrisburg.* 1852.] 8vo, pp. 4. 61555

Communication to the Sectional Boards from the Committee on the Equalization of the Salaries of Teachers, ... June 24, 1848. *Philadelphia.* 1848. 8vo, pp. 24. 61556

A Confession of Faith put forth by the Elders and Brethren of many Congregations of Christians. *Philadelphia.* 1798. 16mo. 61557

Considerations addressed to the Members of the Yearly Meeting of Friends, of Philadelphia. ... *Philadelphia: John Penning-ton.* 1846. 8vo, pp. 86. 61558

For another edition, *see* Vol. IV., No. 15938. This elicited: An Appeal ... . Commended to the Readers of ... "Considerations addressed to the Members of the Yearly

Meeting of Friends, of Philadelphia." ... *Philadelphia: C. Sherman, Printer.* 1846. 8vo, pp. 16.

The Constitution and Ordinances of ... Philadelphia. *Philadelphia: Printed by Hall & Sellers.* MDCCXC. 12mo, pp. xxxii, 87.

Constitution of the Democratic Association ... . [n. p. 1844.] Folio, 2 leaves. 61560

By-Laws and ... Resolutions of the Controllers of the Public Schools of the First School District of Pennsylvania. *Philadelphia.* 1852. 8vo, pp. 44. + *Philadelphia.* 1864. 8vo, pp. 23. 61561

Also: First Annual Report of the Controllers ... with their accounts. Also an abstract of the Law of March 6th, 1818, providing for the Public Education ... . *Philadelphia.* 1819. 8vo, pp. 16. Continued.—Report to the Controllers ... on the ... Central High-School of Philadelphia ... . [n. p. 1840.] 8vo, pp. 52, folded leaf. —Rules and Regulations made by the Controllers ... . *Philadelphia.* 1819. Folio, 1 leaf. *See also* Board of Controllers, *supra.*

First Report of the Managers of the Cooper Shop Soldiers' Home ... . *Philadelphia.* 1865. 8vo, pp. 29, (1). Continued.

Copies of Sundry Petitions, &c. presented by Isaac Austin, setting forth His Claim to the New Ferry, in ... Philadelphia. As also, Copies of Sundry Petitions, &c. from George A. Baker, drawn forth In Consequence of the Claim of said Isaac Austin. *Philadelphia: Printed by Francis Bailey* ... . MDCCLXXXIV. 8vo, pp. 35. P. 61563

Relates to tory estates, the university, and private claims.

Copy of a Letter addressed to each Member of Congress by the Delegates from the Committee appointed at a meeting of the Merchants of Philadelphia. [n. p. 1824.] 8vo, pp. 8. 61564

A Copy of the Acts ... passed by the ... Borough of West Philadelphia. ... *Philadelphia.* 1837. 8vo, pp. 39. 61565

Correspondence ... with the Schuylkill Navigation Company, in relation to The Fair Mount Water Works ... . *Philadelphia.* 1833. 8vo, pp. 47. 61566

A Council held at Philadelphia. *See* Vol. IX., No. 34660.

Daguerreotype Sketches of the Members of First Common Council, after Consolidation ... . By [Thos. M. Coleman] a Reporter for Common Council. *Philadelphia: W. H. Sickels, Printer.* 1855. 8vo, pp. 148. 61567

... The Deed of Settlement of the Society for insuring of Houses, in and near Philadelphia. [*B. Franklin and D. Hall.* 1751?] 4to, pp. 8. P. 61568

See also Philadelphia Contributionship, *infra.*

An Act to Incorporate the Delaware and Schuylkill Basin Company in ... Philadelphia, March 9, 1855. *Philadelphia.* 1855. 8vo, pp. 18. 61569

The Delinquent Tax Bill. Its History, Passage and Provisions. [n. p. 1870.] 8vo, pp. 8. 61570

The Democratic Celebration in Independence Square, on the Fourth of July, 1859. *Philadelphia.* 1859. 8vo, pp. 16.

Address of the Democratic Hickory Club ... of Philadelphia, recommending Martin Van Buren ... [n. p. 1844.] 8vo, pp. 16. 61572

Also: Resolutions of the Democratic Hickory Club of Philadelphia, relative to the nomination of Van Buren. [n. p. 1844.] Folio, 1 leaf.

The Democratic Medley, or Sayings and Doings, with the History of One Day, to which is added the Whig's Light-House, and a Trip through the Custom-House & Post Office. Calculated for the Meredian of Philadelphia ... . *Philadelphia.* [1840.] 12mo, pp. 34. 61573

Principles, Articles, and Regulations, agreed upon by the members of the Democratic Society in Philadelphia, May 30th, 1793. *Philadelphia: E. Oswald.* M,DCC,XCIII. 8vo, pp. 8.

Two Addresses of the Democratic Society ... of Philadelphia, to their Democratic Brethren. ... *Philadelphia: John Binns.* 1811. 8vo, pp. 19. 61575

Address of the Democratic Whig Association of ... Philadelphia, to the People of Pennsylvania. April, 1839. *Philadelphia.* 1839. 12mo, pp. (2), 26, Facts for the People, 16, (2).

Department of Arms and Trophies, Great Central Fair. Catalogue of the Museum of Flags, Trophies, and Relics, relating to the Revolution, War of 1812, Mexican War, and the Present Rebellion, ... to be exhibited at Philadelphia, June 7th, 1864, ... for the Benefit of the U. S. Sanitary Commission. *Philadelphia: Crissy & Markley.* 1864. 8vo, pp. 32. 61577

See also Vol. V., No. 19617.

Description of the New Ledger Building, ... Philadelphia. ... *Philadelphia.* 1867. 8vo, pp. 32. 61578

A Descriptive Sketch of Philadelphia, for 1832, given in a letter from an old Printer. [n. p. n. d.] 8vo, pp. 12. 61579

Dessert to the True American, Newspaper. June, 1798, to January, 1799. [n. p. n. d.] 4to. 61580

Devises, Bequests, and Grants to the Corporation. *Philadelphia.* 1832. 8vo. B. 61581

Dialogue, &c. For the Commencement in the College of Philadelphia, May 30th, 1765. [n. p. 1765.] 12mo, pp. 4.

Digest in force January 1, 1856. Compiled and edited under authority of the City Councils by William Duane, William B. Hood and Leonard Myers. *Philadelphia.* 1856. 8vo. 61583

A Digest of Laws relating to ... Philadelphia, from its Territorial Extension, ... February 2d, 1854, until the close of the Extra Session of the Legislature in 1861. ... *Philadelphia: King & Baird.* 1861. 8vo, pp. (2), xiv, 125. 61584

A Digest of Laws relating to ... Philadelphia, from ... 1854, until ... 1865. With an appendix ... . *Philadelphia: King & Baird.* 1865. 8vo, pp. xiv, 172. 61585

A Digest of Laws relating to ... Philadelphia, from ... 1854, until ... 1866. ... Prepared by David W. Sellers. 1866. *Philadelphia: King & Baird.* 1867. 8vo, pp. xv, 208, (2), 178.

A Digest of the Acts of Assembly, and the Ordinances of the ... Incorporated District of the Northern Liberties; ... By John Miles. ... *Philadelphia: Printed by Joseph Rakestraw.* 1830. 8vo, pp. 220. 61587

A Digest of the Acts of Assembly, and the Ordinances, ... of the Kensington District ... . *Philadelphia: Joseph Rakestraw.* 1832. 8vo, pp. (2), 160. 61588

A Digest of the Acts of Assembly, and of the Ordinances ... of the District of Spring Garden ... . *Philadelphia: Printed by William Brown.* 1833. 8vo, pp. vii, 191. + [*Ibid.*] 1841. 8vo.

Digest of Acts of Assembly relating to the Kensington District ... . *Philadelphia: Perry, Printer.* 1844. 8vo, pp. (4), 286. + *Philadelphia: Isaac Ashmead, Printer.* 1847. 8vo, pp. vii, (1), 9–312. 61590

A Digest of the Acts of Assembly and Ordinances of the District of Moyamensing ... . [*Philadelphia:*] *Bernard J. M'-Cann, Printer.* 1848. 8vo, pp. xv, (1), 9–289. 61591

A Digest of Acts of Assembly, relating to the ... Northern Liberties; ... *Philadelphia: Printed by Fayette Pierson.* 1847. 8vo, pp. 341. 61592

Digest of the Acts of Assembly relating to ... Philadelphia. ... *Philadelphia: Crissy & Markley.* 1860. 8vo, pp. 320. 61593

A Digest of the Laws ... relating to the Police of ... Philadelphia; with Some Account of the History of the Police Forces ... from ... 1682, to the present time: ... added a Copy of the Charter ... Granted by William Penn in 1701. ... *Philadelphia: Crissy & Markley.* 1851. 8vo, pp. vi, 46. 61594

A Digest of the Laws and Ordinances, relating to ... Philadelphia, in force ... 1868. *Philadelphia: King & Baird.* 1869. 8vo, pp. vi, 682. C. 61595

A Digest of the Ordinances of ... Philadelphia, and the Acts of Assembly relating thereto. By John C. Lowber and C. S. Miller. *Philadelphia.* 1822. 8vo. + Digest ... By C. S. Miller. [*Ibid.*] 1828. 8vo. C. + [*Ibid.*] 1834. 8vo. + [*Ibid.*] 1841. 8vo. + [*Ibid.*] 1859. 8vo. C. 61596

A Digest of the Ordinances of the Borough of Frankford ... . *Philadelphia: Joseph Metcalfe & Co.* 1836. 12mo, pp. 68.

Dinner given by the Philadelphia Bar to the Judiciary at the Continental Hotel Philadelphia January 8th 1867 *Philadelphia* MDCCCLXVII 8vo, pp. 80. 61598

Directions For Manouvres, to be Performed by the Brigade composed of the Three City Battalions, on Tuesday, the Fourteenth of November, 1775. [n. p. n. d.] Folio, 1 leaf. H.S.P.

Directory. The Philadelphia Directory, by Francis White ... . To which are annexed, A valuable, ... Table of ... Coins, ... in such order, ... as to render an exchange or comparison ... plain and easy. *Philadelphia: Printed by Young, Stewart, and M'Culloch,* ... M,DCC,LXXXV. 8vo, pp. (4), 98, (2). 61600

On page 22 will be found the following: "Franklin Benjamin, his Excellency, President of Pennsylvania, Market St."

Macpherson's Directory for the City and Suburbs of Philadelphia ... . Published October 1st, 1785, And to be Corrected and Republished Annually. Containing, an Alphabetical List of the Names and Places of Abode of the Inhabitants. *Philadelphia: Printed by Francis Bailey* ... . M,DCC,LXXXV. 8vo, pp. (4), 159.

The Philadelphia Directory. By Clement Biddle. *Philadelphia: Printed by James & Johnson* ... . M,DCC,XCI. 8vo, pp. xviii, (1), 187, (1). H.S.P. 61602

The Philadelphia Directory and Register: ... By James Hardie, A.M. *Philadelphia: T. Dobson.* 1793. 8vo, pp. xii, 234. + The Second Edition. ... *Philadelphia: Printed ... by Jacob Johnson & Co.* ... MDCCXCIV. 8vo, pp. (6), 232. Map. P. 61603

Stephens's Philadelphia Directory, For 1796; ... *Philadelphia: Printed for Thomas Stephens, ... by W. Woodward.* [n. d.] 12mo, pp. 19, (1), 286, 69. Map. B., C., P. 61604

The Philadelphia Directory, for 1797: ... By Cornelius William Stafford. [*Philadelphia:*] *Printed ... by William W. Woodward,* ... 1797. 8vo, pp. (4), 203, 76. Map. + [*Ibid.*] 1798. 8vo, pp. 166, 77, (1). + [*Ibid.*] 1799. 8vo, pp. 159, 78. + [*Ibid.*] 1800. 8vo, pp. 151, 80. + [*Ibid.*] 1801. 8vo, pp. 260, 32.

Robinson's Philadelphia Register and City Directory, for 1799: ... By James Robinson. *Philadelphia: Printed by John Bioren,* ... 1799. 12mo, pp. 16, (154), 17–50, (24). P. 61606

A copy sold at the Mickley sale, in 1878, for $30, was resold in 1880, at the Phillips sale, for $55.

The New Trade Directory, for Philadelphia, Anno 1800 ... . To which is added an Alphabetical List of all the Streets, Alleys and Lanes ... . *Philadelphia: Printed ... by Way & Groff.* 1799. 12mo, pp. xii, 216.

The Philadelphia Directory, City and County Register, for 1802. ... By James Robinson [n. p.:] *Printed ... by William W. Woodward.* [n. d.] 12mo, pp. 279, folded leaf, xxxvi, (12). + 1803. [*Ibid.*] 12mo, pp. 285, lx, (12), Table. + 1804. [n. p.:] *Printed ... by John H. Oswald.* [n. d.] 12mo. + 1805. *Printed for the Publisher.* [n. d.] + 1806. [*Ibid.*] + 1807, '08, '09, '10, '11.

Census Directory For 1811. ... *Philadelphia: Printed by Jane Aitken.* 1811. 12mo, pp. 484, (1).

The Philadelphia Directory and Register for 1813: ... By John A. Paxton ... . [n. p.:] *B. & T. Kite.* [n. d.] 12mo.

Kite's Philadelphia Directory for 1814: ... [n. p.:] *B. & T. Kite.* [n. d.] 12mo.

The Philadelphia Directory for 1816 ... . By James Robinson. [n. p. n. d.] 12mo.

XIV. Edition. Robinson's Original Annual Directory for 1817, being an alphabetical list of more than 22,000 Merchants, Mechanicks, Traders, &c. of Philadelphia and Suburbs; ... *Printed at Whitehall* ... [n. d.] 16mo, pp. 524.

The Philadelphia Directory for 1817 ... . By Edward Dawes. ... [n. p. n. d.] 12mo, pp. (34), 467, (1).

The Philadelphia Directory and Register, for 1818: ... By John Adams Paxton, ... [n. p. n. d.] 12mo. + 1819. 12mo. + Supplement, ... for 1820. 12mo, pp. 22.

The Philadelphia Directory and Register for 1820. ... By Edward Whitely. [n. p.:] *M'Carty & Davis, Printers.* [n. d.] 12mo. + 1821. [A supplement of 31 leaves to Whitely's Directory for 1820.] + 1822. [A supplement of 37 leaves to the Directory for 1820.]

The Philadelphia Index or Directory for 1823: ... By Robert Desilver. [n. p. n. d.] 12mo.

The Philadelphia Directory for 1824: ... By Robert Desilver. [n. p. n. d.] 12mo.

The Philadelphia Directory and Stranger's Guide, for 1825; ... Thomas Wilson, Editor. *Philadelphia: Thomas Wilson, & Wm. D. Vanbaun, John Bioren, Printer.* ... 1825. 8vo, pp. (2), 160, xl.

Desilver's Philadelphia Directory and Stranger's Guide, For 1828. ... *Philadelphia: Robert Desilver* .... 1828. 8vo. Continued to 1837.

A. M'Elroy's Philadelphia Directory, for 1837. ... Published by A. M'Elroy. *Philadelphia: Printed by Rackliff & Jones.* 1837. 8vo. Continued to 1867.

The Philadelphia Circulating Business Directory. For 1838. ... Arranged by J. R. Savage. ... *Philadelphia.* [n. d.] Imp. 8vo, pp. xv, 207.

O'Brien's Wholesale Business Intelligencer and Southern and Western Merchants' Pocket Directory ... for 1838–39. *Philadelphia: John G. O'Brien.* [n. d.] 18mo.

O'Brien's United States Advertising Circular, and ... Merchants' Directory, to ... Philadelphia, for ... 1843. ... *Philadelphia: King & Baird, Printers.* 1843. 16mo, pp. 164.

O'Brien's Philadelphia Wholesale Business Directory, for ... 1844. ... *Philadelphia: King & Baird.* 1844. 16mo. Continued to 1849.

Bywater's Philadelphia Business Directory ... for ... 1849. ... *Philadelphia: Maurice Bywater.* [n. d.] 16mo, pp. 162. Map.

Rae's Philadelphia Pictorial Directory & Panoramic Advertiser. Chestnut Street, from Second to Tenth Streets. *Julio H. Rae, ... Philadelphia.* 1851. Oblong 4to, pp. (66). 16 Plates.

O'Brien's Philadelphia Wholesale Business Merchants and Manufacturers' Directory and Eastern, Western & Southern Circular, for ... 1852. *Philadelphia: John G. O'Brien.* [1852.] 8vo.

Philadelphia Wholesale Merchants' and Artisans' Business Directory, for 1853. By T. Ellwood Chapman. *Philadelphia: T. E. Chapman & Co.* [1852.] 18mo.

The Philadelphia Merchants' & Manufacturers' Business Directory for 1856–7. ... Prepared ... by Griswold & Co. ... *Philadelphia.* [n. d.] 4to, pp. xvi, 402, 100. Map.

McElroy's Wholesale Business Directory, of the ... Mercantile Houses ... 1857. *Philadelphia: H. B. Ashmead.* [1857.] 8vo. + 1859. [*Ibid.*] 8vo.

Philadelphia Complete Directory for 1857. *Philadelphia: William F. Bartlett & Co.* [n. d.] 8vo.

Twitt's Directory of Prominent Business Men ... . Published Semi-Annually. ... [n. p.] 1857. 4to, pp. (5), 60.

Boyd's Philadelphia City Business Directory, ... 1858. Compiled by Wm. H. Boyd. ... *Philadelphia: T. K. Collins, Jr.* [n. d.] 12mo, pp. 360. Continued to 1884.

Cohen's ... Directory ... for 1860. *Philadelphia: Hamelin & Co.* ... [n. d.] 8vo. Map.

E. M. Cross & Co.'s Philadelphia City Business Directory, 1863–64. Compiled by Henry R. Hellier. *Philadelphia: E. M. Cross & Co.* [1863.] 16mo, pp. 328.

McElroy and Co.'s City Business Directory, ... 1867–68. *Philadelphia: McElroy & Co.* 1868. 16mo, pp. 350.

Gopsill's Philadelphia City and Business Directory for 1867–8. Compiled by Isaac Costa. *Philadelphia: James Gopsill.* 1867. 8vo, pp. 1690, cxxviii. Map. Continued to 1884.

Hotel Rooms Business Directory of the leading ... Business Houses ... for 1870. *Philadelphia: J. Berr.* 1870. 16mo.

A Disertation [*sic*] on the Laws of Excise, in answer to Publicus. [*Philadelphia: J. Dunlap.* 1773.] Folio. 61607

The Dorcas Society of the Tenth Presbyterian Church, Philadelphia. *Philadelphia.* 1861. 16mo, pp. 19. 61608

Preamble and Constitution of the DYOTTVILLE APPRENTICES' LIBRARY COMPANY. To which is added the Rules and Regulations of the Glass Factory, with the Report of the Committee ... to investigate the Internal Regulations of the place. *Philadelphia.* 1834. 32mo, pp. 27. 61609

Earnest Call, occasioned by the Alarming Pestilential Contagion, to the Inhabitants of Philadelphia. *Philadelphia: Jones, Hoff & Derrick.* 1793. 12mo, pp. 36. P. 61610

Education of Idiots. An Appeal to the Citizens of Philadelphia. ... *Philadelphia.* 1853. 8vo, pp. 8. 61611

The Election, a Medley, Humbly Inscribed to Squire Lilliput, Professor of Scurrility. [n. p. n. d.] Large folio, 1 leaf.

Engraved on copper, with a view of the election at the top. This is different from the following.

The Election. Humbly Inscribed to the Saturday-Night Club, in Lodge Alley. [n. p. 1765.] Folio, 1 leaf. H.S.P. 61613

Corrected title of our No. 22109, Vol. VI. One hundred and thirty-two lines of poetry, and an advertisement of twenty-one lines, divided into four columns, with a large illustration at the top. The whole engraved on copper, without doubt by Henry Dawkins.

Elections by the Select and Common Councils ... . *Philadelphia.* 1852. 12mo, pp. 12. 61614

Report of the Executive Committee to the ... Directors of the EMIGRANT'S FRIEND SOCIETY, established April, 1848. [n. p. 1848.] 8vo, pp. 16. 61615

Also: ... American Citizen and Emigrant Adviser. ... *Philadelphia.* 1850. 8vo.

Report to the Trustees of the EMLEN INSTITUTION for the Education of Children of African or Indian Descent. *Philadelphia: Printed by Joseph & William Kite.* 1842. 8vo, pp. 26.

Relates to a proposition to transfer the institution to Ohio.

Engineer's Report ... of the ... Direct Route between Philadelphia and Norfolk; ... November, 1858. *Philadelphia.* 1859. 8vo, pp. 30. Map. 61617

An Enquiry into the Condition and Influence of the Brothels in connection with the Theatres of Philadelphia. ... By a Friend of the Drama. ... *Philadelphia.* 1834. 8vo, pp. 24. 61618

Proceedings of the ENTOMOLOGICAL SOCIETY of Philadelphia. March, 1861, to December, 1862. *Philadelphia.* 1862. 8vo, pp. 311. Continued. 61619

Also: Charter and By-Laws ... . *Philadelphia.* 1862. 8vo, pp. 11.

First Annual Report of the ... EPISCOPAL MISSIONARY SOCIETY of Philadelphia. ... [n. p.:] *Printed by John Bioren.* 1817. 12mo, pp. 26. 61620

An Epistle from our General Spring Meeting of Ministers and Elders for Pennsylvania and New-Jersey, held at Philadelphia, from the 29th of the Third Month to the 1st of the Fourth Month, inclusive, 1755. To Friends on the Continent of America. [n. p. n. d.] Folio, pp. 4. 61621

An Epistle from our Yearly Meeting at Burlington, For the Jersey and Pennsylvania, &c. Held ... from the Nineteenth to the Twenty-third Day of Seventh Month 1724. To the Quarterly and Monthly-Meetings of Friends. [Colophon:] *Philadelphia: Printed by Andrew Bradford* ... . MDCCXXIV. Folio, pp. 4. + MDCCXXVII. Folio, pp. 3. + MDCCXXXIV. Folio, pp. 4. + [n. p. 1746.] Folio, pp. 4. 61622

Improved title of our No. 22692, Vol. VI.

An Epistle from our Yearly-Meeting, Held at Philadelphia ... from the 24th ... 9th Month, to the 1st of the 10th Month, inclusive, 1774. To our Friends and Brethren in these ... Provinces. [*Philadelphia: J. Crukshank.* 1774.] Folio, pp. 4.

An Epistle from our Yearly-Meeting, Held at Philadelphia, for Pennsylvania and New-Jersey, ... from the 24th Day of the 9th Month, to the 1st of the 10th Month, inclusive, 1774. [n. p. n. d.] Folio, pp. 4. 61624

Corrected title of our No. 22693, Vol. VI.

An Epistle from the Meeting of Sufferings, Held in Philadelphia for Pennsylvania and New-Jersey, the 5th Day of the First-Month, 1775; To our Friends and Brethren in these and the adjacent Provinces. [n. p. n. d.] Folio, pp. 3. 61625

An Epistle from the three Monthly Meetings of Friends of Philadelphia, to the Members of our Religious Society, in the

City and Neighbourhood. *Philadelphia: Printed by Benjamin & Jacob Johnson.* 1799. 8vo, pp. 8. 61626

The Epistle from the Yearly-Meeting in London, Held ... from the 27th of the Fifth Month to the 1st of the Sixth Month, 1776, inclusive. To the Quarterly and Monthly Meetings of Friends and Brethren in Great Britain, Ireland, and elsewhere. [n. p. n. d.] 4to, pp. 4. 61627

The third and fourth pages contain the Epistle to the Yearly-Meeting at Philadelphia.

An Epistle from the Yearly Meeting ... held in Philadelphia, 4th month, 1821. [n. p.] 1821. Folio, 1 leaf. 61628

An Epistle from the Yearly Meeting of Friends, held in Philadelphia ... 1827 ... . *Philadelphia.* 1827. 12mo, pp. 10.

An Epistle from the Yearly Meeting of Friends, held in Philadelphia, ... 1829. To the ... Friends, ... of America and elsewhere. *Philadelphia: C. Alexander, Printer.* 1829. 12mo, pp. 11

Epistle from the Yearly Meeting of Friends, held in Philadelphia, to the Yearly Meeting of Friends, held in London. Also an Epistle from the Yearly Meeting of Friends, held in New York, ... to their Subordinate Meetings. ... *Dublin: Printed by Thomas J. White.* MDCCCXXXI. 12mo, pp. 14. 61631

Epistle from the Yearly Meeting of Friends, held in Philadelphia, . . 15th of the Fourth Month ... 1861; Addressed to its Members. *Philadelphia: ... C. Sherman & Son, Printers.* 1861. 8vo, pp. 19. 61632

An Epistle of Caution to Friends in General Relating to the Solemn Affirmation ... [*Philadelphia: Andrew Bradford.* 1722.] Folio, pp. 3. 61633

An Epistle of ... Caution and Counsel, addressed to its Members by the Yearly Meeting of Friends, held in Philadelphia ... 1853 ... . *Philadelphia.* 1853. 8vo, pp. 36. 61634

An Epistle of Tender Caution and Counsel, from the Monthly Meetings of Friends of Philadelphia, affectionately addressed to ... our Religious Society, in the said City. *Philadelphia: Printed by Joseph Crukshank.* [1788.] 12mo, pp. 16. + *Leeds.* 1791. 8vo, pp. 16. 61635

Epistle to the Members of the Yearly Meeting of Friends held in Philadelphia. *Philadelphia: Printed by William K. Bellows.* 1863. 12mo, pp. 12. 61636

Constitution and By-Laws of the EVANGELICAL HOME MISSION SOCIETY of Kensington. *Philadelphia.* 1852. 12mo, pp. 8

Address of the Managers of the Mission Tract and Book Society of the EVANGELICAL LUTHERAN CHURCH OF ST. JOHN. *Philadelphia.* 1851. 12mo, pp. 40. S. 61638

Also: Historical Sketch of the Sunday School of the Evangelical Lutheran Church of St. John ... . *Philadelphia.* 1857. 8vo, pp. 21.

Charter and Fundamental Articles of the EVANGELICAL REFORMED CONGREGATION ... of Philadelphia. *Philadelphia: Printea by Conrad Zentler.* 1810. 8vo, pp. 19. 61639

Evening Schools and District Libraries: An Appeal to Philadelphians, in behalf of Improved Means of Education ... for Apprentices and Young Workmen. *Philadelphia.* 1850. 8vo, pp. 26, (1). 61640

Every Philadelphian's Book. ... *Philadelphia.* 1846. 12mo, pp. (2), xxxvi, (2). 61641

An Exercise; Containing a Dialogue and Two Odes Set to Music, for the Public Commencement, in the College of Philadelphia, May 17th, 1775. *Philadelphia: Printed by Joseph Crukshank.* MDCCLXXV. 8vo, pp. 8. 61642

An Exercise, containing a Dialogue and two Odes Performed at the public Commencement in the College of Philadelphia, May 20th, 1766. *Philadelphia: Printed by W. Dunlap.* M,DCC,LXVI. Sm. 4to, pp. 8. 61643

The *Pennsylvania Journal*, June 5, 1766, says, this was chiefly written by Thomas Hopkinson. *See also* Vol. VI., Nos. 23387–89.

An Exhortation & Caution. *See* Vol. IX., No. 37193.

Experiments and Observations. *See* [Rush (Benjamin)].

Extract of a Letter from several Friends in Philadelphia, to John Fothergill, ... and [others] requesting assistance in a time of scarcity, Philadelphia, 12th month 16, 1777. [n. p.] 1777. 4to, pp. 4. 61644

Extracts from the Minutes of the Yearly Meeting of Friends, held in Philadelphia, ... 1827. *Philadelphia.* 1827. 12mo, pp. 10. Continued. 61645

Fac Simile of the Autographs of the Merchants ... of Philadelphia, as subscribed to the Non-Importation Resolutions, October 25, 1765. [*Philadelphia.* n. d.] Folio, 1 sheet. 61646

Facts and Observations. *See* College of Physicians, No. 61548

Facts for the People. ... Philadelphia, September, 1832. [n. p. n. d.] 8vo, pp. (8). 61647

Facts in relation to the Introduction of Gas Light into ... Philadelphia. With a Plan of a Company ... . [n. p. 1824.] 8vo, pp. 12. 61648

Facts in relation to the ... prospects, of Philadelphia ... . *Philadelphia.* 1838. 8vo. 61649

Acts of Assembly relating to FAIRMOUNT PARK. *Philadelphia.* 1868. 8vo, pp. 19, (1). + [*Ibid.*] 1869. 8vo, pp. 24. 61650

Also: Description of Plan for the Improvement of Fairmount Park, by Sidney & Adams. ... *Philadelphia.* 1859. 8vo, pp. 24. Map.—Extracts from the Report of Committee on Fairmount Park Contribution. [n. p. 1856.] 8vo, pp. 10. Map.—Fairmount Park Contribution. ... *Philadelphia.* 1856. 8vo, pp. 8. Plate. + [*Ibid.*] 1856. 8vo, pp. 36. Map.—Fairmount Park Contribution. Sedgely Park Estate, and its Acceptance by the City ... . *Philadelphia.* 1857. 8vo, pp. 16.—First Annual Report of the Commissioners ... . *Philadelphia.* 1869. 8vo, pp. 56. Map. Continued.—Report. [n. p. 1851.] 8vo, pp. 7.—Report of a Special Committee ... . *Philadelphia.* 1867. 8vo, pp. 24.—Report of the Committee on Plans ... upon the Extension of the Park. *Philadelphia.* 1868. 8vo, pp. 31. Map.—Report of the Joint Committee ... on the Extension of Fairmount Park. ... *Philadelphia.* [1860?] 8vo, pp. (2), 9, (1). Map.—Reports upon the Plan of Re-constructing the Fairmount Dam. [n. p. 1842.] 8vo, pp. 16. *See also* [Keyser (Charles S.)], Vol. IX., No. 37695.

Constitution ... of the FAME HOSE COMPANY ... . Revised ... 1820. ... *Philadelphia: Printed by John Young.* [1828.] 16mo, pp. 28. 61651

Federal Tontine Association. *See* Vol. IV., No. 16092.

Fellow Citizens, and Countrymen. [n. p. 1772.] Folio, 1 l.

An election circular, dated Oct. 1, 1772, recommending Dickinson, Hillegas, Parker, etc., as representatives of the city in the assembly.

The Constitution of the FEMALE ASSOCIATION of Philadelphia, for the Relief of Women ... . *Whitehall: Printed by William Young.* 1801. 8vo, pp. 31, (1). + *Philadelphia.* 1803. 8vo, pp. 32. + *Philadelphia: Printed by William F. Geddes.* 1834. 12mo, pp. 24. 61653

Also: Annual Report of the ... Association ... *Philadelphia.* 1801. 8vo. Continued.

The First Report of the FEMALE BIBLE SOCIETY of Philadelphia. ... *Philadelphia: William Fry, Printer.* 1815. 8vo, pp. 31.

First Annual Report of the ... FEMALE DOMESTIC MISSIONARY SOCIETY ... . *Philadelphia.* [1817.] 8vo, pp. 20. Cont'd.

Articles of Association of the FEMALE HOSPITAL SOCIETY; ... *Philadelphia: ... William Fry, Printer.* 1814. 12mo, pp. 20.

Also: Articles of Association, Act of Incorporation, and ... Transactions of the ... Society ... . *Philadelphia: Printed by Lydia R. Bailey.* 1831. 8vo, pp. (2), 58.

A Few Reasons in favour of Vendues. [*Philadelphia.* 1772.] Folio, 1 leaf. + [*Ibid.* 1775.] Folio, 1 leaf. 61657

Charter of the Trustees of the FIRE ASSOCIATION of Philadelphia. ... *Philadelphia.* 1826. 12mo, pp. 12. + *Philadelphia.* 1833. 12mo, pp. 12. + *Philadelphia.* 1856. 12mo, pp. 34. + *Philadelphia.* 1867. 12mo, pp. 44. 61658

Report of the Chief Engineer of the FIRE DEPARTMENT ... for ... 1855. *Philadelphia.* 1855. 8vo, pp. 14. Continued.

First Annual Report of the FIRE MARSHAL to the Mayor ... *Philadelphia.* 1859. 8vo, pp. 45. Continued. 61660

The Firemen's Songster. *Philadelphia.* [1855.] 16mo, pp. 94, (2). 61661

The running title is "The Philadelphia Firemen's Songster."

The Confession of Faith, and Rules ... of the FIRST FREE CHURCH, Philadelphia. *Philadelphia.* 1840. 12mo, pp. 16.

First Letter to the Citizens of ... Pennsylvania, by the [Democratic] Committee ... of Philadelphia. [n. p. 1834.] 8vo, pp. 6

Contains second and third letters. Also: Fourth Letter. ... [n. p. 1834.] 8vo, pp. 4.

Discipline and Rules of the FIRST MORAVIAN CHURCH, Philadelphia. ... [*Philadelphia.* 1810?] 16mo, pp. 18. + A New and Revised Edition. *Philadelphia.* 1860. 12mo, pp. 23.

Address to the Members of the FIRST PRESBYTERIAN CONGREGATION in Philadelphia. In which is stated the advantages ... by ... remaining ... in High Street: Also the ... disadvantages that attend the destruction of the present building ... . [n. p. 1820.] 8vo, pp. 30. 61665

Also: Address of the First Presbyterian ... Congregation, ... to the Ministers and People of Presbyterian Churches ... . *Philadelphia.* 1836. 8vo, pp. 11.—Historical Notes of the First Presbyterian Church ... . [n. p. n. d.] 12mo, pp. 66.

First Presbyterian Church of Southwark. [n. p. 1828.] 12mo, pp. 3. 61666

Constitution adopted by the FIRST SOCIETY OF UNITARIAN CHRISTIANS, Philadelphia, August 23, 1807; with Observations. *Philadelphia: Bartram & Reynolds.* 1807. 8vo, pp. 24. 61667

See also [Eddowes (Ralph)], Vol. VI., No. 21802, *and* [Searson (John)].

By-Laws, Muster-Roll, and Papers selected from the Archives of the FIRST TROOP Philadelphia City Cavalry, from November 17th, 1774 to September 7th, 1815. *Philadelphia.* 1815. 12mo, pp. 54. + From November 17, 1774, to January 1, 1840. *Philadelphia.* 1840. 8vo, pp. 64. + From November 17, 1774, to March 1, 1856. *Philadelphia.* 1856. 8vo, pp. 82. 61668

The Charter, ... of the FIRST UNIVERSALIST CHURCH. *Philadelphia.* 1842. 16mo, pp. 16. 61669

The following | Address | Was read at a Meeting of the Merchants, at the Lodge, in Philadelphia, on Monday, | the 25th of April, 1768. | [*Philadelphia: W. & T. Bradford.* 1768.] Folio, 1 leaf. 61670

In favor of uniting with the merchants of New York and Boston in a renewal of the non-importation agreement.

The following Remonstrance, was this Day presented to the President and Council, by ... their Secretary. To the President and Council of Pennsylvania. The Remonstrance of Israel Pemberton, John Hunt, and Samuel Pleasants. [n. p.:] *Printed by Robert Bell.* [n. d.] Folio, 1 leaf. 61671

From the imprisoned loyalists, dated 4th. 9th mo. 1777. *See* "To the President and Council" *and* "To the Congress," *infra.*

The Foretokens of the Pestilence and Sickness which befel [*sic*] the Philadelphians, as it was warned to a pious inhabitant of this State, many years ago, and rewarned again some time past. Also, Signs and Tokens of its Awful Approach. To which is added a List of the Daily Burials from the commencement to the conclusion of the Yellow Fever ... . *Philadelphia: Printed ... by Ormroa and Conrad.* [1793?] 12mo, pp. 10, (2). H.S.P. 61672

Franklin Cemetery. [n. p. 1839?] 12mo, pp. 12. 61673

Charter and By-Laws of the FRANKLIN FIRE CO. ... Instituted ... 1792. ... *Philadelphia.* 1865. 32mo, pp. 39. 61674

Act of Incorporation, ... of the FRANKLIN FIRE INSURANCE COMPANY ... . [n. p. 1829.] 8vo, pp. 12. 61675

Also: The Franklin Fire Insurance Company ... . The Public are ... informed, that this Company will make Insurance ... . [n. p. 1829.] 8vo, pp. 8.

Franklin Institute. *See* Vol. VII., Nos. 25654–56.

A Freeholder to the Freeholders, etc., of Philadelphia, Sept. 26, 1770. [n. p. n. d.] Folio, 1 leaf. 61676

The Freeholders, and other Electors ... Are requested to attend ... at the State House. [n. p. 1774.] 4to, 1 leaf. 61677

Notice of a public meeting to choose a committee agreeable to the resolve of Congress.

The Freemen of ... Philadelphia are desired to attend at the State House This Day, at two o'Clock ... to consider of proper Instructions to be given to our Representatives on the present alarming and critical Situation of these Colonies. [n. p. n. d.] Folio, 1 leaf. 61678

Dated "Philadelphia, Saturday, July 30, 1768."

Preamble and Constitution of the FRIENDLY ASSOCIATION for Mutual Interests. *Philadelphia.* 1826. 12mo, pp. 8. 61679

Circular and Catalogue of FRIENDS' SCHOOL, Germantown, Philadelphia. ... [n. p. 1870.] 16mo, pp. 8. 61680

Friends, Countrymen, and Fellow-Electors. [n. p. 1774.] Folio, 1 leaf. 61681

An election address. *See also* Vol. V., No. 20041, *and* Vol. VII., No. 25953.

Bye Laws of the FRIENDSHIP FIRE COMPANY. *Philadelphia: Printed by Zachariah Poulson, Jun.* ... MDCCXCV. 24mo, pp. 12.

From our General Spring Meeting of Ministers and Elders, held at Philadelphia, ... from the 21st of the Third Month to the 24th of the same, inclusive, 1778. To our Friends and Brethren in Religious Profession. [n. p. n. d.] Folio, pp. 2. 61683

From our Yearly-Meeting, Held at Philadelphia, for Pennsylvania and New-Jersey, from the 17th to the 21st Day of the 7th Month, 1737. To the Quarterly and Monthly Meetings. [Colophon:] *Philadelphia: Printed by Andrew Bradford.* 1737. Folio, pp. 3. 61684

Improved title of our No. 26006, Vol. VII.

From our Yearly Meeting held at Philadelphia ... the 22d of the Ninth Month, to the 28th of the same (inclusive) 1759. To the Quarterly and Monthly Meetings of Friends belonging to the said Yearly Meeting. [n. p. n. d.] Folio, pp. 3. 61685

From our Yearly-Meeting, Held in London ... Fifth Month 1768 ... To the ensuing Yearly-Meeting of Friends, for Penn-

sylvania and New-Jersey. [Colophon:] *Philadelphia: Printed by D. Hall and W. Sellers.* [n. d.] Folio, pp. 2. 61686

From the Meeting for Sufferings, In London the 10th Day of the Third Month, 1769. To Friends in ... North America. [n. p. n. d.] Folio, pp. 2. 61687

Page 2 contains an epistle "From our Meeting for Sufferings, held at Philadelphia, ... 1st Day of the Ninth Month, 1769."

From the Merchants and Traders Of Philadelphia, in the Province of Pennsylvania; to the Merchants and Manufacturers Of Great Britain. [n. p. 1766.] Folio. 61688

Reasons, etc., for non-importation.

Constitution of the FUEL SAVINGS SOCIETY of the City and Liberties of Philadelphia, (Instituted May, 1821.) ... *Philadelphia.* 1831. 8vo, pp. 8. + [*Ibid.*] 1838. 12mo, pp. 12. + [*Ibid.*] 1846. 61689

A Full and Complete Account of the late Awful Riots in Philadelphia. ... *Philadelphia: John B. Perry* ... . [1844.] 16mo, pp. 60, (2), 36. 61690

Fundamental Rules and Regulations of the Stockholders in the New Theatre, in ... Philadelphia ... . [n. p.:] *Printed by Thomas Desilver.* 1822. 16mo, pp. 8. 61691

Further Hints, on the expediency of a railroad from Philadelphia to Pittsburg. ... to ... the Legislature of Pennsylvania. [n. p. 1828?] 8vo, pp. 9. 61692

General Organization for the Relief of the Poor. A Plan for the Consolidation of Charities. *Philadelphia.* 1855. 12mo, pp. 12

A General Report in relation to the Market Department, the removal of the Market Street Sheds, and a Railroad on Market Street. ... *Philadelphia.* 1856. 8vo, pp. 32. 61694

The Gentlemen, Merchants and Citizens are requested to meet on Business of Importance, This Eveninig. [n. p. n. d.] 4to, 1 leaf. 61695

Dated May 25, 1778.

A German Freeholder, to his Countrymen. [*Philadelphia: W. Goddard.* 1770.] 4to, 1 leaf. P. 61696

An anti-Galloway election circular. *See also* our Vol. VII., No. 27147.

Charter, ... of the GERMAN REFORMED CONGREGATION, in ... Philadelphia. ... [n. p.] 1847. 12mo, pp. 24. 61697

German Society. *See* Vol. VII., No. 27151.

Constitution and By-Laws of the GERMANTOWN BLUES. *Philadelphia: Printed by S. Roberts.* 1819. 18mo, pp. 11. 61698

See also Vol. VII., Nos. 27153–62.

Rules of the GERMANTOWN CLUB. ... [n. p.] 1864. 16mo, pp. 11. 61699

Girard College. *See* Vol. VII., Nos. 27491–95.

Charter of the GIRARD LIFE INSURANCE, Annuity and Trust Company of Philadelphia; ... *Philadelphia: A. Waldie, printer.* 1836. 8vo, pp. 14. B. 61700

By-Laws of GLENWOOD CEMETERY COMPANY ... . *Philadelphia.* 1849. 8vo, pp. 20. 61701

Constitution and By-Laws of the GOOD INTENT BENEFICIAL SOCIETY, of ... Philadelphia. Instituted 1824. ... *Philadelphia: Printed by Joseph Rakestraw.* 1829. 16mo, pp. 24. 61702

A Grand Chorus. *See* Vol. VII., No. 28258.

A Graphic Account of the Alarming Riots at St. Mary's Church, in April of 1822, together with the most important extracts from the Decisions of Chief Justices Tilghman, Duncan and Gibson, relative to the Charter of said Church, including letters from Hon. J. R. Ingersol & Thomas Kittera, Esq. ... [n. p.] *June,* 1844. 8vo, pp. 16. 61703

Laws of the ... Officers First Regiment, "GRAY RESERVE." Constitution and By-Laws, Company A. ... *Philadelphia.* 1861. 16mo, pp. 38. 61704

Catalogue of Paintings ... Etc. of the Art Department in the GREAT CENTRAL FAIR held in Logan Square, June 1864 ... . *Philadelphia.* [n. d.] 8vo, pp. 30. + Second Edition with Additions ... . [*Ibid.* n. d.] 8vo, pp. 32. 61705

Also: List of the Committees of The Great Central Fair for the U. S. Sanitary Commission. Held in Philadelphia, June, 1864. *Philadelphia: Henry B. Ashmead,* ... *Printer.* [n. d.] 8vo, pp. 55, (1).

The Great Fire. Sworn Testimony of the Witnesses examined ... in reference to the ... Fire at Patterson's Bonded Warehouse. ... *Philadelphia.* 1869. 8vo, pp. 120. 61706

Great Meeting of Irishmen. *See* note to No. 35391, Vol. IX.

Great Public Meeting. Ship Pennsylvania—Navy Yard. [n. p. 1837.] 8vo, pp. 8. P. 61707

Recommending the completion of the "Pennsylvania" and the enlargement of the navy yard.

Great Union Meeting in Philadelphia, ... November, 1851. [n. p. n. d.] 8vo, pp. 7. 61708

Guide to Laurel Hill Cemetery ... . *Philadelphia.* 1854. 12mo, pp. 155, 62. 61709

See also Vol. X., No. 39255.

A Guide to the Lions of Philadelphia ... . A Pocket Cicerone for Strangers. *Philadelphia: Thomas T. Ash and Co.* 1837. 12mo, pp. 96. Map and Illustrations. H. 61710

Guide to the Philadelphia Museum. [*Philadelphia.* 1804.] 8vo. 61711

Guide to the Places of Interest in Philadelphia. ... [n. p. n. d.] 24mo, pp. (2), 29. 61712

Report of the ... Managers of the GURNEY EVENING SCHOOL. *Philadelphia.* 1850. 8vo, pp. 11. 61713

A Hand-Book for the Stranger in Philadelphia. Containing Descriptions of all the objects of interest in the City and its Environs. With Views of the Public Buildings. By a Philadelphian. *Philadelphia: George S. Appleton.* 1846. 24mo, pp. 113. Map. 61714

See also Vol. VIII., No. 30212.

Catalogue of the HANNAH MORE ACADEMY. *Philadelphia.* 1855. 8vo. 61715

Address of the HARMONIA SACRED MUSIC SOCIETY ... with its Constitution and By-Laws. *Philadelphia.* 1852. 8vo, pp. 16

Health Law. An Act for Establishing An Health Office, and to Secure the City and Port of Philadelphia from the Introduction of Pestilential and Contagious Fevers. *Philadelphia: Wm. Duane.* 1806. 8vo, pp. 33. 61717

Report of the First Annual Dinner in aid of the HEBREW CHARITABLE FUND, ... Feb. 23, 1853. ... *Philadelphia.* 1853. 8vo, pp. 39. 61718

Statement and Testimony, ... by the HIBERNIA FIRE COMPANY to the ... Directors of the Fire Department, in Opposition to the Claim of the Hand-in-Hand Fire Company, as to Seniority. ... *Philadelphia: F. Vallee, printer.* 1857. 12mo, pp. 443.

Act of Incorporation, By-Laws, &c. of the HIBERNIAN PROVIDENT SOCIETY, for the Relief of Emigrants from Ireland. *Philadelphia.* 1813. 12mo, pp. 16. 61720

Act of Incorporation, ... &c. of the HIBERNIAN SOCIETY, for the Relief of Emigrants ... . *Philadelphia.* 1845. 8vo, pp. 28, (1). + *Philadelphia.* 1858. 8vo, pp. 31. + *Philadelphia.* 1870. 8vo, pp. 33, (1).

Hints on the Subject of Interments within the City ... Addressed to the serious consideration of the members of Councils, ... and Citizens generally. By Atticus. *Philadelphia: William Brown, Printer.* 1838. 8vo, pp. 22. 61721

Historical Catalogue of the Paintings in the Philadelphia Museum, consisting chiefly of Portraits of Revolutionary Patriots, and other Distinguished Characters, 1813. [n. p. n. d.] 8vo, pp. 56. 61722

A History of Philadelphia. *See* [Bowen (D.)], Vol. II. 7048.

An Account of the Laying of the Corner Stone of the HOLMESBURG PUBLIC SCHOOL, ... 1846 ... . *Philadelphia.* 1846. 8vo, pp. 15. 61723

Constitution, ... and Rules of the HOME FOR AGED and Infirm Colored Persons ... . Also, the Proceedings ... First mo. (January) 12, 1865. ... *Philadelphia.* 1865. 8vo, pp. 16. 61724

First Annual Report of the HOME FOR DESTITUTE Colored Children. ... *Philadelphia.* 1856. 8vo, pp. 16. Continued.

The Hospital of the Protestant Episcopal Church, Philadelphia: ... *Philadelphia.* 1869. 12mo, pp. 47. 8 Plates. 61726

Also: An Account of the Proceedings at the Laying of the Corner-Stone of Hospital of the Protestant Episcopal Church, ... May 24th, ... 1860. *Philadelphia.* 1860. 8vo, pp. 91. 3 Plates and 1 Plan.— ... Report, Charter, &c. *Philadelphia.* 1851. 12mo, pp. 23.—Report of the ... Hospital ... . *Philadelphia.* 1858. 8vo, pp. 35. s.

Report of Committee of the HOUSE OF CORRECTION and Employment, on Plan of Organization and Permanent Operation. ... *Philadelphia.* 1854. 8vo, pp. 26. 61727

Also: Report of the Joint Committee on the Erection of a House of Correction *Philadelphia.* 1861. 8vo, pp. 28. Plate.

The Act Incorporating the HOUSE OF REFUGE, and Laws relative thereto. Together with the Rules and Regulations for its Government, and List of Officers, Managers, &c. *Philadelphia: J. Harding, Printer.* 1829. 8vo, pp. 24, (1). 61728

An Address from the Managers of the House of Refuge, to their Fellow-Citizens. *Philadelphia: Printed ... by D. & S. Neall.* 1826. 8vo, pp. 18. + *Philadelphia: Printed by Solomon W. Conrad.* 1828. 8vo, pp. 8. 61729

Also: By-Laws, Rules and Regulations ... of the House of Refuge. ... *Philadelphia.* 1860. 8vo, pp. 48.—The Design and Advantages of the House of Refuge. ... *Philadelphia.* 1835. 8vo, pp. 20. + 1840. 8vo, pp. 27. + 1850. 8vo, pp. 48. + 1854. 8vo, pp. 48.—The First Annual Report ... . *Philadelphia.* 1829. 8vo, pp. 35. Plate. Continued.—Memorial of the ... Directors ... to the ... Councils ... . *Philadelphia.* 1855. 4to, pp. 19. Plan and 2 Plates.

An Appeal to the Public on behalf of a House of Refuge for Coloured Juvenile Delinquents. *Philadelphia.* 1846. 8vo, pp. 11

This elicited: A Review of a Pamphlet, entitled An Appeal to the Public on behalf of a House of Refuge for Colored Juvenile Delinquents. *Philadelphia: W. H. Brisbane, Printer.* 1847. 12mo, pp. 15.

Constitution and By-Laws of the HUNT FEMALE BENEFICIAL SOCIETY ... Philadelphia. ... *Philadelphia: E. W. Conner, Printer.* 1838. 18mo, pp. 12. 61731

Impositions and Frauds in Philadelphia. By a Citizen. *Philadelphia.* 1837. 8vo, pp. 24. 61732

In Committee Chamber, May 16, 1776. [n. p. n. d.] 4to, 1 leaf. 61733

Recommending "all the Inhabitants of this City to forbear any kind of Insult to Quakers who will not observe the Fast recommended by Congress."

In Committee, December 14, 1774. ... Jonathan B. Smith, Secretary. [n. p. n. d.] 4to, 1 leaf. P. 61734

Resolution of the Committee of the City's Liberties of Philadelphia, in encouragement of sheep-breeding.

In Committee of Inspection and Observation, February 5th. 1776. [n. p. n. d.] 4to, 1 leaf. 61735

"This Committee ... hold up to the World, ... John Drinker, Thomas and Samuel Fisher as Enemies to their Country."

Income Tax of the Residents of Philadelphia and Bucks County. For ... 1865. ... *Philadelphia.* 1865. 8vo, pp. 76.

Income Tax of the Residents of Philadelphia, Income of 1865 and 1866 ... . *Philadelphia.* [n. d.] 8vo, pp. 9–79. 61737

Either a preface or advertisements were withdrawn.

Index to the New Plan of Philadelphia and Adjoining Districts, with References to find the Streets, Public Buildings, etc. *Philadelphia.* 1830. 16mo, pp. 44. 61738

Constitution of "The INDIGENT WIDOWS and Single Women's Society;" with Rules ... . *Philadelphia: Printed by Lydia R. Bailey.* 1828. 8vo, pp. 12. + 1832. 8vo, pp. 12. + 1847. 8vo, pp. 12. 61739

Also: Annual Report for ... 1817 of the ... Society, with ... the Contributors, Managers and Officers. *Philadelphia: Printed ... by S. Merritt.* 1818. 8vo, pp. 22. Continued.

First Report of the INDUSTRIAL HOME for the Instruction of Girls in the Arts of Housewifery ... . *Philadelphia.* 1859. 8vo, pp. 8. Continued. 61740

Constitution of the INFANT SCHOOL SOCIETY of the Northern Liberties ... . *Philadelphia: Printed by D. & S. Neall.* [1828?] 16mo, pp. 8. 61741

Inhabitants of Pennsylvania. [n. p. 1773.] 4to, 1 leaf.

Call for a public meeting to prevent the landing of tea, dated Oct. 13, 1773.

The Institute for Colored Youth. ... *Philadelphia: Ringwalt & Brown.* 18—. 16mo, pp. 19. 61743

Also: Catalogue of the Library ... of the Institute ... . *Philadelphia.* 1853. 12mo, pp. 36.—Objects and Regulations of the Institute ... . *Philadelphia.* 1859. 12mo, pp. 27. Continued.

Constitution ... of the IRVING LIBRARY INSTITUTE, organized ... 1856. *Philadelphia.* 1859. 16mo, pp. 19. 61744

Jackson and the Veto. [n. p. 1832.] Folio, 1 leaf. 61745

The Memorial of the Medical Faculty of JEFFERSON COLLEGE, in reply to the Memorial of the Trustees of the University of Pennsylvania. *Philadelphia: R. Wright, Printer.* 1826. 8vo, pp. 7. 61746

Also: Annual Announcement of Lectures, ... by the Trustees ... of the Jefferson Medical College, Philadelphia: For ... MDCCCXXXII. *Philadelphia.* 1832. 8vo, pp. 16. Continued.—A Catalogue of the Graduates of the ... College ... from ... 1826 to ... 1856 ... . *Philadelphia.* 1856. 8vo, pp. 32.

First Annual Report of the JEWISH FOSTER HOME SOCIETY ... *Philadelphia.* 1856. 8vo. Continued. 61747

Journal of the Common Council of ... Philadelphia, for ... 1835. *Philadelphia.* 1835. 8vo. Continued. 61748

Journal of the Select Council, beginning ... 1835, ending ... 1836. *Philadelphia: Printed by Charles Alexander.* 1836. 8vo, pp. 309. Continued. 61749

A Just and True Account of the Prison of ... Philadelphia; ... By a person who has been an Eye Witness, for a considerable length of time. *Philadelphia:* ... *D. M'Kenzie.* 1820. 12mo, pp. 12. 61750

Just published and now selling, at Bell's Book-Store, ... a Catalogue of a large Collection of new and Old Books, in Arts, Sciences and Entertainment, for Persons of all denominations. ... *Philadelphia: Printed by Robert Bell.* MDCCLXXXIII. 8vo, pp. 88.

Report of the Managers of the KENSINGTON and Penn Township Rail-Road Company, ... January 9th, 1837. *Philadelphia: Joseph & William Kite, Printers.* 1837. 8vo, pp. 17. Map.

First Annual Report of the LADIES' AID SOCIETY of Philadelphia. *Philadelphia.* [1861.] 8vo, pp. 15. Continued.

The Second Annual Report of the LADIES' ASSOCIATION, auxiliary to the American Colonization Society. ... *Philadelphia.* 1834. 8vo, pp. 16. 61754

First Report of the LADIES' ASSOCIATION FOR SOLDIERS' RELIEF. *Philadelphia.* 1863. 8vo, pp. 26. B. 61755

First Annual Report of the LADIES' CHINESE ASSOCIATION of Philadelphia. *Philadelphia.* 1845. 8vo, pp. 12. Continued.

The First Annual Report of the Managers of the LADIES' DEPOSITORY; with ... the Officers and Managers ... . *Philadelphia.* 1834. 8vo, pp. 11. 61757

The Monument to Bishop White. The Twentieth Annual Report of the LADIES' MISSIONARY ASSOCIATION of Christ Church ... . 1850. [n. p. n. d.] 8vo, pp. 15. 61758

The only printed report of this association.

Ladies Philadelphia Shopping Guide & Housekeeper's Companion. *Philadelphia.* 1859. 16mo, pp. xi, (1), 119. 61759

Ninth Annual Report of the LADIES' UNION CITY MISSION, ... [n. p.] 1856. 12mo, pp. 23. Continued. 61760

Third Annual Report of the LADIES' UNITED AID SOCIETY of the Methodist Episcopal Church in ... Philadelphia, ... for ... 1869–'70. ... *Philadelphia*. 1870. 8vo, pp. (2), 32. Continued.

Constitution of the LANSDOWN LAND COMPANY. ... [n. p. 1855.] 8vo, pp. 8. Map. 61762

The Latter Part of the Charge Delivered from the Bench to the Grand Inquest, at a Court of Oyer and Terminer and Gaol Delivery ... at Philadelphia, the 24th day of September, 1733 ... [*Philadelphia*. 1733.] Folio, pp. 3. H.S.P. 61763

By James Logan. Very rare. Printed either by Andrew Bradford or Benjamin Franklin, probably the former.

Rules and Regulations of the LAUREL HILL CEMETERY, near Philadelphia; together with a List of Lot-Holders, to November, 1864. *Philadelphia*. 1865. 8vo, pp. 43, 37, (1). 61764

See also Vol. x., No. 39255, *note*.

Charter, Constitution and By-Laws of the LAW ACADEMY of Philadelphia. *Philadelphia*. MDCCCXLVII. 8vo, pp. 44. + 1848. 8vo, pp. 29. + 1858. 8vo, pp. 40. + 1867. 8vo, pp. 43, (2).

Also: Constitution and By-Laws of the Law Academy ... . *Philadelphia: Thomas H. Palmer*. 1822. 12mo, pp. 16. + *Philadelphia: Mifflin & Parry, Printers*. 1827. 12mo, pp. 14, (2).

A Catalogue of Books belonging to the LAW ASSOCIATION, to which are added the Charter, Regulations, and a List of Members. [n. p. 1828.] 8vo, pp. 40. + *Philadelphia*. 1846. 8vo, pp. 53. + 1849. 8vo, pp. 64. + 1857. 8vo, pp. 74. + 1861. 8vo, pp. viii, 113. 61766

Also: Charter of 1849. [n. p. n. d.] 8vo, pp. 9. — . . Proceedings at the Annual Meeting, ... 1842. [n. p. 1843.] 8vo, pp. 8.

The Constitution and Bye-Laws of the LAW INSTITUTE. *Philadelphia: Printed by Thomas Kite & Co.* 1833. 12mo, pp. 8.

Catalogue of the Books belonging to the LAW LIBRARY COMPANY ... . [n. p.:] *Printed by James Humphreys*. 1805. 12mo, pp. (24). + [n. p.:] *Printed by J. Maxwell*. 1811. 12mo, pp. 35

The Laws relating to the Relief and Employment of the Poor ... of Philadelphia ... . *Philadelphia: ... William Brown, Printer*. 1835. 8vo, pp. 72, x. 61769

Laws relative to the Board of Wardens ... of Philadelphia, and the Regulation of Pilots and Pilotages ... . *Philadelphia*. 1848. 8vo, pp. 87, (1). 61770

Rules for the ... LAZARETTO of ... Philadelphia. [n. p.] 1833. 8vo, pp. 7. 61771

Leaves from a Century Plant. Report of the Centennial Celebration of Old Pine Street Church, ... May 29, 1868. Edited by Rev. R. H. Allen, Pastor. *Philadelphia: Henry B. Ashmead*. 1870. 12mo, pp. 215, (1). 12 Plates. 61772

Lemon Hill. *See* [Keyser (C. S.)], Vol. IX., No. 37696.

A Letter from a Gentleman in England to his Friend in Philadelphia, giving him his Opinion of the College in that City. *Philadelphia: Printed by Andrew Steuart*. 1762. 8vo. 61773

Improved title of our Vol. x., No. 40285.

A Letter From a Gentleman in Philadelphia to his Friend in Bucks. [*Philadelphia: Andrew Bradford*. 1728.] Folio, pp. 4.

A Letter From a Gentleman in Philadelphia, to a Freeholder in the County of Northampton. [n. p. 1757.] Folio, pp. 2.

A Letter From a Gentleman travelling through Bucks County, to his Friend in Town. [n. p. 1770.] Folio, 1 leaf. 61776

See also our Vol. x., No. 40297.

A Letter From one in the Country to his Friend in the City, On Occasion of the Law of Summons. [Colophon:] *Philadelphia: Printed and Sold by S. Keimer*. [1723.] Folio, pp. 3.

A Letter to Certain Bank Directors from a Merchant ... *Philadelphia: The Author*. 1796. 8vo, pp. 23. P. 61778

A Letter to John Jones ... [and others] on ... the Right and Power of ... Philadelphia to subscribe for Stock in the Pennsylvania Railroad Company. By John Doe, Esq. *Philadelphia*. 1846. 8vo, pp. 8. 61779

Letter to the Directors of the Bank of Philadelphia on the Curtailment of Discounts and the Effects of the Organization of the Bank of the United States. *Philadelphia*. 1816. 8vo.

The Letters of Junius [Wm. R. Dickerson]; exposing to the Public, ... the mal-practices on the administration of the Law, the corruption in the Offices in the State House row, in ... Philadelphia ... . Written by an Experienced Member of the Philada. Bar. *Philadelphia*. 1848. 8vo, pp. 48. 61781

Letters on the Condition of the Poor: ... Instances of Intense Suffering in Philadelphia ... . By a Citizen of Philadelphia. Second Edition ... . *Philadelphia: Printed by Haswell & Barrington*. 1835. 8vo, pp. 20. 61782

Letters, To the Merchants Committee of Philadelphia, Submitted to the Consideration of The Public. [n. p. n. d.] Folio, 1 leaf. 61783

In favor of non-importation.

A | Catalogue | of | Books | belonging to the | LIBRARY COMPANY | of Philadelphia. | ... | *Philadelphia: Printed by B. Franklin*, 1741. Sm. 8vo, pp. 55, (1). P. 61784

A Catalogue of the Books, belonging to the Library Company ... to which is prefixed a Short Account of the Institution, with the Charter, Laws and Regulations. *Philadelphia: Printed by Zachariah Poulson, Junior*. MDCCLXXXIX. 8vo, pp. xl, 406, (2). + *Philadelphia*. MDCCXCIII. 8vo, pp. 406. + Supplement ... . [*Ibid.*] 8vo, pp. 38. + *Philadelphia*. 1799. 8vo, pp. 471. + *Philadelphia: Printed by Bartram & Reynolds*. 1807. 8vo, pp. xl, 616. + *Philadelphia: C. Sherman & Co., Printers*. 1835–56. 3 vols., 8vo, pp. xxxix, 2104. 61785

Also various supplements.

The | Charter | of the | Library Company | of | Philadelphia. | *Philadelphia: | Printed by B. Franklin*, M,DCCXLVI. | 8vo, pp. 8.

This library was the first chartered in the United States, and the second established. The Redwood Library, Newport, R. I., was established one year earlier (1730), but was not chartered until five years later (1747).

Books | Added to the | Library | since the Year 1741. [n. p. n. d.] 12mo, pp. 22, Rules, (4). 61787

The Charter, Laws, and Catalogue of Books of the Library Company ... . *Philadelphia: Printed by B. Franklin and D. Hall*. MDCCLVII. 8vo, pp. 23, 132. + [*Ibid.*] M,DCC,LXIV. 4to, pp. 26, 150. + With a Short Account of the Library prefixed. ... *Philadelphia: Printed by Joseph Crukshank*. M,DCC,LXX. 8vo, pp. 38, (316). + The Second Part of the Catalogue ... . *Philadelphia: Printed by R. Aitken*. M,DCC,LXXV. 8vo, pp. 67. 61788

Also: Laws of the Library Company of Philadelphia, made in Pursuance of their Charter, At a General Meeting, held in the Library, on the Third Day of May, 1742. *Philadelphia: Printed by B. Franklin*. M,DCC,XLVI. 8vo, pp. 15. — Many Members of the Library Company of Philadelphia ... . [n. p. 1771.] Folio, 1 leaf. Concerning a hall for the company. — Notes for a History of the Library Company ... . [n. p. 1835.] 8vo, pp. 8. — The Original Articles of Association of the Library Company

... Now first printed: together with the Charter, etc. etc. *Philadelphia*. 1869. 8vo, pp. 20.

Constitution and By-Laws of the LIGHT ARTILLERY CORPS of Washington Grays. *Philadelphia*. 1828. 12mo, pp. 12.

Charter and By-Laws of the LINCOLN INSTITUTION. ... *Philadelphia*. 1870. 16mo, pp. 24. 61790

Also: First Annual Report of the Managers of the "Lincoln Institution." ... *Philadelphia*. 1867. 12mo, pp. 20.

List of Committees held in Philadelphia, June, 1864. *Philadelphia: Henry B. Ashmead*. [1864.] 8vo, pp. 56. 61791

A List of some of the Benevolent Institutions of ... Philadelphia, and their Legal Titles ... . *Philadelphia*. 1859. 8vo, pp. 36

A List of Streets, Roads, Lanes, Alleys, &c.; with References to the Plan of Philadelphia. *Philadelphia*. 1824. 16mo. M.

List of the Sub-Committees appointed by the Committee for the city and liberties of Philadelphia, to superintend the several districts of said city, &c. [n. p. 1776.] Folio, 1 leaf. 61794

Signed "Jonathan B. Smith, Secretary," and dated Feb. 26. 1776.

The Little Wanderer. Published at the Home for Little Wanderers, ... Philadelphia. [n. p.] 1867. 8vo, pp. 24. Continued. 61795

Report of the Committee on the LOGAN EVENING SCHOOL for Young Men ... 1849–50. *Philadelphia*. 1850. 8vo, pp. 13.

Catalogus | BIBLIOTHECA LOGANIAE: | Being | A choice Collection of Books, | as well in the Oriental, Greek and | Latin, as in the English, Italian, | Spanish, French and other Lan- | guages. | Given by the late | James Logan, Esq; | Of Philadelphia for the Use of the Publick. | ... | *Philadelphia, Printed by Peter Miller & Comp.* | *in the Year* 1760. 8vo, pp. (2), 116. 61797

Catalogue of the Books belonging to the Loganian Library; to which is prefixed a Short Account of the Institution, with the Law for annexing the said Library to that belonging to "The Library Company of Philadelphia" ... . *Philadelphia: Printed by Zachariah Poulson, Junior*. MDCCXCV. 8vo, pp. 220. + *Philadelphia: J. Dobson*. 1828. 8vo, pp. 245. + *Philadelphia: C. Sherman and Co., Printers*. 1837. 8vo, pp. xvi, 450. + First Supplement. ... *Philadelphia: Collins, Printer*. 1867. 8vo, pp. xxiii, (2), 32. 61798

Charter and By-Laws of the MACHPELAH CEMETERY ... of Philadelphia. Instituted in 1830. ... *Philadelphia*. 1832. 16mo, pp. 14. 61799

Report of the Managers of the MAGDALEN ASYLUM, for ... 1835. *Philadelphia*. 1836. 8vo. Continued. B. 61800

An Act incorporating the MAGDALEN SOCIETY ... . *Philadelphia*. 1802. 12mo, pp. 12. + [*Ibid.*] 1808. 12mo, pp. 12.

Also: The Constitution of the Magdalen Society ... . *Philadelphia*. 1800. 8vo, pp. 11. + [*Ibid.*] 1809. 8vo, pp. 7. — To the Members of the Magdalen Society. [n. p. 1818?] 8vo, pp. 4.

Manual for Councils, containing a list of the Officers and Members of the ... Councils of ... Philadelphia, with the Rules ... *Philadelphia: King & Baird, Printers*. 1859. 16mo, pp. (18), 171. Continued. 61802

Manual of Court Forms, containing the Forms most in use In the Supreme Court, District Court, Court of Common Pleas, Courts of Quarter Sessions and Mayor's Court. *Philadelphia: Printed ... A. Walker, Agt.* 1828. 8vo, pp. xii, 7–248. 61803

Manufacturers of Philadelphia. Census of 1860. *Philadelphia*. 1861. 4to, pp. 21. 61804

The Mariner's Church, Philadelphia. *Philadelphia*. 1824. 8vo, pp. 8. + *New York*. 1824. 8vo, pp. 24. + *Philadelphia*. 1826. 8vo, pp. 24. 61805

Also: Report of the Proceedings of the Seventh Year of the Mariners' Church in ... Philadelphia ... . *Philadelphia: Printed by J. W. Allen*. 1826. 8vo, pp. 17. Continued. — Statement Read at the Anniversary of the Opening of the Mariners' Church, October 16th, 1825. [n. p. n. d.] 8vo. Continued as "Report of ... the Mariners' Church."

First Semi-Annual Report of the MARSHAL OF POLICE, to the Board of Police ... . *Philadelphia*. 1851. 12mo, pp. 12.

May 29. 1773. To the Freemen, Citizens of Philadelphia. [n. p. 1773.] Folio, 1 leaf. 61807

"A Philadelphian" in support of the project to erect market sheds in Market St.

The Mayor. [n. p. 1836?] 8vo, pp. 4. 61808

Election address on the conduct of Mayor Swift.

Constitution and By-Laws of the MEDICAL COLLEGE of Philadelphia. *Philadelphia: Printed by J. Thompson*. 1836. 8vo, pp. 19. + [n. p.] 1840. 8vo, pp. 24. 61809

Report of the Committee of the MEDICAL SOCIETY of Philadelphia, on Epidemic Cholera ... . *Philadelphia: Printed by Lydia R. Bailey*. 1832. 8vo, pp. 17, (1). 61810

See also Philadelphia Medical Society, *infra*.

Constitution and By-Laws of the MEDICO-CHIRURGICAL COLLEGE, of Philadelphia. ... *Philadelphia*. 1849. 12mo, pp. 12.

Members of the Common Council of ... Philadelphia, 1704 to 1776. *Philadelphia*. 1847. 8vo. 61812

Memoirs and Auto-Biography of some of the Wealthy Citizens of Philadelphia ... . With an Appendix: Containing particular accounts of the Lives of Stephen Girard, Jacob Ridgway and Obed Coleman ... . By a Merchant of Philadelphia. *Philadelphia*. 1846. 8vo, pp. 80. 61813

Memorial and Resolutions of Citizens of Philadelphia ... . Against a Further Increase of Duties on Imported Manufactures, ... *Washington: Printed by Gales & Seaton*. 1828. 8vo, pp. 15.

Memorial and Statement of the Philadelphia Bar, in relation to the Salaries of the Judges and the business of the Courts of ... Philadelphia. *Philadelphia: King and Baird*. 1859. 8vo, pp. 22. 61815

Memorial of Inhabitants of Philadelphia, praying that the Baltimore and Ohio Rail Road Company may not be permitted to Import Iron Free of Duty. ... *Washington: Gales & Seaton*. 1828. 8vo, pp. 6. 61816

Memorial ... in Relation to the Delaware Avenue. [n. p. 1833.] 8vo, pp. 25. 61817

The Memorial of ... Citizens ... of Philadelphia [to Congress in favor of protective duties. Second Edition.] [n. p. 1827.] 12mo, pp. 12. 61818

Memorial of Richard A. Gilpin, relative to the construction of a Tunnel under the River Schuylkill: ... to the ... Councils ... of Philadelphia. [n. p. 1836.] 8vo, pp. 12. 61819

Memorial of Sundry Citizens of ... Philadelphia. ... *Washington: Gales & Seaton*. 1824. 8vo. 61820

Memorial of Sundry Citizens of Philadelphia, praying to be protected from the injurious operation of the Auction System, &c. [n. p. 1828.] 8vo, pp. 2. 61821

Memorial of Sundry Manufacturers of Hats, in ... Philadelphia. [*Washington*. 1806.] 8vo. 61822

Relates to the Indian fur trade, etc.

Memorial of sundry Umbrella-Makers of Philadelphia, praying that protection may be extended to the Manufacture of Cotton Umbrellas. ... *Washington: Duff Green*. 1828. 8vo, pp. 3.

Memorial of the American Philosophical Society, and of the Historical Society of Philadelphia, recommending the publication of certain ancient records; and the Report of a Committee of the House of Representatives, upon the same subject. ... *Harrisburg: Samuel D. Patterson*. 1836. 8vo, pp. 8. 61824

Memorial of the Auctioneers of Philadelphia. To ... Congress ... [against legislative interference.] [n. p. 1824.] 8vo, pp. 16. 61825

Memorial of the Commissioners of ... Philadelphia to the Legislature upon ... the Laws Exempting certain Property from Taxation ... . Prepared ... by Elihu D. Tarr ... . *Philadelphia*. 1851. 8vo, pp. 51. 61826

Memorial of the Manufacturers of Hardware, ... of ... Philadelphia. ... *Washington*. 1828. 8vo, pp. 8. 61827

Memorial of the Merchants and Traders of ... Philadelphia. January 16, 1806. ... *Washington: A. & G. Way*. 1806. 8vo, pp. 12. 61828

Memorial of the Owners ... of Wharf Property on the River Delaware, within the Limits of ... Philadelphia, to the ... Councils ... in relation to the Delaware Avenue. [n. p. n. d.] 8vo, pp. 25. 61829

Memorial of the Subscribers ... Philadelphia, Mechanics employed in the Manufacture of Iron ... to Congress. [n. p. 1830?] 8vo, pp. 4. S. 61830

The Memorial of 30,000 Disfranchised Citizens of Philadelphia. To the Senate and House of Representatives. *Philadelphia*. 1855. 8vo. 61831

Memorial passed at a meeting of Certain Manufacturers of Philadelphia, and others ... in favor of an Increase of Duties on Imports ... . *Washington: Duff Green*. 1828. 8vo, pp. 4.

Memorial to the Legislature of ... Pennsylvania, Against the Navy Yard, Broad Street and Fairmount Rail Road Company, ... *Philadelphia*. 1863. 8vo, pp. (2), 79. 61833

Memorial. To the Senate and House of Representatives of ... Pennsylvania [in favor of consolidation]. [n. p. 1850.] 8vo, pp. 18. 61834

Memorials concerning Deceased Friends. *See* Vol. XII. 47737

Rules and Regulations of the MERCANTILE CLUB. *Philadelphia*. 1858. Sq. 16mo, pp. 15. 61835

Catalogue of the MERCANTILE LIBRARY COMPANY of Philadelphia. *Philadelphia*. 1850. 8vo. + [*Ibid.*] 1856. 8vo. + [*Ibid.*] 1870. 8vo, pp. (8), 707. 61836

Also: Annual Report of the Mercantile Library Company ... . *Philadelphia*. 1824. 8vo. Continued. — An Essay on the History and Growth of the Mercantile Library Company ... and on its Capabilities for future usefulness. *Philadelphia*. 1867. 8vo. — Historical Sketch of the Mercantile Library Company ... with the Charter, By-Laws and Regulations. *Philadelphia*. 1850. 8vo, pp. 24.

The Mercantile Register, or Business Man's Guide. Containing a list of the Principal Business Establishments, including Hotels and Public Institutions in Philadelphia. [n. p.] 1846. 8vo, pp. 284. 61837

The Merchants of this City are earnestly requested ... . Saturday, February 4, 1769. [n. p. n. d.] Folio, 1 leaf. P. 61838

A call for a meeting, which appears to have been to further the growth of wool in America.

Message of Robert T. Conrad, Mayor of ... Philadelphia, with ... Documents. ... *Philadelphia: Crissy & Markley*. 1855. 8vo, pp. 120. Continued. 61839

A Minority Report of a Select Committee, appointed to examine the Accounts of the District of Kensington. ... Sept. 7th, 1852. *Philadelphia: King & Baird*. 1852. 8vo, pp. (2), 8.

Minority Report of the Finance Committee. To the ... Councils: [n. p. 1850.] 8vo, pp. 4. 61841

Minority Report of the Select Committee, on the ... Consolidation of ... Philadelphia, with enlarged boundaries. [n. p. 1851.] 8vo, pp. 32. 61842

Minutes of the Proceedings of the Committee, Appointed on the 14th September, 1793, by the Citizens of Philadelphia, the

Northern Liberties and the District of Southwark, to attend to and alleviate the sufferings of the afflicted with the Malignant Fever, prevalent in the city and its vicinity. With an Appendix. *Philadelphia: Printed by R. Aitken & Son* ... . M.DCC.XCIV. 8vo, pp. (2), 223. + Printed by order of the ... Council of the City. *Philadelphia.* 1848. 8vo, pp. 243, List of Interments, 1 folded leaf. c. 61843

An improved title of our No. 49378, Vol. XII.

The Missionaries and the State of Georgia. Address of the Democratic Committee of ... Philadelphia. [n. p. 1832.] 8vo, pp. 4. 61844

A modest Reply to the Speech of Isaac Norris, Esq; delivered from the Bench in the Court of Common Pleas, held for the City and County of Philadelphia, the 11th Day of September, 1727, and afterwards Printed. [n. p.: *Printed by Andrew Bradford?* 1727.] Folio, pp. 4. 61845

Act of Incorporation, By-Laws, Rules and Regulations, Officers and Members, of the MONUMENT CEMETERY of Philadelphia. *Philadelphia.* 1838. 8vo, pp. 18. 61846

See also Vol. XII., No. 50234. Also: Articles of Association of the Monument Cemetery ... . *Philadelphia.* 1837. 12mo, pp. 20.—Communications and Reports, relative to the Affairs of the Monument Cemetery ... published at the request of Lot Holders, January, 1847. *Philadelphia.* [1847.] 8vo, pp. 20. Continued.—Monument Cemetery. By-Laws of the ... Managers for 1838–9. [n. p. n. d.] 8vo, pp. 4. Continued.—The Monument Cemetery of Philadelphia. (Late Pere La Chaise.) Containing several Scientific Essays on the subject of Rural Cemeteries ... . *Philadelphia.* 1837. 8vo, pp. 38. Map.

A Report upon the Property of the MOUNT LEBANON CEMETERY COMPANY. *Philadelphia.* 1858. 8vo, pp. 4. Map.

The Charter, By-Laws and Regulations of the MOUNT MORIAH CEMETERY ASSOCIATION. ... March, 1855. *Philadelphia.* [1855.] 8vo, pp. 16. 61848

Also: [Prospectus] Mount Moriah Cemetery. [n. p. n. d.] 12mo, pp. 12.

By-Laws ... of the MOUNT VERNON CEMETERY COMPANY, at Laurel Hill in ... Philadelphia; and the Act of Incorporation ... in 1856. *Philadelphia.* 1864. 8vo, pp. 20. Folded Plan. + 1873. 8vo, pp. 30. Folded Plan. 61849

Constitution of the MOUNT ZION TABERNACLE, No. 3 ... . *Philadelphia.* 1859. 12mo, pp. 12. 61850

First Annual Report of the MOYAMENSING UNION SCHOOL, and Children's Home. ... *Philadelphia: Wm. F. Geddes.* 1850. 8vo, pp. 16. 61851

Municipal Subscriptions made by the City ... and the ... Districts of Spring Garden, Richmond, and the Northern Liberties, in the County of Philadelphia, to the Capital Stock of the North Pennsylvania Rail Road Company. *Philadelphia.* 1854. 8vo, pp. 40. 61852

Constitution of the MUSICAL FUND SOCIETY of Philadelphia. Established February 29, 1820. *Philadelphia: Printed by Thomas H. Palmer.* 1822. 12mo, pp. 33. 61853

Also: Act of Incorporation, By-Laws, and Orchestral Regulations of the Musical Fund Society ... . *Philadelphia: Printed by Jesper Harding.* 1826. 12mo, pp. 23. + 1831. 12mo, pp. 21. + 1835. 12mo, pp. 21. + 1846. 12mo, pp. 22. + 1849. 12mo, pp. 20.—Report of the Joint Board of Officers to the Musical Fund Society of Philadelphia, at the ... Meeting, May 6, 1856. ... To which is prefixed a brief account of the History, Objects and Condition of the Society: ... *Philadelphia.* 1856. 12mo, pp. 10, (1).

The Deed of Settlement of the MUTUAL ASSURANCE COMPANY, for Insuring Houses from Losses by Fire, in ... Philadelphia. ... *Philadelphia: Printed by William W. Woodward.* 1801. 12mo, pp. 12. + *Philadelphia: Printed by W. Fry.* 1818. 8vo, pp. 15. + *Philadelphia: F. & R. Bailey.* [n. d.] 4to, pp. 8.

Names and Residences of the Directors of Public Schools of ... Philadelphia. 1854. *Philadelphia.* 1854. 8vo, pp. 15.

Address of the NATIONAL CONVENTION of Business Men ... Philadelphia, ... Nov. 15, 1837 ... . *Philadelphia.* 1837. 8vo, pp. 6. 61856

Also: Proceedings of the ... Convention ... . *Philadelphia.* 1837. 8vo, pp. 16.

Proceedings of the NATIONAL CONVENTION of the Soldiers of the War of 1812, held ... in ... Philadelphia, ... 1854. *Philadelphia: Brown's ... Printing Office,* 1854. 8vo, pp. 32. 61857

Articles of Association and Constitution of the NATIONAL UNION CLUB of ... Philadelphia. *Philadelphia: King & Baird.* 1863. 12mo, pp. 12. 61858

Rules for the Government of the NATIONAL UNION PARTY of Philadelphia. *Philadelphia.* 1863. 8vo, pp. 16. 61859

Resolutions adopted by the NATIVE AMERICAN ASSOCIATION of Unincorporated N. Liberties. [n. p. 1845?] 8vo, pp. 4.

Constitution and By-Laws of the NATIVE AMERICAN HALL Co. of Cedar Ward, A.D. 1845. *Philadelphia: Charles Brigham.* 1849. 18mo, pp. 12. 61861

Native American Party. [n. p. 1845.] 8vo, 1 leaf. 61862

Anti-Native American circular.

A New Guide to the Public Buildings ... of Philadelphia, and adjoining District: ... *Philadelphia: H. Tanner, Jun'r.* 1840. 24mo, pp. 36. Map. 61863

A New Picture of Philadelphia, or the Stranger's Guide ... . By H. S. Tanner. Second Edition. *Philadelphia: H. Tanner, Jun'r.* ... 1841. 16mo, pp. 156. Map. 61864

First Report of the NEWSBOYS' AID SOCIETY. *Philadelphia.* 1859. 16mo, pp. 16. 61865

Continued until changed in 1862 to: Fourth Annual Report of the Young Men's Home ... . [n. p. 1862.] 16mo, pp. 16.

No Person whatever is to presume to remove any Merchandise or Goods of any Kind out of the City, without ... obtaining Leave ... [n. p. 1777.] 4to, 1 leaf. 61866

Dated October 1, 1777.

No. 1. Philadelphia, June 10th, 1773. *See* Marvell (A.), Vol. XI., Nos. 45021–221.

Annual Report of the Principal of the NORMAL SCHOOL ... 1850. *Philadelphia.* 1850. 8vo, pp. 32. Continued. 61867

Charter of "The NORTH PHILADELPHIA PLANK ROAD Co." ... *Philadelphia: Evans, Printer.* 1858. 8vo, pp. 22. 61868

Act of Incorporation ... of the NORTHERN DISPENSARY for the ... Poor ... . *Philadelphia.* 1841. 12mo, pp. 16. 61869

Also: Rules, ... of the Northern Dispensary ... . With ... the Annual Report, for 1839. [n. p. 1840.] 12mo, pp. 35.

First Annual Report of the NORTHERN HOME for Friendless Children. ... *Philadelphia.* 1854. 8vo, pp. 32. Continued.

Also: Constitution ... of the Northern Home for Friendless Children. *Philadelphia: William S. Young, Printer.* 1854. 16mo, pp. 20.

Constitution, ... of the NORTHERN MEDICAL ASSOCIATION of Philadelphia. ... *Philadelphia: Thompson, Printer.* 1847. 16mo, pp. 16. 61871

Plan and Charter of the NORTHWOOD CEMETERY COMPANY, ... *Philadelphia.* 1868. 8vo, pp. (2), 6. Map. 61872

Nosum Nosorum: or, A New Treatise on Large Noses. *Philadelphia: Printed [by Andrew Steuart] for the Society of Noses.* M.DCC.LXII. Sm. 8vo, pp. 8. 61873

A satire on the Presbyterians and Quakers.

Notice Is hereby Given To the Merchants, Adventurers, and Masters of Vessels that a Report of their Cargoes is to be made to the Quarter-Master-General ... before they land any Part of it ... *Philadelphia: Printed by James Humphreys, junr.* [1777.] 4to, 1 leaf. 61874

Notice of a Committee Meeting at Carpenter's Hall. Philadelphia, 23 August, 1774. [n. p. n. d.] Folio, 1 leaf. 61875

Notice of a Committee Meeting at Philosophcal Hall. Philadelphia, Sept. 23, 1774. [n. p. n. d.] Folio, 1 leaf.—Notice of a Public Meeting, Philadelphia, Dec. 27, 1773, on occasion of the Arrival of the Tea Ship. [n. p. n. d.] Folio, 1 leaf.

A Number of the Inhabitants of this City, desirous of encouraging the Poor ... . [n. p. n. d.] Folio, pp. (2). P. 61876

Proposals for a linen factory at Philadelphia, about December 12, 1765.

Charter, Constitution and By-Laws of the NUMISMATIC and Antiquarian Society of Philadelphia. ... *Philadelphia.* 1865. 8vo, pp. 16. 61877

Also: Proceedings of the Numismatic and Antiquarian Society ... from ... 1865, to ... 1866. *Philadelphia.* 1867. 8vo, pp. 160.

Constitution and By-Laws of the NUMISMATIC SOCIETY of Philadelphia. ... *Philadelphia.* 1858. 12mo, pp. 11. 61878

Second Annual Report of the NURSE CHARITY ... . *Philadelphia: L. R. Bailey.* 1840. 12mo, pp. 12. Continued. 61879

Objections to the Approval by the City Councils of the Charter of the Central Passenger Railroad Company authorizing the Construction of a Railway on Chestnut and Walnut Streets, in ... Philadelphia. *Philadelphia: Jackson, Printer.* 1858. 8vo, pp. 21. 61880

Observations on the late Law for regulating the Nightly Watch, fixing Lamps, and taking care of the Pumps, in the City of Philadelphia—humbly offered to the Consideration of the Inhabitants of the said City. ... [n. p. n. d.] Folio, 1 leaf. P.

Dated Philadelphia, January 10, 1771. *See* Remarks *and* To the Citizens, *infra.*

Act of Incorporation, By-Laws, Rules and Regulations of the ODD FELLOWS' CEMETERY COMPANY of Philadelphia; ... *Philadelphia: Printed by John Boyle.* 1850. 8vo, pp. 40. Plan and Woodcut. 61882

Official Proceedings of a Town Meeting ... in relation to the establishment of a Dry Dock, and the Defences of the Delaware River; containing the speech of Col. James Page, resolutions passed by the Meeting ... . *Philadelphia: Printed by Florence & Severns.* 1846. 8vo, pp. 11. 61883

Annual Report of the Managers of the OLD MAN'S HOME, ... *Philadelphia.* 1866. 12mo, pp. 16. Continued. 61884

Old Pine Street Church. Manual of the Third Presbyterian Church, in ... Philadelphia. *Philadelphia: William F. Geddes.* 1859. 8vo, pp. 64. Plate. 61885

Report of the Centennial Celebration of Old Pine Street Church, Philadelphia, May 29th, 1868. *Philadelphia.* 1870. 8vo. Portrait and Plates. 61886

On Monday, the Twenty-sixth Instant, at the Theatre in Southwark ... . [n. p. n. d.] Folio, 1 leaf. P. 61887

Notice of dramatic performances by the British officers at Philadelphia, in January, 1778. Printed by J. Humphreys. *See also* Nos. 57271–74, *supra.*

On the Prisons. *See* [La Rochefoucauld-Liancourt], Vol. X.

Charter and Prospectus of the OPERA HOUSE, or American Academy of Music. *Philadelphia.* 1852. 8vo, pp. 16. 61888

Also: History and Description of the Opera House or American Academy of Music, ... Designed ... by N. Le Brun and G. Runge ... . *Philadelphia: G. André & Co.* ... [1857.] 8vo, pp. 20.

Opinion of Counsel on the Liabilities of ... Philadelphia to the Schuylkill Navigation Company ... in ... 1869. *Philadelphia.* 1869. 8vo, pp. 14. 61889

Opinion of Council on the Right of the Schuylkill Navigation Company to make Another Lock and Canal for the use of the Navigation at the Fair Mount Dam. *Philadelphia: Printed by James Kay, Jun. & Co.* 1833. 8vo, pp. 34.

Opinion of Horace Binney, Esq. upon the Right of the City Councils to Subscribe for Stock in the Pennsylvania Rail-Road Company. July, 1846. *Philadelphia: C. Sherman, Printer.* 1846. 8vo, pp. 32. 61890

Opinion of John M. Read, Esquire, against the Right of the City Councils to Subscribe for Stock in the Pennsylvania Railroad Company, and to Increase the City Debt and Taxes for that purpose. *Philadelphia.* 1846. 8vo, pp. 30. 61891

Opinions of Messrs. Eli K. Price, Wm. M. Meredith, and Wm. L. Hirst, Relative to the Liability of the City ... for the amount of bill for Publishing the List of Non Tax-Payers for ... 1854. [n. p. n. d.] 8vo, pp. 16. 61892

Order of Service to be performed at the Consecration of the Synagogue Beth Israel, ... Philadelphia, ... Nissan the 6th, corresponding with March 29th, 5609. *New York: Printed by J. M. Jackson.* [1849.] 12mo, pp. (24). 61893

Order of Service at the Consecration of the Synagogue Roudafe Sholum, of Philadelphia ... 12 April, 1843. *Philadelphia.* 5603. 12mo, pp. 24. s. 61894

An Ordinance for the Appointment of a Beadle. [n. p. n. d.] Folio, 1 leaf. 61895

An Ordinance Providing for the raising ... of Money for supplying ... Philadelphia with Wholesome Water. ... *Philadelphia: Printed by Zachariah Poulson, Junior.* 1799. 8vo, pp. 7. 61896

An Ordinance to Change the Names of Certain Streets, ... &c., in ... Philadelphia. ... *Philadelphia: Bicking & Guilbert.* 1858. 8vo, pp. (2), 66. 61897

Ordinances and Joint Resolutions of the ... Councils ... 1858. *Philadelphia.* 1858. 8vo. 61898

Ordinances for the Regulation ... of Southwark ... . *Philadelphia: Daniel Humphreys.* 1806. 8vo, pp. 17. 61899

The Ordinances of the City ... . To which are prefixed, the Act of incorporation, and the Several Supplements thereto; together with The Address of George Washington ... . *Philadelphia: ... Zachariah Poulson, Junior.* 1798. 8vo, pp. 166.

The Ordinances ... passed since the Nineteenth day of July, ... one thousand seven hundred and ninety-eight. ... *Philadelphia: ... Zachariah Poulson, Junior.* 1800. 8vo, pp. 46. 61901

The Ordinances of the Corporation ... to which are prefixed the Act of Incorporation, and ... Supplements ... with other Acts of the Assembly now in force ... . *Philadelphia.* 1805. 8vo.

Ordinances of the Corporation ... of Philadelphia; ... the Original Charter, the Act of Incorporation, and other Acts ... . By John C. Lowber. *Philadelphia: ... J. Maxwell, Printer.* 1812. 8vo, pp. (4), 312. Plan. Continued. 61903

The Ordinances of the Corporation of the Borough of Frankford, ... the Act of Incorporation, and ... Supplements thereto, &c. *Frankford: Printed by John F. Gilbert.* [1814.] 12mo, pp. 33. 61904

Ordinances of the Corporation of ... Southwark and the Acts of Assembly relating thereto. ... *Philadelphia: ... Thomas Town.* 1829. 8vo, pp. 182. 61905

Ordinances of ... Moyamensing. *Philadelphia.* 1838. 8vo.

Ordinances relative to the Northern Liberties Gas Works; with the Names of the Trustees, their Organization, By-Laws, &c. *Philadelphia: E. G. Dorsey.* 1838. 8vo, pp. 17. 61907

Olympic Theatre. Proceedings, ... Articles and Plan of Association of the Proprietors ... . *Philadelphia: William Fry, Printer.* 1819. 16mo, pp. 38. 61908

Also: Alterations and Amendments in the Articles and Plan of Association of the Proprietors ... . *Philadelphia: Printed by Thomas Desilver.* 1821. 16mo, pp. 15.

Constitution and By-Laws, of the ORPHAN SOCIETY of Philadelphia. ... *Philadelphia: ... William Fry, Printer.* 1815. 8vo, pp. 25. 61909

See also Philadelphia Orphan Society, *infra.*

Our Daily Fare. ... *Philadelphia.* 1864. 4to. 61910

Thirteen numbers were printed at the Sanitary Fair at Philadelphia.

Over de Gevangenhuizen. *See* [La Rochefoucauld-Liancourt].

Paid Fire Department. To the Independent Voters of ... Philadelphia. [n. p. n. d.] 8vo, pp. 16. 61911

Paid Fire Department. Letters to the Judges ... and the Marshal of Police, and Report of the Board of Trade. ... *Philadelphia.* 1853. 8vo, pp. 16. 61912

Panorama and Views of Philadelphia, and its Vicinity. Embracing a Collection of Twenty Views, Drawn of Stone, by J. C. Wild ... . With Poetical Illustrations ... by Andrew M'Makin. Published by J. B. Chevalier ... . *Philadelphia.* 1838. Sm. folio, pp. (22). 24 Plates. 61913

... Paper Book of the City of Philadelphia. *Philadelphia: King & Baird.* 1862. 4to, pp. 104. 5 Plans. 61914

Relates to the erection of a bridge at Chestnut street, and the consequent closing of the Schuylkill to navigation.

Die Artikel | der | PATRIOTISCHEN GESELLSCHAFT | der Stadt und Caunty Philadelphia. ... *Philadelphia: Gedruckt bey Henrich Miller.* [1772.] Folio, 1 leaf. P. 61915

Philadelphia, May 19, 1766. To the Printers of the Pennsylvania Gazette. [*Philadelphia: Hall & Sellers.* n. d.] 4to, 1 l.

Statement of Samuel Garrigues of his quarrel with John Macpherson.

Philadelphia, Wednesday, November 6, 1765. Your attendance at the Court-House tomorrow Evening, at Four O'Clock, is earnestly requested ... . [n. p. n. d.] 12mo, 1 leaf. P. 61917

Philadelphia, November 7, 1765. At a General Meeting of the Merchants and Traders of this City ... . [n. p. n. d.] Folio, 1 leaf. P. 61918

A resolve to import no more goods from England till the repeal of the stamp-act.

Philadelphia, Saturday, July 30, 1768. The Freemen ... . [n. p. n. d.] 12mo, 1 leaf. P. 61919

Call for a public meeting to instruct the representatives, etc.

Philadelphia, November 21, 1769. To the Philharmonical Merchants, and others. [n. p. n. d.] Folio, 1 leaf. P. 61920

Notice of concerts, etc., by John Gualdo. Printed entirely in red.

Philadelphia, May 22, 1770. The Tradesmen, Artificers ... [n. p. n. d.] 12mo, 1 leaf. P. 61921

Call for a non-importation meeting on May 23, 1770.

Philadelphia, July 12, 1770. The Inhabitants of the City of New York, having broke their Non-Importation Agreement, ... [n. p. n. d.] 4to, 1 leaf. P. 61922

Call for a patriotic public meeting.

Philadelphia, Thursday, Sept. 27, 1770 ... . [n. p. n. d.] 4to, 1 leaf. P. 61923

Resolutions in favor of non-importation.

Philadelphia, September 23, 1771. Mr. Faulks, the Noted Performer in Horsemanship ... . [n. p. n. d.] 4to, 1 leaf. P.

Advertisement of Faulk's performances.

Philadelphia, 25th January, 1773. Observations relative to the Manufactures of Paper and Printed Books in the Province of Pennsylvania. [n. p. n. d.] Folio, 1 leaf. P. 61925

Philadelphia, June [24], 1773. You are earnestly requested to meet a Number of the Freeholders of this City, at John Little's, in Fourth-Street, at [6 O'clock this Evening] in Order to Consider of the best Method, to prevent the Mayor and Commonalty from carrying their present Intentions, of erecting Shambles in High-Street, into Execution. To [Mr. Jacob Morgan]. [n. p. n. d.] 12mo, 1 leaf. P. 61926

The parts of title in brackets are in manuscript. The government of Philadelphia, resolving to erect the present market-houses on High street, met with a warm opposition, as being an infraction of the charter, and for some time mobs of citizens prevented any progress being made in the design. This is a call to a secret meeting for this end.

Philadelphia, 9th of December, 1773. By the Medium of the Curious Numerical Machine, invented by the ingenious Mr. Cox, are to be disposed of, the following Two Hundred and Fifty Lots of ornamented rich Plated Goods, (just imported by Samuel Bogle) &c. [n. p. n. d.] Folio, 1 leaf. P. 61927

Philadelphia, January 17th, 1774. Memorandum. [n. p. n. d.] Folio, pp. 2. P. 61928

Advocates book-sales by auction.

Philadelphia, October 1, 1777. ... [n. p. n. d.] 4to, 1 leaf. 61929

Prohibits removal of goods, etc. Printed by J. Humphreys.

Philadelphia, October 10, 1777. Advertisement ... . [n. p. n. d.] 4to, 1 leaf. P. 61930

Calls for a return of horses, etc., to the royal quarter-master-general. Printed by J. Humphreys.

Philadelphia, October 10, 1777. ... [n. p. n. d.] 4to, 1 leaf. 61931

Advertisement of Capt. J. Watt, of H. B. M. ship Delaware, for recruits. Printed by J. Humphreys.

Philadelphia, October 31, 1777. ... [n. p. n. d.] 4to, 1 leaf. 61932

One hundred copies printed by J. Humphreys. Advertisement for loan or purchase of blankets for the king's troops.

Philadelphia, November 24, 1777. ... [n. p. n. d.] 4to, 1 leaf 61933

Printed by J. Humphreys. Orders returns of cargoes, etc., to the king's quarter-master-general.

Philadelphia, December 8, 1777. ... [n. p. n. d.] 4to, 1 leaf. 61934

Regulations for purchase of spirits, molasses, salt and medicines. Signed (by order of Sir W. Howe): Jos. Galloway, Superintendent General.

Philadelphia, 11th Month, 18th, 1793. Respected Friend ... [n. p. n. d.] Folio, 1 leaf. 61935

A circular to their correspondents from Samuel and Miers Fisher, describing the progress of the yellow fever.

Philadelphia, 6th of 12th mo. 1793. A Committee of Friends this day attended each House of the Legislature of this State, with the following Address and Petition.—"To the Senate and House of Representatives of the Commonwealth of Pennsylvania. The Address and Petition of the People called Quakers." —Signed in and on behalf of a meeting appointed to represent our religious Society in Pennsylvania, &c. held the 2nd day of the 12th mo. 1793, by John Drinker, Clerk. [n. p. 1793.] Folio, 1 leaf. + [Another Edition, smaller type. n. p. 1793.] 4to, pp. 4. 61936

To the Committee on Plans for the PHILADELPHIA ACADEMY OF MUSIC. [n. p. n. d.] 8vo, pp. 5. 61937

Philadelphia Album ... . *Philadelphia.* 1830. 4to. 61938

Philadelphia Album and Ladies' Literary Portfolio. *Philadelphia.* 1831. 8vo. Continued. 61939

Philadelphia Almanack for ... 1776. *Philadelphia.* [n. d.] 24mo. 61940

Continued to 1841?

The Philadelphia Almanack For the Year 1778 Calculated For Pennsylvania and the neighbouring Parts To which is Added some useful Tables. [n. p. 1777?] 8vo, pp. 20. Folded Plan of the city. H.S.P. 61941

Engraved on copper by J. Norman.

The Philadelphia Almanac and General Business Directory for ... 1848. ... *Philadelphia.* [n. d.] 16mo, pp. 153. Plate. 61942

Charter and By-Laws of the PHILADELPHIA AND ATLANTIC Steam Navigation Company. *Philadelphia.* 1851. 8vo. 61943

Also: Letter to the Stockholders of the Philadelphia & Atlantic Steam Navigation Co. By John H. Linton, December 30th, 1851. Circular, with Postscript, issued by the Directors, dated January 1st, 1852. Answer to the Same, by John H. Linton, January 12th, 1852. *Philadelphia.* 1852. 8vo, pp. 36.

Annual Report of the President and Directors of the PHILADELPHIA AND BALTIMORE Central Railroad Co. ... 1856. *Philadelphia: McLaughlin Brothers.* 1856. 8vo, pp. 24. Map. Continued. 61944

Philadelphia and Columbia Railroad. Superintendent's Report for ... 1853. [n. p. n. d.] 8vo, pp. 30. Continued to 1856. 61945

Charter, Supplements, ... and ... Officers, of the PHILADELPHIA AND DARBY Rail Road Company. *Philadelphia.* 1859. 8vo, pp. 23, (1). 61946

Proceedings of the Annual Meeting of the Stockholders of the PHILADELPHIA AND ERIE Rail Road Company, ... with the Reports ... *Philadelphia.* 1862. 8vo, pp. 31. 61947

Also: Resources of the Philadelphia and Erie Railroad Region ... . *Erie, Pa.* 1868. 12mo, pp. 179.

Act of Incorporation of the PHILADELPHIA AND READING Rail Road Company. ... *Philadelphia: Thomas Kite & Co.* 1833. 12mo, pp. 19. + Together with a Supplement thereto ... . *Philadelphia: Joseph & Wm. Kite.* 1836. 12mo, pp. 25. + *Philadelphia: Moss & Brother.* 1848. 12mo, pp. 34. 61948

Also: Annual Report of the Philadelphia and Reading Railroad Company. ... *Philadelphia: Isaac M. Moss.* 1844. 8vo, pp. 28. Continued.—Philadelphia and Reading Rail Road. [n. p. 1833.] 8vo, pp. 10.—Report of a Committee of Investigation ... . *Boston.* 1846. 8vo, pp. 60.—Report of the Engineer and General Superintendent ... . *Philadelphia: John C. Clark, Printer.* 1843. 8vo, pp. 12.—Report of the Engineers ... . *Philadelphia.* 1838. 8vo, pp. 14. + [Report, 1839.] *Philadelphia.* 1839. 8vo, pp. 14.—Report of the President and Managers ... to the Stockholders. *Philadelphia.* 1849. 8vo. Continued.—Report on the ... Road, as surveyed by Moncure Robinson ... . *Philadelphia.* 1834. 8vo, pp. 15.—Supplements to the Charter ... *Philadelphia.* 1841. 12mo, pp. 9, (2). + *Philadelphia.* 1848. 12mo, pp. 19.

Report of the ... Directors of the PHILADELPHIA AND SUNBURY RAILROAD ... . *Philadelphia: McLaughlin Brothers.* 1856. 8vo, pp. 39, (1). 2 Maps. 61949

Philadelphia and the Lakes. Address to the Citizens of Pennsylvania, in favor of a Railroad to Connect Philadelphia with the Lakes. [n. p. 1852?] 8vo, pp. 8. 61950

Philadelphia and the North-East Valleys. Address to the Citizens of Philadelphia, in favor of the Philadelphia, Easton and Water Gap Rail-Road. [n. p. 1852.] 8vo, pp. 8. Map. 61951

Constitution of the PHILADELPHIA ANTI-SLAVERY SOCIETY. ... *Philadelphia: Printed by Thomas Town.* MDCCCXXXIV. 12mo, pp. 12. 61952

Also: First Annual Report of the ... Managers of the Philadelphia Anti-Slavery Society, ... July 4th, 1835. *Philadelphia.* 1835. 8vo, pp. 15, (1).

An Act to Incorporate the Stockholders of the PHILADELPHIA ARCADE. [n. p. 1828.] 16mo, pp. 8. 61953

Philadelphia Art Union Reporter. Vol. I. *Philadelphia.* 1852. 8vo, pp. 156. 61954

Philadelphia as it is ... . *Philadelphia: ... P. J. Gray.* 1833. 12mo, pp. 204. Map. + [*Ibid.*] 1834. 12mo. + *Philadelphia: George S. Appleton.* 1845. 18mo, pp. 114. Map. B., C. 61955

Sixteenth Annual Report of the ... Trustees of the PHILADELPHIA ASSOCIATION for the Relief of Disabled Firemen ... . *Philadelphia.* 1851. 12mo, pp. 24. 61956

Fifth Annual Report of the PHILADELPHIA ASSOCIATION in aid of the Swiss Mission in Canada. ... *Philadelphia: Lydia R. Bailey.* 1845. 12mo, pp. 12. 61957

The Origin and Proceedings of the PHILADELPHIA ASSOCIATION of Friends for the Education of Poor Children. ... [n. p.] 1832. 12mo. + Together with the Constitution, By-Laws, &c. *Philadelphia: Printed by Joseph & William Kite.* 1839. 12mo, pp. 19. Continued. 61958

Constitution of PHILADELPHIA ASSOCIATION of the Defenders of the Country, in the War of 1812. ... *Philadelphia: John B. Springer.* 1862. 8vo, pp. 14. 61959

Constitution ... of the PHILADELPHIA ASYLUM for the Deaf and Dumb. *Philadelphia: J. Harding.* 1825. 8vo, pp. 14. 61960

Statement of the Accounts of the PHILADELPHIA BANK. [n. p. 1822.] 12mo, pp. 23. 61961

Minutes of the PHILADELPHIA BAPTIST ASSOCIATION, ... Oct. 6, 1789. *Philadelphia.* [1789.] 4to, pp. 8. Continued. 61962

See also our Vol. VII., No. 27407; Baptist Association, No. 61497, *supra*, and Philadelphian Association, *infra*.

First Annual Report of the ... PHILADELPHIA BAPTIST INSTITUTE, 1859. *Philadelphia.* 1860. 8vo, pp. 23. Continued. 61963

Address of the PHILADELPHIA BAPTIST ORPHAN SOCIETY. [n. p. n. d.] 8vo, pp. 8. 61964

The Philadelphia Bar. A Complete Catalogue of Members from 1776 to 1868. *Philadelphia.* 1868. 8vo, pp. 53. 61965

Address of the Managers of the PHILADELPHIA BIBLE SOCIETY, to the Inhabitants of ... Pennsylvania. *Philadelphia: Printed by Clark & Raser.* 1827. 8vo, pp. 15. 61966

Continued as "Report of the Bible Society of Philadelphia," etc., until about 1840, when the title was changed to "The Pennsylvania Bible Society."

Sixth Annual Report of the PHILADELPHIA BIBLE SOCIETY. *Philadelphia.* 1844. 8vo, pp. 27. Continued. 61967

Also: The Charter and By-Laws of the Philadelphia Bible Society. *Philadelphia.* 1848. 16mo, pp. 12.

Second Annual Report of the PHILADELPHIA BIBLE UNION, ... With the Constitution ... and ... Minutes of the Annual Meeting ... . *Philadelphia.* 1854. 8vo, pp. 47, (1). 61968

The Philadelphia Blue Book: Containing a Complete List of all the Appointments under the New National Administration, ... *Philadelphia: Wm. White Smith.* 1861. 12mo, pp. 35. 61969

An Act to incorporate the PHILADELPHIA BOARD OF TRADE: ... *Philadelphia.* 1841. 18mo, pp. 18. + [*Ibid.*] 1851. 12mo, pp. 19. 61970

Also: Articles of Association of the Philadelphia Board of Trade. [n. p. n. d.] 8vo, pp. 8.—Communication from the Board of Trade ... to the Committee on Finance of the Senate of the United States, proposing a plan of equitable taxation ... . *Philadelphia.* 1862. 8vo, pp. 13.—Legal Restrictions upon the Commerce in Money. Memorial of the ... Board of Trade. [*Washington.* 186–.] 8vo.—Narrative of the Excursion to the West made by the Delegation of the Board of Trade ... . *Philadelphia.* 1860. 8vo, pp. 24.—Report of a Special Committee ... on National Finances and Taxation ... . *Philadelphia.* 1862. 8vo, pp. 15, (1).—Report ... in relation to the Delaware Rail Road, and its connection with ... Philadelphia. ... *Philadelphia.* M.D.CCC.LVI. 8vo, pp. 8. Map.—Report of the Committee on Inland Transportation ... on the Commerce of the Lakes, and the importance of a connection with Lake Ontario at Sodus Bay, May, 1856. ... *Philadelphia.* 1856. 8vo, pp. 18. + *Philadelphia.* 1858. 8vo, pp. 38. 2 Maps.—Report of the Committee ... on the existing Revenue Laws, April 10th, 1860. *Philadelphia.* 1860. 8vo, pp. 43.—Report of the Delegates to the Warren Convention. ... *Philadelphia: Printed by John Thompson.* 1833. 8vo, pp. 20.—Report of the Delegation ... to the Detroit ... Convention, ... July 11th, 1865. *Philadelphia.* 1865. 12mo, pp. (2), 12.—Report of the Excursion Party ... October 15th, 1860. *Philadelphia.* 1860. 8vo, pp. 22.—Twenty-Sixth Annual Report ... prepared for the Executive Council By Lorin Blodget, Secretary, and presented to the Association February 7th, 1859. *Philadelphia: King & Baird, Printers.* 1859. 8vo, pp. viii, 226, (1).

The Philadelphia Book; or Specimens of Metropolitan Literature. *Philadelphia: Key & Biddle.* 1836. 12mo, pp. iv, 13–380 61971

Report of the General Superintendent of the PHILADELPHIA BRANCH of the U. S. Sanitary Commission, to the Executive Committee, February 1st, 1864. *Philadelphia: King & Baird, Printers.* 1864. 8vo, pp. 28. + January 1st, 1865. [*Ibid.*]

1865. 8vo, pp. 51. + January 1st, 1866. [*Ibid.*] 1866. 8vo, pp. 81, (1). 61972

See also "U. S. Sanitary Commission in Philadelphia," *infra.*

Philadelphia Cemetery. Copy of Deed Trust. April 2, 1827. [n. p. n. d.] 8vo, pp. 13. + *Philadelphia: Printed by Henry Young.* 1831. 8vo, pp. 7. + 1845. 8vo, pp. (4), 43. 61973

Articles of Association and Rules of the PHILADELPHIA CHAMBER OF COMMERCE. *Philadelphia: Printed by Zachariah Poulson, Junior.* 1801. 8vo, pp. 8. 61974

Representation of the Philadelphia Chamber of Commerce, signed by order and in behalf of the said Chamber, by Thomas Fitzsimmons, 10 Dec. 1804. [*Washington.* 1804.] 8vo. 61975

Relative to the clearance of armed merchant vessels. Also: Memorial of the ... Chamber of Commerce ... relative to the Bank of the United States. *Washington.* 1810. 8vo.—Memorial of the Chamber of Commerce ... . *Washington: Printed by Gales & Seaton.* 1824. 8vo, pp. 94.—Memorial ... to Congress. *Philadelphia.* 1834. 8vo, pp. 7.

Catalogue of the PHILADELPHIA CIRCULATING LIBRARY: ... *Philadelphia: Printed by Thomas H. Palmer.* 1824. 12mo, pp. (2), 162, 12. 61976

Philadelphia City Guide. 1865. [n. p. n. d.] 18mo, pp. 36. Map. 61977

Appeal to the Public in behalf of the PHILADELPHIA CITY INSTITUTE ... . *Philadelphia: John C. Clark, Printer.* 1853. 8vo, pp. 8. 61978

Also: An Appeal in behalf of the ... Institute, for the Improvement of Young Men. *Philadelphia.* 1855. 8vo, pp. 8.—First Annual Report of the Managers of the ... Institute. ... *Philadelphia: Printed by G. T. Stockdale.* 1856. 8vo, pp. 8.

The First Quarterly Report of the PHILADELPHIA CITY MISSION. ... *Philadelphia: Wm. F. Geddes.* 1831. 12mo, pp. 18. 61979

The First Annual Report of the PHILADELPHIA CITY TRACT SOCIETY ... With the Constitution, By-Laws, and Officers. *Philadelphia: Mifflin & Parry, Printers.* 1828. 8vo, pp. 20. Continued. 61980

END OF VOLUME FOURTEEN.

A DICTIONARY OF BOOKS

RELATING TO AMERICA.

PHILADELPHIA. Rules and Regulations for the ... PHILADELPHIA CLUB. Second Edition. *Philadelphia: Printed by Jesper Harding.* 1847. 16mo, pp. 10, (1). 61981

Also: Charter and By-Laws of the ... Club. *Philadelphia.* 1860. 12mo, pp. 24. + *Philadelphia.* 1863. 12mo, pp. 22.—Charter, By-Laws, Officers and Members ... . *Philadelphia.* 1868. 12mo, pp. 31.—Notice of An Adjourned Meeting ... and the New By-Laws ... . [n. p. 1859.] 12mo, pp. 10.

Annual Announcement of the PHILADELPHIA COLLEGE OF MEDICINE, ... 1847 & 1848. *Philadelphia: Printed by Eyick, Kelly & Co.* 1847. 8vo, pp. 12. B. 61982

Also: List of Graduates in the Philadelphia College of Medicine, for 1847–48 and 1848: With a Catalogue of the Class of 1848, and the Annual Announcement for the Winter Lectures for 1848–49. *Philadelphia: Printed by John H. Gibon.* 1848. 8vo, pp. 13, (1). Continued.

Philadelphia College of Music. 1854. [Prospectus. n. p. n. d.] 8vo, pp. 4. 61983

Charter, Laws and Code of Ethics of the PHILADELPHIA COLLEGE OF PHARMACY, with ... Officers, Members and Graduates. *Philadelphia.* 1856. 8vo, pp. 28. 61984

Also: Journal of the ... College of Pharmacy. ... Vol. I. *Philadelphia.* 1830. 8vo. Continued.

Constitution of the PHILADELPHIA COMPANY OF BOOKSELLERS. Adopted February 18, 1802. [n. p. n. d.] 8vo, pp. (4). 61985

An Act for incorporating the Society, known by the Name and Stile [*sic*] of The PHILADELPHIA CONTRIBUTIONSHIP for the insuring of Houses from Loss by Fire ... . [n. p. 1768.] 8vo, pp. 8. + An Act to amend ... [the same. n. p. 1810.] 8vo, pp. 8. 61986

Also: Centennial Meeting of the Philadelphia Contributionship for the Insurance of Houses from Loss by Fire. ... April, 1852. *Philadelphia: ... C. Sherman, Printer.* 1852. 8vo, pp. 77.—The Charter and Deed of Settlement ... . *Philadelphia: Printed by John C. Clark.* 1836. 8vo, pp. 16.

First Annual Report of the ... Managers of the PHILADELPHIA CORN EXCHANGE ASSOCIATION ... . *Philadelphia: S. N. Winslow & Co., Printers.* 1855. 8vo, pp. 14. 61987

Continued as "Annual Report of the Corn Exchange Association of Philadelphia," until changed in 1868 to the "Report of the Commercial Exchange of Philadelphia."

An Act providing for the appointment of Inspectors of the PHILADELPHIA COUNTY PRISON, and for the Government thereof. ... *Philadelphia: Peter Hay & Co., Printers.* 1835. 8vo. 61988

Also: The First Annual Report of the Inspectors of the ... Prison ... . *Harrisburg, Pa.* 1848. 8vo, pp. 50. Continued.—Reports of the Committee of Investigation to examine and adjust the Books of the ... Prison, appointed January 21, 1854. ... *Philadelphia.* 1854. 8vo, pp. 27.

Articles for the Government of the Second Battalion of PHILADELPHIA COUNTY VOLUNTEERS of the Second Brigade of the First Division, P. M. ... *Philadelphia: King & Baird, Printers.* 1845. 12mo, pp. 10. 61989

Also: Regulations by the Standing Committee of Companies A. B. and C. Adopted June 8th, 1845. *Philadelphia.* 1845. 12mo, pp. 4.

Philadelphia Described ... *Philadelphia.* 1848. 32mo. Map and Plates. 61990

An Account of the PHILADELPHIA DISPENSARY, Instituted ... April 12, 1786. *Philadelphia: Printed by Budd & Bartram.* 1802. 8vo, pp. 20. 61991

Also: Account of the Design, Origin, and Present State of the ... Dispensary. *Philadelphia: Printed by Kimber, Conrad, & Co.* 1805. 16mo, pp. 8.—Plan of the ... Dispensary ... . [*Philadelphia.* 1786.] 8vo, pp. 8.—Rules of the ... Dispensary ... [Report for 1807. n. p. 1808.] 12mo, pp. 11. Continued.

An Act to Establish ... "The PHILADELPHIA, DOVER and Norfolk Steam-Boat and Transportation Company" ... . *Dover: Aug. M. Schee, Printer.* 1825. 8vo, pp. 8. 61992

An Act to incorporate the PHILADELPHIA, EASTON and Water-Gap Railroad Company. [n. p. 1852.] 8vo, pp. 22.

Also: Act of Incorporation ... and the Supplements ... . *Philadelphia.* 1853. 8vo, pp. 23.—Address of the Committee ... 9th of October, 1852. *Philadelphia.* 1852. 8vo, pp. (2), 8. Map.—Memorial of the President and Directors ... to the Councils of ... Philadelphia. ... *Philadelphia.* 1853. 8vo, pp. 12. Map.—Report of the Chief Engineer ... . [n. p. 1852.] 8vo, pp. (2), 8.

Report of the Delegation appointed by the PHILADELPHIA EMIGRANT SOCIETY to enquire into the Nature and Operation of the Emigration Laws in the State of New York. ... *Philadelphia.* 1854. 8vo, pp. 16. 61994

Annual Report of the PHILADELPHIA FEMALE ANTI-SLAVERY SOCIETY. *Philadelphia.* 1835. 8vo. Continued. 61995

The First Annual Report of the PHILADELPHIA FEMALE TRACT SOCIETY ... . *Philadelphia: Printed by Lydia R. Bailey.* 1816. 16mo, pp. 18. Continued. 61996

An Address to the Members of the Religious Society of Friends on ... Slavery and the Slave Trade by the PHILADELPHIA FREE PRODUCE ASSOCIATION of Friends. [n. p.] 1849. 8vo, pp. 16. 61997

Charter of the PHILADELPHIA FIRE AND INLAND Navigation Insurance Company, with ... Supplements. ... *Philadelphia.* 1838. 8vo, pp. 35. 61998

The Philadelphia Fire Marshal Almanac and Underwriters' Advertiser, for ... 1860, containing ... Also the Laws of ... Pennsylvania and the Ordinances ... of Philadelphia, in relation to Fires ... . By Alexander W. Blackburn, ... and William A. Stait ... . *Chandler, Printer, ... Philad'a.* [1859?] 16mo, pp. 320

Report of the Trustees of the PHILADELPHIA GAS WORKS, to the ... Councils of the City ... . *Philadelphia: Printed by J. Crissy.* 1838. 8vo, pp. 16. Continued. 62000

Also: Report of the Trustees ... to the ... Councils ... . To which are prefixed: I. The Reports of Committees of Council ... II. The Report of S. V. Merrick, Esq. ... III. The Ordinances of the ... Councils ... &c. *Philadelphia: Printed by J. Crissy.* 1838. 8vo, pp. (8), xlii, 16, 148. + *Philadelphia: J. H. Jones & Co., Printers.* 1857. 8vo, pp. 604.

Act ... incorporating the PHILADELPHIA, GERMANTOWN, and Norristown Railroad Company. *Philadelphia.* 1831. 8vo, pp. 24. + 1835. 8vo, pp. 39. + 1847. 8vo, pp. 48. 62001

Also: An Act Supplementary to ... an Act to Incorporate the Philadelphia, Germantown and Norristown Rail Road Company. *Philadelphia.* 1832. 8vo, pp. 4. + 1834. 8vo, pp. 7.—Report of the President and Managers ... . *Philadelphia.* 1850. 8vo, pp. 13. Continued.—Reports and Estimates ... . [n. p. 1833.] 8vo, pp. 16. Map.

Report of the ... PHILADELPHIA HOME GUARD. *Philadelphia.* 1861. 8vo. 62002

The Protest of the PHILADELPHIA HOME MISSIONARY SOCIETY, against the recent action of the Executive Committee of the American Home Missionary Society in relation to Churches containing Slaveholding Members, ... April 28, 1857. *Philadelphia.* 1857. 8vo, pp. 16. 62003

Also: The Sixteenth Report of the Philadelphia Home Missionary Society ... . *Philadelphia.* 1856. 8vo, pp. 40. Continued.

Articles and By-Laws of the PHILADELPHIA HOSE COMPANY, revised, July, 1815. ... *Philadelphia: Printed by S. Merritt.* 1815. 18mo, pp. 35. 62004

Also: Historical Sketches of the ... Philadelphia Hose Company. Being the first Hose Company in Philadelphia. December 15, 1803. To which is appended a List of tne Members. *Philadelphia.* 1854. 8vo, pp. 95. P.

Philadelphia in 1824; or, A Brief Account of the various Institutions ... in this Metropolis: being A Complete Guide for Strangers ... . *Philadelphia: H. C. Carey & I. Lea.* 1824. 18mo, pp. xi, (1), 238. Map, Plate and 2 Plans. 62005

Philadelphia in 1830–1: or, a Brief Account of the various Institutions and Public Objects in this Metropolis. ... *Philadelphia: E. L. Carey and A. Hart.* 1830. 12mo, pp. 288. Plate and Map. 62006

See "Picture of Philadelphia," *infra.*

Philadelphia in 1868. A Guide-Book. [n. p. n. d.] 16mo, pp. 64. Map. 62007

Second Annual Report of the PHILADELPHIA INSTITUTE. ... *Philadelphia.* 1833. 12mo, pp. 12. 62008

The Philadelphia Jockey Club. *See* Tickler (Timothy), *pseudon.*

The Philadelphia Journal of Homœopathy. Edited by William A. Gardiner, M.D. ... *Philadelphia.* 18—. 8vo. 62009

The Philadelphia Journal of the Medical and Physical Sciences. ... Edited by N. Chapman, M.D. ... *Philadelphia.* 1820–24. 9 vols., 8vo. + Volume I. New Series. *Philadelphia: H. C. Carey & I. Lea.* 1825. 8vo, pp. (8), 426. Plates. 62010

Continued to 1826 or later. The new series was edited by N. Chapman, M.D., W. P. Dewees, M.D., and John D. Goodman, M.D.

Charter, By-Laws and Rules ... of the PHILADELPHIA LITERARY INSTITUTE. ... *Philadelphia.* 1860. 24mo, pp. 24.

First Annual Report of the Managers to the Contributors to the PHILADELPHIA LYING-IN CHARITY ... . *Philadelphia.* 1833. 8vo, pp. 8. Continued. 62012

Also: Appeal of the Managers of the ... Charity, to their Fellow Citizens ... . *Philadelphia.* 1849. 12mo, pp. 12.—Constitution of the ... Charity. [n. p. 1833.] 12mo, pp. 11.—Philadelphia Lying-In Charity ... . [Charter, etc.] *Philadelphia.* 1832. 8vo, pp. 20.—Report of the Several Branches of the Philadelphia Lying-In Charity and Nurse Society, for ... 1851 ... . *Philadelphia.* 1852. 12mo, pp. 24.

The Philadelphia Magazine for 1788 ... *Philadelphia.* 1788. 8vo. Continued. 62013

The Philadelphia Magazine and Review, or Monthly Repository ... Vol. I. *Philadelphia.* 1799. 8vo, pp. 415. Plates. S.

Philadelphia Malignants Typographed. *See* Tartan, *pseudon.*

The Philadelphia Medical and Physical Journal. Collected and arranged by Benjamin Smith Barton, M.D. ... *John Conrad & Co. Philadelphia;* ... 1804–1809. 3 vols., 8vo, pp. (2), viii, x, 184, (1), vii, 192; (2), xii, 208, ix, 201; viii, 190. Three Supplements, (6), 312. Plates. A. 62015

Improved title of our No. 3822, Vol. I., which see for a note.

The Philadelphia Medical and Surgical Journal. Edited by James Bryan. ... *Philadelphia.* 1855. 8vo. 62016

Act of Incorporation, and Laws of the PHILADELPHIA MEDICAL SOCIETY. *Philadelphia.* 1793. 8vo, pp. 16. M. 62017

Also: The Charter of Incorporation and By-Laws of the Philadelphia Medical Society. ... *Philadelphia.* 1840. 12mo, pp. 23. + *Philadelphia.* 1843. 12mo, pp. 23.

Philadelphia, Monday, May 25, 1840. Great Town Meeting, ... [in favor of] Van Buren and Johnson ... . [n. p. n. d.] 8vo, pp. 32. 62018

The Philadelphia Monthly Magazine, or Universal Repository of Knowledge and Entertainment. Edited by T. Condie. Vol. I. *Philadelphia.* 1798. 8vo. Continued. 62019

The Magazine for March, 1798, contains the national song "Hail Columbia!" under the title of "Patriotic Song, written by J. Hopkinson, Esq. To the tune President's March."

Charter and By-Laws of the PHILADELPHIA MUSEUM COMPANY. *Philadelphia: Printed by James Kay, Jun.* 1828. 12mo, pp. 12. 62020

Also: Charter and Supplement to Charter of the ... Museum Company. *Philadelphia: Printed by William P. Gibbons.* 1836. 12mo, pp. 10. + *Philadelphia: A. Waldie, Printer.* 1840. 12mo, pp. 15.

Philadelphia Newest Almanac for 1775. *Philadelphia: R. Aitken.* [1774.] 12mo. 62021

Prospectus of the PHILADELPHIA OCEAN STEAMSHIP COMPANY. *Philadelphia: King & Baird.* 1859. 8vo, pp. 22.

Philadelphia; or Glances at Lawyers, Physicians, First Circle, &c. &c. ... *Philadelphia: R. H. Small.* 1826. 12mo, pp. (4), 151

Constitution of the PHILADELPHIA ORPHAN SOCIETY; with Rules for the ... Managers and the Asylum. *Philadelphia: Printed by Lydia R. Bailey.* 1827. 8vo, pp. 12. + [*Ibid.*] 1845. 8vo, pp. 12. 62024

Also: First Annual Report of the ... Society. ... *Philadelphia: Printed by William Fry.* 1816. 8vo, pp. 48. Continued.

The Philadelphia Photographer. Edited by E. L. Wilson. ... *Philadelphia.* 1864–65. 8vo. Continued. 62025

The Philadelphia Prayer-Meeting Convention. ... *New York: John F. Trow, Printer.* 1860. 12mo, pp. 56. 62026

The Philadelphia Pursuits. *See* Junius (J.), *pseudon.*, Vol. IX.

The Philadelphia Register, and National Recorder. Vol. I. *Philadelphia.* 1819. Rl. 8vo, pp. 432. Continued. 62027

This periodical was got up on the plan of Niles' "Weekly Register," although somewhat more eclectic.

The Philadelphia Repertory, devoted to Literature and Useful Intelligence. Vol. I. *Philadelphia.* 1810. 4to. Continued.

The Philadelphia Repository and Weekly Register. ... *Philadelphia:* ... *David Hogan.* 1801–1805. 5 vols., 4to. C. 62029

Report of the PHILADELPHIA SABBATH ASSOCIATION. ... *Philadelphia: T. K. & P. G. Collins, Printers.* 1842. 12mo, pp. 15. Continued in 8vo. 62030

Fourth Annual Report of the PHILADELPHIA SABBATH SCHOOL ASSOCIATION ... . *Philadelphia.* 1859. 8vo, pp. 16. Continued. 62031

Prospectus of the PHILADELPHIA SCHOOL OF DESIGN for Women, for ... 1867, and ... report for 1866, with a Catalogue of Art Studies in the ... Institution. ... *Philadelphia: E. C. Markey & Son, Printers.* 1867. 8vo, pp. 25. 62032

A Report of the PHILADELPHIA SEAMEN'S FRIEND SOCIETY, for 1830. *Philadelphia.* 1831. 8vo, pp. 8, (1). 62033

Annual Report of the Acting Committee of the PHILADELPHIA SOCIETY FOR ALLEVIATING the Miseries of Public Prisons. ... *Philadelphia.* 1833. 8vo, pp. 44. 62034

Also: Act of Incorporation and Constitution of the Philadelphia Society for Alleviating the Miseries of Public Prisons. ... *Philadelphia: Jesper Harding, Printer.* 1835. 8vo, pp. 8.—Constitution of the ... Society ... . [n. p. 1787.] 12mo. + *Philadelphia: Printed by Joseph Cruksbank.* 1806. 16mo, pp. 8. + [*Ibid.*] 1808. 12mo, pp. 8. + *Philadelphia: Printed by Solomon W. Conrad.* 1821. 16mo, pp. 15. + *Philadelphia.* 1830. 8vo, pp. 10.—Sketch of the Principal Transactions ... . *Philadelphia.* 1859. 8vo, pp. 32.

First Annual Report of the PHILADELPHIA SOCIETY FOR BETTERING the Condition of the Poor. *Philadelphia: William Stavely.* 1830. 12mo, pp. 11. 62035

Memoirs of the PHILADELPHIA SOCIETY FOR PROMOTING Agriculture. Containing Communications on various subjects in Husbandry & Rural Affairs. To which is added a Statistical Account of the Schuylkill Permanent Bridge. ... *Philadelphia: Printed by Jane Aitken.* 1808, '11, '14, '18, '26. 5 vols., 8vo, pp. lxv, 331, 84, Index, (18), Errata, (2); xvii, 362, (2), vi, Plate, 128, 50, (22); (6), lxxvii, 440, 120, (22), 6 Plates; (8), xxxii, lii, (4), 332, 4 Plates; v, li, 326, 3 Plates. 62036

Also: An Address from the Philadelphia Society for Promoting Agriculture; With A Summary of its Laws; and Premiums offered. [n. p.] M.DCC.LXXXV. 8vo, pp. 16.—Address of the ... Society to the Citizens of Pennsylvania. *Philadelphia.* 1818. 8vo.—Charter and By-Laws of the ... Society ... . *Germantown, Pa.: Printed by P. R. Freas & Co.* 1840. 12mo, pp. 12. + 1858. 8vo, pp. 24.—Laws of the ... Society ... January 10, 1786, with the Premiums proposed, February 5, 1788. To which is prefixed, A List of the Members ... . [n. p.] M.DCC.LXXXVIII. 8vo, pp. 24. + M.DCC.LXXXIX. 12mo, pp. 23.—Minutes of the ... Society ... from its Institution in February, 1785, to March, 1810. *Philadelphia.* 1854. 8vo, pp. (2), 124.—Philadelphia Society for Promoting Agriculture. [Charter, etc. n. p. 1822.] 8vo, pp. 16.—Proceedings of the Annual Exhibition ... held at Rising Sun Village, October 8–9, 1851. *Germantown, Pa.* 1851. 8vo, pp. 27. Continued.—Proceedings of the ... Society ... for ... 1854, 1855 and 1856, ... a Catalogue of the Exhibition of 1855, ... and the Address of Ex-Governor Bigler. ... *Philadelphia.* 1857. 8vo, pp. (4), 122. Plan.—Reports and Letters to the ... Society ... on the proper Season for cutting Timber. ... *Philadelphia.* 1850. 8vo, pp. 16.

Constitution of the PHILADELPHIA SOCIETY FOR THE EMPLOYMENT and Instruction of the Poor. With a Report of a Committee ... on the erection ... of a House of Industry. *Philadelphia.* 1847. 12mo, pp. 12. + *Philadelphia.* 1852. 8vo, pp. 8. 62037

Also: In the Matter of the Application of the Philadelphia Society for the Employment and Instruction of the Poor to the Judges of the Supreme Court to Approve the

Amendments to its Charter. *Philadelphia: Merrihew & Thompson.* 1854. 8vo, pp. (2), 24. + *Philadelphia: Joseph P. Sailer & Co., Printers.* 1855. 12mo, pp. 50.—Report of the ... Society ... . 1847–1848. *Philadelphia.* 1848. 8vo, pp. 16. Continued.

Report of a Committee of the PHILADELPHIA SOCIETY FOR THE ENCOURAGEMENT of Faithful Domestics, ... with the Constitution. *Philadelphia.* 1829. 8vo, pp. 6. M. 62038

Annual Report ... of the PHILADELPHIA SOCIETY FOR THE ESTABLISHMENT and Support of Charity Schools. ... *Philadelphia: Printed by William Fry.* 1820. 8vo, pp. 14. Continued.

Also: The Constitution of the Philadelphia Society, for the Establishment and Support of Charity Schools. ... *Philadelphia: Printed by H. Maxwell.* 1804. 12mo, pp. 16. + *Philadelphia.* 1840. 12mo, pp. 18.—Constitution and Laws ... . With a Historical Sketch of the Institution, and the Life of Christopher Ludwick. *Philadelphia.* 1860. 8vo, pp. 85. Plate.—Report of the ... Managers ... . [n. p. 1812.] 8vo, pp. 12. Continued.

Address of the PHILADELPHIA SOCIETY FOR THE PROMOTION of Domestic Industry to the Citizens of the United States. *Boston: Printed by William W. Clapp.* 1819. 8vo, pp. 116. 62040

Address[es] of the PHILADELPHIA SOCIETY FOR THE PROMOTION of National Industry. ... [n. p. 1819.] 13 Nos., 8vo. + New Series. No. I. [n. p. 1819.] 8vo, pp. 20. + No. II. Second Edition. [n. p. 1819.] 8vo, pp. 32. 62041

Also: Addresses of the Philadelphia Society for the Promotion of National Industry. *Philadelphia: M. Carey & Son.* 1819. 8vo, pp. 280. + Fourth Edition. *Philadelphia.* 1819. 12mo. + Fifth Edition. *Philadelphia: James Maxwell.* 1820. 12mo, pp. 299, (1). + Sixth Edition. *Philadelphia: Carey & Lea.* 1822. 8vo.

Philadelphia Souvenir: a Collection of Fugitive Pieces. [n. p. n. d.] 8vo. 62042

Philadelphia Statistics. [n. p. 1841.] 16mo. 62043

The Second Report of the PHILADELPHIA SUNDAY and Adult School Union: Read at their Annual Meeting ... May 25, 1819. *Philadelphia: Printed ... by Clark & Raser.* 1819. 8vo, pp. 63. Continued. 62044

An Act to incorporate the PHILADELPHIA TIDE LOCK COMPANY ... . *Philadelphia: John C. Clark.* 1838. 8vo, pp. 13.

The Charter and By-Laws of the PHILADELPHIA TYPOGRAPHICAL SOCIETY, with the Members' Names. ... *Philadelphia.* 1843. 16mo, pp. 52. 62046

Constitution of the PHILADELPHIA UNITARY BUILDING ASSOCIATION, with a Lithographic Outline of the Proposed Edifice. *Philadelphia.* 1849. 8vo, pp. 8. Folded Plan. 62047

The Philadelphia Universalist Magazine and Christian Messenger, edited by the Rev. Abner Kneeland. *Philadelphia.* 1821–1822. 2 vols., 8vo. 62048

Philadelphia Vocabulary. *Philadelphia.* 1806. 8vo. 62049

Contains a number of very rude wood-cuts. Early specimen of American wood-engraving.

Philadelphia Wholesale Merchants' and Artizans' Business Directory, for 1853. *Philadelphia.* 1853. 18mo. C. 62050

First Annual Report of the PHILADELPHIA, WILMINGTON and Baltimore Rail Road Company, since the union of the original companies, with the Articles of Union. *Philadelphia.* 1839. 8vo, pp. 16. Continued to 1880. 62051

Also: Acts to amend the Charter of the Philadelphia, Wilmington and Baltimore Railroad Company, passed by the General Assembly of Maryland ... 1853. *Philadelphia: Press of James H. Bryson.* M.DCCC.LIV. 8vo, pp. 16.—Address upon a Proposed Rail Road from Wilmington to the Susquehanna. Together with a Report of the Survey made by William Strickland ... . *Philadelphia.* 1835. 8vo, pp. 18. Map.—Court of Errors and Appeals of the State of Delaware. June Term, 1871. Opinion of the Court ... in re William J. Clarke, Treasurer of ... Delaware, vs. Philadelphia, Wilmington & Baltimore R. R. Co. [In reference to state tax. *Wilmington.* 1871?] 8vo, pp. 17.—Investigation into the Alleged Official Misconduct of the Late Superintendent ... Reported by Arthur Cannon. ... *Philadelphia: James H. Bryson.* M.DCCC.LIV. 2 vols., 8vo, pp. xiv, 1033, lxxii; xv, 273, 383, 229, (1).—Laws incorporating the Philadelphia, Wilmington and Baltimore Rail-Road Company ... [and others]. *Philadelphia: Printed by S. C. Atkinson.* 1836. 8vo, pp. 69.—Letter of Capt. Richard Delafield, ... to Matthew Newkirk, Esq. President of the ... Company, relative to a Rail Road Bridge ... over the Schuylkill at Grey's Ferry. *Philadelphia: Printed by S. C. Atkinson.* 1837. 8vo, pp. 10.—Letter of the President of ... Company to the Secretary of War, in reference to Improved Facilities of Transportation between New York and Washington, ... and Letters and Papers showing the ... services rendered ... by the ... Railroad at the breaking out of the Rebellion. *Washington: Henry Polkinhorn, Printer.* 1862. 8vo, pp. 40.—A Minute Description of ... every object of interest on the whole route ... *Baltimore: John Murphy & Co.* 1850. 18mo, pp. 51.—Mortgage ... to Muncure Robinson, Nathaniel Thayer, Wm. W. Corcoran. [n. p. 1858.] 8vo, pp. (2), 36.—Organization of the United Companies under the name of the Philadelphia, Wilmington and Baltimore Rail Road Company, with the Articles of Union ... . *Philadelphia.* 1838. 8vo, pp. 15.—Philadelphia, Wilmington and Baltimore Railroad Guide: Containing a Description of the ... Objects of Interest along the line of road; ... &c. By Charles P. Dare. Embellished with Four Maps, and Sixty Illustrations engraved by Baxter ... . *Philadelphia: Fitzgibbon & Van Ness.* [1856.] 16mo, pp. 142.—Reply of the President of the ... Railroad in obedience to an order of the House of Delegates. *Annapolis: Thomas E. Martin.* 1853. 8vo, pp. 10.—Report of the Committee to Investigate the Loan made by this State to the Philadelphia, Wilmington and Baltimore Rail Road Company. Presented in the House of Representatives, February 9, 1843. *Dover, Delaware: S. Kimmey, Printer.* 1843. 8vo, pp. 16.—Rules and Regu-

lations for the Management of the Philadelphia, Wilmington and Baltimore, and the Newcastle and Frenchtown, Rail Roads. *Philadelphia: James H. Bryson.* M.DCCC.LIV. 8vo, pp. 40.—Special Meeting of the Stockholders ... held at Wilmington, Delaware, June 28th, 1855. *Philadelphia.* M.DCCC.LV. 8vo, pp. 7.

Constitution, By-Laws, and ... Officers, of the PHILADELPHIA YOUNG MEN'S Bible Society; with an Address ... . Re-organized February, 1840. *Philadelphia:* ... *I. Ashmead.* 1841. 8vo, pp. 16. 62052

Also: The Third Annual Report of the Philadelphia Young Men's Bible Society, being the First since Re-organization, February, 1840. *Philadelphia: Printed by Wm. F. Geddes.* 1841. 8vo, pp. 16.

Constitution, By-Laws and Standing Rules of the PHILADELPHIA YOUNG MEN'S SOCIETY. *Philadelphia:* ... *William F. Geddes.* 1833. 12mo, pp. 23. 62053

Philadelphia's Great North Route. North Pennsylvania Railroad, to connect Philadelphia with North Pennsylvania, Western New York, the Lakes and Canada West. *Philadelphia.* 1853. 8vo, pp. 48. Map. 62054

Constitution of the PHILANTHROPIC SOCIETY, established at Philadelphia, May 6th, 1793. ... *Philadelphia:* ... *James Stackhouse.* 1815. 12mo, pp. 24. 62055

The Constitution and By-Laws of the PHOENIX HOSE COMPANY ... . Instituted ... 1817. ... [n. p. n. d.] 16mo, pp. 30.

Articles of Association of the PHŒNIX INSURANCE COMPANY of Philadelphia. [n. p. 1803?] 8vo, pp. 16. 62057

Picture of Philadelphia, or, a Brief Account of the various Institutions and Public Objects in this Metropolis. ... *Philadelphia: E. L. Carey and A. Hart.* 1835. 12mo, pp. 288, (36). Plate and Map. C., S. 62058

Constitution and By-Laws of the PIKE BENEFICIAL SOCIETY of ... Philadelphia, as ordered to be Printed ... May 22, 1865. ... *Philadelphia: E. C. Markley & Son.* 1865. 12mo, pp. 48.

A Plan for the Government of the Alms-House and for Ordering the Affairs of the Poor in ... Philadelphia, ... Northern Liberties, and ... Southwark. *Philadelphia:* ... *Kimber, Conrad, & Co.* 1805. 8vo, pp. 23. 62060

See also Almshouse, Vol. XIV., No. 61455.

A Plan of Philadelphia, or the Stranger's Guide to the Public Buildings, Places of Amusement, Streets, Alleys, Roads, ... &c.

&c. of ... Philadelphia and adjoining Districts. Being a Complete Guide ... . *Philadelphia: E. L. Carey, & A. Hart.* [1832.] 16mo, pp. 54, (38). 62061

A Plan of the City and Environs of Philadelphia. Engraved and published by M. Alb. Lotter. [n. p.] 1777. Folio.

A Plan of the City and Environs ... Engraved by Wm. Faden. [n. p.] 1777. Folio sheet. 62063

A Plan ... with Works and Encampments of His Majesty's Forces, under Sir William Howe. [n. p.] 1779. Folio.

A Plan of the Improved Part of ... Philadelphia. Surveyed by the late Nicholas Scull. [n. p.] 1762. Folio sheet. 62065

A Plan to Lessen and Equalize the Burthen of Taxation in ... Philadelphia. By a Citizen. *Philadelphia.* 1818. 8vo. W.

Police Manual: Being Rules and Regulations for the Organization and Government of the Consolidated Police of ... Philadelphia. *Philadelphia: King & Baird.* MDCCCLV. 12mo, pp. 72.

Posts at which the Stores are. ... [n. p. n. d.] Folio, 1 leaf.

Form of return of quarter-master's stores; about February, 1779.

Preliminary Report [to Councils] of the Committee on Law relative to the ... more general distribution of Taxation. [n. p. 1871.] 8vo, pp. 9. 62069

Second Annual Report of the Philadelphia Education Society of the PRESBYTERIAN CHURCH. *Philadelphia.* 18—. 8vo.

The Presbyterian Hospital in Philadelphia. History, Charter, and By-Laws. *Philadelphia: ... Alfred Martien.* 1871. 8vo, 42. 62071

The Present State and Condition of the Free People of Color, of ... Philadelphia and adjoining Districts, as exhibited by the Report of a Committee of the Pennsylvania Society for promoting the Abolition of Slavery, &c. ... *Philadelphia: ... Merrihew and Gunn.* 1838. 8vo, pp. 40, 8. 62072

The First Annual Report of the PRISON INSPECTORS and Prison Agent, ... including the Second Annual Report to the Prison Society. *Philadelphia: William S. Young.* 1855. 8vo, pp. 13. Continued. 62073

Prisons de Philadelphie. *See* [La Rochefoucauld-Liancourt], Vol. x. 39053–5, *also* [Moreau (M. L. É.)], Vol. xii. 50576–7.

For "Fourth Edition," in No. 39053, *read* Quatrième Édition. *Chez Madame Huzard, Paris.* 1819. 8vo, pp. xxiv, 99. 3 folded Tables.

Prize Essays on Juvenile Delinquency. Published under the direction of the ... Managers of the House of Refuge ... . *Philadelphia: Edward C. & John Biddle.* 1855. 8vo, pp. 159.

Proceedings and Resolutions of City Councils, Saturday, April 15, 1865, and Thursday, April 20, 1865, on the Death of A. Lincoln. [n. p. n. d.] 8vo, pp. 8. 62076

Proceedings in the City of Philadelphia, respecting the nomination of Henry Clay as a Candidate for the Presidency ... . *Philadelphia: Joseph R. A. Skerrett.*. 1824. 8vo, pp. 8. 62077

Proceedings of a meeting. *See* [Penn (W.)], No. 59745.

Proceedings of a Town Meeting ... Philadelphia, Dec. 28, 1825. With a View to memorialising Congress for an Appropriation for Constructing a Breakwater in the Delaware Bay; with the Memorial ... . *Philadelphia: William Fry, Printer.* 1826. 8vo, pp. 7. 62078

Proceedings of a Town Meeting of the Citizens ... of Philadelphia, without distinction of party, held ... December 6, 1837, to hear the Report of their Delegates to the National Convention of Business Men. ... *Philadelphia: Printed by John Wiltbank.* 1837. 8vo, pp. 16. 62079

Proceedings of Meetings on the 9th November and 4th December, and Report of the Committee of Twelve concerning the Plans of the Proposed Operatic and Dramatic House, the Interest and Security of the Investment, etc. *Philadelphia: T. Thompson, Printer.* 1839. 8vo, pp. (2), 15, (1), folded leaf.

Proceedings of the Bar of Philadelphia, on the ... Increase in the Number and Compensation of the Judges, and the erection of New Court Houses. *Philadelphia: King & Baird.* 1866. 8vo, pp. 8. 62081

Proceedings of the Citizens of Philadelphia relative to the Rail Road to Erie, and of the Convention at Williamsport, Lycoming County, Pa. ... *Philadelphia: Printed by J. Thompson.* 1836. 8vo, pp. 31. Map. 62082

Proceedings of the Committee of Councils of Philadelphia on the Western Canal. *Philadelphia.* 1835. 8vo. 62083

Proceedings of the Committee to alleviate the Sufferings of the Afflicted with Malignant Fever, 1792. *Philadelphia.* 1848. 8vo. B. 62084

Proceedings of the Fœderal Convention, Held at Philadelphia, In the Year 1787, And the Twelfth Year of American Independence. *Philadelphia: Printed by T. Bradford* ... . M.DCC.-LXXXVII. 8vo, pp. 15. 62085

Proceedings of the General Town Meeting Held in the State-House Yard in ... Philadelphia, on Monday the Twenty-sixth and by adjournment to Tuesday the Twenty-seventh of July last. [n. p.:] *Printed by Francis Bailey.* 1779. 8vo, pp. 26. 62086

Proceedings of the Government and Citizens of Philadelphia, on the Reduction of the Hours of Labor and Increase of Wages. *Boston.* 1835. 8vo, pp. 12. 62087

Proceedings of the Great Union Meeting held in ... Philadelphia, On the 21st of November, 1850. Under a Call signed by upwards of Five Thousand Citizens, whose Names are Appended to the Proceedings. ... *Philadelphia: B. Mifflin, Printer.* 1850. 8vo, pp. 83. 62088

Proceedings of the Manufacturers, Mechanics, Merchants, Traders, and Others, of the City and County of Philadelphia, signers of the Memorial to Congress, asking for the return of the Government Deposites to the Bank of the United States. *Philadelphia.* 1834. 8vo, pp. 15. 62089

Proceedings of the Meeting of the Citizens ... of Philadelphia, in relation to the Great Pennsylvania Railroad, from Philadelphia via Harrisburg to Pittsburgh: with the Address of the Committee to the People of Pennsylvania. *Philadelphia.* 1846. 8vo, pp. 16. + *Philadelphia.* 1846. 8vo, pp. 20. 62090

Proceedings of the Special Committee of the Select and Common Councils ... to report upon the ... Western Canal. [n. p. 1835.] 8vo, pp. 21. 62091

Proceedings of two meetings of Citizens of Philadelphia respecting Col. Clark's Plan for Ascending Rapids in Rivers, and thereby improving the navigation of the River Delaware, beyond Trenton. To which is prefixed a Brief Description of

the Plan, with a Plate. *Philadelphia: ... Joseph R. A. Skerrett.* 1824. 8vo, pp. 15. Plate. 62092

Proceedings on the Occasion of Laying the Corner-Stone of the New Hospital in Belment, Philadelphia, including the Addresses of the Right Rev. Alonzo Potter, ... and Rev. Benjamin Dorr, D.D. ... *Philadelphia: E. C. and J. Biddle.* 1856. 8vo, pp. 23. 62093

Proceedings relative to the Formation of an Anti-Slavery Church in ... Philadelphia. *Philadelphia.* 1839. 12mo, pp. 10.

Proclamation [requiring the Inhabitants to obtain arms to defend themselves against the Indians]. *Philadelphia: Printed by Andrew Bradford.* 1728. Folio, 1 leaf. P. 62095

Record of the PROGRESSIVE GARDNERS' SOCIETY of Philadelphia: Being the First Annual Report ... . *Philadelphia.* 1861. 8vo, pp. 129. 62096

Proofs of the Origin of the Yellow Fever, in Philadelphia & Kensington, in the year 1797, from Domestic Exhalation; and from the foul air of the Snow Navigation, from Marseilles: and from that of the Ship Huldah, from Hamburgh, in Two Letters, Addressed to the Governor of the Commonwealth of Pennsylvania, by the Academy of Medicine of Philadelphia. *Philadelphia: Printed by Thomas & Samuel F. Bradford.* 1798. 8vo, pp. (4), 49. 62097

A Proposal for Altering the Eastern Front. *See* [Beck (Paul), *Jr.*], Vol. i., No. 4236.

The Prospect of Philadelphia, and Check on the next Directory. Part i. ... By Edmund Hogan. *Philadelphia: Printed by Francis & Robert Bailey* ... M,DCC,XCV. 8vo, pp. 180. + Second Edition. *Philadelphia: Printed by John Turner, ... for Edmund Hogan.* M,DCC,XCVI. 8vo, pp. 180. 62098

See also our No. 32419, Vol. viii.

Prospectus de l'Académie Classique et Militaire de Mantua, (Village situé a 2½ milles, Ouest de Philadelphie,) derigée par Victor Value. *Philadelphie: P. M. Lafourcade, Imprimeur.* 1828. 12mo, pp. 12. 62099

A Protest Against closing the River Schuylkill at South Street, by the Construction of a Bridge without a Draw. ... *Philada.* [1867.] 8vo, pp. (2), 19. Map. 62100

Directory of the PROTESTANT EPISCOPAL CHURCH and Church Institutions in Philadelphia. Together with a History of the Episcopal Hospital. *Philadelphia: M'Calla & Stavely.* 1870. 8vo, pp. 50, folded leaf. 62101

See also Hospital of the Prot. Epis. Church," Vol. xiv., No. 61726.

Fundamental Laws, Charter of Incorporation, and supplement thereto, of the Trustees of the Academy of the Protestant Episcopal Church in ... Philadelphia. Together with Bishop White's Narrative of the Establishment of the said Academy ... . *Philadelphia.* 1841. 8vo, pp. 27. 62102

Yearly Annals of the Protestant Episcopal Church of the Evangelists, Southwark, Philadelphia, 1845. ... *Philadelphia: King & Baird.* 1846. 12mo, pp. 18. 62103

Report of the PROTESTANT EPISCOPAL SUNDAY and Adult School Society ... . 1821. Together with the Constitution of the Society and the By-Laws of the ... Managers. *Philadelphia: J. Harding, Printer.* 1822. 8vo, pp. 16. Continued. 62104

Constitution of the PROTESTANT EPISCOPAL SUNDAY SCHOOL SOCIETY ... . *Philadelphia.* 1818. 8vo, pp. 7. 62105

A | Protestation | presented to | the Synod | of | Philadelphia, | June 1, 1741. | *Philadelphia: Printed and Sold* | *by B. Franklin.* 1741. | Sm. 8vo, pp. 16. 62106

First Report of the PROVIDENT SOCIETY for the Employment of the Poor, presented ... January 11, 1825. ... *Philadelphia: Printed by Lydia R. Bailey.* 1825. 8vo, pp. 16. Continued.

Also: Philada. Jan. 21, 1824. Provident Society ... . Address to the Citizens of ... Philadelphia, and Constitution. [n. p. 1824.] 8vo, pp. 8.

Constitutions of the PUBLICK ACADEMY in the City of Philadelphia. [*Philadelphia: B. Franklin & D. Hall.* 1749.] Folio, pp. 4. 62108

Signed "Nov. 13, 1749."

Public Ledger Building, Philadelphia ... . [n. p. 1867.] 8vo, pp. 55, (1). 62109

Description of the building, opening ceremonies, etc.

The Public Ledger Building, Philadelphia; with an Account of the Proceedings connected with its Opening, June 20, 1867. *Philadelphia: G. W. Childs.* 1868. 12mo, pp. ix, 186. 2 Plates.

The Public Press and the Action of Councils relative to ... Dummy Engines On Street ... Cars ... *Philadelphia: Stein & Jones.* 1863. 8vo, pp. 10, and cover. 62111

Read and Circulate. City Missions. ... [n. p. n. d.] 8vo, pp. 8. 62112

Dated, Philadelphia, June 4, 1855. Report upon the establishment of a city mission by the Baptist Church.

Register of Trades of the Colored People in ... Philadelphia and Districts. *Philadelphia: Merrihew and Gunn.* 1838. 8vo.

Constitution of the RELIGIOUS TRACT SOCIETY ... . *Printed by Thos. & William Bradford,* ... *Philadelphia.* 1815. 12mo, pp. 4

Remarks of Mr. John Welsh, Chairman of a Committee appointed by certain Citizens of Philadelphia, addressed to a Special Committee of the House of Representatives of Pennsylvania, ... to which was referred the Senate bill, giving permission to the Councils ... to authorize the erection on the Penn Squares, of buildings for the promotion of Natural Science, Literature, the Fine Arts, and the Mechanic Arts. February 26, 1868. [n. p. n. d.] 8vo, pp. 7. 62115

Remarks On a second Publication of B. Henry Latrobe, Engineer, said to be printed by Order of the Committee of the Councils [of the City] [*sic*] and distributed among the members of the Legislature. [n. p. 1799.] 8vo. 62116

Said to be by Rev. Dr. Wm. Smith.

Remarks on the Greenwich Land and Building Association. *Philadelphia.* 1854. 8vo, pp. 7, (1). 62117

Reminiscences of Carpenters' Hall, in ... Philadelphia, and extracts from the ancient Minutes of the Proceedings of the Carpenters' Company ... of Philadelphia. ... *Philadelphia: Crissy & Markley.* 1858. 8vo, pp. 41. 2 Plates. 62118

Reply to an Answer to "Taxation of Learning, Charity, and Religion." *Philadelphia.* 1851. 8vo, pp. 10. 62119

A Reply to the Communication signed D. H. Mulvany: ... in the Norristown Free Press, of October 25, 1835. [n. p. n. d.] 8vo, pp. 28. 62120

Relates to Philadelphia, Germantown and Norristown Railroad. A corrected title of our No. 8239, Vol. ii.

Report from the Committee of Superintendence for the Relief of the Poor. [n. p. 1829.] 8vo, pp. 8. 62121

Report of a Committee appointed at a Meeting held ... December 3rd, 1852, to consider the propriety of ... a Paid Fire Department. *Philadelphia: Moran & Sickels.* 1853. 8vo, pp. 20.

Report of a Committee appointed to investigate the evils of Lotteries, in ... Pennsylvania, and to suggest a Remedy ... . *Philadelphia.* 1831. 8vo, pp. 16. 62123

Report of a Committee of the Select Council of Philadelphia. Read November 10th, 1796. *Philadelphia: Printed by Zachariah Poulson, Junior.* 1796. 8vo, pp. 24. 62124

On the city finances.

Report of a Joint Special Committee of Select and Common Councils, ... to whom was referred certain queries ... from the American Medical Association on ... Public Hygiene. ... *Philadelphia.* 1849. 8vo, pp. 39. 62125

Report of Committee on Police. [n. p. 1847.] Folio, 1 leaf.

Report of Committee on Public Highways. [n. p. 1848.] Folio, 1 leaf. 62127

Report of Jury, Filed January 2d, 1866, with the Testimony Submitted to them. *Philadelphia: King & Baird.* 1866. 4to, pp. (2), 107. 62128

The cover-title reads: "The Addition to Fairmount Park and the preservation of the Purity of the Water Supply, as secured by Ordinance of June 28th, 1864."

Report of the City Bounty Fund Commission, December 31, 1864. [n. p. n. d.] 8vo, pp. 16. + Report ... July 1, 1865. [n. p. n. d.] 8vo, pp. 15. 62129

Report of the City Solicitor on the Mode of Adjusting Taxation on Rural Property. [n. p. 1858.] 8vo, pp. 4. 62130

Report of the Commission appointed by the Sanitary Board of the City Councils to visit Canada, for the investigation of the Epidemic Cholera, prevailing in Montreal and Quebec. *Philadelphia: Mifflin & Parry.* 1832. 8vo, pp. (4), 37. 62131

Report of the Commissioners and Views of the Minority. *Philadelphia.* 1835. 8vo, pp. 12. 62132

Relates to a railroad on Broad street.

Report of the Committee appointed at a Town Meeting of the Citizens of ... Philadelphia, ... 23d of July, 1827, to consider the ... Pauper System of the City and Districts, and to report Remedies for its Defects. *Philadelphia: Clark & Raser.* 1827. 8vo, pp. 28, (6). 62133

Report of the Committee Appointed to Enquire concerning the Complaint of George Logan against Samuel W. Fisher, on a Breach of Privilege: With the Documents accompanying the same. *Lancaster: Printed by Francis & Robert Bailey* ... [1800.] 8vo, pp. 56. 62134

Report of the Committee appointed to inquire into the Expediency of Lighting the City with Gas. *Philadelphia.* 1833. 8vo, pp. 20. 62135

Report of the Committee appointed to Investigate the Affairs of the Philadelphia Savings Institution. Mr. Reed, Chairman. Read in the House of Representatives, March 25, 1836. *Harrisburg.* 1836. 8vo, pp. 12. 62136

Report of the Committee appointed to investigate the Condition of the Sufferers by the Fire at Ninth and Washington Sts., Philada., on ... Feb. 8th, 1865. *Philadelphia: King & Baird.* 1865. 8vo, pp. 12. 62137

Report of the Committee for the Gradual Civilization. *See* Vol. ix., No. 34669.

Report of the Committee of ... Councils of Philadelphia, on the Navigation of the River Schuylkill. *Philadelphia.* 1832. 8vo, pp. 28. 62138

Report of the Committee of Fifteen Citizens, appointed ... May 9th and 18th, 1848, to "Investigate and Report upon the Corruptions in the Administration of Law, the taking of Illegal Fees, and Extortion practiced by Public Officers, etc. Also, The Proceedings of the two Public Meetings ... . *Philadelphia.* 1849. 8vo. + Second Edition. ... [*Ibid.*] 1849. 8vo, pp. 36.

Report of the Committee on a Paid Fire Department, Made to Common Council, May 5th, 1859. ... *Philadelphia.* 1859. 8vo, pp. (2), 109. 62140

Report of the Committee on Finance to the ... Councils, upon the Income and Expenditure of the City ... within the year

1844. *Philadelphia: L. R. Bailey.* 1844. 8vo, pp. 12. Continued. 62141

Report of the Committee on Highways, etc., on the Removal of the Third Street Railroad. *Philadelphia: J. H. Jones & Co.* 1854. 8vo, pp. 12. 62142

Report of the Committee on Legacies and Truants, made ... April 27, 1837. ... *Philadelphia.* 1837. 8vo, pp. 28. Contin'd.

Report of the Committee on Police, on the circumstances ... connected with the destruction of the Pennsylvania Hall, and other consequent Disturbances of the Peace. ... *Philadelphia.* 1838. 8vo, pp. 39. 62144

Report of the Committee on Police and Fire Alarm Telegraphs; together with Propositions for Construction of the Same. ... *Philadelphia.* 1855. 8vo, pp. 20. 62145

Report of the Committee on Qualification of Teachers on the Examinations, ... May ... 1863 ... . *Philadelphia.* 1863. 8vo, pp. 12, (4). Continued annually. 62146

Report of the Committee on Railroads ... October 5th, 1854. *Philadelphia.* 1854. 8vo, pp. 19. 62147

Report of the Committee on Roads and Bridges of the County Board, on the ... proposed Purchase of Penn's Treaty Ground for Public Use. ... *Philadelphia.* 1852. 8vo, pp. 19. Map.

Report of the Committee on the Subject of Judge Symme's Purchase. *Philadelphia.* 1800. 8vo. 62149

Report of the Committee to whom was referred Sundry Memorials against Lighting the City with Gas. *Philadelphia.* 1833. 8vo, pp. 39. 62150

Report of the Committee to whom were referred Sundry Petitions, praying that the Schuylkill Permanent Bridge should be made a Free Bridge. ... April 8, 1834. *Harrisburg.* 1834. 8vo, pp. 11. 62151

Report of the General Executive Committee ... of Philadelphia, appointed by the Town Meeting of February 17, 1847, to provide means to relieve the Sufferings in Ireland. *Philadelphia.* 1847. 8vo, pp. 38, (2). 62152

Report of the Joint Committee appointed by the ... Councils, on the subject of Steam Boats. [n. p. 1817.] 8vo, pp. 13.

Report of the Joint Committee of Councils, relative to the Malignant or Pestilential Disease of Summer and Autumn of 1820, in ... Philadelphia. *Philadelphia: Printed by Lydia R. Bailey.* 1821. 8vo, pp. 55. 62154

Report of the Joint-Committee of the Select and Common Councils, on the City Debts and Expenditures ... . *Philadelphia: Printed by Zachariah Poulson, Junior.* 1801. Folio, pp. 8.

Continued in 8vo.

Report of the Joint Special Committee [of City Councils] in relation to the Pennsylvania Railroad. [n. p. 1846.] 8vo, pp. 55

In favor of subscribing for the stock of the company.

Report of the Joint Special Committees of ... Councils on the Communication from the North Pennsylvania R. Road. [n. p. 1856.] 8vo, pp. 8. 62157

Report of the Joint Special Committee on ... a Proposed Subscription by the Councils ... of Philadelphia to the Capital Stock of the Sunbury and Erie Rail Road Company ... . January 1853. *Philadelphia.* 1853. 8vo, pp. 58. 62158

Also: Report of the Joint Special Committee of Councils in favor of subscribing to the stock of the Sunbury and Erie Railroad. [n. p. 1854.] 8vo, pp. 24.

Report of the Joint Special Committee of ... Councils, on ... Removing the Railway on High, Third, and Dock Streets. ... December 31st, 1840. *Philadelphia.* 1841. 8vo, pp. 35.

Report of the Joint Special Committee of the ... Councils on Steam Fire Engines. November 2, 1854. *Philadelphia.* 1854. 8vo, pp. 7. 62160

A Report of the Meeting for Sufferings, adopted by the Yearly Meeting of Friends, held in Philadelphia, in Relation to the Facts and Causes of the Division, which occurred in New England Yearly Meeting ... 1845. *Boston: T. R. Marvin.* 1849. 8vo, pp. 42. H. 62161

Report of the Philadelphia Committee on ... Transatlantic Steam Navigation, February 7, 1839. *Philadelphia.* 1839. 8vo, pp. 16. 62162

Report of the Philadelphia Relief Committee to collect Funds for the Sufferers by Yellow Fever, at Norfolk and Portsmouth, Va., 1855. *Philadelphia.* 1856. 8vo, pp. (6), 136. Plate.

Improved title of our No. 55482, Vol. XIII.

Report of the Proceedings of a Convention composed of Delegates from the Thirteen Original United States, held in Independence Hall on ... the fifth, and ... sixth of July, 1852, for the purpose of considering the propriety of erecting one or more Monuments in Independence Square, Philadelphia—in commemoration of the Declaration of Independence, July 4, 1776, and in honor of the signers thereof, ... submitted by A. G. Waterman, Esq., of the Select Council, and adopted by both branches of councils September 25, 1851. *Philadelphia: Crissy & Markley, Printers.* 1852. 8vo, pp. 74, Errata, 4 lines. 62164

Report of the Proceedings of a Meeting held ... Philadelphia ... November 3, 1863, to take into Consideration the Condition of the Freed People of the South. *Philadelphia.* 1863. 8vo, pp. 24. 62165

Report of the Proceedings of the Town Meeting in the City of Philadelphia. July 7, 1828. [n. p. n. d.] 8vo, pp. (2), 22.

Report of the Secretary of the Treasury on the Memorial of sundry Merchants of Philadelphia, respecting the erection of Piers in the river Delaware. *Philadelphia.* 1798. 8vo. 62167

First Report of the Solicitor of the Protective War Claim and Pension Agency, of the U. S. Sanitary Commission, in Philadelphia, to the Board of Directors, January 1st, 1865. *Philadelphia.* 1865. 8vo, pp. 24. 62168

Report of the Special Committee, appointed by Select Council, ... to examine the Books, etc., of the Sunbury and Erie Railroad Company. *Philadelphia.* 1855. 8vo, pp. 91. 62169

Report of the Special Committee appointed for the purpose of examining all Books, Papers, Vouchers, Warrants, &c. &c. of the City Treasurer's Office ... . *Philadelphia.* 1856. 8vo, pp. (2), 28. 62170

Report of the Special Committee of Common Council in relation to the Sunbury and Erie Railroad, presented 14th September, 1854. *Philadelphia.* 1854. 8vo, pp. (2), 119. 62171

Report of the Special Committee of the County Board on Public Schools. September 23, 1850. *Philadelphia.* 1850. 8vo, pp. 22. 62172

Relates to the expenditures for schools in Philadelphia.

Report of the Special Committee on Communications from Messrs. Vogdes & Gerard. Together with the Testimony. ... reported by Wm. J. Crowell, A.B. *Philadelphia.* 1862. 8vo, pp. 139. 62173

Also: Report of the Special Committee [of the Controllers of the Public Schools] on Communications from Messrs. Vogdes & Gerard. ... *Philadelphia.* 1862. 8vo, pp. (2), 7.

Report of the Special Committee on Opening Eleventh St. [n. p. 1835.] 8vo, pp. 8. 62174

Report of the Special Committee to investigate the Management ... of the Philadelphia Gas Works ... . *Philadelphia.* 1867. 8vo, pp. 395. 62175

Report of the Special Relief Committee, March 1, 1865. [n. p. n. d.] 8vo, pp. 4. 62176

Report of the Sub-Committee deputed to visit Erie, etc. on the ... Proposed Subscription by the Councils of ... Philadelphia to the Capital Stock of the Sunbury and Erie Rail Road Company. Submitted to the General Joint Special Committee of Councils, December 14, 1852. *Philadelphia.* 1852. 8vo, pp. 92. Map. 62177

Report of the Sub-Committee on Cleansing the City, ... relative to the best means of securing the health and cleanliness of the City. *Philadelphia.* 1849. 8vo, pp. 48. 62178

Report of the Survey of a Section of the River Delaware, from One Mile below Chester, to Richmond, above Philadelphia. Taken by order of the Councils. By David M'Clure. ... *Philadelphia: Printed by Lydia R. Bailey.* 1820. 8vo, pp. 47. Map. 62179

Report of the Topographical Commissioners, appointed ... To Make a Survey of the region of Dock Street, ... to ascertain the best System of Drainage. ... July 5th, 1849. [n. p. n. d.] 8vo, pp. 8. 62180

Report of the Trial for Riot on October 13, 1831, Arising out of a Protestant Procession, July 12. *Philadelphia.* 1831. 8vo, pp. 104. 62181

Report of the Watering Committee, to the Select & Common Councils of ... Philadelphia, relative to the Fair Mount Water Works. Read January 9, 1823. *Philadelphia: Printed by Lydia R. Bailey.* 1823. 8vo, pp. 22. 3 Plates. 62182

Report on Drainage and Sewerage made to the ... Councils of ... Philadelphia, May 9, 1853, by Samuel H. Kneass ... . *Philadelphia.* 1853. 8vo, pp. 22. 62183

Report on the Agency of Intemperance in the Production of Pauperism. *Philadelphia: J. Van Court, Printer.* 1836. 8vo, pp. 16. 62184

Report on the Establishment ... in Philadelphia ... of "Ragged Schools." *Philadelphia.* 1847. 8vo. S. 62185

Report on the Memorial of Sundry Merchants and Traders ... of Philadelphia. April 13, 1798. [n. p. n. d.] 8vo, pp. 8.

Report on the Organization of an Evening School for Male Youths and Adults. [n. p. 1849?] 8vo, pp. 23. 62187

Report. To the Select Council: ... [n. p. 1854.] 8vo, pp. 3.

On changing the name of Carter's Alley to Jayne's street.

Reports to the Yearly Meeting. *See* Vol. IX., No. 34679.

The Representation and Petition of divers Religious Denominations of ... Philadelphia, to the Legislature of ... Pennsylvania. *Philadelphia: Printed by R. Aitken.* 1798. 8vo, pp. 16. 62189

The parsons of that day were disturbed during service by the passing carriages, and wanted permission to put chains across the streets on Sundays.

Resolutions of the Committee of Philadelphia, in regard to the sale of goods. [n. p. n. d.] 4to, 1 leaf. 62190

Dated, December 6, 1774.

Resolutions passed by the ... Councils, June 26th, 1851, fixing the Election Precincts in the City ... . [n. p. n. d.] 8vo, pp. 15. 62191

A Review of a Pamphlet. *See* House of Refuge, Vol. XIV., No. 61730, *note.*

Review of "An Address to the Citizens of Philadelphia, on the subject of Fancy Fairs." *Philadelphia: Printed by M. Fithian.* 1834. 8vo, pp. 8. 62192

Revision of the Delegate System. Rules ... of the Democratic Delegation ... of Philadelphia ... . [n. p. 1842.] Folio, 1 leaf. 62193

"The Rich Men of Philadelphia." Income Tax of the Residents of Philadelphia and Bucks County. For the Year ending April 30, 1865. *Philadelphia.* [n. d.] Rl. 8vo. 62194

Ridge Turnpike. An act to enable the Governor to incorporate a company for making an artificial road ... Vine and Tenth streets, Philadelphia, ... to the Perkiomen Bridge. ... [n. p. 1811.] 8vo, pp. 17. + [n. p. 1815.] 8vo, pp. 22, (1). + *Philadelphia: King & Baird.* 1852. 8vo, pp. 28. 62195

Robert's Second Edition of the Secret "Customs," and Revenue of the Sheriff's Office. "The Customs of the Office" 'are true as the existence of time, and certain as perpetual duration.' *Philadelphia: ... Sylvester Roberts.* 1817. 8vo, pp. 29.

Report of the ROMAN CATHOLIC SOCIETY OF ST. JOSEPH; for Educating ... Poor Orphan Children, for the year ending March 19, 1851. ... *Philadelphia: James Fullerton, Printer.* 1851. 12mo, pp. 16. 62197

Constitution and Address of the ROSINE ASSOCIATION. [n. p. 1847.] 12mo, pp. (2), 12. 62198

Also: Constitution and Report of the Managers of the Rosine Association, with a list of the Annual Subscribers and Contributors. *Philadelphia.* 1848. 12mo, pp. 24. Continued.—Reports and Realities from the Sketch-Book of a Manager of the ... Association, December, 1855. *Philadelphia: John Duross, Printer.* 1855. 12mo, pp. 380.—Semi-Annual Report of the Managers ... . [n. p. 1848.] 8vo, pp. (2), 15.

The Royal Road to Wealth, an Illustrated History of the Successful Business Houses of Philadelphia. *Philadelphia: Published by Samuel Loag, Edited by I. L. Vansant.* [1869.] 8vo, pp. 144. 10 Plates. 62199

Rules and Orders for the Regulation of the Corporation when met in Common Council. [n. p. n. d.] Folio, 1 leaf. 62200

Rules and Regulations for the ... Public Schools, with advice to the Parents and Guardians of Pupils ... . [n. p.] 1820. 8vo, 1 leaf. 62201

Rules of Discipline of the Yearly Meeting of Friends, held in Philadelphia. ... *Philadelphia: Printed by Kimber, Conrad & Co.* 1806. 8vo. 62202

Also: Rules of Discipline of the Yearly Meeting of Philadelphia. [n. p.] 1825. 12mo.—Rules of Discipline of the Yearly Meeting of Friends, held in Philadelphia. ... *Philadelphia: T. Ellwood Chapman.* 1856. 8vo.

Rules for the Government of the Democratic Party of ... Philadelphia, as revised and adopted, June 28th, 1864, and amended July 24th, 1866. ... *Philadelphia.* 1867. 24mo, pp. 48. + As adopted in Convention, August 10, 1869. ... *Philadelphia.* 1869. 16mo, pp. 50. 62203

Rules for the Government of the Select Council. ... *Philadelphia: Printed by Wm. Duane,* ... 1804. 16mo, pp. 10. 62204

Rules for the Government of the Select and Common Councils of ... Philadelphia; ... November 22, 1832. *Philadelphia.* 1832. 8vo, pp. 24. 62205

First Annual Report of the Parochial Meeting of ST. ANDREW'S CHURCH, Philadelphia. ... [n. p. 1865.] 8vo, pp. 18. Continued. 62206

Also: Catalogue of the Parish Library of St. Andrew's Church ... . *Philadelphia.* 1865. 8vo, pp. 53.—St. Andrew's Church Allotment, Woodlands Cemetery. *Philadelphia.* 1846. 8vo, pp. (2), 4. Plan.

Charter of the ST. ANDREW'S SOCIETY of Philadelphia. With a List of Members' Names. ... *Philadelphia: Printed ... by Bain and Orr.* 1837. 12mo, pp. 24, 12. 62207

The Constitution and Rules of the St. Andrew's Society ... . *Philadelphia: D. Hall & W. Sellers.* 1769. 8vo, pp. 19. P. + *Philadelphia: Printed by Hall & Sellers.* MDCCXCI. 8vo, pp. 12.

List of the Resident Members of St. Andrew's Society ... . June, 1840. ... *Philadelphia: Printed by A. Waldie.* [n. d.] 12mo, pp. 12. 62209

Rules for the St. Andrew's Society in Philadelphia. *Philadelphia: Printed by B. Franklin, and D. Hall.* MDCCLI. 8vo, pp. 16.

Report of the ... Managers of the ST. JOHN'S ORPHAN ASYLUM. ... *Philadelphia: Printed by Peter McKenna.* 1851. 12mo, pp. 12. Continued. 62211

The Charter, By-Laws and Rules, of the ST. JOSEPH'S HOSPITAL. ... *Philadelphia.* 1849. 8vo, pp. 16. 62212

Also: First Annual Report of the Managers of St. Joseph's Hospital. March 19, 1850. *Philadelphia: L. R. Bailey.* 1850. 8vo, pp. 20. Continued.—Report of St. Joseph's Hospital, ... from January 1st, 1859 to January 1st, 1866. By Robert B. Cruice, M.D. *Philadelphia: Collins, Printer.* 1866. 8vo, pp. 16. Plate. Continued annually.

Lay Co-Operation in ST. MARK'S CHURCH, Frankford, Philadelphia. January, 1861. *Philadelphia: King & Baird.* 1861. 8vo, pp. (2), 20. 62213

Address of the Committee of ST. MARY'S CHURCH, of Philadelphia, to their Brethren of the Roman Catholic Faith throughout the United States of America, on the subject of a Reform of Sundry Abuses in the Administration of Our Church Discipline. *New York: J. Kingsland & Co., Printers.* 1821. 8vo, pp. 15.

Also: Address of the Ladies of St. Mary's Congregation presented at the meeting in Washington Hall, ... Feb. 14, 1821. [n. p. n. d.] Folio, 1 leaf.—Address of the Lay Trustees to the Congregation of St. Mary's Church, on the approaching Election. *Philadelphia.* 1822. 8vo, pp. 25.—Address of the Trustees of St. Mary's Church to their Fellow-Citizens; containing a Correspondence between them and the Right Reverend Bishop Conwell, on a Late Attempt at a Reconciliation between the Contending Parties of the Congregation of said Church. *Philaaelphia: Printed by Lydia R. Bailey.* 1823. 8vo, pp. 25.—Appendix to the Address of the Lay Trustees of St. Mary's Church, to their Fellow Citizens. [n. p. n. d.] 8vo, pp. 15.—Address of the Trustees ... to the Congregation. *Phihadelphia.* 1831. 8vo.—Address to the Right Rev. Bishop Conwell and the Members of St. Mary's Congregation. *Philadelphia, Feb.* 14, 1821. 8vo, pp. 4.—Address to the Right Rev. the Bishop of Pennsylvania, and the Members of St. Mary's Congregation. [By Rev. William Hogan.] *Philadelphia, Dec.* 21, 1820. 8vo, pp. 4.—An Address to the Roman Catholics of the United States, by a Layman of St. Mary's Congregation ... . [n. p.:] *July,* 1821. 8vo, pp. 48.—An Answer to an "Address by a Catholic Layman to the Roman Catholics of the United States." By a Member of St. Mary's Church. *Philadelphia, July 27th,* 1821. 8vo, pp. 22.—A Brief Reply to a Ludicrous Pamphlet compiled from the Affidavits, Letters, and Assertions of a number of Theologians, with the signature of Henry, Bishop, and entitled Sundry Documents, addressed to St. Mary's Congregation. [By the Rev. William Hogan.] [n. p. 1821.] 8vo, pp. 54.—An nquiry into the Causes which led to the Dissentions actually existing in the Congregation of St. Mary's, and observations on the mode best calculated to prevent its increase. By a Layman of the Congregation. [n. p. 1821.] 12mo, pp. 12.—Last Appeal to the Congregation of St. Mary's Church. [n. p. 1821.] 8vo, pp. 4.—A Pastoral Charge, delivered by the Right Rev. Henry, Bishop of Philadelphia. [n. p.:] *February 11th,* 1821. 12mo, pp. 11. A burlesque in the interest of the Hogan party.—Sundry Documents addressed to St. Mary's Congregation. *Philadelphia: Bernard Dornin.* 1821. 8vo, pp. 30.—Sundry Documents submitted to the Consideration of the Pewholders of St. Mary's Church, by the Trustees of that Church. *Philadelphia: Printed by Lydia R. Bailey.* 1812. 8vo, pp. 26, 3.—Thoughts upon the Administration of Justice in St. Mary's Church. *Philadelphia.* 1809. 8vo.—To the Congregation of St. Mary's, On the Banks of the Rubicon. [n. p.:] *May* 10, 1821. Folio, 1 leaf.—To the Members of St. Mary's Congregation. [n. p. 1821.] 4to, 1 leaf. Anti Hogan.—To the ... Senate and House of Representatives ... of Pennsylvania: The Memorial of ... Members of the Roman Catholic ... Church of St. Mary's, in ... Philadelphia. [n. p. 1822?] 8vo, pp. 46. Against proposed amendments of the charter.—To the Members of St. Mary's Congregation. [n. p.:] *April* 19, 1814. Folio, 1 leaf.—The True Sentiments of the Writer of the Last Appeal to the Congregation of St. Mary's Church. *Philadelphia: Bernard Dornin.* 1821. 8vo, pp. 8.

Second Annual Report of the Vestry to the Congregation of the Church of ST. MATTHIAS. ... *Philadelphia: Jackson, Printer.* 1859. 8vo, pp. 20. Continued. 62215

Zum Andenken an die hundertjährige Jubelfeier in der deutschen evangel. luther. SCT. MICHAELIS-KIRCHE in Philadelphia, am 14 Junius, 1843. Dem Druck übergeben, auf Verlangen des Kirchenrathes der Gemeinde. Der Ertrag ist unsern deutschen Brüdern im Westen bestimmt. *Philadelphia: Gedruckt bei Conrad Zentler.* [n. d.] 12mo, pp. 104. 62216

The Constitution of the ST. PATRICK BENEVOLENT SOCIETY. [n. p. 1804?] 8vo, pp. 8. + By-Laws ... 8vo, pp. 8. 62217

Letter from a Member of ST. PAUL'S, shewing the Source of the present Wranglings in that Congregation. *Philadelphia.* 1764. 8vo. P. 62218

Also: A Letter in reply ... . *Philadelphia.* 1764. 8vo. P.

An Historical Sketch of ST. PETER'S CHURCH, Great Valley, Chester County, Pa. *John Hodgson, Printer, West Chester.* 1850. 8vo, pp. 8. 62219

Report of the Committee appointed at a Special Meeting of the Vestry of ST. STEPHEN'S CHURCH, held May 21, 1861, to prepare a Plan for the Organization and Management of the Burd Orphan Asylum of St. Stephen's Church. [n. p. n. d.] 8vo, pp. 7. 62220

Sanitary Committee. ... Report of the Medical Commission appointed to visit Montreal and Quebec ... . [n. p. 1832.] 8vo, pp. 4. 62221

Report of the SANITARY COMMITTEE of the Councils of Philadelphia, ... September 27, 1849. [n. p. n. d.] 8vo, pp. 3.

Sanitary Fair Catalogue and Guide. *Philadelphia: Magee.* 1854. 4to, pp. 30. 62223

Saturday, February 28, 1778. Theatre. ... [n. p. n. d.] 4to, 1 leaf. P. 62224

A postponement of the performances of the British officers, etc. Eight hundred copies printed by J. Humphreys, Philadelphia.

Articles of Association of the SAVING FUND SOCIETY, with Tables. *Philadelphia.* 1817. 8vo. P. 62225

Schedule of the Real Estate owned by the Corporation of ... Philadelphia, Nov. 22, 1832. *Philadelphia.* 1832. 8vo. P.

The School Fund. [n. p. 1854.] 8vo, pp. 8. 62227

School of Design. [n. p. 1852.] 4to, 1 leaf. 62228

Appeal for an endowment fund.

Answer of the Committee of the ... Directors of the ... Company for erecting a permanent bridge over the SCHUYLKILL at or near ... Philadelphia, to the Questions propounded by the Committee of Councils appointed to inquire into the expediency of making the ... bridge a Free Bridge. *Philadelphia.* 1833. 8vo, pp. 12. 62229

By-Laws, Rules and Regulations of the Corporation ... for erecting a permanent bridge over the ... Schuylkill, at or near ... Philadelphia. To which are prefixed the Act of ... Incorporation, and the Supplement thereto. ... *Philadelphia: Printed by William Fry.* 1822. 16mo, pp. 40. 62230

Memorial of the President ... and Company for erecting a Permanent Bridge over the River Schuylkill at ... Philadelphia, remonstrating against certain alterations prayed for by the West Philadelphia Canal Company ... . *Harrisburg: Henry Welsh.* 1833. 8vo, pp. 26. 62231

Also: Report of the Committee appointed to inquire into the Expediency of making the Schuylkill Permanent Bridge a Free Bridge. *Philadelphia: Lydia R. Bailey.* 1833. 8vo, pp. 16.—Report on the Viaduct across the Schuylkill at Chestnut St. By Thomas S. Stewart. *Philadelphia.* 1855. 8vo.—Report ... Schuylkill Permanent Bridge ... . By Mr. Goodman, April 8, 1834. *Harrisburg.* 1834. 8vo, pp. 11.—... Schuylkill Permanent Bridge. Dec. 12, 1833. [n. p. n. d.] 8vo, pp. 16.—Statement by the President, Directors, and Company for erecting a Permanent Bridge over the River Schuylkill, at or near ... Philadelphia. *Philadelphia: L. R. Bailey.* 1838. 8vo, pp. 17.—Statement of Facts, relative to the Origin and Causes of the present attempt to Free the Schuylkill Permanent Bridge. [n. p. 1831?] 8vo, pp. 36.—To the Public. Schuylkill Permanent Bridge. [n. p. 1834.] 8vo, pp. 16. In favor of freeing the bridge. *See also* Schuylkill Navigation Company.

Charter, By-Laws, Rules and Regulations, of the SCHUYLKILL FISHING COMPANY. Instituted May 1, 1732. Incorporated April 27, 1844. As Amended ... at the October Meeting, 1859. ... *State in Schuylkill: Philadelphia.* 1860. 8vo, pp. 25. 62232

Constitution of the SCOTS THISTLE SOCIETY of Philadelphia. ... *Philadelphia: Printed by John Bioren.* 1799. 8vo, pp. 28.

Also: Alterations and Amendments of the Laws of the Scots Thistle Society. [n. p. 1811?] 8vo, pp. 7.—Laws and Constitution of the Scots Thistle Society of Philadelphia. ... [n. p.:] *Printed ... by Adam Waldie.* 1832. 24mo, pp. 66.

Seaman's Lyceum of Philadelphia. *Philadelphia: William Brown, Printer.* 1836. 12mo, pp. 22. 62234

Act of Incorporation and By-Laws of the SECOND AND THIRD Street Passenger Railway Co. *Philadelphia.* 1858. 8vo.

The Secret "Customs," and Revenue of the Sheriff's Office. ... *Philadelphia: Sylvester Roberts.* 1819. 8vo, pp. 29. 62236

The Sedgely Park Scheme. Reasons of Andrew Miller for voting in Common Council against the ... "Ordinance to pay interest due to Justice Cox, Trustee." *Philadelphia: Gibbons, Printer.* 1857. 8vo, pp. 7. 62237

Also: Special Report of the Committee on City Property, relative to Sedgely Park. [n. p. 1857.] 8vo, pp. 20.

Seven Hints For all who will take them. By a Church of England-Man. [n. p. 1770.] Folio, 1 leaf. 62238

Against non-importation agreements, signed J. S.

The Shakspere Society of Philadelphia. *Philadelphia: Printed ... by King and Baird.* MDCCCLX. 8vo, pp. 16. 62239

Address to the Pupils of SHARON BOARDING SCHOOL, by the Female Principal at the close of the Session 1849. *Philadelphia.* [1849.] 12mo, pp. 22. 62240

Short History of the Yellow Fever, ... in ... Philadelphia, in July, 1797: with a List of the Dead; of the Donations for the Relief of the Poor ... . *Philadelphia: Printed by Richard Folwell.* M. DCC. XCVII. 8vo, pp. 36, 46–64, (16). + Second Edition. [*Ibid.*] M. DCC. XCVIII. 8vo, pp. 64, (16). 62241

A Short History of T. E. Sickels' Connection as Chief Engineer with the West Chester and Philadelphia Rail-Road. [n. p. 1854?] 8vo, pp. 16. 62242

Report of the Committee on the SINKING FUND, made 1830. *Philadelphia.* 1830. Folio. Continued. W. 62243

Sketch of the U. S. Dry Docks at Philadelphia ... *New York.* 1849. 8vo. Plates. 62244

Sketches of Fairmount, Lemon Hill and the adjoining grounds as a Public Park. *Philadelphia.* 1855. 8vo. Map. P. 62245

Sketches of the Higher Classes of Colored Society in Philadelphia. By a Southerner. *Philadelphia: Merrihew and Thompson, Printers.* 1841. 12mo, pp. 116. C. 62246

Constitution de la SOCIÉTÉ FRANÇAISE de Bienfaisance. *Philadelphie: De l'imprimerie de John C. Clark.* 1835. 12mo, pp. 25 [for 35]. + *New York: De l'imprimerie du Courrier des États-Unis.* 1849. 12mo, pp. 24. 62247

Constitution et Règlements ou By-Laws de la Société Française de Bienfaisance de Philadelphie, précédés d'une Esquisse Historique sur son Origine et sa Marche. *Philadelphie: De l'imprimerie de J. B. Chandler.* 1862. 8vo, pp. 43. 62248

Also: Société Française de Bienfaisance de Philadelphie. ... Rapport ... . *Philadelphie: Imprimerie de James B. Chandler.* 1858. 12mo, pp. 23. Continued.

Rules and Regulations of the SOCIETY FOR POLITICAL ENQUIRIES. Established at Philadelphia, 9th February, 1787. *Philadelphia: Printed by Robert Aitken.* M.DCC.LXXXVII. 16mo, pp. 18

Constitution and Laws of the SOCIETY FOR SUPPLYING the Poor with Soup. ... *Philadelphia.* 1857. 8vo, pp. 16. 62250

Constitution of the SOCIETY FOR THE ATTAINMENT of Useful Knowledge. ... *Philadelphia: Printed by Zachariah Poulson, junr.* MDCCXCIV. 24mo, pp. (12). 62251

Constitution of the SOCIETY FOR THE DEFENCE of the Catholic Religion from Calumny and Abuse. *Philadelphia: Printed by Joseph R. A. Skerrett.* 1827. 12mo, pp. 8. 62252

Report of the Board of Managers of the SOCIETY FOR THE ESTABLISHMENT and Support of Charity Schools, 1840. *Philadelphia.* 1840. 8vo. Continued. B. 62253

Constitution of the SOCIETY FOR THE INSTITUTION and Support of First-Day or Sunday Schools in ... Philadelphia, and the Districts of Southwark and the Northern Liberties. ... And a Summary of the Proceedings of the Society, from its commencement to the Seventh Month, July, 1810 ... . [*Philadelphia:*] *Joseph Crukshank, Printer.* 1810. 12mo, pp. 23, (1). 62254

Rules for the Regulation of the SOCIETY FOR THE RELIEF of Free Negroes, and others, unlawfully held in Bondage. Instituted in Philadelphia, in ... 1784. To which are prefixed, The Acts of the General Assembly of Pennsylvania, respecting the gradual Abolition of Slavery. *Philadelphia: Printed by Joseph Crukshank.* MDCCLXXXIV. 8vo, pp. (2), 16. 62255

Constitution of the SOCIETY OF AMERICAN REPUBLICANS. *Philadelphia: Printed by Thomas T. Stiles.* 1809. 16mo, pp. 8.

The Constitution of the SOCIETY OF ARTISTS of the United States, established at Philadelphia, May, 1810. *Philadelphia: Thomas L. Plowman, Printer.* 1810. 12mo, pp. 12. 62257

The Address of the SOCIETY OF CONSTITUTIONAL REPUBLICANS, ... of Philadelphia, to the Republicans of Pennsylvania. ... adopted ... 10th of June, 1805. *Philadelphia: Printed by William M'Corkle.* 1805. 8vo, pp. 28. 62258

Society of Friendly Sons of St. Patrick. *Philadelphia.* 1844. 12mo. 62259

Rules and Constitutions of the SOCIETY OF THE SONS OF ST. GEORGE, Established at Philadelphia, for the Advice and Assistance of Englishmen in Distress. *Philadelphia: Printed by William Cobbett.* 1797. 12mo, pp. 25. 62260

Also: Annual Report of the Society of the Sons of St. George, ... with a List of its Officers, Members and By-Laws, for 1867. *Philadelphia: William F. Geddes.* [n. d.] 16mo, pp. 20.—Charter and By-Laws of the Society of the Sons of St. George. Together with an Historical Sketch of the Origin and Progress of the Society, List of Officers, Members, etc., etc. *Philadelphia: Printed by Haswell, Barrington and Haswell.* 1840. 8vo, pp. 56.—An Historical Sketch of the Origin and Progress of the Society of the Sons of St. George, also the Charter, By-Laws, and Permanent Resolutions, together with an alphabetical list of the Names of the Members and Associates, List of Officers, etc. From April 23d, 1772 to April 23d, 1872. *Philadelphia: W. W. Bates & Co., Printers.* 1872. 8vo, pp. 112. Plate.—List of Members of the Society of St. George, established at Philadelphia for the Relief of Englishmen in Distress, with the Constitution, By-Laws, etc. in 1796. [n. p. n. d.] 8vo.

Constitutional Rules of the SOCIETY OF UNITARIAN CHRISTIANS at Philadelphia, agreed upon ... the 28th of August, 1796. *Philadelphia: Jos. Gales, Printer.* 1796. 8vo, pp. 7. 62261

Also: Charter, By-Laws, and List of Publications of the First Society of Unitarian Christians. *Philadelphia.* 1814. 12mo.—Constitution of the First Society of Unitarian Christians in ... Philadelphia, adopted Aug. 23, 1807. *Philadelphia.* 1807. 8vo, pp. 24. P.

First Annual Report of the SOLDIERS READING ROOM. ... *Philadelphia: Eckel, Printer.* 1863. 16mo, pp. 21. 62262

Some Account of the Prison at Philadelphia, chiefly extracted From a late American Publication. *London: W. and S. Graves.* 1816. 8vo. 62263

South Broad Street, Philadelphia. [n. p. 1869?] 4to, pp. 7. Map. 62264

The Constitution of the SOUTHERN Christian Home Missionary Society, and the Report of a Committee ... on the Organiza-

tion and Conduct of a House of Industry. *Philadelphia: Printed by Merrihew and Thompson.* 1845. 12mo, pp. 12. 62265

Charter of Incorporation and Rules and Regulations of the SOUTHERN DISPENSARY, for the Medical Relief of the Poor. ... *Philadelphia: M'Farland, Printer.* 1863. 12mo, pp. 12, (2).

Also: Rules of the Southern Dispensary for the Medical Relief of the Poor; with Lists of the Contributors, Managers and Officers for the years 1819, 1820 and 1821. *Philadelphia.* [n. d.] 8vo. + For 1822. + For 1823 and 1824. + For 1825. + For 1826. And the Annual Report, for 1825. [n. p. n. d.] 12mo, pp. 10.

In the Supreme Court ... of Pennsylvania. ... Motion on behalf of the SOUTHWARD RAILROAD COMPANY, ... to restrain the City of Philadelphia, ... from removing the City Railroad on Broad Street. ... *Philadelphia: King & Baird, Printers.* MDCCCLXIII. 8vo, pp. 86. 62267

A Special Report of the Committee on Legacies and Trusts, on the Boudinot Lands: ... [and] on the Fire and Hose Establishments of this City ... . *Philadelphia: Printed by L. R. Bailey.* 1837. 8vo, pp. 16. 62268

Specifications and Contract, for the New Public Buildings, ... *King & Baird, Printers, Philadelphia.* [1860.] 8vo, pp. (2), 31.

Free Reading-Room of SPRING GARDEN, for Young Men and Apprentices. *Philadelphia.* 1850. 8vo, pp. 12. 62270

First Annual Report of the ... Managers of the SPRING GARDEN INSTITUTE. ... *Philadelphia: John Richards, Printer.* 1852. 8vo, pp. 22, (2). 62271

Standing Orders for the Garrison of Philadelphia. [n. p. 1777.] Folio, 1 leaf. 62272

Signed Lewis Nicola, Town Major.

State of the Accounts of William Crispin, Esq. late Collector of Excise for ... Philadelphia. ... *Philadelphia: Printed by F. Bailey.* MDCCLXXIV [for 1784]. 8vo, pp. 16. H.S.P. 62273

State of the Accounts of Samuel Dewees, Esq; late Sub-Lieutenant of Philadelphia County. *Philadelphia: Printed by John Dunlap.* MDCCLXXXIII. 8vo, pp. 23. 62274

State of the Accounts of Peter Richards, Esq; Sub-Lieut. of the County of Philadelphia, in which is exhibited, ... the Amount of the Monies received by Fines, and accounted for in the Fall 1779 and Spring 1780; ... [n. p. n. d.] 8vo, pp. 8. 62275

State of the Accounts of Jacob Engle, Esquire, late a Sub-Lieutenant of Philadelphia County. *Philadelphia: Printed by John Dunlap.* MDCCLXXXIII. 8vo, pp. 128. H.S.P. 62276

State of the Accounts of Archibald Thompson, Esquire, late a Sub-Lieutenant of Philadelphia County. *Philadelphia: Printed by Hall and Sellers.* MDCCLXXXIII. 8vo, pp. 41. H.S.P. 62277

State of the Accounts of Col. George Smith, a Sub-Lieutenant of the County of Philadelphia. In which is exhibited, ... the amount of the Fines received and accounted for by him, between March, 1777, and April 1780; ... *Philadelphia: Printed by F. Bailey.* M.DCC.LXXXIII. 8vo, pp. 72. H.S.P. 62278

State of the Accounts of Wm. Antes, Esq. Sub Lieutenant of Philadelphia County, as they have been settled and adjusted. In which is set forth, ... the Amount of Fines received and accounted for: with Lists ... . [n. p. 1783.] 8vo, pp. 17.

State of the Accounts of William Henry, Esquire, Lieutenant of ... Philadelphia and Districts; From April 1st, 1783, to April 1st, 1785. In which is exhibited an Account of the Monies received by him for Militia Fines, and accounted for: ... *Philadelphia: Printed by Robert Aitken.* M,DCCLXXXV. 8vo, pp. 16.

State of the Accounts of the Lieutenants & Sub Lieutenants of ... Philadelphia, and Liberties. From March 1777, to April 1783. Wherein is exhibited, the amount of the fines paid by the six battalions of infantry, and the artillery battalion, which were incurred within that time, for non-performance of militia duty, and exercise. ... *Philadelphia: Printed by Francis Bailey.* M,DCC,LXXXIV. 8vo, pp. 165. H.S.P. 62281

Statement Addressed by the Association of the Fifth Presbyterian Church in Philadelphia, to the Members ... . [n. p. 1829.] 12mo, pp. 4, 11. 62282

Statement of Devises, Bequests, & Grants to the Corporation ... of Philadelphia. In Trust. ... *Philadelphia: Printed by Lydia R. Bailey.* 1832. 8vo, pp. 34, 36, 7. 2 Maps. 62283

Statement of Devises, ... to the Corporation of ... Philadelphia ... including Girard's Will. ... *Philadelphia.* 1832. 8vo, pp. 34, ix, 36. 62284

Statement of the Committee on Finance, showing the Expenses of the Various Municipal Corporations for ... 1853; ...

for debts contracted by the various corporations prior ... . *Philadelphia.* 1855. 8vo, pp. 8. 62285

Statement of the Deaths, with the Diseases and Ages, In the City and Liberties of Philadelphia, during ... 1834. [n. p. 1835.] Folio, 2 leaves. 62286

Statement of the Expenditures of the City Commissioners for ... 1817. *Philadelphia.* 1818. Folio. Continued. 62287

Statement of the Value of the Property owned by the ... City of Philadelphia, ... with the Revenue ... . *Philadelphia: J. H. Jones & Co., Printers.* 1855. 8vo, pp. 10. 62288

A Statistical Inquiry into the Condition of the People of Colour ... . *Philadelphia: Printed by Kite & Walton.* 1849. 8vo, pp. 44. 62289

Statistical Memoranda of some of the Affairs of the Committee on Police. 1849–1850. [n. p. n. d.] 8vo, pp. 8.

Continued to 1852 or later.

Statistics of Cholera: with the Sanitary Measures adopted by the Board of Health prior to, and during the prevalence of the Epidemic in Philadelphia, in the Summer of 1849, Chronologically arranged. ... *Philadelphia: King and Baird, Printers.* 1849. 8vo, pp. 62, (9). BA. 62291

Statistics of Philadelphia: comprehending A Concise View of all the Public Institutions and the Fire Engine and Hose Companies of ... Philadelphia, ... January, 1842. [*Philadelphia:*] *Printed No. 35 Walnut Street.* [n. d.] 12mo, pp. 38. 62292

Statistics of the Colored People of Philadelphia. Taken by Benjamin C. Bacon, and published by order of the Board of Education of "the Pennsylvania Society for promoting the abolition of Slavery," etc. Second Edition. *Philadelphia: Reprinted by order of the Board of Education.* 1859. 8vo, pp. 24. 62293

For the first edition *see our* No. 2639, Vol. I.

Statistics of the Operations of the Executive Board of Friends' Association of Philadelphia ... for the Relief of Colored Freedmen; with the Report of Samuel R. Shepley, ... of his Visit to the ... Freedmen on the Mississippi River. *Philadelphia.* 1864. 12mo, pp. 33. 62294

The Stranger's Guide in Philadelphia and its Environs. ... With Illustrations. *Philadelphia: Lindsay & Blakiston.* 1852. 18mo, pp. 268. Map. + [*Ibid.*] 1854. + [*Ibid.*] 1855. + [*Ibid.*] 1857. + [*Ibid.*] 1860, '61, '65. 62295

The Stranger's Guide to the Public Buildings, Places of Amusement, Streets, ... etc. of ... Philadelphia and adjoining districts ... . *Philadelphia: H. S. Tanner.* 1828. 24mo, pp. 38, 10. Map and Plate. 62296

See also Paxton (J. A.), Vol. XIV., No. 59263.

Street Talk about an Ordinance ... passed the 11th July, 1844, organizing a Military Force for the Government of Philadelphia. *Philadelphia.* 1844. 8vo, pp. 22. 62297

The Street Sweeping & Fertilizing Co. of Philadelphia. ... Its Objects, Facilities and Prospects of Operation in ... Philadelphia, and other Cities and Towns of the United States. ... *Philadelphia.* 1857. 8vo, pp. 24. 62298

A Report from the SUPERINTENDENT OF TRUSTS, showing the amount to the Credit of the several Trusts vested in the Corporation ... and how invested. *Philadelphia.* 1855. 8vo, pp. 61.

Also: A Report from the Superintendent of Trusts in relation to the Boudinot Lands, situated on the Susquehanna River, ... and Report of the Re-Survey of the Same, by Jos. F. Quay. *Philadelphia: Hufty, Stationer.* 1860. 8vo, pp. 22, (1).

A Supplement to the Digest of the Acts of Assembly, Ordinances and Resolutions of the Inhabitants and Commissioners of the District of Spring Garden ... . *Philadelphia.* 1846. 8vo, pp. 86. 62300

Joel B. Sutherland or James Gowen. Read—and then choose. [n. p. 1822?] 8vo, pp. 7, (1). P. 62301

Democratic election address.

Annual Report of the President of the TEACHERS' INSTITUTE, ... of Philadelphia, for ... 1868 ... . *Philadelphia.* 1868. 8vo, pp. 64, (1). 62302

Also: Proceedings of the Teachers' Institute of ... Philadelphia, for ... 1869. *Philadelphia.* 1869. 8vo, pp. 67. Continued.

Constitution and Address of the TEMPORARY HOME ASSOCIATION. *Philadelphia: John Young, Printer.* 1849. 12mo, pp. 12.

Also: Constitution and Semi-Annual Report of the Temporary Home Association, ... [n. p. 1850.] 12mo, pp. 2, 8. Continued.

Ten Years' Progress: or a Comparison of the State and Condition of the Colored People in ... Philadelphia from 1837 to 1847. Prepared by Edward Needles. *Philadelphia.* 1849. 12mo, pp. 16. 62304

Die Regeln der TEUTSCHEN GESELLSCHAFT in Philadelphia. *Germantown: Gedruckt bey Christoph Saur.* 1766. 8vo, pp. 8. P.

Theatre. ... [n. p. 1778.] Folio, 1 leaf. P. 62306

Postponement of performances, dated "8th Apr. 1778." Printed by J. Humphreys, Philadelphia.

Theatre. ... [n. p. n. d.] Folio, 1 leaf. P. 62307

Postponement in Passion-Week. Dated "Philad'a. Apr. 12. 1778."

Annual Report of the ... THEOLOGICAL SEMINARY of St. Charles Borromeo, of Philadelphia. For ... 1848. *Philadelphia: Printed by M. Fithian.* 1848. 12mo, pp. 82. 62308

Fifth Annual Catalogue of the Students ... of the Annual Curriculum of Lectures of the year ending ... February, 1836: Together with a list of the Graduates in Botany and Therapeutics, ... in the THERAPEUTIC INSTITUTE of Philadelphia. ... *Philadelphia: John Thompson, Printer.* 1836. 8vo, pp. (2), 8, (1).

The Complaint and Petition of the Commissioners of the THIRD PRESBYTERIAN CHURCH to the Synod of Philadelphia. *Philadelphia.* 1814. 8vo. 62310

Also: Ecclesiastical Proceedings relative to the Third Presbyterian Church, and to the Rev. E. S. Ely ... . *Philadelphia.* 1814. 12mo. B. *See our* Vol. VI., No. 22384, *note.*

Thursday, Sept. 27. 1770. Many respectable Freeholders, &c. [n. p. n. d.] 12mo, 1 leaf. P. 62311

Call for a Whig meeting *eo die.*

To our Friends and Brethren in religious Profession in these and the adjacent Province. [n. p. 1776.] 4to, 1 leaf. 62312

"Signed in behalf of the Meeting for Sufferings, Philadelphia the 20th day of the Twelfth Month, 1776, John Pemberton, Clerk." "That we may with Christian firmness and fortitude withstand and refuse to submit to the arbitrary injunctions and ordinances of men, who assume to themselves the power of compelling others either in person or by other assistance to join in carrying on war."

To the Citizens of Philadelphia. [n. p. 1771.] Folio, 1 l.

To the Citizens of ... Philadelphia. [n. p. 1826.] Folio.

Address in favor of charity schools.

To the Citizens of Walnut Ward. [n. p. 1844.] 8vo, 1 l.

Native American address.

To the Citizens of Walnut Ward. [n. p. 1845.] 4to, 1 l.

Whig election circular.

To the Congress. The Remonstrance of the Subscribers, Citizens of Philadelphia ... . [n. p.:] *Printed by Robert Bell.* [n. d.] Folio, 1 leaf. P. 62317

From the loyalists who were arrested in September, 1777. Dated "5th, 9th mo. 1777."

To the Freeholders and Electors of the City and County of Philadelphia. [n. p. 1764.] Folio, pp. 2. P. 62318

An anti-Franklin election address.

To the Freeholders and other Electors for the City and County of Philadelphia, and Counties of Chester and Bucks. [n. p. 1764.] Folio, pp. 2. P. 62319

An anti-proprietory election address.

To the Freeholders, Merchants, Tradesmen and Farmers, of ... Philadelphia. [n. p. n. d.] 4to, 1 leaf. 62320

"A Freeholder" in favor of non-importation, dated "Philad. Sept. 26, 1770." In answer to "To the Tradesmen," etc., Sep. 24, 1770.

To the Freemen, Citizens of Philadelphia. [n. p. n. d.] Folio, 1 leaf. 62321

Protest, signed "A Philadelphian," and dated May 29, 1773, against the erection of a market-house in Market street.

To the Freemen, Citizens of Philadelphia. [n. p. n. d.] Folio, 1 leaf. 62322

An attack on the corporation of Philadelphia. A second address against the new market-houses, signed "A Philadelphian," and dated June 16, 1773.

To the Honourable Patrick Gordon, Esq. Lieutenant Governor of the Province of Pennsylvania, and Counties of New-Castle, Kent and Sussex upon Delaware, the Address of the Mayor and Commonalty of the City of Philadelphia in Council the Sixteenth Day of the Fifth Month, July, anno 1726. The Governor's Answer to the Address. *Philadelphia: Printed ... by Andrew Bradford, at the Sign of the Bible, in the Second Street.* Folio, 1 leaf. 62323

To the Hon. Senate and House of Representatives of the United States. Memorial of the Philadelphia Society for the

promotion of American Manufactures. [*Philadelphia.* 1818.] 8vo. 62324

To the Inhabitants of the City and County of Philadelphia. [n. p. n. d.] 4to, 1 leaf. 62325

Signed "A Pennsylvanian" and dated July 14, 1770, in regard to the non-importation agreement. It begins: "The New Yorkers have betrayed a Meanness and Cowardice in deserting us in the present important juncture, which wants a name. May infamy be their portion. And may the names of Bute, a Greville, a Barnard, a Yorker hereafter be synonimous Words."

To the Inhabitants of Philadelphia. [n. p. 1771.] Folio, 1 l.

To the Inhabitants of the City of Philadelphia, and Parts adjacent. [n. p. n. d.] Folio, 1 leaf. 62327

Protest of the soap-boilers of Philadelphia, against Mr. John Rhea's scheme to make a corner in wood ashes. Dated Philadelphia, 15th February, 1772.

To the Inhabitants of the City and Liberties of Philadelphia. [n. p. 1831.] 8vo, pp. 11. 62328

To the Manufacturers and Mechanics of Philadelphia, the Northern Liberties, and District of Southwark. [n. p. 1774.] 4to, 1 leaf. P. 62329

Call for a public meeting on June 9th, 1774, to consider the Boston Port Bill.

To the Merchants, and Traders, of the City of Philadelphia. [n. p. 1770.] Folio, 1 leaf. 62330

In favor of a non-importation agreement.

To the Merchants Committee, the Dry Goods Merchants, &c. [n. p. 1770.] 4to, 1 leaf. 62331

An American in favor of home manufactures, dated "Philada. May 12, 1770."

To the Non-Commissioned Officers and Privates of the several Companies of Associators, belonging to the City and Liberties of Philadelphia. [n. p. 1775.] Folio, 1 leaf. 62332

Urging them to sign the articles of association prescribed by the Assembly.

To the Public. [n. p. n. d.] Folio, 1 leaf. P. 62333

"Philadelphus" against non-importation, dated "Philadelphia, October the 3d, 1770."

To the Public. ... Philadelphia, January 15, 1772. [n. p. n. d.] 4to, 1 leaf. 62334

On the best routes to the West, proposing a canal between Delaware and Chesapeake, etc. Printed by Franklin and Hall.

To the Public—Philadelphia Gaol, the 12th of the 10th Month, 1772. [n. p. n. d.] Folio, 1 leaf. P. 62335

Complaint of one John Vansant.

To the Public. A few plain facts for gas consumers! Theory of Good Light. How to make Small Gas Bills! [n. p. 1856.] 8vo, pp. 16. 62336

To the Tradesmen, Farmers, and other Inhabitants of ... Philadelphia. [n. p. n. d.] 4to, 1 leaf. 62337

"A Tradesman" in favor of non-importation, dated "Northern Liberties, September 24, 1770." For an answer *see* "To the Freeholders," Sept. 26, 1770.

Town Meeting. [n. p. 1840?] Folio, 1 leaf. 62338

In regard to public buildings on Penn Squares.

Tracts connected with the Progressive Increase, Present Condition and Future Prospects of Philadelphia, as connected with the permanent location of Public Buildings. *Philadelphia.* 1838. 8vo. P. 62339

Tracts for the Times. A Few Facts plainly stated for the Citizens ... . To be Read before they Vote on Tuesday next. [n. p. 1841.] 8vo, pp. 8. 62340

A Tradesman's Address to his Countrymen. [n. p. n. d.] Folio, 1 leaf. 62341

On the "Report that our Assembly have framed an Excise Bill." Dated "Phil. Mch. 2d, 1772."

A Traveler's Sketch. Continental Hotel. *Philadelphia: M'Laughlin Brothers, Printers.* 1861. 16mo, pp. 48. Map and 8 Plates. 62342

Description of the Continental Hotel and guide book.

Treasurer's Report, showing the Receipts and Payments, 1839–40. [n. p. n. d] 8vo. 62343

Constitution ... of the TRUE REPUBLICAN SOCIETY ... of Philadelphia. ... *Philadelphia.* 1830. 16mo, pp. 36. 62344

A True Statement of the First Fire on Sunday Evening, July 7, 1844. *Philadelphia.* 1844. 8vo, pp. 8. 62345

The Truth Unveiled; or, a Calm and Impartial Exposition of the origin and immediate cause of the Terrible Riots in Philadelphia, on May 6th, 7th, and 8th, A.D. 1844. By a Protestant and

a Native Philadelphian. *Philadelphia: Printed by M. Fithian.* 1844. 8vo, pp. 24. 62346

Catalogue of the Trustees, ... of the UNION ACADEMY, of Philadelphia, for ... 1855–6. *Philadelphia.* MDCCCLVI. 12mo, pp. 16. Continued. 62347

Constitution of the UNION BENEVOLENT ASSOCIATION, ... 1831. *Philadelphia: Jesper Harding, Printer.* 1831. 8vo, pp. 12. Continued. 62348

Reflections on the System of the UNION BENEVOLENT ASSOCIATION, stating its Beneficial Effects on the Manners, Habits, Conduct, and Comforts of the Poor; ... By a Citizen of Philadelphia. *Philadelphia: Printed by William F. Geddes.* 1837. 8vo, pp. 12. 62349

Also: First Annual Report of the Executive Board of the Union Benevolent Association. *Philadelphia: J. Harding, Printer.* 1832. 8vo, pp. 12. Continued.—The Quarterly Reports of the Executive Board ... of the Association. ... *Philadelphia.* 1836. 8vo, pp. 16. Continued.—Report of the Ladies' Branch of the ... Association. ... 1839–40. *Philadelphia.* 1840. 8vo, pp. 21.—To the Managers of the ... Society. [n. p. 1834.] 8vo, pp. 4.—Visitors of the ... Association. [n. p. 1835?] 12mo, pp. 20. Continued.

Rules and Regulations of the UNION CLUB of Philadelphia. *Philadelphia.* 1843. 16mo, pp. 11. 62350

An Act to Incorporate "THE UNION INSURANCE COMPANY of Philadelphia." Passed ... February 6, 1804. [n. p. n. d.] 8vo, pp. 16. 62351

Address and Resolutions of the UNION LEAGUE of Philadelphia. September 16, 1863. *Philadelphia: King & Baird.* 1863. 8vo, pp. (2), 8. 62352

Also: Address of the Union League ... to the Citizens of Pennsylvania, in favor of ... Abraham Lincoln. *Philadelphia: King & Baird.* 1864. 8vo, pp. 30.—Address ... at the Opening Celebration, May 9, 1863. By N. B. Brown. Lord Lyons in Council with the Democracy. *Philadelphia.* 1863. 8vo, pp. 16.—Address of the Union League ... to the Citizens of Pennsylvania, ... August 26th, 1868. [n. p. n. d.] 8vo, pp. 8.—Articles of Association and By-Laws ... . *Philadelphia: King & Baird.* 1863. 16mo, pp. 16.—First Annual Report ... of the Union League ... December 14, 1863. *Philadelphia.* 1863. 8vo, pp. 16. Continued.—Officers and Members of the Union League ... October 1st, 1863. ... *Philadelphia.* 1863. 8vo, pp. 19.—Proceedings of the Union League ... regarding the Assassination of Abraham Lincoln ... . *Philadelphia: Henry B. Ashmead.* 1865. 8vo, pp. 22.—Rules adopted by the ... Directors, Rules of the League House, and ... Committees. *Philadelphia: Henry B. Ashmead.* 1865. 8vo, pp. 22.—The Will of the People. [n. p. n. d.] 8vo, pp. 8. *See also* our Vol. VI., No. 22982; Vol. VIII., No. 33277; Vol. XII., No. 51745.

A | Catalogue | of Books | belonging to the | UNION-LIBRARY-COMPANY | of Philadelphia. | To which is prefixed, | the Articles of the Company, with the names of | the present members, and rules observed by the | Clerk in letting out books, &c. | *Philadelphia: | printed by James Chattin.* 1754. | 8vo, pp. 53. P. 62353

Also: A Catalogue of Books, belonging to the Union Library Company of Philadelphia. *Philadelphia: Printed by Henry Miller.* M DCC LXV. 8vo, pp. xxiv, 40.

Charter and By-Laws of the UNION SCHOOL and Children's Home. *Philadelphia.* 1851. 16mo, pp. 15. 62354

Report on the Establishment of one or more UNION SCHOOLS in Philadelphia ... . *Philadelphia.* 1847. 8vo, pp. 30. S. 62355

Constitution and By-Laws of the UNION TEMPORARY HOME for Children. *Philadelphia.* [1861?] 16mo, pp. 16. 62356

Also: First Annual Report of the Union Temporary Home for Children. ... *Philadelphia.* 1857. 8vo, pp. 14, (1).

Charter and By-Laws of the UNITED STATES FIRE Co. of Philadelphia. Instituted, October 29th, 1811. ... *Philadelphia: Printed by M. Fithian.* 1841. 16mo, pp. 29. 62357

United States Sanitary Commission. Philadelphia Associates. An Appeal to the People of Pennsylvania for the Sick and Wounded Soldiers. [n. p. n. d.] 8vo, pp. 40. 62358

Also: List of Officers and Associates of the U. S. Sanitary Commission in Philadelphia, and the Officers and Aids of the Women's Pennsylvania Branch of the U. S. Sanitary Commission. January 1st, 1864. *Philadelphia.* 1864. 8vo, pp. (21). *See also* Philadelphia Branch of the U. S. Sanitary Commission, Vol. XIV., No. 61972.

Charter of the UNITED SWEDISH LUTHERAN CHURCHES of Wiccacoe, Kingussing and Upper Merion, called Gloria Dei, St. James and Christ Church. *Philadelphia.* 1836. 8vo, pp. 16.

Also: Statement of Property belonging to the Corporation of the United Swedish Churches of Wiccacoe, Kingussing and Upper Merion. [n. p. 1836.] 8vo, pp. 8.

Address of the UNIVERSITY OF FREE MEDICINE & Popular Knowledge, to the American Public. *Philadelphia.* 1833. 8vo, pp. 12. 62360

Introductory Lessons practised by the URANIAN SOCIETY, Philadelphia, for promoting the Knowledge of Vocal Music. *Philadelphia.* 1785. 8vo. 62361

Statement of URY HOUSE SCHOOL, Philadelphia, Pa., With the List of the School, 1868–69. *Philadelphia.* 1869. 12mo, pp. 16. 62362

Martin Van Buren. [Address of the Committee of Friends of Van Buren of Philadelphia. n. p. 1844.] 8vo, pp. 7.

Also: Circular of the Van Buren Executive Committee and Constitution of the Democratic Rescue Association of Philadelphia. [n. p. 1844.] Folio, 1 leaf.

A View of the Absurd Practice, in the Yellow, or Bilious Fever, Addressed to the Inhabitants of Philadelphia. ... *Philadelphia: Printed by John Bioren.* 1803. 16mo, pp. 16. 62364

Views in Philadelphia, consisting of 20 small and 4 large Panorama Plates on India Paper, engraved on stone by J. C. Wild, with Descriptions. *Philadelphia.* 1838. 4to. 62365

The four panorama plates are seldom found with the book.

Views of Philadelphia, and its Vicinity. Embracing a Collection of Twenty Views, beautifully colored, from Paintings by J. C. Wild. With poetical illustrations of each subject, by Andrew M'Makin. ... *Philadelphia: ... J. T. Bowen.* 1848. 4to, 11 leaves. 20 Plates. 62366

See also Vol. II., No. 5530, *and* Vol. IV., No. 12731.

A Vindication of the late Pastoral Letter of the Synod of Philadelphia, to the Presbyteries and Churches under their care; Dated, Lancaster, September 20, 1816. [n. p. n. d.] 12mo, pp. 31. + [Another edition. n. p. n. d.] 12mo, pp. 12.

Visiting Committees of the Directors of Public Schools for the First Section of the First School District, appointed for the year, commenced July 1, 1844, with a List of the Teachers in the Grammar, Secondary and Primary Schools. *Philadelphia: J. Crissy, Printer.* 1844. 8vo, pp. 19. Continued annually.

Water, etc. Report to the ... Councils, on the Progress and State of the Water Works, on the 24th of November, 1799. ... *Philadelphia: Printed by Zachariah Poulson, junior.* 1799. 12mo, pp. 44. 62369

Also: Acts of Assembly and Ordinances relating to the Water Works. [n. p. 1823.] 8vo, pp. 20.—An Answer to the Joint Committee of the ... Councils ... on the ... Plan for Supplying the City with Water, &c. [n. p. 1799.] 8vo, pp. 7.—Opinions of Messrs. Meredith & Binney, as to the right of the Corporation ... to the use of the Water ... of the River Schuylkill, at Fair Mount Dam. March, 1843. *Philadelphia: J. Crissy.* 1843. 8vo, pp. 15.—Report of the Committee ... [on] the state of the Water Works. ... *Philadelphia: Printed by William Duane.* 1802. 8vo, pp. 85.—Report of the Committee for the Introduction of Wholesome Water into ... Philadelphia. ... *Philadelphia: Printed by Zachariah Poulson, Junior.* 1801. 8vo, pp. 16.—Report of the Joint Committee of the ... Councils, on ... Bringing Water to the City. *Philadelphia: Printed by Zachariah Poulson, Junior.* 1798. 8vo, pp. 12.—Report of the Joint Committee of the ... Councils, ... on ... Watering the City ...

Philadelphia: Printed by Zachariah Poulson, Junior. 1799. 8vo, pp. 7.—Report of the Joint Committee, ... [on] Superintending and Directing the Water Works. ... *Philadelphia: Printed by Robert Cochran.* 1802. 8vo, pp. 21.— ... Report upon the Extension of the Water Works ... . By Henry P. M. Birkinbine, Chief Engineer. *Philadelphia.* 1864. 8vo, pp. (2), 10.—The Water Works. The Misconduct of the Present City Councils in relation to the Fair Mount Water Works ... . *Philadelphia, September,* 1833. 8vo, pp. 8.

Department for Supplying the City with Water. Report on the Experiments with Turbine Wheels, made 1859–60, at Fairmount Works, Philadelphia, by Henry P. M. Birkinbine ... . *Philadelphia: William F. Geddes, Printer.* 1861. 8vo, pp. 56. 3 Plates. 62370

Also: ... Annual Report ... and Plan of Supplying the City with Water by Aqueduct, from the Perkiomen ... February 15, 1866. *Philadelphia: William F. Geddes, Printer.* 1866. 8vo, pp. 83, 27, (1).— ... History of the Works, and Annual Report of the Chief Engineer of the Water Department ... . *Philadelphia: C. E. Chichester.* 1860. 8vo, pp. 115.—Report of the Chief Engineer ... on the Condition of the Works under his charge. ... *Philadelphia: Crissy & Markley.* 1855. 8vo, pp. 60. Continued.

Report of the Watering Committee to the ... Councils, November 1, 1803. *Philadelphia: Printed by William Duane.* 1803. Folio, pp. 21. 62371

Continued in folio until 1836, and thereafter in 8vo. Reports for 1824 and 1825 reprinted in 8vo.

Also: An Additional Report on Water Power, by the Watering Committee: ... *Philadelphia: Printed by William Fry.* 1819. Folio, pp. 15.—Correspondence of the Watering Committee with the Schuylkill Navigation Company, in relation to the Fair Mount Water Works: ... *Philadelphia: Printed by Lydia R. Bailey.* 1833. 8vo, pp. 47.—Report of the Joint Watering Committee of Northern Liberties & Spring Garden Water Works: ... *Philadelphia: Barrett & Jones.* 1846. 8vo, pp. 24. Continued to 1855.—Report of the Watering Committee of the Agreements with the Schuylkill Navigation Company and White and Gillingham, relating to the Water Power of the river Schuylkill. ... *Philadelphia: Printed by W. Fry.* 1819. 8vo, pp. 23—Report of the Watering Committee to the ... Councils ... of Philadelphia, relative to the Fair Mount Water Works. ... *Philadelphia: Printed by Lydia R. Bailey.* 1823. 8vo, pp. 22. 3 Plates.—Report of the Watering Committee, to the Commissioners of the District of Spring Garden. ... *Philadelphia: Printed by Jacob Frick & Co.* 1827. Sm. 4to, pp. 12, folded leaf.—Report of the Watering Committee of the ... Councils ... relative to the termination of the Columbia and Philadelphia Rail Road. *Philadelphia: Printed by Lydia R. Bailey.* 1830. 8vo, pp. 18.—Report. To the Watering Committee [on water mains, etc. n. p. 1850.] 8vo, pp. 6.

First Annual Announcement of the WAGNER FREE INSTITUTE OF SCIENCE, ... 1855–56. ... *Philadelphia.* 1855. 8vo, pp. 16. Continued. 62372

Manual of the WALNUT STREET PRESBYTERIAN CHURCH, ... April, 1855. *Philadelphia.* [1855.] 12mo, pp. 28. 62373

Charter and By-Laws of the WAREHOUSING COMPANY of Philadelphia. ... *Philadelphia.* 1858. 8vo, pp. 15, (1). 62374

Washington's Birthday. Centennial Celebration. [*Philadelphia.* 1832.] Folio, 1 leaf. 62375

Address of the WASHINGTON MONUMENT ASSOCIATION of the First School District of Pennsylvania; with the Constitution and By-Laws, ... Officers, ... Managers and Standing Committees. *Philadelphia: Crissy & Markley, Printers.* 1859. 8vo, pp. 20, (4). 62376

Wealth and Biography of the Wealthy Citizens of Philadelphia; containing an alphabetical arrangement of Persons estimated to be worth $50,000 and upwards ... . By a Member of the Philadelphia Bar. *Philadelphia: G. B. Zieber and Co.* 1845. 8vo, pp. 23, (1). 62377

The Charter and By-Laws of the WELCH SOCIETY. ... *Philadelphia.* 1852. 18mo, pp. 18. 62378

A Copy of Acts of Assembly and Ordinances, passed by the Council of the Borough of WEST PHILADELPHIA. With By-Laws for the Government of Council. *Philadelphia: King & Baird.* 1845. 8vo, pp. 46. 62379

Also: Contracts with the District of West Philadelphia, for the introduction of Water, Curbing and Paving Washington St. and the Lancaster Turnpike ... and for Surveying and Regulating. ... 11th April, 1853. [n. p. n. d.] 8vo, pp. 16.—Report of the Committee ... of West Philadelphia, to consider Plans for erecting Water Works ... . *Philadelphia: Printed by J. Nelson Torr.* 1853. 8vo, pp. 16.

Tenth Annual Report of the WEST PHILADELPHIA CHILDREN'S HOME ... . *Philadelphia: King & Baird.* 1865. 16mo, pp. 36. Continued. 62380

Constitution and By-Laws of the WEST PHILADELPHIA HOMESTEAD ASSOCIATION. Adopted March 15, 1855. *Philadelphia: John Coates, Printer.* 1855. 16mo, pp. 23. Map. 62381

Annual Report of the ... Managers of the WEST PHILADELPHIA INSTITUTE, ... [and] Treasurer ... . *Philadelphia.* 1854. 8vo, pp. 7, (1). Continued. 62382

An Act to Incorporate the WEST PHILADELPHIA PASSENGER Railway Company. [n. p. 1857?] 8vo, pp. 4. 62383

Also: To the Stockholders of the West Philadelphia Passenger Railway Company. [n. p. 1858.] 8vo. [Reason of C. M. Eakin for resigning its presidency.]

An Act to incorporate the WEST PHILADELPHIA RAIL ROAD COMPANY. [n. p. 1835?] 8vo, pp. 14. 62384

Also: First Annual Report of the West Philadelphia Rail Road Company. [n. p. 1836.] 8vo, pp. 7. Map.

Constitution and By-Laws of the WESTERN ASSOCIATION of Ladies for the Relief and Employment of the Poor. *Philadelphia.* 1847. 12mo, pp. (2), 4. 62385

Also: Report of the Board of the Western Ladies of Philadelphia, for the Relief ... of the Poor. *Philadelphia: Joseph Rakestraw.* 1848. 12mo, pp. 12. Continued.

Act of Incorporation and By-Laws of the WESTERN CLINICAL INFIRMARY, of ... Philadelphia. *Philadelphia.* 1854. 12mo, pp. 12. 62386

Constitution and By-Laws of the WESTERN LIBRARY ASSOCIATION of Philadelphia. ... [n. p.:] *Eckel, Printer.* 1856. 32mo, pp. 12. 62387

Whig Anti-Subscription Council Ticket. To the Whig Voters of ... Philadelphia. [n. p. 1846.] Folio, 1 leaf. 62388

Who shall be our Next Sheriff? ... *Philadelphia.* 1823. 8vo, pp. 8. 62389

Rules and Regulations for ... the WILLS HOSPITAL ... . *Philadelphia.* 1834. 8vo, pp. 24. + 1841. 8vo, pp. 24. 62390

Also: By-Laws and Regulations for ... Wills' Hospital. *Philadelphia: Merrihew & Son.* 1867. 8vo, pp. 32.

Report ... on the WILLS LEGACY and ... the Wills Hospital. *Philadelphia.* 1833. 8vo, pp. 14. 62391

Wind Mill Island Cash Lottery. [n. p. 1774.] Folio, 1 l.

To raise £5,250 for the purchase and improvement of public landing places along the Delaware front of Philadelphia.

Der wöchentliche Philadelphische Staatsbote, mit den neuesten Fremden und Einheimisch Politischen Nachrichten; samt den von Zeit zu Zeit in der Kirche und Gelehrten Welt sich ereignenden Merkwürdigkeiten. Montags, den 7. Merz. [n. p. 1763.] Folio, pp. 2. P. 62393

Published every Monday, by Henrich Miller, till Tuesday, Jan. 5, 1768, when it began to appear on that day. After this, considerable variation in the day. Numbers consecutive to 9,200, May 26, 1779, when it ceased.

The Charter, By-Laws and Regulations of the WOODLANDS CEMETERY COMPANY. *Philadelphia: Printed by T. & G. Town.* 1845. 8vo, pp. (2), 8. + *Philadelphia: Kite & Walton, Printers.* 1853. 8vo, pp. 34. + *Philadelphia: J. B. Chandler, Printer.* 1857. 8vo, pp. 47. Plate. + *Philadelphia: Collins, Printer.* 1868. 8vo, pp. 65. 2 Plates. 62394

Also: Reports relative to The Woodlands Cemetery. *Philadelphia: Printed by C. Alexander.* 1843. 8vo, pp. 15.

The Words of a Grand Selection of Sacred Music, as performed at the Church of St. Augustine, in ... Philadelphia, on the 13th of April, 1814, to aid the funds of the Orphan Asylum ... *Philadelphia: Printed by John Binns.* [n. d.] 16mo, pp. 19.

Yellow Fever. [n. p. 1794?] 8vo, pp. 11. 62396

"This little piece was written about the end of the winter 1793–4, on the ... growing alarm of the yellow fever being again in Philadelphia." This seems from the prefatory note to have been a second edition of a privately printed essay on yellow fever.

Second Annual Report of the YOUNG CHRISTIANS' MISSIONARY ASSOCIATION, ... 1854. *Philadelphia: Clarkson, Printer.* [1854.] 8vo, pp. 10. 62397

The Rise and Progress of the YOUNG-LADIES ACADEMY of Philadelphia: Containing an Account of a Number of Public Examinations and Commencements; The Charter and Bye-Laws; Likewise, A Number of Orations delivered By the Young Ladies, And several by the Trustees of said Institution. *Philadelphia: Printed by Stewart & Cochran.* M,DCC,XCIV. 8vo, pp. 119. 62398

Constitution of the YOUNG MAN'S INSTITUTE; together with the Rules and Regulations relative to District Associations ... . *Philadelphia.* 1850. 8vo, pp. 8. 62399

Also: Annual Report of the ... Trustees of the Young Man's Institute. *Philadelphia.* 1850. 8vo. Continued.

Constitution and By-Laws of the YOUNG MEN'S CENTRAL HOME MISSION. *Philadelphia: T. K. and P. G. Collins, Printers.* 1856. 16mo, pp. 16. 62400

Also: Annual Report of the Young Men's Central Home Mission of the M. E. Church of Philadelphia. *Philadelphia.* 1854. 12mo. Continued.

First Annual Report of the YOUNG MEN'S CHRISTIAN ASSOCIATION of Philadelphia. ... *Philadelphia.* 1855. 8vo, pp. 44. Continued. 62401

Also: Charter of the Young Men's Christian Association Building ... . [n. p.] MDCCCLX. 12mo, pp. 8.—Constitution and By-Laws of the ... Association ... with By-Laws ... of Managers and ... Officers. *Philadelphia.* 1854. 16mo, pp. 26, (2). + *Philadelphia: Samuel Loag.* 1865. 12mo, pp. 24.—Constitution and By-Laws of the ... Association of Germantown ... . *Germantown: Wunder & Wagenseller, Printers.* 1858. 16mo, pp. 23. + *Philadelphia: J. S. Helfenstein, Printer.* 1859. 16mo, pp. 26.—Proceedings of the Twelfth Anniversary ... also, the Names of Officers, &c. *Philadelphia.* 1866. 12mo, pp. 24. Continued in 8vo.

First Annual Report of the YOUNG MEN'S MISSIONARY SOCIETY of St. Andrew's Church ... . *Philadelphia.* 1848. 12mo, pp. 15. 62402

By-Laws and Standing Rules of the Second Division of the YOUNG MEN'S SOCIETY. *Philadelphia.* 1833. 12mo, pp. 10.

The Second Annual Report of the YOUTH'S MISSIONARY SOCIETY ... . *Philadelphia.* 1834. 12mo, pp. 12. 62404

The Third Annual Report of the YOUTHS' TRACT SOCIETY ... [n. p.] *October,* 1829. 8vo. Continued. 62405

The Zane Street Girls' Grammar School, Year Book of Facts. 1861–1862. *Philadelphia.* 1862. 16mo, pp. 88. 62406

An Act to Incorporate the ZOOLOGICAL SOCIETY of Philadelphia. *Philadelphia: Crissy & Markley, Printers.* 1859. 16mo, pp. 7. Map. 62407

PHILADELPHIA. Documents relating to the Capture and Destruction of the Frigate Philadelphia at Tripoli, February, 1804. *Washington.* 1850. 8vo. 62408

The Philadelphiad; or New Pictures of the City. ... *Philadelphia: ... Printed ... by Kline & Reynolds.* 1784. 2 vols., sm. 8vo, pp. 83; 59, (1). 62409

PHILADELPHIAN, *pseudon.* Interesting Essays, chiefly on the subject of the Yellow Fever, interspersed with some remarks on the progress of the preparations for a Permanent Bridge; ... By a Philadelphian. ... *Philadelphia: Printed by Budd & Bartram.* 1802. 8vo, pp. 51. 62410

PHILADELPHIAN, *pseudon.* Occasional Essays on the Yellow Fever, Containing a number of remarkable relative facts, as well as some encouraging ideas, that those cities of America, which for more than ninety successive years, had been generally preserved from the dreadful evil, may by the divine blessing on wise and prudent measures, experience in future, a similar preservation from the dire calamities of a mortal pestilence. ... By a Philadelphian. *Philadelphia: Printed by John Ormrod.* 1800. 8vo, pp. 42

See also Vol. VIII., No. 30212, *and* Vol. XIV., No. 61714.

Minutes of the PHILADELPHIAN ASSOCIATION in MDCCLXIX. *Germantown: Printed by Christopher Saur.* 1769. 4to, pp. 7.

Continued until changed to "Minutes of the Baptist Association," No. 61497, *note.*

This body was organized in the year 1707, and is the oldest Baptist association in the United States. To it Brown University owes its origin, and to its fostering care the Warren Association is greatly indebted. The minutes for this year contain many allusions to Rhode Island.

The Philadelphian Magazine, for April, 1788. [Vol. I. n. p. n. d.] pp. 49–136. P. 62413

PHILADELPHIENSIS, *pseudon.* The Manners of the Times; a Satire. In two Parts. By Philadelphiensis. ... *Philadelphia: Printed ... by William Dunlap.* M,DCC,LXII. 4to, pp. 16. 62414

Philadelphische Zeitung, von allerhand auswärtigen und einheimischen merckwürdigen Sachen. Den 31sten December, 1757. Num. LXVIII. *Philadelphia, gedruckt und zu haben bey B. Francklin, General Postmeister, und A. Armbruster.* [n. d.] Folio, pp. 4. H.S.P. 62415

PHILADELPHUS, *pseudon.* *See* Vol. XIV., No. 60717.

PHILÆNI, *pseudon.* Strictures on the Landed and Commercial Interest of the United States for 1786. By Philæni. *New York: F. Childs.* [1786.] 8vo, pp. 20. N., S. 62416

PHILÆNUS (J.), *pseudon.* *See* Vol. IX., No. 36926.

PHILAGATHOS, *pseudon.* A Poem, Commemorative of Goffe, Whaley, & Dixwell, Three of the Judges of Charles I. Who, at the Restoration, took refuge and died in America. To which is prefixed, an Abstract of their History. By Philagathos. ... *Boston: Printed by Samuel Hall.* MDCCXCIII. 8vo, pp. 28. B., M.

PHILALETHES, *pseudon.* Christian Piety, freed from the many delusions of modern enthusiasts of all denominations. By Philalethes. The third edition. With the Life of Armalle Nicolas. *London: printed. Philadelphia: reprinted by Henry Miller.* MDCCLXVI. 12mo, pp. 22. P. 62418

The Life of A. Nicolas is printed with a separate title-page, etc., in 26 pages, and is sometimes found dated 1767.

PHILALETHES, *pseudon.* The Examiner, | or | Gilbert against Tennent, | Containing a Confutation of the Revd Mr Gilbert | Tennent, & his adherents; Extracted chiefly from | his Own writings & formed upon his Own plan | of comparing the Moravian Principles with the | Standard of Orthodoxy, in distinct columns. | Together with some Strictures on the Preface to the | Revd Mr Tennent's Five Sermons and Appendix lately | published, and subscribed by Six Reverend Ministers of Boston. | The whole

being an Essay towards answering three | important Queries, viz. 1. What is Truth in the present Religious Commotions | in this Land? | 2. What is the shortest Method of finding the whole | Truth? | 3. Whether such as are given to change ought not | in Conscience to make their publick Retractions; according to St. Austin? | The whole Essay is Submitted to the Judgment of | Common Sense. | By Philalethes. | ... | *Boston printed* 1743. | *Philadelphia: Re-printed & Sold by B. Franklin.* [1743.] 8vo, pp. 31, (1). 62419

For the original edition *see* [Hancock (John)], Vol. VIII., No. 30172, and for a reply *see* Tennent (G.)

PHILALETHES, *pseudon.* For the service of Truth, By Philalethes or Lover of Truth, T. M. 1703. An Abstract of George Keith's Letter to Thomas Maule, with an Answer by Philalethes there unto ... . [*Philadelphia: Reynier Jansen?*] *Printed for the Author.* 1703. 4to, pp. 20. L. 62420

By Thomas Maule. Of extreme rarity. *See also* Vol. XI., No. 46934.

PHILALETHES, *pseudon.* Tribute | to | Cæsar, | How paid by the Best Christians, | And to what Purpose. | With | Some Remarks on the late vigorous Expedition | against Canada. | Of Civil Government, | How Inconsistent it is with the Government of Christ | in his Church, | Compared with the Ancient, Just and Righteous Principles of the Quakers, and their Modern | Practice and Doctrine. | With some Notes upon the Discipline of their Church in | this Province, especially at Philadelphia. | By Philalethes. | [*Philadelphia: Jacob Taylor? about* 1712.] Sm. 4to, pp. (6), 29.

By Thomas Maule. Extremely rare. The "Tribute to Cæsar" was the tax for the Canada expedition of 1711.

PHILALETHES, *pseudon.* A Friendly Dialogue between Philalethes and Toletus, upon the Nature of Duty. *Newburyport.* 1784. 12mo, pp. 160, 32. 62422

See also [Mather (C.)], Vol. XI., No. 46377, *and* [Portsmouth (Henry)].

PHILALETHES (D.), *pseudon.* *See* Cuba, Vol. V., No. 17816, and add collation, pp. (2), xii, x, 412. B. 62423

PHILALETHES ELEUTHERUS. Over den Slavenstand; met eenige Aanteekeningen en eén Voorbericht van den uitgever Jan van Geuns. *Leiden.* 1797. 8vo. 62424

PHILALETHIUS (Ireneus), *pseudon.* *See* [Teelinck (W.)]

PHILANAX (Calvin), *pseudon.* *See* [Young (Samuel)].

PHILANDER MISIATRUS, *pseudon.* The | Honour | of the | Gout; | or, | A Rational Discourse, demonstra- | ting that the Gout is one of the greatest | Blessings which can befal Mortal Man; | ... By way of Letter to an Eminent Citizen, Wrote in the heat of a violent Paroxysm, and now publish'd for the Common Good. By Philander Misiatrus. *London printed: Reprinted by B. Franklin in Philadelphia.* 1732. Sm. 12mo, pp. 65, (5). 62425

First published, London, 1699. Nearly half a century after Franklin reprinted it, it served to suggest his witty "Dialogue between Franklin and the Gout." Improved title of our No. 32791, Vol. VIII.

PHILANDROS, *pseudon.* An Astonishing Affair! The Rev. Samuel Arnold cast and tried for his Cruelty, though his cause was advocated in a masterly manner, by the Right Hon. Joseph Almon Clark Pray ... . By Philandros. ... *Concord: Printed by Luther Roby.* 1830. 18mo, pp. 168. Plate. C. 62426

The Philanthropic Results of the War in America, Collected from Official and other Authentic Sources, By An American Citizen. *New York: Press of Wynkoop, Hallenbeck & Thomas.* 1863. 8vo, pp. 59. 62427

By L. P. Brockett. For another edition, *see* Vol. II., No. 8161.

A Philanthropic Tour through the United States; by a Gentleman. *New York.* 1843. 8vo, pp. 12. 62428

PHILANTHROPIST, *pseudon.* *See* Vol. VII., No. 29062.

PHILANTHROPOS, *pseudon.* The | Universal | Peace-Maker, | or | Modern Author's | Instructor. | By Philanthropos. | *Philadelphia: Printed by Anthony Armbruster,* | ... . 1764. | Sm. 8vo, pp. 15. P.

Relates to the Paxton Boys.

PHILANTHROPOS, *pseudon.* A Serious Address to the Clergy by a Minister of the Church of England; ... By Philanthropos. *Boston, N. E.: D. Fowle.* 1756. 8vo, pp. 14. 62430

[PHILANTHROPOS, *pseudon.*] Essays on Capital Punishments, Republished from Poulson's Daily Advertiser. *Philadelphia: Printed by Brown & Merritt.* 1811. 16mo, pp. 24. C. 62431

Signed at the end "Philanthropos."

PHILANTHROPOS, *pseudon.* An Appendix to the Essays on Capital Punishments. By Philanthropos. ... *Philadelphia: Printed by S. Merritt.* 1812. 12mo, pp. 33. P. 62432

PHILANTHROPOS, *pseudon.* A Solemn Appeal to Christians of all Denominations in favor of the Cause of Permanent & Universal Peace. By Philanthropos. *New-York: American Peace Society.* 1834. 8vo, pp. 32. 62433

By William Ladd. *See also* Vol. III., No. 9427; [Ladd (W.)], Vol. x., No. 38522–38528, *and* [Rhees (Morgan)].

The Philatelist's Album for American and Foreign Postage and Revenue Stamps. *New York: J. W. Scott & Co.* [1870?] Obl. 8vo, pp. 200. 62434

PHILBRICK (E. S.) Report of E. S. Philbrick, Trustee, concerning Cotton Lands in South Carolina. For ... 1863. [*Boston.* 1864.] 8vo, pp. 8. B. 62435

PHILBRICK (S.) Facts and Observations, illustrative of Some Recent Transactions in the Society of Friends, at Lynn and Salem, Mass. ... By Samuel Philbrick. ... *Boston: Printed by Henry Bowen.* 1823. 8vo, pp. 68. H. 62436

[PHILELEUTHEROS, *pseudon.*] A Blow at the root of Aristocracy, or An Appeal to matters of Fact, in Support of Religious Freedom. [*Boston.* n. d.] 8vo, pp. 21. BA. 62437

See also Vol. XI., No. 45597.

PHILELUTH. BANGOR, *pseudon.* *See* [Foxcroft (T.)], VI. 25392

"PHILEMON SCANK," *pseudon.* A few Chapters to Brother Jonathan, concerning "Infallibility," etc., or, Strictures on Nathan L. Rice's "Defence of Protestantism," etc. *Bardstown, Ky.* 1835. 12mo. 62438

PHILENIA, *pseudon.* *See* [Morton (S. W. A.)], XII. 51026.

PHILETHES, *pseudon.* Reflections on the Statements and Opinions published in the Free Enquirer. By Philethes. *New York.* 1829. 8vo, pp. 43. 62439

PHILIARCUS, *pseudon.* Letters to a Friend, in reference to some Defects in the Polity of the British Leeward Charibee Islands, inscribed to his Excellency the Captain General, By Philiarcus. [*Jamaica.*] 1815. 8vo. 62440

[PHILIBERT (*l'Abbé*).] *See* Gazaignes (J. A.), VII. 26806.

PHILIP V. Decretum super varias delatas ad regium suum Indiarum consilium adversus Jesuitas in Paraquariae accusationes. Cum citata in eodem Jos. de Peralta episcopus de Buenos Ayres. *Tyrnaviæ.* 1745. 4to. 62441

For other editions *see* Vol. v., Nos. 19208–9.

[PHILIP V.] His Catholick Majesty's Conduct compared with that of His Britannick Majesty, as well with regard to what happened before the Convention of the 14th of Jany. 1739, as to what has been done since, untill the Publication of Reprisals and Declaration of War. [*London.* 1739.] 8vo. 62442

In Spanish and English, and entirely relating to America.

[PHILIP V.] His Catholic Majesty's Manifesto, justifying his Conduct in relation to the late Convention. With his Reasons for not paying the Ninety-five thousand pounds. *London: Robert Arney.* 1739. 8vo, pp. 53. 62443

In French and English. For "An Examination of a Pamphlet" *see* Vol. VI., No. 23350, *and* Vol. XIII., No. 56589.

PHILIP V. Oracion a nuestro S. D. Philippo V ... por el insigne colegio Mayor de Santa Maria de Todos-Santos de Mexico ... por el Senado Mexicano. *Mexico* [*about* 1700]. Folio, 36 leaves. 62444

PHILIP (R.) The Life and Times of the Reverend George Whitefield, M.A. By Robert Philip. *London: George Virtue.* MDCCCXXXVII. 8vo, pp. 588. + [*Ibid.*] MDCCCXXXVIII. + *New York: D. Appleton & Co.* MDCCCXXXVIII. 12mo, pp. 554. Portrait. 62445

PHILIP. Life of Philip. *See* [Savage (Sarah)].

Philip Everhard; or a History of the Baptist Indian Missions in North America, from the Formation of the American Baptist Board of Foreign Missions to the Present Time. *Boston: Massachusetts Sabbath School Union.* 1831. 16mo, pp. 108. C. 62446

Philip, or the Aborigines, a Drama ... . *New York.* 1822. 12mo, pp. 48. 62447

Philip Musgrave. *See* Abbott (J.), Vol. I., No. 30.

PHILIPOT (T.) The Original and Growth | of | The Spanish | Monarchy | United with the House of | Austria. | Extracted from those Chronicles, | Annals, Registers and Genealogies, | that yeild any faithful Representation | how the Houses of Castile, Aragon and | Burgundy became knit and combin'd | into one Body. | To which are added several Discourses of those | Accessions and Improvements in Italy, | Africk, with the East and West-Indies, | that are now annexed by Alliance or Con- | quest to the Diadem

of Spain. | By Thomas Philipot, M.A. | ... | *London, Printed by W. G. for R. Taylor* ... 1664. Sm. 8vo, pp. (8), 264. Portrait.

Pages 97–160 relate to Spanish America. Also: An Historical Discourse of the First Invention of Navigation, and the Additional Improvements of it ... . *London: W. Fisher.* 1661. Sm. 4to, pp. (4), 28. C.

PHILIPPART (J.) Memoirs, &c. &c. of General Moreau; ... By John Philippart, Esq. ... *London: Henry Colburn.* 1814. 8vo, pp. viii, 293, (1). Portrait, Map and Facsimile. + *London: Printed by A. J. Valpy.* 1814. 8vo, pp. viii, 293, (1). Map, Portrait and Facsimile. A. + *Philadelphia.* 1816. 8vo. 62449

PHILIPPI (F.) Geschichte des Freistaats von St. Domingo, (Hayti) von D. Ferdinand Philippi ... . *Dresden: P. G. Hilscher-sche Buchhandlung.* 1826. 3 vols., 16mo, pp. (5), 106; (3), 148; (3), 208. B. + Zweite Auflage. *Dresden.* 1827. 3 vols., 16mo.

PHILIPPI. Geschichte der Vereinigten Freistaaten von Nord-Amerika. Von Ferdinand Philippi. *Dresden.* 1826. 3 vols., 16mo. + Zweite Auflage. *Dresden.* 1827. 3 vols., 16mo.

PHILIPPI (R. A.) Reise durch die Wüste Atacama, auf Befehl der Chilenischen Regierung im Sommer 1853–54 unternommen und beschrieben. Von Doctor Rudolph Amandus Philippi ... *Halle: Edouard Anton.* 1860. 4to, pp. x, 192, 62. Map and 27 Plates. B., C. 62452

Also: Florula Atacamensis sive enumeratio plantarum in deserto Atacamense ... . *Halae.* 1860. 4to. 6 Plates. — Verzeichniss der im Museum von Santiago befindlichen Chilenischen Orthopteren. [*Berlin.* 1863.] 8vo, pp. 29.

PHILIPPUS SECUNDUS. *See* [Puga (Vasco de)].

PHILIPPS (M. W.) Autobiography of M. W. Louie Philipps, of Boston, the Reformed Drunkard. Also, A Lecture, delivered by him before the Young Men's Christian Association ... . *Boston: The Author.* 1869. 12mo, pp. 24. 62453

PHILIPS (E.) Miscellaneous Works, consisting of Essays, Political and Moral. By Erasmus Philips. *London: Waller.* 1751. 8vo, pp. (8), 508. C. 62454

Contains a reprint of "The State of the Nation."

PHILIPS. The State of the Nation in respect to her Commerce, Debts, and Money. By Erasmus Philips. *London: Woodman & Lyon.* 1725. 8vo, pp. (16), 152. C. + Second Edition. [*Ibid.*] 1726. 8vo. 62455

Contains the notorious "Assiento" for the slave trade.

[PHILIPS (George).] Travels in North America. *Dublin: C. Bentham.* 1822. 24mo, pp. 184. + *Dublin: Printed by John Jones.* 1824. 18mo, pp. 180. + *Dublin: Printed by Brett Smith.* 1824. 18mo, pp. 180. + *Dublin: Printed by P. D. Hardy.* [n. d.] 18mo. 62456

PHILIPS (G.) Private Case before the House of Lords, between Gillam Philips, Brother of Henry Philips deceased, Hannah Philips his widow, Habijah Savage and Hannah his wife, Arthur Savage and Faith his wife, representatives of Mary Butler, sister of Henry Philips, relative to the division of the Estates of the said H. Philips, in the Province of Massachusetts Bay. *London.* 1737. 2 parts, folio. 62457

PHILIPS (J.) An Authentic Journal Of the late Expedition Under the Command of Commodore Anson. Containing A Regular and Exact Account of the whole Proceedings and several Transactions thereof: Particularly at Madeira, St. Catharine's, St. Julian's, St. Juan Fernandez; their Manner of Living here upon Sea-Lions, Sea-Dogs, &c. the taking of Payta; their cruizing on the Coast of Acapulco, Chequatan Bay, Tenian, one of the Ladrone Islands, and Macao; the taking of the rich Spanish Galleon, called the Nuestro, Signora de Cabodongo, from Acapulco bound to Manila, commanded by Don Geronimo Montero, a Portuguese; their going to Canton in China, &c. To which is added, A Narrative of the extraordinary Hardships suffered by the Adventures in this Voyage. By John Philips, Midshipman of the Centurion. *London: J. Robinson.* 1744. 8vo, pp. 516. S. + *Hull.* 1745. 8vo. 62458

PHILIPS (J. A.) Report on the Property of the California Borax Company. By John Arthur Philips. [With] Review by the Company. *San Francisco: Towne & Bacon.* 1866. 8vo, pp. 12, 14. C. 62459

PHILIPS (M.) The Voyages and Adventures of Miles Philips, A West-Country Sailor. Containing A Relation of his various Fortune both by Sea and Land; the inhumane Usage he met with from the Spaniards at Mexico, and the Salvage Indians of Canada and other barbarous Nations; and the Sufferings he and his Companions underwent by their Confinement and Sentence in the Spanish Inquisition. Together with A Natural Description of the Countries he visited, and particular Observations on the Religion, Customs and Manners of their respective Inhab-

itants. Written by Himself in the plain Stile of an English Sailor. *London: T. Payne.* 1724. 12mo, pp. (12), 216. 62460

PHILIPSBURG, *Pa.* A Description of The Philipsburg Estate, consisting of 70,000 Acres, situate in the Counties of Centre, Cambria and Clearfield, in ... Pennsylvania; with a statement of its ... Coal Field. *New-York: Printed by Bell & Gould.* 1848. 8vo, pp. 16. 62461

First Annual Report of the PHILIPSBURG AND JUNIATA RAIL-ROAD COMPANY, to the Stockholders. *New York: G. F. Hopkins & Son.* 1833. 8vo, pp. 38. Map. 62462

PHILLIMORE (J. G.) Case of the Seizure of the Southern Envoys. Reprinted, with additions from the "Saturday Review." By J. G. Phillimore. *London.* 1861. 8vo. 62463

PHILLIMORE (R.) Memoirs and Correspondence of George, Lord Lyttelton, From 1734 to 1773. Compiled and Edited by Robert Phillimore ... . *London: James Ridgway.* 1845. 2 vols., 8vo, pp. vi, (2), 424; (4), 425–816. A. 62464

Includes some American topics. *See our* Vol. x., Nos. 42889–93.

PHILLIMORE. A Statement of the ... Controversy between ... Great Britain and Paraguay, and Opinion of Robert Phillimore ... thereupon. *Washington: William H. Moore, Printer.* 1860. 8vo, pp. 19. H. 62465

Also: The Case of the Creole considered, in a Second Letter to the Right Hon. Lord Ashburton. *London.* 1842. 8vo. — Letter to Lord Ashburton, suggested by Questions of International Law raised in the Message of the American President. *London.* 1842. 8vo. *See also our* Vol. v., No. 17471.

PHILLIO (C.) Calvin Phillio's Light on Masonry and Anti-Masonry, and a Renunciation of Both, with undissembled esteem for Masons and Anti-Masons. *Providence, R. I.* 1831. 12mo, pp. 23. W. 62466

[PHILLIP (William).] The True and perfect Description. *See* [Veer (G. de)].

PHILLIPIAD. [n. p. n. d.] 8vo. H. 62467

Relates to Phillips Academy, Andover, Mass.

PHILLIPPO (J. M.) Jamaica: its Past and Present State. By James M. Phillippo, of Spanish Town, Jamaica, twenty years a Baptist Minister in that Island. ... *London: John Snow.* MDCCCXLIII. 12mo, pp. xvi, 487, (1). 10 Plates. A. + *Philadelphia: James M. Campbell & Co.* 1843. 8vo, pp. 176. B. 62468

PHILLIPPO. Services at the Designation of Mr. James Phillippo, as a Missionary to the Island of Jamaica: ... *Bradford: Printed for the Authors.* [1823.] 8vo, pp. 67. 62469

PHILLIPPO. The United States and Cuba. By James M. Phillippo ... . *London: Pewtress & Co.* MDCCCLVII. 12mo, pp. xi, 476. A., B. 62470

[PHILLIPS (A.)] Appeal to the Candid of all Parties, respecting the Religious Difficulties in Princeton [Mass.]. [n. p. 1835.] 12mo, pp. 26. 62471

PHILLIPS (A. E.) Statement of A. E. Phillips, late acting United States Consul at ... St. Jago de Cuba, showing the circumstances ... which forced him to seek protection at Jamaica ... from ... a Spanish mob. [*Washington.* 1870.] 8vo, pp. 13.

PHILLIPS (B.) Navy Yard Exposition and Navy Yard Abuses. By B. Phillips. *Philadelphia.* 1820. 8vo, pp. 4. 62473

PHILLIPS (C.) Memoirs of the Life of Catherine Phillips: to which are added some of her Epistles. *London: James Phillips and Son.* 1797. 8vo. 62474

Chapter IV. contains minutes of travels, labors and sufferings in America, etc.

PHILLIPS. Reasons why the People called Quakers, cannot so fully unite with the Methodists, in their Missions to the Negroes in the West India Islands and Africa, as freely to contribute thereto; ... By Catherine Phillips. *London: Printed by James Phillips.* 1792. 8vo, pp. 22. + Second Edition. [*Ibid.*] 1793. 8vo. 62475

PHILLIPS (C.) A Tribute to the Memory of the late General Washington, ... by Charles Phillips, in Answer to a Toast given at a Dinner near Killarney, where Mr. Phillips and Mr. Payne the American Actor were present. *London.* [n. d.] 8vo, pp. 12.

PHILLIPS. A Tribute to the Memory of General Washington ... . By Charles Phillips, Esq. *New-York: O. Wilder and Jas. M. Campbell.* 1823. 12mo, pp. 11. 62477

See also Mitchell (E.), Vol. XII., No. 49685.

PHILLIPS (Daniel). Extracts from the Writings of D. Phillips and Wm. Penn, ... shewing the Analogy between George Keith and the opposers of Elias Hicks. *New York.* 1830. 8vo.

PHILLIPS (D. W.) Puritanical Freedom. An Address ... in North Wrentham, July 4, 1848. By Daniel W. Phillips ... . *Boston: John Putnam, Printer.* 1848. 8vo, pp. 27. H. 62479

Also: Discourse on Temperance, April 6, 1848. ... *Boston.* 1848. 8vo. B.

PHILLIPS (E.) A Sermon, delivered at Bridge-Hampton, (L. I.), April 25th, [5th] 1821. Occasioned by the death of Rev. Aaron Woolworth, D.D. Pastor of the Church in that place ... . By Ebenezer Phillips, Pastor of the Church in East-Hampton. *Jamaica: Printed by Henry C. Sleight.* 1821. 8vo, pp. 16. S.

[PHILLIPS (Edwin D.)] Texas, and its Late Military Occupation and Evacuation. By an Officer of the Army. *New York: D. Van Nostrand.* 1862. 8vo, pp. 35. B. 62481

PHILLIPS (Ezra), *jun.*, Executor, *vs.* Sylvanus Emerson. Account of the Tract of a Territory called the Major's Purchase, in Hanson, Mass. ... [n. p.] 1853. Folio, pp. 5. M. 62482

PHILLIPS (G.) A | Reply | to a | Confutation | of some Grounds for | Infants Baptisme: | as also, | Concerning the form of a Church, | put forth against mee by one | Thomas Lamb. | Hereunto is added, | a Discourse of the Verity and Validity of Infants | Baptisme, wherein I endevour to clear it in it self. As also in | the Ministery administring it, and the manner of administration, | by Sprinkling, and not Dipping; with sundry other | particulars handled herein. | By George Phillips of Watertown in New England. | ... | *London,* | *Printed by Matthew Simmons, for Henry Overton, and are to be sold at* | *his Shop in Popes-head Alley.* 1645. | 4to, pp. (16), 154. C., W. 62483

"To the Reader," by Thomas Shepard, 10 pages. Very rare. The only published work of the first minister of Watertown, Mass. *See* Sprague's "Annals," I. 15–17.

PHILLIPS (G. S.) The American Republic and Human Liberty foreshadowed in Scripture. By Rev. George S. Phillips, ... *Cincinnati: Poe & Hitchcock.* 1864. 12mo, pp. 236. B., C.

PHILLIPS. Chicago and her Churches. By George S. Phillips ... . *Chicago: E. B. Myers & Chandler.* 1868. 16mo, pp. 568. B. 62485

PHILLIPS (H.) Trial of Henry Phillips for the Murder of Gaspard Dennegri. ... Boston, January 9, 1817. [*Boston: Thos. C. Bangs.* 1817.] 8vo, pp. 24. C., W. 62486

PHILLIPS (H.), *Jr.* A Catalogue of the New Jersey Bills of Credit, comprising their Amounts, Denominations, and the

Names of the Persons appointed to sign them, from 1723 to 1786. By Henry Phillips, Jr. ... *Philadelphia: A. C. Kline.* 1863. 8vo, pp. 8. H. 62487

PHILLIPS. Historical Sketches of the Paper Currency of the American Colonies, prior to the Adoption of the Federal Constitution. First Series. By Henry Phillips, Jr., A.M. ... *Printed for W. Elliot Woodward. Roxbury, Mass.* 1865. Sm. 4to, pp. (4), 233. 62488

The second volume appeared with the following title:

PHILLIPS. Continental Paper Money. Historical Sketches of American Paper Currency. Second Series. By Henry Phillips, Jr., A.M. ... *Printed for W. Elliot Woodward. Roxbury, Mass.* 1866. Sm. 4to, pp. 264. 62489

Form Nos. V. and VI. of "Woodward's Historical Series." Two hundred and fifty copies printed on small paper, fifty copies on large paper, and three copies on Whatman's drawing paper in royal 8vo.

[PHILLIPS.] A Review of the Article on Continental Money, in Harper's Magazine for March 1863. [n. p.] *Privately printed.* 1863. 8vo, pp. 8. H. 62490

Signed "Antiquarian."

PHILLIPS. Some Observations on Early Currency of Maryland. A Paper read before "The Numismatic and Antiquarian Society of Philadelphia." ... June 7, 1865. By Henry Phillips, Jr. *Philadelphia: Henry B. Ashmead, Printer.* 1867. 8vo, pp. 8.

See also Vol. VIII., No. 32085.

PHILLIPS (H. M.) Admission of Kansas. Speech of the Hon. Henry M. Phillips, of Pennsylvania, ... March 9, 1858, on the admission of Kansas as a State ... . [*Washington.* 1858.] 8vo, pp. 8. H. 62492

Also: Speech ... on the Expenditure and Revenues of the Nation ... June 12, 1858. *Washington.* 1858. 8vo, pp. 7.

PHILLIPS (I.) An Impartial Examination of the Case of Captain Isaac Phillips, late of the Navy, and Commander of the United States Sloop-of-War Baltimore, in 1798: Compiled from Original Documents and Records, with the Proceedings upon his Application to be restored to his rank in the U. S. Navy. *Baltimore: Printed by Benjamin Edes.* 1825. 8vo, pp. 119. C., H.

PHILLIPS (J.) A General History of Inland Navigation, Foreign and Domestic: containing a Complete Account of the Canals already executed in England, with considerations on those projected. ... By J. Phillips. *London: I. and J. Taylor.* MDCCXCII. 4to, pp. xx, 369, (3). Map and 4 Plates. A. + Addenda. [*Ibid.*] 1794. 4to. + Fourth Edition [abridged and continued]. *London.* 1803. 8vo. 62494

Contains an account of the canals of North and South America.

PHILLIPS (J.) A Narrative, shewing why the Rev. John Phillips is not in connexion with the Episcopalian Methodists, ... *Charleston.* 1796. 8vo, pp. 36. N. 62495

PHILLIPS (J.) An Oration, ... July 4, 1794, at ... Boston, in Commemoration of ... American Independence. By John Phillips. ... *Boston: Printed by Benjamin Edes.* 1794. 8vo, pp. 19

PHILLIPS. Biography of Deacon John Phillips, with Addresses, ... on his One Hundredth Birthday. *Southbridge, Mass.* 1860. 8vo. 62497

PHILLIPS (J.) Mexico Illustrated: with Descriptive Letterpress in English and Spanish. By John Phillips. *London.* 1848. Folio. 26 lithographed Plates. + [*Ibid.*] 1849. Folio. 62498

The plates are from drawings by William Rider. A limited number, with the plates colored to resemble original drawings, was issued at ten guineas.

PHILLIPS (J. B.) Zamira, a Dramatic Sketch, and other Poems. By Jonas B. Phillips. *New York* 1835. 24mo, pp. 142. 62499

PHILLIPS (J. M.) Lecture on the Condition of the Country, ... Lyceum Hall, Woburn, May 8th, 1863. By J. M. Phillips. ... *Woburn: Edward T. Moody, Printer.* 1863. 8vo, pp. 18. H.

PHILLIPS (J. V.) Boston and Missouri Lead Company. Report of ... J. V. Phillips ... 1863. *Boston: Wright & Potter, Printers.* 1863. 8vo, pp. 18. 3 Maps. H. 62501

Also: Report on the Geology of the Mineral Districts contiguous to the Iron Mountain Railroad. ... *St. Louis: M. Niedner, Printer.* 1859. 8vo, pp. 14. Map.

[PHILLIPS (Jonathan).] An Appeal to the People, on the Causes and Consequences of a War with Great Britain. *Boston: Printed by T. B. Wait and Company.* 1811. 8vo, pp. 36. BA.

PHILLIPS (J.) West India Question. The Outline of a Plan for the total ... Abolition of Slavery throughout the British Colonies. By Joseph Phillips ... . *London: J. & A. Arch.* 1833. 8vo, pp. 14. B., S. 62503

PHILLIPS (N.) An Eulogium to the Memory of the Rev. Gershom Mendes Seixas, ... 13th July, 1816. By Naphtali Phillips. *New York.* 1816. 8vo, pp. 13. N. 62504

PHILLIPS (N.) Phillips's United States Diary, or an Almanac, ... 1798. ... *Printed at Warren, R. I., by Nathaniel Phillips.* [n. d.] 12mo. 62505

[PHILLIPS (*Sir* R.)] A Collection of Modern and Contemporary Voyages & Travels; containing, I. Translations from Foreign Languages, of Voyages and Travels never before translated. II. Original Voyages and Travels never before published. III. Analyses of New Voyages and Travels published in England. *London: Sir Richard Phillips.* 1805–10. 11 vols., 8vo. Maps and Plates. 62506

Generally known as Phillips's Collection. It was issued in monthly parts, and comprises fifty-four different works, with separate titles and paginations, but with a general title-page to each of the eleven volumes. It is often found incomplete, and some copies vary in the arrangement. It includes Michaux's Travels, Turnbull's Voyage round the World, Depons's South America, Sarytschew's Voyage of Discovery, Helms's Travels, Perrin du Lac's Louisiana, Lewis and Clarke's Travels, Heriot's Travels through the Canadas, Bolingbroke's Voyage to the Demerary, Ashe's Travels, Peron's Voyage of Discovery, Keith's Voyage to South America, etc.

[PHILLIPS.] A Collection of Modern and Contemporary Voyages and Travels ... . *London: Sir R. Phillips.* 1810. 6 vols., 8vo. Maps and Plates. 62507

Consists of the remainders of the preceding collection. It contains Depons's South America, Peron's Voyage of Discovery, Bolingbroke's Voyage to the Demerary, Ashe's Travels, Sarytschew's Voyage of Discovery, etc.

PHILLIPS. A Million of Facts connected with the Studies, Pursuits, and Interests of Mankind. By Sir Richard Phillips. *New York.* 1835. 12mo. + Third Edition. *New York.* 1846. 12mo. 62508

These editions contain an Appendix on American History, etc.

[PHILLIPS.] New Voyages and Travels: consisting of Originals, Translations, and Abridgments. ... With Index and Historical Preface. *London: Printed for Sir Richard Phillips and Co.* [1819–23.] 9 vols., 8vo. Maps and Plates. A. 62509

Issued in monthly parts. It comprises sixty-five Voyages and Travels, each with its own title and pagination, and includes Fisher's Journal of a Voyage of Discovery to the Arctic Regions, McKeevor's Hudson's Bay, Freminville's Voyage towards the North Pole, Prior's Voyage, Cordova's Voyage of Discovery, Sanson's Travels in Lower Canada, Cornelius's Tour in Virginia, Brackenridge's Buenos Ayres, Waller's West Indies, Schoolcraft's Journal of a Tour 1818–19, Parry's Voyage in the Western Arctic Sea, Kotzebue's Voyage, Silliman's Tour to Quebec, Roquefeuil's Voyage round the

World, Montule's Voyage to North America, Prince Maximilian's Travels in the Brazils, etc.

[PHILLIPS (Samuel).] An Elegy upon the Deaths of those Excellent and Learned Divines the Reverend Nicholas Noyes, A.M. and the Reverend George Curwin, A.M. the Pastors of the First Church of Christ in Salem. [*Boston.* 1717?] 8vo, pp. 8.

Signed "Samuel Phillips."

PHILLIPS. Gospel-Ministers are the Servants of Christ-Jesus: ... A Sermon ... on the 13th of November, 1751. At the Installment of the Rev. Mr. Samuel Chandler, To the ... First Church ... Gloucester. ... By Samuel Phillips ... . *Boston: Printed by S. Kneeland.* 1752. 12mo, pp. (2), 31. B., W. 62511

PHILLIPS. Political Rulers Authoriz'd and Influenc'd by God our | Saviour, to decree and execute Justice: | A | Sermon | Preached at Boston: | In the Audience of His Honour | Spencer Phips, Esq; | Commander in Chief; | The Honourable | His Majesty's Council, | And the Honourable | House of Representatives, | Of the Province of the | Massachusetts-Bay in New-England, | On May 30th. 1750. | Being the Anniversary for the Election of His Majesty's | Council for the said Province. | By Samuel Phillips, A.M. | And Pastor of the South-Church in Andover. | ... | *Boston; New-England: | Printed by John Draper, Printer to His Honour the Lieutenant | Governour and Council.* 1750. | 8vo, pp. (4), 59. B. 62512

PHILLIPS. Preaching Peace by Jesus Christ ... the principal Design of the Gospel-Ministry. A Sermon delivered in the Audience of the Ministers of ... Massachusetts-Bay ... at their Annual Convention in Boston, on May 31st 1753. By Samuel Phillips ... . *Boston: in New England: Printed by S. Kneeland.* 1753. Sm. 4to, pp, (4), 42. B. 62513

PHILLIPS. The Sin of Suicide contrary to Nature. A Plain Discourse, Occasioned by the late Perpetration Of That heinous Crime: viz. on January 7th, 1767. Delivered ... January 11th. ... By Samuel Phillips ... *Boston: Printed ... by Kneeland and Adams.* MDCCLXVII. 8vo, pp. 48. B., W. 62514

PHILLIPS. Soldiers Counselled and Encouraged. A Sermon preached ... in the Audience of the Ancient and Honourable Artillery-Company in Boston, June 1st, 1741. Being the Day of the Election of their Officers. ... By Samuel Phillips ... . *Boston: Printed by Tho. Fleet.* 1741. 8vo, pp. 53. B., W. 62515

PHILLIPS. Three Plain Practical Discourses, ... at Andover, ... October 29th. 1727. ... The day ... preceding the late ... Earthquake. ... On ... Decemb. 21st. 1727. ... On ... Dec. 24th. ... By Samuel Phillips ... . Prefac'd by the very Reverend Mr. Colman. *Boston: Printed for J. Phillips.* 1728. 18mo, pp. (2), vi, 226, (1). B. 62516

PHILLIPS. Wisdom, an essential Requisite, or a necessary Qualification, for an Evangelical Pastor. A Sermon ... on the Third Day of January, A. D. 1759. Previous to the Ordination Of the Reverend Mr. Nathan Holt, to the Pastoral Care of the Second Church and Congregation in Danvers. ... By Samuel Phillips, A.M. ... *Boston: Printed by S. Kneeland.* 1759. 8vo, pp. (4), 50. M. 62517

Also: Advice to a Child. Or, Young People solemnly warn'd both against enticing, and consenting when enticed to Sin. In a Plain Discourse ... . *Boston: Printed for J. Phillips.* 1729. 12mo, pp. (2), iv, 138. B.—Children Well Imployed and Jesus much delighted, or The Hosannah of Zion's Children very pleasing to Zion's King. ... *Boston.* 1739. 16mo, pp. 109.—The Gospel-Doctrine of Justification by Faith explained and vindicated. A Discourse ... at Boston. In the Audience of the Church ... of ... Doctor Sewall: ... June 1st A.M. 1766. ... *Boston: N. E. Printed by Kneeland and Adams.* 1766. Sm. 4to, pp. 62. B.—The History of our Lord and Saviour Jesus Christ Epitomiz'd: In a Catechetical Way. ... *Boston: Printed by S. Kneeland & T. Green for D. Henchman.* 1738. 12mo, pp. (4), iv, 60, (3). B., C.—The Living Water to be had for Asking. A Plain Discourse Delivered ... at Boston, viz. In the Audience of the Church ... of the Reverend Mr. Samuel Cooper ... June 3d, A.M. 1750. ... *Boston: Printed by S. Kneeland for D. Henchman.* MDCCL. 8vo, pp. (4), 28. B.—The Necessity of God's Drawing, in Order to Man's Coming unto Christ, illustrated ... A Sermon ... at Boston, ... To the Church ... of the Reverend Mr. Samuel Cooper ... . June 3d, p.m. 1753. ... *Boston: Printed by S. Kneeland.* 1753. 8vo, pp. (4), 30. B.—The Orthodox Christian; or, A Child, well instructed in the Principles of the Christian Religion, Exhibited in a Discourse by way of Catechising. ... *Boston: Printed by S. Kneeland and T. Green, for D. Henchman.* 1738. 12mo, pp. (4), viii, 135, (7). B.—Seasonable Advice to a Neighbour, given by way of a Familiar Dialogue. ... *Boston: Printed by S. Kneeland.* 1761. 8vo, pp. (2), xi, (1), 86. M. + *Cambridge.* 1811. 12mo, pp. 96.—A Serious Address to Young People; by Way of a Familiar Conference between a Minister and a Young-Man: ... *Boston: Printed by S. Kneeland.* M,DCC,LXIII. 16mo, pp. 120. B.—The Sinner's Refusal to come unto Christ ... A Sermon Deliver'd at Boston, ... June 3d a.m. 1753. ... *Boston: Printed and Sold by S. Kneeland.* 1753. 8vo, pp. (4), 29. B.—A Word in Season. Or, The Duty of the People to take and keep The Oath of Allegiance to the Glorious God: exhibited in a Plain Discourse ... at Byfield, on Sept. 8th. 1726. ... *Boston: Printed by S. Kneeland & T. Green.* 1727. 12mo, pp. (2), viii, 213, (1). B., C. *See also* Sprague's "Annals," I. 273–275.

PHILLIPS (S. C.) An Address on the Annexation of Texas, and the Aspect of Slavery in the United States, in connection therewith: delivered in Boston November 14 and 18, 1845. By Stephen C. Phillips. *Boston: Wm. Crosby and H. P. Nichols.* 1845. 12mo, pp. 56. B., N. 62518

See also our Vol. XI., No. 45639.

PHILLIPS. Speech of Mr. Phillips, of Massachusetts, upon the Bill for the Relief of the Sufferers by the Fire at New York, delivered ... February 16, 1836. *Washington.* 1836. 8vo, pp. 16

Also: An Address, Introductory to the Second Course of the Franklin Lectures: delivered ... in Boston, October 29, 1832. ... *Boston: Printed by Ford and Damrell.* 1833. 8vo, pp. 16. W.—A Lecture on the Usefulness of Lyceums; ... delivered in Boston before the American Institute of Instruction, August 1831. ... *Boston: Hilliard, Gray, Little and Williams.* 1831. 8vo, pp. 38.—An Oration delivered at the Request of the Young Men of Salem, July 4, 1831. ... *Salem: Printed by Warwick Palfrey, Jun.* 1831. 8vo, pp. 40. H.—Speech delivered at Faneuil Hall on the Case of the Abducted Slave. [*Boston.* n. d.] 4to, pp. 2.

PHILLIPS (W.) Argument of Wendell Phillips, Esq., before the Committee on Federal Relations, (of the Massachusetts Legislature,) in Support of the Petitions for the Removal of Edward Greely Loring from the Office of Judge of Probate, February 20, 1855. *Boston: J. B. Yerrinton & Son, Printers.* 1855. 8vo, pp. 43.

PHILLIPS. The Constitution a Pro-Slavery Compact: or, Extracts from the Madison Papers, etc. Selected by Wendell Phillips. *Boston.* 1844. 8vo. + Second Edition. *New York.* 1845. 8vo. + Third Edition, Enlarged. *New York: American Anti-Slavery Society.* 1856. 12mo, pp. 208. C. 62521

PHILLIPS. The Laws of the Commonwealth—Shall they be enforced? Speech of Wendell Phillips, Esq., before the Legislative Committee, February 28, 1865. *Boston: Wright & Potter, Printers.* 1865. 8vo, pp. 16. 62522

PHILLIPS. No Slave-Hunting in the Old Bay State. Speech of Wendell Phillips, Esq., before the Committee on Federal Relations, in support of the Petitions asking for a Law to prevent the Recapture of Fugitive Slaves, ... February 17, 1859. ... *Boston: R. F. Wallcut.* 1859. 18mo, pp. 31. + *New York.* 1860. 12mo, pp. 23. H. 62523

PHILLIPS. Review of Lysander Spooner's Essay on the Unconstitutionality of Slavery. Reprinted from the "Anti-Slavery Standard," with additions. By Wendell Phillips. *Boston: Printed by Andrews & Prentiss.* 1847. 8vo, pp. 95. B. 62524

PHILLIPS. Review of Webster's Speech on Slavery. By Wendell Phillips. *Boston: American A. S. Society.* 1850. 8vo, pp. 44. A., B. 62525

PHILLIPS. Speeches before the Massachusetts Anti-Slavery Society, January, 1852. By Wendell Phillips. *Boston: Robert F. Wallcut.* 1852. 8vo, pp. 24. B. 62526

PHILLIPS. Speeches, Lectures, and Letters. By Wendell Phillips. *Boston: James Redpath.* 1863. 8vo, pp. v, 562. Portrait. + *Boston: Walker, Wise, and Company.* 1864. 12mo, pp. (2), iv, (2), 562. Portrait. A., H. + *Boston: Lee & Shepard.* 1869. 12mo. 62527

PHILLIPS. ... The War for the Union; A Lecture by Wendell Phillips, Esq., delivered in New York and Boston, December, 1861. *New York: E. D. Barker.* 1862. 12mo, pp. (2), 7–30. B. 62528

Also: An Address, delivered in Tremont Temple, Boston, April 19th, 1865 ... . *Worcester: Printed by Charles Hamilton.* [1865.] 8vo, pp. 8. H.—Argument ... against the Repeal of the Personal Liberty Law, before the Committee of the Legislature ... January 29, 1861 ... *Boston: R. F. Wallcut.* 1861. 12mo, pp. 24. B., H.—... Can Abolitionists Vote or take Office under the United States Constitution? ... *New York.* 1845. 8vo, pp. 39. B.—Disunion: Two Discourses at Music Hall, on January 20th, and February 17th, 1861. ... *Boston: Robert F. Wallcut.* 1861. 12mo, pp. 46.—Fraternity Lecture ... Boston, Oct. 4, 1859. Also, Letter ... to Judge Shaw and Prest. Walker. *Boston: Robert F. Wallcut.* 1859. 18mo, pp. 26. H.—The Infidelity of Abolitionism. ... *New York: American Anti-Slavery Society.* 1860. 12mo, pp. 12.—Kossuth ... Speech ... at the A. S. Bazaar ... Dec. 27th, 1851. [*Boston?* 1852?] Folio, pp. (2).—The Lesson of the Hour. Lecture ... delivered at Brooklyn, N. Y., ... November 1, 1859. [n. p. n. d.] 18mo, pp. 24.—The People Coming to Power! Speech ... at the Salisbury Beach Gathering, September 13, 1871. *Boston: Lee & Shepard.* 1871. 12mo, pp. 24.— ... The Philosophy of the Abolition Movement. ... *New York: American Anti-Slavery Society.* 1860. 12mo, pp. 47.—The Pulpit: A Discourse ... at the Music Hall, Boston, Nov. 18, 1860. ... *Boston.* 1860. 12mo, pp. 26.—Remarks ... at the Mass Meeting of Workingmen in Faneuil Hall, Nov. 2, 1865. *Boston.* 1865. 12mo, pp. 21.—Sketch of the Life of Mrs. Eliza Garnaut. ... [n. p. n. d.] 8vo, pp. 8.— ... Speech ... at the Convention held at Worcester, Oct. 15 and 16, 1851 [to consider the rights of women. n. p. n. d.] 8vo, pp. 24.—Speech ... at the Melodeon, ... Jan. 27, 1853. [*Boston.* 1853.] 8vo, pp. 32, 3, (1).—Speech ... at the Worcester Disunion Convention, January 15, 1857. [*Boston.* 1857.] 8vo, pp. 16. + [Another Edition. *Ibid.* n. d.] 8vo, pp. 16.—Tribute to the Memory of Charles F. Hovey, Esq. [n. p. n. d.] 18mo, pp. 24.—Wendell Phillips, Esq. On a Metropolitan Police. [*Boston.* 1863.] 32mo, pp. 32.

[PHILLIPS (Willard).] An Appeal to the Good Sense of the Democrats and the Public Spirit of the Federalists. By a Citizen of Massachusetts. *Boston: Printed by John Eliot.* 1814. 8vo, pp. 23. B., H. 62529

PHILLIPS. A Manual of Political Economy, with particular reference to the Institutions, Resources, and Condition of the United States. By Willard Phillips. *Boston: Hilliard, Gray, Little, and Williams.* 1828. 8vo, pp. 278. B., C. 62530

PHILLIPS. Propositions concerning Protection and Free Trade. By Willard Phillips. *Boston: Charles C. Little and James Brown.* 1850. 12mo, pp. xv, 233. A., B. 62531

PHILLIPS (W.) The Conquest of Kansas, by Missouri and her Allies. A History of the Troubles in Kansas from the Passage of the Organic Act until the close of July, 1856. By William Phillips. ... *Boston: Phillips, Sampson & Company.* 1856. 12mo, pp. 414. S. 62532

PHILLIPS (William Wirt). Address ... at the Laying of the Corner-Stone of the New Chapel for the use of the Inmates of the Sailors' Snug Harbor on Staten Island. By W. W. Phillips, D.D. ... *New York: Printed by Edward O. Jenkins.* 1855. 18mo, pp. 33. S. 62533

[PHILLIPS.] Memorial of the Goodness of God. In Two Discourses, delivered at the Opening of the First Presbyterian Church in the City of New York, Jan. 11, 1846. By the Pastor. *New York.* 1846. 12mo, pp. 120. 62534

Also: An Address to the Ministers, Elders, and Members of the Presbyterian Church, in the United States [on the case of A. Barnes, etc.] *New York: Robert Carter.* 1836. 8vo, pp. 41. B.

PHILLIPS ACADEMY. Copy of the Address delivered to the Students of Phillips' Academy, in Andover, ... July 18, 1791. *Exeter: Printed by Henry Ranlett.* 1791. 8vo, pp. 8. M. 62535

Also: Constitution ... . *Andover: Printed by Flagg and Gould.* 1817. 8vo, pp. 13, (1). M.—Order of Exercises for Exhibition, Aug. 22, 1820. [n. p. 1820.] Folio, 1 l.

PHILLIPS EXETER ACADEMY. Catalogue of Officers and Students of Phillips Exeter Academy. *Exeter.* 1838. 12mo, pp. 59. Continued. 62536

Catalogue of the Officers and Students of Phillips Exeter Academy. 1783–1869. With a ... Notice of the History ... of the Academy. *Cambridge: Welch, Bigelow, and Company, Printers.* 1869. 8vo, pp. xix, (1), 131. 62537

See also our Vol. I., No. 1438.

PHILLIS. *See* Wheatley (Phillis), *and* Peters (Phillis).

PHILMONT, *N. Y.* Constitution and By-Laws of Philmont Lodge ... located at Philmont, N. Y. Adopted 1854. *Albany: J. Munsell.* 1854. 18mo, pp. 20. 62538

PHILMORE (J.) Two Dialogues on the Man Trade. ... *London.* 1760. 8vo, pp. 68. 62539

PHILO, *pseudon.* Philo's | Essex Almanack, | For the Year of the Lord Christ, | 1770. | Being the Second after Bissextile, or

Leap-Year. | Calculated for the Meridian of Salem, in | New-England, Lat. 42 D. 35 M. North. | ... | *Salem: | Printed and sold by Samuel Hall,* ... [n. d.] 16mo, pp. (24). 62540

An "Essex" Almanac for 1769 was also printed at Salem. The issues for 1771–3 are by "Philo-Freeman."

PHILO-AFRICANUS, *pseudon.* A Letter to Wm. Wilberforce, Esq. By Philo-Africanus. *London: J. Debrett.* M.DCC.XC. 8vo, pp. (2), 64. C. 62541

PHILO-AFRICANUS, *pseudon.* A Letter to Philo Africanus, upon Slavery in answer to his of the 22d of November, in the General Evening Post; together with the Opinions of Sir John Strange, and other ... Lawyers upon this subject, with the Sentence of Lord Mansfield, in the Case of Somerset and Knowles, 1772, with his Lordship's explanation of that opinion in 1786. *London: W. Brown.* MDCCLXXXVIII. 8vo, pp. (2), 40. 62542

At page 28 signed "Candidus, December 10, 1787." Improved title of our No. 40451, Vol. XI.

PHILO-AMERICANUS, *pseudon.* The American Struggle. An Appeal to the People of the North. By Philo-Americanus. *London: Effingham Wilson.* 1862. 8vo, pp. 32. 62543

See also Vol. I., No. 1783*a*.

The Philobiblion. A Monthly Bibliographical Journal. Containing Critical Notices of, and Extracts from, Rare, Curious, and Valuable Old Books. ... *Geo. P. Philes & Co. ... New York.* MDCCCLXII–MDCCCLXIII. 2 vols., 4to, pp. (1), 5, (1), 288; 4, 290. 62544

Printed on a variety of India paper. Twenty-four numbers were published.

PHILO-BRITAN, *pseudon.* *See* Vol. V., No. 18550.

PHILO-CATO, *pseudon.* The Celebrated Letters of Philo-Cato. With an Introduction to them. By Aristides. *New York.* 1811. 8vo. N. 62545

See also [Davis (M. L.)], Vol. V., No. 18863.

PHILODEMUS, *pseudon.* Conciliatory Hints ... Submitted to the Consideration of the Citizens of the Commonwealth of South-Carolina. By Philodemus. ... *Charleston: A. Timothy.* M.DCCLXXIV. 4to, pp. 34. H. 62546

PHILO DRAMATIS, *pseudon.* The Rights of the Drama; or, An Inquiry into the Origin, Principles, and Consequences of Theatrical Entertainments. By Philo Dramatis. *Boston.* 1792. 8vo, pp. 48. 62547

Philoeunomos, *pseudon.* *See* [Sherman (Roger)].

Philo-Jackson, *pseudon.* The Presidential Election, written for the benefit of the People of the United States, but particularly for those of the State of Kentucky; relating to the Seminole War, and the Vindication of General Jackson. By Philo-Jackson. *Frankfort: The Author.* 1823. 8vo, pp. 35. BA. + (Second Series.) *Louisville: The Author.* 1823. 8vo, pp. 28. + Third Series. *Frankfort: The Author, May,* 1824. 8vo, pp. 48. + Fourth Series. [*Ibid.*] 1824. 8vo, pp. 54. + Fifth Series. [*Ibid.*] 1824. 8vo, pp. vii, 24. + Sixth Series. [*Ibid.*] 1824. 8vo, pp. 47. BA. 62548

An attempt to vindicate General Jackson from the obloquy which followed his entrance upon the territory of a neutral power, seizing and, without color of law, hanging some of its subjects.

Philolethus, *pseudon.* *See* [Lozano (P.)], Vol. x. 42592.

Proceedings of the Philological Society for 1842–43 and 1843–44. Vol. i. *London: Printed by Richard and John E. Taylor.* 1844. 8vo. + *London: George Bell.* 1854. 8vo. A.

Originally issued in monthly numbers, from Nov. 25, 1842, to the close of 1853, forming 6 vols., 8vo, pp. iv, 298, viii, 3 Plates; iv, 298, (1), viii; iv, 260; iv, 270, viii, Plate; iv, 208; iv, 212, (2), 9, (2), 4, clxxvii. Continued under the following title:

Transactions of the Philological Society 1854. ... *George Bell* ... *London.* [n. d.] 8vo, pp. iv, 303. Map. Continued. A.

The Proceedings and Transactions contain valuable papers on the American languages by Howse, Latham, Schomburgk, and others.

Philom's Address to the People of New England, with Remarks on the Plans to Establish Kingcraft and Priestcraft in the United States ... [n. p.] 1817. 8vo. 62551

In opposition to the New England or Massachusetts Charitable Society.

First Semi-Centennial Anniversary of the Philomathean Society. [History of the Society, Poems, Oration, Dinner, ... &c.] *Albany.* 1854. 8vo, pp. 154. 62552

Philomathes, *pseudon.* Almanac for 1775. By Philomathes. *Worcester.* [n. d.] 12mo. 62553

The Philomathesian. Vol. i. Conducted by a Literary Association in Middlebury College. *Middlebury.* 1833–4. 8vo, pp. (4), 380. 62554

Philomela; with the Notes for Morning Prayer. *Boston.* 1720. 12mo, pp. 110. 62555

The Philometer; or, The Guage of his Majesty's [Napoleon's] "Love" towards the Americans. [*Charleston.* n. d.] Folio, 1 leaf. 62556

Philo Pacificus, *pseudon.* *See* [Walcott (R. F.)], *and* [Worcester (Noah)].

Philopatria, *pseudon.* Almanac for 1767. By Philopatria. *Portsmouth, N. H.* [n. d.] 12mo. 62557

Philopatria, *pseudon.* *See* [Paine (T.)], Vol. xiv. 58203.

Philo Patricius, *pseudon.* *See* Vol. xiv., No. 59074.

Philopatrios, *pseudon.* Some Observations on the Two Campaigns against the Cherokee Indians, in 1760 and 1761. In a Second Letter from Philopatrios. *Charleston: Peter Timothy.* 1762. 8vo, pp. 88. Scheme of the Transactions. P. 62558

"A very rare tract—a defense of the S. C. Rangers, against imputations on their courage and efficiency, made by Lieut. Col. James Grant, commander of the expeditions of 1760 and 1761. The S. C. Regiment was under the command of Henry Middleton, and among its officers were Henry Laurens, Wm. Moultrie, Francis Marion, and Isaac Huger. The controversy resulted in a challenge from Middleton to Grant, and a duel, which terminated without bloodshed."—J. H. Trumbull.

[Philopatris, *pseudon.*] Dec. 5, 1723. A most Humble Proposal To ... The Lords Regents of Great Britain, And to ... the Lords of the Admiralty and Board of Trade; For an Effectual Method to Prevent Piracy, and make The Trade of America Safe in Time to come. ... *Printed by a Merchant in London* .... 1723. Sm. 4to, pp. 15, (1). B. 62559

Signed Philopatris on page 13. Improved title of our No. 51095, Vol. xii.

Philopatrus (Andreas), *pseudon.* *See* [Parsons (Robert)], Vol. xiv., No. 58903.

Philo-Pennsylvania, *pseudon.* *See* Vol. xiv., No. 60610.

Philopolites, *pseudon.* A | Memorial | Of the Present Deplorable State of | New-England, | With the many Disadvantages it lyes under, | by the Male-Administration of their | Present Governour, | Joseph Dudley, Esq. | And his Son Paul, &c. | Together with | The several Affidavits of People of Worth, | Relating to several of the said Governour's Mer- | cenary and Illegal Proceedings, but particularly his | private Treacherous Correspondence with Her Ma- | jesty's Enemies the French and Indians. | To which is Added, A Faithful, but Melancholy Account | of several Barbarities lately Committed upon her Majesty's Sub- | jects, by

the said French and Indians, in the East and West Parts | of New-England. | Faithfully Digested from the several Original Letters, Pa- | pers, and MSS. by Philopolites. | [*London:*] *Printed in the Year,* MDCCVII. *and Sold by S. Phillips* | *N. Buttolph, and B. Elliot. Booksellers in Boston.* | Sm. 4to, pp. (4), 41. BM. 62560

A very rare tract, probably written or incited by Cotton Mather, and printed at London. For a reply *see* "A Modest Enquiry," Vol. xii., No. 49822, and for another tract on the same subject *see* "The Deplorable State of New-England," Vol. v., No. 19639. *See also* "Mass. Hist. Soc. Coll.," Fifth Series, Vol. vi., where all three are reprinted.

Philoponus (Honorius), *pseudon.* *See* [Plautius (Caspar)].

[Philophron, *pseudon.*] Columbia and Britannia: | A | Dramatic Piece. | By a Citizen of the United States. | ... | *New-London: Printed by T. Green,* M,DCC,LXXXVI. 8vo, pp. 63. 62561

Fabius is Washington, Perjunis is Benedict Arnold.

ΦΙΛΟΨΥΧΩΝ, *pseudon.* *See* [Shimeall (R. C.)]

Philo Reflector, *pseudon.* *See* Vol. v., No. 17350.

Philosophic Solitude. *See* [Livingston (W.)], Vol. x. 41647.

Philosophical Register, or Annals of Medicine, Natural History and the Arts. Vol. i. *New York.* 1811. 8vo. Continued

To this periodical many of the most eminent men in the country contributed.

Philosophy of Modern Miracles, ... With Especial Reference to the Mysterious Developments at Bridgeport and elsewhere. By a Dweller in the Temple. *New-York: Stringer & Townsend.* 1850. 8vo, pp. 46. 62563

Philotheos Physiologus, *pseudon.* *See* [Tryon (Thomas)], *and* our Vol. vii., No. 25947.

Philo Veritatis, *pseudon.* To Pacificus in reply to his Essay, entitled a Serious Expostulation with the Society of Friends in Pennsylvania and parts adjacent. By Philo Veritatis. *Philadelphia.* 1808. 8vo, pp. 21. 62564

See also Vol. xiv., No. 58094.

Philp [James]. Philp's Washington Described. A Complete View of the American Capital, and the District of Columbia; with many Notices, Historical, Topographical, and Scientific, of the Seat of Government. Edited by William D. Haley. *New York: Rudd & Carleton.* 1861. 12mo, pp. 239. Map.

Phin (J.) Open Air Grape Culture: [with] the Manufacture of Domestic Wine. By John Phin. *New York: Sheldon & Co.* 1867. 12mo, pp. 375. C. 62566

Phinney (E.) Address ... before the Middlesex Society of Husbandmen and Manufacturers, ... Oct. 7, 1830. By Elias Phinney. ... *Charlestown: Printed by William W. Wheildon.* 1830. 8vo, pp. 28. B. + *Charlestown.* 1831. 8vo, pp. 28. 62567

Phinney. History of the Battle at Lexington, on the Morning of the 19th April, 1775. By Elias Phinney. *Boston: Printed by Phelps and Farnham.* 1825. 8vo, pp. 40. A., C. + *Boston: Noyes, Holmes & Co.* 1875. 8vo, pp. 40. 62568

See also Hosmer (R.), Vol. viii., No. 33109.

Phinney's Calendar, or Western Almanac for 1816. *Cooperstown, N. Y.* [n. d.] 12mo. Continued. S. 62569

Phippen (G. D.) Fitzpen or Phippen, and Allied Families. By George D. Phippen, of Salem. [n. p. n. d.] 8vo, pp. 20. Folded Plate. 62570

Phippen. Pedigree of Saltonstall ... Collated and arranged by Geo. D. Phippen. [*Boston.* 1857.] Folio, folded leaf.

Prepared for Mr. Drake's folio edition of the History of Boston, and also issued separately.

Phipps (C. J.) A Voyage towards the North Pole undertaken by his Majesty's Command 1773 By Constantine John Phipps *London; Printed by W. Bowyer and J. Nichols, for J. Nourse.* MDCCLXXIV. 4to, pp. viii, 252, (1). 3 Maps and 12 Plates. A. + *Dublin: Printed for Messrs. Sleater* ... MDCCLXXV. 8vo, pp. viii, 275. Map and Plate. 62572

"An important addition to nautical science which does honor to its author. Besides a journal of the voyage, it contains a descriptive catalogue of the natural productions of Spitzbergen."—*Biog. Univ.* *See* "Monthly Review," LII. 121. Included in Pinkerton's Collection, Vol. I., *and* Mavor's Voyages, Vol. XI.

Phipps. The Journal of a Voyage undertaken by order of His present Majesty, For making Discoveries towards the North Pole, by the Hon. Commodore Phipps, and Captain Lutwidge in His Majesty's Sloops Racehorse and Carcase. To which is prefixed, An Account of the several Voyages undertaken for the Discovery of a North-East Passage to China and Japan. *London: F. Newbery.* MDCCLXXIV. 8vo, pp. (2), 118. 2 Maps, Plate.

The narrative of some member of the expedition, containing particulars not given in the official account.

Phipps. Voyage au Pole Boréal, fait en 1773, par ordre du Roi d'Angleterre, par Constantin-Jean Phipps. Traduit de l'Anglois [par Jean Nicolas Demeunier]. *Paris: Saillant & Nyon.* MDCCLXXV. 4to, pp. xii, 257, (2). 12 Maps and Plates, and 2 Tables. C. 62574

Phipps. Reise nach dem Nordpol. Auf Befehl Ihro Königl. Grossbrittannischen Majestät. Unternommen im Jahr 1773. Von C. J. Phips, aus dem Englischen, mit Zusätzen und Anmerkungen von Herrn Landvogt Engel. ... *Bern: bey der typographischen Gesellschaft.* 1777. 4to, pp. (6), x, 122. Maps and Plates. J.C.B. 62575

Phipps. See-Reisen von Engländern, Holländern, Franzosen, Spaniern, Dänen und Russen auf dem Nordmeer, Nordpol ... *Bern.* 1795. 4to. Maps. 62576

Phipps (W.) A Sermon occasioned by the Death of Mrs. Eunice T. Smith, ... Wife of Rev. John C. Smith, Missionary to Ceylon, delivered in Paxton, Mass., August 7th, 1842 ... By William Phipps ... *Worcester: J. B. Ripley, Printer.* 1842. 8vo, pp. 19. 62577

The Annual Catalogue of ... Phipps Union Female Seminary, for the Year ending June 25, 1857. Albion, Orleans Co., N. Y. *Rochester: Press of Chester P. Dewey.* 1857. 8vo, pp. 24. Plate. Continued. 62578

Phips (S.) Instructions for treating with the Eastern Indians, given to the Commissioners appointed for that Service, By the Hon. Spencer Phips ... In the Year 1752. Now first printed from the Original Manuscript. *Boston: Samuel G. Drake.* 1865. 4to, pp. 8. 62579

Improved title of our No. 34857, Vol. ix. For the treaty, which was made October 13–21, 1752, *see* our Vol. ix., No. 36736.

Phips (W.) *See* Journal, Vol. ix., No. 36731, [Mather (C.)], Vol. xi., No. 46455, *and* Spencer (T.)

Phips (W.) A Breach in Jerusalem's Walls deplored. A Sermon at Oxford, May 31st, 1761, on the Death of the Rev. Mr. John Campbell. By William Phips. *Boston: J. Draper.* 1761. 8vo, pp. 29. 62580

Phiseldek (C. F. v. S.) Europe and America; or, the Relative State of the Civilized World at a Future Period. Trans-

lated from the German of Dr. C. F. Von Schmidt-Phiseldek ... By Joseph Owen. *Copenhagen.* 1820. *Bernhard Schlessinger.* 8vo, pp. 257. C. 62581

For other editions *see* Schmidt-Phiseldek (C. F. v.)

Phlogobombos (Terentius), *pseudon.* *See* Vol. iii., No. 8838, *and* Vol. ix., No. 36829, *note.*

Phocion, *pseudon.* *See* [Hamilton (Alex.)], Vol. viii., Nos. 29962–5, *also* No. 30697, *and* Vol. xiii., No. 52392.

Phœbus (W.) Memoirs of the Rev. Richard Whatcoat, late Bishop of the Methodist Episcopal Church. By William Phœbus, M.D. *New-York: Joseph Allen.* 1828. 12mo, pp. 118. 62582

Also: An Apology for the Right of Ordination in the Evangelical Church of America: (called Methodists) ... *New-York: Author.* 1804. 18mo, pp. 33. Portrait.

Phœnix (John), *pseudon.* *See* [Derby (G. H.)], Vol. v. 19665.

Phœnix (S. W.) The Descendants of John Phœnix, an Early Settler in Kittery, Maine. By S. Whitney Phœnix. ... *New York: Privately Printed.* 1867. Rl. 8vo, pp. vi, 53, (3).

Five copies printed in 4to, and one hundred in 8vo, sixty of which were afterwards destroyed.

Phœnix. The Whitney Family of Connecticut, and its affiliations; being an attempt to trace the Descendants, as well in the Female as the Male Lines, of Henry Whitney, From 1649 to 1878; to which is prefixed some account of the Whitneys of England. By S. Whitney Phœnix. ... *New York: Privately Printed.* 1878. 3 vols., 4to, pp. xxii, 916; (4), 917–1814; (4), 1815–2740. Coat of Arms and numerous folded Pedigrees.

Printed at the Bradstreet Press. "Edition: 500 copies quarto, 10 copies folio. All for presentation."

The History and Government of the Phœnix Social Club. *Philadelphia.* 1810. 8vo. 62585

... A Phonographic Report of the Debates ... of the New England Methodist Centenary Convention, ... Boston, June 5–7, 1866. ... *Boston: B. B. Russell & Co.* 1866. 8vo, pp. 248. BA.

Photographic Sketch Book. *See* Vol. vii., No. 26635.

Photographic Views, illustrative of the Civil War. A Collection of ... Photographic Views, of McClellan's Campaign, The Defence of Mobile and other Scenes and Incidents connected with the late Civil War .... From Negatives taken ... by Geo. N. Barnard .... *New York.* [n. d.] 4to. 285 Photographs.

Gemma Phrysius de | Principiis Astronomiæ et | Cosmographiæ: deque vsu Globi ab eodē editi. Item | de Orbis diuisione, & insulis rebusq̄ nuper inuētis | Eiusdem libellus de locorum describendorum ra | tione. Et de eorum distantiis inueniendis, nunquam | antehac visus. [Woodcut.] *Parisiis* | *Apud Thomam Richardum, sub Bibliis aureis,* | *ex aduerso Collegij Remensis* | M.D.XLVII. | [Colophon:] *Parisiis* | *excvdebat Thomas* | *Richardus* | 1548. | 8vo, pp. (2), 178. + *Paris.* 1556. 8vo, 172 leaves. 62588

Chap. xxix., De insulis nuper inuentis; chap. xxx., De America; chap. xxxi., De Insulis apud Americam. For other editions *see* our Vol. vii., Nos. 26852–6. No. 26852 is erroneously dated 1850: it should be 1530.

Phyle (F. A. J.) The Hermit, or an Account of Francis Adam Joseph Phyle ... who lived without the use of fire for twenty-two years, in a small cave ... near Mount-Holly ... Second Edition. *New Jersey, John Atkinson.* 1811. 18mo, pp. 108. + [Another Edition. *Ibid.*] 1811. 62589

Physic and Physicians: A Medical Sketch Book, Exhibiting the Public and Private Life of the Most Celebrated Medical Men of Former Days; ... *Philadelphia: G. B. Zieber & Co.* 1845. 2 vols., 8vo, pp. 209; 208. 62590

The Physician's Almanac, for ... 1817. ... Containing ... Astronomical Calculations, with Medical and Meteorological Observations. ... *Boston: Printed ... by Tileston & Parmenter.* [n. d.] 12mo, pp. (36). 62591

Pia Disideria. *See* [Mather (C.)], Vol. xi., No. 46454.

Piacenza (D. Carli da). *See* Carli (D.), Vol. iii., No. 10909, and add: + *Bassano.* 1687. 4to.

Piang Pu, *pseudon.* Revolution in Hell, and the establishment of a Democratic Republic on the principle of the Wilmot Proviso. By Piang Pu. *New York.* 1848. 12mo, pp. 108.

Piang Pu, *pseudon.* Revolution in Orcus, and the Establishment of a Democratic Republic headed by the Hero of a Thousand Fights; an Epic. By Piang Pu. *New York: Published for Fun.* 1848. 12mo, pp. 112. Plate. B. 62593

Piano dell' Assedio di Luisburgo colla Descrizione dell Isola Reale o di Capo Breton. *Amsterdam.* 1758. 8vo. 62594

Piatt (J. J.), *and* (S. M. B.) The Nests at Washington, and other Poems. By John James Piatt and Sarah M. Bryan Piatt. *New York: Walter Low.* 1864. 12mo, pp. 150. B.

[Piatt *and* Howells (W. D.)] Poems of Two Friends. *Columbus.* 1860. 12mo, pp. viii, (2), 132. B. 62596

Piatt. Poems in Sunshine and Firelight. By John James Piatt. *Cincinnati: R. W. Carroll & Co.* 1866. 16mo, pp. 127.

Piatt. Western Windows, and other Poems. By John James Piatt. *New-York: Hurd & Houghton.* 1869. 16mo, pp. 231. B. 62598

Picard (A.) ... Le Conflit Américain et sa Solution Probable, Discussion d'un article de M. R. de F., intitulé: La Question Américaine ... par M. A. Picard. *Paris: Chez Dentu.* 1862. 8vo, pp. 32. A. 62599

Strongly in favor of the North.

Picard (B.) Ceremonies | et | Coutumes | Religieuses | des | Peuples Idolatres | Representées par des Figures dessinées de | la main de | Bernard Picard: | Avec une Explication Historique, & quelques | Dissertations curieuses. | Tome Premier, | Premiere Partie, | Qui contient les Ceremonies Religieuses des Peuples des | Indes Occidentales. | *A Amsterdam,* | *Chez J. F. Bernard,* | M.DCCXXIII. | Folio, pp. (4), 211, (1). 34 Plates. Seconde Partie ... Indes Orientales, pp. 49, (3), 150, (2). 11 Plates. A. 62600

This is counted as the sixth volume of "Ceremonies et Coutumes Religieuses de tous les Peuples du Monde." It contains the religious ceremonies of the natives of America. The plates are mostly copied from those in the celebrated series of De Bry, and are engraved with equal excellence. For the complete work *see* [Bernard (J. F.)], Vol. ii., Nos. 4931–4.

Picazo (Miguel de). Regla y Constituciones del Orden Tercero del Real y Militar de Nuestra Señora de la Merced, Redempcion de Cautivos, y Catálogo de sus Gracias, indulgencias Remissiones, y Privilegios concedidos por los SS. PP. Innocencio xi. y Benedicto xii. y otros Summos Pontifices ... . *Mexico.* 1752. Sm. 8vo, pp. (12), 87. + *Mexico.* 1784. 62601

Piccha (G.) Gregorii Picchæ Oratio ad Sixtum v. Pont. Max. aliosque Christianos Principes et Respublicas pro Britannico Bello indicendo. *Romæ.* 1588. 4to. 62602

This rare and most interesting tract relates to the Spanish armada. It also contains notices of Sir Francis Drake.

Piccolomini (Enea Silvio Vicenzo). *See* Neve y Molina (Louis de), Vol. xiii., No. 52412.

Pichardo (E.) Diccionario Provincial casi-razonado de Voces Cubanas, por D. Estéban Pichardo. Segunda edicion, notablemente aumentada y corregida. *Habana: Imprenta de M. Soler.* 1849. Sm. 4to, pp. 258, (2). + Tercera edicion, notablemente aumentada y corregida. *Habana: Imprenta la Antilla.* 1862. Rl. 8vo, pp. xvii, (2), 281. 62603

First published anonymously, *Matanzas*, 1832. 16mo. + [*Ibid.*] 1836. 16mo.

PICHARDO. Geografia de la Isla de Cuba, por Don Esteban Pichardo. ... *Habana: D. M. Soler.* 1854–55. 4 vols., sm. 4to, pp. xlix, 155; 272; 356; 240. c. 62604

PICHARDO. Memoria Justificativa de la Carta Geo-Coro-Topo-Grafica del departamento Occidental de la Isla de Cuba hasta el limite Oriental de Nueva Filipina. *Habana.* [n. d.] 4 parts, 8vo. 62605

PICHARDO. Miscelanea poética por Esteban Pichardo. *Habana: Imprenta de la Universidad, de D. Antonio M. Valdes.* 1828. 8vo, pp. 30. 62606

PICHARDO (Jos. Ant.) Elogio de San Felipe Neri en la Iglesia de su Congregacion de México. *Mexico: Zuniga.* 1803. 4to, pp. (14), 44, 30. 62607

PICHARDO Y TAPIA (F.) Apuntes Biográficos del V. P. Fray José de la Cruz Espi, conocido por el Padre Valencia. Recogidos por Don Francisco Pichardo y Tapia. *Nueva York: M. W. Siebert.* 1863. 18mo, pp. 51. c. 62608

PICHÉ (E. U.) Aux habitans du Comté de Berthier; Réponse aux injures de la Minerve ... Par E. U. Piché. *Toronto.* 1859. 8vo, pp. 55. 62609

[PICHON (Thomas).] Lettres | et | Mémoires | Pour servir à | l'histoire | Naturelle, Civile et Politique | Du Cap Breton, | depuis | Son établissement jusqu'à la reprise de cette Isle par | les Anglois en 1758. | ... | *A La Haye, chez Pierre Gosse,* | *Et se trouve* | *A Londres, chez Jean Nourse,* | MDCCLX. | 12mo, pp. xvi, 327. A.

"Pichon left France for Canada in 1750, as secretary to Compte de Raymond, Governor of Cape Breton, with whom he remained but for a short time. He died in England in 1781."—*Biog. Universelle. See* "Mass. Hist. Soc. Coll.," First Series, Vol. I.

[PICHON.] Genuine Letters and Memoirs relating to the Natural, Civil, and Commercial History Of the Islands of Cape Breton, and Saint John, from the first Settlement there, to the taking of Louisburg by the English, in 1758. In which, among many interesting particulars, the causes and previous events of the present war are explained. By an Impartial Frenchman.

Translated from the Author's original manuscript. *London: J. Nourse.* 1760. 8vo, pp. xvi, 400. c. 62611

"Impartial, instructive, and entertaining."—*Monthly Review*, XXII. 362.

PICHOT (A.) Les Mormons. Par Amédée Pichot. *Paris: Hachette et Cie.* 1854. 12mo. 62612

PICK (J. C.) Copie | Eens Briefs, geschreven | uyt West-Indien, inde Hooft-stadt van Bresilien, ghenaemt | de Todos le Sanctos, den 23 Mey, Anno 1624. | Door den gheleerden Jan Cornelisz Pick, Dienaer | des godlijcken Woords aldaer. | Met consent der Ed: Heeren der Stadt Delff. | *Tot Delff* | *Ghedruckt by Cornelisz Jansz Timmer, woonende aen't* | *Merckt-veld, inden beslaghen Bybel, Anno* 1624. | 4to, pp. 4. 62613

PICKARD (K. E. R.) The Kidnapped and the Ransomed: being the Personal Recollections of Peter Still and his Wife "Vina," after Forty Years of Slavery. By Mrs. Kate E. R. Pickard. With an Introduction by the Rev. Samuel J. May, and an Appendix by the Rev. William H. Furness, D.D. *Syracuse: William T. Hamilton.* 1856. 12mo, pp. 409. 2 Plates. c. + Third Edition. [*Ibid.*] 1856. 12mo, pp. 409. 62614

PICKARD (Samuel). Autobiography of a Pioneer; with Sermons by the Author, and some Account of the Labors of Elder Jacob Knapp. Edited by O. T. Conger. *Chicago.* 1866. 12mo. 62615

PICKELL (J.) A New Chapter in the Early Life of Washington, in connection with the Narrative History of the Potomac Company. By John Pickell. *New York: D. Appleton & Co.* 1856. 8vo, pp. xi, 17–178. 62616

PICKELL (J.) Report of Examinations and Surveys of a Route for a Rail-Road from Canajoharie, ... to ... Catskill ... . Made ... by Lieut. John Pickell, of the 4th Regt. Artillery. To which is annexed, An Act ... incorporating the ... company. *Catskill: Printed by Faxon & Elliott.* 1831. 8vo, pp. 23. s.

Third Annual Report of the President to the Stockholders of the PICKELL MINING COMPANY. *Baltimore: Printed by James Young.* 1856. 8vo, pp. 24. s. 62618

PICKEN (A.) The Canadas, as they at present commend themselves to ... Emigrants, Colonists, and Capitalists. ... Compiled ... from ... documents furnished by John Galt, Esq. ... and

other authentic sources, By Andrew Picken. ... *London.* 1832. *Effingham Wilson.* 12mo, pp. vi, (2), 349, (2), lxxxvii. Map.

[PICKEN.] The Canadas: comprehending Topographical Information concerning the Quality of the Land, in different Districts; and the fullest general information: for the use of Emigrants and Capitalists. Compiled from original Documents furnished by John Galt, Esq. ... Second Edition. *London: Effingham Wilson.* 1836. 12mo, pp. vi, (1), 349, (2), lxxxvii.

PICKENS (Francis W.) Speech of Mr. Pickens, of South Carolina; Delivered ... May 23, 1836, ... on the Fortification Bill. [n. p. n. d.] 8vo, pp. 16. 62621

Also: Oration ... before the Euphradian and Clariosophic Societies ... . *Columbia, S. C.: Press of Gibbes & Johnston.* 1855. 8vo, pp. 23.—Speech ... Jan. 21, 1836, on the Abolition Question ... *Washington.* 1836. 8vo.—Speech on the Bill to Distribute the Proceeds of the Public Lands among the States ... July 2, 1841. *Washington.* 1841. 8vo, pp. 8.—Speech ... June 22, 1842, on the Tariff. *Washington.* 1842. 8vo.

PICKERING (C.) ... The Geographical Distribution of Animals and Plants. By Charles Pickering, M.D. ... *Boston: Little, Brown & Co.* 1854. 4to, pp. (4), 168, Index, (44). A. 62622

Forms Vol. XV. of the United States Exploring Expedition. *See also* "Transactions of the Amer. Philos. Society," New Series, Vol. III.

PICKERING. ... The Races of Man: and their Geographical Distribution. By Charles Pickering, M.D. *Philadelphia: Printed by C. Sherman.* 1848. 4to, pp. 447. Map and 12 colored Plates.

Forms Vol. IX. of the United States Exploring Expedition. Some copies have the imprint, *Boston: Charles C. Little and James Brown*, 1848, and some *London*, 1849.

PICKERING. The Races of Man; and Their Geographical Distribution. By Charles Pickering, M.D. ... New Edition. To which is prefixed, an Analytical Synopsis of the Natural History of Man. By John Charles Hall, M.D. ... *London: H. G. Bohn.* 1850. 12mo, pp. lxxii, (2), 445. Map and 12 Plates. B. + [*Ibid.*] 1851, '54, '63. 12mo. 62624

Some copies have colored plates. Also: Chronological History of Plants: Man's Record of his own existence illustrated through their names, uses, and Companionship. ... *Boston: Little, Brown, and Company.* 1879. 4to, pp. xvi, 1222. Portrait. A.

PICKERING (*Colonel*). *See* Pickering (Timothy).

PICKERING (D.) Address delivered before the Citizens of Providence, ... on the Fifty-Second Anniversary of American Independence. By David Pickering. *Providence: Smith & Parmenter.* 1828. 8vo, pp. 24. W. 62625

PICKERING. A Discourse delivered at the New Universalist Chapel, Providence, R. I., at its Dedication, Dec. 29, 1825. By Rev. David Pickering. *Providence: B. Cranston.* 1825. 8vo, pp. 16. 62626

Also: A Discourse ... in the Universalist Church in Hudson, June 27, 1821. ... *Hudson.* 1821. 8vo, pp. 16.—The Evils of Intemperance. A Discourse delivered ... January 14, 1827 ... . *Providence: Miller & Grattan.* 1827. 8vo, pp. 22. + Second Edition. *Taunton: S. W. Mortimer.* 1827. 12mo, pp. 22.—Reflections for the New Year. A Discourse ... January 7, 1827. ... *Providence.* 1827. 8vo, pp. 15.—Sermon delivered at the Dedication of the Universalist Meeting House in Halifax, Mass. Jan. 1, 1829. ... *Providence, R. I.* 1829. 8vo, pp. 14.—Sermon ... at the Installation of the Rev. Jacob Frieze, ... First Universalist Society, in North Providence, R. I., Dec. 24, 1828. ... *Providence: John S. Greene.* 1829. 8vo, pp. 16.

[PICKERING (Henry).] Athens and other Poems, by the Author of the Ruins of Pæstum. *Salem: Cushing and Appleton.* 1824. 8vo, pp. 84. 62627

[PICKERING.] The Buckwheat Cake, A Poem. *Boston, Massachusetts. Carter, Hendee & Babcock.* MDCCCXXXI. 8vo, pp. 14. Plate. 62628

Privately printed, and very rare.

[PICKERING.] Poems by an American. ... Not Published. *Boston: Massachusetts. Carter and Hendee.* MDCCCXXX. 8vo, pp. vi, 3–84. B. 62629

Twenty-five copies printed from the press of I. R. Butts.

[PICKERING.] The Ruins of Pæstum; and other Compositions in Verse. *Salem, Massachusetts. Cushing and Appleton.* 1822. 8vo, pp. 128. 62630

PICKERING (J.) An Essay on a Uniform Orthography for the Indian Languages of North America, as published in the Memoirs of the American Academy of Arts and Sciences. By John Pickering, A.A.S. *Cambridge: ... Hilliard and Metcalf.* 1820. 4to, pp. (2), 42. 62631

Reprinted from the American Academy, etc., "Memoirs," Vol. IV.

PICKERING. Eulogy on Nathaniel Bowditch, LL.D. ... Including an Analysis of his Scientific Publications. Delivered ... May 29, 1838. By John Pickering ... *Boston: Charles C. Little and James Brown.* 1838. 8vo, pp. (4), 101. + *Cambridge: Folsom, Wells and Thurston, Printers.* 1838. 4to, pp. (4), lxxvi. H.

[PICKERING. A Grammar of the Cherokee Language. ... *Boston: Mission Press.* 1830.] 8vo. 62633

Only four sheets (pp. 9–40) were printed, when it was discontinued on account of the invention of Sequoyah's new Cherokee alphabet.

[PICKERING.] National Rights and State Rights. A Review of the Case of Alexander McLeod; ... By a Member of the Massachusetts Bar. ... *Boston: Bradbury and Soden.* 1841. 8vo, pp. 46. BA. 62634

PICKERING. Remarks on the Indian Languages of North America. By John Pickering. From the Encyclopedia Americana, Volume VI. Published in 1831. Reprinted [*Philadelphia*]. 1836. 8vo, pp. (2), 581–600. 62635

PICKERING. Ueber die Indianischen Sprachen Amerikas. Aus dem Englischen des Nordamerikaners Herrn John Pickering übersetzt und mit Anmerkungen begleitet von Talvj [Mrs. Edward Robinson]. *Leipzig* 1834 *bei Friedr. Christ. Wilh. Vogel.* 8vo, pp. viii, 79, (1). c. 62636

[PICKERING.] A Vocabulary, or Collection of Words and Phrases which have been supposed to be peculiar to the United States: to which is prefixed a Memoir on the Present State of the English Language in the United States. As published in the Memoirs of the American Academy. *Cambridge: Printed by Hilliard and Metcalf.* 1815. 4to, pp. (2), 98. B. 62637

PICKERING. A Vocabulary, or Collection of Words and Phrases which have been supposed to be peculiar to the United States of America. To which is prefixed an Essay on the present state of the English Language in the United States. Originally Published in the Memoirs of the American Academy of Arts and Sciences; and now republished with Corrections and Additions. By John Pickering. ... *Boston: Cummings and Hilliard.* 1816. 8vo, pp. 206, (1). A. 62638

Also: A Lecture on Telegraphic Language; ... before the Boston Marine Society, Feb. 5, 1833. ... *Boston.* 1833. 8vo, pp. 32. 2 Plates.—A Lecture on the Alleged Uncertainty of the Law, before the Boston Society for the Diffusion of Useful Knowledge, March 5, 1830. ... *Boston.* 1834. 8vo, pp. 28.—Memoir on the Language and Inhabitants of Lord North's Island. ... *Cambridge: Metcalf and Company.* 1845. 4to, pp. (2), 205–247.—An Oration delivered on the Fourth of July, 1804, at St. Peter's Church, in Salem, Massachusetts. ... *Salem: Printed by Joshua Cushing.* 1804. 8vo, pp. 24.—Working Man's Political Economy, founded upon the Principle of Immutable Justice, and the Inalienable Rights of Man. ... *Cincinnati.* 1847. 8vo.

PICKERING (J.) Emigration, or No Emigration; being the Narrative of the Author, (an English Farmer) from the year 1824 to 1830; during which time he traversed the United States of America, and the British Province of Canada, with A View to settle as an Emigrant: ... By Joseph Pickering ... . *London: ... Longman ... .* 1830. 12mo, pp. 172. 62639

PICKERING. Inquiries of an Emigrant, Being the Narrative of an English Farmer From the year 1824 to 1830; with the Author's Additions to March 1832; ... By Joseph Pickering ... . Fourth Edition ... . *London: Effingham Wilson.* 1832. 12mo, pp. xvi, 207. 62640

PICKERING. Führer für Auswanderer nach Amerika. ... *Potsdam.* 1832. 12mo. 62641

PICKERING (O.), *and* UPHAM (C. W.) The Life of Timothy Pickering. By his Son, Octavius Pickering. ... *Boston: Little, Brown, and Company.* 1867–73. 4 vols., 8vo, pp. xix, 549, Portrait; xix, 509, Portrait; (4), 499, Plate; (4), 512, Plate and 2 Facsimiles. A. 62642

Volumes II.–IV. are by Charles W. Upham.

PICKERING. Report of the Trial by Impeachment of James Prescott, Esquire, Judge ... for the County of Middlesex, for Misconduct and Maladministration in Office, ... in ... 1821. With an Appendix ... . By Octavius Pickering and William Howard Gardiner ... . *Boston: Daily Advertiser.* 1821. 8vo, pp. 225, (1). 62643

See also our Vol. III., No. 12030.

PICKERING (T.) A Bad Omen To the Churches of New-England: In the Instance of Mr. John Cleaveland's Ordination, so termed, over a Separation in Chebacco-Parish in Ipswich ... 25th of Feb. 1746, 7. ... By Theophilus Pickering. ... *Boston: N. E. Rogers and Fowle.* MDCCXLVII. 4to, pp. 12. 62644

Also: Supplement to a Piece lately printed, entitled a Bad Omen to the Churches, ... *Boston.* 1747. 4to, pp. 4. *See also* Vol. IX., Nos. 35046–7.

[PICKERING.] The Chebacco Narrative. *See* [Cleaveland (John)], Vol. IV., No. 13592.

PICKERING. Mr. Pickering's Letter to Mr. Whitefield: Touching his Relation to the Church of England; his Impulses or Impressions; and the present unhappy State of Things, &c. offered in excuse of Mr. Pickering's Disinclination to open his Pulpit to him in his late visit to Ipswich, &c. Together with Mr. Pickering's Letter to a Neighbouring Minister; exhibiting his Opinion with Respect to the Reception of Mr. Whitefield, upon private satisfaction. *Boston: Printed and Sold by Rogers and Fowle in Queen-street next to the Prison.* 1745. 4to, pp. 8. B.

PICKERING. The Rev. Mr. Pickering's Letters to the Rev. N. Rogers and Mr. D. Rogers of Ipswich; With their Answer

to Mr. Pickering's First Letter; as also, his Letter to the Rev. Mr. Davenport, of Long Island ... . *Boston: Printed by Thomas Fleet.* 1742. 8vo, pp. 20. B. 62646

PICKERING (T.) An Address to the People of the U. States. To which is added, a Letter from the Hon. Timothy Pickering, a Senator of the United States from the State of Massachusetts, exhibiting to his Constituents a view of the imminent danger of an Unnecessary and Ruinous War. Addressed to His Excellency James Sullivan, Governor of the said State. *Northampton, Mass. Printed by William Butler.* 1808. 8vo, pp. 16. 62647

For other editions *see* No. 62652, *infra.*

[PICKERING.] Congress of the United States. In Senate, January the 20th, 1797. The following Message ... communicating the copy of a Letter from the Secretary for the Department of State to the Minister Plenipotentiary from the United States to the Republic of France. [n. p. n. d.] 8vo, pp. 104.

The letter is signed "Timothy Pickering."

PICKERING. An Easy Plan of Discipline for a Militia. By Timothy Pickering, Jun. ... *Salem, New-England: Printed by Samuel and Ebenezer Hall.* 1775. 8vo, pp. 28, 169, 2, (1). 14 Plates. c. 62649

Published in July, 1775. It is rarely found complete, most copies having been used in the War of the Revolution.

[PICKERING.] Instructions ... *See* Vol. IX., Nos. 34865, *and* 34870.

PICKERING. Interesting Correspondence between His Excellency Governour Sullivan and Col. Pickering; in which the latter vindicates himself against the groundless charges and insinuations made by the Governour and others. *Boston: Printed by Greenough and Stebbins.* 1808. 8vo, pp. 32. + Second Edition. [*Ibid.*] 1808. 8vo, pp. 24. N. + *Newburyport: Thomas & Whipple.* 1808. 8vo, pp. 26. s. 62650

PICKERING. (Not published.) A Letter from Colonel Pickering, containing A Narrative of the Outrage committed on him at Wyoming: With an Account of the Controversies respecting the lands claimed by the States of Pennsylvania and Connecticut, which led to that Event. [*Salem: Printed by T. C. Cushing.* 1819.] 8vo, pp. 38, (1). A., B. 62651

Reprinted in Hazard's Register, Vol. VII. *See* "Reply to Colonel Pickering's Attack."

PICKERING. A Letter from the Hon. Timothy Pickering, a Senator of the United States from the State of Massachusetts, exhibiting to his Constituents a View of the Imminent Danger of an Unnecessary and Ruinous War. Addressed to His Excellency James Sullivan, Governor of the said State. *Boston: Printed by Greenough and Stebbins.* 1808. 8vo, pp. 16. + Second Edition. [*Ibid.*] 1808. 8vo, pp. 16. + *Boston, Printed: London, reprinted for John Joseph Stockdale.* 1808. 8vo, pp. 31, (1). A. + *Boston, Printed. New-Haven, Re-printed by Oliver Steele and Co.* 1808. 8vo, pp. 16. + [*New York.*] 1808. 8vo. + *Troy.* 1808. 8vo, pp. 15. + With Governor Sullivan's Answer. *Hartford: Printed by Lincoln and Gleason.* 1808. 8vo, pp. 16. + *Portsmouth.* 1808. 12mo, pp. 12. + *Newburyport.* 1808. 8vo. + To which is added the Speech of Mr. Gardiner, on the Bill supplementary to the Embargo Law. *Carlisle: Alexander & Phillips.* 1808. 12mo, pp. 27. + To which is prefixed an Address of Thousands to the People of the United States. *Northampton (Mass.)* 1808. 8vo. 62652

For another edition *see* No. 62647, *supra.* For Remarks upon this letter *see* Adams (J. Q.), our Vol. I., No. 282. *See also* "Some Remarks and Extracts."

[PICKERING.] Letter from the Secretary of State to Charles C. Pinckney, Esq. In Answer to the Complaints of the French Minister against the ... United States, contained in his notes to the Secretary of State, dated the 27th of October, and 15th of November, 1796. *New-York: Hopkins, Webb & Co.* 1797. 8vo, pp. 53. c., N. 62653

For a French translation *see* our Vol. X., No. 40690.

PICKERING. Letters addressed to the People of the United States of America, on the Conduct of the Past and Present Administrations of the American Government, towards Great Britain and France. By Col. Timothy Pickering, formerly Secretary of State, &c. *London: Longman ...* 1812. 8vo, pp. 168. 62654

See "Monthly Review," LXIX. 259.

PICKERING. Letters from Mr. Pickering, Secretary of State, to the Chevalier de Yrujo, Envoy Extraordinary and Minister Plenipotentiary of His Catholic Majesty to the United States of America. August 8th, 1797. [n. p. 1797.] 8vo, pp. 37. N.

See also Yrujo (*Chevalier de*).

[PICKERING.] Message from the President of the United States, accompanying a Report of the Secretary of State, containing Observations on some of the Documents, communicated by the President on the 18th January, 1799. ... [n. p.:] *Printed by John W. Fenno.* [n. d.] 8vo, pp. 16. S. 62656

The Report is signed "Timothy Pickering."

PICKERING. Observations on the Dispatch. *See* Tanguy de la Boissière.

PICKERING. Political Essays. A Series of Letters Addressed to the People of the United States. By Timothy Pickering ... . *Canandaigua: Printed by J. D. Bemis.* 1812. 12mo, pp. 215. B.

Said to be the first bound book printed in Western New York. *See* "Hist. Mag.," Second Series, I. 193–6.

PICKERING. A Review of the Correspondence between the Hon. John Adams, late President of the United States, and the late Wm. Cunningham, Esq. Beginning in 1803, and ending in 1812. By Timothy Pickering. *Salem: Cushing and Appleton.* 1824. 8vo, pp. (4), 197. + Second Edition. *[Ibid.]* 1824. 8vo, pp. (4), 140. 62658

PICKERING. Mr. Pickering's Speech ... 26th and ... 28th of February, 1814 ... on the Bill to authorize a Loan of Twenty-five Millions of Dollars. *Georgetown: Printed by Robert Alleson.* 1814. 8vo, pp. (2), 72. B., N. 62659

Also: Address to the Essex Agricultural Society, May 5, 1818. ... *Salem.* 1818. 8vo, pp. 27. M.—Address, before the Massachusetts Agricultural Society, at the Brighton Cattle Show. [n. p.] 1822. 8vo.—Correspondence between P. A. Adet, the French Minister to the United States, and T. Pickering, Secretary of State for the United States. . [n. p. 1796.] 8vo, pp. 87. W.—A Discourse ... before the Essex Agricultural Society, ... February 21, 1820. Suggesting some Improvements in the Agriculture of the County. ... *Salem: John D. Cushing, Printer.* 1820. 8vo, pp. 27.—Mr. Pickering's Speech, In the Senate ... December 1, 1808. ... [On] the Resolution offered by Mr. Hillhouse, to repeal the Embargo Acts ... . [n. p. n. d.] 8vo, pp. 12.—Mr. Pickering's Speech ... on the Resolution offered by Mr. Hillhouse to repeal the ... Embargo, November 30, 1808. [n. p.: *Russell & Cutler, Printers.* n. d.] 8vo, pp. 24. W. + [Another Edition. n. p. n. d.] 8vo, pp. 8. M. + *Hanover (N. H.): C. & W. S. Spear, Printers.* [n. d.] 8vo, pp. 20.—Observations Introductory to Reading the Declaration of Independence, at Salem, July 4, 1823. ... *Salem.* 1823. 8vo. *See* our Vol. VIII., Nos. 29982–3 for two tracts which are sometimes attributed to Timothy Pickering. *See also* Secretary of State, *and* War Department.

[PICKERSGILL (*Lieut.*)] A Concise Account of Voyages for the Discovery of a North-West Passage. Undertaken for finding a new way to the East Indies. With Reflections on the Practicability of gaining such a Passage ... . By a Sea Officer. *London: J. Bew.* MDCCLXXXII. 12mo, pp. xxviii, 69. J.C.B.

See "Monthly Review," LXVII. 72.

PICKET (A. *and* J. W.) The Academician. Containing the Elements of Scholastic Science, and ... Philosophic Education

... By Albert Picket, ... and John W. Picket ... . *New-York: Charles N. Baldwin.* 1820. 8vo, pp. iv, 399. A. 62661

PICKET. Geographical Grammar ... . By A. & J. W. Picket, ... *New York: Smith and Forman.* 1816. 8vo, pp. 80. Maps. + Second Edition. *New York: Daniel D. Smith.* 1817. 8vo, pp. 72. 7 Maps. B. 62662

See "The Western Academician."

PICKET (A.), *Sen.* Opening Address at the Sixth Annual Session of the Western Literary Institute. By Albert Picket, Sen. *Cincinnati.* [n. d.] 8vo, pp. 24. 62663

The Picket-Guard. By Aunt Friendly ... . *New York: Evangelical Knowledge Society.* 1864. 18mo, pp. 60. 62664

PICKETT (A.) The Final Answer: or, Brief Statements and Remarks respecting the Present Division in the South Church and Society, Reading, Mass. By Aaron Pickett. ... *Boston: Printed by C. C. P. Moody.* 1848. 8vo, pp. 71. S. 62665

Also: Sermon at the Funeral of Mrs. Lathrop, of Cohasset.—Sermon at the Funeral of Mrs. Bennett, the wife of the Rev. Joseph Bennett, of Woburn, Mass.

PICKETT. A Review of the Reverend Aaron Pickett's "Reply" and "Defence" by Vindex ... . *Boston.* 1848. 8vo, pp. 58.

By G. Allen. The "Reply" and "Defence" appeared in the Boston "Recorder," Oct. 7, 1847, and in the Boston "Reporter," Nov. 25, 1847.

PICKETT (A. J.) Eight Days in New Orleans in February, 1847. By Albert J. Pickett. *Montgomery: The Author.* 1847. 8vo, pp. 40. C. 62667

PICKETT. History of Alabama, and incidentally of Georgia and Mississippi, from the earliest period. By Albert James Pickett ... . *Charleston: Walker and James.* 1851. 2 vols., 12mo, pp. xix, 377; viii, 445. Map, 3 Plans and 8 Plates. + Second Edition. *[Ibid.]* A. + Third Edition. *[Ibid.]* 62668

A model state history. *See* "Historical Magazine," I. 190.

PICKETT. Invasion of the Territory of Alabama by One Thousand Spaniards, under Ferdinand de Soto, in 1540. By Albert J. Pickett. *Montgomery: Printed by Brittan & Wolf.* 1849. 8vo, pp. 41. N. 62669

PICKETT (C. E.) The Existing Revolution; its Causes and Results. By Charles Edward Pickett. *Sacramento.* 1861. 8vo, pp. 24. H. 62670

Also: Gwinism in California. ... *San Francisco.* 1860. 8vo, pp. 8.

PICKETT (J. C.) Address. Subject: General Washington. For February 22, 1867. By Col. J. C. Pickett. *Washington: Printed by John T. Burch.* 1867. 8vo, pp. 23. + *Washington.* 1867. 4to, pp. 16. H. 62671

PICKETT. Letters and Dissertations upon Sundry Subjects. By J. C. Pickett ... . *Washington: William Greer, Printer.* 1848. 8vo, pp. 64, and cover. 62672

Also: Poems on various Subjects. ... [*Washington: The Author.* 1867.] 8vo, pp. 106

Pickings from the Portfolio of the New Orleans "Picayune" ... *New York.* 1845. 12mo. 62673

PICKMAN (B.) An | Oration, | pronounced, | February 22, 1797, | Before the Inhabitants of the Town of | Salem, in Massachusetts, | assembled to commemorate | the Birth-Day | of | George Washington, | ... | By Benjamin Pickman, jun. | ... | *Printed at Salem, by Thomas C. Cushing.* | 1797. | 8vo, pp. 22. C. 62674

PICOLOMINI (F.) Carta de N. P. Francisco Picolomini, Preposito General de la Compañia de Jesus, á los Padres y Hermanos de la misma Compañia. *Mexico.* 1763. 4to. 62675

PICQUENARD (J. B.) Adonis, ou le Bon Negre, Anecdote Coloniale. Par J. B. Picquenard. *A Paris, De l'Imprimerie de Didot Jeune. L'An* VI.–1798. 24mo, pp. 278, 8. 62676

PICQUENARD. Monbars l'Exterminateur, ou la Dernier Chef des Flibustiers, Anecdote du Nouveau Monde. *Paris.* 1807. 3 vols., 12mo. Plate. 62677

PICQUENARD. Zoflora, ou la Bonne Négresse, Anecdote Coloniale. Par J. B. Picquenard. ... *A Paris, de l'Imprimerie de Didot Jeune. L'An* VIII. [1800.] 2 vols., 24mo, pp. 252; 268.

PICTET (C.) Tableau | de la Situation actuelle | des | États-Unis d'Amérique, | d'après | Jedediah Morse | et les | meilleurs auteurs américains, | par C. Pictet ... . *A Paris,* | *Chez Du Pont* ... 1795. 2 vols., 8vo, pp. 360, (2); 340, (2). 2 Maps and Tables. B.

PICTET (M. A.) Description d'un Météore vu dans la Province de Connecticut, aux États-Unis [Décembre, 1807], et Détails Ultérieurs communiqués à l'Institut de France. ... [*Paris.* 1808.] 8vo. M. 62680

PICTON (T.) A Letter addressed to the Rt. Hon. Lord Hobart, ... Secretary of State for the Colonial Department. By

Colonel Thomas Picton, late Governor ... of the Island of Trinidad ... . *London: Printed by D. N. Shury, for E. Lloyd.* 1804 Sm. 4to, pp. (2), vii, 106, (1). S. 62681

Respecting his administration of the Island of Trinidad. *See* "Monthly Review," XLVIII. 222.

PICTON. Inhuman Torture!! Fairburn's Edition of the Trial of Thomas Picton, late Governor of Trinidad, ... for Torturing Louisa Calderon, in the Island of Trinidad, in the Month of December, 1801, by Suspending her by a Rope tied to her Wrist, and a Sharp Spike the only resting-place for her foot, which was Tried at ... Westminster, ... Feb. 24, 1806 ... . *London: John Fairburn.* [1806.] 8vo, pp. 20. Folded Plate. B. 62682

PICTON. The Trial of Thomas Picton, late Governor of Trinidad, ... for inflicting the Torture on Louisa Calderon, by Suspending her by the Wrist to the Ceiling, without any resting place except a Sharp Spike for her Toe. Tried ... Feb. 24, 1806, and found Guilty. Taken in Short-hand by Pierre F. McCallum, Esq. *London.* [1806.] 8vo, pp. 36. Plate. 62683

PICTON. The Trial of Governor T. Picton, for inflicting the Torture on Louisa Calderon, a Free Mulatto, and one of his Britannic Majesty's Subjects in the Island of Trinidad. ... Taken in Short-hand ... on the 24th of Feb. 1806. *London: Crosby & Co.* 1806. 8vo, pp. 126. 62684

See "Monthly Review," XLIX. 332. Also: Sixteen Cases of Gen. Picton's most Horrid Cruelty in Trinidad. [*London: Printed by B. M'Millan.* n. d.] 4to, pp. 28. H. For refutations *see* our Nos. 26153–5. *See also* Vol. III., No. 9885, *and* Vol. V., No. 19149.

Report on Surveys for the PICTON BRANCH RAILWAY; (via Earltown.) With some Remarks on the Trunk Line. ... By James Laurie, Civil Engineer. *Halifax.* 1860. 8vo, pp. 24.

Pictorial History of England. *See* Vol. V., No. 17374.

Pictorial History of Remarkable Events in America. *New York.* 1849. 8vo. 62686

Part I. History of Mexico; Part II. Battles of Mexico; Part III. Life of Millard Filmore; Part IV. Life of Zachary Taylor.

Pictorial History of the American Revolution. *See* [Sears (R.)]

Pictorial View of California. *See* [Letts (J. M.)], IX. 40723.

Pictorial Views of Massachusetts, for the Young. *Worcester.* 1846. 16mo. 62687

The Picture Exhibition; containing the Original Drawings of eighteen Disciples. To which are added Moral and Historical Explanations. Published under the Inspection of Mr. Peter Paul Rubens, Professor of Polite Arts. *Worcester: Isaiah Thomas.* 1788. 32mo, pp. 112. C. 62688

Picture of New York. *See* Vol. XIII., No. 54579, [Mitchill (S. L.)], Vol. XII., No. 49746, *and* [Ruggles (Edward)].

A Picture of Slavery, drawn from the Decisions of Southern Courts. [n. p. n. d.] 8vo, pp. 16. 62689

Against the election of Judge Woodward, the Democratic candidate for Governor of Pennsylvania. *See also* [Bourne (George)], Vol. II., No. 6921.

Pictures of Edgewood. *See* [Mitchell (D. G.)], XII. 49676.

Pictures of the "Peculiar Institution" as it exists in Louisiana and Mississippi. By an Eye Witness. *Boston: J. B. Yerrington.* 1850. 12mo, pp. 24. 62690

... Pictures of the Times; or, a Contrast between the Effects of the True Democratic System, as displayed under Jefferson, Madison and Jackson in former times, and the Effects of the Aristocratic Sub-Treasury System, as displayed in Martin Van Buren's Time. ... *Philadelphia: Croome, Meignelle and Minot.* 1840. 8vo, pp. 16. 62691

Picturesque America; or, the Land we live in. A Delineation by pen and pencil of the Mountains, Rivers, Lakes, Forests, Water-falls, Shores, Cañons, Valleys, Cities, and other Picturesque Features of our Country. With Illustrations on Steel and Wood, by Eminent American Artists. Edited by William Cullen Bryant. ... *New York: D. Appleton and Company.* [1872–1874.] 2 vols., 4to, pp. viii, 568; vi, 576. 49 Plates. A.

First published in forty-eight parts.

The Picturesque Tourist: being A Guide through the State of New York and Upper and Lower Canada, including a Hudson River Guide; giving an accurate description of Cities and Villages, Celebrated Places of Resort, etc. ... *New York: J. Disturnell.* [1858.] 24mo, pp. (2), 296, exclusive of advertising pages. Maps and Woodcuts. B. 62693

[PIDANSAT DE MAIROBERT (Matthieu François).] Discussion sommaire sur les anciennes limites de l'Acadie, et sur les sti-

pulations du Traité d'Utrecht qui y sont relatives. *A Basle, Chez Samuel Thourneisan.* MDCCLV. 12mo, pp. 37. J.C.B. 62694

This gave offense to the English commissaries, who published an answer to it in 1750. *See* Faribault, No. 831.

[PIDANSAT DE MAIROBERT.] L'Observateur anglais ou correspondance secrete entre Milord All'Eye et Milord All'Ear. *A Londres.* 1777–8. 4 vols., 12mo. S. 62695

This was followed by six more volumes, written after his death by an anonymous author, and an eleventh as a supplement; of the ten volumes several editions were published with the following title:

[PIDANSAT DE MAIROBERT.] L'Espion Anglois, ou correspondance secrete entre Milord All'Eye et Milord AllE'ar [*sic*]. Nouvelle édition, revue, corrigée et considérablement augmentée. ... *Londres.* [*Amsterdam?*] 1779–1785. 10 vols., 12mo. BM. + [*Ibid.*] 1782–85. 10 vols., 12mo. S. 62696

[PIDANSAT DE MAIROBERT.] L'Espion Anglais, ou Correspondance entre deux Milords (Milord All'Eye et Milord All'Ear) sur les moeurs publiques et privées des Francais. *Paris.* 1809 2 vols., 8vo. BM. 62697

A selection of articles from the former collection.

PIDGEON (W.) Traditions of De-coo-dah, and Antiquarian Researches: comprising Extensive Explorations, Surveys, and Excavations of the Wonderful and Mysterious Earthen Remains of the Mound-Builders in America; The Traditions of the last Prophet of the Elk Nation relative to their Origin and Use; and the Evidences of an Ancient Population more numerous than the Present Aborigines. By William Pidgeon. ... *Sampson Low, Son, and Co. ... London; Horace Thayer and Co. ... New York.* 1853. 8vo, pp. 334. Map, folded Plate and Woodcuts. + [*Ibid.*] 1854. 8vo, pp. 334. Plate. + *New York: Horace Thayer.* 1858. 8vo, pp. 334. Folded Plate and Woodcuts. A. 62698

The large map is generally lacking. A record of personal examination of a great number of ancient mounds and fortifications, and of the traditions regarding them, obtained from an aged Sioux chief. The author's researches, however, are rendered almost useless by their blending with baseless hypotheses and unreliable traditions. The numerous plates afford very clear illustrations of many remains of Indian structures.

PIDGIN (W.) Two Discourses, on the Sudden Deaths of Joseph Brown and James Jenness, drowned near Rye-Beach, Sept. 9th, 1806. By William Pidgin. *Newburyport.* 1806. 8vo.

Pieces first published in the Public Advertiser. Sketch of the present Reign ... . *London: J. Kearsly.* 1778. 8vo. 62700

See "Monthly Review," LI. 479.

Pieces Justificatives des Mémoires concernant les Limites de l'Acadie. *A Paris, de l'Imprimerie Royale.* M. DCCLIV. 4to, pp. (2), 646. 62701

... Pièces Officielles, messages, instructions, dépêches, &c., Relatives à la Négociation qui a eu lieu en 1797 & 1798, sur les Différens élevés entre le Gouvernement des États-Unis de l'Amérique et le Directoire Exécutif de France. ... Traduites de l'Anglais, Par M. Peltier. *A Londres: T. Baylis.* 1798. 8vo, pp. 70. C. 62702

Improved title of our No. 59593. At the end: "Lettres au Dr. Priestley en Amérique," pp. 20. For the English edition *see* "The Whole Official Correspondence."

Pièces relatives à la Rupture avec l'Espagne, remises devant les deux Chambres du Parliament, le 29 Jan. 1762. Traduit de l'Anglois. *La Haye.* 1762. 8vo, pp. 1277. 62703

PIEDRAHITA (L. F.) [Half title:] Historia | General | de | Las Conqvistas | del | Nuevo Reyno | de | Granada. | *Amberes.* | *Por Juan Baptista Verdussen.* | 1688.] [Engraved title:] Historia | general | de las conqvistas | del Nvevo | Reyno de Granada. | A la S. C. R. M. | De D. Carlos Segvndo, | Rey de las Españas, | y de las Indias. | Por el Doctor D. Lvcas Fernandez | Piedrahita, Chantre de la Iglesia Metropolitana | de Santa Fè de Bogotà Calificador del Santo Oficio | por la Suprema y General Inquisicion, y Obispo | electo de Santa Marta ... . Folio. A. 62704

Collation: Half-title; folded title, engraved by J. Mulder, surrounded by a border containing portraits of Indian chiefs and views of battles; pp. (16), 599, Indice, (7). 2 folded engraved titles, surrounded by portraits, for books I. and III.

A work of the highest importance for the early history of New Granada. Only this first volume, which comes down to the year 1563, was published. The "aprobacion" is dated at Madrid, April 27, 1688; and it has been supposed by some that the volume was really printed there instead of at Amberes. It was compiled chiefly from the manuscripts of the conqueror, Gonzalo Ximenez de Quesada, and is filled with details of the manners and customs of the natives, and the conquest of the country by the Spaniards.

PIERANTONI (Augusto). La Questione Anglo-americana dell' Alabama. Studio di diritto internazionale pubblico e marittimo. ... Per l'Avv. A. Pierantoni. *Firenze: Stabilimento Civelli.* 1870. 8vo, pp. 52. C. 62705

PIÉRARD (A.) Souvenirs de Mexique, par l'abbé Aristide Piérard ... . *Bruxelles.* 1867. 8vo, pp. 235. 62706

PIERCE *and* BACON. Case of Pierce and Bacon. Memorial to Congress. [n. p. n. d.] 8vo, pp. 20. 62707

Relative to the acceptances of J. B. Floyd, Secretary of War.

PIERCE (C.) Haunts of Vice in New York. By Charles Pierce. *New York: The Author.* 186–. 12mo. 62708

PIERCE (E. L.) Effect of Proscriptive or Extreme Legislation against Foreigners in Massachusetts and New England, on Free Labor, Free States, and the Cause of Freedom and Republicanism in the West. Letter of Edward L. Pierce, Esq., of Chicago, containing Important Statistics in regard to the Foreign Vote at the Presidential Election. ... *Boston.* 1857. 8vo, pp. 16.

PIERCE. The Freedmen of Port Royal, South Carolina. Official Reports. *New York.* 1863. 8vo, pp. 21. B. 62710

First appeared in the "Atlantic Monthly," for August, 1863.

PIERCE. The Negroes at Port Royal. Report of E. L. Pierce, Government Agent, to the Hon. Salmon P. Chase, Secretary of the Treasury. *Boston: R. F. Wallcut.* 1862. 12mo, pp. 36. 62711

PIERCE. The Two Systems of Government proposed for the Rebel States. Speech of Edward L. Pierce, at the Town House, Milton, October 31, 1868. ... *Boston: Wright & Potter, Printers.* 1868. 8vo, pp. 34. 62712

Also: The Personal Liberty Laws. Remarks ... before the Committee of the Legislature, ... Feb. 1, 1861. ... *Boston: Printed by Stacy & Richardson.* 1861. 8vo, pp. 36. B.—A Treatise on American Railroad Law. ... *New York.* 1857. 8vo, pp. xlv, 569. + *New York: Baker, Voorhis & Co.* 1867. 8vo, pp. xlv, 569.

PIERCE (F.) Speech of Hon. Franklin Pierce ... May 1, 1840, upon Claims for Seven Years Half Pay. *Washington.* 1840. 8vo. 62713

PIERCE. Speech ... July 1 and 2, 1841, on Buchanan's Resolutions regarding Removals from Office. [n. p. n. d.] 8vo.

PIERCE. Franklin Pierce's Leben und Wirken. Aufruf an die deutschen Wähler. [n. p. 1852.] 8vo, pp. 8. S. 62715

PIERCE *and* KING. Sketches of the Lives of Franklin Pierce and Wm. R. King, Candidates of the Democratic Republican Party for the Presidency and Vice Presidency of the United States. *Boston.* 1852. 8vo, pp. 32. Portrait. 62716

Also: Sketches of the Lives of Franklin Pierce and Wm. R. King. [*Published by Nat. Dem. Exec. Committee.* n. p. 1852.] Rl. 8vo, pp. 36. *See also* our Vol. VIII., No. 31511.

PIERCE [George F.] Devotedness to Christ: A Sermon ... Nashville, Tenn., April 15, 1855, in Memory of the late William

Capers, D.D., one of the Bishops of the Methodist Episcopal Church, South. By Bishop Pierce. *Nashville, Tenn.: E. Stevenson & F. A. Owen.* 1855. 12mo, pp. 24. 62717

PIERCE. Incidents of Western Travel: In a Series of Letters. By George F. Pierce, D.D. Edited by Thomas O. Summers, D.D. *Nashville, Tenn.: Methodist Publishing House.* 1857. 12mo, pp. 249. 62718

Also: Address to the Graduating Class of the Medical College of Georgia, 1844. ... *Augusta.* 1844. 8vo. B.

PIERCE (H. M.) Address to the First Graduating Class of Rutgers Female College: delivered ... June 2d, 1867. By Henry M. Pierce ... . *New York: Agathynian Press.* 1867. 8vo, pp. 19. 62719

Also: Baccalaureate Address to the Graduating Class of 1870, Rutgers Female College, ... June 5th, 1870. *New York: Cushing, Bardua & Co., Printers.* 1870. 8vo, pp. 15.

PIERCE (H. N.) Sermons preached in St. John's Church, Mobile, on the 13th of June, 1861, the National Fast appointed by His Excellency Jefferson Davis, President of the Confederate States of America. By ... Rev. H. N. Pierce. *Mobile: Farrow & Dennett, Printers.* 1861. 8vo, pp. 12. BA. 62720

PIERCE (I. B.) A Discourse preached at Newport, Herkimer County, New York, at the Funeral of Mrs. Sarah Willoughby, ... December 16th, 1838. By Isaac Bliss Pierce ... . *Albany: Printed by Hoffman & White.* 1839. 8vo, pp. 20. S. 62721

PIERCE (James). The Curse Causeless. Sermon at Exon, Jan. 30, 1716–17. ... Third Edition. *Boston.* 1728. 12mo. + Sixth Edition. [*Ibid.*] 1728. 12mo. 62722

PIERCE (J.) An Address at the Opening of the Town Hall, in Brookline, ... 14 October, 1845. By John Pierce, D.D. ... *Boston: White & Potter, Printers.* 1846. 8vo, pp. 52. A., B.

PIERCE. Brookline Jubilee. A Discourse delivered in Brookline, ... on 15 March, 1847, the day, which completed half a century from his ordination, By John Pierce, D.D. ... *Boston: James Munroe and Company.* M DCCC XLVII. 8vo, pp. 72. B.

PIERCE. A Discourse delivered at Brookline, 24 November, 1805, the day, which completed a century from the Incorporation

of the Town. By John Pierce, A.M. ... *Cambridge: Printed by William Hilliard.* 1806. 8vo, pp. 32. S. 62725

See also "Massachusetts Historical Collections," Second Series, Vol. II. 140–161.

PIERCE. A Discourse ... at Dorchester, on 17 June, 1830, To commemorate the completion of the Second Century from its Settlement by our Pilgrim Fathers. By John Pierce, D.D. ... *Boston: ... W. L. Lewis, Printer.* 1830. 8vo, pp. 36. S. 62726

PIERCE. A Discourse ... at the Dedication of the Meeting-house of the First Congregational Society, Burlington, Vt., Jan. 9, 1817. By John Pierce ... . *Burlington.* 1817. 8vo, pp. 20.

PIERCE. A Discourse .. 9 November, 1817, the Lord's Day after the Completion of a Century from the Gathering of the Church in Brookline. By John Pierce ... . *Boston: Printed by John Eliot.* 1818. 8vo, pp. 32. M. 62728

PIERCE. A Eulogy on George Washington the Great and the Good, Delivered, on the Anniversary of his Birth, At Brookline, and published, at the Request of its Inhabitants. By John Pierce, their Pastor. *Boston: Manning & Loring, Printers.* 1800. 8vo, pp. 24, Washington's Farewell Address, 24. BA., C. 62729

PIERCE. Reminiscences of Forty Years, Delivered, 19 March, 1837, the Lord's Day after the Completion of Forty Years from his Settlement in the Ministry, in Brookline, By John Pierce, D.D. ... Printed, but not published ... . *Boston: Minot Pratt, Printer.* 1837. 8vo, pp. 35. A., B. 62730

PIERCE. Requisites to our Country's Glory. A Discourse before His Excellency ... and the Legislature of Massachusetts, at the Annual Election, ... 3 Jan. 1849. By John Pierce, D.D. ... *Boston: Dutton and Wentworth, State Printers.* 1849. 8vo, pp. 62. B. 62731

Contains a bibliography of Massachusetts election sermons.

PIERCE. A Sermon preached at the Installation of the Rev. John Snelling Popkin, ... Newbury, September 19, 1804. By the Rev. John Pierce ... . *Newburyport: Angier March.* 1804. 8vo, pp. 32. B., N. 62732

PIERCE. A Valedictory Sermon, on leaving the Old Meeting House in Brookline, 8 June, 1806; and a Dedicatory Sermon on Entering the New House of Worship, 11 June, 1806. By John Pierce ... . *Cambridge: William Hilliard, Printer.* 1806. 8vo, pp. 33. W. 62733

Also: An Address at the Funeral of the Hon. Thomas A. Davis, Mayor of Boston, delivered ... November 25, 1845 ... . *Boston:* 1845. *J. H. Eastburn, City Printer.* 8vo, pp. 24.—A Discourse ... at Princeton [Mass.], June 18, 1817, at the Ordination of the Rev. Samuel Clark. ... *Worcester: Printed by William Manning, August,* 1817. 8vo, pp. 36. W.—Ministerial Fidelity. A Discourse ... at Canton, Jan. 30, 1822, at the ordination of Rev. Benjamin Huntoon. ... *Boston.* 1822. 8vo, pp. 28. —On the Mystery of Godliness. A Discourse ... at Medfield, October, 1797. ... *Dedham.* 1798. 8vo, pp. 22.—The Right of Private Judgment in Religion ... . Dudleian Lecture, ... Cambridge, Oct. 24, 1821. ... *Cambridge.* 1821. 8vo, pp. 24. —Sermon ... at the Gathering of the Second Congregational Church, in Dorchester, January 1, 1808. ... *Boston: Printed by Belcher and Armstrong.* 1808. 8vo, pp. 38. M.

PIERCE (J.) An Address ... on the 26th ... May, 1836, the Centennial Anniversary of the Settlement of Gorham. By Josiah Pierce. *Portland: Printed by Charles Day & Co.* 1836. 8vo, pp. 36. C. 62734

PIERCE. A History of the Town of Gorham, Maine. Prepared at the Request of the Town. By Josiah Pierce. *Portland: Foster & Cushing.* 1862. 8vo, pp. 239, (1). B. 62735

PIERCE (L. B.) History of the Second Iowa Cavalry. Containing a detailed account of its Organization, Marches and the Battles in which it has participated; also, a complete Roster of each Company. By Sergeant Lyman B. Pierce. ... *Burlington.* 1865. 8vo, pp. 237. 62736

PIERCE (M. B.) Address on the Present Condition and Prospects of the Aboriginal Inhabitants of North America, with particular reference to the Seneca Nation. By M. B. Pierce, A Chief of the Seneca Nation, and a Member of Dartmouth College. [*Buffalo:*] *Steele's Press.* 1838. 8vo, pp. 16. N. + *Philadelphia.* 1839. 12mo, pp. 24. 62737

PIERCE (N. P.) Mental Freedom our Nation's Glory. Thanksgiving Sermon, delivered in ... Brooklyn, November 24, 1853. By Rev. N. P. Pierce ... . *New York: Printed by John A. Gray.* 1853. 8vo, pp. 28. 62738

PIERCE (S. W.) Battle Fields and Camp Fires of the Thirty-Eighth. An Authentic Narrative and Record of the Organization of the Thirty-Eighth Regiment of Wis. Vol. Inf'y, and the part taken by it in the late war, a short biographical sketch of each commissioned officer, and the name, [etc.] ... of every enlisted man, with notes of incidents relating to them, By Lieut. S. W. Pierce. *Milwaukee: Daily Wisconsin Printing House.* 1866. 12mo, pp. 254, (1). 62739

[PIERCE (Thomas).] The Muse of Hesperia. A Poetic Reverie. *Cincinnati: The Philomathic Society.* 1823. 8vo, pp. 52

Relates to the war of 1812. *See also* our No. 59554, Vol. XIV., and for "Peirce" read "Pierce."

PIERCE (W.) A Discourse delivered to the Congregational Society in Foxborough, Ms. Decemb. 3rd, 1835. By Willard Pierce ... *Dedham.* 1836. 8vo, pp. 19. 62741

PIERCE. A Discourse ... at the Dedication of the ... Union Church, ... East Bridgewater, Mass., January 1, 1845. By Willard Pierce. ... *Boston: Press of T. R. Marvin.* 1845. 8vo, pp. 20. W. 62742

Also: A Sermon, preached at Seekonk, Mass. March 12th, 1825, occasioned by the death of Dr. Alva Carpenter, son of Deacon Elihu Carpenter, of Seekonk ... . *Providence: Barnum, Field & Co., Printers.* 1825. 8vo, pp. 14.

PIERCE (W.) An Almanack for the Year of our Lord 1639. Calculated for New England. By Mr. Wm. Pierce, Mariner. *Cambridge: Printed by Stephen Day.* 1639. 16mo. 62743

Improved title of our No. 59555, Vol. XIV. The first almanac and one of the first productions of the press in the British American colonies, being preceded only by the "Freeman's Oath." No copy is known to be extant. *See* Winthrop's "Journal," I. 289; Thomas's "History of Printing," 2d ed., I. 38–43; and note to our No. 25791, Vol. VII. The date to No. 25791 should read 1639.

The following list comprises some of the early New England almanacs:

MDCXLVI. An Almanack for ... 1646. *See* Vol. XI., No. 47209.

MDCXLVII. An Almanack for ... 1647. *See* Danforth (S.), Vol. V., No. 18473.

MDCXLVIII. | An | Almanack | for the Year of our | Lord | 1648 | Calculated for the Longitude of 315 | degr. and Elevation of the Pole Ar-|ctick 42 degr. & 30 min. & may ge-|nerally serve for the most part of | New-England. | By Samuel Danforth of Harvard Colledge | Philomathemat. | *Printed at Cambridge* [*by Matthew Day*]. | 1648 | 16mo, pp. (16). Title within a border composed of figures of lunar phases.

MDCXLIX. | An | Almanack | for the Year of | our Lord | 1649 | Calculated for ... | ... | New-England. | By Samuel Danforth of Harvard Colledge | Philomathemat: | *Printed at Cambridge* [*by Samuel Green*]. | 1649. | 16mo, pp. (16). L.

Probably the first work printed by Samuel Green.

MDCL. | An | Almanack | for the Year of | our Lord | 1650 | Being the third after Leap year | and from the Creation 5582. | Calculated for ... | ... | New-England. | Parvum parva decent: sed inest sua | gratia parvis. | *Printed at Cambridge* [*by Samuel Green*]. | 1650. | 16mo, pp. (16).

By Urian Oakes. "A Lad of small, as he never was of great Stature, he published a little parcel of *Astronomical Calculations* with the apposite Verse in the Title Page, *Parvum parva decent, sed inest sua Gratia parvis.*"—MATHER'S MAGNALIA, book IV., chap. V.

MDCLVI | An | Almanack | for the year of | Our Lord | 1656. | Being first after Leap year, and | from the Creation 5588. | Whose Vulgar Notes are | ... | Calculated for the Longitude of 315 | gr: and 42 gr and 30 min of N. Lat: | and may Generally serve for | the

most part of | New England. | By T. S. Philomathemat: | *Cambridg* | *Printed by Samuel Green* 1656. | 16mo, pp. (16). W.

An | Almanack | for the year of | our Lord | 1657. | Being Second after Leap-year. | The Vulgar Notes whereof are, | ... | By S. B. Philomathemat. | *Cambridg.* | *Printed by Samuel Green* 1657. | 16mo, pp. (16). W.

An Almanack of the Coelestial Motions for this present Year of the Christian Æra 1659, By Zech: Brigden Astrophil: *Cambridg, Printed by Samuel Green,* 1659. 16mo.

An Almanack for the Year of our Lord 1660. By S.[amuel] C.[heever] Philomathemat: *Cambridg, Printed by Samuel Green,* 1660. 16mo. C.

An Almanack for the Year of our Lord 1661. By S.[amuel] C.[heever]. *Cambridg, Printed by S. G. and M. I.,* 1661. 16mo. C.

An Almanack for the year of our Lord, 1662. By Nathaniel Chauncy. *Cambridg, Printed by Samuel Green.* 1662. 16mo. C.

MDCLXIII | An | Almanack | of the Cœlestial Motions for the Year of the | Christian Æra | 1663. | Being (in our Account) Bissextile, or Leap-year, | and from the Creation 5612. | ... | By Israel Chauncy φιλομαθής. | ... | *Cambridge:* | *Printed by S. Green and M. Johnson.* 1663. | 16mo, pp. (16). W.

MDCLXIV. | An | Almanack | of The Cœlestial Motions for the Year of the | Christian Æra | 1664. | Being in our Account first from Leap-year, | and from the Creation 5613. | Whose Vulgar Notes are | ... | Fitted to New-England Longitude | ... | By Israel Chauncy. | ... | *Cambridge:* | *Printed by S. Green and M. Johnson* 1664. | 16mo, pp. (16). W.

An Almanack ... for ... 1665. *See* Nowell (A.), Vol. XIII., No. 56207.

1666. | An | Almanack | or | Astronomical Calculations | Of the most remarkable Celestial Revo|lutions, &c. visible in our Horizon. | Together with the Scripture and Jewish | Names (wherein though we agree not with | their Terms, yet we follow their Order) | for the ensuing Year 1666 | ... | By Josiah Flint φιλομαθής. | ... | *Cambridge:* | *Printed Anno Dom.* 1666. | 16mo, pp. (14). W.

1667. | An | Almanack | For | the Year of our Lord | 1667. | ... | By Samuel Brakenbury Philomath. | *Cambridge* | *Printed by Samuel Green* 1667. | 16mo, pp. (16). W.

MDCLXVIII | An | Almanack | of the Cœlestial Motions for the Year of | the Christian Epocha. | 1668. | ... | By Joseph Dudley Astrophil. | ... | *Cambridge:* | *Printed by Samuel Green* | 1668. | 16mo, pp. (16). W.

1669. | An | Almanack | of | Cœlestiall Motions | For the year of the Christian Æra, | 1669. | Being (in our Account) second after Leap-|year, and from the Creation | 5618. ... | ... | By J. B. Philomathemat. | ... | *Cambridge:* | *Printed by S. G. and M. J.* 1669. | 16mo, pp. (16). W.

Probably by Joseph Browne. Contains a chronological table of memorable occurrences happening in New England.

1670. | An | Almanack | of | Cœlestiall Motions | For the Year of the Christian Æra, | 1670. | ... | By J. R. φιλομαθής. | *Cambridge:* | *Printed by S. G. and M. J.* 1670. | 16mo, pp. (16). W.

1671. An Almanack of Cœlestial Motions for the Year of the Christian Æra, 1671. Being (in our Account) Leap-year, and from the Creation 5620. The vulgar Notes whereof are ... ... Calculated for the Longitude of 315 gr. and 42 gr. 30 m. North Latitude. By D.[aniel] R.[ussell] Philomathemat. *Cambridge: Printed by S. G. and M. J.* 1671. 16mo.

An | Ephemeris | of the | Cœlestial Motions for the year of the | Christian Epocha | 1672. | Whereto are numbered from | The Creation of the World.. 5621 | General Deluge. 3965 | Constitution of the *Julian* Year. 1716 | Passion and Death of Christ. 1639 | Correction of the Calendar by | Pope Gregory. 90 | Planting of the *Massachusetts* Colony. 44 | Bissex-

tile or Leap year. 01 | The Vulgar Notes are | ... | ... | Calculated for the Longitude ... | ... | and may generally serve for | the most part of *New England.* | By Jeremiah Shepard. | φιλομαθής | *Cambridge:* | *Printed by Samuel Green* 1672. | 16mo, pp. (16). W.

1673 | An | Almanack | of | Cœlestial Motions for the Year of the | Christian Æra. | 1673. | Being second after Leap year, and from | the Creation, | 5622. | The Vulgar Notes are | ... | By N.[ehemiah] H.[obart] | *Cambridge:* | *Printed by Samuel Green.* | 1673. | 16mo, pp. (16). W.

Contains the New England chronology, 1668–72.

1674. | An | Almanack. | Of Cœlestial Motions viz. of the Sun and | Planets, with some of their Principal | Aspects, for the Year of the | Christian Æra | 1674 | Being (in our Account) third after Leap | Year, and from the Creation 5623. | The Vulgar Notes whereof are. | ... | Compiled by J. S.[herman] | *Cambridge:* | *Printed by Samuel Green.* 1674. | 16mo, pp. (16). M.

1675. | An | Almanack | of | Cœlestial Motions for the Year of the | Christian Æra | 1675. | Being (in our Account) Leap-Year, | and from the Creation 5624. | ... | By J.[ohn] Foster. | ... | *Cambridge.* | *Printed by Samuel Green.* 1675. | 16mo, pp. (16). W.

Also for 1676, *Boston: Printed by John Foster.* 1676. 16mo.

1676. | An | Almanack | of | Cœlestial Motions of the Sun and Planets, | with some of their Principal Aspects. | For the Year of the Christian Æra | 1676. | Being in our Account the first after Bis|sextile or Leap-year and from the | Creation, 5625. | ... | By J. S.[herman] | ... | *Cambridge Printed by S. Green.* 1676. | 16mo, pp. (16). W.

Also for 1677, *Cambridge: Printed by S. Green.* 1677. 16mo, pp. (16). W.

Sic in se sua per vestigia volvitur annus. Virg. | 1678. | An | Almanack | of | Cœlestial Motions of the Sun and Planets, | with their principal Aspects, | For the Year of the Christian Æra | 1678. | Being in our Account the third after | Leap-year, and from the Creation, | 5627. | ... | By T.[homas] B.[rattle] | ... | *Cambr. Printed by S. Green & S. Green:* | 1678. | 16mo.

1678. | An | Almanack | of | Cœlestial Motions for the year of the | Christian Epocha | 1678. | Being (in our account) third after Leap-year, and from the Creation | 5627. | ... | [By] J. F.[oster] | *Printed by J. Foster, for John Usher of* | *Boston.* 1678. | 16mo, pp. (32). W.

Also for 1679, *Boston: Printed by John Foster, Sold by Henry Phillips in the west end of the Exchange.* 1679. 16mo.

An | Almanack | or | Register of | Cœlestial Configurations &c. | For the Year of our Lord God | 1679. | And of the World | 5628. | Being (in our account) Leap year, And | from the beginning of the Reign of our | Soveraign Lord Charles II. by the | Grace of God, King of great Brittain, France | and Ireland &c: the 31st year. | ... | By J.[ohn] D.[anforth] Philomath. | *Cambridge printed by Samuel Green* 1679. | 16mo, pp. (16). M., W.

Contains the New England chronology, 1673–78.

MDCLXXX. | An | Almanack | of | Cœlestial Motions for the Year of the | Christian Æpocha, | 1680. | Being in our Account first after Leap-year: | And from the Creation, | 5629. | [By John Foster.] | ... | *Printed for, and sold by Henry Phillips in the* | *west end of the Exchange in Boston* 1680. | 16mo, pp. (16). W. + [Another edition.] *Printed for John Usher of Boston.* 1680. 16mo, pp. (16). M.

MDCLXXXI. | An | Almanack | of | Cœlestial Motions for the year of the | Christian Epocha, | 1681. | Being in our Account second after Leap-year: | And from the Creation, | 5630. | ... | By John Foster, Astrophil. | *Boston;* | *Printed by J. F.* 1681. | 16mo, pp. (18). M., W. + [Another edition.] *Boston: Printed by J. F. for Samuel Phillips in the west end of the Exchange.* 1681. 16mo, pp. (18). M.

Unius labor multorum laborem allevat. | An | Ephemeris | of | Cœlestial Motions, Aspects, | Eclipses &c. For the Year of the | Christian Æra 1682. | ... | By W. Brattle Philomath. | *Cambridge* | *Printed by Samuel Green* 1682. | 16mo, pp. (24). M., W.

M.DC.LXXXIII. The Boston Ephemeris. *See* [Mather (Cotton)], XI. 46239.

MDCLXXXIIII. | Cambridge Ephemeris. | An | Almanack | of | Coelestial Motions, Configurations &c. | for the Year of the Christian Æra, | 1684. | ... | Calculated for the Meridian of Cambridg in N. England, | ... | By N. Russel Astrotyr. | ... | *Cambridge:* | *Printed by Samuel Green* 1684. | 16mo, pp. (16). M.

1684, | The Boston Ephemeris. An | Almanack | for | the Year MDCLXXXIV. | and of the Worlds Creation 5633. | Oppidi Inchoati, 55. | Being the first after Leap-year. | Of which the Vulgar Notes are. | ... | Calculated for the Meridian of Boston in New-Engl. | where the North Pole is elevated 42 gr. 30 m. | ... | By Benjamin Gillam Philonauticus. | *Boston in New England,* | *Printed by Samuel Green for Samuel* | *Philips, and are to be sold at his Shop at* | *the West End of the Town-House.* 1684. | 16mo, pp. (16). M.

MDCLXXXV. | Cambridge Ephemeris | An | Almanack | of | The Cœlestial Motions, For the Year | Of the Christian Æra, | 1685. | ... | By W. Williams Philopatr. | *Cambridge,* | *Printed by Samuel Green for the year* | 1685. | 16mo, pp. (16). M., W. + [Another edition.] *Cambridge, Printed by Samuel Green for Samuel Phillips.* 1685. 16mo.

1685. | The Boston Ephemeris. | An | Almanack | of Coelestial Motions of the Sun & | Planets, with some of the principal Aspects | for the Year of the Christian Æra | MDCLXXXV. | Being in our Account the second after | Leap-year, and from the Creation | 5634. | The Vulgar Notes of which are. | ... | Fitted to the Meridian of Boston in New-England, | where the Artick Pole is elevated 42 gr. 21 m. | *Boston in New-England* | *Printed by and for Samuel Green.* 1685. | 16mo, pp. (16). M.

By Nathanael Mather. *See* our Vol. XI., No. 46774 for a note.

The New-England | Almanack | For | The year of our Lord. 1686. | And of the world. 5635. | Since the planting of Massachusets | Colony in New-England. 58. | Since the found. of Harv. Coll. 44. | ... | By S.[amuel] D.[anforth] Philomath. | *Cambridge.* | *Printed by Samuel Green. sen. Printer to Harvard* | *Colledge in New-England. A. D.* 1685. | 16mo, pp. (16). M., W. + [Another edition. *Ibid.*] 1686. 16mo, pp. (16). M.

Corrected title of our No. 52646, Vol. XIII., which see for a note.

1686. | The Boston Ephemeris. | An | Almanack | Of Cœlestial Motions of the Sun & | Planets, with some of the principal Aspects | for the Year of the Christian Æra | MDCLXXXVI. | Being in our Account the third after | Leap-year, and from the Creation | 5635. | The Vulgar Notes of which are. | ... | Calculated for and fitted to the Meridian of Boston in | New-England, where the North Pole is elevated 42 | gr. 21 m. | By Nathanael Mather. | *New-England,* | *Boston, Printed and Sold by Samuel Green,* 1686. | 16mo, pp. (16). M.

MDCLXXXVII. | Cambridge Ephemeris. | An | Almanack | of | Coelestiall Motions and Configurations | for the Year of the Christian Epocha, | 1687. | Being (in our account) Leap Year; | ... | *Cambridge.* | *Printed by S. G. Colledg Printer* 1687. | 16mo, pp. (16). M.

Tulley 1687. | An | Almanack | For the Year of Our Lord, | MDCLXXXVII. | Being the third after Leap-year, | and from the Creation | 5636. | ... | Unto which is annexed a Weather-Glass, whereby the | Change of the Weather may be foreseen. | ... | By John Tulley. | *Boston, Printed by S. Green for Benjamin* | *Harris; and are to be Sold at his* | *Shop, by the Town Pump near the Change* | 1687. | 16mo, pp. (16). M., W.

Continued annually to 1702. In 1691 the imprint reads, *Cambridge: Printed by Samuel Green and B. Green, and are to be sold by Nicholas Buttolph at Gutteridge's Coffee House, in Boston;* in 1692, *Cambridge: Printed by Samuel Green and Bartholomew Green for Samuel Phillips of Boston;* in 1693, *Boston: Printed by Benjamin Harris;* in 1694, *Boston: Printed by B. Green for Samuel Phillips;* in 1695, *Boston: Printed for John Usher;* in 1696, *Boston, N. E. Printed by Bartholomew Green, and John Allen, for John Usher.* The last one of the series is entitled: Tulley's Farewel 1702. An Almanack ... 1702 ... By John Tulley; who dyed as he was finishing this Almanack; and so leaves it as his last Legacy to his Country-men. *Boston: Printed by Bartholomew Green and John Allen* ... . 1702.

Non cessant anni, quamvis cessant homines. | Harvard's Ephemeris, | or | Almanack. | Containing an Account of the Coelestial | Motions, Aspects &c. For the Year | of the Christian Empire. 1690. | ... | Respecting the Meridian of Cambridge in N. E. | ... | By H. Newman. | *Cambridge.* | *Printed by Samuel Green.* 1690. | 16mo, pp. (16). M.

Vt Fluctus fluctum, sic annus annum trudit. | News from the Stars. | An | Almanack | Containing an Account of the Cœlestial Mo|tions, Aspects, &c. For the Year of | the Christian Empire, 1691. | ... | Respecting the Meridian of Boston, in New-| England ... | By Henry Newman, Philomath. | *Printed by R. Pierce for Benjamin Harris at* | *the London Coffee-House in Boston,* 1691. | 16mo, pp. (25). M.

Boston | Almanack | for the | Year of our Lord God 1692. | Being Bissextile or Leap-Year. | ... | Calculated for the Meridian of Boston in | New-England, where the North Pole | is elevated 42 gr. 30 min. | By H B | *Boston, Printed by Benjamin Harris, and* | *John Allen: And are to be Sold at the* | *London-Coffee-House.* 1692. | 16mo, pp. (20). M.

Monthly Observations | and | Predictions, | for the Present Year, 1692. | With | Astrological Judgments | on the Whole Year. | All Taken from Mr. Patridge's | Almanack: | To which is Added, an Account of a | Plot | Which was lately Discovered in England: And | Which was Foretold by the said John | Patridge, in his this Years Almanack. | Published for General Satisfaction. | *Printed at Boston: And are to be Sold by* | *Benj. Harris, at the London-Coffee-House.* | 1692. | 16mo, pp. 16. M.

1694. | An | Almanack | of the Cœlestiall Motions, Aspects | and Eclipses, &c. For the year of | our Lord God, MDCXCIV. | And of the World, | 5643. | ... | By Philo-Mathemat. | *Boston, Printed by B. Green, for Samuel* | *Phillips, near the South-East end of the Ex*|*change, by the Rose and Crown Tavern.* | 1694. | 16mo, pp. (16). M., W.

An Almanack ... for ... 1695 ... By C. Lodowick, Physician. *Boston.* 1695. 16mo.

MDCCXII. | An | Almanack | of the | Cœlestial Motions, Aspects & Eclipses, | for the Year of the Christian Æra, | 1712. | ... | Fitted to the Meridian of the Island of Barbadoes. | ... | By Edward Holyoke, M.A. | Of Harvard College at Cambridge in New England. | *Boston in N. E. Printed by B. Green,* | *for Benjamin Marston Merchant in Salem; for* | *the use of the Island of Barbadoes* 1712. | 16mo, pp. (16). W.

The Young American Ephemeris For the Year 1715 ... By Increase Gatchell, Etat. 16, Apprentice to George Brownell School-Master, who Teacheth Writing, Cyphering, Navigation &c. Also Musick, Dancing &c. *Boston: Printed for George Brownell.* 1715. 16mo.

Also: Almanacs—By Samuel Clough, *Boston,* 1700–08 (*see* Vol. XIII., No. 52647); By a Lover of Astronomy, *Boston: B. Green and J. Allen,* 1703–06 (XIII. 52695); By N. W[hittemore], 1705–07, 1714–29; By Daniel Travis, [n. p.] 1707–23; By Edward Holyoke, *Boston,* 1708–15 (VIII. 32668); By Thomas Robie, *Boston,* 1710–17; By a Lover of the Mathematicks, *America, Printed in the Year* 1713; By Thomas Paine, *Boston,* 1718–19 (VI. 24687 *and* XIV. 58202); By a Native of New England [Nathan Bowen], *Boston,* 1721–37 (XIII. 52670); By Robert Treat, *New London,* 1723–27; By John Hughes, [n. p.] 1726 (VIII. 33587); By Nathaniel Ames, *Boston, Hartford and New London,* 1726–75 (I. 1309); By Poor Robin, *Newport,* 1728–35; By Samuel Maxwell, *Newport,* 1731 (XI. 47053, *note*); By N. Whittemore revived, *Boston,* 1738–40; By Joseph Stafford, *Boston,* 1740–44; By William Nadir [Dr. Douglass], *Boston,* 1743–47 (XII. 51709); By Poor Job, *Newport,* 1750–55; By Roger Sherman, *Boston, New London and New Haven,* 1750–61; By George Wheten, *Boston,* 1753; By James Davis, *New London,* 1755, '58; Almanac for 1757, *Portsmouth, N. H.* 1757; Astronomical Diary, *Portsmouth, N. H.,* 1758; By Poor Joseph, *Boston,* 1759–60; By John Eddy, *Boston,* 1760–61 (VI. 21809); By a Student of Yale College, *New Haven,* 1761–2; By Nathaniel Low, *Boston,* 1762–65, 1767-1827 (X. 42402); By Benjamin West, *Providence, Newport, and Boston,* 1763–80 (XIII. 52648); By Clark Elliott, *New London,* 1767–70; By Philopatria, *Portsmouth, N. H.* 1767; By Mein and

Fleeming, *Boston*, 1767–71 (XI. 47407); Bickerstaff's Boston Almanack, *Boston*, 1768–1854 (II. 5220); By Samuel Stearns, *Boston*, 1769–76 or later (VI. 21833, *and* XIII. 55536, 55539, 55567); Essex Almanack, *Salem*, 1769–73 (VI. 23006, XV. 62540); By Abraham Weatherwise, *Providence*, 1769–1807 or later (XIII. 52752); By John Anderson, *Newport*, 1772–75 (XIII. 55029); Fleeming's Register, *Boston*, 1772–73 (VI. 24685); By Daboll, *New London*, 1773–1873; By Edmund Freebetter, *New London*, 1773–87 (XIII. 52649); Boston Sheet, *Boston*, 1774; By J. Warren, *Woburn*, 1775; By Watson, *Hartford*, 1775; By Isaiah Thomas, *Boston*, 1775, '79–1822. *See also* Vols. VI., No. 24688, XIII. 52650, 55540–43.

PIERCE (W. B.) My Ancestors in America. Compiled, printed and published for gratuitous distribution among near relatives. By Wm. Blake Pierce. *Chicago*. 1864. 8vo, pp. 48.

PIERCE. Tobacco and Internal Revenue. Letter to the Secretary of the Treasury. By W. B. Pierce. *Utica, N. Y.* 1864. 8vo. 62745

[PIERCE (William Leigh).] An Account of the Great Earthquakes, in the Western States, particularly on the Mississippi River: December 16–23, 1811. ... *Newburyport: Printed and sold at the Herald office, and at the Bookstore of Thomas & Whipple.* 1812. 8vo, pp. 16. 62746

PIERCE. The Year: a Poem, in Three Cantoes. By William Leigh Pierce, Esq. ... *New-York: David Longworth.* 1813. 18mo, pp. 191, Appendix, 75, (2). 62747

A poetical review of the principal political occurrences of the year 1812; now scarce. Corrected title of our No. 59556, Vol. XIV. Also: Oration at Savannah, Ga., July 4, 1812. ... *Savannah.* 1812. 8vo.

PIERCE COUNTY, *Wis.* First Annual Review of Pierce County, Wis., Jan. 1st, 1856. *Prescott: Young & Gibbs.* [1856.] 12mo, pp. 46. 62748

General and Statistical Description of Pierce County, Wisconsin. [n. p. 1854.] 8vo, pp. 8. S. 62749

PIÈROLA (F. A. de). Añales de la Iglesia de Puno. ... Tomo I. *Puno.* 1865. 8vo. Portrait. 62750

PIEROLA (N. F. de). Calendario y guia de forasteros de Lima. Por D. Nicolas Fern. de Pierola. *Lima, Impr. de Santa Rosa.* 1827. 12mo, pp. 170. + *Lima, Impr. ... por Juan Ross.* 1828. 12mo, pp. 118, ii. 62751

See also Vol. X., No. 41081.

PIEROTS (R.) Americanische Freybeuter oder Leben Robert Pierots ... . *Copenhagen.* 1772. 4 vols., 12mo. Plate. 62752

PIERPOINT (F. H.) Gov. Pierpoint's Address to the People of Virginia, May 19, 1865. [*Washington.* 1865.] 8vo, pp. 16.

PIERPOINT. Letter of Governor Peirpoint [*sic*], to ... The President ... of the United States ... on the ... Abuse of Military Power in the Command of General Butler in Virginia and North Carolina. *Washington, D. C.: McGill & Witherow, Printers.* 1864. 8vo, pp. 60. 62754

PIERPOINT. Reorganization of Civil Government. Speech of Governor Pierpoint ... in Norfolk, February 16, 1865. [n. p. 1865.] 8vo, pp. 7. 62755

PIERPOINT. To the People of Virginia. [n. p. n. d.] 8vo, pp. 7. 62756

See also Virginia.

PIERPONT. Sundry | False Hopes | of | Heaven, | Discovered | and | Decryed. | In a Sermon Preached at | the North-Assembly in | Boston, 3. d. 4. m. 1711. | By James Pierpont, M.A. | Pastor of New-Haven Church. | With a Preface by the Rd. Dr. [Cotton] Mather. | *Boston, N. E. ... T. Green* ... 1712. 12mo, pp. (2), xxiv, 46. 62757

See also Vol. IV., No. 15447.

PIERPONT (J.) Airs of Palestine; a Poem: By John Pierpont. ... *Baltimore: The Author.* 1816. 8vo, pp. xxiii, 56, engraved title. + Second Edition. *Boston: Wells and Lilly.* 1817. 12mo, pp. 58, engraved title. + Third Edition Revised. [*Ibid.*] 1817. 18mo, pp. vii, 13–66, engraved title. 62758

PIERPONT. Airs of Palestine, and other Poems. By John Pierpont. *Boston: James Munroe and Company.* MDCCCXL. 16mo, pp. xiii, 334. 62759

PIERPONT. The Anti-Slavery Poems of John Pierpont. ... *Boston: Oliver Johnson.* 1843. 16mo, pp. 64. H. 62760

PIERPONT. Cold Water Melodies, and Washingtonian Songster. By John Pierpont. *Boston.* 1842. 18mo. 62761

PIERPONT. A Discourse delivered in Hollis Street Church, Boston, September 2, 1827: occasioned by the Death of Horace Holley, LL.D. late President of Transylvania University. By John Pierpont ... *Boston: ... Stephen Foster, Printer.* 1827. 8vo, pp. 31. B. 62762

PIERPONT. A Discourse on the Covenant with Judas, ... in Hollis-Street Church, Nov. 6, 1842. By John Pierpont. *Boston: Charles C. Little and James Brown.* 1842. 8vo, pp. 39. B.

Relates to the fugitive slave law.

PIERPONT. A Discourse occasioned by the death of William Ellery Channing. Preached ... Oct. 16, 1842. By John Pierpont. *Boston: Printed by Oliver Johnson.* 1842. 12mo, pp. 23.

PIERPONT. The Garden of Graves. By John Pierpont. ... *Dedham: H. Mann, Printer.* 1841. 8vo, pp. 15. H. 62765

Relates to Mount Auburn.

PIERPONT. "Knowledge is Power," or the True Secret of New England's Strength. A Sermon, preached in ... Boston, on Fast Day, April 5, 1827. By John Pierpont. ... *Boston: Hilliard, Gray, Little and Wilkins.* 1827. 8vo, pp. 16. 62766

[PIERPONT.] A Letter from the Pastor of Hollis Street Society, to his Parochial Friends, with their Reply [by Edmund Jackson]. ... October and November, 1841. *Boston: Printed by Samuel N. Dickinson.* 1841. 8vo, pp. 23. B. 62767

PIERPONT. Mr. Pierpont's Remonstrance against the Action of the Ex-parte Council, with his offer of a mutual council; ... Feb. 15–17th, 1841. *Boston: Printed by S. N. Dickinson.* 1841. 8vo, pp. 23. H. 62768

PIERPONT. The Pilgrims of Plymouth: a Poem delivered before the New-England Society, ... New York, ... December 22, 1855. By John Pierpont. *Boston: Crosby, Nichols, and Company.* 1856. 8vo, pp. 30. B. 62769

PIERPONT. Poem, delivered at Litchfield, Conn., on the occasion of the Centennial Celebration, 1851. By John Pierpont. *Hartford.* 1851. 8vo, pp. 32. 62770

PIERPONT. The Portrait. A Poem delivered before the Washington Benevolent Society, of Newburyport, ... October 27, 1812. By John Pierpont, Esq. *Boston: Bradford and Read.* 1812. 8vo, pp. 36. B. 62771

PIERPONT. "Who goeth a Warfare at his own Charges?" A Discourse ... before the Ancient and Honorable Artillery Company of Massachusetts, on the celebration of their 190th Anniversary, Boston, June 2, 1828. By John Pierpont. ... *Boston: Bowles and Dearborn.* 1828. 12mo, pp. 24. B., C. 62772

Also: The "Address to the People," delivered at the Installation of Rev. Henry A. Miles as Pastor of the South Congregational Society in Lowell, ... Dec. 14, 1836. *Lowell.* 1837. 8vo, pp. 8. + Second Edition. *Boston: Printed by White and Potter.* 1849. 8vo, pp. 8. B.—Angelic Ministrations. A Sermon preached ... in Boston, ... April 16, 1837, the spire of the church having been struck by lightning, ... 8th of the month. ... *Boston: Weeks, Jordan & Company.* 1837. 8vo, pp. 17.—As you sow, so must you reap. A Sermon preached at the Ordination of the Rev. Samuel Presbury, over the Second Congregational Society in Northfield, Mass. February 27, 1828. ... Second Edition. *Boston: Bowles & Dearborn.* 1828. 12mo, pp. 24.—The Burning of the Ephesian Letters. A Sermon ... in Hollis Street Church, ... 8th Dec. 1833. ... *Boston: Printed by Ford and Damrell.* 1834. 8vo, pp. 16.—Moral Resurrection. A Sermon, ... at the Ordination of the Rev. Oliver C. Everett, as Pastor of the First Congregational Church in Northfield, ... March 3, 1837. ... *Boston: James Munroe and Co.* 1837. 8vo, pp. 31.—Moral Rule of Political Action. A Discourse, ... in Hollis Street Church, ... January 27, 1839. ... *Boston: James Munroe & Co.* 1839. 12mo, pp. 24.—National Humiliation: A Sermon ... in Hollis Street Church, Fast Day ... April 2, 1840 ... . *Boston: Printed by Samuel N. Dickinson.* 1840. Small 4to, pp. 16.—The Reformer and the Conservative. A Discourse ... in Hollis St. Church, ... 24th November, 1839. ... *Boston: Printed by S. N. Dickinson.* 1840, 8vo, pp. 15.—"The Things that make for Peace." A Sermon ... 3d December, 1837. ... *Boston: Printed by Isaac Knapp.* 1837. 8vo, pp. 15. B.

Also several educational works. The following relate to the Rev. John Pierpont:

Hollis Street Church. Adjourned Meeting, Monday evening, Oct. 14, 1839. [*Boston.* 1839.] 8vo, pp. 4. 62773

Letter of the Boston Association of Congregational Ministers, to Rev. John Pierpont, with his reply. *Boston: Benjamin H. Greene.* 1846. 8vo, pp. 16. B. 62774

Proceedings in the Controversy between a part of the Proprietors and the Pastor of Hollis St. Church, Boston, 1838 and 1839. *Boston.* [1840.] 8vo, pp. 60. 62775

Proceedings of a Meeting of Friends of Rev. John Pierpont, and his Reply to the Charges of the Committee, of Hollis Street Society. October 26th, 1839. *Boston: Printed by S. N. Dickinson.* [1839.] 8vo, pp. 48. B. 62776

Reply of the Friends of Rev. John Pierpont to a Proposal for dissolving the Pastoral Connexion between him, and the Society in Hollis Street. [Jan. 15, 1840. *Boston.* 1840.] 8vo, pp. 8.

Report of the Committee of the Proprietors of the Meeting-House in Hollis St., upon the "Result" of the late Mutual Ecclesiastical Council. [*Boston.* 1839.] 8vo, pp. 24. 62778

Special Meeting of the Proprietors of Hollis Street Meeting House, March 9th, 1840. [*Boston: W. W. Clapp & Son's Press.* 1840.] 8vo, pp. 15. B. 62779

See also our Vol. II., Nos. 6651–3, *and* Washburn (Emory).

PIERPONT (J.), *Jr.* The Christian's Hope. A Sermon ... at the Funeral of Loyal Scranton, ... Savannah, Georgia, ... January 15th, 1854. ... By Rev. John Pierpont, Jr. *Savannah: Printed by John M. Cooper & Co.* 1854. 8vo, pp. 8. H. 62780

PIERPONT. Essex County Washingtonian Extra. Glory and Shame of America. A Sermon ... in Lynn, on Thanksgiving Day, November 30, 1843. By Rev. John Pierpont, Jr. [n. p.: *J. B. Tolman, Printer.* n. d.] 8vo, pp. 8. B. 62781

PIERRE (L. de S.) The Art of Planting and Cultivating the Vine, also of making and preserving Wines, &c. Compiled for American use, and particularly for the Colony of New Bourdeaux. By Louis de S. Pierre of New Bourdeaux, South Carolina. *London.* 1772. 8vo. 62782

PIERREPONT (E.) Argument of Hon. Edwards Pierrepont to the Jury, on the trial of John H. Surratt for the Murder of President Lincoln. *Washington: Government Printing Office.* 1867. 8vo, pp. 122. 62783

PIERREPONT. A Review By Judge Pierrepont of Gen. Butler's Defense, before the House of Representatives, in Relation to the New Orleans Gold. *New York: Wm. C. Bryant & Co., Printers.* 1865. 8vo, pp. 27. 62784

PIERREPONT. Speech of Hon. Edwards Pierrepont, delivered at the Convention and Mass Meeting of the Democracy opposed to the Chicago Platform, ... New York, November 1, 1864. [*New York.* 1864.] 8vo, pp. 11. + *New York: D. Van Nostrand.* 1864. 8vo, pp. 11. 62785

Also: Charge ... to the Jury, in case of Ship Achorn. *New York.* 1859. 8vo.—Speech ... at the Republican Ratification Meeting, at Cooper Institute, November 3, 1870. *New York.* 1870. 8vo.—Speech ... at the Meeting of War Democrats, at Cooper Institute, October 21, 1868. *New York.* 1868. 8vo.—Speech ... before The Republican Mass Meeting, at Wilgus Hall, Ithica [*sic*], N. Y., October 11th, 1872. *New York.* 1872 8vo, pp. 17..

PIERRIE (T. H. G.) Notes of the United States of America, by the Rev. T. H. G. Pierrie. *New York.* 1854. 16mo.

PIERRON (D. Eduardo). Datos para la Geografía del Imperio Mexicano. ... *Mexico.* 1866. 4to. 62787

PIERS (H.) Thanksgiving Sermon [on the victory over the French in Canada]. By Henry Piers. *London.* 1759. 8vo.

Also: Sermon preached ... at Seven Oaks, in Kent, 21st May, 1742. ... Fifth Edition. *New York.* 1766. 8vo. N.

PIERSON (Abraham). *See* Peirson (A.), Vol. XIV. 59561.

[PIERSON (D. H.)] Memorial of David Magie, D.D., late Pastor of the Second Presbyterian Church, at Elizabeth, N. J. [n. p.] 1865. 16mo, pp. 39. 62789

PIERSON (E. C.) Jamie Parker, the Fugitive. By Emily Catharine Pierson. *Hartford: Brockett, Fuller & Co.* 1851. 16mo, pp. 192. C. 62790

PIERSON (H. W.) American Missionary Memorial. Including Biographical and Historical Sketches. Edited by H. W. Pierson. ... *New York: Harper & Brothers.* 1853. 8vo, pp. xv, 504. Plate. C. 62791

PIERSON. Jefferson at Monticello. The Private Life of Thomas Jefferson. From entirely new Materials. With numerous Fac-similes. By Rev. Hamilton W. Pierson, D.D. ... *New York: Charles Scribner.* 1862. 8vo, pp. 138. Plate and 8 Fac-similes. 62792

Drawn chiefly from the statements of Capt. Edmund Bacon, long the business manager of Mr. Jefferson's estate.

Also: Letter ... to Hon. C. Sumner, with Statements of Outrages upon Freedmen in Georgia, etc. *Washington.* 1870. 8vo.

PIERSON (J.) Christ the Son of God, as God-Man Mediator. A Sermon preached at Newark, N. J., May 8, 1751, before the New York Presbytery ... . By John Pierson, A.M. *Boston.* 1751. 8vo, pp. 29. 62793

PIERSON. A Discourse on the nature and benefits of Christ's intercession in Heaven. By John Pierson, A.M. ... *Woodbridge, in New-Jersey: Printed by James Parker.* 1765. 8vo, pp. 23. S.

PIERSON. The Faithful Minister. A Funeral Sermon, Preached at Elizabeth-Town, October 9, 1747. Occasioned by the Death of the Reverend Mr. Jonathan Dickinson, Late Pastor ... Elizabeth-Town. By John Pierson ... . *Woodbridge, New-Jersey: ... James Parker* ... 1748. 4to, pp. 24. 62795

PIERSON (W. S.) Memorial of Abraham Pierson, First Rector of Yale College. ... By William S. Pierson ... *Hartford.* 1870. 8vo, pp. 16. 62796

PIERZ (F.) Die Indianer in Nord-America, ihre Lebensweise, Sitten, Gebräuche u. s. w., nach vieljährigem Aufenthalte und gesammelten Erfahrungen unter den verschiedenen Stämmen,

bearbeitet von Franz Pierz, Katholischen Missionär. *St. Louis, Mo. Druck ... von Franz Saler u. Co.* 1855. 12mo, pp. 130, (2).

PIESCHEL (C.) Die Vulkane der Republik Mexiko. In Skizzen von Carl Pieschel. *Berlin: Dietrich Reimer.* 1856. Oblong 4to, 2 leaves, 18 Plates. A. 62798

Pietas et Gratulatio. *See* Vol. VIII., No. 30754.

Pietas in Patriam. *See* [Mather (C.)], Vol. XI., No. 46455.

Pietas Matutina. *See* [Mather (C.)], Vol. XI., No. 46456.

PIETERSZ (F.) Aanteekening gehouden op het schip de Vrouw Maria, gedestineerd ter Walvisvangst naar Groenland, Commandeur Fred. Pietersz, in het jaar 1769. *Amsterdam: Erven Wed. Jac. v. Egmont.* [1770.] 4to, pp. 24. 62799

Journal of the ship Vrouw Maria at the whale-fishery in Greenland.

PIETERSZ. Journaal of reys-beschryving op het schip de Vrouw Maria gedestineert ter walvisvangst na Groenland, 1769, gehouden door Freerk Pieters. [*Amsterdam:*] *Gedruckt by K. v. Ryschooten.* [1770.] 4to, pp. 24. 62800

The same as the previous pamphlet with a new title-page.

Piezas justificativas de la conducta politica de Yucatan, al observar la del gobierno de Mejico, respecto de los convenios de 14 de Diciembre de 1843. *Merida.* 1846. 8vo, pp. 82.

Piezas oficiales relativas a los acontecimientos de Cartajena, en Julio i Agosto del presente año, conexionados con la persona del Señor Adolfo Barrot Consul Francés en aquella plaza. Y suplemento. *Bogota.* 1833–34. Sm. 4to, pp. 120, 39. 62802

[PIGAFETTA (Antonio).] Le voyage et na- | uigation, faict par les Espaignolz es | Isles de Mollucques. des isles quilz | ont trouue audict voyage, des Roys | dicelles, de leur gouuernement & man- | iere d uiure, avec plusieurs aultres | choses. | Cum Priuilegio. | *On les vend a Paris en la maison de | Simon de Colines, libraire iure de lu | niuersite de Paris, demourāt en la rue | Sainct Jehan de Beauluais, a lensei- | gne du Soleil Dor.* | [*About* 1525.] Sm. 8vo, 76 leaves, Vocabulary and Table, (4) leaves. J.C.B. 62803

Of extreme rarity. The last three lines read: "Cy finit lextrait dudict liure, | translate de Italien en | Francois." This extract or summary of one of the earliest accounts of Magellan's memorable voyage round the world in 1519–22, was translated by a certain Jacques Antoine Fabre, from an original manuscript in Italian, presented by Pigafetta, who was one of the survivors of the expedition, to Louise de Savoy, the mother

of King Francis I. of France. The geographical descriptions, including the accounts of Brazil and the Patagonian giants, are very curious, and exhibit some strange inaccuracies. The leaf following folio 76 contains vocabularies of "isle de Bresil, des geans de Pataghone & du peuple More de Tadore." Pigafetta's first written account of the voyage was a brief diary of occurrences; but he afterwards wrote, in French or Italian, a more complete and full narrative. In a petition to the authorities of Venice, dated August 5, 1524, he says: "ho composto un libreto de tutto el ditto viazo, qual desidero far stampir." A privilege for twenty years was granted to print this *libretto*, and it may have been published; but no copy of such a book has yet been found. Pigafetta died in 1534, and the earliest Italian edition extant—that included in "Il Viaggio fatto da gli Spagnivoli atorno al Mondo," 1536 (*our* No. 47042, Vol. XI.)—appears to be a translation, somewhat abridged, from the French of Fabre. This was reprinted in Ramusio, Vol. I. Extracts are also given in [Huttich's] "Novus Orbis," *Basiliæ*, 1555, pp. 524–538, and in Eden's "History of Trauayle," *London*, 1577. For another account of the same voyage, *see* Maximilian of Transylvania, *our* Vol. XI., Nos. 47038–42. *See also* [Harrisse's] "Bib. Am. Vet.," No. 134, and "Additions," pp. xxviii–xxxiv.

Four early manuscript copies of the complete narrative, including a treatise on the sphere, and accompanied by curious maps and designs, are still extant. These manuscripts, three of which are in French and one in Italian, were written apparently in the early part of the sixteenth century. The French copies are very minute in details; but the Italian, which is carelessly written and full of errors, seems to be only an extract or paraphrase.

The latter manuscript served as the basis of the following edition:

PIGAFETTA. Primo Viaggio Intorno al Globo Terracqueo ossia Ragguaglio della Navigazione alle Indie Orientale per la via d'Occidente fatta dal Cavaliere Antonio Pigafetta Patrizio Vicentino Sulla Squadra del Capit. Magaglianes negli anni 1519–1522. Ora pubblicato per la prima volta, tratto da un Codice MS. della Biblioteca Ambrosiana di Milano e corredato di note da Carlo Amoretti Dottore del Collegio Ambrosiano. Con un Transunto del Trattato di Navigazione dello stesso Autore. *In Milano* MDCCC. *Nella Stamperia di Giuseppe Galeazzi. Con licenza de' Superiori.* 4to, pp. lii, 237. 6 Maps and 10 Vignettes. A.

There are copies on large paper. At the end: "Raccolta di Vocaboli del Brasile, de' Patagoni, delle Isole del Mar Australe." This is a modernized version, with some alterations, of an Italian manuscript of the sixteenth century, belonging to the Ambrosian library at Milan. Fourteen of the curious maps and designs which accompany the manuscript are here reproduced. The work was translated into French with the following title:

PIGAFETTA. Premier Voyage autour du monde, Par Le Chev^{r}. Pigafetta, sur l'Escadre de Magellan, pendant les années 1519, 20, 21, et 22; Suivi de l'extrait du Traité de Navigation du même auteur; et D'une Notice sur le chevalier Martin Behaim, avec la description de son Globe Terrestre. Orné de cartes et de figures. *A Paris, Chez H. J. Jansen. L'An* IX. [1801.] 8vo, pp. lxiv, (4), 415, (1). 9 Maps and Plates. A. 62805

Translated by Dr. Amoretti, the editor of the Italian edition. The notice of Martin Behaim is translated from the German of M. de Murr, by H. J. Jansen.

PIGAFETTA. The First Voyage round the World, by Magellan. Translated from the Accounts of Pigafetta, and other contemporary writers. Accompanied by Original Documents, with Notes and an Introduction, by Lord Stanley of Alderley. *London: Hakluyt Society.* M. DCCC. LXXIV. 8vo, pp. (8), lx, 257, xx. 2 Maps and 6 Plates. A. 62806

This volume contains six contemporary accounts of the expedition, viz.: The Genoese Pilot's Account, Narrative of the Anonymous Portuguese, Pigafetta's Account of the Voyage and Treatise on Navigation, Letter of Maximilian the Transylvan, Log-book of Francisco Alvo or Alvaro, and Gaspar Correa's Account. Another English version is in Pinkerton's Voyages, Vol. XI.

PIGAFETTA. Beschreibung der von Magellan unternommenen ersten Reise um die Welt. Aus einer handschrift der Ambrosianischen Bibliothek zu Mailand von Amoretti zum erstenmal herausgegeben. Aus dem Franzōsischen. *Gotha: J. Perthes.* 1801. 8vo, pp. lxxi, 296. 3 Maps. C. 62807

PIGGOT (A. S.) The Chemistry and Metallurgy of Copper; including a Description of the Principal Copper Mines of the United States .... By A. Snowden Piggot, M.D. ... *Philadelphia.* 1858. 12mo, pp. 381. C. 62808

PIGHIUS (A.) Albertvs Pi|Ghius Campen|sis de œquinoctiorvm sol|stitiorūque inuentione Ad. R. in Christo patrem D Frā|ciscum Molinium Abbatem S. Maximini, a Secretis & cōsilio. R. Francorum Christianiss. & pijs largitionibus eius|dem prœpositum primarium | Eiusdem de ratione Pascha|lis celebrationis, Deque Restitutione ecclesiastici Kalen|darij. Ad Beatissimum Patrem Leonem X Pontificem | Maximum. | *venundantur Parisij| in vico Diui Iacobi sub scuto Basiliensi.* | *Cvm privile|gio ad Trien|nivm.* | [*About* 1520.] Sm. folio, xxiii, (1), xxx leaves. C. + *Paris.* 1543. 8vo. 62809

Reprinted several times. A reference to the discoveries of Vespucius in the New World occurs on verso of folio xxviii of the second part.
The second part was also issued separately as follows:

PIGHIUS. Albertvs Pighi|vs Campensis, De Ratione Pascha|lis Celebrationis, deqve Resti-|tvtione Ecclesiastici Kalen|darii ad Beatissimvm Pa-|trem Leonem Decimvm | Pontificem Ma-|ximvm. | [*Paris.* 1520.] Folio, Title, 1 leaf, Text, xxx leaves.

PIGMAN (*Mr.*) *See* Maryland, XI. 45090, *note*, 45370, *note*.

The Pigmies and the Priests: showing how some dismal Pagans were converted to a lively faith. A Ballad of the Times of

Enchantment. *New York: Baker & Godwin, Printers.* 1863. 12mo, pp. 7. 62811

Signed "Cymon." A burlesque in rhyme on the wedding of the General Tom Thumb, P. T. Barnum, President Lincoln and the war.

PIGOT (G.) A Vindication Of the Practice of the Antient Christian, As well as the Church of England, And other Reformed Churches, In the Observation of Christmas-Day; In Answer to the Uncharitable Reflections of Thomas de Laune, Mr. Whiston, and Mr. John Barnard, of Marblehead: In a Sermon preach'd on the 4th. of January, 1729–30. By George Pigot, W.D.M. at Marblehead. ... *Boston: Printed by T. Fleet.* 1731. 8vo, pp. 41, (1). B., M., W. 62812

PIGOTT (C.) Strictures on the new Political Tenets of the Right Hon. Edmund Burke. Illustrated by Analogy between his different Sentiments on the American and French Revolutions; ... By Charles Pigott, Esq. *London: James Ridgway.* 1791. 8vo, pp. 104. J.C.B. 62813

See "Monthly Review," VII. 96.

PIKE (A.) Nugæ. By Albert Pike. ... Printed for Private Distribution. *Philadelphia: C. Sherman, Printer.* 1854. 12mo, pp. 393. 62814

One hundred and fifty copies printed for presentation to friends.

PIKE. Prose Sketches and Poems, Written in the Western Country. By Albert Pike. *Boston: Light & Horton.* 1834. 12mo, pp. 200. B. 62815

"A Narrative of a Journey in the Prairie," occupies eighty pages.
Also: Kansas State Rights. Appeal to the Democracy of the South. ... *Washington.* 1857. 8vo.—Lecture ... before the M. W. Grand Lodge of Louisiana, at its forty-sixth Annual Communication, held in New Orleans, February, 1858. *New Orleans.* 1858. 8vo, pp. 68.—Letters to the People of the Northern States, on the Nebraska and Kanza Act, and Southern Slavery. ... *Washington.* 1856. 8vo, pp. 38.—National Plan of an Atlantic and Pacific Railroad, and Remarks ... at Memphis, November, 1849. *Little Rock.* [n. d.] 8vo, pp. 16.—State or Province? Bond or Free? Addressed Particularly to the People of Arkansas. ... [n. p.] 1861. 8vo, pp. 40.—The Statutes and Regulations, Institutes, Laws, and Grand Constitutions of the Ancient and Accepted Scottish Rite: Compiled, ... for the Use of the Order .... *New York.* 1859. 8vo, pp. 167. Plate. In French and English. Also other masonic addresses and reports.

[PIKE.] The Life-Wake of The Fine Arkansas Gentleman who Died before his Time. *Washington: Franklin Philp.* 1859. 8vo, pp. 54. 62816

This pamphlet, of which very few were printed, commemorates a reception given to Albert Pike by his friends, subsequent to a premature announcement of his death which

appeared in the Washington newspapers. It contains several stanzas written by him for the occasion.

PIKE (F. A.) Commercial Relations with the British Provinces. Speech of Hon. F. A. Pike, of Maine, In the House of Representatives, June 3, 1862. [*Washington: Scammell & Co., Printers.* 1862.] 8vo, pp. 8. 62817

Also: The Currency and the War. Speech ... in the House of Representatives, February 5, 1862. [n. p. n. d.] 8vo, pp. 8.—Speech ... on the Reciprocity Treaty. ... May 19, 1864. [n. p. n. d.] 8vo, pp. 8.

PIKE [James], *Corporal.* The Scout and Ranger: being the Personal Adventures of Corporal Pike, of the Fourth Ohio Cavalry, as a Texas Ranger in the Indian Wars, delineating Western Adventure; afterward a Scout and Spy, in Tennessee, Alabama, Georgia, and the Carolinas. Fully illustrating the Secret Service. *Cincinnati: J. R. Hawley & Co.* 1865. 8vo, pp. 394, (1). 25 Plates. + [*Ibid.*] 1866. 8vo. 62818

PIKE (J.) Gospel Ministers, Christ's Ambassadors. A Sermon preached before a Convention of Ministers At Newington, in the Province of New Hampshire, October 9, 1750. By James Pike .... *Boston: Printed by D. Fowle.* 1751. 8vo, pp. 31. N.

PIKE (J. S.) The Financial Crisis: Its Evils and their Remedy. By James S. Pike .... *New York: The Author.* 1867. 8vo, pp. 38. 62820

Also: Chief Justice Chase. ... 1873. *New York: Powers, Macgowan & Slipper, Printers.* 1873. 8vo, pp. (2), 18.—Contributions to the Financial Discussion, 1874–1875. ... *New York: Macgowan & Slipper, Printers.* 1875. 8vo, pp. 44.—The Prostrate State; or, South Carolina under Negro Government. ... *New York: D. Appleton & Co.* 1874. 16mo, pp. 279.—The Restoration of the Currency. ... *New York.* 1868. 8vo, pp. 52.

PIKE (J.) Commemorative Services at the Twenty-fifth Anniversary of the Pastorate of the Rev. John Pike, Rowley, Mass., November 19, 22, 23, 1865. *Salem.* 1865. 8vo, pp. 78.

PIKE. A Discourse, ... in the Congregational Church, Rowley, on the Eighth Anniversary of his Settlement, Nov. 19, 1848. By Rev. John Pike. *Newburyport.* 1848. 8vo, pp. 14.

PIKE. A Discourse, ... in the Congregational Church, Rowley, on the Twenty-second Anniversary of his Settlement, November 23, 1862, by Rev. John Pike. *Boston: Press of T. R. Marvin & Son.* 1862. 8vo, pp. 28. 62823

PIKE. A Sermon delivered before His Excellency ... and the Legislature of Massachusetts, at the Annual Election, ... Jan. 7,

1857. By John Pike .... *Boston: William White, Printer.* 1857. 8vo, pp. 37. B. 62824

Also: The Bud, Blossom and Fruit; ... or, Early Piety ... illustrated ... in the Life of Emily J. Goodhue. ... *Boston.* [1858.] 16mo, pp. 252. Plate.—A Discourse ... in Rowley, at the Annual Thanksgiving, November 26, 1846. ... *Boston: Printed by S. N. Dickinson & Co.* 1846. 8vo, pp. 15.

PIKE (J.) An | Epistle | to the | National Meeting | of | Friends, | in | Dublin, | concerning good Order and Discipline | in the Church. | Written by Josph [*sic*] Pike. | *Philadelphia:* | *Re-printed, and Sold by B. Franklin, and* | *D. Hall,* 1757. Sm. 8vo, pp. 23. + *Wilmington* [*Del.*]: *James Adams.* 1783. 12mo, pp. 24. C. + *Philadelphia.* 1822. 8vo. 62825

PIKE (M. S.) Creola: or The Slave & Minstrel. A Poetical Romance .... By Marshall S. Pike. *Boston:* [*J. E. Farwell & Co.*] 1850. 8vo, pp. 53. 62826

This was suppressed, and the edition destroyed.

[PIKE (*Mrs.* Mary H.)] Bond and Free, by the Author of "Caste" .... *London.* 1858. 12mo. 62827

[PIKE.] Caste: A Story of Republican Equality, by Sydney A. Story, Jr. *Boston.* 1856. 12mo. C. 62828

[PIKE.] Ida May, a Story of Things Actual and Possible. By Mary Langdon. *Boston: Phillips, Sampson & Co.* 1854. 12mo. + *London.* 1855. 12mo. 62829

PIKE (N.) A New and Complete System of Arithmetic, composed for the use of the citizens of the United States: By Nicholas Pike, A.M. ... *Newbury-Port:* ... *John Mycall.* MDCCLXXXVIII. 8vo, pp. 512, Errata, (1). C., P. + Second Edition, Enlarged. Revised ... By Ebenezer Adams, A.M. ... *Printed at Worcester, Massachusetts, at the Press of Isaiah Thomas, By Leonara Worcester,* ... 1797. 8vo, pp. 512. S. + Third Edition .... *Worcester: Isaiah Thomas.* 1798. 12mo. 62830

Frequently reprinted.

PIKE (R.) God round about his People: A Sermon, preached Oct. 30, 1853, on the occasion of the Death of Mrs. Abigail Withington. By Richard Pike .... *Boston: Printed by John Wilson & Son.* 1853. 8vo, pp. 23. 62831

Also: A Sermon preached in ... Dorchester ... January 1st, 1860: ... after the Funeral of ... General Moses Whitney, of Milton. ... *Boston:* 1860. *J. H. Eastburn's Press.* 8vo, pp. 20.

PIKE (S.) A Letter to Mr. Robert Sandeman, Jan. 4, 1766. By Samuel Pike. *Portsmouth, N. H.* [1766.] 8vo, pp. 6. M.

[PIKE.] A Plain and Full Account of the Christian Practices observed by the Church in St. Martin's-le-Grand, London .... *Boston.* 1766. 8vo, pp. 28. M. 62833

PIKE (S.) *and* HAYWARD (S.) Some Important Cases of Conscience answered .... By Samuel Pike and S. Hayward .... The Third Edition. *Boston.* 1757. 8vo, pp. 138. + The Fourth Edition. *Boston.* 1760. 8vo, pp. 136. W. + *Philadelphia: W. Bradford.* 1764. 2 vols., 12mo. 62834

Most of the types for the edition of 1760 were set by Isaiah Thomas, then about twelve years old.

PIKE [Z. M.] An Account of a Voyage up the Mississippi River, from St. Louis to its Source; made under the orders of the War Department, by Lieut. Pike, of the United States Army, in the years 1805 and 1806. Compiled from Mr. Pike's Journal. [*Washington.* 1807.] 8vo, pp. 68. P., W. 62835

PIKE. An Account of Expeditions to the Sources of the Mississippi, and through the Western Parts of Louisiana, to the Sources of the Arkansaw, Kans, La Platte, and Pierre Jaun, Rivers; Performed by Order of the Government of the United States during the Years 1805, 1806, and 1807. And a Tour through the Interior Parts of New Spain, when conducted through these Provinces, by order of the Captain-General, in the Year 1807. By Major Z. M. Pike. Illustrated by Maps and Charts. *Philadelphia: C. & A. Conrad & Co.* ... *John Binns, Printer.* 1810. 8vo, pp. 5, (2), 105, (9), 107–277, (2), Appendix, 65, (1), 53, 87. Portrait, 6 Maps, and 3 folded Tables. A. 62836

Some copies are accompanied by the six maps bound separately in a small quarto atlas. This is the only complete edition. Major Pike was the first explorer under the government of the United States, of that vast portion of the republic now forming the States of Arkansas, Texas, and New Mexico. His accounts of the principal features of the country, and of the savage tribes which inhabited it, are accurate and interesting. Six years after completing this tour, he was killed at Little York, in Canada, by the explosion of a magazine in a fort, from which he had just before driven the garrison by assault.

PIKE. Exploratory Travels through the Western Territories of North America: comprising a Voyage from St. Louis, on the Mississippi to the Source of that River, and a Journey through the Interior of Louisiana, and the North-Eastern Provinces of New Spain. Performed in the years 1805, 1806 and 1807, by Order of the Government of the United States. By Zebulon

Montgomery Pike; Major 6th Regt. United States Infantry. *London: Longman* ... 1811. 4to, pp. xx, 436. 2 Maps. C.

PIKE. Voyage au Nouveau-Mexique, a la suite d'une expédition ordonnée par le Gouvernement des États-Unis, pour reconnoître les sources des rivières Arkansas, Kansès, La Plate et Pierre-Jaune, dans l'intérieur de la Louisiane Occidentale. Précédé d'une Excursion aux Sources du Mississippi, pendant les années 1805, 1806 et 1807. Par le Major Z. M. Pike. Traduit de l'Anglais Par M. Breton .... *A Paris, Chez d'Hautel,* ... 1812. 2 vols., 8vo, pp. xiv, (2), 368; 373. 3 Maps. C.

M. Breton, the translator and editor, corrected numerous errors in the Spanish and French names of persons and places.

PIKE. Reise durch die westlichen Gebiete von Nord-America, enthaltend die Tagebücher der Reisen von St. Louis, den Missisippi hinauf bis an die Quellen dieses Flusses; durch das Innere von Louisiana, und durch die nordöstlichen Provinzen von Neu-Spanien, gemacht in den Jahren 1805, 1806 u. 1807, auf Befehl der Regierung der Vereinigten Staaten. Von Zebulon Montgomery Pike, Major der Infanterie. Aus dem Englischen übersetzt von Ph. Ch. Weyland. Mit einer Charte. *Weimar, im Verlage des Landes-Industrie-Comptoirs.* 1813. 8vo, pp. xvi, 556. Map and folded Table. A., C. 62839

PIKE. Reize naar Nieuw-Mexico en de Binnenlanden van Louisiana, voorafgegaan door eenen togt naar de bronnen van de Mississippi. Uit het Engelsch vertaald. *Amsterdam.* 1812. 2 vols., 8vo. 2 Maps. 62840

PIKE COUNTY, *Ill.* Rules, Regulations [etc.] of the ... Agricultural Society ... Tenth Annual Exhibition, 1861. *Pittsfield.* 1861. 8vo. 62841

PIKE'S PEAK. Hints and Information for the use of Emigrants to Pike's Peak, embracing a Concise and Comprehensive Sketch of the Gold Region, the best Routes, Points of Outfit, etc. *Leavenworth, Kansas.* 1860. 8vo, pp. 15. 62842

Pikin A. B. C. boekoe, nanga Wan pihin Leri-Boekoe. *Amsterdam: J. Termeulen.* 1843. 12mo, pp. 44. 62843

An elementary reading book in the negro jargon of the West Indies.

The Pilgrim Fathers. *See* [Clarke (J. F.)], Vol. IV. 13414, *and* [Mourt], Vol. XII. 51201.

PILGRIM JOHN, *pseudon.* The Soldier's Armor of Strength. A Brief Course of ... Devotional Exercises, ... specially adapted to the present calamitous times of Rebellion and Civil War. By Pilgrim John. *Brooklyn, E. D.: D. S. Holmes.* 1863. 12mo, pp. 96. A. + [*Ibid.*] 1865. 12mo, pp. 96. 62844

Pilgrim Jubilee. Celebration in Providence, R. I., of the Two Hundred and Fiftieth Anniversary of Congregationalism in this Country, October 11th, 1870 ... *Central Falls.* 1870. 8vo, pp. 36. 62845

PILGRIM SOCIETY. *See* Plymouth.

A Pilgrimage over the Prairies. By the Author of "The Fortunes of a Colonist." *London: T. Cautley Newby.* 1863. 2 vols., 12mo, pp. (2), 298; (2), 261. C. 62846

The | Pilgrim's Progress | from | this World | to | That which is to come: | Delivered under the Similitude of a | Dream | VVherein is Discovered the manner | of his setting out | His Dangerous Journey | and Safe Arrival at the Desired Countrey. | By John Bunyan. | ... | *Boston in New England* | *Printed by Samuel Green upon As-* | *signment of Samuel Sewall and* | *are to be sold by John Vsher* | *of Boston* 1681. | 16mo, pp. (10), 164? 62847

Title within a double-line border. The only known copy—lacking the last leaf—was in the possession of George Brinley, Esq., of Hartford, Conn. Bunyan probably refers to this edition in the following lines of his preface to the Second Part of the "Pilgrim's Progress," London, 1684:

"'Tis in New-England under such advance,
Receives there so much loving Countenance,
As to be Trim'd, new Cloth'd and Deck't with Gems,
That it might show its Features, and its limbs,
Yet more, so comely doth my Pilgrim walk,
That of him thousands daily sing and talk."

Other editions: *Boston: Reprinted for B. Eliot.* 1706. 12mo. + Part I. With Cuts. *Boston.* 1738. 12mo, pp. 150. + Part II. With Cuts. *Boston.* 1744. 12mo, pp. 160.
The following German translations are worthy of mention:

Eines Christen Reise nach der Seeligen Ewigkeit, in Englischer Sprache beschrieben durch Joh. Bunian, Lehrer in Betford, um seiner fuertrefflichkeit willen in die Hoch Teutsche uebersetzt. ... *Ephrata in Pennsylvania. Drucks und Verlags der Bruederschafft, Anno* 1754. Sm. 8vo, pp. 280; Part II., 263. + *Germantaun: Gedruckt und zu haben bey Peter Leibert.* 1796. Sm. 8vo, pp. 240; Part II., 225; Leben und Sterben von Joh. Bunian, 26. 62848

The 1754 edition is very rare. For a list of some other productions of the Ephrata press *see* note to Van Braght (T. J.) The third part was published with the following title:

Johann Bunians Pilgrims oder Christen Reise ausz dieser Welt nach der Zukuenfftigen. Der Dritte Theil. Uebersetzt aus der 13ten Englischen Auflage, zur Ermunterung der Liebhaber solcher Reise; von einem geringen Mitpilger. *Germantown: Gedruckt und zu finden bey Christoph. Saur,* 1755. Sm. 8vo, pp. 144; Das Angenehme Opfer ... Johann Bunian, 151. 62849

A very rare imprint.

The Pilgrims' Address, and an Improved Mode of Defence against the Bucaniers [*sic*] of the Ocean of every Nation, ... submitted to the ... consideration of the Citizens of the United States, especially to those gentlemen to whom the more immediate care of our seaports are connected. Second Edition. *Philadelphia: The Author.* 1808. 18mo, pp. 24, Supplement, 12. S.

The Pilgrims of Hope: An Oratorio for the Clintonian celebration of the New Year. ... With ... Notes and an Appendix, containing "The Coalition," a political tract, occasioned by the nomination of De Witt Clinton as a Candidate for ... President ... in ... 1812. *Albany: Re-printed by Packard & Van Benthuysen.* 1820. 12mo, pp. 46, 10. S. 62851

An anti-Clintonian poem with very personal notes.

PILKINGTON (*Mrs.* [M. H.]) A Mirror for the Female Sex. Historical Beauties for Young Ladies. ... By Mrs. [Mary Hopkins] Pilkington. ... *Hartford: Oliver D. & I. Cooke.* 1799. 16mo, pp. xxiv, 211. B., C. 62852

A Pill for Porcupine. *See* [Cobbett (W.)], Vol. IV. 14029.

Pillars of Salt. *See* [Mather (C.)], Vol. XI., No. 46459.

PILLOW [Gideon J.] Defence of Major Gen. Pillow before the Court of Inquiry At Frederick, Maryland, against the charges preferred against him by Maj. Gen. Winfield Scott. [n. p. 1848.] 8vo, pp. 64. A., S. 62853

Signed "Gideon J. Pillow." The cover is dated "June, 1848."

PILLOW. Message from the President ... communicating ... the Proceedings of the two Courts of Inquiry in the case of Major General Pillow. [*Washington.* 1848.] 8vo, pp. 635. S.

Pills, Poetical, Political, and Philosophical. Prescribed for the Purpose of purging the Publick of Piddling Philosophers, of Puny Poetasters, of Paltry Politicians, and Petty Partisans. By Peter

Pepper Box, Poet and Physician. *Philadelphia: The Author.* 1809. 8vo, pp. xviii, 136. W. 62855

By Thomas Green Fessenden.

Pillsbury (P.) The Church As It Is: or the Forlorn Hope of Slavery. By Parker Pillsbury. *Boston: A. Forbes, Printer.* 1847. 16mo, pp. 96. + Second Edition — Revised and Improved. *Boston: Bela Marsh.* 1847. 16mo, pp. 90. B. 62856

[Pillsbury.] The "Party of Progress." Letter to a Radical Member of Congress. [*Concord?* 1867.] 8vo, pp. 4. H.

[Pillsbury.] Second Letter to a Radical Member of Congress. [*Concord?* 1867.] 8vo, pp. 4. H. 62858

Pilmore (J.) The Blessings of Peace: A Sermon Preached in Christ's Church, New-York, on the Fourth of July, 1794. At the Joint Request of the Tammany Society, or, Columbian Order, and the Society of Mechanics. By the Rev. Joseph Pilmore. *New-York: Printed by John Buel.* ... MDCCXCIV. 8vo, pp. 32. 62859

Pilmore. A Sermon Preached in St. Paul's Church, Philadelphia, ... 27th December, 1786. ... For the Relief of the Poor: Before the Honourable Fraternity of The Free and Accepted Masons of Pennsylvania. By Rev. Joseph Pilmore. *Philadelphia: Printed by Elezar Oswald.* M.DCC.LXXXVII. 8vo, pp. 23. + *New York: Printed ... by William Durrell.* M.DCC.XCIII. 8vo, pp. 24. N. 62860

Pilon (F.) The Fair American: a Comic Opera, ... As it is performed ... at the Theatre-Royal, Drury-Lane. Written by F. Pilon. Dedicated to the Right Hon. Lord Camden ... . *Dublin: Printed by J. Exshaw* ... . MDCCLXXXV. 12mo, pp. 71.

The Pilot. *See* [Cooper (J. F.)], Vol. IV., No. 16495.

Il pilota dell' Oceano Atlantico o guida per la navigazione dello stretto di Gibilterra a tutta la costa del Brasile, Montevideo e Rio della Plata ... fino a Londra ... con la descrizione di tutte le isole, banchi, scogli, venti e correnti predominanti in tutto questo tratto di oceano. *Trieste.* 1847. 12mo. 62862

Pilote (F.) Le Saguenay en 1851; Histoire du Passé, du Présent et de l'Avenir du Haut Saguenay au point de vue de la Colonisation. Par Rev. F. Pilote. *Québec.* 1852. 8vo, pp. 147.

Le Pilote Américain. *See* [Blunt (E. M.)], Vol. II. 6028.

Le Pilote de l'isle de Saint-Domingue et des debouquemens de cette isle, comprenant une carte de l'isle de Saint-Domingue et une carte des debouquemens, depuis la Caye d'Argent jusqu'à la partie ouest du placet des isles Lucayes. Pûblié par ordre du roi. *Paris, de l'Imprimerie royale.* 1787. Folio, pp. (2), 18. 6 Maps.

Other editions, *Paris*, 1778, 1781.

Le Pilote de la Terre Neuve, ou Recueil de Plans des côtes et des ports de celle île. Pour l'usage des vaisseaux du Roi, et des navires de commerce destinés à la Pêche ... Publié par ... le ministre ... de la Marine. [n. p.] 1784. Folio. 12 Maps. S.

Pilsbury (A.) Biographical Sketch of Amos Pilsbury, and a Brief Account of the Albany County Penitentiary. *Albany: Joel Munsell, Printer.* 1849. 8vo, pp. (2), 24. 62866

Pilsbury. Memorial of Amos Pilsbury, late Warden of the State Prison, to the General Assembly, May Session, 1845. Together with his Report for the nine months ending Dec. 31, 1844. *Hartford.* 1845. 8vo, pp. 34. 62867

Pilsbury. Sketch of the Life and Public Services of Amos Pilsbury, Superintendent of the Albany Penitentiary, and late General Superintendent of the Metropolitan Police. *Albany: Munsell & Rowland.* 1860. 8vo, pp. 44. Portrait. 62868

Pilsbury [Timothy]. Speech of Mr. Pilsbury in Defence of Texas ... in the House of Representatives, ... June 16th, 1846. [n. p.: *J. & G. S. Gideon, Printers.* n. d.] 8vo. H. 62869

Pilsen [John]. Reply of Lieut.-Col. Pilsen to Emil Schalk's Criticisms of the Campaign in the Mountain Department, under Maj.-Gen. J. C. Fremont. [*New York.* 1863.] 8vo, pp. 14.

Pim (B. Capperton Trevylian), *and* Seemann (B.) Dottings on the Roadside, in Panama, Nicaragua, and Mosquito. By Bedford Pim, Captain R. N., and Berthold Seemann, PH.D. ... *London: Chapman and Hall.* 1869. 8vo, pp. xvi, 468. 2 Maps and 6 Plates. C. 62871

Pim. The Gate of the Pacific. By Commander Bedford Pim, R. N. ... *London: Lovell Reeve & Co.* 1863. 8vo, pp. xiii, (1), 432. 7 Maps and 9 Plates. A., B. 62872

Relates to Nicaragua, Honduras, and the Mosquito Shore.

Pim. The Negro and Jamaica. By Commander Bedford Pim. ... *London: Trübner & Co.* 1866. 8vo, pp. vii, 72. C., S.

Also: An Earnest Appeal on behalf of the Missing Arctic Expedition. ... *London.* 1857. 8vo.

Pima Language. *See* Vol. I., No. 2124.

Pimental (D. M.) Sermon Funebre, de Francisco Xavier Lazcano. *Mexico.* 1763. 4to. 62874

Pimentel (A.) Juicio sobre la causa seguida contra ... Andres Pimentel en ... Havana ... *New-Orleans.* 1844. 8vo, pp. 120. B. 62875

Pimentel (E. E. de B.) Relatorio com que o exm. Snr. Dr. Esperidião Eloy de Barros Pimentel, Presidente da Provincia das Alagoas entregou a administração da mesma provincia no dia 19 de abril de 1866 ao 1.º vice-presidente Dr. Galdino Augusto da Natividade e Silva. *Maceio: Typ. do Bacharel, Felix da Costa Moraes.* [n. d.] Folio, pp. (2), 31. 62876

Pimentel (F.) Cuadro Descriptivo y Comparativo de las Lenguas Indígenas de México Por D. Francisco Pimentel Socio de numero de la Sociedad Mexicana de Geografia y Estadistica ... *México, Imprenta de Andrade y Escalante.* 1862–65. 2 vols., 8vo, pp. lii, 539, (1); vi, 427, (3). B., BA., C. + (Segunda Edicion unica completa) ... *Mexico. Tipografia de Isidoro Epstein.* 1874–75. 3 vols., sm. 8vo, pp. xvi, 426; 472; 571. C. 62877

A very important work, in which separate grammatical sketches, with bibliographical notices, are given of more than forty Mexican and Central American languages and dialects. The second and best edition, which was revised and greatly enlarged, treats more fully of the North Mexican languages.

Pimentel. Dictámen de la Comision nombrada por la Sociedad Mexicana de Geografía y Estadística para examinar la obra de D. Francisco Pimentel intitulada Cuadro Descriptivo y Comparativo de las Lenguas indígenas de México. [n. p. n. d.] 8vo, pp. 7. 62878

Dated "Mexico, Marzo 19 de 1863," and signed by José Fernando Ramirez, José Guadalupe Romero and Manuel Orozco y Berra. In consequence of this favorable report, the Mexican Geographical Society awarded its prize medal to Pimentel.

Pimentel. La Economia Politica aplicada a la propriedad territorial en México por D. Francisco Pimentel ... . *México: Ignacio Cumplido.* 1866. 8vo, pp. 265, Table, (2). C. 62879

Pimentel. Memoria sobre las causas que han originado la situacion actual de la Raza indígena de México, y medios de

rémediarla por Don Francisco Pimentel. ... *México: Imprenta de Andrade y Escalante.* 1864. 8vo, pp. 241, (3). B., C. 62880

Also: Disertacion filologica leida en la Sociedad Mexicana de historia natural. ... *Mexico: White.* 1869. 8vo, pp. 36.

Pimentel y Sotomayor (F.) Por D. Franc. Pimentel y Sotomayor, Presidente que fué de la Real Audiencia de las Charcas, vezino de la Ciudad de Lima, en el Pleyto con D. B. Phelipe de Aragon sobre la revocacion de las Sentencias pronunciadas en 5 de Julio de 1727 y 21 de Junio 1729 por el Presidente ... . [*Mexico.* 1729.] Folio. 62881

Pimentel (M.) Arte Practica de Navegar & Roteiro das Viagens & Costas Maritimas do Brasil, Guine, Angola, Indias e Ilhas Orientaes e Occidentaes ... . Por Manoel Pimentel. *Lisboa.* 1699. Folio. 62882

Pimentel. Arte de Navegar ... & Roteiro das viagens e costas maritimas de Guinè, Angola, Brasil, Indias, & Ilhas Occidentaes & Orientaes, Agora novamente emendado & accrescentadas muitas derrotas novas. Por Manoel Pimentel ... . *Lisboa, na Officina Real Deslandesiana.* M.DCCXII. Folio, pp. (12), 576. 21 Plans and Charts. + Novamente emendado ... . *Lisboa: Franc. da Sylva.* 1746. Folio, pp. (10), 604. 21 Charts. + *Lisboa: Miguel Manescal da Costa Impressor.* M.DCC.LXII. Folio, pp. (12), 603, (1). 21 Maps. 62883

Reprinted again in 1819.

Pimentel. The Brazil Pilot; or a Description of the Coast of Brazil. Translated from the Portuguese of Manoel Pimentel, Principal Hydrographer to His Majesty John the Fifth, of Portugal. To which are added, Charts, of some of its most considerable Ports. From MSS. never before published. *London: Longman, Hurst, Rees, and Orme.* 1809. 4to, pp. (4), iv, 78. 15 Maps. H. 62884

Pimienta (F. D.) Relacion del Svcesso Qve | Tvvo Francisco Diaz Pimienta, General de la Real | Armada de las Indias, en la Isla de santa Catalina. Dase cuenta como la | tomò a los enemigos que la posseian, echandolos della, y de la | estimacion de los despojos, y numero de los | prisioneros. | [Colophon:] *Con licencia. En Madrid, Por Iuan Sanchez. Año* 1642. | Folio, pp. (6). 62885

Pimienta. Relacion del svcesso qve tvvo Francisco | Diaz Pimienta, General de la Real Armada de las Indias, en la Is- | la

de S. Catalina. Dase cuenta de como la tomò a los enemigos que | la posseian, èchandolos della, y la estimacion de los despojos y nu- | mero de prisioneros. | [Colophon:] *Con licencia del señor don Miguel de Luna y Arellano, Cavallero del Abito de San- | tiago, del Consejo de su Magestad, y su Oydor en la Real Audiencia de Sevi- | lla lo imprimio Francisco de Lyra, Año* 1642. | 4to, pp. (12). J.C.B.

Pimpeterre (E.) Le Comte d'Eu et la France nouvelle dans l'Amérique du Sud. Par E. Pimpeterre. *Paris.* 1869. 8vo, pp. 32. 62887

Pin (C. du). Ensaio sobre o fabrico do Assucar ... por M. C. du Pin e Almeida. *Bahia.* 1834. 8vo. 62888

See also Vol. VI., Nos. 21362–65.

Piña y Cuevas (Manuel). Exposicion al Tribunal Superior del Distrito Federal. ... *Mexico.* 1861. 8vo. 62889

Pinchback (P. B. S.) Speech of Hon. P. B. S. Pinchback, ... in the Senate of Louisiana, ... February 4, 1869, upon the Civil Rights Bill, to be entitled "An Act to enforce the Thirteenth Article of the Constitution of the State." [n. p. n. d.] 8vo, pp. 4. H. 62890

Also: A Statement of the ... Case of P. B. S. Pinchback claiming a Seat ... as Senator Elect from ... Louisiana. [n. p. 1873.] 8vo, pp. 13. H.

Pinchbeck (W. F.) Witchcraft: or the Art of Fortune-Telling Unveiled: From the low ambition of the celebrated Mary Pitcher, To the more elevated, but equally vague pretensions of the Injudicious Astrologer. Delineated in a Series of Letters, between a Friend and his Correspondent. ... Together with Poetick Compositions on different Subjects. By William Frederick Pinchbeck, Author of "The Expositor, or many Mysteries unravelled." *Boston: The Author.* 1805. 12mo, pp. 108, including Frontispiece. 62891

Pinchinat (——). Réponse de Pinchinat, Député de Saint-Domingue, aux Discours, actes ou écrits des citoyens Leborgne, Garrigou, Lachapelle et Sonthonax, adressée au Corps-Législatif et au Directoire-Exécutif. *A Paris, De l'Imprimerie de J. F. Sobry.* [1797.] 8vo, pp. xvi, 171. J.C.B. 62892

Relates exclusively to the affairs of St. Domingo.

Pinchion (W.) *See* Pynchon (W.)

Pinckard (G.) Notes on the West Indies: written during the Expedition under the Command of the late General Sir Ralph

Abercromby: including Observations on the Island of Barbadoes, and the Settlements captured by the British Troops, upon the Coast of Guiana; likewise Remarks relating to the Creoles and Slaves of the Western Colonies, and the Indians of South America: with occasional hints, regarding The Seasoning, or Yellow Fever of Hot Climates. By George Pinckard, M.D. ... *London: Longman, Hurst, Rees, and Orme.* 1806. 3 vols., 8vo, pp. xxiv, 448; xx, 472; xix, (1), 456. A., S. 62893

See "Edinburgh Review," IX. 304, *and* "Monthly Review," LIII. 169, LXXXVII. 222.

Pinckard. Notes on the West Indies, including Observations relative to the Creoles and Slaves of the Western Colonies and the Indians of South America; interspersed with Remarks upon the Seasoning or Yellow Fever of Hot Climates. Second Edition, with additional letters from Martinique, Jamaica and St. Domingo. By George Pinckard, M.D. ... *London: Baldwin, Cradock & Joy.* 1816. 2 vols., 8vo, pp. xxiii, 537; xvi, 534, (18)

Pinckney (C.) Observations | on the | Plan of Government | submitted to the | Federal Convention, | In Philadelphia, on the 28th of May, 1787. | By Mr. Charles Pinckney, | Delegate from the State of South-Carolina. | Delivered at different Times in the course of their Discussions. | *New York: Printed by Francis Childs.* | [1787.] Sm. 4to, pp. 27. A. 62895

See Madison "Papers" (App. to Deb. VII.) 653.

[Pinckney.] Observations to shew the Propriety of the Nomination of Colonel James Monroe, to the Presidency of the United States. ... By a South-Carolinian. *Charleston.* 1816. 8vo, pp. 52. BA. 62896

Pinckney. Speeches of Charles Pinckney, Esq. in Congress; On the subject of having Impartial Juries, by Lot, in all the Federal Courts ... *Printed in* 1800. 8vo, pp. 135. W. 62897

Pinckney. Three Letters, Written, and Originally Published, under the Signature of A South Carolina Planter. The First, on the Case of Jonathan Robbins; decided under the Twenty-Sixth Article of the Treaty with Great-Britain, in the District Court of the United States, for South Carolina. The Second, on the Recent Captures of American Vessels by British Cruisers, Contrary to the Laws of Nations, and the Treaty between the Two Countries. The Third, on the Right of Expatriation. By Charles Pinckney, Esquire, Senator in Congress, for South-Carolina. To which is added, An Appendix, containing sundry Documents con-

cerning Jonathan Robbins. *Philadelphia: Aurora-Office.* 1799. 8vo, pp. (2), 65. B., C. 62898

Pinckney. Three Letters lately addressed to the People of the United States, which have lately appeared under the signature of a "South Carolina Planter." The first, on the case of Jonathan Robbins. The second, on the recent captures of the British Cruisers, and the right of a Citizen to expatriate himself. The third, on the Claims of the British Creditors, and the proceedings of the British Commissioners under the 6th article of Mr. Jay's Treaty. By Charles Pinckney ... . *Charleston: T. C. Cox.* 1799. 8vo, pp. 69. J.C.B. 62899

Pinckney (C. C.) An Address delivered in Charleston, before the Agricultural Society of South Carolina, ... on 18th of August, 1829. By Charles C. Pinckney. *Charleston.* 1829. 8vo. + Second Edition. [*Ibid.*] 1829. 8vo, pp. 24. H. 62900

[Pinckney.] The Sermon, ... at Pendleton, ... on ... the Death of the Rev. Jasper Adams, D.D. *Charleston: Printed by A. E. Miller.* 1842. 8vo, pp. 7. H. 62901

See "Authentic Copies," our Vol. I., No. 2446. *See also* Vol. IX., No. 34865, *and* No. 62653, *supra.*

Pinckney (C.) The Young Woman's Gift, of Literature, Science and Morality. By Cotesworth Pinckney. *Boston: J. Buffum.* 1851. 18mo, pp. 192. Plate. 62902

Pinckney (*Mrs.* E.) *See* Lucas (E.), Vol. X., No. 42609.

Pinckney (H. L.) An Oration, delivered in St. Michael's Church, before ... the Inhabitants of Charleston, South-Carolina; on the Fourth of July, 1818. In Commemoration of American Independence; by Appointment of the '76 Association ... . By Henry Laurens Pinckney ... . *Charleston: Printed by W. P. Young.* 1818. 8vo, pp. (2), 29. 62903

Pinckney. "The Spirit of the Age." An Address ... before the Two Literary Societies of the University of North Carolina. By Hon. Henry L. Pinckney ... . *Raleigh: Printed by J. Gales & Son.* 1836. 8vo, pp. 30. H. 62904

Also: An Address delivered before the Temperance Society of ... Washington. ... *Washington.* 1836. 8vo. — Address ... before the Bible Society of the University of Virgina. ... March 11, 1835. *Richmond.* 1835. 8vo. — Address ... before the North Carolina University ... *Raleigh.* 1836. 8vo. — Address to the Electors of Charleston District, ... on ... the Abolition of Slavery. *Washington.* 1836. 8vo, pp. 15. H. — An Address to the Electors of Charleston [Congressional] District. ... *Charleston:*

Burges & Honour. 1836. 8vo, pp. 48. — An Oration ... before the Literary Societies of the University of Georgia, August 3, 1837 ... . *Athens.* 1837. 8vo, pp. 23. — Oration ... before the State Rights and Free Trade Party. ... *Charleston.* 1833. 8vo. — Remarks addressed to the Citizens of Charleston on ... Establishing a Public Cemetery. ... *Charleston.* 1839. 8vo, pp. 32, (4). — Remarks ... on the Resolution ... relative to the Abolition of Slavery ... in the House of Representatives. Feb. 8 ... . *Washington: Printed by Gales and Seaton.* 1836. 8vo, pp. 7. — Report of the Select Committee upon ... Slavery in the District of Columbia ... to the House of Representatives, May 18 ... . *Washington: Blair and Rives, Printers.* 1836. 8vo, pp. 16. — Speech ... in the House of Representatives, Feb. 21, 1837. On a proposition ... to establish a Navy Yard and Dry Dock, at Charleston ... . [n. p. n. d.] 8vo, pp. 8. — Speech ... on the Resolutions relating to the Hon. John Quincy Adams, ... in the House of Representatives, February 6 ... . *Washington: Printed by Gales & Seaton.* 1837. 8vo, pp. 12. H.

Pinckney (J. D.) Reminiscences of Catskill. Local Sketches, by the late James D. Pinckney, together with interesting Articles by Thurlow Weed, Edwin Croswell, S. Sherwood Day, and Joseph Hallock, Esqrs. *Catskill: J. B. Hall.* 1868. 8vo, pp. 79

Pinckney (N.) An Appeal to the Congress of the United States, concerning the Relative Rank of the Medical Officers & Pursers of the Navy. By Ninian Pinckney ... February, 1850. *Baltimore: Printed at George M'Gregor's* ... . 1850. 8vo, pp. 10.

Pinckney. "Life and Character of Admiral Collingwood." Lecture ... by Ninian Pinckney ... in the Naval Chapel at Annapolis ... October 30, 1858. *Annapolis: Thomas J. Wilson.* 1858. 8vo, pp. 23. 62907

Pinckney (T.) Memorial of Thomas Pinckney, with the answer of Mr. Hammond, etc. relative to the British Instructions of 8th June, 1793. Printed for the use of the members of the Senate. [*Washington.* 1794.] 8vo, pp. 32. N. 62908

[Pinckney (Thomas).] Reflections, occasioned by the Late Disturbances [by negroes] in Charleston. By Achates. *Charleston: Printed ... by A. E. Miller.* 1822. 8vo, pp. 30. H. 62909

Pindar (C. L.), *pseudon.?* Alleghania; or, Praises of American Heroes. By Christopher Laomedon Pindar. *Philadelphia: J. B. Lippincott & Co.* 1868. 16mo, pp. 148. C. 62910

Pindar (J.), *pseudon.* The Probationary Odes of Jonathan Pindar, Esq., a cousin of Peter's, and Candidate for the Post of Poet Laureate to the C.[ongress of the] U.[nited] S:[tates]. *Philadelphia: Printed for Benjamin Franklin Bache.* 1796. 12mo.

Originally published in Freneau's "Gazette," and attributed to him.

PINDAR (P.) Pindariana; or, Peter's Portfolio; with Extracts from Tragedy, Comedy, Opera, etc. By Peter Pindar, Esq. *Philadelphia.* 1794. 4to. 62912

PINDAR (P.) Letters from Peter Pindar relative to the Sunday Mail. *New York.* 1830. 18mo. 62913

PINDAR. No. 1. The Vagabond, or New Looking-Glass, being an everlasting Magazine of Acrostical Biography. By Peter Pindar. *New York.* 1823. 8vo. 62914

PINDAR (P., *Jr.*), *pseudon.* Parnassus in Philadelphia. A Satire, by Peter Pindar, jr. *Philadelphia: Privately Printed.* 1854. 12mo, pp. 58. 62915

PINDAR. Secession: or "Borrowed Plumes." In Three Acts. By "Peter Pindar, Jr." Second Volunteer Edition. *Aurora: J. Pendleton Snell.* 1861. 8vo, pp. 39. 62916

PINDAR PUFF (*Brevet-Major*), *pseudon.* *See* [Verplanck (Gulian C.)]

Pindari Olympia, Pythia, Nemea, Isthmia, graece et latine, cum commentari amplissimo opera E. Schmidii. *Wittebergae.* 1616. 4to, pp. 1250. 62917

A rare edition, at the end of which is appended: De America, oratiuncula in promotione xxxv. magistrorum anno 1602 habita.

PINDER (R.) Bowells of Compassion towards the scattered Seed, Or a Visitation to all, who hath been seeking the resting place, but hath not found it .... Written to the Scattered people in America ... by Richard Pinder. *London, Printed for M. W. in the 10th month* 1659. 4to. 62918

PINDER. The Captive (that hath long been in Captivity) Visited with the Day-spring from on High. Or the Prisoner (that hath sitten in the Prison-house of woful darkness) freed into the everlasting light and Covenant of God .... Given forth especially for the sake of the scattered people in America, by one who labours for and waits to see the Elect gathered from the four Quarters of the earth, known by the name of Richard Pinder. *London, Printed for Thomas Simmons* ... 1660. Sm. 8vo. 62919

Written in the Island of Bermuda.

PINDER. A Loving Invitation (to Repentance and Amendment of Life) unto all the Inhabitants of the Island Barbados. Before the Lords sore Judgements come upon them, which is

seen to be Nigh, and which they cannot escape, except Fruits meet for Repentance, and Amendment of Life be brought, with Something more particularly to the Heads and Owners of the Several Plantations. By a Friend to the whole Creation, called Richard Pinder. ... *London: Printed for Robert Wilson* ... 1660. 4to. 62920

Written at Barbados the 10th day of the 8th month, 1660.

PINDER. The Spirit of Error, Found and Discovered in the Accounted Pastors and Teachers of the Island Bermuda, in the West-Indies ... in answer to some Queries that were sent unto them by us called Quakers, their deceit unfolded for the people's sake of the Island, by a servant of truth called Richard Pinder. *London, Printed for Robert Wilson* ... 1660. 4to. 62921

PINDLE (B. T.) Miscellaneous Poems. Intended for the Amusement if not the Instruction of those who may read. By B. T. Pindle. *Baltimore.* 1857. 18mo, pp. 201. 62922

[PINE (George).] The Isle of Pines. 1668. *See* Vol. IX., No. 35255.

PINE (G. W.) Beyond the West; containing an account of two years Travel in that other half of our great Continent far beyond the old West, on the Plains, in the Rocky Mountains, and Picturesque Parks of Colorado. Also, Characteristic Features of New Mexico, Arizona, Wyoming, Montana, Idaho, Eastern and Western Oregon, Utah, Nevada, and the Sun set Land, California, the end of the West. ... By George W. Pine. *Utica: T. J. Griffiths.* 1870. 12mo, pp. 444. + Second Edition, revised and enlarged. [*Ibid.*] 1871. 12mo, pp. 483.

Contains a chapter on the Mormons.

PINE (J. W.) The Pilgrim's Hope; and other Poems. By James W. Pine. *Danbury, Conn.* 1867. 16mo, pp. 157, (5).

PINE. Shadows of the Evergreen; or, Poems for the Gay and Merry, and for the Lone and Desponding. By James Wallace Pine. *New York.* 1858. 12mo, pp. 59. 62925

First Annual Report of the Trustees of PINE GROVE CEMETERY .... *Lynn: Press of L. Josselyn.* 1850. 8vo, pp. 16. Continued. H. 62926

See also Vol. X., No. 42845.

The Pine Lands and Lumber Trade of Michigan ... By an Old Resident ... *Detroit: Printed by H. Barns.* 1856. 8vo, pp. 15.

PINEDA (——). Bibliotheca del ex-Coronel Pineda, o Coleccion de las Publicaciones de la imprenta en el Vineirato de Santafe i en las Republicas de 1774–1850, i de varios MSS. *Granada.* 1853. 8vo. 62928

PINEDA (E.) Descripcion Geográfica del Departamento de Chiapas y Soconusco, por Emeterio Pineda ... *Mexico: Imprenta de Ignacio Cumplido.* 1845. 4to. 62929

PINEDA (J. A. y.) Zurribanda logico-critico-nacional, que se sirve dar á Fr. Juan de San Francisco, Secretario y Defensor del R. P. Provincial del Carmen. *Mexico.* 1846. 4to, pp. 56.

Also: Vindicacion del Provincial de Carmelitas. ... *Mexico.* 1846. 4to.

PINEDA (José Laureano). Mensage pronunciado por el Director Supremo del Estado. *Granada.* 1853. 8vo. 62931

PINELO (A. de L.) Qvestion moral si el chocolate quebranta el ayuno eclesiastico. Tratase de otras bebidas j confecciones que se vsan en varias Provincias. Por Antonio de Leon Pinelo. *Madrid, viuda de Juan Gonçalez.* 1636. 4to, pp. (12), 122, (24).

PINELO. Relacion que en el Consejo de Indias ... [*Madrid.*] 1638. Folio. 62933

PINELO. Velos antiguos i modernos en los rostros de las mugeres sus conueniençias i daños. Ilvstracion de la Real Prematica de las Tapadas. *Madrid, Juan Sanchez.* 1641. 4to, engraved title, (29) and 137 leaves. 62934

For other works by this author *see* Leon Pinelo (A. de), Vol. X., Nos. 40050–58.

PINELO (D. de L.) *See* Leon Pinelo, Vol. X., Nos. 40069–70

PINERES (J. G. de). El Oidor. Drama histórico en cinco actos, escrito en verso, por Jerman G. de Pineres. *Bogotá.* 1865. 8vo, pp. 88. 62935

PIÑERES (T. G. de). Los abusos se radican si se toleran los errores; por Piñeres. *Habana: Imprenta de Palmer é bijo.* 1820. 4to. 62936

PIÑERES. Complemento de pruebas contra la conducta pública del Dr. D. Tomás Romay, por el Dr. D. Tomás Gutierrez de Piñerez. *Habana,* 1821, *imprenta de Palmer é bijo.* 4to. 62937

Also: Extraordinaria ocurrencia .... *Habana: Imprenta de Palmer é bijo.* 1820. 4to. —La Junta provincial de Censura no desempeña las funciones con la justicia é imparcialidad que debe .... *Habana: Imprenta de Palmer é bijo.* 1818. 4to, pp. 12.—Justa

respuesta á D. Manuel García Lavin .... *Habana: Imprenta de Palmer.* 1821. 4to.—Mi Opinion sobre los Jueces de letras por el Dr. D. Tomás Gutierrez de Piñeres. *Habana: Imprenta de Palmer é bijo.* 1851. 4to.—Nadie se sobresalte por lo que dije contra el impreso "Nadie se asuste" del Sr. D. José Arango. ... [*Habana.*] 1821. 4to.—Satisfaccion á la vindicacion y manifiesto dado por la Diputacion de esta provincia .... *Habana: Imprenta de Palmer é bijo.* 1820. 4to.—Sobre elecciones parroquiales .... *Habana: Imprenta de Palmer é bijo.* 1821. 4to.—Soliloquio entre el Dr. Piñeres y Justo Festivo (Rafael Quesada) en que le aconseja el respeto á las autoridades. *Habana: Imprenta del Gobierno.* 1812. 4to. *See also* [Suarez (D. Leonardo S.)]

PIÑERES (V. G.) Lirico Heroico a la Batalla de Ayacucho. Canto, por V*** G*** Piñeres. *Cartagena: Tipog. Tormentaria por J. M. Angúlo. Año de* 1833. 12mo, pp. 9, (1). H.

PIÑERO (G.) Santa Catharina de Sena, Virgen seraphica: de la Tercera Orden Dominica: predicada en ... la Ciudad de Guaxaca: en el dia 30 ... mes de Abril de 97. Por el R. P. M. Fr. Gonzalo Piñero. *En la Puebla.* [1697.] 4to, 22 leaves.

See also Gonzalo Pinero, Vol. VII., No. 27825.

PINET (Antoine du). Plantz, Povrtraitz, et Descriptions de plvsievrs Villes et Forteresses, tant de L'Evrope, Asie & Afrique, que des Indes & Terres-Neuves: ... *A Lyon, par Jan D'Ogerolles.* MDLXIIII. Folio. 40 Plates. 62940

This work treats critically of cosmography, and gives a list of atlases and maps. The map of the world is remarkable for the correctness with which South America is delineated.

Piney Woods Tavern. *See* [Hammitt (S. A.)], VIII. 30082.

PIÑEYRO (E.) Biografia del General San Martin. Por Enrique Piñeyro. Pronunciada ... en el Club Cubano de Nueva York, el 23 de Febrero de 1870. ... *Nueva York: Imprenta de "La Revolucion."* 1870. 12mo, pp. (2), 35. A. 62941

PIÑEYRO. Morales Lemus y la Revolucion de Cuba Estudio Historico Por Enrique Piñeyro ... *Nueva York M. M. Zarzamendi, Impresor.* 1871. 12mo, pp. 140. Facsimile. A. 62942

PIÑEYRO (F. Ayuso). Vindicacion Legal y Disertacion Eclesiastica, Canonica, Historica, y Politica. *Trujillo.* 1830. 4to.

PIÑEYRO Y ULLOA (M.) Defensa Juridica, que se propone por el derecho, que assiste á Doña J. A. de Rossal, muger legitima de D. Martin Piñeyro y Ulloa, Thesorero de la Real Caxa de Pachuca: y que primero lo fue del Capitan D. Roque Alfonso de Valverde. [*Mexico.* n. d.] Folio. 62944

PINGEL (Christian). Om Capitain-Lieutenant og Ridder W. A. Graah's Undersögelsesreize til Ostkysten af Grönland i Aarene 1828–31. *Kjöbenhavn.* 1833. 8vo. 62945

PINGERON (*M.*) Description de l'Isle de la Jamaïque et des différents objets remarquables qui s'y trouvent par M. Pingeron, capitaine d'artillerie. *Avignon.* 1782. 8vo, pp. 58. 62946

Pingortitsinermik. [*Druck von J. F. Steinkopf in Stuttgart.*] 1848. 16mo, pp. (2), 8. 62947

A religious tract in the Eskimo language.

PINGRÉ (*M.*) Mémoire sur le Choix et l'État des Lieux Où le passage de Vénus du 3. Juin 1769 pourra être observé avec le plus d'avantage; et principalement sur la Position Géographique des Isles de la Mer du Sud. Par M. Pingré .... *A Paris, Chez P. G. Cavelier* ... M.DCC.LXVII. 4to, pp. (2), 91, (1). Map.

Also: Mémoire sur la position des Isles de la Mer du Sud. ... *Paris.* 1810. 4to. Map.—Mémoires sur les découvertes faites dans la Mer du Sud avant Bougainville et Cook. ... *Paris.* 1778. 4to.

PINHEIRO (Joaquim Caetano Fernandes). Carmes religiosos, dedicados ao ... D. Manuel do Monte Rodrigues de Araujo, bispo do Rio de Janeiro. ... *Rio de Janeiro: Typ. de Silva Lima.* 1850. 8vo, pp. xii, 88. 62949

PINHEIRO. Curso Elementar de Litteratura Nacional. ... *Rio de Janeiro.* 1862. 8vo. 62950

Includes a sketch of Brazilian literature.

PINHEIRO. Melodias campestres, dedicadas á ... D. Gabriela Celestina de Torres Quintilla. ... *Rio de Janeiro: Typ. Brasiliense de Francisco Manuel Ferreira.* 1851. 8vo, pp. 61. 62951

PINHEIRO (J. F. F.) Annaes da Capitania de S. Pedro, pelo Desembargador José Feliciano Fernandes Pinheiro. *Rio de Janeiro: Impressão regia.* 1819. Vol. II. *Lisboa: Imprensa nacional.* 1822. 2 vols., 4to, pp. 162, (2), Map; 126, (2). Map and 4 Tables. 62952

PINHEIRO. Annaes da Provincia de S. Pedro. ... Segunda Edição correcta e augmentada. *Paris: Typ. de Casimir.* 1839. 8vo, pp. xii, 468. 62953

PINHEIRO. Cultura Americana, que contém uma relação dos terrenos, clima, producção e agricultura das colonias britannicas no norte da America, e nas Indias Occidentaes; traduzida do

inglez por José Feliciano Fernandes Pinheiro, e Antonio Carlos Ribeiro de Andrade. *Lisboa.* 1799. 2 vols., 4to. 62954

PINHEIRO. Historia nova e completa da America, colligida de diversos auctores ... Por José Feliciano Fernandes Pinheiro. *Lisboa.* 1800. 4to. 62955

PINILLOS (C. M. de). Meritos y servicios con que el Sr. D. Claudio Martinez de Pinillos ha podido progresar de Oficial Real Tesorero á Intendente Superintendente ... [n. p.] 1822. Folio, 1 leaf. 62956

PINKERTON (J.) A General Collection of the best and most interesting Voyages and Travels in all parts of the World; many of which are now first translated into English. Digested on a new plan. By John Pinkerton .... *London: Longman, Hurst, Rees, and Orme ... and Cadell and Davies.* 1808–1814. 17 vols., 4to. A., BA., C. 62957

Collation: Vol. I. pp. xiv, (2), 851, 10 Plates; II. pp. (6), 833, 11 Plates; III. pp. (4), 919, 15 Plates; IV. pp. (4), 722, 18 Plates; V. pp. (4), 992, 14 Plates; VI. pp. (4), 913, 5 Plates; VII. pp. (4), 821, 13 Plates; VIII. pp. (4), 776, 17 Plates; IX. pp. (4), 828, 9 Plates; X. pp. (4), 770, 8 Plates; XI. pp. (4), 952, 26 Plates; XII. pp. (4), 678, 11 Plates; XIII. pp. (4), 876, 12 Plates; XIV. pp. (4), 881, 14 Plates; XV. pp. (4), 839, 16 Plates; XVI. pp. (4), 917, 2 Plates; XVII. pp. (4), xxxix, 255, Index, 472. The arrangement of the plates is not the same in all copies.

A collection of great merit and importance. Several northern voyages are included in the first volume, and vols. XI. to XIV., which relate mostly to America, contain: F. Colombo's Life of Columbus, Discoveries by the English from the reign of Henry VIII. to that of Queen Elizabeth, Frobisher's three Voyages, 1576-78, Discovery of and Voyages to Virginia, Carthier's Discovery of New France, 1534, John Smith's History of Virginia, New England and the Summer Isles, Lahontan's Travels, Kalm's Travels, Burnaby's Travels, Thierry de Menonville's Travels, Betagh's Peru, Ovalle's Chile, La Condamine's Travels, Bouguer's Voyage to Peru, Ulloa's Voyage, and Nieuhoff's Brazil. Vol. XVII. contains a retrospect of the origin and progress of discovery by sea and land, and an extensive Catalogue of Books of Voyages and Travels. A list of the contents of all the volumes will be found in the catalogue of the Library of Congress, p. 887, and in the catalogue of the Public Library of Boston. The American reprint, *Philadelphia,* 1810–12, 6 vols., 4to, was never completed.

PINKERTON. A General Collection of the Best and Most Interesting Voyages and Travels in Various Parts of America; Many of which are now first Translated into English. Digested on a New Plan. By John Pinkerton .... *London: Longman, Hurst, Rees, Orme and Brown.* 1819. 4 vols., 4to, pp. (4), 952; (4), 678; (4), 876; (4), 881. 51 Plates. N. 62958

This set consists of vols. XI. to XIV. with new title-pages only.

PINKERTON. Modern Geography. A Description of the Empires, Kingdoms, States, and Colonies ... in all parts of the

World; Including the most recent discoveries, and political alterations. ... By John Pinkerton. ... *London: T. Cadell, Jun. and W. Davies* ... 1802. 2 vols., 4to, pp. cvii, (1), 666; viii, 835, (1). 45 Maps. BA. + The Article America corrected and ... enlarged by Dr. Barton of Philadelphia. *Philadelphia: John Conrad & Co.* 1804. 2 vols., 8vo, pp. clxv, 520; 698. C. + A New Edition, greatly enlarged. *London: T. Cadell and W. Davies.* 1807. 3 vols., 4to, pp. cxxxi, (1), 739; (6), lii, 820; (6), 1005. 50 Maps. BA. + A new edition, with additions and corrections to ... 1817. *London: T. Cadell and W. Davies* .... 1817. 2 vols., 4to, pp. (2), vii, v–xxxi, lxxxiii, 778, 773–775, (1); vii, 850. 52 Maps. A. 62959

Also: Modern Geography. ... Abridged. ... Second Edition. ... *London.* 1806. 8vo, pp. 676.—Abrégé de la Géographie Moderne ... Seconde Édition ... *Paris: Dentu.* M.DCCC.VI. 2 vols., 8vo, pp. xxx, 360; (2), 361–924. Maps. A.

PINKERTON ACADEMY, *Derry, N. H.* Commemorative Services at the Semi-Centennial Anniversary ... September 12, 1866. *Concord: Printed by McFarland & Jenks.* 1866. 8vo, pp. 108.

Fifty-Second Annual Catalogue of Pinkerton Academy, Derry, N. H., for ... 1867. *Concord.* 1867. 8vo. 62961

PINKHAM (R. P.) Memoirs of Simeon J. Milliken, Esq. of Mount Desert, Maine .... By Rebekah P. Pinkham. *Boston: J. Loring.* 1836. 16mo, pp. 108. C. 62962

PINKHAM. A Narrative of the Life of Miss Lucy Cole, of Sedgwick, Maine. By Rebekah P. Pinkham. *Boston: J. Loring.* 1830. 18mo, pp. 108. C. 62963

PINKHAM (T. J.) Farming As It Is! An Original Treatise on Agriculture, with the Rights and Duties of Farmers. By T. J. Pinkham. ... *Boston: Bradley, Dayton & Company.* 1860. 8vo, pp. 393. 62964

PINKNEY (E. C.) Poems, by Edward C. Pinkney. *Baltimore: Joseph Robinson.* 1825. 18mo, pp. 76. + [*Ibid.*] 1838. 18mo, pp. 72. 62965

Also reprinted in the series of the Mirror Library entitled "The Rococo" No. 2, with an introduction by N. P. Willis, *New York,* 1844. Rl. 8vo.

[PINKNEY.] Rodolph. *Baltimore.* 1823. 8vo. 62966

PINKNEY (N.) An Appeal to ... Congress ... concerning the Relative Rank of the Medical Officers & Pursers of the Navy.

By Ninian Pinkney ... February, 1850. *Baltimore: Printed at George M'Gregor's* .... 1850. 8vo, pp. 10. H. 62967

PINKNEY. Lecture delivered by Ninian Pinkney, in the Naval Chapel, at Annapolis, ... October 30, 1858. *Annapolis: Thomas J. Wilson.* 1858. 8vo, pp. 23. 62968

On the life and character of Admiral Collingwood.

[PINKNEY (William).] Memorial of the Merchants of Baltimore, on the Violation of our Neutral Rights. [*Washington.* 1806.] 8vo. N. 62969

Relates to the rule of the French and English war of 1756. *See also* our Vol. XII., No. 48065, note.

PINKNEY. Speech of William Pinkney, Esq., in the House of Delegates of Maryland, at their session in November, 1789. *Philadelphia: J. Crukshank.* 1790. 8vo, pp. 22. J.C.B., M.

Against slavery and the slave-trade.

PINKNEY (W.) The Life of William Pinkney, By his Nephew, the Rev. William Pinkney, D.D. ... *New-York: D. Appleton and Company.* MDCCCLIII. 8vo, pp. 407. Portrait. A. + [*Ibid.*] 1859. 62971

See Wheaton (Henry).

PINKNEY. Memoir of John H. Alexander, LL.D. By William Pinkney, D.D. ... Read before the Maryland Historical Society, ... May 2, 1867. [*Baltimore: John Murphy.* 1867.] 8vo, pp. 31, (1). 62972

Contains a list of Dr. Alexander's works published and in manuscript. Also: An Address ... before the Alumni ... of St. John's College. ... *Annapolis.* 1852. 8vo. — ... A Sermon ... at Bladensburg, Maryland, on Thanksgiving-Day, ... 28 Nov., 1856. ... *Baltimore: D. Bruner.* 1851. 8vo, pp. 13.

PINNEO (B.) A Sermon, preached April 17, 1811, at the Dedication of the New Meeting House in North Milford. By Bezeleel Pinneo, Pastor of the First Church of Christ in Milford. *Sidney's Press, New Haven.* 1811. 8vo, pp. 23. S. 62973

[PINNEO (O.) *and* (E. H.)] Memoir of Addison Pinneo, who died in Hanover, N. H., Sept. 17, 1831 .... Second Edition. *Boston: Perkins & Marvin.* 1832. 18mo, pp. 79. Plate. BA. + Third Edition. *Boston.* 1848. 18mo, pp. 79. Plate.

PINNEY (G.) Essay on the Culture and Management of Forest Trees and Native Evergreens. By Rev. George Pinney *Galena.* 1869. 8vo. 62975

Pinney (N.) The Principles of Education as Applied in the Mobile Institute. By Norman Pinney. *Mobile.* 1836. 8vo, pp. 56. 62976

Pinniger (D.) Trial of Col. David Pinniger, Lieut. Col. Wm. P. Maxwell, Maj. Nathan Whiting, and Captain Allen Tillinghast, Officers of the Kentish Guards, before a General Court Martial, ... at Providence, April 27, 1808, for Disobedience of Orders and Neglect of Duty. *Warren: Printed by Nathaniel & John F. Phillips.* 1808. 12mo, pp. 41, (4). s. 62977

Pinnock [William]. Pinnock's Catechisms. A Catechism of the History of America: in Two Parts. ... Third Edition. *London: G. and W. B. Whittaker.* 1823. 2 vols., 12mo, pp. 72; (2), 72. Portrait. + Part ii. Fourth Edition. *[Ibid.]* 1827. 24mo, pp. 72. B. 62978

Also: Panorama of the Old World and the New. Comprising a View of the Present State of the Nations of the World ... . Enlarged, revised and embellished. ... *Philadelphia.* 18—. 8vo.

Pino (P. B.) Exposicion sucinta y sencilla de la provincia del Nuevo Mexico: hecha por su diputado en Córtes. Por Pedro Baptista Pino. *Cádiz: Imprenta del Estado-Mayor-General.* 1812. 4to, pp. 48, (4). J.C.B. 62979

Pino. Noticias Historicas y Estadisticas de la antigua provincia del Nuevo-Mexico, presentadas por su diputada en cortes D. Pedro Bautista Pino, en Cadiz el Año de 1812. Adicionadas por el Lic. D. Antonio Barreiro en 1839; y ultimamente anotadas por el Lic. Don José Augustin de Escudero, para la comi sion de estadistica militar de la Republica Mexicana. *México: Imprenta de Lara.* 1849. 8vo, pp. iv, 98, (4). Map. 62980

Pino y Penuela (R.) Topografia Medica de la Isla de Cuba, por el Dr. D. Ramon Pino y Penuela. *Habana.* 1855. 8vo, pp. 324. 62981

Pinsger (J.) Das ehrwürdige Leben und vil [*sic*] werther Tod der ehrwürdigen Schwester Rosa de Santa-Maria, von Lima gebürtig, durch Johannem Pinsger. *Insprugg: Michael Wagner.* 1667. 4to. 62982

With an appendix of 60 pages. Title from Ternaux, No. 851. *See* our Vol. viii., No. 30252.

[Pintard (John Marsden).] Letters to Timothy Pickering,

Secretary of State, and the President of the U. S. 15th November, 1799. [*New York.* 1800.] 8vo, pp. 35. N. 62983

Pintard's defence of his conduct as United States Consul at Madeira.

[Pinto (Antonio Cerqueira).] Relação dos festivos applausos com que na cidade do Porto se congratularam os felizes desposorios do Ser.mo Sr. D. Joseph Principe do Brazil, e a Sr.a D. Maria Anna Victoria, Infanta de Castilla ... *Lisboa, Off. da Musica.* 1728. 4to, pp. 14. 62984

Pinto (A. de S.) Um Barbeiro politico. Scena comica original de A. de Souza Pinto. *San Luiz.* 1864. 12mo, pp. 14.

Pinto (A. P.) Apontomentos para o direito Internacional ou Collecção completa dos Tratados celebrados pelo Brasil com differentes Nações Estrangeiras ... por Antonio Pereira Pinto ... *Rio de Janeiro: F. L. Pinto & Ca.* 1864. 8vo, pp. xiii, 504, vi, (1). 62986

Pinto (B. J. de O.) Poesias de Basilio José de Oliveira Pinto. *Rio de Janeiro.* 1866. 4to, pp. 56. 62987

[Pinto (Isaac).] Lettre de Mr. * * * * * a Mr. S. B. Docteur en Médicine à Kingston, dans la Jamaique, au sujet des Troubles qui agitent actuellement toute l'Amérique Septentrionale. *A La Haye: Pierre-Frederic Gosse.* MDCCLXXVI. 8vo, pp. 29. N. 62988

Addressed to Mr. S. Barretts.

Pinto. Seconde Lettre de M. de Pinto a l'occasion des troubles des Colonies, contenant des Réflexions politiques sur les suites de ces troubles, et sur l'état actuel de l'Angleterre. *A La Haye: Pierre-Frederic Gosse.* MDCCLXXVI. 8vo, pp. 90, (2). N.

This elicited "Nouvelles Observations," our No. 56095, Vol. xiii.

Pinto. Letters on the American Troubles; translated from the French of M. de Pinto. *London: John Boosey & J. Forbes.* 1776. 8vo, pp. (4), 89. BA., J C.B. 62990

The writer argues that the war against the American colonies was a just one, but is persuaded that America will in the end be free. *See* "Monthly Review," lv. 397. *See* "Observations," Vol. xiii., No. 56470.

Pinto. Réponse de Mr. J. de Pinto, aux Observations d'un homme impartial, Sur sa Lettre à Mr. S. B., Docteur en Médicine à Kingston dans la Jamaique, au sujet des Troubles qui agitent actuellement toute l'Amérique Septentrionale. *A La Haye: Chez Pierre-Frederic Gosse.* MDCCLXXVI. 8vo, pp. 60.

"The author was a Portuguese Jew, living in Holland, who undertook the defense of the measures of the British government for the subjection of the colonies. His two letters are little more than an abstract of Sir John Dalrymple's celebrated pamphlet, 'The Rights of Great Britain asserted,' etc., which he lauds to the skies."—Rich, i. 246.

Pinto (I.) Prayers | for | Shabbath, Rosh-Hashanah, and Kippur, | or | The Sabbath, the Beginning of the Year, | and | The Day of Atonements; | With | The Amidah and Musaph of the Moadim, | or | Solemn Seasons. | According to the Order of the Spanish and Portuguese Jews. | TRANSLATED by *ISAAC PINTO.* | *And for him printed by John Holt, in New-York.* | A.M. 5526. | [1765–6.] Sm. 4to, pp. iv, 190, (1). 62992

In some copies the title-page reads in the fifth line "Begining" instead of "Beginning," and has the thirteenth line printed in different type: "Translated by ISAAC PINTO."

Pinto (J. J.) Copia de la certificacion dada á la ciudad de Lima, de los privilegios que goza esta nobilisima ciudad de Mexico. ... *Mexico.* 1803. 4to, pp. 22. 62993

[Pinto de Sousa (José Carlos).] Bibliotheca Historica de Portugal e seus Dominios Ultramarinos: Na qual se contém varias Historias daquelle, e destes ms. e impressas em prosa, e em verso, só, e juntas com as de outros Estados, escritas por Authores Portuguezes, e Estrangeiros; ... Nova Ediçaõ, correcta, e amplamente augmentada ... . *Lisboa, na Typographia do Arco do Cego.* MDCCCI Sm. 4to, pp. (26), xiii, 408, 100. B. 62994

Includes a large number of Brazilian authors.

Pinto y Quesada (Alphonso). Relacion de las Exequias del Illmo. Sor. D. D. Diego Antonio de Parada, Arzobispo de Lima. Impresa con la Oracion funebre a expensas de los Dr. D. Joseph de Herrera, y D. Antonio Cubero Diaz, curas rectores de la iglesia cathedral. [*Lima:*] *Ano de* 1781. *En los Niños Húerfanos.* 4to, pp. (64), 74, (12). Portrait, Table and Plan. J.C.B. 62995

Pinzon (C.) Catecismo republicano para instruccion popular, por Cerbeleon Pinzon. Segunda edicion. *Bogotá.* 1865. 18mo, pp. 56. 62996

Also: Algunas cuestiones de actualidad. ... *Bogotá.* 1864. 18mo, pp. 140.

Pinzon (M.) Sermon que en los cultos que la ilustre Archicofradia de Ciudadanos de la Santa Veracruz de esta Capital tributa a la Santa Cruz, dijo el R. P. Fr. Manuel Pinzon, el 5 de Mayo de 1837. *Mégico.* 1837. 8vo, pp. 16. 62997

Piomingo, *pseudon.* *See* [Robinson (John)].

The Pioneer, or California Monthly Magazine; Edited by F. C. Ewer. ... *San Francisco.* 1854–55. 4 vols., 8vo. 62998

The first California magazine.

Pioneer Heroes of the New World, comprising the Lives of the most Famous Discoverers, Explorers, and Conquerors of North and South America; an Account of the Foundation of Colonies ... etc. *Boston: M. F. Howe & Co.* 1855. 8vo.

Pioneer Life in the West; comprising the Adventures of Boone, Kenton, Brady, Clark, the Whetzels, and others, in their Fierce Encounters with the Indians. Illustrated. *Philadelphia: G. G. Evans.* 1858. 12mo, pp. 332. + [*Ibid.*] 1860. 63000

Report of the Pioneer Mills Mine, Cabarrus County, North-Carolina. *Albany.* 1856. 8vo. s. 63001

Pioneer Mothers of the West; or, Daring and Heroic Deeds of American Women. Comprising Thrilling Examples of Courage, Fortitude, Devotedness, and Self-Sacrifice. Illustrated. *Boston.* 1869. 12mo, pp. 348. 63002

See also Frost (John), Vol. vii., No. 26030.

The Pioneers. *See* [Cooper (J. F.)], Vol. iv., No. 16502.

Pious Remains of a Young Gentleman lately deceased. *Boston: R. Draper, Jr.* 1764. 8vo, pp. 12. s. 63003

Piper (A. G.) The Loyalist; or, The Channel Scourge. *New York: Beadle & Co.* 1864. 16mo. 63004

Piper (J.) The Echo; or, the Battle of the Shells, a Satirical Parody in Rhyme of the celebrated Letters of Messrs. Guthrie, Bronson & O'Connor. With the Original Letters. By John Piper. [n. p.:] *January,* 1854. 8vo, pp. 44. 63005

Piper (J. J.) Facts and Figures concerning the Hoosac Tunnel. By John J. Piper. *Fitchburg: John J. Piper, Printer.* 1866. 8vo, pp. 54. B. 63006

Piper (R. U.) The Trees of America. By R. U. Piper, ... [*Boston.* 1855–58.] 4to, pp. (3), 64. 16 Plates. BA. 63007

Four numbers only were published.

Piper (S.) Genealogy of the Family of Solomon Piper, of Dublin, N. H. *Boston: Dutton and Wentworth, Printers.* 1849. 8vo, pp. 20. A. 63008

Pipon (J.) A Discourse ... at Newport, April 30, 1811, at the Installation of Newport Royal Arch Chapter ... . By John Pipon ... . *Newport: Rousmaniere & Barber.* 1811. 8vo, pp. 12.

Piquero (Ignacio). Apuntes para la corografia y la estadistica del estado de Michoacan ... . *Mexico: Imprenta de Vicente Garcia Torres.* 1850. 8vo. Map. + *Tampico.* 1850. 8vo, pp. 319. Map. 63010

Piquero. Breve Instruccion sobre las Contribuciones directas establecidas en la nacion desde el año de 1836. Por Ygnacio Piquero. *Mexico.* 1845. 4to. c. 63011

[Piquet (Fr.)] Ionteri8eienstag8a ne tsiatag ori8atogenton ogonha. *Parisiis. Ononthioke Tehoristoraragon D. P. Lefebvre.* 1826. 12mo, pp. 72. 63012

A catechism in the Iroquois language.

Piratas de la America. *See* [Exquemelin (J.)], vi. 23471–4.

The Pirate Doctor; or, the Extraordinary Career of a New York Physician. By a Naval Officer. *New York: Garrett & Co.* [*about* 1850.] 8vo, pp. 126. c. 63013

The Pirate's Almanac. *Philadelphia: Turner & Fisher.* 1844. 12mo. 63014

The Pirates Own Book, or Authentic Narratives of the Lives ... of the most celebrated Sea Robbers. With Historical Sketches of the Joafsamee, Spanish, Ladrone, West India, ... and Algerine Pirates. *Portland: Sanborn & Carter.* 1837. 12mo. + *Boston.* 1837. 12mo. 63015

Piratical Barbarity. *See* [Parker (G. G.)], Vol. xiv. 58670.

Pirckeymer (B.) Germa- | niae ex variis scri | ptoribus perbreuis explicatio. | Authore Bilibaldo Pirckeymero Con | siliario Cæsareo. | *Norembergæ apud Io. Petreium,* | *Anno* M. D. XXX. | Sm. 8vo, 35 leaves. A. 63016

This rare little work, printed throughout in italic type, closes with an account of Hispaniola and the continent of America, which is here called *Sancta Martha.* Mexico and Temistitan are mentioned, "à qua etiam non longe remota est insula Iucatan cum alijs nuper repertis." Pirckeymer, better known as Wilibald Pirkheimer, also translated and edited Ptolemy's geography, 1525, 1535, 1540, and 1541.

Pirckeymer. Ger- | maniae ex vari- | is scriptoribus perbreuis | explicatio. | Authore Bilibaldo Pirckeymero | Consiliario Cæsareo. | *Augustæ apud Hainricum Stai-* | *ner.* *Anno* M. D. XXX. | Sm. 8vo, 35 leaves. J.C.B. 63017

Pirckeymer. Germaniae ex variis scriptoribus perbreuis explicatio. Authore Bilibaldo Pirckeymero ... . Editio Secunda, ab ipso recognita. *Norimbergæ apud Jo. Petreium, Anno* M. D. XXXII. Sm. 8vo, 36 leaves. 63018

Pirckeymer. Germaniæ ex variis Scriptoribus perbreuis explicatio: Authore Bilibaldo Pirckeymero. Germaniæ Inferioris Historiæ et Loca aliquot declarata: authore Gerardo Noviomago. Genealogia Ducum Burgundiæ, Brabantiæ, Flandriæ, Hollandiæ, etc. ab Hectore Trojano ad Carolum v. usque: authore Edmondo Dintero. *Francofurti.* 1532. Sm. 8vo.

A reprint of the preceding edition, with two additional treatises. Other editions, *Antwerp,* 1585, 8vo, and *Hanover,* 1694, 12mo.

Piron [Alexis]. Fernan Cortez, Comédie. ... *Paris.* 1744. 8vo. 63020

Piron. Fernando Cortés: Tragédie. Repésentée ... Janvier 1744. Par M. Piron. *Paris.* 1757. 16mo, pp. 103. s. 63021

A Spanish translation was published, *Madrid,* 1776, 8vo.

Pirscher (*Dr.*) Discovery of America, Conquest of Mexico, and Conquest of Peru, in French; from the best sources: with a Translation of such Passages as may offer the slightest difficulty. ... By Dr. Pirscher. *London.* 1852. 12mo, pp. 46. 63022

Pisani (F.) Lettres sur les États-Unis d'Amérique Par le Lieutenant-Colonel Ferri Pisani ... *Paris: L. Hachette et Cie* 1862. 16mo, pp. (4), 455. A., C. 63023

The Piscataqua Evangelical Magazine. ... *Portsmouth.* 1805–*Amherst.* 1807. 3 vols., 8vo. 63024

Constitution of the Piscataqua Missionary Society: ... with an Address ... *Portsmouth.* 1804. 8vo, pp. 8. N., W.

Pise (C. C.) History of the Church ... By Charles Constantine Pise ... *Baltimore.* 1827–30. 5 vols., 8vo. c. 63026

Chapter 8 contains a short account of Columbus and the missionaries who accompanied him in 1492.

Pise. Oration in honor of the late Charles Carroll of Carrollton, delivered before the Philodemic Society of Georgetown College. By Charles Constantine Pise ... . *Georgetown, D. C.: Printed by Joshua N. Rind.* 1832. 8vo, pp. 24. B. 63027

Also: Zenosius; or the Pilgrim-Convert. ... *New York: E. Dunigan.* 1845. 18mo, pp. 279. Plate.

[Piso (G.) *and* Marcgraf de Liebstad (G.)] Historia Natvralis | Brasiliae, | Auspicio et Beneficio | Illvstriss. I. Mavritii Com. Nassav. | illivs Provinciæ et Maris svmmi Præfecti Adornata: | In qua | Non tantum Plantæ et Animalia, sed et In- | digenarum morbi, ingenia et mores describuntur et | Iconibus supra quingentas illustrantur. | *Lvgdvn. Batavorum,* | *Apud Franciscum Hackium,* | *et* | *Amstelodami,* | *Apud Lud. Elzevirium.* 1648. | [Printed title:] Guilielmi Pisonis, M.D. | Lugduno-Batavi, | De | Medicina Brasiliensi | Libri Qvatvor: | i. De Aëre, Aquis, & Locis. | ii. De Morbis Endemiis. | iii. De Venenatis & Antidotis. | iv. De Facultatibus Simplicium. | Et | GeorgI MarcgravI de Liebstad, | Misnici Germani, | Historiæ | Rervm Natvralivm | Brasiliæ, | Libri Octo: | Quorum | Tres priores agunt de Plantis. | Quartus de Piscibus. | Quintus de Avibus. | Sextus de Quadrupedibus & Serpentibus. | Septimus de Insectis. | Octavus de ipsa Regione, & illius Incolis. | Cvm | Appendice de Tapuyis, et Chilensibvs. | Ioannes De Laet, | Antwerpianus, | In ordinem digessit & Annotationes addidit, & varia ab Auctore | Omissa supplevit & illustravit. | Folio, pp. (12), 122, (2), Georgi Marcgravi de Liebstad, (8), 293, (7). A., B., C. 63028

Illustrated with numerous woodcuts. There are copies on large paper. Piso's work fills the first 122 pages. Pages 260–290 of the second part comprise an account of the inhabitants of Brazil; De lingua Brasiliensium, è Grammatica P. Josephi de Anchieta, with a Brazilian and Latin vocabulary, by Emanuel de Moraes; De Tapuyarum moribus & consuetudinibus, è Relatione Iacobi Rabbi; De Chilensium lingua, & vocabularium dictionum Chilensium, etc.

Piso. Gulielmi Pisonis | Medici Amstelædamensis | de | Indiæ Utriusque | re Naturali et Medica | Libri Qvatvordecim, | Quorum contenta pagina sequens | exhibet. | *Amstelædami,* | *Apud Ludovicum et Danielem* | *Elzevirios.* | *A°.* clɔ Iɔ c LVIII. | [Printed title:] ... | Gvlielmi Pisonis, | Medici Amstelædamensis, | i. De Aëribus, Aquis, & Locis. | ii. De Natura & cura Morborum, Occidentali Indiæ, imprimis | Brasiliæ, familiarium. | iii. De Animalibus, aquatilibus, volatilibus, & terrestibus, edulibus. | iv. De Arboribus, fructibus, & herbis medicis, atque alimentariis, | nascentibus in Brasilia & regionibus vicinis. | v. De Noxiis & venenatis, eorumque Antidotis. Quibus insertæ sunt | Animalium quorundam vivæ sectiones; Tum & aliquot Me- | tamorphoses Insectorum. | vi. Mantissa aromatica &c. Posita post Bontii tractatus. | Georgii Margravii De Liebstadt. | i. Tractatus Topographicus & Meteorologicus Brasiliæ, cum Ob- | servatione Eclipsis Solaris. | ii. Commentarius de Brasiliensium & Chilensium indole ac lingua &c. | Iacobi Bontii, | Bataviæ in majore Java novæ Medici ordinarii, | i.

De Conservanda valetudine. | ii. Methodus medendi. | iii. Observationes in cadaveribus. | iv. Notæ in Garciam ab Orta. v. Historia Animalium. vi. Historia Plantarum. | Quibus sparsim inseruit G. Piso Annotatio- | nes & Additiones quà icones atque res ne- | cessarias. | ... | Folio, pp. (24), 327, (5), Georgii Marcgravii, 39, Jacobi Bontii, 160, Mantissa aromatica, 161–226, (2).

Owing to the fact that a number of the woodcuts in this work are reproduced from the former this is sometimes said to be a second edition. It is in fact a different work, as a comparison of the contents will prove.

Piso. Historia medica Brasiliae. Novam editionem curavit et praefatus est Josephus de Vering. *Vindobonae.* 1817. 8vo.

Pison y Vargas (Juan). La Elmira Tragedia en Cinco Actos, con la Segunda Parte de los Abates Locos, y sú Loa. ... *Mexico.* 1788. 4to. 63031

Pistorius (T.) Korte en Zakelyke Beschryvinge van de Colonie van Zuriname. Waar in te vinden is een omstandig Berigt van de gelegenheid deezer Volkplantinge; derzelver Rivieren, Kreeken, Forten, Bergen, Plantagien, Water-Werken en Houtzageryen; opgemaakt volgens die nieuwste Land-Kaarten. Mitsgaders een koort Verhaal van deszelfs Inwoonderen, inzonderheit de Leevensmanier der Slaven, hunne Huishoudinge, Godsdienst, Huwelyken; zeldzaame gewoonte by het opvoeden hunner Kinderen, en de wonderbaare begravinge van haare Dooden. Als mede eene Beschryvinge van de Vrugt- en andere Boomen; Aard-gewassen, Wilde en Tamme Land- en Water-Dieren; Boom-, Land- en Water-Vogelen, Visschen, Slangen, Venynige en ander Ongedierten. Benevens een omstandig Berigt van de Zuiker-Riet, Zuiker- en Koffy-Plantagien, Moolens, Kookhuizen en meer andere weetenswaardige zaaken, ook eenige Instructien, zeer dienstig voor alle die eenig Bewind over de Plantagien is aanvertrouwt. Waar agter gevoegt is, echt, omstandig en naauwkeurig Verhaal van de gepleegde Moord aan zyne Excell. den Heer van Sommelsdyk, Gouverneur en het doodelyk kwetzen van de Heer L. Verboom, Commandeur van de Colonie van Zuriname. Meestendeel uit eigene langduurige ondervindinge opgemaakt door de Heer Thomas Pistorius, Lit van de Edele Achtbaare Raad van Policie en Crimineele Justitie op de Colonie van Zuriname. Met Plaaten. *Te Amsterdam, By Theodorus Crajenschot, boekverkooper.* MDCCLXIII. Sm. 4to, pp. (10), 160. 4 Plates. C., H. 63032

Pitcher (N.) Pitchero Threnodia, or an Elegiack Poem,

sacred to the memory of the Rev. Nathaniel Pitcher, Pastor of the North Church in Scituate ... . *Boston: B. Green.* 1724. 12mo, pp. 12. 63033

PITCHLYNN (P. P.) Letter of P. P. Pitchlynn to the People of the Choctaw and Chickasaw Nations upon the Question of Sectionizing and Dividing their Lands in Severalty. [*Washington.*] 1870. 8vo, pp. 15. B. 63034

PITCHLYNN. Letter of P. P. Pitchlynne [*sic*], Choctaw Delegate for himself, and Co-Delegates, to the Senate's Committee on the Judiciary. February, 1870. [*Washington.*] 1870. 8vo, pp. 19. B. 63035

PITCHLYNN. Remonstrance, Appeal, and Solemn Protest, of the Choctaw Nation, addressed to the Congress of the United States. [*Washington.* 1870.] 8vo, pp. 21. 63036

[PITCHLYNN, *and others.*] Brief of the Choctaws in regard to the Net Proceeds of the Sales of their Lands East of the Mississippi, ceded to the United States. [n. p. 1869.] 8vo, pp. 2.

PITEZEL (J. H.) The Backwoods Boy who became a Minister: or, the Family and Personal History of Henry Adolph. By Rev. John H. Pitezel ... . *New York: Carlton & Porter.* [1859.] 18mo, pp. 163. C. 63038

PITEZEL. Lights and Shades of Missionary Life: containing Travels, Sketches, Incidents, and Missionary Efforts, during nine years spent in the Region of Lake Superior. By Rev. John H. Pitezel, alias, Wa-zah-wah-wa-doong, or "The Yellow Beard." ... *Cincinnati: R. P. Thompson, Printer.* 1857. 12mo, pp. 431. 4 Plates. C. 63039

PITKIN (J. B.) A Discourse delivered in ... Richmond, Virginia, ... 4th of July, 1833. By J. B. Pitkin. *Richmond: Printed by Thomas W. White.* 1833. 8vo, pp. 15. 63040

Also: Sermons by Rev. J. B. Pitkin, of Richmond, Va., with a Memoir of the Author, by Rev. S. G. Bulfinch. *Boston.* 1837. 12mo. Portrait.

PITKIN (J. R. G.) Letter of J. R. G. Pitkin ... to Hon. B. F. Butler. The Political Aspect of Louisiana. [*New Orleans.* 1868.] 8vo, pp. 16. H. 63041

PITKIN. Speech of Hon. J. R. G. Pitkin, of New Orleans, in Wilmington Institute, Delaware, Oct. 12, 1866. [n. p. n. d.] 8vo, pp. 20. H. 63042

PITKIN (T.) A Sermon ... at Litchfield, at the Execution of John Jacob, an Indian Native, for Murder. By Timothy Pitkin. *Hartford.* 1768. 12mo, pp. 18. 63043

PITKIN. A Sermon ... at New-Cambridge, in Bristol, February 12th, 1789, At the Funeral of the Rev. Samuel Newell ... By Timothy Pitkin, A.M. ... *Hartford: Printed by Hudson and Goodwin.* M.DCC.XC. 8vo, pp. 20. 63044

PITKIN (T.) A Political and Civil History of the United States of America, from ... 1763 to the close of the Administration of President Washington, in March, 1797: including a summary view of the Political and Civil State of the North American Colonies, prior to that period. By Timothy Pitkin. ... *New Haven: Hezekiah Howe and Durrie & Peck.* 1828. 2 vols., 8vo, pp. 528; (2), 8, (2), 9–539. Portrait of Washington. A., N.

Some copies have the date 1831. *See* "North American Review," XXX. I.

PITKIN. A Statistical View of the Commerce of the United States of America: its Connection with Agriculture and Manufactures: and an Account of the Public Debt, Revenues, and Expenditures of the United States. With a Brief Review of the Trade, Agriculture, and Manufactures of the Colonies, previous to their Independence. Accompanied with Tables, Illustrative of the Principles and Objects of the Work. By Timothy Pitkin ... . *Hartford: Printed by Charles Hosmer.* 1816. 8vo, pp. xii, 407, xix, (1). B. + Second Edition, with Additions and Corrections. ... *James Eastburn & Co. New-York. Printed by Hamlen & Newton, Hartford.* 1817. 8vo, pp. xii, 445, vii, (1). B. + Accompanied with numerous tables. *New Haven: Durrie & Peck.* 1835. 8vo, pp. xv, (1), 600. C. 63046

Also: Mr. Pitkin's Motion, December 23d. 1811. ... *Washington City: Printed by R. C. Weightman.* 1811. 8vo, pp. 4.—Mr. Pitkin's Speech on the Loan Bill, delivered in the House of Representatives, February 10th, 1814. ... *Alexandria: Printed by Snowden and Simms.* 1814. 8vo, pp. 19.

PITMAN (B.) *See our* Vol. X., No. 41182, *and* Trials for Treason at Indianapolis.

PITMAN (H.) A | Relation | of the | Great Sufferings | and | Strange Adventures | Of Henry Pitman, | Chyrurgion to the late Duke of Monmouth, contain- | ing an Account; | 1. Of the occasion of his being engaged in the Duke's Service. 2. Of | his Tryal, Condemnation, and Transportation to Barbadoes, with | the most severe and Unchristian Acts made against him and his

Fellow-sufferers, by the | Governour and General Assembly of that Island. 3. How he made his escape in a small | open Boat with some of his fellow Captives, namely, Jo. Whicker, Peter Begwell, William | Woodcock, Jo. Cooke, Jeremiah Atkins, &c. And how miraculously they were preserved | on the Sea. 4. How they went ashore on an uninhabitable Island, where they met | with some Privateers that burnt their Boat, and left them on that desolate place to shift | for themselves. 5. After what manner they lived there for about three Months, until | the said Henry Pitman was taken aboard a Privateer, and at length arrived safe in En- | gland. 6. How his Companions were received aboard another Privateer that was after- | wards taken by the Spaniards, and they all made Slaves; And how aftar six Months | Captivity they were delivered, and returned to England also. | Licensed, June 13th, 1689. | *London, Printed by Andrew Sowle: And are to be Sold by John Taylor, at the Sign | of the Ship in Paul's Church-Yard,* 1689. | 4to, pp. 38, Advertisement, (1). C.H.K. 63047

A very rare tract.

PITMAN (J.) Address to the Alumni Association of Brown University, delivered in Providence, on their first anniversary, September 5, 1843. By John Pitman. ... *Providence: B. Cranston and Company.* 1843. 8vo, pp. 64. A., B. 63048

Mostly biographical and historical of Brown University.

PITMAN. A Discourse ... at Providence, August 5, 1836, in Commemoration of the First Settlement of Rhode-Island and Providence Plantations. Being the Second Centennial Anniversary of the Settlement of Providence. By John Pitman ... . *Providence: B. Cranston & Co.* MDCCCXXXVI. 8vo, pp. 72. A.

Also published anonymously.

PITMAN. A Long Talk, delivered before the Tammany Society or Columbian Order on their Anniversary A.D. 1810: In Providence. By John Pitman, Jun. Esq. *Providence: Jones & Wheeler, Printers.* 1810. 8vo, pp. 26. 63050

PITMAN. An Oration, delivered on the Centennial Anniversary of the Birth of Washington. February 22, 1832. By John Pitman. *Providence: Weeden and Knowles, Printers.* MDCCCXXXII. 8vo, pp. 36. H. 63051

PITMAN. An Oration, pronounced July 4th, 1812, at the Request of the Republicans of the Town of Salem, in Commemoration of the Anniversary of American Independence. By

John Pitman, jun. Esq. ... *Salem: Warwick Palfray, jun.* 1812. 8vo, pp. 23. B. 63052

[PITMAN.] A Reply to the Letter of the Hon. Marcus Morton, late Governor of Massachusetts, on the Rhode-Island Question. By one of the Rhode-Island People. *Providence: Printed by Knowles and Vose.* 1842. 8vo, pp. 32. H. 63053

[PITMAN.] To the Members of the General Assembly of Rhode Island. [n. p. n. d.] 8vo, pp. 24. 63054

Relates to the Question of Suffrage in 1842, etc. Also: An Address ... before the Providence Union Temperance Society, February 24, 1835. ... *Providence: Knowles & Burroughs.* 1835. 12mo, pp. 24.—Annual Address, ... before the Rhode Island Society for the Encouragement of Domestic Industry, October 21, 1828. ... *Providence: Carlile & Parmenter, Printers.* 1829. 8vo, pp. 28. B.—An Oration ... before the ... Federal Adelphi Society, ... September 5, 1805, in ... Providence. ... *Providence: Printed by Heaton & Williams.* [1805.] 8vo, pp. 20.—A Poem, on the Social State and its future progress; ... before the Philermenian Society of Brown University, ... Sept. 3d, A. D. 1811. ... *Providence: Printed by Jones & Wheeler.* [1811.] 12mo, pp. 14. B.

PITMAN (Joseph S.) *See our* Vol. V., No. 20650, *and* Vol. VII., No. 28621.

PITMAN (R. B.) A Succinct View and Analysis of Authentic Information extant in original works, on the practicability of joining the Atlantic and Pacific Oceans, by a Ship Canal across the Isthmus of America. By Robert Birks Pitman. *London: J. M. Richardson.* 1825. 8vo, pp. viii, 229, Errata, (1). Map. A., C.

PITMAN (R. C.) Shall we license or shall we suppress the Liquor Shops of Massachusetts? Argument of Robert C. Pitman on the License Bill, in the Senate of Massachusetts, April 7, 1868. ... *Boston.* 1868. 8vo, pp. 35. H. 63056

PITOU (L. A.) Voyage à Cayenne, dans les deux Amériques, et chez les antropophages. Ouvrage orné de gravures; contenant le tableau général des déportés, la vie et les causes de l'exil de l'auteur; des notions particulières sur Collot et Billaud, sur les îles Sechelles et les déportés de nivose, sur la religion, le commerce et les mœurs des sauvages, des noirs, des créoles et des quakers. Par Louis-Ange Pitou, Déporté à Cayenne, pendant trois ans ... . *A Paris, Chez L'Auteur ... An* XIII.—1805. 2 vols., 8vo, pp. viii, 60, 312; (4), 404. 2 Plates. A., C. 63057

Some copies were issued with the following title:

PITOU. Voyage à Cayenne dans les deux Amériques et chez les Antropophages. Contenant la liste générale des déportés, des

notes particulières sur chacun d'eux; leur vie leur mort ou leur retour; des notions particulières sur Collot et Billaud, sur les déportés de nivôse aux iles Séchelles; le voyage de l'auteur chez les mangeurs d'hommes, les dangers qu'il y court; son retour par les États-Unis; de la religion, des moeurs et de la culture de l'Amérique septentrionale, des Quakers, &c. Par Louis Ange Pitou, dit le chanteur, déporté à Cayenne en 1798, pendant trois Ans, et rendu à la liberté par S. M. l'Empereur. *Paris.* 1805. 2 vols., 8vo. 2 Maps. 63058

The narrative is largely fictitious.

PITOU. Voyage à Cayenne, dans les deux Amériques et chez les Antropophages ... Seconde Édition, Augmentée de notions historiques sur les Antropophages, d'un remercîment et d'une réponse aux observations de MM. les journalistes. Par L. A. Pitou, déporté à Cayenne en 1797, et rendu à la liberté en 1803, ... *Paris, Chez L. A. Pitou.* 1807. 2 vols., 8vo, pp. (2), 10, v–60, 312; (2), 10, 404. 2 Plates. C., H. 63059

PITOU. Louis Ange Pitou's Leben und Verweisung nach Cayenne, nebst ... seiner Reise in das Innre von Amerika mit ... Nachrichten von den dortigen Wilden oder Menschen-fressern ... Aus dem Französischen ... . *Leipzig: Hinrichs.* 1805. 8vo, pp. vi, 391. 2 folded Plates. H. 63060

PITOU. Reise nach Cayenne in Nord und Süd Amerika und zu den Menschenfressern, nebst deszen Leben von ihm selbst beschrieben nach dem Französischen. *Leipzig.* 1838. 8vo. 2 Plates. 63061

PITRAT (J. C.) Americans Warned of Jesuitism, or the Jesuits Unveiled: By John Claudius Pitrat. ... *New York.* 1851. 12mo, pp. 266. + Third Edition. ... *Boston: Edward W. Hinks & Co.* 1855. 12mo, pp. 192. A. 63062

PITRAT. Review of the Speech of Hon. J. R. Chandler, ... on the Political Power of the Pope: Delivered ... January 10, 1855. By John Claudius Pitrat ... . *Boston: Edward W. Hinks and Company.* 1855. 12mo, pp 72. A. 63063

PITT (W.) An Appendix. The Speech of Mr. Pitt, now Earl of Chatham, upon the Stamp Act. Wherein the Arguments of Mr. Gr—v—lle, and others, in favour of the Act, are answered. *Dublin: Shephard.* 1768. 8vo, pp. 29. 63064

[PITT.] Authentic Copy of Lord Ch——m's Speech in the Ho—se of L—ds in Eng—nd in the D—e on the Present State of the Nation, Nov. 22, 1770. *London.* [1770.] 8vo. 63065

[PITT.] The Celebrated Speech of a Celebrated Commoner. *London: Stephen Austin.* 1766. 8vo, pp. (4), 18. + A New Edition Corrected. [*Ibid.*] MDCCLXVI. 8vo, pp. (2), 17. H.

Composed of extracts from one of Mr. Pitt's speeches, relative to the stamp act. For another edition *see* "Political Debates."

PITT. Correspondence of William Pitt, Earl of Chatham. Edited by William Stanhope Taylor, Esq., and Captain John Henry Pringle, Executors of his Son, John, Earl of Chatham, and published from the original manuscripts in their possession. ... *London: John Murray.* MDCCCXXXVIII–MDCCCXL. 4 vols., 8vo, pp. xxiii, (1), 480; xxiii, (1), 471; xxix, (1), 495; xxxi, (1), 572. Facsimiles, pp. 38. A., C., S. 63067

[PITT.] A Faithful Abstract of Lord Chatham's Last Speech in Parliament, on Tuesday, April the 7th, 1778, The Day he was struck with the Illness which terminated in his Death: Copied from Notes taken within the Bar. *London: G. Kearsley.* M,DCC,-LXXVIII. 4to, pp. 15. 63068

[PITT.] Genuine Abstracts from Two Speeches of the late Earl of Chatham: and his Reply to the Earl of Suffolk. With some Introductory Observations and Notes. ... *London: J. Dodsley.* M.DCC.LXXIX. 8vo, pp. viii, 58. H., M. 63069

On American affairs. *See* "Monthly Review," LX. 157.

[PITT.] Lord Chatham's Speech in the British House of Lords, At the Opening of the Session, 20th November, 1777, on the Debate for Addressing the Throne. [*London:*] *Printed A. D.* 1778. 8vo, pp. 31. 63070

[PITT.] Plan | offered by the | Earl of Chatham, | to the | House of Lords, | entitled, | A Provisional Act, for settling the Troubles | in America, and for asserting the Supreme Legisla- | tive Authority and Superintending Power of | Great Britain over the Colonies. | Which was rejected, and not suffered to | lie upon the Table. | *London: | Printed for J. Almon ...* | M.DCC.LXXV. | 4to, pp. 14, (1).

"We cannot but regret that this plan was rejected, as we are convinced that by a few slight alterations it might have been rendered acceptable to the people of America."—*Monthly Review,* LII. 179.

[PITT.] The | Sentiments | of | Lord Chatham | on the | American Measures, | delivered in his | Speech | on the | Provisional Bill. |

(Authentic Copy.) | *Newcastle: | Printed.* MDCCLXXVI. | 12mo, pp. 16. 63072

P[ITT]. The Speech of Mr. P - - - - - - And several others, In a certain august Assembly On a late important Debate: With an Introduction of the Matters preceding it. [*London:*] *Printed in the Year* —66. [1766.] 8vo, pp. 34. 63073

Relates to the stamp act.

[PITT.] The Speech of the Right Honourable the Earl of Chatham in the House of Lords upon reading the Amendments in the Quebec Bill, on ... the 17. of June, 1774. Together with his Lordship's Speech, on the third Reading, ... of the Bill for providing with Quarters, the Officers and Troops in America. *London: Johnson.* 1774. Folio. 63074

See "Monthly Review," LI. 171.

[PITT.] Speech On the 20th of January, 1775. Taken by a Member. *London: T. Freeman.* M.DCC.LXXV. 4to, pp. 18.

[PITT.] The Speech of the Right Honourable the Earl of Chatham, in the House of Lords, on Friday, the 20th of January 1775. A New Edition. *London: G. Kearsly.* M.DCC.LXXV. 4to, pp. 18. BA. 63076

On the motion for removing his Majesty's forces from the town of Boston, etc. Disclaimed by the Earl of Chatham. Reprinted with the following title:

[PITT.] The Speech of the Right Honorable, The Earl of Chatham, in the House of Lords, January 20th, 1775, On a Motion for an Address to His Majesty, to give immediate orders for removing his troops from Boston forthwith, in order to quiet the minds and take away the apprehensions of His good Subjects in America. *Philadelphia: Printed by John Dunlap.* M,DCC,LXXV. 8vo, pp. 16. 63077

[PITT.] The Speeches of the Right Honourable the Earl of Chatham ... . With a Biographical Memoir, and Introductions and Explanatory Notes to the Speeches. New Edition. *London.* 1848. Imp. 8vo. Portrait. 63078

The following works relate to the Earl of Chatham and American affairs in general:

[PITT.] An Address to the Great Man, with Advice to the Public. *London.* 1758. 8vo. 63079

[PITT.] An Address to the People of Great Britain ... Occasioned by the Dismission of William Pitt ... . *Dublin.* 1761. 8vo, pp. 40. 63080

PITT. Anecdotes of the Life of the Right Hon. William Pitt, Earl of Chatham, ... with his Speeches ... from ... 1736 to ... 1778. *Dublin: P. Wogan.* M. DCC. XCII. 2 vols., 8vo, pp. vi, (8), 402; (7), 403. + Fourth Edition. *London.* 1794. 3 vols., 8vo. + Fifth Edition. *London.* 1796. 3 vols., 8vo. + The Sixth Edition, Corrected. *London: L. B. Seeley.* 1797. 3 vols., 8vo, pp. 504; vi, 422; 404. BA. 63081

For other editions *see* Vol. I., No. 949.

[PITT.] Another Account of a Transaction which passed in the beginning of the year 1778. Rather more correct than what is called An Authentic Account of the part taken by the late Earl of Chatham in that Transaction. *London: T. Cadell.* MDCCLXXVIII. 4to, pp. 43, Dr. Addington's Narrative, 3. 63082

[PITT.] The Answer at Large to Mr. P--tt's Speech. *London: W. Nicoll.* MDCCLXVI. 8vo, pp. 22. H. 63083

[PITT.] An Authentic Account of the Part taken by the late Earl of Chatham in a Transaction which passed in the beginning of the year 1778. *London: J. Almon.* 1778. 4to. + Second Edition. *London.* 1778. 4to. 63084

[PITT.] Authentic Memoirs of the Right Honourable the late Earl of Chatham. ... *London: J. Wenman.* M DCC LXXVIII. 8vo, pp. (2), 102. J.C.B. 63085

[PITT.] Candid Answer to the "Enquiry" ... *London.* 1766. 8vo. 63086

[PITT.] A Certain Great Man Vindicated. *London.* 1761. 4to, pp. 4. M. 63087

[PITT.] The Conduct of a R. Hon. Gentleman in resigning the Seals of his Office, justified, by Facts, and upon the Principles of the British Constitution. By a Member of Parliament. *London: J. Newbery.* MDCCLXI. 8vo, pp. (2), 82. + The Second Edition. [*Ibid.*] MDCCLXI. 8vo, pp. (4), 82. B. 63088

On the right of cutting in the Bay of Campeachy, etc.

PITT. An Earnest Address to the People of Great-Britain and Ireland; Occasioned by the Dismission of William Pitt, Esq. from the Office of Secretary of State. *London: W. Owen.* MDCCLXI. 8vo, pp. (4), 52. B., J.C.B. + *Dublin: O. Watson* ... MDCCLXI. 8vo, pp. 40. 63089

Refers to Braddock's expedition, Canada, etc.

[PITT.] An Enquiry into the Conduct of a late right Honourable Commoner. The Second Impression. *London: J. Almon.* MDCCLXVI. 8vo, pp. 72. + The Third Impression, Corrected. [*Ibid.*] 8vo, pp. 72. H. 63090

See Junius, Vol. IX., No. 36902, for the first edition.

[PITT.] An Examination into the Conduct of Mr. P——, on a late Important Affair; in which Two Letters to the Right Honourable the Earl of B——; are fully Considered and Refuted. In a Letter to a Friend. *London: T. Hope.* 1761. 8vo, pp. 56. J.C.B. 63091

Partly relates to Canada.

[PITT.] Genuine Collection of the several pieces of Political Intelligence Extraordinary, Epigrams, Poetry, &c., that have appeared before the Public in Detached Pieces, Carefully selected by an Impartial Hand. *London.* 1766. 8vo. Frontispiece.

Contains an inscription to be put upon the statues preparing to be sent to America, in memory of Willam Pitt, etc.

PITT. The History of the Life of William Pitt, Earl of Chatham. *London: G. Kearsley.* 1783. 8vo. + Second Edition. *London: The Author.* 1783. 8vo, pp. xv, 302. BA. 63093

"Posterity will say much of Lord Chatham, but not a word of this History."—*Monthly Review*, LXVIII. 309.

[PITT.] Lord Ch---am's Prophecy, An Ode; Addressed to Lieutenant General G-ge. With Explanatory and Critical Notes, By the Editor. ... *London: J. Almon.* M,DCC,LXXVI. 4to, pp. 16. BA. 63094

See "Monthly Review," LIV. 504.

PITT. An | Ode, | in | Two Parts, | Humbly Inscrib'd | to the | Right Honourable | William Pitt. | ... | *London,* | *Printed for the Author,* | *And Sold by John Hart,* ... | M DCC LX. | 4to, pp. 19. 63095

Part II. relates to Canada.

See also our Vol. VII., Nos. 25699, 25700; Vol. X., Nos. 40307, 40310, 40368, 40391, 40444, 40467, 40468, 40480, 40533–40535, 42915; *and* "Political Conduct," "Remarks on a Popular Letter," "Review of Mr. Pitt's Administration," "Short Considerations," "Short View," "A Vindication," and "Word to a Right Honourable Commoner."

PITT (W.) The | Speech | of the | Right Honourable | William Pitt, | in the | House | of | Commons | on Friday, February 21, 1783. | *London: J. Debrett.* | MDCCLXXXIII. 8vo, pp. 39. 63096

On the treaties with France, Spain, and the United States, and perhaps the most eloquent of Mr. Pitt's speeches.

PITT. The Speech of ... William Pitt, on ... the Abolition of the Slave Trade, ... the Second of April, 1792. *London: Printed by James Phillips.* M.DCC.XCII. 8vo, pp. 32. BA., S.

PITT. The Life of William Pitt, Late Prime Minister of Great Britain. ... *Philadelphia: John Watts.* 1806. 8vo, pp. 242. Portrait. 63098

PITT. The Speeches of the Right Honourable William Pitt, in the House of Commons. ... *London: Longman, Hurst, Rees and Orme.* 1806. 4 vols., 8vo, pp. xi, 436; (4), 463; iv, 438; (4), 471. A. + Third Edition. [*Ibid.*] 1817. 3 vols., 8vo, pp. xi, 450; iv, 441; iv, 458. B. 63099

PITTENGER (W.) Daring and Suffering: A History of the Great Railroad Adventure. By Lieut. William Pittenger, one of the adventurers. With an Introduction, by Rev. Alexander Clark. ... *Philadelphia: J. W. Daughaday.* 1863. 12mo, pp. 288. Portrait and Plate. + [*Ibid.*] 1864. 12mo, pp. 288. Plates. BA. 63100

PITTENGER. Oratory, Sacred and Secular: ... With Sketches of the most Eminent Speakers of all Ages. By William Pittenger .... *New York: Samuel R. Wells.* 1868. 12mo, pp. 220.

PITTIS (William). History of the Present Parliament, and Convocation; with Debates relating to the Conduct of the War abroad ... *London.* 1711. 8vo. 63102

Some of the debates relate to American topics.

PITTMAN (P.) The | Present State | of the | European Settlements | on the | Missisippi; | with | A Geographical Description of that River. | Illustrated by | Plans and Draughts. | By Captain Philip Pittman. | *London: J. Nourse.* MDCCLXX. 4to, pp. viii, 99. 8 Maps and Plans. A., C., P. 63103

The author resided several years in the countries he describes, and was employed in surveying and exploring the interior parts.

PITTS (F. E.) A Defence of Armageddon, or our great Country foretold in Holy Scriptures; in Two Discourses, delivered ... on the Anniversary of Washington's Birth Day. By F. E. Pitts. *Baltimore.* 1859. 8vo. 63104

PITTSBURGH, *Pa.* Address of a Committee. *See* Vol. XIV., No. 59833.

Address of Working Men of Pittsburgh, to their Fellow Working Men in Pennsylvania. *Pittsburgh: Printed by W. S. Haven.* 1856. 8vo, pp. 8. H. 63105

Address to the Holders of Bonds of the City of Pittsburgh ... *Pittsburgh: Printed by Singerly & Myers.* 1862. 8vo, pp. 16. B.

Address, [etc.] *See* [Burgwin (H.)], Vol. III., No. 9268, *and* Vol. IV., No. 13726.

Second Report of the ... ALLEGHENY CEMETERY, ... with the Funeral Oration. By Wilson M'Candless, Esq. ... *Pittsburgh: Printed by W. S. Haven.* 1857. 8vo, pp. 151. 2 Plates.

Atlas of the Cities of Pittsburgh, Allegheny, and the Adjoining Boroughs ... by G. M. Hopkins & Co. ... *Philadelphia.* 1872. Folio. P. 63108

The Bishop's Address. *See* [Kerfoot (John B.)], IX. 37612.

First Annual Report of the ... BOARD OF TRADE and Merchant's Exchange ... delivered September 7th, 1855. *Pittsburgh: Printed by W. S. Haven.* 1855. 8vo, pp. 24. H. 63109

Annual Address delivered before the Board of Trade of ... Pittsburgh. By Wilson McCandless. *Pittsburgh.* 1841. 8vo, pp. 34. 63110

Report on the Improvement of the Ohio River, made to the Board of Trade of Pittsburgh, by a Committee appointed ... December 4, 1863. *Pittsburgh: Printed by W. S. Haven.* 1864. 8vo, pp. 25. H. 63111

Bye-Laws and Ordinances of the City of Pittsburgh. *Pittsburgh.* 1828. 8vo. 63112

Circular of the National Committee of the Pittsburgh Convention, called Feb. 22, 1856. [n. p. n. d.] 8vo. 63113

Cramer's Pittsburgh Almanack for 1809. *Pittsburgh.* [n. d.] 12mo. 63114

Continued to 1812 or later.

Dedicatory Services of the new edifice of the Third Presbyterian Church of Pittsburgh, Penn'a. With ... the History of the Church ... *Pittsburgh: W. G. Johnston & Co., Printers.* 1869. 8vo, pp. 95. Woodcuts and Plan. B. 63115

A Digest of Acts of Assembly, the Codified Ordinance of the City of Pittsburgh, Adopted October 6, 1859; and a Digest of other Ordinances now in force. Compiled ... by Alexander W. Foster, City Solicitor. *Pittsburgh: W. S. Haven, ... Printer.* 1860. 8vo, pp. iv, (2), 192. A. 63116

Also: A Digest of the Acts of Assembly and a Code of the Ordinances of the City of Pittsburgh, with an Appendix .... Prepared ... by J. F. Slagle .... *Pittsburgh: Printed by Erret, Anderson & Co.* 1869. 8vo, pp. v, (2), 473. B.

Documents relative to a Communication between Pittsburgh and the Ohio Canal. *Pittsburgh: D. and M. Maclean, Printers.* 1833. 8vo, pp. xxxi, 27. Map. 63117

Memorial Sermon and Address on the Death of President Lincoln, St. Andrew's Church, Pittsburgh, ... April 16, and ... 19, 1865. *Pittsburgh: Printed by W. S. Haven* .... 1865. 8vo, pp. 38. 63118

Includes a sermon by Rev. William A. Snively, and an address by Rev. William Preston, D.D.

Memorial to the Government of the United States from the Citizens of Pittsburgh, setting forth the Advantages of that City, as a Site for a National Armory & Foundry. *Pittsburgh: Printed by W. S. Haven.* 1861. 8vo, pp. 16. Map. H. 63119

The Mercantile Register, containing a List of the Principal Business Establishments, and Public Institutions in Pittsburgh. *Philadelphia: H. Orr.* 1846. 8vo, pp. 50. P. 63120

The Minutes of the Proceedings of the Pittsburgh Convention, called by the Signers of the "Act and Testimony." May 14, 1835. *Pittsburgh: White & Grant, Printers.* 1835. 8vo, pp. 22. B. 63121

Ordinances of the Select & Common Councils of ... Pittsburgh, passed from January 7th, 1863, to January 7th, 1864, together with the Acts of Assembly relating to the City, passed during ... 1863, with ... the Report of the City Solicitor ... . *Pittsburgh: David B. Ferguson, ... Printer.* 1864. 8vo, pp. 83.

The Pittsburg Almanac, or Western Ephemeris, for the Year of our Lord 1788, Bissextile, or Leap Year. *Pittsburg: Printed by Scull and Boyd.* [n. d.] 8vo, pp. 40. P. 63123

Perhaps the first piece printed in Pittsburgh.

A Description of the PITTSBURGH AND BALTIMORE COAL, Coke & Iron Co's Lands. Together with the report of J. P

Lesley, Geologist. *Philadelphia: McCalla & Stavely.* 1871. 8vo, pp. 16. P. 63124

Report of the ... PITTSBURGH AND BOSTON Copper Harbor Mining Company ... . *Boston: Printed by S. N. Dickinson and Company.* 1847. 8vo, pp. 48. Plan. Continued. H. 63125

Statement of Benjamin H. Latrobe, Esq., President of the PITTSBURGH AND CONNELLSVILLE Railroad Company, to the Committee on Internal Improvements of ... Baltimore. *Baltimore: James Young.* 1863. 8vo, pp. 24. 63126

Also: Eleventh Annual Report ... to the Stockholders .... *Pittsburgh: W. S. Haven.* 1863. 8vo, pp. 49. Continued.—Defence of a Majority of the City of Baltimore's Directors .... *Baltimore: James Young.* 1863. 8vo, pp. (2), 22.—Extracts from the Journals of the First Branch of the City Council of Baltimore, relating to the Pittsburgh and Connellsville Railroad Company. [n. p. *February,* 1863.] Folio, 1 leaf.—Formal Opening of the Pittsburgh, Washington and Baltimore Railroad (Connellsville Route). ... 1871 ... The Speeches ... at the Grand Banquet. ... *Baltimore.* 1871. 8vo, pp. 63.—Memorial to Congress, asking aid in completion of their road. [n. p. n. d.] 8vo, pp. 6.—Testimony in reference to Charges of Corruption in securing the passage of an Ordinance for the benefit of the Pittsburgh and Connellsville Rail Road Company ... *Baltimore: John Cox, City Printer.* 1868. 8vo, pp. 68. *See also* our Vol. II., No. 7875.

Pittsburgh and Erie Railroad. Report relative to the Surveys of Routes, read by W. Milnor Roberts, July 8, 1856. *Erie.* 1856. 8vo. 63127

Also: Annual Report of the Pittsburgh and Erie Railroad for ... 1856. [n. p. n. d.] 8vo.

Pittsburgh Directory for 1815. *Pittsburgh: J. M. Riddle.* 1815. 16mo, pp. 156. C. 63128

Probably the first directory. *See* Jones (S.), Vol. IX., No. 36603.

Harris' Pittsburgh Business Directory, for ... 1837. ... *Pittsburgh: Isaac Harris.* 1837. 12mo, pp. 340, Advertisements, (128).

Contains a brief history of Pittsburgh.

Harris' Pittsburgh & Allegheny Directory, ... Including the Boroughs of Lawrenceville and Birmingham .... By Isaac Harris. *Pittsburgh: Printed by A. A. Anderson.* 1839. 12mo.

Harris' General Business Directory, of the Cities of Pittsburgh and Allegheny, and also of the most flourishing and important Towns and Cities of Pennsylvania, Ohio, Western New York, Virginia, etc. ... *Pittsburgh: Printed by A. A. Anderson.* 1841. 12mo, pp. 333, (3). H.

Pittsburgh and Allegheny Business Directory. By Isaac Harris. *Pittsburgh: A. A. Anderson.* 1844. 12mo, pp. 105, (50). Continued to 1847 or later.

Woodward & Rowlands' Pittsburgh Directory for 1852. *Pittsburgh.* [1852.] 12mo. Map.

Directory for 1856–'57, of Pittsburgh and Allegheny Cities .... [*Pittsburgh:*] ... *George H. Thurston.* 1856. 8vo, pp. xxvi, (2), 342. H.

Directory of Pittsburgh & Vicinity for 1859–'60. [*Pittsburgh:*] ... *George H. Thurston.* 1859. 8vo, pp. (8), 332. 2 Maps. Also for 1858–9. [*Ibid.*] 1858. 8vo.

Directory of Pittsburgh and Allegheny Cities, the adjoining Boroughs and Villages. Also, Parts of the adjacent Townships, for 1863–64. [*Pittsburgh:*] ... *George H. Thurston.* [n. d.] 8vo, pp. (4), 400, 63. Continued.

Statement of the Trustees relative to the reorganization of the PITTSBURGH, FORT WAYNE and Chicago Railway, and Laws and Documents in connection therewith, and the new securities. *New York: Baker & Godwin, Printers.* 1862. 8vo, pp. 8, Appendix, 95. Map. A. 63129

Also: First Annual Report of the Board of Directors of the Pittsburgh, Ft. Wayne & Chicago Railway Company, to the Stock and Bondholders, for ... 1862. *Pittsburgh: Printed by W. S. Haven.* 1863. 8vo, pp. 77. Continued.

Pittsburgh, her Advantageous Position and Great Resources, as a Manufacturing and Commercial City, embraced in a Notice of Sale of Real Estate. *Johnston & Stockton, ... Pittsburgh.* 1845. 8vo, pp. 40. A., B. 63130

Pittsburgh in 1826. *Pittsburgh.* 1826. 12mo. 63131

Pittsburgh: its Industry and Commerce, embracing Statistics of the Coal, Iron, Glass, Steel, Copper, Petroleum and other Manufacturing Interests of Pittsburgh. *Pittsburgh: Printed by Bau & Myers,* 1870. 4to, pp. 108. P. 63132

Third Annual Catalogue of the PITTSBURGH FEMALE COLLEGE for ... 1857 and 1858 ... . *Pittsburgh: Printed by W. S. Haven.* 1858. 8vo, pp. 20. Plate. H. 63133

Constitution and By-Laws of the PITTSBURGH HORTICULTURAL SOCIETY. 1848. *Pittsburgh: Printed by Geo. Parkin & Co.* 1848. 12mo, pp. 11. H. 63134

First Annual Report of the PITTSBURGH INFIRMARY, ... presented ... Jan. 13, 1851. *Pittsburgh: Printed by W. S. Haven.* 1851. 8vo, pp. 24. Continued. H. 63135

... Memorial on behalf of the PITTSBURGH MANUFACTURING ASSOCIATION. January 3, 1828. ... *Washington: Printed by Duff Green.* 1828. 8vo, pp. 5. H. 63136

Exhibit of the Affairs of the PITTSBURGH, MAYSVILLE and Cincinnati Railroad Company, Geological Reports, ... etc., Oct. 1854. *Cincinnati.* 1854. 8vo. S. 63137

Pittsburgh Quarterly Magazine. Vol. I. *Pittsburgh.* 1867–8. 8vo. 63138

Pittsburgh Quarterly Trade Circular. October, 1858. *Pittsburgh.* 1858. 12mo. 63139

The Pittsburgh Recorder, published under the Patronage of the Members of the Synod of Pittsburgh. *Pittsburgh.* 1822–24. 2 vols., 8vo, pp. 832; 832. S. 63140

First Report, Address and Proceedings of the PITTSBURGH SANITARY COMMITTEE. *Pittsburgh: Printed by W. S. Haven.* 1863. 8vo, pp. 16. P. 63141

Pittsburgh Sanitary Fair, June 1, 1864. [A poem.] By an Old Citizen. [n. p.:] *Printed by W. S. Haven.* [n. d.] 12mo, pp. 12. 63142

The Pittsburgh Town & County Almanac, for Rogues and Honest Folks, 1814. By John Armstrong. *Pittsburgh.* [n. d.] 12mo. 63143

Continued to 1816 or later.

Report of the Army Committee of the United States Christian Commission. Pittsburgh, Pennsylvania. [n. p. n. d.] 12mo, pp. 13. 63144

Report of the Committee appointed by the Citizens ... on the 21st of December, 1816, to Inquire into the State of Manufactures in the City, ... made February 17th, 1817, in House of Representatives of the United States. [n. p. 1817.] 16mo, pp. 16. B., N. 63145

Report of the Fire Marshal to the Judges of the Court of Common Pleas of Allegheny County, for ... 1870. *Pittsburgh: Printed by Bakewell & Marthens.* 1870. 8vo, pp. 8, (12). B.

First Annual Report of the SUPERINTENDENT OF PUBLIC SCHOOLS for ... 1869. *Pittsburgh: Printed by W. G. Johnston.* 1869. 8vo, pp. 96. Plans. Continued. B. 63147

Supplement to the Pittsburgh Gazette, Jan. 9, 1824. Revision of the Tariff. [*Pittsburgh.* 1824.] 12mo, pp. 12.

Contains the proceedings of a meeting of citizens, and the memorial to Congress that was adopted.

1860. Twelfth Annual Report of the YOUNG MEN'S Mercantile Library Association and Mechanics Institute ... of Pittsburgh, ... With a List of Members, and Charter of the Library Hall Company. *Pittsburgh: Printed by W. S. Haven.* 1860. 8vo, pp. 32. A. 63149

Continued to 1872 or later, when it was changed to the "Pittsburgh Library Association."

Also: Catalogue of the ... Institute. *Pittsburgh, Pa.* 1858. 12mo. S.—Constitution and By-Laws of the Young Men's Mercantile Library. *Pittsburgh.* 1847. 18mo.

... Pittsburgh Landing. Battle of 1862. Letter of U. S. Secretary of War, with Reports of Officers in Command, 1862. [*Washington.* 1862.] 8vo, pp. 275. 63150

See also [Victor (O. J.)]

PITTSFIELD, *Mass.* Circular ... of the MENDELSSOHN MUSICAL INSTITUTE ... Pittsfield, ... Mass. April, 1859. ... *Pittsfield, Mass.: Henry Chickering, Printer.* 1859. 8vo, pp. 20. H.

Catalogue of the PITTSFIELD COMMERCIAL & Classical Boarding School. 1841. *New York: George Tibbals, Printer.* [1841.] 12mo, pp. 11. B. 63152

The Pittsfield Directory for 1868. *Pittsfield: J. B. Hawkins.* [n. d.] 12mo, pp. 115. 63153

First Annual Catalogue of the Instructors and Pupils in the PITTSFIELD GYMNASIUM ... . *Pittsfield, Mass.: Printed by Wm. D. Axtell.* 1846. 16mo, pp. 16. B. 63154

Catalogue of Books belonging to the PITTSFIELD LIBRARY. *Pittsfield: D. T. Neal, Printer.* 1865. 16mo, pp. 40. 63155

An Address, by Rev. Henry Neill, and a Poem by O. W. Holmes ... at the Dedication of the PITTSFIELD (RURAL) CEMETERY, Sept. 9th, 1850 ... . *Pittsfield, Mass.: Axtel,* [*etc.*] *Printers.* 1850. 8vo, pp. 64. Plan. B. 63156

First Annual Catalogue of the Instructors and Pupils in the PITTSFIELD YOUNG LADIES' INSTITUTE. July, 1842. *New York: Printed by A. Hanford.* 1842. 8vo, pp. 12. Continued.

Report of the Special Committee appointed by the Board of Education of ... Pittsfield. [n. p. n. d.] 8vo, pp. 7. B. 63158

Reports of the ... Commissioners ... in the Fire District of ... Pittsfield, containing a ... Plan for the Drainage of said District ... By I. C. Chesborough .... [n. p.:] *Printed for the Commissioners.* 1870. 8vo, pp. 28. B. 63159

Septuagenarian Dinner. Report of the Speeches, Poem and other Proceedings at a Dinner, given June 30, 1870, by the Citizens of Pittsfield, Mass., to their Townsmen who had reached the age of 70 years. ... *Albany, N. Y.: Joel Munsell.* 1870. 8vo, pp. 48. H. 63160

See also Vol. II., Nos. 4893–98, *and* Williams College.

PITTSFIELD, *N. H.* Manual of the Congregational Church, Pittsfield, N. H. *Manchester: Abbott, Jenks & Co's ... Press.* 1855. 24mo, pp. 26. B. 63161

The Pitts-Street Chapel Lectures. Delivered in Boston by Clergymen of six different Denominations, during the Winter of 1858. ... *Boston: John P. Jewett and Company.* 1858. 12mo, pp. 366. H. 63162

Lectures by Rev. William R. Clark, Rev. Thomas B. Thayer, Rev. James N. Sykes, Rev. Nehemiah Adams, Rev. George M. Randall, Rev. Orville Dewey, and Rev Thomas Starr King.

PITZINGER (E. A.) Poems by Miss Eliza A. Pitzinger, of San Francisco. *San Francisco.* 1864. 12mo. 63163

PIUS II. Pii II Pont. Max. Asiae Europaeque elegantissima descriptio ... accessit H. Glareani Compendiaria Asiae, Africae, Europaeque descriptio. *Parisiis apud C. Chevallonium.* 1534. 12mo, pp. (16), 522. 63164

A reference to the discovery of America will be found on page 521.

PIUS IV. Bvlla.|Bvlla S. D. N. D. Pii Divina Providen|tia Papæ Quarti, super Confirmatione œcumeni|ic [*sic*] generalis Concilij Tridentini.| [Colophon:] *Fue impressa ẽ la Ciudad de Mexico ẽ casa de pedro ochar|te por mādado del yllustrissimo y reverẽdissimo señor don|Fray Alonso de Montufar, Arçobispo de la dicha Ciudad.|Meritissimo.|* [1565.] 4to, (10) leaves. 63165

The first part (4 pp.) is followed by: Bvlla.|Bvlla S. D. N. D. Pii Divina Providen|tia Papæ Quarti, super declaratione temporis obser-|uādi decreta sacri œcumenici, & generalis|Concilij Tridentini.| (2 pp.); and: Catalogvs Patrvm, Oratorvm|Doctorum Teologorvm, et alio|rvm qvi svb B. PP. Pio Quarto,|interfvervnt sacro|sancto et celebe|rrimo gene-|rali concilio Tridentino.| (14 pp.)

A copy of this very rare tract was sold at the Ramirez sale in 1880 for £16.

PIUS V. Bulla|Confirmationis et Novae con-|cessionis priuilegiorum omnium ordinum Mendicantium.|Cvm certis Declarationibvs De|cretis & Inhibitiōibus. S. D. N. D. Pij Papæ V. Motu pprio.| [Woodcut.]| *Mexici.*| *Apud Antonio de Spinosa.*| *Anno.* 1568.| [Colophon:] *¶ Impresso en Mexico, con licencia de los señores Presidente y|Oydores de la Audiencia Real de la ciudad y del muy yl-|lustre y reuerendissimo señor Arçobispo della en casa de|Antonio de Spinosa impressor a 4 dias del|mes de Junio de* 1568.| 4to, (14) leaves, including woodcut title and printer's device, which is on a separate leaf at the end. 63166

The Fischer copy sold for £8. 10s. and the Ramirez copy for £6. 5s. Another edition was sold at the Ramirez sale which lacked the last leaf, and commenced on Aij as follows: ¶ Pivs Episcopvs Servvs Ser|uorum Dei ad perpetuam Rei memoriam. [Colophon:] ¶ Exemplar auctenticū missum à Roma exhibuit R. P.|Magister Alfonsus à ueracruce, ordi. heremi. S. Augu.| [n. p. n. d.] 4to, (10) leaves (Aij to Avii, followed by four leaves without signature). This was probably printed in Spain and sent to Mexico by P. Vera Cruz some time before his return from Rome in 1573.

PIUS V. ¶ Tabula priuilegiorum, quæ sanctissimus Papa pius quintus, | concessit fratribus mendicantibus: in bulla confirmationis, | & nouæ, concessionis priuilegiorum, ordinum | mēdicantium. Anno. 1567.| [Colophon:] *Mexici.* ¶ *In ædibus Antonij de Spinosa.*|1568.| 4to, (5) leaves, including printer's device on a separate leaf at the end. 63167

Concerning these three extremely rare productions of the Mexican press, *see* Icazbalceta, "Bibliografia Mexicana del Siglo XVI.," Nos. 46, 54 and 55.

PIUS VI. Breve Apostolico de Pio Sexto, y Estatutos Generales para la ereccion y gobierno de las custodias de misioneros Franciscos observantes de Propaganda fide en las provincias internas de Nueva España. *Madrid: Joachin Ibarra.* 1781. 4to, pp. 42. J.C.B. 63168

PIUS VII. Assists the Cause of Liberty in 1797 ... Pius VII. assists Ferdinand VII. against the Patriots of South America and Mexico in 1816 ... *Philadelphia: J. F. Hurtet.* 1817. 8vo, pp. 73. 63169

In Spanish and English.

PIUS IX. Decreto de Pio IX. en que nombra un visitador y delegado apostolico para los Regulares de la Republica Mexicana, ... *Mexico.* 1855. 8vo, pp. 15. 63170

PIUS IX. Proceedings of the Public Demonstration of Sympathy with Pius IX ... in the City of New York. ... Nov. 29th, 1847. *New York: Printed by Wm. Van Norden.* 1847. 8vo.

PIUS IX. Sanctissimi Domini Nostri Pii Divinâ Providentiâ Papae IX. Litterae apostolicae, quibus conventio inter Sanctam Sedem et Præsidem Reipublicae Sancti Salvadoris in America Centrali, Confirmatur. *Romae.* 1864. Folio, pp. xvi. 63172

[PIUS IX.] Il viaggio al Chili da Giovanni Maria Mastai Ferretti. *Velletri.* 1846. 8vo. 63173

PIXERÉCOURT (R. C. Guilbert de). Christophe Colomb, ou la Découverte du Nouveau-Monde, mélodrame historique en trois actes, musique de M. Darondeau, paroles de De Pixerécourt,

représenté à Paris ... le 5 septembre 1815. *Paris.* 1815. 8vo. + [*Paris.* 1820.] 8vo, pp. 96. 63174

Pizarre, ou La Conquête du Pérou, Tragedie-Lyrique en cinq actes; representée ... Le Mardi 3 Mai 1785. *Paris.* M.DCC.LXXX.VI. 4to. 63175

[PIZARRO (Francisco).] Copey etlicher brieff | so ausz Hispania kummē | seindt/ anzaygent die eygenschafft des/ | Newen Lands/ so newlich von Kay. | May. Armadi ausz dem newen Mör gefunden ist worden/ | durch die hispanier. | [n. p.] M.D.XXXV. | [At the end:] Solche zeyttung ist ausz | hyspanischer Sprach/ in die Frantzosische getransfer|tirt worden/ darnach in Nyderlendisch vnd hoch-|teutsch Sprach. Dise zway schyff hat ein glaubwür|diger Mann mit nammen Mayster Adolff Kay-|May. Secretari in Hyspania abladen sehen.| 4to, (4) leaves, verso of the last blank. 63176

Of extreme rarity. A copy was priced by Mr. Ellis of London in 1884 at £21. The text begins with the following words: "Item es ist vor etlichen Jaren, durch Kay. May. beuelch ausz gefaren ausz Hispania, ein Hispanischer Her Francisco de Pysaria," etc. No copies of the original Spanish edition nor of the Flemish translation have yet been found. For another Spanish account *see* "La conquista del Peru," *Sevilla*, 1534, our No. 61097, Vol. XIV., and for an edition of the letters in French *see* No. 63178, *infra*. An Italian edition of the "Lettere di Pizarro," 1534, a small octavo of four unnumbered leaves, with a title-page composed of several lines arranged in a triangular form, and the text printed in Italic characters, was discovered at Augsburg in 1858. It commenced with a list of the treasures sent to Spain from Peru by Pizarro in January, 1534. This unique tract, the exact title of which has not been preserved, came into the possession of M. Edwin Tross of Paris, and was afterwards sent to England, where it is said to have been lost among the waste paper of the binder's shop, where it had been sent to be bound. *See* [Harrisse], "Bib. Am. Vet., Additions," No. 109.

[PIZARRO.] Copia delle Lettere del Prefetto del|la India la nuoua Spagna detta, alla Cesarea Maesta rescritte.| [At the end:] *Finis.*|M.D.XXXIIII.|*Con gratia, et Priuilegio.*| Sm. 4to, pp. (4).

Probably printed at Venice. This very rare tract, addressed to the emperor Charles V. by some unknown officer, contains an account of Pizarro's invasion and conquest of Peru. It appears to be a translation or abridgment from the Spanish, in which it was probably first printed, but no copy of such an edition is known to be extant. It is also appended to the work of Bordone, *Venice*, 1534–47, *our* Nos. 6419–21, Vol. II. Another Italian account is contained in Ramusio, Vol. III. For a German version *see* "Newe Zeytung," 1534, Vol. XIII., No. 54945. *See also* Vol. X., Nos. 40244, 40558–9, *and* Xeres (F. de).

[PIZARRO.] Nouuelles certai|nes des Isles | du Peru | 1534. | [Woodcut.] *On les vend a Lyon ches Frācoys | Juste deuāt Nostre dame | de Confort.*| [Recto of the first leaf:] Sensuyuent les| letres de Francoys Pizarro | gouuerneur du riche pays et prouince nommee le Peru fai-|sant mention des merueilleu-|ses

choses tant veuez par ces | propres yeulx que par letres a | luy enuoyees par ceulx q̃ au mesme pays habitet | aux quelles sont contenues plusieurs choses nou-|uelles tant de richesses en cette prouince trouuees | & dicelluy pays emenees que de plusieurs aultres|marchandises et richesses: & ce depuis le temps ql|monta sur mer iusques a present.| 12mo, (7) leaves. BM. 63178

So rare that I am unable to refer to a copy in the United States. The following tracts also relate to Pizarro and the conquest of Peru:

[PIZARRO.] Copia di vna Lettera: che a scritto|Luigi Gonzales de Merchado, di Vagliadolit, della India, del Porto del|buon' Giesu, al S. Commandatore. S. Stefano Governator di | Vagliadolit: sopra la Presa del' India del Perù, chiamata|la nuoua Castiglia, e della gran Richezza d'Oro|e d'Argento che la si troua l'año 1532.| [Colophon:] *In Firenze, per Antonio Mazochi Cremonese.* [n. d.] Sm. 4to, (4) leaves, the last of which is blank.

Printed in semi-gothic characters, with 46 lines to a full page. The text begins with these words: "Le nuoue et richezze della Terra richa del Perù, do-|ue e Gouernator Francescho Pizarro, vedute per|me," etc. It was probably translated from a Spanish edition, now lost. The only known copy is in the library of Mr. C. H Kalbfleisch of New York.

[PIZARRO.] Copia di una lettera di Sybilia venuta al Signor Don Lope Imbasciadore Cesareo in Venetia. [n. p. 1538?] 8vo, (2) leaves. 63180

The first leaf contains on the recto an ornamented border within which is the double-headed eagle escutcheon, and below it a globe, surrounded with the inscription, "In Omnem Terram Exivit Cesaris Fama et ĩ Fines Orbis Teremandata," and underneath this, "Svb Vmbra Alarvm Tvar." On the verso is a kind of zodiac. The letter begins on the recto of the second leaf and ends on the verso with "Data in Sibilia a di viij di Febraio M. D. xxxviij." Concerning this plaquette, which treats of the discovery of the province of Liniguara by Diego di Almagro, *see* [Harrisse] "Bib. Am. Vet. Additions," pp. 121–124, where it is reprinted, with a facsimile of the engraved frontispiece. The only known copy is in the Magliabechiana Library at Florence.

PIZARRO (F.) Memorial del pleyto entre D. Francisco Pizarro de la ciudad de Truxillo, de la vna parte, y del Fiscal de la otra. [*Lima.* 1621?] 4to, 12 leaves. 63181

This Francisco Pizarro was the son of Hernando Pizarro, brother to Franc. Pizarro, the conqueror of Peru.

PIZARRO (F.) Lima Fundada ó Conquista del Perú, ... Poema Heroico. ... Por Don Francisco Pizarro. Parte segunda. *En Lima, Año de* 1732. Sm. 4to. 63182

PIZARRO (J. A.) A Funeral Oration, to the ... Memory of Mr. Henry E. Dwight ... . By his friend and fellow Professor, José Antonio Pizarro, in December, 1832. Translated ... from

the Spanish, by S. T. Wallis, A.M. ... *Baltimore: J. Robinson.* 1834. 12mo, pp. 18. 63183

PIZARRO (N.) El Monedero. Novela historica, y de costumbres mejicanas, escrita por Nicolas Pizarro. *Mejico.* 1861. Rl. 8vo, pp. 628. 63184

PIZARRO (R.) Reflexiones que con el interesante objeto de la reconsiliacion de la España ultramarina, con la España europea. *Madrid.* 1820. 8vo, pp. 11. 63185

PIZARRO E ARAUJO (José de Sousa Azevedo). Memorias historicas da capitania do Rio de Janeiro, e das provincias annexas á jurisdicção do vice-rei do estado do Brasil. *Rio de Janeiro, na Imp. Regia.* 1820–22. 9 vols., 4to. 63186

A valuable collection of historical material, but very poorly arranged.

PIZARRO Y GARDIN (J.) Informe que sobre el empedrado y limpieza de las calles de la Habana. Presentó ... D. José de Pizarro y Gardin. *Habana.* 1831. 8vo, pp. (2), 26, (2). B.

PIZARRO Y ORELLANA (Fernando). Discurso ... en que se Muestra la Obligacion qui su Magestad tiene en Justicia, Conciencia y Razon a Cumplir y Mandar Executar la Merced que el rey hiso a Don Francisco Pizarro del titulo de Marques con Veinte Mil Vassallos en la parte donde mas bien le Estieviesse como a Descubridor, Conquistador y Pacificador de los Opulentissimos Reynos del Peru en favor y Gracia de los Successores de su casa y Mayorazgo para qui de tan Grandes hechos no se Obscuresca la Memoria. [*Madrid, about* 1630.] Folio. 63188

Reprinted as an appendix to the following work under the title of "Discvrso Legal y Politico."

PIZARRO Y ORELLANA. Varones|Ilvstres del|Nvevo Mvndo. |Descvbridores, Conqvistadores, y Paci-|ficadores del Opvlento, Dilatado, y Pode-|roso Imperio de las Indias Occidentales:|svs Vidas, Virtvd, Valor, Hazañas, y | Claros Blasones. | Ilvstrados | En los Svcessos destas Vidas con Singvlares Obser-|vaciones Politicas, Morales, Iuridicas, Miscelaneas, y Razon de Estado; para|mayor autoridad de la Historia, y demonstracion della,|y su utilissima Leccion.|Con vn Discvrso Legal|de la Obligacion qve tienen los Reyes a | Premiar los Servicios de svs Vassalos; | ò en ellos, ò en sus Descendientes.|...|Escrive|Don Fernando Pizarro y Orellana ... . | *En Madrid, Por Diego Diaz de la Carrera, Año* M.DC.XXXIX.|*A costa de Pedro Coello Mercader de libros.*| Folio.

Collation: Half title, 1 leaf; title, 1 leaf; Señor, 1 leaf; Dedication, 2 leaves; Cen-

sura, etc., 7 leaves; Prefacion, 6 leaves; text, pp. 427; Discvrso Legal y Politico, pp. 72; Indice, 16 leaves.

This work contains biographies of Columbus, Alonso de Ojeda, Cortez, the four Pizarros, Diego de Almagro, and Diego Garcia de Paredes, in which the treachery and brutality of the conquerors in the treatment of the Indians is palliated and defended. It is, in fact, an extended panegyric on the Pizarros; and together with the appended "Discurso Legal y Politico," which is a long memorial to Philip IV., was written for the purpose of stating their services, and soliciting a confirmation of former grants and remuneration to their descendants. The author calls himself a grandson of the daughter of Francisco Pizarro. As an authority the work is of little value. A continuation still remains in manuscript.

Placard des États-généraux des Provinces-Unies relativement à trois vaisseaux ayant péris au Groënland, daté le 1er décembre 1752. [n. p. n. d.] Folio. 63190

Placard donné par les États-généreaux des Provinces-Unies, le 18 Novembre 1720, concernant l'intercommunication avec les habitants de l'étroit de Davis. [n. p. n. d.] Folio, 1 leaf.

Placcaet|By de Hooghmo: Heeren|Staten Generael dēr Vereenighde Nederlanden, | ghemaeckt op 'tbesluyt vande West-| Indissche Compagnie.| *In 'sGraven-Haghe,|By Hillebrant Iacobssz, Ordinaris ende Gheswooren|Drucker vande Ho: Mo: Heeren Staten Generael. Anno* 1621. *Met Previlegie.*| 4to, 4 leaves. 63192

Edict concerning the establishment of a West India Company, dated June 9, 1621.

Placcaet de Staten Generael tot verbod van den handel op West-Indien ... . *'s Gravenhage.* 1624. Folio, 1 leaf. 63193

Not mentioned by Asher. Prohibition to trade within the limits of the West India Company, dated May 24, 1624.

Also: Another edition, dated June 14, 1632. *'s Gravenhage.* 1632. Folo, 1 leaf.

Placcaet. [Van] de Staten Generael der Vereenichde Nederlanden. *Graven-Haghe, Weduwe ... van Hillebrant Iacobssz van Wuow.* 1625. Sm. 4to, folded sheet. C. 63194

Concerning the capture of San Salvador.

Placcaet | Ende Ordonnantie vande|Hoge ende Mog: Heeren Staten Generael der | Vereenichde Nederlanden, tegens Wechloo-|pers die hun indienst van de West-Indische Compaignie begeven hebbende, ver-|loopen, ofte ooc in tijt van noot | haer Schepē verlaten. | *In s'Graven-Haghe,* | *By de Weduwe, ende Erfghenamen van wijlen Hille-|brant Iacobssz van Wouw, Ordinaris Druckers vande Ho:* | *Mo: Heeren Staten Generael. Anno* 1625.| 4to, (3) leaves. 63195

Edict against those who desert from the West India Company's service, and dated March 22, 1625.

Placcaet tegen het: Nootwendich Discours oft Vertooch aende Ho: Mog: Heeren Staten Generael vande Participanten der Oost-Indische Compagnie tegen de Bewinthebbers. *Middelburgh.* 1622. Folio, 1 leaf. 63196

Edict rendered July 17, 1622, against the "Nootwendich Discours," *our* No. 55449, Vol. XIII.

Placcaet|Teghens seecker Fameus|Libel, geintituleert, Nootwendigh discours, ofte|Vertoogh aende Hog: Mog: Heeren Staten | Generael, van de Participanten der | Oost-Indissche Compagnie, te-|gens de Bewinthebberen. | *In's Graven-Haghe,* | *By de Weduwe eñ Erfgenamen van wijlen Hillebrant*| *Iacobssz van Wouw, Ordinaris Druckers vande Ed: Mog:* | *Heeren Staten van Hollandt ende West-Vrieslandt.*| *Anno* 1622. *Met Privilegie.*| 4to, (4) leaves.

Edict dated July 22, 1622, against the "Nootwendich Discours."

Placcaet|Vande Doorluchtige ende|Hoogh-moghende Heeren Staten Generael, | op'tstuck vant verkoopen ende transporteren van Actien|inde Oost ende West Indische Compagnien, daer by een | yder geinterdiceert ende verboden werdt, inde selve Com-| pagnien egeene Actien te mogen verkoopen, ten ware sy-|luyden de selve Actien effectuelijck inde voorseyde Com-|pagnien zijn herederende: Met vorder ordre eñ reglement | op't transporterẽ eñ doen bekent maken vāde selve actien: | Mitsgaders verboth tegen de gene die met Renuntiatien | eñ andere vonden desen Placcate soecken te subterfugierẽ.| *In s'Graven-Haghe,* | *By Hillebrant Iacobssz, Ordinaris ende Gheswooren*| *Drucker vande Ho: Mo: Heeren Staten Generael.* | *Anno* 1621. *Met Previlegie.* | 4to, (4) leaves. 63198

Edict of July 15, 1621, concerning the sale and transfer of shares in the East and West India Company.

Placcaet Vande Doorluchtige ende Hoogh-moghende Heeren Staten Generaal, op 't stuck van 't verkoopen, ende transporteren van Actien inde Oost-Indische Compaignie. *'s Graven-Haghe.* 1623. 4to, 4 leaves. 63199

Edict of June 3, 1623. This and the above are not mentioned by Asher, who cites the following:

Placcaet|Vande Doorluchtighe ende|Hoogh mogende Heeren Staten Generael op't | stuck van't verkoopen ende transporteren van actien inde | West-Indische Compaignie, daer by een yder geinterdiceert | ende verboden werdt, inde selve Compaignie egeene Actien te|mogen verkoopē, ten ware syluiden de selve actien effectue-|lijck inde voorseyde Compaignie zijn herede-

rende. Met vor|der ordre ende reglement op't transporterẽ ende doen bekent maken vander selve Actien, mitsgaders verboth teghen de|ghene die met Renuncatien ende andere vonden desen Plac-|cate subterfugieren. | *In 's Graven-Haghe,* | *Byde Weduwe, ende Erfgenamen van wijlen Hillebrant Iacobsz* | *van Wouw, Ordinaris Druckers vande Ho. Mo. Heeren Staten Generael.*| *Anno* 1630. *Met Privilegie.*| 4to, (4) leaves. 63200

Edict regarding the sale and transfer of shares in the West India Company.

Placaet | van de Doorluchtighe ende | Hoogh-mogende Heeren Staten Generael op 't|stuck van 't verkoopen ende transporteren van Actien inde|Oost ende West-Indische Compagnien/ daer by een yder geinterdi-|ceert ende verboden werdt/ in de selve Compaignie egheene|Actien te moghen verkoopen/ ten waere syluyden de selve | Actien effectuelyck inde voorseijde Compaignie zyn herede-|rende: Met vorder ordre ende reglement op't transporteren|ende doen bekent maken vanden selve Actien: mitsgaders| verboth teghen de ghene die met Renunciatien ende andere|vonden desen Placate subterfugieren.|*In 'sGraven-Haghe,*|*Byde Weduwe, ende Erfgenamen van wijlen Hillebrandt Iacobsz*|*van Wouw, Ordinaris Druckers vande Ho: Mo: Heeren Staten*|*Generael. Anno* 1630. *Met Privilegie.*| 4to, (4) leaves. 63201

Reprint of the foregoing.

Placcaet| ... *In'sGraven-Haghe,*|*By de Weduwe eñ Erfgenamen van wijlen Hillebrant Iacobssz van Wouw* ... . *Anno* 1622. ... Folio, 1 leaf of 47 lines. + [Another edition. *Ibid.*] 1622. Folio, 1 leaf of 51 lines. 63202

Dated June 10, 1622. This publication informs its readers that the trade with Punto d'Arroy has been granted.

Placaet. [n. p. n. d.] Folio 1 leaf.
Dated November 26, 1622. Prohibition to trade within the limits of the Company.

Placaet. *Graven-Hage, Weduwe van Hillebrandt Iacobsz van Wouw.* 1652. Sm. 4to, 1 leaf. C.

With reference to a silver mine in Brazil.

Placaet van de Staten Generael raeckende de navigatie ende het verboth van toevoer ... naer Portugael. *'s Graven-Hage.* 1657. 4to, pp. 12.
Not mentioned in Asher's "Essay." Edict prohibiting the supplying of merchandise to Portugal and her colonies.

Placcaet ... . *'s Graven-Hage.* 1659. Folio, 1 leaf.
Restrictions laid on the navigation to Greenland.

Placcaet ... . *'s Gravenhage.* 1661. Folio, 1 leaf.
Edict of the States General: prohibition of commerce with the Portuguese in Brazil, etc.

Placcaet .... 's *Gravenhage.* 1661, Folio, 1 leaf.

Edict on the whale-fishery and the navigation to Greenland, prohibiting to rent Dutch vessels, etc., to foreign nations for this purpose.

Placcaet .... 's *Gravenhage.*, 1673. Folio, 1 leaf.

Restriction of the whale-fishery and navigation to Greenland. *See also* Vol. VII., No. 28930.

PLACCIUS (V.) Atlantis Retecta, sive de Navigatione prima Christophori Columbi in Americam. Poëma Vincentii Placcii. *Hamburgi, ex Officina Rebenliniana, A. Ch.* M.DC.LIX. 16mo, pp. (84). S. 63203

PLACE (*Mrs.* M.) The Orphan, or a Brief Memoir of Mrs. Place. ... Written by herself. [*Portland?*] *The Author.* 1830. 12mo, pp. 19. H. 63204

The Place of the Ringgold Light Artillery. *See* [Hiesler (W. M.)], Vol. VIII., No. 31733.

Description of the Property and Mine of the PLACENTIA BAY LEAD Co. and Organization of same. *New York: Press of Wynkoop, Hallenbeck & Thomas.* 1863. 8vo, pp. 31. Map. B.

Placide-Justin. *See* Justin (P.), Vol. IX., No. 36956.

PLACIDO, *pseudon.* *See* [Valdes (Gabriel de la Concepcion)]

Plagiarism; or, a Hint at the Case. By a Layman. ... *Albany, April,* 1817. 8vo, pp. 12. B. 63206

A defense of Rev. Hooper Cumming. *See* Vol. V., No. 17909.

Le Plaidoyer. *See* [Walerande (J. B.)]

Plaidoyer pour le syndic des Creanciers des Mr. Lioncey frères contre la Société des Jesuites. *Paris.* 1761. 8vo. 63207

Relates to Martinique.

A Plain Address to Episcopalians on the proposed Meeting at Mechanic-Hall. By an Episcopalian. *New York.* 1812. 8vo, pp. 4. 63208

A Plain and Earnest Address from A Minister to a Parishioner, on the Neglect of the Publick Worship, and Preaching of the Gospel. *Salem.* 1771. 8vo, pp. 26. 63209

A Plain and Friendly Perswasive. *See* [Makemie (F.)], Vol. XII., No. 44081.

A Plain and Full Account. *See* [Pike (S.)], No. 62833.

A plain and full State of the Demands and Pretensions of his Majesty's Colony of New-York, against the Proprietary Colony of Nova-Cæsaria or New Jersey, respecting the Boundary Line ... [Addressed] To His Majesties Commissioners for settling the Partition-Line between the Colonies ... July 18, 1769. [*New York?* 1769.] Folio, pp. 4. 63210

Very rare. Sometimes followed by an amendment of their claim, by the managers on the part of New York, dated "July 26, 1769," 1 page, and a statement presented to the Commissioners by the agents on the part of New Jersey, 9 pages. *See also* Vol. I., No. 1967, Vol. II., No. 7884, Vol. XII., No. 47648, *and* Vol. XIII., Nos. 53153, 53909.

Plain and Important Facts for the Consideration of the Electors of Newhampshire. [*Portsmouth.* 1807?] 8vo, pp. 16. H.

See also [Plumer (W.)]

A | Plain and Seasonable | Address | to the | Freeholders | of | Great-Britain, | on | The Present Posture of Affairs in | America. | *London: Richardson and Urquhart,* MDCCLXVI. 8vo, pp. (2), 21.

"Ridicule of Mr. Pitt, and declamation against the Americans."—*Monthly Review,* XXXIV. 162.

The Plain Dealer: Number II. Being a Tickler, For the Leisure Hour's Amusement of the Author of Cool Thoughts. Wherein the Force of his several Arguments in Favour of a Change of Government is stated in a clear Light and accommodated to the Comprehension of Readers in every Capacity. By X. Y. Z. Gentleman. To be Continued. *Philadelphia: Printed in Second-Street* [*by Andr. Steuart*], ... 1764. Sm. 8vo, pp. 16.

Dated, May 7, 1764. For Numbers I. and III. *see* [Williamson (Hugh)].

The Plain-Dealer. Vol. I. [Edited by William Leggett.] *New York.* 1830–31. Sm. folio. S. 63214

Plain Directions on Domestic Economy ... . Published by Order of the Society for the Prevention of Pauperism. *New-York: Printed by Samuel Wood & Sons.* 1821. 8vo, pp. 16. H.

Plain English. A Letter to the King. [*London.* 1778.] 8vo, pp. xxxvii, 53. J.C.B. 63216

Signed "Sincerus." The preface which is dated July 1, 1778, states that "this Letter was written and printed in October, 1775, according to its date, and was intended for immediate publication; but, it having the ill luck to displease a gentleman to whom I had great obligations, I forbore to have it advertized." Principally a reply to Dr. Johnson's "Taxation no Tyranny."

PLAIN FACT, *pseudon.* An Answer to a Pamphlet, recently addressed to the Episcopalians of Pennsylvania, under the signature of Plain Truth. By Plain Fact. *Philadelphia.* 1827. 8vo, pp. 28. 63217

In reply to our No. 63239, *infra.*

Plain Facts [on West Indian Slavery]. By the Author of "Honesty the best Policy." [*Leicester: A. Cockthaw.* 1827?] Sm. 8vo, pp. 8. B. 63218

... Plain Facts. *See* Vol. II., No. 6541, *and* Vol. III., No. 8864, *note.* 63219

Plain Facts for Plain People; or, Principle against Expediency. By a Democrat of Maryland. *Baltimore: Printed by R. M. & I. D. Cloud.* 1836. 8vo, pp. 22, (1). BA. 63220

In favor of the election of Van Buren to the presidency.

Plain Facts: being An Examination into the Rights of the Indian Nations of America, to their respective Countries; and a Vindication of the Grant, from The Six United Nations of Indians, to the Proprietors of Indiana, against the Decision of the Legislature of Virginia; together with Authentic Documents, proving That the Territory, Westward of the Allegany Mountain, never belonged to Virginia, &c. *Philadelphia: Printed ... by R. Aitken.* M.DCC.LXXXI. 8vo, pp. 164, (1). C., M. 63221

The authorship has been attributed to Benjamin Franklin and to Anthony Benezet. It is an able treatise on the tenure of the Indian claim to the title of lands occupied by them.

A Plain | Historical Account | of the | Tryal, | Between the Honourable | James Annesley, Esq; Plaintiff, | (Who was banish'd into America, by his | cruel Uncle, where he remain'd many | Years in Slavery.) | And the Right Honourable the | Earl of Anglesea, Defendant: | In which the Councils Pleadings on both | Sides are entirely preserved: | with the | Evidence of the most material Witnesses | easily digested, the Law Terms, whe- [*sic*] | Latin or French explain'd; and the | whole free from the Burthen of tedious | and trifling Circumstances, which too | often attend larger Accounts. | *London Printed: And Sold by Richard Winpenny, at the Bible | in Castle-Street, Bristol.* 1744. | 8vo, pp. 227. 63222

Also: The | Case | Of the Honourable | James Annesley, Esq; | Humbly Offered | To all Lovers of Truth and Justice. | [n. p.:] *Printed in the Year* 1756. | 8vo, pp. 38. Privately printed and very rare. *See* Vol. I., Nos. 1599–1603.

A Plain Letter. *See* [Tucker (J.)]

A Plain Narrative of the uncommon Sufferings and Remarkable Deliverance of Thomas Brown, of Charlestown, in New-England; Who returned to his Father's House the Beginning of Jan. 1760, after having been absent three years and about eight months: Containing An Account of the Engagement between a Party of English commanded by Major Rogers, and a Party of French and Indians, in Jan. 1757, in which Capt. Spikeman was kill'd; and the Author ... left for dead on the Field ... How he was taken Captive by the Indians, and carried to Canada, and from thence to the Mississippi ... . The Second Edition. *Boston: Fowle & Draper.* 1760. 8vo, pp. 27. 63223

"Perhaps the rarest of all Narratives of Indian Captivities."—J. H. TRUMBULL.

The Plain Path to Christian Perfection ... . Translated from the French. ... *Philadelphia: Printed by Joseph Crukshank* ... MDCCLXXII. 16mo, pp. xi, 124. 63224

Contains a preface by Anthony Benezet.

The Plain Question upon the Present Dispute with our American Colonies. ... The Second Edition. *London: ... J. Wilkie,* ... M DCC LXXVI. 12mo, pp. 24. N., S. + The Third Edition. [*Ibid.*] M.DCC.LXXVI. 12mo, pp. 24. + *Dublin.* 1776. 12mo, pp. 24. 63225

"One great purpose of this little ministerial handbill, is to prove that there is nothing new or unprecedented in the exercise of parliamentary authority over the colonies. The writer, however, appears to have been very ignorant of the subject, and very badly instructed by his employers."—*Monthly Review,* LIV. 330.

Plain Questions for Mormonites. By One who knows they are not Saints. ... *London: Wertheim and Mackintosh.* 1852. 12mo, pp. 12. B. 63226

Plain Reasons, I. For Dissenting from the ... Church of England. II. Why Dissenters are not, nor can be guilty of Schism, in ... separating from ... the Church of England. And III. Several Common Objections ... against Dissenters, Answer'd. By a True Protestant. The Eighteenth Edition ... . *Boston in N. E. Re-printed for and Sold by Thomas Hancock.* MDCCXXV. Small 8vo, pp. (4), 40. B., BA. 63227

Plain Sense, on National Industry. Addressed to the People of the United States. *New-York: Printed by G. L. Birch & Co.* 1820. 8vo, pp. 51. B. 63228

Signed, "Plain Sense."

Plain Sense, or Sketches of Political Frenzy and Federal Fraud and Folly. *Washington.* 1803. 8vo, pp. 40. W. 63229

A Plain State of the Argument between Great Britain and her Colonies. *London: T. Becket.* 1775. 8vo, pp. 19. H. 63230

A brief recapitulation of the arguments usually employed by the advocates for parliamentary supremacy over America. Perhaps by Dr. Johnson. Reprinted with the following title:

A Plain Statement of the Argument between Great Britain and her Colonies. The Second Edition. *London: T. Becket.* 1776. 8vo, pp. 19. 63231

A Plain Statement addressed to all Honest Democrats. By One of the People. *Boston: John P. Jewett & Company.* 1856. 12mo, pp. 48. + *Boston: Geo. C. Rand & Avery, Printers.* 1868. 12mo, pp. 36. H. 63232

See also Moody (L.), Vol. XII., No. 50318.

A Plain Statement. *See* [Moore (C. C.)], Vol. XII., No. 50337, *and also* Vol. XIII., No. 54580.

A plain Statement for the Consideration of the Friends of the Protestant Episcopal Church, in the Diocese of Illinois, the Rt. Rev. Philander Chase, D.D. Bishop. ... With notes by Observer. *New York: Turner & Lawrence.* 1846. 8vo, pp. 15, (1). H.

Relates to the organization of Jubilee College.

... A Plain Statement of Facts ... descriptive of the Present State of Slavery in the West Indies. *London:* [*Bagster and Thomas, Printers.* n. d.] 12mo, pp. 12. B. 63234

The Negro's Friend, No. 7. *See* Vol. XIII., No. 52274.

A Plain Statement of Matters. *See* Vol. II., No. 8310.

A Plain Statement of the Rights, &c., claimed by our Colonists, under the Charters Granted to them by our Sovereigns ... . *London: Printed by G. Davidson.* 1833. 8vo, pp. (2), 118.

A Plain Statement to the Common Sense of the People [on Slavery. n. p.] 1826. 4to, pp. 4. 63236

A Plain Tale, Supported by Authentic Documents, justifying the Character of General Wilkinson ... . By a Kentuckian. *New York.* 1807. 8vo, pp. 24. C., W. 63237

PLAIN TRUTH, *pseudon.* Letters to William Staughton, D.D. By Plain Truth. ... *Philadelphia: ... The Author.* 1818. 12mo, pp. 48. 63238

Relates to a quarrel among the Baptists in Philadelphia.

PLAIN TRUTH, *pseudon.* A Candid Address to the Episcopalians of Pennsylvania, in relation to the present situation of the affairs of the Diocese. By Plain Truth. [n. p.] April, 1827. 8vo, pp. 32. H. 63239

For an answer *see* "Plain Fact," No. 63217, *supra.*

PLAIN TRUTH, *pseudon.* Three Letters: one to the Committee of Correspondence; one to "Plain Truth, Junior;" and one to "Plain Fact;" in support of the "Candid Address" to the Episcopalians of Pennsylvania on the affairs of the Diocese. By Plain Truth. [n. p.] *May,* 1827. 8vo, pp. 55. BA. 63240

PLAIN TRUTH, JR., *pseudon.* Another Candid Address to the Episcopalians of Pennsylvania, in relation to the present situation of affairs in the Diocese. By Plain Truth, Junior. [*Philadelphia.* 1827.] 8vo, pp. 22. W. 63241

Plain Truth. Volume I. ... *Canandaigua* (*N. Y.*): *Printed by Thomas B. Barnum.* 1822. 8vo, pp. (4), 192. Continued. H.

A semi-monthly, chiefly devoted to opposing the missionary cause. Two volumes were published.

Plain Truth, ... devoted to the defense of Primitive Christianity and to the exposing of Frauds ... New Series, Vol. I. *Rochester, N. Y.* 1828. 8vo. S. 63243

Plain Truth, addressed to the Independent Electors of the State of New-Jersey. *Trenton: Printed by James T. Wilson.* 1808. 8vo, pp. 27. 63244

Plain Truth; Addressed to the Inhabitants of America. *See* Candidus, *pseudon.*, Vol. III., No. 10671.

Corrected list of the imprints and collations of the various editions:

Philadelphia: Printed, and Sold, by R. Bell, ... MDCCLXXVI. 8vo, pp. (8), 84, Advertisement, (2). Mr. Bell's address precedes the work, which is followed by the articles of "Rationalis" and "Cato," pp. 67–84.

Philadelphia: Printed, and Sold, by R. Bell, ... MDCCLXXVI. 8vo, pp. (6), 9–96. Sig. I is mispaged 57–64 (for 65–72). "Rationalis" and "Cato" fill pp. 75–96. Usually followed by "Extract, from the Journal," pp. (6), *our* No. 15526, Vol. IV., and "Additions to Plain Truth; Addressed to the Inhabitants of America, Containing further Remarks on a late Pamphlet, entitled Common Sense ... Written by the Author of Plain Truth. ... *Philadelphia: Printed, and Sold, by R. Bell,* ... MDCCLXXVI." 8vo, pp. (2), 97–136. Some copies are partly printed on bluish paper, with a slip pasted on the verso of the title: "To Every Purchaser. The impossibility of obtaining White, constituted the Law of necessity, for part of these Additions to appear in Blue," etc.

Philadelphia, Printed: London, Reprinted for J. Almon. M.DCC.LXXVI. 8vo, pp. (4), 47, (1).

Second Edition. [*Ibid.*] M.DCC.LXXVI. 8vo, pp. (4), 47, (1). Some copies are dated M.DCC.LXXVII.

Dublin: Reprinted by M. Mills. M,DCC,LXXVI. 8vo, pp. (4), 44.

Probably written by Joseph Galloway. *See* "Magazine of American History," I. 633; II. 59–60.

Plain Truth, in a Series of Numbers: from the New-York Daily Advertiser. *New-York: Printed by Daniel Fanshaw.* 1821. 12mo, pp. 56. BA. 63245

Concerning the United States Bank.

Plain Truth on the Affairs of Grace Church. *Printed by Charles A. Elliott, Philadelphia.* [1836.] 8vo, pp. 15. 63246

Plain Truth. *See* Vol. VII., No. 25563, [Galloway (J.)], No. 26440, *and* Vol. IX., No. 35382.

... Plain Truths, addressed to the People of N. Hampshire, concerning their State Prison ... . [n. p. n. d.] 8vo, pp. 16. B.

A Plain Word, concerning the Late Circular of the Rt. Rev. Manton Eastburn to the Clergy of Massachusetts. *Boston: Printed by S. N. Dickinson & Co.* 1846. 12mo, pp. 12. BA.

Plain Words to Plain People, by a Plain Man, about the War. *Philadelphia: Union League.* 1863. 8vo, pp. 16. 63249

A Plaine Description of the Barmvdas. *See* [C. (W.)], Vol. III., No. 9759.

PLAINFIELD, *N. J.* Catalogue of the Officers and Students of Greenland Family School, at Plainfield, N. J. 1840–1. [n. p. n. d.] 8vo. N. 63250

Report of the Committee ... to investigate ... the Plainfield Bank ... *Trenton.* 1847. 8vo, pp. 32. 63251

Plainte de la Novvelle France. *See* Vol. III., No. 10543.

Plainte portée contre la cour royale de la Guadeloupe, pour crimes de forfaiture, de soustraction fraudulense de pièces, de faux et d'envoi de pièces fausses au ministre de la justice, par un ancien magistrat condamné le 14 mai 1830 à la peine de la censure. *Caen.* 1833. 8vo, pp. 128. 63252

PLAKE (*Mrs.* K.) The Southern Husband outwitted by his Union Wife. By Mrs. Kate Plake. *Philadelphia: Moore & Brother.* 1868. 12mo, pp. 161. Portrait. C. 63253

PLAMONDON (L.) Discours prononcé devant la Société Littéraire de Québec, à l'ouverture de la Séance du 3e Juin. Par Louis Plamondon. *Québec.* 1809. 8vo. 63254

Plan de Colonization. *See* [Jollivet (M.)], Vol. IX. 36421.

Plan de Independencia adoptada por la Diputacion, 7 Nov. 1836. *Monterey.* 1836. 8vo. 63255

Plan de Independencia Californiana, 1836. *Monterey.* 1836. 8vo. 63256

Plan de Propios y Arbitrios para Fondos Municipales, 1834. *Monterey.* 1834. 8vo. 63257

Plan de subsistencia para el ejército presentado á la Diputacion provincial por la Comision encargada de proponer arbitrios para ella, y aprobado por S. E. en esta fecha. *Carácas.* 1821. 8vo, pp. 9. 63258

Plan d'une agence. *See* [Morhard (——)], Vol. XII. 50694.

Plan einer geregelten deutschen Auswanderung und Ansiedelung in den Vereinigten Staaten Nordamerika's. *Darmstadt.* 1848. 8vo. 63259

A Plan for a School. *See* [Biddle (Owen)], Vol. II. 5245.

A Plan for Civilizing the Indians of North America. *London.* 1796. 8vo. 63260

A Plan for Conciliating the Jarring Political Interests of Great Britain and her North American Colonies, And For promoting a general Re-union throughout the Whole of the British Empire. ... *London: ... J. Ridley* ... . 1775. 8vo, pp. xviii. + [Another Edition. *Ibid.*] 1775. 8vo, pp. xviii. P. 63261

"Contains nothing that is likely ever to be adopted."—*Monthly Review,* LII. 87.

Plan for Conducting the Inspector's Department of the United States. *Philadelphia: Printed by David C. Claypoole, Printer to the Honourable the Congress.* [1780.] 8vo, pp. 8. P. 63262

Plan for conducting the Quartermaster General's Department, agreed to in Congress, July 15th, 1780. *Philadelphia: Printed by David C. Claypoole* ... . M.DCC.LXXX. 8vo, pp. 15. P. 63263

Plan for Conquering Treason. Letter to President Lincoln, by a Citizen of Kentucky. [n. p.] 1862. 8vo, pp. 8. 63264

The Plan for Correspondence and Friendly Intercourse, proposed by ... Delegates ... of the Presbyterian Church ... the Dutch Reformed Church and ... the Associate Reformed Church, when met in New York ... June, 1798 ... approved by the General Assembly of the Presbyterian Church, in May, 1799 ... . [*New York.* 1800.] 8vo, pp. 4. B. 63265

A Plan for encouraging Agriculture, and increasing the Value of Farms in the Midland and more Western Counties of Pennsylvania, applicable to several other Parts of that State, and to many Parts of the United States. [n. p. about 1790.] 12mo, pp. 11. 63266

Plan for establishing a Chaplain of the Presbyterian Denomination in the Jail, Hospital, and Bettering House, Philadelphia. *Philadelphia.* 1802. 8vo, pp. 16. M. 63267

Plan for establishing A General Marine Society throughout the United States ... written at sea, in the year 1794. ... *Philadelphia: Printed by John Fenno.* 1798. 8vo, pp. 32. BA. 63268

Preface signed "S. K."

A | Plan | for | Establishing and | Disciplining | a | National Militia | in | Great Britain, | Ireland, | and | In all the British Dominions | of America. | *London:* | *Printed for A. Millar* ... | M DCC XLV. | 8vo, pp. xlvii, 106. C. 63269

Plan for forming a Warehouse Company. *See* [Lombard (A. C.)], Vol. x., No. 41838.

A Plan for Insurance.. *See* [Boardman (W. W.)], II. 6092.

Plan for Laying out Towns and Townships on the new-acquired Lands in the East Indies, America, or elsewhere. *London.* 1794. 8vo. 63270

A Plan for obtaining Presidents. *See* [Nicholas (S. S.)], Vol. XIII., No. 55178.

A Plan for one Uniform Circulating Medium, to be sufficient for our Population, and commensurate with our Property, at all times ... [*Washington, about* 1833.] 3 parts, 8vo, pp. 8, 4, 6.

Signed, Thomas Law.

A Plan for Resuming Specie Payments without changing the Volume of the Currency. *New York.* 1873. 8vo. 63272

Plan for Securing to British North-America a larger share of Emigration from Great Britain, Germany, &c., by the Construction of a Railway between the Atlantic and Pacific Oceans. *Berlin.* 1860. 8vo. 63273

A Plan for Settling the Unhappy Dispute. *See* [Jenings (Edmund)], Vol. IX., No. 35986.

Plan for shortening the Time of Passage between New York and London. *Portland: Harmon and Williams, Printers.* 1850. 8vo, pp. 20. B. + Printed by order of the Legislature of Maine. *Portland.* 1850. 8vo, pp. 24. Map. 63274

Edited by John A. Poor. *See also* our No. 23109, Vol. VI., and add to the collation, 1 Map.

Plan for terminating the War. *See* [Blanchard (J. P.)], Vol. II., No. 5828.

A Plan for the Abolition of Slavery in the West Indies. *London: William Griffin.* MDCCLXXII. 4to, pp. (4), iv, 33. H.

A Plan for the Abolition of Slavery consistent with the Interest of all Parties. *London.* 1827. 12mo. 63276

A Plan for the General Arrangement of the Militia. *See* [Knox (Henry)], Vol. IX., No. 38161.

A Plan for the Maintenance of the Ministers in New England. *Boston.* 1724. 8vo. 63277

A Plan For the Payment of the National Debt, By Means of a National Bank. [*New York.* 1785.] 8vo, pp. 13. + [Another edition.] *New York: Greenleaf.* 1785. 8vo, 8 leaves, 1 blank. 63278

Plan for the Settlement of 552,500 Acres of Land, in the District of Morgan, Wilkes County, North Carolina. [*London.* 1796.] 4to, pp. 4. 63279

Plan général de défense. *See* Vol. VII., No. 29583.

A Plan looking to an Early Resumption of Specie Payments, and to the Extinguishment of the Public Debt. By a New-York Merchant. *New York: George F. Nesbitt & Co., Printers.* 1867. 8vo, pp. 9. H. 63280

Plan of a Code of Laws. *See* [Marriott (J.)], XI. 44690.

Plan of a Currency Agent, intended to obviate the honest objections of all parties, and to meet the views of moderate men of both parties. [n. p.] 1843. 8vo. 63281

The Plan Of a Performance of Solemn Musick, To be in the Hall of the College of Philadelphia, On Wednesday Evening, April 10th, 1765, For the Benefit of the Charity Schools. [n. p. n. d.] 8vo, pp. 4. P. 63282

Improved title of our No. 61547, Vol. XIV.

A Plan of a Proposed Union. *See* [Cooper (Myles)], Vol. IV., No. 16590, *note.*

Plan of a Review for the First Baltimore Battalion to be held ... 9th ... of June, 1796. O. H. Williams, ... General; ... *Baltimore.* 1794. 8vo. 63283

Plan of a Society for the Sale of Lands in America, for which a Subscription is opened, containing a very beneficial speculation, whereby both large and small sums of money may be improved to very great advantage, without any Hazard of Loss. *London: Instituted* 25 *February* 1794. 4to, pp. 12. J.C.B., H. 63284

Plan of a Theological Seminary adopted by the General Assembly. *Philadelphia.* 1811. 8vo. + Second Edition. *Elizabeth-town.* 1816. 8vo. 63285

Plan of a Treaty of Commerce to be entered into between ... the Estates of the Seven United States of Holland, and the Thirteen United States of North America. ... 30 Oct. 1780. [n. p. n. d.] Folio. 63286

Dutch and English text opposite. Official edition of the Preparatory Plan (projected 1778 at Aix-la-Chapelle), with the correspondence relating to it, as it was presented by the Chev. Yorke, as found with the papers of Mr. Laurens, to the Prince of Orange, and sent by the States General to the Provinces. The subscription of the Treaty is changed in *all* the reproductions.—MÜLLER.

The Plan of an American Compact. *See* Vol. XIII. 56558.

Plan of Association of the North American Land Company. *See* Vol. XIII., No. 55548.

Plan of Association of the Territorial Company, established April, 1795. *Philadelphia: R. Aitken & Son.* 1795. 8vo, pp. 21

A Plan of Consociation, Adopted and Recommended by a Convention of Churches in Windham County, November, 1800. *Windham: Printed by John Byrne.* 1800. 8vo, pp. 16. W.

Plan of English Commerce. *See* [Defoe (D.)], v. 19289.

Plan of Exercise for the Militia of Connecticut. *New London.* 1772. 8vo, pp. 71. 63289

See also Vol. XI., Nos. 45547 *and* 45934.

Plan of Organization of the National Soldier's Historical Association. *Cincinnati.* 1865. 18mo. 63290

A Plan of Reconciliation. *See* [Ramsay (Allan)].

A Plan of Reconciliation with America; consistent with the Dignity and Interests of both Countries. Humbly inscribed to the King. ... *London: Printed by J. P. Coghlan, ... and sold by G. Wilkie* ... . MDCCLXXXII. 12mo, pp. (2), 48. BA. 63291

By J. Cawthorne. This plan yields to America everything but the *word* independency. *See* "Monthly Review," LXVI. 226.

Plan of Re-Union, 1778. *See* [Pulteney (R.)]

Plan of the Albany Hospital. [n. p. 1849.] 8vo, pp. 8.

Plan of the English Commerce, a Prospect of Home and Foreign Trade. *London.* 1728. 8vo. 63293

Plan | of the | New Constitution | for the | United States of America, | agreed upon in a | Convention of the States. | With a Preface by the Editor. | *London: J. Debrett.* M DCC LXXXVII. 8vo, pp. (2), 30. + A New Edition, corrected. [*Ibid.*] 1792. 8vo, pp. 32. S. 63294

Plan of the New York Tammanial Tontine Association. *New York.* 1792. 8vo, pp. 12. N. 63295

Plan of the Standing Army. *See* [Poinsett (J. R.)]

Plan of the Theological Seminary, established in the Washington Academy, and Located in the Village of Salem, May 13, 1819. *Salem, N. Y.: Printed by James B. Gibson.* 1819. 8vo, pp. 15. B. 63296

Plan of the Theological Seminary of the Protestant Episcopal Church ... . Together with ... An Appendix ... . *Hartford: Printed by S. Lincoln.* 1820. 8vo, pp. 21. + Second Edition. *Hartford.* 1820. 8vo, pp. 23. 63297

Plan of the Union Theological Seminary ... in Virginia and North Carolina. *Richmond.* 1831. 8vo. 63298

A Plan of Union, for admitting Representatives from the American Colonies, and from Ireland into the British Parliament ... 10th Decemb. 1770. [n. p. n. d.] Folio, pp. 3. P. 63299

A very curious piece, printed probably at Philadelphia. It urges a representation in Parliament of 50 commons and 10 peers from the provinces and the West Indian colonies.

The Plan of Union of 1801, between Presbyterians and Congregationalists, and Reasons why it should be abandoned. *New York.* 1856. 12mo, pp. 12. 63300

A Plan, or Articles of Perpetual Union, Commerce, and Friendship, between Great-Britain and her American Colonies; founded on the solid basis of Justice, and proposed as a medium between the claims of total Independence on the one hand, and those of legal Subjection on the other. *London: Joseph Johnson.* M. DCC. LXXX. 8vo. 63301

"A very well intentioned writer, who proposes 'to split the difference' in the dispute between Great Britain and the colonies."—*Monthly Review*, LXIII. 386.

Plan Propuesto para la Construccion de Un Camino de Madera o de Hierro ... [por Fitz-Gibbon. *San Salvador.* 1853.] 4to, 4 leaves. 63302

A | Plan | to Reconcile | Great Britain & her Colonies, | and preserve the | Dependency | of | America. | *London: J. Almon.* M.DDC.-LXXIV [for 1774]. 8vo, pp. xvi, 40. 63303

Dedicated to the Duke of Northumberland, and signed "Cosmopolite." "The method proposed is, by granting the colonies liberty to have manufactures of their own and a foreign trade in British vessels; under the sanction of their own representation and taxation." *See* "Monthly Review," L. 485.

Plan van Accomodement. *See* Vol. VII., No. 22995.

PLANAS Y CO. Informe del sindico en la cesion de bienes que Simon Planas y Comp. pretenden se les admite. *Carácas.* 1843. 8vo, pp. 36. 63304

PLANCARTE (J. A.) Flores Guadalupanas, ó Sonetos alusivos á la Celestial Imágen de María Santísima ... en su advocacion de Guadalupe ... escritos por un Autor Americano de nombre incierto: revistos y añadidos por ... Joseph Antonio Plancarte. *Mexico.* 1785. 4to. BM. 63305

PLANCARTE. Sermon de gracias que en la exaltacion al trono de N. Católico Monarca D. Carlos IV. y su solemne proclamacion, hecha por la villa de Zamora de esta Nueva España. *Mexico.* 1791. 4to, 16 leaves. 63306

Also: Poema Panegerico ... . *Mexico.* 1790. Sm. 4to.—Recreacion Poetica ... . *Mexico.* 1794. Sm. 4to.

Planos de Bolsillo, de la Isla de Cuba, la ciudad de la Habana, y sus barrios estramuros, tabla de distancias de unos pueblos á otros. ... *Habana: Imprenta del Gobierno.* 1842. 16mo, pp. (5). 7 folded Maps. + [*Ibid.*] 1847. 16mo, pp. (20). 8 folded sheets. B. 63307

Improved title of our No. 17796, Vol. V.

Plans and Progress of Internal Improvement in South Carolina, &c. *Columbia.* 1820. 12mo. 63308

Plans of Various Lakes and Rivers. *See* Vol. III. 10546.

Planta General de los Empleados de las administraciones principales de la Renta del Tabaco ... *Mèxico: Impreso por J. M. Lara.* 1842. 4to, pp. 15. 63309

Signed "Manuel E. de Gorostiza."

[PLANTAGENET (Beauchamp).] A | Description | of | the Province of | New Albion. | And a Direction for Adventurers with small | stock to get two for one, and good land freely: | And for Gentlemen, and all Servants, Labourers, and | Artificers to live plentifully. | And a former Description re-printed of the heal- | thiest, pleasantest, and richest Plantation of New Albion in | North Virginia, proved by thirteen witnesses. | Together with | a Letter from Master Robert Evelin, that lived there | many years, shewing the particularities, and excellency | thereof. | With a briefe of the charge of victuall, and necessaries, to | transport and buy stock for each Planter, or Labourer, | there to get his Master 50 l. per Annum, or more in twelve | trades, at 10 l. charges onely a man. | *Printed in the Year* 1648. | 4to. C.H.K., J.C.B. 63310

Collation: Title, reverse "The Order, Medall, and Riban of the Albion Knights," etc., with three woodcuts of arms; Dedication to Edmund Ployden, "Lord Proprietor, Earl Palatine, Governour and Captain Generall of the Province of New Albion," at the end dated "Middleboro this 5 of Decemb. 1648" and signed "Beauchamp Plantagenet," pp. 3–8; Text, pp. 9–32.

Improved title of our No. 19724, Vol. V. The country described includes portions of Delaware, New Jersey and Long Island. In the dedication of this extremely rare tract Plantagenet refers to "the two former books printed of Albion 1637, and 1642." No copy has been found of the former, and even the title of it seems to be unknown; but the latter is undoubtedly the "former Description re-printed," mentioned in Plantagenet's title-page, and comprising chapter 3, "The Description of Master Robert Evelin and 13 witnesses, printed 7 years since, and now re-printed." *See* No. 63312, *infra.*

[PLANTAGENET.] A | Description | of the | Province | of | New Albion. | And a Direction for Adventurers | with small stock to get two for one, and good land freely. | And for Gentlemen, and all

Servants, Labourers, | and Artificers, to live plentifully. | And a former Description Re-printed of the healthiest, plea- | santest, and richest Plantation of Nevv Albion in | North Virginia, proved by Thirteen Witnesses. | Together with | A Letter from Master Robert Evelin, that lived | there many yeers, shewing the particu- | larities, and ex- | cellency thereof. | With a Brief of the Charge of Victual, and Necessaries, to trans- | port and buy stock for each Planter, or Labourer, there to get | his Master fifty pounds per Annum, or more, in twelve Trades, | and at ten pounds charges onely a man. | *London,* | *Printed by James Moxon, in the Yeer* MDCL. | 4to. C.H.K. 63311

Collation: Title, reverse "The Order," etc., as in the first edition; Dedication, etc., dated "Middleboro this 5 of Decemb. 1641" [for 1648] and signed "Beauchamp Plantagenet," pp. (6); Text, pp. 32.

This second edition is even more rare than the first. *See* Force's "Tracts," Vol. II., where the edition of 1648 is reprinted. *See also* Vol. XIII., No. 52434, XIV., 59667, *and* [Varlo (C.)]

The following also relates to New Albion:

A | Direction | for Adventvrers | With small stock to get two for one, | and good land freely: | And for Gentlemen, and all Servants, Labourers, and | Artificers to live plentifully. | And the true Description of the healthiest, pleasantest, and richest | plantation of new Albion, in North Virginia, proved by thirteen witnesses. | Together with, | A Letter from Master Robert Evelin, that lived there many | yeares, shewing the particularities, and excellency thereof. | With a briefe of the charge of victuall, and necessaries, to transport | and buy stocke for each Planter, or Labourer, there to get his | Master 50 l per Annum, or more in twelve trades, and | at 10 l charges onely a man. | *Printed in the yeare,* 1641. | 4to, 4 leaves. 63312

A tract of the greatest rarity. The only copy I know of is in the library of Mr. C. H. Kalbfleisch of New York. It comprises a brief description of the country, signed by "Captain Brown, Captain Clayborn, Robert Evelin," and ten others, followed by "Master Evelins Letter." It was reprinted by Plantagenet in his "Description," *supra.*

PLANTAGENET SPRING. An Analysis of the Mineral Water from the Plantagenet Spring, in Canada ... . *New York: Baker, Godwin & Co., Printers.* 1853. 8vo, pp. 24. 63313

Plantas en el Real Jardin de Mexico. *Mexico.* 1795. 8vo. Plate. 63314

The Plantation. A Southern Quarterly Journal of Literature, Politics and General Miscellany. Edited by J. A. Turner, of Georgia. Vol. I. *New York: Pudney & Russell.* 1860. 8vo.

"The special feature of this Journal will be a defence of Negro Slavery."

Plantation and Farm Instruction, Regulation, Record, Inventory and Account Book. ... By a Southern Planter. *Richmond, Virginia: J. W. Randolph.* 1852. 4to, pp. 103. B. 63316

This contains, among other matter, a form of agreement with overseers, and rules for the government of negroes.

Plantation Justice, Shewing the Constitution of their Courts, and what sort of Judges they have in them. By which Merchants may see the Occasions of their great Losses in the Plantation Trade: Lawyers may see such a Model of Justice as they could not have thought of; and others may see how those Parts of the World are governed. *London: Printed for A. Baldwin,* ... 1701. 4to, pp. 12. J.C.B. 63317

Plantation Work | the | Work | of this | Generation. | Written in True-Love | To all such as are weightily inclined | to Transplant themselves and Fami- | lies to any of the English Plantati- | ons in | America. | The | Most material Doubts and Objections against it | being removed, they may more cheerfully pro- | ceed to the Glory and Renown of the God of | the whole Earth, who in all Undertakings is to | be looked unto, Praised and Feared for Ever. | ... | *London, Printed for Benjamin Clark in George-Yard in* | *Lombard-street,* 1682. | Small 4to, pp. (2), 18. J.C.B., C. 63318

By William Loddington, and signed "W. L." On pp. 17, 18, "An Abstract of some Passages out of divers Letters from America relating to Pennsylvania,"—from Lewis Morris, New York, to W. Penn, June 3, 1681; Another to W. P. from New York, June 25th; and two others from the Deputy-Governour of Pennsylvania, to his Wife, and to a Friend, in London. Written to promote the settlement of Pennsylvania. Improved title of our No. 41762, Vol. X.

PLANTE (F.) Francisci Plante Brugensis Mavritiados Libri XII. Hoc est: Rerum ab Illustrissimo Heroe Ioanne Mavritio, Comite Nassaviæ etc. In Occidentali Indiâ gestarum Descriptio Poetica. [Vignette.] *Lugduni Batavorum, Ex Officina Ioannis Maire. Anno* CIↃ IↃ CXLVII. *Væneunt Amsterodami apud Ioannem Blavium.* Folio. J.C.B., S. 63319

Collation: Title, 7 unnumbered leaves, pp. 12, 1 unnumbered leaf, pp. 196, 1 leaf for the "Ordo Tabularum." Portrait of Prince Maurice by T. Matham, 4 large Maps of Brazil, and 22 Plates (all taken from Barlaeus). Some copies contain a portrait of the author by J. Suyderhoef.

A poem on the glorious and wise government of the Dutch Prince John Maurice in Brazil.

El Plantel. Directores, Ramon de Palma, y José Antonio Echeverria. Tomo primero. *Habana: R. Oliva.* 1838–39. 4to, pp. 286. Plates. B. 63320

The Planter: or, Thirteen Years in the South. By a Northern Man. ... *Philadelphia: H. Hooker.* 1853. 12mo, pp. 275.

A Planter, *pseudon.* Observations on the Danger of Losing the Trade of the Sugar Colonies ... By a Planter. *London.* 1714. 8vo. 63322

A Planter, *pseudon.* *See* Vol. vii. 29197, *and* Vol. x. 40257

The Planter's Almanac for ... 1832 ... Calculated for the Latitude and Longitude of Mobile ... . *Mobile: Odiorne ana Smith.* [n. d.] 12mo, pp. (32). Continued. H. 63323

The Planters' Objections to the African Trade Bill. [n. p. 1712.] Folio. 63324

The Planter's Plea. *See* [White (John)].

The Planters Speech, 1684. *See* [Tryon (Thomas)].

The Planter's Victim; or, Incidents of American Slavery. Illustrated. *Philadelphia: W. W. Smith.* 1855. 12mo, pp. 365, (1). 63325

... A Planter's View of the Condition of the Negroes in Jamaica in 1824. [*London: Ellerton & Henderson, Printers.* n. d.] 8vo, pp. (16). B. 63326

See Vol. xiii., No. 52269.

Plants (T. A.) Speech of Hon. T. A. Plants, of Ohio, on Reconstruction; ... in the House of Representatives, February 24, 1866. *Washington.* 1866. 8vo, pp. 16. H. 63327

Plasberg (C. L.) Californië; beschrijving van dat land. ... *Arnhem: J. G. [W. H.] Stenfert; Kroese.* 1849. 8vo. 63328

El Plata cientifico y literario. Revista de los Estados del Plata sobre Legislacion, Jurisprudencia, Economía-política, Ciencias Naturales y. Literatura. Publicado bajo la direccion de Miguel Navarro-Viola. ... *Buenos-Aires.* 1854–55. 7 vols., 8vo, pp. 210; 202; 168; 160; 160; 162; 162. C. 63329

Plata. *See* La Plata, Vol. x., pp. 73–75.

An Account, Historical ... of Rio de la Plata. *See* [Nunez (Ignacio)], Vol. xiii., No. 56330.

Biblioteca del Comercio del Plata. *Montevideo.* 1845–6. 3 vols., sm. 4to. 63330

An important collection of historical and geographical documents, edited by F. Varela.

A | Platform of | Church Discipline | gathered out of the Word of God: | and agreed upon by the Elders: | and Messengers of the Churches | assembled in the Synod at Cambridge | in New England | To be presented to the Churches and Generall Court | for their consideration and acceptance, | in the Lord. | The Eight Moneth Anno 1649. | ... | *Printed by S. G. at Cambridge in New England | and are to be sold at Cambridge and Boston | Anno Dom:* 1649. | 4to. J.C.B., W. 63331

Collation: Title, verso blank; The Preface [by John Cotton], pp. 1–10; Text, pp. 1–29, verso blank; "A Table" and "Errata," one page, verso blank.

Extremely rare. The original edition of the celebrated Cambridge Platform—the text-book of New England Congregationalism. A copy was sold at the Brinley sale in 1879 for $155. For an account of the typographical peculiarities of this very early production of the American press, and the earliest known work with the imprint of Samuel Green, *see* Thomas, "History of Printing," i. 252–4. *See also* Dexter, "Congregationalism as seen in its Literature," pp. 438–47. The original manuscript, and also the revised copy from which the work was printed—both in the handwriting of Richard Mather—are still preserved in the library of the American Antiquarian Society at Worcester.

A | Platform | of | Church-Discipline: | Gathered out of the Word of God, | and agreed upon by the Elders and | Messengers of the Churches | assembled in the Synod at | Cambridge | in | New-England: | To be presented to the Churches and General Court | for their Consideration and Acceptance | in the Lord. | ... | *Printed in New-England; and Reprinted in London, for Peter Cole, at | the sign of the Printing-Press in Cornhil, near the | Royal Exhcange* [sic]. 1653. | 4to. B., C., H., W. 63332

Collation: Title, verso blank, one leaf; Epistle "To all that are Faithful in Christ Jesus," etc., signed "Edw. Winslow," (2) pages; "Books Printed by Peter Cole in Leaden-Hall, London," (2) pages; Preface, pp. 1–8; Text, pp. 1–29, on verso of which is the Table of Contents.

In the Epistle to this edition Winslow mentions another London reprint of the "Platform" as follows: "It would be too long for me to insert the many Things that have occasioned the Delay of Reprinting it; But meeting of late with a Coppy therof Reprinted, not only in a disorderly way, but very Falsly, to the great prejudice of the Work; the Proofs in the margent (amongst other gross Errors) not rightly placed, and so not proving the matter against which they are set; I made it therefore my work to Suppress that Impression and have gained a Promise, They shall never come to publick sale."

A | Platform | Of | Church-Discipline | Gathered out of the | Word of God; | And Agreed upon | By the Elders and Messengers of the Churches | Assembled in the | Synod | At Cambridge in N. E. | To be presented to the Churches and General Court, for their Conside- | ration and Acceptance in the Lord, the 8th Month, Anno 1649. | ... | *Cambridge: Printed by Marmaduke Johnson,* 1671. 4to, pp. (12), 33, (2). B., C., H., M., W. 63333

Very rare. W. E. Woodward's copy was sold for $82; Rice's for $85; and Brinley's for $70

A | Platform | Of | Church-Discipline | Gathered out of | The Word Of God, | And Agreed upon by the | Elders and Messengers | of the Churches Assembled in the | Synod. | At Cambridge in N. E. | To be presented to the Churches & General Court | for their Consideration and Acceptance in | the Lord, the 8th. Moneth, Anno. 1649. | ... | *Boston: Printed by John Foster.* 1680. | Sm. 8vo, pp. (24), 64, (3). B., C., H., W. 63334

Very rare. The signatures are continuous with those of "A Confession of Faith," *Boston: Printed by John Foster,* 1680, our No. 15449, Vol. iv., and the order of the General Court for printing both books is prefixed to the "Confession." The collation of our No. 15449 should be: pp. (7), 65.

A | Platform | of | Church-Discipline, | Gathered out of | The Word of God; | And Agreed upon by the | Elders and Messengers | of the Churches Assembled in the | Synod | At Cambridge in N. E. | To be presented to the Churches & General | Court for their Consideration & Acceptance | in the Lord, the 8th. Month, Anno. 1649. | ... | *Boston: Printed by Bartholomew Green, & John Allen.* | *Sold at the Bookseller's Shops.* 1701. | Sm. 8vo, pp. (26), 64, (6). B., BA., J.C.B., H. 63335

"Reprinted for the first Church of Christ in Boston, pursuant to a Vote of that Church, Febr. 10th. 1700–1." Before the title is the order of the General Court, March 19, 1680, for reprinting the "Confession" and "Platform." An appendix (5 pages) contains "Some Collections For the Information of those that are not acquainted with the Principles and Practices of the First and most Eminent Leaders, in the Churches of Christ in New-England."

A | Plat-form | of | Church-Discipline, | Gathered out of the Word of God, and | Agreed upon by the | Elders and Messengers | Of the Churches assembled in the | Synod | At Cambridge in N. E. | To be presented to the Churches and General | Court for their Consideration & Acceptance | in the Lord, the 8th Month, Anno 1649. | ... | *Re-printed by William and Andrew Bradford in | New-York,* 1711. | Sm. 8vo, pp. (22), 52, (7). B., H.S.P., W. 63336

A reprint of the preceding edition, including the appendix of "Some Collections," etc. A very rare imprint. The brief partnership of the two Bradfords was terminated about 1712, when Andrew established his press at Philadelphia. Brinley's copy was sold for $55.

A | Platform | of | Church-Discipline: | Gathered out of the Word of God, | and Agreed upon by the | Elders and Messengers | Of the Churches assembled in the | Synod | At Cambridge in N. E. | To be presented to the Churches and General | Court, for their Consideration & Acceptance in | the Lord, the 8th Month, Anno 1649. | ... | *Boston, Printed by J. Allen, for N. Boone, at the | Sign of the Bible in Cornhill.* 1717. | Sm. 8vo, pp. xvi, 40, (7). M., W.

Also reprinted in "The Results of Three Synods," *Boston,* 1725, pp. 1–49.

A | Platform | of | Church-Discipline: | Gathered out of the Word of God, | and Agreed upon by the | Elders and Messengers | Of the Churches assembled in the | Synod | At Cambridge in N. E. | To be presented to the Churches & General Court, | for their Consideration and Acceptance in the | Lord, the 8th. Month, Anno 1649. | ... | *Boston, New-England,* | *Printed and Sold by Thomas Fleet, at the Sign of | the Heart and Crown, in Cornhill,* 1731. | Sm. 8vo, pp. xv, 36, (3). B., C., W. 63338

A | Platform | of | Church-Discipline, | Gathered out of | The Word of God; | And Agreed upon by the | Elders and Messengers | Of the Churches assembled in the | Synod | At Cambridge, in N. E. | To be presented to the Churches and General Court | for their Consideration and Acceptance in the | Lord, the 8th Month, Anno. 1649. | ... | *Boston: Re-Printed by John Green, for D. Gookin, | in Marlborough-Street.* 1749. | Sm. 8vo, pp. xxii, 55, (6). B., W. 63339

A | Platform | Of | Church-Discipline, | Gathered out of | The Word of God; | And Agreed upon by the | Elders and Messengers | Of the Churches assembled in the | Synod | At Cambridge, in N. E. | To be presented to the Churches and General Court | for their Consideration and Acceptance in the | Lord, the 8th Month, Anno 1649. | ... | *Boston: Re-Printed and Sold by Green and | Russell, in Queen-street, and by J. Winter, | opposite the King's Arms, in Union-street,* 1757. | 18mo, pp. xxii, 55, (6), Confession of Faith, (2), iv, 53. B., H. 63340

A | Platform | of | Church-Discipline: | Gathered out of the Word of God, and agreed upon by the | Elders and Messengers | Of the Churches assembled in the | Synod | at Cambridge, in New-England: | To be presented to the Churches and General Court, for their Consideration | and Acceptance in the Lord, the 8th Month, Anno 1648. | ... | *Boston:* | *Printed and Sold by John Boyles, in Marlborough-Street,* | MDCCLXXII. | Sm. 8vo, pp. 68. BA., M., W.

Also reprinted in Wise's "Vindication of the Government of New-England Churches," *Boston,* 1772.

A Platform of Church Discipline: Gathered out of the Word of God, and agreed upon by the Elders and Messengers of the Churches assembled in the Synod at Cambridge, in New-England: ... *Boston: Belcher and Armstrong.* 1808. 12mo, pp. 118, 36. C., W. 63342

The "Platform" fills the first seventy pages, and is followed by "The Answer of the Elders," etc. pp. 71–118; and "The Confession of Faith," 36 pp. Some copies of the

"Platform" were also issued separately. For another edition, with a different title-page prefixed, *see our* Vol. xiv., No. 57611, and read for imprint, *Boston, Printed. Reprinted for A. Lyman & Co. Portland.* 1812. 12mo, pp. (2), 118, 36.

A Platform of Church Discipline; Gathered out of the Word of God, and agreed upon by the Elders and Messengers of the Churches assembled in The Synod, at Cambridge in New-England; ... *Reading (Mass.): J. Watson.* 1819. 12mo. + *Boston: True and Weston.* 1819. 12mo, pp. 51. 63343

Also: The Cambridge and Saybrook Platforms of Church Discipline, with the Confession of Faith of the New England Churches, adopted in 1680; and the Heads of Agreement assented to by the Presbyterians and Congregationalists in England in 1690. Illustrated with Historical Prefaces and Notes. *Boston: T. R. Marvin, Printer.* 1829. 12mo, pp. 132. W.

See also Vol. iii., No. 10120, Report on Congregationalism, *and* [Wise (John)]. Of No. 10120 there is an edition, *Boston: Perkins & Whipple.* 1850. 12mo, pp. (4) 128.

The Platform of Ecclesiastical Government established by the Lord Jesus Christ. A discourse addressed by a New-England Pastor to his Flock, March 26, 1826. [*Providence.* 1826.] 12mo, pp. 27. H. 63344

By Nathaniel Emmons.

Platform of the American Anti-Slavery Society and its Auxiliaries. *New York: N. Y. Anti-Slavery Society.* 1853. 12mo, pp. 35, (1). + *New York: American Anti-Slavery Society.* 1855. 12mo, pp. 35, (1). + [*Ibid.*] 1860. 12mo, pp. 35, (1).

Platform of the Congregational Churches. *Middletown.* 1843. 18mo. 63346

"The Platforms," containing The Compromise Democratic ... Baltimore, June 1, 1852; The Compromise Whig ... Baltimore, June 16, 1852; The Buffalo ... 1848; and The Independent Democratic ... Pittsburg, August 12, 1852. Also Mr. Hales' Letter of Acceptance of the Pittsburgh Nomination. [n. p. 1852.] 8vo, pp. 8. H. 63347

The Platforms [of the Republican and Democratic Parties, at Baltimore and Chicago. n. p. 1864.] Folio, 1 leaf. 63348

Pláticas de Asmodeo sobre todas las cosas pasadas, presentes y futuras, y las demas que ocurran. De rebus omnibus et quibusdam aliis. Cartas de Juan Agapito Canelo y Cachuto al Señor Diablo Asmodeo. *Carácas.* 1851. 8vo, pp. 72. 63349

La Platine, l'Or Blanc, le Huitieme Métal, Recueil d'Experiences faites dans les Académies Royales de Londres, de Suede,

&c. sur une nouvelle Substance métallique tirée des Mines du Pérou, qui a le poids et la fixite de l'Or. *Paris.* 1758. 12mo

Plato (A.) Essays; including Biographical and Miscellaneous Pieces in Prose and Poetry. By Ann Plato. *Hartford, Ct.* 1841. 16mo, pp. 122. 63351

The writer was also known as the Colored Sappho.

Platt (E. S.) An Argument in the case of Ebenezer Smith Platt, now under confinement for High Treason. By a Gentleman of the Law. To which is added, the Opinion of the Court of King's Bench on a motion to admit Mr. Platt to bail. Delivered on Monday, May 12, 1777. *London: G. Kearsley.* 1777. 4to, pp. 17. J.C.B. 63352

Platt (G. L.) The Conflict of Two Civilizations. An Address ... Red Hook, September 11th, 1864, on occasion of the National Thanksgiving for Recent Victories. By Rev. G. Lewis Platt, Rector. *Poughkeepsie: Hagar's ... Printing Establishment.* 1864. 8vo, pp. 8. 63353

Also: Life Work. A Farewell Sermon ... in the Church of the Mediator ... *Philadelphia.* 1856. 8vo, pp. 24.

Platt (I. L.) Financial. The Currency, the Standard of Value and the Circulating Medium, Financially Considered. By Isaac L. Platt. *New-York: Thomas Holman, Printer.* 1867. 8vo, pp. 11. H. 63354

Platt (J.) Address of Jonas Platt to the People of Oneida County respecting the Location of the Court-House. [n. p.] 1800. 4to. 63355

Platt. In Senate, 21st March, 1811. Mr. Platt's Speech, on the bill for establishing the Western District Bank. [n. p. n. d.] 12mo, pp. 12. S. 63356

Also: Address ... before the Temperance Society of Plattsburgh. ... [n. p.] 1831. 8vo. *See also* Orlandos (J.), Vol. xiv., No. 57622, which is signed by Jonas Platt as chairman of the arbitrators.

Platt (*Mrs.* L. L.) Spiritual Experience of Mrs. Lorin L. Platt, of Newtown, Conn., with Spiritual Impressions annexed. Written while subjected to the Influence of a Circle of Spirits ... *New Haven: Printed by J. H. Benham.* 1852. 8vo, pp. 40. H.

Platt (S. H.) The Martyrs, and the Fugitive; or a Narrative of the Captivity, Sufferings, and Death of an African Family, and the Slavery and Escape of their Son. By Rev. S. H. Platt,

... Published for the Benefit of the Fugitive. *New-York: Printed by Daniel Fanshaw.* 1859. 12mo, pp. 95. B. 63358

Platt (W. H.) Funeral Sermon ... on ... Hon. William R. King. By W. H. Platt. *Selma, Ala.* 1853. 8vo, pp. 12.

Plattes (G.) A Discovery of Subterraneall Treasure, viz. of all manner of Mines and Mineralls from the Gold to the Coale with ... directions ... for the finding ... melting ... and assaying of them, etc. By Mr. Gabriel Plattes. *I. Oakes for J. Emery, London,* 1639. 4to. + *London.* 1653. 4to. + 1679. + 1684. + *Philadelphia.* 1784. 8vo, pp. 38. + *Philadelphia. Printed* M,DCC,XCII. 8vo, pp. 24. H., P. 63360

Contains some interesting notices of the gold and silver mines in Peru, New England, Virginia, the Bermudas, and other parts of America. The author gives a receipt by which he claims to have produced pure gold, but at a cost greater than its value. He finally died in the streets of London of starvation.

Also: A Discovery of Infinite Treasvre, hidden since the Worlds beginning. Whereunto all men ... are ... invited to be sharers with the Discoverer, Gabriel Plattes. *Printed for J. E. ... sold by H. Moseley, London,* 1639. 4to. + *London: G. Hutton.* 1639. 4to, pp. (34), 92. + *London.* 1653. + 1656.

Platteville, *Wis.* Catalogue of the Platteville Academy, for 1848–9. *Galena.* [n. d.] 8vo. Continued. 63361

In 1866 reorganized as the Wisconsin State Normal School.

Plattsburgh. The Battle of Plattsburgh: A Poem, in Three Cantos. By an American Youth. *Montpelier: Printed by E. P. Walton.* 1819. 12mo, pp. 46. 63362

Plattsburgh Republican,—Extra. The Battle of Plattsburgh, 11th September, 1814. An Account of the Celebration of the Anniversary of the Battle of Plattsburgh, by the Citizens of Plattsburgh and the Clinton County Military Association, September 11, 1843. *Plattsburgh: R. G. Stone.* 1843. 12mo, pp. 12

Platzmann (J.) Amerikanisch-asiatische Etymologien via Behring-Strasse "from the East to the West" von Julius Platzmann. *Leipzig: Druck von B. G. Teubner.* 1871. 8vo, pp. (8), 112. Map. A. 63364

An alphabetical list of 1520 American words, compared with Asiatic and other languages, with an appended list of authorities for each specimen.

Platzmann. Verzeichniss einer Auswahl Amerikanischer Grammatiken, Wörterbücher, Katechismen u. s. w. Gesammelt von Julius Platzmann. *Leipzig,* 1876. *K. F. Köhler's Antiquarium.* 8vo, pp. (6), 38. 63365

A very carefully prepared bibliography.

Plausible gozo de la Nueva España por la prision de crueles insurgentes. [*Mexico.* n. d.] 4to. 63366

[Plautius (Caspar).] Nova Typis | Transacta Na- | vigatio. | Novi Orbis Indiæ Occi- | dentalis | Admodvm Re- | verendissimorvm PP. | ac FF. Reverendissimi ac Illustrissimi Domini, | Dn. Bvellii Cataloni Abbatis montis | Serrati, & in vniversam Americam, sive Novum | Orbem Sacræ Sedis Apostolicæ Romanæ à Latere | Legati, Vicarij, ac Patriarchæ: Sociorumq; Mo- | nachorum ex Ordine S. P. N. Benedicti ad suprà | dicti Novi Mundi barbaras gentes Christi S. Evan- | gelium prædicandi gratia delegatorum Sacerdo- | tum. Dimissi per S. D. D. Papam Alexandrum | vi. Anno Christi. 1492. | Nvnc Primvm | E varijs Scriptoribus in vnum colle- | cta, & figuris ornata. | Avthore | Venerando Fr. Don Honorio Philopono | Ordinis S. Benedicti Monacho. [n. p.] 1621. | A., BA., J.C.B. 63367

Collation: Engraved title, containing portraits of "S. Brandanvs" and "Bvell. Catalonvs," and below the date, an oval engraving of the two continents; Dedication, "Vniverso venerabilissimo religiosissimoq; Monachorum cœtui Ordinis S. P. N. Benedicti. Imprimis autem, & cum primis pietatis, ac liberalium Studiosorum gratiosissimo Patrono Admodum Reverendo Domino Dr. Casparo Plavtio, Monasterij Seittenstöttensis in Austria inferiori Abbati dignissimo, Theologo; ac Philosophiæ Doctori clarissimo, Domino Patri meo in Christo observandissimo." etc., signed "Don F. Honorius Philoponus, Monachus S. Benedicti" (4) pages; text, pp. 1–101, on verso of which is a list of the plates entitled "In Annotationem Bibliopolæ." 18 Plates, all numbered excepting the first, which is a full length portrait of Columbus, with a globe or circular map above him, and the inscription "Almirante de nauios para las Indias," engraved by Wolf. Kilian.

There is another edition, with the same title and date, which contains more preliminary and supplementary matter, and an extra plate. Collation: Engraved title, 1621; Dedication as above, followed by "Ad Benevolvm Ordinis Monastici S. Benedicti Lectorem," together (6) pages; Plate of an Owl, with verses above and below, and beneath all, "Ad finem præfationis ad Lectorem;" "Observatio de Magnete Navtico" (4) pages; text, pp. 1–101, followed by "Vaticinivm De Messia. Et Evangelij ipsius Prædicatoribus" on p. 101, and on verso by "In primis," etc. (a list of names); one leaf containing "Ordinis S. P. Benedicti," and below, "In Annotationem Bibliopolæ," followed on verso by "Errata." 18 numbered Plates. Some copies contain at the end of the volume another extra plate of Columbus, dated 1622.

This curious work contains the relations of the early Benedictine missionaries who first came over with Columbus. It is filled with miraculous accounts of their labors, and one of the plates represents St. Brandan celebrating mass on the back of a large fish, where one of the ships had been stranded in mid-ocean. A specimen of Indian music is given on pp. 35–36. Many of the plates represent scenes in aboriginal life. It is supposed that the author was a monk of the convent of Seittenstöt in Lower Austria, named Caspar Plautius or Plautus, and that he wrote the book under the assumed name of Honorius Philoponus—spelled "Philonus" in one of the editions—in order that he might dedicate it to himself.

"This is one of the impudentest books known. The author's real name was Caspar Plautus, a monk at Lintz in Austria. In the most fulsome style, under his assumed name of Philoponus, he inscribes the work to himself in a long and highly complimentary Dedication. He accuses the De Brys, in their great collection of Voyages, of

telling outrageous lies, forgetting apparently his own whackers."—H. STEVENS, *Bibliotheca Historica.*
Concerning the book and its authorship *see* Placcius, "Theatrum Anon. et Pseudon.," Weller, "Index Pseudon.," Humboldt, "Examen Critique," III. 269, *and* Wynkelmann, "Der Americanischen Neuen Welt Beschreibung."

PLAYER-FROWD (J. G.) Six Months in California. By J. G. Player-Frowd. *London: Longmans, Green, and Co.* 1872. 12mo, pp. (6), 164. B., C. 63368

PLAYFAIR (A. W.) A Letter from a Volunteer of 1806 to the Volunteers of 1860, with suggestions on the Defence of England, her weakness and her strength. By A. W. Playfair, ... *Montreal.* 1860. 8vo, pp. 30. 63369

PLAYFAIR. Suggestions on the Defence of the Canadas, on the most Economical Principles of Blood and Treasure. By A. W. Playfair ... With Appendix on the Subject of the Great Lakes ... *Perth, U. C.* 1865. 8vo, pp. 13. 63370

Also: Comparison between the march of the 43rd Light Infantry, in 1837, and that of the late 104th Regiment in 1813, from New Brunswick to Quebec; also Remarks on the best winter route for troops from the British Isles to Canada. ... *Montreal.* 1862. 8vo.—The Pacific Railway on British Territory. ... [n. p.] 1852. 8vo. —Suggestions on the Defence of Canada, by the formation of Flank Companies from the Sedentary Militia. ... *Montreal.* 1861. 8vo, pp. 8.

PLAYFAIR (H.), *pseudon.* Brother Jonathan: or the "Smartest Nation in all Creation." Sketches of American Life and Manners, selected from the Papers of Mr. Hugo Playfair, late an Officer in the Royal Navy of England. Edited by Paul Paterson. ... *London.* 1840–41. 8vo. H. 63371

Issued in monthly numbers, and published collectively as: The Playfair Papers: or the Americans in 1841. By Capt. Playfair, R.N. *London: Saunders & Otley.* 1841. 3 vols., 8vo. Another edition as follows:

PLAYFAIR. Brother Jonathan, the Smartest Nation in all Creation. By Hugo Playfair. *London: Saunders and Otley.* 1844. 3 vols., post 8vo, pp. iv, 311; (2), 339; (2), 311. 9 Plates by Robert Cruikshank. P. 63372

PLAYFAIR (R.) Recollections of a Visit to the United States and British Provinces of North America in the Years 1847, 1848, and 1849. By Robert Playfair. *Edinburgh.* 1856. Cr. 8vo, pp. 266. + [*Ibid.*] 1859. 8vo. 63373

PLAYFAIR (W.) The History of Jacobinism. ... By William Playfair. With an Appendix, by Peter Porcupine, containing a History of the American Jacobins, commonly denoted

Democrats. ... *Philadelphia: Printed for William Cobbett.* 1796. 2 vols., 8vo, pp. 385; 301, xlviii. C., S. 63374

PLAYFAIR. Lineal Arithmetic, applied to show the Progress of the Commerce ... of England, during the Present Century. By William Playfair. ... *London: The Author.* 1798. 8vo.

With curious colored charts showing the progress of the United States.

PLAYTER (G. F.) The History of Methodism in Canada: with an Account of the Rise and Progress of the Work of God among the Canadian Indian Tribes, and Occasional Notices of the Civil Affairs of the Province. By George F. Playter ... *Toronto: Published for the Author by Anson Green.* 1862. 12mo, pp. viii, 413, (1). 63376

Lettered on back "Vol. I." The volume ends with the year 1828. All published.

PLAZA (E. de la). Memoria sobre la Cria de Abejas y Cultivo de la Cera, premiada por la Junta de Gobierno del Real Consulado de ... Havana. ... [Por] Eugenio de la Plaza ... *Havana.* MDCCXCVII. *Impresa A expensas de la misma Junta.* Sm. folio, pp. (8), 51, (5). B. 63377

PLAZA (Jose Antonio de). Memorias para la Historia de la Nueva Granada, desde su descubrimiento hasta el 20 de Julio de 1810. *Bogota: Ramon Gonzales.* 1850. Rl. 8vo, pp. (2), xii, 464, (2). 63378

PLAZA. Compendio de la Historia de la Nueva Granada desde antes de su descubrimiento hasta el 17 Novbr. 1831. *Bogota: Leon Echeveria.* 1850. 8vo, pp. 136. 63379

A Plea before the Ecclesiastical Council At Stockbridge, In the Cause of Mrs. Fisk, who was excommunicated by the Reverend Pastor and Church in that Place, for marrying a Man whom they called immoral and profane.—Delivered the 6th and 7th of October, 1779. ... By a Gentleman of Connecticut. *Boston: Printed by N. Coverly and R. Hodge* ... MDCCLXXXII. 12mo, pp. 130. 63380

By Joseph Huntington. For other editions *see* Vol. IX., No. 33973.

A Plea for Authors and the Rights of Literary Property. By an American ... *New York: Adlard and Saunders.* 1838. 8vo, pp. 32. B., N. 63381

A Plea for Friendship. *See* [McKean (J.)], Vol. XI. 43374.

A Plea for Harvard. *See* [Quincy (J.)]

A Plea for Hospitals [in New York City] ... *New York: Baker, Godwin & Co., Printers.* 1851. 8vo, pp. 21. H. 63382

A Plea for Impartial Suffrage. By a Lawyer of Illinois. *Chicago: Western News Company.* 1868. 8vo, pp. 95. 63383

A Plea for Literature; More especially the Literature of Free States. By a Member of the Old Congress. *Charleston: Harrison & Bowen.* 1793. 12mo, pp. 119. 63384

A Plea for New Mexico. [n. p. 1868?] 8vo. pp. 8. B.

A Plea for our Foreign Commerce. *See* [Hill (H. A.)], Vol. VIII., No. 31824.

A Plea for Peace and a Platform for the Times. *Washington.* 1863. 8vo, pp. 7. 63386

A Plea for Practical Heraldry in the New World, by J. H. L. A. [n. p.:] *Printed by Richard Barrett.* 1860. 8vo, pp. 16.

Plea for Religious Newspapers: A Sermon ... December 29, 1844, by a Connecticut Pastor [J. D. Hall]. *Hartford.* 1845. 8vo. 63388

A Plea for the Copperheads by a true Union Man. [n. p. n. d.] 8vo, pp. 4. 63389

A Plea for the Farmers' College of Hamilton County, Ohio, ... made July 17, 1850. *Cincinnati.* 1850. 8vo, pp. 26. H.

... A Plea for the Gospel Scheme for the Abolition of Slavery ... [n. p. 185–.] 8vo, pp. 4. H. 63391

Plea for the Indians ... Written as a Memorial ... to ... Congress ... [*Hartford.* 1845?] 8vo. BM. 63392

A Plea for the Medical Staff of the Army. [By Assistant Surgeon Bartholow. n. p. 1862?] 8vo, pp. 16. H. 63393

A Plea For the Ministers of New-England. Per Amicum Cleri, et Populi. ... *Boston: Samuel Gerrish.* 1724. 16mo, pp. (2), 14. B., M., S., 63394

By Rev. Jabez Fitch.

A Plea for the Ministers. *See* [Mather (I.)], Vol. XI. 46717.

A Plea for the Poor. An Enquiry how far the Charges against them of improvidence, idleness, and dissipation are founded in

truth. ... By a Citizen of Philadelphia. Second Edition. *Philadelphia.* 1836. 8vo, pp. 16. H. 63395

A Plea for the Poor and Distressed against the Bill for granting an Excise upon Wines and Spirits ... within this Province ... *Boston, Printed in the Year* 1754. 12mo, pp. 14. H., W. 63396

A Plea for the Poor Soldiers. *See* [Webster (Pelatiah)].

A Plea for the Sabbath in War. Sabbath Committee, New York. [n. p. n. d.] 12mo. 63397

A Plea for the Slave. Addressed to all professing Christians in America. [n. p. n. d.] 16mo, pp. 16. B. 63398

A Plea for the South. *London.* [1864.] 8vo. BM. 63399

See also Vol. XI., No. 45539.

A Plea for the West. *See* [Chase (P.)], Vol. III. 12192.

A Plea for Voluntary Societies, and a Defence of the Decisions of the General Assembly of 1836, against ... the Princeton Reviewers and others. By a Member of the Assembly. *New York: John S. Taylor.* 1837. 12mo, pp. 187. H. 63400

A Plea in Vindication of the Connecticut Title. *See* [Trumbull (B.)]

The Plea of the Colonies, On the Charges brought against them by Lord M-------d, and Others, in a Letter to His Lordship. ... *London: J. Almon.* MDCCLXXV. 8vo, pp. 47. C. + [*Ibid.*] MDCCLXXVI. 8vo, pp. 47. B. 63401

Contains animadversions on two speeches delivered by Lord Mansfield in Parliament.

The | Plea | of the | Colonies | On the Charges brought against them by | Lord Mansfield, and Others, | in a Letter to | His Lordship. | By a Native of Pennsylvania. | *London, Printed in the Year* MDCCLXXVI. | *Philadelphia: | Re-printed and Sold by Robert Bell* ... | MDCCLXXVII. | 8vo, pp. (6), 38. Plate. P. 63402

The Plea of The Innocent. *See* [Keith], Vol. IX. 37205.

A Plea with Christians for the Cause of Peace. [n. p. 1851?] 8vo, pp. 32. 63403

Probably by George C. Beckwith.

A Plea: Written for the Fair. [In verse. *Boston.* 1863.] 4to. 63404

Pleas and Proceedings before the Hon. John Cadwalader, Judge of the District Court of the United States, for the Eastern District of Pennsylvania. United States vs. The Brig Herald. [*Philadelphia.* 1862.] 8vo, pp. 114. 63405

PLEAS (E.) Henry County [Indiana]; Past and Present: A Brief History of the County from 1821 to 1871. By Elwood Pleas. *New Castle, Ind.: Pleas Brothers.* 1871. 16mo, pp. iv, 148. 2 Plates. B., C. 63406

The Pleasant Historie. *See* [Gomara (F. L. de)], Vol. VII., Nos. 27751–2.

Pleasant Memories. *See* [Newton (R.)], Vol. XIII. 55083.

A Pleasant Peregrination. *See* [Nicklin (P. H.)], XIII. 55237

An Act to Incorporate the Stockholders of the PLEASANT VALLEY Manufacturing Company, passed March, 1809. *New York.* 1809. 12mo. N. 63407

PLEASANTON (Stephen). The Light Houses, Beacons, and Floating Lights of the United States, in operation on the 1st December, 1839. ... *Washington.* 1839. 8vo, pp. 16. 63408

PLEASANTON. The Light Houses ... in operation on the 1st of July, 1842. ... *Washington.* 1842. 8vo, pp. 22. 63409

PLEASANTS (Julia), *and* BRADLEY (Thomas Bibb). Aphelia; and other Poems. By Two Cousins of the South. *New York: C. Scribner.* 1854. 12mo, pp. viii, 13–272. C. 63410

PLEASANTS. Callamura. ... *Philadelphia.* 1868. 12mo.

"A novel illustrative of life in the Southern States."—ALLIBONE.

The Pleasing Instructor, or Entertaining Moralist. Consisting of Select Essays, Relations, Visions, and Allegories. Collected from the most Eminent English Authors. To which are prefixed, New Thoughts on Education. A New Edition. *Boston: Printed by Joseph Bumstead.* 1795. 12mo, pp. 312. W.

PLEASONTON (A. J.) Report of Brigadier Gen'l A. J. Pleasonton, Commanding the Home Guard of ... Philadelphia, ... describing the Operations of the ... Councils on the Defence ... of the City, and the ... Organization of the Home Guard. For ... 1861. [n. p. n. d.] 8vo. + Second ... Report. 1862. + Third ... Report ... 1863. *Philadelphia: King & Baird, Printers.* 1864. 8vo, pp. 112. + [Another Edition. *Ibid.*] 1864. 8vo, pp. 21. 63413

PLEBIAN, *pseudon.* *See* Vol. XIII., Nos. 53508 *and* 54619.

PLEBS (W.) A Letter to Rt. Rev. Bishop Onderdonk, of New York, by Washington Plebs, Esq. Followed by an Epistle to Rev. Stephen H. Tyng ... *New York.* 1843. 8vo, pp. 24.

PLEISSNER (——). Der Amerikaner. Lustspiel in einem Aufzuge. ... *Frankfurt und Leipzig.* 1783. 8vo. 63415

Plenty of Money, and the United States of America independent of all Foreign Money Markets. By Navillus. *New York: Samuel Colman.* 1840. 8vo, pp. 33. A. 63416

PLESSIS (J. O.) Discours a l'Occasion de la Victoire Remporte'e par les Forces Navales de sa Majeste' Britannique dans la Mediterranne'e le 1 et 2 Aout 1798, sur La Flotte Francoise. Prononce' dans l'Eglise Cathedrale de Quebec le 10 Janvier 1799. Par Messire J. O. Plessis Curé de Quebec ... *A Quebec: Imprimé au Profit des Pauvres de la Paroisse, et se vend à l'imprimerie.* [1799.]. 8vo, pp. (4), 24. 63417

PLEVIER (J.) Oratio de America et Americanarum gentium origine. ... *Zieriz.* 1756. 4to. 63418

PLEYTE (W.) Leiden, voor 300 Jaren en Thans. Photolithographische Afbeelding van een Platte-Grond van 1578 en Chromolithographische Afbeelding van het Chaertbouc van Straten binnen deser Stadt Leyden en Chaertbouc van de Stadts Wateren gemeten bij Mr. Salomon Davidsson van Dulmanhorst, en Jan Pieterssoon Dou ... *Leiden.* 1874. Folio, pp. (2), 114. Plates. 63419

Two hundred copies printed. Illustrated with over one hundred colored plates, among which is a ground-plan of the lot bought by John Robinson and others, in 1611, for church use.

PLINGUET (J. A.) Souvenirs sur les Commencements de l'Union St. Joseph Montréal. *Montréal.* 1866. 8vo, pp. 72.

PLINIUS (C.) Historia Natvral | de Cayo Plinio | Segvndo. | Tradvcida | por el Licienciado Geronomo de Hverta, | Medico y Familiar del Santo | Oficio de la Inqvisicion. | Y ampliada | por el Mismo, con Escolios y Anotaciones, | en que aclara lo escuro y dudoso, y añade lo no sabido hasta estos tiempos. | Dedicada | Al catolico Rey de las Españas y Indias Don Felipe IIII. nuestro Señor. | *En Madrid: Por Luis Sanchez, Impressor del Rey N. S.* | *Año* 1624. | 2 vols., folio, pp. (56), 907, (1); (16), 720, (15). B.

Imprint of vol. II.: *En Madrid: Por Iuan Gonçalez. Año* 1629. At the end of Book VI., vol. I., pp. 233–248, Huerta has added a description of the West Indies.

PLINIUS SECUNDUS, *pseudon.* *See* Vol. III., No. 10414.

[PLINTH (Octavius).] Formula of Prescriptions, and various Instructions, for Service and Guidance of those who have applied, are applying, or shall apply, to the Enemy to Human Diseases: to which is prefixed, a Vindication, concerning the Dietical Abstinence ... By Sylvan, Enemy to Human Diseases. ... *Providence: The Author.* 1812. 8vo, pp. 139, (1). B. + *H. Mann, Printer, Providence.* 1813. 8vo, pp. (4), 137, (1). B. 63422

[PLINTH.] The Works of Sylvan. Being a Confidential Communication, by Sylvan, Enemy to Human Diseases; and Continuation of the Confidential Communication intended for the General Benefit of the Afflicted. *Providence.* 1813–15. 2 vols., 8vo. 63423

Octavius Plinth, known as the Rain-Water Doctor, resided at Dedham, Mass., gravely claiming to have lived upwards of 560 years.

PLINY, *Junior.* *See* Vol. VII., No. 28768.

PLITT (J. K.) God's doings for the Nation. A Sermon Preached in ... Greenwich, New Jersey, on the Day of National Thanksgiving, November 24th, 1864, By Rev. J. K. Plitt, A.M. ... *Easton, Pa.: L. Gordon.* 1864. 8vo, pp. 21. 63424

PLOCKHOY (P. C.) Kort en klaer ontwerp | dienende tot | Een onderling Accoort, | om | Den arbeyd, onrust en moeye- | lijckheyt, van Alderley-hand-wercxs- | luyden te verlichten | door | Een onderlinge Compagnie ofte | Volck-planting (onder de protectie vande H: Mo: | Heeren Staten Generael der vereenigde Neder-lan- | den; en bysonder onder het gunstig gesag van de | Achtbare Magistraten der Stad Amstelre- | dam) aen de Zuyt-revier in Nieu-ne- | der-land op te rechten; Bestaende in | Land-bouwers, | Zee-varende Personen, | Alderhande noodige Ambachts-luyden en Meesters | van goede konsten en wetenschappen. | Steunende op de voor-rechten van hare Acht- | baer-heden (als hier na volgt) tot dien eynde verleent. | t'Samen gestelt | Door Pieter Cornelisz. Plockhoy van Zierck-zee, voor hem selven en andere | Lief-hebbers van Nieu-neder-land. | *t'Amsterdam gedruckt by Otto Barentsz. Smient, Anno* 1662. | 4to, (8) leaves. 63425

This short and clear project of a mutual agreement, in order to relieve the colony to be founded at the South River in New Netherland is excessively rare. The unfortunate colony of Plockhoy was destroyed by the English in 1664. *See* Asher's "Essay," pp. 206–7, *and* Brodhead I., pp. 698–9. It contains a poem by J. Steendam, entitled "Prickel-Vaersen." *See* Steendam (J.)

The Plot. By way of a Burlesk, [*sic*] to turn F[rankli]n out of the Assembly; between H—— and P——; Proprietary Officers, being two of the Wiser [Conrad Weiser] Sort. [n. p.:] *Printed in the Year.* 1764. Narrow folio, 1 leaf. P. 63426

The Plough and the Sickle: or, Rhode Island in the War of the Revolution of 1776. *Providence: B. T. Albro.* 1846. 8vo, pp. 28. 63427

The Plough Boy. From June 5, 1819 to May 27, 1820. Vol. I. *Albany: Printed by John O. Cole.* [n. d.] 4to, pp. (4), 416. B., S. 63428

Edited by Solomon Southwick, and continued weekly to July 15, 1823, forming four volumes. The first 33 numbers have the caption "The Plough Boy. By Henry Homespun, Jr." (*i. e.* Solomon Southwick), and were continued as "The Plough Boy and Journal of the Board of Agriculture. By S. Southwick."

The Plough, the Loom, and the Anvil. Volume I. *Philadelphia.* 1848. 8vo, pp. (2), 782. Continued. B., H., S. 63429

A monthly magazine. Vols. 1–3, *Philadelphia: J. S. Skinner & Son,* 1848–50; vols. 4–10, *New York: Myron Finch,* 1851–57. Vol. X. is entitled "American Farmers' Magazine."

PLOUGHJOFFER (R.), *pseudon.* Inquiry into the Dissenting Institution, by Richard Ploughjoffer. *Boston.* 1759. 8vo.

PLOUGHSHARE (Peter), *pseudon.* *See* Considerations, Vol. IV., No. 15939.

The authorship of this pamphlet has been ascribed to Samuel B. Beach of Utica.

PLOVER (H.), *pseudon.* The Square Egg; being a Cheap Dish for the Times; served up for the Public Health, with Special Reference to Democrats and Whigs. By Hiram Plover, Jr. ... [*Boston:*] *John P. Jewett & Co.* [n. d.] 12mo pp. 12. H.

Against the Fugitive Slave Bill.

Plow Boy's Almanac for 1845. ... *Cincinnati, O.* [n. d.] 12mo, pp. 114. S. 63432

[PLOWDEN (Charles).] A Short Account of the Establishment of the New See of Baltimore in Maryland and of Consecrating the Rev. John Carroll First Bishop thereof. ... *London.* 1790. 12mo. + *Philadelphia: Reprinted by Carey, Stewart & Co.* 1791. 12mo, pp. 20. 63433

Very scarce. Concerning the author *see* Finotti, "Bibl. Cath. Americana," p. 17.

A Plowman's Complaint. *See* [Brooks (S.)], Vol. II. 8368.

Pluchonneau (——) *et* Maillard (H.) Physiologie des Nègres dans leur pays, précédée d'un aperçu de l'état des noirs en esclavage dans les colonies; d'un exposé de la traite et de considérations sur l'affranchissement, par Pluchonneau et H. Maillard. *Paris.* 1842. 18mo, pp. 124. 8 Plates. 63434

Plum (N. G. A.) Eulogy on La Fayette, delivered at Concord, ... on the 17th of June, 1835. By Nathaniel G. A. Plum. *Concord, N. H.* 1835. 8vo. 63435

Plum (W.) The Letters of a Farmer, containing his Thoughts in the ninety-fourth year of his Age. By William Plum. *Middletown (Conn.): The Author.* 1843. 12mo, pp. 294.

Pluma (J. de) Elogio del Sr. D. Alfonso de Viania y Ulloa censor de la Sociedad Patriótica de la Habana por el Pbro. D. Joaquin de Pluma. *Habana: Imprenta de Arazoza y Soler.* 1822. 4to, pp. 10. 63437

Pluma y Aguilera. Respuesta á la manifestacion que hacen Pluma y Aguilera por Cárdenas. *Habana: Imprenta de Campe.* 1820. 4to. 63438

This elicited: Replica á la respuesta por Pluma y Aguilera. *Habana: Imprenta de Campe.* 1820. 4to. Two editions.

[Plumard de Danguel (R. B.)] Remarques sur les avantages et les desavantages de la France et de la Gr. Bretagne, par Rapport au Commerce, et aux autres Sources de la Puissance des Etats. Traduction de l'Anglois du Chevalier John Nickolls. Seconde Edition. *Leyde.* 1754. 8vo. 63439

Notices the Hudson's Bay, Africa, East India, and South Sea companies. It is not a little curious that the original French edition purports to be translated from the English, while the first English edition is said to be translated from the French.

[Plumard de Danguel.] Remarks on the Advantages and Disadvantages of France and of Great-Britain With Respect to Commerce, and To the other Means of encreasing the Wealth and Power of a State. ... Translated from the French Original. *London: T. Osborne.* MDCCLIV. 12mo, pp. xi, 273. BM. 63440

Plumb (D.) Our Banners Set Up. A Discourse ... at the Organization of the Church of Christ, at Utica, ... November 21, 1841. By David Plumb. ... *Fayetteville.* 1842. 12mo, pp. 23. 63441

Also: The Power and Duty of Congress to Enfranchise the Nation. ... *Boston.* 1868. 8vo. — The Slaveholders' Rebellion. ... [A Poem. *New York, May,* 1865.] 8vo, pp. (8).

Plumb (E. W.) Oration ... at Halifax, Vt., on the Fourth of July, 1825. By Elijah W. Plumb. *Greenfield.* 1825. 8vo.

Plumbe (John). Memorial against Mr. Asa Whitney's Railroad Scheme ... . [*Washington:*] *Buell & Blanchard, Printers.* 1851. 8vo, pp. 48. B. 63443

Plumbe (J.), *Jr.* Sketches of Iowa and Wisconsin, taken during a Residence of Three Years in those Territories. By John Plumbe, Jr. *St. Louis: Chambers, Harris & Knapp.* 1839. 12mo, pp. 103. Map. B., C., S. 63444

Plumbensis (Nicolaus). *See* Vol. xiii., No. 55243, and for collation read: pp. (32), 207, (34). Engraved Frontispiece.

Plumer [William]. The speech of Mr. Plumer, at the Bar of the House of Lords, on the Second Reading of the Bill for the Abolition of the Slave-Trade, in Support of the Petition of the West-India Planters and Merchants against that Measure. *London: Printed by C. and W. Galabin.* 1807. 12mo, pp. 31. B.

[Plumer (William).] An Address to the Clergy of New-England, on their Opposition to the Rulers of the United States. By a Layman. ... *Concord, N. H.: Printed by I. and W. R. Hill.* 1814. 12mo, pp. 28. B., N., S. 63447

[Plumer.] Address to the Electors of New-Hampshire. [*Portsmouth: W. & D. Treadwell, Printers.* 1804.] 8vo, pp. 14.

Sometimes attributed to William Plumer. Dated July 30, 1804, and signed "Impartialis."

[Plumer.] An Appeal to the Old Whigs of New Hampshire. [n. p. 1805.] 8vo, pp. 16. W. 63449

See also Vol. xiii., Nos. 52793–5, 52801, *and* No. 63211, *supra.*

[Plumer.] Message from his Excellency the Governor to the New Hampshire Legislature, June, 1817. [n. p. n. d.] 8vo, pp. 11. + 1818. [n. p. n. d.] 8vo, pp. 12. + 1819. [n. p. n. d.] 8vo, pp. 10. 63450

Also: Speech ... before the Legislature of New Hampshire, Nov. 18, 1812. *Concord.* 1812. 8vo. C. — Speech ... before the Legislature—June Session, 1816. [n. p. n. d.] 12mo, pp. 12. H. — Speech ... to the New Hampshire Legislature, Nov. 1816. *Concord.* 1816. 12mo. W. Also several articles under the signature of "Cincinnatus."

Plumer (W.), *Jr.* An Address delivered before the Rockingham Agricultural Society, October 18th, 1821. By William

Plumer, Jr. *Exeter: Printed by John T. Williams.* 1821. 8vo, pp. 24. B., M. 63451

Plumer. An Address ... at Portsmouth, N. H. on the Fourth of July, 1828. By William Plumer, Jr. *Portsmouth: T. H. Miller and C. W. Brewster, Printers.* 1828. 8vo, pp. 24. B., H.

Plumer. Life of William Plumer, by his Son, William Plumer, Junior. Edited, with a Sketch of the Author's Life, by A. P. Peabody. *Boston: Phillips, Sampson, and Company.* 1856. 8vo, pp. xvi, 543. 2 Portraits. + [*Ibid.*] 1857. 8vo, pp. xvi, 543. 2 Portraits. + [*Ibid.*] 1860. 8vo. S. 63453

Also: Lyrica Sacra; or, War-Songs and Ballads from the Old Testament. ... *Boston: Wm. Crosby and H. P. Nichols.* M DCCC XLVI. 16mo, pp. x, (2), 68. — Manhood, or Scenes from the Past; a Series of Poems. ... *Boston: Tappan and Dennet.* 1843. 12mo, pp. 148. — Speech ... on the Missouri Question, ... in the House of Representatives, ... February 21, 1820. [n. p. n. d.] 12mo, pp. 42. — Youth, or Scenes from the Past; and other Poems. ... *Boston: C. C. Little and James Brown.* MDCCCXLI. 12mo, pp. 144. B.

Plumer (W. S.) Thoughts on the Religious Instruction of the Negroes of the Country. By Wm. S. Plumer, D.D. *Savannah: Edward J. Purse, Printer.* 1848. 8vo, pp. 28. 63454

Also: Thoughts on Religious Education and Early Piety. ... *New York.* 1836. 18mo, pp. 113. Plate.

Plumier (C.) Description | des | plantes | de | l'Amérique. | Avec leurs Figures. | Par le R. P. Charles Plumier, Religieux Minime. | *A Paris,* | *de l'imprimerie royale.* | M. DC. XCIII. | [Colophon:] *A Paris,* | *de l'Imprimerie Royale.* | *Par les soins de Jean Anisson, Directeur de ladite* | *Imprimerie.* | M.DC.XCIII. | Folio. BA., H. 63455

Collation: Half title; title; Preface, 2 leaves; text, pp. 94; Index Plantarum, 4 leaves; Colophon, 1 leaf. 108 Plates.

Some copies are dated M.DC.CXIII—probably a typographical error. A copy with this date is in the Library of Congress.

Plumier. Filicetum Americanum, seu Filicum, Polypodiorum, Adiantorum, etc. in America nascentium icones. Authore P. Carolo Plumier. *Paris.* 1703. Folio. 222 Plates. 63456

Plumier. Nova | Plantarum | Americanarum | Genera, | Authore P. Carolo Plumier Ordinis | Minimorum in Provincia Franciæ, & apud Insulas | Americanas Botanico Regio. | *Parisiis,* | *Apud Joannem Boudot, Regis & Regiæ Scientiarum* | *Academiæ Typographum, via Jacobæa, ad Solem Aureum.* | MDCCIII. | *Cum Privilegio Regis.* | 4to, pp. (8), 52, (4), 21, (1). 40 Plates. B., J.C.B., P.

Plumier. Traité | Des | Fougères | de | L'Amérique. | Par le R. P. Charles Plumier, | Minime de la Province de | France, & Bota-

niste du Roy dans les Isles de l'Amérique. | *A Paris.* | *De L'Imprimerie Royale.* | M.DCCV. | [Colophon:] *Parisiis,* | *E Typographia Regia* | *Curante Joanne Anisson, ejusdem Typographiæ* | *Præfecto.* | M.DCCV. | Folio, pp. xxxvi, 146, Table, (5), Index, (4), Colophon, (1). 172 Plates. H., N. 63458

In Latin and French. There are copies on large paper. First published in Latin in 1703. Many of Plumier's drawings remain unpublished in the library of the Jardin des Plantes, at Paris.

Plumier. Plantarum | Americanarum | Fasciculus Primus, | Continens Plantas, quas olim | Carolus Plumierius, | Botanicorum Princeps | Detexit, Eruitque, | Atque in Insulis Antillis ipse depinxit. | Has primum in lucem edidit, | Concinnis descriptionibus, & observationibus, | Æneisque Tabulis illustravit | Joannes Burmannus, M.D. | ... | *Sumtibus Auctoris,* | *Prostant Amstelædami in Horto Medico,* | *Atque* | *Apud Viduam & Filium S. Schouten,* | & *Lugd. Batav.* | *Apud Gerard. Potvliet & Theodor. Haak.* | M. DCC. LV | [–M.DCC.LX.] Folio. A., BA., C. 63459

Collation: Fasciculus Primus, pp. (8), 16; Secundus, M.DCC.LVI, pp. (4), 19–37; Tertius, M.DCC.LVI, pp. (4), 41–64; Quartus, M.DCC.LVI, pp. (4), 67–87; Quintus, M.DCC.LVII, pp. (4), 91–116; Sextus, M.DCC.LVII, pp. (4), 119–142; Septimus, M.DCC.LVIII, pp. (4), 145–168; Octavus, M.DCC.LVIII, pp. (4), 171–194; Nonus, M.DCC.LIX, pp. (4), 197–220; Decimus, M.DCC.LX, pp. (4), 223–262, Index, (4). Portrait of J. Burmann engraved by Houbraken, and cclxii Plates.

Improved title of our No. 9343, Vol. II. The outline plates are from copies of the unpublished drawings of Plumier, which had come into the possession of Dr. Burmann, who edited and described them.

Plumley (G. S.) Piety secures the Nation's Prosperity. A Thanksgiving Discourse, By Rev. G. S. Plumley. Preached in the First Presbyterian Church, Metuchen, New Jersey, ... December 7, 1865. ... *New York: F. Somers, Printer.* 1866. 8vo, pp. 29. B. 63460

[Plumley.] The Presbyterian Church throughout the World: from the Earliest to the Present Times, in a Series of Biographical and Historical Sketches. *New York: De Witt C. Lent & Company.* 1875. 8vo, pp. (4), vii–xiii, (3), 792. Plates.

Plummer (C.) Narrative of the Captivity and extreme Sufferings of Mrs. Clarissa Plummer, Wife of the late Mr. James Plummer, of Franklin County, State of New York; who, with Mrs. Caroline Harris, wife of the late Mr. Richard Harris, were, in the Spring of 1835, with their unfortunate families, surprised and taken prisoners by a party of the Camanche Tribe of Indians, while Emigrating from said Franklin County (N. Y.) to Texas; and after having been nearly two years in captivity, and witnessed

the deaths of their husbands, were redeemed from the hands of the savages by an American Fur Trader, a native of Georgia ... Mrs. Plummer was made a Prisoner and held in bondage at the same time with the unfortunate Mrs. Harris, with whose narrative the public have been recently presented. *New York.* 1838. 8vo, pp. 23, (1). Plates. S. 63462

The same as our Vol. VIII., No. 30466, with a different title-page.

Plummer (Fred.) A Defence of Capital Punishment ... in a Discussion ... with C. C. Burleigh. *Philadelphia.* 1846. 12mo

Plummer (J.) History of the Life and Adventures of J. Plummer. *Newburyport.* 1796. 12mo. 63464

Plummer (Jonathan). A New Psalm and a New Funeral Sermon, on the Deaths of Many People, 1813. [n. p. n. d.] 4to, 1 leaf. M. 63465

Plummer (Rachel). Narrative, 1839. *See* Parker (J. W.), Vol. xiv., No. 58685.

Plummer Farm School. An Appeal to the Public in its behalf; with an Appendix, containing Act of Incorporation and By-Laws ... *Salem: William Ives and George W. Pease, Printers.* 1857. 8vo, pp. 16. B. 63466

Proceedings upon the Dedication of Plummer Hall, at Salem, October 6, 1857: including Rev. Mr. Hoppin's Address and Judge White's Memoir of the Plummer Family. *Salem: Printed by Wm. Ives and Geo. W. Pease.* 1858. 8vo, pp. 97. BA. 63467

Plunkett (T. F.) Money, Panics and Specie Payment. By Thos. F. Plunkett. *Pittsfield, Mass.* 1873. 8vo. 63468

Plu-ri-bus-tah. *See* [Thompson (M.)]

Pluto. *See* [Woensel (P. v.)]

Pluto: Being the Sad Story and Lamentable Fate of the Fair Minthe. [A Poem.] *Raleigh.* 1867. 8vo, pp. 35. 63469

Plymouth, *Conn.* Proceedings of an Ecclesiastical Council, convened at Plymouth, Conn., Jan. 22, 1856. *New-Haven.* 1856. 8vo, pp. 55. S. 63470

Plymouth, *Mass.* An Account of the Pilgrim Celebration at Plymouth, August 1, 1853, containing a list of the Decorations

in the Town, and correct copies of the speeches ... . Revised by the Pilgrim Society. *Boston: Crosby, Nichols, and Company.* 1853. 8vo, pp. 182. BA., S. 63471

Annual Reports for the Town of Plymouth, for ... 1864. *Plymouth.* 1864. 8vo, pp. 78. Continued. H. 63472

The Articles of Faith and Form of Covenant of the Third Congregational Church of Plymouth. *Plymouth.* 1826. 8vo, pp. 15. 63473

Brief Sketch of the Characters and Sufferings of the Pilgrims, who settled at Plymouth, Dec. 1620. *Boston: Printed by John A. Frost.* 1820. 8vo, pp. 8. BA., W. 63474

Descriptive Letter Press to Accompany the Engraving of the Pilgrims Signing the Compact, on board of the May Flower, November 11th, 1620. Painted by T. H. Matteson. Engraved by Gautier. *William Schaus, New York.* [1859.] 8vo, pp. 8.

Directions for sailing in and out of Plymouth Harbour, taken by Moses Bennet, William Rhodes, Thomas Allen, and Nathaniel Green, ... of the Marine Society of Boston, appointed for this Survey by ... a Committee of the General Court ... appointed to build the Light-House on the Gurnet, ... in July 1768. [n. p. n. d.] Folio, 1 leaf. H. 63476

The First Plymouth Patent: granted June 1, 1621. Now first printed from the Original Manuscript. Edited by Charles Deane ... . *Cambridge: Privately Printed.* M DCCC LIV. 4to, pp. 16

One hundred copies separately printed from the Collections of the Massachusetts Historical Society, Fourth Series, Vol. II. Four copies were also printed on vellum.

The Lectures delivered before the American Institute of Instruction, at Plymouth, August, 1846; ... *Boston.* 1847. 8vo, pp. xii, 203. 63478

Memorial of the Citizens of Plymouth and Kingston, Mass., adverse to ... the Woolens Bill. January 21, 1828. *Washington: Printed by Duff Green.* 1828. 8vo, pp. 8. H. 63479

A Patent for Plymouth. *See* Vol. xiv., No. 59034.

Constitution of the Pilgrim Society, as amended May 1836 ... with a list of members ... . *Plymouth: James Thurber, Printer.* 1840. 12mo, pp. (2), 8. H. 63480

The Constitutional Articles of the Pilgrim Society, incorporated February 24, 1820. *Plymouth: Printed by Allen Danforth.* 1823. 12mo, pp. 12. H. 63481

Festival of the Pilgrim Society, Dec. 22, 1820. *Plymouth.* [1820.] Folio, 1 leaf. M. 63482

The Plymouth Almanac, Directory, and Business Advertiser, for 1846. *Plymouth: Timothy Berry.* 1846. 18mo, pp. 76. A.

Catalogue of the Plymouth Library, Plymouth, Mass. 1858. *Plymouth.* 1858. 8vo, pp. 16. B. 63484

The Proceedings at the Celebration by the Pilgrim Society at Plymouth, December 21, 1870, of the Two Hundred and Fiftieth Anniversary of the Landing of the Pilgrims. *Cambridge: Press of John Wilson and Son.* 1871. 8vo, pp. 208. BA. 63485

Imprint on cover: *Boston: A. Williams and Company.* 1871. The oration by Hon. Robert C. Winthrop fills pp. 24–108.

Proceedings at the Consecration of the Cushman Monument. *See* Vol. v., No. 18140.

Proceedings at the Cushman Celebration. *See* [Shurtleff (N. B.)]

Second Annual Report of the Superintendent of the Public Schools of ... Plymouth ... 1857. *Plymouth: Chas. A. S. Perkins, Printer.* 1857. 8vo, pp. 56. Continued. H. 63486

Report of the Water Commissioners elected ... to cause Water to be brought from South Pond ... Feb. 1, 1856. *Plymouth: Chas. A. S. Perkins.* 1856. 8vo, pp. 48. H. 63487

Plymouth Colony. Records of the Colony of New Plymouth in New England. Printed by Order of the Legislature of the Commonwealth of Massachusetts. Edited by Nathaniel B. Shurtleff, M.D. ... *Boston: From the Press of William White.* 1855–61. 12 vols. in 10, rl. 8vo. A. 63488

Collation: I. Court Orders: Vol. I. 1633–1640, pp. (2), xiii, (1), 190; II. Court Orders: Vol. II. 1641–1651, pp. (10), 202; III. Court Orders: Vol. III. 1651–1661, pp. (10), 250; IV. Court Orders: Vol. IV. 1661–1668, pp. (10), 218; V. Court Orders: Vol. V., 1668–1678, pp. (10), 315; VI. Court Orders: Vol. VI. 1678–1691, pp. (10), 300; VII. Judicial Acts. 1636–1692, pp. (10), 339; VIII. Miscellaneous Records. 1633–1689, pp. (10), 283; IX. Acts of the Commissioners of the United Colonies of New England. Vol. I. 1643–1651, pp. (6), ix–xvi, (8), 237; X. Acts of the Commissioners of the United Colonies of New England. Vol. II. 1653–1679, pp. viii, (4), 492; XI. Laws. 1623–1682, pp. xi 274; XII. Deeds, etc. Vol. I. 1620–1651. Book of Indian Records for their Lands, pp. (2), vii, 264.

Improved title of our No. 53388, Vol. XIII. Vols. I.–VIII. were edited by N. B. Shurtleff; Vols. IX.–XII. by David Pulsifer. *See* New Plymouth, Vol. XIII., Nos. 53384–8, *and also* Vol. II., No. 7962.

Plymouth County, *Mass.* An Address to the Citizens of the County of Plymouth, April 29, 1811. [n. p. n. d.] 8vo, pp. 8. M. 63489

Address to the Electors of the County of Plymouth, May 7, 1811. [n. p. n. d.] 8vo, pp. 8. M. 63490

Address to the Electors of the County of Plymouth, by a Committee of Federal Republicans. [n. p.] 1811. 8vo, pp. 8.

Constitution of the Agricultural Society in the County of Plymouth incorporated June 11, 1819. With a List of the Officers and Members. *Plymouth: Printed by Allen Danforth.* 1832. 16mo, pp. 16. + *East Bridgewater: Printed by G. H. Brown.* 1842. 12mo, pp. 12. H. 63492

Transactions of the Plymouth County Agricultural Society, 1846. *Plymouth: Thurber's ... Press.* 1846. 8vo, pp. 24. Continued. B. 63493

Plymouth County Association for the Improvement of Common Schools, Educational Meeting, at Hanover, Sept. 3d. [n. p. 1838?] 18mo, pp. 17. H. 63494

Subject: A Normal School in Plymouth County. From the "Hingham Patriot."

The Plymouth County Directory, and Historical Register of the Old Colony, containing an Historical Sketch of the County, and of each Town in the County; a Roll of Honor, with the Names of all Soldiers of the Army and Navy ... . *Middleboro, Mass.: Stillman B. Pratt & Co.* 1867. 8vo, pp. 160, 148, 92. Map and 2 Plates. B. 63495

Plymouth, *N. H.* Historical Sketch, Articles of Faith and Covenant, Principles and Rules, and Catalogue of Members, Past and Present, of the Congregational Church, Plymouth, N. H. *J. E. Farwell & Company, Printers ... Boston.* 1867. 8vo, pp. 44.

Lettered on the cover: "Manual of the Congregational Church, Plymouth, N. H."

Plymouth, *Wis.* Constitution, By-Laws, ... of Union Lodge No. 71, I. O. O. F. of Plymouth, Wis. *Milwaukee.* 1854. 18mo. 63497

Plymouth Company. An | Answer | to | The Remarks of the Plymouth Company, | or (as they call themselves) the Proprietors of the | Kennebeck Purchase from the late Colony of | New-Plymouth, published by virtue of their | vote of 31st of January last; on the Plan and | Extracts of Deeds published by the Proprietors | of the Township of Brunswick. | Agreeable to their vote of the 4th of January immediately | preceeding. | Wherein, | The many trifling Cavils against said Plan and Extracts are | answered, many Aspersions cast on them wiped off: and | their entire Consistency with each other fully shewn. | And also the Boundaries of the Plymouth Company's Tract | upcn Kennebeck-River are at Large set forth and ascertain'd. | *Boston: in N. E. Printed in the Year* MDCCLIII. 4to, pp. 33. BA., W. 63498

Corrected title of our No. 8764, Vol. III. *See also* Vol. v., No. 19252, *and* "Remarks on the Plan."

POAKPHUNN, *pseudon.* *See* Vol. XII., No. 50887.

Los Poblanos á los habitantes de Mejico. *Puebla.* 1821. Folio.

El Pobre Peregrino. *Vera Cruz.* 1844. Folio. 63500

POCAHONTAS, *pseudon.* *See* [Pearson (*Mrs.* C. H.)], Vol. XIV., No. 59441, and add + Fourth Edition. [*Ibid.*] 1853. 12mo, pp. vii, 259. 4 Plates.

POCAHONTAS: *See* [Owen (R. D.)], Vol. XIV., No. 58021.

This has also been attributed respectively to R. Mackay and Mrs. L. H. Sigourney.

Pocahontas; a Proclamation: with Plates. [*New Haven: J. Clyme.* 1820.] 8vo, pp. 16. 2 Plates. B. 63502

A satire upon American slavery.

POCAHONTAS. The Memory of Pocahontas vindicated against the Erroneous Judgment of the Hon. Waddy Thompson. ... By a Kentuckian. *Washington: Printed by J. and G. S. Gideon.* 1847. 8vo, pp. 39. A., BA. 63503

The prefatory note is signed "P."

Picture of the Baptism of Pocahontas. *Washington.* 1840. 8vo. 63504

POCCIANTI (M.) Catalogvs Scriptorvm Florentinorvm Omnis Generis, ... Avctore ... Michaele Poccianti ... *Florentiæ, apva Philippvm Ivnctain*, M.D.LXXXIX. 4to, pp. (4), 171, (13). BM.

Contains extracts from Vespuccius' letters, and the evidence given by John Vespuccio (Americus's nephew), in the "Informacion." *See* Navarette, Vol. III.

Pocket Almanack for 1770. *Philadelphia: Printed and Sold by John Dunlap.* [n. d.] 32mo. 63506

See Vol. VII., No. 25564, and add to the note: Continued from 1767 to 1775 or later, with the imprint of *D. Hall & W. Sellers.* *See also* Vol. XIV., No. 60350.

A Pocket Almanack for the year ... 1783, being the third year after leap year and the seventh of American Independence, calculated for the use of the Commonwealth of Massachusetts. ... *Boston: T. & J. Fleet.* [1783.] 16mo. Continued. 63507

See also Vol. VI., No. 24688.

The Pocket Almanack for the year 1784, being the ninth of the American Independence. Calculated for the Meridian of Albany. *Albany.* 1784. 32mo, pp. 30. 63508

The Pocket Chronological Directory; or, Compend of General History ... . Published by Andrew Abernethy. First Edition. *Hartford: Printed by Peter B. Gleason & Co.* 1817. 16mo.

A Pocket Commentary. *See* Vol. VIII., No. 31657.

A Pocket Hymn Book ... Ninth Edition ... . *Philadelphia: Printed by Joseph James.* M.DCC.LXXXVIII. 16mo, pp. 257, (2).

Pocket Hymn Book. [Methodist.] *Philadelphia.* 1793. 18mo, pp. 300. 63511

... A Pocket List ... of Commanding Officers, both North and South, ... during the War. By W. Cullmer. *London.* 1865. Folded card. 63512

A Pocket Mirror for North America. [*London?*] 1755. 12mo. 63513

The Pocket Navigator, ... A Collection of the most Select Voyages. ... *London: ... Ann Lemoine* ... [1806.] 4 vols., 12mo.

Contains the voyages of Columbus, Cortez, Pizarro, Drake, Dampier, Rogers, etc.

POCKLINGTON (J.) Altare Christianum: or, The dead Vicars Plea. Wherein the Vicar of Gr.[antham] being dead, yet speaketh, and pleadeth out of Antiquity, against him that hath broken downe his altar. ... By Iohn Pocklington ... . *London: Printed by Richard Badger.* 1637. 4to, pp. (8), 163. BM. + The Second Edition, Corrected & Enlarged ... [*Ibid.*] 1637. 4to, pp. (8), 196. C. 63515

A letter from John Cotton to the Vicar of Grantham is given entire in the margin of Pocklington's Treatise.

POCOCK (I.) Robinson Crusoe: or, the Bold Buccaniers. ...

By Isaac Pocock ... *Thomas Hailes Lacy, London.* [n. d.] 12mo, pp. 41. + *London.* 1817. 8vo, pp. ii, 48. 63516

The scenes and characters are Indian.

Constitution of the POCOMTUCK VALLEY Memorial Association. [*Litchfield.* 1870.] 8vo, pp. (2). 63517

POE (E. A.) Al Aaraaf, Tamerlane, and Minor Poems. By Edgar A. Poe. *Baltimore: Hatch & Dunning.* 1829. 8vo, pp. 71

Very rare. Poe's first *published* work, and the first with his name on the title-page.

POE. The Conchologist's First Book: a System of Testaceous Malacology, Arranged expressly for the Use of Schools, ... By Edgar A. Poe. ... *Philadelphia: Published for the Author, by Haswell, Barrington, and Haswell.* 1839. 12mo, pp. 156. 12 colored Plates. + Second Edition. [*Ibid.*] 1840. 12mo, pp. 166. 12 colored Plates. A. 63519

Said to be a nearly *verbatim* copy of Capt. Thomas Brown's "Text-book of Conchology," *Glasgow*, 1833.—INTERNAT. MAG. I. 340.

POE. Eureka: A Prose Poem. By Edgar A. Poe. *New-York: Geo. P. Putnam.* MDCCCXLVIII. 12mo, pp. 143. + Second Edition. [*Ibid.*] 12mo. 63520

POE. Euréka. Par Edgar Poe. Traduit par Charles Baudelaire. *Paris: Michel Lévy frères.* 1863. 12mo. 63521

POE. The Literati: Some Honest Opinions about Autorial Merits and Demerits, with Occasional Words of Personality. Together with Marginalia, Suggestions, and Essays. By Edgar A. Poe. With a Sketch of the Author, by Rufus Wilmot Griswold. *New-York: J. S. Redfield.* 1850. 12mo, pp. xxxix, 607.

This usually forms Vol. III. of Poe's works.

POE. Mille et Deuxième Nuit. Par Edgar Poe. *Coulommiers.* 1869. 4to. 63523

[POE.] The Narrative of Arthur Gordon Pym, of Nantucket. Comprising the details of a mutiny and atrocious butchery on board the American brig Grampus, on her way to the South Seas, in the month of June, 1827. With an account of the recapture of the vessel by the survivers; their shipwreck and subsequent horrible sufferings from famine; their deliverance by means of the British schooner Jane Guy; the brief cruise of this latter vessel in the Antarctic Ocean; her capture, and the massacre of her crew among a group of islands in the eighty-fourth parallel of

southern latitude; together with the incredible adventures and discoveries still farther south to which that distressing calamity gave rise. *New-York: Harper & Brothers.* 1838. 12mo, pp. 201. 63524

[POE.] The Narrative of Arthur Gordon Pym, of Nantucket, North America: comprising the Details of a Mutiny, Famine, and Shipwreck, during a Voyage to the South Seas; resulting in various Extraordinary Adventures and Discoveries in the Eighty-fourth Parallel of Southern Latitude. *London: Wiley and Putnam .. Whittaker and Co.; and Charles Tilt.* 1838. 12mo, pp. (2), iv, 9–248, Note, 249–252. A. + *London.* 1841. 4to. + *London.* 1859. 8vo. + *London.* 1861. 8vo. 63525

[POE.] The Extraordinary Adventures of Arthur Gordon Pym, Mariner of Nantucket, during a Voyage to the South Seas. ... *London.* 1844. 8vo, pp. 80. 63526

POE. The Wonderful Adventures of A. Gordon Pym. By Edgar Allan Poe. *London: W. Kent & Co.* [1862.] 12mo, pp. 219. 63527

POE. Aventures d'Arthur Gordon Pym Par Edgar Poe Traduction de Charles Baudelaire. *Paris: Michel Lévy frères.* 1858. 12mo. + Deuxième Édition. [*Ibid.*] 1862. 16mo, pp. (4), 280. + [*Ibid.*] 1870. 12mo, pp. (4), 517, (1). 63528

POE. Aventuras de Arturo Gordon Pym. ... *Barcelona.* 1863. 4to. 63529

POE. Nouvelles Choisies. Le Scarabée d'Or.—L'Aéronaute Hollandais. ... *Paris: Hachette et Cie.* 1853. 12mo. 63530

POE. Poems By Edgar A. Poe. ... Second Edition. *New York: Elam Bliss.* 1831. 12mo, pp. 124. 63531

Very rare. For the first edition *see* No. 63518, *supra.*

POE. Poems. By Edgar A. Poe. ... *London.* 1857. 12mo.

With notices of his life and genius by Edmund F. Blanchard.

POE. Poems by Edgar Allan Poe, Complete with an Original Memoir. *New York: W. J. Widdleton.* 1861. 18mo. + [*Ibid.*] M.DCCC.LXIII. 18mo, pp. 278. Portrait. + [*Ibid.*] 1864. 18mo. + [*Ibid.*] 1865. 18mo, pp. 278. + [*Ibid.*] 1866. 18mo, pp. 278. + [*Ibid.*] M. DCCC. LXXII. 18mo, pp. 278. + With an Original Memoir by R. H. Stoddard. [*Ibid.*] 1874. 18mo.

First published *New York: Redfield.* 1859. 18mo.

POE. Memorial Edition. Poems and Essays of Edgar Allan Poe. Including Memoir by John H. Ingram, Tributes ... by Prof. Lowell and N. P. Willis; with the Ceremonies at the Monumental Dedication. *New-York: W. J. Widdleton.* 1876. 12mo, pp. clxxvi, 5–270. 63534

POE. The Poetical Works of Edgar Allan Poe With a Notice of his Life and Genius By James Hannay, Esq. With twenty Illustrations ... *London: T. A. Addey.* MDCCCLII. 16mo, pp. xxx, (2), 144. + [*Ibid.*] MDCCCLIII. 16mo, pp. xxx, (2), 144. + *London: J. & C. Brown and Co.* [n. d.] 16mo, pp. 185, (3). 8 Plates. 63535

Reprinted 1856, 1858, 1859, 1860, 1862, 1863, 1864, and 1865.

POE. The Poetical Works of Edgar Allan Poe and Richard H. Dana. *London: G. Routledge & Co.* 1857. 18mo, pp. 259, (1). + [*Ibid.*] 1860. 18mo. 63536

POE. The Poetical Works of Edgar Allan Poe, with Original Memoir. Illustrated by F. R. Pickersgill, R.A. [and others]. New Illustrated Edition. *London: Sampson, Low Son & Co.* M DCCC LVIII. Rl. 8vo, pp. xxii, 247. + [*Ibid.*] M DCCC LIX. Rl. 8vo. + [*Ibid.*] MDCCCLXVI. Rl. 8vo, pp. xxii, 167.

Some copies of the 1858 edition have a New York imprint.

POE. The Poetical Works of Edgar Allan Poe. Edited by James Hannay, Esq. With Illustrations. ... Complete Edition. *London: Charles Griffin and Company.* [1865.] 16mo, pp. 191.

POE. The Poetical Works of Edgar Allan Poe. Illustrated by Walter H. Paton, ... and other ... Artists ... . *Edinburgh: Alexander Hislop and Company.* [1869.] 4to, pp. 176. 63539

Other editions: *Melbourne*, 1868, 8vo; *Edinburgh*, 1869, 8vo; *London*, 1871, 8vo; *Edinburgh*, 1872, 12mo; *Edinburgh*, 1872, 8vo.

POE. The Prose Romances of Edgar A. Poe. No. I. The Murders in the Rue Morgue and the Man that was used up. *Philadelphia.* 1843. 8vo. 63540

No more published of this edition.

POE. The Prose Tales of Edgar Allan Poe. First Series. *New York: W. J. Widdleton.* 1867. 12mo, pp. 498. + Second Series. [*Ibid.*] 1867. 12mo, pp. 498. 63541

POE. The Raven and Other Poems. By Edgar A. Poe. *New York: Wiley and Putnam.* 1845. 12mo, pp. (8), 91. +

London: Wiley & Putnam. 1846. 12mo, pp. (8), 91. + *New York: W. J. Demorest.* 1870. 16mo. 63542

POE. The Raven. Illustrated by David Scattergood. *Philadelphia.* 1866. 4to. 63543

Partly set to music.

POE. The Raven. By Edgar Allan Poe. *Glasgow: John Thomson.* 1869. 16mo, pp. 8. 63544

[POE.] Le Corbeau. Conte Fantastique. [Traduit par Eugène Goubert. *Paris.* 1869.] 12mo, pp. 8. H. 63545

POE. Le Corbeau. Par Edgar Poe. Traduit par S. Mallarmé. *Paris.* 1875. Folio. 63546

A handsomely illustrated edition.

POE. Der Rabe, die Glocken, und Lenore. ... *Philadelphia.* 1864. 16mo. 63547

POE. Der Rabe. Mit einer Biographischen Skizze. ... *Philadelphia.* 1869. 8vo. 63548

POE. The Raven. By Edgar Allan Poe. Der Rabe. Von Edgar Allan Poe. Uebersetzt von Niclas Müller. [n. p.:] *Verlag von Nic. Müller.* 1874. 8vo, pp. (13). 63549

In German and English.

POE. Selected Poems. The Raven. Edgar A. Poe. *New York: Kilbourne Tomkins* ... 1875. Sq. 12mo, pp. (9). 63550

POE. The Select Works of Edgar Allan Poe. With Memoir. *Leipzig: A. Dürr.* 1854–58. 2 vols., 12mo, pp. 246; 280.

POE. Ausgewählte Werke von E. A. Poe. Aus dem Englischen von W. E. Drugulin. *Leipzig: Kollmann.* 1853–58. 3 vols., 16mo, pp. 200; 214; 197. 63552

POE. Tales By Edgar A. Poe. *New York: Wiley and Putnam.* 1845. 12mo, pp. (6), 228. + [*Ibid.*] 1849. 63553

POE. Tales and Sketches: to which is added the Raven: A Poem. By Edgar A. Poe. *London: George Routledge & Co.* 1852. 12mo, pp. (4), 268. 63554

POE. Tales of Mystery and Imagination. By Edgar A. Poe. *London.* 1853. 2 vols., 12mo. + *London: Ward and Lock.* 1864. 16mo. 63555

POE. Tales of Mystery, Imagination, and Humour. By Edgar Allan Poe. *London: Vizetelly.* 1852. 2 vols., 12mo. + *London: Ward, Lock, and Tyler.* [n. d.] 12mo, pp. (4), 395. + *Leipzig: Payne.* 1855–56. 2 vols., 16mo, (vols. VI. and VII. of "The English Library.") + *Halifax.* 1855. 16mo. 63556

POE. Tales of the Grotesque and Arabesque. By Edgar A. Poe. ... *Philadelphia: Lea and Blanchard.* 1840. 2 vols., 12mo, pp. 243; 228. B., C. + Second Edition. *New York.* 1845. 2 vols., 16mo. 63557

POE. Les Contes d'Edgar Poe. *Paris.* [1846?] 12mo.

POE. Contes Inédits d'Edgar Poe. Traduits de l'anglais par W. L. Hughes. *Paris: Hetzel.* [1862.] 12mo. 63559

POE. Histoires Extraordinaires Par Edgar Poe Traduction de Charles Baudelaire. *Paris: Michel Lévy frères.* 1856. 12mo. + Quatrième Édition. [*Ibid.*] 1862. 16mo, pp. xxxii, 330, (1). + [*Ibid.*] 1869. 12mo, pp. (4), 523, (1). + [*Ibid.*] 1873. 12mo, pp. (4), 523, (1). 63560

POE. Histoires Grotesques et Sérieuses. Par Edgar Poe. Traduits par Charles Baudelaire. *Paris: Michel Lévy frères.* 1865. 12mo. BA. 63561

POE. Nouvelles Histoires Extraordinaires Par Edgar Poe Traduction de Charles Baudelaire. *Paris: Michel Lévy frères.* 1857. 12mo. + Troisième Édition. [*Ibid.*] 1862. 16mo, pp. xxiv, 287. + [*Ibid.*] 1869. 12mo, pp. (4), 544. C. 63562

POE. Edgardo Poe. Historias Estraordinarias, precedidas de un prólogo crítico biográfico, por El Doctor Landa. *Madrid.* 1858. *Imprenta de Luis Garcia, editor.* 16mo, pp. xxviii, 288. BM. + *Madrid.* 1859. 2 vols., 16mo. 63563

POE. Biblioteca de Viaje. Historias Extraordinarias de Edgard Poe ... Viaje à la Luna ... . *Madrid: Imprenta de El Atalaya* ... . 1859. 16mo, pp. (2), 137. H. 63564

POE. Erstaunliche Geschichten und unheimliche Begebenheiten. Von Edgar Allan Poe. *Stuttgart: Scheible.* 1859. 16mo, pp. 456. 63565

POE. Novellen von Edgar Allan Poe. *Leipzig: Payne.* 1855–1858. 2 vols., 16mo, pp. 192; 192. 63566

POE. Unbegreifliche Ereignisse und geheimniszvolle Thaten. In achtzehn der merkwürdigsten Erzählungen. Von Edgar Allan Poe. *Stuttgart: Scheible.* 1861. 16mo, pp. 580. 63567

POE. Racconti Incredibili. ... *Milan.* 1876. 8vo. 63568

[POE.] Tamerlane and other Poems. By a Bostonian. ... *Boston: Calvin F. S. Thomas, Printer.* 1827. 12mo, pp. 40. BM.

Extremely rare. This is Poe's first printed work, and in the 1829 edition of his poems he refers to it as follows: "This poem was printed for publication in Boston, in the year 1827, but suppressed through circumstances of a private nature."

A careful reprint, with a preface by Richard Herne Shepherd, was published in an edition of 100 copies, *London: George Redway.* MDCCCLXXXIV. 16mo, pp. 64.

POE. The Works of the late Edgar Allan Poe: With Notices of his Life and Genius. By N. P. Willis, J. R. Lowell, and R. W. Griswold. In Two Volumes. ... *New-York: J. S. Redfield.* 1850. 2 vols., 12mo, pp. xx, 483; 495. Portrait. + [*Ibid.*] 1850. 3 vols., 12mo. Portrait. + [*Ibid.*] 1853. 4 vols., 12mo. 63570

For first edition of Vol. III. *see* "The Literati," No. 63522, *supra.*

POE. The Works of the late Edgar Allan Poe With a Memoir by Rufus Wilmot Griswold and Notices of his Life and Genius by N. P. Willis and J. R. Lowell. In Four Volumes. ... *Redfield New York* 1856. 4 vols., 12mo, pp. (2), lv, 483; xxvi, 495; iv, 21–607; 447. A. + [*Ibid.*] 1858. + 1861. + *New York: W. J. Widdleton.* 1863. 4 vols., 8vo. + [*Ibid.*] 1864. 63571

Contents: Vol. I., Tales; II., Poems and Sketches; III., The Literati; IV., Arthur Gordon Pym, etc.

POE. The Works of Edgar Allan Poe Including the Choicest of his Critical Essays. ... With a Study on his Life and Writings, from the French of Charles Baudelaire. ... *London: John Camden Hotten.* [1873.] Cr. 8vo, pp. viii, 676. 63572

POE. The Works of Edgar Allan Poe Edited by John H. Ingram ... *Edinburgh Adam and Charles Black* 1874–75 4 vols., 12mo, pp. (2), xcix, 513; vi, 569; vi, (1), 517; (2), vii, 574. Portrait, Plate and 2 Facsimiles. + *New York: W. J. Widdleton.* 1876. 4 vols., 12mo. 63573

POE. The Works of Edgar Allan Poe, including Poetical and Prose Writings. ... *New York: W. J. Widdleton.* 1876. 12mo, pp. viii, 676. A. 63574